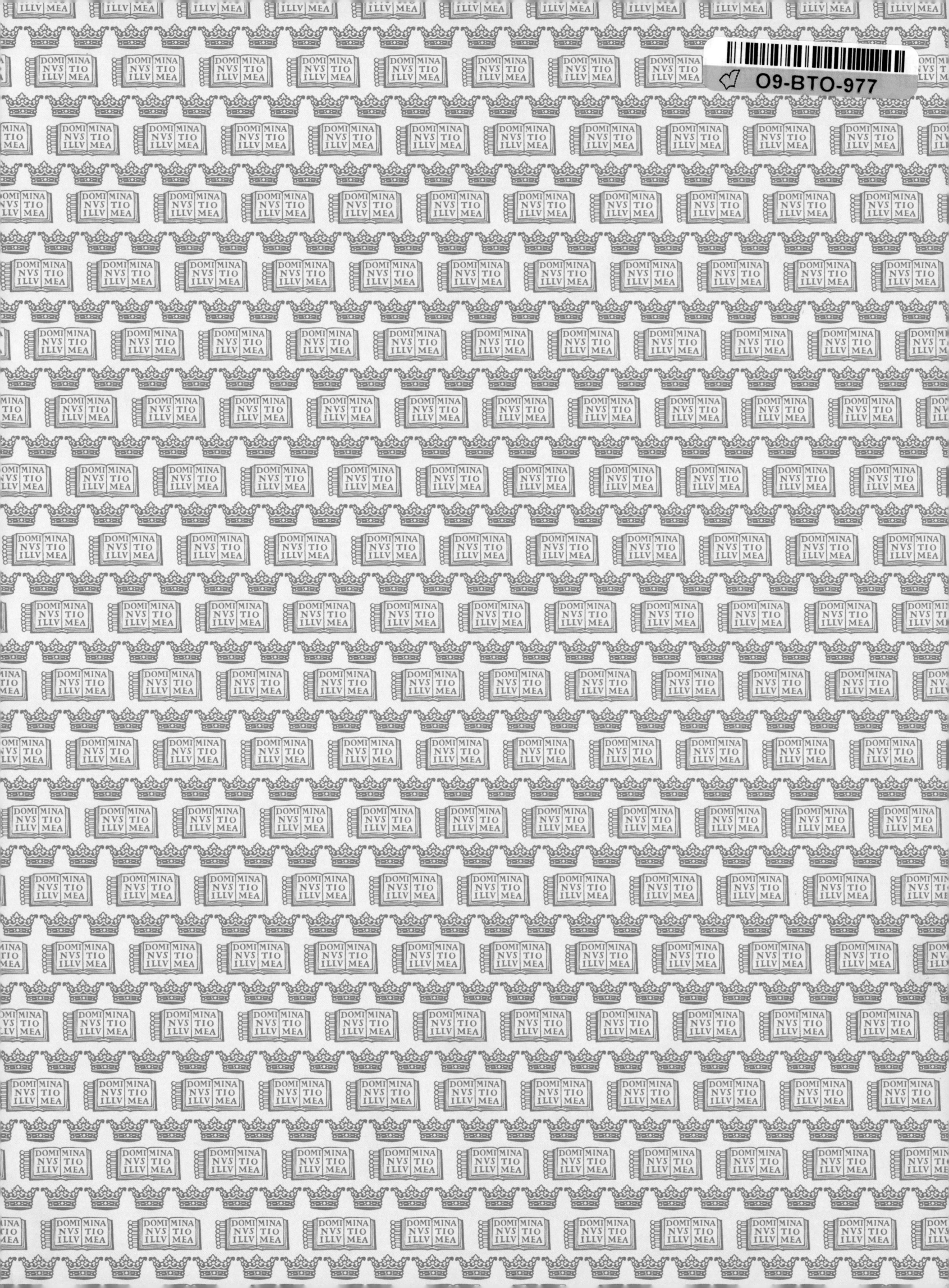

THE OXFORD ENGLISH DICTIONARY

SECOND EDITION

THE OXFORD ENGLISH DICTIONARY

First Edited by

JAMES A. H. MURRAY, HENRY BRADLEY, W. A. CRAIGIE
and C. T. ONIONS

COMBINED WITH

A SUPPLEMENT TO THE OXFORD ENGLISH DICTIONARY

Edited by

R. W. BURCHFIELD

AND RESET WITH CORRECTIONS, REVISIONS
AND ADDITIONAL VOCABULARY

THE OXFORD ENGLISH DICTIONARY

SECOND EDITION

Prepared by

J. A. SIMPSON *and* E. S. C. WEINER

VOLUME XVI

Soot–Styx

CLARENDON PRESS · OXFORD

Oxford University Press, Great Clarendon Street, Oxford OX2 6DP
Oxford New York
Athens Auckland Bangkok Bogotá Buenos Aires Calcutta
Cape Town Chennai Dar es Salaam Delhi Florence Hong Kong Istanbul
Karachi Kuala Lumpur Madrid Melbourne Mexico City Mumbai
Nairobi Paris São Paulo Singapore Taipei Tokyo Toronto Warsaw
and associated companies in
Berlin Ibadan

First published 1989
Reprinted 1991 (with corrections), 1998

British Library Cataloguing in Publication Data
Oxford English dictionary.—2nd ed.
1. English language—Dictionaries
I. Simpson, J. A. (John Andrew), 1953-
II. Weiner, Edmund S. C., 1950-
423
ISBN 0-19-861228-1 (vol. XVI)
ISBN 0-19-861186-2 (set)

Library of Congress Cataloging-in-Publication Data
The Oxford English dictionary.—2nd ed.
prepared by J. A. Simpson and E. S. C. Weiner
Bibliography: p.
ISBN 0-19-861228-1 (vol. XVI)
ISBN 0-19-861186-2 (set)
1. English language—Dictionaries. I. Simpson, J. A.
II. Weiner, E. S. C. III. Oxford University Press.
PE1625.087 1989
423—dc19 88-5330

Data capture by ICC, Fort Washington, Pa.
Text-processing by Oxford University Press
Typesetting by Pindar Graphics Origination, Scarborough, N. Yorks.
Manufactured in the United States of America by
World Color Book Services, Taunton, Mass.

KEY TO THE PRONUNCIATION

THE pronunciations given are those in use in the educated speech of southern England (the so-called 'Received Standard'), and the keywords given are to be understood as pronounced in such speech.

I. *Consonants*

b, d, f, k, l, m, n, p, t, v, z *have their usual English values*

g as in *go* (gəʊ)
h ... *ho!* (həʊ)
r ... *run* (rʌn), te*rr*ier ('tɛrɪə(r))
(r) ... he*r* (hɜː(r))
s ... *s*ee (siː), *success* (sək'sɛs)
w ... *w*ear (wɛə(r))
hw ... *wh*en (hwɛn)
j ... *y*es (jɛs)

θ as in *th*in (θɪn), ba*th* (bɑːθ)
ð ... *th*en (ðɛn), ba*the* (beɪð)
ʃ ... *sh*op (ʃɒp), di*sh* (dɪʃ)
tʃ ... *ch*op (tʃɒp), di*tch* (dɪtʃ)
ʒ ... vi*s*ion ('vɪʒən), dé*j*euner (deʒøne)
dʒ ... *j*u*dge* (dʒʌdʒ)
ŋ ... si*ng*i*ng* ('sɪŋɪŋ), thi*n*k (θiŋk)
ŋg ... fi*ng*er ('fɪŋgə(r))

(FOREIGN AND NON-SOUTHERN)

ʎ as in It. serra*gl*io (ser'raʎo)
ɲ ... Fr. co*gn*ac (kɔɲak)
x ... Ger. a*ch* (ax), Sc. lo*ch* (lɒx), Sp. fri*j*oles (fri'xoles)
ç ... Ger. i*ch* (ɪç), Sc. ni*ch*t (nɪçt)
ɣ ... North Ger. sa*g*en ('zaːɣən)
c ... Afrikaans baardmanne*tj*ie ('baːrtmanəci)
ɥ ... Fr. c*u*isine (kɥizin)

Symbols in parentheses are used to denote elements that may be omitted either by individual speakers or in particular phonetic contexts: e.g. *bottle* ('bɒt(ə)l), *Mercian* ('mɜːʃ(ɪ)ən), *suit* (s(j)uːt), *impromptu* (ɪm'prɒm(p)tjuː), *father* ('fɑːðə(r)).

II. *Vowels and Diphthongs*

SHORT

ɪ as in p*i*t (pɪt), -n*e*ss, (-nɪs)
ɛ ... p*e*t (pɛt), Fr. *sept* (sɛt)
æ ... p*a*t (pæt)
ʌ ... p*u*tt (pʌt)
ɒ ... p*o*t (pɒt)
ʊ ... p*u*t (pʊt)
ə ... *a*noth*er* (ə'nʌðə(r))
(ə) ... beat*e*n ('biːt(ə)n)
i ... Fr. s*i* (si)
e ... Fr. b*é*b*é* (bebe)
a ... Fr. m*a*ri (mari)
ɑ ... Fr. b*â*timent (bɑtimɑ̃)
ɔ ... Fr. h*o*mme (ɔm)
o ... Fr. *eau* (o)
ø ... Fr. p*eu* (pø)
œ ... Fr. b*oeu*f (bœf) c*oeu*r (kœr)
u ... Fr. d*ou*ce (dus)
ʏ ... Ger. M*ü*ller ('mʏlər)
y ... Fr. d*u* (dy)

LONG

iː as in b*ea*n (biːn)
ɑː ... b*ar*n (bɑːn)
ɔː ... b*or*n (bɔːn)
uː ... b*oo*n (buːn)
ɜː ... b*ur*n (bɜːn)
eː ... Ger. Schn*ee* (ʃneː)
ɛː ... Ger. F*äh*re ('fɛːrə)
aː ... Ger. T*a*g (taːk)
oː ... Ger. S*oh*n (zoːn)
øː ... Ger. G*oe*the ('gøːtə)
yː ... Ger. gr*ü*n (gryːn)

NASAL

ɛ̃, æ̃ as in Fr. f*in* (fɛ̃, fæ̃)
ɑ̃ ... Fr. fr*an*c (frɑ̃)
ɔ̃ ... Fr. b*on* (bɔ̃)
œ̃ ... Fr. *un* (œ̃)

DIPHTHONGS, etc.

eɪ as in b*ay* (beɪ)
aɪ ... b*uy* (baɪ)
ɔɪ ... b*oy* (bɔɪ)
əʊ ... n*o* (nəʊ)
aʊ ... n*ow* (naʊ)
ɪə ... p*eer* (pɪə(r))
ɛə ... p*air* (pɛə(r))
ʊə ... t*our* (tʊə(r))
ɔə ... b*oar* (bɔə(r))

aɪə as in f*ier*y ('faɪərɪ)
aʊə ... s*our* (saʊə(r))

The incidence of main stress is shown by a superior stress mark (') preceding the stressed syllable, and a secondary stress by an inferior stress mark (ˌ), e.g. *pronunciation* (prəˌnʌnsɪ'eɪʃ(ə)n).

For further explanation of the transcription used, see *General Explanations*, Volume I.

LIST OF ABBREVIATIONS, SIGNS, ETC.

Some abbreviations listed here in italics are also in certain cases printed in roman type, and vice versa.

a. (in Etym.)	adoption of, adopted from
a (as *a* 1850)	*ante*, 'before', 'not later than'
a.	adjective
abbrev.	abbreviation (of)
abl.	ablative
absol.	absolute, -ly
Abstr.	(in titles) *Abstract, -s*
acc.	accusative
Acct.	(in titles) *Account*
A.D.	*Anno Domini*
ad. (in Etym.)	adaptation of
Add.	Addenda
adj.	adjective
Adv.	(in titles) *Advance, -d, -s*
adv.	adverb
advb.	adverbial, -ly
Advt.	advertisement
Aeronaut.	(as label) in Aeronautics; (in titles) *Aeronautic, -al, -s*
AF., AFr.	Anglo-French
Afr.	Africa, -n
Agric.	(as label) in Agriculture; (in titles) *Agriculture, -al*
Alb.	Albanian
Amer.	American
Amer. Ind.	American Indian
Anat.	(as label) in Anatomy; (in titles) *Anatomy, -ical*
Anc.	(in titles) *Ancient*
Anglo-Ind.	Anglo-Indian
Anglo-Ir.	Anglo-Irish
Ann.	Annals
Anthrop., Anthropol.	(as label) in Anthropology; (in titles) *Anthropology, -ical*
Antiq.	(as label) in Antiquities; (in titles) *Antiquity*
aphet.	aphetic, aphetized
app.	apparently
Appl.	(in titles) *Applied*
Applic.	(in titles) *Application, -s*
appos.	appositive, -ly
Arab.	Arabic
Aram.	Aramaic
Arch.	in Architecture
arch.	archaic
Archæol.	in Archæology
Archit.	(as label) in Architecture; (in titles) *Architecture, -al*
Arm.	Armenian
assoc.	association
Astr.	in Astronomy
Astrol.	in Astrology
Astron.	(in titles) *Astronomy, -ical*
Astronaut.	(in titles) *Astronautic, -s*
attrib.	attributive, -ly
Austral.	Australian
Autobiogr.	(in titles) *Autobiography, -ical*
A.V.	Authorized Version
B.C.	Before Christ
B.C.	(in titles) British Columbia
bef.	before
Bibliogr.	(as label) in Bibliography; (in titles) *Bibliography, -ical*
Biochem.	(as label) in Biochemistry; (in titles) *Biochemistry, -ical*
Biol.	(as label) in Biology; (in titles) *Biology, -ical*
Bk.	*Book*
Bot.	(as label) in Botany; (in titles) *Botany, -ical*
Bp.	Bishop
Brit.	(in titles) *Britain, British*
Bulg.	Bulgarian
Bull.	(in titles) *Bulletin*
c (as *c* 1700)	*circa*, 'about'
c. (as 19th c.)	century
Cal.	(in titles) *Calendar*
Cambr.	(in titles) *Cambridge*
Canad.	Canadian
Cat.	Catalan
catachr.	catachrestically
Catal.	(in titles) *Catalogue*
Celt.	Celtic
Cent.	(in titles) *Century, Central*
Cent. Dict.	*Century Dictionary*
Cf., cf.	*confer*, 'compare'
Ch.	Church
Chem.	(as label) in Chemistry; (in titles) *Chemistry, -ical*
Chr.	(in titles) *Christian*
Chron.	(in titles) *Chronicle*
Chronol.	(in titles) *Chronology, -ical*
Cinemat., Cinematogr.	in Cinematography
Clin.	(in titles) *Clinical*
cl. L.	classical Latin
cogn. w.	cognate with
Col.	(in titles) *Colonel, Colony*
Coll.	(in titles) *Collection*
collect.	collective, -ly
colloq.	colloquial, -ly
comb.	combined, -ing
Comb.	Combinations
Comm.	in Commercial usage
Communic.	in Communications
comp.	compound, composition
Compan.	(in titles) *Companion*
compar.	comparative
compl.	complement
Compl.	(in titles) *Complete*
Conc.	(in titles) *Concise*
Conch.	in Conchology
concr.	concrete, -ly
Conf.	(in titles) *Conference*
Congr.	(in titles) *Congress*
conj.	conjunction
cons.	consonant
const.	construction, construed with
contr.	contrast (with)
Contrib.	(in titles) *Contribution*
Corr.	(in titles) *Correspondence*
corresp.	corresponding (to)
Cotgr.	R. Cotgrave, *Dictionarie of the French and English Tongues*
cpd.	compound
Crit.	(in titles) *Criticism, Critical*
Cryst.	in Crystallography
Cycl.	(in titles) *Cyclopædia, -ic*
Cytol.	(in titles) *Cytology, -ical*
Da.	Danish
D.A.	*Dictionary of Americanisms*
D.A.E.	*Dictionary of American English*
dat.	dative
D.C.	District of Columbia
Deb.	(in titles) *Debate, -s*
def.	definite, -ition
dem.	demonstrative
deriv.	derivative, -ation
derog.	derogatory
Descr.	(in titles) *Description, -tive*
Devel.	(in titles) *Development, -al*
Diagn.	(in titles) *Diagnosis, Diagnostic*
dial.	dialect, -al
Dict.	Dictionary; *spec.*, the *Oxford English Dictionary*
dim.	diminutive
Dis.	(in titles) *Disease*
Diss.	(in titles) *Dissertation*
D.O.S.T.	*Dictionary of the Older Scottish Tongue*
Du.	Dutch
E.	East
Eccl.	(as label) in Ecclesiastical usage; (in titles) *Ecclesiastical*
Ecol.	in Ecology
Econ.	(as label) in Economics; (in titles) *Economy, -ics*
ed.	edition
E.D.D.	*English Dialect Dictionary*
Edin.	(in titles) *Edinburgh*
Educ.	(as label) in Education; (in titles) *Education, -al*
EE.	Early English
e.g.	*exempli gratia*, 'for example'
Electr.	(as label) in Electricity; (in titles) *Electricity, -ical*
Electron.	(in titles) *Electronic, -s*
Elem.	(in titles) *Element, -ary*
ellipt.	elliptical, -ly
Embryol.	in Embryology
e.midl.	east midland (dialect)
Encycl.	(in titles) *Encyclopædia, -ic*
Eng.	England, English
Engin.	in Engineering
Ent.	in Entomology
Entomol.	(in titles) *Entomology, -logical*
erron.	erroneous, -ly
esp.	especially
Ess.	(in titles) *Essay, -s*
et al.	*et alii*, 'and others'
etc.	et cetera
Ethnol.	in Ethnology
etym.	etymology
euphem.	euphemistically
Exam.	(in titles) *Examination*
exc.	except
Exerc.	(in titles) *Exercise, -s*
Exper.	(in titles) *Experiment, -al*
Explor.	(in titles) *Exploration, -s*
f.	feminine
f. (in Etym.)	formed on
f. (in subordinate entries)	form of
F.	French
fem. (*rarely* f.)	feminine
fig.	figurative, -ly
Finn.	Finnish
fl.	*floruit*, 'flourished'
Found.	(in titles) *Foundation, -s*
Fr.	French
freq.	frequent, -ly
Fris.	Frisian
Fund.	(in titles) *Fundamental, -s*
Funk or *Funk's Stand. Dict.*	*Funk and Wagnalls Standard Dictionary*
G.	German
Gael.	Gaelic
Gaz.	(in titles) *Gazette*
gen.	genitive
gen.	general, -ly
Geogr.	(as label) in Geography; (in titles) *Geography, -ical*

Geol.	(as label) in Geology; (in titles) *Geology, -ical*
Geom.	in Geometry
Geomorphol.	in Geomorphology
Ger.	German
Gloss.	Glossary
Gmc.	Germanic
Godef.	F. Godefroy, *Dictionnaire de l'ancienne langue française*
Goth.	Gothic
Govt.	(in titles) *Government*
Gr.	Greek
Gram.	(as label) in Grammar; (in titles) *Grammar, -tical*
Gt.	Great
Heb.	Hebrew
Her.	in Heraldry
Herb.	among herbalists
Hind.	Hindustani
Hist.	(as label) in History; (in titles) *History, -ical*
hist.	historical
Histol.	(in titles) *Histology, -ical*
Hort.	in Horticulture
Househ.	(in titles) *Household*
Housek.	(in titles) *Housekeeping*
Ibid.	*Ibidem*, 'in the same book or passage'
Icel.	Icelandic
Ichthyol.	in Ichthyology
id.	*idem*, 'the same'
i.e.	*id est*, 'that is'
IE.	Indo-European
Illustr.	(in titles) *Illustration, -ted*
imit.	imitative
Immunol.	in Immunology
imp.	imperative
impers.	impersonal
impf.	imperfect
ind.	indicative
indef.	indefinite
Industr.	(in titles) *Industry, -ial*
inf.	infinitive
infl.	influenced
Inorg.	(in titles) *Inorganic*
Ins.	(in titles) *Insurance*
Inst.	(in titles) *Institute, -tion*
int.	interjection
intr.	intransitive
Introd.	(in titles) *Introduction*
Ir.	Irish
irreg.	irregular, -ly
It.	Italian
J., (J.)	(quoted from) Johnson's *Dictionary*
(Jam.)	Jamieson, *Scottish Dict.*
Jap.	Japanese
joc.	jocular, -ly
Jrnl.	(in titles) *Journal*
Jun.	(in titles) *Junior*
Knowl.	(in titles) *Knowledge*
l.	line
L.	Latin
lang.	language
Lect.	(in titles) *Lecture, -s*
Less.	(in titles) *Lesson, -s*
Let., Lett.	letter, letters
LG.	Low German
lit.	literal, -ly
Lit.	Literary
Lith.	Lithuanian
LXX	Septuagint
m.	masculine
Mag.	(in titles) *Magazine*
Magn.	(in titles) *Magnetic, -ism*
Mal.	Malay, Malayan
Man.	(in titles) *Manual*
Managem.	(in titles) *Management*
Manch.	(in titles) *Manchester*
Manuf.	in Manufacture, -ing
Mar.	(in titles) *Marine*
masc. (*rarely* m.)	masculine
Math.	(as label) in Mathematics; (in titles) *Mathematics, -al*
MDu.	Middle Dutch
ME.	Middle English
Mech.	(as label) in Mechanics; (in titles) *Mechanics, -al*
Med.	(as label) in Medicine; (in titles) *Medicine, -ical*
med.L.	medieval Latin
Mem.	(in titles) *Memoir, -s*
Metaph.	in Metaphysics
Meteorol.	(as label) in Meteorology; (in titles) *Meteorology, -ical*
MHG.	Middle High German
midl.	midland (dialect)
Mil.	in military usage
Min.	(as label) in Mineralogy; (in titles) *Ministry*
Mineral.	(in titles) *Mineralogy, -ical*
MLG.	Middle Low German
Misc.	(in titles) *Miscellany, -eous*
mod.	modern
mod.L	modern Latin
(Morris),	(quoted from) E. E. Morris's *Austral English*
Mus.	(as label) in Music; (in titles) *Music, -al; Museum*
Myst.	(in titles) *Mystery*
Mythol.	in Mythology
N.	North
n.	neuter
N. Amer.	North America, -n
N. & Q.	*Notes and Queries*
Narr.	(in titles) *Narrative*
Nat.	(in titles) *Natural*
Nat. Hist.	in Natural History
Naut.	in nautical language
N.E.	North East
N.E.D.	*New English Dictionary*, original title of the *Oxford English Dictionary* (first edition)
Neurol.	in Neurology
neut. (*rarely* n.)	neuter
NF., NFr.	Northern French
No.	Number
nom.	nominative
north.	northern (dialect)
Norw.	Norwegian
n.q.	no quotations
N.T.	New Testament
Nucl.	Nuclear
Numism.	in Numismatics
N.W.	North West
N.Z.	New Zealand
obj.	object
obl.	oblique
Obs., obs.	obsolete
Obstetr.	(in titles) *Obstetrics*
occas.	occasionally
OE.	Old English (= Anglo-Saxon)
OF., OFr.	Old French
OFris.	Old Frisian
OHG.	Old High German
OIr.	Old Irish
ON.	Old Norse
ONF.	Old Northern French
Ophthalm.	in Ophthalmology
opp.	opposed (to), the opposite (of)
Opt.	in Optics
Org.	(in titles) *Organic*
orig.	origin, -al, -ally
Ornith.	(as label) in Ornithology; (in titles) *Ornithology, -ical*
OS.	Old Saxon
OSl.	Old (Church) Slavonic
O.T.	Old Testament
Outl.	(in titles) *Outline*
Oxf.	(in titles) *Oxford*
p.	page
Palæogr.	in Palæography
Palæont.	(as label) in Palæontology; (in titles) *Palæontology, -ical*
pa. pple.	passive participle, past participle
(Partridge),	(quoted from) E. Partridge's *Dictionary of Slang and Unconventional English*
pass.	passive, -ly
pa.t.	past tense
Path.	(as label) in Pathology; (in titles) *Pathology, -ical*
perh.	perhaps
Pers.	Persian
pers.	person, -al
Petrogr.	in Petrography
Petrol.	(as label) in Petrology; (in titles) *Petrology, -ical*
(Pettman),	(quoted from) C. Pettman's *Africanderisms*
pf.	perfect
Pg.	Portuguese
Pharm.	in Pharmacology
Philol.	(as label) in Philology; (in titles) *Philology, -ical*
Philos.	(as label) in Philosophy; (in titles) *Philosophy, -ic*
phonet.	phonetic, -ally
Photogr.	(as label) in Photography; (in titles) *Photography, -ical*
phr.	phrase
Phys.	physical; (*rarely*) in Physiology
Physiol.	(as label) in Physiology; (in titles) *Physiology, -ical*
Pict.	(in titles) *Picture, Pictorial*
pl., plur.	plural
poet.	poetic, -al
Pol.	Polish
Pol.	(as label) in Politics; (in titles) *Politics, -al*
Pol. Econ.	in Political Economy
Polit.	(in titles) *Politics, -al*
pop.	popular, -ly
Porc.	(in titles) *Porcelain*
poss.	possessive
Pott.	(in titles) *Pottery*
ppl. a., pple. adj.	participial adjective
pple.	participle
Pr.	Provençal
pr.	present
Pract.	(in titles) *Practice, -al*
prec.	preceding (word or article)
pred.	predicative
pref.	prefix
pref., Pref.	preface
prep.	preposition
pres.	present
Princ.	(in titles) *Principle, -s*
priv.	privative
prob.	probably
Probl.	(in titles) *Problem*
Proc.	(in titles) *Proceedings*
pron.	pronoun
pronunc.	pronunciation
prop.	properly
Pros.	in Prosody
Prov.	Provençal
pr. pple.	present participle
Psych.	in Psychology
Psychol.	(as label) in Psychology; (in titles) *Psychology, -ical*
Publ.	(in titles) *Publications*
Q.	(in titles) *Quarterly*
quot(s).	quotation(s)
q.v.	*quod vide*, 'which see'
R.	(in titles) *Royal*
Radiol.	in Radiology
R.C.Ch.	Roman Catholic Church
Rec.	(in titles) *Record*
redupl.	reduplicating
Ref.	(in titles) *Reference*
refash.	refashioned, -ing
refl.	reflexive
Reg.	(in titles) *Register*

reg.	regular
rel.	related to
Reminisc.	(in titles) *Reminiscence, -s*
Rep.	(in titles) *Report, -s*
repr.	representative, representing
Res.	(in titles) *Research*
Rev.	(in titles) *Review*
rev.	revised
Rhet.	in Rhetoric
Rom.	Roman, -ce, -ic
Rum.	Rumanian
Russ.	Russian
S.	South
S.Afr.	South Africa, -n
sb.	substantive
sc.	*scilicet*, 'understand' or 'supply'
Sc., Scot.	Scottish
Scand.	(in titles) *Scandinavia, -n*
Sch.	(in titles) *School*
Sc. Nat. Dict.	*Scottish National Dictionary*
Scotl.	(in titles) *Scotland*
Sel.	(in titles) *Selection, -s*
Ser.	Series
sing.	singular
Sk.	(in titles) *Sketch*
Skr.	Sanskrit
Slav.	Slavonic
S.N.D.	*Scottish National Dictionary*
Soc.	(in titles) *Society*
Sociol.	(as label) in Sociology; (in titles) *Sociology, -ical*
Sp.	Spanish
Sp.	(in titles) *Speech, -es*
sp.	spelling
spec.	specifically
Spec.	(in titles) *Specimen*
St.	Saint
Stand.	(in titles) *Standard*
Stanf.	(quoted from) *Stanford Dictionary of Anglicised Words & Phrases*
str.	strong
Struct.	(in titles) *Structure, -al*
Stud.	(in titles) *Studies*
subj.	subject
subord. cl.	subordinate clause
subseq.	subsequent, -ly
subst.	substantively
suff.	suffix
superl.	superlative
Suppl.	Supplement
Surg.	(as label) in Surgery; (in titles) *Surgery, Surgical*
s.v.	*sub voce*, 'under the word'
Sw.	Swedish
s.w.	south-western (dialect)
Syd. Soc. Lex.	Sydenham Society, *Lexicon of Medicine & Allied Sciences*
syll.	syllable
Syr.	Syrian
Syst.	(in titles) *System, -atic*
Taxon.	(in titles) *Taxonomy, -ical*
techn.	technical, -ly
Technol.	(in titles) *Technology, -ical*
Telegr.	in Telegraphy
Teleph.	in Telephony
(Th.),	(quoted from) Thornton's *American Glossary*
Theatr.	in the Theatre, theatrical
Theol.	(as label) in Theology; (in titles) *Theology, -ical*
Theoret.	(in titles) *Theoretical*
Tokh.	Tokharian
tr., transl.	translated, translation
Trans.	(in titles) *Transactions*
trans.	transitive
transf.	transferred sense
Trav.	(in titles) *Travel(s)*
Treas.	(in titles) *Treasury*
Treat.	(in titles) *Treatise*
Treatm.	(in titles) *Treatment*
Trig.	in Trigonometry
Trop.	(in titles) *Tropical*
Turk.	Turkish
Typog., Typogr.	in Typography
ult.	ultimately
Univ.	(in titles) *University*
unkn.	unknown
U.S.	United States
U.S.S.R.	Union of Soviet Socialist Republics
usu.	usually
v., vb.	verb
var(r)., vars.	variant(s) of
vbl. sb.	verbal substantive
Vertebr.	(in titles) *Vertebrate, -s*
Vet.	(as label) in Veterinary Science; (in titles) *Veterinary*
Vet. Sci.	in Veterinary Science
viz.	*videlicet*, 'namely'
Voy.	(in titles) *Voyage, -s*
v.str.	strong verb
vulg.	vulgar
v.w.	weak verb
W.	Welsh; West
wd.	word
Webster	*Webster's* (*New International*) *Dictionary*
Westm.	(in titles) *Westminster*
WGmc.	West Germanic
Wks.	(in titles) *Works*
w.midl.	west midland (dialect)
WS.	West Saxon
(Y.),	(quoted from) Yule & Burnell's *Hobson-Jobson*
Yrs.	(in titles) *Years*
Zoogeogr.	in Zoogeography
Zool.	(as label) in Zoology; (in titles) *Zoology, -ical*

Signs and Other Conventions

Before a word or sense

† = obsolete
‖ = not naturalized, alien
¶ = catachrestic and erroneous uses

In the listing of Forms

1 = before 1100
2 = 12th c. (1100 to 1200)
3 = 13th c. (1200 to 1300), etc.
5–7 = 15th to 17th century
20 = 20th century

In the etymologies

* indicates a word or form not actually found, but of which the existence is inferred
:— = normal development of

The printing of a word in SMALL CAPITALS indicates that further information will be found under the word so referred to.

.. indicates an omitted part of a quotation.

- (in a quotation) indicates a hyphen doubtfully present in the original; (in other text) indicates a hyphen inserted only for the sake of a line-break.

PROPRIETARY NAMES

THIS Dictionary includes some words which are or are asserted to be proprietary names or trade marks. Their inclusion does not imply that they have acquired for legal purposes a non-proprietary or general significance nor any other judgement concerning their legal status. In cases where the editorial staff have established in the records of the Patent Offices of the United Kingdom and of the United States that a word is registered as a proprietary name or trade mark this is indicated, but no judgement concerning the legal status of such words is made or implied thereby.

soot (sʊt), *sb.*[1] Forms: α. 1, 4 sot (2 soth), 4–6 sote, 5 swot, 6 swote; 1, 4– soot (1 sooth, 5 soeth), 5–7 soote. β. 6 sooute, sout(e, sowte, 7 sutt, 7, 9 sut; *Sc.* 6 suit, 6, 8– sute, 9 shute; 9 *dial.* seut, seeat. [OE. *sót*, = MDu. *soet*, *zoet* (Du. dial. *zoet*), NFris. *sött*, *sutt*, ON. and Icel. *sót* (Norw. and Sw. *sot*, Da. *sod*), related to Lith. *sódis* (usually in pl. *sódźei* or *sódźiei*).

The pron. (sʌt), formerly common, is mentioned by Smart in 1836 as no longer used 'by the best speakers'. American dicts. give (suːt) as well as (sʊt).]

1. a. A black carbonaceous substance or deposit consisting of fine particles formed by the combustion of coal, wood, oil, or other fuel.

α. *c*725 *Corpus Gloss.* F 427 *Fuligine*, sooth. *c*1000 *Sax. Leechd.* I. 356 Meng ðærto sot & sealt & sand. *a*1200 *Sidonius Gl.* in *Anecd. Oxon.* Ser. I. v. 36/8 *Fuligo*, soth. *c*1302 *Pol. Songs* (Camden) 195 Hit falleth the Kyng of Fraunce bittrore then the sote. 1387 TREVISA *Higden* (Rolls) VII. 379 Whan al þe chirche was on fuyre, þer fil..noþer sparcle noþer soot uppon Wolston his grave. *c*1420 LYDG. *Assembly of Gods* 618 Hard as any horn, blakker fer then soot. *c*1440 *Pallad. on Husb.* I. 849 Oildreggis fresh for gnattis and for snaylis, Or chamber soot is good to kest aboute. 1530 PALSGR. 273/1 Sote of a chymney, *svÿe.* 1568 WITHALS *Dict.* 46 a/1 Swote, *fuligo.* 1582 BENTLEY *Mon. Matrones* iii. 342 For the time was, when you..liued solitarie, sitting at home among the soote of pots. 1615 CROOKE *Body of Man* 66 Euen as in chimneyes we see by the continuall ascent of soote, long strings of it are gathered as it were into a chaine. 1685 BOYLE *Enq. Notion Nat.* vi. 190 When in a foul chimney, a lump of soot falls into the hearth. 1765 A. DICKSON *Treat. Agric.* (ed. 2) 51 Soot is found to be a very rich manure. 1815 J. SMITH *Panorama Sci. & Art* II. 612 Soot remarkably increases the produce of soils abounding with vegetable matter. 1874 tr. *Lommel's Light* 3 The carbon in fine powder will be deposited upon it, forming a layer of soot.

fig. 1387–8 T. USK *Test. Love* II. ix. (Skeat) l. 38 Al sugre and hony, al minstralsy and melody ben but soot and galle in comparison. 1586 BRIGHT *Melanch.* xxi. 123 Natural actions..are weaker, and as it were smothered with this soote of melancholie.

β. 1541 R. COPLAND *Guydon's Form.* U iij, Some put therto to alter the coloure sute of the chymney. *a*1585 MONTGOMERIE *Flyting* 292 Weil swyld in a swynes skin and smerit ouer with suit. 1590 SPENSER *F.Q.* II. vii. 3 His head and beard with sout were ill bedight. 1648 GAGE *West Ind.* 142 The smoak..filleth the thatch and the rafters..with sut. 1685 in *Verney Mem.* (1907) II. 405 Tis soe foul with sutt, smoke, and Dust. 1729 *Dampier's Voy.* IV. II. 34 The Hodmandods..make themselves Black with Sut [1697 soot]. 1865 DICKENS *Mut. Fr.* I. vi, Distress is for ever a going about, like sut in the air.

†**b.** (See quots. and cf. NILL *sb.*[1]) *Obs.*

[1565 COOPER *Thesaurus*, *Spodium*, a maner of soute rysyng of the trying of brasse.] 1611 COTGR., *Spode*, the heauier foile, soot, or oare of Brasse. 1668 CHARLETON *Onomast.* 300 *Spodos Subterranea*,..Soot of Brass. 1688 HOLME *Armoury* III. 149/2.

2. With *a* and pl. **a.** A particular kind of soot.

1601 HOLLAND *Pliny* II. 324 This is a soueraigne soot to hinder the growth again of haires. 1671 GREW *Anat. Pl.* I. 17 Turpentine,..upon Vstion, sheweth nothing but a black Soot. 1733 CHEYNE *Eng. Malady* II. iii. §4 (1734) 141 The Soots of some..Woods are..of the same Nature and Efficacy. 1796 KIRWAN *Elem. Min.* (ed. 2) II. 43 When burned, it affords a soot and leaves a small quantity of a coaly residuum.

b. A flake of soot; a smut.

1906 *Daily News* 28 May 6 An air unsullied by the soots and scents of London.

3. A substance of a sooty appearance or nature.

1597 MIDDLETON *Wisd. Solomon* xii. 11 Too much seed doth turn to too much soot. 1690 TEMPLE *Ess.* II. *Gardens of Epicurus*, I found my Vines..apt for several years to a Soot or Smuttiness upon their leaves.

4. *transf.* Blackness, darkness.

1789 WOLCOT (P. Pindar) *Subj. for Painters* Wks. 1812 VII. 157 'Tis what the Prince of Soot hath often done.

5. *attrib.* and *Comb.* **a.** Attrib., as ***soot-ashes***, ***-bag***, ***-black***, ***-colour***, ***-door***, ***-dressing***, etc.

1664 EVELYN *Kal. Hort.* (1729) 199 *Soot-Ashes.. prevent Pis-mires..from invading the Fruit. 1798 *Hull Advert.* 18 Aug. 3/3 A chimney-sweeper put the troublesome gentleman into a *soot-bag. 1797 *Encycl. Brit.* (ed. 3) V. 156/2 Lamp-black..is the finest of what are called the *soot-blacks. 1611 COTGR. s.v. *Minimes*, *Couleur de minimes*, a light *soot colour, hauing an eye of a gray in it. 1639 T. DE GRAY *Expert Farrier* 58 Mouse-dunne and such like rusty and sut-colours. 1670 *Caveat to Conventiclers* 2 Clad in a duskish Soot-coloure sort of Shamoy. 1781 LATHAM *Gen. Syn.* I. I. 134 Cinereous Owl... The whole bird appears as if soiled with light soot-colour. 1834 McMURTRIE *Cuvier's Anim. Kingd.* 360 Blackish-bronze or soot-colour and silky above. 1833 LOUDON *Encycl. Archit.* §593 In that case *soot doors would be necessary in the chimney breast. 1854 RONALDS & RICHARDSON *Chem. Technol.* (ed. 2) I. 214 The soot or flue doors, introduced into chimneys for the purposes of cleansing. 1766 *Complete Farmer* s.v. *Lucern*, The preference ought to be given to *soot-dressings. 1722 RAMSAY *Three Bonnets* III. 19 *Soot-draps hang frae his roof and kipples. 1890 *Pall Mall G.* 28 Oct. 1/3 The extremely heavy *sootfall peculiar to the neighbourhood. 1839–52 BAILEY *Festus* 56 Like the *soot-flake upon a burning bar. 1733 W. ELLIS *Chiltern & Vale Farm.* 399 As for Example, if a Person was to dress..his Sands or Gravels in Summer with *Soot-lime, or Pigeons-dung. 1844 H. STEPHENS *Bk. Farm* III. 1249 The operations of the *soot-machine are effected thus [etc.]. 1843 CARLYLE *Past & Pr.* III. xv, To that dingy fuliginous Operative, emerging from his *soot-mill. 1898 *Allbutt's Syst. Med.* V. 3 The *soot-particles lie in the perilobular and interlobular tissue. *a*1722 LISLE *Husb.* (1757) 234 The seed being soaked in *soot-water. 1755 H. WALPOLE *Lett.* (1846) III. 139 Have you no Indian ink, no soot-water? 1882 *The Garden* 22 July 73/2 Soot water is found to be exceedingly beneficial to Pine-apple plants.

b. Similative, as ***soot-black***, ***-brown***, ***-dark***, †***-red*** [cf. OIcel. *sótrauðr*], ***soot-like*** adjs.

1715 *Lond. Gaz.* No. 5375/4 Lost.., two Geldings, the one a *Soote black. 1821 CLARE *Vill. Minstr.* I. 80 The boys through fear in soot-black corners push. 1837 CARLYLE *Fr. Rev.* II. v. iv, Your dark-yellow Mulattoes? And your Slaves soot-black? *c*1843 —— *Hist. Sk. Jas. I* (1898) 244 All soiled *soot-brown, illegible as the letter-press. 1853 C. BRONTE *Villette* xxix, His *soot-dark paletôt. 1789 J. WILLIAMS *Min. Kingd.* I. 211 If you discover a quantity of soft, black, *soot-like matter, you should dig in it. 1837 P. KEITH *Bot. Lex.* 327 The farina of the grain..is converted into a black soot-like powder. *a*1400 *Octouian* 1045 The launce was *swot red and croked.

c. With ppl. adjs., as ***soot-bespeckled***, ***-blackened***, ***-bleakened***, ***-bleared***, ***-clogged***, ***-coated***, ***-grimed***, ***-roughened***, ***-suffused***, etc.

1837 CARLYLE *Fr. Rev.* II. I. ii, In that soot-bleared figure, most earnest of created things. 1839 DICKENS *Nickleby* xvi, A soot-bespeckled prospect of tiles and chimney-pots. 1871 KINGSLEY *At Last* xi, Here and there some huge tree had burnt as it stood, and rose like a soot-grimed tower. 1894 'MARK TWAIN' in *Century Mag.* XLVIII. 17/1 It rained all day..apparently trying its best to wash that soot-blackened town [*sc.* St. Louis] white. 1916 JOYCE *Portrait of Artist* (1969) 115 The soot-coated packet of pictures which he had hidden in the flue of the fireplace. 1921 W. DE LA MARE *Veil* 68 Slow wreathed the grease adown from soot-clogged wick. 1932 W. FAULKNER *Light in August* vi. 111 Memory..knows remembers believes a corridor in a big long garbled cold echoing building of dark red brick sootbleakened by more chimneys than its own. 1947 W. DE LA MARE *Coll. Stories for Children* 122 Chapped, soot-roughened hands. 1956 D. GASCOYNE *Night Thoughts* 23 The soot-suffused sky-canopy. 1977 H. FAST *Immigrants* I. 29 The still half-naked citizens, soot-blackened and homeless, greeted the ruin as they had always greeted their city.

d. Objective, as ***soot-sowing***.

1844 H. STEPHENS *Bk. Farm* III. 1247 The soot-sowing machine.

6. Special combs.: **soot-bag**, a reticule (*Slang Dict.* 1864); **soot-blower**, a device for clearing soot from the flues of a boiler, furnace, etc.; **soot-cancer**, **-dew** (see quots.); **soot house** (see quots.); **soot-wart** (see quot. ? 1810).

1930 *Engineering* 16 May 627/1 Steam driers had met with little success while *soot-blowers had been widely introduced. 1967 *Trans. Inst. Engineers & Shipbuilders in Scotland* CX. 36 Naval boilers, up to the end of the last war, were not normally provided with sootblowers. 1878 WALSHAM *Surg. Pathol.* xiii. 369 From the great frequency with which it occurs in chimney-sweepers, cancer of the scrotum is generally designated the *soot- or sweeps-cancer. 1891 *Cent. Dict.*, **Soot-dew*,..a black, fuliginous coating covering parts of living plants. 1957 E. E. EVANS *Irish Folk Ways* ix. 120 The *soot-houses..whose roofs..were stripped in spring in the days when the whole family migrated to the summer pastures. At any rate the soot-house season runs from October to May... In the Hebrides it was customary to strip the soot-laden thatch of the black-houses annually for use as manure, and the roof was left without a smoke-hole to encourage the deposit of soot. 1966 *Daily Tel.* 21 Apr. 4/7 On Achill Island off the west coast of Ireland are the remains of some small buildings... They are called 'soot houses' and were used for the production of soot for fertilising the potato crop. ? 1810 P. POTT *Obs. Chimney Sweeper's Cancer* 4 It is a disease which always makes its first attack on..the inferior part of the scrotum..: the trade calls it the *soot-wart. 1869 TANNER *Pract. Med.* (ed. 6) I. 126 Since the Act of Parliament made the use of machinery imperative, the soot-wart has been less frequently seen.

soot, variant of SWOTE 'sweat' *Obs.*

†**soot**, *a.* and *sb.*[2] *Obs.* Forms: α. 1 suot, 1–2 swot, 2–5 swote, 3–5 suote, 5 swoote, 7 swoot. β. 4–6 sote. γ. 4–7 soot, 5–6 soote, 6–7 sout(e. [OE. *swót*, var. of *swéte* SWEET *a.*, influenced by *swóte* SOOT *adv.*]

A. *adj.* **1.** Sweet to the smell or taste; sweet-smelling, fragrant.

α. *c*950 *Lindisf. Gosp.* John xii. 3 þæt hus ʒefylled uæs of suot stenc ðæs smirinese. *a*1000 *Passio St. Margaretæ* in Cockayne *Narrat.* 49 Mid swotum wyrtum. *a*1100 in Napier *O.E. Glosses* 226/2 *Odoramentis*, swotum bræðum. *a*1200 *St. Marher.* 4 He is..swotest to smeallen; ne his swote sauur..mei neauer littlin. *c*1275 *Passion our Lord* 561 in *O.E. Misc.*, þo seyh heo þer twey engles myd hwite cloþes and swote. *c*1290 *S. Eng. Leg.* I. 8 A suote smul þare cam of heom. 1362 LANGL. *P. Pl.* A. x. 119 Riht as þe Rose þat red is and swote. ? *a*1366 CHAUCER *Rom. Rose* 60 The erth wexith proude..For swote dewes that on it falle. 1390 GOWER *Conf.* II. 176 With swote drinkes and with softe. *c*1430 *Life St. Kath.* 12 As þe fayre and swoote rose sprygeth amonge þe thornes. *c*1440 *Pallad. on Husb.* XI. 147 Yf me make a knotte on euery roote, They wole be frogh ynough & tender swoote.

β. ? *a*1366 CHAUCER *Rom. Rose* 1425 Thorough moisture of the welle wete Sprong up the sote grene gras. *c*1386 —— *Miller's T.* 19 (Cambr. MS.), A chambre had he..Ful fetously i-dight with erbis sote. 1412–20 LYDG. *Chron. Troy* (1555) I. vi, And them [*sc.* branches]..With sote blosmes freshly to repayre. *c*1420 *Chron. Vilod.* 2083 A sote sauore þe lafte styll þere.

γ. *c*1386 CHAUCER *2nd Nun's T.* 229 Ne never moo ne schul they roten be, Ne leese here soote savour. 1426 LYDG. *De Guil. Pilgr.* 10881 The mor that ther be flourys fayre, Lusty, soote, & fressh off hewe. *a*1450 tr. *De Imitatione* III. lvii. 135 Swetter þan eny soot encence. 1492 RYMAN *Poems* xxxv. 4 in *Archiv Stud. neu. Spr.* LXXXIX. 202 O Iesse rote moost swete and soote. 1555 W. WATREMAN *Fardle Facions* I. v. 78 Wine..wherin are enfused many soote odours and drugges. 1567 GOLDING *Ovid's Met.* VIII. (1593) 114 A roote Of Radish, and a jolly lump of Butter fresh and soote. 1600 FAIRFAX *Tasso* XV. xlvi, The height was greene with herbes and flowrets sout. 1611 COTGR., *Soëf*, sweet,..delicious, delicate, soote.

2. Of persons, qualities, etc.: Pleasant, agreeable, gentle, mild, gracious.

α. *a*1225 *Ancr. R.* 102 þes cos, leoue sustren, is..so unimete swote & swete. *c*1250 *Hymn* in *Trin. Coll. Hom.* App. 256 Leuedi milde, softe & swote, ic crie þe merci. *c*1275 in *O.E. Misc.* 89 For his swete moder luue þat is so veyr and swote. *c*1310 in Wright *Lyric P.* xviii. 57 In myn huerte thou sete a rote Of thi love, that is so swote. *c*1400 *Rom. Rose* 5412 Unto men more profit doth The froward Fortune and contraire, Than the swote and debonaire. *c*1425 *Castle Persev.* 2057 in *Macro Plays*, þerfor, vij systeris swote, lete oure vertus reyne on rote!

β. *c*1374 CHAUCER *Troylus* III. 1194 To whom this tale Sugre be or Sote. *c*1385 —— *L.G.W.* 1077 *Dido*, To sum folk ofte newe thyng is sote. *c*1403 LYDG. *Temple Glas* 1264 And so to ȝow more sote and agreable Shal loue be found. 1477 *Paston Lett.* III. 181 Lest the French Kyng..shuld in eny wise distourbe yow of yowr soft, sote, and sewre slepys. 1503 HAWES *Examp. Virt.* v. 66 With helpe of vertue so swete and sote. 1558 G. CAVENDISH *Poems* (1825) II. 67 Onles that grace have on the rewthe, To plant in the some vertue sote.

b. Of sounds: Melodious; harmonious.

*c*1385 CHAUCER *L.G.W.* 752 *Thisbe*, And on that othir side stod Thesbe The sote soun of othir to resseyue. 1426 LYDG. *De Guil. Pilgr.* 14693 With ther soote mellodye. 1593 BARNES *Parthen.* Sonn. xl, With thy notes harmonious and songs soot. 1614 J. DAVIES (Heref.) *Eclogues* Wks. (Grosart) II. 19 As swoot as Swans thy straines make Thames to ring. *Ibid.* 20 But now ne recke they of soot carrolling.

B. *sb.* That which is sweet; a person of sweet disposition.

*c*1430 *Hymns Virgin* (1867) 29 Me þinkeþ myn herte wole al to-breke Whanne y þinke on þat soote. 1620 BRATHWAIT *Five Senses* in *Archaica* (1815) II. 29 For even by the smell ..do we apprehend all varieties of flowers, sootes, sweets. 1638 —— *Spiritual Spicerie* 227 Nor bee these Soots lesse redolent in odour Which grow by Tiber.

b. In wine-making: (see first quot.).

1682 *Art & Myst. Vintners* (1703) 52 Take 30 gallons of Soot, which is Wine boyled to a Consumption of half, to a Butt of Wine. *Ibid.*, Some instead of Soot make of Sugar Molosses and Honey.

†**soot**, *adv.* *Obs.* Forms: 1–4 swote, 4–5 sote, 4–6 soote. [OE. *swóte*, = MDu. *soete*, *zoete*, OHG. *suozo*, *suazo* (MHG. *suoze*), the adv. corresponding to the adj. *swéte* SWEET.] Sweetly, in various senses.

*c*1000 ÆLFRIC *Gram.* xxxvii. 220 *Oleo*,..ic stince swote. *c*1175 *Lamb. Hom.* 53 He..bret hine [the cheese] for þon þet he scolde swote smelle. *a*1225 *Ancr. R.* 238 Forði þet tu sleptest swote. *a*1300 *Leg. Rood* (1871) 24 Of ech maner frut þat he sei þat smolde also swote. *c*1385 CHAUCER *L.G.W.* 2612 *Hypermnestra*, Thensens out of the fuyr out rekyth sote. 1426 LYDG. *De Guil. Pilgr.* 3459 Spyce & greyn I make to enspyre soote. *c*1450 *Merlin* ix. 133 So swote sauoured.. that fer men shulde fele the odour. 1579 SPENSER *Sheph. Cal.* Apr. 111 They dauncen deffly, and singen soote, in their meriment.

Comb. *c*1425 *St. Mary of Oignies* II. ix. in *Anglia* VIII. 175 þe sote-sauourynge cloþes of þis spouse of Cryste.

soot (sʊt), *v.* [f. SOOT *sb.*[1] Cf. Norw. *sota.*]

1. *trans.* To smear, smudge, or foul with soot; to cover with or as with soot.

1602 MARSTON *Antonio's Rev.* II. ii, The black filth of sinne That soots thy heart. 1634 W. WOOD *New Eng. Prosp.* II. xx. (1865) 108 The young Infant being greased and sooted, wrapt in a Beaver skin [etc.]. 1655 FULLER *Ch. Hist.* 107 The smoake thereof would have sooted his Green suit. 1706 STEVENS *Spanish Dict.* I, *Hollinár*, to soot, to daub with Soot. 1796 WITHERING *Brit. Plants* (ed. 3) I. 82 *Sooty*,.. dark and dirty as if sooted, as are some of the Lichens. *a*1859 DE QUINCEY *Posth. Wks.* (1891) I. 34 He paints himself histrionically; he soots his face.

2. To sprinkle or manure with soot.

1707 MORTIMER *Husb.* (1721) I. 325 Whether it was because the other Land was sooted before, I could never yet find. 1733 W. ELLIS *Chiltern & Vale Farm.* 28 He.. harrowed in his Barly and sooted it on the top. 1778 [W. MARSHALL] *Minutes Agric.* 16 Aug. 1776, Part was dunged; part, sooted; and part, undressed.

3. Sometimes with *up*: to fill or choke with a sooty deposit. Also *fig.*

1903, 1925 [implied in SOOTING *vbl. sb.* below]. 1929 W. E. COLLINSON *Spoken Eng.* 84 The engine is knocking. One of the [sparking] plugs is probably sooted up. 1959 M. PUGH *Chancer* i. 9 London was sooting me up and I couldn't shed it, layer by layer, like the plane-trees in the park.

Hence '**sooting** *vbl. sb.*

1706 STEVENS *Span. Dict.* I, *Tiznadúra*, Smutting, Sooting, Blacking, Smearing. 1903 *Cassell's Suppl.* Add., *Sooting*,..the impregnation of the sparking plug with soot, due to combustion of the explosive mixture when carbureting is bad. 1925 *Morris Owner's Manual* iv. 46 Bad plug insulation is sometimes caused through sooting.

soote, obs. form of SUIT *sb.*

'**sooted**, *ppl. a.* Also 6 **sotyd**. [f. SOOT *v.* or *sb.*] Manured, begrimed, covered, etc., with soot.

1530 [implied in SOOTEDNESS]. 1778 [W. MARSHALL] *Minutes Agric.* 16 Aug. 1776, The dunged [wheat] looked best in winter; the sooted never shewed itself. 1892 *Athenæum* 4 June 739/3 We have no dishonouring business of a sooted leg of mutton—none of those pantomimic tricks.

Hence †**sootedness**, = SOOTINESS. *Obs.*$^{-0}$

1530 PALSGR. 273/1 Sotydnesse, *suyerie.*

sooterkin ('suːtəkɪn). Now *rare*. Forms: 6 suterkyn, 8 -kin; 7 soutterkine, souterkine, soutri-, 8 souterkin; 7– sooterkin. [In sense 1 app. ad. older Du. or Flem. **soetekijn* (cf. Kilian, '*soetken*, dulcis amica, glycerium'), f. *soet* sweet. In sense 2 perh. f. SOOT *sb.*[1]; there is app. no similar term in Dutch.]

†**1.** Sweetheart, mistress. *Obs.*$^{-1}$

1530 *Songs* in *Anglia* XII. 593 This mynyon ys A rutterkyn; non lyke to hym but only Trym hys owne suterkyn.

2. An imaginary kind of afterbirth formerly attributed to Dutch women (see first quot.).

a **1658** CLEVELAND *Char. Diurn. Maker* (1677) 103 There goes a Report of the Holland Women, that together with their Children, they are delivered of a Sooterkin, not unlike to a Rat, which some imagine to be the Off-spring of the Stoves. **1678** BUTLER *Hud.* III. ii. 146 Knaves and Fools b'ing near of Kin, As Dutch-Boors are t' a Sooterkin. **1727** SWIFT *To Delany* Wks. 1755 III. II. 232 There follow'd at his lying-in For after-birth a Sooterkin. **1742** MRS. E. MONTAGU *Lett.* II. 180, I am glad there was a child, but pray was there not a little souterkin for the joy of the Lady's relations. **1748** MARY LEAPOR *Poems* 92 But turn your back, ..Alcidas with a Grin Will vow you're ugly as a Sooterkin. **1862** DRAPER *Intell. Devel. Europe* xviii. (1865) 412 The housewives of Holland no longer bring forth sooterkins by sitting over the lighted chauffers.

b. *transf.* Chiefly applied to persons in allusive senses; sometimes = Dutchman. Also *attrib.*

1680 BETTERTON *The Revenge* III. i, Good morrow, my little Sooterkin; how is't, my prettie Life? **1696** in Maidment *Scottish Pasquils* (1868) 307 For if the Devil assumed thy corpes, And travelled through the Holand Dorps, Thou would terrify the Souterkines. *a* **1704** T. BROWN *Dial. Dead* Wks. 1711 IV. 33 Whilst I was getting Money,..my Wife made it fly like Suterkins at home. **1719** D'URFEY *Pills* II. 219 Ye Jacobites as sharp as Pins, Ye Mounsieurs, and ye Sooterkins, I'll teach you all the Dance. **1746** *Brit. Mag.* 7 Smiling between Anger and Pleasure upon the sniveling Sooterkin. **1795** *Sporting Mag.* V. 136 The highwayman pushed poor Sooterkin [= chimney-sweep] out of the way. **1821** *Blackw. Mag.* IX. 60 Here is the sugar beside, which the hands of the sooterkin negro Reared [etc.].

c. Applied to literary compositions, etc., of a supplementary or imperfect character.

1668 T. ST. SERFE *Tarugo's Wiles* Epil., Besides the Authors true birth [= his play], the Audience will not be satisfied without a Soutterkine. **1728** POPE *Dunc.* I. 126 Fruits of dull Heat, and Sooterkins of Wit. **1777** R. W. Cox in C. F. Hardy *Benenden Lett.* (1901) 152 You can show you are a clever fellow, while poor I..must have my cherubims suffocated, and sooterkins put in the cradle. **1817** CARLYLE *Early Letters* (1886) I. 94 After considerable flourishing, he ventured to produce this child of the Doctor's brain—and truly it seemed a very Sooterkin. **1866** —— *Remin.* (1881) II. 240 It was by her address and invention that I got my sooterkin of a 'study' improved out of its worst blotches.

sooth (su:θ), *sb.* Now *arch.* Forms: 1–2 **soð**, 1, 3–5 **soþ** (3 **soh, seoþ**, 4 **soiþ, sooþ**), 4–6 **soth** (4 **sotht**), 5– **sooth**; 3 **soðe**, 4–5 **soþe**, 4–6 **sothe, southe**, 5–6 **soothe**; *Sc.* (and *north.*) 4–8 **suth** (6 **swth**), 5–7 **suith** (6 **soyt, soith, suythe, suitht**, 7 **suithe**). [OE. *sóð* neut., = OS. *sóđ* (cf. ON. *sannr*, *saðr* masc.), f. the adj.: see next.]

In common use down to the first half of the 17th cent.; after this app. obsolete (except perh. in sense 4c) until revived as a literary archaism, chiefly by Scott and contemporary writers.

I. Without article.

1. Truth, verity. (Cf. SOOTH *a.* 2a.) Also *personif.*

Beowulf 1700 Se þe soð and riht fremeð on folce. *c* **950** *Lindisf. Gosp.* Matt., Int. 1/13 ðif..soð [L. *veritas*] is to soeccenna of moniȝum. *a* **1000** *Elene* 307 (Gr.), Swa ȝe modblinde mengan ongunnon liȝe wið soðe. *a* **1122** *O.E. Chron.* (Laud MS.) an. 1091, Se eorl..litel soðes..of heora forewarde onfand. *c* **1200** ORMIN 14208 To flittenn Fra woh till rihht, fra læs till soþ. *a* **1250** *Owl & Night.* 950 Þe heorte ..so uorleost al his lyht þat ho ne syhþ soþ ne riht. *c* **1300** *Havelok* 36 He louede god..And holi kirke, and soth, ant ricth. *a* **1340** HAMPOLE *Psalter* v. 11 Vndire colour of soth bryngand in falshed. *a* **1400** *Minor Poems fr. Vernon MS.* II. 577 Wraþþe destruyeþ monnes wit, Whon soþ may not beo seiȝene. *c* **1400** *Destr. Troy* 188 Hit was said oft sythes and for sothe holden. **1593** NASHE *Christ's Tears* To Rdr., Wks. (Grosart) IV. 8 They shall be prouided for sumptuously, when sooth and verity may walke melancholy in Marke Lane. **1610** HEYWOOD *Gold. Age* II. i, Simplenesse and sooth, The harmlesse Chace, and strict Virginity Is all our practise. ? **1875** TENNYSON *Holy Grail* 709 Was there sooth in Arthur's prophecy?

b. Used as object to the verbs *say*, *speak*, or *tell*; freq. in the parenthetic phrases *sooth to say*, etc. (Cf. 5b.)

(*a*) *a* **900** CYNEWULF *Crist* 1306 Hwæþer..mon soð þe lyȝe saȝaþ on hine sylfne. *c* **1055** *Byrhtferth's Handboc* in *Anglia* VIII. 300 Ac we heom secgað soð tosoðe. *a* **1200** *Vices & Virtues* 9 Me ne net me noht te forsweriȝen, ac soð te seggen of ðan ðe ic am bicleped. *a* **1250** *Owl & Night.* 217, Vle, heo seyde, seye me soþ, hwi dostu þat vnwihtes doþ. *c* **1300** *Havelok* 2008 Quoth Ubbe, 'Bernard, seyst þou soth?' **1390** GOWER *Conf.* II. 285 Tell me soth And sei the trouthe, if [etc.]. *c* **1450** *Merlin* i. 7 Ye seyde me soth that my suster set but lytill prise of me. **1484** CAXTON *Fables of Æsop* v. xii, My broder, thow sayst soothe, wherfore I thanke the moche. **1594** GREENE & LODGE *Looking Gl.* G.'s Wks. (Rtldg.) 132 Say sooth in secret, Radagon, Is this thy father? **1625** MILTON *On Death Infant* 51 Or wert thou that just Maid who once before Forsook the hated earth, O tell me sooth. **1642** JER. TAYLOR *Episc.* (1647) 196, I am sure I have said sooth, but whether or no it will be thought so, I cannot tell. **1819** SCOTT *Ivanhoe* xxviii, 'Thou art speaking but sooth, Rebecca,' said Isaac. **1897** VOYNICH *Gadfly* (1904) 51/1 So long as I keep to the particular set.., I may speak sooth if the fancy takes me.

(*b*) *c* **1320** *Sir Tristr.* 2206 Tristrem lepe, ywis, þritti fete, soþ to say. *c* **1386** CHAUCER *Wife's Prol.* 601 He was, I trowe, a twenty wynter oold, And I was fourty, if I shal seye sooth. **1508** DUNBAR *Gold. Targe* 198 The salt was all the sarar, suth to sayn. **1577** tr. *Bullinger's Decades* (1592) 653 And to saie sooth, they doe not worship God at all. **1626** R. HARRIS *Hezekiah's Recovery* (1630) 6 To speake sooth, most of us have small reason to glorie in our prayers. **1808** SCOTT *Marm.* I. xxvi, And, sooth to tell, He murmur'd on till morn. **1813** HOGG *Queen's Wake* 24 The wine was served, and, sooth to say, Insensibly it stole away. **1855** H. ROGERS *Ess.* (1874) II. vii. 323 Sooth to tell, the narrative of the achievements here and there draws largely on our faith.

†**c.** ***to come to sooth***, to come true, be fulfilled.

1297 R. GLOUC. (Rolls) 4831 After seint austines day to soþe come al þis [prophecy]. *Ibid.* 6740 Al to soþe it is icome þat sein dunston gan telle.

†**2.** Used adverbially in the genitive singular *sooths*: Of a truth, truly. *Obs.*

c **1000** *Ags. Gosp.* Matt. v. 26 Soþes ic secge þe [etc.]. *a* **1240** *Ureisun* in *O.E. Hom.* I. 185 Nis nan blisse soþes i nan þing þet is utewið þet ne beo to bitter aboht. *Ibid.*, 3e soþes. *Ibid.* 187 Nai soþes, nai. Ne wene hit neuer no mon.

3. In prepositional phrases or constructions having an adverbial force: In truth, truly, really. (See also FORSOOTH *adv.*)

†**a.** ***to** (..) **sooth***. *Obs.*

Beowulf 51 (Gr.), Men ne cunnon secgan to soðe..hwa þæm hlæste onfeng! *c* **1000** *Ags. Ps.* (Thorpe) cxviii. 144 Syle me ða to soðe, and ic syþþan lifiȝe. *c* **1200** ORMIN 10900 Þatt wass, witt tu to fulle soþ, Fullfremedd herrsummnesse. *a* **1225** *Ancr. R.* 190 Wute 3e þet to soðe þet [etc.]. *c* **1305** *St. Kenelm* 277 in *E.E.P.* (1862) 55 Þo þe pope to soþe wiste what was þe tokninge [etc.].

†**b.** ***mid*** or ***with** (..) **sooth***. *Obs.*

c **888** K. ÆLFRED *Boeth.* x, Ne meaht þu no mid soðe ȝetælan þine wyrd. **971** *Blickl. Hom.* 17 He him ȝehet his æriste, swa he þa mid soðe ȝefylde. *c* **1205** LAY. 2181 To gædere comen mid soðe..Locrin & Camber. *a* **1250** *Owl & Night.* 264 Lust hw ich con me bitelle Mid rihte soþe wiþ vte spelle.

c. ***in sooth***.

1390 GOWER *Conf.* I. 315 The Mirour scheweth..As he hadde al the world withinne, And is in soth nothing therinne. **1592** LODGE *Euphues Shadow* C 1 b, Who so thou be that vertue wilt ensew, More sweete in sooth then show in true releefe. **1670** *Moral State Eng.* 62 b, And to shew this is in sooth, I bite this green wax with my Tooth. **1812** BYRON *Ch. Har.* II. lxiii, So sings the Teian, and he sings in sooth.

4. In phrases used expletively or parenthetically to strengthen or emphasize an assertion.

a. ***in*** (or †*to*) ***sooth***.

c **1300** *Beket* 2118 'To Sothe,' quath this holi man, 'prest ich am therto'. *c* **1400** MAUNDEV. (1839) xxiii. 251 And in soothe, o man allone in this Contree wil ete more in a day, than [etc.]. *a* **1450** *Pol., Rel., & L. Poems* (1903) 78 In sothe too me the matire queynte is; For as too hem i toke none hede. **1586** A. DAY *Eng. Secretary* II. (1625) 61 To deliuer ..what hee saw meetest to the purpose, and that in sooth with so deliberate..resolution, as [etc.]. **1596** SHAKS. *1 Hen. IV*, III. i. 259. **1605** CAMDEN *Rem.* 190 But if I haue any skill in South-saying, (as in sooth I haue none). *a* **1652** BROME *Damoiselle* II. i, *Ver*[*mine*]. What canst thou be? *Phil*[*lis*]. Insooth a Gentlewoman. **1771** BEATTIE *Minstr.* I. xxviii, In sooth t'was almost all the shepherd knew. **1808** SCOTT *Marm.* I. xv, Or was the gentle page, in sooth, A gentle paramour? **1871** B. TAYLOR *Faust* (1875) II. II. 141 I've never seen their like, in sooth.

b. ***in good*** or ***very sooth***. Also with ellipsis of *in*.

1577 HARRISON *England* II. v. (1877) I. 132 In good sooth I cannot tell. **1586** B. YOUNG tr. *Guazzo's Civ. Conv.* IV. 220b, Know thou my good gossip, how in good sooth this night my hog is stolen awaie. **1590** SHAKS. *Mids. N.* II. ii. 129 Good troth you do me wrong (good-sooth you do). **1656** SANDERSON *Serm.* (1689) 92 Say now I beseech you in good sooth..at whose door lieth the Superstition? **1808** SCOTT *Marm.* I. xx, 'Now, in good sooth,' Lord Marmion cried. *a* **1839** PRAED *Poems* (1864) I. 6 Or the Dragon had been, in very sooth, No insignificant charmer. **1849** JAMES *Woodman* xi, Good sooth, I know nothing of life. **1872** LONGF. *Wayside Inn* III. *Emma & Eginhard* 73 In good sooth, Its mystery is love.

c. ***by my, your***, etc. (***good***) ***sooth***. Also with ellipsis of *by*.

a **1400–50** *Alexander* 2286 'Sirres, by my sothe,' quod þe segge, 'Sitiles I hiȝt'. **1526** SKELTON *Magnyf.* 354 *Fan.* I trowe, by our lady, I had ben slayne... *Magn.* By your soth? **1596** HARINGTON *Metam. Ajax* (1814) 125 By my good sooth. *a* **1779** D. GRAHAM *Young Coalman's Courtship* ii. (1787) 14 Be me suth it will be the last thing I'll part wi'. **1786** BURNS *To a Louse* v, My sooth! right bauld ye set your nose out. **1789** —— *Willie brew'd* iii, But, by my sooth, she'll wait a wee! **1822** SCOTT *Nigel* xiv, My sooth, they will jump at them in Edinburgh like a cock at a grosart.

II. With article (or pronoun).

5. a. ***the sooth***, the truth; the real or actual facts, circumstances, etc.

Common from *c* 1300 to *c* 1560; now *arch.*

c **897** K. ÆLFRED tr. *Gregory's Past. C.* xlvi. 347 Ne flitað mid eowrum leasungum wið ðæm soðe. *a* **1000** *Sal. & Sat.* 182 (Gr.), Wyrs deð se ðe..ðæs soðes ansæceð! *c* **1200** *Trin. Coll. Hom.* 71 We shule..no þing seien þere þat les beo and no þing of þe soðe forlete. *c* **1250** *Gen. & Ex.* 2036 Ðe wite is hise, ðe right is hire, God al-migtin ðe soðe shire. *a* **1300** *Cursor M.* 777 Þe south fra ȝow wil I noght hide. *c* **1386** CHAUCER *Wife's T.* 75 He goth ful neigh the soth. *c* **1400** MAUNDEV. *Trav.* (1839) xxi. 224 Natheles the Sothe is this, that [etc.]. *c* **1450** *Merlin* ii. 37, I will knowe the soth, whatso-euer it coste. **1562** J. HEYWOOD *Prov. & Epigr.* (1867) 72 It is yll iestyng on the soothe. *a* **1592** GREENE *Jas. IV*, III. iii, Mark the sooth and listen the intent. **1616** W. HAIG in J. Russell *Haigs* (1881) vii. 163 How far my accuser is from the sooth in charging me with this imputation. **1868** MORRIS *Earthly Par.* (1870) I. I. 235 In his face the sooth they might behold.

b. With the verbs *say*, *speak*, *tell*, etc.; freq. in parenthetic phrases. (Cf. 1b.)

(*a*) *a* **1225** *Leg. Kath.* 153 Sone se hire sonde com aȝein, & seide hire þe soðe, heo [etc.]. *a* **1300** *Cursor M.* 3855 Sir, þe soth i wil þe tell. **13..** *Meditations Lord's Supper* 95 The soþe to ȝou y seye, One of ȝow shal me betraye. *c* **1440** *Generydes* 507 Telle me the sothe. *c* **1475** *Rauf Coilȝear* 52 Sen thow speiris, I the tell All the suith hale. *a* **1568** COVERDALE *Ghostly Psalms* Wks. (Parker Soc.) II. 587 Though God make the to saye the soth. **1609** SKENE *Reg. Maj., Treat.* 74 The assisours sal sweir..that they sall the suth say, and na suth conceill.

(*b*) **1338** R. BRUNNE *Chron.* (1810) 28 He ligges at Wynchestre, þe soth it is to seie. ? *a* **1366** CHAUCER *Rom. Rose* 1463 Sprygyng in a marble stone Had nature set, the sothe to telle, Under that pyn tree a welle. *c* **1400** *Sowdone Bab.* 897 This day haue we a ful ille afraye, To saie the south and not to lye. **1513** BRADSHAW *St. Werburge* Prol. 40 Some in contemplacyon, the sothe to say, Some in abstynence [etc.]. **1542** UDALL *Erasm. Apoph.* 166 To bee a thyng out of perauentures hard to dooe, yea and (the south to saye) vtterly vnpossible. **1599** SHAKS. *Hen. V*, III. vi. 151 To say the sooth,..My people are with sicknesse much enfeebled. **1805** SCOTT *Last Minstrel* I. Introd. 57 He thought even yet, the sooth to speak, That, if [etc.].

c. Const. *of* something.

1390 GOWER *Conf.* I. 75 Sche tolde unto hir housebonde The sothe of al the hole tale. **1423** JAS. I *Kingis Q.* 137 The warld..is so double and inconstant, Off quhich the suth is kid be mony assayes. *a* **1500** *Lancelot* 1213 Ther the suth may we Knaw of this thing. *c* **1550** ROLLAND *Crt. Venus* III. 358 Schaw me the suith of this now gif ȝe can. *a* **1592** GREENE *Jas. IV*, I. i. 359 To scorne the sooth of science with contempt. **1870** MORRIS *Earthly Par.* III. IV. 202 The old man doubted not the sooth Of what he said.

†**6.** A true thing or saying; a truth. *Obs.*

sing. *c* **1200** ORMIN 13706 Forr þatt he wollde winnenn Off Cristess muþ summ openn soþ Off hiss goddcunnde mahhte. *c* **1305** *St. Andrew* 39 in *E.E.P.* (1862) 99 If þu woldest þat soþe ihure, and if þu riȝt vnderstode. *c* **1386** CHAUCER *Sqr.'s T.* 166 This is a verray sooth withouten glose. *c* **1430** *Pilgr. Lyf Manhode* I. xliv. (1869) 26 Jrous folk ..mown not discerne cleerliche a sooth for here trowblede vnderstondinge. **1603** HARSNET *Pop. Impost.* 112 The hunting of the Witch heere [is] no fabulous apprehension but a good Catholique Sooth. **1609** SKENE *Reg. Maj., Burrow Lawes* 136 That they sall suth..say, and na suth conceill. **1640–1** *Kirkcudbr. War-Comm. Min. Bk.* (1855) 141 That ilk ane of thame shall the right suithe say and nae suithe conceal.

plur. **13..** *Minor Poems fr. Vernon MS.* lv. xxv. 1 Whon alle soþes ben souht and seene. *c* **1386** CHAUCER *Melib.* ¶211 Thou schalt rather..flee fro the swete wordes of flaterers, then fro the egre wordes of thy frend that saith the thi sothes. *a* **1450** *Knt. de la Tour* (1868) 124 To telle hym his sothes & trouthe withoute flaterie.

†**b.** A certainty *of* a matter. *Obs. rare.*

c **1374** CHAUCER *Troylus* v. 1295 Thorugh whiche thow shalt wel bryngen it aboute To knowe a soth of that thow ert in doute. *Ibid.* 1309.

†**c.** A proverb or adage. *Obs.*$^{-1}$

1655 VAUGHAN *Silex Scint.* II. 179 'Hedges have ears,' saith the old sooth.

†**7.** Soothsaying; prognostication. *Obs.*

1579 SPENSER *Sheph. Cal.* Dec. 87 Tryed time yet taught me greater thinges..: The soothe of byrds by beating of their wings. **1582** STANYHURST *Æneis* III. (Arb.) 85 Post to this prophetesse, let her help and sooth be required.

III. †**8.** Associated with senses of the verb SOOTHE: Blandishment, flattery; a smooth or plausible word or speech. Also *personif.* *Obs.*

1593 SHAKS. *Rich. II*, III. iii. 136 That ere this tongue of mine, That layd the Sentence of dread Banishment On yond prowd man, should take it off againe With words of sooth. **1608** —— *Pericles* I. ii. 44 When *signior* sooth here does proclaime peace, He flatters you, makes warre vpon your life. **1609** B. JONSON *Sil. Woman* v. ii, With a sooth or two more I had effected it.

sooth (su:θ), *a.* Now *arch.* Forms: 1–3 **soð** (2 **sod**), 1, 3–5 **soþ** (3 **soh**, 4 **soiþ, zoþ**), 5 **sooþ**; 3–5 **soth**, 4–7, 9– **sooth** (5 **south**); 3 **soþe** (**seohðe**, 4 **zoþe**), 4–6 **sothe**; *Sc.* and *north.* 4–6 **suth(e**, 5–6 **suith** (6 **soith**), **suythe**, 6 **swth**. [OE. *sóð*, *sóþ*, = OS. *sóđ*, ON. *sannr*, *saðr* (Sw. *sann*, Da. *sand*):—**sǫnþ-* (pre-Teut. *sont-*), related by ablaut to Goth. *sunjis* true, *sunja* truth, and Skr. *satyas* true, real.]

After the first half of the 17th cent. only as a literary archaism, chiefly introduced by Scott and his contemporaries (cf. the note to SOOTH *sb.*).

†**1.** True, veritable, real, genuine: **a.** Of things or qualities. *Obs.*

c **888** K. ÆLFRED *Boeth.* vii. §3 Ælc soþ wela and soþ weorþscipe sindan mine aȝne þeowas. **971** *Blick. Hom.* 25 Mid ælmes-weorcum, & mid soþre hreowe. *c* **1000** *Sax. Leechd.* (Rolls) I. 376 Þis is soð læcæcræft. *c* **1200** *Trin. Coll. Hom.* 191 Swo doð þe werse, þenne he auint mannes heorte emti of rihte bileue and of soðere luue. *c* **1275** *Moral Ode* 362 in *O.E. Misc.*, He is soþ sunne and briht and day bute nyhte. **1297** R. GLOUC. (Rolls) 1264 Vor siker þis is þe soþe wei wiþ oute eni mis-wrenche. **1340** *Ayenb.* 12 In zoþ & guode byleaue. *Ibid.* 126 He his to-delþ..be uour þinges þet zoþ loue makeþ.

†**b.** Of persons, esp. of the Deity. *Obs.*

c **950** *Lindisf. Gosp.* John vii. 40 [Hia] cuoedon ðes is soð uitȝa. *Ibid.* xvii. 3 Ðas..is uutudlice ece lif þætte on-ȝeattað ðec enne soð god. **971** *Blickl. Hom.* 33 He wæs soþ man,.. swylce he wæs soþ God. *a* **1200** *Vices & Virtues* 25 Fader & sune & hali gast is an soþ almihti godd. *c* **1320** *Cast. Love* 648 Ysayȝe..clepede him wonderful for þon, þat he is soþ God and soþ mon.

2. True; in accordance with truth; not false or fictitious: **a.** In predicative use.

Not always clearly distinguishable from SOOTH *sb.* 1.

c **825** *Vesp. Psalter* xviii. 10 Domas godes [sind] soðe. *c* **888** K. ÆLFRED *Boeth.* xxxviii. §2 Ic eom ȝeþafa þæt þæt is soð þæt ðu ær sædest. **971** *Blickl. Hom.* 53 Soþ is þæt ic eow secgge. *c* **1100** *O.E. Chron.* (MS. F) an. 995, Ealla þa wisuste menn..þa cuðan þat soðuste seggan [etc.]. *c* **1175** *Lamb. Hom.* 55 Þet is al soð ful iwis. *c* **1250** *Gen. & Ex.* 2842 He nam so forð, soð it is. *c* **1290** *S. Eng. Leg.* I. 3 Louerd, he seide, ȝif it is soth þat þou man and god beo. **13..** *E.E. Allit. P.* A. 482 Ȝyf hyt be soth þat þou conez saye. *c* **1385** CHAUCER *L.G.W.* Prol. 14 For, god wot, thing is neuer the lasse sooth, Thogh euery wight ne may it nat y-see. *c* **1450** *Bk. Curtasye* 211 in *Babees Book*, A schort worde is comynly sothe þat fyrst slydes fro monnes tothe. ?*a* **1500** *Chester Pl.* XI. 70 Therfore, as it was a-misse, I haue written that souther is. *c* **1550** ROLLAND *Crt. Venus* I. 564 Thay ar richt suith and ar of sentence fow. **1605** SHAKS. *Macb.* V. v. 40 If thy speech be sooth. **1642** JER. TAYLOR *Episc.* (1647) 260 Wee shall find all this to be sooth, and full of order. **1813** BYRON *Br. Abydos* II. x, I have a tale thou hast not dream'd, If sooth— its truth must others rue. **1840** MISS STRICKLAND *Queens Eng.* (1864) I. 160 The kings knew her words to be sooth. **1879** BUTCHER & LANG *Odyssey* 59 The ancient one of the sea, whose speech is sooth.

phr. **13..** *Minor Poems fr. Vernon MS.* xxiii. 796 To seke men is ȝiue þorwh þe An hele, soþ as gospelle. *c* **1386** CHAUCER *Merch. T.* 23 As soth as God is king. *c* **1440** *Partonope* 153 And that hit were as sothe as gospell.

b. In attributive use.

c **1205** LAY. 4652 Sonden commen bi-twenen, þe soðe word me seiden. *c* **1250** *Gen. & Ex.* 17 Cristene men oȝen ben so faȝen..ðan man hem telled soðe tale. **13..** *Cursor M.* 12146 (Gött.), Quarfor þan wil ȝe noght trow, Sother þinges þat i tell ȝu? **1375** BARBOUR *Bruce* I. 9 And suth thyngis that ar likand Tyll mannys heryng, ar plesand. *c* **1400** *Destr. Troy* 11 Sothe stories ben stoken vp, & straught out of mind. **1456** SIR G. HAYE *Law Arms* (S.T.S.) 126 The contrair is the suth opynioun. **1530** PALSGR. 325/1 Sothe, trewe, *veritable*. **1847** MARY HOWITT *Ballads* 238 This book which I had from thee contains the soothest lore. *a* **1869** C. SPENCE *Poems* (1898) 137 The following tale Shall stand a witness, sooth and leal.

prov. **1562** J. HEYWOOD *Prov. & Epigr.* (1867) 72 Sooth bourd is no bourd, in ought that mirth doothe. **1591** HARINGTON *Orl. Fur.* Apol. Poet. P vj, As the old saying is, (sooth boord is no boord). **1721** KELLY *Scot. Prov.* 3.

3. Of persons, etc.: Telling or speaking the truth; truthful. Also const. *in* (speech, etc.), *of* (one's word).

For the ME. phr. *soð cnawes beon* see KNOW *sb.*[1]

a **1250** *Owl & Night.* 698 Vor Alured seyde þat wel cuþe, Euer he spak mid soþe muþe. *a* **1300** *Cursor M.* 24078 Fair he was and fre, mi child, Soth in speche, in maner mild. *c* **1386** CHAUCER *Sqr.'s T.* 13 Pitous and Iust, and ever-more y-liche, Sooth of his word, benigne and honurable. *a* **1568** MONTGOMERIE *Misc. Poems* I. 13, I haif hard oft-tymis suith men say. **1634** MILTON *Comus* 823 Melibœus.., The soothest Shepherd that ere pip't on plains. **1757** DYER *Fleece* I. 630 Hoar-headed Damon.., soothest shepherd of the flow'ry vale. **1810** SCOTT *Lady of L.* I. xxiv, Announced by prophet sooth and old. **1894** *Blackw. Mag.* July 14, I ken a sooth face from a leeing ane.

4. *poet.* Soothing, soft; smooth.

1819 KEATS *To Sleep* 5 O soothest Sleep! if so it please thee, close In midst of this thine hymn my willing eyes. **1820** —— *St. Agnes* xxx, A heap Of candied apple.., With jellies soother than the creamy curd.

sooth (su:θ), *adv.* Now *arch.* and *rare.* Forms: 1 **soðe, soþe,** 5 **sothe;** 3–4 **soþ,** 4 **soth,** 5 **sooþ,** *Sc.* **suth,** 6–7, 9 **sooth.** [OE. *sóðe, sóþe,* f. the adj.: see prec.] Truly; truthfully; in truth.

Beowulf 524 Beot eal wið þe sunu Beanstanes soðe ȝelæste. *c* **1000** *Ags. Ps.* (Thorpe) cxviii. 15 Swa ic þine soðfæstnysse soðe ȝetreowe. *c* **1200** ORMIN 18591 Uss wrat & seȝȝde sikerr soþ Johan þe Goddspell wrihhte, þat [etc.]. *Ibid.* 19729 Forrþi seȝȝdenn þeȝȝ full soþ þatt Crist [etc.]. *a* **1300** *Cursor M.* 14529 Cayphas spak þus in his spa,.. And said wel sother þan he wist. *c* **1386** CHAUCER *Pard. T.* 174 Thou schalt say soth thin othes, and not lye. *c* **1470** HENRY *Wallace* II. 293 And so he told..Quhilk hapnyt suth in mony diuers cace.

b. Used interjectionally.

a **1300** *Cursor M.* 7739 'Es þat,' he said, 'mi sun daui?' 'Ya, soth,' said dauid, 'it es i'. **1470–85** MALORY *Arthur* XVII. xvi. 712 Sothe, sayd he, I am hole of body, thanked be our lord. **1590** SPENSER *F.Q.* III. iii. 13 And sooth, men say that he was not the sonne Of mortall Syre. **1601** SHAKS. *Twel. N.* II. i. 11 *An.* Let me yet know of you, whither you are bound. *Seb.* No sooth sir. **1604** —— *Oth.* III. iii. 52 *Oth.* Went he hence now? *Des.* I [= Ay] sooth. **1834** WHITTIER *Mogg Megone* I. 400 And sooth, 'T were Christian mercy to finish him. **1872** K. H. DIGBY *Ouranogaia* I. xii. 264 And, sooth, the company that take this way No man or woman can for aye admire.

†**sooth-**, representing the adj. or sb. in various obsolete combs., as **soothhead**, truth, verity; **soothquide**, a true word or saying, a truth; a proverb; **soothright(s** *adv.*, truly, verily; **soothsaȝel** *a.*, truthful, veracious; **soothship**, truth; **soothsinger** (see quot.); **soothtell** *a.*, soothsaying.

1340 *Ayenb.* 105 Þet uerste word ous sseweþ þe langnesse of his eurebleuinge;..þe þridde: þe dyepnesse of his *zoþhede. *c* **888** K. ÆLFRED *Boeth.* v. §3 Sona swa hit forlæt *soðcwidas, swa folȝaþ hit leasspellunga. *c* **950** *Lindisf. Gosp.* John x. 6 Ðis soðcuido *vel* ȝedd cuæð ðæm se hælend. *c* **1205** LAY. 9524 Þa cnihtes..cudden him soð quides from Claudien þæm kæisere. *c* **1275** *Ibid.* 13470 Ich wolle telle ou *soþrihtes. *Ibid.* 19068 Nas þar na more sohriht bote þat hit was day-liht. *c* **900** tr. *Baeda's Hist.* III. xvii. (1890) 206 Ic, swa swa *soðsaȝal stærwritere [etc.]. *c* **1200** *Trin. Coll. Hom.* 131 Un-liȝel man selde liȝeð, and soð-saȝel man seið ofte soð. *c* **1320** *Cast. Love* 1020 Ȝif he lyueþ in loue and in boxumnesse, In *soþschupe and in rihtwysnes. **1652** GAULE *Magastrom.* 24 Who is an Inchanter? A *sooth-singer, by canting numbers; or a soothsayer, by calculating numbers. **1582** STANYHURST *Æneis* IV. (Arb.) 108 Now *sothtel Apollo ..A menacing message..vttred.

soothe (su:ð), *v.* Forms: 1 **soðian,** 3 **soðien,** 4, 6 **sothe,** 6 **soth, south,** 6–9 **sooth,** 6– **soothe.** [OE. *sóðian* (also *ȝesóðian* I-SOTHE *v.*), f. *sóð* SOOTH *a.* Cf. ON. (Icel., Norw., Sw.) *sanna* (Da. *sande*).]

†**1.** *trans.* To prove or show (a fact, statement, etc.) to be true; to verify, demonstrate. Also const. *on* (a person). *Obs.*

c **950** *Lindisf. Gosp.* Matt., Int. 7 Ðas..fewer godspelles ..ðæs witȝes boc ec soðeð *vel* fæstnaȝið. *c* **1205** LAY. 8491 Þas weord ich wulle þe treosien,..þat ich hit wulle soðien. *a* **1240** *Sawles Warde* in *O.E. Hom.* I. 261 Þe prophetes þe.. seoð nu al þat isoðet, þat ha hefden longe ear icwiddet of ure lauerd. *c* **1275** LAY. 8315 Ich hit wolle soþi bi mine god treuwe. **1387–8** T. USK *Test. Love* I. v. (Skeat) l. 110 Looke than..thou perserer in my service,..that thilke scorn in thyn enemyes mowe this on thy person be not sothed. **1588** N. TROTTE *Introd. to Hughes' Misfort. Arthur* (1900) 111 They hold the grounds which time & vse hath sooth'd (Though shallow sense conceiue them as conceits).

†**2. a.** To declare (a statement) to be true; to uphold as the truth; to corroborate, support. *Obs.*

a **1553** UDALL *Royster D.* I. ii. (Arb.) 12 Then must I sooth it, what euer it is: For what he sayth or doth can not be amisse, Holde vp his yea and nay [etc.]. **1571** CAMPION *Hist. Irel.* (1809) 57 Verily, being inquisitive of these matters, I could finde no one of them soothed by such persons upon whose relation I am disposed to venture. **1580** LUPTON *Sivquila* 75 For every worde that the riche speaketh is soothed and counted for an Oracle. **1600** *Wisd. Dr. Dodypoll* II. iii. in Bullen *O. Pl.* (1884) III. 118 Do thou but soothe What I my selfe will presently devise. **1616** J. LANE *Contn. Sqr.'s T.* IX. 75 Soothinge his cause, that brave thinges ill begunn Standes recompensd, if held out till rewonn.

†**b.** To maintain or put forward (a lie or untruth) as being true. *Obs.*

1591 SAVILE *Tacitus, Hist.* I. xxxv. 20 Galba yielding to an vntruth so generally soothed, puts on a brest-plate. **1596** WARNER *Alb. Eng.* XII. lxxi. (1602) 297 Vpon my Tongue shall mine Opinion dye, Though should I say to it..Amen, I sooth'd no Lye. **1610** A. COOKE *Pope Joan* 43, *Protestant.* Why may it not be true though it be deliuered with *vt asseritur? Papist.* Why? Because lies are commonly so soothed. **1616** J. LANE *Contn. Sqr.'s T.* VII. 170 For o, but putt this worde (truth) in theire mowth, And laughe for aye, to heere what lies they soothe.

†**3.** To support, or back *up*, (a person) in a statement or assertion. *Obs.*

1544 *St. Papers Hen. VIII*, X. 185 Grandvela wold have denyed the French King to have been taken prysoner by meane of Your Majestie, but Mons[r] de Praet wold not sothe him in it. **1592** KYD *Sp. Trag.* III. x. 19 Deale cunningly; Salue all suspitions, onely sooth me vp. **1610** HEYWOOD *Gold. Age* IV. i, If we get entrance sooth me vp in all things. **1623** MASSINGER *Dk. Milan* V. ii, Sooth me in all I say; There's a main end in it.

†**4. a.** To confirm, encourage, or humour (a person) *in* something by expressing assent or approval.

1568 GRAFTON *Chron.* II. 395 No man durst..aduise hym in any thing, but must sothe him in whatsoeuer he sayd, or did. **1579** LYLY *Euphues* (Arb.) 149 These be they that sooth young youths in al their sayings, that vphold them in al their doings. **1613–8** DANIEL *Coll. Hist. Eng.* (1621) 146 [Princes] are apter to learne to know their greatnesse, then themselues; being euer soothed in all whatsoeuer they doe. **1643** MILTON *Divorce* II. iii. Wks. 1851 IV. 66 If a private friend admonish not,..but if he sooth him, and allow him in his faults [etc.].

refl. **1631** GOUGE *God's Arrows* III. §45. 266 Yet are we not hereupon to sooth our selves too much in our weaknesses.

†**b.** Similarly with *up. Obs.*

1573 G. HARVEY *Letter-bk.* (Camden) 9 If a man feed not there humor, nor sooth them up in there saiings. **1621** BURTON *Anat. Mel.* I. ii. IV. ii. 193 They will not let them bee corrected or controled, but still soothed vp in every thing they doe. **1676** ETHEREDGE *Man of Mode* III. ii, Do not you fall on him, Medley, and snub him. Sooth him up in his extravagance? **1705** STANHOPE *Paraphr.* II. 238 Rendring it an Argument for Presumption to sooth us up in Impenitence and Sloth.

refl. **1588** J. UDALL *Diotrephes* (Arb.) 21 Wel, sooth vp your selfe in your own perswasion, and brag of the multitude of subscribers. **1600** HOOKER *Serm.* ii. 38 Wks. 1888 III. 544, I am not ignorant how ready men are to feed and soothe up themselves in evil. **1622** T. SCOTT *Belg. Pismire* 11 He hateth to be reformed, and doth sooth up him selfe in folly.

†**5. a.** To blandish, cajole, or please (a person) by agreement or assent; to flatter in this way; to humour. *Obs.*

1573 TUSSER *Husb.* (1878) 26 She..sets open the chest, for such as can sooth hir and all away wrest. **1589** PUTTENHAM *Eng. Poesie* III. xv. (Arb.) 183 The yeoman thinking it good manner to soothe his Sergeant, said [etc.]. **1613** PURCHAS *Pilgrimage* (1614) 598 The Cyrenæans to sooth this proud King, which would needs be taken for the sonne of Ammon, stamped his shape in their coynes, with two hornes of a Ram. *a* **1649** DRUMM. OF HAWTH. *Fam. Ep.* Wks. (1711) 152, I can neither love nor sooth any other, be they never so powerful. **1680** OTWAY *Orphan* II. i, The grave dull fellow of small business sooths The Humorist and will needs admire his Wit.

absol. **1583** BABINGTON *Commandm.* (1590) 427 We must smooth it, & sooth it, & carrie two faces vnder one hoode. **1796** LAUDERDALE *Poems* 84 Now-a-days ane canna' phraise, An' sooth, an' lie, an' sweeten.

†**b.** Similarly with *up. Obs.*

1616 *Pasquil & Kath.* v. 80, I thought he was mad in putting me To such an enterprise; and therefore sooth'd him vp With I sir, yes sir, and so sir, at each word. **1652** GAULE *Magastrom.* 22 O ye Hypocrites! that..flatter and sooth up others to a doating presumption [etc.]. **1729** G. ADAMS tr. *Sophocl., Antig.* v. ii. II. 67 Why should I sooth you up with those Tales, wherein at least I shall appear a Liar. *a* **1734** NORTH *Lives* (1826) I. 178 The game lay by soothing up the King, and pushing him on in designs of advancing his prerogative. **1814** NICHOLSON *Poet. Wks.* (1897) 57 A wily, spruce, and nipping blade, Wha..soothed the lasses up wi' baubles.

refl. **1613** DAY *Dyall* iv. (1613) 74 Least upon the hearing thus of sins forgiven, the wicked should soothe up themselves. **1621** BURTON *Anat. Mel.* I. ii. II. vi, They may ..sooth vp themselues with phantasticall humors.

†**c.** Followed by *that* and clause. *Obs.*

1593 NASHE *Christ's T.* 14 b, Hee sootheth him vp, that if God would not haue had him sinne, hee woulde neuer haue giuen him..the meanes to sinne with. **1613** DAY *Dyall* viii. (1614) 169 Let no man sooth up himselfe that he hath a pure and immaculate heart. **1643** MILTON *Divorce* Wks. 1851 IV. 19 Yet I may erre perhaps in soothing my selfe that this present truth [etc.]. *a* **1661** FULLER *Worthies* (1840) II. 359 When soothed up by the servants, 'that not John but some other of his brothers did cry'.

†**d.** With impersonal object. *Obs.*

1592 SHAKS. *Ven. & Ad.* 850 Like shrill-tongued tapsters answering every call, Soothing the humour of fantastic wits. *a* **1656** BP. HALL *Rem. Wks.* (1660) 150 [There are] those that humour, and sooth up corrupt nature. **1669** STURMY *Mariner's Mag.* C iij, [He] commendeth even those things.. which in his heart he doth detest, to the end that he may sooth up the Humour of the Party.

†**6. a.** To smooth or gloss over (an offence, etc.); to render less objectionable or offensive. *Obs.*

1587 GOLDING *De Mornay* i. 11 Some..haue striued to perswade themselues by soothing their owne sinnes, that they haue no Soule at all. **1593** SHAKS. *3 Hen. VI*, III. iii. 175 What? has your King married the Lady Grey? And now to sooth your Forgery, and his, Sends me a Paper to perswade me Patience? **1606** CHAPMAN *Gent. Usher* v. iv. 66 His grosse dotage rather loath'd then sooth'd. *c* **1645** HOWELL *Lett.* I. v. xi, I am of the number of those that had rather commend the Virtue of an Enemy, than sooth the Vices of a Friend.

Comb. *a* **1618** SYLVESTER *Paradox agst. Libertie* 1110 Wks. (Grosart) II. 65 False sooth-sin flatteries, and idle Fairy dreames.

†**b.** Similarly with *up. Obs.*

1592 GREENE *Def. Conny Catching* Wks. (Grosart) XI. 81 Who..to aduaunce his yonger brother..was content to lie, cog, and flatter, and to take any seruile paines, to sooth vp the matter. **1603** FLORIO *Montaigne* III. vii. (1894) 469 We authorize their defects and sooth-up their vices. *a* **1641** BP. MOUNTAGU *Acts & Mon.* (1642) 519 Can wee religiously think the holy Ghost would doe anything to sooth up or countenance a popular error.

7. a. To render (an animal, a person, the feelings) calm or quiet; to restore to a normally peaceful or tranquil condition; to mollify or appease.

1697 DRYDEN *Virg. Georg.* III. 293 If to the Warlike Steed thy Studies bend,..Sooth him with Praise, and make him understand The loud Applauses of his Master's Hand. **1717** POPE *Iliad* IX. 249 With this he sooths his angry Soul. **1777** WATSON *Philip II* XVII. (1839) 351 He may humble himself so far as to soothe us with the hopes of a more mild administration. **1814** JANE AUSTEN *Mansf. Park* (1851) 86 Was he only trying to soothe and pacify her, to make her overlook the previous affront? *a* **1859** MACAULAY *Hist. Eng.* xxiii. V. 22 It was particularly important to soothe Wharton, who had been exasperated [etc.]. **1864** BRYCE *Holy Rom. Emp.* iii. (1875) 14 Ariovistus had been soothed by the title of Friend of the Roman People.

transf. **1710** T. FULLER *Pharm. Extemp.* 146 It [*sc.* the emulsion] sooths up and composeth to quiet, the mad, raging Spirits. **1822** SHELLEY *Fragm. Unf. Drama* 106 Calming me as the loveliness of heaven Soothes the unquiet sea.

b. Const. *to*. Also, to induce *to* do something.

1746 FRANCIS tr. *Horace, Sat.* I. i. 27 As Masters fondly sooth their Boys to read With Cakes and Sweetmeats. **1823** SCOTT *Quentin D.* x, When I walk boldly up to a surly mastiff, and caress him, it is ten to one I soothe him to good temper.

c. With direct speech as object: to say in a soothing manner.

1934 N. MARSH *Man lay Dead* xii. 206 'You shall have every opportunity,' soothed Alleyn. **1976** I. LEVIN *Boys from Brazil* iii. 77 'I agree, Josef, I agree,' the colonel soothed.

8. a. To bring to a calm or composed condition; to affect in a tranquillizing and agreeable manner.

1742 GRAY *Eton* 18 My weary soul they seem to sooth. **1774** GOLDSM. *Nat. Hist.* (1776) V. 26 The male sits near his mate upon some tree, and sooths her by his singing. **1818** KEATS *Endym.* I. 783 Fold A rose leaf round thy finger's taperness, And soothe thy lips. **1869** BROWNING *Ring & Bk.* x. 1645 A cloud may soothe the eye made blind by blaze. **1891** E. PEACOCK *N. Brendon* I. 255 Poetry of a certain kind soothed him.

transf. **1780** COWPER *Progr. Err.* 66 Sweet harmony, that sooths the midnight hour!

b. Const. *to* (a certain state).

1819 BYRON *Juan* II. cxiii, The soft warm hand of youth.. bathing his chill temples, tried to soothe Each pulse to animation. **1870** E. PEACOCK *Ralf Skirl.* III. 82 This monotony soothed her to sleep.

9. a. To reduce the force or intensity of (a passion, pain, etc.); to render less painful or violent; to allay, assuage, mitigate, etc.

1711 ADDISON *Spect.* No. 170 ¶7 An intimate Friend that will..condole their Sufferings, and endeavour to sooth and asswage their secret Resentments. **1742** YOUNG *Nt. Th.* IX. 16 Song soothes our pains; and age has pains to soothe. **1786** BURNS *Vision* II. xvi, Th' adored Name, I taught thee how to pour in song, To soothe thy flame. **1807–8** W. IRVING *Salmag.* (1824) 334 As if anxious to sooth the last moments of his master. **1868** J. H. BLUNT *Ref. Ch. Eng.* I. 402 Soothing agitation or putting an end to discord. **1880** L. STEPHEN *Pope* iv. 92 He was constantly wanting coffee, which seems to have soothed his headaches.

b. To drive *away*, to dispel, by soothing.

1746 FRANCIS tr. *Horace, Epist.* I. ii. 46 Who..with melting Airs Of empty Music sooth away our Cares. **1853** MRS. GASKELL *Ruth* (1855) 208 The deep sense of penitence ..he mistook for earthly shame, which he imagined he could soon soothe away.

c. To soften, tone down, render less harsh or prominent.

1860 HAWTHORNE *Marb. Faun* xvi, Artificial fantasies, which the calm moonlight soothed into better taste than was native to them.

10. *absol.* To have or exercise a soothing or tranquillizing influence.

1728 YOUNG *Love Fame* VI. 194 Ladies supreme among amusements reign; By nature born to sooth, and entertain. **1797** JANE AUSTEN *Sense & Sens.* (1849) 260 Elinor, impatient to soothe, though too honest to flatter. **1809** BYRON *To Florence* xi, 'Twill soothe to be where thou hast been. **1850** TENNYSON *In Mem.* lvi, O for thy voice to soothe and bless! **1871** GARROD *Mat. Med.* (ed. 3) 171 The decoction..is employed as an external application to allay pain and soothe.

Hence **soothed** (suːðd) *ppl. a.*

1599 B. JONSON *Cynthia's Rev.* v. vi, Like an envious wretch, That glitters onely to his soothed selfe. **16..** *The Distracted Emperor* in Bullen *O.P.* III. 184 What will not soothed prynces? **1820** KEATS *St. Agnes* xxvii, The poppied warmth of sleep oppress'd Her soothed limbs. **1839–52** BAILEY *Festus* 379 A rainbow of sweet sounds, Just spanning the soothed sense. **1845** DISRAELI *Sybil* (1863) 241 A warmth which expressed her sense of his kindness and her own soothed feelings.

soothe (suːð), *sb. rare.* [Back-formation f. the vb.] A soothing feeling or effect.

1947 *Landfall* (N.Z.) I. IV. 267 They felt the soothe of the darkness. **1971** J. GARDNER *Every Night's a Bullfight* vii. 170 Close whispering, kissing; the soothe of flesh against flesh.

soother (ˈsuːðə(r)), *sb.* Also 6 souther. [f. SOOTHE *v.*]

†**1.** One who assents or agrees with another; a flatterer. *Obs.*

1553 T. WILSON *Rhet.* 106b, This worlde..hath ouer many such as neuer honest man was, that is to saie, flatterers, fawners, and southers of mennes saiynges. **1593** ABP. BANCROFT *Daungerous Positions* IV. i. 135 An Inn-keeper, (a receiver of all, and a soother of euery man for his gaine). **1612** DRAYTON *Poly-olb.* xvi. 89 But soothers find the way preferment most to win. *a* **1661** HOLYDAY *Juvenal* (1673) 189 Wife, children, and themselves they do distress, They'd tire the soother Cossus.

2. One who or that which soothes, calms, comforts, etc.

1780 S. J. PRATT *Emma Corbett* (ed. 4) III. 137 Dear friend—author of many a comfort—soother of many a care. *c* **1811** MRS. OPIE in A. J. C. Hare *Gurneys of Earlham* (1895) I. 239 Thou goest, sweet soother, every wound to heal. **1824** SCOTT *Ess. on Romance* Misc. Wks. 1870 VI. 164 The professional poet..becomes the companion and soother only of idle and convivial hours. **1865** C. STANFORD *Symb. Christ* vii. 191 Finding in Him the hero of your proud romance, and the soother of your indolence.

3. A soothing thing or influence.

In recent use *spec.* an artificial teat, ring, etc., given to a baby to suck in order to quiet it.

1794 R. J. SULIVAN *View Nat.* I. 19 The warm..affections are in every instance the soothers of melancholy. **1803** JANE PORTER *Thaddeus* (1826) III. xv. 326 Those gentle amiabilities which are the soothers and sweeteners of life. **1841** LYTTON *Nt. & Morn.* I. vi, A pipe is a great soother.

'soother, *v. Ir.* Also soodher. [f. SOOTHE *v.*] *trans.* To blandish, cajole, flatter, etc.

1842 LOVER *Handy Andy* i, 'How can you help it?' 'I'll soother him' [*sc.* a horse]. **1896** F. MATHEW *Wood of Brambles* 183 If they are wantin' to soother you.

soothering, *ppl. a. dial.* and *U.S.* [f. SOOTHER *v.* + -ING².] Blandishing, cajoling.

1866 E. L. LINTON *Lizzie Lorton* II. i. 13 Thee 'se gitten a soothering tongue in thee head, lad. **1884** [see SOFTY *a.*]. **1898** G. BARTRAM *White-Headed Boy* 5 A kind of gentle look in them—a 'soodherin'' look, as we say in Ireland—the way a horse looks at you when he loves you. **1953** *Scots Mag.* Aug. 418 The mither sings a sootherin tune til a waukrif loon.

soothfast (ˈsuːθfɑːst, -æ-), *a.* and *adv.* Now *arch.* [OE. *sóð-, sóþfæst*: see SOOTH *sb.* and FAST *a.*]

Except in Sc. legal use, the word appears to have been obsolete from the beginning of the 17th cent. until its revival by Scott.

A. *adj.* **1.** Of persons: Speaking or adhering to the truth; veracious, truthful; true, faithful, loyal.

c **825** *Vesp. Psalter* lxxxv. 15 Swiðe mildheort & soðfest. *a* **900** CYNEWULF *Crist* 302 Eac we þæt ȝefruȝnon, þæt ȝefyrn bi þe soðfæst sæȝde sum woðbora. **971** *Blickl. Hom.* 187 Þes man is soþfæst & soþsecȝende. *c* **1100** *O.E. Chron.* (MS. D) an. 1065, Her Eadward cing..sende soðfeste saule to Kriste. **1124** *Ibid.* (Laud MS.) an. 1124, Fela soðfeste men sæidon þæt þær wæron maneȝe..ȝespilde. *c* **1205** LAY. 6535 He wes swiðe soðfest [*v.r.* sohfast] and swiðe wel iðæwed. *a* **1300** *Cursor M.* 10189 Was neuer..nan tholmoder in chastite,.. Ne nan soth-faster þan was he. **1340** HAMPOLE *Pr. Consc.* 135 Whar-for ilk man..Suld..knaw..Hou rightwes God es, and how sothefast. *c* **1400** MAUNDEV. (Roxb.) xv. 69 Ʒe schuld..be symple, meke and sothfast. *c* **1440** *Promp. Parv.* 465/2 Sothefast mann or womann, *verax.* **1500–20** DUNBAR *Poems* xxxv. 43 Quhill I hard tell be mony suthfast wy, Fle wald ane abbot vp in to the sky. **1577** *Test. 12 Patriarchs* (1604) 102 Love ye one another with soothfast heart. **1581** MARBECK *Bk. of Notes* 1109 Christ..is called true or soothfast, because he only teacheth vs true, certeine,..& infallible things. **1612** J. DAVIES (Heref.) *Muse's Sacrifice* Wks. (Grosart) II. 36/2, I..weepe for what I want; that is, thy Grace, and Loue. Then, as thou art still soothfast, grant them me. **1816** SCOTT *Antiq.* xxv, Edie was ken'd to me..for a true, loyal, and soothfast man. **1857** EMERSON *Poems* 79 Here am I, here will I abide Forever to myself soothfast.

absol. *c* **825** *Lorica Prayer* in *O.E. Texts* 174 Ðec alle soðfeste fore-ðingiað. *a* **1425** *Cursor M.* 17459 (Trin.), And soþfaste whenne fals is fled Holdeþ forþ his owne sted. **1876** MORRIS *Sigurd* I. 29 Thou shalt know indeed..why the liar gains in a day what the soothfast strives for late.

†**b.** Const. *in* or *of* (word, etc.). *Obs.*

c **1400** tr. *Secreta Secret., Gov. Lordsh.* 103 Þat he be sothfast of wordes. **1422** *Ibid., Priv. Priv.* 211 He sholde bene Sothefaste in worde and dedd. **1559** *Mirr. Mag.* (1563) B j, Abandon all affray, be soothfast in your sawes. **1577** *St. Aug. Manual* (Longman) 70, I know..that he [God] is Soothfast of promise.

2. In accordance or conformity with the truth; true, veracious; †just, equitable.

c **950** *Lindisf. Gosp.* John v. 30 Dom min soðfæst is. *c* **1000** *Ags. Ps.* (Thorpe) lxviii. 28 Hi on þin soðfæst weorc [L. *in justitiam tuam*] syþþan ne gangan. *c* **1205** LAY. 60 Nu bidded Laȝamon alcne æðele mon..þat he þeos soðfeste word segge to sumne. **1375** BARBOUR *Bruce* I. 3 Than suld storys that suthfast wer..Hawe doubill plesance in heryng. *c* **1400** *Pilgr. Sowle* (Caxton, 1483) IV. xxxiii. 82 Shewynge by quyck reson that theyr seynge is sad and sothfast. **1481** in *Eng. Misc.* (Surtees) 39 In defawte of soothfast knowlage. **1513** DOUGLAS *Æneid* VI. i. 174 Scho wes constrenit to schaw all suthfast thingis. **1559** *Mirr. Mag.* (1562) B b j, It was a southfast sentence long ago That hastye men shal never lacke much woe. **1567** TURBERV. *Epit.*, etc. 57b, Thus many yeares were spent with good and soothfast life. **1818** SCOTT *Br. Lamm.* xxii, Soothfast tidings had assured him that this nobleman was..to honour his castle at one in the afternoon. **1829** A. CUNNINGHAM *Magic Bridle, Anniv.* 136 I'll tell a tale. List, ye who glory In truth, and love a soothfast story.

b. Of an oath or evidence. Chiefly *Sc.*

a **1300** *Cursor M.* 6848 Bi fals godds suer yee nan, Athes noiþer sothfast ne man. **1481** *Certificate* in *Eng. Misc.* (Surtees) 39 It is meritable to bere wittenes and suthfast record in any cause. **1502** *Mackintosh Muniments* (1903) 8 Meritable it is to beir leill and suithfast witnessing to the merite. **1561** *Reg. Privy Council Scot.* I. 198 To beir leill and suithfast witnessing in sa fer as thai knaw or shalbe sperit at thame. **1666** *Proclamation* in Wodrow *Hist. Suff. Ch. Scot.* (1830) II. 6 To bear leel and soothfast witnessing, in so far as they know, or shall be spiered at them. **1732** J. LOUTHIAN *Form of Process* (1752) 42 [as in prec.]. **1818** SCOTT *Hrt. Midl.* xv, Why do not you step forward, and bear leal and soothfast evidence in her behalf?

†**c.** Reliable, certain, sure. *Obs.*

a **1400** *Minor Poems fr. Vernon MS.* xxxii. 388 Þen schaltou haue soþfast knowyng, To knowe þi lord in whom is al. *a* **1400** HYLTON *Scala Perf.* II. xlii. (W. de W. 1494), This is a syker felynge & a sothfast. **1593** LODGE *Compl. Elstred* I 2 b, So wiser heads that knew the scourge of warre, Sought soth-fast meanes to mittigate the iarre.

†**3.** Truly or actually that which the name implies; true, real, veritable, very. Said esp. of God or of the persons of the Trinity. *Obs.*

a **1225** *Ancr. R.* 26 Almihti God, Feder, & Sune, & soðfest Holi Gost. *c* **1250** in *O.E. Misc.* 27 Be þet hi offrede gold, þet is cuuenable yeftte to kinge, seawede þet he was soth-fast kink. *c* **1340** HAMPOLE *Pr. Consc.* 8656 For als he es, þai salle him se þan, Sothfast God, and sothfast man. *c* **1374** CHAUCER *Troylus* v. 25 She that was sothfaste croppe, and moore, Of al his lust or joyes here tofore. *c* **1430** *Hymns Virgin* (1867) 47 In þe sooþfast sunne closid it was. **1456** SIR G. HAYE *Law Arms* (S.T.S.) 22 Mony was in that tyme callit papis, and was nocht suthfast. *c* **1470** *Gol. & Gaw.* 1045, I swere be suthfast God, that settis all on sevin!

†**b.** Of qualities, etc. *Obs.*

c **1175** *Lamb. Hom.* 57 Mid al þis haue þu charite, and soðfeste leaue and trowðe lef. *c* **1200** ORMIN 1572 Forr soþfasst lufe bærneþþ azz. *Ibid.* 2659 Þatt wass wiss-soþfasst metleȝȝc. **1377** LANGL. *P. Pl.* B. XIII. 217 Sobrete, and symple speche and sothfaste byleue.

B. *adv.* Soothfastly.

a **1300** *Cursor M.* 22926 All þe flexs þat was o þe man Sothfast sal be raised þan. *c* **1375** *Ibid.* 26961 (Fair.), Þe xv. point hit is þe laste þat þi shrift be made soþ-faste. **1867** EMERSON *May-Day* 26, I care not if the pomps you show Be what they soothfast appear.

'soothfastly, *adv.* Now *arch.* [f. prec.] In a soothfast manner; truthfully, truly, veritably, etc.

a **890** *Charter* in *O.E. Texts* 452 Ic..wille þæt hio sion soðfestliche..ȝetrymed me & minum erfeweardum. *c* **1200** ORMIN 2995 Forr uss birrþ unnderrstanndenn wel & soþfasstlike trowwenn, þatt [etc.]. *a* **1300** *Cursor M.* 9746, I sal on me..O thral tak clething sothfastli. *a* **1340** HAMPOLE *Psalter* x. 6 He anly demes sothfastly of þaire consciens. *a* **1400** HYLTON *Scala Perf.* I. lxviii. (W. de W. 1494), He that is perfytly and sothfastly meke. **1456** SIR G. HAYE *Law Arms* (S.T.S.) 26 The exposicioun of the visioun was suthfastly approvit. *c* **1500** *Lancelot* 1397 Suthfastly I will Ʒour ordynans in euery thing fulfyll. *a* **1555** PHILPOT *Exam. & Writ.* (Parker Soc.) 423 Whiles soothfastly they do confess Christ to be the saviour. **1818** SCOTT *Rob Roy* xxiii, But, if I were to come, wad ye really and soothfastly pay me the siller?

'soothfastness. Now *arch.* [f. SOOTHFAST *a.* + -NESS.]

1. The fact, condition, or quality of being soothfast in various senses; truth; truthfulness or veracity. †*in soothfastness*, in sooth.

c **825** *Vesp. Psalter* v. 10 Nis in muðe heara soðfestnis. *c* **888** K. ÆLFRED *Boeth.* xxxv. §1 Þeah bið simle corn þære soðfæstnesse sæd on þære sawle wuniȝende. **971** *Blickl. Hom.* 17 Drihten sylfa cwæþ, 'Ic eom weȝ soðfæstnesse'. *c* **1200** ORMIN 12920 And tiss iss soþfasstnessess hord þatt all mannkinn birrþ sekenn. *a* **1300** *Cursor M.* 2339 Ai lued he sothfastnes and right. *c* **1386** CHAUCER *Clerk's T.* 740 But now know I in verray sothfastnesse, That in gret lordschip ..Ther is gret servitude. *c* **1412** HOCCLEVE *De Reg. Princ.* 1199 Salamon yafe counseille, men shulden prey Two thynges unto God, in sothefastnesse. **1483** CAXTON *Gold. Leg.* 393/1 Sende thou in to us..the ghoost of sothfastnesse. *c* **1557** PARKER *Ps.* K ij, For as the Lorde is just in worde, so loveth he sothfastnes. **1590** LODGE *Euphues Gold. Leg.* K 3 b, These..are of power no more, Where beautie leanes to wit and soothfastnesse. **1607** WALKINGTON *Opt. Glass* 141 True and full of soothfastnesse. **1881** ROSSETTI *Ball. & Sonn.* 121 For here sit I..In full surrender and soothfastness.

2. With *the.* Also const. *of* (a person, statement, etc.).

c **888** K. ÆLFRED *Boeth.* xxxv. §6 Ne fo we no..on ða bispel for ðara leasena spella lufan, ac forðæmðe we woldon mid ȝebecnan þa soðfæstnesse. **971** *Blickl. Hom.* 55 Se mon se þa soþfæstnesse mid his muþe sprecþ. *c* **1055** *Byrhtferth's Handboc* in *Anglia* VIII. 335 Æfter þære soðfæstnysse þe þa iudeisce witan heoldon. *c* **1175** *Lamb. Hom.* 115 Ðes kingges ..sodfestnesse istaþeleð þes folkes stere. **1375** BARBOUR *Bruce* I. 7 The fyrst plesance is the carpyng, And the tothir the suthfastnes, That schawys the thing rycht as it wes. *c* **1386** CHAUCER *Melib.* ⁋209 To telle yow the sothfastnesse of thinges. *c* **1440** *Registr. Aberdon.* (Maitl. Cl.) I. 249 Þe bischap..askis þat he be distreignyt to schawe his charter for þe suthfastnes to be knawin. **1535** STEWART *Cron. Scot.* II. 558 The suithfastnes thairof rycht sone was schawin. **1571** GOLDING *Calvin on Ps.* ii. 6 The soothfastnesse of the Prophesye was shewed there by the ceremony of solemne consecration. **1830** CHAMBERS *Life Jas. I*, II. x. 278 The question seemed to hinge on the soothfastness of a chamber maid.

3. Personified.

c **897** K. ÆLFRED *Gregory's Past. C.* 409 Ðehieren eac ða.. hwæt sio Soðfæsðnes ðurh hie selfe cwæð. *a* **1300** *Cursor M.* 9545 Þe first o þam was cald merci, þe toþer was hatten sothfastnes. **1377** LANGL. *P. Pl.* B. XVI. 186 Þe secounde of þat sire is sothfastnesse, *filius.* *c* **1400** LOVE *Bonavent. Mirr.* (1908) 17 This douȝter sothfastnesse seith that sche perissheth.

soothful (ˈsuːθfʊl), *a.*¹ *Obs.* or *arch.* Also 4 sothfol, zoþuol; 9 *Sc.* soothfow. [f. SOOTH *a.* + -FUL.] True; truthful, veracious.

13.. *E.E. Allit. P.* A. 498 In sothfol gospel of god almyȝt. **1587** FLEMING *Contn. Holinshed* III. 1339/1 Gods heavenlie grace, and soothful skill reviving Antwerpe newe. **1813** SCOTT *Trierm.* III. xxxiii, Nay, soothful bards have said [etc.]. **1825** JAMIESON *Suppl.*, *A soothfow servant*, one who is not an eye-servant. Loth[ian].

Hence †**'soothfully** *adv.*, truly, really. *Obs.*$^{-1}$

1340 *Ayenb.* 133 Al þet he hedde..he yaf uor þet he wes zoþuolliche poure.

soothful (ˈsuːðfʊl), *a.*² [f. SOOTHE *v.* Cf. SOOTH *a.* 4.] Soothing; restful.

1886 J. ASHBY-STERRY *Lazy Minstrel* (1892) 163 Sweet are the zephyrs, hay-scented and soothful. **1896** —— *Tale Thames* iv. (1903) 28 A picture..agreeable to the eye and soothful to the mind. *Ibid.* 36 There was an indescribably soothful feeling about the place.

soothing (ˈsuːðɪŋ), *vbl. sb.* [f. SOOTHE *v.*] The action of the verb, in various senses.

a **1400** *Minor Poems fr. Vernon MS.* xlix. 185 For ȝif þou woldest hit putte to soþing þat he seyde ouur niȝt vppon þe morwening. *c* **1400** *Destr. Troy* 11495 Thus sotelly with sothyn he set hom a cas, What fortune might falle. *a* **1592** GREENE *Jas. IV*, 1131 Whilst cloking craft with soothing climbes so high. **1607** HIERON *Wks.* I. 430 Secret soothing and flattering of the heart. **1651** HOBBES *Leviath.* II. xxx. 184 The soothing of the people in their unreasonable, or irremediable grievances. **1702** ROWE *Tamerl.* I. i, Away, Deceiver; I will not hear thy Soothing. **1813** SCOTT *Rokeby* IV. x, 'Twas long ere soothing might prevail Upon the child to end the tale. **1847** HELPS *Friends in C.* I. iii. 40 This [trouble] appears..unworthy of having any remedy, or soothing, thought out for it.

b. *pl.* (In first quot. = soothsayings.)

1582 STANYHURST *Æneis* III. (Arb.) 78 Gods, quod he, this messadge turne you to a prosperus omen. Cancel theese menacing soothings, thee godlye reseruing. **1601** DENT *Pathw. Heaven* 372 Whether it bee more meet that I should beleeue the Scriptures, or your soothings iudge you. **1745** W. THOMPSON *Sickness* v. 135 Ideal sounds Soft-wafted on the Zephyr's fancy'd wing, Steal tuneful soothings on the easy ear. **1797** MRS. RADCLIFFE *Italian* xxv, The soothings of sympathy and the delicate arts of benevolence.

soothing (ˈsuːðɪŋ), *ppl. a.* [f. as prec.]

†**1.** Flattering, blandishing; specious, plausible.

1599 SHAKS., etc. *Pass. Pilgr.* i, O, love's best habit is a soothing tongue. **1603** DANIEL *Lady Anne Clifford* 76 The tongues of praise, And troopes of soothing people, that collaud All that we doe. **1644** MILTON *Bucer on Div.* Wks. 1851 IV. 338 Under a false and soothing title of Marriage. **1671** —— *P.R.* III. 6 At length collecting all his Serpent wiles, [he] With soothing words renew'd, him thus accosts.

2. a. That soothes, calms, quietens, etc.; pacifying, mollifying.

1746 FRANCIS tr. *Horace, Epist.* I. i. 49 The Power of Words, and soothing Sounds appease The raging Pain. **1766** FORDYCE *Serm. Yng. Wm.* (1767) II. xiii. 249 From an agreeable young woman..it is incredibly soothing. **1801** SOUTHEY *Thalaba* VI. ix, Lull'd by the soothing and incessant sound, The flow of many waters. **1849** MACAULAY *Hist. Eng.* i. I. 92 Had the King been wise, he would have pursued a cautious and soothing policy towards Scotland. **1872** BLACK *Adv. Phaeton* xii. 160 The soothing influences of dinner had departed.

b. Of medical applications, drugs, etc.; *spec.* *soothing powder* (in quot. *fig.*); *soothing syrup*, a medicinal preparation supposed to calm fretful children; freq. *fig.*, flattery; empty reassurance; merely palliative remedies;

mawkish or sentimental music, emotion, etc.; hence *soothing-syrupy* adj.

1839 *Spirit of Times* 27 Apr. 87/2 Then comes an ague from Canady, vich can't be cured by American Soothing Syrup nor Durham Mustard. **1861** *N.Y. Tribune* 26 Dec. 2/5 Don't fail to procure Mrs. Winslow's Soothing Syrup for children teething. **1896** *Allbutt's Syst. Med.* I. 422 Infants who are being drugged by unscrupulous nurses with 'soothing syrups' or other opiates. **1899** *Allbutt's Syst. Med.* VIII. 597 The affection..disappears in a few weeks under an iron tonic and a soothing application. **1901** W. Churchill *Crisis* II. ix. 193 Senator Bell was their candidate, and they proposed to give the Nation soothing-syrup. *Ibid.* xiv. 246 When the worst comes, the Soothing Syrup men will rally for the Union. **1902** G. H. Lorimer *Lett. Self-Made Merchant* xviii. 261 A lady..in a soothing-sirupy way asked if I would lend it to her. **1914** G. B. Shaw *Translations & Tomfooleries* (1926) 243, I really cannot earn two hundred and fifty guineas by playing soothing syrup to you. **1917** R. Fry *Let.* 20 July (1972) II. 415 My first soothing powder..was to have been a preface but got printed separately. **1926** E. Glyn *Love's Blindness* xvi. 183 If he dispelled..all alarm in Vanessa's imagination, it might possibly be only temporary soothing syrup. **1928** E. O'Neill *Strange Interlude* VIII. 305 Here are passion and hatred and regret and joy and pain and ecstasy, and these are men and women..whose blood is blood and not soothing syrup! **1945** *Richmond* (Va.) *Times-Dispatch* 26 Oct. 5/1 The race between Russia and the United States to obtain strategic bases is fooling no one but the American people—who are still being doped with soothing syrup that differences between ourselves and Russia are those of language and inexperience in foreign affairs. **1963** *Times* 21 Jan. 9/2 Mr. Macmillan and his colleagues must put away the soothing syrup that nothing is really as bad as it seems, that even if all is not quite for the best it automatically will be in the end. **1978** O. White *Silent Reach* xxvi. 268 That's a personal assurance, not official soothing syrup.

'soothingly, *adv.* [f. prec. + -LY².] In a soothing (†plausible, or flattering) manner; so as to soothe, quieten, tranquillize, etc.

1612 Shelton *Quix.* I. 386 Herewithall Anselmo rested the most soothingly and contentedly deceiued, that could be found in the world. **1648** Hexham II, *Smeeckelick*, Flatteringly, Soothingly. **1794** Mrs. Radcliffe *Myst. Udolpho* xxxi, So soothingly beautiful was the scene around her [etc.]. **1817** Shelley *Rev. Islam* I. lviii. 4 An eye of blue Looked into mine, like moonlight, soothingly. **1832** Lytton *Eugene A.* I. vi, 'You do not suffer bodily pain, I trust,' asked Walter, soothingly. **1880** Ruskin *Fors Clav.* lxxxviii. 108 What vexed..me, or returned soothingly to my memory.

'soothingness. *rare.* [f. as prec. + -NESS.] The quality or character of being soothing; a soothing property or feature.

1818 Coleridge *Lett.* (1895) II. 692 She is goodnatured, lively, innocent, but without a soothingness, or something I do not know what that is tender. **1876** Lowell *Among my Bks.* Ser. II. 179 In all this there is soothingness indeed, but no slumberous monotony.

'soothless, *a.* *rare*⁻¹. [f. SOOTH *sb.* + -LESS.] Untruthful; false.

1801 Campbell *Lochiel's Warn.* 78 Down, soothless insulter! I trust not the tale.

†**'soothly**, *a.* *Obs. rare.* [f. SOOTH *a.* + -LY¹.] Soothful, truthful; true, real, etc.

c **888** K. Ælfred *Boeth.* xxxviii. §5 Ne þincð me næfre nanwuht swa soðlic swa me þincað þine spell. *a* **1300** *Cursor M.* 13443 Bot iohn was sothlist in saus. *a* **1400** *Minor Poems fr. Vernon MS.* xlv. 2 Soþeli sawes I wol ȝou telle Of gentyl Ihesu. **1777** Mickle *Syr Martyn* I. xlvi, Dear was the kindlie love which Kathrin bore This crooked Ronion, for in soothly guise She was her genius and her counsellor.

soothly ('suːθlɪ), *adv.* (and *conj.*). Now *arch.* [f. SOOTH *a.* + -LY².]

1. In or with sooth or truth; truly, verily; as a matter of fact; assuredly, certainly, really; indeed.

Freq. in OE. and ME.; from *c* 1450 to *c* 1600 chiefly *Sc.* Very rare in the 17th and 18th centuries.

α. *c* **825** *Vesp. Psalter* lvii. 2 Ȝif soðlice [L. *vere*].. rehtwisnisse spreocað. *c* **950** *Lindisf. Gosp.* Mark xv. 39 Soðlice monn ðes sunu godes wæs. **971** *Blickl. Hom.* 59 Swyþe soþlice we maȝon ȝeþencan þæt hit biþ deaþes ylding. *c* **1175** *Lamb. Hom.* 15 Soðliche me þunched..þet al þas wrake is icumen ouer alle þeode. *c* **1200** Ormin 6445 Þær wass sene þatt ȝho wass Soþlike Godess moderr. *c* **1275** *Sinners Beware* 175 in *O.E. Misc.*, Soþliche betere heom were, þat heo ibore nere. *c* **1300** *Havelok* 276 Soþlike, in a lite[l] þrawe, Al Engelond of him stod awe. **1340** *Ayenb.* 74 Vor huo hier him demþ zoþliche, him ne worþ non hede to by uorlore. **1393** in *Collectanea Topogr.* (1836) III. 256 We ..were confeffes sotheliche in dede sesyd in the Manere of Slaptone. *c* **1430** *Pilgr. Lyf Manhode* I. lxxvi. (1869) 45 Soothliche litel thei wolden preysen my seyinge. **1590** Spenser *F.Q.* III. ii. 14 Ne soothlich it is easie for to read, Where now on earth, or how he may be found.

β. *a* **1300** *Cursor M.* 2552 Our lauerd steuen Sothli till him spak in sueuen. *c* **1384** Chaucer *H. Fame* 364 She wiste sothely he Was forthe vnto his shippes agoon. *c* **1400** Maundev. (Roxb.) vii. 27 Sothely it es noȝt likly þat þai schold be graues. *c* **1449** Pecock *Repr.* I. xi. 53 Sotheli if eny man vnknowith, he schal be vnknowun. **1513** Bradshaw *St. Werburge* 177 Secular prestes expulsed sothely were From diuers monasteries. **1596** Spenser *F.Q.* v. x. 8 For soothly he was one of matchlesse might. **1599** *Broughton's Let.* vi. 20 And soothly so you meant. **1721** Ramsay *To R.H.B.* iii, It soothly shaws them they can spare A rowth to spend. **1826** Hood *Irish Schoolm.* xxvii, So soothly kind is Erin to her own! **1850** Blackie *Æschylus* II. 186 Soothly a worthy deed, a pleasant tale For future years to tell! **1881** Swinburne *Mary Stuart* IV. iii, I would know soothly if your mind be changed.

γ. **1375** Barbour *Bruce* VI. 32 Quhen the Gallowais vist suthly, That he wes with a few menȝhe. *a* **1400-50** *Alexander* 1962 Suthely þou knawes, And wete þou wele [etc.]. *c* **1470** Henry *Wallace* VIII. 877 Yhe may nocht wyn ws suthlie, thocht ye bid. *c* **1550** Rolland *Crt. Venus* Prol. 13 The thrid clepit is Colerike suithlie. **1588** A. King tr. *Canisius' Catech.* 105 Quhilk office suthlie can na maner of vayis appertein to wemen.

b. With *say*, *tell*, etc.

a **1000** *Elene* 317 (Gr.), Weras..þa me soðlice secgan cunnon. *a* **1225** *Ancr. R.* 108 Leorne hit ȝeorne of him þet tu hit kunne, ant muwe soðliche siggen. *c* **1275** Lay. 26210 Ne may no man mid mouþe soþliche segge of haluendeal þan folke. **13..** *Cursor M.* 2398 (Gött.), I can noght say þe sothlier. *c* **1340** Hampole *Pr. Consc.* 6175 Suthly I say yhou, swa yhe wroght. *c* **1386** Chaucer *Knt.'s T.* 341 Whan that oon was deed, sothly to telle, His felawe wente and sought him down in helle. **1426** Audelay *Poems* 19 Thus sayth Marke sothely. *c* **1480** Henryson *Reas. Death & Man* 18 Thay call me deid, Suthly I the declair. **1564** Lady A. Bacon tr. *Jewel's Apol.* v. i. §3 Soothely to saie, no man.. woulde thinke the Jewes lawes..to be newe. **1582** Stanyhurst *Æneis* II. (Arb.) 46 King: mi faith I plight heere, to relate thee veritye soothlye. **1619** H. Hutton *Follie's Anat.* (Percy Soc.) 3 Of this same point I cannot soothly say. *a* **1656** Hales *Gold. Rem.* (1673) 48 He was fain ..to crave aid of his Equivocating Sophistry, and soothly to tell them, I have seen your face as the face of God. **1805** Scott *Last Minstrel* II. i, Then..home returning, soothly swear Was never scene so sad and fair! **1871** Rossetti *Poems, Love's Nocturn* viii, Master, is it soothly said That [etc.]?

†**2.** Used to render L. *autem*, *enim*, *ergo*, etc. *Obs.*

c **825** *Vesp. Psalter* ii. 6 Ic soðlice ȝeseted..eam cyning. *c* **975** *Rushw. Gosp.* Matt. i. 19 Ioseph soþlice hire wer..ne walde [etc.]. *a* **1050** *Liber Scintill.* (1889) 2 Þænne soþlice [L. *tunc enim*] mann fulfremed ys. *a* **1300** *E.E. Psalter* xxxvi. 35 Lauerd soth-like noght lete sal he Him in his hende to be. **1382** Wyclif *Matt.* xii. 15 Sothely Jhesus witynge, wente awey thennes. *c* **1460** *Eng. Reg. Oseney Abbey* (1907) 89 To þe which sothly entente þe forsaide Executours stryffe, saying [etc.].

'soothment. *rare*⁻¹. [f. SOOTHE *v.*] A soothing influence.

1900 *Academy* 28 Apr. 362/1 Oh, the placidity, the soft soul-soothment of living in the country!

†**'soothness.** *Obs.* [f. SOOTH *a.* + -NESS.]

1. The fact, quality, or condition of being true (in various senses); truth or verity; fidelity, faithfulness; reality, fact: **a.** Without article.

c **1275** *Passion our Lord* 365 in *O.E. Misc.*, Þo seyde pilates him to, hwat is soþnesse. **1297** R. Glouc. (Rolls) 988 Vor me mai bet soþnesse of þe moder þan of þe fader iwite. **1387** Trevisa *Higden* (Rolls) I. 71 Fame þat is false..falliþ out of mynde, oþer is despreued by soþenesse i-knowe. *c* **1440** *Eng. Conq. Ireland* 102 He was..of mych speche, & lytel sothnesse. **1530** Palsgr. 273/1 Sothenesse, *uerité*. **1587** Golding *De Mornay* iv. (1592) 43 Verely the most in effect that we can knowe concerning his being,..whether we terme it Soothnesse, or Wisedome,..or Godhead,..it cannot fit him.

personif. **1362** Langl. *P. Pl.* A. II. 163 Soþnesse sauh hem wel and seide bote luyte.

b. *in soothness*, in truth, reality, etc.

c **1386** Chaucer *Sec. Nun's T.* 261 Sayst thou thus to me In sothenes, or in drem I herkne this? *c* **1400** *Apol. Loll.* 27 Wan he is þus iugid & rettid of men, þow he be not so in soþnes. **1412-20** Lydg. *Chron. Troy* I. 330 For in sothnesse of al þer was noon That lyue myȝt by that fatal lawe.

2. With *the*. The truth.

1297 R. Glouc. (Rolls) 7236 Hii wepe & made deol ynou vor hii seye þe soþnesse. **1340** *Ayenb.* 44 Hede þe zoþnesse of þe þinge þet me wyle zelle. *c* **1374** Chaucer *Boeth.* I. pr. vi. (1868) 26 Ne neuer nas ȝit day þat myȝte putte me oute of þe soþenesse of þat sentence.

†**soothsaid**, *ppl. a.* *Obs.*⁻¹ [Cf. SOOTHSAY *v.*] Prophesied, prognosticated.

1582 Stanyhurst *Æneis* I. (Arb.) 18 But this her hole meaning a southsayd mysterie letted That from thee Troians should branch a lineal ofspring.

†**'soothsaw.** *Obs.* Also **sooth saw**. Forms: 1 **soðsaȝu, -saȝe**, 2 **soð-**, 3 **soþ-, sothsaȝe**, 4 **soþsagh**, 5 **sothesaugh**; 3-4 **soþ-**, 4 **soth-**, 4-5 **sothesawe**, 6 **sothsaw**; 4 **sooþ-**, 5 **soothsawe**, 6 **-saw**. [OE. *sóðsaȝu*: see SOOTH *a.* and SAW *sb.*² In later use sometimes not a comb., but a simple collocation of adj. and sb.]

1. The or an act of speaking the truth; (one's) truthfulness, truth.

c **950** *Lindisf. Gosp.* Matt., Int. 7/2 Soðspell *vel* soðsaȝa [= *historia*]. *a* **1023** Wulfstan *Hom.* x. (1883) 74 On manna ȝehwylces mode and muðe soðsaȝu stande. *c* **1380** Wyclif *Treat.* Sel. Wks. III. 6 Aȝein hem þat in blindenes of malice pursuen me for my sooþsawe. *c* **1400** *Rom. Rose* 6125 Though that thou shuldist for thi sothe-sawe Ben al to-beten and to-drawe. *c* **1440** *Gesta Rom.* xlv. 175 (Harl. MS.), My felowe for his sothe sawe, hathe loste his lyf. *c* **1483** Caxton *Epil. Chaucer's H. Fame* d v, This noble man Gefferey Chaucer fynysshyd at the sayd conclusion of the metyng of lesyng and sothsawe.

2. A true saying, statement, or account; a truth.

α. *a* **1250** *Owl & Night.* 1038 Hit was iseid in olde laȝe, An ȝet ilast þilke soþsaȝe [etc.]. *a* **1300** *Cursor M.* 8911 For þe loue o þis soth-sagh. **1362** Langl. *P. Pl.* A. XI. 16 Al þe soþ sawes þat Salamon seide euere. *c* **1384** Chaucer *H. Fame* 2089 A lesynge & a sad soth-sawe. *c* **1430** *Wycliffite Bible* Pref. Ep. ix, For it is an old sothsawe, to the auarouse man as wel lackith the good that he hath, as that he hath not.

β. *c* **1250** *Gen. & Ex.* 14 Ut of latin ðis song is draȝen on engleis speche, on soðe saȝen. *c* **1330** R. Brunne *Chron. Wace* (Rolls) 2298 Sey me þe soþe sawe: How mykel louestou me wyþ wylle? *c* **1384** Chaucer *H. Fame* 676 Thou shalt here..moo tydynges, Bothe sothe sawes and leysinges. **1519** *Interl. Four Elem.* (Percy Soc.) 17, I..gyve the absolucion For thy soth saws; stande up, Jackdaw! *c* **1530** *Hickscorner* (1905) 129, I came..to preach and teach of God's sooth saws Ayenst vice.

soothsay ('suːθseɪ), *sb.* Forms: 6 **sothsay**, 6-7 **southsaye**, 6, 9 **soothsay**, 6 **-saye**. [Back-formation from SOOTHSAYER or SOOTHSAYING *vbl. sb.*: cf. prec. Also written as two words and occas. with hyphen.]

†**1.** A true or wise saying; a proverb, saw. *Obs.*⁻¹

1549 Latimer *Sev. Serm. bef. Edw. VI* (Arb.) 97 An old soth say, but thoughe the sayinge be none of the newist I feare me yet is it one of the trwest.

2. A prediction, prognostication, or prophecy; an omen or portent.

1582 Stanyhurst *Æneis* IV. (Arb.) 96 O the superstitions of beldam trumperye sooth says. **1590** Spenser *F.Q.* II. ix. 51 Shewes, visions, sooth-sayes, and prophesies. **1634** Sir T. Herbert *Trav.* 219 Those foretelling Southsayes.. which without question were knowne unto this Madoc. **1641** Brightman *Predict.* 2 Merlin,..whose South-saies (for so they called them in old time) have proved true even to these latter dayes. **1870** Rossetti *Poems, House of Life* vii, They told me she was sad that day, (Though wherefore tell what love's soothsay, Sooner than they, did register?).

b. Without article. (Good) omen; soothsaying, prognostication. *rare.*

1590 Spenser *F.Q.* III. viii. 50 Aye me,..the signes be sad, And but God turne the same to good soothsay, That Ladies safetie is sore to be drad. **1831** tr. *Tieck's Old Man of Mountain*, etc. 246 Do not you seem to know everything, or else to have learnt it by soothsay?

'soothsay, *v.* *rare.* Also 7 **southsay**. [Back-formation from SOOTHSAYER or SOOTHSAYING *vbl. sb.* Cf. OE. *sóðsecgan* to say or speak truly.] *intr.* To make predictions, to foretell future events; to predict, prophesy. Also with *it*.

1606 Shaks. *Ant. & Cl.* I. ii. 52 Go you wilde Bedfellow, you cannot Soothsay. **1611** Cotgr., *Diviner*, to diuine, presage, soothsay it. **1652** Gaule *Magastrom.* 226 Wherefore suffumigations are wont to be used to them that are about to southsay, for to affect their fancy. **1736** Ainsworth *Lat. Dict.* II, *Vero*,..to soothsay, as wisards, and wise women do. **1850** Blackie *Æschylus* II. 160 Even he soothsaying sings that the Argive camp Holds midnight council to attack the city. **1877** *Daily News* 19 Oct. 6/3 The next fortnight may therefore be pregnant with news, good or evil to the Turkish cause—who will soothsay?

soothsayer ('suːθˌseɪə(r)). Forms: *α.* 4 **zoþ ziggere, sothsegger(e**, 4 **soþ-, sothseyere, -seiere**, 5 **-seyer**, 5-6 **-sayer**, 6 **sothe-, soythsayer**, 6 **soothsaier**, 7- **soothsayer**. *β.* 6 **southeseyer**, 6-7 **southsaier**, 6-8 **-sayer**. [f. SOOTH *sb.* or *a.* + SAYER *sb.*]

†**1.** One who speaks the truth; a truthful or veracious person. *Obs.*

1340 *Ayenb.* 256 Senekes zayþ þet þer ne lackeþ to greate lhordes bote zoþ ziggeres. Vor hi habbeþ lyeȝeres and vlatours to greate cheape and veawe zoþ ziggeres. **1390** Gower *Conf.* III. 164 The Sothseiere tho was lief, Which wolde noght the trouthe spare. *c* **1400** in Herrig *Archiv* CIV. 306 Bettre is chidyng of a soþ-seyere þen deceyuyng of a losyngere. **1642** Milton *Apol. Smect.* Wks. 1851 III. 306 In that which followes, he does not play the Soothsayer but the diabolick slanderer of prayers.

2. One who claims or pretends to the power of foretelling future events; a predictor, prognosticator.

α. **1381** *Rolls of Parlt.* III. 113/ Johannes Say, Soth-seggere. **14..** *Lat.-Eng. Voc.* in Wr.-Wülcker 595 *Mastromaticus*, a sothseyer. *c* **1491** *Chast. Goddes Chyld.* 53 Some sheew prophecye in the spyrite of deuil as ben thise men and wymen whiche men calle dyuynours or sothsayers. **1535** Coverdale *Isaiah* viii. 19 Yf they saye vnto you: aske councel at the soythsayers, witches, charmers and coniurers. **1599** B. Jonson *Cynthia's Rev.* II. v, Sow-gelders, and Sooth-saiers. Gipsies and Iaylers. **1606** Shaks. *Ant. & Cl.* I. ii. 2 Where's the Soothsayer that you prais'd so to th' Queene? **1665** Manley *Grotius' Low C. Wars* 965 While their Sooth-sayers..draw the Peoples minds changable by Superstition, now this way, now that way. **1732** Lediard *Sethos* II. VII. 36 We are guided here by priests and soothsayers. **1791** Cowper *Iliad* II. 1015 Merops, expert in the sooth-sayer's art. **1821** Byron *Sardanap.* II. i, Now were I a soothsayer, I would have boded so much to myself. **1878** J. H. Gray *China* II. xvii. 3 Blind soothsayers are to be met with in all parts of the empire.

β. **1503** *Churchw. Acc. St. Marg., Westm.* (Nichols, 1797) 4 Recieved of the Southeseyer for iv Tapers. *a* **1548** Hall *Chron., Hen. VI*, 27 Jone the Puzel, whom he vsed as an oracle and a southsaier. **1596** Lodge *Divel Coniured* G iij, Some be shepheards, some southsaiers, and so of other crafts and trades. **1621** Burton *Anat. Mel.* I. ii. III. ii. 125 Some Southsayer, wise-man, fortune-teller, or Physition. **1646** Sir T. Browne *Pseud. Ep.* (1650) 12 On this foundation were built the conclusions of Southsayers in their Auguriall and Tripudiary divinations. **1727** De Foe *Syst. Magic* I. i. (1840) 20 By this study they obtained the name of southsayers and astrologers, added to that of magicians.

3. *transf.* An insect of the family *Mantidæ*; a mantis (cf. quot. 1855).

1855 Dallas in *Orr's Circ. Sci., Org. Nat.* II. 359 Another prevalent superstition regarding these creatures is, that if they be asked the way to a place they will immediately indicate the right road by holding one of their legs in that direction,—hence the name of *Soothsayers*, often applied to these insects. *c* **1884** *Cassell's Nat. Hist.* VI. 13 The Mantidæ, Praying Insects, or Soothsayers.

Hence **'soothsaye,ress**, a female soothsayer. **'soothsayership**, prediction, soothsaying, or skill in this.

1648 HEXHAM II, *Een Waerseggeresse, ofte waerseghster*, a Shee-divine, or a Soothsayeresse. **1828** MISS MITFORD *Village* Ser. III. (1863) 118 He had the good fortune to foretell.. the downfal of Napoleon Buonaparte—a piece of soothsayership which has established his reputation. **1875** STEVENSON in Colvin *Lett.* (1901) II. 92 'Yes, my dear,' replied the soothsayeress.

soothsaying ('su:θ,seɪɪŋ), (*vbl.*) *sb.* Also 6 **soythsayenge**, 6–8 **southsaying**. [f. SOOTH *sb.* or *a.* + SAYING (*vbl.*) *sb.*[1]]

1. The practice of foretelling the future or the course of future events; prediction, prognostication.

1535 COVERDALE *Ecclus.* xxxiv. 5 Soythsayenge, witchcraft, sorcery, and dreaminge is but vanyte. *a* **1591** H. SMITH *Wks.* (1867) II. 412 He used soothsaying and divination. **1610** HOLLAND *Camden's Brit.* 652 Wonderfull skilfull in Sooth-saying by the Inspection of Beasts inwards. **1652–62** HEYLIN *Cosmogr.* III. (1682) 21 Famous for Southsaying, and accounted the first Interpreters of dreams. **1727** DE FOE *Syst. Magic* I. iii. (1840) 61 If the wise men.. did not daily produce some new discoveries, it was evident the price and rate of southsaying would come down to nothing. **1850** MAURICE *Mor. & Met. Philos.* (ed. 2) 8 They practise magic and soothsaying: they are the advisers of the king. **1906** J. ORR *Problem of O.T.* xii. 454 Such a view puts prophecy on a level with 'soothsaying'.

2. An instance of this; a prediction or prophecy.

1535 COVERDALE *Micah* v. 12 All witchcraftes will I rote out of thyne hande, there shall no mo soythsayenges be within the. **1585** T. WASHINGTON tr. *Nicholay's Voy.* IV. xix. 134 The art magick, and all other sorts of southsayings. **1629** GAULE *Holy Madn.* 120 At length [he] is content to yield to others Sooth-sayings before the Testimony of his owne Conscience. **1653** HOLCROFT *Procopius, Pers. War* I. 30 Hearkning to impious South-sayings, vainly foretelling to him the Imperiall dignity. **1864** SWINBURNE *Atalanta* 2009 Also for visions that were, And soothsayings spoken in sleep.

So **'sooth,saying** *ppl. a.*, that acts the part of soothsayer; of the nature of, or characterized by, soothsaying. Now *rare*.

1550 W. LYNNE *Carion's Cron.* 24 Sibylla.. signifieth.. a prophetisse or southsayenge woman. **1634** MILTON *Comus* 874 By scaly Tritons winding shell, And old sooth-saying Glaucus spell. **1652** GAULE *Magastrom.* 280 It was a soothsaying divination that provoked to doe the deed. **1727** DE FOE *Syst. Magic* I. iv. (1840) 114 How much were it to be wished, that some of our southsaying wits, who are neither wise men or southsayers [etc.]. **1911** W. W. FOWLER *Relig. Exper. Rom. People* xiii. 296 We hear.. a great deal of wandering soothsayers, soothsaying families, and oracles.

'sootily, *adv.* [f. SOOTY *a.* + -LY[2].] In a sooty manner.

1888 LOWELL *Lett.* (1894) II. x. 405 Silently and sootily pervasive as the fog.

'sootiman. *nonce-wd.* [f. SOOT *sb.*[1] or SOOTY *a.*] A chimney-sweep.

1810 SIR A. BOSWELL *Edinb.* Poet. Wks. (1871) 49 Reckless of the bright Lochaber axe, The sable *sootiman* would dust his sacks.

'sootiness. [f. SOOTY *a.* + -NESS.] The condition or property of being sooty; dirtiness or blackness from, or as from, soot.

1611 COTGR., *Fuligine*, soot, sootinesse; smoakinesse. *c* **1628** DONNE *Serm.* lv. (1640) 557 There growes a blacknesse, a sootinesse upon the soule, by custome in sin. **1727** in BAILEY (vol. II). **1866** *Spectator* 1 Dec. 1339 Every new addition.. is successively hailed.., and then passes into deserved contempt and sootiness. **1892** *Photogr. Ann.* II. 711 That dense sootiness which so frequently spoils collotype work.

'sootish, *a. rare.* [f. SOOT *sb.*[1]] Sooty.

1582 STANYHURST *Æneis* IV. (Arb.) 111 The wyne, in powring, lyke blood black sootish apeered. **1646** SIR T. BROWNE *Pseud. Ep.* 334 Things become blacke by a sootish and fuliginous matter proceeding from the sulphur of bodies torrified.

'sootless, *a.* [f. SOOT *sb.*[1]] Free from soot.

1890 *Nature* 8 May 25 There is nothing to prevent even such towns.. from having atmospheres at least as sootless as that of London.

†**'sootly**, *adv. Obs. rare.* Forms: 2 **swotlice**, 3 **swoteliche, -luche**, 7 **swootly**. [f. *swōt* SOOT *a.* + -LY[2].] In a sweet or pleasant manner; sweetly.

a **1125** in Napier *Contrib. O.E. Lex.* 60 Heo byð swa swotlice ȝefostrede. *a* **1225** *Leg. Kath.* 1392 Ah heo ham onswerede, & swoteliche seide [etc.]. *c* **1230** *Hali Meid.* 41 He vnderfeð bliðeliche, & biclupped swoteluche, þe alre laðlukest. **1614** J. DAVIES *Willy & Wernocke* Wks. (Grosart) II. 20 Chaplets.. To crowne their scalpes that couth most swootly sing.

†**soot-meat.** *Obs.*[−1] [f. SOOT *a.* Cf. OE. *swōtmettas.*] A sweetmeat.

1614 J. DAVIES (Heref.) *Eclogue* 20 Wks. (Grosart) II. 19/1 For, fro thy Makings, milke, and mellie, flowes To feed the Songster-swaines with Arts soot-meats.

†**'sootness.** *Obs.* Forms: 1 **suotnis(se, swotnysse**, 3–4 **swot-**, 4 **swote-, suotnesse**; 4 **sootnes.** [f. SOOT *a.* + -NESS.] The character or quality of being sweet; sweetness.

c **1000** in Cockayne *Shrine* 16 Mycel swotnysse stænc. *c* **1000** *Rituale Eccl. Dunelm.* (Surtees) 88 In stencg svotnisses, *in odore suavitatis. a* **1225** *Ancr. R.* 92 Efter þet me iveleð his swete swotnesse,—efter þet me luueð hine more oðer lesse. *a* **1300** *Leg. Rood* (1871) 28 þe suotnesse þat þer-of com, velde al þat lond. **1382** WYCLIF *Numb.* xv. 3 Brennynge smelle of swetnes [*v.r.* sootnes] to the Lord. —— *Ecclus.* xxiv. 23, I as a vyne frutede swotnesse of smel.

sooty ('sʊtɪ), *a.* Forms: 3 **soti**, 3, 5 **soty**, 4– **sooty**, 6–8 **sootie**; 5 **soyty, sutty**, 6 **swuttie.** [f. SOOT *a.* + -Y. Cf. ON. and Icel. *sótigr, sótugr*, MSw. *sotogher*, Sw. *sotig*.

It is difficult to regard the early south-western *suti* SUTY *a.* as a mere variant of this.]

1. a. Foul or dirty with soot; covered or smeared with soot; full of soot.

a **1250** *Owl & Night.* 578 þu art dim, an of fule howe, An þinchest a lutel soti [*v.r.* soty] clowe. *c* **1386** CHAUCER *Nun's Pr. T.* 12 Ful sooty was hir bour, and eek hir halle. *a* **1400** *Octavian* 800 Clement broghte forthe schelde and spere, .. Soyty [*v.r.* sutty] and alle vnclene. *c* **1440** *Promp. Parv.* 465/2 Soty, or fowlyd wythe soot, *fuliginosus.* **1530** PALSGR. 325/1 Sooty, full of sowte as a chymnay is, *suyeux.* **1599** NASHE *Lenten Stuff* Wks. (Grosart) V. 275 Hee.. hung the residue.. in the sooty roofe of his shad a drying. **1625** K. LONG tr. *Barclay's Argenis* II. xxii. 143 They are still smokie and sootie and in all their colour shew they come from the fire. **1675** HOBBES *Odyssey* (1677) 301 Till from above In thunder Jove his sooty bolt down threw. **1700** T. BROWN tr. *Fresny's Amusem.* 21 Here a Sooty Chimney-Sweeper takes the Wall of a Grave Alderman. **1773** J. BERRIDGE *Wks.* (1864) 96 His own sooty cap is full as good as your rusty bonnet. **1818** SCOTT *Br. Lamm.* xviii, He found that faithful servitor in his sooty and ruinous den. **1895** MEREDITH *Amazing Marriage* viii, When the wind puffs down a sooty chimney the air is filled with little blacks.

transf. **1740** SOMERVILLE *Hobbinol* II. (1749) 133 The furious God In sooty Triumph rides dreadful. **1872** TENNYSON *Gareth & Lynette* 469 So Gareth.. underwent The sooty yoke of kitchen vassalage. **1878** HARE *Walks in Lond.* I. iv. 128 St. Paul's Cathedral.. has a peculiar sooty dignity all its own.

b. Of the soul: Foul with sin.

1655 FULLER *Serm., Best Act Obliv.* 5 How could David's soule in his youth be sooty with sinne? **1680** C. NESSE *Church Hist.* 254 The sooty souls of those nobles.. under their white garments.

c. Of grain: Affected by smut; blackened.

1697 DRYDEN *Virg. Past.* x. 113 Unwholsome Dews.. That blast the sooty Corn.

2. a. Resembling soot in colour; dusky or brownish black.

1593 NASHE *Christ's T.* 61 b, The blacke swuttie visage of the night. **1602** MARSTON *Antonio's Rev.* III. v, Yee sootie coursers of the night. **1640** QUARLES *Sighs* ii. Wks. (Grosart) III. 39 Do'st thou think To glorifie thy Skill In Sooty Characters of Inke? **1766** STERNE in Scoones *Four C. Eng. Lett.* (1880) 249 From the fairest face about St. James's to the sootiest complexion in Africa. **1776** *Addison's Spect.* No. 412 ¶5 The black-bird hence selects her sooty spouse. **1817** BYRON *Beppo* xviii, Not like that sooty devil of Othello's. **1839** LINDLEY *Introd. Bot.* (ed. 3) 478 *Sooty*.., dirty brown, verging upon black. **1845** GOSSE *Ocean* iv. (1849) 164 Their sooty wings horizontally extended. **1964** L. DEIGHTON *Funeral in Berlin* xvii. 105 The girl.. fluttered her big sooty eyes. **1976** 'A. HALL' *Kobra Manifesto* ii. 23 Black hair and a grey face and sooty bags under his eyes.

b. *fig.* or in fig. context. Black, dismal.

1657 R. LIGON *Barbadoes* (1673) 118, I give the Reader but a Sooty Relation of my Maladies. **1659** W. CHAMBERLAYNE *Pharonnida* v. 204 Strook such a terror as if shadow'd by Death's sooty vail. **1673** O. WALKER *Educ.* ix. 78 Better for them to chide even without reason, then store up this sooty humour.

c. In the names of birds, etc., as ***sooty albatross, owl, petrel, tern***, etc.

1777 G. FORSTER *Voy. round World* I. 91 We likewise saw the two before mentioned species of albatrosses.., together with a third,.. which we named the *sooty. **1829** GRIFFITH tr. *Cuvier* VIII. 573 Sooty Albatros. *Diomedea Fuliginosa.* **1872** COUES *N. Amer. Birds* 326 Sooty Albatross. Fuliginous brown, nearly uniform. **1884** *Ibid.* 580 *Canace obscura fuliginosa*, *Sooty Grouse. **1872** *Ibid.* 345 *Sooty Guillemot. **1879** *Sooty mangabey [see MANGABEY]. **1785** PENNANT *Arct. Zool.* II. 232 *Sooty Owl. Cinereous Owl. **1785** LATHAM *Gen. Synop. Birds* III. II. 409 *Sooty Petrel.. inhabits Otaheite. **1802** [see PETREL]. **1891** *Boston* (Mass.) *Jrnl.* 21 Feb. 5/3 These birds were sooty petrels. **1872** COUES *N. Amer. Birds* 331 *Sooty Shearwater. Dark sooty brown. **1785** PENNANT *Arct. Zool.* II. 523 *Sooty Tern,.. crown, hind part of the head and neck, back, and wings, of a sooty blackness. **1870** GILLMORE tr. *Figuier's Reptiles & Birds* 281 The Sooty Tern (*Sterna fuliginosa*) inhabits the bays and gulfs of the Mediterranean. **1801** LATHAM *Gen. Synop. Birds* Suppl. II. 185 *Sooty Thrush... The general colour of the plumage is dark greenish brown. **1783** —— *Gen. Synop. Birds* II. I. 451 *Sooty Warbler, *Motacilla fulicata*. *c* **1880** *Cassell's Nat. Hist.* III. 114 The *Sooty Water Mouse (*Hydromys fuliginosus*) is an inhabitant of Western Australia.

d. *absol.* as a moth-name.

Also ***Old Sooty***, the Devil. *dial.*

1832 J. RENNIE *Consp. Butterfl. & M.* 98 The Sooty (*Acosmetia caliginosa*) appears in June.

e. In the names of plant diseases, as ***sooty blotch***, a fungal disease of apples, pears, and citruses which is caused by *Glœodes pomigena* and gives rise to darkish blotches on the skin of the fruit; ***sooty mould***, any of several fungal diseases of trees and shrubs which cause a dark discoloration of their fruit.

1901 H. M. WARD *Disease in Plants* xxv. 232 [Honeydew] serves as nutritive material for various epiphytic fungi—*e.g.* sooty mould, *Capnodium, Fumago*, and *Antennaria.* **1902** *Ann. Rep. Secretary Connecticut Board Agric. 1901* 132 Among the diseases in this class which prey upon either the fruit or the foliage of the apple.. are the bitter rot.. and the sooty blotch. **1939** Sooty blotch [see *fly-speck* s.v. FLY *sb.*[1] 11]. **1939** *Ann. Bot.* III. 401 The distinction between parasitic and saprophytic 'sooty moulds'.. appears to be valid. **1952** E. RAMSDEN tr. *Gram & Weber's Plant Diseases* ii. 126/2 Sooty mould can be avoided by keeping the tree free from aphides. *Ibid.* 127/1 Associated with *Leptothyrium pomi* is usually the fungus of sooty blotch, *Gloeodes pomigena.* **1969** G. N. AGRIOS *Plant Path.* ii. 19 Certain fungi, e.g., those causing sooty molds, can cause disease by growing on the surface of the plant and feeding on insect excretions rather than by parasitizing the plant.

3. Of colours: Having a dark, dusky, blackish, or dirty tinge.

(*a*) **1597** BP. HALL *Sat.* I. vii, Be shee all sootie-black, or bery-browne, Shee's white as morrows milk. **1730–46** THOMSON *Autumn* 952 Of every hue, from wan declining green To sooty dark. **1796** WITHERING *Brit. Plants* (ed. 3) IV. 296 Gills sooty grey, that is, powdered with black. **1828** STARK *Elem. Nat. Hist.* I. 112 Fur sooty brown above, grayish below. **1855** SMEDLEY *Occult Sciences* 54 Sooty-red was also the colour of Typhon. **1887** W. PHILLIPS *Brit. Discomycetes* 406 The cups are seated on a sooty-black space.

(*b*) **1635** SWAN *Spec. M.* v. §2 (1643) 121 The things which it [lightning] striketh do use to look black, or of a sootie colour. **1658** R. WHITE tr. *Digby's Powd. Symp.* (1660) 39 All the white flowers are sullied with a sooty blackness. **1763** JOHNSON in *Boswell* 25 June (Oxf. ed.) I. 268 By the heat of the sun the skin is scorched, and so acquires a sooty hue. **1785** [see *sooty tern* in 2c]. **1884** NEWTON in *Encycl. Brit.* XVII. 531/1 The plumage [of the noddy] is of a uniform sooty hue.

4. Consisting of soot; of the nature of soot.

1651 CHARLETON & P. M. *Ephes. & Cimm. Matrons* (1668) 49 Gross and sooty Exhalations, such as arise from ardors of the Body. **1683** SNAPE *Anat. Horse* v. ii. (1686) 199 To be vents of the Brain, through which the impure and sooty excrements might exhale or evaporate. **1784** COWPER *Task* IV. 292 The sooty films that play upon the bars, Pendulous. **1789** J. WILLIAMS *Min. Kingd.* I. 211 A quantity of black sooty stuff being thrown up by the spade or the plough. **1846** GREENER *Sci. Gunnery* 179 The barrels must be passed.. through that flame.. until the whole are covered with a black sooty covering. **1902** A. C. HARMSWORTH *Motors & Motor Driving* 140 The interior of the tube becoming blackened by sooty deposit.

5. *Comb.*, as ***sooty-eyed, -faced, -like, -mossed, -mouthed, -plumed*** adjs.

1684 OTWAY *Atheist* III. i, One of those Sooty-fac'd Harlots. **1789** J. WILLIAMS *Min. Kingd.* I. 28 A soft, sooty-like substance. **1806** J. GRAHAME *Birds of Scot.* 58 The sooty-plum'd hedge-sparrow. **1826** *Blackw. Mag.* XX. 512 Let not our readers imagine that this sooty-mouthed Libeller is poor and ignorant. **1874** G. M. HOPKINS *Jrnls. & Papers* (1959) 247 Sooty-mossed boulders in foreground. **1964** L. DEIGHTON *Funeral in Berlin* xvii. 106 The sooty-eyed girl laughed.

Hence **'sootied** *pa. pple.*, made sooty, blackened.

1615 CHAPMAN *Odyss.* XIII. 635 Shirt and coat, all rent Tann'd, and all sootied with noisome smoke.

sooza, obs. form of SOOSY.

sop (sɒp), *sb.*[1] Also 1, 7 **sopp**, 4 (9 *dial.*) **zop**, 4–5, 7 **sope**, 4–7 **soppe**; 8– *Sc.* (*pl.*) **saps.** [OE. *sopp*, *sop-*, app. f. the weak grade of *súpan* SUP *v.*[1] In ME. prob. reinforced by the synonymous OF. *sope, soupe* (see SOUP *sb.*), and in later senses partly from SOP *v.*

The exact relationship of the OE. to the OF. word is not clear. Cf. also MDu. *soppe, zoppe* (WFlem. *zoppe*), *sop*, ON. *soppa* (a foreign word), in the same sense.]

1. A piece of bread or the like dipped or steeped in water, wine, etc., before being eaten or cooked.

a **1100** in Napier *O.E. Glosses* lvi. 10 *Offulam*, sopp. **1340** *Ayenb.* 107 Ase is a zop of hot bryead huanne me hit poteþ in-to wyn. *c* **1375** *Sc. Leg. Saints* iii. (*Andrew*) 375 þane gaf he ilkane a sope with his hand of his awne cope. *c* **1420** *Liber Cocorum* (1862) 53 3et sugurt soppes I nyl forȝete, þou tost shyves of gode manchete [etc.]. *c* **1450** *Two Cookery Bks.* 90 Then cast the same licour vppon þe Soppes, and serue hit forthe fore a good potage. **1484** CAXTON *Fables of Æsop* v. xii, Euery daye the sayd dogge hadde soppes of brede, and of drye breed he hadde ynough. **1520** *Calisto & Melib.* in Hazl. *Dodsley* I. 79 With a toast in wine by the fire I could sit With two dozen sops the colic to quell. **1589** R. HARVEY *Pl. Perc.* (1860) 9 Go to then, and take salt to your soppes, lest sorrow attaint them. **1617** MORYSON *Itin.* III. 117 The fairest Weomen will dine with the same [wine], and a sop of bread dipped in it. *a* **1632** T. TAYLOR *God's Judgem.* II. v. (1642) 68 He would set before his guests onely.. two sops and a few apples. **1697** DRYDEN *Æneid* VI. 567 The prudent Sibyl had before prepar'd A sop, in honey steep'd. **1801** SOUTHEY *St. Patrick's Purgatory* ii, Three sops were brought of bread and wine. **1825** BROCKETT *N.C. Gloss.*, *Sop*, a piece of bread soaked in dripping under the roast. **1862** C. C. ROBINSON *Dial. Leeds* 416 *Sops*, bread broken preparatory to being added to any liquid, or when so added.

attrib. *a* **1000** in Thorpe *Dipl. Angl. Sax.* (1865) 527 Anæ soppcuppan an þrym pundan. **1012** *Ibid.* 553 Ic ann minæn cinæhlafordæ.. anræ sopcuppan.

fig. **1377** LANGL. *P. Pl.* B. xv. 175 If he soupeth, ette but a soppe of *spera-in-deo.* **1631** MASSINGER *Believe as You List* IV. iii, Yf there bee a Cerberus, yf I serve not To make three sopps for his three heads,.. The cur is divelishe hungrie.

†**b.** ***to eat*** (or ***take***) ***a sop***, to make a slight repast. *Obs.*

c **1330** R. BRUNNE *Chron. Wace* (Rolls) 7547 Preyenge ..þat he wolde.. herberwe him wyþ, A day to ete a sop, & drynke, & se his werk. **13..** *Gaw. & Gr. Knt.* 1135 þe leue lorde.. Ete a sop hastyly, when he hade herde masse. *c* **1400** *Laud Troy Bk.* 7932 Than thei ȝede and toke a sop, Thei ete a sop, and afftir dranke. *c* **1440** *Gesta Rom.* xii. 39 (Harl. MS.), If þat ȝe woll voche-safe to take a soppe with me.

c. Const. *in* (or †*of*) the liquid in which the bread, etc., is dipped or steeped.

c **1386** CHAUCER *Prol.* 334 (Harl.), Wel loved he in the morn a sop of [*v.r.* in] wyn. —— *Merch. T.* 631 Thanne he taketh a sope in fyne clarree. *a* **1450** *Knt. de la Tour* (1868)

28 She made euery day dresse..for hem disshes withe soppes of mylke. *c* **1491** *Chast. Goddes Chyld.* 13 Hit is nede that he take a soppe in ale or in wine before mete. *c* **1530** LD. BERNERS *Arth. Lyt. Bryt.* (1814) 363 Suche as wold, toke a sop in wine. *a* **1533** —— *Huon* xiv. 38 They toke a soppe of wyne. **1605** SYLVESTER *Du Bartas* II. iii. III. *Law* 899 Preferring far, Red-Herrings, Rashers, and (some) sops in Tar. **1832** W. STEPHENSON *Gateshead Local Poems* 95 When at the fire they're roasting, We're all to have sops in the grease.

d. ***sop in the pan***, a piece of bread soaked in the dripping from roasting meat. Also *fig.*

1621 FLETCHER *Pilgrim* III. vi, You shall have no more sops i' th' pan else, nor no Porridge. **1786** MRS. A. M. BENNETT *Juvenile Indiscr.* I. 61 A plate of toast and grease, vulgarly called sop in the pan. **1814** SCOTT *Wav.* xxv, This he considered as a mere sop in the pan to stay the appetite of Edward's curiosity.

e. A dish composed of soaked bread.

1845 YOUATT *Dog* ii. 36 Milk at first, and afterwards milk and sop alternately, may be used. **1892** P. H. EMERSON *Son of Fens* xxxii. 334 'What are you going to ha' for breakfast this morning?' mother ax him. 'A baisin of sop.'

2. *transf.* and *fig.* †**a.** Used to denote something of small value. *Obs.*

1377 LANGL. *P. Pl.* B. XIII. 124 [He] hath..sette alle sciences at a soppe saue loue one. **1526** SKELTON *Magnyf.* 2261 Tushe, these maters that ye moue are but soppys in ale.

†**b.** Used of persons in respect of some pervading quality or property. *Obs.*

c **1480** HENRYSON *Test. Cres.* 407 O sop of sorrow, sonken into cair! O Catiue Creisseid! *c* **1550** ROLLAND *Crt. Venus* II. 104 Thair was the sop of science, I suppois: Thair was the flour of fairheid [etc.]. **1605** SHAKS. *Lear* II. ii. 35 For though it be night, yet the Moone shines, Ile make a sop oth' Moonshine of you.

c. A dull or foolish fellow; a milksop.

a **1625** FLETCHER & MASS. *Elder Brother* IV. i, Ye have no more spirit than three sleepy sops. **1859** *Slang Dict.* 58 *Sop*, a soft or foolish man.

d. A person or thing thoroughly soaked or steeped in some way.

1594 SHAKS. *Rich. III*, I. iv. 162 Throw him into the Malmesey-Butte in the next roome... O excellent deuice; and make a sop of him. **1606** —— *Tr. & Cr.* I. iii. 113 The bounded Waters Should..make a soppe of all this solid Globe. **1768–74** TUCKER *Lt. Nat.* (1834) II. 361 Away he goes to make..a sop in the briny broth of Ocean.

e. Something given to appease or pacify the recipient; a bribe.

An allusion to the sop given to Cerberus by Æneas: see CERBERUS.

1665 HOWARD *Committee* IV. i, Do you want some Fees? I'le perish in a dungeon before I'le consume with throwing Sops to such Curs. **1725** SWIFT *Corr.* Wks. 1841 II. 576, I had lately a letter without a name, telling me that I have got a sop to hold my tongue. **1845** BRIGHT *Sp., Irel.* 16 Apr. (1876) 150 This bill..is a sop given to the priests. **1873** SPENCER *Stud. Sociol.* xi. 288, I do not want these sops and gratuities. **1894** *Times* (weekly ed.) 31 Aug. 691/3 This lavish expenditure..is intended as a sop to the disaffected.

3. A tuft of wet green grass amongst hay.

1641 BEST *Farm. Bks.* (Surtees) 33 The many greene soppes that are in it will bee a meanes to make it..moulde in the cocke. *a* **1743** RELPH *Misc. Poems* (1747) 13 A finer hay-day seer was never seen; The greenish sops already luik less green. **1828–** in dial. glossaries (Cumbld., Yks., Lancs., etc.). **1863** MRS. TOOGOOD *Spec. Yorksh. Dial.* (MS.), The hay is not in very good order; there are sops in it.

4. A copious collection or accumulation of some liquid; soppy or soaked state or condition.

1700 *Rector's Bk. Clayworth* (1910) 132 Jan. 20th, a great sop of wett on yᵉ ground. **1856** HAWTHORNE *Eng. Note-bks.* (1879) II. 38 A great pool and sop of blood.

b. A thorough wetting or soaking.

1729 *Dulcinead* 5 One rainy Day t' avoid a Sop, In Church young J——s his Head did pop.

5. In the names of certain fruits: (see SOUR-, SUGAR-, and SWEET-SOP). Also *attrib.*

c **1711** PETIVER *Gazophyl.* VII. lxii, It grows on a sort of Jack or Sop Tree call'd in Luzone Rhymay.

6. A sopper or dipper. *rare*$^{-1}$.

1796 MORSE *Amer. Geogr.* I. 281 The English word that conveys the proper meaning of Tunkers is Sops or Dippers.

sop, *sb.*^{2} Now only *north. dial.* Also 5 **sope**, 5–6 **soppe**. [perh. a. ON. *sopp-r* ball.]

†**1.** A compact body, troop, or company, esp. of fighting men. *Obs.*

1375 BARBOUR *Bruce* III. 47 Samyn in-till a sop held thai. *Ibid.* VII. 567 Sa did thai all.., Syne in a sop assemblit ar. ? *a* **1400** *Morte Arth.* 1493 Sodanly in a soppe they sette in att ones. *c* **1410** *Master of Game* (MS. Digby 182) ii, After..þei put hem in herdes and in soppes with þe rascaile. *c* **1450** *Merlin* xiv. 218 Than thei lepe to horse, and gedered togeder on a soppe. **1513** DOUGLAS *Æneid* X. vii. 31 Quhar ȝondir sop of men thikkis in a rout.

2. †**a.** A cloud *of* mist or smoke. *Obs.*

1513 DOUGLAS *Æneid* I. vi. 176 Venus with ane sop of mist baith tway, And with ane dirk clud closit round about. *Ibid.* V. xii. 5 Thai..gan behald The fyre sparkis wp fleand thik fald In a blak sop of reik.

b. *dial.* (See quot. 1828.)

1828 CARR *Craven Gloss.*, *Sops*, small, detached clouds hanging on the sides of a mountain, which prognosticate rain. **1866** MRS. LYNN LINTON *Lizzie Lorton* I. xii.

3. A lump or mass of blacklead in the ground.

1794 HUTCHINSON *Hist. Cumb.* II. 220 [Blacklead] is sometimes found in *sops* or floats, in a body without branches. **1855** HT. MARTINEAU *Engl. Lakes* 155 'Nests' or 'sops' or 'bellies' of black lead are found in the greenstone.

†**sop**, *sb.*^{3} *Sc. Obs.* [Cf. MDu. and WFris. *sop*, WFlem. *zop*.] Sap.

1513 DOUGLAS *Æneid* IV. ix. 85 Springand herbis..War socht, and with brasin hukis cuttit sone, To get ther mylky sop and vennom blak. **1595** DUNCAN *App. Etym.* (E.D.S.), *Vligo*, the natural sop.

sop (sɒp), *v.* Also 6 **soppy**, **soppe**. [OE. *soppian* f. *sopp* SOP *sb.*^{1} Cf. WFris. *sopje*, MDu. and Du. *soppen* (WFlem. *zoppen*) in sense 1; also WFlem. *zoppen*, Da. dial. *soppe*, in sense 2 a.]

1. a. *trans.* To dip, soak, or steep (bread, etc.) in some liquid. Also *absol.*

c **1000** *Sax. Leechd.* II. 228 Ꝺenim hlaf, ȝeseoð on gate meolce, soppiȝe on suþerne.

a **1529** SKELTON *E. Rummyng* 558 This ale, sayde she, is noppy, Let vs syppe and soppy, And not spyll a droppy. **1570** LEVINS *Manip.* 169/20 To soppe, *offam intingere.* **1597** A. M. tr. *Guillemeau's Fr. Chirurg.* 28/1 We must first let him suppe in a soft dressed egge, or a morsell of breade sopped in wyne. **1610** G. FLETCHER *Christ's Vict.* II. xi, His cheekes as snowie apples, sop't in wine, Had their red roses quencht with lilies white. **1629** MASSINGER *Picture* V. i, For a mess of porridge Well sopped with a bunch of radish and a carrot, I would sell my barony. **1719** DE FOE *Crusoe* I. (Globe) 209, I..let him see me..sop my Bread in it. *a* **1834** LAMB *Months* Misc. Wks. (1871) 399 Everything..is sopped in claret. **1843** JAMES *Forest Days* ii, The peasant sat at the table, sopping his bread in the contents of his jug. **1887** RUSKIN *Præterita* II. 174 One might almost as hopelessly have sopped the Matterhorn as the loaf.

b. To drench with moisture; to soak; also *fig.*, to intoxicate.

1682 D'URFEY *Butler's Ghost* 141 Like Country Vicar,.. at a Wedding, or a Fair, Is sooner sopt than any there. **1683** MOXON *Mech. Exerc.*, *Printing* 391 When a Pressman has taken too much Inck, he is said to Sop the Balls. **1725** *Fam. Dict.* s.v. *June*, The Water is to be supply'd as you find convenient, and no longer, lest it sop your Stem too much. **1788** MARSHALL *Yorksh.* I. 310 The covering moist and feeble, and the sod sopt with wet, fall heavy and flat to the ground. **1820** CLARE *Poems Rural Life* (ed. 3) 127 The dews, brush'd off from grass and flowers, Bemoistening sop his harden'd shoes. **1847** EMERSON *Repr. Men, Montaigne* Wks. (Bohn) I. 348 We have been sopped and drugged with the air, with food [etc.].

c. To carry *away* by soaking.

1853 DICKENS *Bleak Ho.* ii, An arch of the bridge in the park has been sapped and sopped away.

d. With *up*: to soak up, absorb. Also *fig.*

1888 S. O. ADDY *Gloss. Words Sheffield* 229 Come sop up that gravy. **1914** J. GALSWORTHY *Let.* in *Times* 28 Feb. 5/3 The admission or rejection of Tariff Reform, the Disestablishment or preservation of the Welsh Church, I would almost say than the granting or non-granting of Home Rule—questions that sop up *ad infinitum* the energies, the interest, the time of those we elect and pay to manage our business. *a* **1922** T. S. ELIOT *Waste Land Drafts* (1971) 5 Blew in to the Opera Exchange, Sopped up some gin. **1951** D. RIESMAN *Individualism Reconsidered* in A. W. Loos *Religious Faith & World Culture* 73 The everpresent threat of war..used as a rationalization to sop up our 'excessive' comforts. **1962** S. CARPENTER in *Into Orbit* 57 The nose [of the capsule] would sop up much of the friction we were running into and would become quite warm. **1973** J. G. FARRELL *Siege of Krishnapur* ii. 25 The ladies discovered that while sitting in the boat the hems of their dresses had sopped up a certain amount of bilge water. **1977** A. CARTER *Passion of New Eve* x. 158, I sopped up the sauce from the beans with a hunk of bread.

2. *intr.* **a.** To be, or become, soaking wet.

1831 MISS MITFORD in *The Remembrance* 40 Strawberries lay sopping in their beds.

b. Of moisture: To soak *in* or *through*.

1844 DICKENS *Mart. Chuz.* xlvii, Sopping and soaking in among the leaves that formed its pillow; oozing down into the boggy ground,..went a dark, dark stain. **1894** 'TOM COBBLEIGH' (W. Raymond) *Sam & Sabina* i, The water just sops through the turf.

3. [From SOP *sb.*^{1}] **a.** *intr.* To collect sops.

1755 SMOLLETT *Quix.* (1803) II. 139 His necessity is not so great, but that he eats,..though he may feed upon the leavings of the rich, or..go a-sopping, as they term it.

b. *trans.* To propitiate; to bribe.

1837 CARLYLE *Fr. Rev.* II. v. v, Danton and needy corruptible Patriots are sopped with presents of cash.

sop, obs. pa. t. SUP *v.*^{1}

sopar, obs. variant of SUPPER.

sope (səʊp). *Obs.* exc. *north. dial.* Forms: 1 **sopa**, 3– **sope**, 6–7 **soape**, 8 **swoap**, 9 **swope**. [OE. *sopa* (f. weak grade of *súpan* SUP *v.*^{1}), = ON. and Icel. *sopi* (MSw. *sopi*, Norw. dial. *sope*), MLG. *sope*, MDu. *sope* (*zope*), *soop* (Du. *zoop*), older Flem. *sope*, *seupe* (WFlem. *zope*, *zeupe*).] A draught; a small amount of drink, etc.; a sup.

c **1000** *Sax. Leechd.* II. 134 On wearmum wætre drince betonican tyn sopan. *c* **1275** *XI Pains of Hell* 169 in *O.E. Misc.*, Ne moten heo biden neuer o sope. **13..** *E.E. Allit. P.* B. 108 Þyse ilk renkez..Schul neuer sitte in my sale my soper to fele, Ne suppe on sope of my seve. *c* **1400** tr. *Secreta Secret.*, *Gov. Lordsh.* 71 Drynke cler watir with a sope of vynegre. *c* **1450** *St. Cuthbert* (Surtees) 3301 He asked, may I drynk a sope? **1547** BOORDE *Introd. Knowl.* i. (1870) 123 There ale is..smoky and ropye, and neuer a good sope. **1583** STUBBES *Anat. Abus.* (1877) 111 We ought neuer to take morsell of bread, nor sope of drinke, without humble thankes to the Lord. **1673** MRS. BEHN *Dutch Lover* III. ii, But come, t'other turn, and t'other sope, and then for Donna Euphemia. **1684** *Yorks. Dial.* 630 (E.D.S.), I sall send you back by her a soape. **1790** MRS. WHEELER *Westmld. Dial.* 17 She gav a conny swoap oa Milk. **1818** WILBRAHAM *Chesh. Gloss.*, *Sope*, a sup; a sope of rain is a great deal of rain. **1828–** in northern glossaries, etc.

sope, obs. var. SOAP *sb.*; var. SOWP *v. Obs.*

sopeer, soper(e, obs. forms of SUPPER.

sopelalee, var. SOAPOLALLIE.

soph (sɒf). *colloq.* [Abbreviation of SOPHISTER and SOPHOMORE.]

1. = SOPHISTER 3. (In early use also at Oxford.)

1661 K. W. *Conf. Charac.*, *College Butler* (1860) 68 Did you but see him dominere over a freshman,..when they come to be sophs the pump is his reward for his insolencies. **1684** WILDING in *Collect.* (O.H.S.) I. 260 For being created Sen. Soph,..00 00 06. **1691** MRS. D'ANVERS *Academia* 6 These kindly hug young Soph,..And of his Cash t' a Farthing ease him. **1713** BYROM *Rem.* (1854) I. I. 20 There is one Law, a M.A., and Fellow of Emmanuel, has this last week been degraded to a Soph, that is, the Year below a Bachelor. **1740** GRAY in W. Mason *Mem.* I. 266 The furniture much like that of a Soph at Cambridge for convenience and neatness. **1794** *Gentl. Mag.* Dec. 1084 One was a Harry Soph; another a fellow-commoner and senior soph. **1841** PEACOCK *Stat. Cambr.* 146 The exercises in the Sophs' schools for the degree of bachelor of arts have been altogether abandoned. **1871** 'M. LEGRAND' *Cambr. Freshm.* xix. 322 No longer a Freshman proper, but in all the budding dignity of a Junior Soph.

transf. **1860** GEN. P. THOMPSON *Audi Alt.* clxxvii. III. 214 The Romans, senior sophs in their day, ever put their veterans in third line.

2. *U.S.* = SOPHOMORE 1 b.

1778 STILES *Diary* (1901) II. 277, I appointed Stevens a Soph. Waiter in the Hall. **1860** *Macm. Mag.* July 224 These sophomores, or sophimores, or sophs,..have the traditional reputation of being the chief actors in such..larking as goes on at Yale. **1890** GUNTER *Miss Nobody* i. (1891) 8 They have come from Yale by train, singing that old-time glee with which the Sophs used to taunt the Freshes.

sopha, obs. form of SOFA.

sopham, sophem(e, obs. varr. SOPHISM.

sophena, sophene, obs. forms of SAPHENA.

sopheric (səʊˈfɛrɪk), *a.* [f. Heb. *sōphēr* scribe (see SCRIBE *sb.*^{1} 1) + -IC.] Of or pertaining to the Jewish scribes or their teaching. Also **ˈsopherism**, the existence or authority of scribes as a learned class.

1888 *Encycl. Brit.* XXIII. 37/2 A vast amount of Sopheric literature not to be found in the canonical Mishnah. **1890** P. H. HUNTER *After the Exile* II. xii. 241 Sopherism was still a comparatively new phenomenon.

sophester, obs. form of SOPHISTER.

†**ˈsophi.** *Obs.* Also **sophy**. [L. *sophī*, pl. of *sophus*, *sophos*, a. Gr. *σοφός*.] *pl.* Wise men, sages.

1598 MARSTON *Sco. Villanie* I. iii. 181 Now Sophi Ringoes eate, Candi'd Potatoes are Athenians meate. *Ibid.* II. v. 194 Some Sophy say, the Gods sell all for paine.

Sophi: see SOPHY^{1}.

‖**Sophia**^{1} (ˈsɒfɪə). [L. *sophia*, a. Gr. *σοφία*, f. *σοφός* wise. Cf. SOPHY^{2}.]

1. Wisdom, knowledge; *spec.* the Divine Wisdom. (Freq. personified.)

1649 J. ELLISTONE *Behmen's Ep.* Pref. (1886) 5 This knowledge,..this garland, and crown of virgin Sophia. *Ibid.* 117 The fair and noble Sophia..which now at present standeth at the doore of your soule. [**1788** GIBBON *Decl. & F.* xl. IV. 91 The principal church, which was dedicated by the founder of Constantinople to saint Sophia, or the eternal wisdom.] **1840** MILMAN *Hist. Christ.* II. 124 The great mother Sophia, would at length be admitted into the Pleroma or intellectual sphere. **1865** tr. *Hugo's Notre Dame* II. vii. 95 Hermetics, that sophia of all sophias.

2. Used *attrib.* to designate the type of Jewish literature represented by the Wisdom of Solomon, Ecclesiasticus, etc. Hence **ˈSophian** *a.*^{1}

1904 *Expositor* Aug. 117 The influence of the Sophia-literature in S. Luke's Gospel is distinctly marked. *Ibid.*, Undoubtedly a Sophian word from the Apocrypha.

†**Sophia**^{2}, obs. variant of SOPHY^{1}.

1711 *Fingall MSS.* in *10th Rep. Hist. MSS. Comm.* App. V. 118 The grand Signior, or the Sophia of Persia, or the Czar of Russia.

ˈSophian, *a.*^{2} *rare*$^{-1}$. [f. *sophi* SOPHY^{1} + -AN.] Of or pertaining to the Sophy of Persia.

1638 SIR T. HERBERT *Trav.* (ed. 2) 261 Praying for the prosperitie of their King, of the Sophian pedegree.

Sophian, obs. form of SUFIAN *a.*

sophianic (səʊfɪˈænɪk), *a.* *Theol. rare.* [f. SOPHI(A^{1} + *-anic* as in MESSIANIC *a.*] Of or pertaining to wisdom.

1936 *Theology* XXXIII. 317 Karl Pfleger says of this Sophianic mysticism that it is 'extraordinarily profound'. **1970** R. MANHEIM tr. *Corbin's Creative Imagination Ṣūfism* 136 (*heading*) The sophianic poem of a *Fedele d'amore*. *Ibid.* 160 This sophianic intuition is perfectly in keeping with that of the extreme Shī'ites.

sophic (ˈsɒfɪk), *a.* [ad. Gr. *σοφικός*, f. *σοφία* wisdom, *σοφός* wise.]

†**1.** Obtained by some secret process. *Obs.*

1709 *True Light of Alchemy* (heading), The Method and Materials..composing the Sophick Mercury and Transmuting Elixir.

2. Conveying, or full of, wisdom; learned.
a **1773** J. Cunningham *On Death Geo. II*, xxiv. Poems (1810) 461 He'll drop the sword, or shut the sophic page And pensive pay the tributary tear.
3. Pertaining to knowledge or speculation.
1898 J. W. Powell *19th Ann. Rep. Bureau Amer. Ethnol.* p. xlv, The sophic activities so highly developed among the tribes of the arid pueblo region.
So 'sophical *a.*; 'sophically *adv.*
1601 Dolman *La Primaud. Fr. Acad.* iii. 66 It is most certaine, that that which..is in those [regions] aboue, is seene also in this [world] of farre woorse condition, and as it were of a bastard and sophicall nature. **1739** Harris *53rd Ch. Isaiah* 256 (T.), All those books which are called sophical, such as the Wisdom of Sirach, etc. **1888** (*title*), Thesaurus incantatus. The enchanted treasure; or, the Spagyric Quest of Beroaldus Cosmopolita, in which is sophically and mystagorically declared the first matter of the stone.

sophie, obs. form of sophy².

sophi'ology. [f. Gr. σοφία.] **1.** (See quot. 1899.)
1892 J. W. Powell in *Amer. Anthropologist* July 270 For the science of opinions I propose the name *Sophiology*. **1898** —— *19th Ann. Rep. Bureau Amer. Ethnol.* p. xii, The sciences of esthetology, technology, sociology, philology, and sophiology. **1899** —— *Ibid.*, *20th Ann. Rep.* p. clxxi, Sophiology, or the science of activities designed to give instruction.
2. *Theol.* The doctrine of the Divine Wisdom, as serving to explain the relations between God and the world.
1934 *Theology* XXVIII. 23 In his Christology the author [*sc.* Bulgakov] deliberately and openly relies on Sophiology, the doctrine of the eternal and created Wisdom. **1943** E. L. Mascall *He who Is* x. 135 The 'sophiology', or teaching concerning the Divine Wisdom, which looks back to the fourteenth-century mystic of Mount Athos, St Gregory Palamas, and which became prominent in Russian theology in the last century through..Vladimir Solovyev. **1970** R. Manheim tr. *Corbin's Creative Imagination Ṣūfism* 98 From this idea of Creation as theophany..arises the idea of a sophiology, the figure of *Sophia aeterna*.
Hence **sophio'logical** *a.*; **sophi'ologist**.
1933 *Theology* XXVI. 337 This has been related to modern categories of thought by the Russian sophiological school in Paris, especially by Professor S. Bulgakoff. **1937** *Ibid.* XXXV. 92 Such Sophiologists as Bulgakov, Berdyaev, and Solovive.

sophi'ometer. [f. as prec.] (See quot.)
1810 J. Stewart (*title*), The Sophiometer or Regulator of Mental Power, forming the nucleus of the Moral World.

sophism ('sɒfɪz(ə)m). Forms: *α.* 4–5 soffym(e, 5 sofyme; 4 sophim(e, 4–6 sophym(e, 5 -ymme. *β.* 4–6 sopheme (6 -em, 5 soffem-), 5–6 sopham, 7 sophom(e. *γ.* 6–7 sophisme (6 -ysme), 6– sophism. [a. OF. *soff-*, *sophime*, *sof-*, *sophisme* (mod.F. *sophisme*), or ad. L. *sophisma* (Sp. and It. *sofisma*, It. *soff-*, *sofismo*), a. Gr. σόφισμα a clever device, trick, argument, etc., f. σοφίζεσθαι to devise, f. σοφός wise, clever.]
1. A specious but fallacious argument, either used deliberately in order to deceive or mislead, or employed as a means of displaying ingenuity in reasoning.
α. *c* **1350** *Commem. Dead* 218 in Horstm. *Altengl. Leg.* (1881) 149 All þir resons þat þou here sese War my sophims and sotiltese. *c* **1380** Wyclif *Serm.* Sel. Wks. II. 288 Crist and his apostlis weren not moved bi þese sophymes. *Ibid.* III. 227 þis a foul soffyme, a foul and a sotil disceit. *c* **1440** Capgrave *Life St. Kath.* ii. 817 Late be youre sophym! your termes arn but sour! **1474** Caxton *Chesse* iii. iv. (1883) 119 The conclusions and the sophyms of logyque. **1509** Hawes *Past. Pleas.* xi. (Percy Soc.) 42 Seven sophyms full hard and fallacyous. **1530** Palsgr. 173 *Sophisme*, a sophyme.
β. *c* **1386** Chaucer *Sqr.'s T.* 547 Ne couthe man by twenty thousand part Contrefete the sophemes of his art. *c* **1400** *Rom. Rose* 7471 For men may finde alway sopheme The consequence to enveneme. *c* **1470** Henry *Wallace* viii. 1509 Wallace he herd the sophammis euiredeill. **1529** More *Dyalogue* iii. Wks. 216/2 Setting wilkin alone with Simkin disputyng theyr sophem themself. *a* **1570** [see 1 b]. *a* **1603** T. Cartwright *Confut. Rhem. N.T.* (1618) 578 The Apostle had taken the measure of these words from their brawling and bawling Sophomes. **1642** Jer. Taylor *Episc.* (1647) 378 Those few pigmy objections..are but like Sophoms to prove that two and two are not foure.
γ. **1532** More *Confut. Tindale* Wks. 541/1 To tourne their earnest godly sentence into friuolouse cauillacions, & sophismes. **1576** Fleming *Panopl. Epist.* 286 They stand in contention with their sophismes and captious conclusions. **1615** Crooke *Body of Man* 57 A captious Sophisme, made to intrap the ignorant. **1654** Whitlock *Zootomia* 157 How easie to impose Sophismes on one that knoweth no kind of Logick, or form of Reasoning! **1678** Gale *Crt. Gentiles* iv. iii. 199 Here is in this objection a poor sophisme which they cal 'no-cause for a cause'. **1753** Johnson *Adventurer* No. 85 ¶17 To fix the thoughts by writing..is the best method of enabling the mind to detect its own sophisms. **1785** Reid *Intell. Powers* ii. x. 281 Others thought that the argument from revelation was a mere sophism. **1849** Macaulay *Hist. Eng.* v. I. 568 But no sophism is too gross to delude minds distempered by party spirit. **1875** Maine *Hist. Inst.* xiii. 399 The proposition that men are by nature equal he expressly denounced as an anarchical sophism.
†**b.** *spec.* An argument of this kind serving as a University exercise. Also *attrib.* *Obs.*
1566 in Fowler *Hist. Corp. Chr. Coll.* (O.H.S.) 112 Item, he harde no sophisme. *a* **1570** R. Morice in Strype *Eccl. Mem.* xxviii. (1721) III. 233 [Latimer] came into the *Sopham* School, among the Youth, there gathered together of Daily Custom to keep their *Sophams* and Disputations. **1579** Fulke *Heskins' Parl.* 475 Euery boy in Cambridge, that hath but once kept sophisme, would hisse at him for this assertion.
c. Without article: Sophistry.
1768–74 Tucker *Lt. Nat.* (1834) I. 37 Stripping it of all that sophism and equivocation wherewith it has been artfully overclouded. **1830** Herschel *Study Nat. Phil.* ii. iii. 106 To defend their dogmas..by every art of sophism or appeal to passion. **1869** *Pall Mall G.* 16 July 10 Until excess of philosophy, sophism, and theorizing turned every Frenchman into an argumentative lunatic.
†**2.** A device; a scheme. *Obs.*⁻¹
1657 G. Thornley *Daphnis & Chloe* 113 Daphnis, who was of a more projecting wit then she, devised this Sophism to see her.

sophist ('sɒfɪst). [ad. L. *sophista*, *sophistēs*, ad. Gr. σοφιστής, f. σοφίζεσθαι to become wise or learned. Hence also Sp. and It. *sofista*, F. *sophiste*.]
1. In ancient Greece, one specially engaged in the pursuit or communication of knowledge; *esp.* one who undertook to give instruction in intellectual and ethical matters in return for payment.
In the latter sense contrasted with *philosopher*, and freq. used as a term of disparagement.
1542 Udall *Erasm. Apophthegms* 14 b, *Sophistes* at the fyrst begynnyng wer men that professed to bee teachers of wisedome and eloquence, and the name of *Sophistes* was had in honoure and price. **1547** Baldwin *Mor. Philos.* 1 b, The Grecians..naming it first 'sophia', & such as therein were skilled, *sophistes* or wisards. **1605** Bacon *Adv. Learning* ii. 54 b, Not onely in the persons of the Sophists, but euen in Socrates himselfe. **1638** Junius *Paint. Ancients* 98 As well sculpters and painters.., as Sophists and Rhetoricians. **1699** Bentley *Phal.* Introd. 6 The very Sophists themselves ..have declar'd him no Sophist, but a Philosopher. **1763** J. Brown *Poetry & Music* vi. 137 In later Times it became a common Practice for Sophists and Rhetoricians to contend in Prose, at the Olympic Games, for the Crown of Glory. **1835** T. Mitchell *Acharn. of Aristoph.* 717 *note*, Socrates having ironically addressed the two boasting and ridiculous sophists..as gods. *a* **1842** Arnold *Later Hist. Rome* (1846) II. xii. 451 The profession of a Sophist was a legal exemption from the duties of a juryman. **1864** Bowen *Logic* ix. 267 The great use of disputation by the ancient sophists and the Schoolmen, as a logical exercise and a means of education.
2. One who is distinguished for learning; a wise or learned man.
1614 Sylvester *Bethulia's Rescue* ii. 320 Whose prudent Problems, touching every Theam, Draw thousand Sophists to Jerusalem. **1645** Bp. Hall *Treat. Content.* 88 Those Indian sophists who took their name from their nakednesse. **1727** N. Lardner *Wks.* (1838) I. 131 There were in the city two sophists..(or rabbies) who were reckoned exceedingly skilful in the laws of their country. **1794** T. Taylor *Pausanias' Descr. Greece* III. 321 For this god is a sophist, who purifies souls after death. **1812** Byron *Ch. Har.* ii. vi, Can all saint, sage, or sophist ever writ, People this lonely tower, this tenement refit? *a* **1857** R. A. Vaughan *Ess. & Rem.* (1858) I. 46 If we may credit some of our sophists, it [religion] descended from heaven like some of the deified stones of antiquity.
3. One who makes use of fallacious arguments; a specious reasoner.
1581 Pettie tr. *Guazzo's Civ. Conv.* i. (1586) 34 You knowe also that we naturallie hate cauillers and Sophists, who at euerie word will ouerthwart us. **1771** Beattie *Minstr.* i. xli, Hence! ye, who snare and stupify the mind, Sophists, of beauty, virtue, joy, the bane! **1774** Reid *Aristotle's Logic* i. §1 (1788) 5 The pride and vanity of the sophist appear too much in his writings. **1820** L. Hunt *Indicator* No. 26 (1822) I. 201 It is only for sophists to pretend that we, whose eyes contain the fountains of tears, need never give way to them. **1849** Macaulay *Hist. Eng.* vi. II. 7 Nor, it was said, had the speculations of this odious school of sophists [Roman Catholic casuists] been barren of results. **1871** B. Taylor *Faust* (1875) I. xi. 136 Thou art and thou remain'st a sophist, liar.
fig. **1828** Lytton *Pelham* III. ix, Our passions are terrible sophists!
b. *attrib.* or in appositive use.
c **1730** Savage *Character* Wks. 1775 II. 209 Whose savage mind wants sophist-art to draw O'er murder'd virtue specious veils of law. **1847** Emerson *Poems, Good-bye* Wks. (Bohn) I. 416, I laugh..At the sophist schools. **1852** M. Arnold *Empedocles* ii. 29 Before the Sophist brood hath overlaid The last spark of man's consciousness with words. **1875** Jowett *Plato* (ed. 2) III. 43 The style gets the better of the thought in the Sophist-poet Euripides.

sophister ('sɒfɪstə(r)), *sb.* Forms: 4 sofistre, 5 sofister, sof-, sovyster; 4 sophistre, 6 sophystre, -istere, *Sc.* -istar, 6–7 sophyster, 4– sophister. [a. OF. *sophistre*, ad. L. *sophista* sophist.]
†**1.** = sophist 1. *Obs.*
1387 Trevisa *Higden* (Rolls) V. 175 Whanne fendes hadde i-hote hym þe victorie of the Pers, his sophister axede [etc.]. *c* **1440** *Alph. Tales* 26 þer was a yong man þat feste hym at þe scule with Pictagoras, for to be a sophister. **1565** Cooper *Thesaurus* s.v. *Defluo*, Al this came from the fountaines of the sophisters. **1591** Harington *Orl. Fur.* Pref. ¶ij b, The learned Plutarch..tels of a Sophister that made a long and tedious Oration in praise of Hercules. **1609** Holland *Amm. Marcell.* xvi. ii. 56 Hippias Elêus that most quicke and eagre Sophister. **1697** Potter *Antiq. Greece* iv. xi. (1715) 295 There is a story of the Sophister Hermocrates relating to this. **1710** Norris *Chr. Prud.* ii. 93 At first all Artists, and even Philosophers themselves, were call'd Sophisters.
2. = sophist 3.
c **1380** Wyclif *Serm.* Sel. Wks. II. 156 Alȝit a sofistre wolde graunte þat þei lyven wiþouten ende. **1393** Langl. *P. Pl.* C. xviii. 311 A sophistre of sorcerie and *pseudo-propheta*. *c* **1425** *St. Mary of Oignies* i. ix. in *Anglia* VIII. 143/19 In maner of a sofister amonge sum trewe þat traytour enforced hym to medil false. *c* **1430** *Pilgr. Lyf Manhode* i. lxxvi. (1869) 45 Thei wolden..skorne me, and holde me for a sophistre. **1532** More *Confut. Tindale* Wks. 475/2 As though a sophyster woulde with a fonde argumente, proue ..that two egges wer thre. **1549** *Compl. Scot.* xx. 183 Thir freuole sophistaris that marthirs and sklandirs the text of aristotel, deseruis punitione. **1579** W. Wilkinson *Confut. Fam. Love* 39 The Deuill beyng a subtill Sophister beguiled and blynded our graundmother Eue. **1609** C. Butler *Fem. Mon.* (1634) 64 Let no nimble-tongued Sophisters gather a false conclusion from these true premisses. **1650** Baxter *Saints' R.* ii. x. (1662) 284 The ordinary sort of Christians, that are not able to deal with a Sophister. **1703** D. Phillips *Vind. Verit.* iv. 242 The Truth..may easily be defended against the most powerful Batteries of the acutest Sophister. **1764** Reid *Inquiry* i. §8 Let scholastic sophisters entangle themselves in their own cobwebs. **1830** Mackintosh *Progr. Eth. Philos.* Wks. 1846 I. 70 Not to mention Mandeville, the buffoon and sophister of the alehouse. **1892** A. Birrell *Res Judic.* v. 144 The wordy sophister with his oven full of half baked thoughts.
attrib. **1653** Urquhart *Rabelais* i. xiv, Presently they appointed him a great Sophister-Doctor..who taught him his A B C.
b. In the phr. *to play the sophister*.
1550 Bale *Apol.* 122 For now is he dryven to hys uttermost shyfte..to play Jacke Sophystre altogether. **1593** Marlowe *Edw. II*, i. iv. [552] But nephew, do not play the sophister. **1640** Fuller *Abel Rediv.*, *Life Luther* (1867) I. 46 On this point eight days were spent by his playing the sophister. *a* **1659** Bp. Browning *Serm.* (1674) I. xii. 163 He will play the Sophister, and endeavour..to beguil us with subtilties. **1725** [see sophistress].
3. At Cambridge, a student in his second or third year. (Cf. soph 1.) Now *Hist.*
Also in use at Oxford in the latter part of the 17th cent.; cf. soph 1 (quots. 1684 and 1691).
1574 Stokys in Peacock *Stat. Cambr.* (1841) App. A. p. xi, A Sophister provided by the Proctour shall knele before the Responsall sett. **1577** Harrison *England* ii. iii, The first degree, is that of the generall sophisters, from whence..they ascend higher unto the estate of batchelers of art. **1608** Topsell *Serpents* (1658) 778 A number which the meanest Sophister in Cambridge can resolve. **1641** R. Brooke *Eng. Episc.* i. vii. 38 They have practised little, but to wrangle down a Sophister, or to delude a Proctor, in the Vniversity. **1675** Covel in *Early Voy. Levant* (Hakluyt Soc.) 196 They are made like our sophisters' gown, without a cape. **1688** [see sophomore 1]. **1730** in Willis & Clark *Cambr.* (1886) III. 74 The Schools appointed for Batchelors and Sophisters.
b. With distinguishing epithet *junior* or *senior*.
1685 Wood *Life* (O.H.S.) III. 132 This fellow had the impudence before last Act to answer Generalls without a Bachelor or Senior Sophister. **1689** Popple tr. *Locke's 3rd Let. Toleration* L.'s Wks. 1727 II. 396 A Senior Sophister would be laugh'd at for such Logick.
c. Similarly at Harvard and Dartmouth, U.S.A.
1650 in Quincy *Hist. Harvard Univ.* (1840) I. 518 In case any of the sophisters..fail in the premises required at their hands. **1708** S. Sewall *Diary* 27 Sept., He was a Senior Sophister. **1766** in B. Peirce *Hist. Harvard* (1833) 246 That the Senior Sophisters shall attend the Tutor A on Mondays. **1792** J. Belknap *Hist. New Hampsh.* III. 296 The junior sophisters, beside the languages, enter on natural and moral philosophy and composition.
4. At Trinity College, Dublin, a student in his third or fourth year. Also *transf.* and *attrib.*
1841 Lever *C. O'Malley* cv. 510 The columns of attack will be formed by the senior sophisters of the old guard. **1845** W. B. S. Taylor *Univ. Dublin* iv. 147 The science taught..in the third, or junior sophister year, [is] Astronomy and Physics; in the fourth, or senior sophister year, Ethics. *Ibid.*, Junior sophisters are examined in the science taught from the beginning of the second or senior freshman year.
5. *Comb.*, as *sophister-like* adv.
1608 *Sec. Pt. Def. Minist. Reas. Refusal Sub.* 170 [He] changeth the state of the question sophisterlike. **1647** Trapp *Matt.* vii. 24 Putting paralogisms.., tricks and fallacies (sophister-like) upon your own souls.
Hence †'**sophistered** *ppl. a.*, sophisticated. *Obs.*
1567 Maplet *Gr. Forest* 9 It hath bene seene that in stead of a Smaragde some haue had sophistred and counterfayted Glasse.

sophistic (sə'fɪstɪk), *a.* and *sb.* Also 6–8 sophistick, 7 -icke. [ad. L. *sophistic-us*, ad. Gr. σοφιστικός, f. σοφιστής sophist. Hence also Sp. *sofístico*, It. *soff-*, *sofistico*, F. *sophistique*.]
A. *adj.* **1.** Of persons: Given to the use or exercise of sophistry.
1549 *Compl. Scot.* xv. 137, I exort the..rather that thou accuse my tua sophistic brethir. **1711** Shaftesb. *Charac.* (1737) III. 79 The schools of the antient philosophers.. came now to be dissolv'd, and their sophistick teachers became ecclesiastical instructers. **1790** Burke *Fr. Rev.* Wks. 1808 V. 201 The sophistic tyrants of Paris are loud in their declamations against the departed regal tyrants. **1874** K. H. Digby *Temple Memory* (1875) 329 As when sophistic sceptics would cry down Great Anaxagoras.
†**b.** Engaged in speculation. *Obs.*⁻¹
1549 *Compl. Scot.* xvii. 145 At that tyme thai lay al to gydthir in ane cauerne, as dois presently the sophistic egiptiens.
2. Of or pertaining to sophistry or sophists; of the nature of sophistry or specious reasoning.
1591 Sylvester *Du Bartas* i. i. 390 The sandy grounds of their Sophistick brawling. **1612** Webster *White Devil* ii. ii. 7 Some there are, Which by sophisticke tricks, aspire that name..of nigromancer. **1673** Milton *True Relig.* 7 A mystery indeed in their Sophistic Subtilties, but in Scripture a plain Doctrin. *a* **1734** North *Examen* iii. vi. §23 (1740) 439 But he,..by his sophistic Terms, declares the latter only to bear the Bell. **1807** Anna Seward *Lett.* (1811) VI. 348 He who rendered his rare eloquence the sophistic

engine to infatuate his country. **1871** H. B. FORMAN *Our Living Poets* 119 [He] justifies himself to himself with sophistic satisfaction.

b. Pertaining to, characteristic of, the ancient sophists.

1835 T. MITCHELL *Acharn. of Aristoph.* 392 *note*, λεπτὰ, a sophistic word, expressive of whatever is most subtle, ingenious, and acute in mental operation. **1874** MAHAFFY *Soc. Life Greece* xi. 339 The outburst of the sophistic scepticism. **1885** PATER *Marius the Epicurean* I. 219 The undisputed occupant of the sophistic throne.

B. *sb.* **1.** Sophistic argument or speculation as a subject of instruction. Also in pl. form.

1862 MERIVALE *Rom. Emp.* lxvi. (1865) VII. 223 Of the three principal chairs,..that of Sophistics took the first rank. **1865** GROTE *Plato* II. xxii. 96 Sophistic is the shadow or counterfeit of law-giving. **1881** MAHAFFY *Old Greek Educ.* xi. 143 Lecturers in sophistic and rhetoric.

2. Sophistry, deceptiveness.

1868 M. PATTISON *Academ. Org.* v. 222, I reject this as.. reproducing the sophistic of 'Testimonials' in another form.

sophistical (sə'fɪstɪkəl), *a.* Also 5-6 **sophystycal(l**, 6 **-ysticall**, 6-7 **sophisticall.** [See prec. and -AL¹.]

1. = SOPHISTIC *a.* 2.

1483 CAXTON *Gold. Leg.* 390/1 Logyke is deuyded..in demonstratyf, in probable, and in sophystycal. *a* **1513** FABYAN *Chron.* VII. (1811) 649 Whereunto a sophystycall answere was made by the kyng. **1550** BALE *Eng. Votaries* II. 116 b, Wherfore they sought firste of all to bring them vndre by sophistycall sorceryes. **1643** SIR T. BROWNE *Relig. Med.* I. §60 They enforce the condition of God, and in a more sophisticall way doe seeme to challenge Heaven. **1655-87** H. MORE *App. Antid.* (1712) 192 That this perfect Being doth exist, is false and sophistical. **1771** *Junius Lett.* lxi. (1788) 328 The sophistical distinction you attempt to draw between the person injured, and the person injuring. **1825** MCCULLOCH *Pol. Econ.* II. ii. 125 At first sight, this sophistical and delusive statement appears sufficiently conclusive. **1864** BOWEN *Logic* ix. 271 We..take into view all cases of defective and sophistical argumentation.

2. = SOPHISTIC *a.* 1.

1535 COVERDALE *Bible* Prol., All the gloses of oure sophisticall doctours. **1838** THIRLWALL *Greece* IV. xxxii. 259 Aristophanes..regarded the sophistical circles with abhorrence. **1863** COWDEN CLARKE *Shaks. Char.* xviii. 468 He is fluent and sophistical,—a sure token of feeble wisdom and lack of sound argument. **1884** *Daily News* 24 July 4/6 The question..is one which..the most sophistical cannot obscure.

†**3. a.** Employed for the purpose of adulteration or deception. *Obs.*

1558 WARDE tr. *Alexis' Secr.* I. VI. (1580) 110 b, If the woorke bee of Copper, made white by any Sophisticall substaunce. *c* **1645** HOWELL *Lett.* I. vi. 41 There be some that commit Fornication in Chymistry, by heterogeneous and sophistical Citrinations. **1680** C. NESSE *Church Hist.* 272 Not setting out her beauty with sophistical paint.

†**b.** Adulterated; sophisticated. *Obs.*⁻¹

1613 T. GODWYN *Rom. Antiq.* (1658) 180 He that had sold any corrupt or sophistical wares.

Hence †**so'phisticalness.** *Obs.*

1661 in *Phœnix* (1721) I. 68 Having so plainly demonstrated the Sophisticalness of Origen's Arguments. **1727** BAILEY (vol. II), *Sophisticalness*, Captiousness, Deceitfulness; sophistical Quality.

sophistically (sə'fɪstɪkəlɪ), *adv.* Also 4 **sofistically**, 4-5 **-ali**, 5 **-aly**; 5 **sophisticali**, 5-6 **sophystycally**, 7 **sophystically.** [f. prec. + -LY².] In a sophistical manner; fallaciously; with deceptive subtlety.

1382 WYCLIF *Ecclus.* xxxvii. 23 Who sofistically speketh, is hateful. **1471** RIPLEY *Comp. Alch.* VI. ix. in Ashm. (1652) 163 The Mater ys alterate..substancyally, And not.. sophystycally. **1523** FITZHERB. *Husb.* §68 Me semethe, that those men that holde that opinyon, speke sophystycallye. **1584** FENNER *Def. Minist.* (1587) 11 That which by our wordes he can not gather, he sophisticallie inferreth vpon them. **1638** CHILLINGW. *Relig. Prot.* I. iv. §66. 228 You abuse D. Potter.., by taking sophistically without limitation, that which is delivered with limitation. **1697** G. KEITH *2nd Narr. Proc. Turners' Hall* 5 He Defends himself most Sophistically. **1790** BURKE *Fr. Rev.* Wks. V. 92 By these theorists the right of the people is almost always sophistically confounded with their power. **1855** PUSEY *Doctr. Real Presence* iii. (1869) 333 Calvin was far too acute, not to have been conscious, that he was arguing sophistically in both these instances. **1892** *Times* 7 Dec. 9/5 Those who praise the codes of France..often talk loosely and sophistically and unjustly.

sophisticate (sə'fɪstɪkət), *ppl. a.* [ad. med.L. *sophisticāt-us*, pa. pple. of *sophisticāre*: see next.]

†**1.** = SOPHISTICATED *ppl. a.* 1. *Obs.*

c **1400** MAUNDEV. (1839) v. 51 ȝif it be thykke or reed or blak, it is sophisticate, that is to seyne, contrefeted and made lyke it, for disceyt. **1477** NORTON *Ordin. Alch.* v. in Ashm. (1652) 60 Joyne trewe kindes not sophisticate. **1544** PHAER *Pestilence* (1553) M vij, Bole armonyake,..not to brittle, nor to hye coloured, for suche is commonly sophisticate. **1586** LUPTON *1000 Notable Things* (1675) 18 You shall know good and pure Azure from sophisticate and naughty Azure, if [etc.]. **1625** HART *Anat. Ur.* I. i. 11 The countrey..findeth ..good and sufficient stuffe, neither fustie nor sophisticate. **1671** MAYNWARING *Anc. & Mod. Pract. Physick* 66 Yet this cheap sophisticate Medicine..will cost you six times so much.

2. = SOPHISTICATED *ppl. a.* 2.

1599 B. JONSON *Cynthia's Rev.* I. iv, O heaven! that any thing..should suffer these rackt extremities, for the uttering of his sophisticate good parts. **1616** *Pasquil & Kath.* v. 12 O, this Sophisticate friendship, that dissolues With euery heate of Fancie. **1695** LD. PRESTON *Boeth.* III. 127 Thou hast now then the Form and Causes of that adulterate sophisticate Felicity. **1812** CRABBE *Tales* i. 200 'Tis the savage state Is only good, and ours sophisticate! **1850** L. HUNT *Autobiogr.* I. ii. 74 The feeling was true, though the expression was sophisticate and a fashion.

†**3.** = SOPHISTICATED *ppl. a.* 3. *Obs.*

1531 ELYOT *Gov.* III. xi. (1880) II. 279 By the diligent studye of very philosophie (nat that whiche is sophisticate, and consisteth in sophismes). **1629** H. BURTON *Truth's Triumph* 169 Such is his sophisticate sophistry, and frothy wit. **1678** R. R[USSELL] tr. *Geber* II. I. II. iii. 45 They by another Reason thus argue and strengthen their own Sophisticate Opinion.

sophisticate (sə'fɪstɪkeɪt), *v.* Also 6 **sofysticat.** [f. the ppl. stem of med.L. *sophisticāre*, f. *sophisticus* SOPHISTIC *a.* Cf. It. *sofisticare*, Sp. *sofisticar*, F. *sophistiquer*.]

1. *trans.* To mix (commodities) with some foreign or inferior substance; to render impure in this way; to adulterate. Now somewhat *rare*.

c **1400** MAUNDEV. (Roxb.) xviii. 84 It fallez oft tyme þat marchands sophisticatez peper. **1523** SKELTON *Garl. Laurel* 110 Sophisticatid craftely is many a confecture. **1542** BOORDE *Dyetary* x. (1870) 256 They the which do put any other thynge to ale..doth sofysticat theyr ale. **1610** B. JONSON *Alch.* I. iii, He lets me haue good tabacco, and he do's not Sophisticate it, with sack-lees, or oyle. **1662** CHARLETON & P. M. *Myst. Vintners* (1675) 206 Muskadel is sophisticated with the Laggs of Sack, or Malmsey thus. **1756** *Gentl. Mag.* XXVI. 33 It is now..common to sophisticate well known medicines. **1807** T. THOMSON *Chem.* (ed. 3) II. 410 A method of ascertaining whether ether be sophisticated with alcohol. **1853** URE *Dict. Arts* (ed. 4) I. 119 If sophisticated with castor oil, the mixture soon becomes nearly colourless like white honey.

fig. **1591** LAMBARDE *Archeion* (1635) To Rdr., That sweet Odour hee hath left, cannot by their false ingredients be so sophisticated, but may by the judicious bee easily smelt out. **1663** COWLEY *Verses & Ess.* (1669) 100 Our Senses are here feasted with the clear and genuine taste of their Objects; which are all sophisticated there.

b. To deal with in some artificial way.

1611 CORYAT *Crudities* 263 Hauing a looking-glasse before them they sophisticate and dye their haire with the foresaid drugs. **1831** TRELAWNY *Adv. Younger Son* III. 328 His hair, never sophisticated by a comb,..resembled dark sea-weed.

c. To render artificial, to deprive of simplicity, in respect of manners or ideas; to convert *into* something artificial.

1796 MME. D'ARBLAY *Camilla* III. 270 [They were] less sedulously sought by those whom the manners and maxims of the common world had sophisticated. **1820** HAZLITT *Lect. Dram. Lit.* 2 They were not at all sophisticated. The mind of their country was great in them and it prevailed. **1874** LISLE CARR *J. Gwynne* I. vii. 201 They spoke out their thoughts with a rude freedom which..proved that they had not been sophisticated into prigs. **1879** MISS BRADDON *Cloven Foot* iii, Christened plain Sarah or Mary, to be sophisticated later into Celestine or Mariette.

d. To render sophisticated (in senses 2 b, c; in quot. 1947 with weakened sense). Also *refl.*

1947 C. MORGAN *Judge's Story* iv. 17 'But if you have reached the age of twenty-seven without ever having heard of Combined Metallurgical Industries, I am justified.'.. 'Now sophisticate me.' **1956** M. STEWART *Wildfire at Midnight* iii. 33 Three years of my great friend Nicholas.. would sophisticate a Vestal Virgin. **1978** J. I. M. STEWART *Full Term* xxii. 250, I..took to buying..all the paperbacks I could lay my hands on concerning espionage... It was a field that had sophisticated itself since the distant time when Patullo Minor, the Secret Service Boy, had enthralled his school-fellows with his hazardous escapades.

2. To corrupt or spoil by admixture of some baser principle or quality; to render less genuine or honest.

1604 T. WRIGHT *Passions* III. iv. 99 The facultie of eloquence..is sophisticated by many, who couer stincking matters with fragrant flowers. *a* **1626** BP. ANDREWES *Serm.* (1856) 381 It is the manner of the world..to sophisticate ever the best things with hypocrisy. **1692** BENTLEY *Boyle Lect.* v. 155 Lest it should tinge and sophisticate the Light that it lets in by a natural Jaundice. **1845** R. W. HAMILTON *Pop. Educ.* x. (ed. 2) 324 Is not the inference strong, that that party feels..the fallacy of its creed, and must sophisticate it? **1873** M. ARNOLD *Lit. & Dogma* (1876) 242 Those who sophisticate a very simple thing, religion.

3. To corrupt, pervert, mislead (a person, the understanding, etc.).

1597 HOOKER *Eccl. Pol.* v. lxxvii. §14 It alwaies behoueth men to take good heede, lest affection..sophisticate the true and sincere iudgement. **1700** CONGREVE *Way of World* v. ii, Why, have you not been naught? have you not been sophisticated? **1829** SOUTHEY *Sir T. More* (1831) II. 30 Books of casuistry, which sophisticate the understanding and defile the heart. **1847** R. W. HAMILTON *Rewards & Punishm.* viii. (1853) 396 What is it that sophisticates our hopeful youth? **1882** FARRAR *Early Chr.* I. 540 Those who ..sophisticated St. Paul's feeble converts.

refl. **1798** LD. JEFFREY in Cockburn *Life* (1852) I. 101 As it is, I believe I shall go on sophisticating and perverting myself till I become absolutely good for nothing.

4. To falsify by mis-statement or by unauthorized alteration.

1598 SYLVESTER *Du Bartas* II. ii. I *Ark* 173 And thou.. shalt testifie..What now thy shame-lesse lips sophisticate. **1630** PRYNNE *Anti-Armin.* 194 And with all sophisticates and corrupts both the words and meaning of this sacred Text. **1715** BENTLEY *Serm.* x. 338 Not adulterating, not sophisticating the Word. **1774** J. BRYANT *Mythol.* I. 421 The term Trachon seems to have been still farther sophisticated by the Greeks. **1873** F. HALL *Mod. Eng.* 298 As to *demarcation*,..they take the liberty of sophisticating Burke, in making him write *demarkation*.

5. *intr.* To practise sophistication.

1664 OWEN *Vindic. Animad. Fiat Lux* xv, In your following discourse you double and sophisticate. **1791** MRS. RADCLIFFE *Rom. Forest* x, The benevolence of her heart taught her, in this instance, to sophisticate. **1841** MIALL in *Nonconf.* I. 337 Sophisticate and mystify as we will. **1863** COWDEN CLARKE *Shaks. Char.* xiii. 320 We next see him paltering and sophisticating with the truth.

Hence **so'phisticating** *vbl. sb.* and *ppl. a.*

1611 COTGR., *Sofistication*, a sophistication, or sophisticating. **1624** CAPT. SMITH *Virginia* IV. 126 There are so many sofisticating Tobacco-mungers in England. **1651** FRENCH *Distill.* Pref. *4 b, Their sophisticating of Chymical oils with spirit of Turpentine. **1821** LAMB *Elia* I. *Old & New Schoolm.*, The sophisticating medium of moral uses. **1853** URE *Dict. Arts* (ed. 4) I. 378 Leaving the starchy matter, as well as most other sophisticating substances.

sophisticate (sə'fɪstɪkeɪt), *sb.* orig. *U.S.* [Back-formation from the vb.] One who is sophisticated or who has sophisticated tastes. Cf. SOPHISTICATED *ppl. a.* 2 b.

1923 G. ATHERTON *Black Oxen* i. 1 All the Sophisticates (as Clavering had named them, abandoning 'Intellectuals' and 'Intelligentsia' to the Parlor Socialists) were present. **1930** H. S. WALPOLE *Rogue Herries* I. 163 Then Louis of France, making rude gestures, fingers at nose, that he may irritate, polished sophisticate that he is, the barbarian Stanislaus. **1936** 'J. TEY' *Shilling for Candles* xix. 208 Murder and that brittle insincere sophisticate were poles apart. **1942** *Scrutiny* X. 349, I think it is more than an accident that Copland, who started..as a sophisticate of the Big City, should in his mature work have come to express the loneliness..that lies back of all big cities. **1959** *Encounter* Sept. 52/1 For sophisticates, there is a touch of abnormal psychology. **1971** *Hi-Fi Sound* Feb. 25 (Advt.), The simple sophisticate. The Goldring-Lenco GL 69/2 transcription unit.. with much more than 'the basics' for enthusiasts who don't require extreme sophistication of design. **1976** *UCT Stud. in English* (Univ. of Cape Town) Oct. 38 To the sophisticate it is a send-up of the genre in the vein of Chaucer's tale of Sir Thopas.

sophisticated (sə'fɪstɪkeɪtɪd), *ppl. a.* [f. SOPHISTICATE *v.*]

1. Mixed with some foreign substance; adulterated; not pure or genuine.

1607 DEKKER *Wh. Babylon* Wks. 1873 II. 256 The drinke ..they sweare Is wine sophisticated, that does runne Low on the lees of error. **1651** FRENCH *Distill.* Pref. *4 b, They.. have brought a great Odium upon it by carrying about and vending..their sophisticated oils, and salts. **1687** MONTAGU & PRIOR *Hind & Panth. Transv.* 27 To give sophisticated Brewings vent. **1800** HENRY *Epit. Chem.* (1808) 390 The fraud is detected by adding alcohol to the sophisticated spirit. **1897** *Allbutt's Syst. Med.* IV. 371 It is essential that water should be introduced, either pure or sophisticated.

2. a. Altered from, deprived of, primitive simplicity or naturalness. Of a literary text: altered in the course of being copied or printed.

1603 FLORIO *Montaigne* (1632) 301 And truly, Philosophy is nothing else but a sophisticated poesie. **1638** JUNIUS *Paint. Ancients* 119 The sophisticated Art..drew still the eyes and minds of unadvised spectators. **1684** BURNET tr. *More's Utopia* (1716) 118 Among those who pursue these sophisticated Pleasures, they reckon those..who think themselves really the better for having fine Clothes. **1782** V. KNOX *Ess.* vii. 33 He is..pursuing all the sophisticated joys, which succeed to supply the place where Nature is relinquished. **1825** SCOTT *Talism.* x, All this internal chain of feudal dependence is artificial and sophisticated. **1871** L. STEPHEN *Playgr. Eur.* (1894) i. 7 The mountains..are a standing protest against the sophisticated modern taste. **1948** *Studies in Bibliogr.* I. 112 This copy is only a sophisticated version of Stow. **1963** *N. & Q.* Mar. 101/1 We know..that F [of *King Lear*] is a sophisticated text, and it seems..possible that we have an example of sophistication here.

transf. *a* **1652** BROME *Queen & Concubine* III. iii, Where the swoln Courts sophisticated Breath Did but disease my Blood.

b. Of a person: free of naïvety, experienced, worldly-wise; subtle, discriminating, refined, cultured; aware of, versed in, the complexities of a subject or pursuit. Also *transf.* of a play, place, etc., that appeals to a sophisticated person.

Occas. (as in quot. 1952), *Biol.* and *Psychol.* used as opp. NAIVE *a.* 2.

1895 HARDY *Jude* IV. v. 303 Though so sophisticated in many things she was such a child in others that this satisfied her. **1904** J. C. LINCOLN *Cap'n Eri* xii. 230 The only scoffer was the bored Josiah, who, being a sophisticated New Yorker, sat in the best chair and gazed contemptuously upon the entire proceeding. **1915** *New Republic* 13 Feb. 51/2 It is one of those sophisticated melodramas in which a glamor is thrown about the underworld... The dope-fiend, the thief's mistress, the crooked detective, are all exhibited to an audience that apparently prides itself on being 'knowing'. **1933** H. S. WALPOLE *Vanessa* III. 531 Here in these pages was life, the life that so many polished sophisticated writers missed altogether. **1952** *Arch. Ophthalmol.* XLVIII. 607 The sophisticated subject could always distinguish this illusion from the oculogravic illusion. **1954** *Word* X. 236 This conception has cropped up again and again. Even sophisticated thinkers have bent their ingenious efforts to preserving it. **1957** D. ROBINS *Noble One* vii. 71 She preferred smooth sophisticated young men like Keith who amused and flattered *her*. **1962** P. D. STREVENS *Study of Present-Day Eng. Lang.* (1963) 23 The teaching of either language or literature in less educationally and linguistically sophisticated parts of the world. **1969** *Daily Tel.* 18 Oct. 11/5 Its nightclub-restaurant with an 'international' menu and Caribbean band is as sophisticated as you'd find anywhere. **1971** *Ibid.* 17 June 3/3 To the police he showed 'promise' of becoming a sophisticated criminal.

absol. **1952** G. SARTON *Hist. Sci.* I. xvi. 425 It is probable that pederasty was more common in Athens among the aristocrats, the idle rich, and the sophisticated than among the simpler people.

c. Of equipment, techniques, theories, etc.: employing advanced or refined methods or concepts; highly developed or complicated.

1945 C. S. LEWIS *That Hideous Strength* xiv. 384 The man was so very allusive and used gesture so extensively that Mark's less sophisticated modes of communication were almost useless. **1952** G. SARTON *Hist. Sci.* I. xi. 289 He represents a second (or third) and more sophisticated stage in the evolution of Pythagorean astronomy. **1956** *N.Y. Times* 1 Apr. 19/1 Navy scientists are virtually exploring multidimensional space in a time machine in the search for what they call 'sophisticated' high-yield weapons. **1960** *Washington Post* 16 June 20/6 Soviet experts are said to have assisted the Peking regime with advanced nuclear reactors of a sophisticated type. **1966** *Times* 28 Mar. (Austral. Suppl.) p. v/4 Victoria now has many sophisticated industrial complexes. **1970** H. BRAUN *Parish Churches* xvii. 206 The High Gothic font was a sophisticated piece of furniture. **1970** *Daily Tel.* (Colour Suppl.) 28 Aug. 16/4 Laser beams ..are useful to scientists as a sophisticated light-source. **1972** L. ALCOCK *By South Cadbury* viii. 182 The Breiddin had been refortified in the late fourth century with a sophisticated timber defence, in the form of a raised fighting platform and look-out towers. **1972** *Sci. Amer.* Sept. 53/2 One of the most sophisticated of all animal communication systems, the celebrated waggle dance of the honeybee. **1979** *Now!* 14 Sept. 78/1 When they raided the flat the police found two-way pocket radios, explosive substances and what were described as 'sophisticated' timing devices.

3. a. Falsified in a greater or less degree; not plain, honest, or straightforward.

1672 DRYDEN *Assignation* v. iv, I love not a sophisticated truth, With an allay of lye in't. *a* **1806** HORSLEY *Serm.* (1811) 105 Who resist the truth by argument, or..explain it away by sophisticated interpretations. **1835** I. TAYLOR *Spir. Despot.* vii. 329 After ingenious and sophisticated criticism has done its utmost. **1861** HOLLAND *Lessons in Life* v. 69 Our truths are half truths, or exaggerated truths or sophisticated truths.

b. Of a printed book, containing alterations in content, binding, etc. which are intended to deceive.

1862 J. H. BURTON *Book-Hunter* I. 25 His experience.. rendered him the most merciless detector of sophisticated books. Nothing, it might be supposed on first thought, can be a simpler or more easily recognized thing than a book genuine as printed. But in the old-book trade there are opportunities for the exercise of ingenuity. **1952** J. CARTER *ABC for Book-Collectors* 168 Sophisticated..as applied to a book, is simply a polite synonym for doctored or faked-up.

4. *Comb.*, as ***sophisticated-looking***.

1925 T. DREISER *Amer. Tragedy* (1926) I. I. iv. 31 A brisk ..and decidedly sophisticated-looking person.

so'phisticatedly, *adv.* [f. prec. + -LY[2].] In a sophisticated manner.

1956 A. WILSON *Anglo-Saxon Attitudes* I. i. 27 He smiled sophisticatedly to show his superiority to congresses. **1960** E. DAVIES *Beyond Old Bone Trail* i. 2, I was very shy and self-conscious, suffering from what I later found out to be generally and more sophisticatedly known as an inferiority complex. **1971** *Daily Tel.* 1 May 10/2 The work skated sophisticatedly between pastoral musing and a more swinging, jazzy style.

sophistication (səfɪstɪˈkeɪʃən). Also 5 -icac(i)oun, -ycacyon, 5–7 -icacion. [a. OF. *sophistication*, or ad. med.L. *sophisticātio, -ācio*, f. *sophisticāre* SOPHISTICATE *v.*]

1. a. The use or employment of sophistry; the process of investing with specious fallacies or of misleading by means of these; falsification.

c **1400** *Apol. Loll.* 7 And, sin sophisticacoun falliþ ofte in þis matir, feiþful men askyn..þis witnes. **1451** CAPGRAVE *Life St. Aug.* 10 Þe woman..coude not be led oute fro hir trewe beleue with no sophisticacion þat hir son coude make. *c* **1530** MORE *Answ. Frith* Wks. 835/1 For such kind of sophisticacion in arguing, was the very cauillacion and shift that the wicked Arrians vsed. **1597** HOOKER *Eccl. Pol.* v. lxxxi. §2 Bending therevnto their whole endeuour without eyther fraud, sophistication or guyle. **1678** NORRIS *Misc.* (1699) 182 The Law of Nature he only restored and rescued from the Sophistications of ill Principles. **1791** MRS. RADCLIFFE *Rom. Forest* iii, Hers were the arts of cunning practised upon fear, not those of sophistication upon reason. **1846** RUSKIN *Mod. Paint.* II. III. § I. vi. § 8 Happily ignorant of the sophistications of theories and the proprieties of composition. **1882** MISS BRADDON *Mt. Royal* I. i. 29 If you asked her opinion upon any subject you got it, without sophistication.

b. A sophism, a quibble, a fallacious argument.

1491 CAXTON *Vitas Patr.* (W. de W. 1495) II. 176 b/2, The dyuyne scyence Requyreth not to be fulfylled with sophistycacyons nor proposycyons ornate or polyshed. **1548** UDALL, etc. *Erasm. Par. Luke* v. 55 The subtiltees of the Philosophiers sophisticacions. **1581** J. BELL *Haddon's Answ. Osor.* 503 b, The Argument..is worthely rejected in the Logicians Schoole, and is called a meere Sophistication. **1635** SWAN *Spec. M.* i. § 1 (1643) 2 Whose reasons some have called vain sophistications to obscure the truth. *a* **1676** HALE *Prim. Orig. Man.* II. xii. (1677) 244 These Traditions have been admirably dressed by Sophistications and Superadditions. **1783** W. F. MARTYN *Geogr. Mag.* I. 186 Replete with sophistications and interpolations. **1819** L. HUNT *Indicator* No. 6 (1822) I. 46 But they are both as rank sophistications as can be; mere beggings of the question. **1892** W. S. LILLY *Gt. Enigma* 141 If we put aside sophisms and sophistications.

fig. **1618** STUKELEY *Petition* 2 This mans whole life was a meere sophistication. **1630** *Tincker of Turvey, Gentl. T.* 80 He..thought schollers..could deuise many sophistications to make a man a cuckold.

2. a. Disingenuous alteration or perversion *of* something; conversion into some less genuine form; the alteration of a literary text in the course of copying or printing.

1564 *Brief Exam.* *iij b, The sophistication of the arguments of that discourse. **1647** N. WARD *Simple Cobler* 58 The sophistication of Religion and Policie in your time. **1672** DRYDEN *Conq. Granada* Def. Epil. 168 That is a Sophistication of Language, not an improvement of it. **1860** HAWTHORNE *Marble Faun* (1879) II. ii. 25 Before the sophistication of the human intellect formed what we now call language. **1892** T. K. CHEYNE in *Expositor* 217 The sophistication of our native good sense. **1956** *Studies in Bibliogr.* VIII. 10 The paucity of '*em's* in the pages set by Compositor B represents the compositor's sophistication of copy. **1963** [see SOPHISTICATED *ppl. a.* 2 a]. **1981** *Times Lit. Suppl.* 10 July 793/2 It [*sc.* the Folio] also makes numerous minor alterations, many of them literary sophistications.

b. Deceptive modification.

1664 EVELYN tr. *Freart's Archit.* II. viii. 108 This Colossean Structure..had need of some Sophistications from the optiques.

c. The quality or fact of being sophisticated; esp. (*a*) worldly wisdom or experience; subtlety, discrimination, refinement; (*b*) knowledge, expertise, in some technical subject.

1850 L. HUNT *Autobiog.* III. xix. 49 A people who.. preserve in the very midst of their sophistication a frankness distinct from it. **1884** *St. James's Gaz.* 9 Sept. 6/2 No more simple and guileless folk can well be found, in these days of sophistication. **1915** *New Republic* 16 Jan. 27/1 As to semi-education, the assumption is sound enough, and Dr. Burton's chapters on method and structure, on development and climax and ending, are honest first aids to sophistication. **1934** C. LAMBERT *Music Ho!* II. 112 In spite of his dazzling and outward sophistication Stravinsky is essentially primitive and naïve. **1951** R. FIRTH *Elem. Social Organization* v. 163 When we talk..of primitive Greek art ..we are referring..to art that is distinguished primarily by being earlier in time, though it..also bears the character of lack of sophistication. **1964** E. BACH *Introd. Transformational Gram.* vii. 145 The reader of the standard linguistic journals is apt to find articles..that demand considerable mathematical sophistication on his part. **1971** J. B. CARROLL et al. *Word Freq. Bk.* p. xxi/1 Complete understanding of the lognormal model requires considerable mathematical sophistication. **1977** R. WILLIAMS *Marxism & Lit.* II. iv. 99 Mediation, in this range of use, then seems little more than a sophistication of reflection.

d. (*a*) The property or condition (of a thing) of being highly developed or complicated; technical refinement.

1959 *Time* 12 Oct. 67/3 In the past the usual comment was that Russian space vehicles are big and brawny because of more powerful launching rockets, but that U.S. space vehicles, small and elegant, made up for the Russians' gross size by their sophistication. **1972** L. ALCOCK *By South Cadbury* viii. 195 Elaborate arrangements to maintain the defences and their garrisons demonstrate the administrative sophistication of Late Saxon England. **1972** *Practical Motorist* Oct. 162/1 On more modern cars, sophistication is now so far advanced that the linkage would virtually require specialist attention!

(*b*) *concr.* An instance of this; a technically advanced characteristic.

1973 *Nature* 9 Nov. 109/2 The range stretches from relatively simple systems such as bacterial flagella and plant viruses..towards bacterial spores and the more complex sophistications of ribosomes, cell walls and mitochondria. **1976** *Early Music* Oct. 451/2 Instamatics cost..over £50 with built-in light meter and other sophistications.

3. a. An adulterated article; a fraudulently mixed form of something. **b.** A substance used in adulteration.

c **1400** MAUNDEV. (Roxb.) vii. 26 Þe Sarezenes makes swilke sophisticaciouns for to dessayfe Cristen men withall. .. Marchandes also and apothecaries puttes þerto oþer sophisticaciouns. **1620** MELTON *Astrolog.* 7 As meere a Mountebanke, as euer sold Sophistications in Italy or the Low-Countries. **1670** PETTUS *Fodinæ Reg.* 45 They might see and inspect those Impostures and Sophistications so destructive to Commutative Justice. **1683** —— *Fleta Min.* II. 4 Which really are not pure, but mixt with other sophistications. **1875** *Encycl. Brit.* I. 172/1 The chief sophistications of ginger powder are sago-meal, ground rice, and turmeric. **1886** *Daily Telegr.* 20 Mar. (Cassell), The sophistications of or substitutes for butter sold in the metropolitan and urban markets.

4. a. Adulteration (of commodities, etc.).

1540–1 ELYOT *Image Gov.* 74 To haue alway all necessary drougges..without sophistication or other deceite. **1567** MAPLET *Gr. Forest* 9 In this kinde as in al others we must take heed of Sophistication. **1601** HOLLAND *Pliny* II. 86 Nothing is so subject to sophistication as Saffron. **1654** T. WHITAKER *Blood of Grape* (ed. 2) 107 The principal difficulty wilbe in obteining pure wine with out sophistication. **1707** SLOANE *Jamaica* I. 223 Drugsters usually adulterate musk with these, which sophistication is known by its small continuance. **1789** *India Officer's Pocket-Guide Purch. Drugs* (ed. 2) 55 Few drugs are more liable to sophistication than musk. **1823** J. BADCOCK *Dom. Amusem.* 98 Tobacco..is rendered still more pungent by the sophistications..of the manufacturers. **1853** URE *Dict. Arts* (ed. 4) I. 263 The sophistication is easily detected by the microscope. **1871** G. H. NAPHEYS *Prevent. & Cure Dis.* I. ii. 70 Food free from sophistication.

fig. **1593** G. HARVEY *New Lett. Notable Contents* A iij, Publique medicines will admit no sophistication.

b. Const. *of* (an article, etc.).

1562 BULLEIN *Bulwarke, Bk. Simples* 72 b, But there is much craft and sophistication of the Camphor. **1662** CHARLETON & P. M. *Myst. Vintners* (1675) 203 In the close of his chapter touching the Sophistication of wines. **1820** F. ACCUM *Treat. Adult. Food* (title-p.), The Fraudulent Sophistications of Bread, Beer,..and other Articles. **1880** *Daily Telegr.* 24 June, An unscrupulous dealer whose sophistication of silver plate was more ingenious..than the mere forgery of a hall-mark.

so'phisticative, *a. rare*$^{-1}$. [f. SOPHISTICATE *v.*] Characterized by sophistication.

1861 I. TAYLOR *Spir. Hebrew Poet.* 247 A cumbrous, circuitous, and often a sophisticative mode of commenting upon the Prophets.

so'phisticator. [f. SOPHISTICATE *v.*, on Latin types.] One who sophisticates or adulterates.

1605 TIMME *Quersit.* Pref. p. vi, Some readers..are notable sophysticators. **1654** T. WHITAKER *Blood of Grape* (ed. 2) 107, I can cordially commend..that the Sophisticators of wine, may suffer punishment above any ordinary theef. **1680** *Spirit of Popery* Pref. p. vi, I cannot but exhort you..to endeavour to find out this particular Sophisticator. **1720** S. PARKER *Bibliotheca Biblica* I. I. 306 Great Depravers and Sophisticators of Antiquity.

† **'sophistress.** *Obs.* [f. SOPHIST or SOPHISTER: see -ESS.] A female sophist.

1631 MABBE *Celestina* iv. 45 Like a prevaricating Sophistresse..playing the traitour on both sides. **1671** H. M. tr. *Erasm. Colloq.* 243, I think thou art some sophistress thou pratest so wittily. **1725** BAILEY *Erasm. Colloq.* (1878) I. 213 *Ma.* But may I play the Sophister with you now? *Pa.* The Sophistress.

sophistry (ˈsɒfɪstrɪ), *sb.* Forms: 4 **sophestrie**, 4–7 **sophistrie** (5 **-tri**), 5–6 **sophystrye** (6 **-trie**), 5– **sophistry**; 5 **safistre, soffistre, sofystry.** [a. OF. *sophistrie* (mod.F. *sophisterie*, = Sp., It. *sofisteria*), or ad. med.L. *sophistria*: see SOPHIST and -RY.]

1. Specious but fallacious reasoning; employment of arguments which are intentionally deceptive.

1340 *Ayenb.* 65 Ine huyche manyere þet me zuereþ, oþer openliche, oþer stilleliche be art, oþer be sophistrie. **1377** LANGL. *P. Pl.* B. xix. 343 Confessioun & contricioun..Shal be coloured so queyntly and keuered vnder owre sophistrie. **1426** LYDG. *De Guil. Pilgr.* 5767 Tel on, as yt lyth in thy thouht, Wer yt deceyt or sophystrye. **1531** TINDALE *Exp. 1 John* (1537) 8 Can ye..persuade us, thynke ye, with your sophistry? **1582** BENTLEY *Mon. Matrones* 71 Stopping the mouthes of the vnlearned with subtile..persuasions of.. Sophistrie. **1639** HABINGTON *Castara* II. (Arb.) 78 Who will with silent piety confute Atheisticke Sophistry, and by the fruite Approve Religions tree? **1684** BUNYAN *Pilgr.* II. 108 This Maule did use to spoyl young Pilgrims with Sophistry. *c* **1710** POPE *On Silence* 40 The parson's cant, the lawyer's sophistry, Lord's quibble, critic's jest; all end in thee. **1777** PRIESTLEY *Phil. Necess.* 186, I do not profess myself to be master of any uncommon art of detecting sophistry. **1825** LYTTON *Falkland* 65, I feel too well the sophistry of his arguments. **1871** R. H. HUTTON *Ess.* II. 226 Nothing can exceed the tortuous sophistry of this admirable special pleading.

Comb. **1859** HELPS *Friends in C.* Ser. II. II. ii. 25 His wearisome round of..dexterous sophistry-weaving.

b. An instance of this; a sophism.

1673 CAVE *Prim. Chr.* I. i. 9 By their villanies, sophistries, and arts of terrour. **1770** *Junius Lett.* xxxviii. (1788) 209 Perplexed by sophistries, their honest eloquence rises into action. **1856** MISS MULOCK *J. Halifax* II. viii. 195 No sophistries of French philosophy on your part. **1876** FARRAR *Marlb. Serm.* xxxi. 311 To disentangle the soul from the fatal and subtle sophistries of sin.

2. The use or practice of specious reasoning as an art or dialectic exercise.

a **1400–50** *Alexander* 4364 Ne foloȝe we na ficesyens ne philisophour scolis, As sophistri & slik thing to sott wih þe pepill. *c* **1474** *Paston Lett.* III. 408 Item, iij. bokes of soffistre. **1538** BALE *Thre Lawes* 1167 We must haue sophystrye, Phylosophye and Logyck, as scyence necessarye. **1599** B. JONSON *Cynthia's Rev.* v. iv, Though I ..do want (as they say) logicke and sophistrie, and good words, to tell you why it is so. **1617** MORYSON *Itin.* III. 51 The Milanesi are said to excell in the study of the Civill Law ..those of Pavia in Sophistrie. **1677** GALE *Crt. Gentiles* III. 29 Aristotle..rendred his followers more skilful in hatching ..wrangling sophistrie, than true solid Philosophie. **1864** BOWEN *Logic* ix. 267 The great use of disputation by the ancient sophists and the Schoolmen..tended to create a special art of sophistry.

† **3.** Cunning, trickery, craft. *Obs.*

c **1385** CHAUCER *L.G.W.* Prol. 125 The foule cherl [*sc.* the fowler] that for his coueytyse, Hadde hem betrayed with his sophistrye. **1657** G. THORNLEY *Daphnis & Chloe* 110 Others, with all their sophistry, made gins and traps for birds.

4. The type of learning characteristic of the ancient Sophists; the profession of a Sophist.

1837 J. W. DONALDSON *Theat. Grks.* (1849) 97 Euripides was nursed in the lap of sophistry. **1869** A. W. WARD tr. *Curtius' Hist. Greece* II. III. iii. 434 Sophistry became a profitable trade.

Hence † **'sophistry** *v. trans.*, to maintain or argue sophistically. *Obs.*$^{-1}$

1563 FOXE *A. & M.* 268/2 Unto whome the Lorde Cobham thus aunswered, it is well sophistried of you forsoth.

Sophoclean (sɒfəˈkliːən), *a.* [f. L. *Sophoclē-us*, ad. Gr. *Σοφόκλειος*, f. *Σοφοκλῆς*, *-κλέης* (see def.). Cf. F. *Sophocléen.*] Of or pertaining to, characteristic of, Sophocles, the Athenian tragic poet, or his works, style, etc.

1649 QUARLES *Virgin Widow* III. Wks. (Grosart) III. 303/2 Then shall the learned Bayes..Immortalize the Sophoclean Stage. **1746** FRANCIS tr. *Horace, Epist.* II. i. 220 How Æschylus and Thespis form'd the Stage, And what improv'd the Sophoclean Page. **1870** LOWELL *Among my Bks.* Ser. I. (1873) 182 But this is to measure him by a Sophoclean scale. **1880** SWINBURNE *Stud. Shaks.* 46 Rather an Ovidian than a Sophoclean grace of bearing and speech.

sophom(e, obs. forms of SOPHISM.

†**'sophoming**, *ppl. a. Obs.*⁻¹ [f. *sophom* SOPHISM. Cf. SOPHUMER.] Taking part in dialectal exercises.

a **1618** W. BRADSHAW *Unreason. Separ.* (1640) 105 If so be the Syllogisme be true, as every Sophoming boy in the universitie knoweth.

sophomore ('sɒfəmɔə(r)). Now *U.S.* Also 7 **sophy moore**, 8- **sophimore** (8 **soph mor**). [app. f. *sophom* SOPHISM + -OR. Cf. SOPHUMER.]

1. A student of the second year: †**a.** At Cambridge. *Obs.*

1688 HOLME *Armoury* III. 199/1 The several degrees of persons in the University Colledges... Fresh Men, Sophy Moores, Junior Soph, or Sophester. And lastly Senior Soph. **1795** *Gentl. Mag.* Oct. 818 The Freshman's year being expired, the next distinctive appellation conferred is A Soph Mor.

b. In American universities and colleges. Also *transf.* (quot. 1807).

α. **1726** in J. Quincy *Hist. Harvard* (1840) I. 441 The Sophomores recite Burgersdicius's Logic..in the mornings and forenoons. **1766** in B. Peirce *Hist. Harvard* (1833) 246 That the Sophomores shall attend..on Mondays. **1792** BELKNAP *Hist. New Hampsh.* III. 296 The sophomores [at Dartmouth] attend to the languages, geography, logic and mathematics. **1807** W. IRVING *Salmagundi* (1811) II. 41 Three different orders of shavers in New York—those who shave pigs. N.B. Freshmen and Sophomores. **1826** MOTLEY *Corr.* (1889) I. 6 Mr. Cogswell says he should think I might enter Sophomore [at Harvard]. **1865** MRS. WHITNEY *Gayworthys* I. 243 He would have been nearly through a college year by this time; and he had been ready to enter as sophomore. **1892** *Nation* (N.Y.) 22 Sept. 217 Under this system the 'academic' students, *i.e.*, the freshmen and sophomores, work off their required subjects two at a time.

β. *c* **1764** *Freshman Laws* in Woolsey *Hist. Disc. Yale Coll.* (1850) 55 A Senior may take a Freshman from a Sophimore, a Bachelor from a Junior. **1778** STILES *Diary* 15 July (1901) II. 285 [List of] Sophimores. **1804** FESSENDEN *Democracy Unveiled* (1806) II. 42 With all his sophimore's rotundity, With all his semblance of profundity.

2. *attrib.*, passing into adj., as ***sophomore class, society, year***, etc.

1778 STILES *Diary* 25 June (1901) II. 276 Disciplined Cowles & examined & admitted him into the Sophimore Class. **1852** BRISTED *Five Yrs. Eng. Univ.* (ed. 2) 381 Two prizes for problems during the Freshman and Sophomore years. **1883** *Cent. Mag.* XXV. 517/1 Helen was in the Sophomore year of the class..when Robert came home from his first cruise. **1897** FLANDRAU *Harvard Episodes* 95 This fact is..of greater significance than any one..is likely to attach to the sophomore society.

sophomoric (sɒfə'mɒrɪk), *a.* (and *sb.*). Chiefly *U.S.* [f. SOPHOMORE + -IC.] **a.** Of or pertaining to, befitting or resembling, characteristic of, a sophomore; hence, pretentious, bombastic, inflated in style or manner; immature, crude, superficial.

1837 *Harvardiana* IV. 22 Better to face the prowling panther's path Than meet the storm of sophomoric wrath! **1852** T. PARKER *Ten Serm. Relig.* iv. (1863) 68 Our poor pedant, with his sophomoric wit. **1889** W. M. THAYER *Life A. Lincoln* xxiv. 313 It is quite common for an actor to come upon the stage, and, in a sophomoric style, to begin with a flourish.

b. Of persons. Also *ellipt.* as *sb.*

1891 E. FIELD *Truth about Horace, West. Verse* 22 To students sophomoric They'd present as metaphoric What old Horace meant for facts. **1900** *Speaker* 29 Dec. 346/2 A mere sophomoric wordmonger. **1946** AUDEN in *Harvard Alumni Bull.* 15 June 707/1 The sophomoric Who face the future's darkest hints With giggles or with prairie squints.

sopho'morical, *a. U.S.* [f. as prec. + -ICAL.] = prec. Hence **sopho'morically** *adv.*

1847 WELLS & DAVIS *Sketches Williams Coll.* 74 (Thornton), The Professor told me it was rather Sophomorical. Wonder what was intended by that epithet. **1859** BARTLETT *Dict. Amer.* (ed. 2) 429 *Sophomorical*, a term applied to speeches and writings containing high-sounding words and but little sense. **1883** *Science* II. 113/2 The paper is decidedly sophomorical. **1889** *Literary World* (Boston) 21 Dec. 485/2 The question of public worship is discussed rather sophomorically by Rev. D. S. Clark, and more thoughtfully and soberly by an unnamed 'pastor'.

Sophora (səʊ'fɔərə). *Bot.* [mod.L. (Linnæus, 1737).] A genus of leguminous trees, shrubs, or plants, characterized by having odd-pinnate leaves and racemose or paniculate flowers, many species of which are cultivated for their ornamental properties; a tree of this genus.

1753 *Chambers' Cycl.* Suppl., *Sophora*,..the name given by Linnæus to a genus of plants called by Dillenius..*ervi species*. **1826–7** *Encycl. Metrop.* (1845) XVIII. 398/2 This genus [*Edwardsia*] of elegant shrubs has been divided from *Sophora*, from which it is distinguished by its four-winged seed-vessel. **1868** *Rep. U.S. Commissioner Agric.* (1869) 201 The Japan sophora (*Sophora Japonica*), yellow locust (*Robinia pseudacacia*) [etc.]..may be placed in the list of pinnate-foliaged plants. **1883** *Harper's Mag.* Apr. 726/2 The most striking of these is the weeping-sophora, a most graceful..feathery tree, not unlike the locust in form and color of leaf.

Hence **so'phoria, so'phorine** *Chem.* (see quot. 1881).

1878 *Pharmac. Jrnl.* 29 June 1047 Note on the Alkaloid Sophoria. *Ibid.*, In the present state in which it was obtained sophoria is a transparent liquid having a highly alkaline reaction. **1881** WATTS *Dict. Chem.* 3rd Suppl., *Sophorine*, an alkaloïd obtained from the pods of *Sophora speciosa*. It is liquid, and forms a stable chloride.

sopho-spagyric, *a.* [f. Gr. σοφός wise + SPAGYRIC *a.*] Alchemistic.

1893 (*title*), The Hermetic Museum, Restored and Enlarged: most faithfully Instructing all Disciples of the Sopho-spagyric Art, how..the Philosopher's Stone may be found.

'sophronist. *rare*⁻¹. [ad. Gr. σωφρονιστής: see next.] One who seeks to regulate or control.

1904 G. S. HALL *Adolescence* II. 412 Iconoclasm is never better directed than against the literalist, formalist, and sophronist.

'sophronize, *v. rare*⁻¹. [ad. Gr. σωφρονίζειν, f. σωφρον-, σώφρων prudent, self-controlled, etc.] *trans.* To imbue with self-control or sound moral principles.

1827 ARNOLD in Stanley *Life & Corr.* (1844) I. 38 Lest I should get the sons of very great people as my pupils whom it is almost impossible to sophronize.

sophrosyne (səʊ'frɒzɪniː). Also **sophrosune.** [ad. Gr. σωφροσύνη prudence, moderation, f. σώφρων of sound mind, prudent.] Soundness of mind, moderation, prudence, self-control.

1889 *Cent. Dict.*, Sophrosyne. **1944** AUDEN *For Time Being* 89, I am that star most dreaded by the wise, For they are drawn against their will to me, Yet read in my procession through the skies The doom of orthodox sophrosyne [1945 *U.K. ed.* suphrosyne]. **1947** *Mind* LVI. 363 Lord Russell gives us to understand that he has no use for *sophrosyne*. *a* **1963** C. S. LEWIS *Poems* (1964) 3 Thus with magistral hand the Puritan Sophrosune Cooled and schooled and tempered our uneasy motions. **1970** J. GARDNER *Wreckage of Agathon* 153 Even when his ideas were crazy, the man had sophrosyne, as they used to call it in the old days.

†**'sophumer.** *Obs.*⁻¹ [f. *sophum* SOPHISM. Cf. SOPHOMING.] = SOPHOMORE 1 a.

1653 GATAKER *Vind. Annot. Jer.* 131 Your Argument..is so sillie, as that not some exq[u]isite Sophister, but any punie Sophumer may at first sight discover the feeblenesse of it.

Sophy¹ ('səʊfɪ). Now *Hist.* or *arch.* Also 6–7 **sophie**, 6–9 **sophi** (7 **sofi**). [ad. Pers. *çafī* (also *çafawī*), the surname of the ruling dynasty of Persia from *c* 1500 to 1736, derived from the Arabic epithet *çafī-ud-dīn* 'purity of religion', given to an ancestor of Ismail Safī, the founder of the dynasty. Not related to SUFI¹, with which it has freq. been associated.]

1. A former title or designation of the supreme ruler of Persia; the Shah. Also ***Grand Sophy.***

α. **1539** CROMWELL in Merriman *Life & Lett.* (1902) II. 218 His declaracion was..that the Sophy King of Perse had an oratour with the Turke. **1547** BOORDE *Introd. Knowl.* xxxvii. (1870) 214 The great Turke..hath obtayned the Sophyes lond. **1601** SHAKS. *Twel. N.* II. v. 197, I will not giue my part of this sport for a pension of thousands to be paid from the Sophy. **1667** *Lond. Gaz.* No. 209/2 The Grand Sophy of Persia having observed the Grand Sultan to have his hands fully employed in the Siege of Candia. **1686** tr. *Chardin's Coronat. Solyman* 49–51, I cannot but laugh when I find in their writings the Grand Sophy, the Sophy of Persia, and the Sovereign Sophy. For the Kings of Persia are neither called Sophies in general, nor in particular. **1707** *Curios. in Husb. & Gard.* 216 Revenues, which that Commerce brings into the Treasury of the Sophy. **1762–71** WALPOLE *Vertue's Anecd. Paint.* (1786) II. 113 The Sophy of Persia and his court were extremely surprized at the art of engraving so hard a jewel. **1899** R. WHITEING *5 John St.* 299 The great tent..suggests a State pavilion of the Sophy.

transf. **1865** KINGSLEY *Herew.* ii, Marry the Sophy of Egypt's daughter?

β. **1549** W. THOMAS *Hist. Italie* 108 b, Vsnucassan kyng of Persia (whose successour is nowe called Sophie). **1555** EDEN *Decades* (Arb.) 311 Ismael the Sophi and kynge of Persia. **1600** E. BLOUNT tr. *Conestaggio* 24 The Turke against the Sophi, and the King against the Rebels in Flaunders. **1698** FRYER *Acc. E. India & P.* 301 At Cormoot we met a Lion and a Spotted Deer carrying up as Presents to the Sophi from the Mogul. **1769** ROBERTSON *Chas. V*, XI. Wks. 1851 IV. 456 He had discovered a negociation which had been carried on with the sophi of Persia. **1818** RANKEN *Hist. France* V. II. ii. 285 That ambitious warrior had..defeated the sophi of Persia. **1837** M. DONOVAN *Dom. Econ.* II. 13 The sophi of Persia, his lords, and some ambassadors.

2. With *a* and pl. A Persian monarch or king.

1606 SYLVESTER *Du Bartas* II. iv. II. *Magnificence* 106 Wert thou a Sophy; yet with Vertue's luster Thou ought'st (at least) thy Greatnesse to illuster. **1636** R. GRIFFIN in *Ann. Dubrensia* (1877) 53 Grave as a Persian Sophie. **1753** *Scots Mag.* Jan. 2/1 The last of the ancient race of Sophys who wore the Persian crown. **1761** *Ann. Reg.* 147 Erivan, the ancient seat of the sophis. **1823** BYRON *Juan* IX. xxxiii, Like Nadir Shah, that costive sophy.

b. *transf.* A ruler; a great person.

1599 NASHE *Lenten Stuffe* (1871) 31 Our redoubtable sophy, of the floating kingdom of Pisces. **1606** DEKKER *News fr. Hell* Wks. (Grosart) II. 95 None but fooles therefore will maruell, how I and this Grand Sophy of the whore of Babylon came to bee so familiar together.

sophy² ('sɒfɪ). Also 5–6 **sophie.** [In sense 1 ad. L. *sophia* SOPHIA¹. In sense 2 from the second element in *philosophy, theosophy*, etc.]

†**1.** Wisdom, knowledge. *Obs.*

c **1440** CAPGRAVE *Life St. Kath.* v. 1020 It had ben beter to haue kepte the same sophie Whiche þat youre maysteris lerned you first in scole! **1557** GRIMALD in *Tottel's Misc.* (Arb.) 121 Coom fight with mee,..that, in my shield, The seuenfold sophie of Minerue contein. **1588** J. HARVEY *Disc. Probl.* 10 Who knoweth not the difference betweene.. semblance, and assurance; docosophy, and sophy?

2. One or other of the various sciences, departments of study, etc.

a **1843** SOUTHEY *Comm.-pl. Bk.* (1851) IV. 578 The various sophy's—cosmosophy, kerdosophy. **1869** *Contemp. Rev.* XI. 456 Moyen..would sometimes utter himself in their particular sophy.

†**'sophy**³. *Obs.* [Orig. in pl. *sophies*, f. L. *sophi* SOPHI.] A wise or learned man; a sage.

1587 GOLDING *De Mornay* Pref. (1592) p. viii, Some small sparkes of..wisdome,..the which they haue afterward taught vnto others, and for so doing haue bene called Sophies and Philosophers. **1596** H. CLAPHAM *Briefe Bible* II. 127 These Sophies finde with the Babe Iesus, onely Marie. **1610** G. FLETCHER *Christ's Vict.* I. lxxxii, To see their King, the Kingly Sophies come. **1654** WHITLOCK *Zootomia* 47 It were to be wisht their Ideas..were undisputable among the Sophies themselves in Physick. **1678** BUTLER *Hud.* III. i. 1423 Sir, (quoth the Voice) y' are no such Sophy As you would have the World judge of ye.

b. With the epithet *grand* (after SOPHY¹).

a **1635** RANDOLPH *Poems* (1652) 3 You that nothing have Like Schollars but a Beard and Gowne, for me May pass for good grand Sophies. **1638** SANDERSON *Serm.* (1681) II. 127 Whereof Plato and Aristotle and all the other grand sophies among them were ignorant. **1688** W. BATES *Harmony Div. Attrib.* (ed. 3) v. 96 The grand Sophies of the World esteemed it absurd and unreasonable [etc.].

c. In disparaging or sarcastic use.

1649 COL. LE STRANGE in *Plume MSS.* (Maldon, Essex), And like those sophies who would drown a fish I am condemn'd to suffer what I wish.

sopi, obs. variant of SUP *v.*²

‖**'sopie.** Also 9 **soopie, soopje, sopi, sopje; soupie, soupii, soupje, supje.** [ad. Du. *zoopje* (or a. Cape Du. *sopie*) dram, sip, dim. of *zope* (now dial.) SOPE *sb.*] A drink of spirits; a dram.

1696 W. MOUNTAGU *Holland* 38 The common Dutch are satisfied with a sopie of Brandy-Wine. **1790** E. HELME tr. *Le Vaillant's Trav. Afr.* I. v. 90 Those who enter a house are always presented with a *sopi*, that is to say, a glass of rack or gin, or rather of French brandy. **1810** *Barrington's Voy. N.S.W.* I. 179 He never forgoes the luxury of smoking except to give him time to swallow his sopie, or a glass of strong ardent spirit. **1812** A. PLUMPTRE tr. *Lichtenstein's Trav. S. Afr.* I. II. xii. 167 Whatever Mr. Barrow may say of the *Soopje* as the favourite drink of the colonists, I can very safely affirm, that I never..saw three Africans born, in liquor. **1824** W. J. BURCHELL *Trav. S. Afr.* II. x. 287 Muchunka..was..stopped from drinking it all off at once as he had seen the others drink their *sopje* (sopy) or dram. **1827** G. THOMPSON *Trav. & Adventures S. Afr.* I. iii. 33, I alighted and partook of a cup of coffee or a dram (*soopie*) with the hospitable boors. **1834** PRINGLE *Afr. Sk.* ii. 143 They produced their provisions for supper,..which they seasoned with a moderate sopie, or dram. **1835** C. L. STRETCH *Jrnl.* 13 May in *Voorloper* (1976) 743 The glass or cup..was presented to the Chief who previously to giving it to the person intended sipped out some portion and as several soupies were given in this way Macamo naturally became quite overcome with the strength of the Brandy. **1849** E. E. NAPIER *Excursions Southern Afr.* I. vii. 115 A 'Totty', to this day, will share his last sixpence,..or his last 'soupje', with a comrade. **1861** in *Life at Cape* (1973) 37 We ordered a halt to rest a bit, to take a 'soopie', [etc.]. **1862** L. DUFF GORDON *Let.* 2 Mar. in *Lett. from Cape* (1925) 131 Though he declined wine or Cape smoke 'soopjes' (drams) with aversion. **1863** W. C. BALDWIN *Afr. Hunting* vi. 163 There being lots of visitors every day, and a soupii, or a glass of Cape brandy, for every one. **1876** F. BOYLE *Savage Life* 277 After a while, from his lonely cottage by the ford, came to us the boer farmer in quest of supje (Mercian suppy), of raw spirits and a gossip. **1899** WARNER *Capt. Locusts* 19 Fortifying himself against the temperature by means of a cigar and occasional *supjes*. **1939** F. B. YOUNG *City of Gold* I. iii. 95 'Come along, Peruvian,' he shouted. 'Just in time for a sopie.' **1981** A. PATON *Towards Mountain* xv. 117 Part of the remuneration of the ['Cape Coloured'] farm workers is the 'sopie', the draught of sour inferior wine that is given them three or four times a day... The sopie has been condemned by generation after generation of social workers, teachers, and ministers of religion.

sopient ('səʊpɪənt), *a.* and *sb. Med.* [f. L. *sōpient-*, *sōpiens*, pres. pple. of *sōpīre* SOPITE *v.*]

a. *adj.* Having a dulling or deadening effect. **b.** *sb.* A soporific (*Cent. Dict.* 1891).

1804 *Med. Jrnl.* XII. 523 By the use of sopient mucilaginous potions..the symptoms greatly diminished.

†**'sopit**, *pa. pple. Sc. Obs.* Also **sopeit.** [app. ad. L. *sōpīt-us*, pa. pple. of *sōpīre* SOPITE *v.*, but see also SOWP *v.*] Rendered dull or sluggish; sunk *in* sleep, sorrow, etc.

1528 LYNDESAY *Dreme* 998 My hart was wounder sarye, Quhen comoun weill so sopit was in sorrow. **1535** STEWART *Cron. Scot.* II. 228 The Britis all..War sopit so with sensualitie, With gluttony and lichorus appetyte. **1549** *Compl. Scot.* vi. 68, I beand in this sad solitar soune sopit in sleipe. *Ibid.* vii. 68 In my dullit dreyme ande sopit visione.

sopite (səʊ'paɪt), *v.* Now *rare.* Also 6 **sopyte.** [f. L. *sōpīt-*, ppl. stem of *sōpīre* to deprive of sense, render unconscious, put to sleep, etc.]

1. *trans.* To put or lull to sleep; to render drowsy, dull, or inactive. Also *transf.* (with reference to the mental or moral faculties).

1542 BOORDE *Dyetary* ix. (1870) 250 Dyuers tymes some be so sopytyd, that the malt worme playeth the deuyll so fast in the heade [etc.]. **1656** BLOUNT *Glossogr.*, *Sopited*, laid to sleep, being at rest. **1697** tr. *Burgersdicius' Logic* II. xxii. 105 You may demonstrate that an animal sleeps because the common sense is sopited or drown'd by vapours. **1740**

CHEYNE *Regimen* 11 These Natural Powers may be sopited, ..as we see they are in sound Sleep. **1864** A. LEIGHTON *Myst. Leg. Edinb.* (1886) 203 They could not be heard by reason of their having been 'clean gane', or at least sopited in sweet slumber. **1871** BLACKIE *Four Phases Mor.* i. 58 His knowing faculty was blinded and sopited, dosed and drugged by his passions.

2. To put an end to, to settle (a dispute, question, etc.) in some way. Also, to pass over or suppress (something discreditable).

1628 in Birch *Crt. & Times Chas. I* (1848) I. 451 On Friday last there was a meeting of the bishops..about sopiting, as they term it, the controversies of this present time. **1659** FULLER *Appeal Injured Innoc.* I. 49 Being loath to enlarge on so odious a difference, sopited in good measure. **1722** WODROW *Corr.* (1843) II. 675 It grieves me to hear that the differences betwixt Subscribers and Non-subscribers are, after they seemed to be sopited, breaking out again. **1746** TURNBULL *Justinian* XII. xiii, Certainly there was treason in the case, the infamy of which was sopited by his successors. **1818** SCOTT *Br. Lamm.* xv, If such a union would sopite the heavier part of his unadjusted claims. **1849–50** ALISON *Hist. Europe* (1859) VIII. 14 If any disputes did occur they were in general sopited by a bribe to the Mandarins.

Hence **'sopited** *ppl. a.*, **'sopiting** *vbl. sb.*

1646 R. BAILLIE *Anabaptism* (1647) 139 Among many more exploded and sopited errors. **1659** H. L'ESTRANGE *Alliance Div. Off.* 23 A conference should shortly be had for the sopiting and quieting of those disputes. **1818** SCOTT *Br. Lamm.* xviii, The sopiting of a very dangerous claim.

sopite (səʊ'paɪt), *pa. pple. rare.* [f. as prec. Cf. SOPIT *pa. pple.*] Put to rest or sleep; settled.

c **1460** *Reg. Oseney* (1907) 205 All playntys and stryfys.. bitwene the foresaide parties..for ever frendely ben i-cesyd or sospite [*sic*]. **1784** *Irvine Presbyt. Records* in Dobie *Mem. W. Wilson of Crummock* (1896) 57 [Mr. Gemmel craved his wife might be absolved from her scandal,] seeing it is of ane old date and almost sopite. **1877** BLACKIE *Wise Men* 293 Loveliest flowers, whose seeds long summers there Lay sunless and sopite. **1883** R. W. DIXON *Mano* IV. vi. 153 But when, cut off from sense, in sleep sopite, The soul..takes her own instruments.

†**sopition.** *Obs. rare.* [f. L. *sōpīt-*, ppl. stem of *sōpīre*: see SOPITE *v.*] The action of putting to sleep, rendering inactive, etc.

1646 SIR T. BROWNE *Pseud. Ep.* v. xxii. 270 But as for dementation, sopition of reason, and the diviner particle from drinke,..Christian morality and the Doctrine of Christ will not allow.

†**sopitive,** *a. Obs.*$^{-0}$ [ad. med.L. *sōpītīvus.*] 'Causing sleep' (Bailey, 1727, vol. II).

†**'sopless,** *a. Obs. rare*$^{-1}$. In 7 sopelesse. [f. SOP *sb.*[3]] Sapless.

1651 SIR W. MURE *Ps.* XXII. xv. Wks. (S.T.S.) II. 88 My moisture as a sopelesse sheard Is quite consum'd and ceast.

sopor ('səʊpə(r)). Also 7 sopour. [a. L. *sopor* deep sleep, lethargy, related to *somnus* sleep.]

1. A deep, lethargic, or unnatural sleep or state of sleep. In later use *Path.*

1675 R. BURTHOGGE *Causa Dei* 22 Having drunk there their Fill, Benummed with a Mortal Sopor, and consequently Irrecoverably losing and forgetting All they did. **1681** H. MORE *Exp. Dan.* iii. 77 My Spirits retiring as in those that are in a deep Sopor, as if they were half dead. **1707** FLOYER *Physic. Pulse-Watch* 107 When the Pulse becomes more frequent, it turns to a..Sincope; when more rare, to a Sopor or Convulsion. **1720** DE FOE *D. Campbell* 274 Sennertus, in his *Institutio Medica*, writes of the Daemoniacal Sopor of Witches. **1803** *Med. Jrnl.* X. 437 Violent gripings, lassitude, stupor and sopor, which continued a whole day. **1843** R. J. GRAVES *Syst. Clin. Med.* v. 71 The patient was in such a profound sopor, that apparently nothing but warmth remained to indicate that life had not already become extinct. **1899** *Allbutt's Syst. Med.* VII. 282 The sopor deepened until the death of the patient.

†**2.** *fig.* A state of mental or moral lethargy or deadness. *Obs.*

1658 BP. REYNOLDS *Van. Creat.* Wks. (1677) 45, I found that that was but a sopor, a benumb'dness, which was in my apprehension a death of sin. **1681** H. MORE *Exp. Dan.* App. III. 311 Into how deep a sopor therefore or lethargy is their wit and judgment cast? **1693** R. FLEMING *Fulfilling Script.* (1801) App. I. 439 That spiritual sopor and stupidity which hath seized on others.

†**'soporal,** *a. Obs. rare.* [f. L. *sopor* SOPOR.]

1. = CAROTID *a.* 1. (Cf. SOPORIFIC *a.* 1 d.)

1706 PHILLIPS (ed. Kersey), *Soporal Arteries*,..the Carotid Arteries, so call'd because if they be tied, they immediately incline the Person to Sleep. [Copying Blancard *Phys. Dict.* (1693) s.v. *Carotidis.*]

2. Of or pertaining to sleep.

1719 BAYNARD *Health* (1740) 27 When all the faculties of th' mind Are to their (soporal) cells confin'd.

†**'soporate,** *v. Obs.* [f. L. *sopōrāt-*, ppl. stem of *sopōrāre* to put asleep, lull, stupefy, etc., f. *sopor* sleep.] *trans.* To put to sleep; to dull, stupefy.

1623 COCKERAM I, *Soporate*, to bring asleepe. **1657** TOMLINSON *Renou's Disp.* 199 [Frontals] indeed are very expetible which..gently soporate the senses, and roborate the brain. **1678** CUDWORTH *Intell. Syst.* 795 The Soul seeming not to be Thoroughly Awake here, but as it were Soporated, with the..Opiatick Vapours of this gross Body.

Hence **'soporated** *ppl. a.*

1684 tr. *Bonet's Merc. Compit.* VI. 199 And especially soporated Patients awake upon taking a Vomit.

†**sopo'ration.** *Obs. rare.* [ad. late L. *sopōrātiōnem*, noun of action f. *sopōrāre.*] A putting or lulling to sleep.

? *a* **1500** *Creacion of Eve* 12 in *Non-Cycle Myst. Plays* (1909) 8 To assyst us..A slepe in to man be soporacion to sende. **1658** in PHILLIPS.

†**soporative,** *a.* and *sb. Obs.* [f. L. *sopōrāt-*, ppl. stem of *sopōrāre* to SOPORATE. Cf. F. *soporatif, -ive* (Godef.).] = SOPORIFIC *a.* and *sb.*

1628 GAULE *Pract. The.* (1629) 294 Such Potions (whether inebriatiue, soporatiue, or stupefying) may be.. admininstred. **1707** *Curios. in Husb. & Gard.* 256 A Narcotick and Soporative Virtue. **1770** LANGHORNE *Plutarch* (1879) I. 275/2 The debauch threw him into violent pain; to allay which, he asked for a soporative.

soporiferous (səʊpə'rɪfərəs, sɒp-), *a.* Now *rare.* [f. L. *sopōrifer* (f. *sopor* sleep + *-fer* bearing): see -FEROUS. Cf. F. *soporifère*, Sp., Pg., It. *soporifero.*]

†**1.** Of a disease, morbid state, etc.: Characterized by unnatural or excessive sleep; soporose; lethargic. *Obs.*

1590 BARROUGH *Meth. Physick* I. xvii. (1639) 26 Losse of memory..is caused of the Lethargy and other soporiferous diseases. **1597** A. M. tr. *Guillemeau's Fr. Chirurg.* 35 b/1 Shee is as if she hadde the soporiferous dissease, without all strength, clene layed a-longe. **1681** H. MORE *Exp. Dan.* v. 141 It made him fall down into a soporiferous swound.

†**b.** Affected with numbness or 'sleep'. *Obs.*$^{-1}$

1599 A. M. tr. *Gabelhouer's Bk. Physicke* 209 Bath heer-with oftentimes the soporiferous Ioyncte.

2. a. = SOPORIFIC *a.* 1 a.

1601 HOLLAND *Pliny* II. 113 That venomous creature, which by a soporiferous power that it hath..casteth a man into a deadly sleep. **1657** FULLER *Comm. Jonah* (1868) 202 Supposing there was some opium or soporiferous virtue therein. **1710** T. FULLER *Pharm. Extemp.* 408 The whole Body of Physicians hath..attributed to this Plant [*sc.* hounds-tongue] a soporiferous Quality. **1767** J. PENN *Sleepy Serm.* 7 The preacher who delivers himself in such a spiritless, soporiferous manner. **1803** in *Spirit Public Jrnls.* VII. 360 The soporiferous and sudorific properties of this truly inestimable opiate. **1825** SCOTT *Talism.* viii, The invalid,..resisting no longer the soporiferous operation of the elixir, sunk down in a gentle sleep.

b. = SOPORIFIC *a.* 1 b. ? *Obs.* (Common in the 17th c.)

1601 HOLLAND *Pliny* II. 112 Halicacabus..is more soporiferous than Opium, and sooner casteth a man into a dead sleepe. **1626** BACON *Sylva* §96 Soporiferous Medecines applyed unto them, provoke sleep. **1678** GALE *Crt. Gentiles* IV. III. 91 Some soporiferous stupifying wine, or potion, or medicine, which being given to a man, or sprinkled on him, casts him into a deep sleep. **1732** ARBUTHNOT *Rules of Diet* in *Aliments*, etc. 315 The Air perfum'd with the Smell of Soporiferous Plants, as Poppies. **1785** ARNOT *Crim. Trials* 143 They also applied to Kennedy for intoxicating or soporiferous draughts.

fig. **1664** H. MORE *Myst. Iniq.* xx. 75 A lusty draught of that Soporiferous potion that will make him repose himself wholly on the faith of his Priest. **1711** *Vind. Sacheverell* 17 Soporiferous Draughts of Moderation.

c. = SOPORIFIC *a.* 1 c.

1694 MOTTEUX *Rabelais* v. (1737) Prol. p. lvii, Books.. dull, soporiferous.

†**3.** = SOPORIFIC *a.* 3.

1602 MIDDLETON *Phœnix* III. i. 7 Hark, you sluggish soporiferous villains! **1624** R. SKYNNER in *Ussher's Lett.* (1686) 349 Awake you sleepers from your sleep, and ye soporiferous sluggards, arise from your drowsiness.

Hence **sopo'riferously** *adv.* (Webster, 1847); **sopo'riferousness**, the state or quality of being soporiferous; sleepy or lethargic condition.

1597 A. M. tr. *Guillemeau's Fr. Chirurg.* 29 b/1 This vayne is opened agaynst the soporiferousnes and payne in the foreheade. **1727** BAILEY (vol. II), *Soporiferousness*, Sleep-causing Quality. **1838** *Blackw. Mag.* XLIV. 639 A sort of soporiferousness laid hold of me. **1888** *Harper's Mag.* Aug. 343 The very air seems inimical to thought; it is heavy with soporiferousness.

soporific (səʊpə'rɪfɪk, sɒp-), *a.* and *sb.* [f. L. type **sopōrific-us* (f. *sopor* sleep: see -FIC), = F. *soporifique* (1687), Sp., Pg., It. *soporifico.*]

A. *adj.* **1.** Inducing or tending to induce sleep; causing a person to sleep or slumber.

a. Of qualities, etc. (Cf. SOPORIFEROUS *a.* 2 a.)

1690 LOCKE *Hum. Underst.* II. xxiii. §8 The colour and taste of opium,..as well as its soporific or anodyne virtues. **1763** C. JOHNSTON *Reverie* II. II. i. 149 A phlegm,..which here seemed to have extended its soporifick influence over all present. **1765** GOLDSM. *New Simile* 38 Its soporific virtue's such, Though ne'er so much awake before, That quickly they begin to snore. **1848** DICKENS *Dombey* xi, Coaxed to sleep by the soporific agency of sweetbreads. **1879** MᶜCARTHY *Own Times* xxvii. II. 297 Most of those who tried to listen found the soporific influence irresistible.

b. Of medicaments, drugs, etc. (Cf. SOPORIFEROUS *a.* 2 b.)

1775 ADAIR *Amer. Ind.* 173 *note*, He acquiesced because of the soporific dose I gave him. **1828** SCOTT *F.M. Perth* xv, He began to experience the incipient effects of his soporific draught. **1832** BREWSTER *Nat. Magic* i. 3 The influence of drugs and soporific embrocations on the human frame. **1883** *Law Reports 11 Q.B.D.* 588 Charged..with having unlawfully administered soporific drugs to the plaintiff's servants.

c. Of books, writings, talk, etc., or of persons in respect of these.

1727 SOMERVILLE *Fortune Hunter* iv. Poems (1810) 222 Hibernian matrons thus of old, Their soporific stories told. **1760** FOOTE *Minor* I. i, The soporific twang of the tabernacle of Tottenham court road. **1822** BYRON *Juan* VIII. lxxxix, To quote Too much of one sort would be soporific. **1856** R. A. VAUGHAN *Mystics* (1860) I. 108 Dionysius in the East, then, is soporific. **1870** R. W. DALE *Week-day Serm.* viii. 155 Soporific talk begins to flow.

d. In other contexts.

With quot. 1822–7 cf. SOPORAL *a.* 1.

1822–7 GOOD *Study Med.* (1829) I. 546 Hence the name of carotids, or soporific vessels,..was given to the arteries, whose ligature was supposed to produce this very singular result. **1834** SOUTHEY *Doctor* i, I thought of all sleepy sounds, and all soporific things. **1856** R. A. VAUGHAN *Mystics* (1860) I. 69 She lifts the lid, and there steals out a soporific vapour.

2. Of the nature of, characterized by, belonging to, sleep or sleepiness.

1754 *Gray's Inn Jrnl.* No. 76, That soporific Awe, with which they behold Personages of this Cast. **1755** H. WALPOLE *Lett.* (1846) III. 136, I must own I see no blame in thinking an active age more agreeable to live in, than a soporific one. **1896** J. LAMB *Ann. West Kilbride* vi. 161 The soporific tendencies of..a portion of the congregation.

3. Of persons: Drowsy, sleepy, somnolent; = SOPORIFEROUS 3.

1841 CAROLINE FOX *Old Friends* (1882) 64 In vain did the soporific Transcendentalist demand the reason; he was to dress first and know after.

B. *sb.* **1.** A substance, esp. a medicament, which induces sleep.

1722–7 BOYER *Dict. Royal* I, *Un soporatif*, a soporifick. *a* **1746** HOLDSWORTH *Rem. Virgil* (1768) 47 A strong medicine; and, in particular, a strong soporific. **1752** HUME *Ess. & Treat.* (1777) II. 63 Nor has rhubarb always proved a purge, or opium a soporific. **1842** *Penny Cycl.* XXII. 259 Soporifics (Anodynes; Narcotics). **1896** *Allbutt's Syst. Med.* I. 242 The use of soporifics is limited by the extent of their other pharmacological effects.

transf. and *fig.* **1811** MISS L. M. HAWKINS *C'tess & Gertr.* I. Introd., That soporific of houshold care, called 'board-wages'. **1821** LAMB *Elia* Ser. I. *Imperf. Sympathies*, The question operated as a soporific on my moral feeling.

2. A sleepy or somnolent person. *rare.*

1808 W. WILSON *Hist. Diss. Ch.* II. 92 This zealous writer forgot that every charge which he brought against Mr. Pike and his five soporifics, falls with additional weight on himself.

Hence **sopo'rifical** *a.*, **sopo'rifically** *adv.*

1807–8 W. IRVING *Salmag.* (1824) 138 Another gentleman ..proses away most soporifically. **1837** *New Monthly Mag.* LI. 365 We are becoming anatomical and soporifical.

soporose (səʊpə'rəʊs, sɒp-), *a. Med.* [f. L. *sopor* sleep + -OSE[1].] Of diseases, states, etc.: Marked or characterized by morbid sleep or stupor.

1710 T. FULLER *Pharm. Extemp.* 39 The Spirits being oppress'd grow Stupid and Sluggish, as in Soporose Cases. *Ibid.* 352 Shave the Head, and apply it all over in Soporose Distempers. **1825** *Ann. Reg.* 242* She lay in a soporose state, deprived of all sense and power of motion. **1822–7** GOOD *Study Med.* (1829) II. 129 It is chiefly to be found united with syncopal and soporose affections. **1899** *Allbutt's Syst. Med.* VII. 282 Soporose hysteria might have been diagnosed.

'soporous, *a.* Now *rare.* [f. as prec. + -OUS, or ad. F. *soporeux, -euse.* Cf. also L. *sopōrus.*]

1. = SOPOROSE *a.* ? *Obs.*

1684 tr. *Bonet's Merc. Compit.* I. 23 It is an excellent tart Water, much to be desired in all..Soporous cases. *a* **1691** BAXTER in *Reliq. B.* (1696) I. II. 199, I was then under.. Soporous or Scotomatical Ilness of my Head. **1707** FLOYER *Physic. Pulse-Watch* 193 In Apoplexies, Palsies, and soporous Affections, the Spirits are oppress'd. **1730** *Phil. Trans.* XXXVI. 352 Soporous and cataleptick Diseases. **1762** *Ibid.* LII. 454, I..found him in the same soporous, apoplectic state.

2. Soporific; sleep-bringing.

1866 [SHANKS] *Elgin* 55 They may now resign themselves to the soporous sheets without a shudder.

sopose, obs. form of SUPPOSE *v.*

sopped (sɒpt), *ppl. a.* [f. SOP *v.* + -ED[1].] Soaked or steeped in some liquid; saturated or drenched with water or rain.

1822–7 GOOD *Study Med.* (1829) I. 187 A single morsel of sopped biscuit. **1824** MISS MITFORD *Village* Ser. I. (1863) 178 Talking alternately..of lost matches and sopped hay. **1897** MARY KINGSLEY *W. Africa* 81 The captain offered him suits of his own clothes to change his sopped ones for.

'sopper. *rare.* [f. SOP *v.*] One who sops.

1611 COTGR., *Souppier*, a sopper, or browis-belly; one that is euer dipping his bread in the beefe-pot. **1648** HEXHAM II, *Een Zopper*.., a Sopper. **1755** JOHNSON, *Sopper*, one that steeps any thing in liquor.

sopper, obs. variant of SUPPER.

'soppet. *rare*$^{-1}$. In 7 soppitt. [Diminutive of SOP *sb.*[1]] A little sop; a sippet.

1664 in *Maitl. Cl. Misc.* (1840) II. 520 For bread at dinner to be soppittis.

soppily ('sɒpɪlɪ), *adv.* [f. SOPPY *a.* + -LY[2].] In a soppy or sentimental manner.

1977 *Listener* 21 Apr. 527/1 This soppily indulgent account of..shallow suburbanites. **1980** *N.Y. Times* 15 June VII. 14/1 Caroline thinks Ivan is arrogant, which he is; he thinks she is soppily emotional, which she is.

soppiness ('sɒpɪnɪs). [f. SOPPY *a.*]

1. The state or condition of being soppy; wetness.

1895 *Daily News* 25 Feb. 6/7 The heavy frosts and gradual thaw had brought the grounds to a condition of absolute soppiness. **1899** *Played on* 38, I thought you would like to order the carriage at once, and get out of all this soppiness.

2. Mawkish sentiment, facile emotion.

1974 I. MURDOCH *Sacred & Profane Love Machine* 202 Harriet was..fearing tears, a kind of soppiness which might embarrass her dignified friend. **1978** *Times Lit. Suppl.* 1 Dec. 1392/4 Soppiness vies with winsomeness in an exhibition of these postcards at the Bethnal Green Museum.

sopping (ˈsɒpɪŋ), *vbl. sb.* [f. SOP *v.*] The action of the vb. in various senses; a thorough soaking or wetting.

1532 MORE *Confut. Tindale* Wks. 687/2 By bibbing, & sipping, & sopping, & quaffing. **1633** W. AMES *Fresh Suite* II. 37 Sopping of bread in wine..was no signe instituted as an instrument of grace. **1675** H. WOOLLEY *Gentlew. Compan.* 71 Be not over-forward in dipping or sopping in the dish. **1824** MISS MITFORD *Village* Ser. I. (1863) 159 The whole story of the sopping, the drying, the clothes-spoiling. **1888** H. R. REYNOLDS in *Life* xvii. (1898) 414 The delightful rambles and soppings and jolly evening symposia.

ˈsopping, *ppl. a.* [f. as prec.] Soaking; drenched; saturated with water or rain.

1877 W. S. GILBERT *Foggerty's Fairy* (1892) 182 Two sopping females have quartered themselves on two dry bachelors. **1886** J. ASHBY-STERRY *Lazy Minstrel* (1892) 78 The sopping sky is leaden grey.

b. Quasi-*adv.*, as ***sopping sad, wet.***

Freq. in recent use: cf. WFlem. *zoppende nat.*

1866 R. R. BEALEY *Poems, Mally* 30 An' then turn'd soppin sad. **1897** MRS. C. CARR *Cottage Folk* 144 Why's your feet soppin' wet?

soppy (ˈsɒpɪ), *a.* [f. SOP *sb.*[1] or *v.* + -Y.]

†**1.** Full of or containing sops. *Obs.*$^{-0}$

1611 COTGR., *Offeux*,..Soppie; or full of lumpes, or gobbets.

2. Soaked or saturated with water or rain; soft or thoroughly wet with moisture; drenched, sodden.

a. Of land, grass, etc.

1823 E. MOOR *Suffolk Words*, *Soppy*, wet, boggy, swampy; applied to land. **1850** DICKENS *Dav. Copp.* iii, It [Yarmouth] looked rather spongey and soppy, I thought, as I carried my eye over the great dull waste. **1889** JESSOPP *Coming of Friars* v. 211 The level of the street..is in some cases five or six feet below the soppy sod..within the old enclosures.

b. Of things.

1859 R. F. BURTON *Centr. Afr.* in *Jrnl. Geogr. Soc.* XXIX. 78 Clothes feel limp and damp, paper—soft and soppy by the loss of glazing—acts as a blotter. **1892** 'MERRIMAN' *Slave of Lamp* xix, His..dress-clothes were clinging to him with a soppy hindrance.

3. Of the season or weather: Very wet or rainy.

1872 R. HEATH in *Golden Hours* 22 May be..; as it's been so soppy, there'll be some [trout] catched to-day. **1891** *Cent. Dict.* s.v., A soppy day.

4. Sloppy, slovenly.

1899 *Daily News* 12 Jan. 2/1 They may learn the fact, not in any of your foolish, soppy, theoretical ways, but in a hard, practical manner.

5. Full of mawkish sentiment; foolishly affectionate; inane, indulgent; occas. used affectionately. Also *to be soppy on*, to be infatuated with (a person). *colloq.*

1918 H. G. WELLS *Joan & Peter* xi. 369 What Joan knew surely to be lovely, Highmorton denounced as 'soppy'. 'Soppy' was a terrible word in boys' schools and girls' schools alike, a flail for all romance. **1920** H. G. HIBBERT *Playgoer's Mem.* xxxi. 257 The music halls were filled up with the precipitated baseness of pantomime—the puns, the 'unprincipalled' boy, the soppy-sentimental heroine. **1923** C. MACKENZIE *Parson's Progress* x. 121 Everyone will be singing for ever and ever and waving palms and playing harps and all that... I reckon Heaven's soppy, I do. **1929** H. WILLIAMSON *Beautiful Years* xx. 139 'Isn't fair, is it, man?' 'Hush, don't let 'em hear us. They'll think us soppy.' **1930** 'E. BRAMAH' *Little Flutter* xix. 218, I may as well make up my mind that I'm soppy on the blighter. **1935, 1959** [see DATE *sb.*[1] 1 b]. **1961** *Daily Tel.* 2 Dec. 1/5 Lord Parker, Lord Chief Justice, said yesterday he deplored the tendency towards 'soppy and sentimental' treatment of children in juvenile courts. **1974** J. COOPER *Women & Super Women* 16 Being photographed for the *Tatler* with a soppy expression on her face. **1977** *New Yorker* 8 Aug. 11/1 Side benefits include a Chinese Legionnaire who sings soppy Irish ballads.

soppy, obs. form of SOP *v.*

sopra bianco: see BIANCO SOPRA BIANCO.

†**sopraguard**. *Obs. rare.* [ad. It. *sopragguardia*, f. *sopra* above + *guardia* guard.] The chief guard of a camp, army, etc., or a member of this.

1591 *Garrard's Art Warre* 76 When the sopraguardes be many and of sundrie nations.

sopranino (sopraˈnino), *sb.* and *a.* [a. It. *sopranino*, dim. of SOPRANO *sb.* (and *a.*).]

A. *sb.* An instrument (usu. wind) of higher pitch than a soprano (see SOPRANO 3 b). **B.** *adj.* Of or pertaining to such an instrument, as a recorder.

1907 T. S. WOTTON *Dict. Mus. Terms* 185 *Sopranino*, the diminutive of Soprano, a term applied to an instrument of higher pitch than that defined as soprano. **1938** *Oxf. Compan. Music* 785/2 The 'Flauto Piccolo' of Handel in *Acis and Galatea* is the little sopranino recorder, an octave above the treble one (or possibly the flageolet was used). *Ibid.* 832/1 *Sopranino Saxhorn in E Flat (or F)*: also called *Soprano Saxhorn*; also often miscalled *Soprano Flügelhorn* or *Flügelhorn Piccolo*. **1939** A. CARSE *Musical Wind Instruments* xiii. 177 Each group [of saxophones] was in seven sizes... 1. Sopranino..2. Soprano [etc.]. **1954** [see PARDESSUS 2]. **1964** S. MARCUSE *Mus. Instruments* (1966) 485/2 *Sopranino clarinet*, clarinet pitched between the ordinary C clarinet and the piccolo clarinet in high A♭. *Ibid.*, The sopranino in D was in use in 18th- and 19th-c. orchestras. **1968** *Observer* (Colour Suppl.) 19 May 40/5 His nice Irish wife..warms up the sopraninas (very small recorders) by cradling them inside her blouse. **1977** *Times* 27 May 16/4 A new type of violin, the 11½ in sopranino, with strings of such high tension that when they were first used in the United States, the player wore protective goggles in case they snapped.

sopranist (səʊˈprɑːnɪst). [f. SOPRAN-O + -IST.] A soprano singer. Also *attrib.*

1864 *Reader* 6 Feb. 179/3 A French paper mentions a M. Bollaert, a sopranist, as singing at a concert in Paris. **1883** *Grove's Dict. Mus.* III. 461 One of the most famous of the *sopranist* singers who flourished in the last century.

soprano (səʊˈprɑːnəʊ), *sb.* (and *a.*) *Mus.* Pl. **sopranos**, also **soprani**. [a. It. *soprano*, f. *sopra* above.]

1. a. The highest singing voice in women and boys, having a compass from about middle C to two octaves above it; the quality or range of this voice.

1730 [see 3]. **1774** 'J. COLLIER' *Mus. Trav.* (1776) 32 He could not sing only bass and treble,..and soprano to admiration; but also squeak like a pig. **1854** *Orr's Circ. Sci., Org. Nat.* I. 132 It is not yet clearly understood what is the cause of the different qualities of voice, as exhibited in the tenor and bass, and the contralto and soprano. **1899** E. E. HALE *Lowell & His Friends* vi. 76 Then a clear soprano or tenor would be heard.

b. A part for or sung by such a voice. Also *fig.*

1801 BUSBY *Dict. Mus.*, *Soprano*, the treble or higher voice part, or parts. **1848** GEO. ELIOT *Let.* 8 Mar. (1954) I. 253, I should have written a soprano to your Jubilate.

2. A singer having a soprano voice; one who sings the soprano part.

1738 CHESTERF. in *Misc. Wks.* (1777) I. 81 *Sopranos* being the objects of the attention, and raptures of the ladies. **1817** BYRON *Beppo* xxxii, Soprano, basso, even the contra-alto, Wish'd him five fathom under the Rialto. **1834** BECKFORD *Italy* II. 31 Little madam whisks about the Botanic Garden with..a troop of sopranos. **1883** *Grove's Dict. Mus.* III. 635 Many mezzo-soprani can sing higher notes than many soprani. **1892** E. REEVES *Homeward Bound* 187 He..is a dark-haired, stout, youthful-looking male soprano.

3. *attrib.* or as *adj.* **a.** Of persons: Having a soprano voice; singing a soprano part.

1730 OWEN SWINY in Colmon *Posth. Lett.* (1820) 25 We must provide a Soprano Man and a Contrealt Woman. **1854** *Orr's Circ. Sci., Org. Nat.* I. 132 The contralto not unfrequently sings the high notes like soprano singers. **1873** H. C. BANISTER *Music* 217 Solo Tenor and Soprano singers will exceed the altitude here specified.

b. *transf.* Of certain musical instruments, as ***soprano cornet, trombone***; **soprano saxophone**, the second highest member of the saxophone family, usually pitched in B flat; abbrev. **soprano sax**.

1856 BERLIOZ *Instrum.* 151 The Soprano Trombone.. exists still in some parts of Germany. **1859** C. MANDEL *Treat. on Instrumentation Military Bands* 18 The Saxophone. This instrument is made in various keys, viz.:- 1. The B flat soprano-saxophone. **1961** J. A. MACGILLIVRAY in A. Baines *Mus. Instruments* x. 261 The *Tarogato* is a Hungarian instrument resembling a soprano saxophone of wood. **1971** *Guardian* 28 Sept. 10/6 The music is for..flute, trumpet, soprano sax, two basses, and percussion.

4. Of or belonging to the soprano.

soprano clef, the C-clef upon the first line of the treble stave.

1801 BUSBY *Dict. Mus.* Introd. p. xxiii, The Soprano-cliff is used for the second class of the higher species of voice. **1833** WISEMAN in W. Ward *Life* I. v, Possessing a strong soprano voice up to A, and sometimes C. **1845** E. HOLMES *Mozart* 166 The soprano solo was doubtless intended for the Weber. **1883** *Grove's Dict. Mus.* III. 635 That part of the scale upon which even a limited soprano part is written. **1883** *Harper's Mag.* Mar. 551/1 The far-off soprano strains ..become triumphant.

5. *ellipt.* = *soprano saxophone*, sense 3 b above.

1876 [see BARITONE]. **1934** S. R. NELSON *All about Jazz* ii. 57 The other saxophones in common use in the band are the tenor, baritone, soprano and bass. **1967** *Sat. Rev.* (U.S.) 15 Apr. 55/2 Bechet, adjusting the reed of his soprano, looked at him.

‖**sopra-vest**. *rare*$^{-1}$. [ad. It. *sopravesta* or *-veste*, = Sp. *sobrevesta*.] = SOBRE-VEST.

1838 PRESCOTT *Ferd. & Is.* I. xi, A sopra-vest of the same materials concealed his cuirass.

sops-in-wine. Also 8 sopsy-wine, 9 sops of wine. [See SOP *sb.*[1] 1 c. Cf. F. *soupe en vin*, a reddish colour; †the plant lucerne (Cotgr.).]

1. The clove-pink or gillyflower. *Obs.* until revived in 20th cent.

1573 TUSSER *Husb.* (1878) 96 Herbes, branches, and flowers for windowes and pots... Sops in wine. **1579** SPENSER *Sheph. Cal.* May 14 With Hawthorne buds, and swete Eglantine, And girlonds of roses and Sopps in wine. **1594** BARNFIELD *Affect. Sheph.* (Arb.) 10 The Rose, and speckled flowre cald Sops in wine. **1605** SYLVESTER *Du Bartas* II. iii. I. *Vocation* 18 Som July-flowr, or som sweet Sops-in-wine. **1625** B. JONSON *Pan's Anniv.*, Pinks, goulands, king-cups, and sweet sops-in-wine.

1918 'K. MANSFIELD' *Let.* 11 Mar. (1928) I. 152 There is a certain little white pink, striped with dark red, called 'sops-in-wine'. **1972** J. METCALF *Going down Slow* v. 102 What a garden there was at the back of this..inn... Sops in Wine and Floramer, Widow Wail..and deep red damask roses. **1981** T. MCLEAN *Medieval Eng. Gardens* v. 150 Its English name, gillyflower, may be a corruption of July flower, one of its medieval names, others of which were sops-in-wine, queen of delights and..carnation.

2. A variety of apple.

1764 *Museum Rust.* II. x. 37 An apple of very deep red, by some called sopsy-wine, *quasi* sopped in wine. **1860** R. HOGG *Fruit Manual* 25 Sops in Wine... Skin crimson in the shade, stained and striped with purplish crimson next the sun. **1879** BURROUGHS *Locusts & Wild Honey* 11 Bees..will suck themselves tipsy upon varieties like the sops-of-wine.

sopun, obs. pa. pple. SUP *v.*[1]

sopy, obs. form of SOAPY *a.*

sor, sorr, repr. Ir. pronunc. of SIR *sb.* (sense 7 a).

1889 KIPLING *Life's Handicap* (1891) 15 Indirectly, sorr, you have rescued..the peasanthry av a numerous village. **1901** M. FRANKLIN *My Brilliant Career* xix. 162 'How are you enjoying yourself?' 'Treminjous intoirely, sor.' **1914** [see PHWAT]. **1933** E. O'NEILL *Ah, Wilderness!* II. 66 No harm done. Only careful, Norah, careful... Yes, sorr. **1977** M. KENYON *Rapist* v. 54 A fine figure y'are so, if ye'll pardon the unsolicited estimation, sor.

sora (ˈsɔːrə). Also 8 saurer, 8–9 soree. [prob. a native name.] The Carolina rail (*Porzana carolina*). Also *attrib.* with ***gallinule, rail.***

a. **1705** R. BEVERLEY *Virginia* II. vi. (1722) 135 Cranes, Curlews, Herons, Snipes, Woodcocks, Saurers, Ox-eyes, Plover, Larks. **1731** *Phil. Trans.* XXXVII. 175 The Soreè. This Bird is in Virginia as much in Request for the Delicacy of its Flesh, as the Ortulan in Europe. **1785** LATHAM *Gen. Synop. Birds* III. I. 262 Soree Gallinule, *Rallus Carolinus.* **1824** STEPHENS in *Shaw's Gen. Zool.* XII. I. 208 Soree Rail.

β. **1809** A. WILSON in *Poems & Lit. Prose* (1876) I. 172 The Sora was in multitudes at Detroit. **1812** —— *Amer. Ornith.* VI. 28 The Rail or Sora belongs to a genus of birds of which about thirty different species are enumerated by naturalists. **1839** AUDUBON *Ornith. Biog.* V. 572 Sora Rail, *Rallus Carolinus.* **1872** COUES *N. Amer. Birds* 273 *Porzana.* Carolina Rail. Common Rail. Sora. 'Ortolan.'

Sorabe: see next and SORB[2].

Sorabian (səˈreɪbɪən), *a.* and *sb.* [f. med.L. *Sorabi*: see SORB[2].] **a.** *adj.* Of or belonging to the Slavonic race formerly dominant in Saxony; Sorbian. **b.** *sb.* A Sorb; the Sorbian language.

1788 GIBBON *Decl. & F.* lv. V. 544 *note*, Sclavonian captives, not of the Bohemian.., but of Sorabian race. **1851** J. KENNEDY *Nat. Hist. Man* I. 39 The western stem of the Slavonians is composed of the Bohemians, the Poles, the Slovaks, and the Sorabians. **1862** LATHAM *Compar. Philol.* 629 The Sorb, Serb, or Sorabian of Lusatia,..intermediate to the Bohemian and the Polish.

ˈsorage. *Obs.* exc. *arch.* Also 5 sore aage, 7 soreage; 6- soarage. [a. OF. *sorage* (Godefroy; mod.F. *saurage*), f. *sore* SORE *a.*[2] + -AGE (in some instances taken as AGE *sb.*).] The first year of a hawk. Also *attrib.*

?*a* **1400** in Harting *Perfect Bk. Keping of Sparhawkes* (1886) Introd. p. ix, Carry your hauk much, especially in her sorage. **1486** *Bk. St. Albans* a vij b, A Goshawke nor a tercell in thare sore aage haue nott thare mayles named. *Ibid.* b j b, That first yere is calde hir sore aage. **1575** TURBERV. *Faulconrie* 64 There are sundrie of them good in their soarage but beyng once mewed prove nothing worthe. **1620** QUARLES *Feast of Wormes* (1638) 4 Expect no lofty Hagard, ..If in her downy Soreage, she but ruffe So strong a Dove, may it be thought enough. **1684** R. H. *Sch. of Recreat.* 78 And as the Age of these Hawks is, so we name them, as, The first year a Soarage. **1688** HOLME *Armoury* II. 236/2 A Soar Hawk..is called also a Sorage Hawk. [**1852** R. F. BURTON *Falconry Valley Indus* iv. 41 *note*, It becomes..a 'soar-hawk,' or 'soarage' when it has begun to prey for itself.]

soral (ˈsɔːrəl), *a. Bot.* [f. SOR-US + -AL[1].] Of or pertaining to the sori of ferns.

1892 *Athenæum* 12 Nov. 667/3 Showing development of prothalli by soral apospory.

soralium (sɒˈreɪlɪəm). *Bot.* Pl. **-alia**. [mod.L., f. SORAL *a.* + L. *-ium*, neut. sb. ending.] A well-defined area of the thallus in which soredia occur, characteristic of certain lichens.

1921 A. L. SMITH *Lichens* iii. 144 In lichens of foliose and fruticose structure, and in a few crustaceous forms, the soredia are massed together into the compact bodies called soralia. **1938** G. M. SMITH *Cryptogamic Bot.* I. xiv. 518 They [*sc.* the soredia] may develop over the entire surface of a thallus or in localized pustule-like areas (soralia). **1970** *Sci. Jrnl.* Mar. 32/1 Many lichens have small powdery areas called soralia, the shape and location of which are characteristic for each species. The individual grains of powder in the soralia consist of an algal cell surrounded by fungal hyphae, and it is believed that they have a reproductive function. *Ibid.*, Lichens which have abundant fungal fruit bodies rarely form soralia, and vice versa.

†**ˈsorance**. *Obs.* Also 6 soraunce, 7–8 sorrance, 7 soarrance. [f. SORE *a.*[1] + -ANCE, prob. after GRIEVANCE 4.] A sore, or a morbid state producing a sore, in an animal, esp. in a horse.

1523 FITZHERB. *Husb.* §6 If any sorance come to the horse ..than he is lyttell worthe. *Ibid.* §89 The hawe is a sorance in a horse eye. **1577** B. GOOGE *Heresbach's Husb.* III. (1586) 123 A sorance breeding about the ioyntes. **1610** MARKHAM *Masterp.* (title-p.), The curing of all maner of diseases or sorrances in horses. *Ibid.* II. cviii. 390 The maltlong..is a cankerous soarrance aboue the hoofe. **1655** THETFORD *Perf. Horseman* 15 Incurable deformities, gross sorrances, as Spavens, Ringbones,..or the like. *c* **1720** W. GIBSON *Farrier's Guide* II. xxi. (1738) 69 When the Sorance is but in one Eye, it [*sc.* the bandage] ought to reach to the Middle of his Nose. **1749** W. ELLIS *Shep. Guide* 328 These things will afflict them with the nauseous Sorrance.

b. Used with reference to persons. *rare*.
1592 West *1st Pt. Symbol.* §102 Al maner of diseases, griefes and sorances wherewith the said H is now infected. 1601 Holland *Pliny* I. 155 Seldome or neuer complaine they of any sorance in other parts of the body.

c. *fig.* A painful matter; a grievance.
1608 Heywood tr. *Sallust* 35 Their prestinat prerogatives brought passed sorances to remembrance.

sorb (sɔːb), *sb.*[1] [a. F. *sorbe*, or ad. L. *sorbum* service-berry, *sorbus* service-tree. Cf. serve *sb.*[1] So Du. and Flem. *sorbe*, obs. G. *sorbe*, *sorb*.]

1. The fruit of the service-tree (*Pyrus domestica*); a service-berry.
1530 Palsgr. 272/2 Sorbe, a kynde of frute, *sorbe*. 1555 Eden *Decades* ii. i. (Arb.) 110 A certeyne sweetnes myxt with a gentell sharpnes as haue the frutes cauled Sorbes. 1658 Phillips, *Sorb*, a kinde of fruit, called a Service. 1853 Soyer *Pantropheon* 305 Several other kinds of fruits, such as sorbs, medlars, and mulberries. 1889 *Edin. Rev.* Apr. 472 Her native fruits were merely nuts and poor berries, masts, sorbs, and crabs.

2. a. The service-tree (*Pyrus domestica*).
1555 Eden *Decades* ii. i. (Arb.) 110 *note*, Sorbes are cauled in french cormier; they grow not in Englande. 1707 Mortimer *Husb.* 357 The Quick Beam or wild Sorb, by some called the Irish Ash. 1796 Withering *Brit. Plants* (ed. 3) II. 460 True Service, or Sorb. 1845 Browning *Englishman in Italy* 138 [To] strip from the sorbs A treasure so rosy and wondrous, Of hairy gold orbs!

b. = service *sb.* 3, service-tree 2.
1777 Jacob *Cat. Plants* 69 *Cratægus torminalis*, the common or wild Service-tree, or Sorb. 1796 Withering *Brit. Plants* (ed. 3) II. 458 Wild Service-tree, or Sorb.

c. The rowan-tree; = service-tree 3.
1796 W. H. Marshall *W. England* II. 30 The Birch, the Mountain Sorb, and the Larch, if judiciously propagated, would flourish..on the bleakest exposures. 1799 W. Nicol *Pract. Planter* 18 The Mountain Ash, or Sorb, would exuberate here, and assist in nursing the Oak [etc.].

3. *attrib.* and *Comb.*, as *sorb-leaved* adj., *sorb-tree*.
1548 Turner *Names Herbes* 75 Thys tree maye be called in englishe a sorb tree; and the fruite a sorb Appel. 1789 J. Pilkington *View Derbysh.* I. 405 *Sorbus domestica.* True Service, or Sorb-tree. 1845 *Florist Jrnl.* 156 The sorb-leaved spirea is well known as an inhabitant of shrubberies. 1849 J. A. Carlyle tr. *Dante's Inf.* xv, Amongst the tart sorb-trees, it befits not the sweet fig to fructify.

Sorb (sɔːb), *sb.*[2] Also **Sorbe**. [ad. G. *Sorbe*, var. of *Serbe*, representing the national designation *Serb* (pl. *Serbjo*): cf. Serb.
The *o* may be due to the influence of med.L. *Sorabi*: see Sorabian.]

1. A member of the Slavonic race inhabiting Lusatia in the east of Saxony; a Wend.
1843 *Penny Cycl.* XXVI. 206/1 Sorbes or Sorabes, between the rivers Saale and Elbe. 1883 Morfill *Slavonic Lit.* x. 248 The term is still applied to the Sorbs and the Slovenes. 1886 *Encycl. Brit.* XXI. 353/1 The Sorbs had been reduced to a condition of miserable serfdom.

2. The language spoken by this race.
1862 [see Sorabian]. 1887 *Encycl. Brit.* XXII. 147/2 Thus Chekh, Polish, Lower Sorb, *ten*; Upper Sorbish, *ton*.

sorb (sɔːb), *v. Physical Chem.* [Back-formation from sorption, after *absorb*, *absorption*.]

a. *trans.* To collect by sorption. Also *absol.*
1909 J. W. McBain in *Phil. Mag.* XVIII. 918 An idea of the quality of the carbon employed may be obtained from the amount of gas sorbed by it in actual experiment. 1938 *Proc. R. Soc.* A. CLXVII. 407 The two zeolites in the form of three-dimensional networks sorb ammonia copiously without ammoniate formation. 1954 Alexander & Hudson *Wool* viii. 261 When wool is immersed in hydrogen peroxide, some is initially sorbed by the amino and imino groups without reaction. 1970 *New Scientist* 2 July 9/3 Papers with inked designs sorb best on the inked areas. 1972 *Physics Bull.* Oct. 583/1 This has the advantage that exhausted water vapour is not sorbed by the trap on the fine side of the pump.

b. *intr.* for *pass.*
1970 *New Scientist* 2 July 9/3 The SO_2 sorbs strongly to these sweat patches.

Hence **sorbed**, **'sorbing** *ppl. adjs.*; also **'sorbate**[2] [after *distillate*, *filtrate*, etc.], that which is sorbed.
1909 *Phil. Mag.* XVIII. 923 The total amount of sorbed gas is 67·70 c.c. 1921 *Jrnl. Chem. Soc.* CXIX. 454 Experimental results have always been obtained by shaking a certain volume of a solution of known strength with a known amount of sorbing material such as charcoal, and analysing a sample of the remaining solution. 1928 *Phil. Mag.* V. 749 A revised conception of the mutual relations of sorbent and sorbate in cases where the 'power' time-equation holds. 1946 *Nature* 5 Oct. 475/1 Compact, non-porous sorbing media such as wool. 1949 *Discussions Faraday Soc.* VII. 136 Gmelinite and chabazite occlude a still greater variety of sorbates. 1975 *Nature* 28 Aug. 719/1 The Mg ion of dehydrated offretite should have a strong electrostatic field around it, and sorbed molecules should be strongly attracted to form a complex.

sorb-apple. [ad. G. *sorbapfel* (older LG. and Flem. *sorbappel*): see sorb *sb.*[1]] The fruit of the service-tree, or the tree itself.
1548 [see sorb *sb.*[1] 3]. 1562 Turner *Herbal* ii. 143 The sorb appel is very pleasant to be eaten vntill it be rotten. 1578 Lyte *Dodoens* 727 Sorbe Apples or Service beries are much lyke to Medlers. 1611 Cotgr., *Corme*, the Seruice, or Sorb-apple. 1666 J. Davies tr. *Rochefort's Caribby Isles* 35 It tastes like a Sorb-apple. 1725 *Fam. Dict.* s.v. *Service*, There are also two sorts of Sorb-Apples. 1796 H. Hunter *St.-Pierre's Stud. Nat.* (1799) I. 243 The scarlet clusters of the sorb-apple. 1796 C. Marshall *Gardening* xvii. (1813) 287 Service, (sweet) or sorb apple is rarely cultivated for fruit.
attrib. 1578 Lyte *Dodoens* 727 The tree wherupon this fruite groweth is called..in Englishe, Sorbe Apple tree. 1611 Cotgr., *Cormier*, the Seruice tree, Sorb-apple tree.

sorbate[1] ('sɔːbət). *Chem.* [See sorbic *a.* and -ate[1] c.] (See quot. 1823.)
1823 Crabb *Technol. Dict.*, *Sorbate*, a salt formed by the union of sorbic acid with some base. 1860 Hofmann in *Q. Jrnl. Chem. Soc.* XII. 47 Sorbate of silver. 1862 Miller *Elem. Chem.*, *Org.* (ed. 2) v. §4. 411 The sorbates of potash and soda are very soluble, and crystallize with difficulty. 1868 Watts *Dict. Chem.* V. 352 Sorbate of Ammonium crystallises in long needles.

sorbate[2]: see sorb *v.*

sorbefacient (sɔːbɪ'feɪʃ(ɪ)ənt), *a.* and *sb.* [f. L. *sorbē-re* to absorb + -facient.] **a.** *adj.* Causing or promoting absorption. **b.** *sb.* A substance or preparation causing absorption.
1847 in Webster. 1866 A. Flint *Princ. Med.* (1880) 138 Remedies which have been supposed to act as sorbefacients are mercury and iodine.

sorbent ('sɔːbənt), *sb.* (*a.*) *Physical Chem.* [f. sorb *v.*, after *absorbent*.] A material having the property of collecting molecules of a substance by sorption; that which sorbs. Also (and orig.) as *adj.*, having this property.
1909 J. W. McBain in *Phil. Mag.* XVIII. 918 My results show that it [*sc.* a specimen of carbon] is highly sorbent towards hydrogen. 1922 *Chem. Abstr.* XVI. 3017 The sorption isotherms were det[ermine]d..with animal charcoal as the sorbent. 1954 *Trans. Faraday Soc.* L. 981 Montmorillonite has already found various large scale uses as a sorbent. 1973 *Nature* 12 Jan. 92/2 The use of a zirconium oxide sorbent may be an economically realistic method of recovering boron from the sea. 1975 *Petroleum Rev.* XXIX. 239/1 In addition CGA maintains equipment to generate foam having a high sorbent capacity.

sorbet ('sɔːbɪt, 'sɔːbeɪ). Also 8 **sorbette**. [a. F. *sorbet* (Sp. *sorbete*, Pg. *sorvete*), ad. It. *sorbetto*, ad. Turk. *shorbet* (see sherbet), perh. influenced by It. *sorbire* to imbibe. So Du. and Flem. *sorbet*, G. *sorbet(t*.]

1. = sherbet.
1585 T. Washington tr. *Nicholay's Voy.* iii. x, Of the beurage which they do cal Sorbet, they do much vse to drinke in the sommer. [1613 *Haga at Constantinople* 5 Each of the Bassas, and the Ambassadour dranke Sorbetta,.. which is a kinde of drinke made of Water, Suger, and iuyce of Lemonds, mixed with Amber and Muske.] 1682 Wheler *Journ. Greece* ii. 204 Their most ordinary Drink is Water; next, a Sorbet made of Raisins steeped in Water. 1766 Smollett *Trav.* xix. I. 308 Among the refreshments of these warm countries, I ought not to forget mentioning the sorbettes. 1805 *Ann. Rev.* III. 61 Coffee, chocolate, ices, and sorbets are offered beneath the pavilions of the terras. 1834 Beckford *Italy* I. 117 They resorted to drink coffee and sorbet, with laughter and merriment. 1844 tr. *M. T. Asmar's Mem. Babylonian Princ.* II. 27 After some moments spent in mutual civilities, sorbets were served.

2. A variety of sweetmeat or ice.
1864 *Daily Telegr.* 27 Sept., The *menu*..meandered gracefully through fish, flesh, fowl, and truffles, and finally melted away into sorbets. 1885 Mabel Collins *Prettiest Woman* v, The sorbets are delicious sweets of almonds, pistachio, chocolate, or coffee.

Sorbian ('sɔːbɪən), *a.* and *sb.* [f. Sorb *sb.*[2]] = Sorabian *a.* and *sb.*
1836 *Popular Encycl.* VI. i. 138/1 The Sorbians, after 640, settled in the territory deserted by the Hermunduri. *Ibid.* 140/1 The Sorbians, or Wends, in Lusatia. 1877 [see Lusatian *sb.* and *a.*]. 1889 *Cent. Dict.*, *Sorbian*... *a.* Pertaining to the Sorbs or to their language. 1908 [see Lechish *sb.* and *a.*]. 1933, 1972 [see Lusatian *sb.* and *a.*]. 1977 *Language* LIII. 479 Soviet linguists talk about two Sorbian languages (Upper and Lower Sorbian), Western scholars about two Sorbian dialects.

sorbic ('sɔːbɪk), *a. Chem.* [f. sorb *sb.*[1] + -ic.] Contained in, derived from, the berries of the mountain-ash, *Sorbus* (now *Pyrus*) *aucuparia*. Chiefly in *sorbic acid*.
1815 Donovan in *Phil. Trans.* i. 243 Until a better name be devised, I have called it the Sorbic Acid. 1819 Children *Chem. Anal.* 278 Sorbic acid exists in the *sorbus aucuparia*; it is a transparent, colourless, inodorous fluid. 1860 Hofmann in *Q. Jrnl. Chem. Soc.* XII. 43, I propose to designate this beautiful body by the name of sorbic acid, reviving thus a name once used for malic acid. 1862 Miller *Elem. Chem.*, *Org.* (ed. 2) v. §4. 410 The general formula..of the sorbic group. *Ibid.* 411 The substance..becomes crystallized as sorbic acid. 1868 Watts *Dict. Chem.* V. 352 Ethylic Sorbate or Sorbic ether.

† **'sorbicle.** *Obs.*[−1] [f. L. *sorb-ēre* to imbibe.] A preparation which may be drunk.
1657 Tomlinson *Renou's Disp.* 163* Of their cremour may be made a certain sorbicle. [1657 *Physical Dict.*, *Sorbicle*, broth, suppings.]

sorbile ('sɔːbɪl), *a.* [ad. L. *sorbilis*, f. *sorbēre* to drink. Cf. obs. F. *sorbile*.] That may be drunk or supped; liquid.
1620 Venner *Via Recta* viii. 181 Moist and sorbile meats ..are most profitable. 1661 Lovell *Hist. Anim. & Min.* 139 A sorbile egge clarifieth the voice. 1808 Jamieson s.v. *Sop*, This most probably refers to sorbile food, what is vulgarly called spoon-meat.

b. That may be absorbed. *rare*[−1].
1799 W. Taylor in Robberds *Mem.* (1843) I. 289 The phænomena of combustion, respiration, &c. can with equal probability be accounted for..by the hypothesis..of a sorbile principle, or oxygen.

† **'sorbillate**, *v. Obs.*[−0] [f. L. *sorbillāre*.]
1623 Cockeram i, *Sorbillate*, to bib or sup often.

'sorbin. *Chem.* [f. sorb *sb.*[1]] = sorbitol.
1854 *Fownes' Chem.* (ed. 5) 404 Sorbin is, however, no sugar; it is not capable of fermenting. 1857 Miller *Elem. Chem.*, *Org.* ii. §2. 72 Sorbin,..from berries of mountain ash.

Hence **sorbi'nose** *sb.* (See quot.)
1894 *Watts' Dict. Chem.* IV. 497/1 *Sorbinose*,..an unfermentable sugar obtained from the fermented juice of mountain-ash berries.

Sorbish ('sɔːbɪʃ), *a.* [f. Sorb *sb.*[2], after G. *Sorbisch*, *Serbisch*. The native form is *Ser(b)ski*.] The language spoken by the Sorbs.
1883 Morfill *Slavonic Lit.* ix. 242 In the year 1706 Michael Brancel..published a translation of the New Testament into Sorbish. *Ibid.*, This, however, was not the first time that any Sorbish words had been in print.

sorbitan ('sɔːbɪtæn). *Chem.* [f. sorbit(ol + an(hydride.] Any of a number of cyclic ethers which are monoanhydrides of sorbitol; *spec.* the 1,4-anhydride, $CH_2OH{\cdot}CHOH{\cdot}CH{\cdot}(CHOH)_2{\cdot}CH_2O$, a colourless crystalline solid. Freq. *attrib.* in names of fatty-acid esters of these compounds, which are used as emulsifiers and surfactants.
1938 *Industr. & Engin. Chem.* Nov. 1222/2 The inner ether hypothesis was further tested by substituting a mixture of preformed sorbitol inner ethers, or sorbitans, for the sorbitol. 1950 Kirk & Othmer *Encycl. Chem. Technol.* V. 688 Anhydrides of certain hexahydric alcohols and their derivatives, as sorbitan and polyoxyethylene sorbitan esters of fatty acids, are used as emulsifiers and also possess emollient properties. 1958 *Martindale's Extra Pharmacopœia* (ed. 24) 696 The ether-esters, such as sorbitan oleate, are active water-in-oil emulsifying agents, while the polyoxyethylene derivatives mostly produce oil-in-water emulsions. 1969 tr. *Schönfeldt's Surface Active Ethylene Oxide Adducts* iv. 607 A composition containing glycine, phosphoric acid, and, e.g...ethoxylated sorbitan monolaurate as adduct, or sorbitan mono-oleate, is recommended as an antioxidant for fats. 1976 *Nature* 26 Aug. 777/2 By use of surfactants such as sorbitan stearates, water can be emulsified in hydrocarbon solvents and then readily supercooled.

sorbite[1] ('sɔːbaɪt). *Chem.* [f. sorb *sb.*[1] + -ite.] = sorbitol.
1867 *Chambers's Encycl.* IX. 187/2 Sorbin, or Sorbite.., may be obtained in colourless transparent rhombic octahedra. 1868 *Fownes' Chem.* (ed. 10) 638 Sorbin, or Sorbite, is a crystallisable sugar existing in the juice of ripe mountain-ash berries.

Hence **sor'bitic** *a.*[1] (See quot.)
1868 Watts *Dict. Chem.* V. 353 Sorbite when heated gives off acid water, and is converted after some time..into a dark-red mass consisting of sorbitic acid.

sorbite[2] ('sɔːbaɪt). [f. the name of Dr. H. C. *Sorby* (1826–1908).] † **1.** A nitride and carbide of titanium found as red microscopic crystals in pig iron. *Obs.*
1888 H. M. Howe in *Engin. & Mining Jrnl.* 18 Aug. 132 (*table*), Minerals which compose iron. Name suggested here ..Sorbite. *Ibid.* 1 Sept. 177/1 Sorbite has been detected by Sorby in many cast-irons..as beautiful triangles, rhombs, hexagons and complex crosses. 1919 *Mineral. Mag.* XVIII. 376 It [*sc.* cochranite] is formed under the same conditions [as], and sometimes together with, the copper-red cubes of titanium cyano-nitride, $Ti(CN)_2{\cdot}3Ti_3N_2$. This was named sorbite.., a term afterwards withdrawn, as the same name was given..for one of the transition conditions in carbon-steel.

2. A constituent of steel consisting of microscopic granules of cementite in a ferrite matrix, produced esp. when hardened steel is tempered above about 450°C. [a. F. *sorbite* (F. Osmond 1895, in *Bull. de la Soc. d'Encouragement pour l'Industrie Nationale* X. 491).]
1900 *Metallographist* III. 196 The crystallites represent the solid solution of first solidification, from which, during cooling, plates of cementite separated first, then the eutectic, pearlyte or sorbite (the latter if the melting of the cementite was sufficiently complete). 1902 *Encycl. Brit.* XXIX. 572/2 *Austenite*, *troostite*, *sorbite*, and other constituents [of iron] have also been described. 1924 Greaves & Wrighton *Pract. Micros. Metallogr.* vii. 57 Sorbite is the essential constituent of hardened and tempered steels intended for constructional purposes. 1964 H. Hodges *Artifacts* xix. 218 The effect of gently heating a quenched steel is that at low temperatures any martensite present forms troostite, while at higher temperatures..sorbite is produced. 1967 A. H. Cottrell *Introd. Metallurgy* xx. 384 Above about 500°C the cementite particles grow competitively..into larger rounded particles dispersed through the B.C.C. iron matrix, giving a spheroidized structure (sorbite).

Hence **sor'bitic** *a.*[2]
1902 *Jrnl. Iron & Steel Inst.* LXI. 140 Osmond said that probably in future all our steel rails will be made sorbitic. 1904 *Electrochem. Industry* Feb. 51 (Cent.), Stead and Richards in a paper on sorbitic steel rails give a simple method for the production of sorbite in steel. 1927 *Min. Proc. Inst. Civil Engineers* CCXXIV. 319 Photographs indicating the difference between sorbitic and ordinary steel. 1975 *Metals Abstr.* VIII. i. 298/1 The production of

reinforcing wire from grade 80 steel rod with a uniform sorbitic structure is described.

†**sor'bition.** *Obs.* [a. obs. F. *sorbition* or ad. L. *sorbitio*, f. *sorbēre* to imbibe.] The action of imbibing; also, something which may be imbibed.

1623 COCKERAM I, *Sorbition*, a sipping often. **1656** BLOUNT *Glossogr.*, *Sorbition*, a supping, as of broth or pottage. **1684** tr. *Bonet's Merc. Compit.* VI. 234 Chicken broth, tempered with cooling herbs, and sorbitions of the same.

sorbitize ('sɔːbɪtaɪz), *v.* *Metallurgy.* [f. SORBIT(E[2] + -IZE.] *trans.* To convert (steel) into a form containing sorbite. Hence **'sorbitized** *ppl. a.*, **'sorbitizing** *vbl. sb.*; **sorbiti'zation**, the process of sorbitizing.

1918 D. K. BULLENS *Steel* (ed. 2) viii. 167 It required four quenchings to entirely sorbitize the steel. **1927** *Jrnl. Iron & Steel Inst.* CXVI. 582 Conditions of working which tend to keep the oxide content of the bath at a minimum favour the production of sorbitised rails free from hair cracks. **1928** C. J. ALLEN *Steel Highway* I. viii. 97 Another popular means of toughening the steel is by heat treatment, the process known as 'sorbitising' adding considerably to the wearing capacity with but a moderate addition to the cost of the rails. **1930** *Chem. Abstr.* XXIV. 3740 *(heading)* Method of 'sorbitization' of rails used at Nadezhdinsky iron and steel works. **1968** *Metals Abstr.* I. 1266/2 *(heading)* Sorbitizing of rolled wire from the rolling heat. **1975** *Ibid.* VIII. 298/1 *(heading)* Wire-rod sorbitized from its temperature at the end of rolling. **1975** *Chem. Abstr.* July–Aug. 215/1 *(heading)* Sorbitization of carbon steel wire rod during continuous rolling.

sorbitol ('sɔːbɪtɒl). *Chem.* [f. SORBITE[1] + -OL.] A hexahydric alcohol, $CH_2OH{\cdot}(CHOH)_4{\cdot}CH_2OH$, found as a dextrorotatory isomer and crystallizing in the berries of the mountain-ash as colourless needles.

1895 *Naturalist* 24 The unripe berries have much malic acid,..also amygdalin, emulsin, sorbitol. **1898** *Ibid.* 187 Mannite and another alcoholic sugar called sorbitol. **1928** HAAS & HILL *Introd. Chem. Plant Products* (ed. 4) I. 70 Sorbitol occurs in the berries of *Pyrus aucuparia* and also in apple juice. **1955** *Sci. News Let.* 29 Jan. 70/1 A sugary substance called sorbitol..is used to 'entrap' the essential oils and esters that carry the citrus fruit flavor and fragrance. **1964** [see *hexahydric* adj. s.v. HEXA-]. **1975** *Sci. Amer.* Dec. 80 In response to the raised level of glucose in the aqueous humour (as in the blood) that is characteristic of diabetes.. the enzyme catalyzes the reduction of glucose to form the sugar alcohol sorbitol.

Sorbo ('sɔːbəʊ). Also **sorbo.** [Invented name: cf. ABSORB *v.*] The proprietary name of a make of sponge rubber. Usu. *attrib.*, esp. as ***sorbo rubber***. Also *fig.*

1917 *Trade Marks Jrnl.* 15 Aug. 799 Sorbo..Sponge substitutes (India Rubber). Leeson Sponge and Rubber Co. Ltd. **1919** *Ibid.* 7 May 575 Sorbo Rubber-Sponge Products Ltd. **1926–7** *Army & Navy Stores Catal.* 104/2 Sorbo sponges—each 1/3. **1939** *Archit. Rev.* LXXXV. 251 *(caption)* The smaller sketch shows the large rounded sorbo strips fixed to door edges. **1940** *Amat. Radio Handbk.* (ed. 2) 134/1 Most microphones will tend to pick up floor vibrations if rested directly on the table. For this reason they should preferably be placed on a piece of sorbo rubber. **1941** C. KIRKUS *Let's go Climbing* ix. 132, I..put the sorbo mattress underneath my outer clothes, donned gloves and balaclava, and prepared to spend the night. **1941** 'R. WEST' *Black Lamb & Grey Falcon* I. 319 Astra..bounced from the platform like a great sorbo ball to say good-bye. **1942** M. DICKENS *One Pair of Feet* viii. 159 Toots pursed her sorbo lips over the result. **1963** G. FREEMAN *Campaign* vii. 102 Boat-like red slippers with thick, white sorbo soles. **1976** *Lancet* 9 Oct. 801/2 The endangered areas, trochanters and sacrum, are kept free of pressure by placing the patient on a pillow or, better, sorborubber packs.

†**Sor'bonical,** *a. Obs.* [f. SORBONNE. Cf. F. *sorbonique* (16th cent.).] Belonging to, connected with, the Sorbonne.

1543 BALE *Yet a Course Romish Fox* 36 Great bellyed braggers or sorbonycall masters in Parys. **1561** T. NORTON *Calvin's Inst.* III. xv. (1634) 383 The Sorbonicall schooles, the mothers of all errours. **1603** FLORIO *Montaigne* III. xiii. 660 The Sorbonicall or theologicall wine, and their feasts or gaudy dayes, are now come to be proverbially jested-at.

Sorbonist ('sɔːbənɪst). Also 6 **Sorbonest,** 7–9 **Sorbonnist.** [ad. mod.L. *Sorbonista* or F. *Sorboniste*: see SORBONNE.] A doctor or student at the Sorbonne.

α. **1560** DAUS tr. *Sleidane's Comm.* 28 The Sorbonistes condempne Luthers bokes. **1579** FULKE *Conf. Sanders* 674 Claudius de Sanctis, that brauling Sorbonist, woulde proue ..the saide liturgie to be his. **1592** MARLOWE *Massacre Paris* I. ix. 416 Because the blockish Sorbonests Attribute as much vnto their workes As to the seruice of the eternall God. **1631** WEEVER *Anc. Funeral Mon.* 369 He disputed with the Sorbonists in Paris. **1670** G. H. *Hist. Cardinals* I. I. 29 Those censures were made by the Sorbonists. **1751** *Hist. & Crit. Acc. of Hugh Peters* (1818) 27 *note*, The same Sorbonists decreed all those..to be in a mortal Sin. **1820** MILNER *Suppl. Mem. Eng. Cath.* 34 The decision of certain Sorbonists, respecting the lawfulness of the oath. **1886** J. GILLOW *Lit. & Biog. Hist. Eng. Cath.* II. 508 The Sorbonists still stuck to their opinion.

attrib. **1886** *Encycl. Brit.* XX. 195/2 Rabelais had indeed again made for himself protectors whom no clerical or Sorbonist jealousy could touch.

β. **1611** COTGR. s.v. *Ordinaire*, Certaine disputations held among Sorbonnists before they commence Doctors. **1683** *Apol. Prot. France* vi. 78 And upon the return of the Jesuites,..they communicated to the Sorbonnists the Popes Answer. **1757** HUME *Nat. Hist. Religion* 76 'How can you worship leeks and onions?' we shall suppose a Sorbonnist to say to a priest of Sais. **1820** T. MITCHELL *Aristoph.* (1822) II. 22 The Sorbonnists of Paris..in like manner affected to unite peculiar slovenliness and dirtiness with peculiar learning.

b. *transf.* A person of great learning.

1607 R. C[AREW] tr. *Estienne's World Wond.* 340 The grand Negro of all Necromancers (who is also the great Sorbonist of Sorcerers, and maister of Magicians).

Sorbonne (sɔː'bɒn). Also 6–7 **Sorbone.** [F. *Sorbonne*, f. the place-name *Sorbon* (see def.) in the Ardennes.]

1. Orig., a theological college at Paris founded by Robert de Sorbon early in the 13th century; the faculty of theology in the old University of Paris, of great importance down to the 17th century; now, a constituent part of the University of Paris (*Paris IV*), also housing departments from other sections of the University.

The Sorbonne is now the seat of the *Académie* of Paris.

1560 DAUS tr. *Sleidane's Comm.* 270 b, What tyme for the same cause the divines of Sorbone procured him some daunger, he shewed no constancie. **1638** R. BAKER tr. *Balzac's Lett.* (vol. II) 141 Concerning the condition of superiour things, I referre myself to the Sorbone. **1682** *News fr. France* 38 Thus you see how firm the Sorbonne is in this matter. **1728** CHAMBERS *Cycl.* s.v., There are Lodgings in it for 36 Doctors, who are said to be of the Society of the Sorbonne. **1886** *Encycl. Brit.* XX. 195/2 Up to this time Rabelais, despite the condemnation of the Sorbonne,..had experienced nothing like persecution or difficulty.

†**2.** A Sorbonist. *Obs.*[−1]

1631 WEEVER *Anc. Funeral Mon.* 751 He had studied a long time in Oxford, and at Paris amongst the Sorbons.

Hence **Sor'bonnic** *a.* (Cf. SORBONICAL *a.*)

1893 A. LANG *St. Andrews* iv. 105 A writer of the particularly unclassic Latin called Sorbonnic.

sorbose ('sɔːbəʊz, -s). *Chem.* [f. SORB *sb.*[1] + -OSE[2].] A ketohexose sugar obtained esp. from rowan berries as a fermentation product of sorbitol.

1889 *Jrnl. Chem. Soc.* LVI. 480 Sorbose ferments more slowly and less completely. **1913** HAAS & HILL *Introd. Chem. Plant Products* 63 Sorbose is a ketanic sugar produced by the fermentative oxidation of the alcohol sorbite contained in the sap of the mountain ash..; this sugar probably does not exist as such in the plant. **1962** *New Scientist* 5 Apr. 804/2 The fermentations already mentioned, with the less difficult fermentations producing ..sorbose (a key intermediate in the synthesis of vitamin C) .., more or less cover the extent of the British fermentation industry. **1970** *Ibid.* 5 Mar. 462/2 The possible non-nutritive sugars include sorbose (found in Mountain Ash berries), xylose (from oat husks), arabinose [etc.].

‖**Sorbus** ('sɔːbəs). [L. Cf. SORB *sb.*[1]] A Linnæan genus (now placed under *Pyrus*) including the service-tree, mountain-ash, etc.; a tree belonging to this genus. Also *attrib.*

1706 in PHILLIPS (ed. Kersey). **1751** J. HILL *Hist. Plants* 456 The pinnated smooth-leaved Sorbus. **1823** CRABB *Technol. Dict.*, *Sorbus domestica*, seu *Pyrus*, Sorbus Tree, Service, or Sorb.

sorcell, obs. variant of SARCELLE.

†**sorcer.** *Obs. rare.* Also 4, 6 **sorser,** 6 **sorsyer.** [ad. OF. *sorcier* (cf. It. *sortiere*, Sp. *sortero*):—pop. L. **sortiarius*, f. *sort-*, *sors* lot, SORT *sb.*[1]] = next.

13.. *E.E. Allit. P.* B. 1579 Wychez & walkyries wonnen to þat sale,..Sorsers & exorsismus & fele such clerkes. **1502** *Ord. Crysten Men* (W. de W. 1506) IV. ix, The fyfth is of sorcyers and..deuyns. **1549** *Compl. Scot.* xx. 168 Sum sorseris and vytchis, quhilkis ar instramentis of the ald eneme of mankynd.

sorcerer ('sɔːsərə(r)). Also 6 **sorserer, -ar, sosserer,** *Sc.* **socerar.** [f. prec. + -ER.] One who practises sorcery; a wizard, a magician.

α. **1526** TINDALE *Acts* xiii. 6 They founde a certayne sorserer. *Ibid.* 8 The sorserar Elemas..withstode them. **1535** COVERDALE *Isaiah* ii. 6 Whether it be in Sorcerers..or in calkers of mens byrthes, wherof ye haue to many. *a* **1548** HALL *Chron.*, *Edw. IV*, D iiij, Her frendes on the other syde sayd, that she was kept away, and her iorney empeched by Sorcerers and Necromanciers. **1610** SHAKS. *Temp.* III. ii. 49, I am subiect to a Tirant, A Sorcerer, that by his cunning hath cheated me Of the Island. **1651** HOBBES *Leviath.* III. xxxii. 197 The works of the Egyptian Sorcerers..were great miracles. **1727** DE FOE *Syst. Magic* I. i. (1840) 6 Certainly then they did not take those magicians to be..dealers with the Devil, and sorcerers. **1769** BLACKSTONE *Comm.* IV. iv. 60 The civil law punishes with death not only the sorcerers themselves, but also those who consult them. **1816** SINGER *Hist. Cards* 55 The Gipsies..exercised the craft of sorcerers. **1848** GALLENGA *Italy* (1851) 415 The sway exercised by a sorcerer over the demon to whom he has bartered his soul. **1865** J. H. INGRAHAM *Pillar of Fire* (1872) 403 This was the place where the sorcerers and soothsayers held their mystic and fearful rites.

attrib. **1888** MISS RAGOZIN *Media, Babylon, & Persia* x. § 8 (1891) 269 The Shamans or sorcerer-priests of many Turanian tribes.

β. **1552** ABP. HAMILTON *Catech.* (1884) 50 Quhen saevir thow..seikis for ony help at ony wytche, socerar, cowngerar. **1596** R. H. tr. *Lavaterus's Ghostes & Spir.* 28 There haue bene many Magiciens, Sosserers, and Conjurers ..who would easily counterfeit visions.

b. ***sorcerer's apprentice*** [tr. F. *l'apprenti sorcier*, the title of a symphonic poem by Paul Dukas (1897), after *der zauberlehrling*, a ballad by Goethe (1797)], one who, like the apprentice in the ballad with his spells, instigates processes which he is unable to control. Also *attrib.*

1952 E. COXHEAD *Play Toward* iii. 24 Of course there was always a sorcerer's-apprentice element in teaching: but of all their creations, Lance was surely not the one who should be getting out of hand. **1966** J. AIKEN *Trouble with Product X* vi. 115, I wondered if his disciples, like the sorceror's [*sic*] apprentice, had not got out of control. **1967** *Sunday Times* 26 Feb. 2/3 The CIA is not a sorcerer's apprentice that has run wild, but..is under strict government control. **1974** HAWKEY & BINGHAM *Wild Card* xiii. 116 Our first priority should be learning to live with the technology we have already, not acquiring more. Because, like the Sorcerer's Apprentice, we just *ain't* going to be able to handle it.

sorceress ('sɔːsərɪs). Also 6–7 **sorceres.** [a. AF. *sorceresse*, *-esce*: see SORCER and -ESS[1].]

1. A female sorcerer; a witch.

c **1384** CHAUCER *H. Fame* III. 1262 Ther saugh I.. charmeresses, Olde wrecches, Sorceresses, That vse exorsisacions. **1390** GOWER *Conf.* III. 49 Thes queenes were as tuo goddesses Of Art magique Sorceresses. **1470–85** MALORY *Arthur* VI. iv. 187 Sore I am of these quenes sorceresses aferd. **1509** HAWES *Past. Pleas.* xxxvi. (Percy Soc.) 188 The sorceresse, the false roote of doloure, All of golde..Of the best made the head serpentyne. *a* **1548** HALL *Chron.*, *Hen. VI*, 112 Jhon duke of Alaunson and his sorceresse Jone (called the mayde, sent from God). **1638** JUNIUS *Paint. Ancients* 173 Diogenes..witnesseth Medea to have been not a sorceresse, but a woman of knowne wisdome. **1671** MILTON *Samson* 819 How cunningly the sorceress displays Her own transgressions, to upbraid me mine! *a* **1740** WATERLAND *Wks.* (1823) IX. 413 How unlikely is it that God should make use of this sorceress as a prophetess, and should give her the honour of revealing his counsels. **1832** W. IRVING *Alhambra* I. 242 This may be one of those Northern sorceresses of whom we have heard. **1885** PATER *Marius the Epicurean* I. v. 62 In one very remote village lives the sorceress Pamphile.

transf. *a* **1700** KEN *Hymnotheo* Poet. Wks. 1721 III. 95 Much more mysterious is my inbred Lust; In no one thing I can the Sorc'ress trust.

attrib. **1841** W. SPALDING *Italy & It. Isl.* II. 319 Armida, the sorceress-niece of the Sultan of Damascus. **1877** 'RITA' *Vivienne* III. vi, Blanche repaid him with sorceress smiles and false kisses.

b. In playful or familiar use.

c **1800** H. K. WHITE *Lett.* (1837) 282 Sorceress! I cannot burst thy bonds! **1859** GEO. ELIOT *A. Bede* v, Ah! you witch-mother, you sorceress! How is a Christian man to win a game off you?

†**'sorcering,** *vbl. sb. Obs.*[−1] [f. SORCER-ER or SORCER-Y + -ING[1].] The exercise of sorcery.

1614 BP. HALL *Contempl.*, *O.T.* VII. 324 His trade of sorcering had so inured him to receiue voyces from his familiars, in shape of beasts, that this euent seemed not strange to him.

†**'sorcering,** *ppl. a. Obs.* [f. as prec. + -ING[2].] Practising or exercising sorcery.

1583 MELBANCKE *Philotimus* S iv, The sorcering Syrens, who are merrie in tempestes, and heauie in faire weather. **1607** R. C[AREW] tr. *Estienne's World Wond.* 340 This sorcering priest. **1609** HEYWOOD *Brit. Troy* V. lxxxviii, The black spels of this Sorcering witch.

†**'sorcerist.** *Obs.*[−1] [f. as prec. + -IST.] One who practises sorcery; a sorcerer.

1624 HEYWOOD *Gunaik.* II. 77 Moyses made a law that all such as repayred to these jugling sorcerists should be stoned to death.

'sorcerize, *v. rare.* [f. as prec. + -IZE.] *trans.* To transform by sorcery.

1866 FURNIVALL in *Pol., Rel., & L. Poems* 26 *marg.*, A Lombard was sorcerized into a goose. **1972** M. MEAD *Blackberry Winter* xv. 202 The threatening sorcerers of the plains..blackmailed our mild-mannered mountain people by promising temporarily not to sorcerize their relatives, providing they were given food and an adequate supply of trade goods.

sorcerous ('sɔːsərəs), *a.* [f. as prec. + -OUS.]

1. Of the nature of, pertaining to or connected with, sorcery.

1546 BALE *Eng. Votaries* I. 24 He wolde in no wyse commen with them..least they shulde after any sorcerous sort bywytche hym. **1577** HARRISON *England* II. ix. (1877) 178 By sundrie sorcerous and artificiall practises whereby the working of the said elements were restreined. **1605** CHAPMAN *Byron's Trag.* IV. ii, O that in mine Eyes Were all the Sorcerous poyson of my woes. **1646** GAULE *Cases Cons.* 41 Lord! how many are the sorcerous superstitions of the Many? **1698** FRYER *Acc. E. India & P.* 277 Lest an Evil Tongue should have a Sorcerous effect. **1835** J. HARRIS *Gt. Teacher* (1837) 284 In the face of this sorcerous and powerful delusion. **1880** SWINBURNE *Birthday Ode* 207 From fairy-footed fields..And sorcerous woods of Rhineland.

2. Dealing in or exercising sorcery.

1550 BALE *Eng. Votaries* II. 11 Theophylactus..whych after .xv. yeares solde the Papacy to Johan Gracyan hys sorcerouse companyon. **1633** D. R[OGERS] *Treatise of Sacr.* i. 123 Which words..our Saviour did not (as a Sorcerous Priest) murmour over the Bread and Wine.

Hence **'sorcerously** *adv.*, in a sorcerous manner, by means of sorcery.

1646 GAULE *Cases of Consc.* 128 What Act or Instrument of Man..that..may not be sorcerously abused? **1652** —— *Magastrom.* 193 Divination is temptingly and sorcerously sought for.

sorcery (ˈsɔːsərɪ). Forms: α. 4 sorceri, 4–7 sorcerie, 4, 6 sorcerye, 4– sorcery; 4 sorsory(e, 4–6 sorserye, 5 sors(s)ery, sorsry, -rie. β. 5 socerye, 5–6 socery, 6 sossery, -rie. [a. OF. *sorcerie* (f. *sorcier* SORCER), or ad. med.L. *sorceria*. So MDu. *sorcerie, sorserie*.]

1. The use of magic or enchantment; the practice of magic arts; witchcraft.

α. *a* **1300** *Cursor M.* 29255 Crists enemy, þat wiche-craft or sorceri Dos wit ani halud thing. **13..** *K. Alis.* 478 (Laud MS.), þat ilk ni3th, Neptenabus Made so stronge sorcerye. *c* **1386** CHAUCER *Pars. T.* ⁋340 If he were al refreynit by siknes, or by malefice of sorserye. **1422** tr. *Secreta Secret.*, *Priv. Priv.* 199 He..beleuyd swenys and sorsrie. **1470–85** MALORY *Arthur* II. iii. 79 By enchauntement and sorssery she hath ben the destroyer of many good knyghtes. *a* **1548** HALL *Chron., Edw. IV*, I ij b, A seruaunte of the Dukes was sodainly accused..of poysonyng, sorcery, or inchauntment. **1591** SHAKS. *1 Hen. VI*, II. i. 15 To quittance their deceite, Contriu'd by Art, and balefull Sorcerie. **1628** COKE *On Litt.* III. vi, A man was taken in Southwark..with a Book of Sorcery in his Male and was brought into the Kings-Bench. **1844** EMERSON *Misc. P., Tantalus* Wks. (Bohn) III. 322 Alas! the same sorcery has spoiled his skill; no syllable can he shape on his lips. **1878** STUBBS *Const. Hist.* III. xviii. 90 The queen dowager was accused..of an attempt to destroy the king by sorcery.

β. *c* **1460** *Towneley Myst.* xxvi. 129 That may be done thrugh socery. **1500–20** DUNBAR *Poems* l. 6 His mother was ane Farie Queyne, Gottin be sossery. **1511–2** *Act 3 Hen. VIII*, c. 11 Curis..in the which they..use socery and which crafte. **1568** LAUDER *Lam. Pure* 33 Now mony vsis Sosserie.

b. *pl.* Separate forms or instances of this.

1357 *Lay Folks Catech.* (1901) 34 Al mawmetries, Al fals enchaunmentez, and al sorceries. **1542–3** *Act 34 & 35 Hen. VIII*, c. 8 The advoyding of sorceryes, witchecrafte, and other inconveniencies. **1584** R. SCOT *Discov. Witchcr.* (1886) 267 Thereby Ulysses escaped Circes hir sorceries and inchantments. **1648** WILKINS *Math. Magic* II. vii. 201 Simon Magus was eminent for miraculous sorceries. **1671** in *Verney Mem.* (1907) II. 279 Whether she uses any manner of charmes, sorceries, or magic whatever. **1741–2** GRAY *Agrip.* 171 Sorceries, Assassinations, poisonings.

2. *transf.* and *fig.*

1576 FLEMING *Panopl. Epist.* 156, I am not surprised with the incantations and sorceries of vaine glorie. **1592** NASHE *P. Penilesse* 12 b, What drugs, what sorceries, what oiles,..doe our curious Dames vse to inlarge our withered beauties? **1667** MILTON *P.L.* II. 566 Vain wisdom all, and false Philosophie: Yet with a pleasing sorcerie could charm Pain for a while. **1837** CARLYLE *Fr. Rev.* II. III. vi, It is possible, the greatness of this man..might, with most legitimate sorcery, fascinate the volatile Queen. **1880** 'OUIDA' *Moths* III. 262 Personal beauty is a rare sorcery.

sorche, obs. form of SEARCH *v.*

sorcot, obs. form of SURCOAT.

sorcyer: see SORCER.

sord, *sb. Obs.* exc. *arch.* Forms: 5 soorde, sorde, 5–6 sourd(e, 9 sord. [f. SORD *v.*] A flight or flock *of* mallards.

Orig. perhaps the act of taking to wing, but only recorded in the lists of 'proper terms'; in some late copies of these erroneously given as *sore*.

14.. *Harl. MS. 541* fol. 225 in *Phil. Soc. Trans.* (1909) 55 A Soorde of malardes, A Doppyng of herles. *c* **1470** *Hors, Shepe & G.* (Roxb.), A Spryng of teeles, A Sourde of malardes. **1486** *Bk. St. Albans, Hawking* d ij, When ther be in a stobull tyme Sordes of mallardes in the felde. **1801** STRUTT *Sports & Past.* I. ii. 28 A sord or sute of mallards. **1856** 'STONEHENGE' *Brit. Rural Sports* I. ix. 78/1 The following Terms are in Use among Wildfowl-shooters:—A flock of wigeon is termed 'a company'..; of mallards, 'a sord'.

sord, obs. or dial. form of SWARD *sb.*

†**sord**, *v. Obs.*$^{-1}$ [ad. OF. *sordre, sourdre*, etc.:—L. *surgĕre* to rise. Cf. SORD *sb.*] *intr.* To rise or soar *up* in flight.

14.. *Harl. MS. 2340* fol. 49 b. in *Phil. Soc. Trans.* (1909) 28 It spryngyth or sordyth vp sodenly be hym.

sordavalite (ˈsɔːdəvælaɪt). *Min.* Also sordawal(l)ite. [ad. Sw. *sordawalit* (Nordenskiöld, 1820), f. *Sordawala, -vala*, in Finland, its locality.] A vitreous mineral substance found in diabase.

1823 W. PHILLIPS *Min.* (ed. 3) 210 Sordawalite..is described as being nearly black. **1850** ANSTED *Elem. Geol., Min.*, etc. 191 *Sordawalite*, silicate of alumina and magnesia with phosphate of magnesia. **1868** WATTS *Dict. Chem.*, *Sordawallite*, a mineral resembling pit-coal in appearance, forming three layers in trap near Sordawala in Finland. **1882** *Imperial Dict.* (Annandale), *Sordavalite*. [So in later Dicts.]

sorde, obs. form of SWORD.

‖**sordes** (ˈsɔːdiːz). [L. *sordēs* (pl., rare and defective in sing.), filth, uncleanness, etc., related to *sordēre* to be dirty or foul. Cf. SORDS.]

Construed either as singular or plural.

1. Dirt, filth; foul or feculent matter; refuse or rubbish removed or separated by or during the treatment, manufacture, or working of something.

1640 BP. REYNOLDS *Passions* xv. 139 A Sink by an house makes all the house the cleaner, because the Sordes are cast into that. **1657** J. WATTS *A Scribe & his Let. Answ.* Pref. Ep. p. x, You have your eares stuffed and opplete with Kitchinstuffe and such soyl and sordes. **1758** BORLASE *Nat. Hist. Cornw.* 179 The sordes, which settles above the tin, is skimmed off. **1766** SMOLLETT *Trav.* I. 352 The sordes or dirt falls to the bottom, the oil swims a-top. *c* **1800** *State Leslie of Powis* (Jam.), The filth, sordes, dregs, or refuse of a distillery or manufactory. **1837** WHITTOCK *Bk. Trades* (1842) 435 (Tallow-chandler), The prepared tallow, freed by straining from its 'sordes', its adventitious particles and membranaceous envelopment.

fig. **1660** TRAPP *Comm. O.T.* III. 515 Such persons chuse to remain in the *sordes* of their sins. **1780** BENTHAM *Princ. Legisl.* ii. §6 To cleanse itself from the sordes of its impure original it was necessary it should change its name.

2. Filthy or feculent matter attaching to, or collecting on or in, the bodies of persons or animals.

1670 E. BORLASE *Lathom Spaw* 33 In facilitating the passage of the stone and gravel, and abstersing its sordes and minera, I find it very successful. **1790** *Phil. Trans.* LXXX. 391 In the cancerous, as well as in other malignant ulcers, we frequently meet with a white sordes, which closely adheres to the surface of the sore. **1798** W. BLAIR *Soldier's Friend* 51 The copious perspirations..must tend to accumulate filth and sordes upon the skin. **1835** KIRBY *Hab. & Inst. Anim.* II. xx. 316 The bird-louse is probably useful to birds in devouring the sordes which must accumulate at the root of their plumes. **1843** R. J. GRAVES *Syst. Clin. Med.* x. 107 An emetic clears the stomach of offending matters or sordes.

b. Impure matter collecting about the teeth, gums, etc.; *spec.* in *Path.*, the foul crusts formed upon the teeth and lips in typhoid or other fevers.

1746 R. JAMES *Introd.* in *Moufet's Health's Improv.* 48 Putrid Sordes upon the Lips, Teeth, Tongue, Palate, and Fauces. **1811** *Self Instructor* 533 By washing out the gums and natural sordes. **1822–7** GOOD *Study Med.* (1829) II. 242 The lips are furred with a black tenacious sordes. **1876** BRISTOWE *Th. & Pract. Med.* (1878) 109 His lips are dry, black, and probably fissured, his teeth loaded with sordes.

sordet, variant of SOURDET.

sordid (ˈsɔːdɪd), *a.* and *sb.* Also 6–7 sordide, 7 sorded. [a. F. *sordide* (16th c. in Godefroy; = Sp., Pg., It. *sórdido*), or ad. L. *sordid-us* dirty, foul, base, mean, etc., f. *sord-ēre* to be dirty: cf. SORDES.]

A. *adj.* **I. 1.** *Path.* **a.** Of suppurations, etc.: Corrupt, foul, repulsive; of the nature of sordes.

1597 LOWE *Chirurg.* L iij b, The vlcers [are] inequal, sordides [*sic*],..euill fauoured, by reason of the humor, which is most sordide and stinking. **1822–7** GOOD *Study Med.* (1829) II. 163 The skin parched, or soaked with sordid, fetid sweat. *Ibid.* II. 627 There is a dejection of sordid pus in considerable abundance. **1883** J. M. DUNCAN *Lect. Dis. Women* (ed. 2) xvi. 161 An old grey-white accumulation of sordid epithelial detritus.

b. Of an ulcer, wound, etc.: Yielding or discharging matter of this kind.

1597 [see prec.]. **1676** WISEMAN *Surg. Treat.* II. i. 165 There is a second sort of Matter affecting Ulcers that is thick, generated of abundance of gross tough Humours, and rendering the Ulcer foul; whence it is called a *Sordid Vlcer*. **1696** *Phil. Trans.* XIX. 291 The Wound was very sordid; and the inside as well as the outside beset with Slime. **1769** E. BANCROFT *Guiana* 384 The disease corrodes the fingers and toes with a dry, sordid, scabby, and gangrenous ulcer. **1801** *Med. Jrnl.* V. 163 The incision on the left arm, which ..had degenerated into a sordid ulcer. **1822–7** GOOD *Study Med.* (1829) V. 556 In several sordid cutaneous eruptions.

2. a. Dirty, foul, filthy; repellent through want of cleanness or tidiness; in later use, mean and squalid.

1611 COTGR., *Sordide*, sordide, foule, filthie, corrupt. **1627** DONNE *Serm.* xxii. (1640) 223 Sordid, senselesse, namelesse dust. **1655** CULPEPPER, etc. *Riverius* IV. vii. 116 The choller and flegm which is more..impure, swims at the top, and so the blood seems impure and sordid. **1680** OTWAY *Orphan* I. iv, [I will] rather..live on sordid scraps at proud Men's Doors. **1697** DRYDEN *Virg. Georg.* I. 118 [They] sprinkle sordid Ashes all around. **1727–46** THOMSON *Summer* 386 The trout is banish'd by the sordid stream. **1836** EMERSON *Nature, Beauty* Wks. (Bohn) II. 147 In private places, among sordid objects, an act of truth or heroism seems at once to draw to itself the sky as its temple.

b. Of places, houses, etc.

1628 DONNE *Serm.* lxxv. (1640) 762 To finde a languishing wretch in a sordid corner. **1634** SIR T. HERBERT *Trav.* 149 Their houses..within are poore and sordid. **1669** *Phil. Trans.* IV. 1136 The sweepings of the house, any kind of ashes, shovelings of any sordid place. **1821** SHELLEY *Adonais* xxxviii, Whilst thy cold embers choke the sordid hearth of shame. **1864** BURTON *Scot Abr.* I. iii. 122 Stately edifices..were doomed to fall into decay and be succeeded by sordid hovels. **1880** MRS. FORRESTER *Roy & V.* I. 56 She has escaped from her sordid surroundings.

c. Of life, conditions, etc.

1621 BURTON *Anat. Mel.* I. ii. II. v, Through their owne nastinesse & sluttishnesse, & immund sordid maner of life, suffer their aire to putrifie. **1687** A. LOVELL tr. *Thevenot's Trav.* II. 108 The sordid and nasty way that the Ambassadour and all his train lived in. **1691** RAY *Creation* I. (1704) 110 What a Kind of barbarous and sordid Life we must necessarily have lived. **1764** HARMER *Observ.* ii. §13. 70 We..may have imagined..that Abraham lived in a sordid plenty. **1797** GODWIN *Enquirer* II. iv. 206 He can procure a sordid meal. **1850** MRS. JAMESON *Leg. Monast. Ord.* (1863) 253 With tattered raiment and all the outward signs of sordid misery. **1891** KIPLING *Light that Failed* vii. (1900) 112 Dick's experience of the sordid misery of want.

d. Of garments or clothing.

1655 STANLEY *Hist. Philos.* (1687) 136/1 [They] wear the same garment in Winter as in Summer, and that sordid. **1673** W. CAVE *Prim. Christ.* III. v. 366 In a sordid and squalid Habit. **1752** FIELDING *Amelia* (1775) X. 8 The magistrate had too great an honour for truth to suspect that she ever appeared in sordid apparel. **1788** GIBBON *Decl. & Fall* xli. IV. 149 Sordid and scanty were their garments. **1851** TRENCH *Poems* (1862) 183 They put the sordid grave clothes off.

3. †**a.** Of persons (or animals): Dirty or sluttish in habits or appearance. *Obs.*

1613 PURCHAS *Pilgrimage* (1614) 232 They abstaine from swines flesh: neither will that sweete aire of Arabia breath life to that sordide and stinking creature. **1664** H. MORE *Apology* 517 Provided we be not course and sordid, but reverent and comely in our public worship. **1712** ADDISON *Spect.* No. 464 ⁋5 The Person he chanced to see was to Appearance an old sordid blind Man.

b. *Zool.* In the names of a few fishes or birds, in allusion to their dirty-looking colour, as ***sordid chætodon, dragonet, scarus, thrush***.

1803 SHAW *Gen. Zool.* IV. II. 370 *Sordid Chætodon... Dusky-grey Chætodon; native of the Arabian seas. **1769** PENNANT *Brit. Zool.* (1776) III. 147 The *Sordid Dragonet, *Dracunculus*. **1836** YARRELL *Brit. Fishes* I. 266 The Sordid Dragonet..generally occurs of small size. **1881** DAY *Fishes Gt. Brit.* I. 176 Sordid dragonet, dusky skulpin. **1803** SHAW *Gen. Zool.* IV. II. 400 *Sordid Scarus... Brown-ferruginous Scarus. **1801** LATHAM *Gen. Synop. Birds, Suppl.* II. 186 *Sordid Thrush... The plumage in general is greenish ash.

II. †**4.** Of a coarse, gross, or inferior character or nature; befitting or appertaining to a mean person or thing; menial. *Obs.*

1596 SPENSER *F.Q.* v. v. 23 She..in his hand a distaffe to him gaue, That he thereon should spin both flax and tow; A sordid office for a mind so braue. **1605** BACON *Adv. Learn.* II. I. §5 He did thinke much to dispute with any that did alleage such base and sordide instances. *a* **1619** FOTHERBY *Atheom.* II. i. §8 (1686) 195 Not onely in liberall and ingenious Arts, but also in sordide and ignoble. **1655** STANLEY *Hist. Philos.* (1687) 195/2 Modesty teacheth us to decline sordid things. *a* **1701** MAUNDRELL *Journ. Jerus.* 8 Apr. (1707) 107 By which means it was redeem'd from that sordid use. **1751** JOHNSON *Rambler* No. 168 ⁋6 The long habit of connecting a knife with sordid offices.

5. a. Of actions, habits, etc.: Of a low, mean, or despicable character; marked by or proceeding from ignoble motives, esp. of self-interest or monetary gain.

1611 COTGR., *Taquinerie*, sordide miserie,..base pinching. **1639** in *Verney Mem.* (1907) I. 106 His sordide and base dissembling. **1682** BURNET *Rights Princes* ii. 35 The Clergy using all the basest and sordidest Arts possible to draw Legacies from Rich Widows. **1753** RICHARDSON *Grandison* V. ii. 19 We see, in the behaviour, and sordid acquiescence with insults, of these three men, that offensive spirits cannot be true ones. **1781** COWPER *Truth* 76 What is all righteousness that men devise? What—but a sordid bargain for the skies? **1818** BENTHAM *Parl. Reform* 50 That they should sell the attachment of their friends..for dry and sordid gain. **1855** MACAULAY *Hist. Eng.* xviii. IV. 162 His courage, his abilities,..had made him, in spite of his sordid vices, a favourite with his brethren in arms. **1873** DIXON *Two Queens* XVI. ii. III. 193 Though he got her money, he had never ceased repenting of his sordid act.

b. Lacking in refinement; low, coarse, rough.

1668 *Extr. State P. rel. Friends* (1912) III. 278 Edward Wivel..permits their sordid Conventicls to be..kept ther. **1744** AKENSIDE *Pleas. Imag.* II. 15 Long immured In noontide darkness by the glimmering lamp, Each Muse and each fair Science pined away The sordid hours. **1751** JOHNSON *Rambler* No. 168 ⁋3 To him who has passed most of his hours with the delicate and polite, many expressions will seem sordid.

c. *absol.* That which is sordid or mean.

1863 W. MORRIS in Mackail *Life* (1899) I. 21 Whatever there was of sordid about the story had slipped off him. **1902** J. BUCHAN *Watcher by Threshold* 189 Frankly, I hate the sordid and unpleasant.

6. Of persons, their character, etc.: Inclined to what is low, mean, or ignoble; *esp.* moved by selfish or mercenary motives; influenced only by material considerations.

1636 [FREEMAN] tr. *Seneca's Shortn. Life* (1663) 34 He sordid is, who catch'd with rude applause, Grown old, dies wrangling in a worthlesse cause. **1650** BULWER *Anthropomet.* 171 These Nations.., that are so unpolitick, may justly be called wild men, and of a sordid disposition. **1687** WOOD *Life* (O.H.S.) III. 241 He is sordid still, and nothing will change his base humour. **1727** GAY *Fables* I. xix, A Lioncub of sordid mind, Avoided all the lion kind. **1789** BELSHAM *Ess.* II. xli. 561 They are inveighed against as a base and sordid people. **1808** SCOTT *Marm.* II. xxii, Her comrade was a sordid soul. **1840** MISS MITFORD in L'Estrange *Life* (1870) III. vii. 108 The land..will probably be purchased by some sordid person upon the speculation of making us pay an inordinate rent. **1875** MANNING *Mission H. Ghost* viii. 203 All men of the world are sordid, and the more worldly the more sordid.

absol. **1762** COWPER *To Miss Macartney* 54 Thus grief itself has comforts dear, The sordid never know.

7. *Comb.*, as ***sordid-base***; with ppl. adj., as ***sordid-seeming***.

1598 B. JONSON *Ev. Man in Hum.* II. iii, To think a fellow of thy outward presence, Should, in the frame and fashion of his mind, Be so degenerate, and sordid-base. **1920** D. H. LAWRENCE *Lost Girl* xiv. 329 The dreary, to her sordid-seeming Campagna.

B. *sb.* One who is sordid. *rare.*

1959 C. MACINNES *Absolute Beginners* 13 All the old tax-payers know of this absolute, of course, for one thing, the poor old sordids recollect their own glorious teenage days. *Ibid.* 184 It doesn't seem possible such sordids as this lot could frighten you. **1960** N. MITFORD *Don't tell Alfred* ix. 97 My children regarded everybody over the age of thirty as old sordids, old weirdies, ruins, hardly human at all.

†**ˈsordidate**, *v. Obs.*$^{-0}$ [f. L. *sordidāt-us*.] (See quots.) So **ˈsordidated** *ppl. a.*

1604 R. CAWDREY *Table Alph.* (1613), *Sordidated*, defiled, sluttish. **1623** COCKERAM I, *Sordidate*, to make foule. **1656** BLOUNT *Glossogr.*, *Sordidate*, to array sluttishly and filthily.

sor'didity. [f. SORDID *a.*, or a. F. *sordidité* (1573).] Sordidness. **a.** Meanness, miserliness, baseness.

1584 *Leycester's Commonw.* 197 As for valeur, he hath as much as hath a mouse: his magnanimity is base sordiditie. **1621** BURTON *Anat. Mel.* I. ii. III. xii, That greedinesse in getting, tenacity in keeping, sordidity in spending. **1649** EVELYN *Liberty & Serv.* v. Misc. Writ. (1805) 30 The like Sordidityes, which it were a shame to report. **1654** VILVAIN *Theorem. Theol.* vii. 194 So great glory cannot sort or sute with such sordidity. **1917** V. WOOLF *Diary* 22 Nov. (1977) I. 80 Hearing women abuse each other & at the noise others come running with delight—all this sordidity made me think him rather likely to be right. **1923** *Times Lit. Suppl.* 23 Aug. 554/1 His [*sc.* Defoe's] very precise and solid account of licence, adventure, and sordidity [in Roxana]. **1964** A. SWINSON *Six Minutes to Sunset* viii. 150 Carson then switched his attack to the political manœuvring, condemning it for its duplicity and sordidity. **1978** *Times Lit. Suppl.* 1 Dec. 1382/2 Empson seems to insist that one cannot truly admire him without agreeing with him about the sordidity of Englit.

b. Dirtiness, filthiness; dirty or foul matter.

1600 ABBOT *Jonah* 401 The backe shall be disguised with sordidity of sackcloth. **1657** TOMLINSON *Renou's Disp.* 396 A dense gumme conspurcated with no sordidity. **1927** V. WOOLF *Let.* 7 Feb. (1977) III. 326 Here it is pouring; rain coming through the roof; the sordidity too much for me even. **1936** S. SMITH *Novel on Yellow Paper* 152 The lovely deep rich olive green and brown and yellow sordidity of Sickert's London interiors. **1958** *Times Lit. Suppl.* 30 May 291/1 As the inevitable midnight flittings required less and less transport for the furniture and a large family grew up in an atmosphere of increasing poverty, sordidity and even occasional violence, James observed the domestic scene with the eye of an artist.

sordidly ('sɔːdɪdlɪ), *adv.* [f. SORDID *a.* + -LY^2.] In a sordid manner; basely, meanly; mercenarily.

(*a*) *c* **1645** HOWELL *Lett.* (1650) I. 148 This Osman was a man..of excess of courage, but sordidly covetous. **1682** BURNET *Rights Princes* iv. 123 Some came sordidly with the Price or Present in their hands to buy the Bishoprick. **1847** L. HUNT *Men, Women, & B.* I. vii. 27 The most sordidly ridiculous anecdote we remember of a bed-chamber. **1856** *N. Brit. Rev.* XXVI. 237 That Cockburn was sordidly selfish for the promotion of any interests of his.

Comb. **1681** GLANVILL *Sadducismus* II. (1726) 471 A church all over besmear'd with Sordidly-gainful Superstitions.

(*b*) **1656** EARL MONM. tr. *Boccalini's Advts. fr. Parnass.* II. xiv. (1674) 162 A Poet..sordidly apparelled; with his Cloaths all tattered. **1660** R. BLOME *Fanatick Hist.* i. 5 He made holiness to consist in speaking little, and living homely and sordidly.

sordidness ('sɔːdɪdnɪs). [f. as prec. + -NESS.] The state or quality of being sordid.

1. Dirtiness, filthiness; unclean or soiled character; squalor.

1637 SANDERSON *Serm.* (1681) II. 63 To it [*sc.* money].. hath the very name of sordidness been appropriated of old. **1665** NEEDHAM *Med. Medicinæ* 66 Carelesness, Sordidness in neglecting their own Bodies. **1691** RAY *Creation* II. (1704) 357 To deter Men and Women from Sluttishness and Sordidness. **1819** L. HUNT *Indicator* No. 8 (1822) I. 64 He sat looking at his old beard and the wilful sordidness of his hands. **1833** HT. MARTINEAU *Charmed Sea* i. 2 At the first glance the men looked all alike; their heads being shaved, and their dress uniform in its sordidness.

b. Lack of refinement or elegance; coarseness or roughness. *rare.*

1670 CLARENDON *Hist. Reb.* XII. §121 Nor did she prefer the glory of the Church of England before the sordidness of the Kirk of Scotland. **1873** BURTON *Hist. Scot.* VI. lxv. 24 They were offended at the sordidness of the food offered to them.

2. Baseness or meanness; esp. low, mean, or mercenary character or motives; selfish regard for material gain in place of higher interests.

1656 EARL MONM. tr. *Boccalini's Advts. fr. Parnass.* I. xcix. (1674) 133 Keeping continually..hid within the husk of their interest..with so much sordidness and obstinacy never to come out. **1674** tr. *Scheffer's Lapland* ix. 34 Their Priests who..vilify their doctrine by the sordidness of their lives. **1702** ECHARD *Eccl. Hist.* (1710) 403 His chiefest advice to them about him was to abhor all rapine and sordidness. **1746** FRANCIS tr. *Horace, Sat.* I. vi. 90 If none with avarice justly brand my fame, With sordidness, or deeds too vile to name. **1771** FOOTE *Maid of Bath* III. Wks. 1799 II. 236 The sordidness of your mind and manners. **1850** L. HUNT *Autobiog.* I. iii. 106, I blush to remember this..on account of the sordidness of the custom. *Ibid.* II. xi. 55 An extraordinary mixture of..fearlessness with sordidness. **1870** *Pall Mall G.* 24 Dec. 2 The result is but a just retribution on our sordidness and Pharisaism.

†**'sordidous,** *a. Obs.* [f. L. *sordid-us* dirty, abject, base: see -OUS.] Sordid, in various senses.

1602 F. HERING *Anatomyes* 3 The abiect and sordidous scumme, and refuse of the people. **1610** G. CARLETON *Jurisdiction* 217 Those sordidous censures to punish sinne with pecuniary mulcts.

Comb. **1608** TOPSELL *Serpents* (1658) 813 This pusillanimous and sordidous minded man Harpalion.

b. Of an ulcer: = SORDID *a.* 1 b.

1608 TOPSELL *Serpents* 311 The ashes of Earth-Wormes duely prepared, cleanseth Sordi[d]ous, stinking, and rotten Vlcers.

sordine ('sɔːdiːn), *sb.* and *a.* Also 6 surdine; in *mus.* also sordino, *pl.* sordini. [ad. It. *sordina, -dino* (= Sp. *sordina*, Pg. *surdina*), or a. F. **sordine* SOURDINE, f. L. *surd-us* deaf, mute: see SURD *a.*]

A. *sb.* †**1.** A small pipe or mouthpiece placed in a trumpet or bugle in order to muffle or reduce the sound; a trumpet fitted with this. *Obs.*

1591 *Garrard's Art Warre* 343 Lette him make it [*sc.* the alarm] secretly and without striking vp the Drums, or sounding Trompets, but rather vse Drum stickes and Surdines. **1611** COTGR., *Sourdine*, a Sordine, or a kind of hoarse, or low-sounding Trumpet.

2. *Mus.* = MUTE *sb.*^{1} 4 a. Also, = DAMPER 2 a (see also quot. 1907). See also CON SORDINO.

The Ital. form *sordino* is entered in Busby *Dict. Mus.* (1801).

1776 BURNEY *Hist. Mus.* (1789) III. i. 16 The several parts are so thick..that it [the poliphant] has not more tone than a mute or violin with a sordine. **1856** BERLIOZ *Instrument.* 16 The custom is when employing sordines to cause them to be used by all the band of stringed instruments. **1875** KNIGHT *Dict. Mech.* 2246/1 *Sordine*, a little implement placed on the bridge of a stringed instrument, in order to deaden the sonorousness and give it a mournful sound. **1883** GROVE *Dict. Mus.* III. 636/2 The musical terms 'Senza sordini' and 'Con sordini' applied to the damper-stops were used exclusively by Beethoven in his earlier sonatas. **1888** STAINER & BARRETT *Dict. Mus. Terms* (ed. 3) 406/2 *Sordini*. .. (3) Dampers of a pianoforte. **1894** G. DU MAURIER *Trilby* I. i. 42 Gecko..played..in minor, in pizzicato, and in sordino. **1907** T. S. WOTTON *Dict. Mus. Terms* 185 *Senza sordini* is..an indication open to misconstruction in piano music of a certain date, since it may mean 'without dampers' i.e. raising the dampers by means of the damper pedal, or it may mean 'without using the mutes'. **1959** *Collins Mus. Encycl.* 617/2 *Sordino*... (2) Damper (in the piano)... (3) Also applied in the late 18th and 19th cent. to a strip of leather (later felt) used to mute the strings of a piano and controlled by a pedal.

B. *adj.* †**1.** ***sordine trumpet*** (see A. 1). *Obs.*$^{-1}$

1635 J. HAYWARD tr. *Biondi's Banish'd Virg.* 106 Unbraced drummes, sordine trumpets,..and mournefull musick.

2. Muffled, subdued. *rare*$^{-1}$.

1894 'G. EGERTON' *Keynotes* 127 Mutter, mutter—a sordine epic of Hades.

†**'sorditude.** *Obs. rare.* [ad. L. *sorditūdo*, f. *sordes*.] Sordidness.

1623 COCKERAM I, *Sorditude*, filthinesse. **1657** FARINDON *Serm.* 162 To flee from one sin to another, from prodigality to sorditude. **1657** TOMLINSON *Renou's Disp.* 104 That whatever of sorditude is therein may cleave to the cloth.

sordor ('sɔːdə(r)). [a. Latin type **sordor*, corresponding to *sordidus* as *squālor* to *squālidus*, etc.] Physical or moral sordidness.

1823 BYRON *Island* II. iv, The sordor of civilisation, mix'd With all the savage which man's fall hath fix'd. **1836** EMERSON *Nature, Prospects* Wks. (Bohn) II. 173 The sordor and filths of nature. **1874** M. CREIGHTON *Hist. Ess.* i. (1902) 41 The awful background of eternal destiny,..where things lose at once the sordor of common life. **1929** *Oxford Poetry* 28 The world..rises and falls On a wave of confetti and funerals And sordor and stinks and stupid faces. **1934** T. S. ELIOT *After Strange Gods* i. 17 The sordor of the half-dead mill towns of southern New Hampshire and Massachusetts. **1982** *Observer* 10 Oct. 30/8 Budd, as a kid, knew the sordor behind the glamour.

sords. *Obs.* or *dial.* [Anglicizing of L. *sordēs* SORDES.] Dirt, filth; filthiness.

1653 GAUDEN *Hierasp.* 61 There is nothing more delicate and abhorring all sinful sords, than the Ermine of Christian Religion. *Ibid.* 219 Their raggs, sords, and beggery, sufficiently confutes their rare skill. *a* **1825** FORBY *Voc. E. Anglia* 316 *Sords*, filth; washings; off-scourings.

sordume ('sɔːdjuːm). *rare.* [Alteration of SORDUN.] = next.

1955 AUDEN *Shield of Achilles* iii. 76 There I stand in Eden again, welcomed back by the krumhorns, doppions, sordumes of jolly miners.

‖**sordun** (zɔr'duːn). Also sordune. [Ger.] An early form of bassoon, having a cylindrical bore with double reeds.

1876 STAINER & BARRETT *Dict. Mus. Terms* 406/2 *Sordun, Sordono* (It.) (1) An old form of wood wind instrument, having a double reed, with twelve ventages and two keys. **1943** B. MIALL tr. *K. Geiringer's Mus. Instruments* 133 An extremely rare variant of the Bassoon was the *Sordune*... This consisted of a gracefully turned wooden billet containing not merely two but sometimes three parallel cylindrical bores. **1977** *Early Music* Apr. (Advt., recto rear cover), The Sordunes which Praetorius..illustrates in Syntagma Musicum 1619 show a controlled reed instrument of two parallel bores with a bocal tapering towards the end of its length. The Sordune is a useful bridge between the windcap range of instruments, and the controlled reed instruments. **1978** A. BAINES in J. M. Thomson *Future of Early Music in Britain* 22 Once people have spent money on manufactured sorduns and cornamuses, they want their money's worth from them.

sore (sɔə(r)), *sb.*^{1} Forms: α. 1–3 sar (2–3 sær), *north.* and *Sc.* 4 sar, 4–6, 9 sare, 6– sair. β. 3–5 sor (3 seor), 4–5 soor(e (5 soure), 6–7 soare, 7 soar, 4– sore. [OE. *sár* str. neut., = OFris. *sêr* (WFris. *sear*, NFris. *siar*), MDu. *seer*, *zeer* (Du. *zeer*), OS. *sêr* (MLG. *sêr-e*, LG. *ser*, *seer*), OHG., MHG. *sêr* (early mod.G. *sehr*, also masc.), ON. and Icel. *sár* (Sw. *sår*, Da. *saar*), Goth. *sair*: see SORE *a.*

Feminine forms occur in some of the continental langs.: MLG. *sêre*, MHG. *sêre* (early mod.G. *sehre*).]

†**1.** Bodily pain or suffering. *Obs.*

c **825** *Vesp. Psalter* xxx. 11 Asprong in sare lif min. *c* **900** *Baeda's Hist.* IV. xix. (1890) 320 Þy þriddan dæȝe heo wæs eft hefiȝad mid þæm ærrum sarum. **971** *Blickl. Hom.* 59 On synne he bið ȝeeacnod, & on his modor sare he bið acenned. *c* **1000** *Sax. Leechd.* I. 280 Þysse sylfan wyrte syde þæra toþa sar ȝeliðiȝað. *c* **1205** LAY. 12511 We beoð ofte hider ifaren mid wandreðe & mid sare. *a* **1300** *Cursor M.* 628 Vte of his side..Wit-oten sare a rib he tok. **1398** TREVISA *Barth. De P.R.* v. xxx. (Bodl. MS.), Þe touche of senewes haþ no feling of soore and of smerte. *a* **1450** *Le Morte Arth.* 3405 The doughty kynge..For sore myght not hym-self weld. **1484** CAXTON *Fables of Æsop* IV. xiii, My broder and my frend, where aboute is thy sore? **1583** *Leg. Bp. St. Androis* 341 Suppoise the devill maid that graith,..At that tyme, to asswage my sair, I wald have tane it.

†**2.** Sickness, disease; in particularized use, a disease, ailment, or bodily affliction. *Obs.*

a **900** CYNEWULF *Crist* 1356 Þa þe on sare seoce laȝun. *c* **1250** *Gen. & Ex.* 3027 Ðo wex vn-selðe on hem wel hard, dolc, sor, and blein on erue and man. *c* **1300** *Cursor M.* 14147 Þe sare him sekes fra hede to fote. **1377** LANGL. *P. Pl.* B. xx. 96 Kynde come after with many kene sores, As pokkes and pestilences. **1604** SHAKS. *Oth.* IV. ii. 49 Had they rain'd All kind of Sores, and Shames on my bare-head. **1611** BIBLE *2 Chron.* vi. 28 Whatsoeuer sore, or whatsoeuer sicknesse there be. **1648** HEXHAM II, *Roose, ofte de Kole*, S. Anthonies Sore, called the Rose.

3. A bodily injury; a wound. *Obs.* exc. *dial.*

a **1000** *Guthlac* 676 Mec dryhten heht snude ȝesecgan þæt ȝe him sara ȝehwylc hondum ȝehælde. *a* **1200** *12th Cent. Hom.* (1909) 114 Ac þa synfulle men sceolen iseon þa wundæn & þa sar on ure Drihtne. *c* **1380** *Sir Ferumb.* 503 'Me þynkþ þou hast a wonde þere..in þy syde.'.. Olyuer.. turnd him þat sor to hyde. *c* **1400** *Laud Troy Bk.* 5843 He ȝaff Ector an hidous sore. **1513** DOUGLAS *Æneid* XI. xv. 115 The scharp steill heid fixt to the rybbis remanys, In a full deip wound and a grewous sair. **1599** SHAKS., etc. *Pass. Pilgr.* 128 'See, in my thigh,' quoth she, 'here was the sore'. **1785** R. FORBES *Scots Poems Buchan Dial.* 31 He'll suck the poison frae the sair, An' be a noble leech. **1876** *Mid-Yks. Gloss.* 131 *Sore* has the meaning of bruise, or wound, occasionally.

4. A place in an animal body where the skin or flesh is diseased or injured so as to be painfully tender or raw; a sore place, such as that caused by an ulcer.

See *bed-sore* (BED *sb.* 19), *saddle-sore* (SADDLE *sb.* 12).

c **1000** *Sax. Leechd.* I. 134 Wið wunda & wið cancor ȝenim þas ilcan wyrte,..leȝe to þam sare. Ne ȝeþafað heo þæt sar furður wexe. *a* **1300** *Cursor M.* 14012 Þar sco fand ani breck or sare, Wit hir smerl sco smerd þare. *c* **1400** *Lanfranc's Cirurg.* 87 Þe quantite of medicyns þat schulden be leid to þe soor..mai not wiþ lettris be writen. **1474** CAXTON *Chesse* II. v. (1883) 66 And many flyes satte vpon the soores. **1523** FITZHERB. *Husb.* §42 Shede the woll by and by, and laye a lyttell terre thervppon, tyll thou passe the sore. **1592** SHAKS. *Ven. & Ad.* 916 Another [hound] licking of his wound, 'Gainst venom'd sores the only sovereign plaster. **1603** DEKKER *Wonderfull Yeare* Wks. (Grosart) I. 118 Some haue had 18. sores at one time running vpon them. **1682** K. DIGBY *Chymical Secrets* II. 232 Dip a Straw or Feather in it, and touch all round about the borders of the Sore with it. **1755** JOHNSON s.v., To be a sore, there must be an excoriation; a tumour or bruise is not called a sore before some disruption happen. **1784** COWPER *Task* I. 582 They.. vex their flesh with artificial sores. **1826** S. COOPER *First Lines Surg.* (ed. 5) 170 Bruises of the shin so frequently cause sloughing and troublesome sores. **1889** *Science-Gossip* XXV. 193/2 Matter discharged from leprous sores.

5. In fig. and allusive uses, with retention of literal phraseology; esp. coupled with *salve* (see SALVE *sb.*^{1} 2 and *v.*^{1} 1 c).

The sense becomes often coincident with 6 or 7.

c **1350** *Will. Palerne* 598 Ful wel can ich..help ȝow hasteli at al ȝoure hele to gete, ȝif ȝe saie me ȝoure sores. *c* **1374** CHAUCER *Anel. & Arc.* 242 Noon othir helpeþe my soores for to sounde. **1390** GOWER *Conf.* II. 223 Of covoitise if ther be more In love, agropeth out the sore. **1410** in *26 Pol. Poems* ix. 178 Now sumwhat y haue ȝow sayd What is salue to ȝoure sore. **1538** STARKEY *England* II. i. 143 Conuenyent remedys ..to be applyd to such sorys and dyseasys in our polytyke body. **1560** DAUS tr. *Sleidane's Comm.* 304 b, The matter was taken up, yet the sore brake out agayne. **1587** GREENE *Euphues* Wks. (Grosart) VI. 181 That infectious soare of iealowsie. **1610** SHAKS. *Temp.* II. i. 138 You rub the sore, When you should bring the plaister. **1647** N. BACON *Disc. Govt. Eng.* I. lxiv. (1739) 134 The sore between him and his Subjects was not fully cured. **1727** *De Foe's Eng. Tradesman* I. xii. 147 He had got a salve for that sore. **1828** SCOTT *F.M. Perth* vii, It is not for me to put my finger on the sore. **1842** TENNYSON *Walking to Mail* 71 The same old sore breaks out from age to age.

Prov. **1560** DAUS tr. *Sleidane's Comm.* 64 And as the common saiyng is, increase the flamme with oyle, and be as sharpe nayle in the sore. **1562** J. HEYWOOD *Prov. & Epigr.* (1867) 71 It is ill healyng of an olde sore.

†**6.** Mental suffering, pain, or trouble; grief, sorrow, anxiety, or the cause of this. *Obs.*

c **888** K. ÆLFRED *Boeth.* vii. §2 Mið ðæm mæstan sare his modes. *a* **1122** *O.E. Chron.* (Laud MS.) an. 1120, Ðysra deað wæs heora freondan twyfealdlic sar. *c* **1175** *Lamb. Hom.* 121 Lokiað hweðer enies monnes sar beo iliche mine sare. *c* **1205** LAY. 7998 Þer wes Julius Cezar, an heorte he hafde sorȝe & sar. *c* **1250** *Gen. & Ex.* 733 Teres gliden for hertes sor fro loth, and abram, and nachor. *c* **1300** *Havelok* 234 Þer was sobbing, siking, and sor, Handes wringing. *c* **1350** *Will. Palerne* 894 Sikende ful sadly for sor at his hert. *c* **1386** CHAUCER *Knt.'s T.* 596 Who feeleth double soor and heuynesse But Palamon? **1423** JAS. I *Kingis Q.* clxxxii, Euery wicht his awin suete or sore Has maist In mynde. **1523** LD. BERNERS *Froiss.* (1812) I. clxii. 199 Gette vs to the french kynges batayle, for ther lyeth all the sore of the mater [orig. *tout le fort de la besoigne*]. **1575** GASCOIGNE *Glasse*

Governm. Wks. 1910 II. 66 Store is no sore, as the proverbe saith.

†7. Grievous state; affliction, misery. *Obs.*

a 1300 *Cursor M.* 9103 þat sare, þat scam, þat martiring, Was neuer sene on suilk a king! c 1400 *Pride of Life* 406 in *Non-Cycle Myst. Plays* (E.E.T.S.) 101 To sauy þi soul fre sor. 14.. *Tundale's Vis.* 724 Now goo we to a delfull stedde. .. Who schall delyver me from that sore? c 1470 Henry *Wallace* xi. 303 To wyn out off bondage Scotland agayn fra payn and felloun sor.

sore (sɔə(r)), *sb.*² Also 4 sower, 4–6 sowre, 6 soor, 6–7 soare, 9 sor. [Subst. use of sore *a.*²]

†1. *Venery.* A buck in its fourth year. *Obs.*

c 1369 Chaucer *Dethe Blaunche* 429 Of fawnes, sowers [*v.r.* sowres], buckes, does Was ful the wodde. 1486 *Bk. St. Albans* e iv, A sowre at the .iiij. yere. 1523 *North Country Wills* (Surtees) 116 The prior and covent .. clayme of me .. a buck or a soor agaynst Mary Magdaleyn day yerely. 1573 Twyne *Æneid* x. Ffiij b, If he a rowebuck swift .., Or els a sore may find, whose tender hornes begin to ryse. 1588 Shaks. *L.L.L.* iv. ii. 59. 1633 Nabbes *Totenham Court* i. v, A longing Lady in the Strand had a pricket. Then I sent a soare to Barber-Surgeons Hall. 1741 *Compl. Fam.-Piece* ii. i. 310 If any Deer come out that is not weighty, or a Deer of Antlier, which is Buck, Sore, or Sorel. 1774 Goldsm. *Nat. Hist.* ii. v. (1862) I. 329. 1865 [see sorrel *sb.*² 2].

attrib. 1577 in *Middlesex County Rec.* (1886) I. 109 Duos coreos vocatos soreskynnes.

2. *Falconry.* A hawk in its second year. Also *transf.* (quot. a 1613).

1600 [see sore *sb.*⁴]. a 1613 Overbury *Characters, Whore* Wks. (1856) 82 The first yeere of her trade she is an eyesse, .. the second a soare. a 1682 Sir T. Browne *Tracts* (1683) 118 Nor must you expect from high Antiquity the distinctions of Eyess and Ramage Hawks, of Sores and Entermewers, of Hawks of the Lure and the Fist.

sore (sɔə(r)), *sb.*³ *dial.* Forms: 5 sour, sowr(e, soore, 7, 9 saur, 9 soar, sore. [a. ON. *saur-r* (Icel. and Norw. *saur*, MSw. *sör*) mud, dirt, excrement.] Mud; now (in Cheshire and Yorkshire) black mud, liquid manure, drainage.

c 1440 *Promp. Parv.* 460/1 Sloor, or sowr, *cenum, limus. Ibid.* 465/1 Soore, fylthe or sovr (*S., P.* sowre, filthe), .. *lutum.* 1674 Ray *Coll. Words, Saur-pool*, a stinking puddle. 1828 Carr *Craven Gloss.* 98 *Saur*, urine from the cow-house, &c. 1879– in dial. glossaries, etc. (Chesh., Yks.).

†**sore**, *sb.*⁴ *Obs.*⁻¹ [a. older Flem. *sore* 'droogen haerinck, rooden haerinck' (Kilian), a. OF. (*harenc*) *sor*(*e*, now *saur*(*e*: see sore *a.*²] A red herring.

1600 Surflet *Countrie Farme* vii. xliii. 871 Their colour doth diuerslie change according to their mues, which cause them to be called Hagards or Sores, all one with that which is vsuallie done by dryed herings which are called Sores or red herings.

sore, error for sord *sb.*, obs. var. sir *sb.*

sore (sɔə(r)), *a.*¹ Forms: α. 1, 3 sar (2–3 sær, 3 ser); *north.* and *Sc.* 4–5 sar, 4–6, 8 sare (6 sear, seir); 4–5 sayre, 5– 6 sayr, 5– sair (6 saire). β. 3, 5 sor, 5 soor, 5–6 soore, 6 *Sc.* soir, 4– sore (9 *dial.* soor, sooar). *Compar.* 1 sarra, 3–5 sarre, 5 sorrar; 3 sarure, sarer, 6 sarar, sairar, 6, 9 sairer; 4 sorrore, 5– sorer. *Superl.* 1 sarost, 4 sarrest, 6, 9 sairest, 6– sorest. [Common Teut.: OE. *sár*, = OFris. **sêr* (WFris. *sear*, NFris. *siar*, *sîr*), MDu. *seer* (Du. *zeer*), OS. and MLG. *sêr* (LG. *sêr*, *seer*, etc.), OHG. and MHG. *sêr* (obs. and dial. G. *seer*, *sehr*), ON. *sárr* (Icel. *sár*, Norw. *saar*; MSw. *sār*, *saar*):—OTeut. **sairaz* (whence Finnish *sairas* sick, ill). Cf. sore *sb.*¹]

Senses 1–8 are now mainly *arch.* or *dial.*

I. 1. Causing or involving bodily pain; painful, grievous; distressing or severe in this respect:

a. Of wounds, hurts, ailments, or similar causes of physical suffering.

c 897 K. Ælfred *Gregory's Past. C.* xxxviii. (1871) 272 We wieton ðæt sio dieȝle wund bið sarre ðonne sio opene. c 1000 in Thorpe *Laws* II. 278 Se læca þe sceal sare wunda wel ȝehælan, he mot habban gode sealfe þærto. c 1205 Lay. 10423, I þan þridden dæie he sarne dæd þolede. a 1225 *Ancr. R.* 112 Euer so þet flesch is cwickure, so þe pine þerof & þet hurt is more & sarre. a 1300 *Cursor M.* 3478 Hir breding was ful selcut sare, Bot hir chiltting was mikel mare. c 1340 Hampole *Pr. Consc.* 1775 þe payn of dede here es bitter and sare. c 1400 *Pety Job* 293 in *26 Pol. Poems* 130 A man .. With hote and colde, and hungor sore, Turmented ys. 1422 tr. *Secreta Secret., Priv. Priv.* 205 Hit makyth a full heuy and a full Soore wounde. 1539 Bible (Great) *Ps.* xxxviii. 7 My loins are filled with a sore disease. 1593 Shaks. *Lucr.* 1568 'Fool, fool!' quoth she, 'his wounds will not be sore'. a 1629 Hinde *J. Bruen* lxvi. (1641) 219 His weaknesse increased, by reason of a sore stopping in his breast and throate. 1655 Culpepper, etc. *Riverius* xv. iii. 409 The same may also happen after sore labor in child-birth. 1831 J. Wilson *Noctes Ambr.* Wks. 1856 III. 186 You've been suffering under a sair hoast, I hear.

b. Of a blow, bite, weapon, etc.

a 1300 *Cursor M.* 25543 Suet iesu .. sufferd .. dintes sare and smert. c 1340 Hampole *Pr. Consc.* 6972 þai salle .. fele of vermyn bytyng sare. c 1400 *Destr. Troy* 1259 Castor .. suet vnto Sedar with a sore wepyn. c 1470 Henry *Wallace* iii. 215 Thai band thaim fast with wedeis sad and sar. 1500–20 Dunbar *Poems* lxxii. 21 Thai .. gaif him mony buffat sair. 1607 Shaks. *Cor.* ii. i. 268 Cammels .., who haue their Prouand Onely for bearing Burthens, and sore blowes For sinking vnder them. 1611 Bible *Isaiah* xxvii. 1 The Lord with his sore and great and strong sworde.

transf. c 1400 *Apol. Loll.* 38 For ai þe heiar degre, þe sarrar is þe falle.

c. Of sickness.

Passing into the merely intensive sense of 'severe'.

a 1300 *Cursor M.* 8061 In sekenes sar he fand him stad. c 1400 *Brut* 201 þai .. woxen made, or sore sikenesse þai had. 1509 Hawes *Past. Pleas.* xxix. (Percy Soc.) 137 For to haue remedy of his sore sekenes. 1611 Bible *Deut.* xxviii. 59 Sore sicknesses, and of long continuance. 1808 Jamieson s.v. *Sair*, Sair sickness, a sair fever.

2. a. Causing or involving, accompanied by, mental pain, trouble, or distress.

a 1000 *Deor's Compl.* 9 Beadohilde ne wæs hyre broþra deaþ on sefan swa sar swa hyre sylfre þing. a 1000 *Cædmon's Gen.* 425 þæt me is on mode minum swa sar,.. þæt hie heofonrice aȝan to aldre. c 1205 Lay. 7418 þider com tiðende þat him wæs sær [*c* 1275 sor]. a 1300 *Cursor M.* 6443 þis ilk folk .. þat moyses had vnder hand, þai did him selcuth sore trauail. c 1500 *Three Kings' Sons* 44 But ther is o sore point, they that shalle go, knowe not the way. 1568 Grafton *Chron.* II. 765 The tidyngs of this matter came hastily to the Queene .., and that in the sorest wise. 1833 Tennyson *Lotos-Eaters* Choric Song vi, Sore task to hearts worn out by many wars.

b. Of sorrow, repentance, or other feelings.

a 900 Cynewulf *Crist* 209 Nu þu ealle forlæt sare sorȝceare. a 1000 *Cædmon's Gen.* 2029 Abraham .. cwæð, þæt him wære weorce on mode, sorȝa sarost, þæt [etc.]. a 1200 *Vices & Virtues* 21 Mid oðre loke of sare birewnesse. a 1300 *Cursor M.* 9088 For sar it es mi repentance. c 1421 *26 Pol. Poems* xx. 106 Haue mynde of my sorwe sore! c 1470 Henry *Wallace* v. 714 The sayr grewans ramaynyt in his entent. 1871 B. Taylor *Faust* (1875) I. x. 130 Besides his penitence was very sore.

c. Of manifestations of grief: Bitter, painful.

c 1200 *Trin. Coll. Hom.* 83 He ne fecheð noht þe sore siches onneðerward his heorte. 13.. *Cursor M.* 4969 (Gött.), Ioseph herd þair murning sare. c 1400 *Anturs of Arth.* vii, Withe siking sare. 1535 Joye *Apol. Tindale* (Arb.) 41 Paule loked with sore sighes. 1611 Bible *Gen.* l. 10 They mourned with a great and very sore lamentation.

3. a. Involving great hardships, painful exertion, unusual difficulty, etc.

a 900 Cynewulf *Crist* 1418 Ða mec ongon hreowan, þæt .. moncynnes tuddor .. sceolde uncuðne eard cunnian, sare siþas. a 1200 *Moral Ode* 36 Monies monnes sare iswinc habbeð oft unholde. c 1420 *Sir Amadace* (Camden) xxi, God gif him a sore grace, And alle suche waisters as he wasse. c 1475 *Rauf Coilȝear* 637, I haue oft tymes swet in seruice full sair. 1508 Fisher *7 Penit. Ps.* cii. Wks. (1876) 182 Poule .. gate his lyuynge with his owne sore labour. 1605 Shaks. *Macb.* ii. ii. 38 Sleepe, .. The death of each dayes Life, sore Labors Bath. a 1629 Hinde *J. Bruen* xxxii. (1641) 101 His painfulnesse in taking many long and sore journies. 1786 *Har'st Rig* cxiv, In idle dreams they ne'er abound That ha'e sair wark. 1824 Scott *Redgauntlet* let. xi, Sair wark he had to get the siller.

absol. a 1375 *Joseph Arim.* 620 þorw his swete grace þe sarrest is passed. c 1400 *Rom. Rose* 5519 Thei wolen .. chaunge for softe ne for sore.

b. Of battle or other conflicts: Severe, fierce, hot.

c 1400 *Destr. Troy* 5897 The assembly was sorer o þe se banke. 1422 tr. *Secreta Secret., Priv. Priv.* 182 Aftyr many Sore battaillis, .. he flow ouer the See. 1508 Dunbar *Gold. Targe* 198 The salt was all the sarar. 1523 Ld. Berners *Froiss.* I. 180 There was a sore fray, and slayne and drowned mo than sixe hundred frenchmen. 1605 Shaks. *Lear* iii. v. 24 Though the conflict be sore betweene that, and my blood. 1671 Milton *Samson* 287 In that sore battel when so many dy'd. c 1780 Burns '*Ah! woe is me*' i, For sair contention I maun bear. 1816 Scott *Old Mort.* xlii, He has had sair and frequent combats to sustain against the Evil One.

4. a. Pressing hardly upon one; oppressively heavy or severe; difficult to bear or support.

1500–20 Dunbar *Poems* xlix. 30 God schawis the richt With soir vengence. 1535 Coverdale *1 Kings* xii. 14 My father made youre yock sore, but I wyll make it yet sorer vpon you. 1605 Shaks. *Macb.* ii. iv. 3, I haue seene .. things strange: but this sore Night Hath trifled former knowings. 1611 Bible *Ezek.* xiv. 21 How much more when I send my foure sore iudgements vpon Ierusalem. 1714 Prior *Viceroy* xii, On all provisions .. He laid a tax full hard and sore. 1766 Goldsmith *Vicar* xxviii, The hand of Heaven is sore upon us. 1786 Burns *Dream* vi, Your sair taxation does her fleece. 1860 Geo. Eliot *Mill on Fl.* iii. v, It's been a sore chance for you, young man, hasn't it?

b. Of troubles, afflictions, evils, etc.

1563 Winȝet *Wks.* (S.T.S.) I. 101 *marg.*, A dum pastour or a wicious, is a sair scurge on the peple. 1590 Spenser *F.Q.* iii. vi. 53 And for his dearest sake endured sore, Sore trouble of an hainous enimy. 1602 Shaks. *Ham.* v. ii. 241 You must needs haue heard how I am punisht With sore distraction? 1679 C. Nesse *Antichrist* 198 The nature of affliction which is usually sorest at last. 1742 Young *Nt. Th.* iii. 218 Man is to man the sorest, surest ill. 1799 A. Young *Agric. Lincoln.* 341 From 30 to 40 of this stock run in the fen, but to sore loss. 1819 Shelley *Ode West Wind* 52, I would ne'er have striven As thus with thee in prayer in my sore need. 1835 T. Mitchell *Acharn. of Aristoph.* 32 *note*, Those glaring contrasts, which form the sorest ill of poverty. 1871 Palgrave *Lyr. Poems* 101 This is the sorest evil Of evils under the sky.

c. Of trials or temptations.

1572 *Satir. Poems Reform.* xxxi. 78 Now thay cum in freindis clais, Quhilk is ane sairer sey. 1709 Watts *Hymn*, '*With Joy we meditate the Grace*' ii, He knows what sore Temptations mean. 1892 *Photogr. Ann.* II. 893 Each of these advantages must prove a sore temptation to the hand-camera worker.

d. In intensive use: Very great or serious.

1555 in Bonner *Homilies* 5* We shall sone perceyue the offence not lyght, but verye sore and heynous. 1576 Fleming *Panopl. Epist.* 71 The same wil redound to my great blame and sore discredit. 1611 Shaks. *Cymb.* iii. vi. 13 To lapse in Fulnesse Is sorer, then to lye for Neede. 1825 Scott *Talism.* iii, Committing what would have been a sore blot in his shield of arms. 1875 Stubbs *Const. Hist.* II. xiv. 53 Henry was now in sore want of money. 1886 *S.W. Linc. Gloss.* 137 It's a sore shame.

5. Severe, stern, hard, or harsh: †a. Of language, commands, etc. *Obs.*

1526 Tindale *2 Cor.* x. 10 The pistles (sayth he) are sore and strong: but his bodyly presence is weake. 1549 Latimer *Ploughers* (Arb.) 21 A soore word for them that are neglygent. 1610 Shaks. *Temp.* iii. i. 11, I must remoue Some thousands of these Logs, and pile them vp, Vpon a sore iniunction.

b. Of persons. Now *dial.* (Common in 16th c.)

1534 More *Comf. agst. Trib.* ii. Wks. 1171/1, I dare not be so sore as vtterly to forbid it. 1553 T. Wilson *Rhet.* (1580) 123, I call him that is a cruell or mercilesse man, somwhat sore in iudgement. 1567 Maplet *Gr. Forest* 87 b, She is verie extreme and sore towards hir yong. 1901 G. Douglas *Hosue with Green Shutters* 324 Maybe the Lord Jesus Christ'll no' be owre sair on me.

6. Of a strong, severe, or violent character in respect of operation or effect: a. Of feelings.

c 1449 Pecock *Repr.* iii. iv. 295 His .. ouer soor inclinacioun of loue anentis hem. 1611 Bible *Psalm* ii. 5 Then shall hee .. vexe them in his sore displeasure. 1810 Crabbe *Borough* iv. 11 Some, when converted, sigh in sore amaze.

b. Of storms, weather, etc.

1535 Coverdale *Ps.* xvii. 14 He cast sore lighteninges, & destroyed them. 1556 *Chron. Gr. Friars* (Camden) 28 Soch a sore snowe & a frost. 1593 Marlowe *Edw. II*, iv. vi, With awkward windes and sore tempests driuen, To fall on shoare. 1866 Neale *Sequences & Hymns* 36 Brought her through the sorest tempest.

c. Of persons or other agents.

1565 Cooper *Thesaurus, Aduersarius acerrimus*, a very sore and earnest [adversary]. 1592 Timme *Ten Eng. Lepers* B ij, Nimri was a sore driver. 1602 Shaks. *Ham.* v. i. 188 Your water is a sore Decayer of your horson dead body. 1656 Earl Monm. tr. *Boccalini's Advts. fr. Parnass.* i. lxvii. (1674) 85 Princes meet with no sorer enemies, than male-contents. 1688 Holme *Armoury* ii. 122/2 Cattle, Horses, &c. are sore hurts both to Gardens & Orchards.

d. Of actions. *rare*⁻¹.

1563 *Homilies* ii. *Whitsunday* ii, The byshops of Rome haue for a long time made a sore chalenge therunto.

†7. Strong, weighty, valid. *Obs.*

1530 Rastell *Bk. Purgat.* iii. vii, That is a very sore obieccyon that thou hast now put and aledged. 1551 T. Wilson *Logike* (1580) 83 b, To persuade hym the better, he vsed this sore reason.

8. *dial.* = sorry *a.* (See quots.)

In *Destr. Troy* 10445 *sore* appears to have this sense, but may be an error for *sori* sorry *a.*

a 1825 Forby *Voc. E. Anglia* (1830) 316 *Sore*, sorry; vile; worthless... 'He made a sore hand of it!' 1839 Sir G. C. Lewis *Gloss. Heref.* s.v., 'A sore fellow' means a rogue, a rascal. 'A sore time' means a sad time. 1866 Brogden *Prov. Lincs.*, *Sore*, bad, sorry. He's made a sore job of it. 1880 *Antrim & Down Gloss.* 96 *Sore*,.. pitiful or contemptible. 'He's a sore fool.'

II. 9. a. Of parts of the body: In pain; painful, aching. Now *spec.*, having the skin broken or raw.

a 1000 *Riddles* xiv. 6 (Gr.), Ne wæs hyra ænȝum þy wyrs ne side þy sarre. c 1000–1150 *Sax. Leechd.* III. 108 Wið mannes ceola þe byð sær. þisne læce cræft man sceal ðon manne þe byð þe ceola sar. c 1205 Lay. 19501 Me scal lacnien his leomes þat beoð sare. a 1300 *Cursor M.* 15101 O þair fete þat semed sare. a 1352 Minot *Poems* (ed. Hall) i. 15 þai turned ogayn with sides sare. 1387 Trevisa *Higden* (Rolls) I. 51 As a sore membre .. [is parted] from membres þat beeþ hole .. and in good poynt. 1489 *Acc. Ld. High Treas. Scot.* I. 149, vij elne of quhyte to be logouris to the King, the tyme his leg wes sayre. 1526 *Pilgr. Perf.* (W. de W.) 220 b, No parte of our body can be sore or in payne, but al the other partes in maner feleth the same. 1542–3 *Act 34 & 35 Hen. VIII*, c. 8 §1 Suche as ben peined with customable diseases: as womens brestes being sore. 1639 in *Verney Mem.* (1907) I. 104 His gummes are soe sore, he will not yet suffer his nurse to looke into his mouth. 1695 *New Light of Chirurg. put out* 30 The Parts so stiff and sore, as if they never would be well. 1704 F. Fuller *Med. Gymn.* (1711) 57 I'm tyr'd, my Bones are sore. 1774 Burke *Sp. Amer. Tax.* Sel. Wks. I. 112 Your ministerial directors .. then went mumping with a sore leg in America, canting and whining. 1824 Scott *St. Ronan's* xviii, What signifies healing a sore foot when there will be a broken heart in the case? 1847 Marryat *Childr. New Forest* iv, My shoulder is quite sore with the rope. 1881 *Trans. Obstet. Soc. Lond.* XXII. 14 There was no spot sore to touch.

fig. 1725 Pope *Odyss.* iii. 252 Who while my soul is sore Of fresh affronts, are meditating more.

b. Of the eyes, throat, etc.: Painful through inflammation or other morbid condition. ***a sight for sore eyes***: see sight *sb.*¹ 1 d.

(*a*) a 1400 *Stockholm Med. MS.* fol. 128 For sore eyne .. it is preuyd. 1565 J. Halle *Hist. Expost.* (Percy Soc.) 17 Well, .. seyng that you can heale sore eyes, what is an eye? 1606 Shaks. *Tr. & Cr.* v. i. 36 Thou greene Sarcenet flap for a sore eye. c 1680 Beveridge *Serm.* (1729) I. 28 Being troubled with sore eyes. 1765 Gray *Shakespeare Verses* iii, But may not honey's self be turn'd to gall By residence, by marriage, and sore eyes?

fig. 1673 Cave *Prim. Chr.* iii. i. 220 The brightness of his conversation offended the sore eyes of other men.

(*b*) 1686 in *Verney Mem.* (1907) II. 423, I have a cold and a sore Throat. 1719 Quincy *Phys. Dict.* (1722) 13 As they [tonsils] are subject to Inflammation, they frequently are the Occasion of what the common People call a sore Throat. 1787 J. Collins in *Med. Comm.* II. 364 Putrid sore-throat, or angina maligna. 1848 Thackeray *Van. Fair* li, The professional personages .. would leave off their sore throats in order to sing at her parties. 1898 *Syd. Soc. Lex.* s.v., *Sore-throat, clergyman's*, chronic follicular pharyngitis.

(*c*) 1853 Mayne *Expos. Lex.* 73/1 *Aphtha*, .. the disease of infancy, otherwise called thrush, or sore mouth.

c. *Sc.* Of the head: Aching. ***a sore*** (Sc. ***sair***) ***head***, a headache.

1549 *Compl. Scot.* vi. 67 The decoctione of it is remeid for ane sair hede. 1643 *Orkney Witch Trial* in *Abbotsford Club*

Miscell. I. 177 ȝe said also that Bessie Spence hes ay ane sore head, it is ay pained. **1739** A. NICOL *Poems* 52 (Jam.), Syne supperless I go to bed; The morn I wake with a sare head. **1785** BURNS *Death & Dr. Hornbook* xxvi, Tippence-worth to mend her head, When it was sair. **1824** MACTAGGART *Gallovid. Encycl.* 324 A confounded *sair head*, proceeding from the effects of taking the *wee drap*. **1880** *Antrim & Down Gloss.* 96 *Sore head*, a headache.

d. ***a bear with a sore head***, used allusively for a type of sullen irritability, peevishness, or sensitiveness. Cf. SORE-HEAD, -HEADED.

1840 MARRYAT *Poor Jack* xxxviii, As sulky as a bear with a sore head.

e. Colloq. phr. ***dressed*** (or ***done***, etc.) ***up like a sore finger*** (or ***toe***) and varr., overdressed. *Austral.* and *N.Z.*

1919 W. H. DOWNING *Digger Dialects* 46 *Sore finger*, an overdressed person (e.g. 'dolled up like a sore finger'). **1939** K. TENNANT *Foveaux* 430 You ought to a seen us in the ole days when we 'ad a procession every year—done up like a sore toe with banners and floats. **1943** J. A. W. BENNETT in *Amer. Speech* XVIII. 91 'All done up like a sore toe' describes someone dressed over-elaborately; many New Zealand children go barefoot much of the time, and it is with this circumstance in mind that we must interpret the simile. **1958** H. D. WILLIAMSON *Sunlit Plain* 10 Get an eyeful of him! Done up like a sore toe. **1965** P. WHITE *Four Plays* 168 I'm gunna get out of this suit. Dressed up like a sore finger.

f. Colloq. phr. ***to stick*** (or ***stand***) ***out like a sore thumb***, to be very conspicuous or obvious.

1936 E. S. GARDNER *Case of Sleepwalker's Niece* xiii. 128 'No,' he said, 'that's the one thing in the case that stands out like a sore thumb, now that I stop to think of it.' **1941** —— *Case of Haunted Husband* (1942) xvi. 126 A private detective in that atmosphere would stick out like a sore thumb on a waiter serving soup. **1958** *Spectator* 8 Aug. 187/1 A bad officer will stick out like a sore thumb. **1977** *New Yorker* 15 Aug. 42/3 In the strong late-afternoon light the twelve white houses stood out like twelve sore thumbs.

10. Of persons: Suffering pain (from wounds, disease, or other cause). Freq. in alliteration with *sick*. Also *absol.*

1297 R. GLOUC. (Rolls) 6229 In such solas, As folc miȝte þat vorwounded & sor & wery was. *c* **1340** HAMPOLE *Pr. Consc.* 1461 Now er we hale, now seke and sare. *c* **1400** *26 Pol. Poems* xxvi. 109 After he felle foule and sore For luste of women that was hym nygh. **1542-3** *Act 34 & 35 Hen. VIII*, c. 8 §1 In case they [surgeons] wolde minister their cunninge to sore people vnrewarded. **1590** SHAKS. *Com. Err.* III. i. 65 If you went in paine Master, this knaue wold goe sore. **1611** BIBLE *Gen.* xxxiv. 25 On the thirde day when they were sore [after circumcision]. *a* **1700** DRYDEN (J.), While sore of battle, while our wounds are green. **1837** MAJ. RICHARDSON *Brit. Leg.* (ed. 2) II. 291 He was exceedingly sore and faint with the bruises he had received.

11. Afflicted with sorrow or grief; pained, distressed: **a.** Of the heart, etc.

c **1205** LAY. 149 For he nefde nenne sune þe sarure was his heorte. *c* **1250** *Gen. & Ex.* 4044 Manie tiding quad balaam ðor, ðe made balakes herte sor. *c* **1320** *Sir Tristr.* 2141 Markes hert was sare. *c* **1400** *Destr. Troy* 2074 With hoge harmes to haue, & his hert sarre. **1523** LD. BERNERS *Froiss.* I. ccccv. 704 His mynde was so sore therof, that no man coude set hym therfro. *c* **1560** A. SCOTT *Poems* (S.T.S.) xviii. 4, I most departe Frome hir..With hairt full soir. **1721** RAMSAY *Prospect of Plenty* 11 'Till..wi' a heart right sair, He sees the bites grow bein, as he grows bare. **1785** BURNS *Halloween* viii, An' Jean had e'en a sair heart To see't that night. **1834** PRINGLE *Afr. Sk.* xiv. 435 They were brothers—until the herds of the Amakosa increased so as to make the hearts of the Boors sore. **1871** C. GIBBON *Lack of Gold* iii, I think I have made both your hearts sorer than they were before. **1891** FARRAR *Darkn. & Dawn* vii, With a sore conscience [he] was constantly driven to do what he disapproved.

b. Of persons. Now *dial.*

c **1205** LAY. 638 þe king wes on mode sar; þet wes for his monne lure. **13..** R. GLOUC. (1724) 7051 þeruore þe kyng vor hys deþ þe sorrore was. **13..** *Gaw. & Gr. Knt.* 1987 Vche segge as sore, to seuer with hym þere, As þay hade wonde worþyly with þat wlonk euer. **1483** *Cath. Angl.* 349/1 Sore, *dolens*. **1525** LD. BERNERS *Froiss.* II. lxi. [lxiii.] 203 The foresayd knyght helde hymselfe sore of the informacyon of his wyfe. **1876** [ROBINSON] *Whitby Gloss.* 159 'I's varry sair for 't,' sorry for it.

12. a. Of persons or their feelings: Inclined to be irritated or grieved; irritable, sensitive; angry, resentful. Also const. *about*, *on*, and *at*. Now *colloq.* (chiefly *N. Amer.*).

a **1694** TILLOTSON (J.), Malice and hatred are very fretting and vexatious, and apt to make our minds sore and uneasy. **1738** POPE *Epil. Sat.* I. 55 Laugh at your friends, and, if your Friends are sore, So much the better, you may laugh the more. **1815** SCOTT *Guy M.* v, One of the few subjects on which he felt sore. **1849** MACAULAY *Hist. Eng.* ii. I. 233 The public mind was so sore and excitable that these lies readily found credit. **1852** DICKENS in *Househ. Words* V. 307/1 The people were very sore about the French marriage. **1884** G. C. DAVIES *Peter Penniless* xxxii. 230 Everybody was greatly amused at the incident, except Quadling, who was sore about it for a long time. **1904** *N.Y. Even. Post* 13 June 1 Kelly denied the charges and said the patrolman was 'sore' on him. **1923** R. D. PAINE *Comr. Rolling Ocean* xiv. 252 All hands were sore on him, but he couldn't take a hint. **1927** [see HIGH-HAT *v.*]. **1932** WODEHOUSE *Hot Water* xvi. 257 But surely you aren't going to get sore at a little thing like that? **1946** *Sunday Dispatch* 8 Sept. 2/7 They were sore about the decision that had deprived them of complete victory. **1954** [see NAH[1]]. **1975** D. LODGE *Changing Places* iii. 120 Nobody believed him of course, and this made him sore as hell. **1980** *Amer. N. & Q.* Jan. 71/1 Jonson is likely to have been sore about Shakespeare..styling himself gentle.

b. ***sore place, point, spot***, a point or matter in respect of which one is easily vexed or irritated.

1690 W. WALKER *Idiomat. Anglo-Lat.* 426 It is a sore place; i.e. a thing that being touched upon will gall or grieve. **1863** *Bradford Advertiser* 18 July 5/2 Some specially sore point to which you can direct your attack.

c. Similarly with *subject*, etc.

1803 C. WILMOT *Jrnl.* 6 Mar. in T. U. Sadleir *Irish Peer on Continent* (1924) 170 This however is a sore subject, as.. there is scarcely any one that one sees who is not a living victim. **1833** HT. MARTINEAU *Berkeley the Banker* I. viii. 167 It was indeed a sore subject in every house in Haleham. **1871** MEREDITH *H. Richmond* xlviii, There lies the evil of a sore subject among persons of one household. **1886** W. J. TUCKER *E. Europe* 251 Now that they are Christians, the thought of having three of their children interred in a Jewish cemetery is a very sore one with them.

13. *Comb.*, as *sore-foot*, *-footed*, *-hearted* (hence *sore-heartedness*), *-rimmed*, *-toed* adjs.; **sore-back** *attrib.*, (of horses) having a sore back; so **sore-back** *v. trans.*, to give (a horse) a sore back, **sore-backed** *a.*; **sore-eyed** *a.*, having sore eyes; also applied to sheath-billed pigeons, which have reddish caruncles round the eyes.

1835 J. E. ALEXANDER *Sketches in Portugal* x. 224 It [*sc.* a hunting-saddle] sore-backs strange horses, is hard and smooth to the rider, and one can't carry any thing on it in the shape of arms or baggage. **1923** in 'Mark Twain' *Speeches* 9 They have always got a sore-back horse lying around somewhere to sell to the stranger. **1901** KIPLING *Five Nations* (1903) 163 A top of a sore-backed Argentine, with a thirst that you couldn't buy. **1933** J. V. ALLEN *Cowboy Lore* IV. 131 But he went to see the gals on a sore-backed hoss. *a* **1733** in *Prior's Poems* (1733) III. 110 He's dropsical, she is sore-ey'd. **1756** C. SMART tr. *Horace, Epist.* I. ii. (1826) II. 191 To him, that is a slave to desire or to fear, house and estate do just as much good as paintings to a sore-eyed person. **1911** *Blackw. Mag.* Nov. 579/1 We see him arriving sorefoot at the Three Pigeons in Brentford. **1814** JANE AUSTEN *Mansfield Park* II. x. 234 She had only to rise and ..pass quietly away..sore-footed and fatigued. **1927** T. S. ELIOT *Journey of Magi*, And the camels galled, sore-footed, refractory. **1570** *Satir. Poems Reform.* x. 394 Quhilk sycht to se..maid me sair hartit. **1884** D. BOUCICAULT *Shaughraun* III. i. 20/1 Blessings on your path; it always leads to the poor and to the sore-hearted! **1923** D. H. LAWRENCE *Birds, Beasts & Flowers* 55 Open..And red at the core with the last sore-heartedness, Sore-hearted-looking. **1915** —— *Rainbow* xiii. 371 He lifted his face, the sore-rimmed eyes half smiling. **1874** W. CORY *Lett. & Jrnls.* (1897) 364 Men who are a little too sore-toed for marching.

sore, *a.*[2] *Obs.* exc. *Hist.* Also 5 sor, soore, 5–6 sowre, 6–7 soare, 7 sorre, 7–9 soar; *Sc.* 5–6 soyr, 6 soir. [a. AF. (1086 in Domesday Bk.) and OF. *sor*, mod.F. *saur*(*e*, = Prov. *saur*, *sor*, Sp. *soro*, It. *sauro*, med.L. *saurus*, *sorus*, *sorius*, of undetermined origin. Cf. SORE *sb.*[2]]

1. *Falconry.* Applied to a hawk of the first year that has not moulted and still has its red plumage (now called a *red hawk*); hence applied to the plumage itself; occas. extended to other birds of prey, as the kite and eagle.

c **1450** *Godstow Register* 259 A sperehawke sowre. *c* **1481** *Cely Papers* (Camden) 81 The fayreste sor hawke..within aull Yngelond. **1513** DOUGLAS *Æneid* VII. Prol. 125 The soir gled quhislis loud wyth mony ane pew. **1575** TURBERV. *Faulconrie* 69 That hawke that is mewed and hath cast his soare feathers. **1596** SPENSER *Hymn Heav. Beauty* 26 Of the soare faulcon so I learne to fly. **1614** LATHAM *Falconry* 37 The passenger soare-Faulcon is a more choice and tender hawke. **1641** MILTON *Animadv.* Wks. 1851 III. 188 A Soar-Eagle would not stoope at a flye. **1677** *Lond. Gaz.* No. 1180/4 Lost upon Hunslow Heath,..a Sore Tassel Gentle, with the Kings Varvels. **1753** *Chambers' Cycl.* Suppl. s.v. *Falco*, The third [name] is the soar hawk, so called in September, October, and November. **1779** *Encycl. Brit.* (ed. 2) IV. 2901/2 If it be a soar-falcon,..she will indeed be harder to reclaim. **1852** [see SORAGE].

fig. **1614** TOMKIS *Albumazar* III. iv, Fully mued From brown soar feathers of dull yeomanry, To th' glorious bloom of gentry.

†**2.** Of a horse: Of a reddish-brown colour. *Obs.* Cf. SORREL *a.* a.

a **1400** *Sir Degrev.* 76 Fayer stedes in the stallus, Lyard and soore. *c* **1480** HENRYSON *Test. Cress.* 211 (Charteris), Four ȝokkit steidis... The first was soyr, with Mane als reid as Rois. **1513** DOUGLAS *Æneid* XII. Prol. 27 Eous the steid.. Abuf the seyis lyftis furth his heid, Of cullour soyr. **1564** in Raine *Richmondshire Wills* (Surtees) 171, ij fylles, a dappell graye and a sowre baye. **1679** CLAVERHOUSE in *Lauderdale Papers* (1885) III. xcv. 165 With a pitch fork they made..an opening in my sore horses belly.

sore (sɔə(r)), *v.*[1] Also *north.* and *Sc.* 4–6 **sare**, 5–6 **sair**. [f. SORE *a.*[1] Cf. OFris. *sêria*, OS. *sêrian* (MLG. *sêren*), MDu. *seeren* (Du. *zeeren*), OHG., MHG. *sêren* (mod.G. *versehren*), ON. and Icel. *sǽra* (Sw. *såra*, Da. *saare*). OE. had *sárian* to be pained or grieved.]

a. *trans.* To make sore, in various senses; to give (physical or mental) pain to; †to wound.

13.. *Cursor M.* 14147 (Gött.), Al if þai soght fand þai na bote, þe seke him saris fra heued to fote. *c* **1475** *Rauf Coilȝear* 656 He socht in sa sadly, quhill sum of thame he saird. *c* **1489** CAXTON *Sonnes of Aymon* xxvi. 566, I fere to sore the kyng. **1536** BELLENDEN *Cron. Scot.* (1821) II. 109 Ane wolf..quhen scho was sarit with the houndis. [**1583** FULKE *Def. Tr. Script.* i. 56 If wee had a participle in Englishe to say, sored or botched, we woulde vse it.] **1590** SPENSER *F.Q.* III. xii. 38 Her bleeding brest..Was closed vp, as it had not bene sor'd [1596 bor'd]. **1847** H. BUSHNELL *Christian Nurture* iii. (1861) 46 Religion itself, pressed down upon them till they are fatally sored by its impossible claims, becomes [etc.]. **1894** *Harper's Mag.* Feb. 356/1 Some..are on foot, from soring their horses' backs.

b. With *up*. To annoy. *colloq.* (orig. *U.S.*). *rare.*

1929 D. RUNYON in *Hearst's Internat.* July 56/1 It is a sure thing he will get sored up at the second peek. **1963** 'R. EAST' *Pin Men* vi. 162 He sored me up once for all and I left him flat.

†**sore**, *v.*[2] *Venery. Obs.* [Of obscure origin: cf. RESORE.] *intr.* Of the hare: To traverse open ground.

1486 *Bk. St. Albans* e viij b, In the feeldes where he [the hare] gooth no ways beene, Ther he sorth when he steppyth and hit may not be seene. **1576** TURBERV. *Venerie* 239 When a Hare is in playne fieldes, she Soreth. **1602** *2nd Pt. Return fr. Parnass.* II. v. 937 By and by I might see him sore and resore, prick and reprick. **1704** *Dict. Rust.* (1726), *Soring*, the Footing of a Hare in open Field; for then the Huntsmen say, *She Sores*.

sore, obs. variant of SOAR *v.*

sore (sɔə(r)), *adv.* Now chiefly *arch.* and *dial.* Forms: α. 1–3 sare (3 sære); *north.* and *Sc.* 4–5 sar(e, sayre, 4–5, 7 sayr, 4– sair; 8–9 sear. β. 3– sore (3 seore), 4–5 sor, 5–6 soore, 6 *Sc.* soir. *Compar.* 3–5 sarre, 4–5 sarrer, 4 sarare, -er, 5 -arre; 4 sorere, zorer, 6– sorer. *Superl.* 3–4 sarrest, 5 sarest, 3– sorest. [OE. *sáre* (f. *sár* SORE *a.*[1]), = OFris. *sêr*, *seer*, MDu. *seer* (Du. *zeer*), OS. and OHG. *sêro* (MHG. *sêre*, G. *sehr*), MSw. *sāra*, *sāre*, Da. *saare*.]

1. Of striking, wounding, etc.: So as to cause considerable physical pain or bodily injury; violently or severely in this respect.

α. *c* **1000** *Ags. Ps.* (Thorpe) lxxvii. 33 þonne he hi sare sloh, þonne hi sohton hine. *c* **1205** LAY. 27692 Gecron..his spere grap anan and smat Leir þene eorl sære. *a* **1225** *Ancr. R.* 292 þe neiles weren so dulte þet heo..breken þe bones, more þen þurleden, uorte pinen him sarre. *a* **1352** MINOT *Poems* v. 12 It sowed him sare; Sare it þam smerted. **1375** BARBOUR *Bruce* II. 351 Feyle men dede, and woundyt sar. *a* **1450** MYRC 1416 þe herre þat a mon ys in degre, þe sarrer forsoþe falleþ he. **1508** DUNBAR *Tua mariit wemen* 223 Hald abak, and handill me nought sair.

β. *c* **1205** LAY. 27908 Kæi wes forwunded seore. **13..** *Sir Beues* (A.) 407, I schel him smite swiþe sore Upon is hat. **1340** *Ayenb.* 238 Huo þet heȝest ualþ þe zorer he him blecheþ. **1470–85** MALORY *Arth.* x. iii. 416 And fyrst he smote doune my felawe syre Bleoberys & sore wounded hym. *a* **1548** HALL *Chron., Edw. IV*, 200 b, Thei were sore beaten, wounded, and very evil intreated. **1562** J. HEYWOOD *Prov. & Epigr.* (1867) 61 An olde dog byteth sore. But.. tholde bitche biteth sorer. **1653** H. COGAN tr. *Pinto's Trav.* xiv. 44 Seeing ourselves all sore hurt. *a* **1720** SEWEL *Hist. Quakers* (1795) I. II. 130, I did beat you very sore. **1842** LOVER *Handy Andy* l, She..said 'they hurt her sore', and she was 'bleeding a power'.

b. Of sickness or other physical suffering: Severely, dangerously, seriously.

c **1290** *S. Eng. Leg.* I. 231 Longue wenden þis gode men ..þat huy weren of-hongred sore. **1338** R. BRUNNE *Chron.* (1725) 53 þat tyme at Westmynstir Harald sore seke lay. *c* **1350** *Will. Palerne* 593 Seiþth me al ȝour seknesse & what so sore ȝow greuis. **1422** tr. *Secreta Secret., Priv. Priv.* 236 A man..that soore seke is. *c* **1450** *Merlin* xiv. 207 Many ther were throwen to grounde sore bledynge with stroke of speres. **1500–20** DUNBAR *Poems* xliv. 16 Grit pane and wo.. Into thair birth thay suffir sair for ws. **1609** ROWLANDS *Dr. Merrie-man* (Hunterian Cl.) 18 An aged Gentleman sore sicke did lie. **1721** RAMSAY *Prospect of Plenty* 73 Peghing fou sair beneath a lade of fears. **1842** MACAULAY *Horatius* lxi, Fast his blood was flowing; And he was sore in pain. **1878** SPURGEON *Treas. David* Ps. cxviii. 19 Our hero had also in all probability been sore sick.

†**2.** With much suffering; dearly. *Obs.*

Beowulf 1251 Sigon þa to slæpe: sum sare angeald æfenræste. *c* **1205** LAY. 8158 þu me smite bi þon rugge, ah sare þu hit salt a-buggen. *a* **1300** *Cursor M.* 1070 Caym.. Vntil his broþer nith he bare, Allas, þat boght þe sacrilages sare. **1375** BARBOUR *Bruce* XVIII. 514 War it nocht that he war Sic a caytif, he sulde by sair His wourdis. ? **1402** in *Yorksh. Arch. Jrnl.* XX. (1908) 46 Wykked lyf maath [= maketh] a man tabye ful sore.

3. With verbs of grieving, annoying, etc.: So as to cause mental pain or irritation; deeply, intensely.

α. *a* **1000** *Cædmon's Gen.* 1257 (Gr.), Me þæt cynn hafað sare abolgen. *c* **1205** LAY. 4598 þus seide Goðlac, sære him gromede. *c* **1350** *Will. Palerne* 2025 Sche told me a-noþer tale þat me tened sarre. *c* **1400** in *26 Pol. Poems* x. 39 ȝoure gyltes greued god so sare. **1814** SCOTT *Waverley* lxv, But sair, sair angry and affronted wad she hae been.

β. *c* **1200** *Trin. Coll. Hom.* 173 Hie ben sore ofgramede, and wið hem seluen alre sorest. *c* **1330** R. BRUNNE *Chron. Wace* (Rolls) 10286 þan ys þy peryl mykel þe more, þat þou wraþest Crist so sore. *c* **1386** CHAUCER *Sompn. T.* 481 Ne grevith me no thing so sore, As that this elde cherl.. Blasphemed hath our holy covent eeke. **1470–85** MALORY *Arthur* II. vi. 82 The whiche sorowe greued Balyn passyngly sore. **1568** GRAFTON *Chron.* II. 8 For these, and for other sterne and cruell deedes done by hym, the sayde Nobles were sore moued against him. **1671** MILTON *P.R.* IV. 196 Be not so sore offended, Son of God. **1782** COWPER *Gilpin* 54 Although it griev'd him sore. **1870** BRYANT *Iliad* IV. I. 105 Minerva held her peace,..sore displeased with father Jove.

b. Used to intensify the idea of dislike or reluctance, esp. with *against one's will*.

a **1225** *Ancr. R.* 56 Vor þet ec þet he dude hire was iðe frumðe sore hire unðonckes. **1530** PALSGR. 842/1 Sore agaynst my wyll,..*moult enuys*. **1567** *Satir. Poems Reform.* iii. 232 Sa we departit soir againis our will. **1632** LITHGOW *Trav.* x. 449 Then vnhappily came I a shoare..sore agaynst the Generals will. **1782** COWPER *Gilpin* 158 Away went Gilpin,..sore against his will.

4. With great grief, distress, or perturbation of mind; in such a manner or to such an extent as to involve or manifest this. (Passing into a mere intensive.)

a. With verbs of weeping, lamenting, etc.

α. a 900 Cynewulf *Crist* 1572 (Gr.), Hu þa womsceaþan hyra ealdȝestreon..sare greten. a 1000 *Ags. Ps.* (Thorpe) cxxxvi. 1 Ofer Babilone bradum streame, þær we sittað & sare wepað. c 1200 Ormin 7924 Forr iwhillc mann birrþ wepenn her, & sikenn sare. a 1300 *Cursor M.* 9045 Wit bath his eien sar he grett. a 1352 Minot *Poems* (ed. Hall) viii. 60 Þe knightes..Come to sir Edward sare wepeand. a 1400 *Pistill of Susan* 222 Whon we þat semblaunt seiȝ, we siked wel sare. c 1470 *Gol. & Gaw.* 1128 The king..Sair murnand in mude. 1513 Douglas *Æneid* II. xii. 15 The ȝing childring ..Stude all on raw,..About the tresour quhymperand woundir sair. 1567 *Satir. Poems Reform.* iv. 65 Scho come to me..Lamentand sair my greit calamitie. 1778– in northern and Sc. dialect use.

β. c 1200 *Trin. Coll. Hom.* 169 Iob..hefde..his honden to his breste, and sore sihte. a 1250 *Owl & Night.* 885 Vor oþer men hi wepeþ sore. 13.. *Sir Beues* (A.) 1111 Ȝhe fel adoun and wep riȝt sore. 1423 Jas. I *Kingis Q.* lxxi, So sore thus sighit I with my-self allone. 1485 Caxton *Chas. Gt.* 78 Olyuer had so moche compassyon of hym..that he sore wepte. 1535 Coverdale *1 Macc.* ii. 39 When Matathias and his frendes herde this, they mourned for them right sore. 1567 *Satir. Poems Reform.* iii. 3 Ane bony boy was soir makand his mone. 1611 Bible *Judges* xxi. 2 And the people ..lift vp their voices, and wept sore. a 1649 Drumm. of Hawth. *Poems* Wks. (1711) 42 He who did cause her Ill Sore-wailing stood. 1868 Morris *Earthly Par.* (1870) I. I. 394 She turned away lamenting very sore.

b. With verbs of repenting, rueing, etc.

α. a 1000 *Doomsday* 83 (Gr.), þam þe his synna nu sare ȝeþenceþ. c 1175 *Lamb. Hom.* 149 þet him sare roweþ. a 1300 *Cursor M.* 25996 Sua sar þin sakes to for-thingk þat soru thoru þin hert sink. 1375 Barbour *Bruce* IX. 469, I trow ..that him sair repent sall he. c 1470 Henry *Wallace* I. 72 Quhar throuch Scotland rapentyt syne full sar. 1500–20 Dunbar *Poems* ix. 87 In thir pointis, quhair I offendit, sair I rew. 1570 *Satir. Poems Reform.* x. 292 As efterwart thay did repent full sair.

β. a 1200 *Moral Ode* 354 It him mai reuwe sore. c 1250 *Gen. & Ex.* 1166 So sore him reu of ðat bale. c 1290 [see repent *v.* 1]. 13.. *E.E. Allit. P.* B. 290 Sore hit me rwez þat euer I made hem myself. c 1412 Hoccleve *De Reg. Princ.* 663, I now repente wonder sore. 1535 [see forthink *v.* 5 b]. c 1560 A. Scott *Poems* (S.T.S.) iv. 20 Syne..[she] Perchance sall soir repent. 1590 Spenser *F.Q.* III. viii. 47 That all the noble knights..may sore repent with me. 1838 *Wilson's Tales Borders* (1839) V. 15/2 Sore, sore you have rued..that night.

c. With verbs denoting fear, dejection, doubt, etc.

α. c 1200 Ormin 3809 Acc aȝȝ þeȝȝ sinndenn..sare offdredde Off domess daȝess starrke dom. c 1230 *Hali Meid.* 15 Beo sarre offearet to fallen. a 1300 *Cursor M.* 22629 Sair þai sal do for to grise. 1375 Barbour *Bruce* I. 440 He dred sayr his felouny. c 1475 *Rauf Coilȝear* 710, I dreid me sair I be begylit. c 1560 A. Scott *Poems* (S.T.S.) ii. 124 Full sair he dred for blame. 1596 Dalrymple tr. *Leslie's Hist. Scot.* I. 77 Thay feired nocht litle, bot verie sair, that..al sulde succeid verie ill. 1820 Scott *Monast.* iv, Sair, sair my mind misgave me.

β. c 1250 *Gen. & Ex.* 3223 Sore he gunen for-dredde ben. 1297 R. Glouc. (Rolls) 575 Þe king kwakede & is men, so sore hii were agaste. c 1320 *Cast. Love* (Halliw.) 1580 Fulle sore mowe heo then dreden. 1393 Langl. *P. Pl.* C. xxi. 314 'That is soþ,' seide satan, 'bote ich me sore doute'. c 1425 *Eng. Conq. Irel.* vii. 20 (Dubl. MS.), Macmorgh..be-held his men, and saw ham sor amayed. 1484 Caxton *Fables of Æsop* II. v, Whanne the folke sawe that the erthe beganne thus to shake, they were sore aferd. 1508 Dunbar *Gold. Targe* 159 Full sore thay dred to done a violence. a 1591 H. Smith *Wks.* (1867) II. 5 Indeed, this news frighted him sorest. 1611 Bible *1 Sam.* xxviii. 15 Saul answered, I am sore distressed. 1690 W. Walker *Idiomat. Anglo-Lat.* 426, I was sore afraid, you had been gone. 1768–74 Tucker *Lt. Nat.* (1834) II. 636 We are trained up to dread thee sorer by the..customs of the world around us. 1858 Mansel *Bampton Lect.* vii. (1859) 150 In our hearts we believe, yet our thoughts at times are sore troubled.

d. With verbs denoting astonishment or embarrassment.

c 1450 *Merlin* ii. 30 And thei herden hym thus sey, thei were sore a-merveyled. 1470–85 Malory *Arthur* I. iii. 38 Thenne she sore abasshed to yeue ansuer. a 1533 Ld. Berners *Huon* xci. 292 He was stryken fro his horse to the erth sore astonyed, so that he wyst not where he was. 1592 Timme *Ten Eng. Lepers* Ij, They would not wonder so sore at the punishment. 1620 *Frier Rush* 24 At the which they were sore astonished. 1742 Young *Nt. Th.* II. 398 We, sore amaz'd, from out earth's ruins crawl. 1787 Burns *J. Barleycorn* iii, John Barleycorn got up again, And sore surpris'd them all.

5. So as to cause suffering, hardship, or great straits; to a painful or distressing degree; severely, grievously, oppressively.

α. *Beowulf* 2311 Swa hyt lungre wearð on hyra sincȝifan sare ȝeendod. a 1000 *Genesis* 2415 þæt sceal wrecan swefyl & sweart liȝ, sare & grimme. a 1122 *O.E. Chron.* (Laud MS.) an. 1116, Ðis land & þas leodon wurdon..oftrædlice sare ȝeswencte. c 1230 *Hali Meid.* 7 þu..schalt beo sare iderued under hire, as hire þral. c 1440 *York Myst.* xi. 160, I sall send vengeaunce ix. or x., To sewe hym sararre, or I sesse.

β. c 1305 *Mir. St. James* 67 in *E.E.P.* (1862) 59 Þe deuel ȝeode awey, & huld him a-gyled sore. c 1380 Wyclif *Wks.* (1880) 38 Þei ponysche men sorere for breken of here owen lawis þan for brekynge of goddis lawe. a 1400 *Sir Perc.* 349 The lady was never more sore bygone. 1535 Coverdale *1 Macc.* ii. 30 The tyranny increaced so sore vpon them. 1595 G. Markham *Sir R. Grinuile* (Arb.) 85 For his own sake, Whom desperate hazard might indamage sore. 1634 Sir T. Herbert *Trav.* 197 They hate and punish Adultery very sore. 1667 Milton *P.L.* I. 298 The torrid Clime Smote on him sore besides. 1786 Burns *The Lament* viii, Sore-harass'd out, with care and grief. 1806 Surr *Winter in Lond.* III. 7 Unhappy stranger, you have been sore afflicted. 1865 Kingsley *Herew.* vii, The archers shot sore at him from the wall. 1870 Burton *Hist. Scot.* lxviii. VI. 418 His enemies, too, in their hour of triumph, harassed him sore and showed him little mercy.

†**b.** *to sit* (or *set*) *one sore* (see sit *v.* 15). *Obs.*

c 1420 *Sir Amadace* (Camden) xxi, I see a siȝte I thenke on ȝete, That sittus me nowe fulle sore. c 1470 Henry *Wallace* I. 439 Sone, thir tythings sytts me sor. c 1560 A. Scott *Poems* (S.T.S.) xx. 20 Quhat kin thing wes lufe, Quhilk now settis the so sair.

6. To a grievous or serious extent; greatly.

a 1300 *X Commandm.* 38 in *E.E.P.* (1862) 16 Sore and bitter þe soule [it] sal der. 1489 Caxton *Faytes of A.* II. xxxv. 151 Oure lorde sent suche a grete showre of rayne that theyre harneys was sore charged with watre. 1513 in C. Rogers *Coldstream Chartul.* (1879) Pref. 21 Soo soore abewsed with the faire promyses of Fraunce. 1567 *Gude & Godlie B.* (S.T.S.) 37, I knaw that I haif sinnit soir. 1667 Milton *P.L.* IX. 1124 High Passions, Anger, Hate,..shook sore Thir inward State of Mind. 1683 *Yorkshire Dial.* 5 Thur Yowes are Clowclagg'd, they skitter sayr.

b. With reference to physical deterioration.

1523 Fitzherb. *Husb.* §14 All these maner of otes weare the grounde very sore. 1570–6 Lambarde *Peramb. Kent* (1826) 133 This Towne was so sore wasted with fire,..that it was wholly..consumed. 1603 Knolles *Hist. Turks* (1621) 429 The Turkes continuing the batterie had sore shaken the aforesaid tower. a 1668 Lassels *Voy. Italy* (1670) II. 135 Half of it is..sore battered with the aire.

7. With great exertion or effort; laboriously, toilsomely, hard.

a 1300 *Body & Soul* 67 in *Map's Poems* 341 Never ne thouȝtest thow..ho therfore sarrest swonk. 13.. *E.E. Allit. P.* A. 550 Þe fyrst by-gonne to pleny & sayden þat þay hade trauayled sore. c 1550 Cheke *Lett.* 11, J..labor as sore that ye mai thinke [etc.]. 1567 *Reg. Privy Council Scot.* I. 517 Laubourand and travelland sair for his leving. 1620 *Frier Rush* 27 Me thinks you take great paines to worke so sore your selfe. 1795 Macneill *Will & Jean* 1, Will wrought sair, but aye wi' pleasure. 1838 Carlyle *Misc.* (1857) IV. 178 Long and sore had this man thought. 1843 —— *Past & Pr.* III. xiii, To work sore, and yet gain nothing.

b. With great force or vigour; strongly.

(*a*) c 1400 *Laud Troy Bk.* 8681 Thei rode to-gedur wel sare, Many a stalworthe knyȝt thare. 1464 *Paston Lett.* II. 144 The plee by twene Ogan and yow was sore argued. 1523 Ld. Berners *Froiss.* I. cxx. 144 Some of theym..drewe it to them so sore, that they brake the chenes of yron yt helde the bridge. 1527 Andrew *Brunswyke's Distyll. Waters* M ij b, The membre well and sore rubbed therwith.

(*b*) 1542 Udall *Erasm. Apoph.* 199 On a tyme when it thoundreed veray sore. 1560 Daus tr. *Sleidane's Comm.* 94 The wynde blewe sore against the streame. 1656 Bradford *Plymouth Plant.* I. x. (1856) 87 Though it was very darke, and rained sore.

c. With severity or strictness; severely.

1483 Caxton *G. de la Tour* D viij, He had repreued them so sore that they had..grete shame. c 1500 *Lancelot* 1660 Bot schortly thei sall be sar accusit. 1533 More *Answ. Poysoned Bk.* Wks. 1036/2 Of suche bookes, as sore as they bee forbodden, yet are there manye boughte. c 1586 Sidney *Arcadia* II. (1590) 224 Thou heardst even now a young man sneb me sore.

8. Eagerly, earnestly; with great desire or intensity. Chiefly with verbs of longing.

(*a*) 1297 R. Glouc. *Chron.* (Rolls) I. 356/117 Hym longede after veneson þer after longe sore. a 1400–50 *Wars Alex.* 385 Þen kisses he kenely þe quene.., Langis sare to þe layke. c 1420 Lydg. *Assembly of Gods* 1045 He callyd soore for bowes and bade hem shote faste. a 1533 Ld. Berners *Huon* lxi. 211 Ye shall se Huon, whose presence ye so sore desyre. 1575 Gascoigne *Glasse of Governm.* Wks. 1910 II. 78, I long sore to have answere of my letters. 1611 Bible *Gen.* xxxi. 30 Because thou sore longedst after thy fathers house.

(*b*) a 1533 Ld. Berners *Huon* xliii. 143 Then the Admyrall soore [1601 earnestly, Fr. *mout fort*] behelde Huon. 1545 Ascham *Toxoph.* (Arb.) 25 You studie to sore Toxophile. 1611 Bible *Judges* xiv. 17 He tolde her, because shee lay sore vpon him. 1894 Crockett *Raiders* (ed. 3) 284, I urged her sore.

†**9.** Closely, tightly. *Obs.*

Perh. only a contextual variation of sense 10.

1377 Langl. *P. Pl.* B. XI. 219, I conseille alle crystene cleue nouȝte þer-on to sore. 1390 Gower *Conf.* I. 58 That other Ere als faste He stoppeth with his tail so sore, That he the wordes..ne hiereth. 1426 Lydg. *De Guil. Pilgr.* 8797 Sche kepeth hem..Sore shet wyth lok & keye. a 1483 *Liber Niger* in *Househ. Ord.* (1790) 69 Not to boult it soe sore vpon the gurgeones. 1526 *Pilgr. Perf.* (W. de W. 1531) 29 b, It shetteth it self so sore..that..it is not so opened agayne. 1545 Ascham *Toxoph.* (Arb.) 111 The string..beynge sore twined must nedes knap in sunder.

10. To a great extent; greatly, very much.

Chiefly in contexts suggestive of sense 6, but sometimes merely intensive.

c 1440 *Pallad. on Husb.* I. 90 Ne picche hit not to[o] soore into the vale. 1470–85 Malory *Arthur* IV. vi. 126 And anone they felle on slepe, and slepte merueillously sore all the nyght. a 1533 Ld. Berners *Gold. Bk. M. Aurel.* (1546) C ij b, There was a lawe soore vsed and accustomed, and well kepte in the Romayne polycie. 1561 Hollybush *Hom. Apoth.* 34 Seth the Turtel wyth water, salt her not to sore. 1606 G. Woodcock *Hist. Iustine* xxxv. 113 So sore hated was Demetrius among all men. 1611 Shaks. *Cymb.* IV. ii. 225 Oh bill sore shaming Those rich-left-heyres. 1784 Cowper *Task* IV. 343 The wain goes heavily, impeded sore By..loads adhering close To the clogg'd wheels. 1812 Byron *Ch. Har.* I. ii, A shameless wight, Sore given to revel and ungodly glee.

11. With adjs. and advs.: Very, extremely, exceedingly. *Obs.* exc. *dial.*

1474 Caxton *Chesse* III. vii. (1883) 141 The kynge denys had a broder whom he louyd sore well. c 1489 —— *Sonnes of Aymon* iii. 112 That I assaylled theym, it hath cost me sore dere. 1530 *Comp. Old Treat.* in Roy *Rede me* (Arb.) 171 The new testament..set forthe by Master William Tyndale, which they falsely pretende to be sore corrupte. 1596 Dalrymple tr. *Leslie's Hist. Scot.* I. 98 Scheiphouses..of quhais burning thay ar nocht sair solist. 1638 Brathwait *Barnabee's Jrnl.* II. (1818) 61 Where growne surfoot and sore weary, I repos'd. 1860 Geo. Eliot *Mill on Fl.* III. ix, She was sore fond of us children.

12. *Comb.*, as **sore-holding**; **sore-dreaded, -meant, -pressed, -wearied, -won, -worn** adjs.

c 1450 *Merlin* xiv. 222 The haubrekes, that were stronge and sore-holdynge. 1567 *Satir. Poems Reform.* iv. 66 My langsum lyfe and sair tormentit Spirite. 1616 J. Lane *Contn. Sqr.'s T.* x. 330 Ann apparition, which seemd at first to bee some sore ment vision. 1638 Brathwait *Barnabee's Jrnl.* III. 121 Thence to Ferrybrig, sore-wearied Surfoot, but in spirit cheer'd. 1785 Burns *Cotter's Sat. Nt.* iv, To..deposite her sair-won penny-fee. 1787 *Minor* 28 That bedlam,..bedizened in sore-worn flounces. 1843 Bethune *Scottish Fireside Stor.* 279 It was that day..Which brings to sair worn toil a time Of needful peace. 1866 G. Macdonald *Ann. Q. Neighb.* xxviii. (1878) 479 The sore-pressed garrison which had retreated to its last defence. 1870 J. Bruce *Life of Gideon* xviii. 335 Nigh to the spot on which those harnessed and sore-dreaded dreamers lay.

sored, *a.* Chiefly *north.* Also 5 **sorede**, 5–6 **sorde**, 6 **sowerde**, 9 *Sc.* **sorit**. [f. sore *a.*[2]]

1. Of horses, etc.: = sorrel *a.* a. ? *Obs.*

1420 *E.E. Wills* (1882) 53 A sorede horse þat was bought off Henuden. *Ibid.*, þe sorde hors. 1545 *Richmond Wills* (Surtees) 57 Item a sored horse, price xiij s. iiij d. 1587 *Knaresb. Wills* (Surtees) I. 158 A sowerde mare and a fole. 1825 Jamieson *Suppl.*, *Sorit*, of a sorrel colour; as, 'a sorit horse', Clydes[dale].

†**2.** Of colour: = sorrel *a.* c. *Obs.*

1587 *Wills & Inv. N.C.* (Surtees, 1860) 288 One stud mare, of colour bawson sored.

sored, *ppl. a. rare.* [f. sore *v.*[1]] Pained; troubled.

a 1542 Wyatt in *Tottel's Misc.* (Arb.) 73 One onely hope hath stayed my life, apart: Which doth perswade such wordes vnto my sored minde.

soredi- (sə'riːdɪ), comb. form of soredi-um, used in a few terms, as **so'redial** *a.*, of the nature of, pertaining to, a soredium; **so'rediate** *a.*, bearing or characterized by the prevalence of soredia; **soredi(i)ferous** *a.*, bearing soredia; caused by producing soredia; **so'rediform** *a.*, = next; **so'redioid** *a.*, having the appearance, form, or character of a soredium or soredia.

1882 Vines tr. *Sachs' Bot.* 328 *Soredial branches, as they are termed, are thus produced. 1881 *Jrnl. Bot.* X. 115 The *sorediate form of *Pertusaria velata*. 1829 Loudon *Encycl. Plants* (1836) 949 *Ramalina.* Plant cartilaginous,.. somewhat shrubby, mostly *sorediferous. 1856 Lindsay *Pop. Hist. Brit. Lichens* 42 The disc of an apothecium is sometimes rendered abortive by sorediiferous degradation. 1859 Mayne *Expos. Lex.* 1174/2 *Sorediformis*, having the appearance of *soredia*..; *sorediform. 1857 Berkeley *Cryptog. Botany* §459. 418 Many other forms are assumed by the crusts of Lichens;..the *sorediold from the protrusion of groups of gonidia.

‖**soredium** (sə'riːdɪəm). *Bot.* Pl. **soredia.** [mod.L., f. Gr. σωρός a heap. Cf. F. *sorédion.*] A thallus-bud or cell in lichens. Usu. in pl.

1829 Loudon *Encycl. Plants* (1836) 949 *Soredia* are little heaps of free, pulverulent bodies, mostly of a whitish color, placed on various parts of the frond. 1866 *Treas. Bot.* 867/2 The soredia predominating over the crust it assumes the name of *Lepraria*. 1882 Vines tr. *Sachs' Bot.* 327, *A* a simple soredium, consisting of a gonidium covered with a web of hyphæ;..*C* a group of simple soredia.

sorefull, obs. variant of sorrowful.

'**sore-head**, *a.* and *sb.* Also sorehead. [See sore *a.*[1] 9.]

A. *adj.* Irritable or out of temper 'like a bear with a sore head'; discontented, dissatisfied.

1862 *Major Jack Downing* vii. (1867) 61 [He] sed it done very well for some sore-hed Dimmycrat. 1902 *Academy* 22 Mar. 291/1 This is sore-head philosophy.

B. *sb.* **a.** *U.S. political slang.* A dissatisfied or disappointed politician.

1862 *Rocky Mountain News* (Denver) 16 Oct. (Thornton), What will the 'sore-heads' say now? 1878 *N. Amer. Rev.* CXXVI. 402 Each led by a little faction of sore-heads, desperate and reckless. 1888 Bryce *Amer. Commw.* III. lxiii. II. 458 Some discontented magnate objects and threatens to withdraw... If such a 'sore-head' persists, a schism may follow.

b. *slang* (chiefly *N. Amer.*). A discontented, dissatisfied person, a malcontent; a mean, niggardly person.

1848 *Weekly Argus* (Albany, N.Y.) 12 Aug. 253/3 As no other selection could be supposed so well to represent such a conventicle of 'sore heads', it is perhaps quite as well it sho'd take that direction as any other. 1912 J. Sandilands *Western Canad. Dict. & Phrase-bk.*, *Sore-head*, a person who sees trouble and wickedness in everything. 1916 C. J. Dennis *Songs of Sentimental Bloke* 130 *Sore-head*, a curmudgeon. 1934 J. T. Farrell *Young Manhood of Studs Lonigan* iv. 61 'You damn Kike, you got too many horseshoes,' a sore-head said as Davey raked in the pot. 1939 T. Wolfe *Web & Rock* ii. 36 We thought he was a man, but he turns out to be just a little sore-head. 1964 L. Nkosi *Rhythm of Violence* II. i. 23 *Mary*..You two are not to drink until the others arrive! *Jimmy* Rubbish! We have priority claims! *Mary*..Soreheads! What makes you think you have priorities over others! 1978 M. Puzo *Fools Die* xx. 226, I was holding court with a lot of my customers, who were all telling me what a bunch of shit the whole business was, caused by a few soreheads.

So **sore-headed** *a.*, = sore-head *a.*; hence **sore'headedly** *adv.*, **sore'headedness.**

1844 Hood *Tale of Temper* 53 No bear, *sore-headed, could be more cantankerous. 1888 *Pall Mall G.* 19 Dec. 2/1

The men are dissatisfied and 'sore-headed'. **1883** *Ibid.* 8 Jan. 3 *Soreheadedly punctilious about the proper respect paid them. **1860** *Marysville* (Calif.) *Appeal* 31 Mar. 2/2 The patriots of the Customs House [are] suffering from the *sore-headedness which so often follows an unsuccessful attempt at ascendency in the political scale. **1885** W. CORY *Lett. & Jrnls.* (1897) 515 The gossip and the pecking and the sore-headedness of country towns.

Sorelian (sə'rɛlɪən, -'iːlɪən), *a.* [f. the name of Georges *Sorel* (1847–1922), French political philosopher + -IAN.] Of, pertaining to, or characteristic of Sorel or his views on the regeneration of society through proletarian or syndicalist violence.

1921 N. ANGELL *Fruits of Victory* v. 165 The Sorelian philosophy of violence and instinctive pugnacity..gives us the tendency to an infinite splitting of the Labour movement. **1931** R. SOLTAU *French Pol. Thought in Nineteenth Cent.* xiv. 460 Sorelian philosophy can be examined from two aspects. **1936** WIRTH & SHILS tr. *Mannheim's Ideology & Utopia* iii. 125 This attitude takes many forms—appearing first in the anarchism of Bakunin and Proudhon, then in the Sorelien [*sic*] syndicalism, and finally in the fascism of Mussolini. **1970** H. ARENDT *On Violence* iii. 73 The strange revival of the life philosophies of Bergson and Nietzsche in their Sorelian version. **1979** *Dædalus* Winter 19 Pragmatic proposals have replaced the Sorelian myth.

†**sorely**, *a.* *Obs.* In 1, 3 sarlic, 3 sorlich. [OE. *sárlíc* (f. *sár* SORE *a.*[1]), = obs. Flem. *seerlick* (Kilian), OHG. *sêrlîh*; cf. ON. *sárlig-r*, MSw. *sārligh.*] Painful, sorrowful; sad.

Beowulf 842 No his lifȝedal sarlic þuhte secga æneȝum. *c* **888** K. ÆLFRED *Boeth.* xi. §2 Maneȝra sarlicra wita hi ȝewilnodon wið þæm ecan life. **971** *Blickl. Hom.* 123 Se sarlica cwide..þe ure Drihten..to þæm ærestan men cwæþ. *c* **1000** ÆLFRIC *Saints' Lives* II. 140 He..cwæð him to sona mid sarlicre stemne. *c* **1205** LAY. 28457 þa quene læi inne Eouwerwic, næs heo næuere swa sarlic [*v.r.* sorlich].

sorely ('sɔəlɪ), *adv.* Forms: α. 1 sarlice, 3 særliche, 5 sarely; *Sc.* 6 sairlye, -lie, 6- sairly. β. 4 sorly, 5 soreli(e, 5- sorely. [OE. *sárlíce* (f. *sár* SORE *a.*[1]), = OFris. *sêrlîke*, MSw. *sārlika* (*-liga*): cf. ON. *sárliga*.]

In most senses tending to become a mere intensive.

1. In a manner expressive of great pain, grief, or distress.

c **888** K. ÆLFRED *Boeth.* xxvi. §2 Ða onsac se Wisdom sarlice & cwæð [etc.]. **971** *Blickl. Hom.* 225 þa wæron hie ealle sona unrote, & sarlice ȝebærdon. *c* **1000** ÆLFRIC *Gen.* xxi. 16 Heo..sæt hire feorran sarlice wepende. *c* **1055** *Byrhtferth's Handboc* in *Anglia* VIII. 309 Oft seo brodiȝe henn, þeah heo sarlice cloccȝe, heo..þa briddas ȝewyrmð. **1748** THOMSON *Cast. Indol.* I. xxi, They cannot fly, But often each way look, and often sorely sigh. **1841** LONGF. *Childr. Lord's Supper* 348 Each bowed him, weeping full sorely.

2. a. In such a manner as to cause great pain or bodily injury; severely. Also *fig.*

a **900** CYNEWULF *Juliana* 571 [He] sohte..hu he sarlicast þurh þa wyrrestan witu meahte feorhcwale findan. *a* **1000** *Soul & Body* 73 þe sculon her..slitan sarlice swearte wihta. **1553** *Douglas's Æneid* II. (1710) 52/36 Baith hir tendir handes War strenzeit sairly boundin hard with bandes. **1590** SPENSER *F.Q.* III. ix. 29 The wicked engine..secretly did glyde Into his hart, which it did sorely gryde. **1611** SHAKS. *Wint. T.* v. i. 18, I did so: but thou strik'st me Sorely, to say I did. **1650** B. *Discolliminium* 32 Had it once left sucking the Mothers breasts so sorely. **1695** LD. PRESTON *Boeth.* III. 119 Like that angry Insect..they sorely wound th' Enjoyer too. **1870** BRYANT *Iliad* v. I. 173 Wilt thou be angry with me if I drive Mars, sorely wounded, from the battle-field? *Ibid.* XIV. II. 68 These Bore him to Ilium sorely suffering.

b. In a manner involving mental pain, distress, or dissatisfaction.

In OE. the sense 'regrettably, lamentably', occurs.

c **1450** *Godstow Reg.* 633 Hit is vn-semeli..þat contrauersi ..lawfully endid sholde be soreli I-meuid ageine. **1567** *Gude & Godlie B.* (S.T.S.) 61 Rycht sorelie musing in my mynde. **1567** *Satir. Poems Reform.* iv. 157, I speik not but pruife, quhilk I may sairlie rew. **1722** DE FOE *Plague* 75 Sorely I repented of my rashness. **1828** SCOTT *F.M. Perth* xxix, I know my failing, and..so sorely dread that I cannot conquer it. **1865** TROLLOPE *Belton Est.* xxxi. 376 She sorrowed to think that he should want such a thing so sorely. **1870** J. E. T. ROGERS *Hist. Glean.* Ser. II. 134 Sorely against his will, Walpole was at last driven into war.

3. In such a manner as to press hardly or severely upon a person or thing.

c **1205** LAY. 6805 Særliche heo feohte, & fælden heore cnihtes. *c* **1400** *Melayne* 265 þe Sarazene semblede so Sarely þat þay felde faste of oure cheualrye. *c* **1400** *Destr. Troy* 3692 Sodenly þo sailes were sorely bestad. **1606** SHAKS. *Ant. & Cl.* IV. vi. 19, I haue done ill, Of which I do accuse my selfe so sorely, That I will ioy no more. **1613** —— *Hen. VIII*, IV. ii. 14 [He] brought him forward As a man sorely tainted, to his Answer. **1665** MANLEY *Grotius' Low C. Wars* 750 They begirt the Castle, and the sixth day after recovered it, being sorely assaulted and withall wanting of provision. **1725** DE FOE *Voy. round World* (1840) 253, I would be sorely put to it for lodging. **1779** WARNER in Jesse *Selwyn & Contemp.* (1844) IV. 259, I called upon the old duchess, who is 'sorely badly', as they say in Lincolnshire, with her old complaint. **1820** SCOTT *Monast.* xxxvi, Of these most were mounted on steeds which had been sorely jaded. **1846** BROWNING *Soul's Trag.* Wks. 1863 II. 460 The very measures of precaution, which pressed soreliest on himself. **1853** KANE *Grinnell Exp.* xlix. (1856) 465 It is an amorphous mass, so worn that it must have been sorely wrought before its release from the glacier.

4. To a great extent; in a high degree.

1562 WINȜET *Wks.* (S.T.S.) I. 5 Hes not mony..in thair perfite beleif..sairlye stummerit? **1605** SHAKS. *Lear* II. iv. 304 Alacke the night comes on, and the high windes Do sorely ruffle. **1704** SWIFT *Batt. Bks.* Misc. (1711) 239 Who had tore off his Title-Page, sorely defac'd one half his Leaves [etc.]. **1786** BURNS *To a Louse* i, Your impudence protects you sairly. **1831** SCOTT *Ct. Rob.* vii, 'Thou objectest sorely to my complexion,' said the negro. **1855** DICKENS *Lett.* (1880) I. 399 The Association is sorely in want of able men. **1891** FARRAR *Darkn. & Dawn* lv, To stay among them meant death, and his life was sorely needed by the Church of God.

5. *Comb.*, as ***sorely-battered, -needed, -sweated, -tempted, -worn*** adjs.

1870 C. J. VAUGHAN *Earnest Words* (1878) 154 The sorely-tempted soul. **1891** KIPLING *Light that Failed* ii. (1900) 16 A pair of sorely-worn riding-breeches. **1900** W. S. CHURCHILL in *Morning Post* 1 Jan. 6/1 The engine was soon crowded and began to steam homewards—a mournful, sorely-battered locomotive. **1917** —— in M. Gilbert *Winston Churchill* (1977) IV. Compan. I. 87 A mere bluff designed to induce him to dissipate sorely-needed forces on coastal defence. **1952** R. CAMPBELL tr. *Baudelaire's Poems* 129 Who come to waste their sorely-sweated pittance.

†**sorement**, variant of SERMENT 'oath' *Obs.*

a **1400–50** *Alexander* 1464 (MS. A.), When he..soyned him be his sorement þat sare him forthinkis.

soreness ('sɔənɪs). Forms: α. 1 sarnys, -nis, 3 særnes, 4–5 sarnes, 4 sarenes, 6, 8- *Sc.* sairness. β. 4, 6 sorenes, 6 sornes, soare-, 6–7 sorenesse, 7- soreness. [OE. *sárnys* (f. *sár* SORE *a.*[1]), = OFris. *sêrnesse*, MHG. *sêrnisse*.]

1. The condition of being physically sore, in pain, or painful; pain, painfulness.

c **1000** ÆLFRIC *Gen.* iii. 16 On sarnysse þu acenst cild. *c* **1000** —— *Hom.* I. 122 Ure sarnyssa he sylf abær. **13**.. in *Leg. Rood* (1871) 85 All for noght þou feynes þe, All þi sarenes will we se. *c* **1450** *St. Cuthbert* (Surtees) 4236 þe sarnes sone it was astaynt. *c* **1480** HENRYSON *Sum Pract. Med.* 19 Nowdir fevir,..Seiknes nor sairnes. **1495** *Trevisa's Barth. De P.R.* (W. de W.) v. lviii. 175 The marowe heelyth ..the sorenes of the throte and of the breestes. **1562** (*title*), Bulleín's Bulwarke of defence againste all Sicknes, Sornes, and woundes. **1660** BLOUNT *Boscobel* 42 Which..serv'd to encrease rather then asswage the sorenesse of his feet. **1722–7** BOYER *Dict. Royal* II. s.v., Soreness of the Eyes, *Mal des yeux*. **1808** *Med. Jrnl.* XIX. 21 He complained of soreness in his mouth. **1876** BRISTOWE *Th. & Pract. Med.* (1878) 159 The soreness and inflammation of the throat subside.

2. Mental pain, distress, or irritation; irritability, touchiness.

c **1000** ÆLFRIC *Gen.* vi. 6 He..wæs ȝehrepod mid heortan sarnisse wið innan. *a* **1300** *Cursor M.* 26377 Teres falland on þin ei þe sarnes o þin hert to wrei. **1667** *Decay Chr. Piety* vii. 153 Whilest the soreness of his late pangs of conscience remains. **1721** RAMSAY *Keitha* 8 His face speaks out the sairness of his heart. **1796** NELSON 15 July in Nicolas *Disp.* (1845) II. 211, I congratulate you on the soreness which the French feel for your strict blockade of the Port of Toulon. **1832** LYTTON *Eugene A.* I. x, I leave you with more soreness at my late haste than I will acknowledge. **1889** *Law Times* LXXXII. 243/1 The soreness incident to separation has disappeared.

†**3.** Distress, trouble, misfortune. *Obs.*

c **1205** LAY. 13639 Ich eow wulle telle..of muche særnesse þe isiȝen is to londe.

4. Severe or serious character.

a **1586** SIDNEY *Arcadia* IV. (1598) 392 For with the sorenesse of the fall, if she had not had breath giuen her, she had deliuered a foolish soule to Pluto.

Sörensen ('sɜːrənsən). *Chem.* Also Sorensen. The name of Søren P. L. *Sørensen* (1868–1939), Danish biochemist, used *attrib.* and in the possessive to denote a titration method employed in the estimation of amino-acids, consisting in treating the sample with formaldehyde, which combines with the amino groups, and then titrating the carboxylic acid groups against base.

Sørensen first described the method in 1907 (*Compt.-Rend. des Travaux du Lab. de Carlsberg* VII. 1).

1914 J. A. MANDEL tr. *Hammarsten's Text-bk. Physiol. Chem.* (ed. 7) ii. 166 On this behaviour is based Sörensen's formoltitration which serves for the estimation of amino-acids in the urine. **1916** A. P. MATHEWS *Physiol. Chem.* ix. 363 The capacity of the digestive products of combining with formaldehyde steadily increases, as is shown by the Sorensen titration. **1934** W. R. FEARON *Introd. Biochem.* vii. 100 Sörensen's method of formaldehyde titration..is applicable to many amino compounds, including ammonium salts in urine. **1973** BIGGS & WOODSON *Clin. Biochem.* iii. 40 The Sörensen formol titration technique can be used..to obtain accurate titration values.

Soret ('sɔʊreɪ). *Chem.* [The name of Jacques-Louis *Soret* (1827–90), Swiss physicist, who first detected the absorption in a study of blood (*Bibliothèque univ. et Rev. suisse*: *Arch. des Sci. phys. et nat.* (1878) LXI. 347).] ***Soret*** (also †***Soret's***) ***band***, a characteristic intense band at a wavelength of approximately 400 nanometres which occurs in the ultraviolet absorption spectra of porphyrins and their derivatives.

1899 W. D. HALLIBURTON *Essent. Chem. Physiol.* (ed. 3) 148 Oxyhæmoglobin shows a band (Soret's band) between the lines G and H. **1959** *Lancet* 2 May 912/2 The most effective wavelength would be expected to lie in the region of the Soret band, 390–410 mμ, where light absorption is maximal. **1977** *Jrnl. Amer. Chem. Soc.* XCIX. 4191/1 The wavelength of irradiation corresponded to a region of intense Soret band absorption (in tetraarylporphine dications) or to the region of near minimal..absorbance on the long wavelength side of the Soret band (in other species).

‖**sorex.** *rare.* Also *pl.* sorices. [L. *sōrex* (*sōricis*) and *sorex*, related to Gr. ὕραξ.] A shrew-mouse, a shrew. Also *transf.*

1607 TOPSELL *Four-f. Beasts* (1658) 424 Lycinius the Emperor..called them..moths and sorices of the court. **1801** SHAW *Gen. Zool.* II. I. 65 Soricine Mouse..has the general appearance of a Sorex or Shrew.

sorfait, obs. form of SURFEIT *sb.*

sorfeten, obs. form of SURFEIT *v.*

sorfol, -ful, obs. varr. SORROWFUL *a.*

sorgeon, obs. f. SURGEON.

sorgho ('sɔːgəʊ). Also 8 sorgo. [a. F. *sorgho* or It. *sorgo*, also *surgo*, med.L. *surgum, surcum, suricum* (12–13th cent.), of unknown origin.] = SORGHUM (esp. 1 b).

1760 J. LEE *Introd. Bot.* App. 327 Sorgo, *Holcus*. **1862** ANSTED *Channel Isl.* IV. xx. 476 It may be worth stating that the sugar grass, or sorgho, has been cultivated with success as an experimental crop. **1868** WATTS s.v., The glumes.. and stems of sorgho contain red colouring-matters. **1893** WATT *Dict. Econ. Prod. Ind.* VI. III. 277 The Sorgho, which is mainly cultivated on account of sugar.

attrib. **1862** MILLER *Elem. Chem.*, *Org.* (ed. 2) ii. §1. 74 Cane Sugar..is also contained in..the ripe sorgho grass.

b. ***sweet sorgho***, = SORGHUM 1 b.

1861 BENTLEY *Man. Bot.* 697 *Holcus saccharatus*..is called the North China Sugar-cane or Sweet Sorgho.

sorghum ('sɔːgəm). Also 8 sorgum. [mod.L., f. It. *sorgo*: see prec.]

1. a. The cereal plant known as Indian millet, Guinea-corn, durra, etc. (*Andropogon sorghum*, also called *Holcus sorghum* and *Sorghum vulgare*).

1597 GERARDE *Herbal* I. v. 7 At the top..groweth a tuft or eare..like Sorghum. **1673** RAY *Journ. Low C.* 147 We had little other bread than what was made of Sorghum. **1706** PHILLIPS (ed. Kersey), *Sorgum*, a sort of Millet-grain. **1780** *Encycl. Brit.* (ed. 2) V. 3694/2 The most remarkable of the foreign species [of *Holcus*] is the sorghum, or Guinea-corn. **1866** LIVINGSTONE *Last Jrnls.* i. (1874) I. 17 Some sorghum, sem-sem seed, gum-copal, and orchilla weed, constitute the commerce of the port. **1879** LUBBOCK *Addr. Pol. & Educ.* x. 193 Maize and sorghum, a fine tall cereal, which in the distance looks very like maize. **1883** R. HALDANE *Workshop Rec.* Ser. II. 11/1 Rice, maize, wheat, sorghum, and rye are most largely used [for obtaining grain alcohol].

b. The Chinese sugar-cane (*Andropogon saccharatus*, also called *Holcus saccharatus* and *Sorghum saccharatum*). Usually ***sweet sorghum***.

1859 *All Year Round* No. 32. 126 The extensive cultivation of the sorghum, or Chinese sugar-cane, would give a fortune to the cultivator. **1867** A. GRAY *Man. Bot.* (1874) 652 The Sweet Sorghum, and other cultivated races. **1884** tr. *De Candolle's Orig. Cultivated Pl.* 382 Sweet Sorghum..taller than the common sorghum and with a loose panicle.

c. With distinctive names denoting other plants belonging to this genus (see quots.).

1860 *Darlington's Amer. Weeds*, etc. 411 *Sorghum nutans*, ..Nodding Sorghum. Wood Grass. *Ibid.* 412 *S. cernuum*,.. Drooping Sorghum. Guinea Corn.

2. A genus or group of grasses belonging to the tribe *Andropogoneæ* and including the species mentioned above; also, with *a* and pl., a species or variety belonging to this genus.

1842 *Penny Cycl.* XXII. 266 *Sorghum*, a genus of grasses. .. The species form tall grasses with succulent stems. **1884** tr. *De Candolle's Orig. Cultivated Pl.* 380 Botanists are not agreed as to the distinction of several of the species of sorghum. *Ibid.*, A good monograph on the sorghums is needed. **1895–6** *Cal. Univ. Nebraska* 186 New crops, particularly forage crops, and the non-saccharine sorghums.

3. *U.S.* A kind of molasses made from sorghum-juice.

1883 *Chamb. Jrnl.* Apr. 269/1 Maple-sugar and sorghum are unequal to the demand. **1892** *Atlantic Monthly* May 664/2 Jars of lard and jugs of the inevitable 'sorghum' (home-made molasses) were securely tied up and buried in the woods.

4. *attrib.* and *Comb.*, as ***sorghum-crop, -head, -seed, sugar***, etc.

Also ***sorghum-pulling, -tugging*** (De Vere *Americanisms* 287), ***sorghum-evaporator, -knife, -mill, -stripper*** (Knight *Dict. Mech.* 2246), ***sorghum-blight, -midge, -smut***, etc.

1753 *Chambers' Cycl.* Suppl. s.v. *Juncus*, The sharp or pointed Rush, with sorghum heads. **1875** KNIGHT *Dict. Mech.* 443/2 The necessities of the sorghum culture in the United States. **1883** *Times* 30 May 13 A sorghum crop.. which yielded over 2,200 gallons. **1883** *Science* I. 234/1 Others bearing, in all but size, a most striking resemblance to sorghum-seed. **1887** *Encycl. Brit.* XXII. 628/1 The cultivation of sorghum sugar.

b. In the sense 'made of or obtained from sorghum', as ***sorghum beer, flour, molasses, syrup***.

1864 T. D. WELLS *Our Burden* 38 Sorghum molasses, which was not known to this country in 1850. **1865** *Home News* 19 Dec. 5/1 A sample of sorghum flour made of Chinese cane. **1868** *Rep. U.S. Commissioner Agric.* (1869) 401 Strong vinegar can be made from sorghum sirup.

sorgien, -gon, obs. ff. SURGEON.

sorh(ful, obs. varr. SORROW(FUL.

sori, pl. of SORUS.

soricine ('sɒrɪsɪn), *a.* [ad. L. *sōricīn-us*, f. *sōrex* SOREX.] Resembling a shrew-mouse. Freq. in specific names of animals.

1781 PENNANT *Hist. Quadrup.* II. 453 The Soricine Rat.. inhabits the neighborhood of Strasbourg. **1801** SHAW *Gen. Zool.* II. I. 65 Soricine Mouse. *Mus Soricinus*... This is an extremely small species. **1827** GRIFFITH tr. *Cuvier* V. 72 *Vampyrus Soricinus* (Soricine Vampyre of Spix). *c* **1878** *Cassell's Nat. Hist.* I. 333 The Soricine Bat,.. *Glossophaga soricina*... [It] is a small bat.

sorie, obs. form of SORRY.

so'riferous, *a. Bot. rare.* [f. SOR-US + -(I)FEROUS.] Bearing sori.

1859 T. MOORE *Brit. Ferns* (1864) 20 Ferns, the margin of whose frond is soriferous.

†**soring**, *a. Obs.* In 5 sowring. [irreg. f. *sowre* SORE *a.*[2]] = SORE *a.*[2]

c **1450** *Godstow Reg.* 256 Yeldyng therof euery yere to hym .. a spere-hawke sowryng [L. *unum speruarium sorum*] at lammas. *Ibid.* 257 And to the heires of ser Alisaundir of Swereford.. a sowring sperehawke at lammasse.

†**sorite**, Anglicized f. next. *Obs.*[−1]

1656 HOBBES *Liberty, Necess. & Chance* xxiv. 259 To pass by all the other great imperfections, which are to be found in this Sorite [etc.].

‖**sorites** (sə'raɪtiːz). [L. *sōrītēs*, ad. Gr. σωρείτης, f. σωρ-ός a heap.]

1. *Logic.* 'A series of propositions, in which the predicate of each is the subject of the next, the conclusion being formed of the first subject and the last predicate' (Mansel).

In the GOCLENIAN form, 'the subject of each proposition is the predicate of the next, the conclusion being formed of the last subject and the first predicate'.

1551 T. WILSON *Logike* H iij, We ioyne many causes, and many effectes together, wherof is made an argument, called *Sorites*. **1588** FRAUNCE *Lawiers Log.* II. ix. 99 As of many graynes is made a heape of corne, so of many degrees an argument called Sorites by this enthymematicall progression. **1654** Z. COKE *Logick* 148 Sorites is an imperfect Syllogism [etc.]. **1693** DRYDEN *Persius* VI. (1697) 296 *note*, Chrysippus the Stoick invented a kind of Argument, consisting of more than three Propositions; which is call'd *Sorites*, or a Heap. **1838** SIR W. HAMILTON *Logic* xix. (1866) I. 369 The Sorites can be resolved into as many simple syllogisms as there are middle terms between the subject and predicate of the conclusion. **1870** JEVONS *Elem. Logic* xviii. 156 The chain of syllogisms commonly called the Sorites.

b. An instance of this type of syllogism. Also as *pl.* (quot. 1798).

1581 J. BELL *Haddon's Answ. Osor.* 223 b, The Logicians that have described the fourme of a Sorites. **1588** FRAUNCE *Lawiers Log.* II. ix. 99 A sorites [is] but enthymematicall progression by certain degrees. **1620** T. GRANGER *Div. Logike* 285 A Syllogisme many wayes cryptike, is a Dilemma, and a Sorites. **1643** SIR T. BROWNE *Relig. Med.* I. §18 An easie Logick may.. with lesse than a Sorites resolve all things into God. **1725** WATTS *Logic* III. ii. §6 A Sorites is when several middle terms are chosen to connect one another successively [etc.]. **1798** EDGEWORTH *Pract. Educ.* (1811) II. 361 We have seen syllogisms, crocodiles, enthimemas, sorites, &c. explained and tried upon a boy of nine. **1860** H. ROGERS *Ess.* III. 277 An ingenious sorites, by which we may at any time dispense with the positive testimony of an historian. **1870** K. H. DIGBY *Halcyon Hours* 261 No horn'd sorites here would I employ, No captious argument that would annoy.

c. In allusive use.

1711 ADDISON *Spect.* No. 239 ¶10 These Disputants convince their Adversaries with a *Sorites*, commonly called a Pile of Faggots.

2. *transf.* A series, chain, or accumulation *of* some thing or things.

1664 POWER *Exp. Philos.* III. 191 Though Democritus his pit be never so deep, yet by a long Sorites of Observations, and chain of Deductions, we may at last fathom it. *a* **1670** HACKET *Abp. Williams* I. xiii. (1693) 11 Such a long Sorites of Sciences and Tongues. **1875** M. COLLINS in F. Collins *Lett. & Friendsh.* (1877) II. 24 Note this significant fact or sorites of facts.

b. *Math.* (See quots.)

1880 J. J. SYLVESTER in *Coll. Math. Papers* (1909) III. 440 Any such determinate representation of a fractional quantity I shall term a sorites. *Ibid.*, The elements of a sorites are analogous to the partial quotients of a regular continued fraction.

3. A sophistical argument turning on the definition of a 'heap'.

1768–74 TUCKER *Lt. Nat.* (1834) II. 140 The like attack as was made of old by the Academics and Sceptics against the judgment of the senses, with their sophism of the *sorites*, or argument of the 'heap'.

4. A heap, pile.

1871 M. COLLINS *Marq. & Merch.* III. ix. 230 Such sorites of flaming anthracite may possibly cause cephalalgia.

Hence **so'ritic** *a.* [cf. Gr. σωρειτικός], **so'ritical**.

1656 BLOUNT *Glossogr.*, *Soritical*, pertaining to such an Argument [*sc.* Sorites]. *a* **1693** *Urquhart's Rabelais* III. xxxviii. 320 Soritick fool. **1877** BLACKMORE *Cripps* II. v. 73 Nebules of logic, dialectic fogs, and.. the pelting of soritic hail.

†**sorlaque**, obs. variant of *solaque*, SOLAK.

1696 tr. *Du Mont's Voy. Levant* xiv. 175 After 'em came the Sorlaques, or Foot-Guards of the Body.

sorn (sɔːn), *v. Sc.* Also 6 soirn. [f. SORREN.]

†**1.** *trans.* To trouble or harass by exacting free quarters and maintenance; to live upon. *Obs.*

1563 *Reg. Privy Council Scot.* I. 248 The Clangregour.. birnis and slayis the pouer liegis of this realme,.. takis thair gudis, sornis and oppressis thame. **1563–4** *Ibid.* 271 That.. nane of thame sould sorne or oppres our Soverane Ladiis liegis dwelland within the boundis of Stratherne. **1588–9** *Ibid.* IV. 342 Eftir thay had soirned, wracked, and spoilled the saidis haill Illis, thay.. rased fyre.

2. *intr.* To take up free quarters or exact maintenance unjustifiably; to sponge *upon* others for food or lodging.

c **1575** *Balfour's Practicks* (1754) 24 That na persounis heirefter ludge nor sorne in housis or granges pertening to religious or ecclesiasticall men. **1638** H. ADAMSON *Muses Threnodie* (1774) I. 96 The Baliol proud, With English forces.., arrived at Kinghorne, And through the country mightily did sorne. **1725** RAMSAY *Gentle Sheph.* III. iv, He gangs about sornan frae place to place. **1799** J. ROBERTSON *Agric. Perth* 385 Why send the person.. to corrupt, to pilfer and sorn upon your neighbours? **1816** SCOTT *Old Mort.* vi, You pretend to gie entertainments, that canna come by a dinner except by sorning on a carefu' man like me? **1876** EADIE *Thessalonians* 314 The idlers.. had no right to 'sorn' on their friends or burden the funds of the church.

sorname, obs. form of SURNAME.

sorne, obs. f. *sworn*, pa. pple. of SWEAR *v.*

sornee. *nonce-wd.* [f. SORN *v.*] One who is sorned upon; a victim of sorning.

1797 SCOTT *Lett.* (1894) I. 10 As from being a sorner I am becoming a sornee [etc.].

sorner ('sɔːnə(r)). *Sc.* Also 5 sornour, 6 (9) sornar, 7 soroner. [f. SORN *v.*] One who sorns; one who quarters himself upon others; a sponger.

1449 *Sc. Acts, Jas. II* (1814) II. 36/1 The away putting of sorneris, ourlyaris, & masterful beggaris. **1455** *Ibid.* 43/1 Item quhar euer sornoures be ourtane in tyme to cum, þat þai be delieueryt to þe kingis schereffis. **1506** *Exch. Rolls Scotl.* XII. 704 The names of all thevis, pikaris, and sornars that oppress the cuntre. **1575** *Reg. Privy Council Scot.* II. 450 Certane sornaris, vagaboundis and utheris oppressouris of the cuntre. **1609** in Burt *Lett. N. Scotl.* (1818) II. 243 Eating up by sorners (*sturdy beggers*) and idle bellies. **1699** *Records of Elgin* (1903) I. 361 The counsell ordains notorious soroners, wagabonds and strangers to be instantly banished the burgh. **1797** [see SORNEE]. **1821** SCOTT *Pirate* v, This is the house of his Lordship's factor, and no place of reset for thiggers or sorners. **1881** MASSON *De Quincey* ix. 104 The prince of almoners for sorners and beggars.

'sorning, *vbl. sb. Sc.* [f. SORN *v.*] The action or practice of exacting free quarters and maintenance, or of living at the expense of others.

1506 *Exch. Rolls Scotl.* XII. 704 That ye hald courtis.. for stanching of slauchtir, sornyng and oppression. **1563–4** *Reg. Privy Council Scot.* I. 271 Colin Campbell.. sall ansuer him self for the samyn crymes, sornyngis, oppressionis, and offencis. **1669** in *Macfarlane's Geneal. Coll.* (S.H.S.) I. 63 The Outragious Sornings of Glengairrie's Followers. **1678** SIR G. MACKENZIE *Crim. Laws Scot.* I. xxxiv. §iii. (1699) 161 An habitual, and constant trade of Robbing, and sorning, is libelled. **1753** *Scots Mag.* Sept. 468/2 John Gun, for theft and sorning, was sentenced to be hanged. **1754** ERSKINE *Princ. Sc. Law* (1809) 514 Under which class may be included sorning, or the taking of meat and drink by force, without paying for it. **1829** SCOTT *Antiq.* Advert., All laws against sorning, masterful beggary, and every other species of mendicity, being suspended in favour of this privileged class. **1900** R. J. DRUMMOND *Relat. Apost. Teaching* i. 15 Faith was made a plea for indolence and sorning.

So **'sorning** *ppl. a.*

1824 SCOTT *St. Ronan's* viii, A poaching, sorning sort of fallow. **1893** AGNEW *Hered. Sheriffs Galloway* II. xxxi. 65 This sorning band, who had lived for days at free quarters.

soro, obs. form of SORROW.

‖**soroban** ('soroban). [Jap., f. Chinese *suàn-pán* SWAN-PAN.] A kind of abacus used in Japan, adapted from the swan-pan.

1891 A. M. BAKER *Japanese Girls & Women* x. 266 Crowds of clerks sitting upon the matted floors, each with his *soroban*, or adding machine, by his side. **1903** W. DEL MAR *Around World through Japan* xiii. 133 The addition of seven and six presented difficulties unless he had an abacus (*soroban*). **1958** HOSOI SŌ in *Japan* xxii. 612/1 In the beginning of the Edo Era, the *soroban* (abacus) was used by Japanese merchants and engineers for their calculations. The *soroban* was introduced from China. **1965** *Australian* 23 Nov. 12 The appearance of a low-cost, small-type, locally-made electronic computer.. has driven a wedge under the four-century reign of the soroban.

‖**soroche** (so'rotʃe). [Sp., ad. Quechuan *surúči*, name of some mineral to which mountain sickness was attributed, and hence 'mountain sickness'.] A name in the Andes for mountain sickness.

1878 I. L. BIRD *Lady's Life in Rocky Mountains* (1879) iv. 48, I feel a singular lassitude... This is said to be the milder form of the affection known on higher altitudes as *soroche*, or 'mountain sickness'. **1891** E. B. CLARK *Twelve Months in Peru* 104 A headache with a weighty feeling on the brow, vomiting, and breathlessness are the usual symptoms of *sorroche*. **1922** *Glasgow Herald* 4 Jan. 4 In order to minimise the effects of soroche, or mountain sickness, on persons suffering from weak heart the company provides cars with compartments equipped with oxygen. **1963** *Times* 7 June 13/6 Faced with another presidential election this Sunday, the Peruvian people have apparently succumbed to some political equivalent of the *soroche*, the mountain sickness that shortens the breath, softens the will, and enfeebles the body. **1970** *Sci. Amer.* Feb. 56/1 Even mountain natives sometimes lose their acclimatization to high altitude and incur *soroche* (chronic mountain sickness), which is characterized by extreme elevation of the relative number and mass of red cells in the blood.. and ultimately congestive heart failure if the victim remains at high altitude. **1981** L. LEAMER *Assignment* ix. 129 It's great to breathe some real air again... No more *soroche*.

Soroptimist (sə'rɒptɪmɪst), *a.* and *sb.* [f. L. *soror* sister + OPTIMIST *sb.* (*a.*) (prob. after the *Optimist* Club, founded in 1911).] **A.** *adj.* Chiefly in ***Soroptimist Club***, an international service club for professional and business women, founded in California in 1921. Also ***Soroptimist International***. **B.** *sb.* A member of a Soroptimist club.

1921 *Charter* (Soroptimist Club, Oakland, California), Whereas, the persons who [*sic*] names appear at the foot hereof.. having enrolled themselves as Charter Members of the Soroptimist Club (Oakland), [etc.]. **1924** *Glasgow Herald* 8 Mar. 6 The woman publisher who represents her profession in the Soroptimist Club (i.e., women Rotarians). **1924** *British Weekly* 14 Aug. 431/4, I know now what a Soroptimist is. **1930** M. BRADBURY *Cook Bk.* 2 The Soroptimist Club Code of Ethics... As a Soroptimist I pledge my untiring efforts to understand life, my true and right relation to sister Soroptimists and humanity at large, [etc.]. **1955** L. P. HARTLEY *Perfect Woman* iv. 39 Would it be easy, with possibly some Tablers and Soroptimists listening in? **1977** *Times* 6 Apr. 18/7 Among her many activities, Marina devoted a great deal of time to the Soroptimist International organisation. She was president of the National Union of Soroptimist Clubs (Italy) from 1969–1971, when their international golden jubilee was celebrated in Rome.

sororal (sə'rɔərəl), *a.* [f. L. *soror* sister + -AL[1]. Cf. F. *sororal*.]

1. By one's sister; on a sister's side. *rare*[−1].

1654 VILVAIN *Theorem. Theol.* viii. 212 Master John Down a.. sororal Nephew to Bishop Juel.

2. That is a sister. *rare.*

1819 LAMB *Lett.* (1837) II. 55 How do you all do, amanuenses both—marital and sororal?

3. a. Of or pertaining to, characteristic of, a sister or sisters; sisterly.

1858 *Chambers's Jrnl.* IX. 239 Independent of either mother or sister—bound by no authority to either, except.. filial and sororal affection. **1869** MISS MULOCK *Woman's Kingd.* III. 146 To see into what the sororal bond can degenerate, under given circumstances. **1838** SIR W. R. HAMILTON in R. P. Graves *Life* (1885) II. 270 And Ladies, ..With love maternal, or sororal, view Thy gentleness.

b. ***sororal polygyny*** (*Anthrop.*), in some polygamous kinship systems, the custom whereby the first wife's sister(s) are preferred as secondary wives.

1952 A. R. RADCLIFFE-BROWN *Struct. & Funct. in Primitive Soc.* iii. 67 Sororal polygyny (marriage with two or more sisters). **1971** P. B. HAMMOND *Introd. Cultural & Soc. Anthrop.* vi. 159/2 Sometimes the desirability of a man's marrying his wife's sister is stressed, a usage referred to as sororal polygyny. **1977** C. R. & M. EMBER *Cultural Anthrop.* (ed. 2) viii. 154/2 Jealousy.. seems to be lessened if one man is married to two or more sisters (sororal polygyny). *Ibid.*, The Crow Indians practice sororal polygyny, and co-wives usually share the same tepee.

sororate (sɒ'rɔərət). *Anthrop.* [f. L. *soror* sister + -ATE[1], after LEVIRATE.] In some kinship systems a custom whereby, on the death of his wife, a man is expected to marry her (unmarried) sister; also occas. = *sororal polygyny* s.v. SORORAL *a.* 3 b; also *attrib.* Hence **soro'ratic** *a.*, characterized by such a custom.

1910 J. G. FRAZER *Totemism & Exogamy* IV. 140 The other [custom] is the rule which allows or requires a man to marry the younger sisters either of his living or of his deceased wife... The latter custom.. has no distinctive name, but on analogy I propose to call it the *sororate*. **1921** E. WESTERMARCK *Hist. Human Marriage* (ed. 5) xxxi. 263 The sororate, like the levirate, can be.. interpreted as the outcome of existing conditions. **1947** CHAPPLE & COON *Princ. Anthrop.* xiii. 311 The sororate occurs when a man marries two or more sisters. **1952** M. N. SRINIVAS *Relig. & Society among Coorgs* v. 148 As sororatic unions are preferred among the Coorgs, a mother's younger sister steps into the mother's shoes in the event of the mother's death. **1963** W. N. STEPHENS *Family in Cross-Cultural Perspective* i. 27 In many primitive societies broken homes are automatically 'mended' by means of the sororate and levirate. **1970** *Internat. & Compar. Law Q.* XIX. I. 139 The levirate and sororate institutions could perpetuate the inter-kin tie.

sororial (sə'rɔərɪəl), *a.* [f. L. *sorōri-us* sisterly + -AL[1]. Cf. F. *sororial*.] = SORORAL 3 a.

1836 T. HOOK *G. Gurney* (1850) III. iii. 352 'Her brother' ..permitted his approbation of her sororial affection to produce a sort of fraternal acknowledgment. **1877** *World* VII. 7 The gauntlet of sororial criticism which he finds himself compelled to run.

Hence **so'rorially** *adv.*, in a sisterly manner.

1825 T. HOOK *Sayings* Ser. II. I. 23 Taking her *sororially* by the hand, she led her forth from the oak parlour.

†**so'roriant**, *a. Obs.*[−0] [f. L. *sorōriant-*, *sorōrians*, app. f. *soror* sister.] (See quot.)

1656 BLOUNT *Glossogr.*, *Sororiant Virgin*, a yong maid, whose Brests began to be embossed and round, or set out for shew.

So **sorori'ation**. *rare.* (See quots.)

1658 PHILLIPS, *Sororiation*, a swelling, or becoming round, and embossed like a young Virgin's breasts. **1859** MAYNE *Expos. Lex.* 1175/1 *Sororiatio*,.. the equally progressing development of the *mammæ* in the young female: sororiation.

sororicide[1] (sə'rɒrɪsaɪd). [ad. L. *sorōricīda*, f. *soror* sister + *-cīdĕre*: see -CIDE 1. Cf. F. *sororicide*.] One who kills his (or her) sister.

1656 BLOUNT *Glossogr.*, *Sororicide*, a murderer of his own sister. **1721** in BAILEY; and in later Dicts. **1881** *Philadel. Record* No. 3411. 2 Intending sororicides will do well to get this formula fastened in their memories. **1892** BESANT *Ivory Gate* (1893) 195 If the envious man.. denounces a man of reputation as.. a patricide, a sororicide, amicocide.

sororicide[2] (sə'rɒrɪsaɪd). [ad. late L. *sorōricīdium*, f. *soror* + *-cīdĕre*: see -CIDE 2. Cf. F. *sororicide*.] The action of killing one's sister.

1727 BAILEY (vol. II), *Sororicide*, the Killing of a Sister. **1875** J. HUNTER *Man. Bee-keeping* (1876) 115 The Workers prevent this sororicide by setting a guard over the unhatched Queens. **1889** *East. Morn. News* 10 Apr. 3/2 Supposed shocking sororicide.

Hence **sorori'cidal** *a.*

1878 FR. A. KEMBLE *Rec. Girlhood* I. iii. 70 A quite unpremeditated inspiration..—to run away—probably alarmed my parents more than my sororicidal projects.

sorority (sə'rɒrɪtɪ). [ad. med.L. *sororitas*, or f. L. *soror* sister + -ITY, after *fraternity*. Cf. obs. F. *sororité* (Cotgr. 1611).]

1. A body or company of women united for some common object, esp. for devotional purposes; †*U.S.*, the female section of a church congregation.

1532 MORE *Confut. Barnes* VIII. Wks. 761/1 This would he say for the comfort of yͤ whole fraternitie and sororiti in general. **1645** PAGITT *Heresiogr.* (1647) 86 The Synod of New England maketh not only the fraternity but (as they speak) the sorority to be the subject of the.. power of the keyes. **1657** J. WATTS *Dipper Sprinkled* 101 [The care] of the fraternity and sorority within their limits.

2. *U.S.* A women's society in a college or university. Also *attrib.*

1900 *Harper's Mag.* Sept. 490 One saw many of those neat little sorority pins the American girl proudly brings home from boarding-school or college. **1908** G. E. CODY (*title*), Jacquette: a Sorority Girl. **1909** C. W. ELIOT *Univ. Administr.* 223 Sororities have, in general, the same merits and advantages as fraternities. **1911** *Daily Colonist* (Victoria, B.C.) 1 Apr. 2/5 All of the girls lived at a sorority house, 4522 Eighteenth avenue, Northeast. **1948** A. N. KEITH *Three come Home* xiii. 229, I had my sorority pin, which had been specially set in my college days with a diamond. **1977** [see RAT *sb.*[1] 2 e].

'sororize, *v.* Somewhat *rare*. [f. L. *soror* sister + -IZE, after *fraternize*.] *intr.* To associate *with* a person or persons as a sister or sisters; to form a sisterly friendship.

1875 *Temple Bar* Mar. 533 If there be a baby attached to either party, a general sororising is as inevitable as death. *a* **1876** M. COLLINS *Th. in Garden* (1880) II. i. 3 The beautiful girls.. sororising with the rustic maidenhood of their parishes.

†**'sorory**. *Obs.*⁻¹ [f. L. *soror* sister + -Y.] A sisterhood; a sorority.

1600 TOURNEUR *Transf. Metam.* lxviii, The ninefold Sorory themselves exiled, Euen from their natiue home to art's annoy.

sorose, *a. Bot.* = SORIFEROUS *a.*

1891 in *Cent. Dict.*

sorosilicate (sɒrəʊ'sɪlɪkət). *Min.* [a. F. *sorosilicate* (V. Billiet 1945, in *Bull. de la Soc. belge de Géol.* LIII. 182), f. Gr. σωρός heap: see SILICATE.] Any of the group of silicates characterized by isolated pairs of SiO^4 tetrahedra that share an oxygen atom at a common apex.

1947 [see PHYLLOSILICATE]. **1960** *Amer. Mineralogist* XLV. 1 Perrierite is a sorosilicate, with a high number of O-atoms not bonded to silicon. **1972** R. W. FAIRBRIDGE *Encycl. Geochem. & Environmental Sci.* 101/1 In the sorosilicates (two isolated tetrahedra which share one oxygen atom) calcium is present mainly in the epidote group.

‖**sorosis** (sə'rəʊsɪs). [mod.L., f. Gr. σωρός a heap.]

1. *Bot.* (See quot. 1831.)

1831 LINDLEY *Introd. Bot.* I. ii. 180 *Sorosis*,.. a spike or raceme converted into a fleshy fruit by the cohesion in a single mass of the ovaria and floral envelopes. **1845** *Encycl. Metrop.* VI. 122*/1 The fruit [*sc.* mulberry], called a sorosis by botanists, has a peculiar aromatic flavour. **1849** BALFOUR *Man. Bot.* §557 Other instances of a sorosis are the Bread-fruit and Jack-fruit.

2. *U.S.* A women's society or club.

An arbitrary use of the botanical term, adopted as the name of the first club of the kind, founded in 1868.

1869 GEO. ELIOT *Jrnl.* 16 Feb. in *Lett.* (1956) V. 14 The Ladies of the 'Sorosis' at New York.. proposed to make me an honorary member of their society—I declined. **1879** in WEBSTER *Suppl.* **1902** *Out West* May 557 The founding of the first woman's club, Sorosis of New York, was almost simultaneous with the union of the Atlantic and Pacific by the completion of the first transcontinental railway in 1869. **1942** C. MORLEY *Thorofare* xxiii. 98 I've promised to read a paper on my trip abroad to our literary sorosis.

so'rotrochous, *a. Zool.* [f. Gr. σωρός heap: cf. MONOTROCHOUS *a.*] Of rotifers: (see quot.).

a **1843** *Encycl. Metrop.* (1845) VII. 266/1 The Wheel Organs are either *Monotrochous*,.. or the ring is divided or manifold, as in the *Sorotrochous* Infusories. *Ibid.*, Two subdivisions of the Sorotrochous are also observed.

†**sorous**, *a. Obs. rare.* Also 4 sorus. [f. SORE *a.*[1] + -OUS.] **a.** Sorrowful, sad. **b.** Grievous, distressing.

a **1300** *Cursor M.* 16762 + 105 Al creatures for his ded made doil & pite, And þou þat he deed fore cannot sorus be. **1502** ARNOLDE *Chron.* (1811) 129 The most greuous sorous losses, imprisonment, and troubles.

‖**sorpego**, obs. variant of SERPIGO.

1631 T. POWELL *Tom of All Trades* 49 Some of your Clarkly men complaine the moysture of their palmes. Others the Sorpego in their wrists.

sorplers, obs. variant of SURPLICE *sb.*

†**sorporr**, *v. Obs.*⁻⁰ [f. *sor-* SUR- + PORR *v.* 3.] *trans.* To surfeit. Hence **sorporring** *vbl. sb.*

c **1440** *Promp. Parv.* 8/2 Agrotonyd, or sorporryd wyth mete or drynke, *ingurgitatus*. *Ibid.*, Agrotonynge, or sorporrynge, *ingurgitacio*.

sorption ('sɔːpʃən). *Physical Chem.* [Extracted from *absorption* and *adsorption*.] The combined or undifferentiated action of absorption and adsorption. Freq. *attrib.*

1909 J. W. MCBAIN in *Phil. Mag.* XVIII. 916 The non-committal name 'sorption' may be coined to designate the sum of the phenomena, while 'absorption' and 'adsorption' should be restricted to proven cases of the solution or surface condensation respectively. **1932** *Trans. Faraday Soc.* XXVIII. 182 The rate of sorption at constant temperature was very nearly directly proportional to the pressure. **1945** *Electronic Engin.* XVII. 325/1 M. Francis —dealing mainly with the sorption effects of the walls— gives a detailed account of the use of the McLeod gauge with non-permanent gases. **1954** *Thorpe's Dict. Appl. Chem.* (ed. 4) XI. 33/1 In its practical aspects, the term 'sorption' is usually applied to the concentration at solid surfaces of gases and vapours, and of dissolved substances and colloids, and is therefore largely synonymous with adsorption. **1969** *McGraw-Hill Yearbk. Sci. & Technol.* 342/1 Sorption pumping, a process for producing a vacuum in a closed system by the capture and holding of gases by certain solids or liquids, has recently been developed into a practical technique. **1971** [see ROUGH *v.*[1] 7 d]. **1973** *Nature* 12 Jan. 92/1 New work on the sorption of boron compounds may provide a way of isolating the element from seawater. **1978** *Ibid.* 16 Mar. 230/1 It is important in the field of forest products science to know the sorption mechanism of water in wood.

Hence **'sorptive** *a.*, of, pertaining to, or exhibiting sorption.

1921 *Jrnl. Chem. Soc.* CXIX. 928 After each heating, the density was determined and then the sorptive capacity at each of the three temperatures. **1938** *Proc. R. Soc.* A. CLXVII. 392 The paper describes an attempt to relate the sorptive properties [of zeolites] towards permanent gases.. and towards ammonia.. to the structure and properties revealed by the X-ray method.

sorr: see SOR.

sorra, dial. or colloq. f. SORROW *sb.*

sorrance, variant of SORANCE.

†**sorré**. *Cookery. Obs.* Also sore, sorry, surre. [app. a. OF. *soré*, pa. pple. of *sorer* to redden, f. *sore* SORE *a.*[2]] A dish made with chopped eels (or other fish, etc.) spiced and coloured. ***white sorré*** = *blanch-de-sore* (see BLAUNDSORE).

c **1430** *Two Cookery-bks.* 25 Sore Sengle.—Take Elys or Gurnard,.. take Safroun, & caste þer-to,.. take poudere Gyngere, Canelle [etc.]. *c* **1440** *Anc. Cookery* in *Househ. Ord.* (1790) 446 Eles in Sorry. Take eles and cut hom on culpons,.. colour hit withe saunders. *Ibid.* 467 Eles in Surre. *a* **1450** *Tourn. Tottenham* The Feest vii. (Hazlitt *E.P.P.* III. 95), Blobsterdis in white sorre, Was of a nobull curry.

sorrel ('sɒrəl), *sb.*[1] *Bot.* Forms: 4, 6–7 sorell, 5–6 sorel, 6–7 sorrell (6 sowrell), 6– sorrel. [a. OF. *surele* (12th cent.), *sorele*, *surelle* (mod.F. *surelle*), f. OF. *sur* adj., an adoption of the Germanic *sūr* SOUR *a.*]

1. a. One or other of certain small perennial plants belonging to the genus *Rumex*, characterized by a sour taste, and to some extent cultivated for culinary purposes; esp. the common wild species, *R. acetosa*.

Earlier botanical names are *Acedula* (also *Acidula*), *Acetosa*, and *Oxalis*.

c **1440** *Promp. Parv.* 465/1 Sorel, herbe, *surella*. **1530** PALSGR. 272/2 Sorell an herbe, *oseille*. **1548** TURNER *Names Herbes* (E.D.S.) 69 Oxalis, in barbarus latin Acetosa or Acidula, in englishe Sorel or sourdocke. **1578** LYTE *Dodoens* 558 Sorrel is commonly sowen in gardens, and is to be found also growing wylde. **1600** SURFLET *Countrie Farme* II. xv. 222 Sorrell & burnet.. may be sowen in fine ground, and well manured, in the spring time, especially the sorrell. **1653** H. COGAN *Pinto's Trav.* xlvi. 180 Going into the woods we sustained ourselves with a certain herb like unto Sorrell. **1732** ARBUTHNOT *Rules of Diet* in *Aliments*, etc. I. 259 Several Plants known by their Taste, as Sorrel. **1763** MILLS *Pract. Husb.* IV. 131 The seeds of the annual sorts of sorrel should be sown about the latter end of March. **1816** KEATS '*I stood tip-toe*' 98 Her nimble toes Patting against the sorrel as she goes. **1868** *Rep. U.S. Commissioner Agric.* (1869) 394 'Acid' soils,.. indicated by the growth of sorrel.. and other sour plants. **1889** A. R. WALLACE *Darwinism* (1890) 29 The sorrel.. covers hundreds of acres with a sheet of red.

b. With distinguishing epithets, denoting various species of the genus *Rumex*.

For *sheep's*, *tree*, *Welsh sorrel* see these words.

1611 COTGR., *Ozeille petite*,.. *barren Sorrell. **1731** MILLER *Gard. Dict.* s.v. *Acetosa*, The Northern barren Sorrel. **1797** *Encycl. Brit.* (ed. 3) XVII. 610/1 By means of the common *broad-leaved sorrel an excellent black colour is.. given to woollen stuffs. **1855** DELAMER *Kitchen Garden* (1861) 93 The best.. is the Broad-leaved sorrel, of which a marked sub-variety, the Golden Sorrel, is almost exclusively cultivated in the environs of Dunkirk. *c* **1710** PETIVER *Cat. Ray's Eng. Herbal* Tab. iii, *Common Sorrel. **1763** MILLS *Pract. Husb.* IV. 130 The common sorrel, which grows naturally in pasture lands in most parts of England. **1785** MARTYN *Rousseau's Bot.* xviii. (1794) 253 Common.. Sorrel,.. growing in meadows and pastures. **1597** GERARDE *Herbal* II. lxxx. 320 *Oxalis Crispa*, *Curled Sorrell. **1858** A. IRVINE *Handbk. Brit. Plants* 379 *Rumex*,.. *Dock Sorrel. **1886** [see DOCK *sb.*[1] 4]. **1846–50** A. WOOD *Class-bk. Bot.* 477 *Rumex acetosella*. *Field Sorrel. **1681** in *Thanes of Cawdor* (Spald. Club) 352 *French sorrell. **1731** MILLER *Gard. Dict.* s.v. *Acetosa*, The Round-leav'd or French Sorrel. **1819** *Pantologia* s.v. *Rumex*, *R. sentatus*, French sorrel. **1829** [see FRENCH *a.* 5]. **1601** CHESTER *Love's Mart.* lviii, Sage, Scorpiades, and the *garden sorrell. **1855** *Golden sorrel [see *broad-leaved sorrel* above]. **1578** LYTE *Dodoens* v. ix. 559 The fifth kind, which groweth in ditches, is called.. in Englishe, *Great Sorrel, Water Sorrel, and *Horse Sorrel. **1597** GERARDE *Herbal* II. lxxx. 319 *Oxalis tuberosa*, *Knobbed Sorrell. **1731** MILLER *Gard. Dict.* s.v. *Acetosa*, The Common or *Meadow Sorrel. **1753** *Chambers' Cycl.* Suppl. s.v., The great *mountain-sorrel. **1611** COTGR., *Petite salette*, *Pettie Sorrell, sallet Sorrell. **1578** LYTE *Dodoens* v. ix. 558 *Oxalis Romana*, Tours Sorrel or *Romayne Sorrel. **1764** MILLS *Pract. Husb.* IV. 130 The round-leafed garden, or Roman sorrel. **1796** [see ROMAN *a.* 14 b]. **1597** GERARDE *Herbal* II. lxxx. 320 *Oxalis Franca seu Romana*, *Round Sorrell. **1712** tr. *Pomet's Hist. Drugs* I. 25 Others will have the Leaf like round Sorrel. **1731** MILLER *Gard. Dict.* s.v. *Acetosa*, The *Round-leav'd (or French) Sorrel. **1753** *Chambers' Cycl.* Suppl. s.v., The round-leaved garden-sorrel. **1855** DELAMER *Kitchen Garden* (1861) 93 The Round-leaved sorrel.. is not the kind to cultivate, except for variety. **1611** *Salad sorrel [see *petty sorrel* above]. **1597** GERARDE *Herbal* II. lxxx. 321 *Oxalis minor*, *Small Sorrell. **1611** COTGR., *Ozeille sauvage*,.. *sowre Sorrell, the sowre Docke. **1578** *Tours sorrel, *Water sorrel [see *Roman sorrel* and *Great sorrel* above]. **1565** COOPER *Thesaurus*, *Cantherinum lapathum*, *wilde sorell. **1580** HOLLYBAND *Treas. Fr. Tong*, *Ozeille sauvage*, wild sorrell.

2. The leaves of species of *Rumex* (see sense 1) used in cookery or medicine, or as a salad; a decoction or drink made from one or other of these plants.

a **1400** in *Rel. Ant.* I. 51 Drynk sorell, plantayne, and chekyn-mete. *c* **1420** *Liber Cocorum* (1862) 54 With gynger þo pigge eton shalle be, And sorel with þo moton. **1539** ELYOT *Cast. Helthe* 24 Sorell. Being sodden, it louseth the bealy. **1575** GASCOIGNE *Posies* Ep. Yng. Gent., Wks. 1907 I. 12 If the Chirurgian which should seeke Sorrell to rypen an Ulcer, will take Rewe [etc.]. **1620** VENNER *Via Recta* vii. 145 Sorell is good in hot seasons.. for the cholericke. **1696** FLOYER *On the Humours* vi. 68 Cyder, French and Rhenish Wines, Vinegar, Sorrel, Verjuice, Limons. **1746** FRANCIS tr. *Horace*, *Sat.* II. iv. 37 Sorrel and White-Wine, if you costive prove, And Muscles, all Obstructions shall remove. **1747–96** MRS. GLASSE *Cookery* v. 78 Take two handfuls of sorrel, pound it in a mortar.

3. † **a.** ***sorrel de boys***, = WOOD-SORREL. *Obs.*

a **1400** *Stockholm Med. MS.* fol. 95 Alla .i. sorell de boye. **1548** ELYOT, *Acidula*,.. an herbe called sorrell de boys. **1552** HULOET, *Alleluya* herbe, otherwise called *Sorrell de Boys*. **1647** HEXHAM I. (Herbs), Sorell de boyes, or Cuckoes Sorell, *Kockocks Suyringh*.

b. With distinguishing epithets, denoting various species of *Oxalis* (wood-sorrel).

1647 [see prec.]. **1706** PHILLIPS (ed. Kersey), *Alleluja*,.. an Herb otherwise call'd Wood-sorrel, or French Sorrel. *Ibid.*, *Oxalis*, wild Sorrel or Wood-Sorrel, an Herb. **1889** MAIDEN *Usef. Plants* 50 *Oxalis corniculata*,.. 'Clover Sorrel', or 'Sour Grass'. **1909** *Cent. Dict.* Suppl. s.v., Ladies' sorrel, *Oxalis stricta*.

4. With distinguishing epithet: One or other of various plants of other genera in some way resembling sorrel (see quots.).

1864 GRISEBACH *Flora Brit. W. Ind.* 787/2 *Climbing Sorrel, *Begonia scandens*. **1697** *Phil. Trans.* XIX. 375 *Acetosa* (a Plant of the Family with Rhubarb, which will be called The *Indian Sorrel, or Sower Docken). **1753** *Chambers' Cycl.* Suppl. *App.* s.v., *Indian Sorrel*, a name sometimes given to *ketmia*. **1760** J. LEE *Introd. Bot.* App. 327 Sorrel, Indian Red, *Hibiscus*. *Ibid.*, Sorrel, Indian White, *Hibiscus*. **1864** GRISEBACH *Flora Brit. W. Ind.* 787/2 Sorrel, Indian or red, *Hibiscus Sabdarifa*. **1843** BABINGTON *Brit. Bot.* (1847) 273 *Oxyria reniformis*,.. *Mountain Sorrel. **1889** MAIDEN *Usef. Plants* 35 *Hibiscus heterophyllus*,.. '*Queensland Sorrel'. **1829** LOUDON *Encycl. Plants* 586 *note*, H[ibiscus] Sabdariffa.. in the West Indies is called *Red Sorrel. **1864** GRISEBACH *Flora Brit. W. Ind.* 787/2 *Switch Sorrel, *Dodonæa viscosa*. **1887** MOLONEY *Forestry W. Africa* 303 Switch Sorrel of Jamaica.. Shrub or small tree.

5. *pl.* Species of sorrel; sorrel plants.

1596 in *Analecta Scotica* II. 13 The seid of.. sorrelis or sourochis. **1725** *Fam. Dict.* s.v., Alleluya.. has all the same Qualities and the same Taste as the other Sorrels. **1841** *Penny Cycl.* XX. 221/2 Well known as troublesome weeds to the agriculturist, under the name of docks and sorrels. **1866** *Treas. Bot.* 998/2 The Sorrels are considered of great importance in French cookery.

6. ***salt of sorrel***, binoxalate of potash.

1800 tr. *Lagrange's Chem.* II. 209 Oxalic Acidulum, the Salt of Sorrel of the Shops. **1839** URE *Dict. Arts* 192 Two drams of sal-ammoniac, and half a dram of salt of sorrel. **1887** BENTLEY *Man. Bot.* (ed. 5) 654 A potassium salt of oxalic acid, commonly termed salt of sorrel.

7. a. *attrib.*, as ***sorrel-flower***, ***genus***, ***leaf***, ***seed***.

1753 *Chambers' Cycl.* Suppl. s.v., Sorrel seeds.. are esteemed astringent. **1811** A. T. THOMSON *Lond. Disp.* (1818) 350 Sorrel leaves are inodorous, and have a grateful ..acidulous taste. **1845** S. JUDD *Margaret* I. xvii, The snowfields seemed to bloom with glowing sorrel-flowers. **1857** HENFREY *Bot.* 359 *Polygonaceæ.* The Sorrel Order. **1866** *Treas. Bot.* 998/1 *Rumex*, the Dock and Sorrel genus.

b. In the sense 'made from sorrel', as ***sorrel drink, jam, sauce, sops, soup, water.***

1558 WARDE tr. *Alexis' Secr.* 40b, Thre vnces of endiue water, or sorell water. **1589** in H. Hall *Soc. Eliz. Age* (1887) 213 For rostinge the mutton and chickens and sorell soppes for the chickens. **1611** COTGR., *Vinaigrette*, sorrell sawce. **1634** HEYWOOD & BROME *Lanc. Witches* III. H.'s Wks. 1874 IV. 214 Here comes the payre of boyld Lovers in Sorrell sops. **1771** MRS. HAYWOOD *New Present for Maid* 155 Lay it in a dish with some sorrel sauce. **1797** J. WOODFORDE *Diary* 20 Apr. (1931) V. 28 We had for Dinner to day, some Haddocks.. Sorrell Soup, a boiled Tongue & Veal Cutlets. **1855** DELAMER *Kitchen Garden* (1861) 93 It is used.. principally for sorrel-soup. **1862** in Veness *El Dorado* (1866) App. 122 Sorrel jelly,.. sorrel jam, preserved papaws [etc.]. **1863** *Chambers's Encycl.* V. 359/1 *Hibiscus Sabdariffa*.. affords a refreshing beverage, well known in the West Indies as Sorrel Cool Drink.

c. In the names of various plants, etc., as **sorrel-thorn, -vine, -wood** (see quots.). Also SORREL-TREE.

1799 *Med. Jrnl.* II. 80 The irritability inherent in the stamina of the flowers of the sorrel-thorn (*l'épine-vinette*). **1864** GRISEBACH *Flora Brit. W. Ind.* 787/2 Sorrel-vine, *Cissus acida.* **1874** *Treas. Bot.* Suppl. 1343/2 Sorrelwood (N[ew] Zeal[and]), *Oxalis magellanica.*

sorrel ('sɒrəl), *a.* and *sb.*^{2} Forms: 5–8 (9 *arch.*) **sorel, 5 sorelle, sowrell, 5–8 sorell, 6–7 soril; 6–7 sorrell, 7 -ill, 6– sorrel.** [a. OF. *sorel* (*soreal, -eaul, -iel*), f. *sore* SORE *a.*^{2} Hence also med.L. *sorellus.*]

A. *adj.* Of a bright chestnut colour; reddish brown: **a.** Of horses (or other animals).

1469 in *Somerset Med. Wills* (1901) 216, I will that my seruant William Wilson have a sorelle hackney of mine. **1543** *Test. Ebor.* (Surtees) VI. 175 A sorell geldinge. **1570** *Bury Wills* (Camden) 156 My sorrell meare coult. **1634–5** BRERETON *Trav.* (Chetham Soc.) 39 Here, in their stable, four dainty sorrel pied horses. **1680** *Lond. Gaz.* No. 1520/4 A Sorrel, or Bright Chesnut Mare, about 14 Hands and a half high. **1704** SWIFT *Batt. Bks.* Misc. (1711) 252 A sorrel Gelding of a monstrous Size. **1706** *Lond. Gaz.* No. 4190/4 A sorrel chesnut Nag, a little crack winded. **1823** E. MOOR *Suffolk Words, Sorrel*, chestnut-coloured, as applied to a horse. **1852** MRS. STOWE *Uncle Tom's C.* iv. 23 How Mas'r Shelby was thinking of buying a new sorrel colt. **1884** BIBLE *Zech.* i. 8 Behind him there were horses, red, sorrel, and white.

b. Of hair or persons.

1600 BRETON *Pasquils Fooles-cap* xxv, Shee, in a glasse, that sees her Sorrell haire, And straight will put it to the Painters die [etc.]. **1602** —— *Mother's Blessing* lxxv, A sorrell foretop, and a sowish feature. **1634** MASSINGER *Very Woman* III. i, My sorrel slaves are of a lower price, Because the colour's faint. **1664** BUTLER *Hud.* II. i. 696 A Roan-Gelding.., a Lock on's hoof, A sorrel-mane. *a* **1700** B. E. *Dict. Cant. Crew, Sorrel-pate*, red Hair'd. **1708** *Brit. Apollo* No. 36. 2/2 Red Hair'd People, or Carrotty, Sandy, Sorrel, or what you will call them.

c. Of colour or hue.

1534 in *Wells Wills* (1890) 41 Oon mayre of sorell color. **1599** T. M[OUFET] *Silkwormes* 72 How they color change, From blacke to browne, from browne to sorrel bay. **1611** COTGR., *Saurir*, to.. turne into a Sorrell colour. *Ibid.*, Vntill they [*sc.* herrings] haue gotten their Sorrell hue.

d. *Comb.*, as ***sorrel-coloured*** adj.; **sorrel-top** *colloq.* (orig. *U.S.*), a red-haired person.

1887 W. B. YEATS *Let.* 13 Aug. in *Lett. W. B. Yeats to Katherine Tynan* (1953) 37, I enclose these trivial verses... The Fairy Doctor. The fairy doctor comes our way Over the sorrel-coloured wold. **1863** 'E. KIRKE' *My Southern Friends* iv. 58 'Har, you lousy sorrel-top,' said the trader to the red-faced and red-headed bar tender. **1904** 'O. HENRY' in *Everybody's Mag.* Feb. 187/1, I guess they don't raise 74-inch sorrel-tops with romping ways down in his precinct. **1918** G. FRANKAU *One of Them* xix. 145 Once more released to lavish wealth and name On head or blonde or sorrel-top or raven.

B. *sb.* **1. a.** A horse of a bright chestnut or reddish brown colour; also as the name of a horse. (So OF. *Sorel.*)

c **1430** LYDG. *Min. Poems* (Percy Soc.) 202 But on them she wyl have a bonde, As weel of bayard as of brende, And yit for sorelle she wyl stonde. **1482** in *Cely Papers* (Camden) 109 Grett sorell ys in good plyght. **1599** HALL *Sat.* VI. i. 223 Saint Georges Sorrel, or his crosse of blood. **1600** J. M. *New Metamorphosis* (Nares, 1859), Noe holla Jacke, nor Sorrell, hola boye, Will make them stay. **1708** *Brit. Apollo* No. 90. 3/1 O'er Hill and Dale on Sorrel, Noble Steed. **1748** SMOLLETT *R. Random* ix, Sure my Lord's Sorrel is not resty. *Ibid.*, Sorrel, disdaining the rein, sprung forward. **1783–9** T. DAY *Sandford & Merton* (1851) 442, I can assure you they are the true Suffolk sorrels, the first breed of working horses in the kingdom. **1842** BORROW *Bible in Spain* lvi, The horse was small but beautiful, a sorrel with long mane and tail. **1894** *Outing* XXIV. 383/2 At the easy, comfortable pace with which old sorrel jogs him to town on court days.

transf. **1803** J. DAVIS *Trav. Amer.* 378, I am no half-and-half breed; no chesnut-sorrel of a mulatto.

b. In allusive use: (see quot. 1710).

1705 HICKERINGILL *Priest-cr.* II. viii. 82 Those that (Profanely if not Traiterously) Drink a Health to Sorrel. **1710** *Answ. to Sacheverell's Serm.* 15 The King [William III] having.. a fall from his Horse (called Sorrel),.. which was thought to be the cause of his Death, they rejoyced at it, and did usually drink a Health to Sorrel.

2. A buck in its third year. Now *Obs.* or *arch.*

1486 *Bk. St. Albans, Hunting* e iv, And ye speke of the Bucke, the fyrst yere he is A fawne,.. The secunde yere a preket, the iii. yere a sowrell. **1530** PALSGR. 272/2 Sorell, a yonge bucke. **1588** SHAKS. *L.L.L.* IV. ii. 60 The Dogges did yell,.. then Sorell iumps from thicket. **1616** *N. Riding Rec.* II. 122 John Turner presented for breaking the chase of the Rt Hon. Lord Burghley and shooting a sorell there. *a* **1700** EVELYN *Diary* 27 July 1654, I went to the hunting of a sorel deere. **1741** *Compl. Fam.-Piece* II. i. 310 If any Deer come out that is not weighty, or a Deer of Antlier, which is Buck, Sore, or Sorel. **1865** G. F. BERKELEY *Life & Recoll.* II. 256 Doe or buck, pricket, sor or sorel, my orders from the Crown were that every one should be destroyed.

transf. **1612** *Christian turned Turk* (T.), I am but a mere sorell; my head's not hardened yet!

3. A sorrel or reddish-brown colour. Freq. with reference to horses.

1530 PALSGR. 272/2 Sorrell, colour of an horse, *sorrel.* *a* **1586** SIDNEY *Arcadia* (1622) 273 His horse was of a fiery sorrell, with blacke feete. **1611** COTGR., *Alezan toustade*, a darke reddish colour, as of mettall burnt in the fire; a burnt sorrell. **1688** HOLME *Armoury* II. 155/1 *Sorrel*, is more lighter than a light Bay, inclining to a Yellow. **1706** STEVENS *Span. Dict.* I, *Alazán dorádo*, betwixt Roan and Sorrel. **1787** BEST *Angling* (ed. 2) 11 The best colours for lines are sorell, white, and grey. **1828** CARR *Craven Gloss., Sorrel*, a colour between a chestnut and a red. **1860** O. W. HOLMES *Elsie V.* (1887) 111 She was of the shade we call sorrel, or, as an Englishman would perhaps say, chestnut.

† **'sorrelled**, *a. Obs.* Forms: **5 sorelt, 5–6 soreld, 6 sorelyd, sorellyd, -ed, 7 sorreld.** [f. SORREL *a.* + -ED. Cf. SORED *a.*] Of horses: = SORREL *a.* a.

1403 *Nottingham Rec.* II. 22 Item, j. equum sorelt, xij s. **1465** in *Mann. & Househ. Exp. Eng.* (Roxb.) 180 A man that browte the Kynge a fole soreld cowser. **1506** *Paston Lett.* III. 404 My Lord Harry of Stafforth.. rydyng apon a sorellyd courser. **1553** *N. Country Wills* (Surtees) 231 To my cosyn.. my soreld bald geldinge. **1613** *Liber Deposit. Archid. Colcest.* fol. 24, One sorreld mare with a white face.

'sorrel-tree. [SORREL *sb.*^{1}] The sourwood or elk-tree of North America, *Oxydendrum arboreum* (*Andromeda arborea*).

1687 *Phil. Trans.* XLI. 152 The Sorrel-tree bears a Leaf something like a Laurel. **1717** *Petiveriana* III. 247 Sorrel or Sowre-tree. Because its Leaves have that Taste; some are a Foot diameter. **1760** J. LEE *Introd. Bot.* App. 327 Sorrel-tree, *Andromeda.* **1821** W. P. C. BARTON *Flora N. Amer.* I. 107 The sorrel tree itself, however, degenerates into a shrub. **1866** *Treas. Bot.* 472/1 The leaves of *Eubotrys arborea* have an acid flavour, whence the name of Sorrel-tree.

'sorren. *Sc.* and *Ir.* Now *Hist.* Forms: 3–4 **sorthyn, sorchyn, 4 sorryn, sorem, 6 sorehim, sorehon, soren, 7 sorehin, soreine, 9 sorren.** [ad. obs. Irish *sorthan*, explained as synonymous with *coinneamh, coinmheadh* (see COYNYE), 'free quarters, living at free expense'. The Latinized form *sornagium* occurs in the 15th cent. Cf. SORN *v.*] A service formerly required of vassals in Scotland and Ireland, consisting in giving hospitality to the superior or his men; a sum of money or other contribution given in lieu of this.

1289–1308 *Charter* in *Adv. Lib. MS.* 34. 3. 25, p. 194 Volo .. quod dictus dominus Adam, heredes sui vel assignati,.. sint quieti de Sorthyn et Tascal. *Ibid.*, Et volo etiam quod.. habeant sorchyn fascal. *c* **1320** *Reg. Mag. Sig. Scot.* (1912) 533 *note*, Concessimus eidem quod dictas terras habeat.. quiete de Sorem et Freelache. **1364** *Ibid.* 57/1 Quod dicta baronia est libera de sorryn et fathalos.

1596 SPENSER *State Irel.* (1633) 25 Cuddy, Coshery, Bonnaght, Shrah, Sorehin, and such others; the which (I thinke) were customes at first brought in by the English upon the Irish. *Ibid.* 104 They.. exact upon them.. all those kinde of services, yea and the very wilde exactions, Coignie, Livery, Sorehon [etc.]. **1600** DYMMOK *Ireland* (1843) 8 Soren is a kind of allowance over and above the bonaght, which the Galloglass exact upon the poor people,.. viz. 2s. 3d. for a day and a night. **1621** R. BOLTON *Statutes Ireland* 429 If any person or persons.. doe give any Scot or Scots.. being men of warre, any wages, bonaghts, soreine, or any other intertainment. **1856** *Ulster Arch. Jrnl.* IV. 243 He rendered the chief-rents in victual, called *sorren*, to McCarthy More. *Ibid.* 246 The first usage, that of giving *sorren*, grew in course of time into the formal payment of rent.

attrib. **1856** *Ulster Arch. Jrnl.* IV. 243 Land modernly held by *sorren* tenure. *Ibid.* 246 'Sorren land,' probably for most part arable.

So'rrento. The name of an Italian town in the province of Naples, used attrib. in ***Sorrento edge, edging, lace, orange, work*** (see quots.).

1856 MRS. PULLAN *Lady's Dict. Needlework* 25 Sorrento Edge [in Point Lace]. *Ibid.* 28 Sorrento Lace. **1875** KNIGHT *Dict. Mech.* 2246/2 *Sorrento-work*, fret carving, done by a jig-saw. **1882** CAULFEILD & SAWARD *Dict. Needlework* 453/1 Sorrento edging, used in modern Point Lace. **1896** *Daily News* 24 Dec. 3/2 The Neapolitan, or Sorrento orange,.. is not smooth, but rather rough and unprepossessing, and its skin thick.

† **'sorrily**, *a. Obs.*$^{-1}$ In 3 **sorilich.** [f. SORRY *a.* + -LY^{1}.] Sorrowful, sad.

c **1200** *Trin. Coll. Hom.* 185 Sorehful is ure hider cume, and sorilich ure henen sið.

sorrily ('sɒrɪlɪ), *adv.* Forms: α. **2–3 sari-, 3 særiliche, 4 sarili, 4–5 -ly.** β. **2, 4 soriliche, 5 soryly, 5–7 sorily, 7– sorrily.** [f. SORRY *a.* + -LY^{2}. Cf. MHG. *sêrichliken.*]

† **1.** In a sorrowful manner; sadly, sorrowfully. *Obs.*

α. *c* **1175** *Lamb. Hom.* 39 Þu scalt bi-wepen þine sunne.. and ȝeoten þine teres swiðe sariliche. *c* **1205** LAY. 13626 Swiðe he gon to wepen & særiliche siken. *c* **1230** *Hali Meid.* 5 Nis ha þenne sariliche.. akast, & in-to þewdom idrahen. *a* **1300** *Cursor M.* 14252 To fete sco fele him sarili. *c* **1400** *Ywaine & Gaw.* 1791 He luked up ful sarily.

β. *c* **1175** in *Fragm. Ælfric's Gloss.*, etc. (1838) 6 Ȝet sæiþ þeo sowle soriliche to þen licame [etc.]. **1387–8** T. USK *Test. Love* II. iii. (Skeat) l. 60 [To] blobere and wepe til hem list stint, and sorily her mishap complayne. *c* **1400** *Rowland & O.* 459 And all þe lethirs þat þare ware þay assembled soryly. *c* **1450** LOVELICH *Merlin* 2460 Goth forth,.. and axeth the modyr the cause why, why that hire husbond wepeth so soryly. **1606** J. CARPENTER *Solomon's Solace* i. 6 He.. mingled his drinke with his teares,.. sighed sorily, and lamented wofully.

† **2.** So as to cause sorrow; grievously; lamentably, pitiably. *Obs.*

a **1225** *Ancr. R.* 224 Swuðe ofte þer biuoren he hefde iseid him euer soð, uorte biswiken him soriliche on ende. *c* **1330** *Arth. & Merl.* 4810 (Kölbing), What Sarrazin so he mett, Wel soriliche he hem grett. *c* **1400** *Destr. Troy* 754 Þai solast hom samyn.. With venus werkes.. þat sorily dessauis, & men to sorow bringes. *c* **1440** *Jacob's Well* 116 Ȝe be soryly deed wyth þe poysoun of þe feend.

3. In a poor, wretched, or deplorable manner; miserably, wretchedly.

a **1586** SIDNEY *Arcadia* (1622) 73 Thy pipe, O Pan, shall helpe, though I sing sorily. **1586** T. B. *La Primaud. Fr. Acad.* I. (1594) 335 All his possession was but a little farme in the countrie sorily built. *a* **1625** FLETCHER *Nice Valour* II. i, Yet goodness, whose inclosure is but flesh, Holds out oft times but sorrily. **1688** BUNYAN *Jerus. Sinner Saved* (1886) 46 Churches would do but sorrily, if Christ Jesus did not put such converts among them. **1709** J. JOHNSON *Clergym. Vade M.* II. p. xlvi, 'Tis so sorrily related, and by one who lived so many hundred years after. **1768** JOHNSON *Lett.* (1788) I. 10 You serve me very sorrily. **1815** SCOTT *Let.* in *Lockhart* (1837) III. xi. 360 The Brunswickers and Hanoverians behaved very well; the Belgians but sorrily enough. **1856** DORAN *Knights & their Days* xvi. 243 Rough games, that suited but sorrily with their calling. **1875** KINGLAKE *Crimea* (1877) VI. xi. 445 Thus sorrily lagged the males in their undesigned trial of speed.

Comb. **1824** DIBDIN *Libr. Comp.* 607 In the sorrily-printed pages of the original London Post.

'sorriness. Now *rare.* Forms: α. **1 sariᵹnys, 2 -nesse, 1–3 sarinesse, 4–5 sarynes; 3 særinesse, -næsse.** β. **3–4 sorinisse, 3–6 sori-, sorynesse, 4 sorinysche, 6 -nes; 6, 8– sorriness, 7–8 sorryness.** [f. SORRY *a.* + -NESS.]

† **1.** The state of being sorry; sorrow, grief, sadness; = SORROWFULNESS. *Obs.*

α. *c* **1000** ÆLFRIC *Saints' Lives* xxiii. 102 Hwæt mæᵹ beon wop oððe sariᵹnys, ᵹyf þæt næs se mæsta æᵹðres? *c* **1100** *O.E. Chron.* (MS. F) an. 616, Far þare sarinesse ðe he hæfðe far þes cinges unᵹeleauon. *c* **1175** *Lamb. Hom.* 103 Þe fifte sunne is *Tristicia*, þet is þissere worlde sarinesse. *c* **1205** LAY. 27560 Þer wes sarinesse, sorreȝen inoȝe. *a* **1340** HAMPOLE *Psalter* iv. 1 Fra anguys and sarynes þou has broght me. **1483** *Cath. Angl.* 318/2 A Sarynes, *tristicia.*

β. *c* **1200** *Trin. Coll. Hom.* 35 Hwile mid sorinesse, hwile mid werinesse. *c* **1275** LAY. 13639 Ich ȝou telle rouþliche spelles of mochele sorinesse. **13..** *Guy Warw.* (A.) 372 Þe heuinisse, þe sorwe, and þe sorinisse, þat me is on. **1387–8** T. USK *Test. Love* II. xiv. (Skeat) l. 57 Trewly, this is the sorinesse of fayned love. *c* **1440** *Promp. Parv.* 465/1 Sorynesse, or hevynesse, *tristicia.* **1548** R. HUTTEN *Sum Divin.* G ij b, It is feare and sorines of conscience which perceiveth yt god is angry with syn. **1571** GOLDING *Calvin on Ps.* li. 11 So as the sorynesse may settle itself deep in our harts. **1683** CROWNE *City Politiques* II. i, Sorry? what does your sorryness signifie?

† **b.** With *a* and pl. An instance of being sorry.

c **1175** *Lamb. Hom.* 105 Þet þe mon on god blissie bitwuxe þa sorinessen þissere sterke worlde. *c* **1200** *Trin. Coll. Hom.* 71 Alse fele sorinesses swo ich haue on min herte for mine sinnes. *c* **1275** *Sinners Beware* 125 in *O.E. Misc.*, In eche sorinesse His saule he may brynge. **1587** GOLDING *De Mornay* xxix. 464 For the verie repentance of the best men, is but a sorinesse that they cannot be sorie enough.

2. The state or quality of being mean, poor, or paltry; poorness, meanness.

1668 WILKINS *Real Char.* II. i. 32 Indifferency,.. Excellency,.. Sorriness. **1727** BAILEY (vol. II), *Sorryness*,.. Paltriness, Meanness, Lowness of Value. **1891** T. HARDY *Tess* xxxix, The figure near at hand suffers.. because it shows up its sorriness without shade.

sorrip, obs. form of SYRUP.

sorrow ('sɒrəʊ), *sb.* Forms: α. **1 sorh, sorhᵹ, 2–3 sorhe (2 sorhᵹe, 3 seorhe); 1 sorᵹ, 2–4 sorȝe (3 sorge, seorȝe, 4 zorȝe, sorghe); 3 soreȝe (-ege), 5 soroȝe, sorugh(e.** β. **3 serrȝhe, sareȝe; 3–4 serewe, 4–5 serwe, sarow(e; 9** *dial.* **sarrow, sarra(h.** γ. **3 sorw, sorwȝe, seor(u)we, 3–5 sorwe, sorewe.** δ. **4–5 soru, sorou (4 sorouu), 5 soro, 6 sourou; 3–6 sorow(e, 5– sorrow, 6–7 sorrowe; 8–9** *Sc.* **sorro', 9 sorra.** [Common Teut.: OE. *sorh, sorᵹ*, = OFris. **sorge* (WFris. *soarch*, EFris. *sôargh, sûrghe*, NFris. *sörrig, surreg*, etc.), OLFrank. *sorga* (MDu. *sorghe*, Du. *zorg*), OS. *sorga, soraga, soroga* (MLG. *sorge, sorch-*, LG. *sorge, sörge*), OHG. *sorga* (MHG. and G. *sorge*), ON. (Icel., Norw., Sw., Da.) *sorg*, Goth. *saurga* (= **sorga*). Relationship to forms outside of Teutonic is uncertain.]

1. a. Distress of mind caused by loss, suffering, disappointment, etc.; grief, deep sadness or regret; also, that which causes grief or melancholy; affliction, trouble.

In OE. freq. in weaker sense, 'care, anxiety'.

α. *Beowulf* 1322 Ne frin þu æfter sælum; sorh is ᵹeniwod Deniᵹea leodum. *c* **888** K. ÆLFRED *Boeth.* vii. §2 Ða ilcan [ðing].. ðe næfre nanne mon buton sorᵹe ne forlætað. **971** *Blickl. Hom.* 103 Ne biþ þær sar ne ᵹewinn,.. ne sorᵹ ne wop. *c* **1100** *O.E. Chron.* (MS. F) an. 870, Ealne his timan was ȝewinn & sorhȝe ofer England. *c* **1175** *Lamb. Hom.* 63 þe saule of him is forloren and þe sorȝe is him biforen. *c* **1230** *Hali Meid.* 27 Weorldes uanite, þat wurðeð al to sorhe & to care. *c* **1250** *Orison of our Lady* 22 in *O.E. Misc.* 160 Al þis world schal ago Wið seorhe and wið sore. **1340** *Ayenb.* 71 Oþer ine zorȝe oþer ine blisse wyþoute endynge. **1390** GOWER *Conf.* II. 144 His echedaies fantasie Of sorghe is evere aliche grene. *a* **1400–50** *Alexander* 249 Wheþire it be sele or soroȝe. *c* **1450** *Knt. de la Tour* (1868) 1 Fulle of sorughe and gladnesse, as mani lovers ben.

β. *c* **1200** *Moral Ode* 378 (Trin. Coll. MS.), Nis þar sareȝe ne sor non. *c* **1200** ORMIN 4852 þiss.. drifeþþ fra þin herrte, All flæshliȝ care & serrȝhe & sit. *a* **1225** *Ancr. R.* 354 Ine sor & ine seoruw. *a* **1250** *Owl & Night.* 884 Hi ne seoþ her nowiht bute serewe. *a* **1300** *Body & Soul* in *Map's Poems* (Camden) 344 To synne and serwe was thi drauȝt. *a* **1400** *Pist. Susan* 145, I am with serwe biset on eueriche side. *c* **1400** *Apol. Loll.* 108 His trauel schal be-gynne in sarow.

γ. *a* **1200** *Vices & Virtues* 19 Ðar is sorwȝe and sarinesse for ðare muchele ortrewnesse. *a* **1250** *Owl & Night.* 431 Hwanne snouh liþ þikke & wide, & alle wihtes habbeþ sorewe. **1297** R. GLOUC. (Rolls) 5044 Þe king him let ek in sorwe & in siknesse lede. *c* **1320** *Sir Tristr.* 578 Ouer londes he gan fare Wiþ sorwe and reweful chere. *c* **1440** *Jacob's Well* 66 Þou muste haue.. full sorwe in þin herte for þi synne. **1473** WARKW. *Chron.* (Camden) 26 Suche goodes as were gaderide with synne, were loste with sorwe.

δ. *a* **1300** *Cursor M.* 24635 Seke i was and sar for soruu. *a* **1340** HAMPOLE *Psalter* cxxvi. 3 Ȝe þat ete þe bred of sorow, þat is, ȝe þat make sorow in ȝoure pilgrimage. *c* **1375** *Cursor M.* 754 (Fairf.), To saue þaire self.. or ellis in sorou for to lende. *c* **1400** MAUNDEV. (Roxb.) iv. 13 Scho began to crie, as a thing þat had mykill sorowe. *c* **1420** *Chron. Vilod.* 1437 [They] weron in soro & penaunce alle þat nyȝt. **1508** DUNBAR *Flyting* 21 Incres of sorrow, sklander, and evill name. **1559** *Mirr. Mag., Hen. VI*, iv, A silly soule with woe and sorowe souste. **1590** SPENSER *F.Q.* I. vii. 23 For earthly sight can nought but sorrow breed. **1602** SHAKS. *Ham.* I. ii. 232 *Ham.* What, lookt he frowningly? *Hor.* A countenance more in sorrow then in anger. **1690** LOCKE *Hum. Und.* II. xx. (1695) 122 Sorrow is uneasiness in the Mind, upon the thought of a Good lost,.. or the Sense of a present Evil. **1742** GRAY *Adversity* 15 What sorrow was, thou bad'st her know. **1784** COWPER *Task* VI. 46 Sorrow has.. subdu'd and tam'd The playful humour. **1841** HELPS *Ess., Aids Contentm.* (1842) 17 And we may remember that sorrow is at once, the lot, the trial, and the privilege of man. **1891** FARRAR *Darkn. & Dawn* xlii, His face wore a look of sorrow and alarm.

b. In more or less personified use.

13.. *E.E. Allit. P.* B. 1080 Þer was solace & songe wher sorȝ has ay cryed. *c* **1400** *Rom. Rose* 4995 Labour and Travaile Logged ben with Sorwe and Woo, That never out of hir court goo. **1554–9** *Songs & Ball. Philip & Mary* (Roxb.) 1 Sorrowe hath caught me in her sner. **1621** BURTON *Anat. Mel.* I. ii. III. iv, Sorrow,.. the mother and daughter of melancholy. **1757** GRAY *Bard* 62 And sorrow's faded form, and solitude behind. **1812** BYRON *Ch. Har.* II. xcvi, How selfish Sorrow ponders on the past. **1850** TENNYSON *In Mem.* lix, O Sorrow, wilt thou live with me?

c. In proverbs and phrases.

c **1420** *Sir Amadace* (Camden) iii, Bettur sayd soro thenne sene! **1788** *Grose's Dict. Vulg. T.* (ed. 2), Sorrow shall be his sops, he shall repent this. *Ibid.*, Sorrow go by me; a common expletive used by the presbyterians in Ireland.

2. a. With *a* and pl. An instance or cause of grief or sadness; an affliction or trouble.

α. *Beowulf* 149 Torn ȝeþolode wine Scyldinga, weana ȝehwelcne, sidra sorȝa. *a* **900** CYNEWULF *Crist* 86 Swa eal manna bearn sorȝum sawað, swa eft ripað. **971** *Blickl. Hom.* 5 Þæt æȝhwylc man sceolde.. her on sorhȝum beon. *c* **1175** *Lamb. Hom.* 71 Þet lif and saule beon iborȝen and baðe ilesed ut of sorȝen. *c* **1205** LAY. 12332 Ah sone þer æfter sorȝen heom weoren ȝiueðen. *c* **1250** *Gen. & Ex.* 68 Pride.. made ilc sorge, and euerilc bale. **13..** *E.E. Allit. P.* B. 563 Quen þe swemande sorȝe soȝt to his hert.

β. *a* **1300** *Harrow. Hell* (Digby) 28 Harde gates haui gon, Serewes soffred moni hon. *a* **1310** in Wright *Lyric P.* xxx. 89 Nis ther no leche so fyn, oure serewes to bete. *a* **1400** *Minor Poems fr. Vernon MS.* liv. 96 Ȝif eny serwe beo lyk to myn.

γ. *c* **1250** *Gen. & Ex.* 3742 Moyses told hem al ðis answere, And he ben smiten in sorwes dere. **1297** R. GLOUC. (Rolls) 5923 Þe þridde ȝer.. of aildredes kinedom, þe biginning of þis sorwe to engelonde verst com. *c* **1320** *Sir Tristr.* 368 Her sorwen and her care þai witt þat frely fode. **1382** WYCLIF *Ecclus.* xxxviii. 7 In these thingus he.. shal swage sorewen. *c* **1400** *Secreta Secret., Gov. Lordsh.* 60 [It] brynges ynward sorwys to mannys hertys.

δ. *a* **1300** *Cursor M.* 9641 Sua þou wald his sorus slak. **1338** R. BRUNNE *Chron.* (1810) 7 Now of fiue sorowes.. Henry in his writyng telles what þei ware. *c* **1440** *York Myst.* xii. 7 And sithen what sorouse sor warre sene. **1477** EARL RIVERS (Caxton) *Dictes* 8 The wiese men bere their greues & sorowes as they were swete vnto them. **1557** NORTH *Gueuara's Diall Pr.* (1568) 300 There is great difference from the cares and sorrowes of weomen to that of men. **1602** SHAKS. *Ham.* IV. v. 78 When sorrowes come, they come not single spies, But in Battaliaes. **1697** DRYDEN *Æneid* I. 307 The day, but not their sorrows, ended thus. **1713** JOHNSON *Guardian* No. 1 ¶5 All sorrows which can arrive at me are comprehended in the sense of guilt and pain. **1746** FRANCIS tr. *Horace, Epist.* I. ii. 68 Nor House, nor Lands,.. Can.. drive one Sorrow from his anxious Breast. **1827** POLLOK *Course T.* I. (1860) 17 Sorrows remembered sweeten present joy. **1892** WESTCOTT *Gospel of Life* 270 Every sorrow and pain is an element of discipline.

b. ***the Man of Sorrows***, Jesus Christ. (After Isaiah liii. 3.)

a **1853** F. W. ROBERTSON *Serm.* Ser. v. (1890) i. 1 The Human Race typified by the Man of Sorrows. **1857** J. HAMILTON *Less. fr. Gt. Biogr.* 170 The Man of Sorrows was not the man who would upbraid a breaking heart.

c. Applied to persons.

1637 MILTON *Lycidas* 166 Weep no more, For Lycidas your sorrow is not dead. **1821** SHELLEY *Adonais* x, Our love, our hope, our sorrow, is not dead; See, on the silken fringe of his faint eyes [etc.].

3. Used as a term of imprecation, or of mere emphasis, in various phrases and constructions. In later use *Sc.* and *Ir.*, and freq. with *the* = the mischief, the devil.

a. In the phrase ***sorrow on*** (a person or thing).

1325 *Poem Times Edw. II*, 178 in *Pol. Songs* (Camden) 331 Sorwe on that o frere that kepeth come there. **13..** *Minor Poems fr. Vernon MS.* xxxvii. 931 Serwe on heore hedes, but þei wel do! *c* **1440** *York Myst.* xxxii. 362 Now sorowe on such socoure as I haue soght. **1596** SHAKS. *Tam. Shr.* IV. iii. 33 Sorrow on thee, and all the packe of you. **1823** SCOTT *Quentin D.* xvi, To deal with William de la Marck, on whose name be sorrow! **1862** CARLYLE *Fredk. Gt.* XIII. ix. (1872) V. 96 The Duchess Dowager of Würtemburg also came, sorrow on her; a foolish talking woman.

b. In other phrases of imprecation.

13.. *Gaw. & Gr. Knt.* 2383 Of trecherye & vn-trawþe boþe bityde sorȝe & care! *c* **1386** CHAUCER *Wife's Prol.* 308 But tel me wherfor hydestow with sorwe The keyes of thy chist away fro me? *c* **1400** *Gamelyn* 881 Sorwe have that rekke! **1526** *Pilgr. Perf.* (W. de W. 1531) 140 b, Yf than the porter wold come.. & bydde vs walke forth vnthryftes with sorowe. *c* **1560** T. INGELEND *Disobedient Child* C j, God guye the sorow. **1776** BURNS '*O Tibbie, I hae seen the day*' iii, But sorrow tak him that's sae mean. **1831** MISS FERRIER *Destiny* II. xxvi. 352 Aye, that you will, or sorrow take me! **1855** TENNYSON *Maud* I. IV. ii, But sorrow seize me if ever that light be my leading star! **1896** P. A. GRAHAM *Red Scaur* xvii. 258 Sorrow take the chance brought me among you!

c. As an emphatic negative. Chiefly with *a*.

1573 *Satir. Poems Reform.* xxxix. 87 Persauing that, sorrow mair thay socht it. **1583** *Leg. Bp. St. Androis* 791 But sorrow mair the men mycht gett. **17..** RAMSAY *Wyfe of Auchtermuchty* xi, The sorrow crap of butter he gat. **1738** *Scotch Presbyt. Eloquence* 111 The Sorrow a Bit of your Dog will I be. **1818** SCOTT *Br. Lamm.* xxiv, Sorra a bit, if I were him. **1825** CROKER *Fairy Leg. Irel.* I. 152 'Sorrow a know I know,' said Leary. **1865** LEVER *Luttrell of Arran* xviii, The sorrow a word ever crossed your lips.

d. Inserted after *what*, *where*, etc., in impatient questions.

a **1631** BRUCE *Upon Affair of Gowrie* in *Serm.* (1843) 193 The Earl.. said—'What sorrow means all this haste?' *a* **1779** D. GRAHAM *Yng. Coalman's Courtsh.* III. (1787) 22 What a sorrow ails you? **1796** *Twa Cuckolds & Tint Quey* 16 What the sorro' way? D'ye think that I can watch her aye? **1861** R. LEIGHTON *Rhymes & Poems* (ed. 2) 89 'Guid-wife,' quoth John, 'did ye see that moose? Whar sorra was the cat?'

e. In miscellaneous uses with *the*.

1756 MRS. CALDERWOOD in *Coltness Collect.* (Maitl. Club) 178 The holydays play the sorrow with the poor people. **1819** THOMSON *Poems* 131 (E.D.D.), The sorry's i' the cutty. **1839** CARLETON *Fardorougha* iii, Her people's as proud as the very sarra. *Ibid.* v, Tut! go to the sarra. **1887** SERVICE *Life Dr. Duguid* II. viii. 219 She should been brunt, the auld limb o' the sorrow!

4. The outward expression of grief; lamentation, mourning; *poet.*, tears. † In early use esp. ***to make sorrow***.

(*a*) *c* **1340** HAMPOLE *Pr. Consc.* 3218 Grete dole þay mak, somtyme, and sarowe, For þai may nathyng begg ne borowe. **1362** LANGL. *P. Pl.* A. III. 16 Mourne þou not, Meede, ne make þou no serwe. *c* **1400** MAUNDEV. (Roxb.) x. 38 Þe mounkes made mykill sorowe at his dying. **1484** CAXTON *Fables of Æsop* I. xviii, [The lion] beganne to crye and make sorowe. **1523** LD. BERNERS *Froiss.* I. cxlv. 174 Whane they within Calays sawe their kynge depart, thay made great sorowe. **1588** SHAKS. *Tit. A.* III. i. 119 Witnes the sorrow that their sister makes.

(*b*) *a* **1425** *Cursor M.* 10496 (Trin.), Whil she mened þus hir mone Wiþ wepe & sorwes mony one. **1490** CAXTON *Eneydos* lii. 146 Thus lasted the sorowe thre dayes and thre nyghtes, that they neuer dyde ceasse. **1592** SHAKS. *Ven. & Ad.* 963 Where they view'd each other's sorrow, Sorrow that friendly sighs sought still to dry. **1717** POPE *Iliad* IX. 559 Down his white beard a stream of sorrow flows. **1746** FRANCIS tr. *Horace, Sat.* I. v. 106 Where from green wood the smothering flames arise, And with a smoky sorrow fill our eyes. **1820** KEATS *Lamia* II. 67 She nothing said, but, pale and meek, Arose and knelt before him, wept a rain Of sorrows at his words.

†**5. a.** Physical pain or suffering. *Obs.*

1377 LANGL. *P. Pl.* B. xx. 42 He seyde in his sorwe on þe selue Rode, 'Bothe fox & foule [etc.]'. **1382** WYCLIF *Gen.* xxxiv. 25 The thridde day, whanne the sorwe of the woundes is moost greuows. **1388** —— *Rev.* xvi. 11 Thei blasfemyden God of heuene, for sorewis of her woundis. **1398** TREVISA *Barth. De P.R.* XVI. xxx. (Tollem. MS.), Þe reed [celidony] helpeþ.. aȝens woodnesse and aȝens olde sorowe.

†**b.** Mischief; harm, hurt, damage. *Obs.*

c **1430** *Syr Gener.* (Roxb.) 8592 Allas! traied we bene Of the ring bi my modre the Quene..; Som sorow she wirketh, wel wot I. **1599** HAKLUYT *Voy.* II. I. 35 Who yet notwithstanding as he was downe, mangled their feete and legges, and did the Saracens much sorrow.

6. As a term of abuse, reproof, or depreciation applied to persons. Chiefly *north.* and *Sc.*

a **1400–50** *Alexander* 1735 Þou hase sampned.. a sellich nowmbre.. Off laddez & of losyngers & of lityll thefez, Siche sary sorowez as þi-self.

1816 SCOTT *Antiq.* xxvi, Get out o' the gate, ye little sorrow! **1818** —— *Hrt. Midl.* xvi, 'Ye're a leeing auld sorrow then,' replied the fair one. **1839** HOOD *Lost Heir* 53 I'm as hoarse as a crow, with screaming for ye, you young sorrow! **1896** 'L. KEITH' *Indian Uncle* v. 78 'That wee sorra' of a baker's boy with the dinner-rolls.

†**7.** Used in place of SORRY *a.* *Obs.*$^{-1}$

a **1470** H. PARKER *Dives & Pauper* (W. de W. 1496) I. liii. 93/2 Iudas was sorowe therof & grutched.

8. *attrib.*, as ***sorrow-cloud***, ***-mate***, †***-sithe***, ***-smart***. **sorrow song**, a lament; *spec.* a song expressing the sorrows of the American Black people.

A number of attributive compounds occur in OE.

c **1205** LAY. 11109 Monie.. menden to him heore sær & heore sorh-siðes. **1602** MARSTON *Antonio's Rev.* IV. v, Helpe me, good sorrow-mates, to give him grave. **1838** ELIZA COOK *The World* ii, We murmur and droop should a sorrow-cloud stay. **1856** R. A. VAUGHAN *Mystics* (1860) I. 153 Therefore shalt thou.. know no sorrow-smart. **1903** W. E. B. DU BOIS *Souls of Black Folk* xiv. 250 (*heading*) The sorrow songs. *Ibid.*, They that walked in darkness sang songs in the olden days—Sorrow Songs—for they were weary at heart. **1936** A. LOCKE *Negro & his Music* iii. 25 These 'sorrow songs' are more than a priceless heritage from the racial past, they are promising material for the Negro music of the future. **1943** J. COLERIDGE-TAYLOR *Memory Sketch* v. 35 On her return from a South African tour, she [*sc.* Ada Crasby] gave a recital,.. asking my husband to accompany her in his 'Six Sorrow Songs'. **1962** R. E. POOL *Beyond Blues* 18 Marcus Garvey headed a movement of a 'back to Africa' Zionism which was a symptom of race consciousness and of the Negro's awakening discovery of the land of long, long ago: 'All the way from Africa to Georgia, I carried my sorrow songs.'

9. *Comb.* **a.** Instrumental, with pa. pples., as ***sorrow-beaten***, ***-blinded***, ***-bound***, ***-closed***, etc.

1594 *Selimus* in Greene's Wks. (Grosart) XIV. 263 Into whose calmie port My *sorrow-beaten soule ioyes to ariue. **1855** LYNCH *Rivulet* XVI. i, Come, O *sorrow-blinded man. **1842** FABER *Styrian Lake* 39 Why stand ye thus *sorrow-bound. *a* **1586** SIDNEY *Arcadia* (1622) 274 When her breath.. had by sobs gotten into her *sorow-closed breast. *a* **1618** SYLVESTER *Monodia* 79 With sigh-swoln heart and *sorrow-clouded eyes. **1849** M. ARNOLD *Forsaken Merman* 103 And anon there drops a tear From a sorrow-clouded eye. **1598** SYLVESTER *Du Bartas* II. ii. I. *Ark* 71 So, the care-charming hony.. re-advanceth *sorrow-daunted hearts. **1603** J. DAVIES (Heref.) *Microcosmos* Pref., Wks. (Grosart) I. 12/1 With stil-sweating *sorrow-furrowed Browes. **1849** M. ARNOLD *Forsaken Merman* 104 A heart *sorrow-laden. **1645** QUARLES *Sol. Recant.* V. 17 Nor let thy *sorrow-melted heart bemone Thy banisht bondslave. *c* **1595** J. DICKENSON *Sheph. Compl.* (1878) 9 These *sorrow-seasond lines should firme abide. **1647** FULLER *Good Th. in Worse T.* (1841) 156 How many have been *sorrow-shot to their heart! **1812** CRABBE *Tales* v. 628 With *sorrow-shrunken face and hair upright. **1819** J. H. PAYNE *Brutus* V. i. 45 Look upon this *sorrow-stricken form. **1844** LEVER *T. Burke* l. 9 Their grief is low and *sorrow-struck. **1600** *Wisd. Dr. Dodypoll* IV. iii. in Bullen *Old Pl.* (1884) III. 142 Where shall I rest my *sorrow-tired limmes. **1608** SYLVESTER *Du Bartas* II. iv. IV. *Decay* 725 *Sorrow-torn, thus (to himselfe) he cries. **1645** QUARLES *Sol. Recant.* I. 23 To what hopefull end Droyle we our crazy bodies, and expend Our *sorrow-wasted spirits? **1842** CDL. WISEMAN *Prayer & Pr.-Bks.* Ess. 1853 I. 379 The innermost caverns of a hollow, *sorrow-worn breast. ? **1638** WALLER *Lady Rich's Death* 126 Your Tears and *Sorrow-wounded Soul. **1736** *Gentl. Mag.* VI. 615/2 To heal the sorrow-wounded heart! **1588** SHAKS. *Tit. A.* III. ii. 4 Marcus vnknit that *sorrow-wreathen knot.

b. Objective, with pres. pples. and vbl. sbs., as ***sorrow-breathing***, ***bringing***, ***-ceasing***, ***-making***, etc.

1825 D. L. RICHARDSON *Sonnets* 97 Thy lay's sweet flow Of *sorrow-breathing music. **1598** SYLVESTER *Du Bartas* II. i. III. *Furies* 176 The dropsie-breeding, *sorrow-bringing Psylly. **1627** DRAYTON *Agincourt* 32 *Sorrow-ceasing sleepe.. Vpon his Eye-lids stealingly doth creepe. **1470–85** MALORY *Arthur* XXI. xi. 857* Ye dysplese god with suche maner of *sorow makyng. **1820** CLARE *Poems Rural Life* (ed. 3) 142 That sad *sorrow-ripening name—a Man. **1603** DRAYTON *Bar. Wars* VI. xciii. 157 She curs'd her *sorrow-seeing eye. **1601** WEEVER *Mirr. Mart.* (Roxb.) 217 In a *sorrow-sighing extasie. **1596** FITZ-GEFFREY *Sir F. Drake* (1881) 96 The *sorrow-sobbing sighes of extasie. **1720** POPE *Iliad* XXIV. 981 So spoke the fair, with *sorrow-streaming eye.

sorrow ('sɒrəʊ), *v.* Forms: α. 1 **sorȝian, sorhȝian,** 2–3 **sorȝen** (3 **sorgen, sorhen, -in**), 4 **zorȝe,** 5 **soroȝe.** β. 3 **serrȝhenn;** 4 **sarwin, serewe,** 5 **serwe.** γ. 3 **seoruwen, sorewi,** 4–5 **sorewe;** 3–5 **sorwe,** 4 **sorwy,** 4–5 **sorwyn.** δ. 4 **soru(u,** 4–5 **sorou,** 4–6 **sorow(e,** 6 **sorrowe,** 6– **sorrow.** [OE. *sorȝian* (f. *sorȝ*, *sorh* SORROW *sb.*), = OFris. **sorgia* (WFris. *soargje*, NFris. *sörrige*, *surrege*, etc.), OLFrank. *sorgôn* (MDu. *sorghen*, Du. *zorgen*), OS. *sorg-*, *sorag-*, *sorogôn* (MLG. and LG. *sorgen*), OHG. *sorgôn*, usually *sorgên* (MHG. and G. *sorgen*); of different formation are Goth. *saurgan* and ON. *syrgja* (Icel. and Norw. *syrgja*, Sw. *sörja*, Da. *sørge*).]

1. *intr.* To feel sorrow or sadness; to regret or grieve; also, to exhibit signs of grief, to mourn.

In OE. freq. 'to feel care or anxiety, to be anxious'.

α. *Beowulf* 1384 Ne sorȝa, snotor guma! *c* **888** K. ÆLFRED *Boeth* vii. §3 Þa woruldare.. þe þu nu sorȝiende anforlete. **971** *Blickl. Hom.* 97 Þeah hwæþere he sceal winnan & sorȝian, hwonne se dæȝ cume. *c* **1175** *Lamb. Hom.* 103 Þissere worlde sarinesse þenne þe mon sorȝeð alles to swiðe for his hehte lure. *c* **1205** LAY. 5078 Brennes þat isæh & sorȝeden on his heorte. *c* **1230** *Hali Meid.* 27 Moni þing schal ham.. makie to carien, &.. sorhen & siken. **1340** *Ayenb.* 71 [He] nou ine helle wepeþ and gredeþ, yelleþ and zorȝeþ. *a* **1400–50** *Alexander* 4051 Quen he þaire simpilnes sees he soroȝes in his hert.

β. *c* **1200** ORMIN 8950 Whatt wass ȝuw swa to serrȝhenn? *a* **1300** *Cursor M.* 23511 (Edinb.), Ne suld þou nauþir scham ne sarwin. *a* **1400** *Minor Poems fr. Vernon MS.* xxiii. 44 Bihold þe wrecchednesse so rif Of soule þat is serwyng.

γ. *a* **1225** *Ancr. R.* 308 Uour þinges.. muwen makien him to seoruwen, & bittren his heorte. *c* **1330** R. BRUNNE *Chron. Wace* (Rolls) 2439 Þenne bygan Leyr to sorewe, & ment his mone euen & morwe. *c* **1350** *Will. Palerne* 691 But whan he wist it was wast.., he gan to sike & sorwe. *c* **1450** LOVELICH *Merlin* 11794 (E.E.T.S.), Thus ryden they Soreweng, bothe knyht & page.

δ. *a* **1300** *Cursor M.* 23511 Ne sal þou noþer scam ne soruu, Bot haf gret ioi. *Ibid.* 24437, I sagh him dei, i sorud ai. **1375** BARBOUR *Bruce* XX. 484 Lang quhile our hym thai sorowit swa. *c* **1400** *Pilgr. Sowle* (Caxton, 1483) IV. xix. 64 Thenne byganne this fayre tree to wepen and to sorowen. **1474** CAXTON *Chesse* II. v. (1883) 70 They.. sorowe more that wilful pouerte is lost in rome. **1526** *Pilgr. Perf.* (W. de W.

1531) 86b, In all euyll thou mayst fynde cause to mourne and sorowe. **1590** SPENSER *F.Q.* I. ix. 15, I sorrowed all so much, as earst I ioyd. **1667** MILTON *P.L.* XI. 117, I shall.. So send them forth, though sorrowing, yet in peace. **1720** POPE *Iliad* XIX. 134 Stung to the soul, he sorrow'd, and he raged. **1838** LYTTON *Alice* 15 They who have sorrowed may well be reluctant to sadden..those to whom sorrow is yet unknown. **1883** 'OUIDA' *Wanda* I. 34 You have sorrowed and tarried in seclusion long enough.

Prov. **1639** J. CLARKE *Parœmiologia* 220 He that goes a borrowing goes a sorrowing. **1707** MORTIMER *Husb.* (1721) I. 366 Lest, according to the old Saying it proves, 'That he that goes a borrowing goes a sorrowing'.

b. Const. *at*, *for*, *over*.

Examples with *for* and *ymbe* also occur in OE.

1530 PALSGR. 725/1 He soroweth for his fathers deth. **1551** BIBLE *Acts* xx. 38 Sorowing moste of all for the wordes whiche he spake. **1606** SHAKS. *Ant. & Cl.* IV. xv. 52 The miserable change now at my end, Lament nor sorrow at. **1622** R. HAWKINS *Voy. S. Sea* xxx. 69 This I haue sorrowed for many times since. **1671** MILTON *Samson* 1603, I sorrow'd at his captive state. **1797–1805** S. & HT. LEE *Canterb. T.* II. 273 His nature was unequal to sorrowing for more than one object. **1850** TENNYSON *In Mem.* xiv, He should sorrow o'er my state. **1867** 'OUIDA' *C. Castlemaine's Gage* (1879) 17 Sorrowing..for her ruined cause and exiled king. **1875** JOWETT *Plato* (ed. 2) I. 496, I would not have him sorrow at my hard lot.

†**c.** With *for*: To have charge of, look after, provide for. *Obs.*

1481 CAXTON *Reynard* (Arb.) 25 He that sorowed for malperduys was goon his way. And the hows not pourueyed ne vitaylled. **1545** BRINKLOW *Lament.* (1874) 90 Yf ye wolde redresse these thinges,..and sorowe [1542 prouyde] for the poore, so shulde ye be without the clamor of them.

2. *trans.* To think of with sorrow; to feel sorrow on account of; to lament.

a **1340** HAMPOLE *Psalter* iv. 5 ȝe..in ȝoure dennes ere stongen sorowand ȝoure synnes. *Ibid.* xxiv. 17 [The] anlepy is mare lufid, [the] pore is mare sorowid. *c* **1450** *Myrr. our Ladye* 256 The redde rose waxed then pale when the vyrgyn sorowed the dethe of her sonne. **1508** FISHER *7 Penit. Ps.* cxxx. Wks. (1876) 232 Shall not I sorowe the destruccion of .xx. C.M. soules. **1547** J. HARRISON *Exhort. Scottes* a iij, This miserie is muche to be sorowed. **1632** LITHGOW *Trav.* VII. 304 Their time was come, which mortality might sorrow, but..not preuent.

b. With subordinate clause.

Examples with *hwæðer*, *hwylc*, *þæt*, occur in OE.

c **1450** *Myrr. our Ladye* 308 Thy sonne.., whome thou sorowedyst to suffer dethe. **1526** *Pilgr. Perf.* (W. de W. 1531) 290 It is..moche to be sorowed, that [etc.]. **1535** COVERDALE *Judith* iv. 2 They sorowed he shulde do vnto the cite of Ierusalem..as he had done to other cities. **1608** CAPT. SMITH *True Relat.* Wks. (Arb.) 30 Her Father..much sorrowed he could not see me. **1859** TENNYSON *Elaine* 728 She,..sorrowing Lancelot should have stoop'd so low, Marr'd her friend's aim. **1897** HOWELLS *Landl. Lion's Head* 418 He sorrowed that he could not attend a service there.

3. To give pain to; to grieve, make sorrowful.

a **1310** in Wright *Lyric P.* xv. 50 Nou hit sereweth him ful sore, ant bringeth him to grounde. *c* **1394** *P. Pl. Crede* 688 Þat sorweþ myn herte How þei ben cloþed in cloþ. *a* **1425** tr. *Arderne's Treat. Fistula*, etc. 7 ȝif ȝoure soule or mynd couaite þat deliteþ, drinke þe first þat soroweþ or akeþ. **1574** HELLOWES *Gueuara's Fam. Ep.* (1577) 189 The ague that held you, sorroweth me. **1637** HEYWOOD *Royall King* II. iv, It sorrows me that you misprize my love. **1840** *Fraser's Mag.* XXI. 23 The only member of the gentler sex whose name sorrows our obituary, is—Miss Landon. **1890** JEAN MIDDLEMASS *Two False Moves* II. xii. 183 The bitterness of her tone sorrowed him.

Hence **'sorrowed** *ppl. a.*

1607 SHAKS. *Timon* V. i. 152 The publike Body..send forth vs, to make their sorrowed render. **1807** J. BARLOW *Columb.* I. 165 Now raise thy sorrow'd soul to views more bright.

sorrower ('sɒrəʊə(r)). [f. SORROW *v.* + -ER¹.] One who sorrows; a mourner.

1727 *Collect. Epigr.* cdlxii, Take the soft sorrower at her word, and try How deeply rooted woman's vows can lie. **1788** MME. D'ARBLAY *Diary* 19 Nov., My account..was most meekly received by the most patient of sorrowers. **1850** LYNCH *Theoph. Trinal* ii. 19 His wines, that make him for an hour less a sorrower. **1873** MAURICE *Serm. in Co. Churches* 249 We shall ask that..the Comforter may visit us and all the sorrowers of the earth.

sorrowful ('sɒrəʊfʊl), *a.* Forms: α. 1–3 sorhful(l, 3 soreh-, seor(u)hful, sorþfolle; 1 sorȝ-, 3 sorȝ-, 4 sorghful(l, zorȝuol(le; 3–4 sorful, -fol, 4 -uol, zoruol-, 5 sorefull(e, soyrefull. β. 3 serrh-, serehful; 4 serwȝful, 5 serwh-, sereuh-, ser(e)u-, serwful. γ. 3–4 soreuful, 3–5 sorw(e)ful(le. δ. 3–5 soru-, 4–6 soroful(l, 5 sorrofull; 3–6 sorow-, 4–6 sorouful(l, 5– sorrowful (5–7 -full); 6 *Sc.* sorro(w)fow. [OE. *sorh-*, *sorȝful* (f. *sorh*, *sorȝ* SORROW *sb.*), = OHG. *sorgful* (G. *sorgvoll*, usually *sorgenvoll*), ON. *sorgfullr* (Norw. and Sw. *sorgfull*, Da. *-fuld*) and *sorgafullr*, LG. *sörg(e)ful*.]

1. Full of, oppressed by, sorrow or grief; unhappy, sad, regretful.

α. *Beowulf* 2119 Grendeles modor siðode sorhfull. *c* **897** K. ÆLFRED *Gregory's Past. C.* xxvi. 183 Se weleȝa bið eaðmod & sorȝfull. *c* **1000** ÆLFRIC *Judg.* x. 10 Oð þæt hiȝ.. heora synna andetton mid sorhfullum mode. *a* **1200** *Vices & Virtues* 83 Sari and sorhfull am ic. *c* **1205** LAY. 1477 Þe king wes swiðe særi & seorhful on mode. *c* **1250** *Gen. & Ex.* 2326 He..nam ðo breðere euerilk on, And ledde hem sorful a-gon. *c* **1275** LAY. 15489 Þo was sori þe king and sorþfolle þorh alle þing. *c* **1300** *Havelok* 151 Alle þat the writes herden Sorful an sori til him ferden. **1390** GOWER *Conf.* I. 203 This sorghfull king was so bestad, That he schal nevermor be glad. **1422** tr. *Secreta Secret., Priv. Priv.* 199 He became mournynge and Sorefull.

β. *c* **1200** ORMIN 7153 He wass forrdredd & serrhfull inn hiss herrte. *a* **1400** *Pistill of Susan* 144 Þen Susan was serwful, and seide in hire þouȝt. *a* **1400** *Vernon MS.* in *Herrig's Archiv* LVII. 250/1 So sereuhful was þis Bisschope, þat almost he fel in wonhope.

γ. *c* **1300** *Havelok* 1248 Sory and sorwful was she ay. *c* **1385** CHAUCER *L.G.W.* Prol. 390 If so be he may hym nat ascuse [He] axith mercy with a sorweful herte.

δ. *c* **1205** LAY. 167 Þa wes Turnus sari, & soruful on his mode. *a* **1325** *Prose Psalter* l. 18 Þou, God, ne shal nouȝt despisen þe hert sorowful and meke. *a* **1340** HAMPOLE *Psalter* cxlvi. 3 Þai þat offirs til him þe sacrifice of sorouful gast. *c* **1400** *Pilgr. Sowle* (Caxton) I. xxxix. (1859) 43 Ful sorrowful was this Sathanas when he sawe [etc.]. **1495** *Act 11 Hen. VII*, c. 57 Preamble, Your seid Suppliaunt is as sorrowfull and repentant as any creature may be. **1535** COVERDALE *1 Esdras* viii. 71, I rent my holy garmentes, and ..sat me downe sorouful & heuy. **1560** ROLLAND *Seven Sages* 113 Quhairfoir thay war all seuin richt sorrofow. **1579** NORTHBROOKE *Dicing* (1843) 37 Your greate commendation of this sermon maketh me sorrowfull that I had not beene at it. **1676** HALE *Contempl.* II. 107 Whatsoever I love, makes me..Sorrowful in the loss or deprivation of it. **1796** H. HUNTER tr. *St.-Pierre's Stud. Nat.* (1799) II. 365 If I am in a sorrowful mood. **1810** SCOTT *Lady of L.* II. xxix, While, sorrowful, but undismay'd, The Douglas thus his counsel said. **1882** 'OUIDA' *Maremma* I. 13 They were all sorrowful.

b. *absol.* (Chiefly *pl.*)

c **897** K. ÆLFRED *Gregory's Past. C.* 183 Ðætte ða sorȝfullan onȝieten ðæt him becumað ða welan. ? *a* **1400** *Morte Arth.* 953 He saluȝede that sorowfulle with sittande wordez. **1526** *Pilgr. Perf.* (W. de W. 1531) 213 b, How they haue comforted the heuy & sorrowfull. **1556** *Aurelio & Isab.* (1608) M v, Ha poore sorrowfull. **1869** TOZER *Highl. Turkey* II. 324 [Death] coming with a friendly aspect to relieve the sorrowful.

c. *sorrowful tree*, the night-jasmine of India.

1597 GERARDE *Herbal* III. cxxxviii. 1342 *Arbor tristis*, the sad or sorrowfull tree waxeth as bigge as an Oliue tree. *Ibid.* 1343 It is called..in English the Sad or Sorrowfull tree, or the Indian Mourner. **1760** J. LEE *Introd. Bot.* App. 327 Sorrowful-tree, *Nyctanthes.*

2. Indicative or expressive of sorrow or grief.

a **1225** *Ancr. R.* 284 ȝif eni is þet naueð nout þe heorte þus afeited, mid seoruhfule sikes. *c* **1275** LAY. 3410 He mornede swiþe and þeos word seide mid sorfol speche. *c* **1340** HAMPOLE *Pr. Consc.* 503 Al er we born gretand, And makand a sorowful sembland. *a* **1400** *Minor Poems fr. Vernon MS.* liv. 182 Heo caste me mony a serwful loke. **1450** W. LOMNER in *Paston Lett.* I. 124, I.. am right sory of that I shalle sey, and have soo wesshe this litel bille with sorwfulle terys, that [etc.]. **1565** COOPER *Thesaurus* s.v. *Foeditas*, Sorowfull blacke apparell. **1576** GASCOIGNE *Philomene* Ded., I had begonne an Elegye or sorrowefull song, called the Complainte of Phylomene. **1588** SHAKS. *Tit. A.* III. i. 147 His Napkin..Can do no seruice on her sorrowfull cheekes. **1606** —— *Ant. & Cl.* I. iii. 64 Where be the Sacred Violles thou should'st fill With sorrowfull water? **1819** SCOTT *Ivanhoe* xxxii, Her lovely brow, though sorrowful, bore on it a cast of reviving hope. **1877** MRS. FORRESTER *Mignon* I. 225 The poor mother smiles the.. sorrowfulest smile that ever hovered on a woman's lips.

3. Characterized by, involving or inducing, sorrow or grief; distressing, lamentable, doleful.

α, β. *Beowulf* 1278 His modor þa ȝyt..ȝegan wolde sorhfulne sið. *a* **1000** *Phœnix* 417 Þæt hi feor þonan.. drohtað sohton, sorȝfulran ȝesetu. *a* **1122** *O.E. Chron.* (Laud MS.) an. 1112, Hit wæs swiðe hefiȝ tyme & sorhfull þurh ormætne mancwealm. *c* **1200** *Trin. Coll. Hom.* 179 Serehful is ure burde for eues gulte. **1297** R. GLOUC. (Rolls) 823 Þis king adde iwend aboute in such soruol cas. **1340** *Ayenb.* 34 Efter alle þise zorȝuolle poyns of sleuþe him yefþ þe dyeuel. **1370–80** *Visions of St. Paul* 173 in *O.E. Misc.* 228 Þen sauȝ poul a serwȝful siht. **1390** GOWER *Conf.* I. 329 Me is levere forto deie Than live after this sorghful day.

γ, δ. *a* **1300** *Cursor M.* 2785 Þat soruful sin on þam þai thoght..to haue don. *Ibid.* 7861 Saul es slan, þat soroful king. *c* **1400** tr. *Secreta Secret., Gov. Lordsh.* 105, I dye for hunger and sorwfull threst. **1513** DOUGLAS *Æneid* v. xii. 124 In Tartarus, the sorofull hellis pit. **1560** DAUS tr. *Sleidane's Comm.* 123 Fearyng lest this dissention in Religion should come to some sorowfull ende. **1588** SHAKS. *Tit. A.* v. iii. 142 Goe into old Titus sorrowfull house. **1611** BIBLE *Job* vi. 7 The things that my soule refused to touch, are as my sorrowfull meat. **1753** CHALLONER *Cath. Chr. Instr.* 240 The five next are called the dolorous or sorrowful Mysteries. **1788** COWPER *Morning Dream* 32 He..stood looking out for his prey From Africa's sorrowful shore. **1818** SHELLEY *Invoc. Misery* vi, Sounds and odours, sorrowful Because they once were sweet. **1871** ALABASTER *Buddhism* 245 In order that he might teach men how to escape from sorrowful existence.

4. quasi-*adv.* = next.

c **1374** CHAUCER *Anel. & Arc.* 207 Vppon A day full sorouful wepynge. **1871** R. ELLIS tr. *Catullus* lxiv. 202 When from an anguish'd heart these words stream'd sorrowful upwards.

sorrowfully ('sɒrəʊfʊlɪ), *adv.* Forms: (see quots. and prec.). [ME. *sorh-*, *sorȝfulliche*: see prec. and -LY².] In a sorrowful manner; to a distressing extent; sadly, pitiably, etc.

α. *a* **1225** *Ancr. R.* 400 Uorto beon þer deofles hore, schendfulliche & seoruhfulliche world wiðuten ende. *c* **1230** *Hali Meid.* 17 þe engles..þat seoð hare suster swa sorhfulliche afallet. *a* **1300** *Cursor M.* 20896 (Edinb.), Þurȝ saint Petiris orisune Sorfullic þan fel he dune. **1340** *Ayenb.* 90 Hou ssel ich zygge þet hi doþ guod þanne he ssel by þe more zoruollaker ydamned. **1390** GOWER *Conf.* I. 161, I am sorghfully bestad Of that I se an other glad With hire.

β. *a* **1400** *Minor Poems fr. Vernon MS.* xxix. v. 57 Wiþ wepe and wringyng serufoly, To Marie he made his pleynt.

γ. **13..** *Guy Warw.* (A.) 415 Wel sorweful(i)che went Gij In to his chaumber al dreri. *c* **1350** *Will. Palerne* 2971 Sorwfuliche sche siȝt last out schold it lett. *c* **1386** CHAUCER *Frankl. T.* 846 'No, no,' quod he, and sorwfully he siketh. *c* **1430** *Pilgr. Lyf Manhode* III. viii. (1869) 140 Wundringe him and compleyninge him sorwefulliche.

δ. *c* **1375** *Cursor M.* 15355 (Fairf.), Soroufulli þai come togeder. **1483** *Cath. Angl.* 349/1 Sorowfully, *vbi* Sory. **1565** COOPER *Thesaurus* s.v. *Flebiliter*, To singe sorowfully, or as if he wepte. **1580** HOLLYBAND *Treas. Fr. Tong*, *Envy*, sorowfully, against my will. *a* **1648** LD. HERBERT *Hen. VIII* (1649) 471 The matter..he hath sorrowfully lamented. **1794** MRS. RADCLIFFE *Myst. Udolpho* i, The flattering portrait of mankind which..his experience had too sorrowfully corrected. **1839** DICKENS *Nickleby* xii, 'I don't know,' said Smike, shaking his head sorrowfully. **1856** KANE *Arct. Explor.* II. xvi. 175 This was a work.. sorrowfully exhausting to the poor fellows.

sorrowfulness ('sɒrəʊfʊlnɪs). Forms: (see quots. and the adj.). [f. SORROWFUL *a.* + -NESS.] The state of feeling sorrowful; grief, sadness, melancholy.

a **1225** *Ancr. R.* 110 Seoruhfulnesse made him siken sore. *a* **1300** *Cursor M.* 22560 Þan behoves all folk to dei, Thoru sorfulnes þat þai sal drei. **13..** in *Rel. Ant.* II. 226 The day of rykenyng..ys day of wreythe, of wo, of sorowfolnesse. **1382** WYCLIF *2 Macc.* iii. 17 Forsothe sum sorewfulnesse was shed about to the man. **1422** tr. *Secreta Secret., Priv. Priv.* 218 In frenesy, In Dreddys, in Soroufulnesse. **1526** *Pilgr. Perf.* (W. de W. 1531) 277 That we dispose ourselfe in sorowfulnesse of herte to receyue his grace. *a* **1608** DEE *Relat. Spir.* I. (1659) 234 In token of hearty sorrowfulnesse for his fault. **1648** HEXHAM II, *Bedroeftheyt*, Greefe,.. Sorrowfullnesse. **1727** BAILEY (vol. II), *Mournfulness*, sorrowfulness. **1832** L. HUNT *Poems* Pref. p. lv, All are the one common story of sorrowfulness.

sorrowing ('sɒrəʊɪŋ), *vbl. sb.* [f. SORROW *v.*] The action of the verb; mourning, lamentation.

a **1023** WULFSTAN *Hom.* 114 Ðær is sorȝung & sarȝung and a singal heof. *a* **1300** *Cursor M.* 1269, I haue lued so mani a yere Ai in strijf and soruuing stad. *a* **1310** in Wright *Lyric P.* xvi. 53 Sykyng, sorewyng, ant thoht, Tho thre me han in bale broht. **1370–80** *Vis. St. Paul* 223 in *O.E. Misc.* 229 Of heore serwyng was muche wondur. **1482** *Monk of Evesham* (Arb.) 59 Their voycys of wepyng and sorowyng was exaltyd and lyfte vppe. **1530** PALSGR. 273/1 Sorowing or wayling, *deploration.* **1596** SPENSER *F.Q.* VI. iii. 5 They..bring vs bale and bitter sorrowings. **1613** W. BROWNE *Brit. Past.* I. i, Her beauty was the sting, That caused all that instant sorrowing. **1721** WATERLAND *Serm. bef. Sons of Clergy* (1722) 36 Amidst our Sorrowings for the Ravages made by Avarice at Home. **1807** WORDSW. *White Doe* VII. 125 This lovely chronicler of things Long past, delights and sorrowings. **1876** GEO. ELIOT *Dan. Der.* II. xxxi. 278 Sorrowing is your sauce; you can take nothing without it.

sorrowing ('sɒrəʊɪŋ), *ppl. a.* [f. as prec. + -ING².] That sorrows or mourns; mournful.

c **1615** SIR W. MURE *Misc. Poems* xii. 3 My sorowing sighes..do not dispyse. **1705** STANHOPE *Paraphr.* II. 296 The condition of all sorrowing Penitents. **1787** BURNS *Ode Birthday Pr. Chas. Edward* 15 We solemnize this sorrowing natal day, To prove our loyal truth. **1817** SHELLEY *Rev. Islam* II. x, The sorrowing gale Waked in those ruins gray its everlasting wail! **1837** CARLYLE *Fr. Rev.* II. v. ii, Known by and by as *Girondins*, to the sorrowing wonder of the world. **1888** MISS BRADDON *Fatal Three* I. vi, He had not the nerve to go into the cottage and face that sorrowing widow.

Hence **'sorrowingly** *adv.*

1865 *Athenæum* 8 July 43/1 The great admiral then sorrowingly alludes to the difficulty of discharging the ships.

sorrowless ('sɒrəʊlɪs), *a.* Also 1 sorh-, sorȝleas, 5 sorweles, 6 sorowlesse. [f. SORROW *sb.* + -LESS. Cf. MDu. *sorghelos* (Du. *zorgeloos*), MHG. *sorgelôs* (G. *sorglos*, *sorgenlos*), ON. *sorg(a)lauss* (Sw. *sorglös*, Da. *sorgløs*).] Free from sorrow.

Beowulf 1672 Þæt þu on Heorote most sorhleas swefan mid þinra secga ȝedryht. *a* **900** CYNEWULF *Crist* 346 Þær we sorȝlease siþþan motan wuniȝan in wuldre. *c* **1000** *Ags. Gosp.* Matt. xxviii. 14 We læраð hyne, & ȝedoð eow sorhlease. **1412–20** LYDG. *Chron. Troy* IV. 3695 ȝit can þei feyne and salte teris fynde,..And sorweles mornen and compleyne. **1545** JOYE *Exp. Dan.* v. H viij, Taking theyr pleasures in banketting..and playinge so sorowlesse. **1658** HEWYT *Serm., Repentance & Conv.* 23 If their repentance be sorrowless, 'twill prove but a sorry one. **1881** J. RUSSELL *Haigs* xiii. 390 The mourner and the mourned are equally silent and sorrowless.

†**'sorrowly,** *adv.* *Obs. rare.* [f. OE. *sorh*, *sorȝ* SORROW *sb.* + *-líce* -LY².] Sorrowfully.

c **1000** *St. Veronica* in *Cambr. Antiq. Soc.* (1851) 34 He swa sorhlice hys lyf ȝeendode. *c* **1150** *Fragm. Ælfric's Gram.* (1838) 5 Þonne biþ þæt soule hus seoruhliche bereaued. *c* **1205** LAY. 21883 Sorhliche heo gunnen clupien to Arðure þan kinge.

†**'sorrowness.** *Obs. rare.* Sorrowfulness.

13.. *Floriz & Bl.* (A.) 735 Beth non so fair in here gladnesse, Als thai ware in hire sorewenesse. **13..** *Guy Warw.* (A.) 422 Vnder heuen nas þat it ne miȝt haue rewþe Of his sorwenes & of his trewþe.

sorrowy ('sɒrəʊɪ), *a.* Also 4 sorewi, -y. [f. SORROW *sb.*] Sorrowful.

1382 WYCLIF *Ecclus.* xiv. 10 In sorewi slouthe he shal be vp on his bord. —— *Isaiah* xxix. 2, I shal besette aboute Ariel, and it shal be dreri and sorewy. **1850** S. DOBELL *Roman* vii. Poet. Wks. (1875) 144 With thy most sorrowy soul, my harp, remember! **1856** —— *Eng. in Time of War* 198 The sorrowy signal for return.

sorry ('sɒrɪ), *a.* Forms: α. 1 sariȝ, sarȝ-, 1–3 sari, 3 særȝ-, særi, seri; *north.* and *Sc.* 4–5 sari, 4–6, 8 sarie, sary, 8–9 sairy, 6, 9 sairie. β. 3–5 sori, 3–7 sorie, sory, 6 sorye, soarye; 5– sorry, 6–7 sorrie. [OE. *sáriȝ* (f. *sár* SORE *sb.*¹), = OS. *sêrag* (MLG. *sêrich*, LG. *sêrig*), OHG. *sêrag* (MHG. *sêrec*, G.

dial. *sêrich*, etc.), WFris. *searich*, sore, pained, sensitive, etc. In English the change of *ā* to *ō* and subsequent shortening have given the word an apparent connexion with SORROW *sb.*]

1. Pained at heart; distressed, sad; full of grief or sorrow.

In later use freq. in weakened sense, and often employed in the phrase 'I'm sorry' to express mere sympathy or apology.

α. c **888** K. ÆLFRED *Boeth.* xxxv. §7 Ða sceolde se hearpere weorðan swa sariᵹ þæt he ne meahte onᵹemong oðrum monnum bion. c **1000** ÆLFRIC *Gen.* xlviii. 17 Þa Iosep ᵹeseah [etc.],..he wearð swiðe sari. a **1122** *O.E. Chron.* (Laud MS.) an. 1114, Þa wæron hi swa sari swa hi næfre ær ne wæron. a **1200** *Vices & Virtues* 69 Ðies ȝunge mann ȝiede a-wei sari. c **1205** LAY. 28459 Wenhauer þa quene, særȝest wimmonne. c **1250** *Gen. & Ex.* 408 Swilc tiding ðhugte adam god, And sumdel quemeð it his seri mood. a **1300** *Cursor M.* 20378 Sai now broþer, suet iohan, Qui ertu sa sari man? a **1352** MINOT *Poems* (ed. Hall) vii. 88 Ful sari was sir Philip þen. c **1450** *St. Cuthbert* (Surtees) 570 þe childe was sary and þerfore grett. **1500–20** DUNBAR *Poems* xxiv. 37 Lat ws in hairt nevir moir be sary. a **1585** MONTGOMERY *Flyting* 474 Seuin ȝeir, it sat, baith singed and sairie.

β. c **1200** *Trin. Coll. Hom.* 117 He forbed his apostles..þat hie neren noht sorie. c **1275** *Passion our Lord* 147 in *O.E. Misc.*, Þo hi hedden al þis iherd heo were ful sori. c **1320** *Sir Tristr.* 2161 Al sori mark gan go Til he miȝt tristrem kisse. c **1386** CHAUCER *Pars. T.* ¶458 Ay the more strong that the fleisch is, the sorier may the soule be. c **1430** *Syr Gener.* (Roxb.) 6746 No soryer man in erth may dwel Than I. **1470–85** MALORY *Arthur* XVII. xvii. 714* Thenne was not he a lytel sory, for launcelot loued hym. **1535** COVERDALE *2 Esdras* xiii. 13 There came moch people vnto him: some were glad, some were sory. **1582** STANYHURST *Æneis* II. (Arb.) 60 In sight of thee soarye parents hee fel to the groundward. a **1628** F. GREVIL *Cœlica* lxxiv, Sadly clad for Sorrowe's glory, Making joy glad to be sorie. **1780** BURKE *Corr.* (1844) II. 379 As to the party, I do not wonder that they are sorry. **1820** BYRON *Blues* II. 1 Was there ever a man who was married so sorry? **1870** DICKENS *E. Drood* iii, You seem to be sorry, Rosa.

Prov. **14..** *Lat. & Eng. Prov.* (MS. Douce 52) fol. 20 b, As long leuyth a mery man as a sory.

b. *absol.* in sing. or pl.

a **900** CYNEWULF *Crist* 1510 Sarᵹe ᵹe ne sohton. c **1000** *Ags. Psalter* (Thorpe) liv. 1 Ne forseoh æfre sariᵹes bene. a **1300** *Cursor M.* 24861 Þaa sori loked ai sua for-suonken. **1362** LANGL. *P. Pl.* A. XI. 190 Þus bed þe Do-bet,..Sike with þe sory, singe with þe glade.

c. In association with *sick*.

1393 LANGL. *P. Pl.* C. xx. 326 For þer ne is syk ne sory ..þat he ne may [etc.]. **1405** *Lay Folks Mass Bk.* 65 For al that er sek and sary. c **1440** *York Myst.* xlviii. 333 Whanne I was seke and soriest. **1529** FRITH *Antithesis* 303 So that they go away sorrier and sicker in soul and in purse than they were before. **1876** T. HARDY *Ethelberta* (1890) 372 Looking as sick and sorry as a lily with a slug in its stalk.

2. With various constructions:

a. With *at*, *for*, †*of*, = on account of, by reason of; also with *for*, = on behalf of, in sympathy with.

(*a*) c **888** K. ÆLFRED *Boeth.* x, Se is swiðe sariᵹ for ðinum earfoðum. c **1000** ÆLFRIC *Saints' Lives* xxxii. 136 Þæt land-folc..wurdon swiðe sariᵹe for his sleᵹe on mode. c **1205** LAY. 13989 Bruttes weoren særi [*v.r.* sori] for swulchere isihðe. **1297** R. GLOUC. (Rolls) 7051 Þer uore þe king uor is deþ þe soriore was. **1375** BARBOUR *Bruce* II. 65 He wes off his eschap sary. c **1386** CHAUCER *Pars. T.* ¶488 Envye..is sory of alle the bountees of his neighbor. c **1430** *Syr Gener.* (Roxb.) 2068 The pouer wer sory of that dooyng. c **1489** CAXTON *Sonnes of Aymon* xxiv. 515 Moche sori was thadmyrall for the dethe of margaris. a **1548** HALL *Chron.*, *Edw. IV*, 49 b, Yf any man wer sory of the duke of Burgoyns death. **1585** T. WASHINGTON tr. *Nicholay's Voy.* I. v. 4 The captaines..being very sorie for it had restored vnto him that which was taken. **1654–66** EARL ORRERY *Parthen.* (1676) 776, I was sorry at his Death. **1806** *Ann. Rev.* IV. 202 We are sorry at observing references to Bryant. **1879** GLADSTONE *Glean.* II. iii. 168 Much more I am sorrier for my good knight's loss.

(*b*) c **1375** *Cursor M.* 12433 (Fairf.), Ioseph..was ful sary for þe childe. **1484** CAXTON *Fables of Poge* xi, Allas, sayd the mayde, I am sory for yow. **1592** KYD *Span. Trag.* III. v, I am in a sorte sorie for thee. **1675** J. OWEN *Indwelling Sin* xvii. (1732) 229 He considering his Condition, tells him, Alas! I am sorry for you. **1715** DE FOE *Fam. Instruct.* I. iv. (1841) I. 86 Well Sister, I am sorry for you. **1827** SCOTT *Chron. Canongate* iv, The house was old and dilapidated, and looked sorry for itself. **1882** MISS BRADDON *Mt. Royal* I. vi. 157, I think we all feel sorrier for him than for many a better man.

b. With substantive clause.

c **1290** *S. Eng. Leg.* I. 222 Þis monekes..sori were & wroþe ynouȝ, þat we hadde so longe ibeo. **13..** *K. Alis.* 6140 (Laud MS.), Þe kyng was sory..þat he ne miȝth ȝiue hem bataile. c **1385** CHAUCER *L.G.W.* 1082 *Dido*, [She] seyde..that sche sory was That he hath had swych peryl. a **1400–50** *Alexander* 665, I am sary..at þi fourme Is lickenand on na lym..to my selfe. a **1548** HALL *Chron.*, *Hen. V*, 47 b, I am somwhat sory that kyng Henries seruantes of the seller made not maister Enguerant drinke. **1567–8** ABP. PARKER *Corr.* (Parker Soc.) 310 But I am sorry he can so soon conceive displeasantly against me. **1663** S. PATRICK *Parab. Pilgr.* xxxi. (1687) 371 Very sorry they were that it was not possible for them always to accompany him. **1673** DRYDEN *Marr. à la Mode* IV. i, I am sorry we shall not have one course together at the herd. **1797** MRS. A. M. BENNETT *Beggar Girl* (1813) II. 101 She was..sorry Dr. Cameron objected to her maternal arrangements. **1891** FARRAR *Darkn. & Dawn* lviii, I am sorry..that the Emperor's commands admit of no such delay.

c. With infinitive.

1390 GOWER *Conf.* I. 353 Of this aventure..Min herte is sory forto hiere. **1535** STARKEY *Let.* in *England* (1878) p. xix, For sory hys hyghnes wold be to see you not to reche vn-to so manyfest a truthe. **1555** EDEN *Decades* (Arb.) 53 They are sory to occupie the whyppe yf thou mightest otherwyse bee brought to obedience. **1670** LADY M. BERTIE in *12th Rep. Hist. MSS. Comm.* App. V. 21, I am very sorry to heare that the small pox increase. **1769** *Junius Lett.* iii. (1788) 47, I am sorry to tell you..that, in this article, your first fact is false. **1782** MISS BURNEY *Cecilia* VIII. ii, I shall not be sorry to hear it. c **1835** SYD. SMITH *Let. on Sir J. Mackintosh* Wks. 1859 II. 302/1, I am sorry to say I have none to send you. **1861** J. PYCROFT *Agony Point* (1862) 419 There were not a few little ways and snuggeries that they felt sorry to be about to leave.

†**3.** Expressive or suggestive of distress or sorrow.

Beowulf 2447 Þonne he ᵹyd wrece, sariᵹne sang. c **1000** *Ags. Psalter* (Thorpe) lv. 7 Ic..sette on ðinre ᵹesyhðe sariᵹe tearas. **13..** *Cursor M.* 15169 (Gött.), Mani sari sigh..sank tille his herte. c **1386** CHAUCER *Pars. T.* ¶315 Yf he ne hade pitee of mannes soule, a sory song we myght all synge. **1388** WYCLIF *Gen.* xl. 7 Whi is ȝoure face soriere to dai than it ys wont? **1390** GOWER *Conf.* I. 115 With sobbinge and with sory teres This lord goth thanne an humble pas. **1561** NORTON & SACKV. *Gorboduc* IV. ii, But what doth meane The sory chere of her that here doth come? **1567** *Gude & Godlie B.* (S.T.S.) 89 Quhen sall my hart ceis of this sorie sang?

†**4.** Causing distress or sorrow; painful, grievous, dismal. *Obs.*

a **1225** *Ancr. R.* 110 Þe stiche of sori & seoruhful pine. c **1250** *Gen. & Ex.* 1974 Ðo iacob saȝ dat sori writ, He gret. **1297** R. GLOUC. (Rolls) 7296 Þere hii smite to gadere, & made a sori pley. a **1300** *Cursor M.* 2922 Þat sari sight was on to se. c **1350** *Will. Palerne* 3696 So þroli a sori þouȝt þirled min hert. **1390** GOWER *Conf.* II. 47 Thus was the hors in sori plit. a **1400** *King & Hermit* 191, I ne hade neuer so sory a dey, That i ne had a mery nyȝt. c **1450** *St. Cuthbert* (Surtees) 6754 Halfdene kyng of danmarke Made in England sary warke. **1513** DOUGLAS *Æneid* III. iv. 13 The fluid of Stix, that sory place. **1575** GASCOIGNE *Herbes* Wks. (1587) 163, I must indite A wofull case, a chip of sorie chance. **1605** SHAKS. *Macb.* II. ii. 19 This is a sorry sight. *Lady.* A foolish thought, to say a sorry sight.

5. Vile, wretched, worthless, mean, poor; of little account or value: **a.** Of persons, (*a*) in general character or (*b*) in some special respect.

(*a*) c **1250** *Gen. & Ex.* 1074 Ðo sori wrecches of yuel blod wulden him ðor gret strengðe don. c **1325** *Body & Soul* 96 in *Map's Poems* (Camden) 348 Hy shal..tholien harde pinen wyth that sory Judas. c **1380** *Sir Ferumb.* 1252 'Rest,' quaþ sche, 'þow sory wyȝt, god ȝyue yuele chaunce!' a **1400–50** *Alexander* 4417 Loo, sary sottis, slike a sowme of synnars ȝe lufe! c **1500** *Birched Sch.-boy* in *Babees Bk.* (1868) 404 My master lokith as he were madde: 'wher hast thou be, thow sory ladde?' **1560** DAUS tr. *Sleidane's Comm.* 38 What a shame it were..to swarve from that religion..at the motion of a sory Frere. **1579** FULKE *Heskins' Parl.* 445 There is..one sorie boy, that helpeth yᵉ priest to Masse. **1624** GATAKER *Transubst.* 102 Whom they themselves account to be but a sorry obscure fellow. **1673** CAVE *Prim. Chr.* I. iii. 49 The Christians were such a sorry inconsiderable people. **1748** RICHARDSON *Clarissa* (1811) III. 66 Continue Esquire. It is a respectable addition, although every sorry fellow assumes it! **1856** EMERSON *Eng. Traits, Aristocracy* Wks. (Bohn) II. 85 The baron..grew fat and wanton, and a sorry brute. **1886** *Athenæum* 30 Oct. 562/2 His hero is a sorry knave, without principle or rectitude.

(*b*) a **1425** *Cursor M.* 19199 (Trin.), Seruauntis elles be we sory. c **1555** HARPSFIELD *Divorce Hen. VIII* (Camden) 170 A dialogue between a sorry doting divine and a sorry lewd lawyer. **1597** GERARDE *Herbal* II. clxxxvii. §2. 501 A poore sorie Barbar, who had no more skill than he had learned by tradition. **1652–62** HEYLYN *Cosmogr.* II. (1682) 104 A sorry Gainer by the undertaking. **1680** W. ALLEN *Peace & Unity* 81 We know what sorry Saints many of them appear to be. **1706** E. WARD *Wooden World Diss.* (1708) 10 Tho' he's but a very sorry Horse-man, yet he's mightily given to the Chase. **1835** MARRYAT *J. Faithful* xxi, I shall prove but a sorry sweetheart, for I never made love in my life. **1875** JOWETT *Plato* (ed. 2) I. 155, I am a sorry physician, and do but aggravate a disorder which I am seeking to cure.

b. Of things.

a **1300** *Cursor M.* 807 Þe find..said within his sari thoght, 'Ic haue him don to suinc for noght'. **1396–7** in *Eng. Hist. Rev.* (1907) XXII. 296 Pride with his sori genealogie of dedly synnes. c **1450** LOVELICH *Grail* lv. 326 For ho-so entreth in to this place, he may ben siker of sory grace. c **1450** *Knt. de la Tour* (1868) 33 Sori loue haue she that tellithe not the name of hym that last praied her. **1530** PALSGR. 209 Cosshe, a sorie house, *cauerne*. **1565** STAPLETON *Fortr. Faith* 90 It is not inough to make a few sory surmises. **1621** in Foster *Eng. Factories Ind.* (1906) I. 339 A sorrie some for a Governour to borrowe. **1656** JEANES *Mixt. Schol. Div.* 8 Thus, you see, that the feare of men hath..a poore, a sorry, and contemptible object. **1716–8** LADY M. W. MONTAGU *Lett.* I. xviii. 58 It is very good luck to get one sorry room in a miserable tavern. **1771** MACKENZIE *Man Feel.* xiv, I was forced to beg my bread; and a sorry trade I found it. **1825** WATERTON *Wand. S. Amer.* (1882) 163 It makes the historian cut a sorry figure. **1849** MISS MULOCK *Ogilvies* iii, That she now wrote the sorriest hand imaginable. **1889** GRETTON *Memory's Harkback* 153 You can put up with a sorry lodging for yourself, but beware of a bad stable for your steed.

c. Of animals, esp. horses.

c **1480** HENRYSON *Fables, Lion & Mouse* xiii, Unhailsum meit is of ane sarie Mous. **1500–20** DUNBAR *Poems* lv. 18 Sum..Ar now maid tame lyk ony lammis, And settin down lyk sarye crockis. **1523** FITZHERB. *Husb.* §38 Than mayst thou take thy sory weyke ewe awaye, and put her in an other place. **1547** SALESBURY, *Oenyn*, a sory lambe. **1673** CAVE *Prim. Chr.* I. i. 12 Trampled on by the sorriest Creatures, Mice, Swallows, &c. **1742** HUME *Ess.* (1870) xxiii. 158 One man, with a couple of sorry horses. **1760** STERNE *Tr. Shandy* I. x, Mounted..upon a lean, sorry, jack-ass of a horse. **1802** MAR. EDGEWORTH *Moral T.* (1816) I. xi. 92 Sir P. staked his handsome horse against A.'s sorry poney. **1849** E. E. NAPIER *Excur. S. Africa* I. 290 Mounted on very sorry hacks. **1875** COMTE DE PARIS *Civil War Amer.* I. 295 The sorrier the horses the greater the consumption.

6. As *sb.* An exclamation of '(I am) sorry'.

1834 MAR. EDGEWORTH *Helen* xxxv, A too fast hazarded broadside of questions and answers—glads and sorrys in chain-shots that did no execution.

7. *Comb.*, as *sorry-flowered*, *-hearted*, *-looking*. **sorry-go-round** [after MERRY-GO-ROUND: cf. †MERRY-GO-SORRY], a depressing cycle of events.

1382 WYCLIF *Prov.* vii. 7, I beholde the sori hertid ȝunge man. *Ibid.* ix. 17 And to the sory hertid she spac [etc.]. **1786** ABERCROMBIE *Arr.* 51 in *Gard. Assist.*, Miserable, or sorry-flowered [aster]. **1844** LD. HOUGHTON *Poems of Many Years* 242 Without a wish for rest or friends, a sorry-hearted man. **1872** 'MARK TWAIN' *Roughing It* v. 48 The cayote is a..sorry-looking skeleton. **1903** *Daily Chron.* 10 June 9/3 A mangy and altogether sorry-looking object. **1959** V. NABOKOV *Nabokov's Dozen* 1 The blurred Mount St. George..on the picture postcards which since 1910..have been courting the tourist from the sorry-go-round of their prop, among..lumps of rock and..sea shells. **1964** *Punch* 29 Apr. 630/1 It was time to stop the 'sorry-go-round' of inflation.

†**'sorry**, *v.* *Obs.* [f. prec. Cf. OE. *sárᵹian.*] *intr.* To grieve, to sorrow; to provide *for*.

1545 ASCHAM *Toxoph.* (Arb.) 42 If he complayne, they sory with hym. **1553** T. WILSON *Rhet.* 71 b, We rejoyce, we sorie, or we pitie an other mannes happe. **1601** J. WHEELER *Treat Comm.* 57 That those who are traders may be equally and indifferently cared and soried for. **1606** FORD *Fame's Memorial* G iij b, We mourne his death and sorry for his sake.

sorry ('sɒrɪ, 'sʌrɪ), *sb.* *Midlands* and *north dial.* Also **sorrey.** [Var. SIRRAH: cf. SIRREE.] A term of address (now expressing familiarity) for a man or boy.

a **1796** S. PEGGE *Derbycisms* (1896) 65 *Sorry*,..sirrah; in speaking to a boy or lad. **1913** D. H. LAWRENCE *Sons & Lovers* ii. 31 'Shall ter finish, Sorry?' cried Barker, his fellow butty. **1965** BROPHY & PARTRIDGE *Long Trail* 183 *Sorry*, mate, pal, chum. Usually in vocative and chiefly among Yorkshire and Lancashire troops. **1977** SCOLLINS & TITFORD *Ey up, mi Duck!* II. 56 *Sorrey*, the local version of the traditional term 'sirrah'... Nowadays, a term of familiarity, as in: 'Eh up, *sorrey*! Aah's it gooin?' Towards Nottingham the pronunciation sometimes approximates more to 'Surrey'.

'sorryish, *a.* [f. SORRY *a.*] Somewhat sorry.

1793 ANNA SEWARD *Lett.* (1811) III. 330 You would be sorryish to hear, that poor Moll Cobb..is gone to her long home. **1853** G. J. CAYLEY *Las Alforjas* I. 241 The bride-groom..was a sorryish looking individual. **1863** READE *Hard Cash* III. 27 To be sure their idols were sorryish clay, to begin.

†**sorry-mood**, *a.* *Obs.* [OE. *sáriᵹmód*, = OS. *sêragmôd*: see SORRY *a.* and MOOD *sb.*¹] Sorrowful, sad.

Beowulf 2942 Frofor eft ᵹelamp sariᵹmodum. a **1023** WULFSTAN *Hom.* (1883) 133 Sorhful and sariᵹmod ᵹeomriᵹendum mode. c **1205** LAY. 29791 Þa wes he sari-mod and sorhful an heorten. c **1275** *Passion our Lord* 298 in *O.E. Misc.*, [When] Peter..vnder-stod Hwat his louerd hedde iseyd, he wes sori-mod.

†**sort**, *sb.*¹ *Obs.* Also 4–5 **soort**, 5–6 **sorte**. [a. OF. *sort* (mod.F. *sort*, = It. and Pg. *sorte*, Sp. *suerte*), or ad. L. *sort-*, *sors* lot, share, fortune, condition, etc. Cf. next.]

1. a. With possessive pronoun: The fate or lot of a particular person or persons.

c **1250** *Gen. & Ex.* 1186 Abimalech..sente after abraham .., And bi-taȝte him his wif a-non, And his yuel sort was ouer-gon. c **1374** CHAUCER *Troylus* 1754 O lord, right now renneth my sort Fully to dye, or han anoon comfort. **1412–20** LYDG. *Chron. Troy* v. 2643 Ageyn my sort me list not maligne. c **1450** *Merlin* ii. 36 Ye thought to sle hym, be the whiche ye sholde be brought to the deth as be youre sorte. c **1500** *Lancelot* 26 So be such meine fatit was my sort.

b. In more general sense: Destiny, hap, fate, fortune.

c **1386** CHAUCER *Prol.* 844 Anon to drawen every wight began,.. Were it by aventure, or sort, or cas, The soth is this, the cut fil to the knight. c **1450** *St. Cuthbert* (Surtees) 5915 It fell aftir be happe and sort. **1581** MARBECK *Bk. of Notes* 880 That the sorts & lots which appeare most subject to fortune goe so forth by his providence.

2. = LOT *sb.* 1.

13.. *E.E. Allit. P.* C. 193 Sone haf þay her sortes sette & serelych deled, & ay þe lote..lymped on Ionas. **1606** SHAKS. *Tr. & Cr.* I. iii. 376 Make a Lott'ry, And by deuice let blockish Aiax draw The sort to fight with Hector.

b. The casting or drawing of lots; divination by this means. Chiefly in phr. *by sort*, = LOT *sb.* 1 b.

c **1386** CHAUCER *Pars. T.* ¶605 What seye we of hem that bilieven on divinailes, as by flight or by nois of briddes.., or by sort, by geomancie [etc.]? a **1470** HARDING *Chron.* LXVII. ii, Engist and Horsus,..By sort sent out all voyde of Saxonye. **1483** CAXTON *Cato* F j, Thou oughtest not to enquyre by sorte or wytche crafte of that that god wyl doo. c **1500** *Melusine* 110 Ne also sort or enchauntment of art Magique..shul not lette ne greve you. **1525** LD. BERNERS *Froiss.* II. 651 A generall fame..ran vpon her, that all the infyrmiteis the kyng had..came all by hir sortes and artes.

c. The choice resulting from such a casting of lots, = LOT *sb.* 1 c. *rare.*

1382 WYCLIF *Ezek.* xxiv. 6 Woo to the citee of blodis..; soort, or lot, felle not vpon it. —— *Luke* i. 5 Ther was sum prest, Zacharie by name,..of the sort of Abia. **1563–7** BUCHANAN *Reform. St. Andros* Wks. (S.T.S.) 10 That God ..wald send the sort apon hym that war habliast to exerce that estat to hys glore.

3. That which is allotted or assigned; a share or portion. *rare.*

1382 WYCLIF *Josh.* xvii. 18 Thow shalt not haue o soort, but thow shalt passe to the hil. —— *Acts* viii. 21 Part is not to thee, nethir sort, in this word. **1483** CAXTON *Gold. Leg.* 284 b/2 The men took wyues of theyr lignage only, that was by cause the distribucion of the sortes shold not be confounded.

sort (sɔːt), *sb.*[2] Also 4–6 soort, 5 soorte, 5–7 sorte, 5 sortt, sorth. [a. OF. *sorte* (mod.F. *sorte*, = It. *sorta*):—pop. L. **sorta*, alteration of L. *sort-*, *sors*: see prec. Cf. MLG. and G. *sorte*, WFris. *soarte*, Du. *soort*, Da. and Sw. *sort.*]

I. A kind, species, variety, or description of persons or things.

* *Preceded by 'of'.*

1. a. ***of a*** (certain) ***sort***, of a certain kind, etc.
c **1380** WYCLIF *Serm.* Sel. Wks. I. 392 Al þe folk of þis soort is a world þat shal be dampned. **1390** GOWER *Conf.* I. 64 Ther ben lovers of such a sort, That feignen hem an humble port. *c* **1420** LYDG. *Assembly of Gods* 672 What pepyll they were that came to that dysport I shall yow declare of many a sondry sort. **1482** in *Eng. Hist. Rev.* XXV. 122 For every quayre of yᵉ secounde soorte.. he shalle haue viij d. **1545** *Rates of Custome House* b ij b, Fysche of the smalliste sorte. **1574** tr. *Marlorat's Apocalips* 113 The things that are red euery where in the Psalmes and prophets: of which sorte bee these sayings. *a* **1628** PRESTON *New Cov.* (1634) 133 They be not all of one sort, but of divers sorts, some of one sort, some of another sort, but they are all vessels of glory. **1681** DRYDEN *Abs. & Achit.* 682 Surrounded thus with friends of every sort, Deluded Absalom forsakes the court. **1722** DE FOE *Relig. Courtsh.* I. i. (1840) 13, I hope your girls are not of that sort. **1787** MME. D'ARBLAY *Diary* 16 Aug., The moment a topic of that solemn sort is started. **1816** J. SMITH *Panorama Sci. & Art* II. 284 It gives a considerable shock, but has little power of any other sort. **1841** THACKERAY *Gt. Hoggarty Diam.* xiii, Both your son and your daughter-in-law.. are of that uncommon sort. **1875** JOWETT *Plato* (ed. 2) V. 8 He should have a fear of the right sort, as well as a courage of the right sort.

b. ***of*** (various) ***sorts***. (With numerals, etc.)
1459 *Paston Lett.* I. 472, ij. quartelettes, of dyvers sortes. **1482** in *Eng. Hist. Rev.* XXV. 122 Which Bookes bene of iiij. dyuerse manere of soortes. **1519** *Registr. Aberdon.* (Maitl. Cl.) II. 175 Item iiij cusseins of nedyll werk of þre syndry sortis. **1548** TURNER *Names Herbes* (E.D.S.) 24 Centaurium is of two sortes. **1582** HAKLUYT *Divers Voy.* G ij b, An innumerable sort of wilde foule of all sortes. **1651** HOBBES *Leviath.* II. xxiii. 125 Controversies are of two sorts, namely, of Fact and of Law. **1711** ADDISON *Spect.* No. 92 ¶6 Plays of all Sorts have their several Advocates. **1765** *Ann. Reg.* 158 He had.. 33 pegging-awls, 37 awls of other sorts. **1811** WORDSW. in *Mem.* (1851) I. 410 Physical enginery of all sorts. **1843** *Penny Cycl.* XXV. 424/2 The rosettes are of two sorts, fixed and shifting.

2. a. Used of persons, with special reference to character, disposition, or rank. (Cf. 11 b.)
c **1386** CHAUCER *Cook's T.* 17 [He] gadred him a meyne of his sort, To hoppe and synge. *a* **1533** LD. BERNERS *Huon* li. 170 A companyon of your owne sort haue yᵉ founde. **1581** PETTIE tr. *Guazzo's Civ. Conv.* I. (1586) 4 These are for the most part men of good calling, and not of the common sort. **1590** SHAKS. *Mids. N.* III. ii. 159 None of nobler sort Would so offend a Virgin. **1621** ELSING *Debates Ho. Lords* (Camden) 63 For that he hathe made so clere and ingenuous confession, which men of his sorte doe not. **1635** R. N. tr. *Camden's Hist. Eliz.* IV. 409 This Hacket was a man of vulgar sort. **1722** DE FOE *Plague* (1754) 46 Persons of good Sort and Credit. **1749** CHESTERF. *Lett.* ccvii. (1792) II. 289 Worse dressed than people of your sort are. **1781** COWPER *Retirem.* 716 The mind.. Should turn to writers of an abler sort. **1822** SHELLEY *Faust* II. 222 They are too mad for people of my sort.

†**b.** Hence ***of sort***, of (high) quality or rank.
1603 SHAKS. *Meas. for M.* IV. iv. 20 Giue notice to such men of sort and suite as are to meete him. **1606** WARNER *Alb. Eng.* XVI. ci. (1612) 401 For things in some vnseemly are not such to some of Sort. **1624** CAPT. SMITH *Virginia* (1629) 106 His Lordship arrived.., accompanied with Sir Ferdinando Waynman.. and divers other gentlemen of sort.

3. a. ***of a sort***, of the same kind or description. Now *dial.* (also ***of sort***).
1463 *Bury Wills* (Camden) 23, ij lowe candylstikkez of a sorth. **1672** TEMPLE *Ess.*, *Governm.* Wks. 1720 I. 95 The same Countries have generally in all times been used to Forms of Government much of a sort. *a* **1715** BURNET *Own Time* (1766) I. 46 They were men all of a sort. **1839** SIR G. C. LEWIS *Gloss. Heref.* s.v., 'A thing of sort' means a corresponding thing. **1876** BOUND *Prov. Shropsh.*

b. In suggestive use: ***a word of a sort***, a sharp or angry word or reproof. *rare.*
1796 MRS. M. ROBINSON *Angelina* II. 39, I should have given him a word of a sort, I promise you. **1839** SIR G. C. LEWIS *Gloss. Heref.* s.v., 'Words of a sort' means a quarrel.

4. ***of sorts***: **a.** Of different or various kinds. Now *rare.*
1597 in P. H. Hore *Hist. Wexford* (1900) I. 282, 6 yards Canikin, 18 hatts of sorts. **1599** SHAKS. *Hen. V*, I. ii. 190 They [*sc.* bees] haue a King, and Officers of sorts. **1825** T. HOOK *Sayings* Ser. II. *Passion & Princ.* xi. III. 249 At this moment cheeses of sorts were paraded. *c* **1850** *Rudim. Navig.* (Weale) 135 *Nails of sorts* are 4, 6, 8, 10, 24, 30, and 40-penny nails, all of different lengths.. for nailing board, &c.

b. *colloq.* In disparaging use: Of a kind which is not very satisfactory; rather poor. Also without marked disparagement: of some (untypical or unusual) kind, not having the usual characteristics, equipment, facilities, etc.
1902 *Daily Chron.* 20 May 4/6 In the old days Spain provided an outlet of sorts. **1903** MCNEILL *Egregious English* 91 Up to this time you have been an orator of sorts. **1946** D. GWYNN *Bishop Challoner* x. 155 In the Midlands the Franciscans had a school of sorts at Edgbaston. **1959** N. MARSH *False Scent* (1960) i. 21 There's a party of sorts at half-past which I hope may amuse you. **1972** *Times Lit. Suppl.* 4 Aug. 909/4 (Advt.), He is a poetic eye, a visionary of sorts. **1973** *Times* 18 May 22/7 During the Second World War he was a soldier of sorts (he even rose from the ranks).

5. ***something of the sort***, something similar to that previously indicated, mentioned, or specified. ***nothing of the sort***, no such thing.
1839 FR. A. KEMBLE *Resid. in Georgia* (1863) 91 Something of the sort must be done. **1869** MARTINEAU *Ess.* II. 120 Spinoza does nothing of the sort. **1895** *Law Times Rep.* LXXIII. 692/1 With regard to the.. estate in England I disclaim, but I do nothing of the sort as regards the.. estate in America.

** *Followed by 'of'.*

6. a. A particular kind, etc., *of* thing(s) or person(s).
sing. **1529** MORE *Suppl. Souls* Wks. 329/1 Let vs now see whether sort of these twayn might take most harme. **1560** DAUS tr. *Sleidane's Comm.* 63, I knowe that sorte of men ryght well. **1632** LITHGOW *Trav.* III. 102 These Cloysters haue a brauer life.. than any sort of Friers can elsewhere find. **1671** MILTON *Samson* 1323 Have they not.. ev'ry sort Of Gymnic Artists, Wrestlers, Riders, Runners? **1737** BRACKEN *Farriery Impr.* (1757) II. 99 Hay well laid in is the only sort of Fodder for our Horses. **1779** *Mirror* No. 61, From the same sort of feeling has the idea of Home its attraction. **1818** CRUISE *Digest* (ed. 2) III. 478 The second sort of prescription is that which arises from the several statutes of limitation. **1865** TROLLOPE *Belton Est.* xvi. 189 A fair specimen of the sort of letter they ought not to write. **1885** *Truth* 28 May 854/2 He does not appear to be the sort of horse to stand much knocking about.
pl. **1526** *Pilgr. Perf.* (W. de W. 1531) 14 b, These two sortes of the chyldren of Israel. **1590** SIR J. SMYTH *Disc. Weapons* 7 That those sorts of weapons.. may be more readilie.. drawne out. **1656** HAMMOND *Leah & Rachel* (1844) 13 The rivers afford innumerable sortes of choyce fish. **1670** LADY M. BERTIE in *12th Rep. Hist. MSS. Comm.* App. V. 21 The under pettycoatt very richly laced with two or three sorts of lace. **1725** *Fam. Dict.* s.v. *Aristolochy*, There are four sorts of Aristolochies. **1825** T. HOOK *Sayings* Ser. II. *Passion & Princ.* vi, He.. did an infinity of those sorts of things which were not professionally required of him.

b. ***all sorts of*** (things or persons), = 'things or persons of all kinds or descriptions'. (Cf. 7 c.)
1558 WARDE tr. *Alexis' Secr.* 33 b, Take of.. al sortes of Mirabolanes. **1584** R. SCOT *Discov. Witchcr.* II. x. (1886) 27 All sorts of writers,.. learned and unlearned. **1603** *Reg. Mag. Sig. Scot.* 514/1 Ilk hors laid of fische, flesche, cornis and all sortis of viveris. **1687** A. LOVELL tr. *Thevenot's Trav.* I. 143 All sorts of things are sold in this street. **1700** DRYDEN tr. *Ovid's Metam.* XIII. *Acis, Pol. & Gal.* 136 All sorts of Ven'son; and of Birds the best. **1781** T. GILBERT *Plan for Relief Poor* 6 Workhouses are generally inhabited by all Sorts of Persons. **1860** HOLLAND *Miss Gilbert's Career* i. 9 They answered.. to all sorts of questions in geography. **1891** H. HERMAN *His Angel* 238 I've been buying frocks and all sorts of things these days past.
ellipt. **1597** J. KING *On Jonas* (1618) Ep. Ded., Let it receiue favovrable interpretation with all sorts men.

c. With distinguishing adjs. or attrib. phrases.
1590 SIR J. SMYTH *Disc. Weapons* Ded., Others of the most dispost and lustie sort of people of our Nation. **1615** G. SANDYS *Trav.* 120 A number of sheepe; which.. they distribute vnto their slaues and poorer sort of people. **1676** GLANVILL *Ess. Philos. & Relig.* IV. 12 By leaving this whole unintelligible sort of beings out of its accounts. **1705** HEARNE *Collect.* 16 Aug. (O.H.S.) I. 30 Mr. Rymer.. is a very good sort of Man. **1798** CHARLOTTE SMITH *Yng. Philos.* I. 207, I have been tired of such John Trott sort of prosing ever since I was ten years old. **1836** *Backwoods of Canada* 123 We begin to get reconciled to our Robinson Crusoe sort of life. **1861** M. PATTISON *Ess.* (1889) I. 45 A vine or two and some of the finer sorts of fruit. **1885** G. ALLEN *Babylon* xxxviii, Cecca was really not a bad sort of girl.

7. Used collectively: **a.** With *these* or *those*.
1551 RECORDE *Cast. Knowl.* (1556) 86 These sort of people are named of the greke Cosmographers.. Heteroscij. **1563** GOLDING *Cæsar* 76 A great multitude.. of those sorte of rascals whom hope of spoile.. had wythdrawen from husbandrye. **1671** PHILLIPS (ed. 3), *Inchoatives*, in Grammar are those sort of Verbs which express a gradual proceeding in any action. **1691** W. NICHOLS *Answ. Naked Gospel* 15, I do not think we are so much credulous, as these sort of Gentlemen are saucy. **1718** *Entertainer* No. 14. 94 These sort of Mortals are generally.. prepossess'd with a good opinion of themselves. **1798** CHARLOTTE SMITH *Yng. Philos.* II. 29 These sort of details gave my poor father great delight. **1814** SYD. SMITH in Lady Holland *Mem.* (1855) II. 113, I rather suppose it is too far from town for these sort of engagements. **1857** TROLLOPE *Barchester T.* xxxiv, 'Those sort of rules are all gone by now,' said Mr. Arabin. **1872** RUSKIN *Fors Clav.* xxi. 19 What?.. do those sort of people know what love is?

b. With plural verbs or pronouns. Now *rare.*
1568 GRAFTON *Chron.* II. 99 The yonger sort of yᵉ Monkes there gathered themselues together at midnight. **1632** LITHGOW *Trav.* v. 206 The best sort of Mahometans.. call themselues Musilmans. **1647** F. BLAND *Souldiers March* 36 There are yet another sort of Enemies [etc.]. *c* **1671** LOCKE in Ld. King *Life* (1830) II. 284 There are a sort of propositions, passing under the title of maxims. **1704** N. N. tr. *Boccalini's Advts. fr. Parnass.* III. 227 They thought such sort of Showes were not fit to be seen. **1769** BURKE *Obs. late State Nation* 119 There are a sort of middle tints and shades between the two extremes. **1804–6** SYD. SMITH *Mor. Philos.* (1850) 110 Such sort of questions.. are not merely innocent subtleties.

c. With *all.* (Cf. 6 b.) Now *rare* or *Obs.*
1594 R. ASHLEY tr. *Loys de Roy* 10 b, The countrie.. aboundeth with all sort of corne, flesh, and fruit. **1603** *Reg. Mag. Sig. Scot.* 514/2 For mettage of all sort of victuall sauld or mett within the said burgh. **1641** TOMBES *Leaven Phar. Wil-worship* (1643) 14 Al sort of erroneous teachers, and licentious livers, were tolerated. **1709** MRS. MANLEY *Secret Mem.* (1720) III. 121 With all Sort of Address, and artful seeming Sincerity. **1771** T. HULL *Sir W. Harrington* (1797) I. 42 The earl.. has thought fit to drop all sort of correspondence with me. **1804** ANNA SEWARD *Mem. Darwin* 5 He.. supplied their necessities by food, and all sort of charitable assistance.

†**d.** With numerals or partitives. *Obs.*
1594 NASHE *Dido* 1381 Wks. (Grosart) VI. 62 A garden where are.. Musk-roses, and a thousand sort of flowers. **1732** ARBUTHNOT *Rules of Diet* in *Aliments*, etc. (1735) 261 The Nature of most sort of animal Diet may be discovered by Taste and other sensible Qualities.

8. a. In the phr. ***a sort of***.., denoting that some thing, person, quality, etc., is, or may be, included in the specified class, although not typical of it or possessing all its characteristics; = 'something in the nature of'. Cf. KIND *sb.* 14 c.
1703 DE FOE in *15th Rep. Hist. MSS. Comm.* App. IV. 62 Fleeing from her Majesty's justice is a sort of making war against her. **1726** SWIFT *Gulliver* Introd. Let., They use a sort of jabber, and do not go naked. **1780** *Mirror* No. 110, There is a sort of classic privilege in the very names of places in London. **1819** SCOTT *Ivanhoe* i, His legs were cased in a sort of gaiters. **1845** M. PATTISON *Ess.* (1889) I. 14 A moral power.. forcing from them a sort of recognition of its claims. **1853** Sorter [see JACK-LEG, JACKLEG *a.* and *sb.*]. **1884** W. C. SMITH *Kildrostan* 69 We are grown To be a sort of dandies in religion.

b. So ***a*** (or ***some***) ***sort of a***...
1720 SHADWELL *Hasty Wedding* II. iv, I do think him but a sort of a, kind of a,.. sort of a Gentleman. **1766** C. BEATTY *Tour* (1768) 28 We.. put up at some sort of a public house. **1823** SCOTT *Quentin D.* xxxi, The richest heiress in Burgundy has confessed a sort of a—what was I going to say? **1846–9** S. R. MAITLAND *Ess.*, etc. 47 Bishop Burnet is even kind enough to make a sort of an excuse for Sir Thomas More.

c. (*a*) ***sort of, o', a, sorter***, used adverbially: In a way or manner; to some extent or degree, somewhat; in some way, somehow. Hence passing into use as a parenthetic qualifier expressing hesitation, diffidence, or the like, on the speaker's part; also (only in the full form *sort of*) following the statement it qualifies. Chiefly *dial.* and *colloq.*
1790 MRS. WHEELER *Westmld. Dial.* (1821) 63 Its a fine ewnin but its a sort a caad. **1839** MARRYAT *Diary Amer.* Ser. I. II. 218, I bees a sorter courted, and a sorter not; reckon more a sorter yes than a sorter no. **1858** PIRIE *Inq. Hum. Mind* i. 10 One is a sort of bewildered in attempting to discover what it really is which constitutes the obligation. **1833** J. HALL *Legends West* 50 It sort o' stirs one up to hear about old times. **1858** HUGHES *Scour. White Horse* ii. 34 He was sort of proud of them. **1870** B. HARTE *Luck of Roaring Camp* 11 The rosewood cradle.. had, in Stumpy's way of putting it, 'sorter killed the rest of the furniture'.
1903 G. B. SHAW *Man & Superman* II. 67 I'll sort of borrow the money from my dad until I get on my own feet. **1930** A. BENNETT *Imperial Palace* lxiii. 509, I don't believe they sort of understand English people, Italians don't. **1949** *Granta* Christmas 43/2 One of us had to do a big strong man to sort of separate them. **1952** B. MALAMUD *Natural* 126, I hoped she would straighten him out and sorta hold him in the team. **1958** [see BUGGER *v.* 2 c]. **1973** *Art Internat.* Mar. 68/1, I sort of use music as a connection to more of the things I want to be about. **1976** *National Observer* (U.S.) 25 Sept. 17/1 He calls it the 'Icarus Human-Powered Aircraft.' 'It's sort of a cumbersome name.'
1923 J. MANCHON *Le Slang* 283 They hung back in their breeching sort-of, ils s'appuyaient sur l'avaloir, si je puis dire. **1952** M. LASKI *Village* xv. 206 It just happened, sort of, and we couldn't either of us help it. **1959** *Psychiatry* XXII. 293/1 Except I feel like, well, what you're doing anyway is just sitting here and saying all these things just to tease me and to taunt me, sort of. **1976** *National Observer* (U.S.) 28 Feb. 21/4 And it *is* all those things, sort of; and yet it is a really fine book.

d. ***in a sort of*** (***sorta***) ***way***, imperfectly; not exactly, absolutely, or properly.
1875 JOWETT *Plato* (ed. 2) I. 36 The impossibility of a man knowing in a sort of way that which he does not know at all. **1892** T. HARDY *Well-Beloved* I. viii, 'I advised you to go back, Marcie.' 'In a sort of way: not in the right tone.' **1967** E. & M. A. RADFORD *No Reason for Murder* xvii. 115 'He ain't a'goin' to come to life agin, guv'nor.'.. 'I dunno... Mebbe he might—in a sorta way.'

9. ***no sort of***.., used as an emphatic negative phrase to denote the complete absence of anything of the kind specified.
1736 BUTLER *Anal.* I. ii. Wks. 1874 I. 46 There is no sort of ground for being thus presumptuous. **1770** LANGHORNE *Plutarch* (1879) II. 634/2 No sort of harmony could exist between them. **1852** THACKERAY *Esmond* III. xii, The great majority had no sort of inkling of the transaction pending. **1884** *Manch. Exam.* 25 Feb. 4/7 On the part of many, the inclination to work bears no sort of proportion to the inclination to talk.

10. a. ***that*** or ***this sort of thing***, used to denote in a general way a thing, quality, etc., of a like or similar nature to that specified.
1848 THACKERAY *Van. Fair* lxv, She is very unhappy, and —and that sort of thing. *Ibid.* lxvi, 'Pooh! damn; don't let us have this sort of thing!' Jos cried out,.. anxious to get rid of a scene. **1889** JEROME *Three Men in Boat* 103, I would.. lead a blameless, beautiful life,.. and all that sort of thing.

b. ***sort of thing***, used adverbially to indicate the inexactness or indefiniteness of the preceding words. Cf. sense 8 c above. *colloq.*
1935 E. RAYMOND *We, the Accused* v. ii. 572 What he doesn't know about the law isn't worth knowing, sort of thing. **1968** *Guardian* 24 Apr. 9/2, I don't just give him a sharp slap in temper, sort of thing. **1979** A. FOX *Threat Warning Red* xi. 161 A dummy run. Only go through the motions, sort of thing.

*** *In elliptic or absolute use.*

11. a. A particular class, order, or rank of persons.
1529 MORE *Dyalogue* IV. Wks. 287/2 That man.. that would rather send his soule with such a sort as these be, than with all those holy saintes. **1572** J. JONES *Bathes of Bathes Ayde* Ep. Ded. a ij, Hieronymus Montuus.. affirmeth that

of all sortes, Phisike is to bee embraced. **1608** Dod & Cleaver *Expos. Prov.* xi–xii. 128 The one sort are led by the worde and spirit of God, .. the other are led by the flesh, and Sathan. **1667** Milton *P.L.* vi. 376 The other sort in might though wondrous.., Nameless in dark oblivion let them dwell. **1812** Miss Mitford in L'Estrange *Life* (1870) I. 172 The first sort cannot go upon a water-party but you must read an account of it in three full sheets. **1871** Legrand *Cambr. Freshm.* 295 His lordship added, .. they weren't his sort, and he should not have anything to do with 'em. **1878** Browning *Poets Croisic* 44 All sorts and conditions that stood by .. bore witness to the prophecy.

b. With defining or distinguishing adj. (usu. in the comparative). Also (in phr. ***the right sort***) with ref. to one person.

Freq. from *c* 1550 to *c* 1650; now somewhat *rare*.

1548 Turner *Names Herbes* (E.D.S.) 33 Daphnoides, called of the commune sort Laureola. **1549** Allen *Par. Revel. St. John* 11 The spirituall sort, which haue their lyuynge of the gospel, wherunto they are the most extreme enemyes, .. a thousande partes more than the secular and laye sorte. **1576** Gascoigne *Steele Gl.* (Arb.) 82 The yonger sorte, come pyping on apace, .. The elder sorte, go stately stalking on. **1611** Bible *Transl. Pref.* ¶2 This is the lot and portion of the meaner sort onely. **1655** Stanley *Hist. Philos.* i. (1687) 26/1 Laws are like Cobwebs which entangle the lesser sort, the greater break through. *a* **1715** Burnet *Own Time* (1766) I. 295 Sometimes they were fined and the younger sort whipped about the streets. **1760–2** Goldsm. *Cit. W.* xv, The better sort here pretend to the utmost compassion for animals of every kind. **1842** Mrs. Gore *Fascination* 15 You are one of the right sort. **1853** Hickie tr. *Aristoph.* (1872) II. 691 The better sort do not ask for money. *c* **1863** T. Taylor *Ticket-of-Leave Man* iii. 43 But don't look glum, Bob, you're the right sort, you are. **1883** *Daily News* 11 Sept. 3/1 A little knot of those formerly called emphatically 'the right sort'. **1914** G. B. Shaw *Fanny's First Play* i. 173 But hes the right sort: I can see that. **1936** [see right *a.* 8d].

c. So ***a*** (***bad, good,*** etc.) ***sort***, applied to a single person. *colloq.*

c **1869** Taylor & Dubourg *New Men & Old Acres* i. 10 Fanny Bunter—in spite of her Ruskinism-run-mad—isn't half a bad sort. **1875** W. Reade *Outcast* 202 Our host told us the old woman was his mother, and we musn't [*sic*] mind her being cross, she being a real good sort all the same. **1882** J. Sturgis *Dick's Wandering* III. iv. xlii. 82 They cursed and said that Dick was a good sort. **1891** C. Roberts *Adrift Amer.* 165 On the whole he was not a bad sort.

d. Proverb. ***it takes all sorts to make a world***; also ellipt. ***it takes all sorts***.

[**1620** T. Shelton tr. *Cervantes' Hist. Don Quixote* ii. vi. 34 In the world there must bee of all sorts. **1767** Johnson *Let.* 17 Nov. (1952) I. 194 The World, says Locke, has people of all sorts.] **1844** D. W. Jerrold *Story of Feather* xxviii. 161 Click can't get off this time? .. Well, it takes all sorts to make a world. **1908** K. Grahame *Wind in Willows* iv. 89 The Wild Wood is pretty well populated .. with all the usual lot, good, bad, and indifferent... It takes all sorts to make a world. **1940** [see coin *v.*[1] 5d]. **1951** E. Coxhead *One Green Bottle* i. 35 'I daresay it takes all sorts—' conceded Harry vaguely. **1965** J. Fleming *Nothing is Number when you Die* ii. iii. 68 She shrugged. 'It takes all sorts, you know.' **1975** J. I. M. Stewart *Young Pattullo* iii. 71 'My father's a banker during the week and a country gent at week-ends. Takes all sorts you know.' 'Takes all sorts?' 'To make a world.'

e. A girl or young woman; a girl-friend. (Predominantly in male use.) *slang* (orig. *Austral.*).

1933 F. Clune *Try Anything Once* 93 'Look here, George,' I said. 'Lend me a suit of civvies. I've got to meet a great little sort, and her father has a dead nark on soldiers.' **1953** T. A. G. Hungerford *Riverslake* 144 Felix came in after tea and said that his sort could come. **1968** K. Denton *Walk around my Cluttered Mind* 137 They'd told me, 'Don't worry about bringing anything except a bottle. The sorts are laid on.' Even after only ten months I understood this to mean that there would be feminine company. **1970** *Daily Progress* (Charlottesville, Va.) 7-c/3 He [*sc.* a skinhead in the U.K.] wants only to drink, go out with 'sorts', another word for girls, perhaps take pep pills or marijuana. **1972** A. Draper *Death Penalty* ii. 13 Ben .. drove .. to pick up Jeannie—his 'sort' or 'gimpy'. For that was how he described his girl friend.

12. a. A kind, variety, etc., of thing(s).

1523 Fitzherb. *Husb.* §134 Than sorte the trees, the polles by them-selfe, the myddel sorte by them-selfe. **1567** Maplet *Gr. Forest* 2 One of those sortes that is easie to engraue in. **1577** B. Googe *Heresbach's Husb.* ii. (1586) 49 Whereas the Hearbes and Trees are seuered euery sort in their due place. **1633** *Gerarde's Herbal* iii. xcv. 1448 These fiue sorts; the common, the long, .. and the early aprecocke. **1690** Locke *Hum. Und.* iii. iii. (1695) 231 Things are ranked under Names into Sorts or Species, only as they agree to certain abstract Ideas, to which we have annexed those Names. **1776** Cowper *Let.* 12 Nov., One to whom fish is so welcome .. can have no great occasion to distinguish the sorts. **1842** Loudon *Suburban Hort.* 643 According to the richness of the soil and the vigour of the sort. **1861** Dickens *Gt. Expect.* v, May you live a thousand years, and never be a worse judge of the right sort.

b. ***all sorts***, in colloquial or idiomatic uses; as *sb.*: see all E. 13.

1794 Mrs. Radcliffe *Myst. Udolpho* xxxi, There they were, all drinking Tuscany wine and all sorts. **1839** Hood *Our Village* 23 There's a shop of all sorts, that sells every thing. **1863** Mrs. Hawthorne in *N. Hawthorne & Wife* (1885) II. 331, I hope to hear about papa's visit to Rockport, and 'all sorts', as dear Mrs. Browning used to say. **1900** *Westm. Gaz.* 14 Mar. 1/3 Asking how it was possible to have complete transport in stock for an Empire of 'all sorts' like this.

13. † a. *pl.* Spices. *Obs.*$^{-1}$

1530 in Whitaker *Hist. Craven* (1812) 306 Item 2 pounds of sorts of Portugal.

b. *Typog.* One or other of the characters or letters in a fount of type. Usu. in *pl.*

1668–9 in *Cent. Typogr. Univ. Press, Oxford* (1900) 156 Then you will perceiue what sorts your worke runns most vpon and so you must cast ouer such sorts. **1683** Moxon *Mech. Exerc., Printing* 391 The Letters .. in every Box of the Case are .. called Sorts in Printers and Founders Language; Thus a is a Sort, b is a Sort. **1771** Luckombe *Hist. Print.* 248 For example, c, i, m, p, q, u, being Latin Sorts, might be more sparingly cast. **1784** Franklin in Bigelow *Life* (1881) III. 256 The founts, too, must be very scanty, or strangely out of sorts. **1808** Stower *Printers' Gram.* 54 The expense .. in casting a fount of letter with such a number of heavy sorts will be considerable. *Ibid.* 60 The upper case sorts... The lower case sorts. **1839** Hansard *Print. & Type-founding* (1841) 82 Capital letters, figures, accented letters, particular sorts, &c. **1888** Jacobi *Printers' Vocab.* 128 *Sorts*, the general term applied to any particular letter or letters as distinguished from a complete fount.

14. ***out of sorts***: **a.** Not in the usual or normal condition of good health or spirits; in a low-spirited, irritable, or peevish state, esp. through physical discomfort; slightly unwell.

1621 S. Ward *Life of Faith* 46, I wonder .. to see one .. that knowes all must worke for the best, to be at any time out of tune, or out of sorts. **1642** D. Rogers *Naaman* 98 But now .. being defeated, he is out of sorts, and chuseth rather .. to goe away, than to be cured thereby. **1702** S. Parker tr. *Cicero's De Finibus* App. 360 When our Affairs are discouraging, .. we must be at least proportionably Unhappy, and out of Sorts. **1775** Burney *Early Diary* (1889) II. 42 He was extremely out of sorts because there was some company in the room who did not please him. **1801** Ld. Cornwallis in Ld. Stanhope *Life Pitt* (1862) III. xxxi. 354, I am myself out of sorts, lowspirited, and tired of everything. **1857** Dickens *Dorrit* ii. xiii, I am weary and out of sorts to night. **1871** Napheys *Prev. & Cure Dis.* ii. i. 356 The child which is only out of sorts frets itself.

transf. **1815** Scott *Guy M.* xliv, One of the bed-posts .. was broken down, so that the tester and curtains hung forward into the middle of the narrow chamber... 'Never mind that being out o' sorts, Captain.' **1873** Browning *Red Cott. Nt.-Cap* 711 A sense that something is amiss, Something is out of sorts in the display.

b. In literal sense: Out of or without certain kinds of articles or goods. Also *transf.*

1670 Ray *Prov.* 225 Many a man .. coming home from far voyages, may chance to land here, and being out of sorts, is unable for the present time .. to recruit himself with clothes. **1675** V. Alsop *Anti-sozzo* 278 Their unhappiness is, they have not so vast a Stock to set up with, and some-times may be out of Sorts. *Ibid.* 520 He may upon these principles, coyn as many several sorts .. of justifying Faith, as he can possibly spend in seven years time; and as he grows out of sorts, he may stamp as many more.

† 15. Without article: **a.** Rank, class. *Obs.*

1671 Milton *Samson* 1608 With seats where all the Lords and each degree Of sort, might sit in order to behold.

† b. ***in sort***, in various kinds; in variety. *Obs.*

1756 Mrs. Calderwood in *Coltness Collect.* (Maitland Club) 225 As for timber things and kitchen things in sort, smith and wright work were all to sell ready made.

16. ***that's your sort*** (also dial. ***sorts***), as a term of approbation. *slang.*

1792 Holcroft *Road to Ruin* v. i, That's your sort! **1793** *European Mag.* XXIII. 307 A sly old dame, long used to scenes of sport, Cocks her one eye, and snuffles, 'That's your sort'. **1825** Jamieson *Suppl.* s.v., *That's your sorts*! an exclamation used when one is highly pleased with an action or thing. Aberd[een]. **1865** *Slang Dict.* 240 Pitch it into him, that's your sort.

II. † 17. a. A number of persons associated together in some way; a band, company, group, or set of persons (or animals). *Obs.*

In this and the next group not always clearly distinct from senses 6 and 11–12.

c **1400** *Destr. Troy* 3713 The Dukes were drounet, & oþer dere folke. All the sort þat hom suet sunkyn to ground. **1489** Skelton *Death Earl Northumbld.* 212 The heuenly yerarchy, With all the hole sorte of that glorious place. **1500–20** Dunbar *Poems* lxxvii. 46 That seimlie sort, in ordour weill besein, Did meit the quein. *a* **1547** Surrey *Æneid* iv. 276 Paris now with his unmanly sorte. **1583** Stocker *Civ. Warres Lowe C.* i. 2 One sorte of them was burnt, another sort hanged, the thirde drowned, and the fourth sorte had no more hurt but their heades cut off. **1612** W. Sclater *Sick Soul's Salve* 3 An other sort there are, and they as heavily complaine.

† b. ***in sort, on a sort***, in a body or company. ***in sort with***, in common with. *Obs.*

c **1400** *Destr. Troy* 4326 Nawther cercumsiset sothely in sort with the Jewes, Ne comyn with cristenmen. *a* **1400–50** *Alexander* 1555 All þe cite in sorte felowis him eftir. *a* **1536** *Songs, Carols*, etc. (E.E.T.S.) 106, I shall you tell a full good sport, How gossippis gader them on a sort. **1590** Shaks. *Mids. N.* iii. ii. 21 As .. russet-pated choughes, many in sort .., Seuer themselues.

c. Const. *of* (persons or animals).

Common from *c* 1520 to 1650; now *arch.*

1509 Hawes *Past. Pleasure* xxvii. (Percy Soc.) 129 To beholde so fayre and good a sorte Of goodly knyghtes. **1542** Udall *Erasm. Apoph.* 106 A sorte of young striepleynges standing about Diogenes. **1598** B. Jonson *Ev. Man in Hum.* i. v, I was requested to supper, last night, by a sort of gallants. *c* **1611** Chapman *Iliad* iv. 460 The Trojans, like a sort of ewes penn'd in a rich man's fold. **1676** *Life Father Sarpi* in *Brent's Counc. Trent* 28 In the Merchants Street there used to meet a sort of gallant and vertuous Gentlemen to recount their Intelligences, one with another. **1687** Dryden *Hind & P.* iii. 946 A sort of Doves were housed too near their hall.

1828 Scott *F.M. Perth* iv, Here are a sort of knaves breaking peace within burgh. **1865** Swinburne *Chast.* i. i. (1894) 7 What a sort of men Crowd all about the squares! **1880** Webb *Goethe's Faust* i. ii. 57 A soldier, with a sort of gallants round him.

† d. ***all the sort of*** (you, etc.), every one. *Obs.*

1535 Coverdale *Job* xvi. 1 Miserable geuers of comforte are ye, all the sorte of you. **1549** Coverdale, etc. *Erasm. Par. 1 John* 42 Traunsgressions .. doone awaye all the sorte of them by the precious blood of his sonne. **1561** T. Hoby tr. *Castiglione's Courtyer* iii. (1577) R vj b, Ye are all the sort of you too great Clearkes in loue.

† e. A collection, parcel, set, etc., *of* things.

1563 *Homilies* ii. *Agst. Parell Idol.* iii. T t iij, By the space of a sort of hundreth yeares. **1584** Peele *Arraignm. Paris* i. ii, Thou hast a sort of pretty tales in store, Dare say no nymph in Ida woods hath more. **1606** Chapman *Gent. Usher* i. i. 173, I hope youle then stand like a sort of blocks.

18. a. A (great, good, etc.) number or lot of persons or things; a considerable body or quantity; a multitude.

Common from *c* 1530 to 1600; now *dial.*

c **1475** *Mankind* 257 in *Macro Plays* 10 We xall cum euery-chon, Mo þen a goode sorte. ? **1530** Tindale *Exp. Matt.* Prol. 5 b, A great sorte are so feable þat they can nether go forwarde in theyr profession & purpose, nor yet stande. **1551** Turner *Herbal* i. I ij b, If one be set alone .. their wil a great sorte within a shorte space growe of that same roote. **1600** Holland *Livy* xxviii. xi. 676 A great sort were compelled .. to repaire againe into their country habitations. **1650** Stapylton *Strada's Low C. Wars* v. 117 A great sort were drawn in, with the tunes set to the Psalmes, translated .. into French meeter. **1796** W. H. Marshall *Yorksh.* (ed. 2) II. 346 *Sort*, many; 'a good soort', a great many. **1855** [Robinson] *Whitby Gloss.* s.v., There was a good soort there.

† b. Const. *of* (persons or things). *Obs.*

Common *c* 1550–1630, esp. of persons.

1529 More *Dyalogue* i. Wks. 106/2 Of which two thinges I coulde out of .. holy saintes workes gether a good sorte. **1535** Coverdale *Jer.* xliv. 15 All the men .. & a greate sorte off wyues that stode there. **1578** Timme *Calvin on Gen.* 60 The Lord had .. enriched him with an innumerable sorte of benefits. **1600** Abbot *Jonah* 617 Young and old, male and female of reasonable creatures, to a very great sort of thousands. **1637** R. Ashley tr. *Malvezzi's David Persecuted* 257 A great sort of men offend their God in their prosperity, and pray unto him in their adversity. **1681** W. Robertson *Phraseol. Gen.* s.v., A great sort of Ships came from all parts.

19. In the same sense as prec. without qualifying adjective. Now *dial.*

1548 in Strype *Ann. Ref.* (1824) VI. 315 If the world shal turn, A sort of you shal burn. **1564** Becon *Wks.* I. Pref. A v b, Your wisedomes see, what a sort of vnmete men labour dayly to runne hedlong vnto the ministery. **1597** Middleton *Wisd. Solomon* xiv. 26 See what a sort of rebels are in arms. **1823** E. Moor *Suffolk Words*, A sort of loads. **1825** Brockett *N.C. Gloss.*, *Sort*, a lot, a parcel, a number.

† 20. a. A (great, etc.) part or portion *of* a number of persons or things. *Obs.*

1566 Painter *Pal. Pleas.* II. 55 But the greatest soart of the litle infants were slaine out of hand. **1600** Holland *Livy* v. i, He tooke from them the very plaiers and actors, whereof a great sort were his own servants. **1632** Lithgow *Trav.* ii. 70 The greater sort of her mercenary sexe. **1669** Sturmy *Mariner's Mag., Penalties* 7 If any .. Person .. shall permit any sort of the Package therein to be opened, imbezeled, or altered.

† b. ***by a great sort***, by a great deal; by much. *Obs.*$^{-1}$

1579 J. Stubbes *Gaping Gulf* C vij, More loanes of hundred powndes, forty pounds, twenty pounds, .. then were euer payd agayn by a great sort.

III. Manner, method, or way.

21. In phrases with *in*: **a.** Qualified by demonstratives or similar words, as ***in this, that, such, (the) like, what,*** etc., ***sort***. Now *arch.*

Most of these are common from *c* 1550.

1533 Bellenden *Livy* ii. xi. (S.T.S.) I. 169 Thir tithingis movit þe faderis & commouns in diuers maner and sortis. **1560** Daus tr. *Sleidane's Comm.* 350 b, They can fynde none that wyll go in that sorte. **1577** B. Googe *Heresbach's Husb.* i. (1586) 10, I thought in the like sort the wheele of a mill myght be turned. **1601** J. Wheeler *Treat. Comm.* 75 In what sort can her Maiesty .. tolerate or suffer that [etc.]? **1670** Dryden *Conq. Granada* i. i. i, If we treat gallant strangers in this sort, Mankind will shun the inhospitable court. **1713** *Guardian* No. 1 ¶1 Not without some hope of having my Vanity .. indulged in the sort above-mentioned. **1782** Cowper *Gilpin* 93 His horse, who never in that sort Had handled been before. **1800** Wordsw. *Michael* 207 While in this sort the simple household lived From day to day. **1866** Neale *Sequences & Hymns* 11 But in other sort, that midnight round their watch-fires' blaze they feast. **1871** Freeman *Norm. Conq.* IV. xviii. 287 Stores of corn .. men brought together and destroyed in the like sort.

b. With distinguishing adj., as ***in good, honest,*** etc., ***sort***. Now *rare*. †Sometimes with *a*, *any*, *some*, *this*, etc.

(*a*) **1548** Geste *Pr. Masse* 81 Yf the signe be counterfayt and fayned, then nedes must the thing be in semblable sorte whyche is betokened. **1585** T. Washington tr. *Nicholay's Voy.* ii. v. 35, I haue not seen .. a nation .. which studieth more in all honest sorte to obtayne the fauour of straungers. **1600** Hakluyt *Voy.* (1810) III. 568 Wherein is showed in what good sort we liued with our masters. **1634** Sir T. Herbert *Trav.* 79 Hee speedily affronted the Georgians, who receiued him in warlike sort. **1657** Sparrow *Bk. Com. Prayer* (1661) 42 He which prays in due sort, is .. made the more attentive. **1713** Swift *Faggot* Wks. 1755 IV. i. 8 Stewards .. who in solemn sort Appear with slender wands at court. **1784** Cowper *Task* vi. 377 Each animal .. growl'd defiance in such angry sort, As taught him, too, to tremble in his turn. **1813** Scott *Trierm.* ii. xviii, The champions, arm'd in martial sort. **1863** Patmore *Angel in Ho.* II. i. x, According to such nuptial sort As may subsist in the holy court.

(*b*) **1592** Kyd *Sp. Trag.* ii. i. 100 Giue me notice in some secret sort. **1594** Marlowe & Nashe *Dido* i. i, To wear Their bow and quiver in this modest sort. **1642** D. Rogers *Naaman* 29 Jehoram, .. who sent a cursed messenger before him .. (met in a holy sort before God in the judgement of famine). *a* **1704** T. Brown *Two Oxford Scholars* (1730) I. 9 He did not know how to maintain himself and his family in any tolerable sort.

c. ***in some sort***, in a certain undefined or unknown way; to some extent or degree. Freq. in parenthetic use.

1556 *Aurelio & Isab.* (1608) Hiij, The ladies leaste experimentede and wittey be in some sorte the chasteste. **1597** MORLEY *Introd. Mus.* Ded., To notifie vnto your selfe in some sort the entire loue..which I beare vnto you. **1615** W. LAWSON *Country Housew. Gard.* (1626) 7 The Sunne (in some sort) is the life of the world. **1653** H. MORE *Antid. Ath.* Pref., For it is the same Numen in us that moves all things in some sort or other. **1711** STEELE *Spect.* No. 52 ¶3 Our personal Deformities in some sort by you recorded to all Posterity. **1780** *Mirror* No. 97, Having seen Paris,..she thinks that she is authorised, and, in some sort, obliged to speak French. **1865** DICKENS *Mut. Fr.* I. vi, She was named after, or in some sort related to, the Abbey at Westminster. **1894** J. T. FOWLER *Adamnan* Introd. 17 The Christian hierarchy..in some sort succeeded to the Druids and the Brehons.

d. ***in a sort***, in some sort or manner (see prec.); occas. with implication of inefficiency or inadequacy. †Also *in sort*.

1585 in *Eng. Hist. Rev.* Jan. (1913) 55 *note*, So many reasons..did in a sort work in me a confirmation [etc.]. **1592** KYD *Sp. Trag.* III. v. 17, I am in a sorte sorie for thee. *a* **1619** FOTHERBY *Atheom.* II. xi. §5 (1622) 319 Which carried him vp, in a sorte, into Heauen. *c* **1643** LD. HERBERT *Autobiog.* (1824) 62 In Law also the Judge is in a sort superior to his King. **1710** STEELE *Tatler* No. 14 ¶2 The Criminal..was always sure he stood before his Country, and in a Sort before a Parent of it. **1788** *Pict. Tour thro' Pts. Europe* 3 A garden ..wherein the enchantments of that of Armida seem in sort to be realized. **1825** SCOTT *Jrnl.* 6 Dec., H.M...shoots and fishes in a sort even to this day. **1874** BLACKIE *Self-Cult.* 72 Our only chance of becoming great in a sort is by participation in the greatness of the universe.

†**e.** ***in no sort***, in no way, to no extent, not at all. *Obs.*

1570-6 LAMBARDE *Peramb. Kent* (1826) 215 They are in no sorte to be hearde, seeing that by no means they may iustly claime any manner of right in that lande. *a* **1625** JAS. I *Ps.* xxiii. 4 Yea, though I through death's shadow walke, Yet feare I in no sort. **1676** HALE *Contempl.* I. 5 The consideration of our latter end doth in no sort make our lives the shorter. **1708** SWIFT *Sacram. Test* Wks. 1755 II. I. 131 These are, in no sort, a number to carry any point. **1756** C. LUCAS *Ess. Waters* III. 70 They will in no sort mix.

†**f.** ***in sort***, followed by *as* or *that*. *Obs.*

1548 GESTE *Pr. Masse* 83 Gelasius..impugneth the sayd transubstanciation as..uncredyble in sorte as followeth. **1594** CAREW *Huarte's Exam. Wits* vi. (1596) 84 To remaine ..affixed, in sort as the sparrowes are attached to birdlime. **1605** BACON *Adv. Learn.* II. 91 In all causes the first tale possesseth much, in sorte, that the preiudice thereby wrought will bee hardly remooued.

†**g.** ***in all sorts***, altogether, completely. *Obs.*$^{-1}$

1559 in Tytler *Hist. Scot.* (1864) III. 395 Your good mind, ..which as it is in all sorts undeserved on my side, so am I the more affected unto you therefor. **1611** COTGR., *Totalement*, totally,..throughly, in all sorts, altogether.

22. ***after this, what***, etc., ***sort, after a* (..) *sort***, in the preceding senses.

(*a*) **1551** ROBINSON tr. *More's Utopia* I. (1895) 61 After what sorte hooredome..maye be lawfull. **1569** J. SANFORD tr. *Agrippa's Van. Artes* 15 b, After this sorte the Greeke Historiographers..would attribute al thinges to themselves. **1577** B. GOOGE *Heresbach's Husb.* II. (1586) 57 b, The ordering of them is after one sort. **1604** E. G[RIMSTONE] *D'Acosta's Hist. Indies* IV. iv. 212 They drawe golde in those partes, after three sorts.

(*b*) **1551** ROBINSON tr. *More's Utopia* II. (1895) 132 But nowe the houses be curiously builded, after a gorgiouse and gallaunt sort. **1577** HANMER *Anc. Eccl. Hist., Euseb.* I. vi. (1663) 7 It remaineth that we begin after a compendious sort from the coming of our Saviour Christ in the Flesh. **1592** TIMME *Ten Eng. Lepers* Aiij, The generall good..hath moved me, though after a plaine and rude sort, to publish the same. **1857** SUSANNA WINKWORTH tr. *Life Tauler* 67 The Master..received him after a most friendly sort. *a* **1894** CHRISTINA ROSSETTI *Venus' Looking-glass* Poems (1904) 289 Around whose head white doves rose..and cooed after their tender sort.

(*c*) **1557** N. T. (Geneva) *Heb.* xi. 19 Death: from whence he receaued him also after a sort. **1581** E. CAMPION in *Conf.* III. (1584) Z, Man is also the offerer, after a sort. **1610** HOLLAND *Camden's Brit.* (1637) 632 After a sort he surrendered up his Crowne unto him. **1671** H. M. tr. *Erasm. Colloq.* 7 Not so well as I desire; truly I am well after a sort. **1724** A. COLLINS *Gr. Chr. Relig.* 153 The first place of Jeremiah was quoted,..and is still extant after a sort. **1837** CARLYLE *Fr. Rev.* II. II. ii, Captain Dampmartin,..who loves the Reign of Liberty, after a sort. **1879** S. C. BARTLETT *Egypt to Pal.* xii. 267 Into which the hand, with shut fingers, will fit after a sort.

†**23. a.** ***of this sort***, in this way or manner. *Sc. Obs. rare.*

1549 *Compl. Scot.* vi. 38 Of this sort i did spaceir vp ande doune but sleipe. *Ibid.* ix. 79 Of this sort god turnit the hazard of fortoune.

†**b.** So *on such* (*a*) *sort, on this sort*. *Obs.*

1557 *Tottel's Misc.* (Arb.) 136 Happy is he, that liues on such a sort: That nedes not feare such tonges of false report. **1585-6** *Reg. Privy Council Scot.* Ser. I. IV. 50 The saidis personis..on sic sorte persewis the saidis complenaris as thay dar not remane at thair awne duelling houssis. **1597** BEARD *Theatre God's Judgem.* (1612) 191 Permitting him to plague him on this sort, for his amendment. *a* **1632** T. TAYLOR *God's Judgem.* I. II. iv. (1642) 170 But to come to the fact, it was on this sort.

†**c.** ***at all sorts***, at all points. *Obs.*$^{-1}$

1612 W. SHUTE tr. *Fougasses' Venice* IV. vii. II. 13 A thousand Archers from Candy, and another thousand armed at all sortes from the Country of Albania.

†**sort**, *sb.*^{3} *Obs. rare.* Also sortt, soortt. [Perh. identical with prec.] Some measure or weight of figs and raisins.

By Rogers (*Agric. & Prices* IV. 668-9) considered to be equivalent to three frails.

1438-9 *Durham Acc. Rolls* (Surtees) 70 It. in ij Sortez ficuum et racemorum. *Ibid.* 77 Summa rec., ij Sortez et xx lb. **1453-4** *Ibid.* 289 In j soortt ficuum. **1481-90** *Howard Househ. Bks.* (Roxb.) 351 Item, for a sort of fygges, xij. s.

sort (sɔːt), *sb.*^{4} *Computers.* [f. SORT *v.*^{1} II.]

a. The action of arranging items of data in a prescribed sequence.

1956 *Jrnl. Assoc. Computing Machinery* III. 156 Seven passes will effect a complete sort but an eighth pass will be required to collect the items back on to one reel of tape. **1964** C. DENT *Quantity Surveying by Computer* vi. 79 The effect of this sort..will be to arrange the narrative items under their proper headings. **1973** *Computers & Humanities* VII. 202 We decided to remove the umlauts before performing the sort.

b. Special Comb.: **sort key**, a characteristic feature of items of data according to which the data may be arranged; **sort program**, a program written to perform a sort; **sort routine**, a routine written to perform a sort.

1967 D. G. HAYS *Introd. Computational Linguistics* x. 171 The sort has brought together all the contextual spans with a common sort key. Print the first sort key in some obvious place... Then begin printing the contextual spans with that sort key, one after another. **1969** *Computers & Humanities* III. 137 Each letter group, plus the word from which it was derived and the frequency of occurrence of that word..is then sorted in alphabetical order using the letter group as the first sortkey and the position of the first letter of each group..as the second sortkey. **1963** *Communications Assoc. Computing Machinery* VI. 266/2 The tape merging program initially determines an optimum number of merge passes for merging the sorted files produced by the sort program. **1973** *Computers & Humanities* VII. 203 The IBM sort program.. handled eight fields of character or numerical data. **1964** C. DENT *Quantity Surveying by Computer* vi. 79 If we rearrange the keyword so that the trade and heading numbers occupy the most significant position, a standard sort routine with four decks will sort the blocks into the order specified by the trade number plus the heading number. **1969** *Computers & Humanities* III. 137 The letter concordance program accepts the keyword output of the concordance program and generates sort records. These are then sorted by a standard sort routine.

sort (sɔːt), *v.*^{1} Also 5 soortyn, 5-7 sorte, 6 sourt, 9 *dial.* soort, etc. [Partly ad. L. *sortīrī* to divide or obtain by lot, or OF. *sortir* (mod.F. *sortir*, = It. *sortire*, Pg. *sortir*; cf. Pg. and Sp. *sortear*):—pop. L. **sortīre*, f. L. *sors, sort-* lot: see SORT *sb.*^{1} In most senses, however, closely related to SORT *sb.*^{2}, and perh. partly repr. F. *assortir* ASSORT *v.*]

I. †**1. a.** *trans.* To allot, apportion, or assign. Usu. const. *to, for*, or with dat. of person. *Obs.*

c **1374** CHAUCER *Troylus* V. 1827 And forth he wente, shortly for to telle, Ther as Mercurie sorted him to dwelle. **1412-20** LYDG. *Chron. Troy* III. 440 Of our expleit þe troupe to reporte, For whiche part Mars list þe feld to sorte. **1561** NORTON & SACKV. *Gorboduc* IV. ii, What cruell destenie, What frowarde fate hath sorted vs this chaunce? **1583** MELBANCKE *Philotimus* Kj, How many sporting houres were sorted to the Astronomer C. Gallus. **1599** B. JONSON *Cynthia's Rev.* V. iii. [xi], How well Diana can distinguish times? And sort her censures? keeping to herself The doom of gods, leaving the rest to us!

†**b.** To dispose, ordain, order (events). Also *absol. Obs. rare.*

1592 WYRLEY *Armorie* 108 Thus coy fortune sourts, Some now aloft and then cast downe we see. **1594** SHAKS. *Rich. III*, II. iii. 36 All may be well; but if God sort it so, 'Tis more then we deserue or I expect. **1596** —— *Merch. V.* V. 132 But God sort all.

†**2.** *intr.* To exercise or perform divination. *Obs.*$^{-1}$

c **1450** *Merlin* ii. 39 Bringe hethir thy counsell, and the clerkes that sorted of this toure.

†**3.** *trans.* To distribute by lot. *Obs. rare.*

1513 DOUGLAS *Æneid* III. viii. 7 We sort our airis, and chesis rowaris ilk deill. **1582** STANYHURST *Æneis* I. (Arb.) 34 Shee..toyls too pioners by drawcut lotterye sorteth.

†**4.** To obtain as one's lot; to share in, partake of. *Obs. rare.*

1474 CAXTON *Chesse* IV. ii, Thus as in going out first into four poyntes he sorteth the nature of knyghtes. **1483** —— *Gold. Leg.* 209/2 He hath ronne thrououte alle the world and with his prechyng hath purged it and yet he hath not sorted [L. *sortitus est*] heuen.

†**5.** To arrive at, attain to, result in, or reach (an effect, end, etc.). Cf. sense 7 a. *Obs.*

a **1548** HALL *Chron., Edw. IV*, 214 It was almost incredible to se what effect this new imaginacion..sorted and toke. **1593** PEELE *Edw. I*, VI. vi, When the war of rebels sorts an end, None might be prince..But such a one as was their countryman. **1612** SHELTON *Quix.* I. III. xiii. (1620) I. 255 Bidding her to hope firmly, that our good just Desires would sort a wish'd and happy End. **1656** W. COLES *Art Simpl.* 4 Their Medicines oft-times sort not their wished, but sometimes contrary effects.

†**6. a.** *intr.* Of events, etc.: To come about, to fall or turn out, in a certain way or with a certain result. *Obs.*

c **1477** CAXTON *Jason* 113 Sorceries..and.. enchantements, wherof thauenture of the shippe sorted as sayd is. **1589** GREENE *Tullies Love* Wks. (Grosart) VII. 193 Promising all shoulde sort according vnto Lentulus minde. **1598** GRENEWEY *Tacitus, Ann.* XV. vi. (1622) 230 That to the Romans many things had sorted luckily, and some to the Parthians. **1609** DEKKER *Ravens Almanacke* Wks. (Grosart) IV. 241 Which sorted according to their expectations. **1626** BACON *Sylva* §317 The Experiment sorted in this Manner. **1653** H. COGAN tr. *Pinto's Trav.* xxvii. 106 We had recourse to Mercy, which sorted well for us.

†**b.** Similarly with *out*. *Obs.*

1581 RICH *Farew.* (1846) 130 Seyng the matter sorted out as she looked for. **1593** MARLOWE *Edw. II*, II. i, If all things sort out, as I hope they will. *a* **1637** N. FERRAR tr. *Valdes' 110 Consid.* (1638) 15 Having seen that..my determinations sorted out contrary to that which I determined. *a* **1656** USSHER *Ann.* (1658) 158 If things sorted out in this war, as he hoped they would.

†**c.** To come to effect; to be successful. *Obs.*

1613 PURCHAS *Pilgrimage* II. x. I. 137 Intending a plague to the men,..if their working had sorted. **1626** BACON *Sylva* §351 It was tried in a Blowne Bladder..and it sorted not. *Ibid.* §380 Which is a thing of great profit, if it would sort: But vpon Triall..there followed no Effect.

†**7. a.** To come or attain *to* an end, conclusion, effect, etc. *Obs.* (Common *c* 1575-1650.)

1543-4 *Act 35 Hen. VIII*, c. 10 Whiche good and profitable purpose can not sorte to conclusion, nor take good effecte, without the ayde..of parliament. *a* **1548** HALL *Chron., Hen. VII* (1809) 498 The third request..never sorted to any effect or conclusion. **1582** N. LICHEFIELD tr. *Castanheda's Conq. E. Ind.* I. 16 b, Their mischeuous enterprise, which had bene likely to haue..sorted to a sorrowful hap and euent. **1618** *Weakest goeth to Wall* I iij, I will forbeare my knowledge 'till I see To what effect this cause will sort unto. **1659** H. THORNDIKE *Wks.* (1846) II. 540 If there were nothing to help the tenor of such instruments, things contracted would hardly sort to effect.

†**b.** To end in coming or leading *to* a specified result. *Obs.*

1586 A. DAY *Eng. Secretary* II. (1625) 91 Here is head, wit, mind and discretion, all sorting to one thing. **1598** FLORIO To Rdr. b ij, Let..the reapers of the fruites iudge betwixt vs whose paines hath sorted to best perfection. **1620** E. BLOUNT *Horæ Subs.* 216 Euery mans own Method commonly sorteth best to his owne profit. **1624** BP. MOUNTAGU *Immed. Addr.* 51 Were our desires granted vs,.. it would sort vnto our hurt and vtter vndoing.

†**c.** To turn out so as to answer or be agreeable *to* one's wish, desire, etc. *Obs.*

1592 *Soliman & Pers.* II. i. 238 Gentlemen, each thing hath sorted to our wish. **1606** G. WOODCOCK *Hist. Iustine* I. 5 Thinking that..the thing would so come to passe, as.. afterward sorted to their desired wish. **1650** VAUGHAN *Anthroposophia* 2 These Indeavours sorting not to my purpose, I quitted this Booke-businesse.

†**d.** To fall *to* a person as a right or duty. *Obs.*

1622 DRAYTON *Poly-olb.* xxii. 634 To Salsbury it sorts the palm away to bear. *a* **1677** BARROW *Serm.* (1687) I. 142 The duties which upon that occasion are signified to concern people then, do no less now sort to us.

8. *trans.* To answer or correspond to, to befit or suit. Now *rare.*

1587 GOLDING *De Mornay* Ep. Ded., Well sorting your high place and dignitie. **1603** KNOLLES *Hist. Turks* (1621) 360 Which not sorting his desire, the matter was again brought to parle. **1615** BRATHWAIT *Strappado* (1878) 126 To imitate all formes, shapes, habits, tyres Suting the Court, and sorting his desires. **1882** H. S. HOLLAND *Logic & Life* (1885) 12 Certain phenomena..which no other name suits or sorts.

II. 9. a. *trans.* To arrange (things, etc.) according to kind or quality, or after some settled order or system; to separate and put into different sorts or classes; to classify; to assort.

c **1358** [see SORTING *vbl. sb.*]. *c* **1440** *Promp. Parv.* 465/2 Soortyn, or settyn yn a soorte, *sortior*. **1482** *Rolls of Parlt.* VI. 221/2 That the Samon shuld be wele and truly pakked and sorted in the same vessells. **1483** *Act 1 Rich. III*, c. 8 Preamble, Greate quantite of Wolles..which ben sorted the better from the worse, barbed and clakked. **1523** FITZHERB. *Husb.* §134 Than sorte the trees, the polles by them-selfe, the myddel sorte by them-selfe. **1581** MULCASTER *Positions* xxxvii. (1887) 155 The maister..is no absolute potentate.. to sorte mens children, as he liketh best. **1605** HEYWOOD *Know not me* Wks. 1874 I. 285 Past eight a clock, and neither ware sorted, Nor shop swept. **1684** in *3rd Rep. Hist. MSS. Comm.* 427/1 Wee have sorted what papers I could at present find. **1718** *Free-thinker* No. 11. 71 Letters of every Kind come..which I sort according to their different Complexions. **1765** *Phil. Trans.* LV. 206 Mr. Rouse..made a machine for sorting woollen thread upon the same principle with this. **1840** MARRYAT *Poor Jack* xlv, I found her..busy sorting a lot of old bottles. **1888** F. HUME *Mme. Midas* I. ii, When the office was empty, Slivers would go on sorting the scrip on his table.

absol. **1625** B. JONSON *Staple of N.* I. ii, They mannage all at home, and sort, and file, And seale the newes, and issue them. **1847** *Jrnl. R. Agric. Soc.* VIII. I. 7 The breed..was left to chance or the management of shepherds, with whom it could not be a matter of interest to sort or improve.

b. Const. with advs. or preps., as *asunder, in* or *into* (sets or classes, etc.), etc.

1530 PALSGR. 725, I sorte a sonder the good from the badde, *je esplusche*. **1533** MORE *Answ. Poysoned Bk.* Wks. 1087/2 Al whych things I wil sort into theyr places. **1608** WILLET *Hexapla Exod.* 604 The other two curtains were sorted fiue and sixe together. **1644** MILTON *Areop.* (Arb.) 45 Those confused seeds which were impos'd on Psyche as an incessant labour to cull out, and sort asunder. **1688** *Lett. conc. Present State Italy* 99 The People are sorted in several Fraternities. **1885** *Manch. Exam.* 16 Mar. 5/2 A power of analysis..which would equip a mathematician is requisite to sort the material into order.

†**c.** To separate or distinguish (*from* something else). *Obs. rare.*

1551 T. WILSON *Logike* (1580) 61 b, We open the doubtfulnesse..of some woorde or sentence, by makyng a distinction..and seuerally sortyng suche thynges, as then were thought to be euill set together. **1587** FLEMING *Contn. Holinshed* III. 1349/2, I meane so as physicke is now taken separatelie from surgerie, and that part which onelie vseth the hand as it is sorted from the apothecarie. **1599** SHAKS. *Hen. V*, IV. vii. 77 That we may wander ore this bloody field, ..To sort our Nobles from our common men.

10. a. To place in a class or sort; to give a place to; to classify. Also const. *after*, *among*, *as*, *together*.

1486 *Bk. St. Albans, Hawking* d iij, Thay [bells] be passing goode, for thay be wele sortid, well sownded. **1523** SKELTON *Garl. Laurel* 1280 Why shulde she take shame That her goodly name..Shulde be set and sortyd, To be matriculate With ladyes of astate? **1581** MULCASTER *Positions* xxxvi. (1887) 135 That wittes well sorted be most ciuill. **1595** *Locrine* I. i. 136 If thou follow sacred virtue's lore Thou shalt be..Sorted among the glorious happy ones. **1613** CHAPMAN *Maske Inns Crt.* Plays 1873 III. 92 After them were sorted two Cars Triumphall. **1626** BACON *Sylva* §340 Mosse..may be better sorted as a Rudiment of Germination. **1687** TILLOTSON *Barrow's Wks.* I. Pref., The eight following Sermons are likewise sorted together. **1768–74** TUCKER *Lt. Nat.* (1834) I. 124 Sorting them together in a manner not done before.

b. Const. *with*.

1599 DAVIES *Immort. Soul* I. iii. (1714) 20 When she sorts Things present with Things past. **1607** *Scholast. Disc. agst. Antichrist* I. i. 50 The Crosse sorteth vs with the Papists, as much as the Garland sorted the Christians with the Pagans. **1669** STURMY *Mariner's Mag.* VII. iv. 8 This Dial..should be sorted rather with the Æquinoctial Dials, than with the Horizontal. *a* **1703** BURKITT *On N.T.* Mark xv. 37 It had been a sufficient disparagement to our Blessed Saviour to have been sorted with the best of men. **1876** GEO. ELIOT *Dan. Der.* i, A bony, yellow, crab-like hand.., a hand easy to sort with the square gaunt face.

11. a. With *out*. To take *out*, remove, or separate (certain sorts from others).

1534 MORE *Comf. agst. Trib.* II. Wks. 1177/2 The tother kynde is thys whych I rehersed second, and sorttyng out the tother twayne, haue kepte it for the last. **1601** DENT *Pathw. Heaven* 259 Thirdly, let there be sorted out all Hypocrites.. and cold Christians. **1728** CHAMBERS *Cycl.* s.v. *Herring*, These..are carefully sorted out. **1790** BURKE *Fr. Rev.* 187 They will sort out the good from the evil. **1868** LOCKYER *Guillemin's Heavens* (ed. 3) 393 There has not yet been time to sort out the real from the apparent nebulæ.

b. To choose or select in this way. Now *rare* or *Obs.*

1553 BALE *Vocacyon* in *Harl. Misc.* (Malh.) I. 330 God sorted me out, and appointed me from my mothers wombe. **1576** FLEMING *Panopl. Epist.* 441 You shall viewe..comely shapes,..suche as be chosen, picked, and sorted out for the nonce. **1606** DAY *Ile Gulls* I. iii, Sort out but fit time and opportunity. **1818** SCOTT *Hrt. Midl.* xxi, Few folk but mysell could hae sorted ye out a seat like this.

c. To divide or separate *into* smaller parts, etc. *Obs. rare.*

1546 BALE *Eng. Votaries* I. (1560) 12 For of [= by] them ..were the Iles of the Gentiles sorted out into regions. *c* **1582** T. DIGGES in *Archaeol.* XI. 230 That waste vnder the castle, which beinge sorted out into convenient streetes [etc.].

d. To arrange according to sort.

1713 *Guardian* No. 120 (1756) II. 143 Her faculties are employed in shuffling, cutting, dealing, and sorting out a pack of cards. **1852** MRS. STOWE *Uncle Tom's C.* xii. 103 The other lady, sorting out some worsteds on her lap. **1862** SPENCER *First Princ.* II. xxi. §165 (1875) 468 The waves are ever sorting-out and separating the mixed materials against which they break.

e. To reprimand (a person); to deal with (a person) by means of force, repression, etc. *colloq.*

1941 BAKER *Dict. Austral. Slang* 69 *Sort someone out, to*, to reprove a person, put him in his place. **1943** HUNT & PRINGLE *Service Slang* 61 To pick a quarrel and use force is to 'sort out' someone. **1958** J. BLACKBURN *Scent of New-Mown Hay* ii. 24 Get this fellow Kirk sorted out and don't overdo it. **1965** P. ARROWSMITH *Jericho* ix. 92 Let's all go down and sort out that peace pickets' camp. **1974** *Times* 25 Feb. 10/7 Richards came in to sort Willis out and, although Willis prevailed in the end, it was not before Richards had hit him several times for four.

f. To separate out and resolve the complexities of (a problem); to clear up (a confusion or difficulty); to put to rights, deal with. Also, with a person as object: to solve the problems of (someone), 'put (him) straight'. Also *refl.*

1948 'N. SHUTE' *No Highway* v. 128 Will you see if you can get that one sorted out? **1954** J. MASTERS *Bhowani Junction* vi. 51 If I send a message, sort it out between Macaulay and that depilated Sikh assistant of Taylor's. **1962** *Woman's Own* 15 Sept. 69/2 Perhaps you haven't yet decided, assuming this is something which will sort itself out when the time comes. **1963** [see FAVOUR *sb.* 2 b]. **1963** A. ROSS *Australia 63* 17 The two Perth matches..allow the visiting side to sort themselves out. **1973** M. AMIS *Rachel Papers* 46 No, don't tell me she's the very girl to show me what egotistical folly it is to compartmentalize people in this sad way; don't tell me she's going to sort me out, take me on, supply the *cognitio* and comic resolution.

12. *refl.* **a.** To form sets or groups by some process of combination or separation.

1570–6 LAMBARDE *Peramb. Kent* (1826) 338 A Torneament..in which the English men, of a set purpose,.. sorted them-selves against the strangers. **1601** HOLLAND *Pliny* II. 238 For the most part they sort themselues by couples like man and wife. **1692** R. L'ESTRANGE *Josephus, Antiq.* II. v. (1733) 34 They had their times of talking, and sorting themselves together. **1726** DE FOE *Hist. Devil* I. x. (1840) 132 The people necessarily sorted themselves into families and tribes after the confusion of languages. **1760–72** H. BROOKE *Fool of Qual.* (1809) IV. 55 The crowd had sorted themselves, the principals..into one groupe, the young men into another, and the fair maidens into another. **1925** E. F. NORTON *Fight for Everest, 1924* 51 Nearly 300 yak-loads of provision boxes, rolls of bedding and stores of all sorts, dumped higgledy-piggledy off the yaks, began to sort themselves into orderly lines and piles.

b. To associate or consort *with* another or others. (Cf. 19.) Also with *among(st)*. Now *dial.* (freq. in 17th cent.).

1579 TOMSON *Calvin's Serm. Tim.* 1051/1 We see that S. Pauls meaning was by this word Common faith, to sort himself quietly with the rest. **1592** *Conspir. for Pretended Reform.* 1 They..willingly sorted themselues in familiaritie with such. **1642** D. ROGERS *Naaman* 36 Shall I..sort my selfe with such as are enemies? **1691** WOOD *Ath. Oxon.* I. 23 He found out Will. Tyndale in Germany, with whom for a time he sorted himself. *a* **1713** ELLWOOD *Autobiog.* (1714) 7, I always sorted myself with Persons of Ingenuity, Temperance, and Sobriety. **1877** in PEACOCK *Manley Gloss.*

13. a. To adapt, to fit, to make conformable *to* or *with* some thing or person. Now *rare* or *Obs.*

(*a*) **1561** in Tytler *Hist. Scot.* (1864) III. 147 In sorting your entertainment to every person. **1595** GOODWINE *Contin. Blanchardyn* (1890) 216 It hath pleased God to sorte our haps to our harts contentments. **1619** W. SCLATER *Exp. 1 Thess.* (1629) 509 Gods precepts..must be sorted to their seasons. **1822** AINSLIE *Land of Burns* 235 My auld crazy voice is better sorted to hammeart lilts than sic fine springs.

(*b*) **1591** SHAKS. *Two Gent.* I. iii. 63 My will is something sorted with his wish. **1607** DEKKER & WEBSTER *Sir T. Wyatt* D ij b, My lookes (my loue) is sorted with my heart. **1640** tr. *Verdere's Rom. of Rom.* II. 167 If I were at any time to bow unto the affection of a mortall wight, I should never chuse any other to sort my greatnesse withall.

†**b.** To bring *to* an end, effect, etc. *Obs.*

1591 *Troub. Raigne K. John* (1611) 38 Now euery thing is sorted to this end, Let's in. **1597** *Certain Prayers* in *Liturg. Serv. Eliz.* (1847) 677 Lord,..who by thy mighty power sortest to what effect thou wilt the counsels and actions of all men. **1632** LITHGOW *Trav.* III. 117 The diuine Maiestie doth swey the moments of things, and sorteth them in peremptory manner to..vnlooked for effects.

†**14. a.** To choose or select (time, opportunity, etc.) as fitting or suitable. *Obs.*

Freq. passing into the sense of 'to arrange, contrive, find, etc.'

1591 SHAKS. *1 Hen. VI*, II. iii. 27 I'll sort some other time to visit you. **1592** KYD *Sp. Trag.* IV. iv. 103 They had sorted leasure, To take aduantage..Upon my Sonne. **1624** HEYWOOD *Gunaik.* IV. 193 The young man's father, who sorted opportunitie to talke with his sonne. **1634** —— & BROME *Lanc. Witches* II. H.'s Wks. 1874 IV. 192 What times hath she sorted for these journeyes?

†**b.** To choose (a thing or person) from others.

1591 SHAKS. *Two Gent.* III. ii. 92 Let vs into the City presently To sort some Gentlemen, well skil'd in Musicke. **1592** —— *Rom. & Jul.* IV. ii. 34 To helpe me sort such needfull ornaments, As you thinke fit to furnish me. **1638** FORD *Lady's Trial* I. i, Ere now You might have sorted me in your resolves, Companion of your fortunes.

15. To furnish, provide, or supply (a person, etc.) *with* (or *of*) something. In later use only *Sc.*

1598 BARRETT *Theor. Warres* I. i. 4 The strength of the Battaile is the armed Pike, so they be equally sorted with Harquebuze and Musket. *Ibid.* II. i. 26 How would you haue a Companie sorted with weapons? **1600** DYMMOK *Ireland* (1843) 14 It is well sorted with woodes and playnes. **1774** KEITH *Farmer's Ha'* xxvii, He tells them he's weel sorted now Of a' thing gude, and cheap, and new. **1825** JAMIESON *Suppl.* s.v., I can sort ye wi' a knife. **1898** LD. E. HAMILTON *Mawkin* xv. 200, I warrant we'll sort you with another, and as good a yin too.

16. *Sc.* and *north.* in (*a*) to (*d*) and b; *colloq.* in (*e*). (Also with *up*.) To arrange or put in order; to put to rights in some respect.

The leading variations of sense are more fully illustrated in the *Eng. Dial. Dict.*

(*a*) **1827** CARLYLE *Germ. Rom.* IV. 45 Mine host has already in my presence begun sorting the apartment as if I were gone. **1833** LOUDON *Encycl. Archit.* §81 The whole [roofing] to be laid with a sufficient lap, and to be carefully sorted in courses (laid so as that the joints may form regular lines). **1876** ROBINSON *Whitby Gloss.* s.v., 'Get all your things soorted up,' collected together.

absol. **1891** N. DICKSON *Kirk Beadle* 109 The preacher returned to the church and found the beadle busy 'sorting up'.

(*b*) **1816** SCOTT *Antiq.* xliii, The provost's gar'd the beacon light on the Halket-head be sorted up (that suld hae been sorted half a year syne). **1876** WHITEHEAD *Daft Davie*, etc. 121 The wick needed sorting, and the oil was low. **1877** FRASER *Wigtown* 62 Belsher..was once engaged sorting the lock of a cell in the Prison.

(*c*) **1816** SCOTT *Antiq.* xv, The powny hasna gane abune thirty mile the day;—Jock was sorting him up as I came ower by. **1816** —— *Old Mort.* xxxvii, 'Ye may rely on your naig being weel sorted,' said Cuddie; 'I ken weel what belangs to suppering a horse'. **1868** VERNEY *Stone Edge* vii, Lydia was out in the farmyard 'sorting' the cows herself.

(*d*) **1817** *Lintoun Green* 166 Nor he is neither tae sort me right. **1866** MISS MULOCK *Noble Life* iv. 61 She lifted up the poor child, tenderly and carefully—shook his pillows and 'sorted' him. **1890** NISBET *Bail up!* xxviii, Let me sort you up a little.

(*e*) **1950** 'D. DIVINE' *King of Fassarai* x. 82 Take her along to Sergeant Marker. Let him sort it. **1975** M. BRADBURY *History Man* xiii. 220 'Tomorrow will sort itself, Barbara,' says Felicity, 'you'll manage.' **1976** L. HENDERSON *Major Enquiry* ix. 57 They're the boys to get it sorted, all young, keen, and raring to go.

b. To deal effectively with (a person) by way of punishment, repression, etc.

1815 SCOTT *Guy M.* xxxiii, Bid them bring up the prisoner —I trow I'll sort him. **1835–** in Sc. and north dial. glossaries and texts. **1878** A. R. HOPE *My Schoolboy Fr.* 265 'I will sort this Ghost,' said Kennedy.

17. In commercial use: To bring *up* to the usual stock or quantity.

1880 *Daily News* 15 Nov. 3/5 The orders..are merely to enable them to sort up sizes.

III. 18. a. *intr.* To suit, fit, or agree; to be in harmony or conformity. Const. *with*, †*to*, or †*together*. Now *arch.*

(*a*) **1590** SHAKS. *Mids. N.* V. i. 55 That is some Satire keene and criticall, Not sorting with a nuptiall ceremonie. **1599** —— *Hen. V*, IV. i. 63 My name is Pistol call'd. *King.* It sorts well with your fiercenesse. **1610** W. FOLKINGHAM *Art of Survey* I. x. 33 Dry Marle sortes with moist Soiles. *a* **1652** BROME *Queenes Exch.* I. i. Wks. 1873 III. 460 Their Petulances sort not with this place. **1699** PEPYS in *Diary & Corr.* (1879) VI. 215 Of which book it would greatly sort with my Collection that I had a copy. **1709** POPE *Ess. Crit.* 322 For diff'rent styles with diff'rent subjects sort. **1780** COWPER *Progr. Error* 446 The text that sorts not with his darling whim, Though plain to others, is obscure to him. **1827** HARE *Guesses* (1859) 4 The vastness and awfulness of a mere sea-view would ill sort with the other parts of the.. prospect. **1858** H. BUSHNELL *Nature & Supernat.* xi. (1864) 333 The miracles sort with the person of Christ and his mission. **1891** R. W. CHURCH *Oxford Movem.* xi. 178 However ill it might sort with the current language of Protestant controversy.

(*b*) **1590** GREENE *Orl. Fur.* Wks. (Rtldg.) 92 Mine emblem sorteth to another sense. **1604** BP. W. BARLOW *Sum Conf. Hampton Crt.* 27 They appeared before his Maiestie, in Turky gownes, not in their Scholastical habites, sorting to their degrees. **1651** *Sir W. Rawleigh's Ghost* Pref., A careless and pleasurable life, best sorting to our own desires and sensuality. **1709** MRS. MANLEY *Secret Mem.* (1720) II. 248 Yet sorting to his Humour, we will not ask thee to give him too diffusive a Brightness.

(*c*) **1600** HOLLAND *Livy* XLIV. xxiv. 1185 A free citie and a King were,..by nature, enemies that possibly could not sort together. **1641** MILTON *Reform.* II. Wks. 1851 III. 58 Wee see that our Ecclesiall and Politicall choyses may consent and sort as well together..as Christians, and Freeholders.

†**b.** Without const. To be fitting; to accord; to be in place, to exist. *Obs.*

1593 SHAKS. *3 Hen. VI*, II. i. 209 The Queene is comming with a puissant Hoast... *War.* Why then it sorts, braue Warriors, let's away. **1606** —— *Tr. & Cr.* I. i. 110 *Æne.*.. Where-fore not a field? *Troy.* Because not there; this womans answer sorts. For womanish it is to be from thence. **1633** FORD *Broken H.* I. i, Some one, he is assur'd, may now or then (If opportunity but sort) preuaile. **1667** MILTON *P.L.* VIII. 384 Among unequals what societie Can sort, what harmonie or true delight?

c. *Sc.* To come to an agreement or settlement; to come to terms (*on* something).

1685 PEDEN in Walker *Life* (1827) 95 If ye be pleased with the Wares,..he and ye will soon sort on the Price. **1814** SCOTT *Wav.* xviii, I cannot tell you precisely how they sorted; but they agreed sae right that [etc.].

19. To associate, consort, go in company *with* others or *together*. (Cf. 12 b.) Also with *among* and without const. Now *rare* or *dial.*

(*a*) **1592** SHAKS. *Ven. & Ad.* 689 Sometime he runs among a flock of sheep.., And sometime sorteth with a herd of deer. **1612** BACON *Ess., Par. & Childr.* (Arb.) 274 The illiberality of Parents..towards their children..makes them sort with meane companie. **1685** BURNET tr. *More's Utopia* 37 If I should sort with another kind of Ministers. **1720** DE FOE *Capt. Singleton* xiii. (1840) 228 He went over to Captain Avery, and sorted with his people. **1784** COWPER *Tiroc.* 114 Too careless often as our years proceed, What friends we sort with, or what books we read. **1805–6** CARY *Dante, Inf.* xv. 120 A company, with whom I may not sort, Approaches. **1886** ELWORTHY *W. Somerset Word-bk.* 695, I never don't try vor to sort wi' my betters.

transf. **1695** WOODWARD *Nat. Hist. Earth* IV. (1723) 193 Nor do Metalls only sort and herd with Metalls in the Earth.

(*b*) **1601** HOLLAND *Pliny* I. 233 That willingly these little creatures will not sort together vnlesse they were countrimen as it were. *Ibid.* 278 What fowles soeuer haue crooked clawes sort not together in flocks. **1672** EACHARD *Hobbs' State Nat.* 40 Men are apt to sort, to herd. **1709** MRS. MANLEY *Secret Mem.* (1720) II. 253 Thus adorn'd,..what genteel..Company would suffer him to sort among them? **1819** W. TENNANT *Papistry Storm'd* (1827) 77 He did dislike baith Pape and Deil; (Thir twa thegither sortit weil).

†**sort**, *v.*[2] *Sc. Obs.* [ad. F. *sortir*, of doubtful origin.] *intr.* To sally out; to make a sortie.

1571 BANNATYNE *Jrnl.* (1806) 248 They of Edinburgh cvme furth hors and fute..; and they of Leyth also sorted. **1584** HUDSON *Du Bartas' Judith* vi. (1608) 93 The warriours strong, That kept the towne, now sorted forth in throng. *a* **1600** *Hist. Jas. Sext* (Bannatyne Club) 25 Thay sortit from Hammilton upon the 13 day of Maij to pas towart Dumbartan. *Ibid.* 98 The same was so notifeit to the people of Edinburgh, that thair horsemen sortit.

sorta, sorter (ˈsɔːtə), repr. a colloq. pronunc. of the phr. *sort of* (see SORT *sb.*[2] 6, 8).

Formerly also *sort a*, *sort o'*. The examples given here represent SORT *sb.*[2] 6; examples corresponding to sense 8 are entered there.

1790, etc. [see SORT *sb.*[2] 8 c]. **1898** J. D. BRAYSHAW *Slum Silhouettes* 1 Bloomfiel'—never yeard the nime. Wot sorter covey? **1978** J. WAINWRIGHT *Jury People* xxxv. 106 A funny sorta bloody joke. **1981** H. R. F. KEATING *Go West, Inspector Ghote* vii. 85 Come on in here. We got some sorta kook.

ˈ**sortable**, *a.* Also 6 sortible, 9 *dial.* soortable. [a. F. *sortable* (15th cent.), or f. SORT *v.*[1] + -ABLE.]

†**1.** Suitable, appropriate; fit or befitting. Usu. const. *to* (or *unto*). *Obs.*

1586 FERNE *Blaz. Gentrie* 339 To serue him in anye seruice or office,..suche as be sortible to his degree. **1603** HOLLAND *Plutarch's Mor.* 1329 The Moone: which they seeing to be so subject to growing and decreasing,..thought ..to be sortable unto the mutability of the Dæmons kinde. **1621** SANDERSON *Serm.* I. 196 There are generous and ingenuous and liberal employments, sortable to the greatest births and educations. *a* **1663** SIR K. DIGBY *Priv. Mem.* (1827) 17 Recreations..sortable to their age. **1818** SCOTT *Rob Roy* xxxiv, It's a pity his Excellency is a thought eldern.

The like o' yoursell, or my son Hamish, wad be mair sortable in point of years.

2. *north. dial.* Capable of going together.

1641 BEST *Farm. Bks.* (Surtees) 110 In the choise of good deales, . . that they bee sortable, i.e. all of one length, all of one breadth, and all of one thicknesse. **1876** ROBINSON *Whitby Gloss.* 180/1 *Soortable*, accordant or companionable.

†**3.** Of a cargo: Properly assorted; composed of suitable sorts. *Obs.*

1727 DE FOE *Tour Gt. Brit., Scotl.* 90 The Scots Merchants are at no Loss how to make up sortable Cargoes to send with their Ships to the Plantations. **1727** —— *Eng. Tradesm.* viii. (1732) I. 84 When merchants send adventures to our British colonies, 'tis usual with them to make up to each factor what they call a *sortable cargo.* **1818** SCOTT *Rob Roy* xxvi, The facilities which Glasgow possessed of making up *sortable* cargoes for that market.

4. Capable of being sorted or arranged.

1972 *Computers & Humanities* VI. 188 *Description*: Creates sortable tape from card or card-image input, sorts tape, adds . . other information to sorted tape.

Hence † **'sortably** *adv. Obs.*

1607 in Plomer *Abstr. fr. Wills Eng. Printers* (1903) 42 If . . Nicholas Bourne shall . . take so manie books . . sorteable thorough out all my warehouses as they shall arise. **1608** HIERON *Defence* III. 7 Shall not he who is a coheir with Christ at his table cary himselfe sortably to the said person of coheir? **1611** COTGR., *Sortablement*, sortably, fitly.

'sortal, *a.* (and *sb.*) [f. SORT *sb.*^{2} + -AL^1.] Of or belonging to a particular sort or kind. Also as *sb.*

1690 LOCKE *Hum. Und.* III. iii. (1695) 231 That abstract Idea, which the General, or *Sortal* (if I may have leave so to call it from *Sort*, as I do *General* from *Genus*) Name stands for. **1959** P. F. STRAWSON *Individuals* v. 168, I shall draw a rough distinction . . between two kinds of non-relational tie which bind particulars and universals. This is the distinction between *sortal* and *characterizing* universals. **1975** *Times Lit. Suppl.* 28 Feb. 215/3 The orthodox Fregean and Russellian view that the sortals 'man', 'woman', 'cat' are predicables and not names. **1980** D. WIGGINS *Sameness & Substance* 7 Any predicate whose extension consists . . of all the particular things or substances of one particular kind, say horses, or sheep, or pruning knives, will be called here a sortal predicate.

†**sortance.** *Obs.*$^{-1}$ [f. SORT *v.*^{1} + -ANCE.] Agreement, correspondence.

1597 SHAKS. *2 Hen. IV*, IV. i. 11 Here doth hee wish his Person, with such Powers As might hold sortance with his Qualitie, The which hee could not leuie.

‖**sortant,** *a. rare*$^{-0}$. [F., pr. pple. of *sortir* SORT *v.*^{2}] Of an angle: = SALIENT *a.* 4.

1842 GWILT *Archit.* Gloss., *Sortant Angle*, the same as *Salient Angle.*

sortation (sɔːˈteɪʃən). [f. SORT *v.*^{1}: see -ATION.] The action or process of arranging or sorting; arrangement, classification.

1844 *5th Rep. Dep. Kpr. Rec.* 6 The sortation of them has been begun. **1885** J. W. HYDE *Royal Mail* xi. 164 Thus it will be seen that the sortation of letters is no mere mechanical process.

attrib. **1899** J. A. HARVIE-BROWN (*title*), On a Correct Colour Code or Sortation Code in Colours.

sorte, obs. form of SHORT *a.*

sortebrand, obs. form of SURTURBRAND.

sorted ('sɔːtɪd), *ppl. a.* [f. SORT *v.*^{1} Cf. ILL-SORTED *a.*]

1. Picked, chosen, selected.

1547 *Cal. Pat. Rolls Irel.* I. (1861) 154 A convenient number of sorted men for the relief of the Lord Deputy. **1632** HEYWOOD *2nd Pt. Iron Age* Ded., If you persist in the same opinion, when you shall spare some sorted houres to heare it read. **1839** URE *Dict. Arts* 812 The pure ore, or at least the very rich portion, called the *sorted mine.* **1844** MRS. BROWNING *Vis. Poets* cxcv, A company came up the aisle With measured step and sorted smile.

2. Assorted; arranged, classified. Also *sorted-out.*

1697 DRYDEN *Virg. Past.* Pref. (1721) I. 93 A curious Parterre of sorted Flowers. **1722** DE FOE *Col. Jack* (1840) 167 A sorted cargo of goods. **1784** COWPER *Task* III. 634 Grateful mixture of well-match'd And sorted hues. **1891** *Daily News* 2 Mar. 2/2 The sorted papers are thrown into different hoppers. **1927** HALDANE & HUXLEY *Animal Biol.* ii. 64 Each sorted-out pack will be complete in having one card of each kind.

3. *Physical Geogr.* Said of shapes and other features displayed on patterned ground, where the stones forming the patterns are distributed in a way suggesting their having been sorted according to size.

1950 A. L. WASHBURN in *Rev. Canad. de Géogr.* IV. 9 In order to standardize the terminology for the purpose of this paper, the broad classification of patterned ground indicated below has been adopted... Patterns on horizontal ground. Sorted circles. Sorted polygons... Patterns on sloping ground. Sorted stripes. *Ibid.* 13 The stones of sorted stripes range in size from gravel in the narrow stripes to boulders in the largest ones. **1956** —— in *Bull. Geol. Soc. Amer.* LXVII. 830/1 A sorted net is patterned ground whose mesh is intermediate between that of a sorted circle and a sorted polygon and has a sorted appearance commonly due to a border of stones surrounding finer material. **1968** R. W. FAIRBRIDGE *Encycl. Geomorphol.* 374/2 In contrast to circles, sorted polygons . . apparently never develop singly. **1977** A. HALLAM *Planet Earth* 89 The forces generated by freezing and thawing tend to segregate particles of different grain size in the soil to produce sorted polygons, whose margins are outlined by the coarser soil fragments.

sortely, obs. form of SHORTLY *adv.*

sorter ('sɔːtə(r)). [f. SORT *v.*^{1} + -ER.]

1. a. One who sorts, arranges, selects, or classifies; *esp.* a wool-sorter. Also *transf.*

1554 *Act 1 Mary* c. 7 §1 Forcers of Wolles . . and Sorters of Wolles. **1562** J. HEYWOOD *Prov. & Epigr.* (1867) 201 The tounge is assinde, of woordes to be sorter. **1758** JORTIN *Life Erasmus* I. 488 It is plain More wrote it not—and . . he says he was a sorter of that book. **1776** ADAM SMITH *W.N.* I. i. (1869) I. 12 The shepherd, the sorter of the wool, the wool-comber, or carder. **1844** G. DODD *Textile Manuf.* iii. 96 The fingers of the sorter acquire by practice an extraordinary degree of sensitiveness. **1879** *Cassell's Techn. Educ.* IV. 339/2 Wool . . is . . divided into 'sorts' or qualities by experienced sorters or staplers.

b. *spec.* A letter-sorter.

a **1700** B. E. *Dict. Cant. Crew, Sorter*, (at the Post Office) that puts or Digests the Letters into Order or Method. **1737** J. CHAMBERLAYNE *St. Gt. Brit.* II. *List Offices* [in G.P.O.] 690 Sorters 16, of which 14 have 50l. per An. and the two last 40l. **1861** WYNTER *Soc. Bees* 3 Others again . . carry the letters for the general delivery to the tables of the sorters. **1895** *Forum* (U.S.) Oct. 196 A sorter at the post-office . . may accidentally sort one letter of his own out of a million.

2. With advs., as *out.*

1599 *Life More* in C. Wordsworth *Eccl. Biog.* (1817) II. 169, I was onlie a sorter out and placer of principall matters in the same [book] contained. **1881** *Instr. Census Clerks* (1885) 65/3 Worsted Manufacture: . . Sorter out, Spinner.

3. A machine that can sort punched cards into a prescribed order by means of a code punched on selected columns of the cards.

1917 L. R. DICKSEE *Office Machinery* ii. 16 Beyond all question, the most notable . . Sorting Machine is the Hollerith Sorter. **1940** W. J. ECKERT *Punched Card Methods Sci. Computation* 10 The sorter automatically sorts the cards into groups according to the information punched in any chosen column of the cards. The cards to be sorted are placed in the hopper . . and the sorted cards fall into the various receptacles. **1949** [see INTERPRETER 5 a]. **1956** G. A. MONTGOMERIE *Digital Calculating Machines* viii. 146 The second basic piece of equipment is the sorter... A pack of punched cards can be fed into this machine and each card will be automatically examined in turn. **1970** O. DOPPING *Computers & Data Processing* iv. 68 If a deck of cards is to be ordered according to a multi-digit number . . by means of a sorter, it is necessary to let the cards pass through the sorter as many times as the number field has digits.

Hence **'sortership,** the office or position of a letter-sorter.

1886 *Guide Civil Service* 293 Competitive Examination for Female Sorterships in the General Post Office, London.

sorter: see SORTA.

‖**sortes** ('sɔːtiːz, 'sɔːteɪz), *sb. pl.* [L., pl. of *sors* lot, chance.] In phrases ***sortes Virgilianae, Homericae, Biblicae***: divination, or the seeking of guidance, by chance selection of a passage in Virgil, Homer, or the Bible. Also *ellipt.* and *transf.*

a **1586** SIDNEY *Apol. Poet.* (1595) sig. B4, Whereupon grew the worde of *Sortes Virgilianæ*, when by suddaine opening *Virgils* booke, they lighted vpon any verse of hys making. **1646** T. BROWNE *Pseud. Ep.* v. xxi. 272 The first an imitation of *sortes Homericæ*, or *Virgilianæ*, drawing determinations from verses casually occurring. **1700** J. WELWOOD *Memoirs* 100 Lord Falkland, to divert the king, would have his Majesty make a trial of his fortune by the *Sortes Virgilianæ*, which . . was an usual kind of augury some ages past. **1740** H. WALPOLE *Let.* 25 Sept. (1974) XXXVII. 79 In three words I will give you her picture as we drew it in the *Sortes Virgilianæ*—Insanam vatem aspicies. I give you my honour, we did not choose it. **1801** M. EDGEWORTH *Belinda* II. xiii. 25 Several volumes of French plays and novels were lying there, and Clarence Hervey raking up one of them, cried: 'Come, let us try our fate by the sortes Virgilianæ.' **1845** G. E. JEWSBURY in A. Ireland *Sel. Lett. G. E. Jewsbury to J. Welsh Carlyle* (1892) 179, I send it you by way of a 'sortes', and the Bible has as much virtue—that way —as Virgil! **1886** D. C. MURRAY *Cynic Fortune* xv. 183 In the practice of the *sortes* (which was a favourite occupation of his) [he] was elevated or depressed by the text he fell upon. **1897** A. C. BENSON *Diary* June in D. Newsome *On Edge of Paradise* (1980) ii. 63, I took a Sortes Biblicae before refusing. **1947** H. NICOLSON *Diary* 11 Dec. (1968) 118, I consult *sortes Biblicas.* My Bible opens at Ezekiel XL 22. **1969** G. GREENE *Travels with my Aunt* I. xvi. 170 The Sortes Virgilianae—a game my mother considered a little blasphemous unless it was played with the Bible. **1975** V. CANNING *Kingsford Mark* vi. 105 He acknowledged the encouragement of the *sortes.* All the omens were right.

† **'sortfully,** *adv. Obs.*$^{-1}$ [f. SORT *sb.*^{2}] In a suitable or appropriate manner.

1606 CHAPMAN *Gent. Usher* Plays 1873 I. 281 Euery thing About your house so sortfully disposde That . . One vice assists another.

† **'sortiary.** *Obs. rare.* [ad. med.L. *sortiari-us, -a*, f. L. *sors, sort-* SORT *sb.*^{1}]

1. One who practises sortilege.

1652 GAULE *Magastrom.* 333 Numa Pompilius, a Magician or Sortiary not inferior to any. *Ibid.* 342 In France, the magicians, astrologers, sortiaries, sorcerers, wizzards, and witches were so numerous [etc.].

2. = SORTILEGE^1 1.

1653 GATAKER *Vind. Annot. Jer.* 3 No more then it is reqisite for one to be over-much seen in geomancie, palmistrie, sortiarie, auspicie, or aruspicie.

sortie ('sɔːtiː), *sb.* Also 7 sorti. [a. F. *sortie* a going out, etc., f. *sortir* SORT *v.*^{2}]

†**1.** (See quot. 1690.) *Obs.*

1690 ? EVELYN *Mundus Muliebris* 20 *Sorti*, a little Knot of small Ribbon, peeping out between the Pinner and Bonnet. *c* **1691** *Songs & Poems Costume* (Percy Soc.) 200 Her shabbarons next I'll show, Her sortie, and patches of black.

2. a. A dash or sally by a besieged garrison upon an investing force. Freq. in phr. ***to make a sortie.***

1778 H. WALPOLE *Let.* 8 Oct. (1967) XXIV. 413 Before their last *sortie*, one heard nothing but *What news of the fleets?* **1795** SEWARD *Anecd.* II. 217 If the enemy . . thought fit to make any sortie from the town. **1811** WELLINGTON in Gurw. *Desp.* (1837) VII. 285 In case your *sortie* should succeed (which will place the war on its legs again in the best manner). **1843** PRESCOTT *Mexico* VI. vi. (1864) 386 To repel the sorties, made . . by the militia of the capital. **1874** GREEN *Short Hist.* viii. §9 A sortie from Dublin had already broken up Ormond's siege of the capital.

transf. **1827** SCOTT *Jrnl.* 2 Jan., The rheumatism, exasperated by my sortie of yesterday, has seized on my . . knee. **1831** GREVILLE *Mem.* (1875) II. xiii. 119 She was mighty glorious about her *sortie* upon Lambton. **1859** *Once a Week* I. 455 He made a sortie from the box like a lion rushing into the circus.

b. Without article.

1845 D. COSTELLO *Tour Valley Meuse* 156 Subterraneous passages . . used for sortie and retreat by the garrison of the castle.

c. *attrib.*, as ***sortie corvette, party.***

1887 *Pall Mall G.* 11 Jan. 2/1, I am not . . aware that Germany . . proposes to employ 'sortie corvettes' in the absence of guns or submarine mines. **1896** MORRISON *Child Jago* iv, The defeated sortie-party from Jago Court.

d. An operational flight by a military aircraft.

1918 B. HALL *En l'Air* viii. 76 My machine was a single-seated Nieuport biplane... I carried 1,000 rounds of ammunition... An air sortie at dawn! **1941** *Hutchinson's Pictorial Hist. War* 19 Mar.–13 May 64/2 The main target of the R.A.F.'s night sorties is the industrial centre of Emden. **1955** *Times* 29 June 10/3 In the five active days of the test the two sides flew 12,347 sorties and simulated the dropping of over 300 atomic bombs. **1969** G. MACBETH *War Quartet* 37 Then Waking . . we were up . . for New sorties. **1977** *R.A.F. News* 27 Apr.–10 May 11/3 The Phantom has an average sortie capability of more than 1½ hours.

e. *Photogr.* A series of aerial photographs taken during one flight; *transf.*, a photographic session. Also *attrib.*

1953 R. J. C. ATKINSON *Field Archaeology* (ed. 2) i. 24 The unit of classification of prints is the *sortie*, that is, a series of prints taken on a single flight. Each sortie consists of one or more strips of prints, running approximately in an East-West direction, each print overlapping the next to East and West by about two-thirds of its width. *Ibid.*, Each print . . is labelled at the top with the sortie-number. *Ibid.* 25 Sortie plots may be bought separately at the same charge per plot. **1959** N. MAILER *Advts. for Myself* (1961) 229 One sortie when she was photographed sipping a soda she shaped the second straw into a heart. **1963** W. K. KILFORD *Elem. Air Survey* x. 226 When the sortie is complete the film is processed... The relative position of each photograph . . of the sortie is plotted. **1969** G. C. DICKINSON *Maps & Air Photographs* xv. 246 A set of photographs taken during one flight is usually known as a *sortie. Ibid.* 247 More detailed information about coverage is contained on index diagrams, known as sortie plots.

3. a. A sally-port. **b.** An outlet (of a river).

1809 D. THOMPSON *Jrnl.* 18 Aug. (1950) II. 31 The Sortie of the [stream] that falls into the [stream] at Deer's Horns Plains. **1848** LYTTON *Harold* XII. vii, Three sorties, whence the defenders might sally. **1879** *19th Cent.* 1121 The Kalamas has its sortie opposite Corfu.

4. *attrib.* in *Astronautics*, designating spacecraft designed to return to earth after a period; so ***sortie mission.***

1972 *National Observer* (U.S.) 27 May 6/4 NASA also plans a 'sortie module', a laboratory for six scientists and engineers that would be carried in the orbiter's cargo bay for earth-orbit missions lasting from one to four weeks. **1972** *New Scientist* 6 July 3 NASA has offered Europe the 'sortie can'—a pressurised laboratory module that is to swing out from the cargo bay of the orbiting shuttle. **1973** *Times* 15 June 27/7 Here the proposal is that Europe would develop a 'sortie lab' or 'spacelab' module. **1976** LOHMAN & LEE in L. G. Napolitano *Space Activity Impact on Sci. & Technol.* 108 In a series of flights, these aircraft duplicate the observations which would be conducted in a single sortie mission.

'sortie, *v.* Also sorty. [f. prec.] *intr.* To make a sortie; to sally. Hence **'sortieing** *ppl. a.*

1871 *Standard* 27 Jan., Pressing on, the sortying party advanced up the heights. **1899** *Westm. Gaz.* 23 Nov. 7/2 Unsuccessful attempts to sortie are supposed to have been made. **1904** *Daily Chron.* 23 May 5/1 To cover the movements of the sortieing force.

‖**sortie de bal** (sɔrti də bal). [Fr., lit. 'departure from (the) ball'.] A woman's evening cloak with a quilted lining, popular in the late nineteenth century.

1864 M. B. CHESNUT *Diary* 29 Dec. in C. V. Woodward *M. Chesnut's Civil War* (1981) xxxix. 696 Mary was wrapped in a snowy swansdown *sortie de bal.* **1895** [see DOVE *sb.* 1 d]. **1908** A. BENNETT *Old Wives' Tale* III. ii. 296 It was a tall and mature woman who wore over a dress of purplish-black silk a vast flowing *sortie de bal* of vermilion velvet, looped and tasselled with gold.

sortilege^1 ('sɔːtɪlɪdʒ). Also 5 sortylege. [a. OF. *sortilege* (mod.F. *sortilège*, = It., Sp., Pg. *sortilegio*), or ad. med.L. *sortilegium*, f. L. *sortilegus*: see next.]

1. The practice of casting lots in order to decide something or to forecast the future; divination based on this procedure or performed in some other way; †sorcery, magic, witchcraft.

1387 TREVISA *Higden* (Rolls) II. 43 In þat ilond is sortilege and wicchecraft i-vsed. For wommen þere selliþ schip-men wynde. **1430-40** LYDG. *Bochas* VI. iv. (1554) 142 He delited most.. In sortilege and in sorcerye. **1483** CAXTON *Cato* F ij, This cursyd synne of sortylege haboundeth more in wymmen than in men. **1546** BALE *Eng. Votaries* I. 35 b, He sett vp a great scole at Caunterburye.. and taught them.. the art Magyck, Sortilege, Physnomye. **1584** R. SCOT *Discov. Witchcr.* XI. x. (1886) 159 The cousening art of sortilege or lotarie. **1730** BAILEY (fol.), *Sortilege*, a Soothsaying or Divination by Lots; also an Electing by casting of Lots. **1830** SCOTT *Demonol.* ii. 66 They endeavoured by sortilege.. to find as it were a byroad to the secrets of futurity. **1850** MERIVALE *Rom. Emp.* vi. (1865) I. 275 Three times, he related, had lots been drawn;.. each time he had owed his life to the chance of sortilege. **1881** STANLEY *Christ. Instit.* v. 87 Signs of what most Christians now would regard as mere remnants of sortilege and sorcery.

2. An act or instance of divining, choosing, or deciding by the drawing or casting of lots.

1600 HOLLAND *Livy* XLIV. xxii. 1183 As the gods in favour have directed this sortilege, so they will bee present and propitious unto mee. **1795** WYTHE *Decis.* 104 Another lottery, according to which the destiny of every ticket ought to have been decided by a single sortilege. **1819** SCOTT *Ivanhoe* xxxvii, A woman infamous for sortileges and for witcheries. **1842** *Blackw. Mag.* LI. 282 All treasonable assumptions.. commenced in the hopes inspired by auguries, prophecies, or sortileges. **1868** MILMAN *St. Paul's* ii. 20 All sortileges, auspices, divinations, and other works of the devil, were forbidden.

sortilege[2]. *rare.* [ad. L. *sortileg-us* diviner, fortune-teller, f. *sort-*, *sors* lot + *legĕre* to choose. Cf. obs. F. *sortilegue*, It., Sp., Pg. *sortilego*.] One who practises divination or sorcery.

1483 CAXTON *Cato* Contents iv b, Ageynst them that ben sortileges of herbes and of wrytynges for to hele men or horses. *Ibid.* F j b, To the ende that none sette feythe to sortyleges ne to deuyners. **1855** MILMAN *Lat. Chr.* V. XI. ix. 253 He is a sortilege, and consults diviners and fortune-tellers.

'sortileger. Now *rare.* Also 5 sortyloger, -leger. [See prec. and -ER. The form in *-loger* is based upon the med.L. *sortilogus* for *sortilegus*.] One who divines, chooses, or settles by drawing lots or otherwise; a diviner, fortune-teller.

c **1400** *Apol. Loll.* 54 Fraudars, misdoars, sortylogers. *Ibid.* 97 Sortilegeris, and oþer þat are put in þe general sentens and cursing of þe kirk. **1483** CAXTON *Cato* F ij, Often God permytteth and suffreth that, that the sortylegers and devynours maken to come. **1635** HEYWOOD *Hierarchy* I. Comm. 47 We read of three sorts of these Sortilegers or Fortune-tellers. *Ibid.* VII. Comm. 473 Now to speake of those Sortilegers and the effects of their Art. **1864** A. LEIGHTON *Myst. Leg. Edinb.* (1886) 224 All which signs seemed only the opportunity of the devout sortileger, who put her hand upon the Bible.

sorti'legic, *a. rare.* [f. SORTILEGE[1] + -IC.] Dependent upon divination or sortilege.

1896 *17th Ann. Rep. Bureau Amer. Ethnol.* I. 259 The warfare of the Seri is largely sortilegic.

sorti'legious, *a.* ? *Obs.* [f. SORTILEGE[1] or SORTILEGY.] Of the nature of, relating to or connected with, sortilege.

1603 SIR C. HEYDON *Jud. Astrol.* i. 12 Diuinations that were meerely superstitious, sortilegious, and diuellish. **1652** GAULE *Magastrom.* 29 But were all they of Babylon solely and wholly trained up to this sortilegious trade? *a* **1717** DAUBREZ *Rev.* (Lancaster, 1730) 46 Horace.. makes their [*sc.* frogs] Blood an Ingredient in sortilegious Charms.

sortilegist. *rare*[−1]. [f. SORTILEGE[1] + -IST.] One who arranges the drawing of lots.

1865 *Reader* 25 Nov. 598/1 This college sortilegist pretended to be much annoyed at the result he had taken such pains to procure.

‖**sorti'legium.** *rare.* = SORTILEGY 2.

1858 BAILEY *Age* 65 Suppose we try a sortilegium, eh?

sortilegy (sɔː'tɪlədʒɪ, 'sɔːtɪlɛdʒɪ). Also 4–5 sortelegye, -legie (-logie), 6 sortilegie, 7 -ligie. [ad. med.L. *sortilegi-um*: see SORTILEGE[1].]

1. Divination by the casting or drawing of lots or otherwise; = SORTILEGE[1] 1.

1387 TREVISA *Higden* (Rolls) I. 411 Oft gyled was this brood,.. For Merlyns prophecie, And ofte for sortelogie [*v.r.* sortelegie]. **1584** R. SCOT *Discov. Witchcr.* XIII. xxix. (1886) 278 The Aegyptians juggling witchcraft or Sortilegie. **1680** C. NESSE *Ch. Hist.* 269 He had by his sortilegy, or rather sorcery, found out his lucky day. **1839** DE QUINCEY *Mod. Superst.* Wks. 1853 III. 307 That mode of sortilegy which is conducted by throwing open priviledged books at random. **1883** J. PAYN *Thicker than Water* xxviii, Miss Blithers the elder, who believed in sortilegy, presented her with a tract, drawn at random from a whole sheaf of them.

2. An act or instance of this; = SORTILEGE[1] 2.

1643 SIR T. BROWNE *Relig. Med.* I. §18. 39 Even in sortilegies and matters of greatest uncertainty, there is a setled and preordered course of effects. **1656** S. HOLLAND *Zara* (1719) 28 When that venerable Quack sold his Brethrens lives (by a Sortiligie) to save his own.

sorting ('sɔːtɪŋ), *vbl. sb.* Also 4–5 sortyng, 5 *Sc.* -en, 6 soorting. [f. SORT *v.*[1] + -ING[1].]

1. The action of the vb., in various senses; arrangement, classification.

c **1358** *Durham Acc. Rolls* (Surtees) 561 Will'o Randman pro pylyng et sortyng lane. **1485** *Act 1 Hen. VII*, c. 10 §7 The same Wolle shuld be.. clene wounde, withoute any sortyng, barbyng or clakkyng. **1494** *Acc. Ld. High Treas. Scot.* I. 248 Giffyne for sorten of the tymmyr in the ȝard, iij s. iij d. **1554** *Act 1 Mary* c. 7 §1 The.. principall grounde of Clothmakyng ys the true sorting of Wolles. **1599** B. JONSON *Cynthia's Rev.* v. iv, It is the sorting, and the dividing,.. and the decocting, that makes the fumigation. **1625** MARKHAM *Souldier's Accid.* 1 For the Sorting of Armes, it is a good proportion to haue a Companie equally compounded of Armed men and Shot. **1690** LOCKE *Hum. Und.* III. iii. (1695) 230 The Essences of the sorts of Things, and consequently the sorting of Things, is the Workmanship of the Understanding. **1711** ADDISON *Spect.* No. 10 ¶6 The sorting of a Suit of Ribbons. **1765** *Phil. Trans.* LV. 205 In sorting, the skain to be examined is put upon the hook. **1856** DE QUINCEY in 'H. A. Page' *Life* (1877) II. xvii. 51 The separation and sorting of such innumerable papers. **1892** *Athenæum* 23 Apr. 530/1 We have.. a little too much mere sorting of the varied intellectual material.

2. a. With *a* and pl. An instance of this.

1611 COTGR., *Assortissement*,.. a sorting, or suiting of things together. **1764** *Museum Rust.* II. 38, I divide my fruit into three several sorts..; from these three sortings I have.. six several kinds of cyder. **1839** URE *Dict. Arts* 812 The substances.. undergo another *sorting*, with greater or less care. **1871** CARLYLE in *Mrs. C.'s Lett.* (1883) II. 362 He did for me all manner of.. summaries, copyings, sortings.

b. *Sc.* An assortment, supply, stock.

a **1779** D. GRAHAM *Leper the Taylor* I. Writ. 1883 II. 116 Poor Sandy went home with a skinful of terror, and a sorting of sore bones.

3. With advs., as *out*, *up*.

1890 W. J. GORDON *Foundry* 76 Then came a sorting out of the juniors from the seniors. **1890** *Daily News* 16 Dec. 6/4 The higher prices.. have caused a little more sorting up.

4. a. *attrib.*, as *sorting-action*; **sorting-boom, † -cloth** (see quots.); **sorting code** *Banking*, a code number which identifies a branch office in the banking system, and is used to facilitate the processing of cheques and credit transfers; **† sorting-kersey, -machine** (see quots.).

Also, in modern use, with advs., as *sorting-out influence*, *operation*, *process*; *sorting-up business*, *order*, *trade*, etc.

1897 *Geogr. Jrnl.* IX. 278 One of the most remarkable phenomena attending the distribution of earthy materials by wind (or water) is the *sorting action exercised by the fluid. **1877** *Lumberman's Gaz.* 8 Dec. 362 There is a system of '*sorting booms' by which the logs, each bearing a distinguishing mark, are distributed to their several ownerships. **1593** *3rd Rep. Hist. MSS. Comm.* 7/1 Woollen cloths.. called vesses,.. park cloths, or *sorting cloths made in Somersetshire. **1674** JEAKE *Arith.* (1696) 68 One Sack of Wooll.. is accompted to make 4. Standard Clothes of clean Wooll called sorting Clothes. **1847** HALLIW., *Sorting-cloths*, a kind of short cloths, with a blue selvage on both sides of the lists, made in the Eastern counties. **1959** D. S. TRAVERS in *Electronics in Banking* (Institute of Bankers) 50 The cheque of the future... The code appears in five blocks... Block 2—Bank and branch *sorting code. **1965** PERRY & RYDER *Thomson's Dict. Banking* (ed. 11) 524/2 *Sorting code numbers*, a system devised to assist customers of banks who make considerable use of the Credit Transfer system... The number is placed in the box provided on the credit by the customer before passing the credit to the bank. It consists of three groups of two figures each, eg. 20-03-92, the first digits denoting the bank, and the remainder identifying the branch. **1706** PHILLIPS (ed. Kersey), **Sorting-Kersies*, a sort of Cloth so call'd. **1875** KNIGHT *Dict. Mech.* 2246/2 *Sorting-machine.. for gaging leather strips as they are cut from the hide to certain regulated sizes. **1977** *Canad. Jrnl. Linguistics 1976* XXI. II. 149 In (44) the criterion of the *sorting-out operation is P_1. **1960** E. H. GOMBRICH *Art & Illusion* II. iv. 144 Classical art also underwent an evolution, a *sorting-out process after its heroic period.

b. In the sense 'in, at, or on which sorting is done', as ***sorting-board, house, office, siding, table***, etc.; with *adv.*, as ***sorting-out centre***.

1766 ENTICK *London* IV. 191 In which is one of the sorting houses, under the comptrolment of the general penny-post. **1851** J. MILNE *Autobiog.* iv. 109 Aberdeen has become what is termed a sorting office. **1881** A. BATHGATE *Waitaruna* xii. 172 The 'pickers-up' were busy gathering the fleeces.. and carrying them to the sorting table. **1885** BOWMAN *Struct. Wool Fibre* 358 Sorting-board, the table on which wool is sorted. **1899** *Daily News* 4 Mar. 3/2 At Woodford there are extensive sorting sidings. **1952** S. SPENDER *Learning Laughter* vii. 97 The reader should be able to visualize them going to the sorting-out centre near Haifa.

'sorting, *ppl. a.* [f. SORT *v.*[1] + -ING[2].]

1. That corresponds, agrees, or suits (with others of the same class or kind).

1535 *Wardr. Kath. Arragon* 24 in *Camden Misc.* III, Item, fyve pecis of hangings of tapistrye soorting. **1547** *Harl. MS. 1419 A.* lf. 38 Nyne peces sorting.., every of theym lyned with Canvas.

2. That sorts, arranges, or classifies.

1912 *Civil Service Year Bk.* 61 The.. pay of a Sorting Clerk and Telegraphist.

† sortise, *v. Obs.*[−1] [f. OF. *sortiss-*, lengthened stem of *sortir* SORT *v.*[1]] *trans.* To acquire, obtain.

1474 CAXTON *Chesse* IV. ii, But whan he is ones meuyd fro his propre place,.. than he sortiseth the nature of the comyn peple, and thus by good right he hath in hym self the nature of al.

sortition (sɔː'tɪʃən). [ad. L. *sortītio*, f. *sortīrī* to cast or draw lots.]

1. The casting or drawing of lots; selection, choice, or determination by lot.

1597 J. KING *On Jonas* (1618) 120 For so doth Tully define Sortition, that it is nothing else but hap-hazard. **1608** —— *Serm.* 24 Mar. 11 Some reigne by vsurpation,.. some by acquisition,.. some by sortition or augurie. **1659** HAMMOND *On Ps.* xvi. 5 The old way of sortition was by staves or rods. **1790** BURKE *Fr. Rev.* 74 No mode of election operating in the spirit of sortition or rotation. **1849** GROTE *Greece* II. xliv. V. 371 The principle of sortition or choice by lot was never applied.. to all offices at Athens. **1886** *Q. Rev.* July 12 In a certain Arcadian state sortition superseded election.

2. With *a* and pl. An act or instance of determining by lot.

1634 BP. HALL *Contempl.*, *N.T.* IV. 273 The souldiers have.. cast lots upon thy seamlesse coat (those poore spoiles cannot so much inrich them, as glorifie thee; whose Scriptures are fulfilled by their barbarous sortitions). **1634** in *4th Rep. Hist. MSS. Comm.* 127 Whether the advowsons of benefices.. be not passed by balls or sortitions to private residentiaryes. **1830** W. TAYLOR *Hist. Surv. Germ. Poetry* I. 275 The scourging, the crowning with thorns, and the sortition of the garments. **1887** MISS BETHAM-EDWARDS *Next of Kin Wanted* I. xiv. 190 The transfer of the property, by a distribution, sortition, or otherwise.

† 3. An allotted share or portion. *Obs.*

1671 [R. MACWARD] *True Nonconf.* 90 The Lords People.., whether.. termed.. lots, in order to their respective Pastors, whose sortitions, and divisions they are, or as being Gods heritage.

sortli, obs. form of SHORTLY *adv.*

† 'sortly, *a. Obs. rare.* [f. SORT *sb.*[2] + -LY[1].]

1. Of articles: That correspond or form a set.

1459 *Paston Lett.* I. 474, iiij. platers, parcell of ix. platers not sortely. *Ibid.*, v. platers, not sortely.

2. Appropriate; suitable.

1570 *Wit & Science* (1848) 46 Whereby I trust by my good Endever To that good Ladye, so sweete and so sortlye, A maryage betwene them ye shall see shortlye.

† sortly, *adv. Obs. rare.* [f. SORT *sb.*[2] + -LY[2].] So as to agree or correspond; correspondingly, equally.

c **1557** ABP. PARKER *Ps.* cxix. Pref., Here letters all so sortely bound do shew in mysterie Eternall health may sure be found in scripture totally. **1566** —— *Corr.* (Parker Soc.) 278 They be counted sortly learned with the best of them.

† 'sortment. *Obs.* [f. SORT *v.*[1] + -MENT. Cf. It. *sortimento*.]

1. The action or process of sorting, separating, or arranging; sortation, classification.

1598 BARRET *Theor. Warres* 69 The due sortement and matching of these weapons to offend, and defend. **1622** F. MARKHAM *Bk. War* v. iii. 170 The iust number of the Army, together with the true sortment and division of euery weapon. **1755** in JOHNSON. **1778** PRYCE *Min. Cornub.* 233 When it comes to grass they make a sortment of the larger stones from the smaller.

2. A collection of assorted goods or articles; a sorted set or lot; an assortment.

1621 in Foster *Eng. Factories Ind.* (1906) I. 326 To write the bymarke of the sortement of every chest. **1657** in *Thurloe's St. Papers* (1742) VI. 56 In March we expected most of our chiefe merchants to come out for their easter sortment, against which tyme I desired you would be pleased to give orders at Freshford. **1719** W. WOOD *Survey Trade* 246 Manufacturing and making up proper Sortments of Goods. **1766** T. BROOKS *Coins E. Indies* 67 The finest Hysons, and all other Sortments of the Green-Teas.

b. *transf.* A set or number of persons.

1710 MILBOURNE *Meas. Resist.* 4 When a sortment of priests, as he with a peculiar elegance, expresses it, endeavour to bully us into slavery. **1760–72** H. BROOKE *Fool of Qual.* (1809) II. 39 A hundred and fifty visits,.. and through such a sortment too, as your mercers say.

c. A kind or class of things.

1718 QUINCY *Compl. Disp.* 8 The Lightness of this Sortment of Matter. **1720** —— in *Phil. Trans.* XXXI. 76 Thus for all cutaneous Foulnesses.. the Cinnabar, the Æthiops, and all of that Sortment are in readiness.

sort-out. [f. vbl. phr. *to sort out*: see SORT *v.*[1] 11.] **a.** The action or an instance of sorting out (of things or situations that are in disarray). **b.** A fight or dispute.

1937 PARTRIDGE *Dict. Slang* 802/1 *Sort-out*, a fight, a mellay. **1961** *John o' London's* 25 May 591/2 An enlightened attempt at a black-and-white sort-out. **1964** C. WILLOCK *Enormous Zoo* i. 14 Beaton himself had a sort-out with a buffalo bull that tried to overturn his Land-Rover. **1972** *Tel.* (Brisbane) 18 May 18/4 He was the most cantankerous character I have met. I had only been here two days when we had our first sort-out. **1981** G. HAMMOND *Revenge Game* vii. 65 You folk finish the first sort-out downstairs.

sorty ('sɔːtɪ), *a. colloq.* [f. SORT *sb.*[2] + -Y. Cf. WFris. *soartich* of a good sort.]

1. Of one kind or sort; similar, alike.

1885 *Field* 12 Dec. 845/1 Mr. W. Wheeler's cup pigs were .. not quite sorty as to hair, but otherwise a good lot.

2. Consisting of various sorts; mixed.

1899 *Daily News* 3 July 9/7 Phipps,.. usually driving blacks, has got together a very 'sorty' team composed of a skewbald, a chestnut, and bays. *a* **1904** in *Eng. Dial. Dict.* s.v., The water is very sorty this morning—it is much colder at the bottom than on the top.

‖**sorus**[1] ('sɔərəs). Pl. sori ('sɔəraɪ). [mod.L., ad. Gr. σωρός heap.]

1. *Bot.* A cluster of capsules or spore-cases on the under surface of fern-leaves.

1832 LINDLEY *Introd. Bot.* I. iii. 196 In a third tribe the sori occupy the whole of the under surface of the frond. **1857** T. MOORE *Handbk. Brit. Ferns* (ed. 3) 8 The part of the vein on which the sorus is seated. **1876** HARLEY *Royle's Mat. Med.* 360 *Sori* elliptical, imbedded in the substance of the thallus, concave on one side.

2. A similar formation in algæ, lichens, or fungi.

1842 *Penny Cycl.* XXII. 266/2 The term sorus is sometimes applied to mere collections of spores or granules, as seen in many Algæ, of which *Delesseria alata* and *D. sinuosa* are examples. **1874** COOKE *Fungi* 38 The pustules, or sori, break through the cuticle in a similar manner.

†**sorus**[2], obs. variant of SORA.

1775 A. BURNABY *Trav.* 25 They went out into an adjoining marsh to catch soruses... The sorus is not known to be in Virginia, except for about six weeks from the latter end of September.

‖'**sory**, *sb. Obs.* [L. *sōry*, ad. Gr. σῶρυ. Cf. Sp. and It. *sori*.] A kind of mineral ore yielding vitriol; one or other kind of vitriol.

1601 HOLLAND *Pliny* II. 510 As for Sory, that which is brought out of Ægypt is counted best, and farre better than the Cyprian, Spanish, or African. **1657** TOMLINSON *Renou's Disp.* xiii. 27 Many efficacious Poysons also are drawn from Minerals,.. as Quick-silver, red Lead, Parget, Vitriol, Sory, Sandarach [etc.]. [**1728** BAILEY, *Sory*, a kind of Mineral, a sort of Vitriol made of Chalcitis or Cadmia. **1828-32** in WEBSTER. Hence in later Dicts.]

†**sory**, *a. Obs. rare.* Also **soory, sowry.** [f. SORE *sb.*[3] + -Y, or ad. ON. *saurigr* (MSw. *sörogh*).] Filthy, dirty.

c **1440** *Promp. Parv.* 465/1 Soory, or defowlyd yn sowr or fylthe.., *cenosus, cenulentus. Ibid.* 466/2 Sowry, or defowlyd wythe fylthe.

†**soryful**, obs. var. SORROWFUL *a.*

Prob. due to confusion with *sory* SORRY *a.*

c **1550** H. LLOYD *Treas. Health* c ij, Soryful syghes in sharpe agewes be to be fearyd. **1596** DALRYMPLE tr. *Leslie's Hist. Scot.* (S.T.S.) II. 239 Quhilke maid the king sa soryfull .. that [etc.].

soryp, obs. form of SYRUP.

S.O.S. (ˌɛsəʊ'ɛs), *sb.* Also **SOS.** [The letters *s, o* and *s*, chosen because easily transmitted in Morse code.]

1. a. The international radio code-signal of extreme distress, used esp. by ships at sea.

1910 J. A. FLEMING *Princ. Electr. Wave Telegr. & Teleph.* (ed. 2) 882 This signal, S,O,S, has superseded the Marconi Company's original high sea cry for help, which was C,Q,D. **1910** E. LAWTON *Boy Aviators in Nicaragua* 263 S.O.S. is now the wireless distress call. **1924** *Mod. Wireless* III. 310/3 The famous signal 'SOS' was adopted officially by the International Radio Telegraph Convention in July, 1908. **1930** 'SAPPER' *Finger of Fate* 245 The S.O.S. had been picked up by three other boats... The last S.O.S. had broken off abruptly in the middle of the message. **1942** [see DASH *sb.*[1] 7 f].

b. *transf.* An urgent message or appeal for help.

1918 *Punch* 13 Mar. 176 S.O.S. at Suburban Pictures. (In cases of emergency affecting any of the audience messages are sometimes thrown on the screen by the courtesy of the management.) **1931** E. F. BENSON *Mapp & Lucia* iii. 80 There was nothing but helpful sunny cordiality in response to this S.O.S. **1965** D. FRANCIS *Odds Against* xix. 235 You'd sent him to me as a sort of S.O.S.

2. As an abbrev. of various jocular phrases: **a.** 'same old story, stuff', etc. **b.** 'shit on a shingle': chipped beef on toast. *U.S. Mil. slang.*

1918 *Sat. Even. Post* 27 Apr. 62 'What have you got this morning, Thompson? SOS?' 'Yes sir,' returned the striker. 'Same old slum.' **1926** MAINES & GRANT *Wise-Crack Dict.* 14/2 *S.O.S.*, same old story. **1959** I. & P. OPIE *Lore & Lang. Schoolch.* ix. 162 The possessors of young and healthy appetites are lyrical about their food. School dinners are 'muck', 'pig swill'.. 'S.O.S.' (Same Old Slush). **1963** *Amer. Speech* XXXVII. 271 Haskell students do employ the standard American slang initials *S.O.S.*, but.. Girls use them to mean 'same old stuff'... Boys.. refer more specifically to creamed beef on toast.. and this abbreviation stands for either 'same old shit' or 'shit on a shingle'. **1974** *News & Observer* (Raleigh, N. Carolina) 8 July 23/2 The troops still sometimes get S.O.S. for breakfast, whether they want it or not.

3. *attrib.* and *Comb.*, as *S.O.S. call, message, signal*; **S.O.S. redouble** *Bridge* (see quot. 1926[2]); also *ellipt.*

1915 *Daily Mail* 10 May 4/5 The Marconi operators showed magnificent coolness in that hour of trial. They made the 'S.O.S.' call, and they had to make it quickly. **1938** *Encycl. Brit. Bk. of Year* 122/1 S.O.S. and police messages broadcast from all transmitters during the year reached a total of 1,213. **1978** J. THOMSON *Question of Identity* vii. 70 I'd've heard if he was dead.. They'd've put it on the radio; an S.O.S. message. **1926** M. C. WORK *Auction Bridge Compl.* x. 134 The No Trumper resorts to a recently invented signal of acute distress and makes the 'S.O.S. Redouble'. *Ibid.* 498 *S.O.S.* (*redouble*), redouble made to indicate weakness rather than strength. **1939** N. DE V. HART *Bridge Players' Bedside Bk.* 135 If the strong opening No Trumps.. is being played, a redouble by a player who has opened with One No-Trump is not an SOS. **1967** R. L. FREY *Bridge Players' Encycl.* 470/2 In rare circumstances a player may redouble his partner's bid as an SOS instead of his own bid. **1977** C. H. GOREN *Bridge Compl.* (ed. 3) 684 *Redouble*, a call that further increases the scoring value of tricks and penalties after an opposing double; sometimes also used as a request for partner to rescue (S.O.S. redouble). **1917** 'SAPPER' *No Man's Land* 71 A row of grey-painted rockets with a red top, which in case of emergency send up the coloured flares that give the S.O.S. signals to those behind. **1927** H. A. VACHELL *Dew of Sea* 257 He received a letter from the gentleman, regarded (and rightly) by the McCullough as an S.O.S. signal. **1929** C. H. SMITH *Bridge of Life* iv. 83 When one gave an SOS signal all the rest came to his assistance.

S.O.S., *v.* Also **SOS.** [f. prec.] **1.** *intr.* **a.** To make an S.O.S. signal or signals. **b.** *Bridge.* To execute an S.O.S. redouble.

1918 KIPLING *Land & Sea Tales* (1923) 114 Then.. this Baxter-man got busy with his wireless and SOS'ed like winkie. **1926** M. C. WORK *Auction Bridge Compl.* x. 135 In the event of a business pass, the No Trumper can S.O.S. if in need of help. **1975** G. HOWELL *In Vogue* 75/1 We have been passing through the awkward age, when instead of conversing we 'S.O.S.ed' in monosyllabic slang.

2. *trans.* To send an urgent message requesting (someone) *to* do something.

a **1936** KIPLING *Something of Myself* (1937) viii. 221 One of the Captains S.O.S.-ed me to give him 'something to tell these somethinged tourists about it'.

so's: see 's 5.

‖**sosatie** (sɔː'sɑːtɪ). *S. Afr.* Also **sas(s)atie, sas(s)atje, sosaartje,** etc. [Afrikaans, f. S. Afr. Du. *sasaatje*, f. Mal. (Javanese) *sesate* skewered meat.] Curried or spiced meat grilled on a skewer.

1833 *Cape Good Hope Lit. Gaz.* 2 Sept. 138 (Pettman), *Sasaitie*, or cabobs, is really no despicable eating. **1870** *Cape Monthly Mag.* Oct. 224 '*Sosaartjes*', '*smoor-picklaar*', and all sorts of vegetable '*breedies*', are importations from India. **1883** 'R. IRON' *Story Afr. Farm* II. II. iv. 67, I got the Hottentot girl to show me how to make 'sar-sarties' this morning. **1885** L. H. MEURANT *Sixty Years Ago* 29 There existed in those days what we termed 'Sasaatje and Rice' houses, places where a favourite Dutch dish called 'Sasaatjes' was served in the evenings... two sasaatjes (diamond-shaped inch-sized pieces of mutton, curried and about half a dozen stuck upon a bamboo skewer, and then roasted upon a gridiron). **1894** *Cape Argus* 22 Dec. (Pettman), A Hittite.. with a long spear and a very pronounced intention to spit you on it, like a sassatje. *a* **1920** [see BOBOTIE]. **1939** S. CLOETE *Watch for Dawn* xxi. 310 A woman had so much to do with food. Sassaties, bobotee, snysels. **1948** H. V. MORTON *In Search of S. Afr.* 293 Sosaties.. are a popular and delicious grill which can be as simple as veal or mutton cutlets sprinkled with curry powder and roasted on a skewer over a clear wood fire, or as complex as pieces of mutton or pork soaked in wine or vinegar, spiced with coriander, turmeric, pepper, tamarind and grilled in the same way. **1953** *Cape Times* 21 Mar. 3/3 These [South African recipes] are destined for Holland, where they will be needed to prepare *braaivleis* and *sasaties* when the South African *volkspele* team visits Culemborg and holds a *braaivleisaand* there. **1973** *Farmer's Weekly* (S. Afr.) 25 Apr., At a braaivleis the sosaties are eaten straight from the grill.

sose, obs. form of SUSS *sb.*

†**sosh.** *Obs.*[−1] [Imitative. Cf. SOSS *sb.*[2]] A dull, heavy sound; a thud; = SOSS *sb.*[2]

1687 A. LOVELL tr. *Bergerac's Com. Hist.* 8, I fell with a sosh in the Valley below.

‖**soshi** ('səʊʃɪ). Pl. **soshi.** [Jap., lit. 'strong man', a. Chinese *suǒshì*, f. *suǒ* lusty, valiant + *shì* warrior.] A mercenary political agitator or intimidator, a terrorist; a bodyguard.

1891 B. H. CHAMBERLAIN *Things Japanese* (ed. 2) 128 Since 1888, there has sprung up a class of rowdy youths, called *soshi* in Japanese—juvenile agitators who have taken all politics to be their province. **1894** G. N. CURZON *Probl. Far East* ii. 33 The *soshi* or professional rowdies, who are ready, for a consideration, to let out their services to either party in Japan. **1896** L. HEARN *Kokoro* vi. 95 Soshi form one of the modern curses of Japan. They are mostly ex-students who earn a living by hiring themselves out as rowdy terrorists. **1910** LADY LAWSON *Highways & Homes of Japan* xxv. 284 At one time this extraordinary man was a *soshi* or political bully, one of the turbulent class who suffer from too much education and too little to eat. **1930** M. D. KENNEDY *Changing Fabric of Japan* vii. 121 In 1923, meetings in favour of Manhood Suffrage were broken up by gangs of *soshi*. **1977** G. M. BERGER *Parties out of Power in Japan 1931–1941* iv. 147 Nakamizo Tamakichi, a former seiyūkai bodyguard (*sōshi*), organized a group of several hundred toughs.

soskin, variant of SUSKIN.

so so, so-so ('səʊ 'səʊ), *adv.* and *a.* (*sb.*). Also 6 **soo soo, soso,** 6–9 **so, so,** 9 *Sc.* **saesae.** [So *adv.* Cf. G. *so so*, Du. *zoo zoo*, WFris. *sa sa*, in similar use.]

For *so, so*, as a mere exclamation, see SO *adv.* 5 c.

A. *adv.* In an indifferent, mediocre, or passable manner or degree; indifferently, not quite satisfactorily: **a.** With verbs.

1530 PALSGR. 842/1 So so, *tellement quellement.* **1548** UDALL, etc. *Erasm. Par. Luke* vi. 73 b, This thyng, the pharisees could soso awaie withall, because it was a thyng.. of the common vsage. **1553** *Respublica* 647 My ladie, howe doe youe? *Respub.* Even so so, people. **1598** GRENEWEY *Tacitus, Ann.* XII. x. (1622) 171 His wife.. endured the first flight so so, for feare of the enemy and loue of hir husband. **1675** WOOD *Life* (O.H.S.) II. 318 Villerius Bathurst e Coll. Trin. [spoke] well, Philippus Clarke e Coll. Magd. so so. **1872** *Routledge's Ev. Boy's Ann.* 579/1 'And you have succeeded fairly?' 'So-so,' he answered. **1877** H. JAMES *American* vii. 120 'And are you enjoying it?'.. 'Oh, so-so,' he answered.

b. With pa. pples., ppl. adjs., and adjs.

1532 *St. Papers Hen. VIII*, VII. 396 The said old Abbot of Ferfa, reconcyled soo soo to the Pope, hath been of late at Rome. **1548** UDALL, etc. *Erasm. Par. Luke* v. 65 Seeyng the place to be so-so commodious for one to preache the ghospel in. **1600** SHAKS. *A. Y. L.* v. i. 29 *Clo.* Art rich? *Will.* Faith sir, so, so. **1828** SCOTT *Jrnl.* 30 Jan., Am I satisfied with my exertions? So so. **1861** WHYTE MELVILLE *Market Harb.* 41 'I suppose you are very well mounted yourself?' 'So-so,' was the reply.

c. With *but.*

1578 TIMME *Calvin on Gen.* 276 Seeing the Canaanites maintained their life but so so. *a* **1656** USSHER *Ann.* (1658) 151 To see the stipend duly paid.., which yet was but so so performed by him. **1720** C. SHADWELL *Sham Prince* v. i, And so we stitch up one another, and do but so so at the best. **1762** *Crazy Tales* 110 They pass their summers but so so, Drinking as long as they are able. **1820** HOGG *Bridal of Polmood* xvi, The king asked.. how he had passed the night —he thanked his majesty, and said he had been but so so.

B. *adj.* Indifferent, mediocre, of middling quality; neither very good nor very bad, but usu. inclining towards bad. Freq. with *but.*

1. Of things: **a.** In predicative use.

(*a*) **1542** UDALL *Erasm. Apoph.* 313 b, The maister of the feaste had sette upon the table wyne that was but easie and soso. **1576** FLEMING *Panopl. Epist.* 120 If our fortune bee but so so, indifferent (I meane). **1616** R. C. *Times' Whistle* (1871) 63 Your white or Clarret Is but so so; he cares not greatly for it. **1682** D'URFEY *Butler's Ghost* 135 Doubting their luck would be but so-so, And that it would disgrace them all [etc.]. **1827** DE QUINCEY *Murder* Wks. 1854 IV. 9 It is no disparagement to say, that his performance was but so-so.

(*b*) **1591** SPARRY tr. *Cattan's Geomancie* 128 It is so-so for the ayre, for it will raine often times. **1611** COTGR., *Bellastre*, .. fairish, reasonably faire, passable, so so. **1654** WHITLOCK *Zootomia* 260 These Elements to Books Composure go, Some good, some bad, and some So, So. **1712** SWIFT *Jrnl. to Stella* 18 Nov., I dined there t'other day,.. and our meat and drink was very so so. **1771** GOLDSM. *Haunch of Venison* 9 As in some Irish houses, where things are so so, One gammon of bacon hangs up for a show. **1820** BYRON *Blues* II. 77 The taste of the actors at best is so so. **1862** THACKERAY *Philip* xvi, Her pianoforte playing is very so-so indeed. **1871** B. TAYLOR *Faust* (1875) I. v. 90 My wish is great, my power is only so-so.

b. Used attributively.

1767 *Woman of Fashion* II. 48 You will, I fear, make but a so so Figure, as that domestic Animal, a Husband. **1788** WOLCOT (P. Pindar) *Peter's Pension* Wks. 1812 II. 18 Your man-traps.. have had but so-so luck. **1837** BARHAM *Ingol. Leg.* Ser. I. *Grey Dolphin*, After leading but a so-so life. **1862** BURGON *Letters from Rome* 260 Acres of so-so statues, and nameless busts. **1899** A. WERNER *Capt. Locusts* 279 Having got together some very so-so writing materials.

Comb. **1824** MISS FERRIER *Inher.* xviii, Very so-so looking strawberries.

2. Of persons: **a.** In respect of ability, character, position, appearance, etc.

1608 BP. ANDREWES *Serm.* (1841) II. 224 They that have not greatly gone astray, are but even so so. **1663** KILLIGREW *Parson's Wedding* I. ii, Ay marry,.. this is a husband,.. and none of your so-so husbands. **1675** COTTON *Burlesque upon B.* 110 They pretty passable are though (Thank Jove) the Children are so so. **1775** MME. D'ARBLAY *Early Diary* (1889) II. 57 Mrs. Harris—a so-so sort of woman. **1823** BYRON *Juan* XIII. lxxxii, I've seen.. a so-so matron boldly fight Her way back to the world. **1864** *Realm* 22 June 2 No one can deny that among the clergy there is more than a fair percentage of very so-so people.

b. In respect of health or physical condition.

a **1592** GREENE *Jas. IV*, Wks. (Rtldg.) 194 Our king is well, our queen so-so. **1662** J. WILSON *Cheats* I. v, *M.D.* I am afraid you are not well Sir. *Sc.* Yes—I am so, so. **1731** *Gentl. Mag.* I. 349 Howe'er it is, I scarcely know, I find myself but just so so. ?**1800** W. B. RHODES *Bomb. Fur.* i. (1830) 7 We are but middling—that is but so so. **1838** DICKENS *O. Twist* xvii, 'Hoping you find yourself well, sir!' 'So-so, Mrs. Mann,' replied the beadle. **1857** HUGHES *Tom Brown* II. v, 'How 's he?'.. 'So, so; rather done, I think, since his last fall.'

c. In respect of soberness.

1809 MALKIN *Gil Blas* II. iv. ¶4 We drank hard, and returned.. in a pretty pickle, that is to say, so-so in the upper story. **1818** KEATS *Lett.* Wks. 1889 III. 158 Rice may begin to crow, for he got a little so-so at a party of his, and was none the worse for it the next morning.

3. Marked by the excessive use of 'so' in writings or speech.

a **1800** PEGGE *Anecd. Eng. Lang.* (1814) 217 Our Cockney, however, may be supported in this his *so-so* language by respectable Historians.

Hence **so-so-so** *a.* (*nonce-use.*)

1768 MME. D'ARBLAY *Early Diary* (1889) I. 21 We had a large party to the Assembly on Monday, which was *so-so-so.*

so-soish, *a.* Also **so-so-ish.** [f. SO-SO.] Somewhat so-so; rather indifferent.

1819 KEATS *Let.* 15 *Apr.* (1931) II. 353 Do you and the miss Birkbecks get groggy on any thing—a little so so ish so as to be obliged to be seen home with a Lantern[?]. **1826** M. WILMOT *Let.* 13 Jan. (1935) 231 Major F[alconer] goes on so, so, ish, and poor dear Bessy out of spirits. **1835** *Tait's Mag.* II. 475 An imitation of.. an old Scotch ballad—very so-so-ish. **1847** *Illustr. Lond. News* 4 Sept. 158/2 The jumping was only so-so-ish. **1888** FARJEON *Miser Farebrother* xiii, I like him, just a little, in a so-soish way.

Hence **so-soishly** *adv.*

1842 *Civil Eng. & Arch. Jrnl.* V. 236/2 Many.. views being uninteresting in subject,.. and but very *so-soishly* engraved.

†**sospire.** *Obs.*[−1] [prob. ad. It. *sospiro*: see SUSPIRE *sb.*] A sigh.

1575 LANEHAM *Lett.* (1871) 60 With my spanish sospires, my french heighes.

†**sospital**, *a. Obs.*[−0] [ad. L. *sospitālis*, f. *sospit-, sospes* safe, unhurt.] (See quot.) Also †**sospitation** (cf. next).

1656 BLOUNT *Glossogr.*, *Sospital*,.. that is cause of health; medicinable, wholsom, safe, free from danger. **1658** PHILLIPS, *Sospitation*, a keeping safe, and in health, a preserving from danger.

†**sospitator.** *Obs.*⁻¹ [a. L. *sospitātor*, f. *sospitāre* to save: see prec.] A saviour, deliverer.
1643 TRAPP *Comm. Gen.* xl. 20 In honour of God, our Sospitator, for his mercy in our creation.

soss, *sb.*[1] Now *dial.* Also 5 sos, soos, 6 sose, 6–7 sosse. [? Imitative of the sound of lapping.]
1. †**a.** (See quots.) *Obs. rare.*
In many English dialects *soss* is used as a call to dogs and pigs at feeding-time.
c **1440** *Promp. Parv.* 465 Sos, howndysmete,.. *cantabrum.* **1530** PALSGR. 273/1 Sosse or a rewarde for houndes, when they have taken their game, *hvuee.*
b. *Sc.* and *dial.* A sloppy mess or mixture; a dish of food having this character.
1691 RAY *N. Co. Words* (ed. 2) 66 A *Soss*, a mucky Puddle. *a* **1728** *Kennett MSS.* (Halliw.), Of any one that mixes several slops, or makes any place wet and dirty, we say in Kent, he makes a soss. **1802** SIBBALD *Chron. S.P.* IV. Gloss., *Soss*, a large dish of flummery. **1842** J. AITON *Domest. Econ.* (1857) 128 Tea sosses ought not to be endured in the manse kitchen..: porridge is infinitely preferable. **1847** CHAMBERS *Tradit. Edinb.* 164 Lucky could furnish forth a soss—that is stew. **1886** *S.W. Linc. Gloss.* 137 You mak such sosses, for all the world like pigs.
2. A sloven, slut, or slattern.
1611 COTGR., *Halebreda*,.. a luske, a slouch; a sosse. **1901** in *Eng. Dial. Dict.* s.v., A bonny soss o' a wife Nancy Taylor 'ud mak'!

soss (sɒs), *sb.*[2] Chiefly *dial.* [Imitative: cf. SOSS *v.*[2] and SOSH.]
1. The sound made by a heavy, soft body falling upon or otherwise coming in contact with a surface; a heavy, awkward fall. Chiefly in the phr. ***with a soss.***
1718 RAMSAY *Christ's Kirk Gr.* III. iii, And wi' a soss aboon the claiths, Ilk ane their gifts down flang. **1796** W. H. MARSHALL *Yorksh.* (ed. 2) II. 346 'To fall with a soss,' to fall plumb. **1802** SIBBALD *Chron. S.P.* IV. Gloss., *Soss*, noise made by the fall of something heavy and soft. **1825–** in northern glossaries, etc. **1901** A. TROTTER *Earl Galloway Sk.* 59/2 Sandy came and sat down with a 'soss' on a chest by her bedside.
2. The sound made by impact upon water.
1885 *Pall Mall G.* 5 May 4/1 The soss, soss of her bows as she 'punches' the waves asunder.

soss, variant of SASSE *Obs.*

soss, *v.*[1] Now *north. dial.* and *Sc.* [f. SOSS *sb.*[1]]
1. a. *trans.* To make foul or dirty.
1557 TUSSER *100 Points Husb.* lxxii, Their milke slapt in corners, their creame al to sost. **1573** —— *Husb.* (1878) 106 Her milke pan and creame pot, so slabbered and sost.
b. ? To drench, soak.
1587 *Mirr. Mag., Brennus* ix, The cause why so God Neptune did me tosse: Why boyling Seas with surges so me sosse.
2. *intr.* To splash in mud or dirt.
Also *Sc.*, to make or use sloppy food or other messes.
1575 *Gamm. Gurton* I. iv. 26 Cham faine a-brode to dyg and delue, in water, myre and claye, Sossing and possing in the durte. **1876** C. C. ROBINSON *Mid- Yks. Gloss.* 131/2 *Soss*, to.. tread heavily—implying a forceful yielding to pressure, as when.. the feet plash through it [*sc.* mud]. **1951** AUDEN *Nones* (1952) 39 The three wise Maries come, Sossing through seamless waters.
3. *trans.* To lap or lick up. Also with *up.*
1598 R. BERNARD tr. *Terence, Eunuch* v. iv, They will slabber & sosse up browne bread in pottage. **1703** THORESBY *Let. to Ray, Sosse, v.*, [a word] proper to dogs. **1781–** in northern dial. glossaries. **1892** M. C. F. MORRIS *Yorksh. Folk-Talk* 375 T' dog 's sossin all t' cat milk.
Hence '**sossing** *vbl. sb.*
1824 SCOTT *St. Ronan's* xxxii, A wheen cork-headed, barmy-brained gowks! that wunna let puir folk sae muckle as die in quiet, wi' their sossings and their soopings.

soss, *v.*[2] Now *dial.* and *Sc.* [Cf. SOSS *sb.*[2]]
†**1.** *trans.* To put *up* so as to rest softly. *Obs.*
1711 SWIFT *Jrnl. to Stella* 10 March, I went to-day into the City, but in a coach and sossed up my leg on the seat.
†**2.** *intr.* To move gently; to lounge lazily. *Obs.*
1711 SWIFT *Jrnl. to Stella* 7 June, Yes, yes, I remember Berested's bridge; the coach sosses up and down as one goes that way. **1723** —— *Stella at Wood Park* Misc. 1735 V. 209 Poor Stella must pack off to Town:..From whole-some Exercise and Air, To sossing in an easy Chair.
3. To fall with a thud or heavy impact. Also *spec.* in *Mining.*
1789 DAVIDSON *Seasons* 100 Providence oft gets into one scale, To keep the proper poise, when easfu' bliss, Into the other, sosses, overpond'rous. **1825** JAMIESON *Suppl., To Soss*, to fall down as a dead weight, to come to the ground as it were all in a piece. **1883** GRESLEY *Gloss. Coal-m.* 230 *Sos*, to sink into the floor under great pressure from over-lying strata. **1898** C. HYNE *Capt. Kettle* 294 Looks like as if they were going to soss down slap on top of us.
b. To sit *down* heavily.
c **1790** A. WILSON in *Poems & Lit. Prose* (1876) II. 100 We'll hotch awa'.. And soss down on yon sinny stane. **1879** MISS JACKSON *Shropsh. Word-Bk.* 399 'Er sossed down i' the cheer all at wunst.
4. *trans.* To cast or throw heavily.
1855– in dialect glossaries, etc.

soss, *adv.* Now *dial.* [Cf. SOSS *sb.*[2] and *v.*[2]] With a heavy fall or dull thud.
1760 STERNE *Tr. Shandy* III. xxiv, Mrs. Bridget.. fell backwards soss against the bridge. **1862–** in northern glossaries.

soss-, the stem of SOSS *sb.*[1] used attributively in a few combs., with the sense 'fat, dirty, slatternly, etc.', as †*soss-bangle*, †*-belly* (see quots.).
1554 BALE *Declar. Bonner's Articles* xxix. 113 b, What is thy idolatrous mas and lowsye Latine seruice, thou sos-belly swilbol, but the very draf of Antichriste. **1691** RAY *S. & E. Co. Words* 115 A *Sosse-bangle*, a sluttish, slattering, lazy Wench; a Rustic word, only used by the vulgar. [Hence *soss-brangle* in Grose (1788).]

sossage, -ige: see SAUSAGE *sb.*

sossel, -le, *dial.*: see SOZZLE *v.*

'**sossle,** *v. rare.* [? f. SOSS *sb.*[1]] *intr.* To go *about* in an aimless idle manner.
1837 MISS SEDGWICK *Live & Let Live* iii. 31 Your children get such shocking habits sosling about, and doing nothing, and living all in a clutter.

sosteine, sostenaunse, obs. ff. SUSTAIN *v.*, SUSTENANCE.

‖**sostenente.** Also sostinente. [It., pres. pple. of *sostenere* SUSTAIN *v.*] A device or contrivance attached to a pianoforte for the purpose of producing sustained notes like an organ. Also *attrib.*
1840 *Penny Cycl.* XVIII. 142/2 Mr. Mott's *sostinente* was an application of a cylinder and silk loops to an upright piano-forte. The.. tones came forth somewhat like the tones of the seraphine. **1881** *Morning Post* 2 June, Messrs. Brinsmead have patented.. the sostenente sounding board, capable of sustaining sound for 60 seconds. **1885** *Encycl. Brit.* XIX. 76/1 *note*, Mott.. attracted much attention by a piano with sostenente effect.. in 1817. *Ibid.*, But a sostenente piano.. is no longer a true piano.

‖**sostenuto** (sɒste'nuto), *a.* and *sb.* Abbrev. sost. Also 8 sustinuto. [It., pa. pple. of *sostenere* SUSTAIN *v.*]
A. *adj.* **1.** Of music: To be sung or played in a sustained manner. (Cf. quot. 1801.)
1724 *Short Explic. For. Wds. in Mus. Bks.* **1801** BUSBY *Dict. Mus., Sostenuto*, a word implying that the notes of the movement, or passage against which it is placed, are to be sustained or held on to the extremity of their lengths. **1875** in STAINER & BARRETT *Dict. Mus. Terms.* **1955** *Times* 27 July 5/6 Mr. Thomas Matthews, the soloist,.. missed some of its finest effects, chiefly because he under-emphasized its sostenuto spaciousness. **1976** *Gramophone* Sept. 410/1 The *sostenuto* opening and eager staccato continuation are both beautifully judged.
2. Marked or characterized by being sustained or held on.
1826 M. KELLY *Reminisc.* I. 114 He had been the first cantabile singer of his time, and his sostenuto singing was still admirable. **1835** *Court Mag.* VI. 220/2 A kind of Sostenuto or bow effect. **1887** MISS R. H. BUSK *Folksongs Italy* 20 There is probably a sostenuto note in its air.
B. *sb.* A sustained sound or note. Also *fig.*
1757 FOOTE *Author* Epil., Wks. 1799 I. 129 Divine Mingotti! what a swell has she! O! such a sustinuto upon B! **1933** N. DOUGLAS *Looking Back* II. 460 It was September, that wonderful month when the melodies of summer linger on.. in a tranquil *sostenuto*. **1934** C. LAMBERT *Music Ho!* v. 309 His [*sc.* Sibelius's] use of the brass is sparing, concentrating far more on its sostenuto than on its percussive qualities. **1943** D. GASCOYNE *Poems 1937–42* 14 The heart's receptive chalice in pure hands upheld Towards the sostenuto of the sky.

soster(hode, obs. variants of SISTER(HOOD.

so-styled, *ppl. a.* [SO *adv.* 6 a.] Styled or designated by this term or name, but not properly entitled to or correctly described by it; so-called, so-termed.
1844 tr. *M. T. Asmar's Mem. Babylonian Princ.* II. 92 The so-styled civilized daughters of Europe. **1852** THACKERAY *Esmond* II. x, The (so-styled) legitimate representatives of the Viscount Castlewood. **1888** CHILD *Eng. & Sc. Ballads* III. 104/1 *note*, The so-styled Robber Songs of the Russians.

sot (sɒt), *sb.*[1] and *a.* Forms: 1– sot, 1–2, 6–7 sott, 2–7 sotte, 3, 5 sote, 6 soote. [a. OF. *sot* masc., *sote* fem. (mod.F. *sot, sotte*), of unknown origin; the med.L. *sottus* is recorded from *c* 800. Hence also MDu. *sot* (*sod*), *zot* (*zod*; Du. *zot*), MLG. and LG. *sot, sott*, MHG. *sot.*]
A. *sb.* †**1.** A foolish or stupid person; a fool, blockhead, dolt. *Obs.*
c **1000** ÆLFRIC *Saints' Lives* xiii. 132 Ne bið se na wita þe unwislice leofað, ac bið open sott [*v.r.* sot]. *c* **1055** *Byrhtferth's Handboc* in *Anglia* VIII. 313 Seðe his agene spræce awyrt he wyrcð *barbarismus*. Swylce he cweðe þu sot, þær he sceolde cweðan þu sott. *c* **1175** *Lamb. Hom.* 29 Þa iuguleres and þa oðer sottes.. habbeð an þonc. *a* **1250** *Prov. of Alfred* 412 Ne gabbe þu,.. ne chid þu wyþ none sotte. *a* **1300** *Cursor M.* 2457 Þan said abram, þat was na sot, formast til his neueu loth. **1377** LANGL. *P. Pl.* B. x. 8 She.. laughte hym be stylle, With suche wise wordes to wissen any sottes. **1422** tr. *Secreta Secret., Priv. Priv.* 157 Who-so nothynge thynkyth of thyngis y-passet, a sote and a fole he shall be callid. *a* **1500** *Flower & Leaf* 101 (Skeat), So sodainly, that, as it were a sot, I stood astonied. **1509** BARCLAY *Shyp of Folys* (1570) 85 Into the Church then comes another sotte. **1546** J. HEYWOOD *Dial. Wit & Folly* (Percy Soc.) 14 No more dysernythe the sott, at yeres thre score, Then th' ynosent borne within yeres thre before. **1602** J. DAVIES (Heref.) *Mirum in Modum* Wks. (Grosart) I. 25/2 Why hath a wise man, to his Sonne a Sotte? **1641** MILTON *Animadv.* Wks. 1851 III. 235 The one is ever.. a sot, an ideot for any use that mankind can make of him. **1712** STEELE *Spect.* No. 492 ¶1 The Men are such unthinking Sots, that they do not prefer her who restrains all her Passions and Affections [etc.]. *c* **1745** FIELDING *Lucy in Town* Wks. 1784 III. 438 That I should be such a sot as to suffer you!
Prov. a **1250** *Prov. Alfred* 421 Sottes bolt is sone i-schote. *c* **1300** *Prov. Hendyng* in *Rel. Ant.* I. 111 Sottes bolt is sone shote.
Comb. **1610** HEALEY *St. Aug. Citie of God* XX. xxx. 833 Their.. apparelling him [i.e. Christ] with sot-like habites, crowning him with thorne, striking him on the head, with reedes,.. was nothing but a continuate insultation.
2. One who dulls or stupefies himself with drinking; one who commonly or habitually drinks to excess; a soaker.
1592 NASHE *Pierce Penilesse* Wks. (Grosart) II. 43 The Danes are bursten-bellied sots, that are to be confuted with nothing but Tankards or quart pots. **1616** R. C. *Times' Whistle* (1871) 63, I graunt you then a drunken sot may goe For one that is innocuous. **1654** WHITLOCK *Zootomia* 3 He that.. drinketh not all his Wine before the Salt is taken away, and only for Digestion: Such a one is a Drunkard, a Sot, &c. **1693** PRIDEAUX *Lett.* (1875) 160 We are here at a miserable passe with this horrid sot we have got for our Dean. He cannot sleep at night till dosed with drink. **1711** SHAFTESB. *Charac.* (1737) II. 127 One, who abuses himself in this way, is often call'd a sot, but never a debauchee. **1750** BERKELEY *Patriotism* §10 Wks. 1871 III. 455 A sot, a beast, benumbed and stupefied by excess. **1818** SCOTT *Rob Roy* vi, They form a happy compound of sot, game-keeper, bully, horse-jockey, and fool. **1856** EMERSON *Eng. Traits, Ability* Wks. (Bohn) II. 34 Even the pleasure-hunters and sots of England are of a tougher texture. **1870** THORNBURY *Tour rd. Eng.* II. xxii. 112 A poor, clever, worn-out sot.
3. *attrib.*, or in genitive combs., as †**sot-bay, sot's-hof, -hole,** a resort of drinkers; †**sot's cap,** a variety of sea-shell; **sot-weed,** tobacco (*Obs.* exc. *Hist.*).
(*a*) **1532** MORE *Confut. Tindale* Wks. 711/1 A very cold consent of my goffe, that he found and tooke vp at sottes hoffe. **1706** E. WARD *Wooden World Diss.* (1708) 87 His Cruise is over, and he comes to an Anchor in Sot-Bay. **1755** *Gentl. Mag.* XXV. 208 It would not have cost me above four-pence half-penny to have spent my evening at Sots Hole. **1827** HONE *Every-day Bk.* 21 Dec. II. II. 1626 Some 'good fellow', who is good no where but in 'sot's-hole'.
(*b*) **1698** E. WARD *London Spy* I. 9 We had each of us Stuck in our Mouths a lighted Pipe of Sotweed. **1702** T. BROWN, etc. *Lett. fr. Dead* II. Wks. 1707 II. 81 We had every one ramm'd a full charge of Sot-weed into our infernal Guns. **1708** E. COOK (*title*) The sot-weed factor; or, a voyage to Maryland. **1747** *Scheme Equip. Men of War* 35 To add a small Composition of high-flavoured Sot-Weed. **1785** in GROSE *Dict. Vulgar T.* **1961** J. BARTH (*title*) The sot-weed factor. **1965** E. TUNIS *Colonial Craftsmen* iii. 52 Early Americans not only grew a lot of 'sot weed' they also consumed a lot of it.
(*c*) **1713** PETIVER *Aquat. Anim. Amboinæ* Tab. 16/28 *Pectunculus rostratus*,.. Sots-cap.
†**B.** *adj.* Foolish, stupid. *Obs.*
c **1050** *Suppl. Ælfric's Gloss.* in Wr.-Wülcker 171/32 *Hebes*, dwæs, *uel* sott. *a* **1100** *Voc.* Ibid. 316/7 *Stultus*, stunt. *Sottus*, sot. *c* **1200** *Vices & Virtues* 67 'ʒif ʒeure ani,' he seið, 'is healden for wis on ðare woreld, becume sott, and swa he mai bien wis'. *a* **1225** *Leg. Kath.* 107 Luuede heo nane lihte plohen ne nane sotte songes. *c* **1250** *Orison our Lady* 37 in *O.E. Misc.*, And alle mine sot dede Ich bidde hire to me bi-seo. **1648** HEXHAM II, *De Aldersotste*, the Most foolish, or the Sottest.

†**sot,** *sb.*[2] *Obs.*⁻¹ [ad. Sp. *azote.*] A scourge.
1588 PARKE tr. *Mendoza's Hist. China* 261 They began to whippe them vpon the calues of their legges with a sot made of canes.

sot (sɒt), *v.* Also 5–6 sott, 6 sotte. [f. SOT *sb.*[1] (cf. MDu. *sotten, zotten* to be foolish), or aphetic for ASSOT *v.*]
1. *trans.* †**a.** To render foolish or doltish; to stupefy, to besot. *Obs.*
a **1400–50** *Wars Alex.* 4364 Ne foloȝe we na ficesyens ne philisophour scolis, As sophistri & slik thing to sott with þe pepill. **1554** PHILPOT *Exam. & Writ.* (Parker Soc.) 322 The cup of the Whore of Babylon, wherewith she hath sotted and made drunk the most part of Christendom. **1571** GOLDING *Calvin on Ps.* v. 11 He sotteth them with the spirit of drowsynesse and giddynesse. **1600** F. THYNNE *Epig.* (1876) 53 Crisopeia,.. whoe sotts him soe with her bewitchinge sight. **1626** BRETON *Fantastickes* Wks. (Grosart) II. 5/2 Loue.. crosseth wisdome, serueth Beautie, and sotteth folly. *a* **1700** KEN *Edmund* Poet. Wks. 1721 II. 297 Of Wine and Spirits.. They.. should Cellars drain, Which.. should sot the Dane.
†**b.** To blurt *out* stupidly. *Obs.*⁻¹
1608 H. CLAPHAM *Errour Right Hand* 44 He beginnes to puffe,.. and then sotted out this question.
c. With *away.* To waste or squander by sottish conduct.
1746 CHESTERF. *Lett.* cxii. (1792) I. 304, I must.. have destroyed my health and faculties by sotting away the evenings. **1782** *Encycl. Brit.* (ed. 2) IX. 6908/1 Brandy-shops, in which the inhabitants used to sot away their time in drinking strong liquors and smoking tobacco. **1850** *Blackw. Mag.* Nov. 510 The elder son of the forementioned squire had muddled and sotted away much of his share in the Leslie property.
2. *intr.* To play the sot; to drink to excess; to soak. Also with *it.*
1633 MARMION *Antiq.* II. i. (1875) 217 You have been sotting on't all night with wine. **1711** E. WARD *Vulgus Brit.* IX. 99 Where day by day they us'd to sot, At All-fours, Cribidge, or at Put. *a* **1716** SOUTH *Twelve Serm.* (1717) VI. 399 Those, who should have been watching the Motion of the Enemy, were sotting it at their Cups. **1815** W. H. IRELAND *Scribbleomania* 9 Periodical Writers that sot over beer. **1837** DICKENS *Pickw.* vi, Beyond the few.. reckless

vagabonds with whom he..sotted in the alehouse, he had not a single friend.

sot, obs. and dial. pa. t. and pa. pple. of SET *v.*[1]; obs. f. SOOT *sb.*; var. SWOTE (sweat) *Obs.*

Sotadean (səʊtə'diːən), *a.* and *sb.* [f. L. *Sōtadē-us*, f. *Sōtadēs*: see next.] = SOTADIC *a.*
1774 J. PATSALL tr. *Quintilian's Inst.* IX. iv. II. 144 *note*, Sotadean verses consisted sometimes of iambics, sometimes of trochaics, sometimes of dactyls, and sometimes of anapæstics, which being read backwards made another kind of verse. **1830** SEAGER tr. *Hermann's Elem. Doctr. Metres* 96 Among the verses adduced by Hephaestion there are, besides the Sotadean, only two which appear to be really Ionic *à majori.*

Sotadic (səʊ'tædɪk), *a.* and *sb.* Also 8 **Sotadick**. [ad. L. *Sōtadic-us*, f. *Sōtadēs*, Gr. Σωτάδης: see def.]
A. *sb.* **1.** A satire after the manner of Sotades, an ancient Greek poet noted for the coarseness and scurrility of his writings.
1645 MILTON *Colast.* Wks. 1851 IV. 378 Perhaps, as the provocation may bee, I may bee driv'n to curle up this gliding prose into a rough *Sotadic.* **1836** *Fraser's Mag.* XIII. 742 Neither would the keenest bit of satire be a legitimate 'sotadic', without that dash of turbulence in it, and sweeping denunciation.
2. *Pros.* A catalectic tetrameter composed of Ionics *a majore.*
1830 SEAGER tr. *Hermann's Elem. Doctr. Metres* 97 [Plautus] has Sotadics in Aul. ii, 1, 30. sq. iii, 2. Amph. i, 1, 14. sq.
B. *adj.* **1.** Characterized by a coarseness or scurrility like that of Sotades.
1716 M. DAVIES *Athen. Brit.* II. To Rdr. p. xlv, Which favour was..deservedly refus'd to most Necromantick Sotadick and Arian Libels, by the common consent of all Christians.
2. Capable of being read in reverse order; palindromic.
?*a* **1814** T. BROWN in Welsh *Life* vii. (1825) 350 The second syllable is..the sound reversed, like the reading of a Sotadic line. **1862** WHEATLEY *Anagrams* 9 Palindromic verses are also sometimes called Sotadic verses.
3. *Pros.* (See quot. and A. 2.)
1830 SEAGER tr. *Hermann's Elem. Doctr. Metres* 96 The most noted of Ionic verses *à majori* is the Sotadic, constructed for recitation only.
So **So'tadical** *a. rare.*
1610 HEALEY *St. Aug. Citie of God* 642 Sotadicall verses: that is verses backward and forwards.

sotalol ('səʊtəlɒl). *Pharm.* [Etym. unkn.: see -OL.] The compound, $CH_3.NH(SO_2).C_6H_4.CH(OH).CH_2.NH.CH(CH_3)_2$, a beta-adrenergic blocking agent used (in the form of its hydrochloride) in the treatment of cardiac arrhythmias.
1968 *Jrnl. Pharmacol. & Exper. Therapeutics* CLX. 231 The antiinflammatory action of morphine is reversed by nalorphine but not by a *beta* adrenergic blocking agent, sotalol (MJ 1999; 4-(2-isopropylamino-1-hydroxylethyl)-methanesulphonalinide hydrochloride). **1974** R. G. SHANKS et al. in A. G. Snart *Adv. in Beta-Adrenergic Blocking Therapy—Sotalol* I. 24 Sotalol is the only drug which blocks all adrenergic β-receptors and has no membrane stabilizing activity or intrinsic sympathomimetic activity. **1978** *Nature* 19 Oct. 596/2 In contrast, β-adrenergic antagonists lacking the hydrophobicity of propranolol, such as atenolol, practolol and sotalol, are not able to induce meiosis.

‖**so'tana.** [Sp. *sotana.*] A gown or cassock.
1622 MABBE tr. *Aleman's Guzman d'Alf.* II. II. vii. 161, I had furnished my selfe in Milan, with as much rich silke Grogram, as would serue to make mee a cloake, and a Sotana. *a* **1678** MARVELL *Misc. Poems* (1681) 56 Thus armed underneath, he over all Does make a primitive Sotana fall.

†**sotane.** *Obs.*[−1] [ad. It. *sottana.*] = SOUTANE.
1652 HOWELL *Giraffi's Rev. Naples* II. 70 A company of Priests appeared, who went with their Sotanes raised up.

sotch (səʊtʃ). *Physical Geogr.* Pl. sotchs, sotches. [Fr. dialectal word of pre-Latin origin (Robert).] A doline, esp. one in the Causses region of France.
1910 H. R. MILL *Dict. Geogr. Terms* in L. D. Stamp *Gloss. Geogr. Terms* (1961) 426/2 *Sotch*, dolines (*q.v.*) (Causses, France). The term 'cloup' is used in Aquitaine. **1922** *Geol. Mag.* LIX. 394 The only fertile and habitable regions on these barren plateaus are the 'sotches' or hollows, where the red earth formed by the denudation of the limestone is preserved in large funnel-shaped hollows. **1937** *Geogr. Jrnl.* LXXXIX 63 A detailed study of the karst landscape, showing the important part played by the dolinas or 'sotchs' in the dissection of the surface. **1972** M. M. SWEETING *Karst Landforms* iv. 48/2 The sotchs are both circular and elongated, their diameters and depths variable and their topographic situations diverse.

sote, obs. f. SOOT *sb.*; var. SOOT *a.* (sweet), SWOTE (sweat).

sotel(e, -ell(e, sotelnes, -te(e, -y(che, obs. ff. SUBTLE *a.*, SUBTLENESS, etc.

soterial (səʊ'tɪərɪəl), *a. Theol.* [f. Gr. σωτηρία salvation.] Pertaining to salvation.
1879 H. CROSBY *Christian Preacher* ii, The soterial pith of the Gospel is simple and soon exhibited.

†**soteri'alogy.** *Obs. rare.* = SOTERIOLOGY.
1768–74 TUCKER *Lt. Nat.* (1834) II. 421 He established a plan of soterialogy for the restoration and perfection of human nature. *Ibid.* 466, I would call this soterialogy or the plan of salvation.

†**so'terian,** *a. Obs.*[−0] [f. as prec. or f. Gr. σωτήρ saviour.] (See quot.)
1623 COCKERAM I, *Soterian day*, Good-friday.

soteriological (səʊtɪərɪəʊ'lɒdʒɪkəl), *a. Theol.* [ad. G. *soteriologisch*: see next.] Of or pertaining to soteriology or salvation. Also *Comb.*
1879 FARRAR *St. Paul* II. 412 *note*, Lange classes the Epistles as 1. Eschatological. 2. Soteriological [etc.]. **1882–3** SCHAFF *Encycl. Relig. Knowl.* III. 2396/1 Whenever they undertook to remodel..a doctrine, they attached themselves to its anthropological or soteriological bearings. **1890** *Athenæum* 5 July 34/1 The tendency which..may be called the soteriological-Biblical.

soteriology (səʊtɪərɪ'ɒlədʒɪ). [f. Gr. σωτηρία preservation, salvation, or ad. G. *soteriologie*, F. *sotériologie.* Cf. SOTERIALOGY.]
1. (See quot.) *rare*[−0].
1847 WEBSTER, *Soteriology*, a discourse on health, or the science of promoting and preserving health. [Hence in later Dicts.]
2. *Theol.* The doctrine of salvation.
1864 SHEDD *Hist. Chr. Doctr.* II. 204 It was reserved for the Protestant church..to bring the doctrines of Soteriology to a correspondent degree of expansion. *a* **1880** W. L. MCFARLAN in *Scotch Serm.* 237 The whole of the eschatology of the schoolmen,..like their soteriology and their ontology, seems to the modern theologian..untenable.

so-termed, *a.* [SO *adv.* 6 a.] So-called.
1843 R. J. GRAVES *Syst. Clin. Med.* xxvii. 344 They all get well under the (so-termed) antiphlogistic regimen. **1894** H. NISBET *Bush Girl's Rom.* 118 It is only the so-termed free-man who is valueless.

soterology (səʊtə'rɒlədʒɪ). *Theol.* [ad. G. *soterologie*, f. Gr. σωτήρ saviour, f. σω-, stem of σώζειν to save.] (See quot.)
1882–3 *Schaff's Encycl. Relig. Knowl.* III. 2216 [Soteriology] is to be carefully distinguished from soterology, or christology, which treats solely of the person of the Redeemer.

soth(e, obs. ff. SOOT *sb.*[1], SOOTH *sb.*, *a.*, SOOTHE *v.*

sothe, obs. pa. t. and pa. pple. SEETHE *v.*

†**'sothead.** *Obs.* Forms: 3 sothade, 3–4 -hede, 4 -hed, 7 -head; 4 sotthede, -hed(d, soithede (soþede, 5 soþhede). [f. SOT *a.* + -HEAD. Cf. LG. *sottheit*, Du. *zotheid.*] Folly, foolishness, stupidity; a foolish act.
a **1200** *Vices & Virtues* 67 Ðe wise woreld-mann, he halt michel sothade ðat mann forlate..hus and ham. *a* **1250** *Owl & Night.* 1375 Þah heo beo god, me hine may mysfonge, & drawe hine to sothede. *a* **1300** *Cursor M.* 18235 Bot nu þi sothed wel es kydd. *Ibid.* 19194 And sua yee sceu all yur sotthedis. **14..** *Lat.-Eng. Voc.* in Wr.-Wülcker 567 *Baburra*, Sothede. **1690** *Andros Tracts* II. 35 A charge which their most Violent accusers had never yet sothead enough to alledge against them.

sother, obs. f. SOLDER *sb.*[1]

sothern, obs. f. SOUTHERN *a.*

sothero(u)n, obs. ff. SOUTHRON.

†**'sothery,** *a. Obs.*[−1] (Meaning uncertain.)
Perh. the old form of *Surrey* (Skeat).
1540 J. HEYWOOD *Four PP.* 879 Theyr taylles well kempt, and..With sothery butter theyr bodyes anoynted.

sothfast(nes, obs. ff. SOOTHFAST(NESS.

Sothiac ('səʊθɪæk), *a.* [ad. F. *sothiaque*: see SOTHIC *a.* and -AC.]
1. = SOTHIC *a.* 1.
1834 MRS. SOMERVILLE *Connex. Phys. Sci.* xiii. 100 The Egyptians..lost one year in every 14601 [*sic*],—their Sothiac period. **1842** *Penny Cycl.* XXII. 267/1 It is obvious that 1461 years of 365 days each, make 1460 years of 365¼ days. This period of 1460 Julian years was the Sothiac period. **1870** EMERSON *Soc. & Solit.* vii. (1883) 151 The..scholar..who can unearth for me the buried dynasties of Sesostris and Ptolemy, the Sothiac era [etc.].
2. = SOTHIC *a.* 2.
1877 R. S. POOLE in *Encycl. Brit.* VII. 729/2 Consisting of 1460 Sothiac and 1461 vague years. **1887** MAHAFFY & GILMAN *Alexander's Empire* xv. (1890) 158 *note*, This attempted reform of the calendar, by introducing the Sothiac year of 365 days and a quarter, is very interesting.
So **So'thiacal** *a.* [F. *sothiacal.*]
1795 T. MAURICE *Hindostan* (1820) I. I. iii. 101 This cycle of 1461 was called in Egypt the great Canicular year, or Sothiacal period. **1813** PRITCHARD *Phys. Hist. Man* viii. §5. 451 *note*, The cycle of Nabonassar or the Sothiacal year. *Ibid.*, More than the whole Sothiacal period.

Sothic ('sɒθɪk, 'səʊθɪk), *a.* [f. Gr. Σῶθις, an Egyptian name of Sirius, the dog-star.]
1. *Sothic cycle* or *period*, a period of 1460 full years, containing 1461 of the ancient Egyptian ordinary years.
1828 WILKINSON *Materia Hierog.* App. I. p. ii, This period is called 'the Sothic period'. **1860** R. S. POOLE in W. Smith *Dict. Bible* I. 506/1 *Egypt*, The Egyptians are known to have used two great cycles, the Sothic Cycle and the Tropical Cycle. **1892** S. LAING *Human Origins* (1893) 117 They had invented a sothic cycle for the odd quarter of a day.
2. *Sothic year*, a year of 365¼ days, in contrast to the ordinary Egyptian year of 365 days.
1828 WILKINSON *Materia Hierog.* App. I. p. i, As the Egyptian Solar year, in every four years, loses a day of the Sothic. **1860** R. S. POOLE in W. Smith *Dict. Bible* I. 505/2 *Egypt*, There appear to have been at least three years in use with the Egyptians.., the Vague Year, the Tropical Year, and the Sothic Year.

sothly, -ness, -saw, obs. ff. SOOTHLY, etc.

Sotho ('suːtuː). Also **Suthu, Suto**, etc. [Native name.] **A.** *sb.* A subdivision of the Bantu people which includes the Basuto and various other tribes chiefly found in Botswana and the Transvaal; also, the languages spoken by these people. **B.** *adj.* Of or pertaining to this group of peoples or their languages. Cf. SESOTHO.
1928 G. P. LESTRADE *Bantu Tribes S. Afr.* I. I. 14 There has..been..intermarriage between the Bavenda and the Basotho (there was a Sotho invasion of Bavendaland). **1928** *Africa* I. 481 In reality there are two main branches of this group, Chwana spoken in Bechwanaland and the Western Transvaal, and Suto with its main dialects. **1929** [see NGUNI *sb.* and *a.*]. **1936** [see *hill-culture* s.v. HILL *sb.* 4 d]. **1948** M. GUTHRIE *Classification Bantu Lang.* iv. 69 These radicals from Suthu. **1957** C. G. SELIGMAN *Races Afr.* (ed. 2) viii. 120 The Sotho..includes the Southern Sotho of Lesotho.. the Tswana..of Botswana and western Transvaal, and the Northern Sotho..of central and northern Transvaal. **1977** *Times* 7 Sept. 7/4 [The South African] Secretary for Information..gives the population..as..whites,.. Coloureds,..Indians,..Zulus,..Xhosas,..Tswanas,.. North Sothos,..South Sothos, [etc.]. **1979** *Listener* 25 Oct. 545/1 The text Modimo o Lerabu—'God is Love' in the Sotho language. Both Zulu and Sotho are used in the worship.

sothrenwood, obs. f. SOUTHERNWOOD.

sothro(u)n, obs. ff. SOUTHRON.

‖**sotie**[1] (sɔti). Also 4 **sotye**, 5 **sottye**, 9 **sottie**. [OF. *sotie, sottie* (mod.F. *sotie* in sense 2), f. *sot* SOT *a.*]
†**1.** Foolishness, folly. *Obs.*
1390 GOWER *Conf.* I. 60 Than haddest thou the gates stoke Fro such Sotie as comth to winne Thin hertes wit. *Ibid.* II. 209 The grete covoitise Of sotie and of fol emprise. **1483** CAXTON *Gold. Leg.* 360/1 Whan he was yonge he was full of many sottyes and folyes.
2. A species of broad satirical farce, current in France in the 15th and 16th centuries.
1791–1823 D'ISRAELI *Cur. Lit.* (1866) 133 The sotties were more farcical than farce. **1837** *Penny Cycl.* IX. 417/2 Their most celebrated sotie, entitled 'The Abuse of the World',..is attributed to the historian Bouchet. **1879** *Encycl. Brit.* IX. 645/1 These performances..were soon rivalled by the more profane performances of the moralities, the farces, and the soties.

†**sotie**[2]. *Obs.*[−1] [ad. Sp. *azotea*, Pg. *açotea.*] A terrace or flat roof.
1648 GAGE *West Ind.* 47 Cortez desired Montezuma to goe up into the Sotie of his house..and to command his subjects to cease from their heat and fury.

sotil(e, -ill(e, obs. ff. SUBTLE *a.* and *v.*

sotile, var. CITOLE *Obs.*

sotilliche, -ly, -nes, -te(e, obs. ff. SUBTLY, etc.

†**'sotly,** *adv.* and *a.* In 2 sotlice, 3 -liche. [f. SOT *sb.*[1] or *a.* Cf. MDu. *sotte-, zottelike* (Du. *zottelijk*).] **a.** *adv.* Foolishly. **b.** *adj.* Foolish.
1154 *O.E. Chron.* (Laud MS.) an. 1137, He todeld it & scatered sotlice. *c* **1205** LAY. 1970 Heo clepeden hit Cornwaile þurh heora sotliche cure. *a* **1225** *Leg. Kath.* 359 Alle ich iseo þine sahen sotliche isette.

‖**sotnia** ('sɒtnɪə). Now *Hist.* [Russ. *sotnya* hundred, f. *sot-*, related to Skr. *śatam*, L. *centum*, etc.] A squadron of Cossack cavalry.
1863 KINGLAKE *Crimea* II. 212 He had..a brigade of regular cavalry, and nine sotnias of Cossacks. **1878** *N. Amer. Rev.* CXXVI. 150 On the 11th a party of Cossacks reached Pescherna..; one sotnia turned northward.

‖**'sotnik.** Now *Hist.* Also ssotnik, sodnick. [Russ. *sotnik'*, f. *sotnya*: see prec.] A local official among the Cossacks; also, a commander of a sotnia.
1799 W. TOOKE *View Russian Emp.* I. 426 Every stanitza ..has..officers, the atamans, its sotnik [etc.]. **1814** tr. *Klaproth's Trav. Cauc.* 73 In the hundred-towns the Ssotniks..transacted the business. **1854** R. G. LATHAM *Native Races Russian Emp.* 56 Instead of the..Sodnick or head of a certain number of villages—these would have been the native nobles.

‖**Soto** ('səʊtəʊ). [Jap.] One of the three sects of Zen Buddhism. Freq. *attrib.*
1893 S. KURODA *Outlines Mahâyâna* vi. 24 Dôgen introduced the Sôtô sect, 2176 after Buddha, or 1227 A.D. **1894** *Trans. Asiatic Soc. Japan* XXII. 430 The Zen sects.. are divided..into three divisions. The *Rinzai*..from 1168 A.D., the *Sōtō* from 1223 A.D. and the *Obaku* from 1650 A.D. **1917** A. K. REISCHAUER *Stud. in Japanese Buddhism* iii. 117 The chief difference between the Soto and the Rinzai branches of the Zen Sect is that the former puts more weight upon book learning as a subsidiary aid to silent meditation. **1949** C. HUMPHREYS *Zen Buddhism* v. 91 It is in Japan that Zen can best be studied, and although there are three sects of Zen, the Rinzai, Soto and Obaku, there is little difference

between them. **1977** 'E. V. Cunningham' *Case of One-Penny Orange* (1978) iii. 29, I am Zen. The Soto School.

sotol ('səʊtəʊl). [Amer. Sp., f. Nahuatl *tzotolli.*] A plant of dry regions belonging to the genus *Dasylirion* of the family Agavaceæ, native to south-western North America and bearing linear leaves and small white flowers; also, the fibre from the leaves of this plant or the beverage made from the sap.

1881 *Amer. Naturalist* XV. 874 The home of the sotol is Western Texas, Southeastern New Mexico and Northern Chihuahua. **1908** D. T. McDougal *Bot. Features N. Amer. Deserts* 9 This is the typical sotol region. **1942** Castetter & Bell *Pima & Papago Agric.* 213 The mature leaves were dried by the Papago in the sun on a sotol mat. **1964** F. O'Rourke *Mule for Marquesa* 72 The scorched grey of candelilla and guayule, Spanish daggers, sotol with the crowns burned a dirty white by sun and wind. **1976** *Hortus Third* (L. H. Bailey Hortorium) 364/1 An alcoholic beverage, sotol, is extracted from the trunks. **1976** F. A. & D. L. Latorre *Mexican Kickapoo Indians* iii. 44 Two benches..are built and covered with dyed sotol or cattail mats. *Ibid.* v. 64 The favored material used today for

sotraccion, obs. form of subtraction.

†'**sotship.** *Obs.* Forms: 1–3 sotscipe, 3 sothscipe, sotschipe, 4 shotshipe. [f. sot *sb.*[1]] Foolishness, folly.

c **1050** *Suppl. Ælfric's Gloss.* in Wr.-Wülcker 171/33 *Hebetudo*, dwæsnys, *uel* sotscipe. *c* **1131** *O.E. Chron.* (Laud. MS.) an. 1131, þet hi heafdon forloron S' Iohannes mynstre ..þurh his mycele sotscipe. *c* **1205** Lay. 3024 þa ȝet nolde þe leod-king his sothscipe bi-læuen. *a* **1225** *Leg. Kath.* 1961 Swa þet Katerine..swike hire sotschipes, & ure wil wurche. *c* **1300** *Havelok* 2099 Hweþer he sitten nou, and wesseylen, Or of ani shotshipe to-deyle.

†'**sottage.** *Obs. rare.* [f. sot *sb.*[1]] Foolishness, folly, stupidity.

1569 Newton *Cicero's De Senectute* i b, Suche is the.. foolishe sottage and peruerse ouerthwartnes of waywarde people. **1596** Fitz-Geffrey *Sir F. Drake* (1881) 29 Hard yron-ages death-declining sottage.

sotted ('sɒtɪd), *ppl. a.* [f. sot *v.*, or aphetic form of *assotted.*] Rendered sottish or stupid; besotted.

c **1386** Chaucer *Can. Yeom. Prol. & T.* 788 This sotted prest, who was gladder þan he? **1387–8** T. Usk *Test. Love* I. x. (Skeat) l. 18 He..is holde for a foole, and sayd, his wit is but sotted. **1426** Lydg. *De Guil. Pilgr.* 3650 For ouht that I kan se, Ye be sottyd..Off newe. **1574** tr. *Marlorat's Apocalips* 49 The vngodly, being sotted in prosperitie, sleepe a dead sleepe. *c* **1585** [R. Browne] *Answ. Cartwright* 71 It is not a sotted nor wilfull ignorance. **1612** *Two Noble K.* iv. ii. 45, I am sotted, Vtterly lost: My Virgins faith has fled me. *a* **1637** T. Carew *Poems, To B. Jonson* (1870) 84 Thy just chastizing hand Hath fixt upon the sotted age a brand. **1693** Dryden *Juvenal* vi. 798 The potion..turns his brains... The sotted moon-calf gapes. **1826** W. Elliott *The Nun* 101 The dark confines of each sotted breast. **1898** *Daily News* 21 Feb. 3/4 It tried the sotted drunkard to reclaim.

b. Const. *with* (or †*of*).

c **1460** Sir R. Ros *La Belle Dame* 326 So dulle of wyte, so sotyd of folye. **1563** Blundeston *Pref.* in *Googe's Eglogs* (Arb.) 29 Yf the Muse Be sotted so with this graue Study. **1588** Greene *Pandosto* (1843) 18 Having her sences so sotted with care. **1609** Bible (Douay) *Ecclus.* xxiii. 19 Lest..being sotted with thy daily custom, thou suffer reproch. **1681** Dryden *Span. Friar* iv. ii, Had I not been sotted with my zeal, I might have found it sooner.

†**c.** Const. *of, on,* or *upon. Obs.*

1470–85 Malory *Arthur* x. lvi. 508, I merueylle..what eyleth them to be soo mad and soo soted vpon wymmen. **1551** Warwick in Froude *Hist. Eng.* (1860) V. 354 *note*, These men..be so sotted of their wives and children. **1591** Lyly *Endym.* i. i, I hope you be not sotted upon the man in the Moone. **1691** J. Wilson *Belphegor* iii. iv, So sotted on her, he's not himself.

sottely, obs. form of subtly.

'**sotter**, *v. Sc.* and *north. dial.* [Cf. G. dial. *sottern* (also *suttern*) in the same sense.]

a. *intr.* To boil slowly, or with a dull sound.

1781 J. Hutton *Tour to Caves* (ed. 2) Gloss. 96 *Sotter*, to make a noise in boiling as any thick substance does. **1808** in Jamieson. **1819** W. Tennant *Papistry Storm'd* (1827) 39 The broo boils up wi' sotterin' sound.

b. To bubble. Also *poet.*

1834 J. Galt *Lit. Life* III. 51 The blood was sottering out of his shoe mouth. **1886** W. S. McIntosh in D. H. Edwards *Mod. Sc. Poets* IX. 70 This wee burnie sae sottered an' sang. **1951** Auden *Nones* (1952) 64 The sharp streams and sottering springs of A commuter's wish.

†'**sotteran**, *a. Obs.*$^{-1}$ [ad. It. *sotterrano*, f. *sot-* under + *terra* earth.] Subterranean.

1648 J. Raymond *Il Merc. Ital.* 152 The old Poets cald it Aerius, because of the many Sotteran Caves in it.

†'**sottery.** *Obs.* [ad. older (now dial.) F. *sotterie, soterie*, f. *sot* sot *sb.*[1] Hence also MDu. *sotterie* (usually *sotternie*).] A piece of foolishness or folly.

1598 Florio, *Mattarie*, fooleries, madde tricks, sotteries. *a* **1603** T. Cartwright *Confut. Rhem. N.T.* (1618) 564 The reason..is a palpable sottery. **1663** S. Patrick *Parab. Pilgrim* (1687) 437 To accuse the fraud of the first beginners of these Stories, and the folly of them that follow their Sotteries. **1731** Medley *Kolben's Cape G. Hope* II. 46 The Governour..took an infinite pleasure in imposing all the fictions and sotteries he could upon every one.

sotting ('sɒtɪŋ), *vbl. sb.* [f. sot *v.* + -ing[1].] The fact or practice of playing the sot, or of indulging in sottish conduct.

1583 Babington *Commandm.* (1590) 176 An example of vnmeasurable sotting in bed. **1603** Breton *Packet Mad Lett.* i. xxviii, Now for sotting and slauery and for courting in knauery, be perswaded that time will imploy my purse to better purpose. **1707** Hearne *Collect.* (O.H.S.) II. 49 Which Faculty..he..lost by his Idleness and Sotting. **1760** *Cautions & Advices to Officers of Army* 88 Perpetual Sotting cannot fail of blunting your Faculties. **1820** Hazlitt *Table-T.* Ser. ii. xvii. (1869) 358 Nothing could overcome this propensity to low society and sotting. **1869** H. Kingsley *Stretton* II. 206 She was a perfect and absolute mistress of the art of sotting.

‖**sottise** (sɔtiz). [F., f. *sot* sot *a.*] A silly remark or saying; a foolish action. Also *transf.*

1673 Dryden *Marr. à la Mode* iii. i, That's an excellent word to begin withal; as, for example, he or she said a thousand sottises to me. *a* **1734** North *Examen* i. iii. §14 (1740) 131 Which is a Sottise past all Belief. *Ibid.* §23. 136 A Sottise of the lowest Form of Secretaryship. **1952** J. Biggs-Davison *Tory Lives* ii. 48 Tact and flexibility were not often exhibited by the Monarch of whose *sottise* his predecessor was wont to speak. **1963** N. Macrae *Sunshades in October* iii. 39 The Conservative Government.. dismantled two-and-a-half of these three *sottises.* **1977** *Times* 23 Mar. 16/8 The *Daily Mail* Diary..is not slow to criticize errors and *sottises* in rival newspapers.

sottish ('sɒtɪʃ), *a.* Also 6 shottishe. [f. sot *sb.*[1] + -ish.]

†**1.** Foolish, doltish, stupid: **a.** Of persons, or their faculties. *Obs.*

1566 Drant *Horace, Sat.* ii. iii. F viij, Ye shottishe, dotishe, doultishe dawes. **1583** Greene *Mamillia* Wks. (Grosart) II. 292, I meane not to be so..sottish as with free consent to crosse my selfe with perpetuall calamitie. **1621** Burton *Anat. Mel.* i. ii. iii. xiv. (1651) 126 Such are many sottish Princes, brought into a fools Paradise by their parasites. **1678** R. L'Estrange *Seneca's Mor.* i. xi. (1696) 47 The sottish Extract of an ancient Nobility may be preferr'd before a better Man. **1708** Swift *Predict. for 1708* Wks. 1755 II. i. 150 How ignorant those sottish pretenders to astrology are in their own concerns. **1737** Whiston *Josephus, Antiq.* ix. xii. §3 This king was so sottish and thoughtless of what was for his own good, that he would not leave off worshipping the Syrian gods when he was beaten by them.

†**b.** Of things or actions. *Obs.*

1586 A. Day *Eng. Secretary* ii. (1625) 87 What is it that this blinde and sottish love draweth not a man headlong into? **1614** Raleigh *Hist. World* i. 181 It were sottish to conceive, that he would permit the Divell..to raise a Prophet from the dead in Saul's respect. **1641** Milton *Ch. Govt.* ii. ii. Wks. 1851 III. 155 O but..the sottish absurdity of this excuse! **1692** Bentley *Boyle Lect.* ii. 62 It's altogether as reasonable as this sottish opinion of the Atheists. **1755** B. Martin *Mag. Arts & Sci.* 169 'Tis sottish to imagine that they were made to answer no End, but Man's Luxury, Diversion, or Use. **1796** Bp. Watson *Apol. Bible* 207 A style of extreme arrogance, and sottish self-sufficiency.

2. Given or addicted to, characterized or affected by, excessive drinking or coarse self-indulgence. Also *absol.*

1632 Lithgow *Trav.* iii. 92 A right name for so sottish a fellow, for..I neuer saw him..truely sober. **1642** D. Rogers *Naaman* 4 Implunged into a life of sence and sottish sensuality. *a* **1721** Sheffield (Dk. Buckhm.) *Wks.* (1753) II. 160 What else are..the sottish debauches..of Alexander the Great? **1785** Paley *Mor. Philos.* iii. iii. ix, I would make choice of..a town-life, for the mercenary and sottish. **1811** A. T. Thomson *Lond. Disp.* (1818) 292 The effects of opium ..are..loss of appetite and a sottish appearance. **1849** Macaulay *Hist. Eng.* iv. I. 453 People who saw him only over his bottle would have supposed him to be a man gross indeed, sottish, and addicted to low company. **1871** C. Gibbon *Lack of Gold* xii, His face was sallow and sottish.

Comb. **1856** R. A. Vaughan *Mystics* (1860) I. 150 A slip-shod, sottish-looking tailor.

sottishly ('sɒtɪʃlɪ), *adv.* [f. prec. + -ly[2].] In a sottish manner.

1566 Drant *Horace, Sat.* ii. i. E viij, They say that I am subiecte vnto drinke, And shotishely vppon excesse, laye out what so I thynke. **1589** G. Harvey *Pierce's Super.* i. Wks. (Grosart) II. 7, I am none of those, that..sottishly hugge theire owne babyes. **1629** Massinger *Picture* iii. v, I am not So sottishly credulous to believe the devil Hath that way power. **1691** Hartcliffe *Virtues* p. xviii, He breaths short Sighs often, sleeps seldom, till he dyes as sottishly, as he lived. **1702** *Eng. Theophrastus* 274 A man of parts may love indiscreetly but not sottishly. **1828–32** Webster, *Stupidly*, with extreme dullness;..sottishly.

sottishness ('sɒtɪʃnɪs). [f. as prec. + -ness.]

†**1.** Foolishness, folly, stupidity. *Obs.*

Very common in the 17th century.

1589 Fleming *Virg. Georg.* iv. 74 When as a sudden sottishnesse or follie had surprizd And caught th' unwary louer fast. **1604** T. Wright *Passions* iv. i. 108 Silence may proceed sometimes of sottishnesse, because a man knowes not how to reason. **1653** Holcroft *Procopius, Goth. Wars* i. 27 He laughed at their sottishnesse, in hoping to bring their Oxen to their Enemies walls so unadvisedly. **1691** T. H[ale] *Acc. New Invent.* p. xxiii, The idle conceit of the Fish Remora, which mens sottishness hath made a vulgar one. *a* **1758** J. Edwards in Spurgeon *Treas. David* IV. 301 The sottishness of their being insensible of God's all-seeing eye.

2. Condition or conduct typical of a sot: *esp.* indulgence in drinking to excess.

1648 G. Daniel *Eclog* iii. 315 In time depart [thou] From the bewitching Sottishnes of Sin. **1660** Ingelo *Bentiv. & Ur.* ii. (1682) 161 They naturally sink themselves into an unspeakable Sottishness. **1706** Stanhope *Paraphr.* III. 222 The Sottishness of a debauched Understanding. **1785** Paley *Mor. Philos.* iv. ii. (1841) 180 That solitary sottishness which waits neither for company nor invitation. **1855** Maurice *Learning & Working* 322, I cannot conceive how a people, fallen..into feebleness, strife and sottishness, could have escaped the severest punishments. **1860** Pusey *Min. Proph.* 29 The stupid sottishness of the confirmed voluptuary.

‖**sottisier** (sɔtizje). [Fr.] A collection of *sottises*; esp. a list of written stupidities. Also *transf.* and *fig.*

1929 E. Pound *Let.* 1 Feb. (1971) 224 The simplest and briefest form of attack is by a sottisier... Make your sottisier from *Poetry* and the main literary reviews, Sunday supplements, etc. **1944** *Horizon* Sept. 187 Nor is it [sc. *Finnegans Wake*] a mere *sottisier.* **1959** *Observer* 30 Aug. 13/7 A cast-iron certainty for the September *Sottisier* Stakes. **1969** J. Gross *Rise & Fall of Man of Letters* ix. 238 It would be easy to compile a fair-sized sottisier of such remarks, but not very amusing. **1976** *Times Lit. Suppl.* 26 Mar. 345/5 The sloppy editing and the *sottisier* of an index, with its general confusion of names, styles, titles and sexes. **1978** *Times* 22 Mar. 11/8 Ginger Rogers..under-rehearsed commentary is a *sottisier* of all the awful things Americans are supposed to say.

sottle, obs. form of subtle *a.*

‖**sotto voce** ('sotto 'votʃe), *adv., a.,* and *sb.* [It. *sotto* under + *voce* voice.]

1. In a subdued or low voice: **a.** Of speech.

1737 Chesterf. in *Common Sense* 10 Sept. (1738) 226 And in a half Voice, or *Sotto voce*, discusses her solid Trifles in his Ear. **1828** Lytton *Pelham* II. iii, A whole host of hangers-on, who were disputing, by no means *sotto voce*, whether Lady Gander was mad or not? **1853** 'C. Bede' *Verdant Green* ii. vi, 'As though they were bursting with envy—not to say with laughter,' added Mr. Bouncer, *sotto voce.* **1891** Farrar *Darkn. & Dawn* xii, 'Even proverbs warn me against him.' He quoted two, *sotto voce*, to Titus.

b. Of singing (or playing).

1775 *Ann. Reg.* ii. 65 Gabrieli..sung all her airs in what they call *sotto voce*, that is, so low, that they can scarcely be heard. **1780** *Mirror* No. 89, That sort of singing below the full powers of the performer's voice, which the Italians call singing *sotto-voce.* **1801** Busby *Dict. Mus., Sotto Voce*, an expression implying that the movement, or the passage, over which it is written is to be played or sung moderately loud. **1872** C. King *Sierra Nevada* x. 218 Then *sotto voce*, for we were very near, he sang again.

2. *fig.* Quietly, privately.

1819 Scott *Let.* in *Lockhart* (1837) IV. vii. 226 Will you make these enquiries for me *sotto voce?*

3. As *adj.* Uttered, etc., in an undertone.

1809 Malkin *Gil Blas* iv. viii. ¶6 There was not a *sotto voce* passage during the whole visit. **1818** Scott *Rob Roy* viii, 'God forbid!' said the Justice, in a tone of *sotto-voce* deprecation. **1859** Geo. Eliot *A. Bede* liii, David's *sotto voce* performance of 'My love's a rose without a thorn'. **1885** *L'pool Daily Post* 7 May 5/3 There was a suggestion of.. joviality in his *sotto voce* sallies.

4. As *sb.* A remark made in an undertone.

1868 H. A. Stern *Captive Missionary* viii. 185, I only heard from two an ironical *sotto voce*, 'Well, will you walk again?'

sotule, sotyl(e, sotyly, etc., obs. ff. subtle *a.*, subtly *adv.*

‖**sou** (su). Now *Hist.* [F., earlier *soul, sol* sol *sb.*[3] For earlier examples of the pl. *sous*, see souse *sb.*[4]] A French coin, formerly the twentieth part of a livre, subsequently used to designate the five-centime piece.

1814 *Sporting Mag.* XLIV. 60 We gave the postillions ten sous per post extra, to stimulate them to speed. **1823** Byron *Juan* xi. lxxv, They are young, but know not youth,..rich without a sou. **1866** *Cornh. Mag.* Nov. 532 Imagine..that I have been paying thirty-eight sous a pound. **1882** 'Ouida' *Under Two Flags* (1890) 272 He had scarcely a sou in his pocket.

sou, obs. form of sew *v.*, show *v.*, sow *sb.*[1]

souant, variant of suant *a. Obs.*

souari: see saouari.

soubadaree, -y, obs. varr. of subahdary.

soubah, -dar, -ship: see subah, etc.

soubget, -git, obs. forms of subject.

‖**Soubise** (subiz). [From the name of the French general and courtier Charles de Rohan *Soubise* (1715–1787).]

†**1.** A kind of cravat. *Obs.*

1776 Anstey *Election Ball.* (1808) 229 With a shoe like a sauce boat and steeple-clock'd hose And a silken soubise that bob'd up to his nose.

2. A kind of onion-sauce.

Usually *Soubise sauce*, or in F. form *Sauce Soubise.*

1822 Ude *French Cook* (ed. 7) 18 Purée of Onion, or Soubise. **1846** Soyer *Syst. Cookery* 22 *Sauce Soubise.* Peel six large onions [etc.]. **1861** Eliza Acton *Mod. Cookery* 126 Soubise. (English Receipt.)... Soubise. (French Receipt.) **1880** *B'ham Weekly Post* 6 Nov. 1/7 Mutton cutlets, dressed with Soubise sauce, are quite a different thing from mutton cutlets plainly fried.

‖**soubresaut** (subrəso). [F.: see somersault *sb.*] (See quot. 1849.)

1849 R. V. Dixon *Heat* 147 The phenomenon called 'soubresaut', or jumping motion, sometimes observed in liquids when in a state of ebullition. **1863** Grove *Contrib. to Sci.* 420 Boiling like sulphuric acid with soubresauts.

soubrette (su:ˈbrɛt, ‖subrɛt). [a. F., ad. Prov. *soubreto*, fem. of *soubret* coy, reserved, f. *soubra* to set aside.]

1. *Theat.* A maid-servant or lady's maid as a character in a play or opera, usually one of a pert, coquettish, or intriguing character; an actress or singer taking such a part. In extended use, a woman playing a role or roles in light entertainment, e.g. on television or at a seaside variety show, with implications of pertness, coquetry, intrigue, etc.

1753 H. WALPOLE *Lett.* (1840) III. 33 There is a soubrette, called the Niccolina. **1774** *Ibid.* V. 391 A fat woman, rather elderly, who sometimes acted the *soubrette*. *c* **1820** S. ROGERS *Italy* (1839) 57 He prompts the young Soubrette, conning her part. **1839** HALLAM *Hist. Lit.* IV. vi. §52 Congreve has made more use of the all-important soubrette, on whom so much depends in French comedy. **1871** *All Year Round* 24 June 91/1 Tragedy queens and comic soubrettes were alike to her, and she did not present them very differently to her audience. **1905** R. BEACH *Pardners* (1912) i. 33 Variety house, with..two-ton soubrettes, with Barrios diamonds and hand-painted socks. **1951** *Sunday Pictorial* 21 Jan. 6/3 Harriet Cohen has the vivacity and femininity of a soubrette. **1956** *Ann. Reg. 1955* 360 Adele Leigh scored a special success in the soubrette part of Bella. **1958** *Time* 8 Oct. 6/3 His 'wife', Miss Rosita Segovia, takes too soubrette-like a view of this role. **1977** *Listener* 27 Jan. 111/1 By the time she was 18, she was a soubrette at the Gaiety. **1978** *TV Times* 28 Jan.-3 Feb. 26/2 Television's most resilient soubrette, Una Stubbs, can talk about love, marriage and happiness with a twinkle in her eye.

attrib. **1887** *The Lady* 20 Jan. 38/2 Miss Sergisson played the small part of Maid with ease and grace, and wore a very becoming *soubrette* toilette of pink and grey cotton.

2. A lady's maid; a maid-servant.

1824 MISS MITFORD *Village* Ser. I. (1863) 131 She united the pleasant and amusing qualities of a French soubrette, with the solid excellence of an Englishwoman of the old school. **1848** M. W. SAVAGE *Bachelor of the Albany* (1854) 65 The Soubrette leading the way by stating the name of her mistress. **1880** RUSKIN *Bible of Amiens* i. (1884) 4 The little white-capped Amienoise soubrette.

Hence **souˈbrettish** *a.*

1891 E. FIELD *Bk. Western Verse* 198 Soubrettish ways these latter days Invite my praise, but never get it. **1979** J. CROSBY *Party of Year* (1980) xiv. 156 The soubrettish face darkened.

‖**soubriquet** (ˈsu:brɪkeɪ, ‖subrikɛ), *sb.* [a. older F. *soubriquet.*] = SOBRIQUET.

1818 LADY MORGAN *Autobiog.* (1859) 95 That *soubriquet* was given me long after by Mirabeau. **1835** T. MITCHELL *Acharn. of Aristoph.* 121 *note*, The soubriquet of *gapers* appears to have been attached to the citizens of Athens. **1867** TROLLOPE *Chron. Barset* II. xlix. 57 Her name was Susan, but he had always called her Posy, having himself invented for her that soubriquet.

Hence **ˈsoubriquet** *v. trans.*, to nickname.

1880 GORDON *Bk. Chron. Keith* 110 James Henry, soubriqueted the Grammarian from his pedantry.

soubtilite, obs. variant of SUBTILITY.

‖**soucar** (ˈsaʊkɑ:(r)). Also 8 **saucar**, 9 **sahoukar**, **soukar**, **sowcar**, 20 **sahukar**. [ad. Urdū (Hindī) *sāhūkār* great merchant, etc.] A Hindu banker or money-lender.

1785 BURKE *Sp. on Nabob of Arcot's Debts* Wks. VI. 289 When a *saucar*, that is a money dealer, becomes security for any native prince [etc.]. **1799** WELLINGTON *Suppl. Desp.* (1858) I. 378 A debt due by him to a soucar, by name of Rugobah. **1858** J. B. NORTON *Topics* 180 When these new tenants are wealthy soucars..they will not cultivate the soil themselves. **1875** J. WILSON in G. Smith *Life* App. (1878) 633 Money which he had borrowed from Soukars and bankers. **1883** *Madras Mail* 5 Dec. 22/2 The Indian Sowcar has come to possess a notoriety hardly surpassed by that of the European Jew. **1913** J. M. KEYNES *Indian Currency & Finance* iv. 95 Notes, even of the value of Rs. 5, are looked upon with distrust by the village yokels and even by the village sahukars. **1930** *Economist* 12 Apr. 820/1 The majority..consists of rural sahukars, who, though shrewd, are primitive in their methods, and prefer the use of specie and notes to cheques and bills. **1936** J. NEHRU *Autobiogr.* xxxix. 302 The tenant's position was even worse. He was also a *sahukar's* serf.

attrib. **1785** BURKE *Sp. on Nabob of Arcot's Debts* Wks. VI. 237 The right honourable gentleman's favourite soucar cavalry.

Hence **ˈsoucaring**, money-lending.

1785 BURKE *Sp. on Nabob of Arcot's Debts* Wks. VI. 237 The whole art and mystery..of the profession of soucaring.

souccour, obs. f. SUCCOUR *sb.*

†**souce**[1]. *Obs.*$^{-1}$ (Meaning uncertain.)

a **1450** *Fysshynge w. Angle* (1883) 3 With mysfedyng þen schall sche [*sc.* the hawk] haue the frounce, þe Rey, þe Cray, and mony oþer seknes þat brynget hur to þe souce [1496 sowse].

†**souce**[2]. *Obs.*$^{-0}$ (See quot.)

1688 HOLME *Armoury* III. 271/2 A kind of a Drinking Cup ..is by some Gentlemens Buttlers termed a Souce, Goglet, or Goblet.

souce, obs. f. SOUSE *sb.* and *v.*

souch, var. SOUGH *sb.* and *v.*; obs. form of SUCH *a.*

†**souche**, *v. Obs.* In 4 souchy, souche(n), scouche, schoche, 4-5 sowche. [ad. OF. *souchier* (also *sos-*, *suscher*):—L. *suspicāri* to suspect.]

1. *trans.* To suspect, have suspicion of (a thing).

c **1325** *Lay le Freine* 269 Yif ich com hir to More than ichaue y-do, The abbesse wil souchy gile. *c* **1340** HAMPOLE *Pr. Consc.* 788 He souches and trowes sone a thyng, Bot ful late he turnes fra þat trowyng. **1390** GOWER *Conf.* I. 225 If so be myn herte soucheth That oght unto my ladi toucheth [etc.].

2. *intr.* To be suspicious (*of* something). *Obs.*

13.. *Seuyn Sag.* (W.) 1438 He saide nowt,..But euer he souchede him of gile. **1338** R. BRUNNE *Chron.* (1810) 259 Werfore our kyng Edward in þouht fulle wele has souched. *c* **1400** *Laud Troy Bk.* 12596 With foule venym—as alle men souched—His bowe was bent.

souchet: see WATER-SOUCHET.

souchong (su:ˈʃɒŋ). [ad. Chinese *siao-chung* (Cantonese *siu chung*) small sort.] One of the finer varieties of black tea. Also *attrib.*

1760 *Ann. Reg.* 132 The East-India ships..have brought ..62,900 [lb.] of souchong. **1777** ABIGAIL ADAMS in *Fam. Lett.* (1876) 313, I feel as contented when I have breakfasted upon milk as ever I did with Hyson or Souchong. **1803** *Phil. Trans.* XCIII. 268 An ounce of Souchong tea produced 48 grains of tannin. **1850** E. FITZGERALD *Lett.* (1889) I. 208 Now, animated by some very inferior Souchong from the village shop, I continue my letter. **1870** DICKENS *E. Drood* vi, He finished his breakfast as if the flavour of the Superior Family Souchong..were a little on the wane.

soucht, obs. Sc. pa. t. of SEEK *v.*

soucie: see SUSSY *sb.*

†**soucy**. *Obs.*$^{-1}$ [a. older F. *soucie* (mod.F. *souci*), ultimately repr. L. *solsequium.*] = SOLSECLE.

1549 *Compl. Scot.* vi. 57 Ther is ane eirb callit helytropium, the quhilk the vulgaris callis soucye.

soucy: see SUSSY *v.*

soud(e, varr. of SOLD *sb.*[1], *v.*[1], *v.*[2]; Sc. varr. *should*, SHALL *v.*

soudainly, obs. f. SUDDENLY.

soudan(e, obs. ff. SOLDAN.

Soudan, Soudanese: varr. SUDAN, SUDANESE *a.* and *sb.*

soudanly, obs. f. SUDDENLY.

soude, var. SOLD *sb.*[1], etc.; obs. pa. pple. SEW *v.*[1]

†**soudee.** *Obs.*$^{-1}$ [a. OF. *soudee, soldee* :—med.L. *solidāta.*] A solidate.

c **1450** *Godstow Reg.* 158, ij. soudees of rent.

souden, obs. f. SOLDAN.

soudeo(u)r, soudgour, soudiar, -dior, -dioure, obs. ff. SOLDIER.

souder, obs. f. SOLDER, SOLDIER.

soudly: see SUDDLY *a.*

soudon, obs. form of SOLDAN.

soudour, obs. f. SOLDER.

Soudra, var. SUDRA.

soudre, soudur(e, obs. ff. SOLDER.

soudyer, -your(e, -yre, obs. f. SOLDIER.

souel, obs. f. SOWL.

soue(n), obs. ff. SEVEN.

souenyht, obs. f. SEVEN-NIGHT.

soueran(e, etc., obs. ff. SOVEREIGN, etc.

soueþe, obs. f. SEVENTH.

Soufee, obs. f. SUFI[1].

souff, var. SOWFF *Sc.*

souffis(s)ance, -ant, varr. SUFFISANCE, -ANT *Obs.*

‖**souffle** (sufl), *sb.*[1] *Path.* [F.] A murmuring or breathing sound.

1879 WEBSTER *Suppl.* s.v., The uterine *souffle*, a sound heard over the pregnant uterus. **1897** *Allbutt's Syst. Med.* IV. 274 On auscultation, a systolic souffle transmitted from the adjacent aorta is sometimes heard. **1900** *Lancet* 20 Jan. 164/1 The absence of the fœtal heart-sounds and of the uterine souffle is very important.

‖**soufflé** (ˈsu:fleɪ, ‖sufle), *sb.*[2] and *a.* Also 9 soufflet, soufflée. [F., pa. pple. of *souffler*:—L. *sufflāre*, f. *sub* under + *flāre* to blow.

The use of the fem. form *soufflée* is prob. due to its occurrence in *omelette soufflée*.]

A. *sb.* **a.** A light dish, either sweet or savoury, made by mixing materials with white of egg beaten up to a froth, and heating the mixture in an oven until it puffs up.

a. **1813** UDE *French Cook* 195 Soufflé of young Partridges. **1846** SOYER *Cookery* 575 Soufflés when well-made are excellent removes for the winter season. **1847** DISRAELI *Tancred* I. i, I entrusted the soufflées to him. **1883** 'ANNIE THOMAS' *Mod. Housewife* 14 Ducklings and roast pigeons followed, then some pastry and a well-made *soufflé*.

fig. **1888** [see b below]. **1891** MEREDITH *One of our Conq.* xx, Our soufflé of sentiment will be seen subsiding under a breath. **1916** E. POUND *Let.* 27 July (1971) 89 Sometime, certainly, you must have the soufflé of contemporary French poets. **1964** *New Statesman* 1 May 675/3 A girl, her yellow hair in a sort of lacquered soufflé, ran from the police court, crying black tears from the cosmetics of her child's eyes. **1980** T. MORGAN *Somerset Maugham* viii. 202 [The play] *Caroline* was a soufflé whipped up..out of boredom.

β. **1831** *Society* I. 84 Take my plate..for some of the sweets near Miss Bradford. Not the souflet. **1836** B. HALL *Schloss Hainfeld* vii. 104 Last of all, a souflet worthy of Very's or Beauvilliers'.

b. *attrib.*, as ***soufflé-case, -dish***, etc.

1845 E. ACTON *Mod. Cookery* xix. 491 A common soufflé-pan may be purchased for four or five shillings. **1846** SOYER *Cookery* 329 In a common pie-dish or silver soufflée-dish. *Ibid.* 564 A cover large enough for the soufflé-case. **1888** *Athenæum* 22 Sept. 377/3 Mere whipped-egg *soufflé* work of the most artistic kind.

B. *adj.* Of ceramic ware: Having liquid colour applied by means of blowing.

1878 MISS J. J. YOUNG *Ceramic Art* 152 The soufflé decoration is characteristic. **1972** *Trans. Oriental Ceramics Soc.* XXXVIII. 141 The entire vessel covered with *soufflé* gilding.

†**ˈsoufflement.** *Obs.*$^{-1}$ [a. F. *soufflement*, f. *souffler*: see prec.] Breathing, blowing.

1483 CAXTON *Cato* c ij, Platon perceyued..that the pestylence came by the whystelyng and soufflement of the sayd dragons.

†**souffler.** *Obs.*$^{-1}$ [ad. F. *souffleur*, f. *souffler* to blow.] (See quot. and cf. BLOWER[1] 2.)

1674 J. JOSSELYN *Two Voy.* 4 Two mighty Whales we now saw, the one..making a great noise with puffing and blowing; the Seamen called her a Soufler.

‖**souffrante** (sufrɑ̃t), *a.* [Fr., fem. sing. pres. pple. of *souffrir* to suffer.] Of women: delicate, indisposed or ill; prone to anxiety or depression.

1827 E. GROSVENOR in G. Huxley *Lady Elizabeth & Grosvenors* (1965) vii. 141 She is a very interesting person, very handsome, but pale and 'souffrante'. **1877** GEO. ELIOT *Let.* 10 July (1956) VI. 392, I have been *souffrante*, but am content to bear my share of such trouble. **1938** A. THIRKELL *Let.* in M. Strickland *A. Thirkell: Portrait of a Lady Novelist* (1977) vii. 120, I have been so *souffrante* this summer with perpetual headaches. **1977** *Times Lit. Suppl.* 28 Jan. 94/4 A tearful, tortured female, forever *souffrante*, forever worried, forever hoarding and cherishing her sufferings.

souffraunce, obs. f. SUFFERANCE.

‖**souffre-douleur** (sufrədulœr). Also **souffre douleur**. [Fr., lit. 'suffer sorrow'.] One who is in a subservient position and must listen to or share another's troubles; also *spec.* a woman who acts as a paid companion to an older woman.

1845 M. GARDINER *Strathern* II. xvii. 17 The woman on whose arm she leans is her *dame de compagnie*, her *souffre douleur*. **1864** C. M. YONGE *Trail* II. iii. 55 A younger brother and legitimate *souffre douleur*. **1907** M. E. BRADDON *Dead Love has Chains* i. 3 She had her maid and her *souffre-douleur*, a dowerless kinswoman of six-and-twenty. **1962** *Punch* 7 Nov. 684/1 Josephine, employed as Aunt March's *souffre-douleur*. **1981** W. GÉRIN *Anne Thackeray Ritchie* xx. 240 When away from home he always wrote regularly to his 'souffre douleur'.

soufre, obs. form of SULPHUR.

soufrecan, obs. form of SUFFRAGAN.

soufrière (sufriɛr). [Fr., f. *soufre* SULPHUR *sb.* + *-ière* -IER.] = SOLFATARA.

1879 J. W. BODDAM-WHETHAM *Roraima & Brit. Guiana* vi. 53 How pleasant it would be to spend a few days on each of these West Indian islands! To visit their *soufrières*, their mountain forests, their wild hills, and their cultivated estates! **1902** *Pop. Sci. Monthly* July 273 The warm springs and solfataras (or souffrieres [*sic*]) on Martinique and other islands displayed unwonted activity. **1939** *Nature* 14 Oct. 677/1 The soufrières of Montserrat are considered as having been caused mainly by the penetration of meteoric water to a subterrain of sulphided limestone that had been reheated intensively by uprising magma. **1972** *Whitaker's Almanack 1973* 786/2 Montserrat..contains three active soufrières and several hot springs.

sougan, variant of SUGGAN.

sougee, var. SOOGEE.

sough (sʌf, saʊ, *Sc.* sux), *sb.*[1] Forms: 4-5 **swogh(e, swough(e**, 6 **swouch**, 6- **souch**, 7- **sough** (8 **zough**), 8- **sugh** (9 **seugh, soogh, sooch**, etc.); 4 **swowh**, 4-5 **swow(e**, 5 **sow**, 9 **soo**. [ME. type **swōh, swōȝ*, from the verb *swōȝen*: see SOUGH *v.*[1] From the 16th cent. almost exclusively Sc. and north. dial. until adopted in general literary use in the 19th.

The pron. (sɒf) is given by Smart (1836) and Ogilvie (1850).]

1. A rushing or murmuring sound as of wind, water, or the like, esp. one of a gentle or soothing nature.

c **1381** CHAUCER *Parl. Foules* 247 Of sykys hoote as fuyr I herde a swow that gan a-boute renne. *c* **1384** —— *H. Fame* 1031 Herestow not the grete swogh? ?*a* **1400** *Morte Arth.* 759 With þe swoghe of þe see in swefnynge he felle. **1508** DUNBAR *Tua Mariit Wemen* 519 The soft souch of the swyr ..Myght comfort ony creatur of the kyn of Adam. **1513** DOUGLAS *Æneid* II. xi. 81 Ilk swouch of wynd, and every quhisper..affrayit [me]. **1785** BURNS *Cotter's Sat. Nt.* ii, November chill blaws loud wi' angry sugh. **1792** WORDSW. *Descript. Sketches* 359 Faint wail of eagle.., and pine-wood's steady sugh. **1816** SCOTT *Old Mort.* xxxiii, It is the sough of the wind among the bracken. **1847** C. BRONTË *J. Eyre* xii, That evening calm betrayed alike the tinkle of the nearest streams, the sough of the most remote. **1862** CARLYLE *Fredk. Gt.* XIII. vi. (1872) 73 Whereupon solemn waving of hats; indistinct sough of loyal murmur. **1879** MISS BIRD *Rocky Mount.* 101 The strange sough of gusts moving among the pine tops.

b. *Sc.* A canting or whining manner of speaking, especially in preaching or praying.

1723 MESTON *Knight* Poems (1767) 15 Give them the sough, they can dispense, With either scant or want of sense. *c* **1730** BURT *Lett. N. Scotl.* (1818) I. 171 The prayers are often more like narrations to the Almighty than petitions..; and the sough as it is called (the whine) is unmanly. **1816** SCOTT *Old Mort.* xiv, Never stir, if my auld mither is na at the preaching again! I ken the sough o' her texts. **1894** 'IAN MACLAREN' *Brier Bush* ii. 60 He's a speeritually minded man, Maister Cosh, and has the richt sough.

2. A deep sigh or breath. Also *transf.*

c **1386** CHAUCER *Miller's T.* 433 He siketh, with ful many a sory swough. *a* **1400** *Isumbras* 89 His hirde-mene mett he everylkone With a fulle drery swoghe. **14..** *Chaucer's Troylus* IV. 375 (Cambr. MS.), Among his sobbis & his sowis sore. **1616** B. JONSON *Epigrams* cxxxiii, The well-greas'd wherry now had got betweene, And bad her fare-well sough, vnto the lurden. **1788** *Voc. Bargie* in *Trans. R. Irish Acad.* II. 35 *Zough*, a sigh. **1790** BURNS *Battle of Sherra-Moor* i, My heart, for fear, gae sough for sough. **1885** *Field* 12 Dec. 832/1 From the loch would come the sough of a porpoise or the wild cry of a loon. **1901** G. DOUGLAS *House with Green Shutters* 298 It was hours ere he slept, but at last a heavy sough told her he had found oblivion.

3. A rumour; a report.

1716 WODROW *Corr.* (1843) II. 172 By the souch of members I imagine the Duke of Argyle will be named. **1816** SCOTT *Antiq.* xxix, There was a sough in the country about it, but it was hushed up. **1821** GALT *Annals of Parish* xii, I found..a sough of something extraordinar going on. **1900** STRAIN *Elmslie's Drag-net* 35, I had heard some sough o' a byre at Kelso that had been smitten.

4. *to keep a calm* (or *quiet*) *sough*, to keep quiet, to say little or nothing. *Sc.*

1808 JAMIESON, *Keep a calm souch*, be silent. **1816** SCOTT *Old Mort.* xx, I'se aye keep a calm sough. **1863** MRS. GASKELL *Sylvia's Lovers* (1874) 232 Not that I iver let on to them.., so keep a calm sough, my lad. **1880** MRS. LYNN LINTON *Rebel Family* xiii, So that, on the whole, keeping a calm sough was the best wisdom.

Hence **'soughfully** *adv.*, with a soughing sound; **'soughless** *a.*, silent, noiseless.

1851 W. HAY *Lintie o' Moray* 41 Gentle stream, Wi' soughless waters onward stealin'. **1890** MRS. BARR *Friend Olivia* xx, The trees..talked soughfully among themselves.

sough (sʌf), *sb.*[2] Forms: 4 **sogh, sohw,** 5 **swowȝe, swoughe,** 5- **sough** (6 **soughe,** *Sc.* **souch**), 7 **sowgh, saugh,** 9 *dial.* **sugh;** 8- **suff,** 9 **surf,** *dial.* **souffe, soof.** See also SHEUGH. [Of obscure origin. Cf. Antwerp dial. *zoeg* a small ditch in a meadow.]

1. A boggy or swampy place; a small pool.

a **1300** *Cursor M.* 2501 Þai fled and fell vntill a sogh [*Gött.* sohw], And þar þair faas þam foluand slogh. *a* **1450** *Le Morte Arth.* 875 (Roxb.), In a foreste by a swoughe. **1515** *Scottish Field* 440 in *Chetham Misc.* (1856), On a soughe us beside, there seene we our enemies, Were moving over the mountains. **1612** DRAYTON *Poly-olb.* iv. 168 Then Dulas and Cledaugh, By Morgany doe drive her through her wat'ry saugh. **1869** 'OUIDA' *Puck* vii, The road..went through a shallow 'sough' of water. **1876-** in dial. glossaries (Cumb., Yks., Heref.).

2. A small gutter for draining off water; a drain, a sewer, a trench.

c **1440** *Pallad. on Husb.* I. 515 The length [of the ox-stall is] as from the horn into the sough. **1523** FITZHERB. *Surv.* xxxv. 49 If this maner of dichynge wyll nat make the marres grounde drie, than must you make a sough vnderneth therthe as men do to gette cole. *c* **1570** *Diurn. Occurr.* (Bann. Cl.) 100 The said erle slipit ower ane souch, and tomblit doun the same. **1667** PRIMATT *City & C. Builder* 5 The charge of driving such Soughs or Trenches. **1681** *Rec. Burg. Sheffield* (1897) 217 For making a sough to the pin-fold. **1763** *Ann. Reg.* II. 100/1 At proper distances, soughs are formed near the top of the canal, which prevents it from overflowing during immoderate rains. **1780** *Phil. Trans.* LXX. 346, I shall lay a sough of brick, which will convey it from the pump to the boiler. **1805** R. W. DICKSON *Pract. Agric.* I. 301 The most difficult part of the business consists in laying the sough when in running sands. **1833** *Act 3 & 4 Will. IV*, c. 46 §116 Any water pipe, sough, or watercourse already laid down..in..any of the streets. **1885** *Law Times' Rep.* LII. 356/2 Various old stone soughs, which..received the sewage of a number of houses.

attrib. **1892** EMINSON *Epid. Pneumonia at Scotter* 18 The out-door premises..drained off through some common sough pipes.

3. A subterranean drain to carry off the water in a mine; an adit of a mine.

1619 ATKINSON *Gold Mynes Scotl.* (Bann. Cl.) 15 To frame or make a long sowgh, or scowring place, into which they bringe the streame water. **1653** MANLOVE *Customes Lead Mines* 260 (E.D.S.), Main Rakes, Cross Rakes, Brownhenns, Budles and Soughs. **1686** PLOT *Staffordsh.* 137 This sort of damp..is that they commonly meet with in long Soughs for conveyance of water from the coale. **1747** HOOSON *Miner's Dict.* T ij b, These Addits or Soughs if they prove soft, destroy a great deal of Timber, especially in Sand. **1778** W. PRYCE *Min. Cornub.* 81 The Sough or Adit being one hundred fathoms below the surface. **1851** *Act 14 & 15 Vict.* c. 94 §26 If any Person shall, by virtue of any Sough Engine or other Means, unwater or give Relief to any Mine or Vein which may be under Water. **1882** R. L. GALLOWAY *Coal Mining* 25 The drainage of the mines was effected by means of the horizontal tunnels.., which were variously termed adits, watergates, soughs, surfs.

†**sough,** *sb.*[3] *Obs. rare.* Also 5 **sugh.** [repr. OE. *sulh* plough: see SULL *sb.*] A ploughshare.

1432-50 tr. *Higden* (Rolls) VII. 165 Sche..passede by fulle stappes the ix. cultres or sughes with owte eny hurte. **1598** FLORIO, *Vómere*,..the sough or ploughshare or culter. **1688** HOLME *Armoury* III. 333/2 The Sough..[of a plough] is that as Plows into the Ground.

sough, obs. f. pa. t. SEE *v.*; obs. f. SOW *sb.*[1]

sough (sʌf, saʊ, *Sc.* sux), *v.*[1] Forms: 1 **swoȝan,** 5 **swoghe** (**squoe**), 6 *Sc.* **swouch, suowch, swoch;** 4 **souȝe,** 6 (9) **sowgh, sogh,** 6- **sugh,** 8- **sough** (9 *dial.* **suff**); *Sc.* 6 **sowch,** 6, 8- **souch,** 9 **sooch;** 5 **swowe,** 8 **swoo,** 9 *dial.* **sow, sou(e, soo.** [OE. *swóȝan*, = OS. *swôgan* to move with a rushing sound; related to Goth. *ufswōgjan* (cf. OE. *swéȝan* to sound, etc.; Norw. dial. *søgja* to murmur, rustle) and *swōgatjan* to sigh. Cf. also WFris. *swoegje* to pant.]

1. a. *intr.* To make a rushing, rustling, or murmuring sound.

a **900** CYNEWULF *Crist* 950 On seofon healfa swoȝað windas. *a* **1000** *Genesis* 1375 Drihten..let..eȝorstreamas swearte swoȝan. **13..** *E.E. Allit. P.* C. 140 þe see souȝed ful sore, gret selly to here. *c* **1400** *Anturs of Arth.* 55 By þe stremys so strange, þat swyftly swoghes [*v.r.* squytherly squoes]. *c* **1450** HOLLAND *Howlat* 171 Swannis suowchand full swyth, swetest of swar. **1513** DOUGLAS *Æneid* I. vi. 155 Ther wyngis swochand jolely. *Ibid.* v. iii. 76 The fludis..souchand quhair thai fair, In sondir slydis. **1724** RAMSAY *Royal Archers Shooting* iv, The feather'd arrows drive All soughing thro' the sky. **1728** —— *Robt., Richy, & Sandy* 56 Torn frae its roots adown it souchan fell. **1815** G. BEATTIE *John o' Arnha'* (1826) 25 The wind sough'd mournfu' throw the trees. **1857** THOREAU *Maine W.* i. (1864) 3 The white-pine tree..—its branches soughing with the four winds. **1884** MRS. C. PRAED *Zéro* iv, The wind soughed through the budding branches overhead in long monotonous swell.

b. *trans.* To utter in this manner.

1821 CLARE *Vill. Minstr.* I. 29 Each rude-risen tempest.. Sughing its vengeance through the yellow trees. **1975** W. MCILVANNEY *Docherty* I. xviii. 124 Trees were brooding presences, soughing incantations. Every bush hid an invisible force, frequently malevolent.

2. a. *intr.* To draw the breath heavily or noisily; to sigh deeply.

c **1475** *Partenay* 1944 There gan he to sigh and sowghid for wo. *Ibid.* 2890 He sighed, soghed, wepte with teres many. **1806** R. JAMIESON *Pop. Ballads* II. 338, I hear your mither souch and snore. **1847** H. BUSHNELL *Chr. Nurture* II. iii. (1861) 273 Dosing, all together, and sughing in dull dreams.

b. With *away*: To breathe one's last; to die.

1816 SCOTT *Old Mort.* xxxix, His uncle, poor gentleman, just sough'd awa wi' it in his mouth. **1886** WILLOCK *Rosetty Ends* vi. (1887) 46 He muttered 'Puir Gyp', an' then he soughed awa.

3. *trans.* **a.** To hum (a tune). Also *fig.*

1711 RAMSAY *On Maggy Johnstoun* x, I took a nap, And soucht a' night balillilow, As sound 's a tap. **1721** —— *Elegy on Patie Birnie* iv, His face could mak' you fain, When he did sough, 'O wiltu, wiltu do 't again!' **1805** J. NICOL *Poems* II. 133 (Jam.), I, 'mang many merry fouk, Can..sough a tune, an' crack a jock.

b. To utter in a sighing or whining tone.

1816 SCOTT *Antiq.* xxvii, He hears ane o' the king's Presbyterian chaplains sough out a sermon. **1818** —— *Br. Lamm.* xviii, I hae soughed thae dark words ower to mysell.

sough (sʌf), *v.*[2] [f. SOUGH *sb.*[2]]

1. *trans.* **a.** To face or build up (a ditch) *with* stone, etc. **b.** To make drains in (land); to drain by constructing proper channels. Also *absol.*

1688 *Norris Papers* (Chetham Soc.) 175 That all ditches which convey the water crosse the highway be soughed with wall stone, and well covered throughout. **1797** *Trans. Soc. Arts* XV. 209 This lot of land, considered as enclosed, but not soughed. **1836** *Hull & Selby Rlwy. Act* 6 To bore, dig, cut, embank and sough. **1868** C. W. HATFIELD *Hist. Notices Doncaster* II. 285 Silver-street and French-gate were soughed in 1837-8.

2. *intr.* To reach, or get into, a sough.

1898 *Daily News* 19 Feb. 9/2 Lang Syne again raced by, and was a meritorious winner as the hare soughed.

'soughing, *vbl. sb.*[1] [f. SOUGH *v.*[1]] The action of the verb; a rushing or murmuring sound.

?*a* **1400** *Morte Arth.* 931 Swowynge of watyr, and syngynge of byrdez. *c* **1400** *Destr. Troy* 1061 Swoghyng of swete ayre, Swalyng of briddes. **1582** STANYHURST *Æneis* II. (Arb.) 63 The tre..with sowghing yt grunts, as wounded in hacking. **1713** DERHAM *Phys.-Theol.* IV. iii. 119 Which causeth a confusion in the Hearing, with a certain Murmur or Swooing like the fall of Waters. **1817** *Blackw. Mag.* I. 57 Carefully noticing the formation of the clouds..and the *soughing* of the winds. **1859** MISS MULOCK *Romantic T.* 74 In the soughing of the solemn trees. **1879** SALA *Paris Herself Again* xvii, Then come the distant wailing and soughing of a sea of martial music.

'soughing, *vbl. sb.*[2] [f. SOUGH *v.*[2]] The operation of draining or making drains. Also *attrib.*, as *soughing-tile, tool.*

1807 VANCOUVER *Agric. Devon* (1813) 133 Tunnelling, or soughing under the gateways, will be in proportion to..the facility of procuring soughing-tiles. **1840** *Civil Eng. & Arch. Jrnl.* III. 140/1 Improvements in the manufacture of cofered spades and shovels, soughing and grafting tools. **1868** LADY VERNEY *Stone Edge* xxi, I can't afford to lose back-rent, and present rent, and arrears for soughing.

'soughing, *ppl. a.* [f. SOUGH *v.*[1]] Rushing, rustling, murmuring, etc.

Beowulf 3145 Wudurec astah.., swoȝende leȝ. **1513** DOUGLAS *Æneid* VI. xi. 51 A wod with sowchand bewis schene. *Ibid.* VII. Prol. 74 Every lynde Quhyslyt and brayt of the swouchand wynde. **1806** J. GRAHAME *Birds of Scot.* 18 The dismal soughing wing, the doleful cry. **1859** MRS. GASKELL *Round the Sofa* II. 111 The soughing November wind came with long sweeps over the fells. **1880** *Daily Tel.* 29 Oct., The nearly naked branches crackle and moan with the soughing, storm-presaging wind.

sought (saʊt), *sb. north. dial.* Forms: 4 **soght,** 5 **souȝt,** 7 **sought,** 9 **sowt, soot.** [a. ON. **soht* (later *sótt*, Icel. and Fær. *sótt*, Norw. *sott*, Sw. and Da. *sot*), = Goth. *sauhts*, OS. *suht* (hence once in OE.), OHG. and MHG. *suht* (G. *sucht*), Du. *zucht*: cf. also OEFris. *secht*, OWFris. *siochte*. The stem *suh-, suk-* is an ablaut-variant of *seuk-*: see SICK *a.*] Sickness, illness, disease. In later use *spec.* a disease of sheep or other animals.

See also the combs. GULESOUGHT and LUNGSOUGHT.

a **1300** *Cursor M.* 14157 Wel þai trud þat he moght þair broþer sauue of al his soght. **14..** *MS. Sloane* 7, fol. 73 (H.), For the ȝalow souȝt, that men callin the jaundys. **1621** BRATHWAIT *Nat. Embassie* (1877) 242 Scab, sought, the rot or any kind of murren. **1847** HALLIWELL, *Sowt*, the rot in sheep. *Westm.* **1876** RICHARDSON *Cumbld. Talk* Ser. II. 150 Ye'r sheep dee i' t' seekness or t' sowt. **1878** *Cumbld. Gloss.* 91 *Sowt*, the joint-ill in lambs and calves.

sought (sɔːt), *ppl. a.* [pa. pple. of SEEK *v.*]

a. That is, or has been, searched for, desired, etc.

See also *long-sought* s.v. LONG *adv.* 9 a.

a **1300** *Cursor M.* 3254 To mesopotany suith come he, And son he fand þe soght cite. **1382** WYCLIF *Isaiah* lxii. 12 Thou..shalt be clepid a soȝt cite, and not forsaken. **1632** LITHGOW *Trav.* III. 77 Now Creta comes..To my sought view. **1710** BERKELEY *Princ. Hum. Knowl.* §121 Having found the sought figures. **1725** W. HALFPENNY *Sound Building* 21 Then..you will describe the sought Arches *v z t* and *w t*. *Ibid.* 22. **1883** 'ANNIE THOMAS' *Mod. Housewife* 149 The cleverness which makes her a sought woman in every *coterie*.

b. With *-after* or *-for*.

1605 B. JONSON *Volpone* IV. ii, When he mist His sought-for father. **1778** *The Refutation* 13 The sought-for bribe I doubt you'll never see. **1829** BENTHAM *Justice & Cod. Petit.* 12 Such supposed facts as..may be styled unknown or sought-for facts. **1881** *Trans. Obstet. Soc. Lond.* XXII. 66 He was the fashionable and most sought-after accoucheur. **1944** AUDEN *For Time Being* (1945) 32 Her famous, memorable, sought-after evenings. **1978** *Lancashire Life* Apr. 45/2 Foulridge took umbrage,..continuing to build on its [*sc.* Foulridge's] reputation of being a sought-after spot to live.

soughthistle, obs. f. SOW-THISTLE.

sougi-mougi, var. SOOGEE-MOOGEE.

soujge, souji-mouji, varr. SOOGEE, SOOGEE-MOOGEE.

soujour, obs. f. SOLDIER *sb.*

‖**souk** (suk). Also **sok, sook, soug, suk(h, suq.** [Fr., ad. Arab. *sūḳ* market-place.] An Arab market or market-place, a bazaar (sense 1 a).

1826 DENHAM & CLAPPERTON *Narr. Trav. N. & Cent. Afr.* II. 51 The soug, or market, is well supplied with every necessary and luxury. **1829** J. L. BURCKHARDT *Trav. Arabia* 54 In a row of eight or ten shops are sold rice, onions, butter, dates, and coffee-beans... This is what the Arabs call a *souk*, or market. **1855** R. F. BURTON *Personal Narr. Pilgrimage to El-Medinah* I. 333 There is a large 'Suk', or market-place in the usual form, a long narrow lane darkened by a covering of palm leaves, with little shops let into the walls of the houses on both sides. **1899** A. E. W. MASON *Miranda of Balcony* ii. 24 Every evening he comes down to the Sôk, buys milk and bread. **1909** G. W. FURLONG *Gateway to Sahara* I. 21 One afternoon, I was passing here from the *Suk*..when a ragged, unkempt fellow appeared in the caravan road there, acting most strangely. **1921** *Glasgow Herald* 20 Oct. 4 The suqs or covered streets, which, being screened from the glare of the sun, afford fine shelter for shops and markets. **1926** D. BYRNE *Brother Saul* v. 64 When Anna went abroad..to the sook of the perfumers. **1931** *Observer* 6 Sept. 13 The sun-smitten pavement of the *sukh*. **1959** W. THESIGER *Arabian Sands* xiii. 258 Behind the..houses which lined the water-front were the *suqs*, covered passageways, where merchants sat in the gloom, cross-legged in narrow alcoves among their piled merchandise. **1968** R. HARGREAVES *Bloodybacks* iii. 74 The importation of assorted consignments of *filles du roi*, nubile but dowerless wenches willing to marry anyone in a position to provide them with a home... Their distribution was reminiscent of nothing so much as the disposal of Christian slaves in an Oriental *Sok*. **1978** L. HEREN *Growing up on The Times* iii. 91 The assassins escaped into the souks of the city [*sc.* Damascus], and no more was heard of them. **1981** *Financial Times* 12 Dec. 7/2 The lust for gold..grabs most visitors to Sharjah and Dubai, where the gold souks gleam with the stuff.

souk(e, obs. varr. SUCK.

soukar, obs. Sc. f. SUGAR; variant of SOUCAR.

souker, obs. var. SUCKER.

soul (səʊl), *sb.* Forms: α. 1 sawol, -al, 1–2 sawul, 1, 4 sawel (1 sauwel, 4 saw-, sauwil), 1, 4–6 sawl (5–6 sawll, 9 *dial.* sawl, seawl, zawl, etc.), 2–6 sawle; 1, 4 sauel (4 -il), 3–7 (9 *dial.*) saule (3 sæule, 4 zaule, 5 savle); 1, 4–5, 6–9 *Sc.* and *north.* saul, 5–7 *Sc.* and *north.* saull; 5 sal, saal, 5–6 sale, 5–6 (9 *dial.*) sall (6 salle). β. 2–7 sowle, 5 sowel, 5–6 sowylle, 6 sowll, 8 *Ir.* showl, 9 *dial.* sowl; 3–7 soule (6 zoule, soulle), 5– soul (8 *dial.* saoul); 5 sool (6 sooll), 5–6 solle, 6–8 (9 *dial.*) sole, 7 sol. [Common Teut.: OE. *sáwol*, *sáwel*, *sáwl*, etc., = Goth. *saiwala*; the forms in the other languages show various degrees of contraction, as OHG. *sêula*, *sêla* (MHG. *sêle*, G. *seele*), OS. *sêola* (*siola*; MLG. *sêle*, LG. *seele*, *seel*), OLFrank. *sêla*, *sîla* (MDu. *siel-e*, *ziel-e*, Du. *ziel*), OFris. *sêle* (*siele*; WFris. *siel*, NFris. *seel*, *sial*, etc.); ON. *sála*, *sál* (Icel. *sál*, Norw. dial. *saal*), MSw. *sial*, *siäl*, *siel* (Sw. *själ*, Da. *sjæl*), whence Finn. *sielu*, Lapp. *siello*, etc. The ultimate etymology is uncertain.

For examples of the older genitive form without *-s*, see 18.]

I. † 1. The principle of life in man or animals; animate existence. *Obs.* (freq. in OE. in Scriptural passages).

Beowulf 2820 Him of hreðre ȝewat sawol secean soðfæstra dom. *c* **825** *Vesp. Psalter* lxxvii. 50 [He ne] spearede from deaðe sawlum heara. *c* **1000** *Ags. Ps.* (Thorpe) xxxii. 16 Forþam þæt he ȝefriðie heora sawla fram deaðe, and hi fede on hungres tide. **1382** WYCLIF *Jonah* i. 14 Lord, we bisechen, that we perishe not in the soule of this man. *a* **1450** tr. *De Imitatione* I. xviii. 20 For þei hated her soules, þat is to say, her bodely lyues, þat þei miȝt kepe hem in to lif euer-lasting. **1535** COVERDALE *Judg.* xii. 3 Whan I sawe y[t] there was no helper, I put my soule in my honde, and wente agaynst the children of Ammon. **1611** BIBLE *Gen.* xxxv. 18 As her soule was in departing, (for she died). [**1651** HOBBES *Leviath.* III. xxxviii. 241 Soule and Life in the Scripture, do usually signifie the same thing.] **1697** DRYDEN *Virg. Georg.* III. 744 The thriven Calves..render their sweet Souls before the plenteous Rack.

2. a. The principle of thought and action in man, commonly regarded as an entity distinct from the body; the spiritual part of man in contrast to the purely physical. Also occas., the corresponding or analogous principle in animals. Freq. in connexion with, or in contrast to, *body*.

Sometimes personified, as in the common mediæval dialogues between the soul and the body.

α. *c* **888** K. ÆLFRED *Boeth.* xxxiv. §6 To þære saule & to þæm lichoman, belimpað ealle þas þæs monnes good ȝe gastlicu ȝe lichomlicu. **971** *Blickl. Hom.* 21 Eal swa hwæt swa se ȝesenelica lichama deþ oþþe wyrceþ, eal þæt deþ seo unȝesynelice sawl þurh þone lichoman. *c* **1000** ÆLFRIC *Hom.* I. 16 Se man is ece on anum dæle, þæt is on ðære sawle. *c* **1200** ORMIN 11498 Swa þatt te manness bodiȝ beo Buhsumm forþ wiþþ þe sawle. *a* **1300** *Cursor M.* 21757 (Edin.), þe Sawil it hauis of strenþis þrin. **1340** *Ayenb.* 105 þri þinges þet byeþ ine þe zaule, beþenchinge, onderstondynge, and wyl. *a* **1400–50** *Alexander* 4429 All þe sauour of ȝoure sauls is sattild in ȝour mouthis. **1483** *Cath. Angl.* 319 A Savle, *anima.* **1599** ALEX. HUME *Hymns* i. 21 My sensis, and my saull I saw, Debait a deadly strife. **1737** *Gentl. Mag.* VII. 50 The coward lurks in Jockey's saul.

β. *c* **1175** in *Fragm. Ælfric's Gloss.*, etc. (1838) 6 Ʒet sæiþ þeo sowle soriliche to þen licame [etc.]. **12..** *Moral Ode* 394 To þere blisse us bringe god..þenne he vre soule vn-bint of licames bende. *c* **1386** CHAUCER *Prol.* 656 But if [= unless] a mannes soule were in his purs. **1422** tr. *Secreta Secret., Priv. Priv.* 218 Here is i-prowid that the Sowle sueth the condycionys of the bodyes. *c* **1440** *Jacob's Well* 258 As þi soule is lyif of þi body, so is god lyif of þi soule. *a* **1547** SURREY *Eccl.* iii. Poems (1810) 355 Who can tell yf that the sowle of man ascende, Or with the body of it dye? **1596** SHAKS. *Merch. V.* IV. i. 132 To hold opinion..That soules of Animals infuse themselues Into the trunkes of men. **1621** HAKEWILL *David's Vow* 120 It is..vanity, to thinke that all passions either may be or should be utterly rooted out of the soule. **1681** FLAVEL *Meth. Grace* v. 111 If there be spiritual sense in your souls, there is spiritual life in them. **1716–8** LADY M. W. MONTAGU *Lett.* I. xxxix. 159 Our vulgar notion that they do not own women to have any souls, is a mistake. **1774** GOLDSM. *Nat. Hist.* (1776) II. 207 It must be dreadful, ..since it is sufficient to separate the soul from the body. **1841** DICKENS *Barn. Rudge* iii, The absence of the soul is far more terrible in a living man than in a dead one. **1868** HELPS *Realmah* ix. (1876) 247, I mean that there should be a double soul, taking the word 'soul' to include all powers, both of thought and feeling. **1897** MARY KINGSLEY *W. Africa* 441, I know many people have doubts as to the existence of souls in small boys of this class.

fig. **1829** CARLYLE *Misc.* (1857) II. 106 Thus is the Body-politic, more than ever worshipped and tendered; but the Soul-politic less than ever.

b. Without article.

c **1000** ÆLFRIC *Hom.* I. 276 Fixas and fuȝelas he ȝesceop on flæsce butan sawle. **13..** *E.E Allit. P.* B. 290 Al schal doun & be ded & dryuen out of erþe, þat euer I sette saule inne. *c* **1374** CHAUCER *Troilus* II. 1734, I coniure..On his half, which that sowle us alle sende. *c* **1430** *Hymns Virgin* (1867) 102 In soule oonli þou wente to helle. **1535** COVERDALE *Wisd.* xiv. 29 Idols (which haue nether sole ner vnderstondinge). **1692** BENTLEY *Boyle Lect.* i. 13 That all their Thoughts, and the whole of what they call Soul, are only various Action and Repercussion of small particles of Matter. **1727–46** THOMSON *Summer* 774 There on the breezy summit..let me draw Ethereal soul. **1813** BYRON *Giaour* 93 So coldly sweet, so deadly fair, We start, for soul is wanting there. **1884** BROWNING *Ferishtah, Eagle* 47 God is soul, souls I and thou.

c. Coupled with *body* or *life*. (Without article.)

c **888** K. ÆLFRED *Boeth.* xxxiv §9 Ic wat þæt hit bið sawl & lichoma. *a* **1175** *Cott. Hom.* 221 He warð þa man ȝesceapen on sawle and on lichame. *c* **1200** ORMIN 2544 To wurrþenn filledd..I bodiȝ & i sawle Off Godess Gastess hallȝhe mahht. *a* **1300** *Cursor M.* 23903 (Edin.), Lif and sawel I yeld hir til. *c* **1340** HAMPOLE *Pr. Consc.* 129 How wake man es in saul and body. *c* **1450** HOLLAND *Howlat* 739 Bot all committis to the, Saull and lyf, ladye! **1526** *Pilgr. Perf.* (W. de W. 1531) 25 Whan man offreth hymselfe hole to almyghty god, bothe soule & body. **1567** *Gude & Godlie B.* (S.T.S.) 10 Baith Saule and body to defend. **1753** MISS COLLIER *Art Torment.* II. ii. (1811) 127 By never letting him see you swallow half enough to keep body and soul together. **1831** SCOTT *Cast. Dang.* ix, I can hardly get so much for mine as will hold soul and body together.

Comb. **1817** COLERIDGE *Biog. Lit.* (Bohn) viii. 64 To fall back into the common rank of soul-and-bodyists.

Also in Naut. phr. ***soul and body lashing*** (see quot. 1962).

1903 C. PROTHEROE *Life in Mercantile Marine* 150 The best method of arranging his oil-skins to keep the water out, ..known as a 'soul and body lashing'. **1936** B. ADAMS *Ships & Women* iv. 87 All wore rope yarns tightly tied about wrists and ankles... We call those rope yarns 'soul and body lashings'. **1962** A. G. COURSE *Dict. Naut. Terms* 182 *Soul and body lashings*, rope yarns tied round the waist and sleeves of oilskin jackets, and round the bottom of oilskin trousers, to prevent the water, from seas crashing on board, getting under the oilskins. They also prevented the wind from ballooning up inside the oilskins.

d. ***soul and conscience***: in *Sc. Law*, the formula by which medical testimony in writing is authenticated; also *attrib.* (see quot. 1976).

1892 A. M. ANDERSON *Criminal Law of Scotland* v. xiii. 252 Medical reports are made on soul and conscience, read at the trial, and sworn to as true. **1925** W. J. LEWIS *Manual of Law of Evidence in Scotland* III. ii. 84 Medical certificates on soul and conscience, apparently holograph, appear, in non-contentious matters, to be generally accepted without further evidence. **1976** L. KENNEDY *Presumption of Innocence* III. 147 There was a soul and conscience certificate in relation to Mrs Carmichael; this meant that a doctor had sworn on his soul and conscience that she was unfit to attend the court.

3. a. The seat of the emotions, feelings, or sentiments; the emotional part of man's nature.

For the phr. *heart and soul*, see HEART *sb.* 52.

c **825** *Vesp. Psalter* vi. 4 Ʒedroefed sindun all ban min, & sawl min ȝedroefed is swiðe. *c* **950** *Lindisf. Gosp.* Matt. xxvi. 38 Unrot is sauel min..oð deaðe. **13..** *E.E. Allit. P.* C. 325 When þacces of anguych was hid in my sawle. *c* **1400** *Destr. Troy* 10768 Hit wold haue persit with pyte any pure sawle.. hor torfer to se. *c* **1420** in *26 Pol. Poems* 108 My soul of my self anoyed isse. **1553** GRIMALDE *Cicero's Offices* (1600) A iij, Of the soule, or life endued with sences, pleasures is the ende that it would enioy. **1599** SHAKS. *Much Ado* II. iii. 60 Now is his soule rauisht, is it not strange that sheepes guts should hale soules out of mens bodies? **1667** MILTON *P.L.* II. 556 For Eloquence the Soul, Song charms the Sense. **1697** DRYDEN *Virg. Past.* VIII. 113 Such let the Soul of cruel Daphnis be; Hard to the rest of Women; soft to me. **1794** MRS. RADCLIFFE *Myst. Udolpho* xlviii, Valancourt seemed to be annihilated, and her soul sickened at the blank that remained. **1805** SCOTT *Last Minstrel* VI. i, Breathes there the man, with soul so dead, Who never to himself hath said [etc.]. **1857** MAURICE *Epist. St. John* ii. 24 We say sometimes of a speech which strikes us as very sincere and very powerful, 'The speaker threw his whole soul into it'. **1874** M. CREIGHTON *Hist. Ess.* i. (1902) 2 Shakespeare..became in soul one with the mighty prince as with the lowly peasant.

b. Intellectual or spiritual power; high development of the mental faculties. Also in somewhat weakened use, deep feeling, sensitivity.

1604 SHAKS. *Oth.* I. i. 54 These Fellowes haue some soule. **1702** POPE *Wife of Bath* 299 The mouse that always trusts to one poor hole, Can never be a mouse of any soul. **1748** RICHARDSON *Clarissa* VI. 169, I never saw so much soul in a lady's eyes, as in hers. **1823** BYRON *Don Juan* XIV. lxxi. 150 But there was something wanting on the whole—I don't know what, and therefore cannot tell—Which pretty women —the sweet souls!—call *Soul.* **1828** LYTTON *Pelham* xvi, The women love soul, Monsieur—something intellectual and spiritual always attracts them. **1853** —— *My Novel* III. IX. iii. 22 Oh, no! no picture of miserable, vicious, Parisian life. This is beautiful; there is *soul* here. **1873** M. ARNOLD *Lit. & Dogma* (1876) 49 What man of soul..but would prefer to say [etc.]. **1888** PATER *Appreciations, Style* (1889) 22 As a quality of style,..soul is a fact. **1904** F. H. JACKSON *Mural Painting* 21 Benozzo Gozzoli..filled his long life with the production of the most charming wall-paintings, which, if he had had what is often called 'soul', would have placed him very near the summit of the Palace of Art.

4. a. The emotional or spiritual quality of Black American life and culture, manifested esp. in music (see quot. 1973).

1946 *Ebony* Sept. 34/2 He uses a bewildering, unorthodox technique and his playing is full of what jazzmen refer to as 'soul'. **1954** *Grove's Dict. Mus.* (ed. 5) IV. 600/2 Louis Armstrong declared that 'Anything played with beat and soul is jazz.' **1964** *Amer. Folk Music Occasional* I. 17 It's just really rough what the colored entertainers have to go through sometimes... That's why the colored people sing the blues; that's why they sing with soul. **1973** S. HENDERSON *Understanding New Black Poetry* 74 In the late 1950's the word 'Soul' surfaced in the musical community and quickly spread to the wider Black Community, where it came to mean not only a special kind of popular music..but also..'racial spirit' and 'racial flavor'... The word is losing some of its popularity now.

b. *ellipt.* for *soul music* (*b*), see sense 26 below.

1961 [see FUNK *sb.*[2] 2]. **1968** P. OLIVER *Screening Blues* ii. 46 The distinction between gospel music and the most recent development of blues and rock 'n roll—soul—is one of content rather than style. **1975** *New Yorker* 28 Apr. 6/3 She's lately been branching out from a strict regimen of blues and folk songs..to include some rock, soul, and Nashville-inspired ditties. **1979** *Radio Times* 19 July 60/1 The word 'soul' probably originated with Ray Charles... Soul is the music of experience... It's one person's heart speaking to another person's.

c. *attrib.* passing into *adj.* (*a*) Characteristic of or pertaining to Black people or culture; (*b*) of or pertaining to soul music (sense (*b*)).

1962 *John o' London's* 1 Feb. 113/3 Feldman is not really a soul-merchant. **1968** *N.Y. Times* 17 June 46 Sonny Charles, the organist, took over, singing with a soul appeal that caught up even this predominantly white audience. **1969** C. HIMES *Blind Man with Pistol* xxi. 231 The big white man thought they were talking about him in a secret language known only to soul people. **1971** B. MALAMUD *Tenants* 63, I swear to myself I will be the best writer, the best Soul Writer. *Ibid.* 121 From across the street..Bill spied him and whooped, 'Lesser, man, for Christ's sake, cross on over here. I got some soul people with me.' **1972** *Sat. Rev.* (U.S.) 27 May. 18/1 You'll be surprised how many soul folk speak Dutch and work and play in surprising Amsterdam. **1975** D. PITTS *Target Manhattan* (1976) xxvi. 105 They had..listened to a group of black soul singers. **1976** *Drum* (E. Afr. ed.) June 10/2 Soul language is a language of protest, a language of self-assertion, a language that rejects the white man's values. **1981** *Westindian World* 28 Aug. 5/6 The Crusaders are among the finest exponents of the art of making a good listenable soul record.

5. In various phrases (see quots.); also, ***to have no soul***: to be lacking in sensibility or right feeling; ***to have a soul above*** (something): to be superior to or have higher aspirations than (something); ***to make one's soul***: see MAKE *v.*[1] 47.

a. *c* **1400** *Beryn* 2682 A douȝter, þat he lovid right as his owne saal. **1600** SHAKS. *A.Y.L.* I. ii. 247 My Father lou'd Sir Roland as his soule.

b. **1535** STEWART *Cron. Scot.* II. 109 [They] Skantlie durst say thair saull wes thair awin. *c* **1712** W. KING *Old Cheese* 8 Wks. 1776 III. 144 Slouch could hardly call his Soul his own. **1768–74** TUCKER *Lt. Nat.* (1834) II. 124 He dares not say his soul is his own. **1889** CORBETT *Monk* xi. 155 From that moment he could not call his soul his own.

c. **1594** NASHE *Unfort. Trav.* Wks. (Grosart) V. 168 They basted him with a mixture of Aqua fortis [etc.],..which smarted to the very soule of him. **1602** SHAKS. *Ham.* III. ii. 10 O it offends mee to the Soule, to see [etc.]. **1604** —— *Oth.* I. iii. 196, I am glad at soule, I haue no other Child. **1663** DRYDEN *Rival Ladies* IV. iii, She's an infamous, lewd prostitute: I loathe her at my soul.

d. **1599** SHAKS. *Hen. V*, III. vi. 8 A man that I loue and honour with my soule and my heart. **1687** MIÉGE *Gt. Fr. Dict.* II. s.v., With all my Soul, *de toute mon Ame.* *a* **1700** EVELYN *Diary* 6 Feb. 1685, I cannot..but deplore his losse, which..I do with all my soul. **1736** *Gentl. Mag.* VI. 459/1 Here 'tis with all my Soul. **1828** LYTTON *Pelham* II. xxi, 'I pledge you, with all my soul,' said I, filling my glass to the brim.

e. **1588** SHAKS. *Titus A.* V. iii. 190, I do repent it from my very Soule. **1613** —— *Hen. VIII*, II. iv. 81, I..from my Soule Refuse you for my Iudge. *a* **1700** EVELYN *Diary* 18 Aug. 1688, I wish from my soul..her husband..was as worthy of her. **1768** STERNE *Sent. Journ., Temptation*, I could not from my soul but fasten the buckle in return.

f. **1704** SWIFT *T. Tub* II. 64 That Fellow, cries one, has no Soul; where is his Shoulder-knot? **1850** 'L. LIMNER' *Christmas Comes* 9 He seeks refuge in his organ, much to the annoyance of a little tailor in the attic who has no soul in him. **1919** G. B. SHAW *Inca of Perusalem* in *Heartbreak House* 209 You have no soul for fine art.

g. **1795** G. COLMAN *New Hay at Old Market* 10 My father was an eminent Button-maker..but I had a soul above buttons... I panted for a liberal profession. **1834** F. MARRYAT *Peter Simple* I. i. 2 My father, who was a clergyman..had..a 'soul above buttons'. **1889** E. DOWSON *Let.* 27 Oct. (1967) 112, I have still a soul above tractlets. **1899** G. B. BURGIN *Bread of Tears* I. iii. 51 Miss Mercy Tressock evidently wrote a very bad hand, and she hadn't a soul above blots: they were dotted copiously about on every page. **1909** 'O. HENRY' *Rus in Urbe* in *Hampton's Mag.* Aug. 160/1 She had a soul above ducks—above nightingales.

6. *Metaph.* **a.** The vital, sensitive, or rational principle in plants, animals, or human beings. Freq. with distinguishing adjs., as *vegetative*, *sensible* or *sensitive*, *rational* or *reasonable*. (Cf. these words.)

(*a*) **1398** TREVISA *Barth. De P.R.* III. vii. (1495) 53 In dyuers bodyes ben thre manere soules: vegetabilis, that yeuyth lyfe and noo felinge, as in plantes and rootes; Sensibilis, that yeuyth lyfe and felynge and not reason in vnskylfull beestes; Racionalis, that yeuyth lyf, felyng and reeson in men. *c* **1400** tr. *Secreta Secret., Gov. Lordsh.* 91 þe kendly sowel [of things vegetable] gedyrs to-gedyr all þes propertes. **1587** GOLDING *De Mornay* i. 11 Thou beleeuest that the Plants haue a kinde of Soule, that is to say, a certeine inward power or vertue which maketh them to shoote foorth in their season. **1634** SIR T. HERBERT *Trav.* 209 A soft pith, in which consists the soule and vegetatiue vertue of that tree. **1707** *Curios. in Husb. & Gard.* 27 A Plant..contains within itself a Principle of Life, which we may call Soul; from whence proceed the Operations of each Plant. **1725** WATTS *Logic* I. vi. §3 Our elder Philosophers have generally made use of the Word *Soul* to signify that Principle whereby a Plant grows, and they called it the vegetative Soul.

(*b*) **1398** [see prec.]. *a* **1400–** [see SENSITIVE *a.* 1]. **1587** GOLDING *De Mornay* i. 11 Thou beleeuest that..the Beastes also haue one other kinde of Soule, which maketh them to mooue. **1620** T. GRANGER *Div. Logike* 43 The Brutall soule or spirit is not a power or facultie of the reasonable soule. *a* **1676** HALE *Prim. Orig. Man.* (1677) 33 The sensible Soul of a vast Whale exerciseth its regiment to every part of that huge structure with the same efficacy and facility as the Soul of a Fly or a Mite doth. **1725** WATTS *Logic* I. vi. §3 The Principle of the animal Motion of a Brute has been likewise call'd a Soul, and we have been taught to name it the sensitive Soul. **1775** HARRIS *Philos. Arrangem.* Wks. (1841) 373 The soul perceives those goods which it is conscious that the animal wants. **1875** BOULTBEE *Theol. Ch. Eng.* 36 The animal soul was present; for he ate before the disciples. **1880**

LD. REAY *Social Democ. Germany* 8 The soul with which it [*sc.* a plastidule] is endowed, is called protoplastic soul.

(*c*) *a* **1325** *Prose Psalter* 195 As resonable soule & flesshe is o man. **1390-** [see REASONABLE *a.* 1 b]. **1398** [see (*a*)]. **1587** GOLDING *De Mornay* xv. 238 Auerrhoes, and.. Alexander of Aphrodise,.. vpholde that there is but one vniuersall reasonable Soule or minde, which worketh all our discourses in vs. **1597** MORLEY *Introd. Musicke* Ded., Our maisters,.. by whose directions the faculties of the reasonable soule be stirred vp to enter into contemplation. **1610** HEALEY *St. Aug. Citie of God* v. xi. (1620) 202 Hee that gaue the vnreasonable soule sense, memorie, and appetite; the reasonable besides these, phantasie, vnderstanding and will. **1615** [see RATIONAL *a.* 1]. **1725** WATTS *Logic* I. vi. §3 They distinguish this by the honourable Title of the rational Soul. **1875** BOULTBEE *Theol. Ch. Eng.* 36 The rational soul was there; he reasoned with them out of the Scriptures.

b. Hence ***three souls***, in allusion to the above as combined in human beings.

1601 B. JONSON *Poetaster* v. iii. 160 What? will I turne sharke, vpon my friends?.. I scorne it with my three soules. **1601** SHAKS. *Twel. N.* II. iii. 61 Shall wee rowze the night-Owle in a Catch, that will drawe three soules out of one Weauer? [*c* **1645** HOWELL *Lett.* I. iii. 30 The Embryo is animated with three Souls;.. and these three in Man are like *Trigonus* in *Tetragono*.]

7. ***fig.*** Applied to persons: **a.** As a term of endearment or adoration.

1581 PETTIE tr. *Guazzo's Civ. Conv.* I. (1586) 33 b, Politike louers, who.. tearme her.. sometime the heart of their life, sometime their soule. **1590** SHAKS. *Mids. N.* III. ii. 246 My loue, my life, my soule, faire Helena. **1611** —— *Cymb.* v. v. 263 Hang there like fruite, my soule, Till the Tree dye. **1654** GAYTON *Pleas. Notes* III. xiii. 165 O persevere (soule of my soule) And act according to thy word. **1832** TENNYSON *Œnone* 69 My own Œnone,.. my own soul, Behold this fruit. **1864** BROWNING *Dram. Pers., Prospice*, O thou soul of my soul! I shall clasp thee again.

b. The personification *of* some quality.

1605 *1st Pt. Jeronimo* III. ii. 40 Prince Balthezer,.. The very soule of true nobility. **1607** SHAKS. *Timon* I. ii. 215 O he's the very soule of Bounty. **1766** GOLDSM. *Vicar* xxxi, My brother indeed was the soul of honour. *a* **1902** S. BUTLER *Way of All Flesh* (1903) xiii. 56 He had stuck to his post... He had said to himself: 'I.. am the very soul of honour.' **1976** R. LEHMANN *Sea-Grape Tree* 30 He's the soul of courtesy but he can be a wee bit difficult.

c. The inspirer or leader *of* some business, cause, movement, etc.; the chief agent, prime mover, or leading spirit.

1662 J. DAVIES tr. *Olearius' Voy. Amb.* 366 The Chancellor, who was the President of the King's Council, the Soul of Affairs. **1688** HOLME *Armoury* III. 113/2 The Master Printer.. is the Soul of Printing. **1724** DE FOE *Mem. Cavalier* (1840) 122 The soul of the war was dead. **1769** ROBERTSON *Chas. V*, IX. III. 131 Francis.., whom he considered as the soul and mover of any confederacy. **1808** SCOTT *Marm.* VI. xxxviii, Unnam'd by Hollinshed or Hall, He was the living soul of all. **1855** MACAULAY *Hist. Eng.* xi. III. 15 He was the author and the soul of the European coalition. **1882** SERGT. BALLANTINE *Exper.* xvii. 171 As long as he remained.. he was the soul of the table.

8. ***fig.*** Of things: **a.** The essential, fundamental, or animating part, element, or feature *of* something. Also rarely without article.

(*a*) **1596** SHAKS. *1 Hen. IV*, IV. i. 50 Therein should we reade The very Bottome, and the Soule of Hope. **1602** —— *Ham.* II. ii. 90 Breuitie is the Soule of Wit. **1632** MILTON *L'Allegro* 144 The hidden soul of harmony. *c* **1670** HOBBES *Dial. Com. Laws* (1681) 2 Reason is the Soul of the Law. **1712** ADDISON *Spect.* No. 409 ¶ 10, I could wish there were Authors.. who.. would enter into the very Spirit and Soul of fine Writing. **1775** SCHUYLER in Sparks *Corr. Amer. Rev.* (1853) I. 14 That proper spirit of discipline and subordination, which is the very soul of an army. **1807** J. BARLOW *Columb.* III. 564 Thro' the ranks he breathes the soul of war. **1818** HAZLITT *Eng. Poets* ii. (1870) 38 Nature is the soul of art. **1892** WESTCOTT *Gospel of Life* 100 The religious history of the world is the very soul of history.

(*b*) **1610** FLETCHER *Faithf. Sheph.* IV. iv, I have been woo'd by many with no less Soul of affection. **1634** FORD *Perk. Warbeck* III. i, Money gives soule to action.

b. An element, principle, or trace *of* something.

1599 SHAKS. *Hen. V*, IV. i. 4 There is some soule of goodnesse in things euill. **1862** SPENCER *First Princ.* I. i. §1 (1875) 3 [There is] a soul of truth in things erroneous.

c. ***the soul of the world*** [after L. *anima mundi*, Gr. ψυχὴ τοῦ κόσμου], the animating principle of the world, according to early philosophers.

c **1600** SHAKS. *Sonn.* cvii, The prophetick soule Of the wide world, dreaming on things to come. **1678** CUDWORTH *Intell. Syst.* I. iv. 215 In like manner he resolved that the Soul of the World.. was not made by God out of Nothing neither. **1785** REID *Intell. Powers* I. i. 23 A tract of Timæus the Locrian.. concerning the soul of the world, in which we find the substance of Plato's doctrine concerning ideas.

d. The essential part or quality *of* some material thing.

1658 tr. *Porta's Nat. Magic* VII. ii. 192 A Loadstone wrapt up in burning coles.. lost its quality of its soul that was gone, namely, its attractive vertue. **1662** J. DAVIES tr. *Mandelslo's Trav.* 32 This excellent scent.. may be called the soul of all Perfume. **1704** POPE *Windsor For.* 244 He.. With chymic art exalts the min'ral pow'rs, And draws the aromatic souls of flow'rs. **1821** SCOTT *Kenilw.* i, Your Spaniard is too wise a man to send you the very soul of the grape. **1855** TENNYSON *Maud* I. XXII. vi, The soul of the rose went into my blood. **1890** W. J. GORDON *Foundry* 71 But 'the soul of a ship is her engines'.

II. 9. The spiritual part of man considered in its moral aspect or in relation to God and His precepts.

Freq. with implicit reference to the fate of the soul after death, and so partly belonging to sense 10. ***cure of souls***, see CURE *sb.*[1] 4.

α. *c* **825** *Vesp. Psalter* xviii. 8 Æew dryhtnes [is] untelwirðe, ȝecerrende sawle. *c* **830** in Sweet *O.E. Texts* 446 Suilc man sue hit aweȝe, ðonne se hit on his sawale. *c* **1175** *Lamb. Hom.* 71 Þet lif and saule beon iborȝen. *c* **1200** ORMIN 2921 Swa þatt itt Drihhtin cweme be, & halsumm till hiss sawle. *c* **1230** *Hali Meid.* 15 Ne harmeð hit te nawiht, ne suleð þi sawle. *a* **1300** *Cursor M.* 1568 Al þair luf þai gaue to lust, þai did þair sauls all to rust. **1393** LANGL. *P. Pl.* C. VI. 199 Secheþ seint treuthe in sauacion of ȝoure saules. **1456** SIR G. HAYE *Law Arms* (S.T.S.) 16 The wrang errouris, the quhilkis tynis mony a saule. *c* **1485** *Digby Myst.* (1882) IV. 296 Thou knew ther were no remedy to redeym syn, But a bath of þi blude to bath mans saule in. *a* **1509** HEN. VII in Ellis *Orig. Lett.* Ser. I. I. 44 In all other thyngs that I may knowe should be to youre honour & plesure & weale of youre salle. *c* **1560** A. SCOTT *Poems* xxxvi. 9 Wesche me, and mak my sawle serene From all iniquite. *c* **1615** SIR W. MURE *Misc. Poems* xii. 4 Awalk, my sillie saul, in sin quhich too securely lyes. **1786** BURNS *Twa Dogs* 148 Thrang a parliamentin, For Britain's guid his saul indentin.

β. *c* **1220** *Bestiary* 118 Leren he sal his nede;.. and.. tilen him so ðe sowles fode. *c* **1250** *Gen. & Ex.* 4156 Bi-seke we nu godes miȝt, ðat he make ure sowles briȝt. *c* **1300** *Havelok* 1422 But Grim was wis,.. Wolde he nouth his soule shende. **1390** GOWER *Conf.* I. 19 Thei prechen ous in audience That noman schal his soule empeire. **1450-80** tr. *Secreta Secret.* 9 Vndirstondyng is cheef of the governaunce of man and helthe of thi sowle. **1473-5** in *Cal. Proc. Chanc. Q. Eliz.* II. (1830) Pref. 59 That he stode in grete perell of his sowle lyke to be dampned. **1508** FISHER *7 Penit. Ps.* Wks. (1876) I. 7 Makynge this holy psalme wherby he.. was restored to his soules helth. **1582** CDL. ALLEN *Martyrdom Campion* (1908) 35 His going.. was only for his soule's health, to learn to save his soule. **1603** SHAKS. *Meas. for M.* II. iv. 65 Ile take it as a perill to my soule, It is no sinne at all. **1665** PEPYS *Diary* 26 July, I begin to think of setting things in order, which I pray God enable me to put both as to soul and body. **1758** S. HAYWARD *Serm.* Introd. p. xv, Success.. crowning our imperfect labours in the conversion of souls. **1760-79** [see SIN-SICK *a.*]. **1818** SCOTT *Br. Lamm.* xi, To hazard my soul in telling lees. **1871** MEREDITH *H. Richmond* xii, Labour you will in my vessel, for your soul's health.

10. a. The spiritual part of man regarded as surviving after death and as susceptible of happiness or misery in a future state.

c **825** *Charter* in Sweet *O.E. Texts* 444 Ðæt mon ȝedele to aelmessan aet ðere tide fore mine sawle & Osuulfes. **863** *Ibid.* 440 Ic.. iow fer godes lufe bidde þet ȝe hit minre sawle nyt ȝedeo. *a* **1067** in Kemble *Cod. Diplom.* IV. 206 Ich hit.. Gode ȝeuðe mine saule to helpene. *a* **1122** *O.E. Chron.* (Laud MS.) an. 675, Ic wile on min dæi hit æcon for here sawle & for minre sawle. *a* **1250** *Owl & Night.* 1092 Ihesus his soule do mercy. **1297** R. GLOUC. (Rolls) 7591 An abbeye he let rere.. uor hor soulen þat þere aslawe were. *a* **1352** MINOT *Poems* (ed. Hall) v. 88 God assoyle þaire sawls; sais all, Amen. **1375** BARBOUR *Bruce* xx. 346 To pass.. On goddis fais, that his travale Micht eftir till his saull avale. **1418** *E.E. Wills* (1882) 33 Masses to be songe for my saule & for the saules aforsaide. **1488** *Acc. Ld. High Treas. Scot.* I. 90 To pay.. a prest to sing for the Qwenis sawle. **1536** WRIOTHESLEY *Chron.* (Camden) I. 42 Beseechinge him to have mercye on my sowle. **1606** DEKKER *Newes fr. Hell* Wks. (Grosart) II. 142 The soule sees deathes Barge tarrying for her, she begins to be sorrie for her ante-acted euils.

b. In phrases implying the death of a person.

See also BETAKE *v.* 2, and cf. COMMEND *v.* 1 b.

a **1122** *O.E. Chron.* (Laud MS.) an. 1012 And his þa haliȝan sawle to Godes rice asende. *c* **1275** *Passion our Lord* 482 in *O.E. Misc.* 51 Vader ich myne soule biteche in þyne honde. *a* **1300** *Cursor M.* 210 How our leuedi endid and yald Hir sely saul. *c* **1375** *Sc. Leg. Saints* x. (*Matthew*) 312 Eglippus in til gud elde, to god of hewyne, þe sawle can ȝeld. *a* **1400** *Isumbras* 733 My saule I wyte into thy hande, For I kepe to lyffe no mare! *c* **1470** HENRY *Wallace* II. 175 All weildand God, resawe My petows spreit and sawle. **1516** *Test. Ebor.* (Surtees) VI. 1, I bequeath my soull to the holie Trinitie. **1596** DALRYMPLE tr. *Leslie's Hist. Scot.* II. 130 King Henrie.. his saul commendis to God, and his body to the clay. **1819** [see RESIGN *v.*[1] 1 d].

11. Used in various asseverative phrases or as an exclamation, as ***by, for, on*** or ***upon*** (one's) ***soul***, etc.

The *Eng. Dial. Dict.* gives a number of similar examples.

a. 1362 LANGL. *P. Pl.* A. VIII. 23 For þei sworen bi heore soule—'so God hem moste helpe!' *c* **1386** CHAUCER *Prol.* 781 Now, by my fadres soule, that is deed. **1579** SPENSER *Sheph. Cal.* Sept. 248 Now by my soule Diggon, I lament The haplesse mischief, that has thee hent. **1586** FERNE *Blaz. Gentrie* 22 By my Vather's Zoule they semen most of churles not of gentle blood. *a* **1704** T. BROWN *Dial. Dead* Wks. 1711 IV. 47 Be mee Shoul, and bee Chreest and St. Patrick. **1762** FOOTE *Orator* II. Wks. 1799 I. 216 By my shoul but I will spake. **1800** COLERIDGE *Christabel* II. xxviii, By my mother's soul do I entreat That thou this woman send away! **1825** SCOTT *Talism.* xvii, Now, by King Henry's soul! [etc.].

b. *c* **1386** CHAUCER *Reeve's T.* 343 Thou, Iohn, thou swynesheed, awak For cristes saule. **1728** RAMSAY *Monk & Miller's Wife* 243 Whate'er you see be nought surpriz'd, But for your saul move not your tongue. **1807** SYD. SMITH *Lett. Catholics* Wks. 1859 II. 153/1, I cannot for the soul of me conceive whence this man has gained his notions of Christianity. **1826** DISRAELI *V. Grey* VI. i, For the soul of ye you wouldn't know it from the greenest Tokay. **1894** 'J. S. WINTER' *Red Coats* 63 But for the life and soul of him he could not help thinking about her.

c. *c* **1450** LOVELICH *Graal* liii. 116 Sire,.. vppon Oure sowles þe sothe we scholen ȝow seyne. **1482** *Cely Papers* (Camden) 106 Thay sayd howr mother schulld go on preschesyon on Corpys Kyrste day.. and a my sowyll howr mother whent at that day. *a* **1510** DOUGLAS *K. Hart* II. 100 Now, on my saule, ȝe ar bot lurdanis all! **1604** SHAKS. *Oth.* v. ii. 181 Vpon my Soule, a Lye; a wicked Lye. **1693** CONGREVE *Old Bach.* II. iii, What ever the Matter is, O my Sol, I'm afraid you'l follow evil Courses. **1749** FIELDING *Tom Jones* XIV. vii, Should any fatal Accident follow, as upon my Soul I am afraid will. **1824** SCOTT *St. Ronan's* xxxvi, 'On my soul,' said Mowbray, 'you must mean Solmes!' **1842** LOVER *Handy Andy* ix, But, 'pon my sowl, the next time I go buy hay, I'll take care that Saint Pether hasn't any hand in it. **1878** H. SMART *Play or Pay* viii, 'Upon my soul,' rejoined the Hussar, 'I think' [etc.].

d. 1613 SHAKS. *Hen. VIII*, IV. i. 44 Sir, as I haue a Soule, she is an Angell. **1760-1** SMOLLETT *Launcelot Greaves* I. v, As I'm a precious saoul, a looks as if a saw something.

e. 1796 GALL *Elegy on Pudding Lizzie* viii, Saul! how it sharpen'd ilka ane. **1818** SCOTT *Br. Lamm.* iii, Saul, your honour, and that I am. **1845** DISRAELI *Sybil* (1863) 72 Soul alive, but those.. are rotten, snickey, bad yarns. **1896** 'IAN MACLAREN' *Kate Carnegie* 282 But sall, she focht her battle weel.

III. 12. The disembodied spirit of a (deceased) person, regarded as a separate entity, and as invested with some amount of form and personality:

a. With poss. pron. or gen., or implying this.

971 *Blickl. Hom.* 211 Uton nu biddan Sanctus Michael ..þæt he ure saula ȝelæde on ȝefean. *c* **1050** *O.E. Chron.* (MS. C) an. 1036, Syððan hine man byriȝde,.. on þam suð portice, seo saul is mid Criste. *c* **1205** LAY. 29634 Heofne is þe al ȝaru, þider scal þi saulen uaren. *c* **1250** *Gen. & Ex.* 4136 His bodi was biried wið angeles hond,.. In to lef reste his sowle wond. *c* **1300** *Havelok* 245 Þat God self shulde his soule leden Into heuene. *c* **1385** CHAUCER *L.G.W.* 2493 *Phyllis*, The deuyl sette here soules bothe a fere. *c* **1420** in *26 Pol. Poems* 108 Contrary to godis hest þou purchasest þy saule helle prisoun. **1474** CAXTON *Chesse* II. iv. (1883) 52 They lyue in her sowles gloriously that ben slain.. for the comyn wele. **1560** DAUS tr. *Sleidane's Comm.* 115 b, It was beleved certenly that dead mens soules dyd walke after they were buried. **1599** ALEX. HUME *Hymns* i. 131 Then sall my singing saull reioyce, And flee aboue the skie. **1615** G. SANDYS *Trav.* 266 Saint German.. here found the soule of Pascasus tormented with heate. **1833** TENNYSON *May Queen* III. xi, I know The blessed music went that way my soul will have to go. **1875** JOWETT *Plato* (ed. 2) I. 343 Another world in which the souls of the dead are gathered together.

b. With *a, the*, and in pl.

971 *Blickl. Hom.* 67 Mycelne bite Drihten dyde on helle þa he þyder astaȝ,.. & þa halȝan sauwla þonon alædde. *Ibid.* 209 On ðæm clife hangodan.. maniȝe sweartе saula be heora handum ȝebundne. *c* **1200** *Trin. Coll. Hom.* 115 Þo folȝede ure helende michel feord of englen and of holie soules. *c* **1275** *Passion our Lord* 262 in *O.E. Misc.* 56 Þe veond of helle hedde muchel onde Vor hi by-nomen him saulen. *c* **1330** R. BRUNNE *Chron. Wace* (Rolls) 9184 Payens & Cristen, many were slawen, & many a sowle fro body drawen. *c* **1386** CHAUCER *Prol.* 510 A chaunterie for soules. *c* **1430** *Compend. Old Treat.* in Roy *Rede me* (Arb.) 180 They be cowntable of as many sowlys as dyen in thys default. **1470-85** MALORY *Arthur* XVI. xiii. 681 Thenne oure lord Ihesus Cryste shewed hym vnto yow in the lykenes of a sowle that suffred grete anguysshe. **1513** DOUGLAS *Æneid* VI. xi. 3 Sawlis.. quhilkis wer for to wend To mydle erd, and thair in bodeis ascend. **1596** R. H. tr. *Lavaterus's Ghostes & Spir.* 61 With whome the same soule meeting as it did before, lamented very much. **1616** J. LANE *Contn. Sqr.'s T.* IV. 46 *note*, And in her glasse, white soles ascendinge, spied the narrowe waie to theire Lord glorified. **1683** NORRIS *Plato's Two Cupids* iv. Misc. (1687) 88 So Devils and damned Souls in hell Fry in the fire with which they dwell. **1750** GRAY *Elegy* 89 On some fond breast the parting soul relies. **1812** BRYON *Ch. Har.* II. viii, If.. there be A land of souls beyond that sable shore. **1899** *Daily News* 17 Apr. 4/3 The idea was that the soul was a little bloodless, fleshless thing.

c. ***local.*** (See quots., and cf. ***ghost-moth***.)

1851 *N. & Q.* 1st Ser. III. 220 The country-people used to in my youth.. call night-flying white moths, especially the *Hepialus humuli*,.. 'souls'. **1861** *All Year Round* 1 June 234 To this day, in the north and west of England, the moths that fly into candles are called Saules.

13. a. A person, an individual; †a living thing. Chiefly in enumeration, or with *every*.

[*c* **1000** ÆLFRIC *Gen.* ii. 7 And se man wæs ȝeworht on libbendre sawle.]

c **1320** *Cast. Love* 448 Nis þer nout in world.. þat nis destrued.. But eiȝte soulen þ[t] weren i-ȝemed In þe schup. *c* **1381** CHAUCER *Parl. Foules* 33 Erthe and soulis that thereon dwelle. **1535** COVERDALE *Lev.* xi. 46 All maner of soules y[t] crepe vpon earth. *c* **1550** [? G. WALKER] *Detect. Dice-Play* D iv, He wilbe your cuntry man at least, & peraduenture either of kinne or aly, or some soule sib vnto you. **1632** LITHGOW *Trav.* II. 52 Below the middle part, there was but one body, and aboue the middle there was two liuing soules, each one separated from another. **1672** PETTY *Pol. Anat.* (1691) 18 The number of British slain in 11 years was 112 thousand Souls. **1724** *Briton* No. 24. 104 We have now pretty accurately ascertain'd the Number of Souls.. existing in England. **1776** EARL CARLISLE in Jesse *Selwyn & Contemp.* (1844) III. 158 Not the worse for having levanted every soul at Newmarket. **1819** BYRON *Juan* II. lxi, Nine souls more went in her: the long-boat still Kept above water. **1861** M. PATTISON *Ess.* (1889) I. 38 The frail craft capsized, and Hartmann, with nearly every soul on board, went down in her. **1894** WOLSELEY *Marlb.* I. 245 There were about three hundred souls on board.

b. In negative phrases, esp. ***not a soul***.

1610 SHAKS. *Temp.* I. ii. 209 Not a soule But felt a Feauer. **1759** STERNE *Tr. Shandy* II. v, When you are predetermined to take no one soul's advice. **1775** MME. D'ARBLAY *Early Diary, Let.* 10 June, We had not a soul beyond our own family. **1811** SHELLEY in Hogg *Life* (1858) I. 391, I am what the sailors call 'banyaning'. I do not see a soul. **1857** W. COLLINS *Dead Secret* III. i, He allowed no living soul.. to enter the house. **1897** A. MORRISON *Dorrington Deed-box* i, I shall be all alone, without a soul to say a word to.

c. ***dial.*** Used in the pl. as a form of address: Friends, fellows.

1874 T. HARDY *Far fr. Mad. Crowd* lvii, Come in, souls, and have something to eat and drink. **1892** 'Q.' (QUILLER COUCH) *Three Ships* ii, Well, souls, we was a bit tiddly-winky last Michaelmas.

d. In Tsarist Russia, a serf. Also *transf.*

1806 M. WILMOT *Jrnl.* 17 Aug. in *Russ. Jrnls.* (1934) III. 271 One.. often hears two Ladies.. talking to each other about the sale of Lands, purchase of *Souls* (slaves). **1895** C.

GARNETT tr. *Turgenev's Fathers & Children* i. 2 Nikolai Petrovitch Kirsanov..had..a fine property of two hundred souls, or, as he expressed it—since he had arranged the division of his land with the peasants..of nearly five thousand acres. **1943** E. M. ALMEDINGEN *Frossia* iv. 169 The good Boyarin made it known that her dowry would be ..five hundred souls, all under the age of fifty. **1969** V. G. KIERNAN *Lords of Human Kind* vi. 225 Africans were being disposed of as Europeans were by their princes not long before, when the Congress of Vienna..distributed them in lots of so many thousand 'souls'. **1977** V. S. PRITCHETT *Gentle Barbarian* i. 5 Spasskoye was..a self-sufficient feudal community..an empire numbering 5,000 'souls'.

14. a. Used with defining adj. to denote a person of a particular character or in respect of some quality; freq. with a touch of contempt, compassion, or familiarity.

Common in the 16th and 17th centuries.

1519 *North Co. Wills* (Surtees) 105 Euery yere..to give xd. to x poore soulles. *a* **1548** HALL *Chron., Hen. V*, 60 b, Innumerable sely solles dayly died and hourely starued. **1602** MARSTON *Antonio's Rev.* v. v, Call Julio hither. Where's the little sowle? I sawe him not to-day. **1665** *Extr. Sel. P. rel. Friends* (1912) III. 247 The honest Soules..ar much aflicted to be reuiled..by the bold faction. **1806** J. BERESFORD *Miseries Hum. Life* VII. xix, Paying a long visit at the retired house of a well meaning Soul. **1833** HT. MARTINEAU *Loom & Lugger* I. v, It was very well the poor soul had not had a long illness. **1874** BURNAND *My Time* i. 3 Nurse Davis, the kindest soul in the world, and very fond of my mother.

b. Used parenthetically, or with *like*.

1572 *Satir. Poems Reform.* xxxi. 112 Sillie saulis, thay ar sa daft. **1594** KYD *Cornelia* v. 63 He made his Pyoners (poore weary soules)..to dig..new Trenches. **1663** S. PATRICK *Parab. Pilgr.* xx. (1687) 200 Poor Soul! who puts us upon doing..but knows not what it is to believe. **1782** COWPER *Gilpin* 65 Now mistress Gilpin (careful soul!) Had two stone bottles found. **1811** C. K. SHARPE *Let.* Corr. 1888 I. 493 For his errors, poor soul! were venial. **1850** KINGSLEY *A. Locke* (1876) I. 7 She would have stuffed my ears with cotton, kind careful soul. **1870** DICKENS *E. Drood* i, Ye'll remember like a good soul.

c. With more distinct implication of sense 2 or 3.

1635 QUARLES *Embl.* II. v, What mean dull souls, in this high measure, To haberdash In earth's base wares. **1685** *Gracian's Courtier's Orac.* 154 The least atome of baseness is inconsistent with the generosity of great Souls. **1721** RAMSAY *Prospect of Plenty* 129 Active sauls a stagnant life despise. **1741–2** GRAY *Agrip.* 126 Rough, stubborn souls, That struggle with the yoke. **1841–4** EMERSON *Ess., History* Wks. (Bohn) I. 7 It has been said, that 'common souls pay with what they do—nobler souls with that which they are'. **1871** MORLEY *Carlyle* in *Crit. Misc.* Ser. I. 215 It was not science for headlong and impatient souls.

15. In pregnant use: †**a.** (See quot.) *Obs.*$^{-0}$

a **1700** B. E. *Dict. Cant. Crew, He is a Soul*, or loves Brandy.

b. One in whom the spiritual or intellectual qualities predominate (*rare*). ***The Souls***, a late nineteenth-century aristocratic coterie with predominantly cultural and intellectual interests.

1814 BYRON *Diary* 19 Feb., Just returned from seeing Kean in Richard. By Jove, he is a soul! **1890** B. POTTER *Jrnl.* 31 Dec. (1982) I. 349 Balfour..would crush them in the intervals between a flirtation with one of the 'Souls' and the reading of a French novel. **1895** *Daily News* 9 Dec. 7/1 Brought up by such a mother, the Lady Marcella naturally became something of a Soul. **1934** H. G. WELLS *Exper. Autobiogr.* II. ix. 766 The 'Souls', the Balfour set. **1980** D. NEWSOME *On Edge of Paradise* ii. 47 The young and wealthy aspirants to public eminence and the eligible daughters of leading families... The group to be christened by Lord Charles Beresford in 1888 'the Souls'.

IV. In various special or technical uses.

16. (See later quots.) Now *dial.*

1530 PALSGR. 273/1 Soule of a capon or gose, *ame.* **1591** PERCIVALL *Sp. Dict., Molleja*, the tender parte in any birde, which in a goose we call the soule, *Præcordia.* **1774** GOLDSM. *Nat. Hist.* (1862) II. I. i. 5 Their lungs, which are commonly called the sole, stick fast to the sides of the ribs and back. **1876** MRS. G. L. BANKS *Manch. Man* xliv, One of his favourite tid-bits was that spongy lining of a goose's frame known as the *soul*.

†**17.** The bore of a cannon (see quot. 1571).

So F. *l'âme d'un canon.*

1571 DIGGES *Pantom.* (1591) 176 Forasmuch as by the direction of the hollowe Cylinder..of the Peece, the violence of all shot of great Artillerye is not onely directed but also increased, I call that hollowe Cylinder of the Peece her Soule. **1626** CAPT. SMITH *Accid. Yng. Seamen* 32 Particuler..tearmes for great Ordnances, as the concaue, trunke, cylinder, the soule or bore of a peece. **1669** STURMY *Mariner's Mag.* v. xii. 62, I find..the soule or bore to be 1 inch out of his place.

18. The sound-post of a violin.

1838 *Penny Mag.* 30 June 246/2 This peg is called the *sounding-post*, or, as the French term it, the *soul* of the violin. **1854** BREWER *Sound* 145 The object of this prop, called the sound-post or 'soul' of the violin, is..to make the face and back vibrate in exact unison. **1868** AIRY *Sound* 167.

V. *attrib.* and *Comb.*

19. Genitive combs.: †**a.** With forms representing the OE. gen. sing. *sáwle*, as ***soul-boot, leech***, etc. See also SOUL-HEAL, -HEALTH.

Also with gen. pl. *saulene* for OE. *sáwla*.

c **1200** ORMIN 10194 Hefennlike mahhte, þatt mihhte turrnenn swillke menn To sekenn *sawlebote. *a* **1225** *Ancr. R.* 182 þus is sicnesse *soule leche. **1375** in Horstmann *Altengl. Leg.* (1878) 138/2 Praye we..þat god..Be his soule leche. **1411** *26 Pol. Poems* 42, I..Bycom a man to be ȝoure soule leche. *c* **1200** ORMIN 12621 To lokenn whatt itt tæcheþþ uss Off ure *sawle nede. **13..** *Minor Poems fr. Vernon MS.* xxxvii. 733 He..seiþ hit is þe *soule note þat þe prest seiþ and doþ. *c* **1375** *Sc. Leg. Saints* vi. (*Thomas*) 490 Ve suld set our maste delyte In goddis vord fore *sawle profyte. *c* **1470** *Gol. & Gaw.* 269 Be the pilgramage compleit I pas for *saull prow. *c* **1412** HOCCLEVE *De Reg. Princ.* 4440 His lordes *soule salue he from hym hydith. *c* **1200** ORMIN Pref. 102 Icc wile shæwenn ȝuw Hu mikell *sawle sellþe.. unnderrfoþ..all þatt lede. **13..** *Minor Poems fr. Vernon MS.* xxxvii. 781 Al þat þe bodi lykeþ wel Is aȝeyn þe *soule wille.

b. With the form *soul's*, as ***soul's-city, -darling, friend.***

1593 NASHE *Christ's Tears* Wks. (Grosart) IV. 157 He.. cannot chuse but haue his soules-cittie soone raced. **1605** *1st Pt. Jeronimo* I. ii. 65 Adew, soules friend. **1874** LISLE CARR *J. Gwynne* I. vi. 182 An always erring and very faulty soul's-darling.

20. Simple attrib., as ***soul-affair, -blood, †-case, concern)ment, -minster, -power, -work***, etc.

The number of attributive uses is very large, and in this and the following groups only a few of the older or more important are illustrated.

1672 O. HEYWOOD *Diaries* (1883) III. 198 He..was very stupid about *soul-affaires. **1629** DONNE *Serm.* cix. Wks. 1839 IV. 492 Adam is but..red earth, earth dyed red in blood, in *soul-blood. **1848** BAILEY *Festus* (ed. 3) 41 Corruption..is in Your soul-blood and your soul-bones. **1699** O. HEYWOOD *Diaries* (1885) IV. 195 Elizabeth Sonier came to discourse with me in *soul-cases. **1654** WHITLOCK *Zootomia* 393 The Cures (attempted) by a..ranckerous Spirit, are wounds in this *Soule-chirurgery. **1742–3** *Observ. upon Methodists* 23, I hear some are under *Soul concern. **1675** O. HEYWOOD *Diaries* (1883) III. 165, I talk with them about *soul-concernments. **1619** W. Y. *To Rdr.* in *Hieron's Wks.* II. 424 Gods gracious preseruing from *soule-destruction. **1617** HIERON *Ibid.* 191 One fit of *soule-disturbance will make all those kinds of gladnesse to flee away like a dreame. **1645** RUTHERFORD *Tryal & Tri. Faith* (1845) 93 Christ promiseth *Soul-ease. **1646** JENKYN *Remora* 13 Are your heartiest, your *soul-endeavours set upon Reformation? **1726** WODROW *Corr.* (1843) III. 239 Besides much spiritual *soul exercise, it contained many valuable hints at facts. **1816** SCOTT *Old Mort.* xlii, The Cameronians..boasted frequently of Burley's soul-exercises. *a* **1638** MEDE *Wks.* (1672) 631 This order of Dæmons, or *Soul-gods, as I may call them. **1654** GATAKER *Disc. Apol.* 75 Because he would not dissolv the *soul-harmonie of weak persons. **1645** RUTHERFORD *Tryal & Tri. Faith* (1845) 260 That death, that *soul-hell in the want of Christ. *a* **1618** SYLVESTER *Paradox agst. Libertie* 1089 Wks. (Grosart) II. 65 In *soule idlenesse, to spend so large a time. **1677** J. ELLIOT in Birch *Life of Boyle* Wks. 1772 I. p. xxvi, The Lord's work of *soul-instruction and edification. **1662** HIBBERT *Body Divinity* I. 127 *Soul-light is not enough to make us truly wise. **1937** BLUNDEN *Elegy* 16 Foremost of all a matin hymn From these *soul-minsters leaps aloft. *a* **1930** D. H. LAWRENCE *Phoenix* (1936) v. 607 They combine with their *soul-power some great technical skill. *c* **1620** J. DAVIES (Heref.) *Commendatory Poems, Sylvester* Wks. (Grosart) II. 15/1 Here is stor'd such sweet *Soule-ravishments. **1689** *Mem. Rokeby* (Surtees) 12 A sister that.. has rec[eive]d..much *soule-refreshment. **1581** ALLEN *Apologie* 9 b, *Soul rightes (without which men perish doubtlesse euerlastingly). **1657** F. COCKIN *Div. Blossomes* 12 That which unto *Soul-safety much doth tend. **1648** GAGE *West Ind.* iv. 14 That occasion of some *soul-sanctification. **1641** LD. BROOKE *On Episc.* 97 They have come to cutting off Eares, Cheeks, and have yet struck deeper, and essayed many *Soule-Schismes. **1646** TRAPP *Comm. John* xiii. 25 John.., who knew Christ's *soul-secrets. **1883** JEFFERIES *Story of my Heart* 49 The circumambient ether..is full of soul-secrets. **1656** E. REYNER *Rules Govt. Tongue* 269 Some ..have drunk very deep of the cup of *soul-troubles. **1690** C. NESSE *Hist. O. & N. Test.* I. 142 Idolizing the Virgin Mary.., equalling her milk unto Christs blood for *soul vertue. *a* **1618** SYLVESTER *Mem. Mortalitie* lxxxi. Wks. (Grosart) II. 227 Mock-Saints, whose *Soul-weal on your Works you lay. **1668** R. STEELE *Husbandm. Call.* v. (1672) 85 *Soul-work never goes on, unless we have a mind to work. **1927** D. H. LAWRENCE *Let.* 9 Jan. (1932) 679 Painting is more fun and less *soul-work than writing. **1834** K. H. DIGBY *Mores Cath.* v. iv. 109 It was the reflection of God. It was the invisible world, the *soul world. **1600** W. WATSON *Decacordon* (1602) 268 Respecting the danger of *soule-wracke.

21. With the names of persons, etc. (chiefly agent-nouns), as ***soul carrier, -curer, -mate, -thief, -twister***, etc.

1553 BECON *Jewel of Joy* Pref., The mumbling masses of those lasy *soule cariers. **1598** SHAKS. *Merry W.* III. i. 100 *Soule-Curer, and Body-Curer. **1825** COBBETT *Rur. Rides* (1885) II. 88 There is no parsonage house for a soul-curer to stay in. **1785** GROSE *Dict. Vulgar T.*, **Soul doctor*,..a parson. **1880** W. NEWTON in *Serm. Boys & Girls* (1881) 148 The Pharisees called themselves teachers or soul-doctors. *a* **1700** B. E. *Dict. Cant. Crew*, **Soul-driver*, a Parson. **1682** BUNYAN *Gtness. of Soul* Wks. (Offor) I. 142 This is a *soul-fool, a fool of the biggest size. **1656** E. REYNER *Rules Govt. Tongue* 203 Receive Reprovers as the Angels of God, as our *soul-friends. **1382** WYCLIF *Gen.* iii. 14 Thow shalt be cursid among alle the *soule hauers and beestis of the erthe. *c* **1375** *Sc. Leg. Saints* xxvii. (*Machor*) 1457 All þe folk of þat cyte..to sanct morise but mare ar went, & hyme as fadire & *saule-hyrd Resauit sone. **1682** BUNYAN *Gtness. of Soul* Wks. (Offor) I. 140 Every mouth shall be stopped, and all the world (of *soul losers) become guilty before God. **1822** COLERIDGE *Lett., Convers.*, etc. II. 89 You must have a *Soulmate as well as a House or Yoke-mate. **1915** F. M. HUEFFER *Good Soldier* III. v. 202 He thought that Mrs Basil had been his *soulmate. **1976** BOTHAM & DONNELLY *Valentino* ix. 71 Convinced that he had found the woman who would be his life's soulmate. **1812** COLMAN *Br. Grins, Two Parsons* xiv, Great Britain's principal *Soul-mender Liveth at Lambeth Palace. **1650** TRAPP *Comm. Deut.* xxiv. 7 Of which sort of *soul-merchants, there are now-a-dayes found not a few. **1530** TINDALE *Wks.* (Parker Soc.) 437 If he minister it not truly and freely unto us,..he is a thief and a *soul-murderer. **1825** SCOTT *Talism.* xxviii, 'Oh, procrastination!' exclaimed the Hermit, 'thou art a soul-murderer!' **1854** FABER *Growth in Holiness* (1872) xxii. 430 The Church is a living *soul-saver. **1540** COVERDALE *Fruitful Less.* iii. Wks. (Parker Soc.) I. 357 Therefore are many curates and *soul-shepherds so faint and cold to preach..Christ. **1682** BUNYAN *Gtness. of Soul* Wks. (Offor) I. 143 Choose for thyself good soul-shepherds. **1593** NASHE *Christ's Tears* Wks. (Grosart) IV. 120, I deale more searchingly then common *soule-surgions accustome. **1889** W. B. YEATS *Lett. to New Island* (1934) 195 Perhaps they are evil-spirits, these *soul-thiefs, and not fairies at all. **1928** D. H. LAWRENCE *Phoenix II* (1968) 284 Dmitri Karamazov doesn't go half the lengths of the other Russian *soul-twisters. **1956** D. GASCOYNE *Night Thoughts* 33 This soultwister blisters the paint of the set.

22. With vbl. sbs., as ***soul-craving, -feasting, humbling, -making, -mating, -prompting, -transfiguring***, etc.

1602 J. DAVIES (Heref.) *Mirum in Modum* Wks. (Grosart) I. 11/1 The Spirit of Man..Should not, to such Soule-swillings base decline. *c* **1670** O. HEYWOOD *Diaries* (1881) II. 341 This fasting is soul-feasting. **1685** *Ibid.* (1885) IV. 113 How many sweet sabboths,..how many soul-humblings. **1818** BENTHAM *Church-of-Englandism* 329 The ..maintenance of this corrupt system..on pretence of souls-saving. **1819** KEATS *Lett.* (1958) II. 102 Call the world if you Please 'The vale of Soul-making'. **1875** McLEAN *Gospel in Psalms* 203 The wonder should not deprive us of ..the soul-heartening. **1891** *The Tablet* 7 Nov. 743 Christ by a few words of teaching filled the soul-craving of multitudes. **1922** JOYCE *Ulysses* 138 If aught that the..hand of sculptor has wrought in marble of soultransfigured and of soul-transfiguring deserves to live. *a* **1930** D. H. LAWRENCE *Phoenix* (1936) v. 605 Man just doesn't know how to interpret his own soul-promptings. **1939** A. HUXLEY *After Many a Summer* x. 140 Love, Passion, Soul-mating—all in upper-case letters. **1958** *Times Lit. Suppl.* 21 Feb. 101/2 The mid-Victorian novelists..thought of it [*sc.* Oxford] as a moral testing-ground or 'a vale of soul-making'.

23. With pres. pples. forming object-ive combs., as ***soul-adorning, -amazing, -awakening, -boiling, -deadening, -destroying, -inspiring, -satisfying, -searing, -shattering, -stirring, -testing***, etc., adjs.

The number of these is very great, esp. in the works of John Davies of Hereford and J. Beaumont, who have ***soul-afflicting, -attracting, -blinding, -catching, -cheering, -commanding, -conquering***, etc.

a **1618** SYLVESTER *Panaretus* 839 Of all *Soule-adorning Giftes divine,..the Monarchie is Mine. **1688** BUNYAN *Heavenly Footman* (1886) 139 What a *soul-amazing word will that be. *a* **1822** SHELLEY *Posthumous Poems* (1824) 320 *Soul-awakening music, sweet and strong. **1926** C. BARRY *Detective's Holiday* iv. 33 Suddenly a soul-awakening boom behind him smote his ears. **1606** SYLVESTER *Du Bartas* II. iv. II. *Magnificence* 19 Here in Sonnets, there in Epigrams, Evaporate your sweet *Soule-boyling Flames. **1612** J. DAVIES (Heref.) *Muse's Sacrifice* Ep. Ded., Shapers, and Soules of all *Soule-charming Rimes! **1600** TOURNEUR *Transf. Metam.* x. 68 T'enrich her coffers with *soule-choaking dust. **1591** SHAKS. *Two Gentl.* II. vi. 16 Twenty thousand *soule-confirming oathes. **1601** G. MARKHAM *Mary Magd. Lam.* Pref. 19 Yea, *soule-confounding sinne so far hath crept. **1609** J. DAVIES (Heref.) *Holy Rood* Wks. (Grosart) I. 9/2 T'was time to turne His *Soule-conuerting Eies To thee peruerted Peter. **1868** J. H. NEWMAN *Verses Var. Occas.* 125 So we her flame must trim, Around His soul-converting sign. **1659** PELL *Impr. Sea* 76 *note*, *Soul-corrupting discourse. **1837** SYD. SMITH *Serm. Duties Queen* Wks. 1859 II. 253/1 For all the soul-corrupting homage with which she is met. *a* **1708** BEVERIDGE *Thes. Theol.* (1711) III. 347 Drunkenness..is a *soul-damning sin. **1909** MRS. H. WARD *Daphne* viii. 186 This dull, *soul-deadening English life. **1937** *Atlantic Monthly* CLIX. 57/1 Exact information which really can be taught is despised as soul-deadening. *a* **1626** J. DAVIES (Heref.) *Sonn. Sir E. Dyer* Wks. (Grosart) I. 100/1 Minerua and the Muse ioyes my Soule's sence, Sith *Soule-delighting lines they multiplie. **1677** GALE *Crt. Gentiles* III. 64 The Devil, their great Apollo or *Soul destroying God. **1865** TYLOR *Early Hist. Man.* vii. 159 Graving on a folded tablet many soul-destroying things. **1898** G. B. SHAW *Candida* I1, in *Plays Pleasant* 123 What dreadful—what *soul-destroying cynicism! **1930** *Engineering* 25 July 111/3 A common indictment against modern conditions is that machine tending is 'soul-destroying'. **1976** J. SNOW *Cricket Rebel* 40 It was often soul destroying. On wet wickets or slow ones, I was expected to charge up and down and let it go when I knew I had no earthly chance of getting anything out of the wicket. **1642–4** VICARS *God in Mount* 45 The *soul-devouring corruptions of these Clergy-caterpillers. **1898** W. GRAHAM *Last Links* 116 Eyes fixed with an earnest, soul-devouring gaze upon his companion. **1748** THOMSON *Cast. Indol.* I. xxxix, Aerial music..breathed such *soul-dissolving airs, As did [etc.]. **1603** J. DAVIES (Heref.) *Microcosmos* Pref., O that I had a *Soule-enchanting Tongue. **1680** REYNER *Serm. Funeral Ld. Holles* 20 He was careful therefore to store his mind with all *soul-ennobling vertues. **1868** J. H. NEWMAN *Verses Var. Occas.* 37 This their soul-ennobling gain. **1647** TRAPP *Comm. 1 Cor.* vii. 5 Fasting-days are *soul-fatting days. **1595** SHAKS. *John* II. i. 383 Their *soule-fearing clamours haue braul'd downe The flintie ribbes of this contemptuous Citie. **1600** TOURNEUR *Transf. Metam.* viii. 54 *Soule-frighting horrors. **1648** J. BEAUMONT *Psyche* VIII. cxiii, *Soule-knawing Worms. **1848** BUCKLEY *Iliad* 127 To fight with the strength of soul-gnawing strife. **1748** RICHARDSON *Clarissa* VI. 165 Thy *soul-harrowing intelligence. **1593** NASHE *Christ's Tears* Wks. (Grosart) IV. 225 A *soule imitating deuill. **1794** J. TRUMBULL in *Columbian Muse* 58 And damp'd, alas! thy *soul-inspiring ray, Where Virtue prompted and where Genius soar'd. **1979** 'A. HAILEY' *Overload* II. i. 106, I guess it's real soul-inspiring to work in a ritzy layout like this. **1590** SHAKS. *Com. Err.* I. ii. 100 *Soule-killing Witches, that deforme the bodie. **1866** S. B. JAMES *Duty & Doctrine* (1871) 94 This habit is so enervating, so soul killing. **1690** C. NESSE *Hist. O. & N. Test.* I. 24 Man should be..a life-loving creature,..also a *soul loving creature. *a* **1721** SHEFFIELD (Dk. Buckhm.) *Wks.* (1753) I. 87 No writing lifts exalted man so high, As sacred and *soul-moving poesy. **1816** WORDSW. *'Imagination–ne'er before content'* 68 The deep soul-moving sense Of religious eloquence. **1690** C. NESSE *Hist. O. & N.*

Test. I. 137, I shall one day perish by the hand of those *soul-murthering Sauls. **1648** J. Beaumont *Psyche* viii. xxxvi, This noble Face; by whose *soul-piercing raies The Gentiles.. Admonish'd are to.. tread the open paths of highnoon Light. **1870** J. H. Newman *Grammar of Assent* ii. x. 386 That fearful antagonism brought out with such soul-piercing reality by Lucretius. **1601** Weever *Mirr. Mart.* (Roxb.) 208 My crownd, *soule-pleasing, sweet joy, mirth and plesure. **1697** Congreve *Mourn. Bride* iii. vi, That *soul-racking Thought. **1809–10** Shelley '*Oh! take the pure gem*' 18 Long visions of soul-racking pain. **1650** Baxter *Saints' R.* 716 These spiritual, excellent, *soul-raising duties. **1613–6** W. Browne *Brit. Past.* ii. lii, All-loved Draiton in *soul-raping straines, A genuine noat.. Began to tune. *a* **1618** Sylvester *Tetrastica* lxxii, The Charm Of those *soule-rapting Impes of Acheloes. **1603** J. Davies (Heref.) *An Extasie* Wks. (Grosart) I. 94/1 Maie-bowes.. Where out shal breath *soule-ravishing perfume. **1673** Hickeringill *Greg. F. Greyb.* 264 Those soul-ravishing opportunities. **1782** tr. *Mme. de Gomez's Belle A.* II. 195 With what *soul-rending Agonies was it that [etc.]. **1657** F. Cockin *Div. Blossomes* 48 So sweet, so clean, So *Soul-reviving. **1833** H. Blunt *Lect. Hist. St. Paul* II. 55 Those waters of life.. so soul-reviving and soul-strengthening. *a* **1708** Beveridge *Thes. Theol.* (1711) III. 7 Rejoice in Him .. as a *soul-satisfying God in Himself. **1890** Kipling *Life's Handicap* (1891) 151 He was afraid for the sake of another —which is the most soul-satisfying fear known to man. **1939** F. Scott Fitzgerald *Lett.* (1964) 48 It is not very soul-satisfying because it [*sc.* the cinema] is a business of telling stories fit for children. **1936** *Times Lit. Suppl.* 21 Mar. 242/3 We are.. given a *soul-searing account of a Russian pogrom. **1979** 'A. Hailey' *Overload* iii. xii. 253 A week and a half had passed since the soul-searing night when he learned that Ruth's life was endangered by cancerous cells at large in her body. **1731** A. Hill *Advice to Poets* xi, *Soul-shaking Sovereigns of the Passions. **1899** Kipling *From Sea to Sea* II. xxv. 5 The result is *soul-shattering. **1974** R. Harris *Double Snare* xi. 73 She and I had a soul-shattering row, and weren't on speaking terms. **1688** Bunyan *Jerus. Sinner Saved* (1886) 124 Unreasonable and *soul-sinking doubts. **1609** J. Davies (Heref.) *Holy Rood* Wks. (Grosart) I. 10/1 *Soule-slaying Schismaticke, nor God, nor Man. **1834** *Tait's Mag.* I. 173/2 Honest, upright, amiable, patriotic,.. and *soul-stirring David! **1927** *Granta* 14 Oct. 9/1 He rapidly composed and delivered a few soul-stirring orations. **1648** J. Beaumont *Psyche* xviii. cxl, Whilst yet with Charis's *soulsubduing heat Her melted and convicted heart did beat. **1892** W. S. Lilly *Gt. Enigma* 303 That heart-bewildering soul-subduing problem of evil. **1591** Sylvester *Du Bartas* i. vii. 333 Th' ill humours That vex his most-Saints with *soul-tainting tumours. **1932** Wodehouse *Louder & Funnier* 212 The unmistakable look of a man who has passed through some *soul-testing experience. **1965** J. A. Michener *Source* (1966) 192 Captain Epher's plan of battle required daring from all the Hebrews and soul-testing courage from a few. **1616** Drumm. of Hawth. *Flowers of Sion* (1630) 29 A Sanctuarie from *Soule-thralling Snares. **1598** J. Dickenson *Greene in Conc.* (1878) 104 A sequell of many sorrowes, a Centurie of *sowltyring passions. *a* **1634** Chapman *Rev. for Honour* ii. i. 268 To feed the irregular flames of false suspicions And *soul-tormenting jealousies. **1606** J. Davies (Heref.) *Speculum Proditori* Wks. (Grosart) II. 20/1 None but *soule-wounding words for it are meete. **1703** Quick *Serious Inquiry* 27 These Heart-cutting, Soul-wounding Accidents.

24. With pa. pples., as ***soul-benumbed, -blinded, -born, -felt, -struck, -transfigured***, etc.

1593 Nashe *Christ's Tears* Wks. (Grosart) IV. 173 Others there be of these *soule-benummed Atheists. **1612** Drayton *Poly-olb.* vi. 303 *Soul-blinded sots that creep In dirt. **1797** T. Park *Sonn.* 47 Every *soul-born rapture.. That flows from love sincere. *a* **1635** Sibbes *Confer. Christ & Mary* Pref. (1656) 3 A discourse.. between a *soul-burthened sinner, and a burthen-removing Saviour. **1617** Sir W. Mure *Misc. Poems* xxi. 25 Whome snakie hatred, *soule conceav'd disdaine,.. Did long in long antipathie detaine. **1590** Spenser *F.Q.* i. x. 24 Patience.. comming to that *soule-diseased knight, Could hardly him intreat, to tell his griefe. **1798** Sotheby tr. *Wieland's Oberon* (1826) II. 62 A *soul-felt glance of heavenly joy. **1764** Churchill *Candidate* 144 Let no.. *soul-gall'd Bishop damn me with a note. **1794** Mrs. Radcliffe *Myst. Udolpho* i, Ah, paint her form, her *soul-illumined eyes. **1593** Nashe *Christ's Tears* Ep. Ded., Were it effectually recured, in my *soule-infused lines. **1603** J. Davies (Heref.) *Microcosmos* Wks. (Grosart) I. 14/2 Ladies, and Lords, purse-pinched, and *Soule-pain'd. **1949** Blunden *After Bombing* 3 The child *soul-struck with the yellow flag's new fire. **1632** Lithgow *Trav.* x. 435 The *soule-sunke sorrow of godlesse Epicures and Hypocrites. **1922** *Soul-transfigured [see *soul-transfiguring*, sense 22 above]. **1611** Shaks. *Wint. T.* v. i. 58 One worse [wife].. would make her Sainted Spirit Againe possesse her Corps, and on this Stage.. appeare *Soule-vext. *a* **1618** Sylvester *Little Bartas* 960 Wks. (Grosart) II. 93 How many sin-sick did hee inly cure; And deep *soule-wounded binde-up, and assure!

25. With adjs., as ***soul-blind, -deep, -hydroptic***, etc.

1600 Tourneur *Transf. Metam.* xxxviii. 261 Th' exordium of ech soule-sweet argument. **1616** R. Niccols *Overbury's Vision* (Hunterian Club) 51 Those soule-blind men, whom they doe most betray. *a* **1618** Sylvester *Paradox agst. Libertie* Wks. (Grosart) II. 56/1 That good.. wch soul-wise man must seek. **1704** Norris *Ideal World* ii. xii. 479 It hence follows that this.. immutable truth be the only soul-perfective truth. **1842** Cdl. Wiseman *Prayer & Prayer-Bks.* Ess. 1853 I. 379 Everything is heart-felt, soul-deep. **1855** Browning *Grammar. Funeral* 95 He (soul-hydroptic with a sacred thirst). **1888** R. Buchanan *City of Dream* viii. 161 Then die! soul-sure thou hast not lived in vain.

26. Special combs., as † **soul-ale**, an ale-drinking at the funeral of a person; a dirge ale; **soul-bearer**, among the Akan peoples of West Africa, a person deemed to carry within him the external soul of a ruler or important person; **soul-body** *Spiritualism*, a spiritual body (see spiritual *a.* 4 a); **soul-bolts** *pl.*, 'the bolts which fasten the soul in place', used in var. slang phrases expressive of surprise or shock; cf. *soul-case* below; **soul brother**, (*a*) a spiritual brother; (*b*) orig. *U.S. Blacks*, a fellow Black man; cf. *soul sister* below; **soul-cake**, a specially prepared cake or bun distributed in various northern or north-midland counties on All Souls' Day, esp. to parties of children who go 'souling'; **soul-candle**, (*a*) ? one of several candles placed about the coffin at a funeral service; (*b*) [tr. Yiddish *neshome licht*, f. *neshome* soul (Heb. *nešāmā*) + *licht* light *sb.* (G. *licht*)] in Judaism, a candle lit on the eve of the anniversary of a parent's death, and also on the eve of Yom Kippur (the custom is said to derive from Prov. xx. 27); **soul-case**, † (*a*) *slang*, the body; (*b*) *U.S.* and *Austral. slang*, 'the casing of the soul', chiefly used in slang phrases expressive of hardship or suffering; cf. *soul-bolts* above; **soul-catcher**, among various North American Indian peoples, a hollowed bone tube used by a medicine man to contain the soul of a sick person (see also quot. 1976); † **soul chaplain**, = *soul-priest*; † **soul-charm** *a.*, soul-charming; **Soul City**, an epithet applied to the Harlem area of New York city; also *transf.*; **soul-doctor** *slang*, (*a*) a clergyman; (*b*) a psychiatrist; † **soul-driver**, (*a*) a clergyman; (*b*) *U.S.*, a person who trades the services of convicts, indentured servants, or slaves; **soul food**, (*a*) *fig.* spiritual nourishment; (*b*) orig. *U.S. Blacks*, the kind of food typically eaten by Black people, *spec.* those foodstuffs originating in the southern states of America; **soul-force** = satyagraha; **soul-friend** (see quot. 1891); also in extended use (see quots. 1929, 1979); **soul-house**, a model or representation of a house placed by the ancient Egyptians in a tomb to receive the soul of a dead person; **soul kiss** = *deep kiss* s.v. deep *a.* IV. c; so **soul-kiss** *v. trans.*; hence **soul-kissing** *vbl. sb.*; **soul music**, (*a*) *fig.* (see quot. 1900); (*b*) a type of music popularized by Black singers which incorporates elements of rhythm and blues and gospel music; also *ellipt.*: see sense 4 b; **soul-pence, -pennies**, money subscribed by the members of a guild to pay for soul-masses; † **soul-priest**, a priest having the special function of praying for the souls of the dead; **soul-silver**, = soul-scot; **soul sister** orig. *U.S. Blacks*, a fellow Black woman; cf. *soul-brother* (*b*) above; **soul-sleeper**, one who holds the doctrine of psychopannychism; a psychopannychite; **soul stuff, -substance**, a hypothetical immaterial substance believed to form the 'spirit' or 'self' of each person (in some cultures also of animals and objects), and which is independent of the material body and outlives it.

1577 Harrison *Descr. Eng.* ii. i. (1877) i. 32 The superfluous numbers of idle waks,.. church-ales, helpe-ales, and *soule-ales, called also dirge-ales,.. are well diminished. **1951** E. L. R. Meyerowitz *Sacred State of Akan* ii. 51 Like every king.., the queenmother has her elders, among whom are several spokeswomen, female *akrafo* or *soul-bearers. **1967** *Times* 14 Nov. 17/2 (Advt.), A Baga wood nimba shoulder mask,.. an important large Ashanti gold soul-bearer's disc,.. a large New Ireland Uli. **1961** *Soul body [see exteriorize *v.*]. **1971** *Spiritualist* Oct.–Dec. 6/2 Help each other that your soul-body may rise in beauty and can be admired when you reach the World of Spirit. **1850** H. Melville *White Jacket* II. xliv. 296 Start my *soul-bolts, maties, if any more Blue Peters and sailing signals fly at my fore! **1902** J. Burgess *Some Shetland Folk* 77 If du has, I'll knock the bloomin' sowl-bolts out of him. **1903** 'T. Collins' *Such is Life* vi. 234 'Wouldn't think that horse had a devil in him as big as a bull-dog,' observed the horse-driver. 'Shake the soul-bolt out of a man, s'posen you *do* stick to him.' **1742–3** *Observ. upon Methodists* 18 Our glorious *Soul brother had it revealed to him in Spirit [etc.]. **1970** R. Lowell *Notebook* 151 We were an empire, soul-brothers To Babylon and China. **1978** *Listener* 20 July 90/1 Baudelaire recognised in Poe a soul brother and mirror image. **1959** *Jazz* Fall 291 It's one of those type LPs. I had all 'soul brothers'. **1969** *Listener* 4 Sept. 319/3 And if you think the main feeling being expressed is self-pity (and the self-generated violence and frustrations of self-pity), then so what? This is strictly for soul-brothers. **1973** H. Nielsen *Severed Key* xiv. 144 I've got some soul brothers hustling baggage at LAX. **1686–7** Aubrey *Remains* (1881) 23 There is an old Rhythm or saying, A *Soule-cake, a Soule-cake, Have mercy on all Christen soules for a Soule-cake. **1896** P. H. Ditchfield *Old Eng. Customs* 167 On All Souls' Day.. it is still customary for children to go 'a-souling', and soul-cakes are still offered and eaten in Shropshire on this day. **1389** in *Eng. Gilds* (1870) 184 [Four] *saulecandels [shall be found, and used in the burial services]. **1978** I. B. Singer *Shosha* viii. 141 Toward the evening meal, she lit a large candle stuck in a pot of sand—a 'soul candle'—and put on a silk holiday dress. **1796** *Grose's Dict. Vulgar T.* (ed. 3) s.v., 'He made a hole in his *soul case,' he wounded him. **1835** A. B. Longstreet *Georgia Scenes* 109 When you come to the last half mile of each heat, run his heart, liver, lights, and soul-case out of him. **1896** J. C. Harris *Sister Jane* 277 The way that hoss flung around wi' you was enough to jolt your soul-case loose. **1901** F. J. Gillen *Diary* 15 Apr. (1968) 34 Flies were celebrating some festival all night and worried the very soul cases out of us. **1962** R. Tullipan *March into Morning* 13 Then he got the bright idea of bringin' in orphan kids and working the soulcase off them until they turn eighteen and have to be paid more money. **1932** D. Jenness *Indians of Canada* 333 Peculiar to the medicine-men of the Haida, Tlinkit, and Tsimshian was the use of a special '*soul-catcher', a bone tube, generally carved, for capturing the wandering souls of the sick and restoring them to their bodies. **1969** *Times* 22 Sept. 14/2 One invariably sees a face in the centre of a soul-catcher, a tube of hollowed bone into which the shaman [of the Tsimshian Indians] sucked the soul of a sick man—to keep it safe from harm while the illness lasted. **1976** *Times* 10 Nov. 18/4 A nine-inch bone soul catcher of the Tsimshian tribe reached £12,000... A soul-catcher is a tube within which a medicine man would catch the imp that caused a sickness. **1550** Bale *Eng. Votaries* ii. C iv g, In a winter night a *soule chaplaine of the court laye with her. **1598** Sylvester *Du Bartas* ii. ii. ii. *Babylon* 560 The *soule-charm Image of sweet Eloquence. **1964** *N.Y. Times Mag.* 23 Aug. 62/3 **Soul City*, Harlem. **1971** B. Malamud *Tenants* 89 Lesser descended.. into Soul City by himself. **1977** M. Herr *Dispatches* (1978) 196 Danang was Soul City for many of us, it had showers and drinks. **1785** Grose *Dict. Vulgar Tongue*, **Soul doctor*, or *driver*, a parson. **1962** D. Lessing *Golden Notebook* i. 202 Anna Wulf is sitting on a chair in front of a soul-doctor. **1699** B. E. *New Dict. Canting Crew*, **Soul-driver*, a Parson. **1774** in *Amer. Hist. Rev.* (1900) VI. 77 Among them there was two Soul drivers. They are men who.. drive them [*sc.* servants and convicts] through the Country.. untill they can sell them to advantage. **1818** *Massachusetts Spy* 4 Nov. (Th.), Two men, in the character of soul drivers, lodged in the jail for safe keeping, five negros. **1846** *Swell's Night Guide* 132/2 *Soul driver*, a methodist parson. **1973** A. Dundes *Mother Wit* 230 Individuals who speculated in the purchase and sale of slaves were called 'Negro-drivers' or 'soul-drivers'. *c* **1200** *Trin. Coll. Hom.* 27 Godes word þat is þe *sowle fode. *c* **1275** *Serving Christ* 41 in *O.E. Misc.* 91 We wyþ sunnes geteþ saulene fode. *a* **1340** Hampole *Psalter* cvi. 10 In nede of saule fode. **1920** W. R. Lethaby in *London Mercury* Mar. 575 The history that can be seen and touched is a strong and stimulating soul-food, entirely different from vague and wearying written history. **1964** *N.Y. Times Mag.* 23 Aug. 62/3 *Soul food*, chitterlings, collard greens, ham hocks, grits, black-eyed peas and rice, and the like. **1969** L. Sanders *Anderson Tapes* (1970) xxviii. 71 This soul food crap—knuckles and hocks and greens. **1972** *Times* 15 Nov. 10/5 *Soul food.* Professional chef with knowledge of American Southern food.. wanted for a new restaurant.. in Chelsea. **1978** *Broadcast's Programme Edinburgh TV Festival* 8/3 The social centre of the series is a soul-food grocery owned by a West Indian entrepreneur. **1969** *It* 4–17 July 10/4 With *soul force we'll look to the needs of our brother In a world that's our universal home. **1977** *Arab Times* 14 Dec. 2/5 'The voice of women.. is a special soul-force in the struggle for a non-violent world,' the 36-year-old pacificist leader from strife-torn Northern Ireland declared. **1891** *The Month* LXXIII. 221 He was the Generalissimo's.. '*soul-friend', as a confessor is called in Irish [= Ir. *anam-chara*]. **1896** *Westm. Gaz.* 5 Mar. 3/2 An old priest.. tried.. to play the 'soul-friend' to the bandit. **1929** I. M. Clark *Church Discipline in Scotland* i. 29 Columba had a method of entrusting those who had sinned to the spiritual care of individual monks of his community, who were termed soul-friends and whose duty it was to restore the souls of those penitents. **1979** *Church Times* 11 May 2/3 A special sort of job is being offered to spiritually gifted women in the diocese of Truro. The Bishop.. wants them to train to be 'soul friends'—so that they may give spiritual guidance and direction with his formal backing and recognition. **1907** Petrie *Gizeh & Rifeh* vi. 14/2 The depth of grave below the *soul-house is inversely as the height of soil above it. **1953** H. Waugh *Last seen Wearing* 55 She calls him exciting and lets him *soul-kiss her. **1960** Wentworth & Flexner *Dict. Amer. Slang* 504/1 *Soul kiss*, a long passionate open-mouthed kiss, during which a lover's tongue licks, caresses, or explores the tongue and mouth of the beloved. **1970** R. Davies *Fifth Business* ii. 130 Some of them were experts in what were then called French kisses or soul kisses, which the irreverent called 'swapping spits'. **1973** E. Jong *Fear of Flying* 82, I had the distinct sensation of kissing my own mouth—like when I was nine and used to wet a piece of my pillow with saliva and then kiss it to try to imagine what 'soul-kissing' was like. **1900** W. James *Let.* 20 July (1920) II. 133, I.. sit *thinking of letters*, and of the *soul-music with which they might be filled if my tongue could only utter the thoughts that arise in me to youward. **1961** *Commonweal* 24 Mar. 658 It's called 'soul music' because its practitioners have incorporated some of the backbeat, rhythms, and exclamatory melodic lines of Negro gospel music. **1968** P. Oliver *Screening Blues* 9 Soul music, which exploits the intensity of expression of religious song, the form and instrumental character of the blues and the maudlin sentiments of pop music. **1974** *Black World* Mar. 57/2 Soul music belched from windows where Black women wearing tired faces gazed impassively down at the hopeless street. **1980** *Oxford Times* 8 Feb. 15/1 They get really close to the style and spirit of American soul music. **1870** Toulmin Smith *Eng. Gilds* 181 That *soul-pence will be paid by the bretheren. *Ibid.*, For collecting the *soul-pennies from the bretheren. **1484** Caxton *Fables of Poge* xii, Are ye here a *sowle preest or a paryssh preste? **1577** Fulke *Confut. Purg.* 172 The dead arose.., threatning him, that he should dye for it, if he did not restore them their souleprìest. **1606** *Reg. Mag. Sig. Scot.* 646/2 Advocationem.. capellaniarum vulgo *lie Saull-preistis*.. infra ecclesiam collegiatam de Dumbar. **1355–6** *Abingdon Rolls* (Camden) 5 De *soule-seluer vjs. viijd. **1967** Wentworth & Flexner *Dict. Amer. Slang* Suppl. 705/1 **Soul sister*, a female Negro. *Negro use only.* **1968** *N.Y. Times* 17 June 24 Plate glass in Negro-owned establishments remained intact and displayed the words, 'Soul Brother' or 'Soul Sister'. **1976** *Drum* (E. Afr. ed.) June 10/3 African girls have always plaited their hair, and it was the soul sisters in America who were copying the girls in Africa. **1645** Pagitt *Heresiogr.* (ed. 2) 139 **Soule-Sleepers.* That the soule dyeth with the body is an old and despicable Heresie. **1727** De Foe *Hist. Appar.* v. (1840) 45, I am none of the sect of soul sleepers. **1860** *Southern Enterprise* (Thomasville, Georgia) 13 June 2/5 Soul Sleepers is the name of a new religious sect which has recently made its appearance at Fairfield, Iowa.. They.. think that the soul is a mortal substance, and sleeps within the body until resurrection. **1887** J. Kirkland *Zury* 65 He and Peddicomb had both been connected with the little sect of Christians called 'Soul-sleepers'. **1889** *Cent. Dict.*, *Soul-stuff*.., the hypothetical substance of the soul; psychoplasm. **1909** W. JAMES *Mem. & Stud.* (1911) viii. 202 If there were in the universe a lot of diffuse soul-stuff, unable of itself to get into consistent personal form.. it might get its head into the air, parasitically, so to speak, by profiting by weak spots in the armour of human minds. **1972** D. DAVIES *Dict. Anthropol.* 165/2 *Soul-stuff*, mana. The spiritual power with which every male in primitive societies seeks to enhance his prowess and standing in the tribe. It can only be gained by special feats... It is also thought to be found in the hair. **1890** W. JAMES *Princ. Psychol.* I. x. 318 But what is this abstract numerical principle of identity..? May it be the indivisible *Soul-Substance, in which, according to the orthodox tradition, my faculties inhere? **1924** W. B. SELBIE *Psychol. Relig.* ii. 28 Anthropologists are.. fairly generally agreed that underlying all religions is what they call animism, or belief in a soul substance discoverable not merely in men but in things. **1972** H. J. EYSENCK *Encycl. Psychol.* II. 57/2 Heraclitus.. considered fire as the primary force and 'soul-substance' because it moved and transformed matter.

Hence **'soulhood, 'soulship**, the condition or state of being a soul; soulful quality.

1882 H. C. MERIVALE *Faucit of B.* II. I. xix. 40 Many of these leaden caskets may carry yet, locked within them, some rough gem of Christian soulhood. **1893** *Advance* (Chicago) 15 June, Of the modification of the sinless perfection of Christ, of his ethical soulship. **1933** S. SASSOON *Traveller to his Soul* in *Satirical Poems* (ed. 2) 68 The problem which concerns me most.. Is, bluntly stated, 'Have I got a soul?' And, soulhood granted, while millenniums roll, Will it inhabit some congenial clime.. Anonymous in what we name 'the Whole'? **1940** C. S. LEWIS *Problem of Pain* ix. 129 Supposing, as I do, that the personality of the tame animals is largely the gift of man—that their mere sentience is reborn to soulhood in us as our mere soulhood is reborn to spirituality in Christ—I naturally suppose that very few animals indeed, in their wild state, attain to a 'self' or *ego*.

soul, obs. f. SOLE *sb.*[1] and *a.*, SOWEL (stake); variant of SOWL *sb.*

soul (səʊl), *v.* Also 5, 9 *dial.* sowl. [f. the sb. Cf. OE. *sáwlian* (= ON. and Icel. *sálask*, MSw. *siälas*) to die, whence SOULING *vbl. sb.* 1.]

1. *trans.* †**a.** To endow or endue with a soul. Also *fig. Obs. rare.*

c **1386** CHAUCER *Sec. Nun's T.* 329 The goost that fro the fader gan procede Hath sowled hem with outen any drede. **1646** N. LOCKYER *Serm.* 4 All that was said is resum'd and souled, as I may say.

b. To inspire or animate. *rare*⁻¹.

1891 C. DAWSON *Avonmore* 50 Joy souled the day, and love was seen In winter's storms.

2. *intr.* To go about collecting doles, properly on the eve of All Souls' Day. Chiefly in the phr. *to go (a-)souling*.

a **1779** TOLLET in *Brand's Pop. Antiq.* (1813) I. 309 On All Saints Day, the poor people.. go from parish to parish *a Souling*, as they call it. **1820** WILBRAHAM *Cheshire Gloss.* App. s.v., To go a souling, is to go about as boys do, repeating certain rigmarole verses, and begging cakes or money, in commutation for them, the Eve of All Souls' Day. **1883** MISS BURNE *Shrops. Folk-lore* 381 Up to the present time in many places, poor children, and sometimes men, go out 'souling'.

3. To capture or catch souls. *rare*⁻¹.

1825 J. WILSON *Noct. Ambr.* (1855) I. 3 Fiends ride forth a-souling For the dogs of havoc are yelping and yowling.

soul, obs. or dial. form of SOWL *v.*

†**soulack**, obs. variant of SOLAK.

1636 H. B[LOUNT] *Voy. Levant* 92 There was a Soulack, who is an Officer very eminent about the Emperours person. [Hence in Blount *Glossogr.*]

‖**soulagement** (sulaʒmɑ̃). [Fr. Cf. SOLACE *sb.*[1] and SOLAGEMENT.] Solace, relief.

1777 EARL OF CARLISLE *Let.* 18 Feb. in J. H. Jesse *Geo. Selwyn & Contemporaries* (1844) III. 171, I know our house might be a *soulagement* to you. **1949** H. NICOLSON *Diary* 17 Apr. (1968) 169 All this calm reflects my deep *soulagement* at Vita's improvement in health. **1968** A. COATES *Myself Mandarin* xvii. 245 One of my Secretariat colleagues telephoned me.. to remind me.. to return my instrument. .. With a certain *soulagement* I learned that he was referring merely to a piece of paper—the frightening document on the basis of which it all began.

'soular, *a. rare*⁻¹. [f. SOUL *sb.*] Of or pertaining to the soul.

1825 *Sporting Mag.* XVI. 404 They should be merged indiscriminately in the great soular or spiritual mass.

†**'soulary**, *a.* and *sb. Obs. rare.* [f. SOUL *sb.* + -ARY[1].] **a.** *adj.* Of or pertaining to the theory of the separate existence of the soul after the death of the body. **b.** *sb.* One who holds this theory.

1643 R. O. *Man's Mortality* ii. 7 This Soulary fancy of present reward of beatitude after this life. *Ibid.* v. 39 From this place the Resurrection of the body before the day of Judgment.. may better be proved, then such a present soularie enterance into Heaven or Hell. *Ibid.* vi. 53 All this while we have had to doe with this immortall Soule, [which] we cannot find, or the Soularies tell what it is.

soul bell, soul-bell. [f. SOUL *sb.*] The passing-bell. Also *fig.*

1599 NASHE *Lenten Stuff* Wks. (Grosart) V. 214 The.. Bishop of Norwich.. meant not to forsake them till the soule Bell towld them thence. *a* **1603** T. CARTWRIGHT *Confut. Rhem. N.T.* (1618) 394 It is as it were the soule-bell of your Priestly and un-virginly virginity. **1610** BP. HALL *Apol. Brownists* xliv. 107 We call them soule-bels, for that they signifie the Departure of the soule. **1725** BOURNE in Brand *Pop. Antiq.* (1777) i. 1 Of the Soul-Bell, its Antiquity, the Reason of its Institution. **1777** BRAND *Ibid.* 18 Distinction of Rank is preserved here in the tolling of the Soul-Bell. **1893** *Tablet* 27 May 819 The great Soul Bell of St. Swithun's was sobbing in the winter wind for the death of the bishop. **1906** RAVEN *Bells* 112, Persons recovered after their soul bell had sounded.

soul-cake: see SOUL *sb.* 26.

sould(e, obs. or dial. pa. t. and pa. pple. of SELL *v.*; Sc. and north. pa. t. of SHALL *v.*; obs. ff. SOLD *sb.*[1] and *sb.*[2], *v.*[1] and *v.*[2]

souldan, -en, obs. ff. SOLDAN.

souldeour, obs. f. SOLDIER *sb.*

soulder, obs. f. SOLDER *sb.*[1] and *v.*

souldiar, obs. f. SOLDIER *sb.*

†**souldie.** *Obs. rare.* Also 5 souldye. [ad. OF. *souldee, soldee*, etc. (f. *solde* SOLD *sb.*[1]), or MDu. *souldie, soudie*.] Pay, salary, wages.

1474 CAXTON *Chesse* III. iv. (1481) G j, To answer for hym to the knyghtes and to other persones for theyr wages and souldyes. **1481** —— *Reynard* (Arb.) 39 He wolde paye them their souldye or wagis to fore. **1555** W. WATREMAN *Fardle Facions* II. x. 221 Thei haue no wages for their souldie, yet are thei prest, and ready in all affayres.

soule, obs. f. SOIL *sb.*[3], SOLE *sb.*[1] and *a.*, SOWEL (stake), SOWL, SULL *sb.* (plough).

†**soulé**, variant of SAULEE *Obs.*

1450-80 tr. *Secreta Secret.* 31 Than mayst thou ete a good soule aftir as thyn appetit takith the.

souled (səʊld), *ppl. a.* [f. SOUL *sb.* or *v.*]

†**1.** ? Conferred upon the soul. *Obs.*⁻¹

1387-8 T. USK *Test. Love* III. i. (Skeat) l. 15 Who-so can wel understande is shapen to be saved in souled blisse.

2. Endowed with a soul. *rare*⁻¹.

c **1400** *Apol. Loll.* 10 þe maker of man kynd takyng a soulid body of þe virgyn.

3. With qualifying terms: Endowed with a soul of a specified kind.

See also *great-, high-, large-, mean-*, NARROW-SOULED.

1602 MARSTON *Antonio's Rev.* IV. ii, He that's a vilaine, or but meanely sowl'd, Must.. cling to routes of fooles. **1667** DRYDEN *Maiden Queen* I. iii, Matchless in virtue, And largely souled where'er her bounty gives. **1781** MME. D'ARBLAY *Diary* Aug., Dr. Johnson.. is as great a souled man as a bodied one. **1828** LYTTON *Pelham* II. xii, You whey-faced,.. sleepy-souled Arismanes of bad spirits. *Ibid.* xxvi, I have my refuge and my comforter in the golden-souled and dreaming Plato. **1894** MRS. DYAN *Man's Keeping* (1899) 193 What would they tell that faithful-souled Afghan chief?

†**soulement**, *adv. Obs. rare.* Also 3 sulement. [a. AF. *sule-, soulement* (OF. *sole-, seulement*), f. *sul, soul* SOLE *a.*] Solely, only.

a **1225** *Ancr. R.* 282 Sulement luue his god. *c* **1290** *St. Brandan* 202 in *S. Eng. Leg.* I. 225 We fulle also a-doun.. soulement forto schewe oure louerdes suete miȝt.

souler ('səʊlə(r)). *dial.* [f. SOUL *sb.* or *v.*] One who goes 'souling'.

1813 H. ELLIS in *Brand's Pop. Antiq* I. 310 The Souler's Song in Staffordshire is different from that which Mr. Peck mentions. **1887** *S. Cheshire Gloss.* s.v. *Soul*, Parties of soulers go together to all the larger houses in the neighbourhood singing a souling-song.

†**soulet.** *Obs. rare.* Also **sowlet.** [app. f. SOUL *sb.*] (See quot.)

c **1530** tr. *Godfridus' Bk. Knowl. Thynges* H iv b, Of euerye mans bodye, be iiij pryncypall lymbes, that is to saye, soulet lymbes, small lymbes and norycshande lymbes, and gendrynge lymbes. Sowlet lymbes, be the braynes, and all that are there aboute, downe to the wesande.

'soulful, *sb. rare.* [f. SOUL *sb.* + -FUL 2.] As much as a soul can hold or contain.

1649 in *Select Biogr.* (Wodrow Soc.) I. 406 He did so long (as he said) for his soulful of the well of life. **1902** A. B. DAVIDSON *Called of God* x. 268 Except a man be washed, and have a whole soulful of spiritual faculties awake within him, he cannot see the Kingdom of God.

soulful ('səʊlfʊl), *a.* Also **soul-full.** [f. SOUL *sb.* + -FUL 1.]

1. Full of soul or feeling; of a highly emotional, spiritual, or æsthetic nature or character, or marked by this; also, affectedly or unduly æsthetic or emotional.

1860 PRINCESS VICTORIA *Let.* 6 Feb. in R. Fulford *Dearest Child* (1964) 232 The dear Princess said to Fritz Karl while they were singing something of Mozart 'You are looking soulful.' **1863** GILCHRIST *Blake* xxii, Very striking and soulful is the general effect [of an engraving]. **1882** L. C. LILLIE *Prudence* 48 Who can be soulful and an athlete? **1882** B. HARTE *Flip* iii, The poetic, soulful side of his mission was delicately indicated by a pale blue necktie. **1897** *Naturalist* 84 For all who live by it will be manful, soulful, honest, and without fear. **1931** A. HUXLEY *Music at Night* 18 When the great obvious truth is affirmed.. in a series of soulful close-ups.. the sensitive can only wince. **1951** *Sunday Pictorial* 21 Jan. 6/4 His eyes become deceptively soulful.

transf. **1869** W. CORY *Lett. & Jrnls.* (1897) 263 This bit of the earth's expression, this soul-full bit of the earth, the quiet bay.

2. Expressive or indicative of deep feeling or emotion.

1868 TUCKERMAN *Collector* 312 The soulful glow of expression in the inspired countenance of the Apollo. **1869** MRS. WHITNEY *We Girls* xix, Mother and Madam Pennington looked at each other with soulful eyes. **1878** *The Choir* 16 Nov. 730 One of those soulful tunes which cannot fail to engage attention.

3. Expressive of Black feeling; characteristic of Black music. Also as quasi-*adv.*

1964 *Amer. Folk Music Occasional* I. 46, I sing my song more soulful. **1973** *Black Panther* 15 Sept. 15/1 The audience is encouraged to join hands with their neighbors and all standing sway with the soulful music. **1973** *Black World* Apr. 9/1 'Soul' is a highly valued concept among Afro-Americans. Soulful behavior may be called something else by some Afro-Americans, but its value remains.

Hence **'soulfully** *adv.*, **'soulfulness.**

1880 W. S. GILBERT *Patience* I. 11, I am soulfully intense. **1882** *Advance* (Chicago) 20 Apr. 249 She.. carried the audience by her dignity, earnestness and soulfulness. **1893** *Nation* 9 Feb. LVI. 110/2 Languages vary, as do individuals, in genius or soulfulness. **1922** JOYCE *Ulysses* 279 Bronze, listening by the beer-pull, gazed far away. Soulfully. **1979** *Daily Tel.* 23 Apr. 15/2 Her two daughters, .. one bitter and promiscuous, one soulfully virginal, appeared as remote from everyday living as folklore princesses.

†**soul-heal.** *Obs.* [f. SOUL *sb.* 19 + HEAL *sb.* Cf. WFris. *sieleheil*, Flem. *zieleheil*, G. *seelenheil*, †*seelheil*.] = next. **a.** With possessive pronoun.

[*c* **825** in *O.E. Texts* 443 Fore uncerra saula hela & uncerra bearna.] *a* **1300** *Cursor M.* 25168 For vr praier es vnlele And askes gains vr saul hele. **1362** LANGL. *P. Pl.* A. VI. 22, I haue .. souht goode seyntes for my soule hele. *c* **1375** *Sc. Leg. Saints* xxxiii. (*George*) 378 For dout of dede, ful fele reneyt god & þare saule-hele. **1418** in Ellis *Orig. Lett.* Ser. I. I. 4 ȝe desire principaly vertuous lyvyng and ȝour sowle heele. *c* **1440** *Alph. Tales* 146, I trow ye be in dispayr of my sawle heale. **1560** ROLLAND *Seven Sages* 74 Gif ȝe pleis ony thing for to deill, Into Almus, for my weill and Saull heill.

b. In general sense.

[*a* **1225** *Ancr. R.* 182 (MS. C.) þus is sicnesse saulene heale.] **13..** *Minor Poems fr. Vernon MS.* xxxvii. 355 þou spekest of wraþþe in þi tale And seist hit is aȝeyn soule-hale. *c* **1375** *Sc. Leg. Saints* xviii. (*Egiptian*) 323 Lowyt mot our lorde be þat purchesis þus saule-hele! **1390** GOWER *Conf.* I. 29 Adrian.. preith the grete Charlemeine, For Cristes sake and Soule hele [etc.]. **1429** *Acts Privy Council* III. 331 If ony man wol oonly of devocion and for soule heele goo overe in þe said expedicion. *c* **1440** *Jacob's Well* 156 ȝif men teche hem soule-hele, þei scornyn hem. *c* **1550** COPLAND *Hye Way to Spyttel Ho.* 284 Methynk it is a great soule-heale To help them.

†**soul-health.** *Obs.* [f. SOUL *sb.* + HEALTH *sb.* Cf. prec.] The health of the soul; moral or spiritual well-being; salvation.

a. With possessive pronoun or genitive.

1390 GOWER *Conf.* I. 39 So may he winne worldes welthe And afterward his soules helthe. **1432-50** tr. *Higden* (Rolls) I. 365 His preiers for the sawle healethe of his childe. **1526** *Pilgr. Perf.* (W. de W. 1531) 10 b, Whiche is moost necessary for thy soule helthe. **1587** GOLDING *De Mornay* xxiv. 357 The setting downe of rules for Religion and for mans Soulehealth.

b. Without article.

1432-50 tr. *Higden* (Rolls) I. 371 Seynte Patrik.. studiede to.. brynge to the weye of sawle healethe the sawles of the bestialle peple. *Ibid.* V. 127 Take cownesayle of sawle-healethe. **1556** OLDE *Antichrist* 81 The Germaines wolde not.. ther seke soule helth. **1574** tr. *Marlorat's Apocalips* 14 God will gather togither the remnantes of that forlorne and desperate nation, vnto soulehealth. **1603** J. DAVIES (Heref.) *Microcosmos* Wks. (Grosart) I. 36/2 Affliction's water cooles the heate of sinne, And brings soule-health. *a* **1618** SYLVESTER *Paradox agst. Libertie* 587 Wks. (Grosart) II. 60 Sith, if hee use the same, soule-health it hurteth not.

soulical ('səʊlɪkəl), *a.* [irreg. f. SOUL *sb.*] = PSYCHICAL *a.* 2, SOULISH *a.* 1.

1845 BAILEY *Festus* (ed. 2) 215 Some of these bodies whom I speak of are Pure spirits, others bodies soulical. **1872** HANNA *Resur. Dead* 121 It is a soulish or soulical body. **1875** E. WHITE *Life in Christ* III. xx. (1876) 306 The mortal condition of the unregenerate or 'soulical' man.

†**'soulify**, *v. Obs. rare.* [f. SOUL *sb.* + -(I)FY.] *trans.* To endow with a soul. So **'soulified** *ppl. a.*

1662 J. CHANDLER *Van Helmont's Oriat.* 30 Therefore the Seeds of things that are not soulified, are indeed propagated no otherwise than as light taken from light. *Ibid.* 155 Minerals indeed, have not a seed, with the Image of their Predecessor, after the manner of soulified things.

'souling, *vbl. sb.* Now *dial.* [See SOUL *v.*]

†**1.** The giving up of the soul; dying, death, decease. *Obs. rare.*

c **900** in Cockayne *Shrine* 106 Cwæþ sum haliȝ biscop ða he wæs on sawlenga [etc.]. *c* **1440** *Promp. Parv.* 466/1 Sowlynge, or dyynge, *obitus, vel exalacio*.

2. *dial.* The action of going round soliciting doles on or about All Souls' Day. Also attrib., as *souling-children, -song*.

1851 *N. & Q.* 1st Ser. IV. 506/1 The custom of 'souling' .. is carried on with great zeal.. in this neighbourhood [i.e. Cheshire]. **1878** *Ibid.* 5th Ser. X. 426, I am reminded of her just now by the children who are singing their 'Souling Song' under my window. **1883** MISS BURNE *Shrops. Folk-Lore* 382 Soul-cakes.. to give away to the souling-children.

souliote, variant of SULIOTE.

soulish ('səʊlɪʃ), *a.* Also 6 soulisch, sowlish. [f. SOUL *sb.* + -ISH.]

1. Of or pertaining to, characterized or distinguished by, the soul, esp. in its lower or less spiritual aspects (= PSYCHICAL *a.* 2).

c **1550** CHEKE *Matt.* xii. 17 Calling yᵉ principal part bi yᵉ name of yᵉ hoole, which Saint Poul to yᵉ Corinthes called yᵉ soulisch man, which can not perceiue thinges belonging to god. ? **1554** COVERDALE *Hope of Faithful* xvi. (1574) 133 Thus Paule calleth 'Animale corpus' the soulish body, which is interpreted ye natural body. **1649** J. ELLISTONE tr. *Warning fr. J. Boehme* §29. 19 The Highest Tongue,.. which through the wisedome doth.. reveale to every one, in his eternal soulish Constelation, according to the.. measure as he pleaseth. **1662** SPARROW tr. *Boehme's Rem. Wks., Apol. conc. Perf.* 138 This soulish property hath the Name Jesus receiv'd to it selfe. **1752** W. LAW *Spirit of Love* I. (1816) 52 The entrance of the Deity into the properties of your own soulish life. **1786** A. MACLEAN *Comm. Christ* II. (1847) 111 Such are termed.. soulish, animal, or sensual. **1865** MAURICE *Conflict Good & Evil* 33 He will understand St. Paul's contempt for the mere soulish man, his sympathy with the spiritual man. **1886** J. PULSFORD *Divine Genius in Nature & Man* 27 The soulish body.. begins more rapidly to be purified from all the remains of its fleshly defilement.

2. Of the nature of the soul; soul-like. *rare.*

1581 MULCASTER *Positions* vi. (1887) 48 A part of mans bodie.. which breedeth a sowlish, and life spirite. **1662** SPARROW tr. *Boehme's Rem. Wks., Complex.* 4 The Complexion in the Souls Fire becometh Soulish, or like the Soul.

† **soul-knell.** *Obs.* [f. SOUL *sb.* + KNELL *sb.*] The knell rung or tolled at or after the death of a person. Also *fig.*

a **1300** *Vox & Wolf* 251 in Hazl. *E.P.P.* I. 66 Thi soul-cnul ich wile do ringe, And masse for thine soule singe. *c* **1400** *Laud Troy Bk.* 5796 Thei myȝt haue rongen here soule-knylle... Thei hadde dyed for-sothe both, Ne hadde y-come Ayax. **1515** *Scottish Field* 409 in *Percy's Folio MS.* I. 232 The King of his kindnesse.. saith, 'I will sing him a sowle knell with the sound of my gunnes'. **1575** GASCOIGNE *Posies* Ep. Yng. Gent., Wks. 1907 I. 11 That the Soulknill of M. Edwards was also written in extremitie of sicknesse.

So † **soul-knoll.** *Obs.*⁻¹

c **1500** *Ripon Ch. Acts* (Surtees) 377 The sawll knoll, vj *d.*

soulless ('səʊllɪs), *a.* [f. SOUL *sb.* + -LESS. Cf. OE. *sáwol-*, *sáwel-*, *sáwlléas*, MDu. *sielloos* (Du. *zielloos*), MHG. *sêl(e)lôs* (G. *seellos*, *seelenlos*), Sw. *själlös*.]

1. Having no soul; from whom or which the soul has departed. Also *fig.*

1553 *Short Catech.* in *Lit. & Doc. Edw. VI* (1844) 523 That this godly knowledge decay not in thee, nor lie soulless and dead, as it were, in a tomb. **1599** SANDYS *Europæ Spec.* (1632) 225 In sume their holinesse is the very outwerd work it selfe, being a brainlesse head and a soule-lesse body. **1652** BP. HALL *Height of Eloquence* p. xxv, Like soulelesse carkasses they fall down dead. **1678** CUDWORTH *Intell. Syst.* 215 He resolved that the Soul of the World.. was not made by God.. out of any thing Inanimate and Soulless Preexisting. *c* **1801** C. K. SHARPE in Allardyce *Corr.*, etc. (1888) I. 25 Sage Paine,.. Eager to prove.. Mankind deluded fools and soulless beasts. **1860** PUSEY *Min. Proph.* 137 Apollinarians.. held the Godhead to have been united to a soulless, and so a brute, nature. **1897** MARY KINGSLEY *W. Africa* 178, I verily believe that if I were left alone long enough with such a scene as this.. I should be found soulless and dead.

transf. **1841** BREWSTER *Mart. Sci.* ii. (1856) 24 A vast unblest desert senseless, voiceless and soulless. **1876** 'OUIDA' *Winter City* vi, Monotonous parapets of cast-iron, the heaviest, most soulless thing that is manufactured.

2. Of persons: Destitute of or wanting in the noble qualities of the soul; lacking spirit, courage, or elevation of mind or feeling.

1587 MONTGOMERIE *Sonn.* xxiv. 3 A saulles suinger, seuintie tymes mensuorne. **1594** PEELE *Battle of Alcazar* II. iii, He on whose glorie all thy ioy should stay, Is souleless, glorylesse, and desperate. **1613** MARSTON *Insat. C'tess* IV. Wks. 1856 III. 163 That man is soulelesse that ne'er sinnes on earth. **1702** DE FOE *Mock Mourners* 13 Trembling, and Soul-less half the Nation stood. **1728** RAMSAY *Last Sp. Miser* xvi, They ca'd me slave to usury.. And sauleless wretch. **1812** CRABBE *Tales* vi. 263 Nor shall a formal, rigid, soul-less boy My manners alter. **1847** C. BRONTË *J. Eyre* xxiii, Do you think, because I am poor,.. I am soulless and heartless? **1856** HAWTHORNE *Eng. Note-bks.* (1879) I. 25 They did not appear wicked,.. but only soulless.

absol. **1844** MRS. BROWNING *Drama of Exile* 1271 Sinning against the province of the Soul To rule the soulless.

b. Of the eyes: Lacking animation or expression; dull.

1835 BROWNING *Paracelsus* III. Poems (1905) 458 Having lain long with blank and soulless eyes, He sat up suddenly.

3. Of things, qualities, etc.: Characterized by a lack of animation, ardour, or vivacity; dull, insipid, uninteresting.

1632 I. M. S. in *Shaks. Sec. Folio*, What story coldly tells, ..and picture without braine Senseless and soullesse showes. *a* **1652** J. SMITH *Sel. Disc.* vii. 327 It was nothing else but a soulless and lifeless form of external performances. **1656** W. MOUNTAGUE *Accompl. Woman* 119 Modesty is a powerfull charme, without it beauty is soul-lesse. **1833** HT. MARTINEAU *Charmed Sea* iii. 37, I see things as they are, bleak and bare, and soulless. **1864** PUSEY *Lect. Daniel* (1876) 555 Content with its outward soulless round of observances. **1870** MOZLEY *Univ. Serm.* iii. (1877) 49 There is nothing which so little interests us as soulless earnestness, ardour without faith.

b. Of writings, art, etc.: Devoid of inspiration or feeling.

1856 SMYTH *Roman Family Coins* Introd. p. xxix, Too many of our best recent specimens of art are soulless. **1860** PUSEY *Min. Proph.* 204 Giddy, thoughtless, heartless, soulless versifying. **1887** *St. James's Gaz.* 10 Feb. 7/1 Students find its literature, and above all its poetry, soulless and uninspired.

Hence '**soullessly** *adv.*, '**soullessness.**

1870 *Contemp. Rev.* XIII. 12 A reference to the proverbial soullessness of boards. **1871** TYLOR *Prim. Cult.* II. 325 Those to whom religion means.. religious feeling, may say ..that I have written soullessly of the soul. **1891** *Athenæum* 7 Nov. 614/1 Its characters exhibit.. peculiar soullessness.

soul-like, *a.* and *adv.* [f. SOUL *sb.* + -LIKE.]

A. *adj.* Like or resembling a soul or that of a soul; suggestive of a or the soul.

1654 WHITLOCK *Zootomia* 259, I look not for any Soule-like Composure, among the works of men. **1838** MARG. FULLER *Wom. 19th C.* (1862) 351 The pine-trees sigh with their soul-like sounds for June. **1845** BAILEY *Festus* (ed. 2) 219 The soul-like moon, In passive beauty and receptive light. **1899** A. E. GARVIE *Ritschlian Theol.* ii. 43 He considers himself warranted in making the metaphysical inference.. that things must be soul-like beings.

B. *adv.* After or in the manner of a soul.

1845 BAILEY *Festus* (ed. 2) 223 The temple yet to be rebuilt in Zion.. shall soul-like yet re-rise from ruin.

soul-mass. Now *Hist.* or *dial.* Also 5-6 *Sc.* **sawle mess, saul(e) mes(se,** etc., 6 *north.* **sall messe, sawmos,** 9 **sawmas, saumas,** etc.; 5 **sowlemas(se,** 8 **solmus,** 9 **soulmas(s.** [f. SOUL *sb.* + MASS *sb.*¹ Cf. MDu. *siel-*, *zielmisse* (Du. *zielmis*), MLG. *sêlemisse*, MHG. *sêl(e)messe* (G. *seel-*, *seelenmesse*), ON. *sálumessa*, Sw. *själamessa*, Da. *sjælemesse*.]

1. A mass for the soul of a dead person.

In early use *Sc.* and *north.*

1488 *Acc. Ld. High Treas. Scot.* I. 89 To the King to offir at the Qwenis sawle mess. **1496** *Ibid.* 278 To the Kingis offerand at the Kingis saulmes. **1537** *Registr. Aberdon.* (Maitland) I. 414 To þe viccaris of þe queir.. ȝeirlie in þe day of his decese for derege and sawllmess. *a* **1578** LINDESAY (Pitscottie) *Chron. Scot.* (S.T.S.) I. 369 All thair great blythnes and ioy of hir comming.. war all turnit in saul messes and deriegies. **1675** BROOKS *Gold. Key* Wks. 1867 V. 216 The papists.. who.. for the obtaining of pardon, &c., have appointed penances and pilgrimages, and self-scourgings and soul-masses. **1681** BURNET *Hist. Ref.* II. 25 The use and lawfulness of soul-masses and obits. **1828** SCOTT *F.M. Perth* xxx, Bid the grey monk his soul mass mutter. **1853** ROCK *Ch. of Fathers* IV. xii. 176 The mass for the dead or soul-mass, as our fathers called it, had ritual peculiarities.

2. *Soul-mass Day*, All Souls' Day, 2 Nov. Also *ellipt.* Now *dial.*

c **1450** *Mirk's Festial* 269 þe morow aftyr All-halowday ys euermor Sowlemasse-day. **1461** *Paston Lett.* II. 64 Wretyn in hast, on Sowlemas Daye. **1533** *Test. Ebor.* (Surtees) V. 262 To poor people of All-halowe day and Sawmos day. **1876** ROBINSON *Mid-Yks. Gloss.*, *Saumas*,.. the feast of All Souls, November 2.

3. *attrib.* In a number of dial. uses, as **Soul-mass cake, -loaf** (see quots.); **Soul-mass hiring,** a hiring-fair held on or about All Souls' Day.

1661 BLOUNT *Glossogr.* (ed. 2), *Soul-masse-Cakes*, are certain oaten cakes, which some of the wealthier sort of persons in Lancashire [**1674** *adds* Herefordshire, &c.] use still to give the poor on All-Souls day. *a* **1800** PEGGE *Suppl. Grose, Solmus-loaf*, bread given away on All Souls day. North. **1817** G. YOUNG *Hist. Whitby* II. 882 A lady in Whitby has a soul mass loaf about 100 years old. **1837** THORNBER *Hist. Blackpool* 92 The beggar at the door craving an awmas, or saumas cake, (soulmass cake). **1884** *North Star* 7 Nov., Ripon Hirings. The Soulmas hirings were held yesterday.

Hence † '**soul-,massing** *vbl. sb.*, the action or practice of saying masses for the dead. *Obs.*⁻¹

c **1555** ? BRADFORD *Carrying Christ's Cross* vii. 90 So doeth it cast down al their soule massing and foolish foundacions for such, as be dead.

soul-priest: see SOUL *sb.* 26.

soulsage, obs. form of SAUSAGE *sb.*

'**soul-saving,** *ppl. a.* [f. SOUL *sb.* 23.] That saves the soul.

1609 J. DAVIES (Heref.) *Holy Rood* Wks. (Grosart) I. 7/1 This kinde, most kinde, Soule-sauing Emperick—His owne blood broacheth so your Soules to saue. **1642-4** VICARS *God in Mount* (1844) 45 Preaching on deep points of soul-saving grace. **1755** WESLEY *Wks.* (1872) XIII. 209 Soul-damning clergymen lay me under more difficulties than soul-saving laymen! **1833** H. BLUNT *Lect. Hist. St. Paul* II. 34 A real soul-saving conversion. **1885** *Minutes of Wesleyan Conf.* 20 His ministry was marked.. by evangelical fervour and soul-saving power.

Hence † **soul-savingness.** *Obs.*⁻¹

1673 [R. LEIGH] *Transp. Reh.* 134, I shall only point at some of the nesses.. of the peoples coinage:.. soul-savingness.

soul-scot. *Hist.* Forms: 7 **sawl-scot,** 7-9 **soul-scot;** also 9 **soul-scat.** [f. SOUL *sb.* + SCOT *sb.*², after OE. *sáwlsceat* (see SCAT *sb.*¹) or *sáwul(ȝe)sceot.*] A due paid on behalf of a deceased person to the church of the parish to which he belonged; a mortuary.

[**1664** *Spelman's Gloss.* 501/1 *Saulscot*,.. Animæ symbolum.] **1670** BLOUNT *Glossogr.* (ed. 3), *Soul-scot* (Sax.), money paid to the parish Priest at the opening the grave, for the good and behoof of the deceased's Soul. **1766** BLACKSTONE *Comm.* II. xxviii. 425 The second best chattel was reserved to the church as a mortuary:.. And therefore in the laws of king Canute this mortuary is called soul-scot.. or *symbolum animae.* **1819** SCOTT *Ivanhoe* xlii, For this service a splendid *soul-scat* was paid to the convent of Saint Edmund's by the mother of the deceased. **1874** STUBBS *Const. Hist.* I. viii. 229 The clergy received.. church-scot; and.. soul-scot or mortuary-dues. **1892** J. C. BLOMFIELD *Hist. Heyford* 84 Mortuaries, 'soul-scot' or 'corse-presents', which are a kind of ecclesiastical heriot.

'**soul-search,** *v.* [Back-formation f. SOUL-SEARCHING *ppl. a.*] **a.** *trans.* To examine penetratingly and thoroughly; to make a soul-searching analysis of. *nonce-use.* **b.** *intr.* To engage in examination of one's thoughts, to reflect deeply.

1966 *Economist* 29 Jan. 421/2 Trotsky writing in exile, Mr Alistair Cooke soul-searching the trial of Mr Alger Hiss, Adlai Stevenson eulogising Robert Frost. **1968** A. MARIN *Clash of Distant Thunder* (1969) xv. 114 When we tried Eichmann people used to argue and discuss and soul-search. We Jews are very good at that. **1972** *Daily Tel.* 30 Aug. 11/4 Last week there was the heart-rending case of a man in public life soul-searching about the reasons his son took to drugs.

Also as *sb.*, an act of soul-searching; hence '**soul-searched** *ppl. a.*

1966 *Guardian* 8 July 3/5 (*heading*) Soul-search by the Liberals. **1970** E. M. BRECHER *Sex Researchers* ix. 255 More prolonged eye-contacts, or 'soul-searches'. **1978** *Times* 9 Oct. 18/4 The most honest and soul-searched response of the conclave.

'**soul-searching,** *ppl. a.* [f. SOUL *sb.* 23.] That searches, examines vigorously or severely, penetrates, etc., the soul. Also in extended and trivial use.

1612 J. DAVIES (Heref.) *Muse's Sacrifice* Wks. (Grosart) II. 12/1 Soule-searching Lord, and sole selfe-searching God. **1657** J. WATTS *Vind. of Ch. Eng.* 210 Discreet Soul-searching and examining discourses. **1663** *Aron-bimn.* 66 This Kingdom.. hath need of such a faithful, soul-searching Ministry as this is. **1807** J. BARLOW *Columb.* IV. 489 Soul-searching Freedom! here assume thy stand. *a* **1831** POE *To the River* ii. Poet. Wks. (1853) 134 The beam Of her soul-searching eyes. **1886** W. J. TUCKER *E. Europe* 147 His large dark hazel eyes had a penetrating, soul-searching look in them. **1959** *Economist* 17 Jan. 203/1 After a 'soul-searching' parliamentary debate, an openly penitent Belgian government has announced its plan for dealing with the suddenly agitated Congo. **1960** *News Chron.* 13 Oct. 3/2 The deeply soul-searching: 'What do you think of modern jazz?'

Hence '**soul-searchingly** *adv.*

1938 PARTRIDGE *World of Words* ix. 309 The following sextette, ultimately selected from a much longer list of words that had been soul-searchingly gathered for your delectation.

'**soul-searching,** *vbl. sb.* [f. prec.] Examination of one's soul or conscience, deep reflection; penetrating consideration of a state of affairs.

1948 'E. CRISPIN' *Buried for Pleasure* xvii. 145 The announcement.. is not made without a good deal of preliminary soul-searching. **1953** *Time* 6 July 6/3, I would suggest some honest soul-searching for these unrealistic fathers, and orchids to Father Gerald Murphy and the increasing number of his prototypes among the younger Jesuits. **1974** *Country Life* 18 Apr. 926/2 What has been the subject of.. agitated soul-searching is whether rector and churchwardens.. had any right whatsoever to sell it. **1978** P. G. WINSLOW *Coppergold* 39 It's causing a bit of soul-searching at the Yard.

soul-shot. *Hist.* Also 9 **sawlshot.** [f. SOUL *sb.* + SHOT *sb.*] = SOUL-SCOT.

1647 N. BACON *Disc. Govt. Eng.* I. xi. (1739) 20 Next comes a Fee at the death of the party, which was commonly called Soul-shot, and paid (before the dead body was buried) unto that Church where the dead party's dwelling was. **1726** AYLIFFE *Parergon* 379 There was a Duty paid at Funerals by our Saxon Ancestors, which was call'd the Saxon Soul-shot. **1838** SOAMES *Anglo-Sax. Ch.* (ed. 2) 269 One of their objects also was to provide soul-shot on the death of every member. **1844** LINGARD *Anglo-Sax. Ch.* (1858) II. 46 The body was deposited in the grave; the sawlshot paid. **1896** A. AUSTIN *England's Darling* II. 52 Whoever falls Fighting for England, soul-shot sure shall be.

soul-sick, *a.* [f. SOUL *sb.* 25.]

1. Of persons: **a.** Suffering from spiritual indisposition or depression.

1598 SYLVESTER *Du Bartas* II. i. III. *Furies* 759 Soule-sick Patients care not to be heal'd. **1601** DENT *Pathw. Heaven* (1831) 27 No doubt.. they be shrewd signs that a man is extremely soul-sick and in a very dangerous case. **1641** L. F. *Index Ch. Codex* (title-p.), A speedy Remedy and Speciall Spirituall Receipt for a Soul-Sicke Sainte and Sonne. **1903** *Dublin Rev.* July 185 The masses made blind and soul-sick by materialism and agnosticism.

absol. **1623** H. SYDENHAM *Serm. Sol. Occ.* (1637) 25 To the weake and soule-sicke, the still voice.

b. Sick at heart; deeply dejected or depressed.

1609 MARKHAM *Famous Wh.* (1868) 32 Soule-sick to see my goods and riches waste. **1611** BEAUM. & FL. *Maid's Trag.* IV. i, I am soul-sick.. Till I have got your pardon.

2. Characterized by dejection of spirit.

1880 SWINBURNE *Songs of Spring-t., Thalassius* 30 Death spirit-stricken of soul-sick days. **1899** *Westm. Gaz.* 27 June 3 A soul-sick longing comes over us for the silent heather hill.

So **soul-sickness.**

1662 in *Verney Mem.* (1907) II. 187 Truly souch thowts cause soul-sickness. **1865** SWINBURNE *Chastelard* V. ii. 191, I would have given you mine own blood to drink If that could heal you of your soul-sickness. **1876** GEO. ELIOT *Dan. Der.* viii, This is the sort of faith we live by in our soul-sicknesses.

soul-sickening, *ppl. a.* [f. SOUL *sb.* 23.] Extremely depressing or dejecting.

1825 J. WILSON *Poems* ii. 11 One soul-sickening moment of despair. **1854** GREENWOOD *Haps & Mishaps* 89 All was squalor and tatters, soul-sickening and disgusting. **1891** KIPLING *City Dreadf. Nt.* 5 For diffused, soul-sickening expansiveness, the reek of Calcutta beats both Benares and Peshawur.

soul-silver: see SOUL *sb.* 26 and SOWL *sb.*

soul-sleeper: see SOUL *sb.* 26.

soulter, soultring, soultry, obs. ff. SULTER *v.*, SULTERING *ppl. a.*, SULTRY *a.*

‖**soulx, soulz.** *Obs.* Also 7 soulxe. [OF. *soulx, soulz*, pl. of *soul, sol* SOL *sb.*[3]: see also SOUSE *sb.*[4]] A sou. Also as pl.

1542 RECORDE *Gr. Artes* (1575) 199 Firste of Fraunce:.. their soulx (commonly called sowses) go 9 to our shilling. **1613** TAPP *Pathw. Knowl.* 51 The question is how many Soulxes his 234 pounds comes to, euerie 5 Soulxe French valewing 6 pence sterling. *a* **1625** FLETCHER *Bloody Brother* I. i, If The debtor may be won for a French Crown, To pay a Soulz. **1662** PETTY *Taxes* 77 Base money is there-fore such as Dutch shillings, stivers, French soulz.

'souly, *a.* Also 5 sawly. [f. SOUL *sb.* + -Y[1].]

1. †**a.** Of or pertaining to the soul. *Obs.*

c **1400** tr. *Secreta Secret., Gov. Lordsh.* 96 If þe sawle be þanne perfyt and fulfillyd byfore his departynge fro þe body, it shall þanne be ressayued of all sawly vertu. **1633** W. STRUTHER *True Happines* 132 The sonnes of God, in whom this souly love burneth. **1727** ASGILL *Metam. of Man* I. v. 71 That Souly Part of him..which is thought to survive the Body, and to take its Flight to Heaven.

b. = SOULFUL *a.* 1. *colloq. rare.*

1911 D. H. LAWRENCE *White Peacock* vii. 131 I'm not one of your souly sort.

†**2.** = PSYCHICAL *a.* 2. (Cf. SOULISH *a.* 1.). *Obs.*

1639 H. AINSWORTH *Annot. Pentateuch* 10 This animalitie, or souly state, shall be changed into spirituality. As for the terme of this our souly or naturall life, it dureth while our breath is in us. **1660** NEWTON *Comm. John* xvii. (Nichol, 1867) 371 The animal man, the souly man.. perceives not these things.

†**soum**, *sb.*[1] *Sc. Obs.* In 5 sowme, 5-6 sowm, 6 soume. [a. OF. *soume*, var. of *some, somme*: see SEAM *sb.*[2] and cf. SOME *sb.*[3]] A horse-load; a pack. Also *attrib.* in *soum saddle.*

c **1470** HENRY *Wallace* IV. 24 Wallace..Our tuk the child Schyr Ranaldis sowme couth leid. **1497** *Acc. Ld. High Treas. Scot.* I. 345 For ane hors to bere the Kingis sowme. **1505** *Ibid.* III. 160 For floting of the pannell of the sowm sadill. **1512** *Ibid.* IV. 308 Stoppein, taggein, and mending of ane soume sadill. *c* **1575** *Balfour's Practicks* (1754) 87 Ane horse sowme of the said fish, or dry hering.

soum (sum), *sb.*[2] *Sc.* Now chiefly *Hist.* Forms: 6, 8-9 soume, 6-8 sowm(e; 7 summe, 8 soom, 8- soum. [app. the same as *soum* SUM *sb.* Hence Gael. *suim* in sense 2.]

1. The amount of pasturage which will support one cow or a proportional number of sheep or other stock.

1500 *Reg. Mag. Sig. Scot.* 542/1 Concessit..pratum vulgariter nuncupatum le Grymys Medow, cum communi pastura unius equi et 4 de le sowmoys [*sic*] in dicta villa. **1524** *Ibid.* 222/2 Vendiderunt 2 acras terrarum cum tofta et crofta,..cum 6 le sowmys in pastura. **1606** *Sc. Acts, Jas. VI* (1816) IV. 285/2 Extending in the haill to sextene sowmes for the said four akeris. *c* **1730** BURT *Lett. N. Scotl.* (1818) II. 57 If the tenant is to hire his grazing in the hills he takes it by soumes. **1754** ERSKINE *Princ. Sc. Law* (1809) 57 A glebe, which comprehends four acres of arable land, or sixteen sowms of pasture ground. **1799** J. ROBERTSON *Agric. Perth* 72 Moors and sheep-walks are more frequently rented by the soum, than by the acre.

2. The number of sheep or cattle that can be maintained on a certain amount of pasture. ***a soum of sheep***, a number varying in different places from four to ten.

1508 in Pitcairn *Crim. Trials* I. 58* Of shutting up her 'gudis'—viz. sixty-five 'soumes' furth of her said third part. **1594** *Reg. Mag. Sig. Scot.* 34 *note*, Pasturage of 20 sowmes yeild-guidis, profits of each sowm 20s. **1610** *Ibid.* 202/2 Togidder with the pasture of sax sowmes of nolt..upoun the ground of my landis of Grenelaw. **1700** *Minutes Baron Crt. Stitchill* (S.H.S.) 146 Wher any possessed but one Soum in the Mayns that Soum shall absolutely be a Kow or Oxe and not a sheip. *a* **1724** in *Ramsay's Tea-t. Misc.* (1729) 17 A Kilnfu' of Corn I'll gi'e to thee, Three Soums of Sheep, twa good Milk Ky. **1794** *Statist. Acc. Scotl.* XII. 396 A privilege of pasturage for 72 soums of sheep upon the common, 5 sheep being reckoned to a soum. **1884** *Rep. Crofters' Commission* App. A. 468 In Lews and Harris..a man is entitled to send so many soums to the grazings of his townland.

b. In the phr. ***soum's*** (or ***soums'***) ***grass.***

1574 *Reg. Mag. Sig. Scot.* V. 12/1 Cum pastura 6 animalium lie sex sowmes gers. **1582** *Cal. Laing Charters* (1899) 259 The saidis millaris multraris hes ane certaine land of ws for his soumis girse. **1610** *Reg. Mag. Sig. Scot.* 114/1 Cum pasturagio unius summe lie sowmes-gras. **1621** *Sc. Acts, Jas. VI* (1816) IV. 612/2 Act declairing summes Grasse..to be teyndfrie. **1793** *Statist. Acc. Scotl.* VIII. 104 The glebe..is supposed to be legal as to extent, with 4 soums grass, in common with the cattle of the farm.

soum (sum), *v. Sc. Law.* Also 7-8 sowm. [f. prec.] *trans.* To estimate the amount of (pasture) in terms of the 'soums' it can support.

1679 STAIR *Decisions* 23 Jan. (Dunlop) II. 679 Where divers heritors have a common pasturage in one commontie, no part whereof is ever plowed, the said common pasturage may be Soumed and Roumed. **1793** *Statist. Acc. Scot.* VI. 93 Where there are several small tenants upon one farm, the farm is (what they call) soumed. **1838** W. BELL *Dict. Law Scot.* 932 Strictly speaking, to *sowm* the common, is to ascertain the several *sowms* it may hold; and to *rowm* it, is to portion it out amongst the dominant proprietors.

Hence **'souming** *vbl. sb.*

Chiefly in the phr. *souming and rouming*: see ROOM *v.*[2] 1 b. Also *concr.*, the amount of stock which one person may send to a common pasture.

1681 STAIR *Instit.* II. vii. §14 (1693) 289 It is accustomed in some places, to regulat common Pasturage by Souming and Rouming, which is the determining of the several Soums it may hold by particular Proportion of every Room of the Dominant Tenement. **1754** ERSKINE *Princ. Sc. Law* (1809) 221 Which proportions may be fixed by an action of souming and rouming. **1799** J. ROBERTSON *Agric. Perth* 524 The souming of cattle is not so much attended to as it ought to be. *a* **1856** OUTRAM *Lyrics* (1874) 43 She sune made her fu' purse a toom ane, By raising a Process o' Soumin' an' Roumin'. **1884** *Spectator* 17 May 642 The constable and another man..see that only the proper souming has been brought to the grazing. **1889** *Scott. Leader* 17 May 5 His clients had sufficient stock, according to their present souming, to stock the land applied for.

soum(e, obs. ff. SUM *sb.* and *v.*; Sc. var. SWIM.

Soumak ('su:mæk). Also **Soumac, Sumac**, etc. [Orig. uncertain, perh. a corruption of the Azerbaijan place-name *Shemakha.*] A type of rug or carpet made in the neighbourhood of Shemakha in Azerbaijan, distinguished by a flat, napless surface and loose threads at the back. Freq. *attrib.* Cf. KASHMIR 2.

1904, etc. [see KASHMIR 2]. **1932** D. C. MINTER *Mod. Needlecraft* 228/2 *Knitting Stitch*..sometimes called Sumac or Kelim Stitch..is..a long diagonal stitch. It gives a surface effect like those of various traditional woven rugs. **1959** *Chambers's Encycl.* III. 135/2 There are two main varieties of smooth-faced carpets: Kilim, woven like tapestry, and Soumak, where the pattern weft passes over four and under two warp threads. **1960** H. HAYWARD *Antique Coll.* 261/1 *Soumac rugs*, Caucasian rugs in a tapestry weave with conventional designs. **1974** *Times* 9 Mar. 23/5 Specialists in Kelims, Soumaks and Tribal Rugs.

sou markee (su: mɑ:'ki:). Also **sou marquee, sumarkee**, etc. [ad. Fr. *sou marqué*, lit. 'marked sou'.] A small French coin of the eighteenth century issued for the colonies and circulating esp. in the West Indies and North America. Hence *loosely*, something of little value.

1665-7 J. LAUDER *Jrnls.* in *Publ. Scottish Hist. Soc.* (1900) XXXVI. 92 On the place wheir they make it its sold for a sous marky la livre. **1826** *Massachusetts Spy* 5 July (Th.), Who the d——l would give a sumarkee to read the newspapers after breakfast? **1896** H. G. PARKER *Pomp of Lavilettes* 54 I'll bet he's got nothing more than what he went away with, and that wasn't a sou markee! **1903** A. H. LEWIS *Boss* 181, I don't pony for a sou markee. **1936** J. A. MCKENNA *Black Range Tales* 268 Marshall drifted from one settlement to another, and he likewise died without a sou marquee. **1952** R. M. HAMILTON *Canad. Quotations* 138/2 It's not worth a sou marquee. Phrase common in the Maritime provinces meaning, of trifling value; a reference to French Guiana sous which, counterstamped by other West Indian colonies, were sometimes carried north to Canada. **1977** F. LEIBER *Swords & Ice Magic* 80 'By the beats of Titchubi,' the former breathed, 'this is no *sou marque*, black dog no *chien noir.*'

†**soumer.** *Obs. rare.* [var. of SOMER. Cf. SOUM *sb.*[1]] A sumpter-horse.

c **1470** HENRY *Wallace* IV. 53 Thar tyryt sowmir so left thai in to playne.

soun, obs. form of SON, SOON, SOUND, SUN.

sound (saʊnd), *sb.*[1] Forms: α. 1, 3-4 sund (4-5 sonde), 5-6 sownd(e, sounde, 4- sound. β. 5, 7 sown, 6-7 sowne, 8 *Sc.* soun. [Partly OE. *sund* swimming, water, sea, and partly a. ON. *sund* swimming, strait (Norw. *sund* swimming, swim-bladder, strait, ferry; Sw. and Da. *sund* strait; G. *sund* is a late adoption). The stem *sunda-* represents an early *sumda-*, pre-Teutonic *swm-tó-*, f. the stem of SWIM *v.*]

I. †**1.** The action or power of swimming. *Obs.*

Beowulf 507 Eart þu se Beowulf, se þe wið Brecan wunne, on sidne sæ ymb sund flite. *c* **893** K. ÆLFRED *Oros.* II. iv. 72 þa ʒebeotode an his ðeʒna þæt he mid sunde þa ea oferfaran wolde. *c* **1000** ÆLFRIC *Hom.* (Th.) I. 16 Of wætere he ʒesceop fixas and fuʒelas, and sealde ðam fixum sund, and ðam fuʒelum fliht. *c* **1205** LAY. 21326 He..bi-haldeð hu ligeð i þan stræme stelene fisces, mid sweorde bi-georede, heore sund is awemmed. *a* **1300** *Cursor M.* 621 Fiss on sund, and fouxl on flight. *Ibid.* 1841 þat was na creatur in liue.. Bot it war fisse þat flett on sund.

2. The swimming bladder of certain fish, esp. of cod or sturgeon.

So Norw. *sund*, also *sundmage* (Icel. *sundmagi*), f. *mage* stomach (maw).

α. **1323-4** *Ely Sacr. Rolls* II. 43 In sound. empt. pro pictore, 4*d.* **1341-2** *Ibid.* 117 In..soundes pisc., 4½*d.* **14..** in *Rel. Ant.* I. 163 For to make boke-glewe—Take the sowndys of stok-fysch. *c* **1440** *Promp. Parv.* 466 Sounde, of a fysche.., *ventigina.* **1530** PALSGR. 273/1 Sounde of a fysshe, *cannon.* **1661** PEPYS *Diary* 16 Oct., This day dined..upon a fin of ling and some sounds. **1672** JOSSELYN *New Eng. Rarities* 32 The Sturgeon, of whose Sounds are made Isinglass. **1761** FRANKLIN in *J. Adams's Wks.* (1850) II. 82 *note*, This fish-glue is nothing more than the sounds of cod or other fish, extended and dried in the sun. **1769** MRS. RAFFALD *Eng. Housekpr.* (1778) 23 To dress Cod Sounds. Steep your sounds as you do the salt cod. **1822-7** GOOD *Study Med.* (1829) V. 443 All fishes, possessing a sound or air-bladder, are equally capable of supplying this organ with air. **1859** *Habits of Gd. Society* v. 223 Cod is cut crossways, and a small piece of the sound sent with each helping. **1882** *Knowledge* No. 10. 195 In a herring..the 'sound' may be seen as a silvery, glistening bag, which is removable along with the other organs of the fish when it is 'gutted'.

β. *c* **1475** *Promp. Parv.* 466 (MS. K.), Sown. **1655** MOUFET & BENNET *Health's Improv.* xviii. 148 Cods..have also a thick and gluish substance at the end of their stomach called a sowne. **1701** *Househ.-bk. of Lady G. Baillie* (S.H.S.) Introd. p. xxxix, Two barrils of souns and gullits.

†**3.** *Hunting.* A spring or pool of water. *Obs.*

1581 MARBECK *Bk. of Notes* 474 Our Hunters (I trowe) tearme it not to call it the water Springs, but they call it the Sound. The Stagge saie they, got him to the Sound.

II. 4. A relatively narrow channel or stretch of water, esp. one between the mainland and an island, or connecting two large bodies of water; a strait. Also, an inlet of the sea.

The first quot. may represent the OE. *sund* 'sea, water', but the later use appears to be clearly of Scand. origin. Some writers, associating the word with SOUND *v.*[2], have attempted to limit the application to channels capable of being easily sounded.

a **1300** *K. Horn* 628 (Harl. MS.), Y fond a ship rowen in þe sound byflowen [*v.r.* Mid watere al by flowe]. **1513** DOUGLAS *Æneid* I. iv. 15 In ane braid sownd sovir frome al wyndis blawis, Flowis the schoir deip. *c* **1572** GASCOIGNE *Fruites Warre* cvii, The haste so hoate that (eare they sinke the sowne) They came on ground. **1595** *Drake's Voy.* (Hakl. Soc.) 9 We passed a sounde, though, by our mariners, never passed by fleet afore. **1612** DRAYTON *Poly-olb.* i. 164 Her haven angled so about her harb'rous sound, That in her quiet Bay a hundred ships may ride. **1667** MILTON *P.L.* VII. 399 Forthwith the Sounds and Seas, each Creek & Bay With Frie innumerable swarme. **1725** POPE *Odyss.* I. 93 The bright increase Of Phorcys, dreaded in the sounds and seas. **1774** PENNANT *Tour Scotl. in 1772*, 215 Several little isles, divided by narrow and dangerous sounds. **1820** SCORESBY *Acc. Arctic Reg.* I. 88 Steering then along shore, they opened another large sound. **1847** H. MILLER *First Impr. Eng.* xi. (1857) 176 This region of central England was once a broad ocean sound..: there rose land on both sides of it. **1894** J. T. FOWLER *Adamnan* Introd. 66 [Iona] is separated from the Ross of Mull by a sound or strait about a mile across.

transf. **1721** SWIFT *South Sea* Wks. 1755 III. II. 136 There is a gulph where thousands fell; A narrow sound, though deep as hell.

b. In the names of particular straits or inlets.

14.. *Sailing Directions* (Hakl. Soc.) 18 The sow[n]de of blaskay. *Ibid.* 19 The sounde of Ranseynes. *c* **1595** CAPT. WYATT *Dudley's Voy.* (Hakl. Soc.) 5 Wee..safelie arived in the Sownde of Plimworth on the xix th day. **1600** HOLLAND *Livy* XXII. 438 Certaine ships..were..taken about the sound or haven of Cossa. **1670** J. SMITH *Eng. Improv. Reviv'd* VI. 253 The best and chiefest Sound in Shotland is Brace-sound or Broad-sound. **1814** SCOTT *Lord of Isles* I. vii, To where a turret's airy head..O'erlook'd, dark Mull! thy mighty Sound. **1865** *Reader* 4 Feb. 125/3 Near the entrance of Smith's Sound. **1907** *Trans. Devon Assoc.* 52 The Hamoaze and Plymouth Sound.

c. ***the Sound***, the strait between Denmark and Sweden which connects the Cattegat with the Baltic Sea. Also *attrib.*

1633 SIR J. BURROUGHS *Sov. Brit. Seas* (1651) 83 The King of Denmarke at his Wardhouse in the Sound. *a* **1646** J. GREGORY *Posthuma, Maps & Charts* (1650) 328 It is called by the Danish Sond or Sund: by us the Sound. **1846** A. YOUNG *Naut. Dict.* 289 The strait called the Sound, which connects the North Sea with the Baltic. *Ibid.*, *Sound-dues*, a toll or tribute levied by the King of Denmark on all merchant vessels passing the strait called the Sound. **1852** tr. *Ida Pfeiffer's Journ. Iceland* 40 The blue glistening Sound stretching out of sight between the coasts of Denmark and Sweden.

†**sound**, *sb.*[2] *Obs.* Forms: 3 sunde, 4-5 sound(e, 5 sonde. [f. *sund* SOUND *a.* Cf. MLG. *sunt* (also *gesunt*, G. *gesund*), MSw. *sund.*] Health or soundness; safety or security. In prep. phr. ***in*** or ***on, mid*** or ***with sound.***

c **1205** LAY. 4967 He ferde mid sunde in to þisse londe. *Ibid.* 19703 Lauerd, beo þu on sunde. *c* **1325** *Lai le Freine* 51 Is his leuedi deliuerd with sounde? **13..** *Gaw. & Gr. Knt.* 2489 þus he commes to þe court, knyȝt al in sounde. *c* **1400** *Destr. Troy* 546 [To] put you in plite your purpos to wyn, In sound for to saile home & your sute all.

sound (saʊnd), *sb.*[3] Forms: α. 4 sun(e, 4-5 son(e, 4-5, 6 *Sc.* sovne, 4-6 soun(e, sownn(e, 5-6 sown(e, 6 *Sc.* sounn. β. 5-6 sownd(e, 6 sounde, 5- sound. [a. AF. *soun*, OF. *son* (= Prov. *son, so*, Sp. *son*, Pg. *som*, It. *suono*):—L. *sonum*, acc. of *sonus* sound. Cf. OE. *són*, ON. *sónn*, MDu. *son, soen*, from Latin or early OF.

The form with excrescent *-d* finally established itself in the 16th cent., but is condemned by Stanyhurst as late as 1582 (*Æneid* To Reader, p. 11).]

1. a. The sensation produced in the organs of hearing when the surrounding air is set in vibration in such a way as to affect these; also, that which is or may be heard; the external object of audition, or the property of bodies by which this is produced. Hence also, pressure waves that differ from audible sound only in being of a lower or a higher frequency. Cf. INFRASOUND, ULTRASOUND.

α. **a 1300–1400** *Cursor M.* 17288 + 101 When þat our lord vp-rose þe erthe quoke & made sown. **a 1330** *Roland & V.* 708 As þe harp has þre þinges, Wode & soun & strenges. **c 1384** CHAUCER *H. Fame* 765 (Fairf.), Sovne ys noght but eyre ybroken. **c 1400** *Rom. Rose* 4241 His instrumentis wolde he dight, For to blowe and make sowne. **c 1449** PECOCK *Repr.* II. viii. 187 That is to seie, that speche and soun be mad in the ymage bi an aungel of God. **1513** DOUGLAS *Æneid* I. ii. 4 Ane brudy land of furious stormy sownn.

β. **c 1440** *Promp. Parv.* 466/1 Sownde, or dyne, *sonitus, sonus.* **c 1450** in Aungier *Syon* (1840) 379 Whan they haue any nottes..they schal open them softly..and beware of sownde. **1530** PALSGR. 273/1 Sounde, noyse, *son.* **1590** SPENSER *F.Q.* I. viii. 11 He loudly brayd with beastly yelling sound. **1604** E. G[RIMSTONE] *D'Acosta's Hist. Indies* IV. v. 216 It [silver] passeth golde in brightnesse, beauty and sound, the which is cleere, and agreeable. **1697** DRYDEN *Virg. Georg.* III. 522 Linnets fill the Woods with tuneful Sound. **1744** HARRIS *Three Treat.* Wks. (1841) 30 In music, the fittest subjects of imitation are all such things and incidents as are most eminently characterized by motion and sound. **1815** J. SMITH *Panorama Sci. & Art* II. 64 Over the surface of smooth water, sound is conveyed admirably well. **1874** BEDFORD *Sailor's Pocket Bk.* v. 142 Sound travels at the rate of 1090 feet in a second of time, when the air is at freezing point. **1967** I. M. FREEMAN *All about Sound & Ultrasonics* xiii. 99 Sonar is just one of the many uses that engineers and scientists have found for ultrasonic sound, which is often called ultrasound. These are names for sound that is too high in frequency to be heard. **1973** D. ENSMINGER *Ultrasonics* i. 6 Perhaps the animal that is best known for its use of ultrasonics is the bat. Many scientists have studied these interesting animals and their use of sound to find food. **1978** R. B. MINNIX in Lipscomb & Taylor *Noise Control* i. 30 Infrasound is concerned with very low frequency (below about 20 Hz) longitudinal mechanical waves where sound is felt rather than heard.

†**b.** Music, melody. *Obs.*

c 1320 *Sir Tristr.* 2857 Alle maner soun And gle Of minestrals vp and doun Bifor þe folk so fre. **1501** DOUGLAS *Pal. Hon.* II. xi, Terpsichore the fyft with humbill soun, Makis on psalteris modulatioun. **1559** *Mirr. Mag., Jas. I* ix, In liberall artes, in instrumentale sowne.

c. The music, speech, etc., accompanying film, television broadcasting, or other forms of visual presentation (cf. PICTURE *sb.* 2 f.). ***sound-on-film*** (Cinemat.), the incorporation of the sound track with the film. Freq. *attrib.* Cf. *married print* s.v. MARRIED *ppl. a.* 3.

1928 *Television* Oct. 10/2 A one-act play was..televised..and receiving televisors within a range of four miles tuned in both sight and sound. **1960** [see PICTURE *sb.* 2 f]. **1979** R. JAFFE *Class Reunion* (1980) III. iii. 322 Emma was..watching television, but she had the sound..low.

1931 B. BROWN *Talking Pictures* 270 Sound-on-film recording may be monitored direct from a photo-electric cell in the recording machine. **1957** MANVELL & HUNTLEY *Technique Film Music* ii. 27 The true arrival of the sound film was the arrival of sound-on-film. **1976** *Oxf. Compan. Film* 450/1 In the Vitaphone process the sound came from a disc precariously synchronized with the picture. The limitations of this system were quickly recognized and 'sound-on-film' became standard.

d. *Physics.* Applied to various kinds of wave motion (designated ***zero, second, third,*** etc., ***sound***) that are predicted or observed to occur in superfluids and physically bear some resemblance to ordinary ('first') sound.

1944, etc. [see *second sound* s.v. SECOND *a.* 7 a]. **1957** tr. L. D. Landau in *Soviet Physics JETP* V. 102/1 It is shown..that in a Fermi liquid at absolute zero other waves can be propagated; these differ in nature from ordinary sound, and we shall call them waves of 'zero sound'. **1959** K. R. ATKINS in *Physical Rev.* CXIII. 962 This article discusses the possible existence of two hitherto undetected types of wave propagation in liquid helium II. Third sound is a surface wave of long wavelength on a liquid helium film... Fourth sound may exist in narrow two-sided channels. *Ibid.*, To discuss wave propagation in liquid helium II, it is necessary to write down two separate hydrodynamical equations, one for the superfluid component and the other for the normal component. In first sound the two components move in the same direction in phase, and there is a first-order oscillation of the density but only a second-order oscillation of the temperature. In second sound the two components move in opposite directions out of phase, and the temperature oscillation is then first-order while the density oscillation is only second-order. **1969** W. E. KELLER *Helium-3 & Helium-4* vi. 203 (*caption*) Attenuation and propagation velocity of sound in liquid He^3 showing the characteristics associated with the transition from first sound to zero sound for two frequencies. **1974** D. J. BERGMAN in K. D. Timmerhaus et al. *Low Temperature Physics—LT 13* I. 507 Following our experience with third sound, we may expect that in fourth sound, too, when the channels that hold the helium are sufficiently small so that the normal fluid motion is completely locked out, the only important source of attenuation will be conduction of heat into the walls of the helium channels. **1974** *Nature* 15 Mar. 194/3 The report..that they have observed the propagation of fourth sound in the two newly discovered phases of liquid ^{3}He amounts to the first unequivocal evidence that both of these new phases are superfluids. **1976** *Physics Bull.* Aug. 351/2 'Zero sound'..corresponds to oscillations in shape of the Fermi surface. **1981** *Nature* 2 Apr. 359/2 Second sound is an unusual type of propagating wave mode, which can occur in superfluids, involving fluctuations in the local temperature and entropy of a medium rather than in the local density and pressure as found in a conventional sound wave.

e. ***sound and light*** = SON ET LUMIÈRE 1. Used *attrib.*

1960 *Woman* 23 Jan. 35/3 The pretty little town of Buxton, one of the first in England to stage a 'sound and light' production for summer visitors. **1966** J. PHILIPS *Wings of Madness* (1967) I. i. 9 The Sound and Light program put on..every night..kept tourists in town. **1979** *United States 1980/81* (Penguin Travel Guides) 548 On weekend evenings, a multimedia sound-and-light show using laser beams.

2. a. The particular auditory effect produced by a special cause.

α. **1297** R. GLOUC. (Rolls) 5750 A voys sede as him þoȝte þes wordes þoru þe soun. **c 1340** HAMPOLE *Pr. Consc.* 4971 Fra þe tyme þat þai þe son sal here. **1390** GOWER *Conf.* I. 294 So lowde his belle is runge, That of the noise and of the soun Men feeren hem in al the toun. **c 1400** *Sowdone Bab.* 437 Through the Cite wente the sowne, So lowde than gan he yelle. **c 1500** *Lancelot* 1035 To warnnyng them vp goith the bludy sown. **1542** UDALL *Erasm. Apoph.* 108 By the..plashyng or soune that it gave in the falle.

β. **c 1480** HENRYSON *Orpheus & Eurydice* 140 Throu suetenes of the sound, The dog slepit and fell vnto the ground. **c 1580** J. HOOKER *Life Sir P. Carew* in *Archæologia* XXVIII. 144 The trumpeter, clothed in blacke, soundinge the deade sounde. **1609** DEKKER *Gull's Horn Bk.* Wks. (Grosart) II. 253 Throw the cards..round about the Stage, iust vpon the third sound, as though you had lost. **1697** DRYDEN *Virg. Georg.* III. 78 From Hills and Dales the chearful Cries rebound: For Echo hunts along, and propagates the Sound. **1774** GOLDSM. *Nat. Hist.* VIII. i. (1862) II. 243 It is rather the vibrations of the sound that affect the water by which they are excited, than any sounds that they hear. **1821** SCOTT *Kenilw.* xi, Let us hasten on, for the sound will collect the country to the spot. **1839** G. BIRD *Nat. Philos.* 127 The intensity of sound is modified..by the original direction of the sound.

b. Const. *of*, or with possessives. (Cf. 3 b.)

α. **a 1300** *Cursor M.* 12195 Als a chim or brasin bell, þat noþer can vnderstand ne tell Wat takens þair aun sune. **c 1300** *St. Brandan* 383 (Percy Soc.), The Soun of him [*v.r.* of his wyngen] Murie was. **c 1384** CHAUCER *H. Fame* 1642 This foule trumpes soun. **c 1460** SIR R. ROS *La Belle Dame* 123 Lyke as þe sownne of birdis doth expres whanne thei synge lowde. **1483** CAXTON *Gold. Leg.* 221 b/2, He was said the sone of thondre by cause of the soune of his predycacion. **1542** UDALL *Erasm. Apoph.* 81 b, A potte..well tryed by yᵉ tyncklyng and soune thereof. **1590** SPENSER *F.Q.* I. i. 41 The sowne Of swarming Bees.

β. **1480** *Robt. Devyll* 456 in Hazl. *E.P.P.* I. 236 Of theyr prayers to heauen wente the sownde. **1560** DAUS tr. *Sleidane's Comm.* 120 If they here the sound of the bel, they runne thither streight. **1585** T. WASHINGTON tr. *Nicholay's Voy.* IV. xxvi. 145 Their countenance [is] furious, and the sound of their voyce fearefull. **1617** MORYSON *Itin.* II. 84, I sensibly heard..the sound of the vollies of shot in that skirmish. **1669** DRYDEN *Tyrannic Love* I. i, Like the hoarse murmurs of a trumpet's sound. **1794** MRS. RADCLIFFE *Myst. Udolpho* l, In a low..tone, as if the sound of his own voice frightened him. **1815** SCOTT *Guy M.* xiv, He listened to every noise in the street.., and endeavoured to distinguish in it the sound of hoofs or wheels. **1849** MACAULAY *Hist. Eng.* iii. I. 379 But with boasts like these was mingled the sound of complaint and invective. **1866** G. MACDONALD *Ann. Quiet Neighb.* xxvii. (1878) 466 As soon as I ceased to hear the sound of their progress.

c. Similarly with omission of *the*.

a 1300 *Cursor M.* 1031 Þar..es..Sune of santes þat þar singes. **c 1385** CHAUCER *L.G.W.* 2615 *Hypermnestra*, Ful is the place of soun of menstralsye. **14..** *Lat.-Eng. Voc.* in Wr.-Wülcker 578 *Diaphosia*,..soun of voys. **1500–20** DUNBAR *Poems* xxxiii. 50 Vnto no mess pressit this prelat, For sound of sacring bell nor skellat. **a 1700** EVELYN *Diary* 10 Feb. 1685, After sound of trumpets and silence made. **1707** *Curios. in Husb. & Gard.* Pref. p. iii, Things, which..they ought rather to publish at sound of Trumpet. **1823** SCOTT *Quentin D.* xxvii, With sound of bugles, broaching of barrels, and all the freedom of a silvan meal. **1842** TENNYSON *Godiva* 36 She sent a herald forth, And bade him cry, with sound of trumpet, all The hard condition.

d. The distance or range over which the sound of something is heard. In phr. *in* or *within the sound of* (something).

1617 MINSHEU *Ductor* s.v. *Cockney*, One borne within the sound of Bow-bell. **1712–4** POPE *Rape Lock* IV. 118 Sooner shall grass in Hyde-park Circus grow, And wits take lodgings in the sound of Bow. **1852** M. ARNOLD *The Future* 16 Whether he first sees light Where the river..winds through the plain: Whether in sound of the swallowing sea.

3. a. A particular cause of auditory effect; an instance of the sensation resulting from this. Hence also, a phenomenon identical to an audible sound except that it is inaudible by reason of its frequency (cf. sense 1 a).

α. **a 1300** *Cursor M.* 18320 All þai sang þus, wit a sun. **13..** *K. Alis.* 1183 (W.), He blowith smert and loude sones. **1422** tr. *Secreta Secret., Priv. Priv.* 215 Thou shalte haue many rynnynge engyns to make horribill Sownes to gasten thyn enemys. **1484** CAXTON *Fables of Æsop* II. i, He casted to them a grete pyece of wood, whiche maade a grete sowne and noyse in the water. **1565** COOPER *Thesaurus* s.v. *Sonus*, To heare sownes or noyses. **1590** SPENSER *F.Q.* II. v. 30 A gentle streame, whose murmuring waue..made a sowne, To lull him soft a sleepe.

β. **1483** *Cath. Angl.* 349/2 A Sownde, *crepitaculum, crepitus, crepor.* **1526** *Pilgr. Perf.* (W. de W. 1531) 78 He shall gyue a swete syluer sounde. **1562** WINȜET *Wks.* (S.T.S.) I. 37 Thre sindry soundis blawin almast at ane tyme. **1609** DEKKER *Gull's Horn-bk.* iii. 15 The eares are two Musique roomes into which as well good sounds as bad, descend. **1690** LOCKE *Hum. Und.* II. xiii. (1695) 85 To feign a Knowledge..by making a noise with Sounds, without clear and distinct Significations. **1709** *Tatler* No. 81 ¶ 2 There was heard..a Sound like that of a Trumpet. **1754** GRAY *Progr. Poesy* 76 Ev'ry shade and hallow'd Fountain Murmur'd deep a solemn sound. **1815** BYRON *'My soul is dark'* i, If in this heart a hope be dear, That sound shall charm it forth again. **1851** CARPENTER *Man. Phys.* (ed. 2) 341 Concurrently with the impulse of the heart against the chest, a dull and prolonged sound is heard. **1885** J. PAYN *Talk of Town* I. 156 Mr. Erin muttered an articulate sound such as a bumble-bee makes when imprisoned between two panes of glass. **1950** *Sci. Amer.* Aug. 52/2 The English physiologist H. Hartridge..watched bats flying through darkened rooms and advanced the theory that they might be orienting themselves by means of ultrasonic sounds too high in frequency for human ears to hear. **1976** L. H. SCHAUDINISCHKY *Sound, Man, & Building* i. 8 Above 20 000 Hz extends the 'infinite' supersonic range, the ultrasound. Man is not equipped with an organ capable of directly responding to sounds in that range, but where infrasound is concerned it may be picked up with the aid of a special sense of touch. **1978** J. GOLDSTEIN in P. M. Lipscomb *Noise & Audiol.* i. 6 In order to be heard, a sound must be within a certain frequency range because there are limitations in the frequencies the human ear can perceive.

b. Const. *of*, or with possessives. (Cf. 2 b.)

a 1300 *Cursor M.* 23303 Þan sal þai here þe sunes O nedders bath and of draguns. **c 1320** *Sir Tristr.* 1874 Ich here a menstrel, to say, Of tristrem he haþ a soun. **c 1430** LYDG. *Min. Poems* (Percy Soc.) 51 With a clere sowne of plate and of coyngnage. **1474** CAXTON *Chesse* III. vii. (1883) 141 He herde the sownes of musique right melodious. **c 1500** *Lancelot* 772 The trumpetis..blawen furth ther sownis. **1705** ADDISON *Italy* 3 Oft in the Winds is heard a plaintive Sound Of melancholy Ghosts. **1832** W. IRVING *Alhambra* I. 68 A murmuring sound of water now and then rises from the valley. **1869** TOZER *Highl. Turkey* II. 283 Popular tales..are the lingering sounds of world-old myths.

†**c.** A musical tone. *Obs.*$^{-1}$

1662 PLAYFORD *Music* 9 Making them half a tone or sound lower than they were before.

d. *pl.* Popular music; also in *sing.*, a tune or record. *slang* (orig. *U.S.*).

1955 *Amer. Speech* XXX. 304 Kenton's music is round sounds. **1961** RIGNEY & SMITH *Real Bohemia* p. xvii, *Sounds*, music, mainly jazz. **1968** *Daily Mirror* 27 Aug. 7/5 Together cats don't buy records, they buy *sounds*, and they never blow their cool.

e. A characteristic style of (usu. popular) music indicated by a defining word or words. Cf. *Mersey sound* s.v. MERSEY.

1963 [see GEAR *sb.* 5 e]. **1967** *Radio Times* 21 Dec. 55/4 *The Greek Sound...* Tonight's programme is about the new genre, which in the last eight years has given a new impetus and vitality to Greek popular music. **1970** *Guardian* 15 June 9/5 Steel Bands and the Reggae Sound beloved of skinheads. **1974** *Listener* 13 June 767/1 In 1927, there was an inimitable Ellington sound, and so there was at the end.

4. a. In restricted sense: The auditory effect produced by the operation of the human voice; utterance, speech, or one of the separate articulations of which this is composed.

(*a*) **a 1300** *Cursor M.* 11685 Vnnethe had he said þe sune [= the words], Quen þe tre it boghed dune. **13..** *E.E. Allit. P.* A. 532 He..sayde to hem with sobre soun; 'Wy stonde ȝe ydel þise dayez longe?' **1385** TREVISA *Higden* (Rolls) II. 161 Hit semeþ a greet wonder how..her owne langage and tonge is so dyuerse of sown in þis oon ilond. **c 1420** *Pol., Rel., & L. Poems* (1903) 240 Ȝet þei answerid with dollefulle sone. **1575** GASCOIGNE *Certayne Notes* Wks. 1907 I. 467 Remembre to place every worde in his natural *Emphasis* or sound. **a 1586** SIDNEY *Ps.* XVII. iii, Then by thee, [I] was guiltlesse found From ill word, and ill meaning sound. **1667** MILTON *P.L.* IX. 557 Deni'd To Beasts, whom God on thir Creation-Day Created mute to all articulat sound. **1709** POPE *Ess. Crit.* 365 'Tis not enough no harshness gives offence, The sound must seem an Echo to the sense. **1746** FRANCIS tr. *Horace, Epist.* II. i. 171 He forms the Infant's Tongue to firmer Sound. **c 1825** WHATELY in *Encycl. Metrop.* (1845) I. 279/1 The Choice of words, with a view to their Imitative, or otherwise, Appropriate sound. **1867** *Trans. Philol. Soc.* 82 On the sound of initial *th* in English. *Ibid.*, The..two varieties of sound, which we now represent ..by the digraph *th.*

(*b*) **1593** SHAKS. *Lucr.* 1017 Idle words,..Unprofitable sounds. **1663** S. PATRICK *Parab. Pilgrim* iv. (1687) 13 But when he speaks, his words are more than sounds, and have a sting in them which pierces the very heart. **1815** SCOTT *Guy M.* xli, The remnants of an old prophecy, or song, or rhyme;..it is a strange jingle of sounds. **1867** *Trans. Philol. Soc.* Suppl. I On Palaeotype, or the representation of spoken sounds..by means of the ancient types. **1894** W. LINDSAY *Latin Lang.* I If an alphabet is to express the sounds of a language properly, each nation must construct one for itself.

b. The audible articulation(s) corresponding to a letter, word, name, etc.

c 1400 MAUNDEV. (Roxb.) vii. 27 Þe letters and þaire sounes and þaire names. **1530** PALSGR. 3 *E* in frenche hath never suche a sownde as we use to gyve hym in these wordes [etc.]. **c 1620** A. HUME *Brit. Tongue* (1865) 7 Quhat was the right roman sound of them [the vowels] is hard to judge. **1779** *Mirror* No. 64, My ears were now familiarized with the sounds of *Duke, Marquis, Earl.* **1825** SCOTT *Talism.* xxv, The very sound of the name of a royal maiden. **1892** STEVENSON *Across the Plains* i. 11 None can care for literature in itself who do not take a special pleasure in the sound of names.

c. Used with implication of richness, euphony, or harmony.

1553 T. WILSON *Rhet.* (1580) 116 Woordes that fill the mouthe and haue a sound with them, set forthe a matter verie well. **1614** BREREWOOD *Lang. & Relig.* 131 The last letter of the first word cut off in the Greek pronunciation for sounds sake. **1780** *Mirror* No. 110, Blackfriars-wynd can never vie with Drury-lane in point of sound. **1781** COWPER *Table-T.* 516 If sentiment were sacrific'd to sound, And truth cut short to make a period round.

†**d.** Import, sense, significance. *Obs.*

In modern use there is an approach to this sense in phrases which indicate the mental impression produced by a statement, as in SOUND *v.*^{1} 4 (see sense 4 f).

a 1614 DONNE *Βιαθανατος* (1644) 165 A private man in a just warre, may not onely kill, contrary to the sound of this Commandement, but hee may kill his Father, contrary to another. **a 1656** HALES *Gold. Rem.* I. (1673) 56, I have heard a proverb to this sound [etc.]. **a 1700** EVELYN *Diary* 18 Aug. 1673, [He said] 'No, Mr. E..., I will never see this place, this Citty or Court againe', or words of this sound. **1719** DE FOE *Crusoe* I. (Globe) 95 As for being deliver'd, the Word had no Sound, as I may say, to me.

e. Mere audible effect, without significance or real importance.

1605 Shaks. *Macb.* v. v. 27 A Tale Told by an Ideot, full of sound and fury, Signifying nothing. *a* **1704** Locke (J.), Let us consider this proposition as to its meaning; for it is the sense and not sound that must be the principle. **1775** Johnson *Tax. no Tyr.* 33 That a free man is governed by himself..is a position of mighty sound; but every man that utters it..feels it to be false. **1806** *Med. Jrnl.* XV. 55 The reason..might in *sound* be plausible enough, but it certainly was of no benefit.

f. The impression produced by a statement or report, freq. in phr. ***to like the sound of*** (some person or thing). (See note at sense 4 d.)

1859 Mrs. Gaskell *Let.* 21 Mar. (1966) 543, I like the 'sound' of him extremely, and I hope he will like me when we come to know each other. **1965** R. Sheckley *Game of X* (1966) xxii. 155 'You take care of the piloting, and we will handle the navigating.' Somehow I didn't like the sound of that.

5. a. Fame or knowledge, report or rumour, news or tidings (*of* some thing or person). *Obs.* exc. *arch.*

1413 *26 Pol. Poems* xii. 86 Of noblay þey han lore þe sown. **1436** *Pol. Poems* (Rolls) II. 164 They have also ransonned toune by toune, That into the regnes of bost have ronne here soune. **1545** Joye *Exp. Dan.* ii. D vij, When the sowne of the gospell shall be blowne abroade into every lande. **1586** A. Day *Eng. Secretary* II. (1625) 26 Such odde kinde of reports, ..the least whereof would make you storme to the gale, if a man should but ouer-slip himselfe in giuing any manner of sound of you. **1781** Cowper *Hope* 454 God gives the word —the preachers..spread the glorious sound. **1808** Scott *Marm.* VI. vii, Fame of my fate made various sound. **1817** Shelley *Rev. Islam* II. xiii, Until the mighty sound Of your career shall scatter in its gust The thrones of the oppressor.

b. *dial.* With *a*: A rumour.

1899 Raymond *No Soul above Money* II. i. 180 He had a-heard a sound that there wasn't enough stock on the farm.

6. In elliptical uses. **a.** *Cinemat.* and *Broadcasting.* The department in charge of recording sound. Also, an engineer in this department; the equipment used by him.

a **1940** F. Scott Fitzgerald *Last Tycoon* (1941) iii. 30 Call sound, and if he's been heard from, call him. **1969** M. Steinbeck *On Stage* 165 The voice track on a film is called the sound track. The engineer in charge and the whole unit is referred to simply as 'sound'. The director may call out before a take, 'Is sound ready?' **1972** *Listener* 21 Dec. 852/1 Sequence of calls before a shot. Production Assistant: 'Quiet. Going for a take. Standing by.' Director: 'Right.' Sound: 'Sound running.'

b. = radio *sb.* 2 b. Cf. *sound radio*, sense 8 b below. Also *attrib.*

1949 *Times* 17 Feb. 5/3 The first hundred thousand mark is about to be reached in..television licences..compared with the 11 m. for sound. **1955** *Times* 29 June 11/2 So far not even B.B.C. television has found the way to transfer the aura of the 9 p.m. sound news to television. **1967** 'M. Hunter' *Cambridgeshire Disaster* iv. 28 If necessary he would give up television, ask for a transfer to Sound, anything to get more time at home. **1972** P. Black *Biggest Aspidistra* III. iii. 171 The most obvious effect of the Coronation for television was the demand for sets... Though the BBC still regarded sound as the senior service..the sound audience never again exceeded television's.

7. *attrib.* and *Comb.* **a.** Simple attrib., as ***sound-alarm***, ***-aspect***, ***-association***, ***-change***, ***-clause***, ***-colour***, ***-combination***, ***-complex***, ***-development***, ***distinction***, ***-element***, ***energy***, ***event***, ***-feature***, ***-gesture***, ***-group***, ***-history*** [tr. G. *lautgeschichte*], ***-image***, ***-intensity***, ***-language***, ***level***, ***-mark***, ***-output***, ***-pattern***, ***-picture***, ***poem***, ***power***, ***-quality***, ***-sentence***, ***-sequence***, ***-structure***, ***-symbol***, ***-system***, ***-type***, ***-unit***, ***-value***, ***-wave***, ***-word***, ***-world.***, etc.

Freq. in reference to vocal sound.

1843 *Civil Eng. & Arch. Jrnl.* VI. 146/2 Improvements in breakwaters, beacons, and *sound-alarms. **1936** H. Mulder *Cognition & Volition in Lang.* 46 The life of the language as regards its *sound-aspect. **1954** A. H. Gardiner *Theory of Proper Names* (ed. 2) 73 Even logicians..overlooked the importance of the sound-aspect. **1924** Mawer & Stenton *Introd. to Survey of Eng. Place-Names* ix. 174 Its chief weakness is the remoteness of the *sound-association between the original compound name and the suggested simple derivative. **1866** G. Stephens *Runic Mon.* I. p. xxxvii, The law of *sound-change in certain given dialects or languages at certain given periods. **1912** L. Bloomfield in *Jrnl. Eng. & Gmc. Philol.* XI. 623 S[heffield] confuses the factors—sound-change and analogy—that constitute change in language. **1939** [see palatal *a.* 2 b]. **1962** W. Nowottny *Lang. Poets Use* i. 5 Calling in alliteration's aid and that of a sound-change. *a* **1889** G. M. Hopkins *Jrnls. & Papers* (1959) 273 We may now say of rhythm i.e. verse that it is the recasting of speech into sound-words, *sound-clauses and sound-sentences. **1890** G. B. Shaw in *Star* 9 May 2/5 Marlowe's line was not 'mighty'..but it was tuneful, exquisitely emphasised, and sometimes gorgeous in its *sound color. **1962** *Listener* 9 Aug. 225/1 Schönberg's 'melody of sound-colours' (*Klangfarbenmelodie*). **1924** Mawer & Stenton *Introd. to Survey of Eng. Place-Names* v. 100 An unfamiliar English sound or *sound-combination was altered to suit the Norman pronunciation. **1965** *Language* XLI. 93 First a child learns a sound-combination and then he attaches meaning to it! **1931** G. Stern *Meaning & Change of Meaning* 31 If the *sound-complex is to be apprehended as meaning something..a mental content must accrue to it. **1900** E. Björkman *Scand. Loan-Words in M.E.* I. 30 There are some tests of form which are not based on differences of *sound-development between Scandinavian and English. **1965** *English Studies* XLVI. 141 Surnames, like Johe *Le Roper*..reflect the spoken dialect, but do not necessarily prove indigenous sound-developments. **1884** Sweet in *Philol. Soc. Trans.* 598 The imperfect *sound-distinctions of Saxon Germans. **1884** *Cent. Mag.* XXVII. 819 The highest art in the *sound-element of poetry. **1931** G. O. Russell *Speech & Voice* iv. 21 (*heading*) *Sound-energy not air motion. **1962** A. Nisbett *Technique Sound Studio* 239 They readily remove sound energy from the air at their resonant frequency, and this is then mopped up within the absorber. **1962** P. Strevens *Papers in Lang.* (1965) xii. 146 When *sound events are recorded, the technical standard of recording is important. **1939** *Word Study* Mar. 2/1 Linguistics..deals with the use of a limited number of definable events—the significant *sound-features of a language—occurring in certain definable sequences. **1964** W. R. Lee in D. Abercrombie et al. *Daniel Jones* 292 Sounds and sound-features which belong to neither language. **1938** I. Goldberg *Wonder of Words* iv. 55 *Sound-gesture, such as Paget draws upon in this etymology, is precisely what it is called. **1956** J. Lotz in L. White *Frontiers of Knowl.* xiv. 219 Marginal sound-gestures like the bilabial trill used when shivering: *Brrr*! **1928** O. Jespersen in *Proc. Brit. Acad.* XIV. 352 There are no other words than *switch* and *stretch* beginning and ending with exactly these *sound-groups. **1964** J. Vachek in D. Abercrombie et al. *Daniel Jones* 199 If followed by a vowel, the same sound-group was preserved unimpaired. **1933** O. Jespersen *Essentials Eng. Gram.* vi. 62 The *sound-history of French also serves to explain some striking peculiarities concerning the use of the letter *g* in English spelling. **1964** *English Studies* XLV. 422 A detailed knowledge of sound-history..and sound-substitutions. **1943** tr. M. Buber in H. Read *Educ. through Art* ix. 279 *Sound-image after sound-image..emerges from vibrating throat..into the surrounding air. **1951** A. Gardiner *Theory of Speech & Lang.* 70 It is only the sound-image connected with the words which can be reproduced in a physical copy. **1973** S. Heath in *Screen* Spring/Summer 108 A *langue* is defined by Saussure as a system of signs, a sign being the union of *signifiant* ('sound-image') and *signifié* ('concept'). **1982** *Listener* 16 Dec. 26/3 There's something wrong with the way a taped sound-image remains fixed in eternity. **1934** *Discovery* Dec. 346/1 Noise is a subjective phenomenon and cannot be directly measured. The stimulus causing this impression of sound is a *sound-intensity which can be defined and measured objectively. **1952** *Mind* LXI. 215 It is impossible to imagine a sound-intensity divorced from any definite sound-pitch. **1969** *Gloss. Acoustical Terms* (*B.S.I.*) 16 *Sound intensity*,..the sound energy flux through unit area. **1918** *Amer. Jrnl. Philol.* XXXIX. 89 A Dakota Indian ..would not understand a Neapolitan, even though he would sooner understand the gestures than the *sound-language. **1937** R. A. Wilson *Birth of Lang.* 160 The twenty-six already differentiated elements of sound-language. **1931** S. K. Wolf in L. Cowan *Recording Sound for Motion Pictures* xx. 301 It is necessary to have some means of varying *sound levels in theatres. **1974** *Physics Bull.* June 227/1 Leeds City Council, decided to use its licensing laws to limit sound levels in ballrooms, discotheques and similar places of entertainment. *a* **1892** W. Whitman *Daybks. & Notebks.* (1978) III. 671 One of the first desiderata..is a set of..*sound-marks attached to letters..each mark belonging to that specific sound. **1953** H. Read *True Voice of Feeling* I. viii. 144 The caesura is.. the breaking of the rhythm into sense words of different length from the sound marks. **1978** *Sci. Amer.* Jan. 29/3 We cannot shut our earlids; awake, we are always open to..the old soundmarks we remember and cherish. **1881** *Cassell's Nat. Hist.* V. 298 The existence of *sound-organs,..implies a corresponding development of the sense of hearing. **1937** *Sound output [see *control engineer* s.v. control *sb.* 5]. **1947** Crowther & Whiddington *Science at War* 175 It was found that the sound-output was mainly due to propellers. **1925** *Language* I. 41 One must ascertain if the sound is a typical form or one of the points in its *sound pattern, or is merely a variant of such a form. **1977** P. Strevens *New Orientations Teaching of English* xii. 154 Accent features are manifested in sound-patterns of various kinds. **1903** A. W. Patterson *Schumann* xvi. 186 The whole forms a kind of *sound-picture representing the various personages in the dance. *Ibid.* xvii. 203 What if the tone poet..knew infinitely better than his..advisers what was or was not fitting in the great *sound-poem to which his genius gave birth? **1971** *Guardian* 18 Feb. 10/6 Artaud wrote sound poems. **1947** Crowther & Whiddington *Science at War* iii. 155 A transmitter producing about 50 watts of *sound-power in water was adequate. **1950** D. Jones *Phoneme* 12 An alphabetic system of phonetic transcription consists of letters representing *sound-qualities. **1977** *Broadcast* 28 Nov. 14/2 The singles we get are so badly pressed that we get complaints from listeners about the sound quality. *a* **1889** *Sound-sentence [see *sound-clause* above]. **1914** L. Bloomfield in *Trans. Amer. Philol. Assoc.* XLV. 69 The various parts of this *sound-sequence..have been heard and uttered by the speaker (or the hearer). **1962** F. Behre *Contrib. Eng. Syntax* 134 The sound-sequence..must correlate with certain extra-lingual elements to be inferred from the context. **1888** Clodd *Story Creation* xi. 215 Tribes whose stock of *sound-signs is so limited that they cannot understand each other in the dark. **1871** Tyndall *Fragm. Sci.* (1879) I. x. 307 The necessity of employing *sound-signals in dense fogs. **1959** D. Cooke *Lang. Mus.* v. 234 Music..has now become pure *sound-structure, an intellectual and aesthetic delight. **1936** *Science & Society* I. 38 Certain *sound-symbols are universally attached to the same referent by all members of the community. **1975** *Language for Life* (Dept. Educ. & Sci.) xxvi. 521 The learning of sound-symbol correspondences should take place in the context of whole word recognition and reading for meaning. **1879** H. Sweet in *Trans. Philol. Soc. 1877–9* 544, I am fully conscious that mine is a very inadequate study of an exceptionally difficult *sound-system. **1884** —— in *Trans. Philol. Soc.* 599 The richness of our sound-system. **1897** *Mod. Lang. Notes* XII. 244 Least understood..is the historical development of the sound-systems of modern dialects. **1949** J. R. Firth in *Trans. Philol. Soc. 1948* 132 More detailed notice of 'h' and the *glottal stop* in a variety of languages will reveal the scientific convenience of regarding them as belonging to the prosodic systems of certain langauges rather than to the sound systems. **1977** *Canad. Jrnl. Linguistics 1976* XXI. 177 No information about how they work in the sound system of a language is gained. **1941** *Sound-type [see allophone]. **1964** J. C. Catford in D. Abercrombie et al. *Daniel Jones* 29 The laryngologists have no tradition of systematic..description of phonologically pertinent sound-types. **1934** J. J. Logan *Outl. Eng. Philol.* 24 A syllable, thus, is a *sound-unit. **1920** T. S. Eliot *Sacred Wood* 133 It is an arrangement and choice of words which has a *sound-value and at the same time a coherent comprehensible meaning. **1964** W. R. Lee in D. Abercrombie et al. *Daniel Jones* 288 There is a tendency to give them [*sc.* letters] the sound-values they possess in the learner's mother tongue. **1848** *Trans. R. Irish Acad.* XXI. 65, I proceed now to explain..the circumstances of the great sea wave and of the aërial *sound wave, attending most great earthquakes. **1867** Tyndall *Sound* i. 19 The sound-waves, travelling through a homogeneous atmosphere, reached the ear, undiminished by reflection. *a* **1889** *Sound-word [see *sound-clause* above]. **1961** *Times* 19 June 9/6 Its *sound-world is the old sound-world—parts of it exult in the manner of Richard Strauss. **1976** *Gramophone* Aug. 319/3 Decca and DG engineers help their artists to create a much more limpid and crystalline soundworld.

b. With agent-nouns, vbl. sbs., and pres. pples., as ***sound-carrier***, ***concentrator***, ***-detector***, ***-locator***; ***sound-absorption***, ***-production***; ***sound-absorbent***, ***-absorptive***, ***-imitative*** adjs.; ***sound-conducting***, ***-deadening***, ***-exulting***, ***-making***, ***-producing***, ***-reflecting***, etc.

1961 P. Strevens *Papers in Lang.* (1965) xi. 137 The upper surface..is hard, and therefore probably less *sound-absorbent. **1935** *Discovery* May 126/2 The latest designs and materials for sound-proofing and *sound absorption. **1972** *Lebende Sprachen* XVII. 37/1 *Sound absorption*, 1) the process of dissipating..sound energy. 2) The property possessed by materials..of absorbing sound energy. **1937** *Archit. Rev.* LXXXI. p. lxxii/1 The complete unit is also lined with *sound-absorptive material. **1977** *Chicago Tribune* 2 Oct. VI. 9/2 Rehearsals with empty seats are one thing, performances with every seat..filled with sound-absorptive bodies quite another. **1888** E. Clodd *Story Creation* xi. 216 The..languages of civilised races, the *sound-carriers..of the lofty conceptions which are enshrined in prose and poetry. **1884** Knight *Dict. Mech.* Suppl. 832/1 *Sound Concentrator and Projector. **1853** Markham *Skoda's Auscult.* 93 In consequence of the *sound-conducting power of the tissue being increased by its condensation. **1945** Nelson & Wright *Tomorrow's House* iii. 16/2 The existence of walls lined with books constitutes an excellent *sound-deadening treatment. **1962** A. Nisbett *Technique Sound Studio* ii. 48 Of the various possible sound-deadening systems, it is best to try to avoid those which give a padded-cell effect. **1878** *Chambers's Jrnl.* 29 June 413/1 An extremely delicate *sound detector. **1942** W. Simpson *One of our Pilots is Safe* 54 Chances of escaping detection would be good, either by enemy fighters high above or sound detectors on the ground. **1820** Shelley *Prometh. Unb.* IV. 333 My cloven fire-crags, *sound-exulting fountains Laugh with a vast and inextinguishable laughter. **1921** E. Sapir *Language* 4 The interjections and *sound-imitative words. **1956** J. Lotz in L. White *Frontiers of Knowl.* xiv. 223 Even sound-imitative words vary: thus the English *splash* corresponds to Hungarian *loccsan*. **1919** *Sound-locator [see locator 4]. **1941** D. Masters *So Few* ix. 106 Human ears listening at the sound locators to detect the course [of the aircraft]. **1977** *Jrnl. R. Soc. Arts* CXXV. 419/2 The Sound Locator..greatly assisted the anti-aircraft personnel to plan their defences in advance. **1875** Whitney *Life Lang.* ii. 10 By imitation of the *sound-making persons around him. **1871** Darwin *Desc. Man* II. xi. (1890) 327 In two families of the Homoptera.. the males alone possess *sound-producing organs in an efficient state. **1925** P. Radin tr. *Vendryès's Language* 20 The study of *sound-production, that is to say,..phonation. **1894** *Times* (weekly ed.) 2 Feb. 99/2 The adoption of *sound-reading in the English telegraph offices. **1933** *Archit. Rev.* LXXIII. 232 Only a small area of the walls has a *sound-reflecting surface. **1962** A. Nisbett *Technique Sound Studio* 44 A 'bathroom' acoustic would be provided by a small room with strongly sound-reflecting walls. **1892** Wright *Gothic Primer* §109 The first *sound-shifting, popularly called Grimm's Law. **1876** Douse *Grimm's L.* 151, *K* pure must have been..the original single parent sound from which the impure *K*'s were derived—one by ordinary *sound-weakening, and the other by Reflex Dissimilation.

8. a. Special combs.: **sound-attribute** *Linguistics*, a prosodic feature; **sound-bar** *Mus.* (see quot.); **sound barrier**, the obstacle to supersonic flight posed by such factors as increased drag and reduced controllability, which occur when aircraft not specially designed for such flight approach the speed of sound; also *fig.*; ***to break the sound barrier***, to travel faster than sound; **sound-body** *Mus.*, the hollow part of a stringed instrument which strengthens its sound; **sound-bow**, the thickest part of a bell, against which the hammer strikes; **sound-box**, sound-body; also in a gramophone, the box which carries the reproducing or recording stylus; **sound channel** *Oceanogr.*, a layer of water in which sound is propagated over long distances with minimum energy loss, usu. because of refraction back into this layer from above owing to the temperature gradient, and from below owing to the pressure gradient; **sound-conditioned** *a.* [condition *v.* 9], sound-insulated; having improved acoustic qualities; hence **sound conditioning**; **sound effect**, (*a*) orig. *U.S.* (usu. in *pl.*), a sound typical of an event or evocative of an atmosphere, produced artificially in a play, film, etc. (cf. effect *sb.* 3 c); also *attrib.* and *transf.*; (*b*) the effect produced by the sound of a word; **sound-hand**, a system of shorthand based on a phonetic representation of speech-sounds; **sound-house** (see quot.); **sound-insulated** *a.*, insulated against sound;

also **sound insulation**; **sound-law** *Philol.* [tr. G. *lautgesetz*], a rule stating the regular occurrence of a phonetic change in the history of a language or language family; **sound-lore**, the science of phonology; **sound meter**, an instrument for measuring the intensity of sound; **sound moderator**, a device fitted to a firearm which reduces the noise of report, a silencer; **sound pressure**, the difference between the instantaneous pressure at a point in the presence of a sound wave and the static pressure of the medium; **sound print** = SONOGRAM; **sound-proof** *a.*, preventing the passage of loud or disturbing sound or noise; hence ***sound-proofing*** *vbl. sb.*; **sound-proofed** *a.*, that has been made sound-proof; **sound-ranging** *Mil.* (see quot. 1973); hence **sound-ranger**, one trained in sound-ranging; **soundscape** [SCAPE *sb.*³], (*a*) a musical composition consisting of a texture of sounds; (*b*) the sounds which form an auditory environment; **sound-shift**, *Philol.* = SHIFT *sb.* 14 c; **sound-shifting** [tr. G. *lautverschiebung*]; **sound spectrogram** = SONOGRAM; **sound spectrograph** = SONOGRAPH 1; hence **sound-spectrographic** *a.*; **sound spectrography**; **sound-substitution** *Linguistics*, the replacement of one phoneme by another; hence (as back-formation) **sound-substitute** *v. trans.*, to replace (one phoneme) by another (*rare*); **sound-symbolism** *Linguistics*, the (partial) natural representation of the sense of a word by its sound; hence **sound-symbolic** *a.*, pertaining to or manifesting such symbolism; **sound-tight** *a.* = *sound-proof* adj.

1932 D. JONES *Outl. Eng. Phonetics* (ed. 3) i. 2 The student of spoken English..must learn the proper usage in the matter of the '*sound-attributes' (length, stress, and voice-pitch). **1945–9** *Acta Linguistica* V. 88 The phonemes of a given language are realized in concrete sounds and sound-attributes. **1884** HAWEIS *My Musical Life* I. 225 The *sound-bar is a strip of pine wood running obliquely under the left foot of the bridge [of the violin]. **1939** *Jrnl. R. Aeronaut. Soc.* XLIII. 818 It is noteworthy that the curve, which at first is flat, rises gradually for a while, without the enormous increases which other experimenters have found between M.n. 0·6 and 0·8, and which have made them speak of a concrete '*sound barrier'. **1952** *Times* 8 Sept. 5/2 Their moment of triumph after breaking once more through the sound barrier. *a* **1955** in T. H. Pear *Eng. Social Differences* (1955) iii. 112 Is there a Sound Barrier against your Son? **1955** *Times* 7 July 8/3 The bang that shook London early on Tuesday morning was caused..by a Gloster Javelin breaking the sound barrier. **1963** *Listener* 14 Mar. 457/1 The African rhythmic element is not part of the Asian musical heritage, and there are totally different tonal systems which constitute a kind of 'sound-barrier' which jazz has had to crash. **1973** A. PRICE *October Men* xvi. 231 When the General whispered, people moved..when he growled, they broke the sound barrier. **1976** *Lancs. Evening Post* 7 Dec. 1/4 When we went through the sound barrier I only felt a very slight judder. **1875** STAINER & BARRETT *Dict. Mus. Terms*, *Sound-body. **1688** HOLME *Armoury* III. 462/1 The *Sound Bow, the inner part of the Bell, from the lower ring to the top. **1857** in J. Timbs *Year-bk. Facts* 109 A bell of the usual proportions, in which the thickness of the upper or thin part is one-third of the sound-bow or thickest part. **1875** STAINER & BARRETT *Dict. Mus. Terms*, *Sound-box. **1906** SCRIPTURE *Exper. Phonetics* 16 Experiments made on gramophone sound boxes indicate the necessity of changing the prevalent view of such vibrating diaphragms. **1946** *Bull. Geol. Soc. Amer.* LVII. 928 The velocity of propagation of sound decreases, due to the temperature decrease, from the surface to 4000 feet and then increases, due to pressure increase, from there to bottom. This type of velocity pattern is known as a *sound channel. **1972** M. G. GROSS *Oceanogr.* vii. 200 This sound channel is a typical feature of the open ocean at depths of around 1000 meters at midlatitudes to near the surface in polar regions. **1947** *Sun* (Baltimore) 5 Aug. 6 (Advt.), You travel all the way by the same luxurious Panagra DC-6..air-conditioned and *sound-conditioned for your comfort! **1972** *Fortune* Jan. 8E/2 *Sound conditioning assures privacy in these garden apartments. **1909** *Moving Picture World* 10 July 56/1 (Advt.), Yerkes & Co... Manufacturers of high grade *sound effects for moving pictures. **1911** D. S. HULFISH *Cycl. Motion-Picture Work* II. 191 The orchestra comprises pianist and drummer, and a 'sound effect' man. **1928** *Exhibitor's Herald & Moving Picture World* 28 Apr. 21/2 The experts of Victor ..will..arrange for the synchronized orchestration and sound effects for this picture, in which airplane battles will have an important part. **1942** PARTRIDGE *Usage & Abusage* 298/1 Passing over such obviousness as *bang, crash, hiss*..we see that imitation is most effective when the echoism and sound-effects extend over a succession of words. **1951** W. EMPSON *Structure of Complex Words* 412 *Rebuke* is prim, apparently from the sound-effect. **1958** *Listener* 25 Dec. 1091/3 The studio managers who twiddle the knobs and the sound-effects engineers. **1966** *Ibid.* 24 Feb. 284/1 A meteorite passed across the sky and produced a brilliant light, together with sound effects. **1972** P. BLACK *Biggest Aspidistra* I. iv. 36 Producers deplored the attention their ingenuities received, but the public was and is fascinated by sound effects. **1837** PITMAN (*title*), Stenographic *sound-hand. **1884** KNIGHT *Dict. Mech.* Suppl. 832/2 **Sound-house*, a marine alarm station from which audible alarms or signals are given in foggy weather. **1933** *Sound-insulated [see AIR-CONDITIONING *vbl. sb.*]. **1970** Sound-insulated [see INSULATED *ppl. a.* 3]. **1932** *B.B.C. Year Bk. 1933* 365 (*caption*) Eel grass for *sound-insulation sandwiched in walls of pumice concrete. **1969** *Gloss. Acoustical Terms (B.S.I.)* 49 *Sound insulation*, means taken to reduce the transmission of sound. **1874** H. BENDALL tr. *Schleicher's Compar. Gram.* 12 *Vowel *sound-laws* (*i.e.* influence of vowels and consonants on vowels) were not existent in the original Indo-European language. **1911** L. BLOOMFIELD in *Jrnl. Eng. & Gmc. Philol.* X. 629 Synonymous words might be collected to prove almost any desired sound-law. **1974** R. QUIRK *Linguist & Eng. Lang.* i. 3 There are good historical reasons..for our firmly associating it [*sc.* 'language'] with ..'sound-laws'. **1871** KENNEDY *Public Sch. Lat. Gram.* 4 *Soundlore treats of the sounds and relations of Letters and Syllables. **1928** *Sci. Abstr.* A. XXXI. 39 Discusses the differences between physical and physiological intensity of sound and describes a form of *sound meter for technical use. **1974** *Physics Bull.* Oct. 481/2 Dawe Instruments..has introduced the type 1400H sound-meter which uses a ceramic microphone... Sound levels as low as 24 dB can be measured. **1934** *Rep. Departmental Comm. Statutory Definition & Classification of Firearms & Ammunition* 44 in *Parl. Papers 1934–5* (Cmd. 4758) VIII. 871 There is procurable an appliance known as a silencer or *sound moderator which can be fitted to almost all types of firearms for the purpose of reducing the noise of the explosion of the cartridge. **1953** W. G. B. ALLEN *Pistols, Rifles & Machine Guns* xiii. 172 Silencers are not permitted by law on privately owned weapons, but a 'sound moderator' may be used providing the appropriate endorsement is made on the ..Certificate... The only sound moderators on sale are for .22 in. weapons. **1976** *Shooting Times & Country Mag.* 16–22 Dec. 47/1 (Advt.), Erma Emi semi-automatic carbine, ..sound moderator, 'scope. **1916** *Sci. Abstr.* B. XIX. 514 (*heading*) *Sound pressure. **1930** *Jrnl. Sci. Instruments* VII. 113 The response at a particular frequency is measured by the E.M.F. developed by the microphone per unit sound pressure per unit area. **1976** *Acustica* XXXV. 255/1 The transfer function is subtracted from the harmonic analysis of sound pressure to produce the source spectrum. **1969** R. PETRIE *Despatch of Dove* I. iv. 64 Have you ever seen a *soundprint of your own voice? **1884** *Health Exhib. Catal.* 46/1 Movable *Sound-proof Partitions for dwelling-houses, schools, &c. **1894** *Daily News* 2 May 3/3 Each of the class rooms..is made as far as possible sound proof. **1932** *Times Educ. Suppl.* 20 Aug. 321/4 The divisions between class-rooms are *soundproofed with eelgrass quilting. **1956** N. MAILER *Man who studied Yoga* in *New Short Novels* II. iv. 19 Scream my little one. It will do you no good. The walls are soundproofed. **1978** C. TOMLINSON *Shaft* 39 The sighs that in a giant building rise up trapped between its sound-proofed surfaces. **1884** *Health Exhib. Catal.* 83/2 Models showing application of 'Silicate Cotton' for fireproofing and *soundproofing. **1978** J. B. HILTON *Some run Crooked* ii. 17 They've learned to be radio mechanics, asdic operators, *sound-rangers and flash-spotters. **1919** *Sci. Amer.* 17 May 509/1 Both parties to the late conflict excited their ingenuity ..to improve methods of *sound-ranging, on land and in the air and at sea. **1934** T. E. LAWRENCE *Let.* 19 Mar. (1938) 793 Research..to develop the art of sound-ranging, and anti-aircraft gunnery. **1973** J. QUICK *Dict. Weapons & Mil. Terms* 407/3 *Sound ranging*, a method of locating the source of a sound, such as that of a gun report or a projectile burst, by calculations based on the intervals between the reception of the sound at various previously oriented microphone stations. **1968** *Time* 4 Oct. 6 In this collection, he proved his mastery of the subtle colors, treacherous rhythms, and delicate contrapuntal lines that fashioned Debussy's impressionistic *soundscapes. **1973** *Daily Colonist* (Victoria, B.C.) 22 Sept. 5/5 The world soundscape project ..counted horn blasts at intersections around the world. **1977** *Times Lit. Suppl.* 11 Feb. 144/3 A small number of jazz musicians have..gravitated towards the soundscapes of Varèse and Stockhausen. **1977** *Guardian Weekly* 18 Sept. 18/1 The 'soundscape', Schafer's word to describe our sonic environment, the day-to-day background of our auditory experience. **1911** L. ARMITAGE *Introd. Study Old High German* II. iii. 57 OHG is distinguished from all other W. Gmc. languages by a series of Sound-changes affecting its consonant system, which are usually grouped together under the name of the Second or HG. *Sound-Shift. **1922** O. JESPERSEN *Language* ii. 43 The first book in the 1822 volume [of Grimm's *Grammatik*] contains..his exposition of the 'sound shift' (lautverschiebung), which it has been customary in England since Max Müller to term 'Grimm's Law'. **1965** C. F. HOCKETT *Sound Change* 192 What then of the neat discrete 'speech sounds' of the comparativists? Even more, what of their 'sound shifts'? **1880** A. H. SAYCE *Introd. Sci. Lang.* I. iv. 324 Practically the *sound shiftings [in the Semitic dialects] are confined to the sibilants. **1908** J. WRIGHT *O.E. Grammar* 100 The first sound-shifting, popularly called Grimm's Law, refers to the changes which the Indo-Germanic explosives underwent in the period of the Germanic primitive community. **1945** R. K. POTTER in *Science* 9 Nov. 470/2 The beat of the heart may be recorded slowly and converted to the *sound spectrogram form by high speed reproduction. **1974** *Sci. Amer.* Mar. 86/3 The sound spectrograms of Infant A's cries looked exactly like what we have come to regard as being typical of a normal infant. **1945** *Science* 9 Nov. 465/1 The patterns..were made by an instrument that we have called the *sound spectrograph. **1977** *Time* 21 Mar. 64/3 The most striking evidence came from a sound spectrograph, a machine that reduces speech to electronic 'pictures' called spectrograms or voiceprints. **1947** R. K. POTTER et al. *Visible Speech* i. 4 A *sound spectrographic record of the words '*Visible Speech*' is shown in Fig. 3. **1976** *Word 1971* XXVII. 57 Sound-spectrographic and cineradiographic analysis of neonatal cry and crysound. **1948** *Language* XXIV. 4 That we have reached a crucial point in the development of phonemics is clear from the first published results of *sound spectrography. **1962** *Amer. Speech* XXXVII. 67 Surgical study..using synchronized cineradiography and sound spectrography. **1953** K. JACKSON *Lang. & Hist. in Early Britain* II. 558 A possible case of pre-lenition *b* *sound-substituted by AS. *ƀ*. **1898** *Trans. Amer. Philol. Assoc.* XXIX. 38 It is not always easy to say where *sound-substitution ceases and natural speech begins. **1926** L. BLOOMFIELD in *Language* II. 164 Whoever speaks a foreign language or dialect may in it substitute resemblant features of his native speech... Linguistic substitution of phonemes is *sound-substitution*. **1959** A. CAMPBELL *O.E. Gram.* 200 In early loan-words this would arise by the operation of native sound-changes, but in later ones sound-substitution might produce similar results. **1964** R. H. ROBINS *Gen. Linguistics* 14 The onomatopoeic and '*sound-symbolic' part of language is of great significance. **1977** *Word 1972* XXVIII. 318 A new polar response pair with no relevance to the sound to be considered for membership in one of the sound-symbolic semantic clusters in a phonetic-symbolism experiment. **1901** H. OERTEL *Lect. Study Lang.* 328 It would ..embrace the attempts at word-painting and *sound-symbolism. **1922** O. JESPERSEN *Language* 396 The idea that there is a natural correspondence between sound and sense, and that words acquire their contents and value through a certain sound symbolism, has at all times been a favourite one with linguistic dilettanti. **1957** R. W. ZANDVOORT *Handbk. Eng. Gram.* II. ii. 111 Thus *a man's club* by the side of *a men's club*; *a woman's college* by the side of *a women's college*. This seems to be to some extent a matter of 'sound-symbolism': the singular forms are preferred because they have a more 'manly' sound. **1977** G. W. HEWES in D. M. Rumbaugh *Language Learning by Chimpanzee* i. 48 Sound-symbolism may be explicable on the basis of mouth-gesture. **1932** KIPLING *Limits & Renewals* 81 The door was shut; and it's *sound-tight for reasons connected with the last nights of the condemned.

b. In combinations referring to the mechanical or electrical transmission, broadcasting, or reproduction of sound, as ***sound boom***, ***broadcasting***, ***-crew***, ***engineer***, ***man***, ***negative***, ***programme***, ***radio***, ***record***, ***recorder***, ***recordist***, ***source***, ***studio***, ***system***, ***transmission***; ***sound-recording*** vbl. sb. and ppl. adj.; ***sound-reproducing*** ppl. adj.; **sound archive**, a library in which sound recordings are preserved; **sound-book** *disused*, a book supplied with gramophone records to supplement the text; **sound camera** *Cinemat.* (see quot. 1959); **sound check** *colloq.*, a test of sound equipment before a musical performance to ensure that the sound production is correct; **sound-film** *Cinemat.*, a cinematic film with accompanying recorded sound (see also quots. 1923, 1929); **sound gate** *Cinemat.*, the part of a sound head where the sound track is scanned as the film passes through it; **sound head** *Cinemat.*, the part of a film projector concerned with producing an electrical signal from the sound track (see also quot. 1959); **sound-mix**: see MIX *sb.*² 2; **sound mixer** see MIXER 1 c; hence **sound-mixing** *vbl. sb.*; **sound picture** = *sound-film* above; also, any recording of an auditory event; **Soundscriber**, a machine for the recording and subsequent reproduction of the spoken word (a proprietary term in the U.S.); **sound shop**, a shop which sells equipment for playing, reproducing, or recording music; **sound stage**, a stage having acoustic properties suitable for the recording of sound (*spec.* one used for filming); **sound stripe** *Cinemat.*, a narrow band of magnetic material on the edge of a film, which contains the sound track; **sound-thief** *slang*, an expert in 'bugging' or the installation and operation of concealed microphones; **sound track** *Cinemat.*, the sound constituent of a film, recorded on the edge of the film stock as either an optical or a magnetic band; also, such a record independent of the film; freq. *attrib.*; also *fig.*; hence **sound-track** *v. trans.*, to provide with a sound track; to serve as a sound track for; **sound truck**, (*a*) = *loud-speaker van* s.v. LOUDSPEAKER 2; (*b*) (see quot. 1959²).

1962 (*title*) BBC sound archives recorded programmes library World War 1939–1945. **1977** *Times* 16 May 7/5 In July the Sound Records Department of the Imperial War Museum will be opening to the public... Some have been acquired from..the..BBC sound archives. **1937** *Discovery* Feb. 61/2 *Songs of Wild Birds.* By *E. M. Nicholson* and *L. Koch.* With gramophone records... It is the first sound-book published in Britain. **1938** *Times Lit. Suppl.* 17 Dec. 805/2 The sound-book..seems to be catching on. **1975** *Country Life* 13 Feb. 390/2 Ludwig Koch.. conceived the idea of a sound-book—'a combination of text, picture and sound, the last supplied by gramophone records attached to the book'. **1961** G. MILLERSON *Technique Television Production* i. 14 Another camera and sound boom have taken over. **1929** *Television* Jan. 10/3 (*caption*) The Baird Company's Concert Party and Engineers, photographed in the sight and sound broadcasting studio in Long Acre. **1940** R. S. LAMBERT *Ariel & all his Quality* vii. 183 The coming of War, which would make sound broadcasting.. indispensable..would sound the death-knell of television. **1958** *Listener* 21 Aug. 260/1 One must not imagine that sound broadcasting will fail to be of value to the community for many years to come. **1977** Sound broadcasting [see *television broadcasting* s.v. *TELEVISION 3 b]. **1904** *Science Siftings* 26 Mar. 353/1 A wonderful camera that will photograph noises... With this sound camera, all noises.. can be realistically reproduced. **1958** *New Statesman* 26 July 106/1 ITN's roving reporter, Robin Day, roved as far as Egypt with sound-cameras. **1959** W. S. SHARPS *Dict. Cinematogr.* 130/2 *Sound camera.* (1) A film picture camera that makes no external noise in operation and is therefore suitable for use when sound is being recorded. (2) A camera that records sound on film. **1976** *Oxf. Compan. Film* 646/1 Optical sound cameras are now used only to produce negatives for making married prints of finished films. **1977** *Rolling Stone* 13 Jan. 10/1 He runs his hands through his straw-thatched hair as his new band kicks off the sound check with 'You Wear It Well'. **1961** K. REISZ *Technique Film Editing* xii. 185 Having chosen his topics, the producer must get together his unit—cameraman, editor, script-writer and the sound-crew. **1974** A. MORICE *Killing with Kindness* ii. 14 It was some American production they were recording over here... He and the rest of the sound crew had been given Tuesday off. **1937** *Amer. Speech* XII. 101 Sound effect..refers to the diabolical work of the sound man or, with greater dignity, the sound engineer. **1973** J. Porter *It's Murder with Dover* iv. 34 The TV cameraman.. lowered his camera... A nearby sound engineer agreed. **1923** *Mod. Wireless* I. 418/2 The successful production of such a sound record upon a separate film, the sound-film and the picture-film being run simultaneously. **1927** *Daily Mail* 2 July 8/2 The sound-film of the Walker-Milligan fight which was made by the British Phonofilm Co. **1929** *Times* 30 July 13/2 Contrasting 'dialogue films', which, in imitation of the stage, depend principally on dialogue to tell their story, with 'sound films', which use sound as a supplement to silent technique. **1957** Manvell & Huntley *Film Music* 9 We have tried to show how the first principles of sound film music composition were developed through the imaginative collaboration of composers and film-makers. **1964** N. Marsh *Dead Water* vi. 162 A badly-synchronised sound-film. **1975** G. Howell *In Vogue* 65/2 Sound came in 1927, and by the end of 1928 the worst sound film could outdraw the best silent movie. **1931** G. F. Jones *Sound-Film Reprod.* 12 The film must pass through the sound gate at a uniform speed, in order that the pitch of the music or speech shall not vary. **1960** O. Skilbeck *ABC of Film & TV* 61 The sound gate is the corresponding point—though here the film is in constant flow—in a sound camera or head. **1931** S. K. Wolf in L. Cowan *Recording Sound for Motion Pictures* xx. 289 (*caption*) Schematic diagram of Western Electric sound head. **1959** W. S. Sharps *Dict. Cinematogr.* 131/1 *Sound head*,..the mechanism in a film printing machine that is concerned with the printing of the sound track. **1979** *Amat. Photographer* 10 Jan. 88/1 The sound heads are well screened to reduce hum level and are only brought into contact with the film when the projector is set to 'forward, sound'. **1929** *N.Y. Times* 20 Oct. ix. 8/5 *Playback*.. provides a means for the director, the actors and the sound men to determine in general how a scene will sound immediately after it has been taken. **1935** S. W. Pring tr. *L. Sabaneev's Music for Films* vi. 93 The volume of sound emitted is regulated, not by the conductor, but by the soundman in the monitor room. **1971** D. E. Westlake *I gave at Office* (1972) 12 At noon the engineer and the sound man and the director and I would all leave The Hub. **1932** Sound-mix [see mix *sb.*[2] 2]. **1971** *Sat. Rev.* (U.S.) 25 Dec. 44/1 It was necessary to add quite a lot of traffic noise on the final sound mix. **1938** Sound mixer [see cut *v.* 21 e]. **1972** D. Francis *Smokescreen* i. 9 The sound mixer took off his ear-phones..and fiddled..with the knobs on his Nagra recorder. **1977** *Times* 18 Apr. (Gramophone Suppl.) p. iv/6 The controls of the sound-mixing console. **1929** *N.Y. Times* 20 Oct. ix. 8/6 *Soup*, the developing bath in which a sound negative is developed. **1928** *Times* 24 Dec. 28/1 Either British acoustics or the Anglo-German mechanism will presumably be installed in the Gaumont houses, to the exclusion of U.S. sound pictures. **1955** *Radio Times* 22 Apr. 47/3 A recorded sound picture of the Dutch people's struggle to win new land from the sea. **1979** J. Gardner *Nostradamus Traitor* xi. 37 There was a clean sound picture from almost every part of the flat. **1955** *Radio Times* 22 Apr. 1 Radio Times..BBC Sound and Television Programmes. **1966** R. Williams *Communications* (ed. 2) iii. 68 There are more emphatic differences in the distribution of interests in the various BBC sound programmes. **1938** K. Baily in *Radio Times* 21 Oct. 12/2 With a sound radio system that is chiefly a utility service, and in which listeners are participating, the ultimate fusion of vision with sound will be easily achieved. **1952** *Times* 1 Jan. (Rev. of 1951) p. v/2 Sound radio (wireless declined farther towards archaism) has done much during the year. **1971** M. Lee *Dying for Fun* xxiii. 107 The sound radio producer was supervising the recording of an interview. **1900** R. S. Baker *Boy's Bk. Inventions* vii. 258 The cylinder on which the sound pictures or records were to be made was covered with tin foil. **1977** Sound record [see *sound archive* above]. **1957** J. S. Huxley *Relig. without Revelation* (rev. ed.) vii. 171 The invention of the gramophone and the sound-recorder. **1961** L. van der Post *Heart of Hunter* i. i. 30 Charles Leonard, the mechanic who was also our sound recorder..would like nothing better than to go on recording Bushman music and folklore. **1871** *Eng. Mechanic* 17 Nov. 233/1 In sound-recording, I do not think that electro-magnetism would be of much service. **1931** *Electronics* Apr. 587/1 (*heading*) Effects of optical slits in variable area sound recording. **1933** *Chem. Abstr.* XXVII. 50/3 (*title*) Discharge lamp for use with sound-recording apparatus. **1967** A. L. Lloyd *Folk-Song in Eng.* i. 64 [Cecil] Sharp made the notations by ear without the controlling help of sound-recording. **1975** *Language for Life* (Dept. Educ. & Sci.) xv. 234 Another facility of value to the English department..is a sound recording studio. **1958** *Times* 18 Feb. 5/2 Thomas Arthur Howell.., sound recordist.., Twickenham. **1977** *Broadcast* 4 Apr. 25/3 BBC contract news cameramen and sound recordists spelled out their growing concern over pay and conditions. **1931** L. Cowan *Recording Sound for Motion Pict.* 387 *Sound head*, compartment on the projector which contains sound-reproducing systems and mechanisms for guiding and driving film. **1958** M. Kelly *Christmas Egg* iii. 105 Displays of perfectionists' sound-reproducing equipment. **1969** *Gloss. Acoustical Terms* (*B.S.I.*) 41 *Sound reproducing system*, an apparatus for re-creating sound which has been recorded. **1946** *Sun* (Baltimore) 6 Feb. 13/1 The Soundscriber is a recording device which enables observers to describe the position and actions of their assigned horses during a race. The description can be played back immediately..and compared with the pictures of the race. **1950** *Official Gaz.* (U.S. Patent Office) 24 Oct. 1011/2 *Sound Scriber*...for electric sound recording and reproducing machines... Claims use since Feb. 15, 1936. **1968** C. M. Vines *Little Nut-Brown Man* iv. 73 He dictated into the soundscriber, and handed to me the papers referred to in his dictation. **1972** *Daily Colonist* (Victoria, B.C.) 24 May 21/8 Phil Barker tuning a hi-fi set (he's a salesman in a sound shop). **1962** A. Nisbett *Technique Sound Studio* 247 *Crossfade*, a gradual mix from one sound source or group of sources to another. **1931** L. Cowan *Recording Sound for Motion Pict.* 243 Special buildings—sound stages—had to be constructed in which recording could be carried on. **1958** [see bank *sb.*[2] 10 a]. **1978** S. Sheldon *Bloodline* xvii. 205 Rhys brought Elizabeth to a sound stage, where they made motion pictures for research and for their world-wide advertising and products divisions. **1965** *Focal Encycl. Photogr.* (rev. ed.) I. 1418/1 Recording live sound effects or commentary..may be done on the film actually exposed in the camera (usually containing a magnetic sound stripe) or on a tape recorder. **1979** *Amat. Photographer* 10 Jan. 88/1 One of the main criticisms of sound stripe reproduction has been background hiss and hum picked up at the recording stage. **1929** *Morning Post* 24 May 12/7 There are now 17 sound-studios in New York and Long Island. **1962** A. Nisbett *Technique Sound Studio* 272 *Sound studio*,..any room or hall which is primarily used for microphone work. Its most important properties lie in its size and its acoustics—the way in which sound is diffused and absorbed, and the reverberation time. **1964** M. McLuhan *Understanding Media* xxix. 296 Everyone has at some time wished he were equipped with his own sound system during a movie performance. **1977** 'J. le Carré' *Hon. Schoolboy* iii. 56 Where it was operable, he ran moles and sound-thieves in tandem..[that is], Karla had liked to back up his agent operations with microphones. **1929** *Photoplay* Apr. 31/2 *Sound track*, the narrow band of space along the left side of picture film on which is printed the ribbon-like strip of light and dark lines which constitute the record from which sound is projected. **1946** G. Millar *Horned Pigeon* xiv. 191 He made rude sucking noises with his lips, an exaggerated sound-track for the scene he witnessed through the window. **1949** Sound-track *v.* [see kinescope *v.*]. **1957** Wodehouse *Over Seventy* xvi. 154 This is not always the laughter of a real studio audience. Frequently, it is tinned or bottled. They preserve it on sound tracks, often dating back for years. **1968** *Radio Times* 28 Nov. 57/5 Excerpts from the sound-track album of Finian's Rainbow. **1977** *New Statesman* 2 Sept. 314/1 The mindlessly self-pitying lyrics were just about swallowable if used to soundtrack shots of Kingston's corrugated iron shanty towns. **1982** *London Review Bks.* IV. xxiv. 8/1 When M. Hulot's author balances a soundtrack, the human voice plays a small and outclassed part in the din of the inanimate. **1935** *Discovery* Sept. 278/2 The ultra-short wave sound transmissions will stimulate further perfection of sound-reproducing apparatus. **1969** *Gloss. Acoustical Terms* (*B.S.I.*) 11 *Sound transmission*, the transfer of sound energy from one medium to another. **1936** P. Rotha *Documentary Film* iv. ii. 208 Sound-trucks are essentially large and cumbersome objects. **1940** *Nation* 30 Mar. 432/3 Forbidding..the operation of their own sound trucks, and the presentation of their own movie. **1959** *Economist* 2 May 433/1 In the cities, towns and villages of Japan over the past three weeks, the days..have been rendered hideous by 'sound-trucks' rumbling through the streets. **1959** W. S. Sharps *Dict. Cinematogr.* 132/1 *Sound truck*, a mobile sound recording unit, usually with its own power supply. **1971** *Black Scholar* Dec. 56/1 The first time we went out on the soundtrucks, I was on the soundtrucks, the first leaflet we put out, I wrote, the first demonstration, I made up the pamphlets.

sound (saʊnd), *sb.*[4] Now *dial.* Forms: α. 5–7 **sown(e, 7 soune, sounn.** β. 6 **sounde, soonde,** 6–7 **sownd,** 5– **sound.** [var. *swoun(d* swoon *sb.*]

1. A swoon or fainting-fit. Usually with preps. *in* or *into*. Very common *c* 1530–1650, esp. in *to fall in a sound*.

α. *c* **1400** *Laud Troy Bk.* 10254 By-fore his feet fel sche doun For sorwe & care In a ded sowne. **1480** *Robt. Devyll* 139 in Hazl. *E.P.P.* I. 225 So for dreade thys lady laye in a sowne. **1525** Ld. Berners *Froiss.* II. cxcii. [clxxxviii.] 590 She fell in a sowne, and knightes and ladyes came and comforted her. **1591** Greene *Conny Catching* ii. Wks. (Grosart) X. 115 Alas honest man helpe me, I am not well: and with that [he] suncke downe suddenly in a sowne. **1621** Burton *Anat. Mel.* i. ii. iv. iii. 195 Augusta..fell down dead in a sown. **1678** Wood *Life* (O.H.S.) II. 424 She fell in a soune and there layd.

fig. **1655** Fuller *Ch. Hist.* v. 178 For they beheld him, rather in a Sown, then as yet Dead in the Kings favour.

β. **1471** Ripley *Comp. Alch.* v. vi. in Ashm. (1652) 149 The Woman..Which oftyn for fayntnes wyll fall in a sound. **1509** Hawes *Past. Pleas.* xxxvi. (Percy Soc.) 187 Prostrate we fell..And sodaynly we were cast in a sounde. **1559** *Mirr. Mag.* (1563) V iij, From a sigh he falles into a sounde, And from a sounde lyeth ragyng on the grounde. **1596** H. Clapham *Briefe Bible* i. 77 A man in a foming sounde, is not fit for our Table. *a* **1629** Hinde *J. Bruen* xlvii. (1641) 151 All his men were affraid, and one of them fell into a sownd. **1698** *Phil. Trans.* XX. 247 And so [they] came out of the Convulsive-like Motions, lying as it had been in a Sound. **1766** Goldsm. *Vicar* xi, My Lady fell into a *sound*, but Sir Tomkyn drawing his sword, swore he was hers to the last drop of his blood. **1828–** in Sc., Yks., Leic., and Cornw. glossaries.

fig. *a* **1569** Kingesmyll *Man's Est.* ix. (1574) C vij, Lying still in the sounde of sinne and buried vp in death. **1610** Holland *Camden's Brit.* i. 413 When England..bereft..of vitall breath was readie through Civill Warre to sinke downe and fall in a Sound.

b. Without article.

1513 Douglas *Æneid* vii. vi. *heading*, Juno, persavand the Troianis byg ane town, For greif and dolour lik to suelt in sown. **1590** Spenser *F.Q.* iii. v. Argt., Belphebe finds him almost dead, and reareth out of sownd. **1621** Quarles *Div. Poems, Esther* (1717) 28 Tymissa (new awak'd from sound) replies, Our Castle is begirt with enemies. **1661** Wood *Life* (O.H.S.) I. 379 He, striving too much that his voice might be heard, fell in sounn.

2. *dial.* A deep or sound sleep.

1867 P. Kennedy *Banks Boro* xix. 108 We got into a heavy sound towards morning, when we ought to be thinking about getting up.

sound (saʊnd), *sb.*[5] Also 6 **sounde.** [f. sound *v.*[2], or ad. F. *sonde* (Sp. and Pg. *sonda*) in the same senses, app. f. OE. or ON. *sund* sound *sb.*[1] Cf. OE. *sund-ȝyrd*, *-líne*, *-ráp*, sounding-pole, -line, -rope.]

1. a. An act of sounding with the lead; also *fig.*, power of sounding or investigating. *rare.*

1584 B. R. tr. *Herodotus* ii. 70 b, At euery sounde with the plummet, you shall bringe vppe great store of mud [etc.]. *a* **1624** Bp. M. Smith *Serm.* (1632) 168 Man hath but a shallow sound, and a short reach, and dealeth onely by probabilities and likely-hoods.

b. A sounding-line or -lead.

It is possible that *sonde* in *Chaucer's Dreme* 1149 is to be taken in this sense.

c **1620** Z. Boyd *Zion's Flowers* (1855) 19 Ho! Pilot, cause cast out the sound.., And try how deepe wee draw.

†**2.** A hole or excavation. *Obs.*$^{-1}$

1603 Knolles *Hist. Turks* (1621) 581 The Rhodians.. sunke divers deepe sounds in many places of the citie neere unto the wals, to discover the enemies mines.

3. *Surg.* An instrument for probing parts of the body, usually long and slender and having a slightly enlarged end.

1797 M. Baillie *Morb. Anat.* (1807) 319 The disease may be ascertained by the introduction of the sound into the urethra. **1809** S. Cooper *Dict. Pract. Surg.* 453/1 Having previously introduced a metallic instrument, called a sound, into the bladder, and plainly felt the stone. **1846** Brittan tr. *Malgaigne's Man. Oper. Surg.* 71 Of Cauterization... Heat in the candle a finely-pointed metallic sound. **1895** *Arnold & Sons' Catal. Surg. Instrum.* 444 Uterine Sound and Syringe, combined. *Ibid.* 629 Lithotomy Sound.., auscultatory, with India-rubber tubing and ear mount.

4. ***sound-line***, 'the tow-line carried down by a whale when sounding' (*Cent. Dict.*).

†**sound**, *sb.*[6] *Obs.*$^{-0}$ [Of obscure origin; perh. an error for *squid*.] A cuttle-fish.

1611 Cotgr., *Seche*, the sound, or Cuttle-fish. [Hence in later Dicts.]

sound, obs. form of sand *sb.*[1] and *sb.*[2]

sound (saʊnd), *a.* Forms: 3–4 **sund(e,** 4–5 **sond(e,** 6 **soende;** 3–6 **sounde,** 4–6 **sownd(e** (5 **sowunde);** 3– **sound** (5 **sount),** 9 *dial.* **soun', zound, zoun', soond, soon'.** [ME. *sund*, representing OE. *ȝesund* i-sound *a.* The prefix has also disappeared in some of the Continental languages, as WFris. *soun* (*sûn*, *sûnd*), NFris. *sünn* (*sünj*), MDu. (eastern) *sunt*, *sont*, *sond-*, MLG. *sunt*, *sund-* (LG. *sund*; hence Da. and Sw. *sund*), but remains in Du. *gezond*, G. *gesund*.]

I. 1. a. Of persons, animals, etc.: Free from disease, infirmity, or injury; having or enjoying bodily health; healthy, robust. Usu. predicative.

In ME. the prominent sense was 'unhurt, uninjured, unwounded'. The first group illustrates the frequent usage with another adj. (or adv.): see also safe *a.* 1 b, c, and whole *a.*

(*a*) *c* **1200** Ormin 14818 Godess follc all hal & sund Comm wel þurrh Godd to lande. *c* **1220** *Bestiary* 518 Ðis fis wuneð wið ðe se grund, and liueð ðer eure heil and sund. *a* **1310** in Wright *Lyric P.* xxx. 89 Withoute gold other eny tresor he [man] mai be sound ant sete. *c* **1374** Chaucer *Troylus* iii. 1526 God us graunte sounde and sone to mete! *c* **1400** *Laud Troy Bk.* 16534 He bad god..Brynge hem thedir sound & sone. *c* **1440** *Pallad. on Husb.* i. 55 Yf thou se the puple sounde and fair. **1557** Tusser *100 Points Husb.* lvi, A kow good of milk, big of bulke, hayle and sounde. **1573** —— *Husb.* (1878) 115 Then shall thy cattel be lustie and sound.

(*b*) *a* **1300** *Cursor M.* 4350 Þi luue me has broght to grund, Þat i mai neuer mar be sund. **13..** *Sir Beues* (A.) 231 A stalword man and hardi, While he was sounde. *c* **1450** *Mirk's Festial* 13 Anon he com to hom,..and holpe hom soo, þat þay comen sonde to hauen. **1508** Dunbar *Poems* iv. 10 The stait of man dois change & vary, Now sound, now seik, now blyth, now sary. **1596** Harington *Metam. Ajax* (1814) 47 If your hawk's casting be all black, you shall see and smell she is not sound. **1605** Shaks. *Lear* ii. iv. 113 To take the indispos'd and sickly fit, For the sound man. **1660** F. Brooke tr. *Le Blanc's Trav.* 129 A slave of a high price, of thirty yeares age, beautiful, sound, and jolly. **1722** De Foe *Plague* 150 They were known to be all sound and in good health. **1791** 'G. Gambado' *Ann. Horsem.* x. (1809) 108, I have bought a grey gelding lately,..they assured me he was sound. **1849** Claridge *Cold Water Cure* 84 The sound man has purer tastes, independent of his greater self-command. **1853** *Chambers's Jrnl.* Oct., Here is a very fine boy, seven years of age, warranted sound. **1898** Watts-Dunton *Aylwin* ii. iv, A bird with a broken wing would be always more to you than a sound one!

absol. **1597** Hooker *Eccl. Pol.* v. lxviii. (1611) 368 Sound and sicke remaining both of the same body. **1601** Shaks. *All's Well* iv. iii. 189 The muster file, rotten and sound, vppon my life amounts not to fifteene thousand pole. **1670** Baxter *Cure Ch. Div.* Pref. 1 There are the wise and the foolish, the sound and the sick. **1722** De Foe *Plague* 184 The apothecaries and surgeons knew not how to discover the sick from the sound. **1817** Shelley *Rev. Islam* x. xxii, Some, ere life was spent, Sought..to shed Contagion on the sound.

fig. **1765** Francis tr. *Horace, Odes* (ed. 7) ii. iv. 27 Heart-hold [*sic*] and sound I laud her Charms.

b. Const. *of* or *in* (the limbs, mind, etc.).

sound of all four: cf. four *a.* 2 d.

1471 in *Rep. Hist. MSS. Comm.* Var. Coll. IV. 182 Sownde of mynde, sore wowndede, dredyng the parel of dethe. **1577** B. Googe *Heresbach's Husb.* iii. (1586) 114 b, The Horse that is not sounde of his Feete. **1599** Shaks. *Hen. V*, iii. vi. 27 Bardolph, a Souldier firme and sound of heart. **1636** Massinger *Bashful Lover* iv. i, She's sound of wind and limb. **1697** Dryden *Virg. Georg.* iii. 120 The Colt..Of able Body, sound of Limb and Wind. **1807** Crabbe *Par. Reg.* i. 109 Safe from all want, and sound in every limb. **1889** *Horse & Hound* 24 Aug. 516/2 Horses described as 'good hunters' must not only be sound in 'wind and eyes', but must have been hunted. **1890** Doyle *White Company* x, I am still long of breath and sound in limb.

c. In the phr. ***as sound as a bell***. Also *fig.* of the heart.

See also roach *sb.*[1] 1 b and trout *sb.*

1576 Newton *Lemnie's Complex.* (1633) 175 They be people commonly healthy, and as sound as a Bell. **1599** Shaks. *Much Ado* iii. ii. 13 He hath a heart as sound as a bell. **1608** Topsell *Serpents* (1658) 621 From that time forwards, he remained well and lusty, and as sound as a Bell. **1623** J. Taylor (Water P.) *New Discov.* A v, Blinde Fortune did so happily contriue, That we (as sound as bells) did safe ariue At Douer. **1865** *Sketches fr. Cambr.* 26 As for you, however, you are as sound as a bell. **1898** *Pall Mall Mag.* July 306 A single man..with prospects, an' as sound as a bell,..is not to be had every day.

d. Said of appetite, health, etc.

1591 Sylvester *Du Bartas* I. iv, When wilfully his tasteless Taste delights In things unsavory to sound appetites. **1605** Shaks. *Macb.* v. iii. 52 Finde her Disease, And purge it to a sound and pristine Health. **1856** Kane *Arct. Expl.* I. xvi. 191 In spite of all my efforts to keep up an example of sound bearing I fainted twice on the snow.

2. a. Of parts of the body, the constitution, etc.: Not affected by disease, decay, or injury.

Also † *to make* (a wound) *sound*, to heal or cure.

a **1300** *Cursor M.* 26925 And quils þat neunes es in wonde Es plaster nan mai mak it sond. **1390** Gower *Conf.* II. 266 Sche tok..Of herbes al the beste jus, And poured it into his wounde; That made his veynes fulle and sounde. **1560** Bible (Geneva) *Prov.* xiv. 30 A sound heart is the life of the flesh: but enuie is the rotting of the bones. **1577** B. Googe tr. *Heresbach's Husb.* III. 155 You may geue them..the bones them selues broosed, which wyll make theyr teeth the sounder. **1590** Spenser *F.Q.* III. xii. 38 The wyde wound.. Was closed vp,..And euery part to safety full sound, As she were neuer hurt, was soone restor'd. **1621** T. Williamson tr. *Goulart's Wise Vieillard* 9 Thou art quick of hearing, thy teeth are sound. **1630** *R. Johnson's Kingd. & Commw.* 116 Of stature they are tall, of a sound constitution. **1750** tr. *Leonardus' Mirr. Stones* 83 Coral makes sound the wasted gums. **1779** *Mirror* No. 67, I wished to change it while I had a sound constitution, which I owed to Nature. **1803** *Med. Jrnl.* X. 370 When a broken fragment of bone is driven beneath the sound contiguous part of the cranium. **1843** R. J. Graves *Syst. Clin. Med.* xi. 122 The brain is found to be perfectly sound and normal. **1898** *Allbutt's Syst. Med.* V. 74 Inability to lie on the sound side.

b. Of the mind, heart, etc., with reference to intellectual or moral qualities.

Freq. in citations or echoes of Juvenal *Sat.* x. 356 *Mens sana in corpore sano.*

1531 Tindale *Exp. 1 John* (1537) 97 It is the moost felicite that can be to haue a sounde mynde in a sounde body. **1577** Harrison *England* II. xii. (1877) I. 239 They haue noted three things within their sound remembrance. **1598** Rowlands *Betraying of Christ* 15 Sound conscience well is said like wall of brasse; Corrupted, fit compar'd to broken glasse. **1652** Evelyn *State France* Misc. Writ. (1805) 56 A prince of weak fabric and constitution, but sound intellectuals. **1675** Owen *Indwelling Sin* ix. (1732) 111 To endeavour after a sound and stedfast Mind. **1729** Law *Serious C.* xi. 163 The solid enjoyments, and real happiness of a sound mind. **1780** *Mirror* No. 86, Since a sound mind, according to the well-known apophthegm, is in natural alliance with a sound body. **1820** Scott *Monast.* xxi, I must trust to good sword, strong arm, and sound heart. **1876** Trevelyan *Life & Lett. Ld. Macaulay* II. ix. 122 The promptings of a sound manly heart.

c. Of a place: Morally healthy.

1876 Miss Yonge *Womankind* xxiii. 195 Servants who have once, as young girls, been landed in a kind, sound place, where they are well cared for.

3. a. Free from damage, decay, or special defect; unimpaired, uninjured; in good condition or repair.

c **1290** *St. Dominic* 220 in *S. Eng. Leg.* I. 284 Þe holie manness bokes it weren.., Also sounde huy weren and druye ase huy euer er were. **1398** Trevisa *Barth. De P.R.* XVI. vii. (Bodl. MS.), Quyke siluer..is ful longe ikepte i colde uessels and sownde. *c* **1440** *Pallad. on Husb.* XII. 357 Ther cannes styke; on hem sarmentis plie, With grapes faire & sounde aparty hie. **1555** Eden *Decades* II. II. (Arb.) 111 Of theyr soundeste plankes..they framed a newe carauel. **1594** Shaks. *Rich. III*, v. iii. 65 Look that my Staues be sound, & not too heauy. **1653** Ramesey *Astrol. Restored* 147 The Trees are tall, sound, fruitfull, and good. **1687** A. Lovell tr. *Thevenot's Trav.* I. 113 All the Walls are so sound, that they seem as if they had been but lately built. **1725** De Foe *Voy. round World* (1840) 94 Our men healthy, and our ships sound. **1791** 'G. Gambado' *Ann. Horsem.* vi. (1809) 91 If the gate or stile happens to be in a sound state. **1826** *Art Brewing* (ed. 2) 92 You can use good sound barleys for that purpose, and reject blown, or otherwise injured, goods. **1857** Miller *Elem. Chem., Org.* i. 13 By means of a sound elastic cork. **1887** Jefferies *Amaryllis* xiii, They were all dressed better than her, and without a doubt had sound boots on their feet.

fig. **1588** Shaks. *L.L.L.* v. ii. 415 My loue to thee is sound, *sans* cracke or flaw. **1596** Spenser *State Irel.* Wks. (Globe) 612/2 They reserved theyr titles, tenures, and signioryes whole and sound to themselves. **1607** Tourneur *Rev. Trag.* II. iv, Before his eyes He would ha' seen the execution sound Without corrupted favour. **1618** Fletcher *Women Pleased* I. iii, 'Tis but a Proverb sound, and a neck broken.

b. Of air, liquor, or food: Not spoiled or vitiated in any way; hence, wholesome, good and strong. Also in fig. context.

c **1460** *Play Sacram.* 41 And sythe thay toke y[t] blysed brede so sownde And in a cawdron they ded hym boyle. **1584** Cogan *Haven Health* (1636) 300 Neither is the ayre to bee judged sound as soon as the Plague ceaseth. **1594** Plat *Jewell-ho.* I. 9, I haue also heard it verie crediblie reported, that a side of venison hath byn kept sound and sweet one whole month together. **1604** E. G[rimstone] tr. *D'Acosta's Hist. Indies* II. xiv. 114 There is nothing more agreeable, then to inioy a heaven [= air] that is sound, sweet and pleasant. **1635** Swan *Spec. M.* (1643) 381 The Trout is admirable: for this is so sound in nourishment, that [etc.]. **1818** Scott *Hrt. Midl.* xxviii, Mrs. Bickerton..drank some sound old ale, and a glass of stiff negus. **1821** —— *Kenilw.* i, Having a cellar of sound liquor, a ready wit, and a pretty daughter. **1899** *Allbutt's Syst. Med.* VIII. 748 Sound wine in moderation.

c. Financially solid or safe. Also (orig. *U.S.*) *spec.* of currency: having a fixed or stable value, esp. based on gold. Freq. as ***sound money***.

1601 R. Johnson *Kingd. & Commw.* (1603) 17 Francis the I...left his credite sound with the marchants, and readie money to his sonne. **1833** Ht. Martineau *Berkeley the Banker* I. i. 17 In my country, Scotland, the banks are particularly sound. **1841** J. Tyler in J. D. Richardson *Messages & Papers of Presidents 1789–1897* (1897) IV. 85 The idea..of furnishing a sound paper medium of exchange may be entirely abandoned. **1879** Froude *Cæsar* ix. 91 He lent his money..with sound securities and at usurious interest. **1883** *Daily Tel.* 10 Nov. 5/4 The finances of the colony were in a sound condition. **1895** *Nation* 19 Dec. 438/1 He has astonished the friends of sound money. **1903** R. T. Ely *Studies in Evol. Industrial Society* 482 The Fabians have been in favour of what is called with us sound currency. **1938** H. V. Hodson *Slump & Recovery* vii. 217 The 'sound-money' provision that only unquestionably strong banks should be allowed to reopen. **1958** *Spectator* 8 Aug. 198/2 Are they now Sound Money men, after thirteen years of Tory-Socialist inflation?

d. In proper condition for the purpose.

1883 *Cassell's Fam. Mag.* IX. 760/1 The heat may then.. be reduced a little, still the oven must be 'sound', and kept as near as possible at a uniform temperature.

4. a. Of things or substances: Solid, massive, compact. †Of a wood: Dense.

c **1375** *Sc. Leg. Saints* xvii. (*Martha*) 16 Sa thik & sownd was þe wod Be-twene Arle and Avynone. **1387** Trevisa *Higden* (Rolls) IV. 453 Also þe Est ȝate.., þat was so hevy of sound bras þat twenty men were besy i-now for to tende it, ..opened by hymself. **1551** Recorde *Cast. Knowl.* (1556) 17 A sphere is a round and sound body. **1577** B. Googe tr. *Heresbach's Husb.* 20 Hereunto you may cast ashes,..dust and other thinges raked togeather, but in the middest you must lay some sounde matter. **1825** Scott *Talism.* iv, A small Gothic chapel, hewn..out of the sound and solid rock. **1855** *Orr's Circ. Sci., Inorg. Nat.* 212 The line..should have a naturally sound foundation of rock, well drained, and not liable to destruction from mere exposure.

b. Of land: Dry in subsoil; not boggy or marshy. Now *dial.*

1523 Fitzherb. *Husb.* §18 Lette theym [*sc.* sheep] out of the folde, and dryue theym to the soundest place of the felde. *Ibid.* §39 He that hath noo seuerall and sounde pasture, to put his lambes vnto. **1789** T. Wright *Meth. Watering Meadows* (1790) 9 Its [*sc.* land] herbage, if coarse, is fined; its soil, if swampy, becomes sound. **1873** *N. & Q.* 4th Ser. XI. 57 It is a good sound heaf, with plenty of heather, and good herbage.

†5. Safe, secure; free from danger. *Obs.*

1535 Stewart *Cron. Scot.* II. 492 Suppois the se was neuir so soft and sound: In that passage this ilk Edmund wes dround.

6. a. Of sleep, etc.: Deep, heavy, profound; unbroken or undisturbed.

1548 Elyot s.v. *Arctus, Arctior somnus*, sounde slepe. **1560** Daus tr. *Sleidane's Comm.* 232 He was caste into a marvelous depe and sounde slepe. **1597** Shaks. *2 Hen. IV*, IV. v. 35 This sleepe is sound indeede. **1639** N. N. tr. *Du Bosq's Compl. Woman* II. 19 These slaves seeing their pretended Husbands layd in a sound sleepe, most subtilly stole away their Armes. **1673** *Humours Town* (1693) 2, I could scarce get one sound nap. **1709** Addison *Tatler* No. 97 ¶7 Their Slumbers are sound, and their Wakings chearful. **1804** Abernethy *Surg. Obs.* 176 His sleep was sound and undisturbed. **1833** T. Hook *Parson's Dau.* II. xi, [He] went into a sound nap. **1893** Forbes-Mitchell *Remin. Gt. Mutiny* 126, I..had a sound refreshing sleep.

transf. **1616** *Pasquil & Kath.* v. 133 Once more a blessed chance Hath fetcht againe my spirit from the sownd And languishing despaire of happinesse.

b. Hence with *sleeper*. Also as a moth-name.

For *sound* = 'sound asleep', see sound *adv.* 2 b.

1877 *Reports Prov.* 139 (E.D.D.), Pointing to brown moth, 'tis a sound-sleeper. **1898** Watts-Dunton *Aylwin* xv. i, I was always a sound sleeper.

7. a. Of a solid, substantial, ample, or thorough nature or character.

1565 Cooper *Thesaurus* s.v. *Solidus*, With a name of more glorious shew, then sounde value. **1601** Holland *Pliny* I. 567 The soile..vnderneath..drinks in much moisture..; for many a sound showre..passeth and runneth through it. **1618** Bolton *Florus* (1636) 132 Metellus..tooke a most sound revenge for the losse of Iuventius. *a* **1676** Hale *Prim. Orig. Man.* I. i. (1677) 25 It gives every considering man a sound and full conviction that [etc.]. **1784** Cowper *Tiroc.* 437 School-friendships are not always found..permanent and sound. **1815** J. Smith *Panorama Sci. & Art* II. 593 A light, sandy loam, whose sound dryness is acknowledged. **1863** A. K. H. Boyd *Graver Thoughts Country P.* 209 The greedy farmer will tell many lies to get a sound price for a lame horse. **1897** *Allbutt's Syst. Med.* III. 913 When..the attack passes off the patient makes a sound recovery.

b. Of blows, a beating, etc.: Dealt or given with force or severity.

1607 Brewer *Lingua* III. i, I looked for a sound rap on the pate. **1681** Dryden *Span. Friar* III. ii, Just as when a fellow has got a sound Knock upon the head, they say he's settled. **1728** Ramsay *Monk & Miller's Wife* 246 Be sure to lend him a sound rout. **1821** Scott *Kenilw.* xxx, The porter..started up with his club, and dealt a sound douse or two on each side of him. **1852** Miss Yonge *Cameos* I. iv. 27 He will give you a sound beating. **1887** Hall Caine *Life Coleridge* i. 22 He proceeded to exterminate Voltaire by force of a flogging, which Coleridge feelingly described as sound if not salutary.

II. 8. a. In full accordance with fact, reason, or good sense; founded on true or well-established grounds; free from error, fallacy, or logical defect; good, strong, valid.

The several groups of quotations illustrate some of the principal varieties of context.

(*a*) *c* **1440** Capgrave *Life St. Kath.* v. 1183 Youre counseyll in this is neyther saue ne sounde. **1576** Gascoigne *Steele Gl.* (Arb.) 52 And sound advice might ease hir wearie thoughtes. **1596** *Edw. III*, I. i. 101 The soundest counsell I can giue his grace, Is to surrender ere he be constraynd. **1697** Dryden *Æneid* XII. 42 Sound Advice, proceeding from a heart Sincerely yours.

(*b*) **15..** *Syr Peny* 117 in Hazl. *E.P.P.* I. 166 He makyth the fals to be soende, And ryght puttys to the grounde. **1596** Shaks. *Merch. V.* IV. i. 238 You know the Law, your exposition Hath beene most sound. **1600** —— *A.Y.L.* III. ii. 62 Shallow agen: a more sounder instance, come. **1622** Gataker *Spirituall Watch* (ed. 2) 118 To passe by this, which I take to bee not all out so sound. **1653** Ramesey *Astrol. Restored* 36, I would fain see them pass any sound word or Argument against it. **1711** G. Hickes *Two Treat. Chr. Priesth.* (1847) II. 363 This rigorously exercised supremacy, which our princes have since explained into a sounder sense. **1781** Burke in *Corr.* (1844) II. 445 Mr. Laurens' remarks are as sound as they are acute and ingenious. **1818** Cruise *Digest* (ed. 2) III. 305 There seems to have been no sound reason for this distinction. **1841** Macaulay *Let.* in Trevelyan *Life* (1876) II. ix. 118 Your objection to the lines is quite sound. **1849** —— *Hist. Eng.* x. II. 609 Their old theory, sound or unsound, was at least complete and coherent.

(*c*) **1598** Meres in Ingleby *Shaks. Cent. Praise* 24 The cleanest wit and soundest wisedome. **1706** E. Ward *Wooden World Diss.* (1708) 14 Bubling he says is the Result of sound Reasoning. **1780** Harris *Philol. Enq.* Wks. (1841) 450 Strictly conformable to the rules of sound and ancient criticism. **1802** Mar. Edgeworth *Moral T.* (1816) I. viii. 48 Consistent with sound philosophy. **1855** J. Phillips *Man. Geol.* 11 As a basis of true and sound geology. **1865** Tylor *Early Hist. Man.* i. 2 The growth of sound knowledge. **1899** *Allbutt's Syst. Med.* VIII. 840 The patient instead of adopting the counsel of sound surgery, betakes himself to the perilous resources of quackery.

(*d*) **1697** Dryden *Virgil, Life* (1721) I. 72 He has solv'd more Phænomena of Nature upon sound Principles, than Aristotle in his Physics. **1836** Thirlwall *Hist. Greece* II. 225 It does indeed indicate..larger views, and sounder principles of policy. **1855** *Orr's Circ. Sci., Inorg. Nat.* 127 Without sound general views there can be no safe practical use of any science. **1888** Bryce *Amer. Commw.* xvii. I. 244 Without expressing any opinion as to whether the policy of Protection be or be not sound.

b. Theologically correct; orthodox.

1575 Gascoigne *Glasse Governm.* Wks. 1910 II. 66 All this I confesse also to be good & sound doctrine. **1594** Hooker *Eccl. Pol.* IV. ii. §1 It is out of doubt that..in the prime of Christian religion faith was soundest. **1609** Bible (Douay) *Exod.* xxviii. *comm.*, Bishopes and Priestes must have special vertues,..sound doctrin, and band of union. *a* **1700** Evelyn *Diary* 30 Jan. 1653, He ordinarily preach'd sound doctrine. **1784** Cowper *Tiroc.* 198 [Being] taught.. sound religion sparingly enough. **1837** Pusey in Liddon *Life* (1893) II. i. 16 We have too much to do to keep sound doctrine..to be able to go into the question about dresses. **1858** W. Arnot *Laws fr. Heaven* II. xi. 95 A sound creed will not save a careless liver in the great day. **1870** J. Bruce *Life Gideon* xii. 218 The indissoluble connection between a sound faith and a sincere conscience.

†c. Of a book or writing: Accurate, correct.

1599 Thynne *Animadv.* (1875) 61 The printe must be corrected after those written copies (whiche I yet holde for sounde till I maye disprove them). **1611** Bible *Transl. Pref.* ¶6 That Translation was not so sound and so perfect, but that it needed in many places correction. *a* **1700** Evelyn *Diary* 20 Feb. 1676, A famous..treatise against the corruption in the Cleargie, but not sound as to its quotations.

9. Of judgement, sense, etc.: Based on or characterized by well-grounded principles or good practical knowledge.

1577 B. Googe *Heresbach's Husb.* (1586) 7 Those that are of sounder iudgement, account the husbandmen most happy. **1613** Harcourt *Voy. Guiana* 37 As others also of sound iudgement, and great experience doe hold opinion. **1620** T. Granger *Div. Logike* 2 Instituted or framed according to sound reason. **1718** *Free-thinker* No. 75. 137 It is a Maxim of the soundest Sense. **1790** Burke *Fr. Rev.* 303 The learning which could make judicial discretion.. deserving the appellation of a sound discretion. **1830** Scott *Monast.* Introd., By a transcendent flight, beyond sound reason and common sense. **1847** W. C. L. Martin *The Ox* 166/2 A skilful practitioner, whose knowledge of anatomy will enable him to act with promptness and sound judgment. **1857** Livingstone *Trav.* ii. 38 A most convincing proof of our sound sense.

10. Of persons, disposition, principles, etc.:

a. Morally good; honest, straightforward.

1580 Lyly *Euphues* (Arb.) 461 Knowing that there is nothing that smelleth sweeter to the Lorde, then a sounde spirite. *a* **1586** Sidney *Ps.* XVIII. vii, I walk'd his waies,.. Sound and upright with him, to wickednes not bent. **1687** Miége *Gt. Fr. Dict.* II. s.v., To have sound (honest, or good) Principles. **1695** Congreve *Love for L.* III. iv, *Mrs. Fore*... You are such an universal Jugler,—that I'm afraid you have a great many Confederates. *Scan.* Faith, I'm sound.

b. Sincere, true; not doubtful or disaffected in any way; trusty, loyal.

1581 J. Bell *Haddon's Answ. Osor.* 194, I dare scarsely thinke you to be in any respect a sownde frende thereunto. **1613** Shaks. *Hen. VIII*, III. ii. 274, I..That in the way of Loyaltie, and Truth, Toward the King..Dare mate a sounder man then Surrie can be. **1617** Moryson *Itin.* II. 299 Little to bee feared, if the English-Irish there had sound hearts to the State. **1781** Cowper *Friendship* 15 The requisites that form a friend, A real and a sound one. **1817** *Evans's Parl. Deb.* I. 586 The great body of the labourers.. in that part of the kingdom, he believed to be sound.

c. Having a healthy national or moral tone.

1882 Gen. Stewart (of Garth) *Sk. Highlanders*, etc. II. 257 The mass of the population may, on occasions of trial, be reckoned on as sound and trust-worthy. *a* **1862** Buckle *Civiliz.* (1869) III. iii. 130 As long as the people are sound, there is life. **1879** M. Arnold *Mixed Ess., Democracy* 5 One ..beneficial influence,..the administration of a vigorous and high-minded aristocracy is calculated to exert upon a robust and sound people. **1902** *Daily Chron.* 15 Apr. 3/6 The American, too, is a 'sound' man, jolly good company, and no end of fun.

11. a. Of persons: Holding accepted, approved, solid, or well-grounded opinions or views, esp. in regard to religious belief; orthodox.

pred. **1526** Tindale *Titus* i. 13 Wherefore rebuke them sharply, that they maye be sounde [Gr. ὑγιαίνωσιν] in the fayth. **1613** SHAKS. *Hen. VIII*, v. iii. 81 *Gard.* Doe not I know you for a Fauourer Of this new Sect? Ye are not sound. *Crom.* Not sound? **1704** SWIFT *T. Tub* Concl., A temptation of being witty, upon occasions where I could be neither wise, nor sound, nor anything to the matter in hand. **1855** MACAULAY *Hist. Eng.* xiv. III. 447 The King, too, it was said, was not sound. **1874** *Contemp. Rev.* Oct. 708 He came from Scotland sound as a bell on the five points of Calvinism.

absol. **1682** *2nd Plea for Nonconf.* Ded. A iij b, Distinguish between Preacher and Preacher, between the sound and the unsound.

attrib. **1594** HOOKER *Eccl. Pol.* III. viii. 3 The will of God ..no sound divine in the world ever denied to be [etc.]. **1626** in *Cath. Rec. Soc. Publ.* I. 96 Testifying that he was a sound catholique, & had done them faithful service. **1685** BAXTER *Paraphr. N.T.* Mark iv. 20 All sound Christians are not equally fruitful. **1714** POPE *Wife Bath* 55 For so said Paul, and Paul's a sound divine. **1764** WESLEY *Let. to T. Rankin* Wks. 1830 XII. 305, I hope John Cattermole (a sound man) will come and help you. **1820** SCOTT *Monast.* Introd. Ep., It would ill become me, a sound Protestant, and a servant of government.., to implicate myself [etc.]. **1882** R. G. WILBERFORCE *Life W. Wilberforce* III. vi. 169 'Well, but my Lord, after all, he is a very sound man!' 'He is indeed with a vengeance,' said the Bishop, 'if you mean *vox et præterea nihil*'.

b. Hence ***to be sound on*** (something). Orig. *U.S.* and chiefly *colloq.*

1856 *Knickerbocker Mag.* XLVIII. 287 A slight German accent did not prevent him from being sound, as he said, 'on ter coose question'. **1859** BARTLETT *Dict. Amer.* (ed. 2) 430 *Sound on the goose*, a phrase originating in the Kansas troubles, and signifying true to the cause of slavery. **1872** DE VERE *Americanisms* 267 Now, sound on the goose means simply to be stanch on the party question, whatever that may be for the moment. **1893** F. F. MOORE *I Forbid Banns* (1899) 119 That he was sound even on a seven hours' question.

c. *U.S.* (See quot.)

1872 DE VERE *Americanisms* 266 If he has been in political life before, his record is carefully searched to find out if he is sound, that is, if he has always voted strictly with his party.

12. Of sober or solid judgement; well-grounded in principles or knowledge; thoroughly versed and reliable.

1615 G. SANDYS *Trav.* 218 As sound in iudgement as ripe in experience. **1654** tr. *Scudery's Curia Pol.* 61 It was very difficult to be a sick Patient, and a sound Polititian, to govern the people, being personally weak. **1852** BRISTED *Five Yrs. Eng. Univ.* (ed. 2) 274 Good sound scholars, but not remarkably showy or striking. **1872** RUSKIN *Eagle's N.* i. 3 The least part of the work of any sound art-teacher must be his talking. **1891** E. PEACOCK *N. Brendon* I. 62 You are a sound judge of poetry.

13. *Comb.*, as ***sound-headed***, ***-hearted***, ***-minded***, etc. Also ***sound-heartedness*** and ***sound-sweet*** adj.

1808 SCOTT *Let.* in *Lockhart* (1837) II. vi. 205 He is judicious..and uncommonly *sound-headed. **1856** *N. Brit. Rev.* XXVI. 87 Henry and his Parliament, though still doctrinal Romanists, were sound-headed practical Englishmen. **1608** DOD & CLEAVER *Expos. Prov.* 84 Who thus testifie of themselues, and of all other *sound hearted Christians. **1841** MIALL in *Nonconf.* I. 241 A sound-hearted patriot. *a* **1853** ROBERTSON *Lect.* ii. (1858) 53 The *sound-heartedness and right feeling of the great majority. **1826** E. IRVING *Babylon* II. I. 140 It became a fixed and settled principle with all *sound-minded men. **1856** *N. Brit. Rev.* XXVI. 63 This is enough..to screen this sound-minded Calvinist from all criticism or remark. **1863** COWDEN CLARKE *Shaks. Char.* viii. 208 The most *sound-sensed man of the group. **1591** SYLVESTER *Ivry* 459 Wks. (Grosart) II. 251 Their Leach that fain would cure their harm Applying many *sound-sweet Med'cines fit. **1589** R. HARVEY *Pl. Perc.* (1590) 8 They..were the *soundest winded subiects. **1561** T. NORTON *Calvin's Inst.* IV. 86 To poynt out..what maner of thyng the profession of monkes was..: so as the *soundwitted reders may iudge by the comparison.

sound (saʊnd), *adv.* Also 5 **sounde, sownde,** 6 **sownd.** [f. SOUND *a.*]

†**1.** Without harm or injury; in safety or security; safely. *Obs.*

a **1400–50** *Alexander* 5532 How he miȝt seke doun sounde in-to þe see bothom. *c* **1400** *Destr. Troy* 652 So may ye surely & sounde to myselfe come. *c* **1450** HOLLAND *Howlat* 774 He gart thaim se..Sound saland on the se schippis of towr.

2. ***to sleep sound***, to enjoy deep, unbroken, or undisturbed sleep; to be in a profound sleep.

a **1400** *Octavian* 72 When y am to bedd broght, Y slepe but selden sownde. **1513** DOUGLAS *Æneid* VII. Prol. 111 On slummyr I slaid full sad, and slepit sownd. **1590** SPENSER *F.Q.* I. i. 42 So sound he slept, that nought mought him awake. **1722** DE FOE *Col. Jack* i, Among the coal-ashes where I slept..as sound, and as comfortably as ever I did since. **1770** LANGHORNE *Plutarch* V. 224 Fulvius slept so sound after his wine, that [etc.]. **1852** THACKERAY *Esmond* II. v, Some night he begins to sleep sound.

phr. **1711** RAMSAY *On Maggy Johnstoun* x, I trow I took a nap,..As sound's a tap. **1727** GAY *New Song of New Similes* vi, But she, insensible of that, Sound as a top can sleep.

b. ***sound asleep***, sunk in sleep; fast asleep. Also with ellipse of *asleep*.

1592 SHAKS. *Rom. & Jul.* IV. v. 8 How sound is she a sleepe? I must needs wake her. **1821** SCOTT *Kenilw.* i, He may be found sound asleep on his feather-bed. **1839** DICKENS *Nickleby* xxiii, Asleep she did fall, sound as a church. **1844** W. H. MAXWELL *Sports & Adv. Scot.* vii. (1855) 81 'Sound as a watchman,' [he] hears nothing. **1891** A. GORDON *Garglen* ii. 54 How can you say all this, when you were sound as a trooper?

3. In a sound manner; heartily, soundly.

1598 SHAKS. *Merry W.* IV. iv. 61 Let the supposed Fairies pinch him, sound, And burne him with their Tapers.

b. In various combs., as ***sound-judging***, ***-thinking***; ***sound-set***, ***-stated***, etc.

1598 SYLVESTER *Du Bartas* II. i. I. *Eden* 302 Man (having yet spirit sound-stated) Should dwel elswhere, then where he was created. **1632** LITHGOW *Trav.* VIII. 342 The sound set man..still keepeth his way. **1817** SCOTT *Let.* in *Lockhart* (1837) IV. ii. 72 A set of quiet, unpretending, but sound-judging country gentlemen. **1838** DICKENS *O. Twist* xii, Laws which certain profound and sound-judging philosophers have laid down. **1873** LD. DUFFERIN in A. Lyall *Life* (1905) I. vii. 227 My real sympathies were..with the sound-thinking portion of the nation.

sound (saʊnd), *v.*[1] Forms: *α.* 4 **sune,** 4–5 **sone, sovne,** 4–6 **soun(e, sown(e.** *β.* 5–6 **sounde,** 5–7 **sownd(e,** 5– **sound.** [ad. OF. *suner*, *soner* (mod.F. *sonner*), = Prov. and Sp. *sonar*, Pg. *soar*, It. *sonare*:—L. *sonāre*, f. *sonus* sound.]

I. *intr.* **1. a.** Of things: To make or emit a sound.

Frequently with adverbial or adjectival complement.

α. *a* **1325** *Prose Psalter* xlv[i]. 3 Þe waters souned, and ben trubled. **1362** LANGL. *P. Pl.* A. Prol. 10 As I..lokede on þe watres, I slumberde in a slepyng, hit sownede so murie. **1387** TREVISA *Higden* (Rolls) VII. 73 Water organs þat sowneþ by ayer and water. *c* **1450** *Merlin* x. 154 Where as thei herde the trompe sowne. **1486** *Bk. St. Albans* d iij, And thay be brokyn thay wyll sowne full dulli. *a* **1533** LD. BERNERS *Huon* liii. 181 Trompettes & taboures began to sowne. **1565** COOPER *Thesaurus* s.v. *Lituus*, *Strepunt litui*, the trumpettes sowne.

β. **1483** *Cath. Angl.* 350/1 To sownde, *strepere*. **1530** PALSGR. 726/1 This bell soundeth a mys. *Ibid.*, This horne sowndeth meryly. **1579** *Poore Knights Palace* E iij, Whose harpe did sound almost the silent night. **1662** J. DAVIES tr. *Olearius' Voy. Amb.* 33 The Trumpet alwaies sounding when the meat was carried up. **1749** GRAY *Installat. Ode* 35 But hark! the portals sound. **1794** MRS. RADCLIFFE *Myst. Udolpho* xxxiii, Presently the castle-clock struck twelve, and then a trumpet sounded. **1818** SCOTT *Hrt. Midl.* iii. *note*, No other drum but theirs was allowed to sound on the High Street. **1845** J. COULTER *Adv. in Pacific* xiv. 193 In still weather, you will hear them [war-conches] for miles, they sound so loudly. **1877** FROUDE *Short Stud.* (1883) IV. I. x. 120 From the cathedral tower the vesper bell was beginning to sound.

b. To resound (*to*, *with*, or †*of* something); to be filled with sound.

13.. *Minor Poems fr. Vernon MS.* xxiii. 515 Of whos herying sounen..Heuene, Erþe and See. *c* **1475** *Partenay* 4718 A meruelus cry vp he cast þat stound, All the toure souned when he fill to ground. **1577** HANMER *Anc. Eccl. Hist.* (1619) 177 All sounded of lamentation through-out every narrow lane. **1821** SCOTT *Kenilw.* xxxi, The great hall of the Castle..sounding to strains of soft and delicious music. *a* **1854** H. REED *Lect. Eng. Lit.* iii. (1878) 117 It is one of the noblest languages that the earth has ever sounded with. **1896** HOUSMAN *Shropshire Lad* xxii, The street sounds to the soldiers' tread.

c. Of instruments: To give a call or summons *to* arms, battle, etc. Also without subject.

1705 J. ROBINS *Hero of Age* II. ii. 3 Now first is beat the General Alarm, Now sounds to Horse. **1724** DE FOE *Mem. Cavalier* (1840) 68 The trumpets sounded to horse. **1825** SCOTT *Talism.* vii, When the trumpet sounds to arms, my foot is in the stirrup as soon as any. **1855** MACAULAY *Hist. Eng.* xiv. III. 419 The peal of a trumpet sounding to battle.

2. Of persons: **a.** To make a sound by blowing, or playing upon, some instrument.

1382 WYCLIF *Lev.* xxv. 9 Thow shalt sowne with trompe the seuenthe moneth. **1485** CAXTON *Paris & V.* (1868) 4 The mynstrellys..that sowned at the feste. **1576** GASCOIGNE *Kenelw. Castle* Wks. 1910 II. 92 Sixe Trumpetters..who had..Trumpettes counterfetted, wherein they seemed to sound. **1585** T. WASHINGTON tr. *Nicholay's Voy.* III. i. 69 b, They doe sound vpon a thing very like vnto a Cittern. **1609** BIBLE (Douay) *1 Chron.* ii. 55 The kinredes also of the scribes..singing and sounding [L. *resonantes*]. **1687** WOOD *Life* 2 Nov., Soldiers and trumpeters..drinking healths, and every health they sounded. **1706** PHILLIPS (ed. Kersey), *Siticines*,..those who sounded upon a sort of Trumpet..at their Funeral Solemnities. **1819** SCOTT *Ivanhoe* xl, 'What! sound for aid,' exclaimed the Knight, 'against a score of such *rascaille* as these'. **1859** TENNYSON *Geraint & Enid* 382 Enid ..thought she heard the wild Earl..Sound on a dreadful trumpet.

fig. **1567** MAPLET *Gr. Forest* Introd. A iij b, The verie Instrument which I nowe sound of, is not as I would it were.

†**b.** To utter vocal sounds; to speak, cry, or sing. *Obs.*

c **1340** HAMPOLE *Psalter* lxxvi. 16 Many men þat first sownyd, gaynsaiand til goed lare, sithen ware broght till soth-fastnes. *c* **1500** *Lancelot* 1811 'Welcum be he!' and so the puple soundith. **1577** HANMER *Anc. Eccl. Hist.* (1619) 185 Let us honour him (sounding continually with mouth and mind). **1595** SPENSER *Col. Clout* 20 Sith thy Muse.. Was heard to sound as she was wont on hye.

c. ***to sound off.*** (*a*) Of a band: to strike up (see also quot. 1909). Also *imp. U.S. Mil.*

1909 WEBSTER s.v. *sound*, *to sound off*. *Mil.*, at a certain point in the ceremony of parade or guard mounting in the United States army, to play, usually marching in quick time from right to left of the line and back:—said of the band or field music. **1919** *Review* (N.Y.) 30 Aug. 350/3 The organization of all possible 'errors' in the use of language into categories and hierarchies, and parading them before classes with all the pomp of 'Sound off!' and 'Pass in review!'. **1936** *Amer. Speech* XI. 61 The adjutant commands, 'Sound off!' and the band marches, playing, back and forth before the stationary troops... And so,.. when a man talks loud and long, playing the tune of his own thoughts before uninterested comrades, he is said to be *sounding off*.

(*b*) to speak out, to speak loudly; to complain, protest; to brag; to put forward one's opinion, esp. forcefully and at length. *colloq.* (orig. *U.S.*).

1918 G. E. GRIFFIN *Ballads of Regiment* 39 You low-down, dirty rookey! What in blazes do you mean By sounding off and beefing, not a rag upon you clean. **1920** *Amer. Legion Weekly* 13 Aug. 28 (*caption*) *Sounding off*. But he is sounding off before inspection. You can't blame him because he has been hoping and waiting for the *Weekly*.. but it hasn't come. **1935** C. G. FINNEY *Circus of Dr. Lao* 63 Kate, don't go sounding off that way in front of all these people. **1939** J. STEINBECK *Grapes of Wrath* xiii. 174, I didn' mean to sound off at ya, mister. It's the heat. **1943** *Amer. Mercury* Nov. 554 A guy who *sounds off* (talks too much) is told to *knock it off*. **1951** *Sunday Pictorial* 21 Jan. 10/2 The 'Pic' cites a few examples with the sincere wish that someone will shut them up the next time they sound off. **1960** L. COOPER *Accomplices* II. i. 80 He used to sound off about the chap and blackguard him all ends up. **1972** 'E. LATHEN' *Murder without Icing* (1973) xxii. 195 We thought he was just sounding off. **1979** 'A. HAILEY' *Overload* IV. ix. 340 It adds up to him being an exhibitionist with a need to 'sound off' constantly, even in small ways.

3. a. To strike the ears, to be heard, as a sound. Also with *in* (one's) *ears* and with adjs. or advs.

α. **13..** *E.E. Allit. P.* B. 1670 Er þenne þe souerayn saȝe souned in his eres. **1387** TREVISA *Higden* (Rolls) III. 275 'What have I to doo þerwiþ,' quod he, 'wheþer þis noyse sowne upward oþer dounward'. *a* **1450** tr. *De Imitatione* III. i. 64 Pleinly þo eres are blessid, þat takiþ non hede to þe voice sounyng outwarde. **1485** *St. Wenefryde* (Caxton) 9 A voys from heuen souned in his eres. **1548** ELYOT, *Assono*,..to sowne..agayn lyke to an Ecco. **1568** *Interl. Jacob & Esau* IV. ix, The voice of Jacob sowneth in mine eare.

β. **1530** PALSGR. 726/1 Harke howe her voyce sowndeth scyrle in the ayer. **1586** FERNE *Blaz. Gentrie* 229 Names consisting vpon two or three sillables (especially sounding vpon the french) be most honourable. **1632** MILTON *Il Pens.* 74, I hear the far-off Curfeu sound. **1640** in *Verney Mem.* (1907) I. 109 This is the newes that sounds merrily in our eares. **1818** SCOTT *Br. Lamm.* xii, A din, proceeding from the revels.., sounded half-way down the street. **1823** —— *Quentin D.* xxx, As if the words of an oracle sounded in his ears. **1862** MISS BRADDON *Lady Audley* i, The strange passion..making her voice sound shrill and piercing.

b. To issue *out* as, or with, a sound.

1526 TINDALE *1 Thess.* i. 8 From you sounded out the worde of the lorde. **1837** CARLYLE *Fr. Rev.* I. IV. ii, For always, as it sounds out 'at the market-cross', accompanied with trumpet-blast.

c. To be mentioned or spoken of.

1635 J. HAYWARD tr. *Biondi's Banish'd Virg.* 7 Now the daily newes of the future bridegroome began to sound. **1832** DISRAELI *Cont. Flem.* I. vii. (1853) 26 Wherever I went my name sounded, whatever was done my opinion was quoted. **1842** BORROW *Bible in Spain* xxxiv, The name of Flinter had long sounded amongst the Carlist ranks.

d. *Black English.* = *to play the dozens* s.v. PLAY *v.* 16 e; ***to sound on*** (someone): to taunt, to criticize (someone). Cf. sense 13 below.

1962 R. D. ABRAHAMS in *Jrnl. Amer. Folklore* LXXV. 215 When men do 'sound'..it provides a very different kind of release than when adolescents do. **1971** B. MALAMUD *Tenants* 73 I'm not soundin on you, Lesser, but how can you be so whiteass sure of what you sayin if my book turns out to be two different things than you thought? **1972** W. LABOV *Language in Inner City* p. xxii, Johnny..had a curious bald spot on the top of his head several months ago, since grown over, and he is still sounded on regularly by reference to this bald spot. **1973** E. BULLINS *Theme is Blackness* 107 Hey.. baby..why you got to sound on me like that? **1974** H. L. FOSTER *Ribbin', Jivin', & Playin' Dozens* iv. 160 He knows how to 'run a game', to 'signify', to 'woof'..and to 'sound'.

4. a. To convey a certain impression or idea by the sound; to appear to have a certain signification when heard (or read).

α. *c* **1374** CHAUCER *Troylus* v. 678 In non other place.. Feele I no wynde that souneth so lyke peyne; It seith 'Allas! why twynned be we tweyne?' *c* **1449** PECOCK *Repr.* I. v. 27 My feeling in thilk mater is other wise than the speche sowneth. *c* **1450** *St. Cuthbert* (Surtees) 1554 Þai..red þe text als it sounes. **1533** TINDALE *Supper of the Lord* D iij b, They so vnderstode hym, and he so ment as his wordes sowned. **1538** STARKEY *England* I. ii. 63 Hyt sounyth veray yl..to gyue such powar to blynd fortune in mannys felycyte.

β. **1445** in *Anglia* XXVIII. 273 Of ripe thyngis which sounde sadly thou techist men right aged. ? **1530** TINDALE *Exp. Matt.* v. 43 To turne y[e] other cheke is a maner of spekynge and not to be vnderstand as the words sound. **1590** SHAKS. *Com. Err.* IV. iv. 7, I tell you 'twill sound harshly in her eares. **1639** FULLER *Holy War* I. ix. (1840) 14 Whose entreaties in this case sounded commands in the ears of such as were piously disposed. **1651** HOBBES *Leviath.* III. xxxviii. 239 Which soundeth as if they had said, he should come down [etc.]. **1678** CUDWORTH *Intell. Syst.* 314 This may the better be believed..because Diodorus himself hath some Passages sounding that way. **1789** T. TWINING *Aristotle's Treatise on Poetry* 216 To call them a *slip*, would indeed sound strangely. **1815** SCOTT *Guy M.* ix, That sounds like nonsense, my dear. **1825** —— *Betrothed* xiv, Their very names sound pagan and diabolical. **1851** LANDOR *Popery* 47 This sounds oddly to unmitred ears; but much may depend upon the sounding-board. **1874** BLACKIE *Self-Cult.* 71 That sort of talk sounds big, but is in fact puerile.

b. To have a sound suggestive *of* something.

1646 FULLER *Good Th. in Worse T.* Pref., Controversial writings (sounding somewhat of drums and trumpets).

†**5.** To have a suggestion or touch of, a tendency towards, some connexion or association with, a specified thing. *Obs.* Used with a variety of constructions: **a.** With *in* (see also 6), *into*, *to* (or *unto*), *towards*, etc.

The use with *to* is very common in the 15–16th centuries.

(*a*) *c* **1340** HAMPOLE *Pr. Consc.* 6079 Þat day, sal na man be excused Of nathyng..þat sounes in ille on any manere. *c* **1386** CHAUCER *Prol.* 307 Sownynge in moral vertu was his speche. **1399** *Rolls of Parlt.* III. 451/2 The Answers of thes Lordes..souned in her entent in excusation of hem.

(*b*) *c* **1374** CHAUCER *Troylus* I. 1036 Me were lever to dy, Than she of me oght ellis understode, But that that myghte sownyn into good. *c* **1380** WYCLIF *Serm.* Sel. Wks. II. 226 Whatever þei speken or don it sounneþ in to pees and charite. *c* **1412** HOCCLEVE *De Reg. Princ.* 1947 Write him no thyng þat sowneth in-to vice. *c* **1456** PECOCK *Bk. of Faith*

(1909) 137 Bi a meene sownyng into this, that God never revelid thilk article.

(c) c1380 Wyclif Wks. (1880) 306 Gabbyngis & other iapis þat sounen not to charite. 1393 Langl. P. Pl. C. x. 216 To meschief hit souneþ. 1440 in Wars English in France (Rolls) II. 452 He ne hath nought so doen..withoute notable causes sownyng to the wele of him and of his people. 1451 Capgrave Life St. Gilbert 96 All þat he spak was soundyng on-to grete profit of vertuous gouernauns. 1530 Palsgr. 726/1, I promise you that this matter sowndeth moche to your dishonour. 1558 G. Cavendish Poems (1825) II. 5 Most men have no pleasour or delight In any history, without it sownd to vice. 1589 Puttenham Eng. Poesie III. vi. (Arb.) 164 The meane matters..which sound neither to matters of state nor of warre. 1602 Fulbecke 1st Pt. Parall. 75 When the action soundeth to disceit. a1661 Fuller Worthies, Chester (1662) 291 If the Testators Will were not justly performed, it soundeth to the shame and blame of his Executors.

(d) 1513 Douglas Æneid XI. Prol. 49 The first soundis towart virteu sum deyll. 1535 in Ellis Orig. Lett. Ser. III. II. 343 Certayne words..sowndinge towards thavauncement of the Bysshoppe of Rome. 1614 Brerewood Lang. & Relig. 65 In all the Hebrew writings of the Bible, that countrey is never termed by any name sounding toward Phœnicia, but in the Greek only. a1643 Ld. Falkland, etc. Infallibility (1646) 90 This surely sounds somewhat toward a testimony of Apostolick Tradition.

(e) 1597 Hooker Eccl. Pol. v. ii. §1 It is their endeavour to banish..from their cogitation whatsoever may sound that way.

†b. With simple objective, or *of*. *Obs.*

(a) c1380 Wyclif Wks. (1880) 353 Þis sownes not charite but luciferes pride. c1386 Chaucer Prol. 275 Hise resons he spak ful solempnely, Sownynge alway thencrees of his wynnyng. 1482 Monk of Evesham xxxi. (Arb.) 74 They that spake wordis of reboudye the whiche sounned onclenesse.

(b) 1393 Langl. P. Pl. C. xii. 79 Is no wit worth now bote hit of wynnynge soune. a1548 Hall Chron., Hen. VI, 13 Odious billes and language,..sounyng of insurreccion and rebellion against the kinges peace.

†c. With *against*, *with*, or *for*. *Obs.*

(a) c1449 Pecock Repr. I. xiii. 71 Therfore it is no nede me forto..encerche the writingis of Doctouris sownyng aȝens mi present entent. 1471 Sir J. Fortescue in Wks. (1869) 531 It sownyth gretly ayen the kinges old title to his roialme of Fraunce. 1502 Arnolde Chron. (1811) 88 Examyne all such thingis as sowne wyth or ayenst the comon wele. 1581 Lambarde Eiren. II. ii. (1602) 112 Not meerelie a spirituall offence, but mixed, and sounding some-what against the Peace of the lande.

(b) 1502 [see prec.]. 1578 Banister Hist. Man I. 24 He alloweth this to sound with truth. 1639 Ld. Digby Lett. conc. Relig. (1651) 36 How this will sound with that place of St. Austin upon the 98. Psalm.

(c) 1563 Homilies II. Agst. Idol. II. ii. 56 No sentence in the old doctours and fathers soundyng for Images, ought to be of any aucthoritie. 1578–9 Reg. Privy Council Scot. Ser. I. III. 84 A new consait, not altogidder sounding for the necessitie of the caus.

6. *to sound in damages*, in legal use, to be concerned only with damages. Also *to sound in tort*, *to sound in contract*, etc.

1780 M. Madan Thelyphthora II. 153 There is not one [change] which does not sound in damages, as our lawyers speak. 1798 Bay's Reports (1809) I. 16 The discount law only extended to liquidated accounts and not to matters sounding in damages. 1885 Law Rep. 30 Chanc. Div. 21 This covenant did not create a specifically ascertained debt, but only a claim which sounded in damages. 1918 Law Rep. Appeal Cases 289 Whether it sounds in debt or in damages such a cause of action implies a present obligation to pay simultaneous with its coming into existence. 1947 Law Rep. 23 Aug. 466 An action against a salvor for negligence or misconduct sounds in tort. 1964 Mod. Law Rev. XXVII. III. 264 To juggle with the language of the forms of action and say that the plaintiff's action sounds in tort not contract, cannot alter the fact that the line between liability and non-liability is drawn by seeing whether the act..is, or is not, a breach of contract between two other persons. 1972 N.Y. Law Jrnl. 24 Oct. 20/4 While the action sounds in contract, the complaint sets forth two causes of action for unliquidated amounts.

transf. 1865 Pall Mall G. 16 May 1 His conclusion seems to us..to 'sound in' morality. 1865 Fraser's Mag. Nov. 539 It is that the whole book 'sounds', as the lawyer would say, in persuasion, not in conviction.

II. *trans.* **7.** To cause (an instrument, etc.) to make a sound; to blow, strike, or play on.

a1300 K. Horn 209 (C.), Horn þu lude sune Bi dales & bi dune. c1386 Chaucer Prol. 565 A baggepipe wel koude he blowe and sowne. c1440 Partonope 3755 The mynstrallys here Trumpes gan sowne. 1474 Caxton Chesse II. iv. (1883) 53 Therfore Joab ordeyned whan absalon was slayn he sowned a trompette. a1533 Ld. Berners Huon xciii. 299 He sowned the watch belle. 1554 in Vicary's Anat. (1888) App. III. 176 That no maner of person..sounde eny drume for the gatheringe of eny people within the said Citie. 1585 T. Washington tr. Nicholay's Voy. III. xv. 99b, [They] afterwardes doe sounde all their belles togeather. 1586 Marlowe 1st Pt. Tamburl. I. i, Sound vp the trumpets then. c1614 Sir W. Mure Dido & Æneas I. 184 Mariners..Their chearfull whisles meryly do sownd. 1741–2 Gray Agrip. 121 Or say we sound The trump of liberty. 1794 A. Russell's Aleppo (ed. 2) II. ii. I. 155 Very few of the performers [on the syrinx] can sound it tolerably well. 1806 Wordsw. Horn Egremont Castle 112 A long posterity..Sounded the Horn which they alone could sound. 1862 Ansted Channel Isl. I. ii. 33 A bell is sounded in foggy weather. 1896 Law Times Rep. LXXIII. 615/1 The driver of the approaching train began to sound his whistle.

transf. 1590 Spenser F.Q. I. xii. 5 Whom farre before did march a goodly band Of tall young men, all hable armes to sownd.

8. a. To utter in an audible tone; to pronounce or repeat. Sometimes implying loudness of voice. Also with *forth* or *out*.

α. a1300 Cursor M. 22485 Na word þai sal þo queþer sune, Til þat þai be all fallen dune. c1374 Chaucer Troylus II. 573 To yow rehercyn al his speche, Or alle his woful wordis for to sowne. c1407 Lydg. Reson & Sens. 4413 Wher hys fate was..openly to him declaryd, In greke and hebrew tonge sovnyd. c1477 Caxton Jason 38b, Alle the maronners tremblid for drede in suche wyse that they durste not sowne a worde. 1542 Udall Erasm. Apoph. 250b, She could soune the salutacion so often recited unto hir. 1593 Nashe Christ's T. 89 Hearing these tearmes of hell and eternall, so often souned in our eares.

β. c1450 tr. De Imitatione III. xv. 83 Lorde, þou sowndyst [L. intonas] thi domes upon me. 1509 Barclay Shyp of Folys (1570) 69 This man malicious..Nought els soundeth but the hoorse letter R. 1570 Foxe A. & M. (ed. 2) I. 9/1 He commaundeth all bishops and priestes to sounde out their seruice..with a loud voice. 1579 Lyly Euphues (Arb.) 185 Thou giuest as it were a sigh, which all thy companions..seeme by thee to sounde also. 1684 Contempl. St. Man II. v. (1699) 173 Those Millions of Angels, which will be sounding forth their Hallelujahs. 1823 Scott Quentin D. xx, Hearken..to one note of reason, ere it is sounded into your ear by the death-shot of ruin.

b. To reproduce or express in words. *rare.*

c1386 Chaucer Squire's T. 105 Al be that I kan nat sowne his stile. 1592 Shaks. Rom. & Jul. III. ii. 126 No words can that woe sound.

c. To utter or pronounce in a certain way.

1542 Recorde Gr. Artes B iv b, Augrym for Algorisme, as Arabians sound it. 1611 Cotgr. Appendix, E, when it is thus accented, e,..is called é Masculine, and sounded out, as in the Latine word docére. 1634 Sir T. Herbert Trav. 16 Their words are sounded rather like that of Apes, then men, whereby it's very hard to sound their Dialect. 1736 Ainsworth Latin Dict. II. s.v. C, Neither ought it [the letter c] to be sounded with an aspirate, as the modern Italians do. 1844 Kinglake Eothen vii, I suppose it is scarcely now to be doubted that they were so sounded in ancient times.

9. a. To give intimation of, a signal or order for, (something) by the sound of a trumpet or other instrument; to announce, order, or direct by such means. Also *fig.* or in fig. context.

1568 Grafton Chron. II. 326 The watchmen..perceyued well howe that the Castell was scaled and betrayed, and so sowned in a Trumpet Trahey, Trahey. 1582 Stanyhurst Æneis III. (Arb.) 77 With shril brasse trumpet Misenus sowned alarum. 1631 Gouge God's Arrows III. §56. 288 They at their discretion cause alarms or retraits to be sounded. 1673 S'too him Bayes 11 All this is but hanging forth a picture and sounding a call. 1697 Dryden Dedic. Æneid Ess. (Ker) II. 237 Our author seems to sound a charge, and begins like the clangour of a trumpet. 1734 tr. Rollin's Anc. Hist. I. 392 The besieged sounded a retreat. 1789 J. Williams Min. Kingd. I. 160, I feel in myself a strong reluctance against sounding the alarm to my country in a matter of so much importance. 1825 J. Neal Bro. Jonathan I. 90 As if he were sounding a charge with a tin whistle. 1853 Kingsley Hypatia xxii, The trumpets sounded the attack. 1893 Forbes-Mitchell Remin. Gt. Mutiny 260 Bugles were sounding the assembly.

b. To blow (a blast).

1806 Wordsw. Horn Egremont Castle 16 The blast, Which good Sir Eustace sounded, was the last. 1817 Shelley Pr. Athanase 186 When winter's roar Sounded o'er earth and sea its blast of war.

10. To declare, announce, proclaim; to make known or famous; to celebrate.

1412–20 Lydg. Chron. Troy I. 2815 Whan þat þe cok..þe mydnyȝt hour..Be-gan to sowne. c1449 Pecock Repr. III. iv. 295 Also this present processe sowneth..that Crist here clepid this ȝong man into apostilhode. 1576 Gascoigne Kenelw. Castle Wks. 1910 II. 115 O Muses sound the praise of Jove his mighty name. 1590 Greene Orl. Fur. Wks. (Rtldg.) 90 Swift fame hath sounded to our western seas The matchless beauty of Angelica. 1611 Speed Hist. Gt. Brit. IX. vii. (1623) 531 In pulpits and priuate conferences, sounding nothing but the Crosse and Passion of Christ. 1659 Hammond On Ps. 2 But David..sounds Christ upon the harp. 1709 Pope Ess. Crit. 193 Nations unborn your mighty names shall sound. 1725 —— Odyss. IX. 20 Earth sounds my wisdom, and high heav'n my fame. 1777 Johnson Let. to Mrs. Thrale 27 Oct., Of this great truth, sounded by the knowing to the ignorant,..what evidence have you now before you. 1804 J. Grahame Sabbath 306 To him The Sabbath bell sounds peace. 1849 Macaulay Hist. Eng. ii. I. 155 The Tories still continued..to sound the praise of a national militia.

†11. Of words: To signify or mean; to import or imply. *Obs.*

c1391 Chaucer Astrol. I. §21 Zodia in langage of grek sownyth 'bestes' in latyn tonge. 1422 Capgrave in Life S. Aug., etc. 147 The vij son of Iacob,..hite Simeon, whech soundith in our tonge heuynesse or pencifnesse. 1432–50 tr. Higden (Rolls) II. 63 For caer, after the langage of Britones, sowndethe a cite. a1470 H. Parker Dives & Pauper (W. de W. 1496) VII. lxvi. 283 Stelynge sowneth comonly theeft and robbery, and somtyme it sowneth preuely takynge without wyttynge of the lorde. 1526 Pilgr. Perf. (W. de W. 1531) 279b, For sapere in latyn tonge, soundeth as moche in englysshe as to sauour taste or fele. 1542 Udall Erasm. Apoph. 32b, Lenocinium, whiche souneth in englishe enticyng & alluryng. 1627 W. Sclater Exp. 2 Thess. (1629) 134 Mysterium commonly sounds a Religious secret. 1654 tr. Martini's Conq. China 106 The Sirname of Pingsi, which sounds as much as 'Pacifier of the Western world'. 1671 H. M. tr. Erasm. Colloq. 200 Among the Latines discere to learn, sounds not as much as doctrinam accipere, to receive learning.

12. To examine (a person, etc.) by auscultation; to subject to medical examination.

1817 Ld. Sefton Let. 30 Dec. in Creevey Papers (1903) I. xii. 268 It was put into my hand while a surgeon was sounding my bladder..to ascertain whether I had a stone or not. 1887 in Cassell's Encycl. Dict.

13. To taunt. Cf. sense 3 d above. *U.S. slang. rare.*

1958 H. Salisbury Shook-up Generation iv. 63 He had heart. He would do things no other boy would dare. He would sound a cop on the beat and run away laughing.

sound (saʊnd), *v.*[2] Also 5–6 sownd(e, sounde; 5 sone, soune, 6 sowne. [ad. OF. *sonder* (Sp. and Pg. *sondar*), f. *sonde* SOUND *sb.*[5]]

†1. *intr.* To sink in, penetrate, pierce. *Obs.*

13.. Coer de L. 405 He smote hym on hys basinet A grete dente withouten let; It sounded to hys cheke bone. c1374 Chaucer Troylus II. 533 So sore hath she me woundid..That to myn hertis botme it is ysounded. c1400 Destr. Troy 495 With a Sykyng vnsounde, þat sonet to hir hert. Ibid. 5284 Hit sothely with sorow sounys to my hert.

2. a. *Naut.* To employ the line and lead, or other appropriate means, in order to ascertain the depth of the sea, a channel, etc., or the nature of the bottom. Also *fig.* (quot. 1663).

c1485 Digby Myst. (1882) III. 1397 Her is a fayer haven to se! connyngly In, loke þat ye sownd. 1530 Palsgr. 726/1 Sownde, mariner, let us se what water we have to spare. 1555 Eden Decades I. IX. (Arb.) 97 Soundinge with theyr plummet they founde it to bee .xvi. fathames deepe. 1617 Moryson Itin. I. 60 There sounding with our plummet, sand of Amber stuck thereto. 1663 Butler Hud. I. i. 505 To make them dip themselves, and sound For Christendom in dirty Pond. 1725 De Foe Voy. round World (1840) 331 Men went overboard with poles in their hands, sounding, as we call it, for deeper water. 1836 Marryat Midsh. Easy xxx, A man leaped into the chains, and lowering down the lead, sounded in seven fathoms. 1856 Kane Arct. Expl. II. xxiv. 236 We were compelled..to sound ahead with the boat-hook.

transf. 1649 Lovelace The Scrutinie iii, Like skilfull Minerallists that sound For Treasure in un-plow'd-up ground. 1828 P. Cunningham N.S. Wales (ed. 3) II. 25, I sounded with the ramrod, and finding the charge still in the barrel, forthwith complied with Ben's request. 1972 Science 5 May 464/1 Lightweight ionosondes have been placed in satellites, and these sound from the height of the satellite ..down to the peak of the F layer.

b. *fig.* To make inquiry or investigation.

1793 Jefferson Writ. (1859) IV. 23 They have sent commissioners to England to sound for peace. 1825 T. Hook Sayings Ser. II. Sutherl. I. 33, I have sounded carefully, and happen to know that I am correct in my information. 1825 Carlyle Life Schiller I. (1845) 16 His thoughts..had sounded into the depths of his own nature.

3. a. Of the lead: To go down; to touch bottom.

1610 Shaks. Temp. v. i. 56 And deeper then did euer Plummet sound Ile drowne my booke. 1837 Marryat P. Keene xxxviii, When sixteen fathoms were out the lead sounded.

b. Of a whale: To go deep under water; to dive.

1839 Beale Nat. Hist. Sperm Whale (ed. 2) 164 The whale suddenly disappears; he has 'sounded'. 1845 J. Coulter Adv. in Pacific vii. 86 The whale did not, as usual, sound, but after the breach, made off. 1887 Goode Fisheries U.S. 265 If the whale sounds, the crew lay by awaiting its reappearance upon the surface for respiration.

transf. 1895 Outing XXVII. 223/2 Away sped my salmon, ..and again sounded to the bottom and sulked.

4. a. *trans.* To investigate (water, etc.) by the use of the line and lead or other means, in order to ascertain the depth or the quality of the bottom; to measure or examine in some way resembling this.

c1460 Towneley Myst. iii. 438 Now the water will I sownd. 1557 Burrough in Hakluyt Voy. (1589) 327 Sunday I sounded the barre of Zolatitsa, which the Russes tolde me was a good harborow, but in the best of it I found but 4. foote water. 1584 B. R. tr. Herodotus II. 76 Psammetichus.. sounding the waters with a rope of many miles in length, was vnable to feele any ground or bottome. 1604 E. G[rimstone] D'Acosta's Hist. Indies III. xiii. 159 It is so deepe in some places that it cannot be sounded. 1685 Travestin Acc. Siege Newheusel 33 August the third, we sounded the Ditch, and found on the East side four foot of water yet left. 1748 Anson's Voy. II. xi. 258 Our boats..were ordered out..to sound the harbour and its entrance. 1762 Falconer Shipwr. II. 249 They sound the well, and..Along the line four wetted feet appear. 1836 Penny Cycl. V. 266/1 Persons..whose regular business is to sound the bed of the river. 1863 [W. F. Campbell] Life in Normandy I. 110 He ..found a muddy man sounding a hole with the butt end of a driving whip.

transf. 1581 A. Hall Iliad IX. 171 The wine they weakly sounde, On earth the rest they throwe. 1639 N. N. tr. Du Bosq's Compl. Woman I. 56 Laocoon who tooke his Lance in his hand to sound this Machine, was punished for his Curiositie.

b. To measure (depth) in this way.

1628–9 Digby Voy. Medit. (Camden) 89 We haled out fore sailes vpon the backestayes and sounded the depth of the water. 1681 W. Robertson Phraseol. Gen. 1151 To sound the depth with a sounding line. 1728 Chambers Cycl. s.v. Sounding, Dr. Hook has invented a manner of Sounding the Depth of the deepest Sea, without any Line.

c. With *out*: To survey by means of soundings.

1860 Maury Phys. Geogr. 3 To organize and set on foot.. a plan for 'sounding out' the ocean with the plummet.

5. In fig. contexts: To measure, or ascertain, as by sounding.

1589 Nashe Anat. Absurdity Wks. (Grosart) I. 70 Beginning to sound the infinite depth of these misteries. a1601 Pasquil & Kath. (1878) I. 319 If you haue any weight of judgement, you may easily sound what depth of wits they draw. 1642 Fuller Holy & Prof. St. v. xiv. 412 His wealth is so deep a gulf, no riot can ever sound the bottome of it. 1681 Dryden Abs. & Achit. 467 And who can sound the depth of David's Soul? 1739 Wesley Hymn, 'And can it be' ii, In vain the first-born seraph tries To sound the depths of Love Divine. 1824 W. Irving T. Trav. I. 318 He soon sounded the depth of my character. 1847 Tennyson Princ. II. 159 Two plummets dropt for one to sound the abyss Of science. 1863 Cowden Clarke Shaks. Char. xi. 276 His mind intellectual plumb hath never yet sounded.

refl. 1802 Wordsw. Sonn. Liberty v. 13 Happy is he, who ..can sound himself to know The destiny of Man.

6. a. To approach (a person) with conversation or inquiries intended to elicit his opinion or feeling on some matter; to examine or question in an indirect manner. Also with *out*.

1575 FENTON *Gold. Epist.* (1582) 233 Sounding them, she remayned iudge of their wittes and opinions. **1598** BACON *Ess., Of Negotiating* (Arb.) 90 It is better to sound a person ..a farre off, then to fal vppon the pointe at first. **1619** VISCT. DONCASTER in *England & Germany* (Camden) 118 According to the Comandement I receyved from your Matie I have endevored to sound this Prince your sone. **1645** MILTON *Tetrach.* Wks. 1851 IV. 205 Another time about the punishment of adultery they came to sound him. **1713** ADDISON *Cato* I. iii, I've sounded my Numidians, man by man, And find 'em ripe for a revolt. **1755** WASHINGTON *Lett.* Writ. 1889 I. 216, I wish you would sound him on this head. **1818** SCOTT *Hrt. Midl.* li, He sounded Butler on this subject, asking what he would think of an English living. **1849** MACAULAY *Hist. Eng.* ix. II. 402 Russell opened the design to Shrewsbury. Sidney sounded Halifax. **1885** *Manch. Exam.* 21 July 4/6 Foreign financial agents..have been privately and unofficially sounded on the subject. **1944** E. S. GARDNER *Case of Careless Kitten* ii. 21 He..wants someone to sound out Aunt Matilda on how she'll feel. **1956** A. H. COMPTON *Atomic Quest* 230 Japan was sounding out Russia for her help in negotiating a conditional surrender. **1960** *News Chron.* 25 Feb. 1/2 He had sent a three-man mission to Madrid to sound-out the Spanish.

b. To investigate, to search into, to seek to ascertain (a matter, a person's views, etc.), esp. by cautious or indirect questioning; to make trial of in this way. Also with *out*.

1579 TOMSON *Calvin's Serm. Tim.* 281/1 We must beare with many faultes,..and not sounde out matters of most rigorous sorte. **1596** DRAYTON *Legends* ii. 128 Yet sought he then the King's intent to sound. **1650** R. STAPYLTON *Strada's Low C. Wars* IV. 92 By his Letters sounding the inclination of the Duke and Dutchess. **1667** MILTON *P.L.* v. 700 The false Arch-Angel..casts between Ambiguous words..to sound Or taint integritie. **1734** tr. *Rollin's Anc. Hist.* (1827) VII. XVII. 141 He therefore thought it prudent to despatch an embassy in order to sound their dispositions. **1755** WASHINGTON *Lett.* Writ. 1889 I. 159, I should be glad if you could sound their pulse upon the occasion. **1823** LAMB *Elia* II. *Old Margate Hoy*, He was none of your hesitating, half story-tellers..who go on sounding your belief. **1858** FROUDE *Hist. Eng.* III. xii. 4 Cardinal Granvelle was instructed to sound the disposition of Francis.

c. To find *out* by investigation. *rare*$^{-1}$.

1596 LODGE *Wits Miserie & World's Madn.* N iiij, Yet as subtill as they [*sc.* fiends] are, I haue sounded them out, and ..know them.

†7. To understand; to fathom. *Obs.*

1592 KYD *Sp. Trag.* I. v. 24, I sound not well the misterie. **1631** HEYWOOD *Fair Maid of West* I. III. i, *Besse.* Captaine she is thine owne. *Goodl.* I sound it not. **1655** *Nicholas Papers* (Camden) II. 173 The fleete is said to be gone to sea, but wee cannot sound the designe.

8. *Surg.* To examine by means of a sound, esp. for the stone; †to probe.

1597 [see SOUNDING *vbl. sb.*^{2} 4]. **1640** FULLER *Joseph's Coat, David Repent.* xvii. (1867) 224 Nathan, than whom was none more skilled..with a searching tent To sound the sore. **1738** *Phil. Trans.* XL. 372 But the Night following the Pains return'd, which made him resolve to come to Lisle, to be nearer at Hand to be sounded. **1830** S. COOPER *Dict. Pract. Surg.* (ed. 6) 814 The patient being sounded after the fourth [operation] by one of the most dextrous lithotomists in Paris. **1891** MOULLIN *Surg.* 1209 In sounding a bladder a definite plan should be followed.

†sound, *v.*^{3} *Obs.* [f. SOUND *a.*]

1. *trans.* To make sound or whole; to heal.

c **1374** CHAUCER *Anel. & Arc.* 242 Noon othir helpeþe my soores for to sounde. **1412–20** LYDG. *Chron. Troy* IV. 2705 So mortally, þat þer may no salue Her sores sounde. *c* **1430** *Pilgr. Lyf Manhode* I. cxli. (1869) 73 Thee needeth..a Surgien to sounde and counfort ayen the senewes that ben brused.

2. *intr.* To become sound; to be healed or cured.

c **1402** LYDG. *Compl. Bl. Knt.* xlii, Through-girt with many a wounde That lykly are neer for to sounde. ? *a* **1412** —— *Two Merchants* 227 My bollyng festrith, that it may nat sounde.

sound (saʊnd), *v.*^{4} Now *dial.* Forms: α. 4 sounye (9 soony), 4–6 soune, 6 soun, 9 soon; 5 sownyn, 5–6 sowne, 6–7 sown. β. 6 sownde, 6–7 sounde, 6– sound (6 sund, 8 *dial.* soond). [var. of *swoune* SWOON *v.* Cf. SOUND *sb.*^{4}] *intr.* To swoon, to faint.

α. **1393** LANGL. *P. Pl.* C. XXI. 58 'Consummatum est,' quaþ Crist and comsede for to sounye. *Ibid.* XXIII. 105 Many a louely lady..Sounede and swelte for sorwe of deþes dyntes. **1430–40** LYDG. *Bochas* I. ix. (1554) 19 b, Full oft in the day Jocasta gan to sowne. **1470–85** MALORY *Arthur* VI. xvi. 209 Thenne she souned as though she wold dye. **1545** RAYNALD *Byrth Mankynde* 73 If in this meane whyle the woman faynte or sowne by reason of greate payne. **1591** GREENE *Conny Catching* II. Wks. (Grosart) X. 116 The gentleman euen now..sownd here. **1642** H. MORE *Song of Soul* III. iii. 49 This accursed earth; Whose dull suffusions make her often sown, Orecome with cold. **1681** W. ROBERTSON *Phraseol. Gen.* (1693) 1152 To sown or swoon, or to fall in a swoon. **1888–** in dialect glossaries, etc.

β. **1480** *Robt. Devyll* 232 in Hazl. *E.P.P.* I. 228 Many olde folkes he caused to sounde. **1530** PALSGR. 726/1 Let me nat be by whan you let hym blodde, for I shall sownde than. **1579** LYLY *Euphues* (Arb.) 72 Euphues was surprised with such increadible ioye..that he had almost sounded. **1624** LD. KPR. WILLIAMS in *Fortescue Papers* (Camden) 204, I am still ready to sound at the very thought of any meate. **1678** MRS. BEHN *Sir Patient Fancy* II. ii, Oh! I shall sound with the apprehension on't. **1706** ESTCOURT *Fair Example* I. i, Cards and Dice are her perpetual Diversion, tho' she knows I sound at the very sight of 'em. **1755** *Mem. Capt. P. Drake* I. xv. 150 At this my poor Brother, who was close to the Bar, sounded away, and fell down motionless. **1797** MRS. A. M. BENNETT *Beggar Girl* (1813) V. 252, I thoft as she would have a sounded at that. **1828–** in dialect glossaries (Yorks., Northampt.).

†'soundable, *a.*^{1} *Obs.*$^{-1}$ [f. SOUND *v.*^{1}] Capable of sounding.

1567 MAPLET *Gr. Forest* 4 Of all other Metalles, this [*sc.* brass] is most soundable for his shrill and harde noise.

soundable ('saʊndəb(ə)l), *a.*^{2} *rare.* [f. SOUND *v.*^{2}] Of the sea: Capable of being sounded.

1667 *Phil. Trans.* III. 496 The Sea was there soundable, whereas before it was not so.

†'soundage. *Obs.*$^{-1}$ In 6 sownage. [f. SOUND *v.*^{2} + -AGE.] A due paid for the taking of soundings.

1562 in R. G. Marsden *Sel. Pl. Crt. Adm.* (Selden) II. 64 Towage, sownage, and petye lodemanshippe with all other accustomed averages.

sound-alike. [f. SOUND *v.*^{1}, after *look-alike*.] A person or thing that closely resembles another (or others) in sound or name. Also *attrib.* or as *adj.*

1970 *Sat. Rev.* (U.S.) 31 Oct. 59/1 It is another of those more-of-the-same pieces, like the sound-alikes of another era, written by all those minor contemporary imitators of Haydn and Mozart. **1972** *Eye, Ear, Nose & Throat Monthly* Apr. 142/1 When a pharmacist takes a prescription over the telephone..there is always the possibility that a drug not intended by the prescriber is likely to be dispensed. Such an error could be the result of a 'sound-alike' or a 'read-alike' drug. **1975** *Verbatim* May 12/1 The lost *r* may one day ruin my professional reputation—by converting the word that's meant into an unrelated sound-alike. **1977** *Rolling Stone* 5 May 66/2 Hire a Pendergrass soundalike—David Ebo. **1979** *Logophile* II. v. 10/2 The *Encyclopedia of Homonyms*.. claims to be 'the only complete comprehensive collection of 'sound-alike' words ever published'.

Sounday, obs. form of SUNDAY.

sound-board. Also 6 sownd-borde, sowndebord, 7 sound-boord. [SOUND *sb.*^{3}]

1. A thin board or piece of wood forming part of a musical instrument and placed in such a position as to strengthen or increase its sound.

15.. *Proverbis* in *Antiq. Rep.* (1809) IV. 406 But whoso in that instrumente [*sc.* the harp] hathe no speculacion, What restithe withyn the sownde-bord hath but smale relacion. **1504** in Herrig's *Archiv* CXX. 425 Of þe monacorde..I assayde þe musykes..but none wold speke; þe sownd-borde was to hy. **1611** COTGR., *Trembloer*, the Sound-boord of a Musicall Instrument. **1626** BACON *Sylva* §222 You may try it, without any Sound-board along, but onely Harp-wise, at one end of the strings. **1838** G. F. GRAHAM *The. & Pract. Mus. Comp.* Introd. p. v, In both of these harps the sound-board seems to have been large and sonorous. **1874** TYNDALL *Fragm. Sci.* (1879) II. xi. 244 All are..shaken forth into the air by a second sound-board [in a piano].

attrib. **1889** BRINSMEAD *Hist. Pianoforte* 171 Materially elongating the sound-board bridges.

2. a. In an organ (see quot. 1881).

1611 COTGR., *Canon*,..the sound-boord of an Organ. **1667** MILTON *P.L.* I. 709 As in an Organ from one blast of wind To many a row of Pipes the sound-board breaths. **1733** TULL *Horse-Hoeing Husb.* xxii. 320 The Manner of fastning the Organ-Tongue to its Mortise, is by Parchment and Leather glu'd to its Surface, and also to the Sound-Board. **1781** *Encycl. Brit.* (ed. 2) VIII. 5747 The sound-board..is composed of two parts, the upper board or cover H H H, and the under board H I. **1852** SEIDEL *Organ* 47 The great sound-board and wind-chest are of equal length. **1881** W. E. DICKSON *Pract. Organ-Building* iii. 29 The sound-board is a shallow box, divided internally into as many transverse grooves or channels as there are notes on the key-board.

b. In a harmonium (see quot.).

1879 *Grove's Dict. Music* I. 668/1 Above the bellows-board is the 'pan', sometimes erroneously called the soundboard, a board of graduated thickness in which are the channels..determining..the different *timbres*.

3. = SOUNDING-BOARD 1.

1766 ENTICK *London* IV. 278 The sound-board is pendant from the roof of the church. **1842** GWILT *Archit.* Gloss., *Sound-board*, the same as a canopy or type over a pulpit, to reverberate the voice of the speaker.

transf. **1856** LEVER *Martins of Cro' M.* 165 These thin partitions are only soundboards for the voice.

4. Sound-boarding.

1875 in KNIGHT *Dict. Mech.* 2247/2.

sound-boarding. *Carp.* [SOUND *sb.*^{3}] (See quot. 1842.)

1799 [A. YOUNG] *Agric. Linc.* 30 Sound-boarding, at 16*s.* 6*d.* **1842** GWILT *Archit.* Gloss., *Sound-boarding*, in floors, consists of short boards placed transversely between the joists, and supported by fillets fixed to the sides of the latter for holding pugging, which is any substance that will prevent the transmission of sound from one story to another. [Hence in Knight *Dict. Mech.*, etc.]

'sounded, *ppl. a. rare.* [f. SOUND *sb.*^{3} or *v.*^{1}]

†1. Having a (good or sweet) sound. *Obs. rare.*

c **1450** *Godstow Reg.* 23 Now, Syent Bruce! helpe with þy sownded lute. **1486** *Bk. St. Albans, Hawking* d iij, Thay [*sc.* bells] be wele sortid well sownded, sonowre of Ryngyng in shilnes and passing well lasting.

2. Proclaimed, expressed, etc., by sound.

a **1717** PARNELL *Battle Frogs & Mice* III. 6 The sounded Charge remurmurs o'er the Ground.

sounder^{1} ('saʊndə(r)). Forms: 5 sundyr, sondyr, s(o)undre, 6 sovneder, sowndir, 7 soundor, 7, 9 sownder, 4– sounder. [a. OF. *sundre*, *sonre* (mod. dial. *sonre*), of Germanic origin: cf. OE. *sunor*, *suner*, ON. *sonar-* (in *sonarblót*, *-gǫltr*), Lombard *sonor-* (in *sonorpair* boar), OHG. and MHG. *swaner* (OHG. *swanering*, MHG. *swänre*, boar).]

1. A herd of wild swine.

13.. *Gaw. & Gr. Knt.* 1440 On þe sellokest swyn swenged out þere, Long sythen for þe sounder þat wiȝt for-olde. *c* **1410** *Master of Game* (MS. Digby 182) v, þat men calle a trippe of tame swyne and of wylde swyne it is called a soundre, þat is to say, if þer be passed .v. or vi. togydres. *Ibid.* xxiv, When þei be not of iii. yere, men calleth hem swyne of soundre. **1486** *Bk. St. Albans* e ij b, Twelfe make a Sounder of the wylde swyne, xvi. a medyll Sounder what place thay be inne, A grete sounder of swyne .xx. ye shall call. **1576** TURBERV. *Venerie* 100 Of a bore, when he forsaketh the Sounder and feedeth alone he shall be called a Sanglier. **1582** STANYHURST *Æneis* IV. (Arb.) 100 A sounder of hog-steers, Or thee brownye lion too stalck fro the mounten he wissheth. **1598** MANWOOD *Lawes Forest* iv. 25 b, The first yeere he [i.e. the wild boar] is, a Pigg of the sounder. [**1616–** in BULLOKAR *Eng. Exp.* and later Dicts. **1632** *Guillim's Heraldry* III. xiv. (ed. 3) 177 Skilfull Foresters and good Woodmen Doe vse to say, a Sounder of Swyne [etc.]. **1824** MCCULLOCH *Highlands Scot.* III. 407, I have never spoken of a sownder of swine or a sculk of foxes.] **1840** E. E. NAPIER *Scenes & Sports For. Lands* I. iv. 115 The noble sight of a fine sounder..breaking covert and scouring along the plain. **1880** THARP *Sword of Damocles* II. 219 Almost directly afterwards the whole sounder, of ten or a dozen, emerged into the open.

¶**2.** *erron.* **a.** The lair of a wild boar. *rare*$^{-1}$.

1725 POPE *Odyss.* XIX. 519 Rous'd by the hounds and hunters..cries, The savage from his leafy sounder flies.

b. (See quots.)

1823 SCOTT *Quentin D.* ix, It had so happened that a sounder (*i.e.* in the language of the period, a boar of only two years old) had crossed the track of the proper object of the chase. **1891** C. WISE *Rockingham Castle* vii. 153 A wild Boar of the first year was a 'Sounder'.

sounder^{2} ('saʊndə(r)). [f. SOUND *v.*^{1}]

1. One who makes or utters a sound or sounds; one who causes something, esp. an instrument, to sound.

1591 PERCIVALL *Sp. Dict.*, *Tañedor*, a plaier or sounder of any instrument, *cantor*. **1648** HEXHAM II, *Een Luyder*, *ofte Luyer*, a Ringer, a Sounder. **1809** W. IRVING *Knickerb.* IV. iv. (1849) 216 This sounder of brass..was a lusty bachelor. **1831** SCOTT *Ct. Rob.* xiii, In the front..stood the sounder of the sacred trumpet. **1859** DICKENS *T. Two Cities* II. i, The sounders of three-fourths of the notes in the whole gamut of Crime were put to Death.

2. A telegraphic device which enables the communications or signals to be read by sound.

1860 G. PRESCOTT *Electr. Telegr.* 91 Since the adoption of the method of reading by sound, another apparatus has taken the place of the register, or recording apparatus, called the *sounder*. **1872** POPE *Telegraph* iv. 32 The Sounder consists simply of the electro-magnet, armature and lever fixed upon a base. **1876** PREECE & SIVEWRIGHT *Telegraphy* 246 The Sounder, on account of the extreme simplicity of its mechanism, is less liable to faults than any of the other forms of instruments which are employed.

attrib. **1875** KNIGHT *Dict. Mech.* 2247/2 *Sounder-magnet*, the magnet which operates the sounder in the receiving apparatus.

b. A telegraphist who operates or has experience with this.

1887 *Daily News* 2 May 7/3 Telegraphist (sounder) desires engagement.

3. A device or instrument which gives a signal, etc., by sounding; also, the signal so given.

1884 KNIGHT *Dict. Mech.* Suppl. 832/1 *Sounder*, an alarm or call, made by closing an electric circuit. **1891** *Pall Mall G.* 1 June 7/1 An electric sounder, too, is so arranged that it commences to ring if everything is correct, directly the gun is loaded and in the firing position.

sounder^{3} ('saʊndə(r)). [f. SOUND *v.*^{2}]

1. a. One who sounds the depth of water, etc.

1575 GASCOIGNE *Posies* Wks. 1907 I. 356 And whyles I hearken what the Saylers saye, The sownder sings, fadame two full no more. *a* **1668** DAVENANT *Philosopher's Disquisition* v. Wks. (1673) 326 It is a Plummet to so short a Line, As sounds no deeper then the sounders Eies.

b. One who sounds the intentions, opinions, etc., of a person or persons. *rare*$^{-1}$.

1587 FLEMING *Contn. Holinshed* III. 1371/1 For that himselfe would not be seene to be a sounder of men, least he might..indanger himselfe and the enterprise.

2. An apparatus for sounding the sea.

1811 *Naval Chron.* XXV. 221 This sounder shews..the.. depth of water. **1884** KNIGHT *Dict. Mech.* Suppl. 832 *Sounder*, Sir William Thomson's apparatus for deep-sea sounding while the ship is in motion. **1896** *Westm. Gaz.* 2 Dec. 8/1 Whilst sounding on this ledge the sounder struck ground at 550 fathoms.

3. A surgical sound.

1875 KNIGHT *Dict. Mech.* 1926/1 Sim's uterine repositor consists of a short metallic sounder, rotatable on a long shaft.

soundery, obs. form of SUNDRY.

Soundex ('saʊndɛks). *Information Sci.* [f. SOUND *sb.*^{3}] Used, usu. *attrib.*, with reference to a phonetic coding system intended to suppress spelling variations, used esp. in *Med.* to encode surnames for record linkage. Also *absol.*, material encoded using the Soundex code. Hence **Soundex-code** *v. trans.*, to encode (a name or other data) using this code; **Soundex-coded** *ppl. a.*; **Soundex coding** *vbl. sb.*

1959 *Science* 16 Oct. 955/3 The surnames were first reduced to phonetic codes, consisting in each case of the first letter of the name followed by three numeric digits and known as the Russell Soundex Code. *Ibid.* 958/1 The family names on all cards in both files were Soundex coded by means of the computer. **1967** *Amer. Jrnl. Human Genetics* XIX. 340 The usefulness of surname information in its Soundex coded form can be shown to be considerably greater than that of the full alphabetic surnames. **1968** *Brit. Med. Bull.* XXIV. 207/2 The master file of identities of patients is held on magnetic tape in a quasi-alphabetical sequence, based on the Soundex code of surnames. **1970** *Jrnl. Interdisciplinary Hist.* I. 116 Our data are apparently twice as resistant to Soundex coding as Nitzberg's. *Ibid.* 117 No simple strategy such as 'search one Soundex pocket before and one after' will enable us to effect more linkages. *Ibid.*, We.. first applied our pretreatments to all surnames in our test file.. and then applied the files of Soundex to the pretreated surnames. **1972** *Computers & Humanities* VI. 190 In the first attempt a quasi-alphabetic sequence known as the Soundex code, which has been used in the field of medical record linkage, was utilized. The Soundex system sets aside the least reliable portions of Anglo-Saxon surnames, thus Smith/Smyth/Smythe all are codified the same.

soundful ('saʊndfʊl), *a.* [f. SOUND *sb.*^{3} + -FUL.] Full of sound; †tuneful.

1615 CHAPMAN *Odyss.* VIII. 86 The herald on a pin above his head His soundful harp hung. **1891** *Pall Mall G.* 14 Sept. 3/1 The crowd is as dense and as busy and as soundful as ever.

† '**soundful**, *v. Obs.*$^{-1}$ [ad. OE. (ȝe)*sundfullian*, f. ȝ*esundful* sound, prosperous.] *intr.* To prosper. Also † '**soundful** *adv.* [OE. ȝ*esundfullice*], prosperously. *Obs.*

a **1300** *E.E. Psalter* i. 4 What swa he does sal soundefulle al. *Ibid.* xliv. 5 Soundful [L. *prospere*] ga forth.

sound-hole. [SOUND *sb.*^{3}]

1. *Mus.* (See quots. 1883, 1888.)

1611 COTGR., *Les ouyes d'vne Violle*, the sound-holes of the Violl.

1874 CHAPPELL *Hist. Music* xii. 298 The bridge, the tail-piece, and the sound-holes, are ancient Egyptian. **1883** *Grove's Dict. Music* III. 640 *Soundholes* or *f-Holes*, two curvilinear openings in the belly of a stringed instrument, one on each side of the bridge. **1888** *Encycl. Brit.* XXIV. 246/1 Such sound-holes.. have the property of immediately letting out the vibrations of the small mass of air which lies directly under the bridge.

2. *Arch.* (See quot. 1848.)

1848 RICKMAN *Styles Archit.* 152 The openings [in belfries] filled with tracery, but not glazed, which are found in some districts, especially in Norfolk, and there commonly called sound-holes. **1905** *Athenæum* 23 Sept. 408/1 Wrentham has a singularly fine tower, with good 'sound-holes',.. uncommon in Suffolk.

sounding ('saʊndɪŋ), *vbl. sb.*^{1} [f. SOUND *v.*^{1}]

1. a. The fact of emitting or giving out a sound or sounds, or the power of doing this; the sound produced or given out by something, esp. a bell or trumpet.

α. **1388** WYCLIF *Exod.* XIX. 16 The sownyng of a clarioun made noise ful greetli. **1398** TREVISA *Barth De P.R.* XVI. xxxvi. (Bodl. MS.), Bras accordeþ moste to trumpes and taboures for sownynge and longe duringe þerof. *c* **1450** LOVELICH *Grail* lv. 292 That was the Noyse Of here Sowneng. **1482** *Monk of Evesham* lvii. (Arb.) 110 As al the bellys yn the worlde or what sumeuer ys of sownyng had be rongyn to gedyr at onys. **1540–1** ELYOT *Image Gov.* (1549) 68 Harpes, lutes, organes softe in sownyng. **1557** *Tottel's Misc.* (Arb.) 202 A blast so hye, That made an eckow in the ayer and sowning through the sky.

β. *c* **1440** *Promp. Parv.* 466/1 Soundynge, *sonatus*. *c* **1450** *Bk. Curtasye* 69 in *Babees Bk.*, Ne suppe not with grete sowndynge. **1483** *Cath. Angl.* 350/1 A Sowndynge, *sonoritas*. **1530** PALSGR. 273/1 Soundyng, *sonnerie*. *c* **1595** CAPT. WYATT *Dudley's Voy.* (Hakl. Soc.) 46 The cause that made thease people flie from us.. was the soundinge of our trumpetts. **1662** PLAYFORD *Skill Mus.* 72 A beginner.. shall by this way use only one Sounding, *viz.* an Unison. *a* **1700** EVELYN *Diary* July 1645, The fillings up.. 'twixt the walls were of urnes and earthen pots for the better sounding. **1706** A. BEDFORD *Temple Mus.* ix. 196 The Trumpets sounded their Soundings. **1799** *Instr. & Reg. Cavalry* (1813) 284 These soundings are exactly the same as those of the trumpet. **1821** CLARE *Vill. Minstr.* II. 104 The rustic's ear at leisure dwells On the soft soundings of his village bells. **1882** CHRISTINA ROSSETTI *Poems* (1904) 262/2 The irresponsive sounding of the sea.

fig. *a* **1711** KEN *Christophil* Poet. Wks. 1721 I. 504 For thou Omniscient art, To know the Wants and Soundings of my Heart.

b. With advs., as *again*, *on*.

c **1440** *Promp. Parv.* 466/2 Soundynge a-ȝene (or rebowndynge), *resonatus*, *reboacio*. **1560** BIBLE (Geneva) *Ezek.* vii. 7 The sounding againe of the mountaines. **1578** LYTE *Dodoens* 172 The braying or sounding againe of the Asse. **1852** SEIDEL *Organ* 45 The so-called howling or sounding-on of certain pipes when their respective keys are not pressed down.

2. a. Vocal utterance or pronunciation; resonant or sonorous quality of this.

1387 TREVISA *Higden* (Rolls) II. 163 For men of þe est wiþ men of þe west.. acordeþ more in sownynge of speche. **1398** —— *Barth. De P.R.* v. xxi. (1495) 128 It faryth in children that they spylle and hurte many letters and mayе not haue sownyng. *c* **1400** MAUNDEV. (1839) xiv. 152 The Langage of that Contree is more gret in sownynge, than it is in other parties beȝonde the See. **1599** MINSHEU *Sp. Gram.* 6, G.. hath two maner of soundings according to the vowels which follow it.

b. *Black English.* Playing the dozens (PLAY *v.* 16 e).

1962 R. D. ABRAHAMS in *Jrnl. Amer. Folklore* LXXV. 209 The dozens are commonly called 'playing' or 'sounding'. **1965** *Ibid.* LXXVIII. 343 Sounding, especially Mother-Sounding, demonstrates the second place given to the mother-son bond in comparison to the primary place assigned the clique. **1972** W. LABOV *Language in Inner City* p. xviii, The setting was essentially that of a party.. with card games, eating and drinking, singing and sounding. **1974** H. L. FOSTER *Ribbin', Jivin', & Playin' Dozens* v. 183 In Pottsville, Pennsylvania, the term is sounding... In a Brooklyn, New York, secondary school the terms ranking and sounding are still used.

3. The (or an) act of causing a trumpet, bell, etc., to sound; the blowing *of* a bugle or trumpet, esp. as a signal.

1523 LD. BERNERS *Froiss.* I. xviii. 8b, Euery man was warned to be redy at the fyrst soundyng of the trumpette. **1529** *Registr. Aberdon.* (Maitland) I. 396 Be conuocatioun of our said communitie be þe swndyng of þe bell usit in þis part. **1616** B. JONSON *Poetaster* (Init.), After the second sounding. **1811** *Regul. & Orders Army* 281 Whether perfect in the different Soundings of the Trumpet, and in the Beats of the Drum. **1879** *Scribner's Mag.* XIX. 518/2 Only at the sounding of the second bell did Louisiana escape.. to prepare for dinner.

†**4.** = RINGING *vbl. sb.*^{2} 3. *Obs.*$^{-1}$

1600 SURFLET *Countrie Farme* I. xii. 61 Against the noise and sounding of the eare.

5. The action of examining by percussion; *spec.* auscultation; an instance of this.

1883 GRESLEY *Gloss. Coal-m.* 230 *Sounding*, knocking on the roof, etc., to ascertain if it is sound or safe to work under. **1898** *Syd. Soc. Lex.*, *Sounding*, the operation of examining the chest; auscultation. **1900** E. WALLACE *Writ in Barracks* 72 Didn't mind the Doctor's soundin's.

6. *Comb.*, as ***sounding-bar***, ***-machine***, ***-rod***, ***-string***; **sounding bow**, **-box** (see SOUND *sb.*^{3} 8); **sounding-post**, = SOUND-POST.

1756 *Dict. Arts & Sci.* s.v. *Bell*, The parts of a Bell are (1) The sounding bow, or the inferior circle, which terminates it, growing thinner and thinner. **1838** *Penny Mag.* 30 June 246/2 This peg is called the *sounding post*.. of the violin. **1847** TODD & BOWMAN *Phys. Anat.* II. 97 Müller.. could by means of a sounding-rod.. ascertain the relative intensity of the sonorous vibrations. **1853** HERSCHEL *Pop. Lect. Sci.* vii. §58 (1873) 275 The vibrations which reach the ear from a sounding-string. **1875** WHITNEY *Life Lang.* iv. 59 Above the vibrating reed-apparatus is set, after the fashion of a sounding-box, the cavity of the pharynx. **1881** W. E. DICKSON *Pract. Organ-Building* v. 64 A long screw.. biting well in one of the sounding-bars.

sounding ('saʊndɪŋ), *vbl. sb.*^{2} [f. SOUND *v.*^{2}]

1. a. The action or process of sounding or ascertaining the depth of water by means of the line and lead or (now usu.) by means of echo; an instance of this.

1336 [implied in SOUNDING-LINE]. **1352** *Excheq. Acc. Q.R. 20* No. 27 (Pub. Rec. Office), De ijs. iijd. pro cordis emptis minutis per vices, Anglice lyne pro soundings et toppeline pro eadem. **1485–** [implied in SOUNDING-LEAD]. **1631** MARKHAM *Country Contentm.* I. xi. (ed. 4) 76 That in the sounding of Lakes or Riuers, he may know how many foot or inches each.. contayneth. **1699** DAMPIER *Voy.* II. II. 50 Taking your Sounding from Beef-Island shore. **1704** J. HARRIS *Lex. Techn.* I. s.v., When the Seamen try the Depth of the Water with a Line and Plummet, they call it Sounding. **1769** FALCONER *Dict. Marine* (1780) s.v., Sounding with the hand-lead.. is generally performed by a man who stands in the main-chains to windward. **1860** MAURY *Phys. Geog.* (Low) 4 Nor have any reliable soundings yet been made in water over five miles deep. **1880** *19th Cent.* No. 38. 594 At each of the observing stations a sounding was taken for the determination of the exact depth. **1966** *McGraw-Hill Encycl. Sci. & Technol.* XIII. 216/1 Since about the middle of the 1920s, virtually all deep-sea soundings have been made by echo sounding.

transf. **1891** A. M. CLERKE in *Ann. Rep. Smithsonian Instit.* 106 M. Celoria.. obtained for a 'mean sounding', at the north pole of the milky way, almost identically the same number [of stars] given by Herschel's great reflector.

b. *fig.* Investigation. Also with *out*. ***to take soundings***, to try to find out quietly how matters stand.

1592 SHAKS. *Rom. & Jul.* I. i. 156 To himselfe so secret and so close, So farre from sounding and discouery, As is the bud bit with an enuious worme. **1856** LEVER *Martins of Cro' M.* 217 Old Dan bears you no malice, I'd lay fifty pounds on it! But, if you like, I'll just step in and take soundings. **1898** *Westm. Gaz.* 9 Nov. 4/1 The Liverymen afterwards decide the selection. Soundings may have been taken beforehand. **1969** *Daily Tel.* 11 Nov. 21/4 The secret sounding-out by Plessey and BSR was an effort to clear the hurdle before breathing a word, but a share jump precipitated events.

c. *transf.* The determination of any physical property at a depth in the sea or at a height in the atmosphere; an instance of this.

1875 *Proc. R. Soc.* XXIII. 249 Temperature-soundings were taken on the 28th of September and on the 3rd of October, at depths of 2800 and 1420 fathoms respectively. **1947** *Sci. Progr.* XXXV. 88 These soundings have also shown exceedingly dry layers.. to exist from time to time in the troposphere. **1955** E. BURGESS *Frontier to Space* iii. 24 The use of the rocket for altitude sounding is by no means a new idea. **1974** *Physics Bull.* Jan. 11/3 Further instrumental developments are bound to follow and it may be that balloon and rocket soundings of the atmosphere will soon become obsolete.

d. *Archæol.* A trial boring made on a site to gain preliminary information. Cf. SONDAGE.

1957 K. KENYON *Digging up Jericho* 170 Our excavation at the highest point on the central ridge.. was only a restricted sounding. **1967** *Amer. Anthropologist* LXIX. 401/2 At Chagar Bazar, Huwaish (at which only a seven-day sounding was carried out), and in the rest of Mesopotamia 'religious responsibilities rested with the local secular chiefs'.

2. A place or position at sea where it is possible to reach the bottom with the ordinary deep-sea lead (see quot. 1867). Chiefly *pl.* **a.** In prepositional phrases, as ***in*** or ***into***, ***off*** (***the***) ***soundings***.

The form *sowdyng* of the earliest examples also occurs in 1495 under SOUNDING-LEAD.

sing. **14..** *Sailing Directions* (Hakl. Soc. 1889) 21 And ye gesse you ij. parties ovir the see.. ye must north and by est till ye come into Sowdyng. *Ibid.*, Than go north till ye come into sowdyng of woyse [= ooze].

pl. **1626** CAPT. SMITH *Accid. Yng. Seamen* 18 A shallow water, deepe water, soundings, fadome by the marke. **1694** NARBOROUGH *Voy.* I. 18 The Sea-Water is changed whiter than the usual colour, whence I conjecture, I must be in Soundings. **1748** *Anson's Voy.* III. vi. 347 We frequently brought to, to try if we were in soundings. **1790** BEATSON *Nav. & Mil. Mem.* I. 174 At this time a French squadron was cruizing in the soundings. **1840** MARRYAT *Poor Jack* xxii, We were soon out of soundings, and well into the Bay of Biscay. **1867** SMYTH *Sailor's Word-bk.* s.v., To be in soundings.. is limited in common parlance to parts not far from the shore, and where the depth is about 80 or 100 fathoms.

b. In other uses. ***to strike soundings*** (see quot. 1863).

1701 PENN in *Pennsylv. Hist. Soc. Mem.* IX. 69 We were but twenty-six days from land to soundings. **1748** *Anson's Voy.* I. vi. (ed. 4) 83 We had soundings all along the coast of Patagonia. **1802** SCHOMBERG *Naval Chronology* I. 132 He.. sailed with the rest for England. On the 23d of October the admiral struck soundings in 90 fathoms. **1840** MARRYAT *Poor Jack* xxvi, A large homeward-bound Indiaman, which had just struck soundings. **1863** A. YOUNG *Naut. Dict.* 359 *To strike soundings*, is to find bottom with the deep-sea-lead on coming in from sea. A vessel is then in soundings.

c. *spec.* with *the*. Such places in the mouth of the English Channel. ? *Obs.*

1666 *Lond. Gaz.* No. 39/1 A little off the Soundings she met with ill weather. **1693** LUTTRELL *Brief Rel.* (1857) III. 51 Alymer, after seen the Streights fleet past the soundings, goes on some other design. **1722** DE FOE *Col. Jack* xi, We had tolerable weather.. till we came into the soundings, so they call the mouth of the British Channel. [**1897** LAUGHTON in *Dict. Nat. Biog.* LII. 160/2 On 22 Oct. the fleet came into the soundings.]

d. *U.S.* (See quot.) *rare*$^{-1}$.

1804 C. B. BROWN tr. *Volney's View Soil U.S.* 174 On each side, it forms eddies or counter-currents, which, aided by the depositions of the rivers, forms the muddy stratum or deposit, termed soundings.

3. *pl.* The depths of water in the sea, esp. along the coast, in a harbour, road, etc., or (rarely) in a river, ascertained by sounding (sense 1); also, the entries in a log-book, etc., giving these, together with particulars relating to the nature of the bottom.

1570 DEE *Math. Pref.* a iiij b, The Soundinges.. ought the Hydrographer.. to haue certainly knowen. *c* **1595** CAPT. WYATT *Dudley's Voy.* (Hakl. Soc.) 38, I must confesse that the Captaine did not make anie publike declaracion how hee founde the sowndings. **1661** E. HICKERINGILL (*title*), Jamaica Viewed, with all the Ports, Harbours, and their several Soundings. **1748** *Anson's Voy.* II. viii. 216 A plan of the road.. where the soundings are laid down. **1774** M. MACKENZIE *Maritime Surv.* 79 The Survey of the Coast.. and the Soundings near it. **1841** CAPT. B. HALL *Patchwork* II. i. 4 The leadsman.. singing out the soundings to the anxious pilot. **1869** TOZER *Highl. Turkey* II. 341 From the state of the soundings at the present day,.. the river in Strabo's time must have entered the sea [etc.].

4. *Surg.* The action of examining with a sound or probe. Also *attrib.*, as † ***sounding-iron***.

1597 A. M. tr. *Guillemeau's Fr. Chirurg.* 13/1 The soundinge Iron.. is verye conveniente to sound and serche for bullettes in a wounde. **1695** *New Light Chirurgery put out* 36 He will not allow Sounding by Probe. **1830** S. COOPER *Dict. Pract. Surg.* (ed. 6) 816 The manner of searching for the stone, or as it is now more commonly expressed of sounding.

5. *attrib.*, chiefly in sense 1, as ***sounding-machine***, ***-plumb***, ***-plummet***, ***-pole***, ***-rod***, ***-ship***, ***-twine***; **sounding balloon** = BALLON-SONDE; **sounding rocket**, a rocket designed to carry scientific instruments into the upper atmosphere in order to make measurements during its flight.

Also ***sounding-apparatus***, ***-bottle***, etc. (1875– in Knight *Dict. Mech.* and later Dicts.).

1555 EDEN *Decades* III. VI. (Arb.) 163 He coulde at no tyme touche the grounde with his soundynge plummet. **1575** GASCOIGNE *Posies* Wks. 1907 I. 355 (The sounding plumbe) in haste poste hast must raunge, To trye the depth and goodnesse of our gate. **1611** COTGR., *Sonde*, a Mariners sounding plummet. **1776** G. SEMPLE *Building in Water* 18 A sounding Rod.. marked out in Feet and Inches painted. **1832** DARWIN in *Life & Lett.* (1887) I. 232 It is quite a new thing for a 'sounding ship' to beat a regular man-of-war. **1838** *Civil Eng. & Arch. Jrnl.* I. 148/2 A sounding-rod of iron.. was dropped into it, which rebounding several feet, proved that the solid rock had been reached. **1846** A. YOUNG *Naut. Dict.* 289 Massey's Patent Sounding-Machine is an instrument which ascertains the depth of water, and registers it by means of an index. *Ibid.*, *Sounding rod*, a slight bar of iron marked with a scale of feet and inches, used to ascertain the depth of water that may happen to be in a vessel's hold. **1856** KANE *Arct. Expl.* II. vi. 71 A five-sinnet line of Maury's sounding-twine. **1875** 'MARK TWAIN' in *Atlantic Monthly* May 569/1 You can go and get the sounding-pole. **1894** *Times* 18 Sept. 10/4 Sir William Thomson's sounding machine was on the vessel aft, but witness used the deep sea lead. **1902** Sounding balloon [see *BALLON-SONDE]. **1937** C. G. PHILP *Stratosphere & Rocket Flight* v. 33 By the aid of 'sounding' balloons.. data has been obtained of the earth's atmosphere at a height of over 23 miles. **1947** *Amer. Jrnl. Physics* XV. 139/1 (*caption*) The WAC Corporal sounding rocket, which reached 43 mi altitude. **1962** F. I. ORDWAY et al. *Basic Astronautics* iv. 121 Data obtained from the sounding rockets were correlated with readings from the Explorer 4 artificial satellite. **1965** R. A. CRAIG *Upper Atmosphere* ii. 17 Sounding balloons are most commonly made of neoprene and inflated with helium or hydrogen. **1975** *Islander* (Victoria, B.C.) 23 Feb. 13/2 Tying themselves together like mountain climbers, sounding poles in hand, they forded the river. **1978** PASACHOFF & KUTNER *University Astron.* xxviii. 710 (*caption*) The ultraviolet spectrum of 3C 273, taken with a 40-cm telescope, the largest ever flown on a sounding rocket.

† **'sounding**, *vbl. sb.*^{3} *Obs.* [f. SOUND *v.*^{4}]

1. Swooning, fainting.

c **1380** *Sir Ferumb.* 1134 Wan þe Amyral haþ iherd þe kyng, in sowenyng gan he falle; Ac wan he awok of his soȝnyng, loude he gan to calle. *c* **1435** *Torr. Portugal* 1400 Thries in sownyng fell she thare. **1547** BOORDE *Brev. Health* ccxvi. 74 There be many sodein sickenesses, as the pestilence,..the palsey, and soundynge. **1590** BARROUGH *Meth. Physick* II. xiv. (1639) 94 If sounding be caused through paine, you must diligently enquire the cause. **1620** VENNER *Via Recta* (1650) 143 A water of singular efficacie against sowning.

2. A swoon; a fainting-fit.

1580 FRAMPTON *Bezaar Stone* in *Joyf. News* (1596) 119 The bone of the hart..is of great vertue against venom and soundings of the heart. **1595** LODGE *Fig for Momus* G 4, It causeth sownings, passions of the hart. *a* **1657** SIR J. BALFOUR *Ann. Scot.* Wks. 1825 II. 104 Falling into maney soundinges and paines, and violent fluxes of the belley. *c* **1670** WOOD *Life* (O.H.S.) I. 388 Yet he could hardly keep himself from a second sowning.

3. *attrib.*, as ***sounding ecstasy***, ***fit***, ***trance***.

Freq. in the 17th century.

? **1565** LADY HUNGERFORD in H. Hall *Eliz. Soc.* (1886) 253 Your man..founde me in suche sounding fitts and wekenys. **1582** T. WATSON *Centurie of Love* xi, Sone after into howe sorrowfull a dumpe, or sounden [*sic*] extasie he fell. **1632** LITHGOW *Trav.* x. 467, I fell twice in a sounding trance. **1681** H. MORE *Exp. Dan.* 78 A sounding fit that took him at the hearing the voice of the Angel. **1720** MRS. MANLEY *Power of Love* (1741) 49 An immediate Suffocation..might be improved into an appearance of sounding Fits.

sounding ('saʊndɪŋ), *ppl. a.*^{1} [f. SOUND *v.*^{1}]

1. a. Having a sound; causing, emitting, producing, a sound or sounds, esp. of a loud character; resonant, sonorous; reverberant.

Freq. in 18th cent. poetry.

13.. *E.E. Allit. P.* A. 883 Þat nwe songe þay songen ful cler, In sounande notez a gentyl carpe. *c* **1374** CHAUCER *Boeth.* I. pr. ii. (1868) 8 Þe causes whennes þe sounyng wyndes moeuen and bisien þe smoþe water of þe see. **1483** *Cath. Angl.* 350/1 Sowndynge, *argutus, sonorus.* **1526** TINDALE *1 Cor.* xiii. 1, I were even as soundynge brasse. **1560** BIBLE (Geneva) *2 Chron.* xiii. 12 And beholde, this God is with vs,..& his Priests with the sounding trumpets. **1594** MARLOWE & NASHE *Dido* I. 1, Both barking Scilla, and the sounding Rocks. **1636** B. JONSON *Eng. Gram.* iii. Wks. (Rtldg.) 770/2 When it [the letter *v*] followeth a sounding vowel. **1697** DRYDEN *Virg. Past.* v. 130 Murm'ring Billows on the sounding Shore. **1710** J. CLARKE tr. *Rohault's Nat. Philos.* (1729) I. I. ii. 7 Mankind..are apt to think, that the Sound..is in the Air, or in the sounding Body as they call it. **1798** WORDSW. '*Five years have past*' 76 The sounding cataract Haunted me like a passion. **1825** T. HOOK *Sayings* Ser. II. *Man of Many Fr.* I. 319 As the sounding horn foretels the coming-mail. **1883** STEVENSON *Treas. Isl.* xxvii, He went in with a sounding plunge.

b. Preceded by an adj. or adv., as *clear*, *deep*, *loud sounding*, etc.

c **1325** *Prose Ps.* cl. 5 Herieþ hym in cymbals wele sounand. **1486** *Bk. St. Albans* d iij, Looke also that thay be sonowre and well sowndyng and shil. **1500–20** DUNBAR *Poems* lxxxviii. 44 Blith be thy churches, wele sownyng be thy bellis. **1560–** [see HIGH-SOUNDING *a.*]. **1585** T. WASHINGTON tr. *Nicholay's Voy.* III. xv. 99 b, Cimbals of..cleare sounding mettall. **1592** *Arden of Feversham* III. iii. 16 With that he blew an euill sounding horne. **1606** W. S. *Serm. before King*, With the loud sounding trumpet to rouse and araise them. **1693** [see ILL- 6]. **1781** COWPER *Hope* 554 Beneath well-sounding Greek I slur a name a poet must not speak. **1801** *Lusignan* IV. 28 The shores of the deep sounding main. **1845** [see FINE *a.* D. 2 a]. **1882** FLOYER *Unexpl. Baluchistan* 75 The Divine formulas of Islam are merely fine hearty-sounding words to swear in.

† **c.** Having a sound similar *to* something. *Obs.*$^{-1}$

1563 FOXE *A. & M.* 559/1 The booke..is nother English, Laten, Greke, nor Hebrue, nor Douche, but somewhat soundinge to oure English.

d. ***sounding sand*** = *singing sand* s.v. SINGING *ppl. a.* 4 b.

1884 *Proc. Amer. Assoc. Adv. Sci. 1883* 251 The sounding sand is near the surface only, at the depth of one or two feet the acoustic properties disappear. **1897** G. P. MERRILL *Treat. Rocks, Rock-Weathering & Soils* II. ii. 143 On certain Hawaiian beaches, such sands [*sc.* shell sands] give out a distinct note..when walked over, or even when shaken in a closed vessel, and are popularly known as sounding, or singing, sands. **1976** *Nature* 5 Feb. 368/2 Hardly surprisingly in view of their weird effects, sounding sands are incorporated into folklore and legends going back at least 1,500 years.

2. a. Of language, names, titles, etc.: Having a full, rich, or imposing sound; high-sounding, pompous, bombastic, etc. Also *transf.* of writers.

1683 SOAME & DRYDEN tr. *Boileau's Art Poet.* I. 182 Keep to your subject close in all you say; Nor for a sounding sentence ever stray. **1693** DRYDEN *Juvenal* Dedication (1697) p. lxxxix, We make our Authour at least appear in a Poetique Dress. We have actually made him more Sounding, and more Elegant, than he was before in English. **1711** ADDISON *Spect.* No. 26 ¶ 1 Several Persons mentioned in the Battles of Heroic Poems, who have sounding Names given them. **1775** JOHNSON *Tax. no Tyr.* 11 Before they quit the comforts of a warm home for the sounding some-thing which they think better. **1805** N. NICHOLLS in *Corr. w. Gray* (1843) 36 Milton, who, he said, in parts of his poem, rolls on in sounding words that have but little meaning. **1855** MACAULAY *Hist. Eng.* xix. IV. 321 There was a society..which assumed the sounding name of the Royal Academies Company. **1888** BRYCE *Amer. Commw.* lxxii. II. 594 The orator has been apt to evade them or to deal in sounding commonplaces.

b. Of persons: Loudly demonstrative.

1828 LYTTON *Pelham* III. ix, The disinterested kindness and delicacy..contrasted so deeply with the hollowness of friends more sounding, alike in their profession and their creeds.

† **'sounding**, *ppl. a.*^{2} *Obs.*$^{-1}$ [f. SOUND *v.*^{4}] That swoons; swooning.

1621 BURTON *Anat. Mel.* II. III. iii, For all their Physitians and medicines inforcing Nature, a souning wife, families complaints, friends teares,..he..goes to hell with a guilty conscience.

sounding-board^1. [SOUNDING *vbl. sb.*^{1}]

1. A board or screen placed over or behind a pulpit or similar structure in such a manner as to reflect the speaker's voice towards the audience; = SOUND-BOARD 2.

1766 ENTICK *London* IV. 18 A carved pulpit, a veneered sounding-board. **1784** COWPER *Task* III. 21 Since pulpits fail, and sounding-boards reflect Most part an empty ineffectual sound. **1816** *Gentl. Mag.* LXXXVI. I. 500 The sounding-board and back are much carved; the front of the former bears the date '1634'. **1879** J. C. COX *Ch. Derbysh.* IV. 20 The sounding board of the pulpit, when in its old position, spoilt one of the capitals.

transf. and *fig.* **1837** CARLYLE *Fr. Rev.* III. VI. vi, So sings the prophetic voice; into its Convention sounding-board. **1876** 'OUIDA' *Winter City* ix. 261 The more fanciful feeling which makes Nature a sounding-board to echo all the cries of men. **1890** B. L. GILDERSLEEVE *Ess. & Stud.* 370 A super-elegant sounding-board of a man.

2. *Mus.* = SOUND-BOARD 1.

1776 BURNEY *Hist. Music* I. 219 The lower part of the base of the sounding board [of the lyre]. **1801** BUSBY *Dict. Mus.*, *Sounding-Board*, in a harpsichord or piano-forte, a broad, thin board, horizontally situated, and over which the strings are distended. **1862** *Catal. Internat. Exhib., Brit.* II. No. 3437, Pianoforte with patent tubular sounding-board. *c* **1880** *Oxford Helps Study Bible* 134 [The] 'dulcimer' being an instrument formed of strings tightly stretched..over a rectangular sounding-board or box.

sounding-board^2. *rare*$^{-1}$. [SOUNDING *vbl. sb.*^{2}] A board used to ascertain the depth of water.

1776 G. SEMPLE *Building in Water* 19 Sounding Boards..of Inch Plank 12 or 14 Inches broad, divided into Feet and Inches.

sounding-lead. *Naut.* [SOUNDING *vbl. sb.*^{2}] The lead or plummet attached to the sounding-line.

1485 *Naval Acc. Hen. VII* (1896) 51 Leede lynes, j; Sounding leeds, j. **1495** *Ibid.* 193 Sowdyng ledes, ij. **1530** PALSGR. 709/2, I serche the see with a sowndyng leade to knowe howe depe it is. **1584** B. R. tr. *Herodotus* II. 76 Which..would not suffer the line with the sounding leade to sinke to the bottome. **1639** in Picton *L'pool Munic. Rec.* (1883) I. 226 Two compasses, one sounding lead & one barrell of meale. **1669** STURMY *Mariner's Mag.* IV. 137 Common Navigation requireth the Use of no Instruments but the Compass and Sounding-Lead. **1711** *Milit. & Sea Dict.* s.v., The Sounding-Lead is as the Deep-Sea-Lead for Sounding; but it is commonly only seven Pounds Weight, and about 12 Inches long. **1802** A. DUNCAN *Marin. Chron.* (1805) III. 215 Upon..sounding, the strap of the sounding-lead broke; an accident which very rarely happens. **1888** GOODE *Amer. Fishes* 75 These grounds are found by the use of the sounding-lead.

sounding-line. *Naut.* [SOUNDING *vbl. sb.*^{2}] A line used in sounding the depth of water; also, line or other material forming this.

In early use distinguished from the deep sea line: see DEEP SEA.

1336 *Acc. Exch. K.R.* 19/31 m. 4, In .j. petra cordis de canabo..pro vno soundynglyne inde faciendo. **1627** CAPT. SMITH *Seaman's Gram.* ix. 44 Fetch the Sounding line, this is bigger than the Dipsie line. [Hence in Phillips, etc.] **1777** ROBERTSON *Hist. Amer.* II. (1783) I. 104 As his course lay through seas which had not formerly been visited, the sounding-line, or instruments for observation, were continually in his hands. **1845** GOSSE *Ocean* Introd. (1849) 6 In many places no length of sounding line has yet been able to reach the bottom. **1860** MAURY *Phys. Geog.* (Low) xiii. §567 His sounding-line was an iron wire more than eleven miles in length.

soundingly ('saʊndɪŋlɪ), *adv.* [f. SOUNDING *ppl. a.*^{1} + -LY^2.] In a sounding manner; so as to emit or cause a sound, esp. a loud sound or noise; sonorously, imposingly.

1697 J. SERGEANT *Solid Philos.* 70 Those which by the smart motion of the Ayr, do come in thro' the Drum of the Ear,..do affect it with a kind of vibration, or (as we may say) Soundingly. **1844** DICKENS *Mart. Chuz.* xiii, Ye Pharisees, ..who soundingly appeal to human nature. **1865** —— *Mut. Fr.* xvi, No attendant to slap him soundingly. **1884** J. T. TROWBRIDGE *Farnell's Folly* I. xiii. 141 The said library, so soundingly alluded to, was entirely imaginary.

'soundingness. *rare.* [f. as prec. + -NESS.] The quality or character of being sonorous.

1727 BAILEY (vol. II), *Sonorousness*, Soundingness, Loudness. **1799** W. TAYLOR in Robberds *Mem.* (1843) I. 311 They do not often attain a certain majesty of Soundingness, which is frequent in the Latin hexameter. **1839** DARLEY *Beaum. & Fletcher's Wks.* I. Introd. p. xxxviii, To ensure music, lines must be full of sound, or soundingness.

† **'soundish**, *a.* *Obs.*$^{-0}$ [f. SOUND *sb.*^{3}] Somewhat sounding or sonorous.

1530 PALSGR. 325/1 Sowndysshe or sowndynge, *sonoreux.*

soundless ('saʊndlɪs), *a.*^{1} [f. SOUND *v.*^{2}] Of water, the sea, etc.: That cannot be sounded; unfathomable. Freq. *fig.* or in fig. context.

c **1586** C'TESS PEMBROKE *Ps.* CXLVIII. iv, When heav'n hath prais'd, praise earth anew:..Then soundlesse deepes, and what in you Residing low, or moves, or rests. *c* **1600** SHAKS. *Sonn.* lxxx. 10 Your shallowest helpe will hold me vp a floate, Whilst he vpon your soundlesse deepe doth ride. **1647** HERRICK *Noble Numbers, Hell*, Hell is no other, but a soundlesse pit. **1731** A. HILL *Advice to Poets* xv, In Wit's cold Shallows, wade..no more, Her soundless Ocean tempts you from the Shore. **1823** BYRON *Island* IV. iii, The crag's steep inexorable face, With nought but soundless waters for its base. *a* **1861** T. WOOLNER *My Beautiful Lady, Tolling Bell* xxvi, My lost soul sank adown in soundless seas. **1884** W. H. WHITE *Mark Rutherford's Deliverance* iv, When we consider that we live surrounded by the soundless depths in which the stars repose.

transf. **1614** C. BROOKE *Ghost Rich. III*, Poems (1872) 79 Nor wits, nor chronicles could ere containe, The hell-deepe reaches of my soundlesse braine.

soundless ('saʊndlɪs), *a.*^{2} [f. SOUND *sb.*^{3}]

1. Having, making, emitting, etc., no sound; devoid of sound; quiet, silent.

Freq. in the 19th cent.

1601 SHAKS. *Jul. C.* v. i. 36 Your words..rob the Hibla Bees, And leaue them Hony-lesse,..and soundlesse too: For you haue stolne their buzzing, Antony. **1663** BOYLE *Usef. Exp. Nat. Philos.* I. ii. 49 They celebrate his praises, though with a soundless voice. **1797** MRS. RADCLIFFE *Italian* vi, She glided forward with soundless step. **1826** DISRAELI *V. Grey* v. xv, Once more the attentive ear listening for the soundless breath. **1855** LYNCH *Rivulet* XCIII. ii, Soundless as chariots on the snow. **1883** *Standard* 7 Sept. 5/6 The soundless progress of the apparently animated car.

b. In quasi-adv. use: Soundlessly.

1844 MRS. BROWNING *Drama of Exile* 522 My lips prayed, soundless, to myself. **1879** G. MACDONALD *Sir Gibbie* III. i. 14 The moment the sound of them had ceased, he darted soundless after him.

2. In which no sound is heard; still.

1816 WORDSW. *Sonn. Liberty* II. xxxiv. 38 A soundless waste, a trackless vacancy! **1818** MILMAN *Samor* 63 Vast Germany..Deserts to silence and the beasts of game Her long and soundless forests. **1881** *Macm. Mag.* XLIV. 191 She lingered in the soundless drawing-room long after the fire had gone out.

3. Of the ear: Hearing no sound. *rare*$^{-1}$.

1890 TALMAGE *From Manger to Throne* 297 The world has never seen but one surgeon who could..reconstruct the drum of a soundless ear.

Hence **'soundlessly** *adv.*, **'soundlessness**.

1837 *Blackw. Mag.* XLI. 608 Insinuating its way into the bottom of her pocket, and *soundlessly relieving it of the notes and shillings. **1865** WHITNEY *Gayworthys* xxvi, Skylie clapped her hands again, soundlessly. **1889** *Harper's Mag.* Dec. 117/2 Soundlessly you will tread those shadowy pavements. **1834** *Fraser's Mag.* X. 663 Then comes a sort of moonlight dimness, and a dulled *soundlessness. **1881** H. JAMES *Portr. Lady* xxxix, The soundlessness of her step. **1897** HINDE *Congo Arabs* 77 The same monotony of colour and of soundlessness was above us as in the depths below.

soundly ('saʊndlɪ), *adv.* Also 5–6 **sowndely(e**, 5 **soundely**. [f. SOUND *a.* + -LY^2.]

1. a. In or with safety; safely. *Obs.* exc. *arch.*

c **1400** *Destr. Troy* 1826 Antenor..fast vppon fote ferkyt to shippe,..Sailit on soundly as hym selfe lyket. *c* **1440** *York Myst.* xxxii. 358 Ȝis, certis, we schall saue þame full soundely. **1888** STEVENSON *Black Arrow* II. i. 100 'How ye are to cross Till I know not'... 'I can swim,' returned Throgmorton. 'I will come soundly, fear not.'

b. In a sound or healthy manner. *rare*$^{-0}$.

1611 COTGR., *Sainement*, healthfully, soundly.

c. Securely, closely. *rare*$^{-1}$.

1632 LITHGOW *Trav.* I. 4 Sweete Ambrosian Nectar, soundly wrapt In my lock'd closet.

2. With reference to sleep, etc.: Deeply, profoundly; without disturbance or interruption.

c **1400** *Destr. Troy* 6057 Sore men & seke [he made] soundly to rest. *c* **1400** *Melayne* 1524 Sowndely neuer sall þay slepe. **1548** ELYOT s.v. *Somnus*, I slepte more soundely then I was wont. **1576** TURBERV. *Venerie* 150 They sleepe soundlyer in those two moneths than at any other tyme. **1581** A. HALL *Iliad* IX. 171 Where Phœnix doth alone right soundly sleepe. **1624** HEYWOOD *Gunaik.* IV. 185 You watch the time when he is soundliest asleepe. *c* **1717** PRIOR *Epitaph* 11 They soundly slept the Night away. **1794** MRS. RADCLIFFE *Myst. Udolpho* xlv, 'He sleeps soundly then,' said the count. **1820** R. POLLOK *Course T.* v, And all the winds slept soundly. **1847** C. BRONTË *Jane Eyre* xi, At once weary and content, I slept soon and soundly.

3. In an ample, complete, or thorough manner; thoroughly, properly, to the full.

1577 B. GOOGE *Heresbach's Husb.* II. (1586) 85 For that which is cut being greene and tender, dooth the sooner and the soundlier recouer himselfe. **1581** A. HALL *Iliad* x. 188 These two so valiant Greeks, through toile who soundly swet. **1597** A. M. tr. *Guillemeau's Fr. Chirurg.* 7 b/2 The peeces of bones beinge therein verye sowndelye healed. **1602** MARSTON *Ant. & Mel.* v. Wks. 1856 I. 56 Flatter her soundly. **1642–4** VICARS *God in Mount* (1844) 160 Ours played soundly from Gosport with our Ordnance. **1678** BUNYAN *Pilgr.* I. 87 He was soundly bedabled with that kind of dirt. **1827** CARLYLE *Germ. Rom.* I. 161 The messengers had in the meantime been soundly galloped. **1829** SCOTT *Anne of G.* xxxvi, Having disabled the cannon, and filled the German gunners soundly drunk. **1899** *Allbutt's Syst. Med.* VIII. 843 The wound, aided by skin-grafting, heals over soundly.

b. With verbs of beating, striking, defeating, reproving, etc.: Smartly, strongly, severely.

(*a*) **1596** SHAKS. *Tam. Shr.* I. ii. 31 He bid me knocke him, & rap him soundly sir. **1599** —— *Hen. V*, IV. vii. 136 If I can see my Gloue in his cappe,.. I wil strike it out soundly. **1613** PURCHAS *Pilgrimage* (1614) 483 The Prince caused him to be apprehended, and (being soundly whipped) to be banished. **1679** WOOD *Life* (O.H.S.) II. 473 John Dryeden the poet.. was about 8 at night soundly cudgell'd by 3 men. **1726** SWIFT *Gulliver* II. iii, The dwarf was soundly whipped. **1847** C. BRONTE *Jane Eyre* iv, She shook me most soundly, she boxed both my ears. **1868** *Smith's Dict. Gr. & Rom. Biog.* II. 1086/2 Sallust the historian was soundly scourged by Milo.

(*b*) **1647** DIGGES *Unlawf. Taking Arms* §2. 54 You need not doubt but your enemies wil be soundly worsted. **1718** SWIFT *Left handed Letter* 17 So the French, when our generals soundly did pay 'em, Went triumphant to church, and sang stoutly *Te Deum*. **1851** DICKENS *Hist. Eng.* i. 19 He beat them twice; though not so soundly. **1884** *Daily News* 2 Aug. 5/3 The Players were among the very few teams which defeated them, and that soundly.

(*c*) **1692** E. WALKER tr. *Epictetus' Mor.* liv, Lecture him soundly for it. **1828** CARR *Craven Gloss.* s.v., 'I gav it him soundly,' i.e. I severely reprobated his conduct. **1863** COWDEN CLARKE *Shaks. Char.* viii. 200 She rates Sir Toby, and soundly, about his late hours. **1885** *Manch. Exam.* 17 Mar. 5/4 Lord Salisbury.. rated them soundly on the subject of their desertion of Sir S. Northcote.

c. Dearly, heavily, in respect of payment, etc.

1610 SHAKS. *Temp.* II. ii. 81 Hee shall pay for him that hath him, and that soundly. **1632** LITHGOW *Trav.* I. 38 We had payd soundly for his Leachery. **1642** FULLER *Holy & Prof. St.* III. xxv. 232 Let them soundly suffer for it themselves. **1706** E. WARD *Wooden World Diss.* (1708) 15 Except he pay him soundly for a license.

†**4.** In accordance with the principles of true religion; with sound or orthodox views. *Obs.*

1574 WHITGIFT *Def. Aunsw.* i. 74 If we say that in those poyntes whiche we holde from them, that wee thinke soundlyer than they doe, we are readie to proue it. **1581** R. GOADE in *Conf.* II. (1584) N iij, Shall euery particular point of errour in doctrine depriue a man of saluation, holding soundly yᵉ foundation Christ? **1608** DOWNAME in *Eng. Hist. Rev.* (1909) Apr. 245 This Church of England.. did hold.. all substantiall points of diuinity as soundly as any church in the world. **1676** HALE *Contempl.* I. 171 These be some of those Principal Objects of that Faith that over-cometh the world, being soundly received, and digested.

5. With sound judgement or good practical common-sense; according to sound or well-founded principles; without fallacy or error.

1594 HOOKER *Eccl. Pol.* I. xvi. §2 Soundly to judge of a law. **1621** T. WILLIAMSON tr. *Goulart's Wise Vieillard* 197 Let posteritie iudge more soundly then wee of what wee doe want. **1668** DAVENANT *Man's the Master* I. i, I never found my self so much inclin'd to reasoning, and, if you please, let's consult soundly. **1818** SCOTT *Rob Roy* x, More learned than soundly wise. **1858** STANLEY *Life Arnold* II. ix. 146 The power of seeing truth and judging soundly. **1875** E. WHITE *Life in Christ* II. xiii. (1878) 152 From this it may be soundly inferred that the belief.. was of primeval antiquity. **1884** *Law Rep. 13 Q.B.D.* 448 The discretion of the learned judge was soundly exercised with reference to the question.

soundness ('saʊndnɪs). [f. SOUND *a.*]

1. The quality or state of being sound or free from disease; sound or healthy condition; healthiness.

1398 TREVISA *Barth. De P.R.* VI. vi. (Bodl. MS.), Puella is a name of age, of soundenes without wem, and also of honestee. **1571** GOLDING *Calvin on Ps.* xli. 13 Soundnesse may be referred too the body as to the mynd in this wyse. **1601** SHAKS. *All's Well* I. ii. 24, I would I had that corporall soundnesse now. *a* **1610** HEALEY *Cebes* (1616) 134 The Physician.. corroborates the vitals; and finally confirmeth the body in perfect soundnesse. **1701** STANHOPE *Augustine's Medit.* II. xviii. (1720) 167 There shall be in us all imaginable Soundness and Vigour, without any sort of Disease or Decay. **1768** TUCKER *Lt. Nat.* I. II. 322 Though a man would wish in the first place to enjoy vigour of limbs and soundness of constitution. **1830** R. KNOX *Béclard's Anat.* 372 These tissues resemble the tissues of the human body in a state of soundness. **1866** J. G. MURPHY *Comm., Exod.* xix. 9 The hand changed from soundness to leprosy and again to soundness.

fig. **1643** MILTON *Divorce* Introd., Wks. 1851 IV. 3 A certain big face of pretended learning, mistaken.. for the wholsome habit of soundnesse and good constitution.

b. Of the mind, etc.: (see SOUND *a.* 2 b).

1548 ELYOT, *Sanitas*, helth,.. soundenesse of memorie. **1602** J. DAVIES (Heref.) *Mirum in Modum* Wks. (Grosart) I. 15/1 The Soule can not her soundnesse more bewray, Then when she doth Temptations strong resist. **1639** J. SEDGWICK (*title*), The Bearing and Burden of the Spirit, wherein the Sicknesse and Soundnesse of the Mans Spirit is opened. **1678** (*title*), The Temperate Man or the Right Way of Preserving Life and Health, together with Soundness of the Senses, Judgment, and Memory unto extream Old Age. **1818** CRUISE *Digest* (ed. 2) V. 537 Conclusive evidence of the capacity of such vouchee, as to the soundness of his mind. **1860** PUSEY *Min. Proph.* 36 The minds of the wicked.. lose their soundness as it were without knowing it.

c. Firmness, solidity; freedom from weakness, defect, or damage; goodness of condition or repair. Also *fig.*

1548 ELYOT, *Soliditas*,.. soundenesse. **1565** COOPER *Thes.* s.v. *Firmitas*, The hardenes or soundenes of the matter. **1663** S. PATRICK *Parab. Pilgrim* (1687) 414 He considers not that a crazy state of things cannot be so soon amended and restored to entire soundness. **1685** BAXTER *Paraphr. N.T.* 1 John ii. 5–6 It is they that keep his Word, in whom the Love of God doth shew its soundness and perfection. **1827** FARADAY *Chem. Manip.* xviii. (1842) 484 That rigidity which was so dangerous to the apparatus and fatal to its soundness. **1859** *Act 22–23 Vict.* c. 66 §13 The [gas] Meter shall be tested for Soundness or Leakage only. **1875** MANNING *Mission H. Ghost* xii. 332 If you.. saw before you a bridge the soundness of which was doubtful.

2. Orthodoxy in respect of religious belief, political views, or other opinions.

1583 STUBBES *Anat. Abus.* II. (1882) 91 Persons.. whose soundnesse in religion.. they are not ignorant of. **1631** GOUGE *God's Arrows* III. §30. 236 Cause is given for their prayers to be suspected in regard of the soundnesse of them. **1682** *Sec. Plea for Nonconf.* 2 The Worthiness of their Persons,.. Soundness of their Faith, Exemplary Morals. *a* **1700** EVELYN *Diary* 10 Mar. 1687, The Church of England, whose doctrine for Catholic and soundness he preferr'd to all the Communities.. of Christians in the world. **1872** DE VERE *Americanisms* 266 Often it is not enough to ascertain the soundness of the candidate.

3. The quality or fact of being in harmony with solid or well-established principles or facts:

a. Of judgement, reasoning, etc.

a **1600** HOOKER *Eccles. Pol.* (J.), It may stand then very well with strength and soundness of reason, even thus to answer. **1631** GOUGE *God's Arrows* v. §6. 416 Soundnesse of judgement, Sharpenesse of wit, Quicknesse of conceit. **1782** MISS BURNEY *Cecilia* v. iv, The soundness of her judgment had hitherto guarded her both from error and blame. **1799** J. ROBERTSON *Agric. Perth* 552 They have a soundness of understanding equal to the task. **1818** SCOTT *Hrt. Midl.* xxxiv, The soundness of thinking which she had displayed in conversation. **1885** *Manch. Exam.* 18 Feb. 3/2 In critical soundness and penetration, he is infinitely superior to Johnson.

b. Of views, acts, principles, etc.

1739 WATERLAND *Sacram. Pt. Eucharist Expl.* 18, I will not answer for the Acuteness, much less for the Soundness of his Distinction. **1832** HT. MARTINEAU *Ella of Gar.* vii. 81, I always doubt the soundness of a plea which is urged in such a hurry. **1837** P. KEITH *Bot. Lex.* 275 The soundness of the principle on which the Linnæan nomenclature is founded. **1885** *Law Times* LXXIX. 131/2 The soundness of this decision seems to us beyond doubt.

4. Thoroughness, completeness.

1853 LYNCH *Lett. Scattered* (1872) 357 If he wait long enough, he will be flogged with most efficient soundness.

sound-post. [f. SOUND *sb.*[3] + POST *sb.*[1]] A small peg of wood fixed beneath the bridge of a violin or similar instrument, serving as a support for the belly and as a connecting part between this and the back.

[**1592** SHAKS. *Rom. & Jul.* IV. v. 138 What say you, Iames Sound-Post?] **1687** MIÈGE *Gt. Fr. Dict.* s.v. *Ame*, The sound-posts that stand up within the body of a musical Instrument. **1762** STERNE *Tr. Shandy* v. xv, The bridge is a mile too high, and the sound-post absolutely down. **1833** T. FARDELY tr. *Otto's Treat. Violin* 4 The belly, the bass bar, the sound post, and the six blocks, [are] of Tyrolese deal. **1848** J. BISHOP tr. *Otto's Violin* (1875) 78 The chief function of the sound-post is to render normal the vibrations of the back and belly. **1884** HAWEIS *My Musical Life* I. 95 The sound-post—i.e. the little peg which bears the strain on the belly and back.

soundrie, obs. form of SUNDRY.

soune, obs. var. SON, SOON, SOUND *sb.* and *v.*

soup (su:p), *sb.* Also 7–8 **soupe**, **soop.** [ad. F. *soupe* (OF. also *souppe*, *sope*) sop, broth, = Prov., Sp., Pg. *sopa* (It. *zuppa*): see SOP *sb.*[1] Hence also WFlem. *soepe*, *soupe*, Du. *soep*. The relationship of other Teut. forms is less clear: cf. MHG. (G. and Da.) *suppe* with OHG. *sopha*, *soffa* (MHG. *sophe*), MLG. *sope*, *soppe* (LG. *soppe*; Sw. and Norw. *soppa*), MDu. *sop*, *zop* (Du. and Fris. *sop*).]

1. a. A liquid food prepared by boiling, usually consisting of an extract of meat with other ingredients and seasoning.

Freq. with defining words, as *fish, giblet, gravy, hare, ox-tail, pea, turtle soup*; *clear, thick soup*; etc.

α. **1653** URQUHART *Rabelais* I. li, Then made they ready store of Carbonadoes.. and good fat soupes or brewis with sippets. *a* **1700** B. E. *Dict. Cant. Crew*, *Soupe*, Broth, Porridge. **1716** GAY *Trivia* III. 204 And in the Soupe the slimy Snail is drown'd.

β. **1687** MIÈGE *Gt. Fr. Dict.* I, *Soupe*,.. pottage, or soop. **1688** HOLME *Armoury* III. 84/2 *Soops*, a kind of sweet pleasant Broth, made rich with Fruit and Spices. **1691** *Satyr agst. the French* 16 With Dishes which few Mankind knew beside; With Soops and Fricasies, Ragou's, Pottage. **1730** SWIFT *Panegyrick on Dean* Wks. 1755 IV. I. 142 Instead of wholsome bread and cheese, To dress their soops and fricassees. **1760–72** tr. *Juan & Ulloa's Voy.* (ed. 3) I. 78 To make it an ingredient in their soop.

γ. **1677** MIÈGE *Fr. Dict.* II, Soup, or French pottage. **1729** SWIFT *Direct. Serv.* (1745) 20 Let the Cook daub the Back of his new Livery; or when he is going up with a Dish of Soup, let her follow him softly with a Ladle-full. **1758** JOHNSON *Idler* No. 19 ⁋8 He.. has only time to taste the soup. **1807** *Med. Jrnl.* XVII. 220 The patient.. indicated a desire for a little soup, of which he got over a few spoonfuls. **1837** P. KEITH *Bot. Lex.* 181 The Truffle is much esteemed for the rich and delicate flavour which it imparts to soups and sauces. **1859** *Habits of Gd. Society* xi. 310 A light soup is better than a thick one, which clogs the appetite.

fig. **1859** LEVER *Dav. Dunn* xlvi, Cranberry must have got his soup pretty hot, for he has come abroad. **1876** GEO. ELIOT *Let.* 2 May (1956) VI. 244 Are you not sometimes made rather desponding by the reading of newspapers and periodicals?.. All information is given in a soup of comment. **1977** *Undercurrents* June–July 9/1 The twelve page Corruption Supplement is a rich soup of sex, planning scandals, corruption trials, housing fiddles, [etc.].

(*b*) Phr. *(from) soup to nuts* (U.S. colloq.), from beginning to end, completely; everything.

1910 C. MATHEWSON *Won in Ninth* 143 He knew the game from 'soup to nuts'. **1938** H. ASBURY *Sucker's Progress* 16 For many years a common expression was 'from soda to hock', meaning the whole thing, from soup to nuts. **1946** E. O'NEILL *Iceman Cometh* I. 79, I know all about that game from soup to nuts. **1964** F. O'ROURKE *Mule for Marquesa* 42 'Everything here we asked for?' 'Soup to nuts... Nothing but the best.'

b. *Biol.* A solution rich in organic compounds which, it is believed, formerly made up the oceans or lakes of the earth and was the environment in which cellular life originated. Freq. as ***primordial soup***.

[**1929** J. B. S. HALDANE in *Rationalist Ann.* 8 When ultra-violet light acts on a mixture of water, carbon dioxide, and ammonia, a vast variety of organic substances are made... Before the origin of life they must have accumulated till the primitive oceans reached the consistency of hot dilute soup.] **1956** *Amer. Scientist* XLIV. 356 One plausible explanation is that spontaneous resolution of an *early* biosynthetic intermediate from the primordial nutritional 'soup' of the first organisms led to a monoconfigurational world. **1971** I. G. GASS et al. *Understanding Earth* ix. 126/1 This primitive soup provided a nutrient 'broth' for the first living organisms which finally arose within it. **1976** R. DAWKINS *Selfish Gene* xi. 211 Floating chaotically free in the primeval soup. **1977** *Vole* No. 4. 13/2 We both [*sc.* humans and plants] have common ancestors.. in that pool of organic nutrients known as the primordial soup.

2. *colloq.* or *slang.* **a.** Briefs for prosecutions given to members of the Bar at Quarter Sessions or other courts; the fees attaching to such briefs. Also in pl.

1856 *Law Times* XXVII. 122 But will soup so ladled out, to use the well-known phrase, support a barrister in the criminal courts? **1889** B. C. ROBINSON *Bench & Bar* 160 The brief consisted merely of the depositions, and the important honorarium attached to it was called 'soup'. **1891** *Pall Mall G.* 17 Sept. 5/2 A crowd of unemployed barristers.., waiting to secure these [briefs] which are known in Bar slang as 'soups'.

attrib. **1894** *Daily Tel.* 23 Nov. 5/4 The great 'soup' question is again agitating the minds of barristers at the Old Bailey.

b. *in the soup*, in a difficulty. orig. *U.S.*

1889 *Lisbon* (Dakota) *Star* 26 Apr. 4/2 After collecting a good deal of money, the scoundrels suddenly left town, leaving many persons in the soup. **1898** *Pall Mall Mag.* Nov. 420 Of course he knows we're in the soup—beastly ill luck. **1915** J. BUCHAN *Thirty-Nine Steps* ii. 37, I was in the soup—that was pretty clear. **1917** LLOYD GEORGE *Let.* 31 July (1973) 184 Henderson has now put us into the soup & there is no knowing what will happen. **1925** [see EYEBROW 1 d]. **1939** H. G. WELLS *Holy Terror* I. ii. 38 We're in the soup... We've got to do 1914 over again. **1968** *Listener* 23 May 660/3 You find you may want to move a group of pictures.. to a different part of the building, and if the rooms over there are designed for quite a different kind of picture, you're rather in the soup. **1977** C. MCCULLOUGH *Thorn Birds* xvii. 455, I do feel very sorry for her, and it makes me more determined than ever not to land in the same soup she did.

c. In miscellaneous uses: (see quots.).

1891 *Cent. Dict.*, *Soup*, a kind of picnic in which a great pot of soup is the principal feature. **1911** *Webster's Dict.*, *Soup*, any material injected into a horse with a view to changing its speed or temperament.

d. Fog; thick cloud. Cf. PEA-SOUP a.

1901 *Scotsman* 6 Nov. 10/6 Then the 'soup' begins to get thick. Particles of smoke.. remain suspended. **1941** F. H. JOSEPH *Let.* 7 Apr. in *Britain at War* (1942) 4 It wasn't long .. before we were in the soup again. **1966** E. WEST *Night is Time for Listening* iii. 107 Over the North Sea the soup was dense and threatening; turbulence was marked. **1972** J. GORES *Dead Skip* (1973) xxiii. 161 Ballard watched the taillights recede into the soup.

e. Nitro-glycerine or gelignite.

1902 *N.Y. Tribune* 22 Oct. 8/4 Dynamite or nitro-glycerine is called 'soup'. **1903** I. K. FRIEDMAN *Autobiogr. of Beggar* vii. 218 Louis learned how ter make de 'soup' from a gang of 'yeagers' dat used ter blow de doors off country banks. **1905** *Strand Mag.* XXX. 702/1 That's got enough soup in it to blow the whole court-house into the sky. **1920** 'SAPPER' *Bull-Dog Drummond* x. 265 I've got the soup here —gelignite. **1930** D. L. SAYERS *Strong Poison* xiii. 169 Sam put the soup in at the 'inges and it blowed the 'ole front clean off. **1960** *Observer* 24 Jan. 5/1 The American petermen had started it long before the First World War by using soup, nitro-glycerine in liquid form, to pour through a little plasticine channel to blow the fashionable combination lock safes.

f. *Photogr.* and *Cinemat.* A processing chemical, esp. the developer.

1929 *N.Y. Times* 20 Oct. IX. 8 *Soup*, the developing bath in which a sound negative is developed. **1934** *Tit-Bits* 31 Mar. 12/3 The chemicals in which the film is developed are known as 'soup'. **1969** GISH & PINCHOT *Lilian Gish* ix. 102 Joe showed me how film was developed in the 'soup'. **1978** L. DEIGHTON *SS-GB* xxiii. 220 Any special instructions? Over or under development? Fine grain soup? **1979** *SLR Camera* Dec. 60/1 When you've mixed the soup remember to keep it in a well stoppered dark bottle which has been thoroughly cleaned.

g. *Surfing.* (See quot. 1962.)

1962 T. MASTERS *Surfing made Easy* 65 *Soup*, the foam or broken portion of a wave. **1966** *Weekly News* (N.Z.) 19 Jan. 6/2 When going through waves, point the board directly into the oncoming 'soup'. **1968** *Surfer Mag.* Jan. 24/3 By standing feet parallel, you can float over breaking soup. **1977** *Surfing World* (Austral.) XVII. II. 88 Plow through miles of soup.

3. a. *attrib.*, chiefly with names of utensils, as ***soup-bowl***, ***-dish***, ***-kettle***, ***-ladle***, ***-plate*** (also *fig.*), ***-pot***, ***-tureen***, etc.

1858 T. W. ATKINSON *Oriental & West. Siberia* iii. 41 Take my broth with my two friends from the *same* *soup-bowl I could not. **1755** *Gentl. Mag.* XXV. 416 Vessels like *soup-dishes, supported on three feet. **1852** THACKERAY *Esmond* II. xii, The poor devils had even fled without their *soup-kettles. **1716** *Lond. Gaz.* No. 5437/4, 18 Forks, a *Soop-Ladle. **1847** Emerson *Repr. Men, Plato* Wks. (Bohn) I. 295 Drawing all his illustrations..from pitchers and soup-ladles. **1726** D. Eaton *Let.* 16 Feb. (1971) 46, I.. left directions in writing..what to pack up. I wrote down all manner of herbes, and the *soop plates, &c. **1827** Faraday *Chem. Manip.* xii. (1842) 276 The litmus solution should be poured into a dish or soup-plate. **1900** *Daily News* 2 June 6/7 Some thirty years ago, when soup-plate bonnets and round-brimmed hats were in vogue. **1924** E. M. Forster *Passage to India* I. iii. 28 A sunk soup plate of a lawn. **1939** H. Hodge *Cab, Sir?* 217 The badge itself..is called a 'soup-plate'. **1964** C. Willock *Enormous Zoo* v. 80, I shone my torch..and found a couple of large pink soup-plates glaring back at me—a hippo. **1837** Carlyle *Fr. Rev.* I. vii. xi, An enormous tricolor; large as a *soup-platter, or sun-flower. **1751** H. Glasse *Art of Cookery* (ed. 4) App. 331 Put them with the Fins and Head in a *Soop-pot. **1866** Lady St.-Clair-Erskine *Dainty Dishes* (ed. 2) 5 Put into a soup-pot twelve lbs...of beef. **1705** *Lond. Gaz.* No. 4163/3, 5 *Soop Spoons. **1834** Dickens *Sk. Boz* (1836) 1st Ser. I. 160 Delighted to screen himself behind a *soup tureen. **1840** T. A. Trollope *Summer in Brittany* I. 298 An immense soup-tureen full of boiled milk.

b. In combination with other sbs., as ***soup-and-blanket***, ***soup-and-bully***, ***soup-and-patty***; **soup-and-fish** *slang*, men's evening dress, a dinner suit.

1829 Syd. Smith *Let.* in Lady Holland *Memoir* (1855) II. 299 He had not his usual soup-and-pattie look. **1862** Dickens *Somebody's Luggage* 26 She'd have no more chance again the ice, than a chaney cup again a soup-and-bully tin. **1900** *Westm. Gaz.* 26 Sept. 8/1 Making ground with his electors through the medium of the 'soup and blanket brigade'. **1918** Wodehouse *Piccadilly Jim* i. 26 He took me to supper at some swell joint where they all had the soup-and-fish on but me. **1945** 'A. Gilbert' *Black Stage* xi. 149 What do you do about dinner here? Soup-and-fish or just a clean collar? **1970** H. McLeave *Question of Negligence* (1973) xviii. 141 Get him to take off his soup-and-fish and show us his scar.

4. Special combs., as **soup bunch** *U.S. dial.* (see quot. 1923); **soup-fin (shark)**, a brown or grey shark with large teeth, *Galeorhinus zygopterus*, found off the Pacific coast of North America and once hunted for the value of its liver and fins; **soup gun** *U.S. Mil. slang*, a mobile army kitchen (? *obs.*); **soup-house, soup-kitchen**, an establishment for preparing soup and supplying it to the poor or unemployed, either free or at a very low charge; hence **soup-kitchener**, one who accepts food from a soup-kitchen; **soup line** *U.S.*, a queue of people waiting to be fed at a soup-kitchen; **soup man** *Criminals' slang*, an expert user of nitro-glycerine, etc.; **soup-meat**, meat used for making soup; **soup-shop**, (*a*) a shop where soup is distributed free; (*b*) a house where burglars dispose of silver and gold plate; **soup-stock**, stock used in making soup; **soup-strainer (moustache)** *colloq.*, a long moustache; **soup-ticket**, a ticket given to poor people enabling them to receive soup from a soup-kitchen.

1923 *Dialect Notes* V. 244 **Soup bunch*, a small bundle of vegetables for soup. **1938** *Mississippi* (Federal Writers' Project) 286 The grocery stores and the fruit and vegetable stands sell 'soup bunches' which provide the base for home-cooked vegetable soup. **1905** D. S. Jordan *Guide to Study of Fishes* I. xxx. 541 The *soup-fin shark..is found on the coast of California, where its fins are highly valued by the Chinese. **1941** *Sun* (Baltimore) 25 Nov. 5/3 Tales of big profits in soupfin shark liver fishing sent E. Smith..hustling ..to get his share. **1961** E. S. Herald *Living Fishes of World* 27/2 In 1942 and 1943 about five thousand soupfins were caught..west of Los Angeles. **1975** *Daily Colonist* (Victoria, B.C.) 22 Aug. 16/5 In San Diego the markets call it shark or 'soupfin'. **1975** *Islander* (Victoria, B.C.) 30 Nov. 10/2 One shark hunted to near extinction because of its liver..is the soup fin shark. **1918** C. J. Swan *My Company* 72 The cooks took the '*soup gun', as they immediately nicknamed the kitchen, all apart. **1928** A. C. Havlin *Hist. Company A* 37 In spite of being accompanied by our 'soup gun', we frequently charged the trenches assisted only by coffee and a strip of bacon between two slices of bread. **1861** Clington *Frank O'Donnell* 196 These various sums..were spent..in building *Soup-houses, and erecting boilers. **1839** C. Sinclair *Holiday House* xi. 255 We never had a drop of broth from the *soup-kitchen all winter. **1851** Mayhew *Lond. Lab.* II. 259/1 The National Philanthropic Association, with its eleemosynary soup-kitchens, &c. **1907** G. B. Shaw *Major Barbara* II. 220 You lie, you old *soup-kitchener, you. **1938** C. Himes *Black on Black* (1973) 167 The panic which he had prophesied was on hand and already *soup lines had come into existence. **1980** *TWA Ambassador* Oct. 69/3 We had soup lines and the Depression because men lost confidence in themselves. **1961** B. Knox *Die for Big Betsy* ii. 44 'Denby's a "*soup" man,' he said. 'Specializes in second-rate safe-blowings.' **1841** Thackeray *Gt. Hoggarty Diam.* ix, Tell her on no account to pay more than..4½d. for *soup-meat. **1799** *Manch. Mercury* 8 Jan. 4/5 The plan of the *soup shops at Birmingham might be advantageously followed at Manchester. **1817** Cobbett *Pol. Reg.* XXXII. 83 Reduced to such a state as to be fed at Soup Shops by Subscription! **1854** *London Jrnl.* XIX. 322 By the term soup-shops, the speaker meant those convenient houses where burglars and thieves dispose of any silver or gold plate which may fall into their hands. In such establishments the melting-pots are always kept ready. **1861** Dickens *Gt. Expect.* xxxiii, The air of this chamber, in its strong combination of stable with *soup-stock. **1932** Wodehouse *Hot Water* viii. 153 He did not propose to have a valet hanging around him festooned with fungus and snorting at him all the time from behind a great beastly *soupstrainer. **1962** E. Lucia *Klondike Kate* iii. 86 A soulfully humming male quartet in soup-strainers and sideburns. **1968** *Listener* 1 Aug. 140/1 At the telegraph office we aroused with great difficulty an elderly man with a large grey soup-strainer moustache. **1839** E. Hall *Diary* 29 Jan. in O. A. Sherrard *Two Victorian Girls* (1966) i. 11 Our poor house was besieged by a host of people come for *soup tickets. **1841** Marryat *Poacher* xii, They look like soup-tickets. **1870** Lowell *Among my Bks.* Ser. I. (1873) 300 This soup-ticket to a ladleful of fame.

soup, obs. or dial. variant of sup *sb.*[1]

soup (suːp), *v.* [f. soup *sb.*]

1. *trans.* To provide with soup. See also souper *sb.*[1] and **souping** *ppl. a.*

1857 Reade *Box Tunnel* in *Scrap-Bk.* (1906) Mar. 133 He handed them out—he souped them—he tough-chickened them.

2. [cf. soup *sb.* 2 b.] To place in difficulties, to bring to grief. Usu. in pa. pple. *colloq.*

1895 W. C. Gore in *Inlander* Dec. 114 *Soup.* v., to cause to fail; to bring to grief. **1922** Joyce *Ulysses* 160 Luck I had the presence of mind to dive into Manning's or I was souped. **1964** *Daily Tel.* 16 Jan. 26/4 Admitting that he earned £3,000 a year, Lord Taylor said that if he accepted a junior Ministry he would be 'souped'.

3. [cf. quot. 1911 s.v. soup *sb.* 2 c; perh. infl. by super-.] Orig. and chiefly with *up*. To modify (an engine, aircraft, motor vehicle, etc.) to increase its power and efficiency. Also *transf.* and *fig. colloq.* (orig. *U.S.*).

1931 [implied at souped(-up) *ppl. a.*] **1933** C. K. Stewart *Speech Amer. Airman* 92 *Soup Up*, to supercharge. **1939** *Sun* (Baltimore) 3 Aug. 1/6 We have done this without 'souping up' our engines, without putting alcohol in our gasoline,.. or flying with motors which last only five hours. **1949** A. Hynd *We are Public Enemies* i. 22 Dillinger..bought two new Fords. He souped up the motors... Now he was ready to act as his own getaway driver. *Ibid.* 29 John Dillinger and five other public enemies arrived in three souped-up Ford cars. **1959** *Spectator* 17 Apr. 557/1 The collection is souped up with frantic editorial comments. **1962** *John o' London's* 8 Feb. 140/2, I don't think Mr. Hauser was at his most perceptive in souping-up what was already very funny. **1965** L. Whitten *Progeny of Adder* (1966) 31 The quintet, souped up on sets—tranquilizers and pep pills taken together. **1972** F. Warner *Lying Figures* iii. 35 The coffee soups her up so that she has to take a tranquillizer. **1976** K. Benton *Single Monstrous Act* v. 152 He had lovingly souped up the Escort's engine, and now gave it full throttle. **1979** J. Gardner *Nostradamus Traitor* xxxix. 188 A German car: Opel Kadett, souped, and probably reinforced.

Hence **'souping** *ppl. a.*; **'souped(-up)** *ppl. a.*; **'souping(-up)** *vbl. sb.*

1891 *Daily News* 20 Jan. 6/4 The hypocritical cry raised by a gang of souping parsons. **1902** *Edin. Rev.* July 135 Luke found himself accused of countenancing the 'souping' proselytiser. **1931** *Automotive Industries* 30 May 826/1 Ray Keech's run at Daytona Beach in the White Triplex powered with three 'souped-up' Liberty engines. **1941** *Time* 18 Aug. 76/2 Its hero, Slave Trader Matthew Flood, is built like a souped-up Abraham Lincoln. **1949** [see soup *v.* 3]. **1956** D. Walker *Harry Black* xiii. 196 You're like a souped-up version of my mother. **1957** *New Yorker* 2 Nov. 95/2 Their superb High Fidelity components reproduce all the sounds of the original..with no 'souped-up' tones, squeaks or other distortions. **1960** *News Chron.* 16 June 4/6 Without any souping at all, the Mini-Minor..produces a very useful performance. *Ibid.* 4/7 A specially cast manifold for the souped version of the Mini-Austin. **1961** *Times* 7 Nov. 19/1 In Britain a thriving business has grown up in tuning and modifying the engines of existing models to give more performance. So widespread has this practice (referred to by enthusiasts as 'brewing up', 'souping up', or merely 'hotting up') become, particularly with 'Minis' that the B.M.C. introduced an 'officially hotted up' version last September. **1965** *Listener* 18 Nov. 795/1 As if lacking confidence in his own directorial inventiveness, Visconti takes recourse during one sequence to a modulated version of Fellini's style, and at another juncture provides his audience with souped-up..Antonioni. **1975** B. Garfield *Death Sentence* (1976) ii. 11 A souped-up car with enormous rear tires growled past him. **1980** *SLR Camera* July 7/1 News from the Colonies tells us that Ilford have introduced a 'souped-up' 1D-11 for processing black and white film in the USA.

soup, obs. variant of sup *v.*, swoop *v.*

‖**soupçon** (supsɔ̃). [F., repr. OF. *soupeçon*, *souspeçon*:—pop. L. *suspectiōn-*, *suspectio* for *suspicio* suspicion *sb.*] A suspicion, a suggestion, a very small quantity or slight trace, *of* something.

1766 H. Walpole *Lett.* (1857) V. 16 Wesley is a lean elderly man, fresh-coloured, his hair smoothly combed, but with a *soupçon* of curl at the ends. **1838** Miss Maitland *Let. Madras* (1843) 235 We are now writing dialogues for the natives..on different subjects, just to give them a *soupçon* of sense. **1849** [Eastwick] *Dry Leaves* 170 Any one who has the smallest *soupçon* of justice in his composition. **1884** Sir H. Hawkins in *Law Times Rep.* L. 814/1 Nobody would suppose there was even a *soupçon* of a gambling character about the establishment.

‖**soupe** (sup). The French word for soup *sb.*, usu. used with defining addition, as ***soupe à l'oignon*** (onion soup), etc.

1767 'Coriat Junior' *Another Traveller!* I. ii. xx. 196, I well remember that the good father supt up his *Soupe a l'Oignon.* **1777** P. Thicknesse *Year's Journey* II. xliv. 98 A Frenchman eats his *soupe* and *bouille* at twelve o'clock. **1794** [see soup maigre *attrib.*]. **1863** G. Meredith *Let.* 9 Feb. (1970) I. 210 Soupe, à la sage femme. **1865** M. Eyre *Lady's Walks* xxxi. 330 They..dine, except on fête days, on *soupe aux choux*, or *aux haricots.* **1883** 'Wyvern' *Culinary Jottings for Madras* (ed. 4) xxx. 321 '*Soupe à l'oignon*':—Slice a couple of Bombay onions; powder them well with flour... Grated Parmesan should accompany. **1904** A. Bennett *Great Man* xxvi. 306 The host's first spoonful of *soupe aux moules.* **1952** D. Ames *Murder, Maestro, Please* xvii. 126 She insisted on making *soupe à l'oignon* to go with the contents of the bar. **1975** *New Yorker* 6 Oct. 135/1 Good pastries are still sold, along with such popular dishes as *soupe Chinoise*, a pungent concoction containing shrimp, meat, and vegetables. **1980** E. Leather *Duveen Letter* xiv. 163 The waiter brought the *soupe à l'oignon.*

soupe, obs. form of sup *v.*[1] and *v.*[2]

soupé, var. souper *sb.*[2]

soupen, obs. pa. pple. sup *v.*[1]

souper ('suːpə(r)), *sb.*[1] [f. soup *sb.* or *v.*]

1. In Ireland, a Protestant clergyman seeking to make proselytes by means of dispensing soup in charity. Also *attrib.*

1854 *Tablet* 11 Nov. 713/4 Every Souper, every tyrannical agent, every sworn Orangeman, will be a friend to this new order of things. **1861** Clington *Frank O'Donnell* 205 On this account they were called souper-schools and their ministers soupers. **1890** *Cath. News* 29 Nov. 3/4 Our readers are no doubt aware of the usual falsehoods employed by Soupers for this purpose.

2. One converted to Protestantism by the receipt of soup or other charity.

1871 Froude *Short Stud.* II. 369 In a village below the lake is a congregation of Soupers—Protestant converts. **1896** *Daily News* 20 Jan. 6/4 They cannot believe in any Catholic honestly becoming a Protestant. The convert must be a souper.

Hence **'soupering, 'souperism.**

1861 E. G. K. Browne *Ann. Tract. Movem.* (ed. 3) 241 Who has lately..distinguished himself as a partizan of 'Souperism' at Belmullet. **1896** *Cath. News* 18 Jan. 4/5 He has thought of Irish Church 'missions', and believes that the system of soupering is carried on at Barmouth.

‖**souper** (supe), *sb.*[2] Also soupé. [Fr.] Esp. in France: an evening meal, supper; ***souper intime*** (ɛ̃tim) ['intimate']: for two, in privacy.

1787 H. Maty tr. *Riesbeck's Trav. Germany* I. xx. 238 But, alas! so soon as the body is satisfied here, so soon does the mind long for the friendly *dines* and *soupés* of Paris. **1834** *Baboo* I. i. 10 Those soupers are inestimable, and must not cease. **1851** E. Ruskin *Let.* in W. James *Order of Release* (1948) ix. 169 The monk received us very kindly and soon after we had souper, milk, macaroni, salt fish, fritters and very bad wine. **1967** J. Richardson *Courtesans* iii. 37/2 (*caption*) A courtesan bound for a *souper intime.* **1970** *Guardian* 30 Jan. 9/1 The *souper intime* with..low lights, and music. **1976** *New Yorker* 26 Jan. 40/3 By the time she returned, to give Joey a *souper* of boiled-liver chunks, macaroni, pig's maw, beef kidney, and rice, it was almost midnight.

souper, obs. f. supper.

soupie, varr. sopie, soupy *sb.*

'soupify, *v.* [f. soup *sb.*] *trans.* To convert into soup.

1831 Trelawny *Adv. Younger Son* ii, I passed on, ordering him instantly to come on board, or the Maratti would soupify him.

‖**soupii**, variant of sopie.

soupil(l, obs. varr. supple.

‖**soupirant** (supirɑ̃). [Fr., = sighing (lover), pres. pple. of *soupirer* to sigh.] A male admirer, a suitor.

1849 Thackeray *Pendennis* I. x. 93 And is Sir Derby Oaks ..another *soupirant*?.. Another admirer of Miss Fotheringay? **1969** J. Fowles *French Lieutenant's Woman* lxi. 443 But he no sooner saw that than he saw the reality of such an arrangement—how he would become the secret butt of this corrupt house, the starched *soupirant*, the pet donkey.

soupit (obs. Sc.): see sowp *v.*

soupje, var. sopie.

‖**souple.** [F. *souple* supple *a.*] A fabric made of silk which has been freed from gum by a simple boiling-off. Also ***souple silk.*** Hence **'soupling** *vbl. sb.*, the act or process of partially degumming raw silk which is to be made into souple silk.

1887 *Encycl. Brit.* XXII. 62/2 For..making of gauzes, crapes, flour-bolting cloth, and for what is termed 'souples' —the silk is not scoured. **1888** A. Sansone *Dyeing* I. viii. 159 *Souple Silk*, silk which only loses 5 to 8 per cent of its weight, and is consequently not completely deprived of its gum. *Ibid.* 160 *Soupling*: Work 1½ hours in water, containing 3 to 4 grains of cream of tartar per litre. **1927** Horsfall & Lawrie *Dyeing Textile Fibres* x. 283 In the case of degumming for souple silk, the object is to remove only a portion of the gum... An operation called 'soupling' then follows, when the silk is treated for one and a half hours in a solution containing three to four parts tartar per 1,000. **1964** S. R. Crockett *Dyeing & Printing* ii. 23 Varying grades of degumming are exemplified by ecru silk..souple silk..and boiled-off silk.

souple, Sc. and dial. f. supple.

'soupless, *a.* [f. soup *sb.*] Having no soup.

1821 *Blackw. Mag.* X. 562 Breakfastless, milkless, tealess, soupless, punchless.

soup maigre (su:p'meɪgə(r)). [ad. F. *soupe maigre*: see SOUP *sb.* and MAIGRE *a.*] Thin soup, made chiefly from vegetables or fish.

1754 *Connoisseur* No. 19 ¶9 But what, alas! are the weak endeavours of a few to oppose the daily inroads of fricassees and soup maigres? **1766** MISS M. TOWNSHEND in Jesse *Selwyn & Contemp.* (1843) II. 52 If you could persuade them of the wholesomeness of *soup maigre* and barley bread, it might be of great use to them. **1806** A. HUNTER *Culina* (ed. 3) 67 Its bad effects may in a great measure be taken off by a dinner of mutton broth, or soup maigre, on the following day. **1840** J. B. FRASER *Koordistan* I. xv. 366 A sort of *soup maigre* is poured upon it.

attrib. **1779** WARNER in Jesse *Selwyn & Contemp.* (1844) IV. 30 Such a number of pinch-bellied, woebegone, skin-and-grief, lanthorn-jawed, soup-maigre subjects. **1794** WOLCOT (P. Pindar) *Lousiad* I. Wks. I. 210, I hate each pale *soupe maigre* [**1812** soup-maigre] thief.

So **soup-meagre**. Now *rare* or *Obs.*

1737 FIELDING *Miser* III. iii, Let there be two great dishes of soup-meagre, a good large suet pudding,..and a dish of artichokes. **1799** in *Spirit Public Jrnls.* III. 322 Soup-meagre in the van, and snuff; roast-beef behind. **1833** SANDS *Poems* 53 (E.D.D.), Soup-meagre, kickshaws, or plain calf's-foot jelly. **1842** BARHAM *Ingol. Leg.* Ser. II. *Lay St. Cuthbert*, Here was Morbleu (a French devil) supping soup-meagre.

souppar, -er, obs. forms of SUPPER.

soupy ('su:pɪ), *a.* [f. SOUP *sb.*]

1. Like soup; having the appearance or consistency of soup.

1869 DICKENS *Uncomm. Traveller* (1958) xxxiii. 333 The dirty table-cloths, the stuffy, soupy, airless atmosphere. **1872** JEAN INGELOW *Off Skelligs* xiv, We had a very thick fog ..directly after the thunderstorm—a soupy fog. **1888** JACOBI *Printers' Vocab.* 128 *Soupy*, a term of disparagement applied to thin or poor ink. **1890** *Temple Bar* Aug. 449 Sybilla is eating or drinking something of a soupy nature. **1895** MEREDITH *Amazing Marr.* xxxviii, Stir us to the depths, it will be found that we are poor soupy stuff.

2. Sentimental; mawkish.

1953 R. CRAWSHAY-WILLIAMS *Let.* 1 Aug. in B. Russell *Autobiogr.* (1969) III. ii. 92, I was glad to see..your emphasis..upon the role of power politics rather than ideologies—and also your re-emphasis upon the way in which science and scientific method have conditioned (all that is 'best' in) Western Values. It is maddening the way in which the opposite 'soupy' belief is accepted even by most unsoupy people. **1976** *National Observer* (U.S.) 20 Nov. 24/5 He has included them in the autobiography, along with ..a series of sincerely affectionate, if soupy, tributes to Daddy from family and friends. **1977** *New Yorker* 4 July 82/3 There is the silliness of the movie's plangency: hard to feel soupy about a talented couple giving up their love because of the stardust in their eyes.

Hence **'soupiness**, sentimentality.

1963 WODEHOUSE *Stiff Upper Lip, Jeeves* v. 40 That squashy soupiness of hers, that subtle air she had of being on the point of talking baby-talk. **1977** *Gramophone* Jan. 1153/1 The slow movement brings a hint of soupiness in the tone.

soupy ('su:pɪ), *sb. U.S. Mil. slang.* Also **soupie**. [f. SOUP *sb.* + -Y⁶, -IE.] (A summons to) a meal.

1899 J. R. SKINNER *Hist. Fourth Illinois Volunteers* 26 Answered the familiar call of 'soupy, soupy, soupy,' at 5:30 o'clock. **1918** *Stars & Stripes* 5 July 4, I say 'Yum yum' when 'soupie' blows. **1939** *Amer. Speech* XIV. 30/2 *Soupy*, n., mess call (general U.S. Army usage).

sour (saʊə(r)), *a.* and *sb.*[1] Forms: 1-4 **sur** (5 **sur-**), 3-4 **sure**, 4-8 **soure** (4 **zoure**), 4- **sour**; 4-8 **sowr(e, sower** (5 **sowyr**, 7 **shoowre**), 9 *Sc.* **soor**. [Common Teut.: OE. *súr*, = OFris. *sûr* (mod.Fris. *sûr, sür*), MDu. *suur, suer, soer* (Du. *zuur*), OS. (MLG., LG.), OHG. (MHG.) *sûr* (G. *sauer*), ON. *súrr* (Norw., Sw., Da. *sur*), related to Lett. *sūrs* bitter, saltish, unpleasant, Lith. *sũras* saltish, OSlav. *syrŭ* (Russ. *sýroĭ*) moist, raw (Russ. *surovýĭ* raw, coarse): the ultimate origin is uncertain. The Germanic word is the source of F. *sur* (12th cent.), whence *surelle* SORREL *sb.*[1]

The leading senses of the English word are also prominent in most of the cognate languages.]

A. *adj.* **I. 1. a.** Having a tart or acid taste, such as that which is characteristic of unripe fruits and vinegar. Also said of taste. (Opposed to *sweet*, and distinguished from *bitter*.)

c **1000** *Sax. Leechd.* II. 132 Ðenim surne æppel..& leʒe on. *Ibid.* III. 212 Winberian sure ʒeseon, sace ʒetacnað. *c* **1175** *Lamb. Hom.* 129 Þet ðet weter of egypte wes liðe and swete þan folce of israel þe wes sur and bitere..þon monnen of þan londe. *a* **1310** in Wright *Lyric P.* xlii. 114 Ase fele sythe..As sterres beth in welkne, ant grases sour ant suete. **1340** *Ayenb.* 82 More hi uynt smak in ane zoure epple þanne ine ane huetene lhoue. **1377** LANGL. *P. Pl.* B. XVI. 72 Þanne bereth þe croppe kynde fruite,..swete with-oute swellyng, soure worth it neuere. *c* **1460** *Promp. Parv.* (Winch.), Eggyde, as teth ffor sowr ffrute. **1484** CAXTON *Fables of Æsop* IV. i, [The fox] sayd these raysyns ben sowre. *a* **1529** SKELTON *P. Sparowe* 82 The smokes sowre Of Proserpinas bowre. **1558** BP. WATSON *Sev. Sacram.* xi. 64 They also dyd eate the lambe with wylde and sowre lettes. **1577** B. GOOGE *Heresbach's Husb.* II. (1586) 57 The wylde sortes are both sowrer in taste, and smaller in leafe. **1612** WOODALL *Surg. Mate* Wks. (1653) 306 Add some few drops of oyl Vitriol, to make it some what sower in tast. **1666** BOYLE *Orig. Forms & Qual.* 314 Each of them far more salt then Brine, or more sowr then the strongest Vinegar. **1748** *Anson's Voy.* III. ii. 305 The woods produced sweet and sower oranges. **1799** W. TOOKE *View Russian Emp.* I. 288 Of proper sour waters which are applied to medicinal purposes. **1811** A. T. THOMSON *Lond. Disp.* (1818) 423 These are substances which have a sour taste. **1836-41** BRANDE *Chem.* (ed. 5) 370 Chloric acid is a sour liquid.

b. *transf.* Producing tart or acid fruit.

a **1000** in Birch *Cartul. Sax.* I. 229 A dune on stream of ða suran apældran. **1393** LANGL. *P. Pl.* C. XI. 207 Shal neuere good appel þorw no sotel science on sour stock growe. **1560** PILKINGTON *Expos. Aggeus* (1562) 297 The soure crabtree makes the crabbes bitter, and not the crabbes make the tree evyll. **1687** [see next (*b*)]. **1865** C. F. BROWNE *Artemus Ward: his Travels* 151 A Vigilance Committee, which hangs the more vicious of the pestiferous crowd to a sour apple-tree. **1922** JOYCE *Ulysses* 160 We'll hang Joe Chamberlain on a sourapple tree.

c. In figurative or allusive uses; freq. in connexion with *sauce* (cf. SAUCE *sb.* 1 b).

(*a*) **1377** LANGL. *P. Pl.* B. XIII. 43 Ac her sauce was ouer soure & vnsauourely grounde, In a morter..of many bitter peyne. **1500-20** DUNBAR *Poems* lxvii. 19 Off quhais subchettis sour is the sals. *a* **1548** HALL *Chron., Edw. IV*, 20 These soure sauces he tasted as a penaunce for his wanton liuyng. **1626** PEEKE *Three to One* C j, Thus farre, my Voyage for Oranges sped well, but in the end, prooued sower Sawce to me. *a* **1660** *Contemp. Hist. Irel.* (Ir. Archæol. Soc.) II. 42 Witty speeches loose theire rellish when they are ouerseasoned with the sowre sawce of reprehension. **1687** MIÈGE *Gt. Fr. Dict.* II. s.v. *Sweet*, He has given me sweet Meat, but sowr Sauce, (Prov.).

(*b*) **1415** HOCCLEVE *Sir J. Oldcastle* 292 Thogh it seeme sour To the taast of your detestable errour. **1525** TINDALE *Expos.* (Parker Soc.) 234 Nothing is so sweet that they make not sour with their traditions. *c* **1625** DAVENPORT *K. John & Matilda* III. ii, The sower sweetnesse of a deluded minute. *a* **1652** J. SMITH *Sel. Disc.* i. 15 Their doctrines may taste too sour of the cask they come through. **1687** MIÈGE *Gt. Fr. Dict.* II, To be tied to the sowr Apple-tree, for to have an ill Husband. **1720** RAMSAY *Wealth* 142 If not, fox-like, I'll..ca' your hundred thousand a sour plum. **1721** KELLY *Sc. Prov.* 186 It is a soure Reek, where the good Wife dings the good Man. **1785** BURNS *Twa Herds* v, Nae poisoned sour Arminian stank He let them taste.

2. a. Rendered acid by fermentation or similar processes; fermented; affected or spoiled in this way by being kept or exposed too long.

c **1000** *Sax. Leechd.* II. 34 Ðenim þa readan hofan, awyl on surum swatum oþþe on surum ealað. *c* **1000** ÆLFRIC *Gloss.* in Wr.-Wülcker 129 *Oxygala*, sur meolc. **1390** GOWER *Conf.* I. 167 And thus of that thei brewe soure I drinke swete. *c* **1425** *Eng. Voc.* in Wr.-Wülcker 659 *Seruicia acerba*, sowre ale. *c* **1440** *Promp. Parv.* 466/2 Sowre, as dowe, *fermentatus*. *c* **1480** HENRYSON *Test. Cres.* 441 For waillit Wyne and Meitis thou had tho, Tak mowlit Breid, Peirrie, and Ceder sour. **1508** DUNBAR *Poems* v. 30 To get hir ane fresche drink, þe aill of hevin wes sour. **1561** T. NORTON *Calvin's Inst.* IV. xviii. (1634) 713 As with leaven scattered among it, the whole lumpe of dough waxeth sower. **1669** BOYLE *Contn. New Exp.* II. (1682) 168 This Experiment seems to teach us, that Liquors may grow sowre, though no spirits have evaporated from them. **1691** RAY *N.C. Words* (ed. 2) 137 *Sower-milk*, Butter-milk. Sower from its long standing. **1764** *Ann. Reg.* II. 11 They throw the fresh caviar into it, and leave it there to grow sour. **1826** *Art of Brewing* (ed. 2) 32 It cannot recover itself, but remains sickly, and becomes sour. **1884** *Girl's Own Paper* 4 Oct. 4/2 The great duty..of the girls..in Mongolia is to milk the cattle..and work up the milk into..sour-cheese, butter, and whisky.

Comb. **1661** *Extr. Rec. Glasgow* (Burgh Recs.) 465 The sour milk mercat, quhilk is now keeped at the croce.

b. *fig.* or in fig. context. Esp. in *to go* (or *turn*) *sour* (*on* a person).

a **1340** HAMPOLE *Psalter* Prol., O wondirful suetnes, þe whilk waxis noght soure thurgh þe corupciouns of þis warld. **1611** BIBLE *Hosea* iv. 18 Ephraim is ioyned to idoles:..Their drinke is sowre. **1641** [see LEAVEN *sb.* 2 a]. **1686** tr. *Lemery's Course Chem.* (ed. 2) Ep. Ded., The sowre Leaven of Intestine Rebellion. **1799** [see LEAVEN *sb.* 2 a]. **1837** CARLYLE *Fr. Rev.* II. IV. ii, General Dumouriez..finds all in sour heat of darkness. **1928** *Daily Tel.* 20 Mar. 11/5 Sir Victor Sassoon..advised the House to pass the bill, as there was a danger of the Government, in racing parlance, 'going sour'. **1952** C. DAY LEWIS tr. *Virgil's Aeneid* IX. 194 Let only my luck stay good And not turn sour on me. **1957** A. MACNAB *Bulls of Iberia* xv. 214 He cannot afford to ease up in one or two bulls, or the whole afternoon may go sour on him. **1964** L. NKOSI *Rhythm of Violence* 50 What is a cynic but a romanticist turned sour? **1971** A. SAMPSON *New Anatomy of Britain* 278 It is at the meetings with Treasury men that so many political ideals have been defeated, so many bold promises gone sour. **1981** P. NIESEWAND *Word of Gentleman* i. 14 Moorhouse and his party had wiped the floor with the opposition... Then suddenly everything went sour.

c. Of smell. Also *fig.*

c **1340** HAMPOLE *Pr. Consc.* 657 Of herbes and tres comes swete savour, And of þe comes wlatsome stynk, and sour. **1530** PALSGR. 325/1 Sower of smellyng, *sur*. **1843** SIR C. SCUDAMORE *Med. Visit Grafenberg* 48 A strong sour smell, like mellow apples. **1897** *Allbutt's Syst. Med.* III. 12 Of the sour smell about rheumatic patients there can be no doubt.

d. Of breath, eructations, etc.

1578 LYTE *Dodoens* 239 The wambling of the stomacke, and the sower belkes whiche come from the same. **1591** SHAKS. *Two Gentl.* III. i. 331 That makes amends for her soure breath. **1607** [? BREWER] *Lingua* IV. iv, Sweet ointment for sowre teeth. **1619** FLETCHER, etc. *Knt. Malta* III. ii, Whose husband Tax'd for his sowre breath by his enemy, Condemn'd his wife, for not acquainting him With his infirmity.

3. a. Of land, etc.: Cold and wet; uncongenial through retaining stagnant moisture.

1532 HERVET tr. *Xenophon's Treat. Househ.* (1768) 76 What remedy is there, if the grounde be to weete to sowe in it, or to soure to set trees in it? **1573** TUSSER *Husb.* (1878) 84 Some breaking vp laie soweth otes to begin, to suck out the moisture so sower therein. **1605** SYLVESTER *Du Bartas* II. iii. I. *Vocation* 107 Like some rare Fruit-Tree over-topt with spight Of Briers and Bushes which it sore oppresse With the sowr shadow of their thorny tresse. **1677** PLOT *Oxfordsh.* 241 There is another sort of ground in this County which they call Sour-land. **1707** MORTIMER *Husb.* 63 In Oxfordshire..they give their sour Land a tilt, according to the State and Condition of their Lands. **1759** MILLS tr. *Duhamel's Husb.* I. viii. (1762) 45 The ground underneath must be of a most cold and sour nature. **1815** J. SMITH *Panorama Sci. & Art* II. 613 Salt..sweetens sour pastures. **1858** GLENNY *Everyday Bk.* 189/2 The sour soil that they have been growing in. **1897** MARY KINGSLEY *W. Africa* 641 Other vast tracts of it are miserably poor sour, sandy clay.

fig. **1638** SANDERSON *Serm.* (1681) 109 The heart of man is a sowre piece of clay.

transf. **1859** MEREDITH *R. Feverel* ii, In a country of sour pools, yellow brooks, rank pasturage, desolate heath.

b. Of pasture: Having a harsh, unpleasant taste; coarse, rank. Now *dial.*

1654 in *Verney Mem.* (1907) I. 535 The grass must be mown if it be too sour and long for them. **1673** RAY *Journ. Low Co.* 148 The very Grass which grows under the Trees is sowr and crude. **1828** CARR *Craven Gloss.*, *Sour*, coarse, harsh, applied to grass, which grows on wet land. **1881** EVANS *Leicestersh. Words*, *Sour*,..as applied to herbage, rank and bitter.

c. Of wood, etc.: Green. Now *local.*

c **1475** *Rauf Coilȝear* 910 Sall neuer of sa sour ane brand ane bricht fyre be brocht. **1866** BROGDEN *Prov. Lincs.*, *Sour*, green. The hay is too sour to lead.

4. Of petroleum, natural gas, etc.: containing a relatively high proportion of sulphur. Opp. *sweet*.

1919 E. W. DEAN *Motor Gasoline Properties* (U.S. Bureau of Mines Techn. Paper No. 214) 24 There is a possibility that gasoline 'sour' to the doctor test may have been the cause of certain reported corrosion of metal parts of carburetors. **1925** *Petroleum Age* 1 Jan. 16/2 Sour oils also have a distinctively unpleasant odor which is absent in sweet oils. **1936** W. L. NELSON *Petroleum Refinery Engin.* xxiv. 527 For 'sour' sulfur-bearing light distillates, the doctor treatment must be used. **1967** *Wall St. Jrnl.* 31 Jan. 32/2 Recovery of elemental sulphur from 'sour' gas is expected to materially increase available supplies. **1979** *Economist* 11 Aug. 67/1 There is a sour gas formation under the country's best oil field, Yibal.

II. 5. a. Extremely distasteful or disagreeable; bitter, unpleasant.

c **1200** ORMIN 15208 Forr pine iss sur & biteþþ wiþþ & cwennkeþþ erþliȝ kinde. *a* **1250** *Owl & Night.* 866 Þat him beo sur þat er was swete, þar to ich helpe, god hit wot. *c* **1315** SHOREHAM IV. 422 And her-by þou myȝt, man, y-seo hou here ende hys sour. **1377** LANGL. *P. Pl.* B. XI. 250 Al though it be soure to suffre, þere cometh swete after. *Ibid.* XX. 46, I mote nede abyde, And suffre sorwes ful sowre þat shal to ioye tourne. **1509** HAWES *Past. Pleas.* xxx. (Percy Soc.) 148 To have release of your great paynes sower. **1576** PETTIE *Petite Pallace* (1908) I. 45 This life hath been most loathsome and sour vnto me. **1630** *R. Johnson's Kingd. & Commw.* 439 These prosperous beginnings brought forth sowre ends. **1651** HOBBES *Leviath.* II. xxv. 133 When they are for Execution of soure labour. **1701** COLLIER *M. Aurel.* (1726) 302 If so, he has given himself a sour box on the ear. **1837** CARLYLE *Fr. Rev.* II. III. i, That sweet Federation was of last year; this sour Divulsion is the selfsame substance. **1870** EMERSON *Soc. & Solit.* Wks. (Bohn) III. 3 Michael Angelo had a sad, sour time of it.

b. Of music: out of tune.

[**1593** SHAKS. *Richard II* v. iv. 42 How sowre sweet Musicke is, When Time is broke, and no Proportion kept?] **1937** *Amer. Speech* XII. 48/2 *Sour*, out-of-tune playing. **1976** *Gramophone* Feb. 1356/1 String tone is wirey, even a bit sour in the G minor, especially during loud passages.

6. a. Having a harsh, morose, or peevish disposition; sullen, austere; gloomy, discontented, embittered.

a **1225** *Ancr. R.* 114 Grucchunge of bitter & of sur heorte. **1530** PALSGR. 325/1 Sower, cursed or shrewde as a woman is that lowreth, *malgracieux*. **1592** FLEMING *Contn. of Holinshed* III. 1360 The one of nature affable, the other altogither sowre. **1633** G. HERBERT *Temple, Ephes.* iv. 30 2 And art thou grieved..When I am sowre, And crosse thy love? **1663** S. PATRICK *Parab. Pilgrim* (1687) 478 Do not follow your Saviour with a sowre heart, dejected looks, and faln wings. **1709** STEELE *Tatler* No. 89 ¶8 Don't think me a sour Man, for I love Conversation and my Friends. **1779** *Mirror* No. 61, It is not the melancholy of a sour, unsocial being. **1837** CARLYLE *Fr. Rev.* II. VI. iii, Men's humour is of the sourest. **1849** MACAULAY *Hist. Eng.* ii. I. 172 His temper was sour, arrogant, and impatient of opposition. **1874** MAHAFFY *Soc. Life Greece* iii. 65 We might almost imagine that some sour Attic editor had expunged the advice.

absol. **1871** R. ELLIS tr. *Catullus* xxvii. 6 But dull water, avaunt... Seek the sour, the solemn!

b. Const. *upon* (a person). *rare*⁻¹.

1621-31 LAUD *Serm.* (1847) 179 'Keep unity,' then, and be sour..upon any that shall endeavour to break it.

7. Displaying, expressing, or implying displeasure or discontent; peevish, cross: **a.** Of looks, etc.

c **1440** *Alph. Tales* 1 With a sowr cowntenance and a froward luke. **1530** PALSGR. 225/2 Glumme, a sower loke. **1598** MARSTON *Sco. Villanie* III. ix. 217 Grim-fac't Reproofe,..Bend thy sower browes in my tart poesie. **1642** FULLER *Holy & Prof. State* IV. xix. 339 His little eyes can cast a soure glance. **1720** HEARNE *Collect.* (O.H.S.) VII. 186 He..from his sower Looks is commonly called Vinegar Jones. **1750** GRAY *Long Story* 106 Sour visages, enough to scare ye. **1807** J. BARLOW *Columb.* I. 103 Dissembling friends..Now pass my cell with smiles of sour disdain. **1833** HT. MARTINEAU *Brooke Farm* iii. 29 The sour looks with which the strangers were regarded. **1869** TOZER *Highl. Turkey* II. 73 A woman with a sour countenance but rather handsome features.

b. Of words, discourse, opinions, etc.

a **1557** MRS. M. BASSET tr. *More's Treat. Passion* M.'s Wks. 1384/1 With sweete and sower wordes to laboure..to make good men of badde. **1594** J. DICKENSON *Arisbas* (1878) 28 To shield me..from the sowre censures of the ouer-curious Moralists of our age. **1614** RALEIGH *Hist. World* III. (1634) 81 Nicias and his companions had a sowre message to deliver at Sparta. **1663** J. SPENCER *Prodigies* (1665) 17 That Historian, whom we shall easily perceive not more leavened in mind or writing with this kind of sowrer Superstition.

1709 STEELE *Tatler* No. 54 ¶1 He said a sour Thing to Laura at Dinner the other Day; upon which she burst into Tears. **1761** HUME *Hist. Eng.* lx. (1806) IV. 513 The fanaticism which prevailed, being so full of sour and angry principles. **1851** HELPS *Comp. Solit.* iii. 31 In delivering a sour discourse on the wickedness of the others. **1871** MORLEY *Crit. Misc.*, *Carlyle* 235 A system which has raised monstrous floods of sour cant round about us.

c. Of actions.

1659 T. PECKE tr. *Owen's Epigr.* xiii, Sowre is the exit..of the salacious Cyprian Emperess. **1697** DRYDEN *Æneid* XII. 10 He makes a sour retreat, nor mends his pace. **1725** POPE *Odyss.* XI. 693 Touch'd at his sour retreat,..Through hell's black bounds I had pursued his flight. *a* **1740** WATERLAND *Serm.* iii. (1742) I. 81 God..chuses rather an easy and chearful, than an austere and sower Obedience.

d. Wry; distorted.

1611 COTGR., *Morgueur*, a maker of strange mouthes, or soure faces. **1822** LAMB *Elia* I. *Dissert. on Roast Pig*, Make what sour mouths he would for a pretence.

8. Of weather, etc.: Cold and wet; inclement.

1582 STANYHURST *Æneis* IV. (Arb.) 105 In a winters soure storme must nauye be launched? **1599** B. JONSON *Ev. Man out of Hum.* II. iv, Is now thy walk too sweet? Thou said'st of late, it had sowr airs about it. **1687** A. LOVELL tr. *Thevenot's Trav.* I. 272 The same day [we] had sower gusts of Wind and Rain. **1722** DE FOE *Col. Jack* xi, We had a very sour and rough voyage for the first fortnight. **1773** FERGUSSON *Poems* (1789) II. 56 Simmer's showery blinks and winter's sour. **1837** CARLYLE *Fr. Rev.* III. I. vii, The Earth..weeps and blears itself, in sour rain, and worse. **1895** 'SETOUN' *Sunshine* 28 It was a 'cauld sour day', nothing but drizzle.

9. Of animals: Heavy, coarse, gross.

1713 *Lond. Gaz.* No. 5148/12 A strong, sower Horse of 6 l. Price. **1854** *Jrnl. R. Agric. Soc.* XV. I. 228 They [sheep] are apt to run hairy in the wool, big in the bone, and sour in the head. **1881** EVANS *Leicestersh. Words*, *Sour*, as applied to animals, coarse and gross. **1886** in Peacock *N.W. Linc. Gloss.* s.v., Two..sour, fine-looking mares.

III. 10. *Comb.* **a.** Parasynthetic, as ***sour-blooded***, ***-breathed***, ***-faced***, ***-favoured***, ***-featured***, ***-hearted***, ***-looked***, ***-tongued***, etc.

1862 THORNBURY *Turner* II. 136 Turner was no *sour-blooded recluse. *a* **1586** SIDNEY *Arcadia* III. xiii. (1622) 276 Dametas..had fetched many a *sower-breathed sigh. **1653** WALTON *Angler* To Rdr. A v b, If thou be a severe, *sowr complexioned man. **1610** SHAKS. *Temp.* IV. i. 20 Barraine hate, *Sower-ey'd disdaine, and discord. *a* **1697** AUBREY *Lives* (1813) 511 He had a most remarkable aspect,..long-faced, and *sour eielidded, a kind of pigge-eie. **1589** *Marprel. Epit.* (1843) 28 A *sourfaced knaue. **1883** J. MACKENZIE *Day-dawn in Dark Places* 78 Not even Hendrik was sour-faced a day after. **1916** JOYCE *Portrait of Artist* iv. 187 The face was eyeless and *sourfavoured. **1830** SCOTT *Doom Devorgoil* II. ii, With *sour-featured Whigs the Grass-market was cramm'd. **1679** *Poor Robin's Intelligence* in *Sporting Mag.* XXXIX. 61 *Sour headed, saddle backed, goose rumped. **1697** DRYDEN *Virg. Georg.* III. 88 The Mother Cow must wear a low'ring Look, Sour-headed, strongly-neck'd. **1673** *Lond. Gaz.* No. 834/4 A *sowr lookt and plain Horse. **1727** BAILEY (vol. II), *Torvity*, *sour Lookedness. *c* **1460** *Towneley Myst.* xiii. 102 She is browyd lyke a brystyll, with a *sowre loten chere. *Ibid.* xxi. 123 He is sowre lottyn. **1591** SHAKS. *Two Gentl.* II. iii. 6, I thinke Crab my dog be the *sowrest natured dogge that liues. **1890** 'R. BOLDREWOOD' *Col. Reformer* (1891) 203 A *sour-tempered Skye terrier. **1746** FRANCIS tr. *Horace, Sat.* I. vii. 44 The *sour-tongu'd Mungrel the Dispute renew'd. **1930** BLUNDEN *Summer's Fancy* 22 And black-capped and gowned The sour-tongued master stared and hovered nigh. **1821** SCOTT *Kenilw.* iii, An aged *sour-visaged domestic.

b. With pres. pples., as ***sour-looking***, ***-smelling***.

1611 COTGR., *Rechignard*, a..soure-looking, or grimme fellow. **1799** CAMPBELL *Poems*, *The Harper* iii, When the sour-looking folk sent me heartless away. **1838** T. THOMSON *Chem. Org. Bodies* 544 When copal is kept melted till a sour smelling aromatic odour has ceased to proceed from it. **1855** LEIFCHILD *Cornwall* 21 A lean, sour-looking man.

c. With sbs., forming attributive combs.

1836–48 B. D. WALSH *Aristoph.*, *Acharnians* II. ii, 'Tis really terrible for men to have Such sour-grape tempers. **1881** *Academy* No. 492. 271 Of the sour-zealot order. **1898** *Daily News* 24 Mar. 2/5 A private conviction of the sour grapes order.

11. Special collocations (frequently hyphened), as **sourball**, **sour-ball** *U.S.*, (*a*) a peevish or sour-tempered person; also *attrib.* or as *adj.*; (*b*) a boiled sweet with an acid taste; **sour beef** *U.S. local* = SAUERBRATEN; **sour bread**, †(*a*) leavened bread; (*b*) *U.S.*, sourdough bread; **sour cake**, an oat- or rye-cake made of fermented dough; †**sour cheer**, bitter feeling; **sour cherry**, the common cherry; **sour cream**, *spec.* fresh cream soured by the addition of lactic acid; **sour crop** *Vet. Sci.*, oidiomycosis of chickens, turkeys, or other poultry, producing a crop filled with foul-smelling liquid and often thickened and ulcerated; **sour gourd**, (the fruit of) the Baobab, *Adansonia digitata*, or the related species *A. gregorii*; **sour grapes**: see GRAPE *sb.*[1] 1 a; hence **sour-grapeism**, the action or practice of disparaging something because it is out of one's reach; **sour-grapey** *a.*, disparaging because something is out of reach; **sour-grapiness**; †**sour greme**, bitter grief or anger; **sour gum** (*U.S.*), **kettle**, (see quots.); **sour-mash** *U.S.*, (whisky made from) fermenting grain mash; also *attrib.*; **sour orange**, the Seville orange, *Citrus aurantium* distinguished by its thick skin and bitter pulp; also, the tree bearing this fruit; also *attrib.*; **sour plum** (see quots.); **sourpuss**, **sour-puss** *slang* (orig. *U.S.*) [PUSS *sb.*[2]], a sour-faced person; a grumbler; a killjoy; also *attrib.*; so **sour-pussed** *a.*, sour-faced, miserable; †**sour swig**, sour liquor or drink (*fig.*); **sour tree**, = *sour wood*; **sour veld(t)** *S. Afr.*, grassland covered with coarse grass lacking nutritive value; **sour water**, water soured by fermentation, esp. in the process of starch-making; **sour wood** *U.S.*, the sorrel-tree.

A number of others in dial. use are given in the *Eng. Dial. Dict.*

1900 *Dialect Notes* II. 62 **Sour-ball*, a chronic grumbler. **1933** *Manufacturing Chemist* Nov. 41/1 Assorted Sour Balls (purchased in a railroad depot, Boston, Mass.)... Balls had a coating of grain. **1935** J. O'HARA *Appointment in Samarra* iv. 123 My God, you're sourball tonight. **1962** E. LACY *Freeloaders* vi. 113 You think Gil is nuts? He's been acting the sourball all day. **1964** [see HALVA]. **1976** *N.Y. Rev. Bks.* 15 Apr. 33/1 The witness from those years is overwhelming, and not just from snobbish intellectuals and sourball novelists. **1935** *Evening Sun* (Baltimore) 2 Mar. 18/3 Mrs. Haberkorn was 'a world champion' *sour beef cooker. **1947** *Sun* (Baltimore) 3 Nov. 11/8 (Advt.), Old fashioned sour beef & dumplings. **1968** E. STAEBLER *Food that really Schmecks* 36 Sauerbraten (Sour Beef Pot Roast). *a* **1300** *Cursor M.* 6166 And neuer mar þat dai til ete Na *surbred ne nanoþer mete. *c* **1400** MAUNDEV. (Roxb.) xiii. 59 Þai..makes þe sacrement of þe awter of soure bred as þe Grekes duse. **1597** HOOKER *Eccl. Pol.* V. lxxi. §2 There is no Jewish paschal solemnity nor abstinence from sour bread now required at our hands. **1884** H. A. DWIGHT *Bread-Making* 46 Sour bread is such a common evil that a special chapter should be given to it... Sour bread follows..as a consequence of sour yeast. **1902** W. FAULKNER *Go down, Moses* 196 Then for two weeks he ate the coarse, rapid food—the shapeless sour bread, the wild strange meat. **1977** H. FAST *Immigrants* III. 201 Lunch was homemade sausage meat..and fresh milk as thick as cream, and with it Mary Gallagher's home-baked sour bread and home-churned butter. **1793** D. URE *Hist. Rutherglen* 94 Another ancient custom, for the observance of which Rutherglen has long been famous, is the baking of *sour cakes. **1859** GEO. ELIOT *A. Bede* viii, They..look as if they'd never tasted nothing better than bacon-sword and sour-cake i' their lives. *c* **1400** *Destr. Troy* 9127 With remyng, & rauthe, & myche rife sorow, Sobbyng & *sourcher soght fro þere herttes. *c* **1440** *Promp. Parv.* 466/2 Sowre chere, *acrimonia*. **1884** tr. *De Candolle's Orig. Cultivated Pl.* 207 *Sour Cherry—*Prunus cerasus*. **1855** E. ACTON *Mod. Cookery* (rev. ed.) vi. 143 '*Sour cream' is an ingredient not much approved by English taste, but it enters largely into German cookery. **1961** 'E. LATHEN' *Banking on Death* (1962) iii. 22 Roast beef, baked potato—'For God's sake, no sour cream!' **1978** D. FRANCIS *Trial Run* iii. 45 The object of her curiosity..spooned sour cream into his borsch. **1951**, **1975** *Sour crop [see OIDIOMYCOSIS]. **1975** B. MEYRICK *Behind Light* xv. 199 'Sour crop,' he announced.. as he gently felt the chicken's full crop. **1640** PARKINSON *Theat. Bot.* 1632 The Ethiopian *sowre Gourde..groweth in Mozambique..on a faire great tree. **1760** J. LEE *Introd. Bot.* App. 327 Sour Gourd, Æthiopian, *Adansonia*. **1857** HENFREY *Bot.* 247 The fruit of the Baobab, the Monkey-bread or Ethiopian Sour-gourd, has an agreeable acid pulp. **1887** BENTLEY *Man. Bot.* 481 *A[dansonia] Gregorii*... A native of North Australia, where it is known as Sour-gourd and Cream-of-tartar tree. **1853** MRS. GASKELL *Cranford* i. 5 There, economy was always 'elegant', and money-spending always 'vulgar and ostentatious'; a sort of *sour grapeism which made us very peaceful and satisfied. **1957** R. W. ZANDVOORT *Handbk. Eng. Gram.* IX. ii. 307 The suffix is added to syntactic word groups..in such formations as *sour-grapeism*, [etc.]. **1962** *Punch* 11 Apr. 579/1 It may have sounded a silly and *sour-grapey sort of thing to say. **1980** *Good Housekeeping* Nov. 15/3 Perhaps I'm being a tiny bit sour grapey. **1970** *Guardian* 30 July 9/4 One Amsterdam camp site owner who..almost moulded away with *sour grapiness. *c* **1400** *Destr. Troy* 2053 Soche a sorow & a *sourgreme sanke in his hert. *Ibid.* 9042 For sorow & sorgrym of his sonnys dethe. **1814** PURSH *Flora Amer. Sept.* I. 177 *Nyssa villosa*... This tree is known by the name of *Sour-gum. **1880** BESSEY *Botany* 519 The wood of *Nyssa multiflora*, the Sour Gum, Tupelo, or Peppridge tree of the Eastern United States. **1875** KNIGHT *Dict. Mech.* 2250/1 **Sour-kettle*, a vessel used in souring bleached cloth. **1885** 'C. E. CRADDOCK' *Prophet of Gt. Smoky Mountains* 150 Him an' me run a *sour mash still on the top o' the mounting. **1892** 'MARK TWAIN' *Amer. Claimant* i. 23 Over-confidence and gaiety induced by over-plus of sour-mash. **1958** 'W. HENRY' *Seven Men at Mimbres Springs* 216 The reservation doctor..was definitely given to a rigorous regimen of sourmash Kentucky bond taken internally for pain as self-directed. **1976** T. STOPPARD *Dirty Linen* 65 Big bellied, red-eyed men in white crumpled suits swig from medicine bottles of two-year-old sour mash bourbon. [**1890** E. BONAVIA *Cultivated Oranges & Lemons* pl. vi, The Seville Orange of Kandy..known there by the name of *Amool Dódan* (sour round orange).] **1920** H. J. WEBBER in *Bull. Calif. Agric. Exper. Station* No. 317. 268 An examination of sweet and *sour orange seedling stock..showed the presence of many widely different types. **1926** H. H. HUME *Cultivation of Citrus Fruits* iv. 45 Sour oranges, or bigarades, are distinguished from the sweet varieties by their broadly winged petioles. **1938** M. K. RAWLINGS *Yearling* i. 12 There were..sour orange biscuits. **1973** *Advocate-News* (Barbados) 26 Feb. 5/1 A virus of unknown nature..was found to be infecting sour orange seedlings. **1874** *Treas. Bot.* Suppl. 1324/2 *Owenia venosa* is known by the name of the *Sour Plum amongst the colonists. **1889** MAIDEN *Usef. Plants* 49 *Owenia acidula*,..'Sour Plum', 'Native Peach or Nectarine'. **1898** MORRIS *Austral Eng.* 427 *Sour-Plum*, the Emu-apple. **1937** *Sun* (Baltimore) 28 May 14/7 Hadley doesn't look like the kind of *sour-puss who would do that. **1942** *Penguin New Writing* XV. 92 He pretends to be more interested in the antics of his birds than in the puffings an' blowings of a sourpuss of a council clerk. **1960** *Guardian* 15 Mar. 7/3 It's about time we got away from sourpuss champions. **1966** 'H. MACDIARMID' *Company I've Kept* i. 34 All the Moral Rearmers and other sour-pusses in Scotland. **1980** *Logophile* IV. I. 45/2 He had always been henpecked by his wife, a sourpuss with a waspish temper. **1952** J. STEINBECK *East of Eden* xlvii. 520 Henry was a man who liked fun—needed it. A *sour-pussed associate could make him sick. **1548** UDALL, etc. *Erasm. Par. Luke* vi. 74 Hauing been long accustomed to the olde *soureswyg of Moses lawe. **1717** *Petiveriana* III. 247 Sorrel or *Sowre-tree. Because its Leaves have that Taste. [**1801** Sour veldt: see SOUR GRASS 3.] **1863** J. S. DOBIE *S. Afr. Jrnl.* (1945) 76 On across the Little Tugela..over rank *sour-veldt grass. **1894** T. R. SIM *Sk. Flora Kaffraria* 14 The sour veld..is composed of rank strong growing grasses. **1948** *Star* (Johannesburg) 20 Oct. 3/7 Sourveld management presents formidable problems. **1978** *Jrnl. Afr. Hist.* XIX. 479 Seasonal loss of nutrition of the plateau grasses (i.e. the presence of sourveld). **1816** SMITH *Panorama Sci. & Art* II. 554 Water in which the bran has been allowed to become sour, and which is called *sours*, or **sour water*. **1836–41** BRANDE *Chem.* (ed. 5) 1084 The starch suspended in a very foul acid liquor, called *sour water*. **1856** A. GRAY *Man. Bot.* 254 *Oxydendrum*, Sorrel-tree. *Sour-wood. **1859** BARTLETT *Dict. Amer.* (ed. 2) 430 Sour wood (*Andromeda arborea*), a beautiful tree, which..is sometimes called Sorrel tree. **1880** *New Virgin.* II. 171 There were quantities of the pretty, graceful sourwood—the *Oxydendrum arboreum*.

B. *sb.*[1] **1.** That which is sour, in lit. or fig. senses. Used without article, or with *the*, *a*, etc.

(*a*) *c* **1000** *Sax. Leechd.* II. 56 Sele drincan middeldaʒum, & forga sur & sealtes ʒehwæt. *c* **1400** *Rom. Rose* 5059 He is a wrecche..That loved such one, for swete or soure. *c* **1420** *26 Pol. Poems* xvii. 131 For oure swete, he drank ful soure. *c* **1560** A. SCOTT *Poems* (S.T.S.) i. 107 As waspis ressauis of þe same bot soure, So reprobatis Christis buke dois rebute. **1580** LYLY *Euphues* (Arb.) 242 You haue bene a Trauailer and tasted nothing but sowre. **1612** J. DAVIES (Heref.) *Muse's Sacrifice* Wks. (Grosart) II. 12/2 Mellefluous Sweetnesse..Sweeten my Sowre. **1657** J. TRAPP *Comm. Neh.* i. 8 Sower and sweet maketh best sawce. **1881** D. THOMSON *Musings among Heather* 191 We likewise find Our sour gey aften mix'd wi' sweet.

(*b*) *a* **1300** *Cursor M.* 23979 He dranc þe sure and i þe suete. **1390** GOWER *Conf.* III. 12 Tuo tonnes fulle of love drinke,..of the soure or of the swete. **1448–9** J. METHAM *Wks.* (E.E.T.S.) 52, I be myn one schal bothe the sqwete and the soure For yow endure. **1553** T. WILSON *Rhet.* (1580) 4 Hym cunne I thanke, that bothe can and will, once mingle sweet emong the sower. **1584–7** GREENE *Carde of Fancie* Wks. (Grosart) IV. 110 By the sweete (quoth hee) how should we know the sower? **1656** EARL MONM. tr. *Boccalini's Advts. fr. Parnass.* I. lxix. (1674) 86 The Sower of obeying, and Sweet of commanding. **1684** tr. *Bonet's Merc. Compit.* VI. 177 Many People give their Patients..Conserves of the sowre of Citron. **1724** RAMSAY *Tea-Table Misc.* Ded. vi, Their sangs may ward ye frae the sour, And gaily vacant minutes pass.

(*c*) **13..** *E.E. Allit. P.* B. 820 Wyth no sour ne no salt seruez hym neuer. ? **1402** in *Yorks. Arch. Jrnl.* XX. 47 Thus did God dele, For swete, a sour. **1592** BRETON *C'tess Pembroke's Love* Wks. (Grosart) I. 24/1 Sowing the sweete, that killeth euery sower. **1593** SHAKS. *Lucr.* 867 The sweets we wish for, turne to lothed sowrs. **1634** MASSINGER *Very Woman* IV. ii, We have not an hour of life In which our pleasures relish not some pain, Our sours some sweetness. **1714** MANDEVILLE *Fab. Bees* (1733) I. 107 Loaf sugar.. prevents the injuries which a gnawing sower might do to the bowels. **1816** L. HUNT *Rimini* III. 64 He kept no reckoning with his sweets and sours. **1900** WEYMAN *Sophia* xv, The only sour in his cup..arose from his costume.

2. In bleaching and tanning, a bath or steep of an acid character.

1756 F. HOME *Exper. Bleaching* 28 Sours made with bran, or rye meal, and water, are often used instead of milk. **1778** *Phil. Trans.* LXVIII. 125 The bleachers of linen make use of a sour prepared by diluting the strong spirit of vitriol. **1839** URE *Dict. Arts* 137 They are thence removed to the sours. **1860** TOMLINSON *Usef. Arts, Leather Manuf.* 12 The skins are..immersed for twelve hours in a very weak solution of sulphuric acid, called *sours*. **1873** SPON *Workshop Rec.* Ser. I. 30/2 After being cleaned or scalded, discharge in a hot vitriol sour.

3. *U.S.* An acid drink, usually whisky or other spirit with lemon added.

1862 J. THOMAS *How to mix Drinks* 59 The brandy sour is made with the same ingredients as the brandy fix, omitting all fruits. **1885** *Pall Mall G.* 10 Feb. 2/2, I prefer ..'swapping stories' to sipping 'whisky sours'. **1889** *Ibid.* 20 June 3/2 Sours are made principally with whisky or brandy, or Santa Cruz rum.

sour (saʊə(r)), *sb.*[2] [f. SOUR *v.*] An act of souring, *spec.* in bleaching (see prec. B. 2).

1839 URE *Dict. Arts* 135 If the goods be strong, they will require another boil, steep, and sour.

sour (saʊə(r)), *adv.* Also 4–5 sure, soure, 6–7 sowre. [ME. *sūre*, f. *sūr* SOUR *a.* Cf. MDu. *sure*, *zure*.]

†**1.** Bitterly, dearly; severely. *Obs.*

c **1300** *Havelok* 2005 Þus wolde þe theues me haue reft But God-þank, he hauenet sure keft. **1377** LANGL. *P. Pl.* B. x. 361 It shal bisitten vs ful soure þe siluer þat we kepen. *c* **1386** CHAUCER *Sir Thopas* 111 And yit I hope..That thou schalt with this launcegay Abyen it ful soure. *a* **1400–50** *Alexander* 2313 Þai said, soure suld him sowe bot he þe cite ʒeld.

2. Disagreeably, unpleasantly; crossly, gloomily, unfavourably. Chiefly in phr. to *look sour*.

In some cases perh. the adj. used predicatively.

1500–20 DUNBAR *Poems* liii. 37 God waitt gif that scho loukit sour! **1531** TINDALE *Expos. 1 John* (1537) 33 God hath no rodde in his hande, nor loketh sowre. **1557** N.T. (Geneva) *Matt.* vi. 16 When ye fast, loke not sowre as the hypocrites do. **1629** MAXWELL tr. *Herodian* 49 The Roman Citizens being thus surrounded with direfull Mis-haps,.. began to looke sowre vpon Commodus. **1693** LOCKE *Educ.* 58 When the Father or Mother looks sowre on the Child. **1833** HT. MARTINEAU *Brooke Farm* vi. 73 If anything ever did make him look sour, it was his dinner not being ready. **1837** CARLYLE *Fr. Rev.* I. VI. v, Nor has public speaking declined, though Lafayette and his Patrols look sour on it.

sour (saʊə(r)), *v.* Forms: 4–7 soure (4 zoure), 4–8 sowr(e, 6–8 sower, 7– sour. [f. SOUR *a.* Cf. WFris. *sûrje*, MDu. *suren* (Du. *zuren*), LG. *sûren*, OHG. *sûrên* (MHG. *sûren*, G. *sauern*) to become sour; also MHG. *siuren* (G. *säuern*), LG. *süren*, NFris. *sürre*, MSw. and Sw. *syra* to make sour.]

1. a. *intr.* To become sour; to acquire a sour taste.

13.. [see b]. **1390** GOWER *Conf.* I. 82 Fulofte and thus the swete soureth, Whan it is knowe to the tast. **1442** *Lett. Marg. Anjou & Bp. Beckington* (Camden) 80 Youre wynes shall nother soure nor stande base, for defaulte of drynkers. **1530** PALSGR. 640/1, I do some good in the house, I keep breed from moldyng and drinke from sowryng. **1577** B. GOOGE *Heresbach's Husb.* III. (1586) 147 Made of two sorts of milke,..it soone sowreth. **1600** SURFLET *Countrie Farme* III. xlix. 532 The cyder made of sweete apples, hauing a soft and tender flesh, is more apt to sowre. **1662** R. MATHEW *Unl. Alch.* 155 Neither will the Oyl sowre so soon. **1732** ARBUTHNOT *Rules of Diet* in *Aliments*, etc. I. 268 Milk when it sours on the Stomach. **1776** JOHNSON in *Boswell* 12 Apr. (Oxf. ed.) II. 28 He cannot find in his heart to pour out a bottle of wine; but he would not much care if it should sour. **1825** J. NICHOLSON *Operat. Mechanic* 608 It is absolutely necessary that the lime..be allowed to remain a considerable time macerating or *souring* in water. **1881** SHELDON *Dairy Farming* 314 Used in milk it has the effect of preventing the faintest approach of souring, for at least a week, in the hottest of weather.

fig. **1602** *2nd Pt. Return fr. Parnass.* I. ii. 165 Such barmy heads wil alwaies be working, when as sad vinegar wittes sit souring at the bottome of a barrell. **1657** REEVE *God's Plea* 2 This it is..to lye sowring in the leaven of discontent.

b. *fig.* To change or turn *to* a bitter feeling. Also without const.

13.. *K. Alis.* 7002 (Laud MS.), Hote loue often after wil soure. **1678** DRYDEN *All for Love* II. i, Love once past, is, at the best, forgotten; But oftner sours to Hate. **1742** YOUNG *Nt. Th.* I. 338 Like bosom friendships to resentment sour'd. **1885–94** R. BRIDGES *Eros & Psyche* May xxx, Thy sisters' love, seeing thee honour'd so, Will sour to envy.

c. To become embittered, morose, or peevish.

1748 THOMSON *Cast. Indol.* I. xvii, They hate to mingle in the filthy fray, Where the soul sours, and gradual rancour grows. **1754** RICHARDSON *Grandison* VII. xlii. 202 A single woman..remains solitary and unheeded, in a busy bustling world; perhaps soured to it by her unconnected state. **1842** TENNYSON *Walking to Mail* 53 She sour'd To what she is: a nature never kind! **1893** *Daily News* 29 Sept. 3/1 They sour and degenerate, grow cynical and misanthropic.

d. *to sour on*, to take a dislike or distaste to (a person or thing). Orig. *U.S.*

1862 in Thornton *Amer. Gloss.* s.v., Guess the M.P. will 'sour' on William C., when he has seen him for about fifteen minutes. **1872** DE VERE *Americanisms* 205 The curious expression of *souring* on an unpleasant task or occupation. **1900** *Daily News* 13 Nov. 9/3 Dan soured on Castlereagh boys..forthwith.

2. a. *trans.* Of leaven: To cause fermentation in (dough, etc.).

1340 *Ayenb.* 205 Ase þe leuayne zoureþ þet doȝ and hit draȝþ to smac. **1382** WYCLIF *Exod.* xii. 34 Thanne the puple tok sprengid meel, or it were sowrid. **1526** TINDALE *1 Cor.* v. 6 A lytell leven sowereth the whole lompe of dowe. **1642** J. BALL *Answ. to Can* ii. 34 A little leaven soweth the whole masse. **1872** J. G. MURPHY *Comm. Lev.* ii. 11 Leaven is a portion of sour dough, which, when mingled with the fresh mass, sours it also.

b. *fig.* or in fig. context.

1390 GOWER *Conf.* I. 294 He is the levein of the bred, Which soureth al the past aboute. **1611** BIBLE *Transl. Pref.* ¶9 Such as are, if not frozen in the dregs, yet sowred with the leauen of their superstition. **1647** *Hist. Anabaptists* 17 Seducing many, and sowring the new Lump of the Church with the Leaven of his perverse doctrine. *c* **1730** SWIFT *Serm.* vii. Wks. 1841 II. 156/2 The smallest mixture of that leaven will sour the whole lump.

3. a. To make sour or acid; *esp.* to cause to have a tart or sour taste; to spoil in this way.

c **1460** *Promp. Parv.* (Winch.) 461 Sowryn, or make sowre, *aceo.* **1594** NASHE *Unfort. Trav.* Wks. (Grosart) V. 161 To sowre all the wines in Rome, and turne them to vineger. **1632** SANDERSON *Serm.* 467 A nasty vessell sowreth all that is put into it. *c* **1685** DK. BUCKINGHAM *Conf.* Wks. 1705 II. 45 He..Sours our Palm Wine, spoils our Victuals. **1715** ADDISON *Drummer* I. i, He'll sour all the beer in my barrels. **1746** FRANCIS tr. *Horace, Epist.* I. ii. 77 For tainted Vessels sour what they contain. **1818** SCOTT *Br. Lamm.* xii, In case the thunner should hae soured ours at the castle. **1825** J. NICHOLSON *Operat. Mechanic* 608 Allowing no more lime.. than is just sufficient to macerate or *sour* it with the water. **1903** *Daily Chron.* 12 Jan. 7/1 A germ that was souring each brew of beer in a large brewery.

fig. **1599** B. JONSON *Cynthia's Rev.* v. xi, We not intend to sowre your late delights With harsh expostulation. **1611** SHAKS. *Wint. T.* I. ii. 102 Three crabbed Moneths had sowr'd themselues to death. **1645** QUARLES *Sol. Recant.* v, This sowers all thy sweets, sads all thy Rest. **1682** SIR T. BROWNE *Chr. Mor.* 10 To have other by-ends in good actions sowers laudable performances. **1720** OZELL tr. *Vertot's Rom. Rep.* I. I. 47 Appius..could not help sowering the Usefulness of his Counsels with the Austerity of his Character. **1826** LAMB *Elia* II. *Wedding*, The awful eye of the parson..souring my incipient jest to the tristful severities of a funeral. **1859** J. MARSHALL *Hist. Scottish Affairs* x. 218 Education in him had not sweetened nature, but nature had soured education.

b. To make (land) cold and wet.

1842 J. AITON *Domest. Econ.* (1857) 185 It is drenched, soured, and turned into mire through the winter. **1880** C. R. MARKHAM *Peruv. Bark* 262 To allow any excess of water to drain off into a place where it cannot *sour* the soil.

c. *Bleaching.* To subject to the action of diluted acids. Also with *off.*

1756 F. HOME *Exper. Bleaching* 80 In a bleachfield, when they were drawing a parcel of coarse cloth soured in this manner. **1839** URE *Dict. Arts* 136 After which, they are completely rinsed in pure spring water, and then soured. **1873** SPON *Workshop Rec.* Ser. I. 15/1 Then sour the whole in a bath of sulphuric acid. **1875** F. J. BIRD *Dyer's Hand-bk.* 52 After cleaning goods should be soured off.

4. a. To render sour, gloomy, or morose; to embitter (the mind, temper, etc.).

1599 JONSON *Ev. Man out of Hum.* Introd., This protraction is able to sour the best settled patience in the theatre. **1709** STRYPE *Ann. Ref.* I. lii. 522 To sowre the Minds of the Subjects against the Queen. *a* **1770** JORTIN *Serm.* (1771) I. v. 91 Their piety is of that sort which sours the temper. **1788** GIBBON *Decl. & F.* xxxix. IV. 32 His mind was soured by indignation. **1838** LYTTON *Alice* 133 Whose heart his schemes had prematurely soured. **1856** MACAULAY *Misc. Writ.* (1882) 314 Continued adversity had soured Johnson's temper. **1882** J. H. BLUNT *Ref. Ch. Eng.* II. 261 Physical and mental misery, which soured her disposition.

b. With personal object. In pa. pple., also (*U.S.* and *Austral. colloq.*) const. *on* (the source of embitterment, etc.).

1669 TEMPLE *Lett.* (1700) II. 127 The Suedish Court, sowered by the ill Treatment..of their Ministers, will [etc.]. **1701** W. WOTTON *Hist. Rome* 220 These Losses did exceedingly sowre the People. **1769** ROBERTSON *Chas. V*, x. Wks. 1813 III. 208 Philip, sowered by his disappointment, was sent back to Spain. **1832** HT. MARTINEAU *Homes Abroad* i. 12 What sours..him more than to work and work from year to year in vain? **1878** STUBBS *Const. Hist.* III. xviii. 9 He seems to us a man..whose conscience..had soured him. **1897** *Badminton Mag.* IV. 389 The filly, soured by our recent encounter, reared. **1898** E. N. WESTCOTT *David Harum* xli. 346 He's kind o' soured on the hull thing. **1906** E. DYSON *Fact'ry 'Ands* xvii. 225 'Fact is,' said the packer, 'we're gettin' er bit soured on wimmin.' **1907** *St. Nicholas* XXXIV. 601/2 Maybe if I get any more soured on Hammond I'll skate over with my trunk and try Ferry Hill.

†**c.** To invest with a sour expression. *Obs. rare.*

1592 SHAKS. *Ven. & Ad.* 185 Adonis..Souring his cheeks cries 'Fie, no more of love!' **1593** —— *Rich. II*, II. i. 169.

souray, obs. form of SERAI[2].

source (sɔəs), *sb.* Forms: 4–5 sours, 5–6 surs, 5–7 sourse; 4– source (6 sowrce). [a. OF. *sors*, *surs, *sours masc., and *surse, sourse, source* (mod.F. *source*) fem., substantival uses of the pa. pple. of *sourdre* to rise or spring: see SOURD *v.*]

†**1.** 'A support or underprop' (Gwilt). *Obs.*

1346 in J. T. Smith *Antiq. Westm.* (1807) 209 [In the works of the said chapel for sources to the images under the tabernacles... The columns placed..under the aforesaid sources.] **1359–60** *Ely Sacr. Rolls* II. 194 In stipend. Roberti Burwelle facientis Garguyles et ymagines pro sources ad le blakrode.

†**2. a.** *Hawking.* The act of rising on the wing, on the part of a hawk or other bird. *Obs.*

c **1384** CHAUCER *H. Fame* 544 Me fleynge in a swappe he hente, And with hys sours a-yene vp went. *c* **1386** —— *Sompn. T.* 230 Right as an hauk upon a sours Upspringeth into thaer, right so prayeres..Maken her sours to Goddis eeres tuo. **1513** DOUGLAS *Æneid* v. v. 21 [Ganymede] Quham, with a surs, swiftlie Jovis squyer Caucht in his clukis, and bair up in the air. **1575** TURBERV. *Faulconrie* 127 The Sparowhawkes do vse to kill the fowle at the Sowrce or Souse as the Goshawkes do. **1612** SELDEN *Illustr. Drayton's Poly-olb.* v. D.'s Wks. 1876 I. 145 But the Goshawk, taken at the source by the Falcon, soon fell down at the King's foot.

†**b.** The rising *of* the sun. *Obs.*

? a **1400** *Morte Arth.* 1978 In-to Sessoyne he soughte.. And at the surs of the sonne disseuerez his knyghttez.

†**c.** An assault or attack. *Obs.*

1616 J. LANE *Contn. Sqr.'s T.* IX. 179 He gallantlie receavinge bothe theire sourse, and theie as resolutelie quittinge force.

3. a. The fountain-head or origin of a river or stream; the spring or place from which a flow of water takes its beginning.

c **1386** CHAUCER *Clerk's Prol.* 49 Wher as the Poo out of a welle smal Takith his firste springyng and his sours. **1426** LYDG. *De Guil. Pilg.* 21838 Ryht as a welle hath hys sours Vpward, with water quyk and cler. **1579** SPENSER *Sheph. Cal.* Nov. 126 The flouds do gaspe, for dryed is theyr sourse. **1601** HOLLAND *Pliny* XXXI. iii. 408 The head or source therof ariseth at the foot of the utmost mountains of the Pelignians. **1673** TEMPLE *Obs. United Prov.* Wks. 1720 I. 7 He that would know the Nature of the Water,..must find out its Source, and observe with what Strength it rises. **1687** A. LOVELL tr. *Thevenot's Trav.* II. 46 That River..takes its source about four days Journey from Mardin. **1738** GRAY *Tasso* 51 Of many a flood they view'd the secret source. **1774** GOLDSM. *Nat. Hist.* (1824) I. 86 All rivers have their source either in mountains or elevated lakes. **1808** PIKE *Sources Mississ.* III. App. 6 The river..may be about 1000 miles in length, from its sources to its discharges. **1846** MCCULLOCH *Acc. Brit. Empire* (1854) I. 9 Near the sources of the South Tyne and the Tees. **1878** HUXLEY *Physiogr.* 20 The streams and springs from which a river is popularly said to take its rise are..only its proximate sources.

transf. **1605** SHAKS. *Macb.* II. iii. 104 The Spring, the Head, the Fountaine of your Blood Is stopt, the very Source of it is stopt. **1810** SCOTT *Lady of L.* III. ix, The billow.. That far to seaward finds his source.

attrib. **1881** *Rep. Geol. Explor. New Zealand* 135 The middle part of the Buckler Burn, before breaking up into its source-branches. **1899** *Athenæum* 28 Oct. 585/1 To control the source-region of the Nile.

b. With *a* and pl. A spring; a fountain.

c **1477** CAXTON *Jason* 102 b, Hit semed that hit had ben a sourse or sprynge rennyng oute of his body. **1596** DRAYTON *Legends* iii. 451 Like those that strive to stop some swelling Sourse. **1632** LITHGOW *Trav.* VI. 292 A source or standing Well. *Ibid.* VIII. 373 Their Bestiall are watered with sources. **1662** J. DAVIES tr. *Mandelslo's Trav.* 199 There is, among others, a source of hot-water which hath the taste of Tin, and issues out of a Cave. **1735** SOMERVILLE *Chase* II. 24 Where trickling Streams distil From some penurious Source. **1820** BYRON *Juan* IV. liv, Though sleeping like a lion near a source. **1855** TENNYSON *The Letters* v, Like torrents from a mountain source. **1856** MERIVALE *Rom. Emp.* xl. (1871) V. 19 In the time of Augustus seven aqueducts brought water from distant sources to Rome.

transf. **1589** GREENE *Menaphon* Wks. (Grosart) VI. 43 Yet kissing the pretie infant, shee lightened out smiles from those cheekes that were furrowed with continual sources of teares.

c. In fig. contexts.

1581 T. HOWELL *Deuises* (1879) 205 Whose strayned hart in sowrce of sorrowe swymmes. **1609** DRAYTON *Legend Cromwell* 21 This was to me that ouerflowing sourse, From whence his bounties plentifully spring. **1647** CLARENDON *Hist. Reb.* I. §6 No man can shew me a source from whence these waters of bitterness..have more probably flowed. **1754** GRAY *Pleasure* 54 Near the source whence Pleasure flows. **1754** —— *Progr. Poesy* 94 This can..ope the sacred source of sympathetic Tears. **1835** T. MITCHELL *Acharn. of Aristoph.* 479 *note*, The foundation of Megara was in itself a source of hostile feeling, which was never likely to be wholly dried up.

4. a. *fig.* The chief or prime cause *of* something of a non-material or abstract character; the quarter whence something of this kind originates.

c **1374** CHAUCER *Troylus* v. 1591 O swerd of knighthod, sours of gentilesse! **1390** GOWER *Conf.* I. 46 Sche that is the Source and Welle Of wel or wo. **1412–20** LYDG. *Chron. Troy* III. 5469 Of knyȝthod grounde, of manhod sours & wel. **1613** TAPP *Pathw. Knowledge* 322 This Charracter √ signifieth the source, roote or beginning of any number or quantity whatsoeuer. **1690** LOCKE *Hum. Und.* II. i. §4 This source of ideas, every man has wholly in himself. **1760–2** GOLDSM. *Cit. W.* iv, Pride seems the source not only of their national vices, but of their national virtues also. **1770** *Junius Lett.* xxxix. (1788) 220 The free election of our representatives.. is the source and security of every right and privilege. **1831** SCOTT *Cast. Dang.* viii, It is my duty..to leave no stone unturned by which this business may be traced to the source. **1857** MILLER *Elem. Chem., Org.* ii. §3. 77 Gases of an offensive odour, which are the source of annoyance to the neighbourhood. **1875** MANNING *Mission H. Ghost* xii. 223 This intellectual perversion is the source of a systematic immorality.

b. With *a, this*, etc., or pl.

1642 H. MORE *Song of Soul* I. ii. 147 All strength and livelyhood is from this sourse. **1718** PRIOR *Knowledge* 413 She is oblig'd and forced to see A First, a Source, a Life, a Deity. **1759** ROBERTSON *Hist. Scot.* III. Wks. 1813 I. 197 The sixth article remained the only source of contest and difficulty. **1824** R. STUART *Hist. Steam Engine* 195 The many sources of consolation which were afforded by the circumstances. **1848** DICKENS *Dombey* vii, Something or somebody had superseded him as a source of interest. **1861** BUCKLE *Civiliz.* (1873) II. viii. 559 One source of danger to which they had long been exposed was considerably lessened.

c. The origin, or original stock, *of* a person, family, etc.

1669 DRYDEN *Tyrannic Love* IV. i, And, thy full Term expir'd, without all Pain, Dissolve into thy Astral Source again. **1738** GRAY *Propertius* iii. 58 [To] trace Back to its Source divine the Julian Race. **1748** —— *Alliance* 74 Conscious of the source from whence she springs. **1818** BYRON *Juan* I. ix, He traced his source Through the most Gothic gentlemen of Spain.

d. The originating cause or substance *of* some material thing or physical agency.

1803 *Med. Jrnl.* IX. 257 He enquires into the source of the liquor amnii, and he explains..why this water is accumulated. **1827** FARADAY *Chem. Manip.* xii. (1842) 285 Some of the impure sources of potash and soda used in the arts. **1862** MILLER *Elem. Chem., Org.* (ed. 2) ix. 639 It is largely used in lamps as a source of light.

e. A work, etc., supplying information or evidence (esp. of an original or primary character) as to some fact, event, or series of these. Also, a person supplying information, an informant, a spokesman.

1788 ROBERTSON *Hist. Amer.* Pref., The sources from which I have derived such intelligence. **1828** R. BURNS *Dissert.* in *Wodrow's Hist. Suff.* I. p. ix, The testimony of historians.., and other published sources of evidence. **1848** WORNUM *Lect. Painting* 114 *note*, This celebrated work is said, though not upon very authentic sources, to have been carried to Constantinople. **1882–3** SCHAFF *Encycl. Relig. Knowl.* I. 501 The principal source to his life is Gregory of Tours. **1934** WEBSTER s.v. *source n.*, one who or that which supplies information. **1940** W. FAULKNER *Hamlet* II. i. 131 The Varners would know by now from the one incontrovertible source, the girl herself, that two of them were not guilty. *a* **1961** E. M. MILLS in *Webster* s.v. [1]*source*, Sources close to the chief executive report he is planning to request the Legislature to approve state purchase. **1973** *Atlanta* (Georgia) *Jrnl.* 19 Apr. 17A/1 Deputy White House press secretary Gerald Warren issued the following statement: 'The White House is not prepared to react to a story based on sources.' **1979** E. NEWMAN *Sunday Punch* i. 3 He had pointed me in the direction of a couple of stories —he was a kindly man and, as a source, needed no special motivation.

f. *attrib.*, as (sense 4 e) *source book, data, document, material, study.*

1899 A. B. HART (*title*) *Source-book of American history. *Ibid.* p. xvii, The Source Book is meant to supplement, not to supplant the text-book. **1900** *Univ. Corresp.* 10 Feb. 93/1 We are very deficient in accessible source-books on this side of the Atlantic. **1948** L. MACNEICE *Holes in Sky* 43 We rarely read their poems, Mere source-books now. **1961** J. D. ROSENBERG *Darkening Glass* (1963) v. 101 'The Nature of Gothic'..is the source book for *Unto This Last.* **1974** *Education & Community Relations* Jan. 3 The researchers also included a question on what support teachers would welcome from external sources and seven ideas were suggested, i.e. in-service courses, teachers guides or source books, pupils books, films, TV lessons, radio lessons and visiting speakers. **1982** *N. & Q.* Dec. 535/2 *Le Menagier de Paris* has long been known as an invaluable sourcebook for practical details of everyday life in a reasonably prosperous middle-class household in France in the 1390s. **1971** J. Howlett in B. de Ferranti *Living with Computer* ii. 17 The general principle is to.. use it.. as *source data for a whole series of studies. **1920** A. J. Grieve in A. S. Peake *Commentary on Bible* 725 It has therefore been surmised that the writer has here incorporated an Aramaic (possibly Greek) *source-document. **1977** *New Yorker* 29 Aug. 35/2 Source documents, once put into computer-readable form, tend to become relatively inaccessible, and in some computer systems are even eliminated. **1936** *Time* 21 Sept. 47/1 For most of their *source material the editors relied on second-rate writers. **1955** W. Moore *Bring Jubilee* xix. 182 It is not easy to see behind source material, to visualise state papers, reports, letters, diaries as written by men. **1978** *Early Music* Oct. 597/3 The discussion of the music combines a flair for words with great attention to stylistic interactions and the lessons to be learned from study of the source material. **1964** *English Studies* XLV. 252 Even those readers least interested in *source-study are likely to have their notions of Shakespear's work made altogether more accurate. **1979** *Studies in Eng. Lit.: Eng. Number* (Tokyo) 3 Source study—by this is meant here not a mere source-hunting but a comparative study between words and their sources—is certainly rewarding so far as *Confessio Amantis* is concerned.

5. a. *Physics.* A point or centre from which a fluid or current flows. More widely, any point where, or process by which, energy or some material component enters a physical system; opp. sink *sb.*[1] 8.

Freq. without const., but otherwise not really distinct from sense 4 d.

1855, etc. [see sink *sb.*[1] 8]. **1878** W. K. Clifford *Elem. Dynamic, Kinem.* 214 The point *s* is called a *source* of strength μ when the fluid streams out in all directions; when μ is negative, so that the fluid streams inwards, it is called a *sink*. **1882** Minchin *Unipl. Kinemat.* 258 If a source or a vortex exist at *P'*, there will be a source or a vortex of equal strength at *P*. **1885** Watson & Burbury *Electr. & Magn.* I. 216 The given equipotential regions are in such a case generally termed *electrodes*, and sometimes *sources* or *sinks* of electricity, according to the direction of the current flow from or towards them. **1926** H. Glauert *Elem. Aerofoil & Airscrew Theory* iii. 21 A sink is a negative source or a point at which fluid is disappearing. **1956** E. H. Hutten *Lang. Mod. Physics* iv. 139 The engine is in contact with two heat reservoirs (the boiler and condenser, or the source and sink of energy) at different temperatures. **1971** I. G. Gass et al. *Understanding Earth* xix. 263/1 Boundaries at which the net effect of motion is to generate surface area are here termed sources.

b. *Electronics.* (The material forming) the part of a unipolar transistor which corresponds in function to the cathode of a thermionic valve.

1952 [see gate *sb.*[1] 8 h]. **1962** Simpson & Richards *Physical Princ. Junction Transistors* viii. 173 The source and drain.. are ohmic electrodes attached to the *n*-type body of the device [*sc.* a field-effect transistor]. **1977** *Sci. Amer.* Sept. 74/3 The inversion creates a continuous *n*-type channel from source to drain and large currents can flow.

6. *Comb.*, as (sense 4 e) *source-hunter*, *-hunting*; **source-criticism** *Theol.*, analysis and study of the sources used by the authors of the biblical text; hence **source-critical** *a.*; **source program** *Computers*, a program written in a language other than machine code, usu. a high-level language (cf. *object program* s.v. object *sb.* 10); **source rock** *Geol.*, a rock formation in which a particular mineral material originates; *spec.* a deposit in which petroleum is formed.

1977 J. L. Houlden *Patterns of Faith* iii. 26 This is particularly true of the gospels of Matthew and Luke, where, according to the *source-critical orthodoxy.., visible alterations of the Markan basis could be observed. **1901** J. Moffatt *Historical New Testament* App. 677 No method which neglects source-criticism can satisfactorily explain the doublets [in the Apocalypse]. **1931** K. E. Kirk *Vision of God* 498 An elaborate *source-criticism which must be adjudged.. to be in the main based upon the theory, and therefore to involve a vicious circle. **1977** G. W. H. Lampe *God as Spirit* iv. 102 The Jesus whom historical research tries to reconstruct through the laborious processes of source criticism, form criticism, and redaction criticism. **1964** D. Daiches *Eng. Lit.* iv. 82 An attempt to rescue literary study from the philologists and *source-hunters. **1956** *Canad. Forum* June 67/1 His treatment of sources and analogues lacks the rigorous testing which we require of *source-hunting in literary studies after twenty years of sniping by new critics and old scholars alike. **1979** Source-hunting [see *source study*, sense 4 f]. **1959** M. H. Wrubel *Primer of Programming for Digital Computers* vi. 129 The program can be corrected or modified at the *source program stage and reassembled. **1970** O. Dopping *Computers & Data Processing* xix. 304 Instead of machine instructions, the source program contains statements or symbolic instructions, which the computer then translates to an object program by means of a special program. **1973** C. W. Gear *Introd. Computer Sci.* iv. 158 A language compiler accepts as input a set of statements called a source program. **1931** *Bull. Amer. Assoc. Petroleum Geologists* XV. 161 *Source rocks of petroleum include carbonaceous or 'bituminous' sedimentary deposits, containing aquatic plant and animal remains.. and the products of their biochemical and geochemical alterations. **1965** G. J. Williams *Econ. Geol. N.Z.* xix. 352/1 Early borings at Kotuku.. left little doubt that the oil at Kotuku comes from the Oligocene Cobden Limestone—though this does not necessarily mean that the Limestone is the source rock. **1971** I. G. Gass et al. *Understanding Earth* xxii. 323/2 The concentration of diamond source-rocks in the older cratons.

source, *v.*[1] Also 6–7 **sourse**. [f. prec. or OF. *sours-*, pret. stem of *sourdre* sourd *v.*]

†**1.** *intr.* Of a bird of prey: To rise after seizing its quarry. *Obs.*

1513 Douglas *Æneid* xi. xiv. 74 Evir the sarar this ern strenis his gryp,.. Sammyn wyth hys wyngis soursand in the sky.

†**2.** To rise, surge, or boil up. *Obs.*

1594 Nashe *Terrors of Night* Wks. (Grosart) III. 257 Anie ouerboyling humour which sourseth hiest in our stomackes.

†**3.** To spring or take rise *from* something. *Obs.*

1599 Nashe *Lenten Stuff* Wks. (Grosart) V. 249 They.. neuer leaue roaring it out.. of the freedomes and immunities soursing from him. **1611** Cotgr., *Sourcé*, sourced, sprung or begun from. **1666** G. Harvey *Morb. Angl.* viii. 70 [Consumption] sourceth from an Ulcer in the Lungs.

4. *trans.* **a.** In pass., *to be sourced in*, to originate in, to be based in; to mention as a source.

1941 W. C. Handy *Father of Blues* xxii. 298 Affinities that may be sourced in a common ultimate Oriental origin. **1972** 'J. Godey' *Three Worlds of Johnny Handsome* ii. 23 Mitchell became aware of a rumbling sound vaguely sourced in the floor. **1978** *Maledicta 1977* I. 326 Over twenty of Mr. Tamony's scripts are sourced in H. L. Mencken's *American Language, Supplements* 1 and 2. **1982** *Times Lit. Suppl.* 17 Dec. 1394/1, I also drew on a scientific paper discussing Vittoz's work by the Chicago psychoanalyst, Dr Harry Trosman, which is sourced in my notes.

b. To obtain from a specified source; *spec.* of components (for a vehicle). Chiefly in pa. pple.

1972 *Wall St. Jrnl.* 24 Feb. 1/5 Ford works on stripped-down cars, called 'Asian Model Ts' that could be sourced and assembled anywhere in Asia. **1980** *Times* 20 Mar. 27/5 One component manufacturer said last night: 'Our indications are that less than 10 per cent of the Bounty [*sc.* a new car] will be sourced in the United Kingdom.' **1981** *Times* 6 Feb. 18/2 Counterfeited goods, largely sourced from south east Asia.. have mainly been finding their way into British export markets. *Ibid.* 15 Aug. 15/4 British manufacturers.. have stressed that Nissan should source at least 80 per cent of the contents of the cars it plans to make in the United Kingdom in Europe.

Hence †'**sourcing** *ppl. a. Obs.*; '**sourcing** *vbl. sb.*, *spec.* the obtaining of goods and components from a specified or understood source.

a **1660** *Contemp. Hist. Irel.* (Ir. Archæol. Soc.) II. 117 Like a bankroute or shipe lost on the continent by the furie of sourcinge waves. **1960** *Business Week* 2 Jan. 67/3 Businessmen now refer to imports from foreign plants as 'sourcing'—a term that until recently referred to company purchases from a domestic supplier. **1960** *Wall St. Jrnl.* 15 Mar. 14/5 There is a growing tendency toward foreign 'sourcing', the purchase or production of finished goods or components abroad. **1970** *Daily Tel.* 1 Oct. 2/2 Ford, British Leyland and other manufacturing companies has had to resort to 'dual sourcing' for some components because of this year's unprecedented run of major supplier strikes. **1972** *Wall St. Jrnl.* 24 Feb. 1/5 Experience under the U.S.-Canadian auto pact and in the Common Market has emboldened Detroit to expand multi-national sourcing of parts and components.

†**source**, *v.*[2] *Obs.*[−1] [Alteration of souse *v.*[1]] *trans.* To submerge, plunge, souse.

1616 R. C. *Times' Whistle* (1871) 113 Apollo.. Taking his dayly.. course, His fiery head in Thetis watry brest, Three hundred sixty & five times doth source.

source language. [f. source *sb.* + language *sb.*] **1.** A language from which a translation is made.

1953 *Philos. Sci.* XX. 217 One of the decisive steps in certain methods of machine translation is the determination of the syntactic structure of any given sentence in the source-language (i.e., the language from which we translate). **1964** M. A. K. Halliday et al. *Linguistic Sciences* 123 Translation as activity faces only one way; the translator observes an event in one language, the 'source' language, and performs a related event in another, the 'target' language. **1974** R. Quirk *Linguist & Eng. Lang.* vi. 97 The difficulties vary profoundly according to the manifold combinations of source- and target-languages involved.

2. *Computers.* The programming language in which a program or procedure is written. Cf. object language 3.

1959 *Communications Assoc. Computing Machinery* Feb. 9/2 Sections 2 and 3 give a formal description of the Fortran source language, insofar as arithmetic type statements are concerned. **1963** *Ibid.* VI. 430/1 The debugging system has been implemented for Fortran as the source language and could be easily adapted to other problem-oriented languages. **1975** T. Bartee *Introd. Computer Sci.* xiii. 377 For high-level compiler languages such as Fortran, PL/I, and Algol, there is an attempt to make the source language machine-independent.

sourceless ('sɔəslɪs), *a.* [f. source *sb.*] Having no source.

1848 Bailey *Festus* (ed. 3) 109 The sourceless circular river of Thy love. **1908** *Punch* 25 Sept. 436/1 The unnoticed, sourceless wound. **1981** *Washington Post* 8 July C1 Talent—this sourceless asset that one cannot command to be born.

sourcesse, obs. form of surcease *v.*

sour crout, sour-crout. Also 7 **sower crawt**, 8 **soure crud** (after Du.), 9 **sourcrout**; 8 **sour-krout**, 8– **sour krout**, 9 **sour kraut**. [Anglicized form of sauerkraut.] **1.** A fermented preparation of cabbage.

α. **1617** Moryson *Itin.* iii. ii. iii. 83 They vse to serue in sower crawt or cabbage vpon a voide circle of carved Iron. **1712** Arbuthnot *John Bull* ii. iii, Poor Frog [the Dutch].. his children.. live upon salt herring, sowre crud, and borecole. **1775** *Ann. Reg.* i. 190 Cabbages, made into sour-crout, a kind of pickle, but used, in lieu of common food, in some parts of Germany. **1796** T. Twining *Trav. India*, etc. (1893) 3 The American captains have the reputation of keeping rather an indifferent table—living, it is said, principally on salt beef and sour-crout. **1802** Beddoes *Hygëia* viii. 19 Particular things as sour crout gave the person.. uneasiness. **1834** T. Medwin *Angler in Wales* II. 286 Either are to me as bad as a double dose of sour crout. **1852** Thackeray *Esmond* ii. xiii. (1876) 261 Feeding on train-oil and sour-crout. **1865** tr. *Erckmann-Chatrian's Waterloo* (1870) 60 He set a good dish of sour-crout beside the soup-tureen.

attrib. **1778** Han. More *Let.* in W. Roberts *Mem.* (1834) I. 132, I dined yesterday at Garrick's, with the sour crout party.

β. **1776** Cook in *Phil. Trans.* LXVI. 403 Sour Krout.. is .. highly antiscorbutic. **1777** Forster *Voy. round World* I. 53 The captain had for some weeks past ordered sour-krout (or cabbage sliced and fermented) to be regularly served to the crew. *a* **1845** Hood *Knight & Dragon* xiv, Noble Lord of the soil, Of its corn and its oil,.. Of our cream and sour-kraut, Of our carp and our trout. **1857** Hughes *Tom Brown* i. i, You have seen men and cities, no doubt,.. and know the taste of sour krout. **1870** Dubois *Artistic Cookery* 67 Pheasant with Sour-krout. **1884** Knight *Dict. Mech.* Suppl. 834/1 *Sour Kraut Cutter*, a machine for cutting cabbage for kraut.

2. *U.S. slang.* A German. Cf. sauerkraut 2 and kraut 2.

1841 H. J. Mercier *Life in Man of War* 232 Yes, old sour-crout, and you'd be *dirty too* if you were.. in that infernal shot-locker as long as these fellows have been.

Hence **sour-croutish** *a.*

c **1780** Beckford *Italy* (1834) I. 62 An execrable sour-croutish supper was served up to my majesty. **1862** Miss M. B. Edwards *John & I* xv. (1872) 121 The whole atmosphere is rather beery, sour-krautish, and cigarish.

†**sour crud(e.** [ad. obs. Du. *zuurkruid*: see sauerkraut.] = prec.

1708 *Caldwell Papers* (Maitl. Cl.) I. 209 Breath perfumed with garlick and sour crude, (a stinking kind of kail). **1713** Arbuthnot *John Bull* ii. iii, His Children don't eat a bit of good Victuals from one Year's end to the other, but live upon Salt Herring, sowr Crud, and Bore-cole.

†**sourd**, *a. Obs.*[−0] [a. F. *sourd*, in the same sense:—L. *surd-us* surd *a.*] Dim or dull.

1659 Howell *Vocab. Terms, Arts & Sci.* § xxvi, A sourd, or deaf Emerald, which hath a deadish lustre.

†**sourd**, *v. Obs.* Also 4–6 **sourde**. [ad. OF. *sourdre* (also mod.F.), *sordre*, *surdre*, = Pg. *sordir*, *surdir*, *surgir*, Sp. *surgir*, Prov. *sorger*, *sorzer*, It. *sorgere*:—L. *surgĕre* to rise. Cf. sourdre *v.*]

1. *intr.* Of conditions, events, etc.: To arise, take rise, spring or issue.

c **1386** Chaucer *Pars. T.* ¶ 450 Now myghte men axe, wher-of that pride sourdeth and spryngeth. *Ibid.* ¶ 505 Somtyme grucchyng sourdeth of Enuye. **1399** Langl. *R. Redeles* Prol. 5 Sodeynly þer sourdid selcouþe þingis. *c* **1430** *Pilgr. Lyf Manhode* i. xcix. (1869) 53 But j telle thee that many erroures sourdeden sithe, and many harmes. **1474** Caxton *Chesse* 30 For this cause sourden batailles and discordes. **1483** —— *Gold. Leg.* 41/1 Rumour and grutchyng began to sourde and ryse betwene the herdmen of abram. **1531** Elyot *Gov.* i. ii, Wherby at the last should haue sourded dissencion amonge the people. **1567** Drant *Horace, Ep. Arte Poet.* A ij, And nouell words.. shall better credit bringe, If sparinglye.. they sourde from greekishe springe.

2. Of fountains, etc.: To spring up, to issue from the ground.

1398 Trevisa *Barth. De P.R.* xiv. xii. (1495) 473 Welle stremes sourden and moysten this hylle. **1480** Caxton *Myrr.* i. vi. 30 As a fontayn that contynuelly sourdeth and spryngeth. **1483** —— *Gold. Leg.* 96 b/1 A fontayne of water sourded and sprange up and quenchid it alle. **1606** Warner *Alb. England* xv. xcvii. (1612) 386 Is it probable his Staffe should make three furlongs flight Of selfe accord.. and where as it did light Should sourd a plentious wel, not seen or heard of ere that night?

transf. **1596** Nashe *Saffron Walden* Wks. (Grosart) III. 95 Were the Nectar of his eloquence a thousand times more superabundant incessant sourding.

3. Of persons: To be roused, to become angry. Hence †'**sourding** *vbl. sb. Obs.*

c **1400** *Destr. Troy* 1000 But a Sourdyng with sourgrem sanke in his hert. *Ibid.* 1816 Sodenly he sourdit into soure greme. *Ibid.* 5051 While I se you in certain I sourde full of yre, And bolne at þe brest.

sourd(e, obs. forms of sord, sward.

†**sourdet.** *Obs.* (See quot. and next.)

1611 Cotgr., *Sourdine*, a Sourdet; the little pipe, or tenon put into the mouth of a Trumpet, to make it sound low. [Hence *sordet* in Blount *Glossogr.* s.v. *Sordine.*]

sourdine (suə'diːn), *sb.* and *a.* Somewhat *rare.* [a. F. *sourdine*, f. *sourd* deaf, dull: cf. sordine.]

A. *sb.* **a.** *Early Mus.* A muted trumpet.

a **1678** Marvell *Upon Appleton House* lii. Misc. Poems (1681) 90 Death-Trumpets creak in such a Note, And 'tis the *Sourdine* in their Throat. **1891** C. R. Day *Descr. Catal. Mus. Instruments recently exhibited at R. Mil. Exhibition* v. 96 The combination of a double reed with a cylindrical bore .. presents certain theoretical difficulties... During the 14th, 15th, and 16th centuries instruments thus constructed were in common use. Those most generally met with were the *krumhorn*.. and the *sourdine*. **1941** N. Bessaraboff *Anc. Europ. Mus. Instruments* 80 There were several families of instruments, such as the cromornes, the racketts ('the sausage bassoons'), the sourdines. **1976** D. Munrow

Instruments Middle Ages & Renaissance vi. 45/3 The tone is much softer and more muffled, however, and very similar to that of a rackett; hence the other name given to the instrument..*sourdine* (French).

b. A mute or damper.

c **1779** W. Waring tr. *Rousseau's Dict. Mus.* 384 *Sourdine*, a small instrument of copper or silver, which is applied to the bridge of a violin or violincello, to render the sounds weaker. **1959** *Collins Mus. Encycl.* 618/2 *Sourdine*... (1) Mute (of a string or wind instrument). (2) Damper (in the piano). (3) A device for muting the strings of the piano.

B. *adj.* Muffled, subdued. Also *fig.*

1898 *N.Y. Times* 2 July (Cent.), The art of making a commonplace event striking by telling it in hints, as in the sourdine little tragedy of 'A Modern Melodrama'. **1904** *Windsor Mag.* Dec. 166/2 A singular little tune, half sourdine, half pizzicato.

sour dock, sour-dock. Now *dial.* [sour *a.* and dock *sb.*[1]] Common sorrel (*Rumex acetosa*).

c **1325** *Gloss. W. de Bibbesw.* in Wright *Voc.* 162 [Pour sauce vaut la surele, *glossed*] sour-dokke. *a* **1387** *Sinon. Barthol.* (Anecd. Oxon.) 33 *Oxilapacium, acedula*, soure-dock. **1387-8** T. Usk *Test. Love* iii. vi. (Skeat) l. 7 The frute of the soure docke. *c* **1450** *M.E. Med. Bk.* (Heinrich) 88 Tak a rostede oynen, þe lilie rote, & sowredokkes. **1530** Palsgr. 273/1 Sowerdocke, an herbe. **1548** Turner *Names Herbes* (E.D.S.) 69 *Oxalis*,..in englishe Sorel or sourdocke. **1601** Holland *Pliny* II. 255 They vse to seeth it after the maner of Soure-docke. **1647** Hexham i. (Herbs), Sorell, or sower docke, *Surcker, ofte Suyringh.* **1825-** in many dialect glossaries. **1896** Snowden *Web of Weaver* 6 Getting stuff to eat—pignuts, sour docks.

So **sour docken.** Now *north. dial.*

1697 *Phil. Trans.* XIX. 375 *Acetosa* (a Plant..which may well be called The Indian Sorrel, or Sower Docken). **1788** W. H. Marshall *Yorksh.* II. 354 Sourdocken; *rumex acetosa*; sorrel. **1825-** in northern glossaries.

sour-dough ('saʊədəʊ), *sb.* Forms: (see sour *a.* and dough *sb.*). [Corresponds in sense 1 to WFris. *sûrdaei*, older Flem. *suerdeech, -deegh* (Du. and Flem. *zuurdeeg*), MLG. *sûrdêch*, MHG. *sûrteich* (G. *sauerteig*), MSw. *surdegher* (Sw. *surdeg*), Da. *surdeig*.]

1. a. Leaven. Now *dial.* and *rare.*

α. **1303** R. Brunne *Handl. Synne* 10099 þe paste..ne ogh Be made of any maner of soure dogh. **1382** Wyclif *Exod.* xxiii. 18 Thow shalt not offer vpon sour dowȝ the blood of thi sacrifice. **1398** Trevisa *Barth. De P.R.* xvii. lxviii. (Bodl. MS.), Sowr dowe rereþ paste and brede þ^t is medled þerwiþ. **14..** *Nom.* in Wr.-Wülcker 725 *Hoc fermentum*, surdowght. *c* **1440** *Promp. Parv.* 466/2 Sowre Dowe, *fermentum.* *a* **1529** Skelton *E. Rummyng* 288 Som bryngeth her husbandes hood..; And some brought sowre dowe. **1535** Coverdale *Exod.* xiii. 7 Therfore shalt thou eate vnleuended bred seuen dayes, that there be no sowre dowe, ner sowred bred sene in all thy quarters. **1869** *Lonsdale Gloss.* 78/2 *Sour dough* or *doff*, leaven. **1876** *Mid-Yorks. Gloss.* 132/1 *Sour-dough*, the more homely equivalent of *leaven.*

β. *c* **1425** *Voc.* in Wr.-Wülcker 663 *Hoc fermentum*, surdagh. **1483** *Cath. Angl.* 350/1 Sowre daghe, *fermentum, zima.* *c* **1520** M. Nisbet *Matt.* xiii. 33 The kingdom of heuenis is like to sourdauche.

b. *fig.* of qualities, etc.

c **1380** Wyclif *Wks.* (1880) 2 Crist commandiþ to his disciplis..to vndirstonde & flee þe sowrdow of pharisees. **1398** Trevisa *Barth. De P.R.* ix. xxxi. (Bodl. MS.), Ifedde not with olde souredowe of malice but with pure mete of swetenes. *a* **1400** *Minor Poems fr. Vernon MS.* xxiii. 404 Of þe olde wrecchednesse Holdyng doun sourdouh. *c* **1450** *Myrr. our Ladye* 300 Be made free from the olde sowre dowgh, that ys to say, from synne.

c. *N. Amer.* Fermenting dough, esp. that left over from a previous baking, used as leaven; bread made from this. Also *attrib.*

1868 J. Anderson *Sawney's Lett.*, Gie my respecks to your guid wife; If ever I get hame to Fife, I'll teach her hoo to mak loaf bread, Wi' sour dough. **1922** G. C. F. Pringle *Tillicums* 156 In every old prospector's cabin..you would see a bowl which contained sour dough from the previous making. This was used as yeast to be mixed in with the dough at the next baking. **1931** *Sun* (Baltimore) 5 Mar. 12/3 [Maryland] might be thought wanting in pride in the culinary art for which the State enjoyed well-earned fame when Indiana was eating sour dough and jerked meat. **1959** M. Shand *Summit & Beyond* xi. 197 There was good old sourdough bread, too. **1966** Mrs. L. B. Johnson *White House Diary* 3 Apr. (1970) 380 They had sour-dough biscuits too—although they had trouble making them rise in this high altitude. **1971** *Daily Colonist* (Victoria, B.C.) 23 Apr. 4/7 In early America, a pot of sourdough starter was part of a bride's dowry. **1976** *National Observer* (U.S.) 26 June 8/3 San Francisco sourdough has a character all its own, because there are microscopic organisms in the air here that do funny things to the starter. Some say it's the same wild yeasts that work on the nearby vineyards. **1979** *United States 1980/1* (Penguin Travel Guides) 370 Two-pound Porterhouses..served with sourdough bread and pinto beans.

2. *Amer.* An experienced prospector in Alaska, the Yukon, or the Northwest territories.

In allusion to the use of a piece of sour dough for raising the bread baked during the winter.

1898 *Klondike Nugget* (Dawson, Yukon Terr.) 20 July 1/4 The usual strong expletives had been used expressive of their meeting and Mr. Chee Chaco was not looking for information from his old friend Mr. Sour Dough. **1902** *Daily Chron.* 13 Nov. 5/6 He is what is called a 'sour dough' in the parlance of the Yukon, which means that he..has spent a winter in the frozen North. **1904** E. Robins *Magnetic North* viii. 154 You don't get an old Sour-dough like Dillon to travel at forty degrees [below zero].

Hence (from sense 1) †**sour-dough** *v. trans.*, to leaven. *Obs.*

1382 Wyclif *Hosea* vii. 4 The citee restide a litil in mengyng to gydre of soure dowe, til it were sourdowid all. —— *Amos* iv. 5 Sacrifie ȝe herying of sour dowid [L. *de fermentato*]. *c* **1440** *Promp. Parv.* 466/2 Sowyr dowyn, or menge paste wythe sowyr dowe, *fermento.*

†**sourdre,** *sb. Obs.*$^{-1}$ [OF. *sourdre* inf. (cf. next) used as sb.] Source.

c **1477** Caxton *Jason* 29 That he was the veray sourdre and welle of noblesse.

†**sourdre,** *v. Obs.* [a. OF. *sourdre*: see sourd *v.*] *intr.* To arise or spring.

14.. *Chaucer's Pars. T.* ¶448 (Hengwrt MS.), The especes that sourdren of pride, soothely whan they sourdren of malice [etc.]. **1474** Caxton *Chesse* ii. iv. (1883) 57 For as moche as..rebellion..might sourdre and aryse in oon partye or other. *c* **1477** —— *Jason* 111 b, How wele that shold sourdre therof to me a new sorowe. *c* **1500** *Melusine* 50 The fontayne also whiche sourdred & sprang ther haboundauntly.

soured (saʊəd), *ppl. a.* [f. sour *v.*]

1. Rendered sour or acid; fermented, leavened.

1382 Wyclif *Exod.* xii. 15 Who so euer etith sowred breed. **1535** Coverdale *Exod.* xiii. 7 That there be no..sowred bred sene in all thy quarters. **1659** Gauden *Serm.* (1660) 120 As sowred vinegar is made of the sweetest wine. **1670** Covel in *Early Voy. Levant* (Hakluyt Soc.) 120 With leaven of salt and sower'd honey and oil. **1721** R. Keith tr. *T. à Kempis, Solil. Soul* x. 177, I am like a soured Vessel and wholly unworthy of the Inpouring of thy good Spirit. **1873** Tristram *Moab* xiii. 238 A bowl of soured milk—a most delicious draught on a broiling day.

2. Of persons: Embittered, crabbed.

1848 Thackeray *Van. Fair* l, Miss Clapp..is declared by the soured old lady to be an unbearable and impudent little minx. **1857** W. Collins *Dead Secret* iii. i, He returned to his father's house, a soured man at the outset of life. **1885** Miss Braddon *Wyllard's Weird* II. i. 24 Even a soured old maid such as I could but yield to her charm.

Hence **'souredness.**

1858 Gilfillan in *Wyatt's Poet. Wks.* p. xvi, In his Satires we find what we may call a mellowed souredness of spirit.

'souren, *v. north. dial.* [f. sour *a.*] *intr.* To become sour.

1570 Levins *Manip.* 82 To sowerne, *acescere.* **1878** in *Cumberld. Gloss.*

'sourer. *rare*$^{-1}$. [f. sour *v.*] One who sours or causes sourness.

1737 *Gentl. Mag.* VII. 293/1 There is at least a Pair of them; one a Sweetener, the other a Sourer.

†**'sourfulness.** *Obs.*$^{-1}$ Sourness.

1590 Barrough *Meth. Physick* iii. i. (1639) 100 The meats may be perceived to be changed into the savour of rosting or sowerfulnesse.

sourge, obs. form of surge *sb.* and *v.*

sour grass. Also **sour-grass.** [sour *a.*]

1. A tropical grass of the genus *Paspalum.*

1756 P. Browne *Jamaica* 365 Sour Grass. The roots and leaves of this plant..cure sores and ulcers. **1864** Grisebach *Flora Brit. W. Ind.* 787 Sour-grass, *Paspalum conjugatum.*

2. One or other variety of sorrel (*Rumex* or *Oxalis*). Also *attrib.*

1866 Brogden *Prov. Lincs.*, *Sour-grass, Sour-sauce*, the ground sorrel, *Oxalis pratense.* **1888** 'R. Boldrewood' *Robbery under Arms* xx, The long sour-grass..was dripping with the night dew. **1889** Maiden *Usef. Plants* 50 *Oxalis corniculata*,..'Clover Sorrel', or 'Sour Grass'. **1890** 'R. Boldrewood' *Col. Reformer* (1891) 311 Bred in a 'sour grass' country, far inferior for fattening purposes.

3. *S. Afr.* The coarse grass characteristic of sour veld (see sour *a.* 11).

1801 J. Barrow *Acct. Trav. S. Afr.* I. iii. 110 That division of the district called the *Zuure-veldt*, or Sour Grass plains. **1852** M. B. Hudson *S. Afr. Frontier Life* I. 236 About Graham's Town and Lower Albany is 'the Zuurveld or Sour Grass Country'.

†**'sourhead.** *Obs.*$^{-1}$ Sourness.

a **1400** *Stockholm Med. MS.* ii. 827 in *Anglia* XVIII. 327 Sowr[h]ed of ale it wyl abate.

souring ('saʊərɪŋ), *vbl. sb.* [f. sour *v.* Cf. Du. *zuring* souring, sorrel, G. *säuer-, säurung* souring, NFris. *süring* leaven.]

1. A substance which renders sour or acid; *spec.* leaven, lemon-juice, or vinegar. Also *fig.* Now chiefly *dial.*

14.. *Wycliffite Bible* 1 Cor. v. 7 As ȝe ben therf, or withoute sour thing [*v.r.* sowryng]. **1751** Smollett *Per. Pic.* xci. (1779) IV. 91 A double proportion of sowering was visible in his aspect. **1777** —— *Humph. Cl.* 13 July (1815) 239 Looking at me with a double squeeze of souring in his aspect. **1814** Scott *Wav.* xxix, Mine host..infused a double portion of souring into the pharisaical leaven of his countenance. **1829** Hunter *Hallamshire Gloss.* 84 *Souring*, dough left in the tub from one baking of oat-cakes to another. **1836** Haliburton *Clockm.* Ser. ii. ix, There's another lemon left, squire, 'spose we mix a little more sourin' afore we turn in. **1841** Hartshorne *Salop. Ant.* Gloss., *Souring*, vinegar.

b. A preparation used in bleaching and tanning.

1777 *Phil. Trans.* LXVIII. 124 In the old method, the tanners made use of sourings brewed generally from rye, or some other grain.

2. The process or fact of becoming or making sour.

1579 Fulke *Refut. Rastel* 76 He wil haue no wine for feare of sowering. **1662** Merret in Charleton *Myst. Vintners* (1675) 222 To prevent souring of French Wines. **1673** Boyle *Ess. Effluviums* ii. 30 Talking with her about the remedies of the Sowring of Beer and other drinks by Thunder. **1743** *Lond. & Country Brewer* iv. (ed. 2) 280 Though Yeast naturally tends to the sowering of all Drink it is beat into. **1830** M. Donovan *Dom. Econ.* I. 167 That commencement of acetification or souring called *foxing.* **1886** C. H. Fagge *Princ. & Pract. Med.* I. 21 The lactic acid fermentation or souring of milk.

b. *fig.* with reference to character or temper.

1874 L. Stephen *Hours in Library* (1892) II. iii. 89 Hazlitt's cynicism is the souring of a generous nature. **1901** *Contemp. Rev.* Mar. 453 The well-nigh inevitable souring of the dishoused peasant into guerilla or brigand.

3. *spec.* The process of subjecting cloth, wool, skins, etc., to the action of diluted acids.

1756 F. Home *Exper. Bleaching* 37 The general process of bleaching divides itself into these different parts. 1. Steeping and milling. 2. Bucking and boiling... 4. Souring. **1844** G. Dodd *Textile Manuf.* ii. 51 The process of 'grey souring', in which the cloth passes through a machine..containing very dilute sulphuric acid. **1882** Crookes *Dyeing* 7 Next follows souring, known as the 'lime-sour', or 'grey-sour'.

attrib. **1756** F. Home *Exper. Bleaching* 77 The souring process had been going on for two days. *Ibid.*, In the souring vat. **1875** *Encycl. Brit.* III. 820/1 A souring-well under the souring-box is now filled with water and sulphuric acid.

4. A sourish variety of apple; *dial.* a crab-apple.

1846 J. Baxter *Libr. Pract. Agric.* (ed. 4) I. 59 Fearn's pippin,..Hanwell souring. **1860** R. Hogg *Fruit Manual* 11 Hanwell Souring... Flesh firm, crisp, and briskly acid. **1866** *Treas. Bot.* 1075/1 *Souring*, a country name for the Crab apple. **1896** *Warwicksh. Word-bk.* 221 *Souring*, an apple for winter use.

'souring, *ppl. a.* [f. sour *v.*] That becomes or makes sour.

1710 M. Henry *Christianity No Sect* Wks. 1857 II. 445/1 The leaven of the Pharisees which is both souring and swelling. **1859** Dickens *T. Two Cities* ii. xv, A sour wine, or a souring, for its influence on the mood of those who drank it was to make them gloomy. **1883** Grant White *Washington Adams* 33 Pleasing and picturesque, and yet souring and doughing.

sourish ('saʊərɪʃ), *a.* Also 4-5 sourische, 5 -isshe, -ysshe, 7-8 sowrish (7 -ishe), sowerish. [f. sour *a.* + -ish.] Somewhat sour, in various senses:

a. Of things, taste, or smell.

1398 Trevisa *Barth. De P.R.* xvii, xii. (Bodl. MS.), Wormod is ful scharpe herbe, hote and druye, ful sourische & bitter. **1477** Norton *Ord. Alch.* v. in Ashm. (1652) 74 And so is Sowerish tast called Sapor Pontick. **1598** Bp. Hall *Sat.* v. ii, When pleasing Bourdeaux falls unto his lot, Some sourish Rochelle cuts thy thirsting throat. **1617** Moryson *Itin.* iii. 82 They have a kind of bread brownish and sowrish, and made with aniseeds. **1693** Evelyn *De la Quint. Compl. Gard.* I. 142 The bad Qualities of Plums, are..to have their Pulp tough, mealy, and doughy,..or sharp and sowrish. **1725** *Fam. Dict.* s.v. *Cider*, If it be only a little sowerish. **1807** T. Thomson *Chem.* (ed. 3) II. 268 Muriatic acid is to be added, with constant stirring,..till the mass tastes a little sourish. **1866** *Treas. Bot.* 30/1 The sap above referred to is of a sourish taste. **1884** J. Burroughs *Pepacton* 173 Not so dry, and having a sourish smell.

fig. **1647** Trapp *Comm. Rev.* xii. 12 Grosse, troubled, brackish, and sowrish doctrine.

b. Of persons (or animals), temper, etc.

1688 *Lond. Gaz.* No. 2328/4 A Dapple grey Gelding,..a sowrish Head, a little hollow backt. **1792** in *Ld. Auckland's Corr.* (1861) II. 450 His own sourish disposition being naturally much heightened by such horrid doings. **1889** Johnston *Glenbuckie* xii. 145 A worthy, albeit a sourish person. **1897** *Daily News* 19 Oct. 6/1 A lovable fellow in contrast with the narrow, sourish northerner.

Comb. **1859** Geo. Eliot *A. Bede* xvii, I believe he meant right at bottom; but..he was sourish-tempered.

Hence **'sourishly** *adv.*; **'sourishness.**

1670 W. Simpson *Hydrol. Ess.* 81, I haue tasted one near Chesterfield in Derbyshire, which hath a very strong sowrishness. **1719** London & Wise *Compl. Gard.* 66 'Tis very juicy, and has a smack of Sowrishness. **1846** Landor *Exam. Shaks.* Wks. II. 266 Master Silas..looked sourishly, and cried aloud.

†**'sourkit.** *Sc. Obs.*$^{-1}$ [f. sour *a.* + (?) kit *sb.*[1]] Some form of sour milk or cream.

1549 *Compl. Scot.* vi. 43 Thai maid grit cheir of..curdis and quhaye, sourkittis, fresche buttir ande salt buttir.

†**'sourling.** *Obs.*$^{-1}$ [f. sour *a.*] A person of a sour disposition.

1784 *Unfortunate Sensibility* I. Ded. p. ix, In spite of all such sourlings and grim-faced monsters,..I must, and will subscribe [etc.].

sourly ('saʊəlɪ), *adv.* Also 6-8 sowerly, 6-7 sowr(e)ly(e, 6 sour(e)lie, 7 sourely. [f. sour *a.* Cf. MDu. *suur-, zuurlike*, MSw. *surliga.*]

1. In a sour, peevish, or disagreeable manner:

a. With intransitive verbs, esp. *to look.*

1533 Frith *Judgem. Tracy* (1829) 249 Why look you so sourly, good brethren? **1535** Coverdale *Ecclus.* xxii. 22 Yf he speake sowerly, feare not. **1598** Barckley *Felic. Man* (1631) 660 Who seemed to grind his teeth and to looke sowrely upon him. **1607** Shaks. *Cor.* v. iii. 13 Though I shew'd sowerly to him. **1675** Brooks *Gold. Key* Wks. 1867 V. 196 This truth looks very sourly and frowningly upon all such as deny the godhead of Christ. **1700** Dryden *Pal. & Arc.* ii. 303 To this reply'd the stern Athenian Prince, And sow'rly smild. **1726** Pope *Odyss.* xx. 183 Two dogs of chase..Behind him sourly stalk'd. **1835** Lytton *Rienzi* v. vii, The Cardinal smiled sourly. **1881** Miss Braddon *Asphodel* III. 279 'At eighteen I was not a fool,' replied Mrs. Ferrers sourly.

b. With transitive verbs.

1548 UDALL, etc. *Erasm. Par. Matt.* v. 42 Waye not sowrelye nor extremely whiche is more in faulte. **1583** MELBANCKE *Philotimus* T ij, I..being sourelie rebuked for fawning on thee, am yet as fruitfull in thy loue. **1642** H. MORE *Song of Soul* IV. iv, It did much displease, That any should so sourely him outface. **1697** DRYDEN *Æneid* IX. 52 They keep the strict command, And sourly wait in arms the hostile band. **1847** EMERSON *Poems, Threnody* Wks. (Bohn) I. 491 O richest fortune sourly crossed! Born for the future, to the future lost!

c. With adjectives.

1847 C. BRONTE *Jane Eyre* xviii, Her face grew momently ..more sourly expressive of disappointment. **1884** BROWNING *Ferishtah* Poet. Wks. 1907 XVI. 80 The sourly-Sage, for whom life's best was death.

2. With great dislike or distaste.

a **1548** HALL *Chron., Edw. IV*, 39 b, All the Constables promises were..swetely spoken, and sowerly performed. **1579** TWYNE *Phis. agst. Fortune* II. Ep. Ded. 161 What contention haue children with their bookes and learning, most sowerly sowing that, which they shall reape most sweetlie.

3. With sourness or acidity.

1574 HYLL *Bees* xiii, [One] not breathing sourly or of a stinking breath. **1881** *Standard* 29 Oct. 1/2 I'd try their sourness, if I knew Where those gooseberries sourly grew.

sourmouncie: see SURMOUNCY.

sourness ('saʊənɪs). Also 1 surnes, 5–6 sowrenes, 5–7 -ness(e, sowernes(se, 5 sour-, 6 sourenes, 6–7 -nesse, etc. [f. SOUR *a.*]

1. The quality of being physically sour; acidity, tartness.

c **1050** in Wr.-Wülcker 347 *Acredinis*, surnesse. *c* **1400** *Lanfranc's Cirurg.* 195 An oynement maad of armoniac & with þe sournes of citri. **14..** *Contin. Brut* ccxxiv. 292 þe fruyte of þe erþe..were turned into more saltnes & sournes of sauour. **1532** TINDALE *Exp. Matt. v–vii.* (1550) 67 As thou couldest not se leuen though thou breakest vp a loffe, excepte thou smelledest and tastedeste the sourenesse. **1551** TURNER *Herbal* II. 58 Unrype mulberries besyde theyr tartnes they haue also a sournes. **1605** TIMME *Quersit.* I. iv. 19 Sulphur..doth contemper the sharpnes or sowerness of mercurie. **1697** DRYDEN *Virg. Georg.* IV. 215 He knew to.. tame to Plumbs, the Sourness of the Sloes. **1731** MILLER *Gard. Dict.* s.v. *Malt-dust*, Where the Grounds..have contracted a Sourness and Austerity. **1765** *Universal Mag.* XXXVII. 371/2 Any little sournesses [of stomach] they may have. **1815** J. SMITH *Panorama Sci. & Art* II. 441 It has a slightly saltish taste, but no sourness. **1837** P. KEITH *Bot. Lex.* 6 They excite in the palate the sensation of sourness. **1864** *Hardwich's Phot. Chem.* (ed. 7) 12 The characteristics of acids may be stated to be, intense sourness and corrosiveness.

2. The quality of being sour in temper, disposition, or looks.

1482 *Monk of Evesham* xxx. (Arb.) 72 In thys that sche.. in her herte hylde rancour and sowernes agenste hem, sche gretely offendyd. **1548** ELYOT, *Tetricitas*, sowernesse..of countinaunce. **1608** DOD & CLEAVER *Expos. Prov. ix–x.* 120 Let not our sourenesse and discontentment..be any meanes of their discouragement. **1641** J. JACKSON *True Evang. T.* I. 69 The Millenaries..expect..that all sowernesse amongst Christians shall be absorpt of Charity. **1711** STEELE *Spect.* No. 2 ⁋1 This Humour creates him no Enemies, for he does nothing with Sourness or Obstinacy. **1779** COWPER *Let.* 31 Oct., Some sourness in his temper. **1821** LAMB *Elia.* I. *Old Benchers Inner T.*, His look was uninviting, resembling (but without his sourness) that of our great philanthropist. **1875** JOWETT *Plato* (ed. 2) V. 44 Drink..will mellow the sourness of age.

sourock ('sʊərək). *Sc.* Forms: 5 sowrok, 6 -ak, 7 -ock; 6 sourak, -och, 8– sourock (8 -uck, 9 -ack, -ick, sourrock, surrock, soorock). [f. SOUR *a.* Cf. MDu. *zuric* (Kilian *suerick*), MLG. *sureke* (LG. *sürken, sürk*), WFris. *surk*.] The common sorrel, *Rumex acetosa*; also, sheep's sorrel, *R. acetosella*.

c **1480** HENRYSON *Sum Pract. Med.* 29 Ane medecyne for þe maw,..with sueit satlingis and sowrokis. **1549** *Compl. Scot.* vi. 67, I sau..sourakkis, that vas gude for the blac gulset. **1596** in *Analecta Scotica* II. 13 The seid of..sorrelis or sourochis. **1673** WEDDERBURN *Voc.* 18 (Jam.), *Acetosa*, sowrocks. **1777** LIGHTFOOT *Flora Scotica* II. 1131 *Rumex acetosa*. The Sowruck. *Rumex acetosella*. Sheep's Sowruck. **1823** GALT *Entail* xxxiii, Ye hae been eating sourrocks instead o' lang-kail. *a* **1879** T. ORMOND in Edwards *Modern Sc. Poets* 2nd Ser. (1881) 356 Winnelstraes an' souricks grew On oor lumheid.

attrib. **1568** SKEYNE *Pest* (1860) 37 Mixt with thrid part of vater or with rose, or sowrak vatteris. **1865** JANET HAMILTON *Poems* 222 A bunch o' surrock seed in his haun'.

b. *fig.* A sour-tempered person.

1723 RAMSAY *Fair Assembly* xvi, Ye sourocks, hafflines fool, ha'f knave! Wha hate a dance or sang.

sourquidous, variant of SURQUIDOUS *a.*

soursaut, variant of SURSAULT *Obs.*

†**sourse deorse**, *adv. Obs.*$^{-1}$ [ad. L. *sursus deorsus* or *sursum deorsum*.] Up and down.

1616 J. LANE *Contn. Sqr.'s T.* IV. 200 Behold, amidd the aier, the brazen horse Came in his mayne carryer, of sourse deorse.

soursob ('saʊsɒb). *Austral.* [Alteration of SOUR-SOP, perh. in reference to the acid sap.] A bulbous plant, *Oxalis cernua*, of the family Oxalidaceæ, native to South Africa and widely naturalized as a weed elsewhere, bearing divided leaves and clusters of bright yellow bell-shaped flowers; also called the Bermuda buttercup.

1907 *Jrnl. Dept. Agric. S. Austral.* X. 802 Can anyone tell me to destroy a weed called by some 'Soursob'? **1909** J. M. BLACK *Naturalised Flora S. Austral.* 41 *Oxalis cernua*, Thunb. Soursob. **1961** *Times* 23 May 3/1 (Advt.), Biological control of several important weeds and pests of South African origin, such as cape tulip, spiny emex, soursob,.. white wax scale and black beetle. **1972** *Advertiser* (Adelaide) 2 Sept. 5/7 Never have I met an Englishman who actually grew soursobs or oxalis or whatever they are properly called at home.

sour-sop. *Bot.* Also sour sop, soursop. [f. SOUR *a.* + SOP *sb.*[1]]

1. The fruit of the West Indian tree, *Anona muricata*.

1667 *Phil. Trans.* II. 501 The Sower-sop, a pleasant fruit there, hath a flower with three leaves. **1683** TRYON *Way to Health* 570 Sweet Oranges and Lemmons, Plantans, Coco-Nuts, Sower-Sops, &c. **1703** DAMPIER *Voy.* III. I. 67 The Sour-sop (as we call it) is a large Fruit as big as a Man's Head,..and of a green Colour. **1740** *New Hist. Jamaica* 51 Fruits grow in great Plenty,..Mamies, sour Sops, Papas,.. and several Kind of Berries. *c* **1825** CHOYCE *Log Jack Tar* (1891) 22 We..got plenty and abundance of fruit, such as oranges, limes,..pears, soursops, &c. **1849** BALFOUR *Man. Bot.* §745 The Custard-apples, Sweetsops, and Soursops, of the East and West Indies, are furnished by various species of Anona. **1871** KINGSLEY *At Last* ii, It is the cousin of the prickly sour-sop.

2. The tree bearing this fruit.

1753 *Chambers' Cycl.* Suppl. *App.*, *Soure-sop*, or *Sowre-sop*, in botany, a distinct genus of plants, called by botanists *guanabanus* and *anona*. **1764** GRAINGER *Sugar Cane* I. 598 A neighbouring dell, (Which nature to the Soursop had resign'd). **1824** LOUDON *Encycl. Gard.* (ed. 2) §6732 The following are some of the most remarkable of the economical tropical plants... Sour-sop (*Annona muricata*). **1880** BESSEY *Botany* 561 *A. squamosa*, Sweet Sop, and *A. muricata*, Sour sop,..produce edible fruits.

3. = SOURSOB.

1885 *Garden & Field* (Adelaide) Aug. 29/3 'Amateur' wants to know a remedy for 'soursops', and if gas lime would do. *Ibid.* Sept. 41/1 Now there's a fellow who wants £500 to tell farmers how to kill the Soursops or oxalis. **1930** A. J. EWART *Flora of Victoria* 687 *O[xalis] cernua*..Soursop. A perennial with a brown bulb and a tapering root... A troublesome weed, native to South Africa, originally a garden escape.

4. *attrib.*, as ***sour-sop bird, tree.***

1696 SLOANE *Catal. Plantarum Jamaica* 204 The Sowre-sop Tree. **1756** P. BROWNE *Jamaica* 255 The Soursop Tree. This..is one of the most common plants in every Savanna. **1834** *Penny Cycl.* II. 54/2 The following spirited sketch..of the appearance of the sour sop tree. **1895** *Funk's Stand. Dict.* s.v., *Sour-sop bird*,..tanager (*Calliste versicolor*).

sour-sweet, *a.* and *sb.* [f. the adjs.]

A. *adj.* Sweet with an admixture or aftertaste of sourness. Also *fig.*

1591 SYLVESTER *Du Bartas* I. v. 279 The Scolopendra have suckt-in The sowr-sweet morsell with the barded Pin. **1601** MARKHAM *Mary Magd. Lament.* Pref. 18 They cannot sigh ..With contrite minds such soure-sweete throbs to stain. **1633** G. HERBERT *Temple, Bitter-sweet* ii, All my sowre-sweet dayes I will lament, and love. **1859** MEREDITH *R. Feverel* xxxviii, 'A choice of evils,' said Mrs. Doria's sour-sweet face and shake of the head. **1871** KINGSLEY *At Last* x, He..peels carefully off the skin,..and eats the sour-sweet refreshing pulp.

B. *sb.* Something which is sour-sweet; *spec.* an acid sweetmeat.

1603 J. DAVIES (Heref.) *Microcosmos* Wks. (Grosart) I. 42/2 Sinne's sowre-Sweetes do fleete To make the Mind abhorre her former lust. **1612** —— *Muse's Sacrifice* Ibid. II. 83/1 My Proheme is a Feast, Whereat my Muse doth surfet with sowre-sweetes. **1896** ACKWORTH *Clog Shop Chron.* 227 When Ben had taken his seat, and given a sour-sweet to each of the children.

sourtout, variant of SURTOUT.

†**'soury**, *a. Obs.*$^{-1}$ [f. SOUR *a.*] Sourish.

1647 CLARENDON *State Papers* II. 367 If I had a mind to be so sowery as to make comparisons with you.

‖**sous-** (su, suz), *prefix*, representing OF. and mod.F. *sous* (:—L. *subtus*) 'under', 'sub-', in a few words directly adopted from French, as the ME. †**sous-prior** [OF. *souspriour*, mod.F. *-prieur*], subprior; †**sous-cellarer** [OF. *souscelleriere* fem.], under-cellarer; and the later or modern **sous-basha, -chef, -lieutenant, -ministre, -officier, -prefect, -préfecture, -préfet** [F. *sous-préfet*].

(*a*) **1297** R. GLOUC. (Rolls) 10144 þe souspriour of hor hous þe monekes chose echon. **1426** LYDG. *De Guil. Pilgr.* 22237, I am Sowcelerere Off this place, and Pytauncere.

(*b*) **1687** A. LOVELL tr. *Thevenot's Trav.* I. 279 The Officer whom in Turky they call the *Sous-basha. **1825–40** F. BURNEY *Jrnls. & Lett.* (1980) VIII. 49 M. d'Arblay continued in his humbler office, of **sous chef* to one of the *Bureaux de l'Interieur*. **1902** A. BENNETT *Grand Babylon Hotel* xxi. 238 We have found in our second sous-chef an artist. **1973** *New Society* 15 Nov. 412/2, I gradually pieced together the hierarchy. After the chef..came Jacko, the sous-chef. **1980** N. FREELING *Castang's City* I. 1 Lasserre was a Commissaire... He was the sous-chef, the Chief of Staff. **1841** LEVER *C. O'Malley* I. 267, I was two days ago, *chasseur à cheval*, a *sous-lieutenant in the regiment of my father. **1855** *Chamb. Jrnl.* 24 Feb. 113/1 This Lord Milton was the acting **sous-ministre* for Scotland in the administration of Walpole. **1826** H. D. BESTE *Four Yrs. France* 318 He engaged a *sous-officier to come daily to the house to teach him the manual exercise. **1895** E. DOWSON *Let.* 2 Oct. (1967) 316 Owing to a great demand for lodgings by officiers and sous-officiers, we found it..impossible to find what we wanted. **1972** G. BELL *Villains Galore* vi. 68 He had been a *sous-officier* in the [Foreign] Legion. **1889** GUNTER *That Frenchman* xvii. 215 The imperial guardsman and *sous-prefect of the secret police. **1940** J. JOYCE *Let.* 16 Sept. (1966) III. 487 Our applications..passed through the *sous-préfecture of this department this morning. **1976** N. FREELING *Lake Isle* viii. 43 Soulay was a sous-préfecture, and sub-prefects are small beer. **1865** L. BOOTH in S. Pakenham *Sixty Miles from England* (1967) v. 67 Etiquette expects yearly residents to leave cards on the *Sous-Préfet. **1944** H. NICOLSON *Let.* 27 June (1967) 382 They went to the *souspréfecture*. The *sous-préfet*..had been secretary to Pucheu. **1974** E. AMBLER *Dr Frigo* III. 186 The sous-Préfet assured me of his most distinguished sentiments.

†**'sousant**, *a. Obs.*$^{-1}$ A mock-heraldic term f. SOUSE *v.*[1]

1595 *Enq. Tripe-wife* in Grosart *Eliz. Eng.* (1881) 172 A Chitterling rampant in a field sowsant, two haggas puddings for the supporters.

sousaphone ('suːzəfəʊn). Also Sousaphone. [f. the name of John Philip *Sousa* (1854–1932), American bandmaster and composer, after *saxophone*, etc. (see also quot. 1939).] A large bass wind instrument of the helicon type. Also *attrib.*

1925 *Punch* 27 May 561/3 An instrument called the Sousaphone weighs eighteen pounds and is twenty feet long. **1935** *Ibid.* 23 Oct. 470/2 As it was removed from its case he saw that it was a sousaphone—the instrument that plays the 'oom' in Viennese waltzes while the rest of the orchestra follows with the 'wump wump'. **1939** *Internat. Cycl. Mus.* 1772/2 The first sousaphone was made by C. G. Conn in 1899 expressly for Sousa's band and its bell opened directly upward. The present bell-front type was first made in 1908. **1958** [see EXOTICA]. **1974** P. DE VRIES *Glory of Hummingbird* i. 4 The sousaphone tuba he played in the local marching band.

souse (saʊs), *sb.*[1] Now chiefly *dial.* and *U.S.* Forms: 4 sows, 5–9 sowse (5 sowsse), sowce; 5–8 souce, 5 sovse, 6– souse. [a. OF. *sous* (*souz, soulz, soult*, = Prov. *soutz, sols*), or *souce*, ad. OHG. *sulza*, OS. *sulta*, or directly f. the Germanic stem *sult-* (see SALT *v.*[1] and SILT *sb.*), whence also It. *solcio* pickle, condiment.

The OF. forms, partly given by Godefroy under *soult*, are specially illustrated and discussed by A. Thomas in *Romania* (1909), pp. 579–582.]

1. a. Various parts of a pig or other animal, esp. the feet and ears, prepared or preserved for food by means of pickling.

1391 *Durham Acc. Rolls* (Surtees) 50 In uno dolio emp. pro le sows, ijs. ijd. **14..** *Lat.-Eng. Voc.* in Wr.-Wülcker 614 *Succidium*, Sovse. *c* **1440** *Promp. Parv.* 466/1 Sowce, mete, *succidium*. *c* **1460** J. RUSSELL *Bk. Nurture* 360 in *Babees Bk.* (1868) 139 Salt, sowre, and sowse, alle suche þow set a-side. *a* **1529** SKELTON *Agst. Garnesche* iii. 32 Ye slvfferd vp sowse In my lady Brewsys howse. **1595** *Enq. Tripe-wife* in Grosart *Eliz. Eng.* (1881) 149 Thy tripes were yong, thy neates feete fat and faire, Thy sowse was sweete. *a* **1625** FLETCHER *Woman's Prize* I. iv, I'll tell you in a word, I am sent to lay An Imposition upon Souse and Puddings, Pasties, and penny Custards. **1675** HANNAH WOOLLEY *Gentlew. Comp.* 154 Soust Veal, Lamb, [etc.];..boil it close covered, that the souse may look white. **1706** PHILLIPS (ed. Kersey), *Souce*, ..a kind of Jelly, made of Hogs-Ears and Feet boil'd in Water, and afterwards cut into small Pieces, to be stew'd in Vinegar and Sugar. **1725** *Fam. Dict.* s.v., To make an Intermess of Souse, let Hogs Ears and Feet be boil'd after the usual manner [etc.]. **1829** BROCKETT *N.C. Gloss.* (ed. 2), *Souse*, a dish composed of pig's ears, etc. fried. **1854** H. H. RILEY *Puddleford* 147 [I] can give you mush, souse, slap-jacks, briled pork. **1872** DE VERE *Americanisms* 549 *Souse*.. means in Pennsylvania more generally pigs' feet. **1929** W. J. LOCKE *Ancestor Jorico* viii. 108 We were given..souse, which is the gelatinous parts of a pig pickled in lime-juice. **1952** S. SELVON *Brighter Sun* ii. 23 They make souse—boiled pork, seasoned with lime and pepper and cucumber. **1958** B. HAMILTON *Too Much of Water* iv. 74 A real Barbadian breakfast. 'Maan,' he said, 'I give you flying fish an' pepper-pot, an' pudding and souse.' **1974** *Sunday Advocate-News* (Barbados) 10 Mar. 8/1 She is selling a popular Barbadian delicacy—pudding and souse.

b. *transf.* The ears; also in *sing.*, an ear.

a **1658** CLEVELAND *Model New Rel.* 33 How Quops the Spirit? In what Garb or Air? With Souse erect, or Pendent, Winks, or Haws? **1673** MRS. BEHN *Dutch Lover* III. ii, A slink, greasie Hair..through which a pair of large thin souses appear'd. **1708** *Brit. Apollo* No. 57. 2/2 The Dog their large Sowces soon bit. **1787** GROSE *Prov. Gloss.*, *Souse*, the ear, most properly that of a hog, from its being frequently pickled or sowsed. **1825** JENNINGS *Obs. Dial. W. Eng.* 71 *Souse*,..the ear. *Pigs sousen*, pigs ears. **1895** *Dial. Notes* (Amer. Dial. Soc.) I. 383 'Bounder your souse well' = wash your ears well.

2. a. A liquid employed as a pickle.

1502 ARNOLDE *Chron.* (1811) 189 Take..fenell sede broken and bounde in a clothe and ley it in the same souse for oon day. **1523** FITZHERB. *Husb.* §121 Ready at all tymes to eate in the wynter season, and to be layde in souse. **1620** VENNER *Via Recta* iii. 70 The feete of a Bullocke or Heifer, ..tenderly sodden, and layed in sowce. **1706** PHILLIPS (ed. Kersey), *Souce*, a sort of Pickle for a Collar of Brawn, Pork, &c. **1801** *The Port-Folio* I. 352 (Thornton), Thy ears and feet in Souse shall lie. **1883** 'ANNIE THOMAS' *Mod. Housewife* 102 The savoury 'souses' of vinegar, bay-leaves, and spices into which we plunged the other [fish] when baked.

fig. **1619** FLETCHER, etc. *Knt. Malta* II. i, I am in souce I thank ye; thanke your beauty. **1650** T. B[AYLEY] *Worcester's Apoph.* 101 As a thing newly taken out of the sowse of so many friends blood. **1675** HOBBES *Odyssey* VIII. 331 After he had left Calypso's house Warm and sweet water he had never seen, But roll'd by Neptune always was in souse.

†**b.** *to sell souse*: (see quot.). *Obs.*

1611 Cotgr. s.v. *Groin, Faire le groin*, to powt, lowre, frowne, be sullen, or surlie; to hang the lip, or sell sowce.

3. *attrib.* and *Comb.*, as *souse-ale, -drink, -fish, -kit, meat, -seller, -tub, -wife, -woman.*

In some cases perhaps the verbal stem.

1444 *Compota Domest.* (Abbotsford Club) 25 Liberantur Roberto Cooke pro *sowceale..C lagene (bere). **1653** *Bibliotheca Parl.* 3 A Garden of sweet flowers, or a Senator in *Souce-drink, by Alderman Atkins. **1676** *Phil. Trans.* XI. 600 They were put..in souse-drink, or pickle. **1704** *Dict. Rust.* s.v. *Brawn*, Put them into Souce-drink made of Oatmeal..and bran boyled in fair Water. **1695** Wood *Life* (O.H.S.) III. 495 All sorts of *souse fish (lobsters, crayfish). **1565** *Richmond Wills* (Surtees) 179 In the larder..j *sowse-kytt, and j bread grater. **1578** *Knaresborough Wills* (Surtees) I. 133 Two sousekittes. **1972** E. Wigginton *Foxfire Bk.* 20 *Souse meat. Boy, that's the best stuff I ever eat. **1976** *Washington Post* 7 Nov. KI/5 We will try to re-create the atmosphere of a country store. Sardines,..souse meat and soda crackers. **1648** Hexham I, A *Sowse seller. **1561** *Entert. Temple* in Nicholas *Progr. Q. Eliz.* I. 137 The Clerk of the Kitchen..and the Clark of the *Sowce-tub. **1630** J. Taylor (Water P.) *Gt. Eater Kent* 10 Eighteene yards of blacke puddings..haue suddenly been imprisoned in his sowse-tub. **1706** J. Dunton in *Life & Errors* (1818) II. 451 His brains are in a perpetual souce-tub: the pickle..is only changed from Ale to Wine. **1887** Parish & Shaw *Kentish Gloss.* 156 Sowse-tub. **1592** Greene *Upst. Courtier* Wks. (Grosart) XI. 284 He knoweth..what the *sowse wiues are able to make of the inwards. **1622** Fletcher *Prophetess* I. iii, Ye may be an honest butcher or allied to an honest family of sowse-wives. **1620** Markham *Farew. Husb.* (1668) 46 You shall then deal with Butchers, *Sowse-women, Slaughter-men, scullions and the like.

souse (saʊs), *sb.*[2] Now *dial.* Forms: 5-7 sowce, 6 souce; 5, 7, 9 sowse, 6- souse, 8 souze (9 *dial.* zouse, etc.). [Of obscure origin, perh. imitative; cf. MHG. and MLG. *sûs* (G. *saus*, Du. *gesuis*, etc.), noise, din.]

1. A heavy blow; a thump.

1480 *Robt. Devyll* 228 in Hazl. *E.P.P.* I. 228 Pryuelye behynde them woulde he steale, And geue them a sowce with hys hande. **1567** Golding *Ovid's Met.* v. (1593) 108 To Petales he lendeth such a souse Full in the noddle of the necke. **1596** Spenser *F.Q.* IV. viii. 44 His murdrous mace he vp did reare, That seemed nought the souse thereof could beare. **1638** Heywood *Wise Wom.* II. i, Now what did I? but spying the Watch, went and hit the Constable a good sowse on the Eare. **1653** Urquhart *Rabelais* I. xxvii, To some with a smart souse on the Epigaster he would make their midriff swag. **1778** Miss Burney *Evelina* xxi, I desire he'll give you such another souse as he did before. **1809** T. Donaldson *Poems* 13 I'd daud or gie him weel his souses. **1825-** in many dialect glossaries. **1893** Cozens-Hardy *Brd. Norf.* 5 One boy will give another a clip o' the head or a sowse o' the skull.

b. *souse for souse*, blow for blow.

1575 Turberv. *Faulconrie* 55 The hobby..dares encounter the crowe, and to giue souse for souse and blowe for blowe with him in the ayre. **1581** Rich *Farew.* (1846) 208 There was betweene them souse for souse, and boxe for boxe, that it was harde to judge who should have the victorie.

2. A heavy fall. (Cf. soss *sb.*[2])

1774 D. Graham *Hist. Rebellion* (ed. 3) 70 He first fell on a thatched house, Next on a midden with a *souse*. *c* **1890** Lyttle *Robin Gordon* 79 (E.D.D.), A wud wauken up wi' the souse she cum doon on the grun.'

†**souse**, *sb.*[3] *Hawking. Obs.* Forms: 5-6 souce, 6-7 sowce, souse, 7 sowse. [Alteration of source *sb.* 2 a.]

1. The act, on the part of a bird, of rising from the ground, as giving the hawk an opportunity to strike. Only in phr. *at* (*the*) *souse.*

1486 *Bk. St. Albans, Hawking* d j b, Iff youre hawke nym the fowle a lofte: ye shall say she toke it at the mounte or at the souce. **1575** Turberv. *Faulconrie* 127 The Sparowhawkes do vse to kill the fowle at the Sowrce or Souse, as the Goshawkes do, whiche nature hathe taught them. *c* **1595** Capt. Wyatt *Dudley's Voy.* (Hakl. Soc.) 20 The fowle noe soener is putt of from the ryver for the servinge of her, but præsentlie shee falleth and killeth her praie at sowce. **1618** Latham *Falconry* (1633) 49 That will cause her to..master them, as it were, at the sowce, within a short space, being no way able in that season to make wing, to hold out before such a Hawke. **1620** Fletcher *Chances* IV. i, Her feares creeping upon her, Dead as a fowle at souse, she'll sinke.

fig. **1600** W. Watson *Decacordon* (1602) 145 They [Jesuits] haue, like great fawcons or hawkes of the Tower, firmely seazed vpon the pray, kild, at randon, wing, or souce.

2. The act, on the part of a hawk, of swooping down upon a bird. Also *fig.*

Perh. partly due to confusion with souse *sb.*[2]

1590 Spenser *F.Q.* II. xi. 36 As a Faulcon faire That once hath failed of her souse full neare. *a* **1618** Sylvester *Maiden's Blush* 342 The stout Ger-Faulcon stoopeth at the Herne, With sudden Souse, that many scarce discerne. **1638** Ford *Fancies* III. ii, I presume she is a wanton, And therefore mean to give the sowse whenever I find the game on wing.

†**souse**, *sb.*[4] *Obs.* Forms: (see below). [a. OF. *sous* (also *soux, souz*), pl. of *sout, solt*, later *sol* sol *sb.*[3] and *sou* sou. See also soulx.

Instances in rime show that the usual pron. was (saʊs): cf. Smart (1836) 'in plain vulgar English we say *a sowse*'.]

1. A French coin and money of account, equal to the twentieth part of a livre; a sol or sou.

a. *pl.* α. 6 sousz, 6-8 sous, 7 soues. β. 6 sowse (sowese), 6-7 souse, 6, 8 souce, 7 sowce.

For 19th cent. examples of *sous* see sou.

α. **1502** Arnolde *Chron.* (1811) 190 Item xv. sousz of Burdeux makithe a franke whiche is ij. s. *a* **1513** Fabyan *Chron.* VII. ccxxxv. (1516) 158 They shuld paye to the sayd Abbot & Couent lx. M. Sous. **1600** Surflet *Countrie Farme* I. xxi. 120 The men of old..sold them in the time of the Romaines for ten Sous a peece. **1633** in *Northern N. & Q.* I. 93 My fencin and dansin extendes monthli to 25 lib. 10 soues. **1707** in *Sewall's Diary* (1879) II. 37* Shot..was Sold at 13 Sous per Pound.

β. **1512** *Acc. Ld. High Treas. Scot.* IV. 294 Aucht hundretht foure skoire three frankis xj sowse, spendit be the said Johne Balȝard. *a* **1548** Hall *Chron., Hen. V*, 45 b, A greate part of the women and children he expelled the toune, gevyng to every poore creature five sowse. **1586** T. B. *La Primaud. Fr. Acad.* I. 426 A bill..wherein is set downe 20. souse for two new sleeves to his old dublet. **1600** Hakluyt *Voy.* (1810) III. 258, I thinke all that they had together..was not worth five souce. *a* **1618** Raleigh *Obs.* in *Remains* (1661) 200 The King hath raised his silver four Sowce in the Crown. **1690** Strutton *Relat. Cruelties of French* 27 Here our grand Driver..gave us five Souse a Man. **1759** B. Martin *Nat. Hist.* I. 128 The Plaintiff must allow him five Souce per day.

b. *sing.* α. 6-9 sous. β. 6-7, 9 sowse, 7 sowce; 6-9 souse.

α. *a* **1513** Fabyan *Chron.* VII. ccxxxv. (1516) 158 A sous is in value after starlyng money I.d. ob. **1568** *Satir. Poems Reform.* xlvi. 38 Quhair scho findis a fallow fyne, He wilbe frawcht-fre for a sous. **1611** Cotgr., *Sol*, a Sous, or the French shilling. **1675** H. Nevile tr. *Machiavelli's Wks., State France* 262 A sous or penny a day for their Chamber. **1808** *Sporting Mag.* XXXII. 63 Such a potful, indeed, costs only one sous. **1823** in J. A. Heraud *Voy. & Mem. Midshipman* viii. (1837) 137 Grapes are a sous a pound, and peaches twelve for a sous, which is a halfpenny.

β. **1528** Sir R. Weston in Dillon *Calais & Pale* (1892) 91 Of every cowe or oxe j souse frenche. **1547** Boorde *Introd. Knowl.* xxvii. (1870) 191 A sowse is worth .xii. bras pens. **1624** Heywood *Captives* v. iii. in Bullen *O. Pl.* IV, Tush, offer me a sowse but not in th' eare. **1655** tr. *Sorel's Com. Hist. Francion* v. 10 The Showes at the Fair of St. Germans, which he had seen not long before for a Souse. *a* **1658** Cleveland *Model New Rel.* 21 For Sprats are rose an Omer for a Souse.

c. *pl.* 6 souces, sowces, *Sc.* soussis, sowsis, 6-7 sowses, 7 souses, souzes.

1523 Ld. Berners *Froiss.* I. clv. 187 Labourers and worke-men..shall pay x. souces. **1550** *Records of Elgin* (New Spald. Cl.) I. 103 Ordanit that na persoun..rafuse..sowsis that pass nocht throch the ring and mesour. **1577** in Ellis *Orig. Lett.* Ser. III. IV. 25 The Frenche Kinge hathe coyned newe sowces. **1611** Speed *Hist. Gt. Brit.* IX. xv. 94 A fat Mutton was solde for sixe Souses of Paris money. **1655** tr. *Sorel's Com. Hist. Francion* VIII. 28, I have consented to give six Souses for that which is worth but four.

2. Taken as a type of a small coin or amount, with an expressed or implied negative.

α. **1570** *Satir. Poems Reform.* xx. 78 The murther..thay do deny, And countis ȝow not ane sous. **1677** Otway *Cheats of Scapin* II. i, Not a Sous, damn'd Rascal, let him turn Foot-Soldier and be hang'd. **1709** E. Ward *Rambling Fuddle-Caps* 13 But, Nouns, if the Rake-hell continues thus loose, In Revenge, I'll not leave the young Rebel a Sous. **1761** Churchill *Rosciad* 212 Next came the treasurer of either house; One with full purse, t'other with not a sous. **1805** R. Anderson *Cumbld. Ball.* 31 Silly Tom Linton left nit werth a sous.

β. **1676** D'Urfey *Mme. Fickle* I. i, He has no Money now, not a souse—I know it. **1694** Echard *Plautus* 199 By George, you shan't be a Sowce the better for what's in it. **1708** Mrs. Centlivre *Busie Body* I. i, *Sir Geo.* How cam'st thou by such a liberal Education? *Cha.* Not a Souse out of his Pocket, I assure you. **1782** Miss Burney *Cecilia* VIII. viii, There was your friend,..that shot out his brains without paying any body a souse. **1812** Colman *Br. Grins, Elder Bro.* (1819) 113 To lounge, and chat, not minding time a souse. **1815** W. H. Ireland *Scribbleomania* 157 The first, though at times having scarcely a souse, Talks loudly, forsooth, of her Old Manor House.

souse (saʊs), *sb.*[5] Also 8 souze. [f. souse *v.*[1]]

1. a. An act of sousing; a plunge into, immersion in, or drenching with, water; *dial.*, a wash.

1741 Lady M. W. Montagu *Corr.* (1906) I. 88, I have sent for my bathing Cloaths, and on Sunday night shall take a souze. **1793** *Minstrel* I. 185, I was a little unsensed by my sudden souse into the stream. **1820** Scott *Monast.* v, Still keeping her hand on his collar, she gave him two or three good souses in the watery fluid. **1864** Dk. Manch. *Court & Society* I. 192 A sack and a souse in the river not suiting his tastes. **1889** Gretton *Memory's Harkback* 107, I was once saved from a souse in Milford Haven by the coachman's presence of mind.

b. A heavy drinking-bout. *U.S. slang.*

1903 G. Ade *People you Know* 13 (*heading*) The periodical souse. **1930** E. Wallace *Calendar* xviii. 244 If ever a man had an excuse for a souse, you've got it. **1946** E. O'Neill *Iceman Cometh* III. 199 Bejees, we'll go on a grand old souse together.

2. A sound as of water surging against something.

1883 F. M. Crawford *Mr. Isaacs* x. 212 His voice was again drowned in the swish and souse of the water.

3. A drunkard. *slang* (chiefly *U.S.*).

1915 J. London *Jacket* 213, I remember you mentioned playing chess with that royal souse of an emperor's brother. **1936** Wodehouse *Laughing Gas* i. 11 The lad.., who is pretty generally recognized as London W.1's most prominent souse. **1953** R. Chandler *Long Good-Bye* v. 27 Sylvia is not a souse. When she does get over the edge it's pretty drastic.

souse, *sb.*[6] *Arch.* [AF. *souse* (1395 in Rymer *Fœd.* VII. 794), app. a later form of source *sb.* I.] (See quots. and source *sb.* I.)

1836 Parker *Gloss. Archit.* (1850) I. 431 *Souse*, an old term for a corbel, now become obsolete. **1842** Gwilt *Archit.* Gloss., *Souse* or *Source*, a support or under-prop.

souse (saʊs), *v.*[1] Forms: 4- souse, 4-8 sowse (6 sawse, sewse), 7 souze, 7-8 sowze, 9 *dial.* soose; 5-7 sowce, 6-7, 9 souce. [f. souse *sb.*[1], or ad. OF. **souser*.]

I. *trans.* **1. a.** To prepare or preserve (meat, fish, etc.) by steeping in some kind of pickle, esp. one made with vinegar or other tart liquor.

1387 Trevisa *Higden* (Rolls) VII. 217 Þere Tostius hakked his broþer servantes, and sowsede here lemes, and sente word to þe kyng þat..he schulde have salt mete i-now. *c* **1400** Maundev. (1839) xxiii. 251 Thei sleen hem alle, and kutten of hire Eres, and sowcen hem in Vynegre. *c* **1430** *Two Cookery-bks.* 12 An ȝif it sowsyd be, lete it stepe a whyle in hot water tyl it be tendere. ? *a* **1500** *Chester Pl.* (Shaks. Soc.) I. 123 Loe! heares a sheepes heade sawsed in ale. **1530** Palsgr. 725/2, I souce meate, I laye it in some tarte thynge, as they do brawne or suche lyke. **1597** Breton *Wit's Trenchmour* Wks. (Grosart) II. 11/1 A Tench sowsed, a Smelt fried, and a Shrimp new sodden, are serued in their best kindes. **1641** W. Cartwright *Lady-Errant* v. i, If they catch the Amazons, They sowce 'em straight, as we do pig, by quarters, Or else do pickle 'em up for winter sallads. **1697** *Phil. Trans.* XIX. 618 An excellently well tasted fish, especially when soused. **1771** Mrs. Haywood *New Present for Maid* 268 To souce a Capon. **1782** Miss Burney *Cecilia* v. ix, Got a lobster, and two crabs;..stink already;..forced to souse 'em in vinegar. **1859** Trollope *West Indies* iii. 44 No Horace will teach us..how best to souse our living poultry, so that their fibres when cooked may not offend our teeth.

fig. **1625** B. Jonson *Staple of N.* IV. iv. (1905) 95 Fine Songs, Which we will haue at dinner, steept in claret, And against supper, sowc't in sacke. *a* **1704** T. Brown *Contin. Quaker's Serm.* Wks. 1709 III. II. 4 Sowse us therefore in the Powdering-Tub of thy Mercy, that we may be Tripes fit for the Heavenly Table.

b. *transf.* To steep or soak *in* honey, oil, etc.

1636 Davenant *Wits* (1673) 206 You talk'd too of fat Snails..Sous'd in Luca Oyl. **1658** tr. *Porta's Nat. Magic* IV. ix. 129 Quinces..to be smeared over with wax, and then to be sowsed in honey.

2. a. To plunge or immerse (a person, etc.) deeply or thoroughly *in* or *into* water, etc. Also with other preps. and without const.

(*a*) **1470-85** Malory *Arthur* IX. xix. 366 He sousyd sire Dagonet in that welle. **1530** Palsgr. 725/2 He souced him in the water over heed and eares. **1570** B. Googe *Pop. Kingd.* III. (1880) 31 But such as..unbelieuers be, No pardon haue though ten times in the fludde they sowsed be. **1600** Surflet *Countrie Farme* I. xxviii. 170 To souse him euery day..in sea water, three or fower times a day. **1660** R. Coke *Power & Subj.* 158 To be soused over head and ears in cold water. **1703** Steele *Tender Husb.* III. iii, When I like thee, may I be soused over head and ears in a horse-pond! **1836** Sir G. Head *Home Tour* 418 Twice during the passage, one horse..as narrowly as possible escaped being soused in the canal. **1865** M. Arnold *Ess. Crit.* viii. 267 A blazing caldron in which Beelzebub is sousing the damned.

(*b*) **1616** Surfl. & Markh. *Country Farme* I. lxvii. 328 You shall gently take the Hiue from the stone, and sowse it into a sowe of water. **1709** Steele *Tatler* No. 15 ¶2 He sous'd me Head and Ears into a Pail of Water. **1720** *Pol. Ballads* (1860) II. 203 For now the contrivers are tipt with a fee If they souse the subscribers into the South Sea. **1793** *Regal Rambler* 64 He..overturned Master Tommy..and soused him into a deep ditch. **1807-8** W. Irving *Salmag.* (1824) 328 To ascertain the fact by sousing him into a kettle of hot water.

(*c*) **1596** Nashe *Saffron Walden* 4 Like a horse plunging through the myre in the deep of winter, now soust vp to the saddle, and straight aloft on his tiptoes. **1663** J. Heath *Flagellum* 13 The said Master of Mis-rule perceiving the matter, caused him..to be thrown into a Pond adjoyning to the House, and there to be sous'd over head and ears. **1736** Fielding *Pasquin* IV. Wks. 1784 III. 282 One..tumbled down, And he and all his briefs were sous'd together. **1806** J. Neild in Pettigrew *Mem. Lettsom* (1817) II. 197 On this [chair] the woman was placed, and soused three times under water.

b. In pa. pple. with implication of sense 3.

1508 Fisher *7 Penit. Ps.* cxlii. Wks. (1876) 244 The synner is lyke vnto a sowe sowsed in dyrte & myre. **1580** Blundevil *Horsemanship* IV. xxxvi. 17 b, Take a peece of Sponge sowsed well in strong Vinegar. **1633** P. Fletcher *Purple Isl.* VII. lxxiii, His soul quite sowced lay in grapie bloud. **1712** Arbuthnot *John Bull* (1727) 109 Like Ulysses upon his plank after he had been well soused in salt-water. **1747** Richardson *Clarissa* (1811) II. xxiii. 149 To send her home well soused in..our deepest horse-pond. **1845** Darwin *Voy. Nat.* iv. (1879) 76 My animal fell, and I was well soused in black mire.

c. *fig.* or in fig. context.

1567 *Satir. Poems Reform.* iv. 100 Quhat toung..in silence suir can rest? To se ane saule in sorow sowsit. **1583** Greene *Mamillia* Wks. (Grosart) II. 117 This new betrothed couple..are..soused in the seas of sorrow. **1646** G. Daniel *Poems* Wks. (Grosart) II. 4 Some souce in bitter Inke, The venome which they thinke, To taxe the Times. **1680** Otway *Caius Marius* IV. i, Let us to yon adjacent Village, and sowse our selves in good Falernium. *a* **1734** North *Examen* I. i. §21 (1740) 25 Then comes the Treaty and we know not which way to turn, till the Author souces us down in Intrigue. **1781** C. Johnston *Hist. J. Juniper* II. 236 The poverty I had lately been soused in, sweetened my present affluence. **1897** Mary Kingsley *W. Africa* 146 But the planter tells him all, sousing him in torrents of words.

3. a. To drench or soak with water, etc.

a **1542** Wyatt *Mean & Sure Estate Poems* (1810) 385 The stormy blastes her caue so sore did sowse;..That..She must lye colde, and wet. **1555** Bradford in *Coverdale's Lett. Martyrs* (1564) 281 The showres that ye nowe feele and are soused in. **1594** *Merry Knack to know a Knave* in Hazl. *Dodsley* VI. 565 Sous'd with the surge of Neptune's wat'ry main. **1630** J. Taylor (Water P.) *Discov. by Sea* Wks. II. 22/1 We were enclosed with most dangerous sands. There were we sowsd & slabber'd, wash'd & dash'd. **1786** Mme. D'Arblay *Diary* 6 Oct., After being wet through over head, and soused through under feet,..what lives we do lead!

1810 E. D. Clarke *Trav. Russia* (1839) 34/1, I descended a second time, and was again soused with vessels of water. **1822** Miss Mitford in L'Estrange *Life* (1870) II. vii. 153, I am afraid [he] got soused in the thunder-storm, owing to his gallantry. **1871** Meredith *H. Richmond* xi, Then the engines arrived and soused the burning houses.

b. *fig.* in various senses. †In 18th cent., to impose upon, to swindle, etc.

1545 *Primer Henry VIII* (Parker Soc.) 99 We have now suffered much punishment, being soused with so many wars. **1548** Udall, etc. *Erasm. Par. John* viii. 59 Inwardly in their hertes soused and washed with much more enormious sin. **1608** Middleton *Trick to catch Old One* I. iv. 68, I soused 'em with bills of charges. **1678** Otway *Friendship in F.* IV. i, Death, and the Devil! how that puny Rogue Valentine has souced me? **1778** Foote *Trip Calais* I. Wks. 1799 II. 341, I reckon, your lordships were swingingly sous'd on the road? **1832** Cobbett *Rur. Rides* (1885) II. 383 The Dean and Chapter of Durham.. souse him so often with their fines. **1901** *Daily News* 2 Mar. 3/4 When the guns and pom-poms came into action at a gallop and soused the kopjes with shells.

c. Of rain or water: To drown *out* (a fire).

1891 Baring-Gould *In Troubadour-Land* viii. 110, I found that rain and wind had blown and soused out their little fire.

d. To intoxicate thoroughly. Chiefly in pa. pple. Now *slang*.

1613 [see soused *ppl. a.* 2]. **1902** H. L. Wilson *Spenders* ix. 87, I could see then that he was good and soused. **1953** K. Tennant *Joyful Condemned* xxxi. 306 Grandma used to get a bit soused sometimes, but she fed me O.K. **1976** M. Russell *Double Deal* vi. 46 Ralph's a pro. He's soused every night, and I don't recall an edition going astray yet.

†**4.** With *up*: ? To bring to extremities. *Obs.*

1534 More *Comf. agst. Trib.* I. Wks. 1163/1 Let hym go to no leache craft, nor any maner phisick,.. for sirops shold sowce him vp. *c* **1557** *How a Serjeaunt* 20 in Hazl. *E.P.P.* III. 120 An olde trotte.. With hir phisicke will keepe one sicke, till she haue sowsed him vp.

5. To dash or pour (a quantity of water or something containing this). Const. *into*, *on*, etc.

1859 Geo. Eliot *A. Bede* xxviii, 'Dip my cravat in and souse it on my head'. The water seemed to do him some good. **1901** Buchanan *Poems* 44 (E.D.D.), A pail o' cauld water.. was soosed into my face.

II. *intr.* **6. a.** To soak; to be or become soaked or drenched; to fall with a plunge; to go plunging or sinking in water, etc.

c **1400** Maundev. (Roxb.) xxvi. 123 Þai.. layes þam in vynegre for to sowce. **1584–7** Greene *Carde of Fancie* Wks. (Grosart) IV. 81 Iupiter himselfe,.. if I had sowsed in the roaring Seas,.. would haue prouided some happie Dolphin. **1593** Nashe *Christ's T.* (Grosart) IV. 54 All the sinnes of the first World now welter, souse, and beate vnquietly in the Sea. **1678** Shipman *Hen. III of France* II. ii, Through the lowest Region I flew, Sousing through falling Bogs of Dew. **1679** Alsop *Melius Inq.* II. iii. 256 Men of parts.. are necessitated to sowze over head and ears into Compliance at first Dash. **1781** Mme. D'Arblay *Let. to Mrs. Thrale* 6 Feb., How shall I keep from stepping into a post-chaise, and sousing through Gascoyne Lane to look after you? **1840** Thackeray *Barber Cox* Sept., The vessel rode off a little, the board slipped, and down I soused into the water. **1898** M. Hewlett *Forest Lovers* vi, It's a pity to disturb this baby of mine. Saracen and I had better souse.

b. *dial.* To have a thorough wash.

1895 *Dial. Notes* (Amer. Dial. Soc.) I. 400 I'll go and souse. **1897** Jane *Lordship* xvii. 201 Sousing down to the waist every Sabbath morning.

c. To drink so as to become intoxicated, to carouse. *slang.*

1921 E. O'Neill in *Theatre Arts Mag.* V. 32 Ain't you sousin' with 'em most every day? **1923** M. Watts *Luther Nichols* 43 Just as they're middling honest and don't souse.

†**7.** To flow or fall in copious streams. *Obs.*

1591 Drayton *Harmony of the Church* (Percy Soc.) 14 The surging seas came sousing in againe. **1648** J. Beaumont *Psyche* I. xix, Three times he spew'd Fell sulphur upward: which when on his face It soused back, foul Blasphemy ensu'd. *Ibid.* XIV. clix, That storm in full career Broke down and sous'd directly on His Head.

souse (saʊs), *v.*[2] Now *dial.* Forms: 6 sowse, 6– souse (8 *dial.* **sawse**, 9 *Sc.* **soose**); 6, 8 **souce**, 7 **sowce**. [Related to souse *sb.*[2]]

1. To strike, smite, or beat severely or heavily.

15.. *Parl. Byrdes* 128 in Hazl. *E.P.P.* III. 173 Than prayed all the common house, That some myght the hauke souse. [Cf. 136 To distroy the Hauke and all his blood.] **1575** *Gamm. Gurton* III. iii. 46 Hoyse her, souse her, bounce her, trounce her, pull out her throte-boule. **1596** Spenser *F.Q.* IV. iv. 30 So sore he sowst him on the compast creast. ? *c* **1630** Triplet in Aubrey *Brief Lives* (1898) I. 264 He took up the pillion Of his bouncing maid Jillian, And sowc't her like a baggage. **1703** Thoresby *Lett.*, *Souse*, or *Sawse*, on the ears, *v.* to box. **1725** *New Cant. Dict.*, *To Souse*, to fall upon, to beat cruelly; also to plunder or kill. *a* **1743** Ralph *Misc. Poems* (1747) 4 Up flew her hand to souse the cowren lad. **1787** W. Taylor *Scottish Poems* 112 For soundly did he souse my pate. **1809**– in dial. glossaries, etc.

b. With advs. or preps.: To dash *against*, knock or cast *down*, etc., with or by a heavy blow or impact.

a **1593** Marlowe tr. *1st Bk. Lucan* 296 Souse downe the wals, and make a passage forth. **1789** Mrs. Piozzi *Journ. France* I. 399 The people.. always take delight to souce an Englishman's hat upon his head. *a* **1813** A. Wilson *Foresters* Poet. Wks. (Belfast ed.) 263 Musk-rats and 'possums in each hand he bore;.. And as he soused them down with surly gloom [etc.]. **1828** Moir *Mansie Wauch* xv. 221 The de'il.. soosing her doun frae the lift, she landit in that hole.

†**2.** *absol.* To deliver heavy blows. *Obs.*

1590 Spenser *F.Q.* I. v. 8 As when a Gryfon.. A Dragon fiers encountreth in his flight,.. With hideous horrour both together smight, And souce so sore, that they the heauens affray. **1596** *Ibid.* IV. iii. 25 He stroke, he soust, he foynd, he hewd, he lasht.

3. *intr.* To fall heavily or with some weight.

1596 Spenser *F.Q.* IV. v. 36 About the Andvile standing.. With huge great hammers, that did neuer rest From heaping stroakes, which thereon soused sore. *a* **1600** *Floddan F.* vii. (1664) 72 Them Tennis-balls he sousing sent. **1701** Cibber *Love makes Man* I. i, About eight o'Clock.. flap they all sous'd upon their Knees. **1812** W. Tennant *Anster F.* IV. xxx. 84 Successively they souse and roll along, Till.. the carcase-cumber'd soil Is strewn with havock of the jumping throng. **1825** Brockett *N.C. Gloss.*, *Souse*,.. to fall with violence. **1858** R. S. Surtees *Ask Mamma* xxix. 116 He drew a duplicate chair to the fire,.. and, sousing down in it, prepared for a.. chat.

souse (saʊs), *v.*[3] Now *arch.* Forms: 6– souse, 6–8 sowse (7 sowsse), 7 sowze, sowce. [f. souse *sb.*[3] 2.]

1. *intr.* Of a hawk, etc.: To swoop down; to descend with speed and force. Freq. const. *on* or *upon* (a bird, etc.), and sometimes with *down*.

1589 Warner *Albion's Eng.* II. xxxi. 139 Kind killing Hawkes but wagge the wing, and worke to sowse anon. **1591** Sylvester *Du Bartas* I. v. 1087 But suddenly.. Down soust the Eagle on the blazing wood. **1626** T. H[awkins] *Caussin's Holy Crt.* 63 If the dogges spring some little bird, she [the hobby] sowceth vpon it. **1693** Dryden, etc. *Juvenal* xiv. (1697) 343 The Generous Eaglet, who is taught.. to fly at Hares, and sowse on Kids. **1720** Pope *Iliad* XVII. 765 The sacred eagle.. sousing on the quivering hare. **1762** Beattie *Pigm. & Cranes* 162 A fowl enormous, sousing from above, The gallant chieftain clutch'd. **1806** J. Grahame *Birds of Scot.* 70 Now up she rises, and, with arrowed pinions, Impetuous souses.

b. *transf.* and *fig.* of persons or things.

1583 T. Watson *Poems* (Arb.) 103 For when he first espyde my raunging Heart, He Falcon like came sowsing from aloofe. **1590** Lodge *Euphues Gold. Leg.* H iv, Be blythe and frolicke man, Loue sowseth as low as she soareth high. **1668** Dryden *Even. Love* IV. i, I love to stoop to my prey, and to have it in my power to souse at, when I please. **1670** —— *2nd Pt. Almanzor & Alm.* v, As some huge Rock.. So I—Would sowze upon thy Guards, and dash 'em wide. **1729** Shelvocke *Artillery* v. 351 Mounted on a winged Steed.. and sowsing directly upon the Monster. **1738** Pope *Epil. Satires* II. 15 Come on then, Satire! gen'ral, unconfin'd, Spread thy broad wing, and souse on all the kind. **1769** Burke *Corr.* (1844) I. 206 In the style of Lord Chatham's politics, to keep hovering in the air, over all parties, and to souse down where the prey may prove best. **1808** Scott in *Lockhart* (1839) I. 65, I was not permitted to open my lips without one or two old ladies.. being ready at once to souse upon me.

2. *trans.* **a.** To strike *down* (a bird) by a powerful swoop. *rare*$^{-1}$.

1594 *1st Pt. Contention* II. i, How hie your Hawke did sore? And on a sodaine soust the Partridge downe.

b. To swoop or pounce upon (something) in a hostile manner.

1595 Shaks. *John* v. ii. 150 The gallant Monarch.. like an Eagle, o're his ayerie towres, To sowsse annoyance that comes neere his Nest. **1616** B. Jonson *Devil an Ass* IV. vii, He did fly her home To mine own window: but I think I sou[s]'t him, And rauish'd her away, out of his pownces. [**1898** J. A. Gibbs *Cotswold Vill.* xii. 274 Ere the falcon 'souses' her prey.]

souse (saʊs), *adv.*[1] Now chiefly *dial.* Also 7–8 souce, 8 sowse. [f. souse *sb.*[3] or *v.*[3]]

1. Suddenly; without warning.

1680 *Vind. Conform. Clergy* (ed. 2) 32 He dares not so much as lift up a Finger;.. if he doth, souce, he hath him in the Chops immediately. **1728** Vanbr. & Cib. *Prov. Husb.* I. i, Then sowse! we are all set fast in a Slough.

2. With a direct and rapid course.

1690 Dryden *Amphitryon* I. i, He's coming down souse upon us, and hears as far as he can see too. **1755** Smollett *Quix.* II. III. ix. (1803) IV. 27 We shall come souse upon the kingdom of Candaya, as a saker or jerfaulcon darts down upon a heron.

3. With strong or violent impact; heavily.

1694 Motteux *Rabelais* IV. lxvii. (1737) 276 Vinet lent him.. a swinging stoater with the Pitch-fork souce between the Neck and the Collar. **1730** Young *1st Ep. to Pope* Wks. 1757 I. 186 They,.. looking full on every man they meet, Run souse against his chaps. **1789** Wolcot (P. Pindar) *Expost. Odes* ix. 29 Our world.. Would rather see a fellow.. from the attic story of a house Fall down souse Upon a set of cursed iron spikes. **1818** Scott *Br. Lamm.* xx, I hoped it would have fallen souse on your heads before you were aware of it. **1858** Carlyle *Fredk. Gt.* v. vii. II. 128 Gundling comes souse upon the ice with his sitting-part.

souse (saʊs), *adv.*[2] Also 8 souce, 9 sowse. [f. souse *sb.*[1] or *v.*[1]] With a sudden or deep plunge.

1706–7 Farquhar *Beaux' Strat.* v. iii, Now.. all our fair Machine goes souse into the Sea like the Edistone. **1838** Barham *Ingol. Leg.* Ser. I. *Hand of Glory*, Into Tappington mill-dam souse she goes. **1856** R. A. Vaughan *Mystics* (1860) I. VI. viii. 261 As he flounders about, out tumbles the book; he lets go his staff, and makes after it; and souse he goes, over head and ears in a twinkling. **1882** Serjt. Ballantine *Exper.* xxxiii, Just as he was stepping on board, souse he went into the sea.

fig. **1749** Cleland *Mem. Woman Pleasure* (1894) 2, I go souce into my personal history. **1760** Sterne *Tr. Shandy* II. xii. 51 Here have you got us.. souse into that old subject again. **1824** in *Spirit Pub. Jrnls.* (1825) 129 Into all sorts of subjects, both known and unknown, Mr. Hume goes what one may call souse. **1872** Browning *Fifine* lxv, Foiled by the very effort, sowse, Underneath ducks the soul!

†**souse-crown.** *Obs.*$^{-0}$ (See quot.)

a **1700** B. E. *Dict. Cant. Crew*, *Sowse-crown*, a Fool.

soused (saʊst), *ppl. a.* [f. souse *v.*[1]]

1. Steeped in pickle; pickled.

? *a* **1550** *Freiris Berwik* 260 in *Dunbar's Poems* (1893) 294 Ane sowsit nolt fute, and scheipheid. **1584** Powel *Lloyd's Cambria* 104 He should want no maner of Powdered and Sowsed meats. **1621** Burton *Anat. Mel.* I. ii. II. i. (1651) 68 Dryed, sowced, indurate fish, as Ling,.. Red-herrings. **1676** Shadwell *Libertine* 111, If I serve you not in your kind, then am I a sows'd sturgeon. **1677** Wycherley *Pl. Dealer* III. i, Go, dear Rogue, and succeed; and I'll invite thee, ere it be long, to more souz'd Venison. **1790** Shirrefs *Poems* 210 A' their een were chiefly fixt Upo' soust feet. **1842** Combe *Digestion* 137 At nine o'clock A.M. he breakfasted on soused tripe, pig's feet, bread and coffee.

fig. **1622** Fletcher *Beggar's Bush* IV. i, You shall not sink, for ne'r a sowst Flap-dragon, For ne'r a pickl'd Pilcher of 'em all, Sir.

2. Soaked in liquor.

1613 Beaum. & Fl. *Captain* I. ii, I am of that opinion, and will dye in't, There is no understanding, nor can be In a soust Souldier. **1932** J. T. Farrell *Young Lonigan* i. 34 Coming home, he had almost gotten into a mixup with some soused mick.

‖**sous-entendu** (suzɑ̃tɑ̃dy). [Fr.] Something not expressed but left to be understood by the hearer or reader.

1865 Mill *Exam. Hamilton's Philos.* xxii. 442 No shadow of justification is shown for thus.. adopting into logic a mere *sous-entendu* of common conversation in its most unprecise form. **1907** W. De Morgan *Alice-for-Short* xxxii. 332 She knew well enough that the unheard portions of the conversation were worse than what had reached her ears, and the *sous-entendus* probably still worse than they. **1972** *Times Lit. Suppl.* 31 Mar. 374/3 It is satisfyingly like other such duets, though embellished at least once with an erotic *sous-entendu*.

souser ('saʊsə(r)). *dial.* Also soozer. [f. souse *v.*[1]] A thorough drenching or soaking.

1862 C. C. Robinson *Dial. Leeds* 416. **1866** Mordaunt & Verney *Ann. Warw. Hunt* I. 323 The bank broke, and he got a regular souser.

sousing ('saʊsɪŋ), *vbl. sb.*[1] Also 6 sows(s)ing, 7 sowcing. [f. souse *v.*[1]]

1. The action or process of pickling. Also *attrib.* in ***sousing-drink***, ***-tub***. Now *Obs.* or *dial.*

1551–60 *Invent. Sir H. Parker* in Hall *Eliz. Soc.* (1887) 150 A sowssing Tubb for brawne. **1577** Harrison *Descr. Engl.* 110/1 Changing the sowsing drincke least it should waxe soure. **1601** Yarington *Two Lament. Trag.* III. ii. in Bullen *O. Pl.* IV, Chop of my head to make a Sowsing-tub. **1611** Cotgr., *Solloüoir*, a salting, or sowcing tub. **1617** J. Murrell *Bk. Cookerie* (title-p.), The most commendable fashion of Dressing, or Sowcing, either Flesh, Fish, or Fowle.

2. A drenching; a thorough wetting.

1697 J. Lewis *Mem. Dk. Glocester* (1789) 57 Indeed it proved a good sousing, as he was handsomely wetted from the crown to his feet. **1764** Foote *Mayor of G.* II. Wks. 1799 I. 186 After all his marchings, his sousings, his sweatings. **1832** Miss Mitford *Village* Ser. v. (1863) 499 The satisfactory conclusion of the sousing. **1853** Kane *Grinnell Exp.* xxvii. (1856) 224 After.. some uncomfortable sousings in the snow-dust. **1887** *Pall Mall G.* 12 July 13 This continual sousing.. actually rots the hair and leads to baldness.

'**sousing**, *vbl. sb.*[2] *rare.* [f. souse *v.*[2]] The action of beating severely.

c **1580** [Jefferies] *Bugbears* II. iv. 6 (Bond), With sowcynges, with rowsynges, with bownsynges, with trownsynges. **1788** *Hist. of Schoolboy* 46 Talboy declared it his firm intention to have bestowed upon him.. an effectual sousing.

sousing ('saʊsɪŋ), *ppl. a.*[1] Also 6 sowsing, 7 sowcing. [f. souse *v.*[1]]

1. Of ears: Suitable for sousing; unusually large.

1567 Turberv. *Epit.*, etc. 14 b, Hee had a paire of sowsing eares to shilde him from the raine. **1673** Hickeringill *Greg. F. Greyb.* 302 A dismal monster,.. sowcing great luggs and a mouth greater.

2. Drenching, soaking.

1596 Drayton *Legend Pierce Gaveston* iv. Poems (1619) 353 By many a low Ebbe, many a lustie Tide, Many a smooth Calme, many a sowsing Showre. **1648** J. Beaumont *Psyche* XVII. cxxi, The gravid Vapor breaks.. and pours the sousing weather Down through the gloomy air. **1830** Scott *Jrnl.* 7 July, I returned after two, with a sousing shower for companion. **1876** T. Hardy *Ethelberta* xliv. (1890) 353 The windy, sousing, thwacking.. corner called St. Lucas' Leap.

b. Splashing in water.

1891 T. Hardy *Tess* (1900) 55/2 They disappeared round the curve of the road, and only his sousing footsteps.. told where they were.

3. Strong, vigorous, 'powerful'. Now *dial.*

In later examples perh. from souse *v.*[2]

1735 Bolingbroke *On Parties* 10 The arch Slyness of G—on, the dogmatical Dryness of H——e, or the soucing Prostitution of Sh—k. **1764** Foote *Patron* I. Wks. 1799 I. 335 A good sousing satire now, well powder'd with personal pepper. **1780** *West's Guide Lakes* (E.D.D.), A sousing blow. **1876** Robinson *Mid.-Yks. Gloss.* 132/1 A great sousing fellow. *Ibid.*, A sousing lot.

'**sousing**, *ppl. a.*[2] [f. souse *v.*[3]] Swooping.

1700 Dryden *Theodore & Hon.* 318 They close their trembling Troop; and all attend On whom the sowsing Eagle will descend.

souslik, var. suslik.

sousou, var. susu.

† **souspirable**, *a.* *Obs.*$^{-1}$ [f. older F. *souspirer* (mod.F. *soupirer*) to sigh.] Lamentable.

1594 Kyd *Cornelia* v. 287 Incessantly lamenting th' extreame losse, And souspirable death of so braue souldiers.

† **soussie.** *Obs.*$^{-1}$ [a. OF. *soussie*, var. of *soucie*: see SOUCY.] Marigold.

c **1410** *Master of Game* (MS. Digby 182) xii, And also it is gode forto put þer in of þe soussie, of þe whiche men fyndeth ynogh at þe potycaryes, for þe same sekenesse.

sousteine, obs. form of SUSTAIN *v.*

† **sout**, *v.* *Obs.*$^{-0}$ [Back-formation from SOUTER.] *trans.* To mend or patch (shoes).

1598 Florio, *Sanattare*, to cobble, to mend, or sout old shoes. *Ibid.*, *Tacconare*, to cobble, .. to soute, to piece. **1611** —— *Taberciatiua árte*, the arte of patching .. or souting.

‖ **soutache** (sutaʃ). [F., corruptly ad. Hungarian *szuszak* a pendant curl of hair, etc.] A narrow flat ornamental braid of wool, silk, or the like, usually sewn upon fabrics in fanciful designs.

1856 Mrs. Pullan *Lady's Dict. Needlework* 52 *Soutache*. A French name for very pretty ornamental braids. **1859** *Ladies' Cabinet* Dec. 335/2 When trimmed with gold or silver *soutache*, .. the *Zouave* is eminently graceful and coquettish. **1879** *Sylvia's Embroidery Bk.* 253 The blue medallion is outlined with soutache.

attrib. **1882** Caulfeild & Saward *Dict. Needlew.* 453/2 Soutache Braids .. are very narrow silk braids, .. having an openwork centre.

Hence **'soutached** *a.*, fancifully braided.

1860 *Ladies' Gaz. Fashion* Mar. 22/3 Zouave jackets of cloth soutached with silk.

† **soutage.** *Obs.* Also 6 sowltwyche, soultwhiche, -witch, 7 -wich; 7 soultage, sowtage, -ege. [Of obscure origin.] Coarse cloth or canvas used esp. for packing or as a material for bags.

α. **1532–3** in E. Law *Hampton Crt. Palace* (1885) 351 Paid .. for 2 pecys of sowltwyche, every pece conteynyng 33 ellys. **1545** *Rates of Custom House* ciiij b, Soult-whiche the hundreth elles, .. xxx. s. **1657** *Acts of Interregn.* (1911) II. 1215 Linnen Cloth called .. Soultwich, the hundred Els.

β. **1573** Tusser *Husb.* (1878) 136 Some close them vp drie in a hogshed or fat, yet canuas or soutage is better than that. **1591** *Acts Privy Council* (N.S.) XXII. 169 Duche canvas or counterfaicte borrace, harfordes, soutage or sowtwell and guttings are not sold to make sailes for ships. *c* **1611** Chapman *Iliad* xiv. Comm., That which they call our fustian, their plain writing being stuff nothing so substantial but such gross sowtege, or hairpatch, as every goose may eat oats through. **1631** Mabbe *Celestina* Ep. Ded. (1894) 5, I see no reason why they should .. loath silke, because it is lapt in soultage. **1669** Worlidge *Syst. Agric.* 276 *Soutage*, course Cloath, or Bagging for Hops, or such like.

attrib. **1622** Mabbe tr. *Aleman's Guzman d'Alf.* ii. 215 She hath .. silken words, but sowtage deeds.

‖ **soutane** (sutan). [F. *soutane* (†*sotane*, *sottane*), ad. It. *sottana* (med.L. *sutana*, *subtana*), f. *sotto*:—L. *subtus* under. Cf. SOTANA, -ANE.]

1. A long buttoned gown or frock, with sleeves, forming the ordinary outer garment of Roman Catholic ecclesiastics, and worn under the vestments in religious services; a cassock.

In quot. 1838 erroneously applied to the COTTA.

1838 Miss Pardoe *River & Desert* II. 149 The officiating priests were gorgeous in their crimson robes and point-lace soutanes. **1855** Kingsley *Westw. Ho!* xi, A man of middle age, in the long soutane of a Romish priest. **1876** M. Davies *Unorth. Lond.* 335 The preacher .. was clad in the conventional Hindoo coat, long as a Ritualist's soutane.

2. *transf.* A wearer of the soutane; a priest.

1890 *Times* 19 Dec. 7/2 A confederacy of soutanes and petticoats may do much.

soute, obs. form of SUIT *sb.* and *v.*

soutel, obs. form of SUBTLE *a.*

‖ **souteneur** (sutənœr). [Fr., = protector, f. *soutenir* to sustain.] A man who lives on the earnings of a prostitute or prostitutes under his protection. Also *transf.*

1906 tr. *Weininger's Sex & Character* ii. x. 234 The souteneur is always a criminal, a thief, a fraudulent person, or sometimes even a murderer. **1920** A. Huxley *Limbo* 38 After midnight he would write novels with a feminine pen, earning the money that would make his unproductive male labours possible. A kind of spiritual *souteneur*. **1927** *Observer* 11 Dec. 20/2 The souteneur .. extends some shadowy kind of patronage and protection over the girl in return for a 50 per cent or still higher share of her earnings as prostitute. **1969** *Punch* 26 Mar. 469/1 The death-knell of revolution in Britain was the football match between strikers and the police in 1926. It was the moment when the Russian *souteneurs* of the British Communist Party realised with disgust that revolutions can't be made, they have to happen. **1977** M. T. Bloom *13th Man* viii. 147 The underworld of traffickers, *souteneurs*, and prostitutes .. at Buenos Aires.

‖ **soutenu** (sutəny), *a.* and *sb.* *Ballet.* [Fr., pa. pple. of *soutenir* to sustain.] **A.** *adj.* Of a movement: sustained, performed slowly. **B.** *sb.* A sustained or slowly-performed movement, *spec.* a complete turn on point or half point.

1930 [see PLIÉ]. **1947** N. Nicolaeva-Legat *Ballet Educ.* iv. 63 After *en dedans*, the opposite *soutenu* is performed and the *port-de-bras* executed with the active foot extended in front. **1978** *N.Y. Times* 29 Mar. c19/1 The faint sounds of a tune to dance by are drifting out, then a louder shout. 'All you have there is a little soutenu... You did six counts, she did seven.'

souter ('su:tə(r)). Now *Sc.* and *north. dial.* Forms: α. 1 sutere, 3 sutare, 4–5, 8–9 sutor (5 sutore), 6 sutour, 8 suter; 4, 9 sutter. β. 4 soutere (zout-), 4– souter (6, 9 soutter, 9 sooter); 5 soutare, 5– soutar (9 sootar); 9 soutor. γ. 4–5 sowtere, 4– sowter (6 sowtter); 5 sowtare, 5–6 sowtar (6 sowttar). [OE. *sútere*, ad. L. *sūtor* shoemaker, f. *suěre* to sew, stitch. Of the same origin are OHG. *sûtâri* (MHG. *sûter*), ON. *sútari* (MSw. *sutare*, MDa. *sutæræ*), NFris. *süter*, *sütjer*.]

1. A maker or mender of shoes; a shoemaker or cobbler.

Also *spec.* 'one who makes brogues or shoes of horse-leather' (Jamieson, 1808). In the 16th and 17th cent. the word is freq. used with depreciatory force, esp. to denote a type of workman of little or no education.

α. *c* **1000** Ælfric *Saints' Lives* xv. 23 Sum sutere siwode þæs halȝan weres sceos. *a* **1225** *Ancr. R.* 324 A wummon þet haueð forloren hire nelde, oðer a sutare his el. **1379** *Poll-tax W. Riding* in *Yorks. Archæol. Jrnl.* V. 17 Adam Wild' Sutter. **1474** *Acc. Ld. High Treas. Scot.* I. 38 Item gevin to Hud sutor, for the Quenis schoune. *a* **1682** Sempill *Blythsome Wedding* 13 And there will be Sandie the sutor. **1725** *Fam. Dict.* s.v. *Lithotomy*, This we in England call Cutting upon the Gripe, and is the Method our Suters always cut by. **1808** J. Mayne *Siller Gun* ii. xxiii, Jock Willison, a sutor bred. **1817** *Lintoun Green* 6 The Selkirk Sutors aff their stools .. In dirt haste raise.

β. **1340** *Ayenb.* 66 More zuyfter þanne arwe ulyinde and more boryinde þanne zouteres eles. **1387** Trevisa *Higden* (Rolls) VII. 518 Som men seide that this Harold Harefote was a souters sone. *c* **1400** *Destr. Troy* 1585 Sadlers, souters, Semsteris fyn. **1456** Sir G. Haye *Law Arms* (S.T.S.) 208 A soutare, or a skynnare, or a tailloure. *c* **1566** *Merie Tales of Skelton* S.'s Wks. 1843 I. p. lxv, In the parysshe of Dys .. there dwelled a cobler, beyng halfe a souter. **1584–7** Greene *Carde of Fancie* Wks. (Grosart) IV. 102 If Appelles .. suffer the greasie Souter to take a view of his curious worke. *a* **1641** Bp. Mountagu *Acts & Mon.* (1642) 488 How can it but be a maine absurdity, that a Cooke, a Currier, a Souter, a Potter .. should therefore be accounted noble? **1791** Burns *Tam o' Shanter* 41 And at his elbow, Souter Johnny. *Ibid.* 49 The Souter tauld his queerest stories. **1829** Scott *Jrnl.* II. 217, I .. tugged as hard as ever did soutar to make ends meet. **1880** J. F. S. Gordon *Chron. Keith* 74 Coopers, Sooters, Sweetie-Wives, and Buckie Dulse-Wives, &c.

γ. *c* **1386** Chaucer *Reeve's Prol.* 50 The devyl made .. of a sowter, schipman or a leche. **1387** Trevisa *Higden* (Rolls) IV. 307 A poore sowtere fondede to teche a chouȝh to .. seie þe same salutacioun. *a* **1400** in *Eng. Gilds* (1870) 359 Eueryche sowtere þat makeþ shon of newe roþer leþer. **1454** *Paston Lett.* I. 292 They took a man of Stratford, a sowter, and hys name ys Persoun. **1491** *Acc. Ld. High Treas. Scot.* I. 182 Til a sowtar that sewyt halk hwdis to the King. **1513** More *Rich. III* (1883) 79 And in a stage play all the people know right wel that he that playeth the sowdayne is percase a sowter. **1570** B. Googe *Pop. Kingd.* iii. (1880) 33 Masse brings in dayly gaine, as doth the Sowters arte at neede. **1602** Carew *Cornwall* 86 b, While an ignorant fellow of a sowter becomes a magistrate. **1646** Gataker *Mistake Removed* 22 We have, with Lucian's sowter, dreamed of a great feast. **1688** Holme *Armoury* iii. 193/1 St. Crispin .. the Patron of Sowters, Cordwiners and Shoe-makers Journey-Men. **1855** [Robinson] *Whitby Gloss.* s.v., He grins like an aud sowter.

transf. **1593** G. Harvey *Pierce's Super.* Wks. (Grosart) II. 43 Lauinius against Terence; Cratena against Euripides; Zoilus against Homer, [were] but ranke sowters.

† **b.** Employed as a term of abuse. *Obs.*

1478 *Maldon* (Essex) *Crt. Rolls* Bundle 50, No. 8, Willelmus Cotyngham vocavit Johannem Baker horsoned souter contra statutum hujus burgi et dixit 'Vos, horsoned suters, bere a rewle'. **1575** in W. H. Turner *Select. Rec. Oxford 361* [They] came to the howse of .. a cordwayner, .. and .. called him sowter, and .. gave him .. opprobrious words. *a* **1585** Polwart *Flyting w. Montgomerie* 747 Creishie soutter, shoe cloutter, minch moutter!

2. *attrib.* and *Comb.*, as ***souter-craft***, ***-like*** adj.

c **1400** Maundev. (Roxb.) xxvi. 122 Þai do all maner of craftez, þat es to say talyour craft and sowter craft and swilk oþer. **1500–20** Dunbar *Poems* xxvii. 46 Full sowttar lyk he wes of laitis.

b. Special combs.: **souter's brandy**, buttermilk; **souter's clod**, a roll of coarse bread; **souter's end**, a piece of resined twine.

1773 *Edinb. Wkly. Mag.* 9 Dec. 335 A souter's clod, .. if not a second mess of porridge for dinner. **1790** Shirrefs *Poems* 245 Could he get clods and souter's brandy. **1824** Scott *Redgauntlet* ch. xx, Ye will maybe have nae whey then, nor buttermilk, nor ye couldna exhibit a souter's clod? **1832** Vedder *Orc. Sketches* 110 A clarionet, beautifully enamelled with a kind of twine, called by the vulgar 'Sutor's ends'.

Hence † **'souteress.** *Obs.*$^{-1}$

1377 Langl. *P. Pl.* B. v. 315 Cesse þe souteresse [1362 þe souters wyf] sat on þe benche.

soutering, obs. form of SUITORING.

† **'souterly**, *a.* *Obs.* Also 6–7 sowterly. [f. SOUTER + -LY^1.]

1. Resembling a souter; of a common or vulgar type.

1534 More *Treat. Passion* Wks. 1296/2 The special bassawes of that proude souterly Sowdan. **1568** Fulwell *Like will to Like* B iij, You souterly knaues shew you all your maners at once. **1603** Florio *Montaigne* iii. v. (1632) 483 The burden bearing porter, souterly cobbler, and toile-full labourer. **1617** Collins *Def. Bp. Ely* ii. vii. 252 What should one stand tugging with such a sowterly fellow?

2. Appropriate to, characteristic of, a souter.

1589 ? Lyly *Pappe w. Hatchet* E ij, Hee runnes ouer his fooleries with a knaues gallop, ripping vp the souterlie seames of his Epistle. **1593** Nashe *Strange News* Wks. (Grosart) II. 187 The Doctors proceedings haue thrust vpon mee this sowterly Metaphor. **1609** Paule *Life Of Archbp. Whitgift* 40 A cobler, a choise broker for such souterly wares. **1626** R. Bernard *Isle of Man* (1627) 277 They blasphemously publish, that the Scriptures are .. a dead Letter, sowterly Inke, dumbe Iudges.

souterrain ('su:tərem). [a. F. *souterrain*, f. *sous* under + *terre* earth, after L. *subterrāneus*.] An underground chamber, store-room, passage, etc.

a **1735** Arbuthnot (J.), Defences against extremities of heat, as shade, grottoes, or souterrains, are necessary preservatives of health. **1775** R. Chandler *Trav. Asia M.* (1825) I. 151 By the highest of them is the entrance of a souterrain. **1806** J. Dallaway *Observ. Eng. Archit.* 89 In the souterrain of vaulted stone, the military engines and stores were deposited. **1840** Vyse *Oper. Pyramids Gizeh* II. 76 The general direction of the souterrain, near the Second Pyramid. **1899** R. Munro *Prehist. Scot.* ix. 352 In Ireland underground chambers, generally known as 'souterrains' or 'coves', are to be found all over the country.

transf. **1882** *Times* 5 Feb. 4 Hamilton Park having a souterrain of vast mineral wealth.

south (saʊθ), *adv.*, *prep.*, *sb.*, and *a.* Forms: 1, 3 **suð**, suþ, 3 suþe, 4–5 suthe, 4, 6 suth (6 *Sc.* sutht); 3 soþ, 4 soth, 6 *north.* soyth; 3–5 souþ (4 zouþ), 4–5 souþe, 4 sowþe; 3– south (4 souht, 5 *Sc.* soucht), 4–6 southe (5 *Sc.* souythe), 5–6 sowth(e. [Common Teut.: OE. *súð*, = OFris. *sûth* (WFris. *súd*, NFris. *süd*), OS. *sûth* (MLG. *sût*, LG. *sud*), OHG. *sund-*, *sunt-* (MHG. *sund*), ON. (with *r-* suffix) *suðr* (:—**sunþr*; cf. the compar. *sunnar*:—**sunþar*): the relationship of the stem is uncertain. One or other of these forms (perh. the ON.) is the source of OF. *sur*, *sud*, *su* (F. *sud*), Sp. *sur*, *sud*, Pg. *sul*.

MDu. *suut* (*zuut*), *suyt* (Du. *zuid*) and G. *süd* are not the native forms (which would have been respectively **zond* and **sund*), but are due to Fris., LG., or F. influence. In the Scand. languages there is considerable variety in the later forms, as MSw. *sudher*, *södher*, Sw. *söder*, Norw. *sør*, *sud*, *syd*, *sunn*, *synn* Da. *syd*.

In some senses (as B. 2–4) usually with a capital, in others usually with a small letter, but the practice is not uniform.]

A. *adv.* **1.** Towards, or in the direction of, that part of the earth or heavens which is directly opposite to the north. Also with modifying additions, as ***south by west***, etc.

a. With reference to movement, extent, or direction.

c **900** *O.E. Chron.* (Parker MS.) an. 894, þa þe suð ymbutan foron, ymb-sæton Exancester. *a* **1122** *Ibid.* (Laud MS.) an. 1092, Se cyng Willelm .. ferde norð to Cardeol, .. & syððan hider suð ȝewænde. *c* **1205** Lay. 2133 Locrines mær eode suð & forð. *c* **1290** *S. Eng. Leg.* I. 234 So longe huy wenden euene south, þat [etc.]. **1375** Barbour *Bruce* xvi. 265 Syne thai .. sowth till Lwnyk held thair way. ? *a* **1400** *Morte Arth.* 1039 Bot thow moste seke more southe, sydlyngs a lyttille. **1539** *Reg. Mag. Sig. Scot.* 454 Fra the said croce rycht south to the Mercat-gait. *a* **1670** Spalding *Troub. Chas. I* (1850) I. 27 Mynding to lodge thair all nicht be the get going south. *a* **1700** Evelyn *Diary* 22 Mar. 1652, For more than an hundred yards South. *c* **1743** Woodroofe in Hanway *Trav.* iv. lix. (1762) I. 276 Steering south and south by west. **1816** Scott *Bl. Dwarf* viii, As if the devil was blawing us south. **1855** *Orr's Circ. Sci.*, *Inorg. Nat.* 147 The inclination is sometimes north, and sometimes south. **1880** Ruskin *Bible of Amiens* i. (1884) 32 Clovis' march south against the Visigoths.

b. With reference to place or location; *spec.* (*U.S.*), in or into the southern states. Also † ***south-by***, in the south (*Sc.*).

down south: see DOWN *adv.* 30.

Beowulf 858 Moniȝ oft ȝecwæð, þætte suð ne norð .. oþer næniȝ .. selra nære. *c* **805** *Charter* in *O.E. Texts* 442 ðif hiora oðrum oððe bæm suð forȝelimpe. *a* **1000** *Boeth. Metr.* x. 24 Þæt eow suð oððe norð þa ytmestan eorðbuende .. miclum herien. *c* **1200** Ormin 12125 Þa fowwre daless alle þatt Æst, & Wesst, & Suþ, & Norrþ þiss middelærd bilukenn. *c* **1310** in Wright *Lyric P.* xviii. 59 Whether y be south other west. *c* **1391** Chaucer *Astrol.* i. §17 Tak kep of thise latitudes north and sowth. **1591** [see SOUTH-EASTWARD *adv.*]. **1594** Shaks. *Rich. III*, v. iii. 38 His Regiment lies halfe a Mile .. South, from the mighty Power of the King. **1667** Milton *P.L.* xi. 401 The Realme Of Congo, and Angola fardest South. *a* **1670** Spalding *Troub. Chas. I* (1850) I. 27 The Erll .. wes at this tym south. **1762** Bp. Forbes *Jrnl.* (1886) 216 He asked me how the not-swearing clergy lived now South-by. **1769** Falconer *Dict. Marine* (1780) s.v. *Wind*, Coming to the latitude of four degrees south. **1852** Mrs. Stowe *Uncle Tom's Cabin* i. x. 142 To appreciate the sufferings of the negroes sold south. **1866** *Treas. Bot.* 210/2 The plant .. is found .. from latitude 40° to 44° south. **1936** M. Mitchell *Gone with Wind* iii. 51 The air was always thick with threats of selling slaves south and of direful whippings. **1976** M. G. Eberhart *Family Fortune* (1977) vii. 77 'Suppose Mr Jeff sell me south?' .. 'He can't sell you... You and all the slaves .. were set free.'

c. In the phr. ***south and north***. (See also NORTH *adv.* 1 c.)

c **900** tr. *Baeda's Hist.* i. iii. (1890) 30 þæt is .. twelf mila brad suð & norð. **1596** *Reg. Mag. Sig. Scot.* 194/1 Be the grund of ane auld dyk lyand south and north. **1612** Drayton *Poly-olb.* xiii. 315 The second [way runs] South and North, from Michael's utmost Mount, To Cathnesse. **1838** *Penny Cycl.* XI. 439/2 A large island .. which .. extends about 80 miles south and north.

d. Followed by *of*.

1707 J. Chamberlayne *Pres. St. Gt. Brit.* (1710) 344 Rum lies 4 Leagues South of Sky. **1771** *Encycl. Brit.* III. 942/1

Williamstat [is]..fourteen miles south of Rotterdam. **1868** *Rep. U.S. Commissioner Agric.* (1869) 71 The value of marling south of New Jersey.

2. From the south.

1626 BACON *Sylva* §626 In a Faire and Dry Day,..And when the Wind bloweth not South. **1762** FALCONER *Shipwr.* II. 242 South and by west the threatening demon blew.

3. With a south aspect.

1693 EVELYN *De la Quint. Compl. Gard.* I. 30 When we say that a Garden lyes full South, it is when the Sun shines upon it all the day.

4. quasi-*sb.* = B. 1 a. Freq. with *from* or *to.* †Also *at south*, from the south.

c **1200** ORMIN 11258 All þiss middellærd iss ec O fowwre daless dæledd, Onn Æst, o Wesst, o Suþ, o Norrþ. **1338** R. BRUNNE *Chron.* (1810) 19 Þe kynges..cleymed him for þer chefe..Of North & of South..Fro Kent vntille Berwik. *c* **1391**–*c* **1425** [see NORTH *adv.* 2]. *c* **1470** HENRY *Wallace* XI. 777 Fra south and north mony off Scotland fled. **1592** *Soliman & Pers.* III. iv, Monarch and mightie Emperor of the world, From East to West, from South to Septentrion. **1625** CARPENTER *Geogr. Del.* I. vi. (1635) 135 The Meridians are drawne directly from North to South. **1671** MILTON *P.R.* III. 273 To South the Persian Bay. **1725** DE FOE *Voy. round World* (1840) 128 The wind came off shore, for it blew at south. **1748**- [see NORTH *adv.* 2]. **1821–2** SHELLEY *Chas. I*, II. 419 The rainbow hung over the city..from north to south. **1842** BROWNING *Pied Piper* xiii, He turned from South to West, And to Koppelberg Hill his steps addressed.

†**b.** *by south*, in the south; on the south side.

c **1205** LAY. 30214 Þis iherde Cadwalan, þe king wes bi suððen. *c* **1290** *S. Eng. Leg.* I. 236 Þe feorþe dai heo iseiȝen ane yle albi souþe on heiȝ. **1393** LANGL. *P. Pl.* C. II. 117 Hit is sykerer by southe þer þe sonne regneth. *c* **1420** *Avow. Arth.* xlvii, He sayd, he was knoun and cuthe, And was comun fro bi-southe. *a* **1425** [see NORTH *adv.* 2b]. **1596** SHAKS. *1 Hen. IV*, III. i. 75 England, from Trent, and Seuerne, hitherto By South and East is to my part assign'd. **1600** NASHE *Summers Last Will* 869 Wks. (Grosart) VI. 120 Haruest..by south and south-east, shewe thy selfe like a beast.

c. *by south*: (see BY *prep.* 9 b).

c **1391** CHAUCER *Astrol.* II. §31 Than it is deuided in smale partiez of Azymutz, as est, and est by sowthe. **14..** [see SOUTH-EAST *adv.* 1]. *c* **1440** *Promp. Parv.* 466/2 Sowthely, or sum what be sowthe, *australis.* **1682** WHELER *Journ. Greece* VI. 481, I observed Corinth to lie South-East by South off us. *a* **1701** MAUNDRELL *Journ. Jerus.* (1721) Add. 8 With a Course..South East and by South we arrived at Jan-Bolads. **1713, 1725** [see EAST D. 3]. **1772–84** [see SOUTH-EAST *adv.* 1]. **1837** *Fraser's Mag.* XL. 666 Cape Trafalgar bore east by south.

5. *ellipt.* as *prep.* **a.** Southwards along.

1598 *Reg. Mag. Sig. Scot.* 387/1 Passand south the said balk to the laitch or strype.

b. At, in, or to the south of.

Cf. *a-south* prep., in Henry *Wallace* x. 529.

1607 SHAKS. *Cor.* I. x. 31 Tis South the City Mils. **1611** —— *Cymb.* II. iv. 81 The Chimney Is South the Chamber. **1787** BURNS *Winter Nt.* i, When Phœbus gies a short-liv'd glow'r Far south the lift. **1891** KIPLING *Light that Failed* xi. (1900) 185 In the gray wilderness of South-the-water.

B. *sb.* (Usually with *the.*)

1. a. That one of the four cardinal points which is opposite to the north.

c **1290** *S. Eng. Leg.* I. 345 Abouten eiȝte hondret mile Engelond long is Fram þe South into þe North. *a* **1325** *Prose Psalter* lxxvii. 30 He bare ouer þe wynde of þe souþe fram þe heuen. **1390** GOWER *Conf.* III. 30 As the wyndes of the South Ben most of alle debonaire. **1422** tr. *Secreta Secret., Priv. Priv.* 221 Tho whyche dwellyth towarde the Sowthe..as thay of Ethiopy. *c* **1440** *Alph. Tales* 62, iij wyndows, ane at þe suthe, a noder at þe este, & þe iij at þe weste. **1577** B. GOOGE tr. *Heresbach's Husb.* §120 Therfore your stable must stand toward the south. **1610** HOLLAND *Camden's Brit.* (1637) 244 Another brook from the South runneth into him. **1726–46** THOMSON *Winter* 989 The winds at eve..Blow, hollow-blustering from the south. **1837** P. KEITH *Bot. Lex.* 277 The whole mass of ears nodding, as if with one consent, to the south. **1875** GLADSTONE *Glean.* (1879) VI. 149 If standing at the north end of the holy Table, he faces towards the south.

b. Followed by *of.*

1382 WYCLIF *Ezek.* xlvii. 1 To the south of the auter. **1778** *Encycl. Brit.* (ed. 2) II. 1222/1 A town..to the south of mount Atlas. **1834** *Picture L'pool* 83 To the south of George's Pierhead.

2. The southern part of a country or region; *spec.* **a.** of England (below the Wash), Great Britain, Scotland, or Ireland (in mod. use beyond the border of Northern Ireland); the south country.

1297 R. GLOUC. (Rolls) 172 Fram þe souþ tilþ to þe norþ erninge stret. *c* **1330** R. BRUNNE *Chron. Wace* (Rolls) 2382 Þe Duk of Cornewaille Al þe souþ tyl hym gan taylle. *c* **1400** *Brut* xxii. (1906) 26 Anoþere [way] fram þe North into þe South, þat was callede Ikenyle strete. **1543** *Richmond Wills* (Surtees) 50 My Lord Daykar of the soyth. **1631** WEEVER *Anc. Funeral Mon.* 436 Baron Dacres of the South. **1691** RAY *N. Co. Words* s.v. *Goulans*, In the South we usually call marygolds simply *golds.* **1707** CHAMBERLAYNE *Pres. St. Gt. Brit.* (1710) 307 From the Mull of Galloway in the South to Dungsbay Head..in the North. **1837** LOCKHART *Scott* lii. (1845) 451/2 Letters..which Scott at this time addressed to his friends in the South. **1886** KINGTON OLIPHANT *New English* I. 222 This is still used as a Positive in Scotland, though we of the South can say only 'most likely'. **1913** R. KIPLING *Let.* Dec. in Ld. Birkenhead *Rudyard Kipling* (1978) xvi. 257 Which is the most [*sic*] dangerous enemy? The South playing a game it has not got its heart in, or the North in a blind rage? **1974** D. SEAMAN *Bomb that could Lip-Read* vii. 60 The whole attitude of the South baffled and angered him. Irish politics were beyond him. **1978** D. MURPHY *Place Apart* ii. 33 In Northern Ireland one has a wide choice of names for the rest of the island: the Twenty-six Counties, the Free State, Southern Ireland, the South, Eire and the Republic of Ireland.

b. The southern lands of Europe, etc.

Freq. in and after Biblical use with reference to southern Palestine.

c **1374** CHAUCER *Boeth.* II. met. vi. (1868) 55 Þat is to seyne, alle þe poeples in þe souþe. **1382** WYCLIF *Joshua* xii. 8 In the south was Ethee, and Ammorree. **1535** COVERDALE *Gen.* xiii. 1 So Abram departed out of Egipte..towarde ye south. **1667** MILTON *P.L.* I. 354 When her barbarous Sons Came like a Deluge on the South. **1817** SHELLEY *Rev. Islam* x. iv, In the scorched pastures of the South. **1890** DOYLE *White Company* xxiii, Here rode dark-browed cavaliers from the sunny south.

Comb. **1851** MAYNE REID *Scalp Hunters* xix. 131 The scenes through which we were passing, here soft and south-like, there wild, barren.

c. The southern states of America (cf. NORTH *sb.* 2 c). Orig. *U.S.*

1779 STORER in Jesse *Selwyn & Contemp.* (1844) IV. 268 A ship..brings advice that Clinton is not going to the South as he first intended. **1857** A. GRAY *First Lessons Bot.* (1866) 19 Behind it is a Yucca (called Spanish Bayonet at the South). **1872** DE VERE *Americanisms* 120 Certain features of the landscape in the South and West.

3. The southern part *of* a particular country, etc.; as *South of England*, also (freq. with hyphens) *attrib.*; *South of France*, *spec.* the French Riviera; also *attrib.*

1382 WYCLIF *2 Sam.* xxiv. 7 Thei camen into the sowth of Juda. **1422** tr. *Secreta Secret., Priv. Priv.* 185 The Prynces of the Southe of Irland. **1671** MILTON *P.R.* III. 320 From Atropatia..and the South Of Susiana to Balsara's hav'n. **1741** M. W. MONTAGU *Let.* 29 July (1966) II. 245 They are gone to Marseilles and design passing some months in the South of France. **1773** G. WHITE *Selborne* liii, A species of them is familiar to horsemen in the south of England. **1811** A. T. THOMSON *Lond. Disp.* (1818) 350 Rue is..a native of the South of Europe. **1815** E. FREMANTLE *Diary* 8 Sept. in *Wynne Diaries* (1952) xxxi. 533 We determined to take the former Road, particularly as the South of France is not quite quiet. **1847** C. BRONTË *Jane Eyre* III. iv. 106 A large, fashionable, south-of-England city. **1855** *Orr's Circ. Sci., Inorg. Nat.* 152 The chalk of the South of England. **1872** C. M. YONGE *P's & Q's* ii. 10 At the time of her death, Elspeth and Persis had been in the South of France. **1922** M. ARLEN *Piracy* III. v. 183 We are going to the south of France to-morrow. **1922** E. SITWELL in *New Age* 6 July 120/1, I liked ..the warm, South-of-France feeling about her, and her faded hair that was like dry, powdery mimosa. **1940** 'G. ORWELL' *Inside Whale* 42 Dickens..is a south-of-England man, and a cockney at that. **1971** J. BRUNNER *Honky in Woodpile* ii. 14 I'll start on the Sunday papers and catch their South of England editions. **1980** I. MURDOCH *Nuns & Soldiers* i. 83 Soho in summer was his South of France.

4. *transf.* The inhabitants of a southern region or district.

c **1300** *Havelok* 434 Waried wrthe he of norþ and suth. **1382** WYCLIF *1 Sam.* xxvii. 10 In whom felle thou on to dai? Dauid answerde, Aȝens the south of Jude, and aȝens the south of Yranyel. *c* **1620** A. HUME *Brit. Tongue* (1865) 20 Nurice, from nutrix, quhilk the south calles nurse. **1748** GRAY *Alliance* 52 The prostrate South to the Destroyer yields. **1837** W. E. CHANNING *Annex. Texas* Wks. (1884) 541/2 Strange, that the South should think of securing its 'peculiar institutions' by violent means. **1861** LD. R. MONTAGU *Mirr. Amer.* 91 Between the North and South there will be feelings of implacable hatred.

5. a. The south wind. Chiefly *poet.*

a **1340** HAMPOLE *Psalter* cxxv. 5 Þe south blawand, frosyn strandis lesis and rennys. **1382** WYCLIF *Luke* xii. 55 Whanne ȝe seen the south blowynge, ȝe seyen, For heete schal be. **1587** D. FENNER *Song of Songs* iv. 16 Wake North, and com O South, and on my garden blowe. **1697** DRYDEN *Æneid* I. 756 The South, with mighty roar, Dispers'd and dash'd the rest upon the rocky shore. **1757** W. WILKIE *Epigoniad* III. 69 When the north and stormy south engage. **1819** BYRON *Juan* II. clxviii, Breathing all gently.., As o'er a bed of roses the sweet south. **1871** R. ELLIS tr. *Catullus* xxvi. 2 'Tis not showery south, nor airy wester.

b. A south wind; *esp.* one of the southern gales which occur in the West Indies.

1699 DAMPIER *Voy.* II. III. 60 In the West Indies there are three sorts [of storms], viz. Norths, Souths, and Hurricanes. **1707** SLOANE *Jamaica* I. p. lix, Its being liable to be wash'd off by the violent sea-breezes or Souths. **1841** CLOUGH *Poems* (1892) 18 My wind is turned to bitter north, That was so soft a south before.

6. *Bridge.* The player sitting opposite and partnering north: occas. in conventional printed representations of the game, the player who wins the bidding and plays the hand.

1926 [see EAST *sb.* 4]. **1933** C. VANDYCK *Contract Contracted* iii. 31 South deals and bids 1 Diamond. North seeing the possibilities of a Slam gives a Slam Invitation by bidding 5 Spades. **1958** *Listener* 2 Oct. 541/1 One would expect South to pass. **1964** FREY & TRUSCOTT *Official Encycl. Bridge* 514/2 In bridge writing for general reading, South is, conventionally, the declarer... However, in reporting International Matches, the actual positions at the table are used. **1978** *Country Life* 14 Dec. 2098/2 Most Souths without further thought would bid Three No Trumps.

7. A collective name for the industrially and economically less advanced countries of the world, typically situated to the south of the industrialized nations.

1975 *Economist* 18 Oct. 103/2 North-south dialogue... This week's preliminary get-together [between] the west and the oil and non-oil developing nations..illuminated the snake pit ahead. **1977** *N.Y. Times* 22 Sept. 43 Today, any regional struggle over who is to become managing director of the I.M.F. is far less likely to be one between the United States and Western Europe as between the 'North' and the 'South'—that is, the developed, industrial countries and the so-called developing countries, some oil-rich and others oil-poor; some well on the way to industrialization, and others desperately poor. **1978** *New Internationalist* May 6/1 Present patterns of technology transfers from North to South vindicate Bertrand Russell's view..that 'I am compelled to fear that science will be used to promote the power of dominant groups rather than to make men happy.' **1979** *Newsweek* 19 Nov. 144 The turbulent years of the 1970s have witnessed an uneasy confrontation between the North and the South, and a largely unresolved debate on a whole series of specific economic problems.

C. *adj.* (In early use the stem in combination.)

1. With proper names: **a.** Denoting the southern division of a race, nation, or people.

c **900** tr. *Baeda's Hist.* (1890) 4 Fela he me sæde ymbe Suðseaxe & embe Westseaxe. *c* **1100** *O.E. Chron.* (MS.C.) an. 1052, He ȝespeon him to..þæne East-ende, & Suð-Sexan, & Suðriȝan. *c* **1205** LAY. 7449 Guærtaæt þe mode mid þon Suð Walscen. **1387** TREVISA *Higden* (Rolls) VI. 153 In þe fiȝting of þe Souþ Saxons aȝenst Cedwalla. **1577–87** HOLINSHED *Chron.* I. 118/2 The countrie of the Southmercies,..separated from the Northmercies by the riuer Trent. **1643** R. BAKER *Chron.* (1653) 7 The second Kingdome of the Heptarchy, was of the South Saxons. **1862** BORROW *Wales* lxvii, The old chap who disliked South Welshmen. *Ibid.*, The enemy of the South Welsh.

b. Denoting the southern part of a country, land, town, district, ocean, etc., or the more southerly of two places having the same name. *South Kensington* (colloq. *South Ken*), a district of London noted esp. for the museums and other cultural and scientific institutions located there; also *ellipt.*, any of these institutions. *South-Spain* attrib., designating or pertaining to a South Spainer (see sense 1 c below).

962 in Birch *Cartul. Saxon.* III. 325 Æt Suðhamtune. *c* **1100** *O.E. Chron.* (MS. D) an. 1023, [They] feredon on scype his þone halȝan lichaman..to Suðȝeweorke. *c* **1205** LAY. 29925 Of Suð Wales [was] Margadud, monen alre uæȝerest. *c* **1330** R. BRUNNE *Chron. Wace* (Rolls) 4355 Of South Walys com kyng Ignarcet. *c* **1425** *Eng. Conq. Ireland* 6 He went hym thennes in-to south walys. **1577** EDEN & WILLES *Hist. Trav.* 230 b, Betwyxt the West Indie or South America, and the South continent. **1600** PORY tr. *Leo's Africa* III. 168 What time they were lordes of Granada in south Spaine. **1718** [see BRITAIN *sb.*[1] 1]. **1776** ADAM SMITH *W.N.* v. i. iii. (1904) II. 370 From the port of Sallee, in South Barbary, to Cape Rouge. **1816** SCOTT *Bl. Dwarf* i, What news from the south hielands? **1835** *Penny Cycl.* III. 25/2 The South Atlantic Ocean does not offer any other peculiarity in its formation, but the Northern is distinguished by several. **1845** *Encycl. Metrop.* VIII. 600 (*heading*) South London. **1862** A. J. MUNBY *Diary* 18 Jan. in D. Hudson *Munby* (1972) 114, I walked past the South Kensington Museum and along the Cromwell Road. **1866** *Treas. Bot.* 211/1 *Camptosema rubicundum* [is] a native of South Brazil. *Ibid.* 1044/2 Natives of South Africa. **1882** *Girl's Own Paper* 1 Apr. 432/2 We advise your going direct to the British Museum or South Kensington, and make a study of one gallery after another. **1885** A. EDWARDES *Girton Girl* I. iii. 59 There was no South Kensington, and we never called ourselves art students. **1885** *Encycl. Brit.* XVIII. 119/1 When the 'Challenger' was cruising in the South Pacific..the water was found to be uniformly warmer than the air. **1924** J. BUCHAN *Three Hostages* iii. 50 He was M.P. for a South London division. **1924** W. RUNCIMAN *Before Mast* III. ii. 78 A visit was paid to a very fine South Spain barque. *Ibid.*, As it was a Friday we had presented to us a real South Spain meal, pea soup and pork. **1933** M. ALLINGHAM *Sweet Danger* xiv. 172 If we get away with this we might start on the South Ken. There's a large-size model of a flea there I've always had my eye on. **1933** J. MASEFIELD *Bird of Dawning* 98 All South-Spain ships pass where we pass, going or coming. **1944** W. TEMPLE *Church looks Forward* ii. 17 That, broadly speaking, is the aim of the South India Scheme. **1946** *Whitaker's Almanack 1947* 783/2 South Georgia is permanently inhabited and is an important seat of the whaling industry. **1948** *Times* 11 May 3/3 The Communists continued with their campaign to keep the population of South Korea from voting in today's elections. **1949** O. HAMMERSTEIN (*title of musical*) South Pacific. **1950** *Times* 28 Apr. 5/4 The Federal Government has decided to send a mission..to the island of Amboyna, where the revolt which resulted in the proclamation yesterday of the 'independent Republic of the South Moluccas' originated. **1954** *Times* 21 July 6/1 There will probably be two other enclaves for Viet-minh troops now in the south Viet Nam. **1965** M. ALLINGHAM *Mind Readers* i. 22 Her drawl, which Peggie had known when it was pure South London, was now very Mayfair. **1966** *Times* 22 Jan. 7/1 Both the Yemen Government and the Arab League have welcomed the N.L.F.-O.L.O.S. merger into the new anti-British militant 'Front for the Liberation of Occupied South Yemen' (F.L.O.S.Y.). **1972** F. MACCARTHY *All Things Bright & Beautiful* ii. 44 Lethaby..retired from the Central [School] to concentrate on the South Kensington professorship. **1972** H. KURATH *Studies in Area Linguistics* 54 The South Atlantic States—the Southern and South Midland dialect areas. **1975** *Times* 11 Mar. 13/2 Little girls with South Ken accents. **1982** *Daily Tel.* 11 Oct. 18/4 Spinks of St. James's tell me..that the South Atlantic Medal will be seen.

c. With sbs. and adjs. derived from the names of countries, districts, or peoples. *South Spainer*, formerly, a ship engaged in trade with Spain; a sailor on such a ship. See also SOUTH AFRICAN *sb.* and *a.*, SOUTH AMERICAN *sb.* and *a.*

1612 DRAYTON *Poly-olb.* xi. 215 The high descent of that South-Saxon King. **1808** JAMIESON *Diss.* in *Sc. Dict.* I. 21 The Romans..conquered the South-Britains. **1821** A. ROYALL *Lett. from Alabama* (1830) 137 She married a South Carolinian. **1839** *Dublin Rev.* May 449 'Read Mr. James's book,' said a South Australian colonist to the writer of this article. **1842** *Penny Cycl.* XXII. 270/2 South Polar countries. **1844** LADY DUFF-GORDON tr. *Meinhold's Amber Witch* Introd., His South-German language betrays a foreign origin. **1856** C. NORDHOFF *Merchant Vessel* viii. 97 They hold all manner of foreign vessels, or 'south Spainers', in supreme contempt. **1862** BORROW *Wales* lxvii, The people speak neither English nor Welsh, not even South Welsh as you do. *Ibid.*, Anybody may know you are South Welsh by your English. **1877** *Encycl. Brit.* VII. 188/2 *South Slavic* [dictionary]—Richter and Ballman, Wien, 1839–40.

1881 *Ibid.* XII. 755/2 The South Indian [railway line] (the only one on the narrow gauge), in the extreme south, from Cape Comorin to Madras city. **1889** *N.Y. Semi-Weekly Tribune* 6 Dec. 13/4 Three ballots were put in the box for the South Dakotans to draw from. **1903** H. HOLMES *Life & Adv. on Oceans* 8 There may be truth in the saying that a South Spainer, bound for a warm climate, can put his clothes in a stocking. **1924** W. RUNCIMAN *Before Mast* II. iii. 46 Never a cargo vessel looked cleaner or better cared for than this little South-Spainer. **1936** A. W. CLAPHAM *Romanesque Archit.* iv. 81 The system of barrel-vaults without direct lighting of the aisled nave is general in the south-French school. **1939** South Caucasian [see LAZ]. **1941** C. S. FORESTER *Captain from Connecticut* iii. 57 Hubbard's South Carolinian speech. **1949** *Britannica Bk. of Year* 380/1 An interim agreement was signed calling for some U.S. troops to remain in Korea until South Korean military forces could be well organized. **1950** 'P. WOODRUFF' *Island of Chamba* ii. 43 There will be food in the Persian style as well as Moghul and South Indian. **1951** *Britannica Bk. of Year* 342/2 In East Indonesia some prominent Ambonnese people..on April 25 [1950] seceded and proclaimed a South Moluccan independent republic. **1958** T. HICKINBOTHAM *Aden* xii. 196 The South Arabian League which originally advocated union between the Colony and the Protectorate. **1963** E. HUMPHREYS *Gift* II. i. 207 'No thanks, Stel, love.' With her I tended to talk as if I were a South Walian. **1966** J. CLEARY *High Commissioner* i. 20 The Americans will accuse the Chinese and vice versa. The same with the South Vietnamese and the Viet Cong. **1971** *Guardian* 12 July 7/2 Guiding bewildered Irishmen and rooted South Londoners through the intricacies of Notting Hill Gate. **1972** 'E. PETERS' *Death to Landlords!* ix. 135 You are a South Indian yourself, Mr. Narayanan. **1975** *Amer. Speech 1973* XLVIII. 60 A South Dakotan holds that a wet bituminous road is slippery but an icy road is slick. **1975** *Times* 3 Dec. 1/6 The hijackers, all South Moluccans who demanded the return of the islands. **1977** *Trans. Philol. Soc. 1975* 176 *Cuillem* looks possible, *c* presumably representing South Walian phonetics. **1978** *Amer. Speech* LIII. 41 Three areas of the eastern states provided the bulk of the English-speaking settlers for the North Central states: South Midlanders from the Upland South, [etc.]. **1979** *Guardian* 5 Nov. 11/6 The marvellous Tipi cover by South Dakotan Sioux braves.

2. a. With common nouns: Lying towards the south; situated on the side next the south.

Also *transf.* of a magnet pole: see POLE *sb.*[2] 5.

c **893** K. ÆLFRED *Oros.* I. i. §8 Hiera suþȝemæro licgeað to þæm Readan Sæ. **971** *Blickling Hom.* 201 Ðær wæs seo suðduru hwæt hweȝa hade mare. *a* **1124** EADMER in Rock *Ch. of our Fathers* (1903) I. 178 *note*, Principale hostium ecclesiæ, quod antiquitus ab Anglis et nunc usque Suthdure dicitur. *c* **1205** LAY. 27932 Biburied he wes þere..wið uten þan suð ȝæte. **1382** WYCLIF *Ezek.* xlvi. 9 He that entrith by the waye of the south ȝate. **14..** *Sailing Directions* (Hakluyt Soc., 1889) 14 A south moone makith high watir. **1473** *Rolls of Parlt.* VI. 85/1, xv acres of arable Lond,..liyng in the southfeldes of the seid Cite. **1560** GARGRAVE in J. J. Cartwright *Chapters Hist. Yks.* (1872) 10 At Shefeld, wyche was the sowthyst parte of his commyssyon. **1644** in *Scottish Jrnl. Topog.* (1847) I. 73 The Rebells..are betwixt vs and ye Path of Droone on ye south hand. **1738** *Gentl. Mag.* VIII. 577/1 By taking her Meridian Altitudes, both North and South. **1792** MORSE *Amer. Geog.* (ed. 2) 253 The fort near the south end of the city. **1801** *Farmer's Mag.* Aug. 290 Elgin..situated on the south bank of the Lossie. **1842** *Penny Cycl.* XXIII. 217/1 Off the shore are the North and South roads.

Comb. *c* **1470** HENRY *Wallace* VIII. 747 Abowne the toune, apon the southpart sid. **1862** ANSTED *Channel Isl.* I. i. 5 A south-central group, including Jersey. **1880** *Sat. Rev.* 2 Oct. 424/1 Brighton and other South-coast watering-places.

b. ***South Crown, Fish, Triangle***: (see quots. and SOUTHERN *a.* 3 b).

1594 BLUNDEVIL *Exerc.* IV. xix. (1636) 473 Foure other Images towards the South Pole, as the Crosse.., the South Triangle [etc.]. **1638** CHILMEAD tr. *Hues' Treat. Globes* II. vi, The foureteenth [constellation] is Corona Australis, or South Crowne... The fifteenth is Piscis Austrinus, the South Fish. **1674** MOXON *Tutor Astron.* I. iii. §10 (ed. 3) 19 Constellations..added by Frederico Houtmanno,..who..named them as follows:..7 The Camelion, 8 The South Triangle. **1771** *Encycl. Brit.* I. 487/1 The new Southern Constellations [include]..Triangulum Australis, The South Triangle.

c. ***South Bank***, *spec.* the southern bank of the Thames and the areas adjacent to it, (*a*) noted esp. for the cultural complexes and public gardens developed between Westminster and Blackfriars bridges for and since the Festival of Britain in 1951; also *attrib.* and *ellipt.*, any of these complexes; (*b*) used (freq. *attrib.* and as *adj.*) with reference to the policy of the Anglican diocese of Southwark to re-express traditional beliefs and practices in ways that would make them better suited to contemporary life.

1951 H. NICOLSON *Diary* 4 May (1968) 206 Viti and I go to the South Bank Exhibition. We are entranced. **1961** *Guardian* 19 May 22/5 A glass-and-wood pavilion in best South Bank style. **1963** M. FRAYN in Sissons & French *Age of Austerity* xv. 329 The South Bank site—a derelict slum, low-lying, marshy, and heavily blitzed. *Ibid.* 330 A model of the South Bank made out of toilet rolls. **1963** *Guardian* 8 July 14/3 The problems of the South Bank parishes which this so-called South Bank religion is trying to tackle. **1965** LUNN & LEAN *Cult of Softness* iv. 44 The new predestination exercises a certain attraction on South Bank theologians. **1967** A. LASKI *Seven Other Years* xiii. 179 It may be that I am going a little far in calling it atheism; it might, I suppose, be regarded as an effusion of so-called South Bank Christianity. **1968** J. TURNER *Requiem for Two Sisters* i. 5 The vicar..had never thought it part of his duty to dress in a black suit and dog-collar all the time. Indeed, his opinions were to a great extent South Bank. **1977** 'E. CRISPIN' *Glimpses of Moon* vi. 88 No one takes any notice of the clergy nowadays, except for Humanists waiting to welcome South-Bank bishops into the fold. **1977** *Skateboard Special* Sept. 3/4, I do a lot of riding on the South Bank. **1980** *Times* 22 Oct. 13/7 The National have given us many fine productions... This one lapse of quality does not justify the witch-hunt on the South Bank.

3. Of the wind: Blowing from the south. Also *fig.*

Cf. OE. *súðan wind* and SOUTHEN *a.*

c **725** *Corpus Gloss.* (Hessels) A 951 *Auster*, suðuuind. *c* **950** *Lindisf. Gosp.* Luke xii. 55 Miððy [ȝie ȝeseað] suð wind, ȝie cuoeðas þætte wind bið. *c* **1340** *Nominale* (Skeat) 567 *Vent mouent et vent galerne*, Southwynde, westwynde. **1388** WYCLIF *Ps.* lxxvii. 26 He turnede ouere the south wynde fro heuene. **14..** *Lat.-Eng. Voc.* in Wr.-Wülcker 596 *Ventus meridialis*, Southwynde. **1513** DOUGLAS *Æneid* III. vi. 4 The south wyndis blast Our piggeis and our pinsalis wavit fast. *a* **1593** MARLOWE *Ovid's Elegies* II. viii. 19 Thou Goddesse doest command a warme South-blast. **1667** MILTON *P.L.* XI. 734 Meanwhile the Southwind rose,..with black wings Wide hovering. **1734** POPE tr. *Hor., Sat.* II. ii. 27 Oh blast it, South-winds! till a stench exhale. **1820** SHELLEY *Orpheus* 88, I have seen A fierce south blast tear through the darkened sky. **1847** HELPS *Friends in C.* I. i. 4 The clang of an anvil..came faintly up to us when the wind was south. **1917** N. DOUGLAS *South Wind* ii. 16 For Nepenthe was famous not only for its girls and lobsters, but also for its south wind.

fig. **1937** C. MACKENZIE (*title*) The south wind of love. **1946** L. B. LYON *Rough Walk Home* 28 Ask that for these may blow The hot south rage of life again.

transf. **1611** SHAKS. *Cymb.* II. iii. 136 The South-Fog rot him.

4. Of or pertaining to the south; belonging or native to the south.

Cf. OE. *súðfolc, -mæȝð, -mann.*

c **1470** HENRY *Wallace* XI. 779 The South byschop..Till London past, and tald Eduuard him sell. **1616** *Barbour's Bruce* (Hart) XVII. 843 For the South men wald that he made Arest there. **1719** W. WOOD *Surv. Trade* 281 The Assiento Contract has excluded all the Subjects of Great Britain from Trading to New-Spain, but..the South-Company. **1821** SCOTT *Kenilw.* i, For what says the south proverb. **1973** *Express* (Trinidad & Tobago) 1 Feb. 17/1 Behind the move to promote female calypsonians is well-known south businessman, Mr. Lall Parsotan.

5. Facing the south. Also *Comb.*

1527–8 *Rec. St. Mary at Hill* 343 A pane in oon of the sowth windowse. **1642** FULLER *Holy & Prof. State* III. vii. 167 A South-window in summer is a chimny with a fire in't. **1706** LONDON & WISE *Retir'd Gard.* I. I. xii. 53 A South-aspected Wall in Sussex, or about London. **1797** *Encycl. Brit.* (ed. 3) V. 30/2 A south wall..is proper for training them as wall-trees. **1842** LOUDON *Suburban Hort.* 177 Walls having a south aspect. **1867** AUGUSTA WILSON *Vashti* xx, Carnations and mignonette blooming in the south window.

6. Tending towards the south.

1839 *Penny Cycl.* XIV. 141/1 The south declination of the sun. **1886** C. E. PASCOE *Lond. of To-day* xxxiv. (ed. 3) 303 Within a few steps of Hanover Square, in a south direction.

7. *Oxf. Univ. slang.* (See quot.)

1823 EGAN *Grose's Dict. Vulgar T., South Jeopardy*, terrors of insolvency.

south (saʊθ), *v.* [f. SOUTH *adv.* or *sb.*]

1. *intr.* To cross the meridian of a place.

1659– [see SOUTHING *vbl. sb.* 1 a]. **1828** MOORE *Pract. Navig.* 140 The minutes after noon when she [*sc.* the moon] souths. **1883** R. A. PROCTOR *Great Pyramid* iii. 125 [The star] must have been visible to the naked eye, even when southing in full daylight.

2. To veer, move, or turn towards the south; to blow more from the south.

1725 DE FOE *Voy. round World* (1840) 173, I took the occasion..to keep still on southing. **1864** in WEBSTER. **1898** J. M. FALKNER *Moonfleet* xi, About sun-down the wind southed a point or two.

south, obs. f. SOOTH *a.*, SOOTHE *v.*; var. SOWTH.

south- (saʊθ), *prefix*[1]. Combining form representing SOUTH *sb.* or *adv.*, occurring, with the sense 'to or towards, in or on, the south', in participial combinations, as ***south-facing, -falling, -following, -going, running***, etc.; ***south-bounded, -turned***, etc.

(*a*) **1961** *Times* 23 Dec. 3/4 The aspect is right, that is *south-facing. **1978** 'J. BELL' *Swan-Song Betrayed* ii. 16 Her workroom, small but south-facing. **1632** LITHGOW *Trav.* VI. 281 The devalling side of the *South-falling Syon. **1784** *Phil. Trans.* LXXV. 90 The sextuple or *south following set. **1896** *Westm. Gaz.* 2 May 5/2 The *south-going Irish boat express. **1788** *Phil. Trans.* LXXVIII. 372, 13° 17′ from *south-preceding to north-following the meridian. **1819** SCOTT *Let.* in *Lockhart* (1837) IV. viii. 244 My Highland piper,..who spent a whole Sunday in selecting twelve stones from twelve *south-running streams. **1876** 'OUIDA' *Winter City* vii, The *south-wintering northern swallows.

(*b*) **1598** SYLVESTER *Du Bartas* II. ii. III. *Colonies* 83 Those Realms *South-bounded round with Sun-burnt Guinne. **1870** MORRIS *Earthly Par.* III. IV. 296 Exceeding good Its sunny *south-turned slopes are.

2. Also in *Comb.* with advbs., as **south-about** *adv.*, by a southerly route; also *attrib.*; **south-away** quasi-*sb.*, somewhere to the south.

1958 *Times* 20 Dec. 3/3 Bass frequent the coast from Suffolk south-about to Cheshire. **1961** *Times* 24 Nov. 14/6 So it was decided..to send the ship by the south-about route via Cape Horn. **1954** J. R. R. TOLKIEN *Fellowship of Ring* 16 The folk of the Marish..came..up from south-away.

†**south-** *prefix*[2]. [ad. AF. *suth-*, alteration of OF. *suz-*, *sus-*, *sous-* SOUS-.] An element occurring in a few words, as ***south-bailie***, a sub-bailiff; ***southbarbs***, = SUBURB(S; ***south-bois*** (see quot.); ***southcellarer, -deacon, -dean***, = SUBCELLARER, -DEACON, -DEAN; ***south-lace, -lase***, a beam of wood (cf. LACE *sb.* 4) acting as a support for something. *Obs.*

The AF. *suthbaillif* occurs in 1306 in *Rolls of Parlt.* I. 209/2, and *suthvicar* about 1400 in Higden (Rolls) IX. 134.

c **1325** *Poem temp. Edw. II* (Percy) lxvi, Baylys & *south-bailys Under the shireves. *c* **1450** *Brut* 353 Euery strete & lane yn London & yn þe *sowthbarbez. **1541** *St. Papers Hen. VIII* (1834) III. 322 The late suppressed house of Blak Friers in the southe barbis of the said citie. **1706** PHILLIPS (ed. Kersey) s.v. *Vert*, *Nether-vert*..denotes Under-Woods, and is otherwise call'd **South-bois*, or *Sub-bois*. **14..** *Nom.* in Wr.-Wülcker 681 *Hic succellerarius*, a *sowthselerer. *c* **1400** *Three Kings Cologne* (1886) 152 þe preest and þe dekene and þe *southdekene þei mete togeder on thre partyes. **1563** FOXE *A. & M.* 65/2 The wise man Pandolph the Popes Southdeacon. **1393** LANGL. *P. Pl.* C. III. 187 Somenours and *southdenes þat *supersedeas* takeþ. **1374** in Willis & Clark *Cambridge* (1886) I. 238 Wyndbems, *suchlates [? *read* suthlaces], Asthelers, Corbels. **1448** *Ibid.* II. 8 The sowthelases and the asshelers shull accord in brede with the sparres. **1449** *Ibid.* 10 All the sowtlases, asshalers, walplatz and jopees.

South African, *sb.* and *a.* [f. *South Africa*: see SOUTH *a.* 1, -AN.] **A.** *sb.* **1.** A native or inhabitant of South Africa (see below).

This area of southernmost Africa consisted in the 19th century of a group of British and Boer territories; in 1910, following the British victory in the Boer war (1899–1902), these united to form the Union of South Africa; in 1961 the Republic of South Africa was established.

1806 J. W. JANSSENS *Let.* 17 Jan. in G. M. Theal *Rec. Cape Colony* (1899) V. 298 The interest of the few unfortunate Men who I have the Honor to command, that of the brave and good Dutch South Africans.., put me under the necessity to accept the painful conditions. **1871** J. MACKENZIE *Ten Years North of Orange River* p. v, I would specially direct attention to that part..which describes the results of the past contact of Europeans with South Africans. **1897** G. A. PARKER *S. Afr. Sports* p. xiii, I am glad of this opportunity of dedicating this, the first compilation relating to South African sports, to the foremost South African [*sc.* Cecil Rhodes], and one who has for many years encouraged outdoor games with characteristic liberality. **1913** C. PETTMAN *Africanderisms* 3 As South Africans our lot is cast in a country which..is quite young. **1949** E. POUND *Pisan Cantos* lxxx. 92 And persuaded an Aussie or Zealander or S. African To kneel with him in prayer. **1978** J. BRANFORD *Dict. S. Afr. Eng.* p. xiii, This text..has been written for South Africans of all racial groups.

2. *absol.* uses of the adj.

1930 *Economist* 8 Nov. 866/2 South Africans [*sc.* shares] remained firm. **1969** *Guardian* 24 Oct. 9/5 You will need some medium-dry sherry... You could go for a good South African at about £1.

B. *adj.* Of or pertaining to South Africa or its inhabitants.

1824 (*title of newspaper*) The South African Commercial Advertiser. **1838** W. B. BOYCE *Notes on S. Afr. Affairs from 1834 to 1838* p. xv, Much of the misrepresentation of South African affairs, arises from the fact, that the Colonists labour under the..disadvantage of being..unconnected with the powerful interests, which in England press the claims of the Colonists of other British dependencies upon the attention of Parliament and the Public. **1876** in J. Flint *Cecil Rhodes* (1976) iii. 39 Lord Carnarvon's South African policy. **1894** LYDEKKER *Roy. Nat. Hist.* II. 70 The pretty little South-African weasel (*Pœcilogale albinucha*). **1913** C. PETTMAN *Africanderisms* 8 The words of Portuguese, Indian, and Malay origin, still current in South African Dutch. **1921**, **1925** [see AFRIKAANS *sb.*]. **1949** A. WILSON *Wrong Set* 41 Everyone was anxious to know what Harry thought of the South African hock. **1967** L. MEYNELL *Mauve Front Door* v. 64 South African sherry was absolutely right on that evening. **1978** J. BRANFORD *Dict. S. Afr. Eng.* p. xi, South African English..is in every sense, culturally, lexically, grammatically and phonologically, a 'mixed bag'.

Hence **South Africanism**, (*a*) distinctive South African quality; (*b*) a word or idiom peculiar to or characteristic of South Africa.

1959 *Listener* 29 Oct. 714/2 South Africans..were lulled into thinking the essential South Africanism of General Smuts permanently secure. **1961** *Personality* 16 May 27, I think my favourite South Africanism is 'Bioscope'. **1978** J. BRANFORD *Dict. S. Afr. Eng.* p. xiii, These South Africanisms include..a number of English phrases or usages.

South American, *sb.* and *a.* [f. *South America*, the name of the southern part of the continent of America, excluding Central America: see SOUTH *a.* 1, -AN.] **A.** *sb.* A native or inhabitant of South America.

1775 ADAIR *Amer. Ind.* 199 The simple native South-Americans. **1826** F. B. HEAD *Rough Notes Journeys Pampas & Andes* 306 The Spanish South Americans have certainly become independent of the government of Spain. **1863** T. W. HINCHLIFF *S. Amer. Sk.* viii. 173 Spaniards, Italians and South Americans have a vile habit of using the knife. **1913** A. S. PECK *S. Amer. Tour* xxxiii. 361 The manufacturer..should understand that the South Americans in general are not eager to trade with us. **1943** H. F. ARTUCIO *Nazi Octopus in S. Amer.* I. i. 7 This book is a summing up of experiences and observations which might have been those of any South American who believed in the principles of democracy. **1979** *Guardian* 23 Oct. 28/5 The race got off to a bad start, blamed on Europeans and South Americans surging forward before the signal went off.

B. *adj.* Of or pertaining to South America or its inhabitants.

1820 *Times* 11 Mar. 3/5 (*heading*) South-American affairs. **1833** *Penny Cycl.* I. 448 The empire of Brazil..is the principal South American state washed by the Atlantic. **1869** *Month* Jan. 82 The same operation could be carried on in the South American plains. **1950** T. D. MCCOWN in J. H. Steward *Handbk. S. Amer. Indians* VI. I. 2 The osseous human remains and the artifacts of human manufacture..have been accumulated mainly by European and South

American scientists over a period of about 100 years. **1976** 'A. HALL' *Kobra Manifesto* xi. 153 Half the people in the queue were South American Indians.

southard ('sʌðəd), *adv.* and *sb.* Forms: (see quots.). [Reduced form of SOUTHWARD.] = SOUTHWARD *adv.* and *sb.*

In first quot. perhaps a mere misprint.

1470–85 MALORY *Arthur* IV. xxv. 153 Now torne we vnto syr Marhaus that rode with the damoysel..southard. **1624** in Foster *Eng. Factories Ind.* (1909) III. 14 To the southerd of Tegnapatan some three leages. **1849** *Bentley's Misc.* XXV. 38, I mounted 'Hildebrand', bent on a fortnight's excursion to the south'ard. **1883** STEVENSON *Treas. Isl.* xvii, A strong rippling current running..south'ard.

†southboard. *Obs.*⁻¹ [See SOOTH *a.* 2 b and BOURD *sb.*] A repartee.

c **1800** A. CARLYLE *Autobiog.* (1861) 267 Lindsay was a hussar in raillery, who had no mercy... Monteath was more than his match, for he..[gave] him such southboards as silenced him for the whole evening.

'southbound, *a.* (*sb.*) Also south-bound. [f. SOUTH-¹ + BOUND *ppl. a.*¹] **A.** *adj.* **1.** Bound or directed southwards; travelling south.

1885 H. M. JACKSON *Zeph.* vi. 227, I am going on the south-bound train. **1960** 'E. MCBAIN' *Killer's Payoff* ix. 88 A southbound trip that eventually led back to the city. **1976** W. GREATOREX *Crossover* 170 He ran wildly across the south-bound traffic. **1980** K. FOLLETT *Key to Rebecca* xxvi. 276 Southbound trains are less in demand.

2. Intended for traffic travelling south.

1971 *Daily Tel.* 29 Dec. 1/5 Most of the pile-ups were on the southbound carriageway near the junction of the M1 and M10. **1980** *West Lancs. Even. Gaz.* 1 Mar. 3 Sections of north and southbound carriageways of the M6 near Preston will be closed for at least four hours.

B. *ellipt.* as *sb.* A southbound train.

1903 'O. HENRY' in *Everybody's Mag.* Feb. 173/1 Passengers on the south-bound saw them seated together. **1932** W. FAULKNER *Light in August* xv. 340 Folks..begun to come in and buy tickers for the southbound.

South'cottian, *sb.* and *a.* Also -cotian. [See def.]

A. *sb.* A believer in the claims or teaching of Joanna Southcott (1750–1814), who announced herself as the woman spoken of in Revelation xii.

1842 BRANDE *Dict. Sci.*, etc. 1136/1 Southcottians. **1855** MACAULAY *Hist. Eng.* xvii. IV. 28 It would be most unjust to rank the sect which regards him as its founder with the Muggletonians or the Southcotians. **1899** *Dict. Nat. Biogr.* LIX. 322 The Southcottians would not receive him [John Ward].

B. *adj.* Of or pertaining to Joanna Southcott or her followers.

1843 W. B. HARRISON (title), Correspondence of the Southcottian Church. **1850** P. CROOK *War of Hats* 36 Southcottian dupes—the crazed of unknown tongues.

south country. [SOUTH *a.* 2.] The southern part of any country; the district or region towards the south; *spec.* of Great Britain (south of the Tweed), of England (south of the Wash), or of Scotland (south of the Forth).

1375 BARBOUR *Bruce* XVI. 77 He schupe for till ta His way toward the south cuntre. *c* **1400** *Brut* ccxxviii. 301 In þe same ȝere aboute þe Sowthcuntreys..þere fell..much reyne. **14..** *Sir Beues* (C.) 366 To an erle y schall sende the ..In to the sowthe cuntre. **1562** TURNER *Herbal* II. (1568) 71 The tre whiche we call..in the South countre a quikbeme. **1611** BIBLE *Joshua* xi. 16 Ioshua tooke all that land..and all the South countrey. *a* **1784** *Dick o' the Cow* xli. in Child *Ball.* III. 466/1 Johnë Armstrong, The prettiest man in the south countrey. **1862** BORROW *Wales* xxvi, I took you for a Cumro of the south country.

b. *attrib.* (Frequently hyphened.)

1674 RAY *Coll. Eng. Words* 57 South and East Countrey Words. **1801** *Farmer's Mag.* Nov. 419 Some South-country farmers have lately settled in the neighbourhood. **1884** *Rep. Crofters' Commission* II. 1230 Crossing Shetland cattle with south country cattle.

†southdeal. *Obs.* In 1 suðdæl, 3 suþdale. [See SOUTH *adv.* and DEAL *sb.*¹] The southern part or district (*of* a place).

c **825** *Vesp. Psalter* cxxv. 4 Swe swe burnan in suðdæle. *c* **1000** ÆLFRIC in Assmann *Ags. Hom.* vii. 111 Affrica on suðdælæ ðes chames cynnes. *c* **1200** ORMIN 16418 Suþdale off all þiss werelld iss Mysimmbrion ȝehatenn.

South Devon. [f. SOUTH *a.* 1 + DEVON.] One of a breed of cattle, characterized by its large size and light red or fawn colour, and used for both milk and beef production; also, the breed itself. Also *attrib.*

1897 W. HOUSMAN *Cattle* ii. 59 A breed of cattle, now called the South Devon breed, but long known by the local name of 'South Hams', has sprung up. *Ibid.* 61 The 250 animals of 1893..give the aggregate of 2,961 entries of South Devons. **1946** F. H. GARNER *Brit. Dairying* iii. 161 At maturity the South Devon is..heavier than any other breed. Quite commonly South Devon cows weigh 15 or 16 cwt. **1977** 'E. CRISPIN' *Glimpses of Moon* v. 69 Then came the cows, fourteen-hundredweight yearling South Devons.

Southdown ('saʊθdaʊn). Also South Down, South-down. [See def.]

1. One of a breed of sheep, noted for its short, fine wool and for the good quality of its mutton, originally reared on the South Downs of Sussex and Hampshire. Chiefly in pl.

1787 *Young's Ann. Agric.* VIII. 199 The South Downs.. are, for that point, the best short-woolled sheep which I know in England. **1844** H. STEPHENS *Bk. Farm* II. 99 The Leicester and Southdowns afford the best mutton-chops. **1883** *Science* I. 314/1 An experiment with two mature sheep, a southdown and a merino.

2. This breed of sheep. Chiefly with *the.*

1827 GRIFFITH tr. *Cuvier* IV. 340 The South Down have gray faces and legs, fine bones, long small necks. **1844** H. STEPHENS *Bk. Farm* II. 99 When the piece is large, as of Southdown or Cheviot. **1885** BOWMAN *Struct. Wool Fibre* 85 The Shropshire Speckle-faced Sheep is a cross breed between the original horned sheep and the Southdown.

3. *ellipt.* Mutton from this breed of sheep.

1826 B. R. HAYDON *Let.* 18 Aug. in *Autobiogr. & Mem.* (1927) xxiv. 331 His sly hints as I passed his shop that he had 'a bit of South Down, very fine'. **1859** LEVER *Davenport Dunn* xxxvi, His curdiest salmon declined, his wonderful 'south-down' sent away scarcely tasted.

4. *attrib.*, as ***Southdown breed, ewe, sheep, wether, wool.***

(*a*) **1822** COBBETT *Pol. Reg.* 11 May 336 Offered 17 shillings instead of 37 shillings a-head for his South Down Ewes. **1841** *Penny Cycl.* XXI. 357/2 The average dead-weight of the South Down wether varies from 8 to 11 stones. **1846** J. BAXTER *Libr. Pract. Agric.* (ed. 4) II. p. xxvi, The hardiness of the Southdown breed. **1861** *Times* 11 July, Webb's celebrated flock of Southdown sheep.

(*b*) **1828** in Bischoff *Woollen Manuf.* (1842) II. 106 The low-priced foreign wools do sell at about the same rate as South Down wool. **1885** BOWMAN *Struct. Wool Fibre* 251 A fair illustration of pure Southdown wool.

Hence **south-downer.**

1841 J. T. J. HEWLETT *Parish Clerk* II. 226, I prefer a chop to any thing,..Particularly a real south-downer.

south-east (saʊθ'iːst), *adv.*, *sb.*, and *a.* [OE. *súðéast* (see SOUTH *adv.* and EAST *adv.*), = WFris. *súdeast*, MDu. *suut-* (*zuud-*), *suytoost* (Du. *zuidoost*), OS. *sûthôst* (MLG. *sûtôst*), OHG. *sund-*, *suntôst-* (G. *südost*), Da. *sydost*, Norw. *sudaust*. Cf. also OF. *suest*, F. *sud-est*, Sp. *sudeste*, Pg. *sueste*.]

A. *adv.* **1. a.** In the direction lying midway between south and east. Also with modifications, as *by east*, *by south.*

c **893** K. ÆLFRED *Oros.* I. i. 22 Donua muða þære ea scyt suðeast ut on ðone sæ Euxinus. *a* **1122** *O.E. Chron.* (Laud MS.) an. 1097, Se leoma..wæs swiðe lang ȝeþuht suðeast scinende. **13..** *K. Alis.* 5225 (Laud MS.), Al þat niȝth Hij riden south est riȝth. **14..** *Sailing Directions* (Hakluyt Soc., 1889) 11 Fro Houndeclif fote to Humbre the cours is south est and be south. *c* **1470** HENRY *Wallace* IX. 62 Sowthest he saw..Saxten salis arayit all on raw. **1577** *Reg. Mag. Sig. Scot.* 733/2 Passand southeist as the commoun gait gangis. **1682**, *a* **1701** [see SOUTH *adv.* 4 c]. **1725** DE FOE *Voy. round World* (1840) 145 We..stood off to sea, steering still south-east. **1772–84** *Cook's Voy.* (1790) I. 151 We saw the same land south-east by south four leagues distant. **1849** CUPPLES *Green Hand* xiv. (1856) 143, I held south-east-by-east to the mark.

b. Followed by *of.*

1548 PATTEN *Exped. Scotl.* E iij, Vpon this Fauxsyd Bray .., aboute halfe a myle southeast of them. **1771** *Encycl. Brit.* I. 577/1 Bobbio, a town..about twenty-eight miles south-east of Pavia. **1834–6** *Encycl. Metrop.* (1845) VIII. 414/2 About four miles South-East of Callington. **1896** BADEN-POWELL *Matabele Campaign* x, The district east and south-east of Charter.

2. quasi-*sb.* With preps., as *at*, *by*, *from*, *to.*

1297 R. GLOUC. (Rolls) 175 Fram douere in to chestre tilleþ watelinge stret, Fram souþest to þe norþwest. **1600** [see SOUTH *adv.* 4 b]. **1707** J. CHAMBERLAYNE *Pres. St. Gt. Brit.* (1710) 345 It is faced all round with a steep Rock, except a Bay at South-East. **1789** J. WILLIAMS *Min. Kingd.* I. 102 The bearing of course must be in a line from north-west to south-east. **1868** *Chambers's Encycl.* X. 214/1 Similarly, in the southern tropic, the wind will blow from south-east to north-west. **1879** GEIKIE in *Encycl. Brit.* X. 352/2 The variations in thickness from north-west to south-east.

B. *sb.* **1. a.** The direction or point of the horizon lying between south and east.

1387 TREVISA *Higden* (Rolls) I. 173 A partie þerof hatte Bulgaria, and haþ in þe est side Mesia, in þe souþ est Histria. **1432–50** tr. *Higden* (Rolls) II. 47 Watlingestreete goenge.. from the sowthe este in to the northeweste. **1555** EDEN *Decades* (Arb.) 259 They..folowed the South easte nere vnto a cape of the Iland of Buthuan. **1604** E. G[RIMSTONE] *D'Acosta's Hist. Indies* III. v. 134 They call the North *Tramontana*..; Southeast is by them named *Xirocque.* **1725** DE FOE *Voy. round World* (1840) 315 They should have turned off to the south-east. **1806** A. DUNCAN *Nelson* 61 He made the signal..to..steer to the south-east. **1840** R. H. DANA *Bef. Mast* xviii, The shore is rocky, and directly exposed to the southeast.

†b. ***at the south-east***, from the south-east quarter. *Obs.*⁻¹

1725 DE FOE *Voy. round World* (1840) 212 We met with some very bad weather.., the wind blowing very hard at the south-east.

c. Followed by *of.*

1778 *Encycl. Brit.* (ed. 2) II. 1275/1 Bornholm, an island ..to the south-east of the province of Schonen. **1861** PALEY *Æschylus* (ed. 2) *Supplices* 280 *note*, A tract lying somewhere to the south or south-east of Europe. **1896** BADEN-POWELL *Matabele Campaign* xiii, About a hundred miles to the south-east of this.

2. The south-east wind.

1725 POPE *Odyss.* XII. 388 The south-east blust'ring with a dreadful sound.

3. The south-eastern part of a country.

1778 *Encycl. Brit.* (ed. 2) II. 1274/2 The south-east [of Borneo], for many leagues together, is a stinking morass. **1837** CARLYLE *Fr. Rev.* III. I. i, Gloomy tidings..of Sardinia rising to invade the Southeast. **1968** *Radio Times* 28 Nov. 20/5 A look at some non-broadcast music events taking place in London and the South East. **1972** P. JOHNSON *Offshore Islanders* III. 146 There was an enormous bias in favour of the south-east. Clergymen did not want to serve in the wilder and poorer districts of the north and west.

C. *adj.* **1. a.** Lying or situated in or towards, directed to, the south-east.

Cf. the OE. comb. *súðéastende.*

1548 PATTEN *Exped. Scotl.* L viij, We pyght our fyeld a prik shot on this syde the toun: being on the southest half. **1577** in W. H. Turner *Select. Rec. Oxford* (1880) 395 In the Sowest warde, Mr. Ewen; in the Sowthwest warde, Mr. William Barton. **1626** BACON *Sylva* §405 The Planting of Trees warme vpon a Wall, against the South, or South-East Sunne. **1728** CHAMBERS *Cycl.* s.v. *Compass*, What [has been said] of South-East Amplitudes, holds of North-West Amplitudes. **1820** BELZONI *Egypt & Nubia* III. 307 Mr. Beechey and myself went in a south-east direction. **1855** J. PHILLIPS *Man. Geol.* 115 Other ramifications run both on the south-east and north-west sides of Snowdonia.

b. With proper names, denoting the south-eastern division of a continent, race, etc., and with sbs. and adjs. derived from them.

1893 *Geogr. Jrnl.* Nov. 474 Travel and Adventure in South-east Africa: being the narrative of the last eleven years spent..on the Zambesi. **1909** *Prospectus* (South-East Borneo Rubber Plantations Ltd.) 2 This Company has been formed for the purpose of acquiring and working the Rubber Plantation known as Tanah-Intan..situated in South-East Borneo. **1946** F. OWEN *Campaign in Burma* vii. 44 To complete the picture of South-East Asia Command we must reintroduce Lieutenant-General Joseph Stilwell. **1959** 'M. DERBY' *Tigress* ii. 86 Young South-East Asians at play. **1964** *Whitaker's Almanack 1965* 71/1 South-East England Development Proposals. **1968** O. WYND *Sumatra Seven Zero* v. 57 The South-east Asian male is never turned out burly. **1971** H. TREVELYAN *Worlds Apart* xvii. 193 The Deputy Minister in charge of South-East Asian affairs spoke to me..about the responsibilities of the co-chairman for Vietnam.

2. Of the wind, currents, etc.: Blowing or running from the south-east.

Cf. OE. *súðanéastanwind.*

1398 TREVISA *Barth. De P.R.* XI. iii. (1495) 387 That one is Eestwarde and hyghte Nothus the Southeest winde. **1483** *Cath. Angl.* 350/2 þe Sowthe est wynde, *euriaster*, *nothus.* **1565** COOPER *Thesaurus*, *Euronotus*, a south east wynde. **1611** COTGR., *Siroch*, a South-east wind. *Ibid.*, *Süest*, the Southeast wind. **1728** CHAMBERS *Cycl.* s.v. *Wind*, The North-West Winds succeed the South-East, when the Sun draws near the Tropic of Capricorn. **1868** *Rep. U.S. Commissioner Agric.* (1869) 153 Prevailing winds southeast, northwest, and northeast. **1898** *Jrnl. Sch. Geog.* (U.S.) Oct. 298 The strong southeast swell produced by the southeast trade.

south-'easter. [f. prec. + -ER¹.] A wind or gale blowing from the south-east.

1797 A. BARNARD *Let.* 15 Oct. in *S. Afr. a Century Ago* (1901) 100 What a bold south-easter we have had these two days! **1836** IRVING *Astoria* I. 261 They were wafted steadily up the stream by a strong southeaster. **1847** SIR G. SIMPSON *Round the World* I. 372 The south-easter's usual accompaniment of thick and rainy weather. **1884** BEDFORD *Sailor's Handbk.* 221 Simon's Bay is a safe anchorage.., for vessels ride safely with heavy south-easters.

attrib. **1840** R. H. DANA *Bef. Mast* ix, During the southeaster season. *Ibid.* xxiv, With slip-ropes on our cables, in the old southeaster style of last winter.

south-'easterly, *a.* and *adv.* [f. SOUTH + EASTERLY.]

A. *adj.* **a.** Lying, etc., in the direction of south-east. **b.** Blowing or running from the south-east.

1708 SEWEL *Du. Dict.* II, *Zuydoostelyk*, south-easterly. **1716** *Lond. Gaz.* No. 5478/3 The Wind continues South-Easterly. **1846** WORCESTER (citing Hildreth), *South-easterly*, *a.*, being between the south and east. **1884** BEDFORD *Sailor's Handbk.* 192 From October to May..a south-easterly current is experienced.

B. *adv.* Towards the south-east.

1884 *Encycl. Brit.* XVII. 275/2 The course should be east, ..then south-easterly across the north-east trade. **1890** *Cent. Mag.* Feb. 590/1 The route..led him Southeasterly along the river.

south-'eastern, *a.* [f. SOUTH + EASTERN. Cf. OE. *súðéasterne*, OHG. *sund-*, *suntôstrôni.*]

1. Lying on the south-east side; situated in the south-east.

1577 EDEN & WILLES *Hist. Trav.* 230 b, The South-eastern way rounde about Affrike by the cape of Good hope. **1618** in Foster *Eng. Factories India* (1906) I. 11 Those southerne and south-easterne countries. **1632** LITHGOW *Trav.* III. 105 These South-easterne Iles in Summer are extreame hot. **1694** [see PORTUGUESE *sb.* 1]. **1814** SCOTT *Diary* 9 Aug., The extreme south-eastern point of Zetland. **1875** WHITNEY *Life Lang.* viii. 143 Certain communities in southeastern Europe.

b. Of or pertaining to the south-east of England.

1886 KINGTON OLIPHANT *New English* I. 151 [In Trevisa's Chronicle] the South-Eastern form *ie* replaces *eaȝ* in *die* (tingere).

2. Of the wind: Blowing from the south-east.

Cf. OE. *súðéasterne*, *súþanéastern wind.*

1842 *Penny Cycl.* XXII. 286/2 During the south-eastern wind, which is called the *solano*, the thermometer frequently rises to 90°. **1855** KINGSLEY *Westw. Ho!* i, Far below, upon the soft south-eastern breeze, the stately ships go sliding out to sea.

south-'easterner. [f. SOUTH-EASTERN *a.* + -ER¹.] An inhabitant or native of the south-eastern part of a country.

1960 G. ASHE *From Caesar to Arthur* v. 115 The resulting cleavage between Vortigern and the south-easterners whom he aspired to govern was widened by the Pelagian heresy. **1964** *New Society* 26 Mar. 3/2 At present two out of three southeasterners live within 40 miles of Charing Cross.

south-'easternmost, *a.* [f. SOUTH-EASTERN *a.* + -MOST.] Lying furthest to the south-east.

1837 *Penny Cycl.* VIII. 398/1 A range of hills..runs from the north-easternmost point to the south-easternmost at Svenborg. **1845** J. COULTER *Adv. in Pacific* xvii. 278 The south-easternmost part of Tahiti.

south-'eastward, *adv.*, *sb.*, and *a.* [f. SOUTH-EAST + -WARD.]

A. *adv.* In a south-easterly direction; towards the south-east.

1528 in Froude *Hist. Eng.* (1856) II. 63 Master Garret.. fled in a tawny coat south-eastward. **1591** G. FLETCHER *Russ. Commw.* 65 b, The Chrim Tartar..that lieth South, and Southeastward from Russia. **1725** DE FOE *Voy. round World* (1840) 230 Most of those rivers ran rather south-eastward than northward. **1845** *Encycl. Metrop.* VI. 584 The strata sink with a very regular inclination Eastward or South-Eastward. **1896** BADEN-POWELL *Matabele Campaign* xiv, Making its own way, south-eastward towards the Belingwe district.

B. *sb.* The south-east quarter or direction.

1555 EDEN *Decades* (Arb.) 381 To the Southeastwarde, lyeth a hed lande. *Ibid.*, To the southeastwarde of that rocke. **1820** SCORESBY *Acc. Arc. Reg.* II. 345 They had rowed many hours to the south-eastward. **1860** *Merc. Marine Mag.* VII. 172 Some others to the south-eastward are quite out of the way. **1884** BEDFORD *Sailor's Handbk.* 146 Vessels..would do well to stand boldly to the south-eastward with these winds.

C. *adj.* Situated towards or leading to the south-east.

1766 ENTICK *London* IV. 60 The arms of London [are] on the south-eastward pillar. **1796** MORSE *Amer. Geog.* (ed. 3) I. 550 In a southeastward direction.

So **south-'eastwards** *adv.*

1879 GEIKIE in *Encycl. Brit.* X. 366/1 They [*sc.* striæ] run ..eastwards or south-eastwards across the lower grounds of Sweden. **1897** MARY KINGSLEY *W. Africa* 407 The Ogowé's chief affluent..cuts through it again from Samba south-eastwards.

south-'eastwardly, *adv.* [f. SOUTH-EASTWARD + -LY[2].] Towards the south-east; on the south-east side.

1792 MORSE *Amer. Geog.* 194 Bounded..south-eastwardly by the Atlantic Ocean. **1861** *Rep. Miss. River* 56 The Big Horn..flows southeastwardly..through a narrow bottom land. **1890** TALMAGE *From Manger to Throne* 401 Jesus..traveled southeastwardly along the Lebanon mountains.

†**southen**, *a. Obs.* Forms: 1–3 **suðen**, 5 **soþen**; 4 **southen**, 5, 6 *Sc.*, **southyn**. [f. SOUTH *adv.* + -EN[4], or repr. OE. *súðan* adv. (= MDu. and MLG. *suden*, OHG. *sundan*, ON. *sunnan*) 'from the south', in the comb. *súðanwind*.] Of the wind: South, southerly.

c **1000** ÆLFRIC *Voc.* in Wr.-Wülcker 143 *Auster, uel nothus*, suðen wind. *c* **1150** *Canterbury Ps.* lxxvii. 26 And he æwehte suðenwind [*Vesp. Ps.* suðanwind] of heofonum. *c* **1250** *Gen. & Ex.* 3084 A suðen wind is fliȝt up-wond, And blew ðat day. *a* **1300** *E.E. Psalter* lxxvii. 30 He forth-broght southenwind fra heuen. **1398** TREVISA *Barth. De P.R.* XVII. lxi. (Bodl. MS.), The norþen winde greueth þe fige tree more þan þe soþen winde. **14..** in Hartshorne *Anc. Met. Tales* 128 Southyn wyndys that som tyme blowe, Makyn mastys to bowen. **1549** *Compl. Scot.* vi. 61 Auster or meridional vynd, quhilk the vulgaris callis southyn vynd.

†**'southen**, *adv. Obs.*[−1] In 3 **suðen**. [Misuse of OE. *súðan*, or error for *suð*.] Southwards.

c **1250** *Gen. & Ex.* 1167 Suðen he wente & wunede in geraris.

†**south-end**. *Obs.* [ME. *sūðende* (cf. OE. *norðende*), = MDu. *suut-*, *zuutende*, MLG. *sûtende*.] The south of England.

c **1205** LAY. 3372 Forhd þe king wende in to þan suð ende. **1338** R. BRUNNE *Chron.* (1810) 32 Alle þe North ende was in his kepyng, & alle þe South ende tille Edmunde þei drouh.

souther ('sauθə(r)), *sb.* [f. SOUTH *a.* + -ER[1].] A south wind or gale.

1851 *Austral. & N.Z. Gaz.* XXX. 483 During the night a 'stiff souther' put [the *Pauline*] again on shore. **1862** HOPKINS *Hawaii* 10 In the roadstead..there is excellent anchorage except during a Souther or 'Kona'. **1884** J. BURROUGHS *Locusts & Wild H.* 120 A north-easter in one place may be..a souther in some other locality.

†**'souther**, *a. Obs.* Forms: 1 **syþera**, **suþera**, **suðra**, 3 **souþere**, 5 **southir**, 6–7 **souther**. [OE. *sýþera*, *súðera* (f. *súð* SOUTH *adv.*), = MDu. and MLG. *süder*, ON. *syðri* (MSw. *syþre*, *södhre*, Sw. *södre*) and *synnri* (MSw. *sundre*, Da. *sønder-*). Cf. also the combining forms OS. *sûdar-*, Du. *zuider-*, MHG. *sûder-* (G. *süder-*); OHG. *sundar-* (MHG. *sunder-*).] The more southerly of two things or places; situated or lying to the south.

c **900** in Birch *Cartul. Saxon.* II. 242 On þone syþeran stæþ. **931** *Ibid.* II. 371 Andlang þæs suþeran weȝes. *c* **1000** *Sax. Leechd.* III. 270 þone suðran steorran we ne ȝeseoð næfre. *c* **1290** *S. Eng. Leg.* I. 442 In þe oþur half of þe churche, al in þe souþere side. **14..** *Sailing Directions* (Hakluyt Soc. 1889) 16 The groundes on the southir side lyen ferr oute. **1594** R. ASHLEY tr. *Loys le Roy* 12 b, For the inhabitants of our land situated in an aquilonarie quadrant, which are subiect to Souther parellels. **1622** R. HAWKINS *Voy. S. Sea* (1847) 40 The chiefe towne..is on the souther side of the Madera.

souther ('sʌðə(r)), *v.* [f. SOUTH *adv.* + -ER[5].] *intr.* To shift, turn, or fly to the south; of the wind, to south or southern.

1628–9 DIGBY *Voyage Medit.* (Camden) 89 The wind.. towardes night..did souther a litle. *c* **1800** H. K. WHITE *Clift Gr.* 237 When the wild duck, southering, hither rides. **1886** *Field* 25 Sept. 452/1 On chance of the wind southering.

Hence **'southering** *ppl. a.*

1868 MORRIS *Earthly Par.* (1870) II. III. 278 The well-fenced vine, Whose clusters hung upon the southering side Of the fair hill. **1893** *Leisure Hour* Sept. 706 The long fair grass-tufts which the sun In southering glory looked upon.

souther, dial. variant of SOLDER *v.*

'southerling. *rare*[−1]. [f. SOUTH. Cf. EASTERLING.] A native or inhabitant of the south.

1609 J. DOWLAND *Ornithop. Microl.* 80 They thinke he [God] is gone to the South-side of heauen, and therefore cannot so easily heare both the Easterlings and the Southerlings.

southerly ('sʌðəlɪ), *a.* and *sb.* [f. SOUTH; cf. *northerly*, *easterly*.]

A. *adj.* **1.** Situated in or towards the south; southern.

1551 RECORDE *Cast. Knowl.* (1556) 263 The one sorte are called Northerlye constellations, the other sorte Southerly constellations. **1577** B. GOOGE *Heresbach's Husb.* II. (1586) 58 b, In hote and Southerlie Countreis. **1613** PURCHAS *Pilgrimage* (1614) 691 The Southerliest Nations of Africa. **1635** PAGITT *Christianogr.* 35 In the more Southerly part of the great Promontory. **1768** G. WHITE *Selborne* xiii, On account of my living in the most southerly county. **1814** SCOTT *Diary* 22 Aug. in *Lockhart*, The southerly line of what is called the Long Island. **1865** W. G. PALGRAVE *Journ. thro' Arabia* II. 79 We found the southerly plateau more.. uneven than the northern. **1869** DUNKIN *Midn. Sky* 32 Regulus is the most southerly.

2. Of the wind: Blowing from the south. ***southerly burster, buster*** (see BURSTER 2, BUSTER 3 a).

1602 SHAKS. *Ham.* II. ii. 397 When the Winde is Southerly, I know a Hawke from a Handsaw. **1617** MORYSON *Itin.* II. 141 They were enforced to stay by a contrary wind, being Southerly. **1721** *Lond. Gaz.* No. 5966/1 The Southerly and Westerly Winds keep the Fleets still at Elsenab. **1769** FALCONER *Dict. Marine* (1780) s.v. *Wind*, Along the coast of Guinea,..the southerly and south-west winds blow perpetually. *a* **1822** SHELLEY *On an Icicle* i, Where southerly breezes Waft repose to some bosom as faithful as fair. **1850** B. C. PECK *Recollections of Sydney* viii. 132 It is almost a corollary, that the evening of a hot-wind day brings up a 'southerly buster', as we have heard the vulgar call it, very chill indeed..as this wind comes from the southerly region of the Australian Alps. **1878** HUXLEY *Physiogr.* 47 In the greater part of Europe the southerly and westerly winds bring rain.

3. Of distance: Extending southwards.

1669 STURMY *Mariner's Mag.* IV. iii. 153 The Southerly Distance is 172..Leagues.

4. Tending or facing southwards.

1789 J. WILLIAMS *Min. Kingd.* I. 136 They are turned from the south-west to a southerly direction. **1857** GRINDON *Life: its Nature* (ed. 2) iii. 31 No dwellings are so pleasant.. as those which have a southerly aspect. **1869** TOZER *Highl. Turkey* I. 243 We mounted on the other side of the valley in a southerly direction.

B. *sb.* A wind blowing from the south; a southerly buster. *Austral.* and *N.Z.*

1943 K. TENNANT *Ride on Stranger* viii. 79 When the Southerly blew, the stiff leaves..twisted rim-on to the blast. **1964** R. BRADDON *Year Angry Rabbit* xiv. 123 What use is it being able to guarantee fine weather, or rain, or a cool southerly only on the coast? **1973** P. WHITE *Eye of Storm* i. 65 How exotic, how naked her body felt when the southerly began to blow at the end of a sticky summer's day, caressing her inside her dresses.

Hence **'southerliness**, 'the being on or toward the South' (Bailey, 1727, vol. II).

southerly ('sʌðəlɪ), *adv.* [Cf. prec. and -LY[2].]

1. To the southward; in or towards the south; on the south side.

1577 EDEN & WILLES *Hist. Trav.* 233 b, The..streict.. openeth southerly more and more, vntyll it come vnder the tropike of Cancer. **1601** HOLLAND *Pliny* II. xcvii. 43 When she is Northerly, and retired higher and farther from the earth, the tides are more gentle, than when shee is gone Southerly. **1669** STURMY *Mariner's Mag.* IV. iii. 148 You have altered the Latitude, that is..you are more Southerly or Northerly. **1725** DE FOE *Voy. round World* (1840) 145 Then we steered away more southerly for six or eight days. **1756** P. BROWNE *Jamaica* 27 The place, where it is observed, is a pleasant vale situated southerly. **1832** DE LA BECHE *Geol. Man.* 95 A strong current sets from the Polar Seas.. southerly down the coast of America. **1885** *Manch. Exam.* 10 Feb. 5/2 Crossing the hills.., he made his way southerly to Bangkok.

2. From the direction of the south.

a **1642** SIR W. MONSON *Naval Tracts* II. (1704) 260/1 The Wind chop'd up Southerly. **1725** DE FOE *Voy. round World* (1840) 175 The wind still holding southerly,..we could easily perceive the climate to change. **1769** FALCONER *Dict. Marine* (1780) s.v. *Wind*, Along the coasts of Cambodia and China..the Monsoons blow northerly and southerly.

'southermost, *a.* Now *rare*. [f. SOUTHER *a.* Cf. SOUTHMOST *a.*] Most southerly; southernmost.

1555 EDEN *Decades* (Arb.) 381 The southermost [is] lyke vnto a iebet. **1626** VAUGHAN *Gold. Fleece* (title-p.), The Southermost Part of the Iland, commonly called the Newfovndland. **1653** W. RAMESAY *Astrol. Restored* 94 The southermost of the 2 hindermost stars in the brest of the Whale. **1719** DE FOE *Crusoe* I. (Globe) 254 The Southermost End of the Island. **1761** *Phil. Trans.* LII. 174 The consequent and southermost limb of the sun. **1814** SCOTT *Diary* 31 Aug. in *Lockhart*, United to the continent by a key ..built along the southermost channel. *c* **1850** *Rudim. Nav.* (Weale) 78 The southermost vessel..will have the wind veering.

southern ('sʌðən), *a.* and *sb.* Forms: 1, 3 **suðerne**, 1 **suþerne**, 4 **soþern**, **sotherin**, 5 **sothryn**, **-(e)ren**, **soþeren**, **-erne**; 4 **souþerne**, **-erin**, **-eren**, 4–7 **southerne** (5 **sow-**), 5– **southern**; 5–6 **southrene**, 5–7 **southren**, 7 **-rine**. [OE. *súðerne* (f. *súð* SOUTH *adv.* + -ERN), = ON. *suðrœnn*, OHG. *sundrôni*. See also SOUTHRON.]

A. *adj.* **1. a.** Of persons: Living or originating in, coming from, the south, esp. of Great Britain (= English), of England, or of Europe.

c **950** *Lindisf. Gosp.* Matt., Int. 19 Ðy cwoen suðerne ȝemyndȝade. *c* **1386** CHAUCER *Parson's Prol.* 42 But trusteth wel, I am a southren man. **1610** [see NORTHERN *a.* 1]. **1646** J. HALL *Poems* I. 10 As feathers on a Southern-hacneys head. **1802** G. ELLIS *Let.* in Lockhart *Scott* (1837) I. x. 346 In the only situation which can enable a Southern reader to estimate their merits. **1871** SKEAT in *Joseph of Arimathie* p. xi, The southern forms in the poem being due to a southern scribe.

b. *U.S.* Belonging to the Southern States. ***Southern Baptist***, a Baptist who is a member of a church belonging to the Southern Baptist Convention, first organized in 1845; also *attrib.*

1789 *Deb. Congress U.S.* 28 Apr. (1834) 215 Suppose a member from Massachusetts was to propose an impost on negroes, what would you hear from the Southern gentlemen, if fifty dollars was the sum to be laid? **1839** W. E. CHANNING *Wks.* (1884) 553/1 Congress must be an arena in which Northern and Southern parties will be arrayed against each other. **1846** J. SOULE in *Jrnls. Gen. Conf. Methodist Episcopal Church, South* (1851) I. 105 Southern Methodists were able so far to conciliate public opinion, and quiet popular apprehension, as to carry on..the ordinary operations of church enterprise and discipline. **1849** [see NORTHERN *a.* 1 b]. **1866** in W. L. Flemming *Documentary Hist. Reconstruction* (1907) II. 247 In 1845, when the Southern Baptist Convention was organized,..in proportion to the population there were more negroes than white people who were members of our churches. **1888** GUNTER *Mr. Potter* xii. 144 The most desperate charge ever made in the war by Southern troops. **1932** *N.Y. Times* 3 Nov. 19/3 The Southern Baptist handbook for 1932 declares Southern Baptists are 'still wasting money in riotous living'. **1936** M. MITCHELL *Gone with Wind* ix. 195 A delicately nurtured Southern belle with her Irish up. **1964** 'E. MCBAIN' *Ax* ii. 32 A simpering smile on her lips, as though she were a Southern belle waiting to be asked for a dance. **1978** N. LONGMATE *Hungry Mills* i. 21 The 'Southern gentlemen', a breed already famous for their independence and arrogance, owned the large plantations. **1979** *Arizona Daily Star* 1 Apr. E7/4 Television station WFAA, which aired his program, said Robison's remarks crossed over from religious to political proselytizing and then canceled the half-hour program. The result has been a wave of support for the popular Southern Baptist evangelist.

2. Of the wind: Blowing from the south.

c **888** K. ÆLFRED *Boeth.* vi, Swa eac se suðerna wind hwilum mid miclum storme ȝedrefeð þa sæ. *c* **1000** *Sax. Leechd.* III. 276 Ealne ðone cwyld ðe se suðerna wind auster acænð. *c* **1205** LAY. 32038 Com þe wind suðerne, þa sæt an heore wille. *c* **1290** *S. Eng. Leg.* I. 232 þo cam sone a souþerne wynd, þat northþe-ward drof heom faste. **1382** WYCLIF *Ps.* lxxvii. 26 He..broȝte in his vertue the southerne wynd. *c* **1440** *Pallad. on Husb.* I. 1104 The southern wynd is best, as wist Is wel. **1548** ELYOT, *Notus*, the southerne wynde. **1565** COOPER *Thesaurus* s.v. *Notus*, The southerne windes puffe vp the sayles. **1626** BACON *Sylva* §217 The Thinner or Drier Aire, carrieth not the Sound so well, as the more Dense: As appeareth..in moist Weather, and Southern Winds. **1697** DRYDEN *Æneid* III. 96 But southern gales invite us to the main. **1748** *Anson's Voy.* II. i. 116 The southern winds..blow off the land in violent gusts.., which seems to be owing to the obstruction of the southern gale, by the hills in the neighbourhood. **1835** *Penny Cycl.* III. 27/1 The southern trade-wind..always preserves its direction.

3. a. Situated or lying to the southward or in the south; having a position relatively south.

c **1000** ÆLFRIC *Hom.* II. 584 Heo..com fram ðam suðernum ȝemærum to Salomone binnon Hierusalem. **1594** [see SOUTHERNLY *adv.* 1]. **1604** E. G[RIMSTONE] *D'Acosta's Hist. Indies* I. 5 The other Antarticke or Southerne Pole. **1658** DRYDEN *Stanzas O. Cromwell* xxxi, We boldly cross'd the Line, And bravely fought where Southern Stars arise. **1713** POPE *Windsor Forest* 391 Under southern skies. **1774** GOLDSM. *Nat. Hist.* (1776) IV. 49 The Agouti..is found in great abundance in the southern parts of America. **1841** ELPHINSTONE *Hist. Ind.* I. 475 The disappearance of the Greeks after the overthrow of their southern kingdom. **1868** *Rep. U.S. Commissioner Agric.* (1869) 21 A large proportion of this advance was in the southern States.

Comb. **1719** DE FOE *Crusoe* I. (Globe) 193 The Current.. did not so hurry me as the Southern Side Current had done.

b. *Astr.* In the names of constellations, as ***Southern Crown, Fish, Triangle. Southern Cross***: also *transf.*, the Australian national flag.

1594 BLUNDEVIL *Exerc.* IV. xix. (1597) 223 b, The Southerne Crowne, called Corona Australis. *Ibid.* 224 The hinder part of the Southerne fish hauing diuers starres without name. **1700-** [see CROSS *sb.* 12]. **1771** *Encycl. Brit.* I. 487 The ancient Constellations [include]..Corona Australis, The Southern Crown,..[and] Piscis Australis, The Southern Fish. **1845** GOSSE *Ocean* iv. (1849) 178 Of all the constellations that stud the sky of the southern hemisphere, there is none that more strikes a stranger than the Southern Cross. **1855** R. CARBONI *Eureka Stockade* xxxvii. 50 There is no flag in old Europe half so beautiful as the 'Southern Cross' of the Ballaarat miners. **1875** *Encycl. Brit.* II. 817/1 The constellations added by Hevelius [include]..Sextans, The Sextant;..Triangulum Australe, The Southern Triangle. **1917** 'H. H. RICHARDSON' *Richard Mahoney* II. i. 96 The 'Southern Cross' hoisted—a blue bunting that bore the silver stars of the constellation after which it was named.

4. a. Of things: Pertaining or belonging to, produced by, found in, characteristic of, the south.

c **1000** *Sax. Leechd.* II. 224 þæt is suþerne læcedom. *c* **1000** ÆLFRIC *Hom.* II. 584 And hire olfendas bæron suðerne wyrta, and deorwurðe gymstanas. *a* **1300** *Cursor M.* 20061 In a writt þis ilk i fand... In sotherin englis was it draun. **1387** [see B. 1]. *c* **1440** *Promp. Parv.* 467/1 Sowtherne, *idem quod* sowthely. *a* **1548** HALL *Chron., Hen. VI*, 101 Meanynge to haue..a southerne byl, to conteruayle a Northren bastard. **1591** SYLVESTER *Du Bartas* I. v. 877 To seek adventure In Southren Climates for a milder Winter. **1622** in Foster *Eng. Factories Ind.* (1908) II. 43 Which.. brings them quantetyes of southrine commodities. **1709** POPE *Ess. Crit.* 400 That sun..not alone the southern wit sublimes, But ripens spirits in cold northern climes. **1748** [see NORTHERN *a.* 3]. **1801** *Farmer's Mag.* Jan. 108 The great demand for the southern markets in the Autumn. **1886** KINGTON OLIPHANT *New English* I. 68 A curious medley of Northern and Southern pronouns.

b. ***southern lights***, the Aurora Australis.

1775 *Phil. Trans.* LXVIII. 409 Some Southern lights, very rare and motionless. **1777** G. FORSTER *Voy. round World* I. 116 The stars were sometimes hid by..these southern lights (*aurora australis*). **1867** SMYTH *Sailor's Word-bk.* 62 Cook was the first navigator who recorded the southern lights.

c. *U.S. spec.* Pertaining to or belonging to the southern States of America (cf. SOUTH *sb.* 2 c). ***Southern Comfort***, the proprietary name of a brand of alcoholic drink, based on whisky and orig. manufactured in the U.S.

1819 D. THOMAS *Trav. through Western Country* 100 The mistress..treated us to milk, in the true spirit of southern hospitality. **1836** *Southern Lit. Messenger* II. 111/2 We have known a New Englander laugh at the Southern use of the word clever. **1860** *Charleston* (S. Carolina) *Mercury* 15 Nov. 2/5 The 'Lone Star' was very suggestive of the additions which may hereafter be made to the Independent Southern Confederacy. **1877** C. HALLOCK *Sportsman's Gazetteer* 96 The Southern Fox Squirrel inhabits the Southern States from North Carolina to Texas. **1880** 'MARK TWAIN' *Tramp Abroad* xlix. 574 Hot wheat-bread, Southern style. **1925** G. P. KRAPP *Eng. Lang. in Amer.* I. 40 It is..much easier for an American to call up in his mind a kind of image of the Eastern and Southern types of American speech than of the Western or General type. **1934** *Official Gaz.* (U.S. Patent Office) 24 July 786/2 Midland Distilleries, Incorporated, St. Louis, Mo... *Southern Comfort*. For Cordial. **1947** *Trade Marks Jrnl.* 12 Nov. 707/1 *Southern Comfort* B647,105. Wines, spirits (beverages) and liqueurs. Southern Comfort Corporation.., 2121, Olive Street, St. Louis,..Missouri, United States of America; Manufacturers. **1962** A. LURIE *Love & Friendship* iv. 60 He had a slight Southern accent. **1978** M. G. EBERHART *Nine O'Clock Tide* i. 21 I'll take a little drink..Southern Comfort. **1979** *United States 1980/81* (Penguin Travel Guides) 280 The corn bread, fried chicken..and the like are served buffet-style in a big Southern-style mansion. **1980** *Blair & Ketchum's Country Jrnl.* Oct. 142 (Advt.), Grandma Johnston's southern fruit cake.

5. a. In the specific names of animals, birds, or fishes: (see quots. and the sbs.).

Other examples occur in *Shaw's Gen. Zool.* (1800–24) and in Lydekker's *Roy. Nat. Hist.* (1894–96).

1813 SHAW *Nat. Misc.* XXIV. 1058 The *Southern Apteryx. **1690** *Lond. Gaz.* No. 2614/4 A Pack of *Southern Beagles to be sold. **1781** LATHAM *Gen. Synop. Birds* I. I. 264 *Southern Brown Parrot... Inhabits New Zealand. *c* **1880** *Cassell's Nat. Hist.* III. 264 The *Southern Caracaras (*Ibycter australis*) are said to run with extreme quickness. *Ibid.* 144 The *Southern Cavy (*Cavia australis*)..inhabits Patagonia. **1890** *Cent. Dict.*, *Micropterus*... Bass of this genus are variously known as..white-trout, *southern or Roanoke chub [etc.]. **1790** J. WHITE *Jrnl. Voy. N.S. Wales* 266 *Southern Cottus, *Cottus Australis*... This fish did not exceed four inches in length. *c* **1880** *Cassell's Nat. Hist.* III. 116 The little *Southern Field Vole (*Arvicola arvalis*). **1843** *Penny Cycl.* XXVII. 283/1 The bifid cæcum in the *Southern Manatee. **1882** JORDAN & GILBERT *Syn. Fishes N. Amer.* 929 *Argyrops chrysops*, *Southern Porgee. **1785** LATHAM *Gen. Synop. Birds* III. I. 187 *Southern Sandpiper ..inhabits Cayenne. *Ibid.* II. 365 *Southern Tern..inhabits Christmas Island. **1823** —— *Gen. Hist. Birds* VI. 322 *Southern Wagtail... Inhabits New-Holland, and has the air and manners of our Common Wagtail. **1868** *Chambers's Encycl.* X. 151/2 The *Southern or Cape Whale (*Balæna australis*) is now regarded as a distinct species.

b. In the specific names of plants. ***southern beech*** = NOTHOFAGUS.

Cf. OE. *sūðerne popiʒ, rædic, wermód.*

1914 W. J. BEAN *Trees & Shrubs Hardy in Brit. Isles* II. 97 The *southern beeches are only adapted for the milder parts of the country. **1957** M. HADFIELD *Brit. Trees* 189 The so-called 'southern beeches'..represent the beech family in South America, south-east Australia, and New Zealand. **1974** [see NOTHOFAGUS]. **1856** A. GRAY *Man. Bot.* (1860) 267 *Bumelia lycioides*... *Southern Buckthorn... Moist ground, S[outh] Kentucky and southward. *Ibid.* 78 *Vitis vulpina*. Muscadine or *Southern Fox-Grape. **1845–50** MRS. LINCOLN *Lect. Bot.* App. 121/1 *Lilium catesbæi*, *Southern lily. **1607** MARKHAM *Cavelarie* III. 17 Not like your *southerne Oates light and emptie, which in the north wee call skeggs. **1840** *Penny Cycl.* XVIII. 171/2 The *southern Pine (*Pinus australis* or *P. palustris*)... A native of Virginia and the neighbouring states of America. **1856** A. GRAY *Man. Bot.* (1860) 470 *Lilium Catesbæi*, *Southern Red Lily.

6. Facing or directed towards the south.

1706 LONDON & WISE *Retir'd Gard'ner* 19 What fruit best agrees with a Southern Wall. *Ibid.* 20 The Southern Exposition. **1781** COWPER *Retirem.* 494 There, prison'd in a parlour snug and small, Like bottled wasps upon a southern wall. **1900** BP. W. HOW *Lighter Moments* 37 A very good garden with a southern slope.

7. Performed or done in the south.

1748 *Anson's Voy.* I. ix. 92 This..would render all that southern navigation infinitely securer than at present.

8. As *adv.* Towards the south.

1678 DRYDEN *All for Love* I. i, All Southern, from yon Hills, the Roman Camp Hangs o'er us black and threatning.

9. *Comb.*, as ***southern-headed, -shaped, -tinted***; **southern-fried** *U.S.*, cooked in a manner characteristic of the southern states; also *fig.*

1972 *St. Louis Post-Dispatch* 5 Nov. c1/4 'Ah sure thought we were gonna win,' he said in his Southern-fried drawl. 'Ah really did.' **1973** *Sat. Rev. World* (U.S.) 6 Nov. 43/1 Southern-fried chicken..with bananas, sweet corn, and tomatoes. **1976** N. THORNBURG *Cutter & Bone* vi. 142 Not hillbilly really. Just a good ole boy, southern fried. **1982** *Times* 19 June 7/5 Southern fried chicken really is a speciality. **1678** *Lond. Gaz.* No. 1308/4 A broad squot white beagle Bitch,..southern-headed. **1922** D. H. LAWRENCE *Aaron's Rod* xiv. 195 There was..something inhuman and possessed-looking in their foreign, southern-shaped faces, so much more formed and demon-looking than northern faces. **1890** 'R. BOLDREWOOD' *Col. Reformer* (1891) 341 The nut-brown maid, blushing through her southern-tinted skin in a very visible manner.

B. *sb.* **1.** Southern men. *rare.*

1387 TREVISA *Higden* (Rolls) II. 163 Men of myddel Engelond..vnderstondeþ bettre þe side langages, norþerne and souþerne, þan norþerne and souþerne vnderstondeþ eiþer oþer. *c* **1470** HENRY *Wallace* IV. 609 Ane awfull salt the Sothren son began. *Ibid.* 665 Thocht Sotheren had it suorn. **1622** DRAYTON *Poly-olb.* xxii. 903 The Southern on this side, for Yorke 'a Warwicke' cry. *Ibid.* 1127 The Southern expert were, in all to war belong. **1818** SCOTT *Hrt. Midl.* viii, A sturdy Scotsman, with all sort of prejudices against the southern, and the spawn of the southern.

2. A native of the south: **a.** Of Great Britain, or of parts of the United Kingdom.

1721 RAMSAY *Prospect of Plenty* 82 The Southerns will with pith your project bauk. **1814** SCOTT *Lord Isles* VI. xxvi, Both Southern fierce and hardy Scot. *a* **1849** H. COLERIDGE *Ess.* (1851) I. 190 The Southerns, and some of you Northerns too, have a strange idea of the lakes. **1874** S. WILBERFORCE *Ess.* I. 26 Poor stay-at-home Southerns whose nerves were not being braced by the invigorating air of the eastern Highlands.

b. Of Europe.

1830 H. N. COLERIDGE *Greek Poets* 18 That the old Greek and Roman poets were..Southerns, or Inhabitants of the South of Europe. **1856** *N. Brit. Rev.* XXVI. 127 Vegetable oil in lamps lights the Southerns now as in old classical days. **1870** MISS L. TOULMIN SMITH *Eng. Gilds* Introd. p. lxxiii, When..these Southerns brought Christianity into the North.

c. In general use.

1846 G. WARBURTON *Hochelaga* II. 314 There were Hamburg Jews, Spaniards from the Havannah, Northerns and Southerns, Westerns, English, Canadians, and a few who had no country in particular. **1885** SIR H. TAYLOR *Autobiog.* I. 353 The trading interests of the Southerns [of China] were identical with our own.

3. *U.S.* The dialect of English spoken in the southern states.

1935, 1951 [see NEW ENGLAND a]. **1975** *New Yorker* 21 Apr. 33/3, I listened to the Governor's lady talking for some minutes to some of her South Delaware friends, and they *were* talking Southern. **1981** J. SCOTT *Distant View of Death* x. 147 Saying in her comedy Southern: 'Why, *Colonel*..you jest *spoil* lil' ol' me.'

Hence **'southern** *v.*, to become more southerly.

1870 *Daily News* 12 May, At 7.30 a.m. the wind was S.E., but southerning fast. **1894** *Times* 6 Aug. 5/2 The breeze southerned and came fresher.

southerner ('sʌðənə(r)). [f. SOUTHERN *a.*]

1. An inhabitant or native of the south, or of the southern part of any country; freq., a native of southern England.

1833 NEWMAN *Lett.* (1891) I. 394, I have letters of introduction to Messina, Catania... Have I told you of the inconsistencies of these Southerners? **1886** KINGTON OLIPHANT *New English* I. 74 The Southerner, on entering Leeds, still reads the old Northern names of Kirkgate and Briggate on two great thoroughfares.

2. One belonging to the southern States of America.

1836 HALIBURTON *Clockm.* Ser. I. xiii, There's so many rich southerners and strangers there that have more money than wit. **1862** J. SPENCE *Amer. Union* 261 From his youth, the Southerner is habituated to command others. **1875** *N. Amer. Rev.* CXX. 65 The Southerners had every guaranty they could desire that they should not be interfered with at home.

'southernism. Also Southernism. [f. SOUTHERN *a.* + -ISM.]

1. a. An idiom, expression, or word peculiar to the southern States of America. Orig. *U.S.*

1882 *Amer. Mission.* Apr. 108 Aside from African features .., and some Southernisms in voice and expression. **1886** *Academy* 11 Sept. 174/3 Among words classed as Southernisms, or as having peculiar Southern uses.

b. An idiom, expression, or word peculiar to a more southerly part of Britain, esp. to the South of England.

1967 P. J. BAWCUTT *Shorter Poems of Gavin Douglas* p. lxxv, The absence of the southernisms and archaic verbal inflections that are found in Douglas, side by side with the regular Middle Scots forms. **1978** *Trans. Yorks. Dial. Soc.* LXXVIII. 9 More definitely attributable to error is the intrusion of Southernisms such as *hond* for hand, *darter* for daughter and, grammatically, *she* for her as object pronoun.

2. The quality of being southern in character.

1861 *N.Y. Tribune* 15 July 6/4 Southernism has raised the standard and gage of social condition absolutely; and those who are so unfortunate as not to be high-born—i.e., born at the South—are given to feel that they must eke out their shortcomings with an extra amount of Southern ardor and Pro-Slavery talk. **1911** *Q. Reg. Panpresbyt. Ch.* Nov. 479 New Orleans has its solid *Southernism* before, during, and since the war.

southernization (,sʌðənaɪ'zeɪʃən). [f. SOUTHERNIZE *v.*: see -ATION.] The act of making southern in respect of character.

1976 *Time* 27 Sept. 98/2 These developments helped to modify the old stereotypes and mitigate fear of Southernization in the North. **1976** *National Observer* (U.S.) 6 Nov. 14/2 Great pains were taken to ensure the success of this historic occasion, otherwise known as 'The Southernization of Central Park'.

southernize ('sʌðənaɪz), *v.* [f. SOUTHERN *a.*]

1. *trans.* To make southern in respect of language, form, character, etc.

1867 *Hymns Virgin* Pref. p. x, Some of the poems bear traces of having been southernized from a Northern original. **1887** *Athenæum* 15 Jan. 92/3 A copy, partially southernized in language, of a work originally written in pure northern dialect.

2. *intr.* To become southern in respect of quality or character (*Cent. Dict.* 1891).

Hence **'southernized, 'southernizing** *ppl. adjs.*

1871 SKEAT in *Joseph of Arimathie* p. xi, The southernizing tendencies of the scribe. **1873** *Athenæum* 23 Aug. 243/2 A slightly more southernized copy of the Trinity MS. **1890** GURNHILL *Monogr. Gainsborough Par. Reg.* 26 'Churchmaster' is a southernized form of Kirk-master.

southernly ('sʌðənlɪ), *a.* [f. SOUTHERN *a.* + -LY[1].] = SOUTHERLY *a.*

1594 BLUNDEVIL *Exerc.* III. II. viii. (1597) 186 If the declination..be Southernly. **1620** E. BLOUNT *Horæ Subs.* 136 More Sowtherneiy people..vpon extraordinarie businesses driuen to the towne. **1655** CULPEPPER, etc. *Riverius* IX. lxxviii. 265 The External Causes, are.. Southernly weather, or infectious Air. **1658** W. BURTON *Comment. Itin. Antoninus* 218 The Town from the Southernly situation is at this day Southanton. **1803** VISCT. STRANGFORD *Poems of Camoens* (1810) 68 Thy branches still wave to the southernly sigh. **1865** CARLYLE *Fredk. Gt.* XVIII. xiii. (1872) VIII. 48 Wind a mere lull, but southernly if any.

Hence **'southernliness**, the 'state of being southernly' (Ogilvie, 1850).

† **'southernly,** *adv. Obs.* [f. as prec. + -LY[2].] = SOUTHERLY *adv.*

1594 BLUNDEVIL *Exerc.* VI. xxx. (1597) 310 Euery degree of any of the southerne signes riseth Southernly. **1613** PURCHAS *Pilgrimage* (1614) 60 These Northernely are seene, which they attribute to the liuing: those Southernely are hidden. **1636** H. B[LOUNT] *Voy. Levant* 72 Winds which in those parts..in Summer, sit Northernly, and in Winter Southernly. **1658** W. BURTON *Comment. Itin. Antoninus* 120 The Military Port way hence tending somewhat more Southernly.

'southernmost, *a.* [f. as prec. + -MOST.] Most southerly; furthest south.

1725 DE FOE *Voy. round World* (1840) 91 The southernmost point of the isthmus of Malacca. **1758** BORLASE *Nat. Hist. Cornw.* 11 Our latitude..is the southernmost of all England. *c* **1850** *Rudim. Navig.* (Weale) 78 The southernmost vessel..will have the wind veering. **1882** DE WINDT *Equator* 24 Along the south-west coast of Borneo from its southernmost boundary, Cape Datu.

'southernness. [f. as prec. + -NESS.] The property or quality of being southern in character.

1891 *Harper's Mag.* Sept. 640/2 It is all very Southern, and nicely differentiated in its Kentucky Southernness from ..Louisianian life. **1903** *Westm. Gaz.* 11 Feb. 2/1, I understood the Southernness of Brive..in this characteristic. **1931** BLUNDEN *Votive Tablets* 210 The weaknesses of his verse,..the exuberant southernness of so much of it might be effeminate. **1966** *Listener* 10 Mar. 357/3 Cleanth Brooks's recent book on the Southernness of Faulkner. **1973** D. AARON *Unwritten War* vii. 118 Charleston, the hatchery of rebellion and quintessence of Southernness. **1980** T. HOLME *Neapolitan Streak* 10 He had never shown..prejudice against Peroni's southern-ness as most northerners invariably did.

southernwood ('sʌðənwʊd). *Bot.* Forms: (see SOUTHERN *a.* and WOOD *sb.*); also 3 **southren-**, 5 **sothren-, sutherne-**, 5–6 **sothern-**, 7 **soothern-, south-hern-**. *β.* 2 **suþer-**, 5 **soþer-, sother-**. [OE. *súðerne* SOUTHERN *a.* 5 b, and *wudu* WOOD *sb.*]

1. A hardy deciduous shrub or plant, *Artemisia Abrotanum*, having a fragrant aromatic smell and a sour taste, orig. native to the south of Europe, and formerly much cultivated for medicinal purposes. Also, the genus of *Compositæ* of which this is the type.

α. *c* **1000** *Sax. Leechd.* I. 250 Ðeos wyrt þe man abrotanum, & oðrum naman suðerne wuda nemneþ, ys tweʒea cynna. *a* **1387** *Sinon. Barthol.* (Anecd. Oxon.) 12 *Averoyn*, southrenwode. *a* **1400** *Stockh. Med. MS.* i. 12 in *Anglia* XVIII. 295 Aueroyne he take..Queche is callyd soþernwode also. **14..** *Voc.* in Wr.-Wülcker 571 *Caruca*, suthernewode. *c* **1440** *Promp. Parv.* 467/1 Sowtherne woode, herbe,..*abrotonum*. **1548** TURNER *Names Herbes* 7 Sotherwood is hote and dry in the thirde degree. *c* **1550** H. LLOYD *Treas. Health* X iij, Sothernewood & freshe grece..

do drawe oute spriges, thornes, and other thinges. **1614** GORGES *Lucan* IX. 406 That which Southernwood we call, Whose smoake the serpents so distast. **1671** J. WEBSTER *Metallogr.* xv. 211 Resembling the shrub Southernwood, thick set with little twigs leaning one to another. **1718** QUINCY *Compl. Disp.* 121 Southern-wood..is now almost out of use in Medicine. **1785** MARTYN *Rousseau's Bot.* xxvi. (1794) 386 Southernwood is shrubby, erect, and has setaceous leaves very much branched. **1833** TENNYSON *Mariana in South* Poems 20 Not a breath..moved the dusty southernwood. **1867** H. MACMILLAN *Bible Teach.* vii. (1870) 144 Some leaves consist of little more than veins, as in.. fennel and southernwood.

β. *c* **1150** *Voc.* in Wr.-Wülcker 544 *Abrotanum*, suþerwude. *a* **1400** *Sqr. lowe Degre* 33 The sother-wood, and sykamoure. *c* **1460** *Promp. Parv.* (Winch. MS.) 426 Sotherwode, herbe, *abrotanum*.

b. With distinguishing epithets, denoting various species of *Artemisia*, or plants resembling these (see quots.).

1577 B. GOOGE *Heresbach's Husb.* II. (1586) 66b, Some call it *Santonia*, and female Southernewood. **1578** LYTE *Dodoens* I There be two sortes of Sothrenwood (as Dioscorides sayth) the one called female Sothrenwood, or the great Sothrenwood, the other is the male kinde. *c* **1710** PETIVER *Cat. Ray's Eng. Herbal* Tab. xx, Wild Southernwood. **1731** MILLER *Gard. Dict.* s.v. *Abrotanum*, The Lesser and Narrower-leav'd Southernwood. **1753** *Chambers' Cycl.* Suppl., *Santolina*, female southernwood. *Ibid.* s.v. *Santolina*, The male southernwood. **1771** *Encycl. Brit.* I. 428/1 There are 23 species of artemisia, only 4 of which are natives of Britain, *viz.* the campestris, or field-southernwood [etc.]. **1796** WITHERING *Brit. Plants* (ed. 3) III. 709 *Artemisia maritima*. Sea Southernwood. Sea Wormwood. **1853** MAYNE *Expos. Lex.* 89/1 *Artemisia Santonica*,..the Tartarian southern-wood, or wormwood, or the worm-seed plant. **1857** HENFREY *Bot.* 320 *Artemisia Abrotanum* is Garden Southern-wood.

2. *attrib.* and *Comb.*, as ***southernwood-leaved, twig.***

1822 *Hortus Anglicus* II. 389 *S. Abrotanifolius*. Southernwood-leaved Groundsel. **1849** *Diss. Silk Manuf.* (Shanghae) 10 The southern-wood twigs are of a cooling nature. **1887** D. C. MURRAY & HERMAN *Traveller Returns* vii. 98 In each bowl a bound bunch of southernwood twigs.

So †**'southernwort.** *Obs.*

1510 STANBRIDGE *Vocabula* (W. de W.) D ij b, *Abrotinum*, sotherne worte. **1530** PALSGR. 273/2 Southerne-worthe. **1610** MARKHAM *Masterp.* II. clxxiii. 482 *Abrotanum*, which we cal in English southernwort.

Southeyan ('sʌðɪən), *a.* [f. the name of the English poet and prose writer Robert *Southey* (1774–1843) + -AN.] Of, pertaining to or characteristic of the writings of Southey. Hence **Southe'yana** [-ANA *suff.*], writings, etc., relating to Southey.

1817 KEATS *Let.* 11 May (1931) I. 32, I am very near agreeing with Hazlitt that Shakespeare is enough for us. By the by what a tremendous Southean [*sic*] article his last was. **1931** BLUNDEN *Votive Tablets* 191 A modern house would not contain a collection of Southeyana. *Ibid.* 198 The last sentences of the extract show the Southeyan good sense. **1974** R. HOLMES *Shelley* ix. 207 The prose notes are constantly more powerful and effective than the long-drawn Miltonic or Southeyan rhetoric of the verse.

†**south-half.** *Obs.* [OE. *súðhealf* (see SOUTH *adv.* and HALF *sb.*), = MDu. *suuthalf*, ON. *suðrhálfa*, OHG. *sund(ar)halba.*] The south side or part; the south. In later use ellipt. as *prep.*

c **893** K. ÆLFRED *Oros.* I. i, þara landa norþȝemæro sindon æt ðæm beorȝum Caucasus, & on suþhealfe se Reada Sæ. *a* **1122** *O.E. Chron.* (Laud MS.) an. 1016, [Hie] dulfon þa ane mycele dic on ða suðhealfe. *c* **1205** LAY. 15937 þe an [dragon] is a norð half, þe oðer a suð half. *c* **1290** *St. Edmund* 381 in *S. Eng. Leg.* I. 442 In þe southhalf þoruȝ al þe heiȝe strete it [*sc.* rain] leide on for wod. **1439** *Charters*, etc. *of Edinb.* (1871) 64 Lyande in the toune off Leicht..on Soucht halfe the vatir. **1473** *Acc. Ld. High Treas. Scot.* I. 43 Passande with lettres on Southalue for the ditte and the garde. **1474** *Ibid.* 50 Ane vthir curour passande on southalue Forth. **1524** *Ibid.* V. 236, xj lettres..direct to all the Shereffis on south half Forth.

southing ('saʊθɪŋ), *vbl. sb.* [f. SOUTH *adv.* or *v.* + -ING[1].]

1. Of heavenly bodies: The action of crossing or approaching the meridian of a place.

1659 J. MOXON *Globes* II. liv. (1674) 105 The Time of her Rising, Southing, Setting, and Shining. **1697** DRYDEN *Æneid* v. 33 If I observ'd aright The southing of the Stars and Polar Light. **1786–7** BONNYCASTLE *Astron.* 435 *Southing* of the stars, the time when they culminate or come to the meridian. **1834** KEITH *Globes* (1843) Cont. p. xxiii, To find the time of the Moon's southing..on any given day of the month. **1859** R. F. BURTON *Centr. Afr.* in *Jrnl. Geog. Soc.* XXIX. 207 The gradual refrigeration of the ground, and the southing of the sun, produce..the north-east monsoon. **1890** *Science-Gossip* XXVI. 39 Rising, Southing, and Setting of the Principal Planets, at intervals of Seven Days, for February.

2. Progress, movement, or deviation towards the south made in sailing, travelling, etc.; difference in latitude due to moving southward. Chiefly in *Navigation.*

1669 STURMY *Mariner's Mag.* IV. xvii. 202 In the..tenth and eleventh Columns, set down the Northing, Southing, Easting, and Westing. **1690** LEYBOURN *Curs. Math.* 641 Subtract the Lesser Northing or Southing from the Greater. **1712** E. COOKE *Voy. S. Sea* 30 A strong Current..oblig'd us to correct our Southing considerably. **1771** *Encycl. Brit.* III. 370/2 Then they sum up all the northings, and all the southings. **1857** LIVINGSTONE *Trav.* v. 95 The prevailing winds..are easterly, with a little southing. **1868** *Contemp. Rev.* Apr. 600 In 1486 Diaz found the final southing of the protracted African coast-line.

b. Freq. in the phr. ***to make* (..) *southing.***

1803 NELSON 23 May in Nicolas *Disp.* (1845) V. 74 He would certainly make Southing with his Westing. **1844** KINGLAKE *Eothen* ii, After Adrianople I had made more southing than I knew for. **1899** F. T. BULLEN *Log Seawaif* 178 We had always managed to make some Southing each day.

'southing, *ppl. a. rare.* [f. as prec.] Moving or tending towards the south.

1697 DRYDEN *Virg. Georg.* IV. 577 When next the Southing Sun inflames the Day.

southistel, obs. form of SOW-THISTLE.

'southland. Also south land, south-land. [OE. *súðland* (see SOUTH *adv.* and LAND *sb.*[1]), = ON. *suðrland*, Du. *zuidland*, G. *südland.*]

1. A land lying in or towards the south. Now *arch.* or *poet.*

c **1000** ÆLFRIC *Gen.* xxiv. 62 He eardode soðlice on þam suðlandum. **1398** TREVISA *Barth. De P.R.* XIV. ii. (Bodl. MS.), Men of souþe londes beþ contrarye to men of norþe londes in stature. **1535** COVERDALE *Judg.* i. 15 Thou hast geuen me a south & drye londe. **1611** BIBLE *Josh.* xv. 19 Thou hast giuen mee a South-land, giue me also springs of water. **1868** MORRIS *Earthly Par.* (1870) II. III. 335 In a strange land and barren, far removed From southlands and their bliss. **1890** DOYLE *White Company* viii, Yet the king hath given me a living here in the southlands.

2. The southern part of a country or district; the South; †the southern bank.

c **1100** *O.E. Chron.* (MS. D) an. 1052, Hy..heoldan þurh þa brycge aa bi þæm suþlande. *c* **1205** LAY. 2111 þat suð lond þat æfter him Locres wes icleped. *Ibid.* 3741 Scottlondes kinge..hehte þane duc stronge heriȝen in suð londe. **1382** WYCLIF *Josh.* xi. 16 So Josue took al..the south loond, and Gosen. *c* **1470** HENRY *Wallace* IX. 1308 Till the south land with glaid hartis thai socht. *a* **1578** LINDESAY (Pitscottie) *Chron. Scot.* (S.T.S.) II. 21 Mony wther wastland men and clans of the southland. **1849** J. G. WHITTIER in *National Era* 1 Nov. 174/4 The South land hath its fields of cane, The Prairie boasts its heavy grain. **1872** TENNYSON *Gar. & Lynette* 1161 Baken meats and good red wine Of Southland. **1899** MACKAIL *W. Morris* I. 261 To get back into the Southland without again traversing the wilderness. **1905** *Florida Times-Union* 7 May II. 8/1 Yet is this place rich in its treasured holdings of art, its clustered memories and traditions of the Old South or the southland of ante-bellum days. **1956** G. P. KURATH in A. F. C. Wallace *Men & Cultures* (1960) 153 The Charleston, after seething in the Southland as a Negro round dance, was discovered in 1923. **1974** P. MCCUTCHAN *Call for Simon Shard* iv. 32 He entered the Southland..unofficially, no fanfares, no men from Canberra. **1978** *Guardian Weekly* 1 Oct. 9/1, I believe in the Southland... I believe in the people from South Carolina.. and I believe in the people of Georgia.

3. *attrib.* or as *adj.* Also **Southland beech** = *silver beech* s.v. SILVER *sb.* and *a.* 21e, in reference to the region of New Zealand on the west coast of the South Island.

c **1470** HENRY *Wallace* I. 442 Thir Southland hors latt se gif I can ride. *a* **1578** LINDESAY (Pitscottie) *Chron. Scot.* (S.T.S.) I. 348 Money southland men..appeillit wther in barras to fight in singular battell. *a* **1670** SPALDING *Troub. Chas. I* (1850) II. 337 Quhilk wold give the Southland men aneuche ado. *a* **1724** in Ramsay *Tea-t. Misc.* (1876) I. 192 A Southland Jenny..Had for a suitor norland Jonny. **1813** HOGG *Queen's Wake, Introd.* (1814) 9 Her ringlets pale Wide waving in the southland gale. **1819** SCOTT *Leg. Montrose* iv, Southland though they be, they'll scarce eat up all the cattle. **1873** MORRIS *Love is enough* 61 Of many such tales..the Southland folk told us. **1947** J. C. S. BROUGH *Timbers for Woodwork* xvi. 138 Imported beeches are..Red beech..and Southland, or 'Silver' beech. **1966** G. W. TURNER *Eng. Lang. Austral. & N.Z.* viii. 166 The Southland beech is not really a beech.

Hence **'southlander,** a southerner.

1823 SCORESBY *Jrnl.* p. xxxi, A Southlander..wintered at the colony in the year 1757. **1827** SCOTT *Two Drovers* ii, 'May good betide us,' said the Southlander. **1860** (*title*), The Southlanders, an account of an expedition to the interior of New Holland.

†**'southly,** *a. Obs.* [f. SOUTH + -LY[1]. Cf. MDu. *zude-, zuydelic*, Du. *zuidelijk*, WFris. *súdlik*, G. *südlich*, Da. *sydlig.*] Southern, southerly.

c **1440** *Promp. Parv.* 466/2 Sowthely, or sum what be sowthe, *australis.* **1570** LEVINS *Manip.* 100 Southly, *australis.* ? **1579** *Sheldon Tapestry Map* (in Bodl. Libr.), This sowthly part which hear below towards Glocester fall.

†**'southly,** *adv. Obs.* [f. SOUTH + -LY[2]. So Du. *zuidelijk*, G. *südlich.*] Towards or in the south; facing or from the south.

1538 LELAND *Itin.* (1768) II. 38 The Closis..that lye Southly on the Toun. **1573** TUSSER *Husb.* (1878) 40 Place hiue in good ayer, set southly and warme. **1590** MASCALL *Bk. Fishing* 4 When the winde bloweth southly from the South or West.

southly, obs. form of SOOTHLY *adv.*

southmost ('saʊθməst, -məʊst), *a.* Also 1 **suðmest**, *Sc.* 5 **southmaist**, 6 **-mest**. [f. SOUTH *adv.*: see -MOST.] Most southerly; southernmost.

c **893** K. ÆLFRED *Oros.* I. vii. 40 Ða suðmestan Æthiopian hæfdon bryne for ðære hæte. *c* **1470** HENRY *Wallace* VIII. 1091 The southmaist part off Ingland we sall se. **1535** STEWART *Cron. Scot.* II. 626 The southmest part la narrest France that tyde, This ilk Canutus gat. **1623** WHITBOURNE *Newfoundland* 4 It lies the Southmost of any Harbor. **1667** MILTON *P.L.* I. 408 From Aroer to Nebo, and the wild Of Southmost Abarim. **1756** J. WILLME *Sepherah Shelosh* 201 His Nativity happened in the Southmost middle Part of Lancashire. **1789** J. WILLIAMS *Min. Kingd.* I. 123 The greatest number of the edge-seams decline much about the angle forty-five, though some of the southmost of the coals are higher. **1855** BAILEY *Mystic*, etc. 116 To hills of heaven, and southmost shores Unbroken, of peninsular Malay. **1896** G. A. SMITH *Bk. Twelve Prophets* I. 312 Hermon, the southmost..summits of Anti-Lebanon.

'southness. [f. SOUTH + -NESS.] The quality of indicating the south; the state of being relatively south.

1854 *Orr's Circ. Sci., Chem.* 397 The functions of northness and southness in magnetic..relations.

southpaw ('saʊθ,pɔː), *sb.* (*a.*) *colloq.* (orig. *U.S.*, in *Baseball*). [f. SOUTH *a.* + PAW *sb.*[1]]

1. A person's left hand. (In quot. 1848, a punch or blow with the left hand.)

1848 *Democratic B-hoy*, 'I say, Lewy, give him a sockdologer!' 'Curse the Old Hoss, what a south-paw he has given me!' **1885** *Sporting Life* 14 Jan. 4/3 They had always been accustomed to having their opponents hug their bases pretty close, out of respect for Morris' quick throw over to first with that south-paw of his. **1942** BERREY & VAN DEN BARK *Amer. Thes. Slang* §121/53 *Southpaw, wrong hand* or *fist*, the left hand or fist. **1948** *Chicago Tribune* 20 Apr. I. 20/5 He waved his big south-paw and ducked under the roof.

2. One who pitches or throws with the left hand; a left-handed person.

In *Boxing*, a southpaw leads with his right hand.

1891 *Chicago Herald* 24 July 6/1 The new south-paw.. came to town yesterday. **1911** *Daily Colonist* (Victoria, B.C.) 15 Apr. 8/5 Davis came up to bat... He faced the twirler right-handed. He always does with southpaws. **1932** *Ring* Apr. 5/2 McCoy was a slow southpaw who had proved just a good workout for Joe Chip. **1942** BERREY & VAN DEN BARK *Amer. Thes. Slang* §430/10 Left-handed person,..*south-paw.* **1947** J. GUNTHER *Inside U.S.A.* xl. 657 Ah won't even go to the Polo Grounds unless a southpaw's pitchin'. **1951** *Sport* 6–12 Apr. 8/2 On the same bill, Joe Lucy, the young southpaw, meets South African lightweight Gerald Dreyer. **1955** *Sci. News Let.* 14 May 310/2 The family cat may have a preferred paw.., and pussy is most often a southpaw when she is not ambidextrous. **1959** *Sunday Times* 8 Nov. 32/6 In the ball parks all over the United States the so-called 'diamond', formed by the track between the bases, is always oriented to the same points of the compass, so that in whatever park a team is playing the pitcher on his mound will always have his right hand on the north side of his body; hence a left-hander is a 'southpaw'. **1967** *Boston Sunday Herald* 26 Mar. II. 7/1 Rocket Rod Laver leads the greatest tennis show on earth into Boston Garden Monday night... The freckle-faced southpaw is the top-seeded player. **1970** H. MCLEAVE *Question of Negligence* (1973) vi. 48 'Nobody told me he was a southpaw.' Even the psychiatrist had.. forgotten that the surgeon cut with his left hand. **1976** *Billings* (Montana) *Gaz.* 26 June 1-B/2 The 6–0 lefthander, the only southpaw listed on the Angels' roster, struck out six and walked the same number. **1976** 'A. BURGESS' *Beard's Roman Women* (1977) v. 110 Donatella, a south-paw, animated this [*sc.* her left shoulder-blade] while lifting the one remaining chair from the front room. **1978** M. KENYON *Deep Pocket* ix. 103 He wore shorts and boxing gloves. ''E's a southpaw,' Peckover said.

3. *attrib.* or as *adj.* Left-handed; also *transf.*, left-footed, and *fig.*

1891 *Cricket* 29 Oct. 463/1 The Germantown man returned the ball like a flash to the wicket, and the 'south-paw' batsman was run out. **1932** J. T. FARRELL *Young Lonigan* iii. 126 It was swell for Studs to play,..knowing he had made that good kick,..to run back and pick one of Helen's southpaw kicks out of the air. **1949** *Sun* (Baltimore) 3 June 18/8 They would have been bunched against southpaw pitching. **1957** R. WATSON-WATT *Three Steps to Victory* xliii. 245 This was, however, a south-paw kind of compliment. **1969** *New Scientist* 6 Nov. 277/2 Jack Bodell has just become the first south-paw heavyweight champion in British boxing history.

Hence **'southpaw** *v. trans.*, to pitch with the left hand; **'southpawing** *vbl. sb.*, the action of pitching with the left hand.

1928 *Daily Ardmoreite* (Ardmore, Okla.) 12 Apr. 8/1 Herb Pennock southpawed his way the route for the Yankees. **1938** *Chicago Tribune* 4 Apr. 21/1 The White Sox positively refused to be awed today by the south-pawing of Larry French. **1951** *Sun* (Baltimore) 23 Aug. 20/1 Jim Burns southpawed his eighth straight triumph.

†**southright,** *adv. Obs.* [OE. *súþryhte*, f. SOUTH *adv.* + -RIGHT.] Due south.

c **1205** LAY. 20608 Hit was to þere middel-niht; þe mone scæn scan suð riht [*v.r.* souþriht].

Southron ('sʌðrən), *a.* and *sb.* Orig. *Sc.* (and *north.*). Forms: 5 sothroun, -ron, 8 suthron, 9 southron; 6 su-, sotheroun, 6–7 southeroun, 6, 9 sotheron, 8–9 southeron; 6 sudroun, suddroun, -rone, 8 soudron. Also with lower-case initial. [Alteration of *southren* SOUTHERN *a.*; the ending was probably modified on the analogy of *Briton*, *Saxon*.]

A. *adj.* **1.** Belonging to or dwelling in the south, esp. of Britain; southern; *esp.* English as distinguished from Scottish. Chiefly *Sc.*

c **1470** HENRY *Wallace* IV. 494 Or Sothron men suld sege him in that place. *Ibid.* x. 664 Then ferdly fled full mony Sotheroun syr. **1785** BURNS *To W. S[impso]n* x, Where glorious Wallace Aft bure the gree.. Frae Suthron billies. **1810** JANE PORTER *Sc. Chiefs* xxxvii, When the Southron lords delegate a messenger to me. **1892** *Athenæum* 8 Oct. 475/1 Church politics..still possess an interest for Scotland which is perfectly amazing to the Southron observer.

2. Of or pertaining to, characteristic of, the south; situated in or on the south: **a.** In or after Scottish use (= English).

c **1470** HENRY *Wallace* II. 10 To se thaim sched the byrnand Sothroun blude. **1570** *Henry's Wallace* v. 930 On Sutheroun syde full greit slauchter þai maid. **1571** *Satir. Poems Reform.* xxv. 48 By slicht & suddrone bloud. **1807** BYRON *The Adieu* iii, Why did I quit my Highland cave..To seek a Sotheron home! **1858** MACAULAY *Hist. Eng.* vii. II. 183 The French monarchy was to him..what the Southron [*earlier edd.* southern] domination was to Wallace. **1891** BARRIE *Little Minister* xxv, A southron mode of speech.

b. In other uses. Also *transf.*

1828 *Free Press* (Tarboro, N. Carolina) 9 Nov., I am a Republican in principle, and a Southron in feeling. **1831** J. J. AUDUBON *Ornith. Biogr.* I. 110 When those [mocking birds] which had gone to the Eastern States..have returned, they are instantly known by the 'southrons' who attack them on all occasions. **1845** FORD *Handbk. Spain* 773 The wants and wishes of a credulous southron people. **1891** *Cent. Dict.*, *Southron*, pertaining or belonging to the southern United States.

B. *sb.* **1. a.** A native of the south of Great Britain; an Englishman.

c **1470** HENRY *Wallace* II. 304 Bot othir a Scott wald do a Sothroun teyne, Or he till him. **1771** J. MACPHERSON *Introd. Hist. Grt. Brit.* 129 The appellation of Southerons and Norlands are not hitherto totally extinguished among the Scots. **1810** JANE PORTER *Sc. Chiefs* ii, The Southrons are at the gates and we shall be lost. **1879** HUXLEY *Hume* 40 These same Southrons added a passionate admiration for Lord Chatham.

b. In pl. sense, = Englishmen. Freq. with *the*.

c **1470** HENRY *Wallace* I. 188 He saw the Sothroun multipliand mayr. *Ibid.* III. 270 Sothroun to sla he thinkis it na syne. *a* **1795** *Outlaw Murray* xxii. in Child *Ballads* V. 192/1 Frae Soudron I this forest wan. **1820** SCOTT *Monast.* iv, But wha is to haud back the Southron, then? **1849** MACAULAY *Hist. Eng.* vi. (ed. 5) II. 130 In Ireland Scot and Southron were strongly bound together by their common Saxon origin.

†**c.** *Sc.* The English tongue or language. *Obs.*

1513 DOUGLAS *Æneid* I. Prol. 111 Kepand na sudroun bot our awin langage, And speikis as I lernit quhen I was page. **1563** WINȜET *Wks.* (S.T.S.) I. 138, I am nocht acquyntit with ȝour Southeroun. **1581** HAMILTON in *Cath. Tract.* (S.T.S.) 105 James the fyft..hering ane of his subiectis knap suddrone, declarit him ane trateur.

2. a. A native or inhabitant of the south of England, of Europe, etc.

1857 MRS. GASKELL *C. Bronte* (1860) 253 Those nearer to the spot..were sure, from the..accuracy of the writing, that the writer was no Southron. **1868** MILMAN *St. Paul's* 48 The Southron [*sc.* an Italian legate] was to spend his winter in cold London. **1891** J. WINSOR *Columbus* 658 The wisdom in their employment of the aborigines was as eminent as with the Southrons [*sc.* Spaniards] it was lacking.

b. *U.S.* = SOUTHERNER 2.

1848 in Bartlett *Dict. Amer.* 410 He will prevent the nomination of Gen. Butler, or any other Southron. **1878** *N. Amer. Rev.* CXXVI. 84 The Southron was a better fighter than the Northerner.

Hence **'Southrony**, the English. *pseudo-arch.*

a **1795** *Outlaw Murray* xxxiii. in Child *Ballads* V. 192/2 He says yon forest is his ain, He wan it from the Soudronie. *c* **1802** J. MARRIOTT *Feast of Spurs* xiii. in Scott *Minstrelsy*, Intull your saddles, scour awa', And ranshakle the Southronie.

South Sea. [Cf. MDu. *suutsee*, *zuutzee*, the Mediterranean; Du. *zuidzee*, G. *südsee* the Pacific.]

†**1. a.** The sea to the south of Europe; the Mediterranean. *Obs.*

1398 TREVISA *Barth. De P.R.* XIV. ii. (Bodl. MS.), Hote vapoure and moiste comeþ oute of þe souþe see.

†**b.** The English Channel. *Obs.*

[**1432-50** tr. *Higden* (Rolls) II. 37 The side of the sowthe see of Briteyne.] **1478** *Itin. Will. de Worcestre* (Nasmith, 1778) 90 Branston, per 8 miliaria de Axmynster, et per 4 miliaria de le south-see.

2. *pl.* The seas of the southern hemisphere; *esp.* the South Pacific Ocean.

c **1528** R. THORNE *Let. Hen. VIII* in *Hakluyt* (1589) 251 Vntill they come to the..South Seas of the Indies Occidentall. **1601-** [see NORTH SEA 3]. **1622** DRAYTON *Poly-olb.* xix. 365 Brave Candish..through the South Seas pass'd, about this earthly ball. **1719** DE FOE *Crusoe* II. (Globe) 544 To sail from the Phillippine Islands, away to the South-Seas. **1745** P. THOMAS (*title*), A Voyage to the South Seas..in H.M.S. Centurion. **1802** PINKERTON *Mod. Geogr.* II. 506 The Grecian..forms, given by artists..to the people of the South seas,..are totally false. **1866** *Treas. Bot.* 1119/1 Arrowroot..is a favourite ingredient for puddings and cakes in the South Seas.

3. a. The South Pacific Ocean; †the Pacific Ocean as a whole (*obs.*).

1555 EDEN *Decades* III. iii. (Arb.) 251 The Spanyardes thought that by this ryuer they myght haue passed into the south sea. **1638** J. CHILMEAD tr. *Hues' Treat. Globes* III. i. (Hakl. Soc.) 79 America..is terminated..on the West with ..the South Sea. **1771** *Encycl. Brit.* III. 449/1 [The] Pacific ..was called south-sea, because the Spaniards crossed the isthmus of Darien from north to south, when they first discovered it. **1840** *Penny Cycl.* XVII. 116/2 The Pacific.. is also called the South Sea, because vessels sailing from Europe can only enter it after a long southerly course. *Ibid.* 117/1 The name of South Sea has been limited in later times to the southern portion of the Pacific. **1845** DARWIN *Voy. Nat.* (1901) 510 The introduction of Christianity throughout the South Sea.

fig. **1600** SHAKS. *A.Y.L.* III. ii. 207 One inch of delay more, is a South-sea of discouerie. **1721** SWIFT *Ess. Eng. Bubbles*, The ambitious citizens..plunged deep in the wealthy whirlpool of the South Sea.

b. *ellipt.* for 'South Sea bonds, scheme', etc.

1717 MRS. CENTLIVRE *Bold Stroke for Wife* IV. i, 1 *Stock.* South Sea at seven eighths; who buys? **1721** SWIFT *South Sea Project* Wks. 1841 I. 622/1 The nation then too late will find..Directors' promises but wind, South Sea, at best, a mighty bubble. **1856** BAGEHOT *Lit. Studies* II. 1 The real founder was the grandfather of the historian [Gibbon], who lived in the times of the 'South Sea'.

†**4.** *Cant.* (See quots.) Also *attrib. Obs.*$^{-0}$

1725 *New Cant. Dict.*, *South-Sea*, a strong distill'd Liquor, so called by the Inhabitants and Clients of Newgate, &c. *Ibid.*, *South-Sea Mountain*, Geneva.

5. *attrib.* **a. South Sea bubble**, = *South Sea scheme*; **South Sea Company**, a company incorporated in 1711 for the purpose of exclusive trade with the South Seas, and of taking up the unfunded National Debt; **South Sea scheme**, a stock-jobbing scheme which was inaugurated by this Company in 1720 for taking up the whole National Debt, but collapsed in the same year. Also ***South Sea bonds, dream, fund, stock***, etc.

1711 (*title*), A View of the Coasts, Countries and Islands Within the Limits of the South-Sea-Company. **1711** *View Coasts*, etc., *of South-Sea-Coy.* 207 Of the..Countries and Islands within the Limits of the South-Sea-Act. **1720** A. HUTCHESON (*title*), A Collection of Calculations and Remarks relating to the South Sea Scheme & Stock. **1721** AMHERST *Terræ Fil.* No. 12 (1726) 60, I conceive the sum of the charge against the South-sea directors to be this. **1742** YOUNG *Nt. Th.* IV. 76 As wealthy as a South-sea dream. **1771** *Encycl. Brit.* III. 632/2 Things were in this situation, when..the South Sea bubble was projected. **1809** R. LANGFORD *Introd. Trade* 57 South sea stock 89 means, that 89*l.* will purchase 100*l.* of this stock. **1857** GEO. ELIOT *Ess.* (1884) 54 South-Sea dreams and illegal percentage.

b. In specific names, etc. (see quots.).

1866 *Treas. Bot.* 1119/1 The..tubers [of *Tacca pinnatifida*]..contain a great deal of starch known as *South-sea Arrowroot. **1884** MILLER *Plant-n.* 254/1 *Tacca pinnatifida*, Otaheita Salep-plant, Pi-plant, South-Sea-Arrow-root-plant. **1797** *Encycl. Brit.* (ed. 3) V. 407/1 Having..been furnished with *South Sea cloth from the ship, he equipped himself with great quickness. **1753** *Chambers' Cycl.* Suppl. *App.* s.v. *Rose*, **South-Sea Rose*, a name sometimes given to the *Nerion* of botanists. **1866** *Treas. Bot.* 991 South Sea rose, of Jamaica, *Nerium Oleander*. **1728** CHAMBERS *Cycl.*, *Paraguay*, or *Paragoue*,.. a celebrated Plant,..better known, of late, among us, under the Denomination of *South-Sea Tea. **1760** J. LEE *Introd. Bot.* App. 327 Southsea Thea, *Ilex*. **1872** DE VERE *Americanisms* 396 South-sea-tea or Yopon (Ilex vomitoria) occurs North and South.

c. In miscellaneous uses.

1797 *Encycl. Brit.* (ed. 3) V. 391/1 While Mr. Cook proceeded to visit others of the South Sea Islands. **1813** PRICHARD *Phys. Hist. Man* vi. §6. 312 He [Cook] regarded their dialect as a branch of the South Sea language. **1832** A. EARLE *Narr. Residence N.Z.* (1966) 58, I am persuaded that these South Sea islanders, though so nearly of the same complexion, still are not of the same race. **1847** TENNYSON *Princess* III. 261 Cramp'd under worse than South-sea-isle taboo. **1897** FLORA SHAW *Story Australia* iii. 22 A delicacy ..altogether wanting in other South Sea tribes. **1913** C. MACKENZIE *Sinister Street* I. II. ii. 173 That belt of yours, Michael, would give a South Sea Islander a headache. **1974** J. POPE-HENNESSY *R. L. Stevenson* xi. 211 Louis..was as brown as a South Sea Islander.

Hence **South-seaman**, a vessel trading in the South Seas.

1805 *Naval Chron.* XIV. 169 One Store-ship, and a captured English South Seaman. **1839** T. BEALE *Nat. Hist. Sperm Whale* 293 Those very people have massacred nearly the whole of the crew of a South-seaman. **1898** F. T. BULLEN *Cruise Cachalot* vi. 51 The clear and sweet oil.. landed from a south-seaman.

south-side. [Originally repr. ME. *sūðside*, = MDu. *suutside*, *zuutzide* (Du. *zuidzijde*), MLG. *sûtsîde*, G. *südseite*, Da. *sydside*. In later use felt merely as a collocation of SOUTH *a.* and SIDE *sb.*[1]]

a. The side situated in or lying towards the south. Also *attrib.*

1338 R. BRUNNE *Chron.* (1810) 59 Toward þe South side turned þei þar flete. **1387** TREVISA *Higden* (Rolls) V. 297 Andresleg is a greet wode on þe souþ side of Kent. **1417** *E.E. Wills* 27 As men goth ouer in-to þe church at þe South Syde. **1480** [see CHOIR *sb.* 2]. **1535** COVERDALE *Numb.* ii. 10 On the South side shall lye the pauylions..of Ruben. **1560** BIBLE (Genev.) *Numb.* iii. 29 The families of the sonnes of Kohath shal pitch on the Southside of the Tabernacle. **1610** HOLLAND *Camden's Brit.* (1637) 633 On the South side a great part of the Wall standeth. **1670-1** NARBOROUGH *Jrnl.* in *Acc. Sev. Late Voy.* I. (1694) 39, I went a-shore on the South-side to the peeked Rock. **1707** J. CHAMBERLAYNE *Pres. St. Gt. Brit.* (1710) 460 On the South-side [of Holyrood Palace] lies the Queen's Park. **1808** SCOTT in *Lockhart* (1837) I. i. 12 A pond, or old quarry-hole,..on the south side of the square. **1869** *Bradshaw's Railway Man.* XXI. 58 The railway..joins the Glasgow and South Western and the Caledonian (southside branches), on the south side of the city. **1896** BADEN-POWELL *Matabele Campaign* xvii, Lord Grey's party shot to northward of the road, and the south side was our preserve. **1937** H. G. WELLS *Star Begotten* vi. 105 The Punic Wars..he presented as a gigantic necessary struggle between noble north-side soldiers and revengeful, obdurate but extremely competent south-side loanmongers. **1955** KEEPNEWS & GRAUER *Pict. Hist. of Jazz* iii. 43 Pianist Blythe, who died in 1930, was.. in the forefront of the 'South Side style', which meant small-band recordings and jobs at small, rough clubs. **1979** *Irish Times* 28 Sept. 12/6 If the northside area described here is compared with a southside suburb the differences become more marked.

†**b.** In const. without *of*. Also as *adv.*, on the south part; southward. *Obs.*

1489 *Acc. Ld. High Treas. Scot.* I. 125 To pas on the suthsyd the watter. **1726** in W. Wing *Ann. Steeple Aston* (1875) 54 The land heretofore of William Wing southside, and John Bates northward.

south-south-east, *adv.*, etc. [Cf. older Flem. *suydsuydoost* (Kilian), Du. *zuidzuidoost*, G. *südsüdost*.] In or from the direction lying midway between south and south-east. Also as *sb.* and *adj.*

14.. *Sailing Directions* (Hakl. Soc. 1889) 11 Fro Leyrnes to the Hedelonde the cours is north northwest and south south est. **1555** EDEN *Decades* (Arb.) 380 And to the south southeaste [lay] a lowe longe lande. **1598** W. PHILLIP tr. *Linschoten* 165 We held our course south south East. **1638** CHILMEAD tr. *Hues' Treat. Globes* v. (Hakl. Soc.) 140, I finde it to be the North norwest, and South southeast Rumbe. *a* **1691** BOYLE *Hist. Air* (1692) 192 A little island, which bare off us south-south-east some four leagues. **1725** DE FOE *Voy. round World* (1840) 264 [The valley] went winding away..to the south-east, and so to south-south-east. **1839** DE LA BECHE *Rep. Geol. Cornwall*, etc. i. 5 About eight miles in a..south-south-east direction. **1842** *Penny Cycl.* XXIII. 216/2 One principal street, running from south-south-east to north-north-west. **1893** *Times* 8 July 14/2 The wind had southerned a little..and was about south-south-east.

Hence **south-south-'easterly, -'eastward** *advs.* and *adjs.*

1784 *Phil. Trans.* LXXIV. 203, 30° or 20° south-south-eastward. **1796** MORSE *Amer. Geog.* (ed. 3) I. 711 The bank and highland..ranges nearly northerly and south-southeasterly. *Ibid.* 714 The high lands lie northeastward and south southeastward.

south-'southerly. *Amer.* [Imitative: see first quot.] The long-tailed duck, *Harelda glacialis*.

1814 A. WILSON *Amer. Ornith.* VIII. 93 Known along the shores of the Chesapeake Bay by the name of South Southerly, from the singularity of its cry, something imitative of the sound of those words. **1872** COUES *N. Amer. Birds* 291. **1878** A. M. ROSS *Catal. Mammals Canada* 8/1.

south-south-west, *adv.*, etc. [Cf. MLG. *sûtsûtwest*, older Flem. *suydsuydwest*, Du. *zuidzuidwest*, G. *südsüdwest*.] In or from the direction situated midway between south and south-west. Also as *sb.* and *adj.*

1513 DOUGLAS *Æneid* Wks. 1874 II. 284 And Affricus is takin for plat west wynd, that is bot sowth sowthwest. **1555** EDEN *Decades* III. iii. (Arb.) 260 [It] runneth to the quarter of south southwest and north northeast. **1638** CHILMEAD tr. *Hues' Treat. Globes* v. (Hakl. Soc.) 141 You must saile..to the Canary Islands by the South South-west Rumbe. *a* **1701** MAUNDRELL *Journ. Jerus.* (1721) Add. 6 Its Course is South South West. **1772-84** *Cook's Voy.* (1790) I. 151 We discovered land from the mast head, bearing south-south-west. **1827** J. HOLMES *Hist. United Brethren* ii. (ed. 2) 101 The coast..now turned to the south-south-west. **1842** *Penny Cycl.* XXIII. 215/2, 18 miles south-south-west from Bury. **1900** *Westm. Gaz.* 22 Aug. 10/1 The south-south-west of Natal.

Hence **south-south-'westerly, -'western** *adjs.*

1837 *Penny Cycl.* VIII. 204/2 Always with south-south-westerly winds. **1840** *Ibid.* XVI. 325/1 Flowing..in a south-south-western direction. **1850** ANSTED *Elem. Geol., Min.*, etc. §124 A south-south-westerly wind.

South Suffolk. [f. SOUTH(DOWN + SUFFOLK.] One of a breed of sheep, developed in New Zealand by crossing Suffolk and Southdown sheep and used to produce lean meat and short, fine wool. Also *attrib.*

1950 *N.Z. Jrnl. Agric.* Feb. 144/3 Two instances of fresh development with sheep breeds may be mentioned: First, the aim of some breeders in the South Island '..to establish a new breed by crossing Suffolk and Southdown with a view to producing a sheep having Southdown characteristics with a maximum of lean meat'—the South Suffolk. **1956** G. BOWEN *Wool Away!* (ed. 2) xii. 148 South Suffolk. This is a New Zealand type derived from crossing Southdowns with Suffolks, and is being very widely used..in Canterbury and is spreading rapidly to other parts of New Zealand. **1977** *N.Z. Herald* 8 Jan. 4-8/6 (Advt.), 23 South Suffolk ewes.

souðen, variant of SITHEN *Obs.*

south thystell, obs. form of SOW-THISTLE.

Sou'thumbrian, *sb.* and *a. Hist.* [repr. OE. *Súð(an)hymbre*: cf. NORTHUMBRIAN.]

A. *sb.* A native or inhabitant of the northern part of the early English kingdom of Mercia.

1823 INGRAM tr. *Saxon Chron.* 37/2 Oswald..was slain by Penda, king of the Southumbrians [in 642]. **1853** C. D. YONGE tr. *Matt. Westminster* I. 333 The Mercians, who are also called the Southumbrians, that is to say, that part of the Mercians..north of the river Trent. **1899** PLUMMER *Sax. Chron.* II. 440/2 Penda a Southumbrian.

B. *adj.* Of or pertaining to northern Mercia.

1887 *Dict. Nat. Biogr.* XI. 213 A reaction against the Southumbrian party. **1899** PLUMMER *Sax. Chron.* II. 35 Extent of the Southumbrian kingdom.

southward ('saυθwəd, *naut.* 'sʌðəd), *adv.*, *sb.*, and *a.* Forms: 1 **suþ-**, **suðweard**, 3 **suþ-**, **suð-**, 4– **southward**, 5-6 **-warde**, *Sc.* 5-7 **-wart**, 4, 7 **sowthward.** See also SOUTHARD. [OE. *súðweard*, f. SOUTH *adv.* + -WARD. Cf. MDu. *suut-*, *sude-*, *zuytwaert*, MLG. *sûdwart*, *-wert*.]

A. *adv.* **1.** Towards the south; in a southern direction: **a.** Of motion or direction.

c **893** K. ÆLFRED *Oros.* I. i. §10 þær of þæm beorȝum wilþ seo ea suþweard Eufrates. *c* **1000** *Sax. Leechd.* III. 250 Heo [*sc.* the sun] cyrð ðær ongean eft suðweard. *a* **1122** *O.E.*

Chron. (Laud MS.) an. 1095, þa het he makian ænne castel, ..& syððan suðweard for. *c* **1205** LAY. 29543 Swa he droh suð-ward, þat he com to Dorchestre. *c* **1290** *S. Eng. Leg.* I. 234 þo tornede þe wynd in-to þe North, and drof heom south-ward faste. *c* **1391** CHAUCER *Astrol.* I. §17 His Moeuyng is clepid sowth-ward as fro the equinoxial. *c* **1450** *Contin. Brut* 533 Whan he had taried a while in þe Northe.. he retorned Southwarde. **1535** COVERDALE *Numb.* xiii. 17 Go vp southwarde..and loke vpon the londe how it is. **1598** SYLVESTER *Du Bartas* II. ii. IV. *Columnes* 391 Then Southward Sol doth retrograde. **1603** *Reg. Mag. Sig. Scot.* 506/1 Passand ovir the streit..southwart to the loch. **1697** DRYDEN *Virg. Georg.* III. 437 They take their Flight;..Nor Southward to the Rainy Regions run, But boring to the West. **1726-46** THOMSON *Winter* 920 Life..from the dreary months Flies conscious southward. **1841** W. SPALDING *Italy & It. Isl.* II. 32 The apostle..fled from Rome southward. **1872** TENNYSON *Gar. & Lynette* 179 Southward they set their faces.

b. Of relative position.

1390 GOWER *Conf.* III. 127 After hem [*sc.* constellations] I finde thus, Southward from Alisandre forth Tho Signes [etc.]. **1412-20** LYDG. *Chron. Troy* I. 1518 Phebus southward was reised in his arke. **1610** HOLLAND *Camden's Brit.* (1637) 631 Beneath Brecknock and Hereford-shire Southward, lyeth the County of Monmouth. **1669** STURMY *Mariner's Mag.* VII. xvi. 25 Those that live 90 deg. from us Northward or Southward. **1726** in W. Wing *Ann. Steeple Aston* (1875) 54 The land..of Mr. Belcher, lying northward, and of Brazenose College southward.

c. Followed by *of*.

1630 CAPT. SMITH *Wks.* (Arb.) 953 The best Countries.. of the world, both Northward and Southward of the line. **1649** DAVENANT *Love & Hon.* II. i. 701 In a cloud, Southward of yonder star. **1738** *Gentl. Mag.* VIII. 164/1, 20 Leagues Southward of Porto Rico. **1771** *Encycl. Brit.* III. 379/1 Because Port-Royal is southward of the Lizard. **1814** SCOTT *Diary* 26 Aug. in *Lockhart*, Southward of both lies Muick, or Muck. **1896** BADEN-POWELL *Matabele Campaign* ii, Half a mile southward of the town lies a bush-covered rising ground.

d. *Comb.*, as ***southward-facing***, ***-looking***, etc.

1853 M. ARNOLD *Scholar Gypsy* xxiv, The fringes of a southward-facing brow. **1871** MORRIS *Earthly Par.* IV. 88 The southward-looking hill. **1885-94** R. BRIDGES *Eros & Psyche* March 23 The southward stretching margin of a bay.

2. quasi-*sb.* = next.

1842 MACAULAY *Regillus* xxiii, So came he far to southward. **1884** BEDFORD *Sailor's Handbk.* 101 The land wind comes off moderately from southward.

B. *sb.* That direction or part which lies to the south of a place, etc.

1555 EDEN *Decades* (Arb.) 382 Wee had the wynde more easterly to the southwarde then before. **1618** in Foster *Eng. Factories India* (1906) I. 3 Some new way to have a ship from the sowthward. **1707** *Lond. Gaz.* No. 4386/2 Several other light Colliers..are this Day come hither from the Southward. **1748** *Anson's Voy.* I. vi. 66 The wild cattle.. have spread..from Buenos Ayres towards the southward. **1820** SCORESBY *Acc. Arctic Reg.* II. 210 Any situation in a lower latitude than 78°, is called the 'southward'. **1840** R. H. DANA *Bef. Mast* x, It looked black at the southward and eastward. **1883** STEVENSON *Treas. Isl.* xxiii, I made sure she also was wheeling to the southward.

b. Const. *of* (a place, thing, etc.).

1624 *Capt. Smith's Wks.* (Arb.) 762 To trade to the Southward of Cape Cod. **1650** BULWER *Anthropomet.* xi. (1653) 179 The people on the southward of Tinda. **1748** *Anson's Voy.* II. i. 116 The highlands on the southward of the bay. **1801** SIR H. PARKER in A. Duncan *Nelson* (1806) 140 The wind veered..to the southward of the west. **1854** W. OSBURN *Mon. Hist. Egypt* II. ii. 54 A little to the southward of Melawi.

C. *adj.* That has a southerly situation or direction; lying, facing, moving, etc., towards the south.

1611 SHAKS. *Wint. T.* IV. iv. 819 The Sunne looking with a South-ward eye vpon him. **1638** CHILMEAD tr. *Hues' Treat. Globes* I. ii. (Hakl. Soc.) 31 The bright Starre..in the end of the taile (which is also the most Southward of all). **1736** AINSWORTH II, *Australis*, adj., southward, southern. **1820** SCORESBY *Acc. Arctic Reg.* II. 211 A number have been taken in the southward fishing stations. **1864** KERR *Gentlem. Ho.* 290 A southward aspect is..advantageous. **1882** SWINBURNE *Tristr.* (1899) 237 With the southward swallow.

'southwardly, *adv.* and *a.* [f. prec. + -LY².]

A. *adv.* **1.** From the south.

1596 DALRYMPLE tr. *Leslie's Hist. Scot.* (S.T.S.) I. 25 This guse ȝeirlie in the spring tyme returnes to ws: quhair-fra can na man tell: bot southwardlie. **1704** S. SEWALL *Diary* 25 Aug., The wind was Southwardly.

2. In a southward direction; to or towards the south.

1632 LITHGOW *Trav.* x. 443 A large prospect Southwardly towards the Evenise mountaines. **1667** *Lond. Gaz.* No. 189/1 A Fleet of 36 laden Colliers put to Sea from this place Southwardly bound. **1738** G. WHITEFIELD in *Life & Jrnls.* (1756) 90 A Town situated southwardly above an hundred Miles from Savannah. **1796** MORSE *Amer. Geog.* (ed. 3) I. 215 Few of them winter there on their return southwardly. **1810** VINCE *Astron.* xx. 191 The star passed still more southwardly. **1880** L. WALLACE *Ben-Hur* 173 It curved southwardly out of view.

B. *adj.* Situated in or directed towards the south; of the wind, blowing from the south.

c **1682** J. COLLINS *Salt & Fishery* 103 Fir for Exportation to Spain or other Southwardly Countries. **1704** *Phil. Trans.* XXV. 1657 The morning serene.., with small Southwardly Breezes. **1805** *Ibid.* XCVI. 244 The southwardly wind blew fresh. **1858** *Merc. Marine Mag.* V. 208 A southwardly course..would be a proper course.

'southwards, *adv.*, *sb.*, and *a.* Also 1 **suðweardes,** 5 *Sc.* **southwardis,** 6 **-wardys,** 7 **sowards.** [OE. *súðweardes*: see SOUTH *adv.* and -WARDS. So MDu. *sutwarts*, *zuytwerts*, Du. *zuidwaarts*, G. *südwärts*.]

A. *adv.* = SOUTHWARD *adv.* Also quasi-*sb.*

a **1000** *Boeth. Metr.* i. 4 Setton suðweardes siȝeþeoda twa. **1375** BARBOUR *Bruce* XIV. 250 And thai southwardis thair wais raid. **1517** TORKINGTON *Pilgr.* (1884) 38 The londe.. marcheth..Southwardys to the londe of Egipte. **1619** in Foster *Eng. Factories Ind.* (1906) I. 55 They usually have had good quantety..from sowards. **1687** MIÉGE *Gt. Fr. Dict.* I, *Du côté du Midi*, southwards. **1707** J. CHAMBERLAYNE *Pres. St. Gt. Brit.* (1710) 342 All those Islands lie in a Row Southwards one of the other. **1797** *Encycl. Brit.* (ed. 3) XVIII. 861/1 Bending gradually, as we advance southwards,..to the south-west. **1837** LOCKHART *Scott* I. viii. 265 Proceeding southwards, the tourists visited Carlisle. **1875** CROLL *Climate & T.* xiv. 230 Deflected southwards into the Antarctic Sea.

fig. **1857** GRINDON *Life: its Nature* (ed. 2) iii. 31 That the heart should look southwards.

B. *sb.* = SOUTHWARD *sb.*

1618 in Foster *Eng. Factories Ind.* (1906) I. 31, I ymployed the Fraunces..to the southwards the better to discover the coast. **1669** STURMY *Mariner's Mag.* IV. iii. 148 The Ship is to the Southwards of the Place she departed [from]. **1728** CHAMBERS *Cycl.* s.v. *Wind*, In South Latitudes to the Southwards thereof [*sc.* the equator].

C. *adj.* Directed towards the south. *rare*⁻¹.

1842 WHEWELL in Mrs. S. Douglas *Life* (1881) 262 The next time that you make your southwards move.

south-west (saʊθ'wɛst), *adv.*, *sb.*, and *a.* [OE. *súðwest* (see SOUTH and WEST), = OFris. *súdwest*, MDu. *suut-*, *suytwest* (Du. *zuidwest*), OS. *sûthuuest* (MLG. *sûtwest*), OHG. *suntwest* (G. *südwest*), Da. *sydvest*. Cf. OF. *suroest*, F. *sud-ouest*, Sp. *sudoeste*, Pg. *sudueste*.]

A. *adv.* **1. a.** In the direction situated midway between south and west. Also followed by *of*.

c **893** K. ÆLFRED *Oros.* I. i. 24 An ðæra garena lið suð-west ongean þæt iȝland þe Gades hatte. *a* **1122** *O.E. Chron.* (Laud MS.) an. 1097, Ða..ætywde an selcuð steorra... He wæs ȝesewen suðweast. **14..** *Sailing Directions* (Hakl. Soc. 1889) 12 Fro Orfordnesse to Orwell waynys the cours is southwest. *c* **1440** *Pallad. on Husb.* II. 164 Yf they do, turne hem southwest or west. **1574** in *Reg. Mag. Sig. Scot.* 263/1 Passand linialie southwest thruch the mos. **1610** SANDYS *Relat. Journ.* (1637) 22 Foure miles south-west from the foresaid place. **1633** T. JAMES *Voy.* 24 Wee stood South-west. **1719** DE FOE *Crusoe* II. (Globe) 466 His Comrades.. came on Southward, and South-West. **1771** *Encycl. Brit.* III. 942/1 Winchester [is]..sixty-five miles south-west of London. **1849** CUPPLES *Green Hand* ii. (1856) 16 'How does she head just now, Jacobs?' 'Sou'-west-and-by-south, sir.' **1870** MORRIS *Earthly Par.* III. IV. 88 The rook still flies South-west before the wind.

b. From this direction.

1725 DE FOE *Voy. round World* (1840) 306 The little wind that blew being south-west-by-south.

2. quasi-*sb.* **a.** ***at south-west***, = prec. sense. **b.** = next sense.

1555 EDEN *Decades* (Arb.) 258 Directynge theyr course towarde Southewest, they came to an other Ilande. **1591** RALEIGH *Last Fight Revenge* (Arb.) 32 They came into the height of 35. degrees,..where they found the winde at South-west. **1638** CHILMEAD tr. *Hues' Treat. Globes* IV. iii. (Hakl. Soc.) 100 Betwixt South west and bywest. **1671** MILTON *P.R.* IV. 237 Look once more e're we leave this specular Mount Westward, much nearer by Southwest, behold Where [etc.]. **1777** G. WHITE *Selborne* lxxviii, The wind at south-west, and the thermometer at 58½. **1865** KINGSLEY *Herew.* xxxviii, The vast forest which ringed London round from north-east to south-west. **1884** BEDFORD *Sailor's Handbk.* 192 The current runs to the north-west with winds south of south-west.

B. *sb.* **1. a.** The direction, district, or region situated between south and west.

a **1122** *O.E. Chron.* (Laud MS.) an. 1106, Se steorra ætywde innon þæt suðwest. **1387** TREVISA *Higden* (Rolls) I. 173 Mesia..ioyneþ in þe..south west to Dalmatia. **1517** TORKINGTON *Pilgr.* (1884) 61 The wynde Rose in the Suth-weste. **1577** HARRISON *Descr. Brit.* xii. in *Holinshed*, Erin riseth of sundrie heads, and..peninsulateth Seleseie towne on the southwest. **1611** BIBLE *Acts* xxvii. 12 Phenice..lieth toward the Southwest. **1731** MILLER *Gard. Dict.* s.v. *Wind*, The Wind..is like to be in the South or South-west. **1789** J. WILLIAMS *Min. Kingd.* I. 102 You advance..with your face towards the southwest. **1837** CARLYLE *Fr. Rev.* II. v. iii, Such is the combustion of Avignon and the South-west. **1855** *Orr's Circ. Sci., Inorg. Nat.* 117 Represented by soft sands..in the south-west of France.

b. *U.S.* The south-western states.

1835 J. H. OTEY in W. M. Green *Mem. J. H. Otey* (1885) 15 Connected with my journey to the South-West, was an ardent desire to forward..a projected plan of a *Literary and Theological Seminary*, to meet the wants of Episcopalians in Tennessee and Mississippi and Louisiana. **1897** *Sears, Roebuck Catal.* 342/2 The best specimens of broad burlesque for which the Southwest is so distinguished. **1925** C. F. LUMMIS (*title*) Mesa, cañon and pueblo; our wonderland of the Southwest. **1935** A. G. MACDONELL *Visit to America* ix. 142 It must have been from the Spanish south-west..that the first prospectors came..into Montana. **1976** 'R. MACDONALD' *Blue Hammer* xv. 83 Mildred was the most beautiful woman in the South-west. **1979** G. MACDONALD *Camera* ix. 130/2 In the South-West the pueblo Indians..were..much photographed.

c. *ellipt.* for South West Africa (now Namibia).

1976 J. MCCLURE *Rogue Eagle* i. 22 Ma..said she'd write to her family in South West, but he said that was just another Bantustan these days. **1978** S. NAIPAUL *North of South* II. vi. 245 Abraham had been in Namibia ('South-West')... It was in South-West..that he and Tessa had met.

2. The (or a) south-west wind.

1610 SHAKS. *Temp.* I. ii. 323 A Southwest blow on yee, And blister you all ore. **1725** POPE *Odyss.* XII. 343 Should the fierce south-west..toss with rising storms the watery way. **1859** TENNYSON *Geraint & Enid* 935 As the south-west that blowing Bala lake Fills all the Sacred Dee.

C. *adj.* **1.** Of the wind: Blowing from the south-west.

1377 LANGL. *P. Pl.* B. v. 14 þe southwest wynde..Was pertliche for pure pryde, and for no poynt elles. **1483** *Cath. Angl.* 350/2 þe Sowthe west wynde, *fauonius*, *affricus*. **1526** TINDALE *Acts* xxvii. 12 Whych haven..servith to the soughwest and northwest wynde. **1597** A. M. tr. *Guillemeau's Fr. Chirurg.* 51 b/1 A south-west wind, with warmishe showres of rayne. **1608** SHAKS. *Pericles* IV. i. 51 Is this wind westerly that blows? *Leon.* South-west. **1731** MILLER *Gard. Dict.* s.v. *Barometer*, A long continu'd Storm of South-west Wind. **1829** *Chapters Phys. Sci.* 428 The great rains which deluge the whole of India during the south-west monsoon. **1884** BEDFORD *Sailor's Handbk.* 146 From that latitude.., much south-west wind is experienced.

2. a. Lying in or situated to the south-west.

c **1440** *Astron. Cal.* (MS. Ashm. 391), A sowþe weste moone and a norþe Est moone maken an high flode at london brigge. **1540** *Test. Ebor.* (Surtees) VI. 120 To be buried in the churche yerde..in the southe weste corner. **1573** TUSSER *Husb.* (1878) 117 The sunne southwest for hopyard is best. **1663** BUTLER *Hud.* I. i. 68 He could..divide A Hair 'twixt South and South-West side. **1728** CHAMBERS *Cycl.* s.v. *Compass*, What has been said of North-East Amplitudes, holds also of South-West Amplitudes. **1797** *Encycl. Brit.* (ed. 3) II. 624 The south-west side of the island. **1837** P. KEITH *Bot. Lex.* 14 The south-west and south-east coasts [of North America]..being..the more flat. **1886** STEVENSON *Kidnapped* xiii, The reef..was close in under the south-west end of Mull.

b. With proper names, denoting the south-western division of a city, country, continent, etc.

1858 *1st Rep. South-West London Protestant Inst.* 3 *Rules.* 1. That this Society be called 'The South-West London Protestant Institute'. **1899** *Geogr. Jrnl.* May 563 A notice of Dr. Rehbock's work on irrigation in German South-West Africa. **1946** *Whitaker's Almanack 1947* 789 The *Orange*.. is the principal river of the south,..flowing into the Atlantic between the Protectorate of South-West Africa and the Cape of Good Hope. **1950** H. BRIERCLIFFE *Southern England* p. iii, There is necessarily some overlapping with..South-west England and the Midlands. **1968** *Ann. Reg. 1967* 326 The South African Government remained completely unmoved by United Nations' efforts to plan the implementation of the 1966 General Assembly resolution that South West Africa be removed from South African control. **1980** *Times* 14 June 1/8 The Middle East, or south-west Asia as the Americans now call it.

3. Directed towards the south-west.

1756 F. HOME *Exper. Bleaching* 67, I exposed, in a south-west window, half an oz. of Castile soap. **1812** *New Botanic Gard.* I. 61 A wall which had a south-west aspect. **1825** *Greenhouse Comp.* I. 11 A green-house with a west or even south-west aspect.

south-'wester, *sb.* Also **southwester.** [f. prec. + -ER¹. Cf. SOU'-WESTER.]

1. A wind or gale blowing from the south-west.

1833 T. HOOK *Parson's Dau.* III. xi, He felt a longing hope that he might fall in with the Dolly in the Channel, although the prevalence of the south-westers rendered it improbable. **1855** KINGSLEY *Westw. Ho!* viii, The south-wester freshened, and blew three parts of a gale dead into the bay. **1868** *Rep. U.S. Commissioner Agric.* (1869) 176 Logs of all sizes lie..where they are thrown upon the shore by the October southwesters.

2. a. A large oilskin or waterproof hat or cap worn by seamen to protect the head and neck during rough or wet weather.

So Du. *zuidwester*, G. *südwester*.

1836 R. S. SURTEES *Let.* in A. Mathews *Mem. Charles Mathews* (1839) IV. ix. 193 Throwing aside his hat, he put on one of the boatman's 'south-westers'. **1840** R. H. DANA *Bef. Mast* iv, We were glad to..put on our thick clothing, boots, and southwesters. **1845** DISRAELI *Sybil* II. xiv, [He] was shaking the wet off an oilskin hat known by the name of a 'south-wester'. **1883** *Cent. Mag.* XXVI. 947 The six oil-jackets and south-westers.

b. *attrib.* with *cap*, *hat*.

1831 *Ann. Reg.* 113 He wore a smock frock..and a south-wester cap. **1840** R. H. DANA *Bef. Mast* x, We had on oil-cloth suits and southwester caps.

3. A (White) inhabitant of Namibia (formerly known as South West Africa).

1976 *Times* 21 Aug. 13/3 South Africa's original plans to break up South West Africa into eight or nine mini-states, of which the only viable ones would be a 'ranchistan' containing the 99,000 rich German, Afrikaans and English-speaking 'Southwesters', and Ovamboland. **1978** *Guardian Weekly* 7 May 6/2 The Teutonic calm of Windhoek... Like their White Rhodesian counterparts most 'Southwesters' as they call themselves have yet to grasp the dimension of the change.

south-'wester, *v.* *rare*⁻¹. [f. SOUTH-WEST *adv.*] *intr.* To move towards the south-west.

a **1861** A. H. CLOUGH *Poems* (1888) 95 [The sun] Scuth-westering now, thro' windows plainly glassed, On the inside face his radiance keen hath cast.

south-'westerly, *a.* and *adv.* [f. SOUTH-WEST, after WESTERLY.]

A. *adj.* **a.** Of the wind: Blowing from the south-west. **b.** Tending south-westward.

1708 SEWEL *Du. Dict.* II, *Zuydwestelyk*, south-westerly. **1731** MILLER *Gard. Dict.* s.v. *Wind*, The North-East Trade Wind below will be attended with a South-Westerly above. **1840** R. H. DANA *Bef. Mast* vii, A steady though light southwesterly wind. **1869** DUNKIN *Midn. Sky* 59 A south-westerly direction.

transf. **1883** *Harper's Mag.* Aug. 441/2 One murky south-westerly Saturday night.

B. *adv.* South-westwardly.

1792 MORSE *Amer. Geog.* 50 These mountains extend north-easterly and south-westerly. **1883** *American* VII. 168 The party now headed southwesterly for the Siberian coast.

south-'western, *a.* and *sb.* [OE. *sūðwesterne* (see SOUTH *adv.* and WESTERN *a.*), = OHG. *sundwestrôni*.]

A. *adj.* **1.** Of the wind: Blowing from the south-west.

c **1000** *Apollonius of Tyre* (Thorpe) 11 Se angrislica suð-westerna wind him ongean stod. **1362** LANGL. *P. Pl.* A. v. 14 þis souþ-Westerne wynt on a Seterday at euen. **1835** MRS. SOMERVILLE *Connex. Phys. Sci.* xv. (ed. 2) 147 The western and south-western gales, so prevalent in our latitudes. **1894** GLADSTONE *Horace, Odes* I. xiv. 19 Seest not? thy mast How rent by stiff southwestern blast?

2. a. Situated or extending towards the south-west; of or pertaining to the south-west.

1828–32 WEBSTER s.v., To sail a southwestern course. **1839** *Penny Cycl.* XV. 345/1 The south-western coast of the island of Sumatra. **1863** W. BARNES *Dorset Gloss.* 9 The main marks of south-western English. **1888** MISS BRADDON *Fatal Three* I. v, It is too warm in this south-western country.

b. *U.S.* Of, pertaining to, or characteristic of the south-western states.

1806 *New Eng. Palladium* (Boston) 30 July 2/1 The President appoints the Legislative Councils in our South-western Territories. **1832** *Jrnl. Gen. Convention Prot. Episc. Church* 51 Delegates have been chosen to co-operate with Alabama and Louisiana in organizing the contemplated South-Western Diocese. **1973** J. M. WHITE *Garden Game* 150 The walls were whitewashed in simple, South-Western style.

B. *sb.* A wave from the south-west. *rare*$^{-1}$.

1872 TENNYSON *Gar. & Lynette* 1117 Gareth..could not wholly bring him under, more Than loud Southwesterns, rolling ridge on ridge, The buoy that rides at sea.

Hence **south-'westerner**, one belonging to the south-west (of the United States, etc.). Also **south-'westernmost** *adv.*

1862 ANSTED *Channel Isl.* I. iii. 49 The south-westernmost angle. **1888** *Encycl. Brit.* XXIII. 799/1 The south-westernmost portion of the region. **1888** *Cent. Mag.* Feb. 502/2 The bulk of the cowboys..are South-westerners.

south-'westward, *adv.*, *sb.*, and *a.* [f. SOUTH-WEST + -WARD. So MDu. *suytwestwairt*.]

A. *adv.* = SOUTH-WEST *adv.*

1548 PATTEN *Exped. Scotl.* M vj, Thear stode southwestward about a quarter of a mile from our campe, a monasterie. **1553** EDEN *Treat. New Ind.* (Arb.) 28 He sayled by the costes of the Ilande Southweste warde. **1612** DRAYTON *Poly-olb.* viii. 3 Clear Sabrine..South-westward casts her course. **1792** MORSE *Amer. Geog.* 48 The..mountains which run south-westward through Pennsylvania. **1820** KEATS *Lamia* I. 179 That other ridge..Stretches..South-westward to Cleone. **1876** MEREDITH *Beauch. Career* xxxv, Save where a quarry south-westward gaped at the evening sun. **1884** BEDFORD *Sailor's Handbk.* 441 The anchorage for large vessels is south-westward of Little Sea Hill.

B. *sb.* = SOUTH-WEST *sb.*

1775 *Phil. Trans.* LXVIII. 392 When the ship's head was to the Southwestward. **1831** SCOTT *Cast. Dang.* i, Coming from the south-westward. **1884** BEDFORD *Sailor's Handbk.* 411 [The currents] often run with great velocity to the south-westward.

C. *adj.* Tending or flowing towards the south-west.

1796 MORSE *Amer. Geog.* (ed. 3) I. 384 The river Kennebeck takes a southwestward course. **1972** *Science* 19 May 791/1 The southwestward flow of cold drier air is suggested to account for two aspects.

So **south-'westwards** *adv.*

1745 tr. *Egede's Descr. Greenland* 39 The Current..running along the Shore, South-Westwards. **1879** GEIKIE in *Encycl. Brit.* X. 339/2 From the mouth of the St. Lawrence south-westwards into Alabama.

south-'westwardly, *adv.* and *a.* [f. SOUTH-WESTWARD.] = SOUTH-WESTWARD *adv.* and *a.*

1796 *Phil. Trans.* LXXXVI. 350 Under which it is to be extended south-westwardly by a subterraneous cut or tunnel. **1807** VANCOUVER *Agric. Devon* (1813) 43 Sand-hills extend south-westwardly from the mouth of the river Axe. **1858** MAURY *Phys. Geog.* i. §53 We find the current..taking a southwestwardly direction.

†**southwort.** *Obs. rare*$^{-1}$. In 3 suþewurt. = SOUTHERNWORT.

c **1265** *Voc. Plants* in Wr.-Wülcker 554 *Abrotanum*,..suþewurt.

soutilete, obs. variant of SUBTILITY.

souvenir (suːvəˈnɪə(r)), *sb.* [a. F. *souvenir* memory, keepsake, subst. use of the inf. *souvenir*:—L. *subvenīre* to come into the mind.]

1. a. A remembrance, a memory.

1775 H. WALPOLE *Lett.* (1857) VI. 284 You have always been so good to me, Madam, and I am so grateful that if my *souvenirs* were marked with cups, there would be many more than mile-stones from hence to Ampthill. **1777** C'TESS UPPER OSSORY in Jesse *Selwyn & Contemp.* (1844) III. 188 These are the words of our friend the Quaker, and the substantial proofs of this *souvenir* you will soon receive.

b. A slight trace *of* something. *rare*$^{-1}$.

1883 *Harper's Mag.* Nov. 971/1, I would recommend this lavender Ducape, with only just a souvenir of sorrow in it.

2. a. A token of remembrance; something (usually a small article of some value bestowed as a gift) which reminds one of some person, place, or event; a keepsake.

1782 J. DOUGLAS *Trav. Anecd.* (1786) 41 The youngest of the two girls..asked if she was certain, that the little *souvenir* she gave her was safe in her pocket. **1803** MAR. EDGEWORTH *E. de Coulanges* (1832) 217 She intended to offer souvenirs to her English friends. **1838** STEPHEN *Trav. Russia* 75/1 He gave me his last painting..as a souvenir for his sister. **1885** R. BUCHANAN *Annan Water* xxiii, She saw the gentle old pastor counting his souvenirs within.

b. As the title of a work intended as a gift-book, *spec.* of an illustrated annual publication (see first quot.).

1825 (*title*), The Literary Souvenir, or Cabinet of Poetry and Romance. **1835** HOOD *Poetry, Prose, & Worse* xxxvii, How sweet if the bill..But enrich'd, as a copy of verses, The Gem, or a new Souvenir! **1840** —— *Kilmansegg, Educ.* x, Her 'Early Lessons' of every sort, Looked like Souvenirs.

c. *Mil. slang.* In the 1914–18 war, a jocular term for a bullet or shell.

1915 D. O. BARNETT *Let.* 17 May 140 They kept sending their big black souvenirs over. **1929** *Papers Mich. Acad. Sci. Arts & Lett.* X. 324 *Souvenirs*, shells.

3. *attrib.*, as ***souvenir card***, ***-hunter***, ***programme***, ***shop***, ***spoon***.

1900 *Daily News* 15 Nov. 5/2 The presentation of a silver trophy to each corps and of a souvenir card to each Volunteer. **1923** KIPLING *Irish Guards in Gt. War* I. 131 Being a hardened souvenir-hunter, he is reported to have removed the official German name-board of the establishment. **1976** B. JACKSON *Flameout* (1977) iii. 40 Souvenir hunters were a menace..stealing bits of metal that could, if left in position, help determine the cause of the crash. **1962** L. DEIGHTON *Ipcress File* ii. 22 A cigarette-girl..tried to sell me a souvenir programme. **1950** J. FLANNER in *New Yorker* 25 Feb. 84/2 The best souvenir shops for the pilgrims are in the Via della Conciliazione. **1980** J. GARDNER *Garden of Weapons* III. iii. 246 From the souvenir shop the coach party went..for a drink. **1893** *Outing* XXII. 160 When the souvenir spoon became a fad, As a gift to be highly prized.

souvenir (suːvəˈnɪə(r)), *v.* [f. the sb.]

1. *trans.* To pierce with a bullet or shell. Cf. sense 2c of the sb. *Mil. slang* (in the war of 1914–18).

1915 *Chambers's Jrnl.* Oct. 663/1 Our periscope was 'souvenired' later on with a rifle-bullet clean through the tin sides.

2. To provide with or constitute a souvenir of (something). *rare.*

1917 W. OWEN *Let.* 25 Nov. (1967) 510 How much better than a photograph does it [*sc.* a poem] souvenir that day! **1976** *Vogue* Jan. 7/2 The Tate..is issuing a special Constable diary..and a Constable paper-weight. So the exhibition will be fully souvenired.

3. To take as a 'souvenir'; to appropriate; to pilfer, steal. Also *absol. slang* (orig. *Mil.*).

1919 W. H. DOWNING *Digger Dialects* 46 *Souvenir*,..to steal, find, capture, etc. **1920** *Punch* 28 Jan. 65/1 The Major ..set the ladies souveniring among old water-tin stoppers, which he alleged to be the plugs of hand-grenades. **1944** F. CLUNE *Red Heart* 19, I dug up his body, souvenired his false teeth. **1956** S. HOPE *Diggers' Paradise* ix. 83 But early, too, numbers of youngsters show that tendency to 'souvenir' which is the euphonious term for pilfering. **1969** I. BROWN *Rhapsody of Words* 120 Silver spoons and jewellery souvenired from rooms with open windows. **1975** J. I. M. STEWART *Gaudy* vii. 116 It's possible that people sometimes souvenir such things.

Hence **souveˈniring** *vbl. sb.*

1969 'M. INNES' *Family Affair* xiii. 145 It had been lifted much as somebody might lift a china gnome..from a suburban garden. Souveniring, as they say. **1972** *Guardian* 15 May 1/4 The House of Commons is determined to end the 'souveniring' of cutlery... All crests will be removed from the cutlery in some of the visitors' cafeterias.

‖**souvlaki** (suː-, sʊvˈlɑːkɪ). Pl. **souvlakia.** [mod.Gr. σουβλάκι, f. σοῦβλα skewer.] A Greek dish consisting of pieces of meat grilled on a skewer. Also *attrib.* Cf. KEBAB.

1958 R. LIDDELL *Morea* II. vii. 171 They had bought *souvlakia* or bread and cheese at every halt. **1963** J. M. STUBBS *Home Bk. Greek Cookery* vii. 97 The best *souvlakia* I have eaten in Greece are those sold..at Antirhion. **1972** J. AIKEN *Butterfly Picnic* i. 19 Lamb grilled on skewers, souvlakia, and all the different forms of mince that the Greeks delight in. **1979** M. A. SHARP *Sunflower* iii. 30 The building..was..sandwiched between a *souvlaki* stand and a tiny hotel.

souwarrow, obs. form of SAOUARI.

souwe, obs. form of SEW *v.*

sou'-west: see SOUTH-WEST.

sou'-'wester. Also **sou'wester**, **sou-wester.** [Reduced form of SOUTH-WESTER *sb.*]

1. = SOUTH-WESTER *sb.* 1.

1838 COL. HAWKER *Diary* (1893) II. 157 Frost ended in a set in of dirty sou'-wester, with a constant batch of wind and rain. **1894** W. E. NORRIS *St. Ann's* I. 180 One of those steady, relentless sou'-westers, accompanied by sheets of rain.

2. = SOUTH-WESTER *sb.* 2.

1837 COL. HAWKER *Diary* (1893) II. 130, I shipped my sou-wester and went fishing. **1848** DICKENS *Dombey* xxxii, He also provided Rob with a species of hat,..which is usually termed a sou'wester. **1870** THORNBURY *Tour rd. Eng.* II. xxviii. 239 [The] men have their shiny-yellow sou'-westers pulled down over their brows.

b. *attrib.*, = SOUTH-WESTER *sb.* 2b.

1842 DICKENS *Amer. Notes* (1850) 13/1 When the captain comes down again, in a sou'-wester hat tied under his chin, and a pilot-coat. **1860** C. A. COLLINS *Eyewitness* 120 It is a neighbourhood of canvas trousers and sou'-wester hats.

3. *Naut.* (See quot., and cf. NOR'-WESTER 2.)

1848 B. D. WALSH *Aristoph.* 40 *note*, Half-and-half was equivalent to what seamen call a sou'-wester, that is to say, half rum and the rest rum-and-water.

Hence **sou'-'westered** *a.*, wearing a sou'-wester.

1891 *Harper's Mag.* July 179/1 That unseasonably sou'-westered man at the wheel.

souzalite (ˈsuːzəlaɪt). *Min.* [f. the name of A. J. A. de *Souza*, 20th-c. Brazilian mining administrator: see -ITE[1].] A hydrated basic phosphate of aluminium, iron, and magnesium, found in association with scorzalite as fibrous masses of green crystals.

1947 PECORA & FAHEY in *Bull. Geol. Soc. Amer.* LVIII. 1217 The new minerals are named in honor of Dr. Evarists Scorza and Dr. Antonio José Alves de Souza... Souzalite is a fibrous, green hydrous iron magnesium aluminum phosphate. **1951** C. PALACHE et al. *Dana's Syst. Min.* (ed. 7) II. 911 Scorzalite is known from the Corrego Frio pegmatite, Minas Geraes, Brazil, where it occurs with souzalite and brazilianite. **1970** *Amer. Mineralogist* LV. 152 Souzalite is a hydrothermally reworked product of scorzalite and occurs as bluish-green aggregates of polysynthetically twinned prismatic crystals.

souze, variant of SOUSE *sb.* and *v.*

sov[1] (sɒv), colloq. abbrev. of SOVEREIGN *sb.*

1829 P. EGAN *Boxiana* 2nd Ser. II. 492 'Come,' said an old ring-goer, 'here's my *sov.* to begin.' **1846** *Swell's Night Guide* 101 But of whatever size if a known gentleman and some liberality (as nothing less than five sovs would be any inducement) you may perhaps get admittance in the absence of her keeper. **1850** *New Monthly Mag.* XC. 310 As to the purse, there weren't above three or four sovs in it. **1857** HUGHES *Tom Brown* I. v, She gave me half-a-sov this half. **1883** *Harper's Mag.* Mar. 647/2, I slipped a sov. in the paw of the major-general.

Sov[2] (sɒv), colloq. abbrev. of SOVIET *sb.* 2. Usu. in *pl.* with *the.*

1967 [see CHICOM *sb.* and *a.*]. **1969** H. H. COOPER *Cave with Two Exits* II. 163 Their only worry would be that Washington might think the Sovs had done it. **1977** *Time* 28 Feb. 23/3 Certainly in every case I know of, the opposition —usually the Sovs but sometimes the Chicoms—were involved up to their eyeballs on the other side. **1981** P. FOX *Satan's Messenger* ix. 68 'Comeback from the Sovs?' 'Never heard of you.'

sove(n, obs. forms of SEVEN.

†**sovenance.** *Obs.* Forms: 5 sou(u)enaunce, 6–7 souv-, souenance. [a. OF. *sov-*, *souvenance* (F. *souvenance*, It. *sovvenenza*) f. *so(u)venir*: see SOUVENIR *sb.*] Remembrance; memory.

c **1477** CAXTON *Jason* 19 The souenaunce of his lady presented her into his memorie. **1483** —— *Gold. Leg.* 363/2 As she hadde alwey souuenaunce and mynde of Jhesu Cryst. *c* **1550** ROLLAND *Crt. Venus* II. 1026 3e haifand of vs the souenance, With hand we may not make hir resistance. **1590** SPENSER *F.Q.* II. vi. 8 Of his way he had no souenaunce, Nor care of vow'd reuenge. **1614** J. DAVIES (Heref.) *Eclogue* 116 Whan wee wenden till an other place, Our souenance may here ay-gayly wonne. **1625** LISLE *Du Bartas, Noe* 100 Like a forrest wide where..the learned Souvenance Itself entangled is.

soveniht, **-niȝt**, **-nyȝt**, obs. ff. SENNIGHT.

†**sover**, *a.* and *adv.* *Sc. Obs.* Also 4 souar (5 suffer), 5–6 souir, 6 souer, sovir, sowir, seuver. [ad. OF. *soür*, var. of *seür* (mod.F. *sûr*) SURE *a.*, with intrusive *v.*]

A. *adj.* Sure, secure, safe, sound.

1396 in *Scott. Antiq.* XIV. 218 Gif yt sal happyn the..erle til pay the forsaid soume othirways in ony souar maner. **1429** *Sc. Acts, Jas. I* (1814) II. 18 þe ȝeman..sall haif a gude souer hat for his hede, & a doublat of fence. *c* **1470** HENRY *Wallace* III. 84 Gude souir weide dayly on him he wour. *Ibid.* VI. 484 He..said he was baith suffer [*v.r.* sober], wys and trew. *c* **1520** *Reg. Aberdon.* (Maitland Cl.) I. 385 As your Lordship may geit sowir informacion. **1533** BELLENDEN *Livy* II. xiv. (S.T.S.) I. 183 The pepill..garnist þare tentis with maist sovir trinschis & fowseis. **1568** *Satir. Poems Reform.* xlviii. 59 ȝit is my claith seuver for sadillis to ceuver, Suppois the sessioun raid thameself.

B. *adv.* Surely, securely.

c **1550** ROLLAND *Crt. Venus* I. 92 With precious Perle, and gold was souer set. *Ibid.* II. 698 Weill souer set with diuers christall stane.

†**sover**, *v.* *Sc. Obs.* In 5–6 souer, 5 suffer. [Cf. prec. and SURE *v.*, ASSURE *v.*]

1. *intr.* To trust *in* something.

c **1470** *Gol. & Gaw.* 1105 Ane wounder peralous poynt.. To souer in thi gentrice, but signete or sele.

2. *trans.* To render safe from attack or injury, esp. by a formal pledge.

c **1470** HENRY *Wallace* VII. 1188 The hardy Scottis..Set on the laiff with strakis sad and sar, Off thaim thar our as than souerit thai war. *Ibid.* IX. 277 Thai..rasauit him in the toun, And sufferyt [*v.r.* souerit] thaim, for all that he had brocht. *a* **1557** *Diurn. Occurr.* (Bann. Cl.) 26 George Dowglas was souerit to cume and speak with the Governour.

†**soverance.** *Sc. Obs.* Also 5-6 souerance, 6 souerans(e, souuirance. [Cf. prec. and SURANCE *sb.*] Assurance; safe-conduct; truce.

c **1470** HENRY *Wallace* XI. 881 Bot..souerance he wald nocht grant, Thocht thai ȝoldin wald cum as recreant. *c* **1475** *Rauf Coilȝear* 880 Thy self maid me neuer sa affraid, That I for souerance wald haue praid. **1525** EARL OF ANGUS in *St. Papers Hen. VIII* (1836) IV. 378 Richtsa the soverance, takin in Parliament betuix Hir Grace and me,..I have observit and kepit in all poyntis. **1596** DALRYMPLE tr. *Leslie's Hist. Scot.* II. 13 With Ingland thay take nocht a Souerans abone four ȝeiris.

soverance, obs. Sc. f. SUFFERANCE.

sovereign (ˈsɒvrɪn), *sb.* and *a.* Forms: (see below). [a. OF. *soverain, souverein*, etc. (mod.F. *souverain*), = It. *sovrano* (see SOVRAN), Sp. and Pg. *soberano*:—pop.L. **superānus*, f. *super* above. Cf. MDu. *sov(e)rein, souverein, soferein.*]

A. Forms.

1. *α.* 3-5 souerein (4 -eine, 6, 8 sov-), 3-6 souereyn(e, 5 souereeyne, souureyn), 4-6 sovereyn(e, 4 sovreyn); 4-6 sou-, 4-7 soverain(e, 4 souorain), 4-6 sou-, soverayn(e, 5 souereayn).

β. 4-7 souereign(e, 4 soeuereigne, 5 souerign, -ygne), 4-7 sovereigne, 4- sovereign; 4-6 soueraigne (4 souuer-), 5- 6 soueraygne (6 sov-), 6-7 soveraigne, 6-8 soveraign (6 sovar-, 7 -aing).

γ. (Chiefly *Sc.*) 4-7 soueran(e, 4 sowu-, 5 sow-), 5-6 soveran(e.

[For examples of these forms see the senses below.]

δ. 4-5 soueryn, 5 soueren, -eng, -yng(e, 6 -eyng; 5 souerant-, soveraynt-, 6 soverand(e.

1390-1440 *R. Gloucester's Chron.* 5183 (Harl. MS.), þat folc..vnderuonge þere Kyng Egbryȝt to her soueryn. *c* **1400** *Destr. Troy* 11459 In faith of þo faire soueryn. **1421** *Cov. Leet Bk.* 36 Masturs & souerens of this wurthy Cite. *c* **1460** FORTESCUE *Abs. & Lim. Mon.* (1714) 61 More Richesse than his Soveryng Lord. **1535** BOORDE *Let.* in *Introd. Knowl.* (1870) 53 Our most..gracyose souereyng lord the Kynge. **1537** in *Lett. Suppress. Monast.* (Camden) 153 Our soverand lord kyng Henrie. **1548** *Act 2 & 3 Edw. VI*, c. 38 §4 The King or Soverande Lorde.

2. *α.* 4 sufrayn, 5 suffrayn, -ein, 6 -ayne, 6-7 -ain; 5-6 sufferayne, 6 -ayn, -aine, -ein, -aigne, -eigne; 5 sofferayn, sofereyn, 6 -ayne, 5 sofreyn.

a **1340** HAMPOLE *Psalter* 514 Ask..þi sufrayns. *c* **1400** *Destr. Troy* 5055 Diamede..said to þat suffrayn. *c* **1440** *York Myst.* xiv. 46 He is sufferayne of all thyng. **1452** *Cal. Anc. Rec. Dublin* (1889) 277 Our sofferayn lorde the Kyng. **1528** *Star Chamber Cases* (Selden) II. 168 In the xixth yere of our sofreyn lord kyng henry the viijth. **1534** in Peacock *Eng. Ch. Furniture* (1866) 191 With a sufferayn of golde thereto nailed. **1551** TURNER *Herbal* II. 123 A soferayne medicine. **1567** MAPLET *Gr. Forest* (title-p.), The most sufferaigne Vertues in all the whole kinde of Stones & Mettals. **1596** DAWSON *Good Hus-wifes Iewell* 50 A sufferaine ointment for shrunken sinewes.

β. 5 soferan, 5 suffirane, 5-6 sufferan, suffran, *Sc.* -ane; 5 sufferen, 6 suffren, sufferyn.

c **1400** *Destr. Troy* 4817 Plenty of Setis..in a serkyll þe soferan before. *c* **1426** *Abraham's Sacrifice* 273 in *Non-Cycle Myst. Plays* (1909) 33 A, sufferen lord, þi wille be fulfilled. **1515** A. WILLIAMSON in *Douglas's Wks.* (1874) I. Introd. p. xxii, The Quene my mastres and suffrane. **1540** *North Co. Wills* (Surtees) 172 To Mr. John Danyell..oon sufferyn. **1553** BALE *Vocacyon* 5 b, The good suffren of kylkennie.. brought me thyder in the night.

γ. 5 soferand, sufferande, suffraynd; 5-6 sufferante (6 *pl.* -aunce), sufferent(e.

1432 in Burton & Raine *Hemingbrough* (1888) 383 To my sufferante lorde Prior of Durham. *c* **1440** *York Myst.* x. 163 Gude god oure suffraynd syre. *c* **1460** *Towneley Myst.* viii. 22 Take tent to me, youre soferand syre. *a* **1500-34** *Cov. Corpus Chr. Plays* (1902) 2 Loo! sufferentis, now ma you be glad. **1553** *Request true harted Englysheman* 12 All our olde angelles..and our newe sufferantes. **1562** BULLEIN *Bulwarke, Bk. Simples* 7 Sufferente against all hote diseases.

δ. 6 suffaryng; 6- suffering. Now only *dial.*, or *slang.*

1538 *Lichfield Gild Ord.* (E.E.T.S.) 15 Our suffaryng lorde kyng henry the viijth. **1594** DEE *Priv. Diary* (Camden) 50 The Archbishop gave me a payre of sufferings to drinke. **1836** [see BLANK *sb.* 12]. **1914** E. PUGH *Cockney at Home* 221 I've..played..till twelve at night, and then not made half a suffering.

B. Signification.

I. *sb.* **1.** One who has supremacy or rank above, or authority over, others; a superior; a ruler, governor, lord, or master (*of* persons, etc.). Freq. applied to the Deity in relation to created things. In later use suggestive of sense 2 a.

α. *c* **1290** *S. Eng. Leg.* I. 74 For, sire king, þou art mi souerein, and þe erchebischop al-so. *c* **1315** SHOREHAM IV. 262 Who yst þat neuer nas rebel Aȝeins hys souerayn? *c* **1386** CHAUCER *Pars. T.* ¶506 Murmuryng eek is ofte among servauntz, that grucchen whan here soverayns bidden hem to doon leeful things. *c* **1449** *Paston Lett.* I. 78 To my Sovereyn, John Paston. *a* **1470** H. PARKER *Dives & Pauper* (W. de W. 1496) clxxxvi. 181, I suppose that my lege lorde the kynge byddе me do a thynge, and my mayster or my souerayn bydde me do the contrarye. **1559** *Mirr. Mag., Edw. IV*, v. 83 b, For I am departed vntill doomes day: But love you that lord that is soveraine of all.

β. **1377** LANGL. *P. Pl.* B. XII. 200 þo þat seten atte syde table or with þe souereignes of þe halle. **1400** in Ellis *Orig. Lett.* Ser. II. I. 4, But God that is our elder sovereigne gife you long lyve. **1496** *Act 12 Hen. VII*, c. vii, If any laie persone hereaftir purpensidly murder their Lord Maister or Sovereign immediate that they be not admytted to their Clergie. **1588** KYD *Househ. Phil.* 897 Wks. (1901) 262 This distinction of Soueraigne, Ruler, Gouernour, or Maister, is first founded vpon Nature. **1596** SHAKS. *Tam. Shr.* v. ii. 147 Thy husband is thy Lord, thy life, thy keeper, Thy head, thy soueraigne. **16..** MIDDLETON, etc. *Old Law* v. i, The Duke! As he is my sovereign, I do give him two crowns for it. **1673** CAVE *Prim. Chr.* I. i. 15 The Soveraign of the whole Creation. **1734** tr. *Rollin's Anc. Hist.* (1827) I. Pref. 7 Those haughty merchants, who thought themselves Kings of the sea, and sovereigns over crowned heads. **1775** JOHNSON *Lett.* (1788) I. 293 Lucy says I must not go this week... The Lady at Stowhill says, how comes Lucy to be such a sovereign? **1820** BYRON *Mar. Fal.* I. ii, Why, that's my uncle! The leader, and the statesman, and the chief Of commonwealths, and sovereign of himself! **1859** MILL *Liberty* i. 22 Over himself, over his own body and mind, the individual is Sovereign.

γ. *c* **1450** HOLLAND *Howlat* 7 So soft was the sessoun our Souerane dovne sent. **1567** *Gude & Godlie B.* (S.T.S.) 79 Christ our cheif and Souerane.

†**b.** A husband in relation to his wife. *Obs.*

1390 GOWER *Conf.* I. 71 The Prestes tho gon hom ayein, And sche goth to hire sovereign. *a* **1400** *Pistill of Susan* 223 We siked wel sore, For sert of hire souereyn and for hire owne sake. *c* **1450** LOVELICH *Merlin* 6336 To hire lord & souerayn seide sche than: 'My sovereyn,' sche seide, 'ȝowre owne am J'.

c. A person or thing which excels or surpasses others of the kind. Now *rare.*

1500-20 DUNBAR *Poems* xlviii. 170 Haill, of all flouris quene and souerane. **1523** LD. BERNERS *Froiss.* I. ii. 2 They in all theyr dedis were so valyant that they ought to be reputed as soueraignes in all chyualry. **1635** A. STAFFORD *Fem. Glory* (1869) 75 This Soveraigne of her Sexe. **1695** LD. PRESTON *Boeth.* III. 96 We have already defined Happiness to be the Soveraign of Goods.

†**d.** A free citizen or voter of America. *U.S. Obs.*

1846 in *Indiana Hist. Soc. Publ.* (1905) III. 412 Thousands of children in our state have not received even the trifling aid which these [public] funds afford... This fact illustrates the situation of thousands of the future sovereigns of our beloved State. **1861** *Harpers' Mag.* Mar. 570/1 Deacon E—— lived out West... The 'sovereigns' of that section met in caucus to appoint delegates to a County Convention. **1869** 'MARK TWAIN' *Innoc. Abr.* xi. 110, I am a free-born sovereign, sir, an American.

2. *spec.* **a.** The recognized supreme ruler of a people or country under monarchical government; a monarch; a king or queen.

α. **1297** R. GLOUC. (Rolls) 5183 þat folc of estangle vnderuenge þere King egbriȝt to hor souereyn. *a* **1340** HAMPOLE *Psalter* lxviii. 28 Sugetis þat ere folouers of þaire soueraynes. *c* **1400** *Destr. Troy* 1669 For the souerayn hym selfe was a sete rioll. *c* **1440** *Generydes* 94 In Surre.., Where my fader is kyng and souerayne. **1590** SPENSER *F.Q.* II. x. 58 Who after long debate..Was of the Britons first crownd Soueraine. **1741** C. MIDDLETON *Cicero* I. v. 380 Clodius.. granted this Priesthood to one Brogitarus, a petty Soverein in those parts, to whom he had before given the title of King.

β. *c* **1400** *Anturs of Arth.* vi, Thus with solance þay semelede,..And sew to þe soueraygne. **1584** POWEL *Lloyd's Cambria* 11 Inas King of Wessex to be their soueraigne. **1594** BARNFIELD *Sheph. Cont.* (Arb.) 26 When bad subiects gainst their Soueraigne..vnnaturally rebell. *a* **1652** BROME *Queenes Exch.* I. Wks. 1873 III. 459 How darst thou thus oppose thy Soveraignes will. **1665** BOYLE *Occas. Refl.* IV. xii. (1848) 243 'Tis the only thing wherein Subjects can punish their Soveraigns. **1710** ADDISON *Whig Exam.* No. 5 ¶3 The relation between the soveraign and the subject. **1780** *Mirror* No. 82, The Sovereign may be misinformed as to the deservings of those whom he is pleased to honour. **1835** THIRLWALL *Greece* V. I. 131 The Attic king Erechtheus and the Thracian Eumolpus, who had become sovereign of Eleusis. **1865** KINGSLEY *Herew.* ix, They brought down on themselves the wrath of their nominal sovereigns.

transf. **1787** J. ADAMS *Def. Constit. Gov. U.S.A.* (1794) I. 26 The sovereign is the whole country. **1794** *Brookes' Gazetteer* (ed. 8) s.v. *Lucern*, The former [council] is the nominal sovereign.

γ. *a* **1400-50** *Alexander* 2774 A noble prince, þat certified his souerane þir saȝes in a pistill. **1456** SIR G. HAYE *Law Arms* (S.T.S.) 110 Thare suld na subject obey till his soverane to werrey agaynis his God. **1562** WINȜET *Wks.* (S.T.S.) I. 2 The maist excellent and gracius Souerane, Marie Quene of Scottis. **1596** DALRYMPLE tr. *Leslie's Hist. Scot.* I. 296 Maist illustre and bountifull souerane.

b. In fig. applications.

1588 SHAKS. *L.L.L.* III. i. 184 Don Cupid, Regent of Louerimes,..Th' annointed soueraigne of sighes and groanes. **1592** KYD *Sp. Trag.* III. xiv, Come, Bel-imperia,.. My sorrowes ease and soueraigne of my blisse. **1616** T. SCOT *Philomythie* II. Bvb, The knight..they crown The Soueraigne of glory and renowne. **1821** SHELLEY *Epipsych.* 592 Weak Verses, go, kneel at your Sovereign's feet.

†**3.** **a.** A mayor or provost of a town, in later use esp. in Ireland. *Obs.*

a **1325** *MS. Rawl. B.* 520 fol. 32 þat..anquestes..ben imad in tounes þoru him þat is souerein of þe toune. **1399** LANGL. *Rich. Redeles* IV. 32 Whanne it drowe to þe day..þat souereynes were semblid, and þe schire-knyȝtis. *c* **1450** *Cal. Lett. Bk. 'D' Lond.* 205 Diligent execucioun of all that ye shall be chargid of be your sovereynys of this Cite, ye shall performe. **1538** in P. H. Hore *Hist. Wexford* (1900) I. 237 When the Suffrain herde herof he soghte for the said Watkyne..who..bade the Suffrayne take the offendors. **1587** GOLDING *De Mornay* ii. 18 If any man tell of many Magistrates; wee will by and by inquire for the soueraigne. **1617** MORYSON *Itin.* II. 287 The 26 day his Lordship wrote to the Soveraigne of Wexford. **1696** *Lond. Gaz.* No. 3178/4 The Association of the Soveraign, Burgesses, and Commonalty of the Borough of Carlingford in Ireland. **1713** in P. H. Hore *Hist. Wexford* (1900) I. 104 John Ivory, the present Sovereign of the town of New Ross, and his Successors Sovereigns of the said Town. **1762** WESLEY *Wks.* (1872) III. 90 A dancing-master was busily employed in the ..market house [at Belfast]; till at twelve the sovereign put him out, by holding his court there.

†**b.** The Superior of a monastery of other conventual establishment. *Obs.*

14.. *Rule Syon Monast.* liii. in *Collect. Topogr.* (1834) I. 31 The sovereyne..owthe to se that none have more than nedethe nor lasse. *c* **1450** *Myrr. our Ladye* 2 Obedyence to the byddynges of god, and of youre reule, and of youre soueraynes. **1534** *Act 26 Hen. VIII*, c. 3 §8 At the.. pleasures of their masters & soueraines of the monasteries and priories. **1544** tr. *Littleton's Tenures* (1574) 42 b, So may the lorde haue an action agaynste the soueraigne of the house that taketh and admitteth his villeine to be professed.

4. **a.** A gold coin minted in England from the time of Henry VII to Charles I, originally of the value of 22*s.* 6*d.* but subsequently worth only 10*s.* or 11*s.*

There were also ***double*** and ***treble sovereigns***. The first group of quotations exhibits some of the enactments relative to the coin, or indications of its value at different dates. See also HALF-SOVEREIGN.

(*a*) **1503-4** *Act 19 Hen. VII*, c. 5 §1 All maner of Gold of the Coynes of a Sovereyn, Halfe Sovereyn, Riall, half Ryall ..shall go and be curraunt in payment through all this.. Realme. **1526** *Lett. & P. Hen. VIII*, IV. II. 1149 [The King intends..to order by proclamation that the angel..shall be current for 7s. 6d.,..the sovereign 22s. 6d., the demy-sovereign 11s. 3d.] **1542** RECORDE *Gr. Artes* Kij b, A Souerayn is the greatest englishe coyne, and conteyneth..4 crownes and an halfe, that is to say 22s. 6d. **1551** in Strype *Eccl. Mem.* (1822) III. 45 The old sovereign of fine gold which shall be current for thirty shillings of lawful money of England... A whole sovereign of crown gold which shall be current for twenty shillings. **1591** *Wills & Inv. N.C.* (Surtees, 1860) 190 To Mr. Doctor Colmore a trible severignt, beinge thirtie shilling peyce. **1611** in Birch *Crt. & Times Jas. I* (1848) I. 147 Raising..the angel and sovereign to eleven shillings, and the Jacobite piece to two and twenty. **1688** HOLME *Armoury* III. 29/1 The Soveraign, Coined by Henry the Eighth, Edward the Sixth, Queen Elizabeth, King James,..passed for eleven shillings. **1726-31** TINDAL *Rapin's Hist. Eng.* (1743) II. XVII. 157 By an Indenture of 2d. of Elizabeth, a pound weight of Gold..was coined..into 24 Sovereigns, at thirty Shillings a piece. *Ibid.*, A pound weight of Crown Gold of 22 Carats fine, and 2 Carats alloy, was coined into..33 Sovereigns at twenty Shillings a piece. **1853** HUMPHREYS *Coin-coll. Man.* II. 446 To distinguish it from the previous rial, it was determined to call it a 'sovereign'. *Ibid.* 449 [etc.].

(*b*) **1514** *Visit. Dioc. Norwich* (Camden) 120 Johannes Smythe ostendit in camera..iij soveryns. *a* **1548** HALL *Chron., Hen. VIII*, 238 The Merchantes of the Staple.. presented her with an .C. sovereyns of golde in a ryche purse. **1599** B. JONSON *Ev. Man out of Hum.* v. x. 172, I gaue him some soueraignes for his paines. **1607** DEKKER & WEBSTER *Westw. Hoe* I. ii. D.'s Wks. 1873 II. 289 And you will stay till to morrow you shall haue it all in new soueraignes. **1615** J. STEPHENS *Satyr. Ess.* (1857) 233 She hath old harry soveraignes, that saw no sunne in fiftie yeares.

transf. **1660** in J. Simon *Ess. Irish Coins* (1749) 126 The Spanish Suffrain of gold, the Spanish Half-suffrain.

b. A British gold coin of the (nominal) value of one pound. Also *attrib.* as ***sovereign purse, scales.***

1817 *Royal Proclam.* 1 July, That certain pieces of gold money should be coined, which should be called 'sovereigns or twenty shilling pieces'. **1828** P. CUNNINGHAM *N.S. Wales* (ed. 3) II. 156 Sovereigns are the next most advisable articles, and lastly dollars. **1840** HOOD *Up Rhine* 26 I'd give a guinea, that's to say a sovereign, to know what it is. **1882** J. PARKER *Apost. Life* I. 142 What a 'wonder' it would be for some of us to ever give a sovereign to any good cause upon earth!

attrib. **1859** F. S. COOPER *Ironmongers' Catal.* 140 Sovereign Scales, Mint Weights, ⅛ extra. **1907** *Yesterday's Shopping* (1969) 402/1 Gentlemen's sovereign purses, Russia leather..4/6. **1977** *Lancashire Life* Dec. 59/1 Years afterwards I showed him a sovereign purse containing a solitary half sovereign.

†**5.** A variety of pear. *Obs.*$^{-1}$

1664 EVELYN *Kal. Hort.* (1729) 213 Pears. Windsor, Sovereign, Orange, Bergamot [etc.].

II. *adj.* †**1.** Of persons: Standing out above others or excelling in some respect. *Obs.*

c **1330** R. BRUNNE *Chron. Wace* (Rolls) 13214 Souereyne knyghtes þey were, hit seys. *c* **1386** CHAUCER *Man of Law's T.* 991 To him that is so soverayn of honour. **1402** *Pol. Poems* (Rolls) II. 60 Seraphin he is the sovereynest, in charite he brennith. *c* **1491** *Chast. Goddes Chyld.* 44 It is yeuen and sende us fro our louyng fader and fro our souereeyne leche. **1547** *Bk. Marchauntes* cvj, He [*sc.* a cardinal] is alredy in the way and nygh to be hymself the great hatmaker, or souerayn haberdasher. **1576** GASCOIGNE *Kenelw. Cast.* Wks. 1910 II. 104 And that the maide released be, by sovereigne maidens might. **1688** COLLIER *Several Disc.* (1725) 243 As there is one Being sovereign to all the rest, and upon whom they all depend.

2. Of things, qualities, etc.: Supreme, paramount; principal, greatest, or most notable.

α. *c* **1340** HAMPOLE *Pr. Consc.* 7860 Bot þe mast soverayne ioy of alle Es þe syght of Godes bryght face. *c* **1383** in *Eng. Hist. Rev.* Oct. (1911) 748 Prestis owen to make þe sacramentis of holi chirche wiþ souerayn deuocioun. **1450-80** tr. *Secreta Secret.* xx. 17 The sovereyne wisdome of god hath ordeynyd the coldes and the hetis. **1485** CAXTON *Paris & V.* (1868) 30 Of whose comyng messyr Jaques had Souerayn playsyr. *a* **1533** LD. BERNERS *Gold. Bk. M. Aurel.* (1546) Ee b, Me think it shulde be a souerayn foly. **1590** SPENSER *F.Q.* II. vii. 16 The antique world..The guifts of soueraine bounty did embrace. **1648** J. BEAUMONT *Psyche* VI. xliii, A Realm..Where every Ejulation, every Pain Alas, is too too truly Soverain.

β. **1377** LANGL. *P. Pl.* B. XVIII. 217 For-þi god of his goodnesse þe fyrste gome Adam, Sette hym in solace & in souereigne myrthe. **1387** TREVISA *Higden* (Rolls) VII. 111 þe kyng hadde Englisshemen in sovereigne worschippe. *a* **1513** FABYAN *Chron.* III. (1811) 38 When this Coilus had reygned in Soueraygne peace, by the terme of liiii. yeres. **1576** FLEMING *Panopl. Epist.* 19 Whose substance..may be to my person a singular ornament, and a soueraigne safegarde. **1605** BACON *Adv. Learn.* I. i. §3 This corrective spice, the mixture whereof maketh knowledge so soveraigne. **1642** ROGERS *Naaman* 9 Free and soveraigne mercy and compassion might only be ascribed to God. **1683** *Brit. Spec.* 25 It is but just, that Man should pay a Sovereign Adoration and Respect to this bounteous Creator. **1706** E. Ward *Wooden World Diss.* (1708) 99 This is his sovereign Charm against Fear in an Engagement. **1829** I. Taylor *Enthus.* ix. 223 The good of his soul, is the sovereign object of his cares. **1891** Baring-Gould *In Troub. Land* viii. 111 They laughed over their troubles as though it were a sovereign joke.

γ. **1375** Barbour *Bruce* x. 274 Of so souerane gret bounte. *c* **1400** *Destr. Troy* 1125 Iff it be worship & wit wisdom to shewe, Hit is sothely more soueran to see it in werke. **1508** Dunbar *Tua Mariit Wemen* 507 Tha..said, thai suld exampill tak of her souerane teching.

b. Qualifying *good.* (Freq. = *summum bonum.*)

a **1340** Hampole *Psalter* iv. 8 A souereyn goed þai may noght se. *c* **1380** *Antecrist* in Todd *Three Treat. Wyclif* (1851) 118 In þe first boke of souereynest good. **1474** Caxton *Chesse* iii. ii. (1883) 86 Fayth is a souerayn good and cometh of the good wyll of the herte. **1594** T. B. *La Primaud. Fr. Acad.* II. 5 All things belonging to the saluation and soueraigne good of men. **1625** Bacon *Ess., Of Truth* (Arb.) 500 The knowledge of Truth..is the Soueraigne Good of humane Nature. **1692** Dryden *St. Euremont's Ess.* 333 Of all the Opinions of Philosophers concerning the Sovereign Good. **1744** Harris *Three Treat.* Wks. (1841) 45 The sovereign good is that, the possession of which renders us happy. *a* **1871** Grote *Eth. Fragm.* v. (1876) 137 To promote the accomplishment of his supreme purpose—the Sovereign Good of the Community.

c. Of contempt: Supreme, unmitigated.

1749 Fielding *Tom Jones* ii. vii, Which at last ended, on the part of the Lady, in a sovereign contempt for her husband. **1794** Mrs. Radcliffe *Myst. Udolpho* xxx, You hold in sovereign contempt these common failings of your sex. **1825** T. Hook *Sayings* Ser. ii. I. 125 The respect.. turned into the most sovereign contempt for his meanness. **1876** F. Harrison *Choice Bks.* iv. (1886) 88 The great books ..are treated by collectors and librarians with sovereign contempt.

3. Of remedies, etc.: Efficacious or potent in a superlative degree. Freq. in fig. use.

a. **1377** Langl. *P. Pl.* B. xx. 370 þe soureynest salue for alkyn synnes. **1390** Gower *Conf.* III. 131 Of Planteine He hath his herbe sovereine. **1422** tr. *Secreta Secret., Priv. Priv.* 197 Oryson is Souerayn remedy in euery trybulacion. *c* **1491** *Chast. Goddes Chyld.* 13 And this is a souerayn medicyn to al temptacions. **1549** E. Allen *Par. Rev. John* 37 The leaves, frute and sappe of these holy trees, were very holesome and sovereine. **1588** Greene *Perimedes* Wks. (Grosart) VII. 20 A soueraine simple against disquiet and feare. **1633** Bp. Hall *Hard Texts, N.T.* 327 But how soveraine soever it [the Gospel] was of it selfe, yet it was not at all available to the good of many of them. **1662** J. Davies tr. *Olearius' Voy. Amb.* 200 There is also in this Province a Drug very soverain against the Worms.

β. **1578** Lyte *Dodoens* ii. xx. 172 Belfloure..is soveraigne to cure the payne..of the necke. **1596** Shaks. *1 Hen. IV*, i. iii. 57 Telling me, the Soueraign'st thing on earth Was Parmacity, for an inward bruise. **1632** Lithgow *Trav.* iii. 97 The soueraigne minerall against infections. **1679** *Phil. Trans.* XIX. 729 This Giben is..a soveraign Remedy for Coughs and Green Wounds. **1744** Berkeley *Siris* §83, I have found it of sovereign use as well during the smallpox as before it. **1793** Cowper *Let.* Wks. 1836 VII. 330, I conclude that it..may therefore be sovereign in cases where the eyelids are ulcerated. **1839** *Morning Post* 17 Oct., The sovereignest thing on earth for rendering the people wise. **1888** Besant *Eulogy R. Jeffries* 85 That kind of belief..is sovereign against low spirits, carelessness, and inactivity.

γ. **1600** Holland *Livy* viii. xviii. 294 Souerane medicines and holsome for the bodie of man.

†**4.** In literal sense: Lofty. *Obs.*$^{-1}$

1388 Wyclif *Prov.* viii. 2 Whether wisdom crieth not ofte ..In souereyneste and hiȝ coppis.

5. Of persons: Having superior or supreme rank or power; *spec.* holding the position of a ruler or monarch.

a. **1340** *Ayenb.* 189 Þanne ssel he keste his greate manzinge as þe heȝe bissop an souerayn pope. **1340–70** *Alex. & Dind.* 811 Þus dindimus..god by-secheþ to saue þe soueraine prinse. *c* **1400** Maundev. (Roxb.) xiii. 56 Þai schall com.. before Godd þe soueraygne Iugge. **1472–3** *Rolls of Parlt.* VI. 5/2 The soverayn Ruler or Keper of such Castell, Towne,.. or other place. **1563** *Homilies* ii. *Of Repentance* ii, Our sauiour Jesus Christ..beynge our soueravne Byshop. **1598** Yong *Diana* 456 O soueraine God! that once I might but knowe Greefe without hope to sease vpon thy soule.

β. **1390** Gower *Conf.* I. 9 As he which is king sovereign Of al the worldes governaunce. *Ibid.* II. 52 To thee, which art god sovereign. **1600** Holland *Livy* iii. 109 The twelve knitches of rods were born by the Lictors before the soveraigne judge. **1611** Cotgr., *Sultane*,..a Sultannesse; or soueraigne Princesse. **1678** Sir G. Mackenzie *Crim. Laws Scot.* ii. xv. §ii. (1699) 212 The Justice-Court of old, was the only Soveraing Court of the Nation. **1711** Shaftesb. *Charac.* (1737) I. 327 The prince..abhor'd the profanation offer'd to his sovereign-empress. *a* **1763** W. King *Lit. & Polit. Anecd.* (1819) 132 He..hath been introduced to most of the sovereign princes. **1825** Bentham *Ration. Reward* 16 Partly because, being members of the sovereign body, they would have it so. **1839** Thirlwall *Greece* VI. 123 Evagoras ..claimed to be treated as a sovereign prince, the great king's equal in rank and title. **1877** Northcote *Rom. Catacombs* ii. vi. 109 To the Sovereign Pontiffs..we are principally indebted for whatever fragments have been preserved.

γ. *c* **1375** *Sc. Leg. Saints* vi. (*Thomas*) 155 For chastite is souerane quene of al vertuise euir bedene. **1456** Sir G. Haye *Law Arms* (S.T.S.) 109 The pape is soverane to the Emperour, and the Emperour subject to the pape. **1508** Dunbar *Flyting Kennedie* 104 Sen thow with wirschep wald sa fane be styld, Haill, souerane senȝeour!

b. Freq. as a qualification of *lord* or *lady*.

a. *c* **1350** *Will. Palerne* 3954, I sette ȝou for no soudiour but for souerayn lord, to lede al þis lordschip as ȝou likes euer. *c* **1374** Chaucer *Anel. & Arc.* 252 Me þat ye callid your mastresse, Youre soverayne ladye. **1414** *Rolls of Parlt.* IV. 22 Oure soverain Lord, youre humble and trewe lieges [etc.]. **1459** *Ibid.* V. 369/2 The seid Lord had sent his servaunt to oure Soverayne Lady the Quene. **1530** Palsgr. 478/2 She hath ben his soverayne lady. **1590** Spenser *F.Q.* ii. x. 14 Locrine was left the soueraine Lord of all.

β. *c* **1430** Lydg. *Min. Poems* (Percy Soc.) 10 Sovereigne lord, welcome to youre citee! **1474** *Cov. Leet Bk.* 405 Oure Souerygne lady, the Quene. **1558** in Strype *Ann. Ref.* I. ii. App. i. 399 She beinge our sovaraigne lord and ladie, other kinges..ought to paye tribute unto her. **1614** Selden *Titles Honor* 125 What now is one of our particular Notes of Maiestie, not giuen to any but the supreme, I mean Soueraign Lord or Lady. **1678** Bunyan *Pilgr.* i. (1862) 78 Shall I entertain thee against my sovereign Lord? **1727** Gay *Fables* i. xxxvi. 34 When heaven the world with creatures stor'd, Man was ordain'd their sovereign lord. **1820** Scott *Monast.* xxxvi, There rides a faithful servant of his most beautiful and Sovereign Lady. **1832** [see lady *sb.* 2].

γ. **1482** *Eng. Misc.* (Surtees) 41 Ye xxj yer of our soveran lorde kyng Edward the fourth. **1529** *Registr. Aberdon.* (Maitland) I. 395 For commond weill of owre soverane lordis legis. **1581** J. Hamilton in *Cath. Tract.* (S.T.S.) 73 To..my seuerane ladye Marie the Quenis maiestie of Scotland.

c. Of states, communities, etc.

1595 Shaks. *John* v. ii. 82, I am too high-borne to be.. Instrument To any Soueraigne State throughout the world. **1682** A. Mudie *Pres. St. Scotl.* ii. 23 The King is..a free Prince of Sovereign Power. **1771** *Ann. Reg.* i. 67 The Baron ..has been condemned by the sovereign courts to be kept 15 days in prison. **1819** J. Marshall *Const. Opin.* (1839) 160 The defendant, a sovereign state, denies the obligation of a law enacted by the legislature of the union [etc.]. **1835** T. Mitchell *Acharn. of Aristoph.* 448 *note*, Athens had still its law of libel, by which the majesty of the sovereign people was protected. **1868** Cooley *Const. Lim.* i, A State is called a *sovereign State* when this supreme power resides within itself.

d. *Banking.* Designating or pertaining to a commercial loan made to a sovereign state.

1977 *47th Ann. Rep. Bank Internat. Settlements* 102 This ..may have improved the quality of the banks' loan portfolio..but what about the corresponding rise in the country of 'sovereign' risks? **1982** *Daily Tel.* 8 Dec. 21/4 Only £26 million was set aside as a general provision, which is where the bank is believed to take account of sovereign loans. **1983** *Times* 3 Mar. 17/3 The report calls for much greater availability of information about sovereign lending.

6. Of power, authority, etc.: Supreme.

c **1532** Du Wes *Introd. Fr.* in *Palsgr.* 1019 Most redouted imperiall myght, and soverayne majesty. **1595** Markham *Sir R. Grinuile* lii, Shee giues him soueraigne rule, and publique right. **1643** Prynne *Sov. Power Parl.* i. (ed. 2) 101 That the Soveraignest power and jurisdiction..resides in the whole Kingdom and Parliament. **1676** Dryden *Aurengz.* i. i. 60 In change of Government, The Rabble.. Do Sovereign Justice. **1759** Robertson *Hist. Scotl.* iii. Wks. 1813 I. 181 The sovereign authority was by this treaty transferred wholly into the hands of the congregation. **1851** Dixon *W. Penn* xxii. (1872) 193 The sovereign power resides in the governor and freemen of the province. **1878** Stewart & Tait *Unseen Univ.* Introd. 14 This sovereign and paramount influence.

7. Of or belonging to, characteristic of, supremacy or superiority.

c **1600** Shaks. *Sonn.* xxxiii, Full many a glorious morning haue I seene, Flatter the mountaine tops with soueraine eie. **1725** Pope *Odyss.* i. 171 He led the goddess to the sovereign seat. **1850** L. Hunt *Autobiog.* II. xiv. 141 Disobedience.. was an offence doubly irritating to his nature on account of his sovereign habits as a jailer. **1870** Lowell *Among my Bks.* Ser. i. (1873) 324 He really sees things with their sovereign eye.

†**'sovereign,** *v. Obs.*$^{-1}$ [f. prec.] *trans.* To deal with as a sovereign.

1585 R. Williams in Motley *Netherl.* (1860) I. 333 Unless her Majesty do sovereign them presently.

†**'sovereigness.** *Obs.* Also 6 soueraignnesse, 7 sou-, soveraign-, sovereignesse. [f. sovereign *sb.* + -ess.] A female sovereign.

1600 Dekker *Fortunatus* Wks. 1873 I. 90 Most pow'rfull Queene of chaunce, dread soueraignnesse. **1630** Brathwait *Eng. Gentlem.* (1641) 67 Whence it grew that the Roman empire became absolute Sovereignesse of many other ample Dominions. **1686** tr. *Chardin's Coronat. Solyman* 83 There remained another sister of Habas II..who in the Kings absence was as it were Sovereigness of the Place.

†**'sovereignful,** *a. Obs.*$^{-1}$ In 5 soueranefull. [f. sovereign *sb.*] Noble.

c **1470** *Gol. & Gaw.* 1304 This is ane soueranefull thing, be Ihesu! think I.

†**sovereignity.** *Obs.* Forms: 6 souer-, 6–7 soveraignitie; 6–7 souer-, 7–8 soveraignity, -eignity; 6 soueranitie, -enitie, 7 soveranitie. [f. sovereign *a.* + -ity. Cf. OF. *suvrenitet*, It. *sovranità*.] = sovereignty.

c **1560** A. Scott *Poems* (S.T.S.) vi. 22 As prowd princely luve express Is to haif souerenitie. **1584** D. Fenner *Def. Ministers* (1587) 75 Her iust and holy Soueraignitie. **1632** Lithgow *Trav.* Dedic., A homely and familiar Stile; no wayes fit for Soueraignity to peruse. **1671** [R. MacWard] *True Nonconf.* 28 The Soveraignity of Christian Princes can-not give them a contrary privilege. **1722** De Foe *Plague* (1884) 21 My Maker had an undisputed Right of Soveraignity. **1784** D. Herd *Let.* in *Songs* (1904) 50, I am sorry you are already tir'd of the sovereignity.

†**'sovereignize,** *v. Obs.* Also 7 soueraignise, -ize, soveraignize, -eignize; souer-, soveranize, -ise. [f. sovereign *sb.* + -ize. Cf. Pg. *soberanizar.*] *intr.* To exercise supreme power; to rule as a sovereign. (Common in 17th cent.)

1601 Chester *Love's Mart.*, etc. (1878) 3 Her princely eyes..That ore the day and night do soueraignize. **1661** *Sir A. Haslerig's Last Will & Test.* 1 O Bishoprick, where in my Regality I so much Soveraigniz'd, or, as some will have it, Tyranniz'd. **1680** Morden *Geog. Rect., Arabia* (1685) 369 Nimrod Sovereignizing at Babylon.

b. Similarly with *it.*

1656 S. H. *Gold. Law* 39 Every several Sect, Church, and Faction are in Arms..to Rule and Soveraignize it if they can.

Hence †**'sovereignizing** *ppl. a. Obs.*

1621 Lady M. Wroth *Urania* 463 Intreated by the soueraignizing Queen to make relation of her end. **1630** Brathwait *Eng. Gentlew.* (1641) 363 Soveraignizing Saladin..called his Chiefetaine or Generall before him.

'sovereignly, *a. rare*$^{-1}$. [f. sovereign *sb.*] Befitting a sovereign.

1884 J. Parker *Apost. Life* III. 298 He quietly, with sovereignly tone, says, 'Not now'.

sovereignly ('sɒvrɪnlɪ), *adv.* Forms: (see sovereign *sb.* and *a.*). [f. sovereign *a.* + -ly².] In a sovereign manner.

1. In a supreme degree; in a surpassing or pre-eminent manner.

a. *c* **1340** Hampole *Pr. Consc.* 8777 And þat land es cald soverayn ly þe kyngdom of God alle-myghty. **1377** Langl. *P. Pl.* B. xi. 176 [Christ] comaundeth eche creature..hym to louye, And souereynelyche pore poeple. *c* **1400** tr. *Secreta Secret., Gov. Lordsh.* 99 þe kynde of þe þinges abown shall drawe hym souerayn ly to þe craft þat accordes to hem. **1447** Bokenham *Seyntys* (Roxb.) 9 Many spyrtys it counfortyth souereynly. *a* **1536** *Songs, Carols*, etc. (E.E.T.S.) 2 Soueraynly in mynd she is with me. **1577** *St. Aug. Manual* (Longman) 5 Thou art good without qualitie, and therefore ..sovereinly good.

β. *c* **1430** *Syr Gener.* (Roxb.) 457 Al his hert..To loue hir was sett soueraignelie. **1525** Ld. Berners *Froiss.* II. clxxxi. [clxxvii.] 549 Soueraygnely there ought none to enterprise any mater there. **1586** Warner *Alb. Eng.* ii. viii. (1592) 31 But soueraignlie the Sonne of Ioue bestird him in the presse. **1611** Shaks. *Wint. T.* i. ii. 323, I cannot Beleeue this Crack to be in my dread Mistresse (So soueraignely being Honorable). **1648** Boyle *Seraph. Love* ii. (1700) 15 He was Soveraignly Lovely in Himself. **1715** Ash *Serm. for S.P.G.* 9 The other more exalted charity..sovereignly heals all the maladies and infirmities of a corrupt nature. **1768** *Woman of Honor* II. 38 She possesses sovereignly the talent of declining offers without offence. **1834** Mar. Edgeworth *Helen* iii. xii, An expression which had sovereignly taken her fancy. **1856** Doran *Knights & their Days* 182 Alien knights who were expected to render obedience, and could not sovereignly exert it. **1891** Meredith *One of our Conq.* xxxviii, She was a girl sovereignly pure, angelically tender.

γ. **1375** Barbour *Bruce* x. 299 He, for his dedis worthy, Suld weill be prisit soueranly. *c* **1400** Love *Bonavent. Mirr.* (1908) 91 The whiche clennes we oweth souerenly to desire. **1432** *Test. Ebor.* (Surtees) II. 19 þat it may be pleasauns and louyng to hym soueranly.

δ. **1389** in *Eng. Gilds* (1870) 45 In þe worchep..souerengly of þe Noble confessour seynt Antony. **1422** tr. *Secreta Secret., Priv. Priv.* 135 Therfor good rennoune is Souerantly to be desyrid. ? *a* **1500** *Chester Pl.* i. 57 Wee thanke the lorde, full soverayntlie that us hath formed so cleane and cleare.

2. With supremacy or supreme power; royally; as a sovereign.

c **1375** *Leg. Rood* (1871) 124 A nobill king..Was gouernowre of grete empire Souerainly als lord and syre. **1412–20** Lydg. *Chron. Troy* ii. 1064 Wher I hym leue in his royal sete Souereynly regnynge in quiete. **1471** Fortescue *Wks.* (1869) 533, I wrote how that me semyd no woman ought soveranly or suppremely to reynge vpon man. **1611** Cotgr. s.v. *Presidial*, Courts of Iustice..wherein ciuile causes are heard, and adiudged, Soueraignely, and with-out Appeales. **1643** *Case Affairs Law, Relig.*, etc. 12 The superiority that is but subordinately in them is soveraignely in the Parliament. **1692** S. Patrick *Answ. Touchstone* 96 None but God can absolutely and sovereignly forgive sin. **1738** Warburton *Div. Legat.* II. 410 A King who should determine sovereignly and command their armies. **1793** Holcroft tr. *Lavater's Physiog.* xxxiv. 176 [Women] often rule more effectually, more sovreignly than man. **1883** *Mem. Vol. Rev. Alex. Maclean* 231 How sovereignly the Lord of Misrule sways his sceptre.

†**'sovereignness.** *Obs.* [f. sovereign *a.*] The state or condition of being sovereign.

1387–8 T. Usk *Test. Love* ii. ii. (Skeat) I. 85 But soverainnesse ayenward shulde thinke in this wyse: 'I am servaunt of these creatures to me delivered'. **1615** Brathwait *Strappado* (1878) 190 The body is the couer, and in it The minds internall soueraignnesse doth sit As a great Princesse. *a* **1661** Fuller *Worthies, Warwicksh.* iii. (1662) 115, I confess its far short in Sovereignness against Serpents of the Italian Ash.

'sovereignship. *rare.* [f. sovereign *sb.*] **a.** The personality of a sovereign. **b.** Sovereignty.

a **1668** Davenant *Play-ho. to Let* Wks. (1673) 74 Tell him, the Wise are not at leisure now To hear his Sov'raignship. **1817** Jas. Mill *Brit. India* I. ii. x. 438 The idea of the universal sovereignship of India.

†**'sovereigntess.** *Obs.* Forms: 6 souraintess, 7 -tesse; 6 sourantesse, -entisse, 7 soufrentesse. [f. sovereign *sb.* The intrusive *t* is probably due to the influence of *sovereignty.*] = sovereigness.

1586 Warner *Alb. Eng.* iii. xviii. (1592) 76 One seemed to haue passed Stix, and entring Plutos gate, Saw Hecat new canonized the Sourantisse of hell. **1591** Sylvester *Du Bartas* i. iv. 718 Sea's Soueraintess, Sleep-bringer, Pilgrim's guide. **1592** Warner *Alb. Eng.* vii. xxxvi. 154 Anatomize my braine, And ore my senses see your selfe the Sourentesse [**1612** Soufrentesse] to raigne. **1613** Heywood *Silver Age* i. i, To lay the least grosse imputation Upon the Queene, my beauteous Soueraintesse.

sovereignty ('sɒvrɪntɪ). Forms: (see sovereign *sb.* and *a.*). [a. AF. *sovereyneté, soverentee*, = OF. *souveraineté* (mod.F. *souveraineté*): see

SOVEREIGN and -TY.] The quality or condition of being sovereign.

1. Supremacy or pre-eminence in respect of excellence or efficacy.

c **1340** HAMPOLE *Prose Tr.* 14 þe ende and þe soueraynte of perfeccione standes in a verray anehede of Godd. *c* **1403** LYDG. *Curia Sap.* (Caxton) a ij, I symple shall extoll theyr soueraynte And my rudenes shall shewe theyr subtylyte. **1430–40** —— *Bochas* IV. Prol., Which..dyd excel In Rethorike by suffreinte of style. **1567** MAPLET *Gr. Forest* 4 b, His suffeaigntie is, that being..borne aboute a man, [it] keepeth him safe. **1588** SHAKS. *L.L.L.* IV. iii. 234 Of all complexions the cul'd soueraignty, Doe meet as at a faire in her faire cheeke. **1601** —— *All's Well* I. iii. 230 Some prescriptions Of rare and prou'd effects, such as his reading ..had collected For generall soueraigntie. **1610** GUILLIM *Heraldry* II. iii. (1660) 53 By the soveraignty of these partitions being interposed between them.

2. Supremacy in respect of power, domination, or rank; supreme dominion, authority, or rule.

a. *c* **1374** CHAUCER *Troylus* III. 171 Ye shul no more have sovereynte Of my love, than right in this cas is. **1390** GOWER *Conf.* I. 104 Till I hadde wonne The love and sovereinete Of what knyht that..Alle othre passeth. *c* **1430** LYDG. Min. Poems (Percy Soc.) 46 Crafft may shewe a foreyn apparence; But nature ay must have the sovereynte. **1475** *Bk. Noblesse* (Roxb.) 51 God hathe gyve that souvereynte in mannys soule. **1530** PALSGR. 273/2 Soverayntе that a lorde or a superiour hath, *souveraintė*. **1570–6** LAMBARDE *Peramb. Kent* (1826) 143 The Pryor of Christes Church pretended to have..a Soverainty over St. Martines.

β. *c* **1550** H. RHODES *Bk. Nurture* in *Babees Book* (1868) 97 Prease not thy selfe, if thou be wyse, to haue the soueraygntye. **1579** E. K. *Gloss. to Spenser's Sheph. Cal.* Apr. 122 The chiefedome and soueraigntye of al flowres. **1607** SHAKS. *Cor.* IV. vii. 35 As is the Aspray to the Fish, who takes it By Soueraignty of Nature. **1639** T. DE GRAY *Compl. Horsem.* 355 Which causeth choller to have soveraignty and dominion over the other humours. **1697** DRYDEN *Virg. Georg.* II. 398 Jove's own Tree, That holds the Woods in awful Sov'raignty. **1718** *Free-thinker* No. 60. 33 The Romans..had acquired the Sovereignty of the Sea. **1754** EDWARDS *Freedom Will* IV. vii. 233 The Sovereignty of God is his Ability and Authority to do whatever pleases him. **1821** SHELLEY *Hellas* 159 The sage..May have attained to sovereignty and science Over those strong and secret things. **1860** EMERSON *Cond. Life, Power* Wks. (Bohn) II. 334 As long as our people quote English standards, they will miss the sovereignty of power.

γ. **14..** in *Tundale's Vis.* (1903) 200 Where neest thi son thou hast souerente. *c* **1440** *Promp. Parv.* 466/1 Soverente, *superioritas*. **1447** BOKENHAM *Seyntys* (Roxb.) 51 O lorde almyhte which hast overe al Soverente.

δ. **1460** *Pol., Rel., & L. Poems* (1903) 200 More-ouer I yave the suffrauntė that alle Bestis shoulde bowe þe vntyll. **1486** *Eng. Misc.* (Surtees) 54 Unto whome..all other floures shall lowte, and evidently yeve suffranti. **1513** BRADSHAW *St. Werburge* I. 2165 Bycause that Werburge in order was senyoure, Her mother Ermenylde gaue her the sufferaynte.

3. *spec.* The position, rank, or power of a supreme ruler or monarch; royal authority or dominion.

a. **1387** TREVISA *Higden* (Rolls) VIII. 279 þe Scottes seide þat þey knewe non suche sovereynte þat longed to þe kyng of Engelond. *a* **1400–50** *Alexander* 1859 So sadly in soueraynete he set neuire his hope. **1457** HARDYNG *Chron.* i. in *Eng. Hist. Rev.* Oct. (1912) 741 Youre Fadir gafe me in commaundement In Scotlonde ryde..To seke his ryght thar for his souereynte. **1530** PALSGR. 273/2 Soverayntе of a kyng, *regalitė*. **1590** SPENSER *F.Q.* II. x. 48 Had not Androgeus,..enuious of Vncles soueraintie, Betrayd his contrey. **1601** SIR W. CORNWALLIS *Disc. Seneca* (1631) 2 Then must Soverainty nourish feare in subjection.

β. *a* **1548** HALL *Chron., Edw. V*, 4 Manye princes by a longe continued soueraingtee, decline to a proud porte and behaueour. **1598** BARKCLEY *Felic. Man* (1631) 143 Semiramis..desired the King her husband that she might raigne with Soveraignty one onely day. **1625** CARPENTER *Geogr. Del.* II. xiv. (1635) 238 Hee wanne the soueraignty not meerely by the Sword. *c* **1670** HOBBES *Dial. Com. Laws* (1681) 39 This Doctrine concerning the rights of soveraignty..is the Antient Common-Law. **1727** DE FOE *Syst. Magic* I. ii. (1840) 38 Yet this diminutive rank of sovereignty remained many ages in the world. **1777** R. WATSON *Philip II*, IX. (1839) 173 To grant him the title and dignity of the king of Tunis, in compensation for the sovereignty of Greece. **1791** PAINE *Rights of Man* (ed. 4) 168 Monarchical sovereignty, the enemy of mankind, and the source of misery, is abolished. **1878** LECKY *Eng. in 18th C.* I. i. 71 It placed the sovereignty entirely apart from the category of mere human institutions.

fig. **1884** *Pall Mall G.* 16 Oct. 1/1 He taught Democracy the sovereignty of Duty.

b. *transf.* The supreme controlling power in communities not under monarchical government; absolute and independent authority.

1860 MILL *Repr. Govt.* (1865) 21/2 That [form of government] in which the sovereignty, or supreme controlling power in the last resort, is vested in the entire aggregate of the community. **1861** *Morn. Post* 27 Nov., The 'sovereignty' of every State was subsequently acknowledged in express terms, and is a favourite doctrine of every American writer. **1872** DE VERE *Americanisms* 265 Popular sovereignty is naturally the fundamental doctrine of the republic.

4. A territory under the rule of a sovereign, or existing as an independent state.

1715 *Lond. Gaz.* No. 5345/3 On pretence of their being situate in the Soveraignty of Alsace. **1748** HARTLEY *Observ. Man* II. ii. 115 There were many petty Sovereignties in the Neighbourhood of Canada. **1849** COBDEN *Speeches* 72 The United States, with thirty governors, for thirty independent sovereignties. **1867** FREEMAN *Norm. Conq.* (1877) I. iii. 123 Divided among three quite distinct sovereignties.

† **'sovereigntyship.** *Obs.*$^{-1}$ = SOVEREIGNSHIP a.

1575 G. HARVEY *Letter-bk.* (Camden) 92 It doth my harte good..to use your soveraynetieshippes gaye and new-fashionid words.

† **'soverly,** *adv. Sc. Obs.* [f. SOVER *a.*] Surely; securely.

1513 DOUGLAS *Æneid* II. x. 107, I sal be with the sovirlie and full quoye. **1535** STEWART *Cron. Scot.* III. 159 Quhair tha war keipit in ane presoun strang Richt souerlie.

† **'soverty.** *Sc. Obs.* Also 5–6 **souerte**, 6 **-tee, -tie, souirte**, 6–7 **sovertie**. [Cf. SOVER *a.* and SURETY.]

1. Surety.

c **1470** HENRY *Wallace* III. 414 A herald..chargyt him tak souerte of Wallas, [that] He suld him kepe fra merket toune or fair. **1501** *Acc. Ld. High Treas. Scot.* II. 116 Giffin to Ternway pursewant passand with lettrez to tak souertee of the Lord Cathkerth,..xiiij s. **1552** LYNDESAY *Monarche* 4731 Thare it moste remane ane quhyle, Tyll thay gett sufficient souerte For thare kirk rycht and dewite. **1651** D. CALDERWOOD *Hist. Kirk* (1843) II. 230 Patrik Cranstoun and Andrew Armestrang were summouned to find sovertie to underly the law. **1678** SIR G. MACKENZIE *Crim. Laws Scot.* II. (1699) 235 Six days being by-past, and the Soverty not being found. **1752** J. LOUTHIAN *Form of Process* (ed. 2) 86 That he come and find the said Caution and Soverty, acted in Manner foresaid.

2. A person who becomes surety.

1517 *Acc. Ld. High Treas. Scot.* V. 98 Item,..to Eicht, messinger, to ryd agane to Coldinghame, Duns, and Laudar, to cers and sek George Howme with souerties undir payne of hornyng. **1566** MARY Q. SCOTS in *6th Rep. Hist. MSS. Comm.* 609/2 The souirties ye knaw mon be Lawland men and not of the gretast of our nobilitie. **1580** *Excheq. Rolls Scot.* XXI. 543 Mathow Stewart..as cautioner and sovertie for Johne Cuninghame.

sovethe, obs. f. SEVENTH.

Soviet ('səʊvɪɛt, 'sɒvɪɛt, -j-, -ət), *sb.* and *a.* Also **soviet.** [a. Russ. *sovét* council.] **A.** *sb.* **1. a.** In the U.S.S.R.: one of a number of elected councils which operate at all levels of government, having legislative and executive functions.

The term was also applied to various revolutionary councils set up prior to the establishment of socialist rule in 1917.

1917 *Times* 27 July 6/4 (*heading*) Hostile vote against the Soviet. *Ibid.* 8 Sept. 6/4 A meeting of the Central Committee of the Soviet was held..at which the situation on the front was considered. **1920** *Edin. Rev.* July 59 Soviets, *i.e.*, councils or committees of workmen's and soldiers' delegates, are elected in every township, village or rural district for the purpose of local administration. **1930** *Times Lit. Suppl.* 30 Oct. 880/1 The chairman of the village soviet..may in theory be master in his own limited sphere; in practice he is the servant of a Communist 'cell'. **1941** E. STRAUSS *Soviet Russia* iv. 33 Workers and soldiers..organized their own Councils or Soviets. **1953** B. MIALL tr. *Delbars's Real Stalin* vii. 48 The first Soviets of working-class deputies were formed. The president of the Soviet of St. Petersburg was a Menshevik. **1965** B. PEARCE tr. *Preobrazhensky's New Economics* 191 No more workers and office-workers are employed by the state, the local soviets, and the co-operatives than are employed in private industry, private trade, and agriculture. **1979** O. SELA *Petrograd Consignment* 20 During the 1905 uprising in St. Petersburg, together with Rakovsky and Trotsky he [*sc.* Helphand] had led the Soviet.

b. In other countries: a similar council organized on socialist principles.

1918 *Daily Mirror* 12 Nov. 2/4 (*heading*) Berlin Soviet Meets... The first sitting of the Workers' and Soldiers' Council in Berlin was held..this evening in..the Reichstag. **1934** *Fundamental Laws Chinese Soviet Republic* vi. 79 The First All-China Congress of Soviets of Workers..calls upon the Chinese workers and peasants..to fight resolutely against Sun Yat-Sen. **1977** J. CLEARY *High Road to China* ii. 45 The Bolshevists..in Saxony..have taken over some of the towns, declared soviets.

c. *transf.* and *fig.*

1945 *Tee Emm* (Air Ministry) V. 40 Pistons, connecting rods, and other vitals cease to follow the paths their designer intended and form a sort of Soviet of miscellaneous salvage. **1947** CROWTHER & WHIDDINGTON *Science at War* 86 Owing to their character of complete equality and outspokenness, these meetings were called 'Sunday Soviets'. **1972** *History Workshop Pamphlet* No. 6. 26 The cavilling system..was an embryo of workers' control... It was a little Soviet which had grown up within the capitalist system.

2. A citizen of the U.S.S.R. Chiefly in *pl.* (hence *loosely*, = Soviet Union or its leaders).

1920 *Commercial & Financial Chron.* 24 Jan. 288/1 He [*sc.* Clemenceau] insisted upon writing the final paragraph, 'affirming that the Allies had not changed their attitude towards the Soviets'. **1930** *Amer. Speech* VI. 121 (*heading*) Jailed Soviets go on hunger strike. **1943** W. S. CHURCHILL *End of Beginning* 221 The Soviets had to repel the terrific onslaught of Germany. **1959** *Daily Tel.* 7 Feb. 11/4 President Eisenhower, seeking one word to cover citizens of the Soviet Union, has braved the criticism of purists and adopted the term 'Soviets'. **1964** R. A. BUTLER in *Listener* 13 Aug. 222/2, I am sure that the Soviets are not plotting a war against us, or anything like that, at the present time. **1977** C. MCCARRY *Secret Lovers* iii. 34 'Who did Bülow meet in Dresden?'.. 'A Soviet, an Army captain named Kalmyk.'

B. *adj.* **1.** Of, pertaining to, or having, a system of government based on soviets; ***Soviet Union***: the Union of Soviet Socialist Republics.

1918 *Decrees issued by Revolutionary Peoples Govt.* I. 11 The Soviet Government does not look backward, but forward. **1920** *Glasgow Herald* 9 Mar. 8 The [American] Government has virtually decided to permit the resumption of trade relations with Soviet Russia. **1925** A. J. TOYNBEE *Survey Internat. Affairs 1920–3* 369 The new 'Red' Army of Soviet Armenia. **1928** H. N. BRAILSFORD *How Soviets Work* vii. 99 What the Soviet Union has done on a small scale for backward races like the Tartars and Bashkirs may one day have immense significance for..Central Asia. **1946** *Ann. Reg. 1945* 193 It was agreed that the Soviet Union's claims for reparations should be met by removals from the Russian zone in Germany. **1965** M. MICHAEL tr. *J. Myrdal's Rep. Chinese Village* I. 4 In the early 1930s the peasants of northern Shensi..set up their own soviet republic. **1974** tr. *Sniečkus's Soviet Lithuania* 16 The congress called for a socialist revolution in Lithuania and the establishment of Soviet power.

2. Of, pertaining to, under the influence of, or living in the U.S.S.R.

1920 *Russian Economist* I. 89 This is the secret of 'bourgeois' diplomacy, and this riddle is being solved by Soviet diplomacy and with it by all the Russian-speaking people. **1932** *Sun* (Baltimore) 27 Jan. 12/7 If what is Russia is now known as the Soviet Republic, we should have some adjective similar to 'French', 'American', etc... 'Soviet'..has been regularly used—Soviet literature, Soviet morals, and so on. **1935** A. HUXLEY *Let.* June (1969) 397 The thing simply turned out to be a series of public meetings organized by the French Communist writers..and by the Russians as a piece of Soviet propaganda. **1961** *Ann. Reg. 1960* 499 New trade agreements were negotiated also with several countries in the 'Soviet block'. **1964** V. NABOKOV *Defence* xiv. 223 She ..bought the latest numbers of émigré magazines and—for comparison—several Soviet magazines and newspapers. **1977** *Times* 14 June 16/7 He is a Soviet Jew whose family has been refused an exit visa to go to Israel.

Comb. **1920** *Glasgow Herald* 3 Nov. 13 Fifty-two French citizens..reached Paris yesterday from Sovietland. **1945** *Salt* July 17/2 A Jap-Russian conflict would encourage the Soviet-hating 'Nationalist' (formerly 'isolationist') group. **1962** *Times* 1 Jan. 11/6 The Albanian party lacks the intellectual conditioning of a Soviet-trained leadership. **1964** T. B. BOTTOMORE *Elites & Society* vi. 111 The unified elite in Soviet-type societies is contrasted with the plurality of elites in Western-type societies. **1978** *Detroit Free Press* 5 Mar. (Parade Suppl.) 14/4 Romanov would crack down on the mishmash of more than 100 government ministries and independent agencies that create confusion in Sovietland.

3. In combination with adjs. designating another country or people in the sense 'Soviet and..', as ***Soviet-American, -Chinese, -German***, etc.

1939 W. S. CHURCHILL in *Daily Mirror* 24 Aug. 14/2 In view of the Soviet-German intrigue and all other information to hand it is becoming increasingly difficult to see how war can be averted. **1958** *Listener* 28 Aug. 295/2 The theme of Soviet-Arab friendship. **1965** H. KAHN *On Escalation* xiii. 249 The U.S. in fact was carefully concerned to limit, if not avoid direct Soviet-American confrontations. **1971** H. TREVELYAN *Worlds Apart* xvi. 177 In Moscow we saw little prospect of any new initiative being successful at that moment when Soviet-Chinese relations were in an uncertain phase of manœuvre. **1978** F. MACLEAN *Take Nine Spies* iv. 158 The Soviet-German Pact of August 1939.

Hence **Sovi'etic** *a.* (now *rare*), of or pertaining to the (Russian) Soviet system; **'Sovietism**, the (Russian) Soviet system; **'Sovietist** *rare*, an adherent of the Soviet system; **Sovi'etophile** *a.*, that loves the Soviet Union; **ˌSovieto'phobia**, fear of the Soviet Union (cf. *Russophobia* s.v. RUSSO- b); hence **Sovi'etophobe**.

1919 E. E. CUMMINGS *Let.* 7 Nov. (1969) 62 All N.Y.'s radicals are throwing up their hats in celebration of the anniversary of Sovietism. **1920** W. T. GOODE *Bolshevism at Work* 68 The order existing in Sovietic Moscow. **1920** *Glasgow Herald* 19 Aug. 7 All Russia, apart from the Sovietists, bears no ill to Poland. **1934** Sovietic [see *dope-dream* s.v. DOPE *sb.* 5]. **1950** *Sun* (Baltimore) 4 Jan. 1/8 Controversy over what the Truman Administration..can do to keep Sovietism in China from engulfing Formosa, the last refuge of the Nationalists. **1955** *Bull. Atomic Sci.* Jan. 35/3 The strong wine of Sovietophobia on which most of the contributors had dined was just milk for babes at the Burnham table. **1957** V. NABOKOV *Pnin* iii. 71 Only another Russian could understand the reactionary and Sovietophile blend presented by the pseudo-colorful Komarovs. **1966** *Listener* 3 Mar. 325/1 This bloody love..which must go on vitiating all our attempts at Sovietophobia. **1976** *Survey* Summer-Autumn 237 After 1968 Sartre discovered that ultimately his philosophy was more likely to culminate in anarchy than in Sovietism. **1980** *Daily Tel.* 8 July 14 Should not the British media sort out this phobia? Otherwise 'Sovietophobes' might well be in danger of alienating the most convinced of their potential allies, i.e. the Russians.

Sovietize (səʊ-, 'sɒvɪətaɪz), *v.* Also **sovietize.** [f. SOVIET *sb.* and *a.* + -IZE.] *trans.* To convert to a Soviet system of government; to bring into conformity with soviet, communist or Marxist principles; to subject to the influence or control of the Soviet Union.

1920 *Glasgow Herald* 18 Aug. 7 Lenin's attempt to Sovietise the..countries possessed by the Cossacks of the Don, Terek, and Kuban. **1922** *Ibid.* 29 July 8 Not long since the Bolshevists succeeded in Sovietising Bokhara. **1928** *Daily Express* 1 Nov. 9 The izvoschiks (cabdrivers) of Moscow are to be organised, their hours of work regulated, and..their cabs equipped with meters. The task of 'Sovietising' the izvoschik will not be an easy one. **1936** *Sun* (Baltimore) 15 Sept. 13/8 Owners of Lille textile mills, fearful lest their factories 'be Sovietized', tonight defied Government efforts to grant a forty-hour week to labor. Owners of the mills..demanded the right to prevent 'establishment of Soviets' in their plants. **1954** A. KOESTLER *Invisible Writing* 138 Bokhara the noble was being sovietised more ruthlessly than any other Asiatic town. **1968** J. M. WHITE *Nightclimber* xvi. 108 [He] assisted Panchevski, the Defence Minister, to Sovietize the army. **1980** *English World-Wide* I. i. 20 Yiddish spelling was proletarianized, declericalized, and 'Sovietized' in the U.S.S.R.

Hence ˌ**Sovieti'zation**. Also, more *rarely*, '**Sovietizer**; '**Sovietized** *ppl. a.*, '**Sovietizing** *vbl. sb.* and *ppl. a.*

1920 *Glasgow Herald* 12 Aug. 7 A Sovietised Poland subject to the Moscow Government. **1921** *Ibid.* 17 Jan. 11 It remains to be seen how the Persian Court will take to the idea of Sovietisation. **1922** *Ibid.* 29 July 8 The Amir.. cannot but view the Sovietising of this region with great disfavour. **1925** *Ibid.* 26 Mar. 8 The principal virtue of wireless is its sovietising power. **1939** *Sun* (Baltimore) 29 May 13/2 An effort by the medical profession to brand socialized medicine, 'Sovietized medicine' has failed. **1939** *War Illustr.* 9 Dec. 392/3 In Russian Poland conditions were on the whole rather better... The process of Sovietization was carried out gradually. **1948** J. Towster *Political Power in U.S.S.R.* I. iv. 70 The People's Commissariat for the Affairs of the Nationalities..operated as watchdog, organizer, sovietizer, and protector of the nationalities. **1949** F. Maclean *Eastern Approaches* I. vi. 70 At Talgar we boarded a lorry full of highly Sovietized Kazakh girl students. **1955** *Times* 16 Aug. 9/7 As constituent units of the U.S.S.R., the process of sovietization has been applied to the Baltic States without mercy. **1968** V. V. Aspaturian in A. Kassof *Prospects for Soviet Society* vii. 159 Sovietization is here defined as the process of modernization and industrialization within the Marxist-Leninist norms of social, economic, and political behavior. **1974** V. Nabokov *Look at Harlequins* III. i. 132 The President of Quirn.. timorously sympathized with the fashionable Sovietizers. **1982** *Daily Tel.* 30 July 12 If the Western alliance splits and the Russians establish military supremacy in Europe,.. we should fear..'Sovietisation'.

Sovietology (səʊ-, ˌsɒvɪə'tɒlədʒɪ). Also **sovietology**. [f. Soviet *sb.* and *a.* + -ology.] The study and analysis of affairs and events in the U.S.S.R. So ˌ**Sovie'tologist**, a student of Soviet affairs; ˌ**Sovieto'logical** *a.*; ˌ**Sovieto'logically** *adv.*

1958 *Spectator* 3 Jan. 10/2 The Sovietologist really can help his listeners by explaining what has happened. *Ibid.* 13/3 A complete service with serious Sovietological analysis. **1958** *Times Lit. Suppl.* 17 Oct. 595/2 Many works of fuller and more detailed scholarship are.. already becoming available as 'Sovietology' develops more and more into a major industry. **1963** *Ibid.* 4 Jan. 3/1 Mr. Dudinstev's brief excursion into fantasy may be sovietologically significant. **1968** *Soviet Studies* XIX. 467 The change in the function of Soviet ideology..could then be matched by a change in the function of Sovietology, at least in the field of theoretical-ideological controversy. **1971** H. Trevelyan *Worlds Apart* xx. 237 The Sovietologists of the Western press, working on the documents in London or Washington, were forced by the nature of their occupation to draw conclusions, not always justified by the facts. **1976** *Daily Tel.* 21 Oct. 16/6 A newspaper photograph showing the arrival of President Tsedenbal of Mongolia at Moscow Airport has been examined in detail by the 'Way of the World' Sovietological department. **1979** *Dædalus* Winter 121 There are cracks in sovietology as well as in the Soviet monolith itself.

‖**sovkhoz** ('sɒvkɒz). Also **sovhoz, sovkhos**, etc. Pl. **sovkhoz, sovkhozes, sovkhozy**. [Russ., f. *sov(étskoe khoz(yáĭstvo* Soviet farm.] In the U.S.S.R.: a state-owned farm. Also *attrib.* Cf. kolkhoz.

1921 *Russian Economist* I. 385 Sovkhoses, i.e., Soviet farms, that include agriculture of industrial workmen as well as the States' farms proper. **1926** *Spectator* 29 May 922/1 In Soviet Russia any estate is liable to be turned into a *Sovkhos*, a government model farm. **1932** H. G. Wells *Work, Wealth & Happiness of Mankind* iv. 184 The Sovkhoz is a state plantation, a really scientifically planned and directed modern large-scale organization of production... The Sovkhozy have to take up lands hitherto uncultivated. **1938** *Nature* Mar. 453/2 The 'organization of the sovkhozes' (large-scale State agricultural enterprises). **1943** E. M. Almedingen *Frossia* v. 219 New tractors..meant help for thousands of our Sovhoz farms. **1953** O. Caroe *Soviet Empire* xi. 175 Land and water had been nationalized and, after taking a large share for the *Sovkhozes* or state farms, redistributed in an arbitrary fashion. **1955** H. Hodgkinson *Doubletalk* 28 The collective farms are not to be confused with the State farms or *sovkhoz*..which are owned by the State and worked by government employees. **1967** *Bull. Inst. Study USSR* (Munich) June 15 A wave of sovkhoz development followed which, beginning in 1954, did not recede until 1964. **1977** tr. *Le Monde* in *Guardian Weekly* 27 Nov. 12/5 They..lay siege to the stores in search of rare or common articles which cannot be found in their *kolkhoz* or *sovkhoz* (state farm) general stores.

sovly: see sowly *a.*

‖**sovnarkhoz** ('sɒvnɑːkɒz). Also **Sovnarkhoz**. Pl. **sovnarkhozy, sovnarkhozie**. [Russ. *sovnarkhóz*, abbrev. of *sovét naródnovo khozyáĭstva*, council of national economy.] In the U.S.S.R.: a regional council for the local regulation of the economy.

These councils were introduced in 1957 and abandoned in 1965.

1958 *Ann. Reg. 1957* 207 The country was split into 105 'economic regions', in each of which an 'economic council' (*sovnarkhoz*) was established, responsible to the Republican Government. **1962** *Economist* 3 Mar. 788/3 The 107 smaller economic sub-divisions and their councils, or *sovnarkhozy*. **1964** *Ann. Reg. 1963* 211 The most important decisions were now taken by the Party's new Central Asian Bureau or the single regional *sovnarkhoz*. **1964** *Times Rev. Industry* Mar. 90/1 The programme included visits to the Moscow and Leningrad Sovnarkhozie (Councils of National Economy). **1964** *Economist* 12 Dec. 1242/2 The system of regional councils, or Sovnarkhozy, introduced by Mr Khrushchev in 1957.

Sovnarkom ('sɒvnɑːkɒm). [a. Russ. *sovnarkóm*, abbrev. of *sovét naródnykh komissárov*, council of people's commissars.] The highest executive and administrative organ of government of the U.S.S.R. (renamed the Council of Ministers in 1946). Also, a council having analogous functions in one of the republics of the U.S.S.R.

1938 *Ann. Reg. 1937* 196 The Sovnarkom ordered the Gosplan to finish the schedule for the third five-year period. **1939** G. B. Shaw *Geneva* I. 21, I am Commissar Posky of the Sovnarkom and Politbureau, Soviet delegate to the League Council. **1948** J. Towster *Political Power in U.S.S.R.* 248 The central executive committees and sovnarkoms of the constituent republics. **1959** *Times Lit. Suppl.* 2 Oct. 553/3 His [*sc.* Trotsky's] refusal of an offer by Lenin in 1922, twice repeated, that he should be appointed a vice-president of Sovnarkom. **1959** E. H. Carr *Socialism in One Country* II. iv. xx. 244 Even in the domain of treaty-making Sovnarkom acquired independent constitutional powers.

Sovnday, obs. Sc. variant of Sunday.

sovran ('sɒvrən), *a.* and *sb.* Chiefly *poet.* Also 7 soveran. [Milton's spelling of sovereign, after It. *sovrano*.]

A. *adj.* = sovereign *a.*

1634 Milton *Comus* 41 By quick command from Soveran Jove I was dispatcht for their defence. **1648** —— *Tenure Kings* 10 The titles of Sovran Lord, naturall Lord, and the like. **1751** G. West *Educ.* xxxix, While Senates, Priests and Kings his sovran Sceptre own. *Ibid.* liii, His sovran Sway. **1794** Coleridge *Relig. Musings* 19 Nor high grove,..Nor the starred azure, nor the sovran sun. **1802** —— *Hymn Sunrise Chamouni* 3 So long he seems to pause On thy bald awful head, O sovran Blanc! *a* **1834** Lamb *Misc. Poems, Lines on Picture by Leonardo da Vinci*, He..had read all the sovran schemes and divine riddles there. **1887** Mahaffy & Gilman *Alexander's Empire* xxxii. (1890) 300 When circumstances, as it were, thrust upon them sovran authority.

B. *sb.* = sovereign *sb.*

1648 Milton *Tenure Kings* 20 Yet Eglon by the Jewes had bin acknowledged as thir Sovran. **1667** —— *P.L.* I. 246 Since hee Who now is Sovran can dispose and bid What shall be right. **1802** Coleridge *Hymn Sunrise Chamouni* 29 Thou first and chief, sole Sovran of the Vale! **1824** Landor *Imag. Conv.* Wks. 1853 I. 2/1 The scrip across my saddlebow contains a full receipt for the discharge of my sovran. **1887** Mahaffy & Gilman *Alexander's Empire* vi. (1890) 57 By armed interference, which was not unfrequent under these sovrans.

Hence '**sovranly** *adv.*

1833 Tennyson *Œnone* Poems 56 The imperial Olympian With archèd eyebrow smiling sovranly. **1880** W. Watson *Prince's Quest* 14 To see that royal maiden..Unto her palace riding sovranly.

sovranty ('sɒvrəntɪ). Chiefly *poet.* [f. sovran *a.* + -ty.] Sovereignty.

1667 Milton *P.L.* II. 446, I should ill become this Throne ..And this Imperial Sov'ranty. **1830** Tennyson *Poems* 119 Bitter grief Doth hold the other half in sovranty. **1859** FitzGerald *Omar* xii, 'How sweet is mortal Sovranty!'—think some. **1894** Mahaffy in *19th Cent.* May 856 A priestly despotism, a condottiere sovranty.

sow (saʊ), *sb.*[1] Forms: *α.* 1 **suȝu, suȝa**, 3 **suȝe-**, 4 **zoȝe**, 5 **sogh(e, sowhe**, 5, 7, 9 **sough**. *β.* 2 **suwa**, 3 **suwe**, 3–4 **souwe**, 4–6 **soowe**, 4–7 **sowe**, 4– **sow**, 6, 9 *Sc.* **sou**. *γ.* *north. dial.* 5–7, 9 **sew**. *δ.* 6, 9 *dial.* **soo**. [OE. *suȝu*, = WFris. *sûch*, NFris. *sögg, su*, MDu. *soge, seuge* (Du. *zeug*) and *soch, such* (Du. *zog*), MLG. *soge, suge* (LG. *soge*), related to OHG. and MHG. *sû* (G. *sau*) and ON. *sý-r* (acc. *sú*; MSw., Sw., and Da. *so*), also L. *sūs*, Gr. ὗς, Zend *hu*. The stem *su-*, of doubtful origin, also appears in swine.]

1. **a.** The female of swine; an adult or full-grown female pig, esp. a domestic one used for breeding.

α. *c* **725** *Corpus Gloss.* (Hessels) S 172 *Scroffa*, suȝu. *c* **897** K. Ælfred *Gregory's Past. C.* liv. 419 Sio suȝu hi wille sylian on hire sole æfterðæmðe hio aðwæȝen bið. **1340** *Ayenb.* 61 Hy byeþ anlicned to þe zoȝe huanne hi heþ yuarȝed. **1426** Lydg. *De Guil. Pilgr.* 13358, I logge..As a sowhe, in donge and clay. *c* **1460** *Towneley Myst.* xii. 274 And it were for a sogh Ther is drynk enogh.

β. *c* **1150** *Voc.* in Wr.-Wülcker 543 *Scroffa*, suwa. *a* **1225** *Ancr. R.* 204 Þe Suwe of ȝiuernesse, þet is, Glutunie, haueð pigges þus inemned. *c* **1290** *S. Eng. Leg.* I. 62 A-mong alle bestes..A-corsed þou beo, luþere souwe. *c* **1340** *Nominale* (Skeat) 731 *Sengler, troie, et suel*, Bor, sowe, and gilte. *c* **1374** Chaucer *Boeth.* iv. pr. iii. (1868) 122 He is wiþholden in þe foule delices of þe foule soowe. **14..** *Sir Beues* (C.) 2509 Hys heere was as þe brystels of a sowe. *a* **1450** *Knt. de la Tour* (1868) 43 In the pathe he saw a gret blacke swyne and a sowe. **1523** Fitzherb. *Husb.* §121 Let them be bores and sowes all, and no hogges. **1573** Tusser *Husb.* (1878) 74 Good faring sow holds profit with cow. **1605** Shaks. *Macb.* iv. i. 64 Powre in Sowes blood, that hath eaten Her nine Farrow. **1661** Lovell *Hist. Anim. & Min.* 117 The large sided sow is best. **1764** *Museum Rust.* I. 476 When I have a parcel of young pigs in winter, I find these sows will fat them better. **1820** Shelley *Œd. Tyr.* ii. i. 36 The lean Sows and Boars collect about her. **1847** Tennyson *Princ.* I. 191 All the swine were sows. **1871** B. Taylor *Faust* (1875) I. xxi. 183 A tough old sow, and the mother thereon, Then follow the witches every one.

γ. *c* **1440** *Alph. Tales* 187 On a tyme þer was a man þat stale his neghbur sew. **1557** *Richmond Wills* (Surtees) 101 Hoggs, v sewes and one boore. **1684** [cf. sense 2]. **1807** R. Anderson *Cumbld. Ball.* (*c* 1850) 151 Twee braid-backt tips, and a bonny sew. **1883** *Almondbury Gloss.*, *Sew, Soo*, or *Seoo*, a sow.

δ. **1561** Hollybush *Hom. Apoth.* 35 Geue him the milke of a Soo. **1883** [see *γ*].

†**b.** ***my sow's pigged***, a former card-game. *Obs.*

Some other dial. uses are given in the *Eng. Dial. Dict.*

1621 J. Taylor (Water P.) *Motto* D iv, At Primefisto, Post and payre, Primero,..he's a lib'rall Hero; At My-Sow-pigg'd, and (Reader neuer doubt ye, He's skil'd in all games, except) Looke about ye. **1642** *Tom Nash His Ghost* A iv, For your Religions you may (many of you) cast Crosse and Pile, and for your iust dealing you may play at my Sow ha's Pigg'd. **1734** *Poor Robin's Almanack* C vj, The Lawyers play at Beggar my Neighbour; the School-masters play at Questions and Commands; the Farmers play at My Sow's pigg'd. **1883** *Almondbury Gloss.* 115 'My sow's pigg'd' was a game at cards played in this neighbourhood some forty-five years ago.

2. Applied to persons (male or female) as a term of abuse, opprobrium, or reproach, esp. to a fat, clumsy, or slovenly woman.

1508 Kennedie *Flyting w. Dunbar* 321 Insensuat sow, cesse fals Eustase air! *a* **1585** Polwart *Flyting w. Montgomerie* 743 Sweir sow, doyld kow, ay fow, foull fall thy banes! **1630** *Cosin's Corresp.* (Surtees) I. 174 You tore her sleeve, with these reprochfull words, 'Can ye not stand, ye lazie sowes?' **1684** *Yorks. Dial.* 13 (E.D.S.), Ise ding thy Harnes out, thou base mucky Sew. **1696** Phillips (ed. 5), *Sow*,..a term of Reproach given many times to a fat, lazy, rank, big breasted Woman. **1725** Bailey *Erasm. Colloq.* (1878) I. 387 The Wife [has been called] Sow, Fool, dirty Drab. **1785** Grose *Dict. Vulgar T.*, *Sow*, a fat woman. **1803** Boswell *Songs* 5 Ye're a sow, auld man, Ye get fou, auld man. **1825** Brockett *N.C. Gloss.*, *Sow*, an inelegant female, a dirty wench.

3. In various phrases or proverbial uses: **a.** ***to get, have,*** or ***take the*** (or †*a*) ***wrong*** (or ***right***) ***sow by the ear***, or variants of this: To get hold of, hit upon, the wrong (or right) person or thing; to take an incorrect (or correct) view; to arrive at a wrong (or right) conclusion, solution, etc.

1562 J. Heywood *Prov. & Epigr.* (1867) 75 Ye may see, ye tooke The wrong way to wood, and the wrong sow by theare. **1570** Foxe *A. & M.* (ed. 2) 2034/1, I perceiue..that that man hath the sow by the right eare. **1630** J. Taylor (Water P.) *Wit & Mirth* Wks. II. 180/2, I knew when he first medled with your Ladyship, that hee had a wrong Sow by the eare. **1697** Vanbrugh *Æsop* II, He that goes to a courtier in hope to get fairly rid of 'em may be said, in our country-dialect, to take the wrong sow by the ear. **1761** *Brit. Mag.* II. 463 Crabshaw..told her he believed she had got the right sow by the ear. **1841** Hood *T. of Trumpet* 681 The sow that ought By the ear is caught—And the sin to the sinful door is brought. **1852** De Quincey *Schlosser's Lit. Hist.* Wks. 1858 VIII. 60 When he finds that he has not only got the wrong sow by the ear, but actually sold the sow to a bookseller.

b. In other allusive phrases.

See also silk *sb.* 6 and still *a.*

1546 J. Heywood *Prov.* (1867) 24 Littell knoweth the fat sow, what the leane dooth meane. *Ibid.* 32 What should we (quoth I) grease the fat sow in thars. **1562** —— *Prov. & Epigr.* 64 God haue mercy hors, a pyg of mine owne sow. **1567** Maplet *Gr. Forest* Pref., Not to teach or shew the learned, howe in this point Nature hath wrought (for that were as the prouerb is, ye Sow to Minerua). **1607** Topsell *Four-f. Beasts* (1658) 523 In Latin they say *Sus Minervam*, when an unlearned dunce goeth about to teach his better or a more learned man,..or as we say in English, the foul Sow teach the fair Lady to spin.

c. In comparative phrases, esp. ***as drunk as David's sow*** or ***as a sow*** (cf. quots.).

1562 J. Heywood *Prov. & Epigr.* (1867) 43 As meete as a sowe to beare a saddle. *c* **1590** Greene *Fr. Bacon* (1630) E iv b, I am as seruiceable at a table, as a Sow is vnder an Apple tree. **1727** Gay *New Song of New Similes* ii, For, though as drunk as David's sow, I love her still the better. **1816** *Sporting Mag.* XLVIII. 39 A man is said to be..when he cannot see, 'as drunk as a sow'. **1877** E. Peacock *N.W. Linc. Gloss.* 233 'As happy as a sow i' muck,' or 'in a muck-hill'; a phrase setting forth the contented state of those who live for sensual pleasure. *Ibid.*, 'As drunk as David's sow' is a simile conveying the idea of the deepest state of intoxication.

4. **a.** *Mil.* A movable structure having a strong roof, used to cover men advancing to the walls of a besieged town or fortress, and to protect them while engaged in sapping and mining or other operations. Now *Hist.*

[*c* **1125** William of Malmesb. *De Gestis Reg.* iv. (Rolls) II. 426 Unum fuit machinamentum quod nostri suem, veteres vineam vocant; quod machina..protegit in se subsidentes, qui, quasi more suis, ad murorum suffodienda penetrant fundamenta.]

1297 R. Glouc. (Rolls) 8480 A gyn þat me sowe clupeþ hii made ek wel strong, Muche folc inne vor to be boþe wid & long. **1375** Barbour *Bruce* xvii. 597 Of gret gestis ane sow thai maid, That stalward heling owth it had, With armyt men enew thar-in. **1412–20** Lydg. *Chron. Troy* II. 6434 What with gynnys..And gonnys grete, for to caste stonys .., And large sowis lowe for to myne. **1486** *Excheq. Rolls Scot.* IX. 434 Willelmo Andirson, carpentario, pro factura unius instrumenti bellici vocati le sow. **1535** Stewart *Cron. Scot.* III. 342 Than pik and tar, talloun and brynt stane,.. Vpoun that sow richt suddantlie leit fall, Quhilk..scaldit her richt mony than to deid Within the sow. **1610** W. Folkingham *Art of Survey* I. xiii. 45 Engines..Militarie; as Battering-Rams, Sowes, Horses, Tortuses. **1633** T. Stafford *Pac. Hib.* I. x. 68 The Castle therefore they besiege, and placed an Engine (well knowen in this Countrey), called a Sow (to the Wals thereof) to supp [*sic*] the same. **1694** Motteux *Rabelais* iv. xl. (1737) 159 The Engineers..fitted up the great Sow. **1788** Grose *Milit. Antiq.* II. 307 Two machines, the one called the boar, the other the sow, were employed by the parliamentarians in the siege of Corfe castle. **1828–43** Tytler *Hist. Scot.* (1864) I. 137 It was determined to undermine the walls; and for this purpose a huge machine was constructed... From its shape and covering, this formidable engine was called a sow. **1866** KINGSLEY *Herew.* xxviii, They made a floating-sow, and thrust it on before them as they worked across the stream. **1893** H. J. MOULE *Old Dorset* 211 The Parliamentarians took the trouble to bring this ponderous affair, called a 'sow', close to the Castle.

b. *U.S.* 'A movable shed used as a protection by miners' (1895 *Funk's Stand. Dict.*).

5. a. A wood-louse or sow-bug. Now chiefly *dial.*

14.. in *Rel. Antiq.* I. 204 Geve hym of these sowes that crepe with many fete, and falle oute of howce rovys. **1558** WARDE tr. *Alexis' Secr.* 23 b, Then take twelue or fiftene of these litle beastes called Monkes peason or sowes. **1572** MASCALL *Planting & Graffing* 50 There be little beastes called Sowes, which haue many legs. **1600** SURFLET *Countrie Farme* I. viii. 39 If wals be full of sowes and such other like vermine. **1668** CHARLETON *Onomast.* 50 *Asellus*, the Tylers Lowse, or, Sow. **1725** *Fam. Dict.* s.v. *Ulcer*, For Ulcers.., Take Millepedes, call'd by some in English Wood-Lice, and by others Sows. *a* **1825-** in dial. glossaries (E. Anglia, Linc., Leic., Northants, Nottingham, etc.). **1877** F. P. PASCOE *Zool. Class.* 62 Some of the Oniscidæ are land animals, and are known as hog-lice, sows, &c.

b. ***sea-sow***: see SEA *sb.* 23 d.

6. *techn.* A large oblong mass of solidified metal as obtained from the blast- or smelting-furnace:

a. Of lead. Now *Obs.* or *rare.*

So MDu. *soge* in a document of 1445.

1481-90 *Howard Househ. Bks.* (Roxb.) 311 My Lord paied to Geffrey Blower for ij. sowes lede..weying..xvj. c. iij. quarters and xiiij. lb. *a* **1529** SKELTON *E. Rummyng* 72 With clothes vpon her hed That wey a sowe of led. **1546** in W. H. Turner *Select. Rec. Oxford* (1880) 182 For meltyng of the leade.., and castyng into sowes. **1610** HOLLAND *Camden's Brit.* (1637) 611 Twenty sowes of lead long in forme, but foure square. **1668** *Phil. Trans.* III. 770 It is cast into Sand, and runs into those Sowes (as they call them) which they sell. **1688** HOLME *Armoury* III. 260/2 A Pig or Sow of Lead, is generally about three hundred pounds apiece. **1700** J. BROME *Trav.* i. (1707) 34 The [Lead] Ore..being.. afterwards melted down into Pigs and Sows, as they are there call'd.

b. Of iron. (See note to PIG *sb.*[1] 7 and quots.)

1539 in *Hist. Sussex* (Victoria Co. Hist.) II. 245/2 To melt the Sowes in ij forges or Fynories ther must be iiij persones. **1612** S. STURTEVANT *Metallica* (1854) 113 The second kind of Metallar is the Sowe of iron. **1645-52** BOATE *Ireland's Nat. Hist.* (1860) 113 The molten Iron..turning into a hard and stiff mass, which masses are called Sowes by the workmen. **1676** HOBBES *Iliad* XXIII. 817 And then of Iron he brought out a Sough Such as at first it from the Fornace came. *a* **1744** LUCAS in *Trans. Cumb. & Westm. Archaeol. Soc.* (N.S.) VIII. 38 They break the Sow and Pigs off from one another, and the Sow into the same Lengths with the Piggs. **1837** WHITTOCK *Bk. Trades* (1842) 408 (*Smith*), The price of iron, in bars, pigs, and 'sows', has been upon the advance. **1894** *Harper's Mag.* Jan. 418 When the metal cools, the larger masses are called 'sows', and the smaller 'pigs'.

c. In general use: A bar or mass of metal; an ingot. Now *rare* or *Obs.*

1570-6 LAMBARDE *Peramb. Kent* (1826) p. v, By fire to trie out the Metall and to cast it into certeine rude lumps, which they call Sowze. **1590** WEBBE *Trav.* (Arb.) 23 A place.. where they had great store of Treasure and Sowes of Silver. *a* **1656** USSHER *Ann.* (1658) 225 Diodorus reckons upward of 400 thousand talents of silver, and gold in sowes and wedges. **1702** C. MATHER *Magn. Chr.* II. App. (1852) 172 Upon further diving the Indian fetcht up a sow, as they stiled it, or a lump of silver.

d. *fig.* or in fig. context.

1570-6 LAMBARDE *Peramb. Kent* (1826) 474 If any man shall like to take this mettall, drawen by me out of a fewe Sowes into many sheetes. **1599** NASHE *Lenten Stuffe* Wks. (Grosart) V. 293 This vnciuill Norman hotpotch, this sow of lead, that hath neuer a ring at the end to lift it vp by.

e. One of the larger channels, or the main channel, in the hearth of an iron-smelting furnace, serving as a feeder to the smaller channels or 'pigs' (see quots.).

1843 HOLTZAPFFEL *Turning* I. 371 The metal is led from the furnace, through a gutter lined with sand, into a large trough or sow, the end of which is closed with a shuttle. **1884** W. H. GREENWOOD *Steel & Iron* 129 These feeders or sows are themselves put in connection with a common main channel, *d*, leading from the tap-hole to the lower end of the sand- or pig-bed.

f. (See quot.)

1871 *Trans. Amer. Inst. Mining Eng.* I. 112 Metallic iron, not finding heat enough in a lead-furnace to keep it sufficiently fluid to run out with the slag, congeals in the hearth, and forms what smelters term 'sows', 'bears', 'horses', or 'salamanders'.

7. *Sc.* and *north.* A large oblong-shaped rick or stack, esp. of hay.

1659 A. HAY *Diary* (S.H.S.) 155 My whole hey was a great ruck of the Lawes meadow, and 3 litle rucks,.. all which I did put in one sow in the yaird. **1756** MRS. CALDERWOOD in *Coltness Collect.* (Maitl. Club) 166 Severall great sows of hay were on the cannall..; it looked very odd to see a hay sow, perhaps fifty or sixty foot long,..sailing along. **1799** J. ROBERTSON *Agric. Perth* 220 The stack is frequently made in an oblong form, which is vulgarly called a sow. **1833** J. S. SANDS *Poems* 168 (E.D.D.), Like the donkey wi' the sous Of hay. **1871** C. GIBBON *Lack of Gold* viii, Behind was the farm-yard, and well-stocked with fat stacks of grain and hay 'sows'.

8. *attrib.* and *Comb.* (chiefly in sense 1), as *sowcunt* (*coarse nonce-wd.*), *-feeder*, *-hair*, *-herd*, *-pap*, *-skin*, *-sticking*, *-tail*, *-teat*, etc.; *sow-dugged adj.*; *sow-like* adv.; **sow-belly** *U.S. slang*, (salted) side of pork; **sow-drunk** *a.* (see sense 3 c); †**sow-guard**, = sense 4; **sow-libber** *Sc.*, a sow-gelder; **sow-louse**, a wood-louse, sow-bug (now *dial.*). See also SOW-GELDER, -IRON, -METAL.

1867 W. L. GOSS *Soldier's Story of his Captivity* 205 My captor presented to me a generous slice of '*sow-belly'. **1945** B. MACDONALD *Egg & I* (1946) III. viii. 97 Tits fed this baby pickles, beer, sow-belly and cabbage. **1976** G. EWART *No Fool* III. 69 To go into your South, a different life. Sow-belly and cornbread with syrup poured over it. **1922** JOYCE *Ulysses* 541 (*Her *sowcunt barks.*) Fohracht! **1509** BARCLAY *Shyp Folys* (1570) 33 Some *sowe dronke, swalowing meate without measure, Some maudlayne dronke, mourning loudly and hye. **1522** MORE *De quat. Noviss.* Wks. 82/2 Yet shal ye find mo y[t] drink themself sow drunk of pride to be called good felowes, than for luste of the drink self. **1880** TENNYSON *Northern Cobbler* iv, Soa sow-droonk that tha doesn not touch thy 'at to the Squire. **1960** AUDEN *Homage to Clio* 55 Steatopygous, *sow-dugged and owl-headed. **1960** *Farmer & Stockbreeder* 16 Feb. (Suppl.) 37/2 Such an arrangement with individual *sow-feeders, allows for better attention to each sow. **1582** STANYHURST *Æneis* II. (Arb.) 58 They clinge thee scalinges too wals, and vnder a *sowgard They clymb. **1597** DELONEY *Gentle Craft* I. iv, The Aule steele and tackes, the *Sow-haires beside. **1565** COOPER *Thesaurus*, *Scrofipascus*,.. a *sow hearde. *a* **1682** SEMPILL *Blythsome Wedding* 22 There will be *Sow-libber Peatie. **1603** J. DAVIES (Heref.) *Microcosmos* Wks. (Grosart) I. 65/1 For, to dismount from true loue's loftie pitch..Is, *Sow-like, to lie mired in the ditch Of lowest Hell. **1658** ROWLAND tr. *Moufet's Theat. Ins.* 932 Flyes, Gnats, *Sowlice, Fleas, that do much hurt and do no good. **1866** BROGDEN *Prov. Lincs.*, *Sow-louse*, the wood-louse. *c* **1440** *Alph. Tales* 437 þan he garte caste it emang swyne at þai mott devowr it; and þer it was nurisshid on a *sew papp. **1611** SHAKS. *Wint. T.* IV. iii. 20 If Tinkers may haue leaue to liue, and beare the *Sow-skin Bowget. **1823** *Spirit Public Jrnls.* 459 He instantly crammed it back again into the sow-skin purse from which he had taken it. **1883** *Longman's Mag.* Apr. 649 At the *sow-sticking..the neighbours lend helping hands. **1787** BURNS *Halloween* iv, A runt was like a *sow-tail, Sae bow't that night. *a* **1661** HOLYDAY *Juvenal* (1673) 216 Trypherus the learned, who Carves large *sow-teats.

b. In plant-names, as †**sowbane**, goosefoot (*Chenopodium*); †**sow-fennel**, sulphur-wort; **sow-tit**, the wood-strawberry; **sow-wort**, = SOW-BREAD. See also SOW-THISTLE.

Some others are current in dialects or *U.S.*

1657 W. COLES *Adam in Eden* cccix. 577 Goose-foot or *Sowbane. **1796** WITHERING *Brit. Plants* (ed. 3) II. 271 Red Goosefoot. Sowbane. **1578** LYTE *Dodoens* 298 It is called.. in Englishe also Peucedanum, Horestrong,..*Sowe fenill, and of some Sulphurwurt. **1611** COTGR., *Fenouil de porceau*, Sow-fennell, Hogs-fennell. **1788** M. CUTLER in *Life*, etc. (1888) I. 410 It is on a plain..covered with trees—a white oak four feet in diameter near the summit—cavity in the middle covered with *sow-tits. **1838** T. THOMSON *Chem. Org. Bodies* 708 M. Saladin found in the root of the *Cyclamen Europeum*, or *sow wort, a peculiar bitter principle.

c. With the names of animals, etc., in the sense of 'female', as ***sow beaver***, ***-cat*** (also *transf.*), †***-child***, ***grizzly bear***, ***-hog***, ***-swine***; **sow-wasp** *dial.*, a queen wasp. See also SOW-PIG.

1959 E. COLLIER *Three against Wilderness* xxi. 210 She was an old *sow beaver who could be reckoned upon to give birth to four or five sturdy kits. **1676** *Phil. Trans.* XI. 592 A Chat Pard (supposed to be engendred by a Leopard and a *Sow-catt). **1689** N. LEE *Princ. Cleves* III. i, *St. A.* For there's two ravenous Sow-Cats will Eat you. *El.* Your Wives you mean. **1875** PARISH *Dict. Sussex Dial.* 108 I'll give that old sow-cat o' yourn a sock aside the head. *a* **1700** B. E. *Dict. Cant. Crew*, **Sow-child*, a Female Child. **1976** *Telegraph-Journal* (St. John, New Brunswick) 12 Aug. 12/4 A *sow grizzly bear that..mauled him..was only trying to protect her young. **1648** HEXHAM II, *Een Zoch*, a *Sowe-hogge. **1822** SHELLEY *Faust* II. 154 Upon a *sow-swine, whose farrows were nine, Old Baubo rideth alone. **1875** PARISH *Dict. Sussex Dial.* 110 In some parts of the county a reward of sixpence is offered for each *sow-waps killed in the spring.

d. Genitival combs., as **sow's-baby**, *slang* and *Cant* (see quots.); **sow's-back**, *local* (see quot. 1789); †**sow's bread**, = SOW-BREAD; †**sow's thistle**, = SOW-THISTLE.

a **1400** *Stockholm Med. MS.* fol. 198 Sowesthystyl, *labrum*. **1558** WARDE tr. *Alexis' Secrets* (1562) 13 Take an herbe called..in Englishe sowes breade. *a* **1700** B. E. *Dict. Cant. Crew*, *Sow's baby*, a Pig. **1785** GROSE *Dict. Vulgar T.*, *Sow's baby*, a sucking pig. **1789** J. WILLIAMS *Min. Kingd.* I. 107 We..bring up a level mine under the pavement of the coal, quite through the ridge, in order to level the coal upon the other side of it. Some of the Scots colliers call this a ridge, others of them call it a hirst, and some of them call it a sow's-back. **1859** *Slang Dict.* 98 *Sow's baby*,..sixpence.

sow (saʊ), *sb.*[2] Now *dial.* Also sowe (9 *dial.* sou, saa). [app. distinct from SOUGH *sb.*[2], and perh. identical with Flem. dial. *zou* (†*souwe*, *soeuwe* in Plantin and Kilian) drain.] A drain; a channel or run of water.

1316 in *Rep. MSS. Ld. Middleton* (1911) 88 Predicti Adam et socii sui gutturam, que dicitur 'le sowe',.. reparabunt. **1669** W. SIMPSON *Hydrol. Chym.* 359 A kind of ocre..falls to the bottom of the chanels of all..mineral springs, whether sowes or others. **1670** —— *Hydrol. Ess.* 133 All spaws, whether vitrioline from sowes or aluminous. **1709** THORESBY *Diary* (1830) II. 50 Both days entirely spent with labourers, directing and overseeing the sowes to drain water. *c* **1800** STAGG *Bridewain* ix. Misc. Poems (1808) 5 Owr hill an' knowe, thro' seugh an' sowe, Comes tiftan many o' couple. **1824-** in Yorkshire and Cumberld. glossaries.

sow, *sb.*[3] *rare.* In 4 sau, saw. [f. SOW *v.*[1]] An act of sowing.

a **1300** *Cursor M.* 6378 He þam ledd..And fand þam fode in þair nede, Wit-vten ani sau [*v.r.* saw] o sede.

sow (saʊ), *sb.*[4] *Obs.* exc. *dial.* Also 4 sowe. [Of obscure origin.] A blow or stroke.

a **1400** *Sir Eglamour* 317 Syr Egyllamowre hys swerde owt drowe, And to the yeant he gafe a sowe, And blyndyd hym in that tyde. **1869-** in dial. glossaries (Cheshire, Lanc., and Westmld.).

sow, *sb.*[5] *Sc. rare.* [Of obscure origin.]

1. A bride's outfit of clothes; a trousseau.

168. in Morison *Decis. Crt. Sess.* 10436 Andrew Littlejohn pursues the Duchess of Monmouth her curator for payment of a taylor's account taken off by the Duchess for her marriage sow. **1887** *Jamieson's Suppl.* Add., *Sou, sowe*, a bride's outfit or braws... This term is now used only by the fisher-folk of the N.E. of Scot. from Nairn to Buckie.

2. A burial garment; a shroud.

1763 'INSULANUS' *Second Sight* 18 The same girl died of a fever, and as there was no linen in the place but what was unbleached, it was made use of for her sowe.

†**sow**, obs. variant of/or error for SOLE *sb.*[3] 2.

1688 HOLME *Armoury* II. 173/2 The Sow, is the Yoke, which is put about the Cow or Ox-Neck to tye him to the Boosey. *Ibid.* III. 327/2.

sow, obs. variant of SOE, tub.

sow (səʊ), *v.*[1] Pa. t. **sowed**, Pa. pple. **sowed**, **sown**. Forms: (see below). [Common Teut., but presenting considerable variation in form, and changes of conjugation; the chief forms are OE. *sáwan*, OFris. **siâ* (NFris. *sîn*, *se*, EFris. *sâi*), MDu. *saeyen*, *zaeyen* (Du. *zaaien*), OS. *sâian* (MLG. *seien*, *seigen*, *segen*, LG. *seien*, *saien*), OHG. *sâjan*, *sâhen*, *sâen* (MHG. *sæjen*, *sæhen*, *sæn*, G. *säen*) and *sâwen* (MHG. *sæwen*, *sêwen*), ON. and Icel. *sá* (Norw. and Da. *saa*, Sw. *så*), Goth. *saian*. The Teut. root **sæ-* (cf. SEED *sb.*) has counterparts in Lith. *sėti*, OSlav. *sejati*, L. *serĕre* (perf. *sēvi*) to sow, and perh. in Gr. ἵημι.

The original reduplicating conjugation is retained in the Goth. pa. t. *saisō*, ON. pa. t. *sera*, pa. pple. *sáinn* (MSw. *sāin*), OE. pa. t. *séow*, pa. pple. *ȝesáwen*, OS. pa. t. *sêu* (once), OFris. pa. pple. *esên*. Transference to the weak conjugation has taken place in all the continental languages (as OHG. *sâta*, OS. *sâida*, late ON. *sáða*); in English the pa. t. has become weak, the pa. pple. still commonly retains the strong form.]

A. Illustration of forms.

1. *Inf.* (and Pres. stem). *α.* 1-2 **sawan** (2 **sæwæn**), 2-3 **sawen** (**sewen**), 4 **zawen**; 2, 4-6 **sawe**, 4, 6 *Sc.* **sau**, 5- *Sc.* (and *north.*) **saw** (5 *Sc.* **say**); also 5 *Sc.* **schau**, **schaw(e**.

c **825-** [see examples in B]. *c* **1200** *Trin. Coll. Hom.* 147 Hie hiden wepende and sewende. *a* **1300** *Cursor M.* 6839 Your land yee sal sau seuen yeir. **1340** *Ayenb.* 214 Huo þanne ssolde erye and zawe. *c* **1375** *Sc. Leg. Saints* xxvii. (*Machor*) 906 Prechand & sawand godis sed. *Ibid.* xl. (*Ninian*) 133 To schau his seiyde. *c* **1400** MAUNDEV. (Roxb.) xxxii. 147 þe folk ..sawez na land. *c* **1440** *Registr. Aberdon.* (Maitl. Cl.) I. 250 Alsmekill land as a celdr of atis will schawe. *c* **1480** HENRYSON *Aganis Haisty Credence* 41 O wicket tung, sawand dissentioun. **1570** LEVINS *Manip.* 45 To Sawe corne, *seminare*. **1581** J. HAMILTON *Cath. Traict.* in *Cath. Tract.* (S.T.S.) 74 To sau..pernicious heresie. *c* **1639** SIR W. MURE *Ps.* cvii. 37 The feilds they saw. **1785** BURNS *Halloween* xviii, Hemp-seed I saw thee. **1818** SCOTT *Hrt. Midl.* viii, They..might be for sawing the craft wi' aits.

β. 3-4 **sowen** (3 **souin**), 4 **souwen**, 5 **sowyn**; 3-7 **sowe**, 4 **soghe**, 6 **soue**, 6- **sow** (8 **sew**).

c **1200** *Trin. Coll. Hom.* 155 To sowen þe holie sed. *a* **1250** *Prov. Ælfred* in *O.E. Misc.* 108 His sedes to sowen [*v.r.* souin]. **1297** R. GLOUC. (Rolls) 10259 Ne þat bailif..ne soffrede hom nower come, To sowe. **13..** *E.E. Allit. P.* C. 67 In þat cete my saȝes soghe alle aboute. **1362** LANGL. *P. Pl.* A. VII. 59, I wol souwen hit my-self. **1382** WYCLIF *Matt.* xiii. 3 He that sowith, goth out to sowe his seed. *c* **1440** *Promp. Parv.* 466/1 Sowyn corne or oþer sedys, *semino*, *sero*. **1530** PALSGR. 725/2, I sowe corne. **1532** *Galway Arch.* in *10th Rep. Hist. MSS. Comm.* App. V. 405 Whatsoever man ..shall..soue any varyaunce. **1635** R. N. tr. *Camden's Hist. Eliz.* I. 21 To sow Religion. **1697** DRYDEN *Virg. Georg.* I. 2 When to sowe the Corn.

2. *Past Tense.* **a.** *Strong.* 1-2 **seow** (1 **seawu**), 1, 3-7, 8 *dial.* **sew** (3 **siew**, 5 **seew**), 4-5, 7 **sewe** (9 *Sc.* **shewe**), 3-4 **seuȝ** (4 **seeuȝh**, **segh**), 3-4, 6 **seu**, 4 **sue**; *pl.* 1 **seowun**, **-on**, **-an**, **sewon**, 3 **seowen**, **sowen**, 3-5 **sewen**; 3 **seowe**, **sew**, 4-7 **sewe**.

c **825** [see B. 2]. *c* **950** *Lindisf. Gosp.* Matt. xiii. 39 Ðe fiond, ..seðe sawes *vel* seawu, ða is diowl. **971** *Blickl. Hom.* 133 Se Halȝa Gast seow þæt clæne sæd. *c* **1175** *Lamb. Hom.* 133 A riche mon ferde ut and seow. *c* **1200** *Trin. Coll. Hom.* 151 [He] siew þo on wowe. *Ibid.*, þe sed þat he sew. *c* **1250** *Hymn* Ibid. 256 þe holi gost hire on þe seuȝ. *c* **1275** *Moral Ode* 23 in *O.E. Misc.* 59 Hwenne alle men repen schule þat heo ear seowe. *c* **1330** R. BRUNNE *Chron. Wace* (Rolls) 8048 Hym þat þis child on me sew. *c* **1380** WYCLIF *Sel. Wks.* I. 259 God repiþ many þingis þat he sue not. *c* **1430** *Pilgr. Lyf Manhode* I. lxxiv. (1869) 43 She brouhte the greyn..and seew it. **1513** DOUGLAS *Æneid* XII. ix. 47 His fader eyrit and sew ane peice of feild. **1565** *Wills & Inv. N.C.* (Surtees, 1835) 244 Because I seu no winter corne ther. **1641** BEST *Farm. Bks.* (Surtees) 56 Wee sewe nothing but onely our In-field. *a* **1800** PEGGE *Anecd. Eng. Lang.* (1803) 105, I sew..my corn.

b. *Weak.* *α.* 4 **sceued**, 4, 9 *Sc.* **sawed**, 4 **sawit**.

[*c* **950** *Lindisf. Gosp.* Matt. xiii. 25 Ofer-ȝeseawu *vel* ȝeseawde. —— *Luke* xix. 21 þæt ðu ne ȝesaudesd.] *a* **1300** *Cursor M.* 21226 O godds word he sceued þe sede. *c* **1375** *Ibid.* 12323 (Fairf.), þe quete..at ihesus sawed. **1820** SCOTT *Monast.* xiii, About the last barley ye sawed.

β. 4 **sowid(e**, 6- **sowed**, 7 **sowd**.

1382 WYCLIF *Gen.* xxvi. 12 Isaac forsothe sowide in that loond. **1535** COVERDALE *Deut.* xi. 10 Where thou sowedest thy sede. **1560** DAUS tr. *Sleidane's Comm.* 91 The Arrians..

sowed abroade their opinions. 1667 MILTON *P.L.* VII. 358 He..sowd with Starrs the Heav'n.

3. *Past Participle.* **a.** *Strong.* α. 1 **ȝesauen, ȝi-,** 1–2 **ȝesawen,** 4 **y-zawe;** 1, 4–6 **sawen,** 3 **sauen (saȝin),** 4 **sau(u)n,** 4, 6 *Sc.* **sawin,** 5 *Sc.* **sawyn(e, -ing,** 5, 9 *Sc.* and *north.* **sawn,** 6–7 *Sc.* **sawne;** 4 **sewe,** 6 *Sc.* **saw.**

c950 *Lindisf. Gosp.* Mark iv. 15 Seðe ymb woeȝ ðer bið ȝesauen [*Rushw.* ȝisawen] word. 971 *Blickl. Hom.* 133 Þa wæs heora lar sawen. a1300 *Cursor M.* 28174 O strif oft haue i sauun þe sede. 1340 *Ayenb.* 255 Yef hit ys hol oþer aboue y-zawe [= F. *sursemée*]. c1340 HAMPOLE *Pr. Consc.* 445 Vile sede of man with syn sawen. c1375 *Sc. Leg. Saints* xl. (*Ninian*) 203 Þare he saw sawyne il seide. c1440 *Alph. Tales* 420 A man þat had lande to be sawen. c1470 HENRY *Wallace* XI. 1226 Feill off that kyn, in Scotland than was sawyn. 1513 DOUGLAS *Æneid* IV. Prol. 8 In fragill flesche ȝour fekill seid is saw. 1570 LEVINS *Manip.* 62 Sawen, *satus.* c1629 SIR W. MURE *Sonn.* iv. Wks. (S.T.S.) I. 302 If once the seed of true Repentance sawne. 1876 ROBINSON *Whitby Gloss.* s.v., *Sawn*, sown as grain.

β. 3–4 **i-,** 4–5 **y-sowe,** 4–5 **sowe;** 3 **i-,** 4–5 **y-sowen,** 3–7 **sowen,** 5 **sowun,** 5–7 **sowne,** 4, 6– **sown.**

a1250 *Owl & Night.* 1129 Þar newe sedes beoþ isowe. c1330 *Arth. & Merl.* 4537 (Kölbing), No corn no was ysowe. 1382 WYCLIF *Lev.* xxvii. 16 If..the feelde is sowun. c1440 *Pallad. on Husb.* I. 165 Rie of whete ysowen wul vp growe. ?c1450 *Songs, Carols*, etc. (1907) 81 The sede of synne so thyke ys sowe. 1523 FITZHERB. *Husb.* §10 That.. styffe grounde..wolde be sowen with bigge stuffe. 1590 SPENSER *F.Q.* I. ix. 16 True Loues are often sown. 1608 DOD & CLEAVER *Expos. Prov. ix–x.* 29 Some is sowne before others,..some is sowen after others. 1697 DRYDEN *Virg. Georg.* Ess., The Precepts..are sown so very thick. 1774 GOLDSM. *Nat. Hist.* (1776) VII. 353 A furrow which has been newly sown. 1837 P. KEITH *Bot. Lex.* 23 Wheat sown in the spring lives but six months.

b. *Weak.* 4 **i-sowed,** 5 **sowid,** 5, 7– **sowed,** 6 **sowd,** 7–8 **sow'd.**

1362 LANGL. *P. Pl.* A. VI. 34, I haue..I-sowed his seed. 1382 WYCLIF *Num.* xx. 5 This worst place, that may not be sowid. 1596 SPENSER *Hymn Heav. Beauty* 53 The house of blessed Gods,..All sowd with glistring stars. 1656 A. WRIGHT *Five Serm.* 126 The seed sowed in good ground. 1759 R. BROWN *Compl. Farmer* 119 Your corn should be sowed on broad ridges. 1844 S. WILBERFORCE *Hist. Prot. Episc. Ch. Amer.* (1846) 63 It was ploughed and sowed.

B. Signification.

1. *intr.* or *absol.* To perform the action of scattering or depositing seed on or in the ground so that it may grow. Also *fig.* and in fig. context.

c825 *Vesp. Psalter* cxxv. 5 Ða sawað in tearum, in ȝefian hie reopað. c950 *Lindisf. Gosp.* Matt. xxv. 24 Ðu hripes ðer ðu ne sawes. c1000 *Ags. Gosp.* Matt. vi. 26 Behealdað heofonan fuȝlas, forþam þe hiȝ ne sawað ne hiȝ ne ripað. c1175 *Lamb. Hom.* 131 Þe ðe saweð on blescunge he scal mawen of blescunge. c1205 LAY. 10032 Heo tileden, heo seowen, heo repen, heo meowen. a1250 *Owl & Night.* 1039 Hit wes isayd..þat mon schal eryen & sowe, þar he weneþ after god mowe. 1362 LANGL. *P. Pl.* A. VIII. 6 Al þat euere hulpen him to heren or to sowen. c1460 *Towneley Myst.* ii. 124 When I shuld saw, & wantyd seyde. c1500 *God speed the Plough* (Skeat) 2 As I me walked ouer feldis wide When men began to Ere and to Sowe. 1579 LYLY *Euphues* (Arb.) 92 As thou hast reaped where an other hath sowen. 1591 HARINGTON *Orl. Fur.* Pref. ¶ix b, For as men vse to sow with the hand and not with the whole sacke. 1663 S. PATRICK *Parab. Pilgr.* xxxiii. (1687) 404 The birds..who neither sow nor reap. 1687 AYRES *Lyric Poems* (1906) 306, [I] Plough water, sow on rocks, and reap the wind. 1785 BURNS *Death & Dr. Hornbook* viii, Hae ye been mawin, When ither folk are busy sawin? 1842 LOUDON *Suburban Hort.* 623 For a late summer and autumn crop, sow in the end of February. 1865 RUSKIN *Sesame* ii. §95 The path-sides where He has sown.

2. a. *trans.* To scatter seed on or upon (land, etc.) in order that it may grow; to supply with seed. Also, *to sow* (land) *to* (a crop). Cf. PUT *v.*[1] 26 b, PLANT *v.* 6 a.

c825 *Vesp. Psalter* cvi. 37 [Hie] seowun lond. c888 K. ÆLFRED *Boeth.* xxiii, Swa hwa swa wille sawan westmbære land. c1000 ÆLFRIC *Lev.* xix. 19 Ne saw þu þinne æcyr mid ȝemengedum sæde. a1250 *Prov. Ælfred* 123 Þey o mon ahte huntseuenti Acres, and he hi hadde isowen alle myd reade golde. And þat gold greowe [etc.]. 1297 R. GLOUC. (Rolls) 10195 Þe king þo..vorbed þat me ne ssolde non of is lond sowe. a1340 HAMPOLE *Psalter* cvi. 37 Þai sew feldis and þai plantid vyners. 1382 WYCLIF *Gen.* xlvii. 23 Takith seedis, and sowith feeldis, that ȝe mowen han lyuelodis. 1456–70 in *Acts Parlt. Scot.* (1875) XII. 26/2 The lardis of Meldrum has gart eyre and saw owr said landis of Canty. 1526 *Pilgr. Perf.* (W. de W. 1531) 23 After that he tempereth it with dong, than eareth it, soweth it, and haroweth it. 1577 B. GOOGE tr. *Heresbach's Husb.* 45 When you meane to let your ground lye againe for Meddowe or Pasture, your best is to sowe it with Oates. 1660 in *Verney Mem.* (1907) II. 158, I shall want a little hay dust to sow the holes in the parsnage yard. 1735 JOHNSON *Lobo's Abyssinia* Descr. i. 47 They neither Sow their Lands, nor improve them by any kind of Culture. 1801 *Farmer's Mag.* Aug. 298 Cost and Profit of Clearing and Sowing with Wheat 10 Acres of Intervale Land. 1846 J. BAXTER *Libr. Pract. Agric.* (ed. 4) I. 177 In a field of eleven acres,..the whole was sowed with barley. 1939 *Sun* (Baltimore) 4 July 16/2 There will be no possibility of spreading the galls to land that is sown to wheat or rye. 1972 *Morning Star* 4 Jan. 4/1 This was cattle-breeding country, with a dairy produce industry and with only about 75,000 acres sown to grain.

transf. and *fig.* c1420 LYDG. *Assembly of Gods* 1023 Sensualyte..sewe the felde with hys vnkynde seede That causyd Vertu aftyr mykyll woo to feele. 1607 SHAKS. *Timon* IV. i. 29 Itches, Blaines, Sowe all th' Athenian bosomes. 1615 W. BEDWELL tr. *Moham. Impost.* II. §70 Euery man doth sow his wife. 1819 SHELLEY *Mask of Anarchy* lxix, The daily strife..Which sows the human heart with tares.

b. To strew or sprinkle (land, etc.) *with* something as in the sowing of seed. Also *fig.*

1611 BIBLE *Judges* ix. 45 And Abimelech..beat downe the citie and sowed it with salt. 1759 R. BROWN *Compl. Farmer* 113 If once in four or five years you sow it with soot, it will increase it very much. 1831 SCOTT *Ct. Rob.* xxi, The whole mad crew..will return with fire and sword to burn down Constantinople, and sow with salt the place where it stood. 1838 LYTTON *Alice* X. iii, He urged on the horses—he sowed the road with gold.

c. Of seed: To be sufficient for (a certain area).

c1440 [see A. 1]. 1685 W. PENN *Furth. Acc. Pennsylv.* 7 The Land requires less seed: Three Pecks of Wheat sow an Acre. 1761 *Descr. of S. Carolina* 70 About a Gallon of Indian Corn sows an Acre.

3. To cover or strew (a place, etc.) thickly *with* (also †*of*) something. Chiefly in pa. pple.: Thickly strewn or dotted *with* something.

(*a*) c1400 *Pilgr. Sowle* v. v. (1859) 75 This corowne is ful sowen of precious stones. 1426 LYDG. *De. Guil. Pilgr.* 18284 Withe lesyngs, (who lyst know,) vp and downe it is y-sowe. c1500 *Melusine* xxxvi. 288 They thenne departed,..& fond in theire way the feldes sowen with sarasyns deed. c1611 CHAPMAN *Iliad* VI. (1887) 92 When..he leaves the conquered field Sown with his slaughters. 1658 DRYDEN *Cromwell* xiv, Thick as the Galaxy with Stars is sown. 1687 A. LOVELL tr. *Thevenot's Trav.* II. 132 Beyond that, there is hardly any thing to be found but Desarts sowed with stones. 1759 *Ann. Reg.* 52 All this sea is sown thick with sands and shoals. 1847 TENNYSON *Princ.* Prol. 55 For all the sloping pasture murmur'd, sown With happy faces and with holiday. 1864 —— *Aylmer's Field* 158 A close-set robe of jasmine sown with stars.

(*b*) 1613 DONNE *Poems* (1633) 124 [It] sowes the Court with starres. 1700 S. L. tr. *Fryke's Voy. E. Ind.* 88 We.. made the place so hot for 'em, and sowed the ground so thick with their dead Bodies. 1850 TENNYSON *In Mem.* lxxii, Whirl the ungarner'd sheaf afar, And sow the sky with flying boughs.

4. a. To scatter or deposit (seed) on or in the ground, etc., for growth, usually by the action of the hand; to place or put (seed) in the ground; to plant (a crop) in this way.

to sow one's wild oats: see OAT *sb.* 4.

c1000 *Sax. Leechd.* II. 22 Ȝenim tuncersan sio þe self weaxeð & mon ne sæwð. a1100 *Gerefa* in *Anglia* IX. 262 Beana sawan. a1250 *Prov. Ælfred* 93 Þat..þe cheorl beo in fryþ his sedes to sowen. a1300 *Cursor M.* 12325 O quete a littel sede, Apon þe feld he-self it seu. 1387 TREVISA *Higden* (Rolls) VIII. 139 Sedes þat were i-sowe fordried in þe erþe. c1440 *Pallad. on Husb.* XIII. 15 The letuse in this moone is so to sowe. 1523 FITZHERB. *Husb.* §12 It is necessarye to declare, howe all maner of corne shuld be sowen. 1573 TUSSER *Husb.* (1878) 31 Cleane rie that sowes, the better crop mowes. 1604 E. G[RIMSTONE] *D'Acosta's Hist. Indies* III. xx. 186 The want they have of bread, is countervailed with the rootes they sowe. 1697 DRYDEN *Virg. Georg.* I. 2 When to turn The fruitful Soil, and when to sowe the Corn. 1750 W. ELLIS *Mod. Husbandm.* I. ii. 50 They sow [horse-beans] first broad-cast over the ground, and then plow them in: this, as we call it, being sown under furrow. 1816 J. SMITH *Panorama Sci. & Art* II. 681 Sow spinach; earth up celery and broccoli. 1850 McCOSH *Div. Govt.* II. ii. (1874) 200 He is a husbandman and about to sow the crops which are to be his sustenance. 1908 [MISS FOWLER] *Betw. Trent & Ancholme* 21 We sowed and planted Wall-flowers and Stone-crop upon it.

refl. 1842 TENNYSON *Gardener's Dau.* 65 A crowd of hopes, That sought to sow themselves like winged seeds.

b. *transf.* with reference to fish, bacilli, etc.

1854 BADHAM *Halieut.* 42 See..how gluttony, and a desire to please a dainty tooth, have devised means to *sow fish*, and to stock the sea with strange bread. 1861 HULME tr. *Moquin-Tandon* II. III. 169 As far back as the time of Rondelet the art of 'sowing' these molluscs [*sc.* oysters] was known. 1898 P. MANSON *Trop. Diseases* viii. 148 When [the plague bacillus is] sown on blood serum.., an abundant, moist, yellowish-grey growth is formed.

c. *Mil.* To lay or 'plant' (an explosive mine); *spec.* to drop (mines, etc.) by aircraft into the sea or otherwise. Also *absol.*

1939 *Sun* (Baltimore) 20 Nov. 8/2 In the last conflict the Germans sowed 44,000 mines, 11,000 of them in British home waters. 1943 *Ibid.* 26 Nov. 1/5 After they have dropped their first flares they remain over the target area, keeping it marked by sowing more flares. 1944 K. DOUGLAS *Alamein to Zem Zem* (1946) xiv. 82 Mines were sown in the tracks of vehicles, where other vehicles might be expected to follow. 1974 *Times* 18 Apr. 1/3 A lot of anti-personnel mines sown on the canal banks have slipped into the water. 1979 J. BARNETT *Backfire is Hostile!* xiii. 135 Twenty-four Tu-16 Badgers began..sowing at forty-two thousand feet.

5. a. Used with *seed* (and some other terms) in transf. and fig. senses.

(*a*) 971 *Blickl. Hom.* 3 Se Halȝa Gast seow þæt clæne sæd on þone unbesmitenan innoþ. c1340 HAMPOLE *Pr. Consc.* 445 He was geten..Of vile sede of man with syn sawen. 1567 *Gude & Godlie B.* (S.T.S.) 189 Than suld..nocht sa mekle bastard seid [be] Throw out this cuntrie sawin.

(*b*) c1000 ÆLFRIC *Hom.* II. 534 Ȝif we eow þa gastlican sæd sawaþ, hwonlic biþ þæt we eowere flæsclican þing ripon. c1200 ORMIN 5071 Þatt dæþess laþe sed þatt deofless æfre sawenn..Inn ure sawless wille. a1225 *Juliana* 74 Ant reope we of þat ripe sed þat we seowen. a1300 *Cursor M.* 21226 In all þe stedes quar he yede, O godds word he sceued þe sede. c1375 *Sc. Leg. Saints* xl. (*Ninian*) 203 Þare he saw sawyne il seide, to distroy it he cane hyme spede. a1400–50 *Alexander* 4404 To sawe emang þir simpill men sedis of debate. c1480 HENRYSON *Test. Cress.* 137 The seede of loue was sowen on my face. 1526 *Pilgr. Perf.* (W. de W. 1531) 23 b, To haue great profyte and encrease of our sede, that we haue so sowen for his loue. 1576 FLEMING *Panopl. Epist.* 194, I am in belief (I may peraduenture sowe my seede in the sande) that [etc.]. 1648 *Hunting Fox* 14 The tares of sedition which these envious men had sowen. 1813 W. COXE *Mem. Kings of Spain* I. *29 This celebrated act..sowed the germ of future wars. 1868 FREEMAN *Norm. Conq.* (1877) II. vii. 30 In all this the seeds of the Conquest were sowing.

b. Contrasted with *reap* in fig. uses.

See also quots. c 1000 and a 1225 above. The usage (as in sense 1) is derived from various Biblical passages, e.g. *Hos.* viii. 7, *Galat.* vi. 7. For similar examples with *mow*, see MOW *v.* 1 b.

1382 WYCLIF *Pref. Ep. St. Jerome* vii. 71/1 Aggeus,..the whiche sewe in teres that he repe in ioy. c1421 *26 Pol. Poems* 100 Eche dedly synne is a dedly knyf; For he shal repe þat he sewe. *Ibid.* 113 Man..Makeþ moche of hym-self, sayþe al is oures, And repeth þat he neuere ne sewe. 1588 A. KING tr. *Canisius' Catech.* 185 Quhat so euer a man saues the same sal he raipe, for quha sawes in his flesh he sal sheer corruption of the flesh. 1593 SHAKS. *2 Hen. VI*, III. i. 381 Why then from Ireland come I with my strength, And reape the Haruest which that Rascall sow'd. 1823 LAMB *Elia* II. Pref., He sowed doubtful speeches, and reaped plain, unequivocal hatred. 1878 B. TAYLOR *Deukalion* II. iii. 74 What Darkness sowed the Light shall reap.

6. *fig.* To disseminate or spread; to endeavour to propagate or extend. In various contexts.

(*a*) c888 K. ÆLFRED *Boeth.* xxvii, Se eorðlica anweald næfre ne sæwð þa cræftas, ac..gadrað unðeawas. c1200 *Trin. Coll. Hom.* 155 Ure helend saweð his holie word hwile þurh his haȝen muð hwile þurh his apostles. 13.. *Know Thyself* 58 in *E.E. Poems* (1862) 131 His grace is so wide isowe. c1375 *Sc. Leg. Saints* xi. (*Simon & Jude*) 404 Quhen þe apostolis had al-quhare In þat land sawyne goddis lare. 1552 ABP. HAMILTON *Catech.* (1884) 26 The word that is plantit or sawin amongis yow. 1573 *Satir. Poems Reform.* xlii. 898 Þe richt meanis..Ouir all to haue the Gospell sawin. 1607 HIERON *Wks.* I. 157 Light is sowen for the righteous, and ioy for the vpright in heart. 1839 tr. *Lamartine's Trav.* 72/1 Their voyage to Greece and Italy, to sow the Gospel.

(*b*) c897 K. ÆLFRED *Gregory's Past. C.* 356 Aworpen mon ..on ælce tid saweð wrohte. c1386 CHAUCER *Pars. T.* ¶642 Þe synne of hem þat sowen and maken discord. c1450 *Mirour Saluacioun* (Roxb.) 91 Whilk amanges neghburghs discordes to sawe makes hym bisy. 1526 SKELTON *Magnyf.* 189 Measure and I wyll neuer be deuydyd For no dyscorde than any man can sawe. 1562 WINȜET *Wks.* (S.T.S.) I. 77 *note*, The seditious personis sawis schisme and diuisioun. 1581 *Satir. Poems Reform.* xliv. 83 Sathan..To rais his kingdome tentation did sau Into þe hairtis of men in all degrie. 1663 S. PATRICK *Parab. Pilgr.* xxxvii. (1687) 493 Let not the evil one..sow this jealousie in your heart. 1720 OZELL tr. *Vertot's Rom. Rep.* II. XIV. 327 A Counsel which would sow Division in the contrary Party. a1770 JORTIN *Serm.* (1771) I. iii. 49 Those who teach false doctrines to sew dissension amongst them. 1837 CARLYLE *Fr. Rev.* II. I. xi, Between the best of Peoples and the best of Restorer Kings they would sow grudges. 1878 STUBBS *Const. Hist.* III. xviii. 106 He..attempted to sow discord in his brother's Council.

(*c*) 1523 LD. BERNERS *Froiss.* I. cvx. 137 Also there were wordes sowen through all the towne, howe [etc.]. 1560 J. DAUS tr. *Sleidane's Comm.* 5 Martin Luther.., who soweth newe opinions in Germany. 1628–9 DIGBY *Voy. Medit.* (Camden) 30 Some ill-disposed persons..tooke occasion to sowe mutinous discourses. 1859 TENNYSON *Marriage of Geraint* 450 He sow'd a slander in the common ear. 1877 —— *Harold* IV. i, Who sow'd this fancy here among the people?

(*d*) 1531 ELYOT *Gov.* (1580) 57 The necessities, which fortune soweth among menne that be mortall. 1613 SHAKS. *Hen. VIII*, III. i. 158 We are to cure such sorrowes, not to sowe 'em. 1823 LAMB *Elia* II. *Tombs in Abbey*, The antiquarian spirit..may have been sown in you among those wrecks of splendid mortality. 1849 *Blackw. Mag.* LXVI. 627 Can you believe..that the word of the Third Witch, 'thou shalt be King Hereafter,' sows the murder in Macbeth's heart?

†7. To beget (a child). *Obs. rare.*

c1250 *Long Life* 33 in *O.E. Misc.* 158 Of fole fulþe þu art isowe, Wormes fode þu schald beo. c1330 R. BRUNNE *Chron. Wace* (Rolls) 8048, Y ne sey..Hym þat þis child on me sew. a1425 *Cursor M.* 3424 (Trin.), Þe gode childre geten of grace..whenne þei coom, wel is knowe þat þei of goddes grace are sowe.

8. a. To scatter after the manner of seed; to sprinkle, throw or spread about, in this way.

1387 TREVISA *Higden* (Rolls) I. 125 Abymelech.. destroyed þat place..and sewe salt þerynne, for þe lond schulde na more bere fruit and corne. *Ibid.* 339 Also powder of erþe of þat lond i-sowe in oþer londes vseþ awey wormes. c1400 *Laud Troy Bk.* 12920 Many a knyȝt was ouer-throwen, Her bodies lay thik sawen. 1430–40 LYDG. *Bochas* I. viii. (1554) 11 b, His child dismembred and abrode ysowe. 1509 HAWES *Past. Pleas.* XI. (Percy Soc.) 38 What avayleth evermore to sowe The precyous stones amonge gruntynge hogges? 1513 DOUGLAS *Æneid* VII. x. 28 Armouris, suerdis, speris and scheildis, I sall do saw and strow our all the feyldis. 1668 CULPEPPER & COLE *Barthol. Anat.* I. xv. 38 The Gall-bladder hath received very many small Passages, furnished with sundry little twigs, sowed up and down in the Liver. 1726 SHELVOCKE *Voy. round World* 373 They were astonish'd to see my people so thin sown, our scanty number not making any manner of show. 1837 MARRYAT *Dog Fiend* i, With lank hair very thinly sown upon a head which [etc.]. 1864 TENNYSON *Aylmer's F.* 171 Not sowing hedge-row texts and passing by, Nor dealing goodly counsel from a height.

b. To distribute or disperse. *Obs. rare.*

c1350 *Leg. Rood* (1871) 90 And sethin als wide als þai er saun Has no iew hous of his awyn. 1375 BARBOUR *Bruce* IV. 685 Bot thai prophetis so thyn ar sawin, That thair in erd now nane is knawin. 1382 WYCLIF *Zech.* x. 9, Y shal sowe hem in peplis. 1535 COVERDALE *Ibid.*, I wil sowe them amonge the people.

†9. *Sc.* To shed (blood). *Obs.*$^{-1}$

1535 STEWART *Cron. Scot.* I. 303 Wemen..sall nocht.. draw abak quhair mekill blude is sawin.

Hence **sowed** (səʊd), **'sowing** *ppl. adjs.*

1382 WYCLIF *Matt.* xiii. 18 Therfore heere ȝe the parable of the sowynge man. 1733 W. ELLIS *Chiltern & Vale Farm.* 205 This Mischief happens oftner to the latter sowed Wheat. 1876 MEREDITH *Beauch. Career* xxix, Moveless do they seem to you? Why, so is the earth to the sowing husbandman.

sow, *v.*[2] *north.* and *Sc.* Also 5 sowe, 8–9 *dial.* soo, 9 soue. [Of obscure origin.]

1. *trans.* To affect (a person) with pain; to pain or grieve sorely. Usu. with *sore.*

a **1300** *Cursor M.* 6568 Mikel i haf trauaild for yow..þat suilk a godd all honurs now þat will yow her-after sare sow. *a* **1352** MINOT *Poems* (ed. Hall) v. 12 When he sailed in þe Swin it sowed him sare. *c* **1375** *Sc. Leg. Saints* xxxvii. (*Vincent*) 292 Thinkand he mycht na payne mare do til hyme to sow hyme sare. *a* **1400–50** *Alexander* 2313 And þai said, soure suld him sowe bot he þe cite ȝeld.

2. *intr.* To be painful; to thrill or tingle with pain or exertion.

c **1425** WYNTOUN *Chron.* VIII. 6224 Qwhen he a qwhile had prekyt þar, And sum of þaim he gert sow sare. **1438** *Bk. Alexander Grt.* (Bann) 87 The sydis of sum may sowe full sair. **1535** STEWART *Cron. Scot.* II. 258 Thair scharp schutting maid sydis for till sow. *a* **1586** in Pinkerton *Anc. Sc. Poems* (1786) 201 Scho gars me murne,..And with sair straiks scho gars me sow. **1885** GORDON *Pyotshaw* 297 If that bit race hisna set my lugs a' sooin'.

3. *absol.* To produce a tingling sensation.

1796 W. H. MARSHALL *Yorksh.* (ed. 2) II. 346 To *Soo*, to pain the hand, in striking with a hammer or beetle: to *jar*. **1876** ROBINSON *Whitby Gloss.* s.v. *Soo*, It soues up my arm.

sow, obs. 1st and 3rd sing. ind. pa. t. SEE *v.*

sow, obs. form of SEW *v.*, SUE *v.*

sowable ('səʊəb(ə)l), *a.* [f. SOW *v.*[1] + -ABLE.] That can be sowed; fit for sowing.

1706 STEVENS *Span. Dict.* I, *Semental*, sowable, or fit to be sow'd. **1893** *Black & White* 20 May 505/1 Winter beans a failure, peas not sowable.

sowans, variant of SOWENS.

‖**sowar** (sʌ'wɑː(r)). *Anglo-Indian.* Forms: α. sowar. β. sooar, suwar, sewar. [Urdū (Pers.) *sawār* horseman.] A native horseman or mounted orderly, policeman, etc.; a native trooper, esp. one belonging to the irregular cavalry.

α. **1802** in JAMES *Milit. Dict.* **1827** SCOTT *Surg. Dau.* xiii, The lighted match of the Sowar, or horseman, who rode before him. **1859** J. LANG *Wand. India* 336 When a palanquin is escorted by a sowar, the sowar..rides on and gives notice that a lady, or gentleman,..is coming. **1883** F. M. CRAWFORD *Mr. Isaacs* v. 92 The verandah, however, was crowded with servants and sowars.

β. **1819** *Sporting Mag.* IV. 172 A wild hog, which ran as hard as it could, away from us, pursued by a Sooar. **1834** [PRINSEP] *Baboo* I. viii. 125 My practised ear immediately knew that it was a single Suwar. **1844** *New Monthly Mag.* Mar. 435 A troop of sewars is generally placed under the orders of the collector of each district, for the purpose of carrying despatches, escort duty, &c.

sowarry (sʌ'wɑːrɪ). *Anglo-Indian.* Also 8 **sewarry,** 9 **sewary, sawarry, suwarree, sowarree,** etc. [Urdū (Pers.) *sawārī*, f. prec.] The mounted attendants of a person of high rank, state official, etc.; a number of these forming a cavalcade.

1776 *Trial Nundocomar* 43/2 Bollakey Doss went with his sewarry before us. **1803** WELLINGTON in Gurw. *Desp.* (1835) II. 362 They must have tents, Elephants and other sewary. *Ibid.* (1844) I. 789 Which measure would..put an end to the use of the Company's sepoys as sowarry. **1813** J. FORBES *Oriental Mem.* III. 420, I was..often reprimanded..for leaving the suwarree, or state attendants, at the outer gate of the city. **1827** SCOTT *Surg. Dau.* xiv, Orders were given that on the next day all should be in readiness for the *Sowarree*, a grand procession, when the Prince was to receive the Begum.

sow-back. Chiefly *Sc.* Also sowback. [f. SOW *sb.*[1] Cf. *sow's-back* s.v. SOW *sb.*[1] 8 d.]

1. A woman's cap or head-dress having a raised ridge or fold running from front to back.

1808 JAMIESON, *Frowdie*, a cap for the head;..also called a *sow-back*. **1835** MONTEATH *Dunblane* (1887) 113 Auld Wives o' Dunblane..Wi' their cloaks an' their sowbacks. **1886** S. CARMENT *Mem. J. Carment* iii. 79 The aged women with their white soo-backs.

attrib. **1897** J. WRIGHT *Sc. Life* 18 Attired in a white 'sooback mutch' and in short-gown and drugget coat.

2. *Geol.* A ridge of glacial origin suggestive of the back of a sow.

1874 J. GEIKIE *Gt. Ice Age* ii. 17 The long parallel ridges, or 'sowbacks' and 'drums', as they are termed,..invariably coincide in direction with the valleys or straths in which they lie. *Ibid.* vii. 97 'Sowbacks' being the glacial counter-parts of those broad banks of silt and sand that form here and there upon the beds of rivers.

sow-backed, *a.* [f. SOW *sb.*[1]] Having a back like that of a sow; resembling the back of a sow in shape or formation; ridged like a sow's back. ***sow-backed mutch***, = SOW-BACK I.

(*a*) **1728** BAILEY, *Sow Back'd Horses* (among Farriers), such as have straight Ribs, but good Backs. **1883** *Sunday Mag.* 689 Farther back still is the sow-backed and higher ridge known as the Silla del Moro.

(*b*) **1857** STEWART *Sketches Sc. Character* 18 A sow-backit mutch and an auld-fashioned gown. **1895** OCHILTREE *Redburn* ii, Her hair..was seldom seen from under her long, 'sow-backed mutch'.

sowbpowaylle, variant of SUPPOWELL *Obs.*

sow-bread. Also sowbread. [f. SOW *sb.*[1] + BREAD *sb.*, after med.L. *panis porcinus*, or G. *saubrot*, †*säubrot*, †*sewbrot* (Gesner, 1542), older Flem. *seugenbrood* (Kilian).] A plant of the genus *Cyclamen*, esp. *C. europæum*, the fleshy tuberous root-stocks of which are eaten by swine.

c **1550** H. LLOYD *Treas. Health* B vj b, Let the rote of Rape Vyolet or Sowbread be sodden. **1578** LYTE *Dodoens* 330 Sowbread in moyst and stony shadowy places, underneath trees. **1597** GERARDE *Herbal* II. ccxcvi. 694 The common kinde of Sowbread..hath many greene and round leaues. **1651** FRENCH *Distill.* ii. 47 Adde..Sowbread, Wormwood. **1660** SHARROCK *Vegetables* 27 The seeds of divers sowbreads. *a* **1687** MRS. BEHN tr. *Cowley's Plants* C.'s Wks. 1711 III. 377 The Sow-Bread does afford rich Food for Swine, Physick for Man, and Garlands for the Shrine. **1731** MILLER *Gard. Dict.* s.v. *Cyclamen*, It is call'd Sow-bread, because the Root is round like a Loaf, and the Sows eat it. **1830** LINDLEY *Nat. Syst. Bot.* 226 The root of the Cyclamen is famous for its acridity; yet this is the principal food of the wild boars of Sicily, whence its common name of Sowbread. **1861** BENTLEY *Man. Bot.* 605 The Cyclamens are commonly known under the name of Sow-breads.

attrib. **1639** O. WOOD *Alph. Bk. Secrets* 227 Sowbread root..with honied water, purgeth grosse phlegme and filthy humours.

b. With defining terms, as ***common, ivy-leaved, round, round-leaved sow-bread.***

1578 LYTE *Dodoens* 330 Cyclaminon which we may cal round Sowbread. **1629** PARKINSON *Parad.* xxiv. 198 The Common Sowebread is called by most writers in Latine, *Panis Porcinus*, and by that name it is known in the Apothecaries shops. **1712** tr. *Pomet's Hist. Drugs* I. 51 The Root spreads..after the Nature of round Sowbread. **1731** MILLER *Gard. Dict.* s.v. *Cyclamen*, Round-leav'd Sowbread, with Leaves of a purplish Colour underneath. **1858** A. IRVINE *Brit. Plants* 408 *Cyclamen hederæfolium*,..Ivy-leaved Sow-bread.

sow-bug. [f. SOW *sb.*[1] 5 a.] **a.** A wood-louse of the genus *Oniscus*, esp. *O. asellus*. **b.** *U.S.* A small marine crustacean of the genus *Idotea*.

1750 W. ELLIS *Country Housew. Comp.* 157 Sow-bug or Wood-louse. **1815** KIRBY & SP. *Entomol.* iv. (1818) I. 141 He recommends to his credulous patient to take a certain number of sow-bugs per diem. **1851** *Beck's Florist* 41 One of the pits, that was full of sow-bugs. **1883** *Harper's Mag.* Jan. 186/1 The common sow-bug (idotæa) often illumines the crevices and sea-weeds along our shores.

sowcar, variant of SOUCAR.

sowce, variant of SOUSE *sb.* and *v.*

sowcer, obs. f. SAUCER *sb.*

sowd, sowd-: see SOLD *sb.*[1], *v.*[1], *v.*[2]

sowdaine, -an(e, -ayne, etc., obs. ff. SOLDAN.

sowdan, obs. var. SUDDEN *a.*

sowde, var. SOLD *sb.*[2] *Obs.*

sowdear, -eer, -eour, etc., obs. ff. SOLDIER *sb.*

sowder(e, -oure, obs. or dial. ff. SOLDER *sb.*[1], *v.*

sowdy ('saʊdɪ). *Sc.* Also 7 **soudy,** 9 **sou-, sow-, soodie.** [Of uncertain origin. Cf. POWSOWDY.] A species of broth or hotch-potch. Also *transf.* (quot. *c* 1700).

c **1700** *Bannocks of Bear-Meal* in Hogg *Jacob. Rel.* (1819) I. 20 Where shall ye see such, or find such a soudy? Bannocks of bear meal, cakes of croudy. **1807** TANNAHILL *Poems* (1815) 204 They got naething for crowdy, but runts boil'd to sowdie.

sowdyare, -o(u)r(e, obs. ff. SOLDIER *sb.*

sowe, obs. f. SEW *v.*[1], SUE *v.*

sowed, obs. pa. t. and pa. pple. SEW *v.*

sowede, var. SOLD *sb.*[1] *Obs.*

soweder, obs. f. SOLDER *sb.*

sowedeur, obs. f. SOLDIER *sb.*

sowel. Now *dial.* Forms: 1 saȝol, sahel, 3 saȝel; 2, 9 sowel, 4–5 soul(e, 9 sole, zooul. [OE. *sáȝol*, = MHG. (now Swiss dial.) *seigel* rung of a ladder. Cf. SAIL *sb.*[4]]

†**1.** A stout stick or staff; a pole, cudgel, etc. *Obs.*

c **893** K. ÆLFRED *Oros.* II. vi. 88 Ealle þa consulas.. Claudium þone ænne mid saȝlum ofbeotan. *c* **1000** *Ags. Gosp.* Matt. xxvi. 47 þa com iudas an of þam twelfum & micel folk mid hym mid swurdum & sahlum [*Hatton Gosp.* mid sahlen]. *c* **1150** *Semi-Sax. Voc.* in Wr.-Wülcker 549 *Fustis*, sowel. *c* **1205** LAY. 12280 And ælc bær an honde ænne saȝel [*c* **1275** staf] stronge.

2. A stake sharpened at the end, esp. one used in the construction of a hedge or fence; in later use, a hurdle-stake (cf. quots.).

c **900** WÆRFERTH *Gregory's Dial.* 24 His oðer fot wearð fæst on anum saȝle [*v.rr.* sahle, heȝesahle] þæs ȝeardes. **13..** *Guy Warw.* (A.) 3616 In ich half y-sett arawe, Scharpe soules doun of þe hulle y-drawe. **1398** TREVISA *Barth. De P.R.* XVII. cliv. (Bodl. MS.), Soules & stakes beþ iclensed ere þei be ipiȝt in þe grounde. **1844** BARNES *Poems Rur. Life* (1848) 387 *Sowel*, or *Sole*,..a shore or stake, such as is driven into ground to fasten up hurdles to. **1881** *I. of Wight Words*, *Zooul*, a stake to fasten sheep-hurdles. **1890** *Glouc. Gloss.*, *Sole*, a stake driven into the ground to fasten up hurdles.

sowel, var. SOWL *sb.*, food, etc.

sowen, comb. form of SOWENS; obs. pa. pple. SEW *v.*[1] and SOW *v.*[1]

sowenge, obs. f. SEWING *vbl. sb.*[1]

sowens ('soənz, 'su-), *sb. pl. Sc.* (and *Ir.*). Forms: 6 **sowannis,** 7 **sownis,** 7–9 **sowins,** 8– **sowens, -ings, sewings, sooins, so'ns,** 9 **sowans, sooans, -ens, sones; sweens, swins,** etc. [app. ad. Gael. *súghan, súbhan*, the liquid used in preparing 'sowens' (= Ir. *súghán, subhán* sap, juice), f. *súgh, súbh* sap.]

1. An article of diet formerly in common use in Scotland (and some parts of Ireland), consisting of farinaceous matter extracted from the bran or husks of oats by steeping in water, allowed to ferment slightly, and prepared by boiling.

A number of phrases and idiomatic uses are illustrated in the *Eng. Dial. Dict.*

α. **1582** *Records of Elgin* (New Spald. Cl.) I. 168 Scho wald leiff to sie his bairnis beg thair meit; he culd cun sowannis better nor aill. **1625** *Sc. Acts, Chas. I* (1870) V. 182/2 Actis maid anent the pryceis of sownis and englishe beir. **1677** NICOLSON in *Trans. R. Soc. Lit.* (1870) IX. 319 *Sowins*, outshellings. **1698** M. MARTIN *Voy. St. Kilda* iii. 114 These Sowens (*i.e.* Flummery) being blended together, produce good Yest. **1728** SWIFT *Past. Dial.* Wks. 1755 III. II. 204 See, where Norah with the sowins comes. **1771** SMOLLETT *Humph. Cl.* 15 Sept., At night they sup on sowens or flummery of oatmeal. **1785** BURNS *Halloween* xxviii, Till butter'd So'ns, wi' fragrant lunt, Set a' their gabs a steerin. **1818** SCOTT *Br. Lamm.* xix, I was bred a plain man at my father's frugal table, and I should like well would my.. family permit me to return to my sowens. **1855** [J. D. BURN] *Autobiogr. Beggar Boy* (1859) 49, I had..an excellent supper of sowans with milk, and bread and cheese. **1885** W. ROSS *Aberdour & Inchcolme* II. 26 He found the goodwife busy preparing sowans.

fig. **1818** SCOTT *Hrt. Midl.* xlii, The Christian souls..who were hungering for spiritual manna, having been fed but upon sour Hieland sowens by..the last minister.

β. **1776** J. PRINGLE *Disc. Health Mariners* 18 *note*, This rural food, in the North, is called *sooins*. **1778** *Phil. Trans.* LXVIII. 632 What is called sooins in Scotland, and much used by the common people there. **1827** J. WILSON *Noct. Ambr.* Wks. 1855 I. 334 Extendin your notes, as they ca't, ower your sooens and sma' beer. **1899** SPENCE *Shetl. Folk-Lore* 174 Groats, and *ootsiftins*, from the last of which that delicious food called *sooans*..are made.

2. *attrib.*, as ***sowen-cog, -kit, -mug, -porridge,*** etc. Also **sowens-say**, a sieve for sowens.

1722 RAMSAY *Three Bonnets* II. 1 The supper sowin-cogs and bannocks. **1724** —— *Tea-table Misc.* (1876) I. 174 A milsie, and a sowen-pale. **1725** in Herd *Sc. Songs* (1776) II. 143 A spurtle and a sowen mug. **1729** in Paterson *Hist. Musselburgh* (1857) 164 Although the sowin pot should cool. **1776** *Herd's Sc. Songs* II. 139 'Tis fa'en in the sowen kit. **1793** FULLARTON *View Agric. Ayr.* 114 The spence in which were stored the meal-chest, sowen-tubs, besoms, and saddles. **1808** JAMIESON, *Sowens-porridge*, a dish of pottage, made of..cold sowens, by mixing meal with the sowens, while on the fire. **1822** GALT *Sir A. Wylie* xciv, Something about a sowan-cog. **1825** JAMIESON *Suppl.* s.v. *Say*, The sowens-say is supported by two bars laid across the tub. **1900** *Daily Mail* 2 May 5/3 Sowan porridge, our new delicacy, made from fermented oats.

sower ('səʊə(r)). Forms: 1–2, 4–6 **sawere,** 2 **sæwere,** 4 **sauer,** 4–6, 9 *Sc.* **sawer,** 6 *Sc.* **sawar;** 3–4 **sowere,** 4– **sower.** [f. SOW *v.*[1] + -ER. Cf. MDu. *saeyer, sayer*, etc. (Du. *zaaier*), MLG. and LG. *seiger, seier* (*saier*), OHG. *sâhari, sâari* (MHG. *sejer, seher, sewer*, etc., G. *säer*).]

1. One who sows seed.

c **1000** *Ags. Gosp.* Matt. xiii. 3 Soþlice, ut-eode se sædere [*v.r.* sawere, *Hatton* sæwere] hys sæd to sawenne. *c* **1200** *Trin. Coll. Hom.* 155 Ðo beden þe holi apostles seien hem wat þe sowere bitocneð. **1393** LANGL. *P. Pl.* C. XVIII. 103 Now failleþ þis folke boþe sowers and shupmen. *c* **1400** *Cursor M.* 28839 (Cotton Galba), þaire sede to þe feld bus husbandes bere, Bot þis feld cumes to þe sawere. **1532–3** *Act 24 Hen. VIII*, c. 10 All tillers, husbandes, and sowers of the erth within the same. **1573** TUSSER *Husb* (1878) 37 Good seede and good sower. **1611** BIBLE *Isaiah* lv. 10 That it may giue seed to the sower. **1762** MILLS *Syst. Pract. Husb.* I. 321 The inequality of the handfuls which different sowers grasp. **1822** A. CUNNINGHAM *Tradit. Tales, Mother's Dream* (1887) 119 A humble sower of seed-corn. **1842** BORROW *Bible in Spain* xxiv, I..read to them the parable of the Sower.

b. *fig.* or in fig. context.

c **1175** *Lamb. Hom.* 133 Godes word is sed and crist is þe sawere. **1526** TINDALE *Mark* iv. 14 The sower soweth the worde. **1779** COWPER *The Sower* 3 The Sower is gone forth to sow, And scatter blessings round. **1821** SHELLEY *Hellas* 576 The Greek has reaped The costly harvest his own blood matured, Not the sower, Ali. **1874** W. ST. H. BOURNE *Hymn, 'The sower went forth sowing'* iv. (A. & M.), One day the heavenly Sower Shall reap where He hath sown.

c. A machine or apparatus for sowing seed; a sowing-machine.

1728 CHAMBERS *Cycl.* s.v. *Sembrador*, To remedy this Inconvenience, the *Sembrador* or *Sower*, is invented, which being fastened to the Plough, the whole Business..is done at once. **1844** H. STEPHENS *Bk. Farm* III. 788 A simpler implement than even this has been employed—the hand-flask sower. **1868** *Rep. U.S. Comm. Agric.* (1869) 417 Field No. 1..sown with broadcast sower and cultivator combined.

2. *transf.* One who spreads abroad or disseminates something, esp. what is obnoxious or objectionable; a promoter or propagator *of* discord, sedition, etc.

1380 *Lay Folks Catech.* (Lamb. MS.) 734 Bakbyters and sowers of fals lesynggys. *c* **1386** CHAUCER *Sec. Nun's T.* 192 Almyghty Lord,.. Sower of chaste counseil, herde of us alle. *c* **1450** in *Trevisa's Higden* (Rolls) VIII. 469 The myrroure of ypocrites, the sawer of discorde,.. maister Iohn Wiclif. **1533** BELLENDEN *Livy* III. vii. (S.T.S.) I. 271 Ane cumpany of.. seditious lymmaris, sawaris of discorde. **1583** MELBANCKE *Philotimus* T iv b, Mars the God of discord and sower of all Sedition. **1639** DRUMM. OF HAWTH. *Mem. State* Wks. (1711) 130 Clouis.. caused extirpate that sower of impostures, & all his race. **1855** MACAULAY *Hist. Eng.* xviii. IV. 160 The favourite theme of the sowers of sedition.

sower, obs. f. SEWER *sb.*³, SORE *sb.*² and *sb.*³

sower(ed, etc., obs. forms of SOUR(ED, etc.

Sowetan (sə'wɛtən), *sb.* and *a.* Also **Sowetoan.** [f. *Soweto*, acronym for *So*uth *We*stern *To*wnships, a group of Black African townships outside Johannesburg, S. Africa, which was the focus of much civil unrest in 1976 and subsequent years, + -AN.]

A. *sb.* A native or inhabitant of Soweto.

Also, the name of a Black daily newspaper published in Soweto.

1977 [see SHEBEEN b]. **1978** *Washington Post* 14 Jan. A13/1 Many stayed away out of fear, Sowetans said. **1983** *Economist* 28 May 16/1 Had it not been for the South African police, whose brutality drove some 5,000 young Sowetans abroad.., the ANC would constitute no conceivable threat. **1984** *Financial Times* 20 Feb. (Survey) p. v/7 The West Rand Administration Board.. regulates virtually every part of the Sowetans' existence. **1987** *Christian Science Monitor* 10 Mar. 12/2 Each morning.. about 500,000 Sowetans board trains, buses, or one of some 4,000 privately run mini-bus 'taxis' into Johannesburg.

B. *adj.* Of or pertaining to Soweto or its inhabitants; native to or residing in Soweto.

1977 *Washington Post* 23 Dec. A17/2 Police have picked up steadily increasing numbers of 'shopping bag' or 'suitcase' bombs... Combined with the increasing flow of Sowetan students returning from terrorist training. This makes for a high-risk bomb situation. **1983** *Christian Science Monitor* 1 Aug. 4/3 His watchful Sowetan neighbors look for signs he is 'selling out'. **1987** *Summary World Broadcasts: Middle East* (B.B.C.) 16 Feb. B1 The survey.. found that Sowetan families were best off in the country.

sowff (saʊf), *v. Sc.* Also 8-9 sowf, 9 souf(f. [Later Sc. form of SOLF *v.* See also SOWTH *v.*] *trans.* To sing, hum, or whistle (a tune) softly.

1719 RAMSAY *To Arbuckle* 20, [I] Bang'd up my.. whistle, To sowf ye o'er a short epistle. **1728** —— *Friends in Ireland* 13 Sowfing Sonnets on the Lasses. **1819** R. GALL *Poems* 48 The Scotian Muse.. Wad lead you.. Wi her upo' the knowe to lean An' souf a sang. **1850** W. JAMIE *Stray Effusions* 194 To.. sowff aloud some merry air. **1871** W. ALEXANDER *Johnny Gibb* (1873) 20 [He] began.. to 'sowff' over 'My love she's but a lassie yet'.

sow-gelder. Also 9 -gilder. [f. SOW *sb.*¹] One whose business it is to geld or spay sows.

c **1515** *Cocke Lorell's B.* 4 Here is gylys Iogeler of ayebery, And hym sougelder of lothe bery. **1530** PALSGR. 273/1 Sowe geldre, *chastrevx de trvyes.* **1596** NASHE *Saffron Walden* Wks. (Grosart) III. 169 Vpon euerie stage hee hath beene brought for a Sicophant and a Sow-gelder. *c* **1614** FLETCHER, etc. *Wit at Sev. Weapons* IV. ii, Why thou sawcy issue of some travelling Sow-gelder, What makes love in thy mouth? **1654** WHITLOCK *Zootomia* 131 They never use any of this stuff to their Sow-gelder, or Farrier. *a* **1722** LISLE *Husb.* (1757) 407 A sow-gelder that had cut for me, cut four pigs for a neighbouring farmer. **1749** FIELDING *Tom Jones* IV. viii, Old Echepole, the sowgelder. **1820** SHELLEY *Œd. Tyr.* I. 70 Call in.. Moses the sow-gelder. **1857** BORROW *Romany Rye* xvii, Two respectable-looking individuals, whether farmers or sow-gelders, I know not.

b. In references to the horn blown by the gelder to announce his arrival at a place.

1604 MIDDLETON *Father Hubburd's T.* Wks. (Bullen) VIII. 73 Winding his pipe like a horn.. which must needs make him look like a sow-gelder. **1621** BURTON *Anat. Mel.* III. ii. III. iii. (1651) 472 There needs no more.. but a cryer to go before them.. or for defect a Sowgelder to blow. **1673** [R. LEIGH] *Transp. Reh.* 135 You are disturb'd with the tooting of a sow-gelders horn. **1711** ADDISON *Spect.* No. 251 ¶4 The Sowgelder's Horn has indeed something musical in it, but this is seldom heard within the Liberties.

Hence **sow-geldering** *vbl. sb.*

1664 BUTLER *Hud.* II. i. 718 Semiramis.. Who.. laid foundation Of Sow-geldering operation.

sowing ('səʊɪŋ), *vbl. sb.*¹ [f. SOW *v.*¹]

1. The action of scattering seed.

13.. *Cursor M.* 6378 (Gött.), Moyses.. fand þaim fode in þair nede, widuten sauing of ani sede. **1362** LANGL. *P. Pl.* A. VIII. 102, 'I schal sese of my sowynge,' quod pers, 'and swynke not so harde'. *c* **1440** *Promp. Parv.* 466 Sowynge, of corne and oþer sedys, *sacio,.. seminacio.* **1473** *Rental Bk. Cupar-Angus* (1879) I. 164 In sauyng of quhet, pess, ry and benys. **1523** FITZHERB. *Husb.* §14 Whether it be for the vnseasonablenes of the wether, or for thyn sowynge. **1585** T. WASHINGTON tr. *Nicholay's Voy.* IV. xxxii. 154 b, The sowing of corne was brought in.. by Triptolemus. **1634** SIR T. HERBERT *Travels* 183 The Ananas.. growes nor from Tree nor sowing, but of a root. **1697** DRYDEN *Virg. Georg.* I. 319 Nor cease your sowing till Mid-winter ends. **1767** A. YOUNG *Farmer's Lett. to People* 310 He should attend the culture of the lands, the sowing and harvest. **1841** BROWNING *Pippa Passes* Poems (1905) 185 June reared that bunch of flowers you carry, From seeds of April's sowing. **1896** BADEN-POWELL *Matabele Campaign* viii, The rebels.. are getting tired of war, as it prevents the sowing of next year's crop.

b. In figurative or transf. use.

c **1375** *Sc. Leg. Saints* xxxii. (*Justin*) 337 Woman.. suld man haf hyre make to be, for þe sawyng of þare sede. *c* **1440** *Jacob's Well* 83 Jn þis cornere of wose in þe mowth is sowyng of dyscorde. **1529** MORE *Dyalogue* Pref. A j b, The soweynge & settyng forth of Luthers pestilent heresies in this realme. **1577** HANMER *Anc. Eccl. Hist.* (1619) 538 By sowing of strange doctrine.

2. An instance or occasion of this.

1577 B. GOOGE *Heresbach's Husb.* 42 The grounde must out of hand be plowed.. to make it the meeter for the next sowyng. **1719** LONDON & WISE *Compl. Gard.* 201 The Seeds of the first sowing are generally three Weeks coming up. **1763** MILLS *Pract. Husb.* II. 251 On the eleventh of August I suspended the sowings. **1842** LOUDON *Suburban Hort.* 521 By successive sowings in the open air and on heat. **1899** *Speaker* 25 Nov. 191/2 There can be no cold weather sowings.

fig. and *transf.* **1643** J. CARYL *Expos. Job* I. 287 There is a sowing, which is the work of charity. **1844** THIRLWALL *Greece* lxiv. VIII. 320 So ended the Macedonian war; with a plentiful sowing of the dragon's teeth.

3. That which is sown; the quantity of seed sown at one time.

Not always clearly distinct from sense 2.

1733 W. ELLIS *Chiltern & Vale Farm.* 257 The Salts of the first.. are most agreeable to such late Sowings. **1786** ABERCROMBIE *Gard. Assist.* 334 The earlier sowings are cut off by the frost. **1842** LOUDON *Suburban Hort.* 656 These sowings will come into use in November. **1888** *Cent. Mag.* Oct. 815/1 You could not keep the birds out of the garden. .. They had most of the sowings up.

4. *attrib.* and *Comb.*, as ***sowing-harvest, -season, -time***, etc.

1382 WYCLIF *Lev.* xxvi. 5 The vyndage shal occupie the sowynge tyme. **1532** HERVET *Xenoph. Househ.* 50 b, Whanne .. a man hath chosen his sowynge tyme. **1577** B. GOOGE *Heresbach's Husb.* I. (1586) 23 b, To.. prepare it for the sowing season. *c* **1613** *Social Cond. People Anglesey* (1860) 17 The men go in sowing harvest abroad to begg graine and seed. **1681** *Rector's Bk. Clayworth* (1910) 52 Barley found dry in 3 Fields, having lain so, ever since sowing time. *a* **1722** LISLE *Husb.* (1757) 154 They used not generally to buy their seed-barley, nor seed-oats, but just before sowing-time. **1815** J. SMITH *Panorama Sci. & Art* II. 639 March or April is the sowing season.

b. With the names of seed, in the sense 'suitable or used for sowing', as ***sowing mustard, seed, peas***. Hence *Comm.* in ***sowing orders, requirements***.

1604-5 *Shuttleworths' Acc.* (Chetham Soc.) 160 Towe mettes of sowinge pesen iiij^{s} x^{d}. **1611** BIBLE *Lev.* xi. 37 Any sowing seed which is to be sowen. **1648** HEXHAM II, *Zaet-goedt*, Sowing Seed. **1883** *Daily News* 6 Sept. 2/7 There is a good inquiry for sowing mustard. **1893** *Ibid.* 4 May 7/2 Numerous sowing orders still come to hand.

c. With the names of implements, etc., used in sowing, as ***sowing-gear, -machine, -plough, -sheet***.

1765 *Museum Rust.* IV. 78 A wheat two-wheeled sowing-plough. **1812** SIR J. SINCLAIR *Syst. Husb. Scot.* I. 323 The seed to be deposited by a sowing-machine. **1842** *Penny Cycl.* XXII. 278 The idea.. was followed up.. in the sowing-barrow, an instrument still extensively used for sowing grass-seeds. **1844** H. STEPHENS *Bk. Farm* II. 507 The most convenient form of sowing-sheet. *Ibid.* 535 The sowing-geer of the machine.

† **sowing**, *vbl. sb.*² *Sc. Obs.* [f. SOW *v.*²] Sharp or severe pain.

1375 BARBOUR *Bruce* XVI. 628 Thai that, at the first metyng Of speris, feld so sair sowing.

sowing(e, obs. forms of SEWING *vbl. sb.*¹

† **sow-iron.** *Obs.* [f. SOW *sb.*¹ 6.] Sow-metal. Cf. PIG-IRON.

1608 H. WRIGHT in *Lismore Papers* Ser. II. (1887) I. 127 For the remainder of sowe iron nowe Restinge, there is litle or noe barre Iron made thereof. **1645-52** BOATE *Ireland's Nat. Hist.* (1860) 115 One Tun whereof [*sc.* of merchants-iron] is usually made out of a Tun and a half of Sow-Iron. **1677** YARRANTON *Eng. Impr.* 57 There is yet a most great benefit to the Kingdom in general by the Sow Iron made of the Iron Stone and Roman Cinders in the Forest of Dean. **1709** HEARNE *Collect.* 15 Feb. (O.H.S.) II. 170 The sow Iron [is] the best in the.. world.

'**sowish**, *a. Obs.* [f. SOW *sb.*¹ + -ISH.] Like or resembling (that of) a sow; of a coarse or gross nature.

1570 LEVINS *Manip.* 145 Sowish, *suillus.* **1574** *Life Abp. Canterbury* Pref., To Chr. Rdr., Lest therfore the sowishe papiste off England might walter him wantonly in.. his mirie popishe trumperie. **1602** BRETON *Mother's Blessing* lxxv, A minde that treads good manners vnder feete, A sorrell foretop, and a sowish feature. **1661** GRIFFIN *Doctr. Asse* 7 Perhaps thy sowish Soul hath been a thousand times in the Mire.

sowk(e, obs. variants of SUCK.

sowklar, obs. Sc. variant of SUCKLER.

sowl, *sb.* Now *dial.* Forms: α. 1 sufel, -ol, -ul, 3 suuel, 4 sou(u)el, 5 sowvel, -uel, -fful. β. 4-5 sowel, 5 -il, 4-5 sowyl(le, 5-6 sowell. γ. 3-6, 9 *dial.*, soule, 4, 6, 9 *dial.*, soul, 5 sowlle, 5- sowle, sowl, 6 sole, 7-9 *dial.* sool(e, 8-9 sawl, se(a)wl, etc. [OE. *sufel, sufol*, = MDu. *suvel, zuvel* (Du. *zuivel*), MLG. *suvel*, OHG. *sufil(i* neut., *sufila* fem., ON. *sufl* (Norw. *suvl, sovl, sul*, etc.; MSw. *sufl, sofl*, etc., Sw. *sofvel*, Da. *sul*), of uncertain origin.]

1. Any kind of food eaten with bread, as meat, cheese, etc.; relishing or tasty matter added to liquid or semi-liquid food, or the dish so composed. Also *fig.*

α. *c* **960** *Rule St. Benet* (Schröer) 63 We ȝelyfað þæt ȝenoh sy to dæȝhwamlicum ȝereorde twa ȝesodene sufel for missenlicra manna untrumnesse. *c* **1000** *Ags. Gosp.* John xxi. 5 Cnapan, cweðe ȝe, hæbbe ȝe sufol? *a* **1225** *Ancr. R.* 192 Ne þerf þet meiden sechen nouðer bread, ne suuel, fur þene et his halle. *a* **1300** *Moral Ode* 46 in *E.E.P.* (1862) 23 þider we sended suuel [*sic*] & bred to litel & to selde. *a* **1380** *St. Paula* 38 in Horstm. *Altengl. Leg.* (1878) 4 Oþur souuel vsede heo non But oyle wiþ hire bred alon. *c* **1380** WYCLIF *Sel. Wks.* II. 137 'Children, han ȝe ony sowvel?' þat is, mete to make potage, and to medle among potage. **1382** —— *2 Sam.* xiii. 5 That she ȝyue to me meet, and make sowil [*v.r.* sowfful].

β. *c* **1300** *Havelok* 1143, I ne haue neyþer bred ne sowel. **1382** WYCLIF *Gen.* xxv. 34 So breed takun and the sowil of potage [Esau] ete and dronk and ȝede forth. **14..** *Lat.-Eng. Voc.* in Wr.-Wülcker 579 *Edulia*, sowell. *c* **1475** *Pict. Voc.* Ibid. 788 *Hoc edulium*, sowylle. **1562** TURNER *Herbal* II. (1568) 169 The fyrste grene leaves are sodden for kichin or sowell as other eatable herbes be.

γ. **14..** LANGL. *P. Pl.* B. [xv.] XVI. 11 (MS. Rawl. Poet. 38), To haue my fille of þat fruit [I would] forsake alle other soule. *c* **1425** *Eng. Voc.* in Wr.-Wülcker 661 *Hoc edulium*, sowle. *c* **1440** *Alph. Tales* 201 He had no mor money lefte to by hym with soule vnto his bread bod a peny. **1562** TURNER *Herbal* II. 64 They may be eaten with brede.. for soul or kitchyn. *Ibid.* 66 The most part vse Basil and eate it with oyl & gare sauce for a sowle or kitchen. **1599** T. M[OUFET] *Silkwormes* 54 Feede them therewith (no other soule they craue). **1674** RAY *N. Co. Words* 44 *Sool* or *Sowle*, any thing eaten with bread. **1684** *Yorks. Dial.* 213 (E.D.S.), Here'st Dubler broken, and nowther sowl nor breau. **1775** J. COLLIER (Tim Bobbin) *Misc. Wks.* Introd., Whot wofo Times ar' theese! Pot-baws ar scant, an dear is Seawl and Cheese! **1847-** in dial. glossaries (Pemb., Glamorgan, Derby, Lanc., Yks., etc.).

2. *attrib.* in † ***sowl-pennies, -silver***, money given for the purchase of, or in place of, sowl.

? **1292** *Durham Acc. Rolls* (Surtees) 492 Item servientibus domus pro Soulepen'. **1310-1** *Ibid.* 509 Tribus servientibus ecclesie pro eorum souuelp(enys). **1373-4** *Ibid.* 579 In solucione facta Camerario pro soulesilver servientium suorum. **1460-1** *Ibid.* 90 Johanni Stele,.. pro suo soulesilver. **1522-3** *Ibid.* 255 Pro le metcorn, sowlsilver, et aliis necessariis. **1536-7** *Ibid.* 702 Viginti servientibus infra abbathiam in diebus piscium pro eorum soulsylver.

sowl, obs. or dial. form of SOUL *sb.* and *v.*

† **sowl**, *v.*¹ *Obs. rare.* Also 5 soul-. [Of obscure origin. Cf. WFlem. *sowelen, suwelen* (DeBo), and SOLE *v.*³, SOLL *v.*, SOLWE *v.*] *trans.* To make foul or dirty; to soil. Hence † **sowling** *vbl. sb.*

c **1440** *Promp. Parv.* 466/1 Sowlynge, or solwynge, .. *maculacio.* *a* **1450** *Langland's P. Pl.* B. XIV. 2 (MS. Bodl. 814), þouȝ hit [a suit] be soulid and foul y slepe þerynne on nyȝtis. *Ibid.* 13 þat y ne soulid hit wiþ siȝtte or sum ydil speche.

† **sowl**, *v.*² *Obs.*⁻¹ In 6 soul. [f. SOWL *sb.*] *intr.* To form or serve as a relish.

1589 WARNER *Alb. Eng.* IV. xx. 85, I haue.. a peece of Cheese, as good as tooth may chaw, And bread, and Wildings souling wel.

sowl, *v.*³ Now *dial.* Forms: 7, 9 sole, 8 sol(l, 8-9 sowl(e, soul, 9 soal, s'ool, sool(e, zowl, etc. [Of obscure origin. It is doubtful how far various dialect uses of *soal, soul, sowl*, etc., represent the same word. Cf. SOOL *v.*]

1. *trans.* To pull, seize roughly, etc., *by* the ear or ears. In later use esp. of dogs: To seize (a pig) by the ears.

1607 SHAKS. *Cor.* IV. v. 212 Hee'l go, he sayes, and sole the Porter of Rome Gates by th' eares. **1636** HEYWOOD *Love's Mistress* IV. i, Venus will sole mee by the eares for this. **1671** SKINNER *Etymol. Ling. Angl.*, *To Sowl one by the ears*, vox agro Linc. usitatissima (i.e.) aures summâ vi vellere. [Hence in Ray, Bailey, etc.] **1787-** in dial. glossaries and texts. **1892** M. C. F. MORRIS *Yorks. Folk-T.* 115-6 An irate father threatening to sowle his refractory son 'like a dog sowlin' a pig'.

2. To pull or lug (the ears).

1654 VILVAIN *Epit. Ess.* Pref. a v b, Cynthia bids stay, Lest she should sole my Ears away. **1886** *S.W. Linc. Gloss.* s.v., I'll sowle your ears well for you.

sowld, obs. Sc. var. *should* SHALL *v.*

sowldan, obs. f. SOLDAN.

sowlde, obs. f. SOLD *v.*¹

sowlder, obs. f. SOLDER *sb.*

sowldiour, obs. f. SOLDIER *sb.*

sowle, obs. f. SOLE *sb.*¹ and *a.*, SOUL *sb.*, SOWL *sb.*

sowlth (saʊlt). [ad. Ir. *samhailt* likeness, apparition.] A formless, luminous spectre. Chiefly in the writings of W. B. Yeats.

1829 G. GRIFFIN *Collegians* II. xxviii. 289 The Sowlth was seen upon the Black Lake last week. **1892** W. B. YEATS *Countess Kathleen* iii. 54 Call hither now the sowlths and tevishes. **1895** —— *Poems* 79 Pooka, sowlth, or demon of the pit. **1963** *Times Lit. Suppl.* 1 Feb. 78/4 In the first version [of *The Countess Kathleen*].. there is a naive elaboration, in which 'sheogues', 'tevishies', 'sowlths', and other rustic spirits appear.

sowltwyche, obs. f. SOUTAGE.

† **sowly**, *a. Obs.*⁻¹ In 4 sovly. [Cf. SOWL *v.*¹ and SOLWY *a.*] Dirty, foul, unclean.

13.. *E.E. Allit. P.* B. 1111 Hov schulde þou com to his kyth bot if þou clene were? Nov ar we sore & synful & sovly vch one.

sowm, var. of SOUM *v.*

sowm(e, obs. varr. SOUM *sb.*¹ and *sb.*²; obs. Sc. varr. SUM *sb.*, SWIM *v.*

sow-metal. [f. SOW *sb.*¹ 6. Cf. SOW-IRON.] Cast iron in sows or large ingots as it comes from the blasting- or smelting-furnace.

1674 *Phil. Trans.* XVII. 696 They have of late made it much better than heretofore, by melting the Sow-metal over again. **1746** *Brit. Mag.* 96 The *Nucleus Ferri*, Sow-metal or liquid Iron. **1761** *Ann. Reg.* I. 73/2 His new-invented method of making malleable iron from pig or sow metal. **1839** *Penny Cycl.* XIII. 33/2 The names of *sow metal* and *pig-metal*, which..signify..the blocks of iron which are formed in the large main channels, and..the smaller blocks which are formed in smaller side channels.

attrib. **1676** in *Jrnl. Friends' Hist. Soc.* V. 14 The officers took one mare, and his stithy, and sowmettell pot. **1888** R. LEADER in Addy *Sheffield Gloss.* s.v., The very commonest knives made of it are called sow-metal gudgeons.

sowmir, *Sc.*: see SOUMER *Obs.*

sown (səʊn), *ppl. a.* Also 6–7 sowen. [Pa. pple. of SOW *v.*¹]

1. a. Of seed, etc.: That has been sown, freq. as distinguished from that which has grown of itself.

1578 LYTE *Dodoens* 68 Garden or sowen Woad, brused, is good to be layde upon woundes. **1733** TULL *Horse-Hoeing Husb.* xiv. 196 (Dublin ed.), Poor Slate Land, when it has borne sown St. Foin for six or seven Years,..produces Three Crops of Corn. **1795** BURKE *Th. on Scarcity* Wks. VII. 408 Neither of the sown or natural grass was there.. any remainder. **1837** CARLYLE *Fr. Rev.* I. VII. i, Fires, fevers, sown seeds, chemical mixtures. **1872** C. INNES *Lect. Scot. Legal Antiq.* vi. 242 You will observe that made a late hay harvest compare with our sown grass.

b. With limiting term preceding.

See also *new-sown* s.v. NEW *adv.* 3 a.

1771 *Encycl. Brit.* I. 62/2 The early sown pease have the best chance to produce a crop of corn, and the late sown to produce a crop of straw. **1801** *Farmer's Mag.* Apr. 232 Some of the late sown clover wheats have been attacked by the grub. *Ibid.* Aug. 354 The wheat and rye (Autumn sown crops) are good every where. **1890** *Science-Gossip* XXVI. 167 Our native lark,..busy upon some newly sown grass seed.

2. Of land: Furnished with seed. Also *absol.*, esp. as contrasted with *desert*.

1647 HEXHAM I, Sowne fields, *gezaeyde ackeren.* **1670** PETTUS *Fodinæ Reg.* 87 His fenced Parks, Medows, and sowen Fields. **1801** *Farmer's Mag.* Jan. 94 The later sown fields are only putting forth a braird. *Ibid.* Apr. 228 Some of the sown lands were then but half harrowed. **1859** FITZGERALD *Omar* x, With me along some Strip of Herbage strown That just divides the desert from the sown. **1926** T. E. LAWRENCE *Seven Pillars* (1935) v. lviii. 328 The difference between Hejaz and Syria was the difference between the desert and the sown. **1940** J. BUCHAN *Memory Hold-the-Door* i. 22 We had for our playground both the desert and the sown. **1957** K. KENYON *Digging up Jericho* 29 The age-long struggle of the Desert and the Sown.

sown, obs. f. SOON *adv.* and SOUND; obs. Sc. var. SUN.

sownage: see SOUNDAGE.

sownd, obs. f. SOUND.

Sownday, obs. Sc. var. SUNDAY.

sownde, obs. f. SAND *sb.*¹ and SOUND.

sownder, -ir, obs. ff. SOUNDER; obs. Sc. ff. SUNDER.

sowne, obs. f. SOUND *sb.* and *v.*; obs. Sc. var. SUN *sb.*¹

† **sowne**, *v. Obs.*⁻⁰ [perh. = *sowne*, var. of SOUND *v.*¹] *intr.* (See quot.)

1607 COWELL *Interpreter*, *Sowne*, is a verb neuter, properly belonging to the Exchequer, as a word of their art, signifiing so much, as to be leuiable, or possible to be gathered or collected. For example, estreats that sowne not, are such as the Shyreeue by his industry cannot get, and estreats that sowne, are such as he can gather. [Hence in Phillips, Harris, etc.]

† **sowner.** *Obs.*⁻¹ [app. f. *sowne* SOUND *v.*⁴] ? One who lies in a swoon.

c **1430** *Pilgr. Lyf Manhode* II. xci. (1869) 109 Þat oon hatteth Negligence; þat ooþer is werynesse and letargie þe sownere.

sowp (saʊp), *sb.*¹ *Sc.* and *north. dial.* Also 9 soup, saup. [a. ON. *saup* (cf. Norw. *saup* whey, buttermilk, Icel. *saup* soup), related to *súpa* to sup or sip.] A sup, sip; a small quantity *of* liquor; a drink.

1500–20 DUNBAR *Poems* xl. 27 Off wyne owt of ane choppyne stowp, They drank twa quartis, sowp and sowp. **1721** RAMSAY *Elegy on Patie Birnie* vi, After ilk tune he took a sowp. **1785** BURNS *Earnest Cry & Prayer* xxiv, Wi' sowps o' kail and brats o' claise. **1865** M. R. L[AHEE] *Betty-o'-Yep's Laughable T.* 12 Aw'd a saup o' tea an toast just afore aw seet off. **1873** STANDING *Echoes fr. Lanc. Vale* 22 He were a reg'lar brick for a sowp o' drink. **1877** FRASER *Wigtown* 355 Cud ee spare me a wee sowp o' milk for an unweel wean?

† **sowp**, *sb.*², early Sc. variant of SOUP *sb.*

a **1568** in *Bannatyne MS.* (Hunter. Club) 342/14 He..saw the wyf..sittand at ane fyre..With ane fat sowp, as I hard say.

† **sowp**, *v.*¹ *Sc. Obs.* Forms: 5–6 solp, 6 so(u)p, sowp(e. [Of obscure origin: cf. SOPIT *pa. pple.*]

1. *intr.* To weary, to tire; to become exhausted or worn out.

c **1450** HOLLAND *Howlat* 957 He solpit, he sorowit, in sighingis seir. **1513** DOUGLAS *Æneid* XII. xi. 6 Sum deill or than walxis dolf this syre, Seand his horssis begyn to sowpe and tyre. *c* **1586** *My ladyis pulcritud* 32 in *Montgomerie's Poems* (S.T.S.) 279 For no sair Nor sorrow can I soup.

2. In *pa. pple.* Sunk *in* sorrow, sleep, indolence, etc.; exhausted *with* trouble, travel, etc.; worn out with fatigue or weariness.

(*a*) *c* **1450** HOLLAND *Howlat* 42, I herd ane petuoss appele, with ane pur mane, Solpit in sorowe. *c* **1500** KENNEDIE *Passion of Christ* 1011 My hert is now sowpit in site. **1533** BELLENDEN *Livy* (S.T.S.) II. 7 Icelius, sowpit with hevy teris, went amang the pepil. **1567** *Gude & Godlie B.* (S.T.S.) 118 Thay..hes vs left all solpit in to cair. **1585** JAS. I *Ess. Poesie* (Arb.) 49 Then fra thir newis, in sorrows soped haill. (*b*) **1513** DOUGLAS *Æneid* VI. vii. 1 Thus quhill the portar in sleip sowpit lyis. **1533** BELLENDEN *Livy* I. xii. (S.T.S.) I. 72 Þai war solpit at hame in sleuth and Idilnes. *Ibid.* v. xx. II. 217 Nakit bodyis sowpit full of slepe slane. (*c*) **1515** *Acc. Ld. High Treas. Scot.* V. 39 Thair awne hors sum wes slane, sum wes bursyn, sum crukkit, sum soppit. **1533** BELLENDEN *Livy* I. iii. (S.T.S.) I. 22 Becaus he was sowpit with lang travel, he lay doun in ane..plentuus gerss.

sowp, *v.*² *Obs.* exc. *dial.* [app. related to SOWP *sb.*¹] *trans.* To soak or saturate. Hence **'sowping** *ppl. a.*, drenching, soaking.

1513 DOUGLAS *Æneid* VII. Prol. 35 The soill ysowpit into wattir wak. **1807** J. STAGG *Poems* 19 Fast the patt'ring hail was fa'ing, And the sowping rain as thick. **1855** [ROBINSON] *Whitby Gloss.* s.v., They got fairly sowp'd through.

sowp(e, obs. ff. SUP *v.*¹ and *v.*²

sowper, obs. f. SUPPER.

sowpewaile, var. SUPPOWELL *Obs.*

sow-pig. [f. SOW *sb.*¹ 8 c.] A young female pig, esp. one which has been spayed; a sow.

1548 ELYOT, *Scrofula*,..a littell sow pigge. **1573** TUSSER *Husb.* (1878) 82 One bore pig and sow pig, that sucketh before. **1611** COTGR., *Cochonniere*, a Sow; or Sow-pigge. **1628** FORD *Lover's Mel.* I. ii, There is within a mile or two, a Sow-pig Hath suckt a Brach, and now hunts the Deere.. Aswell as any Hound in Cyprus. *a* **1722** LISLE *Husb.* (1752) 289 A sow-pig will eat well at a month old, but a boar-pig at that age will eat strong. **1760** *Phil. Trans.* LII. 36 The four ..soldiers touching with their swords..a sow-pig, held by an herald. **1838** JAMES *Robber* vi, With a cut in his neck, which has made him bleed like an old sow-pig. **1883** W. G. BLACK *Folk Med.* xii. 198 There the sow-pigs were reared.

sowpil, -le, obs. Sc. var. SUPPLE *a.* and *v.*

sowpowayle, var. SUPPOWELL *Obs.*

sowr, obs. f. SOUR.

† **sowr**, *v. Cant. Obs.*⁻¹ (See quot.)

1725 *New Cant. Dict.*, *Sowr*, to beat violently.

sowre, obs. f. SOAR, SORE *sb.*, SOUR.

sowse, obs. f. SOUCE *sb.*

sowser, obs. f. SAUCER *sb.*

† **sow-stang**, var. of SASTANGE.

1706 PHILLIPS (ed. Kersey), *Sow*, a large Tub with two Ears, carry'd on Mens Shoulders by a Pole or long Stick, call'd a Sow-Stang.

sowter, obs. form of SOUTER.

† **sowth**, *sb. Obs.*⁻¹ [a. ON. *sauð-r* (Icel. *sauður*, Norw. *saud*, *sau*; MSw. *södh*, *söd*, Sw. dial. *sau*, *sö*).] A sheep.

c **1200** ORMIN 15565 Crist..draf hemm alle samenn ut, & nowwt & sowwþess alle.

sowth (saʊθ), *v. Sc.* Also 8 south, 9 sooth. [Alteration of SOWFF *v.*] *trans.* = SOWFF *v.*

? **1784** BURNS in *Wks.* (Globe) 298 To 'south the tune', as our Scotch phrase is, over and over, is the readiest way to catch the inspiration. **1785** —— *Ep. Davie* iv, On braes when we please then, We'll sit and sowth a tune. **1843** *Whistle Binkie* Ser. v. 48 Aye whoo ye, whoo, whoo ye, sowth'd Whistlin' Tam.

sowth, obs. pa. pple. of SEEK *v.*

sowthelase: see *south-lace*, SOUTH-².

sowther, obs. f. SOLDER *sb.* and *v.*

sow-thistle (saʊ'θɪs(ə)l). Also sowthistle, sow thistle. Forms: (see SOW *sb.*¹ and THISTLE *sb.*). [Early ME. *suȝeþistel*, perh. an alteration of the earlier *þuȝe-*, *þúþistel* (see THOW-THISTLE), but cf. also OHG. *sûdistel*, MLG. *sudistel*, *sögedistel*, G. *saudistel*, as the name of various plants. Down to the 17th c. usually written as one word.]

1. One or other of the species of *Sonchus*; a plant belonging to this genus, esp. *S. oleraceus* and *S. asper*, common European weeds characterized by their sharply-toothed thistle-like leaves and milky juice.

a **1250** *MS. Bodley 130* lf. 37 b, *Cardun*, sugeþithstel. *a* **1387** *Sinon. Barthol.* (Anecd. Oxon.) 37 *Rostrum porcinum*, sowethistel. **14..** *Medical MS.* in *Anglia* XIX. 84 Take þe sow-thystill & late hym sethyn in whyt wyn. *c* **1450** *Alphita* (Anecd. Oxon.) 89 *Labrum ueneris*,..sough thistil. *c* **1475** *MS. Bodley 536* lf. 16 b, *Labrum veneris*, sowthestell, when yᵉ [stalk?] is broke he droppes mylke. And he beris ȝowlo floure. **1539** ELYOT *Cast. Helthe* (1541) 28 b, I suppose that Southistel and Dentdelyon, be of like qualities [to cichory]. **1577** B. GOOGE *Heresbach's Husb.* I. (1586) 44 The other that be Sommer Weedes, as Sowthystell, and all other Thystels. **1639** O. WOOD *Alph. Bk. Secrets* 70 Sorrell, Succory, Dandelion, and Sowthistle. **1653** BLITHE *Eng. Improver Impr.* 110 When any of these Rich Lands shall..Over-grow with Weeds, Nettles, Hemlocks, Sow-Thistles, &c. *c* **1711** PETIVER *Gazophyl.* VIII. lxxx, A Sowthistle with purple Flowers. **1770** G. WHITE *Selborne* xxxviii, Milky plants, such as lettuces, dandelions, sow-thistles, are its favourite dish. **1845–50** MRS. LINCOLN *Lect. Bot.* 208 This is very observable in the sowthistle, *Sonchus arvensis.* **1855** DELAMER *Kitchen Garden* (1861) 106 Even although we may be inclined to refuse the sowthistle [as a salad-plant].

fig. **1644** MILTON *Educ.* (1738) 136 We have now to hale and drag our choicest and hopefullest wits to that asinine feast of sowthistles and brambles, which is commonly set before them.

attrib. and *Comb.* **1753** *Chambers' Cycl.* Suppl. s.v. *Thistle*, The purple-flowered field-Cirsium, with..sow-thistle leaves. *Ibid.*, The..sow-thistle-leaved field-Cirsium.

b. Applied to species of the allied genera *Lactuca* and *Prenanthes.* ? *Obs.*

a **1387** *Sinon. Barthol.* (Anecd. Oxon.) 27 *Lactucella*,.. sowethistel. **1760** J. LEE *Introd. Bot.* App. 327 Sow Thistle, *Prenanthes.*

2. With distinguishing or descriptive terms, as ***blue, common, corn, marsh, prickly*** (etc.) ***sow-thistle***; ***broad-, round-, spiny-leaved, blue-, small-, white-flowered sow-thistle*** (see quots.).

1796 WITHERING *Brit. Plants* (ed. 3) III. 674 *Sonchus canadensis.* *Blue Sowthistle. **1597** GERARDE *Herbal* II. xxxi. 231 *Sonchus flore cæruleo.* *Blew flowred Sowthistle. *Ibid.* 230 *Sonchus læuis latifolius.* *Broad leafed Sow-thistle. **1753** *Chambers' Cycl.* Suppl. s.v. *Sonchus*, The *common sowthistle is..recommended..as a refrigerant. **1842** *Penny Cycl.* XXII. 240/2 The most common species is the *Sonchus oleraceus*, the common sow-thistle. **1796** WITHERING *Brit. Plants* (ed. 3) III. 674 *Sonchus arvensis.* *Corn, or Tree Sowthistle. **1855** MISS PRATT *Flower. Plants* III. 200 Corn Sow-thistle, Milk-thistle. **1771** *Encycl. Brit.* III. 617/2 The [sonchus] palustris, or *marsh sow-thistle. **1889** *Science-Gossip* XXV. 45/2, I found the marsh sow-thistle growing abundantly in this district. **1597** GERARDE *Herbal* II. xxxi. 229 *Sonchus asper.* *Prickly Sowthistle. **1725** *Fam. Dict.*, *Sow-Thistle*,..a Plant of which there are two sorts, *viz.* the Hare's-Thistle and prickly Sow-Thistle. **1846–50** A. WOOD *Class-bk. Bot.* 363 *Sonchus asper.* *Rough Sow Thistle. *c* **1710** PETIVER *Cat. Ray's Eng. Herbal* Tab. xiv, *Round leav'd Sowthistle. **1853** MISS PRATT *Flower. Pl.* II. 34 The *Small-flowered Sow-Thistle (*Sonchus Floridanus*). **1597** GERARDE *Herbal* 229 Hares lettuce or *smooth Sow-thistle. **1725** *Fam. Dict.* s.v., The smooth Sow-Thistle has the same Properties as the other. **1758** *Phil. Trans.* L. 513 Smooth or unprickly Sowthistle, Hares Lettuce. **1597** GERARDE *Herbal* II. xxxi. 231 *Sonchus flore niueo.* *Snowe white Sowthistle. **1847** DARLINGTON *Amer. Weeds* (1860) 206 The *Spiny-leaved Sow-thistle (*S. asper*). **1597** GERARDE *Herbal* II. xxxi. 231 *Sonchus arborescens.* *Tree Sowthistle. **1766** *Museum Rust.* VI. 444 Tree Sowthistle [*S. arvensis*]. The root is very creeping, full of milk, and with difficulty eradicated. **1597** GERARDE *Herbal* II. xxxi. 230 *Sonchus læuis flore albo.* *White flowred Sowthistle. *Ibid.* 231 *Sonchus syluaticus.* *Wood Sowthistle.

b. ***downy, Tangier sow-thistle*** (see quots.).

1760 J. LEE *Introd. Bot.* App. 327 Tangier Sow Thistle, *Scorzonera. Ibid.* 329 Downy Sow Thistle, *Andryala.*

sowtlase, var. *south-lace*, see SOUTH-².

sowtwell: see SOUTAGE (quot. 1591).

sox (sɒks), commercial and informal spelling of *socks*, pl. of SOCK *sb.*¹

Also used as the final element in the names of some sports teams, esp. in *U.S. Baseball.*

1905 H. G. WELLS *Kipps* I. ii. 37 He abbreviated every word he could; he would have considered himself the laughing-stock of Wood Street if he had chanced to spell *socks* in any way but 'sox'. **1912** G. FRANKAU *One of Us* v. 41 To dollars deaf, impervious to invective, They plunged profaning hands in shirts and sox. **1942** Z. N. HURSTON in *Amer. Mercury* July 88 Dat broad couldn't make the down payment on a pair of sox. **1948** *Richmond* (Va.) *Times-Dispatch* 11 June 27/1 The Boston Red Sox today socked the Cleveland Indians 15–7. **1965** *Liberator* Aug. 20/1 And Sweet Mac was there; legs crossed, showing his..two-fifty sox. **1977** *West Briton* 25 Aug. 17/7 (Advt.), Assorted nylon plain & fancy short sox.

Soxhlet ('sɒkslət). *Chem.* Also soxhlet. The name of Franz *Soxhlet* (1848–1926), Belgian chemist, used *attrib.* (and † in the possessive) to denote an apparatus and method which he devised for the continuous solvent extraction of a solid.

1889 *Jrnl. Chem. Soc.* LV. 359 When using the ordinary form of Soxhlet extractor, there is always a doubt as to the exact time when the substance is completely extracted, unless the whole apparatus is taken to pieces. **1899** *Jrnl. Physiol.* XXIV. 319, I used casein which had been extracted for a week in Soxhlet's apparatus. **1945** M. F. GLAESSNER *Princ. Micropalaeont.* x. 239 Space and equipment for.. simple porosity and permeability tests, soxhlet extraction of bituminous rock samples, and gas analysis may be provided. **1950** *Jrnl. Org. Chem.* XV. 256 The salt-like product was extracted with butyl alcohol in a Soxhlet apparatus for 6 hours. **1968** R. O. C. NORMAN *Princ. Org. Synthesis* vii. 224 Barium hydroxide is placed in the thimble of a Soxhlet extractor over a flask of boiling acetone.

soy[1] (sɔɪ). Also 7 **souy**. [a. Japanese *soy* (also *shoy*), colloquial form of *shō-yu* or *siyau-yu*, ad. Chinese *shi-yu*, *shi-yau*, etc., f. *shi* salted beans, or the like, used as condiments + *yu* oil. The Japanese form is also the source of Malay *soi*, Du. *soya*, *soja*.]

1. A sauce prepared chiefly in Japan, China, and India, from soybeans, and eaten with fish, etc.

A full account of the method of preparation is given by Ure *Dict. Arts* (1839) 1158.

1696 J. OVINGTON *Voy. Suratt* 397 Souy the choicest of all Sawces. **1699** DAMPIER *Voy.* (1729) II. I. 28, I have been told that Soy is made partly with a fishy Composition.., tho' a Gentleman..told me that it was made only with Wheat, and a Sort of Beans mixt with Water and Salt. **1747–96** MRS. GLASSE *Cookery* x. 174 Dish them up with plain butter and soy. **1779** *Encycl. Brit.* (ed. 2) IV. 2511/2 This legumen.. serves for the preparation of..a pickle celebrated among them [*sc.* the Japanese] under the name of *sooju* or soy. **1817** BYRON *Beppo* vii, From travellers accustom'd from a boy To eat their salmon, at the least, with soy. **1853** *Blackw. Mag.* March 280 She put soy instead of sherry into the soda water compound she was mixing. **1870** YEATS *Nat. Hist. Comm.* II. (1872) 191 A sauce or catsup, as thick as treacle and of a clear black colour, called Soy, which is much esteemed.

2. *Bot.* = SOYBEAN.

1880 BESSEY *Botany* 532 Many more species [of food-plants] are now cultivated in India, such as Chowlee, Black Grain, Soy,..etc. **1884** tr. *De Candolle's Orig. Cultivated Pl.* 330 Soy is also grown in the Malay Archipelago.

3. Equivalent to SOYA 2: *attrib.*, as ***soy biscuit, bottle, flour, jam, oil, protein***; **soy frame**, an ornamental stand with a ring frame used for holding a soy bottle; **soy-sauce** = sense 1. See also SOYBEAN.

1897 *Allbutt's Syst. Med.* III. 225 'Soy' flour..contains about 24 per cent. [of carbo-hydrates],..while some soy biscuits..contain twice as much. **1960** Soy bottle [see *soy frame* below]. **1970** *Canadian Antiques Collector* Oct. 18 (*caption*) Four 12-sided soy bottles with shoulder bands of diamonds cut in high relief. **1788–1815** *Watson & Bradbury Pattern Bk.* in F. Bradbury *Hist. Old Sheffield Plate* (1912) IX. 197 Soy frames... Sugar Tongs... Snuffers. **1912** F. BRADBURY *Hist. Old Sheffield Plate* IX. 271 The soy frames and cruet frames..are sufficiently illustrated here to give a very fair general idea of the different fashions. **1931** E. WENHAM *Domestic Silver* x. 142 Snuffer-trays and soy-frames can be..made into attractive inkstands. **1960** H. HAYWARD *Antique Coll.* 261/2 *Soy frame*, silver or plated oblong or oval stand with ring frame for holding soy or sauce bottles. **1956** B. Y. CHAO *How to cook & eat in Chinese* I. iii. 50 Similar to soy sauce is a *soy jam*, which is much thicker in consistency. **1976** *Billings* (Montana) *Gaz.* 30 June 4-B/1 Soy oil lost some 25 points. **1974** *Sci. Amer.* Feb. 19/1 Soy protein is nutritionally somewhat less complete than meat. **1795** Soy sauce [see SOYBEAN a]. **1818** TODD (transl. Thunberg), *Soy-sauce* is prepared from soy-beans (*dolichos soja*) and salt, mixed with barley or wheat. **1959** R. KIRKBRIDE *Tamiko* vii. 54 They had hors d'oeuvres of raw wild vegetables, sashimi, thin slices of raw tuna and sea bream with soy sauce. **1978** *Nagel's Encycl.-Guide: China* 380 The seven sauces used in the stew are replaced by soy sauce, into which the meat is dipped before being cooked.

†**soy**[2]. *Sc. Obs. rare.* [a. obs. F. *soy* (F. *soie*) silk.] ***silken soy***, silk.

1776 *Gilderoy* in Herd *Sc. Songs* I. 73 His stockings were of silken soy, Wi' garters hanging down. **1783** J. MAYNE *Glasgow* 10 Ev'n little maids..clip, wi' care, the silken soy For Ladies' braws.

soya ('sɔɪə). Also 7 **saio**, 9 **sooja**, **soja**. [a. Du. *soya*, *soja*: see SOY[1].]

1. = SOY[1] 1, 2.

1679 J. LOCKE *Jrnl.* in Ld. King *Life* (1830) I. 249 Mango and saio are two sorts of sauces brought from the East Indies. **1771** J. R. FORSTER tr. *Osbeck's Voy.* I. 253 The Japan Soya is better and dearer than the Chinese. **1842** *Penny Cycl.* XXII. 194/1 The Japanese..likewise prepare with them [seeds of *Soja hispida*] the sauce termed *Sooja*, which has been corrupted into *Soy*. **1866** *Treas. Bot.* 537/1 The Sooja of the Japanese, *G[lycine] Soja*, the only erect species of the genus, a dwarf annual hairy plant. **1905** [see MISO]. **1970** *Times* 20 Apr. 4/5 Liveweight gains in turkeys and pigs..were as good as those with fishmeal or soya.

2. *attrib.*, as ***soya flour, meal, milk, oil***; **soyaburger**, a hamburger made with (beef and) soya beans; also, a mixture of minced beef and soya beans; **soya link** [LINK *sb.*[2] 2 c] = next; **soya sausage**, a sausage made with minced soya beans. Cf. SOYA BEAN.

1953 POHL & KORNBLUTH *Space Merchants* ii. 14 When real meat got scarce, we had soyaburgers ready. **1974** *Globe & Mail* (Toronto) 29 Oct. 15/9 The federal government decided to allow soyaburger products to be marketed. **1930** *Times Lit. Suppl.* 27 Feb. 167/2 Soya flour prepared by the ordinary methods soon turns rancid. **1951** *Good Housek. Home Encycl.* 333/1 Stir in the soya flour. **1965** B. SWEET-ESCOTT *Baker Street Irregular* vii. 200 That unspeakable dish, the soya link, the staple diet of the British in the Mediterranean campaign. **1968** J. W. PURSEGLOVE *Trop. Crops: Dicotyledons* I. 265 Soya meal, the residue after the extraction of the oil, is a very rich protein feeding stuff for livestock. **1977** C. MCFADDEN *Serial* (1978) viii. 22/2 Harvey..drank his soya milk without complaint. **1917** H. A. GARDNER *Paint Researches* xxiii. 316 A series of tests were conducted to determine the rate of drying of soya oil. **1982** *Times* 14 Apr. 11/1 Sunoil, linoil and soyaoil prices appeared to be rising. **1971** D. MEIRING *Wall of Glass* xxiii. 195 They went to the counter. It was soya sausages, potatoes, cabbage.

soya bean. Also †**soja bean**; **soyabean**. [f. SOYA + BEAN.] **a.** = SOYBEAN.

1897 *Publ. Georgia Dept. Agric. 1896* 64 A display of soja beans..a legume of exceptionally fine quality for stock feed. **1905** *Chambers's Jrnl.* Mar. 220/2 Soya beans..are grown all over Japan and in Manchuria. **1930** *Times Lit. Suppl.* 27 Feb. 167/2 The high nutritive value of the soya bean has long been recognized. **1958** *Times Rev. Industry* Apr. 92/2 The 1957 increase was well spread; there were..good crops of soyabeans in the United States. **1968** J. W. PURSEGLOVE *Trop. Crops: Dicotyledons* I. 265 Soya beans are one of the world's most important sources of oil and protein. **1973** *Saint Croix Courier* (St. Stephen, New Brunswick) 26 July 1 Canada is not a big user of soya beans.

b. *attrib.*

1911 *Daily Colonist* (Victoria, B.C.) 6 Apr. 14/2 In the cargo for Victoria was a shipment of 500 tubs of soya bean oil. **1944** V. HODGSON *Diary* 7 May in C. Driver *British at Table* (1983) ii. 16, I have an order with the Dairy for a pound of sausage..of soya bean flour. **1966** GETTENS & STOUT *Painting Materials* 62 Soya Bean Oil... A typical analysis of soya bean oil gives 14 per cent of palmitic acid. **1977** G. SCOTT *Hot Pursuit* iii. 26 Drinking glass after glass of..soya bean milk bought from little carts at every corner.

soybean. Also with hyphen or as two words. [f. SOY[1] + BEAN.]

a. The bean of *Glycine max.*, grown for food.

1795 tr. *C. P. Thunberg's Trav.* IV. 121 Soy-sauce, which is every where and every day used throughout the whole empire,..is prepared from Soy Beans..and salt, mixed with barley or wheat. **1802** PINKERTON *Mod. Geogr.* II. 170 The ginger, the soy bean,..are cultivated here [*sc.* in Japan]. **1882** *Garden* 29 July 93/1 Soy Beans..vary considerably in size, shape, and colour. **1970** *N.Y. Times Encycl. Almanac* 259/2 [Iowa] ranks first in popcorn and oats, and is second in soybeans. **1975** *New Yorker* 26 May 50/3 He said that in the nineteen-sixties the United States 'had excess capacity in corn and soybeans'. **1978** J. IRVING *World according to Garp* xv. 300 A field of corn and a field of soybeans.

b. *attrib.*, esp. as ***soybean oil.***

1935 *Cereal Chemistry* XII. 442 It is only within the last decade that the use of soybean flour for food purposes in this country has been seriously considered. **1938** A. A. HORVATH *Soybean Industry* xiv. 97 Quantities of soybean oil have been used in the manufacture of foundry cores. **1956** B. Y. CHAO *How to cook & eat in Chinese* I. iii. 49 The most important flavourer of Chinese food is *soy-bean sauce* or soy sauce for short. **1967** D. & E. T. RIESMAN *Conversations in Japan* 58 Delicacies such as fresh ginger root, soybean soup, meat and vegetables. **1973** P. THEROUX *Saint Jack* v. 52 Over in an armchair drinking soy-bean milk..sat old Mr. Tan Lim Hock. **1979** C. MACLEOD *Luck runs Out* vii. 76 Her successful campaign to have soybean cutlets put on the menu.

Soyer ('sɔɪə(r)). The name of Alexis Benoît *Soyer* (1809–58), French-born cook to fashionable society in England, subsequently working for Irish famine-relief and with the British army in the Crimea, used *attrib.* and formerly in the possessive, as **Soyer('s) stove**, to designate a table-top cooking-range (the *Magic stove*) developed by him in 1849, or his Field stove invented in 1857. Also *absol.*

1856 A. SOYER *Mod. Housewife* (new ed.) 513 (Advt.), Soyer's Magic Stove and Lilliputian Apparatus, specially adapted for out-door cooking. **1857** —— *Culinary Campaign* 524 These receipts are also applicable for barracks, in camp, or while on the march, by the use of Soyer's New Field Stove, now adopted by the military authorities. **1858** VOLANT & WARREN *Mem. Alexis Soyer* xiii. 157 M. Soyer at once perceived the importance of this little apparatus, and.. it was brought out..as 'Soyer's Magic Stove', to which was added the 'Camp Kitchen'. **1878** *Instructions to Mil. Cooks in Prep. Dinners* 9 The field cooking apparatus in use in the Army are Feetham's and Soyer's stoves... Soyer's stove.. is fitted with a boiler only, and will cook for 50 men. **1941** *Jrnl. R. Army Med. Corps* LXXVII. 274 Soyer stoves or other improvised water heaters. **1981** J. BARNETT *Firing Squad* II. 116 Blackened cauldrons, known in the Army as Soyer stoves, spew thick smoke from tall thin chimneys... The men are offered soup from the Soyers.

soygear, obs. f. SOLDIER *sb.*

soygne, var. of SOIGN *sb.*

soygneusly, -ously, varr. SOIGNOUSLY *adv. Obs.*

soyite, soyittour, obs. Sc. varr. SUIT *sb.*, SUITOR.

soyle, obs. var. SOLE *v.*[2]; obs. f. SOIL(E.

soyne, var. of SOIGN *sb.*; obs. Sc. f. SOON *adv.*

soyny, var. of SOIGN *sb.* and *v.*

soyt(e, obs. Sc. varr. SUIT *sb.*

soytour, obs. Sc. var. SUITOR.

soz- (sɒʊz), **sozo-** ('sɒʊzəʊ), combining forms from Gr. σώζειν, employed in a few modern terms, esp. names given to substances having an antiseptic or preservative character, as ***sozal, sozin, sozol***; ***sozogen*** (hence ***-genetic***), ***-iodol, -iodolate***, etc.

sozzle ('sɒz(ə)l), *sb.* Also **sawzle**, **sorzle**, † **sossle**. [Cf. SOSS *sb.*[1]]

1. *dial.* A sloppy spoon-meat or medicine.

1823 E. MOOR *Suffolk Words* 330 *Sawzles*, slops or drinks, given injudiciously to sick persons. **1892** in *Eng. Dial. Dict.* s.v. *Sossle*, How can she be well? She is always taking one sorzle or other.

2. *U.S.* A slattern; a state of sluttish confusion or disorder.

1848 BARTLETT *Dict. Americanisms* 321 *Sossle*, or *sozzle*, a lazy or sluttish woman. **1854** H. H. RILEY *Puddleford* 119 (Thornton), Mrs. Bird, who was a great sozzle about home. **1867** MRS. WHITNEY *L. Goldthwaite* vii, The woman who.. had always hated..anything like what she called a 'sozzle'.

sozzle ('sɒz(ə)l), *v.* Also **sossel**. [Cf. SOSS *v.*[1]]

1. *trans.* To mix or mingle in a sloppy manner. *dial.*

1836 W. COOPER *Sussex Gloss.* 31 *Sossle*,..to make a slop. **1876** ROBINSON *Whitby Gloss.* 180/2 *Sozzled up*, mingled as mince meats in a mess.

2. *U.S.* **a.** To splash; to wash by splashing.

1845 S. JUDD *Margaret* I. ii, Margaret..sat down and sozzled her feet in the foam. **1892** *Cent. Mag.* Apr. 914 Preparatory to sozzling his face at the sink.

b. (See quot.) Also *intr.*

1848 BARTLETT *Dict. Amer.* 321 *To Sozzle*, to loll; to lounge; to go lazily or sluttishly about the house... 'This woman sozzles up her work.' **1878** ROSE T. COOKE *Happy Dodd* xxxiii. (Thornton), A great lazy sozzlin' girl.

3. *intr.* [Back-formation f. SOZZLED *ppl. a.*] To imbibe intoxicating drink. *slang.*

1937 G. FRANKAU *More of Us* xv. 160 Then Sophie called; and brooding, 'Nice schemozzle If that lot stays to feed as well as sozzle.' **1953** N. FITZGERALD *Midsummer Malice* xx. 242 We can sit here and sozzle gently and enjoy ourselves.

sozzled ('sɒz(ə)ld), *ppl. a. slang.* Also †**sosselled**. [f. SOZZLE *v.*] Intoxicated, drunk; drunken.

1886–96 in Farmer & Henley *Slang* (1903) VI. 301/2 She was thick in the clear, Fairly sosselled on beer. **1904** ADE *True Bills* 26 It was customary to mix Tea,..Egg-nog,..and Straight Goods until..the last Caller was Sozzled. **1921** *Blackw. Mag.* Feb. 157/1, I wasn't what you'd call sozzled. I might have been lit up a bit, but sozzled—no. **1935** D. L. SAYERS *Gaudy Night* xx. 414 He was beautifully sozzled last night. **1951** 'J. WYNDHAM' *Day of Triffids* i. 23 'Gin, blast it! T'hell with gin!'.. The voice gave a sozzled chuckle. **1963** N. MARSH *Dead Water* (1964) i. 13 'She'm sozzled,' said Wally, and indeed, it was so. **1972** E. STAEBLER *Cape Breton Harbour* xiv. 130 With a sozzled smile he began to sing about a little yellow dory.

spa (spɑː, spɔː), *sb.* Also 6, 8 **spau**, 6–9 **spaw**, 7 **spawe**. [A place-name (see sense 1).]

1. With capital. The name of a watering-place in the province of Liège, Belgium, celebrated for the curative properties of its mineral springs. †In early use ***the Spa***.

1565 in Burgon *Life Gresham* (1839) II. 93 And now do I the more feare the danger of this winter, for that I have now lost the comodity..of going to the Spa for this yere. **1590** SPENSER *F.Q.* I. xi. 30 Both Silo this, and Iordan did excell, And th'English Bath, and eke the german Spau. **1619** in *Eng. & Germ.* (Camden) 200 For my health to goe drinke the waters of the Spaw for the few dayes yet remayning of their season. **1665** *Verney Mem.* (1907) II. 243 The first inst. we arrived att the nasty Spaw, and have now begun to drinke the horid sulfer watter. *c* **1723** ARBUTHNOT in *Swift's Lett.* (1766) II. 31, I have of late sent several patients in that case to the Spa, to drink there of the Geronster water, which will not carry from the spot. **1733** COOTE *Ibid.* (1768) IV. 59 A walking-stick, the manufacture of Spa, where she had it made for you. **1780** J. ADAMS *Wks.* (1854) IX. 509, I have received your favour, written after your return from Spa. **1835** *Cycl. Pract. Med.* IV. 475/2 The Geronstere is the most celebrated fountain at Spa after the Pouhon.

b. In generalized sense.

1610 BEAUM. & FL. *Scornf. Lady* III. i, He has yet past cure of Physick, spaw, or any diet, a primitive pox in his bones.

2. a. A medicinal or mineral spring or well.

1626 E. DEANE *Eng. Spaw-Fountain* 9 Doctor Timothy Bright..first gave the name of the *English Spaw* vnto this Fountaine about thirty yeares since, or more. **1652** FRENCH *Yorksh. Spaw* vii. 67 For the better understanding of the nature of this Spaw, I made divers experiments thereof. **1727** W. MATHER *Yng. Man's Comp.* 390 The abundance of Medicinal-Waters.., particularly those of the Spaws in Yorkshire. **1778** W. PRYCE *Mineralog. Cornub.* 8 The migration and egress of Metals and Minerals, is obvious enough in the investigation of Mineral Spaws or Springs. **1843** R. J. GRAVES *Syst. Clin. Med.* xx. 234 Sulphureous waters, such as the Lucan and Harrowgate Spas. **1901** BESANT *Lady of Lynn* vi, The town found itself the possessor of a Spa—and such a Spa!

b. Also ***spa bath, pool***. A health bath containing hot, aerated water. *U.S.*

1974 *Los Angeles Times* 13 Oct. III. 8 (Advt.), The Original Santa Barbara Hotub is a superbly-engineered spa that is beautiful furniture. **1976** *Outdoor Living* (N.Z.) I. II. 59/1 A spa pool is a large, hot bath with aerated water, bubbling softly around, massaging your body. **1977** *Times* 29 Oct. 11/5 The latest craze [in Los Angeles] is bathing with your friends..in a jacuzzi or spa-bath. **1979** *Arizona Daily Star* 8 Apr. J1/5 Spas in or next to the pools are also a hot item. Ragel says he sells spas with about 50 percent of his pools.

3. a. A town, locality, or resort possessing a mineral spring or springs; a watering-place of this kind.

1777 SHERIDAN *Trip Scarb.* I. ii, Even the boors of this northern spa have learned the respect due to a title. **1807** J. BERESFORD *Miseries Hum. Life* xiv. 33 The inland Spa is not a jot behind the Fishing-town in the article of tortures. **1856** MERIVALE *Rom. Emp.* xl. (1865) V. 17 Baiae, the most fashionable of the Roman spas, presented another and more lively spectacle. **1879** T. H. S. ESCOTT *England* I. 175 Bath ..continues..to hold its own as one of the great inland spas of the kingdom.

b. A commercial establishment which offers health and beauty treatment (esp. for women)

through steam baths, exercise equipment, massage, and the like. *U.S.*
1960 *Life* 8 Feb. 111/1 The submerged specter above .. is getting a hydraulic underwater massage at a plush health spa near San Diego called the Golden Gate beauty resort whose customers are usually female. **1976** *Vogue* Dec. 214/1 Most American spas are designed exclusively for women. **1981** W. Safire in *N.Y. Times Mag.* 21 June 10/2 Only fuddy-duddies go to the *gym*, .. the upscale .. crowd goes to the *spa*.

4. *attrib.* and *Comb.*, as ***spa-diet***, ***-drinker***, ***-fountain***, ***-house***, etc. See also SPA-WATER.
1626 E. Deane *Eng. Spaw-Fountain* 26 The most proper season to vndertake this our English *Spaw dyet. **1652** French *Yorksh. Spaw* 100 Of the Dyet to be observed by *Spaw-drinkers. **1626** E. Deane (*title*), Spadacrene Anglica, or, The English *Spaw-Fovntaine. **1630** Hakewill *Apol.* (ed. 2) Z z, Who may perhaps with more benefit .. pertake of this our English Spaw-fountaine. **1812** Bigland in *Beaut. Eng. & Wales* XVI. 355 The *spaw-house is situated on the sea-shore. **1808** Pike *Sources Mississ.* (1810) II. 137 On the west side of said ridge we found *spa springs. **1896** *Allbutt's Syst. Med.* I. 330 The good effects produced by *spa treatment. **1652** French *Yorksh. Spaw* 65 The *Spaw-well near Knares-borow. **1778** *Eng. Gazetteer* (ed. 2) s.v. *Scarborough*, The Spaw-well, as it is improperly called, is a spring a quarter of a mile S. of the town. **1815** Scott *Guy M.* xxxix, At the spaw-well below the craig at Gilsland. **1652** French *Yorksh. Spaw* ix. 83 Giving them such directions for the drinking the waters as the very *Spaw-women themselves laugh at.

Hence **spa** (also **spaa**), *v.* (*a*) *trans.*, to subject to spa-treatment; (*b*) *intr.*, to frequent or visit a spa or spas.
1832 in Medwin *Angler in Wales* (1834) II. 280 Here I am, after being '*spaed*' for a week at Cheltenham. **1847** W. E. Forster in Reid *Life* (1888) I. 206, I have been spaaing in this distinguished company now for three days. I joined them at Matlock on Friday morning.

spa, obs. form of SPAE.

†**spaad.** *Min. Obs.* Also 6–7 spawd(e, 7 spaud. [ad. obs. G. *spad*, *spade*, varr. of *spat* SPATH[1].] A variety of talc, gypsum, or spar, or a powder prepared from one or other of these, mainly used to form moulds for casting metal objects.
1594 Plat *Jewel-ho.* IV. 44, I haue seene oftentimes many good patternes of mettall, cast off very sharpely in spawde alone, but .. you must sprincle the spawd with some moisture. **1651** French *Distill.* v. 172 He that casts them [*sc.* antimony cups] must be skilfull in making his spawde. **1686** Plot *Staffordsh.* 154 [A sand] is sent for by Artists living at a great distance, and used by them as a spaud to cast Metalls with. *a* **1728** Woodward *Fossils* 14 English Talc, of which the coarser Sort is call'd Plaister, or Parget, the finer, Spaad, [or] Earth-Flax. **1738** Chambers *Cycl.* s.v., The various kinds of spaad are found pretty frequently in England and Germany; .. they are all soft, and easily pulverized.

space (speɪs), *sb.*[1] Also 5 sspace, 5–6 spase; *Sc.* 5 spas, 6 spais, spaice, spece, 7 speace. [ad. OF. *espace* (*aspace*, *espasse*, *spaze*, etc., F. *espace*, = Prov. *espaci*, *espazi*, Pg. *espaço*, Sp. *espacio*, It. *spazio*), ad. L. *spatium* (med.L. also *spacium*).]
I. Denoting time or duration.
1. a. Without article: Lapse or extent of time between two definite points, events, etc. Chiefly with adjs., as *little*, *long*, *short*, *small*.
a **1300** *Cursor M.* 6980 Þair faith lasted littel space. **1338** R. Brunne *Chron.* (1810) 213 Grace God gaf him here, þis lond to kepe long space. **1375** Barbour *Bruce* XI. 9 And quhen he herd .. at sic space he had Till purvay hym, he ves rycht glad. *c* **1450** Holland *Howlat* 34 All thar names to nevyn .. war prolixt and lang, and lenthing of space. **1471** Ripley *Comp. Alch.* I. vi. in Ashm. (1652) 130 A yere we take or more for our respyte: For in lesse space our Calxe wyll not be made. *c* **1549** *Registr. Aberdon.* (Maitland) II. 307 With intervale and space necessare of þe law vsit. **1634** Sir T. Herbert *Trav.* 18 They become whole and frolicke, in small space. **1700** Dryden *Sigismunda & Guiscardo* 27 To her Father's Court in little space Restor'd anew. **1782** Cowper *Gilpin* 242 The turnpike gates again Flew open in short space. **1812** Cary *Dante, Parad.* XXIII. 16 Short space ensued; I was not held .. Long in expectance. **1835** T. Mitchell *Acharn. of Aristoph.* 178 A ten years' truce, in short, was .. little more than space allowed for making new preparations for war. **1871** Rossetti *Poems, Staff & Scrip* xxx, O changed in little space! .. O pale that was so red!
†**b.** Delay, deferment. *Obs. rare.*
c **1385** Chaucer *L.G.W.* 440 *Prol.*, [I] al for-ȝeue with oute lengere space. **1540–54** Croke *13 Ps.* (Percy Soc.) 19 Without abode or space Bowe downe thyne ears.
†**c.** ***in space***, after a time or while. *Obs.*
c **1400** *Destr. Troy* 2811 Tyll þai comyn of the cost of Caucleda in spase. **1474** Caxton *Chesse* III. viii. (1883) 148 In space and succession of tyme he departed to them alle his goodes temporell. **1526** *Pilgr. Perf.* (W. de W. 1531) 114 Take muddy water .. & set it alone, .. & in space it wyll waxe clere. **1546**–*a* **1553** [see GRACE *sb.* 15]. *a* **1591** H. Smith *Serm.* (1866) I. 22 In space cometh grace.
†**2.** Time, leisure, or opportunity for doing something. Chiefly in *to have* (or *give*) *space*. *Obs.*
a. Const. *to* (usually with inf.) or *of*.
13.. *Guy Warw.* (1891) p. 556 Berard on þe helme he smot: To stond hadde he no space. *c* **1325** *Body & Soul* in *Map's Poems* (Camden Soc.) 346 A! Ihesu, that us alle hast wrouȝt, .. Of amendement ȝef us space. **1362** Langl. *P. Pl.* A. III. 164 Þenne mornede Meede, and menede hire to þe kyng To haue space to speken, spede ȝif heo mihte. **1445** tr. *Claudian* in *Anglia* XXVIII. 277 The doome of heven also yiveth space to mannys favour in the. **1483** Caxton *Gold. Leg.* 215 b/1 Thenne she prayed .. that she myght haue space to praye. **1508** Kennedie *Flyting w. Dunbar* 373 To eit thy flesch the doggis sall haue na space. **1565** Cooper *Thesaurus* s.v. *Spatium*, They had tyme or space to take aduisement. *a* **1637** B. Jonson *Queen & Huntress*, Give unto the flying hart Space to breathe how short soever. **1675** R. Burthogge *Causa Dei* 102 That very space to Repent .. but confirmeth and emboldens the stubborn and wicked.
b. Without const.
1338 R. Brunne *Chron.* (1810) 86 He may, tille he has space, gif it withouten synnes. **1390** Gower *Conf.* II. 256 Thogh thei hadden litel space, Yit thei acorden in that place. *c* **1430** *How the Good Wijf* in *Babees Bk.* (1868) 42 To compelle a dede to be doon & þere be no space, It is but tyrannye. *c* **1510** More *Picus* Wks. 26 Happly thou shouldest not liue an houre more Thy sinne to clense, and though thou hadst space, Yet paraduenture shouldst thou lacke the grace. **1581** H. Walpole in Allen *Martyrdom Campion* (1908) 46 God graunt they may amend the same while here they have the space. **1601** Shaks. *All's W.* IV. i. 98 Come on, thou art granted space.
c. Coupled with other sbs. denoting time, ability, etc.; esp. in ***time and space***, ***space and time***.
(*a*) *a* **1300** *Assump. Virg.* 172 Þat þu .. ȝef hem boþe wille and space, Hem to amendy er hy beo ded. **1303** R. Brunne *Handl. Synne* 11292, Y þanke þe .. Þat hast lent me wyt and space, Þys yn Englys for to drawe. *a* **1330** *Roland & V.* 127 He bisouȝt ihesu .. To sende him miȝt & space, For to wite þe soþe þere. *c* **1386** Chaucer *Parson's Prol.* 64 For to yeue hym space and audience. *c* **1450** *Godstow Reg.* 18, I cry vn-to ȝow .., That ȝe gete to us repentaunce and space. *c* **1480** *Childe of Bristowe* in Hazl. *E.P.P.* I. 121 And y shal laboure .. to bring your soule in better way, yf y have lyf and space. *c* **1550** Rolland *Crt. Venus* III. 153 Thow sall not aill, and I haif life and space.
(*b*) *c* **1386** Chaucer *Prol.* 35 Whil I haue tyme and space. *c* **1400** *Pilgr. Sowle* (Caxton, 1483) I. xvi. 14 He had space and suffysaunt leyser ynow for to haue enstablysshed procuratours. **1484** Caxton *Fables of Alfonce* iii, Whanne the poure man was before the Juge, he demaunded terme and space for to answere. **1500–20** Dunbar *Poems* xv. 32 Asking wald haif .. Convenient tyme, lasar, and space. [**1821** Scott *Kenilw.* xxxii, 'By my faith, time and space fitting, this were a good tale to tell,' said Leicester.]
3. With *the* (*that*, etc.): **a.** The amount or extent of time comprised or contained in a specified period. Const. *of*, or with preceding genitive.
(*a*) *c* **1340** Hampole *Pr. Consc.* 3933 Þe space of alle ane hale yhere. **1340–70** *Alex. & Dind.* 885 Þe space of hure liuus. *a* **1425** tr. *Arderne's Treat. Fistula*, etc. 91 Late it stande stille without mouyng by þe space of a 'pater noster'. **1484** Caxton *Fables of Alfonce* i, [He] festyed hym by the space of xiiij dayes. **1515** *Sel. Cases Star Chamb.* (Selden) II. 98 He bought the space of xx[ti] yere Irne .. and Retailled the same. **1578** Lyte *Dodoens* 28 The leaves .. dronken in wine by the space of seven dayes healeth the Jaundes. **1604** E. G[rimstone] *D'Acosta's Hist. Indies* III. xvii. 174 In the water whereof, you cannot indure to hold your hand, the space of an *Ave Maria*. **1638** Junius *Paint. Ancients* 99 For the space of many generations it hath been a shop of Arts and Artists. **1726** Swift *Gulliver* III. iii. 197 The former revolves in the space of ten hours. **1793** Smeaton *Edystone L.* §344 In the space of a tide, the salt water has not time to .. return. **1832** Brewster *Nat. Magic* xii. 311 In the space of twenty minutes the eggs were roasted quite hard. **1837** P. Keith *Bot. Lex.* 128 He found that sprigs .. became quite dead in the space of a day.
(*b*) *c* **1386** Chaucer *Man of Law's T.* 916 Duryng the metes space, The child stood lokyng in the kynges face. *c* **1450** *St. Cuthbert* (Surtees) 3617 Before many ȝere space. **1500–20** Dunbar *Poems* xxiii. 26 Thow seis thir wrechis sett .. To gaddir gudis in all thair lyvis space. **1576** Fleming *Panopl. Epist.* 27 Who in seuen dayes space lost two sonnes. **1625** in Foster *Eng. Factories India* (1909) III. 101 Within an howers space shee was burnt to the water. *a* **1648** Ld. Herbert *Hen. VIII* (1683) 45 He had but a Winter's Space; for the War was to begin the next Spring. **1820** Keats *St. Agnes* xvii, In a moment's space. **1825** Scott *Betrothed* xxxi, There was more than three hours' space to the time of rendezvous.
b. The amount of time already specified or indicated, or otherwise determined.
1338 R. Brunne *Chron.* (1810) 305 Bituex prime & none alle voide was þe place. Þe bataile slayn & done alle with-in þat space. **1382** Wyclif *Eccl.* iii. 1 Alle thingus han time, and in ther spaces passen alle thingus vnder the sunne. *c* **1430** Lydg. *Min. Poems* (Percy Soc.) 142 Al the space the masse was seyeng. **1545** *Reg. Privy Council Scot.* I. 16 For payment of the saidis horsemen during the said space. **1586** A. Day *Eng. Secretary* II. (1625) 27, I thought .. I might in this space haue found a season conuenient. **1688** Holme *Armoury* III. 221 Their [*sc.* Jews] Custome is before Marriage to be contracted and after some space to be Married. **1712** W. Fleetwood *Four Serm.* Pref. p. viii, That precious Life, had it pleased God to have prolonged it to the usual Space. **1737** *Gentl. Mag.* VII. 690/2 The Expence of the Fleet within the same Space, exceeded 270,000*l.* **1823** Scott *Quentin D.* xxiv, In less than the space we have mentioned, the Count .. came back to the verge of the forest. **1851** Longf. *Gold. Leg.* ii. Poems (1910) 467 Forty years .. Have I been Prior .., But for that space Never have I beheld thy face!
†**c.** ***in the mean space***, meantime, meanwhile. *Obs.* (Cf. MEAN *a.*[2] 2.)
1538 Elyot, *Interim*, in the mean space or time, in the mean season. **1585** T. Washington tr. *Nicholay's Voy.* I. xx. 26 In the mean space .. we went to see the towne. **1612** Shelton *Quix.* I. I. vi, In the mean Space, Gossip, you may keep them at your House. *a* **1656** Ussher *Ann.* vii. (1658) 815 In the mean space Piso went about in vain, to assaile the Navy. **1760–72** H. Brooke *Fool of Qual.* (1809) IV. 70 God was pleased, in the mean space, to cut off all debate.
ellipt. **1600–6** [see MEAN *a.*[2] 2]. **1637** Heywood *Pleas. Dial.* i. Wks. 1874 VI. 99 Meane space, What did the passengers? **1675** Hobbes *Odyssey* x. 537 Mean space Circe a Ram and black Ewe there had ty'd.
4. a. With *a* and pl.: A period or interval of time.
When used without adj. usually implying a period of short duration.
13.. *Coer de L.* 6123 Withinne a lytyl space .. The castel become on a fyr al. *c* **1374** Chaucer *Troylus* I. 505 But whan he had a space left frome his care, Thus to hymsilf full ofte he ganne complaine. *c* **1400** *Destr. Troy* 10131 A space for his spilt men spedely to graue. *c* **1450** Holland *Howlat* 112 To schape me a schand bird in a schort space. *c* **1475** *Rauf Coilȝear* 334 He kneillit doun in the place. Thankand God ane greit space. **1526** Tindale *Acts* xv. 33 After they hadde taryed there a certayne space. **1568** Grafton *Chron.* II. 259 He and his defended themselues .. a long space. **1633** *Verney Mem.* (1907) I. 77 God hath afflicted you with many sad crosses within a short space. **1697** Dryden *Virg. Georg.* III. 117 Like Diligence requires the Courser's Race; In early Choice; and for a longer Space. **1719** in W. S. Perry *Hist. Coll. Amer. Col. Ch.* I. 219 For a considerable space no one could be heard. **1779** *Mirror* No. 8, After a space, I tired of walking by the Red Sea. **1833** *Act 3 & 4 Will. IV*, c. 46 §80 For any space not exceeding thirty days. **1852** Mrs. Stowe *Uncle Tom's C.* ix, When she found a space to say something to her husband. **1873** Hamerton *Intell. Life* I. v. 28 The incompatibility .. is often very marked if you look at small spaces of time only; but if you consider broader spaces, such as a lifetime, then the incompatibility is not so marked.
b. With *of*. (Freq. ***a space of time***.)
c **1340** Hampole *Pr. Consc.* 436 Þer þre partes er þre spaces talde Of þe lyf of ilk man. *c* **1386** Chaucer *Clerk's T.* 47, I dar the better ask of yow a space Of audience. *c* **1500** *Melusine* 335 Nerbonne where he rested hym a lytel space of tyme. **1565** Cooper *Thesaurus* s.v. *Intercapedo*, After a space of time. **1602** Patericke tr. *Gentillet's Disc.* 90 In this contestation .. remained their affaires by a long and great space of yeares. **1657** Sparrow *Bk. Com. Prayer* (1661) 244 A good space of time to do it in. **1708** Swift *Proc. Bickerstaff* Wks. 1755 II. I. 166 After a competent space of staring at me. **1818** Scott *Br. Lamm.* x, The intervention of an unusual space of sobriety. **1831** —— *Cast. Dang.* ix, An intermediate space of punishment. **1880** Sayce *Introd. Sci. Lang.* I. 230 The number of the vibrations in any given space of time.
c. In the advb. phr. (*for*) ***a space***.
(*a*) *c* **1340** *York Myst.* xiv. 97 A starne to be schynyng a space. **1515** Barclay *Egloges* iii. (1570) B vj/2 Els must he rise and walke him selfe a space. *a* **1548** Hall *Chron.*, *Hen. VIII*, 238 b, She with all the Ladyes entered the tentes, and there warmed them a space. **1667** Milton *P.L.* II. 717 Hov'ring a space, till Winds the signal blow. **1720** Pope *Iliad* XVIII. 389 Yet a space I stay, Then swift pursue thee on the darksome way. **1814** Scott *Lord of Isles* v. xxxiii, He paused a space, his brow he cross'd. **1883** *Longman's Mag.* July 270 Knights! .. leave him lying here a space.
(*b*) **1575** *Mirr. Mag.*, *Q. Cordila* xxv, If I departed for a space withall. ? **1690** T. Watson in Spurgeon *Treas. Dav.* Ps. cxxxvii. 1 The other leaves .. for a space hang down their heads. **1818** Keats *Lett.* Wks. 1889 III. 142, I have had one or two intimations of your going to Hampstead for a space. **1877** 'H. A. Page' *De Quincy* I. ii. 26 Meantime deep peace fell for a space on the family.
†**d.** A period of delay. *Obs.*[−1]
1430–40 Lydg. *Bochas* I. ii. (1554) 56 They departed made no lengar spaces, .. And gan to chose them new dwellyng places.
†**e.** A spell of writing or narration. *Obs.*[−1]
c **1440** *Ipomydon* 528 Of chyld Ipomydon here is a space.
II. Denoting area or extension.
* *Without article, in generalized sense.*
5. a. Linear distance; interval between two or more points or objects.
Freq. with more or less suggestion of sense 6.
1390 Gower *Conf.* III. 107 Astronomie .. makth a man have knowlechinge Of Sterres .. And what betwen hem is of space. **1534** More *Comf. agst. Trib.* I. (1553) A ij, Neyther one fynger breadth of space, nor one minute of tyme from you. **1565** Cooper *Thesaurus* s.v. *Spatium*, *Aequali spatio distare*, to be like space asunder. **1606** Shaks. *Ant. & Cl.* II. iii. 23 Therefore Make space enough betweene you. **1667** Milton *P.L.* VI. 104 'Twixt Host and Host but narrow space was left, A dreadful interval. **1690** Locke *Hum. Und.* II. xiii. §3 This Space, considered barely in length between any two beings, without considering anything else between them, is called distance. **1751** Harris *Hermes* Wks. (1841) 145 Between London and Salisbury there is the extension of space. **1808** Stower *Printer's Gram.* 161 Less space is required after a sloping letter than a perpendicular one. **1876** Voyle & Stevenson *Milit. Dict.* 394/1 *Space*, .. the interval between troops when drawn up in line or column. **1892** A. Oldfield *Man. Typog.* iii, When space is required, a mark similar to a sharp in music should be made.
†**b.** Proper place or relationship. *Obs.*[−1]
1390 Gower *Conf.* II. 24 Min herte .. Som time of hire is sore adrad, And som time it is overglad, Al out of reule and out of space.
6. a. Superficial extent or area; also, extent in three dimensions.
1387 Trevisa *Higden* (Rolls) I. 51 Also Affrica in his kynde haþ lasse space. *c* **1450** *St. Cuthbert* (Surtees) 8130 Also Crayke þai him gaue, With thre myle space aboute to haue. **1451** Capgrave *Life St. Aug.* 3 Asia .. conteyneth as mech in space as do þe othir too parties. **1602** Shaks. *Ham.* II. ii. 261, I could .. count my selfe a King of infinite space; were it not that I haue bad dreames. **1687** A. Lovell tr. *Thevenot's Trav.* II. 78 Large Houses .. which take up a great deal of space because of the spaciousness of the Gardens. **1728** Chambers *Cycl.*, *Space*, in Geometry, is the Area of any Figure. **1815** J. Smith *Panorama Sci. & Art* II. 42 The more it is heated, the more space it takes up. **1845** Stoddart *Gram.* in *Encycl. Metrop.* I. 7/1 We are so constituted, that we cannot conceive certain objects otherwise than as occupying space.
b. Extent or area sufficient for some purpose; room. Also const. *to* with inf.
c **1374** Chaucer *Troylus* I. 714 Certeynly no more hard grace May sit on me, for why? there is no space. *c* **1385** —— *L.G.W.* 1999 *Ariadne*, [He] hath Rovme and eke space To welde an axe or swerde. **1573–80** Tusser *Husb.* (1878) 91 Leaue space and roome, to hillock to coome. **1610** Shaks. *Temp.* I. ii. 492 Might I but through my prison once a day Behold this Mayd: .. space enough Haue I in such a prison.

1671 MILTON *P.R.* II. 339 Our Saviour..beheld In ample space under the broadest shade A Table richly spred. **1842** TENNYSON '*You ask me why*' iv, Where..The strength of some diffusive thought Hath time and space to work and spread. **1869** J. G. HOLLAND *Kathrina, Childhood & Youth* 49 The foul demon who would drive my soul To crime that leaves no space for penitence!

c. Extent or room in a letter, periodical, book, etc., available for, or occupied by, written or printed matter.

c **1530** *Pol., Rel., & L. Poems* (1866) 40, I write no more to you, for lacke of space. **1697** DRYDEN *Virg. Georg.* IV. 218 But streighten'd in my Space, I must forsake This Task. **1774** GOLDSM. *Nat. Hist.* (1776) II. 298 With a studied brevity, his system comprehends the greatest variety, in the smallest space. **1866** *Chambers's Encycl.* VIII. 7/2 Various expressive adjectives,..into the consideration of which our space will not permit us to enter. **1885** *Encycl. Brit.* XVIII. 165/1 In the marginal glosses, where it was an object to save space. **1892** *Photogr. Ann.* II. 279 Nothing has been omitted on the score of space.

d. ***on space***, paid according to the extent occupied by accepted contributions. orig. *U.S.*

1894 E. L. SHUMAN *Steps into Journalism* 83 Articles by the beginner are nearly always submitted 'on space'. **1902** ELIZ. BANKS *Newspaper Girl* 202 The woman..if she is 'on space' will soon find the editors with 'no work on hand to-day—sorry—hope something will turn up to-morrow' attitudes. **1933** E. WAUGH *Scoop* III. i. 259 I've only been on the paper three weeks... It is the first time I've drawn any money... I'm 'on space', you see. **1971** D. AVERST *Guardian* xxv. 357 Williams represented the *Guardian* in St Petersburg at first on a small salary..and then..on space.

e. Room in a newspaper, periodical, etc., or on some other medium, which may be acquired for a specific purpose, esp. advertising.

1930 *Economist* 29 Nov. 1003/2 In advertising Britain is far behind America in buying space. **1940** R. S. LAMBERT *Ariel & All his Quality* vii. 168 Selling 'space'..breeds a very different outlook from providing programmes. **1950** *Times* 7 Feb. 5/5 In the last election, one company gave space to the Communist Party and the Commonwealth Party, but the main newsreels adhered to the general agreement that space should be given only to the main parties.

7. *Metaph.* Continuous, unbounded, or unlimited extension in every direction, regarded as void of matter, or without reference to this. Freq. coupled with *time*.

1656 tr. *Hobbes' Elem. Philos.* (1839) 94 Space is the phantasm of a thing existing without the mind simply. **1734** J. KIRKBY tr. *Barrow's Math. Lect.* x. 176 Space is nothing else but the mere Power, Capacity, Ponibility, or..Interponibility of Magnitude. **1799** *Med. Jrnl.* I. 369 The necessary condition of our intuitive knowledge, i.e. that of space and time. **1892** WESTCOTT *Gospel of Life* 184 All our conceptions are defined by conditions of time and space.

8. *Astr.*, etc. **a.** The immeasurable expanse in which the solar and stellar systems, nebulæ, etc., are situated; the stellar depths.

1667 MILTON *P.L.* I. 650 Space may produce new Worlds. *Ibid.* VII. 89 This which yeelds or fills All space. **1816** SHELLEY *Daemon* I. 251 Each [orb] with undeviating aim..through the depths of space Pursued its wondrous way. **1829** *Chapters Phys. Sci.* 411 They recede so far from us, as to be lost in the immensity of space. **1870** PROCTOR *Other Worlds than Ours* ii. 36 Our earth is as a minute island placed within the ocean of space. **1901**, etc. [see *outer space* s.v. OUTER *a.* 3]. **1924** R. GRAVES *Mock Beggar Hall* 40 May not Space be housing and sheltering millions of other beings like us, or different from us? **1959** *Daily Tel.* 23 Feb. 11/6 For the human body, space begins about 12 miles up, where there is not enough air left to burn a candle. **1961** 'C. E. MAINE' *Man who owned World* vii. 86 Such is human psychology that a living man returning from space attracts less attention than a dead man not returning. **1962** F. I. ORDWAY et al. *Basic Astronautics* ii. 26 On April 12, 1961, a 27-year old Russian air force pilot Yuri Gagarin..whirled once around the earth in an orbit at an average altitude of 158 miles. Some 108 minutes after launching, he had returned to earth the first man to travel in space.

b. In the phrase ***into space***. Also *fig.*

1837 CARLYLE *Fr. Rev.* I. I. i, All Dubarrydom rushes off, with tumult, into infinite Space. **1873** HELPS *Anim. & Mast.* i. (1875) 6 The pamphlet has vanished into space. **1892** *Spectator* 2 Apr. 451/2 He broke away,..and plunged, with a few followers, apparently into space!

c. In more limited sense: Extension in all directions, esp. from a given point.

1827 FARADAY *Chem. Manip.* xxiii. (1842) 586 It is with equal difficulty that they throw off their heat by radiation into space or to other bodies. **1854** TOMLINSON *Arago's Astron.* 95 Suppose the body A is projected..into free space. **1885** LEUDESDORF *Cremona's Proj. Geom.* 33 In the above the geometric forms are supposed to lie in space.

*** In particularized or limited senses.*

9. A certain stretch, extent, or area of ground, surface, sky, etc.; an expanse.

13.. *K. Alis.* 7146 (Laud MS.), On a pleyne he chesep a place, þat biclippeþ a mychel space. **1382** WYCLIF *Josh.* xvii. 18 But thow shalt passe to the hil,..and purge spacis to dwelle. **1432–50** tr. *Higden* (Rolls) I. 51 Þerfore men..folowede not the measures of spaces but reasons of diuision. **1565** COOPER *Thesaurus* s.v. *Spatium*, Great and large spaces in wide roomes. **1577** B. GOOGE tr. *Heresbach's Husb.* 42 Though the Corne be laide..in the floores, yet let there be a space left in the middest. **1600** J. PORY tr. *Leo's Africa* App. 368 In which space is comprehended the fairest, fruitfullest,..and most ciuill part of all Africk. **1651** HOBBES *Leviath.* II. xxi. 107 The water..that otherwise would spread it selfe into a larger space. **1713** tr. *Gregory's Astron.* (1726) I. 154 The Stars.., if they were ever more than seventeen in this Space, pass'd away into Comets. **1794** MRS. RADCLIFFE *Myst. Udolpho* l, The space around the building was silent, and apparently forsaken. **1812** BYRON *Ch. Har.* I. lxxii, The lists are oped, the spacious area clear'd,..No vacant space for lated wight is found. **1841** *Penny Cycl.* XXI. 171/1 A general change of temperature in the earth itself, or communicated from the planetary spaces around it. **1878** BROWNING *La Saisiaz* 6 No blue space in its outspread..challenged my emerging head.

fig. **1592** TIMME *Ten Eng. Lepers* C ij, In religion there is both a centre and a space. **1727** BOLINGBROKE in *Occasional Writer* II. 28 Thus Avarice and Prodigality are at an immense distance; but there is a Space marked out by Virtue between them, where Frugality and Generosity reside together. **1856** *N. Brit. Rev.* XXVI. 57 These free spaces are found as well within the Established Church, as among the dissident bodies.

b. Const. *of* (ground, sea, etc.).

1565 COOPER *Thesaurus, Raucus tractus*, a long space of the sea makynge an hoarse noyse. **1665** MANLEY *Grotius' Low-C. Wars* 797 Taking into their Works..a great space of Ground without the Town. **1697** DRYDEN *Virg. Georg.* III. 531 So vast a Space Of Wilds unknown..Allures their Eyes. **1708** J. PHILIPS *Cyder* I. 459 Sailing the Spaces of the boundless Deep. **1746** FRANCIS tr. *Horace, Sat.* II. vi. 204 And now the Night, elaps'd Eleven, Possess'd the middle Space of Heaven. **1815** SHELLEY *Alastor* 405 A little space of green expanse. **1833** TENNYSON *Lady of Shalott* I. ii, Four gray towers Overlook a space of flowers. **1891** FARRAR *Darkn. & Dawn* xxxvii, The *graffito* scrawled upon every blank space of wall in Rome.

fig. **1601** SHAKS. *Jul. C.* IV. iii. 25 Shall we..sell the mighty space of our large Honors For so much trash. **1605** —— *Lear* IV. vi. 278 Oh indistinguish'd space of Womans will. **1818** SHELLEY *Rosalind* 952 And then I sunk in his embrace, Enclosing there a mighty space Of love. *a* **1854** H. REED *Lect. Brit. Poets* xv. (1857) 355 The vast spaces of our English poetry.

†**c.** With poss. pron. The place where one takes up a position, residence, etc. *Obs. rare.*

c **1460** *Play Sacram.* 461 Yea goo we to than & take owr space & looke owr daggaris be sharpe & kene. **1606** SHAKS. *Ant. & Cl.* I. i. 34 Let..the wide Arch Of the raing'd Empire fall: Heere is my space.

d. *ellipt.* in pl. (Cf. sense 8.)

1821 SHELLEY *Hellas* Prol. 75 The senate of the Gods is met, Each in his rank and station set; There is silence in the spaces. **1871** B. TAYLOR *Faust* (1875) II. 6 But if there burst from these eternal spaces A flood of flame, we stand confounded ever.

e. = *living space* (a) s.v. LIVING *vbl. sb.* 7 a. *slang* (chiefly *N. Amer.*).

1976 *New Times* 19 Mar. 36 Werner Erhard through est, has created the 'space' for them to 'be' and given them the 'opportunity' to 'take responsibility' for their lives. **1977** C. MCFADDEN *Serial* (1978) iii. 13/2 Leonard had a lot going for him otherwise, and Kate liked the space he was in. **1980** G. B. TRUDEAU *Tad Overweight*, Seriously, I think I know where you're coming from, and I'd like to share that space. **1981** *Gossip* (Holiday Special) 31/3 The reason why I can say that so boldly is because they give me my space. They let me be me.

10. a. A more or less limited area or extent; a small portion of space (in sense 6 a or 8 c).

c **1380** *Sir Ferumb.* 2247 Neymes..3yf him a strok ounride wiþ-inne þe neckes space. *c* **1391** CHAUCER *Astrol.* I. §2 This ring rennyth..in so Rowm a space þat hit desturbith nat the instrument. **14..** *Nom.* in Wr.-Wülcker 675 *Hoc intercilium*, the space betwene the eyn. **1483** *Cath. Angl.* 351/1 Þe Space be-twene sculders, *jnterscapulum*. **1530** PALSGR. 273/2 Space bytwene the eyes, *entroeil*. **1577** B. GOOGE tr. *Heresbach's Husb.* 42 Leauing open a space for twoo doores. **1594** T. B. *La Primaud. Fr. Acad.* II. 150 That there might bee a more free and easie space for the motion of the animal spirite. **1706** PHILLIPS (ed. Kersey) *Vacuum Disseminatum*, or *Interspersum*, *i.e.* small void Spaces spread about between the Particles of Bodies. **1728** CHAMBERS *Cycl.* s.v. *Area*, The Elliptic Space PSD being drawn equal to the other ASB. **1827** FARADAY *Chem. Manip.* vi. (1842) 179 Even the space left open round the neck may be closed when desirable. **1845** LINDLEY *Sch. Bot.* (1854) 16 A viscid secreting space called the stigma. **1879** HARLAN *Eyesight* iii. 37 The most sensitive portion is a small space directly in the line of vision, called the yellow spot.

b. A part or portion marked off in some way; a division, section.

c **1391** CHAUCER *Astrol.* I. §20 Next thise azymutz..ben ther 12 deuysiouns embelif,..þat shewen the spaces of the howres of planetes. **1398** TREVISA *Barth. De P.R.* VIII. xvi. (1495) 322 As the cercle that hyghte Zodiacus is dystyngued in xii spaces,..so the cercle of the sonne is distingued in xii spaces. **1474** CAXTON *Chesse* IV. ii. (1883) 166 He may not meue but in to one space or poynt. **1625** N. CARPENTER *Geogr. Delin.* I. ix. (1635) 202 Spaces are portions in the Spheare bounded by the Parallel circles. **1669** STURMY *Mariner's Mag.* VII. xxix. 44 Take a short space of a Ruler or Transom, and saw in one side of it a Notch. **1825** J. NICHOLSON *Operat. Mechanic* 129 Set those six spaces off upon a straight line for a base..; set off three spaces upon the perpendicular.

c. A void or empty place or part.

1837 P. KEITH *Bot. Lex.* 95 The..rudiment of the future seed, not yet inclosing a space. **1850** H. REED *Lect. Eng. Lit.* iv. (1855) 140 His human heart had large spaces to hold his fellow-beings in. **1888** ROLLESTON & JACKSON *Anim. Life* 131 The cilia..cause the currents of water to flow..into the interlamellar spaces.

d. A portion of a page (in a newspaper, etc.) available for a specific purpose, esp. advertising; a period or interval of broadcasting time available to or occupied by a particular programme or advertising 'slot'. Esp. in injuction ***watch this space!*** (freq. *transf.*). Cf. sense 6 e above.

1917 *B.E.F. Times* 20 Jan. 15/2 (Advt.), Watch this Space. **1956** *B.B.C. Handbk. 1957* 78 Plays from the West End..are often heard in the more 'popular' programme spaces. **1972** *Sci. Amer.* Feb. 114/1 Kant's own book was discussed in this space a couple of years ago from the paper-back edition issued by the University of Michigan Press. **1979** J. RATHBONE *Euro-Killers* iv. 44 Where is he? Watch this space for exciting revelations in the next few days.

11. a. An interval; a length of way; a distance.

1382 WYCLIF *Gen.* xxxii. 16 Goo 3e bifore me, and be there a space bitwixe flok and flok. **14..** *Sir Beues* (M.) 1130 And Beues rode forth swith harde Towarde the cite of Damas, That was a full feyre space. **1481–90** *Howard Househ. Bks.* (Roxb.) 200 The space to be a fote and halffe betwene the stodes. *a* **1533** LD. BERNERS *Huon* lviii. 198 He was a grete space before all his company. **1585** T. WASHINGTON tr. *Nicholay's Voy.* III. viii. 82 [They] go backwarde a certeine space. **1604** E. G[RIMSTONE] *D'Acosta's Hist. Indies* I. vi. 20 The firme land runnes an infinite space. **1634** SIR T. HERBERT *Trav.* 29 The space from one Boa [buoy] to another, is an hundred paces or more. **1743** W. EMERSON *Fluxions* 109 That is, the Space is always as the Square of the Time. **1807** WORDSW. *White Doe* VI. 161 Apart, some little space, was made The grave where Francis must be laid. **1810** SCOTT *Let.* in *Lockhart* (1837) II. viii. 304 It corresponds..very commonly with the proper and usual space between comma and comma. **1842** THORNTON *Mod. Cabinet Arts* 159 An appreciable difference in the space which separates the stars.

b. Const. *of* (the precise distance).

1382 WYCLIF *Gen.* xxx. 36 He..putte a space of thre daies weye bitwix hem and his dow3tir husbonde. *c* **1440** *Ipomydon* 1466 He had not slepyd..Not the space of a myle [etc.]. **1483** *Sc. Acts, Jas. III* (1875) XII. 32/2 He sal nocht cum..to þe space of sex myle neir þe place. **1526** TINDALE *Rev.* xiv. 20 Bloud cam out..by the space off a thowsande and iiij score furlongs. **1627** *Reg. Privy Council Scot.* Ser. II. VIII. 402 He wes caryed doun in the streame thairof abone ane pair of buttis space.

c. ***from space to space***, at (regular) intervals.

1763 MILLS *Pract. Husb.* IV. 368 To hang upon the vines, from space to space (the nearer the better), phials half filled with sugared water. **1814** SCOTT *Wav.* ix, A heavy balustrade, ornamented from space to space with huge grotesque figures of animals. **1831** —— *Ct. Rob.* xvii, A long,..arched passage, well supplied with air from space to space.

d. A short distance.

1813 SCOTT *Rokeby* I. vii, Now Oswald stood a space aside. **1836** J. H. NEWMAN *Par. Serm.* III. vii. 105 He did not merely approach a space, and then stand as a coward.

†**12.** Course, custom, procedure. *Obs. rare.*

13.. *E.E. Allit. P.* B. 755, I schal my þro steke, & spare spakly of spyt in space of my þewez. *c* **1386** CHAUCER *Prol.* 176 This ilke monk leet olde thinges pace, And helde after the newe world the space.

13. The dimensional extent occupied by a body or lying within certain limits.

1530 PALSGR. 273/2 Space of ones body, *corpsage*. **1675** R. BURTHOGGE *Causa Dei* 28 Some of the Platonists..affirmed that the Place of Hell was all that space between the Moon ..and This. **1678** HOBBES *Decam.* Wks. 1845 VII. 91 They cannot be parted except the air..can enter and fill the space made by their dirempition. **1715** tr. *Gregory's Astron.* (1726) II. 702 That all the Air..is compress'd into the Space *ABZX*. **1823** LAMB *Elia* II. *Old Margate Hoy*, The things do not fill up that space, which the idea of them seemed to take up in his mind. **1842** LOUDON *Suburban Hort.* 193 If we..take the space rendered opaque by the wood at 21 per cent.

14. *Mus.* One or other of the degrees or intervals between the lines of a staff.

1597 MORLEY *Introd. Mus.* 4 You must then recken downe from the Cliefe,..assigning to euerie space and rule a seuerall Keye. **1662** PLAYFORD *Skill Mus.* I. i. 3 The Gamut is drawn upon fourteen Rules, and their Spaces. **1728** CHAMBERS *Cycl.* s.v. *Staff*, Each Line and Space he [Guido Aretino] mark'd at the beginning of the Staff with Gregory's Seven Letters. **1782** MISS BURNEY *Cecilia* X. x, All that torment of first and second position, and E upon the first line, and F upon the first space! **1848** RIMBAULT *Pianoforte* 15 The additional lines and spaces above and below the staff. **1883** *Grove's Dict. Mus.* III. 647/2 The spaces in the treble stave make the word *face*.

15. a. An interval or blank between words, or lines, in printed or written matter.

1676 J. MOXON *Print Lett.* 7 The Distance between one word and another is called a Space. **1706** PHILLIPS (ed. Kersey) *A Blank*, a void space in Writing. **1791** BOSWELL *Johnson* an. 1748 (Oxf. ed.) I. 128 The words..having been first written down with spaces left between them, he delivered in writing their etymologies [etc.]. **1849** CRAIG, *Leads*..[do] not make any impression in printing, but leave a white space where placed. **1908** [MISS FOWLER] *Betw. Trent & Ancholme* 21 Leaving a space for his own name.

b. *Typog.* One or other of certain small pieces of cast-metal, of various thicknesses and shorter than a type, used to separate words (or letters in a word), and also to justify the line.

1676 MOXON *Print Lett.* 11 You must indent your Line four Spaces at least. **1683** —— *Mech. Exerc., Printing* xxii. ¶4 Thin-spaces being..Cast only that the Compositer may Justifie his Lines the Truer. **1771** LUCKOMBE *Hist. Print.* 278 We may count four sorts of Spaces for composing,..besides Spaces for justifying, called Hair Spaces. **1808** STOWER *Printer's Gram.* 161 Spaces are cast to such a regular gradation, that no excuse can be offered..for irregular spacing. **1892** A. OLDFIELD *Man. Typog.* ii, There are five kinds of spaces: the en quadrat; thick space..; middle or 4-em spaces..; thin or 5-em spaces..; and hair spaces.

c. *Telecommunications.* An interval between consecutive marks in a mark-space signalling system such as telegraphy. Opp. MARK *sb.*[1] 13 e.

1859, etc. [see MARK *sb.*[1] 13 e]. **1906** A. E. KENNELLY *Wireless Telegr.* xi. 153 A dash has the length of three dots, and the space separating dots or dashes in a letter are [*sic*] of dot length... The space separating adjacent letters is three dots long and the space separating words, six dots long. **1954** *Electronic Engin.* XXVI. 230/1 The principle..is to explore the centre of each received signal element..to determine whether it is 'mark' or 'space', and use the information so obtained to initiate new signals of correct length. **1968** D. C. GREEN *Radio & Line Transmission (A)* xvi. 292 [In the Murray code] each character is represented by a combination of five signal elements that may be either a mark or a space. In Great Britain a mark is represented by a negative potential or the presence of a tone and a space is represented by a positive potential or the absence of a tone.

16. In specific uses (see quots.).

For *half-*, *quarter-space* see HALF- II. n, QUARTER *sb.* 31. **1846** *Jrnl. R. Agric. Soc.* VII. 207 (Short-horns), The part commonly called 'the space' from the hip to the rib is generally recommended to be short. **1883** M. P. BALE *Saw-Mills* 336 *Space*, the space is the distance from one saw tooth to another, measured at the points. **1884** COUES *N. Amer. Birds* 87 The former places [on a bird's skin] are called tracts or pterylæ.., the latter, spaces or apteria. **1899** *Allbutt's Syst. Med.* VI. 10 In some cases a distinct pulsation may also be felt in the second left [intercostal] space.

17. *Math.* An instance of any of various mathematical concepts, usu. regarded as a set of points having some specified structure; cf. *metric space*, *topological space*, *vector space*.

1911 *Trans. Amer. Math. Soc.* XII. 287 It is not always necessary to set up a definition of distance for the Hilbert space; for other domains of objects to do so might be very difficult or even impossible. **1927** *Bull. Amer. Math. Soc.* XXXIII. 14 The Hilbert space of infinitely many dimensions in which the coordinates $x_1, x_2, x_3, \ldots, x_n, \ldots$ of each point are subject to the condition that the sum of their squares be a convergent series is a metric space in which distance is defined by the formula [etc.]. **1932** M. H. STONE *Linear Transformations in Hilbert Space* i. 1 The word 'space' has gradually acquired a mathematical significance so broad that it is virtually equivalent to the word 'class', as used in logic. **1964** A. P. & W. ROBERTSON *Topological Vector Spaces* i. 5 A topological space is a set provided with a structure that enables convergence and continuity to be considered. **1968** P. A. P. MORAN *Introd. Probability Theory* i. 2 The experiment can turn out in one of a..number of exclusive ways which we denote as $E_1, E_2, E_3, \ldots$, and which we call the 'elementary events'. The set of all such events is called the 'space' of elementary events.

III. *attrib.* and *Comb.*

18. Simple attrib. **a.** In the sense of 'used for spacing (in printing, typing, etc.)', as *space-band*, *-bar*, *-gauge*, *-key*, *-line*, *-rule*; also 'used for holding spaces', as *space-barge*, *-box*, *-paper*.

1771 LUCKOMBE *Hist. Print.* 282 Care should be taken by a Founder to cast Space rules to a true Straight-line. **1798** THORNE *Spec. Printing Types*, Space lines, 4 to english and 4 to pica. **1825** HANSARD *Typographia* Index, Leads or metal space lines. **1858** SIMMONDS *Dict. Trade*, *Space-lines*, printers' leads for justifying, or filling up lines or words, made from 4 to 12 in pica. *Ibid.*, *Space-rule*, a thin piece of metal, type-height, of different lengths, used by compositors for making a delicate line in algebraic and other formulæ. **1875** KNIGHT *Dict. Mech.* 2677/1 By holding the space-key [of a type-writer] down while an 'I' and 'S' are struck. **1888** JACOBI *Printers' Vocab.* 129. **1888** J. HARRISON *Man. Type-Writer* 18 In front of the four banks of keys there is a narrow strip of wood which is called the 'space-bar'. *Ibid.* 25 The 'space-gauge' is a little thumb-piece at the extreme right of the carriage. **1895** E. COLLYNS *Typists' Man.* 17 The space between the lines is regulated by the 'Space Gauge'. **1904** C. T. JACOBI *Printing* (ed. 3) x. 132 A stationary box..contains a series of space-bands. **1919** B. DE BEAR *Typewriting* 22 You depress the space-bar whenever you want to leave a space in a line of the work. **1930** *Daily Express* 23 May 4/6 Spacebands are pushed up to fill out the line to the required width, and then the whole line is automatically conveyed to the face of a mould and filled with molten metal. **1957** *Encycl. Brit.* XVIII. 502/2 By touching another key, a double wedge spaceband is placed between the words. **1962** *Which?* Dec. 359/2 The space bar ..moved the carriage exactly half a space when depressed, the other half when released.

b. Relating to space as a general concept or relation, as *space-consciousness*, *continuum*, *-effect*, *-element*, *harmony*, *-image*, *music*, *-occupancy*, *-perception*, *-relation*, *-sensation*, *-sense*, *-symmetry*, *-value*, etc.

1862 SPENCER *First Princ.* II. v. §59 (1875) 189 We can mentally diminish the velocity or space-element of motion. **1865** S. HODGSON *Time & Space* ii. 65 Their space-relations are not capable of analysis into relations of time. *Ibid.* 75 The space-senses sight and touch..are brought into play simultaneously with the other senses. **1871** SPENCER *Princ. Psychol.* (1872) II. VI. xiv. 194 The various structures fitting the infant for apprehensions of space-relations. *Ibid.* 196 Some space-consciousness accompanies the sensation of taste. **1872** GREEN *Lett.* (1901) 338 The most wonderful church in point of space-effect (if I may coin the word) I ever saw. **1875** G. H. LEWES *Probl. Life & Mind* II. 278 What is signified in speaking of material extension is space-occupancy. **1884** tr. *Lotze's Metaph.* 286 It is essential that the directions..should be unmistakably distinguished in the space-image. **1886** W. JAMES *Let.* 12 Sept. in R. B. Perry *Tht. & Char. W. James* (1935) I. 604 Of already written things I have a long-finished article on space perception, [etc.]. **1890** —— *Princ. Psychol.* II. xx. 195 Let the movement *bc*, of a certain joint, derive its absolute space-value from the cutaneous feeling it is always capable of engendering. *Ibid.* 219 We must..seek to discover *by what means* the circumstances can so have transformed a space-sensation. **1893** *Month* Apr. 483 It is contrary to all our experience of space-occupancy. **1911** W. JAMES *Some Probl. Philos.* xi. 182 God, as the orthodox believe, created the space-continuum, with its infinite parts already standing in it, by an instantaneous *fiat*. **1924** R. M. OGDEN tr. *Koffka's Growth of Mind* 72 Psychology of space-perception. **1932** F. L. WRIGHT *Autobiogr.* II. 145 Freedom of floorspace and elimination of useless heights worked a miracle in the new dwelling place... An entirely new sense of space values in architecture came home. **1933** H. READ *Art Now* ii. 78 At our period the artist..had to infer the extension of plane surfaces..the placing of all objects in a space continuum. **1957** —— *Tenth Muse* xxxi. 279 A distinction between an aesthetic consciousness determined by time-sense (music and poetry) and an aesthetic consciousness determined by space-sense (the plastic arts). **1963** *Times* 30 Apr. 15/1 A 'poème plastique', written in 1918, uses the very up-to-date idea of instrumental units separated in space; a kind of early stereophonic, space music. **1965** W. LAMB *Posture & Gesture* iv. 56 The process of variation, sometimes under the heading Narrow-Wide, is recognized and figures as a component in 'Space Harmonies'. **1977** 'J. LE CARRÉ' *Hon. Schoolboy* xix. 467 Jerry..walked into the reception room. ..Space music was playing and there was even conversation under it. **1979** *Nature* 11 Oct. 433/1 Depending on the symmetry of the lattice and of the arrangement of the atoms within each cell, a crystal is assigned to one of the 230 possible space-symmetry groups.

c. In applied mathematics, as *space-centrode*, *-coordinate*, *-derivative*, *-integral*, *-inversion*, *-locus*, *-path*, *-point*, etc.

1873 J. C. MAXWELL *Electr. & Magnetism* II. 187 The work done by the force *J* 1 during the impulse is the space integral of the force. **1881** *Ibid.* (ed. 2) I. 16, I shall call the vector *J* the space-variation of the scalar function ψ. **1882** MINCHIN *Unipl. Kinemat.* 41 Notation for Space-Points and for Body-Points. *Ibid.* 87 The rolling of the Body Centrode on the Space Centrode. **1888** *Rep. Brit. Assoc. Adv. Sci. 1887* 507 Certain relations which held between the fluid velocities *u, v, w*, and their space-derivatives at any point of a rigid boundary. **1967** CONDON & ODISHAW *Handbk. Physics* (ed. 2) II. vi. 41/1 The Minkowski matrix η is a Lorentz matrix which defines the space-inversion transformation $x' = -x, y' = -y, z' = -z, t' = -t$. **1968** M. S. LIVINGSTON *Particle Physics* vii. 137 Scientists, philosophers, and others have been interested in the significance of space-inversion invariance. **1970** G. K. WOODGATE *Elem. Atomic Struct.* iii. 41 And r_i is the space-co-ordinate of the incident wave at the position of the *i*th electron.

d. orig. *U.S.* In the sense 'paid by or calculated upon the extent of space occupied', as *space-artist*, *-writer*; *space-bill*, *rate*, *writing*; relating to the purchase of (advertising, etc.) space, as *space-buyer*, *salesman*.

1887 *Westm. Rev.* Oct. 858 The general substitution of 'space writing' for the work of salaried reporters. **1895** S. R. HOLE *Tour Amer.* 190 News editors, copy-readers, and space-writers. **1902** E. BANKS *Autobiogr. Newspaper Girl* 207 [By] the 'guarantee space' system..a member of the staff is guaranteed a stipulated sum of money every week, and as much over that amount as he or she makes by writing at ordinary or special space-rates. *Ibid.* 233 Space artists get paid two dollars a single-column cut. **1934** S. BECKETT *More Pricks than Kicks* 92 'Well' insisted the space-writer. **1939** F. M. FORD *Let.* 14 Mar. (1965) 316 You can be certain of occupying a certain space in the pages of the Review and being paid at the usual..space rates. **1948** G. V. GALWEY *Lift & Drop* i. 11 Mrs Lawson, the space-buyer of Rooster's. **1954** KOESTLER *Invisible Writing* IV. xxxv. 377 Dr. Magnus..was now space-salesman for an obscure little Polish gazette. **1972** G. BROMLEY *In Absence of Body* iii. 41 He's the chief space buyer. **1979** *Amer. Film* July–Aug. 55/1 'Now who in the audience will know what a space salesman is?' quizzed Jaffe; a space salesman sells advertising space in a magazine.

e. In sense 8 a, outer space regarded as a field for human activity; (many of these formations are modelled on analogous uses of *air*, *air-*): *space agency*, *biology*, *bus*, *conquest*, *-crew*, *doctor*, *exploration*, *explorer*, *journey*, *law*, *lifeboat*, *liner*, *museum*, *navigation*, *navigator*, *pilot*, *relay*, *research*, *science*, *scientist*, *taxi*, *technology*, *travel*, *traveller*, *tug*, etc.

1958 *Science* 11 Apr. 807/2 Herbert F. York..has been named chief scientist of the Defense Department's new space agency. **1970** *Times* 15 Apr. 1/5 This firm decision was taken today by the space agency in preference to the much riskier feat of attempting a landing a day earlier after a faster return. **1960** *IRE Trans. Military Electronics* IV. 284/2 To gain some insight into the problems..ultimately to be studied in space biology, using these missiles as experimental tools. **1977** J. TODD in S. Brand *Space Colonies* 49/2 During the hey-day of interest in space exploration (summer 1962) a symposium on the ecological aspects of space biology was convened. **1961** *New Scientist* 27 July 216 Ultimately, the space bus named *Ranger* will find its way to the moon, running on electric power drawn from the sun. **1967** *Boston Sunday Globe* 23 Apr. 1/4 Komarov, 40, spent 24 hours 17 minutes in space Oct. 12–13, 1964, aboard the Voshkod 1 'space bus'. **1949** E. F. RUSSELL in 'E. Crispin' *Best SF* (1955) 209 The biped tribes..need all their unity to cope with space-conquest. **1951** A. C. CLARKE *Sands of Mars* x. 126 Visiting space-crews..soon got bored if they had nothing to do between trips. **1974** *Sci. & Technical Aerospace Rep.* XII. 1600/2 Aeromedical problems of weightlessness and the transfer of spacecrews between Soyuz and Apollo spacecrafts are discussed. **1953** J. N. LEONARD *Flight into Space* xi. 103 Using the scientific method of dissecting a many-sided problem into its separate parts, the space doctors discuss and study the dangers of space individually. **1964** *Skylights* Mar. 1 Pulmonary atelectasis—collapse of the small lung sacs—was feared by space doctors, but did not appear during the 17-day test span. **1957** *IRE Trans. Mil. Electronics* I. 43 (*heading*) Space exploration—the new challenge to the electronics industry. **1969** *Guardian* 7 June 2/8 Russia was spending a significantly higher percentage..on space exploration. **1959** K. VONNEGUT *Sirens of Titan* i. 30 The state of mind on Earth with regard to space exploration was much like the state of mind in Europe..before Christopher Columbus set out... The monsters between space explorers and their goals were not imaginary. **1975** *New Yorker* 21 Apr. 108/2 It has turned out that our real space explorers have necessarily been practical men. **1901** H. G. WELLS *First Men in Moon* xx. 248 All through the major portion of that vast space journey I hung thinking of such immaterial things. **1961** *Daily Tel.* 6 May 8/2 Cdr. Shepard's successful space journey is an immense relief not only to the Americans but the entire free world. **1955** A. G. HALEY in *Jet Propulsion* (1956) XXVI. 951/1 We have about as clear a vision of the space law that will prevail one or two centuries from now as Hammurabi in the 22nd century B.C. **1960** *Daily Tel.* 17 Aug. 13/3 Mr Shawcross also announced that he would resign as chairman of the organising committee on space law, recently set up in London. **1980** *Oxf. Compan. Law* 1165/2 *Space law*, principles of law accepted by nations as binding on them and their nationals in engaging in activities in outer space..and in relation to celestial bodies. **1966** *Observer* 4 Dec. 2/7 American scientists are planning 'space lifeboats' to rescue the crews of disabled spaceships. **1944** E. COLLINS *Mariners of Space* i. 14 Earth's new Space Liner..leaves Croydon to-day at noon. **1982** A. HEMINGWAY *Pzyche* i. 16 The castaway..was a former waiter on a spaceliner. **1977** SACHS & JAHN *Celestial Passengers* xxxii. 190 A new space museum is being developed a mile from Disneyland in Anaheim, California. **1931** J. M. WALSH *Vandals of Void* iv. 40 A ticklish job..is this of space navigation. **1976** *Internat. Aerospace Abstr.* XVI. 23/2 Time intervals in problems of space navigation and communication are often obtained be determining the phase of binary signals. **1936** *Forum & Century* July 36/2 Suppose that a breed of space navigators has begun to appear on earth. **1951** A. C. CLARKE *Exploration of Space* 82 His position is, clearly, only one of the things a space-navigator would want to know. **1962** *Amer. Speech* XXXVII. 43 Before April 12, 1961, the concept expressed by *cosmonaut*, in reference to both American and Soviet space flights, was rendered in the American press by such terms as *astronaut*, *spaceman*,..*space navigator*. **1944** E. COLLINS *Mariners of Space* iii. 21 Space pilots and their mechanics buzzed bee-like in and out of their quarters. **1978** *Space Picture Library Holiday Special* 6 The man who rushed forward..could do little more than break the space-pilot's fall. **1958** *Listener* 4 Dec. 910/1 The result implied that the moon could be used as a space relay for transatlantic radio communication. **1957** *IRE Trans. Mil. Electronics* I. 43/1 The development of a system to control remotely a space-research vehicle. **1982** M. DUKE *Flashpoint* xv. 108 We've already had benefits from space research. **1957** D. J. ENRIGHT *Apothecary's Shop* 232 At least one writer, Robert Conquest, is exploring space-science as a subject for his poetry. **1978** *Nature* 16 Feb. 599/1 If the future facing space science 20 years ago lay full of hope and promise, the symposium indicated how confused and uncertain the picture is today. **1953** M. O. HYDE *Flight Today & Tomorrow* 100 Space scientists look to the rocket to carry them beyond the earth. **1969** *Times* 2 May 16/4 Space scientists have discovered six concentrations of dense material below the surface of the moon. **1952** W. LEY in C. Ryan *Across Space Frontier* 114 The space station..is always spinning, and obviously it cannot be stopped just to enable a space taxi to enter one of the turrets. **1970** N. ARMSTRONG et al. *First on Moon* xiv. 369 An orbiting space station and the 'space taxi'..to take astronauts there and back. **1958** *Science* 11 Apr. 803/1 To be strong and bold in space technology will enhance the prestige of the United States among the peoples of the world. **1972** *Guardian* 10 July 11/7 France..and West Gemany [are] eager to embrace the most advanced of space technologies. [**1929** Space travel: see *space station*, sense 20 below]. **1931** J. M. WALSH *Vandals of Void* i. 23 In the early days of space travel more than one ship was pirated. **1951** 'J. WYNDHAM' in *Best of John Wyndham* (1973) 196 The question of continued space-travel ships of the present types becomes grave. **1978** I. WATSON in C. Priest *Anticipations* 13 What kind of space travel..? Well, they can only be going to the stars. **1930** *Science Wonder Q.* Spring 342/2 (*caption*) Illustrating the journey of the space travelers from Astropol to Venus. **1949** 'M. INNES' *Journeying Boy* iv. 39 So might the earth's first space-traveller exclaim as his rocket took off for the moon. **1976** *Listener* 22 July 83/3 A journey of merely five light years would take about 500,000 years... 15,000 generations of men and women..would successively replace the original crew of stellar space-travellers en route. **1961** *Aeroplane* C. 184/1 The one-man 'space tug' would be used for assembling a large space-station in orbit. **1970** *Physics Bull.* Apr. 145/2 A manned moon station is fore-seen, as are..a 'space shuttle' for commuting between the earth and vehicles in low earth orbit, and a 'space tug' for transport to Mars in the 1980s.

f. Applied to sprays designed to produce droplets that will remain suspended in the air for a long period.

1956 *Aerosol Age* June 70/2 This opens up some interesting possibilities in the lower cost, non-toxic pressurized space sprays. **1958** HERZKA & PICKTHALL *Pressurized Packaging* xiv. 271 Although it is possible to produce a space deodorant which employs only deodorant perfume and propellant..it is better to use the perfume in conjuction with glycols. **1973** J. B. WILKINSON et al. *Harry's Cosmeticology* (ed 6) xliv. 764 A good example of the functional use of space sprays is the aerosol room deodorant. **1974** M. O. JOHNSON in Sciarra & Stoller *Sci. & Technol. Aerosol Packaging* xx. 541 (*heading*) Air fresheners and space bactericides.

19. *Comb.* **a.** With adjs. and ppl. adjs., as *space-based*, *-cramped*, *-dependent*, *-embosomed*, *-spanned*, *-spread*, *-thick*.

1683 MOXON *Mech. Exerc., Printing* xiii. ¶ 1 *Space thick*; that is, one quarter so thick as the Body is high. **1845** BAILEY *Festus* (ed. 2) 207 Visiting The spirits in their space-embosomed homes. *Ibid.* 217 The shade Of Death's dark valley And his space-spread wings. **1891** *Pall Mall G.* 26 Jan. 3/1 Our extracts, space-cramped as they necessarily are. **1931** C. DAY LEWIS *From Feathers to Iron* 45 Space-spanned, God-girdled, love will keep Its form, being planned of bone. **1958** I. ASIMOV *Naked Sun* viii. 107 Try getting rid of me against my will and you'll be looking down the throats of space-based artillery. **1962** CORSON & LORRAIN *Introd. Electromagn. Fields* 534 Space-dependent functions can also be represented with the exponential notation. **1972** *Guardian* 9 Feb. 3/8 The US is evolving..an entire space-based defence network.

b. With ppl. adjs., as *space-devouring*, *-filling*, *-occupying*, *-penetrating*, *-travelling*, *-wasting*, etc. Also with (formally identical) vbl. sbs.

1799 *Phil. Trans.* XC. 81 The space-penetrating power is no higher than what will suffice for the purpose. **1817** COLERIDGE *Biogr. Lit.* (Bohn) 62 The soul was a thinking substance, and the body a space-filling substance. **1839** BAILEY *Festus* 326 Space-pervading, oh! ye must be, Spirit-like, infinite. **1848** *Ibid.* (ed. 3) 222 Space-piercing shadow alighting on the face Of some fair planet. **1862** Spencer *First Princ.* II. vi. §60 (1875) 191 The space-occupying kind of force. **1871** Fraser *Life Berkeley* x. 392 The presumed ontological antithesis between what is conscious and what is space-occupying. **1907** W. James *Let.* 14 Feb. (1920) II. 265 The magnificent space-devouring Subway roaring me back and forth. **1934** C. Lambert *Music Ho!* II. 108 His time travelling is like the space travelling of a character like Douglas Fairbanks. **1938** *Times Lit. Suppl.* 1 Oct. 625/3 The space-travelling itself forces a more direct comparison with ..'The First Men in the Moon'. **1949** E. Muir *Coll. Poems* (1960) 177 Its space-devouring eyes Pass me and hurry on. **1962** F. W. Householder in Householder & Saporta *Probl. Lexicogr.* 281 Others objected to them as (a) space-wasting, (b) often irrelevant and unhelpful. **1979** J. Paton *Sea of Rings* xv. 122 We've never encountered any other space-travelling civilisation.

c. In adjectival phr., as ***space-to-ground.***

1958 C. C. Adams *Space Flight* 144 Whether bombing or space-to-ground missile attacks would be any more effective from such a [space] station has not been established. **1967** *Economist* 29 Apr. 479/1 A Soviet space ship that, according to some reports, was having a variety of troubles with attitude control, power consumption and space-to-ground communication.

20. Special combs.: **space age**, the period of human exploration and exploitation of space; freq. *attrib.*, applied to products supposed to be characteristic of this age; hence (*nonce-wds.*) **space-ager**, one living in this age; **space-agey** *a.*, characteristic of this age; **space-averaged** *a. Physics*, averaged over a region of space; **space blanket**, a light metal-coated plastic sheet designed to retain heat; **space-borne** *a.*, carried through space; also, carried out in space or by means of instruments in space; **space-bound** *a.*, bound or limited by the properties of space; **space cabin**, a chamber designed to support human life in space; **space cadet**, a trainee spaceman; also *transf.*, esp. a (young) enthusiast for space travel; **space capsule**, a small spacecraft containing the instruments or crew relating to the purpose of a space flight; **space chamber**, a chamber in which conditions in space or a spacecraft can be simulated; **space charge** *Electronics*, a collection of particles with a net electric charge occupying a volume, either in free space or in a device; freq. *attrib.* and in *Comb.*, as ***space-charge-limited*** adj.; **space club**, a group of nations that has launched or intends to launch spacecraft; *spec.* a consortium of European nations formed to cooperate in space research and development; **space colony**, a large group of people imagined as living and working in a space station or on another planet; **space curve** *Geom.*, a curve that is not confined to any one plane; **space density** *Astr.*, frequency of occurrence per specified volume of space; **space fiction**, science fiction set in space or on other worlds, or involving space travel; so **space-fictional** *a.*; **space-filler**, something that serves to occupy an otherwise vacant space; *spec.* a brief or insignificant item in a newspaper or magazine; **space fleet** *Science Fiction*, a fleet of spacecraft; **space flight**, a journey or travel through space; **space flyer**, (*a*) a spacecraft; (*b*) an astronaut; **space frame** *Engin.*, a three-dimensional structural framework which is designed to behave as an integral unit and to withstand loads applied at any point; †**space-government**, an interim government, an interregnum; **space gun**, (*a*) a large gun which projects a spacecraft into space; (*b*) a hand-held gun whose recoil is used by an astronaut or spaceman to propel himself; **space heater**, any self-contained appliance for heating an enclosed space within a building; also **space heating**; **space helmet**, a helmet worn in space to protect the head and provide air; also *transf.*; also **space-helmeted** *a.*; **space industry**, the sector of industry which manufactures goods and materials in connection with space flight; **Space Invaders**, the name of an animated computer game in which a player attempts to defend himself against a fleet of enemy spaceships; also, the attacking force itself; **space lab, spacelab** = *space laboratory*; *spec.* (with capital initial(s)) as a proper name (see quot. 1980); **space laboratory**, a laboratory in space, esp. a spacecraft equipped as a laboratory; **space lattice**, *Cryst.*, a regular, indefinitely repeated array of points in three dimensions in which the points lie at the intersections of three sets of parallel equidistant planes and every point is surrounded by the same pattern of points in the same orientation; a three-dimensional Bravais lattice; **space launcher**, a rocket used to lift spacecraft into space; **space lift, spacelift** [after air-lift 2], an act of transporting goods or personnel in space; **space medicine**, the branch of science concerned with the medical effects of being in space; **space myopia** (see quot. 1973); **space needle**, a small rod or fibre of conducting material in orbit about a planet; **space-nerve** (see quot.); **space observatory**, an astronomical observatory in space; **space-occupying lesion** *Path.*, a mass, freq. a tumour, which has displaced brain tissue; **space opera** chiefly *U.S.* [cf. *horse opera*, soap opera], space fiction, esp. of a primitive and extravagant kind; an example of this genre; **space-order**, an ordering of points or events in space; **space physics**, the physics of extraterrestrial phenomena and bodies, esp. within the solar system; **space-plane**, (*a*) (see quot. 1961); (*b*) = shuttle *sb.*[1] 8c; **space platform** = *space station* below; **space-port**, a base from which spacecraft are launched; (in fiction) a base at which spaceships take off and land; **space probe**, an unmanned spacecraft for research or reconnaissance; **space programme**, a programme of exploration of space and development of space technology; **space race**, the competition between nations to be first to achieve various objectives in the exploration of space; **space-reddening** *vbl. sb. Astr.*, the reddening of starlight as a result of wavelength-dependent absorption and scattering by interstellar dust; also **space-reddened** *ppl. a.*; **space rocket**, a rocket designed to travel beyond the earth's atmosphere; **space satellite** = satellite *sb.* 2c; **space-saving** *a.*, that uses space economically or tends to the better use of available room; also as *sb.* and **space saver**, a device or appliance designed to this end; **space shot**, the launch of a spacecraft and its subsequent progress in space; **space shuttle**: see shuttle *sb.*[1] 8c; **space sick, space-sick** *a.*, sick from the effects of space flight; hence **space sickness**; **space simulator**, a device which simulates the conditions of space, or of the interior of a spacecraft; **space-speak** [-speak], the jargon of space technologists, considered as a corruption of standard English; **space stage** *Theatr.*, a modern stage on which the significant action alone is lighted, the rest remaining in darkness; hence **space staging**; **space station**, a large artificial satellite used as a base for operations in space; **space suit**, a garment designed to protect the wearer against the conditions of space; so **space-suited** *a.*, wearing such clothing; **space-telegrapher**, one concerned or connected with space-telegraphy; **space-telegraphy**, wireless telegraphy; **space vehicle**, a spacecraft, esp. a large one; **space velocity** *Astr.*, the velocity in space of a star relative to the sun, equal to the vector sum of its proper motion and its radial velocity; **spacewalk, space walk**, an act or spell of physical activity undertaken in space outside a spacecraft; also as *v. intr.*; hence **spacewalking** *vbl. sb.* and *ppl. a.*; also **spacewalker**; **space warp**, an imaginary distortion of space-time that is conceived as enabling space travellers to make journeys that would otherwise be contrary to the known laws of nature; **space-washer**, a washer serving to keep parts of machinery, etc., at a fixed distance apart; **space wave** *Radio* [tr. G. *raumwelle* (A. Sommerfeld 1911, in *Jahrb. der drahtl. Telegr.* IV. 166)], the radio wave that passes from a transmitter to a receiver either directly through space without reflection or with reflection from the ground; **spaceway** *Science Fiction*, an established route of space travellers; usu. *pl.*

1946 H. Harper *Dawn of Space Age* I. i. 5 We have had an age of steam-power, an age of electricity and of the petrol engine, and an age of the air, and now with the coming of atomic power the world should, in due course, find itself in the *space age. **1960** K. Amis *New Maps of Hell* iii. 80 The outset of the space age and the immense technological effort involved in it are obviously the propelling force of much science fiction today. **1963** *New Yorker* 8 June 96 The space-age, space-tested material that makes possible this smart, new look in luggage. **1980** *Times Lit. Suppl.* 7 Nov. 1258/4 Our space-age Palace of History—the new computerized Public Record Office at Kew. **1959** *Times* 9 Mar. 13/5 One of the rockets, the *space-ager firmly believes, will have him aboard. **1962** *Punch* 28 Nov. 781/1 A modern caravan..trying to look zippy and *space-agey. **1946** *Nature* 26 Oct. 582/2 Such time- or *space-averaged statistical structures are becoming increasingly familiar to X-ray crystallographers. **1962** Corson & Lorrain *Introd. Electromagn. Fields* iii. 91 (*caption*) To find the space-averaged field intensity produced by the dipoles, we calculate the field intensity at *O*..and then repeat this calculation for many other points *O′*. **1972** *Brit. Med. Jrnl.* 29 Jan. 293/2 The body temperature should be slowly raised to normal, using a '*space blanket' and heating pads if necessary, in a warm room. **1953** J. N. Leonard *Flight into Space* 157 Undoubtedly one of the great preoccupations of the *space-borne astronomers will be to study the moon and the planets. **1965** *New Scientist* 26 Aug. 485/1 One would have thought that the bugs could have been eliminated from the fuel cell system before it ever became space-borne. **1968** *Ibid.* 28 Mar. 680 In spite of considerable lobbying to make optical astronomy a space-borne science, many practising observers show little enthusiasm for the idea. **1975** *Nature* 22 May 287/1 With the shuttle taking up an ever-increasing share of the space budget, there is likely to be little money to spare for expanding space-borne astronomy. **1960** *Analog Science Fact & Fiction* Nov. 14/2 He banged it shut behind him and, feeling that he might as well continue with his *spacebound existence, walked all the way to the elevator. **1958** D. G. Simons in M. Alperin et al. *Vistas in Astronautics* I. vi. 301 The systems and controls required to establish a *space cabin capsule. **1961** *Guardian* 10 Mar. 1/5 As on previous occasions in this series of Russian experiments, the space cabin, as it is called, weighed 4·5 tons. **1974** *Sci. & Technical Aerospace Rep.* XII. 1013/1 (*heading*) Survival of infectious microorganisms in space cabin environments. **1952** *Newsweek* 13 Oct. 39/2 (*caption*) Test pilot A. M. 'Tex' Johnston..resembles a *space cadet in the new high-altitude helmet and suit designed to protect pilots in the upper air. **1957** P. Moore *Science & Fiction* i. 18 Lucian's seamen are the logical ancestors of the rocketeers and space-cadets of to-day. **1958** C. C. Adams *Space Flight* p. vii, There have been space books for children—our present space cadets and future rocket pilots. **1979** *Harvard Mag.* May–June 15 How can I be one of the first to see these new worlds in detail and not be crawling with gooseflesh? Me, an original space cadet? **1959** *Listener* 15 Jan. 118/1 An American firm is given a contract to build a *space-capsule designed to put a man into orbit round the earth. **1963** *Ann. Reg. 1962* 398 The larger two-man Gemini space capsules, orbiting for a fortnight on end. **1977** G. Scott *Hot Pursuit* x. 88 It starts..with the space capsule... A Russian satellite, one of the Cosmos series. **1959** *Daily Tel.* 23 Feb. 11/7 Col. Steinkamp and his colleagues have been carrying out interesting tests, lasting from four hours to a week, in a sealed '*space chamber'. **1966** *Science World* 7 Jan. 10 The Air Force has been testing the ability of men to live for long periods in a new gas mixture that may be used in space ships... There have been two short tests in 'space chambers'. **1913** *Physical Rev.* II. 450 (*heading*) The effect of *space charge and the residual gases on thermionic currents in high vacuum. **1921** *Ibid.* XVIII. 56 The maximum space-charge limited current was the same for each [tube]. **1956** *Nature* 11 Feb. 285/2 The corresponding current..for maximum space-charged-limited pulsed emission from the surface of the oxide coat is 8 amp. per sq. cm. **1962** Simpson & Richards *Physical Princ. Junction Transistors* iv. 54 For this reason the region AB is often referred to as the space-charge or depletion region. **1980** J. W. Hill *Intermediate Physics* xxii. 210 In the Maltese cross tube and the deflection tube, the space charge formed by the filament is attracted towards the positively-charged anode and accelerated. **1961** *Economist* 14 Jan. 116/2 West Germany agreed by the 1954 treaties not to manufacture long-range missiles. Participation in a *space club with a military potential would take the erosion of the treaties a stage further. **1970** *Daily Tel.* 3 Sept. 5 Britain failed to join the 'space club' yesterday because of a fault in the second stage of the Black Arrow rocket fired from Woomera, Australia. **1974** *N.Y. Times* 19 May IV. 6 The *space colonies..would provide an alternative to earth if the earth's resources ever reach the point of depletion. **1971** *Proc. Nat. Acad. Sci.* LXVIII. 815/1 Our interest here is in *space curves that are the central curves of elastic rods. **1931** *Astrophysical Jrnl.* LXXIV. 268 (*heading*) A numerical method of determining the *space density of stars. **1978** *Nature* 10 Aug. 569/1 *RS Canum venaticorum* systems are the most plentiful binary stars known, having a space density of at least 10^{-6} systems pc^{-3}. **1952** *Space Science Fiction* May 2/1 We like good *space fiction, and we intend to bring you the best of it... The space-opera of flashing rayguns and invincible heroes has long since been overdone. **1960** *Guardian* 19 Aug. 5/4 A frantic urge for escape, but where to? Astrology, necromancy, space-fiction? **1979** *Daily Tel.* 14 Dec. 13/3 Star Trek is the latest in an increasing number of space fiction films which..tend to find individuality. **1963** V. Gielgud *Goggle-Box Affair* xviii. 191 *Space-fictional horrors. **1911** H. S. Harrison *Queed* xviii. 232 There's a little squib about the college that may serve as a *space-filler. **1956** *Nature* 17 Mar. 530/2 Into the large centre well 3–4 drops of anti-serum are deposited and a glass or aluminium plug... The latter serves merely as a space-filler to spare anti-serum. **1972** *Sci. Amer.* July 13/3, I have written some poetry, mostly nonserious, that has found its way into medical journals as space-filler. **1944** E. Collins *Mariners of Space* iii. 25 Space-Captain Jan Marthus of the Martian *Space Fleet steered his friend into the restaurant. **1979** J. Paton *Sea of Rings* 23 William Robert Mahony, ex-Captain, Space Fleet, aged 46. **1931** *Wonder Stories* Jan. 900/1 We know now what conditions are necessary for a *space flight... After all space flying is too great a matter to be limited by national pride and jealousy. **1949** A. C. Clarke *Across Sea of Stars* (1959) 76 There is a timelessness about space-flight..unmatched by any other experience of man. **1978** J. Updike *Coup* (1979) v. 183 The hollow head with which a mummified Pharaoh is helmeted for *his* space-flight. **1911** *Mod. Electrics* Nov. 516/1 He knew now that Fernand 60O 10 had carried off his sweetheart in a *space-flyer and that the machine by this time was probably far out from the earth's boundary. **1931** *Wonder Stores* Feb. 958 To old and seasoned space-fliers like Professor Galloway and myself, there was something ludicrous in all this emotional bustle..over a little hop to the Moon. **1962** M. V. Glenny tr. *Gartmann's Space Travel* 130/1 The space flyer will.. encounter two opposed physical conditions: pressure and weightlessness. **1962** *Listener* 1 Mar. 368/2 All three American space-fliers had had to be landed in the sea. **1912** A. Morley *Theory of Structures* xiii. 380 (*heading*) *Space frames. **1967** *Jane's Surface Skimmer Systems 1967–68* 48/1 The craft is of lightweight space-frame construction in marine aluminium. **1974** *Times Lit. Suppl.* 4 Jan. 14/4 The debased standards of theatre design today and..artists who think 'empty space, lighting, and maybe an aluminium space frame' are enough. **1600** E. Blount tr. *Conestaggio* 261 Knowing there was a *space-gouernement, with likelihood of warre. **1935** H. G. Wells *Things to Come* 12 The stormy victory of the new ideas as the *Space Gun fires and the moon cylinder starts on its momentous journey. **1954** K. W. Gatland *Devel. Guided Missile* (ed. 2) 197 All the propellant could be consumed in the first second of take-off—as Jules Verne proposed in his famous 'space-gun'. **1968** *Amer. Speech* XLIII. 166 *Space gun*, a handheld instrument used to propel an astronaut outside the capsule. **1970** N. ARMSTRONG et al. *First on Moon* viii. 180 This was where I had to use the little space gun. **1976** P. MOORE *Next Fifty Years in Space* i. 16 It is not impossible that the space-gun principle may have its uses in the future, but it will be confined to firing non-fragile payloads off airless worlds. **1925** *Sci. Amer.* Mar. 162/3 *Space heaters. **1951** *Good Housek. Home Encycl.* 203/1 The stove..is primarily designed as a boiling ring but it will also serve as a space heater. **1980** *Amat. Gardening* 25 Oct. 9/1 Electrical space heaters are extremely expensive to run at high temperatures. **1934** *Jrnl. Inst. Heating & Ventilating Engineers* XIII. 234 The open fire is still..the most widely-used domestic *space-heating appliance. **1973** *Guardian* 17 Mar 12/5 What is especially intolerable..is that..electricity with a starting efficiency of only 20 per cent or so is allowed to be sold for space heating, a role particularly suitable for the 80 per cent of low grade heat that has been thrown away. **1954** *Newsweek* 6 Dec. 108/1 It is significant, too, that the American kid of 1954, dazzled by *space helmets and death-ray guns, has time in his daily make-believe for the mustang and the six-shooter. **1973** *Times* 29 Aug. 3/2 Scientists are developing a 'space helmet' respirator to protect miners against dust. **1979** R. JAFFE *Class Reunion* (1980) II. ii. 191 Her blonde, teased, sprayed bubble hairdo..looked like a space helmet. **1957** *Time* 22 July 52/1 From a sealed chamber like the cabin of a rocket ship, and from *space-helmeted human guinea pigs who live in it, medical researchers..hope to learn answers to some fundamental questions about the body's consumption of fuel and oxygen. **1982** D. MACKENZIE *Raven's Revenge* x. 94 A space-helmeted motorcyclist. **1962** M. V. GLENNY tr. *Gartmann's Space Travel* 9 The *space industry..has plans for huge multi-purpose earth satellites. **1972** *Guardian* 10 July 11/2 The unhappy fragmental European space industry. **1979** *Los Angeles Times* 23 Sept. VII. 17/1 Nobody likes to be a loser, but when playing *Space Invaders, most gamesters don't seem to mind. **1980** *Guardian* 2 Feb. 8/3 Driven out of the BR station buffet by bleeping Space Invaders. **1980** *Washington Post* 2 Sept. B1 A world-class Space Invaders player can keep the machine going for an hour. **1982** *London Rev. Bks.* IV. XXIV. 7/1 The advent of the Space Invaders can't mean anything except that new inventions bring new possibilities. **1966** *Electronics* 31 Oct. 134 Although the Gemini computers are highly flexible.., they are not versatile enough for *space labs. **1975** K. GATLAND *Missiles & Rockets* xv. 246 Hatches on top of the cargo compartment will open to permit Space Lab to be hinged out into space. **1979** *Fortune* 29 Jan. 77 In the microgravity of an orbiting spacelab, NASA will make crystals, alloys, and medicines never seen on earth. **1980** T. FURNISS *Space Satellites* 30/2 One of the payloads the Shuttle carries is the Spacelab research station. Spacelab is built in Europe by the member countries of the European Space Agency. **1960** *Space-laboratory [see *meteor bumper* s.v. METEOR]. **1973** *Guardian* 28 May 2/2 The battered American space laboratory, Skylab, cooling parasol now clutched tightly over her gold-foiled head. **1895** *Space-lattice [see LATTICE *sb.* 4 a]. **1923** GLAZEBROOK *Dict. Appl. Physics.* IV. 18/2 In the crystals of very simple chemical compounds..the space-lattice is directly formed by the chemical atoms. In the more complicated crystalline substances..the space-lattice points are surrounded or replaced by groups of atoms. **1973** J. G. TWEEDDALE *Materials Technol.* I. iii. 59 Although there are countless varieties of crystals, there can be only 14 types of space lattice. **1961** *Daily Tel.* 1 Feb. 16/4 (*heading*) Joint effort for *space 'launcher'. **1963** *Guardian* 9 Nov. 7/7 The Soviet Union has now apparently agreed that Governments should be allowed to license private space-launchers. **1954** 'J. CHRISTOPHER' *22nd Cent.* 65 As many as possible would be got away to those planets by a full *space lift. **1964** *Yearbk. Astron. 1965* 142 What then might be realized is a joint use of the nationally developed space hardware in a space-lift of supplies to obtain the first firm footholds on the Moon in the shape of a scientific base. **1949** *Time* 12 Sept. 29/2 The U.S. Air Force's School of Aviation Medicine.. has set up an interplanetary research section, [and] named it the Department of *Space Medicine. **1962** F. I. ORDWAY et al. *Basic Astronautics* xiii. 539 This centrifuge is unique among those used in space medicine research. *Ibid.* xii. 474 Other visual phenomena associated with space flight include *space myopia... Looking out into the darkness of space, the astronaut would not know whether his eyes were focused at infinity or only a few feet from his ship. **1973** *Gloss. Aeronaut. & Astronaut. Terms.* (*B.S.I.*) XVII. 1 *Space myopia*, the tendency of the human eye to accommodate for a distance commonly of the order of six feet when in a featureless environment, resulting in potential failure to perceive objects at considerably greater distance. **1961** *Daily Tel.* 23 Oct. 1/3 (*heading*) *Space needles begin to form radio band. **1964** Space needle [see DIPOLE 2]. **1895** *Funk's Stand. Dict.*, **Space-nerve*, the portion of the auditory nerve that supplies the semicircular canals of the inner ear. **1952** F. L. WHIPPLE in C. Ryan *Across Space Frontier* 136 Our *space observatory can give us vital information as to how some stars die in a spectacular blaze of glory. **1972** *Guardian* 22 Aug. 2/4 A space observatory, Copernicus, was launched here today, the fourth to be put in orbit. **1961** *Lancet* 9 Sept. 570/1 The patients reported in this paper had small pretectal *space-occupying lesions demonstrated both clinically and radiologically. **1978** *Jrnl. R. Soc. Med.* LXXI. 226 These cases illustrate some atypical presentations of tuberculosis—as epilepsy, cranial nerve palsy,..or space-occupying lesion. **1949** *Sat. Rev. Lit.* (U.S.) 24 Dec. 7/3 No less than eight of this year's crop of science-fiction novels are what is known in the trade as '*space operas'—books built round the theme of interplanetary travel. **1952** [see *space fiction* above]. **1960** K. AMIS *New Maps of Hell* ii. 44 In space-opera, Mars takes the place of Arizona with a few physical alterations, the hero totes a blaster instead of a six-gun. **1969** H. WARNER *All our Yesterdays* ii. 41 [Wilson] Tucker is responsible for the use of 'space opera', which he proposed in the January, 1941, *Le Zombie* as a name for the 'hacky, grinding, stinking, outworn spaceship yarn'. **1978** *Broadcast* 31 July 24/1 The Seven-Up [TV advertisement] series..is meant as a space opera send up. **1890** W. JAMES *Princ. Psychol.* II. xx. 276 The obvious objection is that mere serial order is a *genus*, and *space-order a very peculiar species of that *genus*. **1927** B. RUSSELL *Outl. Philos.* iv. 50 A written word is a series of pieces of matter, having an essential space-order. **1961** *Adv. Astronaut. Sci.* VI. 779 *Space physics. **1962** F. I. ORDWAY et al. *Basic Astronautics* iv. 117 An important characteristic of space physics is that it is closely related to two aspects of geophysics, namely atmospheric physics and ionospherics. **1980** *Jrnl. R. Soc. Arts* May 357/1 The College has now built more instruments..making thereby vast additions to space-physics knowledge. **1961** *Aeroplane* C. 597 A *spaceplane is an aircraft capable of entry into orbit, using for propulsion purposes the atmosphere through which it has passed. **1978** *N.Y. Times Mag.* 29 Jan. 26 Designed to take off like a rocket, fly in orbit like a spacecraft, and return to a runway landing like a glider, these huge spaceplanes are expected to make the near reaches of space more accessible than ever before. **1958** F. A. WARREN *Rocket Propellants* xi. 196 Thought of *space platforms, space ships, satellite stations, and high-altitude exploratory rockets overshadows consideration of other rocket uses. **1980** M. BABSON *Dangerous to Know* vii. 47 She'd crashed like a chunk of rubble from an abandoned space platform. **1935** *Amer. Speech* X. 54/1 *Spaceport. **1943** *Astounding Science-Fiction* Feb. 9/1 Carew had landed him at one of the less expensive spaceports. **1962** *Daily Progress* (Charlottesville, Va.) 23 Feb. 11 After these few words, Glenn set out for the ride through brilliant sunshine to this space port—where it all began—and his meeting with President Kennedy. **1977** *Time* 30 May 45/2 For one scene, set in a brawling space-port bar, the casting director went to a London firm called Uglies, Ltd. **1977** *Daily Tel.* 28 July 1/6 The small spaceport at Kagoshima, at the southern tip of Japan, looked more like a station for amateur rocketry than a serious rival to Cape Canaveral. [**1955** E. BURGESS *Frontier to Space* viii. 152 We would then have the deep-space probe.] **1958** *Listener* 20 Nov. 822/1 Direct contact between some form of *space probe and the moon..must be close at hand. **1977** *Whitaker's Almanack 1978* 158/2 A Russian space probe has revealed that the lower layers [of Venus] are extremely dense. **1958** *New Statesman* 6 Sept. 263/2 It was Congress, rather than the President, that took the initiative in pushing a *space programme. **1977** B. LANGLEY *Death Stalk* ii. 23 A number of senators had a vested interest in seeing that the space programme continued. **1959** *Listener* 29 Jan. 226/2 The possible nature of Britain's contribution to the *space race. **1967** M. KENYON *Whole Hog* iii. 31 If you've got something which could keep the same men..in the capsules ..the space race would be won. **1978** *Nature* 9 Mar. 119/2 Czechoslovakia has won the 'little space race' for the third nation to put a citizen into orbit. **1959** *Listener* 24 Dec. 1111/2 The stars are said to be *space-reddened. In the same way atmospheric dust causes the sun to appear red at sunset. **1931** *Astrophysical Jrnl.* LXXV. 392 The differential absorption or *space reddening at 1000 parsecs in the galactic plane is unquestionably real. **1937** Space reddening [see INTERSTELLAR *a.*]. **1928** *Discovery* June 190/1 The arguments used in regard to objections so far raised meet the case in respect of *space-rocket machines. **1936** 'J. BEYNON' *Planet Plane* iv. 36 You can be sure that if they were building a space rocket anywhere we'd have heard of it. **1958** *Listener* 16 Oct. 606/1 A space-rocket, aimed towards the moon, is successfully launched from Cape Canaveral. **1977** 'J. FRASER' *Hearts Ease in Death* vii. 76 Mark Dunton's bed..looked like some sort of space rocket, with tubes connecting various parts of Mark's body to pieces of apparatus. **1954** *Jrnl. Brit. Interplanetary Soc.* XIII. 165 Since it is theoretically possible today to design and build instrumented rocket vehicles for both orbital and escape missions, one is often asked whether there is not justification for a *space-satellite programme, such as the Americans suggested in 1948. **1962** E. SNOW *Red China Today* (1963) lxxxvi. 723 The development of space satellite espionage and electronic detection devices had so far advanced that all essential information needed to guarantee against surprise attacks would soon be in possession of both sides. **1974** P. CATTERMOLE *All about Space Exploration* vi. 74 Unmanned space satellites had been approved by the U.S. Government. **1970** *Toronto Daily Star* 24 Sept. 5/2 (Advt.), Just out on sale!.. New..*Space-saver Consolette [television]. **1921** *Sci. Amer.* 30 July 79/1 Home Building..Many unique *space-saving devices are now being used. **1934** WEBSTER, *Spacesaving*, n. **1936** *Punch* 11 Mar. 287/1 For space-saving reasons, [I] have exchanged the old edition of the D.N.B. for its India paper form. **1964** E. BACH *Introd. Transformational Gram.* ii. 17 The latter notation is useful as a space-saving device. **1978** M. & N. WARD *Home in Twenties & Thirties* 23 Cost saving was one necessity, space saving another. **1961** *Guardian* 29 Mar. 1/6 Russia did not give advance notice of *space shots. **1969** *Times* 19 Feb. 13/4 Between now and April, Mars lies in a favourable position for space shots. **1977** D. BAGLEY *Enemy* xxxii. 259 Designing a trajectory for a space shot to Pluto. **1949** A. C. CLARKE *Across Sea of Stars* (1959) 93, I was sure I'd never be *space sick. **1971** *New Yorker* 27 Feb. 32 If an astronaut were made to move his hand repeatedly in the wrong direction in relation to the spin, he could easily get spacesick. **1951** A. C. CLARKE *Sands of Mars* i. 3 *Space-sickness was a thing of the past. **1969** *New Scientist* 2 Oct. 28/1 The Russian cosmonaut Titov was the first to complain of space sickness in 1961. **1959** *IRE Trans. Mil. Electronics* III. 96/1 For the first *space simulator, it is proposed to use a combination of visual references and cabin motion to give a hint or illusion of 'g' forces. **1974** *Sci. & Technical Aerospace Rep.* XII. 37 (*heading*) Radiometer for measuring a wide range of irradiances in space simulators. **1966** *Science* 13 May 875/1 We read of '*space speak' on every hand. Newspapers and magazines discuss it in their science columns, and popular fancy seems to have been captured by it. The belief is that the space effort has given us, in addition to the possibility of going to the moon, a new linguistic phenomenon. **1982** M. LEAPMAN *Yankee Doodles* III. 175 Transiting is a typical piece of spacespeak in that it makes a verb out of a noun. **1928** J. DOLMAN *Art of Play Production* xviii. 397 Three types of modern stages have..been reasonably successful in accomplishing the true purpose of formalism. One is..the so-called '*space stage', the essential feature of which is light, so controlled as to reveal only the significant action and to suppress the background altogether in a void of darkness. The methods of the space stage are..adaptable to the purposes of expressionism. **1961** *Twentieth Cent.* Feb. 121 A space stage..a broad platform with no barrier between audience and performer. **1959** *Listener* 9 July 73/1 A television equivalent to Brechtian '*space staging'. [**1929** *Science Wonder Stories* Sept. 365 (*heading*) The spatial station as a basis for spatial travel.] **1936** P. E. CLEATOR *Rockets through Space* vi. 141 So great are the possibilities of the *space-station that von Pirquet is of the opinion that the achievement of interplanetary travel ..must depend upon the construction of such a station. **1956** J. G. PORTER in A. Pryce-Jones *New Outl. Mod. Knowl.* 135 We are to visualize a space station, a sort of artificial satellite of the earth which is to act as a landing stage for all space ships. **1969** *Sci. Jrnl.* Feb. 66/1 Although any manned satellite might literally be called a manned space station, the term is usually restricted to spacecraft which remain in orbit for long periods and which carry relatively large crews. **1929** *Science Wonder Stories* July 175/1 Normal communication by speech would be impossible. Of course, this is not true of enclosed, air-filled rooms... But it is true when one is out 'in the open' (in the *space suit). **1962** J. GLENN et al. in *Into Orbit* 244 G-suits are not to be confused with pressure suits (or, now, spacesuits) which the Astronaut wears during space flight to maintain atmospheric pressure at high altitudes. **1979** D. ADAMS *Hitch-Hiker's Guide to Galaxy* iii. 25 He will automatically assume he is also in possession of a toothbrush,..space suit etc., etc. **1951** COGGINS & PRATT *Rockets, Jets, Guided Missiles & Spaceships* v. (*caption*) Switching off the electromagnets in his boots, the *space-suited chief engineer kicks off for a look at his project. **1977** *Daily Mirror* 10 May 19/2 A Staffordshire housewife..saw two Space-suited people with long blonde hair looking down at her from a craft above her house. **1899** *Nature* 12 Jan. 249 The problem is now fair game for the *space-telegraphers. **1898** *Engineering Mag.* XVI. 118/1 The methods of *space-telegraphy. **1946** *N.Y. Times* 29 July 1/2 They are to serve as pioneers for the long-range guided missiles and '*space' vehicles. **1959** *Daily Tel.* 23 Feb. 11/7 Protective clothing..will be needed to help guard a man against the heavy G forces imposed on him because of the great thrust upwards that a space vehicle will develop. **1959** *Times* 15 Sept. 11/3 In putting a space vehicle on to the moon the Russians have provided the most complete.. proof of the length of the lead that they now hold. **1977** 'M. UNDERWOOD' *Fatal Trip* xx. 117 We can often track a load of porn..as successfully as the Americans track a space vehicle..to Mars. **1921** *Bull. Nat. Res. Council Nat. Acad. Sci.* II. 196 Average *space velocities vary from 10 to 30km/sec., there being a well-marked increase in average space velocity as one proceeds from the bluer to the redder stars. **1927** H. N. RUSSELL et al. *Astronomy* II. xix. 652 The space velocity, being found from the proper motion, parallax, and radial velocity, demands for its determination the combination of observations made in very different ways. **1978** PASACHOFF & KUTNER *University Astron.* iii. 62 We can combine the values of velocity in the plane of the sky and in the radial direction to find the actual velocity of the star in space, the space velocity. **1965** *Newsweek* 14 June 30/3 Thirteen new layers had been added [to his spacesuit] ..to protect his torso and legs against micro-meteorites and the extreme temperatures on his *spacewalk. **1969** *Daily Tel.* 17 Jan. 1/2 The link-up was controlled manually by the cosmonauts. The two who made the space 'walk' reported 'feeling fine' after their feat. **1970** *Guardian* 8 July 20/7 Astronaut figures, 12 ft high, will 'space walk' over a quarter-mile section of Blackpool promenade in this autumn's illuminations. **1978** *Nature* 19 Jan. 201/3 The work aboard Salyut-6 is more interesting than his previous mission on Salyut-4, since the cosmonauts can now go for spacewalks. **1979** M. COLLINS *Flying to Moon* vi. 44 We would fly alongside the second Agena, and I would space walk over to it. **1965** *Newsweek* 14 June 30/1 *Spacewalker White had trouble sleeping, due to the excitement. **1965** *Ibid.* 21 June 24/1 He was firmly convinced that *spacewalking is an easily mastered art. **1970** *Daily Tel.* (Colour Suppl.) 10 Apr. 9/4 Theoretically we could now send a space-walking astronaut as an electric repair man to one of these satellites if anything went wrong. **1947** *Jrnl. Brit. Interplanetary Soc.* VI. 138 The next step is to explain that matter and energy are mutually convertible..and from this it is an easy process to pass to the 'invention' of a plausible device which produces a '*space-warp' in the opposite sense to the normal one, by means of the expenditure of energy in some form. Bodies in the region of this artificial 'space-warp' therefore acquire a negative weight—what could be simpler? **1953** *Galaxy Sci. Fiction* Nov. 53/2 He read the next one..about a star-ship that hit a space warp and got hurled into another universe. **1974** G. BUTLER *Coffin for Canary* ix. 108 Don't unnerve me, boss. *You* don't believe in space-warps and voyagers back from another age. **1913** *Rep. Brit. Assoc. Adv. Sci. 1912* 403 His theory leads to the conclusion that there are not only *space-waves (*Raumwellen*) in these media, but also surface-waves (*Oberflächenwallen*) at the boundary surface. **1943** F. E. TERMAN *Radio Engineers' Handbk.* x. 674 The ground wave can conveniently be divided into two components, a surface wave and a space wave. **1974** HARVEY & BOHLMAN *Stereo F.M. Radio Handbk.* vii. 145 The range of the space-wave is chiefly determined by the height of the transmitting and receiving aerials. **1947** *Astounding Sci. Fiction* Sept. 171 You can't believe..your eyes... It was a platitude of the *spaceways. **1979** *Daily Tel.* 1 Feb. 15/2 Everyone loves Harry Harrison; the genre would be poorer without this Monty Python of the spaceways.

†**space**, *sb.*² *Sc. Obs. rare.* [ad. F. *espèce*: see SPECE.] A species or kind (*of* money, etc.).

1591 *Sc. Acts, Jas. VI* (1814) III. 526/1 The diuersitie and chois of sindry space of money current within the same [*sc.* realm]. *Ibid.*, In ressauing and geving furth..all spaces of gold and siluer. *Ibid.*, Ane siluer space of money.

space (speɪs), *v.* Also 6 spase. [f. SPACE *sb.*¹, or ad. F. *espacer* (†*espacier, espatier*) to space, etc., = Sp. *espaciar*, Pg. *espaçar*, It. *spaziare*, L. *spatiārī* to walk, to extend.]

†**1.** *trans.* ? To pave or lay. *Obs.*⁻¹

1538 LELAND *Itin.* (1769) VII. 71 Ther is a very large Courte buildyd about with Tymbar and spacyd withe Brike.

2. To limit or bound in respect of space; to make of a certain extent.

1548 GESTE *Pr. Masse* 86 Not placely as ther placed, spaced, and mesured, but ghostly as ther unplaced, unspaced, and not measured. **1578** *Gorg. Gallery Gallant Inv.* I, Her forehead seemely spaste, wherin doo shine her eyes. *a* **1628** F. GREVIL *Cælica* Prol. 2 A place there is.. Deepe vnder depthes..; darke, infinitely spaced; Pluto the King. **1835** *Fraser's Mag.* XII. 416 In so far as Lamarck has defined nature to be motion,..space, and time, without reference to a being moving or moved,..or being timed and spaced.

3. †**a.** To divide into spaces or sections. Also const. *by* or *with*. *Obs. rare.*

1578 LYTE *Dodoens* 333 Dwarf Gentian hath rounde stalkes..spaced with certayne knottie ioyntes. *Ibid.* 564 The stalke is crested, holowe within, spaced by joyntes or knobbes. **1578** WHETSTONE *Promos & Cass.* II. I. iv, So space your roomes, as the nyne worthyes may Be so instauld, as best may please the eye.

b. *dial.* To measure (ground, etc.) by pacing.

1808 in JAMIESON. **1823-** in dial. glossaries, etc.

4. To set or place, to arrange or put, at determinate intervals or distances.

1703 T. N. *City & C. Purchaser* 186 All Rafters are not spaced alike. **1715** LEONI *Palladio's Archit.* (1742) I. 16 This manner of spacing the Columns, is..call'd *Diastylos.* **1776** G. SEMPLE *Building in Water* 115 The flooring Joists..are to be.. spaced at 18 Inches asunder. **1891** *Pall Mall G.* 23 Oct. 5/1 Each spar was spaced 8 ft. apart.

absol. **1875** KNIGHT *Dict. Mech.* 299/2 Some of the [blind-stile] machines space as well as bore or mortise.

b. Similarly with *out*.

1712 J. JAMES tr. *Le Blond's Gardening* 156 You space out and range all the others by them. *Ibid.* 160 The Plants are spaced out..at three Foot Distances. **1896** H. WOODWARD *Guide Fossil Reptiles Brit. Mus.* 119 *Sparnodus*..is an extinct genus [of fish].., having the teeth somewhat 'spaced out'. **1899** *Daily News* 19 Dec. 5/1 Ice..must..be thicker than that if it is to support a body of troops, or the men must be properly spaced out.

c. *refl.* (Also with *out*.)

1700 J. MONRO *Let.* in *Misc. Curiosa* (1708) III. 399 There is provided a noble and a vast convenience full of variety for the others, to space themselves freely and with pleasure in. **1896** C. K. PAUL tr. *Huysman's En Route* II. iv. 219 Mortifications space themselves out, fatigues are distributed over years and, on the whole, are easily borne.

d. *intr.* With *out*. To experience a drug-induced state of euphoria; to become disoriented by the use of narcotic stimulus. Cf. SPACED *ppl. a.* 4. *U.S. slang.*

1968-70 *Current Slang* (Univ. S. Dakota) III-IV. 116 *Space out, v.* To achieve an euphoric state because of drug use... To lose one's train of thought while under the influence of a drug. **1970** *New York* 16 Nov. 48/3 Karenga ..looks like he's going crazy or spacing out on dope.

5. *Typog.* **a.** With *out*: To extend to a required length by inserting additional space between the words (or lines).

1683 MOXON *Mech. Exerc., Printing* xxii. ¶8 He intends to Space-out the rest if it were not too Wide Set at first. *Ibid.*, Unless his Matter was..so Wide Set that he can Space out no more. **1816** SINGER *Hist. Cards* 132 The improved method of spacing out the lines. **1892** A. OLDFIELD *Man. Typog.* ii. 25 [It is advisable] to read copy whilst spacing out the line.

b. To separate (words, letters, or lines) by means of a space or spaces; occas. = prec.

In recent use also with ref. to typewriting.

1771 LUCKOMBE *Hist. Printing* 249 The care the Compositor took in spacing his matter. *Ibid.* 251 Small Capitals are generally Spaced, as well as Large Capitals. **1808** STOWER *Printer's Gram.* vi. 160 Where a line is even spaced, and yet requires justification. **1875** LIGHTFOOT *Comm. Col.* 231/1 This idea is..expressed..in the words which are spaced.

absol. **1771** LUCKOMBE *Hist. Printing* 398 To space open and wide, is no advantage to a Compositor.

†**6.** *intr.* To walk, ramble, or roam. *Obs.*

a **1572** KNOX *Hist. Reform.* Wks. 1846 I. 137 The said Maister George spaced up and doune behynd the hie altar more then half ane houre. **1596** SPENSER *F.Q.* IV. viii. 54 That he sometimes may space And walke about her gardens of delight. *a* **1599** *Ibid.* VII. vi. 55 That Wolues, where she was wont to space, Should harbour'd be.

spacearium (speɪ'sɛərɪəm). [f. SPACE *sb.*[1] + PLANET)ARIUM.] A large room arranged so that scenes representing space may be projected on to its interior; a planetarium.

1962 *Times* 18 Apr. 11/7 Five separate exhibits..will include such things as the 'Spacearium'. **1976** *Nature* 16 Sept. 180/1 At his disposal is a team of 250, a vast archive, a huge 'spacearium', an enormous theatre with a 55-foot high screen, scores of audio-visual aids and, of course, hundreds of artefacts—which means aircraft and spacecraft.

spacecraft ('speɪskrɑːft, -æ-). Also **space-craft, space craft.** Pl. **spacecraft.** [SPACE *sb.*[1]] Any vehicle designed to travel in space.

1930 *Sci. Amer.* Aug. 142/1 Valier was the principal proponent of working toward the space craft from the known forms of surface or air craft. **1932** D. LASSER *Conquest of Space* xvii. 279 Our experience with cosmic speeds and distances is not equal to the task of guiding a space-craft on its perilous journey. **1946** [see ARTIFICIAL *a.* 1 c]. **1959** *Observer* 2 Aug. 11/5 In the next few days, 40,000 ft. above the Californian desert, the world's first manned spacecraft will switch on its rocket engines for the first time. **1960** *New Statesman* 13 Feb. 214/2 One..complains bitterly of the 'world-wide conspiracy in operation throughout this planet which has succeeded in suppressing *almost all* knowledge of, and discussion of the space-craft known to terrestrials as "Flying Saucers"'. **1960** *Guardian* 15 Dec. 9/5 An American attempt to put a 388 lb spacecraft into orbit around the moon. **1968** *Times* 12 Oct. 18/6 They suggest that the altitude measurement made by the Russian space craft as it approached the surface of Venus was almost exactly half what it should have been. **1976** A. DAVIS *Television: First Forty Years* 47 There are graphics departments..and props departments that can build models of, say, spacecraft.

spaced (speɪst), *ppl. a.* [f. SPACE *sb.*[1] or *v.*]

1. Of printed or typed matter: having the words or lines separated by (a specified mode of) spacing. Also *double-, single-spaced*, qq. v. under the first element.

1808 STOWER *Printer's Gram.* vi. 160 Not in a greater degree than a middling and thin space to a thick spaced line. **1892** A. OLDFIELD *Man. Typog.* ii. 20 Thin spaces..are very useful in a close-spaced line.

2. a. Set at intervals or distances; *fig.* measured, regulated.

1873 F. JENKIN *Electr. & Magn.* xxii. §12 Uniformly spaced central holes serve to move the paper on at a constant speed. **1898** *Westm. Gaz.* 1 Apr. 2/1 Between strangers.., a spaced, even a distant, courtesy is essential to develop lasting friendship. **1920** *Wireless World* 12 June 200 (*heading*) Spaced loop aerial. **1949** G. A. BRIGGS *Sound Reproduction* iii. 35 Sound is picked up by 3 spaced microphones, recorded on separate channels, and played back through 3 spaced speakers. **1959** K. HENNEY *Radio Engin. Handbk.* (ed. 5) xxvi. 27 Analysis..indicates that, regardless of the value of the incident and polarization angles, the spaced-loop output voltage goes through a null when the directions of propagation are contained in the planes of the loop antennas. **1968** *Times* 29 Nov. (Sound of Leisure Suppl.) p. vi/5 The spaced microphone technique (using microphones a few inches or several feet apart, according to taste) relies both on volume and time of arrival differences. **1978** *Geophysical Research Lett.* V. 917/1 Observations of the troposphere with a VHF radar using a large antenna for transmission and small spaced antennas for reception.

b. With *out*.

1937 'M. INNES' *Hamlet, Revenge* III. v. 295 The number of spaced-out acts committed by the criminal. **1952** C. DAY LEWIS tr. *Virgil's Aeneid* IX. 200 Where the ring of defenders was thinnest and daylight showed Between their spaced-out bodies. **1976** 'J. ROSS' *I know what it's like to Die* xxxi. 203 The spaced-out drops of water from the tap.

c. Of children: born or conceived at intervals (of a kind denoted by qualifying advb.).

1939 [see EXPECT *v.* 4 e (b)]. **1965** M. STEWART *Airs above Ground* i. 10 She acquired a wealthy London banker..the kind of man..safely ensconced in the Jaguar belt with three carefully spaced children away at carefully chosen schools. **1976** *Times* 25 Feb. 16/5 The advantages of a smaller or adequately spaced family.

3. Of braid, etc.: Woven or worked in spaces or divisions.

1882 CAULFEILD & SAWARD *Dict. Needlew.* 454/1 *Spaced Braid*... The spaces or divisions into which the two patterns are severally woven are alternately thick, or close and narrow, and comparatively wide and open. *Ibid.*, *Spaced Braid Work*, a variety of Modern Point Lace, but made without fancy stitches and with braids outlined with cord.

4. In a state of drug-induced euphoria, 'high'; removed from actuality or disoriented, by narcotic stimulus. Also *transf.* Freq. with *out*. *slang* (orig. *U.S.*).

1968-70 *Current Slang* (Univ. S. Dakota) III-IV. 116 *Spaced out*, adj., mentally deficient; strange; absent-minded. **1969** *Negro Digest* Sept. 10 Spaced poems say that our ancestors are in the air and will communicate with us. **1969** *Time* 26 Sept. 41 The culture has its own in-group argot: ..'straights' (everyone else), 'heat' (the police)..and being 'spaced out' (in a drug daze). **1971** J. MANDELKAU *Buttons* v. 68, I remember being really spaced out and someone handing me a ladybird—telling me how nice they tasted. **1974** A. LURIE *War between Tates* vi. 131 'You look exhausted.' 'I am sorta spaced out.' **1975** *New Yorker* 5 May 6/1 Vibraharpist Mike Mainieri and pianist Warren Bernhardt play some heavily lyrical and spaced-out duets. **1977** C. McFADDEN *Serial* (1978) xx. 47/1 She just sort of stood there, feeling totally spaced, because the whole number was nothing short of *unreal*.

spacefaring ('speɪsfɛərɪŋ), *vbl. sb.* and *ppl. a.* [f. SPACE *sb.*[1], after *seafaring*.] **A.** *vbl. sb.* Space travel. **B.** *ppl. a.* That engages in space travel.

1959 P. ANDERSON *Virgin Planet* (1969) iii. 20 Who had ever begun the idea that spacefaring was one long wild adventure? **1962** *New Scientist* 1 Mar. 489 The leaders of the two spacefaring countries. **1973** *Sci. News* 3 Nov. 283 My own view..was that they [*sc.* pulsars] were perfect interstellar navigation beacons, the sort of markers that an interstellar spacefaring society would want to place throughout the galaxy. **1978** D. R. MASON *Mission to Pactolus R* i. 11 A long session in a Fingalnan brothel would set them up for another stint of spacefaring.

Also **'spacefarer**, one who travels in space.

1974 *New Scientist* 27 June 772 Such an asteroid-ark might one day encounter spacefarers of another civilisation, members of an intellectual brotherhood of the stars.

spaceful ('speɪsfʊl), *a. rare.* [f. SPACE *sb.*[1] + -FUL.] Spacious, commodious; wide, extensive.

1621 G. SANDYS *Ovid's Met.* III. (1626) 63 The ship in those profound And spacefull Seas, so stuck as on drie ground. **1906** MRS. HARKER *Paul & Fiammetta* xi, 'It's so spaceful, Janey,' she said.

space group. *Cryst.* [f. SPACE *sb.*[1] + GROUP *sb.*, tr. G. *raumgruppe* (A. Schoenflies 1891, in *Krystallsyst. und Krystallstruct.* II. iv. 359).] Any of the 230 sets of symmetry operations, derived from the point groups by the inclusion of translations, glide planes, and screw axes, which are used to classify crystal structures.

1901 *Rep. Brit. Assoc. Adv. Sci. 1901* 322 [Schoenflies] calls the groups of operations, whether those of Jordan or those added by himself, 'space-groups' (*Raumgruppen*). **1903** H. HILTON *Math. Crystallogr.* xvii. 159 Every space-group is isomorphous with one of the thirty-two point-groups consistent with the law of rational indices. **1934** W. P. DAVEY *Study of Crystal Struct.* viii. 240 The 230 space-groups are listed..giving..the Schoenflies code for the derivation of the space-group. **1974** *Nature* 11 Jan. 85/2 Dark-field observation could establish the presence of centres of symmetry, glide planes and screw axes, which could lead to the establishment of the space group.

spacelate, obs. form of SPHACELATE *v.*

spaceless ('speɪslɪs), *a.* [f. SPACE *sb.*[1] + -LESS.]

1. That is not subject to or limited by space; infinite, boundless. Freq. coupled with *timeless*.

1606 J. DAVIES (Heref.) *Sir T. Overbury* Concl., Wks. (Grosart) II. 20/1 They can giue no grace Beyond the span of life: Poore spacelesse-space! *a* **1618** SYLVESTER *Little Bartas* 564 Wks. (Grosart) II. 90 Nor may wee aske, What th' eviternall-One, That space-lesse Space could find to doe alone. **1819** *Blackw. Mag.* V. 323 There timeless, spaceless, dwells the Eternal One. **1874** *Contemp. Rev.* XXIII. 403 The timeless and spaceless Essence. **1880** H. DRUMMOND *Ideal Life*, etc. (1897) 69 By going away He was in a spaceless land and in a timeless eternity.

2. Occupying no space.

1825 COLERIDGE *Aids Refl.* (1858) I. 394 If we exclude space.., the time remains as a spaceless point. **1874** GEO. ELIOT *Coll. Breakf.-P.* 116 A need That spaceless stays where sharp analysis Has a shown a plenum filled without it.

Hence **'spacelessly** *adv.*; **'spacelessness**, the quality or condition of being unbounded by space, or of lacking space.

1895 G. MACDONALD *Lilith* xxxix. 286 We were not in the outer darkness; had we been, we could not have been *with* her; we should have been timelessly, spacelessly, absolutely apart. **1920** S. ALEXANDER *Space, Time, & Deity* I. 342 To possess spacelessness or timelessness (eternity). **1981** M. SPARK *Listening with Intent* v. 91 The spacelessness of this room where I lived..with..a bed for sitting and sleeping on.

'space-like, *a. Physics.* [f. SPACE *sb.*[1] + -LIKE.] Resembling or having the properties of space; *spec.* being or related to an interval between two points in space-time that lie outside one another's light cones (so that no signal or observer can pass from one to the other).

1914 [see *four-vector* s.v. FOUR C. 2]. **1920** A. S. EDDINGTON *Space, Time & Gravit.* iii. 60 Even if the discovery of a new ray led us to modify the reckoning of time and space, it would still be necessary in the study of material systems to preserve the *present* absolute distinction of time-like and space-like intervals. **1934** A. HUXLEY *Beyond Mexique Bay* 215 It may be possible to think of vast durations as composed of space-like fragments. **1955** L. ROSENFELD in W. Pauli *Niels Bohr* 87 An arbitrary family of space-like surfaces. **1964** *Cambr. Rev.* 24 Oct. 51/2 The commutativity..of the field operators at spacelike distances. **1978** PASACHOFF & KUTNER *University Astron.* xxvii. 694 The distance between the events is greater than the distance that light can travel in the time between the events. Such an interval is called spacelike.

spaceman ('speɪsmən). Also **space-man.** [SPACE *sb.*[1]]

1. A journalist paid according to the extent of space occupied by his writing (cf. SPACE *sb.* 18 d).

1892 HOWELLS *Mercy* 116 He felt that as a space-man.. his duty to his family required him to use every means for making copy. **1935** G. GREENE *England made Me* II. 80 He's News... I'm a space man... I can't afford to miss a thing.

2. One who travels in space or comes from another planet.

1942 *Thrilling Wonder Stories* Apr. 110/1 Maybe Lambert was a spaceman. Maybe he wasn't, but if he knew anything at all about spaceman's lingo he'd have to give now. **1944** F. BROWN in B. Aldiss *Introducing SF* (1964) 69 Earth's armada, all ten thousand ships and half-million fighting spacemen. **1956** 'J. WYNDHAM' *Seeds of Time* 81 Whither thou goest, I will go... It was all right for a tribe of nomads, but nowadays the wives of soldiers, sailors, pilots, spacemen—. **1962** A. LURIE *Love & Friendship* xiii. 250 Amateur experts..Visitors from another world... They think they're space men. **1977** P. CARTER *Under Goliath* iv. 21, I was reading a good book all about spacemen.

Hence **'spacemanship**.

1957 *Economist* 2 Mar. 400/1 Dr von Braun has always entertained, and shared with the public, the most ambitious ideals of spacemanship. **1966** *Life* 7 Jan. 32 (*caption*) Down from adventure and spacemanship, Stafford and Schirra pop out for an eye-level look at the sea.

spacer[1] ('speɪsə(r)). [f. SPACE *v.* + -ER[1].]

1. a. A device or piece of mechanism for spacing words; a piece of metal, etc., for making a space, interval, or division.

1884 KNIGHT *Dict. Mech.* Suppl. 911/2 By touching now the justifying-key, he caused the spacer to draw the line into another part of the [type-composing] machine to be justified. **1904** in *Cent. Dict. Suppl.* s.v., These ventilating spaces are obtained by means of metal spacers. **1916** *Chambers's Jrnl.* July 480/1 A new unit in roofing called a spacer allows of ordinary plain tiles or slates being laid wider apart than usual. **1943** *Sun* (Baltimore) 15 Apr. 26/3 She figured out a way to save countless man-hours in the manufacture of spacers—small rubber rings used in Rolls Royce airplane engines. **1954** *Automobile Engineer* XLIV. 508/3 A tubular spacer and two thrust washers round the shaft separate the roller bearings. **1962** *Which?* July 197/2 The second type [of life-jacket]..used *sealed-in air* between inner and outer coverings..which are held apart by 'spacers' of absorbent foam plastic. **1976** *Shooting Mag.* Dec. 12 (Advt.), It's a quality production gun, with one major difference. You can adjust the stock and insert various 'spacers' to achieve the perfect cast and drop.

b. *Archæol.* In full, *spacer plate.* A flat bead perforated with several holes in the same plane, by which the threads of a primitive multi-strand necklace are held apart.

1924 D. RANDALL-MACIVER *Villanovans & Early Etruscans* vi. 173 Fusiform and spherical gold beads, white and blue glass cylinders and small perforated spacers of amber formed the other elements of the necklace. **1940** V. G. CHILDE *Prehist. Communities of British Isles* vii. 124 In Ireland..the crescentic necklace was translated into a crescentic collar, cut out of a sheet of native gold and relieved with designs in panels, imitating the spacer-plates of the necklaces. **1958** *Antiquity* XXXII. 209 The complex-bored amber spacers from Hagenau. **1980** J. J. TAYLOR *Bronze Age Gold Work* iii. 41 The spacer-plate motif can be found in the Beaker repertoire pre-dating Wessex, to which the earliest dated spacer-plate is likely to belong.

2. One who or that which spaces, or allows space, in a particular manner.

1888 *Encycl. Brit.* XXIV. 698/2 It [the cylindrical typewriting machine] is a variable spacer, giving more space to..m and w than to..i, t, and l.

3. *Biol.* A section of DNA which is not represented in the final RNA transcript, separating two sections which are.

1970 O. L. MILLER et al. in *Cold Spring Harbor Symp. Quantitative Biol.* XXXV. 505/2 Non-matrix segments of varying lengths (spacers) are intercalated between matrix units. **1974** *New Scientist* 9 May 329 Chemists..have succeeded in synthesising a nucleotide complementary to a definite part of a small bacteriophage.., a part regarded as a spacer. **1982** W. I. P. MAINWARING et al. *Nucleic Acid Biochem. & Molecular Biol.* vii. 258 There are spacer regions between genes which *may or may not* be transcribed. If transcribed, their contribution to the RNA transcript is removed by an excision process during the maturation of the RNA.

4. Special Comb.: **spacer gel**, a part of the gel used in electrophoresis (see quot. 1975).

1968 J. R. SARGENT *Methods in Zone Electrophoresis* vii. 90 It is possible to eliminate the sample gel and the spacer gels ..and to apply the sample directly on top of the main gel. **1975** DAVIS & SIMPKINS in Williams & Wilson *Biologist's Guide to Princ. & Techniques Pract. Biochem.* iv. 115 The upper third of the gel consists of a large pore 'stacking' or 'spacer' gel, and the lower portion of smaller pore 'running' or 'separating' gel. The function of the stacking gel is to concentrate the sample as it moves through the gel, so that on entering the running gel it is an extremely narrow band.

spacer[2] ('speɪsə(r)). *Science Fiction.* [f. SPACE *sb.*[1] + -ER[1].] **1.** = SPACEMAN 2.

1955 C. M. KORNBLUTH *Mindworm* 59 'I'm a spacer,' he said... 'Venus.' **1958** I. ASIMOV *Naked Sun* i. 11 The Galaxy was closed to Earthmen. It was pre-empted by the Spacers, whose ancestors had been Earthmen centuries before.

2. A spaceship, spacecraft.

1962 *New Worlds Sci. Fiction* Sept. 50 The spacer broke through the low hanging layer of clouds above. **1978** D. R. MASON *Mission to Pactolus R* i. 5 A Fingalnan voice spoke into the quiet command cabin of the hurrying spacer.

spaceship ('speɪsʃɪp). Also **space ship, space-ship.** [SPACE *sb.*[1]] **1.** A spacecraft; esp. a manned one under the control of its crew.

1894 J. J. ASTOR *Journey in Other Worlds* I. vi. 93 'What sort of space-ship do you propose to have?' asked the vice-president.
1929 *Sci. Wonder Q.* I. 65/2 Since the space ship..was circling freely in space..the proximity of the moon was no hindrance to leaving the ship. **1936** *Jrnl. Brit. Interplanetary Soc.* III. 26 It is essential that the space-ship should be in constant communication with its base station. **1938** C. S. LEWIS *Out of Silent Planet* iv. 38 All he ever remembered of his first meal in the space-ship was the tyranny of heat and light. **1948** 'N. SHUTE' *No Highway* ix. 226 Designs for a rocket-propelled Space Ship, I think he called it, for a projected journey to the moon. **1951** A. C. CLARKE *Sands of Mars* i. 9 Sleek, streamlined spaceships..had been the dream of the early twentieth century. **1962** F. I. ORDWAY et al. *Basic Astronautics* i. 2 The spaceship is stimulating the study of space navigation. **1970** N. ARMSTRONG et al. *First on Moon* xiv. 338 If you're going to run a spaceship you've got to be pretty cautious about how you use your resources. **1977** P. CARTER *Under Goliath* vi. 29 It's from Mars... It's a spaceship from Mars.

2. *spaceship earth* (also with capital initials), a phr. used to draw attention to the finite nature of the earth's resources.

1966 B. WARD *(title)* Space ship earth. **1969** R. B. FULLER *Operating Man. Spaceship Earth* iv. 52 We have not been seeing our Spaceship Earth as an integrally-designed machine which to be persistently successful must be comprehended and serviced in total. **1976** *Conservation News* Sept./Oct. 12/1 There is a growing awareness of the need to conserve the life-support systems of spaceship earth. **1981** *Nature* 5 Nov. 41/3 All species on 'Spaceship Earth' have an equal right to exist.

space-time (ˌspeɪs'taɪm), *adj. phr.* and *sb.* Also **spacetime, space time.** [SPACE *sb.*[1]]

A. *adj. phr.* Pertaining to or situated in both space and time.

1905 R. B. PERRY *Approach to Philos.* 131 An experimentally verifiable system must contain space-time variables. **1938** *Harper's Mag.* Jan. 151/2 If you denounce him as a 'Jew', apart from his space-time characteristics, you perform a monstrous act. **1965** *Math. in Biol. & Med.* (Med. Res. Council) v. 227 For many years leukaemia has been alleged to occur in clusters, though the evidence has been largely anecdotal and its interpretation intuitive because of the difficulties..of formulating the hypothesis of space-time clustering in precise and testable terms. **1973** *Nature* 27 July 214/2 The projection of the most recent seismic migration wave to the latitude of maximum recurrence of earthquakes provides the basis for setting the space-time bounds on the next earthquake greater than magnitude 5.

B. *sb. Physics.* [tr. G. *raumzeit.*] Time and three-dimensional space regarded as fused in a four-dimensional continuum containing all events. Also *attrib.*

1915 E. CUNNINGHAM *Relativity* 9 *(heading)* The space-time transformations. *Ibid.* 10 Newtonian Relativity consists in the fact that either (*x*, *y*, *z*, *t*) or (*x'*, *y'*, *z'*, *t'*) are equally valid as space-time coordinates. **1927** S. ERTZ *Now East, now West* viii. 117 I've got quite drunk on theories about the space-time continuum. **1930** *Morning Post* 17 June 13/1 The 'metrical structure' of space-time now adopted by Einstein is based on the assumption that there is a meaning in saying that two short lines are equal in length, that they are parallel, and that the angle between them is not altered when they are moved so as to remain parallel to themselves. **1934** E. MUIR *Coll. Poems* (1960) 44 Lengthening league by league The ghastly thin anatomy of Space Time Stripped to the nerve. **1940** W. EMPSON *Gathering Storm* 18 But if it parts Into uncommunicable spacetimes. **1956** *Nature* 10 Mar. 458/1 He [*sc.* H. Weyl] discovered the first 'unified field theory' in which the Maxwell field appears along with the gravitational field as a geometrical property of space-time. **1967** G. STEINER *Lang. Silence* 283 We are imprisoned in the unexamined assumption or unconscious illusion of a homogeneous, forward-flowing space-time continuum. **1978** PASACHOFF & KUTNER *University Astron.* xxvii. 695 The basic conclusion of the general theory [of relativity] is that gravitational fields change the geometry of spacetime. We say that in the presence of gravitational fields, spacetime becomes curved.

spacewoman ('speɪswʊmən). [f. SPACE *sb.*[1], after SPACEMAN.] A female traveller in space; a woman who comes from another planet.

1962 N. MITCHISON *(title)* Memoirs of a spacewoman. **1963** *Daily Tel.* 18 Oct. 23/3 *(caption)* Russia's first space woman, Valentina Tereshkova, 26, waving at Prestwick yesterday when her plane made a two-hour refuelling stop. **1978** G. HOUSEHOLD *Last Two Weeks of Georges Rivac* i. 14 It doesn't matter which way up I'm put. I ought to be a spacewoman.

spaceworthy ('speɪswɜːðɪ), *a.* [f. SPACE *sb.*[1] + WORTHY *a.*] In a fit condition for space travel. Also **'spaceworthiness.**

1959 'WYNDHAM' & PARKES *Outward Urge* iv. 156 She reclaimed the damaged Satellites, and made three of them spaceworthy again. **1959** J. BLISH *Clash of Cymbals* ii. 39 The unending demands of the city's spaceworthiness. **1960** *New Statesman* 30 Jan. 146/2 Apparently no other proofs were needed to demonstrate the efficacy of their measures to ensure the space-worthiness of the cosmic vehicle. **1968** *Daily Tel.* 16 Dec. 1/8 Russia's unmanned Zond 5 and 6 made successful 'boomerang' flights round the moon, and Soyuz 3 has been proved space-worthy for four days.

spacey, var. SPACY *a.*

spachi, obs. form of SPAHI.

spacial(ity, -ly, varr. of SPATIAL(ITY, -LY.

†**spacie.** *Obs. rare.* [ad. med.L. *spaci-um*, L. *spatium*: see SPACE *sb.*[1]] = SPACE *sb.*[1] 3 a.

1540 *Test. Ebor.* (Surtees) VI. 125 By the spacie of viij[th] yeres. **1541** *Ibid.* 135 To burne the spacie of xij days.

†**spacier**, *v. Sc. Obs.* [ad. OF. *espacier*: see SPACE *v.* and cf. MDu. *spaceren, -ieren*, MHG. and G. *spazieren.*] *intr.* To walk or stroll.

1549 *Compl. Scotl.* vi. (1801) 58 Of this sort I did spaceir vp and doune but sleipe. [**1819** W. TENNANT *Papistry Storm'd* (1827) 109 They spacier'd back and fore in bands.]

spacing ('speɪsɪŋ), *vbl. sb.* [f. SPACE *v.*]

1. The action of the verb, in various senses, or the result of this action. Also with *out.* **a.** In printing, writing, or typing.

1683 MOXON *Mech. Exerc., Printing* xxii. ⁋8 With too great Spacing-out or too Close Setting, he..may save himself a great deal of Labour. **1771** LUCKOMBE *Hist. Printing* 396 Spacing consists in putting a proper distance between words. *Ibid.*, In common Roman Matter, a moderate equal distance between word and word, is counted True Spacing. **1808** STOWER *Printer's Gram.* vi. 159 Close spacing is as unpleasant to the sight as wide spacing. **1862** *Macm. Mag.* Nov. 15 Where the printer can help by means of large letters and spacing. **1871** *Spectator* 22 Apr. 474 The difference between huddling and spacing out is one which depends partly on character.., very few men..spacing out their letters exactly alike.

b. In general use. Also *attrib.* as *spacing collar, lace, machine, washer.*

1874 THEARLE *Naval Archit.* 129 The sizes and spacing of the rivets must be regulated accordingly. **1879** *Cassell's Techn. Educ.* IV. 31/2 The spacing of the beams depends largely upon the positions of the hatchways. **1895** *Jrnl. R. Inst. Brit. Archit.* 14 Mar. 349 There are other points of difference between the spacing out of the pictures.
attrib. **1875** KNIGHT *Dict. Mech.* 2251 *Spacing and Boring Machine*, (Wood-working,) a machine for boring blind-stiles, sashes, etc., at accurately equal distances. **1882** CAULFEILD & SAWARD *Dict. Needlew.* 442/2 *Spacing Lace*.. does not intimate a particular kind of lace, but lace used for a certain purpose. **1916** *Automobile Engineer* VI. 92/2 *(caption)* Adjustable spacing collar for milling cutters. **1923** *Popular Wireless* 27 Oct. 294/1 (Advt.), Spacing washers, large...per doz. 2½d. **1971** *Buck & Hickman Tool Buyer's Guide* 96 Spacing Washers also supplied 1½ in. bore × 2¼ in. dia. *Ibid.*, Spacing collars and washers for milling machine arbors.

2. *Med.* Period of time, esp. between the attacks of malarial fever.

1898 P. MANSON *Trop. Diseases* ii. 48 The fever.., except in the matter of the spacing, which is one of forty-eight hours, resembles that caused by the quartan parasite. **1899** *Allbutt's Syst. Med.* VIII. 207 The intervals between words —the spacing or order in time of utterance—may be irregular.

3. Breadth of treatment; spaciousness.

1877 MORLEY *Crit. Misc.* Ser. II. 257 If we are now and then conscious in the book of a certain want of spacing,..a sense of being too narrowly enclosed.

†**spaciosity.** *Obs. rare.* Also 7 spat-. [ad. F. *spaciosité* (also †*spatiosité*, = It. *spaziosità*, Sp. *espaciosidad*) or late L. *spatiōsitas*, f. *spatiōsus* SPACIOUS *a.*] **a.** A hollow or cavity. **b.** Spaciousness; extensiveness.

1541 R. COPLAND *Guydon's Quest. Chirurg.* L iv b, In depe woundes that haue nede to be serched for the lycour that assembleth in the botome of the spaciosite. **1620** SHELTON *Quix.* II. IV. xvi. 204 That you may behold..the Knitting of the Muscles, and the Spaciosity and Breadth of the Veins. **1694** R. BURTHOGGE *Reason* v. §1. 108 Of spatiosity or extension..I shall have occasion to discourse hereafter, when I come to speak of quantity.

spacious ('speɪʃəs), *a.* Also 4–5 **spaciouse**, 5 **-yous**, 6–7 **spatious.** [ad. L. *spatiōsus* (med.L. *spaciōsus*), f. *spatium* SPACE *sb.*[1], or OF. *spacios, spacieux* (F. *spacieux*, = It. *spazioso*, Sp. and Pg. *espacioso*).]

1. Of lands, etc.: Of vast, large, or indefinite superficial extent or area; wide, widely extended, extensive.

1382 WYCLIF *Isaiah* xxii. 18 He shal sende thee in to a brod lond and spacious. *Ibid.* xxviii. 2 Sent out vp on the spaciouse erthe. **1480** CAXTON *Myrr.* III. xx. 179 The firmamente..is so spacyous, so noble and so large. **1590** SPENSER *F.Q.* III. i. 20 But faire before the gate a spatious plaine, Mantled with greene, it selfe did spredden wyde. **1602** MARSTON *Antonio's Rev.* I. v, That's a large lye, as vast as spatious hell. **1697** DRYDEN *Virg. Georg.* II. 571 Commend the large Excess Of spacious Vineyards; cultivate the less. **1748** GRAY *Alliance* 22 This spacious animated scene survey. **1784** COWPER *Task* I. 164 Ouse, slow winding through a level plain Of spacious meads. **1884** *Marshall's Tennis Cuts* 171 The spacious grounds were looking lovely.
transf. and *fig.* **1602** SHAKS. *Ham.* v. ii. 90 He hath much Land, and fertile;..'tis a Chowgh; but as I saw spacious in the possession of dirt. **1606** —— *Tr. & Cr.* II. iii. 261 Thy wisdome, Which..confines Thy spacious and dilated parts. **1821** SHELLEY *Adonais* xlvii, Dart thy spirit's light.., until its spacious might Satiate the void circumference.

b. Covering a considerable distance.

1607 TOPSELL *Four-f. Beasts* (1658) 242 It is better to qualifie their rage in long and spacious direct journies then in often windings and turnings. **1638** JUNIUS *Paint. Ancients* 226 Mettled horses are best knowne by a spacious race. **1695** LD. PRESTON *Boeth.* IV. 162 And when this spatious Course is run, She to the outmost Sphere doth come.

†**c.** Wide-spread; widely spoken. *Obs.*

c **1645** HOWELL *Lett.* II. lvi. (1892) 463 The High-Dutch or Teutonic Tongue is one of the prime and most spacious maternal Languages of Europe. *Ibid.* lx. 477 The most spacious Dialect of the Hebrew is the Syriac.

2. Of dwellings, rooms, etc.: Having or affording ample space or room; large, roomy, commodious.

1382 WYCLIF *Jer.* xxii. 14, I shal bilde vp to me a large hous, and spacious souping places. **1597** HOOKER *Eccl. Pol.* v. xv. §3 The former buildings which were but of mean and small estate contented them not, spacious and ample churches they erected throughout every city. **1610** HOLLAND *Camden's Brit.* (1637) 294* King Stephen erected a spacious Castle. **1687** MIÈGE *Gt. Fr. Dict.* II. s.v., A spacious Building... A spacious Room. **1770** LANGHORNE *Plutarch* (1851) II. 587/1 [He] hid himself in a spacious cave there. **1794** MRS. RADCLIFFE *Myst. Udolpho* xlii, They presently entered a spacious and ancient chamber. **1832** LYTTON *Eugene A.* I. v. 26 Though it was summer.., the log burnt on the spacious hearth. **1844** H. H. WILSON *Brit. India* I. 117 Spacious barracks were severally appropriated to the use of the European and native troops. **1880** MISS BRADDON *Just as I am* vii, The drawing-room was a spacious and lofty room.

b. Similarly of roads, streets, courts, etc.

1588 SHAKS. *Titus A.* II. i. 114 The Forrest walkes are wide and spacious. **1607** DEKKER *Knt.'s Conjur.* (1842) 22 The wayes are delicate, euen, spatious, and very faire. **1673** RAY *Journ. Low C.* 21 Middleburgh is the capital City of Zealand,..having spatious Streets. **1767** LADY M. W. MONTAGU *Lett.* II. xlvi. 33 The court leading into it is very spacious. **1796** MORSE *Amer. Geog.* I. 155 The streets are spacious and regular. **1809–10** COLERIDGE *Friend* (1865) 18 The spacious outer court was crowded with men and women.

c. quasi-*adv.* Spaciously.

1667 MILTON *P.L.* VIII. 102 Let it speak The Makers high magnificence, who built So spacious.

3. Of things: Presenting, having, or covering a comparatively wide surface; large, ample, expansive.

1631 WEEVER *Anc. Funeral Mon.* 743 Where this spacious Grauestone lies couched. **1663** BUTLER *Hud.* I. iii. 1303 Or that his snout and spacious Ears Do hold proportion with a Bear's. **1727** SWIFT *Market Hill Thorn* Wks. 1755 IV. I. 87 There stood..A spacious thorn before the gate. **1819** SHELLEY *Peter Bell 3rd* IV. xv, Then Peter..smoothed his spacious forehead down With his broad palm. **1847** C. BRONTE *Jane Eyre* i, Thick lineaments in a spacious visage, heavy limbs and large extremities.

b. Of large size; bulky.

1655 VAUGHAN *Silex Scint.* II. 153 The comely, spacious whale. **1867** F. H. LUDLOW *Little Brother* 44 After sundry hustlings, from hurrying men, spacious lounging ladies and busy workmen.

c. Roomy, capacious.

1819 BYRON *Juan* II. clx, They furnish'd him..With a clean shirt, and very spacious breeches.

4. Great, extensive, ample.
1595–7 DANIEL *Civ. Wars* IV. xviii, They, being so mightie, and so popular, And their command so spacious as it was, Might..forget [etc.]. **1605** SHAKS. *Macb.* IV. iii. 71 You may Conuey your pleasures in a spacious plenty, And yet seeme cold. **1607** MIDDLETON *Michaelmas Term* II. i. 101 It seems..your credit [is] very spacious here i' th' city. **1651** tr. *De-las-Coveras' Don Fenise* 280 Charitie was altogether charmed with these spatious consolations. **1704** SWIFT *Tale Tub* Introd., Being a type, a sign,..bearing analogy to the spacious Commonwealth of writers. **1870** LOWELL *Among my Bks.* Ser. I. (1873) 253 What a subject would that have been for a person of Mr. Masson's spacious predilections!

†**b.** That is such on a large scale. *Obs.*$^{-1}$
1599 B. JONSON *Ev. Man out of Hum.* I. iii, Is't possible that such a spacious villaine should live, and not be plagu'd?

5. Characterized by greatness, breadth, or comprehensiveness of views or sympathies.
c **1600** SHAKS. *Sonn.* cxxxv, Thou whose will is large and spatious. **1635** SHIRLEY *Lady of Pleasure* v. i, They have souls more spacious than Kings. **1697** W. MOLYNEUX in *Locke's Lett.* (1708) 214 Your chapter concerning the conduct of the understanding must needs be very sublime and spacious. **1833** TENNYSON *Dream Fair Women* ii, Those melodious bursts that fill The spacious times of great Elizabeth With sounds that echo still. **1875** LOWELL *Spenser* Prose Wks. 1890 IV. 307 In this eclogue he gives hints of that spacious style which was to distinguish him. **1894** *Macm. Mag.* June 160/2 Of the few great men I have known ..Kossuth's [was] the most spacious nature.

6. Prolonged; occupying a considerable time.
1642 MILTON *Apol. Smect.* Wks. 1851 III. 254 Neglecting the maine bulk of all that spacious antiquity, which might stunne children, but not men. **1647** HEXHAM I, A spacious time, *een langen tijdt*.

spaciously (ˈspeɪʃəslɪ), *adv.* Also 7 **spatiously.** [f. prec. + -LY[2].]

1. In a spacious house or place.
1382 WYCLIF *Isaiah* xxx. 23 Ther shul be fed in thi possessioun in that day the lomb spaciously [L. *spatiose*]. **1651** DAVENANT *Gondibert* I. vi. 38 Most spaciously we dwell. **1726** LEONI *Alberti's Archit.* I. 98/2 He can..receive strangers handsomely and spaciously.

2. Amply; largely.
1608 MIDDLETON *Mad World* II. i, Your honour is most spaciously welcome. *a* **1668** DAVENANT *Distresses* IV. i, Though not spaciously Possess'd of Lands, his Honor.. May equal any Mans.

3. At great length; with great fulness.
1605 CAMDEN *Rem.* (1623) 12 Good Lord, how spaciously might a learned pen walke in this argument? **1652** NEEDHAM tr. *Selden's Mare Cl.* 29 So spaciously did Chizzola dilate in speaking of the opinion of the Lawyers. **1715** M. DAVIES *Athen. Brit.* I. 8 Those News-mongers were oblig'd to write spaciously, or a great deal.

4. So as to comprehend or cover much space; extensively.
1603 KNOLLES *Hist. Turks* (1638) 2 A rough and desart country..spaciously extended euen as far as vnto the Arympheians. **1687** MIÉGE *Gt. Fr. Dict.* II. s.v., A Thing that spreads spaciously. **1846** DANA *Zooph.* (1848) 625 Membranaceous and internally spatiously cellular.

5. With largeness of manner.
1865 DICKENS *Mut. Fr.* I. xi, 'How Do You Like London? .. You find it Very Large?' said Mr. Podsnap, spaciously.

spaciousness (ˈspeɪʃəsnɪs). Also 7 **spatiousness(e.** [f. as prec. + -NESS.]

1. The state or quality of being wide, spacious, or commodious; extensiveness of area or dimensions; roominess.
1601 R. JOHNSON *Kingd. & Commw.* (1603) 168 Numbers which may be imagined by the spaciousnes of his dominions. **1631** GOUGE *God's Arrows* v. §15. 427 How farre do they exceed in spaciousnesse the Kingdome of Jehosaphat. **1715** *Lond. Gaz.* No. 5336/2 The Apartments of the States of Brabant..are the finest..for their Spaciousness. **1759** JOHNSON *Rasselas* I. xiii. 95 Yonder palace was raised by single stones, yet you see its height and spaciousness. **1798** *Monthly Rev.* XXVI. 248 A profuse employment of columns gives to his original model an inviting spaciousness. **1864** KERR *Gentlem. House* 83 Somewhat opposed to spaciousness..is the exquisite quality of compactness. **1885** *Manch. Exam.* 8 Apr. 5/1 The spaciousness and stately sweep of Sackville-street.
transf. **1841** MYERS *Cath. Th.* IV. §34. 352 A certain roundness of numbers, and spaciousness of margin.

2. Largeness or breadth of mind, views, etc.
1657 W. COLES *Adam in Eden* To Rdr., So great was that spatiousnesse of mind that God had bestowed on him.

spacistor (speɪˈsɪstə(r)). *Electronics.* [f. SPACE *sb.*[1] + TRANS)ISTOR.] A kind of semiconductor device (see quot. 1957).
1957 STATZ & PUCEL in *Proc. IRE* XLV. 317/1 New devices are considered in which electrons or holes are injected directly into space-charge regions of reverse-biased junctions avoiding the diffusion of carriers through field-free regions. The case considered is one in which the junction is biased at a voltage such that the injected carriers are multiplied by the avalanche process. A device of this type shall be called a spacistor. **1962** SIMPSON & RICHARDS *Physical Princ. Junction Transistors* viii. 175 The spacistor can have input and output impedances of the order of tens of megohms and the coupling between input and output terminals is almost purely capacitative. **1969** A. MARCUS *Electronics for Technicians* viii. 160 There is not, as yet, general agreement upon a symbol for the spacistor transistor.

spack, *a.* and *adv. Obs.* exc. *dial.* Also 3–4 **spac,** 4 **spak, spake;** 7 **spackt,** 9 **spact.** [a. ON. *spak-r* (MSw. *spaker*, Norw. and Sw. *spak*, Da. *spag*) quiet, gentle, wise, clever.]

A. *adj.* **1.** Of persons: Quick, prompt, ready; intelligent, clever. Now *dial.*
c **1200** *Trin. Coll. Hom.* 183 To gode þu ware slau and let, and to euele spac and hwat. *a* **1240** *Lofsong* in *O.E. Hom.* I. 205 Ich habbe..inumen mis, and mis etholden ofte, tovel spac, and slow to Godd. **13..** *E.E. Allit. P.* C. 169 Þenne bispeke þe spakest dispayred wel nere. **1674** RAY *N.C. Words* 44 A *Spackt* Lad or Wench: apt to learn, ingenious. **1818–** in dial. glossaries (Chesh., Derby, Leics., etc.). *a* **1904** in *Eng. Dial. Dict.* s.v., [In Bedfordshire] a child is said to be 'not very spack'.

†**2.** Gentle, quiet, tame. *Obs. rare.*
1303 R. BRUNNE *Handl. Synne* 319 Y sagh hyt [*sc.* the Spirit] so mylde and spake, þat with my hande y myght hyt take. *Ibid.* 7486 For hyt [*sc.* the bird] sate by hym so spake [*gloss.* tame].

†**B.** *adv.* Quickly, promptly, speedily. *Obs.*
13.. *Orfeo* 305 (Auchinleck MS.), His schlauain he dede on, al so spac, And henge his harp opon his bac. *c* **1330** *King of Tars* 774 The soudan com in that was so blak, The child heo schewed him also spak. **13..** *E.E. Allit. P.* C. 104 [The sailors] sprude spak to þe sprete þe spare bawe-lyne.

Spackle (ˈspæk(ə)l). *N. Amer.* Also **spackle.** [Cf. SPARKLE *v.*[2] 4 b and G. *spachtel* putty knife, mastic, filler.] A proprietary name for a compound used to fill cracks in plaster and produce a smooth surface before decoration.
1928 *Official Gaz.* (U.S. Patent Office) 7 Feb. 17/1 *Spackle*... A surfacing compound for filling imperfection so as to bring up to a smooth and level surface areas that are to be painted or decorated. Claims use since Aug. 1, 1927. **1951** *Home Painting, Wallpapering & Decorating* ii. 34 You must be sure there is paint on the surface upon which you are going to put the spackle. **1971** *Black World* Mar. 65/2 After he did that he mixed the spackle with water and spread it as evenly as he could over the crack. **1975** *Amer. Speech* 1969 XLIV. 26 *Spackle, n.*, a prepared paste that, when mixed with water, is used to repair cracks and holes in plaster or gypsum wallboard.

Hence as *v. trans.*, to repair or fill with Spackle (see also quot. 1940); **ˈspackling** *vbl. sb.*
1940 R. MAYER *Artist's Hand-bk. Materials & Techniques* xii. 506 *Spackling* or *Sparkling* (probably from the German *spachteln*, to putty up). The rectifying of a defect in plaster or a mural painting by digging out the defective spot and filling it in with a plastic gesso, plaster of Paris, Keene's cement, or other similar material. **1941** *Pop. Science* July 149 In addition to patching plaster, other prepared powders or so-called 'spachtling [*sic*] compounds' are sold for patching, filling, and smoothing purposes. **1971** H. SMITH *View from Chivo* vii. 69 Then he coated each wire with a spackling compound. **1971** *Black World* Mar. 67/1 People who could watch for him if Death came suddenly sweeping through the crack in the kitchen wall that he hadn't spackled properly. **1980** *Redbook* Oct. 58/3 She cooked better than I and it was a fact that I Spackled the walls better than she.

†**spackly,** *adv. Obs.* Forms: 4 **spacli,** 5 **-ly,** 4 **spakli (-liy),** 4–5 **-ly,** 5 **spakely;** 4 **spaclyche, spaklich(e.** [f. SPACK *a.* Cf. ON. *spakliga*, MSw. *spaklika*.]

1. Speedily, quickly; actively.
Freq. in 14th cent. poetry; in some examples the sense is not quite clear.
c **1310** in Wright *Lyric P.* x. 37 Such reed me myhte spaclyche reowe. *c* **1350** *Will. Palerne* 5456 þe king of spayne spacli spedde him þan to horse. **1377** LANGL. *P. Pl.* B. XVII. 81 And spes spaklich hym spedde, spede if he myȝte, To ouertake hym. *a* **1400–50** *Alexander* 2975 With þat he.. Sparis out spacly as sparke out of gledes.

2. Prudently, knowingly, wisely.
c **1350** *Will. Palerne* 19 þe child..was..breme of his age, For spakly speke it couþe tho, & spedeliche to-wawe. *c* **1400** *Sege Jerus.* 784 Or y wende fro þis walle, ȝe schul wordes schewe & efte spakloker spele.

spackyll, spacle, obs. varr. SPECKLE *v.*

spacy (ˈspeɪsɪ), *a.* Also **spacey.** [f. SPACE *sb.*[1] + -Y.]

1. Large, roomy, spacious. Hence **ˈspaciness.**
1885 *Art Jrnl.* 189/2 A sense of spaciness in the picture. **1891** C. JAMES *Rom. Rigmarole* vii. 62 My study lamp.. throwing a mellow light upon my desk, [and] my spacy blotting-pad.

2. In a heightened state of consciousness; disoriented from reality, = SPACED *ppl. a.* 4. *slang* (chiefly *U.S.*).
1968–70 *Current Slang* (Univ. S. Dakota) III–IV. 117 *Spacey*, adj, appearing to be functioning on a level higher than normal. **1972** *Last Whole Earth Catalog* (Portola Inst.) 67/3 Her expression was very spacy... Her eyes were so weird it was hard to read anything very definite in her face. .. She..sat on the curb in the lotus posture and stared off into the east. **1975** *Globe & Mail* (Toronto) 12 July 32/6 'You get pretty spacey after doing a lot of interviews,' she said. 'One time someone asked me if Dylan had changed a lot and I was so spacey I said, "Well, he doesn't bum drinks any more."' **1977** C. MCFADDEN *Serial* (1978) ii. 10/2 She spotted Martha's ex-husband-once-removed with his spacy new old lady. **1980** J. A. CARVER *Panglor* (1981) viii. 138 His head felt large, and a little spacey, and he felt a heightened sense of geometry, of perspective.

3. Of, pertaining to, or purportedly characteristic of (conditions in) outer space; esp. used in connection with electronic music.
1971 *It* 2–16 June 19/2 A good studio-produced album sounding very live and certainly spacey. **1977** *Rolling Stone* 13 Jan. 62/5 Terje Rypdal,..spun spacey riffs clothed in lots of distortion. **1980** *Radio Times* 27 Sept.–3 Oct. 89/3 For 18 years Ron Grainger's tune gave the programme [*sc.* 'Dr. Who'] an eerie, spacey feel.

spad[1] (spæd). orig. *U.S.* [Var. of SPUD *sb.*] A spike with a flattened end containing a hole to support a plumb-line, so that it can be driven into a tunnel roof to provide a marker.
1908 L. W. TRUMBULL *Man. Underground Surveying* iii. 93 A majority of the mines of the United States are using punched horseshoe nails known as 'spads'. The head of the horseshoe nail..is hammered flat and a hole punched through it. **1957** R. C. A. HOOPER *Winiberg's Metalliferous Mine Surveying* (ed. 4) ix. 186 Some surveyors prefer to have the width of the spad along the longitudinal axis of a drive rather than at right angles. **1973** B. A. BARRY *Construction Measurements* xvi. 220 Line is carried forward in tunneling by tape and theodolite to marks placed either on the floor or side or roof of the tunnel. Driving plugs and spads into the roof to serve as horizontal control (traverse) points keeps them free from traffic damage or disturbance.

Spad[2] (spæd). [f. the initials of S*ociété* p*our* A*viation et ses* D*érivés*, the designers.] Any of several types of French aircraft, esp. a biplane fighter much used in the war of 1914–18. Also *attrib.*
1917 *Sci. Amer.* Oct. 249/1 Still faster is the 'Spad', a tiny biplane. **1918** J. M. GRIDER *War Birds* (1927) 60 They have Pups and Spads and Avros. *Ibid.* 88 There were three Spads so Capt. Foggin asked for Spad pilots. **1920** A. J. L. SCOTT *Hist. Sixty Squadron, R.A.F.* ii. 15 Foot..was given a 'Spad', on which he did great execution during the autumn. **1926** J. L. PRITCHARD *Bk. Aeroplane* xii. 230 Spad machines were recognised as among the fastest..used by the Allies during the war. **1929** HALL & NILES *One Man's War* 170 In very high, thin air the Nieuports manœuvred very well, better perhaps than the Spads did, because the Spad was a heavier machine. **1970** *Word Watching* Apr. 7/1 *Spad*, A-1 fighter-bomber escort for rescue helicopters. **1973** D. LEES *Rape of Quiet Town* vi. 101 Vague memories of anti-aircraft drill from the days of Spads and Fokkers.

spadaite (ˈspɑːdəaɪt). *Min.* [ad. G. *spadait* (F. von Kobell 1843, in *Jrnl. für prakt. Chem.* XXX. 467), f. the name of Lavinio *Spada* de Medici (1801–63), Italian writer, politician, and mineralogist: see -ITE[1].] A hydrated magnesium silicate, $MgSiO_3.2H_2O$, found as an alteration product in lavas, and occurring as amorphous masses coloured red by impurities.
1848 J. D. DANA *Man. Mineral.* 149 Spadaite. A flesh-red mineral, near Schiller spar. **1931** *Amer. Mineralogist* XVI. 232 Spadaite occurs only in the ore shoots, associated with the silicates mentioned, quartz, various sulphides (chiefly chalcopyrite and bornite) and their oxidation products, and small quantities of native gold. **1968** I. KOSTOV *Mineral.* 334 Spadaite, $MgSiO_3.2H_2O$,..corresponds to hydrated enstatite.

†**ˈspaddle.** *Obs. rare.* [Alteration of PADDLE *sb.*[1] 1, after SPADE *sb.*[1] Cf. SPATTLE *sb.*]
a. A small spade.
1669 WORLIDGE *Syst. Agric.* 193 Others destroy them [*sc.* moles] very expeditiously by a Spaddle, waiting in the mornings when they usually stir. **1835** H. C. TODD *Notes upon Canada & U.S.A.* 8 Jonathan..[uses] *spaddle*, for spade.
b. = SPATTLE *sb.*[2] 1.
1861 MRS. BEETON *Bk. Househ. Managem.* 760 The principal utensils required for making ice-creams are ice-tubs, freezing-pots, spaddles, and a cellaret. The use of the spaddle is to stir up..the cream.

spade (speɪd), *sb.*[1] Also 4, 7 **spad;** *Sc.* 6–7 **sped,** 6–7 **spaid.** [OE. *spadu*, *spædu* fem., and *spade* fem. or *spada* masc., = OFris. *spada* (EFris. *spâde*, NFris. *spade*, *spâ*, *spaar*), MDu. *spade* (Du. *spade*, *spa*), OS. *spado* masc. (MLG. *spade*, LG. *spade-n*, *spâ*), G. *spaten* (†*spate*, *spat*; not recorded in OHG. or MHG., and perh. from LG., which is the source of MDa. *spade*, *spaade*, MSw. *spadhe*, Da., Sw., Norw. *spade*, Icel. *spaði*). Closely related to Gr. σπάθη wooden blade, paddle, sword, etc., whence L. *spatha*: see SPADE *sb.*[2] and SPATHE.]

1. a. A tool for digging, paring, or cutting ground, turf, etc., now usually consisting of a flattish rectangular iron blade socketed on a wooden handle which has a grip or cross-piece at the upper end, the whole being adapted for grasping with both hands while the blade is pressed into the ground with the foot.
In more primitive forms, or for special purposes, the blade also may be wholly or partly made of wood, and its lower extremity is sometimes rounded or pointed.
c **725** *Corpus Gloss.* U 13 *Uangas*, spadan. *c* **1000** ÆLFRIC *Saints' Lives* II. 50 Ic nat mid hwi ic delfe, nu me swa wana is æȝþer ȝe spadu ȝe mattuc. *a* **1100** *Gerefa* in *Anglia* IX. 263 Siðe, sicol, weodhoc, spade, scofle. *c* **1150** *Voc.* in Wr.-Wülcker 550 *Uanga, uel fossorium*, spade. *a* **1225** *Ancr. R.* 384 Ȝif eax ne kurue, ne þe spade ne dulue, ne þe suluh ne erede, hwo kepte ham uorte holden? *c* **1290** *S. Eng. Leg.* I. 270 þe eorþe was hard,..and none spade he nadde. *a* **1300** *Cursor M.* 1239 For-wroght wit his hak and spad Of him-self he wex al sad. **1390** GOWER *Conf.* II. 128 So that in stede of schovele and spade The scharpe swerd was take on honde. *c* **1440** *Alph. Tales* cxix. 84 With a spade he smate hur in sonder. **1474** CAXTON *Chesse* III. i. (1883) 76 The spade or shouell is for to delue & labour ther-with the erthe. **1523** FITZHERB. *Husb.* §17 He wyll with a shouell, or a spade, caste out all that is fallen in the rygge. **1591** SPENSER *Virg. Gnat* 653 His yron headed spade tho making cleene, To dig vp sods out of the flowrie grasse. **1630** *R. Johnson's Kingd. & Commw.* 33 The gunne hath brought all weapons to an equality... Nothing resists it but the spade. **1671** MILTON

P.R. III. 331 Of labouring Pioners A multitude with Spades and Axes arm'd. **1729** SWIFT *Corr.* Wks. 1841 II. 626, I knew an old lord..who amused himself with mending pitchforks and spades for his tenants *gratis.* **1784** COWPER *Task* III. 636 Strength may wield the pond'rous spade. **1842** LOUDON *Suburban Hort.* 315 They were so tender as to be much injured by the spade in the process of lifting. **1866** ROGERS *Agric. & Prices* I. xxi. 540 The spade of the Middle Ages was generally a wooden frame tipped with iron.

fig. **1340** *Ayenb.* 108 þanne nymþ he his pic and his spade and beginþ to delue and to myny, and geþ in-to his herte. **1594** *Selimus* Greene's Wks. (Grosart) XIV. 203 Good sir, your wisedomes ouerflowing wit, Digs deepe with learnings wonder-working spade. **1890** R. BRIDGES *Shorter Poems* III. 13 The heartless spade of death.

b. The depth of a spade-blade; a spit.

1674 N. FAIRFAX *Bulk & Selv.* 186 You cannot dig many spades in mold or growthsom earth, before you come at a dead soyl. **1764** *Museum Rust.* II. 377 After I have got through the surface, which is about a spade and half deep. **1786** ABERCROMBIE *Gard. Assist.* 13 Let borders for wall-trees..be well trenched, two spades deep. **1812** SIR J. SINCLAIR *Syst. Husb. Scot.* I. Add. 8 Beginning at one end of the place where the earth is to be taken, and..taking off a spade deep (about eight inches).

c. The length of a spade with its handle.

1825 CROKER *Trad. S. Ireland* 250 'Tis about ten spades from this to the cross. **1827** STEUART *Planter's G.* (1828) 193 The dimensions are then to be marked out..at two 'Spades' and a half distant from the stake, or about eighteen feet diameter.

2. a. Phr. ***to call a spade a spade***, to call things by their real names, without any euphemism or mincing of matters; to use plain or blunt language; to be straightforward to the verge of rudeness.

In the ultimate source of the first quotation, Plutarch's *Apophthegmata* 178 B, the Greek words are τὴν σκάφην σκάφην λέγοντας. There is no evidence that σκάφη (a trough, basin, bowl, boat, etc.) had the sense of 'spade'; in rendering it by *ligo* Erasmus evidently confused it with σκαφεῖον or other derivatives from the stem of σκάπτειν to dig. Lucian *De Hist. Conscr.* 41 gives a fuller form of the phrase, τὰ σῦκα σῦκα, τὴν σκάφην δὲ σκάφην ὀνομάσων.

1542 UDALL *Erasm. Apoph.* 167 Philippus aunswered, that the Macedonians wer feloes of no fyne witte in their termes but altogether grosse, clubbyshe, and rusticall, as they whiche had not the witte to calle a spade by any other name then a spade. **1580** GIFFORD *Posie of Gilloflowers* Wks. (Grosart) 101, I cannot say the crow is white, But needes must call a spade a spade. **1589** *Marprel. Epit.* A ij, I am plaine, I must needs call a Spade a Spade. **1630** *Pathomachia* IV. ii. 34, I am a plaine Macedonian, I must need call a Spade, a Spade. **1647** TRAPP *Marrow Gd. Authors* in *Comm. Ep.* 641 Gods people shall not spare to call a spade a spade, a niggard a niggard. **1706** E. WARD *Hud. Rediv.* I. vii. 11 This is not Time of Day For Truth to be so obvious made, We must not call a Spade, a Spade. **1731–8** SWIFT *Polite Conv.* 199, I am old Tell-Truth; I love to call a Spade a Spade. **1837** W. IRVING *Capt. Bonneville* III. 115 They are the most unsavory vagabonds in their ordinary colloquies; they make no hesitation to call a spade a spade. **1884** *Punch* 15 Nov. 229/2 If it is absolutely necessary to call a spade a spade then it must be done in a whisper.

b. In allusions to the above phrase.

1677 W. HUGHES *Man of Sin* III. iii. 57 As surely as a Spade is a Spade, and ought so to be called. **1728–31** *Lett. from Fog's Jrnl.* (1732) I. 258 A Spade with me was always a Spade, and Coscia a blundering Knave. **1816** J. W. CROKER in *C. Papers* (1884) I. iii. 98 Everything goes by its proper name; a spade is a spade; and a bayonet a bayonet. **1859** TROLLOPE *West Indies* ix. 123 A spade is a spade, and it is worse than useless to say that it is something else.

c. More forcefully, in colloq. phr. ***to call a spade a (bloody) shovel***: to speak with great or unnecessary bluntness.

1919 W. S. MAUGHAM *Moon & Sixpence* iii. 12 We did not think it hypocritical to draw over our vagaries the curtain of a decent silence. The spade was not invariably called a bloody shovel. **1945** N. BALCHIN *Mine Own Executioner* ii. 34 Sometimes..I get so fed up with all the mumbo-jumbo and abracadabra and making of holy mysteries about simple things that I like to call a spade a shovel. **1978** CADOGAN & CRAIG *Women & Children First* ii. 48 As a literary starting-off point, the determination to call a spade a bloody shovel has imposed a fundamental limitation... Outspokenness.. is simply not enough.

3. An implement resembling a spade in form or use: **a.** One or other of various spade-like knives used by whalers, esp. one employed in flensing a whale; a blubber-spade.

1820 SCORESBY *Acc. Arctic Reg.* II. 511 Wood for harpoon and lance-stocks; handles of knives, spades, prickers [etc.]. **1845** J. COULTER *Adv. in Pacific* vii. 75 They each have long spades, and cut the blubber the proper breadth spirally from the base of the head to the flukes. **1887** GOODE *Fisheries U.S.* 264 The officer of the boat..would thrust the sharp-edged spade into the 'small'.

b. A tool used in seal-engraving to remove irregularities of surface.

1850 HOLTZAPFFEL *Turning* III. 1368 A tool called a spade, consisting of a piece of soft iron about 3 or 4 inches long, the end of which is filed at an angle of 45 degrees, and charged with diamond powder. The spade is held in the fingers like a pencil.

c. A spade-like attachment serving to increase the grip of a wheel, retard the motion of a conical pendulum, check the recoil of a gun-carriage, etc.

1862 *London Rev.* 23 Aug. 176 Up to this time the plain surface of the wheels only had been in use, and now..the engine-driver brought in the auxiliary power of the spades, and protruding them a short distance through the wheels, at once doubled the powers of the engine. **1884** F. J. BRITTEN *Watch & Clockm.* 67 In a conical pendulum there is generally a spade attached to and revolving with the pendulum bob, so arranged that..the spade dips deeper into a vessel containing glycerine. **1898** E. S. MAY *Field Artillery* 294 The first round fired forces the spade into the ground. *Ibid.* 328 A spade..is attached to the end of the trail and checks the recoil of the lower carriage.

4. *attrib.* and *Comb.* **a.** With sbs., in attrib. or other relations, as ***spade attachment, -carrier, -cultivation, cutting***, etc.; ***spade-type*** adj.

1899 *Westm. Gaz.* 29 Dec. 5/2 The quick-firing *spade attachment..fitted to all our gun carriages in South Africa. **1895** *Daily News* 15 Feb. 6/4 He speaks casually of seeing the *spade-carriers erecting some earthworks to shelter the outlying Circassians. **1846** MCCULLOCH *Acc. Brit. Empire* (1854) I. 381 *Spade cultivation general. **1859** CORNWALLIS *New World* I. 105 We passed several gangs of men levelling it by *spade-cutting. **1875** KNIGHT *Dict. Mech.* 702/2 Fig. 1654 represents one kind [of digging-machine] in which the *spade-handles pass through guide-slots in an upper bar. **1832** HT. MARTINEAU *Homes Abroad* ii. 27 The soil shall be improved to the utmost by *spade-husbandry. **1771** in *Monthly Messenger* July (1906) 192/1 Richard Lumley, *spademaker in Swalwell. **1843** HOLTZAPFFEL *Turning* I. 210 Much heavier hammers..are used by the spade-makers for planishing. **1885** S. LANE-POOL *Coins & Medals* 202 Of the *tch'ang*, or adze or *spade-pattern, we know..that some were cast specially for the purpose of currency. **1832** *Planting* 37 (L.U.K.), *Spade planting applies to land prepared for the reception of the plants by trenching. **1868** *Rep. U.S. Commissioner Agric.* (1869) 252 A mode of setting Osage thorn quicks, known as *spade-setting, consists in opening a line of slits in the surface soil..with a long, narrow spade. **1542** *Acc. Ld. High Treas. Scot.* VIII. 132 Item, for vj *spaid schaftis deliverit to Johnne Drummond. **1960** *Farmer & Stockbreeder* 29 Mar. 57/2 Most impressive do I find these new *spade-type rotary cultivators which have been imported from the Continent. **1967** *Jane's Surface Skimmer Systems 1967–68* 31/1 The steering gear comprises twin balanced spade-type rudders.

b. With adjs. and pa. pples., as ***spade-armed, -cut, -deep, -dug, -footed, -handed, -like, -proud***, etc. Also ***spade-wise*** adv.

1782 J. TRUMBULL *M'Fingal* III. 61 Till looking back he spied in rear The *spade-arm'd chief. **1962** E. SNOW *Red China Today* (1963) lxvii. 508 Battalions, whole divisions, of spade-armed peasants in this general area have been working on a plan. **1891** S. C. SCRIVENER *Our Fields & Cities* 138 A section of the exposed *spade-cut surface. **1823** J. BADCOCK *Dom. Amusem.* 29 A *spade-deep excision for the planks..to rest upon. **1842** LANCE *Cottage Farmer* 11 Other corn crops..if *spade dug, dibbled, and hoed, will be equally profitable. **1867** *Amer. Naturalist* I. 108 The *Spade-footed Toads..are more uncertain in their appearance, being governed entirely by the dampness or dryness of the season. **1891** *Cent. Dict.* s.v. *Scaphiopodinæ*, A sub-family..containing the American spade-footed toads. **1901** GADOW *Amphibia & Reptiles* 162 The 'Spade-footed Toad', which occurs throughout the whole of Central Europe. **1898** *Westm. Gaz.* 1 Sept. 3/2 The oft so-called *spade-fronted sort of Eton coatie. **1934** DYLAN THOMAS *18 Poems* 25 When blood, *spade-handed, and the logic time Drive children up like bruises to the thumb. **1611** COTGR., *Louchet*, a..*spade-like instrument, halfe headed with yron. **1850** E. CLARK *Britannia & Conway Bridges* II. 597 The flat spade-like portion of the bolt. **1897** *Allbutt's Syst. Med.* IV. 472 The condition of the hands..has been aptly described as spade-like by Sir William Gull. **1941** L. B. LYON *Tomorrow is Revealing* 24 It hurt me, the efficient, *spade-proud hole, That earth-room with its tapestry of boughs. **1783** BARBUT *Gen. Vermium* 93/1 The *Spade-shaped Sea Urchin. **1876** J. H. KIDDER *Kerguelen Isl.* II. 74 (Smithsonian Misc. Collect.), Mouth shields broad, spade-shaped. **1891** *Daily News* 15 Sept. 3/1 One acre of *spade trenched land of average quality. **1646** J. HALL *Poems* I. 5 Whether he Did cut his beard *spadwise or like a T. **1655** MARQ. WORCESTER *Cent. Inv.* 92 The bottom made of Iron-plate Spade-wise.

5. Special combs.: **spade-arm**, the arm used in holding the hand-grip of a spade; **spade-bayonet** (see quot.); **spade-bit** *dial.*, a spit of earth; **spade-bolt**, a form of bolt used in ironwork; **spade-chisel**, a chisel having a broad spade-shaped end; **spade-coin**, = *spade money*; **spade-farm**, a farm cultivated by manual labour with the spade; hence ***spade-farming***; **spade-fish**, a fish resembling a spade in form; now *spec.* the moon-fish, *Chætodipterus faber*; **spade-foot**, (*a*) the foot used in pressing a spade into the ground; (*b*) an enlargement on a chair-leg, etc., resembling a spade; (*c*) a toad having a foot specially adapted for digging; also *attrib.*; **spade-guinea**, a guinea coined from 1787 to 1799, on which the shield bearing the arms has the form of a pointed spade; **spade-hind** (see quot.); **spade lug** *Agric.*, each of a number of metal lugs that are bolted to the rim of a tractor wheel so as to project radially outwards and give an improved grip; hence **spade-lugged** *a.*; **spade-money**, early Chinese bronze money made in the form of spades; †**spade-peak**, a spade-beard; **spade-peat** (see quot.); **spade-press**, *Austr.* a wool-press in which fleeces are compressed by means of a spade; †**spade-silver**, *Sc.* payment for spade-work; †**spade-staff**, a plough-staff, a pattle; †**spade-stale**, **spade-tree** (now *dial.*), a spade-handle; **spade terminal** *Electr.*, a flat, spade-shaped piece of metal having a slot or hole in it for fixing under a nut or bolt to make an electrical connection; **spade-trench** *v.*, to dig deeply with a spade; **spade-wheel**, the wheel in a digging machine which carries the spades; **spade-work**, (*a*) work done with a spade for the preparation of ground; (*b*) *fig.*, preliminary work, difficult or laborious preparation, pioneering research; hence (*rarely*) **spade-worker**.

1801 MAR. EDGEWORTH *Contract* (1832) 157, I should not well be able to manage it with the rheumatism in my *spade-arm. **1875** KNIGHT *Dict. Mech.* 2252/1 **Spade-bayonet*, a broad-bladed bayonet, which may be used in digging shelter-holes or rifle-pits. **1790** W. H. MARSHALL *Rur. Econ. Midl.* II. 442 **Spade-bit*, the quantity of soil raised by one effort of the spade. **1850** E. CLARK *Britannia & Conway Bridges* II. 597 These bolts are 3 inches in diameter, and have been technically called '*spade-bolts'; they are attached..by means of the flat spade-like portion of the bolt. **1895** E. ROWE *Chip Carving* 29 The simplest way..is to use the *spade chisel. **1892** TERRIEN DE LACOUPERIE *Catal. Chinese Coins* Introd. p. xxxviii, The classification and identification of these *spade-coins. **1851** KINGSLEY *Yeast* vi, Among..*spade farms, and model smell-traps. **1871** —— *At Last* xvi, He has not..handiness enough for the more delicate work of a little spade-farm. *Ibid.*, Garden-tillage and *spade-farming are not learnt in a day. **1704** T. POCOCK in *Torrington Mem.* (Camden) 184 We took up this morning a *spade fish... The spade-fish was fry'd. **1805** T. M. HARRIS *State of Ohio* 116 (Thornton), There is a curious fish called the Spade-Fish,..with a bony weapon projecting from the nose.. like a narrow shovel. **1884** GOODE *Nat. Hist. Aquat. Anim.* 445 The Moon-fish, *Chætodipterus faber*. .. In the northern parts of the Gulf of Mexico it is called the 'Spade-fish'. **1891** SIR D. WILSON *Right Hand* 170, I believe every boy will hop on his *spade foot. **1897** K. W. CLOUSTON *Chippendale Period in Eng. Furn.* 154 By using the 'spade foot', as the square excrescence at the thin end of the leg is called. **1899** *Proc. Zool. Soc.* 790 On the American Spade-foot (*Scaphiopus solitarius*). **1901** GADOW *Amphibia & Reptiles* 163 *Pelobates cultripes*, this is the Spade-foot of the whole of Spain and Portugal and of the southern and western parts of France. *Ibid.* 164 *Pelobates cultripes*, Spade-foot Toad. **1853** H. N. HUMPHREYS *Coin Collector's Man.* II. 496 In 1787, a new gold coinage took place, and the guineas, known as *spade guineas, appeared. **1887** JEFFERIES *Amaryllis* viii, It was understood that there were twenty thousand spade guineas in an iron box under his bed. **1844** H. STEPHENS *Bk. Farm* I. 224 The hedger, the *spade-hind, the spadesman, as he is indifferently called, is a useful servant on a farm. **1921** *Trans. Amer. Soc. Agric. Engin.* XV. 175 The tri-spade lugs were cast with three spades on each casting..and were staggered on the wheel when in place similar to the bolt on *spade lugs. **1950** *Engineering* 5 May 506/1 The use of spade lugs in place of plain steel rims and strakes gradually reduced the tractor weight per drawbar-horse-power. **1967** J. OATES *Farm Machinery* xi. 77 Spade lugs and strake bars are used to bite more deeply into the ground. **1945** H. J. HINE *Tractors on Farm* (ed. 2) iv. 38 With *spade-lugged steel wheels the spaces between the lugs must be cleaned out from time to time with a paddle. **1892** TERRIEN DE LACOUPERIE *Catal. Chinese Coins* Introd. p. xiii, *Spade-money of two sizes form chiefly the currency outside Ts'i and Tchou. They consist of little spades with hollow handles, weighing 20 to the higher standard unit of weight. **1592** NASHE *Pierce Penilesse* Wks. (Grosart) II. 27 He *spade peake is as sharpe as if he had been a Pioner before the walles of Roan. **1801** *Farmer's Mag.* Jan. 6 The cutting up of turf, or *spade-peats, from the clay or earthen surfaces of the pasturage, is surely no matter of necessity. **1890** 'R. BOLDREWOOD' *Col. Reformer* xvii. (1891) 202 We devoted the next few days..to fixing the *spade-press—that friendly adjunct to the pioneer-squatter's humble woolshed. **1606** *Reg. Mag. Sig. Scot.* 634/1 Cum lie *spaid-silver pro effossione petarum. **1612** *Ibid.* 238/1 Cum lie spaid-silver pro lucrando lie turvis et devottis. **1706** PHILLIPS (ed. Kersey), *Sull-Paddle*, a small *Spade-staff, or Tool to cleanse the Plough from the Clods of Earth. **1653** BLITHE *Eng. Improver Impr.* 67 A piece of the best tough Willow, about the bigness of a *Spade-Stayle. **1968** *Wireless World* Feb. 133/1 (Advt.), Heavy duty terminals... Black only will take *spade terminals and wander plug. **1976** *Gramophone* May 1841/1 A twin phono-plug low capacitance signal cable is supplied, plus a green spade terminal earth wire. **1411** *Nottingham Rec.* II. 86, j. *spadetree, j d. **1490** *Churchw. Acc. St. Dunstan's, Canterb.*, Item payde for a spade tre, j d ob. **1534** *MS. Acc. St. John's Hosp., Canterb.*, For a spade tre, j d. **1893** *S.E. Worc. Gloss.* 37 *Spade-tree*, the wooden shaft of a spade. **1840** *Penny Cycl.* XVIII. 467/1 The lazy-bed practice repeated for three years will completely *spade-trench the entire land. **1875** KNIGHT *Dict. Mech.* 703 In the rotary machine (Fig. 1655) the ground-wheel *b* drives the *spade-wheel L[1] through the intervention of gearing. **1778** *Encycl. Brit.* (ed. 2) I. 145/1 An iron plough..drawn by a horse..will save much *spade-work. **1837** CARLYLE *Fr. Rev.* II. I. xi, He that has four limbs and a French heart can do spadework. **1901** LD. ROSEBERY *Nat. Policy* (1902) *note on cover*, Political energy must work and entrench. I want some of this spadework on behalf of this policy. **1912** H. G. ALDIS in *Cambr. Hist. Eng. Lit.* IX. xiii. 346 Brian Twyne, a diligent Oxford antiquary who had done much pioneer spade-work in the same field. **1927** *Daily Tel.* 12 July 9/1 The discovery of a helpful blood-test for cancer may be placed among the important advances the near future may give us as a result of spade-work already carried out. **1931** E. F. BENSON *Mapp & Lucia* iv. 93 Lucia..had insisted that all the credit was due to Drake's wife, who had planned everything (or nearly) and had done all the spade-work. **1951** *Sport* 27 Apr.–3 May 8/3 Ernie's crafty spadework has been responsible for many of the goals netted by Jack Milburn and George Robledo. **1977** A. CLARKE *Letter from Dead* ix. 105, I did a bit of spadework on him yesterday.. and he seemed to be thawing a little. **1912** 'SAKI' *Chron. Clovis* 267 'Where I think you political *spade-workers are so silly,' said the Duke, 'is in the misdirection of your efforts.'

spade (speɪd), *sb.*[2] [ad. It. *spade*, pl. of *spada* (Sp. and Pg. *espada*) sword (see SPADO[2]), used as a mark on playing-cards. Cf. G. *spadi* from the same source.

In British and other cards ultimately of French origin the mark has a form resembling that of a pointed spade, so that there is a natural association with SPADE *sb.*[1] Cf. G. dial. *spaten*, Da. and Sw. *spader* (pl.).]

1. a. One or other of the black spade-shaped marks by which one of the four suits in a pack of playing-cards is distinguished; hence *pl.*, the cards belonging to or forming this suit.

1598 FLORIO, *Cáppari*,..those markes vpon the playing cards called spades. **1651** *Pleas. Hist. Miller Mansfield* 19 With Ladies and their Maids like to the Queene of Spades. **1680** COTTON *Compl. Gamester* (ed. 2) 107 The Ace of Spades. **1712–4** POPE *Rape Lock* III. 46 'Let Spades be trumps!' she said. **1784** COWPER *Task* IV. 219 Ensanguin'd hearts, clubs typical of strife, And spades, the emblem of untimely graves. **1850** *Bohn's Hand-bk. Games* (1867) 220 You are to discard..the knave, nine, and seven of spades.

b. *attrib.* in *sing.*

1904 'O. HENRY' *Cabbages & Kings* vi. 105 The invitations to the musicale came sliding in by pairs and threes and spade flushes. **1973** *Country Life* 10 May 1331/1 West led the Spade Knave, which I took with dummy's Ace.

c. *fig.* in advb. phr. ***in spades***, very much, in abundance, extremely. (Spades is the highest ranking suit in Bridge.) *colloq.* (chiefly *U.S.*).

1929 D. RUNYON in *Hearst's International* Oct. 62/2, I always hear the same thing about every bum on Broadway, male and female, including some I know are bums, in spades, right from taw. **1964** WODEHOUSE *Frozen Assets* I. 19 'It's the law I'm beefing about. You didn't make the law.' 'But I administer it.' 'I'll say you do. In spades.' **1972** R. NIXON *Diary* in *Mem.* (1978) 619 Anybody who gets to the top in the Communist hierarchy and stays at the top has to have a great deal of political ability and a great deal of toughness. All three of the Soviet leaders have this in spades.

2. A card belonging to the spade-suit.

1745 HOYLE *Quadrille* (1746) 13 One small Club, Knave and two small Spades. **1828** PRAED *Arr. at Watering-pl.* i. Poems 1864 II. 188, I play a spade. **1879** 'CAVENDISH' *Card Ess.*, etc. 109 Alcippe again plays badly in throwing the ace of hearts to the last spade.

3. a. A Black person, a Negro, esp. male: freq. in White use, as a term of contempt or casual reference. Formerly among U.S. Blacks, a very dark-skinned Negro. *slang* (orig. *U.S.*).

1928 C. MCKAY *Home to Harlem* vi. 56 Jake is such a fool spade. Don't know how to handle the womens. **1929** W. THURMAN *Blacker the Berry* I. 34 Wonder where all the spades keep themselves? **1945** L. SHELLY *Jive talk Dict.* 17 *Spade*, colored person. **1957** C. MACINNES *City of Spades* II. ii. 118 A British lady with a wild love of Spades, and a horrid habit of touching you on the shoulder because she says 'to stroke a darkie brings you luck.' **1969** [see DINGE *sb.*^{3}]. **1971** N. SAUNDERS *Alternative London* xxviii. 263 On Saturdays try Brixton market—nearly as big, more genuine, lots of spades. **1978** J. A. MICHENER *Chesapeake* 678 The four Turlocks hated Negroes and never hestitated in voicing their disgust. 'Goddamned spades killed my cousin Captain Matt—one of them gets out of line with me, he's dead.'

b. *attrib.* or as *adj.*

1928 C. MCKAY *Home to Harlem* vi. 56 She was of the complexion known among Negroes as spade or chocolate-to-the-bone. **1952** C. BROSSARD *Who walk in Darkness* x. 61 These spade intellectuals really think they've made it when they get a white girl. **1964** *Negro Digest* Feb. 55/1, I can't see why no colored man'd want to marry no white chick... Not when there's so many fine spade chicks around. **1978** M. PUZO *Fools Die* liv. 568 Two spade hookers went gliding by arm in arm.

Hence ˈ**spadelet** *nonce-wd.* [-LET], a Black child.

1959 C. MACINNES *Absolute Beginners* 62, I passed a crocodile of infants, and among them a number of little Spadelets.

spade (speɪd), *sb.*^{3} Now *dial.* [OE. *sped*, of unknown origin.] The gummy or wax-like matter secreted at the corner of the eye.

c **725** *Corpus Gloss.* P 375 *Petuita*, sped. *a* **1100** in Napier *O.E. Glosses* I. 1728 *Glaucoma*, sped. **1656** W. DU GARD tr. *Comenius' Gate Lat. Unl.* §204. 57 The eyes—whose corners often times sweat tears, every day spade or filth. **1825** BRITTON *Beauties Wilts* III. 378 *Spade*, the congealed gum of the eye. **1888–93** in Berks, Wilts, and Glouc. glossaries.

†**spade**, *sb.*^{4} *Obs.*$^{-1}$ [ad. L. *spado* SPADO^1.] A eunuch.

Spade in Blount *Glossogr.* (1656) and hence in Phillips and some later Dicts., properly belongs to SPAYED *ppl. a.*

1680 C. NESSE *Church Hist.* 497 Till pimp, or punk, or jade or spade, I do resolve to be.

spade, variant of SPAYD *Obs.*

spade (speɪd), *v.*^{1} [f. SPADE *sb.*^{1} Cf. MDu. (Du.) and MLG. (LG.) *spaden* (LG. also *spâen*), Da. *spade*, Sw. dial. *spa(da)*, G. *spaten*, *-späten*.]

1. *trans.* To cut in the form of a spade. *rare*$^{-1}$.

1594 NASHE *Terrors of Night* Ep. Ded., Wks. (Grosart) III. 214 To let some vnskilfull pen-man or Nouerint-maker startch his ruffe & new spade his beard with the benefite he made of them.

2. a. To dig up, to remove, with a spade.

1647 HEXHAM I, To Spade and delve, *spaden ende delven*. **1755** J. ISMAY in *Yorks. N. & Q.* I. 208 Some sour marshy ground is made arable by spading the turf from the surface and then burning it in heaps. **1795** *Trans. Soc. Arts* XIII. 136, I was advised..to get it [*sc.* the land] dug or spaded. **1807** J. BARLOW *Columb.* II. 632 They form to different arts the hand of toil, To whirl the spindle and to spade the soil. **1844** EMERSON *Lect. New Eng. Ref.* Wks. (Bohn) I. 259 The hundred acres of the farm must be spaded. **1889** *Harper's Mag.* Sept. 570/2 Spading the garden faithfully every spring.

b. To dig *up*, lift *out*, take *off*, with the spade.

1785 G. WASHINGTON *Diary* 5 Sept. (1925) II. 410 Began to spade up the Lawn in front of the Court yard. **1817–8** COBBETT *Resid. U.S.* (1822) 6 Spaded up a corner of ground. **1836** MRS. BRAY *Descr. Tamar & Tavy* I. xx. 348 The slight layer of turf which is spaded off the land. **1854** THOREAU *Walden* i. (1886) 54, I spaded up all the land which I required. **1877** C. TAIT *Let.* in Benham *Cath. & C. Tait* (1879) 557 The grain is spaded out of trucks.

3. To cut or flense with a whaling-spade.

1887 GOODE *Fisheries U.S.* 265 Spading flukes is one of the lost arts of fishery.

4. *intr.* To work with a spade; to dig.

1869 BLACKMORE *Lorna D.* v, Young men would not spade or plough by reason of noble lineage.

Hence ˈ**spaded** *ppl. a.*^{1}

1807 VANCOUVER *Agric. Devon* (1813) 140 The manure [being] thus applied upon the spaded land, the field is next ploughed. **1877** BLACKMORE *Cripps* iii, The patches of spaded mould.

†**spade**, *v.*^{2} *Obs.* [f. *spaid*, *spayed*, pa. pple. of SPAY *v.*, perh. associated with L. *spado*: see SPADE *sb.*^{4}] *trans.* To spay.

1611 CHAPMAN *Widowes T.* Wks. 1873 III. 83 I'll have all young widows spaded for marrying again. **1650** BULWER *Anthropomet.* 208 The women of Egypt were sometimes spaded. **1710** *London's Med. Informer* 32 Women may be Spaded by Sow-Gelders.

Hence †ˈ**spaded** *ppl. a.*^{2}; ˈ**spader**; ˈ**spading** *vbl. sb. Obs.*

1648 HEXHAM II, *Gelte*,.. a spaded Hogge, a barrow Hogge, or a Sowe. *Ibid.*, *Een Lubber*, a Gelder, or a Spader. *Een Lubbinge*, a Gelding or a Spading. **1655** MOUFET & BENNET *Health's Improv.* (1746) 143 If some shall..object, that gelding and spading be unnatural Actions. *Ibid.* 148 Concerning Pork and Hog's Flesh made of a spaded Sow, or a Hog gelded. **1816** *Sporting Mag.* XLVII. 204 Those spaded bitches appeared to have been *grunes* or greyhounds.

spade-beard. [f. SPADE *sb.*^{1} + BEARD *sb.*] A spade-shaped beard; a beard cut or trimmed to the shape of a (pointed or broad) spade-blade.

1598 E. GUILPIN *Skial.* D, He with a spade-beard can full mannerly Leade the olde measures. **1679** *Answ. to Appeal fr. Country to City* 31 An Old fellow with a bald pate, and a spade-beard. **1693** DRYDEN, etc. *Juvenal* xvi. (1697) 387 With their long Spade-Beards, and matted Hair. **1858** CARLYLE *Fredk. Gt.* III. vi. I. 180 A man with high bald brow; magnificent spade-beard.

spade-bone. Chiefly *dial.* [app. f. SPADE *sb.*^{1}, but perh. for *spaude-* or *spalde-bone*: see SPAULD.] The shoulder-blade.

1612 DRAYTON *Poly-olb.* v. 266 A diuination strange.., By th' shoulder of a Ram,.. Which vsuallie they boile, the spade-boane beeing bar'd. **1671** SKINNER *Etymol. Ling. Angl.*, *Spade-bone*, vox agro Lincoln. usitatissima. **1790** W. H. MARSHALL *Rur. Econ. Midl.* II. 443 *Spade-bone*, the shoulder bone; the blade bone. **1823–** in dial. glossaries (chiefly northern and eastern). **1844** BORROW in Knapp *Life* (1899) I. 394 Mahomet,..it is said, wrote his Coran on mutton spade bones.

spadeful (ˈspeɪdfʊl). Also -full. [f. SPADE *sb.*^{1} + -FUL.] A quantity that fills a spade; as much as a spade can hold or take up at one time.

1643 TRAPP *Comm. Gen.* xxx. 27 His mouth shall be filled with a spade-ful of mould. **1720** *Lond. Gaz.* No. 5865/2 His Excellency was to raise the first Spadeful of Earth at the opening of the Dyke. **1796** MORSE *Amer. Geog.* II. 311 Five or six spadefuls of snow. **1826** W. A. MILES *Deverel Barrow* 18 Every spadeful of earth presented a mixture of pottery, charcoal, and flints. **1890** *Science-Gossip* XXVI. 161 When we had dug out one or two spadefuls of soil.

fig. **1886** STEVENSON *Lett.* (1899) II. 13 It is painful, yet very pleasant to dig into the past of a dead friend, and find him, at every spadeful, shine brighter.

spade-graft. Also 3 -graf, 6 -graffe, 7- spade's graft. [f. SPADE *sb.*^{1} + GRAFT *sb.*^{3}]

1. A spade's depth; a spit.

α. **1252** *Cart. de Rameseia* (Rolls) I. 299 Unam perticam fossati..habentis profunditatem duorum spadegrafs. **1523** FITZHERB. *Husb.* §124 Dygge vp the muldes a spade-graffe depe. **1671** J. WEBSTER *Metallogr.* iii. 45 They usually leave one depth of Spade-graft of that Earth. **1688** HOLME *Armoury* II. 115/1 Delfe, or Spadegraft, [is] a digging into the Earth as deep as a spade can go at once. **1765** *Museum Rust.* III. 11 He takes the earth..two spade-grafts deep. **1837** HOWITT *Rur. Life* v. iv. (1862) 390 Every spadegraft of your cultivation annihilates the habitats..of animals, insects, and plants. **1891** ATKINSON *Moorland Par.* 214 Half a spade-graft of mould.

β. **1620** [see GRAFT *sb.*^{3} 1]. **1653** BLITHE *Eng. Improver Impr.* 117 The depth may be two Spades graft or more. **1660** SHARROCK *Vegetables* 95 Thou must goe half one spades graft deep. **1792** [see GRAFT *sb.*^{3} 1]. **1844** *Proc. Soc. Antiq.* I. 30 They were discovered in 1827 near Guisborough, at a depth of about a 'spade's graft' beneath the surface.

¶**2.** The handle of a spade. *Obs.*

Evelyn is copied or followed by the *Dict. Rusticum* (1704), Mortimer *Husb.* (1721) II. 27, etc.

1664 EVELYN *Sylva* v. 21 The Beech serves for various Uses of the House-wife;..likewise for the Wheeler,..for the Bellows-maker, and Husbandman his Shovel and Spade-graffs.

spade-iron. Now *rare*. Also 4 spadierne, -yrin, 5 -yrne, 6 spadeierne, *Sc.* spaid irne. [SPADE *sb.*^{1}] The iron part, the blade or shoeing, of a spade.

1356 in Riley *Mem. Lond.* (1868) 283 [One] spadierne, [and 2 iron] auugeres. **1383–4** *Durham Acc. Rolls* (Surtees) 390 It. in uno spadyrin empt. **1472** *Fabric Rolls York Minster* (Surtees) 78, iij dos. hespes et vj spadyrnes et iij dos. snekes. **1502–3** *Durham Acc. Rolls* (Surtees) 102 Pro iiij spadeiernys, vjd. **1545** *Acc. Ld. High Treas. Scot.* VIII. 360 Item, for foure spaid irnis. **1825–7** BERRY *Encycl. Her.*, *Spade-Iron*, or the shoeing of a spade.

spademan (ˈspeɪdmən). Also **spadesman.** [SPADE *sb.*^{1}] One who uses a spade; a labourer accustomed to work with a spade.

α. **1559** LD. COBHAM in Boys *Sandwich* (1792) 738 Over every x spade men muste be one clercke. **1647** HEXHAM I, A spade-man or spader, *een spader, spitter ofte delver*. **1812** SIR J. SINCLAIR *Syst. Husb. Scot.* I. 49 It is necessary also to employ spade-men..to clear out the small drains. **1854** W. R. WILLIAMS *Relig. Progr.* iii. 59 The spademan who digs the canal. **1864** *Realm* 17 Feb. 7 From his bowels the armed spademen keep issuing evermore.

β. **1826** SCOTT *Woodst.* xxxiii, We are wretched spadesmen enough. **1844** H. STEPHENS *Bk. Farm* I. 224 The spadesman ..is a useful servant on a farm. **1865** *Pall Mall G.* 15 Dec. 3 In Sardinia they can obtain no spadesmen, the Sards having a distaste for performing the continuous work of navvies.

spader (ˈspeɪdə(r)). [f. SPADE *v.*^{1} + -ER^1.] One who works with a spade; an implement which digs, etc., by means of spades; also *dial.*, a breast-plough.

1647 HEXHAM I, A spade-man or spader. **1867** WHITMAN in *Galaxy* IV. 608 The rotary spader did its work well. **1875** KNIGHT *Dict. Mech.* 703 Other forms of spaders have blades thrust out and retracted as the machine advances. **1903** J. H. BRIDGE *Hist. Carnegie Steel Co.* vii. 114 Idly watching the spaders and waterers and trimmers.

spades graft, -man: see SPADE-GRAFT, -MAN.

spadger (ˈspædʒə(r)). *dial.* or *colloq.* [Fanciful alteration of SPARROW.]

1. A sparrow. Also *attrib.*

1862 C. C. ROBINSON *Dial. Leeds* 417 'Spadger-pie' is an article of diet occasionally. **1892** 'SON OF MARSHES' *Within Hour of Lond.* 59 The sparrow, or 'spadger', is a friend to the farmer.

2. *transf.* A boy. *colloq. rare.*

1899 *Captain* II. 273/2 If we've got to take these three young spadgers..we shall want something bigger'n this here gig. **1978** K. BONFIGLIOLI *All Tea in China* I. iii. 29 'See here, young spadger,' he said..'if you should be a little short of tin..come and spend a night or two at Great Coram Street.'

Hence as *v. intr.* (*rare*), (*a*) to catch sparrows or other small birds, to go sparrow-netting; (*b*) *fig.*, to play or frolic *about* in the manner of a sparrow.

1939 F. THOMPSON *Lark Rise* ix. 171 In winter in the 'eighties the youths and big boys of the hamlet would go out on dark nights 'spadgering'. For this a large net upon four poles was carried... When they came to a spot where a flock of sparrows or other small birds was roosting, the net was dropped over the hedge..and the birds enclosed were slaughtered. **1967** *Listener* 7 Sept. 315/2 Tommy Steele spadgered larkily about among the zoomorphs.

spadgers, var. SPAGGERS.

†**spadiard.** *Obs.* Also 7 spador, 8 spadier. [Explained by Holland (*Camden's Brit.* 185) as f. SPADE *sb.*^{1}, but perh. an error for SPALLIARD^1.] A labourer in the Cornish tin-mines.

1610 HOLLAND *Camden's Brit.* To Rdr. 3 A Spadiard that worketh in mines, who while he..followeth the maine vaines, seeth not the hidden small fillets. *c* **1630** RISDON *Surv. Devon* (1811) 11 There are also labourers, that serve for daily wages, whereof be two sorts: the one is called a spadiard, a daily labourer in tin works. **1630** T. WESTCOTE *View Devon.* I. xi. (1845) 53 Of these last are two sorts; one named a spador or searcher for tin. [**1661** BLOUNT *Glossogr.* (ed. 2), *Spadiards*, Laborers in the Tin-mines of Cornwall. **1706** PHILLIPS (ed. Kersey), *Spadiers*, Labourers that dig in the Mines in Cornwall.]

spadiceous (speɪˈdɪʃəs), *a.* Now *Bot.* [ad. mod.L. *spadiceus*, f. L. *spādīc-*, *spādīx* SPADIX.]

1. Of a reddish or brownish colour.

Applied to various shades by different writers.

1646 SIR T. BROWNE *Pseud. Ep.* 167 Of those five [horns] which Scaliger beheld, though one spadiceous, or of a light red, and two inclining to red. **1678** RAY *Willughby's Ornith.* III. ii. §16. 371 The Wings are of a dark spadiceous colour. **1683** SALMON *Doron Med.* II. 350 An oyl..of..a spadicious [*sic*] or light red colour. **1871** W. A. LEIGHTON *Lichen-Flora* 124 Under-surface black or spadiceous towards the margins. **1887** W. PHILLIPS *Brit. Discomycetes* 376 Hymenium milk-white, farinose, becoming spadiceous.

2. Having the nature or form of a spadix.

1760 J. LEE *Introd. Bot.* I. xix. (1765) 52 A Spadiceous aggregate Flower is, when there is a Receptacle common to many Florets placed within a Spatha or Sheathe. **1793** MARTYN *Lang. Bot.* s.v. *Spadix*, A spadiceous flower. A sort of aggregate flower [etc.]. **1830** LINDLEY *Nat. Syst. Bot.* 252 As many of them are arranged in a spadix, and as most of them have a distinct tendency to that kind of inflorescence, the form is called *Spadiceous*. **1858** A. IRVINE *Handbk. Brit. Pl.* 280 The following Orders..have the common character of spadiceous, and generally spathaceous inflorescence.

spadici- (speɪˈdaɪsɪ-), combining form of SPADIX, used in a few terms of *Bot.*, as ***spadiciˈfloral***, ***-ˈflorous***, ***-form*** adjs.

1857 HENFREY *Bot.* 391 The spadiciform peduncle does not represent this structure very clearly. *Ibid.* 397 The inflorescence is moreover hardly spadiciflorous. **1872** OLIVER *Elem. Bot.* I. v. 58 Monocotyledons have their flowers..arranged upon a spadix, hence called Spadicifloral.

ˈ**spadicose**, *a. Bot. rare.* [f. L. *spādīc-* SPADIX.] = SPADICEOUS *a.* 2.

1847 *Nat. Encycl.* I. 125 A small natural order of spadicose Endogens.

‖**spadille** (spəˈdɪl). Also 8 spadil. [F. *spadille*, ad. Sp. *espadilla* (Pg. *espadilha*, It. *spadiglia*), dim. of *espada* sword, SPADE *sb.*[2]: cf. next.] The ace of spades in ombre and quadrille.

1728 YOUNG *Love Fame* VI. 516 Imaginary ruin charms her still; Her happy lord is cuckol'd by spadil. **1773** GOLDSM. *Stoops to Conq.* Epil., She sits all night at cards, and ogles at spadille. **1794** *Sporting Mag.* IV. 201 The ace of spades, called spadille, is always highest trump. **1816** SCOTT *Bl. Dwarf* v, Love and its absurdities in youth—spadille and basto in age. **1851** THACKERAY *Eng. Hum.* iv, About as much time as ladies of that age spent over spadille and manille. **1900** F. F. MOORE *Nell Gwyn* v, What brings you down here from the midst of your routs..and your spadille tables?

‖**spa'dillo.** *Obs.* Also 8 spadillio. [ad. Sp. *espadilla*: see prec.] = SPADILLE.

1680 COTTON *Compl. Gamester* (ed. 2) 71 There are two suits, Black and Red; of the Black there is first the *Spadillo*, or Ace of Spades. **1712–4** POPE *Rape Lock* III. 49 Spadillio first, unconquerable Lord! Led off two captive trumps, and swept the board. **1728** SWIFT *Jrnl. Mod. Lady* Wks. 1755 III. II. 190 She slipt spadillo in her breast.

spading (ˈspeɪdɪŋ), *vbl. sb.*[1] [f. SPADE *v.*[1]] The action of digging, working, striking, etc., with a spade; the quantity of earth that may be lifted with a spade; a spade's depth *of* earth.

1647 HEXHAM I, A spading, *een spittinge ofte delvinge.* **1793** FULLARTON *View Agric. Ayr* (1891) 111 To half trench an acre, with one spading and a shoveling. **1796** W. H. MARSHALL *Rur. Econ. West Eng.* I. 143 The price for 'spading' is about three halfpence, a square perch. **1801** *Farmer's Mag.* Aug. 279 To allow of the removal of perhaps a spading of earth all along. **1842** J. AITON *Domest. Econ.* (1857) 161 The first spading being rich soil taken from the trench, should be buried in the centre of the dike. **1888** *Daily News* 21 Nov. 5/7 Had the League anything to do with the spading and shooting of Colletty? **1891** MALDEN *Tillage* 82 Another method of planting potatoes which is carried out very successfully is known as spading in.

attrib. **1875** KNIGHT *Dict. Mech.* 702/2 A spading-machine for loosening and turning the soil.

spading, *vbl. sb.*[2]: see under SPADE *v.*[2]

‖**spadix** (ˈspeɪdɪks). Pl. spadices (speɪˈdaɪsiːz) and ˈspadixes. [L. *spādīx*, a. Gr. σπάδιξ palm-branch, palm-coloured. Cf. F. *spadice*.]

1. *Bot.* A form of inflorescence consisting of a thick fleshy spike, closely set with flowers, and enclosed in a spathe; a succulent spike, whether enclosed in a spathe or not.

1760 J. LEE *Introd. Bot.* I. viii. (1765) 18 *Spadix* is the Receptacle of a Palm produced within a Spatha, or Sheath, on the Branches that bear Fruit. **1785** MARTYN *Lett. on Bot.* x. (1794) 107 All..growing upon a spadix. [*Note.*] The spadix is the receptacle in this tribe, and has no English name. **1793** —— *Lang. Bot.* s.v. *Spatha*, The calyx of a spadix. *Ibid.*, Some flowers which have no spadix. **1830** LINDLEY *Nat. Syst. Bot.* 285 Flowers unisexual, arranged upon a naked spadix. **1847** W. E. STEELE *Field Bot.* 204 Sterile and fertile spadices cylindrical. **1871** KINGSLEY *At Last* vii, Round our feet are Arums, with snow-white spadixes and hoods. **1897** J. C. WILLIS *Flower. Plants & Ferns* II. 17 They are often so deceived as to lay their eggs on the spadix.

2. *Zool.* A part in cephalopods and hydrozoans having some analogy to a spadix in plants.

1871 ALLMAN *Monogr. Gymnoblastic Hydroids* I. p. xv, *Spadix*,..the hollow body which projects from the floor of the sporosac into its cavity, and round which the generative elements are developed. **1877** HUXLEY *Anat. Inv. Anim.* viii. 534 On the left side, the four tentacles of the posterior division..are converted into a peculiar organ termed the *spadix*. **1883** *Encycl. Brit.* XVI. 674/2 The spadix is in fact the hectocotylized portion of the fore-foot of the male Nautilus. **1888** ROLLESTON & JACKSON *Anim. Life* 762 The term 'spadix' is applied to the central closed endodermic structure representing the manubrial cavity in a gonophore or sporosac.

‖**spado**[1]. [Lat. *spado*, ad. Gr. σπάδων eunuch. Cf. SPADE *sb.*[4]] A eunuch; a castrated person.

c **1430** LYDG. *Min. Poems* (Percy Soc.) 166 Whan that spado lovithe paramouris. **1646** SIR T. BROWNE *Pseud. Ep.* 124 They live longest in every kinde that exercise it not at all, and this is true not onely in Eunuches by nature, but spadoes by Art. **1650** BULWER *Anthropomet.* 207 Castrated animals in any kind & Spado's by Art, live longer then they that retain their Virilities.

‖**spado**[2]. *Obs.* [ad. It. *spada* or Sp. *espada*:—L. *spatha*, ad. Gr. σπάθη: see SPADE *sb.*[1] and *sb.*[2]] A cut-and-thrust sword.

1711 E. WARD *Quix.* I. 105 Drawing forth his Trusty Spado Which was a Rusty old Toledo. **1751** *Narr. of H.M.S. 'Wager'* 9 Every Fellow has his Spado or Dagger that he struts about with. **1785** G. A. BELLAMY *Apology* (ed. 3) II. 9 The Spaniard..seemed glad to have an opportunity of laying by his long spado for some hours every day.

spadona (spəˈdəʊnə). *S. Afr.* [ad. It. *spadone* large sword.] An imperfectly developed feather taken from a young ostrich in its first year.

1881 in A. Douglass *Ostrich Farming in S. Afr.* xiv. 91 Light Spadona..white Boos. **1896** R. WALLACE *Farming Industries of Cape Colony* xi. 235 Spadonas..are pointed like a sword, hence the name, which comes from the Italian. **1955** G. ARCHMAN in Saron & Hotz *Jews in S. Afr.* vii. 130 The different types of feathers that the ostrich produces—chicks, wings, bodies, tails, spadonas..bloods, and female bodies.

spa'droon. *Obs.* exc. *Hist.* [ad. Genevan dial. *espadron*, = F. *espadon* ESPADON.] 'A sword much lighter than a broadsword, and made both to cut and thrust' (James). Also *attrib.*

1798 C. ROWORTH (*title*), The Art of Defence on foot with the broad sword and sabre... To which are added remarks on the spadroon. **1802** JAMES *Milit. Dict.*, *Spadroon Guard*, a guard sometimes used with the cut and thrust sword, and also with the broad sword. **1826** SCOTT *Woodst.* xxiii, Poniard, back-sword, spadroon.

†**spady,** *a. Obs.*[−1] [ad. obs. G. **spadig*, var. of *spathig*, *spatig*: see SPAAD and SPATH[1].] Of the nature of or containing spar.

1683 PETTUS *Fleta Min.* I. III. i. 230 There appertains to the harsh flowing copper Oars,..and what is splendy, mis-pickly, glimery or spady [etc.].

spae (speɪ), *sb. rare.* Also 4 *north.* spa, 6 *Sc.* spe. [a. ON. *spá*: cf. next.] Prediction, prophecy; augury, omen.

a **1300** *Cursor M.* 14526 Cayphas spak þus in his spa, Wordes suilk and oþer maa. **1596** DALRYMPLE tr. *Leslie's Hist. Scot.* (S.T.S.) II. 5 This victorie with the scotis was estemet as a spe or gud tukne of happie succes to follow. **1863** BARING-GOULD *Iceland* 136 The Finns' spae is come true, so here we shall settle.

spae (speɪ), *v.* Orig. *north.* and *Sc.* Also 4 **spa,** 6 **spai, spay.** [a. ON. *spá* (Icel. *spá*, Norw. *spaa*; MSw. *spā*, Sw. *spå*, Da. *spaa*, †*spo*; also NFris. *spoai*, *spuai*, *spui* from Danish), of uncertain origin.] To foretell, to prophesy. Chiefly *trans.* with direct object or with *that.*

a **1300** *Cursor M.* 18988 O propheci..sal þai speke,..And o mi gast I sal a streme To suain and womman gife alsua, At cum wit propheci to spa. **1513** DOUGLAS *Æneid* II. iv. 89 Thocht scho spayit the suitht, and maid na bourd. *Ibid.* III. vi. 28 The Harpy Celeno Spais onto ws a feirfull takin of wo. **1721** RAMSAY *Prospect of Plenty* 76 Does Tam the Rhimer spae oughtlins of this? *a* **1774** FERGUSSON *Farmer's Ingle* Poems (1845) 36 Fu' hale and healthy wad they pass the day; ..Nor doctor need their weary life to spae. **1785** BURNS *Halloween* xiv, [To] seek the foul Thief onie place, For him to spae your fortune. **1815** SCOTT *Guy M.* iii, Tell me the very minute o' the hour the wean's born, and I'll spae its fortune. **1841** BORROW *Zincali* I. iv. 78 A Gypsy sibyl..spaed the good fortune to his daughters. **1863** BARING-GOULD *Iceland* 136 Ingimund left Norway because some Finns had spaed that he should settle in Iceland. **1876** A. LAING *Lindores Abbey* xxvi. 382 The spaewife might now spae in vain.

Hence **'spaeing** *vbl. sb.* (also *attrib.*) and *ppl. a.*; **spaer**, one who foretells.

c **1480** HENRYSON *Orph. & Euryd.* 588 Wichcraft, Spaying, and sorsery. **1513** DOUGLAS *Æneid* I. vi. 148 Les than [= unless] my parentis taucht me spaying craft fals. **1725** RAMSAY *Gentle Sheph.* III. ii, May your spaeing happen soon and weel. **1790** SHIRREFS *Poems* 122 And sae it is with a' the spaeing crew. *Ibid.* 123 Before they enter on the spaeing part. **1820** *Blackw. Mag.* May 161 A seller o' horn spoons, and a spaer o' poor folks' fortunes.

spae-, the verbal stem in comb. (cf. SPAEMAN), as **spae-book, -craft, -woman, -work, -wright.**

1802 LEYDEN *Lord Soulis* lvi, The black *spae-book from his breast he took. **1724** RAMSAY *Evergreen* (1761) I. 135 Suthe I forsie, if *Spae-craft had [= hold], Frae Hethir-Muirs sall ryse a lad. **1889** H. JOHNSTON *Chron. Glenbuckie* 11 Whether the recipient..was a believer in spae-craft or not. **1828** MOIR *Mansie Wauch* xx, Beds at twopence a-night to..dumb *spaewomen. **1815** SCOTT *Guy M.* xi, There was some *spae-wark gaed on—I aye heard that. **1876** MORRIS *Sigurd* I. 16 In peace will I go to his bidding, let the *spae-wrights ban or bless.

'spaedom. [f. SPAE *sb.* or *v.* Cf. ON. and Icel. *spádómr*, MSw. *spādom*, Sw. *spådom*, Da. *spaadom*.] Prophecy.

1862 WINGATE *Poems, Spae Craft* ix, Oh, never again.. The dark, sinfu' regions o' spaedom I'll dare. **1891** ATKINSON *Last of Giant-killers* 115 The old prophecy or spaedom I have mentioned.

'spaeman. *Sc.* Also 5–6 spay-, spaman. [a. ON. *spámann* (nom. *-maðr*; MSw. *spāmann*, Sw. *spåman*, Norw. *spaamann*, Da. *-mand*), f. *spá* SPAE *v.*] A prophet, soothsayer, fortune-teller, wizard.

c **1480** HENRYSON *Orph. & Euryd.* 436 This Theseus.. sett his entencion To fynd the craft of diuinacion, And lerit it vnto the spamen all. **1513** DOUGLAS *Æneid* IV. ii. 29 O walaway! of spamen and diuinis The blind myndis. **1536** BELLENDEN *Cron. Scot.* (1821) I. 121 The spaymen said, thir prodigies signifyit gret damage appering to Romanis. **1725** RAMSAY *Gentle Sheph.* III. ii, Spae-men! the truth of a' their saws I doubt. **1790** SHIRREFS *Poems* 124, I never, a' my days, Had meikle faith in spaemen, or their says. **1830** SCOTT *Demonol.* ix. 315 Pretending..to possess the power of a spaeman. **1867** PEARSON *Hist. Eng.* I. 32 *note*, Either the 'spae man' of the district or the priest of an imported religion.

attrib. **1513** DOUGLAS *Æneid* VI. iii. 77 Praying thus, eftir the spamen werd.

Spaetlese, var. SPÄTLESE.

'spaewife. *Sc.* [f. SPAE- + WIFE *sb.* Cf. ON. and Icel. *spákona*, Da. *spaakone*, Sw. *spåqvinna*; NFris. *spuaiwüf*.] A female fortune-teller; a sybil; a witch.

a **1774** FERGUSSON *Hallow-Fair* iv. Poems (1789) II. 27 What cairds and tinklers come,..An' spae-wives fenzying to be dumb. **1818** SCOTT *Hrt. Midl.* li, Many remembered that Annaple Bailzou wandered through the country as a beggar and fortune-teller, or spae-wife. **1872** KINGSLEY *Poems, Little Baltung* xxvi, Oh a spae-wife laid a doom on me. **1876** A. LAING *Lindores Abbey* xxvi. 382 He was going to consult a spaewife in the neighbourhood.

spag (spæg). Slang abbrev. of SPAGHETTI 1 a. Also **spag bol** (bɒl), spaghetti Bolognese.

1948 PARTRIDGE *Dict. Forces' Slang* 176 *Spag*, spaghetti. (Italian front.) **1969** *Southerly* XXIX. 308 'I'll shout you a plate of steak and spag,' I said. 'It's only a buck.' **1970** D. CLARK *Deadly Pattern* iv. 86 To eat oxtail and spag bol properly, you've got to be stripped to the waist.

spaggers (ˈspægəz). Also **spadgers**. Slang abbrev. of SPAGHETTI 1 a. Cf. -ER[6] and prec.

1960 I. JEFFERIES *Dignity & Purity* v. 96 Thinking of the spaggers I would have rustled up, left to myself. **1980** I. MURDOCH *Nuns & Soldiers* ii. 127 'You said you were tired of spaghetti and potatoes and—' 'Spuds and spadgers fill you up at least.'

spaghetti (spəˈgɛtɪ). [It., pl. of *spaghetto* thin string, twine.]

1. a. A variety of pasta made in long thin strings. Occas., a dish of spaghetti.

1849 E. ACTON *Mod. Cookery* (ed. 8) p. xxxii, *Sparghetti* [sic]—Naples vermicelli. **1888** MRS. BEETON *Bk. Househ. Managem.* §2952 Maccheroni, or Spaghetti, a smaller kind of macaroni,..generally follows the soup. **1921** F. SWINNERTON *Coquette* II. xvi. 175 The waitress approached, bearing two large plates piled high with spaghetti. **1931** B. STARKE *Touch & Go* iv. 51 A..schoolteacher took us to lunch in Avon and showed us how to manage yards of spaghetti by rolling it up on our forks. **1949** J. MORE *Land of Italy* 4 A capacity to eat..*pasta* is an essential requirement... The principal varieties..are the rope-like spaghetti of Naples, the pipe-like macaroni,..and the omelet-like cannelloni. **1956** N. DE LA FÈRE *Italian Bouquet* vi. 66 He slipped the menu under my eyes... I..refused to admit that the only recognisable word was 'spaghetti'. **1965** C. K. STEAD in *N.Z. Short Stories* (1966) 337 Julian came into Gomeo's and asked for a spaghetti. **1981** M. NABB *Death of Englishman* II. iii. 97 Old men..munching slowly at their *spaghetti* with toothless gums.

b. *fig.* and *transf.*

1935 A. HUXLEY *Let.* 17 Feb. (1969) 391 Orlo Williams.. has read every inch of spaghetti that has ever emerged from the Italian presses. **1940** O. NASH *Face is Familiar* 195 And they give you a look that implies that your spine is spaghetti and your soul is lard. **1946** F. HAMANN *Air Words* 50 *Spaghetti*, (1) electric wiring; (2) strings of sealing compound. **1960** COOKE & MARKUS *Electronics & Nucleonics Dict.* 446/2 *Spaghetti*, insulating tubing used over bare wires or as a sleeve for holding two or more insulated wires together. The tubing is usually made of varnished cloth or a plastic. **1973** C. WILLIAMS *Man on Leash* (1974) viii. 119 He was always..experimenting and lashing up nutty pieces of electronic spaghetti. **1981** T. BARLING *Bikini Red North* xiii. 276 His vasectomy could be reversed. 'New techniques. .. We can join up all that miniature spaghetti with incredible accuracy.'

2. An Italian: usu. contemptuous. *slang.*

1931 'D. STIFF' *Milk & Honey Route* iii. 38 Italian hobos are equally rare. They are the 'wops' or 'spaghettis'. **1977** *New Society* 29 Sept. 651/1 When the war criminal, Herbert Kappler, who served a life sentence for having commanded an execution squad that massacred 335 Italian civilians, was spirited out of a military hospital in Rome by his wife, this was generally welcomed [in Germany] with an almost racialist feeling of superiority vis-a-vis those doting spaghettis.

3. Complex roadways forming a multi-level junction, esp. on a motorway. *colloq.*

1963 *Lebende Sprachen* VIII. 166/1 Driver talk..Plenty of spaghetti. **1966** *Guardian* 4 June 14/2 Details of one of the biggest pieces of motorway spaghetti so far designed in Britain were published... It is the Gravelly Hill interchange on the M6. **1972** *Daily Tel.* 19 June 19/3 The transport profession has produced its own jargon... Multi-level motorway-junctions are 'plates of spaghetti'. **1976** *Times Lit. Suppl.* 20 Feb. 184/5 The best-known examples [of three-dimensional mazes] are motorway spaghetti, aesthetically unpleasing and disturbing to drive through.

4. *attrib.* and *Comb.* ***spaghetti house, joint, sauce, tongs***; ***spaghetti-like*** adj.; **spaghetti Bolognese**, spaghetti served with a sauce of which the principal ingredients are beef and tomato; **spaghetti bowl**, a network of pipelines constructed to carry materials between petrochemical companies on the Gulf Coast of the U.S.; also *transf.*; **spaghetti junction** *colloq.*, a complex junction of roads at different levels; applied *spec.* to a major interchange on the M6 near Birmingham; also *fig.*; **spaghetti (shoulder) strap**, a thin cord-like shoulder strap for a dress or the like; **spaghetti tubing** *colloq.*, tubular insulation for electrical wire; **spaghetti Western**, a 'Western' (WESTERN *sb.* 4) or film set in the U.S. 'old west', but made in Italy or by Italians, esp. cheaply.

[**1947** L. P. DE GOUY *Gold Cookery Bk.* 760 (*heading*) Spaghetti alla Bolognese.] **1950** E. DAVID *Bk. Mediterranean Food* 93 If you are serving the classic spaghetti *Bolognese*..see that it is highly flavoured. **1973** 'M. UNDERWOOD' *Reward for Defector* vii. 56 [He] reached out for everything he needed to make himself a plateful of spaghetti bolognese. **1958** *Houston* Apr. 16/1 The mighty petrochemical industry today is feeding from an overflowing 'Spaghetti Bowl'. *Ibid.* 16/3 Industrial Sales Engineer G. R. Walton of the Houston Pipe Line Company (the man who coined the term 'Spaghetti Bowl' about two years ago). **1970** *Chem. & Engin. News* 26 Oct. 30 Mention 'the spaghetti bowl' and most West European petrochemical producers would probably think of the pipeline system in the Gulf Coast of the U.S. rather than the maze being developed in their own back yard. **1962** I. FLEMING *Spy who loved Me* I. ii. 34 Derek took me right across London to a spaghetti house called 'The Bamboo'. **1900** ADE *Fables in Slang* 158 He knew his Works were good, because all the Free and Untrammeled Souls in the Spaghetti Joint told him so. **1982** H. ENGEL *Murder on Location* (1983) ix. 87, I could see a spaghetti joint across the street. **1971** *Evening News* (Worcester) 15 Nov. 7/4 Worcester will have its own 'spaghetti junction' if the big multi-level interchange is ever constructed in the Arboretum. **1978** *Listener* 5 Jan. 25/4 We pass abruptly from the *proprium* to the *ordinarium*—from the winding country road into a great spaghetti junction of criss-cross melodies. **1980** S. BRETT *Dead Side of Mike* xi. 125 He got held up.. under the spaghetti junction between the M23 and M25 because of road works. **1979** K. BONFIGLIOLI *After You with Pistol* vi. 25 We parted in a spaghetti-like tangle of insincere matiness. **1953** A. BONI *Talisman Italian Cook Bk.* xiii. 222 (*heading*) Spaghetti sauce home style. **1968** C. DRUMMOND *Death & Leaping Ladies* v. 111 He was neatly avoiding spilling spaghetti sauce over a very snappy jacket. **1980** B. FREEMANTLE *Charlie Muffin's Uncle Sam* vii. 73 The man hadn't changed his shirt... There was spaghetti sauce on the collar. **1972** *New Yorker* 30 Sept. 81/1 Black cocktail dresses with sparkling spaghetti straps. **1977** *Lancashire Life* Dec. 104/3 The demure look from Elizabeth Hayes consists of a lace-trimmed polyester satin bedjacket which, when taken off, reveals a sexy nightdress with spaghetti shoulder straps. **1980** *Times* 12 Feb. 7/5 A natty little camisole top with spaghetti shoulder straps topped with an amazing sort of opened up tube of knitting which seals your arms and then blossoms into a shrug for the back and shoulders. Do not ask me how it is done. **1972** *House & Garden* Feb. 78/1 Spaghetti tongs, 85p. **1977** 'E. MCBAIN' *Long Time no See* iii. 32 Knives and forks piled haphazardly.. paper napkins, spaghetti tongs, a corkscrew. **1922** *Science & Invention Mag.* May (Advt., rear cover), Spaghetti Tubing, black or yellow in 2½-ft. lengths.. 18 cents per length. **1969** M. PEI *Words in Sheep's Clothing* (1970) iii. 22 'Spaghetti Western' and 'Sukiyaki Western' are terms applied to cheap Westerns produced in Italy and Japan. **1973** J. SUSANN *Once is not Enough* i. 34 It started with the flop of Melba's picture... When your kid is busted into pieces, you can't worry about a spaghetti western. **1977** G. MARTON *Alarum* 56, I wanted to see a Spaghetti Western movie.

‖**spaghettini** (spaget'tini). [It.] A thin variety of spaghetti.

1953 A. BONI *Talisman Italian Cook Bk.* ix. 156 Bring water and salt to boil, add spaghettini and cook 12 minutes. **1974** *Encycl. Brit. Micropædia* VII. 789/3 Among the popular cord forms [of pasta] are spaghetti ('little string'), a finer type called spaghettini, and the very fine vermicelli. **1977** D. E. WESTLAKE *Nobody's Perfect* (1978) II. v. 120 You can buy me spaghettini with clam sauce.

spagnel, obs. form of SPANIEL.

†**spagnolet**. *Obs.*⁻¹ [ad. F. *espagnolette*, f. *espagnol(e* Spanish.] 'A kind of narrow-sleeved gown, a la Spagnole' (*Fop Dict.* 1690).

1690 ? EVELYN *Mundus Muliebris* 2 Nor demy Sultane, Spagnolet, Nor Fringe to sweep the Mall forget.

Spagnolize(d, obs. f. SPANIOLIZE(D.

spagyric (spə'dʒɪrɪk), *sb.* and *a.* *Obs.* exc. *Hist.* Forms: α. 6 **spagirique**, 7- **spagiric** (7 **-ick**); 6-7 **spagericke**, 7 **spargerick**. β. 7-8 **spagyrick**, 7- **spagyric**. [ad. early mod.L. *spagiricus* (used, and prob. invented, by Paracelsus), whence also F. *spagirique* (†*spargirique* Cotgr.), It. *spargirico*, *-ica*, Sp. and Pg. *espagirico*, *-ica*.]

A. *sb.* †1. The science of alchemy or chemistry.

1593 G. HARVEY *Pierce's Super.* 29 Yet who such monarches for Phisique, Chirurgery, Spagirique,.. as some of these arrant impostors? **1605** TIMME *Quersit.* III. 183 Alchymie or Spagyrick.. is the inuenter and schoolmistresse of distillation.

2. An alchemist.

1593 G. HARVEY *Pierce's Super.* Wks. (Grosart) II. 251 The greatest Empiriques, Spagiriques, Cabalists,.. and occult Philosophers. **1613** DRUMM. OF HAWTH. *Cypress Grove* Wks. (1711) 127 Can the spagyrick by his art restore, for a Space, to the dry and withered Rose, the natural Purple and Blush. **1645** BP. HALL *Discontentm.* §4. 14 Like to some cunning Spagirick, that can intend or remit the heat of his furnace according to occasion. **1867** *Cornh. Mag.* Mar. 369 A traveller who saw the celebrated spagyric at the Hague, represents him as still adhering to his old spiritual tricks.

B. *adj.* Pertaining to alchemy; alchemical.

α. **1596** J. HESTER tr. *Paracelsus' Exper. & Cures* F, The Spagericke Antidotarie of the preparation and making of medicines against Goonshot. **1605** TIMME *Quersit.* III. 153 They which are but meanely seene in the spargerick art, and haue been chymists a very short time. **1656** W. DU GARD tr. *Comenius' Gate Lat. Unl.* §706. 227 At this day Spagirick (or Hermetick) Physic is in request. **1681** tr. *Willis' Rem. Med. Wks.* Vocab., *Spagiric*, belonging to alchymie, or to the chymical art. **1737** BRACKEN *Farriery Impr.* (1757) II. 280 Skilful in the Spagiric Art, as well as the Art of Medicine. **1833** CARLYLE *Misc. Ess.* (1872) V. 106 He is distributing spagiric food, medicine for the poor. **1856** R. A. VAUGHAN *Mystics* (1860) II. 103 Medical practitioners of the old school, who denounced the spagiric method. **1891** *Q. Rev.* Oct. 408 The pretension to 'spagiric' immortality of Cagliostro.

β. *c* **1643** LD. HERBERT *Autobiog.* (1824) 49 As for the Chymic or Spagyric Medicines, I cannot commend them to the use of my posterity. **1660** J. H[ARDING] *Basil. Valent. Chariot Antim.* 67 Antimony.. being by Spagyrick Art transmuted, becomes medicinal. **1716** M. DAVIES *Athen. Brit.* II. 395 Medicinally Charitable to the Publick by his Spagyrick Repository. **1844** HECKER *Epid. Middle Ages* 273 The severe metallic remedies of the Spagyric school. **1899** *Literature* 18 Feb. 181 The sages, those who practised the true spagyric art.

spa'gyrical, *a.* Also 6-7 **spagirical(l**, 7 **spagericall**. [f. as prec. + -AL¹.]

1. Of or pertaining to alchemy.

α. **1594** PLAT *Jewell-ho.* II. 20 The perfecting of this branch of the spagirical art. *Ibid.* III. 89 An infinite number of spagiricall experiments. **1651** WITTIE tr. *Primrose's Pop. Err.* IV. i. 204 It is certaine, that by this spagiricall art, the most unruly medicaments are made serviceable. **1654** GAYTON *Pleas. Notes* Pref. Verses, Which.. was done With a Spagericall discretion.

β. **1627** HAKEWILL *Apol.* III. vii. §5 The use of Hermeticall, Spagyricall, or Chymicall physicke. **1651** FRENCH *Distill.* v. 118 The matter will be turned into a spagyricall bloud, and flesh, like an Embryo. **1698** FRYER *Acc. E. India & P.* 306 These Waters of Genoe, as far as I could gather by Spagyrical Solutions, have to their Sulphur an Addition both of Antimony and Nitre. **1747** T. BIRCH *Serm. bef. Coll. Phys.* 22 To discern them may require no mean skill in spagyrical principles and operations.

2. Of persons: Given to the study or practice of alchemy; believing in alchemy.

1652 (*title*), A Hermeticall Banqvet drest by a Spagiricall Cook, for the better preservation of the Microcosme. **1661** BOYLE *Scept. Chem.* I. 56 So justly did the Spagyricall Poet somewhere exclaim [etc.]. **1667** —— *Orig. Forms & Qual.* (ed. 2) 338 If a Spagyrical Physician were Judge.

spa'gyrically, *adv.* Also **spagirically**. [f. prec.] In a spagyric manner; in accordance with spagyric principles.

1621 BURTON *Anat. Mel.* II. v. I. v, If you will have them spagirically prefaced look in Oswaldus Crollius. **1662** MERRETT tr. *Neri's Art of Glass* xxxi, The manner of making Vitriol of Venus, without corrosives, Spagirically. **1670** G. TONSTALL (*title*), Scarbrough Spaw Spagyrically Anatomized. **1694** SALMON *Bate's Dispens.* (1713) 640/2 If such are the Vertues of the gross Flesh, what would it be if it was Spagyrically prepar'd?

'**spagyrist**. Also 7-8 **spagirist**. [ad. mod.L. *spagirista* (F. *spagiriste*): see SPAGYRIC *a.*] An alchemist.

α. **1652** J. WRIGHT tr. *Camus' Nat. Paradox* XI. 280 The Spagirists in seeking the Union of Essences have.. found out the dissolving of all naturall Bodies. **1660** J. H[ARDING] *Basil. Valent. Chariot Antim.* 1 A brief admonition concerning some *Præcognita*, which a Spagirist.. ought to be acquainted with. **1706** PHILLIPS (ed. Kersey).

β. **1661** BOYLE (*title*), The Sceptical Chymist: or Chymico-Physical Doubts & Paradoxes, Touching the Spagyrists' Principles Commonly call'd Hypostatical. **1675** *Phil. Trans.* X. 516 Those Spagyrists that possess or aspire to the nobler Arcana of Gold and Mercury. **1756** AMORY *J. Buncle* (1825) I. 266 A man of great skill in the labours and operations of spagyrists.

So '**spagyrite**. *rare*.

1666 BOYLE *Orig. Forms & Qual.* 58 Other things which Spagyrites obtaine from mixt Bodies. **1697** EVELYN *Numismata* ix. 328 A troop of Spagirits.

‖**spahi** ('spɑːhiː). Forms: 6-7 **spachi**, 7 **spahei**, 7-8 **spahy**, 7-9 **spahee**, 7- **spahi**. [ad. Turkish (Persian) *sipāhī*: see SEPOY.]

1. A horseman forming one of a body of cavalry which formerly constituted an important part of the Turkish army and was to some extent organized on a feudal basis. Now *Hist.*

1562 J. SHUTE tr. *Cambini's Turk. Wars* 53 The Spachi, and other ordres of horsemen. **1585** T. WASHINGTON tr. *Nicholay's Voy.* II. xix. 53 Hys Spachis, or other officers. **1617** MORYSON *Itin.* I. 217 It happened that a Spachi (or Horse-man under the great Turkes pay).. suddenly turned towards us. **1634** SIR T. HERBERT *Trav.* 71 The Great Turke.. gaue.. treasure there, to the Ianizaries and Spaheis. **1728** ELIZA HEYWOOD tr. *Mme. de Gomez's Belle A.* (1732) II. 255 A large Body of Janizaries, with other Infantry, join'd to a considerable Number of *Spahi's*, which are reputed the best Cavalry in the Empire. **1773** *Gentl. Mag.* XLIII. 457 When the Russian columns advanced.. they were furiously assailed by the Spahis that were in ambuscades. **1816** BYRON *Siege Corinth* xxii, Tartar, and Spahi, and Turcoman, Strike your tents, and throng to the van. *c* **1828** LANDOR *Imag. Conv.* Wks. 1876 VI. 150 Every sort of dress that janisary and spahi.. ought to put on in gala. **1854** CHURCH *Misc. Writ.* (1891) I. 352 The Spahis of the house of Othman reared that blood-red banner.

2. A native Algerian horseman serving under the French government.

1863 KINGLAKE *Crimea* II. xvi. 270 In the morning he had ridden forward, escorted by a few Spahis, to reconnoitre the ground. **1864** J. ORMSBY *Rambles N. Africa* 214 The Spahis, on the other hand, are a highly-organised and efficient body. **1882** 'OUIDA' *Under Two Flags* (1890) 231 His height rose far above the French soldiers, and above most even of the lofty-statured Spahis.

spaid, var. SPAYD *Obs.*; obs. f. SPAYED *ppl. a.*

spaier, var. SPARE *sb.*²

spaight, dial. f. SPATE *sb.*

Spaignarde, -nell, obs. ff. SPANIARD, SPANIEL.

spaik, Sc. f. SPOKE *sb.*

spail, var. SPALE *sb.*²

Spain (speɪn). Forms: α. 3-7 **Spaine**, **Spayne**, 4 **Spaigne**, 5 **Speyne**, 6 **Espayne**, 6- **Spain**; 5-6 *Sc.* **Spane**. β. *Sc.* 5 **Spanȝhe**, 5-6 **Spanȝe**, 6 **-ȝie**, **Spaneȝe**, **Spangyie**, 9 **Spainyie**; 5-6 **Spenȝe**, 6 **-ȝee**, **-ȝie**, **Speinȝie**, 9 **Spengyie**. [ad. AF. *Espayne*, *Espaigne* (mod.F. *Espagne*, = Sp. *España*, Pg. *Hespanha*, It. *Spagna*):—late L. *Spānia* (Gr. *Σπανία*) for earlier *Hispānia* (*Ispānia*).

The usual form in OE. is *Ispania*, but in the dat. plur. the aphetic forms *Spenum* and *Spaneum* occur. The dropping of the initial vowel of OF. *Espaigne* is in accordance with English usage: cf. MDu. *Spaengen*, *-gien* (Du. *Spanje*), MHG. *Spanje*, *Spangen-* (G. *Spanien*), ON. *Spánn* (and *Spánland*). The later Sc. forms show the usual change of *nȝ* into *ngy* or *ng*.]

1. The country which together with Portugal occupies the south-western peninsula of Europe.

α. *c* **1205** LAY. 1394 Heo ferden from Spaine riht toward Brutaine. **1297** R. GLOUC. (Rolls) 3915 Þer nas bituene þis & spayne no prince.. þat nas at þis rounde table. *c* **1330** R. BRUNNE *Chron. Wace* (Rolls) 1482 Whan þeyr fflote.. Turnede fro þe lond of Spaigne. **1387** TREVISA *Higden* (Rolls) I. 299 But þere beeþ tweye Spaynes; þe hyder.. þe ȝonder Spayne. **1436** *Libel Eng. Policy* 99 The wolle of Spayne hit cometh not to preffe, But if it be.. menged welle Amonges Englysshe wolle. **1486** *Bk. St. Albans, Hawking* b vi b, Take Oyle of spayne and tempere it with clere wyne. **1501** DOUGLAS *Pal. Hon.* II. xxxv, Now in the realme of Trace, and now in Spane. **1547** BOORDE *Introd. Knowl.* xxx. (1870) 198 Spayne is a very poore countrey. **1550** J. COKE *Eng. & Fr. Heralds* §208 Commodities of Espayne and not of Fraunce. **1605** CAMDEN *Rem.* (1623) 2 Asia serueth thee with silke and purple,.. Spaine with Gold, and Germanie with Siluer. **1706** STEVENS *Sp. & Eng. Dict.* Pref., The long continuance of the Moors in Spain. **1838** PRESCOTT *Ferd. & Isabella* I. ii. (1854) I. 93 The combined forces of France and Spain.

β. **1375** BARBOUR *Bruce* III. 688 The.. strait off Marrok in-to Spanȝe. *c* **1425** WYNTOUN *Cron.* III. ix. 1050 Wiþe-in þe kynrik of Spanȝhe hail. **1561** *Reg. Privy Council Scot.* I. 177 All writtin in the language of Spangyie.

b. *New Spain*, the region including Mexico and Central America. Now *Hist.*

1719 W. WOOD *Surv. Trade* 281 The Assiento Contract has excluded.. Great Britain from Trading to New Spain. **1777** ROBERTSON *Hist. Amer.* III. (1851) I. 231 Grijalva.. called it New Spain, the name which still distinguishes this extensive and opulent province of the Spanish empire in America. **1843** PRESCOTT *Mexico* VII ii. (1850) III. 215 Vera Cruz.. has remained ever since the great commercial capital of New Spain. *a* **1845** *Encycl. Metrop.* XIII. 716/2 Of these disturbances, that of New Spain seemed to threaten the worst consequences.

c. *the Spains*, Spain in Europe and New Spain in America.

1847 DE QUINCEY *Sp. Mil. Nun* Wks. 1862 III. 64 The King of the Spains and the Indies.

d. *fig.* A quantity such as Spain can produce.

1866 HOWELLS *Venetian Life* xvii. 256 Whole Hollands of cabbage, and Spains of onions.

2. *attrib.* in Sc. use: = SPANISH *a.*

Also ellipt. *Spainyie*, *Spengyie*, Spanish cane.

1494 *Acc. Ld. High Treas. Scot.* I. 250 A wall of Spenȝe erne. **1502** *Ibid.* II. 270 For vj waw of Spanȝe irne to the werk in Halyrudhous. *a* **1520** DUNBAR *Poems* lv. 30 Quhill that thai gatt the Spanȝie pockis. **1546** *Acc. Ld. High Treas. Scot.* IX. 42 Tua ellis and ane half Spanȝe freis. **1550** *Ibid.* 399 Thre fyne Spanȝe skynnis. **1565** in Hay Fleming *Reform. Scotl.* (1910) 611 Twa breistis of Spenȝee cattis and twa mantillingis of Spenȝie cattis. *a* **1585** MONTGOMERIE *Flyting* 314 The feavers, the fearcie, with the speinȝie flees. **1825** JAMIESON *Suppl.*, *Spainyie Flees*,.. cantharides.

spain, variant of SPANE *v.*, to wean.

†'**Spainol**. *Obs.* In 4-5 **Spaynol**, 5 **-al**. [ad. AF. type **Espaynol*, = OF. *Espaignol* (see SPANIEL²), Sp. *Español*, Pg. *Hespanhol*, It. *Spagnuolo* :—Romanic **Spaniolus*, f. *Spania* SPAIN.] A Spaniard.

c **1350** *Will. Palerne* 3399 Þe spaynoles speiȝed he was slayne. *Ibid.* 3529 Of þe spaynolus wol I speke. **14..** *Trevisa's Higden* (Rolls) IV. 419 Of Spaynols and of Galles. *c* **1425** WYNTOUN *Cron.* II. ix. 782 Thare schyppys he fand thretty Wytht off Spaynalys a cumpany. *c* **1450** LYDG. *Secrees* 605 He.. Was callyd Iohn, And of nacyoun A spaynol born. **1482** CAXTON *Trevisa's Higden* II. vii. 80 b, Men of the West breketh her Wordes bitwene the teth as spaynols and Romayns.

spair, obs. Sc. f. SPARE *v.*; obs. f. SPEAR *sb.*¹

spairge, Sc. variant of SPARGE *sb.* and *v.*

spait, spaive, variants of SPATE, SPAVE.

spak, obs. or Sc. f. pa. t. of SPEAK *v.*

†**spake**, *v.* *Obs. rare.* In 3 **spakie**, 5 **spak-**. [f. *spak-* SPACK *a.* Cf. ON. and Icel. *spekja*, Norw. dial. *spekkja*, *spækje*, MSw. *späkia*, Da. *spæge* to quieten, tame, etc.]

1. *intr.* To hasten (*to* do something).

12.. *Prayer to our Lady* 14 in *O.E. Misc.*, Hwo se understant wel his ende-dai wel ȝeorne he mot spakie to donde sunne awei fram him, and fele almesse makie.

2. *refl.* To calm oneself, become calm.

a **1400-50** *Alexander* 237 Þat myld.. hire spakid with his speche & spird of him wordis.

spake (speɪk), *sb.* *S. Wales.* [Of unknown origin: perh. var. SPOKE *sb.*] A string of rail-mounted wagons or trolleys used in coal mines to transport men.

1935 *Trans. Inst. Mining Engineers* LXXXVIII. 384 In mines where the men are brought out in spakes, provision should be made for their protection from the cold intake air. *Ibid.* XC. 140 A spake is composed of a number of flat trolleys fitted with wooden seats placed at intervals at right angles to the length of the trolley, and consequently at right angles to the slant. **1971** *Guardian* 6 July 1/5 A colliery accident in which an underground train ran out of control. .. It was remarkable the train—known as a spake—did not leave the rails. **1979** *Times* 29 Dec. 12/5 The seams lay, in places, three miles below ground. To reach them by 'spake', the man-carrying wagons, entailed a journey of half an hour.

spake, obs. var. SPACK *a.*; obs., poet., or arch. f. pa. t. of SPEAK *v.*; Sc. f. SPOKE *sb.*

†**spaked,** *ppl. a. Obs.* Also 5 *Sc.* **spakit.** [ad. LG. *spaket*, pa. pple. of *spaken* (also *verspaken*) to mould, decay, etc.] Moulded, blemished, decayed, rotten.

1438 *Extr. Burgh Rec. Edinb.* (1869) I. 5 The frauchtismen sall specifie in the frauchting of the schip and in the chartour pairtie that thair be na gude woll nor skynnis spakit no schorne, na hyddis kippit to be schorne vp. **1584** B. R. tr. *Herodotus* II. 106 A man..may clearly perceiue, that their hands fel off for very age, by reason that the wood through long continuance of time was spaked and perished. **1615** T. ADAMS *Leaven* 118 What cares a good market-man how fayre the fleece or the flesh looke, if the liver be spak'd. **1688** BUNYAN *Saints' Priv. & Profit* Wks. 1855 I. 662 They looking upon it..do find it spaked and defective.

spakely, variant of SPACKLY *adv.*

spakle, etc., obs. variants of SPECKLE *v.*

†**'spaky,** *a. Obs.*⁻¹ In 6 **spakey.** [ad. LG. *spakig* (NFris. *spaakig*): see SPAKED *ppl. a.*] Mouldy.

1589 R. HARVEY *Pl. Perc.* 19 One spakey Apple will make the whole hourd smel.

spal, obs. form of SPAWL *v.*, to spit.

†**spalch,** *v. Obs. rare.* [ad. OF. *espelucher*, *esplucher* (mod.F. *éplucher*), f. *pelucher* of uncertain origin.] *refl.* Of a hawk: To clean (itself) with the beak.

c **1450** *Bk. Hawking* in *Rel. Ant.* I. 298 Put her oute a-gayn to prowne and spalch herself. **1486** *Bk. St. Albans, Hawking* b vii b, When she begynnyth to penne, and plumyth, and spalchith and pikith her selfe.

spald, var. SPAULD, shoulder; SPAWL, spittle.

spald, *v. north.* and *Sc.* Forms: α. 5, 9 **spald,** 9 **spauld.** β. 5 **spawde,** 9 **spaud, spaad, spoad.** [ad. MLG. *spalden*, = obs. WFris. *spâlde*, MDu. *spouden* (Du. *spouwen*; WFris. *spoude*, *spouwe*), OHG. *spaltan* (MHG. and G. *spalten*), to split. A different grade of the stem is represented by Goth. *spilda*, ON. *speld*, *spjald*, tablet, OE. *speld*, MHG. and G. dial. *spelte* splinter.

Eng. dialects have also the sb. *spald*, *spaud*, corresponding to MLG. *spalde* and *spald* (G. *spalte*, *spalt*), and the derivative verb *spalder*, *spauder* (cf. SPALDERLING), = MLG. *spalderen*.]

a. *trans.* To splinter, split, break up, lay open or flat. **b.** *intr.* To go apart, to splay out.

? *a* **1400** *Morte Arth.* 3699 Be thane speris whare [= were] spronngene, spalddyd [? in] chippys. *c* **1400** *Destr. Troy* 12692 þer were spaudit [*printed* spandit] & spilt in a spase litill, Two hundreth hede schippis in a hond qwile. **1483** *Cath. Angl.* 352/1 To Spawde, *dissoluere*. *Ibid.*, Spawdyd as a schep (*A.* Spawdit as a shippe), *dissolutus*. **1513** DOUGLAS *Æneid* XI. ii. 73 [He] oft down fallis spaldit on the erd. *Ibid.* XII. v. 204 On the erd he spaldit him all flat. **1828–** in northern glossaries.

Hence **'spalding,** a split and dried fish, a speldring; **spalding-knife,** a knife for splitting fish.

1354 in *Priory of Finchale* (Surtees) p. xxxvii, Item j spaldyngknyf. **1776** *Sempill's Blythsome Bridal* in Herd *Sc. Songs* II. 25 And there will be partens and buckies, And whytens and spaldings enew. **1790** WOLCOT (P. Pindar) *Compl. Ep. to Bruce* Ep. Ded. p. ii, Spaldings (*alias* dried whitings). **1867** SMYTH *Sailor's Word-bk.*, *Spaldings*, a north-country name for whitings and other small fish, split and dried. *Ibid.*, *Spalding-knife*, a knife used for splitting fish in Newfoundland.

†**'spalderling.** *Obs.* [f. *spalder* to split (see SPALD *v.*) + -LING. Cf. G. *spälterling* a split piece of wood.] A split and dried fish.

c **1340** *Durh. Acc. Rolls* (Surtees) 38 In viij spalderlyngg' empt. prec. ijd. qᵃ. **1366** *Ibid.* 45 In lx spaldirlinges empt. *Ibid.*, In xviij spalderlenges. **1403** *Ibid.* 51.

†**spale,** *sb.*¹ *Obs.*⁻¹ [OE. *spala* substitute: see SPELE *v.*] Sparing; respite or rest.

a **1250** *Owl & Night.* 258 þu mihtest bet hote galegale, Vor þu hauest to monye tale. Let þine tunge habbe spale.

spale (speɪl), *sb.*² *Sc.* and *north.* Forms: 5–6, 9 **spale,** 5–6, 8–9 **spail,** 6 **spaile, spaill,** 8–9 **speal,** 9 *north.* **spial, spyel.** [Of uncertain origin: cf. SPALL *sb.*¹ and SPEEL *sb.*

There is resemblance in form to ON. *spal-*, *spǫlr* bar, rod, short piece, MHG. (and G. dial.) *spale* rung of a ladder, G. dial. *spale*, *spal* wooden spit, wedge; but real connexion with these is doubtful.]

1. A splinter or chip, a thin piece or strip, of wood.

c **1470** *Gol. & Gaw.* 629 The spalis and the sparkis spedely out sprang. *Ibid.* 983 Half ane span at ane spail..He hewit attanis. *a* **1500** *Ratis Raving* 57 With stikis, and with spalys small, To byge vp chalmer, spens & hall. **1535** STEWART *Cron. Scot.* II. 283 Quhill speris brak, and all in spalis sprang Aboue thair heid. **1570** LEVINS *Manip.* 17 A spale, chip, *assula*. *a* **1578** LINDESAY (Pitscottie) *Chron. Scot.* (S.T.S.) II. 161 The king of France was ewill hurt in the face witht the spaill of ane speir. **1710** RUDDIMAN *Gloss. Douglas' Æneis* s.v. *Spalis*, We use..*speals* for chips of wood, or small splinters. **1781** J. HUTTON *Tour to Caves* (ed. 2) Gloss. 96 *Speals*, chips, or small split sticks. **1786** BURNS *Address of Beelzebub* 39 But smash them! crash them a' to spails! **1839** URE *Dict. Arts* 472 This multiplication of tools becomes unnecessary, by laying against the cutting part of the bit, slips of wood, called spales. **1854** H. MILLER *Sch. & Schm.* (1858) 14 The poor Friendship lies in spales on the bar of Findhorn. **1865** G. MACDONALD *A. Forbes* 50 The floor was covered with shavings or spales, as they are called by northern consent.

b. In proverbial phrases.

1535 STEWART *Cron. Scot.* I. 654 To huif ouir hie, Quhill that the spaill fell into thair ee. *a* **1585** MONTGOMERIE *Cherry & Slae* 184 To late I knaw, quha hewis to hie, The spail sall fall into his eie. **1670** RAY *Prov.* (1678) 369 He that hews over hie, the spail will fall into his eye. **1862** HISLOP *Prov. Scot.* 88 He's no the best wright that casts maist spails. **1894** P. H. HUNTER *J. Inwick* iv. 48 Hew abüne your heid, an' ye'll get a spale in your ee.

2. *transf.* (See quot. 1824.)

1824 MACTAGGART *Gallovid. Encycl.* 432 *Spales o' the cannle*, little curls of tallow, which sometimes appear on a burning candle. **1897** RAMPINI *Hist. Moray & Nairn* vi. 333 A 'spale' or 'waste' on a burning candle indicates an approaching death.

3. *attrib.*, as ***spale-basket, -board, -box.***

1830 J. WILSON *Noct. Ambr.* Wks. 1856 III. 19 Has the dowg swallowed the spale-box o' pills? **1857** MRS. CARLYLE *Lett.* II. 316 In a little oval spale-box. **1877** FRASER *Wigtown* 304 To..have nothing but a bit of a spale-boord between him an' etarnity. **1894** HESLOP *Northumb. Gloss.* 681 *Spyel-basket*, a basket made of wooden *spails*, oak preferred, for carrying food to cattle on a farm.

spale, *sb.*³ [Cf. SPALL *sb.*³] (See quot. and CROSS-SPALE.)

1867 SMYTH *Sailor's Word-bk.*, *Spales*, in naval architecture, internal strengthening by cross artificial beams.

spale (speɪl), *v. Cornish dial.* [Of obscure origin.] *trans.* To fine for absence, lateness, or breach of rules.

1854 *N. & Q.* 1st Ser. X. 419/2 *Spile*, which miners pronounce *spaël*; to inflict a fine or penalty for late attendance at work. **1865** R. HUNT *Pop. Rom. W. Eng.* Ser. II. 125 It isn't worth while to be spaled for any such foolishness.

spale, dial. variant of SPELE *v.*

'spaling, *vbl. sb.* (See quot. 1846.)

1805 *Shipwright's Vade-M.* 238 Upon the cross-spales is marked the middle line and the breadth of the ship at the place of spaling. **1846** A. YOUNG *Naut. Dict.* 289 *Spaling*, or *Baulking*, in shipbuilding, means keeping the frames to their proper breadths by cross-spales or baulks, which should so remain till some of the deck beam knees are bolted.

spall (spɔːl), *sb.*¹ Also 5 **spalle, spolle,** 8– **spawl.** [Of doubtful origin: perh. related to G. *spellen* to split, but cf. SPALE *sb.*²] A chip or splinter, esp. of stone or ore.

α. *c* **1440** *Promp. Parv.* 467/1 Spalle, or chyppe (*K.* spolle), *quisquilia*, *assula*. **1585** HIGINS tr. *Junius' Nomencl.* 411/2 *Segmenta*, the spalls or broken peeces of marble comming off in grauing and hewing. **1611** COTGR., *Retailles*, the spalls, or shards; the peeces which flie from stone in the hewing thereof. **1706** PHILLIPS (ed. Kersey), *Spalls*, Chips of Wood. **1875** KNIGHT *Dict. Mech.* 2252/1 *Spall*, a chip of stone, removed by the hammer. **1892** *Daily News* 22 Oct. 5/4 A stock of granite spalls could be had in.

β. **1793** SMEATON *Edystone L.* §35 The great tendency of the Laminæ whereof the rock is composed, to rise in spawls. *Ibid.* §112 *note*, Observing how soon the quarrymen would cut half a ton of Spawls from an unformed block. **1897** T. HARDY *Well-Beloved* 8 Like all the gardens in the isle it was surrounded by a wall of dry-jointed spawls.

spall, *sb.*² *rare.* [ad. It. *spalla*, or (in quot. 1827) var. of Sc. *spaul* SPAULD.] Shoulder.

1590 SPENSER *F.Q.* II. vi. 29 Their mightie strokes their haberieons dismayld, And naked made each others manly spalles. **1827** CARLYLE *Germ. Rom.* I. 60, [I] catch the noodle by the spall,..and pack him out of doors.

spall (spɔːl), *sb.*³ Also **spawl.** [Of obscure origin: cf. SPALE *sb.*³] A cross-spall; a cross-piece used in staging.

1895 *Whitby Gaz.* 12 July 4/1 Boys frequently went up the spawls instead of the gangway because it was a shorter way on to the ship. **1898** *Westm. Gaz.* 23 June 5/2 These were fixed together at the top by spalls, and strengthened by struts.

spall (spɔːl), *v.*¹ Also 8 **spal,** 9 **spaul, spawl.** [Related to SPALL *sb.*¹]

1. *trans.* **a.** *Mining.* To break (ore) into smaller pieces.

1758 [see SPALLING *vbl. sb.* 1]. **1778** PRYCE *Min. Cornub.* 215 Tin-stuff..is first spalled or broken to the size of a man's fist or less. *Ibid.* 233 They..spal or break them [*sc.* the larger stones] to a less size. **1855** [J. R. LEIFCHILD] *Cornwall* 52 The ore..is..drawn up, after being 'spalled' or broken. **1875** J. H. COLLINS *Met. Mining* 106 The ores, if in large masses, are first 'spalled', or broken up by means of heavy 'spalling hammers'.

absol. **1855** [J. R. LEIFCHILD] *Cornwall* 164 There they sit, 'spalling, jigging,' 'buddling and trunking,' and doing all manner of mining mysteries.

b. To dress (stones) roughly with a hammer.

1793– [see SPALLED *ppl. a.*]. *a* **1925** F. S. ANTHONY *Follow Call* (1936) ii. 22, I landed..on a patch of broken stone I had spalled up..for metalling in front of the stand.

2. a. To split or chip; also, to detach as small fragments or particles. Also with *off*.

1841 HARTSHORNE *Salop. Ant.* Gloss., *Spauled*, split, cleft, as wood. **1846** HOLTZAPFFEL *Turning* II. 501 Should the fibres have been split, or spalled off in shooting the ends, the removal of the edge *b*..would correct the evil. **1971** *Sci. Amer.* June 29/2 As the shock wave traversed a gas bubble some of its energy would go into spalling liquid from the inner surface of the bubble and projecting it through the void to strike the bubble wall at the other side. **1973** J. G. TWEEDDALE *Materials Technol.* II. vi. 154 Thermal fracturing is a somewhat crude way in which material may be 'spalled' off the surface of a brittle material which has low thermal-shock resistance. **1980** M. NAPIER *Blind Chance* xii. 109 She looked at the huge chip of stone spalled off by a bullet.

b. *Nuclear Physics.* To cause spallation of (a nucleus).

1976 *Nature* 16 Sept. 201/1 Stronger shock waves..spall nearly all the nuclei to free nucleons.

3. *intr.* To break *off* in fragments or chips. Also without *off*.

1853 KANE *Grinnell Exp.* xl. (1856) 363 Spawling off under the axe in dangerous little chips. **1881** YOUNG *Every Man his own Mechanic* §423 If this precaution is not taken the corners will 'spawl' off. **1940** K. REXROTH *In what Hour* 33 Novelty emerges after centuries, a rock spalls from the cliff. **1968** *Engineering* 26 July 171/3 These alloys would spall after enamelling. **1977** *Sci. Amer.* Feb. 35/1 High-energy impacts cause large pieces of the target to spall off. **1980** *National Trust* Autumn 14/2 Damp has penetrated the stone..and the corners have broken off or spalled.

spall (spɔːl), *v.*² [Related to SPALL *sb.*³] *trans.* To fix (ship-frames) at the proper breadth by means of cross-spalls.

c **1850** *Rudim. Navig.* (Weale) 112 The main and top-timber breadths are the heights mostly taken for spalling the frames.

spall, obs. form of SPAWL, to spit.

spallard, dial. form of ESPALIER.

spallation (spə'leɪʃən). [f. SPALL *v.*¹ + -ATION.]

1. *Nuclear Physics.* The detachment of a number of nucleons or small nuclei from a larger nucleus, esp. as a result of the impact of an energetic nucleon or other particle. Freq. *attrib.*, as ***spallation product.***

1948 LAPP & ANDREWS *Nuclear Radiation Physics* xiii. 305 When a high-energy neutron strikes a target nucleus, a reaction known as spallation may occur. **1950** GLASSTONE *Sourcebk. Atomic Energy* x. 259/2 They do not undergo fission and break up into two, more or less equal, parts. Instead, such nuclei emit various numbers..of nucleons, leaving a series of products of lower mass and atomic number. The name *spallation* has been proposed for reactions of this kind. [*Note*] This term is based on the verb 'to spall', meaning to break up by chipping off small fragments, which was suggested as appropriate by W. H. Sullivan. **1953** *Ann. Rev. Nuclear Sci.* II. 401 O'Connor & Seaborg..bombarded uranium with 380-Mev α-particles and then analyzed radiochemically for spallation and fission products. **1962** B. G. HARVEY *Introd. Nuclear Physics & Chem.* ix. 183 Reactions in which several particles are emitted are often called 'spallation', regardless of the mechanism by which they take place. **1979** *Nature* 15 Feb. 519/1, ^{18}C can be produced fairly readily in heavy ion collisions, or as a spallation product of heavy nuclei.

2. *gen.* Spalling.

1971 *New Scientist* 8 Apr. 72/3 An outer spallation zone due to the interaction of shock waves with the rock surface. **1974** HAWKEY & BINGHAM *Wild Card* xv. 133 The crash guys..look for recrystallization at micropromontories, Neumann banding, parallel banding, spallation.

spalled (spɔːld), *ppl. a.* Also **spauled, spawled.** [f. SPALL *v.*¹]

1. Dressed or broken with the hammer. More widely, broken off or chipped by spalling. Also ***spalled-off.***

1793 SMEATON *Edystone L.* 194 The spawled parts, parallel to the grain of the Rock. **1867** *Ure's Dict. Arts* II. 66 In the process of cobbing either ragged or spalled work, the greatest care..should be given [etc.]. **1931** G. W. TYRRELL *Volcanoes* ii. 67 Such rocks..may be distinguished from agglomerate by the..occurrence of fragments of spalled-off scoria in the interstices between the blocks. **1971** *Ann. Rep. Delegates Sci. Area Univ. Oxford* 67 Coke ash slag on spalled ends of Steetley tarred dolomite blocks. **1975** *Country Life* 9 Oct. 924/3 Spalled and fractured brickwork was cut out and replaced.

2. ***spalled rubble*** (see quot. 1839).

1839 *Sat. Mag.* 16 Feb. 58/1 That kind of careful masonry, called [in Ireland] *Spauled Rubble*; in which small stones shaped by the hammer..are placed in every interstice of the larger stones. **1888** STOKES *Celtic Ch.* 233 The tower is externally of ashlar or spawled rubble work.

spaller ('spɔːlə(r)). [f. SPALL *v.*¹]

1. A person employed in spalling.

1843 HOLTZAPFFEL *Turning* I. 171 The spallers employ heavy axe-formed or muckle-hammers, for spalling or scaling off smaller flakes. **1884** C. G. W. LOCK *Workshop Receipts* Ser. III. 51/2 The poor ore of the spallers is subjected to the cobbling process. **1894** *Labour Commission* Gloss., *Spallers*, women who, with a mallet, break the tin-ore as it comes from the mine-shaft into small pieces.

2. A spalling-machine.

1877 RAYMOND *Statist. Mines & Mining* 37 The quartz can be delivered at the 'spaller' for less than $2 per ton.

†'**spalliard**[1]. *Obs. rare.* Also 7 spaliard, 9 spallier. [Of obscure origin: cf. SPADIARD.] A labourer engaged in tin-mining.
1625 *Laws Stannaries* xii. (1808) 21 A labouring tinner, a blower, owner of blowing-houses, a spalliard, or adventurer. **1630** DODRIDGE *Dutchy of Cornewall* 93 The laborious search for Tynne in those dayes, euen as it is vsed by the Spaliard at this day with great industrie and paines. [**1836** R. POLWHELE *Hist. Cornw.* Gloss. 91/2 *Spallier*, a labourer in tin-works. See Acts of the Stannary Parliaments.]

spalliard[2], dial. form of ESPALIER.
1886 F. T. ELWORTHY *W. Somerset Word-Bk.* 696 *Spalliard* (spaal·yurd), *sb.*, espalier, a trained fruit tree. I think, sir, we must dig up that *spalliard* plum. **1920** [see PLEACH *sb.*].

spalling ('spɔːlɪŋ), *vbl. sb.* Also **spauling, spawling.** [f. SPALL *v.*[1]]
1. The action of breaking ore into small pieces, or of dressing stones, etc., with the hammer.
1758 BORLASE *Nat. Hist. Cornw.* 203 The best is broken small with hammers, which they call Spalling. **1778** PRYCE *Min. Cornub.* 193 Raising, spaling, and dividing, o. 8. o. **1855** [J. R. LEIFCHILD] *Cornwall* 268 The whole processes of spalling, buddling, jigging. **1875** BRASH *Eccl. Arch. Ireland* 79 The masonry is..of large-sized blocks, fitted without spawling. **1884** C. G. W. LOCK *Workshop Receipts* Ser. III. 50/1 Cleaning is commenced by separating the large from the small stuff, for 'spalling'.
attrib. **1871** MORGANS *Man. Min. Tools* 67 The 'spalling hammer' is used for breaking up lumps of orey mineral for sorting before crushing and stamping. **1875** J. H. COLLINS *Met. Mining* 107 The result of the spalling process is the production of a pile of best ore, a pile of seconds,..and a pile of 'deads'.
2. The process of chipping or splitting *off*.
1842 *Civil Eng. & Arch. Jrnl.* V. 363/1, I noticed a splintering, or spalling off, of the stones supporting the feet of some of the arches. **1875** KNIGHT *Dict. Mech.* 370/2 In order to prevent the brick from *spalling*.

spalme, obs. erron. form of PSALM.

spalpeen (spæl'piːn). *Irish.* [a. Ir. *spailpín*, f. *spailp-* of uncertain origin and meaning + *-in* dim. suffix. The etym. given in quot. 1780 is fanciful.]
1. A common workman or labourer; a farm-worker or harvester.
1780 A. YOUNG *Tour Irel.* 57 Connaught labourers; they are called spalpeens: *spal*, in Irish, is a scythe, and *peen* a penny; that is, a mower for a penny a day. *Ibid.* 333 Spalpeens going from hence decline much. **1807** HOARE *Tour in Ireland* 318, I have heard these boys [i.e. peasant's sons] called Spalpeens. **1818** LADY MORGAN *Fl. Macarthy* (1819) II. 3 Surrounded by petitioning, whining, wretched cotters, spalpeans, road makers, and labourers. **1837** *Boston Advert.* 17 Jan. 4/4 Peter Murphy, late spalpeen in Kerry.
2. Used contemptuously: A low or mean fellow; a scamp, a rascal.
1815 MAR. EDGEWORTH *Love & Law* I. iv, The spalpeen! turned into a buckeen, that would be a squireen,—but can't. **1856** LEVER *Martins of Cro' M.* xv, The dirty, mean spalpeens. **1857** KINGSLEY *Two Y. Ago* xix, I've brought away the poor spalpeen of a priest.
3. A youngster, a boy.
1891 B. STOKER *Snake's Pass* v, I remimber it..a lot higher up the mountain whin I was a spalpeen. **1901** JANE BARLOW *Land Shamrock* 206 If her brother Patrick was a couple of year or so oulder,..but he's only a spalpeen yet.

†**spalt**, *sb.*[1] *Obs. rare.* [Of obscure origin.] A silly or foolish person.
1639 N. N. tr. *Du Bosq's Compl. Woman* I. 26, I can no wayes excuse those Gossips..who are rapt in the companie of certaine Spalts [F. *impertinés*], so they have good clothes, or talk but of the Queene or Princesse. *Ibid.* II. 59 What they only do of purpose to take some Spalt [F. *insensé*].

†**spalt**, *sb.*[2] *Obs.*[−0] [a. G. *spalt*: see SPALD *v.*] (See quots.)
1668 WILKINS *Real Char.* II. iii. §3. 66 Metal[s]..used for ..Making of Soder, being like Tinn, but more hard and brittle: Spelter, Zink, Spalt. **1728** CHAMBERS *Cycl.*, *Spalt* or *Spelt*, a white, scaly, shining Stone, frequently used to promote the Fusion of Metals... The English Spalt is generally very hard. [Hence in Bailey, etc.]

spalt, *a.* Now *dial.* Also 8– **spolt, spoult.** [Related to SPALT *v.*] Of wood: Brittle, short-grained; breaking easily through dryness or decay.
In some dialects also applied to other things.
1567 GOLDING *Ovid's Met.* x. 100 Nor hazle spalt, nor ash whereof the shafts of speares made bee. **1577** HARRISON *England* II. xxii. (1877) I. 341 The parke oke is the softest, and far more spalt and brickle than the hedge oke. **1733** W. ELLIS *Chiltern & Vale Farm.* 113 The Beech is more spalt and short in it self than many others be. *Ibid.* 154 The Wind's Damage, that is often fatal to some of the Arms of this spalt, brittle Wood. **1787** GROSE *Prov. Gloss.* s.v. *Spolt*, The rafters of the church of Norwich are said to be spolt. **1787**– in East Anglian glossaries (in form *spouit*). **1875** PARISH *Sussex Dial.* 110.

spalt (spɔːlt), *v. dial.* Also 8 **spault.** [prob. ad. Du. and Flem. *spalte* (WFris. *spjalte*), = G. *spalzen*, related to SPALD *v.*] *intr.* and *trans.* To split, tear, splinter, etc. Hence '**spalting** *vbl. sb.*
1733 TULL *Horse-Hoeing Husb.* xx. 291 It *Spaults* up from below the Staple. *Ibid.* 296 The Danger of tearing (or spaulting) up of the Under-Stratum along with the Staple. **1854** MISS BAKER *Northampt. Gloss.*, *Spalt*,..to chip, to splint. *Ibid.*, *Spaltings*, branches of trees that are broken off, or riven by the wind. **1876** *Surrey Gloss.* s.v., I must get a mattick,..and spalt they old stubs off.

†**spaltam.** *Obs. rare.* Also 8 'spaltham. [ad. med.L. *aspaltum*, var. *asphaltum*.] Asphalt or bitumen used as a varnish. Also *attrib.*
1532 in E. Law *Hampton Crt. Pal.* (1885) I. 363 Payd to Henry Burd, groser of London, for 12 lb. of white lead,..2 lb. of spaltain [*sic*]. **1777** FOOTE *Taste* I. i, By the addition of your lumber-room dirt, and the salutary application of the 'spaltham pot, it became a Guido.

spalter ('spɔːltə(r)), *v. dial.* [f. prec. + -ER[5]. Cf. *spalder* s.v. SPALD *v.*] (See quots.)
1844 *Civil Eng. & Arch. Jrnl.* VII. 429/2 A hard frost often causes glazed tiles or pots, when exposed to the weather, to chip or spalter. **1854** MISS BAKER *Northampt. Gloss.*, *Spaltered*, split off.

spalter, obs. erron. form of PSALTER.

Spam (spæm). Also **spam.** [App. blend of SP(ICED *ppl. a.* + H)AM *sb.*[1], but see also quot. 1937[1].] **1.** The proprietary name of a type of tinned meat consisting chiefly of pork; also (with small initial) applied *loosely* to other types of tinned luncheon meat.
1937 *Squeal* 1 July 1/2 In the last month Geo. A. Hormel & Co...launched the product *Spam*... The 'think-up' of the name [is] credited to Kenneth Daigneau, New York actor... Seems as if he had considered the word a good memorable trade-name for some time, had only waited for a product to attach it to. **1937** *Official Gaz.* (U.S. Patent Office) 26 Oct. 750/2 Geo. A. Hormel & Company, Austin, Minn... Spam..For Canned Meats—Namely, Spiced Ham. Claims use since May 11, 1937. **1939** J. STEINBECK *Grapes of Wrath* v. 49 The tractor driver stopped..and opened his lunch: sandwiches wrapped in waxed paper, white bread, pickle, cheese, Spam. **1942** *Yank* 28 Oct. 8 There, arrayed in all their glory, were slices of ham, spam, bologna and potato salad. **1951** 'A. GARVE' *Murder in Moscow* xiii. 127, I received..four tins of meat—spam, I think it was called. **1957** H. ROOSENBURG *Walls came tumbling Down* ix. 199 We were offered Spam sandwiches. **1971** C. BONINGTON *Annapurna South Face* xi. 134 That night he made supper, a magnificent concoction of fried Spam and fried new potatoes. **1981** G. MACBETH *Kind of Treason* iv. 41 A plate of Molly's best Spam sandwiches.
fig. **1958** *Listener* 6 Nov. 750/2 An actor can only turn the quite unconscious richness of it [*sc.* the Hoxton voice] into —spam.
2. *Comb.* **Spam can** *slang*, a streamlined steam locomotive formerly used on the Southern Region of British Rail; **Spam Medal** *Mil. slang*, a medal awarded to all the members of a force (see also quot. 1962).
1967 G. F. FIENNES *I tried to run Railway* v. 54 We borrowed from the Southern for trials two Battle of Britain class engines..We took these Spam Cans out. **1971** D. J. SMITH *Discovery Railwayana* x. 59 *Spam can*, streamlined locomotive of the SR. **1945** PARTRIDGE *Dict. R.A.F. Slang* 40 Naffy gong 1939–45 star (medal). Since late 1943... It is also called *the spam medal*. **1959** *Legionary* Mar. 11/1 As all of us overseas at the time were volunteers, it meant that everybody wore one and so, in patronizing fashion, we tagged it [*sc.* the Canadian Volunteer Service Medal] the Spam Medal. **1962** GRANVILLE *Dict. Sailors' Slang* 110 *Spam medal*, 1939–45 star whose ribbon has the same colours as the NAAFI girls' arm flash. As *spam*, a kind of *spiced-ham*, was sold in the NAAFI canteen, what more obvious term could suggest itself?
Hence '**spammy** *a.*, consisting or tasting chiefly of (bland) luncheon meat; also *fig.*, commonplace, mediocre, unexciting.
1959 *Observer* 11 Jan. 18/3 Skipton is toned down to scale with our spammy age. **1960** J. STROUD *Shorn Lamb* i. 13 We got a spammy sort of meal.

span (spæn), *sb.*[1] Forms: 1 span(n, spon(n; 4 sponne, 4–7 spanne, 4–5 spane (5 spayn); 4– span, 6 spann, 8 spand. [OE. *span(n, spon(n*, = WFris. *span*, EFris. *sponne*, MDu. (and Du.) *spanne*, MLG. *spen(ne*, OHG. *spanna* (MHG. and G. *spanne, spann*), ON. *spann-, spǫnn* (Icel. *spönn*, Norw. dial. *spann, sponn*; Sw. *spann*, Da. *spand*), app. related to *spannan* SPAN *v.*[2]
The Germanic word is the source of med.L. *spannus* and *spanna* (*spanga, spana*), It. *spanna*, OF. *espanne, espane*, and *espan* (mod.F. *empan*). In OE. the word is very scantily recorded, and its currency after 1300 may be partly due to OF. influence. The form *spayn*, which also occurs in the vb., is abnormal, unless it represents an OF. *espain* which occurs as a variant of *espan*.]
1. a. The distance from the tip of the thumb to the tip of the little finger, or sometimes to the tip of the forefinger, when the hand is fully extended; the space equivalent to this taken as a measure of length, averaging nine inches.
Freq. followed by a positive or comparative adj.
*c***900** tr. *Baeda's Hist.* IV. xi. (1890) 296 þa wæs se lichoma sponne [*v.r.* spanne] lengra þære þryh. *c***1000** ÆLFRIC *Gloss.* in Wr.-Wülcker 158 *Palmus*, span *uel* handbred. *a***1310** in Wright *Lyric P.* ix. 35 Swannes swyre swythe wel y-sette, A sponne lengore then y-mette. *c***1380** *Sir Ferumb.* 1607 Þe swerd..clef him þanne, Til it hadde in-to is bodi i-soȝt by-nythe is brest a spanne. *c***1386** CHAUCER *Prol.* 155 Sche hadde a fair forheed. It was almost a spanne brood, I trowe. **14..** *Sir Beues* (S.) 2509 A span long þey [i.e. bristles] were, wel rowe. *c***1440** *Promp. Parv.* 467/1 Spanne, mesure of the hand, *palmus*,..*palmata*. **1483** *Cath. Angl.* 351 A Spayn (*A.* Spane), *palmus*. **1535** COVERDALE *Judges* iii. 16 Ehud made him a two edged dagger of a spanne longe. **1577–87** HOLINSHED *Chron.* I. 92/1 The space of his forehead betwixt his two eies was a span broad. **1660** BOYLE *New Exp. Phys. Mech.* ix. (1682) 39 There happen'd in the great Receiver a crack of about a Span long. **1671** J. WEBSTER *Metallogr.* xi. 158 They go no deeper than a span or two. **1718** *Free-thinker* No. 47. 343 Pharao..was a Dwarf, but seven Spans high. **1756–7** tr. *Keysler's Trav.* (1760) II. 276 The diameter..is twelve common spans, or near eight feet. **1811** A. T. THOMSON *Lond. Disp.* (1818) 36 The stems trailing, about a span in length. **1862** DRAPER *Intell. Devel. Europe* xiii. (1865) 303 In which there are walking about men, a span long.
*fig. a***1350** *Geburt Jesu* 40 in Horstm. *Altengl. Leg.* (1875) 66 Þe tyme hem þoȝte longe Inouȝ, ech vnche hem þouȝte a sponne. *a***1586** SIDNEY *Ps.* XXXIX. iii, Lo, thou a spanns length mad'st my living line. **1672** SIR T. BROWNE *Let. Friend* §28 If we reckon up only those days which God hath accepted of our lives, a life of good years will hardly be a span long.
†**b.** In collective sing. with numerals. *Obs.*
*a***1300–1400** *Cursor M.* 17288 + 138 So heghe be thre spane no nother graf þer is. *c***1400** MAUNDEV. (Roxb.) xi. 43 Þai had cherubyn of gold xii. span lang. *c***1440** *Jacob's Well* 194 Þis handle muste be iiij. spanne in lengthe.
c. Const. *of* (the hand) or with possessive.
1607 TOPSELL *Four-f. Beasts* (1658) 186 The ears of it are large and broad,..being at the least as broad as a mans span. **1649** JER. TAYLOR *Gt. Exemp.* III. Disc. 15. 34 So must we take the measures of eternity by the span of a mans hand. **1855** BAIN *Senses & Int.* II. ii. §12, I can appreciate a distance of six or eight inches by stretching the thumb away from the fingers, as in the span of the hand.
d. *fig.* Capability of spanning or grasping.
*c***1800** H. K. WHITE *Lett.* (1837) 284 Below the span of my auditory nerve.
2. The hand with the thumb and fingers extended, esp. as a means of measuring. *Obs.* exc. *arch.*
1535 COVERDALE *Isaiah* xl. 12 Who hath measured heauen with his spanne, and hath comprehended all the earth of yᵉ worlde in thre fyngers? **1867** LONGF. *Dante, Inf.* vi. 25 My Conductor, with his spans extended, Took of the earth.
3. A thing, piece, etc., of the length of a span; a very small extent or space.
13.. *Sir Beues* 815 A spanne of þe groin be-forn Wiþ is swerd he haþ of schoren. **1633** G. HERBERT *Temple, Pulley* i, Let the worlds riches, which dispersed lie, Contract into a span. **1635** QUARLES *Embl.* II. xiv. (1718) 118 Lord, what a nothing is this little span We call a Man! **1738** POPE *Universal Prayer* vi, Yet not to Earth's contracted Span Thy Goodness let me bound. **1746** HERVEY *Medit.* (1818) 217 The landscape, large and spacious,..shrinks into a span. **1798** FERRIAR *Certain Var. Man* 198 It was not enough..to shorten a whole nation to three spans. **1841** ELPHINSTONE *Hist. Ind.* II. 242 There was not a span free from cultivation. **1850** TENNYSON *In Mem.* cxvii, Every grain of sand that runs, And every span of shade that steals.
4. a. A short space of time, esp. as the duration of human life; the (short) time during which a person lives.
Cf. Coverdale *Ps.* xxxviii. 6 Thou hast made my dayes a spanne longe.
1599 DAVIES *Immort. Soul* Introd. xlv. (1742) 12, I know my Life's a Pain, and but a Span. **1607** SHAKS. *Timon* v. iii. 3 Tymon is dead, who hath out-stretcht his span. **1613** —— *Hen. VIII*, III. ii. 140 You haue scarse time To steale from Spirituall leysure a briefe span. **1728** YOUNG *Ode to King* xvii, Jove mark'd for man A scanty span. **1742** —— *Nt. Th.* II. 115–6 We censure nature for a span too short; That span too short, we tax as tedious too. **1788** BURNS *Written in Friars-Carse Hermitage* 37 Did many talents gild thy span? **1812** BYRON *Ch. Har.* II. lxiii, Through their mortal span, In bloodier acts conclude those who with blood began. **1850** ROBERTSON *Serm.* Ser. III. xiv. (1853) 176 The span granted to the butterfly the child of a single Summer, may be long. **1870** MORRIS *Earthly Par.* (1890) 307/1 So strangely shift men's lives in little span.
b. Const. *of* life, etc.
1633 G. HERBERT *Temple, Ch. Porch* lxxvii, Lifes poore span Make not an ell, by trifling in thy wo. **1683** KENNETT tr. *Erasm. on Folly* 81 In so short a space, as the small Span of Life. **1771** BEATTIE *Minstr.* I. xxv, Nor lessen of his life the little span! **1840** MRS. SOMERVILLE *Connex. Phys. Sci.* (ed. 5) xii. 101 In the short span of human life. **1867** FREEMAN *Norm. Conq.* (1877) I. iv. 255 Whose lives were really prolonged beyond the common span of human existence.
5. a. The distance or space between the abutments of an arch, the supports of a beam, the piers of a bridge, the walls carrying a roof, etc.; the stretch or extent of this.
α. **1725** W. HALFPENNY *Sound Building* Pref., For want of knowing, when the Arch of either Spand being given, what must be the Arch of the other. *Ibid.* 20 Set off the Spand of the Intersecting Arch from *v.* to *t.* **1751** —— *New Designs Chinese Bridges* I. 7 A double truss'd Timber Bridge, whose Spand between the top of the Butment is 45 Feet.
β. **1736** HAWKSMOOR *London Bridge* 35 The five Arches are in their Span as followeth. *Ibid.* 42 The two Bridges are very large in their Span. **1753** *Chambers' Cycl.* Suppl. s.v. *Bridge*, The span of the next arch is 56 feet. **1815** J. SMITH *Panorama Sci. & Art* I. 248 The Trustees..having used it for beams in a new warehouse at Liverpool, of more than thirty feet clear span. **1832** G. DOWNES *Lett. Cont. Countries* I. 484 Owing to its height, the great span of the arch is not so perceptible. **1869** RANKINE *Machine & Hand-tools* Pl. F 12, The span between the standards, A, A, being 16 feet. **1874** MICKLETHWAITE *Mod. Par. Churches* 128 York Minster, with its choir of fifty feet span.
transf. **1853** SIR H. DOUGLAS *Milit. Bridges* (ed. 3) 288 The Russians resorted to..difficult applications of carpentry to repair this breach, which, being of considerable span [etc.]. **1887** RUSKIN *Præterita* II. 59 About the span of an English lane that would allow two carts to pass.
fig. **1858** O. W. HOLMES *Aut. Breakf.-t.* (1891) 14 The great minds are those with a wide span, which couple truths related to, but far removed from, each other. **1889** *Spectator* 5 Oct., Congresses might be dismissed on the ground that it is impossible they can do anything to widen the span of knowledge.

b. (See first quot.) *rare.*

1856 'STONEHENGE' *Brit. Rural Sports* I. I. x. § 1. 82 The three first [antlers] are termed the *rights*;..the horn itself, the *beam*; the width, the *span.* **1873** BLACK *Pr. Thule* xxv. 414 You will discourse..of the span and the pearls, of the antlers and the crockets.

c. *Psychol.* Mental extent; the amount of information that the mind can be conscious of at a given moment, or the number of items it can reproduce after one presentation; esp. const. *of*, as ***span of apprehension***, ***attention***, ***consciousness***, etc. Cf. *memory span* s.v. MEMORY 12.

1887 *Mind* XII. 76 The highest number correctly reproduced is to be regarded as the limit which we wish to find, and which we term here the *span. Ibid.* 79 We might expect that 'span of prehension' should be an important factor in determining mental grasp. **1890** W. JAMES *Princ. Psychol.* I. xi. 405 The question of *the 'span' of consciousness* [*sc.* to how many things can we attend at once] has often been asked and answered. **1922** R. S. WOODWORTH *Psychol.* xi. 262 The 'span of attention' for objects..is measured by discovering how many such objects can be clearly seen, or heard, or felt, in a single instant of time. Measurement of this 'span' is one of the oldest experiments in psychology. **1945** *Mind* LIV. 165 She reduced the number of choices to a range lying within or just within the 'span of attention' of her subjects. **1971** *Jrnl. Gen. Psychol.* Jan. 129 No matter how high the level of luminance, the span of apprehensions will not exceed eight items during the critical interval. **1979** R. JAFFE *Class Reunion* (1980) III. ii. 312 The child was very bright and had a long attention span.

d. The maximum lateral dimension of an aircraft, or of a wing, from wing tip to wing tip.

1909 R. KENNEDY *Flying Machines* ii. 34 It will be difficult to get a monoplane of sufficient span for heavy lifts, together with a strong construction. **1927** C. L. M. BROWN *Conquest of Air* vii. 98 It was a biplane, the two main wings being 32 ft. in frontal width (span) and 5 ft. in depth (chord). **1953** *New Biol.* XIV. 73 A vulture has a broad wing of large surface area as well as large span. **1968** MILLER & SAWERS *Technical Devel. Mod. Aviation* v. 137 For the first time Douglas made a basic change in the wing..and increased the span by 10 feet to give greater lift and fuel capacity.

e. A range of numerical values; the difference between the highest and lowest values in a range.

1962 *Gloss. Terms Automatic Data Processing* (*B.S.I.*) 13 *Range.* 1. All the values which a quantity may have. 2. The difference between the highest and lowest of these values (in mathematics often called the span). **1974** *Physics Bull.* Jan. 31/3 The series covers the temperature range 223 to 573 K in eight spans.

f. ***span of control***: in Business Studies, the area of activity, number of functions or subordinates, etc., for which an individual or organization is responsible.

1937 L. GULICK in Gulick & Urwick *Papers on Sci. of Administration* i. 7 Span of control. Just as the hand of man can span only a limited number of notes on the piano, so the mind and will of man can span but a limited number of immediate managerial contacts. **1956** E. BRIDGES in A. Dunsire *Making of Administrator* 5 He will look to see that too many people are not reporting to any one head—that the 'span of control' or of management as they call it, is not too wide. **1962** *Rep. Comm. Broadcasting 1960* 226 in *Parl. Papers 1961–2* (Cmnd. 1753) IX. 259 Since there might well be some scores of companies, it is highly unlikely that a corporation could exercise its responsibilities effectively; the 'span of control' would be too great. **1976** P. R. WHITE *Planning for Public Transport* i. 20 Operation of private party coach hire or excursions may require frequent decisions on pricing and scheduling, and hence a small span of control for each manager is desirable.

6. a. An arch of a bridge; a section between two piers. Also *transf.*, the vault of the sky.

a **1806** H. K. WHITE *Sonn.* ix, In the drear silence of the polar span Dost thou repose? **1862** *Rep. Direct. E. Midl. Railway Cy.* 18 Six spans of the Keeul Bridge are erected since I last reported on the subject. **1891** LOVETT *U.S. Pictures* 39 The total weight of the whole central span is 6,740 tons.

b. *Naut.* (See quot.)

1846 A. YOUNG *Naut. Dict.* 289 *A Span of Rigging*, implies the length of shrouds from the dead-eyes on one side, over the mast-head, to the dead-eyes on the other side of the ship.

c. A stretch, line, or extent *of* something.

1894 *Outing* XXIII. 374/1 The cocoa-nuts hanging from the long, almost unbroken span of cocoa palms that line the beach.

7. *Math.* That which is generated by the elements of some set. Cf. SPAN *v.*[1] 6.

1968 D. PASSMAN *Permutation Groups* ii. 155 We define the span of A, Span A, to be the subspace of FG spanned by all the functions a_{ij}. We list some basic properties of the span. **1981** *Sci. Amer.* Oct. 153 (*caption*) Their [*sc.* vectors'] span is a plane because any point in the plane can be reached by vectorially adding some scalar multiple of *A* to some scalar multiple of *B*.

8. *attrib.* and *Comb.*, as ***span-breadth***, ***-extent***, ***-girth***, ***-length***, ***-line***; (sense 5 c) ***span test***; ***span-broad***, ***-lived*** adjs.; (*poet.*) ***spanlong***, ***-wide*** adjs.; **span loading** *Aeronaut.*, the gross weight of an aircraft divided by its wing span or, more commonly, by the square of the wing span; also *transf.*, of a bird; **span wire**, each of the series of wires suspended across the route of a tram or trolleybus to carry the overhead electric wire; **span-worm** *U.S.* = LOOPER[1].

1604 E. G[RIMSTONE] *D'Acosta's Hist. Indies* IV. viii. 228 In the largest place they have six foote, and in the narrowest a *spanne bredth. **1599** NASHE *Lenten Stuff* Wks. (Grosart) V. 226 In the correlatiue analagie of the *spanbroad rowse running betwixt. **1655** VAUGHAN *Silex Scint.* I. *Resurr. & Immort.* (1858) 26 At last..She wing'd away, And, proud with life and sence Esteem'd..of two whole Elements As meane, and *span-extents. **1807** CRABBE *Par. Reg.* III. 937 No more his *span-girth shanks and quiv'ring thighs Upheld a body of the smaller size. *c* **1440** *Jacob's Well* 170 þe secunde *spanne lengthe of þe handyll. **1756** NUGENT *Gr. Tour, Germany* II. 335 They make steel chains so prodigious fine of a span length, that [etc.]. **1838** *Penny Cycl.* XI. 325/2 The shorter radii describing the two quadrants at the spring of the arch, are upon the *span-line itself. **1846** PROWETT *Prometh. Bound* 26 Can that *span-lived race avail To succour thee in this distress? **1929** *Jrnl. R. Aeronaut. Soc.* XXXIII. 359 This..depends primarily on '*span loading' that is weight/(span)[2]. **1953** *New Biol.* XIV. 72 The sinking speed is a function of the 'span loading', i.e. weight/wing span. A low sinking speed can only be achieved by having a wing span which is large relative to the weight of the bird. **1983** D. STINTON *Design of Aeroplane* iv. 120 In straight and level flight the lift loading across the span..is equal to..the weight of the aircraft divided by the wingspan. Both are referred to collectively as the span loading. **1957** BLUNDEN *Poems of Many Years* 281 *Spanlong rabbits quite forget danger's eye. **1971** *Jrnl. Gen. Psychol.* Apr. 238 We have here a well-defined figural-span measure which does *not* link with other *span tests. **1943** E. MUIR *Narrow Place* 7 Was this the ground That stretched beyond the *span-wide world-wide ditch. **1891** *Electr. World* 21 Mar. 225/1 In the case of side pole and *span wire, construction poles should be placed at the points represented and a span wire run between them. **1963** A. T. DOVER *Electric Traction* (ed. 4) xxiii. 358 At curves the span wire must be on a level with the trolley wire, otherwise the hangar will be pulled out of the vertical. **1820** *Amer. Farmer* I. 375/3 What can our obliging correspondents tell us about the..best method of destroying that dreadful plague of our orchards, the *span worm. **1903** [see MEASURING *ppl. a.* b]. **1972** SWAN & PAPP *Common Insects N. Amer.* xix. 293 The Bruce spanworm is a major defoliator of aspen in the prairie regions.

span (spæn), *sb.*[2] Also 8–9 spann. [a. Du. and LG. *span* (also MDu. and MLG.; G. *spann*, dial. *span*), f. *spannen* to unite, fasten, etc. Cf. OE. *ȝespan(n*, *ȝespon(n* in related senses.]

1. *Naut.* One or other of various ropes or chains used as fastenings or means of connexion (see quots.).

1769 FALCONER *Dict. Marine* (1780), *Span*, a small line.., the middle of which is usually attached to a stay, from whence the two ends branch outwards to the right and left, and having either a block or thimble attached to their extremities. **1794** *Rigging & Seamanship* 281 Each of these chains has..a large iron ring, to which is fastened a chain, called an up-and-down span. **1841** DANA *Seaman's Man.* 124 *Span*, a rope with both ends made fast, for a purchase to be hooked to its bight. **1846** A. YOUNG *Naut. Dict.* 289 *Span*, ..a double rope with thimbles seized betwixt the two parts, stretched across the rigging as a fair-leader for ropes. *c* **1860** H. STUART *Seaman's Catech.* 8 What tackles are used for hoisting the launch in and out? The stays (fitted with a span) between the fore and main mast. *Ibid.* 55 A chain span is shackled to the bolts, and the slips are rove round the span and shackled to the cable. **1894** *Labour Commission* Gloss. 76 *Span*, a length of chain or wire rope used for suspending 'derricks'..to the masts of ships.

2. *U.S.* and *Canada.* A pair of horses harnessed and driven together, *esp.* a pair as nearly alike in colour and size as possible.

1769 *Boston Gaz.* 2 Oct. (Thornton), Wanted, a Spann of good Horses for a Curricle. **1828** P. CUNNINGHAM *N.S. Wales* (ed. 3) II. 54 A span (pair) of horses is a common expression through all the state of New York, and even as far as Upper Canada. **1840** HALIBURTON *Clockm.* Ser. III. xviii. 248 If any man will show me a hoss that can keep it up as he has done.., I'll give him old Clay for nothin', as a span for him. **1841** CATLIN *N. Amer. Ind.* xlv. (1844) II. 81 A snug span of little horses. **1883** *Harper's Mag.* Mar. 572/1 She had her open landau and her span for summer driving.

transf. **1860** O. W. HOLMES *Prof. Breakf.-t.* vii, I'd as lief undertake to keep a span of elephants.

fig. **1884** *Athenæum* 20 Sept. 364/1 Thus ran this span of printing-houses, driven by Barker, neck and neck.

3. *S. Africa.* A team of oxen or other draught animals consisting of two or more yokes.

1812 A. PLUMTRE *Lichtenstein's S. Africa* I. 192 They could not get on the rest of the way without a double Spann. **1850** R. G. CUMMING *Hunter's Life S. Afr.* (1902) 124/2 My large waggon stuck fast, but was extricated with the help of another span. **1893** SELOUS *Trav. S.E. Africa* 13 The fine span of oxen that had belonged to Mr. Collinson.

4. A fetter or shackle. (Cf. SPAN *v.*[2] 1 b.)

1856 WHITTIER *Panorama* 322 To them the Law is but the iron span That girds the ankles of imbruted man.

span, *sb.*[3] *dial.* and *Hist.* [ad. ON. *spann* (Norw. and Sw. *spann*, Da. *spand*), = MLG. and LG. *spann*, *span* pail, measure.] A certain measure *of* butter (in Orkney and the north of Scotland).

1502 in A. Peterkin *Rentals Orkney* (1820) 4 In butter scat j span. *Ibid.*, In butter scat uther half span. **1861** C. INNES *Sk. Early Scotch Hist.* 77 It was the established usage of Caithness, that for every score of cows a span of butter should be paid to the bishop. **1872** A. P. FORBES *Kalend. Sc. Saints* 262 The usage was to take a span of butter for every twenty cows.

span (spæn), *v.*[1] Also 5 *Sc.* spayn, 7 spanne. [f. SPAN *sb.*[1] Cf. OE. *ymbspannan* and *spanning*; G. *spannen* (rare), Icel., Norw., Sw. *spanna*, ON. *spenna*, OF. *espaner*, in similar senses. The form *spayn* is peculiar: see note to SPAN *sb.*[1]]

I. *trans.* †**1.** To grasp, lay hold of, seize. *Obs.*

1375 BARBOUR *Bruce* III. 582 And newys..That wont to spayn gret speris war, Swa spaynyt aris, that [etc.]. **1398** TREVISA *Barth. De P.R.* XVIII. xxxviii. (Bodl. MS.), [The dragon] lurkeþ in weies where þe Elephaunte goþ and bindeþ and spanneþ his legges and sleeþ hym and strangeleþ hym. *c* **1420** *Avow. Arth.* xiii, Thenne the kinge spanos his spere, Opon that bore for to bere. **1513** DOUGLAS *Æneid* III. iii. 111 Doun fallis sailis, the airis sone we span.

2. a. To measure by means of the outstretched hand; to cover with the hand in this way.

† *to span farthings*, to play at span-farthing.

1560 BIBLE (Geneva) *Isaiah* xlviii. 13 My right hand hathe spanned the heauens. **1570** LEVINS *Manip.* 20 To span, *palmare.* **1621** T. WILLIAMSON tr. *Goulart's Wise V.* 185 That we should take vpon vs to spanne with our fingers, and measure with our arme the miracles of God. **1688** PENTON *Guardian's Instruction* (1897) 50 His main design is to..go home again to spanning farthings. **1706** STEVENS *Span. Dict.* I, *Xéme*, half a Foot, or as much as a Man can span with his Thumb and Fore-finger. **1818** KEATS *Endym.* I. 499 For still, with Delphic emphasis, she spann'd The quick invisible strings [of the lute]. **1866** BROGDEN *Prov. Lincs.*, *Span*, to measure a distance by flattening the hand and stretching the thumb and middle finger. **1899** *N. & Q.* 9th Ser. III. 185/1 So that he could span the distance by the fingers of the hand.

†**b.** To measure in any way. *Obs.*

1641 MILTON *Ch. Govt.* I. Wks. 1851 III. 99 To comprehend the hidden causes of things, and span in his thoughts all the various effects that passion..can worke in mans nature. **1648** —— *Sonn. To H. Lawes*, Harry, whose tuneful and well measur'd Song First taught our English Musick how to span Words with just note and accent. **1717** T. TICKELL *Ep. fr. Lady* 3 Oft on the well-known Spot I fix my Eyes, And Span the Distance that between us lies.

†**c.** To measure out; to set a limit or bound to (life, etc.). *Obs.*

1613 SHAKS. *Hen. VIII*, I. i. 223 My life is spand already: I am the shadow of poore Buckingham. **1633** G. HERBERT *Temple, Bunch of Grapes* ii, For as the Jews of old by God's command Travell'd, and saw no town; So now each Christian hath his journeys spann'd. **1657** BP. H. KING *Elegy on G. Adolphus* Poems (1843) 71 Death hath spann'd thee.

d. To encircle or encompass (the waist, wrist, etc.) with the hand or hands.

1781 COWPER *Truth* 155 She recollects her youth, And tells, not always with an eye to truth, Who spann'd her waist. **1797–1809** COLERIDGE *Three Graves* IV. xi, And oft she said, I'm not grown thin! And then her wrist she spanned. **1830** MARRYAT *King's Own* xxiv, 'If I ever am in your list, I presume it will be for a case of plethora,' replied Jerry, spanning his thin waist. **1841** BROWNING *Pippa Passes* iii. Poet. Wks. 1863 II. 54 How your plump arms..have dropped away! Why, I can span them!

3. a. Of the rainbow, a bridge, etc.: To form an arch across or over (the sky, a river, etc.); to stretch or extend over in the form of an arch; to cross from side to side. Also *transf.* or *fig.*

(*a*) **1633** G. HERBERT *Temple, Content* v, This soul doth span the world, and hang content From either pole unto the centre. **1742** YOUNG *Nt. Th.* IV. 418 He looks down On all that soars; and spans immensity. **1781** COWPER *Table-T.* 702 Fancy, that from the bow that spans the sky Brings colours. **1816** SHELLEY *To Peacock* 12 July, A rainbow spanned the lake. **1866** NEALE *Seq. & Hymns* 123 O, sweet Rainbow,..That some day, One Onely Church shall span. *a* **1881** ROSSETTI *House of Life* xii, Two souls softly spann'd With one o'erarching heaven of smiles and sighs.

(*b*) **1736** N. HAWKSMOOR *London Bridge* 40 The Bridge at Rochester..spans a noble and deep River, 550 Feet wide. **1833** L. RITCHIE *Wand. by Loire* 7 The bridge..spans the stream with nine wide arches. **1853** SIR H. DOUGLAS *Milit. Bridges* (ed. 3) 177 The width [of the river] here was 700 feet, and twenty-seven boats were required to span it. **1869** TOZER *Highl. Turkey* I. 201 Its waters are spanned by a fine stone bridge.

b. *transf.* To reach or extend over (space or time).

1624 DONNE *Devot.* (ed. 2) 63 Our thoughts,..that doe not onely bestride all the Sea, & Land, but span the Sun and Firmament at once. **1872** LIDDON *Some Elem. Relig.* ii. 39 His thought spans the intervening desert. **1879** A. W. WARD *Chaucer* i. 5 Chaucer's life..spans rather more than the latter half of the fourteenth century.

4. a. To stretch *out* (the thumb) as in spanning.

1676 MACE *Musick's Mon.* 74 Bring up your Left-Hand from the Table, bended, just like the Talents of a Hawk; All, excepting your Thumb, which must stand Strait; and Span'd out.

b. To throw as an arch or bridge.

a **1861** T. WOOLNER *My Beautiful Lady, Day Dream* 30 Clutching at rainbows spanned across the sky!

5. a. To throw a bridge across (a river, etc.); to bridge over.

1861 SMILES *Engineers* II. 176 Telford spanned both these straits with suspension road bridges. **1876** ROUTLEDGE *Discoveries* 1 Science has spanned great rivers and estuaries with bridges of form unknown to our fathers.

transf. **1875** JOWETT *Plato* (ed. 2) II. 54 He is the mediator who spans the chasm which divides them. **1876** BLACKIE *Songs Relig.*, etc. 233 Not in vain God with lavish blooms of beauty Spanned the slope, and sowed the plain.

b. To cross (a bridge). *rare*$^{-1}$.

1894 H. GARDNER *Unoff. Patriot* 121 The Long Bridge was spanned and the strange party drove down Pennsylvania Avenue.

6. *Math.* To generate. Cf. SPAN *sb.*[1] 7.

1941 BIRKHOFF & MACLANE *Survey Mod. Algebra* vii. 170 This subspace is evidently the smallest subspace containing all the given vectors; hence it is called the subspace generated or spanned by them. **1964** A. P. & W. ROBERTSON *Topological Vector Spaces* i. 3 If L is a linearly independent subset of a vector space E and if S is a subset containing L and spanning E, there is a base B of E with $L \subset B \subset S$. **1981** *Sci. Amer.* Oct. 156/2 For example, the *u*-*v* plane is a vector space that can be spanned by two vectors directed along the positive *u* and *v* axes.

II. *absol.* **7.** To make a span *over* something; to reach with or as with a span; to stretch or range *from* one place or point *to* another. Chiefly *fig.*

1535 COVERDALE *Isaiah* xlviii. 13 My honde is the foundacion of the earth, & my right honde spanneth ouer the heauens. **1592** LYLY *Midas* v. iii. 104 Though my hande bee golde, yet I must not thinke to span ouer the maine Ocean. *a* **1652** J. SMITH *Sel. Disc.* VI. xiii. (1821) 300 The prophetical spirit..is most quick, spanning as it were from the centre to the circumference. **1657** BP. H. KING *Elegy on G. Adolphus* Poems (1843) 71 Thou might'st Vienna reach, and after span From Mulda to the Baltick Ocean. **1899** *N. & Q.* 9th Ser. III. 185/1 If he..spanned accordingly, the button of the first player became his. **1976** *Offshore Platforms & Pipelining* 151/1 Any relatively stiff pipeline laid in a wavy seabed will span in places.

8. *Whaling.* (See quot.)

1888 *Encycl. Brit.* XXIV. 526/2 If the whale is 'spanning', i.e., swimming in a decided direction and appearing at the surface at intervals more or less regular.

span (spæn), *v.*² [ad. Flem., Du., or LG. (also MDu. and MLG.) *spannen*, = OHG. *spannan* (G. *spannen*), OFris. *spanna, sponna*, OE. *spannan* to fix or fasten, to join, to draw tight, etc. Cf. also It. *spannare*, from Germanic.]

1. a. *trans.* To harness or yoke (oxen, horses, etc.); to attach to a vehicle. Also with *in* and *out*: see INSPAN *v.* and OUTSPAN *v.*¹ (Cf. SPANG *v.*³) Also *absol.*

In later use chiefly from S. African Dutch.

1550 COVERDALE *Spir. Perle* vi. (1588) 70 He spanneth hys oxen, and goeth to the field. **1644** [WALSINGHAM] *Effigies True Fortitude* 15 Whil'st horses were span'd in to draw off the peices. **1656** DAVENANT *Siege of Rhodes* Wks. (1672) 23 Those Horses to that Carriage span! Drive, drive! **1793** J. BAXTER *Jrnl.* 2 Feb. in *Amer. Speech* XL. (1965) 199, I and John Schenck spaned in together. **1836** A. F. GARDINER *Journ. Zoolu Country* 303 We left Berea, and spanned out on the flat. **1858** SIMMONDS *Dict. Trade, Span*, ..to attach draught cattle to a wagon. **1894** *Westm. Gaz.* 11 Sept. 8/1 So one day he spanned-in his mules..and leisurely trekked to the widow's homestead.

b. *dial.* To fetter or shackle (a horse).

1847 in HALLIWELL. **1865** R. HUNT *Pop. Rom. W. Eng.* (1871) Ser. I. 112 There, by the roadside, stood an old, bony white horse, spanned with its halter. **1880-** in dial. glossaries (Cornw., Sussex, Kent).

c. *transf.* To enclose or confine.

1844 LOWELL *Fatherland* i, Doth not the yearning spirit scorn In such scant borders to be spanned?

2. a. To stretch, extend, make taut or tight; to draw (a bow). Now *arch.*

The sense appears earlier under SPANNING *vbl. sb.*²

1597 A. M. tr. *Guillemeau's Fr. Chirurg.* 20/1 Where as the inferior parte of the bellye is full of windes, and stiflye stretched out and spanned. *Ibid.* 45 b/1 The Ligature wil in one place be loosened, and in another spanned. **1658** A. FOX *Würtz' Surg.* I. vii. 28 The stitches [in a wound] are so pull'd and spann'd, that they tear out. *Ibid.* II. xxv. 155 With both hands keep it asunder, that the skin be spanned asunder. **1878** B. TAYLOR *Deukalion* III. i. 99 New bows I span, new arrows fill my quiver.

b. *fig.* with *up*.

1655 VAUGHAN *Silex Scint.* I. 53 Be there before the shadows stretch and span up night. *Ibid.* 76 Faith spans up blisse.

3. †**a.** To wind up the wheel-lock of (a pistol or musket) by means of a spanner. *Obs.*

1639 R. WARD *Animadv. Warre* I. 296 In Marching or Trooping through a Towne forget not to have your Peeces spand. *Ibid.* 299 *Span your Pistoll*—This is performed by sinking the Pistoll into his Bridle hand, and taking the Spanner in his right hand, to put it upon the axeltree, and winding about the wheele till it sticke. **1649** C. WALKER *Hist. Independ.* II. 249 A party of Horse..with Swords drawne and their pistols spanned. *c* **1672** *Verney Mem.* (1907) II. 345 Having Pistols before me, I drew one and held it in my hand, so that I could span it in a moment for ffear of a surprise.

b. To screw tight with a spanner.

1859 F. A. GRIFFITHS *Artill. Man.* (ed. 8) 209, 5. Gives shot and wad to 3, runs out, trains, and spans the breeching.

4. *Naut.* To fix, attach, fasten, or draw tight in some way. Also with *in*.

1781 ARCHER in *Naval Chron.* XI. 287 Spaned the booms; saw the boats all made fast. **1820** SCORESBY *Arc. Regions* II. 231 A harpoon thus prepared with foreganger and stock, is said to be 'spanned in'. **1852** BURN *Naval & Mil. Dict.* II. s.v., To span in the rigging. *Ibid.*, To span the runners. **1867** SMYTH *Sailor's Word-bk.* 640 *Spanning a harpoon*, fixing the line which connects the harpoon and its staff. *Ibid.*, *To span in the rigging*, to draw the upper parts of the shrouds together by tackles, in order to seize on the catharping legs.

5. *intr.* Of horses: To form a span or pair; to match in colour and size. *U.S.*

1828 WEBSTER s.v., The horses span well. (New England.)

†**span**, *v.*³ *Obs.*⁻¹ [repr. OE. *spanan*, = OS. and OHG. *spanan*, MDu. and MLG. *spanen*, etc. Cf. FORSPAN *v.*] *trans.* To allure, entice, or draw away (a person).

a **1250** *Owl & Night.* 1490 To mysdo one gode manne & his ibedde from him spanne.

span, *a.*: see SPICK AND SPAN.

span-, the stem of SPAN *v.*¹ and SPAN *v.*², used in a number of special combs., chiefly of a technical character, as **span-beam, -block, -dog, -gutter, -lashing, -piece, -saw** [cf. Du. *spanzaag*, G. *spannsäge*, Sw. *-såg*], **-shackle** (see quots.); **span-waist**, a slender waist; **span-wire, -worm** *U.S.* (see quots.).

1847 HALLIWELL, **Span-beam*, the great beam..in a barn. **1860** *Eng. & For. Mining Gloss.* (ed. 2) 23 *Span beam*, the horizontal beam passing over the whim in which the upper pivot of the perpendicular axis moves. **1883** GRESLEY *Gloss. Coal-m.* 230 *Span-beam*, a long wooden beam supporting the head pivot of the drum axle of a gin, and resting at the extremities upon inclined legs. **1860** H. STUART *Seaman's Catech.* 23 Reeve it..through the *span block on the top-mast cap. **1867** SMYTH *Sailor's Word-bk.* 640 *Span-blocks*, blocks seized into each bight of a strap, long enough to go across a cap, and allow the blocks to hang clear on each side. *Ibid.* 255 **Span-dogs.* Used to lift timber. A pair of dogs linked together, and being hooked at an extended angle, press home with greater strain. **1841** HARTSHORNE *Salop. Ant.* Gloss., **Span-gutter*, a drain in a coal mine, formed by one brick being placed flat, and one at either end to keep the soil from falling in. **1891** *Cent. Dict.*, **Span-lashing*, a lashing used to secure together two ropes or spars a short distance apart. **1836** PARKER *Gloss. Archit.* (1850) I. 431 **Span-piece*, the name given to the Collar-beam of a roof in Lincolnshire, Wiltshire, and other districts. **1875** KNIGHT *Dict. Mech.* 2253/2 **Span-saw*, a frame-saw. **1750** BLANCKLEY *Nav. Expos.* 155 **Spanshakle* is a large Clasp of Iron, which goes round the End of the Davit upon the Fore-Castle, having a large Bolt, which goes through a Fore-Castle Beam. **1846** A. YOUNG *Naut. Dict.* 290 *Span-shackle*, a large bolt with a triangular ring attached to it for lashing anchors or spars thereto. **1871** *Figure-Training* 56 A fashionable *span waist ought not to exceed fourteen inches round. **1897** *Pall Mall G.* 30 Oct. 6/2 The current..passes out to the main conductor, or overhead wire, which is supported over the centre of the track by insulators attached to *span wires extending from uprights placed on either side of the roadway. **1852** T. W. HARRIS *Treat. Ins. New Eng.* (1862) 458 The caterpillars of the *Geometræ* of Linnæus,.. or geometers, *span-worms, and loopers, have received these several names from their peculiar manner of moving. **1885** H. C. MCCOOK *Tenants of Old Farm* 104 A very familiar race of caterpillars, the Geometers, or span-worms.

‖**spanæmia** (spæˈniːmɪə). *Path.* Also **-emia.** [mod.L., f. Gr. σπανο-, comb. form of σπανός (usually σπάν-ιος) scarce, scanty + -αιμία (as in ἀναιμία ANÆMIA), f. αἷμα blood. Cf. F. *spanémie.*] A morbid condition of the blood characterized by a deficiency of red corpuscles; poorness of the blood.

1845 G. E. DAY tr. *Simon's Anim. Chem.* I. 306 The hypinosis speedily merges into spanæmia. [*Footnote*] We prefer this term to anæmia, because the latter is used to represent a morbid condition of the blood subordinate to spanæmia. **1853** MARKHAM *Skoda's Auscult.* xvi, It does not appear to be a sign of anaemia or spanaemia. **1897** *Hutchinson's Arch. Surg.* VIII. 199 There was no evidence of spanæmia.

Hence **spaˈnæmic** *a.*, of or relating to, inducing spanæmia; also *sb.*, a medicine inducing spanæmia.

1882 in *Ogilvie's Imp. Dict.*

spanandry (ˈspænændrɪ). *Zool.* [ad. F. *spanandrie* (P. Marchal 1913, in *Ann. des Sci. Nat.: Zool.* XVIII. 268), ad. Patristic Gr. σπανανδρία scarcity of population, f. Gr. σπάνις scarcity + ἀνήρ, ἀνδρ- man: see -Y³.] Lack or extreme scarcity of males in a population. Hence **spaˈnandric** *a.*

1924 *Nature* 14 June 880/1 A. Vandel: Geographical spanandry in a Branchiopod Crustacean, *Lepidarus apus.* **1967** *Science* 28 Apr. 483/3 Polygamy is extreme, but, since this follows from the fact that males are produced in much smaller numbers than females, *spanandry* seems a better term, and is used here. **1976** *Bull. Entomol. Res.* LXVI. 179 (*heading*) The identity of the greenhouse thrips *Heliothrips haemorrhoidalis* (Bouché) (Thysanoptera) and the taxonomic significance of spanandric males. **1976** *Entomol. Meddelelser* XLIV. 60 The major types of parthenogenesis: thelytoky, cyclical parthenogenesis,..and spanandry are reviewed.

spancel (ˈspænsɪl), *sb.* Also 7 **spanciall**, 8 **spancill**, 9 *dial.* **spenchil, -shel**, etc. [ad. Flem., Du., or LG. *spansel* (in Kilian *spanssel*), f. *spannen* SPAN *v.*² Cf. SPANNEL, and ON. *spennsl* (Norw. *spensl*, MSw. *spenszel*) clasp, tie.] A rope or fetter for hobbling cattle, horses, etc.; *esp.* a short, noosed rope used for fettering the hind legs of a cow during milking. Also *transf.*

1610 [implied in SPANCEL *v.*]. **1674** RAY *N. Co. Words* 44 A *Spancel*, a Rope to tye a Cows hinder Legs. [Hence in Grose and later glossaries.] **1689** *Irish Hudibras* 84 See'st thou that Monster with the Tail, That ugly Monaghan Spanci-all [*marg.* Fetterd] The worst of all the Devils? **1784** SMYTH *Tour in U.S.* I. 172 The horses are turned loose in the woods, only with leather spancills or fetters on two of their legs. **1841** MRS. S. C. HALL *Ireland* I. 114 Upon the neighbouring bushes and wooden crosses hang fragments of clothes, or halters and spancels. **1882** *Blackw. Mag.* LI. 253 He snatched up a spancel that hung at the dairy window.

spancel (ˈspænsɪl), *v.* Also 9 **spansel, spencill.** [f. prec.]

1. *trans.* To fetter or hobble with a spancel or spancels.

1610 GUILLIM *Heraldry* III. xxvi. 184 He beareth Sable a Horse passant Argent, Spanceled on both legs of the neerer side. *Ibid.*, Albeit this Horse be now Spanceled as you see. **1820** J. OXLEY *Jrnls. Two Exped. into Australia* 47 The animals [horses] were all spencilled, but such is the scarcity of both water and grass, that they will wander in search of each. **1825** CROKER *Fairy Leg. Irel.* I. 333 Neither could his neighbours' cattle have been guilty of the trespass, for they were spancelled. **1882** MRS. HECKFORD *Lady Trader in Transvaal* 260 It is the fashion in Africa to spancel a horse by tying its head to one of its legs.

fig. **1844** SIR C. NAPIER *Let. to H. Napier* in *Life* (1862) III. 153 Gough himself is all right, only spancelled by his staff; they wanted to tie my legs too, but I kicked the pail over, and spoiled the milking.

2. *transf.* (See quot.) *U.S.*

1859 BARTLETT *Dict. Amer.* (ed. 2) 431 *To spancel*,..to prevent a crab from biting, by sticking the point of a leg into the base of each movable claw.

Hence **ˈspancelled** *ppl. a.* and *pa. pple.* Also *fig.*

1835 *Fraser's Mag.* XI. 142 We should be about as much in a fit state..as..a spancelled pig to run a race with a greyhound. **1899** SOMERVILLE & MARTIN *Irish R.M.* 267 Driving two brace of coupled and spancelled goats. **1910** J. M. SYNGE *Deirdre of Sorrows* II. 35 You're seven years spancelled with Naisi and the Pair. **1965** *New Statesman* 26 Nov. 848/1 In England it is the wives who regard themselves as the spancelled party. **1980** *Times Lit. Suppl.* 20 June 688/4 He was..spancelled by a lack of money that meant he could never be apprenticed to a leading London surgeon.

†**span-counter.** *Obs.* [f. SPAN *sb.*¹ or *v.*¹ and COUNTER *sb.*³ Cf. SPAN-FARTHING.] A game in which the object of one player was to throw his counters so close to those of his opponent that the distance between them could be spanned with the hand.

Common in the early part of the 17th c.

1566 DRANT *Horace, Sat.* III. G vj, A man that..is gladde To playe at quoytes, or spancounter. **1593** SHAKS. *2 Hen. VI*, IV. ii. 166 Henry the fift, (in whose time boyes went to Span-counter for French Crownes). **1600** NASHE *Summer's Last Will* 1589 Wks. (Grosart) VI. 149, I was close vnder a hedge, or vnder a barne wall, playing at spanne Counter, or Iacke in a boxe. **1647** PEACHAM *Worth of a Penny* 32, I would wish them to venture at Span-Counter and Dust-Point with schole-boyes. **1675** COTTON *Burlesque upon B.* 50 To play at Cat, Trap, Span-counter. [**1815** SCOTT *Guy M.* xii, Rich enough to play at span-counter with moidores.]

Spandau (ˈspændaʊ). Also **spandau.** [f. *Spandau*, name of a district of (West) Berlin.]

a. A German machine-gun used during the war of 1914–18 (see quot. 1966). **b.** Applied to other machine-guns of German design, esp. the MG34 and MG42 of the war of 1939–45. Freq. *attrib.* as ***Spandau (machine) gun.***

a **1918** J. T. B. MCCUDDEN *Five Years in Royal Flying Corps* (1919) v. xii. 241, I distinctly noticed the red-yellow flashes from his parallel Spandau guns. **1929** E. W. SPRINGS *Above Bright Blue Sky* 221 He was suddenly cold as he awaited the crack of the spandaus. **1938** G. S. HUTCHINSON *Machine Guns* xii. 333 The British were armed with Vickers, the Germans with Spandaus. **1944** K. DOUGLAS *Alamein to Zem Zem* (1946) iv. 29 In their pit lay a Spandau machine-gun. **1966** T. R. FUNDERBURK *Fighters* 27 The Maxim gun was manufactured in England..as a Vickers gun. The same gun was manufactured under license by the German Weapons and Munitions Factory, a state arsenal at Spandau, Berlin, and was known as a Spandau gun. A light version..was developed by the Germans for the use of aerial gunners and known as a Parabellum. **1968** A. DIMENT *Bang Bang Birds* vi. 97 Vitconne is crouched behind a Spandau lent to him by a friendly German officer. **1971** F. W. A. HOBART *Pictorial Hist. Machine Gun* 228 (*caption*) First German Airborne Corps defending Cassino... The MG-42 was a very effective dual purpose machine gun. The Germans used it a lot on a tripod to produce fixed line fire. The British troops called it the 'Spandau'.

spander-new, *a. phr.* Now *dial.* Also **spanther-new.** [Alteration of SPAN-NEW.]

1706 E. WARD *Wooden World Dis.* (1708) 19 A first Rate Taylor, when his spander new Fashion takes at St. James's. [**1855** Cf. *brandspandernew* s.v. BRAND-NEW *a.*] **1876** ROBINSON *Mid-Yks. Gloss.*, Spanther-new or Spander-new.

Spandex (ˈspændɛks). orig. *U.S.* Also **spandex.** [Arbitrarily f. EXPAND *v.*]

a. A synthetic elastomeric fibre composed largely of polyurethane. **b.** A proprietary name for certain fabrics made from this fibre.

1959 *Federal Register* 10 Feb. 981/3 The following generic names for manufactured fibers..are hereby established... *Spandex*, a manufactured fiber in which the fiber-forming substance is a long chain synthetic elastomer comprised of at least 85 percent of a segmented polyurethane. **1962** *New Scientist* 22 Mar. 697/1 As materials classified as spandex may have 15 per cent of some other compound to be introduced with the polyurethane, wide variations in fibre properties are possible. **1968** *Trade Marks Jrnl.* 7 Feb. 176/2 *Spandex*... All goods included in Class 22 made wholly or substantially of spandex fibres. Monsanto Chemical Company..U.S.A.; manufacturers.—4th Sept. 1964. **1972** *Brazilian Bull.* (Brazilian Trade Centre, London) Apr. 3 The Brazilian subsidiary of the U.S. Du Pont company is to build a factory at Paulinia..for the production of Lycra Spandex fibre. **1973** *Materials & Technology* VI. iv. 334 The illustration shows cross-sections through three well-known brands of spandex fibre, these being 'Lycra'.., 'Spanzelle'.., and 'Vyrene'. **1978** *Neiman-Marcus Christmas Bk.* 26 Nylon and spandex maillot.

spandite (ˈspændaɪt). *Min.* [Blend of SPESSARTITE and ANDRADITE.] A manganiferous garnet resembling spessartine but containing more iron and calcium.

1907 *Rec. Geol. Survey India* XXXV. 22 The garnet is intermediate in composition between spessartite and andradite, and..Mr. Fermor proposes to introduce the term spessart-andradite, which may be shortened for convenience in general use to spandite. **1955** BROWN & DEY *India's Mineral Wealth* (ed. 3) 606 Spandite, a garnet intermediate in composition between spessartite and andradite, occurs in the Kodurite series of the Srikakulam district of Andhra. It varies in colour from deep orange to brown orange-red and blood-red and never displays the lighter orange shades of the true spessartite. **1972** *Mineral.*

Abstr. XXXIII. 121/1 X-ray data for hiddenite diopside, [etc.]..and a probable spandite are given.

spandrel ('spændrɪl). *Arch.* Forms: α. 5 spaundrell, 6 splandrell, 7, 9 spandrell, 8– spandrel. β. 8–9 spandril. [app. a diminutive of AF. *spaundre, -dere* (1395), of doubtful origin; perh. identical with *(e)spandre* to expand, extend.]

1. a. The triangular space between the outer curve of an arch and the rectangle formed by the mouldings enclosing it, frequently filled in with ornamental work; any similar space between an arch and a straight-sided figure bounding it; also, the space included between the shoulders of two contiguous arches and the moulding or string-course above them.

α. **1477–8** *MS. Exch. K.R. Acc.* 496 No. 17 Pro mandacione et embosyng xviij Spaundrell'. **1532** in BAYLEY *Hist. Tower Lond.* I. App. p. xxxii, A portall wt panells of drapery worke, wt ij. dores, wt a crest of antyk upon the hed, and ij. splandrellys for the caryng of the dore. **1634** in Willis & Clark *Cambridge* (1886) II. 699 For carving the spandrells of the doores. **1712** J. JAMES tr. *Le Blond's Gardening* 73 A great Arch, with a..Pedament over it..sustain'd at the Ends by Spandrels and Scrolls. **1739** LABELYE *Piers Westm. Bridge* 78 As to the Spandrels of the Arches,..they should be filled with..Rubble. **1837** *Civil Eng. & Arch. Jrnl.* I. 14/2 Every time a load passed over the bridge, the vibration was transferred through the loose rubbish to the spandrel. **1847** LEITCH tr. *C. O. Müller's Anc. Art* §276. 266 The Ionic capitals..with a honey-suckle in the spandrel between the spirals of the volute. *a* **1878** SIR G. SCOTT *Lect. Archit.* (1879) II. 52 There are plain windows again over their spandrels.

β. **1750** WREN *Parentalia* 357 It is evident that the Spandrils, or loading of the diagonal Cross-arches, where two cylindrical Vaults meet, must be an inverted Pyramid. **1833** LOUDON *Encycl. Archit.* §237 The steps and the coping of the spandril..together with the coping of the piers..of the stairs..to be of York quarry stone. **1843** *Ecclesiologist* II. 57 The wall pieces, spandrils and hammer-beams are plain. **1897** F. J. BURGOYNE *Library Construction* 233 Greek honeysuckle ornaments in the spandrils.

b. *transf.* The support of a set of steps; the material with which the space between a stair and the floor is filled in.

1833 LOUDON *Encycl. Archit.* §79 To build nine-inch brick spandrils and steps to the front door... (The.. spandrils for door steps are the arches, or the walls, which support the ends of the steps.) *Ibid.* §239 To put..one inch and a quarter square framed spandril to enclose the cellar stairs.

c. On oriental patterned rugs or carpets: one of the spaces between the central field and the border, or between an arch motif and its frame.

1900 J. K. MUMFORD *Oriental Rugs* x. 147 In the spandrels over the arch of the prayer rugs there is a repetition of the pear patterns. **1931** A. U. DILLEY *Oriental Rugs & Carpets* iii. 63 Large central medallions, brilliant pendants, traceried spandrels and graceful floral scrolls. **1962** C. W. JACOBSEN *Oriental Rugs* II. 264 Mudjars have a definite prayer arch design... Many of these have panels above the spandrel with van dykes designs. **1967** *Times* 26 Jan. 22 (Advt.), A *Silk Heriz* with all over blue spandrels on an old mellowed field, classical rust medallion, floral border.

2. 'An inner frame or border for a picture' (Knight *Dict. Mech.* Suppl.).

1862 *Catal. Internat. Exhib., Brit.* II. No. 5696, Gilt picture frames, with spandril and an oval frame.

3. *attrib.*, as ***spandrel bracketing, -conoid, decoration, space, wall***, etc.

1830 WHEWELL *Archit. Notes German Ch.* p. xxxi, This space I will call the spandrel-conoid. **1838** *Civil Eng. & Arch. Jrnl.* I. 127/1 The spaces between the arches were crossed by spandrell walls. **1840** *Ibid.* III. 133/2 In winter the arch contracting descended and the spandril joints opened. **1842** GWILT *Archit.* Gloss., *Spandrel Bracketing*, a cradling of brackets fixed between one or more curves, each in a vertical plane. **1850** T. INKERSLEY *Inq. Rom. & Pointed Arch. France* 311 The spandrel spaces are occupied by a trefoil. **1851** RUSKIN *Stones Ven.* I. xxvi. §ix, One of the spandril decorations of Bayeux Cathedral.

Hence **'spandrelled** *a.*, having or provided with spandrels.

1813 M. EDGEWORTH *Let.* 1 May (1971) 37 The beauty of the spandrilled ceiling with all its rich, and light ornaments. **1838** in *Gentl. Mag. Libr., Eng. Topogr.* (1901) XIII. 266 It had an amply spandrelled fireplace on the northern side. **1890** *Archaeol. Jrnl.* XLVII. 93 The latter beam having curved and spandrelled braces at the ends.

'spandy, *a. U.S.* [? var. of *spander* in SPANDER-NEW.] Very good or fine; smart. Also ***spandy-clean***, quite clean; ***spandy-bright, spandy new***.

1838 'T. TITTERWELL' *Yankee Notions* 116, I have heard of a ghost that always came in a new coat..and a spandy clean dickey. **1848** BARTLETT *Dict. Amer.*, *Spandy-clean*, very clean; perfectly clean. **1863** MISS ALCOTT *Hospital Sk.* 319 (Cent. Dict.), Thirty gentlemen with spandy clean faces and hands. **1868** —— *Little Women* ix, My silk stockings and two pairs of spandy gloves are my comfort. **1903** K. D. WIGGIN *Rebecca of Sunnybrook Farm* i. 14 The trouble is to get the shoes... These are spandy new I've got on. **1968** J. UPDIKE *Couples* iii. 227 Ben's lank hairs ran together to make black seams, like sores downrunning into the tops of his comically new top-siders, cup-soled, spandy-bright. **1973** E.-J. BAHR *Nice Neighbourhood* ii. 23 Don has this very definite fixation that I am going to bang up our spandy new car.

spane, *sb.* [a. ON. *spán-n*, Du. *spaan*, or G. *span* (†*spane*), = OE. *spón* chip: see SPOON *sb.*] A chip or slip of wood.

1602 *Shuttleworths' Acc.* (Chetham Soc.) 146 Spygotts and fawset and for wood spanes, iijd. **1891** BARING-GOULD *Urith* I. vii. 105 At the fire-breast burnt, what was called a 'spane', that is, a slip of deal steeped in resin, which lighted the housewife at her operations at the fire.

spane (speɪn), *v. north.* and *Sc.* Also 4 **spone**, 5–7 **spayn**, 6, 8–9 **spain**, 9 **spaan**, **span**. See also SPEAN *v.* [ad. OF. *espanir* or MDu. and MLG. *spanen* (MLG. also *sponen*), app. related to OE. *spana, spona*, G. dial. *span*, teat: cf. SPEAN *sb.*]

1. *trans.* To wean (an infant, lamb, etc.). Also *fig.* and in fig. context.

a **1300** *Cursor M.* 3018 Quen he [Isaac] was spaned [*Fairf.* sponed] fra þe pap, His fader..made a fest. *a* **1340** HAMPOLE *Psalter* cxxx. 4 As a childe þat has nede to be on his modur kne and fostird wiþ hur mylke perisch if he be wenyd [*v.r.* spaned] & takyn fro mylke. *c* **1440** *Alph. Tales* 107 A womman when sho will spane hur child. **1483** *Cath. Angl.* 351/1 To Spayn (*A.* Spane), *ablactare.* **1509** in *Mem. Fountains* (Surtees) 235, xl yews with their lames to [= until] they be spaned. **1549** D. MONRO in *Macfarlane's Geogr. Collect.* (S.H.S.) III. 293 The Lambes of that end of the countrey uses to be fed, and spained fra the ȝowes. **1570** LEVINS *Manip.* 19 To spane, weane, *ablactare, depellere.* **1653** in Laing *Lindores Abbey* (1876) 224 Their-after the chyld was spayned. **1674** RAY *N. Co. Words* 44 To *Spane* a Child; to wean it. [Hence in Bailey and later Dicts.] **1781–** in various northern and Sc. dial. glossaries and texts. **1819** W. TENNANT *Papistry Storm'd* (1827) 12 The sinfu' bodies o' the Elie Were spain'd frae image-worship hailly. **1896** *Pall Mall Mag.* Apr. 515 To help the old shepherd in 'spaning' the lambs.

†**b.** *Sc.* To suspend, as a punishment. *Obs.*

1516 [see the *vbl. sb.*]. **1529** *Extr. Burgh Rec. Edinb.* (1871) 5 To..spane thame fra the operatione for yer and day.

2. *intr.* Of corn: To begin to take root and cast off the seed.

Cf. WFlem. *spanen, spenen, spennen*, to set (of fruit).

[**1828** CARR *Craven Gloss.*, Corn is said to be in spane or spaan, when it just begins to shoot its roots or to detach itself from the parent grain.] **1843** *Jrnl. R. Agric. Soc.* IV. I. 186 That state of transition, in which it cannot be said whether it derives its food from the seed, the soil, or the atmosphere (the state in which it is commonly said to be 'spaining'). **1863** MRS. TOOGOOD *Yorksh. Dial.* (MS.), The corn is looking yellow; it is just beginning to spane.

Hence **'spaned** *ppl. a.* Also †**'spaneling**, a weaned pig or other animal.

1500–20 DUNBAR *Poems* lxxv. 24 My new spanit howffing fra the sowk. **1560** *Knaresb. Wills* (Surtees) I. 86 A spaned calf. **1563** *Wills & Inv. N.C.* (Surtees, 1835) 210, xiij spaned calves. **1577** *Ibid.* 417, ij sues, iiijor spainlings, & one boare. **1894** P. H. HUNTER *J. Inwick* xx. 251 I'll süne hae to stay my stamack wi' sappy meat, like a spained wean.

spane, obs. Sc. pa. t. SPIN *v.*

†**span-farthing.** *Obs.* [f. SPAN *sb.*1 or *v.*1 and FARTHING *sb.*] A game played with farthings after the same manner as span-counter.

1688 HOLME *Armoury* III. xvi. (Roxb.) 82/1 Playes with Instruments... Span Farthing. **1693** LOCKE *Educ.* Wks. 1727 III. 25 Learning to wrangle at Trap, or rook at Span-farthing. **1720** SWIFT *Mod. Educ.* Wks. 1755 II. II. 36 His chief solace is to steal down, and play at span-farthing with the page, or young black-a-moor. **1764** BP. HURD *Dial. Uses For. Trav.* 70 You might as well..advance him directly to the boy's top and span-farthing, as [etc.]. **1777** *Gamblers* 6 Span-farthing, Hustle-cap, their joy and sport.

spang, *sb.*1 Also 5–6 **spange**. [Probably ad. MDu. *spange* (*spaenge*, Du. *spang*), = OHG. *spanga* (MHG. and G. *spange*), OS. **spanga* (see sense 3), OFris. **spange* (NFris. *spung, spōng*), ON. *spang-, spǫng* (Norw. *spong*; MSw. and MDa. *spang*) clasp, buckle, brooch, spangle, etc.]

†**1.** A small glittering ornament; a spangle. *Obs.*

1423 JAS. I *Kingis Q.* xlvii, A chaplet fresch of hewe, Off plumys..Full of quaking spangis bryght as gold. **1480** *Wardr. Acc. Edw. IV* (1830) 115, vj coursour harneis.. embrowdered and wroght with..spanges of silver and gilt. *c* **1534** in Lewis *Life Fisher* (1855) II. 297 A swett of vestments of rede clothe of gold with spangs and crossys in the myddyst. *a* **1548** HALL *Chron., Hen. VIII*, 76 The same horse Harneis were sette full of tremblyng spanges. **1602** MARSTON *Ant. & Mel.* III. Wks. 1856 I. 34 The other glistering copper spangs That glisten in the tyer of the Court. **1616** DRUMM. OF HAWTH. *Poems, Urania* iii, To spreade the azure Canopie of Heauen, And make it twinckle all with Spanges of Gold. **1625** BACON *Ess., Masques & Triumphs* (Arb.) 540 And Oes, or Spangs, as they are of no great Cost, so they are of most Glory.

2. *techn.* A stain. (See quot.)

1839 URE *Dict. Arts* 136 The stains which come out upon maddered goods, in consequence of defective bleaching, are called in this country *spangs*.

3. *arch.* A clasp or buckle.

After OE. *spang*, occurring once in the OS. part of *Genesis* (l. 445).

1892 BROOKE *Early Eng. Lit.* II. xxii. 106 [He] Set on's head a hollow helm, and..Spanned it down with spangs.

spang (spæŋ), *sb.*2 Chiefly *Sc.* and *north.* [Cf. SPANG *v.*2 In 1 b perh. purely imitative.]

1. A jerk; a sudden and violent movement of a thing. Also in phr. ***to play spang***.

1513 DOUGLAS *Æneid* v. ix. 59 Acestes..Schawand his craft and his big bowis mycht, That lowsit of the takil with a spang. *Ibid.* VII. ix. 50 The flayne flaw fast wyth ane spang fra the string. *a* **1657** SIR W. MURE *Hist. Ho. Rowallane* Wks. (S.T.S.) II. 253 The king.., as he offered swa to doe, dang out his eye with the spang of ane Cocle-shell. **1826** J. WILSON *Noct. Ambr.* Wks. 1855 I. 134, I wadna grudge geein a jug o' toddy to see ane play spang upon you frae a distance o' twenty yards.

b. A sound resulting from such movement.

1883 G. C. DAVIES *Norfolk Broads* xxiii. 160 We heard a loud *spang* behind us, and on turning round saw a large mullet floundering in the jolly.

†**2.** A fillip; a smart rap. *Obs. rare.*

1595 DUNCAN *App. Etym.* (E.D.S.), *Talitrum*, a spang, a chicknawd. **1710** RUDDIMAN *Gloss. Douglas' Æneis* s.v.

3. a. A spring, a bound, a leap.

1818 SCOTT *Rob Roy* xxviii, Set roasted beef and pudding on the opposite side o' the pit o' Tophet, and an Englishman will mak a spang at it. **1842** J. WILSON *Chr. North* (1857) I. 26 See, see how Tickler clears that twenty-feet moss-hag at a single spang like a bird. **1894** CROCKETT *Raiders* iv. 39 Jerry..came up the hill in great spangs.

b. A strong kick.

1863 READE *Hard Cash* xli, He went swinging by the rope back to the main stem of the tree, gave it a fierce spang with his feet, and..got an inch nearer the window. **1867** P. KENNEDY *Banks Boro* xl. 307 You're like our *miel* cow that gives a pail full of milk, and then spills all with a *spang* of her foot.

4. The spring-pole of a centre lathe. ? *Obs.*

1797 *Encyl. Brit.* (ed. 3) XVIII. 608/1 The two ends of the cord, both that which is fixed to the spang and to the foot-board.

†**spang**, *sb.*3 *Obs.* [Of doubtful origin: cf. ON. *spang-, spǫng* (Norw. *spong*; MSw. *spang*, Sw. *spång*) narrow bridge, perh. identical with SPANG *sb.*1] A narrow strip (*of* land or ground).

1610 HOLLAND *Camden's Brit.* II. 220 The West part of it joyneth to the East side by a very small spange of land. **1747** in *Rep. Comm. Inq. Charities* (1830) XXVIII. 145 A small spang of ground.

†**spang**, *v.*1 *Obs.* [f. SPANG *sb.*1 Cf. G. *spängen*, MHG. *spengen*, ON. *spengja*, to stud, etc.] *trans.* To spangle; to ornament as with spangles.

1552 in Money *Par. Ch. Goods Berks.* (1879) 8 Redd veluett spanged with gould. **1590** R. WILSON *Three Lords Lond.* G iij, Queene Junoe's Bird, Whose traine is spangd with Argus hundred eies. **1595** BARNFIELD *Cassandra* D iij b, A Hunters hat, Of crimson veluet, spangd with stars of gold. **1621** SANDYS *Ovid's Met.* II. (1626) 224 Night spangs the skie with starres.

spang (spæŋ), *v.*2 orig. and chiefly *Sc.* and *north.* [Of obscure origin.]

1. *intr.* To spring, leap, bound; to move rapidly. Also with cognate object (quot. 1684). Also *fig.*

1513 DOUGLAS *Æneid* v. ix. 29 Ȝoung Hippocoon..A quhidderand arrow leit spang fra the string. **1596** DALRYMPLE tr. *Leslie's Hist. Scot.* I. 145 Ouir dykes and dubis..they sould spang and leip. *Ibid.* 163 King Gald selfe ..spangis vpe on horse back. **1684** *Yorks. Dial.* 39 (E.D.S.), Lett's spang our geates [= ways], for it is varra snithe. **17..** RAMSAY *To R. Yarde* 97 But when they spang o'er reason's fence, We smart for 't at our ain expence. *a* **1779** D. GRAHAM *Hist. Buck-Haven* III. (1782) 21 Rob spang'd and jump'd over the boat several times. **1816** SCOTT *Old Mort.* vii, An I could but hae gotten some decent claes in, I wad hae spanged out o' bed. **1833** J. RENNIE *Alph. Angling* p. xiv, The trout slipped off, spanged down the bank, and in an instant..was lost. **1966** *If, Worlds of Sci. Fiction* Dec. 39/2 [He] kneed the screen door open so that it spanged against the outside wall. **1976** L. SANDERS *Hamlet Warning* (1977) xix. 165 A stream of bullets spanged off the metal around him. **1979** *Observer* 4 Feb. 4/7 We shared champagne and Coke with the nurses. Thank God spanged out on all sides.

2. *trans.* To cast, throw, jerk, bang. Also const. *about, down, up.*

1513 DOUGLAS *Æneid* XII. vi. 76 His swyft stedis hovis.. Spangit vp the bludy sparkis our the bent. **1662** in Pitcairn *Crim. Trials* III. 607 We haw no bow to shoot with, but spang them from of the naillis of our thowmbes. **1678** J. BROWN *Life of Faith* (1824) I. vii. 134 If the enemy did but spang his fingers end on you, as we say, it struck a knell to his heart. **1856** READE *Never too Late* lxv, She came up to the table with a fantastic spring and spanged down the sparkling mass on it. **1864–** in Yorks. and Linc. dial. use.

3. In combs., as **spang-cockle, -toad.**

1824 MACTAGGART *Gallovid. Encycl.* 432 *Spang-tade*, a deadly trick played on the poor toad. **1828** SCOTT *F.M. Perth* xi, 'Can you play at spang-cockle, my lord?' said the Prince, placing a nut on the second joint of his fore-finger, and spinning it off by a smart application of the thumb.

Hence **spanging-tree**, = SPANG *sb.*2 4.

1797 *Encycl. Brit.* (ed. 3) XVIII. 607/2 One of the most simple kinds of lathe,..in which *a* is the footstool,..*f* the spanging-tree.

†**spang**, *v.*3 *Obs. rare.* [app. an alteration of SPAN *v.*2] *trans.* To attach or yoke (horses).

1580 HOLLYBAND *Treas. Fr. Tong*, *Atteler les chevaux*, to spang horses, or fasten them to the chariote. **1600** SURFLET *Countrie Farme* v. x. 674 There are required..three horses to a plough,..but not so coupled and spanged as..where they vse to plow with mares. **1625** WODROEPHE *Marrow Fr. Tongue* 174 Haue you spanged (or yoaked) my horses to the chariot?

spang, *adv.* orig. and chiefly *U.S.* [Cf. SPANG *v.*2] With a sudden spring or impetus; slap, smack. ***right spang***, entirely, quite; exactly, fair.

1843–8 in Thornton *Amer. Gloss.* s.v. **1884** J. C. HARRIS *Nights Uncle Remus* 196 He drapt right spang in de middle er de fier. **1901** *Munsey's Mag.* XXIV. 806/2 Crack went the trigger, and spang went the ball. **1921** D. CANFIELD *Brimming Cup* I. v. 65 The brooks were.. all running spang full to the very edge with snow-water. **1925** WODEHOUSE *Sam the Sudden* xiii. 91 If he thinks a young bride's going to stand for that sort of conduct right plumb spang in the middle of what you might call the honeymoon, [etc.]. **1936** M. MITCHELL *Gone with Wind* xxxii. 547 So you needs a spang new pretty dress. **1962** *Punch* 26 Dec. 943/1 With its superb flair for the nostalgic and traditional the BBC has put this year's Christmas spang in the middle of its dramatised version of The Old Curiosity Shop. **1971** 'D. CORY' *Sunburst* xiii. 212 Will you *look* at that?.. Spang in the middle of the bloody road.

spanged, *ppl. a. north. dial.* Also spenged. [f. SPANG *v.*[1]] Spangled, flecked, variegated, etc. Usu. of cattle.

1582 *Durham Wills* (Surtees) II. 65, I gyue to Roland Sympson one spangit whye. **1583** *Wills & Inv. N.C.* (Surtees, 1860) 75 To my sonne William a spangde cowe. **1621** *Shuttleworths' Acc.* (Chetham Soc.) 249 For an odde oxe that was spanged. *Ibid.*, For a yolke of oxen called Little Spanged Oxe and his felowe. **1788** W. H. MARSHALL *Yorksh.* II. 354 *Speng'd*, pied, as cattle. **1828-** in dial. glossaries (Yks., Lanc., Cumbld., etc.). **1876** ROBINSON *Whitby Gloss.*, *Spenged.*

spangel(l, obs. forms of SPANGLE, SPANIEL.

spanghew ('spæŋhjuː), *v. dial.* Also spangwhew, -hue. [f. SPANG *v.*[2], with obscure second element.] *trans.* To throw or jerk violently; *spec.* to cause (a toad or frog) to fly into the air.

1781 J. HUTTON *Tour to Caves* (ed. 2) Gloss. 96 *Spangwhew*, to throw up into the air. **1811** WILLAN in *Archaeologia* XVII. 158 *Spangwhew*, to toss with violence. **1853** R. S. SURTEES *Sponge's Sp. Tour* (1893) 18 Hercules had 'spanghewed' so many triers. **1862-** in northern and Sc. use.

spangle ('spæŋg(ə)l), *sb.*[1] Also 5 spangele, -yll, 5-6 spangell(e, 6 spangel, spangill(e. [f. SPANG *sb.*[1] + -LE. Cf. G. *spängel.*]

1. a. A small round thin piece of glittering metal (usually brass) with a hole in the centre to pass a thread through, used for the decoration of textile fabrics and other materials of various sorts.

c **1420** LYDG. *Assembly of Gods* 277 Of goldsmythes werke with spanglys wrought be-dene. *c* **1440** *Promp. Parv.* 467/1 Spangele, or losange.., *lorale.* **1485** *Mat. ill. Reign Hen. VII* (Rolls) II. 17 Item, xi[xx] vnces in spangell for vii. gownes and plackardes for the henxmen. **1535** *Wardr. Kath. Arragon* 35 in *Camden Misc.* III, Garnysshid.. withe spangilles of silver and gilte. *a* **1586** SIDNEY *Arcadia* III. xviii. (1912) 462 His attiring.. all cutte in starres, which made of cloath of silver, and silver spangles, each way seemed to cast many aspects. **1617** MORYSON *Itin.* III. 168 Many of the said Virgines have their neckbands set with spangles, such as some children with us weare. **1693** *Phil. Trans.* XVII. 862 As thin, as the thinnest Spangle you ever saw. **1726** SWIFT *Gulliver* I. vi, Their greatest gold coin, about the bigness of a spangle. **1818** SCOTT *Hrt. Midl.* xxxi, A tawdry scarf of yellow silk, trimmed with tinsel and spangles. **1870** ROCK *Text. Fab.* Introd. p. civ, Silver-gilt spangles wrought to figure six-petalled flowers.

fig. **1647** TRAPP *Comm., Rom.* viii. 28 God changeth our grisly wounds into spangles of beauty. **1652** N. CULVERWEL *Lt. Nature* I. xi. (1661) 84 Are not many Souls guilty, defiled, miserable Beings? and are they all this while spangles of a Deity? *Ibid.* xvi. 145 The least Spangle of Happiness is better, then a Globe of Temporals. *a* **1667** COWLEY *Hymn to Light* ix. Poems (1905) 445 Nor.. dost thou scorn The humble Glow-worms to adorn, And with those living spangles gild.. the Bushes of the Field.

b. *transf.* A star.

1591 SYLVESTER *Du Bartas* I. i. 603 Those bright spangles that the heav'ns adorn. **1614** —— *Bethulia's Rescue* I. 351 Twinkling Spangles nightly brightly roule On sabled Circles of the whirling Pole. **1652** CRASHAW *Mary Magdalene* Wks. (1904) 259 They but seem to fall, As Heavn's other spangles doe. **1728** POPE *Dunc.* III. 61 See round the Poles where keener spangles shine. **1825** SCOTT *Betrothed* viii, The thousand spangles that deck the firmament.

c. A glitter as of spangles. *rare.*

1830 TENNYSON *Sea-Fairies* 24 The spangle dances in bight and bay. **1893** *Cornh. Mag.* Nov. 484 Not a breath of air was stirring; everywhere overhead was the spangle of the stars.

2. a. A condensed particle reflecting light, as of hoar-frost, snow, or dew.

1590 SPENSER *F.Q.* I. x. 48 As hoarie frost with spangles doth attire The mossy braunches of an Oke halfe ded. *a* **1691** BOYLE *Hist. Air* (1692) 193 We took notice of the icy spangles in the air, flying about like atoms in the sun's beams. **1776** MICKLE tr. *Camoens' Lusiad* III. 88 On the rude cliffs with frosty spangles grey, Weak as the twilight gleams the solar ray. **1862** TYNDALL *Mountaineer.* viii. 67 The wintry clouds, as you know, drop spangles on the mountains. **1863** —— *Heat* v. §181 (1870) 146, I have also seen snow flakes descending so softly, as not to hurt the fragile spangles of which they were composed.

b. A glittering point or speck of light.

1821 CLARE *Vill. Minstr.* II. 75 The sun now sinks behind the woodland green, And twittering spangles glow the leaves between. **1841** CAPT. B. HALL *Patchwork* II. viii. 146 The moon.. scattering along the surface of the sea a bright.. chain of spangles.

3. A small or minute glittering particle, esp. of a mineral substance.

1611 COTGR., *Pailles*,.. the flakes, or spangles that flie from hammered, and red-hot yron, &c. **1624** CAPT. SMITH *Virginia* III. v. 58 We saw it was a claie sand so mingled with yeallow spangles as if [etc.]. **1796** KIRWAN *Elem. Min.* (ed. 2) II. 93 Found either in compact masses, or in spangles. **1806** J. BERESFORD *Miseries Hum. Life* II. xxiii, Liquid spangles of powder and pomatum. **1839** URE *Dict. Arts* 606 It occurs there principally in spangles among the alluvial earths. **1877** RAYMOND *Statist. Mines & Mining* 388 Spangles are formed which scintillate and sparkle.

4. a. A scale, spot, marking, etc., suggestive of a spangle.

1796 WITHERING *Brit. Plants* (ed. 3) II. 271 No shining spangles upon them or the calyx. **1797** *Encycl. Brit.* (ed. 3) III. 441/2 A bractea, spangle, or floral leaf, differing in its appearance from the other leaves of the plant. **1854** MEALL *Moubray's Poultry* 157 These spangles,.. in true-feathered birds, are formed perfectly whole and clearly defined. **1867** DK. ARGYLL *Reign of Law* v. (1871) 236 A species of *Lophornis* with a tippet of emerald spangles.

b. An oak-spangle. (See OAK 9.)

1842 SELBY *Brit. Forest Trees* 288 Those beautiful little excrescences so common upon the under side of the leaves of the oak and known by the name of spangles. **1873** TEGETMEIER *Pheasants* 5 Among the more singular articles of food that form part of the pheasants' very varied dietary may be mentioned the spangles of the oak leaf.

c. A fowl or pigeon belonging to a variety distinguished by speckled plumage.

1854 *Poultry Chron.* II. 66/1 Eighteen pens of beautiful silver spangles added to the old laurels of Mr. Vivian. **1855** *Ibid.* III. 175/2 The Toys [*sc.* pigeons] are as follows: Suabians or Spangles, [etc.]. *Ibid.* 355/2 The third kind is what the old breeders of Game fowls call 'Spangles'. The cock is red and white in the hackle and saddle, and black and white in the tail and breast. The hens are partridge-colour, spotted with white. **1948** G. O. RICKWOOD *Constable's Country* 14 The.. 'King's Arms'.. was a rendezvous of cock-fighters in days when the 'feeders' of the birds—Shropshire reds, Staffordshire jet-blacks,.. spangles and other noted breeds—were.. important personages in the hierarchy of the sport.

5. *Cant.* A seven-shilling piece.

1811 *Lexicon-Balatronicum.* **1823** EGAN *Grose's Dict. Vulg. T.*

6. *U.S.* (See quot.)

1875 KNIGHT *Dict. Mech.* 2252/2 The clasps or spangles by which the wires and tapes of hoop-skirts are secured together.

7. *attrib.* and *Comb.*, as ***spangle embroidery, gold, -maker, -stone, -work***; † **spangle-baby**, a fop or dandy; **spangle-gall**, = sense 4 b; † **spangle-wort**, a species of sea-weed.

1602 DEKKER *Satirom.* Wks. 1873 I. 212 We must haue false fiers to amaze these spangle babies, these true heires of Ma. Justice Shallow. **1611** COTGR., *Or de paillole*, spangle gold; or gold thinne-beaten for spangles. *Ibid.*, *Pailleteur*, a Spangle-maker. **1648** HERRICK *Hesp.*, *Temple* 65 The Fringe.. Is Spangle-work of trembling dew. **1681** GREW *Musæum* II. §v. ii. 247 Flat Coralline, as it may be called, or Spangle-Wort. **1708** MOTTEUX *Rabelais* v. (1737) 216 Trash-mongers and Spangle-makers. **1803** SARRETT *New Pict. Lond.* 114 A great variety of Micæ or spangle stones. **1864-5** J. G. WOOD *Homes without H.* xxv. (1868) 493 The curious little galls.. which are appropriately called Spangle-galls, because they are as circular and nearly as flat as metallic spangles. **1874** H. H. COLE *Catal. Ind. Art S. Kens. Mus.* 251 The black ground is covered with gold lace and spangle embroidery.

'**spangle**, *sb.*[2] *Sc.* and *Ir.* ? *Obs.* [Of obscure origin.] A measure of yarn.

1705 SPREULL *Acc. Current betw. Scot. & Eng.* Misc. Writ. (1882) 12 Out of a Pound weight of Lint that grew at home, there was six Spangle of fine Yarn Spun or got out of it. **1780** A. YOUNG *Tour Irel.* I. 166 The 8 lb. [of flax] will spin into.. 20 hanks or 5 spangles fit for a ten hundred cloth. **1865** *Irel. & her Staple Manuf.* (E.D.D.), Every hank contained a dozen cuts,.. and four hanks were counted as a spangle.

spangle ('spæŋg(ə)l), *v.* [f. SPANGLE *sb.*[1] Cf. G. *spängeln*, †*spengeln.*]

1. *trans.* To decorate (a garment or the like) with spangles.

a **1548** HALL *Chron., Hen. VIII*, 16 Russet satyn, spangled with spangels of fine gold. **1572** in Feuillerat *Revels Q. Eliz.* (1908) 180 To John Bettes and his wyfe for one daye and one nighte spangling of the headpeeces. **1611** COTGR., *Pailleter*, to spangle, to bespangle, to trimme, or decke, with spangles. **1784** *Ann. Reg., Chron.* 183/2 They were all five in Spanish dresses.. of white crape spangled with gold. **1807-8** W. IRVING *Salmag.* (1824) 355 The young ladies are industriously spangling muslins. **1874** H. H. COLE *Catal. Ind. Art S. Kens. Mus.* 269 The muslin.. has a very gay appearance, as if spangled. **1904** MRS. ALEC TWEEDIE *Behind Footlights* xi. 210 Women.. trimming headgear, others spangling ribbon.

fig. **1607** SHAKS. *Timon* III. vi. 101 This is Timons last Who stucke and spangled with your Flatteries, Washes it off.

b. To adorn as with spangles; to cause to glitter as if so decorated. Const. *with.*

1591 SYLVESTER *Du Bartas* I. iv. 79 He th' Azure Tester trimm'd with golden marks, And richly spangled with bright glistring-sparks. *a* **1649** DRUMM. OF HAWTH. *Poems* (1656) 63 To spread the Azure Canopy of Heaven, And Spangle it all with Sparkes of burning Gold. **1814** SCOTT *Lord of Isles* I. xxiii, A hundred torches play'd, Spangling the wave with lights. **1839** BAILEY *Festus* 253 The finger of that hand Which spangled o'er infinity with suns. **1883** SYMONDS *Ital. Byways* i. 1 There had been a hard frost, spangling the meadows with rime-crystals.

fig. **1647** N. WARD *Simple Cobler* (1843) 89 It is in fashion with you to spangle your speeches with new quodled words. **1748** RICHARDSON *Clarissa* (1811) VIII. 327 They spangle over their productions with metaphors.

2. Of things: To dot or cover (something) after the manner of spangles.

1596 SHAKS. *Tam. Shr.* IV. v. 31 What stars do spangle heauen with such beautie? **1667** MILTON *P.L.* VII. 384 With thousand thousand Starres, that then appeer'd Spangling the Hemisphere. **1795** COLERIDGE *To Author of Poems* 36 With stars, unseen before, spangling her robe of night! **1831** TRELAWNY *Adv. Younger Son* cxvii, The Sunda islands, which spangle the eastern ocean. **1860** TYNDALL *Glac.* I. iv. 34 Innumerable plates of mica spangled the fine sand.

3. In passive: To present an appearance as if decorated with spangles; to be dotted or spotted *with* something suggestive of spangles.

1667 MILTON *P.L.* XI. 130 Four faces each Had..; all thir shape Spangl'd with eyes. **1756** C. LUCAS *Ess. Waters* II. 136 This lawn is.. in the season spangled with autumnal colchicum. **1775** SHERIDAN *The Duenna* II. i, Her skin.. being spangled here and there with a golden freckle. **1840** THACKERAY *George Cruikshank* (1869) 305 The pew.. wadded, and stuffed, and spangled over with brass nails. **1849** KINGSLEY *Misc.* (1859) II. 299 These bright grey granite rocks, spangled with black glittering mica and golden lichens. **1874** SYMONDS *Sk. Italy & Greece* (1898) I. 13 The meadows, spangled with yellow flowers.

b. In fig. applications.

1589 NASHE *Martin Marprelate* Wks. (Grosart) I. 95 That worke shall come out of the Presse like a bride from her chamber, spangled and trapt. **1828** DUPPA *Trav. Italy*, etc. 84 Rich and varied scenery, spangled at once with the comforts and refinements of life. **1893** MCCARTHY *Dictator* I. 79 Long letters spangled with stirring allusions to the Empire.

c. To be dotted or scattered *about*, like spangles.

1740 RICHARDSON *Pamela* xliv. (1824) I. 368 The villages that lie spangled about this vast circumference.

4. *intr.* To glitter or sparkle with, or in the manner of, spangles.

1639 MAYNE *City Match* To Rdr., Masquers.. spangle, & glitter for the time, but tis through tinsell. **1665** BUNYAN *Holy Citie* 177 All these things will spangle in the New Jerusalem. *a* **1770** CHATTERTON *Bristowe Tragedy* lxvii, Tassils spanglynge ynne the sunne, Muche glorious to beholde. **1854** *Fraser's Mag.* L. 47 A contrast to all the other objects which spangle in the starry vault. **1857** S. WILBERFORCE *Sp. Missions* (1874) 315 Just as.. you see the sparks flashing and spangling.

spangled ('spæŋg(ə)ld), *ppl. a.* [f. prec. + -ED[1].]

1. Adorned or covered with or as with spangles.

1584 LODGE *Alarum* (Shaks. Soc.) 52 Spangled hobbie horses are for children. **1599** B. JONSON *Cynthia's Rev.* III. iv, Here stalkes me by a proud, and spangled sir. **1624** CAPT. SMITH *Virginia* III. v. 58 Diuers places where the waters had.. left a tinctured spangled skurfe. **1698** FRYER *Acc. E. India & P.* 330 No Green Meadows or spangled Fields are here expected. **1743** FRANCIS tr. *Hor.*, *Epodes* xvii. 54 Or shall I.. Teach Thee, a golden Star, to rise, And deathless walk the spangled Skies? **1769** SIR W. JONES *Palace Fortune* Poems (1777) 9 Straight the gay birds display'd their spangled train. **1824** W. IRVING *T. Trav.* I. 280 A majestic plume towered from an old spangled black bonnet. **1886** W. J. TUCKER *E. Europe* 52 In the fantastic, spangled costume of the Wallachian maidens.

fig. **1695** J. EDWARDS *Perfect. Script.* 23 Epictetus and Seneca with all their spangled sayings. **1920** E. SITWELL *Wooden Pegasus* 13 Flickered down the street together In the spangled weather. **1943** L. B. LYON *Evening in Stepney* 17 By spangled weirs we pass the gas-works. **1977** [see RHINESTONE b].

2. Speckled.

1586 MARLOWE *1st Pt. Tamburl.* IV. i, On his siluer crest, A snowy Feather spangled white he beares. **1600** *Knaresb. Wills* (Surtees) I. 223 One spangled cowe with a broken horne. **1753** *Chambers' Cycl.* Suppl. s.v. *Red*, A peculiarly coloured china ware of a spangled red. **1849** BROWNE *Amer. Poultry Yard* (1855) 58 The spangled Hamburghs may be comprised under two varieties. **1859** [see SPANGLING *vbl. sb.*]. **1868** DARWIN *Anim. & Pl.* I. 244 *Spangled* feathers have a dark mark, properly crescent-shaped, on their tips; whilst *pencilled* feathers have several transverse bars.

spangler ('spæŋglə(r)). [f. as prec. + -ER[1].] One who or that which spangles; †one adorned with spangles.

1638 MAYNE *Lucian* (1664) 10, I remember he told a story of one of those spanglers, and glittering men, who come to Athens.. variously apparelled. **1817** KEATS *I stood tip-toe* 118 Spangler of clouds, halo of crystal rivers. **1901** *Daily Chron.* 6 May 9/4 Bonnets.—Good spanglers and fitters.

spanglet ('spæŋglɪt). [f. SPANGLE *sb.*[1] + -ET[1].] A little spangle.

1610 G. FLETCHER *Christ's Vict.* II. x, The watry picture of his beautie proude, Throwes all abroad his sparkling spangelets. **1633** P. FLETCHER *Purple Isl.* XII. lxix, Frozen snow, Whose silver spanglets sparkle 'gainst the day. *a* **1806** H. K. WHITE *Christiad* xiv, To tear the spanglets from yon gaudy plain. **1811** SHELLEY *To a Star* 3 Sweet star,.. Spanglet of light on evening's shadowy veil.

spangling ('spæŋglɪŋ), *vbl. sb.* [f. SPANGLE *v.* + -ING[1].] The action of the vb. in various senses. Also *attrib.*, as ***spangling-machine*** (Knight, 1875).

1576 in Feuillerat *Revels Q. Eliz.* (1908) 276 For the mending and spangling of 4 fethers. *a* **1591** H. SMITH *Wks.* (1867) II. 61 If the proud would leave.. their excess in spangling, their fantastical feathers. **1856** RUSKIN *Mod. Paint.* IV. v. xvi. §17. 245 One of those little flakes of mica-sand, hurried in tremulous spangling along the bottom of the ancient river. **1859** B. P. BRENT *Pigeon Bk.* 62 The Suabian Spangled Pigeon... This Pigeon derives its name from the beautiful and peculiar spotting or spangling of its plumage.

spangling ('spæŋglɪŋ), *ppl. a.* [f. as prec. + -ING[2].] That spangle(s); sparkling, glistening.

1665 BUNYAN *Holy Citie* 25 O the Grace, the Light and Glory, that will strike with spangling Beams from this City. **1712** J. MORTON *Nat. Hist. Northampt.* 294 The Powder..

exhibited a few Spangling Particles, tho' we cou'd not discern any such in it at the first. **1792** S. ROGERS *Pleas. Mem., Ep. to Friend* 153 His spangling shower when Frost the Wizard flings. **1817** SHELLEY *Rev. Islam* IV. i, Upon whose floor the spangling sands were strown. **1843** LE FEVRE *Life Trav. Phys.* II. II. vi. 241 The surface of the ground is one white spangling carpet.

Spanglish ('spæŋglɪʃ). [Blend of SPANISH *sb.*[1] + ENGLISH *sb.*] A type of Spanish contaminated by English words and forms of expression, spoken in Latin America.

[**1954** S. TÍO *A. Fuego Lento* 62 Esta lengua nueva se llamará el 'Espanglish'. La etimología es clara. Viene de español y de english.] **1967** *Time* 7 Apr. 12 A historical pageant known as a 'Texas Fandangle'—border-country Spanglish for fandango, the frenetic Mexican dance. **1972** *Daily Tel.* 28 Nov. 13/8 Argentina is not alone in falling victim to 'Spanglish'. Chilean housewives who have problems with the plumbing call for el gasfitter. **1974** *Amer. Speech 1970* XLV. 230 Spanglish may be characterized as a gradual relexification of Puerto Rican Spanish through borrowings, adaptations, and innovations. **1976** M. MILLAR *Ask for me Tomorrow* (1977) vi. 43 A mixture of Spanish and English slang sometimes called Spanglish.

spangly ('spæŋglɪ), *a.* [f. SPANGLE *sb.*[1] + -Y[1].] Resembling spangles; covered with spangles.

1818 KEATS *Endym.* I. 569 Visions all about my sight Of colours, wings, and bursts of spangly light. **1844** A. PARK *Silent Love* in *Harp Renfrewsh.* Ser. II. (1873) 205 The spangly dew that on the violet lies. **1883** *Nature* XXVII. 351 Black spangly particles.

spang-new *dial.*: see SPAN-NEW.

spangolite ('spæŋgəlaɪt). *Min.* [f. the name of Norman *Spang*, 19th-cent. U.S. mineral collector + *-ol-* + -ITE[1].] A hydrated basic sulphate and chloride of copper and aluminium, $Cu_6AlSO_4(OH)_{12}Cl.3H_2O$, which is a secondary mineral found as pale green, prismatic or tabular, rhombohedral crystals.

1890 S. L. PENFIELD in *Amer. Jrnl. Sci.* CXXXIX. 371, I take pleasure in not only expressing at this time my thanks to Mr. Spang for his kindness but also in naming the mineral ..Spangolite after him. **1949** *Amer. Mineralogist* XXXIV. 182 A few months ago, Mr. Hatfield Goudey..found a new occurrence of spangolite at Majuba Hill, Pershing County, Nevada. **1968** I. KOSTOV *Mineralogy* 514 Spangolite is ditrigonal-pyramidal.., also with perfect {001} cleavage.

spang-whew, variant of SPANGHEW.

Spaniard ('spænjəd), *sb.* (and *a.*). Forms: α. 5 **Spaignarde, Spaynard(e, -erde, Spaynnarde,** 6 **Spaynerd;** 5 **Spayneyarde,** 6 **Spaynyard** (*Sc.* **-ʒard**), **Spainierd** (*Sc.* **-ʒerd, -ʒeard**). β. 5 *Sc.* **Spanʒeart,** 6 **Spanyard(e,** *Sc.* **-ʒard**), 6–7 **Spanyard,** 6– **Spaniard.** [ad. OF. *Espaignart, Espaniard*, f. *Espaigne* SPAIN: see -ARD. So MHG. *Span(n)igerd.*]

1. A native of Spain; a member of the Spanish people. Sometimes (with *the*) in collective sing. = the Spanish nation or people.

α. *c* **1400** *Brut* cxcvii. 220 þe grete lordes..were mellede wiþ oþere nacions,..somme Frenchemen, somme Normans, somme Spaignardes. *c* **1420** *Contin. Brut* ccxxxv. 325 In þis comyng oppon of þe Spaynardes, all þe Englissh men..were take or slayn. **1484** CAXTON *Fables of Alfonce* ii, The spaynard was wonderly wrothe. **1596** DALRYMPLE tr. *Leslie's Hist. Scot.* I. 73 That maist ancient toung of the alde Spaynʒards. *Ibid.* II. 130 Against the spaynerds of portugal.

β. **1491** *Acc. Ld. High Treas. Scot.* I. 179 To the Spanʒeartis that dansyt before the Kyng. **1522** SKELTON *Why not to Court?* 921 Our nobles are gone Amonge the Burgonyons, and Spanyardes onyons. **1592** G. HARVEY *Four Lett.* Wks. (Grosart) I. 175 The Spanyard..will bee aduised before he entangle himselfe with more warres attonce. **1617** MORYSON *Itin.* II. 164 Who entertained a very hot skirmish with the Spaniards. **1649** BP. HALL *Cases Consc.* III. viii. (1654) 247 The poor Indians..profest they would not goe to heaven if any Spanyards were there. **1713** ADDISON *Count Tariff* §22 He found him a true Spaniard, nothing but show and beggary. **1777** R. WATSON *Philip II*, I. (1812) I. 14 He was too much a Spaniard to relish anything that was not Spanish. **1832** MACAULAY *Armada* 39 Far on the deep the Spaniard saw..those twinkling points of fire. **1891** SKEAT *Princ. Eng. Etymol.* Ser. II. 317 The real place of meeting between the Englishman and the Spaniard was in the western world and on the open sea.

2. A Spanish ship or vessel.

1537 *Adm. Crt. Exempl.* I. No. 174 Seeing a ship coming somewhat rome with theym,..Mr. Payne toke it ffor a Spanyard. **1689** in *Cal. Treas. P.* I. Pref. 37 The French has taken 5 Dutch West Indiamen.., also a very rich Spaniard that came from Portabello. **1710** *Lond. Gaz.* No. 4710/3 This Day sailed a Spaniard for Amsterdam. **1761** *Ann. Reg., Chron.* 157/1 Near the Spaniard below the Nore. **1806** A. DUNCAN *Nelson* 36 The Spaniard's mizen-mast fell. **1908** *Pall Mall G.* 20 Apr. 1/3 To be told at breakfast..that 'a Spaniard' was on the rocks.

3. a. The New Zealand plant *Aciphylla Colensoi*, characterized by its long prickly grass-like leaves; New Zealand bayonet- or spear-grass.

1851 in R. B. Paul *Lett. fr. Canterb.* (1857) 108 The country through which I have passed has been most savage, one mass of Spaniards and spear grass. **1882** POTTS *Out in the Open* 287 (Morris), Carefully avoiding contact with the long-armed leaves of Spaniards.

b. A species of sallow or willow (see quots.).

1871 W. SCALING *Salix or Willow* (ed. 2) Descr. Cat. 5 *Salix Legustriana*, known as Common Spaniard. **1875** *Encycl. Brit.* III. 422/1 In the third class, which are known in the trade as 'Spaniards' or Spanish willows, are included about thirty varieties which are classed under *Salix amygdalina*. *Ibid.*, The 'Spaniards' comprise some of the most useful basket-willows.

c. The jack-spaniard (see JACK *sb.*[1] 38).

1909 in *Cent. Dict.* Suppl.

4. *attrib.* (or as *adj.*) and *Comb.*, as ***Spaniard governor, ship; Spaniard-aping, -hunting; Spaniard-like*** adv.; **Spaniard's beard**, Spanish beard.

1485 *Naval Acc. Hen. VII* (1896) 27 Paid..to the Boteswayne of a Spaynard ship. **1488** *Ibid.* 79, iij Spaynard Shippes. **1583** MELBANCKE *Philotimus* Xj, Spanyerdlike [she] was as careles as he. **1611** COTGR., *Espagnolé*,..made Spanish, or Spaniard-like. **1719** DE FOE *Crusoe* II. (Globe) 373 When the Spaniard Governour heard this, he calls to William Atkins. **1855** KINGSLEY *Westw. Ho!* xxv, He asked them whether they would go Spaniard-hunting with him. **1892** STEVENSON *Across the Plains* 79 Long aisles of pine-trees hung with Spaniard's Beard.

Hence (chiefly in modern journalistic use) **Spaniar'dess**, a Spanish woman; **'Spaniardism**, Spanish methods or practice; **,Spaniardi'zation**, the making of a place or thing Spanish; **'Spaniardize** *v. trans.*, to make Spanish; hence **'*Spaniardizing*** vbl. sb. and ppl. a.; **'Spaniardly** *adv.*, in a manner typical of the Spanish; **'Spaniardship**, used as a mock title in speaking of a Spaniard.

1733 FIELDING *Quix. in Eng.* I. i, If your master does not pay me, I shall lay his Spaniardship fast in a place, which [etc.]. **1880** *Daily News* 6 May 5/8 We combat..that Spaniardism he has ushered in. **1886** SYMONDS *Renaiss. It., Cath. React.* (1898) VII. xi. 183 Italian society..beneath the shadow of a score of Spaniardising princelings. **1899** *Westm. Gaz.* 29 Sept. 2/3 Signs of the Spaniardisation of Sloane-street. **1909** KIPLING *Rewards & Fairies* (1910) 42 De Avila ..very Spaniardly hung them all for heretics. **1931** O. NASH *Hard Lines* 93 The bashful Spaniardess apparently finds the amorous Spaniard..menacing to her virtue.

† **Spaniardo.** *Obs.*[−1] A Spaniard.

1598 CHAPMAN *Blinde Beg. Alexandria* Plays 1873 I. 14, I am signeor Braggadino the Martiall Spaniardo, the aide of Ægypt in her present wars.

spaniel ('spænjəl), *sb.*[1] (and *a.*) Forms: α. 4–5 **spaynel,** 5–6 **-ell** (5 **-yel,** 6 **-iel**). β. 5 **spanʒelle, -ʒeall,** 6 **-ʒell,** **-ʒeoll;** 5–6 **spanyel(l,** 6 **-yelle, spannyell, -iell,** 7 **-iel,** 6–7 **spaniell,** 7 **spaniele, spani'el,** 6– **spaniel.** γ. 5 **spayngyel, spanegeole, spangel,** 6–7 **-gell.** δ. 5 **speygn-, spaygn-, spaignol,** 6 **spaignell,** 7 **spagnel.** ε. 6 **span(n)el,** 7 **span(n)ell,** 9 *dial.* or *vulgar* **spanil.** [ad. OF. *espaignol, espaigneul* (mod.F. *épagneul*) 'Spanish dog': see SPANIEL *sb.*[2] So MDu. *spanjoel, -goel, spaelgoen*, etc.]

1. A variety of dog characterized by large drooping ears, long silky hair, keen scent, and affectionate nature, some breeds of which are used for sporting purposes, esp. for starting and retrieving game, while others are favourite pet- or toy-dogs.

α. *c* **1386** CHAUCER *Wife's Prol.* 267 For, as a spaynel, she wol on hym lepe. *c* **1410** *Master of Game* (MS. Digby 182) xvi, A goode spaynel shulde not be to rough, but his taile shulde be rough. **1425** *Rolls of Parlt.* IV. 298/1 By þe Rees of a Spaynell, þere was on a nyght taken..a man. **1484** CAXTON *Fables of Poge* iv, A fayr yong man..whiche..had with hym two fayre spaynels.

β. *c* **1450** *Bk. Hawking* in *Rel. Ant.* I. 297 Lete the spanyell flusch up the covey. **1489** *Acc. Ld. High Treas. Scot.* I. 112 Joly Johne..that brocht ij spanʒeallis to the King. **1519** *Presentm. Juries* in *Surtees Misc.* (1890) 32 That no man kepe no hown, grewand, nor spanʒell. **1557** R. EDGEWORTH *Serm.* vi. 56 It is natural..to a spaniell to be gentle & familiar. **1589** ? LYLY *Pappe w. Hatchet* E ij, There is not a better Spanniell in England to spring a couie. **1621** BURTON *Anat. Mel.* Democr. to Rdr. 4 Like a ranging Spaniel that barkes at euery bird hee sees. **1675** COCKER *Morals* (1694) 5 Beware of that sly Sycophant's Dogg-Tricks, Who, like a Spanniel flatters, fawns, and licks. **1704** POPE *Windsor For.* 99 Before his lord the ready spaniel bounds. **1789** WOLCOT (P. Pindar) *Expost. Ode* xi. Wks. 1812 II. 239 Like crouching Spaniels, down black Lords must lie, Whene'er admitted to the Royal eye. **1840** BLAINE *Encycl. Rural Sports* §2550 The varieties of the spaniel are numerous... A popular distinction made between them by many writers is into springers, cockers, and water spaniels. **1877** *Encycl. Brit.* VII. 328 The Spaniel is the favourite of the sportsman.

γ. *c* **1410** *Master of Game* (MS. Digby 182) Prol., First y will begynn at Racches..and after at Spayngyels. *c* **1425** *Seven Sages* (P.) 1448, I hadde a spangel good of plyght. **1533** *Presentm. Juries* in *Surtees Misc.* (1890) 33 Neither hownde, spangell, ne grewend.

δ. **14..** *Master of Game* (MS. Royal 17. B. xli) xvi, Off Houndes that men calle Spaygnell. **1553** [see 1 c]. **1607** TOPSELL *Four-f. Beasts* (1658) 107 Some are smaller which are called Hounds,..House-curs, Spagnels both for the Water and Land.

ε. **1575** TURBERV. *Faulconrie* Prol., The calling Spanels quest. **1589** *Gold. Mirr.* (1851) 51, I calde my Spannels, and to the field I went. **1616** SURFL. & MARKHAM *Countrey Farme* 679 When you make choice of any spannell, you shall chuse him by his shape, beautie, mettall, and cunning hunting. **1624** CAPT. SMITH *Virginia* VI. 232 Hauing a mastiue Bitch and a Spanell with them. **1640** GENT *Knave in Gr.* I. i. B iv, I think I am little kin to a Spannell, the more I am beaten, the better I affect.

b. With distinguishing terms to denote different varieties or breeds, as ***Alpine, Blenheim, English, King Charles, Norfolk*** (etc.) ***spaniel.*** Also † ***spaniel gentle*** (see first quot.).

See also *land-spaniel* LAND *sb.*[1] 11 b, WATER-SPANIEL.

1576 FLEMING tr. *Caius' Dogs* (1880) 14 Of the delicate neate, and pretty kind of dogges called the Spaniel gentle, or the comforter, in Latine *Melitæus.* **1778** *Encycl. Brit.* (ed. 2) III. 1618/2 They [*Canis Hispaniolus*] are still distinguished by the name of English Spaniels. **1833** W. H. MAXWELL *Field Bk.* 497 King Charles's spaniel, *Can[is] brevipilis. Ibid.*, The hunting spaniel or cocker..*Can[is] index. Ibid.*, The Alpine spaniel. **1845** YOUATT *Dog* 44 The King Charles's Spaniel, so called from the fondness of Charles II for it,..belongs likewise to the cockers. *Ibid.* 45 The Norfolk Spaniel. *Ibid.*, The Blenheim Spaniel. *Ibid.* 51 The Alpine Spaniel, or Bernardine Dog, is a breed almost peculiar to the Alps. **1894** *Daily News* 11 Apr. 6/4 There are the usual number of King Charles, ruby spaniels, and Italian greyhounds.

†**c.** In allusive use. *Obs.*

1553 *Respublica* (Brandl) I. iii. 187 *Adul[acio].* Doe but whistle for me, and I comme foorth with all... *Avar[icia].* Y[t] is myne owne good spaignell Rigg. *a* **1553** UDALL *Royster D.* II. iii. (Arb.) 36 Ye shall see hir glide and swimme, Not lumperdee clumperdee like our spaniell Rig. **1599** T. NASHE *Lenten Stuffe* 43 Fate is a spaniel that you cannot beate from you. **1605** *1st Pt. Jeronimo* I. iii. 1 Come, my soules spaniell, my lifes ietty substance, Whats thy name? **1613** SHAKS. *Hen. VIII*, v. iii. 126 You play the Spaniell, And thinke with wagging of your tongue to win me.

2. *fig.* **a.** One who pries into, or searches out, something.

1562 PILKINGTON *Expos. Abdyas* 56 The papistes..be diligent spayniels to seek al wayes possible to set up that vyle podell of idolatrie. **1646** QUARLES *Sheph. Oracles* Egl. iv. Wks. (Grosart) III. 214/1 These are the generous Spaniels that retrive Imperiall Crownes, and swallow Kings alive. **1647** CLEVELAND *Char. Lond.-Diurn.* 2 Suteable to their plots are their Informers; Skippers and Taylours; Spaniells both for the Land and the Water.

b. A submissive, cringing, or fawning person.

1592 *Nobody & Someb.* in Simpson *Sch. Shaks.* (1878) I. 315 Time was, base spaniell, thou didst fawne as much On me, as now thou strivest to flatter her. **1598** BARNFIELD *Compl. Poetrie* Poems (Arb.) 102 And herein happie, I areade the poore; No flattring Spanyels fawne on them for meate. **1600** HEYWOOD *1st Pt. Edw. IV*, I. i, I, I, you are the Spaniels of the court. **1848** DICKENS *Dombey* xlvi, Have you nothing, Spaniel, to complain of in him? **1852** WHITTIER *Astræa* iii, Perish shall all which makes A spaniel of the man!

3. *attrib.* and *Comb.*, as ***spaniel bitch, dog, eye, group***, etc.; ***spaniel-eyed*** adj.; ***spaniel-like*** adj. and adv.; **spanielship**, a state of mean or fawning submission.

1687 MIÉGE *Gt. Fr. Dict.* II, A *Spaniel-bitch. **1818** SCOTT *Rob Roy* xxxvii, A black spaniel bitch. *c* **1620** Z. BOYD *Zion's Flowers* (1855) 25 The *spaniel dog he loves his Masters eye. **1694** *Acc. Sev. Late Voy.* (1711) I. 17 They were as big as an ordinary Spaniel-dog. **1828** SCOTT *F.M. Perth* xi, A little French spaniel dog sat beside them. **1852** THACKERAY *Esmond* I. viii, Little Beatrix..sat at the farther end of the room..playing with a spaniel dog. **1958** M. KELLY *Christmas Egg* III. 125 Brett could well imagine his assumed *spaniel eyes of reproach. **1975** T. ALLBEURY *Special Collection* xi. 79 Felinski wondered what women would make of those liquid, spaniel eyes. **1963** P. FLEMING *Kolchak* vii. 84 A plump, *spaniel-eyed, ineffective little man. **1840** BLAINE *Encycl. Rural Sports* §2538 The *spaniel group includes the setter, the common spaniel, the Newfoundland dog, and the retriever. *c* **1410** *Master of Game* (MS. Digby 182) xvi, Of the *Spaynell Houndes. **1591** SHAKS. *Two Gentl.* IV. ii. 14 Yet (*Spaniel-like) the more she spurnes my loue, The more it..fawneth on her still. **1834** *Tait's Mag.* I. 385/2 The mere spaniel-like instinct of obedience. **1833** W. H. MAXWELL *Field Bk.* 497 The name of the *spaniel race. **1832** CARLYLE *Misc.* (1872) IV. 77 His devout Discipleship seemed nothing more than a mean *Spanielship.

b. Passing into *adj.* in the sense 'meanly submissive, cringing, fawning', etc.

1601 SHAKS. *Jul. C.* III. i. 43 Low-crooked-curtsies, and base Spaniell fawning. **1606** DEKKER *Double P.P.* Wks. (Grosart) II. 172 He..can creepe into credit,..And (by his Spaniell-fawning) saue his neck. **1681** DRYDEN *Epil. to Lee's P'cess Cleves* 13 The Spaniel Lover, like a sneaking Fop, Lies at our Feet. **1796** SOUTHEY *Hymn to Penates* Poet. Wks. 1837 II. 277 A spaniel race That lick the hand that beats them, or tear all Alike in frenzy. **1875** TENNYSON *Q. Mary* III. iii, These spaniel-Spaniard English of the time.

† **Spaniel**, *sb.*[2] *Obs.* Forms: 4–5 **Spaynyel(l,** 5 **Spayn(h)ell,** *Sc.* **Spanʒell.** [ad. OF. *Espaignol* (cf. SPANIEL *sb.*[1] (and *a.*) and SPAINOL).] A Spaniard.

1387 TREVISA *Higden* (Rolls) IV. 419 Galba Servius regnede aftir Nero..i-chose of Spaynyellus and of Galles. *Ibid.* V. 235 þe Spaynelles, Galles, and Romayns. *c* **1425** WYNTOUN *Cron.* II. ix. 778 (Cott.), þar schippis he fande thretty Wiþe of Spanʒellis in company.

spaniel ('spænjəl), *v. rare.* [f. SPANIEL *sb.*[1]]

a. *intr.* (also with *it*). To act like a spaniel; to be meanly submissive or subservient. **b.** *trans.* To follow, or fawn upon, like a spaniel.

1599 PORTER *Angry Wom. Abingt.* (Percy Soc.) 101 How he would spaniell it, and shake himselfe when he comes out of the pond! **1606** SHAKS. *Ant. & Cl.* IV. xii. 21 The hearts That pannelled [*Hanmer* (1743–4) *emend.* spaniel'd] me at heeles, to whom I gaue Their wishes. **1763** CHURCHILL *Conference* 4 Let Fortune change, and Prudence changes too, Supple and pliant a new system feels, Throws up her Cap, and spaniels at his heels. **1812** W. TENNANT *Anster F.* (1814) I. xvi. 4 By such a pack of men, in am'rous quest, Fawningly spaniel'd to bestow her hand. **1924** GALSWORTHY *Forest* II. i. 33 Devoted to him; spaniels round him all the time. **1958** 'W. HENRY' *Seven Men at Mimbres Springs* vii. 80 With that reference to the gun, Sparhawk began spanielling again, obsequious as ever.

'spanieless. [f. SPANIEL *sb.*[1]] A female spaniel.
1853 C. BRONTE *Villette* xxxviii, He spoke no more to the pupils,..but gave many an endearing word to a small spanieless (if one may coin a word).

'spanielize, *v. rare.* Also 7 spanniolize. [f. SPANIEL *sb.*[1]] *intr.* (also with *it*). To act like a spaniel; to be submissive or fawning.
1641 *Wits Recreations* §498, I cannot spanniolize it week by week, Or wait a moneth to kisse your hand or cheek. **1687** MIÈGE *Gt. Fr. Dict.* II, To Spanielize, or fawn like a Spaniel, *caresser, comme font les Epagneux.*

†**'Spanify,** *v. Obs.* [f. *Span-* (as in SPANIARD, etc.) + -(I)FY.] *trans.* To make Spanish; to Spaniolize. Hence †**'Spanified** *ppl. a.*
1599 in *Archpriest Controv.* (Camden) I. 214 The ruine of our poore country whiche we greately feared by that Spanified league. **1600** W. WATSON *Decacordon* (1602) 350 Those honors they meane of, are throughly spanified. **1601** —— *Import. Consid.* (1831) 15 Utterly refusing to applaud to Parson's Spanified Title. **1602** in *Archpriest Controv.* (Camden) II. 184 Some greate persons are Spanified.

'spaning, *vbl. sb. north.* and *Sc.* [f. SPANE *v.*] The action of weaning, suspending, etc.
*c*1440 *Promp. Parv.* 467/1 Spanynge, or wenynge of chylder, *ablactacio.* *c*1440 *Alph. Tales* 23 When þe childe was att spanyng, þis brewster doghter broght it vnto hym & lefte it with hym. **1516** *Burgh Rec. Edinburgh* (1869) I. 164 Vnder the payne of spayning fra the occupatioun for yeir and day. **1529** *Ibid.* (1871) II. 6 [For] the thrid falt, spanyng of thar operatione. **1565** J. KNOX *Sermon* 24 b, This weaning (or spaning as we terme it) from worldly pleasure, is a thing straunge to the flesh. **1653** in Laing *Lindores Abbey* (1876) 224 Took as weill w[t] the spaining..as any bairne could doe. **1898** LD. E. HAMILTON *Mawkin* ix. 107 The spaning of the lambs was by with.

b. *attrib.*, as ***spaning-lamb, -time***; **spaning brash**, weaning-brash; also *transf.*, a disease which attacks corn in the early stages of its growth.
1416–7 *Durham Acc. Rolls* (Surtees) 317 Pro spanyng lambes. **1447** *Ibid.* 319 Cum ij spanynglamez et j Antonlam. **1549** *York Wills* (Surtees) VI. 296 To..my servaunte, one spaninge quie calf. **1562** *Will of Benson* (Somerset Ho.), A lamb at spanyng tyme. **1582** *Durham Wills* (Surtees) II. 58, xx lambes, to be delivered the next spaninge tyme after my deathe. **1721** RAMSAY *Richy & Sandy* 40 At spaining time, or at our Lambmass feast. **1828** MOIR *Mansie Wauch* xxiii, All the dunts and tumbles of infancy—to say nothing of the spaining-brash and the teeth-cutting.

Spaniolate ('spænɪəleɪt), *v. rare.* Also 6 Spanyol-. [f. *Spaniol-* Spanish (see SPAINOL) + -ATE[3]. Cf. obs. F. *espagnoler*, Sp. *españolar*, and HISPANIOLATE *v.*] *trans.* To Spaniolize. Hence **'Spaniolated** *ppl. a.*
1577 SIDNEY *Lett.* Misc. Wks. (1829) 302 His Brother Earnest, muche lyke him in disposition... Bothe extreemely Spaniolated. **1583** STOCKER *Civ. Warres Lowe C.* III. 109 b *note*, Other letters sent from the Spaniolated Hollanders to Leyden. *Ibid.* 110 *note*, The Spanyolated John le Hutter. **1855** KINGSLEY *Westw. Ho!* xxvii, As Cary said to him once, using a cant phrase of Sidney's,..all heaven and earth were 'spaniolated' to him. **1907** *Athenæum* 25 May 635/3 The poor Spaniolated prince then holding the title.

Spaniolize ('spænɪəlaɪz), *v.* Now *rare.* Also 7 Spagn(i)ol-. [f. as prec. + -IZE. Cf. obs. F. *espagnoliser*, and ESPANOLIZE *v.*, HISPANIOLIZE *v.*] *trans.* To make Spanish; to imbue with Spanish notions or tendencies; to cause to follow Spanish fashions. (Chiefly in pa. pple.)
1598 DALLINGTON *Meth. Trav.* F iv, Like Traitors falsly hearted, or Frenchmen truly Spaniolized. **1625** PURCHAS *Pilgrims* IV. 1485 Their phrase was much mixt with Spanish, for now they are all Spaniolized. **1662** J. BARGRAVE *Pope Alex. VII* (1867) 73 He himself seemeth to be neutral; yet most think that upon occasion he would prove Spaniolized. *a*1743 OZELL tr. *Brantome's Sp. Rhodom.* (1744) 16 He was a Gascon but perfectly Spanioliz'd.
Hence **'Spaniolized, 'Spaniolizing** *ppl. adjs.*
1600 O. E. *Repl. Libel* Pref. p. iv, The trecherie of Spaniolized papistes. **1603** FLORIO *Montaigne* (1634) 133 To become slender in wast, and to have a straight spagnolized body. **1627** H. BURTON *Baiting of Pope's Bull* To Reader 3 A fawning spanolizing Spaniell, silenced with a fat morsell, or a little spettle. **1641** MILTON *Ch. Govt.* II. Wks. 1851 III. 47 A Tympany of Spanioliz'd Bishops swaggering in the fore-top of the State. **1670** G. H. *Hist. Cardinals* II. II. 157 He makes himself notorious by his defending the interest of Spain, he being one of the most Spanioliz'd Cardinals of them all. **1888** *Sat. Rev.* 20 Oct. 1 The stronger but ruder stock of the already Spaniolized Hapsburgs.

Spanish ('spænɪʃ), *a.* (*adv.*) and *sb.*[1] Forms: α. 3 Spainisce, 5 Spaynessh(e, -ysshe, -ish, Spainysshe, 6 Spaynisshe, -ysch, Spaynes, *Sc.* Spaines, 9 *Sc.* Spainish. β. 5–6 Spanyshe, 6 -yssh(e, -ische, -issh, -ys, Spenyes, Spannishe, *Sc.* Spanes, 8 Spannish, 6– Spanish. [f. SPAIN + -ISH, with later shortening of the first element. Cf. OE. *Speonisc* (Ælfric), MDu. *Spaensch, Spaens*, Du. *Spaansch*), G. *Spanisch*, Da. and Sw. *Spansk.*]

A. *adj.* **1. a.** Of or pertaining to Spain or its people; inhabiting, native to, characteristic of, Spain.
*c*1205 LAY. 30703 Heo hahten hine Kinebord ut of Spainisce [*v.r.* Spaynes] ard. **1382** *Wycliffite Bible* Pref. Epp. ix. (1850) I. 76 Spanyshe songes upon deed men [L. *Hiberas nænias*]. *c*1400 *Brut* ccxxix. (1908) 304 When þe Spaynesshe vessellis & nauey were closid yn al about. *a*1533 LD. BERNERS *Huon* cxvii. 415 He coude very wel speke the spanysshe languag. **1585** T. WASHINGTON tr. *Nicholay's Voy.* I. ii. 2 b, [We] sailed through the Spanish Seas towards the Iles Baleares. **1642** HOWELL *For. Trav.* (Arb.) 64 The Spanish Traveller, who was so habituated to hyperbolize,.. that he became ridiculous in all companies. **1684** BUNYAN *Pilgr.* II. 18 All the Gold in the Spanish Mines. **1723** CHAMBERS tr. *Le Clerc's Archit.* I. 56 The Spanish Order.. is more elegant than the Roman. **1774** GOLDSM. *Nat. Hist.* (1776) II. 344 Even those [wild horses] which are found in America are of a Spanish breed. **1796** H. HUNTER tr. *St.-Pierre's Stud. Nat.* (1799) III. 537 In 1566, it constrained the Dutch to shake off the Spanish yoke. **1812** BYRON *Ch. Har.* I. lxxxi, Who late so free as Spanish girls were seen? **1871** EARLE *Philol. Eng. Tongue* 304 Round by the Spanish peninsula have also come to us those English..nouns which are derived from Arabic.

b. ***Spanish Main***, the mainland of America adjacent to the Caribbean Sea, esp. that portion of the coast stretching from the Isthmus of Panama to the mouth of the Orinoco; in later use also, the sea contiguous to this, or the route traversed by the Spanish register ships. Now *Hist.*
1725 SLOANE *Jamaica* II. 297 This is brought from the Spanish Main, or Continent of America. **1765** *Phil. Trans.* LV. 50 The portrait of a child born of negro parents upon the Spanish main. **1803** J. BURNEY *Disc. in South Sea* I. i. 7 That part of the continent, since known by the names of *Terra Firma*, and the Spanish Main. **1839** LONGF. *Wreck Hesperus* iv, Then..spake an old Sailor, Had sailed the Spanish Main. **1890** J. CORBETT *Drake* viii. 110 Cartagena was the capital of the Spanish Main.

c. ***Spanish March*** (see first quot.).
1788 GIBBON *Decl. & F.* xlix. V. 141 In his absence he [Charlemagne] instituted the Spanish march, which extended from the Pyrenees to the river Ebro. *Ibid.* note, The governors or counts of the Spanish march. **1845** *Encycl. Metrop.* XI. 296/1.

d. Of a Jew or Jewish institution: of or belonging to the Sephardim; hence ***Spanish-Jewish*** adj.; also ***Spanish-Hebrew, Spanish (and) Portuguese*** (cf. PORTUGUESE *a.* a).
1817 M. EDGEWORTH *Harrington* iv. 88 This Spanish Jew must..be a most accomplished and amiable person. **1851** [see SEPHARDI]. **1876** GEO. ELIOT *D. Deronda* VII. lv. 238 His mind went to the synagogue..and heard the Spanish-Hebrew liturgy. **1892** [see ASHKENAZIM]. **1894** I. ZANGWILL *King of Schnorrers* v. 105 The Mahamad..administered the affairs of the Spanish-Portuguese community. **1902** G. E. MITTON *Hampstead & Marylebone* 80 In Bryanston Street there is a synagogue which was built for the Spanish and Portuguese Jews. **1932** C. ROTH *Hist. of Marranos* xii. 315 On his death in 1762, he left..a legacy of £1,000 to the Spanish and Portuguese community. **1949** 'R. WEST' *Meaning of Treason* I. vi. 122 That slender and distinguished old gentleman of Spanish Jewish descent, Mr Salzedo. **1977** *Early Music* Apr. 262 Basil Douglas Ltd. presents.. Sephardic Romances from before the expulsion of the Spanish Jews (1492). **1981** *Times* 16 Oct. 9/1 Elias Canetti ..was born in Bulgaria, of Spanish-Jewish descent. **1982** *Times* 26 Jan. 11/5 Sir Moses Montefiore..was an intensely loyal Englishman. The Spanish Portuguese Jewish Congregation..refused a request to transfer the remains to Israel.

2. a. Of things: Of actual or attributed Spanish origin; made, manufactured, or produced in Spain (or Spanish America); associated or connected with Spain on this account.
1485 *Naval Acc. Hen. VII* (1896) 39 Forest billes.., Spaynish dartes. **1486** *Bk. St. Albans, Hawking* c v, Take yolkys of Egges rawe,..put therto spanyshe salte. **1592** *Shuttleworths' Acc.* (Chetham Soc.) 75 Towe ovnsies of blake spenyes sylke to be boughte at Chester, iiij[s]. **1598** *Sc. Acts, Jas. VI* (1816) IV. 169/1 Euerie erle be armit and furnist wth corslet of pruif, heid peces, vanbraces, teslettis, and ane spanische pik. **1615** MARKHAM *Eng. Housew.* II. iv. (1668) 116 If it be Spanish Cute, two gallons will go further than five gallons of Candy Cute. **1649** *Eng. Farrier* xiii, Make your shooe of spruse or Spanish Iron. **1688** HOLME *Armoury* III. xxii. (Roxb.) 274/1 Spanish tobacco, the wreath about a finger thickness. **1794** MRS. RADCLIFFE *Myst. Udolpho* l, Some flasks of rich Spanish wine. **1821** S. F. AUSTIN *Jrnl.* 8 July in *Texas Hist. Assoc. Q.* (1904) VII. 287 Swapped away Wilsons Horse & an old Grey..for a mule, & exchanged a french saddle for a Spanish one. **1829** LOUDON *Encycl. Plants* 205 S[alsola] sativa..affords all the best soda consumed in Europe. It is called by us Spanish or Alicant soda. **1846** BAXTER *Libr. Pract. Agric.* (ed. 4) I. 202 Spanish annotta is unquestionably the best ingredient for colouring cheese. **1880** J. DUNBAR *Pract. Papermaker* 35 Spanish Esparto,..Oran Esparto. **1897** E. HOUGH *Story of Cowboy* 67 The Spanish saddles of the Southwest were often heavily decorated with silver. **1945** *Elk Mountain Pilot* (Crested Butte, Colorado) 19 July 3/1 (Advt.), For Sale... A Spanish Saddle, excellent condition.
Comb. **1654** GAYTON *Pleas. Notes* To Friend, Thou 'dst turn'd the Pyrrhick Galliard of the Times Into inchanted Spanish-Pavin Rimes. **1796** WITHERING *Brit. Plants* (ed. 3) IV. 283 Buffy brown or Spanish snuff colour.

b. Esp. ***Spanish leather, mahogany, needle, soap, -wool*** (see also 7).
1483 in *Antiq. Rep.* (1807) I. 42, viij paire of botews of *Spaynysh leder. **1576** GASCOIGNE *Steele Glas* 373 Wks. 1910 II. 152 Our knit silke stockes, and spanish lether shoes. **1626** L. OWEN *Speculum Jesuiticum* (1629) 9 Our Spanish-leather Saint had a diuine reuelation of the blessed Trinitie. **1693** DRYDEN *Juvenal* vi. (1697) 134 The several Suits Of Armour, and the Spanish Leather Boots! **1711** *Lond. Gaz.* No. 4862/4 Every..Spanish Leather-dresser, and all other Dressers of Hides. **1858** SIMMONDS *Dict. Trade*, *Spanish-leather maker*, a manufacturer of Cordovan-leather. **1837** W. B. ADAMS *Pleasure Carriages* 75 There are two kinds of mahogany, known as '*Spanish' and 'Honduras'. **1869** RANKINE *Machine & Hand-tools* App. 69 Spanish mahogany is the more highly valued for ornamental purposes. **1584** in Feuillerat *Revels Q. Eliz.* (1908) 368 For *spanishe needles iii[d]. **1605** *Tryall Chev.* II. i. in Bullen *Old Pl.* (1884) III. 286 Sitting upon the poynt of a Spanish needle. **1615** MARKHAM *Country Contentm.* I. x, The best substance whereof to make Angling hooks, is either old Spanish needles, or else strong wier. *c*1450 *M.E. Med. Bk.* (Heinrich) 134 Take harde *spaynessh sepe and a litul stale ale. **1572** GASCOIGNE *Councell to Withipoll* 78 Some may present thee with a pounde or twaine Of Spanishe soape to washe thy lynnen white. **1789** H. BUCHAN *Dom. Med.* (1790) 453 Such as cannot bear the asafœtida may substitute Spanish soap in its place. **1870** YEATS *Nat. Hist. Comm.* 206 Spanish or Castile soap is made by mixing olive oil and soda. **1436** *Libel English Policy* in *Polit. Poems* (Rolls) II. 162 Ffor *Spayneshe wolle in Fflaundres draped is. **1728** CHAMBERS *Cycl.* s.v. *Wool*, The goodness of the Spanish Wools is owing to a few English Sheep sent over into Spain. **1797** *Encycl. Brit.* (ed. 3) XVII. 343/2 The wool..is used for mixing with Spanish wool in some of their finest cloths.

c. Of articles of dress, etc.: Made in Spain, of Spanish materials, or after the Spanish fashion.
1530 PALSGR. 273/2 Spaynisshe bagge, *bauldrier.* *c*1534 in Lewis *Life Fisher* (1855) II. 297, 2 Spanyshe napkyns wroght wythe sylke and gold. **1542** *Nottingham Rec.* III. 220 One Spaynes cloke of frysado. **1610** B. JONSON *Alch.* IV. vii, His Spanish slops. *Ana.* They are profane..and idolatrous breeches. **1634** W. TIRWHYT tr. *Balzac's Lett.* 120 A Nose ..against which there is no possible defence but Spanish Gloves. **1652** *News fr. Lowe-Countr.* 2 Sometimes, forsooth, the Spanish Hose Doth trick him up, and there He goes. **1805** SCOTT *Last Minstrel* II. xix, A palmer's amice..With a wrought Spanish baldric bound. **1925** G. GREENE *Babbling April* 17 And the night was so hot, And no one can see in the dark, And a rent in the Spanish shawl. **1967** A. WILSON *No Laughing Matter* II. 92 A grand piano on which [is] a white Spanish shawl with red and green embroidered roses. **1975** 'R. PLAYER' *Let's talk of Graves* iii. 77 The year '54..the year of the largest crinolines... Thrown over them..were.. large Spanish shawls.

d. *Needlework.* (See quots.)
1640 J. TAYLOR (Water P.) *Praise Needle* A 2 The Spanish-stitch, Rosemary-stitch, and Mowse-stitch. **1882** CAULFEILD & SAWARD *Dict. Needlew.* 454/1 Spanish embroidery, a modern work, and closely resembling Darning on Muslin. *Ibid.* 455/1 Some of the Spanish Points are not raised, but are formed with a pattern worked out in Buttonhole Stitches. **1893** MISS MASTERS *Art Needlework* 41 Several specimens of the embroidery executed by this queen [Katharine of Aragon]..are still known as 'Spanish work'.

e. (*a*) Denoting a style of art or architecture native to or characteristic of Spain; (*b*) denoting a style of decoration or architecture imitative of that of Spain. Also ***Spanish-style*** adj.
1927 *Sunset Mag.* May 87/1 Many builders and real estate men are masquerading whole city blocks of houses under the name of Spanish. **1931** S. SITWELL (*title*) Spanish Baroque art. **1937** J. LAVER *Taste & Fashion* xviii. 258 The style of his interior decoration may be shortly described as Spanish 'baroque'. **1950** A. WILSON *Such Darling Dodos* 159 There were Regency bedrooms, a Spanish Baroque dining room. **1953** S. BEDFORD *Sudden View* I. i. 20 The dining-car.. turned out to be..decorated with machine-carved Spanish Renaissance woodwork of astonishing gloom. **1960** *Encounter* Apr. 3/2 There is something ancient and unfamiliar about its [*sc.* a skyscraper's] situation among Spanish-style San Francisco homes. **1970** H. BRAUN *Parish Churches* xi. 148 It [*sc.* the arch] is often four-centred or, in some of the more opulent examples, the three-centred 'Spanish' arch. **1976** *Liverpool Echo* 22 Nov. 14/2 (Advt.), Hall, lounge, Spanish arch to dining room, [etc.]. **1977** *N.Z. Herald* 8 Jan. 4-3/1 (Advt.), $5000 deposit will secure this charming Spanish bungalow in New Windsor. **1979** *Arizona Daily Star* 1 Apr. (Advt. Section) 19/5 Enter this custom Spanish territorial home over a wooden bridge. **1979** N. HARTLEY *Quicksilver* vi. 77 Several Spanish-style interior patios.

3. a. Of a type or kind characteristic of, or exemplified by, the Spaniards.
In quot. 1584, 'deceitful, perfidious, treacherous'.
1530 PALSGR. 225/1 Gyrdell for a purse of the spaynisshe facyon. **1584** WALSINGHAM in *Cott. Libr. Catal.* 8 The French king..will mislike, that, by any Spanish practice, she should be drawn to violate her faith. **1592** G. HARVEY *Four Lett.* Wks. (Grosart) I. 192 Be thinke your selues of the olde Romane Discipline, and the newe Spanish industry. *a*1628 F. GREVILLE *Sidney* iii. (1652) 37 His Spanish haughture. **1693** W. FREKE *Sel. Ess.* Apol. 5, I shall not cramp myself to a Spanish Cutt to do it. **1806** A. HUNTER *Culina* 159 To stew Vegetables in the Spanish manner. **1891** FARRAR *Darkn. & Dawn* xvii, Your poem..is crude in parts. It is too Spanish and provincial.

b. ***an old Spanish custom***: phr. used *joc.* to justify a long-standing practice which is unauthorized or otherwise irregular.
1932 *N. & Q.* 13 Feb. 122/1 Could any reader tell me the origin of the phrase, 'An old Spanish custom,' as applied, in a jocular sense, to any unauthorised practice? **1966** M. TORRIE *Heavy as Lead* x. 115 Giving Sir Ganymede lunch at the pub..appeared by this time to have become an old Spanish custom. **1982** *Listener* 25 Nov. 13/2 The December issue of *Encounter*..lifts some lids on the 'old Spanish customs' of Fleet Street print unions.

4. In the names of various diseases.
1583–91 [see POX *sb.*[1] b]. **1600** PORY tr. *Leo's Africa* I. 39 This they were most certainly perswaded of, that the same disease came first from Spaine; wherefore they..call it, The Spanish poxe. **1608** [see POX *sb.* 1 e]. **1681** [see POCK *sb.* 2 a α]. *a*1700 *Dict. Cant. Crew*, *Spanish-gout*, the Pox. *c*1720 W. GIBSON *Farrier's Dispens.* xiv. (1734) 271 The disease of the Head, which he [Solleysell] calls the Spanish-evil,..affected the Head with a Delirium or Madness. **1868** *Rep. U.S. Commissioner Agric.* (1869) 38 Five western cattle died of Spanish fever at Millerton,..New York, where they were quarantined.

5. Of or pertaining to, dealing or connected with, the language or literature of Spain.
1599 MINSHEU (*title*), A Spanish Grammar, first collected ..by R. Percivale,..now augmented..by J. Minsheu. **1706**

STEVENS *Spanish & Eng. Dict.* Pref., The Spanish Diminutives are much more numerous than the Substantives. **1706** —— *New Spanish Grammar* 3, I shall enter immediately upon the Spanish Alphabet. **1728** CHAMBERS *Cycl.* s.v. *Bible*, Where he explains the Hebrew Words by Spanish Words. **1842** *Penny Cycl.* XXII. 302/1 A Spanish grammar for the use of English students. **1887** *Encycl. Brit.* XXII. 352/2 The law of Spanish accentuation. *Ibid.*, A treatise on Spanish 'doublets' by Mme. Carolina Michaelis. **1888** JACOBI *Printers' Vocab.* 129 Spanish n, a capital or lower case n with a curly accent, thus—ñ.

6. In combination with other proper names, as ***Spanish-American***, ***-Arab(ic***, ***-Indian***, ***-Mexican***, etc.

1705 R. BEVERLEY *Virginia* 51 By their Accounts, we suppose him to have come from the Spanish Indians, somewhere near Mexico, or the Mines of St. Barbe. **1727** E. DORRINGTON *Hermit* I. i. 1, I accidentally fell into Discourse with a Spanish Mexican Inhabitant, named Alvarado. **1797** *Encycl. Brit.* (ed. 3) I. 494/2 The Bastulian or Spanish Phœnician [alphabet]. **1811** *Niles' Reg.* I. 14/2 The Creoles —Spanish Americans—i.e. the descendants of Spaniards born in this country. **1838** PRESCOTT *Ferd. & Is.* Pref., The literal version..of the Spanish-Arab chronicles. **1866** *Treas. Bot.* 821/2 The Spanish-Americans use the leaves as a condiment. **1871** KINGSLEY *At Last* x, One of the old Spanish-Indian jungle tracks. **1886** *Encycl. Brit.* XXI. 653/2 We possess a few literary works written in Spanish Arabic. **1935** E. FARJEON *Nursery in Nineties* II. iii. 91 A beautiful Spanish-Mexican girl who smoked cigarettes. **1980** *Amer. Speech* LV. 39 Geographic names of Spanish linguistic origin [are] utilized..to determine the sphere of Spanish-Mexican influence in California.

7. Special collocations: † **Spanish ashes**, = BARILLA 2. **Spanish biscuit, black** (see quots.). **Spanish bowline** (see quot. 1968). **Spanish brown**, a kind of earth having a reddish-brown colour (due to peroxide of iron), used as a pigment; also, the colour which this imparts. **Spanish burn, burton**, *Naut.* (see quots.). † **Spanish chalk**, a variety of steatite found in Spain. **Spanish Civil War**, the civil war in Spain (1936–9), espoused on both sides as a popular 'cause' throughout Europe and America, in which Nationalist rebel forces, with Fascist support, overcame the Republican Government and its anti-Fascist allies (cf. *International Brigade* s.v. INTERNATIONAL *a.* 2). **Spanish clew**, *Naut.* (see quot.). † **Spanish coal**, an aromatic composition [Sp. *pebete*] burned as a perfume. † **Spanish coin**, *slang* (see quot.). **Spanish-Colonial** *a.*, designating a style of architecture characteristic of the former Spanish colonies in the Americas; also *absol.* **Spanish comb**, a decorative comb having a deep top, worn in the hair. **Spanish dance**, the traditional dance form of Spain, of gypsy origin and characterized by elaborate heel-work and freq. involving the use of castanets; hence **Spanish dancer, dancing.** † **Spanish fig** (see FIG *sb.* 2). **Spanish flu** *colloq.* = *Spanish influenza* below. **Spanish foot**, a foot (of a chair or other piece of furniture) of a scroll form with vertical ribs. **Spanish fox**, *Naut.* (see FOX *sb.* 8). † **Spanish green**, verdigris. **Spanish guitar**, the standard six-stringed (orig. five-stringed) non-electric guitar, used for both folk and classical music. **Spanish hat** (see quot. 1960). **Spanish influenza**, a popular name for influenza caused by an influenza virus of type A; *esp.* that of the pandemic which began in 1918. **Spanish juice, liquorice** (see LIQUORICE 1). **Spanish march**, † **Spanish money**, *slang* (see quots.). **Spanish omelette**, an omelette containing a selection of tomatoes, onions, potatoes, and other vegetables. **Spanish padlock**, *slang* (see quot.). † **Spanish paint, paper**, cosmetics coming from or used in Spain. † **Spanish pike**, a needle (cf. sense 2 b). **Spanish red**, an ochre resembling Venetian red, but slightly yellower (Fairholt, 1854). **Spanish reef**, *Naut.* (see quot.). **Spanish spoon**, a kind of long-handled scoop used for removing the earth in the excavation of holes for telegraph posts. **Spanish stripes**, a kind of woollen fabric (Knight, 1875). † **Spanish sword**, a rapier. **Spanish tile** *Building*, (*a*) a roofing tile that is curved cylindrically and slightly tapered, to be laid alternately convex and concave so as to overlap at both sides; (*b*) *U.S.*, a curved roofing tile that is laid convex upwards and overlaps at one side only by means of a straight projection. **Spanish trot, trumpeter** (see quots.). **Spanish tummy** *colloq.*, a stomach upset of a type freq. experienced by visitors to Spain. **Spanish War** = *Spanish Civil War* above. **Spanish wave** (after G. or Du. use as an intensive: see quot. 1852). **Spanish white**, (*a*) finely powdered chalk used as a pigment or for its cleansing properties; (*b*) a fine quality of flour (see quot. 1882). **Spanish windlass**, *Naut.* (see quot. 1846). **Spanish wood**, Spanish mahogany. **Spanish wool**, a variety of rouge (see also 2 b). † **Spanish worm** (see quot.).

1727 DE FOE *Eng. Tradesm.* iii. (1841) I. 20 These ashes they call *Spanish. **1763** LEWIS *Phil. Comm. Arts* 596 The ashes..are brought to us, under the name of Spanish ashes or *bariglia*. **1769** MRS. RAFFALD *Eng. Housekpr.* (1778) 275 To make *Spanish Biscuits. [Recipe follows.] **1839** URE *Dict. Arts* 341 When this cork [*sc.* the white cork of France] is burned in close vessels it forms the pigment called *Spanish black. **1968** E. FRANKLIN *Dict. Knots* 26 **Spanish bowline*, a double loop knot that is tied in the bight in which the two loops are splayed. **1974** *Maclean's Mag.* May 10/2 Spanish bowlines to make slings for scaffolding. **1660** *Albert Durer Revived* 15 *Spanish Brown is a dirty brown colour. **1703** R. NEVE *City & C. Purchaser* 215 Timber-works that are expos'd to the Weather, ought..to be Prim'd with Spanish-brown. **1732** J. PEELE *Water-Colours* 63 Shadow your Vermilion with Spanish brown. **1850** HOLTZAPFFEL *Turning* III. 1313 The cement is..hardened with red ochre, or Spanish brown and whiting. **1867** SMYTH *Sailor's Word-bk.* 640 **Spanish-Burn*, a specious method of hiding defects in timber, by chopping it in pieces. **1829** *Nat. Philos., Mechanics* II. viii. 36 (L.U.K.), In figs. 65, 66, are represented systems with two ropes and two moveable pullies, called *Spanish burtons. **1846** A. YOUNG *Naut. Dict.* 55 A single Spanish burton, has three single blocks; or two single blocks and a hook fixed to one of the bights of the standing part of the tackle. A double Spanish burton, has one double and two single blocks. **1759** *Phil. Trans.* LI. 41 *note*, My friend Mr. Dacosta shewed me a piece of *Spanish chalk. **1796** KIRWAN *Elem. Min.* (ed. 2) I. 154 The steatites of China..is often called Spanish Chalk. **1936** C. PRIETO *Spanish Front* xi. 80 It is hardly necessary in this book to give a detailed description of the *Spanish Civil War. **1981** A. PRICE *Soldier no More* xi. 144 He'd subscribed to all sorts of causes, from the Spanish Civil War onwards. **1893** ALSTON & WALKER *Seamanship* (ed. 3) 116 **Spanish Clews*.. are made by serving the nettles round below the seizing, leaving one out on each side, at regular intervals. **1616** B. JONSON *Devil an Ass* IV. iv, [To] aske for your *piueti*, *Spanish-cole, To burne, and sweeten a roome. **1785** GROSE *Dict. Vulgar T.*, **Spanish coin*, fair words, and compliments. **1927** *Sunset Mag.* May 15/2 The popular desire seems to be to call this architecture Spanish. Architects are inclined to call it *Spanish-Colonial. **1937** R. NEWCOMB *Spanish-Colonial Archit. in U.S.* viii. 37 Many in these states have wished to build in the Spanish Colonial rather than in the American Colonial. **1973** G. SIMS *Hunters Point* xiii. 114 It's what they call Spanish Colonial style with wooden columns and a roof of heavily twisted tiles. **1977** H. FAST *Immigrants* I. 39 There was much substance if little taste all through the dining room,..a curious and uninspiring marriage of Spanish Colonial and Victorian. **1873** *Young Englishwoman* Mar. 131/2 Diadem plaits or torsade, fastened with a *Spanish comb. **1923** M. KENNEDY *Ladies of Lyndon* iv. 234 Could you find my Spanish comb? And..that black lace shawl. **1975** *Times* 23 Aug. 7/2 She hoped her mother would let her wear a Spanish comb she had rashly bought. **1931** K. BOYLE *Plagued by Nightingale* xvi. 137 He was doing a lively *Spanish dance to the piercing screams of their laughter. **1974** W. FOLEY *Child in Forest* 20 Our elder sister..once did a 'Spanish' dance on the end of the bed, with a cracked soap-dish for a castanet. **1948** 'LA MERI' *Spanish Dancing* i. 1 There are great *Spanish dancers, male and female, who are not Spanish. **1980** A. CORNELISEN *Torregreca* vi. 129 At *Carnevale*..Maria made 'Spanish dancers'' dresses for herself and her little brother. **1948** 'LA MERI' *Spanish Dancing* i. 4 Hermetic Spain is that promised land to which we go to find..the greatest..*Spanish dancing in the world. **1594** NASHE *Unfort. Trav.* Wks. (Grosart) V. 143 To see poore English asses how soberly they swallow *Spanish figges, deuour any hooke baited for them. **1918** W. OWEN *Let.* 24 June (1967) 560 About 30 officers are smitten with the *Spanish Flu. **1937** K. BLIXEN *Out of Africa* II. v. 161 When we had the Spanish Flu on the farm, Farah was.. shivering with fever. **1979** D. WILLIAMS *Genesis & Exodus* xi. 213 Those who had survived 1914–18 and the plague of Spanish flu that followed. **1902** F. C. MORSE *Furnit. of Olden Time* vi. 151 The chair..is of the style called Queen Anne. It has *Spanish feet. **1923** J. C. ROGERS *English Furnit.* II. ii. 56 Legs also were given a sudden broadening like an inverted cup... In some cases there was the carved 'Spanish' foot. **1975** *Country Life* 29 May (Suppl.) 40h (Advt.), Early 16th century Virginia walnut gateleg table with..Spanish feet. **1611** COTGR., *Verd de gris*, verdigrease, a *Spanish greene. **1648** HEXHAM II, *Spaensch Groen*, Spanish Greene. **1862** G. BORROW *Wild Wales* i. 10 Playing remarkably well on the guitar—not the trumpery German thing so called—but the real *Spanish guitar. **1934** S. R. NELSON *All about Jazz* ii. 54 The Spanish Guitar, with its resonant tone and range, has created a minor revolution in the ranks of the fretted instrument players. **1961** A. BIRCH in A. Baines *Mus. Instruments through Ages* vii. 168 At some point during the sixteenth century a fifth course became standard for guitar in Spain... It was this new five-course instrument which was to carry the name of 'Spanish guitar'. **1784** E. SHERIDAN *Jrnl.* 1 Oct. (1960) 26, I found a *Spanish hat was what I must bye... Even silk Balloons are almost out —I have not seen a Cap since I came. **1840** THACKERAY in *Fraser's Mag.* XXI. 688/1 A ricketty lay-figure, in a Spanish hat and cloak. **1882** C. M. YONGE *Unknown to History* II. iv. 47 Captain Fortescue..a long plume in his Spanish hat. **1960** C. W. CUNNINGTON et al. *Dict. Eng. Costume* 201/2 *Spanish hat*,..a large hat of velvet, satin or sarcenet, the brim evasé, trimmed with feathers. **1980** A. CRAWLEY *Dial 200–200* xi. 119 Maria, looking fabulous in her white satin bolero, tight trousers and black Spanish hat. **1918** *Policeman's Monthly* Oct. 4/2 The members of the Hartford department comprise the motor-cycle squad, one of whom was a victim of *Spanish influenza this week. **1940** *N. & Q.* 30 Mar. 218/1 The ravages of the 'Spanish influenza' which, between 1918 and 1922, caused four times as many deaths as those caused by the last war. **1976** BOTHAM & DONNELLY *Valentino* viii. 64 The worst Spanish influenza epidemic since the turn of the century had swept through California. **1803** *Med. Jrnl.* X. 166 The insertion in the Schedule [of the Medicine Act of 1802] of such names as *Spanish juice, refined liquorice [etc.]. **1872** OLIVER *Elem. Bot.* II. 166 Spanish juice is the sweet extract of the Liquorice-root.. evaporated to dryness. **1750–** *Spanish liquorice [see LIQUORICE 1]. **1884** E. L. ANDERSON *Mod. Horsem.* II. xvii. 145 The *Spanish march should be practised at a very slow walk, and the horse well supported by the hand. *a* **1700** B. E. *Dict. Cant. Crew*, **Spanish-money*, fair Words and Compliments. **1886** S. T. RORER *Mrs. Rorer's Philadelphia Cook Bk.* 260 (*heading*) *Spanish omelet. **1935** S. LEWIS *It can't happen Here* xxv. 270 One eye was..so surrounded with bruised flesh that..it looked like a Spanish omelet. **1974** A. WILLIAMS *Gentleman Traitor* xv. 248 He..had the African cook prepare him a Spanish omelette. **1788** GROSE *Dict. Vulgar T.* (ed. 2), **Spanish Padlock*, a kind of girdle contrived by jealous husbands of that nation, to secure the chastity of their wives. **1668** CHARLETON *Onomast.* 303 *Bianca Alexandrina*,..*Spanish Paint for Ladies. **1650** BULWER *Anthropomet.* 155 The women of Spaine are also great painters, other Nations having learnt from them the use of *Spanish-paper. *Ibid.* 156 [see RUBRIC *sb.* 1 b]. **1624** FORD *Sun's Darling* II. i, A French Gentleman that trayls a *Spanish pike, a Tailor. **1867** SMYTH *Sailor's Word-bk.* 640 **Spanish Reef*, the yards lowered on the cap. Also, a knot tied in the head of the jib. **1876** PREECE & SIVEWRIGHT *Telegraphy* 191 For light lines, on which the poles need not be inserted to a greater depth than four feet, the *Spanish Spoon answers the purpose..very fairly. *c* **1532** DU WES *Introd. Fr.* in *Palsgr.* 908 The *spanische sworde, *la rapiere.* [**1904** F. E. KIDDER *Architect's & Builder's Pocket-bk.* (ed. 14) III. 1430 Galvanized-iron tiles of the 'Spanish' pattern.] **1913** —— *Building-Construction & Superintendence* (ed. 9) II. iv. 278 The rafters..are covered with Ludovici interlocking *Spanish tiles set on the 'shiplap' roof-boarding. **1956** E. MOLLOY *Builders' & Decorators' Ref. Bk.* XVII. 3 The English pantile..is a descendant of the Spanish tile.., also called the over-and-under tile. **1979** *Tucson* (Arizona) *Citizen* (Advt. Suppl.) 28 Apr. 16/4 High beamed ceilings, brick floors, French doors, and Spanish tile all help in adding southwestern flavor to a contemporary look. **1884** E. L. ANDERSON *Mod. Horsemanship* II. xvii. 143 The *Spanish Trot is an exaggerated action in which, at each stride, a fore-leg is thrust boldly to the front, and there is a poise or half halt as the horse is in air. **1785** GROSE *Dict. Vulgar T.*, **Spanish*, or *King of Spain's Trumpeter*, an ass when braying. **1967** *Sunday Times* (Colour Suppl.) 21 May 39 They never seem to get *Spanish tummy, and their children are never overtired brats. **1968** A. BROWN *Slay me Suddenly* ix. 129 'Where's Herbert?' 'Vomiting... Spanish tummy, I suppose.' **1937** H. NICOLSON *Diary* 27 July (1966) 310 He [*sc.* Anthony Eden] thinks that the *Spanish War will last another year. **1977** C. MCCARRY *Secret Lovers* x. 130 Is it a good book? You said you were in the Spanish war. **1852** tr. *Ida Pfeiffer's Journ. Iceland* 56 Our decks were washed by a great many *Spanish waves. *Note.* The large waves which approach from the westward are called by the sailors Spanish waves or billows. **1857** DUFFERIN *Lett. High Lat.* (ed. 3) 22 Tumbling about on the top of the great Atlantic rollers—or Spanish waves, as they are called—until I thought the ship would roll the masts out of her. **1546** *Invent. Ch. Goods Sussex* 106 For *Spaynysch whytt, vj[s] vj[d]. **1686** *Phil. Trans.* XVI. 26 Spanish white made of Chalk and Alum burnt together. **1799** G. SMITH *Laboratory* I. 313 This is the magistery of bismuth, used by ladies for a cosmetic; and is termed, by artists, Spanish white. **1825** J. NICHOLSON *Operat. Mechanic* 755 The varnish,..when quite dry, [is] cleaned with starch or Spanish white. **1882** *Notes on Cerem.* (ed. 2) 44 *note*, The very best white flour,.. either that known as 'Spanish whites', or else 'Hungarian flour'. **1846** A. YOUNG *Naut. Dict.* 290 **Spanish-windlass*, a wooden roller having a rope wound about it, through the bight of which rope an iron bolt is inserted as a lever for heaving it round. *c* **1860** H. STUART *Seaman's Catech.* 29 Heave both parts of the strop together with a Spanish windlass. **1875** *Carpentry & Join.* 15 The mahogany being what is often called cedar, to distinguish it from the very hard *Spanish wood. **1892** *Photogr. Ann.* II. 301 This camera is..made of Spanish wood. **1678** PHILLIPS (ed. 4), **Spanish-Wool*, a parcel of Wool so coloured by Spanish Art, and therefore so called, that it imparts its tincture to Ladies [etc.]. **1838** *Penny Mag.* 1 Dec. 467/2 Two other preparations, called Spanish wool and Oriental wool, have been long known to..the dealers and consumers of rouge. **1785** GROSE *Dict. Vulgar T.*, **Spanish worm*, a nail, so called by carpenters when they meet one in a board they are sawing.

8. a. In the specific names or designations of animals, birds, fish, etc. **Spanish Merino** = MERINO 1; **Spanish sheep**, (*a*) = MERINO 1; (*b*) = JACOB 4.

A number of others, chiefly West Indian and Bermudan fish names, are given in American Dicts.

(*a*) **1668** CHARLETON *Onomast.* 74 *Perdix Ruffa*..the Spanish Partridge. *a* **1705** RAY *Syn. Avium & Piscium* (1713) 184 Icterus minor nidum suspendens... The Watchy Picket, or Spanish Nightingale. The Amerian Hang-nest. **1731** ALBIN *Nat. Hist. Birds* I. 87 The Spanish Goose, or Swan Goose. *Anser cygnoides.* **1781** PENNANT *Genera Birds* Pl. 13 Spanish Duck. **1849** D. J. BROWNE *Amer. Poultry Yd.* 25 In the Spanish fowl, the comb is more developed than in any other breed. **1854** MEALL *Moubray's Poultry* 248 Spanish Runt.—Described as the largest of the Runts. **1894–5** LYDEKKER *Roy. Nat. Hist.* III. 393 The Spanish sparrow (*Passer hispaniolensis*) replaces the English bird in many parts of the Mediterranean region.

(*b*) **1648** HEXHAM II, *Een Spaensche Zee-katte*, a Spanish Cat. *a* **1672**– Spanish mackerel [see MACKEREL[1] 2]. **1836** YARRELL *Brit. Fishes* I. 104 The Spanish Bream, *Pagellus erythrinus*. **1882** JORDAN & GILBERT *Syn. Fishes N. Amer.* 669 *Sebastodes rubrivinctus*, Spanish Flag. *Ibid.* 887 *Clupea pseudohispanica*, Spanish Sardine. *Ibid.* 939 *Scarus radians*, Spanish Porgy. **1885** LADY BRASSEY *In the Trades* xvii, The ..little blue and yellow Spanish angel-fish [*Holocanthus tricolor*]. **1888** GOODE *Amer. Fishes* 205 In this limpid pool were many gorgeously-colored species,..the rainbow-fish, the Spanish-lady [*Bodianus rufus*].

(*c*) **1787** *Young's Ann. Agric.* VIII. 197 Four shepherds, and from four to six large Spanish dogs. **1788** W. B. CONYNGHAM *Let.* 28 June in H. B. Carter *His Majesty's Spanish Flock* (1964) iii. 60 In answer to what Evidence I have relative to the success of my Cross from the Spanish sheep I have..the greatest Reason to believe that the Breed may be greatly improved. **1801** SHAW *Gen. Zool.* II. II. 391 The principal distinction of the Spanish Sheep is the fineness of the fleece, and the horizontally extended spire of the horns. **1802** F. L. HUMPHREYS *Life D. Humphreys* II. 346 A Gold Medal..is presented to you..for your patriotic exertions in introducing into New-England one hundred of the Spanish Merino breed of Sheep. 1827 Griffith tr. *Cuvier* V. 172 Spanish Cat... Fur short; feet and lips flesh-colour. 1831 *Ibid.* IX. Syn. 35 Spanish Lizard, *Lacerta (Psammodromus) Hispanicus.* 1837 [see pointer 4]. 1884 Goode *Nat. Hist. Aquat. Anim.* 837 We are informed by a large importer that the Spanish Leech was a small green Leech brought here occasionally.. by sea-captains. 1891 R. Wallace *Rural Economy Austral. & N.Z.* xxvi. 357 The Spanish Merino is a sheep of large size, producing a superior quality of strong combing wool. 1894 Lydekker *Roy. Nat. Hist.* II. 237 The Spanish wild goat inhabits the Pyrenees [etc.]. 1896 *Ibid.* V. 71 The Spanish terrapin (*Clemmys leprosa*), of Spain and North-Western Africa. 1913 Spanish sheep [see Jacob 4]. 1964 H. B. Carter *His Majesty's Spanish Flock* p. x, These were the men who.. transformed the Spanish Merino from an envied monopoly of one nation into the essential foundation of the modern world trade in wool. 1974 *Times* 25 Nov. 3/3 There are now about 150 registered flocks [of Jacob sheep] in Britain, comprising 3,000 spotty sheep, also known as Spanish or piebald.

b. Esp. ***Spanish fly***, = cantharides. Also *fig.*

So Du. *spaansche vlieg*, G. *spanische fliege*, F. *mouche d'Espagne*, etc.

a 1634 Chapman *Alphonsus* iii. i. 179 Drink not, Prince Palatine, throw it on the ground. It is not good to trust his Spanish flies. 1681 Grew *Musæum* i. §vii. ii. 168 The common slender Spanish-Fly. *Cantharis vulgaris.* 1712 Arbuthnot *John Bull* Postscr., He procured Spanish flies to blister his neighbours. 1815 Kirby & Sp. *Entomol.* x. (1818) I. 317 Another species of Mylabris.., which is fully as efficacious as the common Spanish fly. 1842 Loudon *Suburban Hort.* 105 The Canthárides, or Spanish blister-flies, are an essential article of medicine. 1861 Hulme tr. *Moquin-Tandon* ii. iii. iii. 128 Common Cantharides:.. commonly called Cantharides of the shops, Spanish Fly, Cantharides Fly.

transf. 1823 Byron *Juan* ix. xxviii, None, save the Spanish fly and Attic bee, As yet are strongly stinging to be free.

9. In the names of plants, trees, etc., denoting either varieties or distinct species found in Spain or Spanish America (esp. the West Indies), as ***Spanish arbor-vine, ash, briar, campion, cane, cardon, catchfly, coffee, oak, onion***, etc. **Spanish bayonet** (see bayonet *sb.* 5). **Spanish bean**, (*a*) a variety of broad bean; (*b*) *U.S.*, the scarlet runner (*Cent. Dict.* 1891). **Spanish beard**, *U.S.*, the epiphytic plant, *Tillandsia usneoides*, of the Southern States; long-beard. † **Spanish bell**, some garden flower, ? *Campanula hispanica* (cf. G. *spanische glocke*). **Spanish bluebell** = *Spanish squill* below. **Spanish cedar**, a species of Central American cedar, esp. *Cedrela mexicana*, or its timber. **Spanish chestnut, cress** (see quots.). **Spanish dagger** (see quot. 1866); also more generally, one of several species of *Yucca*, esp. *Y. gloriosa*. **Spanish elm**, an evergreen timber-tree (*Cordia Geraschanthus*) of the West Indies. **Spanish garlic**, the rocambole. **Spanish grass**, Esparto grass. **Spanish harebell** = *Spanish squill* below. **Spanish hedge-nettle** (see quot.). **Spanish iris**, a bulbous iris of the genus *Xiphium*, esp. *X. vulgare* (formerly *Iris Xiphium*). **Spanish moss**, = *Spanish beard*. **Spanish needles**, the American plant *Bidens bipinnata* or its prickly fruit. **Spanish nut**, (*a*) an iridaceous plant, *Moræa sisyrinchium*, the bulbs of which are eaten in Spain; (*b*) a variety of hazel-nut, *Corylus colurna*. † **Spanish pick-tooth** (see quot.). **Spanish plum** = plum *sb.* 3 b. **Spanish potato**: (see potato *sb.* 3 a). **Spanish soldier**, = Spaniard 3 a. **Spanish squill**, a bulbous plant, *Endymion hispanicus* (formerly *Scilla hispanica*), bearing loose racemes of blue, pink, or white bell-shaped flowers. **Spanish stopper** = *gurgeon stopper* s.v. gurgeon; cf. stopper *sb.* 8. † **Spanish trumpet**, the jonquil. **Spanish viper's grass**, scorzonera, esp. *S. hispanica* or black salsify. See also Spanish broom.

A number of others are given in American Dicts., as ***Spanish berries, bluebell, buckeye***, etc.

1731 Miller *Gard. Dict.* s.v. *Convolvulus*, Great American Bindweed.., commonly call'd *Spanish Arbor-Vine, or Spanish Woodbind. 1846 Lindley *Veg. Kingd.* 631 *Ipomœa tuberosa*, the Spanish Arbour Vine of Jamaica. 1716 *Petiveriana* i. 178 *Spanish Ash... *Caroba Barbad.* 1856 A. Gray *Man. Bot.* 472 *Yucca gloriosa* and *Y. aloifolia* (*Spanish Bayonet). 1865- [see bayonet *sb.* 5]. 1706 London & Wise *Retir'd Gard.* 96 *Spanish, Sandwich, Windsor Beans. 1763 tr. *La Page du Pratz's Hist. Louisiana* II. iv. 37 The other excrescence is commonly found upon trees near the banks of rivers and lakes. It is called *Spanish beard. 1784 Smyth *Tour in U.S.* I. 372 Another very singular and striking appearance is a kind of Moss, here [Mississippi] called Spanish Beards. 1812 Brackenridge *Views of Louisiana* (1814) 42 The long moss, or Spanish beard, begins to be seen below the Arkansas. 1867 Latham *Black & White* 118 The white oaks and cypresses in the swamps are hung with 'Indian moss', also called 'Spanish beard', a grey pendent lichen. 1664 Evelyn *Kal. Hort.* (1729) 215 August. Flowers in Prime, or yet lasting... *Spanish Bells [etc.]. 1924 L. H. Bailey *Man. Cultivated Plants* 164 *Spanish Bluebell.. fl[ower]s blue to rose-purple, usually a dozen or more, ascending or nodding in an open raceme. 1979 *Guardian* 5 June 10/1 Large white butterflies.. thrusting their long tongues into the Spanish bluebells. 1716 *Petiveriana* i. 177 Barbadoes *Spanish Briar. 1731 Miller *Gard. Dict.* s.v. *Lychnis*, *Spanish Campion, with a red Valerian Leaf, and a purplish Flower. 1703 *Art's Improv.* I. 63 A slip of hollow *Spannish-Cane, brought to a smooth and sharp edge. 1699 Evelyn *Acetaria* 10 The *Spanish Cardon, a wild and smaller Artichoak, with sharp pointed Leaves. 1707 Mortimer *Husb.* 450 Cardons Spanish are only propagated by Seed that is of a longish Oval form. 1738 *Phil. Trans.* XL. 457 *Lychnis Viscosa... Anglicè* *Spanish Catch-fly. 1907 *Spanish cedar [see *cigar-box* s.v. cigar 2]. 1947 J. C. Rich *Materials & Methods of Sculpture* x. 287 Spanish cedar is not a true cedar variety, but the wood is favored by some sculptors for carving. 1972 *Handbk. of Hardwoods* (Forest Prod. Res. Lab.) (ed. 2) 53 'Central American cedar' is sometimes called 'Spanish cedar' in reference to the former Spanish colonies. 1664 Evelyn *Kal. Hort.* (1729) 207 Cherries.., the Common Cherry, *Spanish Black. 1733 W. Ellis *Chiltern & Vale Farm.* 145 There are many sorts of Cherries, as the.. Spanish, Amber, Nonsuch. 1699 Evelyn *Acetaria* 18 The sweet aromatick *Spanish Chervile. 1762 *Ann. Reg.* i. 119 For sowing the greatest number of *Spanish chesnut-trees. 1843 Holtzapffel *Turning* I. 80 The sweet, or Spanish chesnut, is very much like oak. 1880 Bessey *Botany* 478 *Castanea vesca*, the so-called Spanish Chestnut, is a native of Asia Minor and the region eastward to the Himalayas. 1831 Audubon *Ornith.* I. 181 The wild *Spanish Coffee (*Cassia occidentalis*).. grows chiefly in old fields in the Southern States. 1887 Bentley *Man. Bot.* 567 Peeled Colocynth.. is commonly known as Turkey Colocynth, but that imported from France and Spain is sometimes distinguished as French and *Spanish Colocynth. 1823 Crabb *Techn. Dict.* II. s.v., *Spanish Cress, the *Vella annua*, an annual. 1829 Loudon *Encycl. Plants* 552 *Lepidium Cardamines*, Spanish Cress. 1859 A. Van Buren *Sojourn in South* 108 A tall '*Spanish dagger' stood leaning its crested head. 1866 *Treas. Bot.* 1075/2 *Spanish dagger*, a West Indian name for *Yucca aloifolia.* 1939 G. B. Pickwell *Deserts* 25/1 Spanish daggers bloom in deserts. 1975 *Islander* (Victoria, B.C.) 3 Aug. 3/4 The Spanish Dagger, with fruits that are eaten raw, baked on hot stones, made into jelly or dried for winter use. 1758 P. Browne *Jamaica* 170 *Spanish Elm or Prince-wood ..is..one of the best timber woods [etc.]. 1829 Loudon *Encycl. Plants* 150 *Cordia Geraschanthus*, Spanish-elm. 1707 Mortimer *Husb.* (1721) II. 163 Rocamboles are a sort of wild Garlick, otherwise called *Spanish Garlick. 1852 G. W. Johnson *Cott. Gard. Dict.* 781 Rocambole,.. sometimes called Spanish Garlic. 1884 *De Candolle's Orig. Cultivated Pl.* 250 The principal varieties of *Cucurbita maxima* are the great yellow gourd,.. the *Spanish gourd, the turban gourd. 1867 *Ure's Dict. Arts* (ed. 6) II. 237 Esparto or *Spanish Grass. 1808 *Curtis's Bot. Mag.* XXVIII. 1102 (*heading*) *Spanish Harebell. 1823 Crabb *Techn. Dict.* II. s.v., *Spanish Hedge Nettle, the *Prasium*, a shrub. 1863 *Chambers' Encycl.* V. 629/2 *I. xiphium*, sometimes called *Spanish I[ris]. 1880 *Encycl. Brit.* XIII. 276/2 The garden plants known as the Spanish iris and the English iris are both of Spanish origin. 1664 Evelyn *Kal. Hort.* (1729) 201 Prune now your *Spanish Jasmine. 1707 [see jasmine 1 a. β]. 1842 Loudon *Suburban Hort.* 617 The *Spanish lentil, and the tuberous Lathyrus. 1706 London & Wise *Retir'd Gard.* 95 Red *Spanish Lettuce. 1753 *Chambers' Cycl.* Suppl. s.v. *Lychnis*, The capillaceous leaved *Spanish lychnis. 1823 E. James *Acct. Exped. Rocky Mts.* III. 220 The *Spanish moss disappears northwardly of the 33d degree of north latitude. 1856 Olmsted *Slave States* 373 The long, waving drapery of the tyllindria [*sic*], or Spanish moss. 1884 *Evangelical Mag.* Feb. 60 We have the 'Old Man's Beard', or Spanish Moss of American Forests. 1846-50 A. Wood *Class-bk. Bot.* 346 *Bidens bipinnata*, *Spanish Needles. 1866 *Treas. Bot.* 1075/2 *Spanish needles*, a name given in the West Indies to the fruits of a species of *Bidens.* 1597 Gerarde *Herbal* i. lxviii. 94 *Spanish Nut hath smal grassie leaues. 1664 Evelyn *Kal. Hort.* (1729) 205 Ladies Slipper, Stock Gilly Flower, Spanish Nut [etc.]. 1760 J. Lee *Introd. Bot.* App. 320 Nut, Spanish, *Iris.* 1785 Martyn *Lett. Elem. Bot.* xxviii. (1794) 442 The stipules.. of the Byzantine or Spanish nut, which Linnæus gives as a distinct species, are linear. 1829 Loudon *Encycl. Plants* 46 *Moræa sisyrinchium*, Spanish-nut. 1716 *Petiveriana* i. 179 *Spanish Oak... *Caroba Barbad tetraphylla.* 1717 *Ibid.* iii. 204 Spanish Oak. Splits very well into Clap-boards and Ladders. 1852 Morfit *Tanning & Currying* (1853) 98 *Quercus Falcata*..[is] known in Delaware, Maryland and Virginia by the name of Spanish oak. 1706 London & Wise *Retir'd Gard.* 93 Red [and] white *Spanish Onion. 1763 Mills *System Pract. Husb.* IV. 34 The Spanish onion is most esteemed for it's mildness as well as size. 1806 A. Hunter *Culina* (ed. 3) 159 Take four Spanish.. onions. 1647 Hexham i. (Herbs), Pepper wort, or *Spanish Pepper. 1842 Loudon *Suburban Hort.* 607 The annual capsicum, the Spanish, or Guinea pepper, *C. ánnuum* L., a native of South America. 1706 Phillips (ed. Kersey), **Spanish Pick-tooth*, a sort of Herb. 1823 Crabb *Techn. Dict.* II. s.v. *Spondias*, The species are trees, as the.. Purple Hog-Plum, or *Spanish Plum. 1864 Grisebach *Flora Brit. W. Ind.* 787/2 Spanish-plum, *Spondias purpurea.* 1706 London & Wise *Retir'd Gard.* 93 Black [and] White *Spanish Radish. 1731 Miller *Gard. Dict.* s.v. *Raphanus*, Great round black Radish, commonly call'd The Spanish Radish. 1786 Abercrombie *Gard. Assist.* 238 Cuttings of common, or *Spanish reed. 1767 —— *Ev. Man his own Gardener* (1803) 671 *Apples...* Italian apple, *Spanish rennet, Canada rennet [etc.]. 1707 *Spanish salsify [see salsify b]. 1819 *Pantologia* X. s.v. *Scorzonera*, *Spanish scorzonera, or garden viper's-grass. 1901 *Gardener* 12 Jan. 1048 Close by.. is a *Spanish Soldier.., stiff and pointed with its three-cornered stem-like leaves. 1790 *Curtis's Bot. Mag.* IV. 128 (*heading*) *Spanish Squill. 1882 *Garden* 27 Sept. 372/1 Two or three others.. continue in beauty till the first flowers of the Spanish Squill expand. 1977 *Chicago Tribune* 2 Oct. xi. 13/2 Late—Spanish squill.. and double late tulips. 1883 G. O. Shields *Rustlings in Rockies* xxi. 195 Within the space of this five acres may be found.. *Spanish stoppor [*sic*]. 1908, 1921 Spanish stopper [see gurgeon]. 1822 *Hortus Anglicus* II. 104 *Thymus Zygis.* White *Spanish Thyme. 1591 Percivall *Span. Dict.*, *Mielgas*, *spanish trefoyle, *Herba medica.* 1623 Minsheu, *Mielgas*, an herbe called Spanish trefoile, or three leafed grasse. 1664 Evelyn *Kal. Hort.* (1729) 198 March Flowers in Prime, or yet lasting,.. *Spanish Trumpets or Junquils [etc.]. 1852 G. W. Johnson *Cott. Gard. Dict.* 837 *Spanish Viper's Grass, *Scorzonera.* 1875 *Spanish willow [see Spaniard 3 b]. 1731 *Spanish woodbine [see *S. arbor-vine* above].

10. *Comb.*, as ***Spanish-barrelled, -born, -built, -looking, -speaking, -surnamed*** adjs.

a 1628 F. Grevil *Life Sidney* (1907) 104 Resolutely oppose those Spanish-born, or Spanish-sworn Tyrannies. *c* 1677 in Marvell *Growth Popery* (1678) 61 A Spanish built Ship. 1812 Scott *Let.* in *Lockhart* (1839) III. 390, I have got Rob Roy's gun, a long Spanish-barrelled piece. 1818 —— *Rob Roy* xxxi, Levelling their long Spanish-barrelled guns. 1871 Kingsley *At Last* x, A shrewd Spanish-speaking school-master. 1875 Ruskin *Fors Clav.* lvi, Mr. Peter Domecq was, I believe, Spanish born. 1944 N. Coward *Star Quality* (1951) 85 Rather a good Spanish-looking sideboard. 1976 *Billings* (Montana) *Gaz.* 20 June 2-a/1 In what was called the first tabulation of Latino 'segregation trends', the study also said segregation of Spanish-surnamed pupils increased in the 1970s in all regions of the nation. 1981 R. Rendell *Put on by Cunning* vii. 65 A dark, Spanish-looking girl.

B. *sb.* or *ellipt.* **1.** The Spanish language.

1485 Caxton *Malory's Arthur* Pref. 2 Bookes.. as wel in duche, ytalyen, spaynysshe, and grekysshe as in frensshe. 1545 Raynald *Byrth Mankynde* Prol. C viii, To speke dutche, frenche, spanissh, and dyuers other langages. *a* 1568 Ascham *Scholem.* ii. (Arb.) 147 Translating the Vlisses of Homer out of Greke into Spanish. 1623 Minsheu *Span. Gram.* Proem, Spanish is a speech, whereof in times past (in Spaine) there hath beene foure kinds vsed. 1642 Howell *For. Trav.* (Arb.) 39 The Spanish is nought else but mere Latine, take a few Morisco words away. 1706 Stevens *Sp. & Eng. Dict.* Pref., Neither can I allow Spanish to be as generally call'd a Corruption of Latin. 1797 *Encycl. Brit.* (ed. 3) XIV. 564/1 In Spanish, we have many old Gothic words. 1842 Borrow *Bible in Spain* iii, The magnificent tones of the Spanish sounded to great advantage amidst the shrill squeaking dialect of Portugal.

2. In various elliptical or absolute uses:

a. Spanish persons or people; Spaniards. † **b.** Spanish snuff, usually ***plain Spanish***. *Obs.* **c.** (*the*) ***Spanish***, hard cash, money. *slang.* **d.** Spanish bonds or stock.

a. 1660 F. Brooke tr. *Le Blanc's Trav.* 347 There is a large river.. which some Spanish were about to crosse. 1832 W. Irving in P. M. Irving *Life & Lett. Washington Irving* (1863) III. 43 The levee.. presents the most whimsical groups of people of all nations, castes, and colors—French, Spanish, half-breeds, [etc.]. 1880 *News & Press* (Cimarron, New Mexico) 24 June 2/2 The famous Pecos Church, built by the Spanish in 1680. 1932 [see moment *sb.* 1 d]. 1962 *Amer. Speech* XXXVII. 207 English speakers [in northern Colorado] refer to Spanish speakers as *Spanish.* The word *Spaniard* is not used.

b. 1681 Colvil *Whigs Supplic.* (1751) 119 Then hope triumphs, and fear doth vanish, Like grief, when it's expell'd by Spanish. 1698 Farquhar *Love & a Bottle* ii. ii. Wks. 1892 I. 35 The three divisions of his head were filled with orangery, bergamot, and plain Spanish. 1709 Steele *Tatler* No. 1 ¶3 Allowing him some Plain Spanish. 1748 Smollett *R. Random* xxxix, Her upper-lip contained a large quantity of plain Spanish.

c. 1788 Grose *Dict. Vulgar T.* (ed. 2), *Spanish*, the Spanish; ready money. 1806 Surr *Winter in Lond.* II. 122 He helps the flats out of their Spanish. 1811 *Sporting Mag.* XXXVII. 303 After extracting the Spanish from all his sporting acquaintance. *a* 1814 *Sailors' Ret.* ii. iii. in *New Brit. Theatre* II. 342, I wish you would rather give the hard Spanish. 1869 *Punch* 10 July 11/2.

d. 1841 Thackeray *Gt. Hoggarty Diamond* ii, The young stockbrokers used to tell us of immense bargains in Spanish, Greek, and Columbians.

C. *adv.* ***to walk Spanish***, to (cause to) walk under compulsion, properly with some one holding the collar and the seat of the trousers. *U.S.*

1848 Lowell *Biglow P.* Ser. i. No. ii, To.. walk him Spanish clean right out o' all his homes an' houses. 1890 *Voice* (N.Y.) 14 Aug., [They] were hustled out of the country on an hour's notice, made to 'walk Spanish' in fact.

Hence 'Spanishness, 'Spanishry, the quality of being Spanish; 'Spanishy *a.*, of a Spanish type or character.

1922 Joyce *Ulysses* 273 Big Spanishy eyes goggling at nothing. 1957 *American Anthropologist* LIX. 818 Spanish-speaking Venezuelans and 'Spanishy' local-born people. 1960 L. Durrell in *N.Y. Times Bk. Rev.* 12 June vii. 1/1 We travel really to try and get to grips with this mysterious quality of 'Greekness' or 'Spanishness'. 1963 *Times Lit. Suppl.* 17 May 356/5 This intense 'Spanishry' of Unamuno's.. may be a reason.. for his comparative neglect in this country. 1965 *Listener* 25 Nov. 873/2 In the company of the desolate *Gigues*, even Iberia takes on a less obvious Spanishry. 1977 V. S. Pritchett *Gentle Barbarian* iii. 41 Her Spanishness had its Islamic roots. 1979 B. Malamud *Dubin's Lives* vii. 228 She's been reading Spanish love poems... Her voice sounds Spanishy.

† '**Spanish**, *sb.*[2] *Obs. rare.* [Of obscure origin.] Earth or clay unfit for brick-making.

1725 *Act 12 Geo. I*, c. 35 Several Persons.. continue to make Bricks of bad Stuff and unsizeable Dimensions, and do not well burn the same; and in making thereof mix great Quantities of Soil called Spanish. *Ibid.*, No Spanish at any time.. shall be.. mixed with any Brick, Earth, or Clay.

† '**spanish**, *v.*[1] *Obs. rare.* Also **spannish, spanys.** [f. OF. *espaniss-*, lengthened stem of *espanir* (mod.F. *épanouir*) to expand, spread out.] *intr.* Of a flower: To expand or open. So † **spanished** *ppl. a.*, † **spanishing** *vbl. sb.*

c 1375 *Sc. Leg. Saints* xliii. (*Cecilia*) 138 Twa cronis mad wynnly of spanyst rose & quhyt lely. *c* 1400 *Rom. Rose* 3633, I saugh that thurgh the leves grene The rose spredde to spannishyng. *c* 1425 Wyntoun *Cron.* i. Prol. 127, I seke the sawowre of that ros That spanysys, spredys, and evyre spryngys In plesans of the Kyng of Kyngis.

† '**spanish**, *v.*[2] *Obs.*$^{-1}$ [Spanish *sb.*[2]] *trans.* ? To mix (brick-earth) with other material.

1714 *Lond. Gaz.* No. 5209/4 Together with two Stools of Brick-Earth ready dug and spanished.

Spanish broom. [SPANISH *a.* 9.] The plant *Spartium junceum* (or *Cytisus junceus*), common to the Mediterranean region, the rush-like branches or twigs of which are used in basket-work and yield a fibre employed in the manufacture of cords, coarse cloth, etc.

The resemblance of the generic name *Spartium* to L. *spartum* (see SPART^{1}), and misunderstanding of passages in Pliny, has led to occasional confusion between Spanish broom and esparto grass.

1562 TURNER *Herbal* II. 144 The sede and floures of Spanish brome are good to be dronken wyth mede..to pourge strongly. **1676** GREW *Anat. Flowers* II. ii. §8 Spanish Broome, Dulcamara, and others. **1731** MILLER *Gard. Dict.* s.v. *Spartium*, The white Spanish Broom. **1785** MARTYN *Lett. Elem. Bot.* xxv. (1794) 350 Spanish Broom, with some other species, has simple leaves. **1861** BENTLEY *Man. Bot.* 527 *Sarothamnus* (*Cytisus*) *scoparius*, is the common Broom. .. *Sarothamnus junceus*, the Spanish Broom, has similar properties. **1882** *Garden* 29 Apr. 297/1 Pale sulphur-coloured Spanish Broom.

Spanished, *ppl. a.* [f. SPANISH *a.*] (See quot.)

1815 *Zeluca* I. 140 'How do you name Miss Delvayne's vestment, or whatever I ought to stile it?' asked he... 'Why the milinery people..call it Spanished—and are indebted to Wellington for disposing of an expensive dress to almost everybody.'

Spanisher ('spænɪʃə(r)). *colloq. rare.* [f. SPANISH *a.* + -ER^{1}.] A Spaniard.

1910 KIPLING *Rewards & Fairies* 293 The Spanishers had shut down all their Dutch ports against us English. **1940** [see AIM *v.* 5 b].

†'**Spanishify,** *v. Obs. rare*$^{-1}$. [f. SPANISH *a.*] *trans.* To make Spanish; to Spaniolize.

1612 in Birch *Crt. & Times Jas. I* (1848) I. 214 Mr. Rossingham came some three weeks since out of Spain, so Spanishified, that I scant knew him till he saluted me.

Spanishly ('spænɪʃlɪ), *adv.* [f. SPANISH *a.* + -LY^{2}.] Towards Spain or Spanish policy; like Spanish; in a characteristically Spanish manner.

a **1641** FINETT *For. Embass.* (1656) 65 He desired that (if the place were so equall, as some Spanishly inclined pretended) he might have the first choyce. **1717** DE FOE *Mem. Ch. Scot.* II. 128 To excommunicate the Popish and Spanishly affected Nobility, so they then called them. **1882** STEVENSON *Merry Men* i. in *Cornh. Mag.* XLV. 679 The name..of the ship..sounded, in my ears, Spanishly. The Espirito Santo they called it. **1907** *Westm. Gaz.* 3 June 2/1 Its cathedral rising solemnly, Spanishly, greyly above all else.

spank (spæŋk), *sb.*^{1} *dial.* or *colloq.* [f. SPANK *v.*^{1}]

1. A smart or sounding blow, esp. one given with the open hand; a slap or smack.

1785 GROSE *Dict. Vulgar T.*, *Spanks*,..blows with the open hand. **1812** H. & J. SMITH *Horace in Lond.* 140 When ice encrusts the slippery bank, The tallest fall with heaviest spank. **1858** HUGHES *Scour. White Horse* iv. 78 Said Joe, giving me a great spank on the back. **1889** *Cent. Mag.* Mar. 743/1 My mother..lifted me cleverly, planted two spanks behind, and passed me to the hands of Mme. Levicq.

b. The sharp noise or sound produced by this.

1833 M. SCOTT *Tom Cringle* xix, [The snake] let the smaller [tree] go with a loud spank that shook the dew off the neighbouring branches. **1860** O. W. HOLMES *Prof. Breakf.-t.* iii. 64 A clean, straight, hard hit which took effect with a spank like the explosion of a percussion cap.

†**2.** *Cant.* (See SPANK *v.*^{1} 2.) *Obs.*

spank (spæŋk), *sb.*^{2} [f. SPANK *v.*^{2}]

a. The action or fact of spanking or moving along rapidly and sharply.

1801 tr. *Gabrielli's Myst. Husb.* III. 286 Having got her between me and Madame we dashed off full spank.

b. A quick or smart bound or leap.

1882 in *Jamieson's Sc. Dict.* **1886** B. BRIERLEY *Cast upon World* i. 10 A spank..that seemed to have the lithesomeness of a deerhound.

†**spank,** *sb.*^{3} *Cant. Obs.*$^{-0}$ = SPANKER^{1} 1.

1725 *New Cant. Dict.*, *Spanks*, Money, Gold or Silver.

spank (spæŋk), *v.*^{1} *dial.* or *colloq.* [Probably imitative of the sound.]

1. a. *trans.* To slap or smack (a person, esp. a child) with the open hand. Also *absol.*

1727 BAILEY (vol. II), *To Spank*, to slap with the open Hand. **1786** *European Mag.* IX. 292 The Science of Nothing even dunces have taught, Without spanking a pupil, or spending a thought. **1862** F. W. ROBINSON *Owen, a Waif* I. 82 'You're sorry for your mother.'.. 'I think so.., but she spanked hard.' **1867** *Lond. Rev.* 15 June 673/1 This baby.. as a last resource is spanked into a voiceless rage by the mother. **1872** DE VERE *Americanisms* 321 If the sufferer be a child, it is *spanked*, that is, punished by slapping with the open hand.

fig. **1882** *Punch* 11 Mar. 112 House of Lords spanked by 300 against 167.

b. To crack (a whip). *rare*$^{-1}$.

1834 M. SCOTT *Cruise Midge* (1859) 417 The mule drivers ..were stringing into the yard and spanking their whips.

c. To bring down, thrust, etc., with a slap.

1880 TENNYSON *Northern Cobbler* xv, An' 'e spanks 'is 'and into mine.

d. *N.Z. colloq.* To milk (a cow).

1897 I. SCOTT *How I stole 10,000 Sheep* ii. 8 We got on pretty well and spanked, *i.e.* milked, his cows for him night and morning. **1948** D. W. BALLANTYNE *Cunninghams* II. ix. 199 They spanked cows and built fences.

†**2.** *Cant.* (See quot.) *Obs.*

1812 J. H. VAUX *Flash Dict.* s.v., To *spank a glaze*, is to break a pane of glass in a shop window, and make a sudden snatch at some article of value within your reach. *Ibid.*, To *spank* a place is to rob it 'upon the spank'; a *spank* is a robbery effected by the above means.

3. *intr.* **a.** To drop or fall with a spank or smack.

1800 HURDIS *Fav. Village* 61 The sullen shower from the drench'd eaves Drips fast, and on the..pavement spanks.

b. Of a boat: To pound, beat, or slap the water in sailing.

1891 *Cent. Dict.* (citing J. A. Henshall).

4. The vbl. stem used adverbially: With a spank or smack. *rare*$^{-1}$.

1810 *Splendid Follies* III. 8 Spank flew another revoke card from the hand of Samuelina.

Hence **spanked** (spæŋkt) *ppl. a.*

1864 *Daily Tel.* 27 Sept., That back-yards should re-echo to the howling of spanked children.

spank (spæŋk), *v.*^{2} *dial.* and *colloq.* [prob. a back-formation from SPANKING *ppl. a.* 2.]

1. *intr.* To move or travel with speed and elasticity; to go quickly and vigorously; to ride or drive at a sharp trot and in a smart or stylish manner. Usually const. with adverbs or preps., esp. with *along*: **a.** Of animals, in general use.

1807–10 TANNAHILL *Poems* (1846) 20, I saw the dragon spankin o'er the fiels. **1808–** in numerous dial. glossaries and texts (Sc., E. Angl., Northants., Warw., Som., etc.). *a* **1825** FORBY *Voc. E. Anglia* s.v., How he did spank along. **1886** C. SCOTT *Sheep-farming* 200 His dog darts off like a greyhound. We watch him spanking across the glen. **1902** *Daily Chron.* 13 Nov. 8/5 Reynard..came away right-handed and spanked along for Kenwick-park.

b. *spec.* Of horses, or of persons driving or riding these. Also with *it*.

1811 *Lexicon-Balatronicum*, *Spank* (*Whip*). To run neatly along, between a trot and gallop. **1824** SCOTT *St. Ronan's* viii, 'I suppose so, sir,' said the groom... 'Zounds! she can spank it over wet and dry.' **1843** LE FEVRE *Life Trav. Phys.* II. I. xiv. 36 At this season they [the roads] were good, so that we spanked along merrily. **1860** THACKERAY *Lovel* iii, A gentleman in a natty gig, with a high-trotting horse, came spanking towards us.

c. Of ships: To sail quickly and smartly; to bowl *along*.

1834 H. MILLER *Scenes & Leg.* xiii. (1857) 195, I found myself aboard Robinson's lugger, spanking down the frith. **1841** CAPT. B. HALL *Patchwork* II. xiii. 251 When..we did get to sea..we spanked along. **1894** CROCKETT *Raiders* x. (ed. 3) 93 The Ariel was at that moment spanking away to the south'ard.

2. *trans.* To drive (horses) quickly and smartly.

1825 C. WESTMACOTT *Eng. Spy* I. 205 Where Gwydin spanks his fours along. **1840** THACKERAY *Shabby-genteel Story* v, How knowingly did he spank the horses along.

spanker^{1} ('spæŋkə(r)). [Related to SPANKING *ppl. a.* or (in later use) f. SPANK *v.*^{2}]

†**1.** *slang.* A gold coin; usually in *pl.*, coin, money. *Obs.*

1663 COWLEY *Cutter Coleman St.* II. v, Mean time, thou pretty little Smith o' my good fortune, beat hard upon the Anvil of your Plot, I'l go and provide the Spankers. *a* **1668** DENHAM *Dialogue* Poems (1771) 77 Your cure too costs you but a spanker. *a* **1680** BUTLER *Rem.* (1759) I. 269 Tho' he can produce more Spankers Than all the Usurers and Bankers. **1708** MOTTEUX *Rabelais, Pant. Progn.* vi, Old Gold, such as your Double Ducats, Rose-Nobles, Angels, Spankers, Spur-Royals. **1760** FOOTE *Minor* II. Wks. 1799 I. 250 Procure you the spankers, my boy. I have a broker, that.. shall take off your bargain. **1785** in GROSE.

2. a. *dial.* and *colloq.* Anything exceptionally large or fine; a person, animal, or thing of superior quality or character.

1751 SMOLLETT *Per. Pic.* xcv, To turn me adrift in the dark with such a spanker. **1838** W. H. MAXWELL *Stories Waterloo* I. 208 Miss O'Brien was what Rattigan called *a spanker*. **1844** DICKENS *Mart. Chuz.* xvi, Her passage either way, is almost certain to eventuate a spanker! **1865** —— *Mut. Fr.* I. xv, Your new establishment:..it's to be a spanker. **1888** W. ROGERS *Mem. West* ii. 32 [We] are soon rewarded by a brace or so of spankers [*sc.* fish], whose appearance in our basket [etc.].

b. A heavy blow or smack.

1772 BRIDGES *Burlesque Homer* 491 (Farmer), Ajax gave him two such spankers, They smarted worse than nodes and shankers. **1894** MEREDITH *Ld. Ormont* i, Matey's sure aim.. relieving J. Masner of a foremost assailant with a spanker on the nob.

3. *Naut.* **a.** A fore-and-aft sail, set with a gaff and boom at the aftermost part of the ship. Cf. also DRIVER 5 and MIZEN 1.

1794 *Rigging & Seamanship* 162 The Driver-boom, on which the foot of the driver, or spanker, is extended. **1804** *Log 'Victory'* 15 June in Nicolas *Disp. Nelson* (1846) VI. 72 Wore and set the mainsail and spanker. **1840** R. H. DANA *Bef. Mast* xxv, There was no sail now on the ship but the spanker and the close-reefed main topsail. **1894** CLARK RUSSELL *Good Ship Mohock* I. 55 He..told the officer..to brail up the spanker.

attrib. **1794** *Rigging & Seamanship* 217 The Driver or Spanker Sail is bent as a temporary matter. **1840** R. H. DANA *Bef. Mast* xxiii, One boy at the spanker-sheet and guy. **1840** F. D. BENNETT *Whaling Voy.* II. 66 A frigate bird alighted on the spanker-gaff. **1894** C. N. ROBINSON *Brit. Fleet* 251 The last decade of the last century, when the spanker-gaff and boom came in.

b. In full ***spanker mast***. The fourth (or fifth) mast of a ship with four or more masts.

1853 D. MCLEAN *Great Republic* 17 The ship has 4 masts, the after one named the spanker mast. **1892** *Nautical Mag.* June 546 During the first four years of the four-posters, the 'after mizzen' and 'spanker mast' were sometimes heard of. **1902** [see PUSHER 2 b]. **1946** *Amer. Neptune* VI. 138/1 Mr. Bush called the fourth mast the 'jigger' and the fifth the 'spanker', the reverse of the usual nomenclature. **1970** H. CHEVALIER *Last Voyage of Rosamond* 37 We soon not only learned the names of the four masts—the foremast, the mainmast, the mizzen and the spanker.

4. *dial.* (See quots.)

1808 JAMIESON, *Spanker*, one who walks in a quick and elastic way. **1811** WILLAN in *Archaeologia* XVII. 159 *Spanker*, a tall, and active young person. *a* **1825** FORBY *Voc. E. Anglia*, *Spanker*, a person who takes long steps with agility.

5. *dial.* and *colloq.* A horse which travels quickly and smartly; a fast-going horse.

1814 SCOTT *Wav.* xxxix, And ye wanted a spanker that would lead the field,..I would serve ye easy. **1836** HALIBURTON *Clockm.* I. xix, That are horse goes etarnal fast. .. He's a spanker you may depend. **1870** THORNBURY *Tour rd. Eng.* I. ii. 31 The spankers strike out and away they do go ..from Hounslow to Staines.

6. *U.S.* A light cart suitable for rapid travelling.

1831 in A. E. Lee *Hist. Columbus* (1892) I. 318 Our vehicle, which in the dialect of the country was called a spanker, was intended for four persons.

'**spanker**^{2}. [f. SPANK *v.*^{1}] One who, or that which, spanks or slaps.

1892 *Newcastle Daily Jrnl.* 1 Jan. 8/3 A wonderful invention to serve three purposes—a self-rocking cradle, a clothes wringer, and a baby spanker.' **1931** K. BOYLE *Plagued by Nightingale* iv. 28 Washer-women bending over the stream..and with wooden spankers beating the life out of dish-cloths.

'**spanker-boom.** *Naut.* [SPANKER^{1} 3.] The boom on which the spanker is set.

1813 *Examiner* 26 Apr. 261/2 Spanker-boom, gaff, and trysail-mast. **1834** MARRYAT *P. Simple* (1863) 244 Perch yourself upon the spanker-boom, and let me know when you've rode to London. **1854** MISS C. L. BALFOUR *Working Women* 155 The next minute the spanker boom, an immense piece of timber, snapped like a reed.

attrib. **1849** CUPPLES *Green Hand* vii. (1856) 70 Men.. hauling on the spanker-boom guys. **1891** C. ROBERTS *Adrift Amer.* 231, I crawled right aft to the taffrail, and quietly put the end of the spanker boom sheet over.

spanker-eel. *north. dial.* The lamprey.

1846 in BROCKETT (ed. 3). **1883** DAY *Fishes Gt. Brit.* II. 360 Lampern,..cunning, and spanker-eel, Northumberland.

'**spankily,** *adv. rare*$^{-1}$. [f. SPANK *sb.*^{2} or *v.*^{2}] Spankingly.

1842 *Tait's Mag.* IX. 370 We soon arrived spankily at the open hall door.

spanking ('spæŋkɪŋ), *vbl. sb.* [f. SPANK *v.*^{1}] The action of beating or slapping with the open hand by way of punishment. Also *fig.*

1854 MISS BAKER *Northampt. Gloss.* **1859** *Slang Dict.* 98 *Spanking*, a good beating. **1868** in *Sat. Rev.* (1869) 30 Jan., I gave her what some American friends call 'a spanking', sharp, short and effectual. **1885** SALA *Let.* in *Queen* 26 Sept. 307/3 The American lady doctor..suggested 'spanking' all round as a cure for the evil.

attrib. **1899** *Westm. Gaz.* 1 June 5/3 The Warden of Denver Penitentiary has introduced a 'spanking chair' into the list of punishments permitted in the State prison.

fig. **1922** H. CRANE *Let.* 25 Feb. (1965) 80 Your translations amuse me without interesting me as thoroughly as your nicely administered spanking of McAlmon. **1978** *Times Lit. Suppl.* 1 Dec. 1393/1 A. A. Milne's Winnie-the-Pooh stories receive a monstrous spanking for their promotion of snobbery and imperialist values.

spanking ('spæŋkɪŋ), *ppl. a.* Chiefly *dial.* and *colloq.* [Of doubtful origin. Cf. Da. (and NFris.) *spanke* to strut.]

1. Very big, large, or fine; exceptionally good in some respect, freq. with implication of showiness or smartness.

a **1666** FANSHAWE *Love for Love's sake* II. (1671) 64 What a spanking Labradora! **1706** PHILLIPS (ed. Kersey), *Spanking*, spruce, fine, jolly; as *A spanking Lass.* **1772** BRIDGES *Burlesque Homer* 501 (Farmer), A table..Whereon she placed a spanking dish. **1780** in W. Beckford *Italy* (1834) I. 16 The worthy dignitary..enjoys a spanking revenue. **1791** O'KEEFFE *Wild Oats* IV. i, Now for a spanking lie, to continue her in the belief that Jack is the man she thinks him. **1837** MISS MITFORD *Country Stories* (1850) 118 We must see what can be done for that boy—he's a fine spanking fellow. **1842** LOVER *Handy Andy* iv. 40 We'll have some spanking sport.

2. a. Of horses; *esp.* in later use: Moving or travelling at a rapid pace and in a smart and vigorous manner. (Cf. SPANK *v.*^{2} 1 b.)

1738 BRACKEN *Farriery Impr.* (1756) II. 167 He goes by the Name of Spanking Roger. **1802** COLMAN *Poor Gentleman* IV. i, There are four spanking greys..here, that shall whisk us to town in a minute. **1863** SALA *About Shrimpington* 110 As the 'spanking tits', which..were on this occasion more 'spanked' themselves than 'spanking', clattered along. **1897** W. H. THORNTON *Remin. of West-Co. Clergym.* iii. 96 We had a spanking sixteen-hands-high mare in a dogcart.

b. Of persons: Dashing, lively, boisterous.

1801 MAR. EDGEWORTH *Mlle. Panache* II. Wks. 1832 III. 254 This spanking horsewoman has frightened us all out of our senses.

3. Of a breeze: Blowing strongly or briskly; rattling.

1849 CUPPLES *Green Hand* ii. (1856) 23 They..struck up the 'Buffalo', that finest of chants for the weather forecastle with a spanking breeze. **1862** *Lond. Rev.* 16 Aug. 139 We are rushing through the water with a spanking breeze on our quarter. **1888** *Boston* (Mass.) *Jrnl.* 14 Aug. 1/2 Spanking Breeze for the Yachts.

4. Of a pace, rate, etc.: Rapid, smart, vigorous.

1857 HUGHES *Tom Brown* I. v, The wheelers in a spanking trot, and leaders cantering. **1882** SERGT. BALLANTINE *Exper.* xxiii. 230 We went at a spanking pace until suddenly brought to a stand-still. **1899** F. T. BULLEN *Log Sea-waif* 39 A large canoe..was coming off to us at a spanking rate.
fig. **1858** BAILEY *Age* 61 He lives at what folks call a spanking rate.

5. Used as *adv.* Very, exceedingly; esp. as ***spanking new***, brand-new. Cf. SPAN-NEW *a. colloq.*

1886 H. BAUMANN *Londinismen* 188/2 A spanking fine dinner. **1905** *Dial. Notes* III. 71 *Bran spankin' new*,.. absolutely new. **1925** F. SCOTT FITZGERALD *Great Gatsby* i. 6 The [house]..on my right was a colossal affair..spanking new under a thin beard of raw ivy. **1959** *Weekly Times* (Melbourne) 30 Sept. 1 (Advt.), Imagine that great day.. when you take delivery of your new working partner: a spanking new Ferguson 35. **1972** *Newsweek* 10 Jan. 34/2 The spanking new city of Brasília was carved painfully out of the wilderness. **1977** *Time* 19 Dec. 12/1 The spanking-white train chugged into Reading station. **1979** *Radio Times* 5–11 May 4/1 Luxurious surroundings at Lewisham's spanking new leisure centre. **1979** W. STYRON *Sophie's Choice* vii. 164 On the driveway there now rested a spanking clean and polished Cadillac sedan.

Hence **ˈspankingly** *adv.*, at a spanking pace; in a rapid and smart manner.

1803 COUPER *Tourifications* II. 16 A country lad, mounted on a spirited pretty galloway, came spankingly along. **1830** *Fraser's Mag.* II. 439 The time put on his seven-leagued boots, and went spankingly away so rapidly that [etc.]. **1866** *Lond. Rev.* 23 June 697/1 You are told how his reverence rode spankingly to church.

† **ˈspankled** *ppl. a.*, var. of SPANGLED *ppl. a.*

1703 *Lond. Gaz.* No. 3945/4 Stolen.., a sorrel Strawberry Mare..with a bald Face,..and spankled about the Jaws. **1777** MME. D'ARBLAY *Early Diary* 7 Apr., She had on a lilac negligée, gauze cuffs, trimmed richly with flowers and spangles, spankled shoes [etc.]. **1866** G. M. HOPKINS *Jrnls. & Papers* (1959) 143 Carnations..have their tongue-shaped petals powdered with spankled red glister.

† **spank span-new**, *adj. phr. Obs.*$^{-1}$ [Intensified form of SPAN-NEW. Cf. Sc. and north. dial. *spang-new, spanker-new.*] Perfectly new.

1775 S. J. PRATT *Liberal Opin.* lix. (1783) II. 189, I took out a spank span new half-crown piece.

spanless (ˈspænlɪs), *a.* [f. SPAN *v.*[1]] That cannot be spanned.

1847 TENNYSON *Princ.* VI. 20 The little seed..Has risen and cleft the soil, and grown a bulk Of spanless girth.

span-long, *a.* [f. SPAN *sb.*[1] + LONG *a.*] Having the length of a span; hence, brief, short.

1593 NASHE *Christ's T.* Wks. (Grosart) IV. 214 Though our span long youthly prime, blossomes foorth eye-banquetting flowers,..yet in the graue shall we rotte. **1637** B. JONSON *Sad Shepherd* II. ii, There..white faies do dwell, And span-long elves that dance about a pool. **1790** BURNS *Tam o' Shanter* 132 Twa span-lang, wee, unchristen'd bairns. **1878** BROWNING *Poets Croisic* 4 While—never mind who..—Sank stifled span-long brightness in the birth.
Comb. **1654** WHITLOCK *Zootomia* 283 In the apprehension of us Momentanean Ephemeri, and span-long-lived Accountants.

spanned (spænd), *ppl. a.* [f. SPAN *v.*[1] and *v.*[2]] That is or has been spanned or drawn tight.

1597 A. M. tr. *Guillemeau's Fr. Chirurg.* 24/1 The tunge being hindred by a certayne ligament which we call the spanned vayne. **1741** RICHARDSON *Pamela* I. Introd. p. xxvi, He made a too tight-laced Objection, where he quarrels with the spann'd Waist of Pamela.

spanned (spænd), *a. Biol.* [f. SPAN *sb.*[1] + -ED[2].] Of a culture of cells or micro-organisms: having a restricted lifespan; unable to propagate asexually without limit.

1968 *Exper. Cell Res.* XLIX. 116 To produce 'spanned' amoebae the nutritional state of amoebae must be altered for a protracted period. **1971** J. Z. YOUNG *Introd. Study Man* xxii. 293 Transfer of a normal nucleus into spanned cytoplasm produced resumed logarithmic growth, and a spanned nucleus in normal cytoplasm produced the spanned condition. **1973** *Nature* 22 June 444/1 The switch from a 'spanned' culture to one that is 'immortal' does not necessarily signify a qualitative change in other cellular properties.

† **spannel.** *Obs.*$^{-1}$ [f. OE. *spann-an* to fasten + -EL[1].] A spancel.

1398 TREVISA *Barth. De P.R.* XVIII. xiv. (Bodl. MS.), An oxe heerde..bindeþ here feete with lange holdeþ [1495 langhaldes] and spannels.

spannel(l, obs. forms of SPANIEL *sb.*[1]

spanner[1] (ˈspænə(r)). [ad. G. *spanner* (also *spänner*, Sw. *spännare*), f. *spannen* SPAN *v.*[2]]

† **1.** An instrument by which the spring in a wheel-lock firearm was spanned or wound up. *Obs.*

Phillips (ed. Kersey, 1706) has '*Spanner*, the Cock of a Carbine or Fusee'; hence in later Dicts., as Bailey (1721), Johnson (1755), with 'Lock' in place of 'Cock'.

1639 R. WARD *Animadv. Warre* I. 293 A case of good Firelocke Pistolles,..with his Spanner and flaske boxes. **1644** HOWELL *England's Tears for Pres. Wars* in *Dodona's Grove* 169 My Prince his Court is now full of nothing but Buff-Coats, Spanners, and Musket Rests. **1688** HOLME *Armoury* III. xx. (Roxb.) 243/2 The second is called a Spanner; it is a thing made of Iron, haueing a square hole in the bending part of it, by which the springs of wheele locks are wound vp. [**1863** W. THORNBURY *True as Steel* II. 29 He then took the spanner..and bent the spring which communicated with the axis-pin of his wheel-lock.]

2. a. A hand-tool, usually consisting of a small bar of steel, having an opening, grip, or jaw at the end which fits over or clasps the nut of a screw, a bolt, coupling, etc., and turns it or holds it in position; a wrench.

There are several makes of spanner, and they vary greatly in shape and size, some having one opening, others two; some taking one size of nut, etc., others being adjustable to nuts of different sizes.

1790 W. H. MARSHALL *Rur. Econ. Midl.* II. 443 *Spanner*, a wrench; a nut screw-driver. **1831** J. HOLLAND *Manuf. Metal* I. 215 A screw attached to a spanner or lever. **1858** GREENER *Gunnery* 101 Wood carriage complete, with wrought iron screw and spanner for elevating mortar. **1888** RUTLEY *Rock-forming Min.* 22 A nut which screws on to the end of the spindle and is tightened up by means of a spanner.
attrib. and *Comb.* **1830** G. R. AINSLIE *Anglo-French Coinage* 66 Two spanner-like towers. **1902** MARSHALL *Metal Tools* 69 The small worm shown in the spanner head.

b. Colloq. phr. ***to throw a spanner in the works*** and varr.: to cause disruption, to interfere with the smooth running of something. Cf. *monkey-wrench* s.v. MONKEY *sb.* 18 a.

1934 WODEHOUSE *Right Ho, Jeeves* xi. 142 He should have had sense enough to see that he was throwing a spanner into the works. **1939** A. RANSOME *Secret Water* i. 18 We can't go. It's all off. The First Lord's chucked a spanner in the works. **1946** D. L. SAYERS *Unpopular Opinions* 111 She was in love with Leicester—why didn't she marry him? Well, for the very same reason that numberless kings have not married their lovers—because it would have thrown a spanner into the wheels of the State machine. **1959** *News Chron.* 10 July 4/1 Mr. Cousins has thrown a spanner into the Labour Party's works. **1960** R. EAST *Kingston Black* ix. 90 My department might be able to throw a spanner into the works—if necessary. **1977** *Time Out* 17–23 June 5/4 Either way, the 60 workers occupying the factory have put a spanner in the works.

3. *Mech.* **a.** A bar or lever for opening the valves of a steam-engine (see quots.).

1773 W. EMERSON *Mechanics* (ed. 3) 230 The horizontal piece *h* 3, called the spanner; so that moving *h* back and forward, moves the plate 45 over the hole 2, and back again. **1824** STUART *Hist. Steam Engine* 175 Two valves, which are moved alternately by levers acted on on the outside from the revolution of a spanner or lever attached to the hollow axle. **1869** RANKINE *Machine & Hand-tools* Pl. F 1. 2 Lower down on this spindle..is keyed a duplex spanner or rocking lever 1, one end of which is attached..to the valve rod of the small engine.

b. In a parallel-motion steam-engine (see quots.).

1846 A. YOUNG *Naut. Dict.* 306 The lever *e* is called the Spanner or Lever of Parallel Motion. **1867** SMYTH *Sailor's Word-bk.* 640 *Spanner*, an important balance in forming the radius of parallel motion in a steam-engine, since it reconciles the curved sweep which the side levers describe with the perpendicular movement of the piston-rod, by means of which they are driven.

4. *attrib.* and *Comb.*, as **spanner tight** *a.*, of a nut: as tight as can be secured manually with a spanner; **spanner wrench** *U.S.*, a non-adjustable spanner.

1925 *Morris Owner's Man.* 53 The nuts should always be kept (small) spanner tight. **1931** *Daily Express* 31 Jan. 3/6 Even where the nut was absolutely spanner tight. **1940** *Sun* (Baltimore) 30 Mar. 20/1 The fuel door..was bolted closed the night before the ship sank, but was found open with a spanner wrench beside it when salvagers examined the sunken vessel. **1969** *Publ. Amer. Dial Soc.* LII. 35 *Spanner wrench*,..a wrench having a fixed distance between its jaws which fits on the hose couplings and is used to tighten or loosen connections.

† **spanner**[2]. *Obs.* (Origin and meaning obscure.)

1653 (*title*), The Total Rout, or a Brief Discovery Of a Pack of Knaves and Drabs, intituled Pimps, Panders, Hectors, Trapans, Nappers, Mobs, and Spanners.

ˈspanner[3]. *rare.* [f. SPAN *v.*[1]] A rib forming part of a roof-span.

1862 *Macm. Mag.* Apr. 527/2 A spanner like the rib of a groined roof springs from each to unite with its antagonist from the other side of the roof-ridge;..similar, but smaller, spanners perform the same office for the aisle roofs.

spanners (ˈspænəz), *sb. pl.* Chiefly *dial.* [Pl. of *spanner*, f. SPAN *sb.*[1] or *v.*[1] + -ER[1]: cf. SPANNER[3].] A game of marbles (see quot. 1881). Also **ˈspannims.**

1847 J. O. HALLIWELL *Dict. Archaic & Provinc. Words* II. 779/1 *Spannims*, a game at marbles played in the eastern parts of England. **1881** *Cassell's Bk. Sports & Pastimes* 250 Spanners. This is a good simple game for two players. Player No. 1 shoots off his taw, player No. 2 following suit, it being his object either to hit his opponent's taw with his own, or to place his own within a span of it. **1903** *J. Strutt's Sports & Pastimes of People of England* (new ed.) IV. iv. 304 The following is a list of the present (1902) best known marble games:—Bounce About,..Handers,..Pyramid,.. Spanners. **1948** J. L. BAILES *Vocab. Marbles* in *Trans. Yorks. Dial. Soc.* VIII. 23 *Spannims*, sb., E. Ang., the game of hundreds.

span-new (ˈspænnjuː), *a.* Now chiefly *dial.* Also **span new.** [ad. ON. *spán-nýr*, f. *spán-n* chip + *ný-r* new, with normal shortening of the first element. Cf. SPON-NEW *a.*

Dial. variants are *spander-* (*spanther-*), *spanker-*, *spang-new*. See also *bran-span-new* BRAND-NEW; SPANK SPAN-NEW; and SPICK AND SPAN.]

Quite or perfectly new: **a.** Of things, esp. clothes.

c **1300** *Havelok* 968 þe cok bigan of him to rewe, and bouthe him cloþes, al spannewe. **13..** *K. Alis.* 4055 (Laud MS.), Richelich he dooþ hym shrede In span newe kniȝtten wede. *c* **1374** CHAUCER *Troylus* III. 1665 This tale was ay span new to byginne Til at the nyght departed hem atwynne. **1463–4** SIR J. HOWARD *Expenses* in *Manners & Househ. Exp.* (Roxb.) 160 A new jakett off purpylle that was made ffor my mastyr..and itt is spanne new. **1579** G. HARVEY *Letter-bk.* (Camden) 59 Let me borrowe on crackd groate of your purse for this same span new pamflett. **1598** MARSTON *Sco. Villanie* III. xi. 229 The news he tels you, is of some newe flesh, Lately brooke vp, span newe, hote piping fresh. **1626** in Birch *Crt. & Times Chas. I* (1848) I. 158, I have lighted upon a span new proclamation, which I send you in time. **1655** FULLER *Ch. Hist.* II. 60 Therefore [he] would not wear an Old Title, but have a span-New Arch-Bishops Chaire carved out for himself. **1691** RAY *S. & E. Co. Words* 114 *Span New*, very new: that was never worn or used. **1822** COBBETT *Weekly Reg.* 2 Feb. 260 A maker of span-new governments and religions. **1849** CUPPLES *Green Hand* i. (1856) 6 Up the side he scrambles,..all togged out to the nines in a span-new blue jacket. **1879** A. TAYLOR *Guienne* 55 The span-new..nineteenth century miracle.

b. Of persons, etc. Also *Comb.*

1598 MARSTON *Sco. Villanie* Prol., Some spruce pedant, or some Span-new come fry Of Innes a-court. **1619** FLETCHER & MASS. *False One* III. ii, Am I not totally a span-new Gallant, Fit for the choycest eyes? **1648** *Petit. Eastern Assoc.* 24 Such..conditions, as their pride, and span-new Gentries will not indure. **1846** D. JERROLD *Chron. Clovernook* Wks. 1864 IV. 409 Most of the children, however, lost by degrees the errors and weaknesses of their former days, and in time became span-new creatures.

ˈspanning, *vbl. sb.*[1] [f. SPAN *v.*[1]] The action of measuring, bridging, etc., with a span.

1775 ASH *Suppl.*, *Spanning*, the act of measuring with a finger and thumb. **1883** *Athenæum* 24 Nov. 662/3 Increasing skill in the spanning of wide roofs. **1909** *Q. Rev.* Apr. 344 The chasm yawned unspanned... A price..had to be paid for its spanning.

ˈspanning, *vbl. sb.*[2] [f. SPAN *v.*[2]]

† **1.** The action of drawing tight, making close, etc.; the result of this. *Obs.*

1527 ANDREW *Brunswyke's Distyll. Waters* L ij, The same water..is good agaynst the spannyng of the harte. **1592** *Shuttleworths' Acc.* (Chetham Soc.) 74 Houpinge and spannynge of the vesseles, xij^{d}; the porteres for loding the same wyne, vj^{d}. **1597** A. M. tr. *Guillemeau's Fr. Chirurg.* 21 b/2 These swellings cause noe payne, vnles it weare great spanninge of that parte might chaunce.

2. The action of fastening, harnessing, or yoking. Also with *on.*

1874 A. H. MARKHAM *Whaling Cruise Baffin's B.* 25 All hands have been as busy as bees, employed in the operation of *spanning on*, which literally means attaching the lines to the harpoons. **1882** SCHAFF *Encycl. Relig. Knowl.* I. 87 Ritualistic..considerations forbade the spanning of different species of animals.

ˈspanning, *ppl. a.* [f. SPAN *v.*[1]]

1. Extending or crossing as a span.

1823 P. NICHOLSON *Pract. Build.* 122 The rafters were the sides of an equilateral triangle, of which the spanning line was the base. **1825** J. NICHOLSON *Operat. Mechanic* 539 The height, or rise of the arch, is a line drawn at right angles from the middle of the chord, or spanning line, to the intrados. **1881** W. R. W. STEPHENS *Selsey-Chichester* 155 Broad spanning arches, and high massive towers. **1889** C. C. R. *Up for Season* 269 Where..you can gaze far away On the wide-spanning bridge.

2. *Math.* Of a subgraph, esp. one that is a tree: that includes and connects every vertex of a graph.

1956 *Proc. Amer. Math. Soc.* VII. 49 The set of edges eventually chosen must form a spanning tree of *G*, and in fact it forms a shortest spanning tree. **1965** BUSACKER & SAATY *Finite Graphs & Networks* i. 20 A spanning tree is a maximal subgraph of a connected graph which contains no circuits and is a minimal subgraph which joins all vertices. **1972** R. J. WILSON *Introd. Graph Theory* iv. 46 Given any connected graph *G*, we can choose a circuit and remove one of its edges, the resulting graph remaining connected... We repeat this procedure with one of the remaining circuits, continuing until there are no circuits left. The graph which remains will be a tree which connects all the vertices of *G*; it is called a spanning tree of *G*... More generally, if *G* now denotes an arbitrary graph with..*k* components, we can carry out the above procedure on each component of *G*, the result being called a spanning forest (or skeleton).

spanniolize, variant of SPANIELIZE *v.*

span-roof (ˈspænruːf). [SPAN *sb.*[1]] A roof consisting of two inclined sides.

1823 P. NICHOLSON *Pract. Build.* 593. **1881** YOUNG *Every Man his own Mech.* § 1304 When a building..has been made with a span-roof, sloping on both sides. **1901** *J. Black's Carp. & Build.* 22 If the structure be independent or stand alone a 'span' roof (fig. 7) will be needed.
attrib. **1851** *B'ham & Midl. Gardeners' Mag.* May 65 A span-roof pit is the most suitable for this purpose. **1881** BLACKMORE *Christowell* i, It was a long, low, span-roof house. *Ibid.* vii, His span-roof forcing-house.

Hence **ˈspan-roofed** *a.*, having a span-roof.

1836 Parker *Gloss. Archit.* (1850) I. 432 The body of a church is span-roofed and its aisles shed-roofed. **1842** Loudon *Suburban Hort.* 611 They may also be grown as standards in a span-roofed house. **1860** T. Rivers *Orchard House* 20 A span-roofed orchard house, 30 feet long, 14 feet wide.

spanspek (ˈspænspɛk). *S. Afr.* Also **spanspec, sponspe(c)k.** [ad. Afrikaans *spaanspek* sweet melon, f. Du. *Spaans(ch)e* Spanish + *spek* bacon.] = cantaloup.

[**1731** G. Medley tr. *Kolb's Descr. Cape Good Hope* II. 277 *Melo Hispanicus.* i.e. The Spanish or Musk-Melon. The Musk Melons, produc'd at the Cape, are as good as those produc'd in Spain. The Cape-Europeans call 'em Spanish Bacon.] **1886** G. A. Farini *Through Kalahari Desert* v. 61 Mr. Barlett came and asked if I would like to buy any musk-melons (*spanspeck*). **1913** J. J. Doke *Secret City* 78 The ground was cumbered by watermelons and spanspeks. **1951** R. Campbell *Light on Dark Horse* iv. 70 The district is.. scarcely excelled for the size and succulence of its.. spanspec, watermelons, strawberries, [etc.]. **1958** *Cape Times* 12 Dec. 11/4 The always-popular sweet melon—spanspek—is not expected in quantities till the New Year. **1971** *Fair Lady* 10 Nov. 111 Baked egg custard/or Medium slice sponspek melon. **1975** *Cape Times* 13 Jan. 2 A Paarl spanspek exporter said in an interview at the weekend that these prices.. were paid only at the beginning of the season.

Spansule (ˈspænsjuːl). Also **spansule.** [f. span *sb.*[1] + cap)sule.] A proprietary name for a capsule that when swallowed releases a drug steadily for several hours, or that releases various drugs at prearranged times. Cf. *sustained-release* s.v. sustained *ppl. a.* 1 c.

1954 *Official Gaz.* (U.S. Patent Office) 2 Mar. 18/2 Smith Kline & French Laboratories, Philadelphia... *Spansule*... For capsules containing multiples of specially coated globules.. and providing for the gradual release of a medicament in the gastro-intestinal tract. **1954** *Trade Marks Jrnl.* 6 Oct. 1000/1 *Spansule*... Pharmaceutical preparations... Smith, Kline & French International Co. **1955** Osol & Farrar *Dispensatory of U.S.A.* (ed. 25) 89/1 Dexedrine Sulfate Spansules contain 15 mg. of the dextro salt in the form of tiny pellets, of which there are over a hundred in each capsule, having varying disintegration times so as to release the drug uniformly over a period of 8 to 10 hours. **1971** C. Williams *And Deep Blue Sea* (1972) ix. 102 Our labs came up several years ago with a timed-release spansule; the opiate takes effect in about twenty minutes and then an aphrodisiac eight hours later. **1974** 'J. Black' *Oil* (1975) iv. viii. 349 The two men had stayed up the remainder of the night, swallowing Dexamyl spansules while they meticulously went over all that Needham would have to do.

spanwise (ˈspænwaɪz), *a. Aeronaut.* [f. span *sb.*[1] + -wise.] Following the direction of the span of a wing or other aerofoil.

1946 *Jrnl. Brit. Interplanetary Soc.* VI. 95 The phenomenon of tip stall is brought about by spanwise drift in the boundary layer over a swept wing. **1955** J. Shapiro *Princ. Helicopter Engin.* vi. 360 Spanwise mass distribution in uniform section blades.. gives rise to considerable bending moments when the blade is stiff. **1967** *Jane's Surface Skimmer Systems 1967–8* 121/2 A drive pad.. enables the engines of a multi-engined aircraft to be coupled together by spanwise shafting. **1977** *Jrnl. R. Soc. Arts* CXXV. 350/1 A swept wing was made with narrow spanwise slots on the surface.

Spanyard(e, obs. forms of Spaniard.

spanyell(e, obs. forms of spaniel *sb.*[1]

spar (spɑː(r)), *sb.*[1] Also 4 **sperr,** 4–6 **sperre;** 4–7 **sparre,** 4, 6–8 **sparr.** [A word of Continental origin, appearing in the following forms: MDu. *sparre, spar, spaer* (Du. and WFris. *spar*), MLG. *sparre, spare, spar* (LG. *spar, spaar*), OHG. *sparro* (MHG. *sparre,* G. *sparren,* †*sparre,* †*sparr*), ON. *sparri* (Norw., Sw., Da. *sparre*); also MDu. and WFlem. *sperre, sper,* ON. (Icel. and Norw.) *sperra* (older Da. *sperre*), NFris. *spêr, spär.* The type *sparre* is the source of OF. *esparre* (mod.F. dial. *épare*), which may partly have contributed to the adoption of the word in English.]

1. a. One of the common rafters of a roof. Now chiefly *dial.*

a **1300** *Cursor M.* 8796 We haf soght forest bath ner and ferr For to sek a maister sparr [*Gött.* sperr]. *c* **1340** *Nominale* (Skeat) 443 *Cumble, heez et cheueroun,* Roof, firstre and sparre. *c* **1386** Chaucer *Knt.'s T.* 132 He wan the cite aftur, And rente doun bothe wal, and sparre, and raftur. **1402** *Pol. Poems* (Rolls) II. 77 Envie.. reuyd hath oure houses, that unnethes the hillinge hangith on the sparres. *a* **1490** Botoner *Itin.* (Nasmith, 1778) 260 Item the yerdys called sparres of the halle ryalle contenyth yn length about 45 fete of hole pece. *a* **1547** Surrey *Æneid* ii. 580 The gilt sparres, and the beames then threw they down. **1598** Bp. Hall *Sat.* v. i, A silly cote, Whose thatched spars are furred with sluttish soot. **1647** Herrick *Noble Numb., Thanksgiving to God,* A little house, whose humble Roof Is weather-proof; Under the sparres of which I lie Both soft, and drie. **1666** Spurstowe *Wiles of Satan* 24 What shall the spars and rafters do, if the pillars of the building tremble. **1833** Loudon *Encycl. Archit.* §985 The laths to be well nailed to spars (common rafters). **1846** J. Baxter *Libr. Pract. Agric.* (ed. 4) II. 125 Height of the wall.. to the sill, 6 ft. Length of the spars, 15 ft. **1854-** in dial. glossaries (Northampt., Chesh., Northumbld.).

†**b.** *Her.* = chevron *sb.*[1] 2. *Obs.*

1486 *Bk. St. Albans, Her.* f j b, We haue sotheli in armys certan signys the wich ar calde Cheuerons in french.. and in english a cowpull of sparris.

2. a. A pole or piece of timber of some length and moderate thickness; *spec.* an undressed stem of fir or similar wood under six inches in diameter.

1388 in Nicolas *Hist. Royal Navy* (1847) II. 476, xx. sparres de keyne, xiiii. plankes & shelles de keynes. **1392** *Earl Derby's Exp.* (Camden) 156 Pro x hurdell, ij sparrez, ij bulters pro officio suo in naue. *c* **1450** *Merlin* xxv. 460 He caught a sparre of Oke with bothe hondes. *c* **1460** *Towneley Myst.* iii. 130 Thou must spend many a spar this wark or thou wyn To end fully. **1513** *Acc. Ld. High Treas. Scotl.* IV. 481 For.. sperris to mak hand spakis of. **1526** Skelton *Magnyf.* 1047 Of a spyndell I wyll make a sparre. **1615** Chapman *Odyss.* ix. 138 Who tooke the Oliue sparre, made keene before, And plung'd it in his eye. **1664** Evelyn *Sylva* (1679) 27 Mr. Blith makes Sparrs, and small building-Timber of Oaks of eleven years growth. **1708** J. C. *Compl. Collier* (1845) 15 We must have either Oaken Spars, or Firr bawks. **1795** *Phil. Trans.* LXXXV. 579 These platforms.. were always made horizontal at the time of levelling, by means of a mahogany spar, or straight-edge. **1848** Layard *Nineveh* ix. (1850) 239 Loading a small raft with spars and skins for the construction of a larger. **1876** Voyle & Stevenson *Milit. Dict.* 139/2 *Fishing Spars,* in artillery material, consist of spars of wood placed parallel to the spars to be strengthened, by lashing them to one another.

fig. **1648** J. Beaumont *Psyche* xv. cccxxvi, Their Eyes will know no Lid, But make the beams recoil, the spars retreat.

b. Without article, as a material.

1794 *Rigging & Seamanship* 25 The trestle-trees.. are confined in a temporary manner by pieces of spar.

3. †**a.** A bar of wood used to fasten a gate or door. *Obs.* (Cf. spar *v.*[1])

1596 Spenser *F.Q.* v. xi. 4 The Prince.. opening streight the Sparre, forth to him came. **1611** Cotgr., *Barre,* a barre, or sparre, for a doore. **1647** Hexham i, The sparre or bolt of a doore. **1668** Wilkins *Real Char.* ii. x. §4. 257 Bolt, Barr, Sparr.

†**b.** *fig.* A prop or support. *Obs.*[−1]

1630 Lord *Banians* 80 He gained great fame, whereunto his divining fortunes became such a sparre that he was made King of Delee.

c. A spoke, bar, or cross-bar.

In Scotland commonly applied to the bars or rails of a wooden fence or gate.

1687 Miége *Gt. Fr. Dict.* ii, The Spars of a spinning Wheel. **1706** Phillips (ed. Kersey), *Spars* are also the spokes of a Spinning-wheel. **1825** Jamieson *Suppl., Dogrung,* one of the spars which connect the stilts of a plough. **1882** Stevenson *New Arab. Nts.* (1884) 306 'What's all this?' cried the.. host through the spars of the gate.

4. a. *Naut.* 'The general term for all masts, yards, booms, gaffs, etc.' (Young, 1846).

The comb. cant-spar is found somewhat earlier (1611).

1640 in Entick *London* (1766) II. 170 Spars: Bonnispars [*sic*]. Cantspars. Small spars. **1794** *Rigging & Seamanship* 43 Cant Spars, Ratling Spars, Boom Spars, Middling Spars, Small Spars. **1840** R. H. Dana *Bef. Mast* xvii, We next sent ashore our spare spars and rigging. **1863** P. Barry *Dockyard Econ.* 226 The spars will be slight, sufficient merely to give steadiness to the ship at sea. **1878** T. L. Cuyler *Pointed Papers* 173 When the first blow of the cyclone tears our canvas from the spars.

fig. **1848** Thackeray *Van. Fair* xvii, Three young stock-brokers.. sent this little spar out of the wreck.. to good Mrs. Sedley. **1848** Dickens *Dombey* i, Thus clinging fast to that slight spar within her arms, the mother drifted out upon the dark and unknown sea.

b. *Aeronaut.* Each of the main members of a wing on older aircraft, which run transversely to the fuselage and carry the ribs.

1866 *1st Rep. Aëronaut. Soc.* 35 But with all such arrangements the apparatus must fail—*length of wing is indispensable!* and a spar thirty feet long must be strong, heavy, and cumbrous. **1895** *Amer. Engineer & Railroad Jrnl.* Aug. 387/2 Being caught by a side puff, the machine was blown over, and the front starboard spar was too much broken to mend on the field. **1919**, etc. [see rib *sb.*[1] 11 e]. **1930** Nayler & Ower *Aviation of To-Day* vii. 154 The modern steel spar of an aeroplane wing.. can be treated by calculation. **1960** C. H. Gibbs-Smith *Aeroplane* xiii. 96 In 1919, he [*sc.* Adolph Rohrbach] started building smooth-skinned metal surfaces, combined with metal box-spar construction in the wings, thus allowing more stresses to be borne by the surfaces.

5. *Oil Industry.* Also **Spar, SPAR.** An installation intended to float above a submarine well-head and provide large storage tanks and various service facilities, esp. for loading tankers.

1973 *Times* 31 Oct. (Offshore Supply Suppl.) p. iii/2 The concrete spar is anchored above a submarine manifold with pipelines from production platforms. The lower part of the spar is a 300,000-barrel capacity storage chamber. **1975** *Offshore Progress—Technol. & Costs* (Shell Briefing Service) 18 One of the newest deep water concepts is the Spar—floating storage and loading terminal all in one. **1976** *Offshore Platforms & Pipelining* 218 The SPAR has been designed to maintain a constant draft in both the loaded and ballasted conditions. **1979** *North Sea Progress* (Shell Internat. Petroleum Co.) 8 Other methods involve.. the use of custom-built SPAR-type semi-submersible production units.

6. *attrib.* and *Comb.*, as ***spar-batten, -bridge, -pole, -raft, -wood; spar-maker.***

1504 in Gage *Hist. & Antiq. Suffolk* 140 The rofes to be sper batens, and jopies. **1578** in Feuillerat *Revels Q. Eliz.* (1908) 306 Longe sparre poles of ffurre. **1752** *Records Elgin* (New Spald. Cl.) I. 464 Ilk cart load.. of sparwood or logs. **1798** *Survey of Province of Moray* 100 Spar-wood.. about 7 inches diameter, is sold at 7d. the solid foot. **1860** *Sat. Rev.* 28 July 110/1 The master spar-maker, master blacksmith, and timber inspector. **1876** Voyle & Stevenson *Milit. Dict.* 394/2 *Spar Bridge,* a light bridge for crossing broken arches, rivers with steep banks, &c. **1880** *Northwestern Lumberman* 24 Jan., More than the usual number of spar rafts will be prepared this winter.

7. Special combs., as **spar-buoy** (see quot. 1883); † **spar-dry** *a.*, perfectly dry (land); **spar-dust** (see quot.); † **spar foot,** a horizontal piece of wood supporting the lower end of a rafter; **spar-naked** *a.*, stark naked; **spar-piece** (see quot.); **spar shed** a ship-building shed in which spars are stored; **spar torpedo,** a torpedo fastened on the end of a spar projecting from the bows of the boat; **spar tree** *Forestry,* a tree or other tall structure to which cables are attached for hauling logs; **spar-yard** a yard in which ship-spars are prepared.

1860 *Merc. Marine Mag.* VII. 94 A *spar-buoy moored in 11 feet. **1883** *Chambers's Jrnl.* 8 Dec. 772/1 A spar-buoy.. is so designed that a spar or mast stands almost perpendicularly out of the water. **13..** *E.E. Allit. P.* C. 338 Thenne oure fader to þe fysch ferslych biddez, þat he hym sput spakly vpon *spare drye. *a* **1825** Forby *Voc. E. Anglia,* **Spar-dust,* powder of post; dust produced in wood by the depredation of boring insects. **1579** in Willis & Clark *Cambr.* (1886) I. 311, xliiij copple of *sparr feete eche.. iiij foote longe. **1849** *Blackw. Mag.* LXV. 610 The poor fellow was *spar-naked. **1842** Gwilt *Archit.* Gloss., **Spar-piece,* a name given in some places to the collar beam of a roof. **1883** *Daily News* 4 July 5/4 The scene at the *spar shed where the bodies are laid out for identification. **1878** *N. Amer. Rev.* CXXVII. 384 Armed with the *spar-torpedo. **1925** *Spar tree [see *high lead* s.v. high *a.* 21]. **1965** [see *high line* s.v. high *a.* 21]. **1980** *Beautiful Brit. Columbia* Fall 40 Atop the cliff stands a long-disused spar tree; close by the bay are the broken bricks, cement and tile that testify to a long-abandoned project here. **1868** Whitman *Poems, Song of the Broad-Axe* iii, Spar-makers in the *spar-yard.

spar (spɑː(r)), *sb.*[2] *Min.* Also 6–7 **sparr.** [ad. MLG. *spar, sper* (also in combs. *sparglas, -kalk,* MHG. *sparchalch*), related to OE. *spæren* gypsum, *spærstán* spar-stone.]

1. A general term for a number of crystalline minerals more or less lustrous in appearance and admitting of easy cleavage.

A large number of varieties are distinguished by special epithets, as *bitter, Bolognian, brown, calcareous, Derbyshire, Iceland, pearl, ponderous, rhomb, tabular:* see these words and calc-, feld-, fluor-, heavy spar.

1581 in *Trans. Jewish Hist. Soc. Eng.* (1903) IV. 96 In our copper ures were.. a kinde of black stone (wherin the copper groweth), and a kinde of white stone named sparr. **1631** Jorden *Nat. Bathes* vii. (1669) 45 Sparr, which the Dutch call Sput or Querts, shoots into points like Diamonds. **1653** Manlove *Customs Lead-mines* 265 (E.D.S.), Cauke, Sparr, Lid-stones, Twitches, Daulings, and Pees. **1672** Boyle *Ess. Gems* 91 The clear Spar, which in most of our Western Lead-Mines in England is found next to the Metalline Veins. **1756** C. Lucas *Ess. Waters* III. 236 All perfectly petrified; some into bright crystallised spar. **1774** Goldsm. *Nat. Hist.* (1776) I. 66 The pendent rocks were glazed with spar. **1832** Tennyson *Œnone* 82 in *Poems* (1833) 55 Within the green hillside.. Is an ingoing grotto, strown with spar. **1867** Baker *Nile Trib.* xvii. (1872) 304 Immense quantities of very beautiful spar lay upon the surface in all directions.

b. *pl.* Different varieties of this.

1668 Charleton *Onomast.* 274 *Fluores,*.. Spars. **1695** Woodward *Nat. Hist. Earth* iv. 179 Gemms or Stones that are here shot into Cubes.., the Bristow-Stones, Crystallized Sparrs, the Iris,.. and several others. **1797** *Monthly Mag.* III. 203 Matlock is much noted for its.. curious spars and fossils. **1814** Scott *Lord of Isles* iii. xxviii, And o'er his head the dazzling spars Gleam like a firmament of stars! **1823** Byron *Island* ii. vii, Or cavern sparkling with its native spars.

2. a. A fragment or particle of spar. Also *transf.*

1855 [Miss Cobbe] *Ess. Intuitive Morals* 117 The waters of our spiritual life.. stand in need of rocks and falls or at least of spars or pebbles, to freshen them by their resistance. **1873** Dixon *Two Queens* xvi. i. III. 186 Love, romance, generosity, were as foreign to the soul of Charles as to a spar of ice.

b. An ornament made of spar.

1851 Mayhew *Lond. Lab.* I. 370/2 'Spars,' as spar ornaments are called by the street-sellers. *Ibid.* 371/1 Some street-sellers have their spars in covered barrows.

3. *attrib.* and *Comb.*, as ***spar-like*** adj., ***-lode, ornament, -rider, -seller.***

1700 ? Mackworth *Disc. Mine-Adventure, 2nd Abstract* 12 We are Sumping and driving in the new Work in good firm.. Oar, and the Spar-rider continues to under cut in Oar. **1778** W. Pryce *Min. Cornub.* 91 This being a hard unmetallick petrifaction, thence called a Spar Lode by those unacquainted with real Spar. **1797** *Encycl. Brit.* (ed. 3) VI. 230/1 The spar-like gypsum, *marmor metallicum.* **1851** Mayhew *Lond. Lab.* I. 370/2 The spar-sellers carried their goods.. in strong baskets on their heads. *Ibid.* 371/1 Some of the spar ornaments are plain, white, and smooth.

spar (spɑː(r)), *sb.*[3] [f. spar *v.*[2]]

†**1.** A thrust. *Obs.*[−1]

c **1400** *Destr. Troy* 10684 Menestaus.. Presit Polidamas & put hym of horse, With a spar of a speire.

2. A boxing-match; a display of boxing; a motion of sparring.

1814 *Monthly Mag.* XXXVIII. 439 He's coming: I know the white steed from afar; He is not a man to be late at a spar. **1901** *Oxford Times* 16 Mar. 4/2 Boxing: an interesting exhibition spar was given by.. two boys.

3. A cock-fight.

1849 D. J. Browne *Amer. Poultry Yd.* (1855) 45 Many of the handsomest game cocks.. are already trimmed, (in the comb at least,) in case they should be wanted in a hurry for a private spar.

4. *transf.* A wordy contest or dispute.

1836–7 DICKENS *Sk. Boz, Tales* x, Mr. Timson..kept up a running spar with Mr. Watkins Tottle. **1841** HOOD *Tale of Trumpet* 661 Such wrangle, and jangle, and miff, and tiff, And spar, and jar. **1861** MRS. RIDDELL *City & Suburb* 207 Ruby faced out, and had a spar with him.

5. *Comb.*, as **sparmate** *U.S.*, a sparring partner.

1937 *Sun* (Baltimore) 30 Aug. 15/2 Ten days ago one of his sparmates opened up a deep cut under his eye with a punch. **1950** J. DEMPSEY *Championship Fighting* 15, I found plenty of kid sparmates. **1974** *Los Angeles Times* 13 Oct. III. 13/3 Chartchai, three-time world flyweight champion, has been staying at a Tokyo hotel,..with his wife and his manager and his wife, sparmate and trainer.

spar (spɑː(r)), *sb.*^{4} *dial.* [Of doubtful origin: cf. the variant SPEAR *sb.*^{4}] A pointed and doubled rod used in securing thatch.

1746 *B.N.C. Muniments, Estates 43. 45*, Sept. 7, Paid for one day worke of thacing, 1*s.* 6*d.* Paid for 500 of sparies, 1*s.* 3*d.* **1748** *Ibid.* Feb. 26, Paid for 4500 of sparis, 11*s.* 3*d.* **1796** W. H. MARSHALL *Rur. Econ. W. Eng.* I. 330 *Spars*, thatching rods. **1825** JENNINGS *Obs. Dial. W. Eng.* 71 The pointed sticks, doubled and twisted in the middle, and used for fixing the thatch of a roof, are called *spars*: they are commonly made of split willow rods. **1874** T. HARDY *Far fr. Mad. Crowd* xxxvi, The dull thuds of the beetle which drove in the spars.

b. *attrib.*, as *spar-gad, -hook, -house, -rod.*

1844 BARNES *Poems Rur. Life* (1848) 387. **1863** MONCRIEFF *Dream* in *I. of Wight Gloss.* (E.D.S.) 52 He skulks through the copses for sparods and ledgers. **1886** T. HARDY *Woodlanders* ii, A bundle of the straight, smooth hazel rods called spar-gads. *Ibid.* iv, [He] crossed over to the spar-house where some journey-men were already at work.

†**spar**, *sb.*^{5} *Obs.* In 5–6 **spare, sparr(e,** 6 **sper-, spear-, speyr.** [Irregular var. of SPARTH^1.] A long-handled axe; a soldier armed with this.

c **1440** *Eng. Conq. Ireland* (Rawl. MS.) 17 Speris and sparris. *Ibid.* 83 He..broght two Spares faste on his shelde. **1515** *St. Papers Hen. VIII*, II. 5 The armye of every region excede not 200 sperys and 600 kerne. **1534** *Ibid.* 185, 8 score fotmen, called kern, 10 scor spearys, callid gallagloghis; which 10 score sparris amountith to 20 score men. **1543** *Ibid.* III. 444 Ther footemen..having every of them his weapon, callyd a sparre, moche like axe of the Towre, and they be named galloglasse. **1600** DYMMOK *Ireland* (1843) 7 He is named a spare of his weapon so called, 80 of which spares make a battell of Galloglass.

attrib. **1539** *St. Papers Hen. VIII*, III. 142 His armie..be but chorles and plowmen, and..his sparr men went from hym.

†**spar**, *sb.*^{6} *Obs.*$^{-1}$ [f. SPAR *v.*^{1}] A check or impediment.

1613 DAY *Dyall* ix. (1614) 263 First that this Kingdome of Grace be not hindred by many spars and lets that it hath what with the World, the Flesh, and the Divell.

†**spar**, *sb.*^{7} *Obs.*$^{-0}$ In 7 **sparre.** [Of obscure origin.] The purre or stint.

1668 CHARLETON *Onomast.* 108 *Junco*,..the Stint, or Sparre, or Perr.

spar, *sb.*^{8} Anglicized form of SPARUS.

1881 RAWLINSON *Hist. Anc. Egypt* I. ii. 84 Among other delicate fish produced by the Nile may be mentioned..the spar (*Sparus Niloticus*).

spar (spɑː(r)), *v.*^{1} Forms: α. 3 **sperren,** 4–6 **sperre,** 5 **sper,** 7 **sperr.** β. 4–7 **sparre,** 4 **sparr,** 5– **spar.** [In the α-forms app. ad. MDu. *sperren* (Du. *sperren*), = OHG. *sperran* (MHG. and G. *sperren*; hence Da. *spærre*, Sw. *spärra*), f. the stem *sparr-* SPAR *sb.*^{1} The β-forms may be a normal alteration of this, or may represent the base of OE. *ȝesparrian* and *besparrian* BESPAR *v.* For further variants in ME. and later use see SPARE *v.*^{2} and SPEAR *v.*^{1}]

1. *trans.* To fasten (a door or gate) with a bar or bolt; to shut or close firmly or securely. Also occas. with *up*. Now *arch.*

α. *c* **1200** ORMIN 4122 Forr swa..Wass Paradisess ȝate sperrd ȝæn all mannkinn onn eorþe. **1338** R. BRUNNE *Chron.* (1810) 240 To maynten forth þe werre..þe entres did þei sperre, & hold þam in Snowdoun. *c* **1450** *Cursor M.* 10420 (Laud), She sperrid her doris and wept sore. *c* **1462** *Paston Lett.* II. 87 The yates of Lynne..weren fast sperred. **1483** *Cath. Angl.* 354/1 To Sperre, *claudere.* **1579** SPENSER *Sheph. Cal.* May 224 If he chaunce come when I am abroade, Sperre the yate fast for feare of fraude. **1596** —— *F.Q.* v. x. 37 The other which was entred, laboured fast To sperre the gate.

β. *a* **1300** *Cursor M.* 2788 Fast þe dors þan did he sparr [*Gött.* bar]. *a* **1400** N. T. (Paues) *Acts* xii. 14 Sche..lefte þo ȝhate sparde, ande tolde hem þat Peter stondes bifore þe ȝate. **1484** *Cal. Letter-Bks. Lond.* 'L' 202 b, That every nyght..thei Shitte and Sparre their doores at the hour of ix^c of the Clok. *a* **1529** SKELTON *Ware the Hauke* 91 The church dores were sparred, Fast boltyd and barryd. **1555** EDEN *Decades* (Arb.) 143 Excepte they take good heede that the doores bee well sparde. **1614** GORGES *Lucan* I. 5 So when all iarres doe end their dates, Ianus may sparre his Iron gates. **1626** B. JONSON *Staple of N.* II. iv. (1905) 47, I haue heard you..cauke your windores, spar up all your doores. **1674** RAY *N. Co. Words* 44 To *Spar* the Door, to bolt, bar, pin, or shut it... This word is also used in Norfolk. **1825** in JAMIESON *Suppl.* **1888** DOUGHTY *Arabia Deserta* I. 193 The gate was sparred, and the old man made no speed to come down and undo for us.

b. In fig. contexts. Also *absol.*

c **1400** *Apol. Loll.* 34 He closiþ, and þan no man opuniþ; he opuniþ, and þan no man sperriþ. **1435** MISYN *Fire of Love* 16 þai treuly sal haue power to spar heuen to þame. **1555** LATIMER *Let.* in *Serm. & Rem.* (1845) 437 Or else the doors [of heaven] will be shut up [*v.r.* sparred up before ye come], that ye cannot go in. **1612** J. DAVIES (Heref.) *Muse's Sacrifice* Wks. (Grosart) II. 56/1 Thus shall each pious person pray to thee in fitting time (yer Mercies Gate be sparr'd).

†**2.** In general use: To close, fasten, secure, lock, etc. Also with *up*.

c **1200** ORMIN Ded. 261 He sahh..an boc Bisett wiþþ seffne innseȝȝless, & sperrd swa swiþe wel þatt itt Ne mihhte nan wihht oppnenn. *Ibid.* 12155 Forr Cristess þohht wass sperrd..Wiþþinnenn & wiþþutenn. *c* **1400** *Rom. Rose* 3320 He tought it [my heart] so hym for to obey, That he it sparrede with a key. *a* **1425** tr. *Arderne's Treat. Fistula*, etc. 14 Aftirward it [*sc.* the fistula] is opned by itself, and renneþ as it is seid afore, and aftirward it is sperred. **1430–40** LYDG. *Bochas* IX. xxxv. (1554) 215 b, [He] Closed hys booke, and shet it in his chest, But ere he might sperre it with the keye [etc.]. **1615** T. ADAMS *Black Devil* 19 He lockes the doores after him, sparres up the heart with security, that his treasure be not stolne.

†**3.** To confine, enclose, or imprison, to shut *up*, in a place. *Obs.*

a **1240** *Wohunge* in *O.E. Hom.* I. 285 Mi bodi henge wið þi bodi neiled o rode, sperred querfaste wið-inne fowr wahes. *c* **1330** R. BRUNNE *Chron. Wace* (Rolls) 9501 3yf he wyþ sege sperre me her-yn. *Ibid.* 11824 As wyþ þe Romayns for to werre, þat alle men in þer daunger sperre. *a* **1400** HYLTON *Scala Perf.* I. xvi. (W. de W. 1494), And therefore as a wretche & outcaste..art sperred in a hous alone. *c* **1440** *Alph. Tales* 3 Sho was sparred in a cloce cell iij yere. **1583** MELBANCKE *Philotimus* Bbj, He..caused him to bee sparred faste in the same tower. **1586** WARNER *Alb. Eng.* II. xii. (1589) 50 There sparred vp in gates, The valiant Thæbane..a following fight awaites. *a* **1600** *Floddan Field* (1664) I. 10 Our startling Nags in Stables sparde, Are waxen wild with too much rest.

refl. **1535** COVERDALE *Ezek.* iii. 24 Go thy waye, and sparre thy selff in thyne house.

†**4.** To shut (a person or thing) *out* or *in*. *Obs.*

c **1430** *Life St. Kath.* (1884) 66 Sorwyng þat mankynde was spard out..from þe delytes of paradyse. *c* **1460** *Towneley Myst.* iii. 128 Anoynt thi ship with pik and tar.., The water out to spar. **1483** *Cath. Angl.* 354/1 To Sperre jn, *jncludere. Ibid.*, To Sperre oute, *excludere.* **1530** PALSGR. 728/1 What meanyth this woman, she sperryth me out, she callyth me agayne. **1535** COVERDALE *1 Sam.* xxi. 7 But the same daye was there a man sparred in before the Lorde.

†**5.** To fix or fasten *together* or *down*. *Obs.*

1591 FLETCHER *Russe Commonw.* (Hakl. Soc.) 78 They haue drummes besides of a huge bignesse, which they carry ..on foure horses, that are sparred together with chaines. *a* **1722** LISLE *Husb.* (1757) 202 It is very good husbandry to top hay or corn-reeks with well wetted helms, that they may be well sparred down.

spar (spɑː(r)), *v.*^{2} Also 5–6 **sparre,** 7–8 **sparr.** [Of obscure origin.]

†**1.** *intr.* To dart or spring; to strike or thrust rapidly. *Obs.*

a **1400–50** *Alexander* 2975 With þat he brochis his blonke þat þe blode fames, Sparis [*v.r.* Sparrys] out spacly as sparke out of gledes. *c* **1400** *Destr. Troy* 6690 Teuser, with tene turnyt to Ector, Sparrit to hym with a speire. *Ibid.* 6914 He put hym to Paris.., Sparrit at hym with a spere.

2. Of cocks: To strike with the feet or spurs; to fight.

1570 LEVINS *Manip.* 29 To sparre, as cocks do, *confligere.* **1686** R. BLOME *Gentl. Recreat.* II. 279/1 Your Cocks having Sparred sufficiently. **1696** R. H. *Sch. Recreat.* 144 Let him Sparr with another Cock. **1710** PALMER *Proverbs* 255, 'I'll teach you to sparr at your lady!' and in a moment [she] twisted off his neck. **1776** G. WHITE *Selborne* lxxiii, A young cock will spar at his adversary before his spurs are grown. **1828** in Blaine *Encycl. Rural Sports* (1840) 1208 The practice of permitting the stags and younger chickens to spar occasionally.

b. *trans.* To cause (a cock) to spar; to exercise in sparring.

1686 R. BLOME *Gentl. Recreat.* II. 279/1 The Day following Spar him again. **1696** R. H. *Sch. Recreat.* 145 The second Fortnight, twice a Week will be enough to Chase or Spar your Cock. **1832** MARRYAT *N. Forster* xlv, They..fed and sparred them [cocks] to get them into wind.

3. To engage in or practise boxing; to make the motions of attack and defence with the arms and fists; to box. Also const. *at*.

1755 JOHNSON, *Spar*, to fight with prelusive strokes. **1825** C. WESTMACOTT *Eng. Spy* I. 85 Big George can teach the use of fives,..Or spar or keep the game alive [etc.]. **1833** NYREN *Yng. Cricketer's Tutor* 38 The position of the wicket keeper in his standing, should be that of a man preparing to spar. **1847** ALB. SMITH *Chr. Tadpole* xli. (1879) 355 It appeared that two pugilists who were advertised to spar had not yet arrived.

fig. **1809** MALKIN *Gil Blas* IV. xi. ¶6 We..suspended the fray to spar a little with the flagon.

b. *trans.* With cognate object.

1901 *Oxford Times* 16 Mar. 4/2 He..sparred a bye, in which the boxing was only of a light character.

4. To dispute; to bandy words.

1698 COLLIER *Immor. Stage* iv. §5. 147 Jacinta spars again and says, I would have thee to know, thou graceless old Man, that I defy a Nunnery. **1741** RICHARDSON *Pamela* III. 346 What! sparring and jangling again, you Sluts! **1752** CHESTERF. *Lett.* ccxci. III. 336 Only women and little minds pout and spar for the entertainment of the company. **1854** THACKERAY *Wolves & Lamb* Wks. 1899 XII. 30 They spar so every night they meet. **1880** MRS. RIDDELL *Myst. Palace Gardens* xxvi, She liked to hear the two sparring.

b. *trans.* To argue or debate (questions).

a **1734** NORTH *Lives* (1826) III. 336 Among his virtuoso friends and acquaintances he loved to spar questions and foment disputes.

spar (spɑː(r)), *v.*^{3} [f. SPAR *sb.*^{1} Cf. MDu. and MHG. *sparren*, ON. and MSw. *sparra*, older Da. *sparre*, in sense 1.]

1. *trans.* To furnish, make, or close *in*, with spars. Also *fig.*

1657–8 in Willis & Clark *Cambridge* (1886) II. 97 Extraordinary repaires..for slating and sparring ye chappell. **1805** R. W. DICKSON *Pract. Agric.* I. 52 For these purposes, one or more stalls may be sparred to the top. *a* **1851** MOIR *Snow* xii. Poet. Wks. 1852 II. 388 The mill-wheel sparr'd with icicles, Reflects her silver ray. **1894** STEVENSON *Lett.* (1899) II. 333, I have a room now, a part of the twelve-foot verandah sparred in, at the most inaccessible end of the house.

2. *Naut.* **a.** In pa. pple.: Provided with spars.

1840 R. H. DANA *Bef. Mast* xxxiv, She..[was] heavily sparred, with sails cut to a *t*. **1894** *Times* 12 May 9/3 The vessel..was snugly sparred and canvased for the passage.

b. To fix spars across (the rigging) preparatory to rattling down.

c **1860** H. STUART *Seaman's Catech.* 35 Commence sparring the rigging.

c. *U.S.* 'To aid (a vessel) over a shallow bar by the use of spars and tackles' (*Cent. Dict.*). Also with *off*.

1843 T. TALBOT *Jrnls.* (1931) 4 [We became] finally the prey of an insidious sand-bar, where after hours of sparring, ..we again resume the slow ascent. **1875** 'MARK TWAIN' in *Atlantic Mag.* May 568/1 Maybe she 'strikes and swings'. Then she has to while away several hours (or days) sparring herself off. **1883** *American* VI. 40 At low water, the vessel has often to be sparred over sand-bars.

sparable ('spærəb(ə)l). Also 7 **sparabile, sperrable,** 9 **sparrable, -bil.** [Reduced form of SPARROW-BILL.]

1. A small headless wedge-shaped iron nail (stouter than a *sprig*), used in the soles and heels of boots and shoes.

α. *a* **1627** H. SHIRLEY *Mart. Soldier* III. i. in Bullen *Old Pl.*, He would put Sparabiles into the soules then? **1706** PHILLIPS (ed. Kersey), *Sparables* or *Sparrow-Bills*, a sort of small Iron nails, which some Country-People wear in their Shooes. *c* **1780** in C. Coleridge *Life C. M. Yonge* 3 [A letter ..complaining that he had been sent to Oxford with] sparables in his shoes. **1827** FARADAY *Chem. Manip.* xxiv. (1842) 605 Burn a cast-iron sparable in the same manner. **1839** CARLETON *Fardorougha* vii, Why did you get..three rows of sparables in the soles o' them? **1877** BLACKMORE *Cripps* (1887) 356 His heels had their sparables as good as new.

β. **1648** HERRICK *Hesper., Upon Cob, Epig.* 266 His thumb-nailes-par'd afford him sperrables. **1828** CARR *Craven Gloss.*, *Sparrables*, short nails without heads, used by shoe-makers. **1831** J. HOLLAND *Manuf. Metals* I. 216 The portions chopped off would be sparrables. **1893** MOIRA O'NEILL *Dimpses* 42 You could have counted the sparrabils in the soles.

2. *attrib.* and *Comb.*, as *sparable-cutter*, *-paved* adj.; **sparable-tin** (see quot.).

1824 MACTAGGART *Gallovid. Encycl.* 79 The mowdieman's shoon being sparrable paved. **1864** SMYTH *Cat. Min. Coll.* 17 Cassiterite, in ditetragonally terminated crystals, locally termed 'Sparable Tin'. **1884** *Times* 8 Jan. 2/6 A 'sparable-cutter' is a personage well known among the nailers of Cradley and Halesowen.

†**sparadrap.** *Med. Obs.* Also 6 **-drappe, -drape,** 7 **-drop, sparrowdrope.** [a. F. *sparadrap* (†*spadadrap*), = It. *sparadrappo*, Sp. *esparadrapo*, Pg. *sparadrapo*, *esparadrà*, med.L. *sparadrapum* (*spandarapum*), of unknown origin. The second element may be F. *drap* cloth: cf. SPASMADRAP.] A piece of linen or other cloth dipped in, or spread with, some ointment or medicament for use as a bandage or plaster.

1543 TRAHERON *Vigo's Chirurg.* 268 b/2 Dyppe cloutes therein, in the fourme of a sparadrap. **1599** A. M. tr. *Gabelhouer's Bk. Physicke* 212/2 Applye as then theron a Sparadrape, which must in this sorte be made. **1612** WOODALL *Surg. Mate* Wks. (1653) 153 Dipping a course canvas therein in forme of a sparrowdrope. **1635** A. READ *Tumors & Vlcers* 272 Above the unguents you are to apply Sparadrops made onely of wax. **1683** SALMON *Doron Med.* III. 693 Take a sufficient quantity, mix, melt, and make a Sparadrap according to art. **1728** CHAMBERS *Cycl.* s.v., There are as many different Kinds of Sparadrap, as there are of Plaisters for the Cloth to be dipp'd in. [**1755** in JOHNSON (citing Wiseman), and in later Dicts.]

†'**sparage.** *Obs.* [a. OF. *sparage* (= It. *sparagio*), ad. L. *asparagus*: cf. SPERAGE.] Asparagus. Also *attrib.*

1565 COOPER, *Asparagus*,..in English Sparage. *Ibid.*, *Corruda*, an hearbe called wylde sparage. **1592** NASHE *P. Penilesse* Wks. (Grosart) II. 34 Yet am I not against it, that these men..should come to be sparage gentlemen & chuff-headed Burghomasters. **1607** TOPSELL *Four-f. Beasts* (1658) 399 Sea Onions, Scammony, wilde Sparage. **1612** PEACHAM *Gentl. Exerc.* III. ix. (1634) 151 Sparage, Fennell, and white Ellebore.

sparagmite ('spærəgmaɪt). *Geol.* [ad. G. *sparagmit* (J. Esmark *Reise von Christiania nach Drontheim*, etc. (1829) 25), f. Gr. σπάραγμα fragment, piece torn off: see -ITE^1.] A generic term for the feldspathic sandstones (chiefly arkoses), conglomerates, and other fragmental rocks which occur in late Pre-Cambrian formations in Scandinavia.

[**1866** *Geol. Mag.* III. 384 (*table*) 'Spragmitic' strata—conglomerates, Schists, Dolomitic beds.] **1882** A. GEIKIE

Text-bk. Geol. 657 In central and northern Norway the Archæan gneiss is overlaid by reddish and grey sandstones and conglomerates (Sparagmite), with schists, quartzites, and limestones. **1930** PEACH & HORNE *Geol. Scotland* iii. 72 The Sparagmite of Scandinavia is an arkose resembling the dominant type of the Torridon Sandstone. **1979** *Nature* 25 Jan. 290/1 Micaceous meta-arkoses (sparagmites) have, in places, a basal conglomerate resting unconformably on the Basal gneisses.

‖**sparagmos** (spə'rægmɒs). [a. Gr. σπαραγμός tearing, rending.] The tearing apart of a hero, or his ritualized death in an analogous manner as represented in some tragedies or myths when it symbolizes part of the cycle of death and rebirth. Also *fig.*

1949 F. FERGUSSON *Idea of Theater* i. 32 The ritual had.. its *Sparagmos*, in which the royal victim was literally or symbolically torn asunder. **1957** N. FRYE *Anat. of Criticism* iii. 192 The disappearance of the hero, a theme which often takes the form of *sparagmos* or tearing to pieces. Sometimes the hero's body is divided among his followers. **1961** J. HOLLOWAY *Story of Night* vii. 130 The death of Coriolanus is almost as much a *sparagmos* of the ritual victim by the whole social group as was possible on the stage. **1977** *Dædalus* Summer 62 Not that conferences alone can do this, but they are signals that the reconstitution of anthropology at a higher level under the aegis of processualism is under way. Otherwise the centrifugal drift, indeed, the suicidal sparagmos, will go on and on.

sparagrass, obs. variant of SPARROWGRASS.

†'**sparagus.** *Obs.* Also 7 sparragus, 7–8 'sparagus, 8 speragas. [a. med.L. *sparagus*, aphetic form of ASPARAGUS.] Asparagus.

1543 TRAHERON *Vigo's Chirurg.* 196 b/1 Sparagus is hoote and drye. **1607** DEKKER *Iests to make you merry* Wks. (Grosart) II. 304 The flower *sparagus*, that growes out of euery mans dunge, and contemned of euery man. **1611–40** [see ASPARAGUS 1 δ]. **1669** COKAINE *Poems* 247 What delicate Sparagus you have growing there. *c* **1711** PETIVER *Gazophyl.* VI. lvii, Prickly tern-feathered Cape Sparagus. **1711** TEMPEST *Cryes of London* 27 Ripe Speragas. **1785** COWPER *Lett.*, In May we shall have 'sparagus.

attrib. **1640** R. BROME (*title*), The Sparagus Garden. **1668** PEPYS *Diary* 22 Apr., Over to the 'sparagus garden.

sparanaro, variant of SPERONARA.

‖**Sparaxis** (spə'ræksɪs). *Bot.* [mod.L. (1805), a. Gr. σπάραξις tearing, laceration.] A genus of S. African iridaceous plants (related to the genus *Ixia* and characterized by a lacerated spathe), species of which are cultivated for their showy flowers; a plant or bulb of this genus.

1829 LOUDON *Encycl. Pl.* 40. **1841** DUNCAN *Hist. Guernsey* 557 The innumerable species of ixia, sparaxis, and other cognate genera of Cape bulbs. *Ibid.* 559 The ixia, too, and the sparaxis, have lately been observed to hybridise. **1852** JOHNSON *Cottage Gard. Dict.* 517/1 The true Ixias are known from *Sparaxis* by not having, like it, a jagged sheath.

sparble, variant of SPARPLE *v. Obs.*

sparch, *v.*[1] *rare.* [Related to PARCH *v.*] *trans.* and *intr.* To scorch.

1532–3 *Act 24 Hen. VIII*, c. 1 §6 Every Coriar shall well and sufficiently corie & blacke the said Lether tanned.. & not craftely to bourne ne sparche the said Lether. **1894** HALL CAINE *Manxman* III. 156 While the oatcake crackled and sparched and went black.

sparch, *v.*[2], variant of SPARGE *v.*

1894 HALL CAINE *Manxman* v. iii. 287 The net boiler sparched drops of hot water at intervals.

sparch (to parget): see SPARGET *v.*

sparcle, obs. or dial. f. SPARKLE *sb.* and *v.*[1]

spar-deck. Also 6, 8 sparr-, 7–8 spare-deck. [f. SPAR *sb.*[1] Hence G. and F. *spardeck.*] A light upper deck in a vessel.

α. **1570** GOOGE *Pop. Kingd.* III. 40 b, Hir fraught was only Friers and Monkes, and on the spardeckes hie Were all the chiefest members of the wicked papacie. **1599** DALLAM in *Early Voy. Levant* (Hakl. Soc.) 9 Than the booteson of our ship stod upon our spar decke,.. commanding them to come under our Lee side. *a* **1618** RALEIGH *Invent. Shipping* 29 Needing no other addition of building, then a slight spar Decke, fore and afte as the Seamen call it. **1688** HOLME *Armoury* III. xiv. (Roxb.) 35/1 The spar deck, which is the vpermost, betwixt the two masts and is made very slight. **1716** B. CHURCH *Hist. Philip's War* (1867) II. 42 He must take some of the open Sloops, and make Spar-Decks to them. **1769** FALCONER *Dict. Marine* (1780) s.v. *Decks*, Frigates, sloops, &c. with one gun-deck and a half, with a spar deck below to lodge the crew. **1847** H. MELVILLE *Omoo* xxix, On the spar-deck, also, are carronades of enormous calibre. **1887** J. BALL *Nat. S. Amer.* 31 A spar-deck carried flush from stem to stern.

attrib. **1893** *Naut. Mag.* May 396 The spar-deck ship is of character intermediate between the awning-deck ship and the three-deck ship.

β. *a* **1642** SIR W. MONSON *Naval Tracts* II. (1704) 253/2 To have all the spare Decks and other Things of weight taken down. **1706** PHILLIPS (ed. Kersey), *Spare-Deck* or *Sparr-deck*, the uppermost Deck in some great Ships, which lies between the Main and Missen Masts.

Hence **spar-decked** *a.*, fitted with a spar-deck; **spar-decker**, a spar-decked vessel.

1877 SIR C. W. THOMSON *Voy. Challenger* I. i. 9 The 'Challenger', a spar-decked corvette. **1885** LADY BRASSEY *The Trades* 19 The 'Norham Castle' is a spar-decked ship. **1893** *Naut. Mag.* May 397 No allowance should be made for deck erections in a spar-decker.

spare (spɛə(r)), *sb.*[1] Also 5 spar. [f. SPARE *v.*[1] and *a.* Cf. Norw. and obs. G. *spar* the act of sparing or saving.]

†**1.** The fact of leaving unhurt or unharmed; sparing; leniency, mercy. In the phrases ***without spare*** and ***to make*** (***no***, etc.) ***spare***. *Obs.*

(*a*) *a* **1300** *Cursor M.* 2909 Bot þan com dome [= doom] witouten spare, To þaa þat lang was spared are. *c* **1380** *Antecrist* 136 in Todd *Three Treat. Wyclif* (1851), If þai wil noght turn til his lare, He sal þam sla wituten spare. *a* **1425** *Cursor M.* 3974 (Trin.), Iacob dred esau sare, For he was fel wiþouten spare. **1609** HOLLAND *Amm. Marcell.* 139 To wipe away all shamefull dishonour, as whetting their anger against such.. perfidious enemies, without spare.

(*b*) **1591** in Bacon *Genesis New Eng. Ch.* (1874) 127 They have made no spare or conscience to accuse.. and punish us. **1609** HOLLAND *Amm. Marcell.* 80 Our souldiors.. rifled rich villages full of corne and cattell, making spare of none. **1620** tr. *Boccaccio's Decam.* 4 Little lesse spare was made in the villages round about. **1633** BP. HALL *Hard T.* 421 Cut them off.. and make no spare of any of them.

2. a. The exercise of economy, frugality, or moderation. Chiefly in the phrase ***to make*** (***no***, etc.) ***spare***.

1577 GRANGE *Golden Aphrod.*, etc. Pj, To spende and make no spare, he must himselfe incline. **1590** SPENSER *F.Q.* III. i. 51 Whiles fruitfull Ceres, and Lyæus fat, Pourd out their plenty, without spight or spare. **1643** TRAPP *Comm. Gen.* xlvii. 14 Bidden to eate.. what he pleased, and make no spare. **1850** F. S. MERRYWEATHER *Glimmerings in Dark* 36 The canons of the Church.. injoined them to be bountiful in their charity and to use no spare in their hospitality. **1891** *Spectator* 19 Sept. 377/2 We may be able to make shift with 19 million quarters of foreign and Colonial Wheat. It is certainly desirable to make spare, as we may do if we have an abundant potato-crop.

b. Const. *of*. (Common *c* 1600–40.)

1577 KNEWSTUB *Confut.* Rj, He hath plentifully powred out, and made no spare of it, thorow out the whole yeare. **1579** TWYNE *Phis. agst. Fortune* II. xliii. 218 b, There must be no spare of the rod. **1626** BACON *New Atl.* (1650) 1 By which time our Victuals failed us, though we had made good spare of them. **1648** J. GOODWIN *Right & Might well met* 8 They made no spare of their owne deare lives. **1655** tr. *Sorel's Com. Hist. Francion* II. 32 At our meal there was no spare of liquor. **1832** tr. *Tour German Prince* IV. 77 There are a thousand men and two hundred horses in action, and no spare of gunpowder.

†**c.** ***at spare***, with poor or little food or entertainment; poorly, frugally. *Obs.*[−1]

1585 EARL LEYCESTER *Corr.* (Camden) 462 Most of the noblemen and gentlemen lodged that night at spare in Harwiche.

3. a. In various elliptical uses of the adj.: A spare or reserve sum of money; a spare room; a spare part, tool, tyre, etc., carried esp. by motorists to replace a breakage or supply a sudden emergency. Also *spec.* in *pl.*, spare parts.

1642 FULLER *Holy & Prof. St.* IV. xvi. 321 Reserving a spare for all events and accidentall occasions. **1868** DICKENS in *Lett.* (1880) II. 355 To provide and lay down new Brussels carpets in the front spare and the two top spares. **1906** *Daily Chron.* 24 Apr. 3/3 He recommends.. a complete spare magneto. I wonder if he has ever really carried such a 'spare'. **1907** C. W. BROWN *Petrol Engine* i. 11 The manufacture is simplified and the number of 'spares' which the owner of a car is called upon to carry considerably reduced. **1908** *Motor Boat* 5 Mar. 133/1 The best method of dealing with spares is to have a chest made to carry all the spares you require. **1914** *Vanity Fair* Jan. 95/1 Some ingenious modifications have been devised for taking care of the 'spare'. **1930** A. P. HERBERT *Water Gipsies* xxiii. 334 I'll put you to bed in the spare, and let nobody come near you. **1957** *Practical Wireless* XXXIII. 701/2 A suitable piece of aluminium can probably be found in almost any spares box. **1976** M. MAGUIRE *Scratchproof* v. 66 Did it usually take him an hour to put on the spare? Would he mind if I looked at the punctured tyre? **1979** B. PARVIN *Deadly Dyke* v. 23 A small room with a single bed.. had never been used... It would have been thought of as the spare.

b. *slang.* An unattached woman, esp. one available for casual sex. Freq. in phr. ***a bit of spare.***

1969 J. BOLAND *Shakespeare Curse* xxi. 169 Kelley was a man whose wife was in an advanced state of pregnancy. You think he'd turn down a bit of spare if it was offered to him? **1974** P. CAVE *Dirtiest Picture Postcard* x. 61 The men would not have to bother with the married girls anyway. There's plenty of spare about. **1978** R. BUSBY *Garvey's Code* iv. 44, I.. got the impression Maurice was.. on the look-out for a bit of spare... Some of the girls we get in here.. don't leave much to the imagination.

4. orig. *U.S.* In ten-pins and skittles: The knocking down of all the pins with two bowls (thus leaving one 'to spare'), or with the first bowl (= ***double spare***); the score for doing this.

1843 *Knickerbocker* XXII. 327 His bowling at ninepins was the very perfection of carelessness. He was never guilty of a 'spare'. **1879** *Daily News* 2 Sept. 3/1 Younger people.. sought out the American ten-pin alleys,.. and, in striving for 'spares' and 'double-spares', esteemed themselves far in advance of their wise elders. **1884** *Harper's Mag.* Jan. 299/2 Strikes and spares were less common. **1976** *Bridgwater Mercury* 21 Dec., Keith Pollard, whose top-of-the-board 84 included four spares, led Alleycats to a runaway home win.. in a first division Puriton and District Skittles League Game.

†**spare**, *sb.*[2] *Obs.* Forms: 4 spaier, 5 spayere, speyer, speyr(e, 5–6 spayre, 6 sparre, 5–6 (8–9) spare. [Of obscure origin.] An opening or slit in a gown, robe, etc., in later use in a woman's gown (see quot. 1597).

Jamieson (1808) has also 'the slit or opening, formerly used in the fore-part of breeches'.

a **1300** *Cursor M.* 5825 He put it [his hand] eft in his spaier, And vte he drogh it, hale and fere. ? *a* **1400** *Morte Arth.* 2060 A-bowne the spayre a spanne, emange the schortte rybbys. *c* **1430** *Pilgr. Lyf Manhode* II. ix. (1869) 78 And than Resoun putte hire hond in to hire bosom bi a spayere. *c* **1440** *Jacob's Well* 115 His clothyng was lynen, & full of spayerys, & in euery spayere hyng a crewett. *a* **1529** SKELTON *P. Sparowe* 345 My byrde.. That was wont to.. go in at my spayre, And crepe in at my gore Of my gowne before. **1530** PALSGR. 273/2 Sparre of a gowne, *fente de la robe.* **1597** SKENE *De Verb. Sign.* s.v. *Bastardus*, That part of weemens claiths, sik as of their gown, or petticot, quhilk vnder the belt, and before, is open, commonlie is called, the spare. ? *a* **1700** *Jew's Daughter* in Motherwell *Minstrelsy* (1827) 52 She took out a little pen-knife, Hung low down by her spare. [Also in other ballads.]

spare, *sb.*[3] Anglicized form of SPARUS.

1803 SHAW *Gen. Zool.* IV. II. 407 Rose-red Spare, with silvery abdomen. *Ibid.* 419 Silvery Spare [etc.].

spare, *sb.*[4] *Coal-mining.* (See quot.)

1849 GREENWELL *Coal-trade Terms, Northumb. & Durh.* 49 *Spare.*—A piece of wood, 6 or 8 inches long, 6 inches broad, cut from 1 inch Scotch deal, with one of the flat sides tapered off to the end;.. the baff-end is put in first,.. and the spare driven between the baff-end and the crib, in the manner of a wedge.

†**spare**, obs. variant of SPAR *sb.*[1]

Examples of the pl. *spares*, *sparis* in the 15–16th cent. probably belong to SPAR.

1688 HOLME *Armoury* III. 100/1 *Raile*,.. is a piece of Timber, 6, 7, 8, 9, 10 foot or more long,.. and an inch or more thick... *Spare*, is two inches thick, and four inches broad; in some places it is termed a single Quarter.

spare (spɛə(r)), *a.* and *adv.* Also 5 spar. [Connected with SPARE *v.*[1] Cf. ON. *sparr* (to be) spared; OE. *spær*, OHG. *spar*, MDu. *spaer*, MSw. and Norw. *spar* sparing; also Du. *spaar-*, G. and Sw. *spar-*, Da. *spare-*, Icel. *spari-* in combs.]

I. 1. Not in actual or regular use at the time spoken of, but carried, held, or kept in reserve for future use or to supply an emergency; esp. *Naut.* (see quot. 1769); additional, extra.

a. In attributive use. Also ***spare room***, a room not regularly used, esp. a bedroom reserved for visitors. ***spare tyre***, (*a*) an extra tyre carried in a motor vehicle for emergencies; similarly, ***spare wheel***; (*b*) *transf.*, a roll of fat around the stomach (*colloq.*).

The various types of context are illustrated by the different groups of quotations.

(*a*) **13..** *E.E. Allit. P.* C. 104 Cables þay fasten,.. weȝen her ankres, Sprude spak to þe sprete þe spare bawe-lyne. *c* **1450** *Bk. Curtasye* 792 in *Babees Bk.*, The keruer anon.. Into þe couertoure wyn he powres owt, Or in-to a spare pece, with-outen doute. **1497** *Naval Acc. Hen. VII* (1896) 110 Spare extrees for faucons,.. v. **1573** *Richmond Wills* (Surtees) 242, v. ireon teames,.. ij spare crooks. **1590** SHAKS. *Com. Err.* I. i. 80 A small spare Mast, Such as sea-faring men prouide for stormes. **1602** MARSTON *Ant. & Mel.* II. Wks. 1856 I. 23 If you have any spare paire of silver spurs. **1691** T. H[ALE] *Acc. New Invent.* 43 A spare Set thereof [i.e. rudder-irons] sent to Sea with every Lead-sheathed Ship. **1709** *Lond. Gaz.* No. 4521/2 One of the Flukes of the Spare-Anchor [was].. shot off. **1769** FALCONER *Dict. Marine* (1780), *Spare*, an epithet applied to any part of a ship's.. furniture, that lies in reserve, to supply the place of such as may be lost, or rendered incapable of service. Hence we say, spare top-masts, spare sails, spare rigging, &c. **1811** *Regul. & Orders Army* 276 All Spare Ammunition is given in to the nearest Ordnance Depôt. **1856** KANE *Arct. Expl.* II. xvi. 173 We carried spare tins, in case the others should burn out. **1893** KIPLING *Many Invent.* 2 We've just sent our regular engine to London, and this spare one's not.. so accurate. **1917** —— *Diversity of Creatures* 162 The policeman laid his hand on the rim of the right driving-door (Woodhouse carries his spare tyres aft). **1920** 'O. DOUGLAS' *Penny Plain* xxiii. 267 It was a tyre gone... Stark put on the spare wheel and they started again. **1961** *Harper's Bazaar* Dec. 43/1 The deep diaphragm section slims you... That 'spare-tyre' has vanished! **1971** D. DEVINE *Dead Trouble* v. 48 My spare tyre keeps me warm. You're too skinny. **1972** *Country Life* 7 Dec. 1592/3 The luggage boot is.. fairly well filled by the spare wheel. **1977** *Lancashire Life* Nov. 153/1 There is no need for a spare tyre to clutter up the Mini's limited boot space.

(*b*) *a* **1548** HALL *Chron., Hen. VIII*, 29 The master of hys horse folowed him with a spare horse. **1613** PURCHAS *Pilgrimage* (1614) 420 They bring with them three moneths victuall,.. and a spare Horse for food, besides a better for seruice. **1708** J. C. *Compl. Collier* (1845) 33 The Charge of maintaining a spare Shift of Horses. **1781** GIBBON *Decl. & F.* xviii. II. 90 The custom of their warriors, to lead in their hand one or two spare horses, enabled them to advance and to retreat with a rapid diligence. **1822–56** DE QUINCEY *Confess.* (1862) 76 Here's a spare dromedary. **1850** R. G. CUMMING *Hunter's Life S. Afr.* I. 105 A horseman.. accompanied by an after-rider leading a spare horse.

(*c*) *a* **1687** PETTY *Pol. Arith.* (1690) 107 There are spare Hands among the King's Subjects, to earn two Millions more than they do. **1897** *Daily News* 27 May 8/5 Driver R. Wilcockson, a spare driver,.. gave evidence in regard to the irregular hours of the 'spare' men.

(*d*) **1702** *Guide for Constables* 12 He shall keep one or more spare beds for lodging of strangers. **1811** SCOTT *Let.* in *Lockhart* (1837) II. xi. 361 My present intention is to have only two spare bed-rooms. **1814** JANE AUSTEN *Mansfield Park* I. iii. 54 The absolute necessity of a spare-room for a friend was now never forgotten. **1827** SCOTT *Surg. Dau.* i, A spare apartment, in which Doctor Gray occasionally accommodated..patients. **1837** *Southern Lit. Messenger* III. 333 One of the third-story rooms we must keep for a spare room. **1855** *Knickerbocker* XLVI. 380 They have stolen away into the spare-room, otherwise, parlor. **1881** Young *Every Man his own Mechanic* §806. 371 A spare bed which may be put up anywhere in a few minutes. **1904** A. Dale *Wanted: a Cook* 332 The wine-cellar was under the bed in the spare-room. **1928** Galsworthy *Swan Song* III. ix. 280 He spied a spare-room window open at the top. **1953** E. Simon *Past Masters* III. 169 The spare room, newly done up, was frequently inhabited by..distinguished visitors. **1977** J. Porter *Who the Heck is Sylvia?* ix. 79 Her habit of knocking on the spare-room door before entering.

b. In predicative use. Now *rare*.

1497 *Naval Acc. Hen. VII* (1896) 87, ij pair wheles & a pair of hynder wheles spare. **1600** Dymmok *Ireland* (1843) 7 His horse of service is alwaies led spare. **1621** Lady M. Wroth *Urania* 460 They only riding in one Coach, two other went spare. *a* **1642** Sir W. Monson *Naval Tracts* III. (1704) 324/1 Anchors lying spare at the River side. **1899** *Westm. Gaz.* 7 Dec. 5/2 Their ponies were running about spare all over the place.

†**c.** Of land, ground, etc.: Uncultivated, unoccupied, vacant. *Obs.* (exc. in sense 1 a or 2).

c **1470** *Gol. & Gaw.* 112 Sped hym on spedely on the spare mure. **1577** B. Googe *Heresbach's Husb.* I. (1586) 24 The ground that is yeerely sowen, and that hath lyne spare, is to be plowed thryse. **1665** Sir T. Herbert *Trav.* (1677) 221 The number of Gardens, Cemeteries [etc.],..take up much more spare place than London doth. **1669** Worlidge *Syst. Agric.* 93 You may raise these Pollards in Hedge-rows, and spare places.

†**d.** Of a leaf: Blank. *Obs.*$^{-1}$

1705 Hearne *Collect.* 13 July (O.H.S.) I. 5 A spare leafe, before a 4to Book of tracts.

e. *colloq.* Of persons: off-duty, idle (cf. sense 1 a (*c*)). Also, useless, superfluous.

1919 *Athenæum* 1 Aug. 695/2 'To be spare' is to be temporarily off duty. **1925** Fraser & Gibbons *Soldier & Sailor Words & Phrases* 266 *Spare, to look,* to be idle: not engaged on any particular job. **1936** J. Curtis *Gilt Kid* xv. 154 We can't stand around here spare... Come on. **1970** 'D. Halliday' *Dolly & Cookie Bird* viii. 117 Janey stayed there with her manicured hand on his brow..and I felt a bit spare.

f. Phr. *to go spare*: (*a*) to be unemployed; (*b*) to become infuriated or distraught. *colloq.*

c **1942** R. Dimbleby *Let.* in J. Dimbleby *Richard Dimbleby* (1975) vii. 163 I'd be grateful if your team would remember an at least practised broadcaster who appears to be 'going spare'! **1958** F. Norman *Bang to Rights* 169 When he saw what I had done he went spare. **1969** J. N. Smith *Is he Dead, Miss ffinch?* xv. 95 The train had just gone. His lordship nearly went spare. **1975** T. Heald *Deadline* iv. 68 What's the time? Monica will be going spare.

2. a. That can be spared, dispensed with, or given away, as being in excess of actual requirements; superfluous. †Rarely as predicate.

a **1553** Udall *Royster D.* (Arb.) 28 She shall haue the first day a whole pecke of argent... A pecke? *Nomine patris,* haue ye so much spare? **1613** Beaum. & Fl. *Captain* I. iii, When I..have enough spare gold To boil away, you shall be welcome to me. **1783** Burke *Rep. Aff. India* Wks. 1842 II. 49 The supply destined for the London market is proportioned to the spare tonnage. **1816** Tuckey *Narr. Exped. R. Zaire* iv. (1818) 141 The very little spare provisions the natives seem to have at this season. **1849** Sir F. B. Head *Stokers & Pokers* v. (1851) 53 A few of the..men who had spare cash purchased the greater portion of these articles. **1856** Kane *Arct. Expl.* I. xiii. 149 All the spare morsels, the cast-off delicacies of the mess.

b. Of time: Not employed or taken up by one's ordinary or usual duties or occupations; leisure.

a **1610** Healey *Epictetus* (1636) 69 If thou hast any spare time, go. *c* **1643** Ld. Herbert *Autobiog.* (1824) 240 All the spare hours which I could get from my visits and negotiations. **1711** Addison *Spect.* (J.), The female world..have more spare time upon their hands, and lead a more sedentary life. **1885** G. Allen *Babylon* xvi, Minna was working hard in all her spare hours. **1885** 'Mrs. Alexander' *At Bay* iv, The earliest spare moment he could find was devoted to Lady Gethin.

transf. **1633** G. Herbert *Temple, Sunday* iv, The other dayes fill up the spare And hollow room with vanities.

II. †**3.** Of speech: Sparing; marked by reticence or reserve. *Obs. rare.*

13.. *Gaw. & Gr. Knt.* 901 þenne was spyed & spured vpon spare wyse, Bi preue poyntez of þat prynce [etc.]. *c* **1460** *Towneley Myst.* xx. 294 This spekyng must be spar, and neuen it neuer..; let no man wyt where that we war.

4. a. Of persons, their limbs, etc.: Having little flesh; not fat or plump; lean, thin.

a **1548** Hall *Chron., Hen. VII,* 60 b, He was a man of body but leane and spare. **1597** Shaks. *2 Hen. IV,* III. ii. 287 O, giue me the spare men, and spare me the great ones. **1614** Rowlands *Fooles Bolt* (Hunterian Cl.) 34 Thou worthy leane spare Gentleman. **1667** Milton *P.L.* x. 511 His Visage drawn he felt to sharp and spare. **1709** *Tatler* No. 93 ¶4 As I am spare, I am also very tall. **1716** Swift *Progr. Poetry* Wks. 1755 III. II. 162 Hard exercise and harder fare Soon make my dame grow lank and spare. **1808** Scott *Marm.* II. iv, Her cheek was pale, her form was spare. **1844** W. Irving *Goldsmith* xiv. (1850) 172 He was upwards of six feet high, and very spare. **1885** *Spectator* 25 July 971/1 A man of spare figure, with a shrewd, humorous face.

transf. **1848** Dickens *Dombey* lvii, Mrs. Miff assents with a spare nod of her mortified bonnet. **1865** —— *Mut. Fr.* I. xv, The staircase, balustrades, and rails, had a spare look.

b. Const. *in* or *of* (flesh).

1632 Sherwood, Spare (of flesh), *desnué de chair.* **1842** Tennyson *Talk. Oak* 92, I hold them [fairies] exquisitely knit, But far too spare of flesh. **1871** Napheys *Prev. & Cure Dis.* I. i. 45 Spare in flesh.

c. Lacking body or substance; flimsy, thin.

1602 Warner *Alb. Eng.* XIII. lxxix. (1612) 325 But all effects, and names to God his Essence come more short Than Sun-shine to the Suns-selfe, than to action spare report. **1858** Lowell *Vis. Sir Launfal* II. iii, Sir Launfal's raiment thin and spare Was idle mail 'gainst barbed air.

d. *poet.* Growing thinly or sparsely.

1815 Shelley *Alastor* 527 Grey rocks did peep from the spare moss.

e. Of style: unadorned, bare, simple.

1965 *Listener* 7 Oct. 552/2 The narrative..was spare, precise, almost a little cold, and made its tale of muddle and butchery thereby the more devastating. **1966** *Ibid.* 12 May 702/2 We feel the participants to be in agony and it is impossible to remain indifferent to them. This achievement has something to do with the spare, angular dialogue. **1977** *Times* 23 May 25/1 Tom Courtenay gives a frighteningly spare performance in One Day in the Life of Ivan Denisovich.

†**5. a.** Of persons: Sparing, temperate, or moderate *of* or *in* something, esp. diet or speech. *Obs.*

(*a*) **1563** Foxe *A. & M.* 1050/1 He [Hooper] was..spare of dyet, sparer of wordes, and sparest of tyme. **1615** Brathwait *Strappado* (1878) 183 Another may we see, though spare of speech, And temporate in discourse, yet he may teach By his effectual words the rasher sort. **1658–9** in *Burton's Diary* (1828) III. 341, I am very spare of speaking. **1697** Dryden *Virgil, Life* (1721) I. 61 He was..spare of Dyet, and hardly drank any Wine.

(*b*) **1581** Pettie tr. *Guazzo's Civ. Conv.* II. (1586) 71 b, We must be spare in speaking of things which are not easily beleeued. **1589** Puttenham *Eng. Poesie* III. (Arb.) 298 A man to be in giuing free, in asking spare. **1599** Shaks. *Hen. V,* II. ii. 131 Are they spare in diet, Free from grosse passion.

†**b.** Not lavish, liberal, or profuse, esp. in expenditure or living; frugal, niggardly, parsimonious; abstemious. *Obs.*

1577 Hanmer *Anc. Eccles. Hist.* VII. xxxi. (1619) 143 Pierius was proved a spare man of life, and singular in Philosophy. **1583** Stubbes *Anat. Abus.* I ij b, But as some be ouer largeous, so other some are spare enough. **1633** P. Fletcher *Poet. Misc.* 58 Oh happy pair, where nothing wants to either,..Fortune and nature being spare to neither!

c. *dial.* Displaying little exertion or energy; slow, dilatory.

1746– in south-western dial. glossaries, etc.

6. a. Characterized by meanness, bareness, economy, or frugality, esp. in regard to food.

1560 Abp. Parker *Corr.* (Parker Soc.) 133 The unclean or negligent order and spare-keeping of the house of prayer. **1600** Shaks. *A.Y.L.* III. ii. 20 As it is a spare life.., it fits my humor well: but as there is no more plentie in it, it goes much against my stomacke. **1634** Milton *Comus* 767 She.. Means her provision onely to the good, That live according to her sober laws, And holy dictate of spare Temperance. **1876** Geo. Eliot *Dan. Der.* xxiv, To order the whole establishment on the sparest footing possible.

b. Of diet, fare, meals, etc.: Consisting of a comparatively small amount of food, esp. of a plain kind; not abundant or plentiful.

1570 Jewel *View of Seditious Bull* (1582) 29 So that the quantitie be smal, and fit for sober and spare diet. **1607** Rowlands *Earl of Warwick* (Hunterian Cl.) 66 His diet of the meanest, hard and spare. *c* **1665** Mrs. Hutchinson *Mem. Col. Hutchinson* (1846) 24 He was not talkative, yet free of discourse; of a very spare diet. *a* **1721** Prior *Wand. Pilgr.* 13 Spare diet, and spring-water clear, Physicians hold are good. **1784** Cowper *Task* IV. 173 When her patriots.. Enjoy'd—spare feast!—a radish and an egg! **1841** Barham *Ingol. Leg.* Ser. II. *Nell Cook,* The Priory fare was scant and spare. **1842** Combe *Digestion* 203 He was unable for study till five or six hours after even a very spare dinner.

transf. **1893** Stevenson *Catriona* xxv. (1902) 306, I drink nothing else but spare, cold water.

c. *poet.* Scanty, meagre, rare.

1813 Shelley *Q. Mab* v. 202 Some servile souls, Whom cowardice itself might safely chain, Or the spare mite of avarice could bribe. **1842** Tennyson *St. S. Styl.* 77 Eating not, Except the spare chance-gift of those that came To touch my body. **1888** *Cent. Mag.* May 26 Even now the reaper-beams appear, And gather in the clouds' spare aftermath.

7. As *adv.* Sparely; with spare diet. *rare.*

1813 Scott *Trierm.* III. iv, Yet still his watch the warrior keeps, Feeds hard and spare, and seldom sleeps.

III. 8. *Comb.,* chiefly parasynthetic, as ***spare-bodied, -built, -fed*** adjs.; †**spare-handed** *adj.,* having a sparing hand; **spare-time** *a.,* that is done in one's spare time; operating in or occupying spare time.

1626 J. Yates *Ibis ad Cæsarem* I. 1 God is ample in Predestination unto life, but in the death of sinners sparehanded. **1742** Jarvis *Don Quix.* i, He was of a robust constitution, spare-bodied, of a meagre visage. **1813** Scott *Rokeby* II. xxii, His stately form, spare-built and tall. **1837** Lockhart *Scott* IV. v. 157 For 'early to rise', unless in the case of spare-fed anchorites, takes for granted 'early to bed'. **1895** Scully *Kafir Stories* 133 Whitson was a sallow-faced, spare-built man of short stature. **1931** Spare-time [see part-time *a.*]. **1936** 'M. Innes' *Death at President's Lodging* ii. 39 The spare-bodied man that he was. **1955** Blunden *Addresses on General Subjects* 24 This poet [*sc.* Shelley] almost achieved, as one of his spare-time labours, the establishment of the first steamship service in the Mediterranean. **1973** A. Holden *Girl on Beach* 143 He really is a professional lawyer after all, and merely a spare-time amateur art critic. **1978** *Nagel's Encycl.-Guide: China* 320 The 'Spare Time Industrial University' at Shanghai.

spare (spɛə(r)), *v.*^{1} Forms: 1 **sparian, spear-, spærian,** 3 **sparien, spearien,** 3–4 **sparie** (4 **-ye**), 3–5 **spary;** 4–5 **sparen,** 4– **spare,** 5–8 *Sc.* **spair** (6 **spaare, spaer,** 7 **spayer,** 9 *dial.* **spaar**). [Common Teutonic: OE. *sparian* (also *a-*, *ȝesparian*), = OFris. *sparia* (WFris. *sparje*, †*sparje*, NFris. *spari, spāri*), OS. and OHG. *sparôn* (MLG. and LG., MDu. and Du., MHG. and G. *sparen*), ON. *spara* (Icel., Norw., Sw. *spara*, Da. *spare*), f. a stem *spar-* (see spare *a.*) of uncertain relationship. The Teutonic word is the base of OF. *espargner* (mod.F. *épargner*), It. *sparagnare* and *sparmiare*.]

I. 1. a. *trans.* To leave (a person) unhurt, unharmed, or uninjured; to refrain from inflicting injury or punishment upon; to allow to escape, go free, or live. Usually with personal subject.

c **825** *Vesp. Psalter* lxxi. 13 God..spearað dearfan & weðlan. *c* **897** K. Ælfred *Gregory's Past. C.* xlvi. 352 Hie ne sparodon ða synnfullan, ac sloȝon. *c* **1100** in Cockayne *Shrine* 17 Ne spareð nu se fæder þan sune ne nan mann oðren; Ac ælc man winð onȝean oðren. *a* **1122** *O.E. Chron.* (Laud MS.) an. 1086, He sætte.. þæȝnas on cweartern, & æt nextan he ne sparode his aȝenne broðor. *c* **1175** *Lamb. Hom.* 121 þa he na sparede na ihesu crist his aȝene sune. *c* **1205** Lay. 27487 Nuste nan kempe whæm he sculde slæn on, and wham he sculde sparien. **1297** R. Glouc. (Rolls) 8830 Sparie he wolde Mildemen & harde chasty þe proute. **1375** Barbour *Bruce* IX. 297 He..gert his men burn all Bouchane ..and sparit nane. *c* **1400** Maundev. (Roxb.) xxxi. 142 þare es nane spared þat es taken with a trespas. **1474** Caxton *Chesse* II. iv. (1883) 53 To spare them & gyue hem her lyf. **1589** ? Lyly *Pappe w. Hatchet* (1844) 19, I am like death, Ile spare none. **1596** Shaks. *Tam. Shr.* IV. iii. 153 Take thou the bill, giue me thy meat-yard, and spare not me. *a* **1628** Preston *New Covt.* (1634) 364 If men could have entered into Covenant and kept the Law, Christ had beene spared. **1697** Dryden *Virg. Georg.* IV. 758 Whom ev'n the savage Beasts had spar'd, they kill'd. **1780** Cowper *Fable* 34 An earthquake may be bid to spare The man that's strangled by a hair. **1825** Scott *Talism.* iii, Saladin had issued particular orders that he should be spared and protected. **1891** Farrar *Darkn. & Dawn* xlii, They..demanded that there should be a trial, and that the innocent should be spared.

refl. **1297** R. Glouc. (Rolls) 1609 Vor woch dede a man ssolde..Lese is on eye, & he him sulf ne sparde him sulue noȝt, Ac let pulte out is owe eye. *a* **1300** *Cursor M.* 26718 þis man will we spare, For noght he spard him-self are.

b. With impersonal object (but implying or suggesting a person or persons). (Cf. 4.)

c **825** *Vesp. Psalter* lxxvii. 50 [He] ne spearede from deaðe sawlum heara. **1362** Langl. *P. Pl.* A. VII. 11 Spynneth it spedily, spareþ noght ȝour fyngres. **1605** Shaks. *Lear* II. ii. 72 Spare my gray-beard, you wagtaile? **1725** Pope *Odyss.* xv. 303 Receive the suppliant! spare my destin'd blood. **1757** Gray *Bard* 107 Visions of glory, spare my aching sight. **1817** Shelley *Rev. Islam* x. xxiv. 1 Famine had spared the palace of the king.

(*b*) ***spare me*** (or ***my***) ***days!*** an exclamatory ejaculation (*Austral.* and *N.Z. colloq.*).

1916 C. J. Dennis *Songs of Sentimental Bloke* 16 The music of the sorft an' barmy breeze... Aw, spare me days! *c* **1926** 'Mixer' *Transport Workers' Song Bk.* 13 Yet you'll find when work is busy, Spare me days, we're slipping back. **1967** *Coast to Coast 1965–6* 134 Spare me days, you go and toil your guts out [etc.]. **1970** K. Giles *Death in Church* iv. 101 He..gave me one and, spare me days, I almost certainly have it.

c. To allow to be free or exempt *from* (or †*of*) some task, etc. Also *refl.* without const.

1375 Barbour *Bruce* v. 362 He him sparit na kyn thing, Bot prufit swa his fors..That throu his vorschip [etc.]. **1398** Trevisa *Barth. De P.R.* XVIII. cix. (Bodl. MS.), The more scheo [i.e. a cow] is forbore and spared fro [**1495** of] trauaile, þe more slowe [s]he is. **1596** Bacon *Max. & Use Com. Law* II. (1635) 7 By which the Earles were spared of their toyles and labours, and that was laid upon the Sheriffes. **1794** Mrs. Radcliffe *Myst. Udolpho* xxxv, [The] house-keeper, now spared from further attendance by the entrance of the count.

d. To refrain from denouncing or exposing in strong terms; to deal gently or leniently with.

1535 Coverdale *Job* xxxii. 21, I wil open my lyppes, and make answere. I will regarde no maner of personne, no man wil I spare. **1607** Shaks. *Cor.* II. iii. 243 *Sici*[*nus*]. Lay the fault on vs. *Brut*[*us*]. I, spare vs not. **1649** Milton *Eikon.* B 2, As he hath not spar'd his Adversaries, so to him will be us'd no more Courtship then he uses. **1728** T. Sheridan tr. *Persius* (1739) Ded. p. iv, I never did once either distinguish or spare you. **1771** *Junius Lett.* liv. (1788) 295 What public question have I declined? What villain have I spared? **1821** Scott *Kenilw.* xli, As Varney..had been studious to spare the character of his patron. **1852** Thackeray *Esmond* I. iv, My lady used not to spare Colonel Esmond in talking of him. **1891** Farrar *Darkn. & Dawn* lxii. 295 He shrank from eliciting a keenness of wit which had not spared the bloodstained Sylla.

e. To refrain from afflicting or distressing.

1794 Mrs. Radcliffe *Myst. Udolpho* xxxviii, Emily..was followed by the Lady Blanche,..whom she entreated to spare her on the subject of her distress. **1819** Shelley *Cenci* v. ii. 108 Oh, spare me! Speak to me no more!.. Those solemn tones Have sounded worse than torture. **1856** Capern *Poems* (ed. 2) 143 Spare, oh, spare thy tender feelings.

2. *absol.* To exercise or show mercy, forbearance, or leniency.

a **1225** *Juliana* (Royal MS.) 70 A stalewurðe men ne sparie ȝe nawiht; ha haueð us alle scheome idon. *a* **1300** *Cursor M.* 3974 Esau ai he dred ful sare, For he was fel and wald noght spare. **1382** Wyclif *Job* xxvii. 22 He shal senden out vp on hym, and not sparen. *c* **1420** *Prymer* 78 God, to whom it is proprid to haue merci & to spare euer more. **1422** tr. *Secreta Secret., Priv. Priv.* 181 He that is a gouernoure in tymes he shall Spare, and in tymes vengeaunse take. **1535** Coverdale *Job* vi. 10, I wolde desyre him in my payne, that he shulde not spare. **1611** Bible *Prov.* vi. 34 He will not spare in the day of vengeance. **1736** *Gentl. Mag.* VI. 678 Spare, charmer spare! in prudence do! **1761** Gray *Fatal Sisters* 34 Ours to kill, and ours to spare. **1825** Scott *Talism.* xxii, The lion Richard will spare when he has conquered. **1871** Grosart *H. Vaughan's Wks.* I. Ded. p. iv, Available and destined for the same august post (God sparing).

†**b.** Const. *to.* (After L. *parcere.*) *Obs.*

c **1340** HAMPOLE *Psalter* xviii. 13 Of myn hid [trespasses] make me clene, and of oþer spare til þi seruaunte. **1382** WYCLIF *Wisd.* xii. 16 To alle thou makest thee to sparen. *c* **1420** *Prymer* 47 Spare, lord, spare to þe puple.

3. *trans.* †**a.** To refrain from violating, infringing, or breaking. *Obs.*

1303 R. BRUNNE *Handl. Synne* 806 Of al þe festys þat yn holy chyrche are Holy sunday men oght to spare. **1387** TREVISA *Higden* (Rolls) VIII. 129 No privelege of persoun wheþer of holy cherche noþer fredom was i-spared.

b. To abstain from visiting (a sin, etc.) with due punishment; to forgive or pardon.

1388 WYCLIF *Job* xiv. 16 Sotheli thou hast noumbrid my steppis; but spare thou my synnes. *a* **1450** tr. *De Imitatione* III. lv. 132, I þonke þe þat þou hast not spared myn eueles. **1500–20** DUNBAR *Poems* lxx. 27 Thow, that on rude ws ransomit,..Spair our trespas. **1782** COWPER *Mut. Forbearance* 44 If infirmities..Are crimes so little to be spar'd.

c. To preserve or save (life) in place of destroying; to allow to continue or last.

1594 KYD *Cornelia* v. 445 To spare Thy worthles life that yet must one day perish. **1605** SHAKS. *Lear* II. ii. 66 This ancient Ruffian Sir, whose life I haue spar'd at sute of his gray-beard. **1781** COWPER *Expost.* 623 Those holy men.. could not..spare a life too short to reach the skies. **1823** SCOTT *Quentin D.* xix, With what face darest thou ask any guerdon beyond my sparing thy worthless life? **1865** TROLLOPE *Belton Est.* i. 8 He hoped that the squire's life would be long spared. **1890** *Science-Gossip* XXVI. 167 Poor pussy began to purr, and that decided the verdict in favour of her life being spared.

4. a. To abstain from destroying, removing, damaging, or injuring (a thing).

c **897** K. ÆLFRED *Gregory's Past. C.* xviii. 140 Swæ sindon ða loccas to sparianne ðæm sacerde ðæt hie ða hyd behelizen. *c* **900** tr. *Baeda's Hist.* IV. xxvii, Cyricum ne mynstrum seo herehand sparode ne ne arode. **1338** R. BRUNNE *Chron.* (1810) 248 Holy who salle spare,..Whan þo þat hedes are do þer to no gode. **1382** WYCLIF *Rom.* xi. 21 Forsothe if God sparide not the kyndely braunchis, lest perauenture he spare not thee. *c* **1400** *Brut* li. 45 [They] destroyede al þing þat þai fonde; and no þing þai ne sparede. **1480** *Cov. Leet Bk.* 446 In their shotyng called rovyng, ..[they] nother sparen corn ne grasse, but distroyen & defowlen hem. *a* **1586** SIDNEY *Arcadia* (1622) 368 Shee.. was now about to put out his eyes, which all this while were spared. **1643** DENHAM *Cooper's H.* 155 What does he think our Sacriledge would spare, When such th' effects of our Devotion are? **1648** MILTON *Sonn.* viii. 10 The great Emathian Conqueror bid spare The house of Pindarus. **1759** JOHNSON *Rasselas* xxix, From the wonders which time has spared we may conjecture..what it has destroyed. **1794** MRS. RADCLIFFE *Myst. Udolpho* xlv, The beauty..of its delicate carvings, determined the count to spare this door. **1839** THIRLWALL *Greece* VI. 165 It was believed that Alexander..was induced to spare it by the hope that it would soon surrender. **1879** S. C. BARTLETT *Egypt to Pal.* x. 225 Usually a large part of their branches had been cut off, even when the tree itself had been spared.

b. To save or protect (a thing) from damage, wear, or undue strain in some way.

1817 LADY MORGAN *France* I. (1818) I. 63, I remember our having alighted from our carriage to spare its springs in a sort of 'crack-scull-common' road.

II. 5. a. To refrain from using or consuming; to use in a frugal or economical manner. Now *rare*.

c **1000** ÆLFRIC *Hom.* (Thorpe) II. 70 He sparode þæt gode win oð his azenum to-cyme. *a* **1300** *Cursor M.* 7927 For to spar his aun aght þis pouer mans scep he laght. **1398** TREVISA *Barth. De P.R.* VI. xiv. (Bodl. MS.), [A father] spareþ his owne mete to fede his chyld with. *c* **1440** *Jacob's Well* 143 þou my3t so spare þi purse, þat þou my3t forfare þi-self. **1477** EARL RIVERS (Caxton) *Dictes* 14 It satisfieth not to spare metes and do euill dedis. *c* **1550** N. SMYTH tr. *Herodian* II. 19 He..also teacheth others to be frugall, and spare that them selues gette. **1589** GREENE *Menaphon* (Arb.) 34 She sparde no euening milke, but went amongst the cream bowles, and made him a posset. **1635–56** COWLEY *Davideis* I. 869 Free Natures bounty thriftily they spent, And spared the Stock. **1651** HOBBES *Leviath.* II. xxx. 181 He which laboureth much, and sparing the fruits of his labour, consumeth little [etc.]. **1726** SWIFT *Gulliver* III. i, Being resolved to spare my provisions as much as I could. **1743** FRANCIS tr. *Hor., Odes* II. vii. 26 Thy Limbs from Toils of Warfare free, Nor spare the Casks reserv'd for Thee.

†**b.** To save, hoard, or store up. *Obs.*

c **1400** *Gamelyn* 320 My brother is a niggoun.., And we wil spende largely that he hath spared yore. **1483** CAXTON *Cato* F iij b, For men hath dyspended..in lytel tyme that whiche men hath acquyred and spared wyth grete labour. **1500–20** DUNBAR *Poems* xxxvi. 25 Sum grit gud gadderis and ay it spairis. **1579** SPENSER *Sheph. Cal.* May 84 The sonne of his loines why should he regard To leaue enriched with that he hath spard? **1648** GAGE *West Ind.* 160 What monies they have spared, after their own and their servants lawful maintenance. **1683** D. A. *Art Converse* 116 They can inform you of Twenty Arts how to gain and spare a Peny.

c. *absol.* To use or practise economy or frugality; to be parsimonious or niggardly; to live or act sparingly.

1377 LANGL. *P. Pl.* B. XII. 53 And riche renkes ri3t so gaderen and sparen. *c* **1420** *Sir Amadace* (Camden) ii, I my3te lung spare, Or alle these godus qwitte ware, And haue no3te to spend. *c* **1475** *Rauf Coil3ear* 202 Thairfoir sic [good fare] as thow seis, spend on, and not spair. *a* **1513** FABYAN *Chron.* VI. (1811) 234 He..gaue parte vnto suche knyghtes as he fauoured, and spared to theym that hadde wele deserued. **1573** TUSSER *Husb.* (1878) 204 For lordlie bent Must learne to spare. **1621** T. WILLIAMSON tr. *Goulart's Wise Vieillard* 73 It is a pleasing.. excuse among men..to alledge that they spare for their children. **1667** MILTON *P.L.* v. 320 Where Nature..by disburd'ning grows More fruitful, which instructs us not to spare. **1737** POPE tr. *Hor., Epist.* II. ii. 290, I, who at some times spend, at others spare. **1792** BURNS *Country Lassie* iv, But some will spend, and some will spare. **1866** HOWELLS *Venetian Life* 325 Those people who attempt to maintain a certain appearance upon insufficient means,..and who spare in every possible way. **1889** —— *Hazard New Fortunes* 94 They must spare in carriage hire at any rate.

prov. **1562** J. HEYWOOD *Prov. & Epigr.* (1867) 54 Euer spare and euer bare. **1573** TUSSER *Husb.* (1878) 23 Some spareth too late,..the foole at the bottom, the wise at the brim. **1677** MIÉGE *Fr. Dict.* II. s.v., To spare at the spiggot, and let it run out at the bung-hole. **1681** W. ROBERTSON *Phraseol. Gen.* s.v., Better spare at the brim, than at the bottom, *sera est in fundo parsimonia* [Seneca *Ep.* I. 5]. **1736** AINSWORTH I. s.v., It is too late to spare, when all is spent.

d. In passive: To be left over or unused.

1577 GOOGE *Heresbach's Husb.* § 149 You must feede them often by hand, when meate fayles abroade,..and not so much as Barly spared. **1793** SMEATON *Edystone L.* §237 The mason took the mortar out of the bucket; and if any was spared, he still kept on beating. **1799** [A. YOUNG] *Agric. Linc.* 25 All that may be spared at night, should be thrown to the common mortar heap, and fresh stucco made in the morning. **1868** ATKINSON *Cleveland Gloss.* 481 Eat what thee likes, an' what's spared tak' awa' yamm fur t' bairns.

6. To abstain or refrain from using, employing, exercising, etc.; to forbear, omit, or avoid the use or occasion of; also, to use, or deal in, with moderation, economy, or restraint:

a. In various special contexts.

(*a*) *c* **1000** ÆLFRIC *Hom.* II. 324 Se ðe sparað his zyrde, he hatað his cild. *a* **1250** *Prov. Ælfred* 451 in *O.E. Misc.*, þe mon þe spareþ yeorde.., þat him schal on ealde sore reowe. **1393** LANGL. *P. Pl.* C. VI. 139 Ho so spareþ þe spring spilleþ hus children. *c* **1430** *Stans Puer ad Mensam* 91 (Lamb. MS.), Who þat sparíþ þe rodde [*v.r.* the yerd] al uertues settíþ a-side. **1526** SKELTON *Magnyf.* 1955 There is nothynge that more dyspleaseth God Than from theyr chyldren to spare the rod Of correccyon. **1535** COVERDALE *Prov.* xiii. 24 He that spareth the rodde, hateth his sonne. **1664** BUTLER *Hud.* II. i. 844 Love is a Boy, by Poets styl'd, Then Spare the Rod, and spill the Child. **1841** LYTTON *Nt. & Morn.* II. iii, Spare the rod and spoil the child. **1855** THACKERAY *Newcomes* iii, I have a brother to whom my poor mother spared the rod, and who..has turned out but a spoilt child.

(*b*) *a* **1225** *Leg. Kath.* 807 Lure ow is to leosen ower swinkes lan, þe leoteð se lutel of, & sparieð ower speche. *a* **1300** *Cursor M.* 16110 Sai me iesus, qui dos þou þus? to me na soth þou spare. *c* **1386** CHAUCER *Sompn. T.* 55 Tel forth thy tale, and spare it not at al. *c* **1400** *Pilgr. Sowle* (Caxton, 1483) IV. xxx. 78 Flaterers and forgeours that sparen the soothe ben nothynge profitable. **1481** CAXTON *Reynard* xxxiv. (Arb.) 100 Yf ye wyl spare the trouth and lye grete lesynges. **1508** DUNBAR *Tua mariit wemen* 40 Syne thai spak more spedelie, and sparit no materis. **1617** MORYSON *Itin.* II. 72 He might doe well to spare the rest of his speech. **1663** S. PATRICK *Parab. Pilgr.* xii. (1687) 79 Your blushes bid me spare this language. **1731** SWIFT *Death Dr. Swift* Wks. 1841 I. 657/2 Had he but spared his tongue and pen, He might have rose like other men. **1753** RICHARDSON *Grandison* V. iv. 27, I am put upon a task that grieves me, Ease my heart, by sparing my speech. **1820** SCOTT *Monast.* xxxvii, 'Spare your threats,' said Murray. **1848** THACKERAY *Van. Fair* xxix, Much painful and unavailing talk between them was spared. **1864–8** BROWNING *J. Lee's Wife* II. iii, Spare the curse!

(*c*) *a* **1440** *Found. St. Bartholomew's* (E.E.T.S.) 19 Whane thou cummyste yn to the Iewes strete, spare thy sporys, lose thy brydyll, lette thyn hors to my gouernaunce. *c* **1470** *Gol. & Gaw.* 305 Thayr wes na spurris to spair, spedely thai spring. **1575** GASCOIGNE *Glasse of Govt.* Wks. 1910 II. 26 But yet where youth is prone to follow ill, There spare the spurre, and use the brydell still. **1735** SOMERVILLE *Chase* III. 85 Flourish the Whip, nor spare the galling Spur. **1782** MISS BURNEY *Cecilia* VIII. i, Why, Sir, you have not spared the spur! **1831** SCOTT *Ct. Rob.* xvi, Come along..like a good fellow, and for once I shall spare the whip.

b. In miscellaneous (partly *obs.*) uses.

a **1300** *Cursor M.* 5867 Dathait qua werkes on þam spar! þan held þai þam harder þan ar. **1388** WYCLIF *Jer.* l. 14 Ouercome 3e it [*sc.* Babylon], spare 3e not arowis, for it synnede to the Lord. **1515** *Plumpton Corr.* (Camden) 212, [I] entreated them to spare distreyning, till such tyme as I had sent unto you [etc.]. **1553** *Reg. Privy Council Scot.* I. 141 It is maist convenient and best to spair puneisment for the said cryme. **1573** TUSSER *Husb.* (1878) 97 Spare meadow at Gregorie, marshes at Pask, for feare of drie Sommer. **1687** A. LOVELL tr. *Thevenot's Trav.* I. 59 They spare not now and then a blow with a Cudgel by the by. **1831** SCOTT *Ct. Rob.* xxxiii, Count Robert spared putting forth some part of the military skill for which he was celebrated. **1884** F. TEMPLE *Relat. Relig. & Sci.* v. (1885) 142 We recognise that we are bound to spare pain to all creatures that can feel.

c. Const. *to* and infinitive.

Freq. from the 14th to the 17th century; now *rare*.

a **1225** *Juliana* 26 Ant..wa wurðe him wurst þat te mest sparie wondreðe to donne. **13..** *Sir Beues* 4482 Sire Miles.. Lep vpon a dromedary, To prike wolde he nou3t spary. **1377** LANGL. *P. Pl.* B. III. 51 Wist I that..I wolde nou3t spare For to be 3owre frende. *c* **1386** CHAUCER *Merch. T.* 1065, I schal not spare for no curtesye To speke him harm, that wold us vilonye. *c* **1440** *Partonope* 1707 Ye spared not in-to my bedde Homely to gonne. **1479** *Cov. Leet Bk.* 423 Not sparyng to do therin as lawe will for eny persone..what-so-euer. **1526** *Pilgr. Perf.* (W. de W. 1531) 18 Some spare not to make insurrecyon and rebell agaynst theyr prelates and heddes. **1575** GASCOIGNE *Glasse of Govt.* Wks. 1910 II. 16 Spare not to commaund my service. **1637** BP. REYNOLDS *Serm.* (1638) 34, I shall spare to bee so injurious to your patience, and to the businesse wee attend upon. **1686** tr. *Chardin's Coronat. Solyman* 75 The Controller..would not spare to inform the worst he could against him. **1808** SCOTT *Marm.* I. iv, And, from the platform, spare ye not To fire a noble salvo-shot. **1893** STEVENSON *Catriona* xxix. (1902) 346 Using travellers' freedom, we spared to wait for James More.

prov. **14..** *Lat. & Eng. Prov.* (MS. Douce 52) fol. 16 b, Who so sparyth to speke sparyth to spede. **1509** HAWES *Past. Pleas.* XVI. (Percy Soc.) 91 Who spareth to speke he to spede doth spare. **1546** HEYWOOD *Prov. & Epigr.* (1867) 31 Spare to speake spare to speede. **1567** TURBERV. *Epit.*, etc. (1837) 308 My Spencer, spare to speake, and euer spare to speed. **1748** SMOLLETT *R. Random* xxxiv, Remembering the old proverb, 'Spare to speak, spare to speed', [he] resolved to solicit the new captain's interest immediately. **1789** BURNS *Blue-eyed Lassie* ii. **1887** in *Eng. Dial. Dict.* s.v., He that spares to speyk, spares to speed.

d. In elliptical use: To refrain from doing something. Now *rare* or *Obs.*

c **1386** CHAUCER *Friar's T.* 39 Now telleth forth,..Ne spareth nought, myn owne maister deere. *c* **1400** *Destr. Troy* 12736 Sho spilt hade hir spousaile, sparit ho noght. **1530** TINDALE *Wks.* (Parker Soc.) 343, I could more deeply have entered into the practice of our cardinal, but I spare for divers considerations. **1557** TUSSER *100 Points Husb.* lxxxi, In June washe thy shepe,..and kepe them from dust... Then share them and spare not. **1610** SHAKS. *Temp.* II. i. 24 *Alon.* I pre-thee spare. *Gon.* Well, I haue done. *a* **1620** J. DYKE *Right Receiv. Christ* (1640) 161 Talke and spare not.

†**e.** *absol.* To refrain from or forbear the use or exercise *of* something. *Obs. rare.*

c **1470** *Gol. & Gaw.* 274 A! lord, sparis of sic speche, quhill ye speir more. **1481** *Cov. Leet Bk.* 489 To commaunde vs to respite & spare for a season of callyng furth oure seid retynue.

7. a. To avoid incurring or being involved in, to save (expense or labour).

(*a*) *a* **1325** [see (*b*) below]. *c* **1400** *Cursor M.* 29060 (Cott. Galba), If þou fast þi spens to spare, thrise for to ete better þe ware. *c* **1420** *Avow. Arth.* xlviii, Ther was no spense for to spare, Burdes thay were neuyr bare. **1491** *Act 7 Hen. VII*, c. 22 Preamble, Put to your hand and spare no cost. **1548** ELYOT, *Parcere impensæ*, to spare coste. **1617** MORYSON *Itin.* I. 9 This fortification, wherein he hath spared no cost. **1621** in W. H. Hale *Prec. Causes of Office* (1841) 50 He said they haue no nede of popish reliques and that the parishe may spare their money for such thinges. **1693** in Willis & Clark *Cambridge* (1886) II. 376 It being necessary to retrench the expences, it was thought proper to spare the charge of the Organist. **1819** SCOTT *Ivanhoe* xxxiv, The gold thou shalt spare in her cause. **1848** THACKERAY *Van. Fair* lvi, A famous tailor..was summoned to ornament little George's person, and was told to spare no expense in so doing.

(*b*) *a* **1325** *MS. Rawl. B. 520* lf. 30 b, þe king hath igraunted for te sparen trauail and despense of his men. **1526** *Pilgr. Perf.* (W. de W. 1531) 2 b, They..spared no labours neyther by see ne yet by lande. **1560** DAUS tr. *Sleidane's Comm.* 126 They wil spare neyther paynes nor peryl. **1603** KNOLLES *Hist. Turks* (1621) 1154 Meaning..by this means to spare their pouder, shot, and paines, and to reserue them to their better vses. **1675** J. OWEN *Indwelling Sin* xvi. (1732) 216 To spare the trouble in the Education of their Children. **1780** *Mirror* No. 101, These I spared no pains to cultivate and improve. **1827** FARADAY *Chem. Manip.* ix. (1842) 238 He should not spare pains to procure the best possible [filtering-paper]. **1832** HT. MARTINEAU *Life in Wilds* vi. 80 We must spare labour to the utmost till we can get a stock of labourers. **1892** *Photogr. Ann.* II. 601 No time, trouble, or expense has been spared in the matter.

b. To avoid, shun, keep clear of. Now *rare*.

c **1380** *Sir Ferumb.* 1553 Faste þay passede ouer al þe weys..; Ne sparede þay hulles, noþer valeys, bote prikede forþ with bost. **1387** TREVISA *Higden* (Rolls) VI. 39 He hated wyn dronkenes, ribaudye, and harlottie; uppon caas for hete of þe contray he wolde have it i-spared. **1483** CAXTON *Gold. Leg.* 121 b/2 Haue pyte on thy self..that y^{u} mayst..wynne to spare the tormentes that ben yet to come. **1523** LD. BERNERS *Froiss.* I. ccx. 252 They spared nat the dangerous maresses, but went through them. **1590** SHAKS. *Mids. N.* II. i. 142 Shun me and I will spare your haunts. **1821** SHELLEY *Epipsych.* 183 And we know not How much..Of pleasure may be gained, of sorrow spared.

8. a. To dispense with from one's stock or supply, or from a number, quantity, etc.; to part with, to give or grant, lend, etc., to another or others, esp. without inconvenience or loss to oneself; to do without.

Also const. *to* (a person or persons), *from* or *out of* (a stock or store, etc.).

a **1225** *Ancr. R.* 416 3if heo mei sparien eni poure schreaden, sende ham al derneliche ut of hire woanes. *a* **1300** *Cursor M.* 29057 þe mete þat þou þi-self suld ete..þou sal it to þe pouer spare. *a* **1400** *Minor Poems fr. Vernon MS.* lv. i. 67 3it of þi good woldestou not spare. **1481** *Cov. Leet Bk.* 484 To knowe..what able persones & howe many the Towne myght spare ouer þe seid iij^{xx} men. *a* **1548** HALL *Chron., Edw. IV*, 31 b, The lord Beauchampe toke from her rere-ward, more ordinance then she might haue wel spared. **1560** DAUS tr. *Sleidane's Comm.* 398 b, No parte of that wheate, whiche is in the citie, can be spared. **1601** in Moryson *Itin.* (1617) II. 145 At this time he cannot well be spared from hence. **1613** PURCHAS *Pilgrimage* (1614) 516 He is Collector or Treasurer to the King of Ternate in those parts, and sends him what he can spare. **1651** HOBBES *Leviath.* II. xxiv. 129 It is necessary, that men distribute that which they can spare. **1769** JOHNSON *Lett.* (1788) I. 20, I..can easily spare the pine-apple. **1769** FALCONER *Dict. Marine* (1780), *Donner un grand hunier*, to spare a main top-sail to some other ship in company. **1827** FARADAY *Chem. Manip.* xvii. (1842) 463 When a drop only of the fluid can be spared, a glass plate.. will support it. **1855** MACAULAY *Hist. Eng.* xii. III. 241 Kirke could spare no soldiers; but he had sent..some experienced officers. **1879** FROUDE *Cæsar* xx. 337 Cæsar and Pompey must each spare a legion for the East.

b. To reserve, retain, set aside or store up *for* some particular use or purpose; to keep in reserve.

a **1300** *Cursor M.* 5394 þai had noþer worth ne ware þat þai moght for þair mete spare. [*Trin. MS.* þei hadde no þing 3are þat þei my3te to her lyuelode spare.] *c* **1400** *Destr. Troy* 6502 The tother speire þat he sparit, [he] spent vpon hym. **1573** TUSSER *Husb.* (1878) 90 Land meadow that yeerly is spared for hay, now fence it and spare it. **1610** GUILLIM *Heraldry* I. iii. (1660) 19 It is taken up and spared for necessary purposes. **1795** *Gentl. Mag.* 542/2, I request you will spare room for one tribute more to his memory. **1886** C. E. PASCOE *Lond. of To-day* xxvii. (ed. 3) 251 The proper description of which would require more space than we can conveniently spare for the purpose.

c. To set apart, save, or give (time) from one's usual or ordinary duties or avocations; to have free, unoccupied, or unemployed.

a **1548** HALL *Chron., Hen. VI*, 82 b, This..pollitique Capitayne lost not one houre, nor spared one mynet, till he came before the citie of Burdeaux. **1565** COOPER s.v. *Succisiuus*, Time spared from other businesse. *c* **1643** LD. HERBERT *Autobiog.* (1824) 71 That Exercise taking up more time than can be spared from a studious man to get Knowledge. **1741–3** WESLEY *Extr. Jrnl.* (1749) 59, I take such a proportion of time as I can spare every night, to discourse with each child apart. **1788** G. KEATE *Pelew Isl.* xxiii. 297 The portion of time which they could spare from providing for their natural wants. **1833** HT. MARTINEAU *Tale of Tyne* vii. 126 Can you spare a minute, just to look out of this window? **1875** JOWETT *Plato* (ed. 2) V. 423 Let all the citizens who can spare time hear..such causes.

d. In prec. senses as complement to the verbs *have* or *be*, or with ellipse of these.

1390 GOWER *Conf.* II. 396 Whan Somer hath lost al his grene And is with Wynter wast and bare, That him is left nothing to spare. **1530** PALSGR. 726/1 Sownde, mariner, let us se what water we have to spare. **1550** CROWLEY *Last Trumpet* 1198 Thou haste no tyme to spare, and spende in bankettyng. **1633** G. HERBERT *Temple, Ch. Porch* xii, For we have wit to mark them, and to spare. **1654** BRAMHALL *Just Vind.* v. (1661) 102 These [bishops] were few enough for their own province, and none to spare for Britain. **1705** DE FOE in *Lett. Lit. Men* (Camden) 322, I know your Lordship has but few minutes to spare. **1771** FRANKLIN *Autobiog.* Wks. 1840 I. 94 She brought me word she had no such sum to spare. **1836** MARRYAT *Japhet* xlvi, I had an hour to spare, before the coach started. **1863** W. C. BALDWIN *Afr. Hunting* v. 133, I won both events.., with three bullets to spare. **1878** *Masque Poets* 13 If we had only time to spare To taste the glories of the Spring.

9. With direct and indirect object: **a.** To give or grant; to supply (a person) with (something) out of a stock, quantity, etc.

1593 SHAKS. *3 Hen. VI*, II. vi. 78 Then the world go's hard When Clifford cannot spare his Friends an oath. *a* **1616** BEAUM. & FL. *Wit without M.* I. ii, She may spare me her misen, and her bonnets, strike her main Petticoat, and yet outsail me. *c* **1643** LD. HERBERT *Autobiog.* (1824) 138, I was without any meat but what my Footman spared me out of his pocket. **1711** *London Gaz.* No. 4887/3 They outrunning us so very much, that they spared us half their Sails. **1784** COWPER *Task* I. 262 He spares me yet These chesnuts rang'd in corresponding lines. **1821** SCOTT *Kenilw.* xvii, Your nobleness will willingly spare your old servitor his crib and his mess. **1847** TENNYSON *Princ.* VI. 242 And now A word, but one,..Not one to spare her; out upon you, flint!

†**b.** To allow (one) to utter (a word). Also *ellipt. Obs.*

1660 *Trial Regic.* 24 Spare me but one Word. **1710** PALMER *Proverbs* 189 Out comes two or three 'If you'll give me leave's', as many 'Spare me's', 'with submission's', and 'I humbly conceive's'.

c. To save or relieve (a person, one's feelings, etc.) from (something).

1681 DRYDEN *Span. Friar* v. i, Spare my sight the pain Of seeing what a world of Tears it cost you. **1794** MRS. RADCLIFFE *Myst. Udolpho* xxxix, Spare me the necessity of mentioning those circumstances. *Ibid.* xlvi, Adding that he would spare her any difficulties that might occur. **1802** MAR. EDGEWORTH *Moral T.* (1816) I. 216, I shall spare you..the reflections I have made on this occasion. **1856** KANE *Arct. Expl.* II. xxix. 287, I had a set of signals..which spared us the noise of the voice. **1893** SLOANE-STANLEY *Remin. Midshipm. Life* vi. 82, I was, however, spared this infliction. *refl.* **1717** LADY M. W. MONTAGU *Let. to Pope* 1 Apr., I might spare myself the trouble. **1781** COWPER *Charity* 626, I might spare myself the pains to show What few can learn. **1841** W. SPALDING *Italy & It. Isl.* II. 102 We may spare ourselves the labour of looking for its essence. **1848** THACKERAY *Van. Fair* ii, Minerva thought wisely she could spare herself the expense of a master. **1884** *Manch. Exam.* 11 Oct. 5/1 They wrench off cupboard doors to spare themselves the trouble of closing them.

III. *intr.* **10.** *to spare for*: **a.** To desist or refrain from some action because or on account of (difficulty, opposition, loss, etc.).

Freq. *c* 1400; usually with a negative. Now *arch.*

a **1300** *Beket* (Percy Soc.) 62 Heo wende alone..And ne sparede for no sorewe that miȝte come hire to. *c* **1330** *King of Tars* 905 Bid him com hider with his ost,..For no thyng that he ne spare. *c* **1400** *Pilgr. Sowle* (Caxton) v. xiv. (1859) 81 For blandyssyng, for manace, ne for drede They spared not, but stoden by the trouthe. *c* **1430** *How Good Wife taught Dau.* 12 in *Babees Bk.*, Go to chirche whanne þou may, Loke þou spare for no reyn. *a* **1585** MONTGOMERIE *Cherrie & Slae* 370 He is bot daft that hes ado, And spairis for euery speiche. **1810** SCOTT *Lady of L.* v. xxxii, Spare not for spoiling of thy steed. **1823** —— *Quentin D.* x, Throw down the screen—spare not for cup or goblet.

b. With negative: To refrain from action in order to avoid or save (expense, trouble, etc.); to be sparing of or in (something).

c **1400** *Destr. Troy* 233, I shall spare for no spence & þu spede wele. **14..** *Sir Beues* (E.) 3310 þey sparyd neyþer for syluyr ne golde. **1535** LYNDESAY *Satyre* 52 And sie the burgessis spair not for expence, Bot speid thame heir. **1593** MARLOWE *Edw. II*, I. iv, Spare for no cost. **1599** SHAKS. *Much Ado* III. v. 66 And we must doe it wisely. *Dogb.* Wee will spare for no witte I warrant you. **1657** EARL MONM. tr. *Paruta's Pol. Disc.* 55 Cæsar never spared for any labour by which he might hope to purchase renown and glory. **1681** HICKERINGILL *Sin Man-Catching* Wks. 1716 I. 178 They plot their Work,..spare for no pains, no cost, not daunted with any ill success. **1723** *Briton* No. 12 (1724) 54 Crassus.. spared for no Expence to purchase Voices. **1726** LEONI *Alberti's Archit.* II. 53 No Columns or Pilasters were spared for. **1793** SMEATON *Edystone L.* §305 They did not spare for cold water to throw in my face and upon me.

IV. 11. Combs. with the verbal stem, as ***spare-good, -penny, -thrift***; also † **spare-chest**, a chest for spare money, a reserve fund.

1611 COTGR. s.v. *Manger, Il est à table, & n'ose manger*; (Applyable to a miserable spare-good). **1707** J. STEVENS tr. *Quevedo's Com. Wks.* (1709) 298 The Retentive Knight: containing much wholesome Advice for saving the Ready, and being free of good Words. Dedicated to the Society of Spare-Pennies. **1768** *Ann. Reg.* I. 117 The extraordinary expences occasioned by his Sicilian majesty's marriage.. will not be levied upon the state, but defrayed out of the savings of the spare-chest. **1803** *Ann. Rev.* I. 423 The manufacturer has to deal..with the spendthrift and the sparethrift.

spare, *v.*^{2} *north.* and †*Sc.* Also 5 spayr, 6 spair. [var. of SPAR *v.*^{1} Cf. SPEAR *v.*^{2}

Spareð, given as a variant in the *Ancr. R.* 70, is perh. an error for *spereð*.]

1. *trans.* To bar, bolt, or secure (a door or gate).

1375 BARBOUR *Bruce* v. 389 The ȝettis than he gert thame spare, And sat and ete at all lasare. *c* **1375** *Sc. Leg. Saints* xxvi. (*Nicholas*) 363 þocht þe ȝet wes before sparyt, with strinth he enterit In. *c* **1450** *St. Cuthbert* (Surtees) 5067 He fande þe mynster ȝatis spared; As a wodeman he fared. **1583** *Durham Dep.* (Surtees) 314 The said Edward doore was spaired all the tyme the said geis was in eatyng. **1677** NICOLSON in *Trans. R. Soc. Lit.* (1870) IX. 319 *Spare the dure*, shut to the door. **1825** BROCKETT *N.C. Gloss.*, *Spare*, to shut, to close. **1894** HESLOP *Northumbld. Gloss.* 674 'Spare the yett,' 'Spare the door,' are still in common use.

†**2.** To close (the lips or eyes) firmly. *Obs.*

c **1400** *Rule St. Benet* (Verse) 107 And spayr þi lipes, & hald þam still, So þat þay opyn noght with ill! *c* **1450** *St. Cuthbert* (Surtees) 3847 He spared his eghen and lay still.

†**3.** To shut up; to keep *out*. *Obs.*

c **1450** *St. Cuthbert* (Surtees) 4123 As a man in prisoun sparde. **1482** *Monk of Evesham* lv. (Arb.) 107 The crosse.. was lettyn done ageyne, and so sparyd other oute that wuld haue commyn in.

spareable ('spɛərəb(ə)l), *a.* [f. SPARE *v.*^{1}] That can be spared, in various senses of the verb.

1688–9 in Cobbett *Parl. Hist. Eng.* (1809) V. 173 You cannot doubt but the spareable part will be treasured up for the good of the subject. **1821** *Blackw. Mag.* X. 89 We intend shipping a cargo of our worst and most spareable puns on board the next whaler. **1887** BLACKMORE *Springhaven* (ed. 4) III. xix. 270 His great desire..was never to destroy his enemies, by the number of one man spareable.

spared (spɛəd), *ppl. a.* [f. as prec.] Saved up, reserved; not wasted or destroyed, etc.

1580 G. HARVEY *Three Lett.* 40 And my poore Muse hath spent hir spared store, Yet little good hath got. **1623** WODROEPHE (*title*), The spared houres of a Souldier in his travels. **1657** S. PURCHAS *Pol. Flying-Ins.* 189 They breed.. most commonly in Meadows, and spared layes, or else in a hole in the ground. **1874** W. BRUCE *Hebrew Odes* 41 The spared remnant of His host. **1894** H. NISBET *Bush Girl's Rom.* 194 The only spared man of that camp darted towards the bush.

† **spare-dry**: see SPAR *sb.*^{1} 7.

† **'spareful**, *a. Obs.* [f. SPARE *sb.*^{1} or *v.*^{1}] Sparing, frugal.

1565 STAPLETON tr. *Bede's Hist. Ch. Eng.* 107 How sparefull personnes he and his predecessours were,..euen the place, where he bare rule, did witnesse. **1599** *Life More* in C. Wordsw. *Eccl. Biog.* (1853) II. 112 She was also spare-full, and somewhat given to niggardliness. **1600** FAIRFAX *Tasso* IV. xxx, Her sparefull eie to spread his beames denaies.

Hence † **'sparefully** *adv.*; † **'sparefulness**.

1570 JEWEL *View Seditious Bull* (1582) 53 They labour truely, they liue sparefully. *a* **1586** SIDNEY *Arcadia* (1622) 214 Largesse his hands could neuer skill of sparefulnesse. **1618** RYVES in *Camden's Lett.* (1691) 236 We know how sparefully S. Augustine speaketh of them in his books De civitate Dei.

spareless ('spɛəlɪs), *a.* and *adv.* [f. as prec.]

†**1.** Unstinted, unlimited. *Obs.*

a **1400–50** *Alexander* 5467 Sum spends on him of sponges a sparles nounbre.

2. Unsparing, merciless.

1589 *Rare Triumphes Loue & Fortune* I. in J. P. Collier *Five O. Pl.* (Roxb.) 87 What I have promist doubt not to be perfourmed; The sparelesse destinies my will affoorde: Let this defend thee, like a trusty swoord. **1605** SYLVESTER *Du Bartas* II. iii. II. *Fathers* 140 Alas! I could not but even dye for griefe, Should I but yeeld mine Age's sweet reliefe..Into the hands of hang-men's spare-lesse spight. **1826** R. S. HAWKER *Cornish Ball.*, etc. (1904) 220 Thy spareless foe Bears the fell shaft and fatal blow. *a* **1851** MOIR *Unknown Grave* vi. Poet. Wks. II. 346 When all the friends..Were vanish'd..; Pluck'd one by one by spareless Time.

3. As *adv.* Without stint.

1567 PAINTER *Pal. Pleas.* II. 427 With a fashion of attire to garnish their inward parts, so well as (sparelesse) they imploy vpon the vanishing pompe.

sparely ('spɛəlɪ), *adv.* [f. SPARE *a.* Cf. OE. *spærlice*, MDu. *spare-*, *spaerlike*, MLG. *sparlike*, OHG. *sparalîhho* (MHG. *sperlîche*, G. *spärlich*), ON. *sparliga* (MSw. *sparlika*).]

1. In a sparing, frugal, or stinted manner; not fully, amply, or copiously.

1559 *Decl. Doctr.* in Strype *Ann. Ref.* (1709) I. viii. 118 Indeed we do think that discreet ministers will speak sparely and circumspectly of them. **1571** GOLDING *Calvin on Ps.* xxxvii. 25 By their lyving sparely, they have alwais enough. **1601** HOLLAND *Pliny* I. 98 It is drunke vp, and therefore floweth more sparely. **1637** MILTON *Lycidas* 138 Ye valleys low..On whose fresh lap the swart Star sparely looks. **1784** COWPER *Task* IV. 379 They..find at eve, Ill clad and fed but sparely, time to cool. **1840** HOOD *Kilmansegg, Honeymoon* xxx, He drank—the reverse of sparely. **1867** A. BARRY *Sir C. Barry* iv. 101 Ornament is sparely applied.

2. Thinly; sparsely.

1836 [JAS. GRANT] *Recoll. Ho. of Lords* viii. 153 He is thin and sparely made, with a sallow complexion. **1841** C. MACKAY *Longbeard* ii, His hair..hung sparely over his temples.

spareness ('spɛənɪs). [f. SPARE *a.* Cf. OE. *spærnes* frugality, etc.] The quality of being spare, in various senses of the adj.

1648 HEXHAM II, *Magerheydt*, Leanenesse, or Sparenesse. **1649** HAMMOND *Chr. Obligations* 36 Returning the grosse habit of sin to a sparenesse and slendernesse of stature. **1822** GALT *Provost* viii. 55 He was, notwithstanding the spareness of his abilities, a prideful creature. **1826** HOOD *Recipe for Civilization* 142 She saw the spareness of her habits. **1897** *Allbutt's Syst. Med.* IV. 608 After the age of forty years persons either diverge into spareness or become more or less obese.

spare part. [f. SPARE *a.* + PART *sb.*]

1. A duplicate of a part of a machine kept in readiness to replace a loss, failure, or breakage. Freq. *pl.*

1888 J. G. HORNER *Lockwood's Dict. Mech. Engin.* 336 It is customary to include spare parts with work which is despatched to the colonies and with sea-going engines. **1904** *C. B. Fry's Mag.* June 294/2 In addition to the actual trying of the racing car..there is a great deal of detail work in connection with supplies of..spare parts. **1931** *Proc. Inst. Automobile Engineers* XXV. 106 In some cases spare-part lists hardly exist, very largely due no doubt to rapid change of design. **1936** E. WAUGH *Waugh in Abyssinia* v. 182 We would not take the lorry until it was fully equipped... He could not get the spare parts on credit. **1971** *Engineering* Apr. 31/1 Quick and easy over-haul and spare-part replacement. **1972** *Guardian* 18 Oct. 14/2 Some agent for British cars abroad is heard complaining..that he can make no profit because he sells no spare parts.

2. *transf.* A visceral organ or other bodily part from a donor, or a prosthetic device, which is to be used to replace a defective organ, etc., in a person. Freq. *attrib.*, as ***spare-part(s) surgery***. *colloq.*

1944 [see BANK *sb.*^{3} 7 f]. **1960** S. PLATH *Colossus* 87 The storerooms are full of hearts. This is the city of spare parts. **1963** *Daily Tel.* 21 Sept. 9/5 Spare part surgery is still in its infancy. **1967** *New Scientist* 25 May 449/1 With the technique of kidney transplantation now firmly established ..spare-part surgeons are now turning their attention to other organs in the body. **1968** *Guardian* 6 May 8/1 Spare parts surgery is too important to be left to the surgeons alone. **1970** D. J. MARLOWE in *Mystery Writers' Choice 1977* (1977) 4 'Well, what about your body?' I still didn't care for the idea about being used for spare parts. **1977** B. PYM *Quartet in Autumn* ii. 20 She could donate certain organs to assist in research or spare-part surgery.

sparer ('spɛərə(r)). Also 5 sparare. [f. SPARE *v.*^{1} Cf. MLG. and G. *sparer*.]

1. A sparing, frugal, or thrifty person; one who spares in using anything.

c **1440** *Promp. Parv.* 467/1 Sparare, or he þat sparythe, *parcus, parca*. **1542** UDALL *Erasm. Apoph.* 73 b, Plato was a frugall man and a great sparer or housband. **1555** W. WATREMAN *Fardle Facions* II. i. 118 The Nabatheens of all other arabiens are the beste husbandes, and thriftiest sparers. **1601** HOLLAND *Pliny* XI. xix. 321 For otherwise they [bees] are very thriftie and overgreat sparers. **1635** J. GORE *Way to Well-doing* 25 A good sparer makes a good spender. **1816** SCOTT *Old Mort.* i, I am in general a sparer of the rod. **1882** *Pall Mall G.* 14 June 4/2 The Turk has slaves in plenty, and is no sparer of their labour.

b. A thing or substance which aids in sparing or saving.

a **1613** OVERBURY *A Wife*, etc. (1616) K vj b, Hee cannot away with Tobacco; for hee is perswaded (and not much amisse) that tis a sparer of bread-corne. **19..** *Buck's Handbk. Med. Sci.* V. 564 (*Cent. Dict. Suppl.*), The great power as proteid sparers which the carbohydrates exercise.

2. One who refrains from injuring or destroying.

1572 BOSSEWELL *Armorie* II. 78 b, He is the auenger, he is also the sparer. **1607** LLOYD *Pilgr. Princes* 37 b, His sodaine chaunge..from a spoyler of all places, to be a sparer now of his subjects. **1853** *Zoologist* II. 4011 The humane sparer of the poor hedgehog in the midst of his many foes.

spare-rib. Also 8 spear-rib. *β.* 7 sparrib, 8 sparib, 8–9 spar-rib. [prob. ad. MLG. *ribbespêr* (see RIBSPARE) with transposition of the two elements, and subsequent association with SPARE *a.*] A cut of meat, esp. of pork, consisting of part of the ribs somewhat closely trimmed. Also *fig.*

α. **1596** NASHE *Saffron Walden* 48 Let's haue halfe a dozen spare ribs of his rethorique, with tart sauce of taunts correspondent. **1709** W. KING *Cookery* ix, Spear-ribs, surloins, chines, and barons. **1749** FIELDING *Tom Jones* (1775) III. 113, I have bespoke a shoulder of mutton..and a spare-rib of pork. **1834** MARRYAT *P. Simple* xxvii, There was plenty of pork,..a roast sparerib with the crackling on, ..and pig's pettitoes. **1844** H. STEPHENS *Bk. Farm* II. 99 The ribs [of the sheep] are here left exposed at the part from which the shoulder has been removed, and constitute what are called the *spare-ribs*. **1887** JEFFERIES *Amaryllis* xii, Pig-meat—such as spare-rib, griskin, blade-bone, and that mysterious morsel, the 'mouse'.

β. **1607** BREWER *Lingua* II. i, Traile no speares, but sparribs of Porke. **1611** COTGR., *Cotis*, the sparribs of a porke. **1706** S. SEWALL *Diary* 24 Dec. (1879) II. 175 Din'd on Salt Fish and a Spar-Rib. **1748** *Anson's Voy.* III. v. (ed. 4) 449 There was a great quantity of provisions, particularly salted sparibs of pork. **1867** WAUGH *Tattlin' Matty* i. 11 They'n bin killin' a pig; an' hoo's brought me a bit o' spar-rib.

b. *attrib.*, as *spare-rib feast*, etc.

1737 *Ochtertyre Ho. Bks.* (S.H.S.) 90 The sparrib rost peices. **1867** G. EASTON *Autobiog.* i. (ed. 2) 18 The Spare-rib Feast.. took place immediately after the fatted ox had been killed.

spare royal: see SPUR-ROYAL.

'sparesome, *a.* [ad. G. *sparsam.*] Economical.

1864 MAYHEW *German Life* I. 285 We must be sparesome now, the feast days are near at hand.

sparewe, obs. form of SPARROW.

†**sparewort**, obs. variant of SPEARWORT.

1579 W. LANGHAM *Garden of Health* 614 Sparewort, stampe it and apply it.. to the sciatica, to reare a blister.

'sparfle, *v.* *Sc. rare.* In 6 sparfal, 9 sperfle. [Alteration of SPARPLE *v.*] *trans.* To scatter or disperse; to squander.

Sparfeled in Greene's *Orpharion* (1599) 48 is prob. an error for *sparpeled*.

c **1575** *Diurn. Occurr.* (Bann. Cl.) 194 Bot or this tyme, the said men of weare hade sparfallit the best of thame. **1808–25** in JAMIESON (in form *sperfle*).

‖**sparga'nosis.** *Path.* [a. Gr. σπαργάνωσις (Dioscorides 2. 129 in old editions; but in 3. 41 σπάργωσις SPARGOSIS), for σπάργησις, f. σπαργᾶν to swell.]

†**1.** (See quot.) *Obs.*$^{-0}$

1693 tr. *Blancard's Phys. Dict.* (ed. 2), *Sparganosis*, a Distention of the Breasts, occasioned by too much Milk. [Also in Phillips (1706), Bailey, Chambers (1753), etc.]

†**2.** Puerperal swelling of the legs. *Obs.*

1822–7 GOOD *Study Med.* (1829) II. 633 This.. was an instance of erratic or metastatic rheumatism rather than sparganosis. *Ibid.* V. 612 In a singular enlargement of the lower extremity produced by a puerperal sparganosis.

3. Infection with larval tapeworms of the genus *Sparganum*.

1928 *Proc. Soc. Exper. Biol. & Med.* XXVI. 254 Sparganosis results from applying frogs infected with these spargana to inflamed and ulcerated areas of the body. **1954** *Amer. Jrnl. Tropical Med. & Hygiene* III. 123 It is probable that human sparganosis is acquired in Korea by the consumption of raw snake, which is a fairly common practice in this area. **1976** EDINGTON & GILLES *Path. in Tropics* (ed. 2) iii. 210 Sparganosis has been reported in man from many tropical countries such as South East Asia, Africa, Madagascar, China, and South America.

sparge (spɑːdʒ), *sb.* Also *Sc.* spairge. [f. next.]

1. The act of sprinkling or splashing; a sprinkle or slight dash (of liquor, etc.).

1808 in JAMIESON. **1819** W. TENNANT *Papistry Storm'd* (1827) 56 Chariots and horse-hoofs round did scatter Scamander's sand wi' spairge and splatter. **1867** G. W. DONALD *Poems* (1879) 72/2 A spairge may put us in repair When coughs an' caulds our stammacks pester.

2. *Brewing.* A spray of warm water sprinkled over the malt.

1839 URE *Dict. Arts* 107 The malt is exhausted by eight or ten successive sprinklings of liquor.., which are termed in the vernacular tongue, *sparges*. **1869** W. MOLYNEUX *Burton-on-Trent* 244 The 'sparge' is set to run on the malt an additional quantity of water.

3. *attrib.*, as **sparge arm** *Brewing*, a sparge pipe used to sprinkle hot water over the malt, usu. arranged to rotate above the tun; **sparge pipe**, a horizontal perforated pipe used to sprinkle or spray water or other liquids, esp. one used to flush a slab urinal.

1947 *Brewing* (ed. 2) ii. 23 The holes in the actual sparge arms have to be made much larger. **1971** J. S. HOUGH et al. *Malting & Brewing Sci.* x. 261 Other rotating machinery within the mash tun comprises sparge arms (which are moved by water pressure) for spraying liquor evenly over the goods. **1910** MAXWELL & BROWN *Encycl. Municipal & Sanitary Engin.* 444/2 *Sparge pipe*, a pipe having fine holes drilled throughout its length so as to deliver a spray of water as is required for flushing. **1948** *Archit. Rev.* CIV. 289 A sparge pipe on the sky-light ridge cools the glass by water spray in summer. *c* **1972** *Shanks* (Barrhead) *Catal.* 93 Chromium plated flush and sparge pipes with clips.

sparge (spɑːdʒ), *v.* Also 8–9 *Sc.* spairge. [app. ad. OF. *espargier* or L. *spargĕre* to sprinkle; but in sense 1 answering to PARGET *v.* and having the earlier variants SPARGEN and SPARGET.]

1. *trans.* To plaster; to rough-cast.

1560 *Edinb. Burgh Recs.* 62 To reparrall the kirk, to lay the throwchis thairof of new and sparge the samyn. **1597** *Rec. Elgin* (1908) II. 48 The haill eldaris hes promeist a boll lyme ilk ane of thame to sparge the kirk withall. *a* **1670** J. LAMONT *Diary* (1810) 156 Att this time also, the fore-pairt of the house was sparged, with the tower-head. **1883** *Almondbury Gloss.* 125 *Sparge*, to point or plaster the inside of a chimney.

2. To bespatter, besprinkle. Also *fig.*

1786 BURNS *A Dream* vii, An' Will's a true guid fallow's get, A Name not Envy spairges. **1821** LIDDLE *Poems* 127 Auld Cloot at last may spairge ye lightly.

3. To dash, splash, or sprinkle (water, etc.) about. Also *fig.*

1785–6 BURNS *Address to Deil* i, O thou!.. Wha.. Spairges about the brunstane cootie To scaud poor wretches! **1808** JAMIESON, *Spairge*, to dash; as, to spairge water. **1875** G. MACDONALD *Malcolm* I. i. 5 Nobody..'at wad gang and spairge sic havers aboot her.

4. a. *Brewing.* To sprinkle (malt) with hot water. Also *absol.*

1839 URE *Dict. Arts* 107 It would keep up an uniform temperature in the goods, without requiring them to be sparged with very hot liquor. **1885** *Civilian* 3 Jan. 133/1 He, too, sparges for small beer with hot liquor.

b. To aerate (a liquid) with air (in quot. *absol.*).

1973 *Nature* 23 Feb. 534/1 The *p*H was adjusted to 3·8 with concentrated HCl and aeration and mixing accomplished by sparging with air.

Hence **'sparging** *vbl. sb.* Also *attrib.*

1590 in Pitcairn *Crim. Trials* (Bann. Cl.) I. III. 210 Quha had offendit him in nocht spargeing of his chalmer. **1836** *Penny Cycl.* V. 404/2 If sparging or sprinkling the water over the goods should be adopted.. instead of mashing. **1839** URE *Dict. Arts* 107 The only serious objection to the sparging system is the loss of time by the successive drainages. **1869** W. MOLYNEUX *Burton-on-Trent* 245 The malt has had its regulated series of spargings. **1876** *Encycl. Brit.* IV. 274/2 The heat of the sparging water.. must be modified by circumstances.

sparge'faction. *rare*$^{-1}$. [f. L. *spargĕ-re* to sprinkle: see -FACTION.] = next.

1704 SWIFT *T. Tub* Wks. 1768 I. 86 The operation was performed by Spargefaction in a proper time of the Moon.

spargefi'cation. Also -ification. [f. as prec.: see -FICATION.] The action of sprinkling or scattering.

1835 MARRYAT *J. Faithful* ii, Wiping off his share of my liberal spargefication from his coat and waistcoat. **1836** E. HOWARD *R. Reefer* xiii, There was much spargefication of powder. **1892** *Sat. Rev.* 27 Aug. 257/1 There is a liberal spargification of melted butter over divers of the author's contemporaries.

'spargelstone. *rare*$^{-1}$. [ad. G. *spargelstein*, f. *spargel* asparagus.] Asparagus-stone.

1804 R. JAMESON *Min.* I. 540 Asparagus, or Spargel Stone.

†**spargen**, *v.* *Sc. Obs.* In 6 spargein, -eon. [Cf. PARGEN *v.* and SPARGE *v.* 1.] *trans.* To parget.

1512 *Acc. Ld. High Treas. Scot.* IV. 284 For xvj puncheonis plaister,.. send to Dingwall to spargein the wallis tharof. **1562** WINȜET *Wks.* (S.T.S.) I. 14 The prophetis of it, spargeonit thaim with vntemperit morter.

Hence †**'spargener**, a pargeter. *Obs.*

1600 *Rec. Convent. Roy. Burghs* II. 89 Masouns, sklatteris, painteris, spargeneris. **1641** *Acts Parl. Scot.*, *Chas. I* (1870) V. 562/2 The haill Friemen of Masones,.. spargineres, painteres.

sparger ('spɑːdʒə(r)). [f. SPARGE *v.*] An appliance for sprinkling water, esp. in brewing. Also, one used for sprinkling a liquid other than water, or for aerating a liquid with air.

1858 SIMMONDS *Dict. Trade*, *Sparger*, a copper cylinder, used by brewers for dashing or sprinkling. **1875** KNIGHT *Dict. Mech.* 2254/1 *Sparger*, a sprinkler; usually a cup with a perforated lid, or a pipe with a perforated nozzle. **1888** *Wine, Sp. & Beer* 8 Mar. 141/2 The rake mash machine is driven from underneath, so that nothing impedes the action of the rotary sparger. **1949** E. CHAIN in H. W. Florey et al. *Antibiotics* II. xvii. 700 The fermenters.. were made of steel; they contained a sparger for air distribution. *Ibid.*, The air sparger consisted of a ⅜-in. stainless steel pipe bent to form a 12-in. square. **1963** ECKENFELDER & MCCABE *Biol. Waste Treatment* 183 Spargers, each with four 5/16 in. diameter holes radiating horizontally from the center were checked for oxygen absorption efficiency. **1976** *IEEE Spectrum* May 54/2 An early example of.. fatigue failure was that of the liquid boron, or 'poison', sparger at the Garigliano Plant of Ente Nazionale per l'Energia Electrica.. in Cessa Aurunca, Italy, in 1964.

†**sparget**, *v.* *Obs.*$^{-0}$ [var. of PARGET *v.* Cf. SPARGE *v.* 1 and SPARGEN *v.*] *trans.* To parget.

Two MSS. have *sparchyn*, which may belong to SPARGE *v.*

c **1440** *Promp. Parv.* 467 Spargettyn, or pargette wallys.., *gipso*, *limo*. *Ibid.*, Spargettynge, or pargettynge.

spargification: see SPARGEFICATION.

‖**spar'gosis.** *Path.* [Gr. σπάργωσις: see SPARGANOSIS.] (See quot. 1867.) Also *fig.*

1867 [W. J.] E. WILSON *Dis. Skin* (ed. 6) 914 *Spargosis*,.. a substantive term applicable to elephantiasis Arabum, and boucnemia... We prefer spargosis to sparganosis. **1934** 'H. MACDIARMID' *Stony Limits & Other Poems* 23 In open country.. watching an aching spargosis of stars.

sparhawk ('spɑːhɔːk). Now *arch.* or *dial.* Forms: *α.* 1 **spaerhabuc**, **spearhafoc**, 4–7 **sparhauk(e**, 5–6 *Sc.* **-halk**, 5–7 **-hawke**, 6– **sparhawk**. *β.* 4–6 **sperhauk(e**, 5–7 **-hawk(e**. *γ.* 4, 6 **sparehauk(e**, 5 **-hawk**, 7 **-haucke**. *δ.* 4, 6 **sperehauke**, 5 **-hawk(e**. [OE. *spearhafoc*, f. the stem of *spearwa* SPARROW + *hafoc* HAWK: so ON. *sparrhaukr*.] A sparrowhawk.

α. *c* **725** *Corpus Gloss.* A. 432 *Alietum*, spaerhabuc. *c* **1000** ÆLFRIC *Gloss.* in Wr.-Wülcker 132 *Accipiter, uel raptor*, spearhafoc. *a* **1300** *Cursor M.* 1789 Þe sparhauk flough be þe sterling. *c* **1374** CHAUCER *Troylus* III. 1192 What might or may the sely larke seie, Whanne that this sparhauk hath it in his foote? **1438** *Bk. Alexander Grt.* (Bann.) 12 It semis thay sparhalkis war & we lawrokis that durst bot dar. **1483** CAXTON *Cato* h vj b, It is sayd in a comyn prouerbe that crafte is better than the Sparhawke. **1560** ROLLAND *Seven Sages* 28 The Sparhalk is als swyft of flicht As the Griffoun. **1598** BP. HALL *Sat.* IV. iv. 88 Gallio may.. tend his sparhauke mantling in her mew. **1639** MASSINGER *Unnatural Combat* v. i, How her heart beats! Much like a partridge in a sparhawk's foot. **1661** J. CHILDREY *Brit. Bacon.* 13 Sparhawks, the most useless of Hawks. **1700** TYRRELL *Hist. Eng.* II. 820 The Ayries of Hawks, of Spar-Hawks. **1842** TENNYSON *Sir Launc. & Q. Guinevere* ii, Sometimes the sparhawk wheel'd along. **1865** KINGSLEY *Herew.* iv, In the first [copse] there built an eagle, in the second there built a sparhawk. **1891** 'SON OF MARSHES' *Surrey Hills* (1894) 44 Spar'hawk, the woodmen call him.

β. **1377** LANGL. *P. Pl.* B. VI. 199 What pieres preyed hem to do as prest as a sperhauke. **1387** TREVISA *Higden* (Rolls) I. 335 Þere is grete plente of.. sperhaukes. **1456** SIR G. HAYE *Law Arms* (S.T.S.) 299 That he be lord of his subjectis, as to the quaile the sper-hauk. *c* **1489** CAXTON *Sonnes of Aymon* vi. 152 The kyng gaaf to hym a sper-hawke. **1539** FITZHERB. *Survey*. xi. 26 Except it be an entiere rent, as a sperhauke or a hors. **1555** EDEN *Decades* (Arb.) 300 Haukes, as faulcons, gerfalcons, lanners, and sperhaukes. **1602** L. LLOYD *Briefe Conf. Divers Lawes* 32 The feather of a sperhawke in their caps.

γ. *a* **1400** MAUNDEV. (1839) xxii. 238 Gerfacouns, Sparehaukes, Faukons gentyls. **1486** *Bk. St. Albans* c viij b, She may be also callid a spare hawke for .ij. Resones, oon is she sparith goshawkys and tercellys both. **1550** J. COKE *Eng. & Fr. Heralds* §8 (1877) 60 Also we have hawkes of the towre, .. lykewyse goshawkes, and sparehawkes for ladyes. **1587** GOLDING *De Mornay* xxvi. (1592) 416 The Woolfe, the Foxe,.. the Sparehauke, the Kyte & so foorth. **1612** *Shuttleworths' Acc.* (Chetham Soc.) 201 Foure spare-haucke hoodes, xij^{d}. **1890** J. WATSON *Nat. & Woodcraft* viii, The Gamekeeper.. will record a black and bloody list of depredations against the 'spare'-hawk.

δ. **1398** TREVISA *Barth. De P.R.* XII. iv. (Bodl. MS.), Hereby it semeþ þ^{t} *alietus* and a litel sperehauke is all one. *c* **1440** *Promp. Parv.* 468/2 Sperehawke.., *nisus*. *c* **1500** *Melusine* xxiv. 175 His enemyes fled byfore hym as the partrych doth byfore the sperehauke.

†**'sparily**, *adv.* *Obs.* [f. SPARY *a.*] Sparingly; moderately; with restraint.

1603 HOLLAND *Plutarch's Mor.* 1289 Otherwise the priests drinke thereof but sparily. **1606** —— *Sueton.* 56 He granted the freedom of the City of Rome, most sparily. **1633** D. R[OGERS] *Treat. Sacr.* ii. 51 Using liberty sparily. **1642** —— *Naaman* 36, I will more sparily touch forraine nations and Churches.

sparing ('spɛərɪŋ), *vbl. sb.* [f. SPARE *v.*[1]]

1. The action of saving, economizing, or using with frugality.

c **1386** CHAUCER *Pars. T.* ¶835 Sparyng also þat restreyneth þe delicate ease to sitte long at his mete. *c* **1440** *Promp. Parv.* 467/2 Sparynge, *parcimonia*. **1565** COOPER *Thesaurus* s.v. *Circunscribo*, To limite riote within the boundes of thriftie sparyng. **1588** KYD *Househ. Phil.* Wks. (1901) 252 With industrie, sparing, and good husbandry [I] did much augment it. **1621** T. WILLIAMSON tr. *Goulart's Wise Vieillard* 72 Couetousnes.. knowes no meane in sparing or spending. **1640** BP. HALL *Chr. Moder.* (Ward) 5/1 As too much bounty is prodigality, so too much sparing is niggardliness.

attrib. **1560** ROLLAND *Seven Sages* 96 Put spairing dayis and thame togidder, And sa small sall ȝe tyne. **1579–80** NORTH *Plutarch* (1895) III. 346 There was such store of gold and silver in the sparing cofers of their treasurie.

b. Const. *of* (the thing spared).

1377 LANGL. *P. Pl.* B. v. 442 In speche and in sparynge of speche. **1390** GOWER *Conf.* II. 287 For sparinge of a litel cost Fulofte time a man hath lost The large cote for the hod. **1573** TUSSER *Husb.* (1878) 38 A Jack for to saw vpon fewell for fier, for sparing of firewood. **1607** DOD & CLEAVER *Expos. Prov. xi–xii.* 177 This sparing of speech, when men reserue themselues for fit occasions. **1617** MORYSON *Itin.* II. 238 We haue vsed a great kind of sparing of the victuals in the store.

c. *pl.* That which is saved by economy; savings.

1628 GAULE *Pract. The.* (1629) Ep. Ded., The Sparings of want haue euer beene held more acceptable, then the Fallings of abundance. **1647** R. STAPYLTON *Juvenal* XIV. 141 First Poor little sparings, then th' insatiate thirst Of Getting. **1760** *Cautions & Adv. to Officers of Army* 124 Here is another Deduction to be made out of your Sparings. **1866** HOWELLS *Venetian Life* 66 The sparings for the whole week .. are spent for this evening's amusement.

2. The action of leaving unhurt or uninjured, of showing mercy or forbearance, etc.

1375 BARBOUR *Bruce* VIII. 483 Thai.. strak on thame forout sparing. **1422** tr. *Secreta Secret.*, *Priv. Priv.* 181 The vertue of mekenesse kepyth the mene betwene Sparynge and vengeaunce. **1490** CAXTON *Eneydos* lxii. 162 They.. drewe out theyre sharpe swerdes. Thenne was there noo sparynge. *c* **1526** *Plumpton Corr.* (Camden) 226, I pray you be contented to give sparing to the next head Cort at Spoforth. **1585** T. WASHINGTON tr. *Nicholay's Voy.* III. 110 b, [They] cast vpon the head of euery one of them three small buckets full, without sparing of their clothes. *c* **1611** CHAPMAN *Iliad* v. 205 The Reason I laid down Was but the sparing of my horse. **1910** *Daily Chron.* 22 Jan. 3/2 They appear to kill all they can, leaving the sparing to some other time.

†**b.** Respite, delay. *Obs. rare.*

a **1513** FABYAN *Chron.* VII. (1811) 344 The mayre and the cytezyns.. desyred a sparynge of ye lordys tyll they myght speke w^{t} the Kynge. **1531** *Dial. on Laws Eng.* II. xiv. 37, I pray the gyue a lytle sparynge & procede now for this tyme to som othe[r] questyon.

sparing ('spɛərɪŋ), *ppl. a.* and *adv.* [f. as prec.]

1. Inclined to save; exercising economy or frugality in using or spending; niggard.

pred. *c* **1386** CHAUCER *Melib.* ¶633 Ye schul use the richesses.. in such a maner, that men holde yow not skarce ne to sparynge. *c* **1400** *Rom. Rose* 5363 The riche men are loved ay, And namely tho that sparand bene. *c* **1440** *Alph. Tales* 66 Sho was so sparand, at sho wolde giff nothyng.. vnto pure folke. **1568** GRAFTON *Chron.* II. 11 He was so couetous and sparing, that he woulde spende nothing more than he needes must. **1592** SHAKS. *Ven. & Ad.* 1147 It [*sc.* love] shall be sparing and too full of riot. **1807** CRABBE *Par. Reg.* I. 447 The wise frugality, that.. saves to live; Sparing, not pinching, mindful though not mean.

attrib. *c* **1440** *Alph. Tales* 245 When he was a monke, he was a passand hard man, & a sparand. **1590** SHAKS. *Com. Err.* III. i. 27 A niggardly Host, and more sparing guest. **1601** F. GODWIN *Bps. Eng.* 94 He was a very frugal and sparing man, neuer esteeming pompe or outward brauery. **1639** J. CLARKE *Parœmiologia* 261 A sparing father, and a spending son. **1759** FRANKLIN *Ess.* Wks. 1840 III. 256, I most earnestly entreat you will not delay the supplies, nor deal them out with a sparing hand.

transf. **1766** JOHNSON *Let.* 14 Jan. in *Boswell*, The reasons, good or bad, which have made me such a sparing and ungrateful correspondent.

b. Observing economy or moderation, avoiding excess, in some specified respect. Const. *in*, *of*, †*for*, or †*to* (with inf.).

(*a*) **1604** E. G[RIMSTONE] *D'Acosta's Hist. Indies* IV. v. 217 Nature seemes more sparing in bringing it foorth. **1665** MANLEY *Grotius' Low-C. Wars* 151 The People..are very sparing in imposing and granting Subsidies. *a* **1682** SIR T. BROWNE *Tracts* (1683) 98 The Books of Scripture..are often silent, or very sparing, in the particular Names of Fishes. **1756** C. LUCAS *Ess. Waters* I. 154 The ancient Romans were very sparing in the use of wine. **1797–1805** S. & HT. LEE *Canterb. T.* II. 447 [She was] sparing in all she provided for herself. **1849** MACAULAY *Hist. Eng.* iii. I. 389 It was no longer necessary for the King to be sparing in the use of..his undoubted prerogative. *a* **1862** BUCKLE *Civiliz.* (1873) III. ii. 71 And they, who had the power, were not sparing in the use of it.

(*b*) **1615** DAY *Festivals* x. 120 Giue me one that is greedy, and Covetous & to to sparing of expences. **1683** D. A. *Art Converse* 55 Be sparing of your complements before his rivals. **1735** BERKELEY *Free-think. in Mathem.* §34 Wks. 1871 III. 320, I advise you to be more sparing of hard words. **1758** JOHNSON *Idler* No. 1 ⁋7 He is now grown sparing of communication. **1824** MISS L. M. HAWKINS *Annaline* I. 33 He is as sparing of his letters as a brewer of his malt. **1880** RUSKIN *Bible Amiens* i. (1884) 4 [One] neither wasteful of his time nor sparing of it.

(*c*) **1656** EARL MONM. tr. *Boccalini's Advts. fr. Parnass.* I. lxxv. (1674) 92 [He] was not sparing for any pains, in procuring that the Sentence might be favourable. **1690** LOCKE *Hum. Und.* I. iii. §14 Those who talk so confidently of them are so sparing to tell us which they are.

2. a. Characterized by reticence or restraint in discourse or statement.

1568 E. DERING (*title*), A sparing Restraint of many lauishe Vntruthes. **1594** SHAKS. *Rich. III*, III. vii. 194 For reuerence to some aliue I giue a sparing limit to my Tongue. **1601** W. W[ATSON] (*title*), A Sparing Discoverie of our English Jesuits. **1701** NORRIS *Ideal World* I. vi. 364 A very sparing and reserved allegation of a great authority. **1901** *Harper's Mag.* CII. 805/2 A certain sparing touch, with which he presents situation and character by mere statement of fact.

b. Marked by economy or frugality.

1611 COTGR., *Taillé d'espargne*, cut with sparing worke. **1748** *Anson's Voy.* III. iii. (ed. 4) 438 To make the most of their jerked beef, by a very sparing distribution of it.

3. Small in amount, quantity, or extent; not lavish, liberal, or profuse; scanty, limited.

1602 BRETON *Mother's Blessing* xxiii, The sparing diet is the spirits feast. **1634** SIR T. HERBERT *Trav.* 147 Mouthes rather large then sparing. **1672** GREW *Anat. Pl., Idea* 10 The supplies from the Root being yet but slow and sparing. **1730–46** THOMSON *Autumn* 355 Be mindful of that sparing board, Which covers yours with luxury profuse. **1815** J. SMITH *Panorama Sci. & Art* II. 595 Where only the sparing use of lime is admissible, it should be used to the coping. **1857** MILLER *Elem. Chem., Org.* iii. §5. 187 The sparing solubility of chloroform in water.

b. With agent-nouns: Slight, very moderate.

1860 SMILES *Self-Help* x. 273 Many of our most energetic and useful workers have been but sparing readers. **1883** V. STUART *Egypt* 230 He was a wonderfully sparing sleeper.

4. Forbearing; merciful, considerate.

c **1375** *Sc. Leg. Saints* xviii. (*Egiptian*) 733 To god ay lowynge be, þat..sparand Is to wrak of synful. **1605** SHAKS. *Lucr.* 1687 Let the traitor die; For sparing justice feeds iniquity. *a* **1626** BACON (J.), Their king..was sparing and compassionate towards his subjects. **1658–9** in *Burton's Diary* (1828) III. 329 It is easy to misconstrue the debates of this House if we be not sparing one with the other. **1786** BURNS *Holy Fair* xxi, Black Russell is na spairan: His piercin words like Highlan swords Divide the joints an' marrow.

5. As *adv.* Sparingly.

1623 PENKETHMAN *Handf. Hon.* II. xvii, Thy gaines vse sparing. **1627** FELTHAM *Resolves* II. xxiii. Wks. (1677) 42, I will never censure any man,..but sparing, and with modesty. **1742** YOUNG *Nt. Th.* II. 49 Part with it as with money, sparing.

sparingly ('spɛərɪŋlɪ), *adv.* [f. prec. + -LY².]

1. In a sparing or saving manner; frugally, economically.

c **1440** *Jacob's Well* 206 þi wyif & chyld muste sparyngly as hem nedyth spendyn of þi euyl getyn good. **1571** GOLDING *Calvin on Ps.* xxxvii. 19 He teacheth us thriftynesse, by dealing out sparingly. **1598** R. BERNARD tr. *Terence, Andr.* I. i, *Si.* At the first she lived chastely, sparingly, and hardly, earning her living by wooll and webbe. **1611** COTGR., *Frugalement*, frugally, thriftily, sparingly. **1776** ADAM SMITH *W.N.* II. i. (1869) I. 275 He consumes his stock as sparingly as he can. **1781** COWPER *Hope* 521 He..Is sober, meek, benevolent, and prays, Feeds sparingly. **1873** SYMONDS *Grk. Poets* xi. 368 Your goods enjoy, as if about to die; As if about to live, use sparingly.

2. In a restricted or limited manner; very moderately, scantily, slightly.

1555 *Lydgate's Chron. Troy* To Rdr., He shall be compelled to put on..theyr fantasye, and yet..sparinglye. **1588** A. KING tr. *Canisius' Catech.* 175 He quha saues sparinglie sal scheer sparinglie, as the Apostle witnessis. **1617** MORYSON *Itin.* I. 36 We passed..through a Fenny ground and woods of Oake, yeelding some corne, but sparingly. **1684–5** BOYLE *Min. Waters* 79 To make some estimate, how copiously or sparingly the Liquor is impregnated with it. *a* **1722** LISLE *Husb.* (1757) 236 The clover has not come up at all, or but very sparingly. **1784** COWPER *Tiroc.* 198 And taught at schools much mythologic stuff, But sound religion sparingly enough. **1812** *New Botanic Gard.* I. 42 They should be often but sparingly watered. **1843** R. J. GRAVES *Syst. Clin. Med.* xxvi. 331 Cases where the chancre had..suppurated sparingly. **1871** L. STEPHEN *Playgr. Eur.* (1894) ii. 54 A bit of rough scenery.. might be admitted into descriptions, though sparingly.

b. Of eating or drinking: In great moderation; abstemiously.

1574 NEWTON *Health Mag.* 37 All kindes of Shelfishes.. are seldom and sparingelie to be eaten. **1630** *R. Johnson's Kingd. & Commw.* 52 Their Wines..are hurtfull to all,.. except sparingly taken. **1668** H. MORE *Div. Dial.* v. i. (1713) 400 But both you and Philotheus ate so sparingly. **1717** L. HOWEL *Desiderius* (ed. 3) 171 Pray, how must I tast or eat this Fruit? Very sparingly, says he. **1760** *Phil. Trans.* LI. 849 By.. his living sparingly, and being confined to his bed, he became much emaciated. **1805** SOUTHEY *Madoc* II. iv, Sparingly Drink, for it hath a strength to stir the brain. **1865** *Cornh. Mag.* XI. 489 He sipped sparingly the other in acknowledgment of our politeness.

c. Of speaking, etc.: With reserve or restraint; not fully or copiously.

1576 FLEMING *Panopl. Epist.* 80, I wrote of you (by my credite and honestie) sparingly and timorously. **1583** G. BABINGTON *Commandm.* (1590) 402 When a man speaketh of himselfe, let him speak sparinglie, but not falsely. **1605** EARL STIRLING *Alexandr. Trag.* II. ii, Speake sparingly of vice, praise virtue much. **1681** FLAVEL *Meth. Grace* vii. 145 Though there be such a thing as an explicit faith sometimes spoken of among them, yet it is very sparingly discoursed. **1754** CHATHAM *Lett. Neph.* iv. 21 Deliver your own opinions sparingly, and with proper diffidence. **1796** H. HUNTER tr. *St.-Pierre's Stud. Nat.* (1799) III. 111 They reasoned sparingly on the subject of those Sacred Books. **1825** LYTTON *Falkland* 39 Which in modern writings have been so sparingly exposed.

d. To a slight extent; in a small degree.

1796 WITHERING *Brit. Plants* (ed. 3) III. 565 Stalks naked: leaves sparingly serrated. **1804** *Phil. Trans.* XCIV. 428 Octaedral crystals.., that are very sparingly soluble in water. **1835** J. DUNCAN *Beetles* (Nat. Lib.) 268 The head and thorax are black and shining, the latter sparingly punctured. **1855** SCOFFERN in *Orr's Circ. Sci., Elem. Chem.* 502 Silver is sparingly attacked by strong hydrochloric acid. **1871** GARROD & BAXTER *Mat. Med.* (ed. 3) 47 Soluble in water, more sparingly in spirit.

3. With restriction to a few occasions; seldom, infrequently.

1590 SWINBURNE *Testaments* 13 When Codicilles were first inuented, they were vsed very sparinglie. *c* **1643** LD. HERBERT *Autobiog.* (1824) 89 As for hunting in his Forests I told him I should use it sparingly. **1666** DRYDEN *Ann. Mirab.* Pref. (1910) 21 A grave Sentence, affected by Lucan, but more sparingly used by Virgil. **1748** HARTLEY *Observ. Man* I. iv. §1. 426 Discords..sparingly introduced so as to make a strong Contrast. **1803** *Med. Jrnl.* 271 The lancet, however, was more sparingly employed. **1849** MACAULAY *Hist. Eng.* iii. I. 297 Military punishments were doubtless inflicted..; but they were inflicted very sparingly. **1876** FREEMAN *Norm. Conq.* V. xxiv. 389 The Parliament of England has, for some ages, but sparingly exercised its right of personal election.

4. Leniently, gently.

1863 MISS BRADDON *Aurora Floyd* i. 5 Autumn's red finger has been lightly laid upon the foliage—sparingly.

sparingness ('spɛərɪŋnɪs). [f. SPARING *ppl. a.*] The quality of being sparing: **a.** In respect of diet, living, expenditure, etc.

1579 TWYNE *Phis. agst. Fortune* I. xlii. 61 They are most agreable to the auncient sparyngnesse, and the manners of the Romanes. *a* **1603** T. CARTWRIGHT *Confut. Rhem. N.T.* (1618) 370 To the end, that (by the sparingnesse and homelinesse of their diet,) they..might serue for figures of our Sauiour. **1653** HOLCROFT *Procopius, Goth. Wars* III. 82 With a provident sparingnesse he gave them food more scarcely then according to their appetite. **1682** NORRIS *Hierocles* 98 Too much Sparingness [will slide] into Sordidness and Slovenliness. **1726** SHELVOCKE *Voy. round World* 411 By these exercises, and the sparingness of their diet. **1731** *Rape of Helen* Pref. p. v, The few books of English poetry which thro' sparingness I have purchased. **1853** RUSKIN *Stones Ven.* II. vii. §11. 240 A lightness of form and sparingness of material. **1873** HELPS *Anim. & Mast.* iii. (1875) 65 It affords a beautiful illustration of the prudence and sparingness of what we call Nature.

b. In other connexions.

1617 MORYSON *Itin.* II. 50 In secrecy, and in sparingnesse of speech. **1671** [R. MACWARD] *True Nonconf.* 189 For all your sparingness in passing judgment. **1717** L. HOWEL *Desiderius* (ed. 3) 138 Courtesy, and Affability, justly modified with Slowness and Sparingness of Words. **1828** MISS MITFORD *Village* Ser. III. (1863) 60 A prodigality of words which the fair poetess endeavoured to counterbalance by a corresponding sparingness of idea. **1904** *Athenæum* 2 Apr. 423/3 The artistic selection and sparingness of their inclusions.

spark (spɑːk), *sb.*¹ Forms: α. 1 spærca, spearca, 3–7 sparke (4 spearke), 6 sparcke; 3 spærc, 3–4 sparc, 4– spark (5 *Sc.* sprak, 6 sparck). β. 3–5 sperke, 5, 9 *Sc.* sperk. [OE. *spærca*, *spearca*, = MDu. *sparke*, *spaerke* (WFlem. *sparke*, *sperke*), MLG. and LG. *sparke*, of obscure origin and not represented in the other Teutonic languages. With most of the senses compare those of SPARKLE *sb.*]

1. a. A small particle of fire, an ignited fleck or fragment, thrown off from a burning body or remaining in one almost extinguished, or produced by the impact of one hard body on another.

c **725** *Corpus Gloss.* (Hessels) S 192 *Scintella*, spærca. *a* **900** *O.E. Martyrol.* 25 Aug. 152 þa eaȝan wæron swylce fyren iren, ond him sprungon spearcan of þam muðe. *c* **1055** *Byrhtferth's Handboc* in *Anglia* VIII. 320 Hyt beoð spearcan of þam rodere þurh þæs windes blæs. *a* **1225** *Juliana* (Royal MS.) 68 An engel..iþat ferliche fur amidden riht lihte, ant hit cwenchte anan, euer euch sperke [*Bodl. MS.* sparke]. *a* **1300** *Cursor M.* 25756 Na mar þan a sparc in see, Mai sin agains his merci be. *c* **1384** CHAUCER *H. Fame* 2079 As fire ys wont to quyk and goo From a sparke. *c* **1470** *Gol. & Gaw.* 629 Thai hewit on hard steil..Quhil the spalis and the sparkis spedely out sprang. **1570** LEVINS *Manip.* 81 A sperke, *scintilla.* **1596** DRAYTON *Legends* ii. 545 A little sparke extinguish'd to the Eye, That glowes againe e'r suddenly it dye. **1667** MILTON *P.L.* IV. 814 As when a spark Lights on a heap of nitrous Powder. **1774** GOLDSM. *Nat. Hist.* (1776) I. 83 Spirits of wine will flame with a candle, but not with a spark. **1836–41** BRANDE *Chem.* (ed. 5) 230 If we apply a spark to a small heap of gunpowder, it is instantly dissipated in the gaseous form. **1888** F. HUME *Mme. Midas* I. v, Every blow of the pick sent forth showers of sparks in all directions.

b. With *of* (fire, etc.).

c **1400** *Laud Troy Bk.* 7732 He fferd, as he scholde men haue brent With spark of fire that fro him glent. **1423** JAS. I. *Kingis Q.* 48 A ruby..That, as a sperk of lowe,..Semyt birnyng vpon hir quhyte throte. **1560** BIBLE (Geneva) *Job* xli. 10 Out of his mouth go lampes, and sparkes of fyre leape out. **1613** SHAKS. *Hen. VIII*, II. iv. 73 My drops of teares Ile turne to sparkes of fire. **1726** SWIFT *Gulliver* II. vii, The smallest spark of fire..would kindle the whole. **1827** FARADAY *Chem. Manip.* xxiv. (1842) 638 A splinter of wood, with a spark of fire at the extremity.

c. In similes or comparisons.

c **1205** LAY. 21482 Cador sprong to horse swa spærc him doh of fure. *c* **1300** *Havelok* 91 Of knith ne hauede he neuere drede, þat he ne sprong forth so sparke of glede. *c* **1386** CHAUCER *Sir Thopas* 194 Forþ vppon his way [he] glode As sparke out of þe bronde. **1390** GOWER *Conf.* I. 258 Bot such conseil ther mai be non,..That it nys lich the Sparke fyred Up in the Rof. **1535** COVERDALE *Ecclus.* xlii. 22 O how amiable are all his workes, & as a sparke to loke vpon? *a* **1591** H. SMITH *Serm.* (1637) 199 His was but a momentary kingdome, like a sparke which riseth from the fire, and falleth into the fire againe. **1611** BIBLE *Job* v. 7 Yet man is borne vnto trouble, as the sparkes flie vpward. **1891** FARRAR *Darkn. & Dawn* xiii, The grace of God still lived as a faint spark, not wholly quenched, under the whitening embers of his life.

d. *fig.* and in fig. context; freq. with allusion to the beginning or immediate cause of a fire or conflagration.

c **888** K. ÆLFRED *Boeth.* v. §3 Of ðæm lytlan spearcan þe þu mid ðære tyndran ȝefenge, lifes leoht þe onlyhte. *a* **1225** *Ancr. R.* 296 ȝif hit out stureð þe, cwench hit mid teares of watere,..þeo hwule þet hit nis buten a sperke. **1340** *Ayenb.* 137 Huet am ich bote esssse, and spearken, and hor, and stench. **1480** CAXTON *Chron. Eng.* III. (1520) 20/2 The power of god to the whiche power all other ben but a sperke and dust. **1560** DAUS tr. *Sleidane's Comm.* 134 b, For Sathan can rayse up a great flamme through Gods permission, of a verey small sparke. **1609** in *Harl. Misc.* (Malh.) III. 87 That Illustrious Sparke of Honor and Vertue, Sir Robert Sherley. **1631** GOUGE *God's Arrows* IV. §13. 391 Yet were..the sparkes of that fire so blowne up, as dazled the eyes of the Papists. **1655** FULLER *Ch. Hist.* VI. 302 Hereat, that King who was a spark in Himself, was enflamed to that designe by this Prelates perswasion. **1752** HUME *Ess. & Treat.* (1777) II. 134 The smallest spark may here kindle into the greatest flame. **1781** COWPER *Conversat.* 148 Their want of light and intellect supplied By sparks absurdity strikes out of pride. **1845** DISRAELI *Sybil* VI. ix, Left alone they might have remained quiet; but they only wanted the spark. **1857** BUCKLE *Civiliz.* I. x. 600 To put them in a state where, the train being laid, the slightest spark sufficed to kindle a conflagration.

e. ***a spark in one's throat*** (see quot. 1785). *slang.*

1721 KELLY *Sc. Prov.* 334 The Smith has ay a Spark in his Haise [= halse]. And they often take pains to quench it. **1785** GROSE *Dict. Vulgar T.* s.v., A man that is always thirsty, is said to have a spark in his throat. **1820** J. HODGSON in Raine *Mem.* (1857) I. 292 He has a spark in his throat which often requires to be cooled. **1842** TENNYSON *Will Waterproof* 109 She lit the spark within my throat, To make my blood run quicker.

f. Phr. ***sparks fly*** and varr.: heated words are spoken, friction or excited action occurs.

[**1732** T. FULLER *Gnomologia* 244 When the Heart is a fire, some Sparks will fly out of the Mouth.] **1929** *Amer. Speech* V. 124 It was also said of an angry woman that she will 'make the sparks fly'. **1950** F. STARK *Traveller's Prelude* 182 My sister never hurried and never scolded..while the effect of 'sparks flying' in the next ward reacted on all the men. **1977** *Western Morning News* 1 Sept. 10/3 Robertson scored from the spot, and then sparks really began to fly.

2. a. A small trace, indication, or portion *of* some quality, feeling, sentiment, etc., in some way comparable to a spark, esp. in respect of its latent possibilities.

c **888** K. ÆLFRED *Boeth.* xxxv. §5 Sum spearca.. soðfæstnesse. *Ibid.* xxxviii. §7 ðif ðu ða scyldȝan æniȝne spearcan wisdomes hæfden.

1500–20 DUNBAR *Poems* lxx. 11 Ane spark of thy hie excellent prudence Giff ws. **1581** J. BELL *Haddon's Answ. Osor.* 388 Not a sparcke so much of Reason, example, or proofe. **1601** J. WHEELER *Treat. Comm.* 101 For the which they neuer shewed any sparke of thankfulnesse. **1697** J. POTTER *Antiq. Greece* I. x. (1715) 58 All Sparks of Generosity and Man-hood. *a* **1770** JORTIN *Serm.* (1771) I. iii. 41 Whilst any spark of spiritual life remains. **1775** SHERIDAN *Duenna* II. iii, If any sparks of anger had remained. **1820** W. IRVING *Sketch Bk.* I. 110 They still kept alive the sparks of future friendship. **1868** FREEMAN *Norm. Conq.* (1877) II. vii. 22 The King who reigned without a spark of English feeling.

b. A small remnant, fragment, piece, atom, or amount, *of* something.

1548 ELYOT s.v. *Scintilla*, That no sparke of that moste cruell warre be lefte. *a* **1568** in *Bannatyne MS.* (Hunter. Club) 344 He het the milk our hett, And sorrow spark of it wald yyrne. **1581** J. BELL *Haddon's Answ. Osor.* 150 b, It is neither the cause it selfe, nor any sparcke of the cause. **1638**

R. Baker tr. *Balzac's Lett.* (vol. III) 9 From whom in fifteene days I have received but one small sparke of a letter.

c. A speck or spot upon a ground or in a substance of a different colour.

1686 Plot *Staffordsh.* 158 Though it seem to be a white marble fill'd with black sparks. **1873** Spon *Workshop Rec.* Ser. I. 401/2 To make the ink fly off in sparks over the edges of the book.

d. A trace or dash of spirit, courage, etc. (cf. sense 6 b). ***to get a spark up*** (N.Z. colloq.): to fortify one's spirits with alcohol.

1939 C. Belton *Outside Law in N.Z.* 50 Today young men who intend going to a dance drink until closing time.. just to get a spark up, they say. **1942** *Sun* (Baltimore) 30 Nov. 15/4 Navy had a spark plug in Hamberg and another in Hume that Army lacked. There was no man on Army's squad able to supply this needed spark. **1949** J. R. Cole *It was so Late* 15 Can't get a spark up on beer tonight. **1977** *Sniffin' Glue* July 11 The estates are dismal but anyone who's got any spark is alive enough to get active and out.

3. a. The vital or animating principle in man; a trace *of* life or vitality. Freq. in ***vital spark, spark of life***.

1382 Wyclif *2 Sam.* xiv. 7 Thei sechen to quench my spark that is laft. *c* **1440** *Alph. Tales* 495 Go away fro me, womman, ffor yit þer is a sparke of lyfe in me. **1592** Kyd *Sp. Trag.* II. v. 17 O speak, if any sparke of life remaine. **1700** Rowe *Amb. Step-Moth.* I. i. 218 From whose bright Beings Those active Sparks were struck which move our Clay. **1712** Pope *Dying Chr.* 1 Vital spark of heav'nly flame! **1794** Mrs. Radcliffe *Myst. Udolpho* xxix, She lay so long insensible that Emily began to fear that the spark of life was extinguished. **1817** *Gentl. Mag.* Aug. 174/1 The vital spark was extinct before the body was picked up. *a* **1892** Tennyson *God & the Universe* i, Will my tiny spark of being wholly vanish in your deeps and heights?

b. ***divine spark***: a trace of the divine nature in man. Also in trivial use.

1853 Lytton *My Novel* II. VI. xxi. 180 The divine spark had fled from the human face; the Beast is everywhere growing more and more out of the thing that had been Man. **1920** H. J. Laski *Let.* 15 May in *Holmes-Laski Letters* (1953) I. 263 They may be stupid, lazy, what you will; but ninety-nine out of every hundred have a divine spark in them somewhere which sympathy and enthusiasm is sure to light. **1932** *Week-End Rev.* 9 Jan. 46/2 She felt she had not got into touch, had not given herself, had not transmitted the divine spark. **1957** *Oxf. Dict. Chr. Ch.* 1218/1 As originally formed, man was a powerless entity who wriggled on the ground like a worm..until a Divine spark set him on his feet. **1968** F. Lundberg *Rich & Super-Rich* xv. 632 (*heading*) The divine spark among the rich.

4. a. A small diamond (†or other precious stone). Originally ***diamond*** (or ***ruby***) ***spark*** and ***spark of diamond***, etc.

(*a*) **1508** Dunbar *Gold. Targe* 24 Hevinly beriall droppis, ..birnyng as ruby sperkis. *c* **1550** Rolland *Crt. Venus* I. 111 With Rubie sparkis ane greit number to se. **1632** Lithgow *Trav.* III. 85 Being the goodliest plot, the Diamond sparke, and the Honny spot of all Candy. **1701** *Lond. Gaz.* No. 3718/4 A Gold Twisted Tooth Pick Case set with Diamond Sparks. **1748** Smollett *R. Random* lix, A ring set with a ruby..surrounded by diamond sparks. **1813** Scott *Rokeby* I. xxi, Ingot of gold and diamond spark. **1869** Tennyson *Passing Arth.* 224 For all the haft twinkled with diamond sparks.

(*b*) **1551** Sir J. Williams *Accompte* (Abbotsf. Club) 50 Balaces, small sparkes of emeraldes, and small course perles. **1577** in Nichols *Progr. Q. Eliz.* (1788) II. 14 Item,..xvi small rubyes being but sparcks, and v sparcks of dyamonds. **1629** Massinger *Picture* II. ii, Good Madam what shall he doe with a hoop ring, And a sparke of diamond in it? *a* **1694** Tillotson *Serm.* ccxiii. (1744) XI. 4785 The little and short sayings of wise and excellent men are of great value, like the dust of gold, or the least sparks of diamond. **1756–7** tr. *Keysler's Trav.* (1760) II. 275 The Florentine work.. consists of sparks of gems and small pieces of the finest marble. *a* **1774** Goldsm. *Surv. Exp. Philos.* (1776) I. 379 As for those things which cannot be thus weighed, such as quicksilver, small sparks of diamond, and such like.

(*c*) **1599** *George a Greene* I. iv, A chaplet..Set with choice rubies, sparkes, and diamonds. **1614** in *Archaeol.* XLII. 350 A hoope ringe with 9 sparkes. **1675** *Lond. Gaz.* No. 987/4 A Diamond Ring with three very large stones, and some sparks. **1710** Steele *Tatler* No. 245 ¶2 Another [ring] set round with small Rubies and Sparks. **1771** T. Hull *Sir W. Harrington* (1797) II. 239 The lockets are..one,..with the cyphers of her name put on it, set with very small sparks. **1874** *Slang Dict.* 303 *Sparks*, diamonds. Term much in use among the lower orders, and generally applied to stones in rings and pins.

fig. **1758** S. Hayward *Serm.* xvi. 470 The sparks of this crown are perfect holiness and a conformity to God.

b. A (glittering) fragment or particle *of* some metal, ore, or mineral. Also *transf.*

1560 Whitehorne *Ord. Souldiours* (1588) 44 b, If you will make it parfiter, put to it a few stamped brickes, and sparkes of yron. **1581** Stafford *Exam. Compl.* ii. (1876) 51 To trie out the sandes..to get amonge them after much labour small sparkes of gold. **1653** Manlove *Customs Lead Mines* 273 Trunks and Sparks of oar. *a* **1701** Maundrell *Journ. Jerus.* (1721) Add. 10 Tho' it had the sparks and particles of Salt, yet it had perfectly lost its Savour. **1796** Morse *Amer. Geog.* I. 522 This bluish stone was filled with sparks of virgin copper.

5. a. A bright or glittering emanation, flash, or gleam of light. Also *transf.*, a bright glance.

a **1542** Wyatt in *Anglia* XVIII. 479 The lyuely sparkes that issue from those Iyes. **1611** Cotgr., *Bluette*, a little streake, or sparke of heat, in the aire, when the season is verie hot. **1687** A. Lovell tr. *Thevenot's Trav.* II. 195 At first I took them for sparks that are many times seen to flash out of the Sea, when the water is very rough. **1746** Hervey *Medit.* (1818) 256 Abundance of living sparks glitter in the lanes, and twinkle under the hedges. **1750** tr. *Leonardus' Mirr. Stones* 86 Of this stone there is one kind, of a gold colour, with some burning sparks. **1814** Scott *Lord of Isles* v. xii, Beneath their oars the ocean's might Was dash'd to sparks of glimmering light. **1889** *Pall Mall G.* 16 Nov. 3/1 At the sound of her native tongue, a spark came into her dark eyes.

Comb. **1602** Marston *Ant. & Mel.* II. Wks. 1856 I. 20 Delicate, delicious, spark eyed, sleek skind, slender wasted, clean legd, rarely shapt.

b. *Med.* In *pl.*, the glittering caused by the gathering of particles of cholesterin upon the eye in sparkling synchisis.

1899 *Allbutt's Syst. Med.* VIII. 42 It is conceivable that sparks or similar subjective phenomena, may appear from sudden and powerful contraction of the orbicularis palpebrarum compressing the globe.

6. *Electr.* **a.** A brilliant streak or flash of light produced by a discontinuous discharge of electricity between two conductors at a short or moderate distance apart.

[**1742** Desaguliers *Diss. Electricity* 7 If the Room be darken'd when you make these Experiments, you will see Sparks of Light where-ever the Tube snaps.] **1748** Franklin *Lett.*, etc. Wks. 1840 V. 205 That thimble in passing by, receives a spark, and thereby being electrified is repelled. **1788** *Phil. Trans.* LXXVIII. 271 Now, when the machine worked well, Mr. Gilpin supposes he got about two or three hundred sparks a minute. **1827** Faraday *Chem. Manip.* xvii. (1842) 435 Upon putting the prime conductor into its place,..sparks two or three inches in length should fly rapidly from it to the knuckle. **1873** J. C. Maxwell *Electr. & Magn.* (1881) I. 57 The discharge, when it occurs, usually takes the form of a spark.

b. More fully in ***electric(al) spark***. Also *transf.* and *fig.*

1771 *Encycl. Brit.* II. 480/1 The electric spark will strike a hole through a quire of paper. **1831** Brewster *Optics* x. 86 Similar bands are perceived in the light..of the electric spark. **1840** *Brit. Florist* (1846) I. 72 The flowers of this genus may be seen..to emit small electrical sparks or threads of light. **1846** Grote *Greece* I. xvii. (1862) I. 401 Animated by the electric spark of genius.

c. *pl.* usu. const. as *sing.* One who works with electrical equipment: a radio operator, an electrician, etc. *slang.*

1914 *Dialect Notes* IV. 151 *Sparks*, wireless operator. **1917** *Wireless World* V. 37 In the Service the regular nickname for wireless telegraphists is graphically expressed as 'Sparks'. **1922** P. F. Westerman *Wireless Officer* iii. 25 A burly, jovial-featured man..greeted Mostyn as he stepped off the gang-plank. 'Hello, you're our Sparks, aren't you?' **1934** *Sun* (Baltimore) 31 Jan. 20/3 'Sparks', the radio operator, was busy at his key. **1938** H. Borust *In Plain Clothes* xii. 184 Scene shifters, 'sparks' (light men), wardrobe-keepers. **1971** *Guardian* 24 Sept. 12/4, I went to Manchester as a spark's mate—an electrician's mate. **1975** *Listener* 10 Apr. 461/3 Lord Sneaker tells his sparks to wrap up the lights. **1977** M. Babson *Murder, murder, Little Star* viii. 56 The Technical Crew were called by the names of the jobs they did... Sparks was the electrician, Props was the property master, Camera the cameraman. **1980** R. Mitton *Master & Son* i. 9 Meet Ulrica Halsted..the sexiest Spark that ever went to sea.

d. Short for ***spark telegraphy*** (cf. senses 7 b, d).

1921 *Wireless World* 2 Apr. 21/1 Commencing by pointing out the advantages and disadvantages of various circuits for the reception of Spark, C. W. and Telephony, Captain Tingey gave many useful hints. **1922** *Ibid.* 15 Apr. 76/2 One ought to..switch that connection on to different places when one is receiving spark or telephony. **1925** *Weekly Dispatch* 22 Nov. 8/2 If the Government were to replace spark by continuous wave the loss on old apparatus could be set aside by the revenue from wireless licences.

7. *attrib.* and *Comb.* **a.** In the names of contrivances for the arresting, etc., of sparks in locomotive funnels or in chimneys, as ***spark-arrester, -baffler, guard, plate, trap***.

Also, in recent use, *spark-condenser, -consumer*, etc.

1833 Loudon *Encycl. Archit.* §799 What is called a spark plate (a broad plate of cast iron, to reflect back the sparks, and prevent their reaching up to the hops). **1838** *Civil Eng. & Arch. Jrnl.* I. 134/1 The adaptation of this contrivance, and also the spark arrester, is very much called for. **1873** Medley *Autumn Tour U.S. & Canada* ix. 142 The locomotives are generally provided with spark-bafflers to the funnels. **1879** *Cassell's Techn. Educ.* I. 145/2 In American locomotives the top of the funnel is..fitted with a contrivance known as a 'spark-trap' or 'spark-arrester'. **1901** *Scotsman* 7 Mar. 6/1 To force railway companies to attach spark guards to locomotive engines.

b. In the names of electrical apparatus, devices in internal-combustion motors, etc. as ***spark-chronograph, -condenser, discharge(r), frequency, -gap*** (also *attrib.*), ***-recorder, source, station, tester, transmitter***.

1889 *Anthony's Photogr. Bull.* II. 294 The time..I had calculated exactly by means of *spark-chronographs. **1875** Knight *Dict. Mech.* 2254/1 **Spark-condenser* (Electricity), an instrument..used for burning metals or obtaining the spectra of gases. **1848** *Patent Jrnl.* 5 Aug. 266/1 In frictional *spark discharges, the consequent shock, light, and other peculiarities are in part owing to waves of..polarization. **1973** L. R. Lentz et al. in *Automotive Electr. Equipment* (Inst. Mech. Engineers) 63/2 The fuel mixture is ignited prior to the occurrence of the normal spark discharge. **1921** E. E. Bucher *Pract. Wireless Telegr.* 101 *Spark dischargers for radio-telegraphy. **1906** J. A. Fleming *Princ. Electric Wave Telegr.* ii. 157 The author has..devised the following appliances for measuring *spark frequency. **1925** W. Greenwood *Wireless Telegr. & Teleph.* iv. 75 If a low spark frequency is required the alternator circuit can be tuned to the alternator frequency, and the spark gap lengthened. **1889** *Telegr. Jrnl.* 10 May 550/2 An insulated rod, with an induction coil and *spark gap. **1905** *Electrician* Feb. 614/1 Measurements of spark-gap resistance in wireless telegraph senders. **1935** *Discovery* Aug. 226/1 There are two different types of short-wave generator in actual use, the valve and the spark-gap oscillators. **1967** *New Scientist* 14 Dec. 671/1 The operator closes the discharge switch, and the electric charge in the capacitors leaps across the spark gap. **1888** *Encycl. Brit.* XXIII. 124/2 The *spark recorder in some respects foreshadowed the more perfect instrument—the siphon recorder. **1944** *Jrnl. Optical Soc. Amer.* XXXIV. 773/2 A type of interrupted *spark source involving no mechanical parts has been developed for use in quantitative spectrographic analysis. **1956** *Nature* 4 Feb. 222/1 A high-precision spark source and an optical arrangement containing a rotating mirror are needed. **1913** *Year-Bk. Wireless Telegr. & Teleph.* 401 It does not follow..that a continuous-wave station is immune from interference by a *spark station. **1925** *Sci. Abstr.* B. XXVIII. 232 (*heading*) International measurements of the wave-lengths of spark stations. **1925** *Morris Owner's Man.* 84 The motorist should try each plug in turn with the aid of a '*spark tester'. **1916** J. A. Fleming *Princ. Electric Wave Telegr.* (ed. 3) 671 The types of transmitter employing such condenser discharges are called *spark transmitters. **1934** A. L. Albert *Electr. Communication* xv. 426 The reception of damped waves from a spark transmitter..is very simple.

c. In other uses, as ***spark guard, -pistol, -shower, -storm; spark-gushing, -sprayed*** adjs.

1916 *Daily Colonist* (Victoria, B.C.) 11 July 13/5 (Advt.), Furniture and furnishings..including..fender and *spark guard. **1972** *Oxford Times* 14 Jan. 2 A spark guard—of close wire mesh—will prevent sparks from flying out. **1938** S. Leslie *Film of Memory* 131 The *spark-gushing engine passed underfoot. **1938** S. Beckett *Murphy* ix. 171 Firing a *spark-pistol with a kind of despair. **1938** S. Spender *Trial of Judge* I. 16 We..motored out..Skidding—*spark-showers at corners. **1950** D. Gascoyne *Vagrant* 28 Till all night's *spark-sprayed dome is stunned with quick air-quakes of gold. **1969** G. Macbeth *War Quartet* 47 Here, unspilled, The blood of London lay enchaliced, rich Over the *spark-storm.

d. Special Combs.: **spark ball**, a sphere forming one side of a spark gap; **spark chamber** *Physics*, a form of spark counter in which many closely spaced electrodes are used to enable the path of an ionizing particle to be determined; **spark coil**, an induction coil that generates high-voltage pulses from an interrupted low-voltage source, used esp. to energize the sparking plugs in an internal-combustion engine; **spark counter** *Physics* [tr. G. *funkenzähler* (H. Greinacher 1935, in *Helv. Physica Acta* VIII. 266)], a detector for charged particles consisting of two charged electrodes separated by a gas that is ionized by the passage of the particle; **spark erosion** *Engin.*, a method of machining metal in which a series of electric sparks is used to remove droplets from the piece; freq. *attrib.*; hence **spark-erode** *v. trans.*, to machine (a piece) by spark erosion; **spark line**, a spectral line corresponding to an atom in a given state of ionization; **spark machining** *Engin.* = *spark erosion* above; **spark-prop** *Criminals' slang*, a diamond pin, a tie-pin; **spark spectrum**, a spectrum produced by an atom in a given state of ionization, commonly excited under laboratory conditions by an electric spark; **spark telegraphy**, an early method of radio-telegraphy in which high-frequency oscillations are set up in a transmitting aerial by the discharge of a highly charged capacitor through a spark gap in series with an inductance connected to the aerial; hence **spark telegraph**.

1902 *Encycl. Brit.* XXXIII. 230/2 The distance at which the effects of the oscillatory spark could be perceived by the aid of the coherer was closely connected with the height of this air-wire or aerial connected to the *spark balls and coherer. **1924** O. Lodge *Harmsworth's Wireless Encycl.* III. 1864/2 The object of replacing the pointed ends of the wires by spark balls is to prevent the gradual leaking discharge. **1961** *Rev. Sci. Instruments* XXXII. 482/1 The *spark chamber is a direct outgrowth of an older detector called the spark counter. **1974** Frauenfelder & Henley *Subatomic Physics* iv. 56 Spark chambers have many of the advantages of bubble chambers, and they can be triggered. [**1868** *Spark coil: see Sprengel.] **1900** G. D. Hiscox *Horseless Vehicles* vii. 121 The Edison spark coil..is a short, thick coil, which will give a hot, bright spark, and yet will have an instantaneous discharge. **1902** *How to make Things* 3/2 A half-inch spark coil will give very good results. **1922** [see *jump-spark, jump spark* s.v. Jump-]. **1971** *Sci. Amer.* May 86/2 The ordinary automobile spark coil..is the commonest version of the induction coil. **1935** *Sci. Abstr.* XXXVIII. 718 The general name '*spark counter' is proposed for the new counters devised by the author. **1970** *Nucl. Instruments & Methods* LXXXVII. 181/1 Cylindrical spark counters have been designed that employ boron nitride disks as converters. **1980** J. W. Hill *Intermediate Physics* xxiii. 220 (*heading*) The spark counter. **1960** *Metal Treatment* XXVII. 206/1 When a die showed signs of wear, one must be able to take it out, *spark-erode it and replace it. **1955** *Aircraft Production* XVII. 421/1 The process of *spark-erosion machining is becoming widely used for special purposes, such as machining holes in tungsten-carbide. **1977** R. B. Ross *Handbk. Metal Treatments & Testing* 360 Spark erosion is extremely useful where shapes are required in hardened or difficult to machine materials. **1980** *West Lancs. Evening Gaz.* 4 Jan. 10 (Advt.), Familiarity with close tolerance machining and bench work is essential and some experience of spark erosion machining would be an advantage. **1879** *Proc. R. Soc.* XXX. 27 The *spark lines are in the sun, but the less refrangible member of the wide triplet and the blue line seen in the flame are absent. **1932** *Ibid.* CXXXIV. 611 It is proposed to give a complete catalogue of the spark lines of arsenic. **1950** *Jrnl. Optical Soc. Amer.* XL. 180/1 By adjusting the conditions of discharge either arc or spark lines may be made to predominate. **1954** *Engineer* 2 July 12/2 Although *spark machining may, in theory, be carried out with electrode and workpiece separated only by air, in practice a liquid dielectric is used. **1973** J. G. TWEEDDALE *Materials Technol.* II. vi. 152 Spark machining is applicable only to electrically conducting materials. **1879** *Macmillan's Mag.* Oct. 506/1 My pal said, 'Pipe his *spark prop' (diamond pin). **1923** J. C. GOODWIN *Sidelights on Criminal Matters* iii. 32 To steal a tie-pin, or 'spark prop' as it is termed in the slang of thieves, [etc.]. **1873** *Phil. Trans. R. Soc.* CLXIII. 266 *(table)* The *spark-spectrum of the chloride. **1905** E. C. C. BALY *Spectroscopy* 374 The induction coil is used..for the production of the so-called spark spectra of substances. **1970** G. K. WOODGATE *Elem. Atomic Struct.* vi. 105 Na I is also called the arc spectrum of sodium, Mg II the first spark spectrum of magnesium and Al III the second spark spectrum of aluminium. **1934** A. L. ALBERT *Electr. Communication* xv. 426/1 *(caption)* The generation of damped waves with a *spark telegraph set. **1898** *Ludgate* VII. 78/1 Mr. Marconi, in July, 1897, came to England to introduce his new plan of '*Spark Telegraphy'. **1908** *Rep. Brit. Assoc. Adv. Sci. 1907* 730 A movement which much more nearly corresponds with the actual current in the vertical wire as used in spark telegraphy.

spark (spɑːk), *sb.*^{2} [prob. a figurative use of prec.: cf. 1 d, quot. 1609.]

1. A woman of great beauty, elegance, or wit.

1575 R. B. *Appius & Virginia* in Hazl. *Dodsley* IV. 112 But stay: behold the peerless sparks, whereof my tongue did talk, Approach. **1611** CHAPMAN *Widowes T.* I. i, I will wed thee To my great widdowes Daughter and sole Heire, The louely sparke, the bright Laodice. **1676** ETHEREDGE *Man of Mode* I. i, The Vizard is a spark and has a genius that makes her worthy of your self, Dorimant. **1873** BROWNING *Red Cott. Nt.-Cap* 181 The poor mutilated figure, once The gay and glancing fortunate young spark, Miranda.

2. A young man of an elegant or foppish character; one who affects smartness or display in dress and manners. Chiefly in more or less depreciatory use.

c **1600** *Timon* II. iii. (1842) 30 Theis noble sparkes desires your company. **1627** N. BURLEY in Capt. Smith *Seaman's Gram.* a ij, The Galley Iason built, that Græcian sparke. **1685** LUTTRELL *Brief Rel.* (1857) I. 339 Mr. Cradock the mercer, a highflown spark, died lately of a St. Anthonies fire. **1709** POPE *Ess. Crit.* 329 These sparks with awkward vanity display What the fine gentlemen wore yesterday. **1782** WOLCOTT (P. Pindar) *Ode to R. A.'s* Wks. 1812 I. 35 Some young roving Military Spark. **1818** *Sporting Mag.* (N.S.) II. 170 Another dapper spark took the place of the prosecutor. **1852** THACKERAY *Esmond* III. iii, She invited the agreeable young spark to visit her if ever he came to London. **1884** J. GILMOUR *Mongols* 227 The young spark did not relish his rebuke much, but he did not dare to disobey.

b. Used with *my* (see MY *poss. adj.* 1 c).

1700 S. L. tr. *Fryke's Voy. E. Ind.* 207 When I came to go, I found my Spark gone, and was told he was gone off half an Hour before. **1710** STEELE *Tatler* No. 2 ¶1 How-ever, my young Spark ventures upon her like a Man of Quality. **1778** MISS BURNEY *Evelina* xxxvii, Hark'ee, my spark, none of your grinning!

3. A beau, lover, or suitor. Freq. with poss. pron.

1706–7 FARQUHAR *Beaux' Strat.* IV. ii, Had my Spark call'd me a Venus directly, I shou'd have believ'd him a Footman in good earnest. **1747** HOADLY *Suspicious Husband* II. i, I and my Spark have been long acquainted. **1812** CRABBE *Tales* iv. 266 Am I forsaken for a trimmer spark? **1839** MARRYAT *Diary Amer.* Ser. I. I. 141 The first time I ever heard ladies complain of having too many sparks about them. **1871** BROWNING *Balaust.* 1553 The poor poltroon A very woman worsted, daring death Just for the sake of thee, her handsome spark!

4. *attrib.*, as ***spark spirit***, ***wit***.

1602 MARSTON *Ant. & Mel.* v. Wks. 1856 I. 59 Sparke spirit, how like you his voice? **1642** D. ROGERS *Naaman* 238 Your sparke wits, ripe heads, experience and abilities.

spark, *sb.*^{3} *s.w. dial.* [Back-formation from SPARKED *ppl. a.*] 'A spotted or parti-coloured bullock.'

1798 *Young's Annals Agric.* XXX. 314 He objects to sparks. **1888** ELWORTHY *W. Somerset Word-bk.* 697.

spark (spɑːk), *v.*^{1} Also 5 sparkyn, 6–7 sparke, 6 *Sc.* sperk. [Related to SPARK *sb.*^{1}, and agreeing in form with MDu. *sparken*, *spaerken*, *sperken*, (WFlem. *sparken*, *sperken*, WFris. *sparkje*), MLG. *sparken*. The OE. vb. was *spircan*, *spyrcan* (:—**spiẹrcan*), but **spearcade* is a plausible emendation of *sweartade* in *Satan* 78.]

1. a. *intr.* To emit or give forth a spark or sparks; to sparkle. *spec.* in *Electr.* To produce or emit an electric spark or sparks by ionization of the medium separating two conductors at different potentials. Also *transf.* and *fig.* Phr. *to **spark on all cylinders*** = to *function* (etc.) *on all cylinders* s.v. CYLINDER *sb.* 6.

c **1300** *Havelok* 2144 It sparkede, and ful brith shon, So doth þe gode charbucle ston. **1398** TREVISA *Barth. De P.R.* XVII. cxlix, þornes..beþ sone itende in þe fuyre..and sparkeþ and crakkeþ and makeþ moche noyse. *c* **1460** *Promp. Parv.* (Winch. MS.) 462 Sparkyn, *sintillo*. **1562** J. HEYWOOD *Prov. & Epigr.* (1867) 99, I neuer heard thy fyre once sparke. **1611** COTGR., *Estinceller*, to sparke, to sparkle, as fire. **1763** C. BERKELEY in Jesse *Selwyn & Contemp.* (1843) I. 244 Her temper is like charcoal, which kindles soon, and sparks to the top of the house. **1884** S. P. THOMPSON *Dynamo-Electr. Machinery* 60 Any dynamo in which the curve of potentials at the commutator presented such irregularities..would probably spark excessively at the collector. **1905** T. H. HAWLEY *Motor Ignition Appliances* iv. 20 If our charge fails to explode or the plug to spark, the fault must usually be sought for elsewhere. **1926** R. W. HUTCHINSON *Wireless* 112 The spark gap consists of two small spheres sparking across the diameters of two large ones. **1967** L. BACON in L. Holmes *Odhams New Motor Man.* iii. 81 One simple check can clear the whole of the ignition circuit—are the plugs sparking? **1977** M. HINXMAN *One-Way Cemetery* viii. 55 John realized his inspector was sparking on all cylinders. He looked a damned sight fresher than Waller felt.

b. *transf.* Of the eyes, or in reference to these.

1594 SPENSER *Amoretti* lxxxi, Fayre is my loue, when..in her eyes the fyre of loue does sparke. **1631** QUARLES *Samson* xix, Her eyes did sparke, At every glance, like Diamonds in the darke. **1827** HOOD *Hero & Leander* ix, Their cheeks are white.., And those fair mirrors where their joys did spark, All dim.

c. With *over*. To be crossed or connected by a spark as a result of a breakdown in insulation. Also *fig.*

1915 *Standardization Rules Amer. Inst. Electr. Engineers* 48 The voltage at which a given gap sparks over is found by taking the voltage corresponding to the spacing..and multiplying by the correction factor. **1966** R. ARDREY *Territorial Imperative* iii. 88 When antagonists face each other..inhibited from further attack..their energy ..'sparks over'—another ethologist's term—into a third instinctual channel which will cause no damage. **1974** *Sci. Amer.* Feb. 78/2 Since the magnets were not designed to work under water many of them sparked over and failed when power was fed into them.

2. a. To issue, come forth, fall, etc., as or in the manner of sparks. Also *transf.*

1513 DOUGLAS *Æneid* III. viii. 132 The blak laithly smuke ..With gledis sperkand as the haill als thik. **1873** BLACK *Pr. Thule* 13 The sunlight that..sparked on his teeth when he laughed. **1897** CROCKETT *Lad's Love* viii, The anger fair sparked and blazed from her dark, indignant eyes.

b. With advs., as *off*, *out*.

1833 M. SCOTT *Tom Cringle* iii, Every now and then a flying fish would spark out from the unruffled bosom of the heaving water. **1889** *Pall Mall G.* 11 Nov. 6/1 If the phosphorus 'sparks' off, as it is apt to do.

c. To go *out*, be extinguished, like sparks.

1845 BAILEY *Festus* (ed. 2) 269 These have died, are dying, and shall die; Yea, copyists shall die, spark out and out.

3. *trans.* **a.** To send *out*, or emit, in or as sparks.

1596 SPENSER *F.Q.* VI. xi. 21 To sparke out litle beames, like starres in foggie night. **1610** HEYWOOD *Gold. Age* III. i, Threaten your worst! let all your eyes spark fire!

b. To illuminate or enlighten feebly.

1835 E. ELLIOTT *Wonders of the Lane* xxiv. Poems III. 77 Oh, God of terrors! what are we?—Poor insects, spark'd with thought!

c. *Electr.* To affect, act or operate upon, by the emission or transmission of electrical sparks. Also *absol.*, to send a spark *across*, etc.

1889 *Philos. Mag.* Ser. v. XXVII. 339 Whenever a large Leyden jar is sparked through the coil. **1895** *Daily Chron.* 13 Apr. 3/5 Professor Ramsay saw..that he had some gas, and was eager to 'spark' it. **1905** *Brit. Med. Jrnl.* 1 July 14 Whenever this [gap] is sparked across, the tube is softened slightly by the regulator.

d. *fig.* To fire, to inspire; to kindle, to set in motion; ***to spark off***, to be the immediate cause of (something hard to control). orig. *U.S.*

1912 L. J. VANCE *Destroying Angel* ii. 21 Abrupt inspiration sparked the imagination of Peter Stark, and he began to sputter with enthusiasm. **1941** *Sun* (Baltimore) 24 Apr. 15/2 He is the type [of ballplayer] that sparks an infield and hustles all of the time. **1947** *Richmond* (Va.) *Times-Dispatch* 1 Dec. 10/1 We hope that circumstances which might well spark another world conflict will not rise in Palestine. **1957** *Economist* 26 Oct. 287/2 Any encroachment on vital western interests is liable to spark off the sort of war that would incinerate communism along with communists. **1962** *Listener* 4 Oct. 501/1 A story has come out of California and sparked the November election campaign, which is now beginning to smoulder and crackle. **1964** *Ann. Reg. 1963* 100 The final decision to end Federation sparked off immediately a new constitutional controversy. **1970** S. L. BARRACLOUGH in I. L. Horowitz *Masses in Lat. Amer.* iv. 158 The more widely distributed post-reform incomes help spark development by changing propensities to invest. **1978** *Dumfries Courier* 20 Oct. 5/1 The club has taken no stand against this sort of behaviour, which can spark off bad behaviour among the spectators. **1979** *IEEE Trans. Professional Communication* XXII. 70/1 Man has always been intrigued by the elusive nature of the brain mechanisms which spark new and unexpected ideas to solve problems. **1981** *Times* 24 July 23/1 Stocks on the New York Stock Exchange closed higher due to a late afternoon rally, sparked by bargain hunting among oil stocks and blue chip issues.

4. *Sc.* and *north. dial.* **a.** To spatter (dirt, etc.).

1637 RUTHERFORD *Lett.* (1862) I. clxiii. 379 My desire is to ride fair and not to spark dirt..in the face of my..well-beloved.

b. To bespatter or spot with mud, etc. Also *fig.*

1806 DOUGLAS *Poems* 81 Young lasses' fame, my dainty joe, Is unco easy sparkit. **1808** JAMIESON App., *To Spark*,.. to soil by throwing up small spots of mire. **1894** HESLOP *Northumb. Gloss.* 674 The coach gan past sparkt us.

spark (spɑːk), *v.*^{2} [f. SPARK *sb.*^{2}]

† 1. *intr.* With *it*. To play the spark or gallant; to make a display, show off. *Obs.*

1676 ETHEREDGE *Man of Mode* I. i, That she may spark it in a Box, And do honour to her profession. **1688** SHADWELL *Sqr. Alsatia* I. i, Enough [money] to set thee up to spark it in thy brother's face. **1709** MRS. MANLEY *Secret Mem.* I. 164 To purchase..a Back-place in their Coach, that they may spark it in the Prado.

2. *U.S.* To engage in courtship; to play the suitor, wooer, or beau. Also with *it*.

1807–8 W. IRVING *Salmag.* (1824) 276 Whenever he went a sparking amongst the rosy country girls of the neighbouring farms. **1848** BARTLETT *Dict. Amer.* 322 (with quots.). **1862** LOWELL *Biglow P.* Ser. II. *Courtin'* ix, He'd sparked it with full twenty gals. **1884** *Harper's Mag.* Feb. 410/2 He used to go sparkin' round among the girls.

b. *trans.* To make love or pay attentions to; to court.

1888 GUNTER *Mr. Potter* xiv. 176, I've heard as how young Errol is a sparking your daughter. **1893** *Harper's Mag.* Feb. 372/2 The parents..sit in the room while he 'sparks' the ravisher of his heart.

sparked, *ppl. a. s.w. dial.* (and *U.S.*). Also 6 sparkyd, 8–9 -it. [app. f. SPARK *sb.*^{1}; cf. sense 2 c there.]

1. Of cattle, etc., or their colour: Mottled, dappled; parti-coloured.

[**1457** in *Somerset Med. Wills* (1901) 172 Boviculum sparcatum.] **1552** *Will J. Harte* (Somerset Ho.), An oxe of sparkyd colour. **1603–4** in *Wilts. Archaeol. Mag.* (1885) XXII. 225 Quatuor vaccas quarum due color sparked. **1811** T. DAVIS *Agric. Wilts.* 260 Neat Cattle... Colours—Sparked, of two colours, mottled. **1871** PULMAN *Rustic Sketches* (ed. 3) 30 Thee must watch the sparkid hen, Or her'll goo lay astray. **1888** ELWORTHY *W. Somerset Word-bk.* 697 A sparked cat—i.e. a tortoise-shell cat.

b. ***sparked back*** (***plover***), the common turnstone or sea-dotterel. *U.S. local.*

1888 TRUMBULL *Names*, etc., *of Birds* 186 At Falmouth, Sparked-Back, Streaked-Back and Bishop Plover.

2. Specked or spotted *with* gold, silver, etc. (Cf. SPARKY *a.* 1.) *rare.*

1552 in Money *Par. Ch. Goods Berks.* (1879) 46 One Corporas beinge of Red velvete sparked w^t golde. **1860** G. P. R. PULMAN *Song Solomon* i. 11 We'll mek vor thee eydgin's o' gould, all a-sparkid wi' zelver.

†'sparkefy, *v. Obs.*$^{-1}$ [f. SPARK *sb.*^{2} + -FY.] *trans.* To make into a spark or gallant.

1667 LD. DIGBY *Elvira* III. 36 A sharp pointed Hat.. Appears not so ridiculous, as Yonker, Without a love Intreegue, to Introduce, And sparkefy him there.

sparker. [f. SPARK *sb.*^{1} or *v.*^{1} + -ER.]

1. A spark-arrester.

1864 WEBSTER, *Sparker*, a contrivance [in a locomotive-chimney] to prevent the escape of sparks, while it allows the passage of gas.

2. A kind of miniature firework.

1908 *Daily Chron.* 31 Oct. 3/3 When discharged the sparker created a flare and emitted sparks.

3. A powerful form of sonar apparatus used to investigate solid structures underlying sediment on the sea bed.

1961 *Ann. Reg. 1960* 406 The whole area was surveyed by the newly developed 'sparker' technique, an extension of the echo-sounding method used for charting the sea-bottom. The sparker used an intense sound source (a spark) which enabled the sound wave to penetrate the sea bottom. The sound waves were reflected from the interfaces between different kinds of rock. **1969** J. MAVOR *Voyage to Atlantis* II. iii. 84 The 'sparker' and line hydrophone for listening to the reflected sound signals were the most powerful in the world but required a depth of 60 feet and 150 yards of towline astern. **1974** *Nature* 26 Apr. 745/1 An 8 kJ sparker was also used.

sparket(ting: see SPIRKET(TING.

† sparkful, *a. Obs.*$^{-1}$ [f. SPARK *sb.*^{1}] Smart.

1605 CAMDEN *Rem.*, *Languages* 18 Hitherto will our sparkefull Youth laugh at their great grandfathers English.

† sparkin. *Obs.*$^{-1}$ [f. SPAR *sb.*^{1} + -KIN.] A small spar.

1408 *Crt.-roll Great Waltham* (Essex) Nov., Dicunt quod Johannes atte Rothe sine licencia succidit lx. quercuncl. vocat. Sparkynes, pret. v s.

'sparkiness. *rare.* [f. SPARKY *a.*]

1. Sparkling quality.

1641 TRAPPE *Theol. Theol.* iii. 50 As wine the oftner it is poured from vessell to vessell, the more it loseth of its spirits and sparkinesse.

2. The quality of being mottled or parti-coloured.

1868 *Jrnl. R. Agric. Soc.* Ser. II. IV. II. 284 Sparkiness is not liked, but still it does not constitute a valid objection.

sparking ('spɑːkɪŋ), *vbl. sb.*^{1} [f. SPARK *v.*^{1}]

a. The action of emitting sparks; *spec.* in *Electr.*, the production or emission of electric sparks at points where the continuity of a current is broken or interrupted.

1611 COTGR., *Scintillation*, a sparking, or sparkling. **1883** *Daily News* 29 Sept. 7/1 It is, perhaps, owing to this arrangement that there is so little sparking to be seen at the brushes of the machine. **1894** *Westm. Gaz.* 15 Jan. 3/1 None of the electric supply companies can prevent sparking from their cables.

b. *attrib.*, as ***sparking arrangement***, ***distance***, ***knob***, etc. Special Combs.: **sparking coil** = *spark coil* s.v. SPARK *sb.*^{1} 7 d; **sparking plug**, a device that is fitted to the cylinder head of an internal-combustion engine and used to ignite the explosive mixture in the cylinder by the discharge of a spark between two electrodes at its end.

1881 *Nature* No. 624. 572 As soon as the cloud by its motion comes within sparking distance. **1891** *Dublin Rev.* Oct. 421 The sparking arrangement is placed inside an ordinary projection lantern. **1897** G. D. HISCOX *Gas, Gasoline, & Oil Vapor Engines* x. 74 The sparking coil.. consists of a bundle of iron wire, insulated and wrapped with insulated copper wire. **1900** *Knowledge* 1 Oct. 234/2 If the electric bell was placed on the same table as the sparking knobs. **1902** *Daily Chron.* 5 Sept. 7/5 Only when I got to the very top did I find the last sparking plug cracked. **1908** tr.

Lieckfeld's Oil Motors v. 85 A further improvement in electric ignition was introduced by the French firm [*sc.* de Dion et Bouton] when they brought out the sparking plug. **1929** *Proc. Inst. Automobile Engineers* XXIII. 252 If the sparking coil and plug gap be so balanced that the spark is just able to pass without a following arc, then the least widening of the gap will result in a failure of the spark to pass. **1929** E. LINKLATER *Poet's Pub* xxvi. 279 The life of a sparking-plug is a fierce tropical existence. **1970** K. BALL *Fiat 600, 600D Autobook* iii. 35/2 For the best performance, sparking plugs should be renewed every 10,000 miles.

'sparking, *vbl. sb.*² *U.S.* [f. SPARK *v.*²] Courting, paying attentions. Also *attrib.*

a **1859** MCCLINTOCK *Beadle's Crtship.* (Bartlett), If I ever ..had any dealings with the feminine gender again, in the sparking line. **1888** EGGLESTON *Graysons* xxxiii, The boys that do a good deal of sparking, and the girls that have a lot of beaux.

'sparking, *ppl. a.* [f. SPARK *v.*¹]

1. That emits sparks; filled with sparks.

a **1300** *Cursor M.* 2925 Wit sparcand reke.. Als it war a brinand ouen. **1826** J. WILSON *Noct. Ambr.* Wks. 1855 I. 152 Then there is naething but sparking ashes. **1904** *Westm. Gaz.* 21 Sept. 1/1 About as comfortable a seat as a barrel of gunpowder in a sparking smithy.

2. *Sc.* That gives off spots; spattering.

1873 A. G. MURDOCH *Doric Lyre* 57 Noo I maun dicht my sparkin' pen.

sparkish ('spɑːkɪʃ), *a.* [f. SPARK *sb.*² + -ISH.]

1. Of persons: Having the character, airs, or manners of a spark or gallant.

1641 J. JOHNSON *Acad. Love* 89 If it were not for some of the old out-of-date grandames.. the young sparkish girles would read in Shakespeere day and night. **1675** WYCHERLEY *Country Wife* IV. ii, I have been detained by a sparkish coxcomb, who pretended a visit to me. **1694** R. L'ESTRANGE *Fables* 32 A daw that had a mind to be sparkish tricked himself with all the gay feathers he could muster. *a* **1718** PENN *Life* in *Wks.* (1726) I. 159 A Rich, Young, Neat, Sparkish Husband. **1767** S. PATERSON *Anoth. Trav.* I. 55 Genteel! Ha! Sparkish! A good bit! Admirable. **1830** *Fraser's Mag.* II. 458 The place of the sparkish Templar, the wit about town, was then in the pit of a theatre. *a* **1857** D. JERROLD *J. Applejohn* xviii, Several sparkish holyday makers broke through the press.

2. Of things: Characteristic of, or appropriate to, a spark; of a smart or elegant make.

1657 MAY *Life Satyr. Puppy* 5 The Gentleman marking my sparkish behaviour.. earnestly enquires after my name. **1667** WOOD *Life* (O.H.S.) II. 116 Mr. Aubrey was then in a sparkish garb. **1687** *Reflect. on Hind & Panther* 17 And indeed he hath done it in the Sparkishest Poem that ever was seen. **1704** SWIFT *T. Tub* ii, Observe how sparkish a periwig adorns the head of a beech. **1884** J. SHARMAN *Hist. Swearing* 5 Some [pipes] were light and sparkish, others ponderous and clumsy.

Hence **'sparkishness**.

1687 MRS. BEHN *Lucky Chance* Prol., Who thinks good usage for the sex unfit, And slights ye, out of sparkishness and wit. **1727** BAILEY (vol. II), *Sparkishness*, Gaiety, Briskness, Spruceness, &c.

sparkishly ('spɑːkɪʃlɪ), *adv.* [f. prec. + -LY².] Like a spark or gallant; in a sparkish manner.

1676 ETHEREDGE *Man of Mode* I. i, Who.. has adorn'd her baldness with a large white Freez, that she may look sparkishly in the forefront of the King's-box. **1686** F. SPENCE tr. *Varillas' Ho. Medicis* 183 The king of Naples answer'd sparkishly. **1812** W. TENNANT *Anster F.* II. xlvii, Each buttonhole, and skirt, and hem is seen Sparkishly edg'd with lace of yellow gold. **1851** D. JERROLD *St. Giles* xi. 110 A young man sparkishly drest suddenly looked in.

sparkle ('spɑːk(ə)l), *sb.* Forms: α. 4– sparkle, 4–7, 9 *dial.* sparcle (6 -ckle); 5, 7 sparkel, 5 -ele, 5–6 -ell, 5 sparkull, 6 -ul, 5 sparkil, 6 -yl(l. β. 4–6, 9 *Sc.* sperkle, 5 sperkyl(l, 6 -kil, 5–6 spercle. [f. SPARK *sb.*¹ + -LE I, perh. on the analogy of the vb. The earlier senses run parallel with those of *spark.*]

1. A small spark; an ignited or luminous particle.

α. *c* **1330** R. BRUNNE *Chron. Wace* (Rolls) 8544 Þe sparkles fleye as fir of flyntes. *c* **1407** LYDG. *Reson & Sens.* 1579 A firy bronde, Castyng sparklys fer a-broode. **1482** *Monk of Evesham* xvii. (Arb.) 40 They were bore vppe an hy by the grete vyolente flamys of fier as sparclys byn of a brennyng fornece. **1532** MORE *Confut. Barnes* VIII. Wks. 757/2 We be sure by the smoke & the sparcles that there is fyre in the chymneye. **1589** R. HARVEY *Pl. Perc.* (1860) 29 When the steele and the flint be knockde togither, a man may light his match by the sparkle. **1620** T. GRANGER *Div. Logike* 126 A sparkle hath the same vertue that fire hath. **1667** MILTON *P.L.* VI. 766 Fierce Effusion.. Of smoak and bickering flame, and sparkles dire. **1758** REID tr. *Macquer's Chym.* I. 362 You will see a great many sparkles darted up from the surface of the metal. **1818** SCOTT *Rob Roy* xxxiii, I remained ..gazing after them, as if endeavouring to count the sparkles which flew from the horses' hoofs. **1870** BRYANT *Iliad* IV. I. 108 A radiant meteor scattering sparkles round.

β. **1382** WYCLIF *Gen.* xix. 28 Abraham.. saw a multitude of sparkis [*v.r.* sperklis] steiynge vp fro the erthe. **1490** CAXTON *Eneydos* xii. 43 Thynke it not nomore than the sperkell yssuyng oute of the fyre wyth the smoke. **1508** STANBRIDGE *Vulgaria* (W. de W.) A vj b, *Fauilla*, a sperkle. **15..** *Adam Bel* 133 in Hazl. *E.P.P.* II. 144 The spercles brent, and fell hym on. **1570** LEVINS *Manip.* 125 A sperkil, *scintilla*.

Prov. **1382** WYCLIF *Ecclus.* xi. 34 Of oo sparcle fyr is eechid. **1398** TREVISA *Barth. De P.R.* X. viii. (1495) 379 Of a lytill sperkyll in an hepe of towe or of tyndyr cometh sodaynly a grete fyre. ?*c* **1470** G. ASHBY *Active Policy* 426 For of a litle sparkel a grete fyre Comyth, displeasaunt to many a sire. *a* **1536** *Proverbs* in *Songs, Carols*, etc. (E.E.T.S.) 130 Of a lytill sparkyll, commeth a gret fyre.

b. With *of* (fire, etc.).

c **1422** HOCCLEVE *Minor P.* xxiii. 702 Right as sparcles of fyr aboute sprede Whan þat a greet toun set is on a lowe. **1491** CAXTON *Vitas Patr.* (W. de W. 1495) I. xlii. 68/1 Noo thynge fantastyque, but a sparcle of fyre. **1597** J. KING *On Jonas* (1618) 10 Quenching a sparkle of wild-fire. **1615** G. SANDYS *Trav.* 202 The aire appeared as if full of sparkles of fire.

c. In similes or comparisons, and in allusive use.

c **1330** *King of Tars* 194 Whon he was brouht uppon his stede, He sprong as sparkle doth of glede. **1382** WYCLIF *Wisd.* iii. 7 As sparcles in reeddy places thei shuln renne hider and thider. **14..** *Sir Beues* (M.) 1884 Vp he sterte also right As sperkyll oute of fire right. **1660** W. SECKER *Nonsuch Prof.* 342 A man that carries Gun-powder about him, can never stand too far from Sparkles.

d. *fig.* and in fig. context; freq. with allusion to the kindling of a fire or conflagration.

(*a*) **1382** WYCLIF *Wisd.* ii. 2 Sermoun of [*read* is] a sparcle to stirn togidere oure herte. *c* **1386** CHAUCER *Prol. Reeve's T.* 31 Foure gleedes han we..: Avauntyng, liyng, Anger, Coueitise, Thise foure sparkles [*v.r.* sperkles] longen vn to eelde. **1483** CAXTON *Gold. Leg.* 249 b/1 How be hit that the membres were bounden in the hete of the Sparcles, the force of the feith was not corrupt. **1581** J. BELL *Haddon's Answ. Osor.* 263 It shal be as easie a matter for a man to finde as much Relligion in Tullies Officies.. as this your Relligion is, ..a fewe sparckles onely except. **1607** *Scholast. Disc. agst. Antichrist* I. i. 38 We must nourish her sparcles least her light bee quite extinguished. **1629** H. BURTON *Babel no Bethel* 119 Considering them as sparkles leaping out of the boyling brest of juvenile ardour. **1687** DRYDEN *Hind & P.* I. 75 When their glimps was gone, My pride struck out new sparkles of her own. **1707** *Curios. in Husb. & Gard.* 323 Seeds.. contain an Atom of Life, a sparkle of celestial Fire. **1819** SCOTT *Ivanhoe* xxxii, A sparkle hath been quenched by his blood, which no human breath can again rekindle!

(*b*) **1515** BARCLAY *Egloges* II. (1570) Bj/2 A small sparcle may kindle loue certayne. *a* **1548** HALL *Chron., Edw. IV*, 210 Which small sparcle had growen to a greater flame, if the erle of Warwycke.. had not sodaynly quenched it. **1600** HOLLAND *Livy* XXIX. xxxi. 732 Unlesse they put out this sparkle of fire betimes,.. it will be their chaunce to be caught therewith. **1656** EARL MONM. tr. *Boccalini's Advts. fr. Parnass.* II. vi. 207 That every least despised sparkle is apt to occasion great combustions. **1779** JOHNSON *L.P., Addison* ¶45 Some unlucky sparkle from a Tory paper set Steele's politicks on fire. **1859** TENNYSON *Geraint & Enid* 833 To make My nature's prideful sparkle in the blood Break into furious flame.

2. A slight beginning, trace, indication, or manifestation *of* something.

c **1380** WYCLIF *Serm.* Sel. Wks. I. 279 Sparclis of grace þat we felen. **1430–40** LYDG. *Bochas* III. xix. (1554) 91 b/2 The sparcle of vengeance is quicked.. by windes foure. *c* **1450** METHAM *Wks.* 39 With-in Amoryus the sparkyl off loue so rootyd gan be. **1548** UDALL, etc. *Erasm. Par. Mark* Pref. 5 What sparcle of shame remayneth. **1577** HANMER *Anc. Eccl. Hist.* (1619) 150 They had not one sparkle of compassion on us. **1606** J. CARPENTER *Solomon's Solace* iii. 12 He.. giueth not so much as any sparkle or shew of a meeny conceit. **1675** TRAHERNE *Chr. Ethics* 415 Now all these sparkles of joy.. meet together in humility. **1718** BP. HUTCHINSON *Witchcraft* 40 He said he had never found one Sparkle of Truth. **1768–74** TUCKER *Lt. Nat.* (1834) II. 531 Their frictions.. struck out the first sparkles of judgment and forecast. **1825** SCOTT *Betrothed* xxii, Pleased to shew some sparkles of his ancient military education. **1856** EMERSON *Eng. Traits* vii. *Truth* Wks. (Bohn) II. 55 It is an unlucky moment to remember these sparkles of solitary virtue.

3. A vital or animating principle. *rare.*

1388 WYCLIF *2 Sam.* xiv. 7 Thei seken to quenche my sparcle whych is lefte. **1599** DAVIES *Immort. Soul* 3 How can we hope, that.. This dying Sparkle.. Can recollect these beames of knowledge cleare?

†**4.** A small ruby or diamond. *Obs. rare.*

1480 in *Cal. Doc. Rel. Scotl.* (1888) IV. 297 Sparkyllys [called] rubees. **1687** DRYDEN *Hind & P.* II. 528 Entire, one solid shining Diamond, Not Sparkles shattered into Sects like you. **1704** E. ARWAKER *Embassy fr. Heaven* xxxiv. 14 His Chrystal Coach in Di'mond Sparkles burn'd.

5. A glittering or flashing point of light.

1490 CAXTON *Eneydos* xiii. 48 The sterres launchynge theyr bryghte sparkeles, excyte the appetyte of slepe. **1543** TRAHERON *Vigo's Chirurg.* Interpr. Wds., When it is broken, it sendeth out the golden sparcles shinynge like sterres. *c* **1590** GREENE *Fr. Bacon* III. iii, As the Moone Darkneth the brightest sparkles of the night. **1634** MILTON *Comus* 80 Swift as the Sparkle of a glancing Star. **1652** N. CULVERWEL *Lt. Nature* I. xvi. (1661) 136 The Sun.. with its golden Scepter rules all created Sparkles. **1713** *Phil. Trans.* XXVIII. 231 Those Sparkles of Light. **1824** MISS L. M. HAWKINS *Annaline* II. 169, I have witnessed at night.. sparkles which adhered to the adjoining ropes. **1846** RUSKIN *Mod. Paint.* II. III. §2. v. §21 The sparkles streaming from their purple wings like the glitter of many suns upon a sounding sea. **1871** L. STEPHEN *Playgr. Eur.* (1894) v. 128 A few green sparkles just pointing out the Lake of Thun.

fig. **1538** STARKEY *England* II. i. 144 We haue conceyuyd some sparkyl of the celestyal lyght. **1583** BABINGTON *Commandm.* (1590) 82 These were but sparcles as it were of His glorie and maiestie that they sawe. **1606** J. CLAPHAM *Hist. Gt. Brit.* I. I. xii. 34 [The] Christian Religion.. began to cast forth some small sparkles of her brightnesse. *a* **1672** STERRY *Rise & Race Kingd. God in Soul Man* 212 A glance and sparkle of this Eternal Image of essential beauty. **1816** MOORE *Sacred Songs, 'Oh, Thou! who dry'st'* ii. (1849) 247 Hope that threw A moment's sparkle o'er our tears, Is dimm'd and vanished too. **1888** DOUGHTY *Trav. Arabia Deserta* I. vii. 196 These sallies are never unwelcome to Arabs, being as sparkles struck upon their own natural hearts.

b. A flashing or fiery glance.

1590 SPENSER *F.Q.* I. iv. 33 His eies did hurle forth sparcles fiery red. **1721** RAMSAY *Keitha* 41 Her een, which did with heav'nly sparkles low. **1823** ROSCOE tr. *Sismondi's Lit. Eur.* (1846) II. xxxviii. 509 While dark red sparkles from his eye-balls rolled.

6. Glittering or flashing appearance or quality; lively brightness.

1589 GREENE *Menaphon* (Arb.) 34 If the sparkle of her eyes appeare in the night, the starres blush at her brightnesse. **1639** SALTMARSH *Policy* A vij b, Like those jewels which have their matter from earth, their sparkle from heaven. **1820** SCOTT *Monast.* xxxvii, The occasional sparkle of the long line of spears. **1832** W. IRVING *Alhambra* II. 116 His ever-watchful eye caught the sparkle of a diamond. **1885** F. MILLER *Glass-Painting* 53 By rubbing off some of the colour, a wonderful brilliancy and sparkle is imparted.

b. Brightness or liveliness of spirit; smartness; wittiness.

1611 SPEED *Hist. Gt. Brit.* IX. viii. §30 How a King of any royall sparkle, could brooke such Sea and Land Tempests.. I cannot conceiue. **1789** CHARLOTTE SMITH *Ethelinde* (1814) II. 144 The sparkle of spirit and the languish of tenderness. **1828** LYTTON *Pelham* iii, Beside him was a quick, sharp little woman, all sparkle and bustle. **1876** F. E. TROLLOPE *A Charming Fellow* I. xvii. 234 [He] surprised himself by the amount of fun and sparkle he contrived to elicit. **1894** J. CARTWRIGHT *Madame* I The vivacity and sparkle which she inherited from her mother.

c. *spec.* The appearance characteristic of certain wines, due to the presence of carbonic-acid gas.

1833 C. REDDING *Mod. Wines* v. 72 The Sillery has no sparkle at all. **1856** KANE *Arct. Expl.* I. xxxii. 445 If this solitary relic of festival days had lost its sparkle, we had not.

7. A small piece, part, spot, etc., *of* something; a (glittering) particle.

c **1570** FOXE *Serm. 2 Cor. v.* 18 A breeder of sinne, or (as we may call it) a privy sparcle of the Serpents seede. **1585** PARSONS *Chr. Exer.* I. x. 131 All the pleasures.. in the worlde, being onely sparkles and parcelles sent out from God. **1769** *St. James's Chron.* 12–14 Sept. 1/3 A Peasant, into whose Eye flew a Sparkle of Iron. **1818** *Gentl. Mag.* 343/2 An aerolite is of a grey colour, and sprinkled with metallic sparkles. **1822** SHELLEY tr. *Calderon's Mag. Prodig.* ii. 61 Sparkles of blood on the white foam are cast.

8. *Comb.*, as *sparkle-blazing, -drifting, -eyed.*

1614 GORGES *Lucan* I. 35 An vgly Fiend (that in her hand Did hold a sparkle-blazing brand). **1648** HEXHAM II, *Kat-oogigh*, Cat-eyed, or sparkel-eyed like a Cat. **1845** MRS. NORTON *Child of Islands* (1846) 178 Hammer the sparkle-drifting iron straight.

sparkle ('spɑːk(ə)l), *v.*¹ Forms: 3 sperklen, 5, 9 *Sc.* spercle; 5 sparklyn, 5–6 spark(e)l-, 6 -kil(l, -kyll, sparcle; 4– sparkle. [f. SPARK *sb.*¹ + -LE 3. Cf. MDu. *spaer-*, *sparkelen* (Du. and Flem. *sparkelen*, WFlem. also *sperkelen*; WFris. *sparkelje*).]

I. *intr.* **1.** To issue, to fly or spring *out* or *forth*, in sparkles or small particles. Also *fig.*

a **1200** *St. Marher.* 9 Of his spetewile muð sperklede fur ut. *c* **1450** *Myrr. our Ladye* 47 As it had bene a clowde of fyer sparkelyng & dropyng vpon his hed, & vpon all his body. **1587** GOLDING *De Mornay* ix. (1592) 124 The trueth will sparcle out of the Contrarietie of vntruthes, as fire sparcles out of the knocking of one Flintstone against another. **1608** TOPSELL *Serpents* (1658) 621 The spirits.. hastily leaping out as it were, and quickly sparkling forth. **1620** MARKHAM *Farew. Husb.* II. xvii. (1668) 75 As the Pigeons or Crows tear up the straw, the Lime or ashes will sparkle into their eyes and nares. **1649** JER. TAYLOR *Gt. Exemp.* II. Disc. ix. 122 If like a flint he sends a sparke out, it must as soon be extinguished as shewes, and cool as soon as sparkle. **1805** WORDSW. *Prelude* VIII. 409 A diamond light.. was seen Sparkling from out a copse-clad bank. **1864** TENNYSON *Aylmer's F.* 705 When some heat of difference sparkled out.

2. a. To emit or send out sparks or sparkles of fire. Also *fig.*

1480 CAXTON *Myrr.* II. xxviii. 121 This that maketh the clowdes to sparkle and lyghtne whan the thondre is herde. **1530** PALSGR. 726/2 Ware your face, this fier sparkilleth apace. **1590** GREENE *Neuer too Late* Wks. (Grosart) VIII. 107 Their eies like comets, that when they sparkle foretell some fatall disparagement. **1692** SIR T. P. BLOUNT *Ess.* 153 And so, like two Flints struck together, they will be continually sparkling and spitting fire at one another. **1769** *Junius Lett.* xxxv. (1788) 177 The coldest bodies warm with opposition, the hardest sparkle in collision. **1794** WORDSW. *Guilt & Sorrow* xx, Till on a stone, that sparkled to his feet, Struck.. the troubled horse. **1839** BAILEY *Festus* 73, I will rub them backwards like a cat; And you shall see them spit and sparkle up. **1886** *S.W. Linc. Gloss.* 138 Larch-branches sparkle about so, they're dangerous for childer.

b. To throw off small particles; to crackle.

1495 *Trevisa's Barth. De P.R.* XV. cxlix. 542 In the see of Sicilia is.. a wonder maner salt, for it meltyth in fyre and sparklith in water. **1611** COTGR., *La lumiere petille*, the candle sparkles, or spits.

c. Of the eyes: To flash with anger or rage.

1593 SHAKS. *2 Hen. VI*, III. ii. 317 Mine eyes should sparkle like the beaten Flint. —— *3 Hen. VI*, II. v. 131 With fiery eyes, sparkling for very wrath. **1667** MILTON *P.L.* I. 194 With.. Eyes That sparkling blaz'd. **1697** DRYDEN *Virg. Georg.* IV. 652 The Seer.. Rowl'd his green Eyes, that sparkled with his Rage.

3. a. To reflect or emit numerous separate rays or points of light; to glitter or flash.

c **1386** CHAUCER *Knt.'s T.* 1306 A mantelet.. Bret-ful of rubies reed, as fir sparclyng. **1560** BIBLE (Geneva) *Ezek.* i. 7 They sparkled like the appearance of bright brasse. **1611** SHAKS. *Cymb.* II. iv. 40 Sparkles this Stone as it was wont, or is't not Too dull for your good wearing? **1697** DAMPIER *Voy.* (1699) 414 The Sea seemed all of a Fire about us; for every Sea that broke sparkled like Lightning. **1719** YOUNG *Busiris* III. i, Conquest and crowns shall sparkle in her sight. **1794** MRS. RADCLIFFE *Myst. Udolpho* xxxvi, She saw.. the wide sea sparkling in the morning rays. **1821** SCOTT *Kenilw.* xli, Those stately towers.. which still, in some places, sparkled with lights. **1859** JEPHSON *Brittany* ii. 16 The white villas sparkled in the morning sun. **1894** Mrs. F. Elliot *Roman Gossip* iii. 84 An emerald ring..sparkled on one finger.

b. *fig.* or in fig. context.

1667 L. Stuckley *Gospel Glass* ix. 75 We have not sparkled so much the more in an holy Zeal. **1690** Temple *Ess., Poetry* Wks. 1720 I. 247 'Tis something to sparkle among Diamonds, but to shine among Pebbles is neither Credit nor Value worth the pretending. *a* **1764** Lloyd *Poet* Poet. Wks. 1774 II. 32 Who can a hearty praise bestow, If merit sparkles in a foe. **1781** Cowper *Expost.* 483 It [the language] sparkles with the gems he left behind. **1827** Hare *Guesses* (1859) 42 Chaucer sparkles with the dew of morning. **1981** *Times* 10 June 20 Banks and insurances sparkle. An initial flurry of activity was seen in banks and insurances.

c. *fig.* To be extremely bright or lively in conversation or writing; to abound or excel in lively sallies of wit.

1698 Collier *Immor. Stage* 224 Miss Hoyden sparkles too much in Conversation. **1699** J. Dunton *Conv. Ireland* in *Dubl. Scuffle* 382 His Wit sparkles as well as his Eyes. **1744** Berkeley *Siris* §338 Those exalted notions and fine hints that sparkle and shine throughout his writings. **1841** D'Israeli *Amen. Lit.* (1867) 352 They display an original comic invention, and sparkle with the most lively sallies. **1851** Willmott *Pleas. Lit.* (1852) vii. 40 Boccaccio sparkles over a grim treatise of Calvin. **1893** Liddon *Life Pusey* I. xiii. 309 These hints..sparkle with the dry and clear acuteness characteristic of the writer.

d. To move, proceed, flow, etc., in a glittering or sparkling manner. Const. with preps. and advs.

1823 Lamb *Elia* II, *Amicus Rediv.*, To trace your salutary waters sparkling through green Hertfordshire. **1841** Browning *Pippa Passes* Poems (1905) 185 See how that beetle burnishes in the path! There sparkles he along the dust! **1885** Rider Haggard *K. Solomon's Mines* iii, There are the deep kloofs..down which the rivers sparkle.

4. Of wines, etc.: To effervesce with small glittering bubbles, due to the presence or rising of carbonic-acid gas.

1422 [see sparkling *ppl. a.*[1] 3c]. **1671** Milton *Samson* 544 Nor did the dancing Rubie Sparkling, out-powr'd, the flavor, or the smell,..Allure thee from the cool Crystalline stream. **1706** Phillips (ed. Kersey), To *Sparkle*,..to send forth small Bubbles, as strong Wine does in a Glass. **1782** *Phil. Trans.* LXXII. 431 The water sparkled, as does Seltzer water, by the vessel being shook. **1826** *Art of Brewing* (ed. 2) 42 Sparkling in the glass like the finest bottled ale. **1833** Redding *Mod. Wines* v. 116 The white Crose is a light, delicate wine... It sparkles like Champagne.

5. a. Of feelings, etc.: To appear or be evident *in* (or *through*) the eyes by the brightness or animation of these.

1592 Shaks. *Rom. & Jul.* I. i. 197 A fire sparkling in Louers eyes. **1599** —— *Much Ado* III. i. 51 Disdaine and Scorne ride sparkling in her eyes. *a* **1645** Milton *Arcades* 27, I see bright honour sparkle through your eyes. **1667** —— *P.L.* II. 388 Joy Sparkl'd in all thir eyes. **1704** Swift *Batt. Bks.* Wks. 1841 I. 132/2 Rage sparkled in his eyes. **1817** Jas. Mill *Brit. India* II. v. v. 543 With nothing but victory sparkling in his eye. **1848** Dickens *Dombey* liv, Intense abhorrence sparkling in her eyes.

b. Of the eyes: To be bright or animated; to shine, to glisten.

1700 Dryden *To Duchess of Ormond* 10 Inspir'd by two fair Eyes that sparkled like your own. **1782** Miss Burney *Cecilia* VIII. iii, Her eyes sparkling with joy, and her cheeks glowing with pleasure. **1820** Scott *Monast.* xxvii, His eyes sparkled, his frame was agitated. **1883** S. C. Hall *Retrospect* I. 323 A burly man..whose little eyes seemed always sparkling with unclerical humour.

transf. **1833** Ht. Martineau *Berkeley* I. i. 21 Hester blushed, and sparkled, and looked quite ready to communicate something. **1885** 'Mrs. Alexander' *At Bay* iii, A bright happy smile sparkled over her countenance.

†**c.** To entertain a strong desire *for* something.

1665 Brathwait *Comment Two Tales* (1901) 46 You tax me of pride, and tell me, high blood ever sparkles for good Cloathes.

II. *trans.* **6.** To cause to sparkle or glitter.

In early use in pa. pple., and not quite separable from sparkle *v.*[2] 4.

1553 Eden *Treat. New Ind.* (Arb.) 31 A mountayne, whose sande is sparkeled with gold. **1580** Hollyband *Treas. Fr. Tong* s.v. *Brochée*, A gowne all sparkeled with gold, or aglets. **1619** Williams *Serm. Apparell* (1620) 16 In picking their rockes for diamonds to sparkle him. **1716** Pope *Iliad* VIII. 2 Aurora now..Sparkled with rosy light the dewy lawn. **1809** W. Irving *Knickerb.* VI. iv. (1849) 332 The jovial sun..sparkling the landscape with a thousand dewy gems. **1821–30** Ld. Cockburn *Mem.* (1856) iv. 264 The war sparkled us with military gaiety and parade.

7. a. To emit, eject, or throw out (fire, etc.) as or like sparks. Also *transf.*

1588 Shaks. *L.L.L.* IV. iii. 351 Womens eyes..sparcle still the right promethean fire. **1590** Spenser *F.Q.* III. i. 32 The bright glister of their beames cleare Did sparckle forth great light. **1601** Holland *Pliny* I. 13 Mercury sparkeling his raies. **1652** J. Wright tr. *Camus' Nat. Paradox* x. 244, I fore-see then, replied Miestas (sparkling Fire out of his Eyes) that you and I must have a quarrell.

b. Of the eyes: To indicate or betoken (a feeling) by brightness or animation.

a **1601** *Pasquil & Kath.* (1878) I. 224 Your eye Sparkles not spirit as 't was wont to doe. **1602** Marston *Antonio's Rev.* IV. iii, Your eyes should sparkle joy. **1682** C. Irvine *Hist. Scot. Nomencl.* Ded. *iv, Our faces then shone with joy, and our eyes sparkled gladness.

c. In various fig. uses.

1610 Jonson *Alch.* IV. i, A certaine touch, or aire, That sparkles a diuinitie, beyond An earthly beautie! **1615** Chapman *Odyss.* XVIII. 311 Thy younger blood Did sparkle choicer spirits. **1667** O. Heywood *Heart-Treas.* vii, The working forge of men's wicked hearts doth sparkle forth suitable imaginations. **1742** Young *Nt. Th.* v. 781 Her gaiety..That, like the Jews fam'd oracle of gems, Sparkles instruction.

8. With *down*: To dispel (gloom) by cheerful behaviour or spirits.

1840 Lady C. Bury *Hist. of Flirt* iv, His endeavours to sparkle down the gloom on his sister's countenance.

'sparkle, *v.*[2] *Obs.* or *dial.* Forms: 5–6 **sperkel-**, **-kle**, 6 **-cle**; 5–6 **sparkyl-**, 6 **sparkel-**, **-kyll**, 5–6 **sparcle** (6 **-ckle**), 5– **sparkle**. [Alteration of sparple *v.* Cf. disparkle *v.*]

1. *intr.* Of persons: To separate, scatter, or disperse. Freq. with *abroad.*

c **1440** *Generydes* 6049 A bak thei drewe, and sperkelyd her and þer. *c* **1477** Caxton *Jason* 9 The other..were anon so discoraged that they sparklid abrode. **1523** Ld. Berners *Froiss.* I. ccxix. 281 Than they sparcled abrode lyke men y[t] were discomfyted and chased. **1568** Grafton *Chron.* II. 341 Assone as this proclamation was made, they sparkled abroade, euery man to their awne homes.

2. *trans.* To cause to scatter or disperse; to drive in different directions. Also ***sparkle away*** (quot. 1703).

a **1470** Harding *Chron.* CLXXIV. iii, Then went the kyng..and sparcled them then so That North they went. *c* **1489** Caxton *Sonnes of Aymon* xiv. 352 To thende ye maye gader agen togyder your folke that be soo sperkled abrode. **1506** in *Mem. Hen. VII* (Rolls) 282 All his other ships were sparkled, some to Rye..; some were drowned. **1555** W. Watreman *Fardle Facions* I. ii. 31 They ware diuersely sparckled in diuers partes of the world. **1618** Fletcher *Loyal Subj.* I. v, Beaten, and't please your Grace, And all his Forces sparkled. **1703** Thoresby *Let. to Ray, Sparkle away*, to disperse, spend, waste. **1836** Wilbraham *Cheshire Gloss.* (ed. 2) 111 *Sparkle*,..to disperse.

3. To cast abroad; to scatter, sprinkle, or strew.

c **1440** *Gesta Rom.* xxvi. 100 And so is þe blode sperkelid aboute the cradil. **1548** Elyot, *Conspergo*, to scatter or sparcle about abundantly, to strawe. **1555** Eden *Decades* I. III. (Arb.) 77 As thowgh mele had byn sparkeled throwgh owte al that sea.

transf. **1538** Starkey *England* II. i. 157 The cure therof ys sparkylyd in the cure of al other.

b. *dial.* To spatter (liquid, etc.) *over* one.

1787 Grose *Prov. Gloss.* s.v., He sparkled the water all over me. **1854** Miss Baker *Northampt. Gloss.* II. 270 He rode so fast he sparkled the mud all over me.

4. To sprinkle, bestrew, or bespatter *with* (also *in*) something; to dot thickly.

14.. *Sir Beues* 350 (Camb. MS. Ff. ii. 38), The chyldys clothys, ryche and gode, He had sparkylde with that blode. **1555** Eden *Decades* (Arb.) 196 The pauement of the temple is all sparcled with bludde. **1578** Lyte *Dodoens* 586 The fruite foloweth after, which is long, the outside thereof sparckled, and set full of little bowles or bosses. **1625** Purchas *Pilgrims* II. IX. 1495 Who being sparkled therewith, dieth by force of the poyson. **1629** in *Capt. Smith's Wks.* (Arb.) II. 819 To see bright honour sparkled all in gore, Would steele a spirit that ne're fought before.

fig. **1570** Foxe *A. & M.* (ed. 2) 1152/2 Such as had fresh wyttes sparcled with Gods grace.

b. *techn.* To overlay or daub with cement or the like. (Cf. sparkling *vbl. sb.*[2] 2.)

1805 R. W. Dickson *Pract. Agric.* I. 89 Pan-tiling, with small-sized deal lath, and sparkled within side.

5. To disseminate or diffuse; to spread or circulate.

c **1532** Du Wes *Introd. Fr.* in *Palsgr.* 922 Of it to sparcle the beames through all the worlde. *a* **1547** Surrey *Æneid* II. 199 Lefull be it to sparcle in the ayre Their secretes all. **1577–87** Holinshed *Scot. Chron.* (1806) II. 206 Ill seed of sedition, sparkled and scattered in the cruel civil wares before.

sparkleberry. *U.S.* A shrub or small tree, *Vaccinium arboreum*, of the southern United States; the farkleberry.

1891 in *Cent. Dict.* **1908** R. W. Chambers *Firing Line* viii, A superb butterfly..came flitting about the sparkle-berry bloom.

'sparkled, *ppl. a.*[1] [f. sparkle *sb.* or *v.*[1]]

1. Speckled, spotted. Now *dial.*

1480 *Trevisa's Higden* (Caxton) I. 51 b/2 In the welmes after than ones Ben founde reed sperclid [*Rolls ed.* splekked] stones. **1787** [see sparky *a.* 1 b]. **1873** Williams & Jones *Somerset Gloss.* 35 *Sparcled, Sparked*,..speckled.

2. Filled with sparkles. *rare*[−1].

a **1547** Surrey *Æneid* II. 220 But she gan stare with sparcled eyes of flame.

†**'sparkled,** *ppl. a.*[2] *Obs.* [f. sparkle *v.*[2]] Scattered, dispersed; dishevelled.

a **1547** Surrey *Æneid* II. 517 Cassandra..From Pallas chirch was drawn with sparkled tresse. —— *Eccles.* v. 46, I saw..The plenteous houses sackt; the owners end with shame, Their sparkled goods. **1608** Heywood *Lucrece* I. ii, Did not this monster..Make her unwilling charioteer..crush her father's bones..and dash his sparkled brains Upon the pavements?

sparkler ('spɑːklə(r)). [f. sparkle *v.*[1] + -er.]

1. One who sparkles or shines in respect of beauty or accomplishments; *esp.* a vivacious, witty, or pretty young woman.

1713 Addison *Guardian* No. 120 §1 What wou'd you say, should you see the Sparkler..thumping the Table with a Dice-Box? **1772** *Town & County Mag.* 67 He called her his sparkler, and commended her person and accomplishments. **1800** Weems *Life Washington* (1810) i. 6 To wheeze and cough by themselves, and not depress the..spirits of the young sparklers. **1849** Cupples *Green Hand* vi. (1856) 58 'No doubt,' says Bill, 'she's what I call a exact sparkler!'

2. A bright or sparkling eye. Chiefly *pl.* Latterly *colloq.* or *slang.*

1746 Hervey *Medit.* (1818) 59 The eye, that outshone the diamond's brilliancy,..where is it? where shall we find the rolling sparkler? **1775** Sheridan *Duenna* II. ii, One glance of those roguish sparklers would fix me again. **1804** *Sporting Mag.* XXIII. 284 A very beautiful woman, with a pair of bright sparklers. **1854** Ainsworth *Flitch of Bacon* II. iii. 135 As to her eyes, they shine, like—I don't know what..; though they don't come up to the lustre of Bab's sparklers.

3. A sparkling gem; a diamond.

1822 Byron *Werner* III. i. 328 Oh, thou sweet sparkler! Thou more than stone of the philosopher! **1860** *All Year Round* No. 46. 459 Amber mouthpieces filleted with 'sparklers', as the English cracksman affectionately calls diamonds. **1893** McCarthy *Red Diamonds* I. ii. 47 Pretty sparklers, ain't they?

4. An insect having a shining or sparkling appearance; *spec.* any beetle of the family *Cicindelidæ*, a tiger-beetle.

1860 Piesse *Lab. Chem. Wonders* 2 Cicindela or sparkler. *c* **1860** J. Carlin *To Fireflies* i. in *Harper's Mag.* (1884) Mar. 590/1 Awake, ye sparklers, bright and gay.

5. A sparkling wine.

1868 *Rep. U.S. Commissioner Agric.* (1869) 575 In France the manufacturers of sparkling wine..have to increase its effervescence by mixing it with the wine grown in Champagne, which is a natural sparkler. **1975** *Country Life* 2 Oct. 839/3 Other sparklers made by the champagne method can be excellent: notably Sparkling Saumur and Seyssel from Savoy. **1981** *Times* 6 Mar. (Bride & Home Suppl.) p. vi/4 There are lots of good sparkling wines.. Blanquette de Limoux or the Spanish sparklers.

6. Something which shines or sparkles; a sparkling firework.

1879 Warren *Astron.* vi. 113 [Mercury] keeps so near the sun that very few people have ever seen the brilliant sparkler. **1894** *Westm. Gaz.* 3 Nov. 3/2 The most popular and novel among these [fireworks] are the electric sparkler [etc.].

sparkless ('spɑːklɪs), *a.* [f. spark *sb.*[1] + -less.] Free from or devoid of sparks; emitting no sparks.

1821 Shelley *Adonais* xl, Nor, when the spirit's self has ceased to burn, With sparkless ashes load an unlamented urn. **1851** Mrs. Browning *Casa Guidi Wind.* II. 290 Like an anvil black And sparkless. **1881** *Standard* 14 Sept. 3/1 The engine should be..smokeless, as noiseless as possible, but sparkless is imperative.

b. *spec.* in *Electr.*

c **1865** *Wylde's Circ. Sciences* I. 272/1 The relays are 'sparkless'. **1890** *Telegr. Jrnl.* 21 Feb. 203/2 The impossibility of making a sparkless commutator.

Hence **'sparklessly** *adv.*

1891 in *Cent. Dict.* **1906** H. M. Hobart *Elem. Princ. Continuous-Current Dynamo Design* iv. 106 Prior to coming into the position of short-circuit under the brush, it has been carrying a current of, say, 100 ampères in one direction. Immediately after emerging from the position of short-circuit, it will be carrying a current of 100 ampères in the opposite position. The change must take place sparklessly.

sparklet ('spɑːklɪt). [f. spark *sb.*[1] + -let.]

1. A small spark or sparkle. Also *transf.*

1689 Cotton *Poems, Night* ii, Spread o'er the Earth thy Sable Veil, Heaven's twinckling sparklets to conceal. **1824** *Blackw. Mag.* XV. 429 The glimmering worm..Whose sparklet of dim radiance [etc.]. **1877** [May Laffan] *Hon. Miss Ferrard* III. iv. 185 A pale yellowish mist, in which here and there a tiny sparklet was visible.

fig. **1830** W. Taylor *Hist. Surv. Germ. Poetry* II. 176 The steel, with which The great Creator of all truth bestows On the dead tinder of futurity, The first live sparklet. **1856** Miss Yonge *Daisy Chain* I. xxiv. (1879) 256 The first little gleam, little bit of a sparklet of the meaning. **1872** Havergal *Minist. Song* (ed. 3) 15 A praise all morning sunshine, And sparklets of the spring.

2. A small sparkling ornament for a dress.

1902 *Daily Chron.* 2 May 8/3 Mother-of-pearl paillettes are the latest sparklet introduced for the glorification of chiffon dresses.

3. Properly **Sparklet**, with capital initial. The proprietary name of a metal capsule containing carbon dioxide under pressure, used to carbonate the water in a siphon; the siphon or bottle containing such a capsule; the carbonated water produced by this device. Freq. *attrib.*

1896 *Trade Marks Jrnl.* 23 Dec. 1102 *Sparklets.* 198134. Metal capsules to contain compressed gases. Aerators, Limited,..London; Manufacturers. **1902** Kipling in *Collier's* 6 Dec. 8/1 Captain Mankelton..fed me canned beef and biscuits and give me a cigar—a Henry Clay—and a whiskey and sparklet. **1903** M. A. Stein *Sand-Buried Ruins Khotan* ix. 158 The water from the well..tasted extremely brackish, and neither filtering nor the lavish use of 'Sparklets' could make it palatable. **1905** [see aerate *v.* 3]. **1911** *T. Eaton & Co. Catal.* Spring & Summer 175/2 Fresh soda water at a minimum cost with a Sparklet Bottle and a Sparklet Bulb. **1920** *Blackw. Mag.* Apr. 542/2 His particular fancy in drinks—usually whisky and sparklet. **1929** J. Buchan *Courts of Morning* II. xii. 271 A mess-servant brought him a long drink of lime-juice and sparklets. **1933** J. Cary *American Visitor* v. 51 He bustled to fetch glass and sparklet bottle. Bewsher was famous for his hospitality. **1971** R. Dentry *Encounter at Kharmel* iii. 54 He squirted soda water from the sparklet syphon into the generous measure of whisky.

spark-like, *a.* and *adv.* [f. spark *sb.*[1] + -like.]

A. *adj.* Like or resembling a spark.

a **1814** *Mermaid* II. ii. in *New Brit. Theatre* II. 479 Her quick and sparklike eyes appear So kindled with malign intelligence. **1868** Morris *Earthly Par.* (1870) II. III. 278 And sparklike gems glitter from many a hand.

B. *adv.* After the manner of a spark.

1845 BAILEY *Festus* (ed. 2) 316 Thou shalt be Dashed from creation spark-like from a hand Scarless.

sparkliness: see SPARKLINGNESS (quot. *a* 1697).

sparkling (ˈspɑːklɪŋ), *vbl. sb.*[1] [f. SPARKLE *v.*[1]]

1. The action of sending out sparks or sparkles, or of glittering with light; scintillation. *c* **1440** *Promp. Parv.* 467/2 Spartlynge [*Winch.* Sparkelyng]. **1548** ELYOT, *Scintillatio*, a sparkelyng vp of fire. **1614** DRUMM. OF HAWTH. *Poems* (1616) I j, Her Eyes such Beames sent foorth, that but with Paine Here, weaker Sights their sparckling could sustaine. **1667** *Inform. Fire Lond.* in Somers *Tracts* VII. 619 He saw something..like wild-fire by the sparkling and spitting. **1701** G. STANHOPE *Pious Breath.* III. xiv. (1704) 225 Thou hast not..the sparkling of Precious Stones, nor the Harmony of Musick. **1728** BAILEY, *Scintillation*, a sparkling as Fire. **1811** PINKERTON *Petral.* II. 557 Stones thrown bounding into this furnace, produced flaming eruptions with sparkling. **1884** *Pall Mall G.* 8 Apr. 4/1 A sparkling of gold, silver, or the dull lustre of a bronze.

fig. **1613** DRUMM. OF HAWTH. *Cypress Grove* Wks. (1711) 117 From the sparkling of God in the soul, or from the god-like sparkles of the soul.

b. *attrib.* with *relay* (cf. SPARKING *vbl. sb.*[1]). *c* **1865** *Wylde's Circ. Sci.* I. 272 The sparkling relay of other makers compels them to use only a very moderate power.

2. With pl. An instance of this; a shower of sparks; a spark or fiery particle; a gleam, a sparkle. *a* **1529** SKELTON *P. Sparowe* 80 Phyllypes soule to kepe.. from her fyry sparklynges, For burnynge of his wynges. **1558** PHAER *Æneid* v. O ij, They themselues beholding spie, The sparcklings rising broad. **1582** STANYHURST *Æneis* I. (Arb.) 23 First on flint smiting soom sparcklinges sprinckled Achates. **1710** J. CLARKE tr. *Rohault's Nat. Philos.* (1729) I. I. ii. 10 If any one looks full upon the Sun, and immediately goes into a dark Place, he will see the Sun there, and some Sparklings of it. **1799** G. SMITH *Laboratory* I. 181 You may perceive by the increase of the sparklings of the iron bars, how your work goes in. **1820** WORDSW. *River Duddon* Sonn. xxv, The waters seem to waste Their vocal charm; their sparklings cease to please. **1848** CLOUGH *Bothie* III. 52 Here, the delight of the bather, you roll in beaded sparklings.

fig. **1641** R. BROOKE *Eng. Episc.* II. vii. 104 Are there not some sparklings of this Truth, even amongst us in England? **1776** LOVE *Diary* 22 Sept. in *Mem.* (1857) I. v. 198, I have had some sparklings of shame now and then.

ˈsparkling, *vbl. sb.*[2] *Obs.* or *dial.* [f. SPARKLE *v.*[2]]

1. The action of dispersing or scattering. *c* **1460** *Promp. Parv.* (Winch.) 426 Sparkelyng, ..*discipacio.* **1530** PALSGR. 273/2 Sparclyng abrode, *dispertion.* *a* **1616** BEAUM. & FL. *Bonduca* III. ii, March close, and sudden like a tempest: all executions Done without sparkling of the Body.

2. *techn.* (See quot. and cf. SPARKLE *v.*[2] 4 b.) **1787** W. H. MARSHALL *E. Norfolk* (1795) II. 388 *Sparkling.* Claying between the spars to cover the thatch of cottages.

sparkling (ˈspɑːklɪŋ), *ppl. a.*[1] Also 3 **sperclinde**, 5-6 **sperkelynge**; 5 **sprakelynge**. [f. SPARKLE *v.*[1]]

1. That emits sparks or sparkles. Also *fig.* and in fig. context. *a* **1225** *Ancr. R.* 34 þer in sperclinde luue biclupped oure leofmon. **1422** tr. *Secreta Secret., Priv. Priv.* 230 Tho that haue even like ly of fyre brandynge and sprakelynge, bene angry and shameles. **1493** *Festivall* (W. de W. 1515) 45 Tongues muste speke wordes of fyre that is sharpe and sperkelynge. **1599** *George a Greene* I. iv, Wherein two sapphires burne like sparkling fire. **1625** JACKSON *Creed* v. li. 455 The light of truth will suddainly burst out, as from a sparkling fire. **1816** SCOTT *Bl. Dwarf* iii, A large sparkling fire of turf and bog-wood.

transf. **1648** CRASHAW *Delights Muses* Wks. (1904) 121 In the close murmur of a sparkling noyse.

b. *transf.* Of heat. *c* **1700** KENNETT *MS. Lansdowne 1033*, fol. 388 (Halliw.), A sparkling or welding heat, used to weld barrs or pieces of iron. **1815** J. SMITH *Panorama Sci. & Art* I. 11 The sparkling or welding heat is used, by which the metal is brought nearly to a state of fusion.

c. *sparkling synchisis*: (see first quot.). **1859** MAYNE *Expos. Lex.* 1239/1 *Sparkling Synchysis*,.. term for a species of Synchysis, in which sparks are seen flashing before the eyes. **1898** *Hutchinson's Arch. Surg.* IX. 335 This attack had resulted in detachment of retina, sparkling synchisis, and loss of perception of light.

2. Of the eyes: Flashing, bright, animated. **1422** [cf. 1]. **1591** SHAKS. *1 Hen. VI*, I. i. 12 His sparkling Eyes, repleat with wrathfull fire. **1611** COTGR. s.v. *Petiller*, A sparkling, or often-twinckling eye. **1719** DE FOE *Crusoe* I. (Globe) 209 A great Vivacity and sparkling Sharpness in his Eyes. **1784** COWPER *Task* I. 405 A sparkling eye beneath a wrinkled front The vet'ran shows. **1822** SCOTT *Nigel* xi, A thin bronzed visage,..and a pair of sparkling black eyes.

Comb. **1801** CATH. HOOD *Remonstr.*, etc. 26 Sparkling-ey'd health, fair innocence, and peace.

transf. **1837** CARLYLE *Fr. Rev.* II. III. i, With a sparkling briskness of glance.

3. Reflecting or emitting rays of light; flashing, glittering, brilliant, resplendent. **1590** SPENSER *F.Q.* I. viii. 22 His sparkling blade about his head he blest. *c* **1600** SHAKS. *Sonn.* xxviii, When sparkling stars twire not, thou guild'st the eauen. **1661** BOYLE *Style of Script.* 51 What the Diamond is amongst stones, the pretiousest, and the sparklingest, the most apt to scatter light. **1784** COWPER *Task* I. 112 The sparkling trees And shrubs of fairy land. **1812** J. WILSON *Isle of Palms* I. 3 While many a sparkling star..Far down within the watery sky reposes. **1850** R. G. CUMMING *Hunter's Life S. Afr.* (1902) 57/1 A mixture of fat and a grey sparkling ore, having the appearance of mica.

b. Of water, the sea, etc. **1782** *Phil. Trans.* LXXII. 430 The sparkling quality of the water did not cease entirely till the vegetable was quite deprived of its life. **1794** MRS. RADCLIFFE *Myst. Udolpho* iv, Sometimes a torrent poured its sparkling flood high among the woods. **1825** SCOTT *Talism.* ii, They had now arrived at ..the fountain which welled out..in sparkling profusion. **1891** FARRAR *Darkn. & Dawn* xxxii, Its glorious vineyards by that blue and sparkling sea.

fig. **1806** WORDSW. *A Complaint* 10 That consecrated fount Of murmuring, sparkling, living love.

c. Of wines, etc.: (see SPARKLE *v.*[1] 4). **1422** tr. *Secreta Secret., Priv. Priv.* 244 Drynke grene wyne, clere, sharpe, and sparklynge in tempure. **1697** DRYDEN *Virg. Past.* v. 108 Two Goblets will I crown with sparkling Wine. **1757** GRAY *Bard* 77 Fill high the sparkling bowl. **1825** T. HOOK *Sayings* Ser. II. *Passion & Princ.* ix. III. 162 Those to whom the sparkling champagne..was a novelty. **1833** REDDING *Mod. Wines* v. 71 Champagne wines are divided into sparkling.., demi sparkling.., and still wines. **1888** *Encycl. Brit.* XXIV. 606 The sparkling champagnes are made from both white and red grapes.

transf. **1826** *Art of Brewing* (ed. 2) 27 A pungent agreeable flavour, and a brilliant sparkling appearance.

d. Effervescent. **1844** G. BIRD *Urin. Deposits* (1857) 170 This mixture evolves enough carbonic acid to be 'sparkling', and is generally taken with readiness.

e. In certain bird names, as ***sparkling pheasant, -tail*** (see quots.). **1861** GOULD *Trochilidæ* III. pl. 168 *Tryphæna Duponti*, Sparkling-tail. The tail is rendered remarkably sparkling by the decided contrasts of its colours. **1867** —— *Birds Asia* VII. pl. 38 *Phasianus Scintillans*, Sparkling Pheasant.

4. Of talk, writing, etc.: Characterized by brilliancy and liveliness. **1647** CLARENDON *Hist. Reb.* I. §129 His person beautiful, and graceful..; his wit pleasant, sparkling, and sublime. **1701** DE FOE *Trueborn Eng.* 35 It makes their Wit as sparkling as their Wine. **1795–1814** WORDSW. *Excurs.* II. 282 And he continued, when worse days were come, To deal about his sparkling eloquence. **1828** CARLYLE *Misc.* (1857) I. 214 A piece of sparkling rhetoric. **1856** *N. Brit. Rev.* XXVI. 229 Another lively chronicle..; which sketches with ..sparkling vivacity the virtues, the follies, and the shams of our own day. **1884** L. J. JENNINGS *Croker Papers* I. Pref. p. iii, Mr. Croker's own letters were written in a singularly light and sparkling vein.

transf. **1859** GULLICK & TIMBS *Paint.* 268 The vigorous and sparkling touch adopted by Velasquez. **1887** *Encycl. Brit.* XXIII. 710/1 The modern characters..have finer strokes and serifs, and produce in the page a more regular and sparkling general effect.

5. Of persons: Brilliant, animated, sprightly. *a* **1704** T. BROWN *To Belinda* v. Wks. 1711 IV. 100 Tho' she's as sparkling, and as fine As Jests, and Gemms, and Paint can make her. **1746** HERVEY *Medit.* (1818) 269 The voice which so lately pronounced the sparkling pair husband and wife.

6. Of pleasure: Characterized by a high degree of delight or enjoyment. **1789** BURNS *Let. to Mrs. McMurdo* 2 May, Never did little Miss with more sparkling pleasure shew her applauded Samplar to partial Mama. **1842** LOVER *Handy Andy* xlvii, Privation one day, profusion the next, darkling dangers, and sparkling joys!

†ˈsparkling, *ppl. a.*[2] *Obs.*[-1] In 4 **sperkelande**. [f. SPARKLE *v.*[2]] Dispersing, scattering. **1387–8** T. USK *Test. Love* I. ii. (Skeat) l. 75 Wottest thou not wel..that every shepherde ought by reson to seke his sperkelande sheep.

ˈsparklingly, *adv.* [f. SPARKLING *ppl. a.*[1]] In a sparkling or vivacious manner; with sparkling brightness or brilliancy; brilliantly. **1669** BOYLE *Certain Physiol. Ess.* (ed. 2) *Absol. Rest Bodies* 18 Some Diamonds of hers, which sometimes would look more sparklingly than they were wont, and sometimes far more dull than ordinary. **1820** WIFFEN *Aonian Hours* (ed. 2) 13 In whose glass All things look sparklingly. **1854** *Tait's Mag.* XXI. 260 Spurted the splinters sparklingly, saw scraped, and hammer rung. **1879** MEREDITH *Egoist* vii, She assured him sparklingly that she was well.

So **ˈsparklingness.** *rare.* *a* **1691** BOYLE *Ess. Intestine Motions Quiescent Solids* Wks. 1744 I. 286/2, I have..seemed to my self to observe a manifestly greater clearness and sparklingness at some times than at others. *a* **1697** AUBREY *Lives* (1898) II. 245 He threw his reparties about the table with so much sparklingness [ed. 1813 sparkliness] and gentileness of witt.

sparkly (ˈspɑːklɪ), *a.* [f. SPARKLE *sb.* or *v.*[1] + -Y[1].] Sparkling; that sparkles. Also *fig.*, lively. **1922** *Glasgow Herald* 18 Dec. 8 Among the shiny, sparkly rings. **1957** J. FRAME *Owls do Cry* 124 Evening bags covered with sparkly beads. **1978** *Detroit Free Press* 5 Mar. 14 (Parade Suppl.) 14E/3 (Advt.), A wee bouquet—jewel-bright & sparkly as springtime! **1979** *Rescue News* Sept. 8/3 The shop needs a good facelift and more positive selling policy with a wider range of goods and a sparklier range of staff.

spark out, *predic. a.* (and *adv.*) *dial.* and *colloq.* [perh. f. SPARK *sb.*[1] + OUT *adv.*; cf. SPARK *v.*[1] 2 c.]

a. Utterly extinguished. **b.** *fig.* Forgotten; (completely) unconscious. Also as *adv.* **1880** J. HARTLEY *Halifax Clock Almanack* 17 Th' fire wor spark aght. **1882** NODAL & MILNER *Gloss. Lancs. Dial.* 249 He'll goo spark-out—*i.e.* be entirely lost or forgotten. **1936** J. CURTIS *Gilt Kid* v. 51 Eileen..was drunk, proper lit up and had passed spark out. **1952** M. ALLINGHAM *Tiger in Smoke* xi. 172 He's spark out, only just breathin'. Bin like that two days. **1966** A. PRIOR *Operators* xvi. 264 When she goes out, she's spark out. For three hours at least. **1971** F. NORMAN *Dodgem-Greaser* iii. 32 He keeled over like a felled tree and crashed to the canvas, spark out. **1977** *Zigzag* Aug. 5/1 If she tried to physically stop me doing something I would knock her spark out.

ˈsparkover. Also **spark-over**. [f. vbl. phr. *to spark over*: see SPARK *v.*[1] 1 c.] = FLASH-OVER. **1915** *Standardization Rules Amer. Inst. Electr. Engineers* 48 The Spark-over voltage, for a given gap, decreases with decreasing barometric pressure and increasing temperature. **1936** *Nature* 19 Sept. 509/1 The crackling sound of more or less prolonged duration finishes with a loud crack coincident with the final sparkover. **1942** [see ACCELERATING *vbl. sb.*]. **1946** *Nature* 2 Nov. 603/2 The sparkover voltage of different electrode arrangements in air.

spark plug, *sb.* Also (chiefly in *fig.* use) **sparkplug, spark-plug.** [f. SPARK *sb.*[1] or *v.*[1] + PLUG *sb.*]

1. = *sparking plug* s.v. SPARKING *vbl. sb.*[1] b. Cf. PLUG *sb.* 2 m. **1903** *Motor* 3 June 376/1 A small stiff bristle tooth brush ..is very convenient for cleaning the porcelain of a spark plug. **1914** F. STRICKLAND *Petrol Motors* (ed. 2) 55 The high-tension leads and spark plug. **1920** J. D. MORGAN *Electr. Spark Ignition* iv. 43 A natural starting point for the study of spark plugs..is the voltage required to produce sparking. **1931** J. A. POLSON *Internal Combustion Engines* xii. 250 Deposits of carbon on spark plugs may cause failure by providing a path from the central electrode to the shell. **1973** V. CANNING *Flight of Grey Goose* ix. 171 He can't use ours [*sc.* a boat]... I got the spark plug in me pocket.

2. *fig.* One who or that which initiates or is the driving force behind any activity or undertaking. *colloq.* (chiefly *U.S.*). **1941** *Sun* (Baltimore) 24 Aug. 15/2 Introducing Hal Sieling... He's sparkplug of infield. **1953** M. MCCARTHY *Groves of Academe* viii. 159 In an experimental college like our own..a teacher's excitement is the spark-plug behind the whole system. **1958** [see LIQUIDITY 1 d]. **1977** *Time* 14 Mar. 53/3 Lillee is the Australian sparkplug.

Hence **ˈspark-plug** *v. trans.*, to inspire, encourage, or lead (some activity). *U.S. colloq.* **1945** *Sun* (Baltimore) 22 Sept. 4-0/2 Our own reconversion directors have just taken the lid off the construction industry with the hope..that a boom here will help sparkplug a general re-employment drive over the reconversion badlands. **1956** A. H. COMPTON *Atomic Quest* 322 It is important that our government spark-plug the advance of nuclear power. **1961** *Time* 7 July 63/2 Ray Stevens, 67, who sparkplugged the company's diversification, was president from 1956 to 1960.

†ˈsparky, *sb. Obs.*[-1] [f. SPARK *sb.*[2] + -Y.] A spark or gallant. **1756** MRS. CALDERWOOD in *Coltness Collect.* (Maitland Club) 196 Miss Collier the cousine is a well-looked little lassie, and severall little sparkies were in love with her.

sparky (ˈspɑːkɪ), *a.* [f. SPARK *sb.*[1] or *v.*[1]]

1. †**a.** Of velvet: Spotted with gold or some similar material. *Obs.*[-1] Cf. SPARKED *ppl. a.* 2, and 'sparke of veluet Sackets' in Dekker *Work for Armourers* (1608) G ij. **1620** in Blunt *Ch. Chester-le-Street* (1884) 85 Paid for twelve yeards of sparkie velvett for the pulpitt cloth, as 4s. y[e] yearde, 48s.

b. *dial.* Of cattle: Mottled; = SPARKED *ppl. a.* 1. **1787** GROSE *Prov. Gloss.*, *Sparkey*, or *Sparkled*, spotted, sprinkled. A sparkey cow. **1837–** in dial. glossaries (Devon, Somerset, Wilts.). **1869** *Daily News* 8 Dec., The second pure Devon in the young class..showed in fine contrast with the very 'sparky' one in the older class.

2. Emitting sparks; also, lively, vivacious. **1827** CARLYLE *Germ. Rom.* II. 298 The Archivarius caught these lilies blazing in sparky fire and dashed them on the witch. *c* **1865** G. M. HOPKINS *Poems* (1967) 147 Thus he ..Gilds with some sparky fancies his black night. **1883** in W. W. Peyton *Life H. Miller* ii. 21 Few like him for sport, a stirring, sparkie callant. **1928** D. H. LAWRENCE *Lady Chatterley's Lover* x. 134 Pure, sparky, fearless new life! **1979** *Daily Tel.* 6 Apr. 15/2 If they [*sc.* the films] are all as sparky as these larks they deserve support.

sparling (ˈspɑːlɪŋ). Now chiefly *north.* and *Sc.* Forms: α. 4-6 **sperlyng(e, -linge,** 4-6, 8-9 **sperling.** β. 5-6 **sparlynge,** 6 **-lyng,** 6- **sparling,** 7 **sparlin.** [ad. OF. *esperlinge* (later *esperlan*, mod.F. *éperlan*), of Teutonic origin, = MDu. and MLG. *spirlinc*, LG. and G. *spierling* (also G. and Du. *spiering*). Cf. SPIRLING and SPURLING.]

1. The common European smelt, *Osmerus eperlanus.* (Used either as a generic or collective name, or of single fish.) α. **1307–8** *Durh. Acc. Rolls* (Surtees) 3 In..ccc sperlinges. *c* **1325** *Metr. Hom.* 136 Riht als sturioun etes merling, And lobbekeling etes sperling. *a* **1377** *Abingdon Rolls* (Camden) 38 In sperlyng xiijs, xjd. *c* **1420** *Liber Cocorum* (1862) 54 Smalle fysshe þou take þer with, als trouȝte, sperlynges and menwus withal. **1489** *Churchw. Acc. Walberswick, Suffolk* (Nicholls, 1797) 183 The sed 2 men to gef a rekenynge of the heryngs and sperlinges. **1500** *Maldon* (Essex) *Crt. Rolls* Bundle 59, No. 2 b, Per iii barell. heryng, iii cad. heryng, et ii meyse sperling. *a* **1536** *Songs, Carols*, etc. (E.E.T.S.) 114 Whan..sperlyngis rone with speris in harnes to defence. **1587** *Shuttleworths' Acc.* (Chetham Soc.) 43 A querter of a freshe samonde and foure salte ielles iij[s]; sperlinges iij[d]. **1596–7** *Ibid.* 108 Sperlynges. **1754** T. GARDNER *Hist. Dunwich* 145 Fishing-Boats for full and shotten Herrings, Sperlings, or Sprats. *a* **1869** C. SPENCE *From Braes of Carse* (1898) 52 Ye catch a sperling, and I catch a fluke.

β. **14..** *Lat.-Eng. Voc.* in Wr.-Wülcker 609 *Sardallus*, a sparlynge. *c* **1460** J. RUSSELL *Bk. Nurture* 833 in *Babees Book* (1868) 163 Salt fysche, salt Congur, samoun, with sparlynge. **1517** *Sel. Cases Star Chamb.* (Selden) II. 120 Thomas..came with..ix[c] last of heryng..and iiij last of Sparlyng. **1591** SYLVESTER *Du Bartas* I. v. 330 The gilden Sparlings, when cold Winter's blast Begins to threat, themselves together cast. **1651** in W. M. Myddelton *Chirk Castle Acc.* (1908) 34 For sparlings & other fish at Chester. **1653** W. LAUSON *Comm. Dennys' Secrets Angling* II. No. 17 *n.*, [The gudgeon] is a dainty fish, like, or neere as good as the Sparlin. **1782** *Encycl. Brit.* (ed. 2) IX. 6934 Smelts are often sold in the streets of London split and dried. They are called *dried sparlings.* **1793** *Statist. Acc. Scotl.* VII. 54 The smelt or sparling, a very rare fish, is also found in the Cree. **1804** GALLOWAY *Poems* 73 While Forth yields her sa'mon and sparling. **1886** *Field* 23 Jan. 105/3 The fine net..was used for sparling, eels, &c.

†**b.** *fig.* As a term of endearment. *Obs.*$^{-1}$

1570 *Wit & Science* (1848) 38, I wylbe bolde wyth my nowne darlyng, Cum now, a bas, my nowne proper sparlyng.

2. Applied to other small fish: †**a.** The sprat, *Clupea sprattus. Obs.*

1740 R. BROOKES *Art of Angling* II. xxxvii. 153 Of the Sprat or Sparling. A Sprat is so like a Herring in every Particular, that [etc.].

b. *U.S.* A young or immature herring.

1884 GOODE *Nat. Hist. Aquat. Anim.* 550 Certain local names for the Herring which..designate certain conditions and ages. To this class belongs the name 'Sperling', employed by our own fishermen of Cape Ann to denote the young herrings. **1888** EARLL in Goode *Amer. Fishes* 342 The pasture school remained within a few miles of a large school of sperling without being drawn after them.

3. *attrib.* and *Comb.*, as ***sparling-boat, fishing***, etc.; †**sparling-fisher, -fowl**, the (female) goosander, *Mergus merganser*.

1678 RAY *Willughby's Ornith.* 333 The Dun-Diver or Sparlin-fowl: *Merganser fœmina.* **1700** C. LEIGH *Nat. Hist. Lancs.*, etc. I. 161 The Sparling-Fisher..is about the Bigness of a Duck, and by a wonderful Activity in Diving catches its Prey. **1710** SIBBALD *Hist. Fife* II. 49 The Female of it [*sc.* goosander] is by some thought to be the Mergus Cinereus, the Sparling-Fowl. **1754** T. GARDNER *Hist. Dunwich* 20 Each Sperling-Boat, five shillings on presenting Days. **1902** *Stirling Nat. Hist. & Arch. Soc. Jrnl.* 29 The sparling is one of the fishes of the Forth, and sparling fishing is still prosecuted in the river.

†**sparlire.** *Obs.* Forms: *α.* 1 spærlira (etc.), 4 sparlire, sperlire, 4–5 sparlyr(e. *β.* 4–5 sparlyver, -uer, 5 sperlyver. [OE. *spær-, spearlira* (also *sper-, speoru-*), f. *spearwa* calf of the leg + *líra* LIRE *sb.*[1] The later change of *-lire* to *-liver* is irregular.] The calf of the leg.

α. *c* **1000** ÆLFRIC *Deut.* xxviii. 35 Slea þe drihten mid þam wirstan yfele on cneowum and on spearlirum. **13..** *Sir Beues* 2487 Be þe riȝt leg ȝhe him grep,..þat neȝ ȝhe braide out is sparlire. **13..** *Gaw. & Gr. Knt.* 158 Heme wel haled, hose of þat same grene, þat spenet on his sparlyr & clene spures vnder. *a* **1400** *Octouian* 330 The ape hym boot full ylle Thorgh the sparlyre.

β. *c* **1380** WYCLIF *Sel. Wks.* III. 92 Þe Lord schal smyte þee wiþ moost yvel biel in knees and in sparlyveris. **1387** TREVISA *Higden* (Rolls) V. 355 For þat tyme þe Longobardes usede strapeles wiþ brode laces doun to þe sparlyver. **14..** *Parts Body* in Wr.-Wülcker 632 *Musculus*, the sperlyver.

sparm(e, obs. ff. SPERM.

sparmacetye, obs. f. SPERMACETI.

spar-maker: see SPAR *sb.*[1] 6.

sparmannia (spɑːˈmænɪə). [mod.L. (Linnæus filius *Supplementum Plantarum* (1782) 41), f. the name of Andres *Sparrman* (1748–1820), Swedish traveller + -IA[1].] A large hairy shrub of the genus *Sparmannia* (family Tiliaceæ) native to southern Africa, and bearing toothed heart-shaped leaves and clusters of white flowers, esp. *S. africana*.

1801 *Curtis's Bot. Mag.* XV. 516 African Sparmannia... This beautiful shrub is a native of the Cape of Good Hope. **1818** M. EDGEWORTH *Let.* Sept. (1971) 101, I wish I could get a Sparmania [*sic*] for Lady Lansdowne. **1885** T. BAINES *Greenhouse & Stove Plants* 317/2 Most of the insects that are troublesome on indoor plants will live on this Sparmannia. **1956** X. FIELD *Housewife Bk. House Plants* III. 84 The sparmannia likes plenty of elbow room and is inclined to swamp its neighbours. **1976** *Homes & Gardens* Aug. 75/3 Bold foliage plants that will fill out your glass-enclosed jungle include..sparmannia.

sparmaticall, -tyke, obs. ff. SPERMATIC(AL.

sparoid (ˈspærɔɪd, ˈspeɪrɔɪd), *a.* and *sb. Ichth.* [ad. mod.L. *Sparoidēs*, f. *sparus* SPARUS.]

A. *adj.* Of or belonging to, characteristic of, the *Sparidæ* or sea-bream family.

1836 J. RICHARDSON *Fauna Bor. Amer.* III. 71 No one Sparoid species is known to exist on both sides of the Atlantic. **1842** *Penny Cycl.* XXII. 310 The genus *Pentapus* is founded upon certain Sparoid fishes found in the Indian Seas. **1862** COUCH *Brit. Fishes* I. 220 The Sparoid Family, or Sea Breams.

b. Of scales: (see quots.).

a **1856** YARRELL *Brit. Fishes* (1859) II. 135 Sparoid scales are..thin, broader than long, with the centre of growth near their posterior border. **1880** GUNTHER *Fishes* 46 Scales, the free surface of which is spiny, and which have no denticulation on the Margin, have been termed Sparoid scales.

B. *sb.* A fish of this family.

1842 BRANDE *Dict. Sci.*, etc. 1136/2 Sparoids, *Sparoides*, the name of a tribe of Acanthopterygian fishes of which the genus *Sparus* is the type. **1851** MANTELL *Petrifactions* v. § I. 412 Sparoids, or Breams. **1884** GOODE *Nat. Hist. Aquat. Anim.* 394 Californian Sparoids.

sparonaro, obs. variant of SPERONARA.

sparoo, -ov, -ow(e, obs. forms of SPARROW.

†**sparple**, *v. Obs.* Forms: *α.* 4, 6 sparpil(l, 5 sparpeyll, 5–6 sparpyll(e, 6 -el(l, 6–7 -al(l, 4–6 (9) sparple; 4–5 sparpoil, 6 -ole; 5 sperpule, 5–6 sperpele, -ale, -ole, sperple. *β.* 4–6 sparble, 6 sparbel-. (See also SPARFLE *v.*, SPARKLE *v.*[2], and SPARTLE *v.*[1]) [ad. OF. *esparpeillier* (12th c.; mod.F. *éparpiller*), = Prov. *esparpalhar*, Catal. *esparpillar*, It. *sparpagliare*, to scatter, disperse, send in all directions: of uncertain origin, cf. DISPARPLE *v.*]

1. *intr.* To go or run in different directions; to disperse or scatter.

α. *c* **1330** R. BRUNNE *Chron. Wace* (Rolls) 8488 Fele were slayn als þey fledde, & fleyng þey sparplyed & spredde. *c* **1420** *Wars Alex.* (Prose) 39 (E.E.T.S.), Wate þou noȝte wele þat a wolfe chasez a grete floke of schepe & gerse þam sparple. *c* **1450** *St. Cuthbert* (Surtees) 7826 On þe ferth day þai sparpylled. *c* **1475** *Rauf Coilȝear* 26 Ilk ane tuik ane seir way, And sperpellit full fer.

β. *c* **1440** *Partonope* 1076 (Roxb. Cl.), For Partanope made hym sparble wyde. *c* **1450** *Merlin* xvii. 274 Than sparbled the saisnes and turned bakke towarde her chyuachie.

2. *trans.* To cast or throw here and there or in different directions; to scatter; to disperse or separate unduly or improperly.

a **1350** *John Bapt.* 222 in Horstm. *Altengl. Leg.* (1881) 126 Þe banes þat þai fand Sparpilled þai wide in þe land. **1398** TREVISA *Barth. De P.R.* XIX. cxxxi. (1495) 942 The rough voyc is hose and sparplyd by smalle and dyuers brethynge. *a* **1400–50** *Alexander* 4162 Þan ferd þai forth..& freschly assemblis All at was sperpolid on þe spene & spilt with þe blastis. **1487** *Sc. Acts Parlt.* (1814) II. 178 Nor the merchandis gudis be strikin vp nor vnresonably sperpalit. **1513** DOUGLAS *Æneid* XI. xii. 50 With sik rebound and rewyne wonder sayr That he his lyfe hes sparpellit in the ayr. **1542** *St. Papers Hen. VIII*, III. 374 The Kinges Majesties Judges..wer so sperplid or severid from other, not two in one housse. **1566** DRANT tr. *Hor.*, *Sat.* I. i. A iij, If that thou spende and sparple it, no dodkin wyll abyde. **1819** W. TENNANT *Papistry Storm'd* v. (1827) 152 The heukle-banies black That sparpled lay about like wrack Or tangles on a shore.

b. To disperse by distribution or division among persons. Chiefly *Sc.*

1435 MISYN *Fire of Love* 24 Gudes þe whilk he has ouer his nede, to þame þat it nedis he sparpyll. **1533** BELLENDEN *Livy* II. iii. 138 The faderis has dividit þe croun amang þame self, and sparpellit his riches and guddis amang þe pepill. **1581** *Reg. Privy Council Scot.* III. 414 The guidis and geir of the foirsaidis rebellis..ar sparpallit and devidit in the handes of sindre personis. **1615** *Ibid.* X. 343 [They have] sparpallit and disponit upoun the same gold and silver at thair pleasour.

3. To break up, scatter, disperse (an assembly, army, fleet, etc.) by superior force. Freq. with *abroad*.

α. **1382** WYCLIF *2 Sam.* xviii. 8 Forsothe there was the batail sparpoild vpon the face of al the loond. *c* **1420** *Wars Alex.* (Prose) 74 (E.E.T.S.), Thare na gouernour es þe folke are sparpled belyfe als schepe þat ere wit owtten ane hirde. **1489** CAXTON *Faytes of A.* I. xxiv. 74 So were they in parell to be broken and sparpeylled abrode. *c* **1500** *Melusine* 165, I ..shal shew you of the viii vessels that were sparpylled by the tempeste. **1549** THOMAS *Hist. Italy* 186 Andrew and his men behaued them selfes so valiauntly, that they sparpled the imperiall army abrode. **1582** N. LICHEFIELD tr. *Castanheda's Conq. E. Ind.* I. lviii. 121 b, There was made a great slaughter, yea, farre greater then in the fieldes, for that there they were sperpeled and heere they tooke them altogether in their streets.

β. *a* **1513** FABYAN *Chron.* VII. (1811) 375 Where thorough that symple feleshyp whiche named theym self shepherdes, was disseueryd and sparbelyd. *Ibid.* 636 The Kynges hoost was sparbled and chasyd.

4. To disperse in a more or less regular or methodical manner.

c **1400** *Lanfranc's Cirurg.* 158 Þe veyne arisynge comeþ to þe mydrif; & sum partie of hir is sparpoiled þoruȝ þe mydrif & þe lymes of þe brest. **1536** BELLENDEN *Cron. Scot.* (1821) I. 48 King Rewtha brocht all maner of craftis-men out of othir contres, and sparpellit thaim in sindry schiris of his realme. **1553** T. WILSON *Rhet.* 90 There is another kind of exornacion that is not equally sparpled throughout the whole oration.

5. To spread *abroad* or disseminate (rumours, news, etc.).

1536–7 EARL OF DERBY in *6th Report Hist. MSS. Commission* 445/2 Which letters and devises they sparple abroad. **1548** UDALL, etc. *Erasm. Par. John* vii. 52 These sayinges were by secrete whisperinges sperpled abrode. **1582** J. MELVILL *Autobiog.* (Wodrow Soc.) 132 Newes war sparpelit athort the countrey, that the Ministers war all to be thair massacred.

†**sparpled**, *ppl. a. Obs.* [f. prec.] Dispersed, scattered.

1432 *Wednesdayes Faste* (W. de W.), Wherfore his shepe sparpled to folde he can brynge. **1483** *Cath. Angl.* 352/1 Sparpyllde, *sparsus, diuisus.* *c* **1557** ABP. PARKER *Ps.* xliv. 129 Thou letst us all as sparpled sheepe, to be devoured quyte. **1609** HEYWOOD *Brit. Troy* XIII. xcix, With the next [stroke] his sparpled braines appeare. *Ibid.* xv. xc, Ihoues sparpled Alters licke the blood Of slaughtred Priam.

†**sparpling**, *vbl. sb. Obs.* [f. as prec.] The action of the verb; dispersing, scattering. Also, mental or spiritual distraction.

1434 MISYN *Mending Life* 110 All þe sparpilyngis of his hart fest he in on[e] desyre. *Ibid.* 118 Sparpillynge sumtyme comys, & wauyrynge of hart. **1483** *Cath. Angl.* 352/1 A Sparpyllynge, *sparsio, diuisio.* **1557** LD. WARTON in Strype *Ann. Ref.* (1824) VII. 382 Our men being not of power to encounter them held them close from sparpling abroad to destroy the country.

So †ˈ**sparpling** *ppl. a.*, distracting. *Obs.*$^{-1}$

1435 MISYN *Fire of Love* 66 Sturbyld he settis in pesse, & all noyse sparpilland he wastis.

sparre, obs. variant of SPEER *v.*

sparred (spɑːd), (*ppl.*) *a.* [f. SPAR *sb.*[1] or *v.*[3]]

1. Made or constructed of, having or fitted with, spars, narrow boards, or planks, set with intervals or spaces between them.

1805 R. W. DICKSON *Pract. Agric.* I. Pl. 18, Calf pens with sparred floors. **1834** M. SCOTT *Cruise Midge* (1859) 369 A passage..on each side of which were sparred partitions of unpainted pine boards. **1844** J. T. HEWLETT *Parsons & W.* liii, A heavy sparred gate, which ever stood open. **1880** J. DUNBAR *Pract. Papermaker* 49 On the floor of the pit a sparred bottom should be placed.

2. Having spar-like markings.

1827 GRIFFITH tr. *Cuvier* V. 98 The Blue Wing Bat, the Black Back Bat, the Sparred Bat.

3. Of a ship: Furnished with masts, yards, etc.

1905 *Westm. Gaz.* 10 Aug. 9/2 At other points the sparred Indiaman or Colonial traders..lay moored to quay or buoy.

sparrer[1] (ˈspɑːrə(r)). *colloq.* [f. SPAR *v.*[2]] One who spars or boxes. Also *fig.*

1814 *Sporting Mag.* XLIV. 92 The parties were rival sparrers in the North. **1818** COBBETT *Pol. Reg.* XXXIII. 2 The 'Courier' and..the 'Morning Chronicle', those sparrers in double-padded gloves. **1862** THACKERAY *Philip* vii, Cinqbars was a pretty sparrer—but no stamina. **1886** B. SHAW *Cash. Byron's Prof.* Prol. iii, He says you're only a sparrer, and that you'd fall down with fright if you was put into a twenty-four foot ring.

sparrer[2] (ˈspærə(r)), repr. dial. pronunc. of SPARROW; also as first element of SPARROW-GRASS.

1884 [see NEGRO 1 d]. **1935** in Z. N. Hurston *Mules & Men* I. vii. 153 He seen a sparrer sittin' on a dead limb of a tree. **1961** *John o' London's* 19 Oct. 447/1 Cloak-and-dagger intellectuals, or game little cockney sparrers. **1970** N. STREATFEILD *Thursday's Child* xxiii. 156 That Ebeneezer we 'ave to 'elp..'asn't got no more brains than a sparrer. **1979** R. CASSILIS *Arrow of God* III. ix. 78 A dark-skinned..dhoti-clad cockney sparrer.

†ˈ**sparret.** *Obs.*$^{-1}$ [Diminutive of SPAR *sb.*[1]] A small spar or bar.

1632 LITHGOW *Trav.* I. 32 He and I going in to see the inravled image with sparrets of iron.

spar-rib, variant of SPARE-RIB.

ˈ**sparriness.** *rare*$^{-1}$. [f. SPARRY *a.*[2]] Sparry quality or condition.

1841 LD. COCKBURN *Circuit Journ.* (1888) 120 Its stalactites were unbroken... Now that not one remains, the whole charm, which was in its sparriness, is gone.

ˈ**sparring**, *vbl. sb.*[1] [f. SPAR *v.*[1]] The action of closing, fastening, or securing.

1564–78 BULLEIN *Dial. agst. Pest* (1888) 57 The diggyng vp of graues, the sparring in of windowes.

sparring (ˈspɑːrɪŋ), *vbl. sb.*[2] [f. SPAR *sb.*[1] or *v.*[3]] The action of fitting or providing with spars, in various senses.

1459–60 *Durh. Acc. Rolls* (Surtees) 88 Pro..le Watlyng et sparryng unius domus. **1606** *Shuttleworths' Acc.* (Chetham Soc.) 166 For bynding, rearinge, sparringe, lattinge, and making of iiij dowers in the said barne, vj^{li}. **1627** CAPT. SMITH *Seaman's Gram.* ii. 14 For clamps,..they shall be all of six inch planke... The rest for the sparring vp of the workes of square three inch planke. **1873** [W. COOPER] (*title*), Yachts and Yachting... Being a treatise on building, sparring, canvassing, sailing, and the general management of yachts, etc.

sparring (ˈspɑːrɪŋ), *vbl. sb.*[3] [f. SPAR *v.*[2]]

1. The action of fighting or encountering in a special manner (see the vb.) on the part of cocks and pugilists. Also *transf.*, skirmishing.

1686 R. BLOME *Gentl. Recreat.* II. 278/2 After they have been thus fed,..take them out of their Pens, and putting a pair of Hots upon each of their Heals,..let them fight, and buffet each other a good while, provided they do not wound or draw Blood of each other, and this is called Sparring of Cocks. **1728** CHAMBERS *Cycl.*, *Sparring*, among Cock-fighters, is the fighting a Cock with another to breathe him. **1734** tr. *Rollin's Ancient Hist.* (1827) I. 76 Endeavouring by that sparring to keep off their enemy. **1797** *Sporting Mag.* X. 320 Nor is the glory of sparring extinguished for ever. **1811** *Ibid.* XXXVII. 99 A manly stand-up fight, to the exclusion altogether of sparring and shifting. **1861** HUGHES *Tom Brown at Oxf.* viii, The fighting man was..there, stripped for sparring. **1885** *New Bk. of Sports* 127 Fifty years ago sparring with the gloves was regarded chiefly as a means to an end.

2. *transf.* Verbal hitting or skirmishing; engagement in argument or dispute; bandying of words.

1755 J. SHEBBEARE *Lydia* (1769) II. 32 She knew the conversation of the evening would turn upon the subject of the earl's marriage: and that some gentle sparrings might probably be aimed at her ladyship. **1825** JEFFERSON *Autobiog.* Wks. 1859 I. 11 These gentlemen had had some sparrings in debate before. **1861** *Illust. Lond. N.* 18 May 476/3 A little amusing sparring took place between the lecturer and Mr. Sexton. **1891** CLARK RUSSELL *Curatica* 81 But let us have done with sparring, and come to business.

3. In attributive uses, as ***sparring-academy, -lesson, -match, -room***, etc.; †**sparring-blow** (see quots. *a* 1700, 1785), also, a hard or severe blow; **sparring partner**, a boxer employed to practise with another in training for a contest; also *transf.* and *fig.*, esp. a person with whom one enjoys arguing.

a **1700** B. E. *Dict. Cant. Crew, Sparring-blows*, the first Strokes to try the goodness of young Cocks Heels; also those in a Battel before the Cocks come to Mouth it. **1701** RUSHW. *Hist. Coll.* IV. I. 139 This Year [1645] had generally been very fatal to his Majesty's Interests, so it concluded with such a Sparring-Blow as destroy'd almost all hopes of Resource. **1704** *Lond. Gaz.* No. 4063/4 The..Pens are.. very convenient to the sparring and stiving Rooms. **1785** GROSE *Dict. Vulgar T., Sparring blows*, blows given by cocks before they close, or as the term is, mouth it, used figuratively for words previous to a quarrel. **1807** J. BERESFORD *Miseries Hum. Life* (ed. 3) II. xviii. 208 This sparring match is quite a Comedy to me. **1847** ALB. SMITH *Chr. Tadpole* xxix. (1879) 261 I've got a gent up stairs for a sparring lesson. **1853** 'C. BEDE' *Verdant Green* I. xvi, He would have..referred him to his spacious..Sparring Academy. **1908** *Captain* Sept. 530/2 Jack was the best sparring partner he could have. **1930** *Daily Express* 8 Sept. 2/3 Cal Barton (Birmingham), Jack Hood's sparring partner. **1958** *Victorian Studies* I. 248 Mill..is used with the utmost disrespect as a sort of punch-drunk sparring-partner. **1971** H. WILSON *Labour Govt.* xxv. 493 Mr Mikoyan, my old sparring-partner and friend of the 1947 trade talks, now in honourable retirement, was waiting for us. **1977** 'E. MCBAIN' *Long Time No See* iv. 60, I was workin [*sic*] with Warren and a sparring partner... Warren's got a fight Tuesday night.

sparrow (ˈspærəʊ). Forms: α. 1 spearu(u)a, spearwa, 4 sperwe, 4–5 sparwe; 1 spearewa, 3–5 sparewe. β. 1 spearuwa, 3 speruwe, 5 sperow, sperrowe; 3 sparuwe, 4–6 sparowe, (4, 6–7 sparr-), sparow, 4, 6 sparou (4 sparov, sparu, sparw, 5 sparoo), 6– sparrow. [OE. *spearwa*, etc., = Goth. *sparwa*, MHG. *sparwe, sparbe, sperwe*, older Da. *sparwe, sporwe, spørwe* (Da. *spurv*, Norw. dial. *sporv, sparv*, Sw. *sparf*; also obs. Da. *spurg, sporig*, NFris. *sparreg*). The original *w* of the stem has disappeared in OHG. *sparo* (MHG. *spare, spar*, G. dial. *spar*; cf. MHG. *sperlinc*, G. *sperling*) and ON. *spǫrr* (Norw. dial. *sporr, spør*, obs. Da. *sparre, spurre*). Outside of Teutonic the stem seems to occur in OPruss. *spurglis* sparrow, *spergla-wanags* sparrow-hawk.

The forms *speara* in the Vesp. Ps. lxxxiii. 4 and *spare* in the earlier Wycliffite Ps. ci. 8, although similar to the Continental forms without *w*, are so isolated in Eng. that they may be mere scribal errors.]

1. a. A small brownish-grey bird of the family *Fringillidae*, indigenous to Europe, where it is very common, and naturalized in various other countries; esp. the house-sparrow *Passer domesticus*.

α. *c* **725** *Corpus Gloss.* F 128 *Fenus*, spearua. *c* **825** *Vesp. Psalter* ci. 8 Ȝeworden ic eam swe swe spearwa..in timbre. *c* **900** tr. *Baeda's Hist.* II. xiii. (1890) 136 Cume an spearwa & hrædlice þæt hus þurhfleo. *c* **1100** *O.E. Chron.* (MS. D) an. 1067, He..sæið þæt..an spearwa on gryn ne mæȝ befeallan forutan his foresceawunge. *c* **1205** LAY. 29274 He lette forð wenden swiðe ueole sparewen; þa sparwen heore flut no-men [etc.]. *a* **1325** *Prose Psalter* x. 1 Wende þou in-to heuen as a sparwe? *c* **1340** *Nominale* (Skeat) 390 [Man] takith sperwe in nette. *c* **1380** WYCLIF *Sel. Wks.* I. 195 þei ben betere þan many sparewis. *c* **1400** *Brut* xcv. 94 þai.. token peces of tunder..and bonde to sparwe feet.

β. *c* **1000** *Ags. Ps.* (Thorpe) ci. 5 Ic spearuwan..gelice ȝe-wearð. *a* **1225** *Ancr. R.* 152 Ȝet is ancre iefned her to sparuwe þet is one under roue. *Ibid.*, Ich am..ase spearuwe þet is one. *a* **1300** *Cursor M.* 11986 Wit handes made he sparus tuelue. *a* **1340** HAMPOLE *Psalter* cxxiii. 6 We ere takyn out as sparow þat flees þe snare. **14..** *Sir Beues* (M.) 2526 Euery man callyd me a sparoo. **1456** SIR G. HAYE *Law Arms* (S.T.S.) 12 The sparow is a lytill foule janglare. *a* **1529** SKELTON *P. Sparowe* 266 But my sparowe dyd pas All sparowes of the wode. **1555** EDEN *Decades* II. VII. (Arb.) 129 There is no lesse plentie of popingiais, then with vs of dooues or sparous. **1616** R. C. *Times' Whistle* (1871) 87 Fine gellies of decocted sparrowes bones. **1708** PRIOR *Turtle & Sparrow* 5 The Sparrow..(A Bird that loves to chirp and talk). **1784** COWPER *Task* v. 65 The sparrows peep, and quit the shelt'ring eaves. **1802** BINGLEY *Anim. Biog.* (1813) II. 169 No bird is better known in every part of Great Britain than the Sparrow. **1897** *Times* 5 Jan. 10/5 Few small birds, with the exception of the robin, will face the sparrow.

b. Used as a term of endearment.

c **1600** *Timon* II. i. (1842) 24 Lett me but kisse thyne eyes, my sweete delight, My sparrow,..my duck, my cony.

c. *slang.* (See quots.)

1879 *Gd. Words* 739 There are their 'sparrows' (beer or beer money), given by householders [to the dustmen] when their dust-holes are emptied. **1902** *Daily Chron.* 6 Dec. 3/7, I should like to say a few words about the milkman's secret customers, otherwise 'sparrows'.

d. A chirpy, quick-witted person; used *spec.* of a Londoner, in *cockney sparrow*, etc.

1861 C. M. YONGE *Stokesley Secret* iv. 62 'A cock-sparrow for her London manners.'.. 'A London-bred sparrow; a pert forward chit.' **1892** —— *That Stick* I. ix. 95, I care about my neighbours..after a sort, but the jolly city sparrows of the slums for me! **1961** [see SPARRER[2]]. **1969** J. GARDNER *Compl. State of Death* vi. 116 'Your mother's English?' 'Yes. Ma's a little cockney sparrow.' **1969** G. BUTLER *Coffin's Dark Number* xii. 151 She recognized her for what she was, one of those sharp little London sparrows. **1977** *Zigzag* Aug. 4/1 There are never any low class twits, only cockney sparrows and 'characters'.

2. With distinguishing terms, denoting varieties of the true sparrow, or other small birds in some way resembling these.

See also *field-, house-, Java, mountain-, ring-, Savannah, swamp-sparrow*, and HEDGE-, REED-, SONG-, TREE-SPARROW. Many other names, which have obtained little or no currency, are given in the ornithologies of Edwards, Latham, and Wilson.

1668 [see SPECKLED *ppl. a.*]. **1678** RAY *Willughby's Ornith.* 385 The foolish Sparrow..is a Sea fowl, and feeds upon fish. It hath the cry of a Jay. *a* **1705** —— *Syn. Avium* (1713) 187 Green Sparrow, or Green Humming Bird. **1767** tr. *Cranz' Greenland* I. 85 The akpalliarsuk, or sea-sparrow,..is no larger than a fieldfare. **1771** *Encycl. Brit.* II. 633/2 The black fringilla..is the American black sparrow with red eyes. *Ibid.* 634/1 The black fringilla, with a white belly, is the American snow-sparrow of Catesby. **1810** WILSON *Amer. Ornith.* II. 128 The Chipping sparrow is five inches and a quarter long. **1842** J. B. FRASER *Mesopot. & Assyria* xv. 368 The becafico is called the fig-sparrow. **1899** W. T. GREENE *Cage-Birds* 59 The Diamond Sparrow, also an Australian, but inhabiting further south than the Zebra Finch.

3. *attrib.* and *Comb.*, as ***sparrow-chatter, -hole, -kind, -legs, -pest, -shot, -trap, -tribe***; ***sparrow-billed, coloured, -footed, -legged*** adjs.

1841 J. T. HEWLETT *Parish Clerk* I. 288 Cormorants,.. and the *sparrow-billed puffins. **1851** W. ANDERSON *Expos. Popery* (1878) 125 Such is the *sparrow-chatter of a degenerate..generation. **1815** STEPHENS in *Shaw's Gen. Zool.* IX. II. 385 *Sparrow-coloured Bunting. **1601** HOLLAND *Pliny* I. 156 The women [have feet] so short & smal, that there-upon they be called Struthopodes, *i.* *sparrow footed. *a* **1722** LISLE *Husb.* (1757) 193 *Sparrow-holes under the eaves of a reek. **1774** GOLDSM. *Nat. Hist.* (1776) V. 299 Of Birds of the *Sparrow Kind in General. **1886** W. J. TUCKER *E. Europe* 385 A very little man, with a very big abdomen, on *sparrow legs. **1965** F. SARGESON *Memoirs of Peon* vi. 173 Two young *sparrow-legged ruffians. **1884** *York Herald* 26 Aug. 6/5 The Chester Farmers' Club met..to discuss the *sparrow pest and its remedies. **1761** STERNE *Tr. Shandy* III. x. 33 Small curses.. upon great occasions..are but so much waste of our strength... They are like *sparrow shot..fired against a bastion. **1955** L. DURRELL *Tree of Idleness* 48 Under rain, that rattles down the leaves like sparrow-shot. **1876** SMILES *Sc. Natur.* ii. (ed. 4) 38 A few..boys preparing *sparrow-traps. **1842** LOUDON *Suburban Hort.* 107 Among birds of the *sparrow tribe, the starling deserves particular notice.

4. a. Special combs.: **sparrow-beak**, *dial.* (see quot.); **sparrow-bottle**, a jar suspended on a wall to serve as a nesting-place for sparrows; **sparrow-brain** *colloq.*, (a person with) a tiny brain, (a person of) limited intelligence or perception; **sparrow-bub** *dial.*, a fledgling sparrow; **sparrow club**, a society formed for destroying sparrows; **sparrow cop** *U.S. slang* (see quots.); **sparrow-fall** *poet.* (cf. SHAKES. *Ham.* v. ii. 233), a sparrow's death; hence *gen.* mortality; also *attrib.*; **sparrow-fart**, (*a*) *dial.* and *slang*, break of day, very early morning; also *pl.*; (*b*) *rare*, a person of no consequence; **sparrow-hail**, the smallest kind of shot; **sparrow-mumbling**, the action of holding a cock-sparrow's wing in the mouth, and attempting to draw in the head by movement of the lips; **sparrow-net**, a net fixed on a pole, used for catching sparrows living in the eaves of houses or in grain-stacks; **sparrow-picked** *a.*, marked with small indentations; **sparrow-pie**, a dish proverbially supposed to make the eater sharp-witted; **sparrow-pot**, = *sparrow-bottle*; **sparrow-pudding**, = *sparrow-pie*; **sparrow-tail**, a long narrow coat-tail; also *attrib.*

1854 MISS BAKER *Northampt. Gloss.*, **Sparrow-beaks*, fossil shark's teeth: called also birds' beaks. **1881** *N. & Q.* 6th Ser. IV. 456 *Sparrow bottles..of red ware..are continually used by most of the farmers in Thorney Fen. **1930** V. SACKVILLE-WEST *Edwardians* v. 241, I don't suppose it satisfies anyone, except perhaps a *sparrow-brain like mother. **1975** H. FLEETWOOD *Picture of Innocence* iii. 45 She didn't actually *care* about her, and even, with her sparrow brain, despised her. **1917** D. H. LAWRENCE *Look! We have come Through!* 159 Curious long-legged foals, and wide-eared calves, and naked *sparrow-bubs. **1886** *Pall Mall G.* 29 May 4 Clubs, known as '*sparrow clubs', were formed expressly with a view to their utter and speedy extermination. **1896** *Harper's Mag.* June 104/1 The boys do call a park policeman a *sparrow-cop, don't they? **1935** A. J. POLLOCK *Underworld Speaks* 111/1 *Sparrow cop*, police or motorcycle officer who patrols parks and boulevards (petty thefts and petting parties). **1960** WENTWORTH & FLEXNER *Dict. Amer. Slang* 506/2 *Sparrow cop*, a policeman in disfavor with his superiors and assigned to a park to guard the grass. **1946** DYLAN THOMAS *Deaths & Entrances* 40 Mammoth and *sparrowfall Everybody's earth. **1970** T. HUGHES *Crow* 32 An old man..Gazed towards the nearby polished shoes And slowly forgot the deaths in Homer The sparrowfall natural economy Of the dark simple curtain. **1886** R. HOLLAND *Cheshire Gloss.* 331 **Sparrowfarts*, very early morning 'Tha mun be up by *sparrowfarts* or tha'll be too late.' **1922** JOYCE *Ulysses* 747 Miss This Miss That Miss Theother lot of sparrowfarts skitting around talking about politics they know as much about as my backside. **1947** D. M. DAVIN *Gorse blooms Pale* 194 There we were as usual this morning at Sparrowfart, me with the jeep pulled up in front of the General's caravan. **1974** H. MCLEAVE *Only Gentlemen can Play* (1975) II. i. 92 It was important enough to bring you out here at sparrow fart. **1859** *J. Watson's Bards Border* 53 Some *sparrow-hail wad best despatch him. **1868** W. R. TRENCH *Realities Irish Life* (1869) 22 Some flasks of gunpowder and a quantity of 'sparrow hail'. **1852** HAWKER *Cornish Ball.* (1899) 147 Among them, swallowing living mice and *sparrow-mumbling had frequent place. **1621** MARKHAM *Hungers Prev.* 101 The Engine or *Sparrow-nette..must carry this fashion or proportion. **1688** HOLME *Armoury* III. xxii. (Roxb.) 278/1 That on the sinister chief is termed an Eve or Easing nett, or a Sparrow nett or Purse nett. **1707** MORTIMER *Husb.* (1721) I. 323 Many ways are made use of to destroy them; but none more effectual than the large folding Sparrow Net. **1898** F. W. MACEY *Specifications* 130 Granite may be roughly axed, finely axed, *sparrow-picked, or polished. **1881** BLACKMORE *Cristowell* xxxvii, How sharp you are! You've been eating *sparrow-pie. **1886** P. ROBINSON *Valley Teet. Trees* 87 Introduce another British novelty—and try sparrow-pie. **1831** RENNIE *Montagu's Ornith. Dict.* 486 Unless they multiply their *Sparrow pots yearly. **1833** LOUDON *Encycl. Archit.* §550 The use of these sparrow pots is, to prevent the birds from dirtying the walls or windows with what falls from their nests. **1896** *Daily News* 3 Nov. 7/2 The heckler..must rise very early in the morning and dine very liberally off '*sparrow-pudding'. **1888** EGGLESTON *Graysons* xxvi, The lawyers in their blue *sparrow-tail coats with brass buttons, which constituted then [about 1840] a kind of professional uniform.

b. In names of animals and plants: **sparrow-bunting** (see quot.); †**sparrow-camel**, the ostrich; **sparrow-duck**, *dial.* the hooded crow; **sparrow-owl**, one or other of various small owls, esp. of the genus *Glaucidium*; †**sparrow parrot**, a small species of parrot; †**sparrow's toadflax** (see quot. and *sparrow-wort*); **sparrow's-tongue**, the knot-grass, *Polygonum aviculare*; **sparrow-wort** (see quots.).

1894–5 LYDEKKER *Roy. Nat. Hist.* III. 416 The *sparrow-bunting (*Zonotrichia albicollis*),..differs from the true buntings by the exposed nostrils. **1646** SIR T. BROWNE *Pseud. Ep.* 163 The common opinion of the Oestridge, Struthio-camelus, or *Sparrow-Camell conceives that it digesteth Iron. **1895** P. H. EMERSON *Birds* xlix. 140 Kentishmen are sold and eaten as '*sparrow-duck'. **1831** RENNIE *Montagu's Ornith. Dict.* 488 The *Sparrow Owl is a very rare species in England. **1870** GILLMORE tr. *Figuier's Reptiles & Birds* 553 Sparrow Owls are of small size. **1787** LATHAM *Syn. Birds* Suppl. II. 93 *Psittacus fringillaceus.* *Sparrow Parrot... General colour green, head blue. **1597** GERARDE *Herbal* II. clvi. 443 *Passerina linaria.* *Sparrowes Tode flaxe. This plant also for resemblance sake is referred vnto the Linaries, bicause his leaues be like Linaria. *a* **1400** *Stockholm Med. MS.* in *Archaeol.* XXX. 413 *Sparwys-tungge,..*Centenodium*. **1597** GERARDE *Herbal* Table Eng. Names, Sparrowes toong, that is Knotgrasse. **1760** J. LEE *Introd. Bot.* App. 327 *Sparrow-wort, *Passerina*. *Ibid.*, Sparrow-wort, Tragus's, *Stellera*. **1852** G. JOHNSON *Cott. Gard. Dict.* 681/2 *Passerina*. Sparrow-wort... Greenhouse evergreens, white-flowered, and from the Cape of Good Hope.

Hence **'sparrowcide**, the destruction of sparrows; **'sparrowdom**, the region of sparrows; **'sparrower**, one who snares or kills sparrows; **'sparrowhood**, the condition of being a sparrow; **'sparrowish** *a.*, characteristic of a sparrow; **'sparrowless**, devoid of sparrows; **'sparrowling**, a young sparrow; **'sparrowy** *a.*, (*a*) abounding in, frequented by, sparrows; (*b*) characteristic of or resembling a sparrow; so ***sparrowy-looking*** adj.

1865 *St. James' Mag.* Feb. 375 *Sparrowcide is not a modern crime, but was extensively practised by our forefathers. **1880** *Fraser's Mag.* Jan. 49 At least, when we get outside the cities we get outside of *Sparrowdom. **1830** tr. *Aristophanes' Birds* 226 Should any one of you slay Philocrates the *Sparrower, he shall receive a talent. **1869** *Echo* 2 Sept., The sparrows, so soon as ever they grow from the callow state to mature *sparrowhood, become..dark and rusty. **1641** *True Char. of Untrue Bishop* 4 Witnesse his many *Sparrowish, Wrenlike wanton extravagances. **1848** W. STIRLING *Artists of Spain* I. 371 In these *sparrowless shades, Factor spent much of his time. **1849** *Fraser's Mag.* XXXIX. 573 A poor, unfledged, twittering *sparrowling. **1891** MEREDITH *One of our Conq.* II. iv. 85 London of the *sparrowy roadways and wearisome pavements. **1926** S. SITWELL *All Summer in Day* I. i. 18 The sun, also, was very sparrowy in voice, and both sun and birds seemed satisfied for the moment. **1948** I. BROWN *No Idle Words* 31 Were they [*sc.* buntings] bunters in the perky..sparrowy sense. **1953** D. A. BANNERMAN *Birds Brit. Isles* I. 300 The female is a sparrowy-looking little bird at all seasons. **1955** R. GRAVES *Greek Myths* I. lxxiv. 252 Castor and Polydeuces..come darting on 'sparrowy wings' through the upper air. **1976** A. J. RUSSELL *Pour Hemlock* vii. 63 She clutched steno pad to sparrowy chest.

'sparrow-bill. [f. prec.] = SPARABLE 1.

The application in quot. 1834–6 is irregular, a sparrow-bill being properly distinct from a brad, and having no projection.

1629 DEKKER *London's Tempe* iv. Wks. 1873 IV. 123 Hob-nailes to serve the man i' th' moone, And sparrowbils to cloute Pan's shoone. **1688** HOLME *Armoury* III. 300/1 *Sparrow Bills*, Nails to clout Shooes withal. **1706** [see SPARABLE 1]. **1834–6** P. BARLOW in *Encycl. Metrop.* (1845) VIII. 671/1 The kind of brads called sparrow-bills, (which have a small projection from one side of their heads). **1879** *Cassell's Techn. Educ.* IV. 12/1 Those small tacks called sparrowbills, which are much used by shoemakers.

attrib. and *Comb.* **1859** SALA *Gas-light & D.* xxxiii. 387 White drawers and stockings, flaring waist-handkerchiefs and sparrow-bill shoes. **1881** *Instr. Census Clerks* (1885) 91 Sparrow-bill Cutter, Maker.

†**sparrow-blasted**, *a.* *Obs.* [Cf. next.] Balefully stricken or blighted; thunderstruck, dumbfounded.

a **1652** BROME *Queenes Exch.* v. i, What art thow that canst look thus Piepickt, Crowtrod, or Sparrow-blasted? ha! **1682** BUNYAN *Holy War* (1905) 337 Will you never shake off your timorousness? are you afraid of being sparrow-blasted? who hath hurt you? **1823** GALT *Entail* lxxiii, 'Eh! Megsty me! I'm sparrow-blasted!' exclaimed the Leddy,..lifting both her hands and eyes in wonderment.

† **sparrow-blasting.** *Obs.* [f. SPARROW, with jocular or contemptuous force.] The fact of being blasted or blighted by some mysterious power, sceptically regarded as unimportant or non-existent.

1589 ? NASHE *Martin's Months Mind* Ep. to Rdr. B j b, No more praying against thunder and lightning, than against sparrowe blasting. **1593** *Tell-Troth's N.Y. Gift* (1876) 35 To lock vp ones wife for fear of sparrow-blasting. **1617** J. TAYLOR (Water P.) *Trav. to Hamburgh* E 2 b, Which two precious relickes, I brought home with me to defend me and all my friends from sparrow blasting. **1633** T. ADAMS *Exp. 2 Peter* ii. 6 Otherwise they say, we pray against sparrow-blasting.

'sparrow-grass, 'sparrowgrass. Now *dial.* or *vulgar.* Also 7–9 **sparagrass** (7 **sparragras**), 8 **-gras(se.** [Corruption of SPARAGUS, assimilated to SPARROW and GRASS.] Asparagus.

a. **1664** F. HAWKINS *Youths Behav.* II. 178 Prauns, or Sparagrass. *Ibid.*, A dish of Sparagrass. **1711** in Leader *Rec. Burgery Sheffield* (1897) 334 Paid a messinger for bringing sparagrasse from Doncaster. **1723** *Pres. St. Russia* I. 151 Roses, Gilliflowers, and well-tasted Sparagras. **1764** FOOTE *Mayor of G.* II. Wks. 1799 I. 181, I should recommend the opening a new branch of trade; sparagrass, gentlemen, the manufacturing of sparagrass. **1801** SOUTHEY in C. Southey *Life* II. 154 Sparagrass (it ought to be spelt so) and artichokes, good with plain butter.

β. **1649** [see ASPARAGUS 1 δ]. *c* **1685** *Three Merry Trav.* in *Bagford Ball.* 52 Both Chickens and sparrow grass she did provide. **1712** ADDISON *Spect.* No. 371 ¶4 The Ducklins and Sparrow-grass were very good. **1734** [see ASPARAGUS 1 δ]. **1819** 'RABELAIS THE YOUNGER' *Abeillard & Heloisa* 5 Some score hundred sparrow-grass, As it's now call'd by every ass. **1860** O. W. HOLMES *Elsie V.* xxxii, Mind me now, and take the tops of your sparrowgrass. **1865** 'C. BEDE' *Rook's Gard.*, etc. 96, I have heard the word sparrowgrass from the lips of a real Lady—but then she was in her seventies.

b. *attrib.*, as ***sparrow-grass bed, green, plant.***

1658 in W. M. Myddelton *Chirk Castle Acc.* (1908) 78 Paid..his gardiner that came with sparrowgrasse plants. *c* **1700** T. HOUGHTON in *Essex Rev.* (1906) XV. 170 The side of the dwelling house which looks toward the sparagrass beds. **1796** KIRWAN *Elem. Min.* (ed. 2) I. 28 Sparrow grass green—pale yellowish green with a mixture of grey and brown.

'sparrow-hawk. Also 5 **sparowhawke** (6 **-hauke**). [f. SPARROW: cf. SPARHAWK. So Sw. *sparfhök*, Norw. dial. *sporvehauk.*]

1. A species of hawk (*Accipiter nisus*) which preys on small birds, common in the British Islands and widely distributed in northern Europe and Asia. Occas., one or other species of hawk resembling this.

14.. *Metr. Voc.* in Wr.-Wülcker 625 *Nisus*, sparowhawke. *c* **1450** *Mirk's Festial* 43 A byrd þat couthe speke..went out of his cage, and a sparow-hawke wold haue slayne hym. *a* **1548** HALL *Chron., Hen. V*, 58 b, The Normans fled as fast as..the sely Partridge before the Sparowhauke. **1611** BEAUM. & FL. *Philaster* II. i, Use exercise, and keep a Sparrow-hawk. **1642** FULLER *Holy & Prof. St.* IV. xvi. 322 An Embassadour should not as a sparrow-hawk flie outright to his prey. **1752** J. HILL *Hist. Anim.* v. 341 *The Sparrow hawk.* The yellow-legged Falco, with a white, undulated breast, and a fasciated brown tail. **1768** PENNANT *Brit. Zool.* I. 151 The difference between the size of the male and female sparrow hawks is more disproportionate than in most other birds of prey. **1843** YARRELL *Brit. Birds* I. 63 The Sparrow-Hawk is another short-winged Hawk. **1870** GILLMORE tr. *Figuier's Reptiles & Birds* 590 The Sparrow-hawks are distinguished from the preceding birds by the slenderness of their tarsi. **1880** A. NEWTON in *Encycl. Brit.* XI. 534/2 The so-called 'Sparrow-Hawk' of New Zealand (*Hieracidea*) does not belong to this group of birds at all.

fig. **1820** SCOTT *Monast.* xxxv, Thou art a bold sparrow-hawk, to match thee so early with such a kite as Piercie Shafton. **1859** TENNYSON *Marr. Geraint* 444 The second was your foe, the sparrow-hawk, My curse, my nephew.

b. With distinguishing epithets.

1787 LATHAM *Syn. Birds* Suppl. II. 51 *Falco Nisus*,..New Holland Sparrow-Hawk. *Ibid.*, Speckled Sparrow-Hawk. **1807** SHAW *Gen. Zool.* VII. I. 190 Great-Billed Sparrow-Hawk. *Falco magnirostris.* **1810** A. WILSON *Amer. Ornith.* II. 117 American Sparrow Hawk, *Falco sparverius.* **1870** GILLMORE tr. *Figuier's Reptiles & Birds* (1892) 591 Africa possesses..the Dwarf Sparrow-hawk (*Accipiter minullus*).

2. A small anvil used in silver-working.

1869 *Routledge's Ev. Boy's Ann.* 309 The sparrow-hawk, which is a kind of miniature anvil. **1877** G. GEE *Silversm. Hdbk.* 119 The bezil all the time gradually working round the pointed end of the sparrow-hawk.

'sparrow-like, *a.* [f. SPARROW.] Resembling a sparrow or that of a sparrow.

1611 COTGR., *Passerin*, sparrow-like; of..a Sparrow. **1829** GRIFFITH tr. *Cuvier* VI. 82 Sparrow-like Owl, *Strix passerinoides.* **1851** G. H. KINGSLEY *Sp. & Trav.* (1900) v. 116 Small clouds of sparrow-like snow-birds. **1896** *Lloyd's Nat. Hist.* 87 The second type of egg is Sparrow-like.

† **'sparrow-mouth.** *Obs.* [Cf. next.] A wide mouth suggestive of that of a sparrow.

1673 HICKERINGILL *Greg. F. Greyb.* 314 Split jaws, sparrow mouths, grunting, lyons faces, hems, haws. **1699** R. L'ESTRANGE *Fables* II. lvi. (1715) II. 55 Why what a Hawk's Nose have we got here! and what a Sparrow-Mouth! **1700** S. PARKER *Six Philos. Ess.* 25 To me it seems a Miracle that all Hypocrites don't squint, but come off without inverted Pupils, Sparrow-Mouths and blubber'd Lips. [**1756** AMORY *Buncle* (1770) III. 215 His nose hooked like a buzzard, wide nostrils like a horse and his mouth sparrow.]

† **'sparrow-mouthed,** *a. Obs.* [SPARROW 3.] Having a wide mouth.

1611 COTGR. s.v. *Fendu, Bien fendu de gueule*, wide-mouthed, sparrow-mouthed, mouthed vp to the eares. **1621** BURTON *Anat. Mel.* III. ii. IV. i. (1651) 519 Every Lover admires his Mistress, though she be..squint-eyed, sparrow-mouthed, Persean hook-nosed. *a* **1700** B. E. *Dict. Cant. Crew, Sparrow-mouth'd*, a Mouth o Heavenly wide, as Sir P. Sidney calls it. **1725** BAILEY *Erasm. Colloq.* (1878) I. 44 Can you fancy that..Snub-nos'd, Sparrow-mouth'd, Paunch-belly'd Creature? **1785** GROSE *Dict. Vulgar T., Sparrow mouth'd*, wide mouth'd.

'sparry, *a.*[1] [Cf. SPEARY *a.*[1] 1.] ? Hard, stiff.

1641 BEST *Farm. Bks.* (Surtees) 28 Whearas most of the grasse..is a small, sparrie, and dry grasse, and sheepe doe not like it.

sparry ('spɑːrɪ), *a.*[2] [f. SPAR *sb.*[2]]

1. Consisting of, abounding in, spar; of the nature of spar.

1695 WOODWARD *Nat. Hist. Earth* IV. 192 The Water..taking the Sparry Particles as they lay dispersedly mingled with the Sand. **1713** DERHAM *Phys.-Theol.* 64 *note*, One or more vast Stones, which..are incrustated with this Sparry, Stalactical Substance, if not wholly made of it. **1749** *Phil. Trans.* XLVI. 276 Among the great Numbers of sparry Productions which I saw in this Mine. **1778** PRYCE *Min. Cornub.* 28 Neither have we yet seen a perfect Sparry Rhomb in Cornwall. **1812** BRACKENRIDGE *Views Louisiana* (1814) 66, I have seen some pieces penetrated with sparry matter. **1851** MANTELL *Petrifactions* vi. §6. 482 Upon breaking through the sparry floor [of the cave] the ossiferous deposit is exposed. **1877** LE CONTE *Elem. Geol.* II. (1879) 225 Certain mineral matters..in a purer and more sparry form than they exist in the rocks.

b. Impregnated with spar.

1724 J. MACKY *Journ. thr. Eng.* II. xii. 201 From it continually drops a sparry water, which..petrifies. **1782** *Phil. Trans.* LXXII. 203 Nor is there an instance of any earth rendered permanently fluid by any means, except in sparry air.

c. Of places: Rich in spar.

1789 E. DARWIN *Bot. Gard.* I. (1791) 130 Graces and Loves..On venturous step her sparry caves explore. **1806** MOORE '*I stole along the flowery bank*' ii. 9 Oh for a Naiad's sparry bower, To shade me in that glowing hour! **1847** DISRAELI *Tancred* v. v, With pendants hanging like stalactites from some sparry cavern. **1886** RUSKIN *Præterita* I. v. 152 The sparry walks at Matlock.

2. In specific terms denoting mineral substances of the nature of, or containing spar, as ***sparry iron*** (***ore***).

1796 KIRWAN *Elem. Min.* (ed. 2) II. 190 Calcareous, or Sparry Iron Ore. **1797** *Encycl. Brit.* (ed. 3) XV. 751/2 The sparry quartz, which is the scarcest of the whole. **1800** tr. *Lagrange's Chem.* II. 95 Bog iron-ore and sparry-ore appear, in a great measure, to be formed by this combination. **1805** R. JAMESON *Min.* II. 308 Sparry Ironstone... Colour light yellowish-grey. **1816** P. CLEAVELAND *Min.* 552 Thus it is associated with..gray copper, sparry iron, &c. **1854** tr. *Pereira's Polarized Light* (ed. 2) 128 Selenite, or sparry gypsum, is the native crystallised hydrated sulphate of lime. **1868** JOYNSON *Metals* 6 The spathose ores—'chalybeate', 'sparry carbonite of iron'. **1875** CROLL *Climate & T.* xviii. 308 The rock in which they are found is a sparry iron ore.

b. ***sparry acid***, hydrofluoric acid.

1796 KIRWAN *Elem. Min.* (ed. 2) II. 3 The sparry acid exists principally in fluor spar.

3. Of lustre, etc.: Resembling that of spar.

1792 S. ROGERS *Pleas. Mem.* II. 251 A cool sequestered grot From its rich roof a sparry lustre shot. **1820** *Blackw. Mag.* VI. 385 Icicles..gleam in the sunshine with a sparry light. *c* **1830** N. P. WILLIS *Schol. Thebet Ben Khorat* 65 The sparry glinting of the Morning Star. **1845** BAILEY *Festus* (ed. 2) 266 Full of all sparkling sparry loveliness.

sparse (spɑːs), *a.* (*adv.*) [ad. L. *spars-us*, pa. pple. of *spargĕre* to scatter. Cf. It. *sparso*, Pg. *esparso*, OF. *espars(e*, F. *épars(e*.]

1. *Sc.* Of writing: Having wide spaces between the words; widely spaced or spread out.

1727 WODROW *Corr.* (1843) III. 288 These were produced on Tuesday the 18th, and are four or five sheets of sparse write, yet not so long as I expected. **1785** J. BEATTIE *Scoticisms* (1787) 85 The writing is *sparse.*—Loose. Not close. Takes up too much room. **1800** *Monthly Mag.* IX. 237 When much space is occupied by few words, the Scotch, especially the lawyers, say, 'the writing is sparse'. **1825** JAMIESON *Suppl.*, 'Sparse writing' is wide open writing, occupying a large space.

2. Separated by fairly wide intervals or spaces; thinly dispersed, distributed, or scattered; placed, set, etc., here and there over a relatively extensive area; not crowded, close, or dense.

In some instances passing into the sense of 'scanty, few, meagre'.

a. *Bot.* = SCATTERED *ppl. a.* 4 a.

Also (in recent Dicts.) *Zool.* of spots, markings, etc.

1753 *Chambers' Cycl.* Suppl. s.v. *Leaf, Sparse Leaves*, those which are placed irregularly over the several parts of the plant. *c* **1789** *Encycl. Brit.* (ed. 3) III. 443 The Situation of the Parts of a Plant is..Sparse, placed without any certain order. **1866** *Treas. Bot.* 1076/2 *Sparse*, scattered, irregularly distributed.

b. Of population, an assembly, etc., or of persons composing this.

In this sense orig. *U.S.*, and commented upon as an Americanism in the *Penny Cycl.* (1833) I. 449/1.

(*a*) **1828–32** WEBSTER s.v., A sparse population. **1841** EMERSON *Ess., History* Wks. (Bohn) I. 10 A sparse population and want make every man his own valet, cook, butcher, and soldier. **1863** READE *Hard Cash* v, Next day she was at evening church: the congregation was very sparse. **1870** LUBBOCK *Orig. Civiliz.* App. 345 It is my belief that the great continents were already occupied by a wide-spread though sparse population.

(*b*) **1850** *N. & Q.* 1st Ser. I. 215/1 A sparse and hardy race of horsemen. **1879** BROWNING *Halbert & Hob* 11 Thus were they found by the few sparse folk of the country-side. **1890** *Spectator* 21 June, There are..kingdoms where the inhabitants are as 'sparse' as the Maories were when the first ship-captain landed in New Zealand.

c. Of things.

1861 J. H. BENNET *Shores of Medit.* I. i. (1875) 20 [The] Olive-tree..is often as large as a fine old oak, but with fewer limbs and a more sparse foliage. **1864** BROWNING *Dram. Pers., Gold Hair* iii, Smiles might be sparse on her cheek so spare. **1875** MISS BRADDON *Strange World* i, A man with sparse grey hair. **1884** *Fortn. Rev.* Jan. 23 Such efforts as have been made in this direction are sparse.

3. a. Characterized by wide distribution or intervals.

1801 JEFFERSON *Writ.* (1830) III. 462 The great extent of our republic is new. Its sparse habitation is new. **1861** *Press Newsp.* IX. 889/2 It was composed of matter so amazingly sparse, that the whole substance of a comet could be compressed into a single square inch of earthy matter. **1863** MARY HOWITT *F. Bremer's Greece* I. iv. 102 Nearly the whole of our way lay through sparse olive-woods. **1872** HOWELLS *Wedding Journ.* (1892) 288 The village..grows sparser as you draw near the Falls.

b. Thinly occupied or populated.

1851 NICHOL *Archit. Heav.* 267 Situated exclusively within that sparse district,..they composed but a few even of the orbs which are scattered there.

c. Characterized by sparseness or scantiness.

1871 *Echo* 23 Jan., The average German uniform is less showy than the British on account of the sparser use of gold lace. **1889** *Spectator* 14 Dec. 850 The gleaning has been somewhat sparse.

4. In adverbial use: Sparsely. Also *Comb.*

1725 ARMSTRONG *Imit. Shaks. & Spenser* Misc. 1770 I. 150 The bleak puffing winds, that seem to spit Their foam sparse thro' the welkin. **1870** J. R. LOWELL in *Atlantic Monthly* Jan. 8 And thrust far off The Heaven..To voids sparse-sown with alienated stars. **1872** BLACKIE *Lays Highl.* 162 Through the lone sparse-peopled glen. **1883** STEVENSON *Silverado Sq.* (1886) 38 A lawn, sparse planted like an orchard. **1923** D. H. LAWRENCE *Birds, Beasts, & Flowers* 172 What would they do, those..sparse-haired elephants slowly following? **1924** J. MASEFIELD *Sard Harker* III. 201 He held on across the foothills through the sparse-growing sage.

† **sparse,** *v. Obs.* Also 6 **sparce.** [f. L. *spars-*, ppl. stem of *spargĕre* to scatter, sprinkle, strew, etc. Cf. prec. and OF. *esparser*, *-cer*, MDu. *sparsen*, *spaersen* (WFlem. *spaarzen*). See also SPERSE *v.*]

1. *absol.* To distribute or scatter *abroad* in giving.

1535 COVERDALE *Ps.* cxi. 9 He hath sparsed abrode, & geuen to the poore. [So in later versions, commentaries, etc.] **1612** T. TAYLOR *Comm. Titus* i. 8 Hereby thou art like God, he sparseth abroad, he vnweariably giveth good, to good and bad. **1614** T. ADAMS in Spurgeon *Treas. Dav.* VII. 23 Sparse abroad with a full hand, like a seedsman in a broad field.

2. *trans.* To spread or disseminate (a rumour, doctrine, etc.). Freq. with *abroad.*

(*a*) **1536** *Rem. Sedition* F j, They began properly to sparse pretye rumours in the North. *a* **1572** KNOX *Hist. Ref.* Wks. 1846 I. 119 Sparsing a false bruyt, 'That the said Johnne..had broken his awin craig'. **1651** CALDERWOOD *Hist. Kirk* (1843) II. 17 Diversitie of rumors which Satan sparseth against us.

(*b*) **1548** UDALL, etc. *Erasm. Par. Acts* vi. 27 The doctrine of Christes Gospel was sparsed euery daye further abrode. **1585** FLEETWOOD in Ellis *Orig. Lett.* Ser. I. II. 298 For sparcinge abroad certen lewed, sedicious, and traytorous bookes. **1606** HIERON *Wks.* I. 47 Dangerous and infectious bookes, which..are sparsed abroad into all parts.

3. To break up, scatter, send in all directions.

1549–62 STERNHOLD & H. *Ps.* xliv. 10 Our enemies robb'd and spoyld our goods, While we were sparst abroad. **1600** FAIRFAX *Tasso* v. lxxxviii, That many Christians haue they falsly slaine, And like a raging flood they sparsed ar. *c* **1611** CHAPMAN *Iliad* XI. 268 When the hollow flood of aire, in Zephyres cheeks doth swell, And sparseth all the gatherd clouds, white Notus power did draw.

b. To dispose, sprinkle, throw, etc., in a scattered manner. Const. *into* or *upon* (something).

c **1550** H. LLOYD *Treas. Health* P v, Ashes made of a dogges head sparsyd vpon yᵉ holownes of the breste. **1614** GORGES *Lucan* II. 78 To set free the bay againe, And sparse these workes into the maine.

c. To distribute, place, etc., here and there or dispersedly *in* a book or writing. Chiefly in *pa. pple.* Also without const.

1608 PARKE *Fal Babel* B 2 b, I would not heape vp al I could saie at once, but sparse and let them fall here some and there some, the better to profit. **1608** H. CLAPHAM *Errour Left Hand* A iv b, With diuers of the heades sparsed in my Bibles briefe. **1631** R. BYFIELD *Doctr. Sabb.* 118 This hath been anciently taught, and still is sparsed in the writings of the..learned. **1657** J. WATTS *Vind. Ch. Eng.* 42 Though sparsed up and down in your Sheets.

sparsed (spɑːst), *ppl. adj.* [f. prec. + -ED[1].]

† **1.** Dispersed, scattered, spread about or abroad, etc. *Obs.*

1590 H. BARROW in Greenwood *Coll. Art.* D ij b, I haue..bene..accused, by sparsed articles, printed priuiledged books. **1600** FAIRFAX *Tasso* XII. xlvi, There the blustring winds adde strength and might, And gather close the sparsed flames about. *a* **1608** DEE *Relat. Spir.* I. (1659) 410 One..whose nether parts are in a cloud of fire, with his haire sparsed, his arms naked. **1614** GORGES *Lucan* IX. 359 Then flittes hee ouer all the maine, Where flotes the sparsed Nauies traine.

2. *Bot.* = SPARSE *a.* 2 a.

1697 *Phil. Trans.* XIX. 685 Towards the ripening of the Seed, the Burs in which they are included grow more spars'd, or at greater distance. **1725** *Fam. Dict.* s.v. *Umbel*, A sparsed or thin Umbel is, when they [*sc.* flowers] stand at a distance from one another, yet all of an equal Height. **1760** J. LEE *Introd. Bot.* (1765), *Teucrium*, with sparsed Leaves. **1853** MACDONALD & ALLAN *Botanist's Word-Bk.*, *Sparsed*, ..numerous, but without fixed order.

'sparsedly, *adv.* Now *rare.* [f. prec. + -LY[2].] In a dispersed or scattered manner; sparsely.

1570 FOXE *A. & M.* (ed. 2) I. 1/2 The which Church, because it is vniuersall, and sparsedlye through all countries dilated [etc.]. **1640** PARKINSON *Theat. Plants* 4 Branches, slenderly or sparsedly set with two narrow leaves at each joynt. **1664** EVELYN *Pomona* Pref. (1729) 53 There are doubtless many such soils sparsedly throughout this Nation. **1668** WILKINS *Real Char.* II. iv. §4. 100 That which bears larger flowers growing more sparsedly. **1889** STEVENSON *Edinb.* 140 A star or two set sparsedly in the vault of heaven.

† **'sparsedness.** *Obs.*$^{-1}$ [f. as prec.] The condition or quality of being sparsed.

1633 *Gerarde's Herbal* I. xviii. 25 This sometimes varies in the largenesse of the whole Plant, as also in the greatnesse, sparsednesse, and compactnesse of the eare.

sparsely ('spɑːslɪ), *adv.* [f. SPARSE *a.* + -LY[2].]

1. In a sparse manner; not closely or densely; thinly.

1796 MORSE *Amer. Geog.* I. 191 It grows sparsely in the N. England and middle States. **1800** *Monthly Mag.* IX. 237 The paper is sparsely written. **1851** NICHOL *Archit. Heav.* 35 Strewn comparatively sparsely through the neighbouring spaces. **1867** BAKER *Nile Trib.* xix. (1872) 327 A vast plain sparsely covered with small trees.

b. Thinly with respect to inhabitants.

1857 OLMSTED *Journ. Texas* 365 The country is sparsely settled, containing less than one inhabitant to the square mile. **1863** GEO. ELIOT *Romola* II. i, The hill was sparsely inhabited, and covered chiefly by gardens. **1879** H. GEORGE *Progr. & Pov.* II. ii. (1881) 98 The earth as a whole is yet most sparsely populated.

2. At rare or infrequent intervals of time. *rare*$^{-1}$.

1867 MRS. CARLYLE in *C. Reminis.* (1881) II. 153 In summer we had sparsely visitors, now and then her mother, or my own.

3. *Comb.* with ppl. adjs. (usually hyphened), as ***sparsely-bushed***, ***-foliaged***, ***-populated***, etc.

Freq. in recent use.

1880 SPALDING *Eliz. Demonol.* 129 The sparsely populated country sides. **1882** O'DONOVAN *Merv Oasis* I. 330 Sparsely-sprinkled gardens..tremble in the mirage. **1895** J. G. MILLAIS *Breath fr. Veldt* (1899) 300 We all knew the country—a great sparsely-bushed plain. **1897** MARY KINGSLEY *W. Africa* 587 A clump of gnarled sparsely-foliaged trees.

sparseness ('spɑːsnɪs). [f. SPARSE *a.*] The quality of being sparse; sparsity.

1833 J. STORY *Comm. Constit. U.S.* III. ix. II. 70 The concentration or sparseness of the population. **1852** NICOLAY in Visct. Ingestre *Meliora* 52 The 'sparseness', to use an Americanism, of the population. **1887** *Courier* 7 July 9/4 One advantage..resulted from the sparseness of the attendance.

'sparsile, *a. rare*$^{-0}$. [ad. late L. *sparsil-is*, f. *spars-us*: see SPARSE *v.*] Of a star: Not included in any constellation.

1891 in *Cent. Dict.*

‖**sparsim** ('spɑːsɪm), *adv.* [L.] In various places; here and there; sparsely.

1586 J. HOOKER *Conq. Irel.* Ep. Ded. in *Holinshed*, Men.. whose vertues are highlie recorded sparsim in the chronicles of England. **1626** BACON *Sylva* §839 See principally our *Abecedarium Naturæ*; And otherwise Sparsim in this in our *Sylua Syluarum.* **1733** TULL *Horse-hoeing Husb.* 71 (Dubl.), Corn standing irregular and *sparsim.* **1872** LANGE *Comment. O.T.*, *Eccl.* iii. 15. 73 It appears in the Old Testament Ps. i. 5..; Job xxi. 30..; Proverbs and Prophets sparsim.

† **'sparsion.** *Obs.*$^{-0}$ [ad. L. *sparsiōn-em*, f. *spars-us*: see SPARSE *v.*] (See quot.)

1656 BLOUNT *Glossogr.*, *Sparsion*,..a sprinkling, especially of water, coloured with Saffron out of some Pipe.

sparsity ('spɑːsɪtɪ). [f. SPARSE *a.* + -ITY.] Sparse or scattered state or condition; comparative scarcity or fewness.

1865 *Intell. Observ.* No. 37. 35 The density or sparsity of their growth. **1866** HOWELLS *Venetian Life* xx. 330 At receptions where the sparsity of the company permits the lady of the house to be seen. **1883** F. DAY *Indian Fish* 23 While the sparsity or the reverse of the population has also to be taken into account.

spar-stone. *Obs.* exc. *dial.* Also 1 **spærstan**, 2 **-ston**, 4 **sperstane**, 5 **sparre stone**. [In sense 1 repr. OE. *spærstān*: see SPAR *sb.*[2] In sense 2 directly f. the latter word.]

† **1.** Gypsum; plaster. *Obs.*

c **1000** ÆLFRIC *Voc.* in Wr.-Wülcker 146 *Creta argentea*, spærstan. *c* **1050** *Voc.* Ibid. 334 *Gipsum*, spærstan. *c* **1150** *Voc.* Ibid. 550 *Gipsum*, spærston. **1394-6** *Cartul. Abb. de Whiteby* (Surtees) 623 Item pro sperstane et ratonbrede emptis, 11 s. 11 d. **1481** in *Ripon Ch. Acts* (Surtees) 345 Usque ad quandam querruram de plaster vocatam Sparre stone.

2. A stone or rock having a crystalline appearance; quartz, spar.

1694 SALMON *Bate's Dispens.* (1713) 655/1 If you cannot get the *Lapis Judaicus*, our English Spar-stone, (which is plentiful enough in those Countries where there are Leaden-mines) may supply the place. **1880** *Cornw. Gloss.* 53 A man of penetration he, For through a spar-stone he could see.

spart[1] (spɑːt). [ad. L. *spart-um* or Sp. *esparto.* Cf. SPARTO and SPARTUM.]

1. Esparto. Also ***spart-grass***.

In quot. 1601 *ship-sparts* are simply 'cables', Pliny's *navium sparta* being a direct citation of the Homeric νεῶν σπάρτα (*Iliad* ii. 135).

1600 HOLLAND *Livy* XXII. xx. 444 They found great store of Spart (to make cables) provided and laid up there by Asdruball to serve the navie. **1601** —— *Pliny* II. 188, I wot not well whether Homer meant it, when he said, that the ship-sparts were vntwisted and loose. For this is certain, that neither the spart of Africk, ne yet the Spanish spart was as yet in any vse. **1809** tr. *Laborde's View Spain* i. 9 A plain ..fertile in flax and spart, or sea-rush. **1866** *Treas. Bot.* 1076/2 *Spart*, the Esparto. **1909** *Eng. Rev.* Feb. 462 Discussing the while the olive harvest, the price of spart-grass and the chances of the bull-ring.

¶ **2.** Spanish broom. Also ***spart-broom***. *Obs.*

1601 HOLLAND *Pliny* II. 6 The nature of Spart or Spanish broome. **1603** —— *Plutarch's Mor.* 156 The Roper.. suffereth an asse behind him to gnaw and eate a rope as fast as he twisteth it of the Spartbroome. **1611** FLORIO, *Genêstra*, Spart or Spanish-broome. **1726** LEONI *Alberti's Archit.* I. 58 Under these we ought to lay Fern, or Spart, to keep the mortar from rotting the Timber. *Ibid.* 93 Spart and rushes shred small.

spart[2] (spɑːt). *north. dial.* (and *Sc.*). [app. a metathetic form of SPRAT in the same sense.] A dwarf rush; a coarse rushy grass.

1614 *Mem. St. Giles's, Durham* (Surtees) 44 For one thrave of spartes to the Bull house. **1792** *Trans. Soc. Arts* X. 127 Wild marshy grass, rushes, sparts, bents, brambles and brushwood. **1829** BROCKETT *N.C. Gloss.* (ed. 2), *Spart*, a dwarf rush; common on the Northern moors and wastes.

† **spart**[3]. *Obs.*$^{-1}$ App. a term of abuse, of obscure origin.

c **1460** *Towneley Myst.* xii. 271 Godys forbot, thou spart, and thou drynk euery deyll.

Spartacist ('spɑːtəsɪst, -kɪst). Also **Spartakist**. [ad. G. *Spartakist*, f. *Spartakus* SPARTACUS, the name of a Thracian slave-leader in the Gladiatorial War (73–71 B.C.) against Rome, adopted as a pseudonym by K. Liebknecht (see below) in his political tracts: see -IST.] A member of a German radical socialist group formed in 1916 by Karl Liebknecht (1871–1919), Rosa Luxemburg (1870–1919), and Franz Mehring (1846–1919) and dedicated to ending the war of 1914–18 through revolution and to establishing a socialist government. Also *attrib.* or as *adj.*

1919 W. R. INGE *Outspoken Ess.* i. 18 The 'Spartacist' scoundrels who have betrayed and ruined their country. **1920** *19th Cent.* Mar. 560 The extreme Left wing of the Independents, known as Spartacists. **1925** *Contemp. Rev.* Dec. 715 The movement which a few Spartakists originated in the hope of establishing Soviet rule in Germany. **1965** *Listener* 4 Nov. 700/2 Otto Neurath..had been a member of the short-lived revolutionary Spartacist government in Munich. **1974** J. WHITE tr. *Poulantzas's Fascism & Dictatorship* IV. ii. 168 The process followed particular steps ...1918–19. Failure of the German revolution and defeat of the Spartakist militants.

So **'Spartacan** (-kən) *rare* = SPARTACIST; **'Spartacism** (-siz(ə)m, -kiz(ə)m), the policy and principles of the Spartacists.

1918 *N.Y. Times* 15 Dec. I. 3/5 Spartacism appeared in Munich openly..when 'the bloody events in Berlin and the guilt of the Government' were discussed. *Ibid.*, Premier Eisner visited the meeting and defied the Spartacan leaders. **1919** *Nation* (N.Y.) 19 Apr. 632 The Programme of the Spartacans. **1919** J. M. KEYNES *Econ. Conseq. Peace* 271 A victory of Spartacism in Germany might well be the prelude to Revolution everywhere. **1920** *Glasgow Herald* 9 Apr. 9 Spartacism in Germany is a domestic matter for the German Government to deal with.

spartacle, -icle, dial. forms of SPECTACLE.

Spartacus ('spɑːtəkəs). [See SPARTACIST.] Used *attrib.* in ***Spartacus group, league*** [tr. G. *Spartakusbund*], the Spartacists.

1918 *Spectator* 30 Nov. 607/1 The Spartacus group—the wild adherents to Liebknecht and Rosa Luxemburg. **1974** *Encycl. Brit. Macropædia* XI. 205/2 Rosa Luxemburg..in an alliance with Karl Liebknecht and other like-minded radicals..formed the..Spartacus League.

Spartakist, var. SPARTACIST.

spartalite ('spɑːtəlaɪt). *Min.* [f. *Sparta* in New Jersey, its locality, + -LITE.] Red oxide of zinc; zincite.

1843 *Penny Cycl.* XXVII. 781/2 Oxide of Zinc and Oxide of Manganese;..Spartalite.—Occurs in embedded small nodules and massive. **1856** DANA *Min.* (ed. 3) 136 Spartalite ..occurs in lamellar masses and grains of a fine deep red colour.

Spartan ('spɑːtən), *sb.* and *a.* Also 5 **Spert-**, **Spartane**, 7 **Sparton**. [ad. L. *Spartān-us*, f. *Sparta* (Gr. Σπάρτα, Σπάρτη), the capital of the ancient Doric state of Laconia in the Peloponnesus.]

A. *sb.* **1.** A native or inhabitant of Sparta; a Laconian or Lacedæmonian.

Coverdale (1535) has *Sparcians* in 1 Macc. xii, xiv.

c **1425** WYNTOUN *Cron.* IV. 825 þe Spertanys wiþe outtyn chas þar fais wyncust in þat plasse. **1432-50** tr. *Higden* (Rolls) IV. 127 Ionathas renewede frendeschippe after that with the Romanes and Spartanes. **1718** POPE *Iliad* XV. 680 The fiery Spartan..Warms the bold son of Nestor in his cause. **1770** LANGHORNE *Plutarch, Pyrrhus* III. 99 He was neither loved nor trusted by the Spartans. **1836** THIRLWALL *Greece* XV. II. 264 The Persians would not treat them less like brothers than the Spartans. **1845** MAURICE *Mor. Philos.* in *Encycl. Metrop.* II. 570/1 Terse sentences, such as the Spartan delighted in.

2. One who resembles the ancient Spartans in character.

1810 CRABBE *Borough* xviii. 194 Here nature's outrage serves no cause to aid; The ill is felt, but not the Spartan made.

B. *adj.* **1.** Of or pertaining to Sparta or its inhabitants; Laconian, Lacedæmonian.

1582 STANYHURST *Æneis* I. (Arb.) 28 In weed eke in visage lyke a Spartan virgin in armour. *c* **1611** CHAPMAN *Iliad* III. 271 Paris and the Spartan King. **1625** MILTON *On Death of fair Infant* 26 Young Hyacinth the pride of Spartan land. **1667** —— *P.L.* x. 674 The Spartan Twins [Castor and Pollux]. **1743** FRANCIS tr. *Hor.*, *Odes* II. xi. 32 With her flowing Tresses ty'd, Careless like a Spartan Bride. **1770** LANGHORNE *Plutarch* I. 144 They asked not of them.. troops, but only a Spartan general. **1835** T. MITCHELL *Acharn. of Aristoph.* 120 *note*, A word of Spartan origin. **1847** TENNYSON *Princ.* II. 263 Why should I not play The Spartan Mother with emotion?

b. ***Spartan dog***, etc., a kind of bloodhound. Also *fig.*

1590 SHAKS. *Mids. N.* IV. i. 124 My hounds are bred out of the Spartan kinde. **1604** —— *Oth.* v. ii. 361 Oh Sparton Dogge: More fell then Anguish, Hunger, or the Sea. **1697** DRYDEN *Æneid* IV. 187 The force Of Spartan dogs, and swift Massylian horse.

c. ***Spartan stone***, ? Peloponnesian marble.

a **1700** EVELYN *Diary* June 1645, Adorn'd with porphyrie, ophit, and Spartan stone.

2. Characteristic or typical of Sparta, its inhabitants, or their customs; *esp.* distinguished by simplicity, frugality, courage, or brevity of speech. (Cf. LACONIC *a.* 2.)

1644 MILTON *Areop.* (Arb.) 36 To..mollifie the Spartan surlinesse with his smooth songs and odes. **1711** STEELE *Spect.* No. 6 ¶6 The Athenians being suddenly touched with a Sense of the Spartan Virtue. **1770** LANGHORNE *Plutarch, Agis* V. 124 He kept close to the Spartan simplicity. **1781** COWPER *Expost.* 542 If some Spartan soul a doubt express'd. **1847** HELPS *Friends in C.* I. iii. 41 A man who could bear personal distress of any kind with Spartan indifference. **1885** *Times* (weekly ed.) 25 Sept. 14/4 The fare is Spartan in its extreme frugality. **1886** RUSKIN *Præterita* I. vii. 227 These Spartan brevities of epistle.

Hence **'Spartanhood**, Spartan character or qualities; **Spar'tanic** *a.*, = SPARTAN *a.* 2; **'Spartanism**, discipline, principles, or methods resembling those of Sparta; **'Spartanize** *v.*, *trans.* to render Spartan-like; to imbue with Spartan characteristics; *intr.* to act like a Spartan; **'Spartanlike**, *adv.* like a Spartan, bravely; *adj.* resembling (that of) the Spartans; **'Spartanly** *adv.*, in a Spartan manner; with great endurance, etc.

1880 MISS BROUGHTON *Second Th.* I. I. v. 67 She bears it with senseless *Spartanhood for as long as endurance is possible. **1882** J. WALKER *Jaunt to Auld Reekie* 167 His grace's phiz *Spartanic vigour shows. **1880** *Daily Tel.* 19 Feb., A mock-heroic and spurious *Spartanism. **1884** *Athenæum* 19 July 79/3 The hardy but squalid Spartanism of our older public schools. **1849** *Ainsw. Mag.* Dec. 531 Custom and fate may have *Spartanised the feelings of young ladies in garrison. **1875** BROWNING *Aristoph. Apol.* 124 He Spartanizes, argues, fasts and prates, Denies the plainest rules of life. **1883** LD. LYTTON *Life, Lett.*, etc. *Lytton* I. 102 He had high notions of discipline and prerogative, and wished to Spartanise his household. **1838** THIRLWALL *Greece* IV. xxxvi. 413 Pisander..feels *Spartan-like, sword in hand. **1900** *Daily News* 20 Jan. 6/7 A quiet, sorrowful, but Spartanlike resignation. **1890** *Pall Mall G.* 15 May 3/1 Hunters have told me how *Spartanly he will take the months of temperate discipline imposed by a hunting expedition.

spartarent, -ine: see SPATARENT.

sparteine ('spɑːtɪaɪn). Also **spartein**. [f. mod.L. *Spartium* broom: see -INE[5]. Named by Stenhouse (1851).] An alkaloid obtained from common broom, used to some extent in medicine.

1851 J. STENHOUSE in *Chem. Gaz.* IX. 117 Sparteine appears to be a strong narcotic poison, though much inferior in this respect to either nicotine or coneine. **1875** WOOD *Therapeutics* (1879) 483 Spartein paralyzes the motor nerves. **1898** *Allbutt's Syst. Med.* V. 991 Sparteine has no notable advantage over the broom tea..which contains it.

sparth[1]. *Obs.* exc. *Hist.* Also 4 **sparþe**, 4-7 (9) **sparthe**, 5 **sparreth**, 9 **sperth(e**. [ad. ON. *sparða* of obscure origin, perh. related to OHG. *partâ* (MHG. *barte*), OS. *barda* (MLG. *barde*) of the same meaning. Cf. SPAR *sb.*[5]

Sparke in Spenser *St. Ireland* Wks. (Globe) 676/1 is prob. a misreading for either *sparthe* or *sparre*.]

1. A long-handled broad-bladed battle-axe, used especially by the Irish down to the 16th century.

13.. *Gaw. & Gr. Knt.* 209 An ax in his oþer [hand], a hoge & vn-mete, A spetos sparþe to expoun in spelle quo-so myȝt. *a* **1363** HIGDEN *Polychron.* (Rolls) I. 350 Tres fratres ..usum securium, qui Anglice *sparth* dicitur, ad terram Hiberniæ comportarunt. *c* **1386** CHAUCER *Knt.'s T.* 1662 He hath a sparth of twenti pound of wighte. *a* **1400-50** *Alexander* 1403 Now a schaft, now a schild,.. Now a sparth, now a spere. *Ibid.* 2458 Sparrethis spetous to spend & speris in handis. *c* **1425** *Eng. Conq. Ireland* 16 Al, with wepne ryngynge, speres and sparthes ruthlynge to-geddre. **1530** PALSGR. 273/2 Sparthe, an instrument. **1586** J. HOOKER *Hist. Irel.* in *Holinshed* II. 33/1 The one part giuing a fierce onset with stones and spa[r]ths, & the other defending themselues with bowes and weapons. *a* **1604** HANMER *Chron. Ireland* (1809) 59 Their chiefe armes were Skeynes, Speares, Darts, Slings, and Sparthes (which we call Galloglas Axes). *Ibid.* 170 Of these and the former Norwegians, the Irish took the use of the sparthes, now called Galloglas axes. **1801** SCOTT *Eve St. John* iii, At his saddle-gerthe was a good steel sperthe.

2. *transf.* A fighting-man armed with an axe of this kind; a galloglass.

c **1518** in *Jrnl. Kilkenny Arch. Soc.* Ser. II. IV. 112 The said Brene shull finde on his propre Costes an c Sparthis of Gallogles, on his vitailles and wagges..for a quarter of a yere. **1862** *Ibid.* Note, Every Sparthe or axman was attended by four 'horse boys'.

† **sparth**[2]. *Obs.*[−1] (Meaning obscure.)

c **1480** HENRYSON *Fables, Parl. Beasts* xv, The anteloip, the sparth furth can speid.

Spartiate ('spɑːʃɪət). Also 4-5 **Sparciate**. [ad. L. *Spartiātēs*, a. Gr. Σπαρτιάτης, f. Σπάρτη Sparta.] A Spartan.

1382 WYCLIF *1 Macc.* xii. 6 Jonathas..and other peple of Jewis, to Sparciatis, bretheren, helthe. **1387** TREVISA *Higden* (Rolls) IV. 127 After þat Ionathas renewede frend-schipe.. wiþ þe Sparciates. **1609** BIBLE (Douay) *1 Macc.* xiv. 19 This is a copie of the epistles, that the Spartiates sent. **1884** tr. *Ranke's Univ. Hist.* 366 Aristotle recognises only one thousand families of the ancient Spartiates.

spartina (spɑː'taɪnə, -'tiːnə). [mod.L. (J. C. D. Schreber *Linnæus' Genera Plantarum* (ed. 8, 1789) I. 43), ad. Gr. σπαρτίνη rope.]
= RICEGRASS c.

1836 W. J. HOOKER *Compan. Bot. Mag.* II. 258 Distinguishing characters of both our British Spartinas. **1867** M. PLUES *Brit. Grasses* vii. 192 *Spartina stricta*, Smith. Cord Spartina. **1907** *Bull. Misc. Inf. R. Bot. Gardens Kew* 191 Others regard the three recognisable English Spartinas as varieties. *Ibid.* 193 These Spartina-swamps extend along each side of the river [Beaulieu]. **1925** *Jrnl. Ecol.* XIII. 83 *Spartina* is eagerly devoured by beasts of all kinds. **1934** [see GLYCERIA]. **1943** J. W. DAY *Farming Adventure* xxi. 241 Spartina grass will live and grow in salt water on mud where no other plant could exist. **1965** *Times* 31 Aug. 10/6 Spartina grass..thrives on tidal marshes. **1977** *Birds* Autumn 42/3 The fields of spartina have shrunk to spiky islands which are vanishing fast.

'spartle, *sb.* Now *dial.* Also 7 **spartel**. [Alteration of SPATTLE *sb.*[2] Cf. SPURTLE *sb.*] A spatula.

1682 G. ROSE *Sch. Instruct. Officers Mouth* 130 You may instead of a Scummer put in a Spartle. *Ibid.* 159 Keep them always stirring..with a Spoon or Spartel. **1894** HESLOP *Northumbld. Gloss.* 675 *Spartle*, a wooden spatula..used by thatchers for raising up old thatch in order to insert fresh wisps in repairing the roof.

† **spartle**, *v.*[1] *Obs.* Also **spartel-**. [Alteration of SPARPLE *v.* Cf. SPARKLE *v.*[2]] *trans.* To scatter, disperse. Hence † **'spartling** *vbl. sb.*

c **1475** *Promp. Parv.* (K.) 467/2 Spartelyn, *spergo, dispergo.* *Ibid.*, Spartelynge, sundrynge, *dissipacio.* **1483** CAXTON *Gold. Leg.* 15/2 By cause that..many skulles of heedes were there sparteled all openly they said that it was the place of calvarye.

'spartle, *v.*[2] *Sc.* [ad. (M)Du. or (M)LG. *spartelen* (also *spertelen*) in the same sense.] *intr.* To move the body or limbs in a sprawling or struggling manner.

1710 RUDDIMAN *Gloss. Douglas' Æneis, Sprinkilland*, gliding swiftly, with a tremulous motion..of their tails; Scot. Bor. call it *Spartling.* **1789** DAVIDSON *Seasons* 12 Powheads spartle in the oosy flosh. **1828** *Buchan's Ball.* II. 233 Her bonny bairn Lay spartling by her side. *a* **1878** AINSLIE *Land of Burns* (1892) 283 Our Steenie chiel began to squeal An' spartle 'mang the claes.

† **sparto**, aphetic form of ESPARTO. (Cf. SPART[1].)

1577 HOLINSHED *Descr. Scot.* 15/1 Certes such is the force of Rope made of the skinne of this fishe, that they will holde at a plunge no lesse than the Spanishe *Sparto*. **1591** PERCIVALL *Sp. Dict., Tomiza*, a kinde of small corde made of sparto.

† **sparto-statics**. [ad. mod.L. *spartostatica* (Stevinus, 1605), f. Gr. σπάρτον rope: see STATICS.] The science or study of the strength of ropes.

1672 WALLIS in Rigaud *Corr. Sci. Men* (1841) II. 531 Mr. Townley..may receive satisfaction from Stevinus in his Sparto-statics.

‖ **'spartum**. *rare.* Also 7 *erron.* **spartus**. [L.] = SPART[1].

1555 EDEN *Decades* I. II. (Arb.) 69 Certayne long and toughe rotes much lyke vnto the shrubbe called *Spartum*. **1654** R. CODRINGTON tr. *Iustine* XLIV. 514 There is also abundance of Flax and Spartus. **1673** RAY *Journ. Low C.* 458 Round thin baskets made of Spartum like frails. **1841** H. H. WILSON *Trav. Moorcroft & Trebeck in Himalayan Prov.* I. I. 10 A..swinging bridge..of the construction common in these mountains. The ropes used in its formation are made of a variety of spartum or star-three grass.

sparu, obs. form of SPARROW.

‖ **sparus** ('spɛərəs). Pl. **spari** ('spɛəraɪ). [L., ad. Gr. σπάρος. For Anglicized forms see SPAR *sb.*[8] and SPARE *sb.*[3]] A sea-bream or gilt-head.

Formerly also applied to many different fishes in some way resembling these.

1668 WILKINS *Real Char.* II. v. §5. 138 Gilt-Head, Sea-bream, Sparus. **1752** J. HILL *Hist. Anim.* 252 The silvery-eyed, red Sparus. *Ibid.* 253 The reddish Sparus,..the Sea-bream. **1753** *Chambers' Cycl.* Suppl. s.v., Of the *spari* some have acute and cylindric teeth. **1777** G. FORSTER *Voy. round World* II. 171 They also brought..a fine well-tasted sparus ready dressed in leaves. **1803** SHAW *Gen. Zool.* IV. II. 403 Silvery-blueish Sparus, with gold-coloured brows. *Ibid.* 407 Yellowish Sparus. **1836** YARRELL *Brit. Fishes* I. 111 The four-toothed Sparus, *dentex vulgaris.*

sparuwe, obs. form of SPARROW.

† **'sparver**. *Obs.* Forms: α. 5 **spervyr, spervier, speruer**, 5-7 (9) **sperver**, 6 **spurver**. β. 5-7 (9) **sparver**, 5 *Sc.* **sparwort**, 6 **sparuiour, sparuer, sparvill**, 6-7 **sparvar**. [ad. OF. *espervier* (*esprevier*) 'l'ensemble des pièces qui composent le coucher' (1380 in Godefroy), = obs. It. *sparviere, -eri, -ero.* The forms are those of the OF. and It. names for the sparrow-hawk (see SPERVER), but the connexion is not obvious.] A canopy for a bed (or cradle).

α. **1440-1** *Durh. Acc. Rolls* (Surtees) 627 Et solut. pro j. sperver empt. apud London pro d'no Priore. **1480** *Wardr. Acc. Edw. IV* (1830) 129 Sperver of rede damask with curtyns of sarsynett. **1501** *Bury Wills* (Camden) 91 It[em] a sperver of sylke. **1519** *N. Cy. Wills* (Surtees, 1908) 106 A sperver of whyte with a coverlete.

β. **1444** *Test. Ebor.* (Surtees) II. 112 A sparver w[t] coueryn of lynnyn clothe. **1473-4** *Acc. Ld. High Treas. Scot.* I. 41 For iiij½ elne of tartar for a sparwort abone his creddil. **1494** in *Lett. Rich. III & Hen. VII* (Rolls) I. 390 The parlement chambre, where wer..beddes wiche hadden sparvers. **1519** HORMAN *Vulg.* 167 b, Some haue curteynes: some sparuers aboute the bedde to kepe awey gnattis. **1591** HARINGTON *Orl. Fur.* v. 39 A happie woman..hath as quiet sleeps..in a bed of cloth as vnder a sparuer of tissue. *a* **1612** —— *Epigr.* (1633) IV. vi, At home in silken sparvers, beds of down, We scant can rest. **1641** *Invent.* in *Burlington Mag.* (1911) Nov. 100/1 A greate Sparver round about over the Bed.

b. *fig.* and *transf.*

c **1640** A. TOWNSHEND *Poems & Masks* (1912) 24 Thy sparver, a well tufted tree, Ore heaven itselfe, thy canopy. **1688** HOLME *Armoury* III. 449/2 The several names given to these Moveing Houses... A Tent, or a Sperver. A Hutt. A Booth [etc.].

c. *attrib.*, as ***sparver bed, curtain, tester.*** Also *Comb.*, as ***sparver-wise*** adv.

1475 *Bury Wills* (Camden) 251 A white bedde made sparverwyse. **1501** *Ibid.* 135, vj payre shetes wyth the sparver curtanys of dornykes. **1596** *Unton Invent.* (1841) 4, j sparvill tester of silk. **1610** *Althorp MS.* in Simpkinson *Washingtons* (1860) App. p. ii, One half hed bedsted for a sparvar bed. **1611** COTGR. s.v. *Parement, Lict de parement*,.. a bed of State, or, a great Sparuer bed.

† **sparvise**, *sb. Obs.* [Alteration of prec.] (See quots.) Hence † **sparvise** *v. Obs.*

1598 FLORIO, *Capoletto*,..the sparuise or vallance of a bed. **1611** *Ibid.*, *Cortinággio*, the curtaines or valance, or sparuis, or vailing of a bed or window. *Ibid.*, *Sparuierare*,.. to sparuise a bed or chamber.

sparviter: see SPERVITER *Obs.*

sparwe, obs. form of SPARROW.

† **'spary**, *a. Obs.* Also **sparie**. [f. SPARE *v.*[1] Cf. MDu. and MLG. *sparich*, MHG. *sperig* (obs. G. *spärig, sparig*).] = SPARING *ppl. a.* in various senses.

Peculiar to Holland, and frequent in his works.

1601 HOLLAND *Pliny* II. 25 Very scant and sparie of seed. *Ibid.* 387 They wil indure so a long time,..with abstinence and spary feeding. **1606** —— *Sueton.* 158 But in honouring himselfe he was sparie and caried a civile modestie. **1632** —— *Cyrupædia* 4 They instruct them to bee spary in their meats and drinks.

spas, var. SPAZ.

spasm ('spæz(ə)m), *sb.* Also 5-7 **spasme**. [a. OF. *spasme* (F. *spasme*, = Prov. *espasme*, Sp. and Pg. *espasmo*, It. *spasmo, spasimo*), or ad. L. *spasmus* masc., *spasma* neut., a. Gr. σπασμός, σπάσμα, f. σπᾶν to draw, tug, etc. Cf. SPASMA and SPASMUS.]

1. Sudden and violent muscular contraction of a convulsive or painful character.

c **1400** *Lanfranc's Cirurg.* 160 þanne it is greet drede of þe spasme & aftirward of deeþ,..þe akynge arisiþ vp to þe brayn, & þanne comeþ spasme. **1601** HOLLAND *Pliny* II. 41 It cureth those who have their necks drawne backward to their shoulders with the Spasme. **1667** MILTON *P.L.* XI. 481 All maladies Of gastly Spasm, or racking torture. **1670** COVEL in *Early Voy. Levant* (Hakluyt Soc.) 140 He had very oft (almost every minute) a strange kind of spasme in the muscles of his breast. **1753** *Chambers' Cycl.* Suppl. s.v., The spasm is a much less dangerous complaint than the convulsion. **1799** *Med. Jrnl.* I. 49 The first species of spasm in the stomach originates from extreme debility..and atony in that organ. **1845** BUDD *Dis. Liver* 382 Spasm of the gall-ducts is..something more than a mere hypothesis. **1876** BRISTOWE *Th. & Pract. Med.* (1878) 479 Spasm of the larynx and trachea... Spasm is chiefly known as causing contraction of the rima glottidis.

2. With *a* and pl. An instance of this; a convulsive twitch or throe.

c **1477** CAXTON *Jason* 76 b, She fyll on the erthe al in a spasme and a swoune. **1543** TRAHERON *Vigo's Chirurg.* III. 90 b/1 For the prohibition of a spasme ye shal rubbe often the nuke or marye of the backebone. **1601** HOLLAND *Pliny* Expl. Wds. Art, *Spasmes*, be painefull crampes or pluckings of the sinewes and cords of the Muscles. **1652** CULPEPPER *Eng. Physic.* 79 Such persons as have their bodies drawn together by some Spasme or Convulsion. **1681** tr. *Willis's Rem. Med. Wks.* Vocab., *Spasms*, cramps or convulsions of the nerves. **1718** QUINCY *Compl. Disp.* 112 Such Parts likewise draw the Fibres into Spasms, and keep them too tense. **1756** BURKE *Subl. & B.* IV. xxi, Water is found, when not cold, to be a great resolver of spasms. **1804** ABERNETHY *Surg. Obs.* 178 He came again to the hospital complaining of spasms in his left arm. **1839** DICKENS *Nickleby* iii, Newman's face was curiously twisted as by a spasm. **1891** FARRAR *Darkn. & Dawn* iv, The swollen form of the Emperor heaved with the spasm of a last struggle.

3. *fig.* Any sudden or convulsive movement of a violent character; a convulsion:

a. Of natural agencies or forces.

1817 SHELLEY *Rev. Islam* IX. v, As with an earthquake's spasm. **1860** EMERSON *Cond. Life, Power* Wks. (Bohn) II. 334 Red republicanism, in the father, is a spasm of nature to engender an intolerable tyrant in the next age. **1909** *Contemp. Rev.* Feb. 156 Here is a problem more terrible than any spasm of nature.

b. Of feeling, emotion, etc.

1837 CARLYLE *Fr. Rev.* II. v. ii, In utmost preternatural spasm of madness. **1860** EMERSON *Cond. Life, Power* Wks. (Bohn) II. 340 So in human action, against the spasm of energy we offset the continuity of drill. **1874** SYMONDS *Sk. Italy & Greece* (1898) I. x. 200 A mere spasm of suspicious jealousy. **1880** MEREDITH *Tragic Com.* (1881) 294 He caused her a spasm of anguish.

c. Of political excitement, etc.

1862 CARLYLE *Fred. Gt.* VI. ix. (1872) II. 219 War in Italy, universal spasm of wrestle there. **1879** FROUDE *Cæsar* xxvi. 437 The fears which the final spasm of rebellion had again provoked. **1891** FARRAR *Darkn. & Dawn* lxvi, As for the succeeding Emperors, the spasm of their brief elevation was marked by universal horrors.

4. Special Combs., as **spasm band** *U.S.* (now *Hist.*), a group, freq. of children, playing jazz on home-made musical instruments; **spasm music** *U.S.* (now *Hist.*), music played by spasm bands; **spasm war**, a war in which the combatants use their complete thermo-nuclear capabilities.

1926 WHITEMAN & MCBRIDE *Jazz* xiii. 267 When the last fearful note died, he turned to the leader. 'Stale Bread,' said he [*sc.* a judge], 'you may be a band, but you're a *spasm band. Discharged.' The name stuck and the spasm band went on playing. **1943** I. LANG *Background of Blues* 4 Then there were the spasm bands... The saloons and sidewalks where spasm music and street singers found their most generous audiences were those of the French Quarter and particularly those in Storyville. **1964** HALL & WHANNEL *Pop. Arts* x. 297 In the early decades of the century the 'spasm bands' played a kind of home-made jazz on improvised instruments. **1943** *Spasm music [see *spasm band* above]. **1965** H. KAHN *On Escalation* i. 14 But we need alternatives other than all-out *spasm war or peace at any price. **1967** M. H. HALPERIN *Contemp. Mil. Strategy* (1968) ii. 15 The assumption that a general nuclear war between the United States and the Soviet Union would be an all-out, or 'spasm' war.

spasm ('spæz(ə)m), *v.* [f. the sb.]

a. *intr.* To twitch convulsively; to suffer a spasm. **b.** *trans.* To cause to move convulsively. *rare.*

1900 W. D. HOWELLS *Lit. Friends & Acquaintances* viii. 269 Of a person who had a nervous twitching of the face.. he [*sc.* Henry James Sr.] said 'He *spasmed* to the fellow across the room and introduced him.' **1958** 'W. HENRY' *Seven Men at Mimbres Springs* xii. 142 Frank's gun fell from his spasming fingers. **1962** J. D. MACDONALD *Key to Suite* (1968) ix. 152 He spasmed his body inward, dropped the few remaining inches and landed on the railing. **1970** J. HANSEN *Fadeout* ix. 74 The boy's fine head did its slow, neck-straining roll while the unexpectedly deep voice spasmed and his mouth labored. **1978** J. IRVING *World according to Garp* xv. 304 The prostrate pig..squealed, its short legs spasmed.

‖ **'spasma**. *Obs.* [L. *spasma*, Gr. σπάσμα: see SPASM *sb.*] = SPASM *sb.* 1 and 2.

1541 R. COPLAND *Guydon's Quest. Chirurg.* A iiij, There must he begyn,..for daunger of the spasna [*sic*], which is moste peryllous. **1625** PURCHAS *Pilgrims* I. v. 662 A violent Feuer and Spasma. **1670** J. SMITH *Eng. Improv. Reviv'd* 246 If it fill the Nerves of the Muscles only it becomes the Spasma, or Convulsion. **1728** CHAMBERS *Cycl.* s.v., There are Spasma's peculiar to certain Members, and distinguished by particular Names.

† **spasmadrap**. *Obs.* [app. f. med.L. *spasma* a healing powder (Du Cange) + F. *drap* cloth: cf. SPARADRAP.] A medical plaster.

c **1540** in *Vicary's Anat.* (1888) App. IX. 222 Make thereof a plaster, or a spasmadrappe. [**1826** HORACE SMITH *Tor Hill* I. 106 He [a friar] carried divers pills, spasmadraps, cordials, and drops for his adult patients.]

spas'matic, *a.* Now *rare* or *Obs.* [ad. obs. F. *spasmatique* (Cotgr.), or f. Gr. σπασματ-, stem of σπάσμα spasm + -IC.]

1. Spasmodic.

1603 HOLLAND *Plutarch's Mor.* 124 Anger..resembleth not..the sinewes of the soule, but is like rather to their stretching spreines and spasmatick convulsions. **1746** R. JAMES *Moufet's Health Improv.* 13 Pains, Flatulencies, and spasmatic Contractions of the Intestines. **1824** *Examiner* 548/1 Seized with spasmatic lameness.

2. Liable to, or suffering from, spasms.

1601 HOLLAND *Pliny* II. 44 It is a soveraigne remedie for them that bee bursten or Spasmaticke, that is to say, vexed with the Crampe.

So **spas'matical** *a.* Now *rare.*

c **1645** HOWELL *Lett.* II. xx, The ligaments and sinews of my love..wer never yet subject to such spasmatical shrinkings and Convulsions. **1650** ELDERFIELD *Civ. Right Tythes* 89 Many a paralytical or spasmatical fit. **1879** G. MACDONALD *P. Faber* II. ix. 172 The spirit of life is at war with the spasmatical body of death.

,spasmato'mancy. [f. Gr. σπασματο-, combining form of σπάσμα spasm + -MANCY.] (See quot. 1855.)

1855 SMEDLEY *Occult Sci.* 296 Spasmatomancy..is properly a part of medicine, for it is the art of foretelling from convulsive twitchings of the limbs diseases by which a man is about to be attacked. **1885** *Encycl. Brit.* XIX. 4/2 The treatises also contain occasional digressions on.. podoscopy, spasmatomancy, &c.

spasmed ('spæz(ə)md), *a.* [f. SPASM *sb.* + -ED[2].] Affected with, accompanied by, spasms.

1787 *Generous Attachm.* IV. 148 Now I suppose you are absent again; quite spasmed, quite lame, cracked from head to foot. **1790** J. BYNG *Jrnl.* 27 Aug. in *Torrington Diaries* (1935) II. 284 Otherwise I feel myself very low, and enfeebled, relaxed by day, and spasm'd by night. **1831** YOUATT *Horse* viii. 118 The painful and spasmed stretching of this part. **1845** —— *Dog* vi. 123 The dog had lain slightly spasmed for two or three days.

spasmic ('spæzmɪk), *a.* [f. SPASM *sb.* + -IC.] Spasmodic; convulsive.

1710 T. FULLER *Pharm. Extemp.* 301 The breaking off of a spasmic Paroxysme. **1868** WHITMAN *Chants Democratic* Poems 118 The slender, spasmic blue-white jets. **1894** A. MORRISON *Mean Streets* 66 A pale little fellow with a nasty spasmic cough.

spasmodic (spæz'mɒdɪk), *a.* and *sb.* [ad. med. or mod.L. *spasmodicus*, f. Gr. σπασμώδης, f. σπασμός or σπάσμα: see SPASM. So F. *spasmodique*, It. *spasmodico*, Sp. and Pg. *espasmodico*.]

A. *adj.* **1.** Of the nature of a spasm; characterized by spasms or convulsive twitches; marked by jerkiness or suddenness of muscular movement.

a. *spec.* in *Path.*

1681 tr. *Willis's Rem. Med. Wks.* Vocab., *Spasmodic*, belonging to the cramp or convulsion, or hauling of the sinews. **1728** CHAMBERS *Cycl.* s.v., Hunger..is a Spasmodic Affection of the Fibres of the Stomach. **1786** MISS CLAYTON in *Corr. Mrs. Delany* (1862) Ser. II. III. 415 Mrs. Clayton.. is extremely ill with spasmodic convulsions on her lungs. **1799** *Med. Jrnl.* II. 155 An attorney..was during several days afflicted..with spasmodic colics. **1811** A. T. THOMSON *Lond. Disp.* (1818) 101 The use of ipecacuan in spasmodic asthma. **1842** COMBE *Digestion* 334 This actually happens in spasmodic cholera. **1878** T. BRYANT *Pract. Surg.* I. 591 Spasmodic stricture is usually met with in the young.

b. In general use.

1836-7 DICKENS *Sk. Boz* (1850) 199/1 He had..a somewhat spasmodic expression of countenance. **1851** CARPENTER *Man. Phys.* (ed. 2) 606 Sometimes..the spasmodic action occurs in the pronunciation of vowels, and continuous consonants. **1884** *Marshall's Tennis Cuts* 191, I was startled by his firing at me, as it were a series of spasmodic winks.

2. Employed against spasms; antispasmodic.

1728 CHAMBERS *Cycl.*, *Spasmodic*, something belonging to a Spasm, or Convulsion; as a Spasmodic Medicine.

3. Occurring or proceeding by fits and starts; irregular, intermittent; not sustained or kept up.

1837 CARLYLE *Fr. Rev.* I. II. iii, But indeed may we not regret that such conflict..should usually be so spasmodic? **1856** FROUDE *Hist. Eng.* (1858) II. viii. 243 Acquiescence in disorder would be followed by a spasmodic severity. **1874** STUBBS *Const. Hist.* I. vii. 199 The spasmodic efforts of the Northumbrian Danes were checked.

4. Convulsively furious or violent.

1840 CARLYLE *Heroes* (1858) 288 A noble strength, very different from spasmodic violence. **1866** R. W. DALE *Disc. Spec. Occasions* x. 334 They mistake spasmodic vehemence for strength.

5. Agitated, excited; emotional, high-strung; given to outbursts of excitement; characterized by a disjointed or unequal style of expression.

Spasmodic School, a name given by W. E. Aytoun to a group of poets chiefly represented by Alexander Smith, Philip James Bailey, and Sydney Dobell.

1832 CARLYLE *Let.* 28 Aug. (1977) VI. 211 Were I of the spasmodic School, I could gnash my teeth, now and then, over such a banishment: but..I reflect rather what deluges of Folly and Falsehood I stand safe from. **1848** DICKENS *Dombey* i, Miss Tox immediately became spasmodic. **1854** AYTOUN in *Blackw. Mag.* May 534/1 Let us see what is the practice of the poets of the Spasmodic School. **1865** *Cornh. Mag.* May 640 We would..ask them if they would not desire to see their daughters brought up in a simpler, less spasmodic..and morbid way?

absol. **1861** READE *Cloister & H.* lxi, I would be prose laureat, or professor of the spasmodic, or something, in no time.

B. *sb.* †**1.** *pl.* (See quot.) *Obs.*$^{-0}$

1704 J. HARRIS *Lex. Techn.* I, *Spasmodicks*, are Medicines against Convulsions.

2. *pl.* Spasmodic utterances or ejaculations.

1865 *Sat. Rev.* 11 Nov. 617 Mr. Porter's heroics and spasmodics are only excusable on the supposition that they are intended for a class of readers..who rejoice in Watts's Divine and Moral Songs.

spas'modical, *a.* [-AL[1].] = SPASMODIC *a.*

1766 SMOLLETT *Trav.* I. iii. 23, I knew there was no imposthume in my lungs, and I supposed the stitches were spasmodical. **1864** *Daily Tel.* 29 June, M. von Bismarck, who..made spasmodical exertions to prevent the Diet kindling into martial indignation.

Hence **spas'modicalness**.

1881 BROOKS *Candle of Lord* 130 There are two ideas which belong to the notion of vast power... One is spasmodicalness and the other is waste.

spasmodically (spæz'mɒdɪkəlɪ), *adv.* [-LY[2].]

1. *Path.* By means of, with the accompaniment of, a spasm or spasms.

1710 T. FULLER *Pharm. Extemp.* 251 The use of this [julep] is indicated..when the Spirits..are spasmodically exploded. **1763** *Phil. Trans.* LIII. 11 The Temporal and Masseter muscles..were tense, hard, and spasmodically affected. **1814** J. BURNS *Princ. Midwifery* (ed. 3) 391 The uterus may contract spasmodically. **1879** *St. George's Hosp. Rep.* IX. 683 On attempting to take fluids, they..were.. spasmodically rejected.

2. In a jerky or sudden manner.

1839 DICKENS *Nickleby* xl, Poor Noggs..moved spasmodically in his chair. **1864** F. W. ROBINSON *Mattie, a Stray* III. 114 Causing innumerable articles in the glass cases thereon to jump spasmodically with the shock.

b. With convulsive effort or violence.

1840 CARLYLE *Heroes* (1858) 276 A human soul is seen clinging spasmodically to an Ark of the Covenant. **1851** DE QUINCEY *Ld. Carlisle on Pope* Wks. 1859 XIII. 27 Pope obeyed, spasmodically, an overmastering febrile paroxysm. **1880** FLOR. MARRYAT *Fair Alda* II. i. 23 She clung to him spasmodically.

3. By fits and starts; irregularly, intermittently.

1878 HUXLEY *Physiogr.* 190 The steam generally issues spasmodically. **1882** *Standard* 30 Dec. 2/2 If rates went up for a few days they did so spasmodically. **1897** MARY KINGSLEY *W. Africa* 599 The men then gradually go off to sleep, breaking out now and again spasmodically into little rows over a pipe.

spasmodism ('spæzmədɪz(ə)m). [f. SPASMOD-IC *a.* + -ISM.] Spasmodic feeling or emotion.

1878 T. SINCLAIR *Mount* 242 Spasmodism is a true stage in the growth of a first spirit. **1883** *Mem. Vol. Rev. A. Maclean* 231 A curious mixture of mediæval rigidity and modern spasmodism.

spasmodist ('spæzmədɪst). [f. SPASMOD-IC *a.* + -IST.] One whose work is of a spasmodic character or who affects a spasmodic style; a writer of the 'spasmodic school'.

a **1849** POE *Marginalia* Wks. 1864 III. 505 De Meyer and the rest of the spasmodists. **1854** *Tait's Mag.* XXI. 557 The fine frenzies of the noble new school of Spasmodists. **1878** T. SINCLAIR *Mount* 242 Here is the pitfall of the whole school of spasmodists who would make poetry wild 'speaking i' the air'.

†**'spasmodized**, *ppl. a.* *Obs.*$^{-1}$ [Irreg. f. SPASMODIC *a.*] Affected with spasms.

1819 *Metropolis* I. 219 Lady Mildew had recourse to her aromatic vinegar: she was quite spasmodized.

spasmogen ('spæzmədʒən). *Pharm.* [Back-formation from next.] A spasmogenic drug.

1952 *Brit. Jrnl. Pharmacol. & Chemotherapy* VII. 91 There was little differentiation between the degrees of inhibition of..the 'direct' acting spasmogens, as compared with that shown by atropine. **1961** *Jrnl. Pharm. & Pharmacol.* XIII. 446 Common spasmogens such as histamine and 5-HT. **1974** *Nature* 4 Oct. 427/2 The response of the ileum to spasmogens varied widely at different times of the year.

spasmogenic (spæzməʊ'dʒɛnɪk), *a.* [f. SPASM + -O + -GENIC.] †**1.** *Med.* (See quot.) *Obs.*

1899 CHURCH & PETERSON *Nervous & Mental Dis.* VII. vi. 546 If such a hyperesthetic zone arises from or becomes associated with some mental storm, pressure upon it may serve to revive the memories in question and provoke a hysterical fit. It is then denominated a spasmogenic or hysterogenic point or zone.

2. *Pharm.* Of a drug or other substance: promoting the contraction of smooth muscle.

1913 *Chem. Abstr.* VII. 3163 KCl has definit[e] spasmogenic properties in children. **1942** *Jrnl. Pharmacol. & Exper. Therapeutics* LXXIV. 275 Papaverine antagonizes the spasmogenic agents equally. **1975** *Nature* 13 Mar. 151/2 It can block the spasmogenic effects of 5-HT on the smooth muscle of isolated guinea pig ileum.

†**spas'mology.** *Obs.*$^{-0}$ [ad. mod.L. *spasmologia*. So F. *spasmologie*.] (See quots.)

1681 tr. *Willis's Rem. Med. Wks.* Vocab., *Spasmology*, the doctrine of the convulsion or cramp of the sinews. **1823** CRABB *Technol. Dict.* II, *Spasmology*, a discourse or treatise on spasms. [Hence in later Dicts.]

spasmolytic (spæzmə'lɪtɪk), *a.* and *sb.* *Pharm.* [f. SPASM + -O + -LYTIC.]

A. *adj.* That relieves spasm of smooth muscle.

1937 *Jrnl. Pharmacol. & Exper. Therapeutics* LX. 13 The spasmolytic action of Syntropan exerted through the nerve endings on the isolated rabbit intestine is only about 20 times less than that of Atropine. **1953** [see SERPASIL]. **1964** W. G. SMITH *Allergy & Tissue Metabolism* iv. 56 The effects of high dosage include ganglionic blockage and spasmolytic activity. **1982** *Jrnl. Med. Chem.* XXV. 1358/2 Some of these compounds have intensive spasmolytic activity for colonic motility.

B. *sb.* A spasmolytic drug.

1937 *Brit. Med. Jrnl.* 11 Sept. 560/1 The employment of spasmolytics in obstetrics is useful. **1978** *Acta Neurol. Scandinavica* LVII. 65 The drug is..capable of depressing distressing clonus, and it is concluded that it deserves further testing as a spasmolytic.

Hence **spas'molysis**, the action of such drugs.

1946 *Biol. Abstr.* XX. 1122/1 Although the compounds.. have some papaverine-like action on smooth muscle, spasmolysis results largely from their anticholinergic action. **1964** *Jrnl. Amer. Geriatric Soc.* XII. 1083 *(heading)* Spasmolysis: a new technique for treatment of spasticity. **1977** *Scandinavian Jrnl. Respiratory Dis.* Suppl. No. 98. 47 *(heading)* Sensitization of contracted tracheal smooth muscle to β-adrenergic spasmolysis by subthreshold doses of papaverine.

spasmoneme ('spæzməʊniːm). *Zool.* [ad. G. *spasmonem* (G. Entz 1892, in *Math. und naturwissensch. Berichte aus Ungarn* X. 27), f. Gr. σπασμό-ς pulling, convulsion + νῆμ-α thread.] One of the three strands in the stalk of a vorticellid whose sudden contraction causes the stalk to coil tightly, withdrawing the animal from possible danger.

1901 [see AXONEME]. **1941** BEAMS & KING in Calkins & Summers *Protozoa in Biol. Res.* ii. 94 The spasmoneme does not function like a true muscle but like a modified flagellum. **1978** *Jrnl. Cell Biol.* LXXVII. 358/2 Within the stalk is the contractile organelle, often referred to as the myoneme, though the term spasmoneme is preferable since recent studies indicate that the organelle is biochemically distinct from the myosin- and actin-based contractile systems.

spasmophilia (spæzməʊ'fɪlɪə). *Path.* [f. SPASM + -O + -PHILIA.] Undue tendency of the muscles to contract, *esp.* as caused by a deficiency of systemic calcium.

1859 R. G. MAYNE *Expos. Lex. Med. Sci.* 1177/2 *Spasmophilia*, an epithet by Jos. Frank applied to erratic, spasmodic affections. **1892** D. H. TUKE *Dict. Psychol. Med.* II. 843/1 Hyperæsthesia, with the corresponding hyperkinesis, spasmophilia or convulsions, is the principal symptom of spinal irritation. **1907** *Brit. Jrnl. Children's Dis.* IV. 448 J. Zahorsky includes tetany, carpal spasm, carpopedal spasm, laryngospasm and eclampsia, under the name of spasmophilia. **1953** J. H. EBBS in Gaisford & Lightwood *Paediatrics* I. xxxix. 436 Spasmophilia can be defined as an increased excitability of the neuro-muscular junction. **1976** *Roumanian Jrnl. Med. Endocrinol.* XIV. 249 Normocalcemic spasmophilia is not recognized as a morbid entity but as a minor symptom often associated to neurosis.

Hence **'spasmophile** *rare*$^{-1}$, one who suffers from spasmophilia; **spasmo'philic** *a.*, of, pertaining to, or suffering from spasmophilia.

1908 *Med. Rec.* (N.Y.) 30 May 903/1 The theory..that spasmophilic diathesis is a form of latent tetany. **1930** *Jrnl. Amer. Med. Assoc.* 22 Feb. 525/1 The calcium and inorganic phosphate tended toward spasmophilic levels. **1938** S. BECKETT *Murphy* 49 That schizoidal spasmophile. **1941** *Amer. Jrnl. Dis. Children* LXI. 376 *(heading)* Presentation of a spasmophilic newborn infant.

'spasmous, *a.* *rare*$^{-1}$. [f. SPASM *sb.* + -OUS. Cf. OF. *spasmeux*.] Characterized by spasms.

1559 *Mirr. Mag.* (1563) M ij, That loathed leach, that never wellcum death, Through spasmous humours stopped vp his breth. **1859** MAYNE *Expos. Lex.* 1177/1 *Spasmodes*, having or full of spasm or convulsion; spasmous.

‖**'spasmus.** *Obs.* Pl. spasmi. [L. *spasmus*, a. Gr. σπασμός.] = SPASM *sb.*

c **1400** *Lanfranc's Cirurg.* 357 The xv. c^o is of spasmus. **1591** JAS. I *Poet. Exerc.*, *Furies* D ij, Els Spasmus..strait doth holde The Senewes of weake Adam. **1597** A. M. tr. *Guillemeau's Fr. Chirurg.* 2 b/2 If into anye woundes anye Spasmus happen, that is a bad signe. **1657** G. STARKEY *Helmont's Vind.* 266 The Pleuresie is a most dangerous Feaver, with a Spasmus or Convulsion of the side. **1728** CHAMBERS *Cycl.* s.v., A Spasmus happening after the taking of Hellebore..is mortal. *Ibid.*, Accidental Spasmi are of little Continuance.

spasmy ('spæzmɪ), *a.* [f. SPASM *sb.* + -Y[1].] Affected by spasms.

a **1849** MANGAN *Poems* (1903) 168 Twitching A spasmy face From side to side with a grace Bewitching.

spastic ('spæstɪk), *a.* and *sb.* [ad. L. *spastic-us* (Pliny), a. Gr. σπαστικός, f. σπᾶν to draw: cf. SPASM *sb.* So F. *spastique*.]

A. *adj.* **1.** *Path.* Of the nature of a spasm or sudden contraction; characterized or affected by spasmodic symptoms or movements.

1753 *Chambers' Cycl.* Suppl. s.v. *Gout*, The *podagra* in particular is thus defined to be a spastic and painful affection of the foot. **1755** *Phil. Trans.* XLIX. 243 To compose these spastic motions of the parts. **1822-7** GOOD *Study Med.* (1829) I. 318 The graft of a spastic disease upon a spastic temperament. **1878** HAMILTON *Nervous Dis.* 155 There are occasionally spastic contractions, which last for some little time. **1899** *Allbutt's Syst. Med.* VI. 314 Amentia, in association with..spastic limbs.

b. *spec.* in names of special ailments. *spastic paralysis*, a condition in which some muscles undergo tonic spasm (sometimes resulting in abnormal posture) and resist passive displacement, so that voluntary movement of the part affected is difficult and poorly co-ordinated.

1822-7 GOOD *Study Med.* (1829) IV. 334 Spastic wry-neck. From excess of muscular action on the contracted side. **1876** tr. *Wagner's Gen. Path.* 340 Spastic anæmia of the small and smallest arteries. **1877** tr. W. Erb in *London Med. Rec.* V. 435/1 (*heading*) On spastic spinal paralysis (tabes dorsal spasmodique, Charcot). **1879** *Glasgow Med. Jrnl.* XI. 147 (*heading*) Paraplegia, with great muscular rigidity (Erb's spastic paralysis?). **1889** [see PALSY *sb.* (*a.*) 1 b]. **1891** *Lancet* 15 Aug. 354/1 Among the cases of apparent cure.. were cases of spastic paralysis. **1903** TUBBY & JONES *Surg. Paralyses* II. 203 Examples of Little's disease or spastic paralysis. **1937** E. KENNY *Infantile Paralysis & Cerebral Diplegia* viii. 92 In spastic paralysis, if the patient is asked to do something with the fingers, all the muscles controlling the fingers, as well as all the other muscles of the forearm and those of the arm and shoulder girdle, go into spastic contraction. **1938**, etc. [see LITTLE'S DISEASE]. **1954** S. DUKE-ELDER *Parsons' Dis. Eye* (ed. 12) xxix. 586 Spastic entropion is due to spasm of the orbicularis. **1973** W. BARLOW *Alexander Principle* ix. 141 The diagnosis of 'spastic colon' is very often accompanied by such unnoticed abdominal misuse. **1977** *Lancet* 22 Oct. 844/2 He was hypertonic, with mild spastic diplegia.

2. Performing involuntary contractile movements.

1822-7 GOOD *Study Med.* (1829) IV. 576 Such has been the force of the spastic muscles. **1834** *Good's Study Med.* (ed. 4) IV. 144 The contraction was here a spastic ring bordering immediately on the orifice of the uterus.

3. a. Affected with spastic paralysis.

1903 TUBBY & JONES *Mod. Methods Surgery of Paralyses* II. 228 Transformation of the pronator radii teres and transplantation of the carpal flexors were effected in spastic children. **1937** P. M. GIRARD *Home Treatment Spastic Paralysis* i. 10 As a spastic child later learns to walk, a typical 'scissors gait' is frequently observed. **1977** *Whitaker's Almanack 1978* 26 (Advt.), Jonathan has been severely spastic since birth, and is unable to walk unsupported. He also has difficulty with speaking and writing.

b. In weakened use: uncoordinated, incompetent; foolish, stupid. *slang.*

1981 [see sense b of the sb., below]. **1982** BARR & YORK *Official Sloane Ranger Handbk.* 159/3 *Spastic*, temporarily unintelligent. Sloanes don't consider lack of intelligence should be insulted; one, they are basically kind; two, they are unintellectual themselves.

B. *sb.* **a.** A person with spastic paralysis.

1896 *Pediatrics* II. 194 The staggering, uncertain gait of the spastic, often with knees striking or actually crossed, with knees flexed and heels raised, is well known. **1937** E. R. CARLSON in P. M. Girard *Home Treatment Spastic Paralysis* p. xix, Through repeated exercises.. the spastic gradually acquires muscular coordination. **1953** M. MCCARTHY *Groves of Academe* ii. 22 The male part of the college included an unusual number of child prodigies,.. as well as some spastics and paraplegics. **1976** *National Observer* (U.S.) 25 Sept. 21/1 Christy Brown, you will remember, is the Dubliner.. and almost total spastic who, a few years ago, with his left foot tapped out a novel. **1978** R. B. SCOTT *Price's Textbk. Pract. Med.* (ed. 12) XVI. 1347/2 Even with the most skilled and sympathetic management, the emotional needs and problems of the 'spastic' and of the immediate family may present insoluble problems.

b. In weakened use, esp. contemptuously: one who is uncoordinated or incompetent; a fool. Cf. SPAZ. *slang.*

Although current for some fifteen years or more, it is generally condemned as a tasteless expression, and is not common in print.—R.W.B.

1981 R. A. SPEARS *Slang & Euphemism* 369 *Spastic*, (1) a jerk; a giddy person..; (2) pertaining to a blunderer.

Hence **'spastically** *adv.*, in a spastic manner.

1862 A. MEADOWS *Man. Midwifery* VI. ii. 217 The longer it [*sc.* the placenta] is allowed to remain the more spastically does the uterus contract upon it. **1978** R. LUDLUM *Holcroft Covenant* iii. 39 He arched his back spastically, as if gasping for air.

spasticity (spæ'stɪsɪtɪ). [f. SPASTIC *a.* + -ITY.] Spastic condition or quality.

1822-7 GOOD *Study Med.* (1829) I. 293 Its wandering or universal spasticity. *Ibid.* IV. 435 A spasticity or want of pliancy in the muscular fibres of the heart. **1899** *Allbutt's Syst. Med.* VII. 58 Complete paraplegia, with or without spasticity or contracture. **1964** *Proc. R. Soc. Med.* LVII. 715/2 Spasticity is said to be present when a paretic limb involuntarily resists passive displacement, particularly in one direction of movement. Anti-gravity muscles are often affected, but spasticity is by no means restricted to these muscles. **1974** *Times* 23 Jan. 9/7 Spasticity is the end result of pathological changes which disturb the physiology of the central nervous system.

spat (spæt), *sb.*[1] Also 7 **spatt.** [Of obscure origin; perh. related to SPIT *v.*[1]]

1. a. The spawn of oysters or other shell-fish.

[**1376-7** *Rolls of Parlt.* II. 369/1 Il destruit.. le spat des oistres, musklys, & d'autres Pessons.]

1667 SPRAT *Hist. R. Soc.* 307 In the Month of May the Oysters cast their Spaun (which the Dredgers call their Spat). **1687** *Lond. Gaz.* No. 2272/4 The Laws for the preservation of the Spawn and Spatt of Oysters in the River of Burnham. **1721** *Phil. Trans.* XXXI. 251 From the Spat or Seed of which, it is most probable,.. all the Bottom at length ..became cover'd with Oysters. **1796** *Statist. Acc. Scot.* XVII. 70 In May the oysters cast their spat or spawn. **1817** in J. Evans *Excurs. Windsor* 448 For the preservation of the brood and spat of Oysters, and for otherwise regulating the said fishery. **1826** SIR A. CARLISLE *Hunter. Oration* 19 The whole brood are associated together, by being involved in a viscid slime, and in that state called 'The Spat'. **1879** *Cassell's Techn. Educ.* IV. 76 To save the bulk of the spat when free is the great object of oyster culture.

fig. **1881** *Blackw. Mag.* Mar. 272 Many square miles of the South and West of Ireland are but spawning beds of misery. The spat is nourished by the poor laws.

Comb. **1891** W. K. BROOKS *Oyster* 112 Shells are very effective as spat-collectors.

b. In *pl.* in the same sense.

1667 SPRAT *Hist. R. Soc.* 307 One Shell having many times 20 Spats. **1777** PENNANT *Brit. Zool.* IV. 89 The oysters, or their spats, are brought to convenient places, where they improve in taste and size. **1854** S. P. WOODWARD *Mollusca* II. 254 The oysters spawn in May and June, and the fry ('spats') are extensively collected.

†**2.** The eggs of bees. *Obs.*

1634 J. LEVETT *Ordering of Bees* 14 The Bees haue first brought out the Drone spat, and after that their owne spat. *Ibid.* 61 The spat or brood of the Bees are nourished by honey and water. **1657** S. PURCHAS *Pol. Flying-Ins.* 47 Their young is called spat, that which the bees spit forth or deliver by their mouth.

3. *Comb.*: **spat fall, spatfall,** the settling of the planktonic larvæ of bivalves at the sites where they will develop as adults; the extent of such settling.

1925 *Nature* 26 Sept. 486/2 The spat falls in the three years 1922–24 were failures. **1963** *Washington Post* 2 Oct. B-2 The 1963 fall of spat (young oysters) in the James River seed area has been inadequate to maintain seed stocks for the third successive year. This contrasts sharply with the above average spatfall throughout the rest of Virginia's Chesapeake Bay system. **1972** *Aquaculture* I. 258 The possibility of spatfalls must be recognized if the harbour were heavily stocked with this species.

spat (spæt), *sb.*[2] *rare.* [app. an abbreviation of SPATULE.]

†**1.** (See quots.) *Obs.*[−0]

1647 HEXHAM I. s.v., A Spat or an instrument that Chirurgions use in spreading their salves. **1656** BLOUNT *Glossogr.*, *Spat*,.. a little slice or Splatter, wherewith Surgeons and Apothecaries use to spread their plaisters and salves.

2. A flat implement used in playing ball-games.

1866 *Routledge's Ev. Boy's Ann.* 180 A.. version of racquets, with a 'spat' and an India rubber ball.

†**spat,** *sb.*[3] *Min. Obs. rare.* [a. G. *spat*, also *spath* SPATH[1].] = SPAR *sb.*[2]

1706 PHILLIPS (ed. Kersey), *Spat*,.. a kind of Mineral Stone. **1762** tr. *Busching's Syst. Geog.* I. 41 Spat, or Spar, the species of which are cubic, flaky, granular Spat, and transparent Spat;.. glass spat, and field spat.

spat (spæt), *sb.*[4] Chiefly *dial.* or *colloq.* [Probably imitative: cf. SPAT *v.*[2]]

1. A tiff or dispute; a quarrel. Orig. *U.S.*

1804 *Repertory* (Boston) 27 April (Thornton), [London news] The late spat between Mr. Pitt and Mr. W. Pulteney. **1828** WEBSTER, *Spat*, a petty combat; a little quarrel or dissension. (A vulgar use of the word in New England.) **1869** MRS. STOWE *Old Town* 33 They was pretty apt to have spats. **1898** J. M. HENDERSON *Chron. Kartdale*, etc. 316 Robert and his uncle had a bit o' a spat this morning.

2. A smart blow, smack, or slap. Also *fig.*

1823 CREEVEY in *C. Papers* (1904) II. 62 The first sentence relating to Spain is a regular spat on the face to the Villains of Verona. **1831** *Ibid.* 231, I received rather a smartish spat on my shoulder from an unseen stick. **1840** *Comic Lat. Gram.* 23 More kicks, more boxes on the ear, more spats, more canings. **1899** *Contemp. Rev.* Dec. 881 An attention which she promptly requited by a 'spat' on the nose.

3. A sharp, smacking sound.

1881 MARY H. CATHERWOOD *Craque o' Doom* ix. 74 They heard the spat of boot-soles on the flinty pike behind them. **1893** C. KING *Foes in Ambush* 110 The bullets with furious spat drove deep into the adobe.

spat (spæt), *sb.*[5] [Abbreviation of SPATTERDASH.] **1.** A short gaiter worn over the instep and reaching only a little way above the ankle, usually fastened under the foot by means of a strap. Chiefly in *pl.*

1802 JAMES *Milit. Dict.*, *Spatts*, a small sort of spatter-dashes, that reach only a little above the ancle, called also half gaiters. **1820** HOGG *Shepherd's Cal.* xiv, Take in black spats, and a very narrow-brimmed hat, and you have the figure complete. **1863** MRS. MARCH *Heathside Farm* I. 28 Whose nether man was generally cased in brown spats (*Anglice* gaiters). **1888** *Times* (weekly ed.) 16 Nov. 3/4 He wore a pair of dark spats with light buttons.

2. *Aeronaut.* A streamlined covering for the upper part of the wheel of an aircraft, usu. one with fixed landing gear.

1931 *Flight* 16 Oct. 1047/1 (*caption*) The way in which the radius rod and axle are faired into the 'spat' is shown very clearly in these pictures. **1938** *Jrnl. R. Aeronaut. Soc.* XLII. 442, I have noticed that wheels which have spats covering all but the lower portion often spin quite fast in flight. **1943** [see SPATTED *ppl. a.* b].

spat (spæt), *sb.*[6] [app. a. Du. *spat* in the same sense.] A small splash *of* something.

1876 J. WEISS *Wit, Hum., & Shaks.* ii. 47 When a skilfully distended bubble breaks, and only a thin spat of suds is left. **1897** MARY KINGSLEY *W. Africa* 258 Spats of mud.. came flap, flap among the bushes covering me.

spat (spæt), *v.*[1] [f. SPAT *sb.*[1] The use of the form as a pa. pple. (in quots. 1677) is prob. due to association with SPIT *v.*[1]]

1. *intr.* and *trans.* Of oysters: To spawn.

1667 SPRAT *Hist. R. Soc.* 307 With a knife they gently raise the small brood [of oysters] from the Cultch, and then they throw the Cultch in again, to preserve the ground for the future, unless they be so newly Spat that they cannot be safely severed from the Cultch. *Ibid.* 309 The Oysters are sick after they have spat. **1865** *Rep. Sea Fisheries Comm.* II. 1359/2 Some of the oysters.. spat as late as the end of September. The general time of spatting, however, is much earlier. **1879** *Cassell's Techn. Educ.* IV. 77/1 As oysters.. have been known to spat very late in the year.

†**2.** *intr.* Of bees: To breed. *Obs.*

1634 J. LEVETT *Ordering of Bees* 25 The Bees both spat faster and preserve.. their brood the better. *Ibid.* 61.

spat (spæt), *v.*[2] [Prob. imitative: cf. SPAT *sb.*[4]]

1. *intr.* To start *up* sharply or actively; to engage in a dispute. *U.S.*

1809 KENDALL *Trav.* III. 292, I was answered, 'that the women had not much to say in politics, though now and then they would spat up'. **1848** BARTLETT *Dict. Amer.* 323 *Spat*, to dispute; to quarrel. A low word. New England.

2. *trans.* To clap, slap, or smack.

c **1832** SIR C. LYELL in Mrs. Lyell *Life* (1881) I. 11 We were very angry with him for having *spatted* us all round with a ruler. **1845** S. JUDD *Margaret* (Bartlett), The little Isabel leaped up and down spatting her hands. **1886** *Cent. Mag.* Jan. 429/2 You can't spat a man harder betwixt the eyes than to set back an' not break bread wi' 'im.

b. To beat *down* with a spade or the like.

1845 *Jrnl. R. Agric. Soc.* V. II. 553 It must be.. finally spatted down and smoothed by the spade. **1890** *Lippincott's Mag.* Apr. 579 Shovelled away by dozens and spatted down under neat mounds by the unfeeling spade of the scientific excavator.

3. *intr.* To administer slaps or pats; to strike sharply, to spatter.

1868 MISS ALCOTT *Lit. Women* (1869) I. xv. 231 Amy spatted away energetically. **1894** CROCKETT *Raiders* xl. (ed. 3) 341 Bullets spatted uncomfortably among the rocks.

b. Used adverbially.

1890 L. C. D'OYLE *Notches* 71 Bill fired again,.. and I heard the ball go 'spat!' **1895** *Outing* XXVI. 30/2 Spat-spat, splash! they fell, one big sprig coming down squarely on top of my head.

Hence **'spatting** *vbl. sb.*, a slapping, a smacking.

1840 *Comic Lat. Gram.* 34 A caning... A spatting... A flogging. **1883** C. D. WARNER *Roundabout Journ.* 24 As I approached this sunken place I heard a tremendous spatting, and pounding, and chattering, and laughing.

spat, *ppl. a.* [Pa. t. and pa. pple. of SPIT *v.*[2]] With preps. and advbs., as ***spat-on, -out.***

1922 JOYCE *Ulysses* 167 His gorge rose. Spat on sawdust, warmish cigarette smoke.. the state of ferment. **1948** T. A. M. NASH *Anchau Rural Devel. & Settlement Scheme* 6 Ankle deep in spat-out sugarcane fibre. **1968** *Listener* 11 July 40/1 It was generally conceived in the Labour movement that that old-fashioned and now spat-out word, 'comradeship', mattered an awful lot. **1978** A. J. HUXLEY *Illustr. Hist. Gardening* i. 10 Presumably growing from spat-out seeds, they [*sc.* wild fruits] were nearly always found close to the dwellings.

spatangoid (spæ'tæŋgɔɪd), *sb.* and *a. Zool.* [ad. mod.L. *Spatangoides*, f. *Spatangus* (late L. *spatangius*, Gr. σπατάγγης): see -OID.] **a.** *sb.* A sea-urchin belonging or related to the genus *Spatangus* (heart-urchins). **b.** *adj.* Having the characteristics of this.

1857 AGASSIZ *Contrib. Nat. Hist. U.S.* I. 114 Next come true Echinoids, later only Spatangoids. **1877** *Encycl. Brit.* VII. 630/2 In some Spatangoid genera the corona bears symmetrical bands of minute tubercles with attached spines.

†**spatarent,** *a. Obs. rare.* Also **spartarent, -ine.** [a. obs. F. *spa(r)tarent*, ad. med.L. *spatarenticus* (also *spatarensis*): see Mowat *Alphita* (1887) 159.] ***spatarent soap***, a kind of soap formerly in use.

1526 *Grete Herbal* clvii. (1529) K j b, Confect with spatarent sope or Frensshe sope. *Ibid.* cccxcviii. X vj, The other [sort] is called Iewes sope or spartaryne bycause y[e] Iewes wasshe them therwith. *Ibid.* X vj b, The Iewes sope & spartarent.

†**spatch,** *v. Obs.*[−1] [Aphetic form of DISPATCH *v.*] *trans.* To slay, kill.

1616 J. LANE *Contn. Sqr.'s T.* VII. 60 Vnmake my limbes, vntwiste my guiltie liefe, And quicklie spatche thy griefe-killd Algarsife.

spatch-cock, spatchcock ('spætʃkɒk), *sb.* [See quot. 1785 and DISPATCH *sb.* 12.]

1. A fowl split open and grilled after being killed, plucked, and dressed in a summary fashion. Also *attrib.*

Orig. in Irish use, later chiefly Anglo-Indian.

1785 GROSE *Dict. Vulgar T.*, *Spatch cock*, abbreviation of a dispatch cock, an Irish dish upon any sudden occasion. It is a hen just killed from the roost, or yard, and immediately skinned, split, and broiled. **1819** MOORE *Mem.* (1853) II. 317 We had a good deal of laughing at an Irishman who was of our party, on account of a bull he had made at breakfast, and which we called 'half a nightingale'—a sort of 'spatch-cock nightingale'. **1823** —— *Fables, Holy Alliance* i. 86 Proud Prussia's double bird of prey, Tame as a spatch-cock, slunk away. **1851** R. F. BURTON *Goa* 258 Presently the 'butler' informs you that your breakfast, a spatchcock, or a curry with eggs,.. is awaiting you. **1875** MISS BIRD *Sandwich Isl.* (1880) 99 Supper was ready for us;.. the spatchcock and salmon reminded me of home.

2. (See quot.)

1901 BRADLEY *Highw. & B. Lake District* 62 Any official .. would have run a grave risk of being made a spatchcock of, or in other words, of his head being stuck in a rabbit-hole, and his legs staked to the ground.

spatchcock ('spætʃkɒk), *v.* [f. prec.]

1. *trans.* To cook as, or in the manner of, a spatchcock. Hence **spatchcocked** *ppl. a.*

1865 *Pall Mall G.* 2 Aug. 3 Those who have never eaten spatchcocked grouse can hardly be said to know the real flavour of the bird. **1879** MRS. JAMES *Ind. Househ. Man.* 34 You sit down.. to your fowl—spatch-cocked of course, that being the natives' favourite way of dressing the tempting dish. **1890** *Queen* 11 Jan. 68/3 To split a fowl in two and serve one half à la Marengo, and the other half the next day either spatchcocked with mushrooms, or in any other approved fashion.

2. To insert, interpolate, or sandwich (a phrase, sentence, etc.). Const. *in* or *into*.

1901 GEN. BULLER in *Times* 11 Oct. 10/2, I therefore spatchcocked into the middle of that telegram a sentence in which [etc.]. **1901** *Daily Chron.* 18 Oct. 3/4 Such indifferent performances as 'Catriona'—indifferent in spite of the fine short story 'spatchcock'd' into it. **1903** MAHAFFY in *Cal. St. P., Irel.* Introd. 12 We read phrases of apparent sincere religious fervour spatchcocked in between these bloodthirsty expressions.

b. To add to, or modify, by interpolation.

1901 *Daily Chron.* 24 Oct. 5/6 They knew of the spatch-cocked telegram then. **1901** *Speaker* 16 Nov. 190/1 Generals spatchcock telegrams and receive dismissal.

spate (speɪt), *sb.* Orig. *Sc.* and *north.* Forms: α. 5- **spate**, 5-9 **spait**, 6-7, 9 *dial.* **spaitt**, 6-7 **spat**, 7 **spaite**, 9 **spaight**. β. 6-7 **speate**, 7-9 **speat**, 9 *dial.* **speatt**, **speeat**, **speet**, **spete**, **spyet**, etc. [Of obscure origin: the early spelling and rimes show that the original vowel was *ā*, the later change of which to *ea*, etc., is regular.]

1. A flood or inundation; *esp.* a sudden flood or rising in a river or stream caused by heavy rains or melting snow.

α. *c* **1425** WYNTOUN *Cron.* I. vii[i.] *heading*, The ark and the spate of Noe. *Ibid.* VII. 771 Na spate þan mycht mak þar kneys wate. *c* **1440** *Alph. Tales* 381 þe watur þat was cald Padus rase vp opon a grete spate and owryode all þe feldis. **1522** *Aberdeen Reg.* (1844) I. 105 The sentrice of the brig.. quhilk the spat haid brocht dovne incontinent. **1562** TURNER *Herbal* II. (1568) 35 Great heapes of Stones are casten together wyth the myght of a great spat or floode. **1570** LEVINS *Manip.* 39 A spate, *torrens.* *c* **1614** SIR W. MURE *Dido & Æneas* II. 478 Nor haile, nor sleet, nor wind, nor weit [Atlas] eschewes; Adoune his shoulders raging spates do spowt. **1706** SIBBALD *Hist. Picts* in *Misc. Scot.* I. 97 Others perished in the water, being carried down by the spate. **1725** RAMSAY *Gentle Sheph.* I. ii, The spate may bear away Frae aff the howms your dainty rucks of hay. **1858** GLADSTONE *Homer* III. 158 That he carried away in sudden spates many of the horses that were pastured on his banks. **1889** F. A. KNIGHT *By Leafy Ways* 25 Heaps of drifted rubbish,.. to mark the tide-line of the winter spates.

transf. **1611** SIR W. MURE *Misc. Poems* ii. 60 Wks. (S.T.S.) I. 11 No spaits of teires culd quench ye boyling leede. **1847** MOTHERWELL *Poet. Wks.* (ed. 2) 9 In that spate of blood, how well The headless corpse will swim.

β. **1595** DUNCAN *App. Etym.* (E.D.S.), *Eluvio, diluvium*, a speate of watters. *a* **1670** SPALDING *Troub. Chas. I* (Spalding Cl.) I. 81 Throw ane great speat of the water of Die, occasioned be the.. extraordinar rayne, thir haill four schippis brak louss. **1731** *Morison's Dict. Decis.* (1806) XXXIII. 14524 The prejudice.. did arise.. from the running in of mud and gravel, by speats and land-floods. **1785** BURNS *Brigs of Ayr* 121 While crashing ice, borne on the roaring speat, Sweeps dams, an' mills, an' brigs, a' to the gate. **1818** MISS FERRIER *Marriage* I. 296 A Horse and Cart were drowned at the Ford last Speat. **1863** [W. F. CAMPBELL] *Life in Normandy* I. 54 They [i.e. fish] cannot get into these small rivers without a speat.

b. A sudden heavy downpour or storm *of* rain.

1727 *Life J. Semple* in *Biogr. Presbyteriana* (1827) I. 168 With a Speat of Rain, to raise the Waters. **1793** T. SCOTT *Poems* 389 Routh o' kisses, That fell like speats o' rain. **1825-** in numerous northern dial. glossaries. **1871** *Daily News* 25 Aug., All day long there had been a 'spate' of rain in Inverary.

c. *fig.* A sudden or violent outburst or outpouring *of* some quality, feeling, etc.; a sudden rush or flood, an unusual number or quantity, *of* words, events, etc.

α. *c* **1614** SIR W. MURE *Dido & Æneas* III. 191 Death-bent Dido,.. Transported with a rageing spait of ire. *a* **1689** W. CLELAND *Poems* (1697) 45 Innocence proves no defence, Against this Spait of violence. **1730** T. BOSTON *Mem.* x. 320 The spate ran high for the transportation [to Closeburn] when we came to town. *a* **1796** ? BURNS *Poem on Pastoral Poet.* ix, Nae bombast spates o' nonsense swell. **1826** SCOTT *Jrnl.* 6 Sept., Here is a fine spate of work—a day diddled away, and nothing to show for it. **1890** *Argus* (Melbourne) 17 Dec. 9/2, I already had such a spate of schools to attend that I was unable to accept the invitation.

β. **1629** SIR W. MURE *True Crucifix* 564 Wks. (S.T.S.) I. 221 Thy Crimes the cause, thy sinnes inunding speate. **1634** RUTHERFORD *Lett.* (1862) I. xxxvii. 118 God hath dried up one channel of your love by the removal of your husband. Let now that speat run upon Christ. **1710** RUDDIMAN *Gloss. Douglas' Æneis* s.v. *Flum*, A speat of language. **1731** *Plain Reasons Presbyt. Diss.* 138 The most honest cause is often run down with the torrent and speat of law-quirks. **1834** *Tait's Mag.* I. 428/1 Not a foaming speat, and blether of dictionary words. **1858-61** E. B. RAMSAY *Remin.* vi. (1870) 168 Sic a speat o' praying, and sic a speat o' drinking, I never knew.

2. Without article: Flooding or inundation, swollen condition *of* water, etc.; copious downpouring *of* rain. Now usually without const.

1513 DOUGLAS *Æneid* IX. i. 74 Sevyn swelland ryveris eftyr spait of rayne. **1536** BELLENDEN *Cron. Scot.* (1821) II. 287 In this yeir, al the landis of Godowine, be spait of seis, wes coverit with sandis. **1609** SKENE *Reg. Maj.* 9 Inundation, or spate of water, or anie other suddaine chance or perill. *c* **1630** in Burton *Scot Abr.* (1864) II. 323 For as meikle as a greit part of the playfeild.. is spoiled, broken and carriet away in speat and inundation of water. **1848** CLOUGH *Bothie of Toper-na-Fuosich* I. 7 As sudden torrent in time of speat in the mountain. **1893** K. SIMPSON *Jeanie o' Biggersdale* 51 The water rushed down.. angrily in winter and in times of spate.

b. *in* (or †*on*) *spate*, in flood.

1513 DOUGLAS *Æneid* II. vi. 14 Quhen the burne on spait hurlis doun the bank. **1567** *Gude & Godlie B.* (S.T.S.) 111 Lyke burnis that in spait fast rin. **1610** *Aberdeen Reg.* (1848) II. 299 The said burne, efter great rayne, being in spat, brak out oft and diuerse tymes be vehement force. **1803** JAMIESON *Water-Kelpie* xxi. in Scott *Minstrelsy*, Yestereen the water was in spate. **1860** G. H. K. *Vac. Tour* 133 The burn, high in spate,.. rattles harshly at our feet.

c. Broken or turbulent water characteristic of a river in flood. *rare*⁻¹.

1884 W. SIME *To & Fro* 104 The Ilen.. breaking into rough currents of brown 'spate'.

3. *attrib.* and *Comb.*, as *spate river*, *water*; *spate-created* adj.

1456 SIR G. HAYE *Law Arms* (S.T.S.) 115 The spate wateris of the grete mountanis may sudaynly cum till infest the ost and disloge thame. **1529** *Registr. Aberdon.* (Maitl. Cl.) I. 396 Gif it sall happin þe said brig be.. inundatioun of spaitt water weiring of grund be our inaduertence.. to failȝe. **1901** *Scotsman* 4 Mar. 10/2 Floods are of very short duration on those spate rivers. **1901** *Pall Mall G.* 17 Sept. 6/2 Those spate-created runs at the heads of pools.

Hence **spate** *v. trans.*, to flood, swell; *intr.*, to rain heavily. Also **spated** *ppl. a.*

1827 AIKMAN *Hist. Scot.* III. IV. 374 The speated Tweed came down heavy two days before. **1853** W. WATSON *Poems* 26 (E.D.D.), Sheughs an' deep fur-drains were jawin' To spate the burns. **1866** *Banffshire Gloss.* 230 It spaitit on the hail nicht.

spate-bone, irregular variant of SPADE-BONE.

1655 FULLER *Ch. Hist.* v. 169 To humble the Cardinals pride, some afterwards set up on a window, a painted Mastiff-dog, gnawing the spate-bone of a shoulder of Mutton. *a* **1825** FORBY *Voc. E. Anglia*, *Spate-bone, Spaut-bone*, the shoulder-bone of an animal slain for food.

spatel(le, etc., obs. variant of SPATTLE.

spatewil, variant of SPETEWIL *a. Obs.*

spath[1] (spæθ). Now *rare*. [a. G. *spath*, var. spelling of *spat* (SPAT *sb.*[3]), *spad* (SPAAD), MHG. and MLG. *spat*, *spât*. Hence also Du. *spaath*, Da. and Sw. *spat*; F. *spath*, It. *spato*, Sp. and Pg. *espato*.] = SPAR *sb.*[2]

1763 W. LEWIS *Phil. Comm. Arts* 144 A friable opake stone called white spath, which appears to be a kind of gypsum. **1794** R. J. SULIVAN *View Nat.* I. 73 The crystallizations which are found in granite, are almost always of a siliceous substance, quartz: whereas marble has always spath, which is a calcareous one. **1803** *Med. Jrnl.* IX. 494 These layers imitate.. closely calcareous spath. **1886** *Leeds Mercury* 15 Feb. 5/6 The lens coincides with the principal chrystallographic axis of the Spath.

spath[2], variant of SPATHE.

1834 *Penny Cycl.* II. 371/2 Bows made from the spath (σπαθη) of the palm.., six feet long. **1889** *Science-Gossip* XXV. 184/1 The spath is thrown up from the tuber at a different period.

‖**spatha** (ˈspeɪθə). Pl. **spathæ** (-θiː). [L. *spatha*, ad. Gr. σπάθη broad blade, broad flat piece of wood, stem of a palm-leaf, spatula, etc.]

1. *Bot.* A spathe.

1753 *Chambers' Cycl.* Suppl. s.v., The *spatha* is of very different texture.. in different plants. **1760** [see SPADICEOUS *a.* 2]. **1769** E. BANCROFT *Guiana* 31 A tough ligneous cylindrical stalk.. terminated by a conic, reddish purple spatha. **1796** STEDMAN *Surinam* II. xix. 66 The seed is enclosed in a brownish kind of spatha, that arises from the center of the branches. **1830** LINDLEY *Nat. Syst. Bot.* 175 Flowers.. bursting through an irregularly lacerated spatha. **1850** TYAS *Favourite Field Fl.* Ser. II. 18 The daffodils were showing their.. petals through the transparent spatha.

transf. **1834** tr. *Raspail's Org. Chem.* 283 If.. we examine a feather.. we may.. satisfy ourselves, that its tube is formed and grows by means of spathæ, one within another.

2. A flat blade-shaped implement.

1881 J. ANDERSON *Scot. in Early Chr. T.* Ser. II. i. 32 At its right side lay an iron knife, a weaver's rubbing-bone, and spatha of whalebone.

spathaceous (spəˈθeɪʃəs), *a.*[1] *Bot.* [a. mod.L. *spathaceus*: see SPATHA and -ACEOUS.] Furnished with or enclosed by a spathe; of the nature of or resembling a spathe.

1760 J. LEE *Introd. Bot.* II. vi. (1765) 85 Such as have Spathaceous Flowers. **1830** LINDLEY *Nat. Syst. Bot.* 236 Calyx divided or entire, sometimes spathaceous. **1858** [see SPADICEOUS *a.* 2]. **1872** OLIVER *Elem. Bot.* II. 269 Daffodil.. A bulbous herb, with.. a membranous spathaceous bract.

†**spaˈthaceous**, *a.*[2] *Obs.*⁻¹ [f. SPATH[1].] Spathic, spathose.

1794 R. J. SULIVAN *View Nat.* I. 426 A great variety of forms may be produced by the spathaceous particles.

spathal (ˈspeɪðəl), *a. Bot.* [f. next or SPATHA.] 'Furnished with a spathe; as, *spathal* flowers.'

1864 WEBSTER (citing Howitt).

spathe (speɪð). [ad. L. *spatha* or Gr. σπάθη: see SPATHA and cf. SPATH[2]. So F. *spathe.*]

1. *Bot.* A large bract or sheathing-leaf enveloping the inflorescence (usually a spadix) of certain plants, as arums, palms, etc., in such a way as completely to enclose it before expansion.

1785 MARTYN *Lett. Bot.* xiv. 154 These [genera].. agree in having a *Spathe* or sheath instead of a calyx. **1793** —— *Lang. Bot.* s.v. *Spatha*, A Spathe may be one-valved, or two-valved [etc.]. **1811** A. T. THOMSON *Lond. Disp.* (1818) 61 The spathe is erect,.. covering the fruit till it is nearly ripe, when it drops. **1848** TYAS *Favourite Field Fl.* Ser. I. 3 Near the summit of the flower-stalk is a spathe which originally enveloped the bud. **1870** *Zoologist* Ser. II. V. 2354 A singular species of Arum, with long curling horns extending from its lurid spathes.

attrib. **1882** *Garden* 17 June 424/3 A naked stem, inflated spathe-valves, and somewhat broad leaves.

2. *Zool.* A spatulate or spoon-shaped part, process, etc.

1891 in *Cent. Dict.*

Hence **spathed** *a.*, having a spathe (Webster, 1864); **ˈspatheful**, such a number or quantity as fills a spathe.

1888 G. ALLEN in *Good Words* 385 The entire spatheful of pollen-bearing flowers.

spathe-bill. *rare*⁻¹. [f. SPATHE *sb.*] The spoon-billed sandpiper, *Eurynorhynchus pygmæus*.

1840 *Cuvier's Anim. Kingd.* 245 Near the Sandpipers should apparently be placed the Spathe-bill.., which is distinguished by a depressed bill, widened at the tip somewhat as in the Spoonbills.

†**ˈspather.** *Obs. rare.* [Irregularly f. L. *spatha*, or alteration of SPATTER *sb.*[1]] A spattle or spatula.

1597 GERARDE *Herbal* III. xxxix. 1178 Of this there is made a profitable spather or slice to be vsed in making of compounde plaisters and pessaries. **1657** *Physical Dict.* B iv, *Albation*, is the abstraction of Dust.. with a Hares foot, feather, spather, or such like.

So †**ˈspathern.** *Obs. rare.*

1634 T. JOHNSON *Parey's Chirurg.* III. xxix. 121, I have sometimes seen such passages so open, that they would receive the head of a Spathern [F. *espatule*]. *Ibid.* xv. vi. 567 That bone which is deprest must be lifted up with a spatherne, or little sticke.

spathic (ˈspæθɪk), *a.*[1] *Min.* [f. SPATH[1] + -IC. Cf. F. *spathique.*]

†**1.** = SPATHOSE *a.*[1] 2. *Obs.*⁻¹

1788 JEFFERSON *Writ.* (1859) II. 432 The property of the spathic acid, to corrode flinty substances, has been lately applied by M. Puymaurin to engrave on glass.

2. a. = SPATHOSE *a.*[1] 1 b.

1803 *Med. Jrnl.* IX. 494 Sometimes it is found in spathic layers, semitransparent, of different thickness;.. these layers imitate so closely calcareous spath, that [etc.].

b. = SPATHOSE *a.*[1] 1 a.

1831 J. HOLLAND *Manuf. Metal* I. 265 Bergmann had already asserted that manganese was contained in the white or spathic iron ores. **1855** SCOFFERN in *Orr's Circ. Sci.*, *Elem. Chem.* 442 Native peroxide of iron (spathic iron). **1868** JOYNSON *Metals* 7 At Weardale the spathic ore is often found associated with a brown ore—a hydrated oxide.

ˈspathic, *a.*[2] *Bot.* [ad. mod.L. *spathicus*, f. SPATHA 1.] Of or belonging to a spathe.

1859 MAYNE *Expos. Lex.* 1178/1.

spathiform (ˈspæθɪfɔːm), *a.*[1] *Min.* [f. SPATH[1] + -(I)FORM. Cf. F. *spathiforme.*] Resembling spath or spar in form or appearance; lamellar.

1793 R. KERR *Lavoisier's Elem. Chem.* (1802) I. 268 These [forms of uranite] may be divided into three genera, the ochreous, the spathiform, and the mineralized. *Ibid.* 269 The spathiform, or uranite spar.

ˈspathiform, *a.*[2] *Bot.* (*Zool.*) [f. SPATHA or SPATHE.] Having the form of a spathe.

1859 HUXLEY *Oceanic Hydrozoa* 29 The hydrophyllia spathiform and smooth externally.

spathose (spæˈθəʊs), *a.*[1] *Min.* [f. SPATH[1] + -OSE[2]. Cf. SPATHIC *a.*[1]]

1. Of the nature of or resembling spath or spar; abounding in, consisting of, spar; foliated or lamellar in structure or texture; sparry.

a. *spathose iron*, *iron-ore*, *ore*, = SIDERITE 6.

1776 *Phil. Trans.* LXVI. 620 The first experiment [was with] white spathose iron ore from Bayreuth. **1799** *Hull Advertiser* 7 Sept. 4/2 White or yellowish spathose iron. **1801** *Phil. Trans.* XCI. 190 These cavities are analogous to those which appear in the crystals of the spathose ores of iron. **1823** W. PHILLIPS *Min.* (ed. 3) 236 Spathose iron.. occurs of a wine yellow, brownish yellow, yellowish brown and brown colour. **1868** JOYNSON *Metals* 6 The celebrated 'steel irons' of Siegen, Styria, and Carinthia have always been produced from the spathose ores.

b. In general use.

1802 PLAYFAIR *Illustr. Huttonian Theory* 67 All these stones have a tendency to a spathose structure. **1822** J. PARKINSON *Outl. Oryctol.* 22 Calcareous spathose wood previously bituminized. **1856** S. P. WOODWARD *Mollusca* III. 76 Shell external, spathose layer produced beyond the phragmocone into a long pointed beak.

†**2.** Derived from fluor-spar. *spathose acid*, hydrofluoric acid. *Obs.*

1811 PINKERTON *Petral.* II. 139 The fluor is of various colours;.. yielding much phosphorescence when thrown on hot iron, as well as a spathose acid gas.

spaˈthose, *a.*[2] *Bot. rare.* [f. SPATH-E or SPATH-A + -OSE[2].] = SPATHACEOUS *a.*[1]

1839 G. ROBERTS *Dict. Geol.*, *Spathose*, resembling the covering of the date. **1847** in WEBSTER.

So **ˈspathous** *a.* (Webster, 1828-32).

‖**spathula** (ˈspæθjʊlə). *rare.* [L., var. of SPATULA.] A spatula. Also *Comb.*

The erroneous form *spathulor* occurs in Topsell *Serpents* (1608) 34.

1706 in PHILLIPS (ed. Kersey). **1742** *Phil. Trans.* XLII. 75, I mix them gently..with a Spathula of white Wood. **1826** KIRBY & SP. *Entomol.* III. xxxv. 643 A spathula-shaped diverging process.

spathulate (ˈspæθjʊlət), *a.* [f. prec. + -ATE[2].] Spatulate, spatular. Chiefly *Bot.*

1821 W. P. C. BARTON *Flora N. Amer.* I. 34 Flowers large, petals spathulate. **1826** KIRBY & SP. *Entomol.* III. 647 The shape and figure..of scales are very various,..some nearly round,..others spathulate. **1857** HENFREY *Bot.* §88 When the blade passes still more gradually into a broad-winged stalk, a spathulate form results. **1882** VINES tr. *Sachs' Bot.* 529 The lower ones are entirely free, sickle-shaped and pointed, the upper ones broadly spathulate and coherent at their base.

So ˈ**spathulated** *ppl. a. rare.*

1821 W. P. C. BARTON *Flora N. Amer.* I. 120 Radical leaves numerous, spathulated, ciliated, and slightly pubescent. **1859** MAYNE *Expos. Lex.* 1178/1 The *Spondylus spathuliferus* has its shell charged with many rows of simple and spathulated scales.

†**spathule**, Anglicized var. of SPATHULA.

1658 PHILLIPS, *Spathule*,..an Instrument wherewith Chirurgions and Apothecaries spread their plaisters.

†ˈ**spathy**, *a. Obs. rare.* [ad. G. *spathig*, *spatig* (MHG. *spatic*), f. *spath* SPATH[1].] Sparry.

1757 tr. *J. F. Henckel's Pyritologia* 127 The adhering, interspersed, quartzy, spathy matters. *Ibid.* 314 Calcarious, spathy stone.

spatial (ˈspeɪʃəl), *a.* Also spacial. [f. L. *spati-um* SPACE *sb.*[1] + -AL[1].]

1. Having extension in space; occupying or taking up space; consisting of or characterized by space.

1847 WHEWELL *Philos. Induct. Sci.* II. 447 We contemplate objects as made up of spatial parts. **1862** J. W. DRAPER *Intell. Devel. Europe* iv. (1865) 85 All is composed of points or spacial units, which, taken together, constitute a number. **1863** J. G. MURPHY *Comm., Gen.* i. 20 The expanse is here proved to be aerial or spatial; not solid. **1886** A. WEIR *Hist. Basis Mod. Europe* (1889) 474 An independent spatial world, with minds and matter moving about in it.

2. a. Of, pertaining, or relating to space; subject to, or governed by, the conditions of space. Chiefly *Metaph.* and opposed to *temporal*.

α. **1857** WHEWELL *Hist. Induct. Sci.* (ed. 3) I. 351 There are properties of bodies, of the most intimate kind, which involve such spatial relations as are exhibited in the Regular Solids. **1865** J. GROTE *Moral Ideals* (1876) 188 If we translate the consideration of the mind from spatial to temporal language. **1875** CAYLEY in *Phil. Trans.* CLXV. 675 If..we imagine the spatial distribution as made over an indefinitely thin layer or stratum. **1886** A. WEIR *Hist. Basis Mod. Europe* (1889) 481 Ideas..which have been formed from a vast quantity of temporal and spatial experience.

β. **1871** FRASER *Life Berkeley* x. 364 A mathematical or spacial conception of what is real. *a* **1881** A. BARRATT *Phys. Metempiric* (1883) 107 A temporal principle of unity does exist, but a spacial does not.

b. *spatial-temporal* = SPATIO-TEMPORAL *a.*

1903 A. E. TAYLOR *Elem. Metaphysics* III. iv. 249 We can ..confine our attention to the spatial-temporal system of positions. **1925** *Mind* XXXIV. 44 The spatial-temporal order..is and must be taken for granted as ultimate by common sense and science. **1979** *Amer. Pol. Sci. Rev.* Mar. 157/2 Our language is filled with words whose original reference was to the position of one's body in the spatial-temporal world.

3. Happening or taking place in space; caused or involved by space.

1866 W. R. ALGER *Solitudes Nat. & Man* III. 123 Spatial separation is not spiritual independence. *a* **1870** SIR J. HERSCHEL in Proctor *Other Worlds* xii. 276 *note*, One of the arguments advanced in favour of the spatial extinction of light. **1888** *Linnean Soc. Jrnl.* XX. 232/2 Spatial segregation does not depend upon diversity in the qualities and powers of the organism.

4. Of faculty or sense: Apprehending or perceiving space or extension. *spatial ability* (Psychol.), the measured aptitude for perceiving and comprehending relations involving space or extension.

1886 *Encycl. Brit.* XX. 54/1 *note*, The sensibility of our 'spatial sense'. **1886** SIDGWICK *Hist. Ethics* i. 9 To investigate the origin of the spatial faculty. **1940** R. S. WOODWORTH *Psychol.* (ed. 12) iii. 77 Spatial ability is the ability to grasp and use spatial relations. **1952** M. K. WILSON tr. *Lorenz's King Solomon's Ring* vii. 72 Only a few small passerines..possess enough 'spatial intelligence' to find their way through the windows and doors of a house. **1962** J. TIFFIN *Industr. Psychol.* (rev. ed.) v. 158 The spatial ability tests showed the highest relative validity indexes for structural workers..and for some jobs for which such indexes would not be expected. **1964** M. ARGYLE *Psychol. & Social Probl.* xi. 141 Although spatial and non-verbal intelligence tests do not give a good prediction to success at grammar school, they do predict well to success at technical colleges. **1977** *Psychol. Abstr.* LVIII. 813/2 Factor analysis of the intercorrelation matrices for 14 variables yielded the same 4 factors in each group for space perception and spatial ability.

Hence **spatiality** (speɪʃɪˈælɪtɪ), spatial character, quality, or property.

1887 *Mind* Jan. 10 The existence of the vague form..of spatiality. **1890** A. SETH *Scot. Philos.* (ed. 2) iii. 98 Elements which do not already include the fact of spatiality.

spatialism (ˈspeɪʃəlɪz(ə)m). [f. SPATIAL *a.* + -ISM; in sense 2, ad. Fr. *spatialisme*.]

1. *Philos.* (See quot.) *rare.*

1935 *Mind* XLIV. 363 Pure Spatialism which asserts that matter has only spatial, temporal and causal properties.

2. The name of a movement in experimental French poetry led by Pierre Garnier.

1964 *Times Lit. Suppl.* 3 Sept. 827/2 Les Lettres..is Pierre Garnier's organ for a new 'spatialist' conception of poetry... No. 29 (janvier 1963) contains a preliminary manifesto for Spatialism. **1971** J. SHARKEY *Mindplay* 12 *Les Lettres*..in 1963..tried to bring together all of these [modern poetry movements] under a new term—Spatialism—which would include concepts of time, structure and energy.

spatialist (ˈspeɪʃəlɪst), *sb.* and *a.* [f. as prec. + -IST.] **A.** *sb.* **1.** An adherent of spatialism, in either sense.

1934 J. WISDOM *Problems of Mind & Matter* II. x. 168 The Pure Spatialist. The language of some scientists..when they are trying to do philosophy, suggests that they believe that the internal characters of material things consist wholly of spatio-temporal characters—say size, shape and speed. **1964** *Times Lit. Suppl.* 6 Aug. 696/5 Pierre Garnier's review *les lettres* aims at centering spatialists everywhere.

2. One who is concerned with spatial qualities or relations. *rare.*

1940 J. JOYCE *Let.* 13 Mar. (1966) III. 469, I did not wish to inflict temporal art on a spatialist in asking you to go to the concert.

B. *adj.* Of, pertaining to, or characteristic of spatialism.

1964 *Times Lit. Suppl.* 6 Aug. 697/1 Synthesis of the eye-ear-cybernetic trinity of spatialist manifesto. **1967** S. BANN *Concrete Poetry* 19 Yet there is at least one significant point of contact between Goeritz and Garnier. This lies in their common concern with the wider possibilities of the Concrete (or, in Garnier's case, 'spatialist') idiom. **1971** TAYLOR & LUCIE-SMITH *French Poetry Today* 24 Its legitimate offspring thus include genuinely international movements such as Concrete Poetry and Spatialist Poetry.

spatialize (ˈspeɪʃəlaɪz), *v.* [f. SPATIAL *a.* + -IZE.] *trans.* To make spatial; to think of as spatial; to invest with spatial qualities or relations. So **spatialiˈzation**, ˈ**spatialized** *ppl. a.*, ˈ**spatializing** *vbl. sb.*

1882 B. P. BOWNE *Metaphysics* 209 All forms of external experience are not alike calculated to awaken the mind to react with a spatialization of its objects. **1906** S. S. LAURIE *Synthetica* I. 24 There could be no spatialising or localising at all. **1911** A. MITCHELL tr. *Bergson's Creative Evolution* iii. 225 Deduction is an operation governed by the properties of matter... As long as it turns upon space or spatialized time, it has only to let itself go. **1925** A. N. WHITEHEAD *Science & Mod. World* vii. 177 Thus a duration is spatialised; and by 'spatialised' is meant that the duration is the field for the realized pattern constituting the character of the event. **1934** A. HUXLEY *Beyond Mexique Bay* 220 The time that Vaughan perceived..was not real time..; it was the acceptably spatialized, circular duration of the calendar-makers. **1946** R. G. COLLINGWOOD *Idea of History* 188 It is the clock-time of the external world, a spatialized time in which different times exclude one another, just like parts of space. **1949** *Mind* LVIII. 493 By our substantialising of events and our consequent spatialising of time we make this syntactical similarity still closer. **1973** M. HOLLINGTON in R. Fowler *Dict. Mod. Critical Terms* 183 The contribution of structuralism to the analysis of individual literary works has been hampered by its extreme tendency to spatialize the object of contemplation.

spatially (ˈspeɪʃəlɪ), *adv.* Also spacially. [f. SPATIAL *a.*] As regards, in or with reference to, space; by means of space.

1865 J. GROTE *Explor. Philos.* I. 44 The sensation which we have is rudimentarily perhaps, simply of a colour, how spatially related to us is hard to trace. **1877** E. CAIRD *Philos. Kant* II. ii. 447 All spatially or temporarily determined phenomena. **1882** STALLO *Concepts Mod. Phys.* 228 There is no objectively real thing which is not spacially extended. **1896** JEVONS *Introd. Hist. Relig.* xvii. 230 Gods who are spatially remote from him.

spatiate (ˈspeɪʃɪeɪt), *v.* [f. ppl. stem of L. *spatiārī*, f. *spatium* SPACE *sb.*[1]] *intr.* To walk about; to stroll, wander, range, or roam. Also *fig.*

1626 BACON *Sylva* §720 The Fixing of the Minde upon one Object of Cogitation, whereby it doth not spatiate and transcurre, as it useth. **1656** in BLOUNT *Glossogr.* *a* **1711** KEN *Psyche* Poet. Wks. 1721 IV. 299 The Soul in Vision seem'd from Flesh unloos'd To fly abroad, and spatiate unconfin'd. **1734** WATTS *Reliq. Juv.* (1789) 140 My spirit feels her freedom,..Exults and spatiates o'er a thousand scenes. **1846** *Blackw. Mag.* LIX. 759 Give him room and opportunity.. to spatiate for the good of digestion. **1889** *Jrnl. Archaeol. Inst.* No. 181. 15 We can spatiate at peace and gather in a rich harvest of useful information.

Hence **spatiˈation**. *rare*[−0].

1658 PHILLIPS, *Spatiation*, a walking at length, or in a large compasse.

spatio-temporal (ˌspeɪʃɪəʊˈtɛmpərəl), *a.* [f. *spatio-*, used as comb. form of L. *spatium* SPACE *sb.*[1] + TEMPORAL *a.*[1]] Belonging to both space and time.

1900 B. RUSSELL *Leibniz* v. 57 Two things could not co-exist in one spatio-temporal point. **1920** A. N. WHITEHEAD *Concept of Nature* viii. 173 The spatio-temporal structure of events. *a* **1931** G. H. MEAD *Philos. of Act* (1938) II. xv. 232 Physical identity with distant objects gives functional contemporaneity, while the acts that are going on involve the actual concrete spatiotemporal happenings. **1954** A. J. AYER *Philos. Ess.* i. 3 Spatio-temporal points are individuals, ..but not everyone would allow it to be said that they existed. **1975** I. STEWART *Concepts Mod. Math.* xiv. 208 Depress your foot, and move slightly forward in time, thereby dragging a small loop of string with you in the time direction, though leaving most of the knot in its original spatio-temporal state. **1979** A. R. PEACOCKE *Creation & World of Science* I. i. 24 A more general view that reality consists of two orders..: the natural/the supernatural; the spatio-temporal/the eternal; [etc.].

Hence ˌ**spatio-tempoˈrality**, the quality or fact of being spatio-temporal; ˌ**spatio-temporaliˈzation**, the fact of making or investing with spatio-temporal qualities or relations; ˌ**spatio-ˈtemporalized** *a.*; ˌ**spatio-ˈtemporally** *adv.*, in space and time, with reference to both space and time.

1920 S. ALEXANDER *Space, Time, & Deity* I. 250 Relation ..which unites things, is outside each of them spatially (or rather spatio-temporally). *Ibid.* 269 A category which arises not so much out of the character of spatio-temporality taken as a whole..as out of the 'relation'..between the spatial and the temporal elements in any space-time. **1923** C. D. BROAD *Sci. Thought* x. 403 Science regards the ultimate scientific objects as being spatio-temporally homogeneous. **1940** *Mind* XLIX. 185 The qualitative content must vanish with the abstraction of its spatio-temporality. *Ibid.*, It remains possible to take the quality as the spatio-temporalized appearance of the real action of the 'other' with the 'self'. *Ibid.* 324 Evidently the qualification is a function of the spatio-temporalization. **1959** P. F. STRAWSON *Individuals* I. i. 34 Since spatio-temporally continuous existence is.. observed *neither* in the case where we are inclined to speak of qualitative identity *nor* in the case where we are inclined to speak of numerical identity, by what right do we suppose that there is a fundamental difference between these cases? **1964** P. MEADOWS in I. L. Horowitz *New Sociol.* xxviii. 446 They sought to discern in the sweeping spatio-temporalizations of historic experience..the unfolding 'form'..beyond appearance. **1980** A. QUINTON *Francis Bacon* vii. 62 Causes may be spatio-temporally remote from their effects.

‖**Spätlese** (ˈʃpɛtleːzə). Also **Spaetlese**, and with small initial. Pl. **-lesen**. [Ger., f. *spät* late + *lese* picking, vintage.] A white wine made (esp. in Germany) from grapes gathered later than the general harvest.

[**1926** P. M. SHAND *Bk. of Wine* vi. 185 Where the wine is a selected one..the inscription should terminate with the word *Auslese*.., or *Spätlese*.] **1935** H. R. RUDD *Hocks & Moselles* ii. 24 The grower may..leave some..grapes hanging for a week or two longer... He will make with them casks of 'Spätlese', or 'late gathered'. **1951** S. F. HALLGARTEN *Rhineland Wineland* 52 Sweet white wines, Spaetlesen and Auslesen, are very suitable. **1963** *Times* 8 Feb. 12/5 We shall consider three main groups—the lesser wines; the Spätlesen (made from grapes gathered later than the general harvest) and Auslesen (gathering of selected bunches). **1967** K. GILES *Death & Mr Prettyman* i. 37 My husband sent back a case of Spätlese, six years old, light on the tongue as Epsom salts, just the thing with a bit of smoked fish. **1977** *Times* 2 Apr. 14/8 In such a [good] year all the grapes are..upgraded..so that the simple Qualitätswein.. would be as great as a Spätlese, and so on.

spatour, variant of SPATURE *Obs.*

ˈ**spatous**, *a. Min.* ? *Obs.* [f. SPAT *sb.*[3]] Spathic, spathose.

1803 PLYMLEY *Agric. Shropsh.* 50 The white spatous-ore, and considerable quantity of black-jack. **1811** PINKERTON *Petral.* II. 207 Red felspar, in irregular spots,..in greenish spatous hornblende. **1834** *Gentl. Mag.* CIV. I. 175 The black hornblende is the only constituent which has a.. spatous appearance.

†**spattania**. *Obs.* Also **-ana, -armia, spatania.** [Of obscure origin: connexion with med.L. *spatana* a kind of iris (*c* 1300 in Matth. Sylvat.) is uncertain.] (See quots.)

1583 GREENE *Mamillia* Wks. (Grosart) II. 23 The tallest blade of Spattania hath his full height in one moment. **1589** —— *Menaphon* (Arb.) 83 There is no herbe sooner sprung vp than the Spattarmia nor sooner fadeth. **1590** LODGE *Euphues Gold. Legacy* Q 2, Loue growes not like the hearb Spattana to his perfection in one night.

ˈ**spatted**, *ppl. a.* [f. SPAT *sb.*[5]] **a.** Provided with or wearing spats or short gaiters.

1894 G. DU MAURIER *Trilby* II. 184 Our three friends balmorally-booted or neatly spatted. **1894** HALL CAINE *Manxman* 136 One of his spatted feet was on the break.

b. Of an aircraft or its undercarriage: equipped with spats.

1936 R. BRENARD in J. Hammerton *War in Air* XIX. 606 (*caption*) The latest version..has its three 350 h.p. Gnome-Rhone engines enclosed in low-drag cowlings and faired into a 'spatted' undercarriage. **1943** HUNT & PRINGLE *Service Slang* 61 If the wheels of a 'spatted' plane do not retract, it is said to have 'permanent spats'. **1960** C. H. GIBBS-SMITH *Aeroplane* I. xi. 78 This remarkable three-seater had fully cantilevered wings..and 'spatted' undercarriage.

spattee (spæˈtiː). [f. SPAT *sb.*[5], after *puttee*.] Formerly, an outer stocking or legging worn by women for protection against wet and cold.

1926 *Bulletin* 17 Aug. 4/3 The invention is called the 'Highland spattee' and is a Highlander's stocking made spat-fashion to allow the wearer to slip it easily over her shoes and silk stocking. **1928** *Daily Tel.* 10 Jan. 6 The knitted spattee. **1939** JOYCE *Finnegans Wake* I. 11 All spoiled goods go into her nabsack: curtrages and rattlin buttins, nappy spattees and flasks of all nations.

spatten, obs. f. pa. t. (pl.) and pa. pple. SPIT *v.*

† **'spatter**, *sb.*[1] *Obs.* [Alteration of *spatour* SPATURE.] A spatule.

1569 R. ANDROSE tr. *Alexis' Secr.* IV. II. 40 Worke it with a spatter, vntill it be come vnto the heigth of waxe. *Ibid.* III. 25 Laboring them with the spatter. *Ibid.* 45 Working it alwayes with a spatter. **1590** BARROUGH *Meth. Physick* VIII. (1639) 420 Stirre [the materials]..with a spatter untill they come together. **1668** CULPEPPER & COLE *Barthol. Anat.* III. vi. 143 Having cut the pia Mater, open the sides thereof a little with a Spatter.

spatter ('spætə(r)), *sb.*[2] [f. SPATTER *v.* So WFlem. *spetter.*] **1.** A slight splash or sprinkle; a spattering.

1797 T. PARK *Sonn.* 86 'Tis odds that you escape the spatters. **1850** S. DOBELL *Roman* vi. Poet. Wks. (1875) 102, I would wash that hearthstone in your blood, If but the poorest spatter on the wall Would save my child! **1896** *Daily News* 23 Sept. 5/1 Some spatter of war-fire is, indeed, seen here and there.

2. *Geol.* Magmatic material emitted as small fluid fragments by a vent or fissure associated with a volcano; also, a fragment of this.

1953 *Bull. U.S. Geol. Survey* No. 994. 23 Small steep-sided cones composed very largely of spatter are common on the rift zones of Hualalai volcano. **1969** [see DRIBLET *sb.* 4]. **1971** *New Scientist* 10 June 611/1 Irregular explosions threw bright orange lumps of spatter as high as 20 metres. **1976** G. B. OAKESHOTT *Volcanoes & Earthquakes* vi. 49 Activity had concentrated on the building of a combined cinder-and-spatter cone made up of hardened lava fragments and congealed blobs or spatters.

'spatter, *sb.*[3] *rare.* [Short for SPATTERDASH.] A spatterdash or gaiter.

1898 T. HARDY *Wessex Poems* 94 I've my knapsack, fire-lock, spatters.

spatter ('spætə(r)), *v.* [app. a frequentative of the stem found in Du. and LG. *spatten* to burst, spout, etc.: cf. WFris. *spatterje*, Helgoland *spattere* to spirt, WFlem. *spetteren* to spatter.]

I. *trans.* **1. a.** To scatter or disperse in fragments.

1582 STANYHURST *Æneis* II. (Arb.) 44 But Capys..Did wish thee woodden monster weare drowned,..or ribs too spatter a sunder. **1658** BROMHALL *Treat. Specters* II. 175 [He] did command..to burn all, and to spatter the ruines all about. **1877** TENNYSON *Harold* II. ii, O God, that I were in some wide, waste field With nothing but my battle-axe and him To spatter his brains!

b. With *out*: To sputter, or cause to sputter.

a **1586** SIDNEY *Arcadia* IV. (1598) 396 He without any regard of reseruing it for the Kings knowledge, spattered out the bottome of his stomacke. **1649** G. DANIEL *Trinarch.*, *Hen. V*, xxv, But now the Palsey of the Common Earth Trembles my Quill, and Spatters out my Inke. **1806** H. SIDDONS *Maid, Wife & Widow* III. 76 The indiscriminate censure which every pert would-be witling spatters out against the practice of the law.

c. To dash, cast, send flying, in drops or small particles. Const. with preps. or advs.

1721 BAILEY, *Spatter*, to dash or sprinkle upon. **1841** CATLIN *N. Amer. Ind.* lii. (1844) II. 141 Several others struck so near on each side as to spatter the water into our faces. **1852** HAWTHORNE *Blithedale Rom.* v, The..puffs of wind spattered the snow against the windows. **1889** *Anthony's Photogr. Bull.* II. 308 The person working at the next sink cannot spatter hypo or other chemicals on his neighbor's plate. **1905** [see 7].

2. a. To splash or stain with drops of fluid, mud, etc.; to bespatter; *fig.* to assail with obloquy or detraction.

1645 WITHER *Vox Pacifica* 65 Your Foes..Finde meanes to spatter, and to ruine those, Whom, to defend, you did (with vowes) professe. **1656** LD. HATTON in *Nicholas Papers* (Camden) III. 284 Mr Smith is uery sencible that many little pens will spatter him. **1718** LADY M. W. MONTAGU *Let. to C'tess Mar* 28 Aug., The arms of France over the house of the envoy [were] spattered with dung in the night. **1727** GAY *Fables* I. xiv. 45 Bend all your force to spatter merit. **1879** FROUDE *Cæsar* xviii. 296 As an advocate, he must praise the man whom, a year before, he had spattered with ignominy. **1900** *19th Cent.* XLVIII. 795 They're kicking in that mud-puddle, and trying to spatter your nice white dress.

b. To cover in a dispersed manner.

1647 H. MORE *Cupid's Confl.* xlii, So Natures carelesse pencill dipt in light With sprinkled starres hath spattered the Night. **1841** DICKENS *Barn. Rudge* lxv, Lighted brands came whirling down, spattering the ground with fire. **1864** LOWELL *Fireside Trav.* 240 The walls were spattered with placards.

3. Of fluids, etc.: To fall or strike upon (something) in scattered drops.

1837 CARLYLE *Fr. Rev.* III. I. vi, He dies..; his blood spattering the cheeks of his old Mother. **1860** GOSSE *Rom. Nat. Hist.* 42 Huge drops of warm rain, like blood-drops, are spattering the stones.

II. *intr.* **4. a.** To spring or fly, to spirt, in drops or particles; to throw off drops or small fragments.

1600 SURFLET *Countrie Farme* III. liii. 553 As it is boiling ..it will be spattering and casting vp bubbles. *Ibid.*, If it spatter, there is yet some waterish moisture remaining in it. **1674** RAY *Coll. Wds.*, *Iron Work* 129 If..you cast upon the Iron a piece of Brass it will hinder the metal from working, causing it to spatter about. **1863** TYNDALL *Heat* ii. 38 The liquid metal is seen spattering over the poles of the magnet. **1883** *Harper's Mag.* June 117/2 The mineral ichor rises and dances in clouds of steam; it fumes, it spouts, it spatters.

b. To fall, descend, strike, in heavy drops or with a sound suggestive of these.

1675 HANNAH WOOLLEY *Gentlew. Comp.* 145 Pour your Eggs and Cream very high into the Bason, that it may spatter in it. **1859** HAWTHORNE *Fr. & It. Note-bks.* II. 279 The rain-drops began to spatter down faster. **1869** TOZER *Highl. Turkey* I. 316 We heard their bullets..spatter against the rocks. **1887** BESANT *The World went* v, The musket-balls spattering in the water.

5. a. To eject small drops of saliva or particles of food, etc., from the mouth; to splutter while speaking; to cause spattering in any way.

1618 BRETON *Courtier & Countryman* Wks. (Grosart) II. 14/1 The Seruants..no sooner tasted of it, but they did so spit and spatter as if they had been poysoned. *c* **1645** HOWELL *Lett.* I. 229 The Grave spatter'd and shook his Head, saying, 'Twas the greatest error he had committed since he knew what belonged to a Soldier. **1649** MILTON *Eikon.* 19 That mind must needs be irrecoverably deprav'd, which..tasting but once of one just deed, spatters at it, and abhorrs the relish ever after. **1828** LYTTON *Pelham* xxxiv, The confused hubbub of the little domestic deities, who ate, clattered, spattered, and squabbled around her.

b. To scatter drops of ink.

a **1640** JACKSON *Creed* XI. xlii. Wks. XI. 258 As children often make fair letters while their tutors guide their hands, but spatter and blot and dash after they be left to their own guidance.

6. To walk or tread in some splashy substance.

1806 BLOOMFIELD *Wild Flowers* 9 The mill-brook.., Good creature! how he'd spatter through! **1897** RHOSCOMYL *White Rose Arno* 186 'Well, I must find out where I stand first,' said he to himself as he spattered along in the darkness.

III. 7. In combs., as **spatter-cone, -dock** (see quots.); **spatter rampart** *Geol.*, a wall or ridge formed of spatter along the edge of a fissure in a volcanic area; **spatterware, spatter ware** (see quots. 1959, 1977[2]); **spatter-work**, a method of producing decorative work by spraying ink or other fluid over something (e.g. leaves of plants) laid on paper or other suitable material.

1856 A. GRAY *Man. Bot.* (1860) 23 *Nuphar*... Yellow Pond-Lily. Spatter-dock. **1873** ELIZ. PHELPS *Trotty's Wedding Tour* 224 Gray spatter-work (oak leaves and acorns) on cranberry silk. **1891** KIPLING & BALESTIER *Naulahka* (1892) 21 His collection of..embroideries, and.. sofa-pillows and spatter-work filled his parlour. **1905** CHAMBERLIN & SALISBURY *Geol.* I. 580 A still more subordinate variety consists of 'spatter-cones' formed by small mildly explosive vents that spatter forth little dabs of lava which form chimneys, or cones. **1935** *N.Y. Times* 9 June x. 9/2 'Gaudy Dutch' was the name given to some of the spatterware made in the shape of peacocks and tulips for this area many years ago. **1953** *Bull. U.S. Geol. Survey* No. 994. 6 The common basalts of Hawaii erupt quietly, building only low spatter ramparts and diminutive spatter-and-cinder cones. **1959** L. GROSS *Guide to Antiques* viii. 97 Spatterware is a fairly heavy earthenware with characteristic decoration of color applied with a sponge or spattered on to give a stippled effect. **1967** G. MACDONALD in Hess & Poldervaart *Basalts* I. 53 Spatter ramparts may be several kilometers long, although generally they are not continuous over the entire distance. **1977** A. HALLAM *Planet Earth* 96 Spatter cones and spatter ramparts form around parasitic vents and fissures when eruptions are less violent and the magma more fluid. **1977** FLEMING & HONOUR *Penguin Dict. Decorative Arts* 751/1 *Spatter ware*, C19 wares decorated with bright colours applied with a sponge through a stencil, usually giving a blotchy effect. **1980** *Times* 4 Oct. 14/3 On the Staffordshire 'spatterware', in particular, Sotheby's American experts were out by a factor of 10 on some of their estimates.

Hence **spatte'ration**, spattering. *U.S.*

1853 MOODIE *Life Clearings* 112, I wonder if..this waterfall [has] been underminin' With constant spatteration. **1902** *Westm. Gaz.* 23 June 2/1 For Londoners there is no alternative between spatteration and suffocation.

spatterdash ('spætədæʃ). [f. SPATTER *v.* + DASH *v.* Cf. SPATTER-LASH, -PLASH, and the dial. *splatter-*, *spattle-dash(er).*] A kind of long gaiter or legging of leather, cloth, etc., to keep the trousers or stockings from being spattered, esp. in riding. Chiefly in *pl.*

sing. **1687** E. RAVENSCROFT *Long Vac.*, *Prol. to Titus Andronicus*, Prepare to gallop down on Smithfield Titts, Equip'd with the Heel-Spur and Spatter-dash. **1756** TOLDERVY *Hist. 2 Orphans* III. 122 He generally left his stall,..which one day caused him the loss of two pair of breeches, and a spatterdash. **1778** SHERIDAN *Camp* I. ii, There's a leg for a spatterdash. **1841** BORROW *Zincali* I. v, The legs are protected..by a species of spatterdash, either of cloth or leather.

pl. **1687** [see SPATTER-LASH]. **1694** MOTTEUX *Rabelais* IV. xii, The porter soon found him out, by his large greasy spatterdashes, his..hollow flanked mare [etc.]. *Ibid.* xxxii, Cows Leather Spatter-dashes. **1719** DE FOE *Crusoe* I. (Globe) 151, I had..made me a Pair of some-things..to flap over my Legs, and lace on either Side like Spatter-dashes. **1746** in *Rep. Comm. Ho. Commons* II. 99 (Land Forces), Haversacks,..Frocks to go over the Mens Cloaths, Spatter-dashes, and Watering Caps. **1777** W. DALRYMPLE *Trav. Sp. & Port.* xliii, His waistcoat and breeches are generally leather, with a pair of cloth spatterdashes on his legs. **1807–8** W. IRVING *Salmag.* (1824) 358 Dressed in a man's hat, a cloth overcoat, and spatterdashes. **1858** CARLYLE *Fredk. Gt.* IV. viii. (1872) II. 20 This done, he shall as rapidly as possible get on his shoes and spatterdashes.

b. *Comb.*, as ***spatterdash-maker***, ***-making***.

1768 STERNE *Sent. Journ.* (1902) 30 His talents of drum-beating and spatterdash-making. **1905** *Westm. Gaz.* 1 Apr. 3/1 La Fleur,..ex-drummer and spatterdash-maker.

spatterdashed, *ppl. a.* [f. prec. + -ED[1].] Clad in, provided with, spatterdashes.

1848 THACKERAY *Van. Fair* xlv, Many young gentlemen canter up on thoroughbred hacks, spatterdashed to the knee. **1862** SALA *Seven Sons* I. xi. 274 The dashing [Miss] Southbank, splendid in a scarlet riding-habit, spatterdashed with patent leather.

spatterdasher. *Obs.* exc. *dial.* = SPATTERDASH.

1684 *Yorks. Dial.* 373 (E.D.S.), Wife, what's become of my Spatterdashers? **1711** *Lond. Gaz.* No. 4809/4 A pair of Spatterdashers. **1767** *Connoisseur* No. 79 ¶2 (ed. 5) III. 60 He wore upon his legs something that resembled spatterdashers [1755–61 spatterdashes].

spattered ('spætəd), *ppl. a.* [f. SPATTER *v.*]

1. Dispersed or scattered, esp. in drops or small particles.

1647 H. MORE *Minor Poems*, *Exorcismus* iv. Wks. (Grosart) 178/1 Those Eastern spatterd lights..purpling the gay Night. **1720** POPE *Iliad* XXII. 97 Where famish'd Dogs..Shall lick their mangled Master's spatter'd Gore. **1814** SCOTT *Lord of Isles* III. xxix, The spatter'd brain and bubbling blood Hiss'd on the half-extinguish'd wood.

2. Sprinkled, splashed; covered with spots of liquid matter, mud, etc.

1784 COWPER *Task* IV. 6 He comes..With spatter'd boots, strapp'd waist, and frozen locks. **1794** —— *Needless Alarm* 125 By panting dog, tir'd man, and spatter'd horse. *a* **1813** A. WILSON *Foresters* Poet. Wks. (Belfast ed.) 233 The cow loud bawling fills the spattered door. **1892** *Pall Mall G.* 3 Oct. 2/2 Such is the prospect from my spatter'd pane.

'spatterer. *rare*[-0]. One who spatters.

1611 COTGR., *Cracheur*, a spitter, spawler, spatterer.

'spattering, *vbl. sb.* [f. SPATTER *v.*]

1. The action of splashing or sprinkling, etc.

1604 T. M. *Black Bk.* in *Middleton's Wks.* (Bullen) VIII. 40 The lamentable spattering of his pearl-colour silk stockings. **1611** COTGR., *Crachement*, a spitting, spatling, spattering, spawling. **1788** G. KEATE *Pelew Isl.* (1789) 179 *note*, It is probable that the spattering of it on their naked bodies might create an unpleasant sensation. **1805** A. WILSON *Poems & Lit. Prose* (1876) II. 150 A fleet of ducks ..alarmed with sudden spattering soar. **1856** HAWTHORNE *Eng. Note-bks.* (1879) I. 126 Little spatterings of rain.

† **2.** A smattering. *Obs.*[-1]

a **1662** HEYLIN *Laud* (1668) 317 A small spattering in the Hebrew, made him subject unto some suspicion of Heretical Fancies.

3. A noise (esp. that made by bullets) suggestive of the fall or impact of heavy drops.

1866 *Ann. Reg.* 230 Suddenly..a spattering of musketry breaks out. **1870** *Daily News* 29 Oct., A steady spattering of independent fire, could be heard.

'spattering, *ppl. a.* [f. as prec.] That spatters, in senses of the vb.

1576 NEWTON *Lemnie's Complex.* (1633) 148 His beard sluttish, driveling and filthy, with spattering snevell deformed. **1611** COTGR., *Crache en-ruelle*, a spawling, or spattering fellow. **1667** MILTON *P.L.* x. 567 They..instead of Fruit Chewd bitter Ashes, which th' offended taste With spattering noise rejected. **1708** J. PHILLIPS *Cyder* I. 28 With a writhen mouth and spattering noise He tastes the bitter morsel. **1818** SCOTT *Rob Roy* xxx, A continued spattering fire, in which every shot was multiplied by a thousand echoes. **1849** EASTWICK *Dry Leaves* 27 A sudden squall, which..sprinkled us with a spattering rain. **1883** *Mag. of Art* Sept. 470/2 What heaps of linen! What a spattering fire of blows!

† **spatter-lash, -plash**, varr. SPATTERDASH.

1687 MIÉGE *Gt. Fr. Dict.*, Spatter-dashes, or (as they call em in the West) Spatter-plashes, *guêtres.* **1725** BAILEY *Erasm. Colloq.* 131 Where have you been, with your Spatter Lashes?

spatter-work: see SPATTER *v.* 7.

spatting ('spætɪŋ), *vbl. sb.* [f. SPAT *v.*[1]] Of shell-fish: The action or process of depositing spawn. Also *attrib.*

1864 *Morn. Star* 28 Dec., It is calculated, in spite of the bad spatting of the last three years, that there is a stock of oysters..of the value of upwards of 100,000*l.* **1866** *Cornh. Mag.* Aug. 163 We have not had a very good spatting season since 1860. **1877** *Q. Rev.* CXLIV. 486 The spatting process, or labour of the parental oyster.

spattle ('spæt(ə)l), *sb.*[1] *Obs.* exc. *dial.* Forms: α. 1 spatl (spadl, spaðl), 3 spatel, 5 -ell, -ill, -ylle, 6 -ele, -yll, spattyl (*Sc.* -ill); 6 spattle, 6–7, 9 *dial.*, spattle. β. 3–4 spotle, 3, 9 *dial.*, spottle; 4 spotel(e, 4–5 -il, 5 -ell, -yl(l. [OE. *spátl* (*spádl*, also *spáld* SPOLD), f. **spát-*, stem of *spǽtan* to spit. Cf. MLG. *spêdel*, OFris. *spêdel*, *spêdla*.] Spittle.

α. *c* **897** K. ÆLFRED *Gregory's Past. C.* xxxvi. 261 Se ilca.. se na ne forbeaȝ mid his nebbe ðara triowleasena monna spatl, ðonne hie him on ðæt nebb spætton. *c* **950** *Lindisf. Gosp.* John ix. 6 [He] uorhte lam of ðæm spadle & ahof þæt lam ofer eȝo his. *c* **975** *Rushw. Gosp.* Matt. xxvii. 30 Spittende on him heor spaðl. *c* **1000** *Sax. Leechd.* II. 226 ðif þonne ȝit sio adl eȝle, do spatl to. *a* **1240** *Wohunge* in *O.E. Hom.* I. 279 þat tu mihtes wið þat spatel..wasche mi sawle. *c* **1400** tr. *Secreta Secret.*, *Gov. Lordsh.* 72 þat schalt þow knowe..by þy spatill rennand to þy mouth. *c* **1410** *Master of Game* (MS. Digby 182) xii, Put it in a dysshe wt þe spatell of iii. or iiii. fastynge men. **1483** *Cath. Angl.* 352/1 A Spatylle, *saliua*, *sputum.* *a* **1529** SKELTON *P. Sparowe* 358, I..fed him with my spattyl, With his byll betwene my lyppes. **1555** W. WATREMAN *Fardle Facions* II. xii. 277 He mingleth earthe and his spattle toguether, and smereth the eyes, eares, and nosethrilles of the childe. **1601** DEACON & WALKER *Ans. to Darel* 180 By the touch of Christs finger, and the loosing of his tongue by his spattle. **1664** POWER *Exp. Philos.* I. 10 A Wood Louse..fastened to the object-plate by a little spattle. **1876–** in Yorks. and Som. glossaries.

β. *a* **1225** *Ancr. R.* 288 þauh heo bispeteð hire mid hire blake spotle. *c* **1290** *S. Eng. Leg.* I. 362 Seint Marc with is spottle watte a luyte vrþe on þe grounde. *c* **1380** WYCLIF *Serm.* Sel. Wks. II. 193 Cristis spotel hadde greet vertue. **1387** TREVISA *Higden* (Rolls) I. 195 Men þat heleþ smytynge of serpentes wiþ touche or wiþ spotel. *c* **1440** *Promp. Parv.*

469/2 Spyt, or spotle, *sputum, screa, saliva.* **1460–70** *Bk. Quintessence* II. 19 Mortifie it wiþ fastynge spotil. **1886** *Rochdale Gloss.* 83 *Spottle,* matter (saliva) spit from the mouth.

spattle ('spæt(ə)l), *sb.*^{2} Also 5 spatyl, 6 -yll, 6–7 spatle (7 spatwel). [Anglicized f. SPATULE. Cf. Du., G., Da., and Sw. *spatel.*]

1. A spatula. Now *rare* or *Obs.*

c **1440** *Promp. Parv.* 467/2 Spatyl, instrument to clense wythe soorys, *pessaria.* **1530** PALSGR. 273/2 Spatyll, an instrument. **1576** G. BAKER tr. *Gesner's Jewell of Health* 194 When the same shall begynne to melte..Sturre with a spattle. **1594** PLAT *Jewell-ho.* II. 38 With a woodden spatle or spoone, beat them wel together. **1605** TIMME *Quersit.* III. 155 Stirre it continually with an yron spattle. **1658** A. FOX *Würtz' Surg.* II. ix. 80 Unguentum Mucilaginis put into the wounded Eye with a spattle will clear the sight. **1725** *Fam. Dict.* s.v. *March-Pane,* Let all be afterwards well incorporated, with the Spattle. **1854** PAPPE *Silva Capensis* (1862) 59 *Spathulate,* shaped like a spattle.

2. *techn.* and *dial.* (See quots.)

In first quot. associated with SPATTLE *v.*^{2}

1875 KNIGHT *Dict. Mech.* 2254 *Spattle,*..a tool for mottling a molded article with coloring matter. **1888** ADDY *Sheffield Gloss.* 231 *Spattle,* a wooden spoon used for lifting meal from the meal-tub to the bake-stone. **1899** *Cumbld. Gloss.* 307/2 *Spattle,* a peel..used for putting the loaves into the oven, and for removing them.

'spattle, *sb.*^{3} *dial.* [Alteration of PATTLE *sb.*, perh. after prec.] A plough-spade or other small spade. Also *spattle-hoe.*

1824 MACTAGGART *Gallovid. Encycl.* 460 Another, perhaps, gives the sock, another the stilts, another the spattle. **1834** *Tait's Mag.* I. 528 Farmers became country gentlemen; changing..the spattle-hoe for the riding-whip. **1869–94** in Lanc. and Northumbld. glossaries.

†**'spattle,** *v.*^{1} *Obs.* Also 4–5, 7 spatle, 5 spatel. [OE. *spátlian* (more commonly *spǽtlan, -ian*), f. *spátl* SPATTLE *sb.*^{1}] *intr.* and *trans.* To spit. Also with *out.*

c **1000** ÆLFRIC *Voc.* in Wr.-Wülcker 162 *Pitisso,* ic spatliȝe. *c* **1325** *Old Age* in *E.E.P.* (1862) 149, I spitte, i spatle, in speche i sporne. *c* **1330** R. BRUNNE *Chron. Wace* (Rolls) 8196 [The dragons] Spatled, spouted, belewed, & byten. *c* **1450** LYDG. *Secrees* 1416 Erthe, Autumpnus, and Age accordyn in oon, Slough, malencolye, spatlyng euere among. *a* **1470** H. PARKER *Dives & Pauper* (W. de W. 1496) VIII. xiv. 341/1, I suffered to be beten and bounde, to be spateled and despysed. **1538** BALE *Thre Lawes* 444, I can werke wyles in battle, If I do ones but spattle. **1554** PHILPOT *Examin. & Writ.* (Parker Soc.) 313, I would I had a fountain of spittle to spattle on them. **1601** DENT *Pathw. Heaven* (1617) 160 Would to God..that we were come to such a..loathing of lying, that we should euen spattle at it! **1611** COTGR., *Cracher,* to spit; spawle; spattle, bespatter. *Ibid., Craché,* spet, or spatled out.

spattle ('spæt(ə)l), *v.*^{2} Now *techn.* and *dial.* Also 7 spatle. [Related to SPATTER *v.*] *trans.* To spatter or sprinkle; to mottle.

1611 COTGR., *Enfanger,* to spatle, beray, or durtie all ouer with myre. *Ibid., Entretaché,* spotted (and spatled) here and there. **1875** [see SPATTLING *vbl. sb.*^{2}]. **1879–** in Shropshire and Cheshire glossaries.

†**'spattling,** *vbl. sb.*^{1} *Obs.* [f. SPATTLE *v.*^{1}] Spitting; spittle.

c **1000** ÆLFRIC *Voc.* in Wr.-Wülcker 162 *Pituita, i. minuta saliua,* spatlung. *a* **1240** *Lofsong* in *O.E. Hom.* I. 207 Bi his scornunge and bi his spotlunge and bufettunge. *a* **1240** *Wohung* Ibid. 279, I for þe luue of þe þolede schome and bismere and schomeliche spateling of unwurði ribauz. **1576** NEWTON *Lemnie's Complex.* II. 106 b, Spettle, sweat, sneuel, spattling and Phlegme. **1611** COTGR., *Crachement,* a spitting, spatling, spattering, spawling.

'spattling, *vbl. sb.*^{2} [f. SPATTLE *v.*^{2}] Spattering; mottling.

1611 COTGR., *Papillotage,* a spatling, or spottinesse. *Ibid., Papillottes de boue,* mirie spots, spatlings, bedashings. **1875** KNIGHT *Dict. Mech.* 2254/2 *Spattling-machine,* one for sprinkling earthenware with glaze, or coloured slip, to make party-coloured ware.

'spattling, *ppl. a.* Also 6– spatling. [f. SPATTLE *v.*^{1}] *spattling poppy* (or *campion*), bladder campion. *Obs.* exc. *arch.*

1597 GERARDE *Herbal* II. lxviii. §4. 295 *Papauer spumeum,* which I haue Englished Spatling Poppie. *Ibid.* cxxi. §7. 384 Spatling Campion hath a slender hoarie stalke. **1611** COTGR., *Pavot escumant,* spatling Poppie, frothie Poppie. **1640** PARKINSON *Theat. Bot.* 263 Some with us call it Knapbottle, and others Spatling or Frothy Poppy. *a* **1722** LISLE *Husb.* (1752) 324, I gathered a large handful of spatling-poppy, and held it to the cow. **1758** MRS. DELANY *Life & Corr.* (1861) III. 499 Some sea-holly, and spatling poppy. **1785** MARTYN *Lett. Bot.* xix. (1794) 274 Spatling Poppy is not an uncommon weed among corn and in meadows. **1829** *Glover's Hist. Derby* I. 114 *Silene inflata,* spattling poppy, white bottle or bladder champion.

†**spatul.** *Obs. rare.* Also spatull. [var. of SPATULE: cf. SPATTLE *sb.*^{2}] = SPATULA I.

1600 SURFLET *Countrie Farme* I. xii. 81 Stirring it about many times with a spatull of cleane and faire wood. *Ibid.* 82 Mixe them all togither, and stirre them well with a spatull. *a* **1663** K. DIGBY *Chymical Secrets* (1683) 47 Stirring continually with an Iron Spatul.

‖**spatula** ('spætjʊlə). [L. *spatula,* var. of *spathula* SPATHULA, dim. of *spatha* SPATHA. Cf. Sp. *espatula,* It. *spatola.*

The erroneous form *spattular* occurs in Topsell *Four-f. Beasts* (1607) 511. For Anglicized forms see SPATULE, SPATUL, SPATTLE *sb.*^{2}, SPARTLE *sb.*, also (with change of ending) SPATURE and SPATTER *sb.*^{1}]

1. A simple implement of wood, ivory, or metal, having a flat elongated form with various modifications of shape and size, used for a variety of purposes: **a.** For stirring mixtures (esp. of a medical nature), spreading ointments or plasters, etc.

1525 tr. *Jerome of Brunswick's Surg.* C iv/2 Take a spatula & styrre all these togeder. **1599** A. M. tr. *Gabelhouer's Bk. Physicke* 45/1 Reverberate the same dilligentlye with the spatula, and it will be the better. **1639** T. DE GRAY *Expert Farrier* 305 Laid on a spatula plaister-wise. **1669** W. SIMPSON *Hydrol. Chym.* 187 Over which fume..we directly plac'd a spatula. **1683** PETTUS *Fleta Min.* I. (1686) 162 Stir it about continually with a wooden spatula. **1718** QUINCY *Compl. Disp.* 15 We many times stir the Body that is to be calcin'd with a Spatula, or else mix it with something else. **1799** G. SMITH *Laboratory* I. 40 Take some cotton, and with a spatula..work that, the nitre and the brandy together. **1823** P. NICHOLSON *Pract. Build.* 382 Being stirred with a spatula till the whole becomes incorporated. **1837** *Flemish Husb.* 61 in *L.U.K.* III, The butter..is well washed and worked with..a kind of spatula or flat spoon. **1873** SPON *Workshop Rec.* Ser. I. 18/1 The mixture is removed from the stone by a spatula.

b. For minor surgical operations or for the medical examination of certain organs.

1684 tr. *Bonet's Merc. Compit.* II. 45 This Scab..hath fallen off, by the help onely of a Spatula. **1694** *Phil. Trans.* XVIII. 220 With a small Spatula..she pick'd out five or six Worms at a time. **1755** *Gentl. Mag.* XXV. 39 The tongue..must be loosened with a spatula. **1803** *Med. Jrnl.* X. 330 He ordered the patient to take in his mouth a silver spatula, to which the conducting chain had been adapted. **1853** LOWELL *Lett.* (1894) I. iii. 222 There is no spatula with which you can hold the Public's tongue while you force things down their throat. **1879** T. BRYANT *Pract. Surg.* II. 5 This is best done by introducing the little finger or a spatula into the nostril.

c. For technical operations of various kinds.

1842 LOUDON *Suburban Hort.* 306 The strip of bark..being raised up..by the spatula of the budding-knife. **1865** LUBBOCK *Preh. Times* xi. 358 The pottery was all made by women. Their tools were very simple, consisting of..a flat mallet or spatula for the surface [etc.]. **1883** *Harper's Mag.* Oct. 775 The few..tools of the craft—chisel, hammer, spatula—lay in various places. **1887** D. MAGUIRE *Art Massage* ii. (ed. 4) 22 We give this name [i.e. palette] to a kind of spatula in the shape of a battledoor with a long handle.

2. A ferule. *rare*$^{-1}$.

1830 MRS. BRAY *Fitz of Fitz-ford* iii. (1884) 29 A large birchen rod,..and a wooden spatula, to inflict punishment on the hand.

3. *Ornith.* The roseate spoonbill.

1872 *Routledge's Every Boy's Annual* 138 The rose-coloured spatula, a bird that frequents lakes and rivers [in America], and lives on fish.

4. *attrib.*, as *spatula-hand, -hook*; †**spatula-bird,** a spoonbill.

1750 *London Mag.* May 224/2 As to the Spatula-bird,..it is a kind of water fowl, of the goose or duck kind. **1861** PEARSON *Early & Mid. Ages* vii. 66 The *spatula* hand..is rather that of a mechanician than an artist. **1895** *Arnold & Sons' Catal. Surg. Instrum.* 145 Spatula Hook.., in ivory handle.

5. *Comb.*, as *spatula-like, -shaped.*

1796 WITHERING *Brit. Plants* (ed. 3) IV. 100 The spatula-shaped leaves appear at the end of these branches. **1826** KIRBY & SP. *Entomol.* IV. xlvi. 263 *Spatulate,*..spatula-shaped. Broader and rounded at the apex, linear and narrow at the base. **1834** MCMURTRIE *Cuvier's Anim. Kingd.* 150 Their bill..becoming widened and flattened..so as to form a spatula-like disk. **1880** MISS BIRD *Japan* II. 93 A spatula-shaped shuttle of engraved wood.

spatula'mancy. [ad. med. or mod.L. *spatulamancia,* f. *spatula* shoulder-blade.] Divination by means of the shoulder-blade of an animal. (Cf. SPADE-BONE and SPEAL-BONE.)

In quot. 1652 there is app. some error or omission, as the explanation would more properly apply to **spatilomancy,* f. Gr. σπατίλη excrement, parings of leather.

1652 GAULE *Magastrom.* xix. 166 *Spatalamancy,* [divining] by skins, bones, excrement. **1720** DE FOE *D. Campbell* (1841) 241 If it be by consulting the shoulder-bones of any beast, it goes by the name of spatulamancy. **1887** RIBTON-TURNER *Vagrants & Vagrancy* 78 Spatulamancy.., by reading..the blade bone of a shoulder of mutton well scraped.

spatular ('spætjʊlə(r)), *a.* [f. SPATULA.] Having the form of a spatula. Also *Comb.*

1891 *Cent. Dict., Spatular,* like a spatula in form; spatulate. **1906** ALICE WERNER *Natives Brit. Central Africa* v. 107 She..scraped..the neck..with a little spatular-shaped iron razor.

†**'spatulary,** *a. Obs.*$^{-1}$ [f. med.L. *spatula* shoulder-blade, SPATULA.] (See quot.)

1651 J. F[REAKE] *Agrippa's Occ. Philos.* 66 Whence there arose a spatulary kind of divining (i.e.) by the Shoulder-blades.

spatulate ('spætjʊlət), *a.* [ad. mod.L. *spatulatus,* f. *spatula* SPATULA. Cf. SPATHULATE *a.*] Having a broadened and rounded end like that of a common form of spatula: **a.** *Bot.* Of leaves, etc.

1760 J. LEE *Introd. Bot.* III. v. (1765) 176 *Spatulate,* resembling a Spatula; when the Figure is roundish, but lengthened out by the Addition of a linear Base that is narrower. **1785** MARTYN *Lett. Bot.* xxv. (1794) 354 The leaves have..hairy, spatulate leaflets. **1806** GALPINE *Brit. Bot.* 382 L[eaves] several, spatulate, rough at the apex. **1828** SIR J. E. SMITH *Eng. Flora* II. 94 Leaves linear-lanceolate; ..lowermost stalked, somewhat spatulate. **1850** TYAS *Fav. Field Fl.* Ser. II. 74 The leaves..immediately from the root, ovate or spatulate.

b. *Zool.* Of organs or parts.

1826 KIRBY & SP. *Entomol.* IV. 263. **1838** *Penny Cycl.* XI. 232/2 Lower incisor teeth [of giraffe]..spatulate. **1851** S. P. WOODWARD *Mollusca* I. 69 Pen like loligo, but dilated and spatulate behind. **1877** HUXLEY *Anat. Inv. Animals* vi. 262 The large basal joint..bears a curved, spatulate process.

c. In general use.

1883 FRITH & ALLEN *Chiromancy* 70 A woman with rather spatulate fingers and a small thumb. **1892** *Pall Mall G.* 30 June 6 With the long, spatulate little finger the management of business will result. **1897** *Archaeol.* V. 480 Rods of gilt copper expanded at one end into flat spatulate heads.

Comb. **1885** J. THOMSON *Through Masai Land* ii. 88 Their weapons are a knife, a long, spatulate-shaped sword, and the bow and arrow.

spatulate ('spætjʊleɪt), *v.* [f. SPATUL(A + -ATE^3.]

1. *trans.* To stir or mix with a spatula. Also *absol.*

1923 in L. P. ANTHONY *Dict. Dental Sci.* 269/1. **1954** O. C. APPLEGATE *Essentials of Removable Partial Denture Prosthesis* 261 Spatulate thoroughly to free the mix of contained air. **1956** J. N. ANDERSON *Appl. Dental Materials* xviii. 216 The difficulty of spatulating such a mixture..usually results in overspatulation. **1957** *Jrnl. Amer. Ceramic Soc.* XL. 254/1 The fine powders were spatulated intensively with either pine oil or a commercial screen oil. **1981** *Scand. Jrnl. Dental Res.* LXXXIX. 100/2 Dentists often spatulate for too short a time.

2. *Surg.* To give a spatulate form to (a tubular vessel).

1976 *Ann. Thoracic Surg.* XXII. 235/2 The end of the divided subclavian artery was then spatulated. **1977** *Urologia Internat.* XXXII. 369 The..terminal ureter is amputated as needed and the ureter is spatulated for about 10 mm on its anterior surface.

Hence **'spatulating** *vbl. sb.*

1966 *Brit. Jrnl. Urol.* XXXVIII. 525 An atraumatic catgut suture is then inserted..at the apex of the spatulating incision. **1977** *Urologia Internat.* XXXII. 368 The main differences are the way the submucosal tunnel is prepared, the resection and spatulating of the terminal ureter, [etc.].

'spatulated, *a.* [f. prec. + -ED^1.] = SPATULATE *a.* Also as *ppl. a.*, given a spatulate form.

1777 FORSTER *Voy. round World* I. 437 Many were spatulated, flattish, and pointed. **1893** SELOUS *Trav. S.E. Africa* 48 Their two long tail feathers, broadened out or spatulated at the extremity in the form of a paddle. **1957** *Jrnl. Urol.* LXXVII. 413 The technique of anastomosing the spatulated ends of the ureter was used without the ureterotomy above the site of anastomosis. **1977** *Urologia Internat.* XXXII. 369 The spatulated end of the ureter is spread over the trigonal mucosa.

spatu'lation.

I. [f. SPATULATE *a.*] **1.** The fact or condition of being spatulate; a spatulate formation. *rare.*

1881 NEWTON in *Encycl. Brit.* XII. 359/1 The lateral feathers [of humming birds] may..suddenly enlarge into a terminal spatulation as in the..'Racquet-tails'. **1895** *Ibis* July 399 That in some motmots the spatulation of the tail-feathers may be effected by the bird itself.

II. [f. SPATULATE *v.*] **2.** Chiefly *Dentistry.* The process of stirring or mixing with a spatula.

1939 J. OSBORNE *Dental Mechanics* i. 5 (*heading*) Spatulation time. **1940** E. COVINGTON *Efficient Dental Assistant* iii. 71 Rapid and longer spatulation accelerate [*sic*] setting time with most plasters. **1957** V. J. KEHOE *Technique Film & Television Make-Up* xii. 147 Mix by spatulation until a smooth cream is obtained. **1977** *Jrnl. Biomed. Materials Res.* XI. 863 The spatulation was conducted at approximately 150 rpm, but that rate was difficult to maintain throughout the mixing interval. **1981** *Scand. Jrnl. Dental Res.* LXXXIX. 97/2 Twelve fillings with diameters of 6 mm were made.., varying the spatulation time from 5 to 60 s at 5 s intervals.

3. *Surg.* The procedure of spatulating a tubular vessel; also, the spatulated portion.

1977 *Urologia Internat.* XXXII. 372 We advocate spatulation of the terminal end of the ureter. **1979** *Brit. Jrnl. Urol.* LI. 105/2 The stitch is continued around the upper ends of the spatulations.

spatule ('spætju:l). Also 7 spattule. [a. OF. *spatule* (also mod.F.), ad. L. *spatula* SPATULA. Cf. MDu. *spatule, spatele.*]

1. = SPATULA I.

a **1425** tr. *Arderne's Treat. Fistula,* etc. 40 Anoynt it aboue þe sore wiþ a penne or feþer or wiþ a spatule. **1601** HOLLAND *Pliny* II. 508 Stirring it with spattules or ladles often-times in a day, vntill it be resolued into the vineger. **1658** EVELYN *Fr. Gard.* (1675) 294 Frequently stirring the bottom of your pan with the spatule. **1674** GUIDOTT *Observ. at Bath* in *Harl. Misc.* (Malh.) IV. 130 The very knives, and spatules, [which] I put in to stir some residence in the bottom. **1778** *Ann. Reg.* 124/2 With a kind of wooden spatule he scrapes all the blood. **1905** *Blackw. Mag.* May 630/2 A small 'spatule' in silver..which I acquired.

Comb. *a* **1686** SIR T. BROWNE *Norf. Birds* Wks. 1852 III. 314 They..are..remarkable in their white colour, copped crown, and spoon or spatule-like bill.

2. A spatulate terminal portion in the tail-feathers of a bird; a spatulate formation or part.

1873 *Proc. Zool. Soc.* 430 For a long time its tail had perfect spatules.

'spatuliform, *a. rare.* [f. SPATULA: see -(I)FORM.] Spatula-shaped.

1822 J. Parkinson *Outl. Oryctol.* 43 In soft spatuliform thin plates. **1893** S. Stebbing *Hist. Crustacea* vi. 65 The front is horizontal and not spatuliform.

spatu'lose, *a.* [See next and -OSE.] = next.

1867 Dk. Argyll *Reign of Law* v. 245 Plumes of enormous length, with flat or spatulose terminations. **1885** *Proc. Soc. Ant. Scot.* XIX. 142 The arrow-head is.. spatulose and bevelled at the broad end.

spatulous ('spætjʊləs), *a.* [f. SPATUL-A + -OUS.] Resembling a spatula in form; spatulate.

1828 Stark *Elem. Nat. Hist.* II. 439 Cells..slightly clavate or spatulous. **1865** *Spectator* 14 Jan. 39 The forefinger.., if pointed, shows a tendency to mysticism;..if spreading, or 'spatulous', to a restless, active, religious spirit. **1889** Mrs. Lynn Linton *Thro' Long Night* I. I. ii. 20 Sly may..splash his spatulous fingers in rose-water.

†**spature.** *Obs.* Also 4–5 **spatour.** [ad. OF. *spatule* or L. *spatula*, with change of suffix. Cf. SPATTER *sb.*[1]] A spatula.

1348–9 *Durh. Acc. Rolls* (Surtees) 549 In factura unius spatour pro lectuariis..de pixidibus evellendis, v*d.* *c* **1400** *MS. Sloane 2463* 159 b in *Lanfranc's Cirurg.* 297 Loke thou stere hit euermore with a spature of tre till þat it be thikke as oynement. *a* **1425** tr. *Arderne's Treat. Fistula*, etc. 31 And so euermore mouyng strongly wiþ a spatour, seþe þam on a softe fyre. *Ibid.* 69 With þi fynger or with a spature impressyng it [wool]. **1597** Gerarde *Herbal* III. cxxxi. 1335 A spature or a thing to stir with.

spatyl(l, varr. SPATTLE *sb.*

‖**Spätzle** ('ʃpɛtslə, 'ʃpɛts(ə)l), *sb. pl.* Also **Spatzle, spätzle,** and (anglicized) **-s.** [Ger. dial., lit. 'little sparrows'.] Noodles of a type made in southern Germany.

1933 E. E. Amiet *Palmer House Cook Bk.* 247 Spatzles. Into 3 soup-spoonfuls of flour, beat 1 egg and 3 soup-spoonfuls of milk. Add a pinch of salt, a pinch of pepper and a little ground nutmeg. Set a colander over boiling water and squeeze this mixture through, boil for a minute and pour into a sieve and serve. **1959** M. Crosland tr. *Rovan's Germany* 179 The *Spätzle*, a kind of fresh pasta from Swabia. **1978** J. Irving *World according to Garp* viii. 155 Garp had cooked an elegant Paprika Chicken and spätzle.

spau, obs. f. SPA *sb.*

spaud, var. SPAAD (*Obs.*), SPALD *v.*, SPAULD.

†**spaudeler.** *Obs. rare.* In 4 **spawdeler,** 5 **spaudelere.** [f. OF. *espalde* SPAULD. Cf. MLG. *spoldener*, MHG. *spaldenier*, MDa. *spaldenær*, MSw. *spaldenär*, *spoldener*, etc.] A piece of armour protecting the shoulder; a shoulder plate.

13.. *Coer de L.* 5285 Cowdyrbras..Smot Sere Thomas.. On hys spawdeler off hys scheeld, That it fleygh into the feeld. **14..** *Lat.-Eng. Voc.* in Wr.-Wülcker 588 *Humeralis*, a spaudelere [*printed* spanbelere].

spauen, obs. form of SPAVIN.

spaug (spɔːg). *Anglo-Irish.* [Ir. *spág.*] A clumsy, awkward foot.

1910 P. W. Joyce *English as we speak it in Ireland* 331 *Spaug*, a big clumsy foot:— 'You put your ugly spaug down on my handkerchief. **1922** Joyce *Ulysses* 128 Taking off his flat spaugs and the walk.

†**spaught.** *Obs. rare.* Also 7 **spaut, spowte.** [Of obscure origin.] A youth, lad, or stripling.

1598 R. Bernard tr. *Terence, Eunuch* IV. iv, That other came, being a spaught of sixteene yeeres old. **1641** Best *Farm. Bks.* (Surtees) 133 Wee give usually to a spaught for holdinge of the oxe plough fower nobles or perhaps 30*s.* per annum. **1686** G. Stuart *Joco-ser. Disc.* 42 Sir, here's a Spaught that came fra Taunton. **1691** Ray *N. Co. Words* (ed. 2) 68 A *Spaut* or *Spowte*, a youth.

†**spaul,** *v. Obs. rare.* [In sense 1, ad. OF. *espauler* (mod.F. *épauler*); in sense 2, ad. OF. *espaul(l)ier*, both f. *espaule*, *épaule* shoulder.]

1. *trans.* In *pass.*, of a horse: To be injured *in* the shoulder.

c **1410** *Master of Game* (MS. Digby 182) xii, If he may not be hole for all þis, do to hym as men done to an horse þat is spauled in þe sholder byfore.

2. *intr.* Of the shoulders: To move up and down during walking.

c **1430** *Pilgr. Lyf Manhode* II. cvi. (1869) 115, I go with my shuldren spaulinge [F. *des espaules espauliant*] and with my necke coleyinge.

spaul, var. SPALL *v.*[1]; obs. f. SPAWL *sb.* and *v.*

spauld (spɔːld). Now *Sc.* and *north.* Forms: α. 4, 6, 9 **spald,** 5 **spalde, spaulde,** 4– **spauld.** β. 4–5 **spaude,** 5 **spawd(e,** 9 **spaud.** γ. 5, 8–9 **spaul,** 9 **spawl, spoale, spaw-.** [a. OF. *espalde*, **espaulde*, *espaule*, *espalle* (mod.F. *épaule*, = Prov. *espatla*, Sp., Pg. *espalda*, It. *spalla*) shoulder:—L. *spatula* SPATULA.]

1. The shoulder in man or animals; a shoulder of an animal used for food.

α. **1305–6** in *Cal. Doc. rel. Scotl.* (1888) 392 Pro cxxxvj carcosiis bovium et ij spauld et ccciij baconibus. **1338** *Durh. Acc. Rolls* (Surtees) 35 In spald et brusket' emp., xij*d.* *a* **1400** *Sir Perc.* 796, I kepe nothynge of thi coste Ne noghte of thi spalde. *c* **1430** *Two Cookery-bks.* 59 Spaulde de Motoun. **1513** Douglas *Æneid* X. xii. 60 The bustuus swyne ..With spaldis hard and harsk. *Ibid.* xiv. 157 The knycht.. Foundris fordwart flatlingis on hys spald. *c* **1570** in *Bannatyne MS.* (Hunter. Cl.) 269/37 For sen thay red amang our durris, With splent on spald and rousty spurris. *a* **1585** Montgomerie *Flyting* 304 With bockblood and bean-shaw, speven sprung in the spald. *a* **1802** *Kinmont Willie* xvii. in Scott *Minstr. Sc. Border*, With spur on heel and splent on spauld. **1820** Hogg *Sheph. Cal.* i. (1829) I. 32 Some entire carcasses hung by the neck, some by a spauld. **1873** D. Maclagan in Edwards *Mod. Sc. Poets* (1881) III. 180 Baith strang o' limb an' braid o' spauld.

β. *c* **1320** *Sir Tristr.* 485 Þe spaude [*printed* spande] was þe first brede. *c* **1400** *Lanfranc's Cirurg.* 155 Of woundis of þe spaude... Þe spawde is oon of þe iiij. boonys, þe which þat makþ þe foorme of þe schuldre. *c* **1430** *Two Cookery-bks.* 63 Spawdys de Motoun. *c* **1440** *Promp. Parv.* 467/2 Spawde, *spatula.* **1483** *Cath. Angl.* 352 A Spawde, *armus.*

γ. *c* **1400** *Lanfranc's Cirurg.* 165 If þer go ony breeþ þere, it wole do harme to þe spaulis. **1718** Ramsay *Christ's Kirk Gr.* III. xvi, 'Wae worth ye'r drunken saul,' Quoth she, and lap out o'er a stool, And claught him be the spaul. **1724** —— *Vision* v, A various rainbow-colourt plaid Owre his left spaul he threw. **1788** Picken *Poems* 59 For they, some night,.. Might lug us by the spaul to Satan. **1899** *Cumbld. Gloss.* 309/2 *Spoale*,..a butcher's term for the cut between the neck and the forecrop; the thin or flat portion of the shoulder blade.

2. *transf.* A limb, leg, etc.; any joint of the carcass of a beast or bird.

1500–20 Dunbar *Poems* lxi. 64, I wald be spurrit at everie spald. **1535** Stewart *Cron. Scot.* I. 87 The theif takar suld haif the forder spald. **1570** *Satir. Poems Reform.* xxiv. 47 At euerie port a spald of the to hing, As tratouris sould, for schuitting vnder trest. **1715** Ramsay *Christ's Kirk Gr.* II. xx, Wi' hind and fore spaul of a sheep. **1746** Graham *Hist. Rebellion* (1774) 92 Their Brigadier In every spaul did quake for fear. **1807–10** R. Tannahill *Poems* (1846) 30 She tore poor chucky spawl frae spawl. **1831** J. Wilson *Noct. Ambr.* (1856) III. 214 For half a mile, the bubbly, being longer in the spald, would outstep the gander.

3. ***black spauld***, a disease of cattle; black quarter, quarter-evil, or quarter-ill. *Sc.*

1807 *Prize Ess. & Trans. Highland Soc.* III. 368 Mr. J. Hog says..that it is the same disease with the black spauld, which prevails among the young cattle in the west of Scotland, when the grasses fail.

4. *attrib.*, as **spauld-bone**, the shoulder-bone (cf. SPADE-BONE); **spauld-ill**, quarter-ill (cf. sense 3); **spauld-piece** (see quot. 1828).

c **1400** *Lanfranc's Cirurg.* 155 Þe spawde-boon is þinne & brood twoward þe schuldris & in hise endis gristly. **1793** Ure *Hist. Rutherglen* 191 The Spalliel [*sic*] in young cattle, is sometimes cured by [etc.]. **1828** Carr *Craven Gloss.*, *Spaw-bone*, the blade bone or shoulder bone. Hence, a piece of beef cut from the shoulder with a part of this bone, is called the spaw-piece.

spauld, variant of SPALD *v.*

spaulty ('spɔːltɪ), *a. dial.* Also **spoalty, spoulty.** [f. SPALT *a.* + -Y[1].] Dry and brittle.

1895 J. J. Raven *Hist. Suffolk* xix. 266 When turnips are hard and brittle..they are said to be *spoalty*, which William Ellis (1750) spells *spalt*, and Professor Skeat notes as a Cambridge-Shire word. **1904** *Eng. Dial. Dict.* V. 643/1 Them turnips is spoulty. **1906** Kipling *Puck of Pook's Hill* 238 Did he promise me a set of iron cramps or ties for the roof? They never came to hand, or else they were spaulty or cracked.

spaune, obs. ff. of SPAWN.

spaut, variant of SPAUGHT *Obs.*

spave, *v. Sc.* and *north.* Forms: 8–9 **speave, speeav(e,** 9 **speav(v, spaive,** 7– **spave,** etc. [Alteration of SPAY *v.*] *trans.* To spay. Also *intr.* Of an animal: To undergo spaying.

1671 Skinner *Etymol. Ling. Angl.*, To Spay, Spade or Spave. **1781** Hutton *Tour Caves* Gloss., *Speaved*, gelded, barren. **1788** W. H. Marshall *Yorksh.* II. 354 To *Speeav* (mid. dial. to *spave*); to spay, as a female calf. **1795** *Statist. Acc. Scot.* XV. 85 When cut, or spaved, they then with us obtain the name of heifers. **1824** Mactaggart *Gallovid. Encycl.* 432 Spaivers, persons who libb and spaive cattle. *Ibid.*, A young cow with calf..will not speave. **1825–** in dial. glossaries (N. Cy., Cumbld., Yks., etc.). **1876** Robinson *Whitby Gloss.* 181 A speeav'd whye.

Hence **'spaver**, a spayer.

1824 Mactaggart *Gallovid. Encycl.* 372 Few men would I rather spend an hour with than Mr. Papple, the speaver. *Ibid.* 432 [see above].

'spavie. *Sc.* Also 7, 9 **speavie,** 9 **spaivie, spavy,** etc. [Alteration of next.] The spavin. Freq. *fig.*

1706 in Maidment *Pasquils* (1827) 19 The seventh wife Davie, The seventh give him the spavie. **1785** Burns *Inventory* 19, I play'd my fillie sic a shavie, She's a' be-devil'd wi' the spavie. **1785** —— *2nd Ep. to Davie* viii, She'll never leave ye,..even tho' limpin' wi' the spavie Frae door to door. *a* **1813** A. Wilson *Hogmenae* Poet. Wks. (Belfast ed.) 293 At length the twa carriers appeared, The ne'er a ane then had the spavy.

b. *attrib.* or as *adj.* Spavined. *rare*$^{-1}$.

1693 in Maidment *Pasquils* (1868) 272 Ye spur Your speavie mear too fast.

Hence **'spavied** *a.*, spavined.

1785 Burns *1st Ep. to Davie* xi, My spavet Pegasus will limp, Till ance he's fairly het. **1788** Picken *Poems* 115 The spavy't creature never thrave, Wi' a' his care. **1853** Cadenhead *Bon-Accord* 248 (E.D.D.), Like a spavied horse.

spavin ('spævɪn), *sb.*[1] *Farriery.* Forms: α. 5 **spaueyne, -veyne, spavayne,** 6 **spauain.** β. 6 **spauen, speven,** 6–7 **spaven, -ing, spauin,** 6– **spavin** (9 *Sc.* **spaivin**). [ad. OF. *espavain* (cf. med.L. *spavenus*, It. *spavenio*), var. of *esparvain*, *esprevain*, *esprevin* (mod.F. *éparvin*, *épervin*), of obscure origin.]

1. A hard bony tumour or excrescence formed at the union of the splint-bone and the shank in a horse's leg, and produced by inflammation of the cartilage uniting those bones; a similar tumour caused by inflammation of the small hock bones.

1426 Lydg. *De Guil. Pilgr.* 18226 With that fall..I cawht a great spavayne vpon my lege, whiche made me for to halt. *c* **1440** *Promp. Parv.* 467/2 Spaveyne, horsys maledy. **1523** Fitzherb. *Husbandry* §107 A courbe..appereth..a lyttell benethe the spauen. **1551** T. Wilson *Logike* II. N j b, We can se a spauain, a splent, a ring bone, or suche other disease in a horse. **1596** Shaks. *Tam. Shr.* III. ii. 53 His horse.. troubled with the Lampasse, infected with the fashions, full of Windegalls, sped with Spauins. **1614** Markham *Cheap Husb.* I. lii. (1668) 63 A splent is a bony excression under the knee.., the spaven is the like on the inside of the hinder hough. **1633** Marmion *Fine Companion* IV. i, I am afraid this dancing will breed spavins in my legs. **1678** *Lond. Gaz.* No. 1270/4 A Roan Nag,..a little spavin on the off leg behind. **1741** *Complete Family-Piece* III. 435 The Spavin..appears in like Manner on the Shank Bone behind, not far below the Hough. **1766** *Compl. Farmer* s.v. *Spavin*, When the spavin was pressed hard on the inside of the hough, there was a small tumor on the outside. **1825** C. Westmacott *Eng. Spy* I. 321 Having put out a spavin. **1856** Lever *Martins of Cro' M.* xxv, Sir Peter shows an incipient spavin on the off leg, and I think he'd be well sold. **1896** *Blackw. Mag.* Aug. 262 My attention was drawn..to one of the worst spavins I ever saw on the near hock of one of them.

b. A malady of horses due to the above cause. Also *transf.*

c **1500** *Rowlis Cursing* 52 in Laing *Anc. Poet. Scotl.*, The pokkis, the spaving in the halss, The panefull gravell and the gutt. **1594** Greene & Lodge *Looking Gl.* 265 G.'s Wks. (Grosart) XIV. 18 If he haue outward diseases, as the spavin, splent, ring-bone,..we let him blood. **1601** B. Jonson *Poetaster* I. ii, Now the bots, the spauin, and the glanders, and some dozen diseases more, light on him, and his moyles. **1688** Holme *Armoury* II. 152/2 The Spaven [is] an old Halt, which is left as the Horse warms in Travel. **1706** in Phillips (ed. Kersey). **1831** Youatt *Horse* 270 The lameness of spavin..abates, and sometimes disappears, on exercise. **1874** Sir W. W. Hunter in Skrine *Life* (1901) xiii. 229 A cast cavalry charger who gets rid of his spavin the moment he is drummed out of the regiment.

2. With distinguishing terms, as ***blood spavin***, a soft swelling or enlargement of the hock vein caused by the accumulation of blood; freq. taken as synonymous with ***bog spavin*** (see BOG *sb.*[1] 4); ***bone*** or ***dry spavin*** (see BONE *sb.* 17 and prec. 1); ***through*** or ***wet spavin*** (see THROUGH- 2).

ox-spavin, in some 18th c. works, is a rendering of F. *éparvin de bœuf*, and app. had no real currency in English.

1523, **1565** [see THROUGH- 2]. **1580** Blundevil *Horsemanship* III. 57 b, The drie spauen..is a great hard knob, as big as a Walnut, growing in the inside of the hough, hard vnder the ioint. **1607** Topsell *Four-f. Beasts* 406 Of the Spauen there are two kindes, the one hard the other soft: that is: a bone-Spauen, and a blood-Spauen. **1639** T. de Gray *Expert Farrier* 90 We have two sorts of spavens: the one we call a through, wet, bloud or bog-spaven; the other a dry, or bone-spaven. **1677** *Lond. Gaz.* No. 1346/4 A grey Nag,..a thorow spavin on the fore-leg before. **1831** Youatt *Horse* 179 The distension reaches from this bag as low down as the next valve. This is called a blood-spavin. **1846** J. Baxter *Libr. Pract. Agric.* (ed. 4) I. 449 Constituting puffy swellings, called bog spavin. **1885** *Field* 4 Apr. 453/1 The connection between the 'blood spavin' and the 'thoroughpin' is proved by pressing on the swelling in front.

3. *attrib.*, as †***spavin-joint, -place, -vein***, the joint, etc., usually affected by spavin, or where a spavin commonly occurs.

1523 Fitzherb. *Husb.* §118 If a horse wante wartes behynde, benethe the spauen-place. **1607** Topsell *Four-f. Beasts* 407, I haue knowne diuers..helpt onley by taking vppe the Spauen vaine. **1623** Markham *Cheap Husb.* (ed. 3) 47 For the smals of his hinder legges somewhat below the spauin ioynts. **1682** *Lond. Gaz.* No. 1724/4 A hurt not quite cured on the in-side of the Spaven Joint of the near Leg behind. **1688** *Ibid.* No. 2355/4 A dapple grey,..full jointed in both his hinder Legs, in the Spavin place.

Hence **'spavin** *v. trans.*, to affect with the spavin. *rare*$^{-1}$.

1867 Burton *Hist. Scot.* vi. (1873) I. 215 The village hag who spavins the horse.

spavin ('spævɪn), *sb.*[2] *Coal-mining.* [Of obscure origin.] (See quots.)

1870 *Eng. Mech.* 14 Jan. 423/3 Roots were found in the spavin or under clay. **1883** Gresley *Gloss. Coal-m.* 230 *Spavin*, clunch, or ordinary bottom or underclay.

spavined ('spævɪnd), *a.* Also 5 **spaueyned,** 7 **spavend.** [f. SPAVIN *sb.*[1]] Of horses, etc.: Affected with spavin; having a spavin. Also *absol.* (of persons).

c **1430** *Pilgr. Lyf Manhode* II. civ. (1869) 114 With whiche [garments] queyntisen hem as wel the halte, the boistouse, the spaueyned, the blynde, the embosed, the maymed and oothere. **1684** *Lond. Gaz.* No. 1965/4 A brown bay Gelding, ..a little Spavend of his near Leg behind. **1727** Somerville *Bald Batchelor* Poems (1810) 215/2 A mare,..Though she be spavin'd, old, and blind, With founder'd feet, and broken wind. **1788** J. May *Jrnl. & Lett.* (1873) 19, I observed my horse to be lame... Some said he was hipped, others spavined. **1818** Scott *Rob Roy* xix, He..made a present to Andrew of a broken-winded and spavined pony. **1867** Trollope *Chron. Barset* xiii, [He] had ridden over..on a poor spavined brute belonging to the bishop's stable.

b. *fig.* Lame, halting, maimed, etc.

1647 N. WARD *Simp. Cobbler* 37 If any have a minde to ride poste, he will helpe them with a fresh spavin'd Opinion at every Stage. **1822** BYRON *Vis. Judgem.* xci, Ere the spavin'd dactyls could be spurr'd Into recitative. **1856** KANE *Arct. Expl.* II. ix. 93 After a diversified series of spavined efforts, the mystical number forms its triangle at the table. **1863** *Sat. Rev.* 200 We turn our spavined horses out to grass ..; we are sadly in need of some analogous arrangement for spavined Christians.

spaw, obs. form of SPA *sb.*

spa-water. Also 6–8 **spaw-**. [f. SPA *sb.*] Water derived from mineral springs (orig. from those at Spa itself).

1589 PUTTENHAM *Eng. Poesie* III. (Arb.) 285, I being at the Spaw waters, there lay a Marshall of Fraunce.., to vse those waters for his health. **1636** WOTTON in *Reliq.* (1651) 497 The taste and operation of the Spaw-water. **1652** FRENCH *Yorks. Spaw* xv. 114 Four, or six glasses of the Spaw-water may be drunk. **1709** STEELE *Tatler* No. 107 ¶13 Drink upon them a Bottle of Spaw-Water. **1778** R. JAMES *Diss. Fevers*, etc. (ed. 8) 112 It [i.e. rheumatism] went off.. by bathing in the sea, and drinking the Spaw-water at Scarborough. **1843** R. J. GRAVES *Syst. Clin. Med.* xx. 235 Using a course of chalybeate spa waters. **1897** *Allbutt's Syst. Med.* IV. 621 Treatment [of obesity] by spa-waters.

spawde, var. SPAAD *Obs.*

spawe, obs. f. SPA.

†**spawe.** *Obs.*$^{-1}$ Some kind of bird.

1610 W. FOLKINGHAM *Art of Survey* IV. iii. 83 Gray, Greene and Bastard Plouer, Dottrill, May-Chit, Spawe.

†**spawl**, *sb. Obs.* Also 7 **spaul**. [f. SPAWL *v.*] Spittle.

1642 H. MORE *Song of Soul* III. 77 Lastly into his mouth with filthy spaul He spot. **1646** J. HALL *Poems, To young Authour*, The well drench'd smoaky Jew, That stands in his own spaul above the shooe. **1693** DRYDEN *Persius* II. 63 Th' obscene old Grandam.. first of Spittle a Lustration makes: Then in the Spawl her middle-finger dips.

spawl, var. SPALL *sb.* and *v.*, SPAULD.

spawl (spɔːl), *v. Obs.* exc. *arch.* Forms: 6 **spal**, 7, 9 **spall**; 7 **spaule**, 7–9 **spaul**; 6– **spawl**, 7 **spawle**. [Of obscure origin; both date and form are against direct connexion with OE. *spáld* SPOLD.]

1. *intr.* To spit copiously or coarsely; to expectorate.

1607 DEKKER & WEBSTER *Westw. Hoe* V. i, Pray spawle in another roome: fie, fie, fie. **1649** W. M. *Wander. Jew* (1857) 23 He.. so spawles, and drivells, he has almost made a puddle where he stands. **1730** SWIFT *Traulus* Wks. 1755 IV. I. 122 Why must he sputter, spawl, and slaver it In vain against the people's fav'rite? **1755** *Connoisseur* No. 95 ¶11, I began to spawl, and sputter, and keck. [**1864** BROWNING *Dram. Pers., Sludge* 200 He may strut and fret his hour, Spout, spawl, or spin his target, no one cares!]

fig. **1599** NASHE *Lenten Stuffe* Wks. (Grosart) V. 286 Our Norwich now.. was a poore fisher towne, and the sea spawled and springed vp to her common stayres.

b. Coupled with *spit*.

1598 E. GUILPIN *Skial.* (1878) 20 Talke bawdery and Chrestina spets and spals. **1609** MARKHAM *Famous Whore* (1868) 41 Now are my faculties.. to cough, to spaule, to spit, to raile. **1683** TRYON *Way to Health* 170 Sotting and smoaking ten or twenty Pipes of Tobacco in a day,.. and spitting and spawling. **1721** AMHERST *Terræ Fil.* No. 39 (1726) I. 49 The fellow.. fell a spitting and spawling about the room. **1793** *Laity's Direct.* 20 The unclean trick of hawking, spitting or spawling about the chapel.

c. Const. with preps., as *at, on*. Also *fig.*

1635 QUARLES *Embl.* III. ii, To spit and spaul upon his Sun-bright face. **1638** MAYNE *Lucian* (1664) 84 He presently grows disdainfull, and Spawles at me. **1659** BROUGH *Sacr. Princ.* 405 Nor shouldst thou more spaul on His Name, then spit in His Face.

2. *trans.* To utter in a coarse manner.

1616 EARLE *Elegy on Beaumont* B.'s Wks. 1905 I. p. xxxiii, Such mouthes,.. That twixt a whiffe, a Line or two rehearse, And with their Rheume together spaule a Verse. **1794** GIFFORD *Baviad* (1811) 46 And itching grandams spawl lascivious odes.

Hence **'spawler**, a spitter; **'spawling** *ppl. a.*

1598 SYLVESTER *Du Bartas* II. i. III. *Furies* 402 The spawling Empiem.. With foule impostumes fils his hollow chest. **1603** FLORIO *Montaigne* I. xxxviii. (1632) 120 This man whom.. thou seest.., flegmatike, squalide and spauling. **1611** COTGR., *Cracheur*, a spitter, spawler, spatterer.

'spawling, *vbl. sb.* Now *arch.* [f. SPAWL *v.*]

1. The action of the vb.; expectoration.

1609 DEKKER *Gull's Horn-bk.* Wks. (Grosart) II. 207 The manner of spawling, slauering, spetting and driueling in all places. **1684** tr. *Bonet's Merc. Compit.* XIX. 799 A spontaneous Salivation or spawling preceeds Vomiting. **1727** DE FOE *Protestant Monast.* 10 His spitting and spawling turn'd Madam's Stomach. **1753** MISS COLLIER *Art Torment.* Concl. 228 The constant drumming upon the table ..of another! The hawking and spawlting [*sic*] of a third! **1881** DUFFIELD *Don Quix.* II. 577 By his spawling and clearing his throat [he] is preparing to sing something.

attrib. **1608** SYLVESTER *Du Bartas* II. iv. IV. *Decay* 166 A Visard, newly varnisht o'r With spauling Rheums, hot Fumes, and Ceruses. **1628** GAULE *Pract. The.* (1629) 335 Spite contemnes him, He's made their flapping, flouting, spawling Sport.

2. *pl.* Spittle, spittings, saliva.

1614 SYLVESTER *Tobacco Battered* Wks. (Grosart) II. 270 A Drug for Jews.. who did so foule abuse.. with their Spawlings base, Our loving Saviour's lovely-reverend Face. *Ibid.* 274 How juster will the Heav'nly God.. punish.. Those, that on Earth.. Offend the Eyes, with foul and loathsom spawlings. **1693** CONGREVE in *Dryden's Juvenal* xi. 290 Whose Marble Floors with drunken Spawlings shine; Let him lascivious Songs and Dances have.

spawn (spɔːn), *sb.* Forms: 5–6 **spawne, spaune,** 6 **spaume, spane,** 7 **spaen,** 7– **spawn.** [f. SPAWN *v.*]

†**1.** The milt of a fish. *Obs.*

c **1430** *Two Cookery-bks.* 14 Take.. þe lyuer an þe Spaune, an sethe it y-now in fayre Water. *c* **1450** *Ibid.* 90 Take a Gurnard.. (the lyuer and þe Spawne with-in him).

2. a. The minute eggs of fishes and various other oviparous animals (chiefly aquatic or amphibian), usually extruded in large numbers and forming a more or less coherent or gelatinous mass; also, the young brood hatched from such eggs, while still in an early stage of development.

1491 *Act 7 Hen. VII*, c. 9 Grete multitude of Spawne and broode of all maner fysshes of the See. **1538** LELAND *Itin.* (1769) V. 70 A Kinde of Weedes,.. wherin the Spaune hath Socur, and also the greate Fische. **1545** ELYOT, *Anguilla*, a fyshe called an eele, whiche.. cometh without generacion or spawne. **1570** LEVINS *Manip.* 44 Ye spaune of fishe, *fœtus, auxumæ*. **1600** DALLAM in *Early Voy. Levant* (Hakluyt Soc.) 95 This day we saw greate store of the spane of whales, whearof they make spermacetie. **1656** RIDGLEY *Pract. Physick* 325 Anoint it with the spawn of red Snails. *a* **1676** HALE *Prim. Orig. Man.* IV. v. (1677) 338 The Semina or Spawn of Insects. **1710** *Tatler* No. 236 ¶5 He filled several Barrels with the choicest Spawn of Frogs. **1731** *Gentl. Mag.* I. 12 The first appearance of them is in a sort of Spawn, spread over the Cabbage-leaves. **1774** GOLDSM. *Nat. Hist.* IV. 31 Oysters usually cast their spawn in May. **1833** L. RITCHIE *Wand. by Loire* 191 Eels are also plentiful; and their spawn, while ascending the river.., are caught in vast quantities. **1845** BUDD *Dis. Liver* 400 It is remarkable, too, that their excrement and spawn should not have set up disease in the substance of the liver. **1888** GOODE *Amer. Fishes* 27 The European Bass are said to deposit their spawn near the mouths of rivers.

transf. **1555** EDEN *Decades* (Arb.) 142 Whether perles bee ..the byrthe or spaune of there intrals. **1608** TOPSELL *Serpents* (1653) 594 They bite to cleanse their teeth from all spawn and spume of venom.

b. With *a* and pl. A fish-egg; an undeveloped fish.

1563 B. GOOGE *Eglogs* (Arb.) 105 But Pikes haue Spawnes good stoore in euery Pound. **1584** B. R. tr. *Herodotus* II. 93 These male fishe.. shed theyr seede by the way, which their femals.. deuour, and thereof shortly after breede theyr spawnes. **1610** FLETCHER *Faithf. Sheph.* III, Bare-foot may no Neighbour wade.. When the spawns on stones do lye, To wash their Hemp, and spoil the Fry. **1611** FLORIO, *Alace*, a meate made of spaunes of fishes.

3. A brood; a numerous offspring. Chiefly *fig.*

1590 SPENSER *F.Q.* I. i. 22 She poured forth.. Her fruitfull cursed spawne of serpents small. **1600** LANE *Tom Tel Troth* 127 Bearing a spawne of many new-bred sinnes. ?**1619** S. HIERON *Wks.* II. 473 Such.. are.. not only suffered to remayne within, but to encrease also, so that there is euen a fresh spawne of such euery day. *a* **1740** WATERLAND *Def. Ld. Bp. St. David's* Wks. 1823 VI. 282 Its effects and consequences.. are plainly a spawn of all vices and villanies, a deluge of all mischiefs and outrages upon the earth. **1920** D. H. LAWRENCE *Touch & Go* 6 The plays of A People's Theatre are—oh heaven, what are they?—not popular nor populous nor plebeian nor proletarian nor folk nor parish plays. None of that adjectival spawn.

4. *fig.* **a.** A person contemptuously regarded as the offspring of some parent or stock, or as imbued with some quality or principle. In early use freq. with *a* and pl.

1589 NASHE *Pasquill & Marf.* 16 They are the very Spawnes of the fish Sæpia. **1589** ? LYLY *Pappe w. Hatchet* (1844) 16 Whie are not the spawnes of such a dog-fish hangd? *a* **1627** MIDDLETON *Witch* I. ii, Here's a spawn or two Of that same paddock brood. **1667** DRYDEN & DK. NEWCASTLE *Sir M. Mar-all* IV, Thou spawn of the old serpent, fruitful in nothing but in lies. **1706** E. WARD *Wooden World Diss.* (1708) 67 The Gunner Is commonly a Spawn of the Captain's own Projection. **1817** SOUTHEY *Wat Tyler* III. i, This is that old seditious heretic.. And here the young spawn of rebellion; My orders ar'n't to spare him. **1844** LEVER *T. Burke* II. 164 There was a cry.. to have the child executed also, and many called out that the spawn would be a serpent one day. **1865** KINGSLEY *Herew.* i, 'Oh, apostate!' cries the bell-wether, 'oh, spawn of Beelzebub!'

b. Similarly in collective use.

1601 B. JONSON *Poetaster* Prol., How ere that common spawne of ignorance, Our frie of writers, may beslime his fame. **1625** FLETCHER & SHIRLEY *Nt. Walker* III, The Goblins, Haggs, and the black spawn of darkness, Cannot fright me. **1698** FRYER *Acc. E. India & P.* 83 They are worse Brokers than Jews; if they be not the Spawn of them, the Rechabites, that would drink no Wine. **1729** GAY *Polly* II. xxvii, You ne'er were drawn.. Among the spawn Who practice the frauds of courts. **1737** [S. BERINGTON] *Mem. G. de Lucca* (1738) 117 Other Northern Nations, who have.. over-run the Face of Europe; leaving a Mixture of their Spawn in all Parts of it. **1852** R. S. HAWKER in Byles *Life* xiv. (1905) 228 The wretched Heretics, the spawn of that miscreant John Wesley. **1895** RIDER HAGGARD *Heart of World* xvii, The vengeance of generations [might be] accomplished upon the spawn of the Spaniard.

5. *fig.* A product, result, or effect *of* something.

1624 DONNE *Serm.* Wks. 1839 V. 331 The Spawns of Leviathan, the Seed of Sin,.. reign most in that part of the body. **1646** J. HALL *Horæ Vac.* 45 Libels are her spawns. **1673** CAVE *Prim. Chr.* I. v. 12 The result and spawn of lying fame. *a* **1770** JORTIN *Serm.* (1771) V. xiii. 282 Atheism.. is the annual spawn and the natural effect of the gross superstitions.. of the Romish church. **1789** BELSHAM *Ess.* xxv. II. 17 If this hypothesis be a spawn of the Oriental philosophy, it ought to be rejected. **1857** MAURICE *Mor. & Met. Philos.* IV. ix. §35. 558 In the sentimental spawn which was produced from him. **1869** RUSKIN *Q. of Air* i. 59 The many monstrous and misbegotten fantasies which are the spawn of modern licence.

6. *fig.* The source or origin *of* something.

a **1591** H. SMITH *Wks.* (1867) II. 273 It is called, 'The root of all evil,'.. as if we would say, the spawn of all sin. **1607** HIERON *Wks.* I. 331 Both haue in them the root and seed and (as it were) the spawne and beginning of euery euill. **1650** HUBBERT *Pill Formality* 220 In their birth lies the spawne of all evil. **1667** WATERHOUSE *Fire Lond.* 35 The Primitive Martyrs, which were the Churches Spawn.

7. The mycelium of mushrooms or other fungi.

1731 MILLER *Gard. Dict.* s.v. *Mushrooms*, A Bed thus manag'd, if the Spawn takes kindly, will.. produce great Quantities of Mushrooms. **1763** MILLS *Syst. Pract. Husb.* IV. 187 This seed, or rather this spawn.. should be kept very dry till it is used. **1824** LOUDON *Encycl. Gard.* (ed. 2) §3406 Spawn is a white fibrous substance, running like broken threads, in such dry reduced dung, or other nidus, as is fitted to nourish it. **1845** *Florist Jrnl.* 126 The spawn being thus provided, the next consideration is the preparation of the dung, and the making of the bed. **1867** H. MACMILLAN *Bible Teach.* vi. (1870) 112 The spawn of the mushrooms.. both consume putrescent organized matter, and manure the land.

8. *attrib.* and *Comb.*, as ***spawn-box, -deposit; spawn-feathered, -like*** adjs.; **spawn-brick**, a brick-shaped mass of compost containing mushroom-spawn; **spawn-eater, -pike,** *U.S.* (see quots. 1881–4); †**spawn-stone**, oolite, roe-stone.

1641 DAY *Parl. Bees* v, The greater number of spawn-feathered bees Fly low like kites. **1668** CHARLETON *Onomast.* 252 *Ammonites*,.. Lesser Spawn-stone. *c* **1820** in Loudon *Encycl. Gard.* (1824) §3413, I shall next give directions how to form spawn-bricks. **1853** *Zoologist* XI. 4040, I have also seen young toads, though I never noticed any spawn-deposits. **1862** H. MARRYAT *Year in Sweden* II. 420 In the greenhouse are spawn-boxes. **1881** *Cassell's Nat. Hist.* V. 131 The Spawn-eater, or Smelt (*Leuciscus hudsonicus*), is a silvery fish.. about three inches long, and occurs in Lake Superior. **1884** GOODE *Nat. Hist. Aquat. Anim.* 421 At Vermillion, Ohio, there is caught, early in the spring, what is termed the 'Spawn Pike'. **1938** S. BECKETT *Murphy* 249 The iris was reduced to a thin glaucous rim of spawnlike consistency.

spawn (spɔːn), *v.* Forms: 5 **spawnyn (spanyn),** 5–7 **spawne** (6 **spaune**), 7– **spawn.** [app. for **spaund*, ad. AF. *espaundre*, = OF. *espandre* (mod.F. *épandre*) to shed, spill, pour out:—L. *expandĕre* EXPAND *v.*

The AF. word occurs in the treatise of Walter de Bibbesworth (Wright *Voc.* I. 164) in the line 'Soffret le peysoun en ewe *espaundre*', and is glossed by *scheden his roune*, 'shed his roe' (Skeat), misprinted by Wright as *scheden him frome*.]

I. *intr.* **1.** Of fish, etc.: To cast spawn.

c **1400** *Pilgr. Sowle* (Caxton) v. xiv. (1859) 80 Whiche fisshes he putte in the stewe, where they haue spawned and multyplyed. *c* **1440** *Promp. Parv.* 467/2 Spawnyn, as fyschys (*K.* spanyn), *pisciculo*. **1530** PALSGR. 727/1 Never use to ete fysshes, whan they spawne, for they be nat holsom than. **1570** LEVINS *Manip.* 44 To spaune, *oua gignere*. **1613** PURCHAS *Pilgrimage* (1614) 560 The Arabians and Lybians eat them before they haue spawned. **1674** tr. *Scheffer's Lapland* xvi. 81 The fishermen, at those times when the fishes do spawn, do alwaies live on the side of some river. **1694** MOTTEUX *Rabelais* v. xxxi. (1737) 143, I saw.. Fish milting, spawning. **1771** *Phil. Trans.* LXI. 317 Carp spawn in May, June, or July. **1821** SHELLEY *Adonais* xxix, The sun comes forth, and many reptiles spawn. **1865** HATTON *Bitter Sweets* xxvi, The bream and the tench had spawned in the river.

transf. **1673** TEMPLE *Observ. U. Prov.* Wks. 1720 I. 11 These Nations, which seem'd to spawn in every Age, and.. discharged their own native Countries of so vast Numbers.

2. a. To increase or develop after the manner of spawn; to become reproductive.

1607 R. C[AREW] tr. *Estienne's World Wond.* 151 Seeds of sinne, which naturally breed and (as it were) spawne in our hearts. **1658** A. FOX *Würtz' Surg.* I. iii. 10 Then is that wound in that natural swelling hindered,.. then it begins to spawn and swell. **1702** *Phil. Trans.* XXIII. 1260 These [flower-spikes] are thick set in oblong heads, which sometime spawn or divide at the bottom.

b. To grow or develop *into* something.

1677 GILPIN *Demonol.* (1867) 131 Error.. stops not at one or two falsehoods, but is apt to spawn into many others. **1686** GOAD *Celest. Bodies* II. vii. 243 Navigation had not spawn'd into Sholes, or afterwards. *a* **1930** D. H. LAWRENCE *Last Poems* (1932) 198 Oh I have loved the working class Where I was born, And lived to see them spawn into machine-robots.

3. a. To issue or come forth like or after the manner of spawn.

1657 W. MORICE *Coena quasi Κοινὴ* iii. 136 These dismal Heresies which have lately spawn'd. **1693** LOCKE *Educ.* §124 [Lying] is so ill a Quality, and the mother of so many ill ones that spawn from it.

b. Of persons: To swarm *out*.

1718 RAMSAY *Christ's Kirk Gr.* III. xix, The wives and gytlings a' spawn'd out O'er middings and o'er dykes.

4. To swarm or teem *with* something.

1818 SOUTHEY *Ess.* (1832) II. 137 The infidelity with which some of the Scotch Schools have spawned during the last half century. **1856** EMERSON *Eng. Traits, Land*, The rivers and the surrounding sea spawn with fish.

II. *trans.* **5. a.** To produce or generate as spawn or in large numbers; also, in contemptuous use, to give birth to (a person).

1603 SHAKS. *Meas. for M.* III. ii. 115 Some report, a Sea-maid spawn'd him. Some, that he was begot betweene two Stock-fishes. **1687** MONTAGU & PRIOR *Hind & Panth. Transv.* 9 Or else reforming Corah spawn'd this Class. **1730** SOUTHALL *Treat. Buggs* 24 They generally spawn about fifty at a time. **1784** COWPER *Task* II. 827 A race obscene, Spawn'd in the muddy beds of Nile, came forth, Polluting Egypt. **1847** DISRAELI *Tancred* III. vii, A race spawned perhaps in the morasses of some Northern forest hardly yet cleared. **1867** EMERSON *May-Day & Other Pieces* Wks. (Bohn) III. 442 She spawneth men as mallows fresh. **1891** LOUNSBURY *Stud. Chaucer* III. vii. 198 A poet of the kind the eighteenth century spawned in profusion.

b. With *forth, upon.*

1619 HIERON *Wks.* I. 644 Nature hath (as it were) spawned vs forth into this worldly sea. **1838** LYTTON *Alice* VI. ii, But oh, that a nation which has known a Corneille should ever spawn forth a ——. **1865** J. G. HOLLAND *Plain Talk* i. 31 Then think of multitudes of men spawned upon the country every year by our medical institutions.

6. a. To engender, produce, bring forth, give rise to; *spec.* of tornadoes or the like. Also with *forth* and *out.*

1594 NASHE *Unfort. Trav.* 62 Her eies in their closing seemed to spaune forth in their outward sharpe corners new created seed pearle. **1654** WHITLOCK *Zootomia* 202 But well it were if meer Speculation were onely barren;..In the Church it spawneth Heresies. **1683** KENNETT tr. *Erasm. on Folly* 47 The curiosity of the Greeks spawned so many subtleties. **1708** SWIFT *Sacramental Test* Wks. 1755 II. I. 137 What practices such principles as these..may spawn, when they are laid out to the sun, you may determine at leisure. **1792** BURKE *Let. to Sir H. Langrishe* Wks. 1842 I. 557 That they are not permitted to spawn a hydra of wild republicks, on principles of a pretended natural equality in man. **1863** KINGSLEY *Water-Bab.* 23 The house looked..as if it had been all spawned in a night as mushrooms are. **1955** *Sci. News Let.* 18 June 394/1 The general atmospheric conditions in which hurricanes are spawned are known. **1965** *Listener* 21 Oct. 610/1 Every summer the violent climate of the central United States spawns a series of devastating storms—tornadoes—twisters they call them here. **1976** *Bay City* (Michigan) *Times* 12 July 1/5 Powerful thunderstorms roamed much of the East Sunday spawning tornadoes and flash floods.

b. *spec.* in contemptuous use with reference to literary work, utterances, etc.

1631 A. WILSON *Swisser* V. i. (1904) 89 From kissing a' the hand to cutting a' the throat, Sir, O you shall meet 'em, spawning out the word, With such a Grace. *a* **1661** FULLER *Worthies, Gen.* x. (1662) 29 Books..come swimming into the world like shoals of Fishes, and one edition spawneth another. **1672** MARVELL *Reh. Transp.* I. 87 Of late years Mr. Bayes had regularly spawned his books. *a* **1704** *Friendly Adv. to Dr. Bl*—— in T. Brown *Wks.* (1711) IV. 197 Such vile Heroicks..Were never spawn'd before from Irish Brains. **1713** *Lond. Gaz.* No. 5118/2 The Press..hath Spawn'd so many Blasphemous..Pamphlets. **1820** BYRON *Juan* V. lii, But every fool describes, in these bright days, His wondrous journey.., And spawns his quarto. **1826** in W. Cobbett *Rur. Rides* (1885) II. 107 Cobbett's prophecies were falsified as soon as spawned.

7. To supply with spawn or mycelium.

1786 ABERCROMBIE *Gard. Assist.* 205 Mushroom spawn —for spawning new beds.

8. To extract spawn from (fishes).

1884 DAY *Fishes Gt. Brit.* I. p. cix, The mode of spawning or stripping fish..requires practice.

Hence **spawned** *ppl. a.* (*a*) cast or deposited as spawn; (*b*) that has emitted spawn; spent; also with *out.*

1866 *Banffshire Gloss.* 176 *Speinty*, a spawned fish. **1905** *Westm. Gaz.* 1 Feb. 3/2 Sometimes these spawned salmon resemble the genuine article so closely that only an expert can distinguish the difference. **1972** *Trout & Salmon* June 41/1 Unripe fish as well as spawned-out carcasses and unused roe..are sold in the market. **1972** L. HANCOCK *There's a Seal in my Sleeping Bag* vi. 132 Birds congregated on the salmon river to feed on the spawned-out salmon.

spawner ('spɔːnə(r)). [f. SPAWN *v.* or *sb.*]

1. A female fish, esp. at spawning time.

1601 HOLLAND *Pliny* I. 264 The spawner, when the time serueth for generation, followeth after the male. **1652** NEEDHAM tr. *Selden's Mare Cl.* 90 The Romanes..used none but in-land Fish-ponds, storing them with Spawners of the larger size. **1771** *Phil. Trans.* LXI. 317 As the milter, by a natural instinct, follows the spawner. **1787** BEST *Angling* (ed. 2) 5 With a few Milters and Spawners,..a whole country may be stocked in a short time. **1819** *Sporting Mag.* IV. 266 In stocking ponds, put from three to five spawners to one milter. **1888** GOODE *Amer. Fishes* 59 Many late spawners are occupied with family cares until the last of July.

†**b.** Applied to a woman. *Obs.*

1611 BEAUM. & FL. *Philaster* IV. ii, Yet you may do well to spare your Ladies Bed-fellow, and her you may keep for a Spawner. **1675** COTTON *Burlesque upon B.* 38 By no means meddle with that Spawner. For if thou dost,..A graceless Child will be begot.

2. One who, or that which, spawns, produces, etc., in various senses.

16.. in *Hartlib's Legacy* (1655) 117 The least Spawners from the root will grow. Any twigs cut from the body will grow. **1668** R. L'ESTRANGE *Vis. Quev.* I. (1702) 15 Your corrupt Judges are the great Spawners that supply our Lake. **1839** LADY LYTTON *Cheveley* (ed. 2) II. ii. 58 Every one knew Lord de Clifford.., a spawner of Whig pamphlets, and a crack political writer.

3. A spawn-collector (*Cent. Dict.* 1891).

'spawning, *vbl. sb.* [f. SPAWN *v.*]

1. The action of depositing or laying spawn.

c **1440** *Promp. Parv.* 467/2 Spawnynge, of fysche, *pissiculacio.* **1653** WALTON *Angler* 146 His time of breeding, or spawning. **1753** *Chambers' Cycl.* Suppl. s.v. *Salmo*, In the season for spawning it removes into the fresh waters again. **1774** GOLDSM. *Nat. Hist.* (1824) III. 48 Their [*sc.* lampreys] preparation for spawning is peculiar. **1842** LOUDON *Suburban Hort.* 525 It is always best to repeat the spawning when the heat is on the decline. **1866** LIVINGSTONE *Last Jrnls.* (1873) I. 95 The female becomes large for spawning.

fig. *a* **1662** HEYLIN *Laud* (1668) 368 The Churches cast into the same mould..at the spawning of the second separation.

2. *attrib.*, as ***spawning force, season, time***, etc.

1601 HOLLAND *Pliny* I. 245 If a man do the same with a female in spawning time, hee shall haue as many milters follow after her. **1746** FRANCIS tr. *Horace, Sat.* II. viii. 58 This Fish, Mæcenas, big with Spawn was caught, For after spawning-time its Flesh is naught. **1799** *Monthly Rev.* XXX. 51 To prevent the destruction of this most valuable fish, during the spawning season. **1833** RENNIE *Alph. Angling* 66 It is of much importance for the angler to attend to the spawning time of trout. **1856** EMERSON *Eng. Traits, Race* Wks. (Bohn) II. 20 The spawning force of the [British] race. **1860** —— *Cond. Life, Considerations* Ibid. 415 This spawning productivity is not noxious or needless. **1868** *Rep. U.S. Commissioner Agric.* (1869) 320 Protection is accorded to all fish in the spawning season. **1883** WALLEM *Fish Supply Norway* 6 The codfish..are..of 10 or 11 lbs. weight alive, and their errand seems only to be that of a first spawning-trip.

b. In the sense 'in which spawning is performed', as ***spawning-bed, -ground, -pan, -place, -pond.***

1771 *Phil. Trans.* LXI. 315 The first is called the spawning-pond. *a* **1841** in *Penny Cycl.* XX. 363/2 Three pairs have been seen on the spawning-bed at the same time. **1866** *Chambers's Encycl.* VIII. 446/2 Notable from time immemorial as favourite spawning-places. **1883** WALLEM *Fish Supply Norway* 12 Therefore caplin is used for bait, and is caught only for that purpose on its spawning-grounds. **1883** EARLL in Goode *Fish Indust. U.S.* 77 A few spawning-pans, dippers, and pails, in which to impregnate the eggs.

'spawning, *ppl. a.* [f. as prec.]

1. Of fish, etc.: Engaged in casting spawn.

1579 E. K. *Gloss. to Spenser's Sheph. Cal.* Oct. 14 *Frye*, is a bold Metaphore, forced from the spawning fishes. **1873** *Beeton's Dict. Comm.* s.v. *Norway*, Spawning fish form only a small part of this fishery. **1883** WALLEM *Fish Supply Norway* 15 This fishing of spawning herring has been ruined.

2. *transf.* Fertile; teeming; prolific.

1682 *Lond. Gaz.* No. 1729/3 That late horrid Confederacy,..called by the prolifick spawning name of an Association. **1867** EMERSON *May-Day & Other Pieces* Wks. (Bohn) III. 439 On spawning slime my song prevails. **1878** —— *Misc. Papers, Fort. Republ.* Ibid. 399 Then Illinois and Indiana with their spawning loins must needs be ordinary.

'spawnling. *rare*$^{-1}$. [f. SPAWN *sb.*] The product of a single egg of spawn.

1698 MOTTEUX *Quix.* (1733) I. 168 God's Providence.. provides for..the Wormlings in the Earth and the Spawnlings in the Water.

'spawny, *a. rare.* [f. SPAWN *sb.*] **a.** Like that of spawn. **b.** Resembling spawn. **c.** Spawning.

1669 W. SIMPSON *Hydrol. Chym.* 372 If you pour oyl of tartar upon some of the fresh water, it makes a frisking spawny motion. **1786** ABERCROMBIE *Arr.* in *Gard. Assist.* p. x, Perpetuating its duration by a spawny progeny of the root. **1908** *Daily Rec. & Mail* 9 Mar., It is rather amusing to be told..that 'spawny' herring are unfit for food.

†**spay,** *sb. Obs. rare.* Also spey(e. [a. MFlem. *speye* (14th cent., also in F. texts *espeye*; Kilian *spije*; mod.WFlem. *speie, spei*), related to MFlem. *spoye* (Kilian *spuje*, Flem. and Du. *spui*) in the same sense.] A sluice. (Cf. SPAYER.)

1415 in Riley *Mem. Lond.* (1868) 615 [A watergate, called a] scluys, [or a] speye. **1429** *Cov. Leet Bk.* 121 The residu of the money spended apon the makyng of the Town dyche, & the spey atte Gosford yate. **1451** *Ibid.* 258 The whiche portecoles, Spayes & Cheynes ben made & myche part of the dykes clansed.

spay (speɪ), *v.* Also 5–6 spaie, 6–7 spaye, 7, 9 spey; *pa. pple.* spade. [ad. AF. *espeier*, = OF. *espeer* to cut with a sword, f. *espee* (F. *épée*) sword.]

†**1.** *trans.* To pierce or cut (a deer) so as to kill.

c **1410** *Master of Game* (MS. Digby 182) Prol., And after whann the hert is spaied and dede he vndothe hym. *Ibid.* xxxiii, þen shulde who so be moste maister þere byd somme of þe hunters go spay hym euen behynde þe shulder forwarde to þe herte.

2. To operate upon (a female, esp. the female of certain animals) so as to remove the ovaries and destroy the reproductive power.

c **1410** *Master of Game* (MS. Digby 182) xi, And bycause þei shuld not lese her tyme, men make hem yspayed, saue þose men will kepe open to bere whelpes. **1576** TURBERV. *Venerie* lxvi. 186 The kydneys whiche Gelders take awaye from a bytche..when they spaye hir. **1577** B. GOOGE *Heresbach's Husb.* (1586) 150b, The sowes are spaied by burning the matrixe with an irone. ? *c* **1600** *Distr. Emperor* II. i. in Bullen *O. Pl.* (1884) III. 188 If she had been spayd And all mankynd made Euenucks. **1639** T. DE GRAY *Expert Farrier* Ep. Ded., A gelder who spayes more then a hundred fillies. **1664** BUTLER *Hud.* II. iii. 247 [He] knew..When Sows and Bitches may be spade. **1725** *Fam. Dict.* s.v. *Bitch*, But if you would spay your Bitch, it must be done before ever she has a Litter of Whelps. **1799** [A. YOUNG] *Agric. Linc.* 297 He..spays about half the heifers. **1820** SHELLEY *Œd. Tyr.* I. 72 Out with your knife..and spay those Sows That load the earth with Pigs. **1879** DUNCAN *Clin. Lect. Dis. Women* iv. 48 Lastly, it has of late years frequently been decided to spay women in this disease.

fig. *a* **1658** CLEVELAND *Gen. Poems* (1677) 10 Geld your loose wits, and let your Muse be spade.

spaya(r)d, spayd. Now only *arch.* Forms: *α.* 5 spayer, 5 (7) spayad (7 -ade), 9 spayard, -art. *β.* 6–7 spayde, 7 spaide, 7–8 spaid, 8 spayd; *γ.* 6 spaie, 9– spay. [Of obscure origin: only the earliest quots. are of any value for the genuine form of the word. See also SPIRE *sb.*] A male deer in its third year.

α. *a* **1425** in *Rel. Ant.* I. 151 The fyrst yere he is a calfe, the secunde yere a broket, the .iij. yere a spayer. **1486** *Bk. St. Albans, Hunting* e j b, The secunde yere a Broket... The therde yere a Spayad. **1598** MANWOOD *Lawes Forest* iv. (1615) 42 The third yeere, yow shall call him a Spayad. **1632** *Guillim's Heraldry* III. xiv. (ed. 2) 175 The Third Year, you shall call them Spayade. **1688** HOLME *Armoury* II. 132/1 An Hart, is called 1 yeare a Hind,..3 a Spayade or Spayde. **1859** *Todd's Cycl. Anat.* V. 517 In this condition he is called a 'spayard'. **1886** ELWORTHY *W. Som. Word-bk.* 698 *Spayart*, ..a male deer of three years old.

β. **1576** TURBERV. *Venerie* 237 An Hart is called the firste yeare a Calfe, the seconde a Brocket, the thirde a Spayde. **1602** *2nd Pt. Return Parnass.* II. v. 888 Your Hart is the first yeare a Calfe,..the third yeare a Spade. **1627** J. TAYLOR (Water P.) *Armado* D 1 b, So a Hart is the first yeare a Calfe, ..the third a Spaide. **1678** PHILLIPS, *Spaid*, or *Spayad* [in later dicts. *Spayed, Spayd*], a term used by Hunters, a red male Deer of three years old. **1858** SIMMONDS *Dict. Trade, Spade*,..a deer three years old.

γ. **1577** HARRISON *England* III. iv. 226/1, I find that the yoong male is called in the first yeere a calfe, in the second a broket, the third a spaie. **1906** DOYLE *Sir Nigel* xiii. 163 Great his anxiety lest he confuse a spay with a brocket.

spayed (speɪd), *ppl. a.* Also 6 spaied, spaide, 7 spaid, spead(e, spade, 8 speyed. [f. SPAY *v.*] Having the ovaries excised.

c **1410** *Master of Game* (MS. Digby 182) xi, And also oo spayed bycche lasteth longer in hir bonte þenne oþer two þat be not spayed. **1577** B. GOOGE *Heresbach's Husb.* III. (1586) 154b, The spaide Bitches do bite sorest. **1607** MARKHAM *Cavel.* v. ix. 50 If they be speade or gelte mares, they be the worst of al. *a* **1658** CLEVELAND *Poems* (1677) 39 The Groom is Rampant, but the Bride is Spade. **1684** *Lond. Gaz.* No. 1906/4 Stolen.., a Spaid Bay Mare about 15 hands high. *a* **1722** LISLE *Husb.* (1757) 408 Such a sow was worth less by two shillings..than a spayed sow. **1779** *Phil. Trans.* LXIX. 286 When they are preserved it is..for all the purposes of an ox or spayed heifer. **1813** *Sporting Mag.* XLII. 23 Attended only by his two faithful spayed bitches. **1851** H. STEPHENS *Bk. Farm* (ed. 2) I. 256/2 A quey-calf whose ovaries have been obliterated, to prevent her breeding, is a spayed heifer, or a spayed quey. **1859** *Todd's Cycl. Anat.* V. 573/1 The spayed animal continued to breed until she was six years old.

†**spayer.** *Obs.* Also spayr(e, spyre. [f. SPAY *sb.* + -ER.] A sluice.

1450 *Cov. Leet Bk.* 254 They ordeyn that a spyre be made besides the Gosford-ȝate. **1451** *Ibid.* 257 That ther shulde be made Spayers withe-in the water of Shurburn to holde vp the water. *Ibid.* 260 For rammeng & stoppeng the spayre of ston for the water shuld not issu owt.

spayer (deer): see SPAYA(R)D.

spayer, obs. f. SPARE *v.*[1]

spayer(e, varr. SPARE *sb.*[2] *Obs.*

'spaying, *vbl. sb.* [f. SPAY *v.*] The operation of excising the ovaries in female animals or in women. Also *attrib.*

1576 TURBERV. *Venerie* 18 In spaying of hir, it shal not be good to take away all the rootes or strings of the veynes. **1611** COTGR., *Chastrement*, a gelding, libbing, speying. *a* **1722** LISLE *Husb.* (1757) 407 If pigs be cut..they ought not to be suffered to creep through hedges, lest the thread which sows up the spaying hole be drawn out. **1725** *Fam. Dict.* s.v. *Sow*, As for the Spaying of a Sow, which is the Gelding of that Animal [etc.]. **1805** R. W. DICKSON *Pract. Agric.* II. 988 The spaying of the female calves..is an operation of greater nicety. **1822–7** GOOD *Study Med.* (1829) V. 25 The operation of spaying or excising the ovaries. **1879** DUNCAN *Clin. Lect. Dis. Women* iv. 44 Spaying, an operation which has been introduced recently into gynæcological practice.

Spaynal, -ol, varr. SPAINOL *Obs.*

Spaynard(e, -erd(e, obs. ff. SPANIARD.

spaynel(l, etc., obs. ff. SPANIEL.

spayr, obs. f. SPARE *v.*[2]

spayre, var. SPARE *sb.*[2] *Obs.*; obs. f. SPEAR *sb.*[1]

spaz (spæz). *slang.* Also spas. [Abbrev. of SPASTIC *sb.*] = SPASTIC *sb.* b (see also quot. 1977[1]).

1965 P. KAEL *I lost it at Movies* III. 259 The term that American teen-agers now use as the opposite of 'tough' is 'spaz'. A spaz is a person who is courteous to teachers, plans for a career..and believes in official values. A spaz is something like what adults still call a square. **1975** M. AMIS *Dead Babies* viii. 47, I know how long, you little spaz. **1977** *Amer. Speech* 1975 L. 67 *Spas*,..1: Un-co-ordinated, clumsy person 2: Person regarded as dull, foolish, or stupid 3: Friend (jocular use) 'Hey spas, do we have any homework?' **1977** J. WAMBAUGH *Black Marble* (1978) viii. 117 The man's a spaz! A total spaz! **1982** *Guardian* 26 Oct. 8/4 Come onnnnn—bag your face, you geek, you grody totally shanky spaz.

speach(e, obs. forms of SPEECH *sb.*

spead, obs. form of SPEED.

speak (spiːk), *sb.* Chiefly *Sc.* and *north.* Forms: 3–5 speke (4 spece), 4–5 spek, 5 *Sc.* speike (9 speik), 6–7 speake, 8– speak. [Partly the northern form of ME. *spēche* (OE. *spǽc, sprǽc*) SPEECH *sb.*[1]; partly, in later use, f. SPEAK *v.*

In Laȝamon 1971, *Owl & N.* 13, and Rob. Glouc. 8535, 8643, the forms *speke* and *spek* have obviously been miswritten for *spech(e* through being mistaken for parts of the verb.]

†1. a. The action of speaking; also, manner of speaking. *Obs.*

a 1300 *Cursor M.* 13260 He sermund wit his loueli spek. c 1300 *Havelok* 946 Of alle men was he mest meke, Lauhwinde ay, and bliþe of speke. 1375 BARBOUR *Bruce* I. 393 In spek wlispyt he sum deill. c 1375 *Sc. Leg. Saints* xxvii. (*Machor*) 1164 With þis of spek he mad ending. c 1450 HOLLAND *Howlat* 242 All apperit to the Pape,..Salust his sanctitud with spirituale speike.

†b. The power or faculty of speech. *Obs.*

a 1300 *Cursor M.* 24320 Als ded þai war, wit-vten speke. c 1375 *Sc. Leg. Saints* Prol. 122 As to deff men gyfand herynge,..and spek till oþer at war dum.

†c. A language. *Obs.*

a 1300 *Cursor M.* 2267 Þar war al þe speces delt þat now ouer-alle þe werld er melt.

2. a. Talk, discourse, conversation.

a 1300 *Cursor M.* 2618 Wit hir sli spece gun he spell. c 1375 *Sc. Leg. Saints* ii. (*Paul*) 301 With wismen þare-of [Nero] had spek. 1886 WILLOCK *Rosetty Ends* xii. (1887) 88 The affair caused a hantle o' speak.

b. With *a*, *the*, *this*, etc., or possessive pronouns.

a 1300 *Cursor M.* 12197 Ihesus þan folud on his speke, And þus began his resun eke. c 1300 *Havelok* 1065 Þoruth England yede þe speke [*MS.* speche], Hw he was strong, and ek meke. 1375 BARBOUR *Bruce* I. 72 Thai all concordyt, That all thar spek suld be recordyt Till Schyr Eduuard. a 1400–50 *Alexander* 3318 With þis speke at he spake þe sprete he ȝeldis. a 1779 D. GRAHAM *Writ.* (1883) II. 209, I maun hae ..a quiet speak to hersel about it. 1790 SHIRREFS *Poems* 247 Only foes to common sense Frae sic a speak can tak' offence. 1819 W. TENNANT *Papistry Storm'd* (1827) 5 Notin' down within thy book Ilk motion, gesture, speik, and look. 1883– in dial. glossaries, etc. (Yks., Westmld., Linc., Berks.).

†c. ***a great speak***, an important statement. *Obs.*

1587 GOLDING *De Mornay* xxiv. (1596) 366 They thinke themselues to haue made a greate speake, and hard to be resolued.

3. A formal discourse; a speech.

1567 DRANT *Horace, Ep., Arte Poet.* A vij, A solemne speake, mete for great things. 1576 PETTIE *Petite Pallace* 89 b, Before hym Aristotle..maketh a great speake, saying [etc.]. 1600 O.E. *Repl. to Libel* I. i. 9 Nor doth he applie his common place to his purpose, but leaueth it..without any coherence to the rest of his long speake. 1610 R. DAVIES in *Chester's Triumph* (Chetham Soc.) C 3 b, Is it not harsh to heare a Marmeset squeake Vpon a stage a most vnioynted speake? 1791 J. LEARMONT *Poems* 30 Their unco speaks o' sax hours lang.

4. *Cant.* (See quot.) *Obs.*$^{-0}$

1811 *Lexicon Balatronicum* s.v. *Speak*, He has made a good speak; he has stolen something considerable. 1812 J. H. VAUX *Flash Dict.*, *Speak*, committing any robbery, is called *making a speak*; and if it has been productive you are said to have *made a rum speak*.

5. = SPEAKEASY.

1930 *Bookman* (U.S.) LXXII. 398/1 Better grade speaks in Times Square are dispensing with femme shills and hangers-out. 1952 [see OPEN *a.* 2 c]. 1977 H. FAST *Immigrants* IV. 242 We're just lucky it happened in a speak, because maybe no one will bring any charges.

speak (spiːk), *v.* Forms: (see below). [OE. *sprecan* (pa. t. *spræc, sprǽcon*, pa. pple. *ȝesprecen*), = OFris. *spreka* (WFris. *sprekke*, NFris. *spreek, spreeg*), MDu. (and Du.) *spreken*, OS. *sprekan* (MLG. and LG. *spreken*), OHG. *sprehhan* (MHG. and G. *sprechen*); not recorded in Gothic, and absent in older Scand., the obs. Da. *sprecke, sprække*, Icel. *spreka*, being adoptions from LG.

The later OE. *specan* became common in the 11th cent., and forms with *r* app. did not survive in actual use beyond the middle of the 12th cent. A similar elision of the *r* appears very rarely in MDu. *speken*, OHG. *spehhan*.]

A. Illustration of Forms.

1. *Inf.* α. **1 sprecan, spreocan, spræcan;** *north.* **spreca, spræca, -spreaca; sprecca, spræcca; 2 sprecon.**

c 825 *Vesp. Hymns* iv, Nyllað ȝemoniȝfaldian spreocan. c 897 K. ÆLFRED *Gregory's Past. C.* 89 [Hie] ne durron.. sprecan. a 900 in *O.E. Texts* 178 Hu meahte ic..her spræcan? c 950 *Lindisf. Gosp.* Matt. x. 19 Huætt ȝe spreca scilo. *Ibid.* 20 Huæt ȝie sprecca scilon. c 1075 *O.E. Chron.* (Parker MS.) an. 1070, Umbe þæt hi sprecan woldon. a 1122 *Ibid.* (Laud MS.) an. 1114, He wolde sprecon mid him.

β. **1 specan (2 -on), 1–2 specen, 2–5 speken (3** *Orm.* **spekenn), 5 spekyn; 1–2 spæcon, 2 -en, 3 spæ(c)ken; 2–3 speoken.**

c 1000 in Assmann *Ags. Hom.* xviii. 55 Hy..wið hi specan woldon. c 1000 *Ags. Gosp.* Matt. xii. 46 Secende spæcon [c 1160 *Hatton* spæcen] to him. c 1120 *O.E. Chron.* (MS. H) an. 1113, Swa þæt hiȝ uneaðe specon mihton. c 1175 *Lamb. Hom.* 35 Ȝif he mihte speken. *Ibid.* 89 Heo..on-gunnen to speoken. c 1205 LAY. 14758 He wold spæcken heom wið. c 1250 *Gen. & Ex.* 3400 Ðo cam ietro..To speken him. a 1425 *Cursor M.* 20025 (Trin.), I bigon hir worshepe speken. c 1440 *Promp. Parv.* 468/1 Spekyn, *loquor.*

γ. **3–6 speke, 4–6 spek, 4 spec, speck, 5 speike, 6–7 speake, 6–8** *Sc.* **speik, 6– speak** (*Ir.* 8–9 **spake**).

a 1250 *Owl & Night.* 261 Let me speke. a 1300 *Cursor M.* 24795 (Edinb.), For to spek about sum pais. 13.. *Ibid.* 19176 (Gött.), Quilis þai suld samen speck. c 1400 *Destr. Troy* 4976 By course for to speike. 1483 *Cath. Angl.* 353/1 To Speke,..*loqui.* 1535 COVERDALE *Isaiah* lxvi. 19 The Iles ..that haue not herde speake of me. 1586 LD. BURGHLEY in *Leycester Corr.* (Camden) 450 Some spek of namyng the count Morrice. 1609 SKENE *Reg. Maj.* 95 Na man sall speik. a 1700 in *Cath. Rec. Soc. Publ.* IX. 362 She could not speake french. 1762 FOOTE *Orator* II, By my shoul but I will spake.

2. *Pres. tense sing.* (Early contracted forms.)

a. *2nd pers.* α. **1 sprycst, 1–2 sprecst, 2 spræcst.** β. **1 spycst, 2 spæcst, 3 spekst, 3–4 spext.**

α. 971 *Blickl. Hom.* 183 Forhwon ne sprecst þu? c 1000 *Ags. Gosp.* John iv. 27 Hwæt sprycst [c 1160 *Hatton* sprecst] þu wið hiȝ? c 1160 *Hatton Gosp.* John xix. 10 Hwi ne spræcst þu wið me.

β. c 1000 *Ags. Gosp.* Matt. xiii. 10 For hwiȝ spycst [c 1160 *Hatton* spæcst] þu..mid biȝ-spellum? a 1272 in *O.E. Misc.* 98 Hwat spekstu of eny stone. c 1290 *S. Eng. Leg.* I. 128 Þov spext ase a fol. c 1320 in *Rel. Antiq.* I. 265 Ȝef thou with dede mon spext.

b. *3rd pers.* α. **1 sprycð, 1–2 spricð, sprecð, 2 spræcð.** β. **1 spycð, spycþ, 2–4 specþ, specð (2 specd), 3 spechð, 3–4 spekþ, 4 spekth.**

α. c 897 K. ÆLFRED *Gregory's Past. C.* 380 Ðæs monnes saul þe wel spricð. 971 *Blickl. Hom.* 55 Se þa soþfæstnesse.. sprecþ. c 1000 *Ags. Gosp.* John vii. 18 Se þe be him sylium sprycð [c 1160 *Hatton* spræcð].

β. c 1000 *Ags. Gosp.* John vii. 26 Nu he spycþ openlice. c 1200 *Trin. Coll. Hom.* 51 Dauid specð..sume of þe wordes. a 1250 *Owl & Night.* 1072 Wel viht þat wel spekþ. 1340 *Ayenb.* 126 Huanne he specþ of þise..uirtues. 1390 GOWER *Conf.* I. 366 Solyns spekth of a wonder kinde.

3. *Past tense.* **a.** *sing.* α. **1 sprec, 1–2 spræc (1 spræcc), 2 spreac.**

c 825 *Vesp. Psalter* xcviii. 7 In syle wolcnes [he] sprec to him. a 900 in *O.E. Texts* 178 He spræc to his liornæra sumum. c 950 *Lindisf. Gosp.* Luke ix. 11 [He] spræcc him of ric godes. a 1122 *O.E. Chron.* (Laud MS.) an. 1083, Þe abbot..spræc uppon þa munecas. 1131 *Ibid.* an. 1131, Se abbot..spreac mid þone kyng.

β. **1–3 spæc, 2–4 spec, spek, 4–5 speck.**

a 1000 *Psalm l.* 30 Dauid..ðus wordum spæc. a 1122 *O.E. Chron.* (Laud MS.) an. 1046, Sweȝen..spec wið his feder. c 1175 *Lamb. Hom.* 73 Of ileue spek ure drihten. c 1205 LAY. 12655 He..of gode spæc swide wel. a 1225 *Leg. Kath.* 308 Hwil þet ha spek þus. c 1307 *Elegy Death Edw. I*, vi, The pope..spec a word of gret honour. 13.. *K. Horn* 600 An hound.. spek wordes bolde.

γ. **2–5 spac (3** *Orm.* **spacc), 4–5,** *Sc.* **and** *dial.* **7– spack, 5 spacke, spakke, 3–5,** *Sc.* **and** *north.* **6– spak, 9** *Sc.* **spak'.**

a 1154 *O.E. Chron.* (Laud MS.) an. 1140, Þe biscop..spac wid Rodbert. c 1200 ORMIN 224 Spacc he nohht wiþþ tunge. a 1250 *Owl & Night.* 396 Ho spak boþe right & red. a 1300 *Cursor M.* 12005 Sum him..spack o prise. c 1380 WYCLIF *Sel. Wks.* III. 312 Many þinges þat God spac not. c 1400 *Pilgr. Sowle* (Caxton, 1483) I. xvi. 14 These wordys whiche ..the juge..spack. 1470–85 MALORY *Arthur* I. xxi. 68 Thenne spak Igrayne. 1567 *Gude & Godlie B.* (S.T.S.) 84 Than spak that Virgin fre. c 1614 SIR W. MURE *Dido & Æneas* I. 467 Ne'er word she spak. 1786 BURNS *Holy Fair* iv, Laughan as she spak.

δ. **3 spæke, 3–5 speke, 4 speeke, 5 speek.**

Properly representing the OE. forms *sprǽce, spǽce.*

c 1200 ORMIN 16260 Þeȝȝ wenndenn þatt he spæke..off þeȝȝre temmple. c 1275 LAY. 14316 Þe speche þat þe maide speke. c 1320 *Cast. Love* 458 Pees..þus to hire Fader speek. 1382 WYCLIF *Job* ii. 10 As oon of the fool wymmen thou speeke. c 1420 *Sir Amadace* (Camden) lx, Thenne speke Sir Amadace so fre.

ε. **3–** (now *arch.*, *dial.*, or *poet.*) **spake, 4–5 spaak.** Also *2nd pers.* **5 spakist, 6– spakest, 6 spakst, 7** *poet.* **spak'st.**

a 1300 *K. Horn* 535 Do nu þat þu er of spake. c 1380 WYCLIF *Sel. Wks.* III. 265 He spaak þes wordis. 1388 — *1 Sam.* xxviii. 21 Thi wordis, whiche thou spakist. 1461 *Paston Lett.* II. 14, I..spake Ric. Sothwell. 1509 FISHER *Wks.* (1876) 103 That thou spake them to hym. 1667 MILTON *P.L.* VIII. 444, I, ere thou spak'st, Knew [etc.]. 1781 COWPER *Conversation* 511 They spake of him they lov'd. 1827 [see B. 1 f]. 1848 BARTLETT *Dict. Amer.* 321 *Spake*..is still heard occasionally from the pulpit, as well as in conversation. 1872 TENNYSON *Gareth & Lynette* 472 Lancelot ever spake him pleasantly.

ζ. **6– spoke, 7, 9** *dial.* **spok, 7 spoak(e, spook, 8–9** *dial.* **spock.** Also *2nd pers.* **9 spokest.**

1596 SPENSER *F.Q.* VI. xii. 25 He..blasphemy spoke. 1615 COCKS *Diary* (Hakl. Soc.) I. 18 She spoake Spanish. 1617 *Ibid.* 260 He spok to the Chinas. 1697 J. LEWIS *Mem. Dk. Glocester* (1789) 50 A sweetness..that spoke the inner feelings. 1773 GOLDSM. *Stoops to Conq.* III, He spoke to me. 1802 *Med. Jrnl.* VIII. 194 With whom I spoke here lately. 1848 LYTTON *Harold* I. iii. 41 Thou spokest of Harold.

b. *Plur.* α. **1 sprecun, -on (-an), 1–2 spræcon (1 -un, -an, 2 -en).**

c 825 *Vesp. Psalter* cxviii. 23 Aldermen..wið me sprecun. c 897 K. ÆLFRED *Gregory's Past. C.* 95 Eall ðæt ðæt we ær spræcon. 971 *Blickl. Hom.* 77 Hie..to Criste spræcan. *Ibid.* 99 Þa þe..him olyhtword sprecan. c 1000 *Ags. Gosp.* Luke xxiv. 36 Þa hiȝ þis spræcon [c 1160 *Hatton* spræcen]. 1123 *O.E. Chron.* (Laud MS.) an. 1123, Ða spræcon ða biscopas hem betwenan.

β. **1–2 spæcon, 2 spæcen, 2–3 spæken (3** *Orm.* **-enn); 2 specon, 2–5 speken (5 spekon, -yn), 3–5 speke, 4 spek; 4 speeken, spieken, speeke, spieke.**

c 1000 *Ags. Gosp.* Luke xxiv. 14 And hiȝ spæcon him betwynan. c 1160 *Hatton Gosp.* Luke ix. 30 Ða spæken [*v.r.* spæcen] tweȝen weres wið hine. c 1175 *Lamb. Hom.* 89 Þe apostles speken to þes folkes igederunge. c 1205 LAY. 8249 Þus þe cnihtes him spæken [c 1275 speke] wið. c 1305 *St. Dunstan* 9 in *E.E.P.* (1862) 34 Hi speke ech to oþer. a 1325 *Prose Psalter* xxxvii. 13 Hij..speken uanites. 1382 WYCLIF *Ps.* cxviii. 23 Aȝen me thei speeken. 1390 GOWER *Conf.* I. 235 Therof spieken alle men. *Ibid.* III. 300 Togedre as thei tuo speeke. c 1450 *Merlin* 25 The peple..assembleden, and speken of Vortiger. c 1489 CAXTON *Blanchardyn* 71 The most valiaunt knyght that men euere speke of.

γ. **4–5 spaken, 4–5, 7 spake, 4 space, spac, 4, 6** *Sc.* **spack, 4, 9** *dial.* **spak.**

a 1300 *E.E. Psalter* lxxii. 8 Þai..spake quedenes vnrighte. a 1325 *Prose Psalter* cviii. 2 Hij spaken to me. a 1425 *Cursor M.* 11990 (Trin.), Þei spake to Ioseph. c 1449 PECOCK *Repr.* II. x. 206 Whom prophetis bifore spaken Sauiour. 1596 DALRYMPLE tr. *Leslie's Hist. Scot.* II. 284 Tha spack verie scharpe. 1621 COCKS *Diary* 11 Nov. (1883) II. 218 Those 10 men they spake of.

δ. **3–5 spoken, 4 spokyn; 4, 6– spoke, 5 spook.**

c 1250 *Gen. & Ex.* 2913 Quanne he ðat bodewurd spoken. a 1325 *Prose Psalter* cxviii. 23 For princes..spoken oȝains me. 1377 LANGL. *P. Pl.* B. II. 225 Spiceres spoke with hym. 1470–85 MALORY *Arthur* XVII. viii. 700 As they spoken thus. 1598 SHAKS. *Merry W.* IV. iv. 17 That [way] they spoke of.

4. *Past Participle.* α. **1 ȝesprecen, ȝespecen, 3 i-specken, i-speken, i-spæ(c)ken; 1 sprecen, 2 sprecon; 3–5 speken, 7 speaken, 6 spaken.**

Beowulf 643 Þa wæs eft..þryðword sprecen. c 888 K. ÆLFRED *Boeth.* xviii. § 1 Ða ðis þa ȝesprecen was. c 1050 *Ags. Hom.* (Assmann) 183 Ða þa Tyrus hæfde þus ȝespecen. a 1122 *O.E. Chron.* (Laud MS.) an. 675, Swa swa ȝe hit sprecon hauen. c 1200 *Moral Ode* 9 (Trin. Coll. MS.), Fele idel word ich habbe ispeken. c 1205 LAY. 13643 Ich habbe ..ispæken him wið. c 1300 *Havelok* 2369 Þat ich haue of ofte speken. c 1590 in Ellis *Orig. Lett.* Ser. II. III. 159, I have spaken to Dollyne. 1670 DK. YORK in *3rd Rep. Hist. MSS. Comm.* 421/1 Nor will it be speaken on..till next weeke.

β. **3–4 i-speke, y-speke, 4–5 speke, 4 spek.**

a 1250 *Owl & Night.* 1293 For þe hule swo ispeke hadde. c 1290 *S. Eng. Leg.* I. 228 Þare nas neuere..yspeke..non oþur word. 1340 *Ayenb.* 69 Uor þet hi habbeþ yspeke. c 1350 *Will. Palerne* 4605 Til i speke haue.

γ. **4–5 y-, i-spoken, i-spokyn; 4– spoken (5 -ene, -un), 4–5,** *Sc.* **6 spokin (5** *Sc.* **-ine), 4–6 spokyn, 5 spockyn, 6** *Sc.*, **9** *dial.* **spocken (9** *dial.* **spockin, spawken), 6** *Sc.* **spokne, 7 spokn, spoaken.**

a 1300 *Cursor M.* 1757 Quen he his wil had with him spoken. a 1325 *Prose Psalter* xi. 2 Ichon han i-spoken idel þynges. 1450–80 tr. *Secreta Secret.* 13 Whan that this worthi lord hath þus..spokene. 1530 PALSGR. 727/2 Whan they hadde spokyn..of the matter. 1583 *Leg. Bp. St. Androis* 353 Trowing the teallis befoir was spocken. 1596 DALRYMPLE tr. *Leslie's Hist. Scot.* I. 88 We haue schortlie spokne. 1604 E. G[RIMSTONE] *D'Acosta's Hist. Indies* II. ix. 102 Not so great as they had spoken. 1817 WILBRAHAM in *Archaeol.* (1821) XIX. 38 *Spocken*, participle of the verb to speak.

δ. **4–5 y-spoke, 4 i-spoke; 4–9 spoke, 5, 7 spok, 7 spoak.**

1387 TREVISA *Higden* (Rolls) IV. 123 He hadde proudeliche i-spoke. 1390 GOWER *Conf.* I. 60 As I have spoke. c 1430 *Pilgr. Lyf Manhode* I. xliv. (1869) 26 Whan Nature hadde þus yspoke. 1461 *Paston Lett.* II. 42, I have spok with John Rwsse. 1557 GRIMALD in *Tottel's Misc.* (Arb.) 116 Not more..hath Sparta spoke. 1622 DONNE *Serm. 15 Sept.* 37 Neither is that spoak there. 1664 POWER *Exp. Philos.* I. 2 He would not have spoke so doubtfully. a 1774 GOLDSM. tr. *Scarron's Com. Romance* (1775) I. 63 When she had spoke these last words. 1818 SCOTT *Hrt. Midl.* vii, Nothing was spoke of for some time. 1843 S. R. MAITLAND *Dark Ages* xvi. (1890) 293 That I have..spoke the truth.

ε. **6–7 spake, 9** *Sc.* **spak'.**

c 1500 *Three Kings' Sons* 61 That he had spake to hym. 1616 W. FORDE *Serm.* 17 He had no sooner spake the word. 1632 MASSINGER & FIELD *Fatal Dowry* V. ii, Tho' spake by him That never brake his word. 1812 P. FORBES *Poems* 34 (E.D.D.), Another chield that hadna spak'.

B. Signification.

I. *intr.* **1. a.** To utter or pronounce words or articulate sounds; to use or exercise the faculty of speech; to express one's thoughts by words.

Beowulf 1698 Ða se wisa spræc sunu Healfdenes; swiȝedon ealle. c 888 K. ÆLFRED *Boeth.* iii. § 3 Þa ongan he eft sprecan & cwæð to þan Mode. c 1000 *Ags. Gosp.* Matt. xv. 31 Þa mæneȝu wundredon ȝeseonde dumbe specende, healte gangende. a 1200 *St. Marher.* 16 Swuch farlac ich fele ..þet speoken i ne dar nawt. a 1300 *Cursor M.* 19415 Þe hali spirit vte of him spak. 1377 LANGL. *P. Pl.* B. XIX. 126 For defe..to here & dombe speke he made. 1422 tr. *Secreta Secret., Priv. Priv.* 209 He that hyryth the reysones of many men may lightyr well sayne, than he that erste spake. 1581 PETTIE tr. *Guazzo's Civ. Conv.* II. (1586) 69 b, Not to speake, while an other is in speaking,..before he which speaketh be thorowly understood. 1610 SHAKS. *Temp.* II. i. 65 If but one of his pockets could speake, would it not say he lyes? 1719 DE FOE *Crusoe* I. (Globe) 182, I had taught my Poll, as I noted before, to speak. 1828 LYTTON *Pelham* III. xiv, He spoke with great feeling on the subject for which I was summoned. 1897 GLADSTONE *E. Crisis* 6 It is time to speak with freedom.

transf. 1611 BIBLE *Prov.* vi. 13 He winketh with his eyes, he speaketh with his feete.

b. Said of the mouth, tongue, etc.

c 825 *Vesp. Psalter* xvi. 10 Muð heara spreocende wes in oferhyȝde. c 1000 *Ags. Gosp.* Luke vi. 45 Soðlice se muð spycð [c 1160 specð] swa seo heorte þencð. 1382 WYCLIF *Ps.* lxv. 14 My mouth spac in my tribulacioun. 1535 COVERDALE *Matt.* xii. 34 For of ye abundance of ye hert ye mouth speaketh. 1560 BIBLE (Geneva) *Song Sol.* vii. 9 Which.. causeth the lippes of the ancient to speake. 1611 BIBLE *Isaiah* xxxii. 4 The tongue of the stammerers shall bee readie to speake plainely. 1646 CRASHAW *Steps to Temple Poems* (1904) 74 Christ bids the dumb tongue speak; it speakes. 1841 LANE *Arab. Nts.* I. 95 When I have cut off thy head, will it speak?

c. To hold talk or discourse, to converse, with others or with each other. (Cf. 20.) Also, in mod. use, to be on speaking terms.

971 *Blickl. Hom.* 93 Seo eorþe on þæm norþ-ende & on þam east-ende sprecað him betweonum. c 1000 *Ags. Gosp.* Luke vii. 32 Hi synt ȝelice cildum on stræte sittendum & specendum betwux him. c 1125 *O.E. Chron.* (Laud MS.) an. 1123, Se king..and se biscop..riden þær specende. c 1200 ORMIN 3389 Þa hirdess tokenn sone þuss To spekenn hemm bitwenenn. 1375 [see 3 a]. 1390 GOWER *Conf.* I. 208 Thus as

they lihe abedde and spieke. **1582** N. T. (Rhem.) *Acts* xxvi. 31 Going a side, they spake among them selues, saying [etc.]. **1607** SHAKS. *Cor.* I. iv. 4 They lye in view, but haue not spoke as yet. **1777** CLARA REEVE *Champion of Virtue* 54 While they were speaking, Oswald came to them, and said [etc.]. **1819** SHELLEY *Cenci* v. i. 64 Even whilst we speak The ministers of justice wait below. **1826** DISRAELI *Vivian Grey* II. ii, There is Courtown, but we do not speak. **1865** H. KINGSLEY *Hillyars* III. xxiii. 240 Even their husbands did not speak for a fortnight.

(*b*) *spec.* To speak to another by means of a telephone; —— ***speaking*** (where —— is a speaker on a telephone), phr. used by the speaker to announce his identity.

1885 *List of Subscribers* (United Telephone Co.) p. xiv, 'Who speaks?' came distinctly from the wires into the office. '2577,' was the reply—it was the hotel number. **1925** F. SCOTT FITZGERALD *Great Gatsby* ix. 200 But the connection came through as a man's voice, very thin and far away. 'This is Slagle speaking.'.. 'Yes?' The name was unfamiliar. **1933** 'SAPPER' *Knock-Out* i. 9 Standish.. took the receiver from the other's hand. 'Hullo! Sanderson,' he said. 'Yes—Standish speaking. What now?' **1973** J. WAINWRIGHT *Pride of Pigs* 166 'Quince?' said the voice. 'Speaking.' Quince hooked his fingers through the carrying handle of the Trimphone, telephone hand set... He said: 'Who's that?.. Who's speaking?' **1977** L. MEYNELL *Hooky gets Wooden Spoon* xiii. 151 C.I.D. here.. who is it speaking, please?

d. In various phrases and proverbs.

See also BOOK *sb.* 15 and CARD *sb.*[2] 4 c.

a **1250** *Owl & Night.* 1074 'Wel fiȝt þat wel specþ,' seide Alured. **1381** in *Knighton's Chron.* (Rolls) II. 139 Speke, spende and spede, quoth Jon of Bathon. *a* **1425** *Cursor M.* 23849 (Trin.), Euer to speke & not to spede, Wastyng hit is of goddes sede. **14..** [see SPARE *v.*[1] 6 c]. **1596** SHAKS. *Tam. Shr.* II. i. 66 Mistake me not, I speake but as I finde. *c* **1676** SOUTH *Serm.* (1715) 341 He only now-a-days speaks like an Oracle, who speaks Tricks and Ambiguities. **1748** RICHARDSON *Clarissa* VI. 61 He always loved to speak as he found. **1875** JOWETT *Plato* (ed. 2) I. 482, I am speaking like a book.

e. With reflexive or ethical dative. *rare.*

c **1400** *Anturs of Arth.* l, Bot than hym spake Gallerone to Gawayne þe gude. **1703** ROWE *Ulyss.* I. i. 366 This Wife of him that was my Friend? *Eur.* Thou speak'st me well, of him that was thy Friend. **1839-48** BAILEY *Festus* 60/1 Thou speakest me of visions.

f. To deliver a speech or formal address; to express one's opinions or views in an assembly of any kind.

a **1577** SIR T. SMITH *Commw.* II. ii. (1584) 40 The speaker hath no voice in the house, nor they will not suffer him to speake in any bill to mooue or disswade it. **1601** SHAKS. *Jul. C.* III. ii. 89 Heere, vnder leaue of Brutus, and the rest,.. Come I to speake in Cæsars Funerall. **1689** *Sc. Acts Parlt.* (1875) XII. 59/2 That the members be allowed to speak oftner than twyce if it be done with discreatione. **1738** tr. *Guazzo's Art Convers.* 115 Marius, being to speak before the People of Rome, said [etc.]. **1827** SOUTHEY *Hist. Penins. War* II. 574 Lord Grenville spake in a similar temper. **1849** MACAULAY *Hist. Eng.* vi. II. 18 The Commons were summoned to the bar of the Lords; and the King spoke from the throne. His speech had been composed by himself.

g. *spec.* To propose marriage. Cf. sense 14 d.

1604 SHAKS. *Othello* I. iii. 166 She thank'd me, And bad me, if I had a Friend that lou'd her, I should but teach him how to tell my Story, And that would wooe her. Vpon this hint I spake. **1803** G. COLMAN *John Bull* III. i. 31 *Lady Caroline.* Lard, Mr. Shuffleton!.. You never spoke anything to—that is—to justify such a—. *Shuffleton.* (Aside.) That's as much as to say, speak now. **1858** TROLLOPE *Doctor Thorne* II. vi. 81, I think you may speak now, Frank... She is very fond of you. **1904** H. JAMES *Golden Bowl* I. I. xii. 213 He liked.. to feel that he should be able to 'speak'.. the word itself being romantic. **1932** S. GIBBONS *Cold Comfort Farm* xiv. 195 Flora did not dare to imagine what would happen if they returned from the ball and he had not spoken. He *must* speak! **1964** M. LASKI in S. Nowell-Smith *Edwardian England* iv. 198 An interval might have been found—perhaps in the conservatory, perhaps on a sofa in a dark nook under the stairs— when *he* had spoken and *she* accepted.

2. a. Followed by direct quotation of the words uttered.

More commonly with insertion of 'and said'.

Beowulf 1168 Spræc ða ides Scyldinga: 'Onfoh þissum fulle.' *c* **1000** *Ags. Ps.* (Thorpe) lxiii. 4 Hi.. sare sprecað, 'Hwa ȝesyhð usic?' *a* **1325** *Prose Psalter* xxxviii. 5 Ich spak wyþ my tunge, 'Make, Lord, knowen to me myn endyng'. **1375** in Horstmann *Altengl. Leg.* (1878) 127/1 Adam þo spak ful pitously: 'A, deuel, wo þe be!' **1500-20** DUNBAR *Poems* (S.T.S.) xxxiv. 14 Than spak the Devill.., 'Renunce thy God and cum to me'. **1588** A. KING tr. *Canisius' Catech.* 30 For thou hes spoken.. 'the bread quhilk I sal giue is my fleshe'. **1667** MILTON *P.L.* VII. 339 Again th' Almightie spake: Let there be Lights [etc.]. **1781** COWPER *Hope* 524 Well spake the prophet, Let the desert sing. **1825** SCOTT *Betrothed* vi, He spoke again, and in anxious haste, 'Daughter, we are betrayed!' **1859** TENNYSON *Marr. Geraint* 555 Loudly spake the Prince, 'Forbear: there is a worthier'.

b. In pa. t. used in narrative poetry (after L. *dixit*) at the end of a speech. Cf. SAY *v.*[1] B. 3 e.

1667 MILTON *P.L.* I. 663 He spake: and to confirm his words [etc.]. **1697** DRYDEN *Æneid* v. 218 He spoke, and.. at his stern he saw [etc.]. **1716** POPE *Iliad* v. 351 He spoke, and rising hurl'd his forceful dart. **1757** GRAY *Bard* 143 He spoke, and headlong.. plunged to endless night. **1820** SHELLEY *Hymn Merc.* lxix, He spoke, and bound Stiff withy bands the infant's wrists around.

3. a. With advs. and advb. phrases, as *so*, *thus*, etc. (See also 4 a.)

Speak may also be accompanied by many different adverbs denoting either the tone of voice, the temper or intention of the speaker, or the character of the ideas expressed. For some special instances of these see EVIL *adv.* 1, FAIR *adv.* 2, FALSE *adv.* 1, HOME *adv.* 5, LOW *adv.* 3, PLAIN *adv.* 2 and 3, SOFT *adv.* 4, THICK *adv.* 4, WELL *adv.*

971 *Blickl. Hom.* 227 þa he þa þus spræc, ða ȝeseah he [etc.]. *a* **1225** *Leg. Kath.* 312 He.. feng on þus to speokene. *c* **1250** *Kent. Serm.* in *O.E. Misc.* 27 Herodes.. swo spac te þo þrie kinges. **1375** BARBOUR *Bruce* XIX. 613 Thusgatis spekand, thai held thar way. **1557** *Tottel's Misc.* (Arb.) 216 If guile do guide your wit by silence so to speake. **1611** BIBLE *1 Sam.* xviii. 24 On this manner spake Dauid. **1667** MILTON *P.L.* I. 271 So Satan spake, and him Beelzebub Thus answer'd. **1748** SMOLLETT *R. Random* lvi, While I spoke thus, she concealed her face with her fan. **1819** SCOTT *Ivanhoe* xxviii, Speak not so, my dear father. **1845** S. JUDD *Margaret* I. xiv, I have heard Hash speak so.

b. With advs. of quantity, as *less*, *little*, *more*, *much*.

With these words it is often difficult to distinguish between the intr. and trans. uses of the verb.

a **1300** *Cursor M.* 19115 þe apostels spekand þus and mar, þe preistes come. **1338** R. BRUNNE *Chron.* (1810) 77 Was noiþer more no lesse of þer penance spoken. **1388** WYCLIF *2 Sam.* xix. 29 What spekist thou more? *c* **1400** *Brut* cxiii. 114 When þe Kyng herde speke so miche of here beaute. *c* **1475** *Rauf Coilȝear* 270 Mair the King spak nocht. **1588** SHAKS. *L.L.L.* I. i. 112, I haue for barbarisme spoke more. **1702** *Eng. Theophrastus* 335 It is the character of your half witted fellows to speak much and say little. **1805** SCOTT *Last Minstrel* II. xxxii, Little he ate, and less he spoke. **1848** THACKERAY *Van. Fair* xxxiv, Perhaps rather disappointed that the port wine had not made Jim speak more.

c. With advs. denoting continuation, as *away*, *on*.

1535 COVERDALE *Ecclus.* xxvii. 12 Amonge soch as be wyse, speake on hardely. **1591** SHAKS. *1 Hen. VI*, III. iii. 43 Speake on, but be not ouer-tedious. **1725** RAMSAY *Gentle Sheph.* Song xvii, Speak on,.. and still my grief. **1781** C. JOHNSTON *Hist. J. Juniper* II. 164 If stages were built for them to speak away upon. *a* **1814** *Fam. Politics* v. iii. in *New Brit. Theat.* II. 248 Speak away, girl: we shall halt here some time yet. **1885** 'MRS. ALEXANDER' *At Bay* i, He wanted her to speak on.

d. With advs. having reference to the use of a particular language or style of speech.

1823 SCOTT *Quentin D.* xvi, 'Thou speakest too well for one who hath lived always in thy filthy horde,' said the Scot. **1846** LANDOR *Imag. Conv., Southey & Landor* Wks. 1853 II. 164/1 Varlunga, a pastoral district, in which the people speak differently from both.

4. In various parenthetical and other phrases: **a.** In the infinitive, esp. *so to speak*.

(*a*) **1553** T. WILSON *Rhet.* (1580) 205 All goodnesse (to speake at a worde) goeth awaie. **1595** SHAKS. *John* II. i. 514 Or if you will, to speake more properly, I will enforce it easlie. **1628** GAULE *Pract. The.* (1629) 232 Before Herod (to speake in few) they put vpon him a Fooles Note. **1671** H. M. tr. *Erasm. Colloq.* 494 There was no year, wherein he did not gain a thousand duckats, to speak with the least. **1821** SCOTT *Kenilw.* vii, It would cost me nothing.. to say yes—but, to speak on the square, I must needs say no. **1886** C. E. PASCOE *Lond. of To-day* xl. (ed. 3) 349 To speak by the book, 'Mr. Gunter, cook, confectioner, and fruiterer'.

(*b*) **1824** LONGFELLOW *Let.* 2 Mar. in S. Longfellow *Life H. W. Longfellow* (1886) I. iii. 37 If this were not another building, I should have imagined I occupied the same chamber that you did in former times, for it seemed to be the very highest point of the dwelling, the very *apogee*, so to speak. **1837** CARLYLE *Fr. Rev.* I. III. iii, Notables are, so to speak, organed out. **1888** 'J. S. WINTER' *Bootle's Childr.* v, Pearl.. was the leading spirit of the pair, and led Maud by the nose, so to speak.

attrib. and as *sb.* **1874** *Gentl. Mag.* July 126 In a so to speak unconscious manner. **1893** R. HEATH *Eng. Peasant* 248 This statement of his.. is not to be dismissed as a mere so-to-speak.

b. *as they* (etc.) ***speak***, = as the phrase is.

1595 in J. H. Pollen *Acts Eng. Mart.* (1892) vi. 101 Forthwith was found by the twelve *billa vera*, as they speak. **1665** *Phil. Trans.* I. 80 By letting down shafts from the day (as Miners speak). **1695** WOODWARD *Nat. Hist. Earth* I. (1723) 37 Many of them became petrified, as they speak. **1846** KEBLE *Serm.* xiii. (1848) 335 The same saying fell accidentally (as men speak) on the eye of another rich young man.

c. In pres. pple. with advs., as *broadly*, *correctly*, *generally*, *humanly*, *properly*, *roughly*, *strictly*, etc. (Freq. in modern use.)

1699 T. BROWN *Let. to Dr. Brown at Tunbridge* Wks. 1711 IV. 129 Misfortunes.. of which I can, humanly speaking, see no End. **1826** *Art of Brewing* (ed. 2) 90 Generally speaking, I am an advocate for malt and hops only. **1855** *Orr's Circ. Sci., Inorg. Nat.* 108 Strictly speaking also, there are no beds hitherto found lying above the chalk. **1865** RUSKIN *Sesame* ii. §74 Speaking broadly, a man ought to know any language or science he learns, thoroughly.

5. Of a writer, literary composition, etc.: To make a statement or declaration in words; to state or say.

c **1175** *Lamb. Hom.* 131 Seinte paul.. speceð on þe halie pistle þe me ret to dei. *c* **1205** LAY. 70 Al swa þe boc spekeð þe he to bisne inom. *c* **1340** HAMPOLE *Pr. Consc.* 4529 þai sal be, als þe appocalips spekes, In.. hayres cledde. *c* **1400** LOVE *Bonavent. Mirr.* (1908) 50 Herto accordynge speketh the apostle.. in his pistle ad hebreos. **1585** WASHINGTON tr. *Nicholay's Voy.* II. ix. 42 b, Strabo spake aright, where he sayeth [etc.]. **1631** WEEVER *Anc. Funeral Mon.* 250 My old Anonimall Manuscript speakes.. to the like effect. **1763** C. JOHNSTON *Reverie* I. 42 You are to observe that I speak in the general. **1816** J. SMITH *Panorama Sci. & Art* II. 265 It was admitted that the ancients spoke from justifiable data. **1869** T. C. BARKER *Aryan Civiliz.* x. (1871) 31 A law of the Twelve Tables at Rome speaks to the same effect.

6. *fig.* Of things: To be expressive or significant; to make some revelation or disclosure.

1535 COVERDALE *Heb.* xii. 24 The sprenklynge off bloude, that speaketh better then the bloude of Abel. **1602** MARSTON *Ant. & Mel.* IV. Wks. 1856 I. 54 His grief speakes in his slow-pac't steps. **1667** MILTON *P.L.* III. 267 His words here ended, but his meek aspect Silent yet spake. **1722** WOLLASTON *Relig. Nat.* i. 8 We read of feet, that speak; of a philosopher, who answerd an argument by only getting up and walking. **1813** BYRON *Corsair* I. iii, A sail!—a sail!.. Her nation—flag—how speaks the telescope? **1843** R. J. GRAVES *Syst. Clin. Med.* xiv. 153 His countenance now spoke promisingly. **1885** 'MRS. ALEXANDER' *Valerie's Fate* iv, Never had her heart spoken before.

b. To take effect legally; to be valid.

1837 *Act 7 Will. IV & 1 Vict.* c. 26 §24 That every Will shall be construed.. to speak and take effect as if it had been executed immediately before the Death of the Testator. **1845** WILLIAMS *Real Prop.* x. 154 *marg.*, A will now speaks from the death of testator.

7. *transf.* **a.** Of musical instruments, etc.: To emit a sound; *spec.* to utter a full and proper note. Chiefly *rhet.* or *techn.*

1602 SHAKS. *Ham.* v. ii. 286 Let the Kettle to the Trumpets speake. **1676** MACE *Musick's Mon.* 70 The String lying upon This only Round single Fret, cannot but speak Clear. *a* **1700** EVELYN *Diary* 19 Nov. 1674, He.. made it [a violin] speake like the voice of a man. **1794** MRS. RADCLIFFE *Myst. Udolpho* xliii, Horns and other instruments.. spoke in sweet response to the harmony that proceeded from the pavilion. **1843** *Civil Eng. & Arch. Jrnl.* VI. 108/1 By coupling the pedals with the keys, 87 pipes are made to speak with each pedal. **1884** *Encycl. Brit.* XVII. 833/2 This saves space in the interior [of the organ], and gives the large pipes room to speak.

b. Of natural forces, etc.: To emit noise, make a sound; to reverberate.

1604 SHAKS. *Oth.* II. i. 5 Me thinks, the wind hath spoke aloud at Land. ? **1807-8** WORDSW. *Somnambulist* 4 How softly then Doth Aira-force.. Speak from the woody glen! **1859** MEREDITH *R. Feverel* xlii, All at once the thunder spoke.

c. Of firearms: To emit a report on being fired.

1706 E. WARD *Wooden World Diss.* (1708) 67 He loves dearly to hear his Guns speak. **1875** KINGLAKE *Crimea* (1877) VI. vi. 218 The Coldstream.. could not get their wet rifles to speak. **1896** *Pall Mall G.* 8 Jan. 1/3 The news from the Transvaal, where the rifles have already spoken.

d. Of a hound: To give tongue; to bay.

1826 *Sporting Mag.* (N.S.) XVII. 288 The hounds were speaking in the covert. **1888** ELWORTHY *W. Somerset Word-bk.* 605 The word ['quest'] is never used with hounds; they 'give tongue', 'speak', or 'bay'.

e. *Naut.* (See quot.)

1833 M. SCOTT *Tom Cringle* viii, The sharp little vessel began to *speak*, as the rushing sound through the water is called.

f. *techn.* (See quot.)

1884 F. J. BRITTEN *Watch & Clockm.* 205 When the tool is of proper size the pinion will 'speak' (make a squeaking noise) as the red stuff is drying off.

II. With preps., in more or less specialized uses.

8. speak about—: (see ABOUT *prep.* 7).

Cf. the common OE. *sprecan ymb(e*.

a **1300** *Cursor M.* 24795 For to spek abute sum pais. **1605** SHAKS. *Macb.* I. iii. 83 Were such things here, as we doe speake about? **1671** H. M. tr. *Erasm. Colloq.* 263 He falls on speaking about the success of their business. **1737-** [see 14 b]. **1843** J. H. NEWMAN *Lett.* (1891) II. 430 Sermons which speak more confidently about our position than I inwardly feel.

9. speak again(st—: (see AGAIN *prep.* 6 and AGAINST *prep.* 12).

c **1000** ÆLFRIC *Numb.* xxi. 7 We singodon swiðe, for þan þe we swa spræcon onȝean god & þe. *a* **1250** *Owl & Night.* 678 þar muþ shal speke ayeyn horte. **1388** WYCLIF *Ps.* xlix. 20 Thou sittynge spakist aȝens thi brother. *a* **1425** *Cursor M.* 2928 (Trin.), þer aȝeyn durst he not speke. **1545** ASCHAM *Toxoph.* I. (Arb.) 59, I speake not agaynst greate candelles, but agaynst lytle candels. **1605** SHAKS. *Lear* II. iv. 243 Sith that both charge and danger Speake 'gainst so great a number. **1736** AINSWORTH I. s.v., If he go on to speak lavishly against me. **1847** TENNYSON *Princ.* VII. 112 On the other side Hortensia spoke against the tax. **1908** R. BAGOT *A. Cuthbert* xxvi. 339 Some regretted.. that they spoke against her as an interloper.

10. speak for—. a. To make a speech or plea in place of or on behalf of (a person); in later use *esp.* to plead for. Also, to make representations concerning (a thing). ***speak for yourself***: expressing a desire to dissociate oneself from what another has just said or the assumptions behind it.

a **1300** *K. Horn* 171 Hor[n] spak for hem alle. **1382** WYCLIF *Acts* xxvi. 1 It is suffrid to thee, for to speke for thi silf. **1481** CAXTON *Reynard* iv. (Arb.) 7 How grymbart the dasse.. spack for reynart. **1535** COVERDALE *2 Kings* iv. 13 Hast thou eny matter to be spoken for to the kynge? *c* **1643** LD. HERBERT *Autobiog.* (1824) 139 An unpardonable fault, insomuch that no man would speak for him. **1736** AINSWORTH I. s.v., If ever he do so again, I will never speak for him. **1738** SWIFT *Polite Conversation* I. 16 Pray, sir, speak for yourself. **1777** CLARA REEVE *Champion of Virtue* 102 Take courage and speak for yourself. **1778** BOSWELL in *London Mag.* Feb. 58/1, I remember hearing a late celebrated infidel tell that he was not at all pleased when the infidel wife of his friend, a poet of some eminence, addressed him in a company in London, 'we Deists'.—Speak for yourself, Madam, said he abruptly. **1821** SCOTT *Kenilw.* xxxvi, 'I say, speak not for her!' replied Leicester. **1824** —— *Redgauntlet* III. x. 292 'Speak for yourself, friend,' said Peter, scornfully. **1858** LONGFELLOW *M. Standish* III, Why don't you speak for yourself, John? **1916** G. B. SHAW *Androcles & Lion* Prologue 3 *Megaera*: Everybody knows that the Christians are the very lowest of the low. *Androcles*: Just like us, dear. *Megaera*: Speak for yourself. **1946** L. P. HARTLEY *Sixth Heaven* ii. 46 'Speak for yourself,' said Barbara defiantly. **1976** *Times Lit. Suppl.* 30 Apr. 508/4 We learn that 'when viewing serials.. we feel we know these characters well enough, for example, to say hello to in the street.'.. My reaction to this is to say: speak for yourself!

transf. **1607** SHAKS. *Cor.* III. i. 127 There Mutinies and Reuolts..spoke not for them. **1722–7** BOYER *Dict. Royal* I. s.v. *Parler, Ses Services parlent pour lui*, his Services speak for him. **1770** LANGHORNE *Plutarch* (1879) II. 664/2 He had a very engaging countenance, which spoke for him before he opened his lips. **1859** TENNYSON *Merlin & V.* 466 She ceased,..and let her eyes Speak for her.

b. To beg or request; to ask for.

1560 BIBLE (Geneva) *Song Sol.* viii. 8 What shal we do for our sister..when she shalbe spoken for? **1594** LYLY *Mother Bombie* I. iii, They giue vs pap with a spoon before we can speak, and when wee speake for that wee loue, pap with a hatchet. **1605** SHAKS. *Lear* I. iv. 267 The shame it selfe doth speake For instant remedy.

c. To order; to bespeak; to engage.

1679 BUNYAN *Israel's Hope Encour.* Wks. 1855 I. 583 As your great traders do with the goods that their chapmen have either bought or spoke for. **1730** BAILEY (fol.), *To Bespeak*, to speak for something; to give order for it to be made. **1743** *Lond. & Country Brew.* IV. (ed. 2) 284 The next time he went to the Brew-house to speak for more. **1815** JANE AUSTEN *Emma* xv, The bell was rung, and the carriages spoken for. **1859** MRS. STOWE *Minister's Wooing* xii. 115 Three months beforehand, all her days and nights are spoken for. **1943** *Sun* (Baltimore) 25 Feb. 6/1 (Advt.), We hope to preserve even more food this year. But well over half of this season's pack is already spoken for by the Government. **1971** *Petticoat* 17 July 29/2 He's not married, but he's involved, as they say, spoken for, and has lived with his girlfriend in London for the last few years.

d. To indicate; to betoken.

1832 *Philological Museum* I. 335 The great mass of evidence that speaks for an intimate affinity between the Pelasgians and the Hellenes. **1852** MRS. CRAIK *Head of Family* viii, It may speak very ill for Mr. Græme's knowledge of the world, to confess [etc.]. **1910** HIRTH in *Encycl. Brit.* VI. 191/1 This does not seem to speak for racial consanguinity.

e. *to speak for itself*, to be significant or self-evident. (Cf. 29 c.)

1779 WARNER in Jesse *Selwyn & Contemp.* (1844) IV. 213 The letter was not from any of the family, she said, and that speaks for itself. **1821** SCOTT *Kenilw.* viii, But I need not detail them—the fact speaks for itself. **1869** J. MARTINEAU *Ess.* II. 127 The paragraph..will speak for itself.

11. speak of—. a. To mention, or discourse upon, in speech or writing. (See also 14 b.)

c **825** *Vesp. Psalter* cxviii. 46 [Ic] sprec of cyðnissum ðinum in ȝesihðe cyninga. *c* **950** *Lindisf. Gosp.* Luke ix. 11 [He] spræcc him of ric godes. *c* **1175** *Lamb. Hom.* 73 Of þe halie fulht spec ure drihten on oðer stude. *c* **1200** ORMIN 6784 Goddspellboc ne spekeþþ nohht Off all þatt oþerr genge. *c* **1340** HAMPOLE *Pr. Consc.* 2683 Here es þe thred parte of þis buke spedde þat spekes of þe dede. **1422** *Secreta Secret., Priv. Priv.* 203 Of this Spekyth the boke of Iudyth. **1530** PALSGR. 727/2, I go nowe beyondsee, but if God send me lyfe you shall here speke of me. **1603** PARSONS *Three Convers. Eng.* II. viii. 481, I shall haue occasion to speake againe of these heretiks in the next chapter. **1730** A. GORDON *Maffei's Amphith.* 58 The Theatre..is spoke of by Martial. **1818** SCOTT *Br. Lamm.* xviii, 'And speaking of red-game,' said the young scape-grace, interrupting his father. **1884** tr. *Lotze's Metaph.* 43 A common-place with every philosophy which spoke of Things at all.

transf. **1794** MRS. RADCLIFFE *Myst. Udolpho* xlii, Every object on which her eye fixed seemed to speak of the marchioness. **1833** L. RITCHIE *Wand. by Loire* 180 At Doulon every thing begins to speak of the neighbourhood of a city. **1894** MAX PEMBERTON *Sea Wolves* xi, He..wore sea-boots to his hips, though they spoke of much service and of decay.

b. With advs., as *evil, ill, well.*

c **950** *Lindisf. Gosp.* Mark ix. 39 Seðe..mæȝe recone yfle spreca [L. *male loqui*] of mec. **1382** WYCLIF *Ps.* lxxvii. 19 And euele thei speken of God. **1382** —— *Jer.* xl. 16 Fals forsothe thou spekist of Ismael. *c* **1440** *Jacob's Well* 83 Whan þou spekyst euyll of an-oþer mannys goodnesse. **1530** PALSGR. 727/2 Never speke yl of men behynde their backes. **1535–** [see EVIL *adv.* 1 b]. **1568** GRAFTON *Chron.* II. 598 He was..well spoken of of all men. **1611** BIBLE *Luke* vi. 26 When all men shall speake well of you. **1635** R. N. tr. *Camden's Hist. Eliz.* Introd., Howbeit her dayes have beene ill spoken of. **1807** SOUTHEY *Espriella's Lett.* II. 263 The boys..spake well of their masters.

c. In the phr. *to speak of* (in later use = 'worth mentioning'). Chiefly in negative constructions.

Also (*b*) = 'if mentioned or considered'.

(*a*) **1485** CAXTON *Chas. Gt.* 27 Of hys strengthe is not a lytel thynge to speke of, For [etc.]. **1582** BENTLEY *Mon. Matrones* iii. 269 For that which I haue hitherto done, is nothing at all to speake of. **1610** HOLLAND *Camden's Brit.* (1637) 633 This Towne is not very ancient to speak of. **1654** GATAKER *Disc. Apol.* 47 None out-went me, few to speak of came neer me. **1694** WOOD *Life* 23 Oct., No raine to speak of all Sept. and Oct. **1815** SCOTT *Guy M.* xlv, He had ridden the whole day..without tasting anything 'to speak of'. **1881** FREEMAN in Stephens *Life & Lett.* (1895) II. 244 To-day has come the first snow to speak of.

(*b*) **1580** G. HARVEY *Let. to Spenser* in S.'s Wks. (1912) 628/1 For the Romanes to speake of, are but verye Ciphars in this kinde.

†**d.** *not to be spoken of*, (to be) beyond all description. *Obs.*

1600 NASHE *Summer's Last Will* 989 Wks. (Grosart) VI. 126 As for my Pease and my Fetches, they are famous, and not to be spoken of. **1611** SHAKS. *Wint. T.* v. ii. 47 Then haue you lost a Sight which was to bee seene, cannot bee spoken of.

†**e.** To bespeak; to order. *Obs.*$^{-1}$

1596 SHAKS. *Merch. V*, II. iv. 5 We haue not spoke vs yet of Torch-bearers.

f. With verbal sbs.: To suggest, propose, hint at (doing something).

1586 LD. BURGHLEY in *Leycester Corr.* (Camden) 450 Some spek of namyng the count Morrice. **1611** BIBLE *1 Sam.* xxx. 6 The people spake of stoning him. **1792** BURNS *Duncan Gray* ii, Duncan..Spak o' lowpin' ower a linn.

12. speak on—. †**a.** To address or talk to (a person). *Obs.*

? **1370** *Robt. Cisyle* in Halliw. *Nugæ Poet.* (1844) 58 Lowde on hym he began to speke. *c* **1420** *Sir Amadace* (Camden) xxxvii, So come a mon..And speke on him fulle hastely.

†**b.** = To speak of (see 11 a, b). *Obs.*

1593 SHAKS. *2 Hen. IV*, II. ii. 69 (Q.), I am well spoke on, I can heare it with mine owne eares. **1647** SALTMARSH *Spark. Glory* (1847) 28 The Baptism of Christ..is that one Baptism spoken on in Ephes. 4.

c. To discourse upon (a subject, etc.).

1818 SCOTT *Br. Lamm.* xxix, Mr. Hayston speaks on a subject on which you have long since agreed to give him a favourable hearing. **1876** *Nature* 7 Dec. 128 The Society..has invited Prof. Nordenskjöld to speak on the Kara Sea and Jenissei.

13. speak past—. To talk at cross-purposes with; to speak incomprehensibly to. Cf. G. *vorbeireden.*

1952 G. HIMMELFARB *Lord Acton* i. 2 This historian..ended his life..as a lecturer doomed to speak past his audience. **1975** *United Church Observer* Nov. 15/1 The most important issue..is whether we can speak together and converse together, not *at* each other or *past* each other.

14. speak to—. a. To address words or discourse to (a person); to talk to, converse with.

to speak to (see quot. 1837), so as to have conversation or personal acquaintance with one. Freq. in the phr. 'to know (one) to speak to'.

Beowulf 1171 þu on sælum wes..& to Ȝeatum sprec mildum wordum. *c* **825** *Vesp. Psalter* xlix. 7 [Ic] sprecu to Israhela folce. **971** *Blickl. Hom.* 141 Heo spræc to þæm weorode & cwæþ [etc.]. *c* **1000** *Ags. Gosp.* John x. 25 Ic spece [*c* **1160** speke] to eow & ȝe ne ȝelyfað. *c* **1250** *Gen. & Ex.* 925 After ðis spac god to abram. *a* **1300** *Cursor M.* 11964 Sai þou: i der noght til him speke. **1382** WYCLIF *1 Cor.* xiv. 3 He that prophecieth, spekith to men. *c* **1400** *Pilgr. Sowle* (Caxton, 1483) IV. xxiii. 69, I wold haue spoke to them but I ne myght nought. **1528** ROY *Rede me* (Arb.) 118 Thus to the Cardinall he spake. **1581** PETTIE tr. *Guazzo's Civ. Conv.* I. (1586) 13 b, If..you resalute not a friend, he will speake no more to you. *a* **1635** SIBBES *Confer. Christ & Mary* (1656) 15 When he speaks aloof to her, she answereth aloof to him. **1651** HOBBES *Leviath.* III. xxxv. 216 Commanded by a Voice, as one man speaketh to another. **1751** ELIZA HEYWOOD *Betsy Thoughtless* I. 165 What reply she made I do not know, being speaking to Wildly at the same time. **1837** LOWELL *Lett.* (1894) I. 21 How I remember the first time I ever saw you 'to speak to'. **1908** R. BAGOT *A. Cuthbert* xxvi. 342 It was too late that night to speak to her.

b. With *of, on,* or *about* (a matter, etc.).

c **1200** ORMIN 10466 Þatt fir Þatt Sannt Johan Bapptisste Spacc offe to þa sanderrmenn. *c* **1450** LOVELICH *Merlin* 3204 What scholen we don of this mateer That he to vs spak of now heer? **1530** PALSGR. 727/1, I speke to him of my busynes. **1611** BIBLE *1 Sam.* ix. 17 Behold the man whom I spake to thee of. **1737** *Gentl. Mag.* VII. 492, I have..spoke to the King of England..about your Friend. **1796** H. HUNTER tr. *St.-Pierre's Stud. Nat.* (1799) III. 234 They spake to me of the various Works of Nature. **1804** *Med. Jrnl.* XII. 448, I also spoke to the principal surgeons..on the subject of vaccination. **1888** 'J. S. WINTER' *Bootle's Childr.* iv, Whatever you wish for, you have only to speak to nurse here about it.

c. *transf.* or *fig.*; esp. to appeal to, to influence, affect, or touch.

1604 SHAKS. *Oth.* I. ii. 23 My demerites May speake (vnbonnetted) to as proud a Fortune As this. **1606** —— *Ant. & Cl.* I. ii. 188 More vrgent touches Do strongly speake to vs. **1700** ASTRY tr. *Saavedra-Faxardo* I. 116 b, Elogies inscribed on Tombs, speak not to the Dead, but to the Living. **1734** tr. *Rollin's Anc. Hist.* (1827) II. II. 32 To give a more lively idea of the greatness of the victory, by speaking in some measure to the eye. **1825** T. HOOK *Sayings* Ser. II. *Doubts & F.* vii. II. 231 How strongly it speaks to the heart. **1891** FARRAR *Darkn. & Dawn* xvi, The actor had *spoken* to them in the eloquence of rhythmic gesture.

d. To apply to (a person) for a special purpose, esp. for help or service; to influence or bribe. *spec.* To propose marriage to. Cf. sense 1 g.

1362 LANGL. *P. Pl.* A. v. 130 My Wyf..Spak to þe spinsters for to spinne hit softe. **1535** [see 10 a]. **1610** SHAKS. *Temp.* I. i. 3 Good: Speake to th' Mariners. **1669** R. MONTAGU in *Buccleuch MSS.* I. 430 Their friends having spoke to me to speak for them to the King. **1687** A. LOVELL tr. *Thevenot's Trav.* I. 26 If you would have a lodging room there, you must speak to the Porter of the *Han.* **1809** LD. GRANVILLE *Let.* 14 Nov. in B. Askwith *Piety & Wit* (1982) iv. 64, I spoke to Harriet last night; she was very nervous and so was I... She consented to my speaking to the Duke [her father]. **1840** THACKERAY in *Fraser's Mag.* XXII. 230/1 'Will you marry me?' In fact, this very speech had been taught him by cunning Gann, who saw well enough that Swigby would speak to one or other of his daughters. *c* **1860** *Household Wds.* (Flügel), When judges were corrupt,..and attorney generals were to be 'spoken to'. **1863** MRS. GASKELL *Dark Night's Work* iv. 46 He had some discussion with himself as to whether he should speak to her, and so secure her promise. **1977** G. BUTLER *Brides of Friedberg* i. 12 Next day someone I would *much* rather have accepted spoke to me riding in the Row. But it was too late.

e. To treat of or deal with, to discuss or comment on, (a subject) in speech or writing.

1610 J. DOVE *Advt. Seminaries* 42, I desire them therefore ..to speake to these foure points. **1637** HEYLIN *Answ. Burton* 78, For your charges,..I meane to take them..in order, and speake as briefely to them, as you would desire. **1662** STILLINGFL. *Orig. Sacræ* II. vi. §4 Though it be a subject little spoken to either by Jewish or Christian Writers. **1706** STANHOPE *Paraphr.* III. 555 Part of this Scripture hath already been spoken to. **1724** SWIFT *Drapier's Lett.* Wks. 1755 V. II. 110 A lawyer, who speaks to a cause, when the matter hath been almost exhausted by those who spoke before. **1778** EARL MALMESBURY *Diaries & Corr.* I. 166 Unprepared as he was for such a proposition, he could not, he said, off-hand, speak to it accurately. **1869** *Daily News* 28 Apr., The report..was spoken to by the Most Rev. Chairman..and the Bishop of Derry. **1880** *Ibid.* 19 Mar. 2/3, I wish to call your attention..to..that allegation, and I shall endeavour to speak to it.

f. To give (†or constitute) evidence regarding (a thing); to attest, bear testimony to.

1624 BP. MOUNTAGU *Immed. Addr.* 201 [These] speake indeed to the practise since it was in beginning. **1774** MITFORD *Ess. Harmony Lang.* 195 From the antient Greeks I know of nothing speaking to the sound of the diphthong *ου*. **1776** *Trial Nundocomar* 65/2, I cannot speak to the motions of the army. **1817** JAS. MILL *Brit. India* III. ii. 85 The witness was not allowed to speak to the consultation of that day. **1825** HAZLITT *Spirit of Age* 227 This is a nice criticism, and we cannot speak to its truth. **1888** *Times* (weekly ed.) 2 Nov. 22/4 [He] asked that witnesses might be called to speak to his character.

g. To address with reproof; to admonish.

1753 MISS COLLIER *Art Torment.* I. ii. (1811) 67 Who, she hopes, on being spoke to, will do so no more. **1872** JEAN INGELOW *Off Skelligs* xix, 'Papa,' he exclaimed, in a loud, plaintive voice,..'will you speak to Giles?'

h. *Cant.* To rob (a person or place); to steal.

1799 *Spirit Public Jrnls.* III. 353 Twenty-four highway and footpad robberies,..none of the parties *spoke to* on the road able to swear positively. **1812** J. H. VAUX *Flash Dict.*, To *speak to* a person or place is to rob them, and to *speak to* any article is to steal it.

i. *slang.* (See quot.)

1812 J. H. VAUX *Flash Dict.* s.v. *Spoke*, Upon any great misfortune befalling a man,..his friends will say, Poor fellow, I believe he's *spoke to*, meaning it is all over with him.

j. Of hounds: To give indications of (a fox, scent, etc.) by barking.

1845 YOUATT *Dog* iii. 78 When a hound first speaks in cover to a fox. **1883** *Standard* 10 Aug. 2/1 The hounds could not speak to the line.

15. speak unto—. a. To speak to (= 14 a).

c **1386** CHAUCER *Nun's Priest's T.* 586 In al his drede vnto the fox he spak. *c* **1400** *Brut* ccxviii. 258 He..spake vnto ham of þe Kyngus honour. **1526** TINDALE *1 Cor.* xiv. 3 He that prophesieth, speaketh vnto men. **1640** FULLER *Abel Rediv., Life Abbot* (1867) II. 292 His majesty spake pleasantly unto him. **1684** BUNYAN *Pilgr.* II. (1862) 217 [They were] spoke kindly unto by him. **1839** BAILEY *Festus* 136, I speak unto the young, for I am of them.

†**b.** To discourse upon or deal with (a topic).

1639 LD. DIGBY *Lett. conc. Relig.* (1651) 108 The precedency..is pretended due upon another ground also, which I have yet spoke little unto. **1675** J. OWEN *Indwelling Sin* x. (1732) 117 These and the like things,..which are commonly spoken unto, is the Mind of a Believer obliged to attend..constantly unto.

16. speak upon—, to speak about, of, or on. (Cf. 12 b, c.)

1535 COVERDALE *Isaiah* xix. 17 Who so doth but speake vpon it, shal put them in feare. **1550** tr. *Senonoys' Godly Saiyngs* (1846) 147 The doctrine of the gospell whyche we do professe, shal be evill spoken upon. **1794** MRS. RADCLIFFE *Myst. Udolpho* xxxviii, Remember I do not promise ever to speak upon them.

17. speak with—. a. To converse with, talk to; to consult or confer with.

In OE. and early ME. similarly with *mid.*

971 *Blickl. Hom.* 241 He þæt is se þe wið me spræc. *c* **1000** ÆLFRIC *Exod.* xxxii. 23 þa þu..wið god spæce. *c* **1200** *Trin. Coll. Hom.* 85 Alse wise hire lerden, þanne hie wið hire speken. *a* **1250** *Owl & Night.* 1553 Ne mot no mon wiþ hire speke. *c* **1320** *Sir Tristr.* 811 Wiþ morgan speke wil y And spede. **1426** AUDELAY *Poems* 19 Ȝe spekyn with hym in spirit. **1470–85** MALORY *Arthur* I. x. 48 They spak with the knyghtes & welcomed hem. **1530** PALSGR. 727/2 He shalbe spoken with towchyng your cause. **1622** in Foster *Eng. Factories Ind.* (1908) II. 10 They both retired themselves to there privacy, soe that wee could not then speake with them. **1675** *City Mercury* 18–25 Nov. 2/1 He [a Physician] is any time to be spoke with from eight in the Morning to four in the Afternoon. **1764** FOOTE *Patron* III. Wks. 1799 I. 356 Not to be spoke with! Don't tell me, Sir; he must, he shall. **1816** SCOTT *Old Mort.* xxxvi, Your uncle..has been spoken with, and declines visiting you. **1847** TENNYSON *Princ.* II. 58 Not for three years to speak with any men.

fig. **1663** BP. PATRICK *Parab. Pilgr.* xv. (1687) 134 When any temptation desires to speak with you, let the answer be ready, that there is other company within.

b. *Naut.* To hold communication with (another vessel). Cf. 33 b.

1634 SIR T. HERBERT *Trav.* 182 The expedition bearing vp to speak with vs, the ships fell foule. **1708** *Lond. Gaz.* No. 4422/7 We made Signal to the Commanding Officer..that we would speak with him. **1745** P. THOMAS *Jrnl. Anson's Voy.* 24 On our speaking with her we found she had sprung her Fore-stay. **1775** ROMANS *Florida* App. 6, I need not direct seamen how to proceed, in order to speak with any vessel they chance to see.

c. To communicate with (a place). *rare*$^{-1}$.

1659 PELL *Impr. Sea* 275 In Greenland, and Nova Zembla, &c. which onely in Summer-time may bee spoke with.

†**d.** *Cant.* To have to do with; to steal or rob (cf. 14 h). *Obs.*$^{-0}$

1725 *New Cant. Dict.* s.v., *I will never speak with any thing but Wedge or Cloy*; I'll never steal, or have to do with any thing but Plate, or Money, &c. **1785** GROSE *Dict. Vulgar T.* s.v., I spoke with the cull on the cherry coloured prancer, I robbed the man on the black horse.

III. With advs. in special uses.

18. speak out (cf. 36). **a.** To talk in a loud voice, or so as to be heard distinctly.

1530 PALSGR. 727/2 Speke out that a man may here you. *a* **1533** LD. BERNERS *Huon* lxxxiii. 262 Speke out hyer that ye may the better be herde. **1647** HEXHAM I, To speake out alowd. *Ibid.*, To speak half out, or mumbling. **1712** [see OUT *adv.* 11]. **1908** R. BAGOT *A. Cuthbert* v. 44 Jim stared at him. 'What did you say?' he asked. 'Oh, nothing! Did I speak out loud?'

b. To talk freely or unreservedly.

to speak out in meeting (U.S.), to express one's opinions freely or openly (Thornton).

1694 T. BROWN *Lottery for Ladies & G.* Wks. 1711 IV. 172 Is it not as modest to speak out, as to make broad Signs? **1765** G. WILLIAMS in Jesse *Selwyn & Contemp.* (1843) I. 396 Why do not you speak out as to Lord Gower? Is he to come in or not? **1809** *Med. Jrnl.* XXI. 150 But with all who have the courage to speak out, a difficulty remains. **1830** *Mass. Spy* 23 June 4/1 O dear, I spoke out in meeting. **1842** TENNYSON *Morte d'Arth.* 150 Speak out: what is it thou hast heard, or seen? **1906** *Springfield* (Mass.) *Weekly Republic* 13 Sept. 8, I do not think the president will think any the less of me for speaking right out in meeting and saying that I am not for it.

c. To break into speech.

1792 BURNS *Country Lassie* i, Out spak a dame in wrinkled eild.

d. To be apparent or evident.

1845–6 TRENCH *Huls. Lect.* Ser. II. iii. 183 The sense of this speaks out in every arrangement.

†**19. speak over**, to say too much, to exaggerate. *Obs.* (Cf. OVERSPEAK *v.*)

1610 A. COOKE *Pope Joan* 87 If you bring not some author for the proofe of this point, you must giue me leaue to thinke you speake ouer. **1626** R. HARRIS *Hezekiah's Recov.* 4 The Orator spake not over, when hee intimated that Ingratitude was a kinde of Unjustice.

20. speak together, to hold conference or consultation; to confer.

c **1205** LAY. 3248 Þa ilomp hit . . þat þe Scottene king & þe duk speken to gaðere. **1377** LANGL. *P. Pl.* B. xv. 270 Monkes and mendynauntz . . selden speken togideres. *c* **1400** *New Test.* (Paues) Acts xxvi. 31 [They] wente biside ande speke togider. *c* **1450** LOVELICH *Merlin* 3201 Thanne spoken they to-gederes hem be-twene. **1593** SHAKS. *Rich. II*, II. iii. 29 He was not so resolu'd, when we last spake together. **1677** COLES *Eng.-Lat. Dict.* (ed. 17) 1764 To speak together, *colloquor.* **1859** TENNYSON *Marr. Geraint* 385 While the Prince and Earl Yet spoke together.

21. speak up. a. To speak strongly *for* (= on behalf of, in defence of) a person.

1705 HEARNE *Collect.* 17 Oct. (O.H.S.) I. 57, I spoke up for him. **1844** DICKENS *Mart. Chuz.* xliv, It's all very well for you to speak up for him. . . You'll get a fortune by him.

b. To raise the voice in speaking; to talk boldly or unreservedly; to break into speech.

a **1723** in Child *Ballads* III. 135/2 Speak up, jolly blade, never fear. **1863** MRS. WOOD *Trevlyn Hold* II. 226 Timid Mrs. Chattaway . . spoke up to the rescue. **1865** KINGSLEY *Herew.* i, Out he stepped to your father's side, and spoke right up before the king. **1896** [see SPECKSIONEER].

IV. *trans.* **22. a.** To articulate or utter (a word or words).

to speak not a word of, to make no mention or suggestion of. *to speak a* (*good*) *word for*: see WORD *sb.*

Beowulf 341 Wlanc Wedera leod word æfter spræc. **971** *Blickl. Hom.* 31 Se forhwyrfda gast spræc forhwyrfedlice word. *c* **1000** *Ags. Ps.* (Thorpe) lvii. 3 Syððan . . heo on life lyȝe-word spæcon. *c* **1200** *Moral Ode* 9 (Trin. Coll. MS.), Fele idel word ich habbe ispeken. *a* **1300** *Cursor M.* 4342 Ar i ga þou spek wit me a word or tua. *a* **1400–50** *Alexander* 243 Þou a wirschipfull worde has werpid & spoken. **1470–85** MALORY *Arthur* XVIII. xx. 761 There they fond . . a poure man sittyng in the bargets ende and no word wold he speke. **1542** UDALL *Erasm. Apoph.* II. 176 A sorte of the Grekes . . spake many woordes of reproche by the kyng. **1611** BIBLE *2 Sam.* xix. 10 Why speake ye not a word of bringing the king backe? **1651** HOBBES *Leviath.* III. xxxii. 196 Though the mind be incapable of any Notion at all from the words spoken. **1755** B. MARTIN *Mag. Arts & Sci.* 13, I will follow, when I have spoke a Word to one of the Millers. **1806** WORDSW. *Horn Egremont Castle* 87 Thou hast a dungeon, speak the word! And there he may be lodged, and thou be Lord. **1885** 'MRS. ALEXANDER' *At Bay* ix, Elsie followed her into the hall to speak some last words.

b. With cognate accus.: To utter, make, or deliver (a speech or statement).

c **888** K. ÆLFRED *Boeth.* xxxv. §5 On ða ilcan spræce þe þu ær spræce. *c* **930** *Laws Athelstane* VI. viii. §8 (Liebermann I. 180/1), Maniȝe men specað ȝemahlice spræce. *a* **1300** *K. Horn* 387 He spac faire speche. *c* **1400** *Destr. Troy* 8864 When his speche was spokyn, & sped to þe last. **1590** SHAKS. *Mids. N.* III. i. 77 When you haue spoken your speech, enter into that Brake. **1603** —— *Meas. for M.* v. 265 One that hath spoke most villanous speeches of the Duke. **1712** HEARNE *Collect.* 24 May, He desir'd that he might speak a speech publickly upon that occasion. **1837** CARLYLE *Fr. Rev.* I. v. i, Speeches are spoken; . . audible within doors and without. **1876** 'L. CARROL' *Hunting the Snark* IV. vii, The rest of my speech . . You shall hear when I've leisure to speak it.

c. Similarly with other objects denoting a word, sentence, speech, etc., uttered or recited. ***to speak one's piece***: see PIECE *sb.* 17 g.

a **1300** *Cursor M.* 23945 Spell yeit i wald spek if i cuth. *c* **1375** *Ibid.* 1616 (Fairf.), Þe propheci . . þat spokin was of þat childe dere. *c* **1400** *Rom. Rose* 7519 Thou spak a jape not long ago . . Of a young man. **1553** T. WILSON *Rhet.* (1580) 169 Some will speake Oracles, that a manne can not tell whiche waie to take them. **1598** SHAKS. *Merry W.* III. v. 75 After we had embrast, . . & (as it were) spoke the prologue of our Comedy. **1653** WALTON *Angler* 184, I will speak you a copy of verses. **1795** WOLCOT (P. Pindar) *Pindariana* Wks. 1812 IV. 245 He made many quotations and spoke them with propriety. **1823** SCOTT *Quentin D.* xxxii, The last sentence was spoken in a tone which made all the councillors tremble. **1861** PALEY *Aeschylus* (ed. 2) *Choeph.* 915 *note*, Orestes . . speaks two continuous verses. **1865** MORRIS *Jason* III. 291 Whose name I speak not.

fig. **1599** B. JONSON *Cynthia's Rev.* II. iii, He speakes all creame, skimd. **1634** MILTON *Comus* 804 As when the wrath of Jove Speaks thunder . . To som of Saturns crew.

†**d.** To employ (the voice) in utterance. *Obs.*

1382 WYCLIF *Rev.* x. 3 And whan he hadde cried, seuene thundres spaken her voices. *a* **1586** SIDNEY *Ps.* XVIII. iv, Then thundred heav'nly sire, Then spake he his lowd voice.

23. a. To utter or say (something) by way of a remark or statement.

The object is freq. a pronoun, as *it*, *this*, etc., or a relative clause introduced by *that* (*which*) or *what*.

Beowulf 531 Hwæt þu worn fela . . ymb Brecan spræce. *c* **888** K. ÆLFRED *Boeth.* xxxviii. §3 For oðrum ðincgum ic hit spræc ȝet swiðor. **971** *Blickl. Hom.* 19 Eac is to ȝeþencenne hwæt Drihten spræc. *c* **1000** *Ags. Gosp.* Mark xiii. 11 Specað þæt eow on þære tide ȝe-seald bið. *a* **1122** *O.E. Chron.* (Laud MS.) an. 1048, Eustatius . . spæc wið hine þæt þæt he þa wolde. *c* **1160** *Hatton Gosp.* John xii. 50 Þa þing þe ic sprece ic speke swa se fader me saiȝde. *c* **1205** LAY. 26868 Þis wes al þus ispeken. **13..** *Cursor M.* 19115 (Gött.), Þe apostlis speckand þis and mare, Þe preistes come. **1382** WYCLIF *Mark* xiii. 11 Speke ȝe that thing that schal be ȝouen to ȝou in that our. **1422** tr. *Secreta Secret., Priv. Priv.* 188 What is that, that thou spekyste. **1582** ALLEN *Martyrdom Campion* (1908) 47 He was urged . . to speake what he thought of the said Bull of Pius Quintus. **1622** FLETCHER *Span. Cur.* v. i, I dare tell you . . what I have spoken Freely behind your back. *a* **1662** HEYLIN *Laud* (1668) 378 To speak the matter in a word. **1711** *Spectator* No. 192 ¶6 The most indifferent thing has its Force and Beauty when it is spoke by a kind Father. **1780** *Mirror* No. 99, The account he gives of his own feelings . . is evidently spoken in earnest. **1830** tr. *Aristophanes' Acharn.* 26 Grant me yet thy pardon, if . . I have spoke or triflingly uttered anything. **1871** R. ELLIS tr. *Catullus* li. 2 He, if I dare speak it, ascends above them [the Gods].

b. With objective clause: To state or declare *that*, etc.

Beowulf 1595 Gomele ymb godne on ȝeador spræcon, þæt hiȝ þæs æðelinges eft ne wendon [etc.]. *c* **900** tr. *Baeda's Hist.* III. ii. (1890) 156 Ða ȝehyrde he sumne þara broðra sprecan, þæt he wolde feran to þæm halȝan Cristes mæle. **1560** DAUS tr. *Sleidane's Comm.* 369 Murtherers . . which spake it of theyr own mind, that Fernando Gonzage had waged them to slay Octavius. **1611** SHAKS. *Cymb.* IV. ii. 354 The ruine speakes, that sometime It was a worthy building. **1663** GERBIER *Counsel* 62 Experience speaks that as times change . . prises may alter. **1766** *Complete Farmer* s.v. *Surveying*, The farmer speaks loudly, that . . no more should be measured . . than the plow or scythe can go over.

c. With superlative adjs. as (*one's*) *best*, *last*.

a **1631** DONNE *Poems* (1650) 59 Here dead men speake their last. **1876** TREVELYAN *Macaulay* II. ix. 132 In the set party fights . . he did not speak his best.

24. To utter or express (truth, falsehood, etc.) in words or speech.

Beowulf 2864 Þæt la mæȝ secgan, se ðe wyle soð specan [etc.]. *c* **825** *Vesp. Psalter* v. 7 Ðu forspildes hie ða ða spreocað leasunge. *Ibid.* xxvii. 3 Ða ðe spreocað sibbe mid ðone nestan. **971** *Blickl. Hom.* 223 He a to æȝhwylcum soð & riht sprecende wæs. *c* **1000** *Lambeth Ps.* cxliii. 8 Þara muð specende wæs idelnesse. *a* **1225** *Ancr. R.* 82 Ful speche is as of lecherie, . . þæt unweaschene muðes spekeð oþer hwule. **13..** *Deo Gratias* 68 in *E.E.P.* (1862) 126 Þenne i rede þou rule þe so þat Men may speke worschupe bi þe. **1382** WYCLIF *Jude* 16 The mouth of hem spekith pride. *c* **1400** *Rom. Rose* 7514 For it is better stille be, Than for to speken harme. **1470–85** MALORY *Arthur* X. viii. 425 Alle knyghtes speken of hym worship. **1535** COVERDALE *Eph.* iv. 15 Speake euery man the trueth vnto his neghboure. **1598** SHAKS. *Merry W.* II. i. 129 Beleeue it (Page) he speakes sence. **1646** CRASHAW *Steps to Temple* 74 O, 'tis not Spanish, but 'tis heaven she speaks. **1711** ADDISON *Spect.* No. 35 ¶1 If they speak Nonsense, they believe they are talking Humour. *a* **1766** MRS. F. SHERIDAN *Nourjahad* (1767) 179 Nothing is more certain . . than that Cozro has spoke the truth. **1816** SCOTT *Bl. Dwarf* xii, My cousin Ellieslaw, who speaks treason as if it were a child's nursery rhymes. **1841** BROWNING *Pippa Passes* Poems (1905) 169 Do you think I fear to speak the bare truth once for all?

25. With preps.: To utter or direct (words, remarks, etc.) *against*, *to* (also †*on*, *upon*, etc.) a person. Also *fig.*

c **825** *Vesp. Psalter* cviii. 20 Ða ðe spreocað yfel [L. *mala*] wið sawle minre. *c* **1000** *Lambeth Ps.* cviii. 20 Þa þe specaþ yfelu toȝeanes sawle mine. *c* **1175** *Lamb. Hom.* 13 Ne spec þu aȝein þine nexta nane false witnesse. *a* **1300** *E.E. Psalter* xxvii. 4 Þat spekes pees to neghburgh hisse. *a* **1300** *Cursor M.* 16495 Þai . . sal on me tresun spek. **1338** R. BRUNNE *Chron.* (1810) 63 Forto . . destroie þat kynde, þat ouht to him couth speke. **1535** COVERDALE *Ps.* lxxxiv. 8 He shal speake peace vnto his people. *Ibid.* cviii. 20 Those that speake euell agaynst my soule. **1547** *Homilies* I. *Contention* Tjb, To suffre euery man to speake vpon me what thei list. **1599** SHAKS. *Much Ado* v. i. 21 Men Can . . speake comfort to that griefe, Which they themselues not feele. **1603** —— *Meas. for M.* v. i. 129 For certaine words he spake against your Grace In your retirment. **1821** WORDSW. *Eccl. Sonnets* III. ii, Last night . . that Vision spake Fear to my Soul. **1838** [I. WILLIAMS] *Cathedral* 144 Love . . Speaks peace to fall'n humanity.

26. a. To declare in words: to make known by speech; to tell (of).

to speak one's mind: see MIND *sb.*[1] 9 a.

c **825** *Vesp. Psalter* xvi. 4 Ðætte . . ne sprece muð min wirc monna. *Ibid.* lxxvii. 2 Ic spreocu foresetenisse from fruman weorulde. *c* **1000** *Lambeth Ps.* cxliv. 11 Wuldor rices þines hi cweðaþ . . & mihte þine hi specaþ. *c* **1200** ORMIN 12965 Forr þatt he wollde beldenn hemm To spekenn þeȝȝre nede. *a* **1300** *Cursor M.* 24074 Þat es na tung mai speke wit word . . Hu þat vr stur was strang. **1382** WYCLIF *1 Cor.* ii. 7 We speken the wysdom of God, that is hid in mysterie. **1513** *Bk. Keruynge* A iv, Than serue ye forth the table manerly, y^t euery man may speke your curtesy. **1595** SHAKS. *John* III. i. 39 What other harme haue I . . done, But spoke the harme that is by others done? **1611** TOURNEUR *Ath. Trag.* II. i, Here's one, . . saies hee is newly returned from Ostend, and has some businesse of import to speake. **1693** PRIOR *C'tess Exeter playing on Lute* 17 Your Art no other Art can speak. **1760–72** H. BROOKE *Fool of Qual.* (1809) III. 40 You have, in a few words, spoke the whole of the matter. **1812** CRABBE *Tales* iv. 279 Speak, then, my fate. **1837** CARLYLE *Fr. Rev.* I. III. iii, Bound to speak his opinion. **1852** THACKERAY *Esmond* II. ii, I spoke my business.

b. To state or declare in writing, etc.

a **1225** *Ancr. R.* 48 Þis is nu ðe uorme dole, þet ich habbe ispeken hiderto, of ower seruise. *c* **1449** PECOCK *Repr.* I. x. 51 The firste of the iij. opinions spoken and sett forth . . in the first chapiter. **1562** WINȜET *Wks.* (S.T.S.) I. 4 Albeit the time be schort, sumthing of ȝour prais man we speik. **1604** E. G[RIMSTONE] *D'Acosta's Hist. Indies* III. iii. 127 Of the West, I cannot speake any thing certaine or generall. **1672** in E. B. Jupp *Carpenters' Co.* (1887) 305 The said Statute . . makes no mencion at all nor speakes a tittle of a Joyner. *a* **1763** W. KING *Polit. & Lit. Anecd.* (1819) 121, I speak this upon a supposition that Bing [*sic*] was justly put to death. **1849** ROCK *Ch. of Fathers* I. viii. (1903) III. 45 The monument itself, with its little chantry altar, . . speaks what was his belief while here.

c. *transf.* Of musical instruments: To announce, indicate, or proclaim by sound.

1702 ROWE *Tamerl.* I. i. 120 These Trumpets speak his Presence. **1781** COWPER *Anti-Thelyphth.* 161 The trumpet now spoke Marmadan at hand. **1837** A. TENNENT *Force Imag.* 7 In mournful plaints of sorrow now It [*sc.* the pibroch] speaks the battle's close.

27. To use as a language; to talk.

1297 R. GLOUC. (Rolls) 7539 Þe normans . . speke french as hii dude atom. **1387** TREVISA *Higden* (Rolls) I. 345 Þis Gaythelus kouþe speke many langages and tonges. **1456** SIR G. HAYE *Law Arms* (S.T.S.) 22 [He] coude wele speke the langage of Grece and of Latyne. **1530** PALSGR. 727/1 They speke a pedlars frenche amongest them selfe. **1610** HOLLAND *Camden's Brit.* (1637) 596 Welsh and English speaking both languages. **1720** DE FOE *Capt. Singleton* xvi. (1840) 281 Can they speak Dutch? **1756** MRS. CALDERWOOD in *Coltness Collect.* (Maitl. Club) 204 The collonell . . has been over all Europe, and speaks all the languages. **1849** MACAULAY *Hist. Eng.* vii. II. 225 He knew no language but the English, as it was spoken by the common people. **1910** HAVERFIELD in *Encycl. Brit.* IV. 587/1 By this time the town populations . . spoke Latin.

†**28. a.** To make mention of (a person); to speak of or mention in a certain way; to commend (one) *to* another. *Obs.*

1297 R. GLOUC. (Rolls) 2390 Princes oueral aboute of ech kinedom Speke him vuel & hated him. *a* **1300** *Cursor M.* 12005 Sum him loued and spack o prise. *c* **1375** *Sc. Leg. Saints* iii. (*Andrew*) 975 For men will lichtly spek þe ill. *c* **1449** PECOCK *Repr.* II. x. 203 The King . . whom the lesson of prophetis hath bifore spokun. **1613** SHAKS. *Hen. VIII*, IV. ii. 32 Yet thus farre Griffith, giue me leaue to speake him, And yet with Charity. **1618** SIR D. CARLETON *Lett.* (1775) 259 Who they [the ambassadors] shall be, is not yet fully determined; but count Ernest of Nassau is chiefly spoken. *a* **1657** LOVEDAY *Lett.* (1663) 58, I pray speak me to her in the best Language of affection.

†**b.** To assign or dedicate. *Obs.*$^{-1}$

1502 *Ord. Crysten Men* (W. de W. 1506) I. ii, All these thynges the whiche be spoken and consecrate unto god.

c. To bespeak or order. *rare.*

1508 STANBRIDGE *Vulgaria* (W. de W.) B v, I haue spoken a payre of shone agaynst sondaye. **1936** J. STEINBECK *In Dubious Battle* vi. 97 If the bitch ever whelps, I'd like to speak a pup.

†**d.** To use as a term or phrase. *Obs.*$^{-1}$

1579 E. K. *Gloss. Spenser's Sheph. Cal.* Apr. 118 A beauie of Ladyes, is spoken figuratively for a company or troupe.

29. a. To indicate, denote, or betoken; to reveal, make known.

1588 SHAKS. *Tit. A.* I. 438 Lord Titus, . . Whose fury not dissembled speakes his griefes. **1608** —— *Per.* I. iii. 14 His seal'd commission, left in trust with me, Doth speak sufficiently he's gone to travel. **1662** STILLINGFL. *Orig. Sacræ* II. ii. §7 Two things speak much the wisdom of a Nation; good Laws, and a prudent management of them. **1727** A. HAMILTON *New Acc. E. Ind.* I. x. 100 Some Porches and broken Pillars I have seen, that speak their ancient Grandeur. **1770** GOLDSM. *Des. Vill.* 122 The loud laugh that spoke the vacant mind. **1812** BYRON *Ch. Har.* I. lxxvi, Loud bellowings speak his woes. **1856** EMERSON *Eng. Traits, Land*, The solidity of the structures . . speaks the industry of ages.

refl. **1850** CARLYLE *Latter-d. Pamph.* v. (1872) 166 William the Silent spake himself best in a country liberated.

b. Of the countenance, eyes, etc.: To indicate or manifest by expression.

to speak daggers: see DAGGER *sb.*[1] 3 b.

1601 SHAKS. *All's Well* I. iii. 185 Thine eies See it so grosely showne in thy behauiours, That in their kinde they speake it. **1666** DRYDEN *Ann. Mirab.* lxxiii, His face spake hope, while deep his Sorrows flow. **1792** BURNS *Duncan Gray* iv, And oh! her een, they spak' sic things! **1820** KEATS *Isabella* v, If looks speak love-laws, I will drink her tears. **1859** J. WATSON *Bards Border* 78 Her look spoke affection.

†**c.** *refl.* Of things: To be self-evident. *Obs.* (Cf. 10 e.)

1689 POPPLE tr. *Locke's 1st Let. Toleration* L.'s Wks. 1727 II. 244 Let us apply the last Case . . and the Thing speaks itself. **1693** DRYDEN *Juvenal* iii. Argt., The Story of this Satyr speaks it self.

30. a. To manifest or show (a person, thing, etc.) to be or do a certain thing, or to possess a certain quality or character. Const. with simple complement or with *to be*. Now *arch.*

(*a*) **1605** SHAKS. *Macb.* IV. iii. 159 Sundry Blessings hang about his Throne, That speake him full of Grace. **1666** DRYDEN *Ann. Mirab.* xxiii, Men quit the open air, When Thunder speaks the angry Gods abroad. **1709** STEELE *Tatler* No. 75 ¶3 His whole Person is finely turned, and speaks him a Man of Quality. **1796–7** JANE AUSTEN *Pride & Prej.* (1813) 139 A sudden noise below seemed to speak the whole house in confusion.

(*b*) **1642** FULLER *Holy & Prof. State* II. viii. 79 Which speaks his judgement to be better then his invention. *a* **1701** MAUNDRELL *Journ. Jerus.* (1732) 137 This speaks it self to have been part of some very August Pile. **1774** GOLDSM. *Nat. Hist.* (1862) I. xi. 209 Each of which [varieties] . . speaks the kind seldom to have mixed with any other. **1808** HELEN ST. VICTOR *Ruins of Rigonda* II. 156 His graceful carriage . . spoke him to be a person very different from what his plain garb might naturally denote. **1821** SCOTT *Pirate* xxii, His acquaintance with the English language . . plainly spoke him to be an Englishman.

b. To term or call; to describe as. *rare.*

1617 FLETCHER *Valentinian* v. viii, Mays't thou live ever spoken our Protector. **1825** SCOTT *Talism.* xiv, Report speaks thee one unlikely to return thus from fight.

c. To describe (a person). Now *arch.*

1623 B. JONSON *Underwoods, Celebr. Charis* viii, Make account,..And that quickly, speak your Man. **1662** COKAINE *Trag. Ovid* III. i, You mistake me, I cannot speak her to her merit. **1703** ROWE *Ulyss.* I. i, But be it as it may; it speaks you well. **1780** COWPER *Progr. Error* 460 How shall I speak thee, or thy pow'r address, Thou god of our idolatry, the press? **1819** SCOTT *Ivanhoe* xxxix, Thou hast spoken the Jew,..as the persecution of such as thou art has made him. **1859** TENNYSON *Elaine* 154 To speak him true,..No keener hunter after glory breathes.

31. To express or signify. Now *rare.*

to speak volumes: see VOLUME *sb.*

1645 RUTHERFORD *Tryal & Tri. Faith* (1845) 32 Ramhorns speak not taking of towns in an ordinary providence. **1674** N. FAIRFAX *Bulk & Selv.* 200 And they were so ready to make *World* speak *seculum*, that where we give a much unlike meaning, they still hold to it. **1875** E. WHITE *Life in Christ* II. ix. (1878) 93 Men have compelled the narrative to speak a meaning contrary to its intention.

32. a. To send *to*, to cause to pass or enter *into* (another state, condition, or position) by speaking. Also *refl.* and with adj. complement.

1684 BROOK *Precious Remedies* 5 God can speak or nod you to hell in a moment. **1696** BROOKHOUSE *Temple Opened* Pref. A iv, So Now, the same word..comes to speak the Ataxy or Irregularities of the Four Monarchies into..an Harmonious Frame. **1781** COWPER *Expost.* 256 He will be found..Too just to wink, or speak the guilty clear. **1814** SCOTT *Lord of Isles* IV. xxii, That glance, if guilty, would I dread More than the doom that spoke me dead! **1820** A. A. WATTS in Wiffen *Aonian Hours* (ed. 2) p. x, With gratitude thy bosom swelleth To him—who spoke them into birth! **1833** *New Monthly Mag.* XXXVII. 356 He spoke himself into the Common Council.

†**b.** To create by speaking. *Obs.*⁻¹ (Cf. 36 c.)

1735 S. WESLEY *Hymn, 'The Lord of Sabbath'* iv, 'Twas great to speak the World from Nought, 'Twas greater to redeem.

V. 33. a. To talk or converse with; to address.

c **950** *Lindisf. Gosp.* Matt. xii. 46 Soecende spreca him [L. *loqui ei*]. *c* **1250** *Gen. & Ex.* 3400 Ðo cam ietro to moysen, To speken him and ðo kinnes-men. *c* **1450** LOVELICH *Grail* liv. 28 Welcome..ȝe be, longe haue I desired ȝow to speken & se. **1561** in *Maitl. Cl. Misc.* III. 290 He wald cum to þar chalmer and speik tham. **1581** A. HALL *Iliad* VIII. 140 Thus Hector comforts vp his mates, and speaks his horse. *c* **1690** KIRKTON *Hist. Ch. Scot.* viii. (1817) 330 The two brethren went and spoke the Lord Stair. **1722** DE FOE *Col. Jack* ix, What, do you want to speak with the great master? He can't be spoke by you. **1805** SCOTT *Last Minstrel* VI. xxvi, Like him of whom the story ran, Who spoke the spectre-hound in Man. **1852** BAILEY *Festus* (ed. 4) 331 Speaking him In that instinctive Paradisal tongue.

b. To communicate with (a passing vessel) at sea, by signal, speaking-trumpet, etc. Cf. 17 b.

1792 M. RIDDELL *Voy. Madeira* 20 We spoke several East Indiamen. **1793** NELSON 11 Oct. in Nicholas *Disp.* (1845) I. 331 Yesterday I spoke a Ship from Gibraltar. **1816** TUCKEY *Narr. Exped. R. Zaire* i. (1818) 10 We saw several vessels, but spoke none. **1840** R. H. DANA *Bef. Mast* xxxv, She hove-to for us, seeing that we wished to speak her. **1885** *Times* (weekly ed.) 18 Sept. 14/2 A service of swift yawls..to run out and speak the fishing boats.

transf. **1848** DICKENS *Dombey* xxxix, Two or three stragglers..'spoke him'—so the captain entered it—on the subject of spectacles.

34. a. *to speak* (one) *fair*, to address (a person) courteously or kindly. (Cf. FAIR *adv.* 2.)

c **1375** *Cursor M.* 6836 (Fairf.), Speke ham faire wiþ þi mouþe. **1533** MORE *Apol.* 71 b, I am content to..geue them no wors wordes agayn then yf they speke me fayre. **1583** MELBANCKE *Philotimus* E iij b, They thought it good to..speake him faire while their feete were in his mouth. **1690** DRYDEN *Amphitryon* II. ii, Thou wouldst have a woman of the town..to be always speaking my husband fair! **1818** SCOTT *Hrt. Midl.* xxxiii, I spoke the wretch fair; I appeared to confide in her. **1861** GEO. ELIOT *Silas M.* i, He was worth speaking fair, if it was only to keep him from doing you a mischief.

fig. **1669** DRYDEN *Tyrannic Love* IV. i, Heaven speaks me fair.

b. With other advs.

1871 BROWNING *Balaust.* 1562 If thou speak us ill Many a true and ill thing shalt thou hear! **1872** TENNYSON *Gareth & Lynette* 470 Lancelot ever spake him pleasantly.

VI. With advs. in special senses.

†**35. speak forth**, to utter, declare, proclaim.

1526 TINDALE *Matt.* xiii. 35, I wyll..speake forth thinges whych have bene kepte secrete from the begynnynge off the worlde. **1611** BIBLE *Acts* xxvi. 25, I..speake foorth the words of trueth and sobernesse. **1674** N. FAIRFAX *Bulk & Selv.* 191 It would not..more fully speak forth its boundlessness. **1730** BAILEY (fol.), *To Utter*, to pronounce or speak forth.

36. speak out (cf. 18). **a.** To utter; to make known in words; to declare openly or clearly.

1382 WYCLIF *Acts* xxvi. 25, I speke out the wordus of treuthe and sobrenesse. *c* **1440** *Promp. Parv.* 468/1 Spekyn owte, *exprimo.* *c* **1449** PECOCK *Repr.* III. x. 339 That he meened so myche bi hise..wordis, thouȝ he not alle hem out spake. **1602** SHAKS. *Ham.* II. ii. 545 'Tis well, Ile haue thee speake out the rest, soone. **1648** J. BEAUMONT *Psyche* II. clxiv, I'll make his Dumbness find a Tongue To speak out his imposture. **1676** [see MIND *sb.*¹ 9 a]. **1815** SCOTT *Guy M.* xii, You will often hear it mentioned... I will therefore speak it out. **1855** THACKERAY *Newcomes* II. xxi. 209, I have no right..to hear him speak out his heart, and tell it to any friend. **1889** JESSOPP *Coming of Friars* i. 42 Henry..spoke out his mind and showed that he was not too well-pleased.

b. Of things: To declare, manifest, etc.

1613 SHAKS. *Hen. VIII*, II. iv. 140 If thy rare qualities..could speake thee out. **1675** BROOKS *Gold. Key* Wks. 1867 V. 175 Now what do all these things speak out, but the certainty and reality of Christ's manhood? **1715** CHAPPELOW *Rt. Way to be Rich* (1717) 52 He is the highest bidder, and this speaks him out to be the greatest merchant.

c. *poet.* To create by speaking. *rare.* (Cf. 32 b.)

1635–56 COWLEY *Davideis* I. 783 They sung how God spoke out the worlds vast ball. **1844** MRS. BROWNING *Drama of Exile* 1055, I am the spirit of the harmless earth. God spake me softly out among the stars.

d. To talk out (see TALK *v.* 9).

1893 *Westm. Gaz.* 30 Mar. 2/3 He spoke with the obvious intention of speaking out the Bill.

37. *Comb.* **speak-a-word room**, *Sc.* (see quots.); **speak-back** = TALK-BACK; **speak-box**, an intercom device by a (usu. outside) door which allows a caller to speak to someone elsewhere in the building (cf. *voice-box* (*b*) s.v. VOICE *sb.* 14); **speak-out**, an occasion on which people can speak freely and unreservedly; †**speak-room**, = SPEAK-HOUSE 1; †**speak-truth**, one who tells the truth; **speak-your-weight machine**, a weighing machine which announces one's weight in spoken words.

1614 R. TAILOR *Hog hath lost Pearl* in Dodsley *O. Pl.* (1780) VI. 427 But I do trouble thee too much, therefore Good Speak-truth, farewel. **1756** MRS. CALDERWOOD in *Coltness Collect.* (Maitland Club) 175 The nuns..said they never wore it but when they came to the speak-room. **1825** JAMIESON *Suppl.*, *Speak-a-Word-Room*, a parlour. **1839** CHAMBERS *Tour Holland* 23/1 Then we were whirled down again into a little speak-a-word room. **1940** *Chambers's Techn. Dict.* 788/1 *Speak-back*, the subsidiary microphone-amplifier-reproducer in a motion-picture studio, by which the remote recordist can speak to the director on the sound-stage. **1960** *Guardian* 14 Apr. 8/3 His most recent hero..attempts to teach speak-your-weight machines to sing. **1962** N. FREELING *Love in Amsterdam* II. 106 The buzzer went, and he heard Sophia's voice on the speakbox. **1966** *Illustr. London News* 30 July 11 Kidbrooke has its own T.V. studio which incorporates a 'speak-back'. **1966** L. DEIGHTON *Billion-Dollar Brain* xv. 146 His voice was..like a speak-your-weight machine. **1968** *Guardian* 19 Aug. 14/5 Americans Abroad for McCarthy held a 'speak out' near the Speakers' Corner in a sunlit but swampy Hyde Park yesterday. **1970** W. J. BURLEY *To kill a Cat* ix. 152 He rang the bell. Almost at once he was startled by a woman's voice from close at hand. A speak-box which he hadn't expected. He found the little metal grille and spoke into it. 'Come up, please.' **1977** *Daily Tel.* 25 Oct. 11/4 At the New York 'speak out', women were invited to tell anonymously of abuse suffered from promiscuous or sexually taunting male employers or superiors.

-speak (spiːk), *suffix.* The verb SPEAK used, after Orwell's *Newspeak* and *Oldspeak*, as a substantival suffix (cf. SPEAK *sb.* 1) to denote a particular variety of language or characteristic mode of speaking.

1949, etc. [see NEWSPEAK]. **1949**, etc. [see OLDSPEAK]. **1960** K. AMIS *Take Girl Like You* xi. 140 Charlton, his creep-speak effectively silenced, had departed in protest-march style. **1966** *Science* 13 May 875/1 We read of 'space speak' on every hand. Newspapers and magazines discuss it in their science columns... The belief is that the space effort has given us, in addition to the possibility of going to the moon, a new linguistic phenomenon. **1972** *College English* Jan. 439 (*heading*) Doublespeak: dialectology in the service of Big Brother. **1980** *Times* 27 Feb. 14/2 Such emphasizers as *undoubtedly* (Ponderoso Speak: *indubitably*)..diminish, if they do not actually destroy the assurance of a statement. **1981** *Times* 28 Jan. 7/1 (*heading*) Haigspeak rewrites the grammar. **1981** *Guardian* 1 May 2/4 'I am very sorry that I cannot be with you today... I am most grateful and touched that you have decided to name a locomotive after me,' it [*sc.* a telegram] said in classic royalspeak.

speakable ('spiːkəb(ə)l), *a.* Also 5 **spekabylle**, 6 **spe(a)keable**. [f. SPEAK *v.* + -ABLE.]

1. That may or can be spoken; fit or possible to be expressed in speech.

1483 *Cath. Angl.* 353/1 Spekabylle, *effabilis. Ibid.* 379/1 Tellabylle, *vbi* spekabylle. **1545** ASCHAM *Toxoph.* I. (Arb.) 56 Heaping othes upon othes, one in a nothers necke, moost horrible and not spekeable. **1587** FLEMING *Cont. Holinshed* III. 1318/1 Pining with more than speakeable passions. *a* **1684** LEIGHTON *Comm. 1 Pet.* Wks. (1859) 32/2 The best worldly joys are easily speakable. **1837** CARLYLE *Fr. Rev.* III. VI. iii, If no speakable charge exist against a man. **1889** F. M. CRAWFORD *Greifenstein* II. xiv. 112 This creature for whom no speakable name could be found.

†**2.** Having the power of speech; able to speak. *Obs. rare.*

1667 MILTON *P.L.* IX. 563 Redouble then this miracle, and say, How cam'st thou speakable of mute? **1676** MACE *Musicks Mon.* 109 It will seem to speak the word Tut, so plainly, as if it were a Living Creature, Speakable.

3. Able or fit to be spoken *to.*

1956 'C. BLACKSTOCK' *Dewey Death* x. 227 I'm simply not speakable to this morning. **1979** *Daily Tel.* 20 Sept. 18/3, I don't think he is speakable to at the moment... Could you ring back in 20 minutes?

Hence '**speakably** *adv.*

1845 MRS. BROWNING *Lett.* (1899) I. 4 Mr. Kenyon—who most unspeakably, or only speakably with tears in my eyes—has been my friend.

speakeasy ('spiːkiːzɪ). *slang* (orig. and chiefly *U.S.*). Also **speak-easy**. [f. SPEAK *v.* + EASY *adv.*] A shop or bar where alcoholic liquor is sold illegally. Also *attrib.*

1889 *Voice* (N.Y.) 14 Nov., Hundreds of unlicensed dealers in both cities continued to run under the names of 'clubs' and 'speak-easies'. **1895** L. PENDLETON *Corona of Nantahalas* iv. 45 A sort of rural 'speak easy', where the colourless liquid was poured into the purchasers' bottles from a new and innocent-looking kerosene can. **1903** A. H. LEWIS *Boss* xiii. 162 That..no side-doors or speak-easy racket [should be] stood for. **1922** JOYCE *Ulysses* 418 In the speakeasy. Tight. I shee you, shir. **1946** [see *creep joint* s.v. CREEP *sb.* 6]. **1958** S. TRAILL in P. Gammond *Decca Bk. Jazz* vi. 75 Every cheap speakeasy had its resident piano player. **1961** W. VAUGHAN-THOMAS *Anzio* vii. 138 Inevitably some of these underground caves became 'speak-easy' dens where the local black-marketeers sold *vino* to the troops. **1968** [see *prohibition era* s.v. PROHIBITION 6]. **1982** *Age* (Melbourne) 3 Feb. 6/6 Unable to find a respectable job, she first became a bootlegger during the Prohibition era and ran a speakeasy.

speaker ('spiːkə(r)). Forms: 4–6 **speker**, 4–5 **-ere**, 5 **spekar**, **speiker**, 6 **spiker**, 6– **speaker**. [f. SPEAK *v.* + -ER. Cf. OFris. (*for*)*spreker* (WFris. *sprekker*, NFris. *spreeker, spreeger*), MDu. (Du.) and MLG. (LG.) *spreker*, OHG. *sprehhari, -eri* (MHG. *sprechære*, G. *sprecher*).]

1. a. One who speaks or talks.

1303 R. BRUNNE *Handl. Synne* 8291 Þe foule wurde þe speker dereþ. **1388** WYCLIF *Ezek.* ii. 1, Y herde the vois of a spekere. *c* **1400** *Destr. Troy* 5085 In speche may men spie the speker to know. **1485** CAXTON *Chas. Gt.* 27 Whan one spake to hym, he remembred the manere for to compryse thentencyon of the spekar. **1542** UDALL *Erasm. Apoph.* II. 260 b, It was laied..against hym, that he was a speaker of euill by Cæsar. **1565** *Reg. Privy Council Scot.* I. 394 Thair Majesteis sall require the spekar and delatar to gif his complaint or narratioun in writt. **1605** SHAKS. *Macb.* IV. iii. 175 *Malc.* What's the newest griefe? *Rosse.* That of an houres age, doth hisse the speaker. **1651** HOBBES *Leviath.* III. xxxvi. 222 It may bee understood sometimes of the Speaker. **1725** WATTS *Logic* I. iv. §3 It implies both the Falshood of the Speech, and my Reproach and Censure of the Speaker. **1781** COWPER *Hope* 345 All speakers, yet all language at a loss. **1832** BREWSTER *Nat. Magic* vii. 162 The real speaker was a full-grown woman. **1863** GEO. ELIOT *Romola* II. viii, She started up with anger in her eyes, and faced the speaker.

b. *spec.* One who speaks formally before a number of persons; one who addresses an audience; an orator.

c **1400** *New Test.* (Paues) Acts xiv. 11 Þei called..Poule Mercurye, for he was ledar ande spekar of þo worde. *a* **1533** LD. BERNERS *Huon* lxxxii. 254 'Syr,' quod Gaulter, who was yᵉ fyrst speker, 'me thynke he can scape none other wyse.' **1599** SHAKS. *Hen. V*, V. ii. 166 What? a speaker is but a prater, a Ryme is but a Ballad. **1780** *Mirror* No. 102, Some of our public speakers. **1828** WHATELY *Rhet.* in *Encycl. Metrop.* (1845) I. 262/1 The sentiments..which it is so important that the audience should feel towards the Speaker. **1855** MACAULAY *Hist. Eng.* xxii. IV. 744 He..had scarcely taken his seat when he attained a high place among parliamentary speakers. **1891** FARRAR *Darkn. & Dawn* xvii, When the speaker's voice ceased, a burst of applause came from the lips of the hearers.

2. With distinguishing adjs.: **a.** Denoting moral character, tendency to talk, or manner of speaking, as *evil, fair, false, great, hasty, short,* etc.

a **1340** HAMPOLE *Psalter* xxvi. 18 A wickid spekere delited is in his leghe. **1388** WYCLIF *Job* xvi. 9 A fals spekere is reisid aȝens my face. *a* **1450** tr. *De Imitatione* II. i. 41 Crist had aduersaries & suffrid shreude spekers. **1483** *Cath. Angl.* 353/2 A schort Speker, *micrologus.* A grete Speker, ..*grandiloquus.* **1570** LEVINS *Manip.* 212 Great speaker, *loquax.* **1611** BIBLE *Ps.* cxl. 11 Let not an euill speaker bee established in the earth. **1656** BLOUNT *Glossogr.* s.v. *Sphinx*, His unarticulate voice like that of a hasty speaker. **1784** COWPER *Task* IV. 66 The modest speaker is asham'd and griev'd T'engross a moment's notice.

b. Denoting ability (or the want of it) in the use of speech. †*fair speaker*, an orator.

c **1375** *Sc. Leg. Saints* xxxi. (*Eugenia*) 130 Quhat poetis seis, or fare spekaris. **1387** TREVISA *Higden* (Rolls) IV. 141 Þat was a noble spekere in all manere tonges of witt and of wisdom, and cheef spekere wiþ tonge. *c* **1400** *Destr. Troy* 3806 A freike þat was fre, and a feire speiker. *c* **1440** *Alph. Tales* 236 A passand fayr man & a riche, & ane eloquent speker. **1484** CAXTON *Fables of Alfonce* vii, A rethoryque man or fayr speker. **1613** SHAKS. *Hen. VIII*, I. ii. 111 The Gentleman is Learn'd, and a most rare Speaker. **1720** POPE *Iliad* XIX. 86 Unruly murmurs, or ill-timed applause, Wrong the best speaker, and the justest cause. **1778** MISS BURNEY *Evelina* lxxvii, We of the Lower House..have likewise the most able speakers. **1831** SIR J. SINCLAIR *Corr.* II. 108 The Count de Villele was not only an able speaker, but a real statesman. **1865** DICKENS *Lett.* (1880) II. 247 Almost the worst speaker I ever heard in my life. **1871** R. ELLIS tr. *Catullus* xlix. 1 Greatest speaker of any born a Roman, Marcus Tullius.

3. a. The member of the House of Commons who is chosen by the House itself to act as its representative and to preside over its debates. Also called ***Mr. Speaker*** and † ***Speaker-forth.***

In 1376–7 Sir Thomas de Hungerford, app. the first person formally mentioned as holding the office, 'avoit les paroles pur les Communes d'Engleterre en cest Parlement' (*Rolls of Parlt.* II. 374/1).

c **1400** *Brut* 330 Þis same Piers was chosen to be speker for the communes in þe parlement. **1414** *Rolls of Parlt.* IV. 22 The sentence & the entente axked by the Speker mouthe. *c* **1435** *Chron. Lond.* (1905) 50 Sir John Cheyne excusid him ffor the Speker fforth ffor the Comvnes, ffor dyuers Infirmites..that he hadde. *a* **1513** FABYAN *Chron.* VII. (1811) 486 Wherfore the sayde commons prayed by the mouth of theyr speker [etc.]. *a* **1577** SIR T. SMITH *Commw. Eng.* II. ii. (1584) 40 The speakers office is as brieflie and as plainely as he may to declare the effect thereof to the house. **1641** *King's Sp. to Parlt.* 2 Dec., It is no ways in Answer to Master Speakers learned Speech. **1654** WHITELOCK *Mem.* (1732) 52 [The king] himself entred into the house; at which the speaker rose out of his chair, and stood below. **1707** J. CHAMBERLAYNE *Pres. St. Gt. Brit.* I. II. (1708) 114 Before the choice of a Speaker, all the Members of the House of Commons take the Oaths of Allegiance and Supremacy. **1741** *Johnson's Debates* (1787) II. i. 4 The new House of Commons being met, the Usher came from the House of

Lords, with His Majesty's commands for their immediate attendance, when they were ordered to chuse a Speaker. **1818** *Evans' Parl. Deb.* 16 On a message from the lords, Mr. Speaker and several members attended to hear the speech of the lords commissioners read by the Lord Chancellor. **1840** *Penny Cycl.* XVII. 274/2 As yet he is only Speaker elect, and as such presents himself on the following day, in the house of lords. **1901** COURTNEY *Working Const. U.K.* 90 If any vacancy occurs whilst Parliament is in existence, a writ is issued by Mr. Speaker.

fig. **1589** R. HARVEY *Pl. Perc.* (1860) 7 The chiefe actor in the pageant of my braine, and high speaker in the Parlament of my deuise. **1597** SHAKS. *2 Hen. IV*, IV. ii. 18 The Speaker in his Parliament;..th'imagine Voyce of Heauen it selfe.

b. More fully in ***Speaker of (the) Parliament.***

1460 CAPGRAVE *Chron.* (Rolls) 230 It was answerd be Petir de la Mar, Knyte, and Speker of the Parlement. *a* **1500** *Bale's Chron.* in *Six Town Chron.* (1911) 136 And the comones chosen Sir William Oldhall Knight w[t] þe duk of york speker of the parliament. **1565** COOPER *Thesaurus, Demiurgus*,..an officer that proposed all thinges to the people whervpon they should intreate: as the speaker of the parliament amonge vs. **1696** PHILLIPS (ed. 5), *Speaker of the Parliament*, an Officer in that High Court, who is as it were the common mouth of all the rest.

c. The presiding officer or chairman of the House of Lords, now the Lord Chancellor, or one acting as his deputy or substitute. Also †***Lord Speaker.***

1660 PEPYS *Diary* 26 April, I hear, that about twelve of the Lords met and had chosen my Lord of Manchester Speaker of the House of Lords. **1687** MIÉGE *Gt. Fr. Dict.* II. s.v., The one [is] termed the Lord Speaker of the House of Peers, and the other the Speaker of the House of Commons. **1707** J. CHAMBERLAYNE *Pres. St. Gt. Brit.* (1710) 96 The Lord Chancellor or Keeper (who usually is Speaker of the House of Lords). **1797** *Encycl. Brit.* (ed. 3) XIII. 761/2 The speaker of the house of lords..is the lord chancellor,..or any other appointed by the king's commission [etc.]. **1867** *Chambers's Encycl.* IX. 24/2 The Speaker of the Lords may speak or vote on any question. **1891** *Law Times* XCII. 123/2 The Lord Chancellor need not be a member of the House of Lords of which he is the Speaker.

d. A similar president in other assemblies.

1656 BLOUNT *Glossogr., Proloquutor*,..the Speaker or Chair-man of each Convocation-house, or of a Synod, is so termed. **1728** S. JEAKE *Charters Cinque Ports* 91 In both these Courts,..the Head Officer..sits as Chief, and is called in Speeches addressed to him Mr. Speaker. **1789** *Constit. U.S.* I. §2 The house of representatives shall choose their speaker and other officers.

4. One who speaks in place of, or on behalf of, another or others.

1583 MELBANCKE *Philotimus* G j, Princes you know in parliament houses haue their speakers, to declare their pleasures, and ease themselues. **1782** J. BROWN *Nat. & Rev. Relig.* II. ii. (1796) 129 He is the great Speaker for us to God, in his ancient engagements and his continual intercession.

5. One who proclaims or celebrates. *rare*$^{-1}$.

1613 SHAKS. *Hen. VIII*, IV. ii. 70 After my death, I wish ..No other speaker of my liuing Actions,..But such an honest Chronicler as Griffith.

6. As a title of books containing pieces adapted for recitation or reading aloud.

1774 W. ENFIELD (*title*), The Speaker; or, miscellaneous Pieces, selected from the best English Writers. **1858** SIMMONDS *Dict. Trade, Speaker*,..a book for school-reading. **1879** WEBSTER *Suppl., Speaker*, a book containing selected pieces for declamation. (U.S.)

7. As second element: One who speaks a particular language.

1875 W. D. WHITNEY *Life & Growth of Lang.* iv. 72 The difficulty is one which English-speakers can hardly realize. **1899** *Daily News* 2 Oct. 6/4 A population of industrial English-speakers;..a population of pastoral Dutch-speakers.

8. = LOUD-SPEAKER.

1926 *Jrnl. Franklin Inst.* CCII. 436 This speaker employs a six-inch cone driven by an electromagnetic power unit. **1954** R. DAHL *Someone like You* 66 Maybe the great radio engineer doesn't know how to connect the mike to the speaker? **1978** *Hi-Fi News* Sept. 15 (Advt.), High Fidelity speakers for the discerning ear.

9. *attrib.* and *Comb.*, as (sense 8) ***speaker grille, system***; **speaker-hearer**, a person regarded as a user of language; **speaker-key**, a key fitted to a wind instrument to enable the playing of notes an octave or a twelfth higher (cf. *octave key* s.v. OCTAVE *sb.* (*a.*) 8); **speaker-listener** = *speaker-hearer* above; **speaker-phone** *U.S.*, a telephone receiver which need not be held in the hand; **Speaker's Conference**, a conference, first set up in 1916, whose purpose is to examine electoral law and reform under the chairmanship of the Speaker of the House of Commons; **Speakers' Corner**, the north-east corner of Hyde Park, near Marble Arch, noted as a place where soap-box orators traditionally air their views; also *transf.*

1979 P. WAY *Sunrise* iv. 44 There was a bell push and a *speaker-grille just above it. **1965** N. CHOMSKY *Aspects of Theory of Syntax* i. 4 To study actual linguistic performance, we must consider the interaction of a variety of factors, of which the underlying competence of the *speaker-hearer is only one. **1982** *Amer. Speech* LVII. 16 He must ultimately be willing to make claims about this base with respect to a speaker-hearer's capabilities. **1890** D. J. BLAIKLEY *Acoustics in Relation to Wind Instruments* 31 In one direction advantage is taken..to aid the player in producing certain notes, notably on the clarionet; the thumb,—or *speaker-key of which is designedly used to open a small air-way, thereby introducing a weak place, by which means certain sub-divisions of the air column are aided, and certain others are hindered. **1972** S. RICHMOND *Clarinet & Saxophone Experience* vi. 104 By pressing the speaker key for the second harmonic all notes will sound an octave higher. **1965** N. CHOMSKY *Aspects of Theory of Syntax* i. 3 Linguistic theory is concerned primarily with an ideal *speaker-listener, in a completely homogeneous speech-community. **1978** *Archivum Linguisticum* IX. 10 The ideal speaker-listener of generative theory. **1955** *Sun* (Baltimore) 29 July 8/6 The new 'hands-free' *Speakerphones enable you to take notes, refer to records, have others in the room with you join in the telephone conversation. **1968** *Time* 5 Apr. 54 Emerson, a municipal court judge in Downey, Calif., finds the speakerphone invaluable for getting a brief piece of testimony from a policeman, parole officer or technical expert. [**1916** *Times* 16 Dec. 9/5 The Speaker's Electoral Reform Conference is for the moment in suspense.] **1917** *Times* 18 Jan. 9/5 The recommendations of the *Speaker's Conference on Electoral Reform. **1974** *Times* 5 Mar. 2/3 Electoral reform has always been a matter for Parliament itself, expressing its view by means of free votes on recommendations by a Speaker's Conference. **1980** *Guardian* 18 Feb. 3/7 The last Speaker's Conference on electoral law, which met between 1972 and 1974, recommended..that the minimum age for standing for Parliament should be reduced. **1936** J. C. GOODWIN *One of Crowd* xix. 271 *Speakers' Corner is a mixed grill of apostles and propagators, of oddities and crudities, of fanatics and eccentrics. **1953** EARL WINTERTON *Orders of Day* xxii. 313 'Speakers' Corner' in Hyde Park. **1982** *Times* 16 Mar. 10/2 The crypt of St Paul's cathedral is regaining some of its historical reputation as an ecclesiastical Speakers' Corner. **1938** C. HIMES *Black on Black* (1973) 172 A *speaker system was installed to throw his powerful voice even farther. **1974** *Times* 4 Mar. 1/8 At about 4.40 pm the hijacker in the cockpit announced over the speaker system that the aircraft would be landing at Amsterdam.

speakeress ('spi:kərɪs). [f. prec. + -ESS.] A female speaker; a woman acting as a president or Speaker.

1781 *Westm. Mag.* IX. 16 Here the 'Speakeress' was again obliged to call 'to order'. **1831** *Lincoln Herald* 14 Oct. 3/6 The dowager Duchess of Richmond is the Speakeress, and Lady Jersey first clerk at the table. **1831** CARLYLE in Froude *Life* (1882) II. 177, I sate directly behind a speakeress with tongues. **1897** *Westm. Gaz.* 4 Feb. 2/1 With men and women on the Treasury Bench, and, perhaps, a Speakeress in the chair.

speakerine (spi:kə'ri:n). [a. Fr. *speakerine*, f. *speaker* announcer (f. SPEAKER) + fem. suff. *-ine*.] A woman announcer on radio or television; a television hostess.

1957 *Manch. Guardian* 19 Dec. 5/3 B.B.C. television viewers will see a programme..in which ten European countries will take part... The British contribution is to be the 'finale', in which Sylvia Peters is to introduce the women announcers—known as 'speakerines'—of Europe. **1973** D. MAY *Laughter in Djakarta* v. 97 We're going to hear the news from this lovely speakerine? **1979** J. RATHBONE *Euro-Killers* ix. 96 He..turned on the television. A speakerine was announcing the programme.

'Speakership. [f. SPEAKER + -SHIP.]

1. The office of Speaker in a legislative or other assembly.

1653 in S. Jeake *Charters Cinque Ports* (1728) 91 Whereas by septennary Revolution the Speakership of the Ports is now devolved upon us. **1803** G. ROSE *Diaries* (1860) II. 35 Unless he could be prevailed with to take the Speakership of the House of Lords, separated from the Great Seal. **1844** JESSE *Selwyn & Contemp.* IV. 379 Charles Wolfran Cornwall, Esq., whose appointment to the Speakership of the House of Commons is mentioned..in this letter. **1883** *Harper's Mag.* Feb. 371/1 It was an easy and natural promotion to the Speakership of the Imperial Diet.

2. Oratory.

1887 SAINTSBURY *Manchester* 149 There was room for all kinds of Speakership in the great campaign of the League.

† **'speakful,** *a. Obs.*$^{-1}$ In 3 spekeful. [f. SPEAK *v.* + -FUL. Cf. OE. *sprǽcful*.] Talkative.

a **1225** *Ancr. R.* 100 þis is a cruel word..þet vre Louerd seið..to babelinde, & to spekefule ancren.

speak-house. [f. SPEAK *v.* + HOUSE *sb.* Cf. the earlier *speech-house*.]

† **1.** A room, in a convent or monastery, where conversation was permitted or visitors received; the parlour. *Obs.*

c **1650** in J. Morris *Troubles Cath. Forefathers* (1872) 275 Those Cloisters of this Order..did sometimes invite them to dinner, and made great cheer with plenty of wine in their speakhouse. **1762** B. F. E. tr. *Marin's Perf. Relig.* 5 What can be thought of a Religious who runs with eagerness..to the Speak-house, whenever called.

2. In the South Sea Islands, a large hut used as a place of council.

1893 STEVENSON *Island Nights' Entert.* 4 Getting tabooed, and going down to the Speak House to see and get it taken off. **1901** G. BALFOUR *Life Stevenson* II. iv. 80 A large 'speak-house' at Tuagana, some two hours' sail down the coast.

speakie ('spi:kɪ). *temporary.* [f. SPEAK *v.* + -IE, after MOVIE, TALKIE.] A stage play in contrast to a (silent) film; rarely, = TALKIE. Usu. *pl.*

1921 J. M. BARRIE *Let.* 18 Sept. (1942) 192 The ordinary stage drama he [*sc.* Charlie Chaplin] called the 'Speakies'. **1927** *Observer* 24 Apr. 15/1 She prophesied the downfall of the 'speakies' and the triumphant survival of the 'movies'. **1927** *Daily Tel.* 11 Oct. 6 An innovation last night was the introduction of a real stage set in the middle of the film... Whether this mixture of 'movie' and 'speakie' is desirable may be questioned. **1928** *Sunday Dispatch* 15 July 14 'Talkies' or 'speakies' as they are calling them in Hollywood, have very definitely arrived.

speaking ('spi:kɪŋ), *vbl. sb.* [f. SPEAK *v.*]

1. a. The action of the verb; talking, discoursing.

1303 R. BRUNNE *Handl. Synne* 8285 ȝyt þer ys spekyng of vylanyye þat longeþ vnto lecherye. **1375** BARBOUR *Bruce* III. 181 Sic speking off the king thai maid. *c* **1440** *Alph. Tales* 228 He..dischargid þaim þe company & spekyng with of any strangiers. *c* **1470** HENRY *Wallace* VIII. 1507 Sone thai war brocht to spekyng to Wallace. **1523** LD. BERNERS *Froiss.* I. cxxiii. 148 They fledde away as ferr as they might here spekyng of thenglysshmen. **1630** *R. Johnson's Kingd. & Commw.* 10 From the South hath scarce ever beene attempted a journey worth speaking of, to the indammagement of the North. **1691** T. H[ALE] *Acc. New Invent.* p. cx, These very words of the Captains speaking were Noted down from his Mouth by the Person to whom he spake them. **1780** *Mirror* No. 88, A young gentleman, who, from his correct manner of speaking, I suppose practised the law. **1825** SCOTT *Talism.* xviii, Within an hour from the time of my speaking. **1845** CLOUGH *New Sinai* vi. Poems (1849) 25 The Voice, Whose speaking spoke abroad ..The ancient Truth of God.

b. The delivery of speeches; speech-making.

a **1763** W. KING *Polit. & Lit. Anecd.* (1819) 181 *note*, Indeed our methodists and our enthusiasts of all denominations pretend to the gift of speaking. **1828** WHATELY *Rhet.* in *Encycl. Metrop.* I. 241/1 It is evident that in its primary signification, Rhetoric had reference to public Speaking alone. **1847** HELPS *Friends in C.* I. i. 63 That you would not be so bitter against after-dinner speaking.

2. a. With possessive prons., etc.: Speech, talk; conversation, discourse.

a **1325** *Prose Psalter* cxviii. 50 þi spekyng quikened me. **1375** BARBOUR *Bruce* I. 428 Gyff thow wald kep thi fewte, Thow maid nane sic speking to me. *c* **1400** *Laud Troy Bk.* 2810 He toke then leue at qwene Eleyne, Off here spekyng he was fayne. *c* **1460** *Towneley Myst.* xviii. 190 Sich spekyng will we spare. **1876** MORRIS *Sigurd* (1877) 7 So sweet his speaking sounded. **1885** *Athenæum* 17 Oct. 501/2 He was obliged..to mingle some plain political speaking..with his ethical teaching.

b. An instance or occasion of speech or talk; a discourse, †conference, discussion, etc. Now chiefly *U.S.* ***at this*** (or ***the***) ***present speaking***, at this moment.

c **1275** LAY. 12988 þo comen to Londene alle þeos Bruttes to one speking. **1338** R. BRUNNE *Chron.* (1810) 301 In alle þis spekyng com þe tresorere Fro Edward our kyng. **1389** in *Eng. Gilds* (1870) 52 Also it was ordeynd..for to haue a spekyng to-gedyr thre tymes in þe ȝer. **1481** CAXTON *Reynard* xvii. (Arb.) 43 Assone as this spekyng was don. **1491** —— *Vitas Patr.* (W. de W. 1495) II. 184/2 The good relygyous..was enfourmed of this spekyng. **1611** SHAKS. *Cymb.* v. iv. 148 'Tis still a Dreame: or else..a speaking such As sense cannot vntye. **1650** CROMWELL *Let.* 12 Sept. in Carlyle *Lett. & Sp.*, A speaking to instruction and edification. **1835** J. P. KENNEDY *Horse-Shoe Robinson* I. vi. 78 If I suspicioned a bamboozlement, which I am not far from at this present speaking. **1837** DICKENS *Pickw.* xxxiii, That she was the mother of eight children at that present speaking. **1844** MRS. BROWNING *Lady Geraldine's Courtsh.* xii, When a sudden silver speaking, gravely cadenced, over-rung them. **1863** C. C. HOPLEY *Life in South* I. 57 Then came the 'speaking', as the sermon was called. **1891** M. E. RYAN *Told in Hills* III. v. 205 At the present speaking the days are not picnic days. **1895** 'C. E. CRADDOCK' *Mystery Witch-Face Mt.* 206 Thar war a big crowd at the cross roads ter hear the speakin'. **1942** J. THOMAS *Blue Ridge* v. 155 Men ..will travel miles to a speaking—which may be a political gathering or one for..discussing road building.

†**c.** *pl.* Things spoken; sayings, statements, words. *Obs.*

a **1325** *Prose Psalter* cxviii. 11 Ich hidde þy spekynges in myn hert. **1390** GOWER *Conf.* I. 49, I mot algate..make my spekynges Of love. *c* **1400** tr. *Secreta Secret., Gov. Lordsh.* 42 By tokyns & ensamples, & lyke spekyngges. **1535** COVERDALE *Dan.* viii. 23 A kynge..which shall be wyse in darcke speakinges. **1578** *Reg. Privy Council Scot.* III. 16 To credeit the reportis and speikingis of the saidis personis. **1653** H. MORE *Def. Cabbala* 177 To understand the speakings of God, according as the circumstances of the Matter naturally imply.

3. a. With adjs., as *evil, fair, great, wise*, etc.

1340 *Ayenb.* 50 Ine zenne of kueade tonge, þet is in fole spekinge. *a* **1400** *Minor Poems fr. Vernon MS.* 533/159 Whon he þe makeþ feirest spekyng þen drede þou most his dedes suwyng. **1486** *Bk. St. Albans* e iij, For all the fayre spekyng..Commyth of sechyng and fyndyng of the hare. **1535** COVERDALE *Ephes.* iv. 31 Let all bytternes,..roaringe, & cursed speakynge [**1611** euill speaking] be farre from you. **1605** SHAKS. *Macb.* IV. iii. 130 My first false speaking Was this vpon my selfe. **1611** BIBLE *1 Pet.* ii. 1 Laying aside all malice,..and enuies, and euill speakings. **1721** BAILEY, *Malediction*, an Evil Speaking or cursing.

b. With advs., as *evil, soft, thick*, etc.

1530 PALSGR. 274/1 Spekyng toguyder, *locution*. **1580** HOLLYBAND *Treas. Fr. Tong, Abbaissement de voix*, a speaking soft. **1597** SHAKS. *2 Hen. IV*, II. iii. 24 And speaking thicke (which Nature made his blemish) Became the Accents of the Valiant. **1639** DRUMM. OF HAWTH. *Prophecy* Wks. (1711) 180 If the speaking evil of a King be a Sin before God. **1736** AINSWORTH II, *Pronunciatio*,..a speaking out, or delivery of a speech. **1920** D. H. LAWRENCE *Lost Girl* iv. 54 She began to hate outspokenness and direct speaking-forth of the whole mind.

†**4.** The faculty or power of speech. *Obs.*

c **1375** *Sc. Leg. Saints* xii. (*Matthias*) 386 Defe men he gaf heryngе, alsa to dum þe spekyne. **1526** *Pilgr. Perf.* (W. de W. 1531) 140 Though the frere minour gyue syght to ye blynde,..to the domme spekyng.

5. *attrib.*, as ***speaking acquaintance, distance, engagement, exercise, order, part, point, room, tour, trip, voice***, etc.

1687 MIÉGE *Gt. Fr. Dict.* II. s.v., This Book is a great Help both for the speaking and the reading part. **1751** *Female Foundling* II. 47 Immediately I went down into the Speaking-room [= parlour]. **1852** BRISTED *Five Yrs. Eng.*

Univ. (ed. 2) 289 And our acquaintance with the tongue of Dante never became, to borrow a very old Joe Miller, a speaking acquaintance. 1860 ADLER *Prov. Poet.* x. 216 Rudiger has already arrived within speaking distance of the enemy. 1870 EMERSON *Soc. & Solit.* iv. 55 The eloquence of one stimulates all the rest, some up to the speaking-point. 1870 O. LOGAN *Before Footlights & behind Scenes* iii. 37 By and by I got into 'speaking parts', such as the Duke of York in Richard the Third. 1879 *Law Rep. Appeal Cases* IV. 40 If the Court of Quarter Sessions stated upon the face of the order, by way of recital, that the facts were so and so, and the grounds of its decision were such as were so stated, then the order became upon the face of it, a speaking order. 1897 *Allbutt's Syst. Med.* III. 355 Graduated and methodical speaking exercises. 1908 E. TERRY *Story of My Life* xiv. 355 Melba.. had a bad cold, and therefore a frightful *speaking* voice for the moment. 1924 W. HOLTBY *Crowded Street* xxxvi. 270 Delia.. departed northwards on a speaking tour. 1931 F. L. ALLEN *Only Yesterday* ii. 32 He would win them to his cause, making a speaking trip through the West. 1944 N. STREATFEILD *Curtain Up* viii. 99 Mime.. she loved. Then there were her speaking parts. 1973 'E. MCBAIN' *Hail to Chief* vi. 109, I have a speaking engagement... I'm talking at a women's college. 1977 *Rolling Stone* 5 May 15/4 White, a big man with a rich, resonant speaking voice which turned into a tough growl when he sang. 1978 M. DICKENS *Open Book* xix. 173 On this speaking tour, my engagements fell roughly into two main categories. 1979 LD. DENNING *Discipline of Law* II. i. 66 It was possible to extend it to include not only the order of the Tribunal itself—when it was a 'speaking order'—but in addition all the documents properly before the Tribunal and considered by them.

b. In combs. denoting devices or apparatus for producing or conveying articulate sounds, as ***speaking-apparatus, battery, board, -machine, -pipe, telephone, †trump***, etc.; **speaking front**, an organ-front composed of pipes which actually sound, as contrasted with dummy pipes. See also SPEAKING-TRUMPET, -TUBE.

a 1711 KEN *Hymns Festiv.* Poet. Wks. 1721 I. 315 Up then I saw an Angel take His Speaking-Trump. 1795 *Phil. Trans.* LXXXV. 401 By means of the speaking-pipe the workman may be directed to begin, to stop, to go fast, or slow. 1832 BREWSTER *Nat. Magic* vii. 159 It has been supposed.. that in the ancient speaking-machines the deception is effected by means of ventriloquism. 1837 CARLYLE *Fr. Rev.* I. VI. i, Not a unit of whom but has.. his own speaking-apparatus. 1842 *Penny Cycl.* XXIV. 154/1 Speaking-pipes, or tubes to convey the voice from one place to another. 1879 PRESCOTT *Sp. Telephone* 44 During the past year the articulating or Speaking Telephone has attracted very general interest. 1881 W. E. DICKSON *Pract. Organ-building* iv. 53 It is by these means that 'speaking fronts' are arranged according to any design.

c. *on (upon, †in) speaking terms*: see TERM *sb.* 9 a. (Usually in negative constructions.)

1786 MACKENZIE *Lounger* No. 78 ¶2 One half of the neighbours are scarce in speaking terms with the other. 1801 M. EDGEWORTH *Belinda* I. xii. 370 Lady Delacour is not upon speaking terms with this Mrs. Margaret Delacour; she cannot endure her. 1853 DICKENS *Bleak Ho.* xi, Mrs. Perkins, who has not been for some weeks on speaking terms with Mrs. Piper. 1882 'EDNA LYALL' *Donovan* xli, He was no longer on speaking terms with Stephen.

speaking ('spi:kɪŋ), *ppl. a.* [f. SPEAK *v.*]

1. a. That speaks; capable of articulate speech. †In early use *absol.*

c 1250 *Gen. & Ex.* 2821 Quo made domme, and quo specande? 1382 WYCLIF *Ezek.* ii. 1 A vois of the spekynge. 1568 *Satir. Poems Reform.* xlvii. 102 Callit ane speikand devill. 1685 BOYLE *Enq. Notion Nat.* iv. 84 Of some such sort of speaking images, some learned criticks suppose the Teraphim.. to have been. 1740 J. DYER *Ruins Rome* (1903) 33 Historic urns and breathing statues rise, And speaking busts. 1778–81 WARTON *Hist. Eng. Poetry* xxvii. (1870) 452 The public pageants of this period.. received.. the addition of speaking personages. 1832 BREWSTER *Nat. Magic* i. 4 The speaking head which uttered its oracular responses at Lesbos. 1865 TYLOR *Early Hist. Man.* ii. 19 So the speaking man has no business to meddle with the invention of signs. 1883 *Encycl. Brit.* XV. 208/1 The philosopher Descartes made a speaking figure.

fig. 1549 *Compl. Scot.* xiii. 108 Ther is ane ald prouerb that says, that ane herand damysele, and ane spekand castel, sal neuyr end vith honour. 1644 J. BULWER (*title*), Chirologia; or the Natvrall Langvage of the Hand. Composed of the Speaking Motions, and Discoursing Gestures thereof.

b. As the second element of various combs., as ***evil-, fair-, great-, public-, true-, well-speaking***. †Also *absol.*

a 1325 *Prose Psalter* xliii. 18 Fram þe voice of þe reproceand and þe oȝains spekand. ? *a* 1366 CHAUCER *Rom. Rose* 1268 A knyght.. That worthy was and wel spekyng. 1388 WYCLIF *Ps.* xi. 4 The Lorde destrie.. the greet spekynge tunge. 1422 tr. *Secreta Secret., Priv. Priv.* 211 That he bene corteyse, wel Spekynge, and eloquente. 1570–6 LAMBARDE *Peramb. Kent* (1826) 290 The opinion of any one true speaking man. 1611 COTGR. s.v. *Pendu*, A smooth, glib, eloquent, or well speaking tongue. 1647 CLARENDON *Contempl. on Ps.* Tracts (1727) 517 To grapple with our fair-speaking adversaries. 1837 CARLYLE *Fr. Rev.* I. VII. iii, The public-speaking woman at the Palais Royal.

c. In objective combs. with names of languages.

1865 KINGSLEY *Herew.* Prel., French-speaking knights. 1873– [see ENGLISH *a.* C]. 1899 MACKAIL *W. Morris* I. 179 Among Greek-speaking people.

2. a. In various fig. and transf. senses; *esp.* expressive, significant, eloquent.

c 1586 C'TESS PEMBROKE *Ps.* XLV. i, Thie lipps, as springs, doe flowe with speaking grace. 1635 JACKSON *Creed* VIII. xxxi. 358 A prophecie or speaking picture that the victory.. should be accomplishte upon the crosse. 1653 R. FLECKNOE *Poems of all Sorts* 1 Still borne Silence,.. Admirations speakingst Tongue. 1722 DE FOE *Plague* (1884) 84 'Tis a speaking Sight. 1730 T. BOSTON *Mem.* ix, This recovery.. seemed to be speaking as to the point I was concerned about. 1813 SHELLEY *Q. Mab* IV. 3 The balmiest sigh.. Were discord to the speaking quietude That wraps this moveless scene. 1853 HUMPHREYS *Coin-coll. Man.* I. 262 Supposed to have been adopted as a speaking type. 1876 FREEMAN *Norm. Conq.* V. xxii. 40 The same is of itself a speaking witness to their permanence.

b. Of the eyes, countenance, etc.: Highly expressive.

1592 *Arden of Feversham* I. 259 Loue is the Painters Muse, That makes him frame a speaking countenaunce. 1602 *Kyd's Span. Trag.* III. Wks. (1901) 68 With a speaking looke to my sonne Horatio. 1631 P. FLETCHER *Piscatory Eclog.* II. xx. (1633) 12 Me thinks I heare thy speaking eye Woo me my posting journey to delay. 1726 POPE *Odyss.* XVII. 438 With speaking eyes, and voice of plaintiff sound. 1740 RICHARDSON *Pamela* (1824) I. xxiii. 35 Can the pretty image speak, Mrs. Jervis? I vow she has speaking eyes! 1826 DISRAELI *V. Grey* III. vi, One who takes her answer.. from the speaking lineaments of the face, which are Truth's witnesses. 1842 IS. WILLIAMS *Baptistery* II. xxviii. (1874) 145 Expression varies still each speaking glance. 1885 'MRS. ALEXANDER' *At Bay* ii, Elsie was silent, but a distressed look crept over her speaking face.

3. Of likeness, etc.: Striking; true; faithful.

1582 STANYHURST *Æneis* I. (Arb.) 40 His face goodlye roset, with speaking forgerye feigned. 1844 KINGLAKE *Eothen* xviii, Anybody.. could still draw a speaking, nay scolding, likeness of Keate. 1862 P'CESS ALICE *Mem.* (1884) 40 A most beautiful picture of the Grand Duchess Hélène —quite speaking.

4. Special Combs. ***speaking clock***, a telephone service giving the correct time in words (cf. *talking clock* s.v. TALKING *ppl. a.* 2); ***speaking demurrer***, (see quot.); ***speaking-flame lamp***, a safety lamp which announces the presence of explosive gas by giving out a peculiar sound; ***speaking stop***, a stop key on an organ which permits or prevents the sounding of a rank of pipes.

1934 *P.O. Electr. Engineers' Jrnl.* XXVII. 142/1 For some time past a *speaking clock has been installed in Paris. 1978 'H. CARMICHAEL' *Life Cycle* xiii. 139 If nobody at Scotland Yard has a watch you could've dialled the Speaking Clock. 1887 *Cassell's Encycl. Dict.*, **Speaking-demurrer*, Law, a demurrer in which new facts not appearing upon the face of a bill in equity were introduced to support a demurrer. 1883 GRESLEY *Gloss. Coal-m.* 230 *Speaking-flame lamp. 1938 *Oxf. Compan. Mus.* 660/2 An organ of 168 actual '*speaking stops' (we so call the stops which really sound, as distinct from other devices.) 1977 *Gramophone* Mar. 1444/2 This is a very large Compton organ indeed, with 37 speaking stops on the pedal.

'speakingly, *adv.* [f. prec. + -LY².] In a speaking or eloquent manner; strikingly.

1633 BROME *Antipodes* (1640) v. 4 A Mute is one that acteth speakingly, And yet sayes nothing. 1746 HERVEY *Medit.* (1818) 250 How solemnly they recognize the fate of others, and speakingly remind us of our own. 1765 H. WALPOLE *Otranto* iv. (1798) 75 The judgments which the portents of these days but too speakingly denounce against thy house. 1831 *Fraser's Mag.* IV. 286 It is surprisingly clever, and speakingly characteristic.

So **'speakingness**. *rare.*

1851 J. BROWN *Lett.* (1907) 94 Such a voice for.. sweetness, and power—and a certain speakingness. 1957 E. BOWEN in K. Mansfield *34 Short Stories* 15 Words had but one appeal for her, that of speakingness.

speaking-trumpet. (Also unhyphened.) [SPEAKING *vbl. sb.* 5 b.] A kind of trumpet (chiefly used at sea), so contrived as to carry the voice to a great distance, or to cause it to be heard above loud noises.

1671 SIR S. MORLAND *Tuba Stentoro-phonica* Title-p., The instruments (or Speaking-Trumpets) of all sizes [etc.]. 1671 *Phil. Trans.* VI. 3056 An Account of the Speaking Trumpet, as it hath been contrived and published by Sir Sam. Moreland Knight and Baronet. 1680 *Lond. Gaz.* No. 1520/1 The Twelfth at night, Captain St. Johns, by the help of the Speaking Trumpet, called to us. 1709 *Ibid.* No. 4506/2 They were told (by a Speaking Trumpet from the Castle) that the Enemy had taken the Town. 1773 GOLDSM. *Stoops to Conq.* I. i, He sometimes whoops like a speaking trumpet. 1824 MISS MITFORD *Village* Ser. I. (1863) 127 His voice was loud enough to have hailed a ship at sea without the assistance of a speaking-trumpet. 1887 W. P. FRITH *Autobiogr.* I. v. 60 A very old gentleman.. with a speaking-trumpet under his arm.

fig. and *transf.* 1710 PALMER *Prov.* 145 This is performing the contemptible office of a speaking-trumpet. 1823 SCOTT *Quentin D.* xxx, Reason.. borrows the speaking-trumpet of Necessity, and her voice becomes lordly and imperative.

speaking-tube. (Also unhyphened.) [SPEAKING *vbl. sb.* 5 b.]

1. A tube or pipe for speaking, or communicating orders, from one room, building, etc., to another.

1833 LOUDON *Encycl. Archit.* §1457 Orders being given by the waiter above through a speaking-tube. 1844 T. WEBSTER *Encycl. Dom. Econ.* §4797 These speaking tubes first came into use here.. about thirty-five years ago. 1894 ELIZ. BANKS *Camp. Curiosity* 27 Annie was called to the hall to answer the whistle of the speaking-tube.

attrib. 1884 KNIGHT *Dict. Mech.* Suppl. 834/1 *Speaking Tube Whistle*, a modification of an intonating modulating steam whistle.

2. A speaking-trumpet.

1889 F. COWPER *Capt. of 'Wight'* 304 'You'll be aboard o' us an' you take no more care,' sung out the Master through a speaking-tube.

†'speakless, *a. Obs.*⁻¹ [f. SPEAK *v.* + -LESS.] Unspeakable, indescribable.

1612 FIELD *Woman is a Weathercock* III. ii, But speakless is his plague, that once had store And from superfluous state falls to be poor.

†'speakman. *Obs. rare.* In 4 speke-. [f. SPEAK *v.*] An advocate or spokesman.

1340 *Ayenb.* 60 To þan belongeþ þe zenne of ham þet zechiþ spekemen ham uor to praysi. *Ibid.* 99 Oure guode spekeman and oure zuete mayster Iesu Crist.

speako ('spi:kəʊ). *U.S. slang.* [f. SPEAK(EASY + -O².] = SPEAKEASY.

1931 *Amer. Mercury* Dec. 415/2 There's only one thing in the world that puts a speako over, and that's good will. 1932 *Ibid.* Jan. 11 A brewery which supplied every other speako between Fourteenth and Canal streets. 1941 J. M. CAIN *Mildred Pierce* (1943) i. 29 Making the grand tour of all the speako's he knows.

†'speakworthy, *a. Obs.*⁻¹ In 6 speke-. [f. SPEAK *v.*] Worthy of mention.

1562 TURNER *Herbal* II. (1568) 77 Poppy geueth no spekeworthy norishment vnto the body.

speal, dial. f. SPALE *sb.*²; var. SPEEL *v.*

speal-bone. *Sc.* and *north.* [For dial. *speal-bane*, var. *spule-bane*: see SPULE.] The shoulder-blade, esp. as used in a method of divination.

Pennant is the chief source of later instances.

1771 PENNANT *Tour Scot. 1769*, 154 There is another sort of divination, called Sleinanachd, or reading the speal-bone, or the blade-bone of a shoulder of mutton well scraped. 1802 SIBBALD *Chron. S.P.* Gloss. s.v. *Spald*, 'Reading the speal or spule-bane,' antiently a common mode of divination. 1871 TYLOR *Prim. Cult.* I. 113 A proper English term for it is 'reading the speal-bone'.

speale, var. SPELE *v.*² *Obs.*

spealt, obs. f. SPELT *sb.*¹

spean (spi:n), *sb.*¹ Now *dial.* Forms: α. 6–7 speane, 6–7, 9 spean. β. 6– spene, 8–9 speen, 9 spen. [a. MDu. or MLG. *spene* (Du. and Flem. *speen*, WFris. *spien*, LG. *spene, späne*), = ON. *speni* (MSw. *spene, späne*, etc.; Norw., Sw., obs. Da. *spene*), related to OE. *spana, spona*: see SPANE *v.*]

†1. Swelling of the uvula. *Obs.*⁻¹

1527 ANDREW *Brunswyke's Distyll. Waters* C iv, It is also good to be gargoled agaynste vuala that is the spene in the strote.

2. A teat or nipple, *esp.* of a cow.

α. 1573 TWYNE *Æneid* XI. Ii ij b, To her tendre lippes in milkinge, downe their speanes he raught. 1607 TOPSELL *Four-footed Beasts* 38 A bear.. hath also foure speanes to her Paps. *Ibid.* 126 The Hinde hath vdders betwixt her thighes with foure speanes like a cow. *Ibid.* 138 The females.. haue vnderneath their bellies great paps, with many speanes to sucke at. 1688 HOLME *Armoury* II. 171/2 The Speanes, or the Paps, the four Dugs, by which the Milk is drawn from the Udder. 1873– in dial. glossaries (Surrey, Kent, Yks.).

β. 1674 RAY *S. & E. Co. Words* 76 A Seen [1691 *Speen*] or *spene*: a cows pappe, *Kent*. [Hence in Worlidge (1681), Phillips, etc.] 1736 PEGGE *Kenticisms* (E.D.S.), *Speen*, the teat of a cow. 1846 J. BAXTER *Libr. Pract. Agric.* (ed. 4) II. 104 The maid.. milks two speens, while the calf sucks the other two. 1863– in dial. glossaries, etc. (Kent, Sussex, Hants, Pemb., Wexford, etc.), in forms *spene, speen*, and rarely *spen*.

spean (spi:n), *sb.*² *south. dial.* Also **spane, spen(e, speen.** [Of obscure origin.]

1. A prong of a fork.

18.. *Devon Gloss.* in Halliw. (1847), *Spanes*, the prongs of a peek, or hay-fork, or dung-fork. 1848 *Jrnl. R. Agric. Soc.* IX. II. 550 On stiff soils.. the flatter and broader forks or speens are best. 1889 JEFFERIES *Field & Hedgerow* 79 A two-spean spud, or Canterbury hoe, with points instead of a broad blade.

2. A bar or rail of a gate.

1863–83 in Hampshire glossaries.

spean (spi:n), *v. Sc.* and *north. dial.* Forms: 6 speane, 6, 8–9 spean (8 speean, 9 spene). [Later form of SPANE *v.*, or independently ad. MDu. or MLG. *spenen* (Du. and Flem. *spenen*, LG. *spenen, spänen*), = MHG. *spenen* (G. dial. *spänen*), f. *spene* SPEAN *sb.*¹]

1. *trans.* To wean, in *lit.* and *fig.* senses.

1595 DUNCAN *App. Etym.* (E.D.S.), *Depello*, to put away, to speane, *lacte depellere*. 1599 A. HUME *Poems* (S.T.S.) 87 Thinke not that thou art sufficientlie mortified, and speaned from the world. 1781 J. HUTTON *Tour to Caves* (ed. 2) Gloss. 96 *Spain*, or *spean*, to wean. 1788 W. H. MARSHALL *Yorksh.* II. 354 To *Speean*.., to wean, as calves or pigs. 1808– in Sc. and northern dial. glossaries and texts. 1831 *Sutherland Farm Rep.* 75 *Husb.* (L.U.K.) III, The fields.. not being eaten bare by the sheep, the scythe is passed over them as soon as the lambs have been speaned. 1871 W. ALEXANDER *Johnny Gibb* xxix, The vera winter that Benjie was spean't.

absol. 1831 *Sutherland Farm Rep.* 79 *Husb.* (L.U.K.) III, The sale ewe lot.. which are then brought in to lamb, and, consequently, to spean early.

b. In phrases implying the creation of extreme disgust, repression, etc.

1790 BURNS *Tam o' Shanter* 160 But wither'd beldams, auld and droll, Rigwoodie hags wad spean a foal. 1826 SCOTT *Let.* in *Lockhart* (1839) I. 171 One of the ugliest countenances.., enough as we say to spean weans. 1895 R.

B. C. GRAHAM *Notes on Menteith* i. 13 Slate-roofed cottages, ..hideous enough to spean a bairn.

2. (See quot. and SPANE *v.* 2.)

1829 BROCKETT *N.C. Gloss.* (ed. 2), Young corn is said to be speaned, when the milky..juice of its grain is exhausted, and it is obliged to depend on the nutriment collected by its own roots.

Hence **'speaning** *vbl. sb.*; also *attrib.* in ***speaning brash, time*** (cf. SPANING *vbl. sb.* b).

1831 *Sutherland Farm Rep.* 75 *Husb.* (L.U.K.) III, That the aftermath may be, at speaning time, open to recruit the weakest and worst fed lambs. *Ibid.* 78 The speaning was performed nearly a fortnight sooner than had been formerly practised. 1872 MACMILLAN *True Vine* iii. 122 After a while the field of emerald loveliness looks suddenly sere and yellow... This remarkable change is caused by what the farmers call the 'speanin brash'.

†**'speaning,** *sb. Obs.*$^{-1}$ In 6 spenyng. [Cf. prec. and *spaneling* s.v. SPANE *v.*] A weaned pig.

1536 *Cockersand Chartul.* (Chetham) 1179 Store of swine. Item ix yong Spenynges... Item oone olde Hogge.

spear (spɪə(r)), *sb.*[1] Forms: α. 1–7 spere (3 spære), 3–6 sper (5 sperre), 5–7 speere. β. 5–6 speir, 5 speire, speyre, spayre, 6 spair. γ. 6–7 speare, 7– spear. [OE. *spere*, = OFris. *spiri, spere, sper* (WFris. *spear*), MDu. *spere, speer* (Du. *speer*), OS. and MLG., OHG. and MHG. *sper* (G. *speer*), ON. pl. *spjǫr*; MSw. *spär* and obs. Da. *spær* are from MLG. It is doubtful whether L. *sparus*, hunting-spear, is related.]

I. 1. a. A thrusting weapon consisting of a stout wooden staff of some length, on which a sharp-pointed head, usually of iron or steel, is socketed or otherwise securely fixed; a lance; also, a shorter or lighter weapon of this kind used for throwing.

α. *c* 725 *Corpus Gloss.* (Hessels) C610 *Contos*, speoru. *c* 893 K. ÆLFRED *Oros.* III. xvii. §1 Þa for he..& funde hiene ænne be weʒe licgan mid sperum tosticad. *c* 950 *Lindisf. Gosp.* John xix. 34 An ðara cempa mið spere sidu his untynde. *c* 1000 ÆLFRIC *Saints' Lives* xii. 55 Þæt hors hine bær forð swa þæt spere him eode þurh ut. *c* 1060 *O.E. Chron.* (MS. C) an. 1055, Ær þær wære æniʒ spere ʒescoten, ær fleah ðæt Englisce folc. *a* 1225 *Ancr. R.* 60 Þerefter heo schekeð hire spere, & nehleheð up on hire, &..ʒiueð speres wunden. *c* 1275 *Passion our Lord* 179 in *O.E. Misc.*, Mid speres and myd staues and oþe vele þinge. *c* 1320 *Sir Tristr.* 1446 Wiþ a spere feloun He smot him in þe side. *a* 1400 *Sir Perc.* 191 Off alle hir lordes faire gere Wolde scho noʒte with hir bere, Bot a lyttille Scottes spere. 1470–85 MALORY *Arthur* I. x. 48 Vlfyus and Brastias dressid theire speres and ranne to gyder with grete raundon. 1483 *Cath. Angl.* 354/2 A Sperre for a bayre, *exculpulum, venabulum.* *a* 1548 HALL *Chron., Hen. VIII*, 36 b, The Scottes dayly shipped long speres called Colleyne Clowystes. 1590 SPENSER *F.Q.* I. i. 11 The Champion..to the Dwarfe a while his needlesse spere he gaue.

β. *c* 1400 *Destr. Troy* 6494 Two speirus full dispitus he sparet to cast. 14.. *Trevisa's Barth. De P.R.* XVII. xxxi. (Bodl. MS.), Dartes of reede..so longe..þ[t] þei vse hem in stede of speirs. 1562 WINȜET *Wks.* (S.T.S.) I. 78 That knycht quha peirsit our Lordis syde with the speir. 1596 DALRYMPLE tr. *Leslie's Hist. Scot.* II. 330 The Scotis ouerthrew monie Jnglismen with speiris.

γ. 1524 *St. Papers Hen. VIII*, II. 115 Englishe speares, bowes, and billes. 1560 DAUS tr. *Sleidane's Comm.* 130 The chief Prophet..thrusteth his speare into hym. 1630 *R. Johnson's Kingd. & Commw.* 109 Some after the fashion of Italie, using a Scull, a Iacke, a Sword, and two light Speares. 1667 MILTON *P.L.* I. 292 His Spear, to equal which the tallest Pine Hewn on Norwegian hills..were but a wand. 1756–7 tr. *Keysler's Trav.* (1760) IV. 403 The spears of both these champions are still shewn here. 1813 SCOTT *Trierm.* I. xvii, Four of the train combined to rear The terrors of Tintadgel's spear. 1889 BADEN-POWELL *Pigsticking* 90 The short or 'jobbing' spear is generally used throughout Bengal and Upper India.

b. Without article, freq. coupled with *shield, sword*, etc., and used in a collective sense.

c 1205 LAY. 548 Brutus..mid sweord & mid spere al he todrof þes kinges here. *a* 1250 *Owl & Night.* 1022 He myhte bet teche ane beore To bere scheld and spere. *a* 1300 *Cursor M.* 20817 To be þan for vs sper and scheild. 1377 LANGL. *P. Pl.* B. XVIII. 12 Wyth-oute spores other spere spakliche he loked. *c* 1400 *Rom. Rose* 5823 That she..nyl..smyte a stroke in this bataile, With darte, ne mace, spere, ne knyf. *c* 1470 HENRY *Wallace* IV. 302 All..Off that party that mycht weild bow or sper. 1500–20 DUNBAR *Poems* liv. 16 Quhai for hir saik, with speir and scheld, Preiffis maist mychtelye in the feld [etc.]. 1595 *Reg. Mag. Sig. Scot.* 116/2 With jak, knaipisca, speir and suord. 1611 BIBLE *Jer.* vi. 23 They shall lay hold on bowe and speare. 1725 POPE *Odyssey* x. 169, I climb'd a cliff, with spear and sword in hand. 1810 SCOTT *Lady of Lake* V. xi, And still, from copse and heather deep, Fancy saw spear and broadsword peep. 1849 AYTOUN *Lays Scott. Caval.* 70 Why go you forth..With spear and belted brand?

†**c.** Const. *of* (peace or war). ***spear of peace***, a blunt spear used in jousting. *Obs.*

a 1400 *Sir Degrev.* 1177 Tak ether of ȝow a spere, Bothe of pes and of were. *Ibid.* 1261 To gret sperus of pese Bothe these lordes hem chese. 1508 KENNEDY *Flyting w. Dunbar* 545 Deulbere, thy spere of were, but feir, thou yelde.

†**d.** The sharp head of a pike. *Obs. rare.*

1690 *Exercise of Foot* 121 Trail your Pikes with the Spears behind. *Ibid.* 144 The Pikemen Charge their Pikes to the Front, the Spears in a Line Breast high.

e. *Mil.* One of the transverse spikes or poles of a cheval-de-frise.

1823 CRABB *Technol. Dict.* 1828 SPEARMAN *Brit. Gunner* (ed. 2) 142 Weight, Dimension, &c. of Chevaux-De-Frize... Barrel, Length 9 ft. 5 in. Spears, 20. Length 6 ft. 1834–47 J. S. MACAULAY *Field Fortif.* (1851) 82 The spears of the chevaux-de-frise should be so arranged as to present three rows of points to the enemy. 1876 VOYLE & STEVENSON *Milit. Dict.* (ed. 3) s.v. *Chevaux de frise*, Each length is composed of a barrel or stout beam.., with strong sharp spears driven through it, in two or more different directions.

2. a. In *transf.* and *fig.* uses.

c 897 K. ÆLFRED *Gregory's Past. C.* xxxv. 244 Ða speru ðære soðfæstnesse, ðæt sindon haliȝra ȝewrita manunga. *a* 1300 *Cursor M.* 28046 O licheri agayn þe spere Wit chastite þou sal þe were. *c* 1470 HENRY *Wallace* II. 231 Compleyne for hym that was your aspre sper. 1500–20 DUNBAR *Poems* lxxxiv. 40 Inconstance..; Secreit invy, and of dispyt the speir. 1546 J. HEYWOOD *Prov.* (1867) 29 Will is a shrewde boy... A gentle white spurre, and at neede a sure speare. 1593 SHAKS. *Rich. II*, I. i. 171, I am..Pierc'd to the soule with slanders venom'd speare. 1820 SHELLEY *Prometh. Unb.* I. 31 The crawling glaciers pierce me with the spears Of their moon-freezing crystals. 1873 M. ARNOLD *Lit. & Dogma* (1876) 328 The spear of Butler's reasoning. 1930 R. CAMPBELL *Adamastor* 60 A starved mongrel..From where he crouched, a thrilling spear of pain, Hurled forth his Alleluia to the sky. 1934 T. S. ELIOT *Rock* ii. 78 Encompassed with enemies armed with the spears of mistaken ideals.

b. The 'sack'; dismissal. *Austral. slang.*

1912 in Stewart & Keesing *Old Bush Songs* (1957) 273 I've been many years a shearer and I fancied I could shear, I've shore for Rouse of Guntawung and always missed the spear. 1941 BAKER *Dict. Austral. Slang* 69 *Get the spear*, to be dismissed from a job.

†**3.** In allusive phrases or uses. **a.** ***under a spear***, under one banner, pennon, or flag. *Obs.*$^{-1}$

1297 R. GLOUC. (Rolls) 11861 So þat þer were To & tuenti kniȝtes vnder a spere.

†**b.** ***to sell at the spear, to put***, etc., ***under the spear***, to sell by auction. ***to pass under the spear***, to 'come under the hammer'. *Obs.*

After the common L. phrase *sub hasta vendere*.

1600 HOLLAND *Livy* II. xvii. 55 The rest of the inhabitants were sold at the speare in ouvert market like slaves. *Ibid.* XXIII. xxxii. 496 Their fields he would lay wast; sell their servants in port sale at the speare. 1611 B. JONSON *Catiline* II. i, When you see..that..their Houses, and fine Gardens [are] giuen away, And all their goods, vnder the Speare. 1689 EVELYN *Let. to Pepys* 12 Aug. in *E.'s Diary* (1827) IV. 319 The noblest library that ever pass'd under the speare at outcry. 1709 MRS. MANLEY *Secret Mem.* (1736) IV. 96 They persuaded him to put all the Furniture of the House immediately under the Spear.

†**c.** ***stroke of the spear***: (see quot. and FEATHER *sb.* 11 b).

1753 *Chambers' Cycl.* Suppl. s.v., The feather of a horse, called the *stroke of the spear*, is a mark in the neck, or near the shoulder, of some Barbs [etc.].

4. a. A soldier armed with or carrying a spear; a spearman. Now *arch.*

c 1205 LAY. 7453 Com of Muriene, moni spere kene. *a* 1400 *Sir Degrev.* 319 The best mene that he ledde, He hadd y-lefft home to wedde, With ffyffty spers is he ffledd. *c* 1450 *Contin. Brut* 580 One Watkyn Ruskyn, a gentill man and a gud spere, was slayn at þe wynnyng of þe same bullewerk. 1475 *Bk. Noblesse* (Roxb.) 38 Ser John Chaundos,..whiche had bene in many batailes, and had the governaunce of M[l]. speris. *a* 1548 HALL *Chron., Hen. VI*, 55 The Erle of Huntyngdone,..with twoo M. archers, and foure hundred speres, was sente into Gascoyne. *a* 1578 LINDESAY (Pitscottie) *Chron. Scot.* (S.T.S.) II. 39, ij[c] speiris witht the earle of Angus and ij[c] witht my lord governour. 1618 BOLTON *Florus* (1636) 55 Caius Minutius, a speare in the fourth Legion. 1820 SCOTT *Monast.* xxxv, That plump of spears that are spurring on so fast. 1885 RUSKIN *Pleas. Eng.* 113 He sent..for some German knights, and got five hundred spears.

†**b.** (See quots. and PENSIONER 2.) *Obs.*

1539 CRANMER *Let. to Cromwell* in *Rem.* (1833) I. 296 Edward Askew..is by some nobleman preferred unto the room of one of these new spears in the Court. 1540 WRIOTHESLEY *Chron.* (Camden) I. 112 This yeare [1539] the kinge made many yong gentlemen speres, and gave them 5 l. a peece. *a* 1548 HALL *Chron., Hen. VIII*, 6 Also this yere [1509], the kyng ordeined fiftie Gentle menne to bee speres, euery of theim to haue an Archer, a Dimilaunce and a Custrell, and euery Spere to haue three greate Horses. *Ibid.* 237 b, In December [1539] were appointed to wayte on the kynges hyghnes person fiftie Gentelmen called Pencioners or Speares, lyke as they were in the first yere of the kyng.

c. A hunter or sportsman who uses a spear; a pig-sticker.

1849 EASTWICK *Dry Leaves* 75 One of the best spears who ever chased the wild boar over wide plain and tangled hill. 1863 TREVELYAN *Compet. Wallah* (1866) 139 Mr. Mildred, an indigo planter, a first-rate spear and rough-rider.

5. a. A sharp-pointed weapon used for various purposes; esp. one for catching fish, a leister.

Also with defining terms, as *eel-, fish-, salmon-, trout-spear.*

1551– [see SALMON *sb.*[1] 4]. 1555– [see EEL-SPEAR]. 1611 [see FISH *sb.*[1] 6 b.]. *a* 1700 EVELYN *Diary* 22 July 1654, Abounding in trouts catch'd by speare in the night. 1766 *State of Proc., A. Macdonald* v. *Dk. Gordon* Pursuer's Proof 13 The fish..were killed and taken out by spears. 1774 GOLDSM. *Nat. Hist.* (1776) VI. 208 They renew their attacks, till the whale begins to be quite enfeebled.., when they plunge their longer spears into various parts of its body. 1815 SCOTT *Guy M.* xxvi, This chase, in which the fish is pursued and struck with barbed spears,..is much practised at the mouth of the Esk. 1840 BLAINE *Encycl. Rural Sports* §2889 The salmon is also caught with a spear, which they dart into him as he swims near the surface of the water.

b. A pointed iron bar. *rare.*

1607 DEKKER *Jests* G ij, If they haue..taken note of any casement, without a speere going vp in the middle. *Ibid.* G ij b.

c. A prong *of* a fork. (Cf. SPEER *sb.*[2])

1739 BAKER in *Phil. Trans.* XLI. 135 A Young Woman..received a Wound just in the Pupil of her right Eye, by the Spear of a common Fork. 1748 AERY *Ibid.* XLV. 412 She received a Wound in the Cornea of her right Eye, by the Spear of a common Fork, which also divided the Uvea.

6. a. *pl.* The thorns or prickles of a plant, the spines or spikes of a hedgehog, sharp fins of a fish, etc. Chiefly *poet.*; now *rare.*

[1503 DUNBAR *Thistle & Rose* 130 Vpone the awfull Thrissill scho beheld, And saw him kepit with a busche of speiris.] 1607 TOPSELL *Four-f. Beasts* 279 The Hedghog rowleth vpon the Serpent..and killeth his aduersary, carrying the flesh vpon his speares. 1693 DRYDEN, etc. *Juvenal* iv. (1697) 91 Mark the pointed spears That from thy Hand on his pierc'd Back he wears! *Note.* He makes the Flatterer call the sharp Fins rising on the Fishes back, Spears. 1821 CLARE *Vill. Minstr.* II. 161 The very bramble, weeping 'Neath dewy tear-drops that its spears surround. 1827 —— *Sheph. Cal.* Feb. ix. 23 The hedgehog,..As shepherd-dog his haunt espies,..rolls up in a ball of spears.

b. The sting of a reptile or insect, esp. of a bee. Now *Sussex dial.*

1608 TOPSELL *Serpents* 172 Nor yet he when [he] with his angry mouth Doth byte, such paines and torments bringeth As other Serpents..When with his teeth and speare he stingeth. 1609 C. BUTLER *Fem. Mon.* A iij b, The speere she hath is but little and not halfe so long as the other Bees. *Ibid.* A v b, Hir speere she [the bee] is very loth to vse, if by any other meanes she can shift hir enimy. *a* 1700 KEN *Edmund* Poet. Wks. 1721 II. 90 Into his tendrest Parts..the pertinacious Legion dart their spears. 1721 BRADLEY *Philos. Acc. Wks. Nat.* 149 Our Gnat, which is of the unarmed Kind, having no Spear in its Mouth. 1875 PARISH *Sussex Dial.*, *Spear*, the sting of a bee. 1889 *Longman's Mag.* July 269 The best thing..when you have taken 'the spear' out, is to rub the place with a leek.

7. A beam or ray *of* light.

c 1850 LOWELL *Above & Below* I. iii, 'Tis from these heights alone your eyes The advancing spears of day can see. 1894 HALL CAINE *Manxman* 277 A spear of candle-light shot from her door.

II. *attrib.* and *Comb.*

8. Simple attrib., in the sense 'of or belonging to a spear', as ***spear-blade***, †***-block***, ***-butt***, †***-pile*** (= shaft), ***-tip***, etc.; also denoting distance or measurement, as ***spear-cast***, ***-length***, ***-throw***; and miscellaneous, as ***spear-arm***, ***-forest***, ***-print***, ***-storm***, ***-stroke***, ***surge***, ***-thrust***.

1880 BROWNING *Dram. Idyls, Echetlos* 5 Up, back, out, down—was the *spear-arm play. 1880 F. WITTI *Diary* in J. Hatton *New Ceylon* iv. (1881) 99 To the one end of the blowpipe is always made fast a *spear-blade. 1543 *Acc. Ld. High Treas. Scot.* VIII. 223 For certane *speir blokis boucht ..to his grace in Ayr,..xv li. 1853 KINGSLEY *Hypatia* vi. 73 An obedience which the Roman soldiers could only have compelled by hard blows of the *spear-butt. 1865 MORRIS *Jason* x. 209 As in the stream they lay A *spear-cast from the shore. 1946 S. SPENDER *European Witness* xiv. 217 A country of clustered *spear-forests and gloomy heaths. 13.. *Gaw. & Gr. Knt.* 2316 He sprit forth spenne fote more þen a *spere lenþe. *c* 1400 *Destr. Troy* 3698 Hit spirit vp spitiously fyue speire lenght. 1585 T. WASHINGTON tr. *Nicholay's Voy.* I. viii. 9 The ditch..was only seuen fadomes broade, and twoo speare lengths deep. 1890 DOYLE *White Company* xxxvi, He fell within a spear-length of the English line. 1638 BRATHWAIT *Psalmes Paraphr.* cli, Six hundred iron shekels masse upon my *speare-pile playes. 1911 E. POUND *Canzoni* 4 Deep in my heart that *spear-print stays, That wound I got beyond the waters. 1848 LYTTON *K. Arthur* III. xlviii, May Harold, thus confronting all, Pass from the *spear-storm to the Golden Hall. 1835 *Court Mag.* VI. 35/2 The captive English,..awaiting the *spear-stroke with unblenching fortitude. 1900 CHESTERTON *Wild Knight & Other Poems* 103 The crest of the *spear-surge. 1884 J. COLBORNE *Hicks Pasha* 46 Their many-coloured *spear-tassels dropping on their shoulders. 1892 RIDER HAGGARD *Nada* 28 The men were running..with the length of a *spear-throw between them. 1825 SCOTT *Talism.* xxvi, With sword-cut and *spear-thrust all hack'd and pierced through. 1930 T. S. ELIOT tr. *St.-J. Perse's Anabasis* 43 The horsemen..feeding on their *spear-tips the pure disasters of sunshine. 1857 GOSSE *Omphalos* xii. 362 It falls to the ground before the *spear-touch of our Ithuriel. 1895 *Cath. Mag.* Aug. 210 The *spear-wound in His side.

9. General combs. **a.** With agent-nouns, as ***spear-bearer***, ***-fisher***, ***-fisherman***, ***-hurler***, ***-planer***.

1449 in Sharp *Cov. Myst.* (1825) 193 Item, ij sperberrers ..ij d. *c* 1515 *Cocke Lorell's B.* 10 Tankarde berers,..and spere planers. 1876 G. W. COX *Gen. Hist. Greece* II. i. 103 His spear-bearer Gyges. 1895 JANE MENZIES *Cynewulf's Elene* 25 The great spear-hurler, who the hosts to battle led. 1951 T. C. ROUGHLEY *Fish & Fisheries of Australia* ix. 309 Members will not..seek quarrels with line-fishermen or other spear-fishermen regarding priority rights of fishing at any place. 1962 *Underwater Swimming* ('Know the Game' Ser.) 19/1 The spearfisherman should always carry a knife. *Ibid.*, An added safety device is to have a float anchored in the diving area to which the spearfisher can go to rest or leave his catch. 1982 *Times* 21 July 3/3 Dr Paul Cragg, a biologist, was in favour of resuming grants for spearfishermen.

b. With verbal sbs. (objective or instrumental), as ***spear-bearing***, ***-breaking***, ***-fishing*** (hence, as a back-formation, ***spear-fish*** vb. intr. and trans.), ***-pricking***, etc.; also similative, as ***spear-flashing***.

1861 PALEY *Æschylus* (ed. 2) *Pers.* 149 *note*, Archers, or Persians, are again opposed to *spear-bearing Greeks. 1848 BUCKLEY *Iliad* 265 *Spear-brandishing Polydamas came as an avenger. 1823 SCOTT *Quentin D.* xxvi, I should otherwise have had *spear-breaking between you and my cousin of Orleans. 1962 *Times* 6 Apr. 7/2 Sail, snorkel, skin-dive, *spear-fish in tropical Florida. 1963 *Harper's Bazaar* Jan. 65/1 On the Côte d'Azur, many of the big fish have been.. spear-fished out of sight. 1973 J. JONES *Touch of Danger* xix. 106, I expostulated... Sonny..was no adept with flippers or speargun. 1601 *Reg. Mag. Sig. Scot.* 392/2 Lie cobill, curroch et *speir fischingis super aqua de Spey. **1945** Spear-fishing [see FLIPPER *sb.*² 1 b]. **1960** M. A. GABRIELSEN et al. *Aquatics Handbk.* xiv. 102/1 Spear fishing is becoming a popular competitive as well as recreational sport. **1973** J. JONES *Touch of Danger* xix. 107 Sonny was against spearfishing for sport. **1937** BLUNDEN *Elegy* 78 Against high blue *Spear-flashing white the spire. **1895** SIR H. MAXWELL *Duke Britain* viii. 117 Forced by heavy blows and *spear-prickings to resume progress. **1865** MORRIS *Jason* VI. 485 *Spear-shaking warrior and slim-ankled maid. **1895** K. GRAHAME *Gold. Age* 98 His *spear-splintering crash of tourney. **1828** P. CUNNINGHAM *N.S. Wales* (ed. 3) II. 42 By means of their perpetual wars and the practices of *spear-throwing, child-murder, and concubinage. **1848** BUCKLEY *Iliad* 26 *Spear-wielding auxiliaries from many cities.

c. With past pples. (instrumental), as ***spear-bound, -fallen, -famed, -pierced, -shaken, -stuck, -tipped***, etc.

1816 H. G. KNIGHT *Ilderim* 280 The *spear-bound steeds that ready harness'd fed. **1824** SYMMONS *Agamemnon* 104 The blood-drop..from the *spear-fallen man Drips apace. **1848** BUCKLEY *Iliad* 42 These, *spear-famed Idomeneus commanded. **1863** J. H. NEWMAN *Verses Var. Occas.* 33 Faint shadows of the *spear-pierced side. **1947** S. SPENDER *Poems of Dedication* IV. 56 Above the destroyed city reborn city..Tower of wings climbing *spear-shaken skies. **1848** BUCKLEY *Iliad* 43 He killed Mynetes and *spear-skilled Epistrophus. **1943** D. GASCOYNE *Poems 1937–42* 5 Whose are these hollow red-filmed eyes And thorn-spiked head and *spear-stuck side? **1870** MORRIS *Earthly Par.* III. IV. 364 In forefront of battle let him fall; Or..on some foeman's *spear-swept wall. **1954** W. FAULKNER *Fable* 132 The *spear-tipped iron fence beyond which the three sentries flanked the blank door beneath the three morning-windy flags.

d. With adjs., as ***spear-headed, -pointed, -straight***, etc.

1561 *Burning St. Paul's* ℙ 2 (Camden), A long and a speare pointed flame of fier. **1598** BARRET *Theor. Warres* II. i. 20 A speare-headed staffe, sharpe pointed with iron. **1753** *Chambers' Cycl.* Suppl. s.v. *Phaseolus*, The American *phaseolus*, with a sinuated and spear-pointed leaf. **1777** POTTER *Æschylus* (1779) I. 184 Sev'n chiefs of high command, In arms spear-proof, take their appointed stand. **1846** LANDOR *Exam. Shaks.* Wks. II. 295 Rushes spear high. **1848** J. R. LOWELL *Poems* 2nd Ser. 69 A stem..Standing spear-straight in the waist-deep moss. **1873** SPON *Workshop Rec.* Ser. I. 59/2 No spear-pointed drill can be tempered hard enough not to break. **1919** J. MASEFIELD *Reynard the Fox* II. 107 With spear-straight stern.

e. In some specific names, as ***spear-bill, -billed*** (grebe), ***spear-leaf, -nosed*** (bat).

1827 GRIFFITH tr. *Cuvier* II. 9 We may here add the Lunette,..spear-nosed bat. *Ibid.* V. 69 *Phyllostoma Hastatum* (Spear-leaf Phyllostome, or Javelin Bat). **1884** COUES *N. Amer. Birds* 793 *Æchmophorus*, Spear-bill [*Index*, Spear-billed] Grebes.

10. a. Special combinations, as **spear-axe**, a spear with an axe-shaped head; **spear-carrier**, a carrier of a spear, a spearman: used *transf.* as (*a*) orig. *Theatr. slang*, an actor with a walk-on part; hence, an unimportant participant; (*b*) *U.S. colloq.*, a proponent or 'standard-bearer' (cf. SPEARHEAD 1 b); † **spear-egg-shaped** *a.*, *Bot.* lanceolate-obovate; † **spear-field**, the field of battle; † **spear-foot** (see quot.); **spear gun**, a type of weapon used in spearfishing which operates by firing a detachable harpoon; also *attrib.*; hence **spear-gunner**; **spear-hand**, the hand with which a spear is usually held, thrown, etc.; the right hand or side; **spear-hook**, *U.S.* a kind of snap-hook or spring-hook for taking fish (*Cent. Dict.*); **spear-nail** (see quot.); **spear-play**, exercise or fighting with spears; **spear-pyrites**, *Min.* a variety of marcasite or white iron pyrites; **spear-running**, jousting with spears; now *arch.*; **spear-side** (after OE. *on spere-healfe*), the male line of descent; † **spear silver**, *Sc.* a form of military tax or levy; † **spear-stick**, a spiked walking-stick; **spear tackle** *Austral.*, an illegal tackle in rugby football in which a player is lifted and thrust to the ground head first; hence as *v. trans.*; **spear-thrower**, an implement used to aid the throwing of a spear.

1865 J. H. INGRAHAM *Pillar of Fire* xi. 129 The offensive weapons of the [Egyptian] army are the..*spear-axe [etc.]. **1960** *New Yorker* 13 Aug. 97/1 The 'Quartet' is full of characters who in one novel may seem irritatingly superfluous *spear-carriers,..but who in the 'Quartet' turn out to be members of a literary repertory company. **1963** *Times* 20 May 12/5 Most of those spear-carriers not only don't know where the United States is but they don't know where they are themselves. **1967** *N.Y. Times* 21 May 26/1 Dr. King had 'emerged as the public spear-carrier of a civil disobedience program'. **1976** *Times* 18 Mar. 10 In Wisconsin on the same day Representative Morris Udall, the 'liberal-progressive' spear carrier, will have to win to stay in the race. **1981** N. MARSH *Black Beech & Honeydew* (rev. ed.) x. 215 The students..would begin to accept the enormous challenge of a Shakespeare play and their own real importance, if only as spear-carriers, in doing so. **1982** *Sunday Sun-Times* (Chicago) 20 June 100/1 By the time Breakfast at Wimbledon telecasts are beamed into the United States on Fourth of July weekend, American tennis pros Davis, Dunk and Hardie will have vacated their present lodging and be long gone from the venerable tournament that they graced momentarily as spear-carriers. **1796** WITHERING *Brit. Plants* (ed. 3) I. 82 **Spear egg-shaped*,..shaped like a spear towards the base, and like an egg towards its extremity. *Ibid.* II. 474 Flower-scales spear-eggshaped, in pairs. *c* **1470** *Gol. & Gaw.* 1238 To speid thame our the *spere-feild enspringing thai sprent. **1753** *Chambers' Cycl.* Suppl., **Spear-foot*, of a horse, is the far-foot behind. **1951** T. C. ROUGHLEY *Fish & Fisheries Austral.* ix. 303 The sport of fishing with spears or *spear-guns under water..has had only a brief history. *Ibid.* 304 Most Australian spear-gun fishermen use a gun with rubber as the motive power. **1979** J. LEASOR *Love & Land Beyond* i. 7 The..five-pronged fork of an underwater spear gun. **1951** T. C. ROUGHLEY *Fish & Fisheries Austral.* ix. 308 Those responsible for such an attitude know little of the *spear-gunner's activities. **1728** CHAMBERS *Cycl.* s.v. *Hand*, *Spear-Hand, or Sword-Hand, is used for a Horseman's Right-Hand. **1824** SYMMONS *Agamemnon* 12 On the spear-hand and by the seat of state. **1875** KNIGHT *Dict. Mech.* 2255/2 **Spear-nail*, one with a spear-shaped point. *c* **1640** J. SMYTH *Lives Berkeleys* (1883) I. 325 Given to his Esquiers for to play at *Spearplay at Bristoll, 26ˢ 8ᵈ. **1885** C. J. LYALL *Anc. Arab. Poet.* 96 Steeds, in the spear-play skilled. **1894** *Geogr. Jrnl.* III. 479, I had the pleasure of witnessing a spear-play between two parties. **1837** DANA *Min.* 405 White Iron Pyrites, *Pyrites rhombicus*..*Spear Pyrites. **1865** WATTS *Dict. Chem.* III. 402 White Iron pyrites, Marcasite, Radiated pyrites, Spear pyrites. *c* **1550** ROLLAND *Crt. Venus* IV. 597 Than tuik thay in Iurnayis of Tornament, And *speir rinning, with mony Interpryis. **1823** SCOTT *Quentin D.* xiv, At the spear-running of Strasbourg. **1861** PEARSON *Early & Mid. Ages* 122 In his [Alfred's] will he declares his intention of..leaving his land on the *spear-side. **1870** LOWELL *Study Wind.* 246 Such and such qualities he got from a grandfather on the spear side. **1496** *Acc. Ld. High Treas. Scot.* I. 324 To gadir in the *spere siluer of Perth, Forfare, and Striuelinschire. **1801** tr. *Gabrielli's Myst. Husb.* II. 135 His *spear stick, pelisse, &c. were at the Curate's. **1969** *Sun-Herald* (Sydney) 13 July 36/2 Canterbury were penalised for a *spear tackle on Cavanagh. **1977** *Telegraph* (Brisbane) 8 Nov. 3/3 He was injured after he was allegedly spear-tackled... A player is spear-tackled when an opponent tackles low, lifts the man with the ball high, turns him over and thrusts him into the ground head first. **1871** TYLOR *Prim. Cult.* I. 60 The highest people known to have used the *spear-thrower proper are the Aztecs.

b. In the names of plants, trees, etc., as **spear arum**, † **crowfoot, -fern, -flower, -lily, -(plume) thistle, -wood** (see quots.).

1845–50 MRS. LINCOLN *Lect. Bot.* App. 220/1 *Spear arum, *Rensselaeria*. **1597** GERARDE *Herbal* II. ccclv. 815 Called..in English *Speare Crowfoote, Spearewoort, and Banewoort. **1867** W. W. SMYTH *Coal & Coal-mining* 37 The *Odontopteris*, or tooth-fern, and *Lonchopteris*, or *spear-fern, are [fossil] genera which occur less frequently. **1891** *Cent. Dict.*, **Spear-flower*, a tree or shrub of the large tropical and subtropical genus *Ardisia* of the *Myrsineæ*. **1889** MAIDEN *Usef. Native Pl.* 621 *Doryanthes excelsa*... '*Spear Lily.' 'Giant Lily.' **1855** MISS PRATT *Flower. Pl.* III. 231 (*Spear Plume Thistle.) Heads of flowers large, mostly solitary. **1753** *Chambers' Cycl.* Suppl. s.v. *Thistle*, The broad-leaved *spear-Thistle. **1777** JACOB *Cat. Plants* 19 *Carduus lanceolatus*, Spear-Thistle. **1844** H. STEPHENS *Bk. Farm* III. 1066 The biennial spear-thistle, *Cnicus lanceolatus*, the spines of which breaking in the flesh, give acute pain when touched. **1872** MACMILLAN *True Vine* vii. 320 In the common spear-thistle, each plant produces upwards of a hundred seed-vessels. **1866** *Treas. Bot.* 1077/2 *Spearwood, *Acacia doratoxylon*. **1874** *Ibid.* Suppl. 1343/2 Spearwood, also *Eucalyptus doratoxylon*.

c. In the names of fishes, as **spear-beak, dog, -fish** (see quots.).

1896 LYDEKKER *Roy. Nat. Hist.* V. 507 The extinct Jurassic *spear-beaks (*Aspidorhynchus*) constitute a second family. **1848** *Zoologist* VI. 1975 Picked Dog, *Spear Dog, *Spinax acanthias*. **1882** JORDAN & GILBERT *Syn. Fishes N. Amer.* 119 *Carpiodes cyprinus*... Quillback; *Spear-fish; Sail-fish; Skimback. *Ibid.* 420 *Tetrapturus albidus*, Bill-fish; Spear-fish. **1888** GOODE *Amer. Fishes* 241 In Cuba, the Spear-fishes are called '*Aguja*'.

spear (spɪə(r)), *sb.*² Forms: 5–6 **spere**, 6 **speere**, **speare**, 9 **speer**, 7– **spear**. [Irregular variant of SPIRE *sb.*¹, perh. influenced by prec.]

† **1.** A spire of a church or other building; a pyramid. *Obs.*

a **1490** BOTONER *Itin.* (Nasmith, 1778) 221 Altitudo de le spere..sicut modo fracto continet 200 pedes. [*Ibid.* 241 Spera sive pinaculum cum turri quadrata ecclesiæ Beatæ Mariæ de Radclyff.] **1509** BARCLAY *Shyp of Folys* (1570) 169 Chemnis also, as Diodorus sayes, Builded a speere hye and wonderous... This speere was costly, dere and sumptuous. **1570–6** LAMBARDE *Peramb. Kent* (1826) 260 The speare or steeple of which Churche was fired by lightening. *c* **1605** *Acc. Bk. W. Wray*, in *Antiquary* XXXII. 212 The great spere of St. Wilfrides steple. **1653** H. MORE *Antid. Ath.* I. iv. §2 If you say it consists of Points,..I can demonstrate that every Spear or Spire-Steeple is as thick as it is long. **1663** in Strype *Stow's Surv.* (1754) I. II. vii. 443/1 Your Lordship being the Owner of the greatest Part of the said Speare or Steeple. **1755** *Mem. Capt. P. Drake* II. iii. 79 A great and rich Cloyster,..where there is a very fine Church that has four Spears.

2. a. The plumule or rudimentary shoot of a seed; *spec.* the acrospire of grain.

1647 HERRICK *Noble Numbers, To Finde God* Tell me the motes, dust, sands, and speares Of Corn, when Summer shakes his eares. **1676** M. COOK *Forest-Trees* 63 Watering them [nuts, etc.] may kill them, by making the kernel swell too hastily, and so crack it before the spear causeth it; or it may Mould and stupifie the spear. *a* **1722** LISLE *Husb.* (1757) 91 By the time the spear is shot under ground the corn is well rooted. **1886** ELWORTHY *W. Som. Word-bk.* s.v., In malting or other germination of grain, the *spear* is that sprout which develops into the future stalk, as distinct from the shoots which form rootlets.

b. A blade, shoot, or sprout (*of* grass, etc.).

1841 CATLIN *N. Amer. Ind.* lv. (1844) II. 203 Not a spear of grass is broken or bent by his feet. **1865** *Athenæum* No. 1979. 444/3 Leaves of trees and spears of corn. **1873** JOAQUIN MILLER *Life among the Modocs* xx. 253 He pointed to the new leaves of the trees, [and] the spears that were bursting through the ground. **1896** HOWELLS *Impress. & Exp.* 283 Every spear of grass had been torn from it.

c. Similarly of hair.

1852 MRS. STOWE *Uncle Tom's C.* xxv, If they's to pull every spear o' har out o' my head it wouldn't do no good.

d. The edible shoot, including stem and tip or head, of asparagus or of sprouting broccoli (esp. calabrese).

1952 *Quick Freezing* Jan. 9/1 At a Birds Eye press conference held recently it was stated that three new products have been added to that range. These are: (1) Chicken livers... (2) Broccoli spears, broccoli cuts... (3) Pineapple slices in syrup. **1966** *Harrod's Food News* Sept. 2/1 Brocolli Spears—8 oz. 2/11 *Ibid.* 5/1 Asparagus spears Spanish (5½ in. long)—17 oz. tin 4/9. **1969** *Oxf. Bk. Food Plants* 162/1 Asparagus..is usually considered to be a luxury vegetable. The part eaten is the young shoot or 'spear'. **1974** P. WESTLAND *Taste of Country* ii. 37/2 Cover with the cooked broccoli spears and then the cheese sauce. **1979** *Sunset* Apr. 178/2 A light entrée, it's especially good when accompanied with sliced ham..and additional spears of freshly cooked asparagus.

3. *south. dial.* **a.** *collect.* Reeds, esp. as a material for thatching, or for plastering upon.

1794 *Trans. Soc. Arts* XII. 144 This prevents its being overrun with spear and sedge. **1819** COBBETT *Weekly Reg.* 13 Feb. 658 In England we sometimes thatch with reeds, which in Hampshire, are called *spear*. **1894** *Times* 14 June 14/1 The long coarse herbage which fringes the banks of rivers and other streams, and is locally termed 'spear', makes excellent thatch for hay and corn stacks.

b. A stem or stalk of a reed, osier, etc.

1844 W. BARNES *Poems Rur. Life* (1848) 388 *Spears*,..the stems of the reed *arundo phragmites*, sometimes employed instead of laths to hold plaster. **1905** *Westm. Gaz.* 12 Aug. 5/1 She walked down to the water's edge, through the green osier spears, bareheaded.

c. *attrib.* in ***spear-bed, reed***.

1812 COL. HAWKER *Diary* (1893) I. 46 Second storeys of many houses of spear reed, cemented..with plaster. **1863** WISE *New Forest* 287 The phrase 'spire-bed', or 'spear-bed field', is very common, meaning a particular field, near where the 'spires' grow. **1874** T. HARDY *Far fr. Mad. Crowd* I. xxii. 251, I believe Farmer Boldwood kissed her behind the spear-bed at the sheep-washing.

spear (spɪə(r)), *sb.*³ Also 6 spere. [Variant of SPIRE *sb.*³]

1. A young tree, esp. a young oak; a sapling. Also attrib. in ***spear oak, tree***.

1543 *Mem. Fountains* (Surtees) 412 Yonge saplings, speres of okes and ashes. **1891** *Pall Mall G.* 23 Mar. 3/3 Large numbers of spear trees are destroyed while decaying pollards are left standing. **1895** *Daily News* 20 May 6/5 Bury Wood, which is mainly composed of spear oaks, horn-beam, and blackthorn.

† **b.** *transf.* A stripling, youth. Also *fig. Obs.*

1526 SKELTON *Magnyf.* 947 In faythe, Lyberte is nowe a lusty spere. *a* **1529** —— *Agst. Garnesche* iii. 41 At Gynys when ye ware But a slendyr spere, Dekkyd lewdly in your gere.

2. *techn.* A pump-rod. Also *attrib.*

1729 CAPT. W. WRIGLESWORTH *MS. Log-bk. of the 'Lyell'* 9 Oct., Took in..18 small Sparrs, and 9 Spears. **1731** *Phil. Trans.* XXXVII. 7 The four Necks of the Crank have each an Iron Spear, or Rod, fixed at their upper Ends to the respective Libra, or Lever. **1750** BLANCKLEY *Nav. Expos.* 124 Stave or Spear (Pump Hand) is a long Rod of Iron with an Eye at the upper End, which Hooks to the Brake. **1824** *Mechanic's Mag.* No. 43. 238 Which requires least manual labour in the case of a common ship-pump, a long or a short spear? **1849** GREENWELL *Coal-trade Terms, Northumb. & Durh.* 49 Spears are made of Memel or Norway fir, in lengths of about 40 feet, and joined together by spear-plates. **1862** *Times* 28 Jan., The engine from which the pumps derive their motive power..and the great beam to which their 'spears' or rods were attached.

spear, *sb.*⁴ *Dev.* and *Cornw. dial.* [Variant of SPAR *sb.*⁴] A thatching rod. Also *attrib.*

1837 J. F. PALMER *Dialogue Dev. Dial.* Gloss. 84 *Spears* or *Spear-sticks*, the pointed sticks, doubled and twisted, used for thatching. **1891** *Hartland Gloss.* s.v., Slatting..shoots of withy or nut-halse by means of a spear-hook, which is like a narrow-bladed bill-hook. **1899** BOURNE *Billy Bray* 55 (E.D.D.), I told the farmer to bring three hundred sheaves [of reed]..., and some spears for them.

spear (spɪə(r)), *sb.*⁵ *rare.* [f. SPEAR *v.*³] The act of spearing or striking with a spear, *spec.* in pig-sticking.

1903 SIR M. G. GERARD *Leaves fr. Diaries* vii. 224 The gainer of first spear in the final heat becoming the winner of the Cup. *Ibid.*, The rule is that upon anyone touching the pig and calling 'Spear', should any other man..have reason to question the claim, he must shout 'No spear'.

spear, variant of SPEER *sb.*¹ (screen, etc.).

spear (spɪə(r)), *v.*¹ *Obs.* (exc. *dial.*). Forms: 3 **speren**, 5 **speryn** (**speyryn**); 4–5 **spere**, **sper** (4 **spir-**); 6 **speare** 6, 9 *dial.* **spear**. [a. MLG. *speren* (LG. *speren, speeren, speiren*), related to MDu. *sperren*, OHG. *sperran*: see SPAR *v.*¹

It is clear from rimes and other evidence that the pret. forms *sperde, sperd*, common in the 13th and 14th centuries, usually belong to this verb and not to *sperre* SPAR *v.*¹]

1. *trans.* To shut or close (a door, lid, etc.) firmly or securely; † to bar or block (a way).

c **1250** *Gen. & Ex.* 384 He ben don ut of blisses erd, Cherubin hauet ðe gates sperd. *a* **1300** *Cursor M.* 5618 In þis kist þe barn sco did. Quen it spird was wit þe lid,..Sco laid it on þe water fame. *Ibid.* 18086 Spers [*Gött.* Speris] your yates, þis es na gamen. *c* **1330** R. BRUNNE *Chron. Wace* (Rolls) 13166 Sire Richer saw, & Beduer herde, þat þer enemis þer weyes sperde. *a* **1400–50** *Alexander* 5545 In at a wicket he went & wynly it speris. ? **1449** *Paston Lett.* I. 83 And qhan he com thedder, the dors were fast sperid. **1542** BECON *Potation for Lent* I viij b, Heauen gates were speared agaynst vs for the sin of our first father Adam. *c* **1550** BALE *Image both Ch.* (East) 30 Speared is Gods Temple, when his true worshipping is hid. **1894** in HESLOP *Northumbld. Gloss.*

b. With *up*.

1445 in *Anglia* XXVIII. 275 Where as townys were longe speryd vp, he dare sette wide þe yates. **1538** BALE *Thre Lawes* 1100, I close vp heauen, And speare vp paradyce.

2. In general sense: To close, shut, etc.

a **1225** *Ancr. R.* 80 þet ȝe þertoȝeines..tunen [*C.* speren] ower eiðurles. *a* **1340** HAMPOLE *Psalter* x. 5 His egh lidys ..þat now ere oppynd & now sperd. *Ibid.* cxl. 3 Swa be oure lippis opyn til shrift, and sperd til excusynge of syn. **1387** TREVISA *Higden* (Rolls) VII. 121 For overmoche sorwe the herte is stoken and spered. *a* **1400–50** *Alexander* 3649 Brant vp he sittis, Springis out a spere, sperid all þe platis. *a* **1425** tr. *Arderne's Treat. Fistula*, etc. 39 þe lacertes and þe synowes speryng and opnyng þe lure. *c* **1440** *Promp. Parv.* 283/1 Lacyn, or spere wythe a lace, *fibulo*. *c* **1550** BALE *Image Both Ch.* (Wyer) E v, So was it [a book] afore speared by the decre of God. **1560** BECON *Policy War* Wks. 1564 I. 139 Howe many wynke and speare theyr eyes, because they wyll not se it.

3. To shut up or confine (a person) in a prison or other place. Also *fig.*

c **1250** *Gen. & Ex.* 2194 He dede hem binden, and leden dun, And speren faste in his prisun. *c* **1300** *Havelok* 448 Onon he ferde To þe tour þer he woren sperde. **1375** BARBOUR *Bruce* IV. 14 Thai stythly speryt [thaim] Bath in fetrys and in presoune. *c* **1400** MAUNDEV. (Roxb.) xxiv. 113 He spered him in amanges his tresour withouten mete or drink. *c* **1460** *Play of Sacrament* 46 In an hoote ouyn [they] speryd hym fast. **1542** BECON *Potation for Lent* F iiij, Fastynge speareth vp & encloseth as though it were in a narrowe prison the extraordinary & vnlawfull mocions. **1548** —— *Solace Soul* Wks. 1564 II. 111 Therfore doth he ..snarle him with these fetters and chenes, speareth hym in this prison & dongen.

b. To shut up, put away, or enclose, in some receptacle.

a **1300** *Cursor M.* 6888 Ilk waand þat þai þere bare He sperd wit-in þer santuare. **1303** R. BRUNNE *Handl. Synne* 3656 Cunsel of shryfte sperd yn hys breste, He ne oght for to telle. *Ibid.* 6134 Weyl I ferde Ar y, yn purs, penys sperde. *a* **1400** *Minor Poems fr. Vernon Ms.* xxiv. 195 In þi wombe þou speredest heuene Hele of god, vre mede. *a* **1564** BECON *Art. Chr. Relig. Proved* Wks. 1564 II. 158 When the disciples..dyd receaue his bodye they receiued it neither shutte or speared, or enclosed on ye bread.

c. To unite or join closely.

1545 BALE *Image Both Ch.* C vj, They are speared up together faste unto hym with the shyninge cheane of charite.

4. To exclude; to shut *out*.

a **1300** *Cursor M.* 25183 þat thoru vr liuelade wick we sper fra us þe rightwis demester. **13..** *Seven Penit. Psalms* 72 in *Engl. Stud.* X. 234 In heuene, whan þou holdist alle, Late me not be þer out isperd. *c* **1440** *Jacob's Well* 228 Wo to ȝou þat speryn out of ȝoure herte þe mynde of cristes passioun. *c* **1450** *Cov. Myst.* (Shaks. Soc.) 31 This blysse I spere ffrom ȝow ryth fast.

5. *absol.* To perform the act of closing or shutting.

a **1300** *Cursor M.* 13329 O þaim þou sal þe caiss ber, For to oppen bath and sper. *Ibid.* 17357 þai sperd fast wit lok and kai. *c* **1340** HAMPOLE *Pr. Consc.* 3835 Of wilk þe pape þe kays bers, Whar-with he bathe opens and spers. **1538** BALE *God's Promises* VII, O perfyght keye of David,..whych openest and no man speareth. *c* **1550** —— *Image Both Ch.* (Day) I iij, With all auctorite..to open or to speare.

6. *intr.* To close or shut; to admit of being closed. *rare.*

a **1300** *Cursor M.* 1683 þu sal..Mak a dor wit mesur wide, A windou sperand wel on hei. **1550** BALE *Eng. Votaries* II 38 Whyls the dore..oft tymes opened and speared agayne.

Hence **speared** *ppl. a.*[1]; **'spearing** *vbl. sb.*[1] and *ppl. a.*

a **1300** *Cursor M.* 10091 He com in at þe yatt sperd. *a* **1425** *Ibid.* 1683 (Trin.), þou shalt..Make..A sperynge wyndowe als on heȝe. *c* **1440** *Promp. Parv.* 284/2 Latchynge, or sperynge wythe a lacche, *clitura, pessulatus. Ibid.* 460/1 Sloot, or schytyl of sperynge,..*pessulum*. *c* **1450** *Mirour Saluacioun* (Roxb.) 24 And bot it is merveille and more to passe thorgh spered ȝate. **1542** BECON *Potation for Lent* I viij b, The spearynge of the chyrch dore.

spear (spɪə(r)), *v.*[2] Also 6–7 speer. [Irregular variant of SPIRE *v.* Cf. SPEAR *sb.*[2]] *intr.* Of corn, etc.: To sprout, germinate. Also with *out*.

1573 TUSSER *Husb.* (1878) 174 Malt being well speered, the more it will cast. **1651** R. CHILD in *Hartlib's Legacy* (1655) 91 Rooks, which pluck up in light land, presently after the Corn speareth, much Corn. **1678** *Phil. Trans.* XII. 946 As soon as the Heads begin to shoot or speer within the ground,..howe or pare the ground all over very thin. *a* **1722** LISLE *Husb.* (1757) 114 Fourteen barley-corns of the twenty had put forth roots, but had not speared. *Ibid.* 139 In turning up wet wheat straw..I found..many loose grains speared out. **1763** MILLS *Pract. Husb.* III. 156 That surface must be so fine, and so lightly compressed, that the seed may spear through it. *a* **1825-** in dial. glossaries (Yks., E. Anglia, Kent, Surrey, Sussex, etc.). **1886** *Science* VII. 174 The single blade 'spears' first into three, then into five or more side-shoots.

Hence **speared** *ppl. a.*[2]; **'spearing** *vbl. sb.*[2]

1577–82 BRETON *Toyes* Wks. (Grosart) I. 58/2 What their shiftes should be,..by speered Mault the Bruer soone will see. **1707** MORTIMER *Husb.* (1721) II. 23 You may prepare them for spearing by laying the [Ash-] Keys in Earth or Sand. **1765** *Museum Rust.* III. 151 It would have been better ..if more of it had been grown last year, when the wheat was almost all speared.

spear (spɪə(r)), *v.*[3] [f. SPEAR *sb.*[1] Cf. G. *speeren.*]

1. a. *trans.* To pierce or transfix with a spear.

1755 in JOHNSON. **1774** GOLDSM. *Nat. Hist.* (1824) III. 40 A prodigious ray..was speared by the Negroes at Guadaloupe. **1815** SCOTT *Guy M.* liv, The only light..was a quantity of wood burnt to charcoal in an iron grate, such as they use in spearing salmon by night. **1823** —— *Quentin D.* x, He would questionless have made in, and speared the brute. **1853** KANE *Grinnell Exp.* I. (1856) 480, I have seen them spear the eider on the wing. **1869** FREEMAN *Norm. Conq.* (1875) III. xii. 176 The poet tells us how the King saw his men speared and shot down.

fig. and *transf.* **1843** CARLYLE *Past & Pr.* IV. iii, Spearing down and destroying Falsehood. **1855** TENNYSON *Maud* I. IV. 23 The Mayfly is torn by the swallow, the sparrow spear'd by the shrike.

b. To dismiss. *Austral. slang.* Cf. SPEAR *sb.*[1] 2 b.

1911 'S. RUDD' *Dashwoods* 13 If I was the boss here I would. I'd spear him without warnin'.

c. To cause to move like a spear; to spearhead.

1920 W. CAMP *Football without Coach* v. 85 The ball should be held in the hand and speared through the air by giving the hand a twist as the ball leaves it. **1951** *Daily Progress* (Charlottesville, Va.) 11 Feb. 1/6 The Second Division at the end of its eight-day battle had set the pattern of the Eighth Army's new hunt-and-kill offensive with aggressive tank forces spearing the way. **1969** G. MACBETH *War Quartet* 46 So when I Speared the first squadron in the dawn assault Over the cliffs, that wool..Warmed the heart's beating.

d. To beg; to obtain by begging. *U.S. slang.*

1912 *Railroad Man's Mag.* Apr. 493/1 They had mooched the stem and threw their feet, And speared four-bits on which to eat. **1926** *Amer. Speech* II. 390/1 To *make the grade* or *connect* is to get the amount of money one is after. *Spear* is another word for connecting. **1942** BERREY & VAN DEN BARK *Amer. Thes. Slang* §370/3 Beg; request a loan or gift, ..*spear*.

2. a. *intr.* To rise *up* like a spear.

1822 AINSLIE *Land of Burns* 151 Do ye see a steeple yonner, spearing up frae amang the massy trees? **1891** *Illustr. Lond. News* 7 Feb. 174/1 The two broken masts, swinging and spearing high up under the..heaps of vapour.

b. To move like a spear. *rare.*

1944 *Times* 14 Apr. 4/2 Yesterday the tanks handed over to the infantry, and speared south-east and south-west towards the Crimean mountains.

spear(e, obs. forms of SPEER *v.*[1]

speared, *a.* [f. SPEAR *sb.*[1]] Armed with a spear or spears.

1819 KEATS *Otho* V. v. 160, I will lead your legions forth, Compact in steeled squares, and speared files. **1839** BAILEY *Festus* 150 The speared desires that overran The fairest fields of virtue.

spearer ('spɪərə(r)). [f. SPEAR *sb.*[1] or *v.*[3]] One who is armed with, or strikes with, a spear.

More frequent in Combs., as *eel-, salmon-spearer*.

1573 BARET *Alv.*, *A Pensioner*, a gentilman about a prince alway ready, with his speare: a sperer. **1885** *Sat. Rev.* 21 Nov. 673/1 The spearer [of eels] takes aim.

'spear-grass. Also **speargrass, spear grass.** [f. SPEAR *sb.*[1]]

†**1.** = SPEARWORT 3. *Obs.*

1548 TURNER *Names Herbes* (E.D.S.) 84 Flamula is the herbe whiche we cal in englishe Sperewurte or spergrasse. **1579** T. LUPTON *Notable Things* iii. §91 (1660) 48 Whosoever is tormented with the Sciatica or the Gout, let them take an herb called Speregrasse. **1596** SHAKS. *1 Hen. IV*, II. iv. 340 Yea, and to tickle our Noses with Spear-grasse, to make them bleed.

2. One or other of various British grasses, *esp.* couch-grass (*Triticum repens*, *Agrostis*, etc.).

1784 *Young's Annals Agric.* I. 197 The soil is light and sandy, and consequently very subject to spear-grass (*triticum repens*). **1806** J. GRAHAME *Birds of Scot.* 3 He founds their lowly house, of withered bents And coarsest speargrass. **1820** KEATS *Lamia* II. 228 Let spear-grass and the spiteful thistle wage War on his temples. **1823** E. MOOR *Suffolk Words*, *Spear-grass*, the coarse sour grass..called couch, squitch, and quitch, in other counties. **1825** HOLDICH *Ess. Weeds Agric.* 43 Black-grass (*Alopecurus agrestis*), also called Black-bent, Spear-grass, Slender Foxtail-grass, etc.

3. *Amer.* **a.** One or other of several species of meadow-grass, esp. *Poa pratensis*.

1747 FRANKLIN *Lett.* Wks. 1887 II. 80 The grass which comes in first after ditching is spear-grass and white clover. **1762** MILLS *Syst. Pract. Husb.* I. 152 Mr. Eliot, after draining the swamp [in New England]..., sowed it with grass-seed, such as red clover, spear grass,..and herd grass. **1846–50** A. WOOD *Class-bk. Bot.* 614 *Poa pratensis.* Spear Grass... *P. nemoralis.* Wood Spear Grass... *P. annua.* Annual Spear Grass. **1856** A. GRAY *Man. Bot.* (1860) 561 *Poa annua...* Low Spear-Grass.

b. Some South American grass or plant.

1833 M. SCOTT *Tom Cringle* iv, Impervious underwood of prickly pear, penguin, and speargrass.

c. *sea spear-grass*, a species of manna-grass.

1856 A. GRAY *Man. Bot.* (1860) 560 *Glyceria maritima*,.. Sea Spear-Grass.

4. *Austr.* One or other of various grasses belonging to different genera (see quots.).

1847 LEICHHARDT *Jrnl.* ii. 44 Very disagreeable, however, was the abundance of Burr and of a Spear-grass (*Aristida*). **1865** TENISON-WOODS *Disc. & Expl. Austr.* II. 463 *note*, The settlers call it spear-grass, and it is, I believe, a species of *Anthistiria*. **1874** RANKEN *Dom. Australia* v. 86 Sheep in paddocks cannot be so well kept clear of spear grass. **1889** MAIDEN *Usef. Pl.* 90 *Heteropogon contortus*,..'Spear Grass'. *Ibid.* 110 These grasses are excellent feeding before the appearance of the inflorescence; afterwards they are known as 'Spear Grasses'. **1890** LUMHOLTZ *Cannibals* 23 A nocuous kind of grass, namely the dreaded spear-grass (*Andropogon contortus*), which..rendered sheep-raising impossible.

5. A New Zealand umbelliferous plant of the genus *Aciphylla*.

1851 [see SPANIARD 3 a]. **1863** S. BUTLER *First Year Canterb. Settl.* vi. 81 Spaniard..is sometimes called spear-grass, and grows to about the size of a mole-hill.

6. One or other of several Asiatic grasses or plants.

1864 *Daily Tel.* 15 Aug., A place where an elephant could not crush through the thorn-trees,..the creeping plants, and the spear-grass. **1884** J. GILMOUR *Mongols* 81 Here and there were the ghost-like remnants of last year's growth of spear-grass. **1900** POLLOK & THOM *Sports Burma* 378 Coming in contact with spear grass and the fine hair of the bamboo.

'spear-head, *sb.* Also **spearhead.** [f. SPEAR *sb.*[1]]

1. a. The sharp-pointed head or blade forming the striking or piercing end of a spear.

c **1400** MAUNDEV. (Roxb.) ii. 6 Ane of þe nayles, and þe spere heued, and many oþer reliques er in Fraunce. *c* **1400** *Laud Troy Bk.* 17106 Thei were alle In mochel doute How the spere-hed scholde gon oute With-oute lesyng of his lyff. *c* **1445** LYDG. *Nightingale* II. 158 Thurgh myn hert the sper-hed gan it dresse. **1503** *Acc. Ld. High Treas. Scot.* II. 202 For ane sper hede gilt, xxviij s. **1523** FITZHERB. *Husb.* §54 Ther is a grasse called sperewort, and hath a long narowe leafe, lyke a spere-heed. **1610** HOLLAND *Camden's Brit.* (1637) 188 They found Spear-heads, axes, and swords of brasse. **1638** JUNIUS *Paint. Ancients* 320 Others do but shew their halfe bodies,..their head-pieces, their spear-heads. **1778** *Eng. Gazetteer* (ed. 2) s.v. *Tamworth*, A large trench remains..where bones of men and horses, and spear-heads, have been dug up. **1825** SCOTT *Talism.* xxviii, His lance.. shivered into splinters from the steel spear-head up to the very gauntlet. **1883** in *Fisheries Japan* (Fish. Exhib.) 35 A long bamboo rod..which is tipped at the extremity with an iron-barbed spear-head.

b. *fig.*, esp. the leading part or element (of a thrust, movement, etc.); a person or group leading an attack.

1893 in J. H. Barrow *World's Parlt. Relig.* II. 1540 The Scriptures were to be the spear-head, all other knowledge the well-fitted handle. **1929** *Times* 12 Nov. 17/3 The Belfast members of the society..were made the spearhead of a thrust for an advance of wages for shipyard joiners alone. **1932** *Times* 12 July 6/3 Afterwards they [*sc.* Yorkshire] broke down before the Nottinghamshire attack, with Larwood as its spearhead, and lost seven wickets for 53 runs. **1940** *Hutchinson's Pictorial Hist. War* 10 Apr.–11 June 176 Synchronizing their Blitzkrieg attack with dive-bombers, German tanks acted as the spearhead in the rapid Nazi advance through the Low Countries and Northern France. **1945** L. MUMFORD *City Development* xii. 130 The park system is thus the very spearhead of comprehensive urban planning. **1946** *R.A.F. Jrnl.* May 168 He was called upon to organize the new spearhead for Bomber Command. **1951** 'J. WYNDHAM' *Day of Triffids* xii. 223 When they found that we represented only a group similar to their own, and were not the spearhead of a rescue party on the grand scale their interest would lapse. **1958** *Manch. Guardian* 20 Aug. 4/2 Lord Cameron and his colleagues do not think that the dockers' claim can be fairly regarded as the spearhead of a new national wage movement. **1962** *Times* 27 Nov. 13/2 Mr. W. P. Tapley..told me of..preparations to..keep traffic flowing regardless of the weather. 'Salt,' he said, 'is still the spearhead.' **1970** A. TOFFLER *Future Shock* iii. 40 America, as the spearhead of superindustrialism, represents a new, quicker, and very much unwanted tempo. **1977** 'J. LE CARRÉ' *Honourable Schoolboy* xviii. 442 The spearhead of the operation will be handled by ourselves. If supportive action is required, Martello will supply it.

2. *transf.* A thing having the pointed form characteristic of the head of a spear.

1894 DOYLE *S. Holmes* 33 The sticky spearheads of the chestnuts were just beginning to burst into their fivefold leaves. **1897** QUILLER-COUCH *Stevenson's St. Ives* xxxiii, Yonder was England, with the Solway cleaving the coast —a broad, bright spearhead, slightly bent at the tip.

3. *attrib.* and *Comb.*, as *spear-head army, forces, form, group, -shaped.*

1931 W. S. CHURCHILL *World Crisis* VI. xx. 301 Amid these varying schemes one plain question stood forth. Should Mackensen with the '*spear-head army' go on or stop? **1978** R. V. JONES *Most Secret War* xlix. 486 The enthusiasm of its members was such that they were sometimes ahead of our *spearhead forces. **1897** MARY KINGSLEY *W. Africa* 324 The Fan decorates the bellows with *spearhead forms, the points whereof are directed towards the fire. **1977** M. WALKER *National Front* ii. 39 During 1961, the Special Branch had been aware that the *Spearhead group had been formed. **1865** LUBBOCK *Preh. Times* ix. 274 A weathered hatchet..identical in form with the *spearhead-shaped specimens from Amiens.

Hence **'spear-head** *v. trans.*, to act as the spear-head of, to lead (a movement, attack, etc.).

1938 *Daily News* (Los Angeles) 27 July 8/1 Liberal leader who spearheaded the debate. **1943** *Sun* (Baltimore) 9 July 1/6 He also disclosed that the Marines spearheaded the direct invasion of New Georgia by landing at Segi. **1944** *Times* 19 Feb. 4/7 Spearheaded by our fleet, we have been able to drive the enemy from these bases. **1957** K. A. WITTFOGEL *Oriental Despotism* 8 Those nonbureaucratic groups and strata which, in feudal Europe and Japan, spearheaded the rise of a commercial and industrial society. **1968** P. OLIVER *Screening Blues* ii. 88 Spearheaded by singers like Little Richard Penniman, Ray Charles or B. B. King.., the musical forms which had been held at a distance for so long were allowed to merge. **1980** M. FONTEYN *Magic of Dance* 289 She was such an intelligent artist and fine dancer that she was able to spearhead the ballet reforms, still advancing rather slowly. **1983** *Times* 21 Jan. 16/5 Furniture sales appear to be spearheading the upturn in consumer spending.

spearien, obs. form of SPARE *v.*[1]

'speariness. *rare*⁻¹. [f. SPEARY *a.*[1]] The character of being speary or sharp-pointed.

a **1722** LISLE *Husb.* (1757) 141 The spikiness and speariness of the tops.

spearing ('spɪərɪŋ), *sb.* Chiefly *U.S.* [? ad. Du. and G. *spiering* smelt (see SPARLING).] **a.** *U.S.* The anchovy. **b.** ***ground spearing*** (see quots.).

?**1838** *Encycl. Metrop.* (1845) XXIV. 333/2 *Saurus Myops*, Cuv.;..Mouse-eyed Saury... Is found off St. Helena, and called by the colonists the Ground Spearing. **1884** GOODE *Nat. Hist. Aquat. Anim.* 612 The fishermen distinguish it [Anchovy] from the true 'Whitebait', the young of the herring, calling it 'Spearing'. **1896** JORDAN & EVERMANN *Fishes Amer.* 533 *Trachinocephalus myops*,.. Ground Spearing;..common in West Indies and Brazil.

spearing ('spɪərɪŋ), *vbl. sb.* [f. SPEAR *v.*[3]] The action of piercing, killing, etc., with a spear. Also *attrib.*

1779 COOK *Third Voy.* VI. v. (1784) III. 297 Our diversion was therefore changed to spearing of salmon. **1839** T. C. HOFLAND *Brit. Angler's Man.* xv. (1841) 184 The spearing-ground generally chosen, is a soft, sandy, or grassy bottom. **1876** 'WILDFOWLER' *Shooting & Fishing Trips* II. 263 He resumed his spearing [of eels]. **1900** ISABEL SAVORY *Sportswoman in India* i. 16 Spearing on the near side of a horse is most dangerous, and is not allowed.

†'**spearing**, *ppl. a.* *Obs.*[−1] [f. **spear*, var. of SPIRE *v.*] Rising in a spiral form.

1752 *Phil. Trans.* XLVII. 478 Those, who saw it evaporate, affirm it ascended into the clouds in a long spearing vapour, and at last ended in a fiery stream.

spearke, obs. form of SPARK *sb.*[1]

spear-like ('spɪəlaɪk), *a.* [f. SPEAR *sb.*[1]] Resembling a spear in shape or in sharpness.

1567 MAPLET *Gr. Forest* 35 The Bulrush hath..two kindes: one..verie blunt and the other is rather Spearelike. *a* **1593** MARLOWE tr. *1st Bk. Lucan* 530 Fiery meteors blaz'd in heauen: Now spearlike, long; now like a spreading torch. **1865** TYLOR *Early Hist. Man.* viii. 223 This spear-like fossil. **1872** COUES *N. Amer. Birds* 265 A quick thrust of the spear-like bill. **1884** BOWER & SCOTT *De Bary's Phaner.* 220 Each of these contains a single spear-like crystal.

spearman[1] ('spɪəmən). [f. SPEAR *sb.*[1] Cf. SPEARSMAN.]

1. A soldier or warrior armed with a spear; one who carries a spear as a weapon.

1297 R. GLOUC. (Rolls) 7753 Of kniȝtes & squiers, Speremen auote & bowemen, & al so arblasters. **1375** BARBOUR *Bruce* xv. 220 To the ficht Maknakill then Come with twa hundreth of gude sper-men. *c* **1400** *Laud Troy Bk.* 16671 The speremen ride, the bowemen schote. *c* **1500** *Melusine* 219 Thenne mounted spere men on horsback, and bygane euery man to marche forth in fayre aray. **1591** SAVILE *Tacitus, Hist.* II. xxxiii. 73 A valiant companie..of spearemen and horse departed away. **1665** MANLEY *Grotius' Low C. Wars* 451 Against whom was sent Lewis of Nassau, with 400 Spear-men. **1790** COWPER *Odyss.* III. 504 Beside him, he bade sleep the spearman bold. **1807** WORDSW. *White Doe* VI. 123 A Spearman brought him to the ground. **1865** J. H. INGRAHAM *Pillar of Fire* xi. 128 The Egyptian army consist[s]..of bowmen, spearmen,..and other corps.

b. A royal or civic officer bearing a spear.

c **1640** R. SEMPILL *Piper of Kilbarchan* 29 At fairs he play'd before the Spear-men, All gaily graithed in their gear-men. **1674** BLOUNT *Glossogr.* (ed. 4), *Pensioners*,..are the more noble sort of Guard to the King's Person... In Hen. 8. time they were called *Spearmen.*

2. A spearer of fish.

1815 SCOTT *Guy M.* xxvi, 'The deil's in Gabriel!' said the spearman, as the fragments of glowing wood floated..down the stream.

3. *U.S.* As an insect-name (see quot.).

1868 *Rep. U.S. Commissioner Agric.* (1869) 80 Numbers of the *Lebia grandis*..were taken feeding on the larvæ of the ten-lined spearman (*Doryphora 10-lineata*).

Spearman[2] ('spɪəmən). *Statistics.* The name of Charles Edward *Spearman* (1863–1943), English psychologist, used *attrib.* and in the possessive to designate a coefficient he devised as a measure of the degree of agreement between two rankings, being their product-moment correlation coefficient; symbol ρ or *R*.

1907 *Drapers' Company Res. Mem.* (Biometric Ser.) IV. 22 There is a further very serious indictment to be made against Spearman's R... R retains a constant value for wide variations in ρ_{12}. **1942** *Biometrika* XXXII. 277 The Spearman coefficient ρ may be regarded as a sample grade correlation. *Ibid.* 278 The error involved in using Spearman's ρ from a small sample. **1970** *Jrnl. Gen. Psychol.* LXXXIII. 91 A Spearman rank correlation coefficient.. between the median latency scores on the last day of training and the mean of the median latencies over the three days of testing produced a value of −·3.

spearmint ('spɪəmɪnt). [f. SPEAR *sb.*[1]]

1. a. The common garden mint, *Mentha viridis*, much used in cookery.

1562 TURNER *Herbal* II. (1568) 54 Thys herbe is called with us gardin mynte, and as far as I remembre, it is called spere mynte, and if it be not named so, it may well be called so of the sharpnes of the lefe. **1584** COGAN *Haven Health* xvi. 38 One [kind] most fragrant in sauour..is called Spere Mint, and is vsed to be put in puddings. **1597** GERARDE *Herbal* II. ccxv. 552 The leaues of Speare Mint are long like those of the Willow tree. **1620** VENNER *Via Recta* vii. 153 Of these two, the Speare-Mint is the more excellent. **1666** BOYLE *Orig. Forms & Qual.* 124 *Raphanus Aquaticus*, Spearemint, and even *Ranunculus* it self, did grow..in Viols filld with fair water. **1717** BERKELEY *Jrnl. Tour Italy* Wks. 1871 IV. 552 Air perfumed with spearmint growing over an ample space. **1779** FORREST *Voy. N. Guinea* 247 In this garden he had..onions, parsley, spearment, and the Spanish raddish. **1807** P. GASS *Jrnl.* 103 There is in the bottoms a great quantity of spear-mint and currant bushes. **1811** A. T. THOMSON *Lond. Disp.* (1818) 255 Spearmint is stomachic and carminative. **1882** *Garden* 6 May 320/1 Mint should now be planted, both the Spearmint and Peppermint.

b. With pl. A plant of this.

1539 ELYOT *Cast. Helthe* 78 Mylke, newe mylked, wherin is put..three leaues of good speare myntes. **1620** VENNER *Via Recta* ii. 44 Take..of Speremints, of Balme, of each one handfull.

c. *ellipt.* A piece of chewing-gum flavoured with the oil extracted from this plant.

1920 'SAPPER' *Bull-Dog Drummond* ix. 240 A grim-faced man at the wheel..had apparently felt the seriousness of the occasion so acutely, as to deposit his third piece of spearmint on the underneath side of the steering-wheel for greater safety. **1945** J. STEINBECK *Cannery Row* i. 9 No Abbeville child..knew the lack of a stick of spearmint ever afterward.

2. *attrib.* and *Comb.*, as ***spearmint-leaf, oil, root, water.***

1662 R. MATHEW *Unl. Alch.* 192 Put into it one quart of Rose-water, and one quart of Spermint-water. **1681** GREW *Musæum* I. vii. ii. 165 Not Oval, but rather expressing the figure of a Speer-Mint-Leaf. **1757** A. COOPER *Distiller* II. v. (1760) 126 The simple Waters now commonly made, are Orange-flower-water,..Spear-mint-water [etc.]. **1786** ABERCROMBIE *Gard. Assist.* 306 Plant spear-mint roots in a hot bed. **1857** MILLER *Elem. Chem., Org.* vii. §1. 448 Indifferent oils, such as spearmint oil (C_{20} H_{20} O_2). **1860** WARTER *Sea-board* II. 29 All I could give her was some spearmint water.

spear-point. [f. SPEAR *sb.*[1]]

1. The point of a spear.

c **1450** *Merlin* xvii. 275 The cristin hem receyved at spere poynte. **1584** *Shuttleworths' Acc.* (Chetham Soc.) 13 Payed for makinge a spair poynt, vj[d]. **1597** *Cal. Border Pap.* II. 464 Langriges..did openlie baffell and reprove the said lord Harrise of treason, by bearing his glove upon a speare point. **1753** *Chambers' Cycl.* Suppl. s.v. *Crambe*, A fruit of the shape of a spear point. **1776** MICKLE tr. *Camoens' Lusiad* IX. 78 Like melted gold the brazen spear-points blaze. **1815** SCOTT *Guy M.* xlvii, A staff in her hand, headed with a sort of spear-point. **1856** KINGSLEY *Heroes* IV. ii, Then they hurled their lances at his shield, but the spear-points turned like lead.

attrib. **1862** *Catal. Internat. Exhib., Brit.* II. No. 6490, Table knives and forks, spear point, palette, and butchers' knives. **1930** BLUNDEN *Poems* 55 Like stars in frost as spear-point-bright.

2. *transf.* Something resembling the point of a spear. Also *fig.*

1861 L. L. NOBLE *Icebergs* 169 Where the ice shoots up into thin spear-points. **1902** *Daily Chron.* 1 Apr. 2/1 The ruddy spearpoints of the beech buds..swelling with new life. **1937** R. WARNER in C. Day Lewis *Mind in Chains* 37 Let us utilise this weight without blunting the spearpoint of our advances. **1963** *Times* 15 Jan. 8/4 The spearpoint of aggression has been blunted in Vietnam.

3. A species of moth (see quot.).

1832 J. RENNIE *Consp. Butterfl. & M.* 79 The Spear Point (*Acronycta cuspis*)... Rare. Kent.

spear-rib, obs. form of SPARE-RIB.

spearse, variant of SPERSE *v.*

spear-shaft. Also 1, 3 sperescæft, 4–5 spereschaft(e, 5 spereshafte, speyre-chaft. [f. SPEAR *sb.*[1] Cf. OHG. *sperascaft* (MHG. *sperschaft*, G. *speerschaft*), MSw. *spärsskapt.*] The long shaft or handle to which the spear-head is fixed. Also *transf.* (quot. 1841).

a **900** WÆRFERTH tr. *Gregory's Dial.* 14 Þær hi ealle ongunnon heora hors mid heora sperescæftum þerscan. *c* **1205** LAY. 14752 He nom ænne spere-scæft þe wes long & swiþe stærc. **1382** WYCLIF *1 Chron.* xx. 5 Whos spere schaft was as the beme of websters. **1398** TREVISA *Barth. De P.R.* XII. xxiv, Locusta..haþ longe legges, as a spere schafte. *c* **1420** *Contin. Brut* 337 William Walworth.. slow Iack Straw, and anon ryȝt þere dede smyȝt of his hed, and sette it vp apon a spere-schafte. **1483** *Wardr. Acc.* in *Antiq. Rep.* (1807) I. 49, viij spereshaftes with their chapitulls. *a* **1700** KEN *Edmund* Poet. Wks. 1721 II. 26 Fit barbed Heads for their Spear-shafts to make. **1841** H. MILLER *O.R. Sandst.* vii. 119 They form a continuous convex stratum in the sandstone spear-shaft. **1887** MORRIS *Odyssey* x. 170 As I steadied myself with my spear-shaft.

spear-shaped, *a.* [f. SPEAR *sb.*[1]] Resembling a spear in shape; pointed like a spear.

1763 MILLS *Pract. Husb.* III. 282 The lobes are small, spear-shaped, and hoary on their under side. **1796** WITHERING *Brit. Plants* (ed. 3) I. 203 Petals..spear-shaped, rather flat, but a little bent inwards. *Ibid.* III. 625 Thorns simple and compound: leaves spear-shaped. **1831** SCOTT *Ct. Rob.* xxiii, The tent..was raised upon tall spear-shaped poles. **1837** P. KEITH *Bot. Lex.* 260 Appendages..varying much in form in different species, as awl-shaped, spear-shaped, half-arrow-shaped. **1908** SIR H. JOHNSTON *Grenfell & Congo* II. xxvii. 788 The paddles along the main course of the Congo are generally spear-shaped.

spearsman. [f. SPEAR *sb.*[1]] = SPEARMAN[1].

1836 MRS. TRAILL *Backw. Canada* 159 He is considered very skilful as a spearsman. **1885** *Manch. Exam.* 13 Feb. 5/4 They are specially marked out by the Arab marksmen and spearsmen.

spear-staff. [f. SPEAR *sb.*[1]] The staff or shaft of a spear; = SPEAR-SHAFT. Also *transf.*

1530 PALSGR. 274/1 Speare staffe, *fust de lance.* **1565** COOPER *Thesaurus, Hastile*, a speare staffe. **1653** W. RAMESEY *Astrol. Restored* 100 The fixed Stars in Libra..are in number Twenty-five...20. The calf of the right leg of Bootes. 21. The Spear-staff Incalurus of Bootes. **1687** MIÈGE *Gt. Fr. Dict.* II, Spear-staff, *la hampe.* **1736** AINSWORTH II, *Hasta pura*, a spear staff without an iron head. **1776** MICKLE tr. *Camoens' Lusiad* I. 274 [Mars] Strikes his tall spear-staff on the sounding ground. **1878** GOSSE *Rivers Bible* 376 His spear-staff was 'like a weaver's beam'.

spearwort ('spɪəwɜːt). Forms: 1 sperewyrt, 3 -wurt, 5 -wourt(h, 5–7 -wort, 6 -wurte; 4–5 sperwort, 6 sperworte; 8 speerwort; 6 spearewoort (7 -wort), 6– spearwort. [f. SPEAR *sb.*[1] Cf. G. *speerkraut, -wurz.*]

†**1.** Elecampane (*Inula Helenium*). *Obs.*

c **1000** *Sax. Leechd.* I. 210 Ðenim þas wyrte þe man hinnula campana, & oþrum naman spere wyrte nemneþ. *a* **1100** in Wr.-Wülcker 299 *Innule campane*, sperewyrt. *c* **1265** *Voc. Plants* Ibid. 558 *Hinnula campana*, sperewurt.

†**2.** = NEP *sb.*[2] *Obs.*

c **1000** ÆLFRIC *Gloss.* in Wr.-Wülcker 135 *Nap siluatica*, sperewyrt, *uel* wilde næp.

3. One or other of several species of ranunculus, esp. *R. Flammula* (lesser or small spearwort) and *R. Lingua* (great spearwort).

The identity of the plant in quot. *c* 1450 is doubtful.

a **1387** *Sinon. Barthol.* (Anecd. Oxon.) 21 *Flammula*, i. sperwort, calidus est et siccus in quarto gradu. *a* **1400** *Stockholm Med. MS.* 185 Sperewourt or launcelef. *Ibid.* 189 Þe lesse sperewourth. *c* **1450** *Alphita* (Anecd. Oxon.) 23 *Borith*, nonaclum cirurgie, lanceolata aquatica idem,.. sperewort. **1523** FITZHERB. *Husb.* §54 Ther is a grasse called sperewort, and hath a long narowe leafe, lyke a sperehead, and it wyll growe a fote hyghe, and beareth a yelowe floure. **1597** GERARDE *Herbal* II. ccclv. 815 Spearewoort is like to the other Crowfootes in facultie, it is hot in the mouth or biting, it exulcerateth and raiseth blisters. **1614** MARKHAM *Cheap Husb.* I. xxx. 79 The grasse which is vnwholesome for Sheepe, is that which hath growing amongst it, Spearewort, Pennywort, or Penny-grasse. **1635** SWAN *Spec. M.* (1670) 219 Spear-wort, or Banewort, is an herb which if it be taken inwardly, is deadly. *c* **1710** PETIVER *Cat. Ray's Eng. Herbal* Tab. xxxix, Great Spear-wort. Small Spear-wort. **1763** MILLS *Pract. Husb.* III. 312 The hairy wood grass, the lesser spearwort,..have evidently suspicious marks. **1848** JOHNS *Week at Lizard* 210 Lined..with..aquatic plants, among which the great spear-wort..is..conspicuous. **1865** *Reader* No. 153. 628/2 The little dwarf spearwort. **1890** *Science Gossip* XXVI. 44/1 It is a well-known variety of the lesser spearwort.., which I have found in a very fine condition in Sussex.

b. Mentioned as used by beggars to produce artificial blisters or sores.

1567 HARMAN *Caveat* (1869) 44 All for the most parte.. wil either lay to their legs an herb called Sperewort, eyther Arsnicke, which is called Ratesbane. **1608** DEKKER *Belman of London* Wks. (Grosart) III. 99 With Sperewort or Arsenick will they in one night poyson their leg be it neuer so sound, and raise a blister, which at their pleasure they can take off againe. **1673** R. HEAD *Canting Acad.* 74 Sperewort or Arsnick..will draw blisters.

Hence '**spearworty** *a.*, diseased through the eating of spearwort. ? *Obs.*

1736 PEGGE *Kenticisms* (E.D.S.) 48 The liver of a rotten sheep, when it is full of white knots, is said to be speerworty.

speary ('spɪərɪ), *a.*[1] [f. SPEAR *sb.*[1]]

†**1.** Of grass: Hard and stiff. *Obs.*

1577 HARRISON *England* 37b/2 Where..blewe claye aboundeth..there the grasse is speary, rough, and very apt for bushes. **1653** BLITHE *Eng. Improver Impr.* 11 They bear little, or no grass, a little wild Time, and speary harsh grass, that Cattell eat not.

2. Resembling a spear or spears; slender and sharp-pointed; keen.

1820 HOGG in *Blackw. Mag.* VI. 464 The speary wood Groans to the blast. **1822** MOIR *Ibid.* XI. 305 The bordering reeds exalt higher their speary summits. **1855** *Fraser's Mag.* LI. 95 Speary sleet and driving snow. **1872** HOWELLS *Wedding Journ.* (1892) 143 Dark evergreens that..point their speary tops above the crest of bluffs.

3. Consisting of spears; waged with spears.

1810 W. TAYLOR in *Monthly Mag.* XXIX. 417 Thread of Roman entrails twin'd In the speary loom they strain. **1888** DOUGHTY *Arabia Deserta* I. 25 Better him were to comb his beard..at home, than show his fine skin to..their speary warfare.

'**speary**, *a.*[2] [perh. f. SPEAR *sb.*[2], but cf. prec.] Slender, spindly.

1821 CLARE *Village Minstr.* II. 104 Speary barley bowing down with dew. **1854** MISS BAKER *Northampt. Gloss.*, *Speary*, shooting up long and slender. **1899** *Jrnl. R. Agric. Soc.* Mar. 114 Too close planting induces to speary growth.

speat, var. SPATE *sb.*

speate, obs. f. SPIT *sb.*

speave, var. SPAVE *v.*

speawe, obs. f. SPEW *v.*

spec (spɛk), *sb.*[1] *colloq.* and *slang.* [Short for SPECULATION; orig. American, but in English use from *c* 1825.]

1. a. A commercial speculation or venture.

Freq. with qualifying adj. as *bad, good.*

1794 J. ADAMS *Wks.* (1856) I. 469 Many merchants have already made a noble *spec.* of the embargo by raising their prices. **1819** W. FAUX *Mem. Days Amer.* (1823) 37 By way of turning a penny, or as they say, of making a good *spec.* of it. **1824** in *Spirit Public Jrnls.* (1825) 204 And the Hunts —a bad spec.,..Have published some posthumous trash of Byshe Shelly. **1851** MAYHEW *Lond. Labour* I. 378, I have already sold enough to pay me well enough for my spec. **1872** A. H. HUTCHINSON *Try Cracow* (ed. 2) v. 93 A Prussian banker..who purchased the property..as a kind of spec to form into a limited company.

transf. **1829** in Knapp *Life G. Borrow* (1899) I. 140 Do not enter the army; it is a bad spec. **1855** DELAMER *Kitchen Garden* (1861) 177 Sow a few dwarf kidney beans as a spec.

b. *on spec*, on the chance of obtaining some advantage, gaining some profit, etc. In recent use more generally, as a gamble, on the off chance.

1832 MARRYAT *N. Forster* xlvi, Both..came out on spec. **1837** DICKENS *Pickw.* xxxiii, They said what a wery gen'rous thing it was o' them to have taken up the case on spec. **1857** KINGSLEY *Two Y. Ago* xxv, If tradesmen will run up houses on spec in a water-meadow, who can stop them? **1928** R. CAMPBELL *Wayzgoose* ii. 36 Some came on spec and others came on bikes. **1938** F. D. SHARPE *Sharpe of Flying Squad* xxv. 256 He never tries anywhere on spec., and never does more than two houses a night. **1970** G. GREER *Female Eunuch* 178 The third book bought on that same day was bought on spec. **1978** *New York* 3 Apr. 36/3 Franklin Thomas remembers starting the center on spec with an analysis that projected a 50–50 chance of succeeding. **1981** B. HINES *Looks & Smiles* 197 'Is he expecting you?' 'No, we just came on spec.'

2. *Winchester slang.* A good or enjoyable thing or occasion. Also *on spec*.

1891 WRENCH *Winch. Wordbk.* (1901) s.v.

spec, *sb.*[2] *U.S. slang.* [Short for SPECTACLE *sb.*[1] or SPECTACULAR *sb.*] **a.** In a circus: (see quot. 1926). **b.** An elaborate and expensive television show.

1926 *Amer. Speech* I. 283/1 *Spec.*, the opening spectacle, or grand entry. **1949** *New Yorker* 5 Nov. 61 Mrs. Webster rode an elephant in the 'spec'. **1959** G. MARX *Let.* 7 Dec. in *Groucho Lett.* (1967) 268 Our little play..could possibly be done as a TV spec.

spec, *sb.*[3] *colloq.* [Short for SPECIFICATION.] A detailed working description; a standard of manufacture or construction. Also *transf.* Freq. *pl.*

1956 *Mag. Fantasy & Sci. Fiction* Oct. 20/2 Belle was not only a perfect secretary..she also had personal specs which would have delighted Praxiteles. **1966** *Aviation Week & Space Technology* 5 Dec. 5/3 (Advt.), The reliability requirements are, in many cases, virtually unbelievable. Seemingly, a unit built to these kinds of specs would almost have to work perfectly forever. **1976** J. CARROLL *Madonna Red* (1977) i. 30 The 707 spec sheets she had memorised.. at the Black September training camp. **1979** *Amat. Photographer* 30 May 99/1 The basic specs of these two new OMs remain the same. **1979** *Truck & Bus Transportation* July 20/2 Leyland Australia is basically working within the U.K. spec. to keep costs down.

spec, *sb.*[4] Colloq. abbrev. of SPECIALIST 2c. *U.S.*

1958 *Army-Navy-Air Force Register* 14 June 7 Grade E7. Title, Old: Master Spec. New: Specialist-7. **1969** I. KEMP *Brit. G.I. in Vietnam* iii. 43 Specialist Fourth Class—or Spec. Four—Much, a small man..who talked in a continuous monotone. **1977** 'E. MCBAIN' *Long Time no See* xii. 200 These are designations of rank. An E-3 is a Pfc., a Spec 4 is Specialist 4th Class, a corporal. An E-5 is a three-striper, and so on.

spec, *a. colloq.* [Short for SPECULATIVE *a.*] Of or pertaining to the practice of building houses without prior guarantee of sale, esp. in estate developments. Also as *adv.* Cf. SPECULATIVE *a.* 7a.

1958 *Observer* 2 Mar. 8/4 As 'developers' and L.P.T.B. leap-frogged over each other..far into the Home Counties, we created the vast paradise of spec' building and hire-purchase. **1958** *Spectator* 4 July 13/1 Builder-designed 'spec' houses. *Ibid.* 8 Aug. 193/2 A film snippet of 'spec.' housing. **1962** D. TENCH *Law for Consumers* vii. 100 Where the buyer buys a completed new house from the builder or developer (what is sometimes called a 'spec' built house). **1965** *New Society* 11 Nov. 6/3 How seldom local authorities and spec builders use any research at all. **1970** J. BETJEMAN *Ghastly Good Taste* (new ed.) p. xxv, Spec. builders and advertisement hoardings and litter droppers. **1978** J. WAINWRIGHT *Jury People* lii. 191 That estate..contains ..'high density' housing...'Spec building'—that is, or was, the term used for such estates. **1978** *Listener* 14 Sept. 337/3 The new, spec-built, often neo-Georgian houses.

spec, variant of SPECK *sb.*

†**specary**, *a. Sc. Obs.*[−1] [ad. med.L. **spicarius* (usually *spicatus*), f. L. *spīca* spike.] *Nardus specary*, spikenard.

1535 STEWART *Cron. Scot.* III. 286 The quhilk with spycarie [= spicery] Anoyntit wes, and nardus specarie.

†**spece.** *Obs.* Forms: 4–7 **spece** (5 **speche**), 4, 6 **spiece**, 7 **speece**. [ad. OF. *espece* (mod.F. *espèce*) sort, kind, appearance, etc., ad. L. *speciēs* SPECIES. Cf. SPICE *sb.*]

1. Appearance, form, likeness.

a **1325** *Prose Psalter* xlix. 2 Fram þe sonne arisyng vn-to þe going a-doune, þe spece of his fairnes is of Syon. **1490** CAXTON *Eneydos* xix. 70 The soule of my fader Anchisis.. apyereth byfore me vndre the speche of a terryble ymage.

2. a. A spice; an aromatic vegetable condiment. **b.** A medical substance; a drug.

a **1300** *Body & Soul* in *MS. Laud 108* fol. 200 Ȝwere ben þine cokes snelle, þat scholden gon greiþe þi mete With speces [*written* spetes] swete for to smelle? **1390** GOWER *Conf.* II. 325 With diverse spieces The fleissh..Sche takth, and makth therof a sewe. **1561** HOLLYBUSH *Hom. Apoth.* 15 Nether let him eat any fishes nor speces. **1605** TIMME *Quersit.* III. 177 Take..the speces of diamarg[ariton] frigid., camphor, of each 2 drachmes.

3. A species, kind, sort, or variety.

1303 R. BRUNNE *Handl. Synne* 8319 Ȝyt ys þyr a specyal spece þat doþ leccherye klymbe by a grece. **1357** *Lay Folk's Catech.* 527 (T.), Of this syn comes sum sere speces. **1390** GOWER *Conf.* III. 114 As for wisdom, it is in Grece, Wher is apropred thilke spiece. **1422** tr. *Secreta Secret., Priv. Priv.* 219 More-ouer we sene that euery beest hath his propyr Sowle, and his Propyr body. Of thes Speces neuer faillyth. **1491** CAXTON *Vitas Patr.* (W. de W. 1495) I. i. 3 b/2 Nytree, Whyche is a spece of Salte puryfycatyff. *c* **1530** L. COX *Rhet.* (1899) 44 These thre laste be properly callid speces or kindes or oracions. **1637** B. JONSON *Sad Shepherd* III. i, Tempest shall grow hoarse, Loud thunder dumb, and every speece of storm, Laid in the lap of listening nature, hush'd. **1647** M. HUDSON *Div. Right Govt.* II. ix. 137 Thus much briefly of the nature and spece's of Fundamentall Honour; the other spece of Honour opposite to this is Symbolicall.

4. A part, portion, or share; a touch or trace.

c **1330** R. BRUNNE *Chron. Wace* (Rolls) 904 A bacheler.. born y þe lond of Grece; Of þat blod he hadde a spece, ffor his ffader was Gregeys. **1548** UDALL, etc. *Erasm. Par. Mark* ii. 23 Certain of Johns disciples..were attached with a spiece of humain enuie, for that [etc.].

spece, obs. f. SPACE *sb.*[1], SPEAK *sb.*, SPEECH *sb.*

specefie, -fy(e, obs. ff. SPECIFY *v.*

†**specery.** *Obs.* Also **-eri, -erye.** [ad. OF. *especerie*, var. of *espicerie*.] Spicery.

a **1300** *Cursor M.* 23456 (Edinb.), Swet speceri to..smel. *a* **1400** *Sqr. lowe Degre* 687 She sered that body with specery. **1404** in Ellis *Orig. Lett.* Ser. II. I. 30, vi Schippis owte of Fraunce..wᵗ wyn & specery. **1480** CAXTON *Chron. Eng.* ccxliii. 284 Dyuerse speceryes and baumes.

spech(e, obs. ff. SPEECH *sb.*, SPETCH *sb.*

†**speche.** *Obs.*[−1] [Cf. MLG. *spêke*, MHG. *speiche, speich* (G. *speichel*; Du. *speeksel*).] Spittle.

a **1225** *Ancr. R.* 288 þauh heo bispeteð hire mid hire blake spotle [*C.* speches, *T.* speckes].

specheles(s, etc., obs. ff. SPEECHLESS, etc.

specht, obs. f. SPEIGHT (woodpecker).

special ('spɛʃəl), *a.*, *adv.*, and *sb.* Forms: 3–6 **specyal** (4 **-el**), 4–5 **-alle**, 4–6 **-all**; 3–6 **speciale**, 4 **-ele**, 5 **speceale**; 3– **special** (4 **-el**), 4–6 **-alle**, 4–7 **-all**, 6 **spetiall**, 7 **speaciall**. [ad. OF. *especial* (see ESPECIAL *a.*) or L. *speciālis* individual, particular, f. *speciēs* SPECIES. Cf. It. *speciale, speziale*; MDu. *speciael* (Du. *speciaal*), G. *spec-*, *spezial*, *-iell*.]

A. *adj.* **1.** Of such a kind as to exceed or excel in some way that which is usual or common; exceptional in character, quality, or degree:

a. Of actions, qualities, etc.

a **1225** *Ancr. R.* 56 Nullich þet no mon iseo ou bute he habbe leaue speciale of ower meistre. **1297** R. GLOUC. (Rolls) 8730 Special loue þer adde ibe er..Bituene him & þe kinges doȝter Mold of scotlonde. *c* **1340** HAMPOLE *Pr. Consc.* 2781 For þe saul for ilka penaunce here, Sal haf specyel ioy in heven swa clere. *c* **1384** CHAUCER *H. Fame* 68, I wol make Inuocacion With special deuocion. *c* **1400** MAUNDEV. (Roxb.) xi. 49 Þerfore scho had a speciale gift of Godd. *c* **1430** LYDG. *Min. Poems* (Percy Soc.) 44 Do almesse dedes where nede is specialle. *c* **1449** PECOCK *Repr.* II. xi. 214 Forto make..persoones come into remembraunce of a mater, ymagis & picturis seruen in a specialer maner than bokis doon. **1526** *Pilgr. Perf.* (W. de W. 1531) 2 This treatyse promyseth..thre great prerogatiues or special benefytes. **1573** G. HARVEY *Letter-bk.* (Camden) 1 Harti thanks for the ..special gud wil which you have alwais..shewid me. **1601** SHAKS. *Twel. N.* III. iv. 69 Let some of my people haue a speciall care of him. **1624** USSHER in *Lett. Lit. Men* (Camden) 131 The first bookes that I shall have speciall neede of. **1667** MILTON *P.L.* II. 1033 Mortals..whom God and good Angels guard by special grace. **1717** in *Nairne Peerage Evidence* (1874) 145 With the special advice and consent of his said lady. **1781** COWPER *Expost.* 631 The moles and bats in full assembly find, On special search, the keen-ey'd eagle blind. **1818** SCOTT *Hrt. Midl.* xxxiv, As you say you have special reason to apprehend violence from them. **1857** MILLER *Elem. Chem., Org.* ii. §4. 97 The foregoing facts..have a special interest. **1867** FREEMAN *Norm. Conq.* (1877) I. App. 645 Men of no special celebrity.

b. Of material things, events, etc.

13.. *E.E. Allit. P.* A. 235 Ho profered me speche, þat special spyce. **1340–70** *Alisaunder* 183 Ðer sprong neuer spicerie so speciall in erþe. **1535** COVERDALE *Jer.* xxii. 7, I will prepare a destroyer..to hew downe thy special Cedre trees. **1585** T. WASHINGTON tr. *Nicholay's Voy.* II. v. 35 Thinges most speciall and woorthie of memorie. **1610** HOLLAND *Camden's Brit.* (1637) 335 A speciall fountaine, into which God infused a wonderfull gift and vertue. **1685** R. BURTON *Eng. Emp. Amer.* xxii. 208 They have Horses so plentifull that a special one may be bought for six or seven pound. **1831** SCOTT *Cast. Dang.* i, A few special spots excepted, the soil..was more and more mixed with the pastoral and woodland country. **1833** HT. MARTINEAU *Cinnamon & Pearls* v. 92 A special instrument of forcing the means of production into artificial channels.

c. Of persons.

1461 *Paston Lett.* II. 51, I shuld have had as speciall and as gode a maister of you, as any pour man. **1503** HAWES *Examp. Virt.* xiv. 292 Our Sauyour Ihesu deere and specyall. *a* **1548** HALL *Chron., Edw. V*, 13 b, One of the speciallest contriuers of all thys horrible treason. **1639** FULLER *Holy War* II. xl. 97 These proved excellent souldiers and speciall horsemen, and are called Mammalukes. **1747** HOADLY *Suspicious Husband* I. iii, A special Acquaintance I have made to-day! **1854** MISS BAKER *Northampt. Gloss.* s.v., She's a special favourite. **1904** A. GRIFFITHS *50 Years Public Service* xii. 169 A strong brigade of single workers, 'special' convicts, 'blue dress men' of exemplary conduct.

†**d.** *spec.* Notable, important, distinguished. *Obs.*

1576 FLEMING *Panopl. Epist.* 377 Secrete sciences, which hee did impart but to a verie fewe, the same being special persons. **1591** *Reg. Privy Council Scot.* Ser. I. IV. 623 The speciall and cheif personis of the said parochin. **1602** FULBECKE *Pandects* 32 So did the Thebane state a long time florish..by the wisedome of Pelopidas, Epamondas, and other speciall men. **1631** WEEVER *Anc. Funeral Mon.* 516 These I suppose to be the burials of some special persons.

e. *colloq.* Particularly interested or informed.

1830 GALT *Lawrie T.* II. v. (1849) 56, I ain't special 'bout pedigrees.

2. a. Of friends: Admitted to particular intimacy; held in particular esteem.

a **1300** *Cursor M.* 13365 Þe bridgom did alle þider call His specialiest freindes all. **1387** TREVISA *Higden* (Rolls) I. 9 Þan special frendes þat knewe myn entent..prayed me besiliche, þat [etc.]. **1422** tr. *Secreta Secret., Priv. Priv.* 151 Yestyrday he hadd frendys Speciall, but to-day he haue ham all y-lyke. *c* **1489** CAXTON *Sonnes of Aymon* xiv. 344 Come nere, my specyall frende. **1535** COVERDALE *Acts* x. 24 Cornelius..had called together his kynszfolkes and speciall frendes. **1691** WOOD *Ath. Oxon.* II. 191 This book, as Mr. Ley's special friend hath told me, was written by the said Ley. **1863** BOYD *Graver Th. Country Parson* 240 A Christian man ought never to choose for his special friend a person who, he knows, has no religion.

†**b.** Particularly intimate; closely attached by acquaintance or friendship. Const. *to*, *with*. *Obs.*

a **1300** *Cursor M.* 17626 Þai send forth seuen men o wale, War mast to ioseph speciale. *c* **1325** *Metr. Hom.* 30 An cloyster monk loued him ful wel, And was til him ful speciel. **1375** BARBOUR *Bruce* v. 501 Thai vald nocht persauit be, That thai war speciall to the king. *c* **1450** *St. Cuthbert* (Surtees) 2610 Elfled, þat honorabil abbas, To whaim cuthbert sa special was. *Ibid.* 7885 He was speciall to þe kyng. *c* **1500** *Lancelot* 411 To them that war to hyme most speciall. *Ibid.* 906 For o knycht he send, That was most speciall with the lady kend.

3. a. Marked off from others of the kind by some distinguishing qualities or features; having a distinct or individual character; also, in weakened sense, particular, certain.

1303 R. BRUNNE *Handl. Synne* 8319 Ȝyt ys þyr a specyal spece þat doþ leccherye klymbe by a grece. *c* **1386** CHAUCER *Pars. T.* ¶488 Alle other synnes ben somtyme oonly agains oon special vertu; but certes envye is agayns alle vertues. **1387** TREVISA *Higden* (Rolls) I. 27 Eueriche prouince and londe is descryued for to me come to Britayne þe laste of alle, as most special. **1535** COVERDALE *Zech.* xiv. 8 This shalbe that specyall daye, which is knowne vnto the Lorde. **1561** T. NORTON *Calvin's Inst.* I. 32 Seing it is the purpose of yᵉ Prophet to adorn Christ with such special notes as may builde our Faith vpon him. **1620** T. GRANGER *Div. Logike* 43 Aristotle saith, a man is the most speciall. **1628** T. SPENCER *Logick* 131 That is most speciall, vnto which there can be no other Species inferior. **1725** WATTS *Logic* I. iii. §3 A special Idea is call'd by the Schools, a Species. **1768–74** TUCKER *Lt. Nat.* (1834) I. 474 As well in entire systems as in their sundry parts, yea, members, and more-over, the speciallest species of them. **1841** *Penny Cycl.* XXI. 178/2 Of Special or Local Secretions. *Ibid.*, Secreted in a particular part of plants for a special purpose. **1854** GEO. ELIOT tr. *Feuerbach's Essence Christianity* iii. 44 God as God..has no more significance for religion than a fundamental general principle has for a special science. **1859** BARTLETT *Dict. Amer.* (ed. 2) 432 *Special deposit*, a deposit made in a bank subject to the control of the depositor, and which is not made a part of the funds of the bank to be used by it in its business. **1861** M. PATTISON *Ess.* (1889) I. 48 The Germans ..maintained in it an altar, and had their own masses said in it on special days. **1866** *Weekly New Mexican* (Santa Fe) 22 Dec. 2/2 One of the senators from San Miguel county having resigned, a special election was held. **1884** J. SULLY *Outlines Psychol.* xii. 553 The order of development of the special sensibilities..concerned. **1886** I. M. RITTENHOUSE *Jrnl.* 3 Feb. in *Maud* (1939) xi. 368 Eliza brought me a special delivery letter from my good boy. **1904** *Harper's Mag.* Feb. 462/2 And what a lucky chance that brought me a 'special delivery'. **1907** R. HERMON-HODGE *Let.* 20 Jan. in R. S. Churchill *Winston S. Churchill* (1969) II. Compan. I. 641, I am sure you will agree that while the class of men which provides the Yeomanry with officers must often present 'special cases' such as yours, it would never do to make them precedents. **1908** Special school [see DEFECTIVE *sb.* 2c]. **1911** W. JAMES *Some Probl. Philos.* i. 4 Limited by the omission of the special sciences, the name of philosophy has come more and more to denote ideas of universal scope exclusively. **1921** *Handicapped Children* (Connecticut Board of Educ.) 6 Let us consider those children who are in need of special education because of some degree of mental abnormality. **1929** E. C. THOMAS *Lay Folks' Hist. Liturgy* I. xiv. 62 In addition to the missions mentioned above, there seems to have been a special relationship between Britain and Galicia. **1944** *Act 7 & 8 Geo. VI* c. 31 §228 In fulfilling their duties under this section, a local education authority shall, in particular, have regard..to the need for securing that provision is made for pupils who suffer from any disability of mind or body by providing, either in special schools or otherwise, special educational treatment. **1944** H. A. HODGES *Wilhelm Dilthey* 110 At the close of the Middle Age the emancipation of the special sciences began. **1945** *Hansard Commons* 7 Nov. 1299 We should not abandon our special relationship with the United States and Canada about the atomic bomb. **1957** LD. HAILEY *African Survey 1956* xvii. 1160 The academic standards to be adopted in the new University College in the first instance were to be those of the University of London, and an application to enter into 'special relationship' with the University of London was accepted. **1958** *Times* 4 July 15/1 The new scheme of 'special deposits' to be introduced by the Bank of England will in effect be kept in reserve in case of need. **1961** *Yale Review* LI. 21 If Britain enters 'Europe', the possibly illusory 'special relationship' with the United States will lose much of its plausibility. **1963** *Sunday Express* 7 July 1 There is a faction in Washington which does not share the official United States policy of friendship for Britain, and which dislikes the 'special relationship' between the two countries. **1968** Special class [see PREEMIE]. **1974** *State* (Columbia, S. Carolina) 15 Feb. 22-A/6 The beleaguered Republican candidate in the February 5 special election to replace the late Rep. John Saylor of Pennsylvania. **1974** Special vote [see OVERALL, OVER-ALL *adv.* 1 c]. **1976** *Pacifist* Jan. 4/1 The Secretary of State for Defence insists that defence is a special case—housing, social services, education are not? **1977** Special delivery [see RECORDED *ppl. a.* 1 b]. **1977** *Times Educ. Suppl.* 21 Oct. 47/3 A teacher with experience in Special Education to teach basic subjects to groups of slow-learning children. **1978** *London Clearing Banks* (Committee London Clearing Bankers) 68 From 1958 onwards the Bank was able to supplement its open-market operations with calls for special deposits from the clearing banks; when a call was made, each bank had to lodge at the Bank of England a cash deposit of a specified percentage of its total deposits. **1979** R. JAFFE *Class Reunion* (1980) III. iv. 333 The baby had been sent to a special school because she had been born with a kind of sickness. **1980** *Encounter* May 41/2 The encounters took on a peculiarly symbolic significance at a time when various signs point to the possible demise of Israel's 'special relationship' with West Germany and the United States.

b. In predicative use: Limited or restricted.

1848 J. T. WHITE *Xenophon's Anab.* III. iv. §15 Notes (1872) 174 Zeune refers the term to their imitating the Scythians in the mode of discharging the arrow; but this is too special.

c. Additional to the usual or ordinary.

1840 *Rep. Sel. Comm. Railw. Quest.* 255, I believe this special train was the next. **1847** in *Thames Valley Times* (1887) 22 June 5/3 Special Trains may be engaged for large Parties. **1872** B. JERROLD *London* xx. 177 The news-boy would deliver the special edition. **1882** J. HATTON *Journalistic Lond.* 148 The whole *Morning Standard* is printed in one hour and fifty minutes,..and the special edition in forty-five minutes. **1939** L. MACNEICE *Autumn Jrnl.* v. 23 They are selling and buying the late Special editions snatched and read abruptly. **1957** V. BRITTAIN *Testament of Experience* iv. 162 Newsvendors calling special editions ran up and down.

d. Special collocations: ***Special Air Service***, a special section of the armed forces trained in commando techniques of warfare; cf. *S.A.S.* s.v. S 4 a; ***special area***, a depressed area of high unemployment designated in 1934 (see quot.) for development and improvement; cf. *development area* s.v. DEVELOPMENT 11; ***Special Branch***, a section of the C.I.D. which deals with police matters relating to political security; ***Special Drawing Right***, an additional drawing right allocated to member countries of the International Monetary Fund, allowing them extra powers to purchase foreign currency from the Fund, and so increase their foreign exchange reserves; usu. *pl.*; cf. *SDR* s.v. S 4 a; ***special effect*** (Cinematogr.), a scenic illusion created by props and camera-work (see quot. 1951); usu. *pl.*; ***special interest*** (U.S.), a group or corporation which seeks special advantages for itself, usu. by political means; ***special paper***, an extra advanced examination of the General Certificate of Education, formerly known as a scholarship paper; ***Special Reserve***, special units formed in peacetime to furnish a reserve for the regular army in time of war; ***special stage*** (see quot. 1967).

1942 *We speak from the Air* (Ministry of Information) xvii. 53 There is no better example of co-operation between the services than in the organisation and training of the *Special Air Service troops that has been quietly taking place for some time. **1977** *Proc. R. Soc. Med.* LXX. 504/1 Major I. T. Houghton discussed first aid in the Special Air Service Regiment. This was formed in 1941 by David Stirling for operations behind the enemy lines in North Africa. **1980** *Jrnl. R. Soc. Arts* July 491/1 The Special Air Service..is trained for special tasks and it therefore represents the ready-made anti-hijacking force. **1934** *Act 25 Geo. V* c. 1 §8 (1) This Act may be cited as the *Special Areas (Development and Improvement) Act, 1934. **1945** *Archit. Rev.* XCVII. 109/1 The former Special Areas, now renamed (with adjustments) the Development Areas, are not necessarily economic and social entities. **1979** G. POTTINGER *Secretaries of State for Scotland 1926–76* xiv. 148 The modest incentives dating originally from the Special Areas Acts of 1934 and 1937, and modified by post-war legislation, to persuade firms to move to depressed districts were no longer considered adequate. **1894** J. G. LITTLECHILD *Reminiscences* i. 8 The later years of my service at Scotland Yard were spent in connection with the '*special' branch of the Criminal Investigation Department. **1936** 'N. BLAKE' *Thin Shell of Death* ix. 159 Scotland Yard had got into touch with the Special Branch in Dublin. **1962** *Listener* 15 Mar. 459/2 Warrants of this kind would be normally executed by special branch officers acting under the directions of the Director of Public Prosecutions. **1979** J. WAINWRIGHT *Duty Elsewhere* vii. 30 The Special Branch... Originally, it was the Special *Irish* Branch. Terror met by terror. **1982** *Listener* 16 Dec. 4/1 It is held by those in Special Branch that contact with Security Service is already so close that SB ought to take over primary responsibility for counter-espionage. **1967** *Bankers' Mag.* CCIV. 216 The scheme for creating new 'reserve units'..had already been abandoned for a plan for establishing new special automatic drawing rights with the IMF... The *special drawing rights will be shown as part of the reserves in Britain and the US... The special drawing rights are to be administered by the IMF, but kept separate from its other assets. **1971** H. WILSON *Labour Govt.* xxxv. 726 The IMF Special Drawing Rights scheme ..had come into effect on 28 July [1969]. **1978** *Internat. Relations Dict.* (U.S. Dept. State Library) 23/2 The IMF has created its own international unit of account—the Special Drawing Right (or SDR or 'paper gold'). **1937** *Special effects [see EDITOR *sb.* 5]. **1951** *Jrnl. Soc. Motion Picture & Television Engineers* LVII. 53/1 Studio terminology combines under 'special effects' a large variety of items, materials, equipment and processes which..aid in realistically imitating natural phenomena..which otherwise could be considered only at prohibitive expense or with impossible hazards. **1978** R. HILL *Pinch of Snuff* vii. 65 The special effects department must be getting better. **1910** G. PINCHOT *Fight for Conservation* 134 The people of the United States believe that..the Senate and the House no longer represent the voters by whom they were elected, but the *special interests by whom they are controlled. **1980** *Outdoor Life* (U.S.) (Northeast ed.) Oct. 21/2 It is a measure of the arrogance of the special interests that 53 of the new lease applications are for tracts inside the proposed wilderness area. **1963** *Times Educ. Suppl.* 1 Feb. 197/4 In your issue of November 23 a letter was published concerning the restriction imposed by the S.S.E.C. that no A level candidate may offer more than two of the *special papers which are to replace the scholarship papers. **1976** *Bridgwater Mercury* 21 Dec. 1/5 Karen..passed all of her A level subjects, English, Economics and History at Grade A, as well as gaining a Distinction on the Special Paper in the last subject. **1908** *Times* 11 Apr. 8/2 The second order details the precise conditions of the transfer of all Militia units, except those disbanded, to the *Special Reserve. **1908** *Regs. for Officers of Special Reserve* 1 The Special Reserve of Officers is a branch of the Reserve of Officers, established by Royal Warrant dated the 3rd April, 1908. *Ibid.*, The Special Reserve. Special reservists form part of the first class of the army reserve. **1909** *Army & Navy Gaz.* 19 June 589/2 Mr. Haldane stated that bayonets are now being issued to all infantry units of the Special Reserve which are being armed with the short rifle. **1931** [see CADRE 2]. **1935** *Regs. for Officers & Airmen of Special Reserve serving in R.A.F. Squadrons* (Amendment 5) 1 Applications for the attendance of Special Reserve personnel to give evidence in private lawsuits will be reported at once through the usual channels. **1967** P. MOSS *Story so Far* vi. 65 A lot of international rallies..have special stages, or tests, over the worst bits of road they can find. Not all big rallies have to do this but on those which do it is on these *special stages that the rally is won and lost. **1977** *Belfast Tel.* 27 Jan. 25/4 The other two members of the team have elected him to drive all the competitive sections—or special stages—along the 18,000 mile route.

4. Of persons: **a.** Appointed or employed for a particular purpose or occasion. †Also in predicative use (with *in*).

13.. *K. Alis.* 7609 (Laud MS.), By a speciale messager, I wil hir sende loue drurye. **13..** *E.E. Allit. P.* B. 1492 Bifore þe sancta sanctorum soþefast dryȝtyn Expouned his speche spiritually to special prophetes. *c* **1400** LOVE *Bonavent. Mirr.* (1908) 49 Peraunter gabriel that was special messanger of this werk. **1405** *Rolls of Parlt.* III. 605/1 Our generalls and specialls Attornes and Deputes. *c* **1450** *St. Cuthbert* (Surtees) 843 þai were speciale in his seruyse. **1646** GATAKER *Mistake Removed* 18 Having from the mouth of God, by a special expresse, received a release. **1801–31** [see CONSTABLE 5 e]. **1843** N. SIMONS *Statutes at Large, U.K.* XVI. 131 Commissioners for General Purposes to execute all Matters with respect to the Duties under all the Schedules except such as are directed to be executed by Special or other commissioners. **1856** *Men of the Time* 687 He was deputed to be the special correspondent of the 'Times' in the Crimea. **1865** *Ibid.* 714/2 He was employed as Special Commissioner during the Irish famine. **1926** *Daily Chron.* 13 May 1/3 Measures must be taken to demobilise the special constabulary..and to ensure the speedy return to normal conditions. **1932** AUDEN *Orators* I. 36 Jokes about special constables and conscientious objectors. **1956** in J. Biggs-Davison *Hand is Red* (1973) x. 134 Members of the R.U.C. and B Special Constabulary. **1970** *Britain 1970: an Official Handbk.* (Central Office of Information) 105 All police forces have an attachment of special constables, who are volunteers willing to perform police duties without pay in their spare time. In England and Wales the function of special constables is to act as auxiliary to the regular force when required. In Scotland they are employed only in emergencies, although they may be assigned for duty for training purposes. **1970** P. LAURIE *Scotland Yard* 294 *Special patrol group*, a unit of uniform policemen, about 130 strong, attached to no particular area. They are available for intensive patrolling, searches, guards, raids, etc. **1971** *Halsbury's Statutes England* (ed. 3) XXXIV. 1252 Unlike the General Commissioners..the Special Commissioners are civil servants, and their powers and duties are not limited to any particular area... They do, however, act independently of the Crown. **1980** P. G. WINSLOW *Counsellor Heart* xx. 215 Men were sent to saturate the area. The Special Patrol Group was called in.

b. Devoted to a particular or limited field of study or research.

1899 *Allbutt's Syst. Med.* VIII. 120 Some well-known (and not too special) specialist.

c. ***special buyer***, the bill-broker of the Bank of England in the discount market; ***special partner*** (U.S.) = *limited partner* s.v. LIMITED *ppl. a.* 2 b.

1941 *Economist* 1 Feb. 149/1 The help given to the market last week by the special buyer has made itself more felt. **1965** SELDON & PENNANCE *Dict. Econ.* 311 In Britain open market operations in Treasury Bills are conducted through a firm of discount brokers (the 'Special Buyer') on instructions from the Bank of England. **1822** *Laws of State of New York* ccxliv. 259 That partnerships, to be formed under this act, shall consist of one or more partners, jointly and severally responsible..who shall be called general partners; and one or more partners, who furnish certain funds or capital to the common stock, whose liability shall extend no further than the fund which he or they have furnished to the partnership stock, and who shall be called special partners. **1839** MARRYAT *Diary Amer.* 1st Ser. II. 251 In America, if a person wishes to become a special partner (a sleeping partner) in any concern, he may do so to any extent he pleases. **1889** *Cent. Dict.* 4309/1 If the statute governing partnerships is violated the special partner becomes liable as a general partner.

5. a. Having an individual, particular, or limited application, object, or intention; affecting or concerning a single person, thing, circumstance, etc., or a particular class of these.

special intention: see INTENTION 12 b.

13.. *Coer de L.* 6471 The abbot..brought hym lettres speciele, Aselyd with the barouns sele. *c* **1380** WYCLIF *Sel. Wks.* III. 441 þai say furst, þat speciale prayere..is better þen generale. *c* **1400** *Lanfranc's Cirurg.* 195 þe white morphu is curid..wiþ þis special medicyn. **1444** *Rolls of Parlt.* V. 111/2 That..a speciall Commission be made to the chief Justice of your Benche. **1526** SKELTON *Magnyf.* 2464 From you I receyued a letter, Whiche conteyned in it a specyall clause That I sholde vse Largesse. **1570–6** LAMBARDE *Peramb. Kent* (1826) 329 Of a speciall intent and purpose to pray to God for raine. **1596** SHAKS. *Merch. V.* v. i. 292 There doe I giue to you..a speciall deed of gift. **1613** PURCHAS *Pilgrimage* (1614) 918 On which day this..came.. without any special appointment, to the presse. **1651** HOBBES *Leviath.* II. xxvi. 145 In which case there is no speciall Law ordained. **1764** BURN *Poor Laws* 194 To.. distribute the same, together with other special benefactions, to such as shall have most need. **1790** F. BURNEY *Diary* Jan. (1842) V. III. 85 Mr Fairly's marriage.. was by special licence, and at the house of Sir R— F—. **1802** PALEY *Nat. Theol.* xv. (1819) 242 It is a special purpose, specially consulted throughout. **1825** Special licence [see DROIT[1] 1 b]. **1849** MACAULAY *Hist. Eng.* vi. II. 51 He was sent to London charged with several special commissions of high importance. **1849** *Rep. Sel. Comm. Public Libraries* 138 in *Parl. Papers* XVII. 1 The second description of libraries would be those destined to represent special branches of literature; for instance the Commercial Library, or the Library of Fine Arts, at Hamburgh, would be a most perfect instance of those special libraries. **1862** *Sat. Rev.* 8 Feb. 147 Popular theology dispenses with special knowledge as a key to difficulties. **1892** *Photogr. Ann.* II. 285, I could not very well include it under 'Special Cameras.' **1908** H. CECIL *Let.* 20 Aug. in R. S. Churchill *Winston S. Churchill* (1969) II. Compan. II. 808 A special licence costs a lot of money..so you had better go for an ordinary one or for banns. **1937** *Discovery* June 192/2 At the request of the British Council, the Association of Special Libraries and Information Bureaux had undertaken the compilation of a short list of standard and technical books by British authors. **1954** K. AMIS *Lucky Jim* iii. 27 Have you got that syllabus together ..the list of stuff for your special subject next year? **1966** A. BATTERSBY *Math. in Management* ix. 232 The appeal to elasticity is evident in any retail outlet with price reductions, 'special offers' or trading stamps. **1971** P. D. JAMES *Shroud for Nightingale* vii. 243 He might well have told his special nurse or blurted it out in his delirium. **1973** *Scotsman* 7 Aug. 6/2 The 'wedding' in the registrar's office at Dumfries took place after the couple were granted a special licence in the courthouse only 50 yards away. **1976** *Gloss. Documentation Terms* (*B.S.I.*) 62 *Special library*, a library maintained by an association, government agency, parliament, research institution, learned society, professional association, museum, business firm, industrial organization, chamber of commerce, etc. or other organized group, the greater part of its collection being in a specific field or subject. **1977** *Western Morning News* 1 Sept. 1/1 Instant coffee is to be on 'special offer' in various shops and supermarkets for the next six months.

b. Entering into details or particulars; precise.

1681 *Lond. Gaz.* No. 1648/4 Providing always that the Libel..be special, as to a certain place..; and also be special as to the time. **1876** E. MELLOR *Priesthood* viii. 348 This confession must not only be general, but special, involving a minute description of all the circumstances in which the sins were committed.

c. ***special (theory of) relativity***: see RELATIVITY 2.

6. Having close, intimate, or exclusive connexion or relationship with one person or thing (or set of these); peculiar: **a.** Of persons.

1382 WYCLIF *Deut.* vii. 6 That thow be to hym a special puple. **1456** SIR G. HAYE *Law Arms* (S.T.S.) 253 [The] king of Napples mon..mak..oblissing to the pape as specale lord soverane till him. **1508** KENNEDIE *Flyting w. Dunbar* 417, I am the kingis blude, his trew speciall clerk. **1591** SHAKS. *1 Hen. VI*, I. i. 171 To Eltam will I, where the young King is, Being ordayn'd his speciall Gouernor. **1611** BIBLE *Deut.* vii. 6 The Lord thy God hath chosen thee to be a special people vnto himselfe. **1737** CHALLONER *Cath. Chr. Instr.* (1753) 213 In this Nation we keep the Days of St. Thomas of Canterbury, and of St. George, as our special Patrons. **1898** WATTS-DUNTON *Aylwin* I. ii, I always looked upon him as my special paid henchman.

b. Of things.

1484 CAXTON *Chivalry* 89 The comyn wele is gretter and more necessary than propre good and specyall. **1548** UDALL, etc. *Erasm. Par. Luke* v. 54 b, The propre and moste speciall office of suche an one. **1578** LYTE *Dodoens* II. xliv. 202 Floures..without any speciall smell. **1599** HAKLUYT *Voy.* II. II. 4 Their language was speciall, and not mixed with Romane speech or Arabian. **1673–4** GREW *Anat. Pl., Trunks* (1682) 132 The specifying of the Sap dependeth chiefly on the special Nature of the Parts. **1850** MCCOSH *Div. Govt.* III. i. (1874) 296 Every intuitive principle in our constitution has its special truth to reveal and sanction. **1870** J. YEATS *Nat. Hist. Comm.* 1 Each region has its special treasures. **1884** R. PATON *Scott. Ch.* viii. 81 Columba..had his special cell at Iona, in which he wrote and read.

c. Const. *to*.

1871 RUSKIN *Arrows of Chace* (1880) I. 227 Nearly every great church in France has some merit special to itself. **1894** *Nature's Method in Evol. Life* vii. 77 The new force special to the whale.

7. *Law.* Used with a large number of legal terms to denote particular or distinctive instances or cases of the thing, action, or person in question, as ***special bail***, ***bailiff***, ***bastard(y***, ***heir***, ***magistrate***, ***occupant***, ***order***, ***prosecutor***, ***resolution***, ***tail***, ***term***, ***verdict***.

See also JURY 2 d, and SPECIAL PLEADER, PLEADING.

1495 [see TAIL *sb.*² 3 b]. **1544** tr. *Littleton's Tenures* 4 b, Tenaunt in tayle specyal, is where landes and tenementes be gyuen vnto a man and his wyfe and the heyres of theyr .ii. bodyes begoten. **1665** EVER *Tryals per Pais* xiii. 166 A Special Verdict, or Verdict at large, is so called, because it findeth the special matter at large, and leaveth the Judgement of the Law thereupon, to the Court. **1720** T. WOOD *Inst. Laws Eng.* II. 1009 The Special Pleas are many, as *Per dures*, *Per Minas*. **1768** BLACKSTONE *Comm.* II. 259 There the heir might, and still may, enter and hold possession, and is called in law a special occupant. **1769** *Ibid.* III. 287 In order to arrest the defendant, and make him put in substantial sureties for his appearance, called special bail. **1818** CRUISE *Digest* (ed. 2) VI. 413 With a subsequent devise to the heirs general, or special, or issue, of A. **1835** *Tomlins's Law Dict.* I. s.v. *Bailiff*, Formerly bailiffs of hundreds were the officers to execute writs; but now it is done by special bailiffs, put in with them by the sheriff. *Ibid.* s.v. *Bastard*, Bastardy, in relation to the several manners of its trial, is distinguished into general and special bastardy. **1845** STEPHEN *Comm. Laws Eng.* (1874) II. 176 By 'Special' resolution—i.e., by one passed by a majority in number and three-fourths in value of the creditors present. **1852** *Alabama Reports* XX. 446 The Court of Commissioners of Roads and Revenue in this State has no power to hold special terms, except in cases expressly authorized by law. **1859** *Indiana Reports* XI. 562 The indictment was signed by James F. Suit, as prosecuting attorney; but it appears that he was a special prosecutor elected by the people. **1889** *Cent. Dict.*, *Special orders*, in *law*, those orders which are made only in view of the peculiar circumstances of the case, and require notice to the adversary and a hearing by the court. **1919** *Act 9 & 10 Geo. V* c. 100 §26 Anything which under the Electric Lighting Acts may be effected by a provisional order confirmed by Parliament may be effected by a special order made by the Electricity Commissioners and confirmed by the Board of Trade. **1934** *Northeastern Reporter* CXC. 270/2 'Special term of court' is one not fixed by general statute establishing court terms, but ordinarily called pursuant to power granted by statute. **1936** *Panel* Mar. 3/3 Several thousand additional witnesses have been examined in the office of Mr. Dewey, the Special Prosecutor. **1966** TACHERON & UDALL *Job of Congressman* vii. 198 Special orders are designed primarily to authorize the House to disregard the regular rules of procedure so that a particular matter can be handled with dispatch. **1973** *N.Y. Law Jrnl.* 25 July 12/8 The sole question raised on this appeal is whether or not Special Term erred when it concluded that a 1960 Pontiac convertible..was covered under an automobile insurance policy issued with respect to a 1960 Buick sedan. **1974** *Greenville* (S. Carolina) *News* 22 Apr. 1/3 'The special prosecutor has already indicted and is preparing to try' seven former Nixon campaign or administration aides. **1975** J. P. MORGAN *House of Lords & Labour Govt.* ii. 64 Orders are known in the Lords as Special Orders. **1979** *Internat. Jrnl. Sociol. of Law* VII. 279 The function of the Special Magistrate was 'to represent in his own person the whole policy of Britain'.

8. ***Math.*** Of a group: that can be represented by matrices of unit determinant.

1903 J. E. CAMPBELL *Theory Continuous Groups* i. 17 This group is called the special linear homogeneous group; it is a sub-group of the general linear homogeneous group. **1955** B. HIGMAN *Appl. Group-Theoretic & Matrix Methods* xii. 181 The rotation group in three dimensions is isomorphic with a factor group of the special unitary group in two dimensions containing half the number of elements. **1955**, **1967** [see *SU* s.v. *S* 4 a]. **1968** M. S. LIVINGSTON *Particle Physics* xii. 212 Special unitary group theory based on two fundamental states (known by the symbol SU(2)) leads to the prediction of a multiplet structure in the spectrum of substates. **1971** D. GORENSTEIN in Powell & Higman *Finite Simple Groups* ii. 68 The latter group is the projective special unitary group.

9. ***Comb.*** In collocations used attributively, as ***special agreement***, **-*creation***, **-*interest***, **-*occasion***, **-*procedure***, **-*purpose***, **-*range***, **-*service***, **-*temper***, or derivatives of these, as ***special-creationist***, **-*correspondently*** adv.

1886 SPENCER in *19th Cent.* May 766 The point of view of the special-creationist. **1887** *Pall Mall G.* 10 Jan. 5/1 When the special-service man desires to inculcate caution on the driver of the next train, he affixes a single detonator to the rail. **1891** KIPLING *Life's Handicap* 86 It suited him to talk special-correspondently. **1895** W. H. HUDSON *Intr. Spencer's Philos.* 27 The special-creation hypothesis. **1897** *Outing* XXX. 279/1 A special-temper tool steel. **1901** *Daily Tel.* 9 Mar. 9/3 Two British special service officers have left London for the Abyssinian capital. **1944** *Act 7 & 8 Geo. VI* c. 31 §26 If at any time the managers or governors of an aided school or a special agreement school are unable or unwilling to carry out their obligations..it shall be their duty to apply to the Minister for an order revoking the order by virtue of which the school is an aided school or special agreement school. **1945** NELSON & WRIGHT *Tomorrow's House* vii. 80/1 The living-room..is..turning into a special-purpose room like the study. **1952** *Times* 4 Feb. 2/3, £250,000 for grants in aid towards a new 'special agreement' secondary school, and for works at four aided polytechnics. **1956** ABRAHAM & HAWTREY *Parliamentary Dict.* 188 *Special procedure order*, a term applied by the standing orders of both Houses to an order, made or confirmed by a minister, in relation to which the Statutory Orders (Special Procedure) Act, 1945, applies. **1957** *Times Lit. Suppl.* 8 Nov. 678/5 Instruction covers everything from the regular features of the dinner table to special-occasion items for the buffet or the hors-d'œuvre tray. **1959** W. K. RICHMOND *British Birds of Prey* p. xi, How far, if at all, was it safe to rely on a phraseology which enjoyed no common currency, however acceptable it might be to this or that special-interest group? **1961** *Act 9 & 10 Eliz. II* c. 62 2nd Schedule §2 Where a trust fund includes special-range property,.. the special-range property shall be carried to a separate part of the fund. **1964** D. FOULKES *Introd. Admin. Law* i. 6 The first part of the procedure provides for the proper publication of the order (known as a 'special procedure order') and the making of objections, and the second part for parliamentary scrutiny. **1982** *Time* 8 Nov. 92/2 The special-interest slangs generated then were interminably publicized.

B. *adv.* and in phr. ***in special.***

1. In a special manner; especially, particularly. Now only *colloq.* or *dial.*

a **1300** *Cursor M.* 27972 Speciale þan cals þis sin Wrak o him þat ligges þar-in. **1340** *Ayenb.* 230 Oure lhordes lemman special is yloued þet lokeþ maydenhod. **14..** *Sir Beues* (C) 688 + 3 Sche preyed yow specyalle, To come & speke with hur yn preuyte. **1451** CAPGRAVE *Life St. Aug.* 35 He comendid gretly his cunnyng and special his deuocion. **1513** BRADSHAW *St. Werburge* I. 2460 It [i.e. an exemption] to confyrme and roborate specyall With charters and dedes and seales patent. **1545** RAYNALD *Byrth Mankynde* 124 Sethe them in white wyne, and therein lap the infante, spetiall yf it be not taken ouer great heate. **1600** PORY tr. *Leo's Africa* VI. 278 Great plenty of dates, which..are speciall good. **1613** USSHER *Lett.* (1686) 17 One thing therein I think special worthy of observation. **1670** J. SMITH *Eng. Improv. Reviv'd* 65 The Chesnut is special good Timber for Building. **1765** COWPER *Let.* 5 Nov., They [the Unwins] live in a special good house. **1851** HELPS *Companions of Solit.* vii. 143 A case came on rather unexpectedly..and I was sent for 'special' as we say. **1856** *2nd Rep. Postmaster General* 12 That the Night Mail train should be run special (without passengers). **1859** THACKERAY *Virgin.* ix, The Duke of Marlborough was no special good penman.

†**2.** **in special**: **a.** Specially, especially, particularly. *Obs.*

c **1374** CHAUCER *Troylus* I. 901 Se that thow in special Requere not that is ayens her name. **1390** GOWER *Conf.* I. 7 The world is changed overal, And therof most in special That love is falle into discord. *c* **1400** *Pilgr. Sowle* (Caxton, 1483) IV. xxxiii. 81 Ther ben other counceylours of the kynge that haue for to sene in special to gouernaunce of his propre goodes. *c* **1440** *Gesta Rom.* I. xlviii. 211 The Emperour made a generall feste, to the whiche þe Erle was i-bede in speciall. **1500** in *Exch. Rolls Scotl.* XII. 266 *note*, To all and sindry oure liegis..and in speciale to our custumaris of oure burgh of Abirdene. **1551** ROBINSON tr. *More's Utopia* I. (1895) 33 Chyefelye suche thynges as shalbe profytable to be knowne; as in specyall be thoese decrees and ordinaunces. **1603** BODLEY in *Buccleuch MSS.* (Hist. MSS. Comm.) 44 We have a speech given out, among Papists in special, of a match..between our Prince and the King of Spain's..daughter. **1665** BUNYAN *Holy Citie* (1669) 62 Which Salvation I take in special to signifie our fortification and safety from the wrath of God. **1680** ALLEN *Peace & Unity* 134 He singles out this in special as the matter of his request.

†**b.** In detail; so as to enter into particulars. *Obs.*

c **1386** CHAUCER *Melib.* ¶268 Ȝe han wel & couenably taught me as in general how I shal gouerne me... But now wolde I fayn þat ȝe wolde condescende in special. **1401** *26 Pol. Poems* iii. 49, I speke not in specyale Of oo kyngdom the lawe to telle; I speke hool in generale. *c* **1449** PECOCK *Repr.* V. xv. 562 That y be not ouer long..y speke not of thilk mater in special here. **1573** *Satir. Poems Reform.* xl. 106 That this may be maid mair manifest, I will discurs sum thing in speciall Tuiching this Lamp.

†**c.** In an individual, separate, or distinctive manner. *Obs.*

1390 GOWER *Conf.* I. 18, I wol noght seie in general, For ther ben somme in special In whom that alle vertu duelleth. *Ibid.* 92 Bot such a thing in special, Which to hem alle in general Is most plesant. **1469** *Waterf. Arch.* in *10th Rep. Hist. MSS. Comm.* App. V. 307 If ony suete or chalange be ..so done in commene or in speciall. **1508** DUNBAR *Tua Mariit Wemen* 495 To euery man in speciall speke I sum wordis. *c* **1550** '*Faine wald I, with all diligence*' in *Dunbar's Poems* (1893) 310 And thocht I say in generale, Sum sall it tak in speciale.

C. *sb.* †**1.** **a.** A particularly intimate or favourite friend, associate, or follower. *Obs.*

c **1290** *S. Eng. Leg.* I. 23 þat specials to hym were. **13..** *Coer de L.* 2352 Let him yelde my tresor every dele If he will be my speciele. *a* **1340** HAMPOLE *Psalter* lxvii. 27 [Those] till whaim aungels ere gret specials. *c* **1400** *Destr. Troy* 8830 Thus he spake for his spede his specials vnto. *a* **1450** tr. *De Imitatione* II. viii. 49 Lete ihesu be sool þy derlyng and þy special. **1581** *Satir. Poems Reform.* xliii. 129 Ane of the speciallis [that] did mentene ȝour croun, Ȝour ferme protectour in ȝour tender ȝeiris. **1596** DALRYMPLE tr. *Leslie's Hist. Scot.* II. 84 To require libertie to cum to Scotland with ..his gard of his speciallis. *a* **1660** HAMMOND *Serm. Prov.* i. 22 (1664) 42 The Saviour, that hath promises of long life annexed to some specials of his service.

†**b.** A (female) sweetheart or paramour; a mistress or concubine. *Obs.*

c **1375** in *Rel. Ant.* I. 40 Byhold, my derlyng, speketh to me, arys, come nerre, my special, come. **1388** *Pol. Poems* (Rolls) I. 276 Here specialis yf y kys [*v.r.* Ther special whan thei kis]. **1432–50** tr. *Higden* (Rolls) VI. 449 Hit happede a monke of Seynte Audoen in Roone to goe in a nyȝhte towarde the hows of his specialle. **1473** *Visitation Paper* in *Archaeologia* XLVIII. 250 þe vecar of þe sayde towne has haldyn to hys speciall this vj ȝere and more, and noe correction done. **1554** *Interlude of Youth* C j b, A backe galantes, and loke vnto me, And take me for your speciall.

†**c.** A male sweetheart or lover. *Obs.*

c **1400** *Laud Troy Bk.* 13552 To vysite him ful offte sche went; For sche wiste he toke the falle Off Troyle that was hir specialle. **1432–50** tr. *Higden* (Rolls) VI. 333 After that sche electe into pope..was gete with childe by her specialle. *c* **1489** CAXTON *Blanchardyn* xx. 67 [She] altogydre was of her determyned, to make of Blanchardyn her louer and her specyall. *a* **1500** *Gest Robin Hood* VIII. xxxv, For the loue of a knyght, Syr Roger of Donkesly, That was her owne speciall.

†**2.** A particular person; an individual. *Obs.*

c **1400** *Destr. Troy* 4292 Fals goddes..þat entrid into ymagis,..Spekand to specyals, þat spede for to aske. *Ibid.* 12119 All þai sparit þat speciall to spill at þe tyme.

†**3.** **a.** A particular point, part, detail, concept, or statement. *Obs.*

c **1386** CHAUCER *Melib.* ¶389 Lat us now descende to the special [*v.r.* purpos special]. *c* **1449** PECOCK *Repr.* V. v. 512 This comaundement..is not but a special and a parti of this general and hool comaundement. **1581** *Satir. Poems Reform.* xliii. 25 To pen the speciallis it passis mony a hunder. **1594** T. B. *La Primaud. Fr. Acad.* II. 162 Reason ..descendeth from generalles to specialles, & from them to particulars. **1611** W. SCLATER *Key* (1629) 177 Which generall is farther amplified by the specials. **1628** T. SPENCER *Logick* 204 Of the kindes of Distribution, and first of the Generall into the Speciall.

†**b.** A particular thing or article. *Obs.*

1599 B. JONSON *Ev. Man out of Hum.* II. i[i], To the perfection of the compliment..are required these three specials. **1615** in *Buccleuch MSS.* (Hist. MSS. Comm.) I. 168 Those specials which they appropriate to themselves are the sole and main commodities of the Kingdoms now in question. **1621** BP. MOUNTAGU *Diatribæ* 467 You must shew some reason why *Decimæ* were restrayned vnto some specialls, seeing *Primitiæ* extended themselues vnto all.

†**4.** Species, kind. *Obs.*

1551 T. WILSON *Logike* (1580) 54 Beauis with Alexander, are comprehended under man as their kinde and speciall. **1628** T. SPENCER *Logick* 131 The lowest species, is that which cannot be divided into other specialls. **1654** Z. COKE *Logick* 32 Quality hath four kinds or specials.

5. *ellipt.* **a.** A special constable, correspondent, etc.; an advocate at a special fee.

1833 W. H. BRETON *Excursions in New South Wales* ii. 51 A Government Establishment formerly existed at Wellington Valley..and it was to this place that all the principal convicts, or those called *specials* were sent: that is to say, those of good connections. **1837** DICKENS *Pickw.* xxiv, 'Is the other specials outside, Dubbley?' inquired Mr. Grummer [the chief constable]. **1867** J. MORISON *Australia* ix. 220 A laudable consideration was shown by the Government to a class of convicts belonging to..'the upper classes of society', and who were known by the name 'specials'. **1882** PEBODY *Eng. Journalism* 147 To number among its enterprising band of correspondents the famous special of the *Daily News*. **1893** *Westm. Gaz.* 29 Sept. 1/2 A 'special' is an advocate who is not attached to any particular Court, but who will accept any brief with a special fee of 50 guineas marked upon it. **1939** *War Illustr.* 9 Dec. 393/3 Accompanied by German police, bands of Sudeten 'specials' raided the University and the Czech societies, and many persons were taken to the Gestapo headquarters. **1955** *Times* 20 July 4/3 There were only two police constables on St. Mary's, reinforced for the occasion by four 'specials'. **1972** *Times* 7 Apr. 5/2 (*heading*) Specials platoon fired into crowd.

b. A special train, examination, prize, article, dish, edition, offer, programme, etc.

1866 [G. A. LAWRENCE] *Sans Merci* xvi, They had been warned at the terminus that a 'special' would probably be needed. **1867** *Oregon State Jrnl.* 19 Jan. 2/3 A Washington special says that [etc.]. **1871** M. LEGRAND *Cambr. Freshm.* 298 When the 'special' containing the excursion party.. entered the station. **1890** *Lancet* 11 Oct. 796/1 What are known as 'specials' are being held this week. These are for men who partially failed at the last regular examinations. **1897** *Daily News* 16 June 9/1 It is laid down that the same dog cannot win more than one of these specials. **1899** J. F. FRASER *Round World on a Wheel* xiv. 162, I described..the London evening papers..the 'specials', 'extra specials', and 'second extra specials'. **1914** JOYCE *Dubliners* 115 They went into the parlour at the back and O'Halloran ordered small hot specials all round. **1933** E. WAUGH *Scoop* II. iv. 212 Make up the Irish edition with his morning cable... If the follow-up comes in..run a special. **1939** J. B. PRIESTLEY *Let People Sing* ii. 44 What about ordering the *Ninepenny Special*—steak-and-kidney pudding and peas? **1952** *Hist. Times* IV. I. ix. 415 The leading articles and 'specials' exposing the exaggerations of the 'yellow peril' school published during the year. **1958** *Punch* 1 Jan. 60/3 Accepting one of his hostess's 'specials' at one of her now-famous 'get-together' parties. **1961** *Listener* 28 Dec. 1135/2 There have, however, been single performances and 'specials' worthy to be recalled. **1966** T. PYNCHON *Crying of Lot 49* i. 14 Pink flyers advertising specials at the markets. **1977** B. PYM *Quartet in Autumn* ii. 24 I'll do one of my specials—baked beans on toast with a poached egg on top. **1979** *Tucson* (Arizona) *Citizen* 20 Sept. 7B/6 NBC made a deal with the studio to make a few two-hour 'Buck Rogers' movies, to be shown occasionally as specials. **1980** *Redbook* Oct. 46/1 Before you go to the supermarket, check your newspaper for sales. Watch for patterns: 'specials' usually occur toward the beginning of the month, when supplies are highest.

'special, *v. slang.* [f. the sb.]

1. *intr.* To work as a special correspondent for a newspaper.

1915 T. BURKE *Nights in Town* 318, I have worked on six newspapers... I have done everything, from subbing to specialling.

2. *trans.* Of a member of the staff of a hospital: to attend continuously to (a single patient).

1961 'K. NORWAY' *Waterfront Hospital* vii. 130 She seems determined to special Emlyn Roberts. **1967** *Nursing Times* 27 Jan. 111/1 A nurse will have to 'special' the patient to make the necessary observations. **1978** L. ISENBERG in D. Abse *My Medical School* 207 One night we were asked if someone would 'special' a lady who might require surgery during the night for suspected abdominal trauma.

specialism ('spɛʃəlɪz(ə)m). [f. SPECIAL *a.* + -ISM.]

1. Restriction or devotion to a special branch of study or research; limitation to one department or aspect of a subject.

1856 J. GROTE in *Cambr. Ess.* II. 88 The question of professionalism, or specialism, in education. **1876** GLADSTONE *Homeric Synchr.* 212 This divarication into specialism..is a sign of an old..condition of study and practice. **1891** *Lancet* 3 Oct. 773 This is the true remedy for the evils of specialism [in medicine].

2. With *a* and pl. A special study or investigation; an instance of specializing. Also, a specialized area of knowledge or work; a professional or academic field.

1868 *Lancet* 8 Aug. 171 Medicine is a specialism; but of no narrow kind. **1884** *Athenæum* 7 June 720/2 Hence the book is one of specialisms. The specialisms, however, do not lapse into mere technicalities. **1891** *Daily News* 9 Apr. 3/5 To do it, the work must be made a specialism. **1937** L. Mumford in F. Mackenzie *Planned Society* p. vii, Specialists..cannot plan: for planning involves the job of coordinating specialisms, focussing them in common fields of knowledge, and canalizing them in appropriate channels of commom action. **1950** [see EXPERTISE]. **1967** *Times Rev. Industry* May 125/2 These [*sc.* technical specifications] can be prepared in a fashion likely to impress a group of people of different specialisms, including operating managers, engineers, finance officers and scientists. **1977** *Antiquaries Jrnl.* LVII. 342 But why did the Americanist W. M. Bray find it so difficult to extract a subject from his own specialism?

specialist (ˈspɛʃəlɪst). [f. as prec. + -IST, or ad. F. *spécialiste*.]

Worcester (1846) gives '*Specialist*, a practical man. *Qu. Rev.*' Hence in Ogilvie (1850).

1. A medical practitioner or authority who specially devotes his attention to the study or treatment of a particular disease or class of diseases.

1856 Kane *Arct. Explor.* II. ix. 93 The recital might edify a specialist who was anxious to register the Protean indications of scurvy. **1875** B. Meadows *Clin. Observ.* 11 Has been treated by an eminent specialist, with both arsenic and mercury. **1889** D. C. & H. Murray *Dang. Catspaw* 162 He was a famous nerve specialist when he retired from practice.

2. a. In general use, one who specially or exclusively studies one subject or one particular branch of a subject.

1862 Spencer *First Princ.* II. i. §36 (1867) 130 Even the most limited specialist would not describe as philosophical, an essay which [etc.]. **1877** Sir C. W. Thomson *Voy. Challenger* I. i. 9 To associate with her complement of scientific officers a civilian staff of specialists. **1884** Symonds *Shaks. Predec.* Pref. p. ix, I cannot pretend to be a specialist in this department, nor have I sought to write for specialists.

b. [tr. Russ. *spetsialist*.] In Communist parlance, a person with a specialist knowledge in some area of science, engineering, or culture; an engineer, scientist.

1929 V. M. Molotov *Communist Party Soviet Union* 39 Of course there cannot be many among the ranks of the old specialists who could be taken into the Party... The Shakhty case revealed clearly enough that we have some of the most bitter enemies among the specialists, whose skill we must nevertheless use. **1974** T. P. Whitney tr. *Solzhenitsyn's Gulag Archipelago* I. I. ix. 334 The Case of Glavtop—May, 1921. This case was important because it involved *engineers*—or, as they had been christened in the terminology of the times, 'specialists', or spetsy. **1977** 'S. Leys' *Chinese Shadows* (1978) ii. 101 It [*sc.* the Tower of the Six Harmonies] is such a sturdy building that an army of 'specialists' would have been necessary to demolish it.

c. An enlisted man in the U.S. army employed on specialized duties. Cf. SPEC *sb.*[4]

Freq. prefixed to the name of a soldier. The grades of specialists are modelled on the ranks, from corporal to master sergeant, but do not correspond to them in other respects.

1955 *Army-Navy-Air Force Register* 14 May 1/1 Army personnel in the top four enlisted grades will be separated into two groups, non-commissioned officers and specialists. .. Those who perform non-leadership duties of a technical or administrative nature will be designated 'Specialists'.. and will rank among themselves as Master Specialists (E-7), Specialist First Class (E-6), Specialist Second Class (E-5), and Specialist (E-4). **1969** I. Kemp *Brit. G.I. in Vietnam* iii. 67, I got on particularly well with the new crew chief, Specialist Fifth Class Jaycelon. **1974** *Encycl. Brit. Micropædia* VII. 406/2 *Specialist*, military, any of four enlisted ranks in the U.S. Army corresponding to the grades of corporal (Specialist 4) through sergeant first class (Specialist 7).

3. *Ecol.* A species which is closely adapted, and largely restricted, to a particular mode of life.

1966 *Amer. Naturalist* C. 607 When the gain to a jack-of-all-trades in reduced travelling time makes up for his lower hunting efficiency compared to the patch specialists, then the jack-of-all-trades will outcompete both specialists. **1973** P. A. Colinvaux *Introd. Ecol.* xli. 576 Animals become specialists in eating particular plants; the plants, on an evolutionary time scale, respond with new poisons. **1978** *Nature* 5 Jan. 56/2 *K*-selected species (or 'specialists') exhibit conservative strategies for survival in predictable environments, and are adapted against pressures from predators and inter-specific competition.

4. *attrib.* (of persons or things).

1883 *Fortn. Rev.* July 110 The matters to be dealt with require a specialist knowledge. **1887** D. Maguire *Art Massage* (ed. 4) 15 The specialist doctor who practises therapeutic massage should develop a special action of his own. **1893** F. Adams *New Egypt* xix, I had no specialist acquaintance with the place or the people.

specialistic (spɛʃəˈlɪstɪk), *a.* [f. prec. + -IC.] Of or pertaining to specialism or specialists.

1882 *Athenæum* 7 Jan. 13/1 The specialistic study demanded by modern philology. **1890** *Ibid.* 19 July 87/2 The learned, specialistic mind takes in the facts of one or two creeds or departments. **1893** *Min. 8th Nat. Counc. Cong. Chs. U.S.A.* 220 Encouragement of specialistic investigation on the part of both faculty and students.

‖**spécialité** (spɛsjalite). Also specialité. [Fr.: see SPECIALITY.] A special or distinguishing feature, characteristic, etc.; a specialty. Also ***spécialité de la maison***, a dish which a restaurant considers its speciality, or one for which it is particularly noted. Cf. SPECIALITY 5 c.

1839 W. A. Shee *Jrnl.* Sept. in *My Contemporaries* (1893) iii. 79 The jousts..are..the *specialité* of such a meeting. **1857** Geo. Eliot *Let.* 1 Sept. (1954) II. 379 Every new or renovated journal should have a specialité—do something not yet done, fill up a gap. **1861** K. Stanley *Let.* 1 Feb. in B. & P. Russell *Amberley Papers* (1937) I. iii. 114 Mr. Oliphant..is very anxious that Japan should not be thought his spécialité so he will not learn the language. **1893** Somerville & 'Ross' *Vine Country* ix. 167 The *spécialité* of the town, ordered expressly for us by Monsieur A., the macaroons made at the convent according to an ancient recipe known to the nuns. **1914** 'Saki' *When William Came* xiv. 242 Iced mulberry salad, my dear, it's a *spécialité de la maison*, so to speak; they say the roving husband brought the recipe from Astrakhan, or Seville, or some such outlandish place. **1935** A. E. W. Mason *They wouldn't be Chessmen* xii. 137 He would take his luncheon at a famous restaurant on the Quai which had a specialité de la maison. **1956** R. Macaulay *Towers of Trebizond* xi. 119 We got several good trout, and two odd-shaped fishes which must have been a specialité of that lake, as we had never seen them before. **1957** 'P. Portobello' *Deb's Mum* 18 Old Lady Dolgelly, who made a *spécialité* of housekeeping. **1962** 'R. Simons' *Killing Chase* v. 68 'How about *Specialité de la Maison*?' 'What's that?' 'Cod roes on toast.' **1976** 'M. Innes' *Gay Phoenix* iii. 42 These Paphians, like the restaurants, had their *spécialités*.

speciality (spɛʃɪˈælɪtɪ). Also 5 -itee, 5-6 -ite, 7 -allitye. [ad. OF. *especialité* ESPECIALITY (later *specialité*, mod.F. *spécialité*) or late and med.L. *speciālitās*, f. *speciālis* SPECIAL *a.* Cf. It. *spec-, spezialità*, Sp. *especialidad*, Pg. *-idade*.]

1. A special, particular, or individual point, matter, or item; freq. *pl.*, particulars, details.

1432-50 tr. *Higden* (Rolls) I. 27 Till hit be commen to Breteyne the last prouince, as vn to a specialite moste specialle for whom [t]his present storye was made. **1513** in Halliwell *Lett. Kings Eng.* (1846) I. 216 After rehearsal..of many..injuries, griefs, and damages.., the specialities whereof were superfluous to rehearse. **1560** *Inchaffray Charters* (S.H.S.) 167 Providing that the specialitie heirin expremit mak nocht dirogatioun to the generalite. **1581** Sidney *Apol. Poet.* (Arb.) 31 The generalities that containeth it, and the specialities that are deriued from it. *a*1600 Edmonds *Observ. Cæsar's Comm.* 47 This last Commentarie containeth the specialities of the warre which Cæsar made against all the States of Gallia. **1624** in *Cosin's Corr.* (Surtees) I. 37 These speciallityes I desire, if the thing be printed, may be left out. **1719** Waterland *Vind. Christ's Div.* xxi. 323 The περιχωρησις and interior Generation, are two specialities taught by the Catholicks. **1865** Mill *Comte* 159 A practical position..chains the mind to specialities and details. **1867** Ruskin *Time & Tide* (1872) 5 Yonder sad letter warped me away from the broad inquiry, to this speciality, respecting the present distress of the middle classes.

2. a. The quality of being special, limited, or restricted in some respect (occasionally implying particularity of application or treatment. †***in speciality***, in detail. †***but speciality***, without partiality or favour.

1456 Sir G. Haye *Law Arms* (S.T.S.) 1 The ferde [part shall be] of bataillis in specialitee. *Ibid.* 99 Here he spekis of armes and baneris in specialitee. **1493** *Sc. Acts, Jas. IV* (1814) II. 233/1 A..Juge quhilk sall minister justice to all parteis but specialitie. **1576** Fleming tr. *Caius' Dogs* (1880) 5 Of a singuler specialitie they deserued to bee called.. bloudhounds. **1617** Ussher *Lett.* (1686) 48 Neither doth the speciality of the one any ways abridge the generality of the other. **1619** W. Sclater *Exp. 2 Thess.* (1629) 304 Distinguish ye twixt speciality of loue, and partiality. **1657** S. Sergeant *Schism Dispatch't* 137 This Particularity then, and speciality of schismatical guilt,..makes a man in a.. more special manner faulty. **1829** I. Taylor *Enthus.* iv. (1867) 99 With a completeness and speciality of coincidence. **1847** Grote *Greece* II. xi. III. 181 Some of them are mere general and vague directions, while others again run into the extreme of speciality. **1872** J. G. Murphy *Comm. Lev.* vi. 12-16 In the general ordinances..it would have been out of place because of its speciality.

†**b.** Technical usage. *Obs.*[−1]

1657 Heylin *Ecclesia Vind.* 105 The word so used.. became in fine a word of Art or speciality, amongst the writers of the new [Testament].

c. ***in speciality***, especially, particularly.

1867 Ruskin *Time & Tide* v. §23 There were, in speciality, two thoroughly good pantomime actors.

d. *Biol.* Special development or adaptation to surroundings.

1880 A. R. Wallace *Island Life* 100 The comparative poverty and speciality of their animals. *Ibid.* 323 Cause of Great Speciality in Fishes.

3. a. A special or distinctive quality, property, characteristic, or feature; a peculiarity.

1625 Purchas *Pilgrims* II. 1380 *margin*, The specialities of Horeb. **1794** J. Hutton *Philos. Light* 182 But, there must be specialities in the case,..and, these specialities may form a proper subject for investigation. **1844** Dickens *Mart. Chuz.* lii, Think of this, Sir,..apart from the specialities.. of prejudice. **1868** Visct. Strangford *Selections* (1869) II. 259 The Doctor's Khivan Mollah..will be but an uncertain guide to the specialities of Yarkandi Turkish. **1881** *Nature* No. 627. 4 There is a wonderful similarity between all the chief tribes.., though there are many specialities in habits.

b. With *the*: The distinctive quality, etc., *of* a particular thing or class.

1829 Jas. Mill *Hum. Mind* (1869) II. 40 The special nature of that group or series..constitutes the speciality of the relation predicated. **1855** Bain *Senses & Int.* II. ii. §8 The speciality of the pleasures of light is their endurableness. **1882** F. P. Cobbe *Peak in Darien* 32 It is the speciality of all vice to be selfishly indifferent to the injurious consequences of our actions.

4. *Law.* **a.** = SPECIALTY 7.

1681 *Brasenose Coll. Doc.* M[2] 56, Leases, Chattells and Specialities wherein I have any estate. **1704** J. Harris *Lex. Techn.* I, *Speciality*, in Law, is most commonly taken for a Bond, or Bill, or such like Instrument. **1756** Garrick *Cath. & Petrucio* I. i, Let specialities be therefore drawn between us, That cov'nants may be kept on either hand.

b. A special warrant; also, the officer charged with executing this.

1815 *Ann. Reg., Chron.* 9 James O'Sullivan,..with a speciality from the sheriff, proceeded to his estate... Mr. H., having fired in through a window at the speciality and those on the inside, they quickly returned the fire.

5. a. A special aptitude, skill, occupation, or line of business.

1867 Ruskin *Time & Tide* i. §3 Every nation is fitted..for some particular employments or manufactures; and..it is the true interest of every other nation to encourage it in such speciality. **1879** Miss Braddon *Cloven Foot* III. xiv. 263 It was made by a man who had a speciality for these things. **1886** C. E. Pascoe *Lond. of To-day* xxxix. (ed. 3) 331 This gentleman's speciality [as a bookseller] lies in the department of theology. **1892** *Photogr. Ann.* II. 705 Who make a speciality of publishing maps prepared for cyclists.

b. A special subject of study or research; that branch of scholarly, scientific, or professional work in which one is a specialist.

1858 Kingsley *Misc.* (1859) I. 140 Even men of boundless knowledge..must have had once their speciality, their pet subject. **1867** Mgr. Patterson in Manning *Ess. Relig. & Lit.* Ser. II. 491 Let us..suppose the writer in question to have a speciality; let us suppose him to be a Catholic theological writer. **1880** J. W. Sherer *Conjuror's Dau.* 111 Mr. Cowley..was acquainted with most of the sciences, but his speciality was Entomology.

c. A thing or article specially characteristic of, produced or manufactured by, a particular place, business firm, etc. (Cf. SPECIALTY 8 and SPÉCIALITÉ.)

1863 Dickens *Lett.* (1880) II. 191 The romantic drama.. is the speciality of your theatre. **1863** Sir W. Holmes *Rep.* in Veness *El Dorado* (1866) App. 158 Indeed, rum seems a sort of 'speciality' of that island [Jamaica]. **1892** *Photogr. Ann.* II. 529 The Optical Lantern trade is somewhat different to photography as regards specialities. In the main, most dealers content themselves with selling goods that are not specially their own. **1977** T. Heald *Just Desserts* i. 16 Bognor chose..a speciality of the house called Pollo Sophia Loren. **1980** F. King *Indirect Method* 161 You must try these profiteroles. Speciality of the *maison*. **1982** J. Midgley *Stone Killer* iii. 23 They dined on the restaurant speciality, Sicilian-style macaroni.

6. a. A thing or article of a special kind, as distinguished from what is usual or common.

1867 Latham *Black & White* 84 One is for the routine cooking, which is always the same; the other is for the preparation of the specialities of each day's diet. **1880** *Plain Hints Needlework* 13 Where special materials are insisted on, specimens of these specialities should be at hand for reference.

b. *attrib.*

1930 E. Ferber *Cimarron* xxiii. 373 Fascinating little speciality shops..just like those..on Madison Avenue. **1938** [see BACK *sb.*[1] 25 a]. **1959** *Times* 9 Mar. (Britain's Food Suppl.) p. xiv/4 Dishes produced in the speciality restaurant often surpass..those of establishments that attempt to run the full range. **1967** *Times Rev. Industry* Feb. 31/1 The newly-created group was thus firmly based in three different markets—household and pharmaceutical products and speciality foods. **1979** N. Freeling *Widow* iii. 10 A gigantic supermarket, with a covered gallery of speciality shops all around.

7. *Theatr.* Used *attrib.* to designate a performer or performance, esp. in variety entertainments, of an unusual or specialized character.

1933 P. Godfrey *Back-Stage* xv. 187 The next important subdivision of the chorus consists of the speciality dancing troupe. *Ibid.*, A few speciality solo steps. **1952** W. Granville *Dict. Theatrical Terms* 166 *Speciality artiste*, a vaudeville artiste who specializes in impersonations, juggling, etc. **1962** A. Nisbett *Technique Sound Studio* iii. 69 It is also possible to balance most dance bands and speciality groups on a single microphone provided that sufficient trouble is taken. **1967** *Stage* 2 Mar. 21/4 (Advt.), Wanted for long summer season speciality act, strong male vocal..and two girl dancers. **1970** W. J. Burley *To kill Cat* iii. 58 We had a cabaret artiste of that name... She was a speciality dancer and her art possessed great artistic merit.

specialization (ˌspɛʃəlaɪˈzeɪʃən). [f. SPECIALIZE *v.* + -ATION.] **1.** The action or process of specializing or of becoming specialized.

a. Of language, legislation, etc.

1843 Mill *Logic* IV. v. II. 270 We have seen above, in the words *pagan* and *villain*, remarkable examples of the specialization of the meaning of words. **1864** Max Müller *Sci. Lang.* Ser. II. viii. 352 *note*, The specialization of general roots is more common than the generalization of special roots. **1891** Driver *Introd. Lit. O.T.* (1892) 26 A noticeable difference is the greater specialization and strictness of the provisions contained in the former narrative.

b. *Biol.* Of animals or plants, or of the parts or organs of these.

1862 Dana *Man. Geology* 599 This law of specialization —the general before the special—is the law of all development. **1869** Spencer *Princ. Psychol.* (1872) I. III. vi. 330 Change from a general diffusion of food to a localization of food, involves a further specialization. **1880** A. R. Wallace *Island Life* v. 75 The cause..is, undoubtedly, the extreme specialisation of most insects.

c. Of employments, studies, etc.

1865 Mill *Comte* 94 The increasing specialisation of all employments..is not without inconveniences. **1868** M. Pattison *Academ. Org.* v. 273 The principle of the improvement which appears to me possible in our system of studies is that of specialisation. **1890** GROSS *Gild Merch.* I. 116 The rapid development and specialisation of industry. **1891** *Lancet* 3 Oct. 774 We are opposed to the specialisation of hospitals.

2. *Biol.* A specialized character or adaptive feature in an organism.

1918 F. W. JONES *Probl. Man's Ancestry* 30 Pithecoid specializations vary so much in their manifestations in the different groups of monkeys. **1978** *Nature* 26 Jan. 353/1 It seems that both intermuscular and subcutaneous lipid accumulation and a reduction in skeletal ossification have evolved as specialisations to reduce density in *Pleuragramma*, a pelagic Antarctic fish without a swim bladder.

specialize (ˈspɛʃəlaɪz), *v.* [ad. F. *spécialiser*, = It. *specializzare*, Sp. and Pg. *especializar*: see SPECIAL *a.* and -IZE.]

1. *trans.* To mention or indicate specially; to specify, particularize.

1616 SHELDON *Mir. Antichr.* 261 Our Sauiour specialising and nominating the places in which these false prophets should teach his presence to be. **1657** J. SERGEANT *Schism Dispach't* 66 The proper answer..is to specialize some plea for themselves, which will not as well excuse their Desertours. **1873** FERGUSON *Discourses* 23 Still less has he a right to specialise the sign from heaven by which the proof is to be established. **1874** BLACKIE *Self-Cult.* 61, I will now specialise a few of those virtues the attainment of which should be an object of lofty ambition.

b. *absol.* To enter into particulars or details.

1613 WITHER *Abuses Stript* in *Juvenilia* (1633) 249 First lash the Great-ones; but if thou be wise, In generall and doe not speciallize. **1850** BLACKIE *Æschylus* I. 296 It is quite common with Æschylus to give a general description first, and then specialise.

2. To render special or specific; to invest with a special character or function.

1628 EARLE *Microcosm., Scept. in Relig.* (Arb.) 67 He is at most a confus'd and wild Christian, not specializ'd by any forme, but capable of all. **1701** NORRIS *Ideal World* I. vi. 321 The great difficulty is to specialize this account, to shew in particular what kind of thing truth is. **1850** ROBERTSON *Serm.* Ser. III. v. 73 He specializes what is universal. **1874** MAHAFFY *Soc. Life Greece* xi. 339 A belief in some systematic ruler of the world,..not specialised in form or character. *Ibid.* xii. 362 The Attic legal system..by specialising its courts apparently provided for a prompt and accurate treatment of disputes.

b. *spec.* in *Biol.* In pa. pple.: Adapted to a special function or environment; modified by development tending towards this end.

1851 S. P. WOODWARD *Mollusca* I. 32 Respiration is performed by the mantle, or by a portion of it specialized, and forming a gill. **1874** LUBBOCK *Orig. & Met. Ins.* v. 86 The earliest known Neuroptera and Orthoptera, though in some respects less specialized than existing forms. **1881** TYLOR *Anthrop.* ii. 43 Man's upper and lower extremities have become differentiated or specialised in two opposite ways.

c. To develop (parts) by adaptation to surroundings.

1897 MARY KINGSLEY *W. Africa* 558 If this sort of weather goes on I expect I shall specialise fins and gills myself.

3. To make narrower and more intensive.

1855 M. PATTISON in *Oxford Ess.* 292 The very fact that the new statute has restrained and specialized the subjects in the School of Literae Humaniores. **1868** —— *Academ. Org.* v. 264 The principle I am now contending for goes further still in the direction of specialising study.

4. *intr.* a. To engage in special study or some special line of business, etc.

1881 *Jrnl. Educ.* 1 Mar. 51/1 They will not allow their scholars to specialize. **1888** BRYCE *Amer. Commw.* cii. III. 442 Enabling men to specialize..in matters like history and Oriental or Romance philology. **1897** MARY KINGSLEY *W. Africa* 505 A certain set of men and women then specialise off to study how these spirits can be managed.

b. To develop in a special direction; to assume a special form or function.

1889 *Lancet* 28 Sept. 635/1 That some cells have specialised on the amœboid character is seen in the so-called myeloplaxes.

specialized (ˈspɛʃəlaɪzd), *ppl. a.* [f. prec.]

1. Specially adapted, modified, or developed: a. *Biol.* (Cf. prec. 2 b.)

1853 LEWES *Hist. Philos.* (ed. 2) 254 The operation of some external thing on the specialized nervous system. **1854** OWEN in *Orr's Circ. Sci., Org. Nat.* I. 205 The modified or specialized character of the elements of the cranial vertebræ has gained for them special names. **1870** ROLLESTON *Animal Life* 16 There are no specialized renal arteries in birds. **1889** *Science-Gossip* XXV. 182 If several species of bees are adapted to each specialised flower.

b. In general use.

1865 LUBBOCK *Preh. Times* 280 Numerous and specialised as are our modern instruments, who would care to describe the exact use of a knife? **1874** SIDGWICK *Meth. Ethics* I. iii. 28 The sentiment of veracity, courage, purity, &c. But each such specialized sentiment in its normal state includes..the more general impulse to do right.

2. Rendered special or particular.

1885 MYERS *Ess.* II. 63 Laws of which our highest generalisations may be but the specialised case or the incidental aspect.

3. Specially mentioned or indicated.

1893 F. ADAMS *New Egypt* 157, I fancy..that the very manner of the specialised passage is identic.

specializer (ˈspɛʃəlaɪzə(r)). [f. as prec.] One who specializes.

1878 *Fraser's Mag.* XVII. 267 Minds of the first rank are generalisers; of the second, specialisers.

ˈ**specializing,** *vbl. sb.* [f. as prec.] The action or process of becoming or rendering special in some respect.

1889 SIDGWICK in *Jrnl. Educ.* Feb. 116 Prevented by need of early specialising. **1904** H. BLACK *Pract. Self Cult.* v. 138 Division of labour, or specialising of functon have [*sic*] become essential in modern industry.

ˈ**specializing,** *ppl. a.* [f. as prec.] That specializes, in senses of the verb.

In the first group of quots. the ppl. a. is not clearly separable from attributive uses of the vbl. sb.

(*a*) **1701** NORRIS *Ideal World* I. vi. 326 The great specializing character that distinguishes necessary and eternal truths from those of the opposite order. **1861** H. MACMILLAN *Footn. Page Nat.* 203 In the fungi, however, there is little or nothing of this specializing or differentiating process. **1873** SYMONDS *Grk. Poets* v. 111 We remark a powerful specializing tendency.

(*b*) **1890** *Times* 24 Dec. 7/3 To enable 'specializing' students to follow their courses. **1894** *Nature's Method in Evol. Life* vi. 70 Specialising organs made their appearance.

specially (ˈspɛʃəlɪ), *adv.* Forms: 3–4 **specialliche,** 4– **specially,** 5 **-alli,** 6 **-allie, -allye;** 4 **specialyche, -ich(e, -ali,** 4–5 **-aly,** 6 **-alie;** 4 **specyaly,** 5 **specealy,** 5–6 **specyally** (5 **spes-**); 6 **spetiallye,** 7 **-ally.** [f. SPECIAL *a.* + -LY², after L. *speciāliter* or OF. (*e*)*speciaument*, (*e*)*specialement* (mod.F. *spécialement*). Cf. ESPECIALLY *adv.*]

1. In a special manner; in a degree or to an extent beyond what is usual or customary; particularly.

1297 R. GLOUC. (Rolls) 10220 Þe king of alimayne sende specialliche inou To king Ion þat he wiþdrowe him of is wou. **13..** *Seuyn Sages* (W.) 3547 On God in heuyn ay thinkes he, And specialy he praied him till To help him. **1340** *Ayenb.* 7 Þise þri hestes diȝteþ ous to gode specialliche. **1375** BARBOUR *Bruce* IV. 467 The kyng..sperit syne full specialy, Giff ony man couth tell tithand [etc.]. *c* **1450** *Mirk's Festial* 12 Ȝet childyr dydden hym worschyp spesyaly byfor any oþer seynt. **1486** *Rec. St. Mary at Hill* (1905) 18 The said preest..to..be alwey charged specially & deuoutly to pray daily..for the soule of the said Iohn Nasyng. **1512** *Act 4 Hen. VIII*, c. 20 Preamble, Your said Besecher..was specially requyred to arrest and take the said John. **1548–9** (Mar.) *Bk. Com. Prayer* 127 b, Speciallye we beseche thee to saue and defende thy seruaunt, Edwarde our Kyng. **1590** SIR J. SMITH *Disc. Weapons Ded.* 9 b, They haue vsed diuers waies.., but chieflie two, speciallie to be noted. **1617** MORYSON *Itin.* II. 50 Not so much in secrecy and in sparingnesse of speech..as more specially in Court factions. **1711** in *Nairne Peerage Evidence* (1874) 135 Lykeas by the said first contract..it is specially provided and declared. **1816** A. KNOX *Rem.* (1834) I. 49 The House of Lords and the Established Church are specially united to each other. **1860** TYNDALL *Glac.* II. xvi. 313 Measurements..which bear more specially upon the subject. **1875** JOWETT *Plato* (ed. 2) V. 404 There appears to be a need of some bold man who specially honours plainness of speech.

b. Qualifying adjs. and advs.

1422 tr. *Secreta Secret., Priv. Priv.* 207 A Specialy behouabill Place of Prayynge is a pryue Place. **1530** PALSGR. 842 Specially wel,..*fort bien.* **1535** COVERDALE *Song Sol.* ii. 4 He..loueth me specially well. **1685** BAXTER *Paraphr. N.T.* Matt. iii. 2 Tho' repentance be always a duty, it's specially necessary to..our assurance of pardon. **1847** S. AUSTIN *Ranke's Hist. Ref.* III. 659 That alliance of a specially religious nature. **1867** MITCHELL *Rural Studies* 108 As a hint for better ones, I think it specially good. **1871** FREEMAN *Hist. Ess.* Ser. I. viii. 243 The military results..were not specially glorious.

2. Of special purpose; expressly.

c **1315** SHOREHAM I. 1219 God ches folk specialliche.. Offyce for to fonge. *c* **1340** HAMPOLE *Pr. Consc.* 935 Alle þe world so wyde and brade, Our Lord speciali for man made. *c* **1410** HOCCLEVE *Mother of God* 115 The fadir god gan edifie (By his sone oonly-geten specially) To him an hows.

1842 LOUDON *Suburban Hort.* 502 Mr. Mills invariably raises plants specially for that purpose. **1879** *Cassell's Techn. Educ.* II. 179/2 It is better to make them specially for each patient.

b. By special effort or application.

1882 FREEMAN *Amer. Lect.* 124 The Latin tongue..lives on..as a book-language specially learned.

3. Above or beyond, more than, other things or persons; in a supreme degree; pre-eminently.

c **1340** HAMPOLE *Pr. Consc.* 3603 Þan may þe saules in purgatory, By way of grace specialy, Be delivered of pyn. **1387–8** T. USK *Test. Love* III. ix. (Skeat) l. 15 But specialliche, predestinacion of goodnesse alone is sayd by these grete clerkes. *c* **1400** LOVE *Bonavent. Mirr.* (1908) 160 It is ful perilous..to..haue a name of holynesse, as hauen specially thise recluses. *a* **1548** HALL *Chron., Edw. V*, 9 b, In two places specially, the one at the elbow of the citie, ..& the other in the very bowels. **1596** SHAKS. *Tam. Shr.* I. i. 121 To labour and effect one thing specially.

b. Freq. ***and specially,*** used to introduce a clause following upon a previous statement.

1303 R. BRUNNE *Handl. Synne* 59 To alle crystyn men,.. And speciali, alle be name, Þe felaushepe of Symprynghame. *c* **1380** WYCLIF *Sel. Wks.* III. 101 Wherefore we alle scholde be meke, and specialyche prestes. *c* **1400** MAUNDEV. (Roxb.) xxxiv. 154 Þai can speke wele of þe Bible and specially of þe buke of Genesis. *c* **1430** LYDG. *Min. Poems* (Percy Soc.) 16 God..preserve him in alle manner thing. And specially..In enmyes handis that he nevir ffalle. **1481** CAXTON *Godfrey* xlvii. 88 But oure peple, and specially the Frenssmen, myght not byleue that this Ioye..myght come of ony trayson. **1535** COVERDALE *Isaiah* lx. 9 The Iles also shal gather them vnto me, and specially the shippes of yᵉ see. **1585** T. WASHINGTON tr. *Nicholay's Voy.* II. v. 35 To the great pleasure..of vs.., and specially of the faire dames. **1617** MORYSON *Itin.* IV. 420 Toscany, and more spetially the Citty and State of Florence therein contayned, is noted to yeald men of stronge memorye. **1651** HOBBES *Leviath.* III. xxxv. 216 In the Writings of Divines, and specially in Sermons. **1807** A. KNOX *Rem.* (1834) I. 71 For the attention I have ever received from them, and specially for the invaluable regard of individuals, I trust I am cordially grateful.

c. Similarly without *and.*

1483 CAXTON *Cato* B vj, Thou oughtest not to mocke.. none other, specyally whan thy wyll is to haue companye with hem. **1538** STARKEY *England* I. ii. 30 That thyng wych one callyth lyght knolege..the other callyth ignorance, specyally when hyt ys ouercome wyth the contrary persuasyon. **1577** B. GOOGE *Heresbach's Husb.* i. (1586) 14 b, That the sicke may be..looked vnto, specially yf their diseases be contagious. **1625** BACON *Ess., Wisd. for Man's Self* (Arb.) 183 And be so true to thy Selfe, as thou be not false to Others; Specially to thy King, and Country. **1807** G. CHALMERS *Caledonia* I. III. ix. 451 *Toscheoderach*, an officer, or jurisdiction, not unlike to a baillierie, specially, in the isles. **1878** BROWNING *La Saisiaz* 11 Child's play call it— specially when one descends!

†4. With particularity or detail; not generally or vaguely. *Obs.*

c **1340** HAMPOLE *Pr. Consc.* 7526 Now wille I tylle þe sevend part wende,..þe whilk spekes..Specialy of þe ioyes in heven. *Ibid.* 7875 Now will I specialy shew yhow mare Of seven maners of blysses þare. **1456** SIR G. HAYE *Law Arms* (S.T.S.) 102 Law canoun, and law civile,..determynis specyaly as law and resoun gevis. **1502** *Ord. Crysten Men* (W. de W. 1506) II. viii, Yᵉ whiche thynge ought to be understande generally & specyally. **1544** tr. *Littleton's Tenures* 116 Yif he plede yᵉ release specially. **1620** T. GRANGER *Div. Logike* 43 Whereby men are most specially specificated and individuated.

†5. ***in specially,*** especially. *Obs.* (Cf. INSPECIALLY *adv.* and INESPECIALLY *adv.*)

1503 HAWES *Examp. Virt.* vii. 89 For other nacyons our lawe ne dredeth But our swerd they do in specyally. **1505** in *Mem. Hen. VII* (Rolls) 280 In specially he intendithe ayenst the Kynge of Oran.

6. In, or in regard to, species. *rare.*

1628 T. SPENCER *Logick* 66 Two men are the same specially, because they haue a reasonable soule.

7. *Comb.*, as ***specially-adapted, -arranged,*** etc.

1873 DARWIN *Orig. Spec.* (ed. 6) vii. 190 To break the egg-shell by tapping..with their specially adapted beaks. **1880** GEIKIE *Phys. Geog.* iii. 127 A specially arranged kind of thermometer. **1892** *Photogr. Ann.* II. 610 In newly and specially-erected premises. **1893** J. A. HODGES *Elem. Photogr.* (1907) 139 The specially-prepared plates to which I have referred.

specialness (ˈspɛʃəlnɪs). Also 6 specyal-. [f. as prec. + -NESS.] The quality of being special.

1530 PALSGR. 274/1 Specyalnesse, *specialité.* **1668** WILKINS *Real Char.* II. i. §3. 34. *a* **1679** T. GOODWIN in Spurgeon *Treas. David* Ps. lxxviii. 67–8 The specialness of his love greateneth it, endeareth it to us. **1879** P. BROOKS *Influence Jesus* ii. (1883) 78 It is the depth of His government that makes the specialness of His government. **1900** STODDARD *Evol. Eng. Novel* 177 Specialness in the direction of the purpose-work of the hero.

special pleader¹. [See PLEADER¹.]

1. *Law.* A member of an Inn of Court who devotes himself mainly to the drawing of pleadings, and to attending at Judges' chambers (Wharton).

1804 *Act 44 Geo. III*, c. 98 *Schedule A*, Certificate to be taken out by every Special Pleader. **1870** *Jury Act, Schedule*, Persons exempt from serving on juries... Serjeants, barristers-at-law, certificated conveyancers, and special pleaders if actually practising. **1891** *Stamp Act* §48 (a), The certificates of..conveyancers, special pleaders and draftsmen in Equity in England.

fig. **1901** H. SUTCLIFFE *Willowdene Will* i. 21 They showed clean hoofs to the highwayman's undischarged special pleaders [= pistols].

2. One who uses special pleading; a disingenuous or sophistical disputant.

1809 MALKIN *Gil Blas* IV. iii. ¶4 All the arts of a thorough-bred special pleader.

special pleader². [See PLEADER².] A special plea; a piece of one-sided pleading.

1891 *Pall Mall G.* 30 Sept. 7/2 Nor do we find it so cheap as is stated in Mr. Percy Lindley's special pleader for the cause of those interested in this particular tour.

ˈ**special pleading.** [See PLEADING *vbl. sb.*]

1. A pleading drawn with particular reference to the circumstances of a case, as opposed to general pleading.

1684 A. VIDIAN (*title*), The Exact Pleader; A Book of Entries of Select and Special Pleadings in the Court of King's-Bench. **1685** J. HANSARD (*title*), A Book of Entries of Declarations and other Pleadings general and special.

2. The putting forward of special pleadings; the art or science of drawing pleadings.

1768 BLACKSTONE *Comm.* III. 305 The science of special pleading having been frequently perverted to the purposes of chicane and delay, the courts have of late in some instances..permitted the general issue to be pleaded. **1849** FORSYTH *Hortensius* (1879) 341 Of all the systems that ever were invented to cramp and confine the intellect, that of special pleading seems to have been the most admirably adapted to attain that end. **1864** BOWEN *Logic* ix. 299 In Law the only object of what is called *special pleading* is, to ascertain the precise point at issue.

attrib. **1846** LD. CAMPBELL *Chancellors* V. 81 Carteret.. ridiculed with much pleasantry this piece of special-pleading sophistry. **1896** *Westm. Gaz.* 3 July 2/2 It will enable him to make some capital special-pleading speeches.

b. *fig.* Ex-parte or one-sided argumentation; disingenuous pleading; sophistry.

1872 MURRAY in *Compl. Scotl.* Introd. p. cxiv, His [Leyden's] argument, which is probably one of the most successful pieces of special pleading in existence. **1878** STUBBS *Study Med. & Mod. Hist.* ix. (1886) 217 We all know what an amount of special pleading was thought necessary to justify that [the Norman Conquest].

Hence **special-plead** *v. intr.*, to employ special pleading or sophistical argument.

1848 DK. ARGYLL *Eccles. Hist. Scot.* 232 They [*sc.* the clergy]..misrepresent, conceal, and special-plead.

specialty ('speʃəltɪ). Forms: 4–6 **specyalte** (5 **-allte**), 5–6 **specyaltee**, 6 **-alt(e)y**; 4–5 **specialte**, 5–6 **-tee**, 4–7 **-tie**, 6–7 **-tye**, 6– **specialty** (6 **-allty**); 5 **spetialte**, 7 **specielty**. [ad. OF. *(e)specialté*, f. *(e)special* SPECIAL *a.*: see -TY, and cf. SPECIALITY and ESPECIALTY.]

I. †**1. a.** Special affection, attachment, or favour.

c **1330** R. BRUNNE *Chron. Wace* (Rolls) 5281 + 15 For grete luf & specialte he toke with him sir Androche. **1375** BARBOUR *Bruce* VII. 246 Quhat is he That garris ȝow haue sic specialte Till men that traualis? *a* **1400** *Minor Poems fr. Vernon MS.* 527/75 Drauȝ vppon þe no specialte Of Mon þat is of gret dignite. **1435** MISYN *Fire of Love* 28 þerfore bettyr I trow þere specialte to wante þen in þer handys to fall. *c* **1450–60** in *Babees Book* 330 Thorow affeccion to personys or by specialte.

†**b.** *for* or *in specialty*, as a special mark of favour or esteem. *Obs.*

c **1400** MAUNDEV. (1839) ii. 13 That was ȝoven to me for gret Specyaltee. *c* **1460** *Emaré* 176 For gret loue he ȝaf hyt me, I brynge hyt þe in specyalte.

†**2.** Particularity or detail in description or discussion. Chiefly in phr. *in specialty*. *Obs.*

c **1380** WYCLIF *Sel. Wks.* III. 513 But, to discende doun in specialte, fful mane articlis of reulis of siche sectes ben openly contrarie to þe apostlis reule. *c* **1449** PECOCK *Repr.* I. xx. 130 The othere bokis..schewen the same in specialte. **1526** *Pilgr. Perf.* (W. de W. 1531) 9 After that we shall entreate in a more specyalty..yᵉ holy lyfe of religyon. **1561** T. NORTON *Calvin's Inst.* IV. 47 Before that we beginne to discourse of euery one of these in specialtie. **1577** KNEWSTUB *Confut.* (1579) 5 He hath dealt wisely, to leaue the other chapters without anie specialtie.

3. *in* (also †*by*, †*of*, †*with*) *specialty*, in a special or particular manner or degree.

1451 CAPGRAVE *Life St. Aug.* 32 O þing I pray ȝou of specialte. **1576** FLEMING *Panopl. Epist.* 253 Hee sheweth also, by specialtie, wherein it is good to bee exercised. **1659** W. BROUGH *Sacr. Princ.* 284 The body for which (with specialty) He gave His blood. **1711** *Fingall MSS.* in *10th Rep. Hist. MSS. Comm.* App. V. 122 The episcopal Protestants in specialty triumph the most. **1865** H. BUSHNELL *Vicar. Sacr.* ii. (1868) 65 Taking them as clients in specialty.

4. a. Special or particular character or quality; a special feature or characteristic.

(*a*) **1575** LANEHAM *Let.* (1871) 25 Whear the specialty of the sport waz, to see, how sum for hiz slakness had a good bob with the bag. **1606** SHAKS. *Tr. & Cr.* I. iii. 78 The specialty of Rule hath beene neglected. *a* **1641** BP. MOUNTAGU *Acts & Mon.* (1642) 32 All shall bee then taught by God, which once was the specialty of Prophets. **1837** CARLYLE *Fr. Rev.* I. IV. iv, A man living in falsehood, and on falsehood; yet not what you can call a false man: there is the specialty! **1861** DICKENS *Gt. Expect.* III. 181 The specialty of the occasion caused our talk to be less dry and hard.

(*b*) **1609** W. SCLATER *Threefold Preserv.* (1610) E iv b, A specialty in it belongs to them, that labour in the word and doctrine. **1628** —— *Three Serm.* (1629) 36 Yet who..is not readie to conceit some singular specialtie in their degree and measure of sinning. **1838** W. BELL *Dict. Law Scot.* 849 There were specialties, however, in the case. **1846** GROTE *Greece* II. II. v. 453 The Laconian dialect contained more specialties of its own than any other variety of the Dorian. **1887** RUSKIN *Præterita* II. 265 The house itself had no specialty, either of comfort or inconvenience, to endear it.

(*c*) **1598** MARSTON *Sco. Villanie* I. iv. 186 If he were once but freed from specialty. **1848** BAILEY *Festus* Proem (ed. 3) p. x, Of Him who..one human heart With equal power and specialty inspires.

b. The quality of being limited or determined by special cases or circumstances.

1619 W. SCLATER *Exp. 1 Thess.* (1630) 64 Such the Specialtie of Gods fauour in the distribution. **1623** BP. HALL *Contempl., O.T.* xx. 6 Looke how much more specialtie there is in the charge of God, so much more danger is in violation. **1683** J. CORBET *Free Actions* III. xxxvii. 55 There is always a specialty of Grace towards the Elect. **1859** S. WILBERFORCE *Sp. Missions* (1874) 186 One..who is beckoning me by the specialty of my position to take up..the work which he so nobly began. **1874** FINLAYSON *Divine Gentleness* iv. 80 Any special duty..tends, by its very specialty, to brace us for the doing of it.

c. Special knowledge; tendency to specialism.

1868 M. PATTISON *Academ. Org.* v. 158 An electoral body which shall be competent to look out for and select true eminence in specialty. **1868** *Rep. U.S. Commissioner Agric.* (1869) 141 The favorite charge against the academies is their 'one-sidedness' or specialty.

II. †**5. a.** A thing specially belonging or attached to one person; a special possession, distinction, favour, or charge. *Obs.*

1388 WYCLIF *Ex.* xix. 5 If ȝe schulen here my vois,..ȝe schulen be to me in to a specialte [L. *peculium*] of alle puplis. **1451** CAPGRAVE *Life St. Aug.* 46, I wil þat no man ȝyue to me so precious cloþis whech þat I, as of a specialte a-boue oþir, schuld wer. *c* **1491** *Chast. Goddes Chyld.* x. (Caxton) 26 Some desire..myracles or vysions or reuelacions or some other specyalte. **1628** BP. HALL *Contempl., O.T.* XIX. 1300 Not without some specialty from God doth Elijah follow the campe.

†**b.** *of* or *with a specialty*, especially, particularly. *Obs.*

1686 GOAD *Celest. Bodies* I. xviii. 118 The Wind may Change we know, every Hour, but with a Specialty upon the Hour of the Suns leaving us. **1818** SCOTT *Hrt. Midl.* xlvii, Lady Robertland, whilk got six sure outgates of grace..in times past; and of a specialty, Mr. John Scrimgeour, minister of Kinghorn.

6. a. A special or particular matter, point, or thing.

c **1400** *Pilgr. Sowle* (Caxton, 1483) IV. xxxv. 83 Iustyces of the countrees somme for pees some for other specialte owen to see the gouernaunce of the Countre. **1450** *Rolls of Parlt.* V. 194 The Joyntour of the office of forein Apposer is comprisid under this generaltee, with the specialtee above rehersed. **1502** in *Lett. Rich. III & Hen. VII* (Rolls) II. 108 No specialties of our communicacions, but only the generalties. **1550** BALE *Apol.* 32 God commaunded certen specyaltees to Abraham, Isaac and Jacob. **1588** J. HARVEY *Disc. Probl.* 64 What should I argue the case any farther,..or heape vp more particularities, and specialties, which are so infinitely innumerable? *a* **1619** M. FOTHERBY *Atheom.* II. xiii. §3 (1622) 352 By all which specialties, this Conclusion is proued. *a* **1641** BP. MOUNTAGU *Acts & Mon.* (1642) 418 The Sect of the Pharisees tendered and recommended..to the people many specialties..to bee observed. **1782** MONRO *Compar. Anat.* (ed. 3) 42 We go on to consider the specialties in the *viscera* of each kind. **1820–30** COLERIDGE *Lit. Rem.* (1838) III. 21 Judgment, solid sense, invention in specialties,..in these we can shew giants. **1831** CARLYLE *Sart. Res.* II. viii, Amid these specialties, let us not forget the great generality.

b. A special or separate proviso or article in an agreement, etc.

14.. *Master of Game* (MS. Douce 335) 72 b, If thei haue ony specialte of a certeynn nombre of swynn to go in the forest, ye shul do vs to wete whether thei be rynged or no. **1636** EARL CORK *Diary* in *Lismore Papers* Ser. I. (1886) IV. 199 There is an Indented receipt..wherin all the particuler specielties ar expressed.

7. *Law.* A special contract, obligation, or bond, expressed in an instrument under seal.

c **1482** in *Cal. Proc. Chanc. Q. Eliz.* (1830) II. Pref. 63 Your besecher can have noo remedy by cours of the comen lawe, for asmoche as he hath noo specialte in writyng. **1483** *Cely Papers* (Camden) 134 To receyve yn thys martt all syche specyalltes of yowrs payabull yn thys martt. **1528** in *Lett. Suppress. Monast.* (Camden) 3 Certen munimentes, evidencez, and specialties, tochinge and apperteynynge unto our monastery. **1594** WEST *2nd Pt. Symbol., Chancerie* §120 He neither tooke any specialtie or securitie of him,..nor provided any witnesses to be present. **1621** *Galway Arch.* in *10th Rep. Hist. MSS. Comm.* App. V. 470 Those persons whoe have neglected to produce theire said evidences, grauntes, and specialties, to bee looked into by the Maior. **1644** HOWELL *Twelve Treat.* (1661) 238 There's no legall Instrument, no Bond, Bill, or Specialty can be writ but upon his seal'd paper. **1768** BLACKSTONE *Comm.* III. 154 Where the debt arises upon a specialty, that is, upon a deed or instrument under seal. **1781** M. MADAN *Thelyphthora* III. 309 Marriage-settlements, mortgage-deeds, and specialties of various kinds. **1856** H. BROOM *Comm. Common Law* II. i. 274 A specialty..is distinguished from a simple contract in writing by certain solemnities attendant on its execution—viz. by sealing and delivery. **1883** H. G. WOOD *Limitation of Actions* 64 All instruments under seal of record, and liabilities imposed by statute, are specialties within the meaning of the Stat. 21 James I.

fig. **1606** DANIEL *Queen's Arcadia* II. iii, I..had secur'd her of my constant truth, Vnder so many faithfull specialties. **1640** FULLER *Abel Rediv., Junius* (1867) II. 187 She was bound by the specialty both of nature and grace to provide for her children. **1650** —— *Pisgah* III. xi. 436 But can an acquittance of humane tradition, be valid, against a debt of specialty by God's command?

attrib. **1818** CRUISE *Digest* (ed. 2) II. 176 Legatees are entitled to stand in the place of specialty creditors. **1875** K. E. DIGBY *Real Prop.* v. (1876) 249 Debts..secured by deed (called specialty debts).

8. a. A special line of work or business; a special manufacture or product (characteristic of a certain firm, place, etc.); an article specially dealt in or stocked. (Cf. SPECIALITY 5 c.)

1860 *Sat. Rev.* X. 737/2 Mr. Lovell Reeve..has a specialty—to use a neologism of the day. It is to illustrate books with stereographs. **1873** LELAND *Egypt. Sketch-Bk.* 246 His specialty was inlaid-work of mother-of-pearl and ebony in little diamonds, squares, and triangles. **1883** *Eng. Illustr. Mag.* Nov. 89/1 The brass work of Birmingham has long been one of its specialties. **1891** *Daily News* 16 Feb. 2/7 The better classes of fancy tweeds, choice serges, and specialties.

b. A special subject of study or research.

1861 tr. *Czermak's Uses Laryngoscope* ii. 10 Physicians..who do not intend to make a specialty of laryngoscopy. **1861** *Sat. Rev.* 7 Dec. 591 Mr. Aris Willmott's specialty (to use a very current piece of slang) is with the sacred poets. **1873** MORLEY *Rousseau* I. 150 There is a constant tendency on the part of energetic intellectual workers..to concentrate their energies on a minute specialty. **1883** M. PATTISON *Mem.* (1885) 70 He had selected as his specialty currency and finance.

9. *N. Amer.* = SPECIALITY 6, 7.

1888 G. O. SEILHAMER *Hist. Amer. Theatre* II. 118 Dr. Bayley, a specialty performer..gave entertainments in this country as early as 1752. **1901** *Daily Colonist* (Victoria, B.C.) 3 Nov. 12/3 These expensive attractions in conjunction with a big specialty company of no mean pretensions will go to make up an excellent show. **1915** in S. Marcus *Minding Store* (1974) ii. 23 Twenty-five specialty shops in one building. **1919** [see FOLLY *sb.*[1] 5 b]. **1936** J. STEINBECK *In Dubious Battle* i. 3 Department stores and specialty shops. **1961** BOWMAN & BALL *Theatre Lang.* 338 *Specialty number*, a song not intended to be fully integrated with the rest of the entertainment—Musical comedy. **1968** *Globe & Mail* (Toronto) 17 Feb. B4 Roblin Steel Corp..., maker of specialty steel forgings and castings.., plans to buy privately owned Washburn Co., maker of specialty household products. **1978** *Language* LIV. 189 M & M apparently prefer to leave these rich but page-devouring matters to specialty works.

speciate ('spiːʃɪeɪt), *v. Biol.* [Back-formation from SPECIATION.] *intr.* Of a population of plants or animals: to exhibit evolutionary development leading to the recognition of a new species. Hence **'speciating** *ppl. a.*, showing or inducing speciation.

1964 *Oceanogr. & Marine Biol.* II. 206 C[*odium*] *fragile* appears to be speciating as it moves into waters where these two subspecies are present. **1970** *Watsonia* VIII. 67 The lack of flower-constancy and of other speciating factors in the visitors. **1973** P. A. COLINVAUX *Introd. Ecol.* xli. 579 Man alone can change his niche without speciating. **1981** *Nature* 26 Feb. 743/2 Only rarely will members of the small speciating population be fossilized, so that the lineage will show what are known as 'punctuated equilibria'—a long series of unaltered fossil forms followed by a rapid shift to a new type.

speciation (spiːʃɪ'eɪʃən). *Biol.* [f. SPECI(ES + -ATION.] The formation of new and distinct species in the course of evolution.

1906 O. F. COOK in *Science* 30 Mar. 506/2 Speciation..is the origination or multiplication of species by subdivision, usually..as a result of environmental incidents. **1926** *Nature* 21 Aug. 271/1 Thus *speciation* through continuity stands in contrast with *mutation* through discontinuity. *Ibid.* 272/1 Isolation is the most important factor in the speciation of birds. **1953** J. S. HUXLEY *Evolution in Action* iii. 71 Much of speciation represents a frill of mere diversity. **1978** *Nature* 21 Sept. 255/1 Speciation involves the splitting of a single evolutionary lineage into two or more genetically independent ones.

specie ('spiːʃɪ, 'spiːʃiː, 'spiːʃɪiː). [a. L. *speciē*, abl. sing. of *speciēs* SPECIES, orig. adopted in the phr. *in speciē* (see IN). So MDu. and Du., MHG., Da. and Sw. *specie*.]

I. In the phrase **in specie**.

1. a. In kind; in respect of kind; specifically.

1562 TURNER *Herbal* II. 93 b, Pitiusa is iudged to differ in spicie or kynde from the cypresse spourge. **1600** W. WATSON *Decacordon* (1602) 66 Being of one and the selfe same kind in specie. **1631** B. JONSON *Discoveries* (Rtldg.) 764/2 They differ but in specie: either in the kind is absolute. **1672** BOYLE *Virtues of Gems* 119 The..substance..may be of so small specific gravity, as not to make the Gem at all heavier in specie than Crystal it self. **1704** SWIFT *T. Tub* iii, A sort of Critick, not distinguisht in *specie* from the former, but in Growth or Degree. **1743** D. WATSON *Horace, Sat.* etc. II. *Dissert.* p. xliii, Casaubon therefore is guilty of a palpable Mistake, when he says that the Satires of Lucilius were wholly different in Specie from those of Ennius and Pacuvius. **1802–12** BENTHAM *Ration. Judic. Evid.* (1827) I. 219 The power of the advocate, though in respect of intensity less in *degree* is in *specie* the same with the power of the judge.

†**b.** In a manner or form properly belonging to a species or class; in respect of species, as opposed to individually. *Obs.*

1620 WOTTON in *Reliq.* (1685) 501 Whether visits of respect..being received *in specie*, should be paid *in individuo*. **1651** BAXTER *Inf. Bapt.* 105 Infants in specie (and not those numerically only) should not be forbidden to come.

†**c.** In respect of specific form or manner, as opposed to generally. *Obs.*

1651 BAXTER *Inf. Bapt.* 302, I know meer circumstances are determined of but in general, and left to humane determination in Specie. **1670** —— *Cure Ch. Div.* 83 First, as a Papal Catholick Church... Secondly as particular Congregations in specie.

2. In the real, proper, precise, or actual form; without any kind of substitution. In later use only in *Law*.

1551 CRANMER *Lord's Supper* (1844) 156 As unto the Jews Jesus Christ was given in figures, so to us he is given *in specie*, that is to say, *in rei veritate*, in his very nature. **1659** BAXTER *Key Cath.* II. iii. 431 It is not a Head, but this Head *in specie*, that is, the form of the Church, if any such be. *a* **1683** SIR W. SCROGGS *Courts-leet* (1728) 228, I should have my Things again in Specie, if they may be had. **1760** GILBERT *Cases in Law & Equity* 400 If the Chattel itself be by the Agreement to be returned *in specie*, he can only be said to detain it from me unjustly. **1818** CRUISE *Digest* (ed. 2) I. 235 The covenant will be decreed to be performed in specie. **1886** *Law Rep. 34 Chanc. Div.* 139 The widow is..to possess the leaseholds in specie during her lifetime.

3. †**a.** In the actual coin specified. *Obs.*

1615 in Birch *Crt. & Times Jas. I* (1848) I. 370 Having, besides other gold, above seven thousand Jacobus pieces in specie. **1630** *R. Johnson's Kingd. & Commw.* 209 To pay a Rose-noble of gold, not only in value, but *in specie* for their passage.

†**b.** Of coin or money: In the actual form of minted pieces of metal. *Obs.*

1617 MORYSON *Itin.* I. 276 In respect of the foresaid difficulties to export coyne *In specie*, that is in the kinde. **1622** MALYNES *Anc. Law-Merch.* 477 That the imaginarie moneys..do ouerrule the course and propertie of Reall and Substantiall moneys *in specie*. **1691** LOCKE *Money* Wks. 1727 II. 46 Our Coin.., whether we send it in Specie, or whether we melt it down here to send it in Bullion. **1714** in Somers *Tracts* II. 114 By which means the ancient Method of paying Money in Specie into the Exchequer hath been much laid aside, and a great Part of the Revenue of the Kingdom received in Bank Notes.

c. Of sums or amounts: In actual coin; in money. (Cf. 6.)

1636–7 in Birch *Crt. & Times Chas. I* (1848) II. 264 The other third, by the agreement, was to go over to Dunkirk in specie. **1663** DRYDEN *Wild Gallant* I. ii, But, besides the land here mentioned, he has wealth in specie. **1713** *Guardian* No. 120 (1756) 144 All play-debts must be paid in specie, or by an equivalent. **1756** TOLDERVY *Hist. 2 Orphans* II. 124 That I am poor, is very certain, having in specie only the sum of ten-pence half-penny. **1870** *Pall Mall G.* 23 Sept. 9/1 With forty first-class cabin passengers and 156,395 dols. in specie. **1871** C. DAVIES *Metric Syst.* III. 113 As the balances..could be paid for only in specie.

†**4. a.** Of goods or commodities: In kind. (See KIND *sb.* 15.) *Obs.*

1626 in Birch *Crt. & Times Chas. I* (1848) I. 131 Nor will the country pay money instead of viands *in specie*. **1699** *Laws Nevis* xxiv. (1740) 19 All Masters of Ships..shall pay..One Pound of Pistol Powder (in *Specie*) for each and every Ton. **1738** *Hist. Crt. Excheq.* ii. 28 When they did not deliver their Goods in Specie to the King.

†**b.** *transf.* Of requital or repayment: In a similar fashion; with like treatment. *Obs.*

1632 *Story Bks. Little Gidding* 180 She shall..requite her parents in specie, as Merchants speak, when the payment is made in the self-same Coine. **1678** BUTLER *Hud.* III. ii. 1544 This Worthy, as the World will say, Is paid in Specie, his own way. **1702** *Eng. Theophrastus* 93 Kindnesses are to be paid in Specie as well as Money. **1760–72** H. BROOKE *Fool of Qual.* (1792) II. 223 My husband..loved me with passion; and, as I could not pay him in specie, I endeavoured to supply my want of affection..by my attention.

II. In general use.

†**5.** Form. ***in its proper specie***, = sense 2. *Obs.*

1644 *Doc. Lett. Pat. at Oxf.* (1837) 123 The Moneyes..to be of the same specie, weight, and goodnesse as his Majestys Moneys in the Tower of London. **1698** in *Col. Rec. Pennsylv.* I. 543 That everything you have taken by virtue of the warrant of Replevin, be forth coming in its proper specie.

6. Coin; coined money. (Cf. 3 c.) †Also, a commodity serving as a means of exchange or trade.

1671 in *9th Rep. Hist. MSS. Comm.* App. II. 13/2 Unpurged brown [sugar], being the specie of the country [Barbadoes], pays for the exports from the kingdom. **1710** *Acc. Dist. T. Whigg* II. 19 A Bung-Cart..laden with Specie and Exchequer Bills. **1749** SMOLLETT *Gil Blas* x. x, I sometimes kissed the specie, and contemplated the different pieces with..rapture. **1794** MANN in *Lett. Literary Men* (Camden) 440 They have plundered the Nation..and consequently must possess an immense quantity of specie. **1848** MILL *Pol. Econ.* III. xiii. §1 (1876) 329 Up to this point the effects of a paper currency are substantially the same, whether it be convertible into specie or not. **1864** BOWEN *Logic* ix. 274 Money may mean either specie, or bank-notes, or currency consisting of a mixture of these two.

fig. **1709** MRS. MANLEY *Secret Mem.* (1736) I. 219 He saw Promises were no longer Specie, or would any more pass current with Zara. **1806** H. SIDDONS *Maid, Wife, & Widow* I. 241 Affection is a current coin: every other specie is an infamous alloy. **1864** LOWELL *Fireside Trav.* 107 All of whose wits were about him, current, and redeemable in the specie of action.

7. †**a.** A subordinate division. *Obs.*

1670 MOXON *Pract. Perspective* 1 This Specie of Perspective is many times (alone) called the Opticks. **1750** BEAWES *Lex. Mercat.* (1752) 6 The laws [of trade]..which are long since become a Specie of the law of nations.

b. Species; kind. Now *Obs.* exc. as erron. sing. of SPECIES *sb.* 10.

1711 *Lond. Gaz.* No. 4874/4 To prepare a List of each respective Specie [of bills] which they intend to Subscribe. **1738** [G. SMITH] *Cur. Relat.* II. 558 Such Men who are Plagues to their own Specie. **1747** W. HORSLEY *Fool* (1748) II. 141 Our Hero made Divinities, though of a peculiar Specie. **1800** C. STURT in *Naval Chron.* IV. 396 A very large specie of gull. **1810** *Splendid Follies* III. 193 Such is the specie of game after which Nettletop is now in search. **1858** in Bartlett *Dict. Amer.* (1859) 432 The size of the trap,..and the nature of the bait, depends upon the specie of the animal hunted for. **1974** A. SCOTT-JAMES *Sissinghurst* vi. 74 There are..thickets of specie roses in many odd corners. **1974** *Country Life* 25 Apr. 1033/2 (Advt.), We specialise in Roses (specie & old-fashioned). **1980** *Daily Tel.* 22 Jan. 11/2 Castrated rats and other animals live longer than normal creatures of the specie. **1980** *Pan Am Clipper* Oct. 48/1 Is he [*sc.* man] descended directly from apes, or is he a specie that evolved from an entirely new..branch of the primate tree?

8. *attrib.* (in sense 6), as ***specie* †(*bank*)-*bill*, †*bank-note*, †*book*, *issue*, †*note*, *parcel*, *payment*, *value***; **specie jar**, a large glass or china jar formerly used for storage in chemists' shops and now used only for display; **specie point** = *gold point* s.v. GOLD[1] 10; **specie-room**, a strong-room on a ship in which gold coin was deposited.

1696 *Lond. Gaz.* No. 3242/4 A Specie Bank Note for 300l. payable to John Norton. **1697** *Ibid.* No. 3361/4 A Specie Bank-Bill..for 100l. payable to Jonathan Tabor. **1697** LUTTRELL *Brief Rel.* (1857) IV. 267 They will allow no other interest on specie notes then 2*d.* per day per cent. **1700** G. BROWN (*title*), Specie Book, serving to turne any number of pieces of Silver to pounds Scots or Sterling. **1786** R. KING *Life & Corr.* (1894) I. 5 Reducing the price of the article..by the scale of its specie value. **1808** *Edinb. Rev.* II. 107 To recommend the perpetual stoppage of specie-issues at the Bank. **1845** McCULLOCH *Taxation* II. xi. (1852) 382 The resolution to revert to specie payments at the old standard. **1861** G. J. GOSCHEN *Theory Foreign Exchanges* iv. 50 There would have existed a certain competition..to buy at a heavy discount, much below specie point, in order subsequently to realize at least the specie value. **1884** *Illustr. Lond. News* 11 Oct. 342/1 Daily conveyance of ordinary and specie parcels. **1891** *Scribner's Mag.* Nov. 603/2 In these days of heavy gold shipments, the specie-room on the steamship is a very important institution. **1914** *N. & Q.* 14 Feb. 127/1 The well-known 'specie jars' of chemists' shops. *a* **1929** R. BEDFORD in Murdoch & Drake-Brockman *Austral. Short Stories* (1951) 100 I'll bring dynamite..and blow the specie-room open..and haul out the gold-boxes. **1929** C. J. S. THOMPSON *Myst. Apothecary* xix. 257 The large cylindrical vessels called 'specie jars', with metal or gilded lids, that still decorate some of the chemists' shop-windows. **1966** A. GILPIN *Dict. Econ. Terms* 190 *Specie points or Gold points*, the extreme points of variation in a rate of exchange under the gold standard.

specie-, combining form of L. *speciēs* SPECIES, employed in a few recent terms, as **specie'graphical** *a.*, of or pertaining to the scientific description of species. (Cf. SPECIO-.)

1888 *Nature* 2 Feb. 322/1 A more direct reference to a speciegraphical description of *S*[*almo*] *namaycush* might have been expected.

species ('spiːʃiːz, 'spiːʃɪiːz), *sb.* Pl. species; also 7–9 specieses. [a. L. *speciēs* (abl. sing. *speciē* SPECIE) appearance, form, kind, etc., f. *specĕre* to look, behold; hence also G. *species, spezies*. Within the Romanic languages the word is represented by It. *specie, spezie*, Sp. and Pg. *especie* (and *especia*), OF. *espece* (F. *espèce*) and *espice* (F. *épice*): see SPECE and SPICE *sb.*]

I. †**1. a.** Appearance; outward form. *Obs.*

This sense is partly represented in the legal use of the word: see quots. 1651 and 1765–8 under SPECIFICATION 1 b.

1559 MORWYNG *Evonym.* 400 An other very good wine with the same species, but in other weight. **1651** HOBBES *Leviath.* IV. xliv. 338 A Divinity under their *species*, or likenesse.

b. *Math.* Of geometrical figures (see quot. 1842).

But in earlier quots. taken in sense 9.

1660 BARROW *Euclid* I. xxxii, All right-lined figures of the same species. *Ibid.* VI. vii, The angles C and F are not of the same species or kind. **1715** tr. *Gregory's Astron.* (1726) I. 411 The Methods..for finding the Species and Position of the Orbit of the Earth. **1842** *Penny Cycl.* XXII. 322/2 Euclid..means by figures of the same species those which have the same form, whatever may be their size... The word species is here used in its primitive sense of appearance. **1881** CASEY *Sequel to Euclid* 37 A triangle is said to be given in species when its angles are given.

2. *Eccl.* The visible form of each of the elements of bread and wine used in the sacrament of the Eucharist; one or other of these elements.

Sometimes rendered by 'form', but more commonly (through association with 9) by 'kind': see KIND *sb.* 13 b.

1579 FULKE *Heskins's Parl.* 84 They ceasse to be the body & bloud of Christ, when the species or kinds of bread and wine, are putrified or rotten. **1614** BREREWOOD *Lang. & Relig.* 213 They deny the true body of Christ to be really in the sacrament of the eucharist under the species of bread and wine. **1637** GILLESPIE *Eng. Pop. Cerem.* III. ii. 34 Now that which was under the species, though in their conceit it was Christs body, yet it was indeed Bread. **1671** WOODHEAD *St. Teresa* II. xi. 97 As soon as I had communicated (the Species remaining yet as it were intire). **1737** CHALLONER *Cath. Chr. Instr.* (1753) 99 The Ceremony of mixing a Particle of the Host with the Species of Wine in the Chalice. **1849** ROCK *Ch. of Fathers* I. ii. 101 The sacramental species are no longer bread and wine, but have been changed into the Very Body and Blood of Christ Himself. **1880** LITTLEDALE *Plain Reasons* xxx. 78 *note*, All the acts..took place in relation to the species of bread, and not with regard to the chalice.

†**3. a.** The outward appearance or aspect, the visible form or image, *of* something, as constituting the immediate object of vision. *Obs.* (Common in 17th cent.)

1598 R. HAYDOCKE tr. *Lomatius* Pref. 4 The picture mooveth the eye, and that committeth the species and formes of the things seene to the memory. **1603** H. CROSSE *Vertues Commw.* (1878) 42 Our sight being removed from the obiect and species of things. **1653** URQUHART *Rabelais* I. xliv, As if they had seen the very proper species and forme of death before their eyes. **1699** LD. TARBUT *Let.* in *Pepys' Diary* (1870) 688 That which is generally seen by them is the species of living creatures, and inanimate things, which are in motion.

†**b.** Similarly without *of*. *Obs.*

c **1613** W. BROWNE in *Sir T. Overbury's Wks.* (1856) 12 Yet through thy wounded fame, as thorow these Glasses which multiply the species, We see thy vertues more. **1654** GAYTON *Pleas. Notes* I. viii. 27 For he saw at a convenient distance forty windmills to be the very same, that the species represented them. *a* **1700** KEN *Hymnotheo* Poet. Wks. 1721 III. 355 As the two Eyes, two Species entertain.

†**c.** The image of something as cast upon, or reflected from, a surface; a reflection. *Obs.*

1638 WILKINS *New World* v. (1707) 41 The Light which appears in the Moon at the Eclipses, is nothing else but the second Species of the Sun's Rays. **1669** *Phil. Trans.* IV. 1104 The way of casting the Species of the Sun through a good Telescope of a competent length, on an extended paper. **1697** DRYDEN *Æneid* VIII. 36 The glitt'ring species here and there divide, And cast their dubious beams from side to side. **1737** *Gentl. Mag.* VII. 121/2, I cast the Species of the Sun on a Sheet of Paper..thro' a two-foot Telescope. *c* **1790** IMISON *Sch. Arts* I. 200 The Species of an object is the image or representation thereof made by the rays of light in the Focus, or place where they unite.

†**4.** A thing seen; a spectacle; *esp.* an unreal or imaginary object of sight; a phantom or illusion. *Obs.*

1639 S. DU VERGER tr. *Camus' Admir. Events* 34 We will cause her obsequies to be prepared, and a fantasme, or species to be put into the grave. **1652** J. WRIGHT tr. *Camus' Nat. Paradox* VI. 134 Shee had no sooner opened her Eyes, but the first *species* that formed it self to her sight, was an horrible Serpent of an immense growth. **1661** LOVELL *Hist. Anim. & Min.* 82 It helps against vaine species.

†**5.** *Metaph.* A supposed emission or emanation from outward things, forming the direct object of cognition for the various senses or for the understanding. *Obs.*

The species affecting the senses were classed as *sensible* (divided into *audible, visible*, etc.) and distinguished from the *intelligible*. See also INTENTIONAL *a.* 3.

a. With qualifying adjs.

1614 BP. HALL *No Peace with Rome* §8 (1627) 665 In the same state as the faculty of seeing when a sensible species is absent. **1651** HOBBES *Govt. & Soc.* xiii. §7. 195 We may more truly say..that the sensible, and intelligible species of outward things,..are by the ayre transported to the soule. **1661** BOYLE *Spring of Air* (1682) 108 Because no visual species's could proceed either from it, or through it, unto the eye. **1700** ASTRY tr. *Saavedra-Faxardo* II. 54 The Councils are as 'twere..the Optick Nerves, by which visible Species are transmitted to the Prince. **1707** J. FRAZER *Disc. Second Sight* 17 Visible Ideas, or Species, are emitted from every visible Object to the Organ of the Eye.

b. In general use.

1621 BURTON *Anat. Mel.* I. i. II. vii, Memory layes vp all the Species which the Senses haue brought in, and records them. **1668** CULPEPPER & COLE *Barthol. Anat.* Man. IV. viii. 345 That the Species of odours may with the Air be carried to the..Organs of Smelling. **1683** TRYON *Way to Health* 269 The very Air conveys the Species of diseased People, more especially if there be fit and prepared matter for Diseases. **1756** GIBBON *Autobiog. & Corr.* (1869) 182 If you understand by ideas these chimerical species, the mere fictions of metaphysicians.

c. A mental impression; an idea.

1644 DIGBY *Nat. Bodies* xxxviii. §3. 329 If there be aboundance of specieses of any one kind of obiect then strong in the imagination. **1650** EARL MONM. tr. *Senault's Man bec. Guilty* 244 Imagine..that his soul exercising those species which she by the senses had received, considered the works of God. **1711** SHAFTESB. *Charact.* (1737) III. 33 There are certain moral Species or Appearances so striking, ..that..they bear down all contrary Opinion.

†**6.** In Platonic philosophy, = IDEA *sb.* 1. *Obs.*

1678 CUDWORTH *Intell. Syst.* 261, I suppose, said Socrates, that God and the very Species, Essence or Idea of Life, will be granted by all to be Incorruptible. **1704** NORRIS *Ideal World* II. vi. 315 Plato..supposed besides these corporal things another kind of beings separate from matter and motion, which he called species or ideas. *Ibid.*, That so the soul did not understand those corporal things, but the separate species of those corporal things. **1792** MONBODDO *Language* ix. 110 These perfect ideas of Plato are no other than the specieses of things which were held by Aristotle to exist in the mind of the deity.

II. 7. *Logic.* The second of the five Predicables (q.v.), connoting the common attributes or essential qualities of a class of persons or things as distinguished from the genus on the one hand and the individual on the other.

1551 T. WILSON *Logike* B vj, Species is a common word that is spoken of many whiche differ only in number, as manne is spoken of Socrates,..and of euery proper name belonging to a man. As Socrates is a man. **1567** JEWEL *Def. Apol.* III. v. 343 What adoo was made in daily disputations ..aboute Genus and Species, and the reste of the Vniuersals. **1657** J. SMITH *Myst. Rhet.* A viij b, Species, is a more special title attributed to divers particulars under it: as, Man to William, Thomas, John. **1668** WILKINS *Real Char.* II. i. §3. 26 That common nature which is communicable to several Individuals, is called Species, Sort or special kind. **1725** WATTS *Logic* (1726) 36 A special Idea is call'd by the Schools, a Species; it is one common Nature that agrees to several singular or individual Beings. *Ibid.* 235 All those supposed unknown Parts, Properties or Species are clearly and distinctly perceived to be..contain'd in the known Parts, Properties or general Ideas. **1827** WHATELY *Logic* 138 Whatever Term can be affirmed of several things, must express..their whole essence, which is called a Species. **1857–60** [see DIFFERENCE *sb.* 4 c].

†**b.** The essential quality or specific properties *of* a thing. *Obs.*

1594 T. B. *La Primaud. Fr. Acad.* II. 429 The instruments whereby the *Species* or kinde of any thing is vnited and knit vnto the matter. **1599** B. JONSON *Ev. Man out of Hum.* II. vi, I am come to haue you play the Alchymist with me, and change the species of my land, into that mettall you talke of. **1610** —— *Alch.* II. iii, We..can produce the species of each mettall More perfect thence, then nature doth in earth. **1651** HOBBES *Govt. & Soc.* vii. §1. 109 We have already spoken of a City by institution in its Genus; we now say somewhat of its species.

8. a. A class composed of individuals having some common qualities or characteristics, freq. as a subdivision of a larger class or genus.

1630 PRYNNE *Anti-Armin.* 180 This kinde of argument from euery indiuiduall to the species will not hold. **1653** ? HALES *Brevis Disq.* in *Phenix* (1708) II. 324 Are you not yet sure whether..if you reject all the Species, the whole Genus be taken away? **1690** LOCKE *Hum. Und.* III. vi. §8 The individuals that are ranked into one sort, called by one common name, and so received as being of one species. **1762** KAMES *Elem. Crit.* (1833) 486 A number of individuals considered with respect to qualities that distinguish them from others, is termed a species. **1822** I. TAYLOR *Elem. Educ.* 39 The smaller parcels into which we afterwards divide the whole, are called species. **1843** MILL *Logic* I. vii. §3 In this popular sense any two classes one of which includes the whole of the other and more may be called a genus and a species. **1870** JEVONS *Elem. Logic* xii. 98 A species is any class which is regarded as forming part of the next larger class.

†**b.** *Algebra.* (See quot. 1704.) *Obs.*

'The term was..used by Vieta in its logical sense, as opposed to individual, in designating the algebraical notation which he first distinctly proposed' (*Penny Cycl.* XXII. 322).

1674 JEAKE *Arith.* (1696) 334 Species are Quantities or Magnitudes, denoted by Letters, signifying Numbers, Lines,.. Figures,..&c. **1688** *Lond. Gaz.* No. 2319/4 Together with Arithmetick in Species or Algebra, &c. **1704** J. HARRIS *Lex. Techn.* I, *Species* in Algebra, are those Letters, Notes, Marks, or Symbols, which represent the Quantities in any Equation or Demonstration.

c. Without article, esp. in phr. ***in species***.

1785 REID *Intell. Powers* 28 To differ in species is one thing, to differ in degree another. **1841** LANE *Arab. Nts.* I. 30 It is believed..that the difference between them and the Jinn and Sheytáns is a difference of species.

9. a. A distinct class, sort, or kind, of something specifically mentioned or indicated. Freq. const. *of*.

The separate groups of quotations illustrate the chief varieties of context.

(*a*) **1561** T. HOBY tr. *Castiglione's Courtyer* III. (1900) 223 Both the one and the other is conteined under the Species of *Homo*. **1660** R. COKE *Justice Vind.* 26 If the Scriptures be true,..that since Adam..the species of Mankind was continued by generation. **1697** DRYDEN *Virg. Georg.* III. 830 Sheep, Oxen, Horses fall; and heap'd on high, The diff'ring Species in Confusion lye. *a* **1763** SHENSTONE *Ess.* Wks. 1765 II. 155 Man is not proud as a species, but as an individual. **1799** WASHINGTON *Lett.* Writ. 1893 XIV. 196 To sell the overplus I cannot, because I am principled against this kind of traffic in the human species.

(*b*) **1599** B. JONSON *Cynthia's Rev.* II. iii, Every your most noted species of persons, as your marchant, your scholer, your souldier. **1662** J. DAVIES tr. *Olearius' Voy. Amb.* 170 They were certain Indian Lords... The same Author distinguishes them into four species. *a* **1687** PETTY *Pol. Arith.* (1690) 95 Might not the several Species of the Kings Subjects be equally mixt in their Habitations? **1750** JOHNSON *Rambler* No. 75 ¶2 That species of men whom the ladies generally mention with terror. **1780** BENTHAM *Princ. Legisl.* xviii. §44 *note*, Aristotle..divides mankind into two distinct species: that of freemen and that of slaves. **1867** KINGSLEY *Water Life* vi. (1879) 71 Dante, with his various *bolge*, tenanted each by its various species of sinners.

(*c*) **1581** SIDNEY *Apol. Poet.* (Arb.) 43 Now in his parts, kindes, or *Species*, (as you list to terme them) it is to be noted, that some Poesies haue coupled together two or three kindes. **1759** GOLDSM. *Wks.* (1837) III. 215 Disapproving in one species of composition, what we approve in another! **1780** *Mirror* No. 79, No species of poetry has given occasion to more observation and criticism than what is called *pastoral*. **1801** BUSBY *Dict. Mus.*, *Species*, a subdivision of one of the genera of the ancient music. The genera of the Greeks were three... The Species were called *Chroia*, or colours of the genera. **1826** MACAULAY *Misc. Writ.* (1860) I. 303 No species of fiction is so delightful to us as the old English drama. **1845** M. PATTISON *Ess.* (1889) I. 1 Such history is a distinct species of composition.

(*d*) *a* **1625** SIR H. FINCH *Law* (1636) 252 Wood is the generall of all trees growing, and therefore shall be put in demand before Alders and Willowes which are but *species* of it. **1656** [? J. SERGEANT] tr. *T. White's Peripat. Inst.* 355 By the meeting of different parts, as many kinds and species of Earths,..we see [etc.]. **1727** A. HAMILTON *New Acc. E. Ind.* II. l. 229, I told them what the current Price was in Town for every Species of my Goods. **1794** HUTTON *Philos. Light*, etc. 65 That it is the invisible species of light which is most absorbed by the..glass.

(*e*) **1635** J. HAYWARD tr. *Biondi's Banish'd Virg.* 136 There was not any *species* of simplicity that I counterfeited not affectately. **1644** DIGBY *Nat. Bodies* ii. §8. 14 There remaineth no more to be said of this subiect, but to enumerate the seuerall specieses of Quantity. **1769** E. BANCROFT *Guiana* 368 In this situation they are subjected to many complicated species of misery. **1792** J. BARLOW *Constit. of 1791*, 9 That species of government which offers a premium for wickedness. **1825** MACAULAY *Ess.*, *Milton* (1851) I. 26 He fought for the species of freedom which is the most valuable. **1834** L. RITCHIE *Wand. by Seine* 83 That imaginative species of memory which converts the past into the present.

b. ***a species of***, a kind of (cf. KIND *sb.* 14); also with *the*. †In early use in more definite sense.

1620 T. GRANGER *Div. Logike* xiii. 315 When in the handling of a controuerted question, diuers opinions are recited, it is a part, or species of a narration. **1644** BULWER *Chirol.* 108 For suretiship is a species of bargaining. **1751** JOHNSON *Rambler* No. 87 ¶9 Their gratitude is a species of revenge. **1815** SCOTT *Guy M.* xii, A species of native banditti who were always on the watch for prey. **1839** FR. KEMBLE *Resid. in Georgia* (1863) 12 Under the species of social proscription in which the blacks in your Northern cities exist. **1842** LOUDON *Suburban Hort.* 345 Clipping is a species of pruning that was formerly much more general.

c. Applied to individuals as unique or as typical of a class.

1644 CLEVELAND *Char. Lond. Diurnall* 7 As the Angels, each of them makes a severall *Species*; so every one of his Souldiers is a distinct Church. **1656** COWLEY *Pindar. Odes, Praise of Pindar* i, Pindar is imitable by none; The Phœnix Pindar is a vast Species alone. **1719** YOUNG *Busiris* v. i, I can't complain in common with mankind—But am a wretched species all alone. **1768** JOHNSON *Pref. to Shaks.* Wks. IX. 243 In the writings of other poets a character is too often an individual; in those of Shakespeare it is commonly a species.

d. With possessive pronouns, usually with reference to man or animals.

1706 E. WARD *Wooden World Diss.* (1708) 42 He loves dearly to propagate his Species, even in the very Lands that know him not. **1794** GODWIN *Caleb Williams* 48 You will live deserted in the midst of your species. **1839** RUSKIN *Poetry Arch.* vi. §87 A man who could remain a radical in a wood country is a disgrace to his species.

e. ***the species***, the human race.

1711 ADDISON *Spect.* No. 10 ¶6 Their Amusements seem contrived for them rather as they are Women..; and are more adapted to the Sex, than to the Species. **1728** FIELDING *Love in Sev. Masques* Ded., Wks. 1882 VIII. 3 Those morose schoolmen, who would confine knowledge to the male part of the species. **1797** GODWIN *Enquirer* I. i. 1 If individuals were happy, the species would be happy. **1814** CHALMERS *Evidences* vi. 182 Every great step in the history of the species. **1859** MILL *Liberty* i. 7 In the stage of progress into which the more civilized portions of the Species have now entered.

f. *Chem.* and *Physics*. A particular kind of molecule, ion, free radical, etc.; a distinct kind of atom (esp. a radioactive one) or sub-atomic particle.

[**1857** W. A. MILLER *Elem. Chem.* III. 45 Other remarkable species of compounds which are obtained by substitution, are those in which a portion of the hydrogen of the original body is displaced by chlorine.] **1895** C. S. PALMER tr. *Nernst's Theoret. Chem.* IV. ii. 521 We will select as a further..example of complete heterogeneous equilibrium, a system composed of H_2O and SO_2, i.e. two molecular species. **1948** *Nature* 28 Feb. 291/2 The use of tracer materials, radioactive species, and radiations. **1962** COTTON & WILKINSON *Adv. Inorg. Chem.* xiv. 427 Pure sulfuric acid contains a number of species in equilibrium. **1967** M. CHANDLER *Ceramics in Mod. World* vi. 179 Natural uranium is not a single nuclear species. It contains two isotopes. **1971** *Physics Bull.* Dec. 720/3 Using the techniques of flash photolysis..he has identified the spectra of many new species, like CH_2, CH_3 and NH_2. **1974** *Nature* 13 Dec. 538/1 Whether *n* is considered to be the total number of particles in the Universe or the number of a given species, such as electrons or nucleons, is not important within the accuracy considered here.

10. *Zool.* and *Bot.* A group or class of animals or plants (usually constituting a subdivision of a genus) having certain common and permanent characteristics which clearly distinguish it from other groups.

The exact definition of a species, and the criteria by which species are to be distinguished (esp. in relation to genera or varieties), have been the subject of much discussion.

1608 TOPSELL *Serpents* 126 Some haue taken the word *Crocodilus* for the Genus, and the seuerall Species, they distinguish into the Crocodile of the Earth, and the water. **1676** RAY *Corr.* (1848) 122 In the 'History of the Fero Islands' I find no more *species* of birds than what I have already inserted in the Ornithology. **1695** WOODWARD *Nat. Hist. Earth* VI. (1723) 272 There were then the very same kinds of Animals and Vegetables, and the same subordinate *Species* under each kind that now there is. **1730** MILLER *Gard. Dict.* s.v. *Leontopetalon*, We have but one Species of this Plant in the English Gardens. **1753** *Chambers' Cycl.* Suppl. s.v. *Specific*, The *torpedo maculosa*, and *non maculosa*, seem to express two species different only in the spots. **1807** J. E. SMITH *Phys. Bot.* 462 Of which genus *Phyllachne*..is justly there reckoned a species. **1825** WATERTON *Wand. S. Amer.* I. i. 94 The Humming-birds are chiefly to be found near the flowers at which each of the species of the genus is wont to feed. **1862** JOHNS *Brit. Birds* 415 The American Bittern..seems to differ in no material respect from the European species. **1878** HUXLEY *Physiogr.* 208 Exactly the same kind or species of shell-fish is found to-day living in the Mediterranean.

†11. a. *pl.* The separate materials or ingredients used in compounding a perfume, drug, or similar preparation. *Obs.*

1601 HOLLAND *Pliny* I. 375 The Species that goe to the composition of sweet Perfumes. *Ibid.* II. 289 It is one of the species or ingredients entring into the preseruatiue compositions called Antidotes. **1693** tr. *Blancard's Phys. Dict.* (ed. 2), *Species* of Treacle are those Ingredients of which Treacle is compounded: By the same Name are called the *Species* of ordinary Decoctions.

†b. *pl.* Spices. *Obs.*$^{-1}$

1652 CRASHAW *Carmen Deo Nostro* Wks. (1904) 198 Mountains of myrrh, & Beds of species.

†c. A composition used in embalming. *Obs.*

1767 GOOCH *Treat. Wounds* I. 457 Filled with a *species*, compounded of fragrant herbs, aromatic drugs, and gums reduced to powder.

†12. a. A particular kind or sort of coin or money. *Obs.*

1617 MORYSON *Itin.* I. 275 With covenant to deliver him by his Factor the same [coins], both in the Species or Kind, and in the number. **1699** BENTLEY *Phal.* 440 Dionysius perhaps did not only recoin the money of Syracuse; but alter the Species too and the Names of it. **1704** *Lond. Gaz.* No. 4029/1 The different Rates at which the same Species of Foreign Coins do pass. **1756** MRS. F. BROOKE *Old Maid* No. 20. 171 He gave me a note specifying the sum, and the several species of money of which it consisted.

†b. Coinage, coin, money, bullion. *Obs.*

In this sense it is difficult to distinguish between sing. and pl., and in some cases the pl. of SPECIE may be intended.

a **1618** RALEIGH *Prerog. Parl.* 58 If all be content to pay upon moderation and change of the Species. **1672** PETTY *Pol. Anat.* (1691) 70 What hath been said of the Silver-species, may be said of the Gold-species. **1701** *Lond. Gaz.* No. 3740/3 The melting down of the Species is prohibited. **1748** *Anson's Voy.* (ed. 4) 248 The species on board her was inconsiderable, being principally small silver money. **1788** PRIESTLEY *Lect. Hist.* III. xvi. 138 Their nominal species..being about three times higher than ours. **1804** *Captive of Valence* II. 100 By prohibiting species to be carried out of his kingdom in such small quantities, he will prevent the entry of a sum much more considerable.

†c. Metal (gold or silver) used for coinage. *Obs.*

1790 BURKE *Fr. Rev.* Wks. V. 56 The paper securities..held out as a currency..in lieu of the two great recognized species that represent the lasting conventional credit of mankind.

†13. *pl.* **a.** *Naut.* Sorts of provisions. *Obs.*

[**1699** LUTTRELL *Brief Rel.* (1857) IV. 494 The victualling the Streights fleet without due proofe for the prime costs of the several species of provision.] **1716** *Lond. Gaz.* No. 5464/3 The Goodness of the several Species, and Conditions expected from each Contractor. **1751** *Navy Board Orders* 4 Apr. (MS.), The Kingfisher..to be Victualled to three months of all Species except Beer. **1806** CAPT. MUNDY in *Naval Chron.* XXXIX. 13 Stored and victualled for five months, of all species.

†b. Sorts of produce. *Obs.*

c **1730** BURT *Lett. N. Scotl.* (1818) II. 53 So that if the tenant is not provided with all the species he is to pay, then that which is wanting may be converted into money.

14. *attrib.* and *Comb.*, as ***species-cross***, ***-cycle***, ***diversity***, ***-evolution***, ***-formation***, ***group***, ***-maker***, ***-monger***, ***-preservation***; **species being**, a term [tr. G. *Gattungswesen* (P. C. Reinhard, 1797)] used by Marx to denote man's objective consciousness of life and the mastery of the natural world through work which characterize the human species; man considered in respect to these qualities; **species pair**, a pair of species which are similar, sympatric, and closely related, but distinct; **species-poor**, **-rich** *adjs.*, having a small, or large, number of species; so **species richness**; **species rose**, a rose belonging to a distinct species and not to one of the many varieties produced by hybridization; cf. OLD ROSE; **species sanitation** *Med.*, measures taken against a particular species of mosquito in order to reduce the incidence of malaria; **species-specific** *a.*, found in or characteristic of the members of one species only; hence **species specificity**; **species-uniform** *a.*, consistent throughout a species.

1959 M. MILLIGAN tr. *Marx's Econ. & Philos. MSS of 1844* 75 Conscious life-activity directly distinguishes man from animal life-activity. It is just because of this that he is a *species being. *Ibid.* 76 It is just in the working-up of the objective world, therefore, that man first really proves himself to be a *species being*. **1979** GLASSNER & FREEDMAN *Clinical Sociol.* iv. 95 Workers are alienated from..their 'species being', or from their human capacity for conscious and creative activity. **1926** J. S. HUXLEY *Ess. Pop. Sci.* 25 Where the offspring of *species-crosses are perfectly fertile, [etc.]. **1883** *Encycl. Brit.* XVI. 843/2 The complete series of forms needed to represent the species being the *species-cycle. **1967** *Oceanogr. & Marine Biol.* V. 257 An intuitive character referable to any natural population or assemblage of individuals is *species diversity or biotic diversity. **1972** Species diversity [see *species richness* below]. **1946** F. E. ZEUNER *Dating Past* xii. 355 This genus experienced an episode of abundant *species-evolution from the Eocene to the Miocene, or roughly for 50 million years. **1977** R. HOLLAND *Self & Social Context* viii. 246 Mead's concept of the social-self..never clarifies the relation between species-evolution and individual development. **1941** J. S. HUXLEY *Uniqueness of Man* vi. 155 Chromosome-doubling after crossing is a method of *species-formation in which the isolation is not spatial but genetic. **1975** *Nature* 24 Jan. 290/3 Some hakes, especially the western South American *species-group (*M[erluccius] gayi*), might support a greater fishery than at present. **1851** S. P. WOODWARD *Mollusca* I. 61 Fancying that the genus-maker, and not the *species-maker, should enjoy this privilege. **1849** DARWIN in F. Darwin *Life & Lett.* (1887) I. 366 As long as *species-mongers have their vanity tickled by seeing their own names appended to a species. **1942** J. S. HUXLEY *Evolution* vi. 284 Overlapping *Species Pairs. Numerous puzzling cases are presented by extremely similar species which overlap over much of their range and yet remain distinct. **1959** *New Biol.* XXVIII. 70 Of some sympatric species-pairs, one member releases pollen in the morning and the other in the evening, and the stigmas of each species are receptive only at the appropriate times, so considerably reducing the chances of receiving foreign pollen. **1964** V. J. CHAPMAN *Coastal Veg.* ix. 225 In the absence of grazing a luxuriant and *species-poor Festucetum rubrae develops. **1976** *Jrnl. R. Soc. Arts* CXXIV. 640/1 The Southern Ocean is characterized by a species-rich, productive ecosystem which contrasts sharply with the species-poor, relatively barren terrestrial and freshwater ecosystems of the islands and continental landmass. **1894** H. DRUMMOND *Ascent Man* 24 Obeying the law of *species-preservation, to feed its young. **1973** *Nature* 30 Mar. 344/2 In maintaining or reconstructing types of herbaceous vegetation in which the density of flowering plants exceeds 20 species/m²—the so-called '*species-rich' communities, success is often frustrated by competitive exclusion. **1981** *Country Life* 12 Feb. 376/3 Species-rich hedges were treated sympathetically. **1972** *Ecology* LIII. 279/2 The pattern of bird *species richness (mean number of species per census) was quite similar to the pattern of bird species diversity. **1930** J. N. HART *Rose Growing* ix. 57 The *species roses are actually wild roses, either native..or imported. **1935** N. MITCHISON *We have been Warned* II. 196 There were Penzance briars, and species roses growing unpruned. **1976** LD. HOME *Way Wind Blows* xiv. 200 A very attractive garden to the south and front of the house..had been filled with a wide variety of species roses. **1930** M. F. BOYD *Introd. Malariol.* vi. 418 'Selective control', 'species control' or '*species sanitation', as it is variously designated, *i.e.*, limiting efforts to the control of one species. **1945** *New Biol.* I. 107 The disease can be controlled by applying anti-mosquito measures to these kinds [*sc.* malarial vectors] only. This method of control, species sanitation, was first used, with spectacular results, by Watson in Malaya. **1959** A. A. SANDOSHAM *Malariology* i. 19 The increased knowledge of the systematics and bionomics of local anopheline fauna made it possible to evolve the more scientific and more economic method of mosquito control referred to as 'species-sanitation'. **1924** *Jrnl. Exper. Med.* XL. 106 The question arises whether these antigens are simple *species-specific proteins. **1956** *Nature* 21 Jan. 133/1 The reduction in oxygen consumption appears to be caused by a species-specific antibody in the N'Dama serum. **1980** A. KENNY *Aquinas* iii. 76 Chomsky has argued that it is impossible to explain the rapidity with which children acquire the grammar of a language from the..utterances of their parents unless we postulate a species-specific innate language-learning ability. **1925** *Jrnl. Exper. Med.* XLII. 141 Species specificity of cells is of a different order as opposed to *species specificity of proteins. **1964** H. HYNES *Med. Bacteriol.* (ed. 8) vii. 76 The differences that make a protein molecule a specific antibody are only minor; in chemical structure and species-specificity..it is still a γ-globulin molecule. **1968** R. W. LANGACKER *Lang. & its Structure* ix. 247 The view that linguistic experience serves more to activate language than to shape it accounts for the fact that language is *species uniform and species specific. **1976** *Word 1971* XXVII. 225 If a sign language is treated on a par with an oral language, then language is neither species-specific nor species-uniform, because other species are now known to be capable of learning a sign language.

speciesism (ˈspiːʃiːzɪz(ə)m). [f. SPECIES *sb.* + -ISM.] Discrimination against or exploitation of certain animal species by human beings, based on an assumption of mankind's superiority.

1975 R. D. RYDER *Victims of Sci.* 16, I use the word 'speciesism' to describe the widespread discrimination that is practised by man against other species... Speciesism and racism both overlook or underestimate the similarities between the discriminator and those discriminated against. **1976** *New Society* 3 June 544/1 If racism and sexism are wrong, what abut speciesism? Peter Singer apologises for using this graceless term. **1979** *Listener* 7 June 777/1 'Speciesism' is intended to convey the idea that one animal species, human beings, supposes that it has the right to exploit other species. **1982** *Times* 8 Apr. 13/1 Animals have rights... There are forms of 'speciesism' as corrupting as 'racism' or 'sexism'.

Hence **ˈspeciesist** *a.* and *sb.*

1975 R. D. RYDER *Victims of Sci.* 21 The main speciesist defence of cruelty to animals is that mankind benefits—in terms of knowledge, economy or sport, for example. **1977** *Daily Tel.* 5 May 16 A demonstrating mob of anti-speciesists, perhaps accompanied by species even odder than themselves, may soon be..cawing, roaring and singing ..at your door. **1978** *Nature* 9 Nov. 122/2 Gould is, in general, rather good at puncturing human speciesist vanity, and in particular he will have nothing to do with the myth that evolution represents progress toward man.

specifiable (spɛsɪˈfaɪəb(ə)l), *a.* [f. SPECIFY *v.*] Capable of being specified.

1661 BOYLE *Style Script.* 118 Which otherwise being so near Infinite, as to be Indefinite, are not so easily specifiable in Rules. **1888** *Nature* Oct. 592/1 A minute but specifiable fraction of an original disturbance.

† **specifial,** *a. Obs. rare.* [Irreg. f. SPECIFY *v.*, or error for SPECIFICAL *a.*] Specific.

a **1670** HACKET *Abp. Williams* II. (1692) 151 They..ought first to put in a Specifial Charge, and the *Reus*, or Defendant first be call'd to his Answer. *Ibid.* 176 It took away..the very specifial Form, Essence, and Being of a Parliament.

specific (spɛˈsɪfɪk, spə-), *a.* and *sb.* Also 7 specifique, 7–8 -ick. [ad. med.L. *specific-us*, f. *speci-ēs* SPECIES: see -FIC. Hence also F. *spécifique*, It. *specifico*, Sp. and Pg. *especifico*.]

A. *adj.* **1. a.** Having a special determining quality.

a **1631** DONNE *Poems* (1912) 194 For, God no such specifique poyson hath As kills we know not how. **1650** BULWER *Anthropomet.* 72 Which sentence is..true..of all parts that naturally exist in any specifique body. **1842** LOUDON *Suburban Hort.* 59 Bones are valuable as a specific manure, because they contain phosphate of lime.

† **b.** Having the qualities of a species. *Obs.*

1650 BULWER *Anthropomet.* 129 Man is not at once an Individuum and a specifique Individuum.

2. a. Of qualities, properties, effects, etc.: Specially or peculiarly pertaining to a certain thing or class of things and constituting one of the characteristic features of this.

c **1650** DENHAM *Of Prudence* 16 That thou to Truth the perfect way mayst know, To thee all her specific forms I'll show. **1665** *Phil. Trans.* I. 48 Plants and other Medicinal things, that have specifique Vertues. **1712** ADDISON *Spect.* No. 409 ⁋5 The distinguishing Perfections, or, if I may be allowed to call them so, the Specifick Qualities of the Author whom he peruses. **1744** BERKELEY *Siris* §87 The specific taint or peculiar cause of the malady. **1782** *Phil. Trans.* LXXII. 196 The different portions of elementary fire contained in such substance, and absorbed by it,..and hence called its specific fire. **1804** ABERNETHY *Surg. Obs.* 150 *note*, The specific operation of mercury on the constitution. **1837** P. KEITH *Bot. Lex.* 139 The primitive and specific molecule proper to each organ pre-exists already in the infant embryo. **1863** E. V. NEALE *Anal. Th. & Nat.* 36 Between these unities of quantity there exist relations independent of their specific magnitudes. **1884** BOWER & SCOTT *De Bary's Phaner.* 503 Plants, in which the demarcation of the annual rings is constantly absent as a specific peculiarity.

b. ***specific difference***: see DIFFERENCE *sb.* 4 c.

1649 BULWER *Pathomyot.* I. vi. 32 Al actions equally proceed from the Soul, but receive their Specifique difference from the instruments. **1697** tr. *Burgersdicius' Logic* II. ii. 6 A perfect Definition consists of the next Genus and Specific Difference. **1777** PRIESTLEY *Matt. & Spir.* (1782) I. xxii. 282 It was necessary to find some specific difference between them. **1840** CARLYLE *Heroes* iii. (1904) 82 Where there is no specific difference, as between round and square, all definition must be more or less arbitrary. **1861** MILL *Utilit.* v. (1874) 74 This feature in the case.. constitutes the specific difference between justice, and generosity.

c. Peculiar *to*, characteristic *of*, something.

1667 WATERHOUSE *Fire Lond.* 9 The mediation of concurring circumstances specifique to that Issue. **1874** SYMONDS *Sk. Italy & Greece* 251 Their style..is specific to Italy in the middle of the fifteenth century. **1897** *Allbutt's Syst. Med.* III. 519 Ulcers in the stomach specific of these affections may arise.

d. *Physics.* (i) Of or designating a dimensionless number equal to the ratio of the value of a property of a given substance to the value of the same property of some reference substance (as water) or of vacuum under the same conditions, so providing a relative value for comparison with different substances, as ***specific gravity*** (see GRAVITY 4 c); ***specific heat*** (see HEAT *sb.* 2 d); ***specific inductive capacity*** = *dielectric constant* s.v. DIELECTRIC *a.* 2 b; ***specific viscosity***, the difference between the viscosity of a solution of a given concentration and that of the pure solvent, divided by the viscosity of the pure solvent.

1838 M. FARADAY in *Phil. Trans. R. Soc.* CXXVIII. 33, I feel satisfied that the experiments altogether fully prove the existence of a difference between dielectrics as to their power of favouring an inductive action through them; which difference may..be expressed by the term specific inductive capacity. **1918** *Physical Rev.* XII. 50 One arm was then filled with water, and the other with a mixture of water and ethyl alcohol, the specific inductive capacity of which was known. **1935** *Jrnl. Physical Chem.* XXXIX. 157 Staudinger later adopted the term 'specific viscosity', for the quantity η_r-1. **1944** [see PERMITTIVITY]. **1959** K. HENNEY *Radio Engin. Handbk.* (ed. 5) iv. 2 The dielectric constant K of an insulating material is the ratio of the capacitance C_x of a capacitor using the material as the dielectric to the capacitance C_a using air as the dielectric... This property of the material is sometimes called inductivity or specific inductive capacity. **1966** M. L. MILLER *Struct. Polymers* v. 206 At the highest rate of shear used in these experiments, the reduced specific viscosity was independent of concentration.

(ii) Of or designating a physical quantity that is referred to a unit of mass, volume, or other measure in order to form a number independent of the properties of the particular system studied, and so measuring an inherent property or characteristic that can be scaled to describe a given system or used as an indicator of the effect of an action or process, as ***specific acoustic impedance*** (see IMPEDANCE 2); ***specific activity***, the activity of a given radioisotope per unit mass; ***specifc charge***, the ratio of the charge of an ion or sub-atomic particle to its mass; ***specific conductance, conductivity***, the conductivity of unit length of a material of unit cross-sectional area; the reciprocal of resistivity (see RESISTIVITY 1); ***specific (fuel) consumption***, the weight of fuel consumed by an engine per unit time per unit of power or thrust developed; the reciprocal of specific impulse; ***specific impulse*** (see IMPULSE *sb.* 2 c); ***specific ionization***, the number of ion pairs produced by an ionizing particle per unit path length; ***specific refraction, refractive constant***, a constant relating the refractive index (n) of a material to its density (ρ), given by $(n^2 - 1)/(\rho(n^2 + 2))$; ***specific resistance, resistivity*** = RESISTIVITY 1; ***specific rotation, rotary power***, the angle through which the plane of polarization of light of a specified wavelength is rotated by passage through a column of an optically active substance of given length (usu. 10 cm.) and at unit concentration; ***specific surface***, the surface area per unit volume of a finely-divided substance; ***specific thrust*** = *specific impulse* above; ***specific volume***, the volume of a substance per unit mass; the reciprocal of density.

In mod. use, there is a tendency to restrict the application of *specific* to quantities that are referred to unit mass. Accordingly, alternative terms are being advocated to replace those that do not conform to this narrow definition, as *conductivity* for *specific conductance* and *specific conductivity*, *relative density* for *specific gravity*, *specific heat capacity* (which is referred to unit mass) for *specific heat*, *dielectric constant* or *relative permittivity* for *specific inductive capacity*, and *resistivity* for *specific resistance* and *specific resistivity*.

The examples follow in alphabetical order.

1938 *Nature* 18 June 1098/1 The *specific activity of phosphatide P extracted from human blood corpuscles 24 hours after administration of labelled sodium phosphate was found to be 40 times less than that of plasma inorganic P. **1961** G. R. CHOPPIN *Exper. Nuclear Chem.* xi. 186 Much higher levels of specific activity may be counted with no resolving time losses. **1926** R. W. LAWSON tr. *Hevesy's Man. Radioactivity* i. 6 From the magnitude of the deflexion, combined with similar deflexion experiments in an electric field, we can determine the magnitude of the *specific charge (e/m). **1971** D. F. JACKSON *Concepts of Atomic Physics* ii. 18 The specific charge of the lightest known ion, that of hydrogen, is $9{\cdot}579 \times 10^7$ C. kg^{-1}. **1885, 1886** *Specific conductance [see CONDUCTANCE]. **1924** J. R. PARTINGTON in H. S. Taylor *Treat. Physical Chem.* I. xi. 517 In such cells conductivity water with a specific conductance of $0{\cdot}21 \times 10^{-6}$ ohm^{-1} can be kept 12 hours without change. **1958** CONDON & ODISHAW *Handbk. Physics* IV. ix. 141/1 In terms of Ohm's law, the defining equation..for specific conductance reduces to $\kappa = I/E$..where I is the current and E the potential applied to a centimeter-cube sample of the conductor. **1898** C. L. SPEYERS *Text-bk. Physical Chem.* ix. 166 A 5% aqueous solution of KCl at 0° has a *specific conductivity of $0{\cdot}056617$ mhos. **1957** G. E. HUTCHINSON *Treat. Limnol.* I. viii. 558 (*caption*) Composition of standard bicarbonate waters of varying specific conductivities. **1931** *Automotive Industries* 9 May 726/2 Fig. 10 shows the variation in *specific consumption, power and head temperature of the A70 cylinder, with change in fuel flow. **1946** J. W. VALE *Aviation Mechanic's Engine Man.* ix. 271 At any altitude the specific fuel consumption increases with the increase of power output. **1966** J. H. HORLOCK *Axial Flow Turbines* viii. 214 For the high by-pass ratios..the specific fuel consumption drops rapidly with increasing turbine temperature. **1932** *Physical Rev.* XXXIX. 884 The *specific ionization thus determined does not exceed 32 ion-pairs per cm, in water-saturated air at 68 cm pressure. **1961** G. R. CHOPPIN *Exper. Nuclear Chem.* iii. 23 This specific ionization is a measure of the rate of energy loss. **1940** GLASSTONE *Textbk. Physical Chem.* viii. 524 The difference between the *specific refractions for two wave lengths, e.g., the Hα and Hγ lines, is called the specific dispersivity. **1899** J. WALKER *Introd. Physical Chem.* xiv. 138 Another *specific refractive constant is given by [etc.]. **1899** J. MCCRAE tr. *Reychler's Outl. Physical Chem.* III. ii. 197 In order to determine the *specific resistance of a solution in ohms, we consider a cubical mass of the solution, the length of whose side is 1 centimetre. **1935** WILSON & DOWSE tr. *Holzer's Foundations Short Wave Therapy* 74 The specific resistance is not..a constant, independent of frequency. **1978** P. W. ATKINS *Physical Chem.* xxv. 820 The resistance of a material increases with its length l but decreases with its cross-section A... The proportionality coefficient is called the resistivity, or specific resistance. **1958** *Chambers's Techn. Dict.* 716/1 *Resistivity*, a term denoting volume resistivity, i.e. the resistance of a block of the material in question having unit length and unit cross-sectional area; also called *specific resistivity. **1964** R. F. FICCHI *Electrical Interference* viii. 133, ρ is the specific resistivity of the conductor. **1899** J. WALKER *Introd. Physical Chem.* xv. 150 The *specific rotation of lævorotatory oil of turpentine is 37·01°. **1940** GLASSTONE *Textbk. Physical Chem.* viii. 585 The optical rotatory power of a pure substance, particularly in the liquid state, is generally expressed in terms of its specific rotation or specific rotatory power. **1958** CONDON & ODISHAW *Handbk. Physics* VI. vi. 120/1 The molecular rotation is the product of the specific rotation by the molecular weight M of the active material. **1876** *Jrnl. Chem. Soc.* I. 667 It is proposed to substitute α_D for the *specific rotatory power obtained by means of the sodium ray. **1899** J. WALKER *Introd. Physical Chem.* xiv. 139 The specific rotatory power is usually denoted by the symbol [α]. **1924** *Chem. Abstr.* XVIII. 3507 The *specific surfaces of several varieties of charcoal were measured. **1951** A. E. ALEXANDER *Surface Chem.* i. 4 Colloidal materials such as charcoal and clays show adsorption phenomena very markedly owing to their large specific surfaces..which arises [*sic*] from their fine state of subdivision. **1977** ROWELL & FARINATO in L.-H. Lee *Characterization of Metal & Polymer Surfaces* II. 399 The specific surface of a monodisperse colloid becomes independent of the number concentration and refractive index of the spherical particles. **1949** D. G. SHEPHERD *Introd. Gas Turbine* iii. 78 The curves for *specific thrust are in general of similar shape.., increasing with T_{max} and having in an optimum value at a certain pressure ratio. **1966** J. H. HORLOCK *Axial Flow Turbines* viii. 211 A high value of specific thrust means that small engine weight is required. **1868** JONES & WATTS *Fownes's Man. Chem.* (ed. 10) II. 250 The numbers obtained.., representing the *specific volumes of the various solid and liquid elementary substances, present far more cases of discrepancy than of agreement. **1957** *Amer. Inst. Physics Handbk.* II. 117 Many tables and other aids have been prepared for the routine calculation of density and specific volume of sea water.

3. a. *Med.* Of remedies, etc.: Specially or exclusively efficacious for, or acting upon, a particular ailment or part of the body.

1677 W. HARRIS tr. *Lemery's Chym.* I. xvi. 195 It is esteemed to be specifick for malignant Diseases. **1680–90** TEMPLE *Ess. Health & Long Life* Wks. 1720 I. 285 Garlick ..I believe is..a Specifick Remedy of the Gout. **1704** J. HARRIS *Lex. Techn.* I. s.v., Physitians mention in their Books three kinds of Specifick Medicines. **1778** R. JAMES *Diss. Fevers* (ed. 8) 80 Little can be said in favour of specific medicines, but what is equally applicable to specific methods of cure. **1899** *Allbutt's Syst. Med.* VI. 795 The internal administration of specific remedies.

b. *Path.* Of a distinct or characteristic kind.

1804 ABERNETHY *Surg. Obs.* 166 We must not impute the occurrence of these peculiar sores to mere irritability, but to some specific contagion. **1843** R. J. GRAVES *Syst. Clin. Med.* xx. 234 The specific irritation of the skin termed scabies. **1876** tr. *Wagner's Gen. Path.* 260 Specific-pus, is not distinguished histologically and chemically from common pus. **1898** *Allbutt's Syst. Med.* V. 150 Specific peribronchitis of the trachea and bronchi. **1899** *Ibid.* VII. 685 Some of thses lesions are 'specific' in the sense of being characteristic of syphilis.

4. a. Precise or exact in respect of fulfilment, conditions, or terms; definite, explicit.

1740 J. PENN, etc. (*title*), Upon a Bill to compell a Specifick Execution of Articles of Agreement, entred into between the Partys for setling the Boundarys of the Province of Pensilvania. **1768** BLACKSTONE *Comm.* III. 116 This may ..be effected by a specific delivery or restoration of the subject-matter in dispute to the legal owner. **1856** DOVE *Logic Chr. Faith* v. ii. 317 We do not as yet know the specific commandments of the moral law. **1862** TROLLOPE *Orley F.* ii, She had been specific in her requests, urging him..to settle Orley Farm upon her own boy. **1871** MARKBY *Elem. Law* §109 A command must by its very nature be specific.

b. Exactly named or indicated, or capable of being so; precise, particular.

1766 BLACKSTONE *Comm.* II. 8 What it is that gave a man an exclusive right to retain..that specific land. **1779** BURKE *Corr.* (1844) II. 264 A specific misconduct, brought home to a particular man, is always to be attended to. *c* **1788** —— *Charges agst. W. Hastings* Wks. 1813 XII. 370 Without a publick well-vouched account of the specifick expenditure thereof. **1828** MACKINTOSH *Speech Ho. Commons* Wks. 1846 III. 492 There are..two specific classes of grievances complained of by the Lower-Canadians. **1865** H. PHILLIPS *Amer. Paper Curr.* II. 68 No specific preparations had been made by the states to perform their part of the engagement. **1880** L. STEPHEN *Pope* iv. 103 The specific cause of the quarrel, if cause there was, has not been clearly revealed.

c. Of a duty or tax: assessed on an article or goods according to quantity or amount without reference to value.

1789 *Deb. Congress U.S.* 9 Apr. 107, I shall not pretend to say that there ought not to be specific duties laid upon every one of the articles enumerated. **1845** J. K. POLK *Diary* I Nov. (1929) 23, I had recommended..the abolition of the minimum principle and specific duties. **1901** J. S. NICHOLSON *Pol. Econ.* III. 348 If the tax is specific and not *ad valorem*. **1930** M. CLARK *Home Trade* III. xxii. 187 Specific duties are those which are based on the quantity of the imported produce, i.e. they are so much per lb. or so much per gallon, etc. **1959** *Chambers's Encycl.* V. 512/2 Specific duties are expressed as an amount of money on the unit amount of the product while *ad valorem* duties are expressed as a percentage addition to the selling price.

5. Of or pertaining to, connected with, etc., a distinct species of animals or plants. ***specific epithet*** (chiefly *Bot.* and *Microbiology*), the second (adjectival) element in the Latin name of a species according to the binomial system, which follows the generic name and serves to distinguish a species from others in the same genus; ***specific name***, (*a*) (now chiefly *Zool.*) = *specific epithet* above; (*b*) (now chiefly *Bot.* and *Microbiol.*), the Latin name of a species, which in the binomial system comprises a generic name and a specific epithet.

1753 *Chambers' Cycl.* Suppl. s.v., The more accurate of the modern naturalists have..set about the reformation of the specific names of things. *Ibid.*, But as this holds in all the genus, there can be no use made of it as a specific character. **1775** ROSE *Elem. Bot.* 302 A Plant is said to be compleatly named when it has got both the generic and specific name. **1796** WITHERING *Brit. Plants* (ed. 3) I. p. v, Many of the Specific Characters..are entirely new. **1842** LOUDON *Suburban Hort.* 19 Specific names..often indicate the situation or the county where the plant is found naturally. **1866** DARWIN *Orig. Spec.* (ed. 4) ii. 58 Such characters of course are not of specific value. **1870** HOOKER *Stud. Flora* 147 Scarcely entitled to specific rank. **1871** *Nature* 20 July 221/1 The mistake Cotteau is accused of making of assigning to Desor instead of Agassiz the specific name of *Pseudodiadema hemisphæricum* is entirely unfounded. **1880** A. R. WALLACE *Isl. Life* 359 Thus one great cause of specific modification would be wanting. **1905** *Règles Internat. Nomencl. Zool.* (Congrès Internat. de Zool.) 31 A specific name becomes a subspecific name when the species so named becomes a subspecies. **1906** *Internat. Rules Bot. Nomencl. 1905* 47 When a..species is moved into another genus..the first specific epithet..must be retained. **1926** *Rep. Brit. Assoc. Adv. Sci. 1925* 75 A species [of animal] is a community, or a number of related communities, whose distinctive morphological characters are..sufficiently definite to entitle it, or them, to a specific name. **1945** *Rhodora* XLVII. 274 Binomial nomenclature was not intended by Linnaeus to supersede the polynomial specific name. **1964** *Internat. Code Zool. Nomencl.* ii. 7 The name of a species consists of two words (binomen)..; ..the first word is the generic name, the second word is the specific name. **1966** *Internat. Code Bot. Nomencl.* iii. 27 *Tuber*..was accompanied by binary specific names, e.g. *Tuber cibarium*, and is therefore admissible. *Ibid.* 30 The name of a species is a binary combination consisting of the name of the genus followed by a single specific epithet. **1970** *Watsonia* VIII. 156 The specific epithet *racemosa* is.. not applicable in the genus *Amelanchier*. **1974** *Encycl. Brit. Macropædia* II. 1019/2 Gaspard Bauhin, a Swiss botanist of the late 16th and early 17th centuries, designated plants by a generic and a specific name. **1982** ARMS & CAMP *Biology* (ed. 2) xx. 310 Specific epithets..are adjectives, and the same one may be combined with different generic names and used for a number of unrelated organisms; for example, *Erythronium americanum*, the trout lily; *Euarctos americanus*, the American black bear.

B. *sb.* **1. a.** A specific remedy. (See A. 3 a.)

1661 EVELYN *Fumifugium* 8, I doe assent that both Lime and Sulphur are in some affections Specifics for the lungs. **1671** SALMON *Syn. Med.* III. xxii. 427 Elder-tree..is a specific for the cure of the Dropsie. **1684** tr. *Bonet's Merc. Compit.* VI. 170 Specificks for Fevers seem to have place chiefly in Agues. **1732** ARBUTHNOT *Rules of Diet in Aliments*, etc. I. 429 If there be a Specifick in Aliment it is certainly Whey. **1779** JOHNSON *Lett.* (1788) II. 64 How did you light on your specifick for the tooth-ach? **1843** R. J. GRAVES *Syst. Clin. Med.* xxvii. 351 All specifics lead to a false system of therapeutics. **1873** SPENCER *Study Sociol.* i. (1877) 20 Always you find among people in proportion as they are ignorant, a belief in specifics.

attrib. **1859** MEREDITH *R. Feverel* xxii, Her parties were the dullest in London, and gradually fell into the hands of popular preachers, Specific Doctors, raw Missionaries [etc.].

b. *transf.* and *fig.*

1662 CHARLETON *Myst. Vintners* (1675) 192 Having found out certain Specifics as it were, to palliate the several Vices of Wines of all sorts. *a* **1680** BUTLER *Rem.* (1759) I. 224 For all Defences and Apologies Are but Specifics t' other Frauds and Lies. **1779** J. MOORE *View Soc. Fr.* (1789) I. xviii. 140 A more infallible specific against tedium and fatigue. **1841** HELPS *Ess., Aids Contentm.* (1842) 17, I have no intention of putting forward specifics for real afflictions, or pretending to teach refined methods for avoiding grief. **1860** MILL *Repr. Govt.* (1865) 59/2 Against this evil the system of personal representation..is almost a specific.

2. A specific difference, quality, statement, subject, disease, etc. Usu. *pl.* Also *loosely*, details, particulars.

1697 tr. *Burgersdicius' Logic* II. ii. 7 The Difference is taken from his Form... But because incorporeal Substances have none, and the Specificks of Corporeal, even lye hid [etc.]. **1757** MRS. GRIFFITH *Lett. Henry & Frances* (1767) III. 148 The Phænomenon..is owing to two most uncommon Specifics, in the Constitution of your Mind, and of your Body. **1874** H. W. BEECHER *Lect. Preaching* Ser. III. viii. 153 Generics never take hold of men. It is specifics that take hold of them. **1891** *Daily News* 19 Oct. 6/5 Even in London Board Schools only 20,000 scholars were presented in specifics. **1893** W. R. GOWERS *Dis. Nervous Syst.* (ed. 2) II. 330 Acute specifics, pneumonia, and septicæmia. **1966** *New Statesman* 9 Sept. 350/2 The latter [*sc.* journalism].. considers the specifics of an event, using implicit general principles of behaviour out of necessity. **1972** G. BROMLEY *In Absence of Body* iii. 30 Let's get down to specifics. What can we actually do to help? **1975** *N.Y. Times* 11 Sept. 8/1 Placing this tragedy of a woman's sexual obsession with her stepson within the arresting specifics of this strange setting does at least remove it from the fury-bestrewn never-never-land of the antique Greek drama. **1977** F. BRANSTON *Up & Coming Man* xii. 125 He told us he had been investing in property in London, but he was a bit vague about the specifics. **1980** *Jrnl. R. Soc. Arts* Feb. 152/1 Planning should start..with specifics rather than concepts.

3. A specific word, name, etc., *spec.* in taxonomy or toponymy.

1962 BURRILL & BONSACK in Householder & Saporta *Prob. Lexicogr.* 195 The elements in geographic names that indicate the class of the entity, e.g., in *Red Hill*..or *Lake Erie*.., *Hill* and *Lake*, are the generic elements (or 'generics'). The elements that indentify the particular entity, in the above instances *Red* and *Erie*, are called the specific elements (or 'specifics'). **1969** J. FOWLES *French Lieutenant's Woman* viii. 50 Although many scientists of the day gratefully used her [*sc.* Mary Anning's] finds to establish their own reputation, not one native type bears the specific *anningii*. **1977** *Word 1972* XXVIII. 133 Most of the specifics, or second elements, in such names are demonstrably of Gaelic and not of Pictish origin.

-specific. The adj. used as the final element in combination with sbs. to designate phenomena peculiar to the category indicated by the precedent element: specific to or that specifies (something).

1924, etc. [see *species-specific* adj. s.v. SPECIES *sb.* 14]. **1936**, etc. [see *organ-specific* adj. s.v. ORGAN *sb.*[1] 8]. **1949** K. DAVIS *Human Society* xxi. 600 Age-specific fertility trends show that a stationary or a declining population will soon eventuate. **1965**, etc. [see *language-specific* adj. s.v. LANGUAGE *sb.* 6 b]. **1971** J. Z. YOUNG *Introd. Study Man* v. 84 Study of some brain-specific proteins. **1978** *Dædalus* Fall 7 Herodotus' report..refracts into intensely age-specific opinions. **1979** *Nature* 25 Jan. 251/1 But there is a far less trivial, and far more nation-specific way in which intellectual resources may be used or squandered.

spe'cifical, *a.* and *sb.* Now *rare.* [f. med.L. *specific-us* (see SPECIFIC *a.* and *sb.*) + -AL[1].]

A. *adj.* **1.** = SPECIFIC *a.* 2. †Also of division: Resulting in the separation of species.

1432-50 tr. *Higden* (Rolls) I. 27 In the maner of a diuision genericalle in to a diuision specificalle. **1570** J. DEE *Math. Pref.* B iij b, The specificall order and forme, due to euery seede. **1637** GILLESPIE *Eng. Pop. Cerem.* IV. ii. 4 The specificall nature of that action. **1682** NORRIS *Hierocles* 6 Which so retain their Connexion in their specifical distinction & conjunction. *a* **1703** BURKITT *On. N.T.* 1 Cor. xi. 7 Consider the woman according to her specifical nature. **1751** R. SHIRRA in *Rem.* (1850) 150 The first regeneration is a specifical change—a change from nature to grace. **1815** CHALMERS *Posth. Wks.* (1849) VI. 278 The great and specifical end of that affecting solemnity.

b. = SPECIFIC *a.* 2 b.

1621 BURTON *Anat. Mel.* I. i. III. i. 46 Omitting the specificall difference. **1678** CUDWORTH *Intell. Syst.* 799 According to the best Philosophy, which acknowledges no Essential or Specifical Difference of Matter. **1713** DERHAM *Phys.-Theol.* VIII. vi. 425, I could not perceive any difference, at least, not specifical, between the Flies coming from these two productions.

2. = SPECIFIC *a.* 1.

1610 HEALEY *St. Aug. Citie of God.* VIII. vi. 308 Alcinous saith..that God is incomprehensible,..not definable, nor specificall. **1644** DIGBY *Nat. Bodies* xxiv. (1658) 273 Generation is not made..by a specifical worker within. **1648** MILTON *Tenure Kings* (1650) 39 Having..clad him over, like another specifical thing, with formes and habitudes destructive to the former.

3. *Med.* = SPECIFIC *a.* 3 a.

1604 F. HERING *Mod. Defence* 21 The specificall Antidot of the Pest is yet vnknowen. **1612** WOODALL *Surg. Mate* Wks. (1653) 209 All minerals shew themselves in operation to be specifical. **1660** tr. *Paracelsus' Archidoxis* I. VII. 102 As ..Water quencheth Fire, even so doth the Specifical Anodine extinguish Diseases.

4. = SPECIFIC *a.* 4 a and 4 b.

1768 BLACKSTONE *Comm.* III. ix. 154 The proper remedy is by action of debt, to compel the performance of the contract and recover the specifical sum due. **1781** *Gentl. Mag.* LI. 616 *Matadores* in Spanish are *murderers*, and the specifical cards so called do cut down and *murder* all the rest.

5. *Zool.* and *Bot.* = SPECIFIC *a.* 5.

1761 *Phil. Trans.* LII. 84. I only mention this species, to determine its specifical character. **1790** R. PULTENEY *Hist. Sk. Bot. in Eng.* I. v. 69 Allowing for the time when specifical distinctions were not established,..the number [of plants] he was acquainted with is much beyond what could easily have been imagined.

6. Limited to a special sense.

1778 *Gentl. Mag.* XLVIII. 407/1 It is not uncommon for a general word to become specifical.

B. *sb.* **1.** = SPECIFIC *sb.* 1.

1651 BIGGS *New Disp.* ¶ 134 By adding strong specificals. **1656** RIDGLEY *Pract. Physick* 61 Specificals are, the whitest dung of a Wolf [etc.].

2. A person representing a class.

1651 N. BACON *Disc. Govt. Eng.* II. xl. (1739) 176 This is done in the Convention of States, which in the first times consisted of Individuals, rather than Specificals.

specifi'cality. *rare.* [f. SPECIFICAL *a.*] The quality of being specific.

1660 tr. *Paracelsus' Archidoxis* I. VII. 96 That same Specificality taketh its Original and Rise from External Things. **1756** J. CLUBBE *Misc. Tracts, Physiogn.* (1770) I. 20 They agree indeed so much..that their specificality is swallowed up in their general likeness. **1858** CARLYLE *Fredk. Gt.* IX. iii. (1872) III. 96 Official List of them was drawn-up here, with the fit specificality.

specifically (spɛ'sɪfɪkəlɪ, spə-), *adv.* [f. as prec.]

1. In respect of specific or inherent qualities: **a.** Of likeness or difference.

1624 GATAKER *Transubst.* 48 One thing is said to be another, which cannot be individually or specifically the same. **1628** T. SPENCER *Logick* 209 This hath one kinde of forme, that hath another, therefore this doth specifically differ from that. **1678** CUDWORTH *Intell. Syst.* Pref. 14 There is a substance specifically distinct from body. **1785** REID *Intell. Powers* VI. i. 414 Judgement is an act of the mind, specifically different from simple apprehension. **1859** DARWIN *Orig. Spec.* xi. (1860) 370 During the newer Pliocene period,..and whilst the majority of the inhabitants of the world were specifically the same as now. **1877** E. R. CONDER *Basis Faith* iv. 182 Other minds generically like, but specifically unlike, my own.

b. Of comparative weight.

1692 BENTLEY *Boyle Lect.* iv. 10 If an Axhead be supposed to float upon water, which is specifically much lighter than it. **1725** *Family Dict.* s.v. *Pores*, If they had not [pores], all Bodies would be alike specifically weighty. **1774** PENNANT *Tour Scotl. in 1772*, 331 The waters are said to be specifically lighter than most others. **1800** VINCE *Hydrost.* vii. (1806) 78 The vapours..become specifically heavier than the medium wherein they floated. **1878** HUXLEY *Physiogr.* 152 The cold water becoming specifically lighter and rising to the surface.

c. In other contexts.

a **1676** HALE *Prim. Orig. Man.* I. ii. (1677) 44, I shall not at large discuss those Faculties and Organs which he hath in common with Vegetables and Brutes, but those only that belong to him specifically as Man. **1865** TYLOR *Early Hist. Man.* iii. 54 The gesture language appears not to be specifically affected by differences in the race or climate of those who use it. **1894** J. DENNEY *Stud. Theol.* v. 103 This conjunction of ideas is specially but not specifically Pauline.

2. In a specific or definite form or manner.

1646 SIR T. BROWNE *Pseud. Ep.* 95 [They] seem specifically and in regular shapes to attend the corruption of their bodyes. **1707** *Curios. in Husb. & Gard.* 32 The Plant.. may be specifically discern'd in each..Seed. **1766** BLACKSTONE *Comm.* II. 335 A deed of defeazance..upon events specifically mentioned. **1790** BURKE *Fr. Rev.* 32 The law by which this royal family is specifically destined to the succession. **1837** CARLYLE *Fr. Rev.* III. II. v, Is there any man here that dare specifically accuse me? **1870** J. BRUCE *Life Gideon* xxiii. 419 It is well to have ascertained, thus specifically, how deep-seated..is our spiritual disease. **1891** *Law Times* XCII. 105/2 The lady had contracted specifically with a view to bind definite separate estate.

3. In something of the same kind.

1780 JEFFERSON in Sparks *Corr. Amer. Revol.* (1853) III. 177 These articles shall be either identically or specifically returned, should we prove successful.

4. In a special manner. Chiefly *Med.*

1801 in *Med. Jrnl.* VIII. 90 That all medicines act specifically upon one or more parts of the body. **1829** I. TAYLOR *Enthus.* vi. (1867) 121 A dispensation of moral exercise, specifically adapted to the temper and power of the individual. **1899** *Allbutt's Syst. Med.* VI. 304 Nearly all authors agree that syphilitic arteritis is much more likely to occur in persons who have not been specifically treated.

spe'cificalness. *rare*[−0]. [f. as prec.] 'A specific quality' (Bailey, 1727, vol. II).

spe'cificate, *sb. rare*[−1]. [Cf. next.] Something specified or stated.

1804 COLERIDGE in *Blackw. Mag.* (1882) CXXXI. 124 The imaginative power..acting with its permeative..might on the thoughts, images, specificates of the poet.

specificate (spɛ'sɪfɪkeɪt, spə-), *v.* Now *rare* or *Obs.* [ad. med.L. *specificāt-*, ppl. stem of *specificāre* SPECIFY *v.*]

1. *trans.* To distinguish as belonging to a particular species, group, kind, etc.; to determine specifically.

1620 T. GRANGER *Div. Logike* 43 Whereby men are most specially specificated and individuated. **1637** GILLESPIE *Eng. Pop. Cerem.* IV. iii. 7 An action is said to be specificated by its object, and individuated by its circumstances. **1673-4** GREW *Anat., Trunks* I. ii. 108 The properties, whereby the said Vessels of the Barque are specificated and distinguished one from another.

refl. *c* **1629** DONNE *Serm.* vii. (1640) 69 Life is the character by which Christ specificates and denominates himselfe. **1653** ASHWELL *Fides Apost.* 57 A peculiar Epithite, wherby he specificates himselfe.

2. To apply specifically or especially *to*; to confine or limit *to*.

1631 J. BURGES *Answ. Rejoined* 33 God doth not onely commend Davids affection in generall, but his affection [is] actuated to a deed, and specificated to this deede. *a* **1638** MEDE *Wks.* (1672) 843 That passage being it seems anciently specificated to *Resurrectio Prima*. **1687** J. RENWICK *Pref., Lect., & Serm.* (1776) 446 We must understand that prayer to be specificated to that all for whom he gave himself a ransom.

3. To give specific or explicit details of or concerning; to mention specifically or in detail; to particularize or specify.

1649 JER. TAYLOR *Gt. Exemp. Disc.* Pref. ¶ 25 Those few superadded precepts, in which God did specificate their prime duty. **1654** G. GODDARD in *Burton's Diary* (1828) I. 150 But we shall..labour to specificate our enemies, to know who they be, and are, that seek the very destruction and being of these nations. **1843** *Tait's Mag.* X. 137/1 In beginning the following story, with the same popular phrase, we specificate a very different moment from the arduous struggles of the Pretender. **1847** CARLYLE in *Fraser's Mag.* XXXVI. 632 Of which latter office my Correspondent could not..quite specificate the meaning.

4. To render specific in character or qualities. †Chiefly *Chem.* (common *c* 1650–80).

1650 ASHMOLE *Chym. Coll.* 125 That it might.. communicate its fixt Nature, to the prepared Medicine, which being specificated it might at length become perfect. **1669** W. SIMPSON *Hydrol. Chym.* 257 The vine.. specificates the water..into its own shape. **1694** SALMON *Bate's Dispens.* (1715) 463/2 It is a general Remedy and may be specificated by the addition of several Salts.

1866 *Nation* 4 Oct. 269/1 Words have seemingly contrary and inconsistent tendencies. Now they incline to specificate that which was generic; now to generalize that which was specific.

5. *intr.* To become specific.

1835 COLERIDGE in *Fraser's Mag.* XII. 494 In a crystal we may perceive a tendency to specificate, or become a specific total.

Hence **spe'cificated, spe'cificating** *ppl. adjs.*

1651 FRENCH *Distill.* v. 163 When it hath received its body by becoming a specificated salt. **1657** OWEN *Vindication of Treatise on Schism* ix. 142 Disputes about an implicit and explicit covenant, of specificating forms [etc.]. **1666** BOYLE *Orig. Forms & Qual.* 316 All the Volatile, and Acid, and Lixiviate Salts, that we know of, are of so determinate and specificated a Nature,..that there is no one sort of the three. *a* **1676** HALE *Prim. Orig. Man.* I. i. (1677) 40 Without any particular, specificating, concurrent, new imperate act of the Divine special Providence to every particular determination of his Will. **1763** W. LEWIS *Phil. Comm. Arts* 72 The specificating principles of the metal.

specification (ˌspɛsɪfɪ'keɪʃən). [ad. med.L. *specificātiōn-em*, n. of action f. *specificāre* SPECIFY, or a. F. *spécification* (1341 in Godef. *Compl.*), = It. *specificazione*, Sp. *especificacion*, Pg. *-ação*.]

†**1.** The action of investing with some specific or determinate quality; conversion to something specific. *Obs.*

1615 CROOKE *Body of Man* 285 All formation and specification (for you must giue vs leaue to vse our Schoole-tearmes in these matters of Art) that is, all power to set the seale or figure or difference vpon any thing. **1664** EVELYN *Sylva* (1679) 3 The maturer seeds..freeing themselves from those impediments which hindred their Specification and Nativity. **1701** NORRIS *Ideal World* I. 261 So then the creatures owe their pure being to the power of God, but the specification of their being to his ideality.

b. *Roman* and *Scots Law.* The formation of a new species of property out of material belonging to another by converting it into a different form.

1651 G. W. tr. *Cowel's Inst.* 65 There is also an accession by specification or changing the Species, as if a man create a new Species out of a substance which was anothers, the property shall be in him, that made the Species. **1681** STAIR *Instit.* I. xii. 189 Appropriation by Specification. **1736** in Bell *Comm. Laws Scot* (1826) I. 277 It was found, that the specification by malting did not bar the reduction. **1765–8** ERSKINE *Inst. Law Scot.* II. i. §16 Under accession may be included specification, by which is understood a person's making a new species or subject, from materials belonging to another. **1826** BELL *Comm. Laws Scot.* I. 276 The famous controversy of the Proculeiani and Sabiniani concerning specification. **1869** R. CAMPBELL *Austin's Jurispr.* (ed. 3) II. liv. 904 There are various cases in which a party acquires a right in a thing belonging to another by labour employed upon it; for instance in the Roman Law by specification, that is by giving it a new form.

†**2.** A specific character, quality, or nature. *Obs.*

1628 DONNE *Serm. John xiv.* Wks. 1839 I. 534 His specification, his character, his title, Paracletus, the Comforter, passes through all. **1656** JEANES *Mixt. Schol. Div.* 40 An act ought to be proportioned unto it's object, seeing it takes therefrom it's specification. **1710** W. SALMON (*title*), Botanologia: the English Herbal, or, History of Plants, containing their Names, Species, Descriptions, Qualities, Specifications,..and Uses.

3. Specific definition or description; description by specific or peculiar characters; †a specific name or appellation.

1633 J. ADAMS *Exp. 2 Peter* ii. Wks. 1865 X. 408 Therefore this lust hath the specification: lust of uncleanness. **1651** BAXTER *Inf. Bapt.* 64 It is..either a spirituall Mercy (common or speciall) or else Mercy in the generall without specification. **1660** R. COKE *Justice Vind.* 41 Men..must alter their Terms as they proceed from one thing to another, and add to them in the specifications of them. **1734** WATERLAND *Import. Doctr. Holy Trin.* ii. 37 In short, the Specification of our Worship, and the right Direction of it, are nearly concern'd in this Doctrine. **1879** THOMSON & TAIT *Nat. Phil.* I. I. §218 The second element in the specification of a force is its direction... The third element in the specification of a force is its magnitude. **1879** H. SPENCER *Data Ethics* vi. §39. 100 From the biological point of view, ethical science becomes a specification of the conduct of associated men.

b. *Logic.* (See quots. and DETERMINATION 5 b.)

1864 BOWEN *Logic* iv. 75 The contrary process of descending from higher to lower Concepts through the successive assumption of Marks is called Determination, —more properly Specification, as it expresses the act of becoming a Species. **1877** E. CAIRD *Philos. Kant* II. iv. 273 An endless process of specification which, beginning with the most general and vague determinations,..goes on to determine the object in all its particular relations. **1884** tr. *Lotze's Logic* 185 We may set down any conception *M* as equivalent to any other conception *N* when we have by further specification so changed *N* that it is equal to *M*.

c. Assignment to a (new) species. *rare*$^{-1}$.

1878 DARWIN in *Life & Lett.* (1887) III. 160, I should think nearly perfect separation would greatly aid in their 'specification', to coin a new word.

4. Specific, explicit, or detailed mention, enumeration, or statement *of* something.

1642 JER. TAYLOR *Episc.* (1647) 119 No example in all Scripture of any censure inflicted by any meere Presbyters, either upon Clergy or Laity; no specification of any power that they had so to doe. **1658** T. WALL *Charact. Enemies Ch.* 30 The specification of these other beasts in the text prompts my inclination to this sense. **1719** F. HARE *Ch. Author. Vind.* 27 By demanding a Specification of the powers claimed. **1762–71** H. WALPOLE *Vertue's Anecd. Paint.* (1786) II. 47 *note*, Besides others for very obscure persons, and without specification of place. **1817** JAS. MILL *Brit. India* II. v. ii. 380 The allegation of precipitation and unfairness..he..by a specification of circumstances endeavoured to disprove. **1839** HALLAM *Hist. Lit.* IV. vii. §60 The specification of some public or private library where they may be seen. **1862** MARSH *Eng. Lang.* iii. 59 The specification of the particular colours which he ascribes to the wings of the archangel.

b. Without const.

1767 GOOCH *Treat. Wounds* I. 97 Celsus agrees with Hippocrates, adding some specifications, in respect to the wounded parts. **1794** PALEY *Evid.* II. i. (1825) II. 224 If the prophecies had been composed after the event, there would have been more specification. **1838** PRESCOTT *Ferd. & Is.* (1846) II. xix. 179 This illustrious family..is worthy of specification. **1888** BRYCE *Amer. Commw.* I. I. App. 546 The provisions of the whole fifth section..are in so many State constitutions that no specification is needed for them.

c. *spec.* A document, drawn up by the applicant for a patent and submitted to the proper authority, giving an explicit description of the nature, details, construction, and use of an invention.

1791 *Obs. Utility Patents* 16 The Patentee being under the necessity of describing in his Specification the nature and form of his invention in all its parts. **1815** J. SMITH *Panorama Sci. & Art* II. 140 We shall now take so much from the specification of the patent..as may explain [etc.]. **1854** RONALDS & RICHARDSON *Chem. Technol.* (ed. 2) I. 369 The drawings are taken from Mr. Reece's original specification. **1882** *Engineer* 24 Feb. 138/2 After carefully perusing the defendant's specification,..I am led to think [etc.].

d. *techn.* A detailed description of the particulars of some projected work in building, engineering, or the like, giving the dimensions, materials, quantities, etc., of the work, together with directions to be followed by the builder or constructor; the document containing this.

1833 LOUDON *Encycl. Archit.* §233 Particulars, or Specification and Estimate. *Ibid.*, We shall give the specification, for each trade, in a separate paragraph. **1850** DENISON *Clock & Watch-m.* 272, I have seen a specification ..furnished sometime ago by an eminent architect for an important public clock. **1883** M. P. BALE *Saw-Mills* 67 The author appends a short specification of 30 h.-p. boiler suitable for saw-mill work.

e. A specified article, item, or particular.

1828–32 in WEBSTER. Hence in later Dicts.

†**specificative**, *a. Obs.* [f. SPECIFICATE *v.* + -IVE. Cf. F. *spécificatif*, *-ive* (14th c. in Godef.).] That serves to specify or distinguish; specific.

1641 *Relat. Answ. Earl of Strafford* 54 Treason was a thing of a simple and specificative nature. **1644** HUNTON *Vindic. Treat. Monarchy* iii. 13 It's specificative distinction must be from something which distinguisheth Powers. **1710** tr. *Werenfels's Disc. Logom.* 25 Whether Body, as *natural*, be the Object of its Speculation? And if so, whether the word *As* be reduplicative or specificative.

†**specificatively**, *adv. Obs.* [See prec.] Specifically.

c **1600** *Timon* IV. iii. (1842) 66 The moone may be taken 4 manner of waies; either specificatiuely, or quidditatiuely, or superficially, or catapodially. **1659** H. L'ESTRANGE *Alliance Div. Off.* 134 In thy seed (declaring specificatively in whose) shall all the nations of the earth be blessed. **1678** GALE *Crt. Gentiles* IV. III. ii. 31 *As* here..cannot be taken Reduplicatively, but only Specificatively, as it specifies one and the same Act. **1701** NORRIS *Ideal World* I. iii. 164 Which phrase must be taken specificatively, not objectively.

specificity (spɛsɪ'fɪsɪtɪ). [ad. F. *spécificité*, or f. SPECIFIC *a.* + -ITY.]

1. a. The quality or fact of being specific in operation or effect.

1876 BARTHOLOW *Mat. Medica* (1879) 417 It is not an action of specificity—like quinia in intermittent and remittent fevers. **1884** *Trans. Victoria Inst.* 37 *note*, The specificity of germs is still an unsettled question. **1922** [see DIRECTEDNESS]. **1946** *Scrutiny* XIV. 109 George Eliot's genius appears in the specificity with which she exhibits the accomplishments in Gwendolen of the kind of conscious advantage she resembles Isabel in enjoying. **1977** J. F. FIXX *Compl. Bk. Running* vii. 89 Few runners had supposed it could possibly be so hot on a mid-April day in Massachusetts, so practically nobody had trained properly. As a result, most people's times were terrible. The same specificity principle applies to terrain.

b. The narrowness of the range of substances with which an antibody or other agent acts or is effective.

1896 *Allbutt's Syst. Med.* I. 888 He denies, from experiments of his own, the specificity of protective serum. **1904** G. H. F. NUTTALL *Blood Immunity & Blood Relationship* ix. 381 Wassermann..brought the question of specificity into greater prominence. *Ibid.* 443/1 (Index), Specificity of precipitins. **1935** N. P. SHERWOOD *Immunol.* xii. 274 Two kinds of specificity can be demonstrated by immune reactions, one that applies to species and the second to type variation within a species. **1971** *Sci. Amer.* July 26/1 The specificity, or narrow spectrum, of vaccines is a limitation; it means that a different vaccine is required for each virus or strain of virus.

c. *Biol.* The degree to which a parasite or symbiote is restricted in its range of hosts.

1924 *Rep. Brit. Assoc. Adv. Sci. 1923* 453 They [*sc.* parasitic nematodes] may be divided broadly into a section with more or less strict 'specificity' and a section with members occurring in various hosts, often of quite distantly related groups. **1955** *Sci. Amer.* July 77/1 It is also known that the protein coat determines the specificity of the virus, i.e., whether or not it will attack a certain bacterium. **1965** B. E. FREEMAN tr. *Vandel's Biospeleology* xv. 245 This is more a case of parasitic or symbiotic specificity than cavernicolous specialisation.

2. The fact of being specific in character.

1879 *Brit. Med. Jrnl.* 24 May 785 No one who has studied the clinical history of diphtheria can avoid grave doubts as to its specificity. **1894** *Lancet* 3 Nov. 1058 The doctrine of the invariable specificity of the disease. **1897** *Allbutt's Syst. Med.* III. 633 In determining the specificity of the rheumatic origin. **1928** HARTSHORNE & MAY *Studies in Deceit* II. xii. 221 (*heading*) Specificity of attitudes. **1958** R. WILLIAMS *Culture & Society* III. iii. 231 A principal virtue was always the specificity, not only of definition, but of illustration. **1981** *Times* 16 July 6/1 They also want to avoid 'specificity' because they have not yet formulated fully-fledged policies.

spe'cificize, *v. rare.* [f. SPECIFIC *a.* + -IZE.] *trans.* To make specific.

1885 *Alienist & Neurol.* VI. 483 The richest specificized apparatus of nervous mechanism.

†**spe'cificly**, *adv. Obs.*$^{-1}$ In 7 **-fiquely.** [f. SPECIFIC *a.* Cf. F. *spécifiquement.*] Specifically.

1650 *Descr. Future Hist. Europe* 13 Daniel..doth..most plainly and specifiquely picture the two grand preparations to this spirituall Monarchy of Christs Church.

spe'cificness. *rare.* [f. as prec. + -NESS.] Specific character or quality.

1682 H. MORE *Annot. Glanvill's Lux O.* 233 For a Spirit is nothing else but such a specifick simple Substance or Essence, the Specifickness or whose nature onely is its real intimate Form. **1727** in BAILEY (vol. II). **1852** LYNCH *Lett. to Scattered* 249 There should be much specificness in prayer, yet may too large a portion of our prayer be specific. *Ibid.* 251 Peculiar natural character will give specificness to a man's sins. **1905** W. STEVENS *Let.* 31 Dec. (1967) 85 Reflections..on Japanese life, on specificness,..on my future. **1966** J. ELLIS in C. E. Bazell *In Memory of J. R. Firth* 83 By *register-choice* is meant the particular register out of the performer's range to which the utterance may be assigned..the specificness of the assignment depending on the delicacy of the analysis.

‖**spe'cificum.** *Obs.* [Neuter sing. of med.L. *specific-us* SPECIFIC *a.*] = SPECIFIC *sb.* I.

1651 FRENCH *Distill.* To Rdr. B ij b, A specificum against all distempers of the liver. **1658** A. FOX *Würtz' Surg.* III. vi. 234 Other specifica proper for the head may be used.

'**specified**, *ppl. a.* [f. SPECIFY *v.*] That is or has been definitely or specifically mentioned, determined, fixed, or settled.

1645 *Verney Mem.* (1907) I. 422 That you may add to my fortin the above specifide sum. **1796** *Cavalry Instr.* (1813) 134 All these specified wheelings are in order to make the divisions [etc.]. **1845** MCCULLOCH *Taxation* I. iii. (1852) 126 Their incomes die with themselves or cease at specified periods. **1878** H. S. WILSON *Alpine Ascents* i. 2 Engaged by us as chief guide for a specified time.

'**specifier.** [f. SPECIFY *v.*] **a.** One who specifies; the writer or drawer up of a patent specification.

1758 in *Sixth Rep. Dep. Kpr.* (1845) App. II. 157 Henry Raminger..: For..Bullets of Lead, (made by machines invented by the Specifier). **1787** *Ibid.* 177 An instrument (discovered by the Specifier's father, and by him imparted).

b. That which specifies.

1954 A. J. AYER *Philos. Ess.* iii. 61 Let us say of any two singular referential statements S and S′..that S is a specifier of S′ if and only if S′ is not a component of S, S entails S′, and S′ does not entail S. **1964** E. A. NIDA *Toward Sci. Transl.* xii. 258 As the data are analyzed both semantically and structurally, certain 'specifiers' can be associated with the elements in question, as tags of identification. In the comparison stage, the specifiers of the source-language text are matched with specifiers of the receptor language, so that the corresponding semantic and structural elements are properly identified. **1971** [see INTENSIFIER].

specifique, etc., obs. forms of SPECIFIC, etc.

specify ('spɛsɪfaɪ), *v.* Forms: 4–6 **specyfy** (5–6 **specyfe**), 4–7 **specifie**, 4– **specify** (5–6 **-fe**); 4 **specefie**, 5–6 **-fy**, 6 **-fye** (6 **specief-**, **speesyf-**). [a. OF. *specifier* (13th c.; mod.F. *spécifier*, Prov., Sp. *especificar*, It. *specificare*), ad. med.L. *specificāre* to describe, mention, note particularly or specifically.]

†**1.** *intr.* To speak or make relation *of* some matter fully or in detail. *Obs.*

a **1300** *Cursor M.* 27959 Forthermar o þis lecheri Agh i þe noght to specifie. **1390** GOWER *Conf.* III. 86 If I therof schal specefie So as the Philosophre tolde, Nou herkne. **1487** *Cely Papers* (Camden) 161, I wrate ij letters to yow..specyfying of divers matters of Flaunders. *c* **1489** CAXTON *Blanchardyn* I Whiche boke specyfyeth of the noble actes and fayttes of warre, achyeued by..Blanchardin.

2. *trans.* To mention, speak of, or name (something) definitely or explicitly; to set down or state categorically or particularly; to relate in detail. Usually said of persons, but sometimes of an act, document, etc.

c **1340** HAMPOLE *Pr. Consc.* 3352 Now wille I som syns here specify For whilk þai duelle in purgatory. *c* **1380** WYCLIF *Sel. Wks.* II. 294 Petre specifieþ here mekenes, þat men shulde have bi ensaumple of Crist. *a* **1400** *Harmony Gospels* (MS. Bodl. 771) Prol., Here..beginneþ a table þat specifieþ euery chapitre..in þis book. *c* **1430** LYDG. *Min. Poems* (Percy Soc.) 10 They began to syng..This same roundelle wiche I schalle now specify. **1491** *Rolls of Parlt.* VI. 443/1 Any other greter charge, than in the said acte is specified. 1515 BARCLAY *Egloges* III. (1570) B vj b/2 Then haste thou wretched payne Of colde or of heate, of thirst, hunger and rayne. And mo other paynes then I will specify. 1560 DAUS tr. *Sleidane's Comm.* 233 A terrible tempest was lyke to enswe, as in the seventh booke is specyfied. 1600 E. BLOUNT *Hosp. Incur. Fooles* 39 Yet had he no more in his armie, then we haue specified. 1648 WILKINS *Math. Magic* I. x. 61 It shall not therefore be impertinent..to specifie some of the most remarkable amongst them. 1766 BLACKSTONE *Comm.* II. 319 But then there must many requisites be observed, which the statute specifies, otherwise such leases are not binding. 1827 JARMAN *Powell's Devises* II. 329 If the number specified correspond with the number existing at the date of the will. 1855 PRESCOTT *Philip II*, II. vii. I. 215 The fact that the lords had not specified any particular subject of complaint..gave the king an obvious advantage. 1894 *Solicitors' Jrnl.* XXXIX. 2/2 The..report ..must state that fraud has been committed, though the guilty person need not be specified.

b. With clause as object, freq. introduced by *that*. †Also with *to be* or simple complement.

(*a*) *c* 1380 WYCLIF *Wks.* (1880) 341 How crist specified to petre to ȝyue hym þe keyes of heuen. *c* 1407 LYDG. *Reson & Sens.* 2451 For poetis specifye That goddys..Purposede of presumpsion To wrastle with this Champyon. 1430–40 —— *Bochas* IX. i. (1554) 20 b, To shewe and specifye He was the prophet that called was Messy. 1470–85 MALORY *Arthur* XXI. i. 839 The letters specefyed that Kynge Arthur was slayn in bataylle. 1547 J. HARRISON *Exhort. Scottes* f iij, Our Cronicles specifie yᵗ those .xviii. kinges were in Englande. 1582 T. WATSON *Centurie of Love* lxxii. (Arb.) 108 In this Sonnet The Authour seemeth to specifie, that his Beloued [etc.]. 1834 K. H. DIGBY *Mores Cath.* v. vi. 181 Philippe Augustus, in founding a daily mass.., specifies that it shall be said early in the morning.

(*b*) 1513 BRADSHAW *St. Werburge* I. 288 Saynt Merwalde specyfyed vncle to saint Werburge. 1597 J. PAYNE *Royal Exch.* 47 The..sede of Abraham, specifyed to be lyke in nomber to the starrs.

c. In pa. pple. with limiting adverb preceding (rarely following).

1412–20 LYDG. *Chron. Troy* v. 3599 þat noble myȝti conquerour, Herry þe Fyfþe, to-forn y-specefied. *c* 1460 FORTESCUE *Abs. & Lim. Mon.* (1885) 140 A ffewe regions beffore specified. 1467 in *Eng. Gilds* (1870) 389 In eny of them above specified. 1562 WYNȜET *Wks.* (S.T.S.) I. 9 As we do to the warldly ignorantis abone specifiit. 1576 FLEMING tr. *Caius' Dogs* (1880) 2 There are two sortes of Dogges by whose meanes, the feates within specifyed are wrought. 1651 HOBBES *Leviath.* II. xxx. 175 The essentiall Rights of Soveraignty (specified before in the eighteenth Chapter). 1664 POWER *Exp. Philos.* I. 16, I could not onely see the long bristles formerly specified. 1710 in *Nairne Peerage Evidence* (1874) 153 The severall yearly few dutys above specified payable to us. 1799 G. SMITH *Laboratory* I. 185 Take thereof double the quantity above specified. 1800 *Med. Jrnl.* III. 428 The patient has never suffered the least return of her fits since the time there specified.

d. With omission of direct object, esp. in clauses introduced by *as*.

1390 GOWER *Conf.* II. 86 The ferste, if I schal specefie, Was *lapis vegetabilis*. 1412–20 LYDG. *Chron. Troy* I. 2578 Liche as to ȝow I thenke specifie [*v.r.* to specifie]. 1433 —— *St. Edmund* I. 96 Be sentence of prudent Carnotense In Enteticon where he doth specifie. 1532 MORE *Confut. Barnes* VIII. Wks. 812/1 The very true church of Christ..is ..this one comon well knowen catholyke churche.., as I before haue specyfyed. 1596 SHAKS. *Merch. V.* II. ii. 131 The rich Iewes man that would, sir, as my Father shall specifie. 1709 HEARNE in *R. Glouc. Chron.* II. 597 Accordingly several Editions follow'd with Improvements, as you have particularly specify'd in your Paper.

†**3. a.** To make special mention of (a person); to celebrate. *Obs.*⁻¹

c 1450 HOLLAND *Howlat* 733 Haile speciose, most specifyit with the spiritualis! Haile ordanit or Adam, and ay til indur!

†**b.** To exhibit or show (a quality, etc.) to advantage or in a special manner. *Obs.*⁻¹

a 1575 *Pol. Verg. Eng. Hist.* (Camden) 254 This certis was a singuler and notable fighte, wheerin the Englishe people didd well specifie their manwhode and valiance.

†**4.** To call by a specific name. *Obs.*⁻¹

1652 SELDEN *Domin. Sea* 21 Some of the aforesaid Autors speak with general words, saying the Sea of the Venitians; yet others do specifie it, using the name of the Gulf.

5. To invest with a specific character.

1645 RUTHERFORD *Tryal & Tri. Faith* (1845) 54 An intention to take satisfactory vengeance on the reprobate, specifieth his rod, and maketh it punishment of black wrath. 1676 GALE *Crt. Gentiles* II. IV. 421 An action is specified from its particular cause, not from the first universal cause. 1750 tr. *Leonardus' Mirr. Stones* 59 Only that form which specifies the matter is more powerful than other forms. 1876 F. H. BRADLEY *Ethical Stud.* 71 Be specified in yourself, but not specified by anything foreign to yourself.

†**6.** *intr.* To develop into different species; to vary in kind or character. *Obs.*

1664 EVELYN *Sylva* (1679) 3 Some there are, 'Spring of themselves unforc't by human care,' Specifying according to the various disposition of the Air and Soil.

Hence **'specifying** *vbl. sb.* and *ppl. a.*

1673–4 [see SPECIAL *a.* 6 b]. 1681 BAXTER *Acc. Sherlocke* v. 204 Its species is the specifying Form. 1701 NORRIS *Ideal World* I. iii. 164 How then will you distinguish,..since 'tis himself that is still the specifying object in both? ?1819 CHALMERS *Congregat. Serm.* Wks. 1836 VIII. 368 That.. which impresses on the mercy of the Gospel its essential and specifying characteristic.

specimen (ˈspɛsɪmən). Also 7, 9 *dial.* speciment. [a. L. *specimen*, f. *specĕre* to look, look at. Cf. F. *spécimen*, Sp. *especimen*.

The Latin pl. *specimina* was fairly common in the latter half of the 17th c.]

†**1.** A means of discovering or finding out; an experiment. *Obs.*⁻¹

1610 W. FOLKINGHAM *Art of Survey* I. viii. 17 For deprehending and finding out the taste of the Earth, Vergil prescribes a generall Specimen for triall of salt and bitter soyles.

†**2.** A pattern or model. *Obs.*

1619 R. JONES *Resurrection Rescued* (1659) 67 Our Resurrection shall be like our Saviour's: His and ours make a mutual Aspect; His the Specimen, and ours the Complement. 1647 H. MORE *Poems* 60 It so weakens and disables men That they of manhood give no goodly specimen. 1697 *Observ. Money & Coin* 2 Some Brittish Princes did Coyn some pieces both of Gold and Silver, of which he there exhibits to us the Specimina.

3. An example, instance, or illustration *of* something, from which the character of the whole may be inferred.

1659 BP. WALTON *Consid. Considered* 291 These specimina of his candor and love of truth. 1683 CAVE *Ecclesiastici, Greg.-Naz.* 282 He had scarce given a Speciment of his Learning. 1700 DRYDEN *Fables* Pref. (1721) 21 You have here a specimen of Chaucer's language. 1780 *Mirror* No. 97, The conversations of which I have given you a specimen. 1829 JAS. MILL *Hum. Mind* (1869) I. 133 It is one of those specimens of clear and vigorous statement..in which the Analysis abounds. 1847 EMERSON *Repr. Men, Shaks.* Wks. (Bohn) I. 357 Our English Bible is a wonderful specimen of the strength and music of the English language. 1863 D. G. MITCHELL *Sev. Stor.* 4 It is a fair specimen of what the Roman stationers could do.

4. a. A single thing selected or regarded as typical of its class; a part or piece *of* something taken as representative of the whole.

1654 WHITLOCK *Zootomia* 493 Any one may sooner finde a fault, than mend it, in any Specimens, or performances of Art. 1725 DE FOE *Voy. round World* (1840) 99 Things..of which they had brought specimens. 1765 *Museum Rust.* IV. 239 English workmen, who have made specimens of the several articles of equal goodness with those of the Dutch. 1830 D'ISRAELI *Chas. I*, III. vii. 128 We cannot judge of this concealed genius by many specimens we have of her correspondence. 1853 MAURICE *Proph. & Kings* xix. 335 A very memorable chapter of Micah's prophecy,..which our Church has chosen as a specimen of the whole book. 1887 LOWELL *Democracy*, etc. 96 It was not a bringing of the brick as a specimen of the house.

b. *spec.* An animal, plant, or mineral, a part or portion of some substance or organism, etc., serving as an example of the thing in question for purposes of investigation or scientific study.

1765 *Museum Rust.* IV. 126, I have found and send a specimen of another yellow trefoil. 1797 *Phil. Trans.* LXXXVII. 383, I covered one side of a specimen of Iceland crystal, three inches deep, with black paper. 1802 M. CUTLER in *Life*, etc. (1888) II. 112 Very busy in putting up a box of [botanical] specimens for Mr. Paykull. 1827 FARADAY *Chem. Manip.* xvi. (1842) 431 Such portions of valuable fluids or solids..intended for specimens. 1854 RONALDS & RICHARDSON *Chem. Technol.* (ed. 2) I. 121 This determination of the amount of coke yielded by any specimen of coal. 1878 HUXLEY *Physiogr.* 192 In different specimens, however, the lava exhibits great variations.

transf. 1844 S. WILBERFORCE *Hist. Prot. Episc. Ch. Amer.* (1846) 5 The native thus cruelly kidnapped was not the only specimen they gathered. 1850 HT. MARTINEAU *Hist. Peace* v. xi. (1877) III. 414 He will stand in history as a specimen —dry and curious—but in no way as a vital being.

c. With adjs. denoting the value of the example as a type.

1841 D'ISRAELI *Amen. Lit.* (1867) 463 These complimentary sonnets..are not the happiest specimens in our language of these minor poems. 1849 PARKER *Introd. Stud. Gothic Archit.* v. 197 Lincoln college chapel is also a very favourable specimen of Jacobean Gothic. 1856 DELAMER *Fl. Garden* (1861) 2 If we can show finer and more remarkable specimens than our neighbours, so much the better.

5. Of persons as typical of certain qualities or of the human species. Also *colloq.* or *slang* with derogatory force, chiefly with defining adj., as ***a bright, poor*** (etc.) ***specimen***.

(*a*) 1817 COBBETT *Pol. Reg.* XXXII. 92 Mr. Hickman and Mr. Young..are new specimens of the spirit and the talent, which the times and the cause of freedom have brought forth. 1842 LOVER *Handy Andy* xxi, Growling was looking on in amused wonder at this specimen of vulgar effrontery, whom he had christened 'The Brazen Baggage', the first time he saw her. 1855 MACAULAY *Hist. Eng.* xvi. III. 703 They were perhaps the two most remarkable specimens that the world could show of perverse absurdity.

(*b*) 1837 DICKENS *Pickw.* ii, 'Here you are, sir,' shouted a strange specimen of the human race. 1897 MARY KINGSLEY *W. Africa* 328 Where one continually sees magnificent specimens of human beings.

(*c*) 1854 THOREAU *Walden* (1884) 163 There were some curious specimens among my visitors. 1908 R. BAGOT *A. Cuthbert* ii. 15 What was her husband about?.. He must have been a poor specimen.

†**6.** A brief and incomplete account *of* something in writing; a rough draught or outline serving to show the chief features. *Obs.*

1665 HOOKE *Microgr.* Pref. 2 b, Some specimen of each of which Heads the Reader will find in the subsequent delineations. 1672 *Life Mede* in *M.'s Wks.* (ed. 3) p. xxx, To the same effect he had express'd himself in an early Specimen or first Draught of his Thoughts.

7. (See quot.)

1819 *Act 59 Geo. III*, c. 90 §10 Whereas it is usual for the Officers of Excise to leave on the Premises of the Traders and Manufacturers under their Survey, certain Books or Papers commonly called *Specimens*, for recording therein the Entries in the Books of such Officers of the state of the Manufactory [etc.].

8. *attrib.*, passing into *adj.* (freq. hyphened): Serving as, or intended for, a specimen; typical.

Freq. in recent use and often applied to plants, fish, etc., of an exceptionally large size or fine quality.

1860 ADLER *Prov. Poet.* xviii. 421, I have..produced such specimen-quotations as will serve to give us an idea of the decadence of this poetry. 1870 *Hist. Sketch Anderston Ch.* 9 These specimen facts speak of marvellous changes. 1877 RAYMOND *Statist. Mines & Mining* 251 The highest assay made from specimen rock was $2,000 per ton. 1877 *Academy* 3 Nov. 428/1 The specimen chapter here given us is on Guicciardini's embassy to Spain in 1511. 1896 *Daily News* 7 Sept. 7/5 A number of 'specimen' fish have lately been caught in the Thames.

b. *Comb.*, as ***specimen-hunter, -monger***, etc.; **specimen-book**, a book of specimens or samples; **specimen-box**, a portable box or case specially adapted for carrying botanical or other specimens; **specimen page**, a page submitted by a printer as a sample setting for a book; **specimen tree**, a tree planted on its own, away from other plants of a similar size.

1871 W. BLACKWOOD *Let.* 19 Sept. in *Geo. Eliot Lett.* (1956) V. 190, I also send you by Book Post a *specimen Book from which you will..be able to select the colour for the paper cover. 1896 T. L. DE VINNE *Moxon's Mech. Exerc., Print.* 404 The specimen-book of the Enschedé foundry. 1897 VOYNICH *Gadfly* I. ii. 21 Arthur brought out his *specimen box and plunged into an earnest botanical discussion. 1896 *Westm. Gaz.* 4 Nov. 4/1 It used to be a favourite resort of the entomological *specimen hunter. 1864 C. P. SMITH *Our Inherit. in Gt. Pyramid* 18 The hammers of tourists and the axes of *specimen-mongers. 1835 DICKENS *Let.* 9 Dec. (1965) I. 102, I have received neither *specimen page nor proofs. 1877 W. PATER *Let.* 30 Jan. (1970) 27 Dear Mr. Macmillan..Of the two specimen pages, I enclose the one I think preferable. 1926 S. UNWIN *Truth about Publishing* ii. 37 As soon as the printers' estimate and specimen page are received and have been checked, the estimate has to be completed by the addition of the cost of paper, binding and other items. 1975 J. BUTCHER *Copy-Editing* ii. 13 Specimen pages are intended to show solutions to all the general typographical problems that the printers will meet in the book. 1933 A. OSBORN *Shrubs & Trees for Garden* xxiv. 119 Weeping trees are unsuitable for grouping, but very valuable for planting as *specimen trees on the lawn. 1961 E. WAUGH *Unconditional Surrender* III. ii. 230 Guy took to walking..in the public gardens.. There were winding paths, specimen trees, statuary. 1980 *Amat. Gardening* 25 Oct. 15/1 It makes a shapely specimen tree as well as being good for making a hedge or screen.

Hence **'specimenify** *v. trans.*, to select as a specimen or instance; **'specimenize** *v. trans.*, to show a specimen or sample of; to collect or preserve as a specimen.

1821 LAMB *Lett.* (1888) II. 34 The line you cannot appropriate is Gray's sonnet, specimenifyed by Wordsworth..as mixed of bad and good style. 1832 *Blackw. Mag.* XXXII. 812 A conceited coxcomb..tormented the birds, and poked the beasts, specimenizing fantastically his 'universal knowledge'. 1894 E. H. A[ITKEN] *Naturalist on Prowl* 173, I noticed a lovely little silvery spider, and resolved to specimenize it.

†**spe'ciminal**, *a. Obs.* [f. L. *specimin-*, stem of *specimen* (see prec.) + -AL¹.] Of the nature of a specimen, example, or type.

1664 H. MORE *Myst. Iniq.* 200 The said Reformation is an eminent speciminal completion of the prophecy of the Resurrection of the Witnesses. 1685 —— *Paralip. Prophet.* 483 Christ's partial or speciminal taking again possession of his Kingdom.

specio-, comb. form of L. *species*, employed in a few scientific terms of recent introduction, as ***speciographic, -graphy, -logic, -logy***. (Cf. SPECIE-.)

1882 *Imperial Dict.* IV. 151/1 *Speciology*, the doctrine of species.

†**speciose**, *a. Obs.*⁻¹ [ad. L. *speciōs-us* SPECIOUS *a.*] Beautiful, lovely. In quot. *absol.*

c 1450 HOLLAND *Howlat* 733 Haile speciose, most specifyit with the spiritualis!..Haile our hope and our helpe!

speciosity (spiːʃɪˈɒsɪtɪ). Now *rare*. Also 5 **specioustee**, 6–7 **speciositie**. [ad. late L. *speciōsitās* (= F. *spéciosité*, It. *speziosità*, Sp. *especiosidad*, Pg. *especiosidade*) beauty, good appearance or looks, f. *speciōsus* SPECIOUS *a.*: see -ITY.]

†**1.** The quality of being beautiful; beauty, fair or lovely appearance. Also, a beautiful thing. *Obs.*

a 1470 HARDING *Chron.* ccvii, He had..Iewelles in chestes, and stones of precioustee, And other Marchauntes in specioustee. 1535 STEWART *Cron. Scot.* I. 107 The palice [that] proper wes to se, Poleist perfyte with all speciositie. 1627 SYBTHORPE *Apost. Obed.* 25 Although the commonweale be safest and most beautifull, when it is at unitie in it selfe,..yet, that the speciositie may the better appeare to us, we must survey it by particulars. 1660 H. MORE *Myst. Godl.* IV. xii. 128 The Transfiguration of his person on the top of mount Tabor into so great a glory as all the speciosities of the world could not equalize. 1731 BAILEY (vol. II), *Speciousness, Speciosity*, fairness of show and appearance.

2. The quality of being specious; speciousness.

1608 T. JAMES *Apol. for Wickliffe* 33 He preached against the pretiosity, speciosity, and miraculositie, and sundry other sophistications about images.

1839 CARLYLE *Chartism* v, Speciosity in all departments usurps the place of reality..; instead of performance, there is appearance of performance. 1851 —— *Sterling* I. v. (1872) 35 Professions, built so largely on speciosity instead of performance.

b. *pl.* Specious actions, promises, etc.

1837 CARLYLE *Fr. Rev.* II. v. i, Poor Paris;..enveloped in speciosities, in falsehood which knows itself false. **1858** —— *Fredk. Gt.* I. i. I. 11 The shops declining to take hypocrisies and speciosities any farther.

specious ('spiːʃəs), *a.* Also 5 **specius, speceows,** 5–6 **specyous,** 7 **spetious.** [ad. L. *speciōs-us* fair, beautiful, fair-seeming, f. *speciēs* SPECIES. Hence also F. *spécieux, -euse*, It. *spezioso*, Sp. and Pg. *especioso*.]

1. Fair or pleasing to the eye or sight; beautiful, handsome, lovely; resplendent with beauty. ? *Obs.*

a. Of persons, their parts, etc., or of things.

(*a*) *a* **1400** *Minor Poems fr. Vernon MS.* xxiii. 146 Heil ful of grace, eke Speciouse at al, Mayden wys and þerto Meke. *c* **1425** *St. Elizabeth of Spalbeck* in *Anglia* VIII. 115/45 Hir chere semiþ þen ful specyous and cleer & gracyous. **1526** *Pilgr. Perf.* (W. de W. 1531) 184 Specyous & beautyfull is he aboue all the chylder of men. **1626** T. H[AWKINS] *Caussin's Holy Crt.* 45 Nicephorus relateth certaine lineaments of his stature, colour and proportion of his members,..in all parts louely and specious. **1652** GAULE *Magastrom.* 265 Yet the wise men of Greece were not ashamed to pursue specious boyes. *a* **1670** HACKET *Cent. Sermons* (1675) 422 There is thy Saviour..looking like a specious Bridegroom. **1748** RICHARDSON *Clarissa* (1811) I. xvi. 109 Disagreeable only as another man has a much more specious person. **1791** COWPER *Odyss.* XVII. 547 Gods! how illiberal with that specious form! **1818** HAZLITT *Eng. Poets* i. (1870) 14 The Greek statues are little else than specious forms.

(*b*) **1402** *Pol. Poems* (Rolls) II. 98 The pore man at the specious ȝate praiede to the apostlis to parten of her almes. *c* **1440** *Gesta Rom.* viii. 20 That oþer [way] specius and faire, sett aboute withe lileis and Rosis. **1582** N.T. (Rhem.) *Acts* iii. 10 He which sate for almes at the Specious gate of the temple. **1621** BRATHWAIT *Nat. Embassie* (1877) 188 Smooth to the touch, and specious to the sight. **1651** FRENCH *Distill.* vi. 192 So will the Spirit..be coloured with a very specious blue colour. **1697** AUBREY *Brief Lives* (1898) I. 77 The great Cardinal Richelieu, who lived both to designe and finish that specious towne of Richelieu. **1756** BURKE *Subl. & B.* Wks. 1842 I. 57 When any object partakes of the above mentioned qualities, or of those of beautiful bodies, and is withal of great dimensions, it is full as remote from the idea of mere beauty; I call it *fine* or *specious*.

transf. *c* **1485** *Digby Myst.* (1882) III. 628 To me itt is a Ioye most speceows. **1631** MASSINGER *Emperor East* I. ii, Your specious titles Cannot but take her.

b. Of flowers, birds or their feathers, etc. In later use, having brilliant, gaudy, or showy colouring. Also *transf.*

(*a*) **1513** BRADSHAW *St. Werburge* I. 3456 This rutilant gemme and specious floure [*sc.* the body of St. Werburge]. *a* **1637** B. JONSON *Underwoods, Epitaph Master Corbet* Wks. (1640) 178 And adde his Actions unto these, They were as specious as his Trees. *a* **1682** SIR T. BROWNE *Misc. Tracts* (1684) 93 Successive acquists of fair and specious Plants. **1731** MILLER *Gard. Dict.* s.v. *Saxifraga*, The fourth Sort is propagated for the Sake of its specious Flowers. **1800** ANDREWS *Bot. Rep.* 87 This truly specious Ixia! **1812** *New Botanic Gard.* I. 29 The corolla specious, and purple in colour. **1837** P. KEITH *Bot. Lex.* 265 The novice in botany, who is attracted, perhaps, only by what is specious in the plant or flower.

(*b*) **1688** HOLME *Armoury* II. 287 It can set up specious feathers on the crown of its head like a crest. **1688** *Phil. Trans.* XVII. 996 There be other sorts of Goldfinches variegated with red, orange and yellow Feathers, very specious and beautiful. **1786** S. GOODENOUGH in *Mem. Sir J. E. Smith* (1832) I. 184 Bees, several new ones, one very specious indeed. **1803** SHAW *Gen. Zool.* IV. II. 603 Specious Mackrel, *Scomber Speciosus*. **1809** *Ibid.* VII. II. 364 Specious Jay, *Corvus speciosus*. Crested green Jay.

2. Having a fair or attractive appearance or character, calculated to make a favourable impression on the mind, but in reality devoid of the qualities apparently possessed.

In certain contexts passing into the sense 'merely apparent'.

1612 T. TAYLOR *Comm. Titus* i. 16 Their actions, although neuer so good in themselues, neuer so specious vnto others,..yet are abhominable vnto God. **1644** QUARLES *Judgm. & Mercy* 144 Let not the specious goodness of the end encourage me to the unlawfulness of the means. **1681** DRYDEN *Abs. & Achit.* 746 A smooth pretence Of specious love, and duty to their Prince. **1705** STANHOPE *Paraphr.* II. 264 The most specious Instances,..such as Martyrdom,..are no necessary Proofs of Charity. **1743** FRANCIS tr. *Hor., Odes* II. i. 4 The specious Means, the private Aims,..how fatal to the Roman State! **1774** REID *Aristotle's Logic* iv. §2 (1788) 72 The friends of Aristotle have shown that this improvement of Ramus is more specious than useful. **1807** CRABBE *Birth Flattery* 67 What are these specious gifts, these paltry gains? **1849** MACAULAY *Hist. Eng.* v. I. 599 It appeared that this plan, though specious, was impracticable. **1873** W. H. DIXON *Two Queens* x. v. II. 179 What was done by him in Rome was merely specious.

absol. **1676** DRYDEN *Aurengz.* Ep. Ded. A ij, But somewhat of Specious they must have, to recommend themselves to Princes.

b. Of pretences, pretexts, etc.

1611 SPEED *Hist. Gt. Brit.* IX. viii. 499/2 Traiterous requests..which he was now willing to maske with the specious pretext of iustice and deuotion. **1632** *Galway Arch.* in *10th Rep. Hist. MSS. Comm.* App. V. 478 The specious pretences you made. **1734** *Col. Records Pennsylv.* III. 546 Notwithstanding the specious and ample Professions made by the Governor of Maryland. **1769** ROBERTSON *Chas. V*, x. III. 254 The specious pretexts which had formerly concealed his ambitious designs. **1836** THIRLWALL *Greece* xvii. III. 4 Cimon seized this specious pretext for exterminating the people.

c. Of appearance, show, etc.

a **1628** PRESTON *Effect. Faith* (1631) 74 There be many works that have a specious and faire shew in the view of men; But..God regards them not. **1647** CLARENDON *Hist. Reb.* IV. §172 The law..being neglected or disesteemed (under what specious shews soever). **1729** BUTLER *Serm.* Wks. 1874 II. 65 A discovery..which they..have found out through all the specious appearances to the contrary. **1735** SOMERVILLE *Chase* II. 313 To rob, and to destroy, beneath the Name And specious Guise of War. *a* **1827** WORDSW. *Sonn. Liberty* II. vi. 10 Ere wiles and politic dispute Gave specious colouring to aim and act. **1849** MACAULAY *Hist. Eng.* vii. II. 231 A policy which had a specious show of liberality. **1870** MOZLEY *Univ. Serm.* iv. (1877) 74 We have even in the early Christian Church that specious display of gifts which put aside as secondary the more solid part of religion.

d. Of falsehood, bad qualities, etc.

1665 GLANVIL *Scepsis Sci.* xiv. 79 Such an Infinite of uncertain opinions, bare probabilities, specious falshoods. **1682** DRYDEN *Abs. & Achit.* II. 955 Who Truth from specious falsehood can divide [etc.]. **1728** YOUNG *Love Fame* II. 68 If not to some peculiar end assign'd, Study's the specious trifling of the mind. **1748** MELMOTH *Fitzosborne Lett.* lii. (1749) II. 63 Religion without this sovereign principle [generosity], degenerates into slavish fear, and wisdom into a specious cunning. **1823** SCOTT *Quentin D.* xvii, In whose eyes the sincere devotion of a heathen is more estimable than the specious hypocrisy of a Pharisee. **1866** MRS. H. WOOD *St. Martin's Eve* i. (1874) 4 Be not ensnared by specious deceit.

3. Of language, statements, etc.: Fair, attractive, or plausible, but wanting in genuineness or sincerity.

1651 HOBBES *Leviath.* II. xxi. 110 It is an easy thing, for men to be deceived, by the specious name of Libertie. **1665** MANLEY *Grotius' Low C. Wars* 371 The Prince,..by an evident demonstration, confuting specious words. **1670** MARVELL *Corr.* Wks. (Grosart) II. 338 This motion seemed specious and welcome to the Committee. **1712** ADDISON *Spect.* No. 469 ¶5 Gratifications, Tokens of Thankfulness, Dispatch Money, and the like specious Terms. **1798** S. & HT. LEE *Canterb. T.* II. 230 She then imparted the specious tale of the Marquis's loss at the gaming-table. **1849** MACAULAY *Hist. Eng.* v. I. 568 The meaning latent under this specious phrase. **1855** MOTLEY *Dutch Rep.* v. v. (1866) 748 The specious language of Philip's former letters.

b. Of reasoning, arguments, etc.: Plausible, apparently sound or convincing, but in reality sophistical or fallacious.

1651 HOBBES *Leviath.* I. xv. 73 This specious reasoning is neverthelesse false. **1656** tr. *Hobbes' Elem. Philos.* (1839) 415 For the establishing of vacuum, many and specious arguments and experiments have been brought. **1726** POPE *Odyss.* XIX. 8 To sooth their fears a specious reason feign. **1788** GIBBON *Decl. & F.* xliv. IV. 378 A specious theory is confuted by this free and perfect experiment. **1791** MACKINTOSH *Vind. Gall.* Wks. 1846 III. 107 Many subtle and specious objections are urged. **1856** *N. Brit. Rev.* XXVI. 23 Undoubtedly it is robust good sense which is here brought to bear upon a specious sophism. **1877** GEIKIE *Christ* xxvii. (1879) 308 He was not led away by such suggestions, however specious.

absol. *a* **1850** CALHOUN *Wks.* (1874) III. 274 To this it may be traced, that the Senator prefers the specious to the solid, and the plausible to the true.

†**4.** Apparent, as opposed to real. *Obs.*$^{-1}$

1617 MORYSON *Itin.* II. 64 The Lord Deputie conceived the Earles surprise to bee an evill more spetious then materiall.

5. Of material things: Outwardly or superficially attractive or pleasing, but possessing little intrinsic worth; showy. *rare.*

1816 SIR J. REYNOLDS *Charac. of Painters of Italy* 136 [Michael Angelo] has rejected all the false, though specious ornaments, which disgrace the works even of the most esteemed artists. **1825** MACAULAY *Ess., Milton* (1851) I. 23 We shall, like Bassanio in the play, turn from the specious caskets..., and fix on the plain leaden chest.

6. Of persons: Characterized by conduct, actions, or reasoning, of a specious nature; †outwardly respectable.

1740 RICHARDSON *Pamela* (1824) I. 83 But now I have found you out, you specious hypocrite! **1798** CANNING *New Morality* 84 in *Poetry Anti-Jacobin* (1799) 223 If Vice appal thee..Yet may the specious bastard brood, which claim A spurious homage under Virtue's name,..rouse thee! **1799** W. GILPIN *Serm.* v. 54, I propose next to describe that of the specious or decent man. By the decent man, I mean him, who governs all his actions by appearances. **1841** DICKENS *Barn. Rudge* xl, You are a specious fellow,..and carry two fans under your hood. **1884** *Pall Mall G.* 14 May 5/1 If we were to sum up similarly in one word the chief characteristics of their German rival, we should say that Von Hartmann was specious.

†**7.** Of algebra: = LITERAL *a.* 1 c. *Obs.* (Cf. SPECIES 8 b.)

1670 COLLINS in Rigaud *Corr. Sci. Men* (1841) I. 154 A design to cause Diophantus to be turned into specious algebra. **1673** KERSEY *Algebra* I. i. 2 Algebra is by late Writers divided into two kinds; to wit, Numeral and Literal (or Specious). **1728** CHAMBERS *Cycl.* s.v. *Algebra*, In 1590, Vieta..introduc'd what he call'd his 'Specious Arithmetick', which consists in denoting the Quantities..by Symbols or Letters.

8. *Psychol.* Appearing to be actually known or experienced.

1890 W. JAMES *Princ. Psychol.* I. 642 We are constantly conscious of a certain duration—the specious present—varying in length from a few seconds to probably not more than a minute.

speciously ('spiːʃəslı), *adv.*[1] [f. prec.]

†**1.** So as to present a fair or respectable appearance. *Obs.*

1647 CLARENDON *Hist. Reb.* II. §39 Lashly had placed them by the advantage of that hill so speciously that they had the appearance of a good body of men. *a* **1677** BARROW *Serm.* iv. Wks. 1687 I. 46 To these considerations may be added, that we are commanded to walk εὐσχημόνως (decently, or speciously, which implies a regard to mens opinion). **1698** FRYER *Acc. E. India & P.* 396 To grow Rich, be saluted with Honour, appear magnificently, be accounted Noble and speciously Great,..they will venture on any Evil Enterprize.

2. In a specious manner; attractively or plausibly, but deceptively or fallaciously.

1647 CLARENDON *Contempl. Ps.* Tracts (1727) 405 There can be little said for the defence of the one, which may not be as speciously offered..for the defence of the other. **1699** BURNET *39 Art.* xxii. 234 Contrary..to the Worshipping of Images of all sorts, how speciously soever they may be disguised. **1734** tr. *Rollin's Anc. Hist.* (1827) II. II. 63 Other motives were speciously intended. **1781** GIBBON *Decl. & F.* xix. II. 143 Exasperated, as he might speciously allege, by injuries of a similar nature [etc.]. **1800** COLQUHOUN *Comm. Thames* viii. 261 It has been argued speciously, that Docks will supersede the necessity of a Police. **1872** J. L. SANFORD *Estim. Eng. Kings, Jas. I*, 323 The poverty of his exchequer, to which his policy of abstinence from war has been sometimes speciously attributed.

'**speciously,** *adv.*[2] [Alteration of SPECIALLY *adv.*] Specially, notably, principally.

The form also occurs in mod. dial. (*Eng. Dial. Dict.*).

1598 SHAKS. *Merry W.* III. iv. 113 [*Mrs.*] *Quickly.* I will do what I can for them all three,..and Ile bee as good as my word, but speciously for M. Fenton. *Ibid.* IV. v. 114 *Qui.* Haue not they suffer'd? Yes, I warrant; speciously one of them.

speciousness ('spiːʃəsnıs). [f. SPECIOUS *a.*]

1. The quality of being speciously attractive, plausible, etc.

1648 J. BEAUMONT *Psyche* XX. cclxxi, Never could She find leisure to attend On ceremonious Idelness, nor by The civil speciousness of Visits spend Her precious Time on courteous Vanity. **1663** S. PATRICK *Parab. Pilgrim* xviii. (1687) 174 With much speciousness, and very fair shews of faithful counsel will all this be represented. **1753** JOHNSON *Adventurer* No. 45 ¶1 The numberless projects that have flattered mankind with theoretical speciousness. **1797** *Phil. Trans.* LXXXVII. 181 These objections have at least speciousness to recommend them to our notice. **1824** DE QUINCEY *Idea Univ. Hist.* Wks. 1859 XIII. 146 All good, that is not engrafted upon moral good, is mere show and hollow speciousness. **1885** J. PAYN *Talk of Town* II. 229 The calmness of this reasoning appalled Margaret even more by its speciousness than by its falseness.

†**2.** Fair or elegant appearance. *Obs.*

1650 FULLER *Pisgah* IV. vi. 11 The quickness, speciousness, cheapness, and novelty of the work; not the state, riches, and curiosity thereof. **1731** [see SPECIOSITY 1]. **1756** BURKE *Subl. & B.* III. xxiii. 227 Elegance and Speciousness.

specioustee, obs. variant of SPECIOSITY.

speck (spɛk), *sb.*[1] Forms: 1 **specca,** 5–7 **specke,** 5 **spe(c)kke, speke;** 4, 7, 9 *U.S.* **spec,** 5 **spekk,** 6 **spek,** 7– **speck.** [OE. *specca*, not found in the cognate languages, but cf. SPECKLE *sb.*]

1. a. A small spot of a different colour or substance to that of the material or surface upon which it appears; a minute mark or discoloration. Occas. const. *of* (cf. 2).

c **725** *Corpus Gloss.* (Hessels) N 160 *Notae*, speccan. *c* **1000** *Sax. Leechd.* (Rolls) II. 88 Smire þonne þa speccan mid þære sealfe. **13..** *E.E. Allit. P.* B. 551 On spec of a spote may spede to mysse Of þe syȝte of þe souerayn þat syttez so hyȝe. **1398** TREVISA *Barth. De P.R.* XVI. xciv. (Bodl. MS.), Salte doþ awey speckkes [1495 speckles] in þe face ȝif it is itempered wiþ water camphora. *Ibid.* XVIII. lxxxi, Pantera.. is a beeste paynted wiþ smal rounde speckes [1495 speckles]: so þat al his skynne semeth fulle of yȝen bi diuersite of speckes blacke, white and rede. **1530** PALSGR. 274/1 Specke, marke, *marcque*. **1591** PERCIVALL *Sp. Dict.*, *Peca*, a specke, a spot in the face, *macula, næuus*. **1611** COTGR., *Tacheture*, a spot, specke, or speckle. **1671** GREW *Anat. Pl.* I. (1684) 5 Divers small Specks, of a different colour from that of the Parenchyma,..may be observ'd. **1727** GAY *Fables, Peacock, Turkey & Goose* 2 In beauty faults conspicuous grow, The smallest speck is seen on snow. **1787–9** WORDSW. *Ev. Walk* 356 But now the clear bright Moon her zenith gains, And, rimy without speck, extend the plains. **1815** J. SMITH *Panorama Sci. & Art* II. 745 Give the little speck of light reflected from the pupil of the eye, with pure white. **1868** FREEMAN *Norm. Conq.* (1877) II. vii. 34 Such faults seemed little more than a few specks on a burnished mirror.

b. With adjs. of colour, etc.

c **1050** in Wr.-Wülcker 446 *Maculam pullam*, þone sweartan speccan. **1567** MAPLET *Gr. Forest* 7 Bespotted with Purple speckes and bloud coloured vaines. **1608** WILLET *Hexapla Exod.* 641 The saphir..shineth with golden speckes in it. **1663** BOYLE *Usef. Exp. Nat. Philos.* I. iii. 54 The cicatricula or little whitish speck discernable in the coat of the eggs yolk. **1687** A. LOVELL tr. *Thevenot's Trav.* I. 239 The Skin of it is all spotted black and white, with some yellowish specks. *a* **1701** MAUNDRELL *Journ. Jerus., River Euphr.* (1749) 158 Stone very much resembling Porphyry, being of red ground, with yellow specks and veins, very glossy. **1796** STEDMAN *Surinam* (1813) II. xxviii. 348 The timber brown, variegated or powdered with white specks. **1818–20** E. THOMPSON tr. *Cullen's Nosologia* 325 An efflorescence consisting of small, distinct, purple specks and patches. **1877** HUXLEY & MARTIN *Elem. Biol.* 18 In some *Amœbæ* a clear space makes its appearance... After a while, a small clear speck appears at the same spot.

fig. **1822** LAMB *Elia* I. *Praise Chimney Sweepers*, I have a kindly yearning towards these dim specks—poor blots—innocent blacknesses.

c. Applied to things rendered extremely small by distance or by comparison with their surroundings. (Common in 19th cent.)

1656 COWLEY *Pindar. Odes, Extasie* ii, Where shall I find the noble Brittish Land? Lo, I at last a Northern Spec espie, Which in the Sea does lie! **1815** J. SMITH *Panorama Sci. & Art* II. 723 What the eye sees distinctly at once, is comparatively but a speck in the vast scene. **1819** BYRON *Juan* II. xiii, The town became a speck, From which away so fair and fast they bore. **1868** LOCKYER *Elem. Astron.* §321 We find.. that the whole solar system is but a mere speck in the universe.

d. Applied to a very small or distant cloud. Freq. in fig. context.

1726-46 THOMSON *Summer* 987 Amid the heavens, Falsely serene, deep in a cloudy speck. **1831** D. E. WILLIAMS *Life & Corr. Sir T. Lawrence* II. 73 The speck destined to be the tempest of future life. *a* **1832** MACKINTOSH *Revol. 1688* Wks. 1846 II. 230 Not a speck in the heavens seemed to the common eye to forebode a storm. **1878** STUBBS *Const. Hist.* III. xviii. 211 The solitary speck that clouded the future of the dynasty.

2. a. A small or minute particle *of* something.

a **1400-50** *Alexander* 743 Als sprent of my spittyng a specke on þi chere, þou sall be diȝt to þe deth. **1587** D. FENNER *Song of Songs* i. 10 With speckes of siluer very fine they set about shalbe. **1664** POWER *Exp. Philos.* I. 23 The Gloworm... Her eyes are two small black points or specks of jett. **1839** DE LA BECHE *Rep. Geol. Cornwall*, etc. xi. 327 These bunches frequently containing strings and specks of ore. **1860** TYNDALL *Glac.* II. xxi. 342 We watch the ice.. and find that every speck of dirt upon it retains its position. **1879** HARLAN *Eyesight* v. 52 Specks of iron and steel, how-ever, may often be removed.. by the use of a strong magnet.

fig. **1713** YOUNG *Last Day* III. 251 Call back thy thunders, Lord,.. Nor with a speck of wretchedness engage. **1757** MRS. GRIFFITH *Lett. Henry & Frances* (1767) III. 252 A man of Sense, and Taste, and Virtue,.. who magnifies her every Speck of Merit! **1865** DICKENS *Mut. Fr.* I. iii, The only speck of interest that presents itself to my.. view.

b. Without const. Also *fig.*

1601 HOLLAND *Pliny* I. 310 In these so little bodies (nay pricks and specks rather than bodies indeed). **1712** BLACKMORE *Creation* VI. 282 Each vital Speck, in which remains Th' entire, but rumpled Animal. **1748** *Anson's Voy.* II. vii. 214 Here we struck ground.., and found the bottom to consist of grey sand, with black specks. **1853** KANE *Grinnell Exp.* xxxiv. (1856) 298 An almost constant deposition of crystalline specks, which covered our decks with a sort of hoar-frost. **1855** J. PHILLIPS *Man. Geol.* 201 Coarse sandstone with carbonaceous specks. *a* **1862** BUCKLE *Misc. Wks.* (1872) I. 18 What we have done is but a speck compared to what remains to be done. **1883** S. C. HALL *Retrospect* I. 258 He.. deemed it a duty.. to magnify faults and dwindle virtues to specks.

c. A small piece, portion, etc., of ground or land. Also ***the Speck*** (Austral. colloq.), Tasmania.

1538 LELAND *Itin.* (1769) VII. 31 The hole Foreste of Maxwel except it be a smaul Spek is yn Chestre. **1796** STEDMAN *Surinam* (1813) I. vii. 166 My negroes having made a temporary kind of bridge, to step from the yawl upon a small speck of dry ground. **1800** COLERIDGE *Piccolom.* I. x, Yield them up that dot, that speck of land. **1930** *Bulletin* (Sydney) 11 June 21 N.S.W., V., Q., S.A., W.A. and the Speck. **1949** *Geogr. Mag.* Feb. 373 *Tassie* and *The Speck*, meaning Tasmania. **1963** *Times* 12 Mar. (Austral. Suppl.) p. v/4 Tasmania—affectionately known as 'the speck'.

d. ***not.. a speck***, not at all. *U.S.*

1843 HALIBURTON *S. Slick in Eng.* I. ii. 31, I doubled up my fist, for I didn't like it [the treatment] a spec. **1936** M. MITCHELL *Gone with Wind* xl. 719 You're smart enough about dollars and cents... But you.. aren't a speck smart about folks.

3. a. A small spot as indicative of a defective, diseased, or faulty condition; a blot, blemish, or defect.

1825 J. NICHOLSON *Operat. Mechanic* 636 The best [glass] is that which is.. free of blemishes, as blisters, specks, streaks, &c. **1859** TENNYSON *Merlin & V.* 393 The.. little pitted speck in garner'd fruit, That rotting inward slowly moulders all. **1909** *Cent. Dict.* Suppl. s.v., White speck of tobacco, a disease.. caused by the fungus *Macrosporium tabacinum*.

transf. and *fig.* *c* **1785** COURTENAY in *Boswell's Johnson* (Oxf. ed.) I. 525 Hence not alone are brighter parts display'd, But e'en the specks of character pourtray'd. **1815** MACKINTOSH *Speech* Wks. 1846 III. 317 What is destroyed by the slightest speck of corruption [etc.]. **1825** SCOTT *Talism.* xvii, Can all the pearls of the East atone for a speck upon England's honour? **1878** BROWNING *Poets Croisic* 36 Not a dint Nor speck had damaged 'Ode to Araminte'.

b. *slang.* (See quots. 1851.)

1851 MAYHEW *Lond. Lab.* I. 88/1 The damaged oranges are known as 'specks'. *Ibid.* 117/1 The shrivelled, dwarfish, or damaged fruit—called by the street-traders the 'specks'. **1897** *Daily News* 9 Sept. 3/7 He heard children asking for 'farthingsworths of specks' at defendant's stall.

4. In moth-names (see quots.).

1832 J. RENNIE *Consp. Butterfl. & M.* 89 The White Speck (*Leucania unipuncta*..);.. a minute white dot at the base of the hinder stigma. *Ibid.* 135 The Tawny Speck (*Eupithecia subfulvata*..) appears the beginning of August.

5. *Comb.*, as ***speck-like*** adj.

1917 J. MASEFIELD *Lollingdon Downs* 56 No spark of him is specklike in his glass. **1965** E. BISHOP *Questions of Travel* I. 11 A specklike girl and boy, Alone, but near a specklike house.

speck, *sb.*[2] *north. dial.* Forms: 5 **spekk(e**, **speke**, 6 **specc-**, 6-8 **specke**, 7- **speck**. [Of obscure origin: a common later form is SPETCH.]

1. A patch or piece of leather used in the making or mending of boots or shoes. †Also, a patch of cloth or other material.

c **1440** *Promp. Parv.* 468/1 Spekke, clowte, *pictacium.* **1483** *Cath. Angl.* 353/1 A Spekk (Speke *A.*), *presegmen.* **1570** LEVINS *Manip.* 47 A specke, *cento.* **1609** BIBLE (Douay) *Josh.* ix. 5 And shoes very old which for shew of oldenesse were clouted with speckes. **1664** *Spelman's Gloss.*, *Pictatium*,.. Anglicè a scraw, or a speck, or the clout of a shoe. **17..** *Robin Hood rescuing three Squires* in Child *Ball.* III. 179 Robin did on the old mans cloake, And it was torne in the necke; 'Now, by my faith,' said William Scarlett, 'Heere shold be set a specke'. **1788** W. H. MARSHALL *Yorksh.* II. 354 *Speck*, the heel-piece of a shoe. *a* **1825** FORBY *Voc. E. Anglia*, *Speck*, the sole of a shoe. **1876** ROBINSON *Whitby Gloss.*, *Speck*, the piece put on to the heel or toe of a shoe.

†**2.** A piece, strip, or trimming of undressed hide used in making size. *Obs.*

1496-7 *Durh. Acc. Rolls* (Surtees) 250 Et sol. eidem pro le spekkes et dealbacione aule, xviij *d.* **1531** *Durham Househ. Bk.* (Surtees) 69 Empcio le Whyteledre... Et in mundacione 3 pellium equorum soluti Johanni Grynvill, 2*s.* Et eidem pro 3 speccis, 6*d.* *Ibid.* 84 Et in speccis emptis pro camera de Meryngton, 4*d.* **1611** *Churchw. Acc. Pittington* (Surtees) 161 Paide for fower bushels of speckes to the same [lime], xx d.

†**3.** (See quots.) *Obs. rare.*

1684 *Yorks. Dial.* 39 Thy Father and Hobb, mun gang to th' Smiddy, And fetch the Specks, Sock and Cowlter hither. *Ibid.* Clavis, *Specks*, are long thin pieces of Iron which Husband-men nail upon their Ploughs, to save them from wearing.

speck, *sb.*[3] *E. Anglian dial.* [ad. OF. *espec* or *especque* (mod.Norm. *épec*, Picard *épêque*, F. *épeiche*), ad. MHG. *speck*, *spech*, var. of *specht* SPEIGHT.] A woodpecker.

15.. *Parl. Byrdes* in Hazl. *E.P.P.* III. 176 Than in his hole sayd the Specke [*v.r.* Woodspecke], I woulde the hauke brake his necke. [**1847** HALLIWELL, *Woodspack*, a wood-pecker.] **1855** *Norfolk Wds.* in *Trans. Philol. Soc.* 37 *Specke.* —Woodpecker.

speck (spɛk), *sb.*[4] Now *U.S.* and *S. African.* Also 7 **specke**, 9 **spec**, **spek**. [a. Du. *spek* (†*speck*, MDu. *spec*) or G. *speck* (MHG. *spec*, OHG. *spec*, *spech*; MLG. *speck*, whence MSw. *späk*, Sw. *späck*, Da. *spæk*), related to OE. *spic* SPICK *sb.*[1]]

1. a. Fat meat, esp. bacon or pork. **b.** The fat or blubber of a whale. **c.** The fat of a hippopotamus.

a. **1633** HEYWOOD *Eng. Trav.* I. ii, Adue good Cheese and Oynons, stuffe thy guts With Specke and Barley-pudding for disgestion. **1809** in Thornton *Amer. Gloss.* s.v., He goes out almost every week to eat speck with the country folks; thereby showing that a democratic governor is not to be choaked with fat pork. **1886** *Trans. Amer. Philol. Assoc.* XVII. App. p. xii, 'Speck' is.. the generic term applied [in Pennsylvania] to all kinds of fat meat.

b. **1743** *Univ. Spectator* 25 Sept. 3 About ten Days ago a large Whale run ashore at Whitehills near Banff, from which they have already taken 80 Barrels of Speck. **1825** in JAMIESON *Suppl.* **1856** KANE *Arct. Expl.* I. ii. 23 The spec or blubber is purchased from the natives with the usual articles of exchange.

c. **1863** W. C. BALDWIN *Afr. Hunting* iv. 110 Mothlow shot a sea-cow, and I went down.. to bring up half a wagon-load of speck. **1864** P. L. SCLATER *Guide Zool. Gard.* 53 The layer of fat next the skin makes excellent bacon, technically denominated Hippopotamus speck at the Cape.

2. *attrib.* in the names of tackle or apparatus used in dealing with whale-speck, as ***speck-block***, ***-fall***, ***-purchase***, ***-tackle***, ***-trough*** (see quots.).

1820 SCORESBY *Acc. Arctic Reg.* II. 299 The harpooners.. divide the fat into oblong pieces or 'slips'..; then affixing a 'speck-tackle' to each slip, progressively flay it off, as it is drawn upward. *Ibid.* 306 The 'speck-trough'.. consists of a kind of oblong box or chest, about twelve feet in length. **1846** A. YOUNG *Naut. Dict.* 121 The speck-falls, whereof there are two, for hoisting the blubber and bone off the whale, are ropes rove through two blocks made fast to the blubber-guy. *Ibid.* 290 Speck-block. **1874** A. H. MARKHAM *Whaling Cruise to Baffin's B.* 133 The fish is taken in, in four hoists, with the fore and main spek tackles.

speck (spɛk), *v.*[1] [f. SPECK *sb.*[1], or back-formation from SPECKED *ppl. a.*]

1. a. *trans.* To mark with specks; to dot after the manner of specks.

1580 HOLLYBAND *Treas. Fr. Tong*, *Picoter*, to peckle, to pricke thicke, to specke. **1611** COTGR., *Maculer*, to spot, blot; specke, speckle, bespatter. **1805** SOUTHEY *Madoc* I. vi, A beautiful and populous plain it was;.. And many a single dwelling specking it. **1835** WILLIS *Pencillings* I. xii. 89 Only broken by a few prostrate figures, just specking its wide area. **1853** MRS. GASKELL *Cranford* i, Trim gardens.. without a weed to speck them.

b. In passive: To be covered, marked, or diversified *with* (or *by*) specks or spots.

1667 MILTON *P.L.* IX. 429 Each Flour of slender stalk, whose head though gay Carnation, Purple, Azure, or spect with Gold, Hung drooping unsustained. **1678** *Lond. Gaz.* No. 1337/4 A Little white lap Spaniel Dog,.. his legs speckt with brown. *a* **1732** GAY *Ep.* xiii. Poems 1790 I. 217 When I some antique jar behold, Or white, or blue, or speck'd with gold. **1821** CLARE *Vill. Minstr.* (1823) I. 67 Pasture speck'd with sheep, and horse, and cow. **1845** E. WARBURTON *Crescent & Cross* I. 339 The lake was soon specked by people swimming, or rowing themselves on logs of wood. **1870** ROCK *Text. Fabr.* I. 40 They are specked all over with quatrefoil spots.

2. *intr.* To move or fly *like* specks.

1821 CLARE *Vill. Minstr.* II. 197 The sweeping rack That specks like wool-flocks through the purple sky.

3. *trans.* To go over (a woven fabric) and remove specks or other blemishes.

1895 in *Funk's Standard Dict.*

4. To convert into a mere speck.

1898 MEREDITH *Odes Fr. Hist.* 90 Specked overhead, the imminent vulture wings At poise.

5. *Austral.* [Both this and sense 1 of SPECKING *vbl. sb.* may properly repr. abbrev. of SPECULATE *v.*: cf. SPEC *sb.*[1]] **a.** *intr.* To search for small particles of gold or opal on the surface. **b.** *trans.* To search the surface of (the ground) for traces of gold or opal; to discover (particles of gold, etc.) in this manner.

1888 H. LAWSON *His Father's Mate* in *Stories* (1964) I. 139 A pick and shovel, and a gold dish.. with which he used to go 'a-speckin'' and 'fossickin'' amongst the old mullock heaps. **1903** R. BEDFORD *True Eyes* lviii. 305 With little cries of delight he 'specked' a four-ounce slug of the red gold. *Ibid.* lx. 315 They had sieved and dry-blown and 'specked' the little tongue of auriferous soil. **1926** *Spectator* 14 Aug. 240/2 Went 'specking' in nearby creeks. Got colours of gold but no nuggets. **1936** I. L. IDRIESS *Cattle King* xxiv. 211 Next morning they picked up gold. In trembling excitement they 'specked' piece after piece. **1969** E. WALLER *And there's Opal out There* 116 A couple of tourists specking for bits of potch and opal.

speck, *v.*[2] *north. dial.* [f. SPECK *sb.*[2]] *trans.* To patch or mend (shoes) with 'specks'.

1681 in Magrath *Flemings in Oxf.* (O.H.S.) II. App. M. 313 Paid unto Jo. Thompson of Hawkeshead shoemaker for soaling and Specking of Georges, Michaels, Richards & Rogers shoes, 2*s.* **1876** in ROBINSON *Whitby Gloss.* **1898** in KIRKBY *Lakel. Wds.*

speck and span, variant of SPICK AND SPAN.

1614 TOMKIS *Albumazar* II. ii. (1615) D ij b, Of a starke Clowne I shall appeare speck and span Gentleman. **1767** S. PATERSON *Anoth. Trav.* I. 48, I became desirous of seeing one of the last speck-and-span new things. **1840** THACKERAY *Paris Sk.-bk.* I. 51 No man stepped out so speck and span.. as Major British.

speckboom, obs. form of SPEK-BOOM.

specked (spɛkt), *ppl. a.* [f. SPECK *sb.*[1] or *v.*[1]]

1. Covered or marked with specks or spots; speckled; chequered, dappled, variegated.

1382 WYCLIF *Gen.* xxx. 32 Seuer alle thi speckid sheep, and with speckyd flese, and what euere ȝolow, and speckid, and dyuerse colourid were, as wel in sheep as in geyt, shal be my mede. **1387** TREVISA *Higden* (Rolls) I. 189 Ȝif þey drynken of boþe, þey schulle worþe spekked of dyuers colour. **1398** —— *Barth. De P.R.* XVIII. lxviii. (Bodl. MS.), His backe is diuerslich ischape & specked as þe pard is. *c* **1450** *Nominale* (MS. Harl. 1002) 147 b, *Scutulatus*, speckud. *c* **1460** *Towneley Myst.* xxx. 243 A syde hede and a fare fax, his gowne must be spekytt. **1578** LYTE *Dodoens* 64 The floures are.. specked in the knappes and buddes. **1616** J. LANE *Contn. Sqr.'s T.* IX. 387 Wheare seemd a longe speckd snake, his postern drewe and wrigled, her to stinge with forker blewe. **1654** GAYTON *Pleas. Notes* IV. viii. 227 Sure a pure Chrystall would more pleasant be Than a spect glasse tainted by venemous eye. *a* **1700** B. E. *Dict. Cant. Crew*, *Speckt-wiper*, a colour'd Handkerchief. **1821** CLARE *Vill. Minstr.* II. 204 The speckt throstle never wakes his song. **1886** HOLLAND *Chesh. Gloss.*, *Speckt baw*, a suet dumpling with currants in it.

b. Of fruit: Having specks of decay or disease.

1658 [implied in SPECKEDNESS]. **1882** *Garden* 4 Feb. 72/2 Even when the trees are but slightly affected by either canker or mildew the fruit is sure to be specked and comparatively valueless for market. **1897** *Daily News* 9 Sept. 3/7 'Specked' fruit was fruit damaged, but not necessarily unsound.

†**2.** Of a disease: Characterized by the appearance of specks or spots. *Obs.*$^{-0}$

1648 HEXHAM II, *Ceter, of schorfte als Lazerie*, Specked Leprosie.

Hence **ˈspeckedness**, the state of being specked or covered with specks, blemishes, etc.; a specked or unsound place.

1617 *Rider's Dict.*, *Nævositas*, speckednesse. **1656** BLOUNT *Glossogr.*, *Nevosity*, speckedness, fulness of moles or freckles. **1658** tr. *Porta's Nat. Magick* IV. v. 119 See that [the fruits].. bee sound, without any bruise, or speckednesse.

ˈspeckiness. *rare.* [f. SPECKY *a.*[1]] The state of being specked or specky.

1857 *Ecclesiologist* XVIII. 170 Some quaint speckiness or lininess of detail.

ˈspecking, *vbl. sb.* [f. SPECK *v.*[1] + -ING[1].]

1. *Austral.* The action of searching for surface gold or opal. Cf. sense 5 of SPECK *v.*[1]

1901 M. VIVIENNE *Travels in W. Australia* 171 Almost everyone in the camp went out for an afternoon's specking (looking on the ground for nuggets). **1945** *Walkabout* (Melbourne) 1 Mar. 14 Most of the residents of Lightning Ridge are experts at the art of 'specking'.

2. The discoloration of pottery through contamination of the glaze, or this effect contrived for decoration.

1967 M. CHANDLER *Ceramics in Mod. World* iii. 96 In the case of a glaze mix, it is particularly important to avoid contamination and specking. *a* **1977** *Harrison Mayer Ltd. Catal.* 22/3 Ilmenite... can be used in glazes to obtain specking effects.

speckle (ˈspɛk(ə)l), *sb.* Also 5 **spakle**, **spakkyl**, **spackyll**, **specle**, 6 **speccle**, **speckil**. [Corresponds to MDu. *speckel* (Flem. *spekel*, Du. *spikkel*): see SPECK *sb.*[1] and -LE.]

1. a. A speck, small spot or mark, esp. one occurring on the skin, body, etc.; a natural marking of this nature; a small patch or dot of colour.

c **1440** *Promp. Parv.* 467/1 Spakle (*S.* spakkyl, *P.* spackyll), *scutula.* **1495** [see SPECK *sb.*[1] 1, quots. 1398]. **1530** PALSGR. 274/1 Speccle in ones face, *lentylle.* **1549** E. ALLEN *Erasm. Par. Rev. St. John* xiii, Like unto a cat of the mountayne with her many speckles and spottes. **1591** SPENSER *Virg. Gnat* 250 An huge great Serpent all with speckles pide. **1601** HOLLAND *Pliny* II. 62 With vinegre alone, it [cumin] cureth the blacke spots and speckles appearing in any part of the bodie. *a* **1658** CLEVELAND *Wks.*

(1687) 285 The monstrous Fry Like Serpents with fair Speckles strike the Eye. **1825** SCOTT *Talism.* xvii, A coat or tabard .. made of dressed bull's hide, and stained in the front with many a broad spot and speckle of dull crimson. **1856** MORTON *Cycl. Agric.* II. 575/2 The seeds of a grayish colour, with purple speckles.

b. A small or minute object.

1882 BLACKMORE *Christowell* xvii, The humours of a slippery speckle, just beginning to outgrow a tadpole.

2. a. Speckled colouring, speckling.

1851 HAWTHORNE *Ho. Sev. Gables* x. 114 She curiously examined .. the peculiar speckle of its plumage.

b. A granular appearance seen in images formed by originally coherent light as a result of the interference of waves that have been reflected at a rough surface or have passed through an inhomogeneous medium; also, each of the light or dark areas giving rise to this appearance. Freq. *attrib.*

1965 *Jrnl. Optical Soc. Amer.* LV. 247 Exposing photographic film directly to the backscattered radiation confirms the independent existence of the speckles. *Ibid.* 252/2 Both speckle pattern and diffraction pattern were recorded (photographically) at the same distance from the aperture. **1970** A. LABEYRIE in *Astron. & Astrophysics* VI. 85/1 'Speckle' refers to the grainy structure observed when a laser beam is reflected from a diffusing surface... In large telescopes, the image of point stars also features a speckle pattern, due to seeing induced phase fluctuations on the wavefront. **1975** T. S. MCKECHNIE in J. C. Dainty *Laser Speckle & Related Phenomena* iv. 126 We may reduce speckle by simply reducing the coherence of the illumination. **1976** *Physics Bull.* Aug. 357/2 Objects viewed in highly coherent light acquire a peculiar granular appearance. This is the laser speckle phenomenon. **1977** *McGraw-Hill Encycl. Sci. & Technol.* 397/1 The size of the speckles is equal to the diffraction-limited resolution limit of the telescope, regardless of the resolution limit determined by the turbulent atmosphere. **1979** *Nature* 5 July p. vii/2 A double laser speckle camera which is used for non-destructive stress, vibration, and flaw analysis of engineering components.

3. *attrib.* and *Comb.*, as ***speckle-bellied, -coated, -faced, -starred*** adjs.; **speckle-belly,** (*slang*) a Nonconformist or Dissenter; (*U.S.*) one or other of various birds or fishes having speckled markings on the abdomen; **speckle interferometry,** the analysis of speckle in two or more images, differing only in the instant of exposure, as a means of obtaining information about the source of light or the agent that caused the speckle; so **speckle-interferometric** *a.*; **speckle-wood** (see SPECKLED *ppl. a.* 3 b).

1783 WALDRON *Contin. Ben Jonson's Sad Sheph.* 71 This swoll'n and *speckled-bellied toad. **1874** *Slang Dict.* 303 **Specklebellies*, Dissenters. A term used in Worcester and the North, though the etymology seems unknown in either place. **1884** COUES *N. Amer. Birds* 684 *Anser albifrons gambeli*,.. Speckle-belly. **1888** TRUMBULL *Names Birds* 24 Gadwell,.. Gray Duck,.. is known .. at Moriches [in Long Island] as Speckle-Belly. **1891** *Cent. Dict.*, *Speckle-belly*, a trout or char, as the common brook-trout of the United States, *Salvelinus fontinalis.* **1871** BROWNING *Balaust.* 1321 Round thy lyre, Phoibos, there danced the *speckle-coated fawn. **1885** BOWMAN *Struct. Wool Fibre* 85 The Shropshire *Speckle-faced Sheep is a cross breed between the original horned sheep and the Southdown. **1973** *Astrophysical Jrnl.* CLXXXII. L139 *Speckle interferometric techniques are an effective way of obtaining information about small solar features without the problems of lifting large telescopes above the Earth's atmosphere. **1970** A. LABEYRIE in *Astron. & Astrophysics* VI. 85 Key words: *speckle interferometry. **1972** *Sci. Amer.* Feb. 106 The technique, known as speckle interferometry, can also be used to map local deformations in stressed mechanical parts. **1973** *Astrophysical Jrnl.* CLXXXII. L139 Speckle interferometry is potentially more powerful than two-aperture Michelson stellar interferometry because the entire aperture is used. **1978** PASACHOFF & KUTNER *University Astron.* II. vi. 148 The speckle interferometry technique involves taking photographs of the speckle pattern with very short exposures—on the order of 1/100 second—or using electronic detection devices and then using mathematical techniques and computer assistance to deduce the properties of the starlight that entered the telescope. **1591** SYLVESTER *Du Bartas* I. v. 143 Feast-famous Sturgeons, Lampreys *speckle-starr'd. **1619** J. SCOTT *Hist. & Descr. Amazones* (MS. Bodl. Rawl. A 175) lf. 370b, They Loaded the Ship with Tobacco, Anotta, and *Specklewood. **1669** STURMY *Mariner's Mag., Penalties & Forfeit.* 6 Speckle-wood, Jamaica-wood, Fustick, or any other Dying-wood. **1729** *Cowley's Voy.* 24 The island of Borneo .. is plentifully stored with .. fine wood, as Speckle-wood and Ebony.

†**speckle,** *a. Obs. rare.* Speckled, dappled.

1536 *MS. Acc. St. John's Hosp., Canterb.*, For a spekyll cowe, xvs. iiij d. **1538** *Ibid.*, For a spekyll cowe att crystenmes, xvs. iiij d.

speckle ('spɛk(ə)l), *v.* [f. SPECKLE *sb.* or back-formation from SPECKLED *a.* Cf. MDu. *speckelen, spekelen* (WFlem. *spekelen*, Du. *spikkelen*).]

1. *trans.* To mark with, or as with, speckles; to cover or dot (a surface, etc.) after the manner of speckles.

1570 LEVINS *Manip.* 47 To speckle, *maculare.* **1611** COTGR., *Grivoler*, to peckle, or speckle; to spot with diuers colours. **1648** HEXHAM II, *Spickelen*, to Speckle, or to Spott. **1708** SEWELL II, *Bespikkelen*, to Speckle. **1780** COWPER *Progr. Error* 83 Dawn appears; the sportsman and his train Speckle the bosom of the distant plain. **1834** PRINGLE *Afr. Sk.* vi. 201 So numerous were those herds,.. they literally speckled the face of the country. **1848** THACKERAY *Van. Fair* xli, Squads of them might have been seen, speckling with black the public-house entrances. **1854** DICKENS *Hard T.* III. vi, Beautiful shadows of branches flickered upon it, and speckled it.

transf. **1862** *Catal. Internat. Exhib., Brit.* II. No. 6449, One wonders how on earth needle-making came to speckle such a scene.

2. *intr.* To form speckles; to become speckled; to be dotted about like speckles. *rare.*

1703 tr. *H. van Oosten's Dutch Gardener* IV. ix. 218 If you water them in the Heat of the Sun, the leaves will speckle, and so often lose their Spindel. **1820** CLARE *Poems Rural Life* (ed. 2) 209 And moss and ivy speckling on my eye. **1821** —— *Vill. Minstr.* II. 15 Every thing shines round me just as then, Mole-hills, and trees, and bushes speckling wild. **1973** R. ADAMS *Watership Down* ix. 36 As the plants moved in the breeze, the sunlight dappled and speckled back and forth over the brown soil.

speckled ('spɛk(ə)ld), (*ppl.*) *a.* and *pa. pple.* Also 5 **spac-, spaklyd, spekelede, spekeld, specled,** 6 **spekeled, speckelde,** 7 **speckeld.** [Corresponds to MDu. and WFlem. *spekelde* adj. and *gespekeld* (Du. *gespikkeld*) pa. pple. See SPECKLE *sb.*] Covered, dotted, or marked with (numerous) speckles or specks; variegated or flecked with spots of a different colour from that of the main body; spotted.

1. a. In predicative use.

a **1400** *Stockholm Med. MS.* ii. 658 in *Anglia* XVIII. 323 His stalke is .. Lyke nedderis hyde spaclyd amonge. *c* **1400** MAUNDEV. (Roxb.) xxxi. 143 Þai bene of dyuerse coloures, as rayed, rede, grene and ȝalowe,.. and all spekelede. *c* **1440** *Promp. Parv.* 467/1 Spaklyd, *scutulatus.* **1570** LEVINS *Manip.* 49 Speckled, *maculosus.* **1612** T. TAYLOR *Comm. Titus* i. 15 He is no better than a leper in Gods eies,.. outwardly spotted and speckled like the leopard. **1638** JUNIUS *Paint. Ancients* 138 To have their .. Pigeons speckled and painted after their own phantasie. *a* **1700** EVELYN *Diary* 7 May 1662, He drawing it [his arm] oute we found it all speckled. **1774** GOLDSM. *Nat. Hist.* (1776) V. 265 She usually lays but one [egg], which is speckled. **1796** H. HUNTER tr. *St.-Pierre's Stud. Nat.* (1799) I. 579 They are thus speckled, I admit, only on one side. **1861** PALEY *Æschylus* (ed. 2) *Agam.* 383 *note*, If unskilfully mixed it turns quite black externally, and is liable to become dim and speckled after being polished. **1965** *Jrnl. Optical Soc. Amer.* LV. 247 When a diffuse surface is illuminated by a coherent monochromatic source such as a laser, the illuminated area appears speckled. **1978** PASACHOFF & KUTNER *University Astron.* II. vi. 148 At any one instant, the image of a star through a large telescope looks speckled because different parts of the image are affected by different small turbulent areas in the earth's atmosphere.

fig. **1614** T. ADAMS *Divell's Banket* 25 The Conscience growes more speckled by them, till men become not only spotted, but spots.

b. Const. *with* something, esp. of a colour different from that of the main surface or material.

1483 CAXTON *Gold. Leg.* 353/1 In the sayd welle appiere yet stones bespryncte and specled as it were with blood. *a* **1548** HALL *Chron., Hen. IV*, 12 Some had the mainferres .. dropped and gutted with red and other had them spekeled with grene. **1578** LYTE *Dodoens* 203 Two leaves, speckled with great redde spottes. **1653** W. RAMESEY *Astrol. Restored* 57 The *Heliotropion*, is in colour green like a Jasper, speckled with red. **1735** JOHNSON *Lobo's Abyssinia* Descr. xii. 114 These Serpents .. have .. their bellies speckled with Brown, Black, and Yellow. **1794** MRS. RADCLIFFE *Myst. Udolpho* xxxiv, Its luxuriant plain .. speckled with gardens and magnificent villas. **1825** SCOTT *Betrothed* x, As she beheld that the trophies were speckled with blood. **1891** *Science-Gossip* XXVII. 23 With a dark zone of different shades of brown and black round the small end and speckled with the same colours on the other part.

2. In attrib. use. **a.** Of animals, their skin, parts, etc. ***speckled beauty***, a fine trout.

1482 *Trevisa's Higden* (Caxton) II. xi. 86 Alle the spekeld lammes and kyddes. *a* **1547** SURREY *Æneid* II. B iv, The adder .. Rered for wrath swelling her speckled neck. **1583** MELBANCKE *Philotimus* F iv b, A foxe though he haue not so gawdye a skin as the Leopard, hath more wit then the speckled foole. **1590** SPENSER *F.Q.* I. i. 17 She .. turning fierce, her speckled taile aduaunst. **1634** SIR T. HERBERT *Trav.* 5 [Sharks] are alwayes directed by a little speckled fish, called a pilot fish. **1675** HOBBES *Odyssey* (1677) 166 A goatskin .. Of which a speckled wild goat had been flaid. **1735** SOMERVILLE *Chase* I. 247 His Ears and Legs Fleckt here and there, in gay enamell'd Pride Rival the speckled Pard. **1789** E. DARWIN *Bot. Gard.* II. (1791) 109 Two serpent forms .. ploughed their foamy way with speckled breasts. **1832** LYTTON *Eugene A.* I. v, The speckled trout, fresh from the stream. **1859** GEO. ELIOT *A. Bede* i, A clean old woman .. talking to some speckled fowls. **1873** G. C. DAVIES *Mount. & Mere* xiv. 112 In the mean time I had landed two speckled beauties.

transf. **1598** SYLVESTER *Du Bartas* II. i. III. *Furies* 217 How many loathsome swarms Of speckled poysons .. in close Ambush lurk. **1697** DRYDEN *Virg. Georg.* III. 663 A Snake .. renew'd in all the speckl'd Pride Of pompous Youth. *c* **1760** SMOLLETT *Ode Leven-Water* 13 The springing trout in speckled pride.

b. Of flowers, stone, cloth, garments, etc.

1577 B. GOOGE *Heresbach's Husb.* IV. (1586) 191b, Veronica .. beareth a leafe like the Blackthorne, with a blewish speckled flowre. **1599** HAKLUYT *Voy.* II. 211 Ouer the body they haue built a tombe of speckled stone. **1648** HEXHAM II, *Gespickelt laken*, Speckled or Spotted cloath. **1682** *Lond. Gaz.* No. 1757/4 A dark-colour'd Stuff Riding-Coat,.. and speckled Stockings. **1708** SEWEL II, *Spekkige boter of kaas*, speckled butter or cheese. **1843** J. E. PORTLOCK *Geology* 525 The cavities are lined with green earth, and, from their number and minuteness, give a very speckled appearance to the mass. **1887** BESANT *The World Went* ii. 15 He wore a common speckled shirt like the watermen's children.

c. *fig.* Of sin, vice, etc.: Characterized by, full of, moral blemishes or defects.

1603 DEKKER & CHETTLE *Grissil* (Shaks. Soc.) 8 Before my soul look black with speckled sin My hands shall make me pale death's underling. **1608** DAY *Law Trickes* I. i, Her credit is more foule Than speckled scandall or black murders soule. **1629** MILTON *Hymn Nativ.* xiv, And speckl'd vanity Will sicken soon and die. **1664** DUCHESS OF NEWCASTLE *Sociable Lett.* xv, Being unspotted, and free from that speckled Vice.

d. *colloq.* Of a mixed character or nature; motley.

1845 S. JUDD *Margaret* I. x, It was a singularly freaked and speckled group. **1909** *Daily Chron.* 16 Dec. 7/1 They are certainly not all desirable, taken separately. It must be owned that they are usually a speckled lot.

3. a. In the specific names of birds, fishes, animals, etc. (see quots. and the sbs.).

A number of moth names are given in Rennie *Consp. Butterfl. & Moths* (1832).

(*a*) **1888** TRUMBULL *Names Birds* 11 American White-fronted goose,.. Laughing goose,.. known in various parts of the West as Prairie Brant, *Speckled Belly, and *Speckled Brant. **1781** LATHAM *Gen. Synop. Birds* I. I. 97 *Speckled Buzzard,.. in shape like our common Buzzard. **1884** COUES *N. Amer. Birds* 276 *Catherpes mexicanus conspersus*, *Speckled Cañon Wren. **1678** RAY *Willughby's Ornith.* III. 341 The greatest *speckled Diver or Loon: *Colymbus maximus caudatus.* **1785** LATHAM *Gen. Synop. Birds* III. II. 341 Speckled Diver, *Colymbus stellatus.* **1894** HESLOP *Northumbld. Words*, Speckled-Diver, the young of the red-throated diver, *Colymbus septentrionalis.* **1815** STEPHENS in *Shaw's Gen. Zool.* IX. II. 438 *Speckled Finch (*Fringilla bononiensis*). **1785** LATHAM *Gen. Synop. Birds* III. I. 266 *Speckled Gallinule .. frequents the marshes of Germany. **1678** RAY *Willughby's Ornith.* III. 283 The greater *speckled or red Heron of Aldrovand. **1785** LATHAM *Gen. Synop. Birds* III. II. 341 Greatest *speckled Loon... This bird is pretty frequent in England. **1772** *Phil. Trans.* LXII. 383 *Speckled Partridge Hawk, at Hudson's Bay. The name is derived from its feeding on the birds of the Grous tribe, commonly called partridges, at Hudson's Bay. **1668** CHARLETON *Onomast.* 78 *Passeres Maculatus*,.. the *speckled Sparrow, with a yellow tail. **1783** LATHAM *Gen. Synop. Birds* II. I. 255 Speckled Sparrow... Back, and rump, black, white, and yellowish, mixed. *Ibid.* 87 *Speckled Thrush,.. speckled with small numerous brown spots.

(*b*) **1836** YARRELL *Brit. Fishes* II. 164 The *Speckled Cod is frequently taken in the weirs at Swansea. **1881** DAY *Fishes Gt. Brit.* I. 278 Turton's 'speckled cod' may have been so coloured due to disease. **1804** SHAW *Gen. Zool.* V. II. 417 *Speckled File-fish, *Balistes Punctatus.* **1884** GOODE *Nat. Hist. Aquat. Anim.* 263 *Speckled Garrupa (*Sebastichthys nebulosus*). **1863** COUCH *Brit. Fishes* II. 170 *Speckled Goby (*Gobius reticulatus*, Cuvier) .. is known in the Mediterranean. **1877** C. HALLOCK *Sportsman's Gazetteer* 276 Locally they are .. severally known as yellow perch, .. *speckled hen, etc. **1888** GOODE *Amer. Fishes* 56 'Marsh Bass' .. and 'Speckled Hen' are other names applied to one or both species [of bass]. **1672** *Speckled Hound-fish [see HOUND-FISH 2]. **1876** GOODE *Fishes Bermudas* 72 *Gymnothorax moringa*, *Speckled Maray. **1884** [see MORAY]. **1877** C. HALLOCK *Sportsman's Gazetteer* 378 Silver Perch, or *Speckled Perch. **1888** GOODE *Amer. Fishes* 71 *Pomoxys annularis* .. has other names of local application as .. 'Goggle Eye', 'Speckled Perch'. **1882** JORDAN & GILBERT *Syn. Fishes N. Amer.* 320 *Salvelinus fontinalis*, Brook Trout; *Speckled Trout. **1884** GOODE *Nat. Hist. Aquat. Anim.* 504 The Dolly Varden Trout, *Salvelinus malma*,.. is known in the mountains as 'Lake Trout', 'Bull Trout', 'Speckled Trout'. **1804** SHAW *Gen. Zool.* V. II. 428 *Speckled Trunk-Fish, *Ostracion Meleagris.*

(*c*) **1797** *Encycl. Brit.* (ed. 3) IV. 306/2 The Axis, or *Speckled Deer, has slender trifurcated horns. *c* **1880** *Cassell's Nat. Hist.* IV. 253 China yields the *Speckled Emys. **1802** SHAW *Gen. Zool.* III. II. 581 *Speckled Slow-Worm, *Anguis Meleagris*;.. nearly allied to the common Slow-Worm. *Ibid.* I. 30 *Testudo Europæa*... The *speckled Tortoise is of rather small size. **1831** GRIFFITH tr. *Cuvier* IX. 11 The Speckled Tortoise, *Testudo Europæa.* **1884** GOODE *Nat. Hist. Aquat. Anim.* 158 The 'Spotted Tortoise' or '*Speckled Turtle', *Chelopus guttatus.*

b. speckled wood, (*a*) a variety of wood having speckled markings; *esp.* the South American snake-wood or letter-wood, *Brosimum Aubletii*; (*b*) a brown butterfly with yellowish spots, *Pararge egeria*, found in lightly shaded places in Britain, much of continental Europe, and North Africa. Also ***speckled osier*** (see quot. 1885).

1656 *Act Commw.* c. 20 Rates (1658) 476 Log-wood... Speckled-wood. **1663** GERBIER *Counsel Builders* (1664) 109 What extent of Land about Surrenam is beset with speckled wood. **1703** DAMPIER *Voy.* III. I. 55 Here are Dye-woods, as Fustick, &c. with Woods for other uses, as speckled Wood, Brazil, &c. **1766** M. HARRIS *Aurelian* 132 Speckled wood... It flies in woods. The caterpillar feeds on grass. **1796** MORSE *Amer. Geog.* I. 745 A beautiful piece of speckled wood, made use of in cabinet work. **1843** HOLTZAPFFEL *Turning* I. 106 Snake wood, Letter or Speckled wood, is used at Demerara, Surinam, and along the banks of the Orinoko, for the bows of the Indians. **1885** C. G. W. LOCK *Workshop Rec.* Ser. IV. 277/1 The best variety [of the *Salix viminalis*] is known under several names, as .. the .. blotched osier, and speckled osier. **1974** [see *meadow brown* (*butterfly*) s.v. MEADOW *sb.* 4 b].

c. speckled yellows, a disease of sugar beet characterized by distorted and discoloured leaves, caused by a deficiency of manganese.

1938 *Brit. Sugar Beet Rev.* XII. 77/2 Fields affected with 'Speckled Yellows' can be recognised from a considerable distance. **1959** *New Biol.* XXX. 91 Diseases such as 'grey speck' of oats, 'speckled yellows' of sugar beet and 'marsh spot' of peas are caused by the low availability of manganese in the soil. **1960** *Farmer & Stockbreeder* 15 Mar. 149/2 (*caption*) Sugar Beet leaf—illustrating deficiency of manganese ('speckled yellows').

4. *Comb.*, as *speckled-faced*, *-tailed* adjs.

1884 COUES *N. Amer. Birds* 278 *Thryothorus bewicki spilurus*, Speckled-tailed Wren. **1884** *Daily News* 10 Dec. 3/1 The black or speckled-faced class [of sheep]. **1886** *Pall Mall G.* 7 Dec. 10/2 Fat wether sheep, of any blackfaced or speckledfaced mountain breed.

Hence **ˈspeckledness**, the state of being speckled; spottiness.

1611 COTGR., *Haglure*, the maile (or speckledness) of the coat of a hawke. **1665** HOOKE *Microgr.* 200 The speckledness of his shell. **1727** BAILEY (vol. II), *Speckledness*, Spottedness.

ˈspeckler. *rare.* [f. SPECKLE *v.*] One who or that which speckles.

1798 W. MAVOR *Brit. Tourists* V. 258 A hamlet, the residence of poverty, [may] be a fair speckler of the mountain's brow.

ˈspeckless, *a.* [f. SPECK *sb.*[1]] Having no speck or speckle; free from specks, blemishes, flaws, etc. Also in fig. context.

1788 WOLCOT (P. Pindar) *Peter's Proph.* 41 The beautiful deformities of nature! Birds without heads, and tails, and wings, and legs,.. speckless eggs [etc.]. *a* **1827** WORDSW. *Misc. Sonn.* II. xix, If his thought stand clear,.. Bright, speckless, as a softly-moulded tear. **1833** M. SCOTT *Tom Cringle* xviii, The second sun set—still the horizon was speckless. **1889** C. EDWARDES *Sardinia* 120 The speckless blue of the sky.

b. Free from specks of dirt, dust, etc.; scrupulously or spotlessly clean. Also in fig. context.

1827 PUSEY in Liddon *Life* (1893) I. vii. 137 Viewing their minds in the almost speckless mirror of his own. **1859** GEO. ELIOT *A. Bede* i, The leaded windows were bright and speckless. **1879** MACQUOID *Berksh. Lady* 159 Afraid of soiling his speckless shoes.

Hence **ˈspecklessly** *adv.*, **ˈspecklessness**.

1862 T. A. TROLLOPE *Marietta* I. x. 187 Signor Giuseppe Palli.. equally rigid and bolt upright in his chair, equally specklessly black. **1876** MRS. WHITNEY *Sights & Ins.* xiii. 130 The whole turn-out is specklessly brilliant in finish. **1882** 'F. ANSTEY' *Vice Versa* iv. 64 His dress.. having all the uncreased trimness and specklessness [etc.].

ˈspeckling, *vbl. sb.* [f. SPECKLE *v.*] The action of the vb.; speckled marking or marks.

1611 COTGR., *Tacheture*,.. a spotting, speckling, marking. **1648** HEXHAM II, *Een spickelinge*, a Speckling, or a Spotting. **1872** COUES *N. Amer. Birds* 254 More or less dusky speckling on the throat, breast and sides. **1965** *Jrnl. Optical Soc. Amer.* LV. 247/1 Speckling has.. been observed when viewing a translucent material which is backlighted by a cw [*sc.* continuous wave] laser. **1973** *Astrophysical Jrnl.* CLXXXII. L139 Small, high-contrast features such as umbral dots and faculae near the limb [of the sun] show the speckling most clearly.

So **ˈspeckling** *ppl. a.*, producing speckles or blemishes. In quot. *fig.*

1602 MARSTON *Ant. & Mel.* IV. Wks. 1856 I. 45 O, this is naught but speckling melancholie.

ˈspeckly, *a.* [f. SPECKLE *sb.* Cf. MDu. *speckelich* (Du. *spikkelig*) speckled.] Full of or covered with speckles; speckled, spotted; freckled.

1704 *Phil. Trans.* XXV. 1758 Through which the Spot appeared distinct,.. with an Eliptical Speckly mist about it. **1886** G. ALLEN *Kalee's Shrine* i. 17 The speckly dress and impossible bonnet. **1899** E. PHILLPOTTS *Human Boy* 95 A thick-necked, speckly, stumpy chap like Bray.

specknell, obs. form of SPIGNEL.

specksioneer (spɛkʃəˈnɪə(r)). *Whale-fishing.* Also specktion(e)er, spectioneer, ˈspeckshioner. [ad. Du. *speksnijer*, colloquial form of *speksnijder*, f. *spek* SPECK *sb.*[4] + *snijden* to cut. The Du. *ij* was formerly, and is still locally, pronounced as (iː).] A harpooner, usually the chief harpooner, of a whaler, who directs the operation of flensing the whale or cutting up the blubber.

α. **1820** SCORESBY *Acc. Arctic Reg.* II. 40 The office of specksioneer, as it is called by the English. The specksioneer is now considered the principal harpooner. *Ibid.* 299 The harpooners, directed by the specksioneer, divide the fat into oblong pieces or 'slips'. **1858** SIMMONDS *Dict. Trade*, *Spectioneer*, a whaling name for the first harpooner. **1863** MRS. GASKELL *Sylvia's Lovers* II. 89 They spoke of the specksioneer, with admiration enough for his powers as a harpooner and sailor. **1867** SMYTH *Sailor's Word-bk.* 641 *Specktioneer*, the chief harpooner in a Greenland ship.

β. **1836** *Uncle Philip's Convers. Whale Fishery* 87 There is among the harpooners one man called the specktioner, and as he commands, the harpooners cut the fat into long pieces. **1896** KIPLING *Seven Seas* 24 Up spake the soul of a gray Gothavn 'speckshioner.

†**speckstone.** *Min. Obs.* [ad. G. *speckstein*, f. *speck* SPECK *sb.*[4] + *stein* STONE *sb.*] Soapstone, or the Chinese variety of this; figure-stone.

1794 SCHMEISSER *Syst. Min.* I. 194 To the harder kinds belong.. the Chinese smectis, or speckstone, which takes a fine polish.

speckt, error for *specht* SPEIGHT.

specky (ˈspɛkɪ), *a.*[1] Also 7 speckie, 8 speckey. [f. SPECK *sb.*[1] + -Y.] Covered or marked with specks; speckled, spotted; having specks or spots of disease, discoloration, etc.

1382 WYCLIF *Gen.* xxx. 33 Alle that weren not dyuerse, and speckid [*v.rr.* specky, specke]. **1587** MASCALL *Govt. Cattle, Sheepe* (1596) 206 Although the skinne be specky and spotted of diuers colours. **1763** W. LEWIS *Phil. Comm. Arts* 65 In some parts it appeared specky or full of small holes. **1793** *Trans. Soc. Enc. Arts*, etc. XI. 17 For where the leaves curl, the fruit is always specky. **1856** MORTON *Cycl. Agric.* I. 48/1 When ground with wheat, they render the flour 'specky'. **1865** *Intell. Observ.* No. 37. 18 A turbid or specky appearance. **1884** F. J. BRITTEN *Watch & Clockm.* 34 Pieces [of steel] that have been cleaned in dirty benzine.. will become specky in blueing.

transf. **1858** *Dublin Univ. Mag.* LII. 264 A style which might technically be termed specky and disfigured by some affectations which honest criticism must deplore.

ˈspecky, *a.*[2] *colloq.* [f. SPEC(S + -Y[1].] Bespectacled.

1956 R. JENKINS *Guests of War* IV. i. 167 The unbraw unlovable puke married to yon specky gasping smout of a barber. **1959** I. & P. OPIE *Lore & Lang. Schoolch.* ix. 172 A girl or boy with spectacles is known as 'Four-eyes', 'Specky four-eyes', '*Annie* four eyes'... Occasionally he is 'Eye balls'.. and 'Specky Jock' (Scotland).

specle(d, obs. ff. SPECKLE *sb.*, SPECKLED *ppl. a.*

Speclette (spɛkˈlɛt). [f. SPEC(S + *-lette* (refashioned on Fr. model after -LET): cf. -ETTE.] A pair of spectacles that folds at the bridge (see quot. 1962[1]).

1931 *Illustr. London News* 31 Oct. 707/3 (Advt.), Speclettes the delightful and fashionable folding spectacles. **1962** L. S. SASIENI *Optical Dispensing* viii. 182 In the 'Speclette' the sides are folded in halves on to the lenses and the two halves of the front folded over each other in the plane of the lenses, the one sliding across the other. *Ibid.* 183 (*caption*) 'Speclette' folding spectacles.

specs. Also **specks.** [Dial. or colloq. abbreviation of *spectacles* SPECTACLE *sb.*[1]] Spectacles for the eyes.

α. **1807** HOGG *Mountain Bard* Poet. Wks. 1838 II. 202 The miller.., wi' specks on his nose, To hae an' to view it was wondrous fain. **1815** G. BEATTIE *John o' Arnha'* (1826) 40 Wi' specks on nose,.. The wary fiend loom'd bluff and big. **1882** BLACKMORE *Christowell* xxvii, Must have my thick specks.

β. **1826** J. WILSON *Noct. Ambr.* Wks. 1855 I. 125 Few o' them.. that canna read big prent wi' powerfu' specs. **1853** CARLYLE in Froude *Life C. in Lond.* (1884) II. 127 She reads now with specs in the candlelight, as well as I; uses her mother's specs I perceive. **1873** CARLETON *Farm Ball.* 19 She got her specs from off the mantel-shelf.

†**spect,** *v.*[1] *Obs. rare.* [ad. L. *spect-āre* to look.] *intr.* To look or face in a specified direction.

1585 T. WASHINGTON tr. *Nicholay's Voy.* I. xvi. 17 b, Ther is another port which specteth towards the North. *Ibid.* II. vi. 35 The yle of Chio.. lyeth in the sea Ionique specting Eastwardes.

spect, *v.*[2] Also **spec, speck, 'spect,** etc. Repr. (chiefly U.S.) non-standard pronunc. of (*I*) *expect* or *suspect*.

1839 F. A. KEMBLE *Jrnl. Residence Georgian Plantation* (1863) xii. 118 Good for colored folks, missis; me 'spect not good enough for white people. **1852** MRS. STOWE *Uncle Tom's Cabin* II. xx. 38, I spect I grow'd. Don't think nobody never made me. **1893** H. A. SHANDS *Some Peculiarities of Speech in Mississippi* 59 Speck (spec). Used by negroes for both *expect* and *suspect*. **1914** 'BARTIMEUS' *Naval Occasions* xx. 182 'Spect's you wants yer breakfus'—same's me! **1927** A. P. RANDOLPH in A. Dundes *Mother Wit* (1973) 200 What's th' matter wid you? 'Specks you got dat Randolph fever, too, eh? **1976** *Washington Post* 7 Nov. K2/2 We'll teach them.. how to say: I SPEC (as in 'I spec I will do that.'). **1976** C. DEXTER *Last seen Wearing* xix. 151 'Has the wife got the chips on, Lewis?' 'I 'spect so.' **1977** F. PARRISH *Fire in Barley* x. 106, I 'speck you want me to feed the zoo.

†**spectaˈbility.** *Obs.*[−1] [f. next, or ad. L. *spectābilitās*.] Display, show.

1637 GILLESPIE *Eng. Pop. Cerem.* II. iv. 20 Musculus reprehends Bishops, for.. adding Ceremonies unto Ceremonies in a worldly splendor and spectability.

†**spectable,** *sb. Obs. rare.* [Substituted for SPECTACLE *sb.*[1], after next or OF. *spectable* sb.] A spectacle.

1535 *Goodly Primer, Prayer Lord* C j b, For an effectual example, & spectable of all vertues. **1550** COVERDALE *Spir. Perle* xxviii. (1588) 269 Job, the spectable of patience.

†**spectable,** *a. Obs.* [ad. L. *spectābilis* (f. *spectāre* to look) or a. OF. (also mod.F.) *spectable* (It. *spettabile*, Sp. *espectable*).]

1. Presentable to the sight; worthy of being seen or contemplated.

1432–50 tr. *Higden* (Rolls) I. 5 For in this tyme presente artes and lawes scholde falle vtterly, thexemplares of acciones spectable scholde not be patent. **1489–99** *Inscript. Holloway Chapel, Widcome* in Wood *Life* (O.H.S.) II. 409 Thys chapill floryschyd with formosyte spectabyll In honour of Mary Magdalen prior Cantlow hath edyfyd. **1611** T. HIGGONS *Serm. at Pauls Crosse* 42 My function and office.. was very spectable, yea honourable also. **1635** HEYWOOD *Hierarchy* III. Comm. 150 That by which a woman is made more faire and Spectable. **1665** J. SERGEANT *Sure Footing* 63 Experience of them.., by the venerable Sacraments, by the spectable Majesty of outward Ceremonies.

2. Capable of being seen; visible.

c **1440** *Pallad. on Husb.* IV. 692 Ther are in hem certeyn signys spectable Which is teschewe, and whiche is profitable. **1604** T. WRIGHT *Passions* v. §4. 220 Divers times both proportion, comelinesse, or.. other perfection be more spectable in the reiected, then in the accepted. **1622** *Tom Tell-Troath* in *Harl. Misc.* (1744) II. 405/1 The blasing Starr was not more spectable in our Horizon, nor gave People more Occasion of Talke. *a* **1655** T. ADAMS *Serm.* ix. Wks. 1861 I. 104 Their prayers were at the corners of streets;.. and so more spectable to many passengers.

†**spectabundal,** *a. Obs.*[−1] [f. L. *spect-āre* to look, after adjs. in *-bundus*.] Eager to see.

1652 URQUHART *Jewel* Wks. (1834) 230 By the inchanted transportation of the eyes and ears of its spectabundal auditorie.

spectacle (ˈspɛktək(ə)l), *sb.*[1] Forms: 4– spectacle (5 -acul); 4 spectakil, 5 -akele, -akyl(le, 6 -akle, -akill(e; 7 specktacle, -ikill. [a. OF. *spectacle* (also mod.F.: see next), = It. *spettacolo*, Sp. and Pg. *espectaculo*, or ad. L. *spectāculum* (poet. *-āclum*), f. *spectāre* to look. Hence also G., Da., Sw. *spektakel*.]

I. 1. a. A specially prepared or arranged display of a more or less public nature (esp. one on a large scale), forming an impressive or interesting show or entertainment for those viewing it.

a **1340** HAMPOLE *Psalter* xxxix. 6 Hoppynge & daunceynge of tumblers and herlotis, and oþer spectakils. **1382** WYCLIF *2 Macc.* v. 26 He stranglide togidre alle that camen forth to the spectacle, or biholdyng. **1542** BECON *Pathw. Prayer* A iij b, What an extreme enemy is the worlde... Howe doth it delyghte vs with the beholdyng of the vayne spectacles therof! **1553** EDEN *Treat. New Ind.* (Arb.) 16 The Romaynes.. were wont to put them [*sc.* the elephant and rhinoceros] together vpon the theater or stage, for a spectacle. **1607** TOPSELL *Four-f. Beasts* 315 The noblest horses.. were ioyned together in chariots for races, courses, spectacles, games, and combats. **1617** MORYSON *Itin.* IV. 476 To which and to many musterings and other frequent spectacles, the people flocke in great numbers. **1641** J. JACKSON *True Evang. T.* II. 126 They abhorred Theaters, and publique spectacles, especially of blood. **1763** J. BROWN *Poetry & Music* iv. 43 The gentle Passions, and less affecting Actions, which might fill the Spectacles of a mild and peaceful Nation. **1782** J. WARTON *Ess. Pope* II. viii. 87 What solid reason can we give why the Romans.. could yet never excel in tragedy, though so fond of theatrical spectacles? **1806** J. BERESFORD *Miseries Hum. Life* II. xii, Violent rain coming on, and continuing.. during the whole of the spectacle. *c* **1854** H. REED *Lect. Eng. Lit.* ix. (1855) 290 It was a very fine spectacle, but it was nothing more than a spectacle. **1865** LECKY *Ration.* (1878) I. 324 He had written a treatise dissuading the Christians of his day from frequenting the public spectacles.

b. Without article.

1387 TREVISA *Higden* (Rolls) V. 375 In comyn spectacle þere me stood to beholde playes and som newe þinges. **1607** TOPSELL *Four-f. Beasts* (1658) 374 Cæsar when he was Dictator, presented in spectacle four hundred Lions. **1740** CIBBER *Apol.* 57 Sir William Davenant, therefore,.. to make Head against their Success, was forc'd to add Spectacle and Musick to Action. **1809** PINKNEY *Trav. France* 98 The French.. infinitely excell every other nation in all things connected with spectacle. **1835** LYTTON *Rienzi* X. vi, Gorgeous imagination rather than vanity.. had led the Tribune into spectacle and pomp. **1866** CARLYLE in Froude *Remin.* (1881) II. 215 She was constantly in spectacle there, to her-self and to the sympathetic adorers.

attrib. and *Comb.* **1834** *Edinb. Rev.* LX. 7 The spectacle-loving public of the seventeenth century. **1908** *Stage Year Bk.* 21 An ingeniously conceived.. spectacle play.

2. A person or thing exhibited to, or set before, the public gaze as an object either (*a*) of curiosity or contempt, or (*b*) of marvel or admiration.

In *2 Sam.* xxiii. 21 the later Wycliffite version has the literal rendering 'worthi of spectacle'.

(*a*) *a* **1380** *S. Paula* 67 in Horstm. *Altengl. Leg.* (1878) 4 To gode angeles and to men Spectacle mad forsoþe we ben. **1382** WYCLIF *1 Cor.* iv. 9. **1382** —— *Hebrews* x. 33 In that other ȝe [were] maad a spectacle bi schenschips and tribulaciouns. **1582** N. T. (Rhem.) *1 Cor.* iv. 9 We are made a spectacle to the world, and to Angels and men. **1724** GAY *Captives* v, Let her be led a public spectacle. **1818** SCOTT *Hrt. Midl.* xii, How proud I was o' being made a spectacle to men and angels, having stood on their pillory at the Canongate.

(*b*) **1609** BIBLE (Douay) *2 Sam.* xxiii. 21 He also stroke the Ægyptian, a man worthie to be a spectacle. **1794** GODWIN *Caleb Williams* 110 A man who.. must stand alone the spectacle and admiration of all ages of the world. **1805–6** CARY *Dante, Inf.* XXIX. 130 And his rare wisdom Abbagliato show'd A spectacle for all. **1837** CARLYLE *Fr. Rev.* II. v. xii, There he stands, with unimpeachable passivity,.. a spectacle to men.

3. a. A thing seen or capable of being seen; something presented to the view, esp. of a striking or unusual character; a sight. Also *fig.*

1434 MISYN *Mending Life* 127 Odyr says þat contemplacion is free sight in þe spectakyls of wysdom. **1509** HAWES *Past. Pleas.* xx. (Percy Soc.) 97 Alas! thought I, this is no spectacle To fede myn eyne, whiche ar now all blynde. *a* **1540** BARNES *Wks.* (1573) 346/2 S. Augustine sayth, Let vs not loue any visible spectakilles lest.. by louing shadowes we be brought in to darknes. **1600** SHAKS. *A.Y.L.* II. i. 44 But what said Iaques? Did he not moralize this spectacle? **1648** WILKINS *Math. Magic* I. x. 66 Either of them might joyntly behold the same spectacles. **1784** COWPER *Task* I. 476 The paralytic.. sits, Spectatress both and spectacle, a sad And silent cypher. **1794** R. J. SULIVAN *View Nat.* II. 15 The spectacle has in it something almost supernatural. **1829** *Chapters Phys. Sci.* 315 To observe this spectacle the back of the spectator must be turned towards the sun. **1839** FR. A. KEMBLE *Resid. in Georgia* (1863) 32 How shall I describe to you the spectacle which was presented to me. **1849** MACAULAY *Hist. Eng.* v. I. 645 Lord Stawell.. was punished by having a corpse suspended in chains at his park gate. In such spectacles originated many tales of terror.

b. The sight or view *of* something.

1625 in Foster *Eng. Factories Ind.* (1909) III. 56 Whole rabbles of people, whose revengefull eyes never glutted themselves to behould the spectacle of our mizeries. 1658 in *Verney Mem.* (1907) II. 138 Trobled with the specktikill of a discontented sister. 1780 BENTHAM *Princ. Legisl.* xiv. §1 The spectacle of your suffering gives me at least for a time a feeling of pleasure. 1816 SCOTT *Old Mort.* xxxii, The spectacle of their hurried and harassed retreat. 1852 H. ROGERS *Ecl. Faith* (1853) 3 The spectacle of the interminable controversies..occupied the mind of Germany. 1874 L. STEPHEN *Hours in Library* (1892) I. v. 185 The spectacle of a man tortured by a life-long repentance.

4. a. A sight, show, or exhibition *of* a specified character or description.

1484 CAXTON *Curiall* 5 They only that ben hyest enhaunsed ben after theyr despoyntement as a spectacle of enuye, of detraction, or of hate. 1665 MANLEY *Grotius' Low C. Wars* 681 Both near at hand, and far off, nothing [was seen] but terrible spectacles of horrour and dying. 1671 MILTON *P.R.* I. 415 A poor miserable captive thrall,..A spectacle of ruin or of scorn. 1746 HERVEY *Medit.* (1818) 50 How many dismal hours did that illustrious Sufferer hang, a spectacle of woe to God, to angels, and to men! 1791 BURKE *Corr.* (1844) III. 219 A spectacle of suffering royalty. 1839 FR. A. KEMBLE *Resid. in Georgia* (1863) 65 Such another spectacle of filthy disorder I never beheld.

b. With descriptive adjs. denoting the impression (agreeable, imposing, or otherwise) conveyed by the thing seen.

(*a*) 1560 DAUS tr. *Sleidane's Comm.* 115b, The same woulde be a moste pleasaunt syght, and spectacle for the Lutherians. 1580 LYLY *Euphues* (Arb.) 433 Your eyes being too olde to iudge of so rare a spectacle. 1664 POWER *Exp. Philos.* I. 6 The Gray, or Horse-Fly: Her eye is an incomparable pleasant spectacle. 1698 FRYER *Acc. E. India & P.* 76 In the mean while Nature affords us a pleasant Spectacle for this Season. 1718 LADY M. W. MONTAGU *Let. to Lady Rich* 10 Oct., The shops being all set in rows so regularly well lighted, they made up a very agreeable spectacle. 1845 DARWIN *Voy. Nat.* viii. (1879) 162 The sea presented a wonderful and most beautiful spectacle. 1873 HAMERTON *Intell. Life* I. vi. (1876) 31 The magnificent spectacle of the universe.

(*b*) 1590 SPENSER *F.Q.* II. i. 40 Pitifull spectacle, as euer eye did view. 1602 MARSTON *Antonio's Rev.* v. vi, Whose hand presents this gory spectacle? 1653 H. COGAN tr. *Pinto's Trav.* ix. 30 Which was so dreadful a spectacle to us, as we had not the power to cry out. 1726 SWIFT *Gulliver* II. iv, The beggars..gave me the most horrid spectacles..a European eye beheld. 1740 RICHARDSON *Pamela* (1824) I. 77, I shan't be able to stir out this day or two, for I am a frightful spectacle! 1837 DISRAELI *Venetia* I. ix, Mrs. Cadurcis indeed offered a most ridiculous spectacle. 1863 BRIGHT *Sp., Amer.* 26 Mar. (1876) 125 Privilege has beheld an afflicting spectacle for many years past.

II. †5. a. A means of seeing; something made of glass; a window or mirror. *Obs.*

*c*1430 LYDG. *Lyfe of our Ladye* (MS. Bodl. 75) fol. 19 Riȝt as þe son percyd þorouȝ glas, Thorouȝ crystal beryl or spectacle, Wiþ oute harme. *c*1430 —— *Min. Poems* (Percy Soc.) 140 By his labour was cristened al this lond, Feith of our lord wex moor cleer than spectacle. 1439 in Sir W. Dugdale *Monast. Angl.* (1823) IV. 553/2 We ordeyne..that ye..have no lokyng nor spectacles owte warde, thorght the wiche ye mythe falle in worldly dilectacyone. 1548 ELYOT, *Specularius*, he that maketh glasse windowes or spectacles, a glasiar. 1576 FLEMING *Panopl. Epist.* 49 Should I set before your eyes, as it were a spectacle or looking glasse, men of great noblenesse and passing fame? 1630 *R. Johnson's Kingd. & Commw.* 130 The first is Temperance, with a Diall and Spectacle.

†b. *fig.* A mirror, model, pattern, or standard.

*c*1430 LYDG. *Min. Poems* (E.E.T.S.) 52 To all virgines merour and spectacle, Off hire merites of hevene crownyd queene. 1483 CAXTON *G. de la Tour* e iiij b, Here is a fair spectacle to euery woman to see in, and conceyue the tyme comynge. 1523 LD. BERNERS *Froiss.* I. cccc. 695 This harde and peryllous aduenture myght well be to hym a spectacle all his lyfe after, and an ensample to all other. *a*1548 HALL *Chron., Hen. VI*, 101 The erles..determined first to ryde to London, as the chefe key, and common spectacle to the whole Realme. *a*1575 tr. *Pol. Verg. Eng. Hist.* (Camden, No. 36) 217 Knowing the owld sayde sawe, that preestes weare the spectacle and looking glasse of the whole worlde.

†c. An illustrative instance or example. *Obs.*

1579 W. WILKINSON *Confut. Fam. Love* 65b, Hee [Judas] should be a notable spectacle of God's vengeance. 1632 LITHGOW *Trav.* x. 489 When the Starres of great states decline.., and [are] made the deplored-for spectacles of the inconstancy of fortune. 1656 EARL MONM. tr. *Boccalini's Advts. fr. Parnass.* I. viii. (1674) 10 Through their Masters ingratitude and cruelty..they became the spectacle of all brutish usage.

6. a. A device for assisting defective eyesight, or for protecting the eyes from dust, light, etc., consisting of two glass lenses set in a frame which is supported on the nose, and kept in place by side-pieces passing over the ears. Usually in *pl.*

sing. *c*1386 [see c]. 1415 HOCCLEVE *To Sir J. Oldcastle* 417 Right as a spectacle helpith feeble sighte, Whan a man on the book redith or writ. 1447 BOKENHAM *Seyntys* (Roxb.) 27 Myn eyne bleynte Shuld be, ner helpe of a spectacle. 1589 PUTTENHAM *Eng. Poesie* III. xxv. (Arb.) 311 There be artes and methodes..by which the naturall is in some sorte relieued, as th'eye by his spectacle. 1628 DONNE *Sermons* 289, I thank him..that assists me with a Spectacle when my sight grows old. *c*1640 J. SMYTH *Lives of Berkeleys* (1883) II. 408 Reading much, yet never used spectacle or other help. 1728 CHAMBERS *Cycl.* s.v. *Eye*, This Membrane, like a Kind of Spectacle, covers the Eye.

pl. *c*1430 LYDG. *London Lackpenny* Min. Poems (Percy Soc.) 105 What will you copen or by? Fyne felt hattes, or spectacles to reede? *c*1500 *Blowbol's Test.* 101 in Hazl. *E.P.P.* I. 96 No man may his letters know nor se, Allethough he looke trughe spectacles thre. 1561 T. NORTON *Calvin's Inst.* I. 11b, Being holpen with spectacles,..they begin to read distinctlie. 1617 MORYSON *Itin.* III. 56 And because they cast up sand upon the passengers, some curious men use spectacles of glasse to preserve their eyes. 1656 RIDGLEY *Pract. Physick* 129 Use of Spectacles weakneth the sight, unlesse you wear them for need. 1728 PEMBERTON *Newton's Philos.* 383 Hence may be understood why spectacles made with convex glasses help the sight in old age. 1761 *Phil. Trans.* LII. 124 Plain spectacles..do not appear to have been known till a hundred years after. 1831 BREWSTER *Optics* xxxviii. 320 Spectacles and reading glasses are among the simplest and most useful of optical instruments. 1859 *Habits of Gd. Society* iii. 154, I am one of those people who wear spectacles for fear of seeing anything with the naked eye. 1887 RUSKIN *Præterita* II. 233 Tourists who pass their time mostly in looking at black rocks through blue spectacles.

transf. 1593 SHAKS. *2 Hen. VI*, III. ii. 112, I..bid mine eyes be packing.., And call'd them blinde and duskie Spectacles.

b. In phr. ***a pair of spectacles.*** †Also without *of.*

1423 *Test. Ebor.* (Surtees) III. 75 De xxs receptis pro pare de spectakeles de argento et deaurato. 1463 *Bury Wills* (Camden) 15 A peyre spectaclys of syluir and ouyr gylt. 1529 MORE *Dyaloge* I. Wks. 147/1 And so should the scripture stand them in as good stede, as a paire of spectacles shold stand a blinde freer. 1589 PUTTENHAM *Eng. Poesie* III. xxv. (Arb.) 311 No lesse to be laughed at, then for one that can see well inough, to vse a paire of spectacles. 1666 PEPYS *Diary* 24 Dec., I this evening did buy me a pair of green spectacles, to see whether they will help my eyes or no. 1726 SWIFT *Gulliver* I. ii, A pair of spectacles (which I sometimes use for the weakness of mine eyes). 1756–7 tr. *Keysler's Trav.* (1760) III. 374 On the other side is another cardinal with a large pair of spectacles on his nose. 1827 FARADAY *Chem. Manip.* xxiii. (1842) 590 A pair of spectacles, with side as well as front glasses.

c. *fig.* A means or medium through which anything is viewed or regarded; a point of view, prepossession, prejudice, etc.

*c*1386 CHAUCER *Wife's T.* 347 Povert a spectacle is, as thinkith me, Thurgh which he may his verray frendes se. 1579 W. WILKINSON *Confut. Fam. Love* 16 He that putteth on the Christall spectacles of Gods word. 1598 BARCKLEY *Felic. Man* (1631) 648 We behold our owne faults with spectacles that make things shew lesse. 1606 *Proc. agst. Late Traitors* 356 False informations, which are rightly called the spectacles of error. 1644 JESSOP *Angel Ephesus* 62 One of late looking on his words with an Episcopall paire of spectacles, blesseth himselfe at the reading of them. 1676 HOBBES *Iliad* Pref., They that..look upon it with the oldest spectacles of a Critick, may approve it. 1711 *Countrey-Man's Lett. Curat* 29 All the World hitherto had thought, these Horses and Chariots of Fire had been the Prophets Guard not his Danger; But they have wanted the Doctor's Spectacles. 1861 [see ROSE-COLOURED *a.* 3]. 1869 J. MARTINEAU *Ess.* II. 5 They offer you the spectacles they did not use. 1889 *Spectator* 28 Dec., He early recognised that it is a scholar's duty to interpret what he sees simply, without the spectacles of prepossession.

†d. A device for restricting the view of horses.

In both passages a rendering of It. *occhiali.*

1632 J. HAYWARD tr. *Biondi's Eromena* 3 The horse with his spetacles and covering. 1656 EARL MONM. tr. *Boccalini's Pol. Touchstone* in *Advts. fr. Parnass.* 395 The jealous Spaniards keep..a caveson upon his nose, a bit in his mouth, a spectacle on his eyes, as if they were afraid of him.

7. a. *ellipt.* A species of moth.

1819 SAMOUELLE *Entomol. Compend.* 422 *Noctua triplasea.* The dark Spectacle. *Noctua asclepiades.* The light Spectacle. 1832 J. RENNIE *Consp. Butterfl. & M.* 92 The Dark Spectacle (*Abrostola triplasia*) appears in July. *Ibid.*, The Spectacle (*Abrostola Asclepiadis*) appears the end of July.

b. *Zool.* A marking resembling a pair of spectacles.

1884 COUES *Key N. Amer. Birds* 815 Spectacled Guillemot... A pair of white spectacles on the eyes, and whitish about base of bill. 1908 E. M. GORDON *Indian Folk Tales* viii. (1909) 76 Two varieties of *cobrā*, one with the spectacles and the other without them.

c. *pl.* A batsman's score of two zeros or 'duck's eggs' in a cricket match of two innings. Freq. in ***a pair of spectacles.*** Cf. PAIR *sb.*[1] 2b. †Also (*rarely*) in sing., a score of zero in one innings.

1835 *Bell's Life* 13 Sept. 3/4 Good put a spectacle on him first ball. 1865 *F. Lillywhite's Guide to Cricketers* 27 The ominous 'spectacles' have been worn by the best sighted men. 1892 in W. A. Bettesworth *Chats Cricket Field* (1910) 455. 1893 *Whitaker's Alm.* 613 Unlucky enough to make spectacles for his side against Middlesex. 1898 *Globe* 1 Sept. 5/5 Yesterday in a match..he made a pair of spectacles. 1907 E. V. LUCAS *Hambledon Men* 230 It is believed he never made two noughts, or 'a pair of spectacles', in any match of note! 1979 *Wisden Cricket Monthly* Dec. 21/3 Who got a 'pair of spectacles' for Yorkshire on his first appearance?

8. a. *pl.* The glazed openings in the cab-screen of a locomotive.

1878 F. S. WILLIAMS *Midl. Railw.* 503 We..see through the 'spectacles' of the powerful little engine..that [etc.]. 1896 *B'ham Weekly Post* 15 Feb. 8/7 The lid of the sand-box was blown off, and, rising in the air, was shot through the spectacles of the engine.

b. The device consisting of two frames containing respectively red and green glass worked at night in connexion with a railway semaphore.

1881 *Standard* 17 Dec. 2/5 When we got to the up-distant signal I called..attention to the fact that the arm and spectacle were thickly covered with snow. 1889 G. FINDLAY *Eng. Railway* 68 With the arm is a frame containing coloured glasses, and termed 'spectacles'.

c. A mechanical device attached to a phonograph (see quot.).

1889 *Pall Mall G.* 11 Mar. 1/1, I have just finished some improvements in the spectacle (a term given to the mechanical device holding the receiver and transmitter).

9. *attrib.* and *Comb.* (in sense 6), as ***spectacle-frame, lens, -mark, years; spectacle-seller, -user, -wiper; spectacle-bestrid, -blurred, -less, -like, -shaped*** adjs.

1784 COWPER *Task* II. 439 At conventicle, where worthy men..strain celestial themes Through the prest nostril, *spectacle-bestrid. 1932 W. FAULKNER *Light in August* (1933) xiii. 291 Misshapen, with his gray stubble and his dark *spectacle-blurred eyes. 1879 *Cassell's Techn. Educ.* II. 179/1 In the manufacture of blue steel *spectacle-frames. 1898 WATTS-DUNTON *Aylwin* xv. iii, A strongly marked indented line..made by long-continued pressure of the spectacle frame. 1862 *Catal. Internat. Exhib., Brit.* II. No. 2899 Concave, convex, and meniscus *spectacle lenses. 1889 *Longman's Mag.* Oct. 619 Her brother's helplessness in his *spectacleless condition. 1663 GERBIER *Counsel* 13 Those *Spectacle-like cant Windows, which are of Glasse on all sides. 1796 P. RUSSELL *Indian Serpents Coromandel* 8 The spectacle-like mark on the hood. 1895 *Oracle Encycl.* II. 98 Specimens [of the Cobra] destitute of the *spectacle-mark come from the E. Indies. 1648 HEXHAM II, *Een bril.. verkooper*, a *Spectacle..Seller. 1847 A SMEE *Vision* 50 The knowledge possessed by even the better order of spectacle-sellers. 1802 SHAW *Gen. Zool.* III. I. 409 The neck marked above by a large black and white *spectacle-shaped spot. 1838 WELLINGTON *Lett. to Miss J.* (1890) 102, I return..the *Spectacle Wipers which you was so good as to send me. 1657 R. AUSTEN *Fruit-trees* ii. 10 What a shame is it for a man to begin to learne his letters and to spell at *spectacle yeares!

b. In names of animals or birds having markings round the eyes, or elsewhere, suggestive of a pair of spectacles, as **spectacle bat, owl, snake, thrush, warbler.** (Cf. SPECTACLED *a.* 2.)

1827 GRIFFITH tr. *Cuvier* V. 69 *Phyllostoma Perspicillatum* (*Spectacle Bat). 1787 LATHAM *Suppl. Gen. Syn. Birds* I. 50 *Spectacle Owl..is less stout than the Cinereous Owl. 1829 GRIFFITH tr. *Cuvier* VI. 83 The Spectacle Owl,..*Strix perspicillata.* 1802 SHAW *Gen. Zool.* III. II. 409 *Spectacle Snake... The Coluber Naja, or Cobra de Capello, is a native of India. 1840 *Penny Cycl.* XVI. 60/2 The Asiatic species.., Spectacle-snake of the English,..may be considered as the type of the genus. 1783 LATHAM *Gen. Synop. Birds* II. I. 61 *Spectacle Thrush. *Ibid.* 452 *Spectacle Warbler..[has] a naked yellowish wrinkled skin, which encircles the eye all round, giving the appearance of wearing spectacles.

10. Special combs.: **spectacle-case**, a case of leather or other material in which spectacles are kept when not in use; **spectacle clew**, a form of double clew for a sail; **spectacle eye**, a spectacle glass; **spectacle furnace** (see quot.); **spectacle plate**, = sense 8a; **spectacles-seat**, *slang*, the nose; **†spectacle telescope**, a binocular telescope or field-glass.

1597 *Shuttleworths' Acc.* (Chetham Soc.) 108 A *specta[c]le cace, vj[d]. 1690 *Lond. Gaz.* No. 2079/4 Lost.., a Black Shagreen Spectacle-Case. 1866 J. MARTINEAU *Ess.* I. 47 The spectacle-case may well be empty, if the glasses are already on the nose. 1863 *Appleby's Handbk. Mach. & Iron Work* 92 *Spectacle Clues, all sizes—Black, 35/0 per cwt. 1884 KNIGHT *Dict. Mech.* Suppl. 200/1 Ear-ring clew... Spectacle clew. 1862 *Catal. Internat. Exhib., Brit.* No. 2887 Lump of Brazilian pebble, from which slabs are cut and ground into *spectacle eyes. 1875 KNIGHT *Dict. Mech.* 2257 **Spectacle-furnace*,..a furnace with two tap-holes, one above the other. 1900 *Daily Express* 19 June 5/7 Alongside the driver is a fireman,..frowning..through the *spectacle plate. 1895 MEREDITH *Amazing Marriage* xvi, Ben received a second spanking cracker on the *spectacles-seat. 1728 CHAMBERS *Cycl.* s.v., F. Cherubin, a Capuchin, describes a kind of *Spectacle-Telescopes, for the viewing of remote Objects with both Eyes; hence called Binoculi.

‖**spectacle** (spɛktakl), *sb.*[2] [F.: see prec.]

1. = SPECTACLE *sb.*[1] 1.

1749 CHESTERF. *Lett.* ccviii. (1792) 294 Go to whatever assemblies or *spectacles* people of fashion go to. 1768 EARL CARLISLE in Jesse *Selwyn & Contemp.* (1843) II. 336, I shall go to Fontainbleau on Saturday next. It is to be extremely dull; no *spectacle* at court. 1792 A. YOUNG *Trav. France* 217 If cheapness of living, *spectacles*, and pretty women, are a man's objects.., let him live at Venice. 1801 HELEN M. WILLIAMS *Fr. Rep.* I. xi. 110 The love of a *spectacle* is, you know, the ruling passion of the Parisians. 1837 LOCKHART *Scott* III. xi. 370 So mounted,..he witnessed the great closing *spectacle* on the *Champ de Mars.*

2. *spec.* A piece of stage-display or pageantry, as contrasted with real drama.

1752 T. SCROPE in Jesse *Selwyn & Contemp.* (1843) I. 149 Their *spectacles* were very grand, and their stage far surpasses ours; but their plays, in my opinion, fall as far short. 1835 T. MITCHELL *Acharn. of Aristoph.* 1059 *note*, The progress of the piece evidently requires here some little pageant or *spectacle.* 1860 *Once a Week* 14 July 70/1 The young Thespians..had to appear as Peace and Plenty, amidst a great display of red-light, at the end of a grand *spectacle*, which was drawing uncommonly well.

'**spectacle**, *v. rare.* [f. SPECTACLE *sb.*[1]]

1. *trans.* To scrutinize through spectacles.

*a*1734 NORTH *Lives* (1826) III. 131 The barons, each one after another, spectacled it over and over, and scarce believed their own eyes. 1888 MURDOCH *Readings* Ser. II. 47 Oh, ye may spectacle me as much as ye like, my fine man.

2. To provide with spectacles.

1880 *Sat. Rev.* No. 1295. 235 Of late years the practice of putting children into spectacles has increased with alarming rapidity... Spectacling them may be a wholesome preventive.

spectacled ('spɛktək(ə)ld), *a.* [f. as prec.]

1. Provided with or wearing spectacles.

1607 SHAKS. *Cor.* II. i. 221 All tongues speake of him, and the bleared sights Are spectacled to see him. 1624 MIDDLETON *Game at Chess* II. i, When the Inquisitors came all spectacled To pick out syllables. **1779** *Mirror* No. 8, Those grave personages, whom you may observe daily.. rising in a coffee-house in the full dignity of a spectacled nose. **1818** SCOTT *Hrt. Midl.* vi, Half-scared by the.. spectacled old lady, by whom these tempting stores are watched. **1852** R. S. SURTEES *Sponge's Sp. Tour* xxix. 175, 'I think it will be a fine day,' he said,.. turning his spectacled face up to the clouds. **1886** W. J. TUCKER *E. Europe* 215 A couple of spectacled professional gentlemen.

b. With distinguishing adjs.

1884 G. ALLEN *Philistia* I. 12 There was honesty.. in those hazy blue-spectacled eyes. **1896** *Idler* Mar. 247/2 This innocent-looking little gold-spectacled bald-headed gentleman.

2. In names of birds, animals, etc., having spectacle-shaped markings or the appearance of wearing spectacles (see quots. and SPECTACLE *sb.*[1] 9 b).

1831 GRIFFITH tr. *Cuvier* IX. Syn. 21 *Spectacled Alligator, *Crocodilus (Alligator) Sclerops.* **1835** *Penny Cycl.* IV. 87 The *Spectacled Bear, *Ursus Ornatus* of F. Cuvier, inhabits the Cordilleras of the Andes in Chili. **1894** LYDEKKER *Roy. Nat. Hist.* II. 23 The spectacled bear of the Peruvian Andes.. is a small-sized black species. **1830** GRIFFITH tr. *Cuvier* XI. 188 The *Spectacled Cayman (*Crocodilus Sclerops*) is the most common in Cayenne. **1854** OWEN in *Orr's Circ. Sci., Org. Nat.* I. 197 They sustain a fold of integument, peculiarly coloured in some species—*e.g.*, the *spectacled cobra. *c* **1880** *Cassell's Nat. Hist.* IV. 304 The natives say that the Spectacled Cobra is a Snake of the city or town. **1872** COUES *N. Amer. Birds* 292 *Spectacled Eider,.. a whitish space round eye, bounded by black. **1884** *Ibid.* 815 *Uria carbo*,.. *Spectacled Guillemot. **1896** LYDEKKER *Roy. Nat. Hist.* V. 298 The little *spectacled salamander (*Salamandrina perspicillata*) of Italy. **1831** GRIFFITH tr. *Cuvier* IX. 274 Named *Spectacled Serpent, from a black line drawn on the widened part of its disk in the form of spectacles. **1861** HULME tr. *Moquin-Tandon* II. v. i. 259 The Naia or Spectacled Serpents—called also the Hooded Snakes. **1834** *Encycl. Metrop.* (1845) XXII. 397/1 The Snakemen [of India].. never use in their shows any other poisonous Snake than the *Spectacled Snake. **1871** *Cassell's Nat. Hist.* I. 262 Leaf-like organs, often of the most extraordinary forms (see the Head of the *Spectacled Vampire). **1829** GRIFFITH tr. *Cuvier* VI. 446 *Spectacled Warbler, *Sylvia Conspicillata.* **1894–5** LYDEKKER *Roy. Nat. Hist.* III. 493 The spectacled warbler builds its nest in a small bush about a foot from the ground.

spectacle-glass. [SPECTACLE *sb.*[1]]

1. A lens of a pair of spectacles.

a **1583** in Halliwell *Rara Mathem.* (1841) 40 For makinge of the smallest sorte of them, commonly called spectacle glasses. **1697** *C'tess D'Aunoy's Trav.* (1706) 146 Proportionably as a Man's Fortune rises, he increases in the largeness of his Spectacle-Glasses and wears them higher upon his Nose. **1761–9** tr. *Voltaire's Works* XXVI. 196 (Jod.), A lentular spectacle-glass. **1852** MRS. STOWE *Uncle Tom's C.* ix, He.. seemed particularly busy in clearing his throat and wiping his spectacle-glasses. **1879** *Cassell's Techn. Educ.* II. 177/1 Preference is usually given to bi-convex and bi-concave spectacle glasses.

†**2.** A lens used as, or in, a microscope or telescope. *Obs.*

1671 GREW *Anat. Pl.* I. i. (1682) 2 Magnified with a good Spectacle-Glass. *Ibid.* 20 A lesser sort, which by the help only of a good Spectacle Glass may be observ'd. *a* **1697** AUBREY *Lives* (1898) I. 283 Anno 1678, he [Halley] added a spectacle-glasse to the shadowe-vane of the lesser arch of the sea-quadrant (or back-staffe).

spectacle-maker. [SPECTACLE *sb.*[1] 6, 7 c.]

1. One who makes spectacles.

1530 PALSGR. 274/1 Spectacle maker, *lunettier.* **1611** COTGR., *Besiclier*, a Spectacle-maker. **1674** BOYLE *Excell. Theol.* I. iv. 168 Des-Cartes does acknowledge with other writers, that perspective-glasses were.. first found out.. casually by one Metius, a Dutch spectacle-maker. **1728** CHAMBERS *Cycl.* s.v. *Telescope*, Fifty Years afterwards, a Telescope.. was made.. by a Spectacle-maker of Middlebourg. **1839** *Penny Cycl.* XIV. 119/1 [List of City Companies] Spectacle-makers. **1883** *Encycl. Brit.* XVI. 258/1 Not only were spectacle-makers the first to produce glass magnifiers (or simple microscopes), but [etc.].

2. One who makes no score in either innings in a game of cricket.

1893 *Star* 8 July 4/2 The compiler has been cruel enough to set out a full.. list of spectacle makers during the whole term of years.

spectacular (spɛk'tækjʊlə(r)), *a.* and *sb.* [f. L. *spectacul-um* SPECTACLE *sb.*[1]]

1. a. Of the nature of a spectacle or show; striking or imposing as a display. Also *fig.*

1682 G. HICKES *Serm. bef. Ld. Mayor 30 Jan.* 4 The Spectacular sports were concluded. **1865** *Daily Tel.* 20 Nov. 5/1 The true interests of the drama may in the end be advanced by its separation from merely spectacular entertainments. **1876** BLACK *Madcap Violet* xliv. 382 That was all very well as a spectacular exhibition. **1884** *Nonconf. & Indep.* 13 Nov. 1094/1 The Lord Mayor's Show was a more ambitious and spectacular pageant than ever. **1934** J. B. PRIESTLEY *Eng. Journey* ix. 316 Both my companions knew about this yard, which had been a spectacular failure in which over a million of money had been lost.

b. *absol.* That which appeals to the eye.

1876 J. PARKER *Paracl.* I. xvi. 257 The carnal mind loves the spectacular, the marvellous. **1896** J. M. MANLY *Introd. Macbeth* p. xxiii, The list of plays and masques indicates a growing tendency to the spectacular during the 2nd decade of the 17th century.

2. Pertaining to, characteristic of, spectacles or shows.

1864 *Daily Tel.* 16 Aug., They are fond of spectacular magnificence. **1876** MELLOR *Priesthood* vi. 293 It is easy.. to surround any ceremony.. with a spectacular splendour which captivates the imagination. **1883** E. H. ROLLINS *New Eng. Bygones* 240 That climate.. spread over the landscape a great spectacular glory.

3. Addicted to, fond of, spectacles.

1894 *Daily Tel.* 2 July 7/2 All the glory of uniform and the glow of colour beloved by the most spectacular nation in the world.

4. As *sb.* A spectacular display. Also *spec.* a radio or television programme, entertainment, etc., produced on a lavish or spectacular scale.

1890 *Pall Mall G.* 8 Apr. 7/2 An amphitheatre.. in which spectaculars on a grand scale might be produced before a half-million spectators. **1953** *N.Y. Times* 3 Jan. 8/5 Thirteen 'spectaculars' will be affected, including the giant British Overseas Airways sign, Cunard and Canadian Pacific Lines displays and advertisements for gin, wine, radio and television. **1954** *Ibid.* 28 Mar. x13/1 Its [*sc.* NBC's] big feature.. will be a series of costly and lavish ninety-minute 'spectaculars'—opera, drama, musical comedy, circuses, ice shows, etc. **1958** *Times* 28 Mar. 3/4 A television 'spectacular' transmitted by the National Broadcasting Company. **1966** *Punch* 8 June 858/2 *The Disorderly Knights*, a historical novel of the sixteenth century by Dorothy Dunnett, is a five hundred page spectacular: enormous in every possible way. **1969** *Listener* 20 Feb. 249/3 Radio drama may miss its former purse-power, and the multi-studio 'spectacular' is a fashion of the past. **1971** *Scope* (S. Afr.) 19 Mar. 4/2 It was a golfing spectacular the old pros will talk about for years. **1978** S. BRILL *Teamsters* x. 391 The ceremony and dinner party were followed by an entertainment spectacular put on by.. Barbara McNair, Billy Daniels, Ed McMahon and Frank Sinatra.

Hence **spec,tacu'larity**, spectacular quality or character.

1883 HOWELLS *Woman's Reason* xii, The bare spectacularity of the keeping.. must all be eloquent of a boarding-house. **1891** —— *Imperative Duty* 6 A certain civic grandiosity, a sort of lion-and-unicorn spectacularity.

spec'tacularism. [f. SPECTACULAR *a.* and *sb.* + -ISM.] Spectacular character or quality.

1888 G. B. SHAW in *Star* 18 July 2/4 These are but details, only to be noted at Covent Garden, because so much is there sacrificed to spectacularism on the highest scale. **1931** *Aberdeen Press & Jrnl.* 14 Oct. 6/4 The spectacularism of Noel Coward.

spec'tacularly, *adv.* [f. the adj.] In a spectacular fashion; after the manner of a spectacle.

1859 DICKENS *T. Two Cities* II. i, He was permitted to be seen, spectacularly poring over large books. **1897** *Advance* (Chicago) 14 Jan. 43 The '7,000 free Christmas dinners', spectacularly served in barracks. **1901** *Munsey's Mag.* XXIV. 838/2 They moved slowly and spectacularly up the avenue.

†**spec'taculous**, *a. Obs.*[-1] [f. L. *spectacul-um* SPECTACLE *sb.*[1]] Spectacular.

1632 LITHGOW *Trav.* VI. 271 Setting them on their Altars, O spectaculous Images! adoring them for gods.

'spectant, *a. Her.* [a. L. *spectant-*, stem of *spectans*, pres. pple. of *spectāre* to look.] (See quot.)

1825–7 W. BERRY *Encycl. Her.* I, *Spectant*, at gaze, or looking forward, sometimes termed *in full aspect*. The term is, likewise, applied to any animal looking upwards, with the nose bendwise.

spectate (spɛk'teɪt), *v.* [f. L. *spectāt-*, ppl. stem of *spectāre* to look.]

1. *intr.* and *trans.* To look or gaze (at).

1709 [implied at *spectating ppl. a.* and *vbl. sb.* below]. **1854** DE QUINCEY in 'H. A. Page' *Life* (1877) II. xviii. 88 The thing to be spectated, or in base vulgar, the spectacle.

2. *intr.* [Back-formation from SPECTATOR.] To be a spectator rather than a participant, esp. at a sporting event.

1929 *Amer. Speech* IV. 501 An advertisement in an Iowa paper reads: 'Ladies Only at the Promenade Roller Rink Thursday afternoon, 2:30 to 5. No men will be allowed to skate or to spectate.' **1971** H. C. RAE *Marksman* II. iii. 118 On Sunday afternoons.. the boys meet and play soccer.. Occasionally Gordon went there, to play or to spectate. I'm not sure which. **1974** 'P. B. YUILL' *Bornless Keeper* xiii. 125 He enjoyed spectating at a good snarling-match. **1980** L. BIRNBACH et al. *Official Preppy Handbk.* 90/2 They.. provide entertainment for the Prep women who spectate when they're not flinging a ball about themselves.

Hence **spec'tating** *ppl. a.* and *vbl. sb.*

1709 in Ashton *Social Life Reign Q. Anne* (1882) I. 287 A Gentleman sitting on the Coach, civilly salutes the Spectating Company. **1858** DE QUINCEY *Wks.* VII. App. 329 To the poor spectator (unless paid for spectating) [it] is sympathetically painful. **1942** *Amer. Speech* XVII. 24 'Tackle the shoe problem—shoes for *spectating*' was the heading of an advertisement of a Department Store, Oct. 11, 1941. **1966** *Listener* 12 May 697/2 Only a gigantic comic talent.. could.. communicate the comic grandeur to a spectating, as opposed to a reading, audience. **1978** D. FRANCIS *Trial Run* xix. 234 I'd ridden in races in that state .. so why fret at some gentle spectating.

spec'tation. *rare.* [ad. L. *spectātio*, noun of action f. *spectāre* to look.] The action of beholding, observing, or inspecting.

1638 *Briefe Relat.* 16 The Execution of the Lords Censure in Starre-Chamber,.. at the spectation whereof the number of people was so great [etc.]. **1940** R. G. COLLINGWOOD *Ess. Metaphysics* xxxi. 307 The mere act of spectation could in time generate the idea of a cause.

†**spec'tative**, *a. Obs.*[-0] [ad. L. *spectātīv-us.*] (See quot.)

1656 BLOUNT *Glossogr.*, *Spectative*, that belongs to speculation; speculative, contemplative.

spectator (spɛk'teɪtə(r)). Also 6–7 **spectatour.** [a. L. *spectātor*, agent-noun f. *spectāre* to look, whence also F. *spectateur* (1540), It. *spettatore*, Sp. and Pg. *espectador.*]

1. a. One who sees, or looks on at, some scene or occurrence; a beholder, onlooker, observer.

a **1586** SIDNEY *Arcadia* II. x. (1912) 211 [He] thought no eyes of sufficient credite in such a matter, but his owne; and therefore came him selfe to be actor, and spectator. *c* **1645** HOWELL *Lett.* (1650) II. 27 There is a true saying, 'That the spectator oft times sees more than the gamester'. **1651** HOBBES *Leviath.* II. xxxi. 189 A signe is not a signe to him that giveth it, but to him to whom it is made; that is, to the spectator. **1677** HUBBARD *Narrative* (1865) I. 16 In such Passages as were variously reported by the Actors, or Spectators, that which seemed most probable is only inserted. **1774** GOLDSM. *Nat. Hist.* (1776) II. 205 Even the agonies of the former rather terrify the spectators, than torment the patient. **1794** MRS. RADCLIFFE *Myst. Udolpho* xxxviii, Henri was a silent and astonished spectator of the scene. **1828** LYTTON *Pelham* xvi, There is some trick afloat to which we may as well be spectators. **1841** JAMES *Brigand* xxxii, The hall was totally void of spectators.

†**b.** *spec.* A scientific observer. *Obs. rare.*

1646 SIR T. BROWNE *Pseud. Ep.* I. iv. (1686) 10 They were conceived by the first Spectators to be but one Animal. **1787** *Families of Plants* I. 259 Jacquin, Brown, and other Spectators consider it as a distinct Genus.

2. a. *spec.* One who is present at, and has a view or sight of, anything in the nature of a show or spectacle.

1590 SPENSER *F.Q.* II. iv. 27 The treachour.. Me leading, in a secret corner layd, The sad spectatour of my Tragedie. **1611** SHAKS. *Wint. T.* IV. i. 20 Imagine me (Gentle Spectators) that I now may be In faire Bohemia. **1690** T. BURNET *Theory Earth* II. 214 This being the last act and close of all humane affairs, it ought to.. satisfie the spectators, and end in a general applause. **1716** LADY M. W. MONTAGU *Let. C'tess Mar* 14 Sept., All the men of quality at Vienna were spectators. **1784** COWPER *Task* v. 878 Gods .. that sit Amus'd spectators of this bustling stage. **1814** JANE AUSTEN *Mansf. Park* (1851) 103 Fanny began to be their only audience, and sometimes as prompter, sometimes as spectator, was often very useful. **1855** KINGSLEY *Westw. Ho!* xxvi, He had been a pitying spectator of the tragedy. **1897** 'SARAH TYTLER' *Lady Jean's Son* x. 178 The opposite houses, crowded from top to bottom with spectators.

attrib. **1639** COKAINE *Masque* Dram. Wks. (1874) 13 When they have danced all they intended, the Lar, or one of the Masquers, invites the spectator-ladies with this song to join with them. **1891** *Daily News* 12 Oct. 3/5 The spectator portion of the baths was crowded to its utmost capacity.

b. *spectator sport*, a sport which affords good entertainment for spectators as well as for participants. Also *transf.* and *fig.*

1943 *Amer. Speech* XVIII. 95 The American 'spectator-sports' (of clothes) has been mistranslated in at least one advertisement [in New Zealand] as 'spectacular-sports'. **1944** M. LASKI *Love on Supertax* xi. 109 Burn all those clothes you've got on.. and get back into a decent unpretentious spectator-sports-suit. **1954** *Encounter* Feb. 57/1 The fascination of the great spectator-sports—soccer, athletics, cricket, lawn tennis—is partly due to the effect of the game on its audience. **1969** A. GLYN *Dragon Variation* ix. 268 Well, call this [*sc.* chess] a spectator sport, twenty goddam minutes and nobody's moved a thing. Give me tennis! **1975** *New Yorker* 10 Feb. 110/3 With hard times upon us there may be a question in the minds of even the least dedicated office-holders both here and in Albany about how long their hard-pressed constituents will let them get away with treating representative government as a minor spectator sport. **1979** *Guardian* 12 June 8/1 Watching election coverage all through the night is a great spectator sport.

3. Used as the title of various periodical publications. Also *Comb.*

Freq. with distinguishing epithets, as *The Catholic, Country, Modern, Monthly, Provincial, Temperance Spectator* (published at various dates between 1792 and 1866).

1711–14 ADDISON (*title*), The Spectator. **1711** STEELE *Spect.* No. 20 ¶2 Ever since the *Spectator* appear'd. **1714** ADDISON *Ibid.* No. 567 ¶8, I intend shortly to publish a *Spectator*, that shall not have a single Vowel in it. **1728–37** (*title*), The Universal Spectator, and Weekly Journal. **1744** ELIZA HEYWOOD *Female Spectator* I. 5 Whatever Productions I shall be favour'd with from these Ladies.. will be exhibited under the general Title of *The Female Spectator.* **1755** H. WALPOLE *Lett.* (1846) III. 178 The Spectator-hacked phrases. **1828–** (*title*), The Spectator. A weekly journal of news, politics, literature, and science.

Hence **spec'tatordom**, spectators collectively; **spec'tatorism**, the practice of being a spectator or onlooker at sports or games.

1854 THOREAU *Walden* i. (1863) 49 He was there to represent spectatordom. **1889** *Wykehamist* No. 241. 317/1 There are distinct limits to the use of 'spectatorism'.

spectatorial (spɛktə'tɔərɪəl), *a.* [f. prec.]

1. Pertaining or appropriate to, characteristic of, a spectator.

In earlier examples with reference to SPECTATOR 3.

1712 STEELE *Spect.* No. 336 ¶1, I hope your Spectatorial Authority will give a seasonable Check to the Spread of the Infection. *Ibid.* No. 430 ¶1 All which is submitted to your Spectatorial Vigilance. **1744** ELIZA HEYWOOD *Female Spectator* v. (1748) I. 257 In fine, my spectatorial capacity will permit me to approve of no other entertainments which are paid for. **1889** *Macm. Mag.* May 40 He.. stood in a spectatorial attitude, watching the world through wicked humorous eyes.

2. Forming part of a spectacle.

1783 COLMAN *Prose Sev. Occas.* (1787) III. 73 To introduce a groupe of Spectatorial actors speaking in one part of the Drama and singing in another.

3. Having the characteristics of one or other of the periodicals bearing the title of *Spectator*.

1817 WHEWELL in Todhunter *Acc. Writ.* (1876) II. 21 A magazine or periodical collection of essays upon all subjects, scientific, literary, spectatorial, or any other. **1834** SOUTHEY *Doctor* lxiii. (1848) 134 A painter might describe the facial angle,.. and whether the chin was in the just mean between rueful length and spectatorial brevity. **1891** *Pall Mall G.* 4 Mar. 2/2 Disposing of it in one of those airy generalizations which Spectatorial omniscience is wont to throw off from time to time.

Hence **specta'torially** *adv.*

1930 A. HUXLEY *Brief Candles* 14 People think I'm an excellent psychologist. And I suppose I am. Spectatorially. But I'm a bad experiencer. **1973** *Times Lit. Suppl.* 14 Dec. 1536/5 Our Londoner applauds not a murder, but a representation; and he himself is spectatorially present at a representation, not at a murder. **1980** D. NEWSOME *On Edge of Paradise* vi. 211 Arthur was invited to a number of spectatorially promising occasions.

spectatorship (spɛk'teɪtəʃɪp). [f. as prec.]

† **1.** Presentation to the eyes of spectators. *Obs.*

1607 SHAKS. *Cor.* v. ii. 71 If thou stand'st not i'th state of hanging, or of some death more long in Spectatorship.

2. The state of being a spectator or beholder; the fact of (merely) looking on.

1712 STEELE *Spect.* No. 304 ¶3 Moreover, your first rudimental Essays in Spectatorship were made in your Petitioner's Shop, where you often practised for Hours. **1854** MRS. OLIPHANT *M. Hepburn* III. 248 He stood.. looking forth, if not with the exulting delight of his former spectatorship, at least with..curiosity. **1881** H. JAMES *Portrait of Lady* xv, What is the use of being.. restricted to mere spectatorship at the game of life? **1896** *Eng. Churchm.* 5 Nov. 745/1 England's part in such an event could not.. be one of mere spectatorship.

3. Spectators collectively.

a **1836** CHALMERS *Moral Philos.* vii. Wks. V. 301 It.. will be followed up by the instant and obstreperous glee of a whole host of spectatorship.

spectatory (spɛk'teɪtərɪ). [f. SPECTATOR: see -ORY.]

1. A body of spectators.

1831 *Blackw. Mag.* XXIX. 887 They anticipated or rather turned the tables on the audience or spectatory.

2. The part of a building intended for, or assigned to, spectators.

1829 H. FOOTE *Compan. to Theatres* 135 Such as do not wish to mix in their frolics, may witness them from the spectatory of the theatre. **1836** G. CLARKE *Pompeii* I. 286 Galleries gave access to the spectatory at different elevations. **1837** *Penny Cycl.* IX. 3/2 The spectatory or saloon for the visitors is a rotunda 40 feet in diameter. **1881** P. FITZGERALD *World behind Scenes* I. ii. 21 One of the most difficult questions is how is the *salle* or 'spectatory', as old writers call it—not a bad word either—to be effectively lighted.

spectatress (spɛk'teɪtrɪs). [f. SPECTATOR: see -ESS[1] and cf. next.] A female spectator.

1632 J. HAYWARD tr. *Biondi's Eromena* 101 The Princesse that stood all this while an amazed spectatresse [etc.]. **1703** ROWE *Fair Penit.* v. i, See where she stands! Spectatress of the Mischief which she made. **1759** JOHNSON *Idler* No. 42 ¶5 To be a daily spectatress of his vices. **1799** CAMPBELL *Pleas. Hope* I. 179 She, sad spectatress,.. Watch'd the rude surge his shroudless corse that bore. **1844** *For. Q. Rev.* XXXIII. 440 As soon as she appeared the other spectatresses were eclipsed. **1861** *Sat. Rev.* 21 Dec. 648 Was the Grand Duchess a spectatress of the atrocity?

fig. **1789** E. DARWIN *Bot. Gard.* I. 149 So should young Sympathy, in female form, Climb the tall rock, spectatress of the storm. **1791** COWPER *Iliad* XI. 89 Discord, spectatress terrible. **1836** THIRLWALL *Greece* III. xix. 92 As she had been a quiet spectatress of the fall of Samos.

spectatrix (spɛk'teɪtrɪks). [a. L. *spectātrix*, fem. of *spectātor*. Cf. F. *spectatrice*, It. *spettatrice*.] = SPECTATRESS.

1611 COTGR., *Spectatrice*, a spectatrix. **1615** W. HULL *Mirr. Maiestie* 88 She (good soule) stood by the crosse as a dolefull spectatrix of that wofull Tragedy. **1651** HOWELL *Venice* 4 She [Venice] hath allwayes.. chosen rather to be a Spectatrix or Umpresse, than a Gamestresse. *c* **1710** CELIA FIENNES *Diary* (1888) 15 The discription of the Coronation ..which I received the relation off from a spectatrix. **1781** EARL MALMESBURY *Diaries & Corr.* I. 390 The Dutch Ambassadors.. are leaving nothing untried to prevent Her Imperial Majesty from remaining spectatrix of their quarrel. **1860** MRS. A. CLIVE *Why P. Ferrall* x, She had been spectatrix of the same scene at a play. **1866** J. B. ROSE tr. *Ovid's Met.* 264 Spectatrix of this cruel fate was I.

† **'spectible**, *a. Obs.*[−1] [f. L. *spect-*, ppl. stem of *specĕre* to look.] Visible.

1581 J. BELL *Haddon's Answ. Osor.* 207 Hee added moreover Statutes and Lawes, not onely emprinted within every ones hart, but engraven also outwardly in spectible Tables.

spectinomycin (,spɛktɪnə'maɪsɪn). *Pharm.* [f. mod.L. *spect-ābilis* visible, remarkable (see SPECTABLE *a.*), + -MYCIN.] An antimicrobial substance obtained from the fungus *Streptomyces spectabilis* and used esp. to treat gonorrhœa that is resistant to penicillin.

1964 *Antimicrobial Agents & Chemotherapy* 438/1 The in vitro activity of spectinomycin.. was tested against routine gonococcal isolates and against resistant strains isolated from penicillin therapy failure cases of gonorrhea. **1976** *Lancet* 25 Dec. 1379/2 Spectinomycin succeeded in 21 (95%) of 22 patients treated. **1977** *Maclean's Mag.* Feb. 54 The only cure so far for the new strain is spectinomycin, a drug four times as costly as penicillin and hence not widely applicable in the Far East.

spectioneer, variant of SPECKSIONEER.

spectra, pl. of SPECTRUM.

† **'spectral**, *sb. Obs. rare.* [Cf. next.] An apparition; a spectre.

a **1656** USSHER *Ann.* (1658) Ep. to Rdr., Those things which I produce concerning Preesages, Spectrales, and Oracles. *Ibid.* 705 He expounded to him out of the doctrine of the Epicureans, what was to be thought concerning such spectrals.

spectral ('spɛktrəl), *a.* [ad. L. type **spectrāl-is*, f. *spectrum* SPECTRE and SPECTRUM. So mod.F. *spectral*.]

† **1.** Capable of seeing spectres. *Obs.*

1718 BP. HUTCHINSON *Witchcraft* v. 81 Joseph Ballard.. sent to Salem, for some of these Accusers, who pretended to have the spectral Sight, to tell him who afflicted his Wife.

2. a. Having the character of a spectre or phantom; ghostly, unsubstantial, unreal.

1815 SHELLEY *Alastor* 259 The mountaineer, Encountering on some dizzy precipice That spectral form. **1818** SCOTT *Br. Lamm.* xiii, Some of the spectral appearances which he had heard told of in a winter's evening. **1853** KANE *Grinnell Exp.* xxxiv. (1856) 307 The setting sun.. gave us again the spectral land about Cape Adair, eighty miles off. **1877** BLACK *Green Past.* xlii, We saw through a window a wild vision of a pair of spectral horses apparently in mid-air.

fig. **1829** I. TAYLOR *Enthus.* viii. 191 A spectral resemblance of piety, unsubstantial and cold as the mists of night. **1837** DICKENS *Pickw.* xxiv, A spectral attempt at drollery.

Comb. **1840** MRS. S. C. HALL *Irish Peasantry* (1850) 138 A lean, spectral-looking gray horse.. limped towards them. **1868** BOYD *Less. Middle Age* 315 A mile or two down,.. tall and spectral-white, stands the Cloch lighthouse.

b. Resembling, looking like, suggestive of, a spectre or spectres. Also *spec.* in *Zool.*

1828 LYTTON *Pelham* xviii, The spectral secretary of the embassy. **1843** BETHUNE *Sc. Fireside Stor.* 110 That species of erect tombstone, which some one has somewhere designated 'spectral'. **1851** RUSKIN *Stones Ven.* (1874) I. App. 366 The old spectral Lombard friezes. **1884** COUES *N. Amer. Birds* 509 *Strix cinerea*,.. Spectral Owl. **1896** H. O. FORBES *Hand-bk. Primates* I. 20 The Spectral Tarsier.

3. Characteristic of, appropriate to, a spectre.

1820 BYRON *Mar. Fal.* v. ii, They form'd a spectral voice, Which shook me in a supernatural dream. **1852** MRS. JAMESON *Leg. Madonna* Introd. (1857) 25 Compared with the spectral rigidity, the hard monotony, of the conventional Byzantines. **1898** WATTS-DUNTON *Aylwin* I. vi, Crumbling cliffs, whose jagged points.. had the kind of spectral look peculiar to that coast.

4. Produced merely by the action of light on the eye or on a sensitive medium.

1839 G. BIRD *Nat. Phil.* 398 If the wafer were yellow, and placed on a black surface, the spectral image will be deep violet when viewed on a white ground; in the same manner a white wafer is attended by its black spectral figure.

5. a. Of or pertaining to, appearing or observed in, the spectrum. Also applied to a property or parameter which is being considered as a function of frequency or wave-length, or which pertains to a given frequency range or value within the spectrum. Cf. SPECTRUM 3 a, b.

1832 *Nat. Philos.* (L.U.K.) II. Index 40 Spectral colours, when re-united, produce white. **1849** MRS. SOMERVILLE *Connex. Phys. Sci.* (ed. 8) xxiv. 235 A spectral image obtained by Mr. Hunt on a similar [Daguerreotype] plate. **1866** ATKINSON tr. *Ganot's Physics* (ed. 2) §480. 424 The relative distances of the different spectral lines. **1879** ROOD *Mod. Chromatics* x. 127 By mixing three or more spectral colours no new hues were produced. **1883** *19th Cent.* Nov. 881 Its absorptive capacity for particular spectral tints. **1919** *Sci. Abstr.* A. XXII. 563 Section 2 considers the definition of temperature. This is based upon thermal radiation and spectral distribution. **1950** *Audio Engin.* Aug. 14/2 A knowledge of the spectral characteristics of sound sources will indicate the regions in the frequency scale to which particular attention must be paid in assessing the effect of response changes in the sound system. **1951** *New Biol.* XI. 34 A spectral absorption curve, in which the proportion of light absorbed is plotted against wavelength. **1957** G. E. HUTCHINSON *Treat. Limnol.* I. vi. 376 The spectral composition of the total reflected light when the sun is high is little different from that of the incident. **1964** *Oceanogr. & Marine Biol.* II. 13 The turbulent fluctuations of velocity or of some other property of the water.. may be observed directly, and the spectral distribution of energy.. derived from the observations. **1966** *McGraw-Hill Encycl. Sci. & Technol.* IV. 582/2 Any spectral emissivity value is valid only for a narrow wavelength interval. **1971** *Physics Bull.* July 385/2 Spectral intensity is intensity per unit bandwidth ($W\ sr^{-1}\ Hz^{-1}$). *Ibid.* Nov. 653/3 An investigation of the spectral content, vibrato, attack and sound pressure of vowels sung by male and female students under technical and performing conditions. **1977** I. M. CAMPBELL *Energy & Atmosphere* viii. 272 The spectral absorption characteristics of alkyl nitrates are rather similar to those of nitric acid.

b. Carried out or performed by means of the spectrum.

1879 PROCTOR *Pleas. Ways Sci.* i. 26 The inquiry seems specially suited to the methods of spectral photography pursued by Dr. Draper. **1881** *Times* 11 Mar., Spectral observations on stars.

c. *Math.* Of or pertaining to the spectrum of a transformation (SPECTRUM 6).

1948 P. R. HALMOS *Finite Dimensional Vector Spaces* ii. 80 The characteristic equation, and consequently every other spectral concept such as the proper values and their multiplicities, is invariant under replacing A by BAB^{-1}. **1968** P. A. P. MORAN *Introd. Probability Theory* iii. 118 Hence U and V are non-singular matrices, and we have $P = U^{-1}\Lambda U = V\Lambda V^{-1}$, which is a 'spectral' decomposition of P.

6. Special collocations: ***spectral analysis***, chemical analysis of substances by means of their spectra; analysis of light or another oscillating system into a spectrum; ***spectral index*** (see quot. 1956); ***spectral series*** = SERIES *sb.* 16; ***spectral term***: see TERM *sb.* 11 d; ***spectral type*** (Astr.), any of the types used to classify stellar spectra, each being associated with stars of a characteristic range of temperatures and compositions and designated by a letter or letters.

1862 *Amer. Jrnl. Sci.* Nov. 404 There are few branches of science which promise more magnificent results than the *spectral analysis. **1888** *Phil. Mag.* XXV. 343 (*heading*) Mathematical spectral analysis of magnesium and carbon. **1930** *Proc. IRE* XVIII. 1199 Expression (9) lends itself to spectral analysis into its component frequencies by the following process. **1978** *Nature* 16 Mar. 232/2 As a further step, we carried out a spectral analysis according to the techniques of Blackman and Tukey on the time series for each of our latitude bands. **1956** *Observatory* LXXVI. 181 The usual terminology is adopted, where the flux density S from a discrete source refers to the flux in both polarizations, and the *spectral index x refers to the index in the relationship $S \propto (\text{frequency})^x$. **1967** *Astrophysical Jrnl.* CL. 5 The average spectral index of twenty-six spirals between 40 and 21 cm is $-0{\cdot}83$. **1974** *Nature* 4 Oct. 398/2 The spectral shape of the pulsed emission.. can be approximated by a power law with an energy spectral index of $\alpha \sim 1$ to about a GeV. **1900** *Sci. Abstr.* III. 465 A most useful review of the present state of knowledge respecting *spectral series. **1974** G. REECE tr. *Hund's Hist. Quantum Theory* iv. 61 Several attempts were made to give a theoretical interpretation of the spectral series. **1890** A. M. CLERKE *System of Stars* iii. 37 About eleven-twelfths of all the stars show linear spectra of absorption. They fall into two great divisions, corresponding to Father Secchi's first and second *spectral types. **1924** *Proc. Amer. Acad. Arts & Sci.* LIX. 217 If the stellar density for any spectral type were uniform throughout space, the number of stars visible should double with every increase of half a magnitude in brightness. **1973** SMITH & JACOBS *Introd. Astron. & Astrophysics* x. 268 Since we will have occasion to refer to specific spectral types in the following paragraphs, we give the spectral sequence from hot to cool stars (40,000 K to 3000 K) here: O, B, A, F, G, K, and M. Each spectral class is further divided into ten sub-classes 0 to 9.

Hence **'spectralism**, a spectral or ghostly scene. **spec'trality**, a phantasm; ghostliness. **'spectralness**, the quality or character of being spectral.

1851 CARLYLE in *New Rev.* (1891) Oct. 299 All dreamlike, one *spectralism succeeding another. **1850** —— *Latter-d. Pamph.* i. 50 Traditions now really about extinct;.. still haunting with their *spectralities.. almost all of us! **1880** *Scribner's Mag.* July 326 There is about it a certain vagueness and spectrality. **1892** W. W. PEYTON *Memorab. Jesus* x. 285 A *spectralness, which.. gives you an idea of weirdness.

spectrally ('spɛktrəlɪ), *adv.* [f. SPECTRAL *a.*]

1. In a ghostly manner.

1837 CARLYLE *Fr. Rev.* II. II. vi, This.. did for many months.. walk spectrally,—in all French heads. **1865** DICKENS *Mut. Fr.* III. ii, The steamer's lights moved spectrally a very little.

2. In the form of a spectrum; as regards, or in terms of, the spectrum.

1914 S. E. SHEPPARD *Photo-Chem.* viii. 325 Spectrally dispersed rays. **1971** *Jrnl. Gen. Psychol.* LXXXIV. 95 Spectrally pure stimuli are being produced by passing the output of a xenon arc through narrow-band interference filters. **1973** *Sci. Amer.* Nov. 77/1 The results of this experiment suggest that noise spectrally adjacent to the signal is most effective in masking recognition. **1980** *Ibid.* Oct. 123/1 The light.. is spectrally pure and monochromatic.

spectre ('spɛktə(r)), *sb.* Also 7- specter (now *U.S.*). [a. F. *spectre* (16th cent., = It. *spettro*, Sp. and Pg. *espectro*), or ad. L. *spectrum*, f. *specĕre* to look, see.]

1. a. An apparition, phantom, or ghost, esp. one of a terrifying nature or aspect.

1605 Z. JONES (*title*), A Treatise of Specters or straunge Sights, Visions and Apparitions appearing sensibly unto men. **1641** *Lords Spiritual* 15 Thus this great Goliah being handled, appeareth.. rather a ghost and specter, then a body. **1703** POPE *Thebais* 133 Swift as she pass'd, the flitting ghosts withdrew, And the pale spectres trembled at her view. **1744** HARRIS *Three Treat.* Wks. (1841) 40 The superstitious have not a more previous tendency to be frightened at the sight of spectres,.. than [etc.]. **1813** SCOTT *Trierm.* II. Interlude i, How should I, so humbly born, Endure the graceful spectre's scorn? **1862** *Macm. Mag.* Apr. 507 The simple.. explanation of spectres is that they are our own thoughts. **1871** PALGRAVE *Lyr. Poems* 37 A terror.. As when a sudden spectre at mid-day Meets us.

b. *fig.* An unreal object of thought; a phantasm of the brain.

1711 SHAFTESB. *Charac.* (1737) I. 53 When the mind is taken up in vision, and fixes its view either on any real object, or mere specter of divinity.

c. *fig.* An object or source of dread or terror, imagined as an apparition.

1774 GOLDSM. *Nat. Hist.* (1776) II. 206 Death.. is a spectre which frights us at a distance. **1837** CARLYLE *Fr. Rev.* I. I. iv, That same cloud-capt, fire-breathing Spectre of Democracy. **1856** KINGSLEY *Lett.* (1878) I. 500 The glaring eye of the dark spectre of bereavement. **1893** *Black & White* 29 July 122/2 The Channel Tunnel spectre is laid.

d. *transf.* One whose appearance is suggestive of an apparition or ghost.

1807–8 W. IRVING *Salmag.* (1824) 352 [She is] a mere house-hold spectre, neither giving nor receiving enjoyment. **1825** J. NEAL *Bro. Jonathan* I. 362 A creature like you—a spectre— . . to talk about seeking your fortune! **1891** MARIE A. BROWN tr. *Runeberg's Nadeschda* 50 Ever since a spectre From place to place he wanders.

e. A faint shadow or imitation *of* something.

1849 C. BRONTE *Shirley* xxiv, With the strangest spectre of a laugh.

2. One of the images or semblances supposed by the Epicurean school to emanate from corporeal things.

1785 REID *Intell. Powers* 26 The spectres of Epicurus were composed of a very subtle matter. **1834** SOUTHEY *Doctor* v. 11 The old atomists supposed that the likenesses or spectres of corporeal things . . assail the soul when she ought to be at rest.

3. An image or phantom produced by reflection or other natural cause.

1801 *Encycl. Brit.* Suppl. II. 514/2 Spectre of the Broken, a curious phenomenon observed on the summit of the Broken. **1832** BREWSTER *Natural Magic* vi. 148 It is only within the last forty years that science has brought these atmospherical spectres within the circle of her dominion. **1860** TYNDALL *Glac.* I. ii. 22 Before each of us . . stood a spectral image of a man. . . We stretched forth our arms; the spectres did the same. **1908** [MISS FOWLER] *Betw. Trent & Ancholme* 299, I must look again for this aerial and charming spectre.

4. *Zool.* One or other of the insects or animals distinguished by the epithet *spectre-* (see 7), esp. an insect of the family *Phasmidae*.

1797 *Trans. Linn. Soc.* IV. 190 This singular animal [sc. *Phasma dilatatum*] . . belongs to that tribe of insects which Stoll has called by the title of Spectres. **1815** KIRBY & SP. *Entomol.* iii. (1818) I. 67 *note*, Orthoptera consisting of Cockroaches, Locusts, . . Spectres, Mantes, &c. **1816** *Ibid.* xxiii. (1818) II. 328 The spectres . . are distinguished by tarsi of five joints. **1880** *Encycl. Brit.* XIII. 152/2 *Phasmidæ* (Spectres, or Walking-Sticks).

†**5.** A horrid spectacle or sight. *Obs.*⁻¹

a **1763** SHENSTONE *Elegies* xxii. 68 To see my limbs . . gash'd beneath the daring steel, To crowds a spectre, and to dogs a prey!

6. a. *attrib.* (chiefly in sense 1), as ***spectre-bark***, ***-chimera***, ***-doubt***, ***-fashion***, ***-horse***, etc.

1817 COLERIDGE *Anc. Mar.* III. xiii, Off shot the *spectre-bark. **1837** CARLYLE *Fr. Rev.* III. VI. i, Through some section of History, Nineteen *spectre-chimeras shall flit, . . till Oblivion swallow them. **1799** CAMPBELL *Pleas. Hope* II. 263 Ye *spectre-doubts, that roll Cimmerian darkness on the parting soul! **1822** SCOTT *Nigel* x, It were a shame to my household, thou shouldst glide out into the Strand after such a *spectre-fashion. ? **186.** B. HARTE *Friar Pedro's Ride* in *Fiddletown*, etc. (1873) 112 A phantom friar, on a *spectre horse. **1805** SCOTT *Last Minstrel* VI. xxvi, Like him . . Who spoke the *spectre-hound in Man. *c* **1820** S. ROGERS *Italy* (1839) 118 He had so oft beheld . . The *spectre-knight. **1825** J. WILSON *Poems* II. 305 While stern beneath the chancel high, My country's *spectre monarch stood. **1777** WARTON *Poems* 61 We bid those *spectre-shapes avaunt. **1798** COLERIDGE *Anc. Mar.* III. xiv, Off darts the *Spectre-ship. **1807** BYRON *Childish Recoll.* 7 What grisly forms, the *spectre-train of woe, Bid shuddering Nature shrink beneath the blow. **1816** KIRBY & SP. *Entomol.* xxi. (1818) II. 220 The *Spectre tribe . . go still further in this mimicry. **1817** COLERIDGE *Anc. Mar.* III. x. *marg. note*, The *Spectre-Woman and her Death-mate.

b. *Comb.*, chiefly in similative adjs., as ***spectre-faint***, ***-lean***, ***-like*** (also adv.), ***-looking***, ***-pale***, ***-pallid***, ***-staring***, ***-thin***; also ***spectre-haunted***, ***-mongering*** (adjs.), ***-queller***.

1924 R. GRAVES *Mock Beggar Hall* 5 The exiled Alcibiades Beheld him in the Chersonese, Yet *spectre-faint. **1831** CARLYLE *Sart. Res.* II. viii, At worst as a *spectre-fighting Man, nay who will one day be a Spectre-queller. **1718** ROWE tr. *Lucan* 303 No Swain thy *Spectre-haunted Plain shou'd know. **1873** E. BRENNAN *Witch Nemi*, etc. 78 That dark land and spectre-haunted grove. **1887** MEREDITH *Ballads & P.* 85 He came out of miracle cloud, Lightning-swift and *spectre-lean. **1719** DE FOE *Crusoe* I. (Globe) 258 Not making quite so staring a *Spectre-like Figure as I did. **1834** *Tait's Mag.* I. 726/1 Spectre-like they stray, And soon their steps in distance die away. **1884** J. COLBORNE *Hicks Pasha* 41 The camels glided noiselessly and spectre-like over the track. **1849–50** ALISON *Hist. Europe* VIII. lv. §24. 580 With a few thousand miserable and *spectre-looking followers. **1809** BYRON *Bards & Rev.* 919 Let *spectre-mongering Lewis aim . . To rouse the galleries. **1928** V. WOOLF *Orlando* v. 233 The *spectre-pale beech trees. **1844** HOOD *Haunted House* III. ix, But from their tarnish'd frames dark Figures gaz'd, And Faces *spectre-pallid. **1831** *Spectre-queller [see *spectre-fighting* above]. **1826** MILMAN *A. Boleyn* (1827) 72 Thy tossing, feverish, *spectre-staring midnights. **1820** KEATS *Ode to Nightingale* 26 Where youth grows pale, and *spectre-thin, and dies.

7. Special combs.: **spectre-bat**, a tropical species of bat (*Vespertilio* or *Phyllostoma spectrum*); **spectre-candle** (see quot.); **spectre-crab**, a glass-crab (*Cent. Dict.*); **spectre insect**, an insect of the genus *Phasma* (see 4); **spectre-lemur**, = *spectre tarsier*; **spectre-mantis**, = *spectre insect*; **spectre-shell** (see quot.); **spectre-shrimp**, a slender-bodied amphipod of the genus *Caprella*; **spectre tarsier**, a small lemuroid animal (*Tarsius spectrum*).

1781 PENNANT *Hist. Quadrup.* II. 552 *Spectre Bat. . . Inhabits South America. **1827** GRIFFITH tr. *Cuvier* V. 71 *Phyllostoma Spectrum* (Spectre or true Vampyre Bat). **1835** *Penny Cycl.* IV. 172/2 Belemnite, Thunderstone, or Arrowhead . . : we . . find the term Devil's fingers bestowed on them, and not unfrequently that of *spectre-candles. **1826** KIRBY & SP. *Entomol.* III. 90 The largest egg known . . is that of a *spectre insect (*Phasma dilatatum*), figured in the Linnean Transactions. **1886** GEIKIE *Class-Bk. Geol.* 359 Spectre-insects (*Phasmidæ*) . . have been detected chiefly among the shales and coals of the Coal-measures. **1882** *Spectre-lemur [see TARSIER]. **1840** F. D. BENNETT *Whaling Voy.* I. 343 The insects we found here were the *spectre-mantis; a purple butterfly [etc.]. **1753** *Chambers' Cycl.* Suppl., *Concha spectrorum*, the *spectre shell, a name given by authors to a species of voluta, from some odd figures described on its surface [etc.]. **1882** *Cassell's Nat. Hist.* VI. 212 The popular name of *Spectre, or Skeleton Shrimp, seems very appropriate. **1871** *Ibid.* I. 250 The *Spectre Tarsier, which inhabits the Oriental Archipelago and the Philippine Islands.

Hence **'spectre** *v. trans.*, to fill with spectres; **'spectredom**, the realm or region of spectres.

1849 AYTOUN *Old Camp* ii, It hath a look that makes me old, and spectres time again. **1883** J. S. STALLYBRASS tr. *Grimm's Teutonic Myth.* III. 930 Part and parcel of this heathenish spectredom. **1897** *Daily Tel.* 20 July 7/3 The tyranny of the manager of spectredom.

spectred ('spɛktəd), *a.* [f. SPECTRE *sb.* 1.] Filled with spectres; converted into a spectre; resembling a spectre.

1791 WOLCOT (P. Pindar) *Lousiad* III. Wks. 1794 I. 269 Amidst the spectred solitude of sleep. **1803** T. G. FESSENDEN *Petit. agst. Tract. Trumpery* 2 'Gainst spectred poverty still striving. **1809** E. S. BARRETT *Setting Sun* I. 69 That specter'd elf, Grim death hath seiz'd our father your viceroy.

†**spectrene**, *a. Obs.*⁻¹ [f. as prec.] Spectral.

1652 GAULE *Magastrom.* 355 By malefical incantations there was brought in to him the spectrene apparition of her whom he loved.

spectrey. *nonce-wd.* [f. SPECTRE *sb.* 1.] A place of spectres.

1822 GALT *Sir A. Wylie* I. xxiii. 207, I believe it is a huge old Ann-Radcliffe place, a spectrey surrounded by a rookery.

†**'spectrical**, *a. Obs.*⁻¹ [f. as prec.] Spectral. Hence †**'spectrically** *adv. Obs.*

1609 SIR E. HOBY *Let. to T. H[iggons]* 85 Then are you cruell comforters, who . . do terrifie the departing soule of him . . with such spectricall delusions. **1615** *Curry Combe for a Coxe-Combe* iii. 121 Such is the exposition of the place so spectrically raysed, and so dubitatiuely propounded by the Interpreters themselues.

spectrin ('spɛktrɪn). *Biochem.* [f. SPECTR(E *sb.* + -IN¹; so called because it was isolated from 'ghosts' (sense 11 e) of red blood cells.] A fibrous protein constituent of the membranes of red blood cells, forming a network on the inside of the plasma membrane.

1968 MARCHESI & STEERS in *Science* 12 Jan. 204/2 Because this protein appears to be a new molecular species and is extractable from erythrocyte ghost membranes, we suggest that it be called Spectrin. **1974** *Sci. Amer.* Mar. 27/3 The two heaviest polypeptide components, with molecular weights of 255,000 and 220,000, are collectively known as spectrin. **1978** *Bio Systems* X. 98/1 A variety of proteins other than actin can form filaments (e.g., flagellin, spectrin, spasmoneme filaments, skeletin).

'spectrish, *a. rare*⁻¹. [f. SPECTRE *sb.* + -ISH.] Somewhat spectral or ghostly.

1822 GALT *Sir A. Wylie* I. xx. 170, I am indeed not surprised that you should be somewhat disconcerted, for I believe that I am a little spectrish.

spectro- ('spɛktrəʊ), combining form (on Greek analogies) of SPECTRUM, chiefly employed in a number of recent terms, as ***spectro-bolograph***, ***-bolographic*** adj., ***-bolometer***, ***-bolometric*** adj., ***-colorimetry***, ***-comparator***, ***-microscopical*** adj., ***-photograph(y***, ***-polarigraph***, ***-polariscope***, ***-pyrometer***, ***-telescope***, etc.; **spectro'heliogram**, a photograph obtained with a spectroheliograph; **spectro'heliograph**, (*a*) an instrument which photographs the sun using light of a particular wavelength, *esp.* that of the Balmer α emission line of hydrogen; †(*b*) a spectroheliogram; hence **ˌspectrohelio'graphic** *a.*; **ˌspectroheli'ometer**, a spectrophotometer for use in studying the sun; **spectro'helioscope**, an instrument which provides a directly observable monochromatic image of the sun by means of a rapidly scanning device which transmits light of only one wavelength (which may be modified so that Doppler shifts can be observed); **spectrophone** a device in which a body of gas may be caused to emit sound waves when illuminated by a periodically interrupted beam of electromagnetic radiation (usu. visible or infra-red); hence **spectro'phonic** *a.*; **ˌspectrophospho'rimetry**, the spectrometric study of phosphorescence; so **ˌspectrophospho'rimeter**, a spectrometer designed for this; **ˌspectrophosphori'metric** *a.*; **ˌspectrophotofluo'rometer**, a spectrophotometer designed for the study of fluorescence; hence **ˌspectroˌphotofluoro'metric** *a.*, **-fluoro'metrically** *adv.*; **ˌspectropola'rimeter**, an instrument designed to measure rotation of the plane of polarized light as a function of wavelength; so **ˌspectropolari'metric** *a.*; **ˌspectropola'rimetry**; **ˌspectroradi'ometer**, a combination of a spectroscope and a radiometer, designed to measure the intensity of electromagnetic radiation over a range of wavelengths; so **ˌspectroradio'metric** *a.*; **'spectroradi'ometry**; **'spectrotype** *Immunol.*, the range of antigens to which a given antibody is reactive.

1905 *Astrophysical Jrnl.* XXI. 354 *Spectroheliograms were obtained showing detail in the centre of the disk. **1968** *New Scientist* 11 Jan. 97/1 (*caption*) X-ray spectroheliograms of solar plages obtained with *OSO*-4. **1973** Spectroheliogram [see RASTER *sb.*² a]. **1892** *Athenæum* 16 July 102/1 An instrument called the *spectroheliograph . . , by means of which . . photographs are now made of all the prominences visible round the entire circumference of the sun with a single exposure. **1903** Spectroheliograph [see FLOCCULUS 3 b]. **1907** *Athenæum* 6 Apr. 415/3 Dr. Lockyer showed spectroheliographs of the sun. **1915** [see FLOCCULUS 3 b]. **1965** P. WYLIE *They both were Naked* iv. 152 Big gadgets—telescopes, spectroheliographs, particle accelerators and the like. **1905** *Athenæum* 29 Apr. 535/2 *Spectroheliographic Results explained by Anomalous Dispersion. **1905** *Astrophysical Jrnl.* XXI. 279 Our new explanation of the spectroheliographic results will be founded on the hypothesis that the sun is an unlimited mass of gas in which convection currents . . are continually forming. **1973** *Sci. Amer.* Oct. 76/2 The major experiments of Skylab include a *spectroheliometer from the Harvard College Observatory that is mapping the sun at wavelengths of from 300 to 1,350 angstroms with a resolution of five seconds of arc. **1976** *New Yorker* 6 Sept. 40 The spectroheliometer showed that they extended up from the chromosphere . . into the transition region between the chromosphere and the corona. **1906** *Astrophysical Jrnl.* XXIV. 42 This instrument . . constitutes a *spectrohelioscope, and was intended for the visual study of prominences. **1929** G. E. HALE in *Encycl. Brit.* XXI. 179/2 The spectrohelioscope renders visible to the eye many of the phenomena of the solar atmosphere photographed with the spectroheliograph and also permits their velocities in the line of sight to be measured. **1955** *Sci. Amer.* Sept. 194/2 In 1890 George Ellery Hale and Henri Deslandres independently invented the spectrohelioscope. This instrument utilized the red light of hydrogen to produce an image of the entire disk of the sun. **1885** tr. *Behrens' Micros. in Bot.* V. 139 The *spectro-microscopical apparatus . . has become an important instrument in the investigation of the coloring matter of plants. **1881** A. G. BELL *Sound by Radiant Energy* 41 These substances are put in communication with the ear by means of a hearing-tube, and thus the instrument is converted into a veritable *spectro-phone. **1948** *Chem. Abstr.* XLII. 1467 An app. was constructed for the detn. of gases absorbing in either the infrared or the visible region, on the principle of Bell's spectrophone. **1965** *New Scientist* 21 Oct. 199/3 The collisional phenomenon has recently been investigated . . using a device named the 'spectrophone', in which a sample of gas is subjected to a sequence of pulses of infrared (140 a second) during which the molecules acquire vibrational energy. If they lose that energy by collision, the increase in molecular velocities, and therefore in pressure, is detected by a microphone in the gas, which accordingly registers a 140 c/s note. **1881** A. G. BELL *Sound by Radiant Energy* 41 Suppose we smoke the interior of our *spectrophonic receiver. **1961** *Nature* 8 Apr. 166/1 The measurements with our *spectrophosphorimeter set an upper limit to the lifetime of the pyrene dimer. **1978** *Ibid.* 19 Jan. 236/1 The weak after-glow spectrum is also shown in Fig. 1*a*, at a gain factor of 20 for 100% solid crystalline carbazole at an identical setting of the spectrophosphorimeter. **1968** M. ZANDER *Phosphorimetry* iii. 136 The quantitative *spectrophosphorimetric analysis of mixtures. *Ibid.* 138 The qualitative and quantitative analysis of a mixture is possible by *spectrophosphorimetry. **1974** *Nature* 30 Aug. 763/1 Analysis of the fluorescent material (by chromatography on the adsorbent *in situ* by spectrofluorimetry *in situ*, and by the latter technique and by spectrophosphorimetry after solvent extraction from the adsorbent). **1956** *Rev. Sci. Instruments* XXVII. 664/2 *Spectrophotofluorometer. Continuous activation of compounds and measurement of the resulting fluorescence throughout the visible and ultraviolet regions is provided by this instrument. **1974** *Nature* 1 Feb. 291/1 The continuous formation of NADH:NADH was measured fluorometrically at 37°C with an Aminco Bowman spectrophotofluorometer using an excitation wavelength of 340 nm and an emission wavelength of 460 nm. **1964** *Jrnl. Exper. Med.* CXX. 509 The *spectrophotofluorometric technique of Shore *et al.* . . was used with slight alterations. **1975** *Nature* 17 Apr. 636/1 Cells were centrifuged and the histamine released into the supernatant . . was determined *spectrophotofluorometrically. **1926** *Sci. Abstr.* A. XXIX. 310 (*heading*) A *spectro-polarimeter for the ultra-violet. **1971** *Nature* 16 July 192/1 Circular dichroism was measured at 25°C with a JASCO ORD/UV-5 spectropolarimeter equipped with a CD attachment. **1960** C. DJERASSI *Optical Rotatory Dispersion* iii. 28 These refractive index gradients . . account for the 'blanking-out' phenomenon noted in the *spectropolarimetric examination of ketal formation. *Ibid.* 18 The single most important factor responsible for the renewed interest in rotatory dispersion has been recent advances in ultraviolet *spectropolarimetry. **1881** *Nature* XXIII. 524 The *spectropyrometer is proved practically useful. **1927** *Jrnl. Optical Soc. Amer.* VII. 439 The essential parts of a *spectroradiometer consist of (1) a suitable spectrometer for dispersing thermal radiation into a spectrum, and (2) suitable radiometric instruments for measuring the spectral radiation intensities. **1975** *Nature* 10 Apr. 512/2 Measurements of the spectral energy distributions . . of natural radiation between 400 and 800 nm were made using a spectroradiometer. **1922** *Jrnl. Optical Soc. Amer.* VI. 1021 The transmission screen method should prove useful in supplementing the *spectroradiometric measurements . . on fainter stars. **1951** *Electronics* Jan. 81/3 This is a spectroradiometric curve of a particular color, obtained by measuring . . the number of watts radiated by the source at each wavelength. **1921** *Jrnl. Optical Soc. Amer.* V. 133 The fiducial line in this Bureau's *spectroradiometry is the yellow helium line. **1945** R. A.

SAWYER *Exper. Spectroscopy* xi. 277 The methods used in the investigation of the infrared radiation.. are essentially the methods of spectroradiometry. **1880** *Athenæum* 25 Sept. 405/1 A *spectro-telescope,.. the purpose of which is to enable the observer to survey large portions of the sun's disc at once in homogeneous light. **1974** *Nature* 16 Aug. 532/2 The A5A idiotype has been found to be associated with a particular antibody *spectrotype. **1981** *Exper. Parasitol.* LII. 216/2 When a clone of S1 spectrotype was allowed to establish a relapsing infection on two separate occasions, two variants of different spectrotypes were produced.

spectrochemical (spɛktrəʊ'kɛmɪkəl), *a.* [f. SPECTRO- + CHEMICAL *a.*] Of or pertaining to spectrochemistry; ***spectrochemical series***, a series of ligands arranged in order of magnitude of the ligand field splitting that they cause in the electronic orbitals of a central atom.

1896 *Jrnl. Chem. Soc.* LXX. I. 553 The results of a spectrochemical investigation.. establish the formula. **1938** R. TSUCHIDA in *Bull. Chem. Soc. Japan* XIII. 393 Arranging in the ascending order of *P* [*sc.* 'the work which would be done by the system if the ligand were to approach from infinity to the seat of co-ordination'], we obtain a spectrochemical series for the first band: viz., NH_3, H_2O, F^-, Cl^-, Br^-, I^-. **1960** *Jrnl. Iron & Steel Inst.* CXCV. 375/1 The most satisfactory boron line for spectrochemical use is at 2497.73 Å. **1966** PHILLIPS & WILLIAMS *Inorg. Chem.* II. xxviii. 396 Now when the [crystal-field splitting] energies, *Δ*, obtained from spectra.. are compared for a large number of different cations, it is found that there is an approximately constant ligand series, the Fajans–Tsuchida spectrochemical series: $CO > CN^- > NO^- > .. S^{2-} > Br^- > I^-$. **1975** P. S. BRATERMAN *Metal Carbonyl Spectra* i. 3 Electronic spectra contain *d-d* bands that place CO in the spectrochemical and nephelauxetic series.

Hence **spectro'chemically** *adv.*, as regards spectrochemistry; by spectrochemical methods.

1905 *Nature* 15 June 160/2 Several simple molecules of this kind may be combined into one crystallised particle of the spectrochemically normal diamond. **1966** P. W. J. M. BOUMANS *Spectrochemical Excitation* i. 4 Alloys containing more than two elements.. were investigated spectrochemically.

spectrochemistry (spɛktrəʊ'kɛmɪstrɪ). [f. SPECTRO- + CHEMISTRY.] The branch of chemistry dealing with the chemical application of spectroscopy, esp. in analysis, and with the interpretation of spectra in chemical terms.

1893 *Jrnl. Chem. Soc.* LXIV. I. 254 (*heading*) Spectrochemistry of nitrogen. **1905** *Nature* 15 June 162/1 It is of course of the greatest value to be able to examine the constitution of the bodies without affecting them chemically; and spectrochemistry.. gives us the means of doing so. **1957** *Technology* Sept. 258/2 In the department of applied science.. radio-chemistry, spectro-chemistry and metallurgy are all prominent. **1966** P. W. J. M. BOUMANS *Spectrochemical Excitation* p. viii, This book will.. contribute to further progress in the field of theoretical spectrochemistry.

ˌspectrofluo'rimetry. Also -fluoro-. [f. SPECTRO- + FLUORO-, FLUORIMETRY.] The spectrometric study of fluorescence. So **ˌspectrofluo'rimeter (-fluoro-)**, a spectrometer designed for this; **ˌspectrofluori'metric (-fluoro-)** *a.*, **-'metrically** *adv.*

1957 *Analyst* LXXXII. 611 The sensitivity of the spectrofluorimeter depends not only on the sensitivity of the detector and the intensity of the exciting light, but also on the slit width and aperture of the analysing monochromator. **1961** *Analytical Chem.* XXXIII. 1362/1 The spectrofluorometer has a sensitivity equivalent to 0·01 p.p.m. of quinine sulphate. **1962** *Lancet* 26 May 1130/1 The plasma was analysed spectrofluorometrically for the pharmacologically active spirolactone. **1965** *Analytical Chem.* XXXVII. 137/1 (*heading*) Spectrofluorometric determination of submicrogram amounts of aluminium and beryllium. **1965** *Jrnl. Clin. Path.* XVIII. 375/1 (*heading*) A device for spectrofluorimetry. **1971** *Nature* 2 July 24/2 All the chromosomes in the human complement can be paired by these patterns, which can be analysed most accurately by a quantitative spectrofluorimetric method. **1975** D. H. BURRIN in Williams & Wilson *Biologist's Guide to Princ. & Techniques Pract. Biochem.* v. 147 Spectrofluorimetry is most accurate at very low concentrations. *Ibid.*, Spectrofluorimeters enable the utilization of great spectral selectivity since.. two monochromators may be used. **1957** *N.Y. Times* 8 Nov. 33/4 In the meantime, using spectrofluorometry, thin-layer chromatography and a third technique with iodine, the Coast Guard and the E.P.A. conducted 741 tests at its laboratories in Georgia and Connecticut. **1976** *Nature* 16 Sept. 242/2 The amine was isolated by ion-exchange chromatography.. and estimated spectrofluorimetrically.

'spectrogram. [f. SPECTRO- + -GRAM.] A photograph of a spectrum. Hence, more widely, a visual representation of a spectrum of any kind.

1892 *Pall Mall G.* 17 Feb. 7/2 The spectrograms of the star show two spectra, one above the other. **1900** *Edinb. Rev.* Apr. 474 There must be a suspension of judgement in the matter until spectrograms of nebular nuclei can be produced in evidence. **1939** *Amer. Speech* XIV. 313/2 Examination of eleven subjects singing the vowel 'ah' normally and after hydrogen inhalation... Illustrated with acoustic spectrograms. **1961** *Brit. Birds* LIV. 388 The original spectrograms have a frequency scale from 0 to 10 kilocycles per second. **1975** *Nature* 25 Sept. 295/1 Spectrograms obtained with a Carnegie image tube on the 2·1-m telescope at the Kitt Peak National Observatory have been used to complete the determination of radial velocities for 50 of the 52 galaxies. **1978** *Hi-Fi News* Sept. 175/1 None of these, however, exceeded −70dB ref. 36 V RMS across the load (shown in spectrogram *fig. 2*). **1981** *Amer. Speech* 1977 LII. 237 The degree of centralization was determined by the use of a bilogarithmic scale in measuring the spectrograms of eighty instances of /aɪ/.

'spectrograph. [f. as prec. + -GRAPH.]

1. An instrument used for photographing a spectrum. More widely, any apparatus for producing a visual record of a spectrum (optical or otherwise). Cf. *mass spectrograph* s.v. MASS *sb.*[2] 10 d, *sound spectrograph* s.v. SOUND *sb.*[3] 8.

1884 YOUNG in *Proc. Amer. Acad. Arts & Sci.* 238 In July, 1876, several photographs of the spectrum of Vega were taken with an apparatus which Dr. Draper called the spectrograph. **1889** *Anthony's Photogr. Bull.* II. 394 The color sensitiveness of the plate I find out with the aid of my Quartz spectrograph. **1893** *Nation* 16 Feb. 126/2 With the eleven-inch Draper spectrograph nearly a thousand photographs were taken. **1940** *Geogr. Jrnl.* XCV. 276 My own work was research on the Ozone Layer with a Dobson Spectrograph. **1955** *Times* 15 June 5/5 Such spectrographs are used in laboratories to examine the ions existing in ionized gases, and an American version has been used in rockets. **1967** M. SCHLAUCH *Language* v. 102 There is an instrument called the spectrograph which can record and photograph the complex series of vibrations of the air which convey a sequence of spoken sounds. **1974** *Encycl. Brit. Macropædia* XI. 605/1 The most noteworthy observation made with the parabola spectrograph was the spectrum of rare gases present in the atmosphere... There was a line corresponding to an ion of mass 22 that could not be attributed to any known gas.

2. = SPECTROGRAM.

1891 *Pall Mall G.* 26 Sept. 4/2 A few spectrographs of pure and impure blood. **1898** *Edinb. Rev.* Apr. 306 Rich harvests of photographs and spectrographs were garnered.

Hence **spec'trographer**, one who uses a spectrograph; **spectro'graphic** *a.*, relating to a spectrograph or the observations made with it; **spectro'graphically** *adv.*, in a spectrographic manner; **spec'trography**, the art of using the spectrograph.

1884 *Science* III. 727/1 Spectrographic operations are.. much more sensitive to atmospheric conditions than are visual observations. **1900** *Edinb. Rev.* Apr. 458 'Spectrography' is the complement of spectroscopy. *Ibid.* 460 The spectrographic impression of a hydrogen star. *Ibid.* 474 Having spectrographically surveyed the entire heaven. **1903** AGNES CLERKE *Probl. Astrophys.* 3 Spectroscopic photography, or 'spectrography' dates from Sir William Huggins's adoption of the dry gelatine process in 1876. **1946** *Nature* 20 July 79/1 The result of this selection is a volume from which spectrographers may derive helpful guidance in the correct choice of analytical methods. **1959** E. PULGRAM *Introd. Spectrography of Speech* i. 20 The position, which I have at least in part adopted in consequence of learning to view language spectrographically. *Ibid.* ii. 27 The experimental linguist.., like the spectrographer of speech, is interested in the cultural *and* the physical values of the phenomena at the same time. **1962** *Amer. Speech* XXXVII. 62 Phonemic analysis of the stress-intonation system based on spectrographic analysis of a specific corpus. **1974** *Sci. Amer.* Mar. 86/3 Another promising diagnostic technique for detecting abnormalities in infants, in addition to the spectrographic analysis of the cry, is the measurement of.. changes in brain waves in response to sounds. **1981** *Amer. Speech* 1977 LII. 269 A carefully developed argument, supported with spectrographic evidence.

spectro'logical, *a.* [See next and -LOGICAL.]

1. Pertaining to spectres or apparitions.

1802 *Ann. Reg., Chron.* 387/1 This man stated that he had lately arrived from the Continent and intended to exhibit before the public his deceptions in the spectrological art.

2. 'Of or pertaining to spectrology; performed or determined by spectrology; as, spectrological analysis' (1882 *Imp. Dict.*).

spec'trology. *rare.* [f. SPECTRO- (in senses 1 and 3 of SPECTRUM) + -LOGY.]

1. The science or study of spectres.

1820 W. IRVING *Sketch Bk.* (1821) II. 196 The gloom of religious abstraction, and the wildness of their situation,.. had filled their imaginations with the frightful chimeras of witchcraft and spectrology. **1827** HONE *Table Bk.* I. 710 Spectrology. A Remarkable Narrative.

2. The scientific study of spectra.

1862 *Amer. Jrnl. Sci.* May 440 The attention of the French scientific world is wholly fixed on *spectrology*, for thus do they designate the experiment with the spectroscope of Bunsen and Kirchhof. [Hence in Webster (1864), etc.] **1969** JAMES & STERNBERG *Design of Optical Spectrometers* p. x, Spectroscopy (or *spectrology*, to introduce here a word coined by Fellgett) belongs to this branch of physics.

spec'trometer. [ad. G. *spektrometer* or F. *spectromètre*.] An instrument used for measuring the index of refraction. Now in extended use, any of a wide range of instruments for producing spectra and measuring the positions, etc., of spectral features. Cf. *mass spectrometer* s.v. MASS *sb.*[2] 10 d.

1874 tr. *Lommel's Light* 144 The determination of the index of refraction can be much more conveniently effected by means of Meyerstein's Spectrometer. **1878** *Smithsonian Rep.* 431 The spectrometer stands upon a plate of metal which can be made to revolve so that measurements by repetitions are practicable. **1883** *Knowledge* 18 May 297/1 Professor Clifton of Oxford has brought out a new spectrometer. **1901** *Sci. Abstr.* IV. 930 Universal spectrometer... This instrument can be used for studying any portion of the spectrum, either visually, photographically, or photometrically, with two different dispersions. **1950** *Sci. News* XV. 19 Monochromatic light of chosen wavelength, from a spectrometer, is now used in order to stimulate the retinal receptors. **1958** *Antiquity* XXXII. 124 The characteristics of the trace-elements present are detected by a special Gamma-ray Spectrometer. **1978** P. W. ATKINS *Physical Chem.* xix. 616 The centre of the e.s.r. spectrum of the methyl radical occurs at 329·4 mT when the spectrometer is using 9·233 GHz microwaves.

Hence **spectro'metric** *a.*; **spectro'metrically** *adv.*; **spec'trometrist**, an expert in spectrometry; a person employed to operate a spectrometer; **spec'trometry.**

Cf. F. *spectrométrique*, *-métrie* (Littré).

1891 *Cent. Dict.*, Spectrometric. **1902** WEBSTER *Suppl.*, Spectrometry. **1903** AGNES CLERKE *Probl. Astrophys.* 8 The 'spectrometric' division of photometry consists in the comparative estimation of ray-intensities. **1948** *Physical Rev.* LXXIV. 1222/1 By extending the method.. a higher order mass resolution is obtained which is generally usable in the mass spectrometry of positive ions. **1953** G. P. BARNARD *Mod. Mass Spectrometry* 286 A different method was used.. to determine the half-life of ^{85}Kr mass spectrometrically. **1954** POWELL & ROSS in *Appl. Mass Spectrometry* (Inst. Petroleum) 7 In Raman spectrometry, the material is irradiated with monochromatic light.. and the light scattered at right angles to the incident beam is examined spectrometrically. **1958** *Antiquity* XXXII. 124 The staff consists now of two Senior Scientific Officers, two Research Assistants, three technicians, a secretary and two part-time workers (optical spectrometrist and statistician). *Ibid.*, In Optical Spectrometry, a programme of analysis of prehistoric European bronzes.. is being carried out. **1962** *Oxf. Univ. Gaz.* 9 Mar. 775/2 Continuing his research on the history of British Bronze Age metallurgy, he completed a programme of spectrometric analyses of Early Bronze Age material. **1971** *Nature* 27 Aug. 646/2 Some 3,3-diaryl oxetanes which could not be isolated but only detected spectrometrically in solution. **1973** *Physics Bull.* Feb. 108/1 The term chemi-ionization has unfortunately taken on a different meaning amongst mass spectrometrists. **1975** *McGraw-Hill Yearbk. Sci. & Technol.* 193/1 Flame spectrometry, traditionally a single-element technique, has been advanced recently to include multielement analysis.

spectrophotometer (ˌspɛktrəfəʊ'tɒmɪtə(r)). [f. SPECTRO- + PHOTOMETER.] An instrument designed to measure the relative intensity of light (usu. transmitted or emitted by a substance under study) at different wavelengths in a particular region of the spectrum.

1881 *Nature* XXIV. 552 Photometric comparison of luminous sources of different colours, by M. Crova. He uses a spectrophotometer. **1938** *Jrnl. Optical Soc. Amer.* XXVIII. 18 This spectrophotometer was designed specifically to measure in the visible region the absorption spectrum of visual purple. **1948** *Nature* 21 Feb. 285/2 Total penicillin may be assayed non-biologically with the aid of the.. ultra-violet spectrophotometer. **1966** *McGraw-Hill Encycl. Sci. & Technol.* II. 594 d/1 The split-beam spectrophotometer.. measures the difference in absorption at any given wavelength between two nearly identical cell suspensions. **1976** C. SKEGG tr. *Welz's Atomic Absorption Spectroscopy* v. 84 In modern spectrophotometers a logarithmization of the signal takes place within the instrument, so that the readout on the display is already in absorbance and no conversion is required.

Hence **ˌspectrophoto'metric** *a.*, of, pertaining to, or employing a spectrophotometer; **ˌspectrophoto'metrically** *adv.*; **spectropho'tometry**, the technique of using a spectrophotometer.

1884 *Boston* (Mass.) *Jrnl.* 13 Sept., A 'spectrophotometric study of pigments', by Professor Nicolls. **1897** *Allbutt's Syst. Med.* IV. 285 Normal fresh urines.. examined spectro-photometrically. **1899** *Phil. Mag.* XLVIII. 421 In direct comparisons of white light this latter principle has been successfully applied; but in spectrophotometry the optical difficulties in the way of its use have prevented the obtaining of corresponding results. **1942** *Astrophysical Jrnl.* XCVI. 451 Spectrophotometric observations of the light of the night sky have been made for the stronger lines of the visual region of the spectrum. **1961** *Times* 9 Jan. 2/3 (Advt.), The Physical Assay Division.. is concerned.. with.. application of industrial methods of analysis including ultraviolet and infra-red spectrophotometry. **1972** R. A. JACKSON *Mechanism* iv. 76 If the reaction is followed spectrophotometrically the presence or absence of stable intermediates is often indicated from the changes in the spectrum as the reaction proceeds. **1976** G. THURSTON *Coronership* i. 13 Methods of analysis by chromatography and spectrophotometry enable accurate results to be produced with speed. **1977** I. M. CAMPBELL *Energy & Atmosphere* ix. 307 (*caption*) Concentration profile of O_2.. versus altitude in the upper mesosphere, measured by rocket-borne spectrophotometric detection.

spectroscope ('spɛktrəskəʊp), *sb.* [ad. G. *spektroskop* or a. F. *spectroscope*.] An instrument specially designed for the production and examination of spectra.

1861 *Proc. Amer. Philos. Soc.* VIII. 279 The results obtained by the spectroscope. **1869** ROSCOE *Chem.* 153 The blowpipe flame.. exhibits a characteristic series of bands when examined by means of the spectroscope. **1880** HAUGHTON *Phys. Geogr.* i. 6 By means of the spectroscope, it has been ascertained that the terrestrial elements, found in meteoric stones, may be found also in the sun.

Hence **'spectroscope** *v. trans.*, to examine by means of a spectroscope.

1881 *Standard* 30 Dec. 5/2 It was photographed and spectroscoped. **1886** PIAZZI SMYTH in *Trans. Roy. Soc. Edin.* XXXII. 521 Hence a solar spectroscoping.. might be expected to have some further special interest connected with our own earth.

spectroscopic (spɛktrə'skɒpɪk), *a.* [f. prec. or ad. F. *spectroscopique*.]

1. Performed by means of the spectroscope.

1864 *Athenæum* No. 1929. 500/2 The spectroscopic examinations. **1870** PROCTOR *Other Worlds* ii. 38 So many of the wonders of modern science are associated with spectroscopic analysis. **1878** NEWCOMB *Pop. Astron.* III. ii. 257 Devoting special attention to the spectroscopic observations. **1883** *Science* I. 115/1 The results of spectroscopic work.

2. a. Presented or afforded by, pertaining or belonging to, the spectroscope.

1869 *Eng. Mech.* 31 Dec. 375/1 Data.. with respect to the spectroscopic appearances of comets. **1879** PROCTOR *Pleas. Ways Sci.* i. 7 In some cases, the quantity of a material to give unmistakable spectroscopic evidence is singularly small. **1884** KNIGHT *Dict. Mech.* Suppl. 835/2 *Spectroscopic Eyepiece*,.. an adaptation of the spectroscope to the microscope for the examination of minute substances.

b. ***spectroscopic binary*** (Astr.), a star whose binary nature is revealed only by a study of its spectrum.

1896 *Circular Harvard Univ. Observatory* No. 11, Professor Solon I. Bailey has found that the star μ^1 Scorpii is a spectroscopic binary. **1930** R. H. BAKER *Astron.* viii. 338 Some examples of spectroscopic binaries among the bright stars are: Capella, Spica, Castor, β Aurigae and Algol. **1975** *Sci. Amer.* Mar. 28/2 The normal star associated with Cygnus X-1 is a single-line spectroscopic binary with a period of 5·6 days. The term spectroscopic here means that the presence of two stars is indicated by a periodic Doppler shift of the spectral lines of at least one of the stars as they revolve around a common center of gravity. **1978** PASACHOFF & KUTNER *University Astron.* vi. 134 (*caption*) Alcor and Mizar provide examples of both visual and spectroscopic binaries.

3. Occupied or dealing with spectroscopy.

1871 tr. *Schellen's Spectrum Anal.* Pref. 4, I regret that the author has reversed the practice of the principal spectroscopic authors. **1871** *Daily News* 12 Jan., It is true the spectroscopic party.. at Oran failed totally.

So **spectro'scopical** *a.*

1870 *Eng. Mech.* 11 Feb. 520/2 The nature of the solar atmosphere is ascertained by spectroscopical examinations of the light of the sun. **1882** *Athenæum* 4 Mar. 286/2 An interesting series of spectroscopical observations.

spectro'scopically, *adv.* [f. prec.] By means of the spectroscope; in respect of spectroscopic qualities, etc.

1871 tr. *Schellen's Spectrum Anal.* 16 *note*, When the light of burning magnesium is observed spectroscopically. **1879** PROCTOR *Pleas. Ways Sci.* v. 125 The part of the remaining light spectroscopically most effective. **1903** *Times* 25 Mar. 10/4 Radium.. remains spectroscopically identical after many months of continuous emission of heat.

spectroscopist (spɛk'trɒskəpɪst, 'spɛktrəskəʊpɪst). [f. SPECTROSCOPE *sb.* + -IST.] One who pursues researches with the spectroscope.

1866 *Athenæum* 3 Mar. 304/3 The following will perhaps interest spectroscopists. **1879** PROCTOR *Pleas. Ways Sci.* i. 8 [It] would not affect those rays sufficiently for the spectroscopist to recognize any diminution of their lustre. **1893** SIR R. BALL *Story of Sun* 195 The phenomenon known to spectroscopists as the reversal of the dark lines.

spectroscopy (spɛk'trɒskəpɪ, 'spɛktrəskəʊpɪ). [f. as prec., after forms in *-scopy*, or ad. F. *spectroscopie*.] The art of using the spectroscope; that branch of science which involves the use of the spectroscope. In mod. use, the investigation of spectra by any of various instruments.

1870 W. HUGGINS *Manchester Lect.* 36 This was the state of this newly-born science of Spectroscopy when in 1861 [etc.]. **1881** M. L. KNAPP *Coming Disasters* 17 The progress made within the last few years in spectroscopy. **1955** *Sci. Amer.* Sept. 144/2 The faintness of the aurora and the rapidity with which it changes make spectroscopy difficult, but development of the technique.. has produced beautiful spectrograms of auroras extending.. into the near ultraviolet and the near infrared. **1966** *McGraw-Hill Encycl. Sci. & Technol.* XII. 589/1 The important instruments that are used in spectroscopy include spectroscopes, spectrometers, spectrographs, interferometers, and spectrophotometers. **1978** *Nature* 21 Sept. 199/2 We intend carrying out further spectroscopy on the object, providing that it does not fade too quickly, to monitor spectral variations.

spectrous ('spɛktrəs), *a.* [f. SPECTRE *sb.* 1.] Spectral.

1652 GAULE *Magastrom.* 215 We see that men are really affected and terrified even from spectrous and ludibrious phantasmes. *Ibid.* 298 [He] was haunted mightily with a spectrous apparition of a beautiful woman. **1678** CUDWORTH *Intell. Syst.* I. ii. §2. 61 They could have been nothing else but a certain kind of Aerial and Spectrous Men. **1809** W. BLAKE *Descr. Catal.* 22 The Plowman of Chaucer is Hercules in his supreme eternal state, divested of his spectrous shadow. **1868** SWINBURNE *Blake* 282 These, with all their flock of emanations and spectrous or vegetating shadows, let us leave to the discretion of Los.

spectrum ('spɛktrəm). Pl. **spectra** (also spectrums). [L. *spectrum*: see SPECTRE *sb.*]

1. An apparition or phantom; a spectre.

1611 SPEED *Hist. Gt. Brit.* IX. xiv. (1632) 770 Walsingham hath written of a fatall Spectrum or Apparition,.. where sundry monsters of diuers colours.. were seen. **1649** BULWER *Pathomyot.* II. ii. 140 Feare also, and a Sudden fright or Spectrum,.. hath the same effect sometimes upon the Muscles of the Face. **1684** *Case of Cross in Baptism* 14 Startled at Thunder, taken in a storm, frighted with a spectrum. **1706** BAYNARD *Cold Baths* II. 309 He would sooner believe Witch-Craft and Spectrums. **1728** *Brice's Weekly Jrnl.* 19 July 1 The Maid's seeing his Spectrum, could be no.. *Deceptio Visus*, but.. was a real Apparition of the Deceased. **1809** W. IRVING *Hist. New York* (1861) 182 Subject to bad dreams.. in the night, when the grizzly spectrum of old Keldermeester would stand sentinel by his bedside. **1860** RUSKIN *Mod. Paint.* V. IX. xi. 326 *note*, Fuseli may wander wildly among gray spectra, but Reynolds and Gainsborough must stay in broad daylight, with pure humanity.

fig. **1657** H. PINNELL *Philos. Ref.* 67 The Spectrum, ghost, or fantasie, the Light of Nature. **1674** GREW *Anat. Pl., Disc. Mixture* (1684) 222 Their notions of Mixture.. being.. so many phantastick Spectrums, serving only to affright men from coming near them. **1710** SACHEVERELL *Answ. Bp. Oxford's Sp.* 21, I was.. surpriz'd.. with an Apparition or Spectrum, which the Magi call a Parenthesis. **1866** HUXLEY *Physiol.* x. 247 Many persons are liable to what may be called *auditory spectra*—music of various degrees of complexity sounding in their ears, without any external cause, while they are wide awake.

2. An image or semblance. *rare.*

1693 PENN *Fruits Solitude* II. §197 A jealous man only sees his own spectrum, when he looks upon other men, and gives his character in theirs. **1831** CARLYLE *Sart. Res.* II. viii, Two little visual Spectra of men, hovering.. in the midst of the Unfathomable.

3. a. The coloured band into which a beam of light is decomposed by means of a prism or diffraction grating. Also, a dark band containing bright lines produced similarly; such a (coloured or dark) band, or the pattern of lines in it, as characteristic of the light source; hence, the pattern of absorption or emission of light or other electromagnetic radiation over any range of wavelengths exhibited by a body or substance.

1671 NEWTON in *Phil. Trans.* VI. 3076 Comparing the length of this coloured Spectrum with its breadth, I found it about five times greater. **1674** *Ibid.* IX. 218 The Sunbeams.. passing through a Glass Prism to the opposite Wall, exhibited there a Spectrum of divers colours. **1728** PEMBERTON *Newton's Philos.* 323 These colours shall discover themselves more perfectly.. the larger the spectrum is. **1788** V. KNOX *Winter Even.* I. iii. 27 All the hues of the prismatic spectrum. **1815** J. SMITH *Panorama Sci. & Art* I. 440 It assumes an oblong shape,.. and exhibits seven different colours. This oblong image is called the spectrum, and from its being produced by the prism, the prismatic spectrum. **1824** *Edin. Philos. Jrnl.* X. 39 Lines are also seen in the spectrum of other fixed stars of the first magnitude. **1839** G. BIRD *Nat. Philos.* 326 The solar spectrum may therefore be regarded as composed of three spectra of equal lengths over-lapping each other. **1879** *Cassell's Techn. Educ.* I. 126/1 Most of our sources of artificial light yield spectra without lines. **1879** *Encycl. Brit.* X. 215/1 When the light of a burning metal is examined with a properly-arranged prism, it is seen to give a dark band or spectrum which is traversed by certain vertical bright lines. **1900** *Proc. R. Soc.* LXVI. 45 The expected argon spectrum was almost entirely absent. **1925** G. A. LINDSAY tr. *Siegbahn's Spectroscopy of X-Rays* vi. 195 X-ray spectra afford one of the most direct sources of information concerning the inner structure of the atom. **1966** *McGraw-Hill Encycl. Sci. & Technol.* VIII. 420/2 Microwave spectra of atoms can be used to measure.. nuclear electric and magnetic moments. **1971** *Physics Bull.* July 401/1 The laser spectrum extends from the vacuum ultraviolet to the far infrared. **1978** PASACHOFF & KUTNER *University Astron.* xxviii. 709 All the lines in the spectrum of 3C 48 were shifted by 37 per cent, a still more astounding redshift.

fig. **1860** HOLLAND *Miss Gilbert's Career* iv. 68 All the colors of the spectrum of truth. **1874** H. R. REYNOLDS *John Bapt.* viii. 453 A luminous spectrum lingers for a while in the atmosphere of Judaism.

b. The entire range of wavelengths (or frequencies) of electromagnetic radiation, from the longest radio waves to the shortest gamma rays of which the range of visible light is only a small part; any one part of this larger range.

1888 *Encycl. Brit.* XXIII. 142/1 When a telescope is to be constructed for photographic purposes the aim should be to unite.. the rays near that portion of the spectrum which act most powerfully on the photographic plate. **1923** GLAZEBROOK *Dict. Appl. Physics* IV. 891/1 Beyond the photographic limit, investigation of the infra-red spectrum by means of the heating effect of the rays has been carried on. **1947** *Sci. News* IV. 54 The wave lengths of the visible spectrum, from red over yellow, green, blue to violet, lie between 700 and 350 millionths of a millimetre. **1962** *Rep. Comm. Broadcasting 1960* i. 5 in *Parl. Papers 1961–2* (Cmnd. 1753) IX. 259 The division by international agreement of the frequency spectrum into bands allocated to particular services forms part of the International Radio Regulations. **1978** PASACHOFF & KUTNER *University Astron.* ii. 21 The new ability that astronomers have to study parts of the electromagnetic spectrum other than light waves enables us to increase our knowledge of celestial objects manyfold.

c. An actual or notional arrangement of the component parts of any phenomenon according to frequency, energy, mass, or the like. Cf. *mass spectrum* s.v. MASS *sb.*[2] 10 d, *power spectrum* s.v. POWER *sb.*[1] 18 f.

1887 *Science* 11 Mar. 238/1 It is proposed to analyze a composition by forming what may be called a 'word-spectrum', or 'characteristic curve', which shall be a graphic representation of an arrangement of words according to their length and to the relative frequency of their occurrence. **1897** J. J. THOMSON in *Phil. Mag.* XLIV. 297 When the cathode rays are deflected by the electrostatic field, the phosphorescent band breaks up into several bright bands separated by comparatively dark spaces; the phenomena are exactly analogous to those observed by Birkeland when the cathode rays are deflected by a magnet, and called by him the magnetic spectrum. **1933** *Proc. R. Soc.* A. CXLII. 347 A large number of experiments was made to determine the distribution of α-particles over the whole of the spectrum, which includes α-particles of ranges between 7 cm. and 12 cm. **1939** *Psychol. Rec.* III. 60 Fig. 1 shows the acoustic spectra of three tones of the same singer and vowel, sung at the three different intensity levels at approximately the same frequency. **1962** A. C. GIMSON *Introd. Pronunc. Eng.* iii. 21 The spectrum above 4,000 cps would appear to be largely irrelevant to the recognition of our vowels. **1971** *Nature* 3 Sept. 2/2 The idea.. is that even quite small explosions can be distinguished from earthquakes of comparable size by the high frequency parts of their seismic spectra. **1973** WILLIAMS & FLEMING *Spectrosc. Methods in Inorg. Chem.* (ed. 2) iv. 181 In many cases, convenient starting points for counting the spectrum are the peaks at m/e 28 (N_2^+) and m/e 32 (O_2^+).

d. *fig.* The entire range or extent of something, arranged by degree, quality, etc.

1936 R. CAMPBELL *Mithraic Emblems* 20 Their sistered stridences ignite The spectrum of the poets' lyre. **1952**, etc. [see *broad-spectrum* a. s.v. BROAD D. 2]. **1958** *Listener* 28 Aug. 308/2 At the other end of the political spectrum Lloyd Warner has used similar methods in his nostalgic account of the status system of old New England. **1964** G. L. COHEN *What's Wrong with Hospitals?* i. 18 Theoretically, students remain long enough on each type of ward to give them a spectrum of experience. **1971** *Sci. Amer.* July 25/2 At the polar ends of the age spectrum—children and 'senior citizens'—the trends at the moment are following different courses. **1979** *Practical Woodworking* Mar. 42 P—— hand tools embrace a wide spectrum of products.

4. The image retained for a time on the retina of the eye when turned away after gazing fixedly for some time at a bright coloured object.

1786 *Phil. Trans.* LXXVI. 313 This appearance in the eye we shall call the ocular spectrum of that object. **1829** *Nat. Philos., Optics* xvii. 46 (L.U.K.), One of the most curious affections of the eye, is that in virtue of which it sees what are called ocular spectra, or accidental colours. **1839** G. BIRD *Nat. Philos.* 398 Thus wafers, or other coloured objects, produce spectra of colours complementary to their own. **1854** *Lardner's Mus. Sci. & Art* I. 85 Unreal objects will often be perceived. These are called spectra. *Ibid.*, This object is an optical spectrum.

5. *Ent.* A spectre-insect (*Phasma*).

1838 *Murray's N. Germany* 34 The minerals and insects are also good; among the latter are various specimens of spectrum, nearly a foot long.

6. *Math.* (See quots.)

1948 P. R. HALMOS *Finite Dimensional Vector Spaces* ii. 79 The set on n proper values of A, with multiplicities properly counted, is the spectrum of A. **1972** A. G. HOWSON *Handbk. Terms Algebra & Anal.* xvii. 83 The set of all eigenvalues of a linear transformation *t* of a finite-dimensional vector space *V* is known as the spectrum of *t*.

7. *attrib.* (in sense 3): **a.** ***spectrum analysis*** (cf. SPECTRAL *a.* 6). Also *fig.*

1866 ATKINSON tr. *Ganot's Physics* 425 The method of spectrum-analysis is most readily applied to the alkaline metals. **1871** tr. *Schellen's Spectrum Anal.* Pref. 4 The great merit of the book as a popular treatise on Spectrum Analysis. **1873** FARRAR *Famil. Speech* ii. 39 The microscope and spectrum analysis of Philology.

b. Misc., as ***spectrum allocation, -band, -line, microscope, photography, work***.

1871 tr. *Schellen's Spectrum Anal.* 101 The number of the spectrum-lines of a substance. *Ibid.* 456 Qualitative Analysis.. by means of the spectrum microscope. **1889** *Anthony's Photogr. Bull.* II. 389 The bath plate is less suitable for spectrum photography. **1891** *Ibid.* IV. 357 The yet hardly visible spectrum band. **1899** LOCKYER in *Daily News* 13 Nov. 6/7 For this spectrum work very rapid isochromatic plates.. should be employed. **1960** *McGraw-Hill Encycl. Sci. & Technol.* XI. 260/1 (*caption*) Radio spectrum allocations. **1980** *Sci. Amer.* Feb. 32/1 The control of interference lies at the heart of spectrum allocation, which entails the development of systematic plans for the use of frequencies in radio communication.

8. Special Comb.: **spectrum analyser**, a device which analyses a system of oscillations into its spectral components.

1942 *Radiation Lab.* (Mass. Inst. Technol.) *Man.* No. M-115 (*title*) Spectrum analyzer (Type 103) for pulsed oscillators at 3,000 Mc/sec. **1973** *Times* 14 Dec. 8/8 So far they had spent 150 man-hours in preliminary work, setting up 'spectrum analysers, computers, graphical displays and other advanced equipment'.

'spectry, *a. rare.* [f. SPECTRE *sb.* 1.] Spectral.

1796 TOWNSHEND *Poems* 69 When the cowl'd monk.. Fleets o'er the seat of long past crimes; And spectry forms of cloister'd maids In sorrow bow their pensive heads.

†**'speculable**, *a. Obs. rare.* [ad. L. *speculābilis*, f. *speculārī* to SPECULATE. Cf. It. *speculabile*.]

a. That admits of speculation; speculative. **b.** = SPECULAR *a.* 3.

c **1449** PECOCK *Repr.* II. i. 134 Ech treuthe knowun in mannis vnderstonding is a treuthe considerable or speculable or biholdable oonli. **1592** R. D. *Hypnerotomachia* 68 b, Beeing come to the fift mount they finde it speculable, lyke a mirrour.

specular ('spɛkjʊlə(r)), *a.* [ad. L. *speculāris*, f. *speculum* SPECULUM; or, in senses 6 and 7, f. L. *speculārī* to spy, observe, *specula* watch-tower. Cf. F. *spéculaire* (16th c. in Godef. *Compl.*), Prov. *specular*, It. *speculare, specolare*, Sp. and Pg. *especulario*.]

I. 1. a. ***specular stone*** (after L. *specularis lapis*), a transparent or semi-transparent substance formerly used as glass or for ornamental purposes; a species of mica, selenite, or talc; a piece or flake of this. (Cf. PHENGITE.) *Obs.* exc. *arch.*

1577 HARRISON *England* II. xii. (1877) I. 236, I find obscure mention of the specular stone to haue beene found and applied to this use [*sc.* window-making] in England. **1627** DONNE *Serm.* Wks. 1839 IV. 472 In Temples made of Specular Stone that was transparent as glass or crystal. **1677** PLOT *Oxfordsh.* 68 Unless they are particles of the specular stone, or English Talc. **1715** tr. *Pancirollus' Rerum Mem.* I. I. vi. 15 Specular Stones were a shining kind of Substance, and..transparent like the Air. **1889** tr. *Rénan's Apostles* xi. 168 The decoration of a hall which he wanted to have adorned with specular stones.

†**b.** A piece of this used as a mirror. *Obs.*$^{-1}$

1640 CAREW *Poems* Wks. (1824) 104 Give then no faith to the false specular stone, But let thy beauties by th' effects be knowne.

†**2.** Of vision: Obtained by reflection only; not direct or immediate. *Obs.*

Based upon *1 Cor.* xiii. 12, where the Vulgate has *per speculum in ænigmate* and the Greek δι' ἐσόπτρου ἐν αἰνίγματι.

a **1619** FOTHERBY *Atheom.* II. viii. §5 (1622) 293 Not in a specular, and ænigmaticall vision; but in a cleere, and immediate one. *a* **1677** MANTON *Transfig. Christ* ii. Wks. 1870 I. 349 Not only doth vision or immediate intuition produce this effect, but also spiritual specular vision, or a sight of God in the ordinances. **1704** NORRIS *Ideal World* II. v. 287 St. Paul says..we see through a glass darkly... This has given occasion to the schools to distinguish of a certain ænigmatical or specular vision, in opposition to that vision of God which is by his essence.

3. a. Having the reflecting property of a mirror; presenting a smooth, polished, and reflecting surface; of a brilliant metallic lustre. Now *Min.*

1661 BOYLE *Scept. Chem.* v. 333 From this red Body.. may be obtain'd a Mercury bright and Specular as it was before. **1666** —— *Orig. Forms & Qual.* 235 Divers of these Christals have..Triangles..and other Figures exquisitely Cut on their smooth & specular surfaces; and others, Bodies of Prismatical shapes. **1796** *Phil. Trans.* LXXXVI. 273 It is evident that the particles of bodies are specular. **1796** KIRWAN *Elem. Min.* (ed. 2) I. 36 The laminæ..have not a polished, or at least, nor a specular surface. **1816** P. CLEAVELAND *Min.* 552 Specular native arsenic. This very remarkable variety of Arsenic possesses a metallic brilliancy. **1829** *Chapters Phys. Sci.* 281 Specular bodies are those the surfaces of which, being polished, reflect the rays in the same order as they come from other bodies. **1851** MANTELL *Petrifactions* iii. §1. 144 Iron-glance, or specular oxide, from Elba, Stromboli, Vesuvius.

fig. **1665** BOYLE *Occas. Refl.* III. vi. (1848) 156 The fine Expressions you applaud, are commonly parts of a Sermon that have no specular Virtue in them.

b. *specular iron* or *iron ore*, hæmatite, esp. the brilliant crystalline form of this.

(*a*) **1796** KIRWAN *Elem. Min.* (ed. 2) II. 162 Specular Iron ore. **1803** *Phil. Trans.* XCIII. 336 The primitive form of the slightly attractable oxide of iron, formerly known by the name of specular iron ore. **1859** R. HUNT *Guide Mus. Pract. Geol.* (ed. 2) 153 Specular iron ore is found throughout Asia, Corsica, Germany [etc.]. **1882** FLOYER *Unexpl. Baluchistan* 125 The blocks of specular iron ore are very heavy.

(*b*) **1804** *Phil. Trans.* XCIV. 332 The fine gray specular iron from Sweden. **1854** BAKEWELL *Geol.* 87 Iron presents itself separately as a volcanic product in the peculiar form of brilliant laminæ, called specular iron, which bears a high polish. **1879** RUTLEY *Study Rocks* x. 155 The crystallised variety, specular iron or ironglance, belongs to the rhombohedral system.

c. Designating or pertaining to reflection by a surface in which incident light is reflected as in a mirror.

1863 ATKINSON tr. *Ganot's Physics* 363 The reflection from the surfaces of polished bodies, the laws of which have just been stated, is called the regular or specular reflection. **1927** *Jrnl. Optical Soc. Amer.* XIV. 371 The instrument is so constructed that the identical areas employed in the measurement of specular density may be used without change for the measurement of the diffuse density. **1940** *Chambers's Techn. Dict.* 789/2 *Specular density*, the photographic density in an image measured with parallel light, as contrasted with diffuse density, when the total light passed is measured, including that dispersed. **1967** E. CHAMBERS *Photolitho-Offset* vii. 76 Some surfaces have both specular and diffuse reflection—such as varnished wood. **1974** *Jrnl. Optical Soc. Amer.* LXIV. 546/2 Conventional definitions of reflectance treat the road as a perfectly diffuse surface and entirely omit the specular component of reflectance.

4. Of a telescope: Fitted with a speculum; reflecting.

1676 *Life Paul Sarpi* in *Brent's Counc. Trent* 21 Gio. Battista Porta..makes honourable mention of Padre Paolo as of no ordinary personage, and particularly of his specular perspective.

5. Performed by means of a surgical speculum.

1898 P. MANSON *Trop. Diseases* xviii. 307 In every case in which there is probability of rectal disease digital or specular examination must be made.

II. 6. Of or pertaining to sight or vision; esp. *specular orb* (poet.), the eye.

1656 BLOUNT *Glossogr.*, *Specular*,..belonging to seeing or spying, to Spectacles or glass windows. **1708** J. PHILIPS *Cider* i. 22 Thy Specular Orb Apply to well-dissected Kernels. **1721** D'URFEY *Two Queens Brentford* v. i, Always considering the Design is for specular Instruction. **1810** SOUTHEY *Kehama* XIV. x, In the fiendish joy within his eyes, She knew the hateful Spirit who look'd through Their specular orbs.

7. *poet.* Of heights, etc.: Affording or giving a wide or extensive view. (Cf. SPECULATION 2 c.)

1671 MILTON *P.R.* IV. 236 Look once more e're we leave this specular Mount Westward. **1833** WORDSW. '*Hope smiled when your nativity was cast*', Calm as the Universe, from specular towers Of heaven contemplated by Spirits pure. **1842** IS. WILLIAMS *Baptistery* I. x. (1874) 115 This is Wisdom's specular height, from whence To view as from a watch-tower things of sense. **1890** J. H. STIRLING *Philos. & Theol.* viii. 144 The specular heights of the universal.

specularite ('spɛkjʊləraɪt). *Min.* [f. SPECULAR *a.* + -ITE[1].] = *specular iron ore* s.v. SPECULAR *a.* 3 b.

1892 E. S. DANA *Dana's Syst. Min.* (ed. 6) 213 Specular iron; Red Hematite, Red Ocher. Specularite. **1959** BERRY & MASON *Mineralogy* x. 364 In the variety called specular hematite or specularite the color is black and the luster metallic and splendent. **1959** J. D. CLARK *Prehist. Southern Africa* ix. 244 Specularite (specular iron) was apparently an often sought-after medium for paint in the Later Stone Age. **1970** *Prof. Papers U.S. Geol. Survey* No. 700-c. 103/1 A specularite-bearing conglomeratic sandstone containing minor malachite was noted about 1 mile southeast of the copper locality.

'specularly, *adv.* [f. as SPECULAR *a.*] In a specular manner; by reflection as in a mirror.

1704 J. NORRIS *Ideal World* II. v. 288 If we have no knowledge of God at all, then we do not know him so much as specularly or ænigmatically. **1930** *Jrnl. Optical Soc. Amer.* XX. 23 The smoother the surface, the greater is the intensity of the specularly reflected light and the greater..is the lustre or gloss. **1978** D. N. LAPEDES *McGraw-Hill Dict. Physics & Maths.* 920 *Specular reflection factor*, the ratio of the specularly reflected light to the incident light. **1980** *Rec. Advances Ultrasound Diagnosis* II. 10 Only echoes specularly reflected could be identified with any certainty.

†**'speculary**, *a. Obs. rare.* [ad. F. *spéculaire*: see -ARY[2].] = SPECULAR *a.* 1.

1694 MOTTEUX *Rabelais* v. xliv. 207 She..led him..into a round Chappel made of transparent speculary Stones.

speculate ('spɛkjʊleɪt), *v.* [f. L. *speculāt-*, ppl. stem of *speculārī* to spy out, watch, examine, observe, etc., f. *specula* a look-out, watch-tower, f. *specĕre* to see, look. Cf. It. *speculare*, *specolare*, Sp. and Pg. *especular*, OF. *especuler*, *speculer*, F. *spéculer*.]

1. *trans.* To observe or view mentally; to consider, examine, or reflect upon with close attention; to contemplate; to theorize upon.

Common in the 17th c.; now *rare* or *Obs.*

1599 SANDYS *Europæ Spec.* (1632) 62 Yet notwithstanding these are theorems which few list to speculate. **1632** J. HAYWARD tr. *Biondi's Eromena* 12 To speculate the meanes of negotiating with diversity of persons, and to put the same in practise. **1643** SIR T. BROWNE *Relig. Med.* II. §13 If we do but speculate the folly and indisputable dotage of avarice. *a* **1706** EVELYN *Hist. Relig.* (1850) I. 54 We should not, therefore, wholly consult our senses when we speculate truth. **1788** T. TAYLOR *Proclus* I. 74 It is just, after speculating its whole and entire genus, to consider the differences of its more particular sciences, according to their species. **1793** —— *Sallust* v. 24 Likewise..we should speculate providence, fate and fortune, virtue and vice. **1852** SIR W. HAMILTON *Discuss.* (1853) 21 We..conceit ourselves that we contemplate absolute existence, when we only speculate absolute privation.

b. Said of the soul, understanding, etc.

1604 T. WRIGHT *Passions* IV. ii. §2. 129 A gluttonous stomacke..causeth such a mist before the eyes of the soul, that shee cannot possibly speculate any spirituall matters. *a* **1652** J. SMITH *Sel. Disc.* iv. 87 Whensoever it will speculate truth itself, it will not then listen to the several clamours and votes of these rude senses. **1678** NORRIS *Misc.* (1699) 157 It being..against the Nature of Understanding to make that truth which it speculates. **1816** *Pamphleteer* VIII. 65 Fables are theological which employ nothing corporeal, but speculate the very essences of the gods.

c. With obj. clause introduced by *how*, *what*, *when*.

1856 *N. Brit. Rev.* XXVI. 192 When the company were speculating what lost production of the human mind was most to be regretted. **1857** J. HAMILTON *Less. Gt. Biog.* 296 They were speculating how the stone might be moved away. **1885** 'MRS. ALEXANDER' *At Bay* xi, She had begun to speculate when Glynn would join them.

d. To talk (a matter) *over* conjecturally.

1862 DICKENS *Somebody's Luggage* i, Speculating it over with the Mistress, she informed me that the luggage had been advertised.

2. To look or gaze at (something); to examine, inspect, or observe closely or narrowly. ? *Obs.*

1616 J. LANE *Contn. Sqr.'s T.* VI. 298 The troopes of horse, before, behind, theare, heere, speculates all approches, farr and neere. **1672** MARVELL *Reh. Transp.* I. 66 If he frequented their company it was only to speculate his own Baby in their Eyes. *a* **1734** NORTH *Lives* (1826) III. 350 Every morning he speculated his urine. **1805** *Spirit Public Jrnls.* IX. 244 Louis shall hold a mirror to thine eyes, Wherein thy downfal thou mayst speculate.

b. *spec.* To observe (the stars, heaven, etc.), esp. as an object of study.

1630 SHIRLEY *Grateful Servant* II. i, I shall neuer eat garlike with Diogenes in a Tub, and speculate the Starres without a shirt. **1652** GAULE *Magastrom.* 7 One contemplates them [i.e. the heavens, etc.] devoutly, and constantly;..the other speculates them superstitiously. **1707** *Athenian Sport* (title-p.), The Eye beholds as much when it looks on a Shilling, as when it speculates the whole Heaven. **1890** J. H. STIRLING *Philos. & Theol.* iv. 73 The sun and moon, which, he [Anaxagoras] said, he was born to speculate.

†**3.** *intr.* To exercise spiritual contemplation.

c **1630** C. LEVER in Farr *S. P. Eliz.* (1845) II. 523 Thy heauenly presence is a faire aspect; There doth my soule delight to speculate.

4. To engage in thought or reflection, esp. of a conjectural or theoretical nature, *on* or *upon* a subject.

a **1677** BARROW *Serm.* ii. Wks. 1686 III. 18 For who would not more readily learn..to draw by setting a good Picture before him, than by merely speculating upon the laws of Perspective. **1774** GOLDSM. *Nat. Hist.* (1776) II. 67 It is all this time storing its mind with objects, upon the nature, the properties, and the relations of which future curiosity may speculate. **1790** BURKE *Fr. Rev.* Wks. 1898 II. 7, I certainly take my full share..in speculating on what has been done, or is doing, on the public stage. **1845** BAILEY *Festus* (ed. 2) 138 Here we can speculate on policy, On social manners, fashions, and the news. **1871** C. DAVIES *Metric Syst.* III. 121 Taxation and philosophy now began to speculate, at the same time, upon the weights and measures of England.

b. Const. *about*, *as to*, *concerning*, etc.

1847 HELPS *Friends in C.* I. viii. 133 Nearly every body whose death was worth speculating about. **1855** *Orr's Circ. Sci., Inorg. Nat.* 217 Adaptations, concerning the nature, object, and extent of which it would be equally foolish and impossible to speculate. **1860** TYNDALL *Glac.* I. v. 38 While speculating as to the wisdom of entering the cavern.

5. To engage in the buying and selling of commodities or effects in order to profit by a rise or fall in their market value; to undertake, to take part or invest in, a business enterprise or transaction of a risky nature in the expectation of considerable gain. Also const. *on* or *in*.

1785 JEFFERSON *Corr.* Wks. 1859 I. 472 Should any attempt be made to speculate on these papers [i.e. the public stocks]. **1787** [implied in *Speculating* vbl. sb.]. **1822** BYRON *Let. to Ellice* 12 June, I do not go there to *speculate*, but to settle. **1839** DICKENS *Nickleby* i, Would he be what he is if he hadn't speculated?

transf. **1841** THACKERAY *Gt. Hoggarty Diam.* xiii, I was not over well pleased that his lordship should think me capable of speculating in any way on my wife's beauty.

b. In the game of speculation (q.v.).

1850 *Bohn's Handbk. Games* (1864) 325 The eldest hand shews the uppermost card, which if a trump, the company may speculate on or bid for. *Ibid.*, The company speculating as they please, till all are discovered.

c. To count or reckon *on* something as probable or certain. *rare*$^{-1}$.

1797 COLERIDGE *Lett.* (1895) I. 215 You might safely speculate on twenty pounds a year or more from your compositions.

d. *trans.* To invest (money) in an enterprise which involves considerable risk.

1907 *Westm. Gaz.* 2 Dec. 7/1 They were compelled to own the cars privately because the railways would not speculate the money.

Hence **'speculated** *ppl. a.*, **'speculating** *vbl. sb.* (also *attrib.*) and *ppl. a.*

1787 M. CUTLER in *Life*, etc. (1888) I. 304 The speculating plan concerted between the British in Canada and New Yorkers was now well known. **1812** COMBE *Syntax*, *Picturesque* xxv. 232 We do not bring our learned powers To vex its speculating hours. **1820** SCOTT *Monast.* xxxi, A rash ..interpretation of the Scriptures, wrested according to the private opinion of each speculating heretic. **1865** H. BUSHNELL *Vicar. Sacr.* i. (1868) 49 The innate sense of justice in men has been mocked by the speculated satisfactions of justice.

speculation (spɛkjʊ'leɪʃən). Also 4 speculacioun, 5-6 -cion, 6 -cyon, -tyon, -tione. [ad. late L. *speculātiōn-em*, noun of action f. *speculārī* to SPECULATE. Cf. OF. *speculation* (14th c.), F. *spéculation*, It. *specul-*, *specolazione*, Sp. *especulacion*, Pg. *especulação*.

In English, as in later L. and the Romance languages, the literal senses have been less usual than the transferred, and the earliest examples occur in the latter group.]

I. 1. The faculty or power of seeing; sight, vision, *esp.* intelligent or comprehending vision. Now *arch.*

1471 RIPLEY *Comp. Alch.* in Ashm. (1652) 121 O Hygh Yncomprehensyble and gloryous Mageste, Whose Luminos Bemes obtundyth our Speculation. **1474** *Cov. Leet Bk.* 393 O splendent Creator! In all oure speculacion, More bryghter then Phebus! **1603** BRETON *Packet Mad Lett.* I. xx. Wks. (Grosart) II. 11 Beleeue not your eyes, till they haue a better speculation. **1605** SHAKS. *Macb.* III. iv. 95 Thou hast no speculation in those eyes Which thou dost glare with. **1648** J. BEAUMONT *Psyche* XXI. lxviii, Her Speculation fix'd its Eye Upon the royal Goodness of her Lord. **1821** SHELLEY *Ginevra* 149 Open eyes, whose fixed and glassy light Mocked at the speculation they had owned. **1829** SCOTT *Anne of G.* xxxiv, His horny eye had lost the power of speculation. **1861** LD. LYTTON & FANE *Tannhäuser* 84 Her eyes Wide open, fix'd into a ghastly stare That knew no speculation.

†**2.** The exercise of the faculty of sight; the action, or an act, of seeing, viewing, or looking on or at; examination or observation. *Obs.*

1509 HAWES *Past. Pleas.* VII. (Percy Soc.) 27 Her goodly chambre was set all about With depured myrrours of speculacion. **1530** PALSGR. 274/1 Speculation, beholding, *speculation*. **1599** SHAKS. *Hen. V*, IV. ii. 31 Though we vpon this Mountaines Basis by, Tooke stand for idle speculation. **1648** BOYLE *Seraph. Love* (1660) 13 Whilst they liv'd Exiles here on Earth, 'twas such a speculation..'as seeing Him who is invisible'. **1693** *Phil. Trans.* XVII. 691 The square Tower in the middle fitted with Holes for Speculation. **1711** ADDISON *Spect.* No. 3 ¶1 In one of my late Rambles, or rather Speculations, I looked into the great Hall where the Bank is kept. **1774** JOHNSON in *Boswell* 1 Oct., Wales is so little different from England, that it offers nothing to the speculation of the traveller.

†**b.** Observation of the heavens, stars, etc. *Obs.*

In some quots. with suggestion of sense 4.

1538 ELYOT, *Astrologia*, the speculation and reasonyng concernyng the celestial or heuenly motions. **1601** HOLLAND *Pliny* I. 597 But now to goe on still with our Astrologie and Speculation of Heaven as wee have begun. **1617** MORYSON *Itin.* I. 59 He [Tycho Brahe] had a little round house of great beauty, in which he did exercise his speculation. **1652** GAULE *Magastrom.* 7 What difference betwixt a divine contemplation and a diviners speculation of the heavens!

†**c.** ***top,*** or ***turret, of speculation***, one from which a wide or extensive view is obtained. *Obs.*

After L. *turris speculationis* (Gregory *Moral.* xxxi. §85).

1653 Codrington *Marrow Hist.* Ep. Ded., Here, as from a Turret of Speculation, you may look down upon the Vulgar. **1667** Milton *P.L.* xii. 589 Let us descend now therefore from this top Of Speculation.

†**3. a.** A spectacle or sight; a spectacular entertainment or show. *Obs. rare.*

c **1440** *Gesta Rom.* i. xxvi. 100 (Harl. MS.), As ofte as a man goþe to the Iolytees of worldlye speculacions, & hathe delectacion in hem. *c* **1520** *Mystery Resurr.* in *Rel. Antiq.* II. 151 It pleasid thi Godhed to tak but three To beholde and see the highe speculatioun, Of thy Godly majestye in thy transfyguratioun.

†**b.** An observer or watcher; a spy. *Obs.*$^{-1}$

1605 Shaks. *Lear* iii. i. 24 Seruants,..Which are to France the Spies and Speculations Intelligent of our State.

II. 4. The contemplation, consideration, or profound study *of* some subject.

Freq. in the 17th cent.; now *rare* or *Obs.*

c **1374** Chaucer *Boeth.* v. pr. ii. (1868) 153 þe soules of men moten nedes ben more free whan þei loken hem in þe speculacioun or lokynge of þe deuyne þouȝt. **1549** *Compl. Scotl.* vi. 62 Ane rustic pastour..distitut of vrbanite, and of speculatione of natural philosophe. *c* **1590** Marlowe *Faustus* iii. 114 Ile liue in speculation of this Art, Till Mephastophilis returne againe. **1604** Wright *Passions* i. xi. 45 The motions of our Passions are hidde from our eyes... Yet for the Speculation of this matter, I thinke [etc.]. **1693** Congreve *Old Bach.* iv. vi, Sure it is a good book, and only tends to the speculation of sin. **1788** T. Taylor *Proclus* I. Pref., The great object of ancient philosophy, was an accurate speculation of principles and causes.

b. Without const., or with *in, into, concerning.*

1550 Bale *Eng. Votaries* ii. E iij, Other instructors he had ..whych..were most conning in that speculacyon. **1563** Shute *Groundes Architecture* B ij b, Optica, is properly called perspectiue, and is of a furder speculacion, then therin can or nedeth to be exprest. **1636** Heywood *Challenge Beautie* ii. i, *Bona.* That you may know it is not lust, but love, And the true speculation I have tane, In both these adjuncts, that proclaime you rare. **1669** Clarendon *Ess.* Tracts (1727) 96 The end of this speculation into ourselves and conversation with ourselves. **1674** *Playford's Skill Mus.* iii. 3 This kind of Counterpoint..may appear simple,..yet the right speculation may give much satisfaction even to the most skilful. **1678** Cudworth *Intell. Syst.* i. iv. 416 Furthermore Aristotle declares, that this Speculation concerning the Deity, does constitute a Particular Science by it self. **1715** *(title)*, The Prophecies of Michael Nostradamus... Made English for the Speculation of the Publick.

c. The conjectural anticipation *of* something.

1795 Burke *Th. Scarcity* Wks. 1842 II. 253 Continually in a state of something like a siege, or in the speculation of it.

5. An act of speculating, or the result of this; a conclusion, opinion, view, or series of these, reached by abstract or hypothetical reasoning.

1432–50 tr. *Higden* (Rolls) V. 27 Ptholomeus, a man nobly erudite in speculacions mathematicalle. **1575** Vautrollier *Luther on Ep. Gal.* 16 There is nothing more daungerous then to wander with curious speculations in heauen. **1588** Lambarde *Eiren.* iii. i. 328 These speculations of M. Marrowes reading, are like inough to fall in practise. **1613** Purchas *Pilgrimage* (1614) 512 Such are his speculations of these hidden fires, that he maketh them the causers of Windes [etc.]. **1673** Temple *Let. Duke Florence* Wks. 1720 II. 286 To make the Speculations of Strangers Abroad, part of your own Diversion at Home. **1708** Swift *Sentim. Ch. Eng. Man* Wks. 1755 II. i. 77 It is not a bare speculation that kings may run into such enormities as are above-mentioned. **1769** Burke *Let. Marq. Rockingham* Corr. 1844 I. 219 Not that I rely much on this speculation of my own. **1793** Smeaton *Edystone L.* §344 In consequence of these speculations, I ordered a well to be sunk near the middle of the peninsula. **1816** Mackintosh *Bacon & Locke* Wks. 1846 I. 332 The source of many mistaken speculations on the important subjects of government and education. **1881** *Nature* No. 618. 414 Speculations respecting their ultimate form or structure will have found a place in the science as soon as such speculations have helped to arrange the facts which are known.

†**b.** An aim, purpose, or intention. *Obs.*

1616 B. Jonson *Devil an Ass* ii. v, They may..spend an houre; Two, three, or foure, discoursing with their shaddow: But sure they haue a farther speculation.

c. A conjectural consideration or meditation; an attempt to ascertain or anticipate something by probable reasoning.

1796 Horsley *Serm.* (1811) 189 The populace that were witnesses of the miracle 'wondered': they wondered, and there was an end of their speculations upon the business. **1833** Ht. Martineau *Brooke Farm* xii. 135 Our annual speculations about how so much good cheer was to be consumed. **1841** Dickens *Barn. Rudge* i, The subject of their speculations had done due honour to the house by calling for some drink.

6. Without article: Contemplation of a profound, far-reaching, or subtle character; abstract or hypothetical reasoning on subjects of a deep, abstruse, or conjectural nature.

a **1450** tr. *De Imitatione* iii. lx. 141 Neiþer þe ȝifte of prophecie, ner worching of myracles, ner speculacion, be it neuere so hye, is of eny estimacion wiþouten hir [*i.e.* grace]. *c* **1532** Du Wes *Introd. Fr.* in *Palsgr.* 1062 Abstynence of Danyell, speculation of Hely, experience of saynt Paule. **1565** Hardyng *Confut.* i. 34 The scriptures haue nede of speculation (that is to witte, to be well studied and considered) to the ende the force and power of euery argument may be knowen. **1596** Spenser *Hymn Heavenly Beauty* 134 Thence gathering plumes of perfect speculation, To impe the wings of thy high flying mynd. **1606** Bryskett *Disc. Civill Life* 252 Euen as sapience or wisedom is the guide and gouernesse of speculation. **1708** Swift *Sentim. Ch. Eng. Man* Wks. 1755 II. i. 72 Because slavery is of all things the greatest clog and obstacle to speculation. **1748** Hartley *Observ. Man* ii. i. §4. 17 Men of great Speculation and Refinement may desire to have this analogical Reasoning supported. **1776** Adam Smith *W.N.* i. i. (1869) I. 11 Philosophers or men of speculation, whose trade is not to do anything, but to observe everything. **1828** Lytton *Pelham* xxxiii, If I have any fault, it is too great a love for abstruse speculation and reflection. **1857** Buckle *Civiliz.* i. 5 Habits of speculation..are the essential condition of all real knowledge. **1875** Jowett *Plato* (ed. 2) V. 25 The same desire to base speculation upon history..we find in the Critias.

b. As opposed to *practice, fact, action,* etc.

1530 Lyndesay *Test. Papyngo* 30 Boith in practick and speculatioun. **1597** Morley *Introd. Mus.* iii. 153 Now.. make a lesson as I haue done, and ioine practise with your speculation. **1599** B. Jonson *Cynthia's Rev.* ii. iii, Your courtier theorique, is hee, that..doth now know the court, rather by speculation, then practice. *a* **1676** Hale *Prim. Orig. Man.* (1677) 25 Usefulness in reference to Speculation or Knowledge, and Usefulness in relation to Practice or Exercise. **1777** J. Adams *Wks.* (1854) IX. 470 This is fact, and facts are stubborn things in opposition to speculation. **1800** *Ann. Reg.* 28/1 His talents were much more fitted for action than speculation.

c. In more or less disparaging use, usually with adjs., as *bare, mere, pure,* etc.; also simply = conjecture, surmise.

(*a*) **1575** Vautrollier *Luther on Ep. Gal.* 35 And that which he thinketh him selfe to know, he attaineth only by bare speculation. **1612** Brinsley *Lud. Lit.* Comm. Pref., Neither are these directions of meere speculation, whose promises are commonly as large, as the performance defectiue. **1665** Sir T. Herbert *Trav.* (1677) 196 For that of Abulfæda..is no new discovery;..I know he has it onely by speculation. **1696** Stanhope *Chr. Pattern* (1711) 87 The reason why these things are seen with so useless speculation, is because our minds are not rightly disposed. **1712** Steele *Spect.* No. 450 ¶1 [Partaking] more of the Invention of the Brain, or what is styled Speculation, than of sound Judgment or profitable Observation. **1780** *Mirror* No. 107, In every art and science, practitioners complain how often they are deceived by specious theories and delusive speculation. **1812** Woodhouse *Astron.* xiii. 135 The enquiry into the form, since the theory is complete without it, is one of pure curiosity and speculation. **1861** Ld. Brougham *Brit. Const.* i. (1862) 13 The mere romantic speculation of political dreamers.

(*b*) **1791** Ld. Auckland *Corr.* (1861) II. 396 There is some speculation here that he may look towards the fourth princess.

d. In ***matter, object, subject,*** etc., ***of speculation***. Also *ellipt.* for this.

(*a*) **1665** Glanvill *Def. Van. Dogm.* 75 The little delight I have in matters that are not of very material speculation. **1736** Butler *Anal.* Introd. (1798) 3 This determines the question, even in matters of speculation. **1769** *Junius Lett.* xii. (1788) 75 Let me..consider your character and conduct merely as a subject of curious speculation. **1788** Priestley *Lect. Hist.* v. xlix. 369 The progress of society, is one of the most..useful objects of speculation. **1810** W. Wilson *Hist. Dissent. Ch.* iii. 63 Points of speculation, or party, he studiously avoided. **1832** Brewster *Nat. Magic* xiii. 340 They afford ground of curious speculation. **1847** Helps *Friends in C.* i. i. 4 It was a matter of frequent speculation with us, whether [etc.].

(*b*) **1793** Smeaton *Edystone L.* §111 The various Strata.. would furnish speculation to the curious naturalist.

e. ***in speculation***, in conjecture or theory; not actually or practically; also, under consideration, in contemplation or view.

(*a*) **1638** Mede *Wks.* (1672) 154 This Faith is not barely Historical and in speculation, but a Faith in motion. **1645** Ussher *Body Div.* (1647) 37 Is God every where in speculation only? **1718** *Free-thinker* No. 90. 246 It avails nothing, that a projected Change is, in Speculation, for the Better. **1777** Hamilton *Wks.* (1886) VII. 483 As to their notion.., I apprehend it will do better in speculation than in practice. **1793** Horsley *Serm. Westm.* 29 Whatever preference therefore, in speculation, he might give to the Republican form, he could not, with these principles, be practically an enemy to the Government of Kings.

(*b*) **1811** Sir Wm. Scott *Dodson's Rep.* I. 32 Operations against Buenos Ayres were entirely in speculation, and not finally decided upon.

†**7.** A plan or scheme for some enterprise or undertaking. *Obs.*$^{-1}$

a **1700** Evelyn *Diary* 7 Sept. 1667, Came Sir John Kiviet to article with me about his brick-work speculation.

8. The action or practice of buying and selling goods, land, stocks and shares, etc., in order to profit by the rise or fall in the market value, as distinct from regular trading or investment; engagement in any business enterprise or transaction of a venturesome or risky nature, but offering the chance of great or unusual gain. Also *Comb.*

1774 H. Walpole *Let. to Mann* 1 May, Next to gaming, ..the predominant folly is pictures... Sir George Colbroke, a citizen, and martyr to what is called *speculation*, had his pictures sold by auction last week. **1776** Adam Smith *W.N.* i. x. i. (1904) I. 127 Sudden fortunes, indeed, are sometimes made in such places, by what is called the trade of speculation. *a* **1817** T. Dwight *Trav. New Eng.*, etc. (1821) I. 218 The first cause..of this evil was, if I mistake not, what has been proverbially called in this country *Speculation.* **1834** *Tait's Mag.* I. 408/1 The evils produced by that species of gambling named speculation. **1897** *Daily News* 10 Apr. 5 The speculation-laden air of Johannesburg.

b. ***on speculation***, on chance; on the chance of gain or profit. Cf. spec *sb.*[1] 1 b.

1811 Miss Hawkins *Countess & Gertrude* (1812) II. 162 A distant relation who had married, at fifteen, in the East Indies, sent out on speculation. **1837** Dickens *Pickw.* xxvi, Won't Mr. Dodson and Fogg be wild if the plaintiff shouldn't get it,..when they do it all on speculation?

9. An act or instance of speculating; a commercial venture or undertaking of an enterprising nature, esp. one involving considerable financial risk on the chance of unusual profit. Cf. spec *sb.*[1] 1.

1776 Adam Smith *W.N.* i. x. i. (1904) I. 127 A bold adventurer may sometimes acquire a considerable fortune by two or three successful speculations. **1787** M. Cutler in *Life*, etc. (1888) I. 305 We obtained..the remainder for a private speculation. **1825** Cobbett *Rur. Rides* 327 The talk about 'speculations', that is to say adventurous dealings, or rather commercial gamblings,..is the most miserable nonsense. **1841** W. Spalding *Italy & It. Isl.* III. 393 The government was to undertake a certain part of the speculation, while the remainder of the capital might be given off in shares. **1880** *Austr. Town & Country Jrnl.* 14 Feb. 314/4 A young fellow who had a speculation in pigs on hand.

fig. **1876** J. Parker *Paracl.* ii. Epil. 387 Life itself is a high and solemn speculation.

10. *Cards.* A round game of cards, the chief feature of which is the buying and selling of trump cards, the player who possesses the highest trump in a round winning the pool.

1804 Miss Austen *Watsons* in J. E. A. Leigh *Mem.* (1871) 357 'What's your game?'..'Speculation I believe.' **1839** Dickens *Nickleby* ix, They sat down to play speculation. **1868** Pardon *Card Player* 83 As a merry game for Christmas parties speculation is without a rival.

speculatist ('spɛkjʊleɪtɪst). [f. speculate *v.*]

1. One who speculates, or indulges in abstract reasoning; a professed or habitual speculator; a theorist. (Very common from *c* 1750.)

1613 tr. *Pedro Mexio's Treas. Anc. & Mod. Times* 12/2 The Septuagint..haue commonly traduced it to be in Eden. .. Other speculatis[t]es do affirme it to be in Syria. **1621** Granger *Eccl.* 24 Let the profoundest speculatist, or curious practitioner, turne the edge of his wit which way he will to finde out some new thing. **1714** tr. *T. à Kempis, Chr. Exerc.* x. 15 Either a lofty Speculatist, or a subtil Disputant. **1750** Johnson *Rambler* No. 14 ¶5 The speculatist is only in danger of erroneous reasoning, but the man involved in life has his own passions, and those of others, to encounter. **1780** Cowper *Progr. Error* 490 Fresh confidence the speculatist takes From ev'ry hair-brain'd proselyte he makes. **1807** *Edinb. Rev.* X. 369 We shall..lay before our readers the opinions of this clever speculatist. **1849** Darwin in *Life & Lett.* (1887) II. 37 This confounded variation..is pleasant to me as a speculatist, though odious to me as a systematist. **1886** A. Weir *Hist. Basis Mod. Europe* (1889) 20 The social principles recommended by speculatists.

b. With disparaging adjs.

1693 W. Freke *Sel. Ess.* xxxiv. 223 'Tis the Curse of dreaming Speculatists, that they not only have no taste of real Wisdom, but mispend the time that should lead them to it. **1766** Eliz. Carter *Let. to Mrs. Vesey* 1 July, The most visionary speculatist must sometimes awake to the cares and solicitudes of real life. **1792** W. Roberts *Looker-on* (1794) I. 373 An Utopian speculatist might amuse himself with planning a department..which should be called the office of advice. **1827** G. S. Faber *Orig. Expiat. Sacr.* 262 The notion of its divine institution originated..with some fantastical innovating speculatists among the modern Puritans. **1850** McCosh *Div. Govt.* 217 He is probably an idle dreamer,.. or a wild speculatist. **1893** *Ch. Times* 20 Oct. 1062 The vapid and airy region of third-rate speculatists.

c. As the title of a book or periodical.

1730 *(title)*, The Speculatist. A Collection of Letters and Essays, Moral and Political, Serious and Humourous, upon Various Subjects. [**1787** Sir J. Hawkins *Life Johnson* 538 Concanen, one of the Dunciad heroes, in a paper called 'The Speculatist'.]

d. With adjs. denoting the subject or sphere of speculation.

1802 Beddoes *Hygëia* viii. 92 The hypothesis of any medical speculatist. **1818** Busby *Gram. Music* 167 Among those who succeeded Rameau, as musical speculatists, was the celebrated Tartini. **1837–8** Sir W. Hamilton in *Reid's Wks.* I. 53/2 Some of the recent physiological speculatists of Germany. **1850** Gladstone *Glean.* (1879) V. lxxxiii. 232 In the other case we may as political speculatists either rank with those [etc.].

2. One who speculates in commerce or finance.

1812 *Examiner* 5 Oct. 634/1 The Corn and Mealing Trade has lately got into the hands of Speculatists. **1832** *Fraser's Mag.* V. 653 Among other inducements to the cupidity of the queen and speculatists, he affirmed [etc.]. **1834** H. Miller *Scenes & Leg.* xxx. (1857) 448 The great wealth of the speculatist proved insufficient.

speculative ('spɛkjʊlətɪv), *a.* and *sb.* Also 5 speculatif, -ijf, -iff, -yff, 6 -ife, -yf(e, -yue, 6–7 -iue. [a. OF. *speculatif, -ive* (mod.F. *spéculatif, -ive,* = It. *specul-, specolativo,* Sp. and Pg. *especulativo*), or ad. late L. *speculātīv-us*, f. the ppl. stem of *speculārī* to speculate.]

A. *adj.* **1.** Of the nature of, based upon, characterized by, speculation or theory in contrast to practical or positive knowledge: **a.** Of knowledge.

c **1380** Wyclif *Sel. Wks.* I. 241 Þis cunnyng was not speculatif. **1555** Eden *Decades* (Arb.) 277 They..confessed that the ordinarie pilottes and mariners ignorant in Cosmographi, are not to bee compared to men of speculatiue knowleage. **1585** Blagrave *(title)*, The Mathematical Iewel, ..compiled and published for the Furtherance..of Gentlemen and others desirous of Speculatiue Knowledge. **1612** Brinsley *Lud. Lit.* xxi. (1627) 252 Other speculative or more curious knowledge in Quiddities. *a* **1674** Clarendon *Surv. Leviath.* (1676) 117 From his speculative knowledge of man-kind. **1736** Butler *Anal.* i. v. Wks. 1874 I. 103 A practical sense of things, very different from a mere speculative knowledge. **1748** Richardson *Clarissa* (1811) V. ix. 124 She has a world of knowledge: knowledge speculative, as I may say, but no experience. **1850** C. Daubeny *Atom. The.* i. (ed. 2) 4 One more proof of the benefits arising from experimental science, and of the unexpected advances in speculative knowledge. **1865** Dickens *Mut. Fr.* I. v, His knowledge of its affairs was mostly speculative and all wrong.

b. Of special sciences, or parts of these.

c **1400** *Lanfranc's Cirurg.* 15 Alle þese þingis..ben but techinge of medicyns [*v.r.* medycine] speculatijf. **1561** T. Norton *Calvin's Inst.* Pref., An arte of brawlyng whiche these men call Speculatiue Diuinitie. **1597** Morley *Introd. Mus.* Annot., As for the diuision, Musicke is either speculatiue or practicall. **1601** Holland *Pliny* II. 344 Chrysippus..altered the Theoricke and speculatiue Physicke of Hippocrates and Prodicus, with all their principles. **1665** Boyle *Occas. Refl.* v. i. (1848) 296 The diligent Studies of Speculative and Polemical Divinity. **1730** Chamberlayne *Relig. Philos.* Pref. p. xx, Euclid, Algebra, and other Speculative Parts of the Mathematicks. **1741** Watts *Improv. Mind* (1801) 112 Endeavour to apply every speculative study, as far as possible, to some practical use. **1859** Sir W. Hamilton *Lect.* (1877) I. vii. 111 Theoretical, called likewise speculative,..philosophy has for its highest end mere truth or knowledge. **1881** Froude *Short Stud.* (1883) IV. II. i. 168 The speculative part of it [religion] was accepted because it was assumed to be true.

c. In general use.

a **1483** *Liber Niger* in *Househ. Ord.* (1790) 50 Men of worshipp, endowed with vertues, morall and speculatiff. **1526** *Pilgr. Perf.* (W. de W. 1531) 31 b, As well in matters speculatyue as practyue. **1615** Crooke *Body of Man* 26 Many of these nice and fine points..serue rather for a speculatiue pleasure & admiration, then be of any vse in the art of physick or Chirurgery. **1677** Yarranton *Eng. Improv.* Addr. Ld. Windsor, They have given the World sufficient Tests of the vast difference betwixt Speculative Notions and Practical Experiments. **1708** Swift *Sacram. Test* Wks. 1755 II. I. 127 The bare opinion of his being vicar of Christ is but a speculative point. **1761** Hume *Hist. Eng.* III. xlvi. 24 The king's despotism was more speculative than practical. **1812** Sir H. Davy *Chem. Philos.* 17 The speculative ideas of the Arabians were more or less adopted by their European disciples. **1849** Macaulay *Hist. Eng.* ii. I. 247 He..had a languid speculative liking for republican institutions. **1880** McCarthy *Own Times* xlv. III. 350 Even against speculative dangers a wise people will always take precautions.

2. a. Of persons: Given to speculation; inclined to theorize or indulge in conjectural reasoning.

c **1546** G. Joye in Gardiner *Declar. Joye* (1546) 53 Euery speculatyue pharisay and idle hypocrite. **1555** Eden *Decades* (Arb.) 218 If there bee any dyfference.., it canne not bee perceaued but by the iudgement of speculatiue men. **1609** J. Dowland *Ornith. Microl.* 5 A Speculative Musitian excels the Practick. **1660** Boyle *New Exp. Phys. Mech.* (1682) 123 To dwell upon all the several Reflexions, that a Speculative Wit might make. **1712** Addison *Spect.* No. 305 ¶8 Six Professors, who, it seems, are to be Speculative Statesmen. **1785** Reid *Intell. Powers* I. viii. 245 Why have speculative men laboured so anxiously to analyse our solitary operations? **1813** Sir H. Davy *Agric. Chem.* (1814) 339 He is too speculative a writer to awaken confidence in his results. **1841** Helps *Ess., Pract. Wisd.* (1842) 4 Many persons are considered speculative merely because they are of a searching nature. **1855** Macaulay *Hist. Eng.* xix. IV. 327 The only statesman, indeed, active or speculative, who did not share in the general delusion was Edmund Burke.

absol. **1774** Goldsm. *Nat. Hist.* I. x, The various opinions that have employed the speculative upon this subject.

b. Similarly of the soul, mind, etc.

1570 Dee *Math. Pref.* *j, Ascend, and mount vp (with Speculatiue winges) in spirit. **1599** Nashe *Lenten Stuffe* Wks. (Grosart) V. 300 The grossest kind of fire that.. illumines my speculatiue soule. **1793** T. Beddoes *Math. Evid.* 10 They seem to promise, to speculative minds, a sort of independance upon external things. **1809–10** Coleridge *Friend* (1818) III. 81 A certain number of speculative minds is necessary to a cultivated state of society.

†**c.** Given to pry or search *into* something. *Obs.*

1605 Bacon *Adv. Learn.* I. iii. §7 To be speculatiue into another man, to the end to know how to worke him,.. proceedeth from a heart that is double. **1612** —— *Ess., Counsel* (Arb.) 322 Councellors should not be too speculatiue into their Soueraignes person.

3. Of life, etc.: Spent in, devoted to, speculation.

1579 Lyly *Euphues* (Arb.) 142 A trifold kinde of life, Actiue,..Speculatiue, which is continuall meditation and studie. **1643** Milton *Divorce* II. xix. Wks. 1851 IV. 115 Christ himselfe hath taught us..even for a bodily healing to dispence with that holy and speculative rest of Sabbath. **1670** Clarendon *Ess.* Tracts (1727) 167 An active and practical condition of life, or a speculative repose. **1849** Macaulay *Hist. Eng.* vi. II. 54 There was..no walk of speculative or of active life, in which Jesuits were not to be found.

4. Of faculties, etc.: Adapted for, exercised in, speculation (†or vision).

1604 Shaks. *Oth.* I. iii. 271 When light wing'd Toyes Of feather'd Cupid, seele with wanton dulnesse My speculatiue, and offic'd Instrument. **1605** —— *Macb.* v. iv. 19 Thoughts speculatiue, their vnsure hopes relate. **1678** Cudworth *Intell. Syst.* 408 That Perfect Happiness is a Speculative or Contemplative Energy, may be made manifest from hence. **1703** Atterbury *Serm.* (1734) II. 126 The other, being a mere speculative Power, hath no Contrary in the Mind of Man to struggle with. **1860** Mill *Repr. Govt.* (1865) 6/2 If any one requires to be convinced that speculative thought is one of the chief elements of social power. **1896** Dk. Argyll *Philos. Belief* 11 Our speculative faculties are altogether untrustworthy on such subjects.

†**5.** Pertaining to vision; optical. *Obs.*

1656 Blount *Glossogr., Catopticks*, professors of the Opticks, or art speculative.

6. Suitable for observation or watching; speculatory. Chiefly *poet.*

1709 Pope *Lett.* (1735) I. 81, I have been inform'd, that you have left your speculative Angle in the Widow's Coffee-house. **1782** Cowper *Jackdaw* 13 Fond of the speculative height, Thither he wings his airy flight. **1784** —— *Task* I. 289 Now roves the eye; And, posted on this speculative height, Exults in its command. **1821** Wordsw. *Eclipse Sun* 1 High on her speculative tower Stood Science.

7. a. Of persons: Given to, or engaging in, commercial or financial speculation. ***speculative builder***, a builder who has houses erected without securing buyers in advance. Hence ***speculative-built*** adj. Cf. spec *a.*

1763 Janssen *Smuggling laid open* 28 Several Persons, who go under the Denomination of Speculative Buyers, purchase Teas there, meerly on an Expectation of the Price rising afterwards. **1776** Adam Smith *W.N.* I. x. (1869) I. 119 The speculative merchant exercises no one regular.. business. **1799** *Hull Advertiser* 6 Oct. 3/3 To keep down the price of corn which speculative men were trying to advance. **1813** Scott *Let.* in *Lockhart* (1837) III. ii. 107 Any rare printed book which a speculative bookseller might purchase with a view to re-publication. **1868** *1st Rep. Comm. Employment Children, Young Persons, & Women in Agric.* 35 in *Parl. Papers 1867–8* XVII. 95 Cottages..have been put up by speculative builders of the flimsiest materials. **1902** G. K. Chesterton *Twelve Types* 13 The colossal diagram of streets and houses is..the opium dream of a speculative builder. **1933** *Archit. Rev.* LXXIV. 120 There is a possibility, of course, that the speculative builder who has bought this estate is an intelligent man. **1960** Pidgeon & Crosby *Anthology of Houses* 94, 2-storey, speculative-built terrace houses. **1973** *Listener* 25 Jan. 118/1 The idiocies and crudities permitted to the developer—or, as I prefer to call him, the speculative builder.

b. Of the nature of, characterized by, or involving speculation.

1799 *Hull Advertiser* 6 Oct. 3/3 Articles which ought..to be exempt from all speculative interest. **1848** Mill *Pol. Econ.* III. xxiv. §2 (1876) 395 There are two states of the market, one which may be termed the quiescent state, the other the expectant or speculative state. **1879** H. George *Progr. & Pov.* VIII. iii. (1881) 371 How speculative rent checks production. **1907** *Standard* 19 Jan. 2/4 Heavy speculative transactions have been in progress in tin for weeks past.

c. Forming an object of speculation.

1890 *Daily News* 30 Sept. 2/5 The market for speculative beetroot continues dull and prices to decline.

8. Special collocations: ***speculative fiction*** (see quot. 1953); ***speculative grammar***, a late medieval scholastic grammatical system in which the structure of language is interpreted through scholastic philosophy in terms of our perception and representation of the world by the 'modes of signification' (*modi significandi*) (cf. modistæ); any one of the grammatical theories arising from this analysis.

1953 R. A. Heinlein in *Library Jrnl.* July 1188/1 The term 'speculative fiction' may be defined negatively as being fiction about things that have not happened. **1978** Speculative fiction [see sci-fi]. **1951** R. H. Robins *Anc. & Mediaeval Gram. Theory in Europe* iii. 80 Most of these philosophical or 'speculative' grammars were entitled *De Modis Significandi* (whence the name 'Modistae'), or, as we might put it to-day, 'On Semantics'; they covered a great deal more ground than would now be included in 'grammar' narrowly considered. **1968** J. Lyons *Introd. Theoretical Linguistics* i. 15 It was the task of scientific, or 'speculative', grammar to discover the principles whereby the word, as a 'sign', was related on the one hand to the human intellect and on the other to the thing it represented, or 'signified'. **1972** Hartmann & Stork *Dict. Lang. & Linguistics* 139/1 New in these universal speculative grammars [were]..the refinements in syntactic analysis, e.g. the function of prepositions, the formal criteria of grammatical acceptability, and the concepts of dependency, government and transitivity. **1975** *Canad. Jrnl. Linguistics* XX. 134 Speculative grammar attempted to show how the 'modes of existence' of objects were apprehended by the 'modes of understanding' of the human intellect.

B. *sb.* †**1.** As a book-title, = mirror *sb.* 4. *Obs.*

c **1430** Lydg. *Min. Poems* (Percy Soc.) 63 Vincencius in his speculatif historialle, Of this saide monk makithe ful mencyoune.

2. †**a.** Speculation; hypothetical reasoning; theory. *Obs.*

After late L. *speculātīva* sb. So F. *spéculative.*

1412–20 Lydg. *Chron. Troy* I. 3578 For-dullid is myn ymagynatif, To deme in practik or in speculatif. **1426** —— *De Guil. Pilgr.* 18575 For speculatyff..With-outen good experience Avaylith lytle or ellis nought. **1474** Caxton *Chesse* III. v. (1883) 119 The maistres of rethorique ben the chyef maistres in speculatyf. *a* **1500** in M. Cooke *Hist. Masonry* (1861) 90 Of speculatyfe he was a master and he lovyd well masonry and masons. **1509** Barclay *Shyp Folys* (1570) 102 Such that haue practise and nought of speculatife.

†**b.** *pl.* Speculative matters; the speculative sciences. *Obs.*

1640 Sedgwick *Christ's Counsell* 258 In speculatives be wise to sobriety, in practicals be as good as thou canst. *a* **1670** Rust *Disc. Truth* (1682) 166 As indispensible are the mutual respects and relations of things both in Speculatives and Morals. **1678** Cudworth *Intell. Syst.* 416 Aristotle.. concludes, that as the Speculative Sciences in General, are more Noble and Excellent than the other, so is Theology or Metaphysicks the most Honourable of all the Speculatives.

c. With *the*: That which rests only on speculation.

1877 Sparrow *Serm.* xix. 254 When..we are compelled ..to make a choice between the speculative and the practical we should give preference to the latter.

†**3.** A speculator or speculatist. *Obs.*$^{-1}$

a **1638** Mede *Wks.* (1672) 878 If it were in Latine, it would make some of your German Speculatives half wild.

speculatively ('spɛkjʊlətɪvlɪ), *adv.* [f. prec.]

1. In a speculative manner; in respect of, by means of, speculation.

1570 Dee *Math. Pref.* C iij b, Thus can the Mathematicall minde deale Speculatiuely in his own Arte. **1599** *Life More* in Wordsw. *Eccl. Biog.* (1863) II. 110 As [he] speculatively, so practicallie taught them to embrace vertue. **1631** R. H. *Arraignm. Whole Creature* xii. §6. 166 Salomon, as the wisest of men speculatively: as the best experienced of men, practically. **1693** Norris *Pract. Disc.* (1711) III. 230 If he that is speculatively wise, did but joyn Consideration to his Notion, he would quickly become practically so. **1713** *Guardian* No. 3 ¶1 These Sages of Iniquity are, it seems, themselves, only speculatively wicked. **1793** Burke *Obs. Conduct Minority* Wks. 1842 I. 623 It is not easy to state for what good end..Mr. Fox should be fond of referring to those theories, upon all occasions, even though speculatively they might be true. **1814** D'Israeli *Quarrels Auth.* (1867) 454 No man was more speculatively bold, and more practically timorous. **1855** Macaulay *Hist. Eng.* xv. III. 579 The objection was, beyond all doubt, speculatively just; but..no practical inconvenience was to be apprehended. **1875** Manning *Mission H. Ghost* ii. 37, I will endeavour then to draw this out, not speculatively, but practically.

b. With a speculative or meditative air.

1883 *Harper's Mag.* Sept. 626/1 She looked speculatively at the..linen duster.

2. Towards, by way of, commercial or financial speculation; on speculation.

1847 in Webster. **1898** *Westm. Gaz.* 16 Feb. 8/1 Whether the shares..should command a premium of 250 per cent. is a question best answered by the speculatively-inclined. **1908** *Ibid.* 10 Nov. 2/1 Occasionally a solicitor may be found who will take up his case speculatively.

'speculativeness. [f. as prec.] The quality of being speculative; tendency towards speculation.

1727 Bailey (vol. II), *Speculativeness*, Propenseness to Speculation, Studiousness in Observation: *Speculativeness* is the Opposite to Practicalness. **1828–32** Webster, *Speculativeness*, the state of being speculative, or of consisting in speculation only. **1855** Milman *Lat. Chr.* xiv. ii. VI. 402 The one man who at that period..by the congenial speculativeness of his mind..was qualified to translate into Latin the mysterious doctrines of the Areopagite. **1890** *Nature* 30 Oct. 633 The subject is worked out with all Mr. Seebohm's..energy and speculativeness.

'speculativism. [f. as prec.] Excessive exercise of, or leaning towards, speculation.

1865 *Spect.* 30 Sept. 1094 The characteristic of the sixteenth century was a *speculativism* alike in thought and action, rather than earnest faith and resolute deed. **1878** *Pop. Sci. Monthly* July 269 Built on the quicksand of æsthetics and speculativism which was quickly swept away by the tide of barbarian invasion.

speculator ('spɛkjʊleɪtə(r)). Also 6–7 -our. [a. L. *speculātor*, agent-noun f. *speculārī* to speculate, or ad. F. *spéculateur*, = It. *specul-*, *specolatore*, Sp. and Pg. *especulador*.]

1. One who speculates on abstruse or uncertain matters; one who devotes himself to speculation or theoretical reasoning.

1555 Eden *Decades* (Arb.) 367 The philosophers, speculatours of naturall thynges, saye that it is engendered of substaunce more watery then fyerie. **1646** Sir T. Browne *Pseud. Ep.* III. xiii. 137 The Writers of Minneralls and naturall speculators, are of another beliefe. **1664** Power *Exp. Philos.* III. 193 The old Dogmatists and Notional Speculators, that onely gaz'd at the visible effects and.. Resultances of things. **1798** Malthus *Popul.* (1878) 5 The most enthusiastic speculator cannot suppose a greater increase. **1855** Paley *Aeschylus* Pref. (1861) p. xii, Pythagoras, one of the most deep-minded speculators of the ancient world, speaks in every page of Aeschylus. **1871** C. Davies *Metric Syst.* III. 285 Some philosophical speculators have started doubts whether the metre is really the forty millionth part of the circumference of the earth.

b. Used as the title of periodicals.

1790 [N. Drake, etc.] The Speculator. **1801** The Speculator, containing essays on men and things.

2. A watchman, sentry, or look-out.

1607 Topsell *Four-f. Beasts* (1658) 406 It is reported by a certain Greek writer that, if their speculator do not give them the watch-word,..they tear him in pieces with their teeth. **1661** R. Burney *Κέρδιστον Δῶρον* 104, I am the speculator and sentinel that chase away all evil with my eyes. **1663** Butler *Hud.* I. i. 711 We,..Like Speculators, should foresee From Pharos..Portended Mischiefs [etc.]. **1725** Broome *Observ.* in *Pope's Odyss.* XII. III. 215 All the boats had one speculator in common, to give notice when the fish approach'd. **1820** T. S. Hughes *Trav. Sicily* I. iv. 139 The speculator or man who descries the movements of the fish.

†**3.** One who engages in occult observations or studies. *Obs.*

1652 Gaule *Magastrom.* 9 Diviners, Speculators, Circulators, Prognosticators,..&c. **1658** Sir T. Browne *Pseud. Ep.* (ed. 4) VI. xiv. 416 The Hebrew letters in the heavens, made out of the greater and lesser Stars, which put together do make up words, wherein Cabalistical Speculators conceive they read the events of future things. **1691** Wood *Ath. Oxon.* I. 244 Dee..appointed his Friend Kelley to be his Seer or Skryer or Speculator, that is to take notice what the Spirits did.

†**4.** An observer, spectator. *Obs.*$^{-1}$

1647 Nye *Gunnery* xviii. 95 As they wriggle to and fro, they will pull one another after them, to the speculatour a great deal of content.

5. A messenger sent to consult an oracle. *rare*$^{-1}$.

1794 T. Taylor *Pausanias' Descr. Greece* III. 149 They sent speculators (*theoroi*) to Delphos.

6. One who engages in commercial or financial speculation.

1778 HAMILTON *Wks.* (1886) VII. 560 The speculators in the city have been bidding against the commissaries. **1786** JEFFERSON *Writ.* (1859) I. 578 There are even speculators in America who will purchase it. **1827** HONE *Every-day Bk.* II. 1476 He was a keen.. speculator, well versed in the mystery of the bulls and bears. **1848** DICKENS *Dombey* vi, One or two bold speculators had projected streets. **1884** *Fortn. Rev.* Mar. 346 There are a class of speculators in the fag ends of leases.

specula'torial, *a. rare*$^{-0}$. = SPECULATORY *a.*

1860 WORCESTER (citing Blount and Bailey). Hence in later Dicts.

'speculatory, *sb.* and *a.* Now *rare.* Also 6-7 -orie. [ad. L. *speculātōri-us*: see SPECULATE *v.* and -ORY. In sense 1 of the sb. from the L. fem. *speculātōria* (sc. *ars*): cf. F. *spéculatoire.*]

A. *sb.* †**1.** The observation or study of occult phenomena. *Obs.*

1569 J. SANFORD tr. *Agrippa's Van. Artes* 52 b, Out of the same fundation commeth Speculatorie, which doth enterprete thunder, lightning, and other impressions of the Elementes. **1676** tr. *Agrippa's Van. Arts* (1684) 99 Among the Arts therefore of Fortune-telling vulgarly professed in hope of gain, are Physiognomy,.. Soothsaying, Speculatory, and Interpretation of Dreams.

†**2.** A place of observation. *Obs.*$^{-1}$

1619 J. BAINBRIDGE *Descr. Late Comet* 14 Appearing to our eye on the superficies of this terrestriall speculatorie.

†**3.** = SPECULATOR 2. *Obs.*$^{-1}$

1775 L. SHAW *Hist. Moray* v. 211 By their speculatories or scouts, they had certain intelligence of the King's approach.

B. *adj.* †**1.** Of the nature of, pertaining to, occult speculation. *Obs.*

1588 J. HARVEY *Disc. Probl.* 26 No Opticall, or Speculatorie Theories: no Cabalisticall, or Traditionall Suppositions. **1652** GAULE *Magastrom.* 244 Whether mythology or astrology (the poeticall or the speculatory fable) serves most to make one another good or more significant? **1676** tr. *Agrippa's Van. Arts* (1684) 105 Upon the same Grounds the Art of Speculatory Divination is founded.

†**2.** Inspectorial. *Obs.*$^{-1}$

1634 T. CAREW *Cœlum Brit.* Wks. (1824) 154 My privileges are an ubiquitary, circumambulatory, speculatory, interrogatory, redargutory immunity over all the privy lodgings.

3. Serving for observation; affording an outlook or view.

1781 WARTON *Hist. Kiddington* (1783) 58 Both these [Roman camps] were nothing more than speculatory outposts to the Akeman-street. **1791** W. GILPIN *Forest Scenery* II. 99 Another small fort.. is generally supposed to have been a speculatory station to the grand camp of Buckland. **1837** CARLYLE *Fr. Rev.* II. v. ii, Extreme Left; sitting on the topmost benches, as if aloft on its speculatory Height or Mountain.

speculatrix (spɛkjʊ'leɪtrɪks). [a. L. *speculātrix*, fem. of *speculātor.*] A female speculator, in various senses.

1611 COTGR., *Speculatrice*, a speculatrix; a contemplatiue ..or watchfull woman. **1744** Z. GREY *Butler's Hud.* II. iii. 1093 *note*, This Sarah Jimmers, whom Lilly calls Sarah Shelhorn, a great Speculatrix. **1841** D'ISRAELI *Amen. Lit.* III. 207 Persons even of ordinary rank in life pretended to be what they termed *speculators*, and sometimes women were *speculatrices.* **1908** *Westm. Gaz.* 29 Aug. 7/2 This.. indicates that the exploitress and speculatrix has just obtained an advantage by doing something particularly mean.

†**specule**, *v. Obs.*$^{-1}$ [ad. OF. *speculer*: see SPECULATE *v.*] *trans.* To regard attentively.

1484 CAXTON *Fables of Æsop* v. vi, The he goot.. speculynge and beholdynge his shadowe [in the water].. sayd suche wordes within hym self.

speculist ('spɛkjʊlɪst). [f. SPECUL-ATE *v.* + -IST.] = SPECULATIST.

1707 C. N. *Poem on Union* 18 No more vain Speculists your Fancies Cheat. **1788** G. A. STEVENS (*title*), The Adventures of a Speculist, or, a Journey through London. **1825** N. WOOD *Railroads* 290 The ridiculous expectations, or rather professions, of the enthusiastic speculist. **1861** I. TAYLOR *Spir. Hebrew Poetry* 198 The astute speculist shall be heard quoting the very man—who is quoting Isaiah.

†**'speculous**, *a. Obs.*$^{-1}$ Speculative.

?*c* **1600** *Distr. Emperor* IV. iii. in Bullen *O. Pl.* (1884) III. 236 *Ol.* Thys newe pyle of honor walks as if A would knocke patts with heaven. *Rich.* Tys not unlike Your owne true pryde dothe make you speculous.

‖**speculum** ('spɛkjʊləm). Pl. 'specula and -ums. [L. *speculum*, f. *specĕre* to look (at), observe. So F. *spéculum*, It. *speculo*, *specolo*, Sp. *espéculum.*]

1. A surgical instrument of various forms, used for dilating orifices of the body so as to facilitate examination or operations.

Freq. with Latin genitive of the part for which the instrument is used, as ***speculum oculi, oris***, etc.

1597 A. M. tr. *Guillemeau's Fr. Chirurg.* C ij b/1 A Dilatorye of the Eyeliddes, or the Speculum of the Eye. **1671** PHILLIPS, *Speculum oris*, an Instrument to skrew open the mouth, that the Chirurgion may discern the diseased parts of the throat. **1693** tr. *Blancard's Phys. Dict.* (ed. 2), *Dilatorium*, a Chyrurgeon's Instrument, wherewith the Womb or the Mouth is dilated or opened. It is called likewise *Speculum*, because by it one may see into the Mouth or the Womb. **1752** SMELLIE *Midwifery* Introd. p. xlix, He is the first who gives a draught of the *Speculum Matricis* for dilating the Os Internum. **1800** *Med. Jrnl.* IV. 103 Permit me to offer the model of a Speculum Oculi, for insertion in the Medical and Physical Journal. **1862** *Catal. Internat. Exhib., Brit.* II. No. 3552, *Specula*, an elegant assortment for the eye, ear, vagina, rectum and nose. **1897** *Allbutt's Syst. Med.* III. 983 Under an anæsthetic the speculum may be of service.

2. a. A mirror or reflector (of glass or metal) used for some scientific purpose; †a lens.

1646 SIR T. BROWNE *Pseud. Ep.* VII. xviii. (1686) 312 Archimedes burnt the ships of Marcellus with Speculums of Parabolical figures. **1666** BOYLE *Orig. Formes & Qual.* (1667) 30 The giving to a large Metalline Speculum a concave figure, would never enable it to set wood on fire. **1756-7** tr. *Keysler's Trav.* (1760) I. 401 The notes are written in a very small hand,.. so that they cannot be easily read without a magnifying *speculum.* *c* **1790** IMISON *Sch. Art* I. 218 There are four of these concave specula, of different magnifying powers, to be used as objects to be examined may require. **1825** *Gentl. Mag.* XCV. I. 292/1 On opening it, it was found to contain in the lid a small convex metallic *speculum*, and in the under-part a larger one. **1860** FARADAY *Forces Nat.* (1874) 186 A single small speculum, no larger than a nut, will send it in any direction we please. **1873** SPON *Workshop Rec.* Ser. I. 317/1 Place the speculum, face downwards, in a dish.

fig. **1826** KIRBY & SP. *Entomol.* xlvii. IV. 404 The ultimate object intended to be reflected from this great speculum of creation. **1829** I. TAYLOR *Enthus.* vi. 146 The few individuals in every age to whom it has happened to live, and act, and speak under the focus of the speculum of history.

b. *spec.* A metallic mirror forming part of a reflecting telescope.

1704 NEWTON *Optics* (1721) 97 Such an Instrument,.. if it be six Foot long, (reckoning the length from the Speculum to the Prism, and thence to the Focus T). **1782** J. EDWARDS in *Naut. Almanac* (1787) 52 The Springs at the Back of the great Speculum, which are every Moment varying their Elasticity. **1815** J. SMITH *Panorama Sci. & Art* I. 44 It.. is susceptible of so exquisite a polish, as to be admirably adapted for the speculums of telescopes. *c* **1865** *Wylde's Circ. Sciences* I. 73/2 The speculum is generally made of an alloy composed of variable quantities of copper and tin. **1868** LOCKYER *Elem. Astron.* §481 The largest reflector in the world has been constructed by the late Earl of Rosse; its mirror, or *speculum*, is six feet in diameter.

c. *transf.* A telescope fitted with a speculum.

1789 HERSCHEL in *Phil. Trans.* (1790) LXXX. 10 In hopes of great success with my forty-feet speculum, I deferred the attack upon Saturn till that should be finished.

†**3.** A diagram or drawing. *Obs.*$^{-1}$

1676 COLEY *Clavis Astrol.* (ed. 2) III. 674 A Speculum of the Geniture, or Table of the Radiations of the Planets.

4. *Ornith.* A lustrous mark on the wings of certain birds; = MIRROR *sb.* 6 b.

1804 BEWICK *Brit. Birds* II. 342 The exterior webs.. are glossed with gold green, which forms the speculum or beauty-spot of the wings. **1863** C. ST. JOHN *Nat. Hist. & Sport Moray* 35 The pochard has no speculum or bright bar on the wing. **1871** DARWIN *Desc. Man* I. viii. 291 The beautiful green speculum on the wings is common to both sexes.

5. = *speculum metal* (see sense 6 a).

1912 *Phil. Mag.* XXIV. 321 The gold surface was brought into closer proximity to the speculum surface. **1929** *Bureau of Standards Jrnl. Res.* (U.S.) II. 343 Data are presented on the ultra-violet reflecting power of various metals—beryllium, chromium,.. speculum, stellite, and stain-less steel. **1941** *Proc. Physical Soc.* LIII. 263 It is not without interest to note that speculum has not such a good reflecting power as the three former materials. **1966** *McGraw-Hill Encycl. Sci. & Technol.* XIII. 650/1 Among special cast bronzes are bell metal.. and speculum.

6. *attrib.* **a.** ***speculum metal***, an alloy of copper and tin used for making specula. Also ***speculum steel.***

1796 *Phil. Trans.* LXXXVI. 438 The composition in common use, which contains the greatest proportion of tin, is called speculum metal. **1807-10** TANNAHILL *Poems* (1846) 76 'Twas by the rays' reflected heat, Frae speculum steel. **1818** W. PHILLIPS *Outl. Min. & Geol.* (ed. 3) 46 If the proportion of tin [to copper] amount to one third, it forms speculum metal, used for reflecting telescopes. **1873** SPON *Workshop Rec.* Ser. I. 13/1, 2 lbs. copper, 1 lb. tin, 1 oz. arsenic, form a good speculum metal.

b. ***speculum forceps*** (see quot. 1875).

1875 KNIGHT *Dict. Mech.* 2261/1 *Speculum-forceps*, long, slender forceps, used for dressing wounds or operating on parts not accessible except through speculums. **1881** *Trans. Obstet. Soc. Lond.* XXII. 47 The ovum could generally be removed by the administration of ergot and the ordinary speculum forceps.

sped, *ppl. a.* [Pa. pple. of SPEED *v.*] Discharged, let go.

1891 H. HERMAN *His Angel* 75 No human ingenuity has yet invented the means of recalling the sped bolt.

sped, obs. f. SPADE *sb.*[1] and *sb.*[3], SPEED *sb.*; pret. of SPEED *v.*

spedd(e, obs. pret. of SPEED *v.*

spede, obs. f. SPEED *sb.* and *v.*

spedee, sped(e)ful(le, spedi, etc., obs. ff. SPEEDY *a.*, SPEEDFUL *a.*, etc.

speece, variant of SPECE *Obs.*

speech (spiːtʃ), *sb.*[1] Forms: α. 1-2 spræc, sprec, 2 sprace, spræche. β. 1 spæc, spec, 2 spece, 3 spæche (spache, spiche), 3-6 speche (4 spieche), 4-6 spech, 6- speech, 6-7 speach, speache; *Sc.* 6 speitche, 6-7 speiche. [OE. *spræ̆c, spréc* (later *spǣc, spéc*), = OFris. *sprêke, sprêtse* (NFris. *sprêk, spriak*) and *sprâke* (WFris. *sprake, spraek*, EFris. *sprôk*), MDu. *sprāke, spraec* (Du. *spraak*), OS. *sprâka* (MLG. *sprâke*, LG. *sprâke, sprâk*, etc.; hence Sw. *språk*, Da. *sprog*), OHG. *sprâhha* (MHG. *sprâche*, G. *sprache*), f. *sprǣc-* the pret. pl. stem of *sprecan, specan* SPEAK *v.* As in the verb, the forms with *spr-* did not survive beyond the 12th century.]

I. 1. a. The act of speaking; the natural exercise of the vocal organs; the utterance of words or sentences; oral expression of thought or feeling.

c **725** *Corpus Gloss.* (Hessels) S 299 *Sermo*, spręc. *c* **897** K. ÆLFRED tr. *Gregory's Past. C.* 274 Hit is awriten.. ðætte hwilum sie spræce tiid, hwilum swiȝȝean. *c* **1000** *Ags. Gosp.* Matt. vi. 7 Hiȝ wenað þæt hi sin ȝehyrede on hyra meniȝfealden spæce. *c* **1230** *Hali Meid.* 17 Hire forme fulst is sihðe:.. Speche is hire oðer help. **1297** R. GLOUC. (Rolls) 7197 Stalwarde mon of speche he was. *c* **1330** *Assump. Virg.* (B.M. MS.) 628 Oure mayne þee knewe þat ilke nyȝt Bothe bi speche & by syȝt. *c* **1386** CHAUCER *Prol.* 783 Hold up youre hond withoute more speche. *c* **1400** LOVE *Bonavent. Mirr.* (1908) 53 For moche speche with oute frute is a grete vice and displesynge to god and man. *c* **1470** *Gol. & Gaw.* 261 Than schir Spynagrose with speche spak to the king. **1500-20** DUNBAR *Poems* xx. 4 In mekle speiche is part of vanitie. **1594** T. B. *La Primaud. Fr. Acad.* II. 89 Thus the thoughtes and counsailes of the minde and spirite are discouered and manifested by speach. **1667** MILTON *P.L.* VIII. 377, I with leave of speech implor'd, And humble deprecation thus repli'd. **1690** LOCKE *Hum. Und.* III. vi. (1695) 258 This is adjusted to the true end of Speech, which is to be the easiest and shortest way of communicating our Notions. **1732** BERKELEY *Alciphr.* I. §14 Men.. express their thoughts by speech. **1751** HARRIS *Hermes* Wks. (1841) 117 Since speech, then, is the joint energy of our best and noblest faculties. **1825** SCOTT *Talism.* xxii, A movement.. attended with no speech and very little noise. **1864** *Reader* 14 May 626 The author would define human speech as a method of expressing human thought by audible sounds. **1887** BOWEN *Æneid* VI. 387 He accosts them, and first breaks silence in speech.

fig. **1611** SHAKS. *Wint. T.* V. ii. 14 There was speech in their dumbness, Language in their very gesture.

transf. **1866** B. TAYLOR *Euphorion* 273 The speech of winds. **1904** SWINBURNE *Channel Passage*, etc. 181 The speech of storm, the thunders of the soul.

b. *transf.* The speaking or sounding of a musical instrument, organ-pipe, etc.

1862 *Catal. Internat. Exhib., Brit.* II. No. 3377, Quickness of 'speech', flute-like quality of tone,.. are some of the characteristics of the English harmonium. **1880** *Grove's Dict. Music* II. 578 The manner of testing the 'speech' [of an organ] by blowing the pipe with the mouth in various ways. **1881** W. E. DICKSON *Pract. Organ-building* xii. 146 The speech of the pipe will be entirely unaltered.

†**c.** *fig.* Mouth-piece; organ. *Obs.*$^{-1}$

1578 T. N. tr. *Conq. W. India* (1596) 34 Certainly he was the meane and speech of all their proceedings.

d. *spec.* in *Linguistics.* = PAROLE *sb.* 3.

[**1924**: see *speech-utterance*, sense 12 a below.] **1935** [see PAROLE *sb.* 3]. **1937** J. R. FIRTH *Tongues of Men* 16 De Saussure's famous lectures.. in which the speech-language distinction is regarded as fundamental. **1953** U. WEINREICH *Languages in Contact* ii. 9 The question of merging vs. unmerged coexistence is a problem *par excellence* in speech-language relations. **1964** *English Studies* XLV. (Suppl.) 35 A second aspect of no less importance is the distinction between 'language' (*langue*) and 'speech' (*parole*). **1974** M. TAYLOR in *Metz's Film Lang.* p. ix, *Speech* (parole) is the antithesis, or, rather, correlative, of language system: language system is the social aspect of language, whereas speech is the utterance, the actual practice, of a language system.

2. a. Talk, speaking, or discourse; colloquy, conversation, conference. Commonly const. *with* or *of* (a person), and chiefly occurring in phrases, esp. ***to have speech.***

†*in speech with*, in negotiation with. *Obs.*

(*a*) *c* **900** tr. *Baeda's Hist.* III. xxviii. 248 Osweo.. & Ecgberht.. hæfdon betweoh him spræce & ȝeþeahte, hwæt to donne wære [etc.]. *c* **975** *Rushw. Gosp.* John xi. 47 ðisomnadun.. ða biscopas & æ-larwas to sprece. *c* **1000** ÆLFRIC *Saints' Lives* iv. 342 Se dema.. æfter langsumre spræce let þa modor to þam suna. *c* **1200** ORMIN 12803 Biforenn þatt Filippe toc To clepenn þe to spæche. *c* **1400** *Pilgr. Sowle* (Caxton, 1483) IV. xxiv. 70 We shalle take the right weye to the yonder lady of whiche we ben in speche. **1604** SHAKS. *Oth.* II. iii. 225 Montano and my selfe being in speech, There comes a Fellow. **1667** MILTON *P.L.* IX. 1133 Adam.. Speech intermitted thus to Eve renewd. **1850** TENNYSON *In Mem.* Concl. xxvi, Again the feast, the speech, the glee.

(*b*) *c* **900** tr. *Baeda's Hist.* I. xxvii. 72 Hafa ðu mid þone ilcan biscop sprece & ȝeþeahte hwæt to donne sy. *c* **1000** ÆLFRIC *Hom.* II. 584 Seo cwen ða hæfde spræce wið Salomon. *a* **1122** *O.E. Chron.* (Laud MS) an. 1085, Æfter þisum hæfde se cyng mycel ȝeþeaht & swiðe deope spæce wið his witan ymbe þis land. *c* **1275** *O.E. Misc.* 86 Ich hit am ..þat wiþ þe holde speche. **1489** *Cely Papers* (Camden) 15, I am in speche wyt Hewe Brone.. for money. **1596** HARINGTON in *Metam. Ajax* (1814) p. xiv, To make him come to speech with him. **1601** SHAKS. *All's Well* II. v. 62 He desires Some priuate speech with you. **1653** HOLCROFT *Procopius, Goth. Wars* II. 60 Venetia, where having speech with Vitalius, they repented of their Errour against the Emperour. **1819** SCOTT *Ivanhoe* xliii, When, in speech with each other, they expanded their blubber lips. **1837** CARLYLE *Fr. Rev.* II. II. ii, There is speech of men in uniform with men not in uniform.

(*c*) **1599** SHAKS. *Much Ado* V. ii. 3 Praie thee.. deserue well at my hands, by helping mee to the speech of Beatrice. **1821** SCOTT *Kenilw.* xxxiv, Look to it that none have speech of her. **1858** M. ARNOLD *Merope* 928 A messenger.. Arrived, and of the King had speech but now. **1872** BLACK *Adv. Phaeton* xii. 165 He had come from London to get speech of his sweetheart.

b. With possessive pronoun, or *the* and genitive: The opportunity of speaking or conversing with a person; an audience or interview with one. In phrases *to come, be admitted, bring, to* (one's) *speech*. Now *arch.* or *Obs.*

c **900** tr. *Baeda's Hist.* I. xxv. 58 Se cyning..het Agustinum mid his ȝeferum þider to his spræce cuman. *a* **1122** *O.E. Chron.* (Laud MS.) an. 1093, Ne mihte he beon weorðe..ure cynges spæce. **1123** *Ibid.* an. 1123, Ær hi mihte cumen to þes papes spræce. **1451** CAPGRAVE *Life St. Aug.* 16 Sche is come to lond and to þe speche of hir son. **1560** DAUS tr. *Sleidane's Comm.* 384 b, Being admitted to his speache aboute the begynnynge of December. **1595** RALEIGH *Discov. Guiana* 2 In all that time we came not to the speach of any Indian or Spaniard. **1640** tr. *Verdere's Rom. of Rom.* II. 169, I will bring you to the speech of her whom it represents. **1690** G. FAREWELL in *Andros Tracts* II. 187 He could never obtaine a releasement, or by any meanes come to the speech of any of their Magistrates. **1734** *Col. Records Pennsylv.* III. 548 They were admitted after some time to the Speech of the Prisoners. **1778** *Hist. Eliza Warwick* II. 49 Sir Charles's valet..soon brought her to the speech of him. **1809** MALKIN *Gil Blas* v. i. ⁋65 He found the means of getting to the speech of me in private. **1821** SCOTT *Nigel* xxvii, To the speech of the King you will not come so easily, unless you..meet him alone.

c. Mention *of* a thing. Also with *no*. Now *rare*.

c **1305** *Land Cokayne* 111 in *E.E.P.* (1862) 159 N'is no spech of no drink, Ak take inoȝ wiþ-vte swink. *c* **1440** *Pallad. on Husb.* I. 1115 Conuenyent hit is to knowe, of bathis Whil speche is mad [etc.]. **1565** RANDOLPH in Tytler *Hist. Scot.* (1864) III. 194 The speech of this marriage to any of them all..is so much contrary to their desires that [etc.]. **1592** *Arden of Feversham* IV. iv. 66 But see in any case you make no speache Of the cheare we had at my Lord Cheineis. **1659** H. THORNDIKE *Wks.* (1846) II. 550 Being meant of the vine which he had speech of a little afore that. **1864** TROLLOPE *Can you forgive her?* I. xix. 150 No payment of former loans had been made, nor had there been any speech of such.

†**d.** *to take the speech* [after F. *prendre la parole*], to take one's turn in conversation. *Obs.*$^{-1}$

1612 SHELTON *Quix.* I. IV. xiv. 453 Then she taking the speech, demanded..whether I was a Gentleman.

3. a. Common or general talk; report, rumour, or current mention *of* something. Freq. with *much* or *great*. Now *rare* or *Obs.* (Cf. 9 a.)

c **1200** ORMIN 4877 All onn hæþing & o skarn Off me gaþ eȝȝwhær spæche. *c* **1275** LAY. 4018 Þo was mochel speche ouer al þeos kineriche of Juden þare cwene. **1390** GOWER *Conf.* II. 31 Anon as Demephon it herde, And every man it hadde in speche, His sorwe was noght tho to seche. *c* **1400** *Three Kings Cologne* (1886) 51 Grete speche was in all þe contrey among all þe pepil long tyme after of hem. **1533** MORE *Debell. Salem* Wks. 930/1 And of thys trauail..I herde much speach made almost euery weeke. **1562** *Child-Marriages* 99 He sais he dwellid nere them, & ther was spech of such thinges, but he toke no hede of them. **1601** JONSON *Ev. Man in Hum.* (Q.[1]), III. ii. 35 Doctor Clement, what's he? I haue heard much speech of him. **1622** BACON *Hen. VII*, 211 My Lord, I haue heard much of your Hospitalitie, but I see it is greater then the speach. **1837** CARLYLE *Fr. Rev.* III. II. i, There comes Committee Report on that Decree.., and speech of repealing it.

†**b.** Const. with inf. or clause. *Obs.*

1600 E. BLOUNT *Hosp. Incur. Fooles* 309 Besides there was speech to sende fowre galliasses and twelue galleies. **1616** SIR C. MOUNTAGU in *Buccleuch MSS.* (Hist. MSS. Comm.) I. 250 There is now speech the Lord Chief Baron shall go into the King's Bench. **1677** W. HUBBARD *Narrative* II. 5 In the mean time before there was yet any Speech, or endeavour to settle any other Plantation in those parts.

†**c.** *in speech*, spoken about, mentioned. *Obs.*

1602 SIR H. SAVILE in *Buccleuch MSS.* (Hist. MSS. Comm.) I. 36 A fit man is sought out to be employed.., and yourself already here in speech for that service. **1617–8** SIR D. CARLETON *Lett.* (1775) 233, I have been moved..concerning the residence of our merchant-adventurers, which hath been often attempted, and is now again in speech, to be removed from Middleburg. **1628** HOBBES tr. *Thucydides* (1822) 13 The truest quarrel, though least in speech, I conceive to be the growth of the Athenian power.

II. 4. The form of utterance peculiar to a particular nation, people, or group of persons; a language, tongue, or dialect.

c **888** K. ÆLFRED *Boeth.* xviii. §2 Forðon hiora spræc is todæled on twa & [on] hundseofontiȝ, & ælc þara spræca is todæled on maneȝa þioda. *c* **1000** ÆLFRIC *Gen.* xi. 1 Ealle men spræcon ane spræce. *a* **1122** *O.E. Chron.* (Laud MS.) an. 1095, þa het he makian ænne castel..& hine on his spæce Malueisin het, þæt is on Englisc Yfel nehhebur. *c* **1200** ORMIN Ded. 130 And tærfore hafe icc turrnedd itt Inntill Ennglisshe spæche. *Ibid.* 16057 To spekenn wel Wiþþ alle þede spæchess. *c* **1250** *Gen. & Ex.* 665 Al was on speche ðor bi-foren, ðor woren sundri speches boren. **13..** *Cursor M.* 2270 (Gött.), þat first was bot an and na ma; Nou er þer spechis sexti and tua. **1387** TREVISA *Higden* (Rolls) II. 93 Gildas..turnede þese tweie lawes out of Bretoun speche in to Latyn. *c* **1400** MAUNDEV. (Roxb.) iii. 8 Þare er also many oþer diuerse cuntreezand spechez..obeyand to þe emperour. **1535** COVERDALE *2 Kings* xviii. 26 Speake to thy seruantes in the Syrians language,..and speake not vnto vs in the Iewes speche. **1547** BOORDE *Introd. Knowledge* iv. (1870) 137 In Scotlande they haue two sondry speches. **1603** G. OWEN *Pembrokeshire* (1892) 17 Both the ffleminges and ffrench speach alltogether worne awaie. **1674** tr. *Scheffer's Lapland* 74 When from the original of the People he infers the same of the Speech. **1727** DE FOE *Syst. Magic* I. i. (1840) 17 The several families who understood one another's speech kept together. **1840** HOOD *Up the Rhine* 31 They deal in foreign gestures, And use a foreign speech. **1875** WHITNEY *Life Lang.* iii. 37 There are at least two sounds in the Anglo-Saxon which are unknown in our present speech.

5. The faculty or power of speaking, or of expressing thoughts by articulate sounds.

? *a* **1000** *Laws Ethelb.* §52 (Liebermann), Ȝif spræc awyrd weorð .XII. scillingas. *c* **1000** *Sax. Leechd.* II. 288 Ȝif hwam seo spræc oþfylð. *c* **1053** *O.E. Chron.* (MS. C) an. 1053, þa færinga sah he niðer wið þæs fotsetles spræce benumen. *a* **1175** in Napier *Holy Rood-tree* 8 [Me] iðuht wæs þæt mi spece me ætfeallæn wæs. *c* **1200** ORMIN 7299 Hemm alle beþ o Domess daȝȝ Binumenn muþ & spæche. *a* **1225** *Leg. Kath.* 495 Muð bute speche, ehnen buten sihðe. *c* **1320** *Sir Tristr.* 1489 No ȝede he bot ten stride, His speche les he þar. **1398** TREVISA *Barth. De P.R.* v. xxiii. (Bodl. MS.), Euerich beest þat is with oute lunges is with oute voice and speche. *c* **1420** LYDG. *Assembly of Gods* 517 Yef I may see hys fase, For euer of hys speche I shall hym depryue. **1587** GOLDING *De Mornay* i. 8 When in..man we..consider Speech: must wee not needes say that he was made to communicate himselfe to many? **1676** SOUTH *Serm.* (1715) 342 That Speech was given to the ordinary Sort of Men, whereby to communicate their Mind; but to wise Men, whereby to conceal it. **1732** LEDIARD *Sethos* II. IX. 288 The Governor..had recover'd the use of his speech. **1742** YOUNG *Nt. Th.* II. 469 Had thought been all, sweet speech had been deny'd. **1849** MACAULAY *Hist. Eng.* iv. I. 439 Soon after dawn the speech of the dying man failed. *a* **1854** H. REED *Lect. Eng. Lit.* iii. (1878) 88 Speech, even more than reason, distinguishes man from the brute.

fig. **1664** MARVELL *Corr.* Wks. (Grosart) II. 167 Seeing upon so extraordinary occasions as these, the boldest eloquence would lose its speech.

6. Manner or mode of speaking; *esp.* the method of utterance habitual to a particular person. Usually with possessives.

c **1000** *Ags. Gosp.* Matt. xxvi. 73 Soþlice þu eart of hym, & þin spræc [*Hatt.* sprace] þe ȝeswutelað. *c* **1200** ORMIN 2207 Siþþenn seȝȝde he sone anan Wiþþ all full openn spæche [etc.]. **1297** R. GLOUC. (Rolls) 8535 He was quointe of conseil & speke [*v.r.* speche] & of bodi strong. **1338** R. BRUNNE *Chron.* (1810) 30 No non [was] so faire of face, of spech so lufly. *c* **1386** CHAUCER *Clerk's T.* 797 O goode God! how gentil and how kynde Ye semede by your speche and your visage. **1500–20** DUNBAR *Poems* xviii. 31 And be I ornat in my speiche, Than Towsy sayis [etc.]. **1535** COVERDALE *Mark* xiv. 70 Thou art a Galilean, and thy speach soundeth euen alike. **1598** YONG *Diana* 347 Putting a corner of his handkercher in his mouth, bicause he would not be knowen by his speech. **1644** MILTON *Educ.* (1738) 137 Their Speech is to be fashioned to a distinct and clear pronounciation. **1781** COWPER *Table T.* 346 His speech, his form, his action, full of grace. **1839** FR. A. KEMBLE *Resid. in Georgia* (1863) 67 They are languid in their deportment and speech. **1867** FREEMAN *Norm. Conq.* (1877) I. App. 725 Charmed with the handsome countenance and ready speech of the youth.

III. 7. The result of speaking; that which is spoken or uttered: **a.** With possessives, etc.: One's words, discourse, or talk.

c **897** K. ÆLFRED *Gregory's Past. C.* 192 Ðu bist ðonne ..ȝehæft mid ðinre aȝenre spræce. *c* **950** *Lindisf. Gosp.* John viii. 43 Sprec min ne onȝeattas ȝie. *c* **1000** *Lambeth Ps.* xcviii. 172 Freabodaþ *vel* mærsað tunge min spæce þin. *c* **1075** *O.E. Chron.* (Parker MS.) an. 1070, þa angan Thomas his spæce hu he com to Cantuuarebyri [etc.]. *c* **1200** ORMIN 18736 All þuss he spacc onnȝæness hemm To lihhnenn þeȝȝre spæche. *a* **1250** *Prov. Ælfred* (C.) 22 He was wis on his worde, and war on his speche. *a* **1300** *Cursor M.* 27932 Speche o disur, Rimes vnright, gest of Jogolur. **1382** WYCLIF *John* viii. 43 Whi knowen ȝe not my speche? for ȝe mown not heere my word. *c* **1460** *Vrbanit.* in *Babees Book* (1868) 15 With þy speche þou may þe spylle. **1535** COVERDALE *1 Sam.* xxv. 33 Blessed be thy speach, and blessed be thou. **1552** HULOET *Dict.* Aj, A.A.A which is the primitive Speache or naturall voyce of a Baby. **1605** CAMDEN *Rem.* (1623) 39 You may frame your speech according to the matter you must worke on. **1644** MILTON *Areop.* (Arb.) 31 They who to States and Governours of the Commonwealth direct their Speech. **1779** *Mirror* No. 64, Every one seemed impatient of his neighbour's speech, and eager to have an opportunity of introducing his own. **1821** SCOTT *Kenilw.* xxiii. A man, whose mixed speech of earthly wealth and unearthly..knowledge, hath in it [etc.]. **1860** TRENCH *Serm. Westm. Abbey* ix. 117 We may be quite sure that as our speech is, so we are.

b. In general use.

part of speech: see PART *sb.* 19.

971 *Blickl. Hom.* 225 Ne ȝehyrde næniȝ man on his muþe oht elles nefne Cristes lof & nytte spræce. *a* **1023** WULFSTAN *Hom.* (1883) 299 Haliȝ ȝeþanc and god spæc and fullfremed worc. *a* **1122** *O.E. Chron.* (Laud MS.) an. 1114, He wolde sprecon mid him dærne sprece. *c* **1205** LAY. 445 Pandrasum þene king he grette mid greiðlicre speche. *c* **1275** *Passion our Lord* 257 in *O.E. Misc.*, Vre louerd hym onswerede myd swyþe veyre speche. **1362** LANGL. *P. Pl.* A. II. 23 Fauuel with feir speche haþ brouȝt hem to-gedere. *a* **1400–50** *Alexander* 739 Reviles he þis oþire renke with vnrid speche. **1526** *Pilgr. Perf.* (W. de W. 1531) 92 b, [He] defendeth with hygh and clamorous wordes or speche his opinyon. **1581** LAMBARDE *Eiren.* I. ii. (1588) 11 The Statutes..do all (in playne speach) couple the maintenance of the Peace with the pursuing of suites. **1647** TRAPP *Comm. 1 Tim.* v. 13 The Rabbins have a Proverb, that ten Kabs of speech descended into the world, and the women took away nine of them. **1697** tr. *Burgersdicius' Logic* I. xxiv. 98 Speech is either perfect or imperfect. Perfect is that that absolves the sentence; an imperfect is not. **1821** SHELLEY *Ginevra* 62 If..wildered looks, or words, or evil speech,..can impeach Our love. **1872** HUXLEY *Physiol.* vii. 184 Speech is voice modulated by the throat, tongue, and lips. **1874** SAYCE *Compar. Philol.* i. 14 Speech is uttered thought.

†**c.** = LOGOS. *Obs. rare.*

1587 GOLDING *De Mornay* v. (1592) 50 The same thing which in the Trinitie we call the Sonne, the Word, the Speech.

8. a. A certain number of words uttered by a person at one time; *esp.* a more or less formal utterance or statement with respect to something.

c **888** K. ÆLFRED *Boeth.* xl. §1 Hwæðer ðu nu onȝite hwider þios spræce wille? **971** *Blickl. Hom.* 195 Þa mycclan spræca..weorþaþ him þonne ealle on heaf ȝehwyrfede. *c* **1000** ÆLFRIC *Gen.* xvii. 22 God þa astah upp..siððan he þas spræce ȝeendod hæfde. *a* **1200** *Vices & Virtues* 11 Godes forbode, ðe me forbett alle euele spaches. *a* **1275** *Prov. Ælfred* 353 Gin þu neuere leuen alle monnis spechen. **13..** *Gaw. & Gr. Knt.* 1261 Þe knyȝt with speches skere, Answared to vche a cace. **1362** LANGL. *P. Pl.* A. x. 34 Alle þing at his wille was wrouȝt wiþ a speche. **1508** DUNBAR *Tua Mariit Wemen* 239 Onone quhen this amyable had endit hir speche..the laif allowit hir mekle. **1548** GESTE *Pr. Masse* Gj, Yf thone be through the sayd speche autorysed to sacryfyce christis body, the other is in lyke maner. **1611** BIBLE *Transl. Pref.* ⁋3 He would not suffer it to be broken off for whatsoeuer speaches or practises. **1642** FULLER *Holy & Prof. St.* III. xii. 181 Many have been the wise speeches of fools, though not so many as the foolish speeches of wise men. **1710** *Tatler* No. 266 ⁋3, I began to make him compliments of condolence; but he started from his chair, and said, Isaac, you may spare your speeches. **1794** MRS. RADCLIFFE *Myst. Udolpho* xxxi, His quivering lip and lurking eye made her almost repent the boldness of her speech. **1819** SCOTT *Ivanhoe* xxix, From the speeches of these men who were my warders just now, I learn that I am a prisoner. **1841** DICKENS *Barn. Rudge* ii, The traveller returned no answer to this speech.

†**b.** An account or mention *of* something. *Obs.*

1387 TREVISA *Higden* (Rolls) I. 223 By þat wall is þe bath Byaneus made, of þe whiche baþ was raþer a speche [L. *de quo supra dicitur*].

†**c.** A talk or discourse between persons or *with* another. *Obs.*

1469 *Plumpton Corr.* (Camden) 23 It were well done that ye had a speech with Mr. Midleton of the forme of the pleading. **1483** *Cath. Angl.* 352/2 A Speche, *colloquium*. **1508** DUNBAR *Tua Mariit Wemen* 12, I hard..Ane hie speiche, at my hand, with hautand wourdis. **1633** BP. HALL *Hard Texts* 507 Hitherto I have related the speech which the angel had with me.

d. An address or discourse of a more or less formal character delivered to an audience or assembly; an oration; also, the manuscript or printed copy or report of this. Also †*His Majesty's Speech, Speech from the Throne, King's* (or *Queen's*) *Speech*: a speech delivered by the sovereign (in person or by commission) at the opening or prorogation of Parliament; now *spec.* the speech delivered by the sovereign at the opening of Parliament, written by his or her ministers and setting forth the policies and legislative programme of the Government. Also, a speech delivered by the representative of the sovereign at the opening of the legislative assembly of a member of the Commonwealth.

1583–4 *Reg. Privy Council Scot.* III. 631 Maister Andro Melvile..answerit that, althocht the speitche [*sc.* a sermon] wer alledgit to be treasoun, yit the tryell in the first instance aucht not to be befoir the King, bot befoir the Kirk. **1603** in *Jrnls. House of Commons 1547–1628* I. 146/2 His Majesty's Speech ended, Mr. Speaker..presented himself to his Majesty. **1605** BACON *Adv. Learn.* II. xiii. §7 Demosthenes ..had ready framed a number of prefaces for orations and speeches. **1617** MORYSON *Itin.* II. 71 After him Sir Francis Bacon concluded the accusation with a very eloquent speech. **1641** *Diurnall Occurrences of Parliament 20th Jan.–10th Mar. 1628* 1 M. Selden reported to the House that his Majesties Speech made the last day of the Parliament, in the upper House, is also entred by his Majesties command. *Ibid.* 5 (*heading*) The Kings Speech. **1697** DRYDEN *Virg. Georg.* II. 731 Some Patriot Fools to popular Praise aspire, Of Publick Speeches, which worse Fools admire. **1751** *Parliamentary Hist.* V. 279 Nor, like the former Speech from the Throne, is it mention'd by any Historian. **1758** *Ann. Reg.* 151/2 Four days after the speech was delivered, her royal highness carried it to the assembly of the States General. **1771** *Junius' Lett.* xlii. (1788) 237 The consideration of his Majesty's speech of 13th November 1770, and the subsequent measures of government. **1792** J. WOODFORDE *Diary* 15 Dec. (1927) III. 395 The Kings Speech in the House of Lords, a very long one. **1827** HARE *Guesses* (1859) 427 The difference between a speech and an essay should be something like that between a field of battle and a parade. **1844** ERSKINE MAY *Law of Parl.* vii. 142 The session is opened at once by the Queen's speech. *Ibid.* xxi. 326 On the opening of Parliament, the Queen, in her speech from the throne, addresses the commons. **1855** DICKENS *Lett.* (1880) I. 400 They are going to print my speech in a tract-form. **1897** *Westm. Gaz.* 13 Jan. 1/1 The Council for the settlement of the Speech from the Throne at the opening of Parliament. **1906** *Daily Colonist* (Victoria, B.C.) 11 Jan. 4/1 The opening [of the Legislative Assembly] will be attended with the usual ceremonies, and in the King's Speech will be indicated some of the salient points of the government policy. **1923** J. C. W. REITH in *Radio Times* 23 Nov. 290/3 At the opening of Parliament..our proposal to broadcast the King's Speech was..declined. **1964** ABRAHAM & HAWTREY *Parliamentary Dict.* 165 A Queen's speech is read by the Lord Chancellor on proroguing Parliament, but this is never debated... This speech reviews the session which it concludes. **1971** *Guardian* 17 Aug. 2/1 The traditional Speech from the Throne read in Maltese by the new Governor-General. *a* **1974** R. CROSSMAN *Diaries* (1975) I. 508 As a backbencher I never dreamed of attending the Queen's Speech debates, regarding them as the most boring occasions.

e. A school exercise or composition declaimed or recited upon speech-day.

1886 C. E. PASCOE *London of To-day* xviii. (ed. 3) 173 The proceedings on this anniversary begin with the 'speeches', delivered in 'Upper School', in Greek, Latin [etc.].

†**9. a.** A report or rumour. *Obs.* (Cf. 3.)

c **1000** *Ags. Gosp.* Luke vii. 17 Ða ferde þeos spæc [*v.r.* spræc] be him on ealle iudea. *a* **1400–50** *Alexander* 1884 For þan sall spring vp þe speche & sprede out of mynd, How I haue conquired a kyng þe kidest of þe werd. **1603** KNOLLES *Hist. Turks* (1621) 760 That there was a speech of a marriage to be made betwixt Mustapha and the Persian kings daughter. **1654** *Nicholas Papers* (Camden) II. 145 There is a speech here of many tropes discharged by Cromwells consent. **1660** *Essex Co.* (Mass.) *Crt. Rec.* in *Geneal. Q. Mag.* III. 29 There was a speech that one Mr. Browne..had lost a mare.

†**b.** A current saying or assertion. *Obs.*

1575 GASCOIGNE *Flowers* Wks. 1907 I. 64 The common speech is, spend and God will send. **1577** B. GOOGE *Heresbach's Husb.* I. (1586) 20b, The common people haue a speache, that ground enriched with Chalke, makes a riche father, and a beggerly sonne. **1639** FULLER *Holy War* v. xvii. (1647) 257 It was the common speech that the Holy land had long since been wonne, but for the false Collusion of the Templars..with the Infidels. **1642** tr. *Perkins' Prof. Bk.* v. §411. 177 It is a common speech, That the dower of a woman ought to be assigned unto her by metes and bounds.

†**c.** A phrase, term, or idiom. *Obs.*

1596 SPENSER *State Irel.* Wks. (Globe) 676 For Borh in old Saxon signifyeth a pledge or suretye, and yet it is soe used with us in some speaches, as Chaucer sayeth; St. John to *borrowe*. **1607** TOPSELL *Four-f. Beasts* (1658) 399 In ancient time, a Mouse-killer was taken for an opprobrious speech. **1675** BROOKS *Gold. Key* Wks. 1867 V. 411 Vorsitus thinks it a speech taken from the custom of soldiers or cities.

†**10. a.** A claim, cause, or suit, esp. of a legal nature; a law-plea. *Obs.* (common in OE.).

c **897** K. ÆLFRED *Gregory's Past. C.* xxviii. 196 Ðeah hie ryhte spræce hæbben hiera yfel on him to tælonne. **961** in Thorpe *Charters* 203 þæt þis æfre ȝesett spræc wære. *c* **1000** *Ags. Ps.* (Thorpe) ix. 4 Forðam þu demst minne dom and mine spræce. *c* **1200** *Trin. Coll. Hom.* 179 And ȝief he him [*sc.* his underling] set a speche and mid woȝedome binimeð him his biliue. *a* **1250** *Owl & Night.* 398 Þe nyhtegale..hire ofþuhte þat heo hadde þe speche so feor uorþ iladde. *Ibid.* 545 Yet nis þeos speche ibroht to dome. *c* **1381** CHAUCER *Parl. Foules* 489 Frome the morowe gan this spech last Tyll don-warde went the sonne wonder fast. [Cf. 495 Whan shall your cursyd pledynge haue an ende.] *c* **1450** *Godstow Reg.* 157 The sentence of this covenaunte..was, that the said Abbesse shold withdraw her speche the which she hadde ayenst the said Symond afore the kyngis Iustice.

†**b.** A manorial court in the Forest of Dean (cf. quot. and SPEECH-HOUSE). *Obs.*

1687 *Customs Miners Dean Forest* 15 §26 The Constable.. shall deliver the Miners in six weeks at the Speech, that is the Court for the Wood before the Verderors,..sufficient of Timber [etc.].

11. *slang.* (See quot.)

1874 *Slang Dict.* 303 *Speech*, a tip or wrinkle on any subject. On the turf a man will wait before investing on a horse until he 'gets the speech', as to whether it is going to try, or whether it has a good chance. To 'give the speech', is to communicate any special information of a private nature.

IV. 12. *attrib.* and *Comb.* **a.** Simple attrib., as ***speech-acoustics, act, -apparatus, -behaviour, -break, -breathing, -correctionist, -deafness, defect, -element, -energy, -event, -feeling, -form, -group, -habit, -material, -melody, -movement, -organ, -pattern, -response, -rhythm, science, -situation, -sound, -stuff, -style, -system, -unit, -utterance, -way***, etc. (Freq. in recent use.)

1949 *Archivum Linguisticum* I. I. 42 Philologists are beginning to turn away from phonetics to *speech-acoustics. **1961** *Amer. Speech* XXXVI. 222 A treatment of speech acoustics up to spectrography. **1946** C. MORRIS *Signs, Lang. & Behavior* ii. 37 There is no language.. without the production of sign-vehicles, and it is such production which constitutes a *speech-act. **1955** J. L. AUSTIN *How to do Things with Words* (1962) iv. 40 Here there is an obvious parallel with one element in *lying*, in performing a speech-act of an *assertive* kind. **1974** D. HYMES *Foundations of Socio-Linguistics* ii. 52 A party (speech situation), a conversation during the party (speech event), a joke within the conversation (speech act). **1982** *Papers Dict. Soc. N. Amer. 1977* 86 Speech acts are not predictable from code characteristics either. **1842** *Penny Cycl.* XXII. 430/2 The machinery of respiration, of vocalization, and of enunciation, together constitute the *speech-apparatus. **1931** T. H. PEAR *Voice & Personality* ii. 22 There is the person whose *speech-behaviour adumbrates what would develop if at this point the speaker received encouragement. **1980** *English World-Wide* I. 283 Seven of the essays are by German-writing authors on linguistic problems of German, ranging from urban speech (Vienna) to the speech behaviour of accused in court. **1674** N. FAIRFAX *Bulk & Selv.* To Rdr., The great *Speech-break at Babel. **1955** *Brit. Jrnl. Psychol.* XLVI. 54 Measures of *speech-breathing activity promised to be more immediately relevant to the changing states of tension and affect during interview. **1977** D. FRY *Homo Loquens* iii. 23 An interesting feature of speech breathing is that the moments at which we breathe in are far from being arranged haphazard. **1972** J. L. DILLARD *Black English* vii. 267 *Speech correctionists and educators... One Negro speech correctionist-psychologist..went so far as to indulge in a little too-elementary learning theory: language, being a learned activity, can be learned badly. **1899** *Allbutt's Syst. Med.* VII. 429 To this condition Lichtheim gave the name of 'isolated *speech-deafness'. *Ibid.* 394 Aphasia and other *Speech Defects. **1865** tr. *Strauss' New Life Jesus* I. Introd. 179 In the latest of our Gospels..the overweight is again on the side of the *speech-element. **1943** *Speech energy [see *audio frequency* s.v. AUDIO-]. **1933** L. BLOOMFIELD *Language* ii. 24 We have yet to examine B, the *speech-event in our story. **1948** J. R. FIRTH in *Lingua* I. 400 A *speech event* in a context of situation is therefore a technical abstraction from utterances and occurrences. A *speech event* may be sub-divided into *speech items*. **1976** *Word 1971* XXVII. 197 In my analysis, the communicative process is divided into the threefold gradation proposed by Hymes of *speech situation, speech event*, and *speech act*. **1916** L. BLOOMFIELD in *Trans. Amer. Philol. Assoc.* XLVII. 13 Our *speech-feeling seems to distinguish quite clearly between predicating and non-predicating utterances. **1979** *Amer. Speech 1976* LI. 135 The double negative is both a part of our speech-feeling and a sensible way to strengthen a negative statement. **1863** W. BARNES *Dorset Gloss.* 9 The main marks of south-western English, as it differs from the *speech-forms of the north. **1873** EARLE *Philol. Eng. Tongue* (ed. 2) §320 Grimm bewails this seduction of the *speech-genius from the true path. **1925** L. P. SMITH *Words & Idioms* 245 Linguistically considered, England, the Dominions, and the United States may almost be regarded as one *speech-group. **1964** C. BARBER *Present-Day Eng.* v. 124 There are phase-differences between different speech-groups, and it would be unsafe to assume that the words currently fashionable in a Birmingham rock-and-roll club were simultaneously fashionable in a West End night-club, or that the picturesque phrases used by schoolboys were still fashionable in R.A.F. messes. **1928** O. JESPERSEN *Internat. Lang.* I. 26 Everybody will necessarily transfer some of his *speech-habits to the international language. **1979** M. MILLAR *Murder of Miranda* II. 72 It's a speech habit I picked up from all the teenagers. **1886** TUPPER *Life as Author* 133 As a youth..I was, from the *speech-impediment since overcome, isolated from the gaieties of society. **1912** A. D. SHEFFIELD *Grammar & Thinking* vii. 188 Sentence-study..can profitably keep in view the diverse *speech-material that the pupil meets in his work with foreign languages. **1962** A. J. BLISS in Davis & Wrenn *Eng. & Med. Studies presented to J. R. R. Tolkien* 29 Either a fragment of speech-material has one of the rhythms which are acceptable, in which case *ictus* and stress inevitably coincide; or else it cannot be used in verse at all. **1934** *Essays & Studies* XIX. 141 This *speech-melody of ordinary intercourse. **1970** *English Studies* LI. 278 This latter feature, also known as intonation or speech melody, is of course almost a subject in itself. **1918** R. BRIDGES in *Poems of G. M. Hopkins* 96 It was at one time the author's practice to use a very elaborate system of marks, all indicating the *speech-movement. **1957** C. E. OSGOOD et al. *Measurement of Meaning* i. 12 Little or no correspondence between thought-movements and speech-movements was found. **1842** *Penny Cycl.* XXII. 429/1 The voice..may possess the peculiar conditions of those distinctions which constitute *speech-notes. **1925** GRATTAN & GURREY *Our Living Lang.* p. xxi, Sounds are produced and modified by the position of *speech-organs. **1961** *Amer. Speech* XXXVI. 217 Theory of the syllable must be based on the articulatory movements of speech organs. **1936** G. K. ZIPF *Psycho-Biology of Lang.* v. 195 One infers the nature of *speech-patterns from the exemplifications of the patterns, i.e. the configurations of speech-elements. **1969** M. PUGH *Last Place Left* xxix. 207 His speech patterns were as elaborate as ever, but his voice was no longer so well modulated. **1974** *Howard Jrnl.* XIV. 80 The restricted and elaborate codes which characterize the speech patterns of the lower and middle classes respectively. **1927** G. A. DE LAGUNA *Speech Development* ii. 36 The correlation between the *speech-response and its objective conditions is a correlation between independently variable elements of resonse and independently variable elements of the external situation. **1910** G. SAINTSBURY *Hist. Man. Eng. Prosody* IV. iii. 316 The presence of closely allied forms [of the alliterative line], in the different Scandinavian and Teutonic languages, assumes..a natural rise from some *speech-rhythm or tune-rhythm proper to the race and tongue. **1976** J. LEE *Ninth Man* 275 His poor father with the snicker-provoking Germanic speech rhythms. **1933** *Amer. Speech* VIII. 37/1 Graduate curricula in *speech science, phonetics, speech psychology, and rhetoric. **1977** *Whitaker's Almanack 1978* 530 First degrees..are awarded ..in *Speech Science* by the University of Sheffield. **1953** *English Studies* XXXIV. 258 'Man' and 'garden' in this context denote..definite, individualized concepts... Taken out of the context (or of the *speech-situation) they are semantically colourless. **1980** *English World-Wide* I. I. 99 This is still used..if at least one of the participants in a speech situation has not been educated in English or.. Bahasa Malaysia. **1840** GEO. ELIOT *Let.* 21 Dec. (1954) I. 77 Pray bring Phonarthron—*speech-sound is a boon that I often need—I shall expect from it..a key to the classic Oriental and Sclavonic tongues. **1869** ELLIS *E.E. Pronunc.* I. Introd. 1 In order to write intelligibly on speech sounds, some systematic means of representing them must be adopted. **1934** JOYCE *Let.* 9 Aug. (1966) III. 316 Also why for you make me big *speechstuff about Frankee Doodles? **1936** J. KANTOR *Objective Psychol. Gram.* xi. 156 As a test of the validity of the *speech-style conception we may inquire into its applicability to speech studies. **1978** *Amer. Speech* LIII. 66 Samarin notes that speech styles of glossolalia are socioculturally determined, as are speech styles of English prayers. **1946** H. JACOB *On Choice of Common Lang.* II. ii. 96 Inflected systems are highly resistant to simplification... However, most of the European *speech-systems have progressed considerably in the right direction. **1964** *English Studies* XLV. (Suppl.) 37 Whereas Aristotle started from..'speech' (*parole*), these philosophers had the speech-system (*langue*) in mind. **1820** W. TOOKE *Lucian* I. 230, I can make *speech-traps, in which I catch those who talk with me. **1936** G. K. ZIPF *Psycho-Biology of Lang.* 233 A sentence is a speech-element, or a *speech-unit. **1949** C. E. BAZELL in *Travaux du Cercle Linguistique de Copenhague* V. 77 This succession of speech-units need not answer to anything in the system. **1924** L. BLOOMFIELD in *Mod. Lang. Jrnl.* Feb. 319 Actual *speech-utterance, *la parole*, varies not only as to matters not fixed by the system..but also as to the system itself. **1956** J. WHATMOUGH *Language* 42 There is an inverse relationship between frequency of occurrence and the comparative perspicuity that accompanies the utilization of a speech-utterance. **1842** *Penny Cycl.* XXII. 431/2 Respiration and *speech-voice training will follow. **1931** H. SHENTON *Internat. Communication* I. 46 This approach to the problem might well be called a study of the *speech-ways of mankind. **1955** *English Studies* XXXVI. 17 Current Elizabethan usage, harking back to much older, popular speechways. **1972** H. KURATH *Studies in Area Linguistics* i. 12 Any native speaker's usage is in a large measure representative of the speechways of a social or age group in his community. **1887** MORRIS *Odyssey* IX. 258 Yet even so with *speech-words I answered again and spake.

b. With agent-nouns, verbal sbs., or present pples., as ***speech analyser, -bringer, -trainer, -writer; speech-bereaving, -getting, -making, -shunning, -training***, etc.

1593 NASHE *Christ's T.* Wks. (Grosart) IV. 224 The speech-shunning sores, and sight-acking botches of theyr vnsatiate intemperance. **1608** DAY *Hum. out of Breath* III. ii, If speech-bereaving love will let thee speak. **1717** ROWE *Poems* Wks. 1728 I. 79 That Tyburn-Tribe of speech-making Non-jurors. **1798** COLERIDGE *Tears in Solit.* 57 A vain, speech-mouthing, speech-reporting Guild. **1834** J. S. MILL in *Monthly Repos.* VIII. 419 One of our politicians.. reproached him..with being a λογογράφος, or speech-writer. **1837** CARLYLE *Fr. Rev.* III. I. ii, Their miraculous healer and speech-bringer is rapt away. **1875** WHITNEY *Life Lang.* ii. 13 The whole process of speech-getting. **1933** *Amer. Speech* VIII. 11/1 To complete any gaps there may be in the speech training of the members. **1955** T. H. PEAR *Eng. Social Differences* 99 Many people..flare up at any suggestion (except from a speech-trainer consulted voluntarily) of possible improvements in their speech. **1973** *Canad. Jrnl. Linguistics* XVIII. 90 Using the speech analyzer..we then recorded an intonation curve (in Hz) for each sentence on photo-sensitive paper. **1976** H. WILSON *Governance of Britain* iv. 88 The transatlantic custom of using speech-writers, recently imported into Britain for the use of certain eminent politicians and others, is only to be deplored. **1977** P. STREVENS *New Orientations Teaching of Eng.* vii. 86 Young learners will learn best through mimicry with speech training games for interest and for special points of difficulty, but with little or no use of phonetics.

c. With past pples., as ***speech-bound, -famed, -flooded***.

1761 CHURCHILL *Rosciad* 30 Was speech-fam'd Q——n himself to hear him speak. **1870** ROSSETTI *Poems, House Life* xxii, The speech-bound sea-shell's low importunate strain. **1888** BRYCE *Amer. Commw.* III. lxxiv. II. 611 England has since 1876 become the most speech-flooded country in the world.

13. Special combs.: **speech area**, (*a*) a region of the brain involved in the comprehension or production of speech, a speech-centre; (*b*) a geographical area with a distinct speech type; **speech-centre** (see quots.); **speech chain** *Linguistics*, an utterance regarded as a sequence of elements; **speech clinic**, a centre for the treatment of speech defects; **speech code** *Cryptology*, a simple verbal code formed by the regular substitution of secret words; **speech coil**, a coil that drives the cone of a loud-speaker according to the signal current flowing in it; **speech-community** *Linguistics*, a group of persons sharing a language or variety of a language; **speech-craft**, the knowledge or science of speech; **speech-crier**, one who hawked the 'last dying speeches' of criminals; **speech-day**, the day at the end of the school year upon which exercises are declaimed and the annual prizes distributed in certain public schools; **speech island** *Linguistics*, a small area inhabited by speakers of a language or dialect other than that spoken in the surrounding areas; **speech pathology**, the study and treatment of defective speech; hence **speech pathologist**; **speech physiology**, the study of the physical production of speech sounds; **speech-prefix**, in the text of a play: the name or description of the speaker(s) of a line or lines, set at the head of each speech; **speech psychology**, the study or application of psychological methods and techniques useful in learning to speak a language; also **speech psychologist**; **speech-reading**, the action on the part of deaf and dumb persons of comprehending speech by watching the movements of a speaker's mouth; so ***speech-reader***; **speech recognition**, the process of identifying and interpreting or responding to the sounds produced in human speech; **speech recognizer**, a machine capable of responding to the content of speech; **speech-room**, the room or hall at Harrow School in which speeches are delivered; **speech-song** = SPRECHGESANG; **speech stretcher** *Phonetics* (see quot. 1972); **speech synthesizer**, a machine designed to generate sounds imitative of the human voice and recognizable as meaningful speech; **speech therapy**, the training of patients in the production of a full range of speech sounds; hence **speech therapist**, one who practises this; **speech-to-noise ratio**, the signal-to-noise ratio of speech.

1885 *Harper's Mag.* Mar. 638/2 (*in figure*) *Speech area. **1913** *Q. Rev.* Jan. 124 Over a large portion of the highest level of the brain the special work of each group of cells or 'area' is now known. If our speech-areas are diseased we cannot speak. **1933** [see DIALECT 2b]. **1961** *Amer. Speech* XXXVI. 95 Speech areas can be delineated and sub-divided on the basis of heteroglosses. **1968** PASSMORE & ROBSON *Compan. Med. Stud.* I. xxiv. 52/1 (*caption*) The three speech areas [*sc.* Broca's area, superior area, Wernicke's area] shown on the left cerebral cortex. **1879** *Syd. Soc. Lex.* s.v. *Centre*, **Speech centre*,..a cortical centre situated in the region of the posterior extremity of the third left frontal convolution. **1899** *Allbutt's Syst. Med.* VI. 759 In their opinion this bundle..connects the cortical centre for sight with the auditory speech-centre. **1950** D. JONES *Phoneme* I Nearly every utterance, or '*speech chain', is made up of a large number of small elements. **1953** C. E. BAZELL *Linguistic Form* i. 5 But the smaller the number of choices, at any one point of the speech-chain, the smaller the probability of open juncture. **1963** DENES & PINSON (*title*) The speech chain: the physics and biology of spoken language. **1963** R. I. MCDAVID *Mencken's Amer. Lang.* 320 The spread of technical medical terminology to education, as *clinic* (yielding *reading clinic* and **speech clinic*). **1976** *New Yorker* 15 Nov. 146/2 A young man..who took a Ph.D. in speech pathology at Iowa in 1936 and then left to set up a speech clinic and research centre. **1973** 'A. HALL' *Tango Briefing* xviii. 221 Fred was the standard *speech-code name for any third member of an active cell. **1928** *Wireless World* 6 June 603/2 (*caption*) Various gauges of wire for *speech coil. **1934** *Discovery* Oct. 301/2 The 2-in. speech coil attached to the 11-in. cone works in a flux density of 11,500. **1975** G. J. King *Audio Handbk.* vi. 132 The speech coil is composed of inductance, distributed capacitance and resistance. **1894** G. E. Karsten in *Publ. Mod. Lang. Assoc.* IX. 327 It is pre-eminently the *speech-community which moulds the individual's language. **1911** L. Bloomfield in *Jrnl. Eng. & Gmc. Philol.* X. 629 A language is formed (i.e., a new speech-community is segregated) by definite changes in the outer surroundings of a group of people. **1950** R. A. Hall *Leave your Language Alone!* x. 153 Theoretically, it might be possible to keep an otherwise-normal speech-community hermetically sealed off from all outside sources of borrowing. **1978** K. Hudson *Jargon of Professions* 10 Speech communities are no longer as self-contained as they were. **1573** R. Lever *Arte Reason* 6 The arte of measuring, witcrafte, *speachcraft, starre-crafte, &c. **1878** W. Barnes (*title*), An Outline of English Speech-Craft. **1856** J. Ballantine *Poems* 68 Ilk wee *speech-crier, Ilk lazy ballant singin' idler. **1870** H. Lonsdale *Life R. Knox* vi. 109 Speech-criers of the last horrid doings of Burke and the doctors. **1848** Thackeray *Van. Fair* xxiv, He used to go down on *speech-days..and scatter new shillings among the boys. **1898** G. W. E. Russell *Coll. & Recoll.* xxxv. 482 The budding scholar..declaimed his verses on Speech-day. **1888** M. D. Learned in *Amer. Jrnl. Philol.* IX. 65 We are to seek the causes which have contributed to the formation of this important *speech-island in the domain of German dialects. **1933** [see Lusatian *sb.* and *a.*]. **1957** *Publ. Amer. Dial. Soc.* xxvii. 5 In one instance, that of *stone boat*, there is an additional speech island along the Mississippi, opposite St. Louis. **1978** *Amer. Speech* LIII. 44 A large speech island appears in the German-settlement area of Missouri and Illinois. **1972** J. L. Dillard *Black English* vii. 267 A linguistically sophisticated *speech pathologist like Joan Baratz. **1982** *Amer. Speech* LVII. 213 Speech pathologists, audiologists,..and many others have had some introduction to formal linguistic analysis. **1931** L. E. Travis *Speech Path.* p. vii, *Speech pathology is in its growing pains. **1976** *New Yorker* 15 Nov. 148/2 One of his advisers suggested that he sign up instead for the graduate program in speech pathology at the University of Iowa. **1936** G. K. Zipf *Psycho-Biology of Lang.* iii. 96 The experimental phoneticist ..attempts to determine by his laboratory study of *speech-physiology what changes [in a language] are possible. **1961** *Amer. Speech* XXXVI. 222 A treatment..of speech physiology by means of X-ray stills and films. **1959** *N. & Q.* June 213/1 It is therefore recommended that for the last speech of 'Elder Worthy' on I, 60..the *speech-prefix 'Young Worthy' be substituted. **1978** *Studies in Eng. Lit.: Eng. Number* (Tokyo) 12 There are eleven Latin speech-prefixes. The first five are '*Omn.*' for all the characters on the stage. **1937** Palmer & Hornby *Thousand-Word Eng.* i. 21 It is in the nature of a designed *plateau* (as *speech-psychologists call it), that is..a given stage..at which the learner may pause. **1921** H. E. Palmer *Princ. Lang.-Study* 19 A logical order of progression in accordance with principles of *speech-psychology. **1933** *Amer. Speech* VIII. iv. 37/1 There are graduate curricula in speech science, phonetics, speech psychology, and rhetoric. **1911** J. K. Love *Deaf Child* 161 The best speakers amongst the deaf and dumb are not always the best *speech-readers. **1891** R. Elliott *Elem. Lang. Deaf* Pref. p. v, *Speech and lip-reading should form the medium of communication and explanation. **1953** Fry & Denes in W. Jackson *Communication Theory* xxx. 426 (*heading*) Mechanical *speech recognition. *Ibid.* 427 The reasons for the failure of these..systems becomes clear when the mechanism of human speech recognition is considered. **1970** *New Scientist* 30 Apr. 216/2 Research on speech-recognition devices is still in its extreme infancy. **1980** *TWA Ambassador* Oct. 25/1 A second went to Bell Telephone Laboratories for a computerized speech-recognition system that can respond to human sentences. **1953** W. Jackson *Communication Theory* 431 Any mechanical *speech recognizer requires for its operation a considerable amount of linguistic information. **1970** O. Dopping *Computers & Data Processing* xi. 162 A 'normal' speech recognizer would recognise words regardless of the speaker. **1880** Trevelyan *Hist. C. J. Fox* ii. 50 Fox..was always to the front both in the *speech-room and the debating society. **1884** *Jrnl. Educ.* 1 Sept. 347/2 My memory takes me back some five-and-twenty years to the old speech-room at Harrow. **1909** *Cent. Dict.* Suppl., *Speech-song. [**1925** Song-speech: see Sprechgesang.] **1946** E. Blom *Everyman's Dict. Mus.* 580/1 *Speech-song*,..a term for a kind of singing that approximates to speech and touches the notes, indicated by special signs, without intoning them clearly at the proper pitch. **1959** *Listener* 17 Dec. 1093/2 The Roman practice of narrating during Holy Week the Evangelists' accounts of the Passion in a stylized speech-song (*tonus lectionis*). **1976** P. Stadlen in D. Villiers *Next Year in Jerusalem* 324 The Bible's casual hint at Moses' 'heavy tongue'..[is] realized, by having Moses engage in speech song while..Aaron is made to sing. **1948** M. Joos *Acoustic Phonetics* (Lang. Monogr. No. 23) 129 The usefulness of the *speech stretcher for phonetic demonstration is immense. **1972** Hartmann & Stork *Dict. Lang. & Linguistics* 216/2 *Speech stretcher*, a device used in phonetic research to slow down recorded speech without changing the pitch or distorting it in any other way. **1953** *Jrnl. Acoustical Soc. Amer.* XXV. 735/1 A *speech synthesizer would be required to simulate..closely the actual dimensions of the vocal tract. **1970** *Times Lit. Suppl.* 23 July 787/4 If the zealous phoneticist is dissatisfied with the acoustics of a real human voice he can nowadays, it seems, ring down for a speech synthesizer, couple it up to his computer, and manufacture ideal vowel sounds. **1933** S. M. Stinchfield *Speech Disorders* i. 10 A clinician, psychologist or *speech therapist might suspect that one of the following conditions would be found in such a case. The child may be deaf, or some childhood illness may have slowed up his rate of development. **1975** M. Kenyon *Mr Big* ii. 21 A speech therapist..who'd insisted that correct speech being a matter of breath control for six months he would simply have to learn to breathe. **1933** S. M. Stinchfield *Speech Disorders* vii. 141 It is worthwhile to spend some time in reviewing the more important types of nervous disorders, in order to better understand their implications, in undertaking *speech therapy. **1976** E. Ward *Hanged Man* xl. 267, I took the speech therapy and the office-boy jobs. **1951** *Engineering* 23 Feb. 226/3 Those concerned with the telephone apparatus..have paid much attention to questions of speech intelligibility, but in its broad aspects the matter is of direct interest to most shop executives. It is not their business to design loud speakers, but they are certainly concerned with the *speech-to-noise ratio in workshops. **1981** *Amer. Speech* XXXVI. 221 Monosyllabic, bisyllabic, and trisyllabic words presented for identification in seven different speech-to-noise ratios.

speech, *sb.*^{2} ? *U.S.* [app. repr. an OE. *ȝespǽce, f. *spáce* spoke *sb.*] (See quot.)

1875 Knight *Dict. Mech.* 2261/1 *Speech*, of a wheel, the hub with the spokes, without the fellies and tire.

speech (spiːtʃ), *v.* [f. speech *sb.*^{1}]

†**1.** *trans.* To drive *out* by means of speech. *Obs.*$^{-1}$

1654 Gayton *Pleas. Notes* iii. i. 67 Doe but recount (for I must speech out this timorousnesse from thy head and heart).

2. To say or state in a speech or speeches. *rare.*

1682 T. Flatman *Heraclitus Ridens* No. 54 (1713) II. 90 The Bills of Exclusion and Association (whatever was Speech'd or Resolv'd to the contrary) are not now thought [etc.]. *a* **1734** North *Lives* (1826) I. 229 In speeching to the jury, one and the same matter, over and over again, the waste of time would be so great that..there would scarce be an end.

3. To make a speech to; to address in a speech; *dial.*, to speak or talk to. Also with compl.

1818 Moore *Fudge Fam. Paris* ii. 35 Your Lordship, having speeched to death Some hundreds of your fellow-men, Next speeched to Sovereigns' ears,—and..at last Speeched down the Sovereign of Belfast. **1864** Carlyle *Fredk. Gt.* xv. viii. IV. 119 Upon which I immediately turned about to our own Regiment; speeched them, and made them huzzah. **1877–86** in Linc. glossaries.

4. *intr.* To make or deliver a speech or speeches. Also with *it*. Now *rare.*

(*a*) **1684** Wood *Life* 8 Nov., Mr. Charles Hickman.. speech'd it in laudem Thomae Bodley in the Schola linguarum. *c* **1720** *Fable Widow & Cat* iv. in *Prior's Wks.* (1907) 383 But in a saucy manner He Thus Speech'd it like a Lechmere: 'Must I [etc.].' *a* **1734** North *Lives* (1826) I. 230 He was positive not to permit more than one counsel of a side to speech it to the jury.

(*b*) **1710** *Acc. Last Distemper T. Whigg* i. 9 He stood up upon the Bulks in Westminster-Hall, and speech'd against him from Morning till Night. **1821** *Blackw. Mag.* IX. 82 Lambton speeching till the lights are gone. **1824** in *Spirit Public Jrnls.* (1825) 203 Tom Moore to Lord Lansdown is tipsily speeching. **1835** *Fraser's Mag.* XI. 612 He was fêted and speeched unto at divers and sundry towns. **1864** A. Thomson in *Remin.* (1904) I. xviii. 299 Yesterday I speeched well at St. Andrews.

b. To direct a speech or speeches *at* a person. Also *dial.*, to speak *with* some one.

1826 Scott *Woodst.* xxi, Have I not been speeched at by their orators. **1888** K. Saunders *Diamonds* 30 He hasn't *speeched* wi' me much.

speeched (spiːtʃt), *a.* [f. as prec.] Having or using speech of a specified kind.

1567 Drant tr. *Horace, Ep.* ii. i. G iv, This fayre-speachde queare. **1581** A. Hall *Iliad* ii. 33 Though tongues, yea, fully ten Right good he had, and mouthes like, wel speecht that open were. **1605** *1st Pt. Jeronimo* ii. iv, I could not think you but Andreas selfe, so legd, so facst, so speecht. **1682** *Lond. Gaz.* No. 1731/4 A thin Melancholy Man,..slow Speeched. **1805** T. Holcroft *Mem. B. Perdue* I. 16 Fair-speeched gentlemen as they are.

speecher (ˈspiːtʃə(r)). [f. speech *sb.*^{1} or *v.*]

1. One who makes speeches; a speaker.

1762 Foote *Orator* i. Wks. 1799 I. 194 Here is a man.. that will make thee a *speecher* at once. **1818** Moore *Fudge Fam. Paris* ix. 108 Oh, can we wonder, best of speechers! That [etc.].

2. *Harrow slang.* The speech-room; speech-day.

1894 Wilkins & Vivian *Green Bay Tree* I. 43 When Butler called you up to give you the key in speecher this morning. **1905** H. A. Vachell *The Hill* i, You ought to have been here last Speecher.

speechful (ˈspiːtʃfʊl), *a.* [f. speech *sb.*^{1} Cf. OE. *sprǽcful.*] **a.** Full of speech; possessing the power of speech; loquacious, talkative.

1842 Mrs. Browning *Grk. Chr. Poets* 83 One speechful voice among the silent. **1861** G. E. Maunsell *Poems* 246 Like a blest influence, Speechful, though dumb. **1873** Mrs. Whitney *Other Girls* xxvi, She had..carried him to the nursery, got him on her knee in a speechful condition.

b. Of the eyes, etc.: Full of expression; expressive, speaking. Also const. *of* (some quality).

1820 C. R. Maturin *Melmoth the Wanderer* IV. xxviii. 228 No form of Guido's, hovering in exquisite and speechful undulation between earth and heaven. *a* **1849** Mangan *Poems* (1859) 83, I well could read her speechful eye. **1865** E. Burritt *Walk to Land's End* xii. 407 He could not have made the expression of the central face more speechful of sadness. **1872** Blackie *Lays Highl.* 18 Dost thou see the speechful eyne Of the fond and faithful creature Sorrowed with the swelling brine?

Hence ˈ**speechfulness**.

1880 Meredith *Tragic Com.* (1881) 30 This man's face was the born orator's,..the animated mouth..stamped for speechfulness and enterprise. **190.** *Buck's Handbk. Med. Sci.* I. 414 (Cent. Suppl.), Sensory aphasia is..in the beginning..the aphasia of comparative speechfulness, while motor aphasia in the beginning is usually absolute speechlessness.

speech-house. Now *Hist.* [OE. *sprǽchús* (f. *sprǽc* speech *sb.*^{1}), = OS. *sprâk-hûs*, OHG. *sprâh-hûs* (MHG. *sprâch-hûs*).] A hall, room, or building set apart for speech, conference, etc.; a court-house; †a monastic parlour.

Retained in the place-name Speech-house-Road in the Forest of Dean, Glouc.

c **1050** *Suppl. Ælfric's Gloss.* in Wr.-Wülcker 184 *Auditorium*, spræchus. *Ibid.*, *Curia, uel senatus*, uþwitena spræchus. *c* **1205** Lay. 13036 Þe abbed hit him uðe, & he hine ladde to spæc-huse. *Ibid.* 13123 Whet Vortiger þenchéð in ure spæc-huse þer he spel haldeð. **1640** W. Somner *Antiq. Canterbury* 126 Aforetime it [the Guildhall] was commonly called and knowne by the name of the Speech-house. **1799** Hasted *Hist. Kent* IV. 426. **1838** *Dean Forest Mines Act* ¶ 54 A copy of all the rules [etc.] to be hung in the Speech House within the said Forest.

speechification (ˌspiːtʃɪfɪˈkeɪʃən). [f. speechify *v.*: see -fication.]

1. An instance or occasion of speech-making; a speech, oration, harangue.

1809 *Spirit Public Jrnls.* XIII. 150 Very useful for just seasoning all public speechifications. **1824** Southey *Sir T. More* (1831) I. 361 Quarterly and Annual Meetings, Preachers from a distance, Speechifications. **1851** Huxley in L. Huxley *Life* (1900) I. vii. 89, I made a speechification of some length..about a new animal.

2. The action of making speeches; oratory.

1825 Lockhart in *Scott's Fam. Lett.* (1894) II. 339 Would not he be a goose to indulge Wordsworth with speechification [etc.]? **1853** Conybeare *Ess. Eccles. & Soc.* (1855) 94 Lectures here, addresses there, and speechification everywhere. **1877** Symonds *Renaiss. It.* II. 528 The fifteenth century was the golden age of speechification.

speechifier (ˈspiːtʃɪfaɪə(r)). Also 8 **speechefyer**, 9 **speechifyer**. [f. speechify *v.*] One who speechifies or delivers speeches; one given to, or having some aptitude for, public speaking.

1778 Foote *Trip Calais* i. Wks. 1799 II. 331 The man is ..a pretty good speechefyer. **1794** C. Pigot *Female Jockey Club* 82 As an orator his parliamentary speeches prove him an inimitable, practical speechifier. **1819** *Monthly Mag.* XLVIII. 307 He was no speechifier; but preferred talking over such business in a walk. **1837** Whittock *Bk. Trades* (1842) 322 (*Mariner*), Without which..our overweening public speechifyers..would lose at least one topic of oratorical lamentation. **1886** W. J. Tucker *E. Europe* 259 In all classes amongst us you will find a formidable number of professional chatterboxes and speechifiers.

speechify (ˈspiːtʃɪfaɪ), *v.* [f. speech *sb.*^{1} + -ify.

Noted by Bartlett (1848) as 'a rather low word, and seldom heard except among bar-room politicians'. In ordinary use, together with its derivatives, chiefly employed as a humorous form or with depreciatory suggestion.]

1. *intr.* To make or deliver a speech or speeches; to harangue or 'hold forth'; to speak or talk at some length or with some degree of formality.

1723 [implied in speechifying *vbl. sb.*]. **1762** Foote *Orator* i. Wks. 1799 I. 193 And have you speechified yet? *Ibid.* 194, I did speechify once at a vestry. **1806** *Naval Chron.* XV. 19 Jack made..attempts to *speechify*. **1833** Moore *Mem.* (1854) VI. 341 Lord Lansdowne began to speechify to the German and Frenchman. **1862** Thackeray *Philip* vii, We were free to speechify,..and be as young as we liked.

2. *trans.* To address in a speech or speeches.

1862 *Daily Tel.* 9 Sept., Who entertained the crazy egotist Wilkes,..and 'ovated' and speechified him?

Hence ˈ**speechifying** *ppl. a.*

1803 J. Foster in Ryland *Life* (1846) I. 247 The man who has just conquered his speechifying antagonist. **1817** Mar. Edgeworth *Th. on Bores* Wks. 1848 IX. 213 Of the common parliamentary bore there be two orders; the silent, and the speechifying. **1828** Miss Mitford *Village* Ser. iii. (1863) 109 There was also..a Mrs. Harden, speechifying and civil, and a Miss Harden, her daughter, civiller still.

speechifying (ˈspiːtʃɪfaɪɪŋ), *vbl. sb.* [f. prec.]

1. The action of making or delivering speeches; the practice of oratory.

1723 *Briton* No. 19 (1724) 84 He has an excellent Talent at Speechifying. **1762** Foote *Orator* i. Wks. 1799 I. 193 'Tis all brought about by his speechifying. **1812** Byron *Ch. Har.* ii. xii. *note*, Their little absurdities are as harmless as.. maiden speechifying. **1849** C. Bronte *Shirley* xvi, Then came the feast, and afterwards the meeting, with music and speechifying in the church. **1884** *Chr. Commonw.* 23 Oct. 20/3 The immense volume of speechifying during the recess, on both sides.

b. The action of speaking or talking, esp. in a formal manner or at excessive length.

1777 Mme. D'Arblay *Early Diary* (1889) II. 193 Richard,..after fine speechyfying, walked off. **1782** Eliz. Blower *Geo. Bateman* I. 21, I could stand and hear you talk all day long; to be sure you have a vast fine knack at speechifying. **1853** Miss Yonge *Heir of Redclyffe* xxv, Come, what's past can't be helped, and I have no end of work to be done, so there's speechifying enough for once. **1887** P. McNeill *Blawearie* 131 'No more speechifying, Morris,' shouted the overseer. 'Let us haste to the rescue.'

2. An instance or occasion of public speaking.

1843 F. E. Paget *Warden of Berkingholt* 77 Nothing is to be done without platforms, and meetings, and speechifyings. **1852** H. Newland *Lect. Tractar.* 28 The meetings and the speechifyings and the hard words. **1894** *Brit. Jrnl. Photogr.* XLI. 91 A demonstration, a feasting, a speechifying, and a concert all rolled into one.

speeching (ˈspiːtʃɪŋ), *vbl. sb.* [f. speech *sb.*^{1} or *v.*] The action or practice of making speeches; the art of speaking; a speech.

1664 J. Wilson *A. Commenius* i. i, You've such a knack at speeching. **1702** Rowe *Tamerl.* ii. ii, This vile Speeching,

This After-game of Words is what most irks me. **1771–2** *Ess. fr. Batchelor* (1773) I. 143 For God's sake reserve it for the house, I shall hear more than enough of speeching if ever we meet there. **1820** KEATS *Cap & Bells* iv, An audience had, and speeching done, they gain Their point. **1857** J. BROWN *Lett.* (1907) 113 Have you looked at the speechings of that infinite Swell and Snob?

attrib. **1824** in *Spirit Public Jrnls.* (1825) 288 Had doughty beadles..chaced Ev'ry poor puppy that at greatness scowled, I fear my speeching talent had been waste.

So '**speeching** *ppl. a.*, speech-making.

a **1734** NORTH *Examen* I. ii. §71 (1740) 67 But it seems the House of Peers thought fit to send the four speeching Lords to the Tower. **1808** MOORE *Corruption* ii. 28 A few crank arguments for speeching lords.

speechless ('spiːtʃlɪs), *a.* Also 1 spæcleas, 3–5 specheles (5 -less, 6 -lesse), 6–7 speech(e)les(se. [OE. *spǽcléas* (f. *spǽc* SPEECH *sb.*[1]), = older Flem. *spraeckeloos* (Du. *sprakeloos*), MLG. (and LG.) *sprâkelôs*, OHG. *sprâhhalôs* (MHG. *sprâche-*, G. *sprachlos*).]

1. a. Destitute of, unendowed with, or lacking the faculty of speech; naturally or permanently mute or dumb.

a **1000** *Gloss.* in *Germania* (1878) XI. 398/72 Spæclease *vel* dume, *elinguia*. **1377** LANGL. *P. Pl.* B. xv. 36 Þanne am I spirit specheles and *spiritus* þanne ich hatte. **1530** PALSGR. 325/2 Spechelesse, that can nat speke, *muet*. *c* **1586** C'TESS PEMBROKE *Ps.* CXV. iii, They mouthes, but speechlesse, have: Eyes sightlesse. **1588** SHAKS. *Titus A.* III. ii. 39 Speechlesse complayne[r], I will learne thy thought: In thy dumb action, will I be as perfect As begging Hermits in their holy prayers. **1669** W. HOLDER *Elem. Speech* 115 He that never hears a word spoken, nor can be told what it signifies, it is no wonder if such an one remain speechless. **1746** FRANCIS tr. *Horace, Sat.* I. iii. 134 When the first Mortals crawling rose to Birth, Speechless and wretched, from their Mother-Earth. **1815** SHELLEY *Alastor* 123 He lingered,..through the long burning day Gazed on those speechless shapes. **1889** MIVART *Orig. Hum. Reason* 287 Speaking of his hypothetical speechless-man.

b. Of a state or condition: Characterized by the lack of speech.

1593 SHAKS. *Rich. II*, I. iii. 172 What is thy sentence then, but speechlesse death, Which robs my tongue from breathing natiue breath? **1819** SHELLEY *Cenci* v. ii. 69 She is as pure as speechless infancy!

2. a. Unable to speak on account of illness, injury, or extreme exhaustion.

c **1290** *S. Eng. Leg.* I. 67 Wel longue he lai speche-les þene dethþ forto a-bide. **1470–85** MALORY *Arthur* I. iii. 39 Thenne he fyll passynge sore seke, so that thre dayes & thre nyghtes he was specheles. **1484** in *Cely Papers* (Camden) 155 Old Henley ys wyddowe hath beyn specheless thys daye & a hallfe. **1591** *Troub. Raigne K. John* i. 378 Some powere strike me speechless for a time! **1601** SHAKS. *Jul. C.* I. ii. 255 He fell downe in the Market-place, and foam'd at mouth, and was speechlesse. **1675** HOBBES *Odyssey* (1677) 66 All his body swell'd was: and in fine Speechless and breathless was he, like one dead. **1770** LANGHORNE *Plutarch* (1851) I. 408/1 He lay a long time speechless. **1797** S. & HT. LEE *Canterb. T.* (1799) I. 393 The criminal himself..sank pale, and speechless, into the arms of those nearest. **1857** LONGF. *Santa Filomena* vii, Slow..The speechless sufferer turns to kiss Her shadow.

fig. **1611** SHAKS. *Cymb.* I. v. 52 His Fortunes all lye speechlesse, and his name Is at last gaspe.

b. Deprived for the time being of the power of speech through astonishment, fear, or other emotion; temporarily dumb; unable to answer. Also (*dial.*) as *adv.*

c **1374** CHAUCER *Troylus* IV. 370 And specheles thus ben thise ilke tweye, That neither myght a word for sorwe seye. **1526** TINDALE *Matt.* xxii. 12 Howe camyst thou in..and hast not on a weddyng garment? and he was even spechelesse. **1582** STANYHURST *Æneis* II. (Arb.) 68 Heere with I was daunted, my hear stard, and speechles I stutted. **1608** DAY *Hum. out of Breath* III. ii, If speech-bereaving love will let thee speak, Then, speechless man, speak with the tongue of love. **1667** MILTON *P.L.* IX. 894 Speechless he stood and pale, till thus at length First to himself he inward silence broke. **1711** STEELE *Spect.* No. 113 ¶4, I at last came towards her with such Awe as made me Speechless. **1778** MISS BURNEY *Evelina* lxxviii, Speechless, motionless myself, I attempted not to stop him. **1837** CARLYLE *Fr. Rev.* I. III. viii, An astonished Parlement sits convoked; listens speechless to the speech of D'Espréménil. **1891** FARRAR *Darkn. & Dawn* xlvi, Acte was almost speechless with surprise. **1915** D. H. LAWRENCE *Rainbow* i. 34 The woman's not speechless dumb. She's not clutterin' at the nipple. She's got the right to please herself.

c. Deprived of speech through excessive drinking. Hence *colloq.*, dead drunk.

1881 BESANT & RICE *Chapl. of Fleet* I. 158 Those evenings of riot from which Sir Miles was so often carried home speechless.

3. Refraining from speech; keeping or observing silence; silent. Also, reticent, taciturn.

1390 GOWER *Conf.* I. 85 Thanne is my cause fully schent, For specheles may noman spede. **1530** PALSGR. 325/2 Spechelesse, of fewe wordes, *musart*. **1592** KYD *Sp. Trag.* II. ii, *Bel.* Why stands Horatio speecheles all this while? *Hor.* The lesse I speak, the more I meditate. *a* **1771** GRAY *Dante* 53 On my Children's Eyes Speechless my Sight I fix'd. **1848** DICKENS *Dombey* xxxvi, A bony and speechless female with a fan.

transf. **1602** SHAKS. *Ham.* II. ii. 507 A silence in the Heauens,..The bold windes speechlesse. **1607** —— *Cor.* V. i. 67 Twas very faintly he said Rise: dismiss me Thus with his speechlesse hand.

†4. Not uttered or expressed in speech. *Obs.*

1596 SHAKS. *Merch. V.* I. i. 164 Sometimes from her eyes I did receiue faire speechlesse messages. *c* **1600** —— *Sonn.* viii. 13 [The strings] Whose speechlesse song..Sings this to thee. **1603** —— *Meas. for M.* I. ii. 188 For in her youth There is a prone and speechlesse dialect, Such as moue men.

5. Of an emotion, etc.: Of such a nature as to deprive one temporarily of the power of speech; characterized by loss of speech.

1593 SHAKS. *Lucr.* 1674 Which speechless woe of his poor she attendeth, And his untimely frenzy thus awaketh. **1738** GLOVER *Leonidas* I. 364 In speechless anguish on the hero's breast She sinks. **1761** GRAY *Odin* 75 What virgins these, in speechless woe, That bend to earth their solemn brow? **1794** MRS. RADCLIFFE *Myst. Udolpho* xxxiii, She gave herself up to speechless joy. **1848** DICKENS *Dombey* lxii, Mr. Dombey nods at the Captain, who shines more and more with speechless gratification. **1865** CARLYLE *Fredk. Gt.* XVIII. v. (1872) VII. 164 He surveyed with speechless feeling the small remnant of his Lifeguard of Foot.

6. Marked or characterized by absence of speech; free from, unaccompanied or undisturbed by, speech.

1726 POPE *Odyss.* XIX. 251 A speechless interval of grief ensues. **1738** WESLEY *Ps.* CXXXVII. i, Her we bewail'd in speechless Groans. **1765** WALPOLE *Otranto* iv, [Her mother] seeing Matilda fall at her feet with a flood of speechless tears. **1817** SHELLEY *Rev. Islam* V. liii, As o'er that speechless calm delight and wonder grew. **1855** LONGF. *Hiawatha* xiv. 17 In the great, mysterious darkness Of the speechless days that shall be! **1874** SPURGEON *Treas. David* Ps. xciv. 17 He..would have been wrapped in speechless silence.

7. *poet.* Incapable of expression in or by speech.

1813 SHELLEY *Q. Mab* v. 138 Stifling the speechless longings of his heart, In unremitting drudgery and care! **1817** —— *Rev. Islam* I. xlii, At night, methought in dream A shape of speechless beauty did appear. **1851** MRS. BROWNING *Casa Guidi Wind.* I. 90 As the veil withdrawn 'Twixt the artist's soul and works had left them heirs Of speechless thoughts.

Hence '**speechlessly** *adv.*, without speech or speaking; silently.

1848 THACKERAY *Van. Fair* xiv, The placable and soft-hearted Briggs speechlessly pushed out her hand at this appeal. **1857** W. COLLINS *Dead Secret* (1861) 238 She stood ..looking steadfastly, speechlessly, breathlessly, at her blind husband. **1895** SCULLY *Kafir Stories* 126 He glared speechlessly at Kondwana and Senzanga.

'**speechlessness.** [f. SPEECHLESS *a.*] The state or condition of being speechless; lack or loss of speech.

1581 DEE *Priv. Diary* (Camden) 10 My mervaylous horsnes and in manner spechelesnes toke me. **1638** RAWLEY tr. *Bacon's Life & Death* (1650) 54 The immediate preceding signs of death are..the memory confused, speechelesnesse, cold sweats [etc.]. **1822–7** GOOD *Study Med.* (1829) I. 540 *Aphonia*. Dumbness. Speechlessness. Inability of Speech. **1863** MRS. WHITNEY *Faith Gartney's Girlh.* xvii, Her very speechlessness before him had come from the deep pleasure that his presence had given to her. **1873** B. HARTE *Fiddletown* 17 The monstrous doll, whose very size seemed to give a pathetic significance to its speechlessness.

speechlet ('spiːtʃlɪt). [f. SPEECH *sb.*[1] + -LET.] A short speech.

1881 *Daily News* 28 Nov. 3/5 He speaks in the fashion —I don't know whether I should not call them speechlets —very much of the *feuilletons* of the French romances. **1896** *Westm. Gaz.* 13 Mar. 7/3 Leaving out of account speechlets by Mr. B. L. Thompson,..Lord Carrington [etc.].

So '**speechling.** [-LING[1] 2.]

1880 TROLLOPE *Cicero* I. 226, 'I will send you,' he says, 'the speechlings which you require'.

speech-maker. [SPEECH *sb.*[1]] One who makes or delivers a speech or speeches, esp. in public; an orator.

1710 SWIFT (*title*), The famous Speechmaker of England; or Baron..Lovel's Charge at the Assizes. **1738** *Gentl. Mag.* VIII. 94/2 Their Youth became Witlings, Demi-Criticks, and Speech-makers. **1842** LOVER *Handy Andy* xix, Let me see the speech-maker, and I'll tell you what he says. **1873** SYMONDS *Grk. Poets* i. 30 The consummate skill of professional speech-makers.

speech-making, *vbl. sb.* [f. as prec.] The action or fact of making or delivering speeches.

1718 J. TRAPP tr. *Virgil* Pref. to Æneis (1735) I. p. xl, I do not understand why Speech-making in an Heroick Poem must be called Dramatic. **1820** T. MITCHELL *Aristoph.* I. p. lxiii, When a mania took place in Athens, whether for cock-fighting or speech-making,..it was no slight obstacle that could oppose it. **1870** DISRAELI *Lothair* xlix. 264 Speech-making is a new thing for me. **1876** RUSKIN *St. Mark's Rest* iv. §47 Through sixteen hundred years of effort and speech-making, and fighting.

b. An instance or occasion of this.

1835 J. FOSTER *Life & Corr.* (1846) II. 302 Some of our journals and speech-makings. **1845** DICKENS *Chimes* ii. (ed. 2) 73 Don't look for me to come up into the Park when there's a Birthday, or a fine Speechmaking.

†speechman. *Obs.* Also 6–7 speche-, speachman. [f. SPEECH *sb.*[1]] One who is appointed to speak for others; a spokesman.

c **1530** in *Essex Rev.* (1904) XIII. 22 Who wer messyngers and spechemen for lynsell for ye obtaynyng of ye lese of Macchyng parsonage? **1559** AYLMER *Harborowe* I iv b, Thou shalt be his God and he thy specheman. **1570** B. GOOGE *Pop. Kingd.* III. 35 b, Not seeking Mediators here, nor Speachmen for to pray. **1630** W. SCOT *Apol. Narr.* (1846) 167 Mr. James Melvill..was appointed to be their speechman.

fig. **1564** BECON *God's Word & Man's Invent.* Pref., Wks. II. 388 b, He would..straightwaies (so that money be the Aduocate and spechman)..be more meeke and gentle than a Lambe.

speechment. *nonce-word.* [f. SPEECH *sb.*[1] or *v.*] A speech or oration.

1826 J. O'KEEFE *Recoll.* I. ix. 341 After this grand speechment, it was thought advisable not to let her have any thing at all to say. **1854** HUXLEY in L. Huxley *Life* (1900) I. viii. 113, I am rejoiced you liked my speechment.

speed (spiːd), *sb.* Forms: 1 spoed (spod), 1–6 sped, 3–6 spede, 5–7 speede, 6– speed; 4 spied, 4–8 speid; 5 spyd(e, 6–7 spide. [OE. *spéd*, earlier *spœ́d*, = MDu. *spoed*, *spoet* (Du. *spoed*), OS. *spôd*, *spôt* (MLG. *spôd-*, *spôt*, *spoet*, *spoit*), OHG. *spôt*, *spuot* (MHG. *sput*), f. OE. *spówan*, OHG. *spuon* to prosper, succeed.]

I. †1. Abundance. *Obs.*

Also freq. in OE. 'substance, means, wealth'.

a **900** CYNEWULF *Crist* 604 He us æt ʒiefeð, & æhta sped, welan ofer widlond. *a* **1000** *Genesis* 1084 Tubal Cain, se þurh snytro sped smið cræfteʒa wæs. *c* **1200** ORMIN 12079 Off þatt hemm weorelldahhtess spedd Aȝȝ waxeþþ mare & mare. *Ibid.* 12252 Off laferrddom, off ahhtess sped. *c* **1250** *Gen. & Ex.* 122 Of euerilc ouȝt, of euerilc sed, Was erðe mad moder of sped.

†2. Power, might. *Obs.*

971 *Blickl. Hom.* 179 Þonne syndon on þyssum Simone twa speda, mannes & deofles. *c* **1000** *Ags. Ps.* (Thorpe) lxxxviii. 7 Þu eart mæʒena God,..nis þe ealra ʒelic ahwær on spedum. *c* **1250** *Gen. & Ex.* 25 God..unspered al ðe fendes sped, And halp ðor he saȝ mikel ned. *Ibid.* 2995 Her hem wantede miȝt and sped.

3. a. Success, prosperity, good fortune; profit, advancement, furtherance. *Obs.* exc. *Sc.* or *arch.*

c **725** *Corpus Gloss.* (Hessels) P 707 *Præuentus*, spoed. *Ibid.* S 646 *Successus*, spoed. *a* **900** CYNEWULF *Elene* 1182 He ah æt wiʒʒe sped, siʒor æt sæcce. *c* **1000** *Ags. Ps.* (Thorpe) lv. 4 Ic..on God..ʒelyfe, þæt minre spræce sped folʒie. *c* **1250** *Gen. & Ex.* 2221 [They] hauen it so to iacob broȝt, And tolden him so of here sped. *Ibid.* 3929 Al..is fultum and his sped. *a* **1300** *Cursor M.* 22886 (Edinb.), þe mar man swink him þar aboutin Fra sped þe ferre he sal ben outin. **1390** GOWER *Conf.* II. 11 For Slowthe is mihti to confounde The spied of every mannes werk. *c* **1407** LYDG. *Reson & Sens.* 4906 Now shal ye here..Al the processe of my spede. **1412–20** —— *Chron. Troy* IV. 4662 Myn entent is nat to repreue ȝoure wyse conseil..ȝif it conclude to þe comoun spede Of my peple and sauacioun. **1503–4** *Act 19 Hen. VII*, c. 19 Preamb., For their owne spede and lucre they suffer their ledder to passe untruly coryed. *c* **1510** MORE *Picus* Wks. 32 What seruice maie so desirable bee, As where all turneth to thyne owne spede. **1611** CHAPMAN *Widdowes T.* Wks. 1873 III. 8, I am assured of my speede. **1786** BURNS *Ep. Young Friend* xi, In ploughman phrase 'God send you speed'. **1791** LEARMONT *Poems* 51 We wiss him speed Till he unravel ilka quirk. **1899** GREIG *Logie o' Buchan* xii. 203 Guid-bye than, Jamie; and I wish ye a' speed and forder.

b. With adjs., as *good*, *evil*, etc.: Success, fortune, lot.

c **1250** *Gen. & Ex.* 309 ȝet ic wene I can a red, ðat hem sal bringen iwel sped. **14..** *Sir Beues* (1894) 182/2 God send them evyll spede. **1451** *Rolls of Parlt.* V. 219/2 The good spede of this Act of Resumption. **1535** *Goodly Prymer* S j b, That temyng women may haue ioyfull spede in their labour. **1577–87** HOLINSHED *Chron.* III. 1097/1 In the assistance.. all their hope of prosperous speed consisted. **1634** CANNE *Necess. Separ.* (1849) 221 It is..worth the noting, what ill speed Mr. Dayrell hath still in all his testimonies. **1651** WELDON *Crt. Chas.* 194 Another Parliament was summoned, wherein..there proved no better a good speed and successe than a mere frustration of all hopes on both hands. **1724** DE FOE *Mem. Cavalier* (1840) 113 The king wished us good speed. **1809** MALKIN *Gil Blas* v. i. ¶21 You give way to difficulties with more haste than good speed.

Comb. *a* **1616** BEAUM. & FL. *Little Fr. Lawyer* v. iii, They are men of a charitable vocation,..And put a good speed penny in my purse.

c. *to come* (*good*) *speed*, to be successful. So *to come bad*, or *no*, *speed*, to be more or less unsuccessful. *Sc.*

a **1557** *Diurn. Occurr.* (Bann. Cl.) 19 He come no speid but depairtit with repulse. *c* **1620** Z. BOYD *Zion's Flowers* (1855) 57, I at the market have this day come speede. **1638** A. CANT *Serm. at Edinburgh* (1699) 21 If I had hope to come speed with you. **1756** MRS. CALDERWOOD in *Coltness Collect.* (Maitland Club) 232 There was one came about gathering charity,..but she came very ill speed. **1824** MISS FERRIER *Inher.* xxxii, No wonder he came such bad speed at the courting. *Ibid.*, Somebody has come good speed. **1881** W. GREGOR *Folk-Lore* xxii. 161 Sittin beggars cumna speed.

†4. a. Assistance, aid, help. *Obs.*

c **1340** HAMPOLE *Pr. Consc.* 2882 And þat may be thurgh helpe and spede Of prayer of frendes and almusdede. **13..** *E.E. Allit. P.* B. 1607 Þurȝ þe sped of þe spyryt þat sprad hym with-inne. **1399** *Rolls of Parlt.* III. 451 [To] procede as hym thoght for the best.., for the spede of this nede and of all the Parlement. **1423** *Ibid.* IV. 256 In spede as wele of the Kynges nede, as of his peple. ? *a* **1500** *Chester Pl.* x. 79 Haue here of me, to do thee speede, right a gay garment.

†b. One who, or that which, promotes success or prosperity. *Obs.*

c **1375** *Cursor M.* 21348 (Fairf.), Of þe rode now for to rede, ihesus criste he be mi spede. **1377** *Pol. Poems* (Rolls) I. 215 He that was ur most spede Is selden seye and sone forȝete. *c* **1450** *Godstow Reg.* 4 [Cross] of ihesu criste be euer oure spede. **1577** GRANGE *Golden Aphrod.*, etc. S iv, Adewe therefore, God be thy speede. **1591** *Troub. Raigne K. John* (1611) 54 S. Francis be your speed. **1596** SHAKS. *1 Hen. IV*, III. i. 190 Good-manners be your speede. **1681** W. ROBERTSON *Phraseol. Gen.* (1693) 1158 Christ be our speed.

II. 5. a. Quickness in moving or making progress from one place to another, usually as the result of special exertion; celerity, swiftness; also, power or rate of progress.

In OE. only in the dat. plur. used adverbially. In ME. freq. in advb. phrases, as ***a good speed***, or with preps. (cf. 8 and 9).

a **1000** *Genesis* 2397 Ðewiton him þa ædre ellorfuse æfter þære spræce spedum feran. *c* **1250** *Gen. & Ex.* 1598 Fro bersabe he ferde wið sped. *a* **1300** *Cursor M.* 16597 Him þai can to nede, At tak þe tan end o þe tre, to ga þe better spede. *c* **1350** *Will. Palerne* 1765 William & þe mayde..gon forþ þurȝth þe gardin a wel god spede. *a* **1400** *Sir Perc.* 720 For to rynne scho myȝte not thole Ne folowe hym no spede. *c* **1450** *St. Cuthbert* (Surtees) 1727 For mare spede be ship he went. *c* **1450** HOLLAND *Howlat* 292 He wald nocht spair for to spring on a gud speid. **15..** *Christ's Kirk* 143 in *Bann. Ms.* 287 He suld bene swift that gat him, throw speid. **1596** SHAKS. *Merch. V.* III. iv. 56 Madam, I goe with all conuenient speed. **1667** MILTON *P.L.* II. 700 Back to thy punishment,..and to thy speed add wings. **1697** DRYDEN *Virg. Georg.* III. 305 Thus, form'd for speed, he challenges the Wind. **1758** JOHNSON *Idler* No. 6 ¶ 10 The true causes of her speed were fear and love. **1797** S. & HT. LEE *Canterb. T.* (1799) I. 355 He exerted all the speed fatigue would allow. **1823** SCOTT *Quentin D.* xvii, The Scottish mountaineer was at liberty to put forth a speed which was unrivalled in his own glens. **1847** MARRYAT *Childr. N. Forest* xxii, That's a fine horse you were riding, sir. Has he much speed? **1891** FARRAR *Darkn. & Dawn* xii, Pudens had seen him..run up the steps with a speed which a Roman regarded as very undignified.

b. Of things: Swiftness, rapidity, velocity, of direct or circular movement; rate of motion or revolution.

c **1200** ORMIN 18094 All swa se waterrstræm Aȝȝ fleteþþ forþ & erneþþ Towarrd te sæ wiþþ mikell sped. **1560** DAUS tr. *Sleidane's Comm.* 83 It began at the Ocean sea, &..spred over all Germany, & with unspeakeable spede. **1590** SHAKS. *Com. Err.* I. i. 110 Her part..Was carried with more speed before the winde. **1619** in *Eng. & Germ.* (Camden) 156, I know not whether I should have beene diverted a second time from taking the speede of the river if [etc.]. **1742** GRAY *Eton* 29 What idle progeny succeed To chase the rolling circle's speed? **1823** SCOTT *Quentin D.* xxvii, What has taken some time to narrate, happened, in fact, with the speed of light. **1857** DUFFERIN *Lett. High Lat.* (ed. 3) 410 Then, notwithstanding the slowness of the speed, it requires as much luck as skill to avoid collisions. **1883** M. P. BALE *Saw-Mills* 209 If a sawing or planing machine is driven at a very great rate of speed.

c. With numerals or adjs. forming attrib. combs. Freq. in sense d below; also *ellipt.*, a bicycle having the number of gears indicated.

1871 *Routledge's Ev. Boy's Ann.* Apr. Suppl. 3/2 Three-speed Pulley. **1885** *Field* 31 Jan. 121/3 A 'ten-speed gear' tricycle. **1904** *Westm. Gaz.* 5 July 12/1 Very high-speed passenger trains. **1955** *Radio Times* 22 Apr. 30/1 (Advt.), 6-valve, 3-speed, autochange table radiogram. **1970** 'D. HALLIDAY' *Dolly & Cookie Bird* iii. 26 A runaway self-propelled two-speed-gear lawnmower. **1975** *Sat. Rev.* (U.S.) 3 May 44/1 Then they'll hop onto their sleek 3-, 5-, or 10-speeds and..explore America's city streets.

d. Any of the possible gear ratios of a machine, esp. a bicycle or motor vehicle; the equipment associated with this; = GEAR *sb.* 7b.

1866 *English Mechanic* 22 June 263/1, I think in velocipede construction it is necessary to have two speeds... By pulling the lever A it throws the small wheels out of gear, and the driver can use the large wheels for level ground and the small ones for ascending hills. **1904** KIPLING *Traffics & Discoveries* 304, I was on the point of reversing and working my way back on the second speed ere I ended in some swamp, when I saw sunshine through the tangle ahead and lifted the brake. **1907** G. B. SHAW *John Bull's Other Island* IV. 80 The pig..put in the fourth speed with its right crubeen. **1926** T. E. LAWRENCE *Seven Pillars* (1935) IX. cii. 560 The armoured car was too heavy for the flints, and always she sank in a little, making heavy going on third speed. **1951** N. MITFORD *Blessing* II. ii. 170 I'll get you a bike with three speeds. **1974** *Encycl. Brit. Macropædia* II. 522/2 The simplest automobile transmission is the sliding-spur-gear type with three or four forward speeds and a reverse. **1980** P. LIVELY *Judgement Day* x. 129 A shiny new bike with three speeds.

6. a. Quickness, promptness, or dispatch in the performance of some action or operation. Freq. in the phrase ***with (all) speed***.

For the proverbial contrast with *haste*, see HASTE *sb.* 6.

a **1000** *Genesis* 2667 Spedum sæȝde eorlum Abimeleh.. waldendes word. *c* **1250** *Gen. & Ex.* 1083 Ðo seiden ðis angeles to loth wið sped. *c* **1425** *Abraham's Sacrifice* 376 in *Non-Cycle Myst. Plays* (1909) 51 Thys fyere schall brene a full good spyd. **1526** *Pilgr. Perf.* (W. de W. 1531) 90b, Let vs ryse agayne with all spede. **1577** B. GOOGE *Heresbach's Husb.* §29 Barley..must be geathered with more speede then other graynes. *c* **1614** SIR W. MURE *Dido & Æneas* I. 77 Let vs a navie then prepair with speid. **1663** S. PATRICK *Parab. Pilgr.* xii. (1687) 81 All that surprizes me is..that such feeble words as mine should..with such speed excite so high a degree of Love. **1701** PENN in *Pennsylv. Hist. Soc. Mem.* IX. 51 Get them transcribed by good hands with all speed. **1761** GRAY *Odin* 1 Uprose the King of Men with speed. **1847** HELPS *Friends in C.* I. viii. 128 Insist upon speed in learning... This speed gives the habit of concentrating attention. **1891** FARRAR *Darkn. & Dawn* lv, The execution of the Christians was to be hurried on with all speed.

b. *Photogr.* The relative rapidity with which a plate, film, etc., is acted upon by light or by a developer.

1892 ABNEY *Instr. Photogr.* (ed. 9) 103 Measuring the speed and gradation of plates. **1935** S. C. JOHNSON *Foulsham's Compl. Photographer* iii. 26 The last of the four factors which must be considered in determining the length of an exposure is the speed of the plate or film. **1977** 'J. LE CARRÉ' *Hon. Schoolboy* vi. 123 Loading a cassette into the camera, he set the film speed.

c. *Photogr.* = *shutter speed* s.v. SHUTTER *sb.* 3b.

1917 P. L. ANDERSON *Pictorial Photogr.* v. 95 Of course these high speeds are not necessary for indoor work, where an exposure of less than 1/8 second is practically never desired. **1947** A. RANSOME *Great Northern?* xxiii. 286 He set the aperture at f.11, the speed at a twenty-fifth of a second. **1977** J. HEDGECOE *Photographer's Handbk.* 162 Speeds of 1/500–1/2000 sec allow you to freeze subject action beyond the perception of the eye.

d. The rate, measured in words per minute, at which a person can write shorthand or can type; *spec.* (freq. in *pl.* of both skills) applied to the capacity of a particular person.

1886 *Encycl. Brit.* XXI. 840/2, 180 or 200 words a minute is no uncommon speed in certain styles of speech such as the conversational,—a speed which many [short-hand writers] ..would never acquire. **1933** SMITH & MUNRO *Guide to High Speed Writing in Pitman's Short-hand* i. 10 It is well within the capacity of the majority..to reach a speed of, say, 160 words a minute, and..all writers of the system should make up their minds that that is to be their *minimum* speed. **1957** C. SMITH *Case of Torches* xi. 137 He..said there wouldn't be much shorthand or typing. So I thought—well, I don't want to lose my speeds, then I heard about this job. **1976** H. TRACY *Death in Reserve* i. 14 I'm a sort of secretary. .. I've got high speeds in shorthand and typing.

7. An amphetamine drug, esp. methamphetamine, freq. taken intravenously. Cf. SPEED-BALL 1a. *slang* (orig. *U.S.*).

1967 [see FREAK *sb.*[1] 4c]. **1967** [see METHEDRINE]. **1969** FABIAN & BYRNE *Groupie* viii. 66 Now he was on speed the paranoid fantasies were really beginning. **1970** N. SAUNDERS *Alternative London* xxii. 175 Amphetamines ('speed') are stimulants which can temporarily reduce fatigue, increase mental activity and give you a general feeling of well-being. **1975** J. SYMONS *Three Pipe Problem* ix. 65 'What was he on?' .. 'Speed mostly. Sometimes acid.' **1978** G. VIDAL *Kalki* v. 109 Dr Lowell produced a hypodermic needle. I let him shoot me up... I assumed that he had given me speed.

8. In various prepositional phrases:

†**a.** ***in speed***, with speed, speedily. *Obs.*

c **1250** *Gen. & Ex.* 1221 Abraham rapede him sone in sped for to fulfillen godes reed. *c* **1375** *Sc. Leg. Saints* xxix. (*Placidas*) 800 One þe morn scho went in sped to þe gret maister of þe knychtede. *Ibid.* xxxiii. (*George*) 233 Ta þi horse in spede, & pas in haste fra þis stede. *a* **1586** SIDNEY *Ps.* XXXI. i, Deliver me, deliver me in speed. **1596** SHAKS. *Merch. V.* III. iv. 49 Take this same letter..In speed to Mantua.

b. ***at speed*** (also †***at his speed***, †***on*** or ***upon the speed***), at a rapid rate of movement.

1632 LITHGOW *Trav.* VI. 259 [He] stroke at me with his halfe-pike; but his horse being at his speed, I preuented his cruelty. **1646** EVANCE *Noble Order* 26 They are most upon the speed after [this game]. **1670** MILTON *Hist. Eng.* Wks. 1738 II. 16 Riding on the speed down a steep Hill. **1781** COWPER *Table-T.* 685 Always at speed, and never drawing bit. **1807** SIR R. WILSON *Priv. Diary* (1862) II. viii. 293 We were galloping at speed when an unfortunate marais received my horse. **1865** VISCT. MILTON & W. B. CHEADLE *N.-W. Passage by Land* iv. (1867) 62 We gained on them rapidly, until within about 200 yards, when they went off at speed.

c. ***at*** (or †***on***) ***full speed***, = 9b.

1749 FIELDING *Tom Jones* XI. ii, The young lady looking behind her, saw several horses coming after on full speed. **1784** COWPER *Task* VI. 331 The horse..That skims the spacious meadow at full speed. **1849** MACAULAY *Hist. Eng.* v. I. 610 The waggoners drove off at full speed. **1877** M. M. GRANT *Sun-Maid* ii, The Marquis drove at full speed.

9. In advb. phrases (without article):

†**a.** ***good speed***, speedily, quickly. *Obs.*

a **1300** *Cursor M.* 4786, I sagh caf on þe watur flete;.. dunward flette it wel god spede. **1375** BARBOUR *Bruce* IV. 507 Ȝon is the kyng, but dreid; Ga we furth till hym bettir speid. *c* **1420** *Avow. Arth.* xl, Toward Carlele ryȝte He hies, gode spede. **1500–20** DUNBAR *Poems* xxxiii. 24 He fled away gud speid.

b. ***full speed***, with the utmost speed possible. (Cf. 8c.) Also *attrib.*

1382 WYCLIF *Deut.* iii. 18 Fulspeed goo ȝe before ȝoure britheren. **1654–66** EARL ORRERY *Parthen.* (1676) 343 He thrust himself into the Wood full speed. **1700** S. L. tr. *Fryke's Voy. E. Ind.* 212, I ran full speed towards her to help her. **1737** [S. BERINGTON] *Mem. G. de Lucca* (1738) 69 Ten or a dozen armed Turks came upon us full Speed from the Town. **1835** W. IRVING *Tour Prairies* xxi. 187 Away several of them dashed, full speed. **1860** *Merc. Marine Mag.* VII. 139 The engines are going 'full speed ahead'. **1890** *Times* 18 Sept. 4/2 The Blanche..went out..for her four hours' full-speed trial of her engines.

10. a. ***to make speed***, to hurry, to make haste.

1548 UDALL, etc. *Erasm. Par. Matt.* iii. 30 Jesus left Galile ..& maketh spede vnto Jordane. **1548–9** (Mar.) *Bk. Comm. Prayer, Morn. Prayer*, O God, make spede to saue me. **1635** R. N. tr. *Camden's Hist. Eliz.* I. 60 Though she made but slow speed about it. **1663** *Extr. State P. rel. Friends* (1911) II. 180 Make all possible speed and gett Matts and deales for a Bulke head there if to be had. **1868** FREEMAN *Norm. Conq.* (1877) II. vii. 117 They made good speed with their journey.

†**b.** ***to have,*** or ***get, the speed of***, to outdistance, get ahead of (one). *Obs.*

1605 SHAKS. *Macb.* I. v. 36 Our Thane is comming: One of my fellowes had the speed of him. **1646** FULLER *Good Th. in Worse T.* (1841) 106 The other had got the speed of him, having first accused himself,..and already obtained his pardon.

c. ***to be one's speed***: to suit one's tastes, interests, or abilities; to be one's 'cup of tea' (CUP *sb.* 12b(ii)). *colloq.* (chiefly *U.S.*).

1923 E. L. RICE *Adding Machine* v. 77 'Did you ever carve a leg of lamb?'.. 'No, corned beef was our speed.' **1954** R. BISSELL *High Water* iii. 36 'I'm gonna buy you an Uncle Wiggly book,' I said. 'He'd be just your speed.' **1970** J. SANGSTER *Touchfeather, Too* i. 11 Lesbianism..isn't really my speed at all. I'm a normal type girl.

11. a. An inflammatory disease of cattle.

1704 *Dict. Rust.* s.v., *Speed.* This Distemper in Cattle [1725 *Fam. Dict.*, in Black Cattle] may well be so called, because it either mends or ends in three Days time. *a* **1800** PEGGE *Suppl. Grose*, *Speed*, a disease among young cattle in the Autumn. North. **1834** YOUATT *Cattle* 362 In the West Riding, where from the rapidity with which it runs its course it is called the *speed*, it also generally begins behind. **1881** SHELDON *Dairy Farming* 63/1 Calves are extremely liable to the fatal disease of 'hyant', 'speed'.

b. A section of a cone-pulley giving a particular rate of speed.

1881 YOUNG *Every Man his own Mechanic* §550. 257 The steps or speeds of the cone pulleys are generally flat and driven by a flat leathern belt.

c. (See quot.)

1889 W. MARCROFT *Ups & Downs* 18 The class of machinery first made at the Hartford New Works, Werneth, was called speeds, generally known as roving frames.

12. *attrib.* and *Comb.* **a.** In the names of devices or apparatus for regulating or indicating speed, as ***speed-check***, ***-clock***, ***-cone***, ***-gauge***, ***-meter***, etc.

Descriptions of some of these are given by Knight *Dict. Mech.* (1875–84). The number of such combs. has greatly increased in recent years, as ***speed-band***, ***-board***, ***-brake***, ***-gear***, etc.

1898 *Westm. Gaz.* 18 Nov. 9/1 The Sawyer footbrake—which appears to be a very reliable form of *speed-check. **1862** *Catal. Internat. Exhib., Brit.* II. No. 3220, Watchman's detector clocks, steam or *speed clock. **1869** RANKINE *Machinery & Millwork* 312 The most convenient way of changing the velocity-ratio of rotation of a pair of shafts..is by means of '*speed-cones'. **1843** *Civil Eng. & Arch. Jrnl.* VI. 248/2 The name Sillomêtre..might be well rendered in English *Speed-gauge. **1875** KNIGHT *Dict. Mech.* 2261/2 Osborne's speed-gage is for the purpose of determining the rate of speed at which shafting or wheels are rotating. **1858** SIMMONDS *Dict. Trade*, **Speed-indicator*, a gauge for testing the velocity of steam engines or machines. **1863** A. YOUNG *Naut. Dict.* 244 Tyssen's Ship's Log, or Speed Indicator. **1892** *Photogr. Ann.* II. 341 A roller blind shutter, with outside speed indicator. **1898** KIPLING *Fleet in Being* ii, The Sub watches the *speed-lights of the next ahead, for as those lanterns change so must he adjust his pace. **1938** *Times* 14 Oct. 15/4 The driver of the omnibus.. traversed the evidence of the *speed-meter by pleading that his omnibus was so constructed as to be incapable of travelling at the alleged illegal speed. **1958** *Manch. Guardian* 21 Jan. 6/3 The use of radar speedmeters to enforce the law on the roads promises to be more successful than most efforts to reduce..road accidents. **1875** KNIGHT *Dict. Mech.* 1262 The fly-wheel (of a foot-lathe), on which is the cord passing to the *speed-pulley of the head-stock. *Ibid.* 2262 Such a machine..does not fulfill the conditions of a *speed-recorder. **1880** *Engineer* XLIX. 404 *Speed regulator for light machinery. **1888** JACOBI *Printers' Vocab.* 129 **Speed riggers*, riggers graduated to allow of the driving band being shifted to increase or reduce the running power.

b. Denoting the attainment of, or capacity for, high-speed, as ***speed-bike***, ***bowler***, ***-gallop***, ***launch***, ***-skating*** (hence ***-skater***, ***-skate***).

Also, in recent use, ***speed-car***, ***-lathe***.

1852 R. F. BURTON *Falconry Valley Indus* viii. 81 The four miles of best speed gallop. **1885** *Daily News* 24 Jan. 6/7 The performances of the exponents of speed skating. **1894** *Westm. Gaz.* 6 Jan. 5/2 The tendency is altogether in favour of the 'speed' skate as against the slow, antiquated article. **1897** *Ibid.* 27 Jan. 7/2 Speed-skaters..are thoroughly enjoying themselves. **1904** *Trans. Inst. Naval Archit.* XLVI. 161 The American speed launches. **1950** W. HAMMOND *Cricketers' School* v. 52 No one exemplified better than Larwood the true speed-bowler's action. **1955** S. SPENDER *Coll. Poems 1928–1953* II. 74 Speed-bikes and tracks are real. **1977** *Arab Times* 3 Dec. 10/5 West Indian speed bowlers Andy Roberts and Michael Holding helped bring about the collapse of the Australian 'super test' cricket team.

c. Miscellaneous, as ***speed-capacity***, ***-law***, ***-limit***, ***-praise***, ***-rate***, ***record***, ***-stroke***, ***-trial***, etc.; ***speed-time***, ***-torque*** adjs.; **speed-boat**, a high-speed motor boat; hence **speed-boating**, riding in a speed-boat; **speed bug** [BUG *sb.*[2] 4a] *slang*, one who enjoys travelling at high speed; an addict of speed sports; **speed bump** *colloq.* = *sleeping policeman* s.v. POLICEMAN 1e; **speed cop** *slang*, a policeman or official detailed to enforce traffic laws, esp. a motorcycle patrolman; **speed demon** [DEMON 2e] *slang*, one who likes to travel at great speed, a 'speed bug'; also *transf.*; **speed freak** (orig. *U.S.*), a person addicted to an amphetamine drug (cf. sense 7 above); **speed gun**, a hand-held device for estimating the speed of a moving vehicle (proprietary name in U.S.); see also sense e; **speed hog** [HOG *sb.*[1] 7c] *slang*, one who causes annoyance by exceeding the normal or legal speed limit; **speed king** *slang* (orig. *U.S.*), a motor-racing champion; **speed limit**, (*a*) the maximum speed a vehicle is capable of achieving (quot. 1893); (*b*) the maximum speed permitted by law on certain types of road or to specified classes of vehicle; **speed-man**, a cyclist who rides at a high rate of speed; **speed merchant** *colloq.*, one whose 'business' concerns the use of speed; *spec.* (*a*) *Cricket*, a fast bowler; (*b*) one who enjoys driving or riding at high speed (cf. MERCHANT *sb.* 3); **speed-read** *v. trans.* and *intr.*, to read rapidly by assimilating several phrases or sentences at once; so **speed-reader**, one who speed-reads; **speed-reading** *vbl. sb.*; **speed shop** *slang* (see quot. 1954); **speed trap**, a system operated by the police for detecting motorists exceeding the speed-limit; **Speed-walk** *U.S.*, a proprietary term for a moving walkway for conveying passengers; also (with small initial) in general use; cf. TRAVOLATOR; †**speed while**, a short time; **Speedwriting** orig. *U.S.*, the proprietary name of a form of shorthand which uses the letters of the alphabet; hence **speedwriter**. See also SPEEDBALL, SPEEDWAY.

1911 *New Fry's Mag.* May 224/1 The number of *speed-boats, pure and simple, has grown greatly. **1929** 'Seamark' *Down River* i. 6 Hillary Kittredge..had fallen under the lure of speed-boat racing. **1940** R. Chandler *Farewell, my Lovely* xxxvii. 280 The speedboat scuffed the *Montecito's* ancient sides. **1976** H. Kemelman *Wednesday the Rabbi got Wet* liii. 311 There are houses all around this little lake and each..must have a speedboat or an outboard. **1928** *Sunday Dispatch* 5 Aug. 11/3 The heavy demand for petrol, created by the new sport of '*speed' boating. **1975** *Country Life* 30 Oct. 1129/1 A useful side effect of the speed-boating..was the weed being cut by the propellers of the boats. **1914** *Automobile Topics* XXXIV. 191/1 The trials..were crowded with excitement for the *speed bugs who filled the grandstands. **1928** Speedbug [see AQUAPLANE]. **1975** *Public Works* Aug. 73/1 *Speed bumps had been installed in many apartment complexes and shopping center parking lots. **1978** T. L. Smith *Money War* (1979) I. 59 As he approached the speed bumps, Hogan slowed... They took the bumps gently and then pulled off the road. **1900** *Daily Express* 16 July 1/1 A motor car with a claimed *speed capacity of 85 miles an hour. **1924** *Cape Argus* 12 Jan. 20 These '*speed cops', however, wear uniform and are not got up to appear like ordinary motor-cyclists. **1933** *Amer. Speech* VIII. 72/2 His Grace, on being stopped, demanded 'Are you a speed-cop?' The patriotic magistrates fined him £10. 10s. and suspended his license for three months. **1948** *Sat. Even. Post* 3 July 77/3 Speed cops still speak politely to me. **1941** *Speed demon [see DICE *v.* 1 a]. **1962** A. Lurie *Love & Friend-ship* vii. 113 Helen, the regular cashier, was a speed demon. **1971** *Black Scholar* Jan. 35/1 Jack Johnson..has been called many things, e.g. show off, fool, speed demon. **1967** *Speed-freak [see FREAK *sb.*[1] 4 c]. **1973** R. Mills *Young Outsiders* ii. 63 In the summer of 1970 Jimmy would have been labelled a 'speedfreak' within the circles in which he moved. **1972** *Official Gaz.* (U.S. Patent Office) 1 Aug. TM 29/1 CMI, Incorporated, Minturn, Colo. Filed Feb. 1, 1971. **Speed Gun* for Traffic Radar..First use Dec. 10, 1970. **1972** *Tuscaloosa* (Ala.) *News* 14 Dec. 32/4 The hand-held Digital Doppler, a new tool police are using to catch speeders... The police purchased eight of the devices—also known as 'speed guns'. **1976** *Tel.* (Brisbane) 24 June 1 The speed guns are being used by traffic police mainly in areas of potential traffic hazard. **1928** *Daily Express* 23 Aug. 9/4 The scheme to limit '*speed-hogs'. **1974** *Country Life* 30 May 1360/1, I join issue with the RYA on their objection to.. boat registration... Without it the speed hog..will often continue to go undetected. **1913** *Illustr. Technical World Mag.* June 493/1 (*caption*) Ralph De Palma. The '*speed king' of 1912. **1938** C. Graves *Swiss Summer* 108 German princes, English speed-kings..are usually to be found here. **1976** *Western Mail* (Cardiff) 22 Nov. 3/2 Yesterday's event was held to raise money for the memorial fund to the Welsh speed king who died in a rally incident in the summer. **1926** *Scribner's Mag.* Aug. 152/1, I hear you break *speed-laws as recklessly as hearts. **1893** *Outing* XXII. 104/2 Both assured her owner that she had not touched her *speed limit. **1902** *To-day* 13 Mar. 648 The Automobile Club urges that the existing speed limit should be abolished. **1909** *Chambers' Jrnl.* Mar. 225/1 A speed-limit sometimes as low as..four and three-quarter miles per hour. **1926** *Motor* 26 Oct. 561/1 (*heading*) The speed limit. 35–40 m.p.h. or none at all? **1970** P. Laurie *Scotland Yard* v. 113 Fifty mph..is only ten mph above the speed limit there. **1973** H. McCloy *Change of Heart* i. 6 As for my mother, I can't make her drive ten miles over the speed limit. **1896** *Cycling Times* 10 June 2/4 Smith, who is a '*speed man,' may be able to push the same machine ..to the tune of twenty [miles] an hour. **1913** J. B. Hobbs *How to make Century* xi. 80 The *speed merchant was now sending up such hot samples that his every delivery was more likely to take a wicket than offer a chance of runs. **1923** *Daily Mail* 15 Feb. 6 The goggled 'speed merchant' cannot see so well as usual. **1951** *Ithaca* (N.Y.) *Jrnl.* 9 Aug. 21/1 [He] had a glass arm and he certainly was no speed merchant. **1982** J. B. Hilton *Sunset Law* i. 11 A County Court judge..drove at reckless speed about the highways, menacing speed-merchants with a Smith & Wesson. **1605** Sylvester *Du Bartas* II. iii. I. *Vocation* 861 Thou that thrice ..Losest thy *speed-praise, and thy life beside. **1894** C. H. Cook *Thames Rights* 25 The reasons against fixing a *speed-rate are these. **1960** *Time* 24 Nov. 21 Bagwell taught himself to *speed-read, gulping whole paragraphs at a glance. **1973** *Sat. Rev. World* (U.S.) 20 Nov. 64/2 (*caption*), I speed-read your last book in two minutes and twenty seconds. **1965** *N.Y. Times* 5 June 22 The Evelyn Wood Reading Dynamics Institute..teaches prospective *speed-readers to see every word on the page—but to read three words at once, not one word out of three. **1975** 'S. Marlowe' *Cawthorn Jrnls.* xix. 162 He wished he had something to read... He was a speed-reader. He had an IQ of 140. **1983** *Listener* 20 Jan. 25/2 A library for an extra-terrestrial speed-reader cruising above the British Isles. **1965** G. Jackson *Let.* 3 Oct. in *Soledad Brother* (1971) 89 Be sure to look into the course on *speed reading. **1977** *Time* 3 Jan. 13/3 Having promised to read every bill brought up before the state senate, he ran into 2,300 of them. So he took a speed-reading course and read them all. **1935** P. Frankau *I find Four People* IV. 235 About this time the copywriter accomplished a *speed-record for journalism. **1942** E. Paul *Narrow St.* xvii. 132 The *Bremen* made her maiden trip to New York and set a speed record. **1954** *Amer. Speech* XXIX. 102 **Speed shop*, a parts house, where engine parts and equipment are sold, and sometimes where hot rods are built. **1962** *Punch* 17 Oct. 561/1 Engineering firms and speed shops supply every beefed or stripped refinement. **1977** *Hot Car* Oct. 49/3 You can often pick up reasonable headers off the shelf from a good speed shop. *a* **1618** Sylvester *Mem. Mortalities* ii. Wks. (Grosart) II. 223 Having Death's *speed-stroak undiscerned given. **1917** A. T. Dover *Electric Traction* ii. 8 A *speed-time curve, for a run between two stations, is usually made up of periods of—(1) acceleration; (2) constant speed, or 'free running'..; (3) coasting..; and (4) retardation or braking. **1976** P. R. White *Planning for Public Transport* x. 216 In urban areas, higher rates of acceleration followed by a period of coasting can enable a given schedule to be covered using less energy (this is illustrated with reference to speed-time curves in Chapter 4). **1920** *Whittaker's Electr. Engineer's Pocket-bk.* (ed. 4) 544 For electric traction on railways and tramways, a motor possessing a variable *speed-torque characteristic is preferable to one possessing a constant speed-torque characteristic. **1962** G. A. T. Burdett *Automatic Control Handbk.* I. 2 The motor must often have a speed/torque characteristic to match that of the driven machine. **1927** U. Sinclair *Oil!* 9 'Sit still,' said the man. 'Don't look round. A *speed-trap!' **1980** G. M. Fraser *Mr American* xviii. 344 She had been caught in a police speed trap on the way to Brighton. **1883** W. H. Maw *Rec. Pract. Marine Engineering* I. 286/2 It was not found possible to take indicator diagrams on the full *speed trials, but a considerable number of trials were run at lower speeds progressing up to 11·74 knots per hour. **1885** *Pall Mall G.* 14 Jan. 11/1 The speed trials of the *Umbria*..and the *Collingwood*. **1955** *Britannica Bk. of Year* 490/1 **Speedwalk*, a moving sidewalk. **1956** *Official Gaz.* (U.S. Patent Office) 4 Sept. TM 9 Passenger Belt Conveyors, Inc., Akron, Ohio. .. Speedwalk..For Passenger Belt Conveying Apparatus. First use Mar. 29, 1954. **1960** *Times Rev. Industry* Apr. 28/1 A twin-track passenger-carrying conveyor belt..is being constructed in London... Known as speed-walks.. and travolators, at least two dozen installations are already in use in the United States. **1978** *Jrnl. R. Soc. Arts* CXXVI. 431/1 We can expect to see improvements in short-haul feeder and ancillary systems such as speedwalks, travelators and escalators. **13..** *E.E. Allit. P.* B. 1285 Alle he spoyled spitously in a *sped whyle. **1955** W. Gaddis *Recognitions* III. ii. 740 You didn't send me a *speedwriter down. **1925** *Speedwriting* (Brief Eng. Systems, Inc.) 7 (*caption*) *Speedwriting, the wonderfully efficient new system of shorthand, developed by Miss Emma B. Dearborn, can be written after a few weeks' study, either by pencil or on any make of type-writer. **1927** *Official Gaz.* (U.S. Patent Office) 8 Aug. 242/1 *Speedwriting*... Printed Lessons and Examination Sheets Issued from Time to Time. Claims use since Dec. 29, 1924. **1929** *Radio Times* 8 Nov. 439/2 Speedwriting (The Universal Shorthand). **1938** E. B. White *Quo Vadimus?* 24 They sell a new kind of shorthand course, called the Quigley Method of Intensive Speedwriting. **1962** *New Scientist* 5 July 11/1 Part of the Speedwriting method is to cut out most of the vowels and unnecessary movement in making other letters. **1976** T. Stoppard *Dirty Linen* 24 You do speedwriting I suppose?.. Yes, if I'm given enough time. **1982** Barr & York *Official Sloane Ranger Handbk.* 84/1 Every Sloane secretarial college has a nimbus of girls with their shorthand books or red speed-writing books.

d. With vbl. sbs. and ppl. adjs., as ***speed-making***, ***-mingling***, ***-multiplying***, ***-producing***.

1548 Elyot, *Properantia*, haast, speede makyng. **1611** Cotgr., *Acceleration*, hast, or speedmaking. **1875** Knight *Dict. Mech.* 2262/1 This gearing-up or..speed-multiplying ..is found in many kinds of machinery. *Ibid.* 2262/2 A system of speed-multiplying gear. **1885–94** R. Bridges *Eros & Psyche* Nov. vi, Betwixt the twin speed-mingling fans of gold. **1893** *Outing* XXII. 106 Another great speed-producing son of the same sire. **1901** *Munsey's Mag.* XXV. 737/1 When the colt settled into his stride again, the effort at speed making was continued as before.

e. *Photogr.* In names for an electronic flash-gun, as ***speed flash***, ***gun***, ***lamp***, ***-light***.

1940 A. L. M. Sowerby *Wall's Dict. Photogr.* (ed. 15) 315 Externally, a speed-gun takes the form of a box or casing that can be attached to the camera to make the whole a single unit. **1950** W. F. Berg *Exposure* 339 A special kind of flash lamp is the speed flash, also known as multiple or electronic flash... One of the most important advantages of speed lamps is their exceedingly short flash time. **1953** *Sun* (Baltimore) 10 Jan. 5 (*caption*) A photo snapped of Prime Minister Winston Churchill..showed five-sided 'spots'. It was raining at the time and was attributed to reflections from a speedlight. **1969** A. Feininger *Compl. Colour Photographer* II. 45 Electronic flash or speedlight has.. advantages over conventional flashbulbs. **1979** *SLR Camera* Jan. 36/1 The AE-1 is..an automated system camera. It includes a power winder for auto film transport, a speedlite for auto flash photography and an automatic exposure control.

speed (spiːd), *v.* Forms: 1 **spedan**, 3–5 **speden** (3 **-enn**, 5 **-yn**), 4–5 **sped**, 6 **spede**; 4–7 **speede**, 6– **speed**; 5–6 *Sc.* **speid**, 6 **spead**. *Pa. t.* 2 **spædde**, 2–6 **spedde**, 3 **spede**, 4– **sped**, 4–7 **spedd**. *Pa. pple.* 3–5 **i-sped**, 5 **i-spedde**; 4 **y-sped(d**, **y-spedde**; 3– **sped**, 4–6 **spedd**, 5–6 **spedde**, 8– **speeded**. Also *3rd sing. pres.* 3–4 **spet**, 5 **spette**. [OE. *spédan* (once; otherwise *ȝespédan*, early ME. *i-speden*), = MDu. *spoeden*, *spueden* (Du. *spoeden*), OS. *spôdian* (MLG. and LG. *spôden*), OHG. *spuoten* (G. *spuden*, *sputen*, from LG.), f. the stem **spōd-*: see SPEED *sb.*]

I. 1. a. *intr.* Of persons: To succeed or prosper; to meet with success or good fortune; to attain one's purpose or desire. Now *arch.*

993 *Battle of Maldon* 34 Ne þurfe we us spillan, ȝif ȝe spedaþ to þam. *a* **1122** *O.E. Chron.* (Laud MS.) an. 656, Swa he spedde swa him Crist huðe, swa þet in feuna ȝeare wæs þet mynstre ȝare. **1154** *Ibid.* an. 1140, Eustace..wende to biȝæton Normandi þær þurh, oc he spedde litel. *c* **1200** Ormin 12317 He.. wollde winnenn Crist..All alls he wann Eve & Adam, ȝiff þatt he mihhte spedenn. *c* **1275** *Moral Ode* 258 in *O.E. Misc.*, Ne his poure kunesmen at him ne myhte nouht spede. *a* **1300** *Cursor M.* 734 In his auen schap To sped he hopd haue na hap. **1362** Langl. *P. Pl.* A. III. 164 Menede hire to þe kyng To haue space to speken, spede ȝif heo mihte. *c* **1425** *Brut* 363 So the King come to Engelond ayen, for lesyng of moo of his peple, and þus he spedde not þere. **1456** Sir G. Haye *Law Arms* (S.T.S.) 13 Quhen he sawe that he mycht nocht in that maner spede. **1500–20** Dunbar *Poems* xiii. 24 Some speidis [at law], for he in court hes menis. *a* **1542** Wyatt in *Tottel's Misc.* (Arb.) 53 Soonest he spedes, that most can lye and fayn. **1647** N. Bacon *Disc. Govt. Eng.* I. iv. (1739) 9 [They] sent for aid where they were most like to speed for the present, and left the future to look to it self. *a* **1688** Bunyan *Israel's Hope Encour.* Wks. 1855 I. 614 Wouldst thou be a man that would pray and prevail? Why, pray to God in the faith of the merits of Christ, and speed. **1825** Scott *Betrothed* xxiii, Here we come near to the spot where we hope to speed, or no where. **1835** Browning *Paracelsus* III. 989 This he has done and nobly. Speed that may! **1836** J. Martin *Discourses* 367 It is a thing in which we are sure of speeding.

Prov. *c* **1470** *Gol. & Gaw.* 879 Oft in romanis I reid: Airly sporne, late speid. **1593** R. Harvey *Philad.* 5 He that goeth aspying goeth aspeeding. [See also SPARE *v.*[1] 6 c.]

†**b.** Const. *of*: To succeed in getting, obtaining, or accomplishing. *Obs.*

c **1400** Maundev. (Roxb.) xxxiii. 151 Many grete lordes has assayd diuerse tymes to passe;..bot þai myght noȝt spede of þaire iournee. **1530** *Hickscorner* (1905) 148 But there he could not speed of his prey. **1530** Palsgr. 727/1 And y maye spede of this ones, I care nat and I never sewe to him whyle I lyve. **1573** L. Lloyd *Marrow of Hist.* (1653) 256 Untill she sped of the like chance that Procris did, she could never be quiet. **1600** Pory tr. *Leo's Africa* I. 41 Their young men may goe a wooing to diuers maides, till such time as they haue sped of a wife. **1643** Prynne *Sov. Power Parl.* App. 26 But he sped little of his purpose.

2. a. With advs.: To succeed or fare *well*, *ill*, etc.

a **1122** *O.E. Chron.* (Laud MS.) an. 1114, Sona þær æfter sende se cyng him..to Rome æfter þes ærcb' pallium, & an munec mid him.., & hi þær well spæddon. *c* **1200** Ormin 14242 Swa þatt teȝȝ mihhtenn spedenn wel To winnenn erþlic ahhte. *c* **1250** *Gen. & Ex.* 1585 And ðu salt ðe betre sped, If it beð bi ðin faderes red. *Ibid.* 3314 'Ille,' he seiden, 'haue we sped'. *c* **1330** R. Brunne *Chron. Wace* (Rolls) 4279 Y trowe þou schalt fol euele spede. **1377** Langl. *P. Pl.* B. III. 270 Spille it and spare it nouȝte, þow shalt spede þe bettere. *a* **1425** tr. *Arderne's Treat. Fistula*, etc. 75, I spedde effectuously with sich a clistre þat is þer made. **1483** Caxton *Gold. Leg.* 113 b/1 He answerd that he had euyl spedde. **1573** Tusser *Husb.* (1878) 44 But worse shall he speed, that soweth ill seed. **1577–87** Holinshed *Chron.* I. 128/2 Some warres he had, and sped diuerslie. *a* **1628** Preston *New Cov.* (1634) 86 When we pray best, we speed best. **1676** Hobbes *Iliad* II. 116, I wonder less that we no better speed. **1791** Cowper *Odyss.* VII. 61 For boldest men Speed ever best.

b. With *how* (or *however*).

c **1230** *Hali Meid.* 27 Hwase, of engel, lihteð to iwurðen lahere þen a beast,..loke hu ha spede! *c* **1290** *S. Eng. Leg.* I. 148 Heo tolden þe kinge al heore cas, hov heo hadde i-sped. *a* **1300–1400** *Cursor M.* 17288 + 123 þai..told vnto þer maisters how þat þai hade spedd. *c* **1450** Lovelich *Merlin* 9656 Merlyne hadde hym told..hou that they thanne spedden jn desert. *a* **1533** Ld. Berners *Huon* lxxxi. 247 He demaunded how I had sped in my iourney. **1563** B. Googe *Eglogs*, etc. (Arb.) 114, I entred in, with fearefull Harte, muche doutyng howe to speede. **1617** Moryson *Itin.* II. 109 Not caring how the messengers sped, so the letters were not understood. **1653** in *Hatton Corr.* (Camden) 9 How-ever wee speed heere, 4 of our Est India shipps are taken by the Dutch. **1766** Goldsm. *Vicar* x, Well, my girls, how have you sped? **1814** Southey *Roderick* xxv. 501 Go tell thy father now how thou hast sped With all thy treasons! **1852** Miss Yonge *Cameos* (1877) I. xvii. 129 If she could thus treat a royal uncle, how must not men inferior in rank have sped?

c. With *as* or *thus*.

1649 Milton *Eikon.* 15 In this Warr against the Church hee hath sped as other haughty Monarchs, whom God hath harden'd to the same enterprize. **1653** Holcroft *Procopius*, *Pers. Wars* I. 24 Thus the Romans spedd with these people.

3. *impers.* To go or fare (well or ill) *with* a person, etc. †In early use with dat. or *to*.

c **1205** Lay. 18695 þa iseh Vðer king þat him ne spedde naðing. *Ibid.* 29508 þu scalt..beode þer godes godd-spel; þe scal spede ful wel. **1297** R. Glouc. (Rolls) 8163 þe cristine were of þe sarazins an onywar biset, & vor þe sarazins were ywar, hom spedde wel þe bet. *a* **1325** *Life Adam* 67 in Horstm. *Altengl. Leg.* (1878) 140 To Adam wende we, And loke we hou him spet þat..He brak godes comandment. **1545** Brinklow *Compl.* xxiv. (1874) 69 Comenly it spedeth vnhappyly to that reame, where thei be embassytors. **1610** Guillim *Heraldry* III. xii. 122 Though sometime it speed with them contrary to their Titles. **1854** Ferrier *Inst. Metaph.* Introd. 8 As time has advanced, it has constantly sped worse with philosophy, instead of speeding better.

4. a. Of things: To prove successful; to thrive.

c **1200** Ormin 1765 Godess ennglеþeod Ne maȝȝ nohht unnderrstanndenn Hu mikell Cristess bede maȝȝ Towarrd hiss faderr spedenn. *a* **1300** *Cursor M.* 28317 Oþer mans beginyng of gode dede Oft-sith i letted for to spede. *a* **1586** Sidney *Ps.* XXXVII. iii, Lay all thy trusting On hym, and he will make it speed. **1626** W. Yonge *Diary* (Camden) 93 Arminianism and Pelagianism do much speed abroad, in divers parts of this realm. **1713** Swift *Cadenus & Vanessa* Wks. 1755 III. II. 7 A project..which, if it sped, Wou'd shew the merits of the cause. **1866** *Contemp. Rev.* I. 263 The suits of the Bishop of Salisbury against Dr. Williams and of Dr. Fendall against Mr. Wilson had not sped.

b. With modifying words (as *well*, *ill*, *how*, etc.): To succeed, fare, go (on), make progress, etc.

a **1250** *Owl & Night.* 763 Oft spet wel a lute lyste, þar muche strengþe..myste. *c* **1400** *Gamelyn* 800 'I se wel,' seyde Gamelyn, 'the justice is sette; Go aforn, Adam, and loke how it spette.' *a* **1425** tr. *Arderne's Treat. Fistula*, etc. 95 And so schal it better spede. **1449** in *Cal. Proc. Chanc. Q. Eliz.* (1830) II. 55 The xxvj li. levyng behynde shall be wele and truly paied..unto the forseid Thomas like as the forseid werkes spedyn. **1545** Brinklow *Lament.* A iv b, The Cytie neuer speadeth so euell, as when they so ronne a whore hountinge. **1681** W. Robertson *Phraseol. Gen.* s.v., This business speeds well under our hands. **1733** W. Ellis *Chiltern & Vale Farm.* 79 The Acorn here may speed very well. **1781** Cowper *Conversat.* 316 Relate how many weeks they kept their bed, How an emetic or cathartic sped. **1855** Prescott *Phillip II*, I. viii. I. 114 Philip's suit no longer sped so favorably as before.

†5. To be profitable, expedient, or useful. Chiefly *impers. Obs.*

c **1380** WYCLIF *Serm.* Sel. Wks. II. 109 It spediþ to ȝou þat o man die for þe puple. **1382** —— *Ecclus.* xxxvii. 31 Forsothe not alle thingus to alle speden. **1423** JAS. I. *Kingis Q.* xxviii, Ane wofull wrecche that to no wight may spede. *a* **1425** tr. *Arderne's Treat. Fistula*, etc. 3 For-als-miche in hard thingis it spedith to studiers for to perseuere and abide.

6. a. *trans.* To further or assist (a person); to cause to succeed or prosper. Also *refl.* Now *arch.*

a **1240** *Sawles Warde* in *O.E. Hom.* I. 267 Hwa se þis writ haueð ired, Ant crist him haueð swa isped, Ich bidde.. þet ȝe bidden ofte for me. *a* **1300** *Cursor M.* 29002 Seuen ar þai [*sc.* boons] þat vs mai spede Til al þat euer we haue of nede. *c* **1386** CHAUCER *Reeve's T.* 113, I prey you speed us in al that ye may. *c* **1430** *Syr Tryam.* 1196 Y tryste in God that he schalle me spede. **1503–4** *Act 19 Hen. VII*, c. 28 Preamb., The Kinges Highnes.. is therfor enclyned to here & spede resonably the seid peticioners. **1530** PALSGR. 727/1 Serve God well and he shall spede you in all your busynes. **1601** SHAKS. *Jul. C.* I. ii. 88 For let the Gods so speed mee, as I loue The name of Honor, more then I feare death.

absol. **13..** *E.E. Allit. P.* B. 551 On spec of a spote may spede to mysse Of þe syȝte of þe soueryn þat syttez so hyȝe. **1819** SCOTT *Ivanhoe* xli, Achieving an adventure, with only his good sword, and his good arm to speed.

b. In the phrase ***God speed me, thee***, etc., or variations of this. (Cf. GOD-SPEED.) Also ***God speed the plough***, etc.

(*a*) *c* **1320** *Sir Tristr.* 2266 He may bidde god me spede. **1375** BARBOUR *Bruce* XVIII 389 'Do than,' he said, 'and god the speid!' *c* **1386** CHAUCER *Knt.'s T.* 1700 God spede you; goth forth and ley on faste. *c* **1400** *Gamelyn* 827 God spede me this day at my newe werk. *c* **1470** HENRY *Wallace* II. 93 Go hens,.. the mekill dewill the speid. **1526** TINDALE *Matt.* xxviii. 9 Iesus mett them sayinge: God spede you. **1553** T. WILSON *Rhet.* (1580) 4 As for other that haue no witte, thei wil neuer learne it, therefore God speede them. **1617** in Birch *Crt. & Times Jas. I* (1848) II. 17 God speed him, and send him a better voyage than I even hope for! **1641** MILTON *Reform.* II. Wks. 1851 III. 42 The little adoe.. puts mee into the mood to tell you a tale ere I proceed further; and Menenius Agrippa speed us. **1677** MIÈGE *Fr. Dict.* II. s.v., God speed you well. **1819** SCOTT *Ivanhoe* xxxii, Rowena waved a graceful adieu to him..—the Saxon bade God speed him. **1866–** in Sc. use (*Eng. Dial. Dict.*).

absol. *c* **1586** C'TESS PEMBROKE *Ps.* CXXIX. v, God speed, friendes, God give you joy. **1594** SHAKS. *Rich. III*, II. iii. 6 3 *Cit.* Neighbours, God speed. **1602** [see (*b*)].

(*b*) *c* **1500** *Spede the Plough* 8 I pray to God, spede wele the plough. **1569** T. NORTON *Warning agst. Papists* O iv, Let vs draw.. together, and then say and sing merily, God spede the ploughe of England. **1589** HORSEY *Trav.* (Hakl. Soc.) App. 310 Thearby have they maynatyned their decayed trade.. by meanes of their traffycque. God speed their plowe! **1602** DEKKER *Honest Wh.* xii, *Duke.* God speed, father. *Mad.* God speed the Plow, thou shalt not speed me. **1610** FLETCHER *Faithf. Sheph.* II. i, Great Pan for Syrinx sake bid speed our Plow. **1781** COWPER *Charity* 123 Heav'n speed the canvass, gallantly unfurl'd [etc.].

†**c.** In the adjuration ***so God me speed***, etc. *Obs.*

c **1320** *Sir Tristr.* 1631 þe king swore, so god him spede, þat boþen schuld haue riȝt. **1393** LANGL. *P. Pl.* C. XI. 107 'ȝut sauereþ me nat þi sawe,' quaþ ich, 'so me crist spede'. *c* **1440** [see SO *adv.* 19]. *c* **1460** *Towneley Myst.* x. 194 Whos is that chyld, so god the spede?

†**d.** Const. *of* or *with*: To provide or furnish (one) with something. Chiefly in *pa. pple.* Also *refl. Obs.*

1530 TINDALE *Answ. Sir T. More* Wks. (1573) 249/2 We beleue, we deserue to be sped of all that our blynd hartes desire. **1554** *Interlude of Youth* in Hazl. *Dodsley* II. 17, I can speed thee of a servant of price, That will do thee good service. **1576** PETTIE *Petite Pallace* 36 She.. began to cast in her head how she myght be sped of an other husband. **1600** HOLLAND *Livy* III. xlvi. 119 For this time I am sped of sureties ynough. **1601** —— *Pliny* I. 144 There also a man may be sped with bondslaues. **1665** BRATHWAIT *Comment Two T.* (1901) 56 Of such an one she speeds her self, that it seems his Soul deserv'd well of her.

7. In *pa. pple.* (see also prec.): **a.** Furthered or brought to the end or condition desired; so dealt with as to be satisfied or well situated. (In later use also with *well.*)

13.. *Cursor M.* 24752 (Gött), þat gifs me list of hir to rede, For he es all spedd þat scho will spede. **1390** GOWER *Conf.* I. 94 Er thou be sped, Thou schalt me leve such a wedd, That [etc.]. *c* **1420** LYDG. *Lond. Lyckpeny* v, But, lackyng mony, I could not be sped. *c* **1450** *Reg. Oseney* 111 If hit happe my wife to be i-spedde in child-beryng at Barton. **1566** *Pasquine in Traunce* 35 For the moste part, she that went to bed a Virgin, arose from thence spedde with hir errande. **1571** CAMPION *Hist. Irel.* vi. (1633) 18 And then if they can get a piece of rugge to cover them, they are well sped. **1657** W. RAND tr. *Gassendi's Life Peiresc* I. 110 [He] went on purpose.. into Dauphine; and returned sped, about the beginning of the year following. **1680** H. MORE *Apocal. Apoc.* 208 But they that have obtained their glorified body, .. they are sped already, and are safe from this fate. **1713** *Guardian* No. 100 (1756) II. 78 When the maid was once sped, she was not suffered to tantalize the male part of the commonwealth. **1864** SWINBURNE *Atalanta* 368 That this great hunt with heroes for the hounds May leave thee memorable and us well sped.

b. In contexts implying an evil plight or awkward situation.

c **1530** *Remedy Love* lxxiii. in *Chaucer's Wks.* (1532) 368 b/1 To warne him nowe he is too farre speddе; It is to late him to forbede. **1596** SHAKS. *Tam. Shr.* V. ii. 185 We three are married, but you two are sped. **1601** HOLLAND *Pliny* II. 49 Like as those that be sped with the yellow jaunise. **1616** *Marlowe's Faustus* in M.'s Wks. (1910) 217 *Benu.* 'Zons, hornes againe. *Mart.* Nay chafe not man, we all are sped. **1709** PRIOR *Ladle* 92 Told 'em, for Supper or for Bed They might go on, and be worse sped. **1821** SCOTT *Kenilw.* v, 'We are fairly sped now,' said Foster; 'yonder is thy lord's signal'.

c. Appointed or elected *to* (or as) something. *rare.*

c **1380** WYCLIF *Wks.* (1880) 23 For who so may most gold brynge sunnest schal be sped to grete benefices. **1691** WOOD *Ath. Oxon.* II. 18 His father got him to be sped a Kings-scholar at Westminster. **1903** in Farmer & Henley *Slang Dict.* VI. 307 Sped to New College = elected to a scholarship.

†**d.** Prepared, equipped; skilled or versed *in* something. *Obs.*

a **1450** tr. *De Imitatione* III. xxi. 89 Wherfore be þou spedde & redy to fiȝtyng, if þou wolt haue þe victory. **1526** SKELTON *Magnyf.* 562 Can you a remedy for a tysyke, That sheweth yourselfe thus spedde in physyke? *a* **1529** —— *P. Sparowe* 788 In Chauser I am sped, His tales I haue red.

8. a. To promote or further (a matter); to bring to or towards a successful issue or termination; to accomplish or carry out.

a **1300** *Cursor M.* 23920 Mi will ic hope þou will me spede. *c* **1386** CHAUCER *Sec. Nun's T.* 357 Every maner boone That he God asked, it were sped ful soone. **1390** GOWER *Conf.* I. 162 Thei kepte that non other scholde Touchende of love his cause spede. *a* **1425** tr. *Arderne's Treat. Fistula*, etc. 36 þan, forsoþe, may he.. finaly spede þe forseid cure aboute four & tuenty wekes. *c* **1450** *Merlin* v. 87 And ye haue also wele spedde the entente of Merlin. **1526** *Pilgr. Perf.* (W. de W. 1531) 168 This holy prayer for his ennemyes anone was spedde,.. for it conuerted saynt Paule. **1568** GRAFTON *Chron.* II. 8 The next yere when king William had sped his businesse in the sayde Countrie, he returned into England. **1633** G. HERBERT *Temple, Cross* iv, Ev'n when my hopes seem to be sped, I am to grief alive. **1697** DRYDEN *Virg. Past.* VII. 44 These Branches of a Stag.. Young Mycon offers, Delia, to thy Shrine. But speed his hunting with thy Pow'r divine. **1771** MRS. GRIFFITH *Hist. Lady Barton* II. 218 The only amends we can make you, for having sped our frolic, is to desire the favour of your company to dinner. **1833** MRS. BROWNING *Prometh. Bound* Wks. (1904) 150/1 May no sin be sped in the word that is said. **1847** EMERSON *Poems* (1857) 90 He had so sped his wise affairs That he caught Nature in his snares.

b. *spec.* To promote, expedite, prosecute (a bill, plea, etc.), as a matter of official or legal business.

1429 *Rolls of Parlt.* IV. 343/2 No Bill shal be sped but in the place ordeyned. **1482** in Rymer *Fœdera* (1711) XII. 164/2 In passyng and spedyng Letters of Transsumpt under the Seale of our Office of Mairaltie. **1566** *Reg. Privy Council Scot.* I. 466 Nocht to compone nor speid ony confirmatioun upoun the few abonewrittin. **1591** LAMBARDE *Archeion* (1635) 143 No Bill be sped, but in place ordained for Councell. **1641** *Termes de la Ley* (1659) 94 All plees touching the life or maihem of a man, called Plees of the Crown, are usually held and sped in the King's name. **1726** AYLIFFE *Parergon* 27 All those Writings and Matters, which.. are sped in open Court at the Instance of one or both of the Parties Litigant. **1884** *Law Rep.* 27 *Chanc. Div.* 63 The Plaintiffs ought to undertake to speed the action, that is to prosecute the action with due diligence.

9. †**a.** To treat of, deal with (a matter). *Obs.*

13.. *Cursor M.* 224 (Gött.), For mani [matters] ar þar for to spede. *c* **1374** CHAUCER *Boeth.* V. pr. i. (1868) 149 She hadde.. tournede þe cours of hir resoun to somme oþer þinges to ben tretid and to ben ysped. *Ibid.* pr. iv. 161 ȝit ne haþ it nat ben determined ne yspedd.. diligently of any of yow.

b. To bring to an end; to finish or dispatch.

c **1340** HAMPOLE *Pr. Consc.* 2682 Here es þe thred parte of þis buke spedde. *c* **1400** *Destr. Troy* 7601 When this speche was sped, speke þai no fferre. **1470–85** MALORY *Arthur* III. x. 111 Was there gras, otys, and breed for their horses; soone it was sped, and full hard was their souper. **1764** GOLDSM. *Trav.* 191 At night returning, every labour sped, He sits him down the monarch of a shed. **1825** SCOTT *Talism.* xvii, Go, speed thine office quickly, sirrah.

c. To dispatch, destroy, kill (a person, etc.).

1594 PLAT *Jewell-ho.* III. 74 They [rats] shall not be able to rise.. before you haue sped them. **1605** *Play of Stucley* in Simpson *Sch. Shaks.* (1878) I. 201 Braving braggart, since thou dost seek thy death, Look to thyself; I'll speed thee if I can. **1654** FULLER *Two Serm.* 20 Thus no doubt Herod.. was confident he.. had sped and despatched the Iewish king amongst the rest. **1735** POPE *Prol. Sat.* 31 A dire dilemma! either way I'm sped, If foes, they write, if friends, they read me dead. **1819** SCOTT *Ivanhoe* xxx, But that I wore a shirt of Spanish mail under my plate-coat, I had been fairly sped. **1845** DISRAELI *Sybil* VI. xii. III. 310 'Yes. I am sped,' he said in a faint voice.

II. 10. a. *trans.* To send with speed or haste; to hurry (a person, etc.) *out* or *away*; also, to force to go.

c **1250** *Gen. & Ex.* 3178 Egipte folc hem hauen ut sped. **1634** SIR T. HERBERT *Trav.* (1638) 106 Assaph-chan seeing all as he desired, speeds away a sure post with letters to Curroon. **1678** *Spanish Hist.* II. 15 Eight Ships commanded by our Admiral were speeded out from Cadis. **1770** GOLDSM. *Des. Vill.* 309 If to the city sped—what waits him there? **1781** COWPER *Expost.* 289 The cry in all thy ships is still the same—Speed us away to battle and to fame. **1845** SUMNER *True Grandeur Nations* (1846) 10 The twenty thousand letters, which each fortnight are speeded from this port alone, could not be sent. **1885** *Manch. Exam.* 10 July 5/2 Every soul in that part of the mine would be sped into eternity.

b. To send out, cast, discharge, or direct, with some degree of quickness and force.

a **1569** KINGESMYLL *Godly Adv.* (1580) 13 His tong spedyng wordes no faster then thei may seme wel bestowed. **1791** COWPER *Iliad* III. 436, I sped my spear in vain. **1830** TENNYSON *Poems* 43 His last arrow is sped. **1842** MACAULAY *Horatius* xlv, Through teeth, and skull, and helmet So fierce a thrust he sped. **1891** H. HERMAN *His Angel* xii. 236 The glance he sped towards his betrothed was brimful of expectant love.

†**c.** To recall hastily. *Obs.*$^{-1}$

1606 G. WOODCOCK *Hist. Ivstine* VI. 31 This their intent gaue matter of great mistrust vnto the Lacedemonians, causing them to speed home Agesilaus from his Persyan victories.

d. To enable (a person) to make speed in departing or travelling; to further the going or progress of; sometimes simply, to bid farewell to.

1725 POPE *Odyss.* XV. 84 True friendship's laws are by this rule exprest, Welcome the coming, speed the parting guest. **1732** —— *Hor. Sat.* II. ii. 160 For I, who hold sage Homer's rule the best, Welcome the coming, speed the going guest. **1829** SCOTT *Anne of G.* xxvi, Assuring them, that.. horses and faithful attendants should be ready to speed the youth on his journey to Nancy. **1849** ROCK *Ch. of Fathers* II. 388 Everywhere the brief-bearer was received, treated, and speeded on his way. **1894** B. CHAMBERS *Butterfly* 241 Next morning the host stood once more on the steps, speeding the parting Miss Scropes.

11. a. To give speed to (a course, etc.); to hasten; to cause to be rapid in movement.

a **1300** *Cursor M.* 19076 Up he ras, And to þe temple spede his pas. **1387** TREVISA *Higden* (Rolls) III. 231 þe cours was so i-sped þat the strokes come to-fore þe enemyes. **1577–87** HOLINSHED *Chron.* I. 35/1 So through France [Claudius] sped his iournies till he came to the side of the Ocean sea. **1700** DRYDEN *Iliad* I. 54 The helpless Priest reply'd no more, But sped his Steps along the hoarse-resounding Shore. **1746** FRANCIS tr. *Horace, Art Poet.* 215 To the grand Event he [the poet] speeds his Course. **1807** J. BARLOW *Columb.* III. 16 The king, undaunted in defensive war, Repels their hordes, and speeds their flight afar. **1855** CHAMIER *My Travels* I. vi. 88 There before us passed traveller after traveller, each speeding his way to the hotel. **1885** HOWELLS *Silas Lapham* (1891) I. 35 Let me.. take you out over the Milldam, and speed this mare a little. I'd like to show you what this mare can do.

b. To press or urge on, *esp.* in order to bring to an early result or termination; to expedite.

1390 GOWER *Conf.* I. 180 The Souldan.. In alle haste his cause spedde To sende for the mariage. **1463** *Bury Wills* (Camden) 17 To spede the tyme for yᵉ sarmon. **1535** STEWART *Cron. Scot.* II. 639 Now tarie nocht thairfoir; speid hand, haif done. **1696** RAY in *Lett. Lit. Men* (Camden) 202, I think it best to speed the finishing and fitting my Supplement for the Presse. **1697** DRYDEN *Virg. Past.* IV. 11 O chaste Lucina speed the Mother's pains, And haste the glorious Birth. **1815** SCOTT *Guy M.* xxvii, One of those prayers, or rather spells,.. used by the vulgar and ignorant to speed the passage of a parting spirit. **1870** BRYANT *Iliad* VI. I. 207 Command thy maids to speed the work.

c. To cause (time) to pass (*away*) quickly.

1818 SCOTT *Rob Roy* xxi, The incident.. sped away a part of the time which hung so heavily on my hand. **1851** HAWTHORNE *Snow Image*, etc. (1879) 246 Then he strove to speed away the time.

d. To increase the speed or working rate of. In recent use chiefly with *up*. Also *fig.*

1856 KANE *Arct. Expl.* I. xxvii. 353 Our plans were formed at once; there is nothing like emergency to speed, if not to instruct, the energies. **1894** *Westm. Gaz.* 4 Sept. 7/1 What of machinery? Shall we get that 'speeded up' sufficiently to counterbalance the shorter working day? **1909** C. F. G. MASTERMAN *Condition of England* ii. 23 When life has become 'speeded up' to the motor-car level. **1931** *Times Lit. Suppl.* 3 Dec. 979/3 He brought youth to the theatre; he speeded it up. **1974** A. LURIE *War between Tales* xiv. 277 He has the sense of being slowed down and speeded up alternatively.

e. To give a specified speed to (a machine).

1881 *Eng. Mechanic* No. 874. 376/3 My own 46 in. [wheels] are speeded down to 40 in. for level roads. **1889** *Engineer* LXVIII. 458 When an engine is speeded to run 300 revolutions per minute. **1897** *Daily News* 10 July 4/3 On similar automatic machines, speeded alike.

12. *refl.* **a.** To go with speed; to make haste in passing from one place to another. Now *arch.*

a **1300** *Cursor M.* 10555 Ga to mete him, þou þe spede. *c* **1350** *Will. Palerne* 5169 Now.. speke we of þe spaynols.. hou þei sped hem to spayne. *c* **1400** *Laud Troy Bk.* 17817 Antenor him hamward spedde. *c* **1450** *Merlin* I. 21 So he spedde hym oute of the town till he com to a ryver. **1509** HAWES *Past. Pleas.* XVIII. (Percy Soc.) 77 Venus and she made conjuncyon. Frome the cumbust way she had her so sped. **1560** DAUS tr. *Sleidane's Comm.* 386 They both talking long and much with the Emperor alone, spede them on their journy. **1610** HOLLAND *Camden's Brit.* 374 Severne.. with many windings and turnings in, and out, speedeth him unto the Ocean. **1678** BUNYAN *Pilgr.* I. (1862) 41 Christian suddenly started up and sped him on his way. **1821** SCOTT *Kenilw.* ix, Dickie.. bolted from the cottage, and sped him to the top of a neighbouring rising ground.

b. To act with speed; to make haste in doing, or to do, something. Now *arch.*

a **1300** *Cursor M.* 13538 Fra now behoues þe sun him spede For to do his fader dede. **1390** GOWER *Conf.* II. 256 And he with alle haste him spedde And made him naked and al warm. *c* **1400** *Destr. Troy* 13236 þe worthy.. sped hir full specially my sped for to let. **1447** BOKENHAM *Seyntys* (Roxb.) 35 For to other thyngys I wold spede me. **1526** *Pilgr. Perf.* (W. de W. 1531) 72 b, These thynges.. we shall spede vs.. to declare euery daye by it selfe. **1581** A. HALL *Iliad* v. 86 Iris straight hir spedde To dresse them wel. **1647** N. BACON *Disc. Govt. Eng.* II. xiii. (1739) 71 The Eagle stooped, and sped himself so well, as within six years he fastned upon the Sword and Scepter. **1682** BUNYAN *Holy War* (1905) 329 Then speed you to do that which is written in my Law. **1805** SCOTT *Last Minstrel* II. xxi, Now, speed thee what thou hast to do. **1828** —— *F.M. Perth* ii, Come, Dorothy, speed thee with the food, old woman.

13. *intr.* **a.** To go or move with speed. Also with *it.*

c **1400** *Destr. Troy* 7733 The grete horses.. Sparit for no Spurse, speddyn to the flight. *c* **1470** HENRY *Wallace* IV. 775 'Speid fast,' he said, 'Wallace is lokit in'. **1500–20** DUNBAR *Poems* lxxiii. 11 Walk furth, pilgrame,.. Speid home, forquhy anone cummis the nicht. **1562** WINȜET *Wks.*

(S.T.S.) I. 3 Sum..speidis baith with airis and erect salis [etc.]. **1610** Holland *Camden's Brit.* 696 From Aberford the said Riveret Coc speedeth immediately to the River Wherf. **1637** Heywood *Royall King* I. iii, I'le try to day which of our two good steeds Can speed it best; let the most swift take both. **1697** Dryden *Virg. Past.* IV. 25 The Goats with strutting Dugs shall homeward speed. **1736** Gray *Statius* I. 48 O'er his head, Collecting all his force, the circle sped. **1795** Southey *Joan of Arc* II. 128 From the disastrous plain of Agincourt I speeded homewards. **1835** Lytton *Rienzi* I. i, The vessel thus referred to was speeding rapidly down the river. **1856** Kane *Arct. Expl.* II. xxi. 211 The dogs speed from hut to hut, almost unguided by their drivers. **1860** Tyndall *Glac.* I. vii. 51 Streams sped downwards, falling over the rocks.

fig. **1588** Shaks. *L.L.L.* II. i. 120 Your wit's too hot, it speeds too fast, 'twill tire. **1869** J. Martineau *Ess.* II. 49 We might..have lightly sped across the slippery logic. **1893** Stevenson *Catriona* v. (1902) 51 His eyes speeding here and there without rest.

b. Of time: To advance or pass quickly.

13.. *Sir Beues* (A.) 1475 Whan hit to þat time spedde, þat Yuor scholde þat maide wedde. **1833** Ht. Martineau *Cinnamon & Pearls* i. 1 The brief twilight of the tropics had just sped away. **1858** Sears *Athan.* II. iii. 195 The day speeds on to the great evening. **1891** Farrar *Darkn. & Dawn* xxxv, The hours sped by almost unnoticed.

c. To make haste *to* do something; to be speedy in action.

a **1400** *Pistill of Susan* 103 Spyces speden to spryng, In Erbers enhaled. *a* **1425** *Cursor M.* 13538 (Trin.), Now bi-houeþ þe son to spede For to do his fadir dede. **1480** *Robt. Devyll* 188 in Hazl. *E.P.P.* I. 226 [He] prayed hys sonne, that he woulde spede, For to learne bothe to wryte and reade. **1577** Hanmer *Acc. Eccl. Hist., Socrat.* v. vi. (1619) 341 Being sore sicke, and speeding to baptisme. **1625** Bacon *Ess., Of Delays* (Arb.) 525 First to Watch, and then to Speed.

d. With complement: To attain a speed of.

1900 *Westm. Gaz.* 1 May 6/3 Her engines are twin-screw triple expansion,..and she will speed seventeen knots.

e. To drive a motor vehicle fast, esp. at an illegal speed; to break the speed limit in a motor vehicle.

1931 Galsworthy *Maid-in-Waiting* xiii. 118 'I'm going to speed,' said Jean, looking back. The speedometer rose rapidly. **1941** M. Halsey *Traffic Accidents & Congestion* v. 41 The very word *speed* has come to mean *speeding* or going too fast. **1949** R. A. Byrd *Driving to Live* xi. 156 It becomes ridiculous, in the light of this new discovery [*sc.* road-stare phenomenon], for any driver to brag about his ability to speed. **1954** B. Preston *Focus on Road Accidents* II. 63 If the motorist continued to speed and was caught, several times a day, every day, then he would soon stop speeding. **1969** *New Yorker* 14 June 29/2 If you speed, we'll charge you the same amount we charge anyone. **1979** D. Anthony *Long Hard Cure* viii. 72, I..went back to my car. I sped a little on the way back to town.

f. To be under the influence of an amphetamine drug. Also *fig.* Usu. as *pres. pple.* Cf. sense 7 of the sb. *slang.*

1973 R. Mills *Young Outsiders* ii. 60 If you are speeding you go out and do more things. **1977** *Rolling Stone* 7 Apr. 47/1 'The best diet for the road,' he says, 'is soup for lunch and candy for supper. It keeps the weight off and you're speeding on all that sugar by show time.' **1978** S. George *Screen Test* ii. 18 'You speeding?' He shrugged. 'Yes. Cancels the alcohol.'

'speedball. Also speed-ball, speed ball. [speed *sb.*] **1. a.** A dose of a drug, esp. a mixture of cocaine and morphine or of cocaine and heroin. *slang* (orig. *U.S.*).

1909 R. Beach *Silver Horde* v. 58 You must have fed him a speed-ball, for I never saw a guy gear up so fast... He's developed a remarkable burst of speed. **1935** N. Ersine *Underworld & Prison Slang* 69 Speedball, a mixture of *coke* and *morph* which is much in demand among drug addicts. **1953** W. Burroughs *Junkie* xiv. 139 A shot of morphine would be nice later when I was ready to sleep, or, better, a speedball, half cocaine, half morphine. **1964** *Guardian* 18 Apr. 6/3 To give a nobbler eighteen months for slipping a speedball in a greyhound's breakfast is like tossing up a ball and then punishing it for having the effrontery to bounce. **1974** M. C. Gerald *Pharmacol.* xv. 291 The 'speedball', a mixture of cocaine and heroin, is frequently employed to modulate the extreme feelings of excitement.

b. A glass of wine, *spec.* when strengthened by additional alcohol or spirits. *U.S. slang.*

1926 *Amer. Speech* I. 653 *Speed-balls*, wine. **1931** 'D. Stiff' *Milk & Honey Route* 215 *Speed balls*, sherry wine. These days it may be any wine, even *dago red.* **1931** G. Irwin *Amer. Tramp & Underworld Slang* 178 *Speedball*, a glass of wine, more especially when 'doped' or made stronger by the addition of some alcohol, ether or strong spirits.

2. a. A ball-game resembling soccer, but in which a ball caught in the air may be passed by hand (see quot. 1976). *U.S.*

1923 *Amer. Boy* Jan. 24 (*heading*) Speedball—a new boys' game. *Ibid.* 25/1 Rychener..called out to Coach Mitchell, 'This is certainly a speedy game. Let's call it speedball.' **1928** *Sportswoman* Oct. 22/2 Speedball furnishes exercise for the whole body—legs, trunk, arms. **1933** *Jrnl. Health & Phys. Educ.* Oct. 38/1 Speedball has gained popularity until it is now used by high schools, private schools, teachers' colleges, and universities from coast to coast. **1946** E. D. Mitchell in Fox & Davies *Official Soccer-Speedball Guide* It is fitting that this particular year should be a reminder to me to see what has been happening to Speedball... It was twenty-five years ago in the Fall of 1921, at the University of Michigan, that it was first played. **1961** J. S. Salak *Dict. Amer. Sport* 413 The conversion of a ground ball to an aerial ball is the essential difference between speedball and soccer. **1976** *Webster's Sports Dict.* 410/1 *Speedball*, a game played between 2 teams of 11 players on a football field with the object of kicking a ball between the uprights of the goal or passing the ball over the end line to score and preventing the opposing team from scoring.

b. *Boxing.* A type of small, fast punch-ball.

1955 F. Mills *Learn Boxing with Me* v. 72 The platform pear ball is not an easy ball to punch... The ball to use is the small-type speedball, weighing about nine to ten ounces. The heavier kinds are too slow to be beneficial. **1975** Oliver & Riley *Boxing* ix. 46 Gyms vary in..the amount of equipment..available. Essentially what is needed is a ring, punch-balls, speed-balls, heavy bags and punching-pads.

'speeded, *a.* [f. speed *sb.*] Having a specified speed, as *high-speeded.*

1890 *Jrnl. Franklin Inst.* Mar. 261 Circular saws and other high speeded wood-working machines.

speeded-up, *ppl. a.* [f. speed *v.* + -ed[1] + up *adv.*]

a. Of a film: giving the appearance of rapid motion usu. as a result of being projected at a speed greater than that of original shooting. Cf. speed *v.* 11 d.

1931 J. S. Huxley *What dare I Think?* ii. 54 It is one of the most astonishing spectacles to see, on the speeded-up film, the processes of cell-division, of organization of growth. **1951** A. C. Clarke *Sounds of Mars* xi. 143 You've all seen the films we made—especially the speeded-up colour one showing a complete cycle of Saturn's phases. **1968** A. Diment *Bang Bang Birds* viii. 146 Everything was happening like a speeded up holiday movie. **1976** *Listener* 25 Mar. 381/2 A speeded-up film of a flower opening and closing.

b. *transf.* Having an increased speed.

1962 M. McLuhan *Gutenberg Galaxy* 47 The new institutes for speeded-up reading. **1980** U. Curtiss *Poisoned Orchard* vii. 65 Sarah went to meet her at a speeded-up saunter.

speeder ('spiːdə(r)). Also 5 speder, -ar. [f. speed *v.*]

1. One who speeds, aids, or furthers; a helper or forwarder. Now *arch.*

c **1400** *Laud Troy Bk.* 4798 He made him lord and her leder, And prayed god be her speder. *c* **1440** *York Myst.* i. 110 To spill vs þu was oure spedar. **1616** Chapman *Homer's Hymn Hermes* 52 Speeder of Nights spies And guide of all her dreames obscurities. **1859** G. Meredith *R. Feverel* xxxviii, I ain't a speeder of matrimony, and good's my reason! **1887** Morris *Odyss.* XIII. 41 For now are all things ready.., The speeders and gifts of well-wishers.

†**2.** One who prospers or succeeds, *esp.* in a suit.

1580 Lyly *Euphues* (Arb.) 405 Your wooers [will be] good old Gentlemen before they be speeders. **1592** Greene *Philomela* Wks. (Grosart) XI. 155 He that is a sutor in Ieast, maye be a speeder in earnest. **1611** Cotgr. s.v. *Perdeur*, The miserable pleader is a miserable speeder; the sparing of a fee is often the spoyle of a cause. **1671** H. M. tr. *Erasm. Colloq.* 32 Go thy way advocate, thou wilt come back again a speeder.

transf. **1611** Chapman *Widdowes T.* Wks. 1873 III. 7 My former suites have been all spenders, this shall be a speeder.

3. A device or contrivance for quickening or regulating the speed of machinery; also, a kind of roving-machine used in cotton-manufacture.

1847 *Knickerbocker* XXX. 517 A few [girls] tend the 'warpers', the 'spoolers', and the 'speeders'. **1875** Knight *Dict. Mech.* 2261/1 The twist, which is given in the bobbin and fly frame by the rotation of the spindle and flyer, is given in the speeder by an endless belt.

4. One who cycles, motors, etc., at a high rate of speed; a fast car, horse, etc. Also *spec.* one who exceeds the speed limit in a vehicle.

1891 in *Cent. Dict.* **1893** *Columbus* (Ohio) *Disp.* 6 Sept., A certain good-fellowship has been established between the speeders and the city. **1974** R. B. Parker *God save Child* i. 6 [The police] have to arrest drunks and flag down speeders and break up fights.

5. *N. Amer.* A small vehicle running on railway tracks used for line maintenance, etc., orig. only manually propelled.

1905 J. Outram *In Heart of Canad. Rockies* 152 The top of a box car is the choicest of propelling methods, unless one can get a ride on a hand-car or a speeder, with opportunity to slacken speed or stop whenever one desires. **1934** *Sun* (Baltimore) 6 Aug. 2/1 One hour in advance of the pilot train section men went over the President's route in gasoline 'speeders'. **1947** A. Saunders *Algonquin Story* xi. 128 The husband, apparently a section man, had rushed up the tracks on a three-wheeled 'speeder' to bring Molly back to help. **1960** J. J. Rowlands *Spindrift from House by Sea* ii. 107 They had taken him out with pneumonia..fifty miles on a gasoline speeder..at twenty below zero. **1970** R. & J. Paterson *Cranberry Portage* xxiii. 152 For days I travelled by locomotive, trolley, speeder, anything moving my way.

speedful ('spiːdfʊl), *a.* Also 4-6 sped(e)ful(e, -full(e, 5 spedphull, 5-7 *Sc.* speidful(l, 5 speyd-), 6 speedeful. [f. speed *sb.* + -ful.]

†**1.** Profitable, advantageous, expedient, helpful, efficacious. *Obs.*

1340-70 *Alex. & Dind.* 623 God is spedful in speche & a spryt clene. **1375** Barbour *Bruce* III. 574 Saylys, ayris, and othir thing, That was spedfull to thar passyng. *c* **1394** *P. Pl. Crede* 264 In pouernesse of spyrit is spedfullest hele. *c* **1449** Pecock *Repr.* I. xix. 111 Of which ech bi him silf is a good and a speedful wey. **1456** Sir G. Haye *Law Arms* (S.T.S.) 112 Quhilkis thingis ar maist nedefull to the bataill and spedefull. **1509** Fisher 7 *Penit. Ps.* xxxviii. Wks. (1876) 70 That they myght vse these holy psalmes as..spedefull prayers for remyssyon and forgyuenes. **1573** Tusser *Husb.* (1878) 116 Good store howse needfull well ordred speedfull.

†**b.** Freq. in *it is speedful* or syntactical variations of this. *Obs.*

c **1340** Hampole *Prose Tr.* 23 Vnto these men itt is nedefulle and spedefulle to vse the werkis of Actife liffe als besili as þei may. **1387** Trevisa *Higden* (Rolls) III. 127 It is nouȝt spedeful to us to knowe þat day. **1414** in *Proc. Privy Council* (1834) II. 141 That it were spedefulle to sende swiche ambassiatours. *c* **1449** Pecock *Repr.* I. v. 27 It is profitable and speedful ofte tymes a man forto speke as many vsen forto speke. *c* **1537** De Benese *Measurynge Lande* A iij, It is..not spedefull to mete therewyth a great quantite of lande. *c* **1550** Rolland *Crt. Venus* III. 909 Do as ȝe think speidfull in this proces. **1609** Skene *Reg. Maj.* 170 He..sall assigne to them ane certaine day, to vnderly the law, either in that air, or thereafter quhen he sall think speidfull.

2. Speedy, quick, swift, rapid. Now *rare.*

1387 Trevisa *Higden* (Rolls) II. 167 þese men been speedful boþe on hors and on foote. *c* **1400** tr. *Secreta Secret., Gov. Lordsh.* 80 It gladys þe herte, and makys..þe tonge spedfull. **1545** Raynald *Byrth Mankynde* 59 Geuynge her good hope of a spedeful delyuerance. **1595** Barnfield *Cassandra* D vij b, His sturdie steedes: Whose speedful course the day and night now eeuens. **1615** T. Adams *Lycanthropy* 8 It is not enough to be speedfull, we must also be discreet and faithfull. **1903** L. M. Watt *Communion Table* viii. 65 This speedful fleetingness of all earth's days.

b. Quasi-*adv.* Speedily, quickly.

? *c* **1480** *Ragman Roll* 52 in Hazl. *E.P.P.* I. 71 To moysten ther your appetitys drey, Ful spedful ye rennyn and ful yerne.

†**3.** Of time: Passing quickly; short, brief. *Obs.*

a **1400-50** *Alexander* 971 With þat he bloþirs in þe brest.. in a spedfull space so þe sprete ȝeldis.

Hence **'speedfulness,** speed, swiftness.

1386 *Almanack for Year* (1812) 8 In oþer planetis it hace more spedefulnesse.

'speedfully, *adv.* [f. speedful *a.*] **a.** Speedily, quickly. **b.** Effectively.

1398 Trevisa *Barth. De P.R.* v. xxvii. (Bodl. MS.), þe same bones in here ioyntes meue þe more spedefullich. *c* **1475** *Partenay* 183 Then thay toke ther way wonder spedfullye. **1483** *Cath. Angl.* 353/1 Spedefully, *efficaciter, effectiue.* *a* **1548** Hall *Chron., Hen. V*, 70 We shall labor.. spedefully, diligently, and truly. **1615** T. Adams *Lycanthropy* 9 It is not yet enough to go speedfully and heedfully except also deedfully.

†**'speediful,** *a.* *Obs.*[−1] In 7 speedyfull. [f. speedy *a.*] Speedy, prompt.

1647 *16 New Quæres Prælates* Ded. p. i, Publishing a speedyfull and satisfactory answer to these fewe Questions.

†**speedihead.** *Obs.*[−1] In 5 spedyhed. [f. speedy *a.*] Swiftness, rapidity.

c **1440** *Jacob's Well* 185 þe thridde spanne in þe handyl of þi schryfte muste be spedyhed, wyth-outyn delaying.

speedily ('spiːdɪlɪ), *adv.* Forms: 4 spedili, 4-6 spedily, 6 spedyly, speadilie, *Sc.* spedalie, 6-7 speedilie, 6- speedily. [f. speedy *a.* Cf. OE. *ȝespēdiȝlīce* prosperously. Before the 17th cent. less usual than *spedely* speedly *adv.*] In a speedy manner; with speed or celerity; quickly.

13.. *Cursor M.* 4048 (Gött.), þat loueword had sua spedili spredd. *c* **1400** *Rule St. Benet* (Prose) 1 Gladly take and spedily fulfil þe warnyng of þe meke fadir. *a* **1425** *Cursor M.* 19214 (Trin.), Spedily [*earlier MSS.* sped(e)li] spelled þei goddes word. ? *a* **1550** *Freiris Berwick* 217 in *Dunbar's Poems* (1893) 292 Syn to hir madin spedyly scho spak. **1563** Hyll *Art Garden.* (1593) 16 The seedes sowen in due chosen time ..doth speediliest breake forth and shoote vp. **1605** Shaks. *Lear* IV. ii. 80 You Iustices, that these our neather crimes So speedily can venge. **1659** in *Verney Mem.* (1907) II. 97 Itt being high tyme..speedily to looke out for a place for him. *a* **1700** in *Cath. Rec. Soc. Publ.* IX. 346 To the end she may the speedierly Arrive to Inioy the company of yᵉ Blessed. **1749** *Naval Chron.* III. 93 An opportunity of closing the Line speedilyer. **1779** *Mirror* No. 65, The marriage was speedily concluded. **1837** P. Keith *Bot. Lex.* 28 An example that was speedily followed by that of Dodonæus. **1877** Froude *Short Stud.* (1883) IV. I. x. 117 A short altercation ..ended speedily in high words on both sides.

speediness ('spiːdɪnɪs). Forms: 6 spedynesse, spedi-, speedines, 6-7 speedinesse, 6- speediness (7 speedy-). [f. speedy *a.* Cf. OE. *spēdiȝnes* opulence.] The quality of being speedy; quickness, celerity, promptitude.

1530 Palsgr. 274/1 Spedynesse, *hastifueté.* **1548** Udall, etc. *Erasm. Par. Matt.* ix. 60 Maruelyng at ye great spedines of miracles. **1635** Swan *Spec. M.* vi. §2 (1643) 202 [Waters] yield us an easinesse and speedinesse of conduct and traffick. **1663** S. Patrick *Parab. Pilgr.* xix. (1687) 185 The wounds ..are made more angry, and you hinder the speediness of the Cure. **1770** Langhorne *Plutarch* (1851) I. 279/1 Much lustre did fortune add to the gallantry of their exploits by the speediness of their execution. **1775** Adair *Amer. Ind.* 234 For the certainty, ease, and speediness of cure.

speeding ('spiːdɪŋ), *vbl. sb.* [f. speed *v.*]

1. a. Success, prosperity, good fortune; the fact of being successful or of attaining one's end.

a **1300** *Cursor M.* 23716 þat dos all vr speding spill. *c* **1400** tr. *Secreta Secret., Gov. Lordsh.* 112 It [*sc.* Mercury in mid-heaven] shal shewe spedynge of þe werk & perfeccion. *c* **1460** *Play of Sacrament* 112 In Spayne & in Spruce moche ys my spedyng. *a* **1555** Latimer *Serm. & Rem.* (Parker Soc.) 234 For which like doings we shall have like speedings. **1570** T. Norton tr. *Nowel's Catech.* (1853) 187 Such as pray doubting and uncertain of their speeding. **1608** Shaks. *Per.* II. iii. 116 Each one betake him to his rest; To-morrow all for speeding do their best. **1686** F. Spence tr. *Varillas' Ho. Medicis* 393 Either th'one or t'other of these two conspiracies cou'd not have miss'd of speeding, if the Duke ..had not revealed them. **1713** M. Henry *Ordinat. Serm.* Wks. 1857 II. 503/1 Those who go without sending, will come back without speeding. **1726** S. Willard *Body Div.* 900/1 How we may so ask as not to miss of speeding in it.

b. Lot or hap in respect of success.

1573 Tusser *Husb.* (1878) 9 By practise and ill speeding, these lessons had their breeding. **1599** Shaks., etc. *Pass. Pilgr.* xviii, Heart is bleeding, All help needing, O cruel speeding, Fraughted with gall. **1641** Milton *Ch. Govt.* ii. 37 The not deferring is of great moment to the good speeding.

†**2.** The action of sending out or forth. *Obs.*

1382 Wyclif *Judith* ii. 7 Olofernes..noumbrede men in to the speding [L. *in expeditionem*], as the king comaundede to hym.

3. The action of aiding, furthering, or setting forward.

c **1400** tr. *Secreta Secret., Gov. Lordsh.* 94 Yn spedynge of goodnesse. **1530** Palsgr. 711/2 I set a syde, as counsayloures or judges do all their maters for the hasty spedynge of some one. **1625** Sanderson *Serm.* (1681) I. 125 To give any kind of furtherance to the speeding either of justice in civil, or of judgment in criminal causes. **1672** T. Cory *Course & Pract. Comm.-Pl.* 30 The Plaintiff was not bound to give the Defendant notice of the speeding a Writ of Inquiry of Damages.

4. a. With *up*; The process of increasing the rate of work or production.

1892 *Daily News* 8 Feb. 6/2 One of the most remarkable features of modern industrial enterprise is the great 'speeding up' of industry. **1897** S. & B. Webb *Industr. Democr.* I. viii. 399 This enforced 'speeding up' would be all very well if the old plan of paying by the piece were continued.

b. The act of driving a motor vehicle fast, esp. at an illegal speed. Also *transf.*

1908 *Evening Star* (Washington) in *Daily Chron.* 7 Oct. 4/7 Baby carriages are required to carry lights at night in Chicago. That rapid city may yet find it necessary to provide special police to keep the baby carriages from speeding. **1911** *Daily Colonist* (Victoria, B.C.) 2 Apr. 2/4 It was decided that everything possible would be done to assist the authorities in enforcing reasonable regulations regarding speeding. **1922** J. A. Dunn *Man Trap* ii. 24 Driving a car about the countryside at the expense of many fines for speeding. **1977** E. W. Hildick *Loop* xvii. 115 The copper. .. He's been trying to get you all afternoon... I hope you haven't been doing no speeding.

5. *Comb.* **speeding citation, ticket** *U.S.*, a summons given to a motorist who has violated a speed regulation.

1974 *Marlboro Herald-Advocate* (Bennettsville, S. Carolina) 18 Apr. 1/4 Out of the 228 speeding citations.. there was only one request for a jury trial. **1960** 'E. McBain' *Heckler* v. 70 He had flatly refused to square any raps for them, raps ranging from speeding tickets to disorderly conduct. **1978** R. Ludlum *Holcroft Covenant* ix. 114 If it'll get you out of Rio..I'll go like a greased pig in a slaughterhouse and pay the speeding tickets from my per diem.

speeding ('spi:dɪŋ), *ppl. a.* [f. Speed *v.*]

†**1.** ***well-speeding***, successful. *Obs.*$^{-1}$

1422 tr. *Secreta Secret., Priv. Priv.* 235 Whoso hath the Paas large and slow, he is wyse and wel spedynge in al his dedys.

2. a. Leading with speed; rapid, direct.

c **1611** Chapman *Iliad* xxii. 280 Where th'unequal winding bone..had place, and where there lay The speeding way to death. **1641** H. L'Estrange *God's Sabbath* 81 For (to take a short and speeding course) the most embraced and popular opinion is that [etc.].

b. Causing to move with speed; favouring.

1757 W. Wilkie *Epigoniad* iv. 86 To speeding gales I saw the canvass rise.

c. Moving with speed.

1847 Emerson *Poems, Visit* Wks. (Bohn) I. 404 Speeding Saturn cannot halt. **1884** *Marshall's Tennis Cuts* 269 Till the speeding ball appeared as One continuous flash of lightning.

d. Of motor vehicles, motorists, etc.: travelling fast, esp. at an illegal speed.

1957 R. Matheson *Shores of Space* 156 People who had.. been struck down by speeding cars. **1960** *Daily Tel.* 16 Jan. 1/5 Now the speeding motorist will find things more difficult. **1978** 'M. Yorke' *Point of Murder* xiii. 125 A speeding Mini, in the small hours, might attract notice if a police patrol car were around.

†**3. a.** Dispatching, finishing; deadly, fatal. *Obs.*

?*c* **1600** *Distr. Emperor* ii. i. in Bullen *O. Pl.* (1884) III. 185 Twas a speedinge plott To send me into Spayne. **1621** Lady M. Wroth *Urania* 313 He might chuse the most mischeuing, and most speeding hurt for him. **1660** May *Hen. II*, vi. 419 A speeding feaver seiz'd his vitall part. **1693** Dryden, etc. *Juvenal* xii. 22 A Neck so strong, so large, as wou'd demand The speeding Blow of some uncommon hand.

†**b.** Liable to a fatal wound. *Obs.*

1612 T. James *Jesuits' Downf.* 68 The best weapons the Iesuits haue to defend themselues, and wound their opposits in the speedingst place they can. **1631** Heywood *Fair Maid of West* i. Wks. 1874 II. 278 You hit him in the very speeding place.

†**4.** Effective; decisive. *Obs.*

1612 Webster *White Devil* Wks. (Rtldg.) 36/2 There's no way More speeding than this thought on. **1613** Shaks. *Hen. VIII*, i. iii. 40 The slye whorsons Haue got a speeding tricke to lay downe Ladies. *a* **1641** Bp. Mountagu *Acts & Mon.* (1642) 212 If he could produce but one ancient copy (which is a speeding argument in Scaligers and Casaubons Grammar).

5. Serving to further, advance, or aid.

a **1625** Fletcher *Noble Gent.* iii. i, I am resolv'd my Wife shall up to Court;..that is a speeding course, And cannot chuse but breed a mighty fortune. **1812** Cary *Dante, Paradise* xxii. 41 Such a speeding grace shone over me, That from their impious worship I reclaim'd The dwellers round about.

Hence **'speedingly** *adv.*

1647 N. Ward *Simp. Cobler* 77 Pray speedily therefore, and speedingly.

speedless ('spi:dlɪs), *a.* Also 4 **spedeles**, 6 **speedeles.** [f. Speed *sb.* + -less.]

1. Profitless, ineffectual, unsuccessful.

13.. *S. Erkenwolde* 93 in Horstm. *Altengl. Leg.* (1881) 268 Þer was spedeles space to spyr vsch one oþer Quat body hit myȝt be þat buried wos þer. *a* **1542** Wyatt *Poet. Wks.* (1861) 114 A speedless proof I have endured; And now I leave it to them that lust. **1571** Golding *Calvin on Ps.* xx. 20 David poureth not oute his moninges as vaine and speedlesse. *c* **1611** Chapman *Iliad* xvi. 441 But no such speedless flight Patroclus let his spear perform. **1821** Clare *Vill. Minstr.* II. 71 Till speedless trials prove the doubted elf As skill'd in noise and sounds as Hodge himself.

2. Of persons: Meeting with no success.

1586 Warner *Alb. Eng.* i. vi. (1589) 21 For Lycus, speedles in his lust, against her so had frownde. **1615** Chapman *Odyss.* v. 40 It obeys thy powers; And in their ship returne the speedlesse wowers.

†**'speedly,** *adv. Obs.* Forms: α. 4 **spedlic, -li,** 4–5 **-ly,** 6 **lye,** 7 **speedly.** β. 4 **spedeliche,** 4–6 **-ly,** 6 **-lie, speadely,** 6–7 **speedely(e.** [f. Speed *sb.* Cf. OE. *spēdlīce* successfully, effectually.] = Speedily *adv.*

α. *a* **1300** *Cursor M.* 19214 Spedli [*Edinb.* spedlic, *Gött.* spedeli] þai speld godds word. *c* **1380** Wyclif *Wks.* (1880) 153 Þei..ne wolen spedly lerne..þe gospel & goddis hestis. *c* **1400** *Laud Troy Bk.* 9621 The ffloures sprede & spedly sprynge. **1482** *Monk of Evesham* xxviii. (Arb.) 69 She.. hastyd her spedly gretly profeting on the iorney that goyth to paradyse. **1530** Cromwell in Merriman *Life & Lett.* (1902) I. 334 Beseching your grace spedlye to send hym home. **1618** Bolton *Florus* iii. xxi. (1636) 246 The army of Norbanus was quickly overthrowne and all Scipio's forces.. speedly oppressed.

β. **13..** [see α]. **1387** Trevisa *Higden* (Rolls) III. 199 Þe ȝongelynge dede spedeliche his dedes. *c* **1400** *Destr. Troy* 10942 Two spurres full spedely [she] spent on his helis. *c* **1440** *Jacob's Well* 208 It castyth noȝt oute spedely þe wose of synne fro þe pytt of lustys. **1512** *Act 4 Hen. VIII*, c. 18 Preamb., For the accomptes of the same more spedelie to be taken. **1588** Parke tr. *Mendoza's Hist. China* 38 For that it should be speedelier doone. **1618** in Foster *Eng. Factories India* (1906) I. 17 You must speedelye looke to this maggat.

speedo ('spi:dəʊ), colloq. abbrev. of Speedometer.

1934 *Passing Show* 21 July 19/3 The puzzled eyes of his scarlet face went hopelessly to the speedo. The needle was steady at fifty-five. **1938** L. MacNeice *I crossed Minch* vi. 81 Lever..stepped on the gas, He said,..'Just you watch the speedo climb.' **1960** *News Chron.* 10 Oct. 6/6 The speedo needle does not obscure the mileage indicator. **1969** M. Calthorpe *Defectors* 140 He glanced at the speedo... He'd driven almost five miles. **1976** P. Hill *Hunters* vii. 93 The car [was as] steady as a rock..as the speedo reached up towards its limit.

speedometer (spi:'dɒmɪtə(r)). [f. Speed *sb.* + *-ometer* -meter.] **1. a.** A speed-indicator, esp. one affixed to an automobile.

1904 *Times* 4 Aug. 13/1 His 'speedometer'..showed he was going at only ten miles an hour. **1912** *Motor Man.* (ed. 14) 115 (*caption*) Details of system of friction drive for shaft of speedometer. **1932** *World Today* Feb. 261/1 The noisiest thing about this car was its speedometer, which maintained a noise something between a click and a swish. **1955** L. G. Pringle *Driving Lessons* 35 Chancing to glance at his speedometer, he discovered he was travelling at 45 m.p.h. through a built-up area! **1978** K. Jolly *Driving made Easy* 35 The speedometer shows your speed in miles per hour... It should be checked frequently quickly when on the move.

b. The distance-indicator that is often incorporated in the speed-indicator of a motor vehicle; an odometer. *U.S.*

1929 *Collier's* 12 Jan. 8/2 Don't believe the speedometer of that magnificent limousine. It could have been fixed for sale purposes in twenty minutes. **1938** Palmer & Crooks *Millions on Wheels* v. 87 Several courts have decided..that setting speedometers to indicate lower than actual mileage is a fraudulent practice... The buyer of a used car should therefore not even bother to look at the speedometer mileage. **1942** R. W. Riis *Repairmen will get You* ii. 19 The car has gone at least 20,000 miles, although I think the speedometer doesn't register all the miles.

2. *attrib.*, as ***speedometer needle.***

1909 *Quarterly Rev.* Jan. 148 Men are tempted to feel as if they must be acting rightly when the speedometer needle hovers below the figures 10. **1977** N. Slater *Crossfire* iv. 77 The speedometer needle [was] jumping erratically around the 50 mph mark.

speedster ('spi:dstə(r)). [f. Speed *sb.* + -ster, after *roadster.*] **1.** A fast motor vehicle; a speed-boat.

1918 Webster Addenda, *Speedster*,..a high-speed roadster, usually with low seats, accommodating two persons seated side by side. **1928** *Daily Express* 3 Sept. 5/5 But I'm not telling everyone who comes up in a swell speedster [*sc.* a speed-boat]. **1977** 'J. Gash' *Judas Pair* vi. 72 He lived about fifteen miles off the trunk road... I patted my speedster and swung the handle.

2. a. A motorist who drives fast.

1921 *Daily Colonist* (Victoria, B.C.) 16 Oct. 25/3 As a means of checking up on the speedster, a device has been invented. **1930** *Aberdeen Press & Jrnl.* 17 May 8/5 Lochiel criticised the making of trunk roads for the use of south speedsters. **1974** J. Cleary *Peter's Pence* vii. 197 McBride drove fast: in Rome slow drivers got more attention..than speedsters.

b. More generally, a person who moves or acts very quickly, a fast runner. Also applied to animals.

1947 *Richmond* (Va.) *Times-Dispatch* 9 Nov. B7/7 The 175-pound speedster from Bridgeton, N.J., never quit running until he was across the goalline. **1966** D. Varaday *Gara-Yaka's Domain* iv. 48 The four speedsters made a sudden concentrated rush at the meat-rich tycoon. **1977** *Time* 13 June 21/2 An American track-meet promoter, anxious to lure a top dash man to his indoor meet to increase the gate, called a speedster and promised him $800 plus expenses for joining the field.

speed-up. [f. vbl. phr. *to speed up*: see Speed *v.* 11 d.] **a.** The act or process of increasing the speed or working rate of a thing. Also *attrib.*

1923 *Daily Mail* 3 Mar. 7 Train Speed-up..The speeding up of all services. **1944** *Sun* (Baltimore) 18 May 18/6 (*heading*) Assembly speedup law is planned. **1953** J. S. Huxley *Evolution in Action* i. 33 With a hundred-thousand-fold speed-up [of film]..the overall processes of evolution became visible. **1970** R. Lowell *Notebook* 158, I too in the end will see the things like this, Whatever I've lived assumed in one bright glance Like speed-up reading. **1977** P. Somerville-Large *Eagles near Carcase* v. 102 'Go on,' I said, 'not too fast.'.. The last thing I wanted was a speed-up.

b. The act or process of increasing productivity, esp. without raising rates of pay. orig. and chiefly *U.S.*

1935 *Sun* (Baltimore) 9 Feb. 2/1 Labor unrest..flows from..inequitable hiring and rehiring methods, espionage, speed-up and displacement of workers at an extremely early age. **1938** *Reader's Digest* May 55/2 There is no piecework, no speedup. **1943** *Sun* (Baltimore) 14 June 10/7 The extreme manifestation of management is the ruthless speedup or stretch-out, where production is increased without thought of the health of the working-man. **1959** N. Mailer *Advts. for Myself* (1961) 184 The productive speed-up tends to be replaced by..'feather-bedding'. **1962** E. Snow *Other Side of River* xxxi. 235 In 1955, for example, the *Workers Daily* revealed that alleged gains made in 'speed-up' drives by shocking over-use of labor were more than offset by heavily increased losses in man-power output. **1974** *Time Out* 22 Nov. 64/3 It's a depressing and probably accurate picture of a failure of consciousness in a barely unionised community where speed-ups, piece-work and cheap labour are rife.

'speedway. [Speed *sb.*] **1. a.** *U.S.* A track or road prepared for fast horse-driving. Now *Hist.*

1894 *Voice* (N.Y.) 28 June, New York has millions of dollars to spend upon its uptown parks and speedways. **1968** *N.Y. City* (Michelin Tire Corp.) 97 Trotters were in fashion, and they whipped through the Park to the speedways of Harlem.

b. A road on which motor vehicles may travel fast. Also *gen.*, a motorway. Also *fig.* orig. *U.S.*

1903 *N.Y. Times* 16 Aug. 24/7 The numerous owners of rapid roadsters are devoting no inconsiderable portion of their Summer leisure to spirited brushes on the new speedway. **1919** *Public Opinion* 14 Nov. 471 (*heading*) The Speedway to Prosperity. **1927** [see Autostrada]. **1946** J. W. Day *Harvest Adventure* xiv. 247 The traffic on that concrete speed-way, the Great West Road. **1976** J. van de Wetering *Tumbleweed* xx. 176 Their car..was joining the main traffic on the speedway.

2. *Sport.* **a.** A racing track for motor vehicles. Also *transf.*

1925 *Kansas City* (Missouri) *Star* 31 May 1/1 Here is how they finished..in the thirteenth annual 500-mile motor classic on the Indianapolis speedway yesterday. **1968** D. Braithwaite *Fairground Architecture* 170/1 *Speedway*, a loose term which could refer either to an Ark—mounted with *motor-cycles*, or to a Monte Carlo Rally. **1979** *Arizona Daily Star* 1 Apr. c12/2 USAC's 200-mile race at the Ontario Motor Speedway last weekend turned out better than a lot of people figured.

b. *transf.* A sport in which motorcyclists race several laps about a short oval dirt track. Freq. *attrib.*

1930 S. Elder *Romance of Speedway* i. 9 Now that Speedway Racing has taken its place as one of our national pastimes. *Ibid.* ii. 27 In the first rank among Speedway riders. *Ibid.* 33 Habitual frequenters of Speedway gatherings. **1937** D. W. Harding in *Scrutiny* VI. iii. 254 When we have passed..from the state of idly watching men ..and have accepted the invitation to form part of an audience for jugglers, acrobats..or speedway riders..we may speak of display entertainment. **1950** *Sport* 22–8 Sept. 21/2 The Wembley crowds shot up and speedway in general benefited. **1961** K. Reisz *Technique Film Editing* (ed. 9) ii. 77 Bill Fox (Dirk Bogarde) had been an ace speedway rider before the war. **1977** *Western Morning News* 30 Aug. 12/3 Exeter gave themselves a tremendous boost in their challenge for the Gulf British League speedway title when they snatched a precious point from title rivals Reading.

speedwell ('spi:dwɛl). [app. f. Speed *v.* 1 + Well *adv.*] One or other species of *Veronica*, an extensive genus of small herbaceous plants with leafy stems and small blue (rarely pink or white) flowers; a plant belonging to this genus.

1578 Lyte *Dodoens* 26 Paules Betony, Herbe Fluellyn, or Speedewell. **1646** Sir T. Browne *Pseud. Ep.* 101 An herbe there is commonly called Betonica Pauli, or Paul's Betony .., and is no more then speed well, or Fluellen. **1671** Phillips, *Speedwell*,..in Latin *Betonica Pauli*, and *Veronica Mas*, and *Femina*. **1760** J. Lee *Introd. Bot.* App. 327 Speedwell, *Veronica*. **1833** E. Elliott *Spirits & Men* 22 in *Spl. Village*, etc. 218 While groups of speedwell, with their bright blue eyes,..cluster in the sun. **1850** Tennyson *In Mem.* lxxxiii, Bring orchis, bring the foxglove spire, The little speedwell's darling blue. **1885** R. Buchanan *Annan Water* v, The banks were sprinkled thick with speedwells and primroses.

attrib. *c*1710 PETIVER *Cat. Ray's Eng. Herbal* Tab. xlviii, Speedwell Cress. Hill sides. 1862 MISS YONGE *C'tess Kate* v, The young lady..delicately blue and white, like a speedwell flower.

b. With distinguishing terms.

The number of specific designations is very large: see *Chambers' Cycl.* Suppl. (1753) s.v. *Veronica*, Withering *Brit. Plants* (1796) II. 12–18, *Penny Cycl.* (1843) XXVI. 271, Irvine *Handbk. Brit. Plants* (1858) 439–444.

1611 COTGR., *Veronique masle*, the male Speed-well. 1731 MILLER *Gard. Dict.* s.v. *Veronica*, Common Male Speedwell or Fluellin. *Ibid.*, Narrow-leav'd spik'd Speed-well [etc.]. 1777 JACOB *Cat. Plants* 121 *V[eronica] serpyllifolia*, little, or smooth Speedwell, or Paul's Betony. 1796 WITHERING *Brit. Plants* (ed. 3) II. 17 *Veronica Chamaedrys*... Wild Germander. Germander Speedwell. 1840 HODGSON *Hist. Northumb.* III. II. 360/1 *Veronica scutellata*, Narrow-leafed Marsh Speedwell. 1846–50 A. WOOD *Class-bk. Bot.* 406 *V. arvensis*. Field Veronica. Corn Speedwell... *V. agrestis*. Neckweed. Field Speedwell. 1847 DARLINGTON *Amer. Weeds*, etc. (1860) 227 *V. peregrina*,..Foreign Veronica. Purslane Speedwell. 1855 MISS PRATT *Flower. Pl.* IV. 89 Spiked Speedwell... Gardeners call it Cat's-tail Speedwell. 1882 *Garden* 15 Apr. 263/3 The New Zealand Speedwell, when well grown, is one of the most beautiful of green-house plants. 1898 MORRIS *Austral Eng.* 428 *Native Speed-well*,.. a Tasmanian species, *Veronica formosa*.

speedy ('spiːdɪ), *a.* Forms: 4–5 spedi, 4–6 spedy(e, 6 *Sc.* speidie, spidy (7 spidde); 6–7 speedie, 6– speedy. [f. SPEED *sb.* Cf. OE. *spédiȝ* prosperous, wealthy, powerful, etc.; MDu. *spōd-*, *spoedich* (Du. *spoedig*), MLG. *spôdig*, G. (from LG.) *spudig* (obs.), *sputig*, *spütig*.]

†**1.** Advantageous, expedient, helpful. *Obs.*

*c*1380 WYCLIF *Wks.* (1880) 42 þei schulle see þat it is spedy to here nedy. *c*1400 *Apol. Loll.* 50 It semiþ good, spedi, and meritori, þat þe kirk be honorid. *c*1449 PECOCK *Repr.* II. xii. 220 Therfore this..is a spedi condicioun and a myȝti forto helpe.

2. a. Moving, or able to move, with speed; going or travelling quickly; swift.

1375 BARBOUR *Bruce* VI. 591 He bad fif of his cumpany That..on fut spediast ware..Ryn eftir hym. *c*1470 HENRY *Wallace* I. 230 Wallace was spedy, and gretlye als agast. 1533 BELLENDEN *Livy* I. xi. (S.T.S.) I. 64 Ane knycht come to tullus on ane spedy hors. 1576 FLEMING *Panopl. Epist.* 120 Foure swifte and speedie legions. 1630 *R. Johnson's Kingd. & Commw.* 421 The Barbary Horse is more speedy than the rest. 1641 MILTON *Ch. Govt.* I. vii. 41 They..can best judge how speedy we are to their relief. 1716 POPE *Iliad* v. 54 The speedy javelin drove from back to breast. 1811 *Sporting Mag.* XXXVII. 135 To get not only speedy but lasting racers.

absol. 1742 YOUNG *Nt. Th.* II. 223 Why spur the speedy? Why with levities New-wing thy..day's too rapid flight?

†**b.** *speedy man*, one formerly employed to carry from Oxford to Winchester intimations of vacancies at New College. *Obs.*

1825 C. WESTMACOTT *Eng. Spy* I. 260 A speedy-man by nimbler foe Lies buried in the earth below. *Ibid.* note, Wm. Perkins..the New College Speedy-man.

3. a. Acting with speed; active, prompt, quick.

1504 C'TESS RICHMOND tr. *De Imitatione* IV. vii. (1893) 269 So neglygent vnto the seruyce of god, so spedy to thende therof. 1551 T. WILSON *Logike* (1580) 52 b, The Gospell then required speedie Preachers. 1589 PUTTENHAM *Eng. Poesie* III. (Arb.) 241 *Expeditio*, or the speedie dispatcher. 1627 MAY *Lucan* III. 19 Three sisters speedy hands cannot suffice, For breaking threads has tyr'd the Destinies. 1702 in *Pennsylv. Hist. Soc. Mem.* IX. 125 Thy affairs here require a speedy hand. 1793 SMEATON *Edystone L.* §200 The mixtures..rendered the plaster less speedy in setting. 1821 SCOTT *Kenilw.* xxxiv, Speak out, and be speedy.

b. That quickly becomes so.

1628 FELTHAM *Resolves* II. [I.] iii. 7, I will take heed both of a speedy friend and slow enemy. Love is never lasting that flames before it burns.

4. a. Characterized by speed of motion or progress from one place to another.

1382 WYCLIF *Rom.* i. 10 If by ony maner aftirward sumtyme I haue esy, or spedy, weie in the wille of God of comynge to ȝou. *a*1548 HALL *Chron.*, *Edw. IV*, 14 He then ..beyng well furnished, with spedy iorneys, came safe to his citie of London. 1590 SPENSER *F.Q.* I. i. 39 Making speedy way through spersed ayre. 1618 in Foster *Eng. Factories Ind.* (1906) I. 30 The conveyaunce would bee cheape, secure and speedy. 1685 DRYDEN *Ep. Albion & Albanius* 3 Feign'd Zeal ..set out the speedier Pace; But, the last Heat, Plain Dealing won the Race. *a*1701 MAUNDRELL *Journ. Jerus.* (1732) 144 The nearest and speediest way. 1797 S. & HT. LEE *Canterb. T.* (1799) I. 348 Favourable winds seemed for some time to promise them a speedy navigation. 1825 SCOTT *Talism.* xxii, A horseman..had returned on a speedy gallop to El Hakim. 1860 TYNDALL *Glac.* I. xvi. 118 Our progress was much more speedy than it had been on starting in the morning. *Ibid.* II. ix. 273 The speedier central motion [of the glacier].

b. Of time: Passing rapidly.

1598 YONG *Diana* 123 As she thinkes the howers of her life short and speedie.

5. a. Characterized by speed in operation or action; taking place rapidly or quickly.

1529 *Star Chamber Cases* (Selden) II. 179 The king willing speding [? *read* spedy] remedy for the saide [*sc.* scarceness]. 1577 B. GOOGE *Heresbach's Husb.* III. (1586) 156 b, Wee keepe vp Cattes for the auoiding of the mischiefe, neither is there a speedier remedie. 1602 WILLIS *Stenographie* A ij b, Secondly, in speedie writing: For he that is well practized in this Art, may write Verbatim, as fast as a man can treateably speake. 1653 W. RAMESEY *Astrol. Restored* 128 It denoteth good success and speedy dispatch in the business. 1678 MARVELL *Growth Popery* 21 Another Act for speedier convicting of Papists. 1726 SWIFT *Gulliver* II. vii, The speedy determination of civil and criminal causes. 1764 *Museum Rust.* IV. 5 Therefore some speedy remedy should be applied. *a*1806 H. K. WHITE *Lett.* (1837) 273 The speedier disseminating of the blessed gospel. 1843 SIR C. SCUDAMORE *Med. Visit Gräfenberg* 30 An impatient desire of urging crisis for the sake of a more speedy cure. 1867 FREEMAN *Norm. Conq.* (1877) I. iv. 149 The speedy fusion of Normans and English was greatly promoted by the fact [etc.].

b. Rapidly brought to pass or to an end; quickly accomplished, arrived at, or obtained.

The distinction between this and the prec. sense is often very slight.

1607 SHAKS. *Cor.* I. iii. 87, I will wish her speedy strength. 1648 *Hamilton Papers* (Camden) 184 To expect opportunities to assist and serue you, of which yee will see speedy effects. 1703 T. BROWN *Mourning Poet* Wks. 1711 IV. 215 Neale started first, to raise a speedy Sum, A Million Lottery. 1747 GRAY *Fav. Cat* 33 She mew'd to ev'ry wat'ry God, Some speedy aid to send. 1803 *Med. Jrnl.* X. 274, I flatter myself that the controversy will come to a speedy termination. 1855 MACAULAY *Hist. Eng.* xxii. IV. 701 Unless they could send him a speedy supply, his troops would..desert by thousands. 1895 *Law Times* XCIX. 544/1 There are under the existing rules some facilities for obtaining a speedy decision in such cases.

c. *speedy trial* (U.S. Law), a criminal trial held after a minimum of delay, considered to be a citizen's right; also *attrib.*

[1776 G. MASON *Virginia Decl. Rights* in *Virginia Gaz.* (Williamsburg) 1 June 2/2 In all capital or criminal prosecutions a man hath a right to demand the cause and nature of his accusation, to be confronted with the accusers or witnesses, to call for evidence in his favour, and a speedy trial by an impartial jury. 1789 J. MADISON in T. Lloyd *Congress. Reg.* 4 June 428 In all criminal prosecutions, the accused shall enjoy the right to a speedy and public trial. 1807 J. OVERTON *Tennessee Reports* (1813) I. 253 The 9th section of the bill of rights secures to the citizen a speedy, public trial, and to demand the cause of accusation against him. 1878 *Michigan Reports* XXXVIII. 739 The right to a speedy and public trial in criminal cases by an impartial jury cannot be taken away by legislation.] 1893 *Southeastern Reporter* (1894) XVIII. 284/1 The 'speedy trial', and the policy of the law to expedite the trial of criminal cases, forbid that the person accused of crime shall be detained in prison beyond any term of the court at which he can lawfully be tried. 1901 *Daily Colonist* (Victoria, B.C.) 22 Oct. 1/6 Robt. Cameron, a penitentiary convict, before Judge Bole in the Speedy Trial court today, pleaded guilty to attempting to escape. 1926 J. BLACK *You can't Win* xviii. 262, I..decided to go before the court under the Speedy Trials Act. A defendant electing for a speedy trial dispenses with a jury and saves time and money for the community. 1951 F. H. HELLER *Sixth Amendment* iv. 60 The right to a speedy trial may not be asserted merely in order to forestall the ends of public justice. 1976 *Billings* (Montana) *Gaz.* 30 June 1-c/3 Judge Sorte rejected defense motions to dismiss the charges against the couple on grounds of prejudicial pretrial news coverage and lack of a speedy trial.

6. quasi-*adv.* Speedily.

1601 DOLMAN *La Primaud. Fr. Acad.* (1618) III. 782 To trie who should goe speediest. 1632 J. HAYWARD tr. *Biondi's Eromena* 12 Polimero..had put himselfe in that shippe only to get out the speedier from Birsa. 1756 TOLDERVY *Hist. 2 Orphans* III. 108 Humphry, having some reason to remember those sort of gentry, very speedy escaped into Drury-lane. 1796 J. MOSER *Hermit Caucasus* I. 172 Are causes decided as speedy, and at as small an expence as possible? 1866 S. B. JAMES *Duty & Doctrine* (1871) 61 You in your future, you in your speedy-coming actual experience.

7. *speedy cut*, an injury on the inner side of a horse's fore leg, near the knee, caused by the foot of the opposite leg when in motion. Also as *v. trans.* and *attrib.* (sometimes with ellipse of *cut*).

1692 *Lond. Gaz.* No. 2787/4 Lost,..a sorrel Gelding, full-aged,..speedy-cuts the off Leg before. 1697 *Ibid.* No. 3351/4 A brown bay Nag,..speedy cut. 1831 YOUATT *Horse* 245 The inside of the leg, immediately under the knee,..is subject to injury from what is termed the speedy cut. 1862 *Catal. Internat. Exhib., Brit.* II. No. 4693, Web, Fetlock, Speedy, Splint,..and Strengthening Boots. 1884 KNIGHT *Dict. Mech.* Suppl. 464/1 The upper or speedy-cut boot, which is concaved in front to fit..the hoof-boot.

Hence †'**speedying** *vbl. sb.*, speeding.

1617 EARL ARUNDEL in *Buccleuch MSS.* (Hist. MSS. Comm.) I. 193 For the speedying whereof..I doubt not but your Lordships' persuasions may prevail. 1650 FULLER *Pisgah* II. v. vi. 202 For the speedying of whose conversion he pleased to compose the many different judgments of Christians into one truth.

†**speek**, *sb. Obs.* Also speeke, speake. [Irregular var. SPICK *sb.*³] A large nail; a spike-nail.

1611 COTGR., *Clou d'estoupe*, a speake, or sheathing nayle; vsed in ships. *c*1635 CAPT. N. BOTELER *Dial. Sea Service* (1685) 276 Those nails you call speeks. They are great and long iron nails with flat heads and of divers lengths. Some of the speeks are ragged which cannot be drawn out again. 1671 SKINNER *Etymol. Ling. Angl.*, *Speeks*, vox Naut. sic autem dicuntur magni Clavi ferrei.

attrib. 1633 T. JAMES *Voy.* 108 Their weake Speeke Ships, can hardly long endure it.

Hence †**speek** *v.*¹ *trans.*, to fasten *up* with spikes.

*c*1635 CAPT. N. BOTELER *Dial. Sea Service* (1685) 277 They use with these nails to fasten a Coin..unto the deck, close to the Breech of the carriages of the great Guns to help keep them firm up.., and this is called speeking up of the Ordnance. 1711 *Milit. & Sea Dict.* s.v., In foul Weather they use to speek up the Guns; that is, nail a Quoin to the Deck, close to the Breech of the Carriage, to help keep up the Piece strong to the Ship's side.

†**speek**, *v.*² *Obs.*⁻⁰ = PEAK *v.*³ 1.

1644 MANWARING *Seaman's Dict.* 68 Speek the Missen, (that is, put the yard right up and downe by the mast). 1711 *Milit. & Sea Dict.* s.v. *Spell*, This Word is most commonly us'd to the Mizzen-Sail; for when they take it in, or speek it up, they say spell the Mizzen.

speel, *sb.*¹ Now *dial.* Also 7 speele, 7, 9 spele. [Of Scand. origin: cf. Norw. *spela*, *spila*, Sw. *spjela*, *spjele*, of the same meaning.] A splinter or strip of wood, iron, etc.

*c*1440 *Wycliffite Bible* 2 Kings xviii. 21 The splyndre or speel therof schal entre in to hys hond. 1634 *Lowe's Chirurg.* 185 Boyle all in an earthen pot, and stirre it about with a speele of wood. 1660 M. PARKER *Hist. Arthur* C iv, The speele of a broken launce hapned to pierce his skull. 1676 WISEMAN *Surg. Treat.* 286 During which some small Speels of Bones cast off, and the Ulcer cicatrized without much difficulty. *a*1700 KENNETT *MS. Lansdowne 1033* fol. 388 (Halliw.), A *spele*, a small wand, or switch in Westmorl[and]. 1854 MISS BAKER *Northampt. Gloss.*, *Spele*,..a long, thin slip of wood. 1872 *N. & Q.* 4th Ser. IX. 21/2 He had got a speel in his finger. 1882 *Lancash. Gloss.* 249 *Speel* (Preston), a splinter.

speel, *sb.*² *Sc.* Also spiel. [f. next.] The act of clambering or climbing.

1807–10 TANNAHILL *Poems* (1846) 76 He clamb the heights of Jura's isle, Wi' weary speel. 1885 [J. LUMSDEN] *Rhymes* 31 Steeple-Jack daurna wage a spiel wi' me.

speel (spiːl), *v.*¹ *Sc.* and *north. dial.* Forms: 6 speill, 6, 9 speil, 9 spiel; 6 spel, spele, 8– speel, 9 speal. [Of obscure origin; perh. a back-formation from SPEELER¹.]

1. *intr.* To mount or ascend to a height by climbing; to climb or clamber (*up* or *down*).

1513 DOUGLAS *Æneid* II. viii. 11 Wp to the side wallis mony leddir set is, Quhairon thai preis fast our the ruif to speill. 1530 LYNDESAY *Test. Papyngo* 154 This Bird..began to speill, rycht spedalie. 1560 ROLLAND *Seven Sages* 232 The skipper speillit belyve to the top Mast. 1715 RAMSAY *Christ's Kirk Gr.* II. x, [They] swat like pownies when they speel Up braes. 1816 SCOTT *Old Mort.* x, I could..speel down..weel eneugh. 1818 —— *Hrt. Midl.* xx, The..wolves ..that I used to see spieling up on my bed. 1863 in Robson *Bards of Tyne* 221 So he speal'd up the side.

fig. *a*1586 MONTGOMERIE *Misc. Poems* iii. 31 Then spurgald sporters they begin to speill [at court]. 1825 J. WILSON *Noct. Ambr.* Wks. 1855 I. 2 You'll see who will have speeled to the top of the tree.

b. *transf.* Of the sun, etc.: To move towards the zenith.

1718 RAMSAY *Christ's Kirk Gr.* III. i, The dawn Speel'd westlines up the lift. 1768 ROSS *Helenore* 58 An' neist the sun to the hill heads did speal. 1819 W. TENNANT *Papistry Storm'd* (1827) 43 Phoebus..up the pend at furious rate Gaed spielin'.

2. *trans.* To mount or ascend, to climb or clamber up (a hill, tree, etc.).

1571 *Satir. Poems Reform.* xxviii. 160 The Lord.. Inspyrit thair spreitis, & gart thame speil that heuch. 1785 BURNS *To W. Simpson* iii, My senses wad be in a creel, Should I but dare a hope to speel..The braes o' fame. 1790 A. WILSON *2nd Ep. A. Clark* Poet. Wks. (Belfast ed.) 99 Tired wi'..Speeling stairs, and lifting snecks. 1815 SCOTT *Antiq.* vii, Nae mortal could speel them [*sc.* the cliffs] without a rope. 1894 HESLOP *Northumbld. Gloss.* 676 He speeled the tree like a cat.

fig. 1786 BURNS *To Jas. Smith* xiii, Ance that five an' forty's speel'd.

b. *transf.* Of things.

1790 A. WILSON in *Poems & Lit. Prose* (1876) II. 198 Bonny mornin' speels the eastlin lift. *a*1849 W. NICHOLSON in Edwards *Mod. Scott. Poets* (1881) III. 67 The honeysuckles speel the roof. 1856 R. SIMPSON *Covenanters of South* 429 An ancient Celtic dyke speels the beetling height.

speel, *v.*² *dial.* and *slang.* Also spiel. [Origin obscure: perh. f. SPEEL *v.*¹] **a.** *intr.* To go fast; to run *away*, make off. Chiefly *Austral.* in later use.

*a*1818 W. MIDFORD *Cappy* in T. Thompson *Coll. Songs* (1827) 49 Owre his airm hung a basket—thus onward he speels, And enter'd Newcassel wi' Cap at his heels. 1829 *Sessions Papers at Old Bailey* 9 Apr. 329 The blake come, i spelld away. 1882 *Sydney Slang Dict.* 9/2 Shake this mob, Bill, and speel to the den, and let our lushy shicksters bring the ruin in. 1905 in A. B. Paterson *Old Bush Songs* 56 No more shall we muster the river for fats, Or spiel on the Fifteen-mile plain. *a*1921 G. H. GIBSON in *Penguin Bk. Austral. Ballads* (1964) 207 With a turn o' speed..As can spiel like a four-year brumby. 1945 S. J. BAKER *Austral. Lang.* 70 Horses are said..*to speel* when they travel fast.

†**b.** *trans.* Phr. *to speel the drum* (see quots.). Cf. DRUM *sb.*¹ 9 d. *Obs.*

1839 H. BRANDON in W. A. Miles *Poverty, Mendicity & Crime* 167/2 *To speel the drum*, to run away with the stolen property. 1859 *Slang Dict.* 98 *Speel*, to run away, make off; 'Speel the drum', to go off with stolen property. *North.*

speel-bone. *dial.* Also 4 spile-, 7 speell-. [? f. SPEEL *sb.*¹ Cf. Craven dial. *spell-baan* in the same sense.] The small bone of the leg (†or arm).

1307 *Wakefield Crt. Rolls* (1906) II. 131 [They assaulted and beat her, and broke the] spilebon [of her arm]. 1698 in *Jrnl. Friends' Hist. Soc.* (1912) IX. 193 A fall..broke the speell bone of her leg. 1869–76 in Lonsdale and Whitby glossaries.

†'**speeler**¹. *Sc. Obs.* In 5 spelare, 6 spelair. [prob. ad. older Flem. or LG. *speler* (G. *spieler*) player, actor; formation on SPEEL *v.*¹ is less likely.] A performer; an acrobat.

1496 *Acc. Ld. High Treas. Scot.* I. 322 Item,..giffin to the tawbronar that playit to the King, and the spelare with him, xxvij *s.* 1502 *Ibid.* II. 334 Item, to the spelair, his quartar pensioun, xij li. x s. 1503 *Ibid.* 387 Item, to the Inglis spelair, that playit the supersalt.

'speeler^2. *Sc.* [f. SPEEL *v.*^{1}] One of a pair of spiked irons used in climbing poles or trees.

1869 in Mrs. Gordon *Home Life Brewster* iii. 31 These [firs] the boys ascended, with 'speilers' or iron cramps on their ankles, to reach the crow-nests.

speeler^3. *Austr.* [perh. f. north. dial. *speel* 'to run quickly' (of a horse).] A horse with a turn for speed.

1893 MRS. C. PRAED *Outlaw & Lawmaker* I. 252 He's a bit of a speeler. He'd lick the lot of 'em if he was put into training.

speeler, var. SPIELER, 'sharper'.

speen, var. SPEAN *sb.*; Sc. dial. var. *spune* SPOON *sb.*

Speenhamland ('spi:nəmlænd). Now *Hist.* The name of a village near Newbury, Berks., used *attrib.*, esp. as ***Speenhamland system***, and (rarely) *absol.* of a system of poor relief adopted by the magistrates there in 1795, and subsequently established throughout most of rural England.

[**1797** F. M. EDEN *State of Poor* I. ii. 577 This shews.. what should be the weekly Income of the industrious poor, as settled by the Magistrates for the County of Berks, at a meeting held at Speenhamland, May the 6th, 1795.] **1835** R. HALL *Let.* 10 July in *1st Ann. Rep. Poor Law Commissioners* 208 It is singular that the provisions of the Speenhamland Act of Parliament, as the Berkshire table is called,.. contemplate only the case of the *industrious* poor. **1854** G. NICHOLLS *Hist. Eng. Poor Law* II. xii. 139 The famous Berkshire bread-scale, locally known as the 'Speenhamland Act of Parliament'. **1902** *Encycl. Brit.* XXVI. 665/2 The well-known Speenhamland scale (1795), by which a larger or lesser allowance was given to a family according to its size and the prevailing price of corn. **1925** C. M. WATERS *Econ. Hist. England 1066–1874* VI. i. 332 The enclosures and Speenhamland had quadrupled the poor-rate. **1934** B. RUSSELL *Freedom & Organization 1814–1914* vi. 78 An important step in the development of the Poor Law was taken by the inauguration of what is called the 'Speenhamland' system in 1795. **1959** *Chambers's Encycl.* VII. 550 The 'Speenhamland' system of poor relief.. remained in force until the Poor Law Amendment Act of 1834. **1973** *Listener* 19 Apr. 500/3 Bill Jordan, a sociologist, ..sees the social security system..as a modern Speenhamland system, deepening the division between the rich middle classes and the 'pauperised' poor.

speer (spɪə(r)), *sb.*^{1} Now *dial.* Forms: 4–5 **spere**, 6 **sper**, 7 **speare**, 9 **spear**, 5, 7– **speer**, 6, 9 **speere**. [? a. MLG. *speer*, *sper* spar-work.] A fixed screen for warding off an air-draught; a wooden partition near the door or by the fire-place; a chimney-post.

1379 *Durham Acc. Rolls* (Surtees) 131 In factura unius spere de Estlandbord' in Scakar Hostill. cum ligaturis ferreis et clavis. **1419** *Mem. Ripon* (Surtees) III. 145 Pro dobyng ij sperys j mesuagii in Bondgate pro ij dies. *c* **1440** *Promp. Parv.* 468/2 Spere, or scuw,..*scrineum, ventifuga*. *a* **1470** H. PARKER *Dives & Pauper* (W. de W. 1496) IV. iv. 1641 He was put out of the chambre & layde hym behynde the spere at the halle dore. **1530** PALSGR. 274/1 Speere in a hall, *buffet*. **1538** in Gage *Hist. & Antiq. Hengrave* (1822) 42 Item, yᵉ said hall to have ij coberds; one benethe, at the sper, wᵗ a tremor; and another, at the hygher table's inde, wᵗout a tremor. *a* **1600** *Heir of Linne* 80 in *Percy's MS.* (1867) I. 78 When that he came to Iohn of the Scales, vpp at the speere he looked then. **1674** RAY *N.C. Words* 44 The Speer. Chesh. The Chimney post. **1820** WILBRAHAM *Chesh. Gloss.* 62 *Speer*, the chimney post on each side of the fire-place. **1886** B. BRIERLEY *Cast upon World* i. 9 The first object to be seen after the door was closed was a pinched face at the edge of the 'speer'.

† **speer**, *sb.*^{2} *Obs.* Also 8 **spear**. [var. of SPIRE *sb.*^{1} (cf. SPEAR *sb.*^{2}).] A branch or prong of a deer's horn. (Freq. in Topsell's work.)

1607 TOPSELL *Four-f. Beasts* 327 They [*sc.* the horns] are sharp.., no where smooth but in the tops of the speers. **1658** ROWLAND *Topsell's Four-f. Beasts* 97 These [harts] do excell all other in the beauty of horns,..branching forth into many speers. *Ibid.* 98 At one year old they have nothing but small bunches,..at three years they grow forked into two speers. [Hence in Blome *Gentl. Recreat.* (1686), *Dict. Rust.* (1704) s.v. *Hart*, Chambers *Cycl.* (1728) s.v. *Head*, etc.] **1774** GOLDSM. *Nat. Hist.* III. v. 113 [The stag's] horns are called his head; when simple, the first year they are called broches; the third year, spears.

speer, *sb.*^{3} *Sc. rare.* Also **spier**. [f. SPEER *v.*^{1}] An inquiry, questioning, or interrogation.

1788 MACAULAY *Poems* 134, I..had nae fear O' getting you wi' little spier, Being sure to find you. **1822** GALT *Steam-Boat* x. 257 There was..a wonderful speer and talk about what we had all seen that day at the Coronation.

speer, *sb.*^{4} *rare.* Also *Sc.* **spire**. [Of obscure origin.] Spray.

1825 JAMIESON *Suppl.*, *Spire*, spray. Sea-spire, the spray of the sea. Renfr[ew]. **1902** 'M. FAIRLESS' *Roadmender* 70 The salt and speer of the sea, the companying with great ships, the fresh burden.

speer (spɪə(r)), *v.*^{1} Chiefly *Sc.* and *north.* Also **speir, spier.** Forms: α. 1 **spyrian**, 4 **spury-, spur-**, 5–6 **spure, spur**, 6–7 **spurre**; 1 **spirian**, 4–5 **spire**, 4–6 **spyre**, 4–5, 9 **spir**, 5 **spyr, spirr, spyrr**, 5–6 **spyrre**, 5, 7 **spirre**. β. 4 **sperije**, 5 **speryn**, 4–6, 9 **sper**, 5 **speore**, 5– **speir**, 6 **speire**, 6–8 **spear**, 8– **spier**, 5– **speer**; 5 *Sc.* **spar**, 7 *north.* **sparre**. [Common Teut.: OE. *spyrian*, = OS. **spurian* (cf. the sbs. *spuringa, spurida*), OHG. *spurigen, spurien* (MHG. *spüren, spürn*, G. *spüren*, dial. *spieren, spiren*), ON. (Icel. and Norw.) *spyrja* (Sw. *spörja*, Da. *spørge*, †*spørje*); cf. also MDu. *spören* (Du. *speuren*), LG. *spören, sporen* (hence Da. *spore*, Sw. *spåra*), obs. G. *spören, speuren, spuren*. For the relationship of the stem *spur-*, *spor-* see SPOOR *sb.*

In OE. the original senses of 'to make or follow a track', 'to go in search of', 'to seek after', are fully represented.]

I. *intr.* **1.** To put a question or questions; to make inquiries; to ask. Also with advs. as *about*, *in*.

α. *c* **888** K. ÆLFRED *Boeth.* xxvi. §2 Ʒenoh ryhte þu spyrast; swa hit is swa þu sezst. *a* **1300** *Cursor M.* 11475 'Gais,' he said, 'and spirs well gern'. **13..** *Seuyn Sages* (W.) 3832 The seriantes..spird obowt als he tham bad. **1375** BARBOUR *Bruce* III. 486 And on sic maner spyryt he, That he knew that it wes the king. *c* **1400** *Destr. Troy* 4297, I will tell..How sprittis in hom spake to qwho þat spirre wold. *c* **1475** *Babees Bk.* 37 Yf there be eny worde That yee kenne nouhte, spyrre whils yee yt ken. **1530** PALSGR. 731/1, I spurre, I aske a questyon. **1659** SOMNER *Dict. Sax. Lat.-Angl.* s.v. *Spyrian*, Lanc. *to spirre*.

β. *c* **1375** *Sc. Leg. Saints* xxx. (*Theodera*) 228 þane mad þe kerlyng sum dangere, wittand scho suld þe ȝarnare spere. *c* **1430** *Syr Gener.* (Roxb.) 6820 He that was the maryner Went aboute fast to spere; Of this mariage he herd tel. *c* **1475** *Rauf Coilȝear* 51 Sen thow speiris, I the tell All the suith hale. **1535** STEWART *Cron. Scot.* I. 75 Exploratouris than haif tha send..That was expert, to speir about. **1774** FERGUSSON *Leith Races* Poems (1845) 30 Where do ye win? if ane may speir. *c* **1780** BURNS *Tarbolton Lasses* v, And should ye ride by yon hill-side, Speer in for bonie Bessie. **1808** MAYNE *Siller Gun* III. xix, 'It sets ye weel, indeed, to speer,' The sutor answer'd.

b. Const. *about* or *anent, after, for, into, of* (= concerning).

α. *a* **1300** *Cursor M.* 11444 þai toke þair gesting in þe tun, And spird him efter vp and dun. *Ibid.* 13628 Quar-for spir yee o þat gom? **1338** R. BRUNNE *Chron.* (1810) 112 þe kyng in þat forest A moneth lay, to spire for wod & wilde beste. *c* **1400** *Destr. Troy* 12429 The kynges into councell callit hir þan, To spir of hor spede. *c* **1440** *Alph. Tales* 122 þai went vnto þis clerkis howse & spirrid after þer maister & his suster.

β. **1375** BARBOUR *Bruce* IV. 494 Heir I saw the men, That ȝhe speir eftir, mak luging. *Ibid.* XVI. 21 And he..sperit of his brotheris fair. *c* **1450** *St. Cuthbert* (Surtees) 300 He wendes forthe..Of þis nouelry to sper. *c* **1489** CAXTON *Sonnes of Aymon* xxvii. 573 Whan he founde not his mayster in the chirche he..spered after him. ? *a* **1550** *Freiris Berwik* 59 in *Dunbar's Poems* (1893) 287 Freir Robert sperit eftir the gud man. *a* **1578** LINDESAY (Pitscottie) *Chron. Scot.* (S.T.S.) I. 258 [He] come..cryand and speirand for the king. *a* **1700** ? SEMPILL *Maggie Lauder* v, Gin ye should come to Anster Fair, Spier ye for Maggie Lauder. **1717** RAMSAY *Elegy Lucky Wood* xii, And after ages bairns will spear 'Bout thee and me. **1795** BURNS *Braw Wooer* vii, I speered for my cousin..Gin she had recovered her hearin'. **1815** SCOTT *Guy M.* i, Troth, I kenna, unless ye like to..speer for quarters at the Place. **1824** —— *Redgauntlet* let. xi, Speer as little about him as he does about you. **1866** H. KINGSLEY *Leighton Court* xxxiii, Of whom were ye speiring?

c. Const. *at* (also †*of*) a person. Cf. 4.

a **1300** *Cursor M.* 15899 Gladli wald he spek and sper, Bot at quam he ne wate. **1375** BARBOUR *Bruce* v. 39 The King.. sperit at hym how he had done. **1441** *Plumpton Corr.* (Camden) p. lvi, Sir William Plompton..spirred of the said tenants..of the governance & rule that night. **1470–85** MALORY *Arthur* XXI. viii. 852 Syr Launcelot spyrred of men of douer where was kyng Arthur become. **1500–20** DUNBAR *Poems* xc. 33 Gif..he be blinde, and can nocht at the speir. **1585** JAS. I *Ess. Poesie* (Arb.) 48 I speared at him..What word of Phœnix which was flown away? *a* **1724** in Ramsay *Tea-t. Misc.* (1733) I. 28 He first speer'd at the guidman. **1792** BURNS '*An' O for ane-and-twenty*' ii, At kith or kin I need na spier. **1818** SCOTT *Hrt. Midl.* x, What needs ye be aye speering then at folk? **1903** *Pilot* 22 Aug. 169/1 These things can only be ascertained by 'speiring' at the Colonies themselves.

†**2.** To inquire one's way; to make one's way, proceed or go, *to* a place, etc. *Obs.*

c **1450** *St. Cuthbert* (Surtees) 1606 Be hir tellyng men wer steryd, And diuers to þe saynt speryd, and come in pilgrimage. **1513** DOUGLAS *Æneid* II. vi. 52 To quhilk other forthres sall we speir? *Ibid.* VI. v. 147 Speir to the portis quhilkis Velinos hait. **1615** BRATHWAIT *Strappado* (1878) 131 Heere stood I musing..Till Iockie wha dost thinke speard vp to me.

II. *trans.* **3.** With objective clause: To inquire or ask *how, what, who*, etc.

α. *c* **900** tr. *Baeda's Hist.* xvii. (1722) 499 Hi ða spyredan hwæt and hwonan he wæs. **13..** *K. Alis.* 2569 (W.), He.. spirred whider Darie is went. **1338** R. BRUNNE *Chron.* (1810) 327 He spired as he ȝede, who did suilk trespas. **1390** GOWER *Conf.* I. 198 This lord to spire Began, fro whenne that sche cam. *c* **1440** *Alph. Tales* 264 þan þis duke besoght þaim to spur who did þis trispas. **1483** CAXTON *Gold. Leg.* 77/1 Therfore spyre and aske how thou maist goo to hym.

β. *c* **1325** *Metr. Hom.* 95 The king..sperid in quat time, and quat cyte, That Goddes sun suld born be. **1375** BARBOUR *Bruce* x. 522 Tharfor preuely sperit he Gif ony man mycht fundin be [etc.]. **1456** SIR G. HAYE *Law Arms* (S.T.S.) 1 He speris quhat thing is bataill. *a* **1470** HARDING *Chron.* CXVII. viii, Buryed he was, but where no man durste spere. **1549** *Compl. Scot.* xi. 100 His sone pontius sperit quhou he suld vse hym contrar the romans. *a* **1572** KNOX *Hist. Ref.* Wks. 1846 I. 241 'What sayis thow of the Messe?' spearis the Erle of Huntley. **1637** RUTHERFORD *Lett.* (1862) I. lxxix. 202 Rouse..your soul, and speer how Christ and your soul met together. **1686** G. STUART *Joco-ser. Disc.* 13 I speer'd what news in this gude town. *c* **1770** BEATTIE *To A. Ross* vi, Naebody car'd For anes to speer how Scota far'd. **1818** SCOTT *Rob Roy* xviii, And is't the way to Glasgow ye were speering if I ken'd? **1871** C. GIBBON *Lack of Gold*, xiv, You needna' speir how I ken.

4. To make inquiries concerning, to ask questions regarding (a thing or fact). Also const. *at* or *of* (a person).

13.. *E.E. Allit P.* B. 1606 Alle þat he spured hym..he expowned clene. *c* **1375** *Sc. Leg. Saints* ii. (*Paul*) 229 At þame spere but mare þe cause quhy I gert ȝou cum þare. **14..** *King & Barker* 13 in Hazl. *E.P.P.* I. 4 Howr kyng bad hes men abeyde, And he welde sper of hem the wey. *c* **1450** *St. Cuthbert* (Surtees) 2622 When many thinges sho had speryd. *c* **1500** *Lancelot* 1169 At qwhome ful sone than gan scho to Inquere, And al the maner of the ostis till spere. **1549** *Compl. Scot.* Prol. 15 Gyf ony persone vald speir at me the maneir of the gouernyng of ane battel. **1646** ROW *Hist. Kirk* (Wodrow Soc.) p. xxxiii, To informe of thingis that I sall speir at him. **1686** G. STUART *Joco-ser. Disc.* 14 Ye speer the Gate ye kenn right weel. **1830** GALT *Lawrie T.* IX. viii. (1849) 434 Oh, no great sum; ye needna speer that. **1858–61** E. B. RAMSAY *Remin.* ii. (1870) 21 It's no the day to be speering sic things.

b. With special objects, as *tidings, price*, etc.

to speer (one's) price, to ask one's terms, to ask in marriage.

(*a*) *a* **1300** *Cursor M.* 5682 Moyses..sett him þar a wel bi-side, Tiþand for to spir and bide. **1375** BARBOUR *Bruce* XIX. 599 Ilkane at othir sperit tithing. *a* **1400–50** *Alexander* 237 And þar [she] hire spakid with his speche & spird of him wordis. **1513** DOUGLAS *Æneid* III. ii. 155 My fadir exhortis ws..Apollois ansueir speir. *a* **1585** MONTGOMERIE *Cherry & Slae* 946 Ʒe culd not luck..That all opinions sperit.

(*b*) **1583** *Leg. Bp. St. Androis* 794 For a pair of schone he ast. Bot or he sperit the price to pay them [etc.]. **1785** BURNS *Scotch Drink* xiv, Monie..hardly, in a winter season, E'er spier her price. **1823** GALT *Entail* II. xxviii. 268, I was past thirty before man speer't my price. **1837** LOCKHART *Scott* vi. I. 186 We've stood here an hour by the Tron, hinny, and de'il a ane has speered our price.

c. To request the return of (money); to ask *back*.

1818 SCOTT *Hrt. Midl.* xlix, This siller binds me to naething, and can never be speered back again.

d. To ask for (advice); to beg (leave).

1724 in Ramsay *Tea-t. Misc.* (1733) I. 101 Love speers nae advice Of parents o'er wise. *a* **1835** *Child Maurice* xii. in Child *Ball.* II. 268/1 She maun cum to the merrie greenwud, And speir the leive o nane. **1866** J. YOUNG *Life J. Welsh* 403 'It's right like, Sir,' said she; 'for we never speired his advice'. **1895** CROCKETT *Men of Moss-hags* xxxv. 253 Dinna bide to speer her leave.

5. To trace or find out by inquiry. Usu. with *out*.

c **1375** *Sc. Leg. Saints* vi. (*Thomas*) 10 Bisily fore to spere a man, þat sic palace can make. **1390** GOWER *Conf.* III. 324 He bad his man to gon and spire A place wher sche myhte abyde. **1562** TURNER *Herbal* II. (1568) 39 Perchance som of vs..myght spere it out and fynd it by that name. **1637** RUTHERFORD *Lett.* (1862) I. 434 Oh that people would speer out Christ! **1648** *Burgh Rec. Glasgow* (1881) II. 157 To speir out men fitting to be employet for the Manufactorie. *c* **1746** J. COLLIER (Tim Bobbin) *View Lanc. Dial.* (1775) 41 I soyn sperr'd the Gentlemon's Hoah eawt. **1863** S. S. JONES *Northumbld.* 64/1 Tryin' tae speer oot his station an' character. **1854** MISS BAKER *Northampt. Gloss.* s.v., Speer it out if you can. With us it is almost *obs.*

6. With cognate object (see also 7): To ask (a question).

c **1460** *Towneley Myst.* xxx. 206 Whi spir ye not, sir, no questyons? **1549** *Compl. Scot.* xvi. 143 The preist of peblis speris ane questione in ane beuk that he conpilit. **1581** J. BELL *Haddon's Answ. Osor.* 56 But you begyn here to.. spurre questions at me on all sides. **1816** SCOTT *Old. Mort.* xxxvii, I hae had sae mony questions speered at me in my day. **1889** BARRIE *Window in Thrums* 168 Ye shouldna spier sic annoyin' queistions.

7. To question or interrogate (a person). Usually with const., as *of*, interrogative clause, or cognate object (cf. 6).

Still in Sc. use; also *spec.* to propose marriage to (a woman).

a **1300** *Cursor M.* 3826 He spird þaim queþen þai ware. *c* **1400** *Anturs of Arthur* xx, Of thies sperituale thynges spyre me na mare. **1484** in *Cely Papers* (Camden) 153 He speryd me noo oder questyans. **1568** tr. *Montanus' Inquisit.* 22 b, He shall ride the racke, and there be spurred certeyne questions. **1594** LYLY *Mother Bombie* IV. ii, Ile be so bolde as spurre her, what might a bodie call her name? **1600** HOLLAND *Livy* XXIII. xii. 481 b, Seeing a Senatour bluntly spurreth me the question.

†**b.** To call upon or demand formally. *Obs.*$^{-1}$

1493 *Festivall* (W. de W. 1515) 193 All those..that haue ben spyred thryse in holy chyrche themselfe wyttynge.

c. To invite.

1818 SCOTT *Br. Lamm.* ix, Just that ye suld speer ony gentleman hame to dinner.

Hence **'speerer**, an inquirer. *rare*$^{-1}$.

c **1375** *Sc. Leg. Saints* xxvii. (*Machor*) 1140 þarfor lewe forthir to spere..; for sperer of his maieste fra his Joy sall donne thrungine be.

speer (spɪə(r)), *v.*^{2} *dial.* and *U.S.* [perh. identical with prec., influenced by PEER *v.*] *intr.* To peer. Const. *at, into, out*.

1866 BLACKMORE *Cradock Nowell* xlv. (1873) 293 Out went Eöa, speering around for the tracks of Bob. **1866** J. SLEIGH *Derby Gloss.* (E.D.D.), To speer and pry into any thing. **1885** B. HARTE *Maruja* i, She a flirt, speerin' at men with that modest, downcast air? **1895** *Pall Mall G.* 2 Dec. 3/2 We all speered out to catch a glimpse of the Injiman.

speer, variant of SPERE *a. Obs.*

speer(e, obs. forms of SPEAR, SPHERE.

'speering, *vbl. sb. Sc.* and *north. dial.* [f. SPEER *v.*^{1} Cf. SPURRING *vbl. sb.*^{2}]

1. The action of questioning or inquiring; interrogation, inquiry.

a **1100** in Napier *O.E. Glosses* 132/1 *Adinuentionum,* ȝesmeangum, spyrungum, axungum. *a* **1300** *Cursor M.* 27280 In spiring loke þe preist be sli. **1375** Barbour *Bruce* III. 568 Eftir the mete sone rais the king, Quhen he had lewyt hys speryng. *c* **1400** *Destr. Troy* 12093 He besit hym barly þe burde forto seche,.. Till he aspiet hir.. by speryng of othir. *c* **1440** *York Myst.* xxxiii. 64 For any spirringes in þat space no speche walde he spell. **1552–3** *Reg. Privy Council Scot.* I. 137 Anent the spering.. of every wrang sen the peax bigane. **1816** Chalmers in Hanna *Life* (1851) II. 77, I.. went through a great deal of speering and hand-shaking. **1892** *Edin. Rev.* Jan. 51 He used to reply to his son's eager 'speerings' by such admissions as 'That I do not know' [etc.].

2. Information obtained by inquiry. Also *pl.*

1375 Barbour *Bruce* v. 490 He.. lay still in the castell than, Till he gat spering at [= of] a man Of Carrick. **1814** Scott *Wav.* xxx, If it please my Creator, I will forthwith obtain speirings thereof. **1824** —— *Redgauntlet* let. xi, Ony of the hill-folk he could get speerings of.

speet, obs. f. or var. spit *sb.* and *v.*

Speeton ('spiːtən). *Geol.* The name of a village on the North Yorkshire coast, used *attrib.* with reference to a series of clays of Lower Cretaceous age which outcrop there.

1829 J. Phillips *Geol. Yorkshire* I. iii. 74 From the termination of the white cliffs the coast bends to the northward, and exhibits in succession, rising from beneath the chalk, the Speeton clay and the coralline oolite series. **1882** A. Geikie *Text-bk. Geol.* 816 The marine Neocomian strata of England are well exposed on the cliffs of the Yorkshire coast at Filey, where they occur in a deposit long known as the 'Speeton Clay'. **1946** L. D. Stamp *Britain's Structure & Scenery* xviii. 204 In the northern basin the Lower Greensand is represented by the Speeton Clays, with 'carstone', succeeded by marls and the famous Red Chalk of Hunstanton and Lincolnshire. **1969** Bennison & Wright *Geol. Hist. Brit. Isles* xiv. 323 On the north side of the Yorkshire Wolds a narrow out-crop of clays is found and it extends to the coast near Speeton. These clays, some 300 feet thick and known as the Speeton Series, range in age from the Ryazanian to the Albian.

speget, obs. f. spigot *sb.*

speid, obs. f. speed.

†**speight.** *Obs.* Also 5 *Sc.*, 6–7 **specht**, 6 **speicht**, 6–7 **speyght**, 7 **spight**. [Either repr. an unrecorded OE. ***speht** (***speoht**), or a. MDu. or MLG. *specht* (Du. *specht*, WFris. *specht*, *spjucht*), = OS. *speth* (sic), OHG. *speht* (MHG. *speht*, *speiht*, G. *specht*): cf. Da. *spætte*, Norw. *spetta*, Sw. *hackspett*, and OF. *espoit*, *espois* (from Germanic). The ultimate affinities of the word are uncertain.

Speckt in Johnson (1755) is due to a misprint in Ainsworth (1736) s.v. *Picus*.]

The green woodpecker, *Gecinus viridis.* (Cf. speck *sb.*³ and wood-spite.)

c **1450** Holland *Howlat* 334 The Specht was a purcevant, provde till apper, That raid befor the empriour. **1513** Douglas *Æneid* vii. iv. 91 Ane byrd.. Wyth sprutlit wyngis, clepit a Speicht wyth ws, Quhilk in Latyne hecht *Pycus Marcyus.* **1552** Elyot, *Picus martius,* a birde:.. of this bee three kyndes, the fyrst a specht, the seconde a hecway, the third.. is not in England. **1598** Sylvester *Du Bartas* II. i. iv. *Handicrafts* 157 Eve, walking forth about the Forrests, gathers Speights', Parrots', Peacocks', Estrich' scatt'red feathers. **1601** Holland *Pliny* I. 278 Some little birds there are also that haue hooked clees, as the Spights. **1656** W. Du Gard tr. *Comenius' Gate Lat. Unl.* 43 The Gnat-snapper used to feed on figs; and the Speight on Bees.

†**speild.** *Sc. Obs.*⁻¹ [var. of speld *sb.*] A piece, part, or strip.

1653 in Laing *Lindores Abbey* (1876) 231 He took neither hyd not half ane hyd, but ane speild of ane hyd, and caried it to the house.

Speinȝie, obs. Sc. form of Spain.

†**speir**¹. *Obs.* Forms: 4 **speyr(e**, 4–5 **speire**. [ad. OF. *espeir(e* espeire.] Hope; expectation.

1303 R. Brunne *Handl. Synne* 6476 Þy sone ys now yn þe same speyre; he shal nat þenk þat he shal deye. *c* **1330** —— *Chron. Wace* (Rolls) 5790 To haue a lord þey were in speyr. *c* **1400** *St. Alexius* (MS. Laud 622) 1030 To þi comyng was al my speire, To haue ymade of þee myne eire.

†**speir**². *Obs. rare.* Also 5 **speyr**. [Aphetic f. *despeir* despair *sb.*] Despair; despondency.

13.. *Eufrosyne* 9 in Hortsm. *Altengl. Leg.* (1878) 174 Þis mon was sori and in gret speir, For he hedde of his bodi non heir. **14..** *Tundale's Vis.* 1008 Tundale feld a stynkyng ayr, Then of his lyffe he was in speyr.

speir, var. speer *v.*¹; obs. Sc. f. sphere.

speir(e, obs. ff. spear *sb.*¹

‖**Speisesaal** ('ʃpaɪzəzaːl). [Ger.] In German-speaking countries: a dining room, dining hall.

1871 *Monthly Packet* Christmas 57 The gentlemen betook themselves to the Speise saal, about which a cheerful bustle prevailed. **1929** E. M. Brent-Dyer *Rivals of Chalet School* v. 61 'No walk *this* day!' said that young person, looking sadly out of the window of the *Speisesaal* while they were having hot coffee and biscuits. **1969** J. Eastwood *Come die with Me* (1970) ii. 20 She.. went down to the Speisesal [*sic*].

speiss (spaɪs). Also 8–9 **speis**. [ad. G. *speise* in the same sense, a special use of *speise* (:—pop. Lat. *spēsa*, L. *expensa*) 'food, nourishment'.]

1. An impure metallic compound, containing nickel, cobalt, iron, etc., produced in the smelting of certain ores; *esp.* an arsenide obtained in the manufacture of smalt and used as a source of nickel.

1796 Kirwan *Elem. Min.* (ed. 2) II. 287 It [sulphurated nickel] affords, together with Speis (which is a compound of Nickel and Cobalt) also Copper and Silver. **1839** Ure *Dict. Arts* 302 The latter ores should be but slightly roasted, so as to convert the nickel into speiss. **1850** Fownes *Chem.* (ed. 3) 295 The artificial, or perhaps rather merely fused, product, called *speiss*,.. may be employed as a source of the nickel-salts. **1877** Raymond *Statist. Mines & Mining* 184 The average assay of speiss produced during the year. **1883** *Encycl. Brit.* XVI. 61/2 We can produce a speis which contains only cobalt and nickel.

2. speiss-cobalt, tin-white cobalt; smaltine.

1872 Raymond *Statist. Mines & Mining* 20 Antimonial silver ore with traces of speiss-cobalt. **1877** *Encycl. Brit.* VI. 81/1 Smaltine or speiss cobalt, an arsenide of the isomorphous bases, cobalt, nickel, and iron.

speit, obs. Sc. f. spit *sb.*

spek, obs. f. speak, speck, speke².

‖**spek-boom** ('spɛkboːm). Also **speck-**. [S. African Du., f. *spek* speck *sb.*⁴ + *boom* tree.] The purslane-tree (*Portulacaria Afra*) of South Africa.

1834 Pringle *Afr. Sk.* vi. 209 The spekboom, with its light green leaves and lilac blossoms. *Ibid.* vii. 248 Browsing on the succulent spekboom, which clothed the skirts of the hills. **1850** R. G. Cumming *Hunter's Life S. Afr.* (1902) 12/1 One vast jungle of dwarfish evergreen shrubs and bushes, amongst which the speckboom was predominant. **1879** Atcherley *Trip Boerland* 186 The *spek-boom* grows here in great profusion.

†**speke**¹. *Obs.*⁻¹ [ad. L. *spec-us*.] A cave.

1377 Langl. *P. Pl.* B. xv. 270 Monkes.. In spekes an in spelonkes selden speken togideres.

†**speke**². Also 5 **spek**, 7 **speak**. [a. MDu. or MLG. *spēke* spoke *sb.*]

1. A handspike.

1366 in Nicolas *Hist. Royal Navy* (1847) II. 473 [For one other] wyndas [bought, with four] spekes [pertaining to the same, 12 d.]. **1417** in Riley *Mem. Lond.* (1868) 656 [Taking in his hands a certain staff commonly called a] spek.

2. A wheel-spoke.

? *a* **1400** *Morte Arth.* 3264 The spekes was splentide alle with speltis of siluer. **1483** *Cath. Angl.* 353/1 A Speke (A Speke of a qwele), *radius.* **1485** in *Ripon Ch. Acts* (Surtees) 374, xxj axiltrees,.. x gang de felghes,.. iiij gang de spekes. **1617–8** *Shuttleworths' Acc.* (Chetham Soc.) 228, xj gange of fellice [felloes],.. viij gange of speaks.

speke, etc., obs. f. speak, etc.

spekenardy, obs. var. spikenard.

speknel, obs. f. spignel.

spelæan (spɪ'liːən), *a.* Also **spelean**. [f. mod.L. *spelæ-us*, f. L. *spēlæum*, ad. Gr. σπήλαιον cave.]

1. Inhabiting a cave or caves; frequenting caverns; cave-dwelling.

1839 G. Roberts *Dict. Geol.* 161 *Spelæan,* that frequent caverns. A term applied to the hyæna. **1874** Dawkins *Cave Hunt.* iii. 118 The remains of the spelæan variety of the spotted hyæna were very abundant in the cave-earth. *a* **1882** *Fraser's Mag.* (Imp. Dict.), Those primitive spelæan people who contended against and trapped the mammoth.

2. Of the nature of a cave.

1882 Owen in *Longman's Mag.* I. 67 More satisfactorily.. than in any other spelæan retreat which I have explored.

†**spelch**, *sb. Obs. Sc.* and *north.* [Related to spelk *sb.*]

1. A chip or splinter.

1572 R. Bannatyne *Jrnl.* (1806) 388 The portcullious.. fell down to the ground agane, and a part of a spelch therof fleing of, hurt Harie Balfour in the heid. **1634** *Lowe's Chirurg.* 354 A little part of the bone is superficially separated like unto a little spelch or sclat.

2. (See quot.)

1677 Nicolson in *Trans. R. Soc. Lit.* (1870) IX. 319 *Spelch,* a swathe band.

†**speld**, *sb. Obs.* Also 4–5 **spelde**, 4 **spielde**. [OE. *speld* neut., = ON. *speld*, *spjald* (Norw. *spjeld*, Sw. *spjell*), related to Goth. *spilda* fem., MHG. and G. dial. *spelte* tablet, splinter, chip, etc.: see spald *v.*]

1. A flake or particle of fire; a spark. Also with *of*.

c **1050** *Voc.* in Wr.-Wülcker 529 *Tedasque,* and biernende speld. *c* **1100** in Napier *O.E. Glosses* 161/2 *In fauillam,* on spelde. *c* **1290** *S. Eng. Leg.* I. 210 Wrechche gostes.. he seiȝ Fleo op and doun al brenninde, ase speldene doth of fuyre. *Ibid.* 474 Ake ofte gret fuyr and eke stuyrne wext of a luytel spielde. *c* **1440** *R. Gloucester's Chron.* (Rolls) II. 819 *note,* And þer amydde he cast A litil spelde of fuyre and abowte þe speld fast He by wounde þys tender.

2. A chip or splinter.

1350 *Will. Palerne* 3603 Þe kniȝt spere in speldes altoschiuered. *Ibid.* 3855 So spakli here speres al on speldes went.

speld, *v. Sc.* Also 6 **speild**. [Related to spald *v.* For the vowel cf. prec.]

1. *trans.* To lay flat or extended; to spread out; to split open. Also *refl.*

c **1480** Henryson *Fables, Preach. Swallow* xxvii, Heirefter ȝe sall find als sour as sweit, Quhen ȝe ar speldit [*v.r.* speildit] on ȝone carlis speit. *c* **1480** —— *Orph. & Eurydice* 177 Besyde hym on the bent, He saw speldit a wonder wofull wicht, Nailit full fast. **1513** Douglas *Æneid* v. vii. 19 All flat [he] hym speldit on the dwn sand, In the deid thrawis. **1533** Bellenden *Livy* I. xi. (S.T.S.) I. 68 He.. band þis Mecius speldit betuix þe twa cheriottis. **1710** Ruddiman *Gloss. Douglas' Æneis* s.v., [We] say, 'He spelded himself on the ice'; and 'a spelded herring', and 'speldings', &c. **1866** Edmondston *Gloss. Shetl.* 114 *Speld,* to split up, to lay open, S.

2. To split or crack. *rare*⁻¹.

1616 *Aberdeen Burgh Reg.* (1848) II. 346 The back dyick of the colledge yard.. is creuisched and speldit at the wast neuck thairof, and lick[l]ie to faill.

†**spelder**, *sb. Obs.*⁻¹ [= MLG. *spelder*, MHG. *spelter*: cf. speld *sb.* It is doubtful whether OE. *speldra* pl. belongs here or to *speld*.] A splinter, shiver, or chip.

1530 Palsgr. 274/1 Spelder of woode, *esclat.*

spelder ('spɛldə(r)), *v.*¹ *north. dial.* [ad. OF. ***espeldre** (*espeaudre*, *espialre*; later *espeller*, *espeler*, mod.F. *épeler*), f. the Germanic stem *spell-*: see spell *v.*¹] *trans.* and *intr.* To spell, as words.

c **1200** Ormin 16347 Adamess name Adam iss all Wiþþ fowwre stafess spelldredd. *Ibid.* 16440 And ȝiff þatt tu cannst spelldrenn hemm, Adam þu findesst spelldredd. **1483** *Cath. Angl.* 353/2 To Speldyr, *sillabicare.* **1691** Ray *N.C. Words* (ed.2) 68 *To Spelder,* to Spell. *a* **1743** Relph *Misc. Poems* (1747) 15 Right oft at schuil I've spelder'd owr thy rows. **1788–** in dial. glossaries (Yks., Lanc., N.Cy., Cumbld.).

Hence **'spelderer**; **'speldering** *vbl. sb.*

1483 *Cath. Angl.* 353/2 A Spelderer, *sillabicator.* **1876** Robinson *Whitby Gloss.* 181/1 He's ept at his speldering.

spelder, *v.*² *Sc.* [Cf. speld *v.* and dial. *spalder* (s.v. spald *v.*).]

1. *intr.* To spread or extend oneself, by throwing or stretching out the legs (and arms). Also in *pa. pple.*, stretched out in this manner.

1720 Pennecuik *Screams fr. Helicon* 67 The Doxies turn up their Keels and spelder. **1756** Mrs. Calderwood in *Coltness Collect.* (Maitl. Club) 129 Bowles, who had come from the other cabin,.. was speldring with legs and arms to keep his ballance. **1820** Hogg *Bridal of Polmood* vii, Kimmers, that war lying doveryng.. and spelderyng. **1863** W. Miller *Willie Winkie*, etc. (1902) 1 The dog's spelder'd on the floor.

2. *trans.* To split and spread open (a fish, etc.). Hence **'speldered** *ppl. a.*

1710 Ruddiman *Gloss. Douglas' Æneis* s.v. *Speldit,* We say also *spelder*.. in the same sense. **1808** Jamieson, To *Spelder,* to split, to spread open; as, *to spelder a fish,* to open it up for being dried. **1828** Moir *Mansie Wauch* vii. 61 Splitting the hills as ye would spelder a haddy. **1896** P. A. Graham *Red Scaur* xvii. 260 Never talk o' fightin', you speldered herring!

spelding ('spɛldɪŋ). *Sc.* Also 7–8 **spelden**, 8–9 **-in**, 9 **-ane**. [f. speld *v.* + -ing¹. Cf. next and the earlier spalderling.] A small split fish, preserved by being dried in the sun.

1537 in *Reg. Mag. Sig. Scot.* (1883) 608/1 Reddend. annuatim.. pro Fischarhill 40 sol. pro lie kayn speldingis. **1547** *Acc. Ld. High Treas. Scot.* IX. 106 Item, mair for ane card of speldinges, put in the said castell, price vj li. *a* **1682** Sempill *Blythsome Wedding* 63 And there will be partans, and buckies, Speldens, and haddocks anew. **1722** Ramsay *Three Bonnets* iv. 169 Swift hame and feast upon a spelding. **1785** Boswell *Tour Hebrides* 50, I bought some *speldings*, fish (generally whitings) salted and dried in a particular manner. **1805** McIndoe *Poems* 107 This trout.. was faulded in twa like a speldin. **1883** *Fisheries Exhib. Catal.* 67 Dried Sprats,.. Soft Speldings, Whitebait.

'speldring. *Sc.* Also **-rin**, **-rain**, **-ron**. [f. spelder *v.*²] = prec.

1802 Sibbald *Chron. S.P.* Gloss., *Speldings, Speldrings,* small fish (as haddocks) stretched open and dried in the sun. **1834** J. Wilson *Noctes Ambr.* xxxiv. Wks. 1856 IV. 88 Finnans! Kipper! Speldrins! Herring! **1881** Day *Fishes Gt. Brit.* I. 284 Haddock.. are finnan haddocks, when smoked in a peculiar manner: if simply dried, speldrings.

transf. **1820** *Blackw. Mag.* VIII. 98 Whose place, as soon as he evaporated, was filled by another strange rizzard speldron.

spele, var. speel *sb.* and *v.*

spele, *v.*¹ Now *dial.* and *rare.* Forms: 1 **spelian**, 3 **spelien**, 4 **spelie**, **-ye**; 3 *Orm.* **spelenn**, 4 **spele**, *s.w. dial.* 8 **speal**, 9 **spale**. [OE. *spelian*, related to *ȝespelia* and *spala* substitute (see spale *sb.*¹), of obscure origin.]

1. *trans.* To take or stand in the place of (another); to represent.

c **960** *Rule St. Benet* (Schröer) 114 For Cristes arwurðnysse and for þæs lufe, ðe he spelað. *c* **1000** Ælfric *Gram.* v. 8 *Pronomen* is ðæs naman speliend, se spelað þone naman, þæt ðu ne ðurfe tuwa hine nemnan. *c* **1000** —— *Hom.* II. 62 Næs ðeah Isaac ofslegen, ac se ramm hine spelode. ? *c* **1730** *Dorset Voc.* in *N. & Q.* 6th Ser. (1883) VIII. 45 *Speal,* to spare one and take his place.

2. To spare or save (something); to leave over; to use sparingly or frugally.

c **1200** *Trin. Coll. Hom.* 31 ȝef þu ani þing spelest and leuest, þat þu forlest. *c* **1200** ORMIN 10133 þatt te birrþ hellpenn iwhillc mann.. Wiþþ all þatt tu mihht spelenn wel & libbenn þær wiþþutenn. **1303** R. BRUNNE *Handl. Synne* 1204 Wykkedlyche al þat gode he dyspendyþ þat hys fadyr for godenesse spelyþ. *c* **1330** —— *Chron. Wace* (Rolls) 14470 Schipes he hadde, y ne wot how fele; Alle he tok, & non wold spele. **1393** LANGL. *P. Pl.* C. VII. 432 As an hounde.. so gan ich to brake, And spilde þat ich spele myghte. *c* **1400** *St. Alexius* (Trin.) 208 Al þat he spelye myȝte,.. His pouere feren he delde. **1880** *W. Cornwall Gloss.* 53/2 *Spale*,.. to make anything last a long time. To spare.

absol. **1393** LANGL. *P. Pl.* C. XIV. 77 Boþe [to] spele and spare to spene vpon þe needful.

†**b.** To set aside; to neglect. *Obs.*

1338 R. BRUNNE *Chron.* (1810) 96 He & oþer fele sent vnto Roberd, þat stound suld he not spele, sen he þat tiþing herd.

†**3.** To spare (a person); to leave unpunished or unharmed. *Obs.*

a **1300** *Body & Soul* in *Map's Poems* (Camden) 339 Forlorn wretches that tou miȝtest spele,.. wȝi lestouȝ hem be born? *c* **1330** R. BRUNNE *Chron. Wace* (Rolls) 12428 Arthur.. smot hym sore woundes fele, Nought of hym ne wolde he spele. *c* **1380** *Sir Ferumb.* 458 þar-for y am to þe y-sent to spelie þai doȝty men.

†**b.** To respite *from* death. *Obs.*

13.. *Seuyn Sages* (W.) 542 To-dai tho hast him fram deth i-speled.

Hence †**'speling** *vbl. sb.*, sparing. *Obs.*

c **1420** *Anturs Arth.* xx. (Douce MS.), þes arne þe graceful giftes of þe holy goste, þat enspires iche sprete, withe oute speling.

†**spele**, *v.*[2] *Obs. rare.* Also 7 speale. [ad. OF. *espeler* (mod.F. *épeler*), *espelir*: cf. SPELL *v.*[2]]

1. *trans.* **a.** To interpret or explain as. **b.** To signify or mean.

a **1225** *Ancr. R.* 170 þes nome Assuer is ispeled eadi,.. & bitocneð God: eadi ouer alle. *Ibid.*, Mardocheus speleð 'amare conterens impudentem'.

2. *intr.* To spell.

a **1400** *Minor Poems fr. Vernon MS.* 694/76 Sum leueþ on hit, As children leorneþ for to spele. **1611** COTGR., *Espeler*, to spell, to speale; to ioyne letters, or sillables together. *Ibid.*, *Espelement*, a spelling, or spealing of words.

Hence †**'speler** (in 7 spealer), = SPELLER[2] 1.

1611 COTGR., *Appelleur*, a caller; or spealer.

speleology (spɛliːˈɒlədʒɪ). Also spelæo-. [ad. F. *spéléologie*: see SPELÆAN and -OLOGY.] The scientific study of caves. Also, the hobby of exploring caves.

α. **1895** E. A. MARTEL in *Rep. 6th Geogr. Congr.* (1896) 721 To make of speleology something else than a mere sport. **1899** *Pop. Sci. Monthly* LV. 562 The southern half of Missouri and the Black Hills.. offer.. regions for the study of caves, or speleology. **1937** *Caves & Caving* I. 7/1 The objectives of the British Speleological Association... 1. The promotion of friendship and the exchange of ideas amongst those who are interested in speleology. 2. The study of the geological, hydrological, archaeological and 'sporting' aspects of speleology. **1974** *Islander* (Victoria, B.C.) 8 Dec. 15/4 Press reports.. have promoted public interest in the sport and science of speleology.

β. **1895** *Knowledge* Oct. 223/2 'Spelæology, the Science of Caverns,' was the title of a paper by Mons. E. A. Martel. **1896** *Geogr. Jrnl.* VII. 221 An account of the position of Spelæology, the science of caverns, in geography.

So **speleo'logical** *a.*, of or pertaining to speleology; **spele'ologist**, a student of, or authority on, cave-research; also, an explorer of caves.

1895 *Knowledge* Oct. 223/2 It was shown that *spelæological investigation would be of value to many branches of natural science. **1900** *Geogr. Jrnl.* XV. 78 The progress of speleological exploration in Yorkshire. **1895** MARTEL in *Rep. 6th Geogr. Congr.* (1896) 722, I hope.. that the English *speleologists may be.. incited to renewed investigations. **1895** *Knowledge* Oct. 223/2 Much remains to be done by British spelæologists. **1955** *Times* 20 Aug. 5/3 A team of Spanish speleologists from Pamplona.. have completed a 10-day exploration of the Larra region of the Pyrenees. **1971** *Daily Tel.* 1 May 11/4 Speleologists (or cavemen) should explore the Dove's Nest in Borrowdale.

speleothem (ˈspiːliːəʊθɛm). *Geol.* [f. Gr. σπήλαιον cave + θέμα that which is laid down, deposit.] Any structure which is formed in a cave by the deposition of minerals from water, e.g. a stalactite, stalagmite, etc.

1952 G. W. MOORE in *Nat. Speleol. Soc. News* June 2/1 In an effort to relieve the ambiguities of 'formation', the term speleothem is proposed... It is suggested that the word be used as a general term for secondary mineral deposits formed from water in caves, such as stalactites, helictites, rimstone terraces. **1968** *Nature* 6 July 49/1 Temperature dependent fluctuations in the $^{18}O/^{16}O$ composition of calcite deposited on speleothems could be used to fill this gap in the present understanding of past climates. **1976** W. B. WHITE in Ford & Cullingford *Sci. of Speleology* viii. 271 There is a competition between shapes guided by the flow path of the solution and shapes guided by the particular mineral and its crystal habit. This gives rise to two broad classes of speleothems, drip-stone and flowstone forms and erratic forms. **1980** *Cambr. Encycl. Archaeol.* 53/1 Methods involving the measurement of different isotopes are being widely applied to derive long climatic records from ice cores, cave deposits like stalagmites (speleothems) and tree rings.

speler, var. or obs. f. SPELLER[3].

spelican, var. SPILLIKIN.

spelk (spɛlk), *sb.* Chiefly *north.* (and *Sc.*). Also 1 spelc, 5 spelke, 7 spelck. [OE. *spelc* (also *spilc*), = WFlem. *spelke* (De Bo), Norw. *spjelk*, Icel. *spelka*, †*spjalk*, related to MDu. *spalke* (Kilian *spalcke*), *spalc* (Du. *spalk*), LG. *spalke*, *spalk* splinter, chip.]

1. A surgical splint.

c **1000** *Saxon Leechd.* II. 68 þonne recce he þa ban swa he swiþost mæȝe, do spelc to. **1691** RAY *N.C. Words* (ed. 2) 149 A Spelck, *Fascia.* **1703** in THORESBY *Let. to Ray.* **1855-** in north. dial. glossaries, etc.

2. A splinter or chip; a small strip of wood.

c **1440** *Promp. Parv.* 468/1 Spelke, *fissula.* **1623** MARKHAM *Country Housew. Gard.* x, The lesse your Spelkes are, the lesse is the waste of your hony, and the more easily will they draw, when you take your Bees. **1788-** in northern glossaries. **1894** *Rev. Reviews* Sept. 256 A belated attempt to extract a small spelk from the hand of the Irish peasant. **1899** R. WALLACE *Schoolmaster* 26 A schoolboy carefully gathered up the larger 'spelks' of the tram of the broken vehicle.

3. A thatching-rod; = SPAR *sb.*[4]

1563 *Richmond Wills* (Surtees) 169, iij. spelks and iij. carres, xix d. **1578** *Ibid.* 282 Woodd and bords.. with stangs, hots, and cares, and spelks and latts. **1712** in *Trans. Cumbld. & Westm. Archæol. Soc.* (N.S.) III. 108 For 184 bottles of thatch... For spelks two hundred and twenty seven. **1781** J. HUTTON *Tour to Caves* (ed. 2) Gloss. 96 *Spelks*, small sticks to fix on thatch with. **1828-** in Yorkshire and Lancs. glossaries, etc.

4. In various uses: (see quots.).

1828 CARR *Craven Gloss.*, *Spelk*,.. a spoke of a wheel. **1829** BROCKETT *N.C. Gloss.* (ed. 2), *Spelk*, a little, slender creature; used as a term of reproach. **1875** KNIGHT *Dict. Mech.* 2264/1 *Spelk*,.. a rod in a loom.

spelk (spɛlk), *v.*[1] Now *Sc.* and *north. dial.* Also 1 spelcean, 5 spelkyn, spelke. [OE. *spelcan* (also *spilcan*), = WFlem. *spelken* (Du. *spalken*), OIcel. *spelkja*, Norw. *spjelka*, Sw. *spjälka* (MSw. *spiälca*), f. *spelc*, etc.: see prec.] *trans.* To fasten with a spelk; *esp.* to bind or join (a broken limb, bone, etc.) by means of splints.

c **1000** *Sax. Leechd.* II. 6 ȝif scancan forade synd,.. hu mon spelcean scyle. *c* **1440** *Promp. Parv.* 468/1 Spelte [*v.r.* spelke, spelkyn] broke bonys or oþer þyngys. **1637** RUTHERFORD *Lett.* (1881) ciii. 199 Many broken legs since Adam's day hath He spelked. *c* **1700** KENNETT *MS. Lansdowne 1033* (Halliw.), To *spelk* in Yorkshire, to set a broken bone. **1802** in SIBBALD *Chron. S.P.* Gloss. **1828-** in north. dial. and Sc. glossaries (Yks., Lancs., Shetland). **1889** W. WESTALL *Birch Dene* II. ix. 140 The doctor bound up and spelked his maimed fingers.

Hence **'spelking** *vbl. sb.*

c **1440** *Promp. Parv.* 468/1 Spellynge [*v.r.* spelkynge], broke bonys or oþer thyngys, *fissulatus.*

†**spelk**, *v.*[2] *Obs.*$^{-0}$ [Of obscure origin: cf. SPELT *v.* and Sc. *spilkings* split peas.] *trans.* To bruise (beans).

1483 *Cath. Angl.* 28/1 Benes spelked, *fabefrese. Ibid.* 353/2 Spelkyd benes,.. *fabefrese.* [**1796** S. PEGGE *Derbicisms* Ser. I. 66 (E.D.S.), To *spelch* horse-beans, to bruise them in a mill. Obsolete.]

spell (spɛl), *sb.*[1] Also 1-7 spel, 2-5 spelle. [OE. *spel*, *spell*, = OS. *spel*, *spell-*, MDu. *-spel*, OHG. (and MHG.) *spel*, *spell-* (G. dial. *spill*, *spiell* gossip, G. *-spiel*), ON. *spjall*, Goth. *spill* recital, tale, etc.]

†**1. a.** Without article: Discourse, narration, speech; *occas.* idle talk, fable. *Obs.*

Beowulf 873 Secg eft ongan.. on sped wrecan spel ȝerade. *c* **888** K. ÆLFRED *Boeth.* xiii, þa ongon he eft secgean spel & þus cwæð. *c* **1000** *Sax. Leechd.* III. 232 Ðæt nis to spelle ac elles to rædenne þam þe hit licað. *c* **1175** *Lamb. Hom.* 153 To lusten hoker, & spel, & leow [*read* leoþ], & oðer þing þet boð to-ȝeines godes heste. *c* **1205** LAY. 12093 Nes hit neowhær itald on songe no on spelle. *c* **1290** *S. Eng. Leg.* I. 329 ȝweþer þis beo soth,.. oþur us þinchez ase in metingue, oþur in manere of spelle? *a* **1310** in Wright *Lyric P.* xxv. 68 Thine peynes rykene hit were long, Ne may hem tellen spel ne song. *c* **1375** *Sc. Leg. Saints* xxiii. (*Seven Sleepers*) 362 Wes nane þat euire hard tel of ony of þame in red na spel. *c* **1425** AUDELAY *XI Pains of Hell* 321 þen seide vr lord to hem in spelle.

†**b.** *to set spell on end*, to begin to speak. *Obs.*

a **1300** *Siriz* 62, I shal setten spel on ende, And tellen þe al. *a* **1300** *Cursor M.* 1295 Seth þen sette him spell [*Trin.* tale] on-end And tald warfor þat he was send. *c* **1440** *Alph. Tales* 84 He sett spell on ende & tolde hym all þe cace.

†**2. a.** A discourse or sermon; a narrative or tale; also (OE.), a subject of discourse. *Obs.*

Beowulf 2898 Lyt swiȝode niwra spella.. ac he soðlice sæȝde ofer ealle. *c* **888** K. ÆLFRED *Boeth.* xxvi. §3 Ða se Wisdom ða þis spel asæd hæfde. *Ibid.* xxxi. §1 We ȝeheordon ȝeo ȝeara on ealdum spellum þæt [etc.]. *c* **1000** ÆLFRIC *Gram.* Pref. (Z.) 2 Syððan ic ða twa bec awende on hundeahtatiȝum spellum. *c* **1200** ORMIN 8026 þurrh þatt teȝȝ cwemmdenn Jesu Crist Wiþþ spelless & wiþþ dedess. *a* **1250** *Owl & Night.* 1794 Ne can ic eu na more telle; her nys na more of þisse spelle. *a* **1300** *Cursor M.* 19655 (Edinb.), Mikil he lernid.. Of spellis þat he siþin spac. *c* **1320** *Sir Tristr.* 2768 þe geaunt herd þat spelle, For þi him was ful wa. *a* **1400-50** *Alexander* 3840 ȝit for na spell at he spirid spek wald þai neuire. *a* **1450** MYRC 170 Take gode hede on thys spel. *a* **1500** *Tale of Harper* 4 in Hazl. *E.P.P.* III. 44 A man may dryfe forth the day.. With harpyng and pipyng and other mery spellis.

1612 DEKKER *If it be not Good* Wks. 1873 III. 282 There with holy spels mens soules they cherish. *a* **1617** BAYNE *On Eph.* (1658) 115 The Gospel.. may well bee called a good spell or word. *a* **1653** GOUGE *Comm. Heb.* xiii. 9 Gospel, that is a good spell, a good speech.

†**b.** With possessive pronouns, etc. *Obs.*

a **1000** *Daniel* 479 Ece drihten.. se ðe him dom forȝeaf.. þam þe his spel berað. *c* **1175** *Lamb. Hom.* 27 Bi hulche monna seið drihten in his spelle. *c* **1200** ORMIN 185 To turrnenn.. þe suness þurrh hiss hallȝhe spell Till þeȝȝre faderr herrte. *a* **1300** *Cursor M.* 5332 þe king badd all to listen þan, And þus iacob his spell be-gan. *c* **1386** CHAUCER *Sir Thopas* 182 Now hold your mouth.. And herkneth to my spelle. *a* **1450** MYRC 1443 But he take hyre in hys spelle, þen he may þe name mynge.

1579 E. K. *Gloss. to Spenser's Sheph. Cal.* Mar. 54 And herehence I thinke is named the gospell, as it were Gods spell or worde. **1642** H. MORE *Song of Soul* II. III. iv. 31 So many myriads tumble down to hell, Although partakers of Gods holy spell.

3. a. A set of words, a formula or verse, supposed to possess occult or magical powers; a charm or incantation; a means of accomplishing enchantment or exorcism. (Cf. the earlier NIGHT-SPELL.)

1579 E. K. *Gloss. to Spenser's Sheph. Cal.* Mar. 54 Spell is a kinde of verse or charme, that in elder tymes they vsed often to say ouer euery thing, that they would haue preserued, as the Nightspel for theeues, and the woodspell. **1598** SHAKS. *Merry W.* IV. ii. 185 She workes by Charmes, by Spels, by th'Figure, & such dawbry as this is. **1615** G. SANDYS *Trav.* 28 Where the spirits of the deceassed, by certaine spels.. were accustomed to be raised. **1651** HOBBES *Leviath.* III. xxxvii. 236 If therefore Enchantment be not, as many think it, a working of strange effects by spells, and words; but Imposture [etc.]. **1727** DE FOE *Syst. Magic* I. vi. 153 The diabolical spells and charms of the pagan magicians. **1761** GRAY *Odin* 59 Prophetess, my spell obey. **1810** SCOTT *Lady of L.* III. vi, Whatever tells Of magic, cabala, and spells. **1848** MRS. JAMESON *Sacr. & Leg. Art.* (1850) 138 Hermogenes.. bound Philetus by his diabolical spells, so that he could not move hand or foot. **1894** J. MACINTOSH *Ayrshire Nts. Entert.* iii. 32 The Norwegians believed it to have been raised by the spells of the Scottish witches.

b. *transf.* and *fig.* An occult or mysterious power or influence; a fascinating or enthralling charm.

1592 NASHE *Four Lett. Confut.* 35 His only care was to haue a spel in his purse to coniure vp a good cuppe of wine with at all times. **1599** B. JONSON *Ev. Man out of Hum.* II. vi, Your good face is the witch and your apparell the spells that bring all the pleasures of the world into their circle. **1618** FLETCHER *Loyal Subj.* II. ii, Thinking what strange spells these Rings have, And how they work with some. **1668** COWLEY *Ess. Verses & Pr.*, *Garden* v, These are the Spels that to kind Sleep invite. **1766** FORDYCE *Serm. Yng. Wm.* I. vii. 302 Let it be remembered however, that the triumph of their rivals is commonly.. short. The spell on which it is founded is soon broke. **1784** COWPER *Task* VI. 98 Books are not seldom talismans and spells, By which the magic art of shrewder wits Holds an unthinking multitude enthrall'd. *a* **1817** JANE AUSTEN *Lady Susan* xxxiv. (1879) 279 The spell is removed; I see you as you are. **1856** *N. Brit. Rev.* XXVI. 218 The ordinary devices by which the novelist keeps us under his spell. **1865** KINGSLEY *Herew.* xii, The spell was on him,.. that of woman's tact.

c. A device, trick. *rare*$^{-1}$

1728 RAMSAY *Last Sp. Miser* ix, To hane in candle I had a spell Baith cheap and bright.

4. *attrib.* and *Comb.* **a.** With pa. pples., as ***spell-banned***, ***-caught***, ***-enslaved***, ***-raised***, ***-riveted***, ***-soaked***, etc.

1610 SHAKS. *Temp.* V. i. 61 There stand For you are Spell-stopt. **1649** G. DANIEL *Trinarch.*, *Hen. IV*, ccxxii, Soe you may Vnderstand Spel-Sprung Castles,.. if you haue the Key. **1691** DRYDEN *K. Arthur* III. ii, I cannot stir; I am spell-caught by Philidel. **1805** H. K. WHITE *Let. to C. Lofft* 10 Sept., By dark wood, or hamlet far retired, Spell-struck, with thee I loiter'd. **1817** CAMPBELL *Reullura* in *Theodric*, etc. 146 He.. stood at the statue's foot, Spell-riveted to the spot. **1828** *Blackw. Mag.* XXIV. 481 The gay attire of spell-raised loveliness. **1867** JEAN INGELOW *Story of Doom* VII. 24 Japhet strove Vainly to take away his spell-set eyes. **1896** *Dublin Rev.* Apr. 339 The legions.. dissolved, like a spell-banned host. **1938** DYLAN THOMAS *Let.* 14 Oct. (1966) 210 A still room in a spellsoaked house. **1955** J. R. R. TOLKIEN *Return of King* VI. iv. 227 The creatures of Sauron, orc or troll or beast spell-enslaved, ran hither and thither.

b. With agent-nouns and vbl. sbs., as ***spell-monger***, ***-mutterer***, ***-speaker***; ***spell-casting***, ***-weaving***.

1625 HART *Anat. Ur.* II. xi. 123, I say nothing of our Spel-mongers, curing by characters, figure-casting, with a world of other forbidden trash. **1633** —— *Diet of Diseased* Introd. 22 Many.. have often recourse to Wizards, Spelmongers [etc.]. **1821** SCOTT *Pirate* xxvi, We shall soon see how the old spell-mutterer will receive us. **1845** FORD *Handbk. Spain* I. 48 A person who has visited these spell-casting sites. **1883** STALLYBRASS tr. *Grimm's Teut. Myth.* III. 1109 Many books.. couple together sieve-turners and spell-speakers. **1894** *Westm. Gaz.* 6 Sept. 2/1 The capture and the spell-weaving proceed as usual.

c. With sbs., as ***spell-craft***, ***-glance***, ***-word***, etc.

1817 MOORE *Lalla Rookh*, *Fire Worshippers* (ed. 2) 206 His only spell-word, Liberty! *Ibid.* 249 Like those Peri isles of light, That hang by spell-work in the air. **1817** SCOTT *Harold* II. iii, To its dread aim her spell-glance flew. **1844** *Ayrshire Wreath* 176 Then comes the spell-craft of the mind To knit the soul [etc.].

d. With adjs., as ***spell-free***, ***-like***, ***-proof***.

1799 SHERIDAN *Pizarro* IV. iii, The spell-like arts, by which this hypocrite first undermin'd.. a guileless heart! **1801** LEYDEN *Elfin King* Poems (1875) 168 Except on his faulchion arm Spell-proof he bear.. The holy Trefoil's charm. **1837** CARLYLE *Fr. Rev.* II. VI. i, A France spell-free, a Revolution saved.

spell (spɛl), *sb.*[2] Now *dial.* Also 6-9 spel, 7 spelle. [Perh. a later form of SPELD *sb.*, but cf. G. *spellen* to split, cleave.]

1. A splinter, chip, fragment.

1545 ASCHAM *Toxoph.* II. (Arb.) 121 To swadle a bowe much about wyth bandes, verye seldome dothe anye good, excepte it be to kepe downe a spel in the backe. **1591** HARINGTON *Orl. Fur.* XIX. lxi, The speares in spels and sundry peeces flew As if they had beene little sticks or cane. **1610** MARKHAM *Masterp.* II. cli. 450 This will heale any bone or spell, or any other stubbe. **1612** *Ench. Med.* 100 Remoue the sharpe spels and splinters of bones. **1674** RAY *N. Co. Words* 44 A *Spell* or *speal*, a Splinter. **1811** FAREY *Derbyshire* I. 250 Large Slapits, Spels or fragments fly off, sometimes with loud explosions. **1829-** in northern glossaries.

2. A bar, rail, or rung.

1559 *Dunmow Churchw. MS.* 43 Item, to John Hutt for spells for the bells, iid ob. **1641** BEST *Farm. Bks.* (Surtees) 15 To a barre belongeth two heads,..into which the 4 spelles are to bee putte:..the spelles are usually 6, 7, or sometimes 8 foote in length. **1796** W. H. MARSHALL *Yorksh.* (ed. 2) II. 346 *Spel* (vulg. *speyl*); a bar. **1847-** in dial. glossaries (Linc., Yks., Cumb.). **1864** GILBERT & CHURCHILL *Dolomite Mount.* 230 Upon a face of rock were two long beams of wood, with, instead of spells, notches cut in the timbers at irregular intervals.

3. The trap used in the game of ***spell and knur*** (also ***knor***, ***null***, etc.). Cf. KNUR 3.

1781 J. HUTTON *Tour to Caves* (ed. 2) Gloss. 96 *Spel-and-knor*, the game of trap-stick. *a* **1809** HOLCROFT *Mem.* (1816) I. 61 Spell and null, bandy, prison-bars, and other field games. **1816** *Sporting Mag.* XLVIII. 178 The games most common at Newmarket, were fives, spell and null, marbles, [and] chuck-farthing. **1828** CARR *Craven Gloss.* **1862** C. C. ROBINSON *Dial. Leeds* 338 Underneath, at the four corners, are 'prods' wherewith the 'spell' is fixed into the earth. **1868** *N. & Q.* 4th Ser. I. 325.

spell (spɛl), *sb.*[3] Also 7 **spel**. [Related to SPELL *v.*[3], and perh. directly representing OE. *ȝespelia* substitute (cf. *spala* SPALE *sb.*[1]).]

1. A set of persons taking a turn of work in order to relieve others; a relay, relief-gang, or shift. Now *rare*.

1593 P. NICHOLS *Drake Revived* (1628) 27 Rowing in the eddy..by spels, without ceasing, each company their halfe houre glasse. **1602** CAREW *Cornwall* 10 b, In most places, their toyle is so extreame, as they cannot endure it aboue foure houres in a day, but are succeeded by spels. **1627** CAPT. SMITH *Seaman's Gram.* ii. 9 In pumping they vse to take spels, that is, fresh men to releeue them. **1628-9** DIGBY *Voy. Medit.* (Camden) 87 Yet I sent them an other fresh spell of men. **1851** G. BLYTH *Remin. Mission. Life* II. 108 The fifteen or twenty persons who constituted the spell refused to go on.

2. a. A turn of work taken by a person or set of persons in relief of another.

a **1625** *Nomenclator Navalis* (Harl. MS. 2301) s.v., As when they pump a hundred strokes,..they call it a spell. **1626** CAPT. SMITH *Accid. Yng. Seaman* 30 To row a spell, hold-water, trim the boate. **1644** MANWAYRING *Seaman's Dict.* 79 At a Chaine-Pump, the Spels goe by Glasses. **1683** MOXON *Mech. Exerc., Printing* xxiv. ¶ 15 The First now takes his spell at Pulling: for the First and Second take their spell of Pulling and Beating an agreed number of Tokens. **1769** FALCONER *Dict. Marine* (1780) s.v., Such are the spells, to the hand-lead in sounding; to the pump;..and to steer the ship; which last..is generally called the *trick*. **1838** HOLLOWAY *Prov. Dict., Spell*, a turn, as one workman says to another:—'now you take a spell'. **1849** CUPPLES *Green Hand* xi. (1856) 112, I stays aboard the brig, works my spell in her, an' takes my trick at the hellum. **1886** STEVENSON *Kidnapped* xvi, The men gave way..with a good will, the passengers taking spells to help them.

b. *to give a spell*, to relieve another by taking a turn of work.

1750 BLANCKLEY *Nav. Expos.* 156 To give a Spell, is all one as to say, Work in such a one's Room. **1825** J. NEAL *Bro. Jonathan* II. xviii. 138 One or two..were continually offering to give him a 'spell'—or a 'lift'—or a 'turn' [at counting his money]. **1829** B. HALL *Travels in N.A.* I. 188 A poor old negro..begged to be taken in, and offered to give me a spell when I became tired.

c. Without article, in phr. ***spell and spell*** (***about***), ***spell for spell***; ***to keep*** or ***take spell***.

1797 S. JAMES *Narr. Voy.* 202 They re-bailed out our boat ..spell and spell about. **1799** *Hull Advertiser* 27 July 4/2 His faithful companions..worked incessantly (spell and spell) for nine days. **1828** *Life Planter Jamaica* 36 Plato takes spell after him. *Ibid.*, Langbey was keeping spell, or in other words, had charge of the negroes employed in preparing the sugar. **1837** MARRYAT *Dog Fiend* liv, We plied the pumps, 'twas spell and spell. **1855** [ROBINSON] *Whitby Gloss.* s.v., Spell for spell is fair play.

3. a. A continuous course or period *of* some work, occupation, or employment; a turn or bout *at* something. Also without const.

1706 E. WARD *Wooden World Diss.* (1708) 34 He.. believes there is no more Sin in taking a Spell with a Whore, than in pumping a leaky Vessel. **1804** NELSON 4 Nov. in Nicolas *Disp.* (1846) VI. 257 The Termagant Sloop will be going to Lisbon—she has had a long spell of service. **1824** SOUTHEY in C. C. Southey *Life* (1850) V. 187, I have lately taken a pleasant spell at it, and have something more than a volume ready. **1857** HUGHES *Tom Brown* I. ii, The closeness of the men in action to one another..makes a spell at back-swording a very noble sight. **1885** *Manch. Exam.* 18 Mar. 5/3 Twenty-five years without a holiday except on Sunday is certainly a remarkable spell of assiduous labour.

b. *dial.* and *Austral.* An interval or period of repose or relaxation; a rest.

Examples from 1863 to 1975 may be found in *Dict. Newfoundland English* (1982).

c **1845** J. TUCKER *Ralph Rashleigh* (1929) xi. 146 Both men took a hoe and gave the children a spell. **1847** J. O. HALLIWELL *Dict. Archaic & Provincial Words* 78½ *Spell*, ..pleasure; relaxation. *Somerset*. **1852** MUNDY *Antipodes* (1857) 83 Your carriage horses will be all the better for a 'spell', (a rest). **1862** J. S. DOBIE *Jrnl.* 10 Sept. in *S. Afr. Jrnl.* (1945) 23 Invited to stay and give my horse a day's spell. **1865** TUCKER *Austr. Story* i. 84 The only recompense was..to light his pipe and have a 'spell'. **1867** M. A. BARKER *Station Life in N.Z.* 128 We were all so breathless that a 'spell' (do you know that means 'rest'?) would have been most acceptable. **1900** H. LAWSON *On Track* 107 He did not go back to work that night; he took a spell. **1931** G. L. NUTE *Voyageur* 96 Every five miles or so a halt was made to rest the dogs and to allow the men to smoke. These stops were termed 'spells' or 'pipes', and the voyageurs spoke of a day's journey as being so many spells or pipes. **1940** F. SARGESON *Man & his Wife* (1944) 30 About half-way back to the shore he took a spell. **1954** B. MILES *Stars my Blanket* xix. 141 We stopped for a 'spell' in the sandy bed, spreading out ground-sheets in the shade of the trees that lined the centre of it. **1972** *Regional Lang. Studies Newfoundland* May 9 *Spell*, a period of rest or a short sleep. Used..in Newfoundland and in Anglo-Irish. **1977** *N.Z. Herald* 8 Jan. 1-9/2 Marie Kay has been back racing only a little over a month following a long, enforced spell.

c. ***spell oh!*** (or ***ho!***), used as a call or signal, usu. to rest or cease working; also = prec.

1837 MARRYAT *Dog Fiend* I. ix. 94 'Come now,' said Coble, tossing off his glass, 'spell oh!—let's have a song while they take their breath'. **1841** R. H. DANA *Seaman's Man.* 124 *Spell ho!*..used as an order or request to be relieved at work by another. **1891** MORRIS *News fr. Nowhere* 51 So he stayed his pick and sang out, 'Spell ho, mates! here are neighbours want to get past'. **1900** H. LAWSON *On Track* 97 Bill..was having a spell-oh under the cask when the white rooster crowed.

4. a. A period or space of time of indefinite length; usu. with adjs. denoting duration, as *long*, *short*, etc.

1728 MORGAN *Algiers* II. iv. 265 The Corsairs met with a brisk Reception and were warmly entertained for a good Spell. **1767** GIBBON *Let. to Holroyd* 29 Apr., I hope to take a pretty long spell in town. **1775** ROMANS *Florida* App. 56 Those unlucky persons..have lain that long spell wearing and tearing vessels and rigging. **1836** MARRYAT *Midsh. Easy* xxvi, A hope that Mr. Easy would take his share of the duty, now that he had had such a spell on shore. **1860** MAYNE REID *Hunter's Feast* xxii, It only halted a short spell, and then.. it run up to the carcass. **1870** MISS BRIDGMAN *R. Lynne* I. xii. 184 Thirty years! It is a good spell off a man's life.

b. A period having a certain character or spent in a particular way.

1830 SOUTHEY *Lett.* (1856) IV. 175 The very sight of you ..would go far towards giving these poor girls a spell of better health than..at present. **1885** 'MRS. ALEXANDER' *At Bay* i, Then came a spell of wandering, of high play, of rage for costly excitement, which..beggared him in a few years. **1885** R. W. DIXON *Hist. Ch. Eng.* xix. III. 330 After a grievous spell of eighteen months on board the French galleys.

c. ***by spells***, at intervals, now and again.

1788 *Massachusetts Spy* 4 Sept. 3/2 It had..rained by spells for three days before. **1821** in Cobbett *Rur. Rides* (1885) I. 2 To-day the fog came by spells. **1854** THOREAU *Walden* xiii, I had an old axe..with which by spells in winter days..I played about the stumps. **1883** *Harper's Mag.* Mar. 602/1 All day by 'spells' I have been out helping Jack make the garden.

d. ***for a spell***, for a time. In *U.S.* without prep.; also ***a spell ago***, some time ago.

(*a*) **1834** [SEBA SMITH] *Lett. J. Downing* xxx. (1835) 208 Mahogany was as cheap as pine boards was a spell ago. *c* **1850** 'DOW JR.' in Jerdan *Yankee Hum.* (1853) 88 That woman who broomed me out of the house a spell ago.
(*b*) **1745** D. GIDDINGS *Jrnl.* 27 May in *Essex Inst. Hist. Coll.* (1912) XLVIII. 299, I..continued in ye Trench a Spell. **1834** [SEBA SMITH] *Lett. J. Downing* xxvii. (1835) 179 So I whistled Yankee Doodle a spell. **1848** LOWELL *Biglow P.* Poems 1890 II. 11 He stood a spell on one foot fust, Then stood a spell on tother. **1884** *Harper's Mag.* Feb. 410/2 He tried doctorin' a spell.
(*c*) **1862** TROLLOPE *N. Amer.* I. 186, I wish those masons ..could be driven to the labour market of Western America for a spell. **1890** *Melbourne Argus* 7 June 4/1, I..was told by an honest and sensible doctor to..get out in the bush and work for a spell.

e. *N.Z.* One of the periods into which a game of rugby is divided.

1900 *N.Z. Illustr. Mag.* III. 237/1 Usually in the second spell, when play is getting more exciting. **1934** A. E. MULGAN *Spur of Morning* I. iii. 23 The school won a hard game by six to nil, a try in each spell.

f. *Cricket.* A period or series of overs during a session of play in which a bowler bowls unchanged.

1976 J. SNOW *Cricket Rebel* 77 On that last afternoon at Colchester I took three quick wickets in my first spell. **1977** *World of Cricket Monthly* June 27/3 He was brilliantly caught by Richards at second-slip off Croft's first ball of a new spell.

5. a. A continuous period or stretch *of* a specified kind of weather.

1728 T. SMITH *Jrnl.* (1849) 265 For several days past, there has been a spell of comfortable weather. **1733** *Ibid.* 266 This whole week has been a spell of warm weather. **1775** WASHINGTON *Lett. to J. Reed* (1852) 32 The setting in of a severe spell of cold weather, and a considerable fall of snow. **1808** SOUTHEY in C. C. Southey *Life* (1850) III. 163 We are now having a spell of wind and rain. **1840** R. H. DANA *Bef. Mast* iii, We have now had a long 'spell' of fine weather. **1897** *Jrnl. R. Agric. Soc.* Dec. 663 If a spell of cold wind.. should prevail.

attrib. **1868** *Pall Mall G.* 28 July 4 On the supposition that such 'spell-weather', as the Americans call it, is to last for ever.

b. With adjs., as *cold*, *hot*, *dry*, *wet*, etc.

1740 T. SMITH *Jrnl.* (1849) 268, I believe no man ever knew so winter-like a spell so early in the year. **1797** JEFFERSON *Writ.* (1859) IV. 157 You wish to know the state of the air here during the late cold spell. **1817-8** COBBETT *Resid. U.S.* (1822) 286 The hot spells as well as the cold spells, seldom last more than three days. **1860** MAURY *Phys. Geog.* iv. §241 The phenomena of cold and warm 'spells' are often observed in the United States. **1887** *Boston* (Mass.) *Jrnl.* 23 Aug. 5 Everybody found smoking on the streets.. during the dry spell was liable to be arrested.

6. *U.S.* A period of being indisposed, out of sorts, or irritable; an attack or fit of illness or nervous excitement.

1856 KANE *Arct. Expl.* II. iii. 47 An attack of partial epilepsy; one of those strange indescribable spells, fits, seizures, whatever name the jargon gives them, which indicate deep disturbance. **1869** MRS. STOWE *Oldtown* xvi, When Hepsy does get beat out she has *spells*, and she goes on awful, and they last day arter day. **1889** GUNTER *That Frenchman* xvii. 210 Oh! blues, hysteria, headache, tantrums —any ill that's particularly feminine, we call spells in America.

spell (spɛl), *sb.*[4] *colloq.* [f. SPELL *v.*[2]] A way or mode of spelling a word.

1702 C. MATHER *Magn. Chr.* VII. v. (1852) 546 There were eighteen horrid false spells..in one short note that I received from him. **1801** *Monthly Mag.* XII. 299 Why should this spell (as school children say, and, I think, rightly, for mode of spelling) be authorized?

spell, *sb.*[5] *Cant.* [a. Du. or Flem. *spel* (G. *spiel*), or abbrev. of SPELLKEN.] A playhouse or theatre. Also *attrib.*

1812 J. H. VAUX *Flash Dict., Spell*, the play-house. **1819** —— *Mem.* II. 199 They say, the push, as the push at the spell doors. **1865** *Slang Dict.* 241 'Precious rum squeeze at the spell,' *i.e.* a good evening's work at the theatre.

spell, *v.*[1] *Obs.* or *dial.* Forms: 1 **spellian**, **-iȝan** (**spillian**), 2-4 **spellen**, 3-5 **spelle**, 4-6 **spel**, 4- **spell**. [OE. *spellian* (f. *spel* SPELL *sb.*[1]), = OHG. *-spellôn* (MHG. *spellen*, G. dial. *spellen*, *spillen*), MDu. and MLG. *spellen*, Goth. *spillôn*, ON. *spjalla*, to talk, discourse, etc.

It is doubtful how far some modern dialect uses of *spell* represent this word.]

1. *intr.* To discourse or preach; to talk, converse, or speak.

c **888** K. ÆLFRED *Boeth.* xvi. § 1 Þa ongan he eft spellian & þus cwæþ. *c* **950** *Lindisf. Gosp.* Luke xxiv. 15 Miððy [hia] woeron spellendo *vel* ȝespelledon. *c* **1000** *Sax. Leechd.* III. 202 Mid deadum spellian, ȝestrion hit ȝetacnað. *a* **1200** *Vices & Virtues* 121 Ða ðe Crist gann arst to spellen,..ða sade he [etc.]. *a* **1300** *Cursor M.* 8520 He þat mikel has for to tell þe scortliker he aght to spell. *a* **1375** *Lay Folks Mass Bk.* App. iv. 508 Iesus..dude him aȝeyn in paradis,..Wiþ speche as I ow spelle. *a* **1450** *Le Morte Arth.* 3722 What helpeth lenger for to spelle? *c* **1450** HOLLAND *Howlat* 99 He suld spedely speike, and spair nocht to spell.

b. Const. *of* (the thing spoken of).

c **1200** ORMIN 6389 Þa lifess þatt icc habbe ȝuw Summ del nu spelledd offe. *a* **1300** *Cursor M.* 95 Qua-sa will of hyr fayrnes spell, Find he sal inogh to tell. *c* **1330** R. BRUNNE *Chron. Wace* (Rolls) 10613 Til Domesday men schalle spelle ..of Arthures dedes. *a* **1400-50** *Bk. Curtasye* 379 in *Babees Bk.*, Now of marschalle of halle wylle I spelle, And what falle to hys offyce now wylle y telle. *c* **1450** LOVELICH *Grail* xxxvii. 455 I beleve ryht wel That this is he of whom ȝe spelle. **1530** in Ellis *Orig. Lett.* Ser. III. II. 186 I assure your Grace shall sease and put to sylence sum persons that moche spelyth of the same.

2. *trans.* To utter, declare, relate, tell.

a **1000** *Boeth. Metr.* Proem 4 Him wæs lust micel ðæt he ðiossum leodum leoð spellode. *c* **1200** ORMIN Ded. 311 I wollde..þatt all Ennglisshe lede..Wiþþ tunge shollde spellenn itt. *c* **1290** *S. Eng. Leg.* I. 112 Acke of seint thomas him-selue þat beste cometh nou to spelle. *c* **1320** *Cast. Love* 692 No tonge ne may hit telle, Ne þouȝt þenche, ne mouþ spelle. **1390** GOWER *Conf.* II. 20 I can noght thanne unethes spelle That I wende altherbest have rad. **1426** AUDELAY *Poems* 28 He that spekys and spedys noȝt, he spellys the wynd. *c* **1485** *Digby Myst.* (1882) v. 275 Blessed is that soule that this speche spelles. **1509** HAWES *Past. Pleas.* XVI. (Percy Soc.) 68 Pryvely I did his lesson spel, Sayeng to him, my chance and desteny Of al other is the moste unhappy.

spell (spɛl), *v.*[2] Pa. t. and pa. pple. **spelled**, **spelt**. Also 4-5 **spelle**, 5 **spellyn**; 5-7 **spel**. [ad. OF. *espeller* (also *espeler*, mod.F. *épeler*: see SPELE *v.*[2]), f. the Germanic stem *spell-*: see prec. and SPELL *sb.*[1] The earlier OF. type **espeldre* is represented by SPELDER *v.*[1] Du. and Flem. *spellen*, WFris. *spelle*, *spjelle*, in this sense may also be from French, rather than directly connected with SPELL *v.*[1]]

I. *trans.* **1. a.** To read (a book, etc.) letter by letter; to peruse, or make out, slowly or with difficulty.

a **1300** *Cursor M.* 14692 Your aun bok yee can noght spell. *c* **1400** *Trevisa's Higden* (Rolls) VII. 333 Lanfranc..took hym a þing with letter [L. *abecedarium litterarum*] for to spel. *c* **1440** *Promp. Parv.* 468/1 Spellyn (*S.* letters), *sillabico*. **1530** PALSGR. 728/1 He hath bene at scole thys halfe yere and yet he can nat spell his pater noster. **1687** MIÈGE *Gt. Fr. Dict.* II. s.v., He begins to spell the Letters.

1780 *Mirror* No. 75, What must be the state of him who sits down to spell the newspapers with the determined resolution of believing whatever he sees in print? **1807** CRABBE *Par. Reg.* III. 298 As they approach to spell the age, the name, And all the titles of th' illustrious dame. **1825** T. HOOK *Sayings* Ser. II. *Passion and Princ.* vi, Reading all the newspapers, spelling the red-book and the directory. **1850** THACKERAY *Pendennis* v, He was spelling the paper, with the help of his lips.

b. With *out* or *over*.

c **1813** S. SMITH in Lady Holland *Mem. S. Smith* (1855) I. vii. 157 He..spelt over the county paper on Sundays. **1820** SHELLEY *Witch Atl.* xxvi, All day the wizard lady sate aloof, Spelling out scrolls of dread antiquity. **1864** THACKERAY *D. Duval* i. (1869) 4 It used to be my lot as a boy to spell out my lady Viscountess's letters to her.

c. To make (one's way) letter by letter in reading.

1849 MACAULAY *Hist. Eng.* i. I. 45 Not one man in five hundred could have spelled his way through a psalm.

2. *fig.* **a.** To discover or find out, to guess or suspect, by close study or observation. Also with *out*.

1587 GOLDING *De Mornay* i. 8 A plaine booke laide open to all men..to reade, and (as yee would say) euen to spell God therein. **1635** JACKSON *Creed* VIII. xxii. 252 The babes then did spel the Prophets meaning not amisse. **1691** tr. *Emiliane's Observ. Journ. Naples* 82 Spelling nothing good from it, he went immediately to the Door of the Church. **1707** NORRIS *Treat. Humility* vii. 324 One may make a shift to spell out who is the gentleman, and who it is that would only be thought so. **1879** SPURGEON *Serm.* XXV. 333 That there should be a God, heathens might spell out.

b. To make out, understand, decipher, or comprehend, by study. Also with *out*.

1635 JACKSON *Creed* VIII. xvii. 189 Hee that could rightly spell the severall passages in the forementioned authors. **1671** MILTON *P.R.* IV. 385 By what the Stars..In thir conjunction met, give me to spell. **1681** FLAVEL *Meth. Grace* xi. 238 Christ is an unsearchable mercy: who can spell his wonderful name? **1791** COWPER *Iliad* v. 77 Unskill'd to spell aright The oracles predictive of the woe. **1820** PRAED *Surly Hall* 80 Poems 1864 II. 117 He..spells a horse's teeth divinely. **1842** H. ROGERS *Ess.* (1874) I. i. 36 The arts of spelling out and piecing the mouldering records of antiquity. **1886** DOWDEN *Shelley* (1887) I. ii. 72 Nor was his an intellect that could spell out patiently the lessons of nature.

c. To consider, contemplate, scan intently. Also with *over*.

1633 G. HERBERT *Temple* iv, Will great God measure with a wretch? Shall he thy stature spell? **1654** H. L'ESTRANGE *Chas. I* (1655) 118 So that in short (all circumstances spell'd together) I may safely say [etc.]. **1821** SCOTT *Kenilw.* vii, I will sit on this footstool at thy feet, that I may spell over thy splendour. **1823** —— *Quentin D.* xiii, As if he were in the act of internally spelling and dissecting every lineament and feature. **1859** TENNYSON *Vivien* 217 For still I find Your face is practised when I spell the lines.

d. To turn *out* (literary work or writing) with some difficulty.

1829 SCOTT *Jrnl.* 15 May, I have spelled out some work this day, though I have been rather knocked about.

3. a. To name or set down in order the letters of (a word or syllable); to enunciate or write letter by letter; to denote by certain letters in a particular order.

1588 SHAKS. *L.L.L.* v. i. 50 What is Ab speld backward with the horn on his head? *a* **1595** R. SOUTHWELL *Mæoniæ, Virgin's Salutation*, Spell Eva back and Ave shall you find. **1612** BRINSLEY *Lud. Lit.* 151 Cause also euery one to spel the words which he hath made in Latine,..so as [etc.]. **1693** DRYDEN *Disc. Satire* Ess. (ed. Ker) II. 67 If this be so, then it is false spelled throughout this book. *Ibid.* The French.. never spell it any other way than *satire*. **1750** GRAY *Elegy* 81 Their name, their years, spelt by th' unletter'd Muse, The place of fame and elegy supply. **1784** COWPER *Task* I. 283 Leaving an obscure, rude name, In characters uncouth, and spelt amiss. **1842** *Proc. Philol. Soc.* I. 7 Their mode of spelling the passive participle. **1888** SWEET *Hist. Eng. Sounds* 70 The same word may be spelt in half-a-dozen different ways on the same page.

fig. *a* **1668** LASSELS *Voy. Italy* (1670) I. Pref., Though these things be but the Elements and Alphabet of breeding, yet without them he can never spel *gentleman* rightly.

b. Similarly with *out*.

1867 *Chambers's Encycl.* IX. 52/2 The medium, under spirit-guidance, spelling out the requisite words. **1871** M. LEGRAND *Cambr. Freshm.* 356 The machine was clicking away, and the needle rapidly spelling out its message. **1899** BULLEN *Way Navy* 88 The discordant notes of sirens spelling out each ship's name.

c. Of letters: To form (a word).

1834 MARRYAT *J. Faithful* iv, What doth *c-a-t* spell then? **1852** DICKENS *Bleak Ho.* v, He went on quickly, until he had formed..the word *Jarndyce*... 'What does that spell?' he asked me.

d. *slang.* (See quot.)

1865 *Slang Dict.* 241 *Spell*, to advertise, to put into print.

e. *U.S. to spell* (someone) *down*: to defeat (someone) in a spelling-contest. †**f.** *U.S.* To put to the test in spelling. *Obs.*

1854 B. F. TAYLOR *Jan. & June* 259 They all stand in solid phalanx by schools, and the struggle is, to spell each other down. **1866** C. H. SMITH *Bill Arp* 171 He then spelt him right straight along on all sorts of big words, and little words. **1871** E. EGGLESTON *Hoosier Schoolm.* (1872) iv. 47 Ralph dreaded the loss of influence..if he should be easily spelled down. **1932** *Randolph Enterprise* (Elkins, W. Va.) 18 Feb. 4/5 He was fairly spelled down at close of my school at Job, spring 1882, by a little girl not 7 years old. **1952** T. PYLES *Words & Ways of Amer. Eng.* (1954) v. 82 He who misspelled had to take his seat; the master's purpose was to 'spell down' the pupils.

g. *fig. to spell out* (orig. *U.S.*): to explain (something) step by step; to state explicitly or in detail.

1940 *San Francisco News* 31 Dec. 11 In the interest of clarifying public opinion, these opponents should spell out their position fully. **1952** B. WOLFE *Limbo '90* (1953) xxiv. 390 Spelling out the bald verities to a retarded child. **1956** J. POTTS *Diehard* xiii. 196 If you weren't such a fool you'd know it too. You want me to spell it out in words of one syllable for you? **1960** *Guardian* 1 Nov. 8/5 Dr. Kaldor would apparently have us spell all these things out. But.. there really is a limit to the amount of detail..to which a party in Opposition can commit itself. **1973** G. W. TURNER *Stylistics* vi. 171 An electrician asking which of three wires is 'the earth' clearly means 'the earth(ed) wire' or 'the wire connected with the earth', but hardly needs to spell it out. **1978** J. A. MICHENER *Chesapeake* v. 239 With studied care Thomas Janney spelled out the terms of the deal he had arranged.

4. *fig.* †**a.** *to spell* (one) *backward*, to misrepresent; to pervert. *Obs.*

1599 SHAKS. *Much Ado* III. i. 60, I neuer yet saw man.. But she would spell him backward. **1669** HOPKINS *Serm.* (1685) 42 What is this but to spell the Magistrates backwards and to give him that power over your consciences by his prohibitions, which you deny to his commands?

b. *to spell..short*, to express by a shorter and blunter term.

1830 DE QUINCEY *R. Bentley* Wks. 1857 VII. 76 A dedication..was what the French used to understand by a *pot-de-vin*; in fact, 'spelt short,' it was a bribe.

c. *to spell baker*, to have, or perform, a difficult task. *U.S. colloq.*

1868 LONGFELLOW *Giles Corey* II. i, If an old man will marry a young wife, Why then—why then—why then—he must spell Baker!

5. To amount to; to signify, imply, or involve. (Common in recent use.)

a **1661** FULLER (Webster), The Saxon heptarchy, when seven kings put together did spell but one in effect.

1890 SAINTSBURY in *New Rev.* Feb. 142 There can be no question..that 'Republic' usually spells 'corruption'. **1891** *Spectator* 27 June, To go on trading on these terms would very soon spell ruin.

II. *intr.* **6. a.** To form words by means of letters; to repeat or set down the letters of words; to read off the separate letters forming a word or words.

a **1400–50** *Alexander* 630 He..wonder wele leres, Sped him in a schort space to spell & to rede. **1570** LEVINS *Manip.* 55 To spel, *syllabam coponere.* **1592** SHAKS. *Rom. & Jul.* II. iii. 88 O she knew well, Thy Loue did read by rote, that could not spell. *c* **1645** MILTON *Sonn.* xi, Some in file Stand spelling fals. **1685** BAXTER *Paraphr. N.T.* Matt. xiii. 13, I speak to them in similitudes, as children must be first taught to spell. **1712** SWIFT *Prop. Correcting Eng. Tongue* Wks. 1841 II. 288 A foolish opinion..that we ought to spell exactly as we speak. *a* **1764** LLOYD *Poet* Poet. Wks. 1774 II. 23 Those who cannot spell will Talk. **1816** BYRON *A Sketch* 14 She taught the child to read, and taught so well, That she herself, by teaching, learn'd to spell. **1870** ROGERS *Hist. Gleanings* Ser. II. 137 He never could spell accurately.

b. *fig.* To engage in study or contemplation *of* something. *poet.*

1632 MILTON *Penseroso* 170 The..Mossy Cell, Where I may sit and rightly spell Of every Star that Heav'n doth shew. **1738** GRAY *Propertius* ii. 15 Then let me rightly spell of nature's ways.

7. a. To intimate or suggest a desire *for* something; to ask *for*, either by hints or direct request.

WFlem. *spellen* is similarly used (De Bo).

1790 BENTHAM *Wks.* (1843) X. 230 Was it natural..to spell for such a thing in the most distant manner? **1818** JANE AUSTEN *Persuasion* II. x. 215, I had not the smallest intention of asking him,..but he gave so many hints;..I never saw any body in my life spell harder for an invitation. **1840** J. H. NEWMAN *Lett.* (1891) I. 429 Before I had given him anything, he began to spell for something. **1860** *Ibid.* II. 105 It will be observed..that he 'spelled' for the curacy. **1876** ROBINSON *Whitby Gloss.* 181/2 'He was a good hand at spelling for't,' clever at entreaty.

b. With other constructions.

c **1800** R. CUMBERLAND *John De Lancaster* (1809) II. 52 Nephew David spells hard to borrow him, but I won't lend him to David of all men living. **1821** COMBE *Syntax, Wife* IV. (Chandos Cl.) 339 Syntax with native keenness felt At what the cunning tradesman spelt. **1855** [ROBINSON] *Whitby Gloss.* s.v., 'He spell'd hard in the matter,' he endeavoured perseveringly to gain his point.

spell (spɛl), *v.*[3] [Later form of SPELE *v.*[1] Cf. SPELL *sb.*[3]]

1. *trans.* To take the place of (a person) at some work or labour; to relieve (another) by taking a turn at work. Now *U.S.*

1595 RALEIGH *Discov. Guiana* (1596) 44 Euery gentleman and others taking their turns to row, and to spell one the other at the howers end. **1823** T. ROUGHLEY *Jamaica Planter's Guide* 340 Sometimes there are two ostensible boilers to spell and relieve one another. *Ibid.*, When he is obliged to be spelled, for the purpose of natural rest [etc.]. **1857** GOODRICH *Recoll.* I. 62, I was sometimes permitted.. to spell my father in this favorite employment [*sc.* shelling corn]. **1873** LOWELL *Lett.* (1894) II. 91 He tells me that the Finns recite their poems six or seven hours on the stretch, spelling one another, as we say in New England.

b. To relieve by an interval of rest; to rest (*esp.* a horse). Chiefly *Austr.*

1846 STOKES *Disc. Australia* II. i. 42 In order to spell the oars, we landed at a point on the east side. **1867** H. BUSHNELL *Mor. Uses Dark Th.* 252 Nature is put under a heavy pressure..; spelled by no relaxations, freshened by no play of society. **1885** MRS. C. PRAED *Head Station* xli. III. 202 They are camping at Araluen and spelling the horses.

2. *Naut.* To take a turn or turns of work at (the pump, etc.).

1769 FALCONER *Dict. Marine* (1780) s.v., Thus we say, spell the pump, spell the lead, &c. ?**1782** *Loss of H.M.S. Centaur* 3 The Captain was obliged to turn all hands up to spell the pump.

3. *intr.* **a.** To replace one set of workers by another; to take turns.

1861 MAYHEW *Lond. Lab.* (ed. 2) III. 247 We go on in that way throughout the day, spelling at every 28 tons.

b. *Austr.* To take an interval of rest.

1880 *Victoria in 1880* 114 (Morris), He 'spelled' upon the ground. **1890** *Melbourne Argus* 13 June 6/1 Working a steady stroke through the day, smoking and spelling as they willed. **1893** J. A. BARRY *S. Brown's Bunyip* 2 It was Sunday, and the caravan was spelling for the day.

spell (spɛl), *v.*[4] [f. SPELL *sb.*[1] 3.]

1. *trans.* To charm, fascinate, bewitch, bind by (or as by) a spell; to act as a spell upon.

a **1623** BUCK *Rich. III* (1646) 116 For a time he was much speld with Elianor Talbot. **1682** DRYDEN & LEE *Dk. Guise* IV, He durst not touch me; But aw'd and craven'd as he had been spell'd [etc.]. **1793** MME. D'ARBLAY *Diary* V. IX. 397 Susanna's temporary widowhood..has spelled me with a spell I know not how to break. **1816** KEATS *To a Friend who sent me some Roses* 12 But when..thy roses came to me My sense with their deliciousness was spell'd. **1876** *Good Words* 687 We stayed our walk—spelled to the spot—to watch The sunset glorifying earth and sky.

b. To protect (one) *from*, to drive *away*, by means of a spell or charm.

1691 DRYDEN *K. Arthur* I. ii, Thor, Freya, Woden, hear and spell your Saxons, With sacred Runic rhymes, from death in battle. **1876** *Tinsley's Mag.* XVIII. 240 Thy soft voice spelled away All my dearth.

2. To invest with magical properties.

1697 DRYDEN *Virg. Georg.* III. 445 This, gather'd in the Planetary Hour, With noxious Weeds, and spell'd with Words of Pow'r, Dire Stepdames in the Magick Bowl infuse.

Hence **spelled, spelling** *ppl. adjs.*

1591 SHAKS. *1 Hen. VI*, v. iii. 31 Vnchaine your spirits now with spelling Charmes. **1838** S. BELLAMY *Betrayal* 22 To such end his spell'd appearance wrought.

†**spell**, *v.*[5] *Naut. Obs.* [Of obscure origin; partly confused with SPILL *v.*] (See quots.)

c **1635** N. BOTELER *Dial. Sea Service* (1685) 167 Take in the Missen-mast; or at the least, Peek it up: which Peeking up is called Spelling the Missen. **1704** J. HARRIS *Lex. Techn.* I, *Spell*, a Sea Word signifying to let go the Sheats and Bowlings of a Sail, (chiefly the Missen) and Bracing the weather Brace in the Wind, that the Sail may lie loose in the Wind. **1711** [see SPEEK *v.*[2]].

spell, *v.*[6] *dial.* Also 9 spel. [f. SPELL *sb.*[2]]

1. *trans.* **a.** To fit with bars or cross-pieces. **b.** To put into splints.

1641 BEST *Farm. Bks.* (Surtees) 61 The best way for spellinge of an hive is to putte in the two lowermost spelles aboute 4 wreathes from the bottome of the hive, and the two uppermost spelles just 4 wreathes above them. **1886** *S.W. Linc. Gloss.* 138 The Doctor did not spell it while to-day.

2. *trans.* and *intr.* To splinter.

1811 FAREY *Derbyshire* I. 367 On his return, [he] finds all the Vein-stuff so furrowed, spelled, or slappeted off. **1829** *Glover's Hist. Derby* I. 81 Where the hard 1st toadstone also, in the gates and shafts, thus spels off.

spellable ('spɛləb(ə)l), *a.* [f. SPELL *v.*[2] + -ABLE.] Capable of being spelled or denoted by letters.

1837 CARLYLE *Mirabeau* Misc. Ess. 1857 IV. 69 All manner of reviews and periodical literatures that Europe, in all its spellable dialects, had. **1864** —— *Fredk. Gt.* XV. ii. IV. 21 District not important, not very spellable, though doubtless pronounceable by natives to it. **1896** A. MORRISON *Child Jago* x. 108 There came a hoot or two, a 'Yah!' and other less spellable sounds, expressive of contempt.

spell-bind ('spɛlbaɪnd), *v.* [f. SPELL *sb.*[1] 3, after SPELL-BOUND *a.*] *trans.* To bind by, or as by, a spell; to fascinate, enchant.

1808 SOUTHEY *Chron. Cid* 380 Hermogenes spell-bound him so that he could not move. **1861** J. PYCROFT *Agony Point* (1862) 109 The eye of the experienced physician spell-binds the lunatic. **1877** C. GEIKIE *Christ* xlix. (1879) 590 The power and majesty of His discourse had spell-bound many others.

spellbinder ('spɛlbaɪndə(r)). orig. *U.S.* [f. as prec.] A political speaker capable of holding an audience spell-bound. Also *gen.*

1888 *New York Tribune* 15 Nov. 6/1 The Republican Orators—'Spellbinders'—who worked during the recent campaign. **1888** *Boston* (Mass.) *Jrnl.* 23 Dec. 2/2 The Republican campaign orators..intend forming themselves into a permanent organization to be called the Republican Spellbinders' National Association. **1896** *N.Y. Weekly Witness* 30 Dec. 13/1 Highrollers, as the boss spellbinders are technically called. **1906** *Calgary* (Alberta) *Eye Opener* 6 Oct. 1/3 He is a spell-binder all right. **1932** [see *flesh-creeper* s.v. FLESH *sb.* 12 b]. **1939** *English* II. 245 Coleridge..would seem to have been something of a spell-binder: we have many witnesses..to the potency of the fascination he exerted over those with whom he came in contact. **1969** *N.Y. Rev. Books* 2 Jan. 15/2 'The books of all three are products of men who do not necessarily believe in their thoughts.' The risk is obvious of course—the false prophet, the spellbinder. **1974** P. DE VRIES *Glory of Hummingbird* (1975) ii. 11 A ministry replete enough with intimations.. that he was less than a spellbinder.

Hence **'spellbinding** *vbl. sb.* and *ppl. a.*; **'spellbindingly** *adv.*

1896 *N.Y. Weekly Witness* 30 Dec. 13/1 He prayed to be permitted to try his hand at spellbinding. **1977** *Gramophone* Dec. 1121/3 A group of songs with orchestra..sounded so spellbindingly lovely. **1978** K. J. DOVER *Greek Homosexuality* iii. 164 Philosophy..was not the product of solitary meditation, to be communicated by a spell-binding orator.

spell-bone *dial.*: see SPEEL-BONE.

spell-bound, ('spɛlbaʊnd), *ppl. a.* [f. SPELL *sb.*[1] 3.] Bound by, or as by, a spell; fascinated, enchanted, entranced.

1799 H. GURNEY *Cupid & Psyche* (1800) 17 Spell-bound she own'd thy mild control. **1813** SCOTT *Trierm.* II. xxvii, So lovely seem'd she there, Spell-bound in her ivory chair. **1837** DISRAELI *Venetia* I. ii, It seems a spell-bound place. **1874** L. STEPHEN *Hours in Library* (1892) I. vi. 199 The student who has once submitted to his charm becomes spellbound.

spelldown ('spɛldaʊn). *U.S.* [f. vbl. phr. *to spell down*: see SPELL *v.*² 3 e.] An eliminating contest in spelling.

1943 *Nat. Geogr. Mag.* Dec. 755 Among cherished memories of 'the days of real sport', the old-fashioned 'spelldown' takes high rank. **1951** E. GRAHAM *My Window looks down East* xv. 131 Mrs. Rowen decided to give him another chance and started the 'spelldown' over, but the children were consulted first. They agreed. The spelling started again. **1958** *Time* (Atlantic ed.) 23 June 38/1 In the ..19th round of the spelldown, 13-year-old Betty Morgan, ..choked up on *chiaus*.

†'**speller**¹. *Obs. rare.* [f. SPELL *v.*¹ Cf. MDu. *spelre*; G. dial. *speller* a gossip.] A preacher.

a **1200** *Vices & Virtues* 45 Wile ðu hlesten spelleres and priestes and munekes..ne scalt ðu næure habben god. *a* **1300** *Cursor M.* 20849 Speke we nou o þaa spellers bald, ..þe apostlis þat all wide war spred. *Ibid.* 21179 þir war his discipleis tuelue,..Spellers o trouth.

speller² ('spɛlə(r)). Also 5 -are. [f. SPELL *v.*² So Du. and Flem. *speller.*]

1. One who spells, or spells out, words; one having a specified proficiency in spelling; an authority on spelling.

c **1440** *Promp. Parv.* 468/1 Spellare, *sillabicator.* **1598** CHAPMAN *Sev. Bks. Iliad* To Rdr., I write..to him that will disdaine those easie obiections, which euery speller may put together. **1687** MIÉGE *Gt. Fr. Dict.* s.v., A good Speller, in point of Writing. *Ibid.*, A bad Speller. **1776** *Pennsylv. Even. Post* 28 Mar. 160/2 He..is a poor writer and speller. **1858** CARLYLE *Fredk. Gt.* VI. iii. II. 37 The worst speller ever known. **1882** SCUDDER *Noah Webster* ii. 38 Webster was a moralist as well as a speller.

2. A seeker *after* something.

1796 PAINE *Writ.* (1895) III. 217 John Adams..it is known was always a speller after places and offices.

3. *U.S.* A spelling-book.

1864 in WEBSTER. **1882** SCUDDER *Noah Webster* ii. 70 The popularity of 'the speller' rendered it liable to piracy. **1904** *Westm. Gaz.* 25 May 4/2 The extremely primitive primers and 'spellers'.

'**speller**³. *Obs.* or *arch.* Also 6 speler. [Aphetic f. ESPELER.] (See quots. and SPILLER².)

1576 TURBERV. *Venerie* 238 In a Bucke we say, Burre, Beame, Branche, Aduauncers, Pawlme, and Spelers. **1611** COTGR., *Espois d'un cerf*, the top of a red Deeres head; of a fallow, the Spellers. **1632** *Guillim's Heraldry* (ed. 2) III. xiv. 179 Skilfull Wood-men describing..a bucks head..say..spellers. [Similarly in other writers.] **1659** TORRIANO, *Spéssi*,..those sharp hornes on the top of a Deers Antler called the Spellers. **1686** PLOT *Staffordsh.* 200 Whereof some of the blades are curled round, divided and jagged like the Spellers of a Bucks-head. [**1857** *Fraser's Mag.* LVI. 211 The advancer, palm, and spellers or spillers.]

spellful ('spɛlfʊl), *a.* Also spelful. [f. SPELL *sb.*¹] Full of, abounding in, spells or magical power.

1773–83 HOOLE *Orl. Fur.* xv. 102 Here, while his eyes the learned leaves peruse, Each spelful mystery explain'd he views. **1805** T. HARRAL *Scenes Life* III. 36 You..would fain persuade me, by your spelful art, that I can act. **1865** E. BURRITT *Walk to Land's End* 28 Eyes of every spellful influence. **1889** *Harper's Mag.* Nov. 943 Her accents are spellful as her eye.

spellican, var. SPILLIKIN.

†'**spelling**, *vbl. sb.*¹ *Obs.* [f. SPELL *v.*¹] Speaking, talking, discourse, utterance.

In OE. esp. 'idle or unprofitable talk'.

c **1000** ÆLFRIC *Hom.* (Thorpe) I. 180 Forbuȝað idele spellunge, and dyslice blissa. *c* **1030** *Rule St. Benet* (Logeman) 83 Idelnesse oððe spellingum [L. *otioso aut fabulis*]. *a* **1225** *Ancr. R.* 64 Spellunge & smecchunge beoð ine muðe boðe;..we schulen..speken nu of spellunge. *a* **1300** *Cursor M.* 19951 Petre þam said o spelling þan O baptising þat iohn bigan. **1390** GOWER *Conf.* II. 263 So that with spellinge of hir charmes Sche tok Eson in bothe hire armes.

spelling ('spɛlɪŋ), *vbl. sb.*² [f. SPELL *v.*² So Du., Flem., and WFris. *spelling.*]

1. a. The action, practice, or art of naming the letters of words, of reading letter by letter, or of expressing words by letters.

c **1440** *Promp. Parv.* 468/1 Spellynge, *sillabicacio.* **1451** CAPGRAVE *Life St. Aug.* 8 Thus lerned he þe smale sciences, as spellyng, reding and constrewyng, in his ȝong age. **1551** T. WILSON *Logike* (1580) 17 b, Shewe hym the maner of spellyng before wee teache hym to reade. **1580** HOLLYBAND *Treas. Fr. Tong*, *Espelement des syllables*, a spelling of syllables. **1612** BRINSLEY *Lud. Lit.* 151 The former knowledge of spelling. **1693** LOCKE *Educ.* §143 His eldest Son, yet in Coats, has play'd himself into Spelling with great eagerness. **1758** L. TEMPLE *Sketches* (ed. 2) 18 Of the Modern Art of Spelling. **1771** LUCKOMBE *Hist. Printing* 270 Compositors..never can arrive to one regular way of Spelling. **1809–10** COLERIDGE *Friend* (1837) III. 343 There is one branch of learning without which learning itself cannot be railed at with common decency, namely, spelling. **1871** EARLE *Philol. Eng. Tongue* ii. 121 That which we call a settled orthography is a habit of spelling which admits only of rare modification.

b. *U.S.* A spelling-bee, spelling-test. *rare.*

1860 O. L. JACKSON *Colonel's Diary* (1922) 23 The boys were anxious for a spelling in the evening. **1889** J. W. RILEY *Pipes o' Pan at Zekesbury* 45 How her face used to look in the twilight As I tuck her to spellin'. **1975** *Budget* (Sugarcreek, Ohio) 20 Mar. 14/3 The young folk are having german spellings once a week.

2. a. Manner of expressing or writing words with letters; orthography. Also *fig.*

c **1661** *Marq. Argyle's Last Will* in *Harl. Misc.* (1746) VIII. 29/2 It is most evident, that the right Spelling of *Covenant* is *Covetousness.* **1693** DRYDEN *Disc. Satire* Ess. (ed. Ker) II. 67 In the criticism of spelling, it ought to be with *i*, and not with *y*. **1697** C. LESLIE *Snake in Grass* (ed. 2) 112 By some unusual Spelling of some words. **1770** [SIR D. DALRYMPLE] *Anc. Scottish Poems* 271 From the spelling of the specimens..I incline to think [etc.]. **1855** MACAULAY *Hist. Eng.* xviii. IV. 245 The letter may still be read with all the original bad grammar and bad spelling. **1894** LINDSAY *Latin Lang.* i. §12 However natural it may appear for the Romans to have adopted Greek spelling.

b. A particular instance of this; a special collocation of letters representing a word.

1731–8 SWIFT *Polite Conv.* Introd. 50 Of these Spellings the Publick will meet with many Examples. **1758** L. TEMPLE *Sketches* (ed. 2) 18 An Author seems reduced to great Extremities, who flies to new Spellings to distinguish himself. **1811** SCOTT *Let.* in *Lockhart* (1837) II. x. 351 All the license of using obsolete words and uncommon spellings. **1894** LINDSAY *Latin Lang.* i. §8 The dates at which these spellings are first found on inscriptions.

3. *attrib.*, as ***spelling-bee*** (BEE¹ 4), ***card, -game, -lesson, match, mistake, -reform(er***, etc.; **spelling pronunciation**, the pronunciation of a word according to its written form; **spelling school**, †(*a*) a building in which spelling is taught; (*b*) *U.S.*, a contest in spelling. Also SPELLING-BOOK.

1875 *Ann. Reg.* 111 A *Spelling Bee has been held at the Myddelton Hall, Islington. **1850** C. M. YONGE *Langley School* xviii. 166 'Nobody' left the gate open,..tore the *spelling cards, scratched the slates. **1974** 'J. LE CARRÉ' *Tinker, Tailor, Soldier, Spy* xxii. 186 Spelling cards lay spread over the floor. **1731** T. DYCHE (*title*), The *Spelling Dictionary. **1880–3** (*title*), The *Spelling Experimenter... Conducted by W. R. Evans. **1862** *Catal. Internat. Exhib.*, *Brit.* II. No. 5504, Alphabet and *spelling game, adapted for infant-schools and nurseries. **1815** SCOTT *Guy M.* li, He had ..the strongest desire..to resume *spelling lessons and half-text. **1845** H. GREELEY in *Publ. Mod. Lang. Soc. Amer.* (1941) LVI. 501 It used to be the custom that the head of the first class and the next should choose sides for a '*spelling match'. **1967** B. BANFILL *Pioneer Nurse* xiii. 146 An invitation for all of us to an old-fashioned Spelling Match. **1966** N. MARSH *Black Beech & Honeydew* iii. 74, I won a Navy League Empire Prize..with an essay containing thirty-one *spelling mistakes. **1901** E. KOEPPEL (*title*) *Spelling-pronunciations. **1927** L. BLOOMFIELD in *Amer. Speech* II. 438/1 This last feature is a fairly close parallel to our 'spelling pronunciations', such as the full form *fore-head* for *forrid* and the now perhaps accepted *waist-coat* and *seamstress* for *weskit* and *semstress.* **1944** [see *pronunciation-spelling* s.v. PRONUNCIATION 6]. **1977** P. STREVENS *New Orientations Teaching of English* xii. 153 One further characteristic of American pronunciation that contrasts with British speech is the frequency of 'spelling pronunciations' in both place-names and proper names. **1848** A. J. ELLIS (*title*) A plain statement of the objects and advantages of the *spelling reform. **1873** EARLE *Philol. Eng. Tongue* (ed. 2) 179 Many proposals for spelling-reform have been made in this country and in America. **1849–50** (*title*), The *Spelling Reformer. Edited by A. J. Ellis. **1908** G. K. CHESTERTON *All Things Considered* 220 Some spelling-reformers..do spell his name phonetically. **1936** *Discovery* May 164/2 Unlike many spelling reformers, he respects tradition and the 'look' of a word. **1704** SWIFT *Tale of Tub* 16 There is also, the *Spelling School, a very spacious Building. **1832** E. M. CHAMBERLAIN *Jrnl.* 25 July in *Indiana Mag. Hist.* (1919) XV. 241 In the evening I appointed a spelling school at which I invited all the parents to attend. **1948** E. N. DICK *Dixie Frontier* 138 Backwoods debating societies, spelling schools, story telling, and singing helped to while away the time.

'**spelling**, *vbl. sb.*³ [f. SPELL *v.*⁴] The use or exercise of spells or charms. *rare.*

1664 COTTON *Scarron.* IV. (1741) 115 She'll make a Cowl-staff, by her Spelling, Amble like any double Gelding. **1939** DYLAN THOMAS *Map of Love* 15 Endure burial under the spelling wall.

spelling ('spɛlɪŋ), *vbl. sb.*⁴ [f. SPELL *v.*³]

1. *Sc.* The practice of acting as a substitute for another or taking turns at some work or labour.

1920 *Glasgow Herald* 16 Apr. 7 The Sheriff finds that the custom known as 'spelling' is recognised in the West of Scotland, and in this case the defender's stevedore assented to the pursuer 'spelling' for the regular employee. **1955** *Times* 17 Aug. 5/4 Organized 'spelling'—that is to say, arrangements between members of a gang that they shall take it in turns to leave their work—is still to be found in Glasgow and Liverpool, in spite of many attempts to stamp it out. **1965** *Daily Express* 6 Aug. 4/5 'Spelling' in Glasgow is the same as 'welting' in Liverpool.

2. *Austral.* Resting from work. Also *attrib.*

1911 *Chambers's Jrnl.* Aug. 591/2 Old Davy..settled down on a selection near Grassmere which the Cornet Scrubber,..used as a spelling-place in his spare hours. **1926** B. CRONIN *Red Dawson* ii. 36 There was need for their spelling before they sat in on the game in real earnest.

'**spelling-book.** [SPELLING *vbl. sb.*²] A book designed to teach spelling.

1677 T. LYE (*title*), New Spelling-Book. **1712** STEELE *Spect.* No. 296 ¶1 By the Assistance of a Spelling-Book it's legible. **1714** MANDEVILLE *Fab. Bees* (1733) I. 332 Buried alive in their hall under a great heap of primers and spelling-books. *c* **1775** JOHNSON in *Boswell* (Oxf. ed.) I. 30 Tom Brown..published a spelling-book, and dedicated it to the Universe. **1828** MISS MITFORD *Village* Ser. III. (1863) 7 Superintending the different exercises of the needle, the spelling-book, and the slate. **1852** C. W. HOSKYNS *Talpa* xx. (1854) 177 Nature is a schoolmaster that teaches without spelling-books.

attrib. **1771** LUCKOMBE *Hist. Printing* 270 [The hyphen] has given employment..to a number of Spelling-Book-Authors. **1835** MACAULAY in Trevelyan *Compet. Wallah* (1864) 421 They designate the education which their opponents recommend as a mere spelling-book education.

'**spellingly**, *adv.* [f. *spelling*, pres. pple. of SPELL *v.*²] By dint of spelling; letter by letter.

1644 DIGBY *Nat. Bodies* xix. §7. 171 If then we can but arriue to decypher the first characters of the hidden Alphabet..and can but spellingly reade the first syllabes of it [etc.]. **1847** THACKERAY *Lords & Liv.* iii, Jeames read the ..paper..; not spellingly and with hesitation.

†**spellken.** *Cant. Obs.* [See SPELL *sb.*⁵ and KEN *sb.*²] A theatre.

c **1800** in Byron *Juan* XI. xix. *note*, If you at the spellken can't hustle, You'll be hobbled in making a Clout. **1823** BYRON *Ibid.* XI. xix, Who in a row like Tom could lead the van, Booze in the ken, or at the spellken hustle?

†'**spellman.** *Obs.* Also spelman. [f. SPELL *sb.*¹ 3.] One who employs spells or charms.

1611 H. BROUGHTON *Require of Agreement* 27 At Francfurt a Preacher by occasion of speach against English Spellmen, was aunswered that they were allowed in England. **1641** J. TRAPPE *Theol. Theol.* vi. 250 Balaam, Satan's spelman (as one cals him). **1680** C. NESSE *Church Hist.* 75 He calls for Balaam, the Devils spelman, to curse Israel.

†'**spelly**, *a. Obs.*⁻¹ [f. SPELL *sb.*¹ 3.] Full of spells or charms.

1648 EARL OF WESTMORELAND *Otia Sacra* (1879) 37 By vanquishing the Witchcrafts of the Skies, The Spelly-vaprous mists.

spelonk, variant of SPELUNK *Obs.*

spelt, *sb.*¹ Also 5 spilt, spylt, 6 spelte, 7 spealt. [OE. *spelt*, = MDu. *spelte*, *spelt* (Du. *spelt*, WFris. *spjelte*), OS. *spelta* (MLG. *spelte*), OHG. *spelza* (MHG. *spelze*, *spelte*, G. *spelz*, *spelt*), a. late L. *spelta* (from *c* 400, mentioned as a foreign word answering to the older L. *far*), whence also It. *spelta*, *spelda*, Sp. *espelta*, OF. *spelte*, *spealte*, *spiautre*, *espeltre*, *espiautre*, etc., mod.F. *épeautre*.

The evidence indicates that the word had no continuous history in Eng., and little currency, until the 16th cent.]

1. A species of grain (*Triticum spelta*) related to wheat, formerly much cultivated in southern Europe and still grown in some districts.

a **1000** in Wr.-Wülcker 273 *Faar*, spelt. *Ibid.* 401 *Farris*, hwætes, speltes. *Ibid.* 405 *Far serotina*, spelt samgrene. **1392** *Earl Derby's Exp.* (Camden) 225 Pro spelt per ipsum empt' ibidem [*sc.* at Modon]. **1398** TREVISA *Barth. De P.R.* XVII. lxxxi. (Bodl. MS.), Some greyne is noþer in codde noþer in huole as barlich & spilt [*v.r.* spylt]. **1562** TURNER *Herbal* II. (1568) 85 The stalkes [of Phalaris] ar..much lyke vnto the strawes of spelt. *Ibid.* 133 Semen is called..in Duche speltz; it may in English be called spelt. **1578** LYTE *Dodoens* 164 This plant groweth amongst wheate and Spelte, in good frutefull groundes. **1597** GERARDE *Herbal* I. xlii. 61 Spelt is like to wheate in stalks and eare. *a* **1656** USSHER *Ann.* (1658) 770 He passed it..thorough unbeaten paths, where his food was spelt and dates. **1661** LOVELL *Hist. Anim. & Min.* 55 The meale of spelt, in red Wine helpeth the stingings of Scorpions, applied warme. **1736** BAILEY *Houshold Dict.* s.v. *Brawn*, Bread made of Spelt is hard of digestion. **1762** MILLS *Pract. Husb.* I. 408 Spelt, though commonly reckoned a summer corn, is sowed either in autumn, or in the spring. **1805–6** CARY *Dante, Inf.* XIII. 101 There sprouting, as a grain of spelt, It rises to a sapling. **1855** SINGLETON *Virgil* I. 75 There, upon the season being changed, You'll sow the golden spelt. **1884** *De Candolle's Orig. Cultivated Pl.* 362 Spelt is now hardly cultivated out of south Germany and German-Switzerland.

2. *attrib.*, as ***spelt-cake, -corn, -ridge, -wheat.***

1610 W. FOLKINGHAM *Art of Survey* I. xi. 35 Spelt-corne in a fat moist layer degenerats from bad to better, *viz.* in three yeeres space to Wheat. **1688** HOLME *Armoury* II. 87/1 Spelt-Corn is lesser and blacker than Wheat. **1694** MOTTEUX *Rabelais* II. Let. i. 3 Oats, Spelt-Corn, and Barly. **1753** *Chambers' Cycl.* Suppl. s.v. *Zea*, The bread made of the spelt corn..is lighter and whiter than any other bread. **1832** *Veg. Subst. Food of Man* 35 Spelt Wheat—*Triticum spelta*—is imagined to have been the Triticum of the Romans, and the Zea of the Greeks. **1853** SOYER *Pantropheon* 43 Among other delicate dishes..he had ordered a spelt cake to be made.

spelt, *sb.*² *rare.* Now *dial.* [Connected with SPELT *v.* Cf. SPELD *sb.* and G. *spelze* husk.] A thin piece of wood or metal; *spec.* a board of a book (OE.), a toe- or heel-plate (*dial.*).

c **1000** ÆLFRIC *Gloss.* in Wr.-Wülcker 164 *Quaternio*, cine. *Planca*, spelt... *Membrana*, bocfel. ? *a* **1400** *Morte Arth.* 3265 Abowte cho whirllide a whele... The spekes was splentide alle with speltis of siluer. **1585** HIGINS tr. *Junius' Nomenclator* 143 *Schidia vel schidiæ*,..Chippes or spelts of wood. **1875** PARISH *Sussex Dial.* 111 *Spelts*, iron toes and heels for boots.

spelt, variant of SPALT *sb.*² *Obs.*

spelt (spɛlt), *v.* Now *dial.* [Related to SPELD *v.* in the same way as SPALT *v.* to SPALD *v.* Cf. G. *spelzen* to husk.] *trans.* To husk or pound (grain); to bruise or split (*esp.* beans). Hence '**spelted** *ppl. a.* (Cf. SPELK *v.*²)

1570 LEVINS *Manip.* 58 To spelt corne, *tundere, eglumare.* **1607** MARKHAM *Cavel.* v. (1617) 8 The loues in some places are rould in spelted beanes. **1620** —— *Farew. Husb.* xv. 137 The garden Pease..serue..for pottage, boiling, parching or spelting. **1623** —— *Cheap Husb.* (ed. 3) I. 52 If then you cause those beanes to be spelted vpon a milne, and so mixt with oates, it will recouer him. **1707** MORTIMER *Husb.* (1721) I. 258 Feed them with Oats, spelted Beans, Barley-meal, or Ground-Malt mixed with Milk. **1877** in *N.W. Linc. Gloss.*

spelter ('spɛltə(r)), *sb.* Also 8–9 speltre. [Corresponds to OF. *espeautre*, MDu. *speauter*, Du. and G. *spiauter*, LG. *spialter*, but the immediate source is not clear. Related to PEWTER.]

1. Zinc. (Now only *Comm.*) Also *locally* applied to various ores.

1661 BOYLE *Certain Physiol. Ess.* (1669) 194 Leaving a lump or two of Spelter there for two or three days. **1671** J. WEBSTER *Metallogr.* Pref. B ij b, Ores..of Antimony, Tinglass, Spelter, Talk, and Cinnober. **1733** TULL *Horse-Hoeing Husb.* xxii. 350, I have often made them with a mix'd Metal, of half Pewter and half Spelter. **1758** BORLASE *Nat. Hist. Cornw.* 129 Of bismuth, speltre, zink, naptha,.. I have received specimens from several parts of Cornwall. **1799** G. SMITH *Laboratory* I. 106 Fling into it one ounce of spelter, i.e. zinc. **1835** *Penny Cycl.* IV. 182/2 The articles which Belgium supplies to England are oak-bark,..spelter, and sheeps' wool. **1860** *Ure's Dict. Arts* (ed. 5) III. 1076 The general consumption of Spelter throughout the world is about 67,000 tons per annum. **1912** *Trans. R. Geol. Soc. Cornwall* XIV. 153 In some of the deeper levels..an intimate mixture of chaliopyrite and garnet, which sometimes contains cassiterite also, locally known as 'spelter', has been met with in considerable quantities.

2. An alloy or solder of which zinc is the principal constituent.

1815 J. SMITH *Panorama Sci. & Art* I. 51 The hard solder for copper, is a soft fusible sort of granulated brass, well known to artists under the name of spelter. **1824** *Mechanic's Mag.* No. 26. 415 Method of making spelter for brazing iron, copper, etc. **1854** H. MILLER *Sch. & Schm.* (1858) 392 An elderly tinker..sat admiring a bit of spelter of about a pound weight. It was gold, he said.

3. *attrib.* and *Comb.*, as ***spelter-box, -dust, -heap, -maker, -ore.***

1684 *Lond. Gaz.* No. 1991/4 There is another Watch a Spelter Box and Case all in one. **1758** BORLASE *Nat. Hist. Cornw.* 129 Speltre ore I have had from a mine near St. Columb. **1868** *Q. Rev.* No. 248. 346 Covering acres of ground like the spelter and cinder heaps. **1882** BLACKMORE *Christowell* xlv, Where mine-slag, sparry rocks, and spelter dust combined to glare with intense heat. **1884** C. G. W. LOCK *Workshop Rec.* Ser. III. 18/1 Spelter or zinc statuettes, known in the trade as imitation or French bronze. **1897** *Allbutt's Syst. Med.* II. 940 Spelter workers,..that is, men who smelt zinc ore, occasionally suffer from plumbism.

b. ***spelter solder***, a solder made from zinc and copper.

1671 BOYLE *Usef. Nat. Philos.*, *Trades* 19 Though common Spelter-soder be much cheaper, than that which is made with Silver instead of Spelter. **1797** *Encycl. Brit.* (ed. 3) XVII. 745/1 In this heat soft solder is just ready to melt, and has no tenacity;..even spelter solder is considerably weakened by it. **1843** HOLTZAPFFEL *Turning* I. 268 Soft spelter-solder, suitable for ordinary brass work, is made of equal parts of copper and zinc. **1873** SPON *Workshop Rec.* Ser. I. 365/2 This solder possesses several advantages over the usual spelter solder or brass.

Hence **'spelter** *v. trans.*, to unite with spelter solder.

1861 W. GRAHAM *Brassfounder's Man.* 34 When the work is cleaned, bound, fluxed, and speltered, the whole is subjected to a clear charcoal or coke fire.

speltoid ('spɛltɔɪd), *a.* and *sb. Bot.* [a. G. *speltoid* (H. Nilsson-Ehle 1917, in *Botaniska Notiser* 305), f. *spelt*: see SPELT *sb.*[1] and -OID.]

A. *adj.* Of a wheat: resembling or having certain characteristics of spelt. **B.** *sb.* A speltoid wheat.

1920 *Hereditas* I. 116 A distinctive character of these speltoids..is the short outer glumes, abruptly cut off at the top as in *Triticum spelta*... Speltoid heterozygotes are also characterized by longer straws and longer and more lax spikes than the mother sort. **1932** *Proc. 6th Internat. Congr. Genetics* I. 286 Speltoid and dwarf types..are found in the progeny of treated plants of *Triticum vulgare*. **1939** SANSOME & PHILP *Recent Adv. Plant Genetics* vii. 212 The speltoids differ from the parental type in having lax ears, thick keeled glumes which can only be pulled away from the grain with difficulty, and by the presence of awns. **1975** *Proc. R. Soc.* B. CLXXXVIII. 149 Reasonably uniform lines were available for test crosses with *vulgare* and speltoid tester stocks. *Ibid.* 156 *Spelta* and speltoid cannot be distinguished phenotypically... The low frequency of defectives in F_2's with base-sterile speltoids indicates a high degree of buffering by the polygenic system.

Hence **'speltoidy**, speltoid character.

1944 *Genetics* XXIX. 233 Speltoidy (so called because of the resemblance to *T. spelta*) has been shown..frequently to be due to the effects of a particular monosome. **1958** *Nature* 28 Jan. 1813/1 Okamato..has shown that chromosome IX is in the A genome, and has thus reduced the historical importance of speltoidy and compactoidy.

speluncar (spɛ'lʌŋkɑː(r)), *a.* [f. L. *spelunca*.]

1. Having relation or reference to a cave.

1855 *Ecclesiologist* XVI. 295 What Mr. Scott calls the speluncar idea, is thus fully carried out. **1861** BERESF. HOPE *Eng. Cathedr. 19th C.* iii. 85 Mr. Burges..bases his plan upon what has been called, by a self-explanatory term, the speluncar principle of tropical architecture.

2. Of the nature of a cave.

1865 *Sat. Rev.* 11 Feb. 181 Nor would these speluncar chambers gain much in artistic value..were the point gained.

spe'luncean, *a. rare*[−1]. [f. as prec. + *-ean*.] = SPELUNCAR *a.* 2.

1803 G. S. FABER *Cabiri* II. 380 His opinion, that the ornamented artificial cavern,..and the circular speluncëan temple, were all the legitimate descendants of the Mithratic grotto.

†**spelunk**. *Obs.* Forms: 4–5 spelonk(e; 4–6 spelunc, spelunk(e, 6 speluncke. [ad. L. *spelunca* or OF. *spelonque, spelunque*. Cf. MDu. *spelonke, spelunke* (Du. *spelonk*), MHG. and G. *spelunke*.] A cave or cavern; a grotto.

13.. *S. Erkenwolde* 49 in Horstm. *Altengl. Leg.* (1881) 267 Thre sperlis of þe spelunke..Was metely made of þe marbre. **1377** LANGL. *P. Pl.* B. xv. 270 Monkes and mendynauntz men bi hem-selue, In spekes an in spelonkes selden speken togideres. **1382** WYCLIF *Gen.* xxiii. 9 Preye ȝe for me..that he ȝyue to me the dowble spelunk, or caue. *a* **1400–50** *Alexander* 5392 All spritis in þis spelonk here speke þai to-gedire. **1483** CAXTON *G. de la Tour* d ij b, Not hows of marchaundyse nor pytte or spelonke for theues. **1511** *Guylforde's Pilgr.* (Camden) 24 Into the first of thyse two spelunkes entred the women. **1563** BECON *Reliques of Rome* 53 b, Our recluses haue grates of yron in their spelunckes and dennes.

spelunker (spɛ'lʌŋkə(r)). *N. Amer. slang.* [f. as SPELUNK + -ER[1].] One who explores caves, esp. as a hobby; a caver, a speleologist.

1942 A. F. HARLOW *Weep no More, my Lady* xxiii. 407 A young man named Floyd Collins, a native of the hills a few miles north of the Mammoth, had long been a confirmed 'spelunker', or cave bug. **1946** *Life* 4 Nov. 143 Cave exploring,..which bears the scientific name of speleology, has a group of amateur followers who like to call themselves 'spelunkers'. **1965** P. ORDWAY *Night of Reckoning* (1967) 131 Not being a spelunker at heart, let's hope..there aren't too many bats. **1971** G. G. LUCE *Body Time* ii. 54 A courageous spelunker and geologist, Michel Siffre, who spent two months on a subterranean glacier in the French Alps in 1962. **1980** 'E. MCBAIN' *Ghosts* viii. 155 The cave seemed not in the least bit inviting. He had always considered spelunkers the choicest sorts of maniacs.

Hence (as a back-formation) **spe'lunk** *v. intr.*, to explore caves as a hobby; **spe'lunking** *vbl. sb.*, the practice or hobby of exploring caves.

1946 *Life* 4 Nov. 143 (*heading*) Life goes spelunking. **1959** *Weekend* 12 Sept. 77/2 To take a second look at Cadomin caves *Weekend* organized another spelunking expedition. **1965** R. MCDOWELL *Hound's Tooth* vii. 105 They had no legitimate complaint if he chose to take Jenny spelunking in Hunter's Cave. **1974** *Islander* (Victoria, B.C.) 8 Dec. 15/3 Spelunking..is a sport which has become popular within our time. **1979** *United States 1980/81* (Penguin Travel Guides) 563 You can see these on..walks through the cave, ..and on spelunking tours where you do your own locomoting on all fours.

spelye, obs. variant of SPELE *v.*[1]

†**spen**, *sb. Obs.*[−1] (Meaning obscure.)

13.. *Gaw. & Gr. Knt.* 1074 ȝe schal..cum to þat merk at mydmorn, to make quat yow likez in spenne.

spen, *v.* ? *Obs.* Also 4, 9 spenn. [a. ON. *spenna* (Icel. and Norw. *spenna*, Sw. *spänna*, Da. *spænde*), = MDu. and MLG. *spennen*, NFris. *spên*, *spän*, related to SPAN *v.*[2] Cf. SPEND *v.*[2]]

1. *trans.* To clasp; to fasten by means of clasps or buckles; to button or lace.

13.. *E.E. Allit. P.* A. 49 Bifore þat spot my honde I spennd, For care ful colde þat to me caȝt. **13..** *Gaw. & Gr. Knt.* 587 Wyth ryche cote armure, His gold sporez spend with pryde. *c* **1400** *Destr. Troy.* 10942 Telamon full tyte.. Two spurres full spedely spent on his helis. *c* **1500** *Lancelot* 2806 The maden sone one to his chalmer gos, And sacretly his armour one hyme spent. **1825** JAMIESON *Suppl.*, *To Spenn*,..to button, or to lace one's clothes; as, to spenn the waistcoat.

b. With personal object.

c **1400** *Rowland & O.* 361 Þay spende hym with his gilte sperres, And dressede hym in his armours.

2. *intr.* To fit tightly or closely.

13.. *Gaw. & Gt. Knt.* 158 Hose of þat same grene, þat spenet on his sparlyr, & clene spures vnder.

spen, variant of SPEAN *sb.*

spence[1] (spɛns). Also 5–7 spens(e, 5 spenyse. [Aphetically f. OF. *despense* (mod.F. *dépense*), = Sp. and Pg. *despensa*, It. *dispensa*, med.L. *despensa*, *dispensa* (rarely *spensa*), in the same sense: cf. DISPENSE *sb.*[1] So Swiss dial. *spense*.

The prefix *de-* is similarly dropped in other words; in this case there may have been association with SPENSE *sb.*]

1. A room or separate place in which victuals and liquor are kept; a buttery or pantry; a cupboard. Now *dial.* or *arch.*

α. *c* **1386** CHAUCER *Sompn. T.* 223 Fat as a whale, and walking as a swan; Al vinolent as Botel in the spence. **1426** LYDG. *De Guil. Pilgr.* 23026, I hadd no maner lyberte;..in the seller, nor in the spence, ete nor drynke on no syde. *c* **1460** *Play of Sacram.* 529 He syttyth with sum tapstere in yᵉ spence. **1540** PALSGR. *Acolastus* Q iij, If we..bring out of (the buttery) or spence all the meate that is left. **1600** SURFLET *Countrie Farme* I. v. 22 [A] vaulted roome, which shall also be for the huswifes vse and serue for a spence, to keepe her prouision of victuals in. **1684** *Yorks. Dial.* 183 (E.D.S.), Our Sew hes been 'ith Spence, thrawn down Whigg-Stand. **1720** *Postmaster* 25 Nov. 103 House.. contains Four Chambers,..a Kitchen, with two Spences. **1790** GROSE *Prov. Gloss.* (ed. 2), *Spence*, a small place for setting milk or drink in, made with wainscot, or a lattice. **1814** SCOTT *Wav.* xvii, In one large aperture, which the robber facetiously called his *spence* (or pantry). **1865** R. HUNT *Pop. Rom. W. Eng.* (1871) Ser. i. 110 Nancy must have something to drink before she started for Penzance, and she went to the spence for the bottles.

fig. **1609** HOLLAND *Amm. Marcell.* XIX. xii. 141 These cruell enterludes, which out of a spence or budget of craftie devices he brought forth.

β. **14..** *Lat.-Eng. Voc.* in Wr.-Wülcker 578 *Dispensa*, a spense. *c* **1450** *St. Cuthbert* (Surtees) 1441 He bare þe bordeclath to þe spens. **1519** HORMAN *Vulg.* 151 b, I haue ij spensis: one for euery day: a nother for store of all vitayle, tyll newe come. **1609** SKENE *Reg. Maj.* 6 Hir keyes..of hir spens, hir ark of hir claithing and jewells, or of hir cist or coffer.

2. *Sc.* An inner apartment of a house; a parlour.

a. **1783** BURNS *Poor Mailie's Elegy* iv, Our Bardie, lanely, keeps the spence. **1786** —— *Vision* I. ii, Ben I' the Spence, right pensivelie, I gaed to rest. **1820** SCOTT *Monast.* iv, They rushed into the spence, (a sort of interior apartment in which the family ate their victuals in the summer season,) but there was no one there. **1843** BETHUNE *Sc. Fireside Stor.* 154 Others assisted in conveying the invalid to the spence of the inn, which had been readily offered for the accommodation of the family.

3. *attrib.*, as ***spence-basket, -door.***

1825 JAMIESON *Suppl.*, *Spense-Door*, the door between the kitchen and the spense. **1844** W. H. MAXWELL *Wand. Highl. & Isl.* I. ix. 180 A peg behind the spence door. **1881** CUSSANS *Hist. Hertfordsh.* III. II. 321 *Spence-Basket*, a basket used by waggoners to hold provisions for their journey.

†**spence**[2]. *Obs. rare.* Also 4 spense. [Substituted for SPENCER *sb.*[1], after prec.] A steward.

a **1300** *Cursor M.* 28740 For quat [need] es þat spense [*v.r.* spenser] mai be Nithing þar þe lauerd es fre. *c* **1325** *Metr. Hom.* 165 Hir spense [*v.r.* spensar] knew hir fleysleye. *a* **1568** *Henryson's Twa Myss* xix. in *Bannatyne MS.* (Hunter. Cl.) 963 The spense come in, with keis in his hand. **1644** DIGBY *Nat. Soul* ii. §3. 367 In the scripture we meete with these wordes, the iudge of vniustice, the spence of wickednesse, the man of sinne,..which in our phrase of speaking, do signify an vniust iudge, a wicked spence, and a sinnefull..man.

Spencean (spɛn'siːən), *a.* and *sb.* [f. the name of the political theorist Thomas *Spence* (1750–1814).] **A.** *adj.* Of or pertaining to Thomas Spence or his views.

1817 CASTLEREAGH in *Parl. Deb.* 280 To trace these Hampden and Spencean clubs through all their bearings. *Ibid.*, The great mass received the Spencean doctrines among them. **1866** CHARNOCK *Verba Nom.* 287 *Spencean System*, a plan..by which the human kind could be provided with sustenance without pauperism.

B. *sb.* A follower of Thomas Spence.

1817 W. PONSONBY in *Parl. Deb.* 286 Those foolish and criminal people called the Spenceans. **1817** COLERIDGE *'Blessed are ye'* 132 The poor visionaries called Spenceans.

†**spencer**, *sb.*[1] *Obs.* Also 4 spensere, 4–5 spenser, 6 *Sc.* spensar; 5 spencere. [a. AF. *espenser* (cf. SPENCE[2]), var. of *despenser*, OF. *despencier*, DISPENSER.] One who dispenses or has charge of the provisions in a household; a steward or butler.

α. *a* **1300** *Cursor M.* 4447 Þe spenser and þe botelar bath þe king self wit þaim was wrath. *c* **1380** WYCLIF *Wks.* (1880) 413 Þus a clerk or spenser of a curat may parte þes godis in þe name of hym. **14..** *Lat.-Eng. Voc.* in Wr.-Wülcker 561 *Acellarius*, a spenser. *c* **1480** HENRYSON *Fables, Town & C. Mouse* xix, The spensar come with keyis in his hand.

β. *c* **1400** *Gamelyn* 493 Adam þe spencer toke vp þe clothe. *c* **1420** *Chron. Vilod.* 175 After he was kynge, he wedded hure.., His owne spencers douȝter he [= she] was. **1483** *Cath. Angl.* 354/1 A Spencer, *vbi* A butler. **1580** HOLLYBAND *Treas. Fr. Tong*, *Despensier, qui a la garde de la viande*, a spencer.

spencer ('spɛnsə(r)), *sb.*[2] [From the family name *Spencer*. In sense 1 prob. from that of Charles Spencer, third Earl of Sunderland (1674–1722); in sense 2 from that of George John Spencer, second Earl Spencer (1758–1834); in sense 3 from that of Mr. Knight Spencer (fl. 1803); in sense 5, from the name of Christopher Miner Spencer (1833–1922), U.S. inventor and manufacturer.]

†**1.** A kind of wig. Also *attrib. Obs.*

17.. *Songs & P. on Costume* (Percy Soc.) 206 At us the fribbles may strut and look big, In their spencers, bobs, and ramelies. **1748** SMOLLETT *R. Random* xv, A gold laced hat, a spencer wig, and a silver hilted hanger. **1753** HOGARTH *Anal. Beauty* xvi. 218 The uniform 'diamond' of a card was filled up by the flying dress..of the little capering figure in the spencer-wig.

2. A short double-breasted overcoat without tails worn by men in the latter part of the 18th century and the beginning of the 19th.

Hence G. *spencer*, *spenser*, now *spenzer*, WFlem. *spensel*.

1795 *Sporting Mag.* V. 324/2 Spencers. These fashionable coatlets. *Ibid.* VI. 41/2 A young gentleman then approaching, dressed in a light coat, and a blue spencer. **1796** *Ibid.* VII. 311 The economical garment called a spencer. **1817** J. BRADBURY *Trav. Amer.* 126 This occasioned..on my part a pretended alarm for fear that his coat should become a spencer. **1853** DICKENS *Bleak Ho.* xxiv, A very respectable old gentleman,..dressed in a black spencer and gaiters and a broad-brimmed hat. **1899** C. K. PAUL *Memories* 81 Bethell was the last man who wore a 'spencer', an over-jacket which allowed the tails of a dress-coat to appear below it.

b. A kind of close-fitting jacket or bodice commonly worn by women and children early in the 19th century, and since revived.

1799 J. WOODFORDE *Diary* 19 June (1931) V. 200 Very cold indeed again today, so cold that Mrs. Custance came walking in her Spenser with a Bosom-friend. **1803** WITTMAN *Trav. Turkey* 442 They wear a kind of short spencer of green silk or satin. **1836–7** DICKENS *Sk. Boz, Scenes* xiv, There was a considerable talking among the females in the spencers. **1885** LADY BRASSEY *The Trades* 69 The women were mostly dressed in..some sort of dark jacket or spencer.
attrib. **1883** *Cassell's Mag.* Dec. 43/2 A resuscitation is the Spencer bodice, as much like those of forty years ago as can be.

c. A short coat or jacket.
1831 J. BROWN *Let.* 26 Oct. (1912) 27 Then there is the odd dress of the sailors, with bright yellow worsted spencers and large slouched hats. **1851** MAYNE REID *Scalp Hunt.* xx. 141 Some wore leathern calzoneros, with a spencer or jerkin of the same material. **1879** STEVENSON *Trav. Cevennes* 10 My travelling wear of country velveteen, pilot-coat, and knitted spencer.

d. A type of under-bodice (usu. made of wool) worn esp. by women and girls to provide extra warmth in winter.
1881 in A. Adburgham *Shops & Shopping* (1964) xvii. 189 Light, elastic, inexpensive [hand-knitted clothes], including Jerseys, Cardigans, Vests, Spencers, Combinations, etc. **1924** [see HUG-ME-TIGHT 1]. **1953** 'P. WENTWORTH' *Ivory Dagger* xvii. 69 Miss Silver stood revealed in a slip petticoat of grey artificial silk and a neat white spencer whose high neck and long sleeves had..a narrow crochet edging. **1972** L. HANCOCK *There's a Seal in my Sleeping Bag* viii. 204, I wore two spencers (Australian item of thermal underwear).

3. A form of life-belt.
1803 *Phil. Mag.* XVI. 172 Account of the Marine Spencer for the Preservation of Lives in Cases of Shipwreck. **1806** *Ann. Reg., Usef. Proj.* (1808) 980/2 Swimming spencers, which..consist of a cork girdle.

4. *slang.* (See quot.)
1804 *Sporting Mag.* XXIII. 220 A small glass of gin in St. Giles's [is called] a Spencer.

5. A type of rim-fire repeating rifle or carbine used esp. during the U.S. Civil War. Freq. *attrib.*
1866 'F. KIRKLAND' *Pictorial Bk. Anecdotes & Incidents* 660/1 Harris ordered the skirmish line forward,..with orders to silence the troublesome battery..with the aid of the Spencer rifle. **1873** J. H. BEADLE *Undeveloped West* 545 My horse, bridle, saddle, lariat, gun (a Spencer) and two Navajo blankets cost me two hundred dollars. **1904** *Kynoch Jrnl.* Apr.–June 96 The second repeater—and the one most prominent in the war—was the Spencer, having a magazine in the butt containing seven cartridges. **1923** J. H. COOK *Fifty Yrs. on Old Frontier* 5, I had traded a pistol..for a Spencer carbine. **1949** *Exciting Western* May 36/2 The .52 Spencer he kept under the bunk was a souvenir of Malvern Hill. **1974** *Encycl. Brit. Micropædia* IX. 412/1 *Spencer carbine*, military rifle with a magazine in the buttstock that contained seven cartridges. The cartridges were fed into the chamber by means of a trigger-guard operating lever.

spencer (ˈspɛnsə(r)), *sb.*[3] *Naut.* [Perhaps of similar origin to prec.] A fore-and-aft sail, set with a gaff, serving as a trysail to the fore or main mast of a vessel.
1840 R. H. DANA *Bef. Mast* v, We had got her down to close-reefed topsails, double-reefed trysail, and reefed fore spenser. **1851** KIPLING *Sailmaking* (ed. 2) 5 There are the fore-trysail, main-trysail, and mizen-trysail, or as they are sometimes called the fore-spencer, Duke of York or main-spencer, and storm-mizen. **1860** MAURY *Phys. Geog.* xix. §807 At 8 p.m...hove to under close-reefed main top-sail and spencer.
attrib. **1840** R. H. DANA *Bef. Mast* v, The chief mate..was standing..at the foot of the spenser-mast. *Ibid.* xxv, The captain ordered the fore and main spencer gaffs to be lowered down.

†**ˈspencer,** *v. Obs.*$^{-1}$ (Meaning obscure.)
1831 *Examiner* 278/1 The accomplished Sir Robert Gresley has arrived in Newark, and has offered to display his pugilistic prowess in the Market-place, having been spencered by the people.

Spencerian (spɛnˈsɪərɪən), *a.* and *sb.* Also †Spencerean. **A.** *adj.* **1.** [f. the name of the philosopher Herbert *Spencer* (1820–1903).] Of or pertaining to Herbert Spencer or his philosophical views.
1865 *N.Y. Social Science Rev.* I. 70 Spencerean philosophy will permeate and penetrate the world of thought. **1878** W. JAMES in *Jrnl. Speculative Philos.* XII. 9 This explicit acknowledgement..seems, after all, to bring back unity and simplicity into the Spencerian formula. **1886** *Academy* 28 Aug. 132/3 The Comtian and Spencerian systems. **1900** H. MACPHERSON *H. Spencer* 66 The comprehension of the Spencerian philosophy.

2. [f. the name of the U.S. calligrapher Platt Rogers *Spencer* (1800–64).] **a.** Designating a system of handwriting developed by Spencer. Also *absol.*
1863 *Amer. Jrnl. Educ.* XIII. 876 (Advt.), Spencerian system of penmanship. **1865** *21st Ann. Rep. Board of Trustees Public Schools Washington D.C.* (1866) 19 The committee recommend that the Spencerian System of Penmanship be substituted for that of Potter and Hammond. They deem the Spencerian superior. **1906** *Mod. Writing Master* Sept. & Oct. 5/1 The condemning of the old Spencerian penmanship by the educators..marks the first point at which one can detect sober and serious thought on the subject. The old Spencerian had many faults as a system.

b. Of, pertaining to, or characteristic of the cursive script developed by Spencer and used in his system.
1883 G. A. GASKELL *Penman's Handbk.* 21/2 Spencerian, by P. R. Spencer, 1848. **1892** HOWARD & BROWN *Lessons in Rapid Writing* 8 Use an elastic steel pen with fine and well tempered point. Gillott's No. 604..and Spencerian No. 1, are as good as any pens manufactured. **1895** *Montgomery Ward Catal.* Spring & Summer 118/1 Spencerian Script Ruler, a heavy maple ruler.., copies of penmanship printed on both sides of ruler. **1911** G. S. PORTER *Harvester* xix. 479 That is where Uncle Henry showed his fine Spencerian hand. **1966** H. NIELSEN *After Midnight* (1967) iv. 60 On the sheet of paper one line was written in a severe Spencerian script. **1972** J. MOSEDALE *Football* ii. 16 A document in Spencerian script faded by the years. **1982** 'W. R. DUNCAN' *Queen's Messenger* xii. 153 His script was close to Spencerian at times.

B. *sb.* A follower of Herbert Spencer.
1878 W. JAMES in *Jrnl. Speculative Philos.* XII. 7 Whether any Spencerian would hail with hearty joy their advent is another matter. **1888** *Athenæum* 14 Jan. 47/1 Being somewhat of a Spencerian, Major Ellis looks on their gods as originally spirits.

Hence **Spenˈcerianism**, = next.
1881 LD. ACTON *Lett. to Mary Gladstone* (1904) 89 The doctrine that there is no resisting the priesthood except by definite Spencerianism. **1892** *Nation* 28 Apr. 322/3 The editor appears to be a propagandist of Spencerianism.

Spencerism (ˈspɛnsərɪz(ə)m). [f. *Spencer* (see prec.) + -ISM.] The philosophy of Herbert Spencer, or views in accordance with this.
1880 *Nature* XXI. 406 The propagation of Spencerism and Monism. **1900** H. MACPHERSON *H. Spencer* 66 Spencerism stands on its own merits as the philosophy of the knowable.

So **ˈSpencerite**[1], a Spencerian.
1871 J. MCCOSH *Christianity & Positivism* vii. 182 There is a..set of youths in our day who will become Comtists, or Millites, or Spencerites, or even Huxleyites. **1882** *Advance* (Chicago) 30 Mar. 194 There are such sects as Calvinists and Agnostics, and one..of Spencerites.

spencerite[2] (ˈspɛnsəraɪt). *Min.* [f. the name of L. J. *Spencer* (1870–1959), British mineralogist + -ITE[1].] A hydrated basic zinc phosphate, $Zn_4(PO_4)_2(OH)_2.3H_2O$, found as colourless or white monoclinic crystals, freq. in stalactitic masses, in a zinc mine near Salmo, British Columbia.
1916 *Nature* 29 June 375/1 Prof. T. L. Walker: Spencerite, a new zinc phosphate from British Columbia. **1918** *Univ. of Toronto Studies (Geol. Ser.)* No. 10. 13 The spencerite forms the central part of the stalactitic growths and would appear to have been sealed up by the later shell of calamine. **1972** *Mineral. Mag.* XXXVIII. 690 Spencerite is an example of a mineral containing Zn in both octahedral and tetrahedral co-ordination.

spencite (ˈspɛnsaɪt). *Min.* [f. the name of Hugh S. *Spence* (1885–1978), Canadian mineralogist + -ITE[1].] A metamict borosilicate of rare-earth and other elements (chiefly yttrium and calcium), which is closely related to tritomite and occurs as brownish- or greenish-black grains and irregular masses.
1961 C. FRONDEL in *Canad. Mineralogist* VI. 576 Spencite is a new borate-silicate of calcium and yttrium, $(Ca,Fe)_2(Y,La)_3(B_3Si_4.3Al_7)_8(O,OH,F,Cl)_{20}$... This new mineral was collected by Hugh S. Spence in 1934 from a prospect pit in Cardiff township..and was tentatively identified as thalenite. **1968** I. KOSTOV *Mineral.* 319 Spencite, $Y_3(CeTh)CaBSi_2O_{13}$, is another member [of the tourmaline group] occurring as black grains. **1973** *Canad. Mineralogist* XII. 71/1 Spencite varies widely in its physical properties and chemical composition. **1976** *Mineral. Abstr.* XXVII. 246/2 Spencite (tritomite-Y) is described from nepheline syenite pegmatites in the Dugdu and Kadyros Palaeozoic alkaline massifs.

spency (ˈspɛnsɪ). *dial.* [Of obscure origin.] The stormy petrel, *Procellaria pelagica*.
1813 MONTAGU *Ornith.* Suppl., *Petrel (Stormy)*,..Mitty, Assilag, Spency, Sea-Swallow, Allamotti. **1844** *Zoologist* II. 627 Storm petrel,..the 'Mother Carey's chickens', or 'Spencies', as they are called by sailors. **1899** *Shetland News* 14 Jan. (E.D.D.), The Manx shearwater, or 'lyrie' of our native folk,..and the storm petrel, or 'spencie'.

spend (spɛnd), *sb.*[1] [f. SPEND *v.*[1]]
1. a. The action of spending money; the amount spent.
a **1688** BUNYAN *Israel's Hope Encouraged* Wks. 1855 I. 618 What if I cannot but live upon the spend all my days, yet, if my friend will always supply my need, is it not well for me? *c* **1800** J. NEWTON in R. Cecil *Life* (1853) 169 A man always in society, is one always on the spend. **1904** *Sat. Rev.* 17 Dec. 751 The suggestion that the Government is 'on the spend'. **1976** *Computers in Higher Education & Research: Next Decade* (Dept. Educ. & Sci.) 22 About £21 million should be spent for universities on new machines, buildings and operating costs..with a spend of about £10 million for research councils for similar purposes. **1982** *ICL News* Oct. 4/1 On the hardware side customer spends are relatively high—typically around £3 million for an installation. **1983** *Observer* 16 Jan. 8/4 The battle for advertising spend.

b. *ellipt.* for 'spending money'. Freq. in *pl. colloq.* and *dial.* (chiefly northern).
1970 *Guardian* 9 Dec. 9/2, I can remember when Lancashire children..turned over their unopened wage packet to Mum, who gave them back very modest 'spends'. **1976** *West Lancs. Even. Gaz.* 13 Dec. 6/2 What do other OAPs get for 'spends'. **1977** P. CARTER *Under Goliath* xxiii. 127 Nearly everyone I knew got their spends on Friday night so they would all be at the pictures.

†**2.** *Obs. slang.* Semen, vaginal secretion; ejaculation. Cf. SPEND *v.*[1] 15 c.
1879–80 *Pearl* (1970) 13, I felt her crack deluged with a warm, creamy spend whilst my own juice spurted..in loving sympathy. *Ibid.* 217 You dissembling, bleeding, rotten..lump of shit, rubbed over with a little spend. *c* **1888–94** *My Secret Life* III. 143, I could always go on pushing after a spend in those days, my prick would not loose its stiffness for minutes afterwards. **1891** *Simple Tale of Suzan Aked* (1898) iii. 100 Then, of course, not a drop of spend can get into me, because it is all caught by the letter.

spend, *sb.*[2] *Sc.* [f. SPEND *v.*[3]] A spring, leap, bound. Also *fig.*
1825 in JAMIESON *Suppl.* **1828** MOIR *Mansie Wauch* xix. 277 Making a spend like a greyhound.

spend (spɛnd), *v.*[1] Pa. t. and pa. pple. spent. Forms: *Inf.* 4–7 **spende** (5 **spendyn**), 4– **spend.** *Pa. t.* 3–5 **spende**; 4–5 **spended** (5 **-ide, -yd**; *Sc.* 5 **-yt**, 6 **-it**); 4 **spente,** 5– **spente.** *Pa. pple.* 3–4 **i-spend,** 4–6 **spend(e**; 3 **i-spendet,** 4 **spendet,** 5 **-ut(te,** 6 *Sc.* **-it**; 4 **i-spended,** 4–5 **spendid,** 4–6 **-yd, spended** (5 **-ede**); 2, 5 **i-spent,** 6 **y-spent,** 4– **spent** (6 **spynt**), 5–6 **spente.** [OE. **spendan* (cf. *spendung* and *á-, forspendan*), ad. L. *expendĕre* (cf. It. *spendere*, Sp. *espender*), which was also adopted in other Germanic languages, as OHG. *spendôn, spentôn* (MHG. and G. *spenden*), OS. **spendôn* (MLG. and MDu. *spenden*), ON. *spenna.* The ME. *spende*, however, may also have been formed aphetically from OF. *despendre* DISPEND *v.*: cf. SPENCE. From the early ME. pa. t. and pa. pple. a new inf. SPENE *v.* was formed, on the analogy of such verbs as *wene* ween; the converse process took place in LEND *v.*[2]]

I. *trans.* **1. a.** Of persons: To pay out or away; to disburse or expend; to dispose of, or deprive oneself of, in this way.
The object is usually money, or a particular sum of this, but occas. a more general term denoting property or wealth, esp. in earlier use.
c **1175** *Moral Ode* 28 in *O.E. Hom.* I. 161 Al to muchel ich habbe ispent, to litel ihud in horde. *c* **1280** *Sarmun* 25 in *E.E.P.* (1862) 4 And bot þou hit hab ispend ari3te þe gode þat god þe haþ ilend of ihsu criste þou lesist þe si3t. *a* **1300** *Cursor M.* 17507 þai..gaf þam giftes gret to spend. *c* **1380** WYCLIF *Wks.* (1880) 5 Lest freris ypocrisie and wynnyng be stoppid and þe peples almes betere spendid. **1436** *Pol. Poems* (Rolls) II. 190 Oure money [is] spente alle to lytelle avayle. *c* **1491** *Chast. Goddes Chyld.* (Caxton) 69 Riches and worshippes ben but lente to man for a tyme to yelde rekeninge of hem how they ben spended. *a* **1533** LD. BERNERS *Huon* lx. 211 To seke hym I haue spent all my golde and syluer. **1574** J. DEE in *Lett. Lit. Men* (Camden) 34, I have..spent very many hundred powndes. *c* **1643** LD. HERBERT *Autobiog.* (1824) 5 After he had spent most part of his means, he became a soldier. **1697** DRYDEN *Virg. Georg.* I. 406 The Farmer to full Bowls invites his Friends, And what he got with Pains, with Pleasure spends. **1732** BERKELEY *Alciphr.* II. §2 When money is spent, it is all one to the public who spends it. **1776** ADAM SMITH *W.N.* II. iii. (1904) I. 378 That portion of his revenue which a rich man annually spends. **1827** SCOTT *Chron. Canongate* iii, If I lost the estate, I at least spent the price. **1894** *Temple Bar* CII. 340 She spent his money and led him such a life.
prov. **1548** in Strype *Eccl. Mem.* (1721) II. App. Q. 51 Evil gotten, worse spent. **1562** J. HEYWOOD *Prov. & Epigr.* (1867) 62 Soone gotten, soone spent, yll gotten yll spent. *Ibid.* 154 Lyttle good, soone spended.
fig. **1591** SHAKS. *Two Gent.* II. iv. 41 Sir, if you spend word for word with me, I shall make your wit bankrupt. **1663** DRYDEN *Wild Gallant* Prol., And for Wit, those that boast their own Estate, Forget Fletcher and Ben before them went, Their Elder Brothers, and that vastly spent.

b. Const. with prepositions, as †*about, for, in, on*, or *upon*.
a **1225** *Leg. Kath.* 101 For hare sake ane dale ha etheold of hire ealdrene god & spende al þet oðer in neodfule & in nakede. *c* **1290** *S. Eng. Leg.* I. 101 On leches heo hadde i-spendet Muche del of hire guod. *c* **1325** in *Pol. Songs* (Camden) 69 He spende al is tresour opon swyvyng. *c* **1400** *Brut* clxxiii. 195 His tresoure þat he hade spendede about his werre. *c* **1440** *Gesta Rom.* x. 32 (Harl. MS.), Also he spende ij[d] vpon him selfe. **1528** *Star Chamber Cases* (Selden) II. 177 [He] says he hasse a M[l] pownd to spend in the law ayenst hys Neyburus. **1578** in Feuillerat *Revels Q. Eliz.* (1908) 307 For sondrey parcells by him boughte & brought into the office to be spente about the rock. **1611** BIBLE *Isaiah* lv. 2 Wherefore doe yee spend money for that which is not bread? **1696** PRIDEAUX *Lett.* (Camden) 176 After all y[e] interest he could make and many thousands spent in y[e] canvas. **1706** E. WARD *Wooden World Diss.* (1708) 56 The poor Souls..are oblig'd to spend their Pay upon the very Wine that was assign'd them. **1735** JOHNSON *Lobo's Abyssinia* Descr. i. 45 They.. spent their Wealth in costly Ornaments for Churches, and Vessels for the Altars. **1883** F. M. PEARD *Contrad.* I. 23 She spent a fortune in shoes and gloves. **1897** W. C. HAZLITT *4 Generations* II. 185 When his lordship told her that he had spent upon her enough to build the *Great Eastern*. **1971** *Publishers' Weekly* 4 Oct. 42/2 Countless people..have longed to own the Oxford dictionary and could not afford to spend $300 for it. **1977** H. FAST *Immigrants* 6 Anna persuaded him..to spend two dollars for a heavy jacket.

†**c.** To give away (a garment) in payment. *Obs.*
c **1440** *Jacob's Well* 157 Brynge hedyr þat pilgrym þat spendyd 3ister evyn his slaueyn at þe wyn! **1553** T. WILSON *Rhet.* (1580) 133 He loues women well; he will spende Goddes Coope if he had it. **1575** *Gamm. Gurton* II. iv. 40 By the masse, chil rather spend the cote that is on my backe!

†**d.** To levy charges on (a person). Only in the phrase ***spend me and defend me.*** *Obs.*
1590 PAYNE *Brief Descr. Ireland* (1841) 4 They haue a common saying which I am persuaded they speak vnfeinedly, which is, Defend me and spend me. **1596** SPENSER *State Irel.* Wks. (Globe) 624/1 They..are very loth to yeld any certayne rent, but onely such spendinges, saying commmonly, 'Spend me and defend me'.

†e. With dative of the person whose money is expended. *Obs.*

1609 B. Jonson *Sil. Woman* iv. i, She spends me forty pounds a year in mercury and hogs-bones. **1666** Pepys *Diary* 21 Feb., A little vexed to see myself so beset with people to spend me money.

2. *absol.* To exercise, make, or incur expenditure of money, goods, means, etc.

1297 R. Glouc. (Rolls) 8026 Him ne roȝte hou he spende, ne wat, he was so prout. ?*a***1366** Chaucer *Rom. Rose* 1157 Not Avarice.. Was half to gripe so ententyf, As Largesse is to yeve and spende. *c***1440** *Jacob's Well* 207 þi wyif & chyld muste sparyngly..spendyn of þi euyl getyn good. **1530** Palsgr. 728/1 This gere can nat laste longe, for he spendeth a pace and getteth nothyng. **1595** Lodge *Fig for Momus* H i b, Spend on thy house, to tyle it from the raine. **1652** J. Wright tr. *Camus' Nat. Paradox* vi. 115 These Strangers, ..spending high, and making such cheer as the others were not accustomed to see. **1860** Ruskin *Unto this Last* iv. §72 The vital question for individual and for nation is..'to what purpose do they spend?' **1869** Lowell *Under Willows* 162 To spend in all things else, But of old friends to be most miserly.

prov. **1562** J. Heywood *Prov. & Epigr.* (1867) 54 Spend, and god shall send,..saith tholde ballet. **1636** Sir R. Baker *Cato Variegatus* 32 Tis an old saying; spend, and God will send.

b. In the phrase ***to spend and be spent.***

1611 Bible *2 Cor.* xii. 15 And I wil very gladly spend and bee spent for you. **1694** Penn *Rise & Progr. Quakers* iii. 66 They could have no design to themselves in this Work, thus to expose themselves to Scorn and Abuse; to spend and be spent. **1828** Carlyle *Misc.* (1857) I. 236 Counting it blessedness enough so to spend and be spent.

3. To expend or employ (labour, material, thought, etc.) in some specified way: **a.** Const. *on* or *upon.*

*a***1300** *Cursor M.* 20857 It es na spede our suinc to spend On thing we may noght bring til end. *c***1400** *Destr. Troy* 6502 The tother speire, þat he sparit, [he] spent vpon hym. *c***1440** *Pallad. on Husb.* iv. 541 The plauntys sette is stonys to sustene, And donged lond vpon the rootys spende. **1590** Shaks. *Mids. N.* iii. ii. 74 You spend your passion on a misprisd mood. **1605** Bacon *Adv. Learn.* i. iv. §2 Then did Sturmius spend such infinite and curious paines upon Cicero the Orator. **1662** Stillingfl. *Orig. Sacræ* ii. vii. §1 Their great R. Abravanel, who spends his whole 13 Chapter *de capite fidei* upon it. **1706** E. Ward *Wooden World Diss.* (1708) 19 He spends a great deal of puzzling Thought upon his Boat's Crew. **1707** Mortimer *Husb.* (1721) I. 2 It concerns the judicious Husbandman to consider the Nature of the Land he is to spend his Time, Cost and Labour upon. **1822** Lamb *Elia* i. *Distant Corresp.*, As useless as a passion spent upon the dead. **1875** Jowett *Plato* (ed. 2) I. 170 Why do you spend many words and speak in many ways on this subject?

b. Const. *in.*

*a***1300** *Cursor M.* 28493 O spusail i haf þe halines In lust al spended o my fles. **1500-20** Dunbar *Poems* lxxix. 9 Ȝe neid nocht..paper for to spend, nor ink, In the ressaueing of my soumes. **1588** Shaks. *L.L.L.* ii. i. 19 To be counted wise, In spending your wit in the praise of mine. **1663** *Extr. St. Papers rel. Friends* ii. (1911) 181 All the paines and cost therein spent was casting good money after bad. **1696** Tate & Brady *Ps.* cii. 5, I spend my Breath in Groans. **1728** Pemberton *Newton's Philos.* 319 It will be necessary to spend a few words in explaining what is meant by the refraction of light. **1889** *Nature* 24 Oct. 613 The equivalence of the work spent in overcoming fluid.

c. With other constructions.

*c***1340** Hampole *Pr. Consc.* 2431 Þe byhoves acounte yhelde..how þow has spendyd þi wittes fife. *c***1430** Lydg. *Min. Poems* (Percy Soc.) 224 For the better thy speche thou spende. **1509** Hawes *Past. Pleas.* xliv. (Percy Soc.) 214 And thus in vaine thou hast thy labour spent. *a***1529** Skelton *Agst. Garnesche* iv. 176 My study myght be better spynt. **1619** Fletcher, etc. *Knt. Malta* iii. ii, My last breath cannot Be better spent, than to say I forgive you. **1648** Gage *West Ind.* xx. 175, I would spend my best endeavours for the helping and furthering of them. *a***1763** W. King *Polit. & Lit. Anecd.* (1819) 154 To spend three or four whole pages to prove that this is neither Latin nor sense.

d. To express (an opinion). Now *dial.*

1687 Miège *Gt. Fr. Dict.* ii. s.v., To spend his Verdict, to give one's Opinion. **1902** *Brit. Med. Jrnl.* 19 July 209 An Ulster man will ask his medical adviser to 'spend his opinion' on a case.

4. a. To employ, occupy, use or pass (time, one's life, etc.) *in* or *on* some action, occupation, or state.

*a***1300** *Cursor M.* 28259 Þe tyme þat ic in lijf has lende In idel-nes ic haue it spende. *c***1385** Chaucer *L.G.W.* 650 *Cleopatra*, And thus the longe day in fight they spende. *c***1482** J. Kay tr. *Caoursin's Siege Rhodes* (1870) ¶2 The space of .iii. yeres which were spended and occupped in the conseylyng of thes werkes. **1509** Hawes *Past. Pleas.* xxxi. (Percy Soc.) 150 That you your youth in ydelness wyll spende. **1560** Daus tr. *Sleidane's Comm.* 137 The space of two dayes followyng, was spent in Godly admonitions. **1600** Holland *Livy* x. xxii. 367 Thus in handling of these matters was that day spent. **1669** Sturmy *Mariners' Mag.* ii. ii. 52 Men..spending their spare-time on this Practice. *a***1701** Maundrell *Journ. Jerus.* (1732) 142 After about half an hour spent in surveying this place. **1746** Francis tr. *Horace, Epist.* i. vii. 69 Philip, whose Youth was spent in Feats of War. **1802** Mar. Edgeworth *Moral T.* (1816) I. iv. 19 He spent his time in training horses. **1837** Carlyle *Fr. Rev.* i. i. iii, Christophe de Beaumont, who has spent his life in persecuting hysterical Jansenists. **1859** Jephson *Brittany* viii. 112 The morning..was spent in walking about Morlaix.

b. With other complements.

*a***1400** *Minor Poems fr. Vernon MS.* xxxii. 347 Þenk þenne ..Hou þou hast spendet þi tyme honeste. *a***1440** *Relig. Pieces fr. Thornton MS.* 19 Þan sall þou besyly thynke how þou hase spende þat day (or þat nyghte). **1580** Lyly *Euphues* (Arb.) 243 Would you haue me spend the floure of my youth, as you doe the withered rase of your age? **1621** T. Williamson tr. *Goulart's Wise Vieillard* 46 Young men (for the most part) spend their time badly. **1687** A. Lovell tr. *Thevenot's Trav.* i. 56 They are extreamly Lazy, spending the whole day sitting on a Divan. **1715** De Foe *Fam. Instruct.* i. v. (1841) I. 109 How do they spend the sabbath at your aunt's? **1799** Han. More *Fem. Educ.* (ed. 4) I. 120 They do not scruple to allow their daughters to spend almost the whole of their time exactly like the daughters of worldly people. **1808** Scott in *Lockhart* (1837) I. i. 35 My time with him, though short, was spent greatly to my advantage. **1891** Marie A. Brown tr. *Runeberg's Nadeschda* 13 Many hours had been thus sweetly spent.

c. *ellipt.* To pass (the day, evening, etc.) in social intercourse or entertainment, or as a guest.

1697 J. Lewis *Mem. Dk. Glocester* (1789) 51 Mrs. Atkinson invited Lady Harriot and Lady Anne Churchill one day to dine with her, in her chamber, and spend the day. **1843** Dickens *Christm. Carol* iii, The very lamp-lighter.. was dressed to spend the evening somewhere. **1852** Mrs. Stowe *Uncle Tom's C.* iii, I'm so glad you's come! Missis is gone to spend the afternoon.

5. a. To use up; to exhaust or consume by use; to wear out. In later use freq. with *force, fury,* etc., as object.

1297 R. Glouc. (Rolls) 8332 Þe sarazins wiþoute wuste ..þat no maner liflode ne miȝte to hom wende; So þat þo hii adde ispend þat wiþinne was [etc.]. *a***1375** *Lay Folks Mass-bk.* App. iv. 347 Whon his parchemyn was al spende, He rauhte þe Rolle bi þe ende Wiþ his teth a-non. **1387** Trevisa *Higden* (Rolls) IV. 331 Þey chaungede nevere hosen and schoon, noþer cloþinge, but whan þey were i-tore or i-spend. *c***1440** *Jacob's Well* 206 And it be spendyd or wastyd, þou art noȝt bounde to restore it. **1535** Coverdale *Deut.* xxxii. 23 I wil heape myscheues vpon them, I wil spende all myne arowes at [1611 vpon] them. ?**1580** Lodge *Sch. Abuse* A iv, Did not they spende one candle by seeking another. **1599** Shaks. *Much Ado* i. i. 281 If Cupid haue not spent all his Quiuer in Venice. **1633** G. Herbert *Temple, Ch. Porch* li, If thou be Master-gunner, spend not all That thou canst speak, at once. **1667** Milton *P.L.* i. 176 The Thunder.. Perhaps hath spent his shafts. **1707** Floyer *Physic. Pulse-Watch* 90 A great Contention of the Mind spends the Spirits, but if it be moderate, it only spends the Humidity of the Lympha. **1757** W. Wilkie *Epigoniad* vii. 220 Erring from the course, In mazes wide, the rower spent his force. **1781** J. Moore *View Soc. It.* (1790) I. viii. 87 Having spent their fury in the destruction of the tyrant. **1802** James *Milit. Dict.* s.v., To spend all your ammunition. **1878** Bosw. Smith *Carthage* 285 Meanwhile the war, which seemed for the moment to have spent its force in Italy, had broken out with fresh fury in Sicily.

transf. *a***1656** Ussher *Ann.* vi. (1658) 104 Into them he put all such as he suspected for enemies at home, desiring Cambyses that he would spend them there and never send them home again.

b. To bring to a violent end; to destroy; to consume by destruction or wasting; †to disperse or dissipate; to reduce or convert *into* something.

*c***1435** *Torr. Portugal* 2010 Tho men of armes theder went, Anon they had theyre hors spent, Her guttys oute she rave. **1481** *Cely Papers* (Camden) 80 Aull the whowlschypys ar cwm to Calles savyng vij, qwher of ij be spente. **1502** Arnolde *Chron.* (1811) 133 The saide William W. occupyed the sayde shyppe and spent her att Caleys, in soo moche that alle the gables, sayles, and other takell..he solde them at Caleis. **1570** *Satir. Poems Reform.* xxi. 104 On the countrie of Scotland..Thair is na mendis..With speid till thay be spendit. **1668** Culpepper & Cole *Barthol. Anat.* i. xvii. 47 Each branch..being again divided into other lesser ones, they are at last spent into Veins and Arteries as smal as Hairs. **1672** H. Savile *Engagement with Dutch Fleet* 6 A Fireship [was] taken, and we forced them to Spend most of the rest. **1871** R. Ellis tr. *Catullus* lxiv. 81 When a plague so deadly..Spent that slender city.

†c. Of emotion, action, etc.: To deprive (a person) of energy, strength, or resources; to exhaust or wear out. *Obs.*

1582 T. Watson *Centurie of Love* xix. 55, I whom Loue hath spent. **1616** J. Lane *Contn. Sqr.'s T.* viii. 30 Tell him I will auxiliaries send him, gainst warrs all difficulties, whiche maie spende him. **1674** Flavel *Husb. Spiritual.* Proem 9 It spends a minister to preach, but more to be silent.

d. *refl.* Of persons or things: To exhaust or wear out (oneself or itself); to become incapable of further activity; to cease to operate.

(*a*) *a***1593** Marlowe & Nashe *Dido* i. i, Here is this bush ..will I stand, Whiles my Aeneas spends himself in plaints. **1613** Heywood *Braz. Age* ii. ii. Wks. 1874 III. 208 Why should we..spend ourselues on accidentall wrongs? **1658** T. Langley in *Thurloe Papers* VII. 463 They [Quakers] cry out soe loude in their preachings, that they..spend themselves extremely. **1718** Hickes & Nelson *J. Kettlewell* i. xx. 44 He spending himself..in his Labours of Love. **1823** Mrs. Sherwood *Henry Milner* iii. vii, Suppose you go and spend yourself with a run,..and then we will have some discourse. **1837** Carlyle *Fr. Rev.* ii. iv. viii, Man after man spends himself in this cause. **1868** Nettleship *Ess. Browning* vi. 233 He never rested until he had spent himself in asserting those claims.

(*b*) **1663** S. Patrick *Parab. Pilgrim* xxiii. (1687) 236 This voice was intercepted by a new passion like to the former, though it was not long before it had spent it self. **1664** Power *Exp. Philos.* iii. 155 Camphire, which spends itself by continually Effluviating its own component Particles. **1705** Collier *Ess. Mor. Subj.* iii. *Pain* 25 For Torment like a Storm spends itself, and is destroy'd by its own Force. **1777** Priestley *Matt. & Spir.* Pref. (1782) p. ix, The popular Clamour may have spent itself. **1791** Cowper *Yardley Oak* 86 Thought cannot spend itself, comparing still The great and little of thy lot.

6. a. To suffer the loss of (blood, life, etc.); to allow to be shed or spilt.

[*a***1340** Hampole *Psalter* xx. 1 Swa that..he spend noght his preciouse blode in vayn on vs.] *c***1400** *Rom. Rose* 5440 Wenyng with hym they wolde abide..And also for hem to spende her bloode. **1516** *Acts Parlt. Scotl.* (1875) XII. 37/2 For conservacioun of quhais persoun we are determit to spend oure Livis. **1553** Eden *Treat. New Ind.* (Arb.) 6 Knowing that whereas one death is dewe to nature, the same is more honourably spent in such attemptes as may be to the glorye of God. **1594** Shaks. *Rich. III*, i. iii. 125 To royalize his blood, I spent mine owne. **1751** *Affect. Narr. of Wager* 53 They..would still spend their Lives for his Defence. **1868** Nettleship *Ess. Browning* vi. 158 Money which they had spent no sweat to obtain.

†b. *Naut.* To lose or incur the loss of (a mast, yard, sail, etc.) through bad weather or by some accident. *Obs.* (Freq. in the 17th c.)

1591 *Hon. Actions of E. Glemham* Cij, In which storme he spent his Maine Mast, which had beene before fysht. *c***1635** Capt. N. Boteler *Dial. Sea Services* (1685) 164 When a Mast or Yard is broken down by foul Weather, or any other accident, the Sea-word is, the Mast or Yard is spent. **1665** *Lond. Gaz.* No. 14/3 She was much beaten at Sea by storm, having spent her Main-mast and Fore-mast. **1694** Motteux *Rabelais* v. xviii. 79 Lest we should spend our Topsails.

7. a. To use for food or drink; to consume in this way; to eat or drink.

Common from *c* 1550 to *c* 1700, freq. with the addition *in one's house or family*; now *dial.*

*c***1380** Wyclif *Wks.* (1880) 217 God made alle goode mete & drynke couenable for men schulden spende it & lyue þerby. *a***1425** *Cursor M.* 13410 (Trin.) Þe good drynke shulde furst spende [*Cott.* dispend] And þe weiker at þe ende. *c***1450** Lovelich *Grail* lvi. 74 Of Cornes ȝe haven..gret plente, More thanne be ȝoure howshold spendid schal be. **1468** *Cov. Leet Bk.* 338 Hit is ordeyned þat no house-holder frohensfurth bye no more butter þen he well spend in his owne house. **1551** Ascham *Let.* Wks. 1865 I. ii. 257 Isles.. so full of walnut trees that they cannot be spent with eating, but they make oile of them. **1577** Harrison *England* in *Holinshed* (1587) 170/1 Malt..feedeth vpon the hop,.. which being extinguished the drinke must be spent or else it dieth. **1657** Sparrow *Bk. Com. Prayer* (1661) 279 If any of the Bread And Wine remain,..if consecrated, it is all to be spent..by the Communicants. **1670** J. Smith *Eng. Improv. Reviv'd* 190 Houses for keeping Pheasants, Partidges, and other Fowl to be spent in the Family, or sold at Markets. **1719** London & Wise *Compl. Gard.* 44 So great a quantity of Fruit..that 'twill be all we can do to spend them before the Rottenness..surprizes them. **1743** *Lond. & Country Brewer* ii. (ed. 2) 155 For Beer or Ale that is to be spent presently, two, three, or four, to eight Bushels will suffice. *a***1825** Forby *Voc. E. Anglia* s.v., We spend so much meat, flour, cheese, etc. in our family weekly.

absol. *c***1440** *Pallad. on Husb.* iv. 404 Or let a tonne of barly hem comprende Vchon from other; close hit til thou spende. *c***1475** *Rauf Coilȝear* 202 Thairfoir sic [good fare] as thow seis, spend on, and not spair.

†b. To serve, serve up (a dish, food, etc.). *Obs.*

*c***1350** *Will. Palerne* 4324 Þann were spacli spices spended al a-boute, fulsumli at þe ful to eche freke þer-inne. *c***1420** *Liber Cocorum* (1862) 31 Make hit þyke inowghe þenne, Whenne þou hit spendes byfore gode menne.

c. *Agric.* To use (a crop, hay, etc.) as food or fodder for cattle; to eat off.

1733 Tull *Horse-Hoeing Husb.* x. 104 There are now Three Manners of Spending Turneps with Sheep. **1764** *Museum Rust.* II. lix. 171 When I sow vetches before wheat, I always, in the spending my crop, have regard to the condition of my land. **1789** T. Wright *Meth. Watering Meadows* (1790) 7 The farmer..has an hundred tons of hay to carry off and spend upon his other ground. **1823** E. Moor *Suffolk Words* s.v., To spend all the stover, straw, and turnips on the land.

8. To make use of; to use or employ. Now *rare.*

*a***1400-50** *Alexander* 2458 Sparrethis spetous to spend & speris in handis. *c***1450** *Vrbanitatis* 74 in *Babees Bk.*, In chambur among ladyes bryȝth, Kepe þy tonge & spende þy syȝth. **1570** J. Campion in *Hakluyt's Voy.* (1599) II. i. 117 The oiles which we do spend in England for our cloth, are brought out of Spaine. **1621** in Foster *Eng. Factories Ind.* (1906) I. 259 In other places yt [*i.e.* coral] ys much spent to burne with the dead. *a***1692** Pollexfen *Disc. Trade* (1697) 129 If it be considered that all persons of all degrees, did wear, or spend, some of those Commodities. *a***1700** Evelyn *Diary* 12 Oct. 1641, A Light-horse-man (as they call it) taking us in, we spent our tide as far as Greenwich. **1845** Browning *Time's Revenges* 47 You shall see how the Devil spends A fire God gave for other ends!

9. a. To expend or employ (speech or language); to utter or emit (a word, sound, etc.).

13.. *Gaw. & Gr. Knt.* 410 If I spende no speche, þenne spedez þou þe better. **1362** Langl. *P. Pl.* A. viii. 50 Ac he þat spendeþ his speche and spekeþ for þe pore. **1508** Dunbar *Gold. Targe* 274, I knaw quhat thou of rethorike hes spent. **1576** Gascoigne *Philomene* Wks. 1910 II. 181 The piteous pleasant notes, Which Phylomene doth darkely spend in spring. **1591** Skaks. *1 Hen. VI*, ii. v. 38, I may embrace his Neck, And in his Bosom spend my latter gaspe. **1633** Bp. Hall *Hard Texts, N.T.* 20 However the false pretenders unto Wisdom are ready..to spend their censures thus injuriously.

†b. ***to spend the mouth, tongue,*** etc. Of hunting dogs: To bark or give tongue on finding or seeing the game. Also *fig.* *Obs.*

1590 Cokaine *Treat. Hunting* D ij b, He will vent so oft, and put vp ouer water, at which time the houndes will spend their mouthes verie lustely. **1599** Shaks. *Hen. V*, ii. iv. 70. *a***1627** H. Shirley *Mart. Soldier* iii. i. in Bullen *Old Pl.* (1882) I. 203 A packe of the bravest Spartan Dogges in the world; if they do but once open and spend there gabble, gabble, gabble it will make the Forest ecchoe. **1657** R. Ligon *Barbadoes* 3 The onely difference I finde is, these doe not spend their mouthes, but what they want in that is supplyed by the goodnesse of their noses. **1682** N. O. *Boileau's Lutrin* iv. 228 Nor was it Reason that the gutted Fops Should spend their Tongues, who could not use their Chops.

†c. *absol.* = prec. *Obs.*

1602 *2nd Pt. Return Parnass.* ii. v. 826 Hunters luck Sir, but there was a fault in your Hounds that did not spend well.

1651 CLEVELAND *Poems* 12 The Ven'sons now in view, our hounds spend deeper. **1672** R. WILD *Poet. Licent.* 39 Hanging 's the end By Huntsmen's Rule, of Hounds that will not spend. **1741** *Compl. Fam.-Piece* II. i. 290 Then draw with more Care, checking your Hound, lest he spends when he comes so near as to have him in the Wind.

fig. **1643** SIR T. BROWNE *Relig. Med.* II. §3 For then reason like a bad hound spends upon a false sent. **1682** S. PORDAGE *Medal Rev.* 233 Let the hot Tories, and their Poet Curse, They spend in vain, and you are ne'r the worse.

d. To allow or cause to flow; to shed.

1602 MARSTON *Antonio's Rev.* I. v, If hee is guiltlesse, why should teares be spent? **1697** *Phil. Trans.* XIX. 373 Whether any part of the Tree (as Body, Root, or Branch) will spend it [i.e. gum] being purposely Wounded. **1820** SCOTT *Monast.* xxvi, And you, Sir Knight, think better of us than to suppose you may spend Scottish blood, and reckon for it as for wine spilt in a drunken revel.

10. a. To consume, employ, use superfluously, wastefully, or with undue lavishness; to waste or squander; to throw away.

In some instances the sense is conveyed by the addition of *in vain, to no purpose*, etc.

1390 GOWER *Conf.* II. 395 Many on.. Whiche after felle in gret desese Thurgh wast of love, that thei spente. **1509** HAWES *Past. Pleas.* XXXI. (Percy Soc.) 154 Wo worth love that I do spend in wast. **1530** PALSGR. 728/1, I spende, as men.. wastyth any thyng in vayne, *je consume.* **1590** SIR J. SMYTH *Disc. Weapons* 22 Wherby it commeth to passe, that such quick and hastie Harquebuziers, doo worke no other effect but spend powder, match & shot. **1604** SHAKS. *Oth.* II. iii. 195 What's the matter That you vnlace your reputation thus, And spend your rich opinion, for the Name Of a night-brawler? **1638** JUNIUS *Paint. Ancients* 61 The impatient horses.. do spend before the race thousand and thousand steppes to no purpose. **1827** SCOTT *Highl. Widow* v, I am a fool.. to spend my words upon an idle.. unintelligent boy. **1885** 'MRS. ALEXANDER' *At Bay* xi, The horror and disgust of the creature on whom you spent your life!

b. To waste (time).

a **1604** HANMER *Chron. Ireland* (1809) 123 Brother Lazerianus (saith he) let us not spend time, neither trouble this people with this tedious question. **1658–9** SIR R. TEMPLE in *Burton's Diary* (1828) IV. 44, I am sorry this has spent your time. I do not see what fruit you will have by recommitting it, unless to spend as much more of your time. **1720** J. CLARKE *Educ. Youth* 27 Those vain Amusements that have been found out to make Boys spend their Time at School.

11. To allow (time, one's life, etc.) to pass or go by; to live or stay through (a certain period) to the end. Cf. sense 4.

1423 *Acts Privy Counc.* III. 90 His forsayd retenu.. continued fro yere to yere unto four yer was nere spendid and passid. *c* **1440** *Pallad. on Husb.* XII. 501 Tho iij dayes spende, They vessel hit. **1500–20** DUNBAR *Poems* lxix. 35 Remember thow hes compt to mak Off all thi tyme thow spendit heir. **1565** STAPLETON tr. *Bede's Hist. Ch. Eng.* 191 Spending all the daies of my life, in the mansion of the same monastery. **1617** MORYSON *Itin.* I. 12, I spent this winter at Leipzig. *c* **1643** LD. HERBERT *Autobiog.* (1824) 7 His son.. went to the Low Country Wars, and after some time spent there, came home. **1732** BERKELEY *Alciphr.* I. §1 If you and Dion would spend a week at my house. **1784** COWPER *Task* I. 547 And now she roams The dreary waste; there spends the livelong day. **1854** LD. HOUGHTON in T. W. Reid *Life* (1891) I. xi. 498, I have been spending six weeks in Ireland. **1886** C. E. PASCOE *Lond. of To-day* xx. (ed. 3) 199 A journey into the country affords perhaps the most rational and pleasant way of spending Sunday.

†**12. a.** To cause or involve expenditure of (something). *Obs.*

1616 *Buccleuch MSS.* (Hist. MSS. Comm.) I. 248 The putting off of the arraignments spent much money. **1674** JEAKE *Arith.* (1696) 451, 5 Guns in 2 Days spend 60 Barrels of Powder. **1703** R. N[EVE] *City & C. Purchaser* 276 A great Covering with these spends but little Mortar.. and but little time in laying.

b. To occupy, take up, or waste (time). †Also with double object.

a **1627** DONNE *Lett.* (1651) 172 It spent me so little time after going, that [etc.]. *a* **1631** —— *Six Serm.* i. (1634) 2 That earth and that heaven which spent God himself.. six dayes in finishing. *a* **1649** WINTHROP *New. Eng.* (1825) I. 140 The main business, which spent the most time,.. was about the removal of Newtown.

13. Const. with adverbs, as *away, out, up*, in various senses.

1532 MORE *Confut. Tindale* Wks. 609/2 Therin he spendeth vp that Chapiter. **1542** UDALL *Erasm. Apoph.* 16 b, Some ther bee, that in lyngreyng & drivyng foorth.. spenden out all their life. **1576** FLEMING *Panopl. Epist.* 405, I was fully determined.. to haue spent away the tedious time, in some talke. **1602** CAREW *Cornwall* 157 b, The Cornish forces.. encamped themselues on the greene,.. and there spent out the night. **1650** TRAPP *Comm. Deut.* xxxii. 23, 'I will spend mine arrowes,' which yet cannot be all spent up. **1848** THACKERAY *Van. Fair* lxvii, She.. reproached herself for having flung away such a treasure. It was gone indeed. William had spent it all out.

II. *intr.* †**14.** Of time, the season, etc.: To pass, elapse. *Obs.*

1607 S. COLLINS *Serm.* (1608) 11 To finish this, because the time spendeth so fast. *c* **1614** SIR W. MURE *Dido & Æneas* II. 246 Before the palace all the cowrt attends The Queen's aryvall, whil the morning spends. **1681** R. KNOX *Hist. Ceylon* 120 The time and season of the year spending for the ship to proceed on her voyage.

†**15. a.** To be consumed, dispersed, exhausted, or used up; to pass off or *away*. *Obs.*

1626 BACON *Sylva* §129 The Sound spendeth, and is dissipated in the Open Aire. *Ibid.* §622 The Vines.. are so often cut, and so much digged and dressed, that their Sap spendeth into the Grapes. **1643** J. STEER tr. *Exp. Chyrurg.* vi. 25 He shall diligently take notice how the blacknesse of the powder spendeth away. **1704** N. N. tr. *Boccalini's Advts. fr. Parnass.* III. 247[They] never thought it worth their while to examine how the Oil spent, or the Taper burn'd.

†**b.** Of a storm: To die down, exhaust its force or fury. *Obs.*$^{-1}$

1655 VAUGHAN *Silex Scint.* III. *Thalia Rediv.* 237 Giving the tempest time to spend.

c. To ejaculate; to have an orgasm. *slang.*

1662 PEPYS *Diary* 7 Sept. (1970) 191, I went up to her and played and talked with her and, God forgive me, did feel her; which I am much ashamed of, but I did no more, though I had so much a mind to it that I spent in my breeches. **1714** *Cabinet of Love* 19 For at one instant both together spent. **1763** WILKES & POTTER *Essay on Woman*, Oft when we spend we propagate unknown. **1868** *Index Expurgatorius of Martial* 1 When you say, Hedylus, 'I shall spend, finish if you mean to finish', my flame languishes. **1922** JOYCE *Ulysses* 739 He made me spend the 2nd time tickling me behind with his finger. **1980** R. L. DUNCAN *Brimstone* vii. 163 He felt himself spending at the very moment she contracted around him.

16. a. Of foodstuffs, wheat, hay, etc.: To turn out or prove in use to be of a certain quality; to last or hold out *well*. Now *dial.*

1673 TEMPLE *Ess., Ireland* Wks. 1720 I. 115 They had observed [that] it [i.e. butter] spent as if it came from the richest Soil of the two. **1687** MIÈGE *Gt. Fr. Dict.* s.v., Meat that spends well. **1763** *Museum Rust.* I. 156 It [wheat] was sold in the public markets, and declared.. to spend as well as if it had been of the last year's growth. **1764** *Ibid.* II. 210 Yet did this hay spend as well as if it had been got in never so favourably. **1840** SPURDENS *Suppl. Forby's E. Angl. Gloss* s.v., The meal spends well, i.e. it holds out well; lasts long.

b. *dial.* To produce or yield (*well*).

1854 MISS BAKER *Northampt. Gloss.* s.v., Corn that yields well is said to spend well. **1893** *Wilts. Gloss.* 152 How do your taters spend to-year?

17. Of a liquid: To flow or run. ? *Obs.*

1735 *Dict. Polygraph.* I. S 4 White-lead;.. let it be as stiff as it well can be to spend well from the pencil. **1742** *Lond. & Country Brew.* I. (ed. 4) 28 Taking particular Care.. to return two, three, or more Hand-bowls of Wort into the Mash-tub, that first of all runs off, till it comes absolutely fine and clear, and then it may spend away, or run off for good. **1811** *Self Instructor* 535 Fustic.. spends with or without salts.

spend, *v.*[2] Now *dial.* [Alteration of SPEN *v.*]

†**1.** *trans.* To grasp (a spear). *Obs.*

c **1430** *Syr Tryam.* 828 A spere spendyd he thare; He prekyd to the kyng with fors. *a* **1500** *Chevy Chase* 84 He sawe the Duglas to the deth was dyght; He spendyd a spear, a trusti tre.

2. *dial.* (See quot.)

1877 *N.W. Linc. Gloss.* 234 *Spend up*, to brace up the hames of harness.

spend, *v.*[3] *Sc.* [Of obscure origin.] *intr.* To spring, leap, dash.

1533 BELLENDEN *Livy* I. xviii. (S.T.S.) I. 106 [She] draif þe chariot oure hir faderis body, with sic violence þat.. þe blude of hir faderis body spendit on hir face. **1808** JAMIESON, *Spend*, to spring. **1839** MOIR *Mansie Wauch* (ed. 2) xxii. 275 Holding the naig's head, in case it should spend off, and capsize the concern.

spend, *v.*[4] *Mining.* (See quot. 1860.)

1847 in HALLIWELL. **1860** *Eng. & For. Mining Gloss., Cornw.* (ed. 2) 24 *Spend*, to break ground; to work away.

spendable ('spɛndəb(ə)l), *a.* Also 6 -abyll. [f. SPEND *v.*[1] + -ABLE. Cf. SPENDIBLE *a.*]

†**1.** That may be expended, consumed, or used up for ordinary purposes. Of paper; Suitable for wrapping things in, or similar uses, in contrast to writing-paper. *Obs.*

a **1500** *MS. Sloane 4.* 81 Take spendabyll pauper and clene flesshe of þe hyppys of a catt. **1502** ARNOLDE *Chron.* (1811) 74 Paper scribabil the bale, vi. d'. Paper spendable the reme, q'. **1527** *MS. Acc. R. Gibson* (P.R.O.), Item.. for rebyn poyntis for the kynge and the lordes, iij dosyn and a groose of spendabyll poyntis.

2. That which can be spent for current needs.

1886 *Times* 29 Mar. 8/3 The enormous loss of spendable income thereby occasioned to the landlords. **1893** *Ibid.* 8 Aug. 10/1 The loss of spendable income by farmers owing to crop failures and low prices.

spend-all. Now *rare.* Also spendall, spend all. [f. SPEND *v.*[1] + ALL *sb.*] One who spends all his goods, money, etc.; one who is prodigal, wasteful, or too free in expenditure; a spendthrift.

1553 T. WILSON *Rhet.* (1580) 123, I call a notable flatterer, a faire spoken manne:.. a spende-all, a liberall gentleman. **1566** DRANT *Horace, Sat.* I. ii. A viij, Teschue, and shun the name Of spendall, and of scatter good. **1609** W. M. *Man in Moon* (1849) 29 Thy wife shall be enamored of some spend-all, which shall wast all as licentiously as thou hast heaped together laboriously. **1655** R. YOUNGE *Charge agst. Drunkards* 4 Drunkards are not onely lazie get-nothings; but they are also riotous spend-alls. **1708** *Brit. Apollo* I. No. 5. 3/1 A Sot, a Spend-all, a Gamester. **1870** *Macm. Mag.* July 168/1 A lounging upper world of spend-alls and do-nothings. **1896** MARY BEAUMONT *Joan Seaton* 114, I like a thrifty man, he doesn't backen himself like a spend-all.

transf. **1583** MELBANCKE *Philotimus* A iij, By your folly spendall is your store consumed, and by your God the sendall it may be restored.

†**spender**[1]. *Obs.* In 4 spendere, 5 -are. [Aphetic form of *de-*, DISPENDER.] A steward.

1340 *Ayenb.* 190 He.. het his desspendoure þet he him yeaue uyftene pond of gold. Þe spendere be his couaytise ne yeaf bote vyf. *Ibid.*, Þo he clepede his spendere and him acsede hou moche he hedde y-yeue to þe kniȝte. *c* **1440** *Promp. Parv.* 468/2 Spendare, *dispensator.*

spender[2] ('spɛndə(r)). Also 4 spendour, 5 -are. [f. SPEND *v.*[1] + -ER[1]. Cf. MDu. *spender*, OHG. *spentâri, -eri* (MHG. *spendære, -iere*, G. *spender*).]

1. One who spends; *spec.* one who spends lavishly or wastefully, a spendthrift.

1393 LANGL. *P. Pl.* C. VI. 28 An ydel man þow semest, A spendour þat spende mot oþer a spille-tyme. **1398** TREVISA *Barth. De P.R.* VI. xvi. (Bodl. MS.), He is a greete spender of his lordes good and catel. *c* **1440** *Promp. Parv.* 468/2 Spendare in waast, *prodigus. c* **1450** *Myrr. our Ladye* 114 Ye saye that she ys a prudente and a ware spender and dysposer of goodes. **1562** J. HEYWOOD *Prov. & Epigr.* (1867) 62 Ye are calde.. to great a spender. **1581** SIDNEY *Apol. Poet.* (Arb.) 42 They would let so vnprofitable a spender starue. **1620** T. GRANGER *Div. Logike* 200 Of Spenders there are two sorts, some are Prodigall, some Liberall. **1670** *Moral State Eng.* 90 She is commonly a most extravagant spender. **1760–72** H. BROOKE *Fool of Qual.* (1809) III. 118 An industrious.. man.. is richer in my eye than a spender with thousands. **1844** EMERSON *Lect., Young Amer.* Wks. (Bohn) II. 302 Money is of no value, it cannot spend itself. All depends on the skill of the spender. **1883** *American* VI. 217 Very rich men in England are much freer spenders than they are here.

prov. **1596** BELL *Surv. Popery* I. II. iv. 84 After great getters come great spenders. **1611** COTGR., *Mal soupe qui tout disne*, of a young spender comes an old beggar. **1629** GAULE *Holy Madn.* 438 After a great Getter, then commonly comes a Spender. **1635** J. GORE *Way to Well-doing* 25 A good sparer makes a good spender. **1639** J. CLARKE *Paræmiol.* 262 Great spenders are bad lenders.

transf. **1611** CHAPMAN *Widdowes T.* Wks. 1873 III. 7 My former suites have been all spenders, this shall be my speeder. **1656** DAVENANT *Siege Rhodes* 1st Entry, They Stewards are, Without accompt, to that wild Spender, War.

2. One who, or that which, consumes, employs, or uses up; a consumer or waster *of* something.

1565 COOPER *Thesaurus, Consumptor*, a spender, consumer, or waster. **1600** SIR W. CORNWALLIS *Essays* xviii. Lj b, I will put away this sleepy Humour, for it is an extreme spender. **1675** HAN. WOOLLEY *Gentlw. Comp.* 85 Queen Elizabeth.. was pleased to term Plays the harmless Spenders of time. **1704** SWIFT *Mech. Operat. Spir.* in *Tale Tub* 296 To prevent Perspiration, than which nothing is observed to be a greater Spender of Mechanick Light. *a* **1825** FORBY *Voc. E. Anglia, Spender*, a consumer. A 'small spender' is a person who has very little appetite.

3. *Tanning.* A pit in which the bark is leached. Also *attrib.* in ***spender pit***.

1882 *Encycl. Brit.* XIV. 382/2 The method of leaching commonly adopted in the United Kingdom is to pass the bark through a series of leachers or spender pits. **1897** C. T. DAVIS *Manuf. Leather* iv. (ed. 2) 61 When the material in No. 1 is spent, it is cast and filled with fresh bark, and becomes the best leach,.. No. 2 becoming the spender.

'spendful, *a. rare*$^{-0}$. [f. SPEND *v.*[1]] Inclined to spend; lavish, extravagant.

1611 COTGR., *Despendeux*, spendfull, wastfull. *Ibid.*, *Despensier*, spending,.. spendfull.

†**spend-good.** *Obs. rare.* [f. SPEND *v.*[1] + GOOD *sb.*] A spend-all, spendthrift.

1605 *Play of Stucley* in Simpson *Sch. Shaks.* (1878) 162 He's very wild, a quarreller, a fighter Aye, and I doubt a spend-good too. **1611** COTGR., *Enfans sans soucy*, an vnthrift, spend-good, carelesse companion.

†**'spendible**, *a. Obs.*$^{-0}$ [ad. late L. *spendibilis* (10th c. in Du Cange), f. late L. *spendĕre* to weigh out, expend, etc.] = SPENDABLE *a.* 1.

1483 *Cath. Angl.* 353/2 Spendybylle, *expendibilis.*

'spending, *sb.* ? *Obs.* [prob. f. SPEND *v.*[2]] A cross-bar forming part of the bottom of a coal-corf.

1797 J. CURR *Coal Viewer's Pract. Comp.* 16 Flags for the corf bottom, of Oak..; bars or spendings of Oak. *Ibid.* 19 This plate is nailed under the spending of the corf.

spending ('spɛndɪŋ), *vbl. sb.* [f. SPEND *v.*[1]]

1. a. The disbursing, expending, paying out or away of money, etc.; expenditure. †*at other spending*, at another's expense.

c **1000** ÆLFRIC *Hom.* (Thorpe) II. 556 Sum underfehþ eorðlice æhta, and se sceal ðæs pundes spendunge Gode agifan of his æhtum. **1338** R. BRUNNE *Chron.* (1810) 280 First he was a kyng, now is he soudioure, & is at oþer spendyng bonden in þe toure. **1377** LANGL. *P. Pl.* B. XIV. 197 But owre spences and spendyng sprynge of a trewe wille, Elles is al owre laboure loste. *c* **1430** LYDG. *Min. Poems* (Percy Soc.) 67 [Be] Curteys of language, in spendyng mesurable. **1500–20** DUNBAR *Poems* xli. 5 Be nocht a wreche, nor skerche in ȝour spending. **1582** N. LICHEFIELD tr. *Castanheda's Conq. E. Ind.* I. xxvi. 69 b, Not remembring the trouble of his spirite, neyther yet the spending of his treasure. **1686** tr. *Chardin's Coronat. Solyman* 90 According to the usual rate of their spending. **1719** RAMSAY *To Arbuckle* 111 My income, management, and spending. **1815** SCOTT *Guy M.* xxxii, It wasna for his spending,.. for he just had a mutton-chop and a mug of ale. **1848** THACKERAY *Van. Fair* xxvi, There was a deal of spending in two thousand pounds. **1867** FREEMAN *Norm. Conq.* (1877) I. v. 297 There was nothing.. but.. spending of money.

transf. **1412–20** LYDG. *Chron. Troy* II. 1511 For whom I had.. so gret ado Or I hir gat with spendyng of my blood.

b. An instance or occasion of this; an amount spent.

1617 RICH *Irish Hubbub* 46, 319375. pounds all spent in smoake, besides priuate spendings. **1666** PEPYS *Diary* 31

Dec., My spendings this year have exceeded my spendings the last, by 644*l.*

†**2. a.** That which may be expended or spent; means of support; goods, money, cash. *Obs.* (freq. in the 15th c.).

a **1290** *S. Eustace* 209 in Horstm. *Altengl. Leg.* (1881) 215 Swinken and sweten he moste þo, Wor [= for] his spending wes al at-go. *c* **1325** *Deo Gratias* 33 in *E.E.P.* (1862) 129 Whon .i. hedde spendyng here bifore, þer wolde no felauschupe founde me fro. **1436** *Pol. Poems* (Rolls) II. 166 They loste here goode, here mone, and spendynge. **1470–85** Malory *Arthur* xi. xi. 587 Whanne she was awaked she sente a squyer after them with spendynge ynough. **1500–20** Dunbar *Poems* xxi. 13 Lak of spending dois him spur. **1650** Row *Hist. Kirk* (Wodrow Soc.) 417 The money furnished him spending till he came to London.

†**b.** A supply of some produce or commodity formerly levied by an Irish landlord upon his tenants. *Obs. rare.*

1596 Spenser *State Irel.* Wks. (Globe) 623/2 The which is a common use amongest the Irish landlordes, to have a common spending upon theyr tenauntes. *Ibid.* 624/1 They ..are very loth to yeld any certayne rent, but onely such spendinges. **1612** Davies *Why Ireland*, etc. (1747) 179 Irish exactions,..cuttings, tallages, or spendings.

3. The action of using or employing, of using up or consuming, in later use *esp.* as food.

a **1430** *Octouian* 376 Both thys chylde and thy palfray, Thou most here lete thys ylke day To owre spendyng. **1500–20** Dunbar *Poems* ix. 11 Off the wrang spending of my wittis fyve. **1573** Tusser *Husb.* (1878) 120 Whome fancie persuadeth..to haue for his spending, sufficient of hops. **1648** Gage *West Ind.* 133 Others to bring him wood for his house spending. **1693** Evelyn *De la Quint. Compl. Gard.* I. 77 As for the Fruits that are for the spending both during the End of Autumn, and all the whole Winter. **1709** Dampier *Voy.* III. ii. 24 The Fish or Flesh that they take, besides what serves for present spending, they dry on a Barbacue. **1764** *Museum Rust.* II. ii. 14 They made excellent pork for family spending. **1850** *Jrnl. R. Agric. Soc.* XI. i. 150 The turnip or root land..is ploughed and planted as opportunity offers up to Christmas..; the spending and carting off requiring time.

4. a. The action or fact of losing, destroying, exhausting, etc.

c **1595** Capt. Wyatt *Dudley's Voy.* (Hakl. Soc.) 54 When wee expected nothing less then..breakinge of shrowdes, spendinge of mastes, springinge of plankes. **1598** R. Bernard tr. *Terence, Heavtontim.* Prol., To the spending of my spirits and wasting of my bodie. **1605** *Journ. Earl Nottingham* in *Harl. Misc.* (Malh.) II. 540 Had not the hoy ..by spending of her mast..caused a longer abode. **1680** Burnet *Rochester* (1692) 21 He was fully perswaded that Death was not the spending or dissolution of the soul. **1707** Mortimer *Husb.* (1721) II. 54 Be careful to rub a little dry Earth upon the Wound where you cut them,..to prevent their spending of themselves too much, which these Trees are very subject to do.

†**b.** *Obs. slang.* An orgasm; an ejaculation. Cf. spend *v.*[1] 15 c.

1856 W. Whitman *Leaves of Grass* 242 The babes I beget upon you are to beget babes in their turn, I shall demand perfect men and women out of my love-spendings. **1879–80** *Pearl* (1970) 15 She came again in another luscious flood of spendings.

†**5.** Of dogs: The action of giving tongue. *Obs.*

1615 Markham *Country Contentm.* i. i. 7 If you would have your Kennell for sweetnesse of cry, then you must compound it of some large dogges, that haue deepe solempe mouthes, and are swift in spending, which must as it were beare the base in the consort.

6. The pouring or rushing *of* water.

1847 Emerson *Poems* (1857) 156, I see the inundation sweet, I hear the spending of the stream.

7. *attrib.* in the sense 'used or available for ordinary expenditure or consumption', as ***spending-brass***, ***-silver*** (= spending-money), ***spending income***; **spending-cheese** (see quot. *a* 1825).

1377 Langl. *P. Pl.* B. xi. 278 *Spera in deo* speketh of prestes þat haue no spendyng syluer. *c* **1386** Chaucer *Can. Yeom. T.* 7 And spending silver had he right y-nough. *a* **1500** *Gest Robin Hood* ccxlv. in Child *Ball.*, For of thy spendynge-syluer, monke, Thereof wyll I ryght none. **1815** Scott *Guy M.* xxxviii, I'll take care o' the bits o' claes, and what spending siller she maun hae. *a* **1825** Forby *Voc. E. Anglia*, *Spending-cheese*, a cheese of a middling quality, used for family consumption in the dairy districts of Suffolk. **1862** Trollope *N. America* xi, A man should certainly not apportion more than a seventh of his spending income to his house rent. **1896** Snowden *Web of Weaver* iv, He had a great deal more 'spending-brass' nor I could handle.

b. In the sense 'of or pertaining to expenditure or disbursement', as ***spending-power***, ***spree***, ***tax***.

1930 *Economist* 13 Sept. 477/1 Economy appeared to be denounced as a 'policy of stagnation' and the dangerous line of 'increased spending-power' once more held out as a remedial policy. **1942** *Time* 7 Sept. 94/3 The Senate Finance committee..pondered a new Treasury proposal for a 'spending tax' designed to encourage war savings. **1956** A. Huxley *Adonis & Alphabet* 140 We are now squandering the capital of metallic ores and fossil fuels... How long can this spending spree go on? **1968** *Punch* 23 Oct. 563/1 At the back of my mind there is a tiny doubt about the feasibility of the Spending Tax. **1980** 'R. B. Dominic' *Attending Physician* xvi. 144 You're not going on a spending spree with all that loot, are you?

ˈspending, *ppl. a.* [f. spend *v.*[1]] That spends, in various senses of the verb.

1589 Puttenham *Eng. Poesie* iii. xxiv. (Arb.) 298 It is decent to be..in houshold expence pinching and sparing, in publicke entertainement spending and pompous. **1639** J. Clarke *Paræmiol.* 261 A sparing father, and a spending son. **1674** Flavel *Husb. Spiritual.* xvii. 147 If this were not so, all the self-denial, spending duties and sharp sufferings of the people of God would turn to their damage. **1681** —— *Meth. Grace* ix. 203 Soul troubles are spending and wasting troubles. **1885** *Times* (weekly ed.) 7 Aug. 6/4, I am an industrious man; I am not a spending man.

spending-money. [f. spending *vbl. sb.* 7.] Money used or available for spending; a sum allowed for this purpose; pocket-money.

1598 R. Bernard tr. *Terence, Heavtontim.* i. ii, Allowing them little spending mony. **1600** Dymmok *Ireland* (1843) 8 Soren is a kind of allowance over and above the bonaght, which the Galloglass exact upon the poore by way of spendinge monye. **1632** Massinger *City Madam* i. i, From whom Received you spending-money? **1707** J. Chamberlayne *St. Gt. Brit.* ii. iii. lvi. (1710) 654 The Allowance of 1*s.* 6*d.* per Week for Spending-Money. *a* **1732** T. Boston *Crook in Lot* (1805) 153 The servant at the term gets his fee in a round sum, while the young heir gets but a few pence for spending-money. **1856** Olmsted *Slave States* 102 The slaves have a good many ways of obtaining 'spending money'. **1890** *Spectator* 5 July, Each missionary is therefore mulcted on the average to the extent of £60 a year, a direct reduction..in his total spending-money of nearly one-fourth.

ˈspendless, *a. rare*⁻¹. [f. spend *v.*[1] + -less.] That cannot be spent or consumed.

1600 B. Young in *Eng. Helicon* Kij, An endlesse plaint that shuns all consolation, A spendlesse flame that never is impaired.

ˈspendsavour, *a. nonce-wd.* [f. spend *v.*[1] + savour *sb.*] That has lost its savour.

1879 G. M. Hopkins *Poems* (1967) 81 Are you beam-blind, yet to a fault in a neighbour deft-handed? are you that liar And, cast by conscience out, spendsavour salt?

spendthrift (ˈspɛndθrɪft), *sb.* (and *a.*). Also 7 **spend-thrift.** [f. spend *v.*[1] + thrift *sb.*[1] Cf. the earlier dingthrift.]

1. One who spends money profusely or wastefully; one who wastes his patrimony by foolish or lavish expenditure; an improvident or extravagantly wasteful person (freq. connoting moral worthlessness).

1601 Holland *Pliny* I. 246 What would he have cost our prodigal spendthrifts, if hee had been taken upon our coasts neere Rome? **1670** Dryden *Conq. Granada* i. i, Thus, as some fawning Usurer does feed With present Sums th'unwary Spendthrift's Need. **1750** Johnson *Rambler* No. 53 ¶9 Little satisfaction will be given to the Spendthrift by the encomiums which he purchases. **1776** Adam Smith *W.N.* iv. i. (1904) II. 11 This complaint..of the scarcity of money, is not always confined to improvident spendthrifts. **1852** Thackeray *Esmond* i. xiv, If I fall,..there will only be a spendthrift the less to keep in the world. **1864** Bowen *Logic* ix. 278 An instance of the former is what may be called the Spendthrift's Fallacy.

transf. **1860** Emerson *Cond. Life, Fate* Wks. (Bohn) II. 324 Nature is no spendthrift, but takes the shortest way to her ends.

2. *transf.* One who employs or uses something lavishly or profusely; a prodigal consumer, user up, or waster, *of* something.

1610 Shaks. *Temp.* ii. i. 23 Fie, what a spend-thrift is he of his tongue. **1654** Whitlock *Zootomia* 302 But the Debaucht burner out of his dayes..is an undoubted Spend-thrift of time. **1742** Young *Nt. Th.* ii. 273 Thus, with indulgence most severe, she treats Us spendthrifts of inestimable time. **1825** J. Neal *Bro. Jonathan* III. 297, I have been a prodigal of my best affections; a foolish prodigal —a spendthrift. **1890** *Spectator* 25 Jan., How can a man be proud of his genius without dreading that he may prove a spendthrift of that genius instead of its skilful almoner?

3. *attrib.* passing into *adj.* **a.** Acting as or like, having the qualities of, a spendthrift.

1607 Tourneur *Rev. Trag.* i. i, Within the spend-thrift veynes of a drye Duke. **1647** R. Stapylton *Juvenal* 109 Spend-thrift Fabius,..who in his youth spent his estate, and was thence surnamed the Gulfe or (as our word is) the Spend-thrift. *a* **1704** T. Brown *Walk round Lond., Coffee-Houses* Wks. 1709 III. iii. 40 The Spendthrift Officers. **1834** Lytton *Pompeii* i. i, These rich plebeians are a harvest for us spend-thrift nobles.

fig. **1830** Galt *Lawrie T.* v. ii. (1849) 194 The common wee spendthrift fiddle.

b. Characterized or marked by excessive or improvident expenditure; wasteful.

1790 Burke *Fr. Rev.* 234 Had you no way of turning the revenue to account, but through the improvident resource of a spendthrift sale? **1838** Lytton *Leila* iv. v, The spendthrift violence of the mob was restrained. **1886** W. J. Tucker *E. Europe* vii, As the money-lender is an inevitable figure, where habits are spendthrift and bankruptcy imminent.

Hence **ˈspendˌthriftism**, the state or quality of being spendthrift. **ˈspendˌthrifty** *a.*, prodigal or wasteful in expenditure.

1642 D. Rogers *Naaman* 611 For their spend-thrifty, uncleane and ruffianlike courses. **1862** T. C. Grattan *Beaten Paths* I. 30 The Irish..felt a poor pride in acting down to the degrading level of spendthriftism and bullying.

ˈspendˌthriftiness. *rare.* [f. spendthrifty *a.* + -ness.] The act or quality of being spendthrifty.

1950 H. J. Massingham *Curious Traveller* iv. 76 For such spendthriftiness no honest word can be said. **1959** *Times* 29 June 12/6 The feeling of pleasurable spend-thriftiness.

†**spene,** *sb. Obs.*⁻¹ (Meaning obscure.)

a **1400–50** *Alexander* 4162 þan ferd þai forth..& freschly assemblis All at was sperpolid on þe spene & spilt with þe blastis.

spene, variant of spean *sb.* and *v.*

†**spene,** *v. Obs.* Also 4 **spen.** [Alteration of spend *v.*[1]]

1. *trans.* To spend, expend (money, goods, etc.).

c **1175** *Lamb. Hom.* 31 Nabbe ic nawiht þer-of, ic hit habbe al ispened. *Ibid.* 79 A þe marȝen [he] bitahte him twa peneȝes to spenen on him. *a* **1250** *Owl & Night.* 1525 þat were gulte, þat leof is oþer wymmon to pulte & speneþ on þare al þat he haueþ. *c* **1290** *S. Eng. Leg.* I. 147 He nadde him-sulf nouȝt to spene. **1393** Langl. *P. Pl.* C. xviii. 71 Of þat þat holychurche of þe olde lawe cleymeþ, Priestes on aparail and on purnele spenen. **1400** in Ellis *Orig. Lett.* Ser. ii. I. 6 Rather then I schuld fael he wold spene of his own godde xx. marke.

absol. *c* **1205** Lay. 3302 Andd nowher heo ne spedet and auere heo spened.

b. To exact contributions from (tenants). Cf. spend *v.*[1] 1 d.

1538 *St. Papers Hen. VIII*, III. 48 His servauntes and his kerne dothe spene my tenauntes and fermoris in the barrony of Dunnbrathie.

2. To spend, in other senses; to employ, expend, make use of, use.

c **1200** *Trin. Coll. Hom.* 179 Ðe underlinges þenchen oðe dai hu hie muȝen mest swinken and spenen here flesh and here blod on iuele swinche. *a* **1225** *Ancr. R.* 322 Euerich tide & euerich time schal beon þer irikened, hwu hit was her ispened. *a* **1300** *Sarmun* xlvii. in *E.E.P.* (1862) 6 What is þe ioi þat man sal hab if his lif he spenip wel. **1340–70** *Alex. & Dind.* 876 But ȝe han dainte in dul ȝoure daies to spene. *a* **1400** *Minor Poems fr. Vernon MS.* l. 555 Loke wel in þi mood þi wit to spene wysliche.

Hence †**ˈspening** *vbl. sb.*, spending, expenditure.

1297 R. Glouc. (Rolls) 8001 In speninge he was fol large In herte þoru out prout.

†**spen-foot,** *adv. Obs.*⁻¹ [app. f. spen *v.*] ? With the feet close together.

13.. *Gaw. & Gr. Knt.* 2316 He sprit forth spenne fote more þen a spere lenþe.

spenged, variant of spanged *ppl. a.*

Speȝe(e, -ȝie, obs. Sc. varr. Spain.

Spenglerian (ʃpɛŋˈglɪərɪən), *a.* [f. the name of the German philosopher Oswald *Spengler* (1880–1936) + -ian.] Of, pertaining to, or characteristic of the philosophy of Spengler, esp. as expressed in his work *Der Untergang des Abendlandes* ('The Decline of the West').

1922 *Contemp. Rev.* July 52 Here the Spenglerian antithesis between Apollonian and Faustian is apparent. **1933** *PMLA* XLVIII. 608 It is hardly necessary to refer to Spenglerian pessimism. **1948** A. Toynbee *Civilization on Trial* 12 We do here seem to find a certain measure of Spenglerian uniformity. **1964** P. Worsley in I. L. Horowitz *New Sociology* 373 Spenglerian-cycle schemas. **1978** H. Wouk *War & Remembrance* xvi. 165 They sometimes played chess, and Hesse gloomed over the board in Spenglerian tones about the collapse of European man.

Also (now *rarely*) **ˈSpenglerism**, the philosophy of Spengler or views in accordance with his; **ˈSpenglerist** *a.* and *sb.*

1922 *Contemp. Rev.* July 50 There is no doubt in the minds of the Spenglerists that..from the ruins of Russia will arise a new culture. *Ibid.* 51 He will not have 'Spenglerism' dismissed as mere materialist determinism. *Ibid.* 52 The Spenglerist philosophy has not so far been exploited in the interests of German chauvinism. **1931** *Times Lit. Suppl.* 5 Feb. 93/2 His criticism of Pragmatism, Behaviourism, Spenglerism..are..intellectually acute.

Spengyie, obs. Sc. var. Spain.

spenn(i)e, obs. ff. spinney.

spens, obs. f. spence, spense.

†**spenˈsation,** aphetic f. dispensation.

1618 Belchier *Hans Beer-pot* F, Oh fie on periury, Ile not beleeue spensations of the Pope.

spense (spɛns). Now *dial.* Also 3–4, 6 **spens,** 3–7, 9 *dial.* **spence.** [ad. OF. *espense*, = AF. *expense* expense.]

†**1.** Expense, expenditure; cost. *Obs.*

1297 R. Glouc. (Rolls) 3486 He nadde noȝt wel war-wiþ such menie up to holde, Ac..he þoȝte of þe saxons is spense vp arere. *a* **1350** *St. Cecilia* 459 in Horstm. *Altengl. Leg.* (1881) 164 þe bischop..made a kirk of ful grete spens. **1382** Wyclif *1 Cor.* ix. 18 That I preching the gospel, putte the gospel with oute spence takynge, or sustenaunce therfore. *c* **1400** *Destr. Troy* 233, I shall spare for no spence & þu spede wele. *c* **1460** *Reg. Oseney Abbey* 50 To þe Burgeys spense to such a parlement i-chose. **1523** Ld. Berners *Froiss.* I. ccvi. 243 So that they demaunde no wages, nor for losse of horse nor spence. **1566** Drant *Horace, Sat.* i. ii. Aviij, And fearyng such lyke blame That doth ensue outragiouse spence, he will not geue nor lende One crosse of coyne.

b. *pl.* Charges, costs, items of expense or expenditure; *esp.* in later use = expense 3 c.

1377 Langl. *P. Pl.* B. xiv. 197 But owre spences and spendynge sprynge of a trewe wille. *c* **1380** Wyclif *Sel. Wks.* III. 347 How shulde not þis suffice now for fewer clerkis and lesse of spensis? *c* **1400** *Brut* 328 This tretys lasted twey ȝer, wiþ grete costes & houge spences of boþe parties. **1720** in *Jrnl. Derbysh. Archæol. Soc.* (1905) XXVII. 215 For spenses at Chappell fair, 1 0 0. **1886** Elworthy *W. Somerset Word-bk.* s.v. *Overdrow*, To pay all 'spences.

2. *concr.* That which may be or is spent; money, supplies; *dial.* pocket-money. Also *pl.*

a **1225** *Ancr. R.* 350 Ne he ne bereð no garsum bute gnedeliche his spense. *c* **1290** *Beket* 1365 in *S. Eng. Leg.* 145 Þe king him fond spence i-novȝ to him and alle his. **1303** R. BRUNNE *Handl. Synne* 6857 To þe cyte he was com late, And of spensys had he non. **1387** TREVISA *Higden* (Rolls) VII. 127 Þe duke was prayed of þe emperour for to take costage and spence for the way. *c* **1460** *Towneley Myst.* xxii. 249, I wold spende all my spence To se hym ones skelpt. **1886** H. CUNLIFFE *Rochdale Gloss.*, *Spence*, pocket-money.

†**3.** The expenditure or spending *of* goods, income, etc. *Obs.*

c **1400** *Destr. Troy* 13692 So he sped hym by spies, & spense of his gode. **1538** STARKEY *England* II. iii. 201 Wych..ys the occasyon of the grete spens of the intrat of the monastery. **1567** DRANT *Horace, Ep.* I. xv. Evj, When as with spence of parentes goddes Sir Meui once began..for to be cawld a iolly gentleman.

†**b.** The employing, expending, consuming, or using up *of* something. *Obs.*

1555 J. PROCTOR *Hist. Wyat's Rebellion* 54 b, To aduenture the spense of her royall bloude in defense of them. **1563** FOXE *A. & M.* 745 Many hote argumentes were betwene them,..with muche spence of language. **1594** LODGE *Wounds Civil War* A iv b, The spence of yeares that Marius hath ore-past..Hath taught him this.

spense, obs. form of SPENCE.

†**'spenseful**, *a. Obs.*$^{-1}$ [f. SPENSE.] Extravagant or lavish in expenditure.

1600 SIR R. CECIL in *Carew MSS.* (1869) 445, I think he is but spenceful beyond measure.

spenser, variant of SPENCER[1] *Obs.*

Spenserian (spɛn'sɪərɪən), *a.* and *sb.* [f. the name of the Elizabethan poet Edmund *Spenser* (? 1552–1599) + -IAN.]

A. *adj.* Of or belonging to, characteristic of, Spenser or his work.

Spenserian stanza, the stanza employed by Spenser in the *Faerie Queen*, consisting of eight decasyllabic lines and a final Alexandrine, with the rhyming scheme *ab ab bc bcc*.

1817 COLERIDGE *Biog. Lit.* I. iv. 84 The Spencerian stanza, which always..recalls to the reader's mind Spencer's own style. **1818** SCOTT *Rob Roy* ii, I.. was busy in meditation on the oft-recurring rhymes of the Spenserian stanza. **1853** RUSKIN *Stones Ven.* II. vii. 273 The Spenserian mingling of this mediæval image..is altogether exquisite. **1890** HOSMER *Anglo-Sax. Freedom* 97 The redoubtable Spenserian giant, Kirk-rapine.

B. *sb.* **1.** A Spenserian stanza, or a poem in this metre.

1818 KEATS *Lett.* (1848) I. 133, I see no reason..why I should not have a peep at your Spenserian. **1853** J. NICHOL in Knight *Mem.* (1896) ii. 101, I hope to come nearer it at any rate than in these Spenserians. **1886** *Athenæum* 23 Jan. 131/2 Scarcely any poet since Spenser has written entirely successful Spenserians... Byron..failed altogether in Spenserians.

2. A follower or imitator of Spenser; a poet of Spenser's school.

1894 GOSSE *Jacobean Poets* 47 His [Donne's] were the first poems which protested, in their form alike and their tendency, against the pastoral sweetness of the Spenserians.

So **Spen'seric**, *a.* [-IC.] Spenserian.

1795 ANNA SEWARD *Lett.* (1811) IV. 113 That gay town, which Shenstone, in his Spenseric poem, the Schoolmistress, has so beautifully apostrophized.

spent (spɛnt), *pa. pple.* and *ppl. a.* [SPEND *v.*[1]]

I. In predicative uses.

1. a. Of material things: Expended, consumed, used up completely.

c **1440** *Promp. Parv.* 468/2 Spent, *expensus, dispensatus.* **1450** in *Rep. Hist. MSS. Comm.* Var. Coll. IV. 85 The vitailes of oure seid Towne ben al moste spent & consumed. *a* **1548** HALL *Chron., Hen. V*, 14 b, Their vitaile was in maner al spent, and newe they coulde gette none. **1591** SHAKS. *1 Hen. VI*, II. v. 8 These Eyes, like Lampes, whose wasting Oyle is spent, Waxe dimme. **1632** LITHGOW *Trav.* VII. 329 The..cause of our Arriuall here, was in regard of our fresh Water that was spent. **1664** POWER *Exp. Philos.* I. 34 When the Liquor wherin they swim is almost spent and dried up. **1769** SIR W. JONES *Palace Fortune* Poems (1777) 19 His guards retir'd, his glimmering taper spent. **1837** LOCKHART *Scott* I. xi. 417 When the lamp of his own genius was all but spent. **1849** MACAULAY *Hist. Eng.* v. I. 611 Their powder and ball were spent. **1883** BROWNING *Jocoseria* 116 Our acquist Of life is spent.

†**b.** Wrecked; drowned. *Obs. rare.*

c **1477** CAXTON *Jason* 76 b, And thus by this waye they [i.e. ships] were all lost and spent. **1626** *Whitburn Par. Reg.* 17 July, John Burne of Sheels, being casten forth of a Cobble and spent in the sea.

2. Passed, gone; come to an end; over: **a.** Of time. Also *far spent* (FAR *adv.* 3 c).

1528 GARDINER in Burnet *Hist. Ref., Rec.* I. ii. (Pocock) IV. 127 The day being then spent. **1560** DAUS tr. *Sleidane's Comm.* 182 The time is farre spente. **1593** SHAKS. *Rich. II*, II. i. 154 His time is spent, our pilgrimage must be. **1611** BIBLE *Rom.* xiii. 12 The night is farre spent. **1615** SANDYS *Trav.* 87 January being now well spent, we departed from Constantinople. **1667** MILTON *P.L.* VIII. 206 Day is yet not spent. **1724** GAY *Captives* I. (1772) 19 Is night near spent? **1841** BROWNING *Pippa Passes* Poems (1905) 189 New year's day is over and spent. **1860** TYNDALL *Glac.* I. xi. 79 The day was already far spent.

b. Of things, material and immaterial.

c **1600** SHAKS. *Sonn.* cvii, And thou in this shalt finde thy monument, When tyrants crests and tombs of brasse are spent. **1634** SIR T. HERBERT *Trav.* 7 The raine is spent. **1766** BLACKSTONE *Comm.* II. 237 Till both the immediate bloods of George Stiles, the paternal grandfather, are spent. **1818** CRUISE *Digest* (ed. 2) III. 496 The lease..determined by the estate tail being spent.

3. a. Of persons or animals: Deprived of force or strength; tired or worn out by labour, exertion, hardship, etc.; completely exhausted.

1591 SAVILE *Tacitus, Hist.* I. xii. 7 Galba was spent and feeble for age. **1647** HEXHAM I. (*Hunting*), The Hart, Stagg, Hinde, Buck, or Doe, is spent. **1691** RAY *Creation* I. (1704) 159 Why the Hare when she is near spent makes up a Hill? **1713** ADDISON *Cato* IV. iv, Now thou seest me Spent, overpower'd, despairing of success. **1774** GOLDSM. *Nat. Hist.* (1776) V. 33 Many..quite spent by the fatigues of their flight, drop down into the sea. **1840** DICKENS *Old C. Shop* xlv, So very weak and spent she felt.

transf. **1612** DRAYTON *Poly-olb.* i. 319 When long-renowned Troy lay spent in hostile fire.

b. Const. *with* age, fatigue, toil, etc.

Freq. from *c* 1600 to 1730.

1603 KNOLLES *Hist. Turks* (1621) 137 Ertogrul now spent with age, shortly after died. **1611** SHAKS. *Cymb.* III. vi. 63 Almost spent with hunger, I am falne in this offence. **1703** POPE *Thebais* 537 On the cold marble spent with toil he lies. **1760–72** H. BROOKE *Fool of Qual.* (1809) III. 5 Being spent with fatigue, I..sat me down to die. **1817** SHELLEY *Rev. Islam* x. xxxvii, They will sleep with luxury spent. **1867** F. PARKMAN *Jesuits in N. Amer.* iv. (1875) 26 Spent with travel, and weakened by precarious and unaccustomed fare.

4. a. Of things: Exhausted of the active or effective power or principle.

1596 LODGE *Marg. Amer.* F iv b, Thy sap by course of time is blent, My sence by care and age is spent. **1633** T. JAMES *Voy.* 85 Our tooles were all so spent, that we could cut none. **1665** MANLEY *Grotius' Low C. Wars* 437 For by the..long distance of place, the Shot was spent, before it came to the place, which it was intended to batter. **1697** DAMPIER *Voy.* I. 36 At length when the Creatures strength is spent, they..knock it on the head. *a* **1722** LISLE *Husb.* (1757) 154 The malt is spent and wasted before it is laid in the grounds. **1774** GOLDSM. *Nat. Hist.* (1776) I. 201 If this acquired velocity be quite spent. **1817** SHELLEY *Rev. Islam* IV. xxx, Though their lustre now was spent and faded. **1883** *Manch. Exam.* 28 Nov. 5/1 The vigour and 'go' infused into the party..would show symptoms of being spent.

b. *Naut.* Of the tide or a current.

c **1595** CAPT. WYATT *Dudley's Voy.* (Hakl. Soc.) 3 Our master thought it not good to turne downe the channell, the tide beinge soe far spent. **1616** J. LANE *Contn. Sqr.'s T.* VII. 359 Then in hee bore for land, till th' tyde was spent. **1719** DE FOE *Crusoe* I. (Globe) 143 When I had made some-thing more than a League of Way by the Help of this Current or Eddy, I found it was spent. **1743** BULKELEY & CUMMINS *Voy. S. Seas* 137 And the Tide being spent, we put into a small Cove, and made fast.

II. In attributive uses.

5. a. Of persons or animals: = sense 3.

a **1563** ASCHAM *Schoolm.* (Arb.) 152 The talke of a spent old man. **1605** SHAKS. *Macb.* I. ii. 8 It stood, As two spent Swimmers, that doe cling together. **1715** POPE *Iliad* II. 465 Let..each spent courser at the chariot blow. **1825** HONE *Every-day Bk.* I. 292, I remember the..squire and his..chaplain casting home on spent horses. **1859** JEPHSON *Brittany* xii. 193 The English archers..charged down..upon the now spent and wearied French.

b. Of fish: Exhausted by spawning; having recently spawned. Also *ellipt.* as *sb.*, a spent herring.

1864 *Intell. Observ.* V. 369 After the performance of this function the fish is sickly and weak, and is then called a Shotten or Spent fish. **1866** *Chambers's Encycl.* VIII. 446/2 Salmon, which have completed their spawning, continue for some time..very unfit for the table... They are called 'foul fish', or more distinctively, 'spent fish', or Kelts. **1883** *Fisheries Exhib. Catal.* 69, 1 Barrel Large Full Herrings... 1 Barrel Spent Herrings. **1957** W. C. HODGSON *Herring & its Fishery* ii. 18 In this area [of the North Sea] there are large shoals of small immature herrings of low fat-content mixed with recovered spents that are just beginning to fatten. **1975** *New Yorker* 22 Dec. 55/1 April and May are the slack months, since the spring spawning has by then completed itself, and the herring are what are known as 'spents'—thin, indolent, not worth the catching.

c. *spent gnat*, a kind of artificial fly used in trout fishing.

1867 F. FRANCIS *Angling* vi. (1880) 229 The black drake, or spent gnat, as it is sometimes called. **1894** *Daily News* 9 June 832/1 All kinds were tried, including the spent gnat, but the fish would have none of them.

6. a. Of things: Exhausted, worn out, used up; no longer active, effective, or serviceable.

1697 DRYDEN *Virg. Georg.* I. 108 That the spent Earth may gather heart again; And, better'd by Cessation, bear the Grain. **1830** LYELL *Princ. Geol.* I. 322 If the action of one becomes very great for a century or more, the others assume the appearance of spent volcanos. **1850** WHITTIER *To Avis Keene* 38 Where spent waves glimmer up the beach. **1883** MISS BROUGHTON *Belinda* II. 189, 'I should like to sit down,' says Belinda, in a spent voice.

b. Of arrows, balls, or shot.

1697 DRYDEN *Æneid* IX. 906 Heaps of spent Arrows fall and strew the Ground. **1799** *Naval Chron.* I. 169 A spent ball..hit him. **1802** JAMES *Milit. Dict.* s.v., Spent balls..are frequently fatal in their effects. **1858** CARLYLE *Fredk. Gt.* II. ix. I. 153 [He] declared in solemn Diet, the Pope's ban to be mere spent shot.

c. Of hops, tan, etc., from which the essential properties have been extracted.

1826 *Art of Brewing* (ed. 2) 105 If the disorder do not subside readily, a gyle of spent hops thrown in will generally be advantageous. **1842** LOUDON *Suburban Hort.* 390 Coverings for the surface of the ground include dead leaves, ..spent tan,..rotten dung,..&c. **1857** MILLER *Elem. Chem., Org.* vi. §1. 372 A quantity of common salt is next added to separate the spent leys. **1877** RAYMOND *Statist. Mines & Mining* 390 The spent liquor..is discharged into the stream.

7. In comb. with *out*.

1620 DEKKER *Dream* Wks. (Grosart) III. 18 The Terrestiall Pauement burn'd, In which the Starres to spent-out Snuffes were turnd. **1848** THACKERAY *Van. Fair* lxi, A spent-out, bootless life of defeat and disappointment.

‖**speos** ('spiːɒs). *Egyptol.* [Gr. σπέος cave, grotto.] A cave temple or tomb, esp. one of some architectural importance.

1843 G. WILKINSON *Mod. Egypt & Thebes* v. II. 56 Pasht ..has always the head of a lionness, and the title, 'Lady of the excavation' or 'Speos'. **1888** C. D. BELL *Winter on Nile* xviii. 170 There is a large speos with four massive pillars.

speowen, obs. form of SPEW *v.*

sper, obs. var. SPAR *v.*[1], SPEAR *sb.*[1], *v.*[1], SPEER *v.*, SPHERE.

†**sperable**, *a. Obs.* [ad. L. *spērābilis* (f. *spērāre* to hope) or F. *espérable* (Sp. *esperable*, Pg. *esperavel*, It. *sperabile*).] That may be hoped for; admitting of, giving room for, hope. Of debts: = SPERATE *a.* 1.

1565 SIR W. CECIL in Ellis *Orig. Lett.* Ser. II. II. 297 Wherin suerly perceaving his own cause not sperable, he doth honorably and wisely. **1571** —— in D. Digges *Complete Ambass.* (1655) 164, I am sorry that your health is not more sperable to be speedily recovered. **1591** UNTON *Corr.* (Roxb.) 187 If..you yourselfe shall find the recovery [of Rouen] sperable, then..you may afterwards use the kind of speache. *c* **1615** JAS. I in *Buccleuch MSS.* (Hist. MSS. Comm.) I. 170 Debts before the 30th of Elizabeth, though they be never so sperable.

speragas, variant of SPARAGUS *Obs.*

†**'sperage.** *Obs.* Also 7 spirage, sperrage, 8 spearage. [a. OF. *sperage*, var. of *sparage* SPARAGE.] Asparagus.

c **1440** *Pallad. on Husb.* III. 558 Sperages seed..Is good to sowe hem with,..For cannes & sperage haue oon tylynge. **1545** ELYOT, *Asparagus*, an herbe callyd of common Apotecaries Sparagus, in englishe Sperage. **1577** B. GOOGE tr. *Heresbach's Husb.* 19 Sperage and such like, must be sowen in shaddowy places. **1620** VENNER *Via Recta* vii. 150 Asparagus or Sperage is hot in the beginning of the first degree. **1688** HOLME *Armoury* II. 99/2 Asparagus or Sperage... The Flowers are yellow, consisting of six leaves. **1731** MILLER *Gard. Dict.*, *Asparagus*,..Sparagus or Sperage. **1760** J. LEE *Introd. Bot.* App. 327 Spearage, see Asparagus.

attrib. **1611** COTGR., *Pois à visage*,.. Sperage Beanes, French Beanes,..Kidney Beanes. *a* **1661** HOLYDAY *Juvenal* 77 Thy patrone's fish, Deck'd round with sperage-buds.

b. With distinguishing adjs.

1545 ELYOT, *Corruda*, an herbe called wylde sperage. **1548** TURNER *Names Herbes* (E.D.S.) 17 It maye be called in englishe pricky Sperage, because it is all full of pryckes. **1601** HOLLAND *Pliny* II. 122 The stalke is smooth, and resembleth garden Sperage. *a* **1661** HOLYDAY *Juvenal* 214 Wild sperage too We'll have; my plow-man's wife her spindle threw Aside, to gather it. **1758** BORLASE *Nat. Hist. Cornw.* 233 Marsh-asparagus or sperage, *Asparagus palustris.*

'sperate, *a.* ? *Obs.* [ad. L. *spērāt-us*, pa. pple. of *spērāre* to hope.]

1. Of debts: Having some likelihood of being recovered; not desperate.

1551 *Will of R. Studlaye* (Somerset Ho.), Sperate debtes. *a* **1625** COPE in Gutch *Coll. Cur.* I. 122 Which [debts] were good, which were bad, which sperate, which desperate, no man knew. **1697** in *New Jersey Arch.* Ser. I. (1901) XXIII. 83 A negro maid servant and debts sperate and desperate. **1710** in Ecton *St. Q. Anne's Bounty* (1721) 108 We have therefore spent much Time..in distinguishing between the sperate and desperate Debts of the Clergy. **1798** *Washington's Reports* I. 169 Outstanding debts, distinguishing such as are sperate from such as are supposed to be desperate.

2. In general use: Giving or leaving room for hope; of a promising nature.

1808 LD. ELLENBOROUGH in *10 Rev. Rep.* (1893) 718 If you think there is anything sperate in it, I will save the point. **1824** *Cowen's Rep.* (N.Y. State Supreme Crt.) 106 Every vessel has a point of time at which it passes from a Sperate to a desperate state, or arrives at a situation of unseaworthiness.

†**speratory**, *a. Obs.*$^{-1}$ [See prec. and -ORY.] Resting in hope or expectation.

1629 DONNE *Serm.* cxxxvi. Wks. 1839 V. 442 [Mammon offers] the present and possessory things of this world, God but the future and speratory things of the next.

†**spercil.** *Obs.*$^{-1}$ [app. f. *sper* SPAR *sb.*[1]] ? The spars of a roof.

1570 LEVINS *Manip.* 125 Ye spercil, *subtegulaneum.*

spercle, obs. form of SPARKLE.

spere, obs. form of SPEAR, SPEER, SPHERE.

†**spere**, *a. Obs.* Also speer. [Of obscure origin.] Frail, delicate.

c **1440** *Promp. Parv.* 468 Spere, or fres (*K.* freshe or brityl, *P.* britill or brekyll), *fragilis.* *c* **1440** *Jacob's Well* 221 My chayere is my body of speer brotyl & rotyn bonys, in whiche my soule sytteth. **1486** *Bk. St. Albans, Hawking* e viii b, She may be callid a Spere hawke for of all the hawkys that ther be she is moost spere, that is to say moost tendre to kepe.

†**sperel.** *Obs.* Also sperl-. [prob. of Flem. origin: cf. WFlem. *spèrel*, *sperrel* door-bar, f. *sperren* SPAR *v.*[1]] A means of closing or fastening; a bar or bolt; a book-clasp.

13.. *S. Erkenwolde* 49 in Horstm. *Altengl. Leg.* (1881) 267 Thre sperlis of þe spelunke þat spradde [? *read* sparde] hit o lofte Was metely made of þe marbre. *c* **1440** *Promp. Parv.* 365/1 Ondoynge, or opynynge of schettellys, or sperellys, *apercio. Ibid.* 469/1 Sperel, or closel yn schetynge, ..*firmaculum. Ibid.*, Sperel, of a boke, ..*offendix*, .. *signaculum.*

sperete, obs. form of SPIRIT *sb.*

†**sperge**[1]. *Obs.*[−1] [? ad. OF. *esperge*, var. of *asperge.*] ? Asparagus.

c **1400** *Lanfranc's Cirurg.* 275 He schal ete fenel, ache, persil, sperge, .. & he schal ete no mustard.

†**sperge**[2]. *Obs.*[−1] [Aphetic f. ASPERGE *sb.*] A sprinkler.

1675 EVELYN *Philos. Disc. Earth* (1676) 143 Gently refresh'd with a dewie sperge or brush, not with the watring-pot.

‖**spergula** (ˈspɜːgjʊlə). [med. and mod.L. *Spergula*, of unknown origin.] One or other variety of spurrey.

1829 [see CERASTIUM]. **1882** *Garden* 29 Apr. 297/2 Couch Grass and Spergula are at this season very troublesome. **1884** tr. *De Candolle's Orig. Cultivated Pl.* 115 Agriculturists distinguish a taller variety of spergula.

ˈ**spergulin**. *Chem.* [f. mod.L. *Spergula*: see prec.] (See quot.)

1881 WATTS *Dict. Chem., 3rd Suppl.*, *Spergulin*, a fluorescent body, occurring in the seed-coverings of *Spergula vulgaris* and *S. maxima*, and produced at the time when the seeds blacken and are nearly ripe.

sperie, obs. var. SPURREY.

sperit(e, varr. SPIRIT *sb.*

sperk(e, obs. or Sc. varr. SPARK.

sperket, obs. or dial. f. SPIRKET.

sperling, var. SPARLING.

sperm (spɜːm), *sb.* Forms: 4–7 **sperme**, 6 **spearme, sparme**, 7 **sparm**, 6– **sperm**. [ad. OF. *esperme* (F. *sperme*), *sparme*, or L. *sperma* (hence also It. *sperma*, Sp. and Pg. *esperma*), a. Gr. σπέρμα, f. the stem of σπείρειν to sow.]

I. 1. a. The generative substance or seed of male animals (esp. of vertebrates).

c **1386** CHAUCER *Monk's T.* 19 In the feld of Damassene With goddes owene finger wroght was he And nat bigeten of mannes sperme [*Harl. MS.* sperma] unclene. **1398** TREVISA *Barth. De P.R.* XIII. xxix. (Tollem. MS.), The whale haþ gret plente of sperme, and after þat he gendreþ wiþ þe female, superfluite þerof fleteþ aboue þe water. *a* **1425** tr. *Arderne's Treat. Fistula*, etc. 14 Som-tyme þe sperme goþ oute by þe hole of þe ȝerde infistulate. **1526** *Grete Herball* xxviii. (1529) B v b, Ambre is hote and drye... Some say that it is the sparme of a whale. **1549** *Compl. Scot.* vi. 67, I sau hemp, that coagulis the flux of the sparme. **1605** TIMME *Quersit.* I. xvi. 85 We see, of bread and wine, blood to be made; of blood, sperm or seed. **1646** SIR T. BROWNE *Pseud. Ep.* 330 And thus may it also be in the generation and sperm of Negroes. **1725** *Fam. Dict.* s.v. *Poultry*, The Cock.. rarifies the Egg, and renders it fit to produce its Species by the Sperm or Tread he infuses into it. **1783** JUSTAMOND tr. *Raynal's Hist. Indies* V. 361 It hath since been imagined, that pearls must be the eggs or the sperm of the fish inclosed in the shell. **1822–7** GOOD *Stud. Med.* (1829) V. 6 The male shortly afterwards passes over the spawn or hard roe, and discharges upon it his sperm, which we call soft roe or milt. **1878** F. J. BELL *Gegenbaur's Elem. Comp. Anat.* 53 Receptacles which serve for the collection of the sperm.

b. A spermatozoon.

1904 *Brit. Med. Jrnl.* 15 Oct. 964 Gametes (eggs and sperms). **1905** G. A. REID *Princ. Heredity* xii. 162 If these same sperms reside for a longer time [etc.].

†**2. a.** The eggs of insects. *Obs.*

1615 W. LAWSON *Country Housew. Gard.* (1626) 44 The red peckled butter-flye doth euer put them [i.e. caterpillars], being her sparm, among the tender spraies for better feeding. **1747** W. GOULD *Eng. Ants* 34 A just Description of the Sperm or Eggs (which is entirely answerable to what the Queen lays).

†**b.** Offspring, brood (of persons). *Obs. rare.*

1641 MILTON *Animadv.* Wks. 1851 III. 237 Let not those wretched Fathers thinke they shall impoverish the Church .., though they keep back their sordid sperm begotten in the lustinesse of their avarice.

3. *transf.* The generative matter or source from which anything is formed or takes its origin:

a. Of plants.

1610 J. DAVIES (Heref.) *Commend. Poems, Vaughan* Wks. (Grosart) II. 3/2 His royall Trench (that.. holds the Sperme of Herbage by a Spring). **1620** MARKHAM *Farew. Husb.* (1625) 99 The worme.. deuouring vp the substance or sperm, is the cause that the corne cannot grow. **1642** H. MORE *Song of Soul* II. I. ii. 25 I'll call't form bestiall, It makes a beast added to plantall sperm.

b. Of other material things.

1651 FRENCH *Distill.* v. 108 Water is both the Sperme, and the Menstruum of the world. **1671** J. WEBSTER *Metallogr.* iv. 77 The Sperm of Metals is not different from the sperm of other things, to wit, an humid vapour. **1694** MOTTEUX *Rabelais* IV. i. 3 The Fifth [ship had for its device] a famous Kan made of Sperm of Emerald. **1845** BAILEY *Festus* (ed. 2) 120 The primal sperm and matter of the world.

c. Of qualities, conditions, etc.

1639 G. DANIEL *Ecclus.* xxvi. 91 Infects her mind With the black Sperme of Contradiction. **1659** C. NOBLE *Inexpediency Exped.* 4 The Remedy that is prescribed is the very Seed and Sperm.. and Vivary of that difference. **1820** SHELLEY *Ode Liberty* xv, 'Tis the sperm Of what makes life foul, cankerous, and abhorred.

4. a. *attrib.*, as ***sperm-bag, -ball, -cell, -germ***, etc.; **sperm bank** = *semen bank* s.v. SEMEN 2; hence **sperm banking**; **sperm count**, the number of spermatozoa in the ejaculate or in one millilitre of it; **sperm morula**, a ball of spermatozoa.

1849 *Phil. Trans.* CXXXIX. I. 347 The spermatozoa are distinctly seen in the *sperm-bag. **1887** *Encycl. Brit.* XXII. 424/2 Each cell.. produces a large number of spermatozoa, which occur in spherical clusters or *sperm-balls. **1963** B. RUSSELL *Let.* 10 Mar. in *Autobiogr.* (1969) III. iv. 173 If a *sperm-bank, such as you envisage, had existed during the régime of Hitler, Hitler would have been the sire of all babies born in his time in Germany. **1977** M. SOKOLINSKY tr. *Merle's Virility Factor* vi. 130 Suppose you've had a vasectomy done... The men kept the sperm.. in a sperm bank, in case their wives wanted to be fertilized. **1972** *Science* 7 Apr. 32 Biologist Mark Lappé.. is disturbed that commercial outfits are the first to introduce large-scale *sperm banking. **1851** CARPENTER *Man. Phys.* (ed. 2) 148 In the lower tribes, both of Plants and Animals, we find that '*sperm-cells' and 'germ-cells' are developed in the midst of the ordinary tissues of the body. **1881** MIVART *Cat* 318 The male pro-nucleus is a spermatozoon, which is a part of the nucleus of the original sperm-cell. **1868** WATTS *Dict. Chem.* V. 397 With *sperm-corpuscles, mucus-corpuscles, and epithelium-scales. **1941** *Endocrinology* XXVIII. 783 For approximately 18 days after the fever, the human total *sperm counts remain at a relatively normal level. **1979** *Daily Tel.* 29 Nov. 19/1 Her twin was told she was unlikely to have children because of her husband's low sperm count. **1859** *Todd's Cycl. Anat.* V. [138] Two different organised bodies, which are respectively formed from two different cells; the ovigerm and the *spermgerm. **1856** EMERSON *Eng. Traits, Ability* (1903) 56 Stall-feeding makes *sperm-mills of the cattle. **1889** *Cent. Dict.*, *Sperm morula. **1921** *Nature* 7 July 586/1 The occurrence of developing sperm-morulæ in microscopic sections of.. oysters has.. been already observed. **1936** *Mem. Musée Royal d'Histoire Naturelle de Belgique* (2nd Ser.) III. 1003 Since females on English [oyster] beds nearly always carry some sperm morulae amongst the eggs, self-fertilisation will nearly always be possible. **1826** KIRBY & SP. *Entomol.* IV. xlii. 146 The *Sperm-reservoir (*Spermatheca*) is an organ connecting the vagina with the oviduct. **1883** LANKESTER in *Encycl. Brit.* XVI. 682/2 In other Mollusca.. this formation of '*sperm ropes' is known. **1859** HUXLEY *Oceanic Hydrozoa* 64 The smaller contained a *sperm-sac, with incompletely developed spermatozoa. **1841** T. R. JONES *Anim. Kingd.* 280 Two long auxiliary vessels.., that have been named *sperm-vessels, gluten-vessels, and gum-vessels by different authors.

b. *Comb.*, as ***sperm-forming, -like, -producing, -secreting*** adjs.

1836–9 *Todd's Cycl. Anat.* II. 414/1 The principal forms of the sperm-secreting organs. **1876** BRISTOWE *Th. & Pract. Med.* (1878) 32 Infect them, by either growing parasitically .., or (sperm-like) imparting to them specific properties. **1878** F. J. BELL *Gegenbaur's Elem. Comp. Anat.* 53 The relation of the egg-forming and sperm-forming organs to one another varies greatly. **1927** HALDANE & HUXLEY *Animal Biol.* ii. 52 Their walls are composed of germ-cells (sperm-producing cells).

II. (Short for SPERM WHALE or SPERMACETI.)

5. a. ***sperm oil***, an oil found together with spermaceti in the head of various species of whales.

1839 T. BEALE *Nat. Hist. Sperm Whale* 149 There was still a gradual increase in the importation of sperm oil. **1857** MILLER *Elem. Chem., Org.* vi. §1. 358 The principal drying oils are those of linseed, walnut, hemp,.. and sperm oil. **1883** *Fisheries Exhib. Catal.* 202 Crude and refined Sperm oil, used for illuminating,.. and in the manufacture of spermaceti.

attrib. **1849** CUPPLES *Green Hand* ii. (1856) 18 Trimming up the sperm-oil lights.

b. ***sperm candle***, a spermaceti candle.

1775 in *Essex Inst. Hist. Coll.* (1887) XIII. 202 He heard sperm candles were 3s. **1839** C. F. BRIGGS *Adventures Harry Franco* II. 143 Mrs. Brown's house was brilliantly illuminated with a sperm candle in each side light. **1856** *Orr's Circ. Sci., Pract. Chem.* 458, 15 sperm candles will give the light of 16.5 stearic. **1890** *Daily News* 29 Oct. 3/5 The only clean and tidy candles.. were wax candles and sperm candles.

6. a. A sperm whale. Also *collect.* and *attrib.*

1840 F. D. BENNETT *Narr. Whaling Voy.* II. 185 The commencement of the Sperm Fishery by England. **1854** *Chamb. Jrnl.* 28 Jan. 53/2 See, again! there is a sperm of the largest size, which has just leaped. **1860** MAURY *Phys. Geog.* xviii. 772 The parts of the ocean.. in which the sperm are found. **1895** *Pall Mall G.* 16 Dec. 2/1 He killed as many as five sperms in a single day with one harpoon.

b. ***sperm-bird*** (see quot.).

1840 F. D. BENNETT *Narr. Whaling Voy.* I. 10 Many ocean birds of the high south latitudes were now visible.., as nellies (*Procellaria gigantea*); blue-petrels, or sperm-birds (*Prion pachyptila*), [etc.].

7. Sperm candles or oil.

1856 *Orr's Circ. Sci., Pract. Chem.* 458 If there be any difference, the light of sperm is a little greater, and that of stearic acid a little whiter. **1890** CLARK RUSSELL *Ocean Trag.* I. iv. 68 The soft.. radiance diffused by the burning sperm.

†**sperm**, *v. Obs.*[−1] [f. prec.] *intr.* To spawn.

a **1425** tr. *Arderne's Treat. Fistula*, etc. 41 þei grew to þe liknes of þe womb of a.. creuyse or lopster when he spermeþ or frieþ.

‖ˈ**sperma**. Now *rare.* Pl. **spermata**. [a. L. *sperma* or Gr. σπέρμα: see SPERM *sb.*] Sperm; seed.

14.. [see SPERM *sb.*[1]]. **1527** ANDREW *Brunswyke's Dist. Waters* M iij, The same water is good and multyplyeth the sperma. **1597** A. M. *Guillemeau's Fr. Chirurg.* 3 b/2 The patient can nether retayne his vrine, Sperma, or Stole. **1600** PORY tr. *Leo's Africa* 344 Whether the said Amber be the sperma or the excrement therof, they cannot well determine. **1668** *Phil. Trans.* III. 790 Here have been Sperma-Ceti-Whales driven upon the shore, which Sperma (as they call it) lies all over the Body of those Whales. **1728** CHAMBERS *Cycl.*, *Sperm* or *Sperma*, the Seed whereof an Animal is form'd. **1843** R. J. GRAVES *Syst. Clin. Med.* xxvii. 350 By the mixture and mutual neutralization or solution of different spermata. **1886** *Lond. Q. Rev.* Oct. 129 Basilides is said to have spoken of a 'sperma' or seed-mass, from which all things have been produced.

sperma-, combining form of prec.: see SPERMADUCT, etc., and cf. SPERMATO-, SPERMO-.

spermaceti (spɜːməˈsiːtɪ, -ˈsɛtɪ). Forms: 6–9 **sperma ceti** (5 **cete**, 7 **coeti, cetæ**); 5– **spermaceti** (5 **-cetie**, 7 **-cete, -cæty**, 8 **-cety**); 6 **sparmaceti**. [med.L., from *sperma* sperm + *cēti* gen. sing. of *cētus* (ad. Gr. κῆτος) whale, through an erroneous opinion as to the nature of the substance. Hence also F. *spermaceti*, It. *spermaceti*, Sp. *espermaceti*, Pg. *-cete*. The corrupt form PARMACETY was formerly common.]

1. A fatty substance, which in a purified state has the form of a soft white scaly mass, found in the head (and to some extent in other parts) of the sperm-whale (*Physeter macrocephalus*) and some other whales and dolphins; it is used largely in various medicinal preparations, and in the manufacture of candles.

1471 RIPLEY *Comp. Alch.* in Ashm. (1652) 113 Use.. Sperma Cete ana with redd Wyne when ye wax old. **1525** tr. *Jerome of Brunswick's Surg.* R iij b/2 Take sperma ceti .iij. dragma, mumie an ounce. **1581** RICH *Farew.* T j, The Doctor tooke Sparmaceti, and suche like thynges that bee good for a bruse. **1600** DALLAM in *Early Voy. Levant* (Hakl. Soc.) 95 This day we saw greate store of the spane of whales, whearof they make spermecetie. **1658** A. FOX *Würtz' Surg.* IV. v. 334 When Sperma Cetæ is stale.. it ought not to be used, making the medicine very unpleasant. **1747** WESLEY *Prim. Physick* (1762) 53 Put a Scruple of Sperma-Ceti into the yolk of a new-laid Egg. **1774** GOLDSM. *Nat. Hist.* (1824) III. 27 The first cavity or chamber of the brain, is filled with that spermaceti which is supposed of the greatest purity and highest value. **1811** A. T. THOMSON *Lond. Disp.* (1818) 297 Spermaceti is demulcent and emollient. **1842** LOVER *Handy Andy* ii. 26 All the spermaceti in M'Garry's shop won't cure you. **1897** F. T. BULLEN *Cruise of 'Cachalot'* 51 Spermaceti exists in all the oil, especially that from the dorsal hump.

fig. **1601** B. JONSON *Poetaster* II. i. (1905) 28 Looke here, my sweet wife.., my deare mummia, my balsamum, my *spermacete*. *a* **1613** OVERBURY *Characters, Ord. Fencer* Wks. (1856) 112 For an inward bruise, lambstones and sweet-breads are his onely sperma ceti, which he eats at night next his heart fasting.

2. *attrib.* and *Comb.*, as ***spermaceti-candle, -fat, -fish, manufactory, oil, -ointment, -refiner***.

1738 CHAMBERS *Cycl.* s.v., *Spermaceti candles are of modern manufacture,.. superior to the finest wax-candles. **1758** FRANKLIN *Lett.* Wks. 1887 III. 8 The extinguisher is for spermaceti candles only. **1858** SIMMONDS *Dict. Trade*, *Spermaceti-candles*, fine transparent candles, used as wax lights. **1868** WATTS *Dict. Chem.* V. 397 Sperm-oil appears to be isomeric with *spermaceti-fat or cetin. **1781** *Encycl. Brit.* (ed. 2) VIII. 6171 *Physeter*, or *Spermaceti-fish,.. a genus belonging to the order of cete. **1748** ARMSTRONG *Misc.* (1770) I. 216 Their filthy greasy brains, that were never fit for any thing but the *sperma ceti manufactory. **1765** *Museum Rust.* IV. 76 A taper.. lamp, with four ordinary threads of cotton in the wick, consumes ·1664 oz. of *spermaceti oil in one hour. **1820** SCORESBY *Acc. Arctic Reg.* II. 413 The oil.. is more inflammable than spermaceti-oil. **1843** R. J. GRAVES *Syst. Clin. Med.* ix. 103 A piece of lint smeared with *spermaceti ointment. **1858** SIMMONDS *Dict. Trade*, *Spermaceti-ointment*, a pharmaceutical preparation consisting of lard, spermaceti, and bees'-wax. *Ibid.*, **Spermaceti-refiner*, a person who purifies spermaceti, chiefly by pressure and crystallization.

b. ***spermaceti whale***, the sperm whale.

1658 SIR T. BROWNE *Gard. Cyrus* iii, A better account.. of that prominent jowle of the Sperma Ceti Whale. **1672** *Phil. Trans.* VII. 5021 To heal Bruises and Aches with the Oyl of the Sperma-ceti-Whale. **1763** *Ann. Reg.* I. 116 Two spermaceti whales have been caught on the Essex coast. **1783** *Phil. Trans.* LXXIII. 231 They look for ambergrise in all the spermaceti-whales they catch. **1845** DARWIN *Voy. Nat.* (ed. 2) x. 223 *note*, We saw.. several spermaceti whales jumping upright quite out of the water.

spermacetic (spɜːməˈsiːtɪk), *a. rare*[−1]. [f. SPERMACET(I + -IC.] Of or pertaining to spermaceti; *spermacetic oil* = *spermaceti oil* s.v. SPERMACETI 2 a.

1922 JOYCE *Ulysses* 393 They.. rubbed him all over with spermacetic oil.

spermacide (ˈspɜːməsaɪd). *rare*[−1]. [f. SPERMA- + -CIDE.] = SPERMICIDE.

1908 *Chem. Abstr.* II. 3128 Reports upon Dr. Bamberger's lupina powder, spermacide, and choleysin are given.

ˈ**spermaduct**. *Zool.* [f. SPERMA- + DUCT *sb.* 6 a.] A spermatic or seminal duct or passage in a male animal. Also ˈ**spermagone, sperma**ˈ**gonium**, *Bot.* = SPERMOGONE, -GONIUM. ˈ**spermaphore**, ˈ**spermaphyte**, *Bot.* = SPERMOPHORE, -PHYTE.

1891 *Cent. Dict.*, *Spermaduct*,.. a spermatic duct, or sperm-duct [etc.]. **1905** J. McCABE tr. *Haeckel's Evol. Man* II. 823 In the male they convey the spermatozoa away from the testicles, and are called 'spermaducts', or *vasa deferentia.*

1876 *Encycl. Brit.* IV. 159/1 Embedded in the margin of the thallus in Lichens..certain hollow urn-shaped bodies are found, which have been termed *spermagones (conceptacles). **1861** H. MACMILLAN *Footn. Page Nat.* 73 Minute, blackish, elevated, somewhat gelatinous points called *spermagonia, occurring on various parts of the upper surface of the thallus. **1880** BESSEY *Botany* 299 Minute cells (the *spermatia*), which..are permitted to escape through the small opening at the apex of the spermagonium. **1847** WEBSTER, **Spermaphore*, in botany, that part of the ovary from which the ovules arise; it is synonymous with *Placenta*. **1891** *Cent. Dict.*, **Spermaphyte*. **1897** tr. *Strasburger's Text-bk. Bot.* 432 They are also termed Seed-plants or Spermaphytes.

† **'spermal**, *a. Obs.*$^{-1}$ [f. SPERM *sb.* + -AL[1], or ad. med.L. *spermāl-is*.] Spermatic.

1642 H. MORE *Song of Soul* II. II. i. 9 This is the nourishing Of all; but spermall form, the certain shapening.

spermalege ('spɜːməlɪdʒ). *Ent.* [ad. F. *spermalège* (J. Carayon 1959, in *Rev. de Zool. et de Bot. Africaines* LX. 82), f. L. *sperma* SPERM *sb.* + *legere* to gather, collect.] In female bedbugs, an organ in which sperm are received and stored.

1964 H. E. HINTON in K. C. Highnam *Insect Reproduction* (Symp. R. Entomol. Soc. Lond. No. 2) 101 These cells constitute the mesodermal part of the organ of Ribaga (or Berlese), or, as it is now aptly called by Carayon, the mesodermal part of the spermalege. **1978** H. V. DALY *Introd. Insect Biol.* iv. 62/2 In some bedbugs a spermalege, or specialized organ of the integument, is developed where the puncture normally is made.

‖**spermarium** (spɜː'mɛərɪəm). Pl. **-aria**. [mod.L., f. *sperma* sperm.] = next.

1861 J. R. GREENE *Man. Anim. Kingd., Coelent.* 40 Processes of the body-wall, within which are developed true generative organs, the 'spermaria' and 'ovaria', constitute the reproductive apparatus of the *Hydrozoa*. **1881** LANKESTER in *Encycl. Brit.* XII. 550 Each ovarium and each spermarium represents an aborted generative person.

spermary ('spɜːmərɪ). [Anglicized f. prec: see -ARY[1].] The organ or gland in which spermatozoa are generated in male animals.

1864 in WEBSTER (citing Dana). **1885** S. F. CLARKE in *Riverside Nat. Hist.* (1888) I. 76 In a limited region on the body of *Hydra*,..there appear..small out-growths of the body-wall which prove to be the spermaries.

sperm-aster ('spɜːmæstə(r)). *Biol.* Also **spermaster, sperm aster**. [f. SPERM *sb.* + ASTER 4.] A star-shaped configuration which in some species forms ahead of the sperm nucleus as it enters the egg in fertilization, and which develops into the amphiaster.

1904 *Biol. Bull.* VI. 226 One is the growth and division of the sperm aster, the other the growth of the nucleus. **1925** E. B. WILSON *Cell* (ed. 3) v. 400 In almost all cases the sperm-nucleus, as it advances within the egg, is typically preceded by a sperm-aster which sooner or later divides to form an amphiaster that is the forerunner of the cleavage-amphiaster. **1946** *Nature* 17 Aug. 239/1 Colchicine treatment..inhibits spindle formation as well as the appearance of the spermaster in fertilized eggs and of the monaster in parthenogenesis. **1977** *Jrnl. Embryol. & Exper. Zool.* XL. 194 It would be of the utmost interest to establish whether a causal relationship does also exist between sperm aster formation and the movement and directionality of the female pronucleus.

‖**spermatheca** (spɜːmə'θiːkə). Pl. **-thecae**. [f. SPERMA- + THECA.] A receptacle in the oviduct of female insects and invertebrates, in which fecundation of the ova takes place.

1826 KIRBY & SP. *Entomol.* xlii. IV. 147 *n.*, Perhaps likewise the organ discovered by M. L. Dufour in *Scolia*..may be a *spermatheca*. **1841** T. R. JONES *Anim. Kingd.* 283 The spermatheca has a small accessory vesicle connected with it. **1888** ROLLESTON & JACKSON *Anim. Life* 206 The female apparatus is completed by two pairs of vesicular spermathecae.

Hence **sperma'thecal** *a.*, of or belonging to the spermatheca.

1883 LANKESTER in *Encycl. Brit.* XVI. 658/2 On reaching the point where the spermathecal duct debouches they are impregnated by the spermatozoa. **1900** *Proc. Zool. Soc.* June 169 In the region of the spermathecal apertures.

spermatic (spɜː'mætɪk), *a.* and *sb.* Also 6 **sparmatyke**, 7 **-ique**, 6 **spermaticke**, 6–7 **-ike**, 7 **-ique**, 7–8 **-ick**. [ad. med.L. *spermatic-us*, ad. Gr. σπερματικός, f. σπέρμα sperm, or OF. (also mod.F.) *spermatique* (1314), = It. *spermatico*, Sp. and Pg. *espermatico*.]

1. a. Containing, conveying, or producing sperm or seed; seminiferous.

1539 ELYOT *Cast. Helthe* (1541) 12 Vessels spermatike, wherin mannes seede lyeth. **1597** A. M. tr. *Guillemeau's Fr. Chirurg.* 21 b/2 Not to touch the testicles, nether anye of the spermaticke vessels. **1646** SIR T. BROWNE *Pseud. Ep.* 189 The seminall ejaculation proceeds..from the spermatick glandules. **1730** CHAMBERLAYNE *Relig. Philos.* I. iii. §22 The Spermatic Arteries, coming on each Side out of the great Artery. **1797** M. BAILLIE *Morb. Anat.* (1807) 356 A disease of the spermatic chord which is not uncommon, is an enlargement of its veins. **1857** BULLOCK tr. *Cazeaux' Midwifery* 69 The numerous lymphatic vessels..contribute to the formation of the spermatic plexus. **1881** MIVART *Cat* 243 Within it is a layer of membrane—the spermatic fascia.

b. Full of, abounding in, sperm; generative, productive.

1619 DRAYTON *Owle* Poems 407 There in soft Downe the liquorous Sparrow sat, Pamper'd with meats, full spermatike and fat. **1648** J. BEAUMONT *Psyche* IX. xxxiv, Spermatick Nile, which brings Choise Monsters forth. **1655** T. VAUGHAN *Euphrates* 32 This Primitive spermatic Ocean filled all that space which we now attribute to the Air.

2. a. Of the nature of sperm; resembling sperm.

1541 R. COPLAND *Guydon's Quest. Chirurg.* B iv b, They haue theyr breding and begynnynge of sparmatyke mater. *a* **1631** DONNE *Elegies* viii. 8 Ranke sweaty froth..Like spermatique issue of ripe menstruous boiles. *c* **1645** HOWELL *Lett.* III. xxix, A production of an organicall body out of the spermatic substance. **1693** SIR T. P. BLOUNT *Nat. Hist.* 28 It would sometimes let fall a Spermatick Juice, which..would thereupon produce another coral. **1828** KIRBY & SP. *Entomol.* (ed. 2) IV. xlii. 153 This organ was a reservoir for the spermatic fluid. **1869** H. A. NICHOLSON *Man. Zool.* 22 As a rule, the germ-cell is produced by one individual and the spermatic element by another.

b. *transf.* and *fig.* Resembling sperm, esp. in generative or reproductive power.

1669 GALE *Crt. Gentiles* I. III. iii. 44 The Stoics also held, there was..a spermatic effluorative word, whereby the world was formed. **1671** J. WEBSTER *Metallogr.* x. 142 Having annexed to it some slates and other spermatick matter, which detracts from the goodness of its own nature. **1741** WARBURTON *Div. Legat.* Wks. 1811 III. 168 You will be assumed into the Divine nature, or the spermatick reasons. **1870** EMERSON *Soc. & Solit.* Wks. (Bohn) III. 80, I find certain books vital and spermatic, not leaving the reader what he was.

† **3.** Directly derived from sperm (according to old physiological views). *Obs.*

1548–77 VICARY *Anat.* ii. (1888) 18 The Grystle is a member simple and spermatike, next in hardnes to the bone. **1621** LODGE *Summary Du Bartas* I. 284 *Stomake.* The substance thereof is more spermatique then sanguine. **1670** *Phil. Trans.* V. 2077 The two sorts of Parts of the Body, Spermatick and Sanguineous. **1684** tr. *Bonet's Merc. Compit.* XIV. 498 A Membrane is a Spermatick part, which being consumed is not regenerated. **1728** CHAMBERS *Cycl.* s.v., The Ancients made a general Division of the Parts of the Animal Body into Spermatic and Fleshy.

4. Of qualities: Characteristic of, peculiar to, derived from, sperm.

1642 H. MORE *Song of Soul* II. App. 101 Nought can e'er consume that centrall power Of hid spermatick life. **1669** W. SIMPSON *Hydrol. Chym.* 269 Water..by the spermatick efflorescence of a mineral seed becomes wrought into a mineral juyce. **1706** DE FOE *Jure Div.* Introd., Spermatick Vigour spreads the poison'd Race, Conveys Hereditary Crimes apace. **1866** SHUCKARD *Brit. Bees* 296 This in some cases has a spermatic odour. **1896** *Allbutt's Syst. Med.* I. 204 The first theory..views the growth of a tumour as due to the spermatic influence of certain cells upon those contiguous.

5. Existing in sperm.

1685 J. LOCKE *Jrnl.* 22 June in Ld. King *Life & Lett. John Locke* (1830) I. 309, I saw, at Mr. Lewenhoek's, several microscopical observations..but the best of all his glasses, and those by which he describes his spermatic animals, we did not see. **1837** P. KEITH *Bot. Lex.* 304 According to him, they are animated substances; the analogues of the spermatic animalcules of Leuenhoeck. **1857** BULLOCK tr. *Cazeaux' Midwifery* 96 These minute bodies have been designated as the spermatic animalcules, or the spermatozoa.

6. As *sb.* and *pl.* The spermatic vessels.

1690 in Maidment *Bk. Sc. Pasquils* (1868) 277 Spermaticks sink, true mother of discord, Inflam'd these Hectors. **1719** QUINCY *Phys. Dict.* (1722) s.v. *Semen*, In the Aorta, where the Spermaticks arise. **1857** BULLOCK tr. *Cazeaux' Midwifery* 68 The arteries which supply the ovary are the spermatics, and proceed directly from the aorta. **1859** *Todd's Cycl. Anat.* V. 651/1 This structure is found..in the internal spermatics, and in all the veins of the uterine substances.

† **sper'matical**, *a. Obs.* Also 5 **spermatycall**, 6 **sparmaticall**. [See prec. and -AL[1].]

1. = SPERMATIC *a.* 2.

1471 RIPLEY *Comp. Alch.* VI. xviii. in Ashm. (1652) 165 Yt thus fro thyng to thyng was alterat..; And so our Mater spermatycall wythin one Glas Wythin hyt selfe must turne fro thyng to thyng. **1655** in Hartlib *Ref. Commw. Bees* 22 A tender spermatical milk enclosed in a most tender skin.

2. = SPERMATIC *a.* 3.

1562 BULLEIN *Bulwarke, Dial. betw. Sorenes & Chir.* 22 Members, whiche Phisicians call sparmaticall, beyng ones loosed, will not be ioyned again. **1615** CROOKE *Body of Man* 697 Euery Similar part is either Spermaticall or fleshie. **1633** P. FLETCHER *Purple Isl.* II. xii. *marg. note*, A nerve is a spermaticall part rising from the brain and the pith of the back-bone. **1668** CULPEPPER & COLE *Barthol. Anat.* Introd., All these parts are commonly divided into Spermatical, Sanguine or mixt.

3. Endowed with sperm or semen.

1610 HEALEY *St. Aug. Citie of God* VII. ii. 260 Liber and Libera, [gods] of the distillation of seede in all spermaticall creatures.

4. = SPERMATIC *a.* 1.

1615 CROOKE *Body of Man* 217 The spermaticall vessels which bring the seede from the whole bodye..are foure. *Ibid.* 837 The left Emulgent also is larger then the right, because of the Spermatical veine which was to arise therefrom. **1621** LODGE *Summary Du Bartas* I. 269 The spermaticall, or seede Vessels.

5. = SPERMATIC *a.* 4.

1642 H. MORE *Song of Soul* II. I. ii. 25 Both what hight form spermaticall Hath here a share, as also that we term Soul sensitive. *a* **1652** J. SMITH *Sel. Disc.* VII. iv. (1660) 309 Like the Spermatical virtue of the Heavens, which spreads it self freely upon this Lower World. **1682** H. MORE *Annot. Glanvill's Lux Orient* 119 We have..reason..to suppose this Vital or Spermatical Law is amongst the rest.

sper'matically, *adv.* [f. prec. + -LY[2].] In a spermatic manner; in a way characteristic of sperm; seminally.

1647 TRAPP *Comm. Matt.* i. 20 He..was conceived of the holy Ghost, not spermatically, but operatively. **1682** H. MORE *Annot. Glanvill's Lux Orient* 119 Such a spirit as contains Spermatically or Vitally all the Laws contrived by the Divine Intellect. **1822** T. TAYLOR *Apuleius* 324 The participations subsist in these subjects spermatically.

spermaticide (spɜː'mætɪsaɪd). Now *rare*. [f. SPERMATO-: see -CIDE.] = SPERMICIDE. Hence **sper'maticidal** *a.* = SPERMICIDAL *a.*

1923 M. C. STOPES *Contraception* v. 104 Of all the chemical substances used as spermaticides, undoubtedly quinine is in the most general use. **1931** Spermaticide, spermaticidal [see SPERMICIDE]. **1934** J. ELLISON et al. *Sex Ethics* v. 93 The spermaticidal effect of these pessaries is not very high, and many failures have resulted. *Ibid.*, The use of lactic acid jelly ointment, as a lubricant, will assist in ensuring that all parts of the vagina are covered with spermaticide.

'spermatid. *Biol.* Also **-ide**. [f. L. *spermat-*, stem of *sperma* sperm + -ID.] A seminal cell which develops into a spermatozoon; *spec.* one that is formed by the meiotic division of a secondary spermatocyte and develops into a spermatozoon without dividing again.

1889 GEDDES & THOMSON *Evol. Sex* ix. 113 The sperm or spermatozoon is differentiated from an immature cell or spermatide. **1904** *Biol. Bulletin* Feb. 150 There is the normal number of two chromosomes. The ovotid and the spermatid have each only one. **1924** E. W. MACBRIDE *Study of Heredity* ii. 46 In the case of the male cell each secondary spermatocyte divides into two precisely equal cells called spermatids. **1959** [see *spermatogonium* s.v. SPERMATO- 1]. **1968** *New Scientist* 2 May 218/2 It now appears that the X and the Y chromosomes become genetically inert before the spermatids (the cells from which the spermatozoa develop) are formed.

Hence **sper'matidal** *a.*

1975 *Biochem. & Biophysical Res. Communications* LXVII. 183 Proteins extracted from elongated spermatids..reveal the presence of a new spermatidal basic protein fraction.

sperma'tiferous, *a.* [f. as prec. + -(I)FEROUS.] Bearing or conveying sperm.

1862 ANSTED *Channel Isl.* II. viii. 189 His specimens were covered with spermatiferous spermogones. **1865** M. C. COOKE *Microsc. Fungi* ii. 24 The colour of this spermatiferous matter is commonly orange.

'spermatin. *Chem.* Also **-ine**. [a. F. *spermatine*, f. as prec. + *-ine* -IN[1].] An albuminic constituent of the spermatic fluid.

1836–9 *Todd's Cycl. Anat.* II. 458/2 In the spermatic fluid of the horse, Lassaigne has detected..Peculiar animal matter called spermatine. **1856** *Orr's Circ. Sci., Pract. Chem.* 317 The seminal principle (spermatine), is..nearly analogous to albuminous substances. **1873** RALFE *Phys. Chem.* 176 The peculiar albuminoid substance, spermatin, is probably a mixture of globulin and lecithin.

sper'matio-, comb. form of SPERMATIUM, as in **spermati'ogenous** *a.*, bearing spermatia. **sper'matiophore**, = SPERMATOPHORE 2.

1887 GARNSEY tr. *De Bary's Fungi* v. 241 Some Pyrenomycetes..form layers agreeing in every respect with the spermatiophores. *Ibid.*, They are..cushion-shaped bodies with spermatiogenous surface.

'spermatism. *rare*$^{-0}$. [ad. mod.L. *spermatismus* (Gr. σπερματισμός) or F. *spermatisme*: cf. next.] (See quots.)

1857 DUNGLISON *Med. Dict.*, *Animalculism*, Spermatism. **1882** *Imp. Dict.* IV. 155/1 *Spermatism*,..1. The emission of sperm or seed.—2. The theory that the germ in animals is produced by spermatic animalcules.

'spermatist. [ad. mod.L. **spermatista* or F. *spermatiste*, f. L. *spermat-*, *sperma* sperm + -IST.] One who held the view that the sperm alone was the source of animal life.

1836–9 *Todd's Cycl. Anat.* II. 427/1 According to the..theory..of the Spermatists,..the male semen alone furnished all the vital parts of the new animal. **1899** J. A. THOMSON *Sci. Life* 125 Other observers, nicknamed 'spermatists' or 'animalculists', believed them [*sc.* spermatozoa] to be the earliest stages of the young animal.

‖**spermatium** (spɜː'meɪʃɪəm). *Bot.* Pl. **-atia**. [mod.L., ad. Gr. σπερμάτιον, dim. of σπέρμα seed, SPERM *sb.*] A minute linear sporule forming part of the reproductive system of lichens and fungi. (Chiefly in pl.)

1856 W. L. LINDSAY *Pop. Hist. Brit. Lichens* 75 The fecundating influence of the spermatia or stylospores. **1867** J. HOGG *Microsc.* II. i. 291 The spermatia or contents of the spermagonia never germinate. **1885** GOODALE *Physiol. Bot.* 440 *note*, A branch showing antheridia, *a*, and a carpogonium, *o*, with the trichogyne, *t* (*e*, spermatium).

† **'spermative**, *a. Obs. rare.* Also 6 **sparmatyf**. [ad. med.L. **spermativ-us*.] Spermatic.

1541 R. COPLAND *Guydon's Quest. Chirurg.* C j, I say secondly that no membres sparmatyf after the losse of theyr substaunce maye nat regenerate. **1610** HEALEY *St. Aug. Citie of God* 267 The brain..is the most excellent of the spermative parts.

ˈspermatize, *v.* [ad. F. *spermatiser* or med.L. *spermatizāre*, ad. Gr. σπερματίζειν to sow, etc., f. σπερματ-, stem of σπέρμα SPERM *sb.*]

† **1.** *intr.* To emit or produce sperm. *Obs.*

1611 COTGR., *Spermatiser*, to spermatize; to shed, eiect, or iniect sperme. **1646** SIR T. BROWNE *Pseud. Ep.* 149 Affirming that women do not spermatize,.. he deductively includes both sexes in mankinde. **1725** BOURNE *Antiq. Vulg.* xxvii, In ancient Times the Dragons.. did frequently.. Spermatize in the Wells and Fountains. **1777** BRAND *Pop. Antiq.* xxvii. 281, I have nothing to observe here concerning Mr. Bourne's lustful Dragons, their spermatizing in the Wells,.. &c.!

2. [Back-formation f. SPERMATIZATION.] *trans. Mycology.* To effect spermatization upon. *rare.*

1932 *Mycologia* XXIV. 347 Apothecia are produced only when the isolate from the crocus is used as a source of microconidia to spermatize any of the other six.

Also **spermatiˈzation** (see quot. 1932); **ˈspermatizing** *ppl. a.*

1932 F. L. DRAYTON in *Mycologia* XXIV. 346 The development of apothecia by *Sclerotium Gladioli*.. has been induced by means of placing the microconidia of one thallus on certain structures which develop on another thallus. This process may be called 'spermatization', and it will be so designated throughout this paper. **1945** *Ibid.* XXXVII. 635 He attempted to intercross these four races by the spermatization method. **1967** M. E. HALE *Biol. Lichens* iii. 42 The spermatizing element may be any hypha that can contact the ascogonium. **1970** *Cytologia* XXXV. 427 The mechanism of spermatization in this fungus.. is of a type not so far reported.

spermato- (ˈspɜːmətəʊ), repr. Gr. σπερματο-, combining form of the stem of σπέρμα SPERM *sb.*, employed in a large number of terms (chiefly of recent origin) relating to the reproductive organs or activities of animals and plants.

Some of these are employed only in L. forms, as *spermatocystidium*, *-cystis*, *-cystitis*, etc., and others have had very little currency even in special works. A number have alternative forms in *sperma-* or *spermo-*.

1. In terms denoting special reproductive organs, or parts of these, as ***spermato-blast***, ***-cyst***, ***-gemma***, ***-gone***, ***-mere***, ***-spore***; **spermatocyte**, a cell which gives rise to spermatids by meiosis; the ***primary spermatocyte*** gives rise in meiosis I to two ***secondary spermatocytes***, which each give rise in meiosis II to two spermatids; **spermatogonium**, (*a*) *Bot.* (see quot. 1957); (*b*) *Zool.*, a primordial male reproductive cell which undergoes mitosis and gives rise to primary spermatocytes.

Some of these are the source of adj. forms, as ***spermatoblastic***, ***-cystic***, ***-gonial***, ***-gonic***, etc.

1882 *Imp. Dict.* IV. 155/1 **Spermatoblast*,.. certain stalk-like filaments in the seminal ducts upon which the spermatozoa are developed. **1886** *Encycl. Brit.* XX. 412/1 To the whole prolongation with its lobes he [Von Ebner] applies the term spermatoblast. **1884** *Proc. Boston Soc. Nat. Hist.* 61 The first stages in the development of the *spermatocyst of Hydra. **1886** *Encycl. Brit.* XX. 412/2 One kind.. divide into a mass or spermatogemma of small cells (*spermatocytes). **1920** Spermatocyte [see OOGONIUM 2]. **1959** [see *spermatogonium* below]. **1970** Spermatocyte [see OOCYTE]. **1886** *Encycl. Brit.* XX. 413/1 The *spermatogemma meanwhile is developing a central cavity. **1898** A. S. PACKARD *Text-bk. Entomol.* 499 A colossal cell,.. the *spermatogone, from which the entire contents of the testes originate. **1902** *Biol. Bull.* III. 44 In the case of the accessory chromosome, it has been found advantageous to trace its course through the *spermatogonial divisions in *Brachystola*, and through the spermatocyte changes in *Hippiscus*. **1976** *Nature* 22 Jan. 209/1 After 600 rad of X rays, the mean spermatogonial mutation rate was one-third that of the 7-locus mean. **1861** BENTLEY *Man. Bot.* 384 The spermagonia or *spermatogonia [in Lichens] were first discovered by Tulasne. **1886** *Encycl. Brit.* XX. 412/2 One kind, resembling young ovules, which he [Von La Valette St. George] terms primitive seminal cells or spermatogonia. **1957** SNELL & DICK *Gloss. Mycol.* 144/2 *Spermatogonium*, the proper form for what is called 'spermogonium'.., but seldom used. **1959** W. ANDREW *Textbk. Compar. Histol.* xii. 490 [In fishes] spermatogenesis consists of the same general cytological stages as in the invertebrates: namely, spermatogonia, spermatocytes, spermatids, and spermatozoa. **1968** PASSMORE & ROBSON *Compan. Med. Stud.* I. xxxvii. 27/2 Spermatogonia show little sign of activity until puberty when they begin to multiply rapidly. **1970** [see OOGONIUM]. **1974** *Sci. Amer.* Sept. 56/3 In the course of spermatogenesis the two important objectives are reduction of the chromosome number from the diploid number (46) of the spermatogonium to the haploid number (23) of the spermatozoon and the preparation of the spermatozoon for its role in fertilization. **1886** *Q. Jrnl. Microsc. Sci.* XXVI. 597 The region where the spermatogonia are formed at the expense of their mother-cells or *spermatomeres.

2. In some other sbs. and adjs. with second elements of obvious meaning, as ***spermatoˈspore***; ***spermatoˈphoral***, ***-ˈphorous***, ***-ˈpœic***, ***-ˈrrhœa***, adjs. Also, **spermatoˈcidal** *a.* = SPERMICIDAL *a.*; **ˈspermatocide** = SPERMICIDE; **spermatoˈgenesis**, the formation and development of spermatozoa (cf. SPERMIOGENESIS); so ***spermatogeˈnetic***, ***-ˈgenic***, adjs., ***spermatoˈgenically*** *adv.*; **spermaˈtology**, †(*a*) a treatise on sperm; (*b*) the scientific study of sperm.

1928 *Funk's Stand. Dict.* 2337/3 **Spermatocidal*, checking or killing the motor-power of spermatozoa. **1937** Spermatocidal [see CHINOSOL]. **1949** *New Gould Med. Dict.*, *Spermatocide. **1881** *Athenæum* 11 June 787/1 M. Mathias Duval on *spermatogenesis. **1886** *Encycl. Brit.* XX. 412/1 The process of spermatogenesis in the Bull, Dog, and Rabbit. **1978** P. J. HOGARTH *Biol. Reproduction* ii. 11 The final phase of spermatogenesis in the testes is known as spermiogenesis.., and consists of the progressive conversion, without division, of the spermatids into functional spermatozoa. **1980** Spermatogenesis [see SPERMIOGENESIS]. **1886** *Encycl. Brit.* XX. 412/1 Ascribing *spermatogenetic functions both to the spermatoblasts and to the round cells. **1880** ALLMAN in *Linn. Soc. Jrnl., Zool.* XV. 136 These I regard as the remains of the *spermatogenic tissue. **1980** *Nature* 10 Apr. 548/1 *Spermatogenically active testes. **1833** DUNGLISON *Dict. Med. Sci.* II. 312/2 **Spermatology*, a treatise on sperm. **1851** DUNGLISON *Med. Lex.*, *Spermatology*, a treatise on sperm. **1970** B. A. AFZELIUS in B. Baccetti *Compar. Spermatol.* 568 In spite of the great efforts to solve the problems in comparative spermatology we find ourselves confronted with more questions than answers. **1976** T. SHARPE *Wilt* iv. 32 He got the Nobel prize for spermatology. **1886** HOWES & SCOTT *Huxley's Pract. Biol.* 291 The *spermatophoral gland or flagellum. **1851** DUNGLISON *Med. Lex.*, **Spermatophorous*, sperm-bearing. The cells or granules in the sperm have been so called. **1799** *Monthly Rev.* XXX. 521 A curious restorative and *spermatopoeic sugar-candy of the Japanese. **1858** MAYNE *Expos. Lex.* 1180/2 **Spermatorrhœa*,.. seminal flux. **1879** T. BRYANT *Pract. Surg.* II. 226 Spermatorrhœa doubtless exists as a disease although rare. **1880** *Q. Jrnl. Microsc. Sci.* 83 The term *spermatospore.. is applied to the constituent cells of a testis, derived from the primitive germ-epithelium.

‖**spermatocele** (-siːl). *Path.* [med.L.: see prec. and CELE. So F. *spermatocèle*, Sp. *espermatocela*.] (See quots.)

1693 tr. *Blancard's Phys. Dict.* (ed. 2), *Spermatocele*, a Rupture caused by the Contraction of the Vessel which ejects the Seed, and its falling down into the Scrotum. **1823** CRABB *Technol. Dict.*, *Spermatocele*,.. a swelling of the testes, or epididymis, from an accumulation of semen. **1874** VAN BUREN *Dis. Genit. Org.* 407 Spermatocele is a collection of serous fluid, containing spermatic elements.

spermatogone, **-ˈgonium**: see SPERMATO- 1.

ˈspermatoid, *a. rare*$^{-0}$. [f. *spermat-* sperm + -OID.] Similar to sperm.

1855 DUNGLISON *Med. Lex.*, *Spermatoid*, Gonoides.

spermaˈtoon. *Biol.* Pl. -ˈtoa. [f. SPERMATO- + Gr. ᾠόν egg.] A spermatid.

1875 BRANDE & COX *Dict. Sci.*, etc. III. 530/1 Sometimes the sperm-cell contains a single spermatoon, sometimes several spermatoa.

ˈspermatophore. [f. SPERMATO- + -PHORE.]

1. *Biol.* In certain of the lower forms of animal life, a structure containing a compact mass of spermatozoa.

1847–9 *Todd's Cycl. Anat.* IV. I. 485/1 These fibres in the Cephalopods are.. surrounded.. by peculiar sack-like enclosures or Spermatophores. **1870** ROLLESTON *Anim. Life* 108 A packet of spermatozoa, aggregated in their passage along the convolutions of the vasa deferentia into the so-called 'spermatophore'. **1880** HUXLEY *Crayfish* 351 The filaments are in fact tubular spermatophores.

2. *Bot.* A part of the spermogonium of lichens or fungi, on which the spermatia are borne.

1861 BENTLEY *Man. Bot.* 384 The spermagonium, when mature, has its interior filled with a number of bodies called spermatia.. raised on stalks, termed spermatophores.

Hence **spermatoˈphoric** *a.*

1959 W. ANDREW *Textbk. Compar. Histol.* xii. 475 [In the common squid] peculiarly complicated organs, the spermatophoric organs and sacs, receive the sperm from the vas deferens, pack them into bundles, and cover them with a tunic.. before their ejection as spermatophores by the penis. **1977** M. J. & J. WELLS in Giese & Pearse *Reproduction Marine Invertebrates* IV. vi. 297 In.. the wider initial section of the first spermatophoric gland, the sperm are embedded in a mucin secretion.

ˈspermatophyte. *Bot.* = SPERMOPHYTE.

1897 *Nature* 11 Nov. 46/1 In the pteridophytes and spermatophytes nutritive and assimilatory structures are developed.

spermatoˈzoal, *a. Phys.* [f. SPERMATOZO-ON + -AL[1].] Of or pertaining to spermatozoa; of the nature of a spermatozoon. So **spermatoˈzoan**, **-ˈzoic** *adjs.*

1858 J. W. DRAPER *Human Physiol.* (ed. 2) 518 Spermatozoic filaments, developing in Certhea vulgaris. **1877** HUXLEY *Anat. Inv. Anim.* xii. 661 The ascription of a spermatozoal nature to the striæ of the modified endoplastules is not warranted. **1888** ROLLESTON & JACKSON *Anim. Life* Introd. p. xxv, Fusion of the nuclei, often termed the male (spermatozoal) and female (ovular) pronuclei. **1954** G. I. M. SWYER *Reproduction & Sex* ii. 24 The spermatozoan content of the ejaculate.

spermatoˈzoid. [f. as SPERMATOZOAL *a.* + -ID, or ad. F. *spermatozoïde*.]

1. *Bot.* A minute fertilizing body or cell in Cryptogamia and Algæ.

1857 HENFREY *Bot.* 511 Spermatozoids are filiform bodies of various forms, mostly presenting one or more spiral curves, or minute globules. **1863** M. J. BERKELEY *Brit. Mosses* iii. 18 An oblong sac.. filled with cellular tissue, each ultimate cell of which.. gives birth to a spermatozoid. **1877** HEATH *Fern World* 11 The sperm cells contain minute, active, thread-like bodies called spermatozoids.

2. *Phys.* = next.

1861 T. R. JONES *Anim. Kingd.* (ed. 3) 156 The testicular cæca become filled with granulations,.. but these do not contain spermatozoids. **1870** H. A. NICHOLSON *Man. Zool.* 22 A sperm-cell or spermatozoid.. is enabled to develop itself into a new individual.

‖**spermatozoon** (-ˈzəʊɒn). Pl. **-zoa**. [f. SPERMATO- + Gr. ζῷον living thing, animal.] One of the numerous minute and active filaments present in the seminal fluid, by which the fecundation of the ovum is effected.

1836–9 *Todd's Cycl. Anat.* II. 113/1 The Spermatozoa have been detected.. in the different classes of the Articulate Animals. **1844** G. BIRD *Urin. Deposits* (1857) 376 Mixed with these are generally found round granular bodies, rather larger than the body of a spermatozoon. **1881** MIVART *Cat* 245 The special secretion of the testis consists of certain spermatic filaments or spermatozoa.

spermi-, irregular comb. form of L. *sperma* SPERM *sb.*, as in **spermiˈducal** *a.*, **ˈspermiduct** (= SPERMADUCT), †**spermifiˈcation**, **sperˈmigerous** *a.*

1666 J. SMITH *Old Age* 106, I shall only mention five;.. Chylification, Sanguification, Assimulation, Lactification, and Spermification. **1877** HUXLEY *Anat. Inv. Anim.* v. 240 They frequently play the part of oviducts and spermiducts. *Ibid.* viii. 481 *note*, In the common Oyster the genital cæca ..are found to be either almost all ovigerous or almost all spermigerous. **1897** *Proc. Zool. Soc.* 343 The spermiducal glands are long and coiled.

ˈspermic, *a. rare*$^{-0}$. [ad. F. *spermique*: see SPERM *sb.*] Of or pertaining to sperm or seed.

1858 MAYNE *Expos. Lex.* 1180/2 The interior of the Spermoderm.. he [Richard] terms the *spermic cavity*. **1882** *Imp. Dict.* IV. 155/1.

spermicide (ˈspɜːmɪsaɪd). [f. SPERMI- + -CIDE.] Any substance which kills spermatozoa, esp. one used as a contraceptive. So **spermiˈcidal** *a.* Cf. SPERMACIDE, SPERMATICIDE, and *spermatocide* s.v. SPERMATO-.

1929 *Jrnl. Hygiene* XXIX. 323 The spermicidal powers of the various chemical contraceptives sold to the public have never previously been compared, and no one has been in a position to say that one spermicide is preferable to another. **1931** *Ibid.* XXXI. 190 The words 'spermicide' and 'spermicidal' are preferred, on grounds of euphony, to 'spermaticide' and 'spermaticidal'. **1936** *Discovery* Sept. 277/2 Baker has shown that soap solution is more spermicidal than most chemical contraceptives. **1962** A. HUXLEY *Island* vi. 84 Before the age of rubber and spermicides. **1977** V. COLEMAN *Paper Doctors* ix. 93 There were 15 different types of spermicidal contraceptive waiting to be prescribed. **1977** E. J. TRIMMER et al. *Visual Dict. Sex* (1978) xiv. 135/3 Spermicides.. should not be used alone as a contraceptive method.

spermidine (ˈspɜːmɪdiːn). *Biochem.* [f. SPERM(IN + -IDINE.] A colourless liquid triamine, $H_2N(CH_2)_3NH(CH_2)_4NH_2$, which is found very widely in living tissues, in company with spermine, and has a number of metabolic functions.

1927 H. W. DUDLEY et al. in *Biochem. Jrnl.* XXI. 97 This base has been given the name spermidine since it not only occurs in association with spermine but also has been found to be structurally related to the latter substance. **1964** A. WHITE et al. *Princ. Biochem.* (ed. 3) xxvi. 538 Spermine and spermidine are present in significant amounts in ribosomes and appear to be essential to their structure and function. **1974** *Nature* 17 May 250/1 The polyamines spermine spermidine and their precursor putrescine occur ubiquitously and in high concentrations in animals and plants.

ˈspermine (ˈspɜːmiːn). *Chem.* Also **-in**. [a. F. *spermine*: see SPERM *sb.* and -INE[5].] A toxin extracted from the pancreas and some other parts of the body.

1892 *Lancet* 16 July 175/1 Professor de Poehl.. had succeeded in extracting from the pancreas, thyroid body, ovaries and testes a leucomaine called spermine. **1898** *Allbutt's Syst. Med.* V. 647 A compound of phosphoric acid and a base 'Spermin'. **1899** *Ibid.* VIII. 50 Oppenheim once observed tetany after a spermin injection. **1927** [see SPERMIDINE]. **1937** *Thorpe's Dict. Appl. Chem.* (ed. 4) I. 315/1 The polyamino-compounds are of little interest with the exception of spermine, a tetra-amino derivative of the constitution $NH_2{\cdot}[CH_2]_3{\cdot}NH{\cdot}[CH_2]_4{\cdot}NH{\cdot}[CH_2]_3{\cdot}NH_2$, first isolated from human semen by Schreiner, and occurring in many mammalian organs. **1964**, **1974** [see SPERMIDINE].

spermiogenesis (spɜːmɪəʊˈdʒɛnɪsɪs). *Biol.* [f. SPERMI- + -O + -GENESIS.] The development of spermatozoa; *spec.* the maturation of spermatids into spermatozoa (the last phase of spermatogenesis).

1920 *Biol. Bull.* XXXIX. 333 The general topography of spermiogenesis has been worked out on *Murgantia*. **1956** *Nature* 25 Feb. 387/2 A study of spermiogenesis in the bandicoot.. has shown that an acrosome is indeed present. **1980** D. J. BEGLEY et al. *Human Reproduction* iii. 30/2 Following spermatogenesis and spermiogenesis, which take about 64 days in man, sperm pass through the rete into the epididymis.

spermo-, irregular comb. form (for SPERMATO-) of L. *sperma* or Gr. σπέρμα SPERM *sb.*[1], used in various terms of *Phys.*, *Zool.*, and *Bot.*

The older and more important of these are given below; many others, as ***spermocarp***, ***-centre***, ***-coccus***, ***-cyte***, ***-duct***, ***-lith***, ***-nucleus***, etc., appear in recent Dicts. or special scientific works.

spermoderm ('spɜːməʊdɜːm). *Bot.* [ad. mod.L. *spermoderma, -dermis* (De Candolle) or F. *spermoderme*: see prec. and DERM.] The combined outer and inner integuments of a seed, or the outer of these by itself.
1841 *Penny Cycl.* XXI. 184/1 The external coverings of the seed..are called the testa, perisperm, or spermoderm. **1861** BENTLEY *Man. Bot.* 337 Some writers..use the word testa in a general sense for the two integuments, and call the external one spermoderm. **1864** *New Syd. Soc. Year-bk. Med. & Surg. for 1863* 427 The spermoderm of the bean..is also poisonous.

spermogon-, the stem of SPERMOGON-IUM, occurring in a few derivative adjs., as **spermogo'niferous, sper'mogonoid, sper'mogonous.**
1871 W. A. LEIGHTON *Lichen-Flora* 126 Laciniæ..undulate, and spermogoniferous towards the centre. **1875** M. C. COOKE *Fungi* 200 The fungus never got beyond the spermogonoid stage. **1891** *Cent. Dict., Spermogonous,*..having the character of spermogonia or spermogones.

'spermogone. *Bot.* Anglicized form of next.
1856 W. L. LINDSAY *Pop. Hist. Brit. Lichens* 72 The cavity of the spermogone is usually simple and rounded. **1862** ANSTED *Channel Isl.* II. viii. 189 His specimens were covered with spermatiferous spermogones. **1882** *Encycl. Brit.* XIV. 555/1 The spermogones, which are the presumed male organs of reproduction,..differ in appearance from the apothecia in being very minute corpuscles.

‖**spermogonium** (-'gəʊnɪəm). Pl. -gonia. [mod.L., f. SPERMO- + Gr. γον- stem of γονή, γόνος offspring, etc. Cf. SPERMAGONIUM.]
1. *Bot.* One of the receptacles in lichens and fungi in which the spermatia are produced.
1857 HENFREY *Bot.* 169 Smaller chambers, analogous in structure to the perithecia,..occur in the thallus of all Lichens..; they are called spermogonia. **1866** *Treas. Bot.* 1211/2 The pycnidia or spermogonia of different sporidiiferous lichens. **1887** W. PHILLIPS *Brit. Discomycetes* 349 Spermogonia in the form of minute depressed tubercles.
2. *Phys.* A sperm-cell.
1913 J. W. JENKINSON *Vertebrate Embryol.* 23 In the male sex the primordial germ-cells divide to form small cells, the spermogonia.

†**sper'mologer.** *Obs.*$^{-1}$ [f. Gr. σπερμολόγος gathering seeds, also *fig.* picking up news, gossiping.] A gatherer of seeds. In quot. *fig.*
1676 MARVELL *Mr. Smirke* 38 Whereas there are some Few among the Few, such Spermologers, that unless a grain of Faith fall down, by the by, from Heaven, your seed is Barren.

sper'mologist. *rare*$^{-0}$. [f. as prec. or next: see -IST.] (See quots.)
1727 BAILEY (vol. II), *Spermologist*, a Gatherer of Seed. **1755** JOHNSON, *Spermologist*, one who gathers or treats of seeds. [Hence in later Dicts.].

sper'mology. *rare.* [In sense 1 f. SPERMO- + -LOGY. In sense 2 ad. Gr. σπερμολογία: cf. SPERMOLOGER.]
1. (See quot. and cf. SPERMATOLOGY.)
1882 *Imp. Dict.* IV. 155/1 *Spermology*,..that branch of science which investigates sperm or seeds; a treatise on sperm or seeds.
2. An instance of babbling or trifling talk.
1890 EARLE *Engl. Prose* xii. 485 For historical truth it is on a level with that favorite spermology of the Liberation Society, which seeks to diffuse the notion [etc.].

spermophile ('spɜːməʊfɪl). *Zool.* [ad. mod.L. *Spermophilus* (Cuvier) or a. F. *Spermophile*: see SPERMO- and -PHILE.] A rodent belonging to the squirrel-like genus *Spermophilus*, widely distributed in the northern hemisphere; a pouched marmot.
1824 RICHARDSON in Parry *N.W. Passage* App. 314 We know nothing..whether they are true marmots or spermophiles. **1839** *Penny Cycl.* XV. 517/2 This Spermophile inhabits the barren grounds skirting the sea-coast. **1849** *Sk. Nat. Hist., Mammalia* IV. 18 Besides possessing cheek-pouches, the Spermophiles are distinguished by the closeness of the ears, the slender form of the body,..and the narrowness of the paws. *c* **1880** *Cassell's Nat. Hist.* III. 92 The Spermophiles are Squirrel-like in form and have rather short tails.

'spermophore. *Bot.* [ad. mod.L. *spermophorum* or a. F. *spermophore*: see SPERMO- and -PHORE.] The placenta in plants. Also **'spermophyte** *Bot.*, a seed-bearing plant. **spermo'phytic** *a.*, 'capable of producing true seeds' (1891 *Cent. Dict.*). **'spermospore** *Phys.*, a compound cellular mass from which sperm filaments are developed. **spermo'toxin** *Chem.*, a serum destructive to spermatozoa.
1861 BENTLEY *Man. Bot.* 283 The placenta is called by Schleiden the *spermophore. **1891** *Cent. Dict., Spermophyte,*..a plant producing true seeds. **1881** MIVART *Cat* 245 From these cells the spermatozoa appear to be formed by subdivision of the nucleus of each *spermospore. **1902** *Brit. Med. Jrnl.* 12 Apr. 920 Metchnikoff [deals] with *spermotoxins and leucotoxins.

'spermous, *a. rare*$^{-1}$. [f. SPERM *sb.* + -OUS.] Of the nature of sperm; spermatic.
1822-7 GOOD *Study Med.* (1829) V. 8 The male..afterwards ejecting over them his spermous fluid.

sperm whale. Also **sperm-whale.** [Short for *spermaceti whale*: cf. SPERM *sb.* II.]
1. The spermaceti whale, *Physeter macrocephalus*; = CACHALOT.
1839 T. BEALE *Nat. Hist. Sperm Whale* 3 The sperm whale is one of the most noiseless of marine animals. **1860** GOSSE *Rom. Nat. Hist.* 48 In the midst of this war of the elements appear a pair of sperm-whales. **1884** GOODE *Nat. Hist. Aquat. Anim.* 7 The Sperm Whale..was first described by Clusius in 1605 from specimens cast up on the coast of Holland in 1598 and 1601.
b. Applied, with distinguishing epithets, to species of whales resembling, or related to, this.
1882 *Cassell's Encycl. Dict.* s.v. *Cachalot*, The Mexican Sperm-whale (*Catodon Colneti*). *Ibid.*, The South Sea Sperm-whale, found..in the Southern Ocean. **1891** *Cent. Dict.* s.v., *Porpoise sperm-whale*, a pygmy sperm-whale, or snub-nosed cachalot.
2. *attrib.*, as ***sperm-whale fishery, fishing***, etc.; **sperm-whale porpoise** (see quot. 1884).
1839 T. BEALE *Nat. Hist. Sperm Whale* 136 Rise and Progress of the Sperm Whale Fishery. **1884** GOODE *Nat. Hist. Aquat. Anim.* 18 The Sperm Whale Porpoise, ..*Hyperaodon bidens*. **1887** —— *Fisheries of U.S.* 69 The next important sperm-whale ground to be discovered was the Japan Ground. **1888** *Encycl. Brit.* XXIV. 528/1 American Fisheries..Sperm whale fishing seems to have commenced early in the 18th century.
Hence **sperm-whaler**, a person or vessel engaged in the capture of sperm-whales; **sperm-whaling** *pres. pple.* and *vbl. sb.*
1834 *Tait's Mag.* I. 411/1 The London sperm-whalers are generally large vessels. **1840** F. D. BENNETT *Narr. Whaling Voy.* II. 202 Difficulties that oppose the Sperm-Whaler's success. **1851** *Lit. Gaz.* 11 Jan. 30/3 The graphic accounts of sperm-whaling, by Beale and Bennett. ? **1863** in *Pall Mall G.* (1895) 16 Dec. 2/1 Accidentally killed while sperm-whaling off the Brazil Banks. **1887** GOODE *Fisheries of U.S.* 69 Sperm-whaling at New Zealand and the offshore ground.

'spermy, *a. rare.* [f. SPERM *sb.*] Resembling, of the nature of, sperm; full of sperm. (In quot. 1851, with reference to spermaceti.)
1657 S. PURCHAS *Pol. Flying-Ins.* 29 Into those orbicular cells is injected a spermy matter thick like cream. **1851** H. MELVILLE *Moby Dick* II. xxxviii. 253 If you unload the skull of its spermy heaps..you will be struck by its resemblance to the human skull. **1973** M. AMIS *Rachel Papers* 31, I decided I would ring her when I got back. It would be intelligent to do it while I still felt tolerably spermy and Joycean after my night with Gloria.

†**spermyse.** *Obs.* A kind of cheese.
1542 BOORDE *Dyetary* xiii. (1870) 266 Spermyse is a chese the which is made with curdes and with the iuce of herbes. *Ibid.*, I knowynge the herbes,..coulde tell the operacyon of spermyse chese.

spern, variant of SPURN *sb.*

speromagnetic (ˌspɪərəmæg'nɛtɪk), *a. Physics.* [f. Gr. δια-σπείρειν to scatter + ANTIFERR)O-MAGNETIC *a.*] Applied to an amorphous magnetic material in which the individual electron spins are aligned more or less anti-parallel to their closest neighbours but overall there is a statistical distribution of orientations with no preferred direction. Also **spero'magnetism.**
The form *sperimagnetic* occurred throughout the 1973 coinage paper. This was corrected by Coey et al. in *Physical Rev. Lett.* (1976) XXXVI. 1062.
1973 *Nature* 21–28 Dec. 445/2 The new phenomenon of speromagnetism (or amorphous superparamagnetism) adds a further delectable layer of complexity to what is already a highly elaborate network of phenomena. **1973** COEY & READMAN in *Ibid.* 477/2 Such a configuration, with the spins fixed relative to each other but possessing no overall preferred direction, is illustrated in Fig. 2*c*. It is termed 'sperimagnetic' [*sic*]..and..is probably a fairly common phenomenon in amorphous compounds. **1976** *Physical Rev. Lett.* XXXVI. 1062/1 Speromagnetism may also occur where the anisotropy dominates the exchange, in pure amorphous rare-earth metals, for example. **1976** *Physics Bull.* July 294/3 Speromagnetic ordering may also result when the exchange is distributed about zero with a range of positive and negative values.

‖**speronara** (spero'nara). Forms: α. 8–9 **speronara**, 9 **-aro.** β. 8–9 **speronare.** γ. 8–9 **sparan-, sparonaro,** 9 **sparonara.** [It.] A large rowing and sailing boat used in southern Italy and Malta.
α. **1783** *Phil. Trans.* LXXIII. 175, I had a pleasant voyage in my Maltese Speronara (which are excellent boats, and the boatmen very skilful). **1838** H. G. KNIGHT *Normans in Sicily* 135 The harbour only contains a few fishing-boats and speronaras. **1870** DISRAELI *Lothair* lxxi. 378 The boat was what is called a *speronaro*; an open boat worked with oars, but with a lateen sail at the same time when the breeze served.
β. **1797** HOLCROFT tr. *Stolberg's Trav.* IV. xcii, We went on board a *speronare*. **1836** MARRYAT *Midsh. Easy* xviii, Let's get on board one of the speronares which come with fruit from Sicily. **1887** GUNTER *Mr. Barnes* i. 6 A score or so of feluccas and speronares from Sardinia and Sicily.
γ. **1799** NELSON 22 May in Nicolas *Disp.* (1846) VII. p. clxxxiii, Neither of the two Sparanaroes..having joined, I cannot send this for Palermo. **1823** J. J. BLUNT *Vestiges Anc. Manners Italy* ii. 33 A friend of mine who..had hired a sparonara to convey them from Naples to Rome. **1828** DUPPA *Trav. Italy*, etc. 202 Here we quitted Sicily, and took a Sparanaro to visit Stromboli.

sperow, obs. f. SPARROW.

sperple, var. SPARPLE *v. Obs.*

sperr, obs. var. SPAR *sb.*[1], *v.*[1]

sperrable, obs. var. SPARABLE.

sperre, obs. var. SPAR *sb.*[1], *v.*[1], SPHERE, SPUR.

†**'sperring**, *vbl. sb. Obs.*$^{-1}$ (Meaning obscure.)
1340 *Ayenb.* 53 Þe ilke byeþ properliche glotounes þet al uorzuelȝeþ, ase deþ þe kete of his sperringe.

sperrowe, obs. form of SPARROW.

sperrylite ('spɛrɪlaɪt). *Min.* [f. the name of Francis L. *Sperry* (*c* 1862–1906), U.S. chemist + -ITE[1].] Platinum arsenide, $PtAs_2$, found as opaque greyish-white isometric crystals.
1889 H. L. WELLS in *Amer. Jrnl. Sci.* CXXXVII. 67 (*heading*) Sperrylite, a new mineral. **1902** H. A. MIERS *Mineral.* II. 332 Sperrylite, the only natural compound of platinum, occurs as brilliant microscopic crystals..in a nickeliferous ore consisting of various sulphides, at Sudbury in Ontario. **1926** *Mineral Mag.* XXI. 94 A very fine and unusual crystal of sperrylite..came from a new adit on the Tweefontein farm..about 10 miles NNW. of Potgietersrust, Waterberg district, Transvaal. **1975** *Canad. Mineralogist* XIII. 327/2 Sperrylite is a common mineral in many platinum-bearing deposits.

sperse (spɜːs), *v.* Now *arch.* Also 7 spearse. [Aphetic form of DISPERSE *v.*, prob. in part after It. *sperso*, pa. pple. of *spergere* to scatter.]
1. *trans.* To cause to scatter or disperse; to drive in different directions.
1580 BARET *Alv.* S. 93 That is spersed and scattered out of order. **1591** SPENSER *Visions Bellay* viii, I saw the wrathfull winde..That sperst these cloudes. **1596** —— *F.Q.* v. iii. 37 He..broke his sword in twaine, and all his armour sperst. **1603** DEKKER *Wh. Babylon* (1607) K iv, Are those clowds sperst that stroue to dimme our light? **1614** GORGES *Lucan* II. 77 Rockes..like the sands are spearst abroad, Faster than hands can them vnload. **1642** H. MORE *Song of Soul* xlviii, What then shall hinder but a roscid air With gentle heat eachwhere be 'sperst and sprent.
1845 T. COOPER *Purg. Suicides* (1877) 122 Who, then, shall sperse the dark eternal mists? **1879** J. D. LONG *Æneid* I. 80 Wreck their sinking boats, Or sperse and whelm their corses in the deep.
2. *intr.* To take different directions.
1819 W. TENNANT *Papistry Storm'd* (1827) 125 They..spers'd about in search o' beds.
Hence **spersed** *ppl. a.*
1590 SPENSER *F.Q.* I. i. 39 Making speedy way through spersed ayre. **1642** H. MORE *Song of Soul* II. App. 5 An inward triumph doth my soul up-heave And spread abroad through endlesse 'spersed air.

†**spert.** *Obs.* Also 5–6 sperte. [OE. *sperte, spirte, spyrte*, ad. L. *sporta* basket.]
1. A basket used for holding articles or for catching fish.
c **975** *Rushw. Gosp.* Matt. xv. 37 þara ʒebroca [hie] ʒenomen siofun sperta fulle. *a* **1000** ÆLFRIC *Hom.* II. 402 Spyrte bið..of rixum ʒebroden, oððe of palm-twyʒum. *c* **1000** *Colloq. Ælfric* in Wr.-Wülcker 93 Hu ʒefehst þu fixas? .. Ic wyrpe..spyrtan and swa hwæt swa hiʒ ʒehæftað ic ʒenime. **1406** in *Essex Rev.* (1904) April 74 [Putting] spertes [and other fish-catching devices into the lord's river].
2. A species of willow or osier.
1578 LYTE *Dodoens* 744 That which hath reddish barke, is called..in English Red Withy, and the better sort thereof is called Red Sperte. *Ibid.*, The small lowe Withy is called..the Sperte or twigge Withy. **1611** COTGR., *Siler*, the hearbe ..Hartwort; some also call Spert, or the Osier Withie, so.

spert(e, varr. SPIRT *sb. Obs.*

spertle, obs. var. SPIRTLE *v.*

speruwe, obs. f. SPARROW.

†**sperver.** *Obs. rare.* In 4–5 speruer, -vyr, spreuere. [ad. OF. *espervier, esperver* (mod.F. *épervier*) and *esprevier* (obs. F. *éprevier*), = Prov. *esparvier*, It. *sparviere* (*-eri, -ero*), of Germanic origin (OHG. *sparwari, sperwere*, G. *sperber*).] A sparrow-hawk.
c **1330** *Arth. & Merl.* 5258 (Kölbing), And Agreuein tok þat destrer, & fleiȝe þer on so a speruer. **13..** *King Alis.* 183 (Laud MS.), A speruer þat was honest, So sat on þe lefdyes fyst. *a* **1400** *Octouian* 702 A stowt squyere..bar vpon hys ryght hond gay A fayr spreuere.

†**sperviter.** *Obs. rare.* In 5 sper-, sparuiter (-uyter). [ad. OF. *esperveteur, espreveteur, f. *espervier*: see prec.] A keeper of sparrow-hawks.
1486 *Bk. St. Albans, Hawking* b v b, Tho that kepe Sperhawkys and muskettys ben called Speruiteris. *Ibid.* e viij b, The namys of a Spare hauke as Ostrigers and Sparuiters have determyned.

†**sperware.** *Obs.* (Meaning obscure.)
1434 *Indenture Fotheringey* in Dugdale *Monast.* (1830) VI. III. 1414/1 Til aither isle shall be a sperware enbattailement of free-stoon throwgh out, and both the ends enbattailled butting upon the stepill.

sperwe, obs. f. SPARROW.

spery, obs. var. SPURREY.

sperycall, obs. f. SPHERICAL.

speryt, obs. f. SPIRIT.

‖**spes** (speɪz). *Law.* [L.] A hope or expectancy, esp. of some future benefit. Also in various Latin phrases (see quots. 1959).

1815 *Decisions First & Second Divisions Court of Session* (Faculty of Advocates) 28 Feb. 258 There is a *jus crediti* conferred on the heir of a marriage-contract. It is not a mere *spes successionis*, but a *jus crediti*. **1945** *Law Rep.* 10 May 363 *Sine spe recuperandi*, in the sense of abandoning all hope of his owner recovering the ship. **1952** *Ibid.* 10 July 486 The taxpayer's answer to that is, first of all, that this is not property at all but a mere *spes* or hope of getting something. **1959** JOWITT *Dict. Eng. Law* II. 1664/2 *Spes recuperandi*, the hope of recovery. If it is entertained by a person in danger of death, it makes a declaration by him inadmissible in evidence... *Ibid.*, *Spes successionis*, an expectation of succession, as distinct from a vested right. **1977** JOHNS & GREENFIELD *Dymond's Capital Transfer Tax* ii. 40 The fiction of *Re Scott* does not go so far as to require one to suppose that the beneficiary had more than an interest in expectancy..or indeed a mere *spes*, when he died.

speshul (ˈspɛʃəl), repr. supposed colloq. pronunc. of SPECIAL *a.* and *sb.*

1900 *Times* 7 July 10/1 Boys..trample continually on your toes and screech everlastingly into your ears 'Cigarettes, cigars, chocolates'..'Speshul 'dition—latest cricket scores.' **1979** *Jrnl. Lancs. Dial. Soc.* Jan. 5 His first *buzz* was a *football speshul* to Maine Road.

spessartine (ˈspɛsətiːn). *Min.* [ad. F. *spessartine* (Beudant, 1832), f. *Spessart* a hilly district in north-western Bavaria, where it is found: see -INE[5].] Garnet containing manganese in place of calcium; manganese garnet.

1850 ANSTED *Elem. Geol., Min.*, etc. 190 *Spessartine* is the name given to a deep red garnet in which protoxide of manganese replaces the lime of the usual formula, so that it becomes silicate of alumina and manganese. **1888** RUTLEY *Rock-Forming Min.* 112 Spessartine, or manganese-alumina garnet, occasionally exhibits a red, or yellowish-red colour. **1910** *Encycl. Brit.* XI. 471/1 Spessartite, or spessartine,..is a fine aurora-red garnet, cut for jewelry when sufficiently clear. **1977** A. HALLAM *Planet Earth* 128 An individual [garnet] can be regarded as an intimate mixture of two or more of the following end-members: pyrope (magnesium-aluminum garnet), almandine (iron-aluminum garnet), spessartine (manganese-aluminum garnet), grossularite (calcium-aluminum garnet), andradite (calcium-iron garnet), and uvarovite (calcium-chromium garnet).

spessartite (ˈspɛsətaɪt). [f. as SPESSARTINE: see -ITE[1].] **1.** *Min.* = SPESSARTINE. Chiefly *N. Amer.*

1868 J. D. DANA *Syst. Mineral.* (ed. 5) 268 Manganese-Aluminagarnet; Spessartite. **1910** [see SPESSARTINE]. **1934** G. L. ENGLISH *Getting acquainted with Minerals* II. 228 Some of the fine garnets of Delaware County, Pennsylvania are spessartite. **1953** F. H. POUGH *Field Guide to Rocks & Minerals* II. 296 Spessartite is less common and not often properly identified when it is in a schist. **1971** R. PURVIS *Treasure Hunting in Brit. Columbia* i. 21/2 Spessartite is pink to dark brown.

2. *Petrogr.* [ad. G. *spessartit* (H. Rosenbusch *Mikrosk. Physiogr.* (ed. 3) (1896) II. 529).] A porphyritic lamprophyre in which the feldspar is sodic plagioclase and the phenocrysts consist of an amphibole or pyroxene, usu. green hornblende.

1908 P. MACNAIR *Geol. & Scenery of Grampians* II. x. 64 Dykes and sills of lamprophyre, including kersantites, vogesites, and spessartites, are..to be met with throughout the Highlands. **1930** PEACH & HORNE *Chapters Geol. Scotland* iv. 108 The dark basic sills in the dolomites of the Assynt region..include representations of vogesites and spessartites. **1966** [see *lamprophyre* s.v. LAMPRO-]. **1970** *Jrnl. Geol.* LXXVIII. 742/1 The dikelets probably formed during later stages of crystallization of the spessartite.

spet, *sb.*[1] Now *dial.* [f. SPET *v.*] The or an act of spitting; spit, spittle. Also *Comb.*

1446 LYDG. *Nightingale P.* I. 259 Hogh that the Iewes.. There all defouled with spet his blessed face. **1570** LEVINS *Manip.* 86 Spet or spetting, *sputum*. **1592** NASHE *P. Penilesse* Wks. (Grosart) II. 67 Would you..gesse it were possible for anie shame-swolne toad to haue the spet-proofe face to out liue this disgrace? *a* **1658** LOVELACE *Lucasta, Posth.* 42 The speckl'd Toad..Defies his foe with a fell Spet. **1882** T. HARDY *Two on Tower* xxii, Well, when I found 'twas Sir Blount my spet dried up within me.

spet, *sb.*[2] *U.S.* [a. F. *spet*, = Sp. *espeto(n)*.] A species of barracuda, the *Sphyræna sphyræna* (*S. spet*) of Europe.

1896 D. S. JORDAN & B. W. EVERMANN *Fishes N. & Mid. Amer.* I. 826 *Sphyræna sphyræna* (Linnæus). European Barracuda; Spet; Sennet.

spet, *v.* Now *dial.* [Alteration of SPETE *v.*, after pa. t. and pa. pple. *spet(te.*] To spit, in various senses; to expectorate. (Freq. *c* 1550–*c* 1630.)

a. *intr.*

c **1421** *26 Pol. Poems* 91 She spettes on me, and doþ me fyȝe. **1542** UDALL *Erasm. Apoph.* 147 A certain saucy.. young spryngall..spetted even in the veraye face of hym. **1584** R. SCOT *Discov. Witchcr.* XII. xviii. (1886) 219 Spet into the shoo of your right foote. **1617** MORYSON *Itin.* III. 42 Their sumptuous Churches (in which it is a great trespasse so much as to spet). **1655** CULPEPPER, etc. *Riverius* VI. I. 130 They who have the Tooth-ach, do continually spet. **1867** H. J. DANIEL *Muse in Motley* 43 He wud spet, Iss, spetty like a toad. **1881-** in southern dial. glossaries.

fig. **1621** BP. HALL *Heaven upon Earth* §25 He that sits in heauen..bids his winds spet sometimes in thy face.

b. *trans.* Also const. *in, out, up.* Freq. *fig.*

1532 MORE *Confut. Barnes* Wks. 736/1 All hys deuelyshe lies which he spetteth and speweth oute vpon honest men. **1573** BARET *Alv.* s.v., To spette out his poyson: to speake the worste that he can. **1598** MARSTON *Pygmal., Sat.* ii. 152 Spett in thy poyson theyr fair acts among. **1634** MILTON *Comus* 132 When the Dragon woom Of Stygian darknes spets her thickest gloom. **1639** O. WOOD *Alph. Bk. Secrets* 87 [Let him] spet from him the rhewme in a Bason as often as he needeth. *Ibid.* 115 Then spet it forth. *Ibid.* 167 Spet out the rhewme as it comes. **1697** DRYDEN *Virg. Georg.* IV. 148 A thirsty Train That..spet from their dry Chaps the gather'd dust again. **1895** 'ROSEMARY' *Chilterns* ii. 55 Don't tech it!—that ull spet pison if you do.

Hence **ˈspetter**; **ˈspetting** *vbl. sb.*

c **1460** *Vrbanitatis* 19 in *Babees Bk.*, Fro spettyng & snetyng kepe þe also. **1548** ELYOT, *Excreatio*, a spettyng out. **1580** HOLLYBAND *Treas. Fr. Tong, Cracheur*, a spetter. **1607** TOPSELL *Four-f. Beasts* 550 Those which are molested with corrupt and bloody spettings with retchings. **1648** HEXHAM II, *Een Spouwer*, a Spetter, or a Spuer. **1655** CULPEPPER, etc., *Riverius* VII. vi. 164 Usually the word Hœmoptysis doth signifie al manner of Spetting of blood.

spet, obs. f. SPIT *sb.*[1]; obs. or dial. pa. t. SPIT *v.*[2]

spet(te, obs. pres. t. SPEED *v.*; obs. ff. SPIT *sb.*[1]; see SPIT *v.*[2]

spetch (spɛtʃ), *sb.* Also 7 spech, 9 spitch. [Related to SPECK *sb.*[2]]

1. A piece or strip of undressed leather, a trimming of hide, used in making glue or size.

1611 [see *spetch-grease* below]. **1624** *Naworth Househ. Bk.* (Surtees) 216 Glover's spech, iiij[d]. **16..** *Churchw. Acc. All Saints, York* Ibid., For glovers' spetches to maike syse to wase the wales, 10[d]. **1795** J. PHILLIPS *Hist. Inland Nav.* Add. 40 For every pack or sheet of wool, dried pelts, or spetches, carried the whole length of the canal.., six-pence. **1815** *Pocklington Canal Act* 52 Dried pelts, spetches, and wool. **1858** SIMMONDS *Dict. Trade, Spetches*, a name for glue pieces; the offal of skin and hides. **1883** R. HALDANE *Workshop Rec.* Ser. II. 300/2 The materials..in use for the manufacture of glue are the following:—(*a*) 'Wet' materials: sheep-pieces or 'spetches' from fellmongers.

attrib. and *Comb.* **1611** COTGR., *Surpoinct*,..Spech grease; an oylie grease scummed from peeces of lickored leather sodden in water for that purpose. **1881** *Instr. Census Clerks* (1885) 166 Spitch Dealer (refuse of Hides).

2. *dial.* A piece or patch of leather, esp. one used for making or mending boots, clogs, etc.; also, a patch of cloth.

1828 CARR *Craven Gloss.*, *Spetch*, a patch. **1853** 'TOM TREDDLEHOYLE' *Bairnsla Ann.* 52 Ther [cobbler's] hause floor..is kept cuvard all ovver we leather spetches. **1863-** in Cumbld. and Yks. dial. glossaries and texts.

spetch, *v.* Now *north. dial.* [f. the sb. Cf. SPECK *v.*[2]] *trans.* To patch, mend, or repair (shoes, clogs, etc.) with 'spetches'; to patch (a garment) with cloth.

16.. *York Corp. Min.* in *Naworth Househ. Bk.* (Surtees) 216 *note*, The said shomakers shall not in anywise spetche, clout, or coble any manner of bootes. **1828** CARR *Craven Gloss.*, *Spetch*, to patch. **1862-** in w. Yks. dial. glossaries and texts. **1873** STANDING *Echoes* 13 It's all mendin' and spetchin'—scarce iver aught new: Thur's mi white weddin' shirt's to be patched op wi blue.

†**spete**, *v. Obs.* Forms: *Inf.* 1 spætan, 3 speten, 4–5 spete. *Pa. t.* 1 spætte, 2–5 spette (4 spetide); 3–4 spatte, 4 spat. [OE. *spǽtan*, f. the stem **spǣt-*: cf. SPATTLE *sb.*[1] and *v.*[1] The inf. and pres. forms disappeared in the 15th cent., and the pa. t. and pa. pple. came to be associated with SPIT *v.*[1]] To spit; to expectorate: **a.** *intr.*

c **1000** *Ags. Gosp.* Mark x. 34 Hi him on spætað [*Hatton* spæteð]. *Ibid.* John ix. 6 þa spætte [*Hatton* spette] he on þa eorþan. *a* **1225** *Ancr. R.* 240 þonne spet heo & schekeð þet heaued. *a* **1250** *Owl & Night.* 39 Me luste bet speten þane singe Of þine fule howelynge. *c* **1275** *Passion our Lord* 272 in *O.E. Misc.*, þe Gywes..Blyndfellede and spatten him on. *c* **1300** *Leben Jesu* (Horstm. 1873) 29 He..spatte a luyte on is fingur. **13..** *K. Alis.* 979 Tho thou spettest in my visage. **1382** WYCLIF *Mark* vii. 33 He..spetinge towchide his tunge. **14..** in Wr.-Wülcker 610 *Screo*, to spete.

b. *trans.*

a **1225** *Ancr. R.* 82 þe þet swuch fulðe speteð ut [etc.]. **1398** TREVISA *Barth. De P.R.* v. xxxv. (Bodl. MS.), As it fareþ in ham þat spetynne bloode and quyture. *c* **1400** *Pilgr. Sowle* (Caxton, 1483) v. x. 101 He smote hym in the brest that he spette blood many dayes after.

Hence †**ˈspeting** *vbl. sb. Obs.*

1388 WYCLIF *Lev.* xv. 8 If sich a man castith out spetyng on hym. *a* **1400** *Stockholm Med. MS.* i. 302 in *Anglia* XVIII. 302 It schal drywyn owte all þe peyne Withowte gret spetynge or oþer peyne.

spete, obs. form of SPIT *sb.*[1] and *v.*[2]

†**spetewil**, *a. Obs. rare.* (Of uncertain origin and meaning.) Hence †**spetewiliche** *adv.*

a **1200** *St. Marher.* 9 Of hir spetewile muð sperklede fur ut. *Ibid.* 12 Hwil þet ha spec þus o þet spatewile wiht. *Ibid.* 15 He bigon þus spetewetliche [? *read* spetewiliche] to speokene.

†**spetia.** *Obs. rare.* Also 7 spetya. [? a. It. *spezia* specie.] Actual coin or money, = SPECIE 6.

1620 in Foster *Eng. Factories India* (1906) I. 195 Theye bringe hether either redy spetya or exchanges. **1622** *Ibid.* (1908) II. 43 Mr. Younge with upwards of 5,000 ruppees in ready spetia..departed for Lahore.

spetious, obs. form of SPECIOUS *a.*

spetos, spetous(e, -ly, spetows(le, varr. SPITOUS, -LY *Obs.*

spettell, obs. f. SPETTLE, SPITAL.

spetter, spetting: see SPET *v.*

†**spettle.** *Obs.* Forms: 5 spetil, 6 spettill, spettyl, 7 -ell; 6–7 spetle, spettle. [repr. OE. *spǽtl*, var. of *spátl* SPATTLE *sb.*[1], or modification of *spattle* after SPETE *v.* and SPET *v.* Cf. SPITTLE *sb.*] Spittle, spit. (Freq. *c* 1575–1650.)

1422 tr. *Secreta Secret.*, *Priv. Priv.* 240 Sutil and thyn spetil that descendyth or comyth doune fro the Palete of the mouth. *c* **1520** M. NISBET *John* ix. 6 He spittit into the erd, and made clay of the spettil [**1535** *Coverd.* spetle]. **1584** R. SCOT *Discov. Witchcr.* II. vi. (1886) 22 She will put spettle privilie upon hir cheeks, and seeme to weepe. **1608** SYLVESTER *Du Bartas* II. iv. IV. *Decay* 617 Hee spets at Heav'n, And his owne spettle in his face is driven. **1650** BULWER *Anthropomet.* (1653) A iij b, Thy Cheeks on each side bored through appeare; Thorough whose holes (the slavering spetles vent) The Teeth [etc.]. **1693** DRYDEN *Persius* I. 210 No Blood, from bitten Nails, those Poems drew; But churn'd, like Spettle, from the Lips they flew.

transf. **1555** EDEN *Decades* (Arb.) 294 The swette of heauen or as it were a certeyne spettyl of the starres.

†**ˈspettly**, *a. Obs. rare.* In 6 spettelly, 7 -ely. [f. prec. Cf. SPITTLY *a.*] Spittle-like.

1578 BANISTER *Hist. Man* v. 69 The Glandules..imbrue and washe it [the ventricle] with a certaine spettelly humor. **1634** T. JOHNSON *Parey's Wks.* VI. xii. (1678) 129 Glandules ..which like sponges suck and receive..a waterish and spettely humour.

spettylle, obs. form of SPITAL.

spetuously, variant of SPITOUSLY *Obs.*

†**ˈspeustic**, *a. Obs.*−[0] [ad. L. *speustic-us* (Pliny), ad. Gr. σπευστικός.] (See quot.)

1656 BLOUNT *Glossogr.*, *Speustick*, made in haste or quickly, made and baked on the sudden. [So in Phillips.]

spew (spjuː), *sb.* Also 7–9 spue. [f. the vb.]

1. a. That which is spewed or cast up from the stomach; vomited matter; vomit. Also *fig.* or in fig. context.

1609 MARKHAM *Famous Wh.* (1868) 32 Thus to mine old trade, and spew of hell, Onely for gaine, agen I basely fell. **1642** H. MORE *Song of Soul* I. iii. 29 That foul spue Which the false Dragon casts in every coast. **1660** MILTON *Free Commw.* Wks. 1851 V. 445 The Language of thir infernal Pamphlets, the Spue of every Drunkard, every Ribald. **1705** SWIFT *Salamander* 66 Wks. 1841 I. 607 She soon would find the same effects, Her tainted carcase to pursue, As from the salamander's spew. **1739** R. BULL tr. *Dedekindus' Grobianus* 266 'Twas nothing but his Due, Instead of Laurel to be crown'd with Spue. **1817** JAS. MILL *Brit. India* I. II. iv. 159 Throwing upon another from the navel downwards to his foot, spue, or urine, or ordure.

b. *techn.* (See quot.)

1893 *Labour Commission* Gloss. No. 9, *Spew-out*, the emanation similar to treacle of the glucose from the uppers or leather when kept for a time.

c. Surplus material exuded between the halves of a mould during the manufacture of plastic objects. Freq. *attrib.*

1933 *Industr. & Engin. Chem.* June 647/1 The degree of flow can be readily controlled by the location, size and placement of the spew hole. **1945** A. T. BIRKBY *Phenolic Plastics* iv. 43 Provision should be made for air venting, and, in the case of compression moulds, for spew-ways. *Ibid.* viii. 93 'Flash' or 'spew' soon begins to appear round each press, and unless swept up and removed becomes a nuisance. **1964** WORDINGHAM & REBOUL *Dict. Plastics* 165 *Spew groove*, in moulding operations, the groove in a mould which permits the escape of surplus material.

2. *dial.* The fourth swarm of bees in a season.

1750 W. ELLIS *Mod. Husbandm.* IV. I. 182 The swarm is the first and greatest number, the cast is the next greatest, the colt the next, and the spew the least of all. *Ibid.* II. 115. **1854** in MISS BAKER *Northampt. Gloss.*

3. *dial.* A wet, marshy piece of ground; a place in a field, etc., where water oozes up.

1794 P. FOOT *Agric. Midl.* 45 (E.D.D.), The water.. appears at the foot or in the middle of a declivity, and causes a spew, a squall, or boggy piece of ground. **1868** R. W. HUNTLEY *Gloss. Cotswold* (*Glouc.*) *Dial.*, *Spew*, a spungy piece of ground. **1871** KINGSLEY *At Last* viii, The little pitch wells—'spues' or 'galls', as we should call them in Hampshire.

4. Special Comb.: **spew frost** = *needle ice* s.v. NEEDLE *sb.* 14.

1938 C. F. S. SHARPE *Landslides & Related Phenomena* iii. 27 Growths of frost crystal of this sort are known as spew frost.., feather-ice, or needle-ice..and on the European continent as Pipkrake or Kammeis. **1939** [see *needle ice* s.v. NEEDLE *sb.* 14].

spew (spjuː), *v.* Forms: *α.* 1 spiwan, spywan, spiowan, speowan, 3 speowen; 3– spew, 4–6 spewe, 5 spyw-, 6 speew, speawe. *β.* 4–9 spue (5 spuwe, spw-). [Two OE. forms are here represented: (1) the strong verb *spíwan*, *spýwan* (pa. t. *spáw*, pl. *spiwon*), = OFris. *spîa*, *spiga* (WFris. *spije*, EFris. *spî*, NFris. *spî*, *spei*, *spai*), OS. *spîwan* (MLG. *spîen*, *spîgen*, *spiggen*), OHG. *spîwan* (MHG. *spîwen*, *spîen*, G. *speien*), ON. and Icel. *spýja* (Norw., Sw., Da. *spy*), Goth. *speiwan*; (2) the weak verb *spéowan*, *spiowan* (pa.

t. *spéowde, spíowde*). The strong forms barely survived beyond OE. The Continental languages also show a tendency to adopt weak forms, and exhibit various irregular modifications of the stem, which is found outside of Teutonic in L. *spuĕre*, Gr. πτύειν, Lith. *spiauti*, etc.]

1. *intr.* To bring up and discharge the contents of the stomach through the mouth; to vomit. Not now in polite use.

Also in OE., to spit, to discharge spittle or blood.

a. c **897** K. ÆLFRED *Gregory's Past. C.* v. 45 ȝif hire ðonne se wiðsace, ðonne is cynn ðæt him spiwe ðæt wif on ðæt nebb. *c* **1000** ÆLFRIC *Saints' Lives* xii. 163 Swa þæt he bið þam hunde ȝelic þe spywð, and eft ytt þæt he ær aspaw. *c* **1100** *O.E. Chron.* (MS.F) an. 1003, Ða ȝebræde he hine to spiwenne & cwæd ðæt he seoc wære. *a* **1225** *Juliana* 49 Hare ahne blod ich habbe ofte imaket ham to spitten & to speowen. *c* **1340** *Nominale* (Skeat) 344 *Homme vomyte pur surfet*, [Man] spewith for ouer mykul. *c* **1386** CHAUCER *Melib.* ¶ 451 If thou ete of it out of mesure, thou shalt spewe. *c* **1400** tr. *Secreta Secret., Gov. Lordsh.* 71 þe medicyn ys þys, to drynke cler watir with a sope of vynegre, and spewe. **1530** PALSGR. 728 This felowe is so lothsome that he wolde make one spewe. **1570** LEVINS *Manip.* 214 To speawe, *spuere, vomere.* **1570** GOOGE *Pop. Kingd.* IV. 56 He..holdes their heades that spewing lie. **1607** MIDDLETON *Fam. Love* IV. iii. 93, I will..send him packing, or else he will spew or do worse before me. **1647** TRAPP *Marrow Gd. Authors* in *Comm. Ep.* 687 Such as should make a Christian spew to think on them. **1739** R. BULL tr. *Dedekindus' Grobianus* 42 There, unabash'd, heroically, spew. **1783** GIBBON *Misc. Wks.* (1814) II. 327, I had not the least symptom of sea-sickness, while my companions were spewing round me. **1809** BYRON *Lines to Mr. Hodgson* iii, Passengers their berths are clapt in, Some to grumble, some to spew. **1888–** in dial. glossaries and texts (Som., Norf., Lanc., Yks., Durh., etc.).

transf. **1731** POPE *Ep. Burlington* 154 The rich Buffet well-colour'd serpents grace, And gaping Tritons spew to wash your face.

β. a **1400** TREVISA *Higden* (Rolls) VII. 503 Edricus a fals traytor, feyned for to spuwe, and seide that he was seke. *c* **1460** *Towneley Myst.* xxiv. 82, I spuyd and spyt right in his face. **1509** BARCLAY *Shyp of Folys* (1570) 33 Some spue, some stacker, some vtterly are lame. **1530** PALSGR. 730/2, I spue, I gyve over my gorge, *je gomys.* **1633** P. FLETCHER *Purple Isl.* VII. lxxvii, All drink to spue, and spue again to drink. **1706** J. H. BROWNE *Pipe of Tobacco* Poems (1768) 123 A pot wherein to spit or spue. **1877** in *Holderness Gloss.*

fig. **1586** T. B. *La Primaud. Fr. Acad.* I. 365 Lysander,.. being reviled with many bitter speeches, said to him that offered the injurie: Spue out boldly, my friend; spue out.. and spare not.

†**b.** *trans.* To bespew or bespit. *Obs.*

1526 *Pilgr. Perf.* (W. de W. 1531) 97 b, He was illuded & scorned with garmentes of irrisyon, spewed in yᵉ face.

2. *trans.* To bring up (food or drink) from the stomach and eject through the mouth; to cast up or vomit; to cast out, throw forth, or discharge (blood, poison, etc.) from the mouth. Also in fig. context.

In OE. the object is sometimes in the dative.

971 *Blickl. Hom.* 57 Ne þæt to nahte nyt ne biþ þæt man godne mete ete oþþe þæt betste win..drince, ȝif..he hit eft spiwende anforlæteþ. *a* **1000** *Juliana* 476 (Gr.), Eac ic sume ȝedyde, þæt him banlocan blode spiowedan. *c* **1000** ÆLFRIC *Saint's Lives* xii. 63 He feoll þa æt ðære forman snæde underbecc ȝeswoȝen, and spaw blod. *c* **1200** *Trin. Coll. Hom.* 199 [þe] neddre..speweð hire atter. *c* **1220** *Bestiary* 139 in *O.E. Misc.*, Oc he speweð or al ðe uenim ðat in his brest is bred. *c* **1300** *Havelok* 1819 þe fifte..Gaf he a ful sor dint ok, Bitwen þe sholdres,..þat he speu [*printed* spen] his herte blod. **1387** TREVISA *Higden* (Rolls) IV. 439 Men ete.. filþe þat men hadde y-spewed [*v.r.* yspuwed] and i-cast up. *c* **1400** *Lanfranc's Cirurg.* 118 Or ellis he spewiþ [*v.r.* spyweþ] his mete, or he feliþ to gret akþe in þe heed. **1500–20** DUNBAR *Poems* xxvii. 59 He about the Devillis nek Did spew agane ane quart of blek. **1590** SPENSER *F.Q.* I. i. 20 Therewith she spewd out of her filthy maw A floud of poyson. **1611** SIR W. MURE *Wks.* (S.T.S.) I. 6 Ane spytfull spidar, ewer spewing Ye poysonous potioune of late rewing. **1697** DRYDEN *Virg. Georg.* III. 772 The Steer..dying spews a Flood Of foamy Madness, mix'd with clotted Blood. **1815** G. BEATTIE *John o' Arnha'* (1826) 39 Dæmons, dragons, spectres dire, Spewin' reek, an' riftin' fire.

b. Const. with advs., as *forth, out, up.*

a **900** *O.E. Martyrol.* 23 Mar., He spaw his innoð ut þurh his muð. *c* **1200** *Trin. Coll. Hom.* 37 þe fule man þe foleȝeð his wombes wil..and þe est metes and drinkes ut speweð. *a* **1240** *Sawles Warde* in *O.E. Hom.* I. 251 Iteilede draken.. forswolheð ham ihal, ant speoweð ham eft ut biuoren ant bihinden. **1388** WYCLIF *Job* xx. 15 He schal spue out the richessis, whiche he deuouride. **1632** LITHGOW *Trav.* III. 92 Their Musicke in the end was sound drunkennesse, and their Syncopa turnd to spew vp all. **1655** MOUFET & BENNET *Health's Improv.* (1746) 239 If you shift them into fresh Water or Brine..they will open themselves, and spue out all their Gravel and Filthiness. **1682** N. O. *Boileau's Lutrin* II. 172 Thou look'st as if first eaten, and then spew'd up. **1855** SINGLETON *Virgil* II. 247 But he..from his jaws prodigious smoke..spews forth.

fig. a **1618** RALEIGH *Instr. to Son* (1651) ix. 27, I thought at the last, quoth Diogenes, he would spue out a whole house. **1639** S. DU VERGER tr. *Camus' Admir. Events* 214 Thus they left him in that place, spewing out his soule with his bloud.

c. Freq. in fig. use with reference to abusive or objectionable language. Chiefly const. with advs., as *forth, out, up.* (Freq. *c* 1550–1600.)

a **1225** *Ancr. R.* 86 þe uorme [backbiter] cumeð al openliche, & seið vuel bi anoðer, & speoweð ut his atter. **1532** [see SPET *v.* b]. **1535** JOYE *Apol. Tindale* (Arb.) 39 [He] hathe spewed forthe al his venome and poyson at once vpon me. **1576** FLEMING *Panopl. Epist.* 114 But why shold they spue against me their spiteful stomaches? **1628** WITHER *Brit. Rememb.* II. 171, I doe not grudge mine enemies to spue Their slanders on my name. **1632** LITHGOW *Trav.* x. 472 My sonne, beholde you deserue to be burnt quicke..: Spewing forth also this Fæminine Latine [etc.]. *a* **1704** T. BROWN *Amusem. Ser. & Com., Lond.* Wks. 1709 III. I. 17 There is an Evidence ready to spue up his false Oaths at the sight of the common Executioner. **1718** T. GORDON *Dedic. to Gt. Man* 20 Why must prating Oafs..be for ever suffer'd, without Rebuke, to be spewing up their ill-scented Crudities in the Faces of Men that are either Wise or Brave? **1877** DOWDEN *Shaks. Primer* v. 53 Thersites spews over everything that we had deemed high and sacred, his foul.. insults.

3. To cast *out* († or *up*), to eject or reject, with abhorrence, contempt, or loathing. Also const. *out of* or *forth* (a place). (Freq. *c* 1600.)

(*a*) **1388** WYCLIF *Lev.* xviii. 25 Of which lond Y schal vysyte the grete synnes, that it spewe out hise dwellers. **1526** TINDALE *Rev.* iii. 16 Because thou arte..nether colde ner hott, I will spew the oute of my mought. **1583** STUBBES *Anat. Abus.* (1877) 105 It will spue out many of his Maisters out of dores before it be long. **1601** BACON *Decl. Treas. E. of Essex* Wks. 1879 I. 433 He was thus justly spewed out of the realm. *a* **1652** BROME *Novella* v. i, I shall take for your disgrace an order Shall spue you forth the City. **1692** RAY *Disc.* III. xii. (1732) 421 Heaven would naturally spue out and eject a wicked Person. **1729** W. FLOWER *Let. Swift* S.'s Wks. 1841 II. 624 Bad men..should be spewed out of it with the utmost contempt. **1849** MACAULAY *Hist. Eng.* vii. II. 231 William..would have been pronounced by..bigots on both sides a mere Laodicean,..and fit only to be spewed out.

4. To eject, cast or throw out or up, as if by vomiting. (Freq. in the 17th c.).

1598 SYLVESTER *Du Bartas* II. ii. IV. *Columnes* 224 A Bullet spewd from Brazen Brest. **1613** DRAYTON *Man in the Moone* 240 Others [*sc.* shell-fish] agayn wide open that did yawn, And on the grauell spew'd their orient spawn. **1676** GREW *Musæum, Anat. Stomach & Guts* (1681) vii. 29 The glands of the Guts are likewise of great Use. The Mucus which they spew, serves to make the Guts slippery. **1697** DRYDEN *Virg. Georg.* I. 176 When Earth with Slime and Mud is cover'd o'er, Or hollow Places spue their wat'ry Store. **1707** MORTIMER *Husb.* (1721) II. 120 The Frosts are apt to spew them out of the Ground. **1710** T. FULLER *Pharm. Extemp.* 250 It is useful to..hinder the Lympha's being plentifully spewed out of the Glands.

b. Const. *forth, out, up.*

1610 G. FLETCHER *Christ's Vict.* I. xxii, And, least their pleasant gods should want delight, Neptune spues out the Lady Aphrodite. **1664** EVELYN *Sylva* (1679) 10 Your plants beginning now to peep, should be earthed up,..especially, after breaking of the greater Frosts, and when the swelling mould is apt to spue them forth. **1678** BUNYAN *Pilgr.* I. 13 At such time as this place doth spue out its filth. **1727** EARBERY tr. *Burnet's St. Dead* 127 The Sepulchres open'd their marble Jaws, and spew'd out their Dead. **1855** SINGLETON *Virgil* I. 138 If no high Mansion..Of morning visitants a mighty tide Spews forth from all its halls.

c. *spec.* To eject by volcanic action.

1594 GREENE & LODGE *Looking Gl.* 1382 G.'s Wks. (Grosart) XIV. 62 The hill of Sicely..spues out from below The smoakie brands that Vulcans bellowes driue. **1685** BURNET *Trav.* (1687) II. iv. 27 What can be the fuel of so lasting a burning, that hath calcined so much matter, and spewed out such prodigious quantities. **1690** —— *Theory Earth* II. 86 When the bowels of the earth begin to melt, and the mountains spew out streams of liquid fire. **1717** BERKELEY *Jrnl. Tour Italy* Wks. 1871 IV. 589 It is pretended that in [the year] 31 hot waters were spewed out of the crater. **1847** C. BRONTË *Jane Eyre* xx, A crater-crust which may crack and spue fire any day.

5. *techn.* **a.** To force or cause to ooze out by undue strain or pressure; *spec.* in *Naut.* use (see quot. 1863).

1570–1 *Admiralty Crt. Exam. 18*, 17 Feb., Havinge her okam spewed owte. **1630** *Ibid.* 49, 26 Aug., [A leaky ship] spewed the ocum out of her seames. **1663** GERBIER *Counsel* 28 That which is thin, will cause the work to settle more in one place then in the other, and the joynts to spue out the Morter. **1863** A. YOUNG *Naut. Dict.* 365 A vessel is said to spue the oakum when her straining and labouring at sea forces the oakum out of the seams of her planks.

†**b.** Of a gun: To throw out or drop (powder) instead of consuming it. *Obs.*$^{-1}$

a **1642** SIR W. MONSON *Naval Tracts* III. (1704) 344/1 The shorter Piece will spue her Powder.

6. *intr.* Of water, liquids, etc.: To flow, pour, or run in a more or less copious stream; to ooze or be forced *out* or *up*. Usually const. with adverbs or preps. Now chiefly *dial.*

1670 J. SMITH *Eng. Improv. Reviv'd* 38 Being full of Landsprings (which is Water running within the Earth, and shews it self, or is discovered by breaking out, or spewing up in many places). **1675** WORLIDGE *Syst. Agric.* vii. §10 (ed. 2) 123 The Sap or Gum will also spew out in that place. **1695** WOODWARD *Nat. Hist. Earth* III. (1723) 152 It [water] spues out of Chasmes, opened by the Earthquake, in great Abundance. **1717** BERKELEY in Fraser *Life* (1871) iii. 79 This stuff would sometimes spew over and run down the convex side of the conical hill. **1784** CULLUM *Hist. Hawsted & Hardwick* iii. 171 *Sand-Galls*, spots of sand in a field where water oozes, or, as we say, spews up. **1843** *Jrnl. R. Agric. Soc.* IV. I. 40 The gravel..causes the land-springs to rise and spew out upon the surface. **1892** STEVENSON & L. OSBOURNE *Wrecker* 339 Avalanches of clay, rock, and uprooted forest spewed over the cliffs and fell upon the beach.

b. Of ground: To swell through excess of moisture; to slip or run when left unsupported.

1839 *Civil Eng. & Arch. Jrnl.* II. 27/1 Stratford marshes, where the ground for a depth of eight feet is inclined to 'spew up'. **1860** WORCESTER, *Spew*, v.n., to swell, as wet land affected by frost, so as to throw seed out of the ground; as, 'The ground spews'. **1876** ROBINSON *Mid-Yks. Gloss.* s.v., In constructing a 'sike' for the drainage of land, gravelly earth will often break edge, and spew.

c. *Artill.* (See quot.) *rare*$^{-0}$.

1842 BURN *Nav. & Milit. Techn. Dict.* I, *Saigner du nez*, to spew, run at the mouth; applied to a gun when, from too quick a fire, it bends at the chase, or the muzzle droops.

7. Of bees: To swarm for the fourth time in one season.

1750 W. ELLIS *Mod. Husbandm.* IV. II. 115 Bees will sometimes (but rarely) swarm, cast, colt, and spew, from one and the same old stock of Bees in one Summer.

Hence **spewed** *ppl. a.*; **'spewer**.

c **1000** ÆLFRIC *Gloss.* in Wr.-Wülcker 108 *Uomex, uel uomens*, spiwere. **1606** HOLYOKE *Rider's Dict.* I, *Vomitor*, a spewer, or parbreaker. **1633** P. FLETCHER *Purple Isl.* VII. lxxvii, Insatiate sink, how with so generall stain Thy spu'd-out puddles court, town, fields entice! **1648** HEXHAM II, *Een Braker*, a Vomiter, or Spewer. *Ibid.*, *Een Spouwer*, a Spetter or a Spuer. **1883** *Almondbury & Huddersf. Gloss.*, *Spuers*, squibs; serpents; a kind of fireworks.

spewiness ('spjuːɪnɪs). [f. SPEWY *a.*] *Agric.* Spewy, boggy, or undrained condition (of land).

1653 GAUDEN *Hierasp.* 551 These..would in time bear store of good fruits; if the coldnesse and spewinesse of the soil..did not make them dwindle. **1762** *Tull's Horse-Hoeing Husb.* (ed. 4) xvi. 246 The most prejudiced Farmers agree, that keeping the Lands or Ridges of wet Ground always cross the Descent doth cure its Spewiness.

spewing ('spjuːɪŋ), *vbl. sb.* [f. SPEW *v.* + -ING¹.]

1. The action of the verb in various senses; vomiting; an instance or occasion of this.

a **1000** in Wr.-Wülcker 230 *Euomatio*, speowung. *c* **1000** ÆLFRIC *Gloss.* Ibid. 162 *Euomitio*, spiwingc. **1387** TREVISA *Higden* (Rolls) IV. 393 Also he usede ofte clistories and spuynge. **1398** —— *Barth. De P.R.* XIII. xxi. (Bodl. MS.), þe see..bredeþ drede and feere & heedeache and spuying. *c* **1440** *Promp. Parv.* 471/1 Spwynge, or brakynge (or parbrakynge), *vomitus.* **1500** *Ortus Vocab.*, *Ructus* i. *vomitus, angl'.* a spwynge. **1535** COVERDALE *Hab.* ii. 16 For the cuppe of the Lordes righte honde shall compasse the aboute, and shamefull spewinge in steade of thy worshipe. **1657** H. CROWCH *Welsh Traveller* 4 Then to spewing did her [= she] fall. **1686** J. DUNTON *Lett. fr. New-Eng.* (1867) 23 As often as I view'd the Ocean, or durst peep out of my Cabin, to order Palmer to assist me in my Spewing. **1842** BURN *Naval & Mil. Techn. Dict.* I, *Egueulement*, elliptical enlargement of the bore, called running or spewing at the muzzle, of a gun, occasioned by quick and long continued firing. **1883** *Athenæum* 4 Aug. 146/3 The 'spueing' of the sloppy ink over the edges of the letters.

b. *attrib.*, as ***spewing-fit***, †***-nut*** (see quot.).

1586 LUPTON *1000 Notable Things* (1675) 121 The pouder of Nux Vomica called the Spuing Nut. *a* **1704** T. BROWN *Walk round Lond., Quaker's Meet.* Wks. 1709 III. III. 21 When the Spewing-fit is over, he'll sit down to take a Nod.

2. Matter spewed out or vomited; spew.

c **1380** WYCLIF *Sel. Wks.* II. 330 Houndis..þat after þe tyme þat þei have spued þei turnen aȝen and eeten þe spuynge. **1388** —— *Isaiah* xxviii. 8 Alle bordis weren fillid with spuyng and filthis. **1553** BECON *Reliques of Rome* (1563) 226 If a man by any chaunce of glotony, do spue out yᵉ sacrement, the same spuyng must be brent. **1880** *Antrim & Down Gloss.* 98 *Spuans*, what is vomited.

'spewing, *ppl. a.* [f. as prec.]

1. That spews, in senses of the vb.

1388 WYCLIF *Isaiah* xix. 14 A drunkun man and spuynge. **1560** ROLLAND *Seven Sages* 97 Thow poysonit spewand spout. **1605** SYLVESTER *Du Bartas* II. iii. I. 1306 Earth's exhalations hot Are spewing Ætnas that to Heav'n aspire. **1648** J. BEAUMONT *Psyche* XVIII. clxi, That Simon he outspit in Heresy, And higher than his spewing Father flew. **1856** *Deil's Hallowe'en* 16 (E.D.D.), Some dreepit a' wi' spewin' sairs.

2. *Agric.* Of ground: Characterized by the oozing out of moisture; excessively wet; spewy. Freq. in the 17th c.; now *rare* or *Obs.*

1610 W. FOLKINGHAM *Art of Survey* I. x. 24 Spewing grounds ouer-soaked with sower moisture are well releeued by being sowne with Oates. **1634** W. WOOD *New Eng. Prosp.* (1865) 11 The Soyle is for the generall a warme kinde of earth, there being little cold-spewing land. **1664** EVELYN *Sylva* xvii. 36 In moist, and boggy places they will flourish wonderfully, so the ground be not spewing. *a* **1722** LISLE *Husb.* (1757) 11 Chalk is healing, and therefore proper for clay, cold, and spewing grounds.

3. Issuing as if spewed out.

1616 SURFL. & MARKH. *Country Farme* v. x. 540 These Oxen are fittest for those soyles which are tough and firme, without anie spewing moisture in them. **1675** EVELYN *Philos. Disc. Earth* (1676) 86 Cutting your Furrow..about a foot beneath the spewing water. **1786** BURNS *Vision* iii, The spewing reek That fill'd, wi' hoast-provoking smeek, The auld, clay biggin.

spewy ('spjuːɪ), *a.* Also 7–8 spewey. [f. SPEW *v.*¹ + -Y.]

1. Of ground: Tending to excessive wetness; from which water rises or oozes out. Chiefly *Agric.*

1669 WORLIDGE *Syst. Agric.* iii. §3. 22 Where the ground is moist, cold, clay, spewy, rushy or mossie. **1721** MORTIMER *Husb.* (ed. 3) I. 110 The place was cover'd with a scurf of wet spewy Earth about a Foot thick. **1733** TULL *Horse-Hoeing Husb.* xviii. 251 Hills are made wet and spewy by the Rain-water which falls thereon, and soaks into them as into other Land. **1821** COBBETT *Rural Rides* (1853) 49 A nasty spewy black gravel on the top of a sour clay. **1849** *Jrnl. R. Agric. Soc.* X. II. 437 The wet 'spewy' pastures of the Cotswold Hills. **1879** MISS BRADDON *Vixen* xxvii, They..splashed through a good deal of spewy ground.

b. *transf.* Of literary style: Sloppy, slovenly.

1829 [H. BEST] *Personal & Lit. Mem.* 171 The main cause of the puffy, spungy, spewy, washy style that prevails at the present day.

2. Frothy, effervescent. *rare*$^{-1}$.

1743 *Lond. & Country Brew.* IV. (ed. 2) 279 Whereby any such spewy, creamy Head or Ferments, is entirely kept off.

spey, obs. f. SPAY *v.*

spey(e, varr. SPAY *sb.* (sluice).

speyr(e, varr. SPEIR *Obs.*; obs. forms of SPEAR *sb.*[1], SPEER, SPHERE *sb.*

† **speys.** *Obs. rare.* Also speyes. [ad. OF. *espeisse* (*espesse, espoisse*), f. *espeis* (F. *épais*) thick.] A thick or dense part of a wood.

In quots. perh. taken as a plural form.

c **1410** *Master of Game* (MS. Digby 182) xxx, Howe an hunter shall quest amonge clere speys and amonge hy trees. *Ibid.*, þei abyde amonge clere speyes and in hye wodes. *Ibid.* xxxiii, If it be in thyk speys, bowes or braunches broken as þe dere hath walked, he sholde saye lowde: sy va.

† **sphacel.** *Obs. rare.* [a. older F. *sphacel* (1554), *sphacele* (mod.F. *sphacèle*), ad. med.L. *sphacelus.*] = SPHACELUS.

1634 T. JOHNSON *Parey's Wks.* IX. xv. 335 It [doting] happens..from a Gangreen or Sphacel. *Ibid.* x. xx. 371 There sometimes followes a corruption and Sphacell of the fractured bones of the scull upon wounds of the head. [**1849** in CRAIG.]

† **'sphacelate,** *a. Obs. rare.* [ad. med. or mod.L. *sphacelātus*: see next and cf. F. *sphacélé*, Sp. *esfacelado.*] Sphacelated.

1634 T. JOHNSON *Parey's Wks.* XXVI. xxxi. 1064 Exhalations, lifted or raised up from any part which is gangrenate or sphacelate. **1785** MARTYN *Lett. Bot.* xxvi. 392 Having a cylindric..calyx with the scales sphacelate or seeming mortified at top.

sphacelate ('sfæsɪleɪt), *v. Path.* [f. med. or mod.L. *sphacelāt-*, stem of *sphacelāre*, f. *sphacelus* SPHACELUS. Cf. F. *sphacéler* (16th cent.).]

1. *trans.* To affect with sphacelus; to cause to gangrene or mortify.

1653 URQUHART *Rabelais* I. xxvii, To some others he spoiled the frame of their kidneys, marred their backs,.. sphacelated their shins. **1663** BOYLE *Usef. Exp. Nat. Philos.* II. ii. 38 The inside of the abdomen looked as well neer black, as if it had been sphacelated. **1676** WISEMAN *Surg. Treat.* v. ix. 383 For the most part, the long retention of Matter sp[h]acelates the Brain.

2. *intr.* To become gangrenous or mortified.

1684 tr. *Bonet's Merc. Compit.* XIV. 474 They render their Patients..lame of their Fingers ends, because the Bones do sphacelate. **1707** SLOANE *Jamaica* I. p. cxlvi, It sphacelated more and more and..he died. **1764** *Phil. Trans.* LIV. 242 The lungs..were..here and there upon their surface beginning to sphacelate. **1829** COOPER *Good's Study Med.* (ed. 3) III. 470 Sometimes the whole aneurismal swelling suddenly inflames, and sphacelates. **1899** *Allbutt's Syst. Med.* VIII. 824 The tumour..then sphacelates and drops off.

Hence **'sphacelating** *ppl. a.*

1799 KENTISH in Beddoes *Contrib. Phys. & Med. Knowl.* (1799) 266 The same sphacelating tendency. **1822-7** GOOD *Study Med.* (1829) III. 491 It often alternated from a sphacelating to an erysipelatous inflammation.

'sphacelated, *ppl. a.* [f. prec. + -ED.]

1. *Path.* Mortified, gangrened.

attrib. **1612** WOODALL *Surg. Mate* Wks. (1653) 387 They used to take off the Sphacelated member. **1738** *Phil. Trans.* XL. 9 A separation of the sphacelated sluff. **1783** BENTLEY in *Med. Comm.* I. 258 The sphacelated parts were dressed. **1800** *Med. Jrnl.* IV. 167 The greater portion of the surface ..was in a sphacelated state. **1877** F. T. ROBERTS *Handbk. Med.* (ed. 3) I. 393 The sphacelated portion is expelled. *pred.* **1668** CULPEPPER & COLE *Barthol. Anat.* 374 The lower part of the Arm was gangrenated and sphacelated. **1712** *Phil. Trans.* XXVII. 513 The Liver was intirely sphacelated. **1782** W. HEBERDEN *Comment.* xvi. (1806) 85 The pelvis was sphacelated. **1859** SEMPLE *Diphtheria* 11 All the soft parts..appeared deeply sphacelated.

2. *Bot.* Withered, dead.

1806 J. GALPINE *Brit. Bot.* 409 [Leaves] somewhat sphacelated at the apex. **1821** W. P. C. BARTON *Flora N. Amer.* I. 125 Root..invested at the bottom and upper part with a sphacelated, brownish-black tunic.

sphacelation (sfæsɪ'leɪʃən). *Path.* [f. SPHACELATE *v.*] The fact or process of becoming mortified; the formation of a sphacelus.

1657 *Physical Dict.*, *Sphacelus*, deadness of any part. *Sphacelation*, the same as before. **1665** BOYLE *New Exper. Cold* vi. 204 The Gangrænes and Sphacelations that often rob living men of frozen Toes. **1718** QUINCY *Compl. Disp.* 138 The Insensibility which sometimes the Opium induces, so as to endanger a Sphacelation. **1771** D. LYSONS *Ess. Camphire* 10 Against such violent internal inflammations as are productive of sphacelation. **1826** S. COOPER *First Lines Surg.* (ed. 5) 44 Both during the extension of the disorder, and..when the sphacelation has stopped. **1897** *Allbutt's Syst. Med.* IV. 128 The mass of ulceration and sphacelation in which..the vessels are often involved.

‖**sphacelia** (sfæ'siːlɪə). *Bot.* [mod.L., f. *sphacelus* SPHACELUS, with reference to its effects when eaten.] The first stage of the fungus which produces ergot in rye. Also *attrib.* Hence **spha'celial** *a.*

1879 *Encycl. Brit.* IX. 834/2 The ascospores, on germinating,..give rise again to the sphacelia, which closes the cycle. **1880** BESSEY *Botany* 289 In this stage, which is called the Sphacelia stage, it produces a multitude of conidia. **1882** VINES tr. *Sachs's Bot.* 317 The conidia can germinate at once and immediately again detach conidia, which..again produce a sphacelia in other Grasses. **1909** B. M. DUGGAR *Fungous Dis. Plants* xi. 245 The surface mycelial areas are thrown into folds and numerous short conidiophores arise, bearing small ovate conidia. This is known as the sphacelial stage. **1938** G. M. SMITH *Cryptogamic Bot.* I. xii. 453 This is followed by a progressively upward metamorphosis into compact tissue until the whole mycelium has been changed into a sclerotium that is capped with remnants of the sphacelial tissue. **1976** G. C. AINSWORTH *Introd. Hist. Mycol.* vii. 187 The major contribution of L. R. Tulasne in his classic paper in 1853..was to demonstrate that the sphacelial phase, the sclerotia, and the ascocarps were all stages of one fungus, *Claviceps purpurea.*

sphace'linic, *a. Chem.* [f. prec. or SPHACELUS.] ***sphacelinic*** (or ***sphacelic***) ***acid***: (see quot.).

1897 *Allbutt's Syst. Med.* II. 797 Kolert tells us that ergot contains two poisons; sphacelinic acid, which provokes the gangrene; and cornutine.

'sphacelism. *rare.* [ad. F. *sphacélisme* or mod.L. *sphacelismus* (Gr. σφακελισμός).] (See quot.)

1656 BLOUNT *Glossogr.*, *Sphaselism*, an ulcer eating in the brain.

sphacelous ('sfæsɪləs), *a. Path.* [f. SPHACEL-US + -OUS.] Gangrenous, necrotic.

1682 *Phil. Trans.* XIII. 93 Large and corrupted spleens, sphacelous and corroded tongues. **1728** CHAMBERS *Cycl.* s.v. *Sphacelus*, A Sphacelous Foot..ought to be cut off in the mortified Part, near the live Part. **1824** *Ann. Reg.* 157 The right foot and the lower part of the leg..was sphacelous.

‖**sphacelus** ('sfæsɪləs). *Path.* Also 6 sphacilus. [med. or mod.L., ad. Gr. σφάκελος gangrene, etc. Cf. It. *sfacelo*, Sp. and Pg. *esfacelo*, F. *sphacèle* SPHACEL.]

1. Necrosis, mortification; an instance of this.

1575 BANISTER *Chyrurg.* III. (1585) 488 If the malice of this ulcer..fall a creeping, it turneth to Sphacilus. **1600** SURFLET *Countrie Farme* II. xlii. 256 The flying fire, the ringworme, the leprosie, the Gangrena, and Sphacelus. **1612** WOODALL *Surg. Mate* Wks. (1653) 379 A Gangrene is ever the forerunner of a Sphacelus. **1728** CHAMBERS *Cycl.* s.v., The Sphacelus is distinguished by the Lividness or Blackness of the Part affected. **1782** W. HEBERDEN *Comment.* xxxi. (1806) 154 Ending fatally in a sphacelus of the bowels. **1813** J. THOMSON *Lect. Inflam.* 519 Gangrene, gangrenous inflammation, or inflammation which shows a tendency to terminate in sphacelus. **1878** T. BRYANT *Pract. Surg.* I. 570 General inflammation of the pulp, following sooner or later on the previous condition and resulting in its sphacelus.

2. A mass of mortified tissue; a slough.

1880 A. FLINT *Princ. Med.* 52 A necrosed mass of tissue is called a sphacelus or slough. **1899** *Allbutt's Syst. Med.* VI. 575 The sphacelus becomes black, dry and hard.

sphære, obs. form of SPHERE.

sphæriaceous (sfɪərɪ'eɪʃəs), *a. Bot.* [f. mod.L. *Sphæriace-æ* (see def.) + -OUS.] Belonging to, typical of, the *Sphæriaceæ*, an extensive family of Fungi.

1857 HENFREY *Bot.* 587 Corpuscles..extruded through the pore of the spermogonium, as in the Sphæriaceous Fungi. **1875** M. C. COOKE *Fungi* 35 The majority of so-called species are undoubtedly conditions of sphæriaceous fungi.

'sphæriaform, *a. Bot.* Also sphæriæform. [f. mod.L. *Sphæria* (see def.) + -(I)FORM.] Having a form like that of *Sphæria*, the typical genus of *Sphæriaceæ* (see prec.).

1857 BERKELEY *Cryptog. Botany* §237. 247 Many species of..acrosporous sphæriæform Fungi. **1887** W. PHILLIPS *Brit. Discomycetes* 351 Pycnidia intermixed with the above, sphæriaform.

sphærical, -ick, obs. forms of SPHERIC(AL.

‖**sphæ'ridium.** *Zool.* Pl. -'ridia. Also -ideum. [mod.L. (Lovén), f. *sphæra* SPHERE *sb.*] One of the numerous minute rounded bodies attached to certain parts of sea-urchins.

1877 HUXLEY *Anat. Inv. Anim.* 572 In some genera, these *sphæridea*..are sunk in fossæ of the plate to which they are attached. **1888** ROLLESTON & JACKSON *Anim. Life* 559 Sphaeridia..occur on the peristome and ambulacra... Structurally they are modified spines, spherical or oval in shape.

sphaerite ('sfɪəraɪt). *Min.* [ad. G. *sphärit* (V. von Zepharovich 1867, in *Sitzungsber. der K. Akad. der Wissensch.* (*Math.-Nat. Classe*) LVI. 24), f. *sphärisch* spherical: see -ITE[1].] A hydrous aluminium phosphate now identified with variscite.

1886 J. D. DANA *Syst. Mineral.* (ed. 5) 587 Sphærite... In globular concretions with a drusy faceted surface, without a distinct fibrous or concentric structure. **1921** *Bull. U.S. Geol. Survey* No. 679. 135 Sphaerite... Spherical masses of white fibers. **1950** *Amer. Mineralogist* XXXV. 1059 It appears that sphaerite is wholly identical with variscite.

sphæro- ('sfɪərəʊ), ad. Gr. σφαιρο-, combining form of σφαῖρα ball, SPHERE, employed in a considerable number of terms, esp. *Bot.* and *Zool.*, of which only a few are naturalized in form or have any general currency. **'sphæroblast** *Bot.* (see quot.); **sphæro'cobaltite** *Min.*, 'carbonate of cobalt, found in small spherical masses' (Chester).; cf. *spherocobaltite* s.v. SPHERO-; **'sphærocone** *Palæont.*, an ammonoid with a very involute shell in which the outer whorl conceals the inner one and the whole has a globular form; **sphæro'dactyle,** a species of humming-bird; **'sphærolite,** (*a*) (see quot.); (*b*) obs. var. SPHERULITE; † **sphæ'romachy** (see quot.); **sphærosome,** var. SPHEROSOME; **'sphærospore** *Bot.* (see quot.); **sphæro'stilbite** *Min.*, 'a variety of stilbite, occurring in radiated spheres' (Chester).

1901 H. M. WARD *Diseases in Plants* xxiv. 225 *Woodnodules* or **Sphæroblasts* are curious marble-like masses of wood which protrude with a covering of bark from old trunks of Beeches, etc. **1877** *Mineral. Mag.* I. 267 *Sphœrocobaltite [*sic*]..occurs in spheroidal forms with roselite at Schneeberg, Saxony. **1881** WATTS *Dict. Chem.*, *3rd Suppl.*, *Sphærocobaltite*, or *Cobalt-spar*, is a native carbonate of cobalt belonging to the calcspar-group, black on the outside, red within. **1923** *Sphærocone [see SERPENTICONE]. **1970** R. M. BLACK *Elements Palaeont.* viii. 89 Sphaerocones occur repeatedly during ammonoid history. **1860** GOSSE *Rom. Nat. Hist.* 149 The little *sphærodactyle,—which we might put into a quill-barrel, and carry home in the waistcoat pocket. **1881** WATTS *Dict. Chem.*, *3rd Suppl.*, **Sphærolite*, a volcanic glass from the lava of Antisana. **1658** PHILLIPS, **Sphæromachy*, a playing at bowls, or tennis. **1866** *Treas. Bot.* 1081/1 **Sphærospore*, the quadruple spore of some algals. **1850** DAUBENY *Atom. The.* (ed. 2) xii. 410 The former combinations are called hydro-silicates... Example: *Sphærostilbite.

sphæroid, -al, variants of SPHEROID, -AL[1].

sphærometer, variant of SPHEROMETER.

sphærosiderite (sfɪərəʊ'sɪdəraɪt). *Min.* [f. SPHÆRO- + SIDERITE[1].] 'A variety of siderite occurring in spherical concretions' (Chester).

1837 DANA *Min.* 213 Carbonate of Iron. Sparry Iron... Sphærosiderite. **1878** LAWRENCE tr. *Cotta's Rocks Class.* 50 In the compact state, or when occurring in reniform masses or concretions, this mineral is termed sphærosiderite. **1886** GEIKIE *Class-Bk. Geol.* 181 Sphærosiderite or Clay-ironstone concretions enclosing portion of a fern.

sphærule, -lite, -litic, obs. ff. SPHERULE, etc.

† **sphagian,** *a. Obs.*[−1] [f. Gr. σφάγιος slaying, slaughtering.] Employed in the killing or sacrificing of animals.

1607 TOPSELL *Four-f. Beasts* 88 Then put they vnder him their Sphagian vesselles to receiue his bloud.

† **sphagitid.** *Obs.*[−1] [ad. F. *sphagitide*, ad. Gr. σφαγῖτιδ-, σφαγῖτις (φλέψ) jugular vein, f. σφαγή throat.] (See quot.)

1653 URQUHART *Rabelais* I. xliv, He cut clean through the jugularie veins and the sphagitid or transparent arteries of the neck.

'sphagneous, *a. rare*[−1]. = SPHAGNOUS *a.* 1.

a **1864** GESNER *Coal, Petrol.*, etc. (1865) 53 They contain the remains of sphagneous plants and woody fibre.

sphag'nologist. [f. *sphagn-*, SPHAGNUM: see -OLOGIST.] A special student of, or authority on, the sphagna.

1886 *Jrnl. Roy. Microsc. Soc.* VI. 108 The very great diversity displayed by different sphagnologists in the limitation of species.

So **sphag'nology,** the special study of the sphagna (*Cent. Dict.* 1891).

sphag'nose, *a. rare*[−1]. = SPHAGNOUS *a.* 2.

1818 T. NUTTALL *Genera N. Amer. Plants* I. 250 Growing in sphagnose morasses.

sphagnous ('sfægnəs), *a.* [f. SPHAGN-UM.]

1. Of the nature of, consisting of, sphagnum.

1828-32 WEBSTER (citing Bigelow), *Sphagnous*, pertaining to bog-moss, mossy. **1846** DANA *Zooph.* iv. (1848) 64 Like the sphagnous moss of a peat-swamp, coral zoophytes continue growing at top. **1868** *Rep. U.S. Commissioner Agric.* (1869) 173 The annual moisture..would collect between the impervious clayey soil and its sphagnous covering. **1888** *Pall Mall G.* 29 Aug. 12/1 A marsh lake—whose wide margins were one dense mass of trembling sphagnous moss.

2. Producing, or abounding in, sphagnum.

1845 S. JUDD *Margaret* I. v, Their habitat is sphagnous places, what you call swamps. **1853** G. JOHNSTON *Nat. Hist. E. Bord.* I. 39 Sundew. In sphagnous bogs.

‖**sphagnum** ('sfægnəm). *Bot.* Pl. **sphagna, -ums.** [mod.L. (J. J. Dillenius *Hist. Muscorum* (1741) 240), f. Gr. σφάγνος a kind of moss.]

1. A genus of mosses growing in boggy or swampy places; bog-moss, peat-moss; also, one or other of the species or plants composing this genus.

1741 J. J. DILLENIUS *Hist. Muscorum* 240 The larger soft and hollow-leaf'd Bog Sphagnum. **1753** *Chambers' Cycl.* Suppl. s.v., The sphagna are divided into two orders, the one comprehending the branched kinds, and the other the unbranched ones. **1839** LINDLEY *Introd. Bot.* (ed. 3) 547 The only case of undoubtedly perforated parenchyma with which I am acquainted is in Sphagnum. **1857** HENFREY *Bot.* 443 The *Sphagna* have antheridia like those of *Jungermannia.* **1880** BESSEY *Botany* 351 The adult plant-body in this class, which includes, besides the Sphagnums, all the true Mosses, is always a leafy stem.

attrib. **1839** LINDLEY *Introd. Bot.* (ed. 3) 547 The circular spaces in Sphagnum leaves are openings. **1857** T. MOORE

Handbk. Brit. Ferns (ed. 3) 27 On this a thin layer of sphagnum moss should be spread.

2. The mossy substance of which plants of this genus are composed.

1840 *Florist's Jrnl.* (1846) I. 208 Covered over with dry sphagnum, or bog moss. **1863** LYELL *Antiq. Man* 9 The lowest stratum consists of swamp-peat composed chiefly of moss or sphagnum. **1877** W. H. DALL *Tribes Ext. N.W.* 80 A saucer or dish of stone or clay, with a wick, usually of sphagnum.

3. Special Comb.: **sphagnum bog, swamp**, a bog in which the plant-life consists chiefly of mosses of the genus *Sphagnum*.

1911 C. B. CRAMPTON *Vegetation Caithness* iv. 51 In recent times.. *Sphagnum* bogs have been reduced to their present small proportion in the moorland associations. **1951** V. NABOKOV *Conclusive Evidence* iv. 47 Beyond the lower course of the river.. the vast expanse of a misty-blue sphagnum bog. **1972** DEAN & SMITH *Wisconsin* 78/2 Sphagnum bogs are one stage in the succession from open-water lake to conifer swamp. **1890** *Science-Gossip* XXVI. 60 In the far-off bogs and sphagnum swamps of North Wales. **1941** J. BUCHAN *Sick Heart River* II. 124 A bottomless half-frozen sphagnum swamp.. heaved under his tread.

sphai'ristic, *a. rare*⁻¹. [ad. Gr. σφαιριστικ-ός playing at ball; see next.] Tennis-playing.

1882 *World* 14 June 15 Lawn-tennis has not to answer for many accidents; so that two in a week among the sphairistic ladies of Ireland seems alarming.

sphairistike (sfɛə'rɪstɪkɪ). *Obs.* exc. *Hist.* [ad. Gr. σφαιριστική (τέχνη) (skill) in playing at ball, f. σφαιριστικός: cf. prec. Cf. STICKÉ.] A type of tennis first played in 1873 which was later developed into and renamed lawn-tennis.

1874 G. D. FITZGERALD in *Field* 21 Mar. 270/2 Sir, I have lately seen a new game played which will be a great acquisition as an out-of-door amusement at country houses. The game is called Sphairistike, or Lawn Tennis. **1874** F. KILVERT *Diary* 27 July (1969) III. 55 We began to play 'sphairistike' or lawn tennis. **1927** *Times* 10 June 10/4 Badminton quickly got a certain popularity in England, and from it Major Wingfield invented sphairistike. The net of sphairistike was practically the badminton net, 5 ft. high at the sides, with the same, if a broader, red tape along the top. *Ibid.*, The name 'sphairistike', however, was impossible (if only because people would pronounce it as a word of three syllables to rhyme with 'pike'), and it was soon rechristened. **1965** *Punch* 16 June 895/2 The British invented lawn tennis, though the original name for it, 'sphairistike', didn't catch on. *Ibid.* 896/3 Arthur Balfour.. mildly suggested that a better name for 'sphairistike' would be 'lawn tennis'! **1982** 'J. GASH' *Firefly Gadroon* v. 62 My eyes lit upon a genuine old Sphairistike racquet.

'sphalerite. *Min.* [f. Gr. σφαλερ-ός deceptive + -ITE¹ 2; named by E. F. Glocker (1847).] Zinc-blende.

1868 in WATTS *Dict. Chem.* **1871** *Jrnl. Chem. Soc.* XXIV. 312 (*heading*) On the occurrence of thallium in sphalerite from Geroldseck (Breisgau). **1925** A. S. ALEXANDER *Tramps across Watersheds* v. 235 Some of these minerals and ores are:—gold, silver bloom, galena or lead ore, blende or sphalerite or zinc ore.. and a great variety of quartz. **1952** [see ROBINSONITE]. **1969** BENNISON & WRIGHT *Geol. Hist. Brit. Isles* x. 247 The later, mesothermal, lodes.. carry such minerals as galena and sphalerite with a little uranium ore as well. **1973** *Times* 1 Dec. 11/3 'This piece', he said, indicating a toffee-coloured chunk of sphalerite from Picos de Europa, Santander, Spain, 'was brought up from the mine for me by a local dealer'.

†sphalm. *Obs.*⁻¹ [Anglicized f. next.] An error; an erroneous doctrine or tenet.

1715 M. DAVIES *Athen. Brit.* I. Pref. 29 Both the Romish and Jacobite Schisms and Sphalms are irretrievably laid open and flat to the Ground thereby.

‖'sphalma. *Obs. rare.* Pl. sphalmata(s). [a. Gr. σφάλμα, f. σφάλλειν to err.] An error or slip in writing or copying.

1657 EVELYN *Let.* in *Mem.* (1827) IV. 45 I have been bold to note places with my black-leade where yᵉ Amanuensis has committed some sphalmatas.

sphecid ('sfɛsɪd), *sb.* and *a.* *Ent.* [f. mod.L. family name *Sphecidæ*, f. *Sphex* SPHEX (Linnæus *Systema Naturæ* (ed. 10, 1758) I. 569): see -ID³.]

A. *sb.* A fossorial wasp of the family Sphecidæ. **B.** *adj.* Of or pertaining to an insect of this kind.

1895 J. H. & A. B. COMSTOCK *Man. Study of Insects* xxii. 650 The Sphecids or the Thread-waisted Wasps.. are the most commonly observed of all our digger-wasps as certain species build their mud nests in the attics of our houses. **1926** E. O. ESSIG *Insects Western N. Amer.* xxviii. 871 Sphecid or Thread-Waisted Wasps.. are solitary, nest in the soil, and provision the nests with spiders or insects. **1966** C. SWEENEY *Scurrying Bush* v. 75, I saw a handsome, inch long, metallic blue-black wasp fly out from behind the row of books. It was a sphecid or mud dauber. **1976** R. M. BOHART et al. (*title*) Sphecid wasps of the world. *Ibid.* 1 Adult sphecids feed on a variety of food.

sphecoid ('sfiːkɔɪd), *a.* *Ent.* [f. Gr. σφηκ-, σφήξ wasp (see SPHEX) + -OID.] Wasp-like; *spec.* resembling, or related to, the digger-wasps.

1815 KIRBY & SP. *Entomol.* ix. (1818) I. 263 It is probable that most of the other Vespoid and Sphecoid Hymenoptera .. assist in this great work. **1858** MAYNE *Expos. Lex.* 1183/2 *Sphecoides*,.. resembling a wasp: sphecoid.

‖sphendone ('sfɛndəniː). *Archæol.* [a. Gr. σφενδόνη a sling, head-band, etc.]

1. A head-band or fillet, shaped like a common form of sling, worn by women in ancient Greece.

1850 LEITCH tr. *C. O. Müller's Anc. Art* §363 (ed. 2) 453 On the hair:.. The sphendone surrounded with rays. **1872** HEAD *Sel. Grk. Coins in Electrotype Brit. Mus.* 6 Head of Parthenope, wearing sphendone, to right.

2. An area composed of elongated sloping sides with a rounded end.

1847 LEITCH tr. *C. O. Müller's Anc. Art* §290. 281 The Messenian stadium, which is surrounded by colonnades, has 16 rows of seats in the sphendone.

sphene (sfiːn). *Min.* Also **sphen**. [a. F. *sphène* (Haüy, 1801), f. Gr. σφήν wedge, from the shape of its crystals.] = TITANITE I.

1815 AIKIN *Min.* (ed. 2) 137 Sphen. Rutilite... Colour redish, yellowish, greyish, and blackish brown. **1849** DANA *Geol.* vi. (1850) 347 Some minute crystals of sphene. **1879** RUTLEY *Stud. Rocks* x. 140 Frequently the crystals of sphene appear cloudy or imperfectly translucent.

sphenethmoid (sfɪ'nɛθmɔɪd), *sb.* and *a.* *Zool.* [f. Gr. σφήν wedge (cf. SPHENO-) + ETHMOID.] One of the cranial bones in batrachians, situated at the base of the skull; the girdle bone. Also ***sphenethmoid bone***.

1875 HUXLEY in *Encycl. Brit.* I. 754/1 As it takes the place of the ethmoid, presphenoid, and orbito-sphenoids, it may be termed the *sphen-ethmoid*. **1877** HUXLEY & MARTIN *Elem. Biol.* 218 Appearing at the base of the skull, at the front end of the parasphenoid, is the girdle-bone or sphenethmoid. **1903** *Encycl. Brit.* XXXV. 896 Sphen-ethmoid bone.

spheniscan (sfɪ'nɪskən). *Ornith.* [f. mod.L. *Sphenisc-us* (Brisson) + -AN.] A penguin of the genus *Spheniscus*; a jackass penguin.

1840 *Cuvier's Anim. Kingd.* 255 The Spheniscans.. have a straight and compressed beak. *Ibid.*, The Cape Spheniscan .. chiefly inhabits the neighbourhood of the Cape, where it nestles among the rocks.

So **sphe'nisque**. *rare.*

1826 STEPHENS in *Shaw's Gen. Zool.* XIII. 64 Cape Sphenisque. *Ibid.* 65 Magellanic Sphenisque.

spheno- ('sfiːnəʊ), a. Gr. σφηνο-, combining form of σφήν wedge, employed in a number of scientific terms.

1. *Anat.* In adjs. which designate something pertaining to the sphenoid bone together with the part specified by the second element of the compound, as **spheno-'basilar, -ba'silic, -'frontal, -'malar, -man'dibular, -ma'xillary, -oc'cipital, -'orbital, -'palatine, -pa'rietal, -'temporal.**

Some of these represent Latin formations, as *sphenopalatinus*, *-pharyngæus*, in use from at least the 17th cent. Cf. also F. *sphénobasilaire*, *-maxillaire*, *-palatin*, etc.

1849 CRAIG, *Spheno-basilar. **1904** DUCKWORTH *Stud. Anthropol. Laborat.* 213 The spheno-basilar suture. **1897** *Allbutt's Syst. Med.* IV. 486 Premature synostosis of the *spheno-basilic suture. **1830** R. KNOX *Béclard's Anat.* 280 Of this kind are the *spheno-frontal sutures. **1884** J. E. LEE tr. *Römer's Bone Caves of Ojcow* 29 A synostosis of the spheno-frontal and the lower part of the coronal sutures. **1855** HOLDEN *Hum. Osteol.* 94 Other short sutures, such as the '*spheno-malar', 'spheno-parietal', 'zygomatic',.. speak for themselves. **1893** H. MORRIS *Human Anat.* ii. 190 The *spheno-mandibular ligament (long internal lateral).. is a thin, loose band, situated some little distance from the joint. **1967** G. M. WYBURN et al. *Conc. Anat.* iv. 112/2 The sphenomandibular ligament runs from the spine of the sphenoid to the lingula at the mandibular foramen. **1771** *Encycl. Brit.* I. 227 The inferior orbitary, or *sphenomaxillary fissure. **1831** R. KNOX *Cloquet's Anat.* 107 The Spheno-maxillary Fossa.. is formed by the sphenoid bone behind, the upper maxillary bone before, and by the palate bone to the inside. **1840** E. WILSON *Anat. Vade M.* (1842) 29 The sphenoid, in conjunction with the occipital, was described.. as a single bone, under the name of *spheno-occipital. **1841** *Penny Cycl.* XXI. 158/1 The round aperture is.. confounded with the *spheno-orbital slit. **1831** R. KNOX *Cloquet's Anat.* 107 The *spheno-palatine hole. **1858** H. GRAY *Anat.* 489 The Spheno-Palatine Ganglion (Meckel's), the largest of the cranial ganglia. **1881** MIVART *Cat* 86 The spheno-palatine foramen opens into the nasal cavity. **1831** *Spheno-parietal [see below]. **1884** J. E. LEE tr. *Römer's Bone Caves of Ojcow* 29 The spheno parietal suture .. is also in part completely obliterated. **1831** R. KNOX *Cloquet's Anat.* 89 It is traversed by various sutures, the coronal, the sphenoidal, the *spheno-temporal, the spheno-parietal, and the squamous.

2. In names of minerals, as **'sphenoclase** (see quots.), or of genera of animals or plants, as **'sphenodon, spheno'phyllum, sphe'nopteris.**

Webster (1864) also gives '*Sphenogram*, a cuneiform or arrow-headed character', to which the *Imp. Dict.* (1882) adds *sphe'nographer*, *-'graphic*, *-graphist*, *-graphy*.

1868 WATTS *Dict. Chem.* V. 399 **Sphenoclase*, a mineral occurring in parallel layers.. in a bluish granular limestone .. in Norway. **1896** CHESTER *Dict. Min.*, *Sphenoclase*, a questionable silicate of calcium, etc., of yellowish color. **1878** J. F. BELL *Gegenbauer's Comp. Anat.* 440 This arrangement obtains also in some Saurii (*Sphenodon). *c* **1880** *Cassell's Nat. Hist.* IV. 290 The Tuatera, or Hatteria, or the Sphenodon Lizard. *Ibid.* 341 The remarkable Lizard from New Zealand—the Tuatera, or Sphenodon. **1837** *Penny Cycl.* VII. 294/1 **Sphenophyllum*.. has broad wedge-shaped leaves, the veins of which are forked. **1858** BAIRD *Cycl. Nat. Sci.* 509/2 *Sphenophyllum*, a genus of fossil plants peculiar to the coal measures and the transition formations. **1837** *Penny Cycl.* VII. 292/2 **Sphenopteris* has twice or thrice pinnatifid leaves. **1842** *Ibid.* XXII. 338/2 *Sphenopteris*, a genus of fossil ferns... They are all coal-measure plants. **1851** MANTELL *Petrifactions* i. §2. 32 The other characteristic Wealden plant is the Sphenopteris (*S. Mantelli*), or wedge-leaf fern.

sphenochasm. ('sfiːnəʊkæz(ə)m). *Geol.* [f. SPHENO- + Gr. χάσμ-α CHASM.] (See quot. 1958.)

1958 S. W. CAREY in *Continental Drift* (Geol. Dept., Univ. of Tasmania, Hobart) 193 A Sphenochasm.. is the triangular gap of oceanic crust separating two cratonic blocks with fault margins converging to a point, and interpreted as having originated by the rotation of one of the blocks with respect to the other. **1965** A. HOLMES *Princ. Physical Geol.* (ed. 2) xxix. 1086 The Gulf [of California] sphenochasm appears to have been filled with rheid mantle material in much the same way as the Red Sea. **1971** *Nature* 2 July 21/2 As the Gulf of Honduras sphenochasm completed its opening, the Yucatan and Nicaraguan cratons assumed their modern positions relative to North America.

sphenoid ('sfiːnɔɪd), *a.* and *sb.* Also 8 **sphænoid**, 9 **sphenoïd**. [ad. mod.L. *sphēnoīdēs*, *sphēnoeidēs* (†*sphæno-*), a. Gr. σφηνοειδής, f. σφήν wedge: see -OID. So F. *sphénoïde* (1611).]

A. *adj.* ***sphenoid bone***, a bone of irregular form situated at the base of the skull, where it is wedged in between the other bones of the cranium.

1732 MONRO *Anat.* (ed. 2) 76, I have seen separate.. Bones at the Conjunction.. of the sphenoid and parietal Bones. **1766** *Phil. Trans.* LVII. 119 Portions of medullary substance lying upon the sphænoid bone. **1831** R. KNOX *Cloquet's Anat.* 41 The sphenoid bone is articulated with the frontal, ethmoid, occipital, parietal, and temporal bones. **1884** M. MACKENZIE *Dis. Throat & Nose* II. 232 The posterior third of the roof.. is formed by the body of the sphenoid bone.

B. *sb.* **1.** *Anat.* The sphenoid bone; one or other of the separate parts of this.

1828 STARK *Elem. Nat. Hist.* I. 28 In the fœtus the occiput is divided into four parts, the body of the sphenoid into two. **1841** T. R. JONES *Anim. Kingd.* 638 These two halves may .. be called, respectively, the anterior and posterior sphenoids. **1896** tr. *Boas' Text Bk. Zool.* 362 In the basal and lateral regions in front of the parts just mentioned are the sphenoids (ali-, orbito-, and basi-shenoid).

2. *Cryst.* A wedge-shaped crystal bounded by four equal and similar triangular faces.

1855 *Orr's Circ. Sci., Inorg. Nature* 435 The Rhombic Sphenoid, or, Irregular Tetrahedron, is a hemihedral form, derived from the double four-faced rhombic pyramid. *Ibid.*, A sphenoid may be derived from every one of the pyramids previously described. **1878** GURNEY *Crystallogr.* 78 A closed figure bounded by four similar isosceles triangles.. is sometimes called a sphenoid.

sphenoidal (sfɪ'nɔɪdəl), *a.* *Anat.* Also 8 **sphænoidal**, 8–9 **sphenoïdal**. [ad. mod.L. *sphēnoīdālis* (†*sphæn-*), f. *sphēnoīdēs* SPHENOID. So F. *sphénoïdal* (18th cent.).]

1. ***sphenoidal bone***, the sphenoid bone.

1726 MONRO *Anat.* 88 It is connected to the sphenoidal Bone, by means of that same Suture. **1746** *Phil. Trans.* XLIV. 11 The Hole of the sphænoidal Bone, thro' which the Optic Nerve passes. **1834** MᶜMURTRIE *Cuvier's Anim. Kingd.* 173 A narrow canal which traverses the palatine and sphenoidal bones.

2. Of or pertaining to, connected with, the sphenoid bone.

Chiefly in a number of special collocations, as ***sphenoidal angle, fissure, sinus, suture***, etc.

1726 MONRO *Anat.* 88 The sphenoidal Suture connects it to the Wedge-like Bone. **1728** CHAMBERS *Cycl.*, *Sphenoidal Suture*, in Anatomy, a Suture thus call'd from its encompassing the *Os Sphenoides*. **1808** BARCLAY *Muscular Motions* 505 The frontal, sphenoidal, and maxillary antres. **1822** J. PARKINSON *Outl. Oryctol.* 284 The sphenoidal plates which form a vault over the palate bones. **1854** R. OWEN in *Orr's Circ. Sci., Org. Nature* I. 167 Such cells are called .. 'sphenoidal' and 'ethmoidal sinuses' in man. **1872** MIVART *Anat.* 83 A long but narrow space, termed the sphenoidal fissure.

sphenotic (sfɪ'nɒtɪk), *a.* and *sb.* *Zool.* [f. SPHEN(O)- + OTIC *a.*] **a.** *adj.* Of or pertaining to, formed by combination of, the sphenoid bone and otic structures in certain fishes and in birds. **b.** *sb.* The sphenotic bone or ossification.

1872 MIVART *Anat.* 106 It may also, in Fishes, have added to it a large and distinct ossification, the sphenotic. **1884** COUES *N. Amer. Birds* 156 The post-frontal process, morphologically the post-frontal or sphenotic bone, bounds the rim of the orbit behind. **1885** *Athenæum* 13 June 764/1 He attempted to show.. that the human *lingulæ* are homologous with the sphenotic of the bird. **1895** *Proc. Zool. Soc.* 371 The sphenotic process is also relatively somewhat shorter.

spheral ('sfɪərəl), *a.* Also 6 **-all**. [ad. late L. *sphēr-*, *sphærālis*, f. *sphæra* SPHERE *sb.*: see -AL¹. So It. *sferale*, Pg. *esferal*.]

1. Of or pertaining to a sphere or round body; having the rounded form of a sphere; spherical.

1571 DIGGES *Pantom.* IV. vi. X, Thus also.. ye shal most speedily finde these spheral semidiameters. *Ibid.* xvii. Bbj b, All the sides and diameters both circular and spherall of.. regulare solides. **1690** LEYBOURN *Curs. Math.* 328 In respect of these Bodies Spheral Circumscriptibility. **1766** G. CANNING *Anti-Lucretius* II. 107 These in a form exactly spheral place.

b. *fig.* Symmetrically rounded or perfect.

1841 EMERSON *Ess., Intellect* ¶19 The poet, whose verses are to be spheral and complete. **1844** *Ibid., Nom. & Real.* ¶12 There is somewhat spheral and infinite..in every genius.

2. Of or pertaining to the cosmic spheres or the heavenly bodies: **a.** Of the supposed music of the spheres.

1829 CARLYLE *Misc.* (1857) II. 77 As the Ancients fabled of the Spheral Music. **1845** BAILEY *Festus* (ed. 2) 237 She spake as with the voice Of spheral harmony. **1860** TYNDALL *Glac.* II. i. 239 The ancients had their spheral melodies.

b. In other contexts.

1849 LYTTON *Caxtons* XIV. i, Fortune,..calm and aloft amongst the other angelic powers, revolves her spheral course. **1863** COWDEN CLARKE *Shaks. Char.* xvi. 409 To discuss the Platonic theory of the spheral motion. **1883** *Nature* 8 Feb. 351 As closely contiguous in space as are the molecules of spheral atmospheres.

Hence **sphe'rality**, sphericity. *rare*$^{-0}$.

1891 in *Cent. Dict.*

sphe'ration. *rare.* [f. SPHERE *sb.* + -ATION.] The process of being formed into a sphere; the formation of a sphere or spheres.

1883 *American* VII. 152 A sketch of the life of a nebula not thus broken up, of its rotation, annulation, and final spheration into a nebulous orb.

sphere (sfɪə(r)), *sb.* Forms: *α.* 4-5 sper (5 sperre), speere, 4-6 spere, 6 *Sc.* speir, speyr; 4-5 spire, 5 spyere, *Sc.* spir. *β.* 5- **sphere** (5 sphyre), 6-7 sphear(e, 7 spheere; 6-7 **sphær**, 7 **sphære**, **sphaer**(e. [ad. OF. *espere* (13th c.), later *sphere* (mod.F. *sphère*) or late L. *sphēra*, earlier *sphæra*, ad. Gr. σφαῖρα ball. So It. *sfera*, Sp. and Pg. *esfera*; MDu. *spere*, *speer* (Du. *sfeer*), MHG. *spære*, *spere* (G. *sphäre*).]

I. 1. a. The apparent outward limit of space, conceived as a hollow globe enclosing (and at all points equidistant from) the earth; the visible vault of heaven, in which the celestial bodies appear to have their place.

oblique, parallel, right sphere: see OBLIQUE *a.* 2b, PARALLEL *a.* 1b, RIGHT *a.* 3a.

a **1300** *Cursor M.* 1548 Quen sa fele yeier ar wroken oute þe mikel spere [*Gött.* spire] es rune aboute. *c* **1340** HAMPOLE *Pr. Consc.* 4867 Alle þe fire þat es in þe spere, And under erthe, and aboven erthe here. *c* **1430** LYDG. *Life our Lady* (Harl. MS. 629) fol. 43b, As the svnne dothe in heuen shyne In mydday speere dovn to vs by-lyne. *c* **1470** HENRY *Wallace* VIII. 1186 The mery day sprang fra the oryent... Heich in the sper, the signes maid declayr. **1513** DOUGLAS *Æneid* III. viii. 13 Or [= ere] the speir his owris rollit rycht Sa far about that it wes skars mydnycht. **1590** SPENSER *F.Q.* I. x. 56 He wondred much..What stately building durst so high extend Her loftie towres vnto the starry sphere. **1634** MILTON *Comus* 241 Sweet Echo,..Sweet Queen of Parly, Daughter of the Sphear. **1655** VAUGHAN *Silex Scint.* (1858) 135 If a star Should leave the sphære. **1703** MOXON *Mech. Exerc.* 352 The highest Heaven with all its imagined Circle[s], is called the Sphere. **1727-46** THOMSON *Summer* 204 The face of Nature shines, from where earth seems, Far stretch'd around, to meet the bending sphere. **1847** TENNYSON *Princ.* III. 89 But I An eagle clang an eagle to the sphere. **1854** TOMLINSON *Arago's Astron.* 17 They had remarked that, amidst the general movement of the sphere, one of the stars of the Lesser Bear appeared always to remain in the same position.

fig. **1608** CHAPMAN *Dk. of Byron* III. i. 155 When I appear'd from battle, the whole sphere And full sustainer of the state we bear. *a* **1711** KEN *Psyche* Poet. Wks. 1721 IV. 204 God is our circumambient Sphere.

b. A material representation of the apparent form of the heavens; a globe or other construction illustrating the place and motions of the celestial bodies. (See also ARMILLARY *a.*)

c **1391** CHAUCER *Astrol.* II. §26 The excellence of the spere solide..shewyth Manifeste the diuerse assenciouns of signes in diuerse places. *c* **1400** MAUNDEV. (Roxb.) xxv. 115 Sum has..astrolabres of gold, sum speres of precious stanes. *c* **1532** DU WES *Introd. Fr.* in *Palsgr.* 1039 When I shall teche you the spere. **1551** RECORDE *Cast. Knowl.* (1556) 73 Set your Sphere before you, and first turn it so that bothe the Poles may touch the Horizont. **1674** MOXON *Tutor to Astron. & Geog.* (ed. 3) App. 201 As a Sphear is an Astronomical Instrument, it is a complication of material Circles only, so fitted together that they represent all the imaginary Circles and motions of the eighth Sphear, and the Circles and motions of all the Planets about the Earth. **1701** —— *Math. Instr.* 19 *Sphere*, made of Silver or Brass Hoops, or Rings, representing the Principal Circles of the Sphere (called a material Sphere). **1774** J. BRYANT *Mythol.* I. 341 They had the use of the sphere, and were acquainted with the zodiac. **1821** TURNER *Arts & Sci.* 172 He [Atlas] was..the first who represented the world by a sphere. **1864** SPENCER *Illust. Progress* 172 Then came the sphere of Berosus,..and the quadrant of Ptolemy.

2. a. One or other of the concentric, transparent, hollow globes imagined by the older astronomers as revolving round the earth and respectively carrying with them the several heavenly bodies (moon, sun, planets, and fixed stars).

The number of these was originally supposed to be eight, subsequently increased to nine and finally to ten by the addition of the PRIMUM MOBILE and the ***crystalline sphere*** (see CRYSTALLINE *a.* 5).

c **1374** CHAUCER *Troylus* V. 1809 His lighte gost ful blysfully is went Vp to þe holwghnesse of þe seuenþe spere. *c* **1381** —— *Parl. Foules* 59 After shewede he hym the nyne speris. *c* **1400** tr. *Secreta Secret., Gov. Lordsh.* 65 Yn ordynance of þe heuens and of þe speres, and þe disposicioun of þe planetes. *c* **1450** *Treat. Astrol.* (MS. Ashm. 337) 8b, In the firmament above the viij spere there is a brode cercle ful of sterris. ? *a* **1533** FRITH *Answ. More* (1548) 62 Yᵉ hyghest sphere..with his swift mouying doth violently drawe the inferiour Spheares with him. **1559** W. CUNNINGHAM *Cosmogr. Glasse* 10 This region do in contayne .x. spheres. **1627** FELTHAM *Resolves* I. xxvii. (1628) 86 Some will know Heauen as perfectly, as if they had been hurried about in euery Spheare. **1643** SIR T. BROWNE *Relig. Med.* I. §49, I grant that two bodies placed beyond the tenth Spheare..could not behold each other. **1695** LD. PRESTON *Boeth.* I. (1712) 8 He saw of every wandring Star The various Motions through each Sphear. **1827** POLLOK *Course T.* x, The spheres stood still, and every star Stood still and listened. **1841** LANE *Arab. Nts.* I. 20 This notion of the seven heavens appears to have been taken from the 'seven spheres'.

b. In references to the harmonious sound supposed to be produced by the motion of these spheres; in later use esp. in the phr. ***the music of the spheres***.

c **1381** CHAUCER *Parl. Foules* 61 Aftyr that the melodye herde he That comyth of thilke speris thryes thre. *c* **1400** *Pilgr. Sowle* (Caxton) v. i. (1859) 70 The cause of this melodye is the merueyłous mouyng, and wonderfull tornyng of the spyeres. **1601** SHAKS. *Twel. N.* III. i. 121, I had rather heare you to solicit that, Then Musicke from the spheares. **1606** —— *Ant. & Cl.* V. ii. 84 His voyce was propertied As all the tuned Spheres. **1698** FRYER *Acc. E. India & P.* 191 Our Organs are the Musick of the Spheres to them. **1732** POPE *Ess. Man* I. 202 If nature thunder'd in his op'ning ears, And stunn'd him with the music of the spheres. **1827** POLLOK *Course T.* I, The chiming spheres, By God's own finger touched to harmony. *a* **1882** ROSSETTI *Site Mulberry Tree* 12 Wks. 1886 I. 285 This deaf drudge, to whom no length of ears Sufficed to catch the music of the spheres.

c. Used as a standard of comparison to denote a great difference in rank, intelligence, etc.

1633 MARMION *Fine Companion* IV. i, He may be styl'd a civil gentleman, ten spheres below a fool. **1646** SIR T. BROWNE *Pseud. Ep.* I. iii. (1658) 13 Although their [i.e. tutelary spirits] condition and fortunes may place them many Spheres above the multitude. **1859** MEREDITH *R. Feverel* xv, Erelong he meets Ralph, and discovers that he had distanced him by a sphere.

d. A place of abode different from the present earth or world; a heaven.

1592 *Soliman & Pers.* I. i. 29 *Love.* Now will I vp into the brightsome sphere, From whence I sprung, till [etc.]. **1680** R. GRAHAM *Poems* 2 She..from her lower Circle there Took flight into an higher Sphær. **1817** MOORE *Lalla Rookh, Fireworshippers* IV. 344 If there be some happier sphere, Where fadeless truth like ours is dear. **1863** J. THOMSON *Sunday at Hampstead* II. iv, Being lord in Mohammed's seventh sphere. **1865** LECKY *Ration.* (1878) I. 337 A future sphere, where the injustices of life shall be rectified.

3. One or other of the concentric globes formerly supposed to be formed by the four elements, earth, water, air, and fire; †also, the globe formed by these elements collectively. Now *Hist.*

c **1380** WYCLIF *Sel. Wks.* III. 64 Filosofris..seyn þat undir þe moone is a spere of sotil fier, and in þat is a spere of þe eir, and in eiþer spere of þe watir, and in þe myddil of þe world..spere of þe erþe. *c* **1400** tr. *Secreta Secret., Gov. Lordsh.* 95 þe mone, vinder whom ys þe spere of þe elemenz, þat er fyre, Eyre, water, and erthe. **1423** JAS. I *Kingis Q.* lxxvi, Ascending vpward ay fro spere to spere, Through aire and watere and the hote fyre. *c* **1450** LYDG. *Secrees* 166 To chaunge..from the Erthe the Watir and the Ayr, And parte the Ellementys in ther sperys fayr. **1530** RASTELL *Bk. Purg.* II. xiii, The fyre therin wyll ascend to the proper place and spere of the element of the fyre. **1604** E. G[RIMSTONE] *D'Acosta's Hist. Indies* III. vi. 136 As for the fire, without doubt it hath his sphere (as Aristotle and other Philosophers have held). **1664** POWER *Exp. Philos.* II. 107 By which it most evincingly appears, that water does gravitate in its own Sphære (as they phrase it). **1837** WHEWELL *Hist. Induct. Sci.* I. iii. I. 70 The principle that each element seeks its own place, led to the doctrine, that, the place of fire being the highest, there is, above the air, a sphere of fire.

4. a. With possessive pron. or genitive: The particular sphere (in sense 2) appropriate to, or occupied by, each of the planets (or the fixed stars).

c **1374** CHAUCER *Troylus* III. 1495 Furste schal Phebus falle from his spere. *Ibid.* v. 656 O brighte Lucina,..ren faste aboute thy spere. **1426** LYDG. *De Guil. Pilgr.* 20043 The cours off sterrys alle, Mevnge in ther bryhte sperys. **1430-40** —— *Bochas* IX. xxviii, Lyke Phœbus shyning in his midday spere. **1508** KENNEDIE *Flyting w. Dunbar* 338, I perambalit of Pernaso the montayn, Enspirit wyth Mercury fra his goldyn spere. **1551** RECORDE *Cast. Knowl.* (1556) 7 The Sphere of the Moone whiche is lowest. **1590** SHAKS. *Mids. N.* II. i. 153 Certaine starres shot madly from their Spheares. **1610** —— *Temp.* II. i. 183 You would lift the Moone out of her sphere. **1656** S. HOLLAND *Don Zara* 73, I can call down Luna when I list from her sphere. **1736** GRAY *Statius* i. 55 The sun's pale sister, drawn by magic strain, Deserts precipitant her darken'd sphere. **1764** REID *Inquiry* vi. §1 We can measure the planetary orbs, and make discoveries in the sphere of the fixed stars. **1821** BYRON *Cain* III. i, Suns, moons, and earths, upon their loud-voiced spheres. **1849** M. ARNOLD *The Voice* 4 As the kindling glances..Which the bright moon lances From her tranquil sphere.

transf. **1781** COWPER *Truth* 400 Go—bid the winter cease to chill the year; Replace the wand'ring comet in his sphere.

b. *fig.* Of deities, persons, or things.

c **1500** *Lancelot* 170 The mychty gode of loue, That sitith hie in to his spir abuf. **1509** HAWES *Joyf. Med.* xvi, Now gentyll Jupyter..Sendynge downe trouthe from thy fulgent spere. **1602** SHAKS. *Ham.* I. v. 17 A Tale..whose lightest word Would..Make thy two eyes, like Starres, start from their Spheres. **1621** J. LANE *Tritons Trumpet* (MS. Reg. 17 B 15, fol. 3), But Chaucer shee bidds com downe off his spheare. *c* **1760** SMOLLETT *Ode to Blue-ey'd Ann* 23 When nature from her sphere shall start. **1814** SCOTT *Lord of Isles* VI. xxxvi, He..greeted him 'twixt joy and fear, As being of superior sphere.

c. The orbit of a planet. Also *fig.*

1594 SPENSER *Amoretti* lx, Mars in three score yeares doth run his spheare. *Ibid.*, The spheare of Cupid fourty yeares containes.

5. a. A place, position, or station in society; an aggregate of persons of a certain rank or standing.

In early use directly associated with 4b, and used only of elevated rank.

1601 SHAKS. *All's Well* I. i. 100 He is so aboue me, In his bright radience and colaterall light Must I be comforted, not in his sphere. **1647** CLARENDON *Hist. Reb.* I. §71 Any man who shined in such a sphere in that age in Europe. **1678** *Yng. Man's Call.* 66 You are ready..to..complain, that the orbe and sphære in which you are placed is low and mean. **1724** SWIFT *Drapier's Lett.* vii. Wks. 1761 III. 140, I should think myself obliged in conscience to act in my sphere according to that vote. **1790** BURKE *Fr. Rev.* Sel. Wks. 1898 II. 89 I saw her just above the horizon, decorating and cheering the elevated sphere she just began to move in. **1820** SCOTT *Monast.* xiv, The young lady, who seemed to have dropped amongst them from another sphere of life. **1886** RUSKIN *Præterita* I. vii. 210 The change, for her, was into a higher sphere of society.

b. The group of persons with whom one is directly in contact in society.

1839 J. H. NEWMAN *Par. Sermons* IV. xiii. 235 Each knows little about what goes on in any other sphere than his own. **1848** DICKENS *Dombey* xx, It was an assurance to him that his power extended beyond his own immediate sphere.

6. a. A province or domain in which one's activities or faculties find scope or exercise, or within which they are naturally confined; range or compass of action or study.

1606 SHAKS. *Ant. & Cl.* II. vii. 16 To be call'd into a huge Sphere, and not to be seene to moue in 't. **1635** A. STAFFORD *Fem. Glory* (1869) 167 Divinity not being the spheare wherin my studies move. **1712-4** POPE *Rape Lock* II. 75 Ye know the spheres and various tasks assign'd By laws eternal to th' aërial kind. **1776** ADAM SMITH *W.N.* I. iii. (1904) I. 20 A village is..too narrow a sphere for him. **1853** C. BRONTE *Villette* viii, That school offered for her powers too limited a sphere. **1884** R. PATON *Scott. Ch.* vii. 62 Other labourers in similar spheres had left the gloom unbroken.

b. With possessive pronouns. (Cf. 4.)

1643 R. BAKER *Chron.* (1653) 587 All this while the King had moved within his own Sphear, and had done nothing out of the Realm. **1667** PRIMATT *City & C. Builder* 55 They do buy their materials at cheaper rates than those out of whose sphere it is. **1705** STANHOPE *Paraphr.* II. 266 Not..thrusting into Business above our Capacity and proper Sphere. **1762-71** H. WALPOLE *Vertue's Anecd. Paint.* (1789) IV. 147 Each personage is distinct from the rest, acts in his sphere, and cannot be confounded with any other of the dramatis personæ. **1841** *Penny Cycl.* XXI. 175/1 In his new sphere Seckendorf showed the same activity and good will towards the people as before. **1888** BRYCE *Amer. Commw.* xxxiii. I. 495 Each of which [*sc.* executive and legislative powers] forms its view as to the matters falling within its sphere.

c. In phrases with *in* and *out of*, denoting suitability, or the want of it, to surroundings or environment.

1650 FULLER *Pisgah* IV. i. 10 The Temple, where this glorious Plate shined in its proper sphear. **1670** CLARENDON *Hist. Reb.* XV. §78 He..told them that all the time he was in France he was out of his sphere. **1762-71** H. WALPOLE *Vertue's Anecd. Paint.* (1786) II. 261 He was no sooner at Rome, than he found himself in his sphere. **1832** HT. MARTINEAU *Each & All* i, She is in her own sphere wherever there is grace, wherever there is enjoyment.

7. a. The whole province, domain, or range *of* some quality, thing, etc.

1602 MARSTON *Ant. & Mel.* II. Wks. 1856 I. 25 Ladie, erect your gratious simmetry: Shine in the spheare of sweete affection. *a* **1668** DAVENANT *News fr. Plimouth* I. i, London, the Spheare of Light and harmony. **1704** SWIFT *Mech. Oper. Spirit* Wks. 1768 I. 205 There are three general ways of ejaculating the soul, or transporting it beyond the sphere of matter. **1750** JOHNSON *Rambler* No. 169 ¶5 They see a little, and believe that there is nothing beyond their sphere of vision. **1777** ROBERTSON *Hist. Amer.* (1783) I. 105 In this course, he came within the sphere of the trade wind. **1849** RUSKIN *Sev. Lamps* i. §1. 7 Extending principles which belong altogether to building, into the sphere of architecture proper. **1875** JOWETT *Plato* (ed. 2) IV. 8 The sphere of mind was dark and mysterious to him.

b. Esp. *of* action, activity, operation, etc.

1661 COWLEY *Gov. Oliver Cromwell* Wks. (Grosart) II. 299/2 The bounds of those laws which have been left them, as the sphere of their authority. **1666** DRYDEN *Ann. Mirab.* Pref. *Ess.* (Ker) I. 12 All which, by lengthening of their chain, makes the sphere of their activity the larger. **1729** BUTLER *Serm.* Wks. 1874 II. 154 The sphere of action of..the greatest part of mankind is much narrower than the government they live under. **1783** BURKE *Rep. Aff. India* Wks. 1842 II. 26 The spirit..prevailed not only in Bengal, but seems, more or less, to have diffused itself through the whole sphere of the company's influence. **1836** W. IRVING *Astoria* II. 27 The distrust..had increased in proportion as they approached the sphere of action. **1852** MRS. STOWE *Uncle Tom's C.* xx, Miss Ophelia resolved to confine her sphere of operation and instruction chiefly to her own chamber.

c. Similarly with *a* and pl. Also *ellipt.*

1726 BUTLER *Serm. Rolls Chap.* xv. 309 A Sphere of Knowledge..to our Capacities. **1757** BURKE *Abridgm. Eng. Hist.* II. iii. Wks. (1812) 288 He agreed to an accommodation which..only left to himself a sphere of government. **1862** STANLEY *Jew. Ch.* (1877) I. iii. 61 His history belongs henceforth to a wider sphere. **1867** DK. ARGYLL *Reign of Law* ii. 55 They belong to wholly different spheres of thought. **1879** FROUDE *Cæsar* xiii. 179 Cæsar could only wish for a long absence in some new sphere of usefulness.

d. ***sphere of action, influence,*** or ***interest,*** a region or territory (orig. esp. in Africa or Asia) within which a particular nation claims, or is admitted, to have a special interest for political or economic purposes. Also *ellipt.* and *attrib.*

1885 EARL GRANVILLE in Hertslet *Map of Africa by Treaty* (1894) II. 596 A Memorandum of Agreement for separating and defining the spheres of action of Great Britain and Germany in those parts of Africa where the Colonial interests of the two countries might conflict. *Ibid.* 598 Their respective spheres of influence in the territories on the Gulf of Guinea. **1890** SIR C. W. DILKE *Probl. Greater Britain* v. II. 193 Our South African 'sphere'. **1898** *Westm. Gaz.* 25 July 1/2 There is no necessary opposition between the sphere of influence policy and the 'open-door' policy. **1950** L. FISCHER in R. H. S. Crossman *God that Failed* 223 It provided for a spheres-of-influence division of the areas accessible to Soviet-Nazi aggression. **1973** A. BROINOWSKI *Take One Ambassador* iv. 43 The Japanese themselves are told they can't resort to force, even in what they see as their own sphere of influence. **1981** *Times* 21 Feb. 13/5 A programme of reform [in Poland] sufficiently limited to reassure the Russians that their sphere of influence is safe.

II. 8. a. *Geom.* A figure formed by the complete revolution of a semicircle about its diameter; a round body of which the surface is at all points equidistant from the centre.

1398 TREVISA *Barth. De P.R.* XIX. cxxvii. (1495) 128 The Spere is a fygure shape alle rounde and is pere to Solid in all partyes. *c* **1400** *Pilgr. Sowle* (Caxton, 1483) v. xiv. 107 Alle thre dymensions in a round body nys but the same, and yf ther be ony difference the spere is not parfyte. **1551** RECORDE *Cast. Knowl.* (1556) 17 A Sphere is a sound figure, made by the tournynge of half a circle, tyll it ende where it began to be moued. **1570** BILLINGSLEY *Euclid* XI. def. 12. 316 A Sphere is a figure most apt to all motion, as hauing no base whereon to stay. **1613** PURCHAS *Pilgrimage* I. ii. (1614) 10 Neyther is it yet absolutely round and a perfect sphere. **1698** KEILL *Exam. Th. Earth* (1734) 223 A Sphere.. whose Center of Gravity coincides with its Center of Magnitude. **1753** *Chambers' Cycl.* Suppl. s.v., Parallel planes, which divide the diameter of a sphere into equal parts, divide the surface of the sphere into equal parts at the same time. **1840** LARDNER *Geom.* 204 The diameter..on which the generating circle turns is called the axis of the sphere, and its extremities..are called the poles of the sphere. **1879** *Cassell's Techn. Educ.* I. 394 Draw the complete plan, and project..the external form of the sphere.

†**b.** The containing surface of such a figure or body. *Obs.*$^{-1}$

a **1631** DONNE *Poems* (1650) 7 Shine here to us, and thou art every where; This bed thy center is, these wals, thy spheare.

c. *Math.* The set of all points at a specified distance from a specified point.

1934 C. C. KRIEGER tr. *Sierpiński's Introd. Gen Topology* vi. 77 The set $K(p,r)$ (where $p \in M$, and $r > 0$) is called an open sphere of centre p and radius r. **1959** E. M. PATTERSON *Topology* i. 3 Since all spheres are homeomorphic, we speak of *the* sphere, rather than *a* sphere. **1968** E. T. COPSON *Metric Spaces* iii. 32 If we impose on the set..of all ordered pairs of real numbers the metric $\rho(x,y) = \max\{|x_1 - y_1|, |x_2 - y_2|\}$ the spheres are squares.

9. a. A body of a globular or orbicular form; a globe or ball.

1388 WYCLIF *Isaiah* xxix. 3 And Y schal cumpasse as a round speere, ether trendil, in thi cumpasse. **1432-50** tr. *Higden* (Rolls) I. 227 In the hiȝhte of whom is a spere of brasse conteynenge the bones of Iulyus Cesar. **1575** LANEHAM *Let.* (1871) 49 With obelisks, spheare, and white bearz, all of stone, vpon theyr curioouz basez. **1667** MILTON *P.L.* VII. 355 Of Celestial Bodies first the Sun A mightie Spheare he fram'd. **1747** FRANKLIN *Lett.*, etc. Wks. 1840 V. 188 Our spheres are fixed on iron axes, which pass through them. **1794** MRS. RADCLIFFE *Myst. Udolpho* i, The changing moon forsakes this shadowy sphere. **1831** BREWSTER *Optics* xxviii. 237 If we place a sphere of glass in a glass trough of hot oil. **1842** TENNYSON *Locksley Hall* 164 Lying in dark-purple spheres of sea. **1875** DARWIN *Insectiv. Plants* vi. 95 The fourth [cube] was converted into a minute sphere surrounded by transparent fluid.

fig. **1671** MILTON *Samson* 172 For him I reckon not in high estate Whom long descent of birth Or the sphear of fortune raises. **1701** NORRIS *Ideal World* I. vi. 389 He..can never go out of her sphere, whose center is everywhere, and whose circumference in nowhere. **1853** LYNCH *Self-Improv.* 33 Religion..at last fills the sphere, the eternity of his being.

b. The rounded mass of such a body.

1555 EDEN *Decades* I. I. (Arb.) 67 The iudgement of auncient wryters as touchynge the bignesse of the Sphere and compasse of the Globe. **1663** S. PATRICK *Parab. Pilgr.* xxxvi. (1687) 470 To colour the cheeks of our Apples, and enlarge the Sphere of our Cabbages. **1827** HOOD *Plea Mids. Fairies* i, With a broader sphere The Moon looks down on Ceres and her sheaves. **1830** TENNYSON *Mermaid* 54 All things..Would lean out from the hollow sphere of the sea. **1858** GREENER *Gunnery* 79 Until the flat surface is nearly equal to the diameter of the sphere of the ball.

c. The surface or material of a circular object.

c **1611** CHAPMAN *Iliad* XIV. 154 A girdle, whose rich sphere a hundred studs impress'd.

10. †**a.** = GLOBE *sb.* 4, ORB *sb.*[1] 11. *Obs.*

1387 TREVISA *Higden* (Rolls) I. 235 The riȝt hond holdynge þe spere, þat is þe roundenesse and þe liknesse of þe world. *a* **1548** HALL *Chron., Hen. VIII,* 91 b, A hande of golde holdyng a spere of the worlde.

b. An orb of the mundane system; a planet or star.

1598 MARSTON *Sco. Villanie* x. Hiij b, A hall, a hall, Roome for the Spheres, the Orbes celestiall Will daunce *Kemps Iigge.* **1607** SHAKS. *Timon* I. i. 66 All kinde of Natures That labour on the bosome of this Sphere. **17..** WATTS *Hymn, 'God is a Name of my Soul adores'* ii, Thy Voice produc'd the Sea and Spheres. **1837** BABBAGE *9th Bridgewater Treat.* iii. 57 He has traced the orbits of earth's sister spheres. **1871** BLACKIE *Four Phases Morals* i. 20 We attempt ambitiously to measure the remote movement of the spheres.

III. 11. *attrib.* **a.** In the sense 'of or pertaining to the celestial spheres', as ***sphere-fire, -harmony, -melody, -metal, -music, -song, -tune.***

1609 MARKHAM *Famous Wh.* (1868) 33 Angels learnt their spheare-tunes from my voice. *c* **1630** MILTON *Univ. Carrier* ii. 5 So hung his destiny never to rot,..Made of sphear-metal, never to decay Untill his revolution was at stay. **1820** SHELLEY *Cloud* 71 The sphere-fire above its soft colours wove. **1837** CARLYLE *Fr. Rev.* I. III. vi, The Sphere-music of Parlementary eloquence begins. **1840** —— *Heroes* iii. (1904) 84 The Greeks fabled of Sphere-Harmonies. **1858** SEARS *Athan.* xvii. 143 We..strike out bravely for the sphere-melodies. **1878** BROWNING *La Saisiaz* 24, I shall no more dare to..Pass off human lisp as echo of the sphere-song out of reach.

b. In the sense 'having the form of a sphere', as ***sphere-crystal.***

1882 VINES tr. *Sachs' Bot.* 63 It crystallises in the form of so-called Sphere-crystals,..consisting of crystalline elements disposed in a radiate manner. **1885** GOODALE *Physiol. Bot.* 53 Both forms have been termed Sphæraphides and Sphere-crystals.

12. Comb., as ***sphere-born, -descended, -filled, -found, -headed, -like, -tuned*** adjs; **sphere gap** *Electr.*, a form of spark gap with two spherical electrodes, used esp. in devices for measuring high voltages.

c **1630** MILTON *At a Solemn Music* 2 *Sphear-born harmonious Sisters, Voice, and Vers. **1747** COLLINS *Passions* 95 O Musick! *sphere-descended maid. **1855** BAILEY *Mystic*, etc. 82 The holy image of the *sphere-filled air. **1747** COLLINS *Ode to Liberty* iv. 34 The secret builder knew to choose Each *sphere-found gem of richest hues. **1913** *Trans. Amer. Inst. Electr. Engineers* XXXII. 739 The *sphere gap has been suggested as a standard instrument to be used in the measurement of high voltage. **1962** *Newnes Conc. Encycl. Electr. Engin.* 767/2 The measurement and recording of testing voltages requires either a voltage divider ..or a sphere gap..capable of measuring the peak voltage. **1786** ABERCROMBIE *Arr.* 56 in *Gard. Assist.*, *Sphere headed greater [thistle]. **1567** MAPLET *Gr. Forest* 23 In manner *Spherelike it hath one within an other. **1719** D'URFEY *Pills* V. 119 Last of all there should appear, Seven Eunuchs sphere-like Singing here. **1896** *Pop. Sci. Monthly* Feb. 507 The water..breaks up into spherelike globules. **1636** T. SANFORD in *Ann. Dubrensia* (1877) 50 And how your Swaines will leave Posteritie *Sphære-tuned Sonnets. **1752** H. M[OORE] *To Mem. of Dr. Doddridge* xi, I seem to..catch sweet Music from thy Sphere-tun'd Tongue.

sphere (sfɪə(r)), *v.* Also 7 **sphear.** [f. prec.]

1. *trans.* To enclose in or as in a sphere; to encircle, engirdle, surround. Also with *about.*

1607 CHAPMAN *Bussy d'Ambois* I. i. 31 Spreading all our reaches As if each private arm would sphere the earth. *c* **1611** —— *Iliad* XVIII. 185 When any towne is spher'd With siege of such a foe, as kils mens mindes. **16..** MIDDLETON, etc. *Old Law* v. i, A place at hand we were all strangers in, So spher'd about with music. **1856** MRS. BROWNING *Aur. Leigh* III. 309, I resolved by prose To make a space to sphere my living verse. **1866** W. R. ALGER *Solit. Nat. & Man* II. 43 Mourners, sphered by their dark garb in a sacred and touching solitude.

2. To make into a sphere; to fill up or 'crown' *with* liquor.

1605 B. JONSON *Masque of Blackness* Wks. (Rtldg.) 547/2 An urn sphered with wine. *a* **1849** H. COLERIDGE *Ess.* (1851) I. 272 Who could endure to see the sweet creature take a trumpet and sphere her bias cheeks like fame?

b. *fig.* To form into a rounded or perfect whole.

1615 CHAPMAN *Odyss.* XVIII. 297 That no more my mone Might waste my blood..For want of that accomplisht vertue spher'd In my lou'd Lord. **1622** MASSINGER & DEKKER *Virg. Martyr* IV. i, You, hitherto, Have still had goodness sphered within your eyes, Let not that orb be broken. **1847** TENNYSON *Princ.* IV. 129 Not vassals to be beat,..but living wills, and sphered Whole in ourselves and owed to none.

3. To place in a sphere or among the spheres; to set in the heavens.

1606 SHAKS. *Tr. & Cr.* I. iii. 90 And therefore is the glorious Planet Sol In noble eminence, enthron'd and sphear'd Amid'st the other. **1657** W. MORICE *Coena quasi Κοινὴ* xxii. 215 All that fire which is spheared on high and separate from commixture, is a pure element. **1667** MILTON *P.L.* VII. 247 Light..from her Native East To journie through the airie gloom began, Sphear'd in a radiant Cloud. **1820** SHELLEY *Fiordispina* 26 But thou art as a planet sphered above. **1847** TENNYSON *Princ.* IV. 418, I would have reach'd you had you been Sphered up with Cassiopëia. **1850** —— *In Mem.* ix, Sphere all your lights around, above; Sleep, gentle heavens, before the prow.

b. *fig.* To set aloft or aloof; to place above the common reach.

1615 BRATHWAIT *Strappado* (1878) 190 The minds internall soueraignesse doth sit, As a great Princesse, much admired at, Sphered and reared in her chaire of state. **1649** G. DANIEL *Trinarch., Rich. II,* lxxxii, Maiestie should be sphear'd Beyond the common Eye. **1853** LYTTON *My Novel* VI. iv, The pale reflex and imitation of some bright mind, sphered out of reach and afar. **1861** LD. LYTTON & FANE *Tannhäuser* 14 That so august a spirit, sphered so fair, Should from the starry sessions of his peers Decline.

4. To send *about* in a circle; to turn *round* in all directions.

1648 HERRICK *Hesper., His Age* xix, We'l still sit up, Sphering about the wassail cup, To all those times, Which gave me honour for my Rhimes. **1820** KEATS *Hyperion* I. 117 Open thine eyes eterne, and sphere them round Upon all space.

5. *intr.* To centre *in* something.

1856 MASSON *Ess. Biog. & Crit.* i. 34 The very same soul ..was also related with inordinate keenness and intimacy to all that this life spheres in.

Hence **'sphering** *vbl. sb.* Also *attrib.*

1818 KEATS *Endym.* II. 251 One of those Who, when this planet's sphering time doth close, Will be its high remembrancers. **1877** SYMONDS *Renaiss. It.* vi. 323 How those mighty master spirits watched the sphering of new planets in the spiritual skies.

-sphere, *suffix.* [f. the sb., after *atmosphere.*] Used in names of more or less spherical structures or regions forming part of or associated with the earth (or any celestial object), as BARYSPHERE, BIOSPHERE, IONOSPHERE, MAGNETOSPHERE, etc.

sphered, *ppl. a.* [f. SPHERE *v.* + -ED[1].] Converted into a sphere; formed like a sphere or circle.

1606 SHAKS. *Tr. & Cr.* IV. v. 8 Till thy sphered Bias cheeke Out-swell the collicke of puft Aquilon. **1820** KEATS *Lamia* II. 183 Twelve sphered tables, by silk seats insphered. **1855** M. ARNOLD *To Marguerite* iii, From thy remote and sphered course. **1860** TYNDALL *Glac.* I. xviii. 124 The sphered masses of condensed vapour which issue from a locomotive.

sphereless ('sfɪəlɪs), *a.* [f. SPHERE *sb.* + -LESS.]

a. Having no proper sphere; wandering. **b.** Displaying no spheres; orbless, starless.

1816 SHELLEY *Masque of Anarchy* lxxviii, Let the horsemen's scimitars Wheel and flash, like sphereless stars. **1870-4** J. THOMSON *City Dreadf. Nt.* III. i, When the night its sphereless mantle wears.

sphere'ometer. *rare.* [f. SPHERE *sb.*]

1. *Naut.* (See quots.)

1862 *Catal. Internat. Exhib., Brit.* II. No. 2775, A 'sphereometer', for facilitating the practice of great circle sailing. **1863** A. YOUNG *Naut. Dict.* 361 *Sphereometer,* a contrivance 'for facilitating great circle sailing by obviating abstruse calculations'.

2. = SPHEROMETER (Knight, 1884).

spheric ('sfɛrɪk), *a.* and *sb.* Forms: 6 **spherike,** 6–8 **spherick** (7 **sphear-, sphær-, sphœrick**), 7– **spheric** (8 **sphæric, spherique**). [ad. late L. *sphĕr-, sphæricus,* ad. Gr. *σφαιρικός,* f. *σφαῖρα* SPHERE *sb.*, or F. *sphérique* (14th c.), = It. *sferico,* Sp. and Pg. *esferico.* The sb. corresponds to late L. *sphærica* fem.]

A. *adj.* **1.** Of or relating to the sphere as a geometrical figure. (Cf. SPHERICAL *a.* 2.)

1559 W. CUNNINGHAM *Cosmogr. Glasse* 5, I wil exhort you ..to reade with great diligence..Theodosius of spherike Demonstrations. **1594** DAVIS *Seamans Secrets* II. (1607) 4 Cutting the Equinoctiall at right Spherick Angles. **1704** J. HARRIS *Lex. Techn.* I, *Spherick Geometry*, or *Projection*, is the Art of Describing on a Plane the Circles of the Sphere [etc.]. **1706** W. JONES *Syn. Palmar. Matheseos* 279 Of Spheric Trigonometry. **1798** HUTTON *Course Math.* (1807) II. 51 The spheric segment PFN.

2. = SPHERICAL *a.* 1.

1610 HOLLAND *Camden's Brit.* I. 224 Foure round isles of Sphærick work. **1622** DRAYTON *Poly-olb.* xxviii. 335 Stones of a spherick form. **1673** GREGORY in Rigaud *Corr. Sci. Men* (1841) II. 247, I spoke not so of spheric speculums. **1753** *Chambers' Cycl.* Suppl. s.v. *Lycoperdon,* The blood red sphæric lycoperdon. **1791** E. DARWIN *Bot. Gard.* I. IV. 178 The diving castles, roof'd with spheric glass. **1828** SPEARMAN *Brit. Gunner* (ed. 2) 134 It appears that when the spheric chamber is filled with powder, it has the advantage in point of range. **1855** SINGLETON *Virgil* I. 30 Behold with spheric mass a nodding world. **1883** LANIER *Eng. Novel* 273 The most ravishing combination of tender curves and spheric softness.

3. Of or petaining to, connected with, the spheres or heavenly bodies.

1648 J. BEAUMONT *Psyche* XX. cxl, Those rich Notes.. Whose Comfort makes the spherick melody. **1652** BENLOWES *Theoph.* VII. xlii, No lines, poles, tropicks, zones can thee enthrall, First mover of the Spheardck ball. **1813** T. BUSBY *Lucretius* II. v. 863 What there he [*sc.* the sun] borrows from the spheric skies, To parts opposing his advance supplies. **1844** MRS. BROWNING *Drama of Exile* 2050 We shall leap up..To join the spheric company. **1880** G. MACDONALD *Diary Old Soul* Jan. 20 Then harmony with every spheric song, And conscious power, would give sureness divine.

B. *sb.* (Chiefly *pl.*) The mathematical study or science of the sphere; spherical geometry and trigonometry.

1660 STANLEY *Hist. Philos.* III. I. 53 Geometry is precedent to Sphærick, as Station is to Motion. **1730** CHAMBERLAYNE *Relig. Philos.* III. xxiv. §9 Concerning Spherics, or the Intersections and Angles which the Circles make. **1757** *Phil. Trans.* L. 422 We have (per spherics) sin. AE : 1 (rad) :: co-t. E : co-t. AH. **1820** SHELLEY *Let. M. Gisborne* 94 Conic sections, spherics, logarithms. **1867** BRANDE & COX *Dict. Sci.*, etc. III. 532/1 The practical application of spherics to navigation.

spherical ('sfɛrɪkəl), *a.* and *sb.* Forms: *α.* 6 **sperycall,** 6–7 **sphericall,** 7– **spherical.** *β.* 6–9 **sphærical** (7 **-all**). *γ.* 7 **spheaticall.** [f. as prec. + -AL[1].]

A. *adj.* **1. a.** Having the form of a sphere (or a segment of a sphere); globular.

α. **1523** SKELTON *Garl. Laurel* 1514 Then to the heuyn sperycall vpwarde I gasid. **1570** BILLINGSLEY *Euclid* XI. def. 12. 316 The Sphericall superficies, which is the limite..of a Sphere. **1613** PURCHAS *Pilgrimage* (1614) 508 The Earth being,..at the first forming of it, more perfectly sphericall. **1698** KEILL *Exam. Th. Earth* (1734) 275 He will not suppose ..that the Channel of the Sea is exactly of a Spherical surface. **1753** HOGARTH *Anal. Beauty* 8 Connected circular threads, or lines, forming a true spherical shell. **1805–17** JAMESON *Char. Min.* (ed. 3) 168 Supposing the molecules to be spherical. **1851** S. P. WOODWARD *Mollusca* 38 Completely spherical pearls can only be formed loose in the ..soft parts of the animal. **1871** B. STEWART *Heat* (ed. 2) §67 A kind of flask, either cylindrical or spherical.

β. **1570** DEE *Math. Pref.* Dj b, Perpendiculars drawen to the Sphæricall Superficies of the earth. **1610** HEALEY *St. Aug. Citie of God* 483 A center is that point in the midst of a sphæricall body from whence all lines drawn to the circumference are equal. **1658** SIR T. BROWNE *Gard. Cyrus* iv. 64 Since many..sphæricall seeds arise from angular spindles. ?**1705** BP. BERKELEY in Fraser *Life* (1871) 483 Segments of sphærical surfaces. **1753** *Chambers' Cycl.* Suppl. s.v. *Lycoperdon*, The snow white sphærical lycoperdon.

γ. **1613** *Blundevil's Exerc.* III. II. vi. (ed. 4) 381 Sith the earth and the water..do make together one whole Sphearicall or round body.

b. Of form or figure: Characteristic of a sphere.

1527 THORNE in *Hakluyt* (1589) 257 To set the forme Sphericall of the world in *Plano* after yᵗ true rule of Cosmographie. **1553** EDEN *Treat. New Ind.* (Arb.) 11 Wyth what certayne demonstracions the Astronomers and Geometricians, proue the earth to bee rounde, and the Sphericall or rounde forme to bee mooste perfecte. **1608** TOPSELL *Serpents* 260 They haue eyther a Sphæricall and heauenly, or at least-wise an Ouall forme. **1698** KEILL *Exam. Th. Earth* (1734) 137 The Figure of the Earth which the Theorist rightly affirms not to have been exactly Spherical. **1803** IMISON *Sci. & Art* I. 237 The machine used on this occasion was formed of silk of a spherical figure. **1868** LOCKYER *Guillemin's Heavens* (ed. 3) 96 Its form is not rigorously spherical.

†**c.** *spherical number*, a number whose powers always terminate in the same digit as the number itself. *Obs.* (Cf. CIRCULAR *a.* 10.)

The only spherical numbers are 5, 6, and 10.

1646 SIR T. BROWNE *Pseud. Ep.* 219 As Plato first began, and some have endeavoured since by perfect and sphericall numbers. **1658** —— *Gard. Cyrus* iii. 53 The number of five is remarkable in every Circle, not only as the first sphærical Number, but the measure of sphærical motion. **1704** J. HARRIS *Lex. Techn.* I, *Circular Numbers*, or *Spherical ones*, according to some, are such whose Powers terminate in the Roots themselves.

d. Circular. *rare*⁻¹.

1730 A. GORDON *Maffei's Amphith.* 126 A spherical Building, with Towers at Intervals, as the City Tusculana appears in the Coins of the Sulpician Family.

2. *Math.* **a.** Of lines or figures: Drawn in, or on the surface of, a sphere; esp. ***spherical triangle***.

1571 DIGGES *Pantom.* IV. x. Y i b, The axis and sphericall Diameter of thys Dodecaedron. **1585** BLAGRAVE *Math. Iewel* (title-p.), The whole Artes of Astronomy... Dyalling, Sphericall triangles, Setting figures [etc.]. **1632** J. HAYWARD tr. *Biondi's Eromena* 136 Such like were the reasonings of sundry young Princes of divers Countries, who like sphericall lines came to meete all in one and the same center. **1678** HOBBES *Decam.* Wks. 1845 VII. 162 The arch of a spherical angle is the side opposite to the angle. **1715** tr. *Gregory's Astron.* (1726) I. 476 The spherical Triangle *PLT*. **1824–5** *Encycl. Metrop.* (1845) I. 362/1 A spherical polygon is a portion of the surface of a sphere terminated by several arcs of great circles. **1860** CAYLEY *Math. Papers* (1891) IV. 428 The envelope of XY is a spherical conic. **1861** PARKER *Introd. Gothic Arch.* (ed. 2) Gloss. Ind. 250 *Spherical triangle*, a triangular opening with curved sides, used in clearstory windows. **1886** B. BROWN *Schola to Cathedral* iv. 168 The spherical pendentive, by which dome construction was brought to perfection.

b. Dealing with the properties of the sphere or spherical figures.

1728 CHAMBERS *Cycl.* s.v., Spherical Geometry, the Doctrine of the Sphere. *Ibid.*, Spherical Trigonometry, the Art of resolving Spherical Triangles. **1795** PLAYFAIR *Elem. Geom.* 279 Elements of Plane and Spherical Trigonometry. **1852** BRISTED *Five Yrs. Eng. Univ.* (ed. 2) 220 To make sure of the two questions in Spherical Trigonometry, on the first morning's paper.

c. Of or pertaining to, characteristic of, arising from, the sphere or its properties.

Chiefly in special collocations, as *spherical aberration, excess, harmonic, inversion, projection*, etc.: see the sbs.

3. Of or pertaining to the celestial spheres.

1605 SHAKS. *Lear* I. ii. 134 As if we were..Knaues, Theeues, and Treachers by Sphericall predominance. *a* **1619** FOTHERBY *Atheom.* II. xi. §1 (1622) 310 This sphericall motion of the heauens. **1838** MRS. BROWNING *Isobel's Child* xxxi, A harp whose strings are..tuned to music spherical.

4. ***spherical compasses, lathe***: (see quots.). ***spherical wave***: a wave in which the wave fronts are concentric spheres.

1875 KNIGHT *Dict. Mech.* 2264/2 *Spherical Lathe*, a lathe for turning spheres. **1891** *Cent. Dict.*, *Spherical compasses*, a kind of calipers for measuring globular bodies. **1907** *Chem. Abstr.* I. 1470 The spherical wave of explosion is propagated in a fluid medium according to formulas analogous to those derived for plane waves. **1976** D. ROSS *Mechanics of Underwater Noise* ii. 35 The intensity of a spherical wave is proportional to the square of the pressure.

5. Forming parasynthetic adjs., as ***spherical-bodied, -roofed, -surfaced***.

1804 SHAW *Gen. Zool.* V. II. 432 Spherical-bodied Diodon, with triangular spines. **1946** *Nature* 26 Oct. 26 583/2 The abberations of a spherical mirror are corrected by a single spherical-surfaced meniscus lens. **1977** *N.Y. Rev. Bks.* 13 Oct. 16/1 The spherical-roofed auditorium at CIA headquarters in Langley.

B. *sb.* A spherical body. *rare.*

1652 GAULE *Magastrom.* xxvi. I ij, All these Arts are chiefly conversant about the spherical, or round, whether figure, or number, or motion; they are forced..to confesse, that a perfect round, or spherical, is no where to be found.

sphericality (sfɛrɪˈkælɪtɪ). [f. SPHERICAL *a.*] The quality of being spherical; sphericity.

1669 STURMY *Mariner's Mag.* V. v. 19 The Sphericality of this Terrestial Globe. **1780** HARRIS *Philol. Enq.* Wks. (1841) 362 *note*, Let us, for example, call sphericality (if we may employ such a word) the essential form to a bowl. **1844** G. S. FABER *Eight Dissert.* (1845) II. 250 From an acquaintance with the earth's sphericality. **1878** *N. Amer. Rev.* CXXVI. 375 A knowledge of the sphericality of the earth.

spherically (ˈsfɛrɪkəlɪ), *adv.* Also 6 **sphærically**. [f. SPHERICAL *a.* + -LY².] In a spherical manner; in the form, after the fashion, of a sphere.

1592 T. DIGGES *Descr. Cœlest. Orbs* To Rdr., in L. Digges *Prognost.* M j, The Sunne..giueth lawes of motion to the rest [of the spheres], sphærically dispersing his glorious beames of light through all this sacred Cœlestiall Temple. *a* **1639** WOTTON in *Reliq.* (1651) 215 And it [*sc.* the circle] seemes, besides, to have the approbation of Nature..: For birds do build their nests Spherically. **1690** LEYBOURN *Curs. Math.* 449 It may be concluded..that it is Spherical, because it is Spherically illuminated. **1882** VINES tr. *Sachs' Bot.* 423 The projection..swells up spherically at once.

ˈsphericalness. *rare.* = SPHERICALITY.

1644 DIGBY *Nat. Bodies* iv. §2. 27 Such bodies..do receiue theire figure and limits from such letts as hinder them from attaining to that sphericalnesse they ayme att. **1704** *Phil. Trans.* XXV. 1728 The Sphericalness of the Apple of the Eye in Men. **1730** BAILEY (fol.), *Sphericity*, the Quality of a Sphere;..Sphericalness.

sphericist (ˈsfɛrɪsɪst). *rare.* [f. SPHERIC *a.* + -IST.] (See quot.)

1897 *Athenæum* 29 May 716/1 One long tirade against the sphericists, or those who hold that the earth is round.

sphericity (sfɛˈrɪsɪtɪ). Also 7 **sphæricity**. [ad. mod.L. *sphēr-, sphæricitās*: see SPHERIC *a.* and -ITY. So F. *sphéricité*, It. *sfericità*, Sp. *esfericidad*, Pg. *-idade*.]

†**1.** A spherical body or figure. *Obs.*⁻¹

1625 N. CARPENTER *Geogr. Del.* II. vii. 111 Such a sphericity as hath the same center with the center of the Earth.

2. The quality of being spherical or having the form of a sphere.

1625 N. CARPENTER *Geogr. Del.* I. ii. 38 The reasons..that in generall proue the Sphæricity of the Terrene globe are diuers. *Ibid.* II. v. 70 Forasmuch as this hath little or no proportion to the vast Sphæracity [*sic*] of the Water. **1650** BULWER *Anthropomet.* 20 By some device to have their Heads..rounded, that they may obtain a perfect Sphericity. **1719** *Phil. Trans.* XXX. 1089 The Sphericity of the drops of Rain. **1789** BELSHAM *Ess.* I. xix. 370 Sphericity..is a property belonging to a complete globe. **1809** HUTTON in *Encycl. Metrop.* (1845) III. 476/1 Let two large glasses, of convenient sphericities, be placed at proper distances. **1866** *Cornhill Mag.* Aug. 164 Tastes differ about the colour of pearls... At Bombay those of yellow hue and perfect sphericity are preferred. **1881** *Nature* XXIII. 398 The sphericity characteristic of the liquid state.

b. Of numbers: (see SPHERICAL *a.* 1 c.)

1658 SIR T. BROWNE *Gard. Cyrus* 70 For the stability of this Number, he shall not want the sphericity of its nature, which multiplied in it self, will return into its own denomination.

ˈsphericle. *rare*⁻⁰. [dim. of SPHERE *sb.*, on Latin types.] 'A small sphere' (Webster, 1847).

spherico- (ˈsfɛrɪkəʊ), used as combining form of SPHERIC *a.* in a few terms, as ***spherico-cylindrical, -tetrahedral, -triangular*** adjs.

1778 *Phil. Trans.* LXVIII. 69 The fourth and fifth shots were of a long form, which may be called spherico-cylindrical, as they were cylinders terminated by hemispherical ends. **1839** *Penny Cycl.* XIV. 335/2 Buccal appendages spherico-triangular. **1857** M. J. BERKELEY *Cryptog. Bot.* §636. 556 Sporangia..containing large spherico-tetrahedral spores. **1879** *St. George's Hosp. Rep.* IX. 522 A concavo-convex spherico-cylindrical glass, in preference to a biconvex spherico-cylindrical.

spherics: see SPHERIC B.

spherics, occas. var. SFERICS *sb. pl.*

spheriform (ˈsfɪərɪfɔːm), *a.* Also 7 **sphery-**. [ad. L. type **sphēri-, sphæriformis*: see SPHERE *sb.* and -FORM.] Having the form of a sphere; = SPHERICAL *a.* 1. Also *fig.*

1678 CUDWORTH *Intell. Syst.* I. iv. §20. 378 God was said to be σφαιροειδὴς or Spheryform, by Xenophanes, only..as being..every way like a uniform. **1848** MARTINEAU *Ess. & Addr.* (1891) II. 227 There is something spheriform in the Providence of humanity. **1869** —— *Ess.* II. 176 A thing of spheriform perfection.

ˈspherify, *v. rare.* [Cf. prec. and -FY.] *trans.* To invest with a spherical form; to turn *into* a spherical body. Also **spherifiˈcation**.

1848 POE *Eureka* 74 Several fragments..were..spherified into a moon. *Ibid.* 75 Three moons..having been formed.. by the rupture and general spherification of as many distinct ununiform rings. **1866** R. CHAMBERS *Ess. Fam. & Hum.* Ser. I. 197 The same attractive force which spherifies the tear of morning on the prickle of the thorn.

ˌspherioˈdactyl. *Zool.* Also **-yle**. [a. F. *sphériodactyle* (Cuvier), f. Gr. σφαιρίον, dim. of σφαῖρα sphere + DACTYL.] A gecko belonging to one of Cuvier's subdivisions. Hence **ˌspherioˈdactylous** *a.*

1838 *Encycl. Metrop.* (1845) XXV. 45/2 Spheriodactylous Geckos,..with the tips of the toes terminating in a little smooth pellet. **1840** *Cuvier's Anim. Kingd.* 278 A fifth subdivision is composed of the Spheriodactyles,..which are certain small Geckos [etc.]. **1845** *Encycl. Metrop.* Index, Spheriodactyls.

†**ˈspherist.** *Obs.*⁻¹ [f. SPHERE *sb.* + -IST.] An observer of the spheres.

1604 E. G[RIMSTONE] *D'Acosta's Hist. Indies* VI. iv. 438 Neyther do they call those characters, letters,..but rather ciphers, or remembraunces, as those be which the Spherists or Astronomers do vse.

‖**spheriˈsterion.** *rare.* Also **spheristerium**. [ad. Gr. σφαιριστήριον, f. σφαῖρα ball.] A place for exercise in ball-play. In quot. 1824 *fig.*

1764 R. ADAM *Ruins Palace Spalatro* 11 On the other side of the Cella Media was a Spheristerium.., a room alotted for the different exercises of the ball. **1824** LANDOR *Imag. Conv., Arist. & Callisth.* II. 339 What a spheristerion is opened here to the exercise of informers!

sphero- (ˈsfɪərəʊ), var. of SPHÆRO-, used as combining form of SPHERE *sb.* (cf. F. *sphéro-*) in various terms, chiefly scientific and technical, as **spheroˈcobaltite** *Min.* = *sphærocobaltite* s.v. SPHÆRO-; **spheroˈconic** *Math.*, **spherocyˈlindric** *a.* (see quots.); **sphero-cyˈlindrical** *a.*, (of a lens) having a spherical and a cylindrical surface; **ˈspherogram** *Math.* (see quots.); **ˈspherograph** *Naut.*, a device serving to facilitate the calculation of spherical problems; **spheˈrology**, the science, study, or theory of the sphere; †**spheˈromachy** [L. *sphæromachia*, Gr. σφαιρομαχία] (see quot.); **spheroˈmaniac**, one who is passionately fond of playing at bowls; **spheroˈphyric**, *a. Min.* (see quot.); **ˈspheroplast** *Biol.* [-PLAST], a bacterium or plant cell bound by its plasma membrane, the cell wall being deficient or lacking and the whole having a spherical form; hence **ˈspheroplasting** *vbl. sb.*, treatment (as with an enzyme) that converts cells to spheroplasts; **ˈspheroplasted** *a.*; **spheroˈpolar** *a. Geom.*, **spheroˈquartic** *Math.*, **spheroˈsiderite** *Min.* (see quots.); **sphero-ˈstilbite** *Min.*, a variety of stilbite, having the form of radiated spheres; **spherosyˈmmetrical** *a.*, spherically symmetrical.

Also, in recent works or Dicts., *spherobacteria, -crystal, -mere*, etc.

1889 *Cent. Dict.*, *Spherocobaltite. **1924** *Amer. Mineralogist* IX. 61 Spherocobaltite. **1975** *Soviet Physics—Crystallogr.* XX. 74/1 The reaction involved in the synthesis of $CoCO_2$ has been studied in connection with the problem of growing single crystals of spherocobaltite. **1867** BRANDE & COX *Dict. Sci.*, etc. III. 532/1 **Spheroconic*, the section of a sphere by a quadric cone having its vertex at the centre. **1871** [see *spheroquartic*]. **1825** J. NICHOLSON *Operat. Mechanic* 541 If a cylinder intersect a sphere of greater diameter than the cylinder, the arch is called a *sphero-cylindric arch. **1881** *Sphero-cylindrical [see ASTIGMATIC *a.* 2]. **1962** L. S. SASIENI *Optical Dispensing* x. 264 A toric lens is a curved sphero-cylindrical lens. **1870** CAYLEY *Math. Papers* (1894) VII. 403 In the figures called '*spherograms'..the representation of a hemisphere is all that is required. **1858** *Merc. Marine Mag.* V. 231 The *Spherograph, invented by Mr. Saxby, will shew..the true bearing of the Sun at any time throughout the day. **1867** BRANDE & COX *Dict. Sci.*, etc. III. 532/1 *Spherograph*, an instrument invented for the practical application of spherics to navigation. By its aid any possible spherical triangle can be constructed without dividers or scales. **1656** BLOUNT *Glossogr.*, **Spheromachy*, playing at Tennis, or Bowling. **1906** *Gentl. Mag.* Dec. 631 To us as to all *spheromaniacs, a good game at bowls is the finest sport in the world. **1895** DANA *Man. Geol.* (ed. 4) 77 The kind of mineral is indicated by the terms *orthophyric*, if orthoclase;..**spherophyric*, if containing spherical concretions, etc. **1958** C. HURWITZ et al. *Jrnl. Bacteriol.* LXXVI. 612/2 Lederberg (1956) has referred to these forms as protoplasts. In view of current uncertainty as to the fate of the cell wall in this case, we shall use '*spheroplasts' (McQuillen, 1958, personal communication) as a neutral term. *Ibid.* 613/2 Spheroplasts are osmotically fragile in a hypotonic environment. **1976** *Ann. Rev. Microbiol.* XXX. 42 Conversion of these cells to spheroplasts results in the release of periplasmic proteins into the supernatant. **1973** *Jrnl. Bacteriol.* CXVI. 491/1 *Spheroplasted cells were found to lose endonuclease I from periplasm to surrounding medium. **1965** *Acta Path. Microbiol. Scand.* LXIII. 412 The mechanism of the ..*spheroplasting effect of the incubation temperature is not obvious. **1973** *Jrnl. Bacteriol.* CXVI. 493/2 Spheroplasting does not affect gamma-ray induced DNA degradation in *E. coli CRthy*⁻⁻. **1867** BRANDE & COX *Dict. Sci.*, etc. III. 532/1 **Sphero-polar Reciprocal*, [see] Polar Reciprocal. **1871** CASEY in *Phil. Trans.* CLXI. 585 On this account I have called this species of cyclide..a *sphero-quartic... The sphero-quartic is the intersection of a sphere and a cone. *Ibid.*, A sphero-quartic is the envelope of a variable circle whose centre moves along the sphero-conic, and which cuts the circle J orthogonally. **1836** T. THOMSON *Min., Geol.*, etc. I. 444 Carbonate of Iron. Brownspar, ..*spherosiderite, spathose iron. **1862** DANA *Min.* 247 The globular concretions found in some amygdaloids or lavas have been called spherosiderite. **1843** PORTLOCK *Geol.* 222 At Portrush it [Stilbite] occurs white, (? Spherostilbite,) in implanted globules. **1964** *Progress Reaction Kinetics* II. 299 The ions SO_4^{--} and F^-..both can be considered as fairly *spherosymmetrical.

spherocyte (ˈsfɛrəʊsaɪt, ˈsfɪərəʊ-). *Med.* [f. SPHERO- + -CYTE.] A red blood cell which is biconvex instead of biconcave.

1908 CHRISTOPHERS & BENTLEY in *Sci. Mem. Officers Med. & Sanitary Dept. Govt. India* XXXV. 77 As such cells..are a sign of most important pathological changes, we have thought it desirable to have a name to designate the condition and have termed them spherocytes. **1947** *Amer. Jrnl. Med. Sci.* CCXIV. 255/1 The increased hemolysis seems due to the fact that spherocytes and ovalocytes are removed by the spleen more readily than are normal biconcave disks. **1977** *Lancet* 12 Nov. 1025/2 The blood smear showed many fragmented red bloodcells and some spherocytes.

Hence **sphero'cytic** *a.*, of, pertaining to, or characterized by the presence of spherocytes; **spherocy'tosis**, any spherocytic condition.

1933 F. W. PRICE et al. *Textbk. Pract. Med.* (ed. 4) XI. 775 Acholuric jaundice. Synonyms.—Spherocytosis; congenital hæmolytic anæmia. **1937** E. B. KRUMBHAAR in R. L. Cecil *Textbk. Med.* (ed. 4) 1266 Hemolytic Jaundice. (Congenital, Familial,..Spherocytic Anemia, [etc.]). **1947** *Amer. Jrnl. Med. Sci.* CCXIV. 255/1, 2 families which have a characteristic history and the clinical findings of hereditary spherocytic hemolytic icterus but show no spherocytosis. **1970** PASSMORE & ROBSON *Compan. Med. Stud.* II. xxxi. 3/2 The specific abnormality underlying spherocytic haemolytic anaemia is unknown. **1977** *Lancet* 6 Aug. 305/1 Repeated phagocytosis in lymphoreticular tissues is a feature of many hæmatological disorders, of which hereditary spherocytosis is an example *par excellence*.

spheroid (ˈsfɪərɔɪd), *sb.* and *a.* Also 7–9 **sphæroid**, 8 **spheroide**. [ad. L. *sphæroīdēs*, ad. Gr. σφαιροειδής, f. σφαῖρα ball: see -OID. So F. *sphéröde* (1556), It. *sferoide*, Sp. and Pg. *esferoide*.]

A. *sb.* A body approaching in shape to a sphere, *esp.* one formed by the revolution of an ellipse about one of its axes. ***oblate, prolate spheroid***: see the adjs.

1664 BARROW in Rigaud *Corr. Sci. Men* (1841) II. 39 Were I to compute the portions of a sphere or spheroid, I should only use these rules, out of Archimedes. **1698** KEILL *Exam. Th. Earth* (1734) 95 After the fashion of a broad spheroid which is generated by the rotation of a semi Ellipsis round its lesser Axis. **1777** *Phil. Trans.* LVII. 285 Conceive now a spherical surface..to be carried about with the revolving spheroid. **1829** *Chapters Phys. Sci.* 41 In all cases, the centre of gravity tends towards the centre of the terrestrial spheroid, or to a point very near to it. **1854** MURCHISON *Siluria* vi. 134 [Mudstone] has a tendency to run into large spheroids. **1881** LE CONTE *Sight* 52 The form of a perfect eye is that of a spheroid of revolution about the optic axis.

B. *adj.* = SPHEROIDAL *a.*

1767 *Phil. Trans.* LVIII. 32 As no two measurements.. make the earth of the same spheroid figure. **1875** COOKE *Fungi* 62 Afterwards small sphæroid projections appear at certain points on the mycelium. **1884** JEFFERIES *Red Deer* iii. 42 The spheroid form concentrates more substance in a given measurement than any other.

spheroidal (sfɛˈrɔɪdəl), *a.* Also **sphæroidal**. [f. SPHEROID *sb.* + -AL[1]. So F. *sphéroïdal*, Sp. and Pg. *esferoidal*.]

1. a. Of form, figure, etc.: Characteristic of a spheroid; approximately spherical.

1781 *Phil. Trans.* LXXI. 503 Allowing for the spheroidal figure of the earth. **1802** PLAYFAIR *Illustr. Huttonian The.* 493 To account for its assuming the spheroidal figure. **1845** TODD & BOWMAN *Phys. Anat.* I. 138 The spheroidal form of the cranium. **1890** *Science-Gossip* XXVI. 49/1 While the heavier portions..were being drawn together so as to acquire a spheroidal contour.

b. ***spheroidal condition*** or ***state***: (see quots. 1860 and 1871).

1855 SCOFFERN in *Orr's Circ. Sci., Elem. Chem.* 190 If it be projected upon a capsule of platinum, maintained at a red heat, the salt..will assume the spheroidal condition. **1860** *Ure's Dict. Arts* (ed. 5) III. 732 *Spheroidal state*, the name given by Boutigny to the condition assumed by water when projected into red hot vessels. **1871** B. STEWART *Heat* (ed. 2) §110 Vaporization in the Spheroidal Condition, where a liquid evaporates slowly although in apparent contact with a very hot substance.

2. a. Having the form of a spheroid.

1798 HUTTON *Course Math.* (1807) II. 348 The spheroidal hollow in the bottom of the bore. **1822** J. PARKINSON *Outlines Oryctol.* 77 A stony polypifer, fixed, in a simple hemi-sphærical or sphæroidal mass. **1867** J. HOGG *Microsc.* II. i. 271 A splitting up..into six or eight masses, which become spheroidal sporules. **1878** NEWCOMB *Pop. Astron.* IV. iii. 998 A constant flattening of the spheroidal atmosphere.

Comb. **1891** MOULLIN *Surg.* 138 Spheroidal-celled Cancer ..occurs in the breast,..nose, and palate.

b. In special applications (see quots.).

1805–17 R. JAMESON *Char. Min.* (ed. 3) 209 Spheroidal, when its surface consists of forty-eight convex faces, as in the diamond. **1842** GWILT *Archit.* Gloss., *Spheroidal Bracketing*, that formed to receive the plastering of a spheroid. **1881** MIVART *Cat* 26 Or they may be rounded, forming spheroidal epithelium. **1897** *Allbutt's Syst. Med.* III. 977 Spheroidal carcinoma is rare in the large intestine.

c. *Metallurgy.* = NODULAR *a.* 4.

1920 *Jrnl. Iron & Steel Inst.* CII. 261 The present experiments were undertaken to clear up the cause of the formation of the spheroidal cementite. **1957** *Technology* July 172/3 To-day, nodular or spheroidal graphite cast iron is an article of commercial manufacture. **1977** *Metals Abstr.* X. 1801/1 Tests were made on boronizing spheroidal graphite cast iron (SGCI) to improve surface hardness and wear resistance.

3. Dealing with the properties of spheroids.

1876–7 CAYLEY *Math. Papers* (1896) IX. 197 The fundamental formulæ of Spheroidal Trigonometry are those which belong to a right-angled triangle.

Hence **sphe'roidally** *adv.*, after a spheroidal manner; so as to form spheroids.

1888 *Q. Jrnl. Geol. Soc.* XLIV. 450 The great mass of Mynydd-y-Rhiw..is largely built up of spheroidally jointed rock.

spheroidical (sfɛˈrɔɪdɪkəl), *a.* [f. SPHEROID *sb.* + -ICAL.]

1. = SPHEROIDAL *a.* 2.

1698 *Phil. Trans.* XXXIII. 254 Because..I have already shew'd that the Surface of the Ocean is spheroidical and not spherical. **1713** DERHAM *Phys.-Theol.* VIII. vi. (1752) 378 Its leaves expanded, minister to the germination of globular, and other spheroidical balls. **1787** *Gentl. Mag.* Nov. 993/1 The barrows..are..in general nearly spheroidical. **1823** DE QUINCEY *Lett. Lang.* (1860) 128 Any whatever of the larger spheroidical fruits. **1831** H. LLOYD *Light & Vision* III. i. 265 The bounding surfaces of the refracting media, however, are not spherical,..but spheroidical.

2. = SPHEROIDAL *a.* 1.

1708 J. KEILL *Anim. Secret.* 163 The Globule would be pressed into a Spheroidical Form. **1710** *Brit. Apollo* III. No. 118. 1/2 The Spheroidical Figure of the Earth. **1845** HERSCHEL *Ess.* (1857) 666 The change of spheroidical form.

Hence **sphe'roidically** *adv.*, spheroidally.

1786 JEFFERSON *Writ.* (1859) II. 69 We may, therefore, conclude it impossible for the poles of the earth to shift, if it was made spheroidically.

ˌspheroi'dicity. [Cf. prec. and -ICITY.] The state or character of being spheroidal.

1855 SCOFFERN in *Orr's Circ. Sci., Elem. Chem.* 189 The phenomenon of *spheroidicity*, or calefaction,..must have been noticed. **1867** DENISON *Astron. without Math.* 7 The spheroidicity of the earth or any other planet is usually called its ellipticity.

ˈspheroidism. *rare.* [f. SPHEROID *sb.* + -ISM.] The fact of being a spheroid.

1728 CHAMBERS *Cycl.* s.v. *Earth*, Mons. Cassini has found, that the Degrees of a Meridian grow larger, the further we go towards the Line by one Eight hundredth Part of every Degree; which puts the Spheroidism of the Earth past Question. **1903** *Engineer* 9 Jan. 42/3 Most makers of flash boilers repudiate the idea that spheroidism manifests itself.

†sphe'roidity. *Obs. rare.* [f. SPHEROID *a.* + -ITY.] Spheroidicity.

1740 CHEYNE *Regimen* 5 The Rotundity, or at least the Spheroidity of its constituent particles. **1794** G. ADAMS *Nat. & Exp. Philos.* IV. xlii. 133 The orbit of the earth has an eccentricity, more than double in proportion to the spheroidity of its globe.

spheroidize (ˈsfɪərɔɪdaɪz), *v. Metallurgy.* [f. SPHEROID *sb.* + -IZE.] **a.** *intr.* Of grains, esp. of graphite in cast iron or steel: to undergo conversion into spheroids.

1912 in A. Sauveur *Metallogr. Iron & Steel* App. II. 6 On long heating the pro-eutectoid and pearlitic cementite spheroidize slowly, and neighboring particles merge. **1936** G. F. C. GORDON *Elem. Metallurgy* (ed. 2) ix. 125 The effect of annealing hyper-eutectoid steel, if done with great care, is to cause the network of free cementite to 'spheroidise'. **1939** E. C. ROLLASON *Metallurgy for Engineers* viii. 112 Prolonged annealing induces greater ductility at the expense of strength, owing to the tendency of the cementite in the strained pearlite to 'ball-up' or spheroidize.

b. *trans.* To convert (grains) into spheroids.

1918 *Jrnl. Iron & Steel Inst.* XCVII. 433 The cementite is completely spherodised [*sic*] into round-shaped globules. **1958** *Times Rev. Industry* July 48/3 The high carbon chrome tubes..have to be 'spheroidized' to get them into a good machinable condition. **1978** *Nature* 20 July 237/1 One hypothesis is that the BeO particles were spheroidised (grain refining agents should be angular and sharp-cornered) either during the hot isostatic pressing or during the time when molten.

Hence **'spheroidized** *ppl. a.*, **'spheroidizing** *vbl. sb.*; **spheroidi'zation**, the process of converting to spheroids.

1912 A. SAUVEUR *Metallogr. Iron & Steel* xii. 15 It may well be asked whether..the spheroidizing of pearlite is due to excessively slow cooling. *Ibid.*, Spheroidized pearlite is softer, less tenacious, and more ductile than lamellar pearlite. **1920** *Jrnl. Iron & Steel Inst.* CII. 267 The temperature interval of spheroidisation in low carbon steels is very small, extending only to about 20°. **1923** GLAZEBROOK *Dict. Appl. Physics* V. 341/1 Pearlite which has undergone spheroidising is known as granular pearlite. **1939** E. C. ROLLASON *Metall. Engineers* viii. 118 During subsequent hardening operations the time required to dissolve fine spheroidised cementite is less than for the lamellar type. **1944** GREGORY & SIMONS *Heat-Treatment of Steel* xv. 181 The reheating temperature is below the lower critical or transformation point, as in the spheroidization of the carbide particles in high carbon tool steels. **1958** *Times Rev. Industry* July 48/3 To soften them they are heat treated in spheroidizing furnaces. **1967** A. H. COTTRELL *Introd. Metallurgy* xx. 384 Above about 500°C the cementite particles grow competitively..into larger rounded particles dispersed through the B.C.C. iron matrix, giving a spheroidized structure (Sorbite). **1977** *Industr. & Engin. Chem. Process Design & Development* XVI. 108/1 The process involves the melting and spheroidization of 44–125-μ magnetite grit.

spherometer (sfɛˈrɒmɪtə(r)). Also **sphærometer**. [ad. F. *sphéromètre*: see SPHERO- and -METER.] An instrument for measuring the sphericality or curvature of bodies or surfaces.

1827–8 HERSCHEL in *Encycl. Metrop.* (1845) IV. 567 The 'Spherometer', a delicate species of *calibre* contrived by M. Biot. **1830** —— *Study Nat. Philos.* 355 The elegant invention of the sphræometer,..substituting the sense of touch for that of sight in the measurement of minute objects. **1876** *Catal. Sci. App. S. Kens.* 29 Spherometer for measuring spherical curves, with true gun-metal plane.

Comb. **1903** *Nature* 12 March 442/2 The spherometer-calliper, which, we believe, was used with success in the testing of the instruments employed in the transit of Venus expeditions.

spherosome (ˈsfɪərəʊsəʊm). *Biol.* Also **sphæro-**. [ad. F. *sphérome* (P.-A. Dangeard 1919, in *Compt. Rend.* CLXIX. 1008): see SPHERO- and -SOME[4].] A cytoplasmic liquid droplet or cell organelle found in plant tissues, often associated with hydrolytic enzymic activity; the plant structure answering to the lysosome in animal tissues. Hence **sphero'somal** *a.*

1954 *Biol. Abstr.* XXVIII. 2398/1 The sphaerosomes are real and permanent cytoplasmic structures, and..are neither artifacts nor temporary storage droplets of fat or other lipoids. **1958** *Exper. Cell Res.* XV. 611 The spherosomes are seen as opaque white globules 0·7 μ in diameter, or as dark-rimmed spheres. **1966** *Protoplasma* LXII. 220 In the cells studied..spherosomal motion is rapid during the first 24 hr. **1976** BELL & COOMBE tr. *Strasburger's Textbk. Bot.* (rev. ed.) 16 The nucleus, plastids, mitochondria, spherosomes and golgi bodies remain throughout within the cytoplasm.

spherular (ˈsfɛr(j)ʊlə(r)), *a.* [f. SPHERULE *sb.* + -AR[1].] Having the form of a spherule.

1820 SCORESBY *Acc. Arctic Reg.* I. 429 Having a spherular nucleus, giving rise to radii in all directions. **1822–7** GOOD *Study Med.* (1829) II. 54 Instead of being annular wheels with iron axles, they are spherular wheels with iron tiers. **1889** *Nature* XXXIX. 315/2 Spherular bodies consisting of radially-aggregated fibres of a single mineral.

'spherulate, *a. Ent. rare*[−0]. [ad. mod.L. *sphærulāt-us*.] (See quot.)

1826 KIRBY & SP. *Entomol.* IV. xlvi. 274 *Spherulate*,.. having one or more rows of minute tubercles.

spherule (ˈsfɛr(j)uːl). Also 8 **sphærule**. [ad. L. *sphēr-, sphærula*, dim. of *sphæra* SPHERE *sb.* Cf. F. *sphérule*.]

1. A little sphere; a small or minute spherical or globular body.

1665 HOOKE *Microgr.* 85 A Spherule or Globe. **1713** DERHAM *Phys.-Theol.* 79 *note*, The Particles of Water thus mounted up by the Heat, are visibly Sphærules of Water, if viewed with a Microscope. **1752** *Phil. Trans.* XLVII. 457 Each..was composed of ten or twelve angular and chrystalline spherules. **1813** T. BUSBY *Lucretius* II. VI. Comm. p. vii, The density of the spherules is less and less as the parts recede from the centre. **1852** DANA *Crust.* I. 642 Minute, ruby-red spherules. **1875** M. COLLINS *Sweet & Twenty* I. x, A fountain..throwing its showers of perennial spherules into the air untiringly.

attrib. *c*1790 IMISON *Sch. Arts* I. 215 In using these spherule microscopes, the objects are to be placed in one focus, and the eye in the other.

2. *Bot.* 'A globose peridium, with a central opening, through which sporidia are emitted' (Lindley).

1796 WITHERING *Brit. Plants* (ed. 3) IV. 391 Spherules in heaps, but not confluent, globular, very small.

3. Special Comb. **spherule cell** *Ent.*, a kind of cell in the hæmolymph of certain insects (see quot. 1969).

1935 R. E. SNODGRASS *Princ. Insect Morphol.* xiv. 394 The spherule cells of caterpillars differ in many ways from those of Coleoptera, but they appear to be cells of the same type. **1969** R. F. CHAPMAN *Insects* xxxiii. 677 Spherule cells, found in Lepidoptera and Diptera, are round or oval cells with large, non-refringent, usually acidophilic inclusions filling the whole cell. **1974** [see *œnocytoid* s.v. ŒNO-].

spherulite (ˈsfɛr(j)ʊlaɪt). Also 9 **sphærolite, spherolite, sphærulite**. [f. L. *sphærula* SPHERULE + -ITE[1] 2 a and 2 b; in sense 1, ad. G. *sphærolit* (now *sphärolit*) (A. G. Werner, *a* 1816: see W. G. W. Becker *Journal einer Bergmännischen Reise* (1816) II. p. vi).]

1. †a. *Min.* A concretionary substance found in small spherular masses in certain rocks. *Obs.*

1823 W. PHILLIPS *Min.* (ed. 3) 209 Sphærulite..occurs in small roundish masses, sometimes aggregated in the botryoidal form. *c*1840 *Encycl. Metrop.* VI. 516/1 Sphærulite..occurs in small spheroidal and botryoidal masses imbedded in pearlstone and pitchstone. **1862** DANA *Min.* 357 Spherulite is a kind of pearlstone, occuring in small globules in massive pearlstone. **1889** *Science-Gossip* XXV. 47 Spherulite and pitchstone from Arran.

b. *Geol.* A small spheroidal mass found in rock; *spec.* one consisting of many crystals which have grown radially from a point.

1829 *Trans. Geol. Soc.* II. 202 A previous separation had taken place of the feldspathose spherolites. **1844** C. DARWIN *Geol. Observations on Volcanic Islands* iii. 58 The sphærulites are either white and translucent, or brown and opaque. **1856** *Q. Jrnl. Geol. Soc.* XII. 340 The multiplication and confusion of these crystallites or sphærulites ultimately destroy the glassy character of the substance altogether. **1863** DANA *Man. Geol.* §8. 88 [Pearlstone] often contains spherical concretions, called spherulites, which consist of feldspar with an excess of quartz. **1868** *Mem. California Acad. Sci.* I. 52 Small globular grains, from the size of a pin-head to that of a rifle bullet, called 'sphærolites' by Beudant. **1886** GEIKIE *Class-Bk. Geol.* 214 In some obsidians, little sphærulites of a dull grey enamel-like substance have made their appearance. **1909** J. P. IDDINGS *Igneous Rocks* I. vi. 230 Such spherulites

..consist of radiating prisms of alkali feldspar with submicroscopic graphic intergrowths of quartz. **1931** [see ORBICULE]. **1939** W. H. TWENHOFEL *Princ. Sedimentation* xv. 570 Spherulites with radiate structure are evidently a form of crystal aggregate, whereas those with amorphous internal structure are either excremental particles or colloidal aggregates as glauconite, greenalite, or chamoisite. **1974** A. C. TENNISSEN *Nature of Earth Materials* v. 280 Spherulites have a radial type of internal structure.

c. A small spheroidal mass of crystals or fibrils of any substance, esp. a polymer.

1893 *Mineral. Mag.* X. 97 (*table*) $LiNaSO_4$... Spherulitic... Some of the spherulites have a radial structure. **1911** *Chem. Abstr.* V. 1052 The author describes the peculiar structure of spherulites obtained in cholesterol and β-naphthalene benzoate. **1933** *Bureau of Standards Jrnl. Res.* (U.S.) X. 488 The microscopical examination of the crystals of rubber hydrocarbon indicates that they are spherulites composed of many fine needles. **1963** *New Scientist* 7 Nov. 334/1 Some polymers, like nylon and polystyrene are highly crystalline. They do not normally form single crystals, however, but produce so-called spherulites which are clusters of plate-like or needle-like individual crystals. **1975** *Sci. Amer.* Dec. 99/1 The spherulite, or 'sunburst' microstructure normally results from crystallization under quiescent conditions.

2. *Palæont.* (With capital initial.) A genus of fossil molluscs.

In early use in L. form *Sphærulītēs*.

1834 GRIFFITH tr. *Cuvier* XII. 92 Sphærulites,..where the valves are roughened by irregularly raised plates. **1841** MILLER *O.R. Sandst.* viii. 153 The hippurites, sphærulites, and nummulites of the same formations, in Greece, Italy, and Spain. **1847** ANSTED *Anc. World* x. 241 One such genus is called Sphærulite... They seem most nearly allied to the inhabitants of those univalve shells of which the limpet is the present representative.

spherulitic (sfɛr(j)ʊˈlɪtɪk), *a.* *Geol.* and *Min.* Also **sphærulitic**, †**spherolitic**. [f. prec. (sense 1) + -IC.]

1. Of rocks and other substances: Containing, or composed of, spherulites. Cf. SPHERULITE 1 c.

1833–4 J. PHILLIPS *Geol.* in *Encycl. Metrop.* VI. 761/1 That concretionary structure which reminds us of some kinds of obsidian and sphærulitic traps. **1863** DANA *Man. Geol.* §6. 88 Spherulitic obsidian. Contains small feldspathic concretions. **1889** *Science-Gossip* XXV. 216 Pitchstone (ordinary, banded, and spherulitic). **1893** [see SPHERULITE 1 c]. **1975** *Sci. Amer.* Dec. 100/2 The microstructure of spherulitic polymers is also significantly affected by the phenomenon of secondary crystallization.

2. Pertaining to, characteristic of, spherulites.

1829 *Trans. Geol. Soc.* II. 202 Even where no traces of spherolitic structure are visible, the ribboned arrangement of the rock is owing to the mass of matter having been drawn out in the direction of the zones while still liquid. **1878** LAWRENCE tr. *Cotta's Rocks Class.* 86 Spherulitic or Globuliferous. A texture so named, somewhat similar to the oolitic. **1879** RUTLEY *Stud. Rocks* xi. 184 Spherulitic structure is sometimes developed in artificial glass. **1945** *Trans. Faraday Soc.* XLI. 321 One of the clearest demonstrations of the spherulitic structure was provided by a specimen of polythene. **1962** F. W. BILLMEYER *Textbk. Polymer Sci.* v. 149 The point of initiation of spherulitic growth, its nucleus, may be a foreign particle..or may arise spontaneously in the melt.

3. Having the form or character of a spherulite.

1844 C. DARWIN *Geol. Observations of Volcanic Islands* iii. 64 The little brown sphærulitic globules of the rocks of Ascension. **1888** RUTLEY *Rock-Forming Min.* 130 Sections passing through the centres of these spherulitic bodies. **1933** *Bureau of Standards Jrnl. Res.* (U.S.) X. 486 The appearance and properties of the spherulitic clusters did not depend upon the sample of ammoniated latex from which they had been prepared.

Hence **spheruˈlitically** *adv.*

1975 *Sci. Amer.* Dec. 104/2 A spherulitically crystallized polymer.

spherulitize (ˈsfɛr(j)ʊlɪtaɪz), *v.* *Geol.* [f. SPHERULITE.] *trans.* To render spherulitic.

1889 *Q. Jrnl. Geol. Soc.* XLV. 250 The milk-white fragments of felstone..are, at places, spherulitized, and contain abundant microliths.

ˈspherulitoid, *a.* *Geol.* [f. as prec. + -OID.] More or less spherulitic in structure.

1889 *Q. Jrnl. Geol. Soc.* XLV. 248 Chains of stellate spherulitoid enclosures along the curved surface of a crack.

sphery (ˈsfɪərɪ), *a.* Also 6 **spherie**, 7 **spheary**, 9 **spherey**. [f. SPHERE *sb.*]

1. Of or pertaining to, connected with, the spheres or heavenly bodies; sphere-like.

1590 SHAKS. *Mids. N.* II. ii. 99 What wicked and dissembling glasse of mine, Made me compare with Hermias sphery eyne? **1634** MILTON *Comus* 1021 Love vertue,..She can teach ye how to clime Higher than the Spheary chime. **1816** KEATS *Ep. to Bro. George* 4 In seasons when I've thought No spherey strains by me could e'er be caught From the blue dome. **1818** —— *Endym.* III. 33 A thousand Powers..Hold sphery sessions for a season due. **1867** JEAN INGELOW *Christ's Resurr.* xxii, Hurrying down the sphery way Night flies. **1882** SYMONDS *Animi Figura* 121 Discord that jars upon the sphery tune.

2. Having the form of a sphere. Also *Comb.*

1600 LANE *Tom Tel-troth* 183 Astronomie..hath lost By cruell fate her starre-embroidred coate; Her spherie globe in dangers seas is tost, And in mishap her instruments doe floate. **1871** B. TAYLOR *Faust* III. (1886) 274 This way, ye gloomy, sphery-bodied, monster throng [of phantoms]!

spheterize (ˈsfɛtəraɪz), *v.* *rare.* [ad. Gr. σφετερίζειν, f. σφέτερος one's own.] *trans.* To make one's own; to appropriate.

1779 SIR W. JONES *Let.* in *Parr's Wks.* (1828) I. 109 Remember to reserve for me a copy of your book..I am resolved to *spheterize* some passages of it. **1895** *Academy* 30 Mar. 279/1 By filching a purse or spheterizing a neighbour's spoons.

‖ **Sphex** (sfɛks). *Ent.* Pl. **ˈSpheges** (ˈsfiːdʒiːz) [a. Gr. σφήξ (pl. σφῆκες) wasp.] A genus of digger-wasps; a wasp of this genus.

1797 *Encycl. Brit.* (ed. 3) XVII. 689/2 Sphex, Ichneumon Wasp, or Savage. **1805** BINGLEY *Zool.* (ed. 3) III. 354 Many species of the Sphex are common in England;..their larvæ feed on dead insects, in the bodies of which the parent Spheges lay their eggs. **1857** GOSSE *Omphalos* 319 Immense tribes of solitary Bees, Wasps, and Spheges. **1881** DARWIN *Veg. Mould* 93 A sphex..stocks its nest with paralysed grasshoppers.

attrib. **1807** J. E. SMITH *Phys. Bot.* 196 An insect of the Sphex or Ichneumon kind. **1815** KIRBY & SP. *Entomol.* xi. (1818) I. 351 Similar laborious exertions are not confined to the bee or Sphex tribe. **1897** *Contemp. Rev.* June 869 A sphex-wasp stings into helplessness the caterpillars it has selected.

Hence **ˈsphexide**, a wasp belonging or related to the genus *Sphex*.

1828 STARK *Elem. Nat. Hist.* II. 230 In the Hymenoptera, such as wasps, bees, sphexides, &c. the extremity of the abdomen incloses a sting, calculated for attack or defence.

sphincter (ˈsfɪŋktə(r)). *Anat.* Also 7 **sphyncter**. [a. L. *sphincter*, ad. Gr. σφιγκτήρ band, contractile muscle, f. σφίγγειν to bind tight. So F. *sphincter*, It. *sfintere*, Sp. and Pg. *esfinter*.]

1. a. A contractile muscular ring by which an orifice of the body (in man or animals) is normally kept closed.

Sometimes with Latin genitive of the part, as ***sphincter ani, vaginæ, vesicæ***.

1578 BANISTER *Hist. Man* VII. 97 Some [Arteries] together with certaine Ueynes of *Vena caua*, do flowe to the Muscles called the Sphincter. **1594** T. B. *La Primaud. Fr. Acad.* II. 352 This straight gutte hath this muscle, which the physicions call sphincter. **1623** HART *Arraignm. Ur.* ii. 4 The two muscles called Sphyncters. **1691** *Phil. Trans.* XVII. 819 The Fibres that compose the Sphincter of the Bladder. **1740–1** BERKELEY in Fraser *Life* (1871) viii. 263, I have also known tow, dipped in brandy and thrust into the fundament, to be effectual in strengthening that sphincter. **1759** GOLDSM. *Bee* No. 4 ¶ 26 A glutinous liquid, which..it spins into thread, coarser or finer as it chooses to contract or dilate its sphincter. **1807** *Med. Jrnl.* XVII. 421 In the lower part [of the pupil], the divided fibres of the sphincter receded. **1851** G. F. RICHARDSON *Geol.* (1855) 245 A lung.. which opens and shuts, at the will of the animal, by the action of a muscular sphincter. **1872** HUXLEY *Physiol.* 145 The muscular fibres are so disposed as to form a sort of sphincter around the aperture of communication.

b. *transf.* and *fig.*

1737 M. GREEN *Spleen* 697 Debarr'd the pleasure to impart By av'rice, sphincter of the heart. **1752** *Phil. Trans.* XLVII. 455 The animal [i.e. a coral-insect], when it wanted to come forth from its niche, forced the sphincter at its entrance. **1837** P. KEITH *Bot. Lex.* 335 Their edge has the appearance of being a sort of thickened sphincter capable of opening and shutting.

2. a. *attrib.*, as ***sphincter control, -fibre, -power***; also **sphincter-muscle**, = sense 1.

1615 CROOKE *Body of Man* 422 Euen the muscles haue a motion which we call *Tonicum motum*,..especially the two sphincter muscles. **1676** *Phil. Trans.* XI. 603 His sence was ..that they might be rather numerous, though small, Sphincter-muscles. **1774** GOLDSM. *Nat. Hist.* (1824) III. 15 A bony partition, which is closed by a sphincter muscle on the inside. **1808** BARCLAY *Musc. Motions* 463 Sphincter muscles cannot open themselves. **1876** CURLING *Dis. Rectum* 169 A large part of the sphincter muscle may be excised without seriously weakening the retentive power of the anus. **1879** *St. George's Hosp. Rep.* IX. 348 The margin of this opening possessed slight sphincter power. **1897** *Allbutt's Syst. Med.* III. 365 A spasm of the sphincter fibres at the lower end of the circular coat of the œsophagus. **1949** M. MEAD *Male & Female* v. 115 They [*sc.* Samoan children] do not need to fear that they themselves, by their unsteady sphincter control,..will endanger the normal order of existence. **1957** *Psychoanal. Rev.* XLIV. 121 The attainment of anal sphincter control in childhood is so fundamental in human socialization that the surgical destruction of anal sphincter control must result in a severe emotional and social disruption.

b. *Comb.*, as ***sphincter-contracting, -inhibitory, -like*** adjs.

1841 *Penny Cycl.* XXI. 160/1 The closing appears to be effected by sphincter-like muscles. **1899** *Allbutt's Syst. Med.* VI. 775 A sphincter-contracting centre, closely associated with a sphincter-inhibitory centre.

Hence **ˈsphinctered** *a.*, possessing a sphincter (of a specified kind); **sphincˈteric**, **sphincˈterial**, **ˈsphinctrate** *adjs.*, of or pertaining to, of the nature of, a sphincter.

Recent Dicts. give *ˈsphincteral*.

1883 DUNCAN *Clin. Lect. Dis. Women* (ed. 2) viii. 54 This is a sphincteric opening, and during the child-bearing period of life it must open and close. **1884** C. B. KELSEY *Dis. Rectum & Anus* v. 106 No amount of sphincteric contraction would close it. **1887** SOLLAS in *Encycl. Brit.* XXII. 415 Which communicates through a sphinctrate aperture. **1889** *Cent. Dict.*, Sphincterial. **1963** R. P. DALES *Annelids* i. 32 A terminal bladder or vesicle closed by means of a sphinctered nephridiopore. **1965** AUDEN *About House* (1966) 27 A second childhood, petulant, weak-sphinctered In a cheap hotel. **1976** R. POUND *A. P. Herbert* xxvi. 298 Its equability, with or without the reinforcement of vitamins, deep breathing, and the eccentric sphincterial discipline, may have added to his length of days.

sphincterotomy (sfɪŋktəˈrɒtəmɪ). *Surg.* [f. SPHINCTER: see -TOMY.] The surgical cutting of or into a sphincter.

1890 in BILLINGS *Med. Dict.* **1892** A. DUANE tr. *Fuchs's Textbk. Ophthalm.* IV. iii. 726 Stellwag's operation is called oblique blepharotomy or sphincterotomy. **1922** J. JOYCE *Let.* 4 Oct. (1966) III. 67 He says that..a slight operation —not iridectomy or iridotomy but sphincterotomy will probably restore a great part of former vision. **1977** *Proc. R. Soc. Med.* LXX. 160/2, I do not think this particular technique is suitable for simple procedures such as cholecystectomy or sphincterotomy.

ˈsphingal, *a.* *rare.* [f. *sphing-* stem of SPHINX.] Resembling that of a sphinx.

1851 B. W. BALL *Elfin-Land* I. 21 No sphingal countenance more calm, Than his majestic face.

†**ˈsphingian**, *a.* *Obs.*[−1] In 7 **sphyngian**. [f. as prec.] = SPHINXIAN *a.*

1620 BP. HALL *Hon. Marr. Clergy* I. iv. (1628) 744 These sphyngian riddles are for better heads.

sphingid (ˈsfɪndʒɪd), *sb.* and *a.* *Ent.* [f. mod.L. family name *Sphingidæ*, f. *Sphinx* SPHINX, adopted as a generic name by Linnæus (*Systema Naturæ* (ed. 6, 1748) 63): see -ID[1].] **A.** *sb.* A hawk-moth of the family Sphingidæ. **B.** *adj.* Of or pertaining to an insect of this kind.

1911 *Trans. Zool. Soc. London* XX. 85 Almost the entire surface is thinly coated with fine, short, white hair, an exceptional feature with Sphingid larvæ. *Ibid.* 95 *Erinnyis ello*... The commonest Sphingid of tropical America. **1930** *Proc. Entomol. Soc.* V. 24 The caudal horn was movable in many Sphingid caterpillars. **1933** *Discovery* Apr. 125/1 Eye-spots..occur particularly in sphingids. **1973** *Nature* 16 Mar. 205/2 Recently internal ocelli have been reported in several adult sphingids. **1981** G. KEYNES *Gates of Memory* iii. 41 A boy in another House had been fortunate enough to catch a specimen of an extremely rare immigrant sphingid moth.

Sphingine (ˈsfɪndʒaɪn), *a.* *rare*[−1]. [f. *sphing-* stem of SPHINX + -INE[1].] Sphinx-like; characteristic of a Sphinx; enigmatic, inscrutable.

1925 A. HUXLEY *Those Barren Leaves* II. i. 86, I would put on..my most Sphingine smile.

sphingo- (ˈsfɪŋgəʊ). *Biochem.* Comb. form of Gr. Σφίγξ, stem Σφιγγ- SPHINX (see quot. 1881 for *sphingosin*), used in the names of a number of related compounds isolated from the brain and nervous tissue, as **sphingoˈlipid(e**, any naturally occurring fatty acid derivative of a sphingosine; hence **ˌsphingolipiˈdosis** (see quot. 1962); **sphingoˈmyelin** [MYELO-], any of a number of complex phospholipids which are phosphoryl choline derivatives of *N*-acyl sphingosines; **ˈsphingosine** (formerly -**in**), a colourless crystalline base, $C_{18}H_{37}NO_2$, or any of various homologues and derivatives of this, which combined as sphingolipids occur widely in brain and nervous tissue.

1947 H. E. CARTER et al. in *Jrnl. Biol. Chem.* CLXIX. 77 Among the lipide constituents [of nerve tissue] there are at least three, the cerebrosides.., sphingomyelins.., and gangliosides.., which are derivatives of the organic base sphingosine. Sphingosine may also be present in other compounds... As a matter of convenience it is proposed that the term sphingolipide be used to designate these substances. **1978** J. R. HOLUM *Org. & Biol. Chem.* xi. 225 The acyl units in the acylamido parts of the sphingolipids are not the usual fatty acids found in neutral fats. **1962** KNUDSON & KAPLAN in Aronson & Volk *Cerebral Sphingolipidoses* 395 The sphingolipidoses are hereditary diseases in which there is an accumulation of sphingolipids in one or more tissues of the body... There are at least three enzyme defects among the sphingolipidoses. **1976** *Adv. Exper. Med. & Biol.* LXVIII. 9 (*caption*) Examples of early prenatal diagnoses carried out with the present microtechniques in pregnancies at risk for sphingolipidoses. **1883** J. L. W. THUDICHUM in *12th Ann. Rep. Local Govt. Board 1882–3*: *Rep. Med. Officer 1882* App. B. No. 3. 221, I have for the purposes of the present research isolated and analysed two representatives of this remarkable class of bodies, one *amidomyelin*..another *sphingomyelin*, which was found to be..a genuine educt and principle of the brain. **1920** [see CEPHALIN[2]]. **1946** *Biol. Rev.* XXVI. 285 Sphingomyelins are phosphatides in which the sphingosine or a closely related base is bound by an NH−CO linkage to a fatty acid..and by an ester linkage to choline phosphoric acid. **1973** Sphingomyelin [see LECITHIN]. **1881** J. L. W. THUDICHUM in *Ann. Chem. Med.* II. 18 A body remained insoluble which was of an alkaloidal nature, and to which, in commemoration of the many enigmas which it presented to the inquirer, I have given the name of *Sphingosin*. **1908** HALL & DEFREN tr. *Abderhalden's Text-bk. Physiol. Chem.* ii. 20 On being subjected to hydrolysis this substance took up two molecules of water and formed one molecule of cerebronic acid, one of sphingosine and one of galactose. **1957** [see CEREBROSIDE]. **1968** A. WHITE et al. *Princ. Biochem.* (ed. 4) iv. 73 Although the above C_{18} sphingosines are most abundant in sphingolipids, other homologous C_{16}, C_{17}, C_{19}, and C_{20} sphingosines also are found among the naturally occurring sphingolipids.

†**sphingture**, obs. variant of SPHINCTER.

1612 WOODALL *Surg. Mate* Wks. (1653) 6 The Sphingtures or gathering muscles of the fundament, will not of themselves without resistance be opened.

Sphinx (sfɪŋks). Pl. **sphinges** (ˈsfɪndʒiːz), **sphinxes**. Also 5 **spynx**, 7–8 (9) **sphynx**. [a. L. *Sphinx*, a. Gr. *Σφίγξ* (stem *Σφιγγ-*), app. f. *σφίγγειν* to draw tight. So F. *sphinx*, It. *sfinge*, Sp. and Pg. *esfinge*.]

In generalized senses usually with small initial; otherwise with capital S.

1. a. *Gr. Mythol.* A hybrid monster, usually described as having the head of a woman and the (winged) body of a lion, which infested Thebes until the riddle it propounded was solved by Œdipus; also, any monster of a similar form and character.

1420–2 LYDG. *Thebes* I. 624 And as I rede, Spynx this monstre hight. *Ibid.* II. 2158 At thylke mount wher that Spynx was slawe. **1581** SIDNEY *Apol. Poet.* (Arb.) 55 What that before tyme was, I thinke scarcely Sphinx can tell. **1588** SHAKS. *L.L.L.* IV. iii. 342 Subtill as Sphinx, as sweet and musicall, As bright Apollos Lute. **1615** G. SANDYS *Trav.* 131 The vpper part of a Sphinx resembled a maide, and the lower a Lion. **1649** DRUMM. OF HAWTH. *Poems* Wks. (1711) 40/2 Geryons, Harpyes, Dragons, Sphinges Strange, Wheel, where in spacious gires the fume doth range. **1729** MANDEVILLE *Fab. Bees* II. 266 Do you lay any Stress upon Sphinxes, Basilisks, flying Dragons, and Bulls that spit Fire? **1756–7** tr. *Keysler's Trav.* (1760) III. 146 Several relievo's of plaster, representing a sphynx, a griffin, and other imaginary animals. **1820** SHELLEY *Prometh. Unb.* I. 347 Thou Sphinx, subtlest of fiends Who ministered to Thebes.. unnatural love, and more unnatural hate. **1883** *Fortn. Rev.* Feb. 193 The sphinx had an awkward habit of swallowing up those who could not guess her riddles.

b. *transf.* A person characterized by some quality of the Sphinx; *esp.* one who propounds or presents a difficult question or problem.

1603 B. JONSON *Sejanus* II. iii. [III. i.], I am not Oedipus inough, To vnderstand this Sphynx. **1611** SPEED *Hist. Gt. Brit.* IX. xii. §8. 670/1 The Sphynx, who is said to be the Author of this ambiguous Riddle,.. was Adam de Torleton. **1808** *Sporting Mag.* XXX. 209 A lady named Gibson, one of the sphynxes of Fleet-market. **1857** KINGSLEY *Ten Y. Ago* xxvii, He was a sphinx, a chimera, a lunatic broke loose, who took unintelligible delight in getting wet, and dirty. **1884** *Bath Herald* 25 Oct. 3/2 Mr. Dodson has for many years been a political sphinx.

c. *fig.* A thing or subject of a mysterious or inscrutable nature.

a **1610** HEALEY *Cebes* (1636) 110 For ignorance is a Sphynx unto man. **1678** *Yng. Man's Call.* 46 It is the philosophers sphinx, which however it may seem to propound toyes, yet devoureth all (as that did) who fall unwisely into its imbraces. **1856** R. A. VAUGHAN *Mystics* (1860) I. 13 History fairly questioned is no Sphinx.

2. a. A sculptured, carved, or moulded figure of an imaginary creature having a human head and breast combined with the body of a lion.

The Egyptian sphinxes usually exhibit male heads and wingless bodies; in the usual Greek type the head is female and the body winged.

α. **1579–80** NORTH *Plutarch* (1896) V. 320 He had a Sphinx of Yvory geven him by Verres. **1738** LD. CHESTERF. in *Common Sense* 4 Mar. (1739) 33 A Sphynx of curious Workmanship and of inestimable Value. **1789** MRS. PIOZZI *Journ. France* I. 405 There is a sphinx upon it.. mighty clearly expressed. **1865** LIVINGSTONE *Zambesi* iv. 97 The southern end of the range rises in the form of an unfinished sphinx. **1877** AMELIA B. EDWARDS *Up Nile* Pref. p. xv, The stone lips of a colossal Sphinx, buried to the neck in sand.

β. **1603** HOLLAND *Plutarch's Mor.* 1290 Setting up ordinarily before the.. gates of their temples, certaine Sphinges. **1678** CUDWORTH *Intell. Syst.* 315 With which agreeth also the Testimony of Plutarch, he adding a further Confirmation thereof from the Egyptian Sphinges. **1863** LD. LYTTON *Ring Amasis* II. 32 The beautiful serious sphinges, with their smooth lion-limbs, and serene human faces. **1877** *Times* 17 Feb. 4/5 There are handles ornamented with bull's heads, winged sphinges [etc.].

γ. **1651** CLEVELAND *Poems* 31 As Temples use to have their Porches wrought With Sphynxes, creatures of an antick draught. **1766** WALPOLE *Lett.* (1857) IV. 492 Two sphynxes in stone, with their heads coquetly reclined. **1814** HEYNE *Tracts on India* 336 In the Conjeveram pagoda there are pillars resting on sphynxes. **1888** F. HUME *Mme. Midas* I. iii, The motionless calm which the old Egyptians gave to their sphinxes.

b. *spec.* The colossal stone image of this kind near the pyramids of El-Gizeh in Egypt.

1613 PURCHAS *Pilgrimage* VI. i. I. 467 Not farre hence is that Sphynx, a huge Colosse, with the head of a Maid, and bodie of a Lion. **1687** A. LOVELL tr. *Thevenot's Trav.* I. II. v. 134 It is said, that this Sphynx, so soon as the Sun was up, gave responses to any thing it was consulted about. **1797** *Encycl. Brit.* (ed. 3) XV. 681/2 The great sphynx was in his [Pliny's] time upwards of 62 feet above the surface of the ground. **1820** KEATS *Hyperion* I. 31 Her face was large as that of Memphian sphinx. **1869** RAWLINSON *Anc. Hist.* 68 Thothmes IV, who cut the great sphinx near the Pyramids. **1879** LOFTIE *Ride in Egypt* 162 To some the Sphinx is part of the great 'Time-passage' theory.

3. A kind of ape; in mod. use, a sphinx-baboon.

1607 TOPSELL *Four-f. Beasts* 17 The Sphinx or Sphinga is of the kinde of Apes... In the promontory of the farthest Arabia, neer Dira, are Sphinges, and.. Lyons. **1613** PURCHAS *Pilgrimage* VI. i. I. 466 Other Apes there are store, .. Satyres with feet like Goats, and Sphynges, with breasts like women and hairie. **1871** *Cassell's Nat. Hist.* I. 148 This excited the indignation of the Sphinx, who trotted off to the further end of his cage.

4. An insect belonging to the lepidopterous genus *Sphinx* or to the family represented by this, so called from the attitude frequently assumed by the caterpillar.

1753 *Chambers' Cycl.* Suppl., *Sphinx*,.. a name given by Mr. Reaumur to a very singular species of caterpillar. **1816** KIRBY & SP. *Entomol.* xxiii. (1818) II. 369 The most remarkable insects in this respect are the sphinxes, and from this they doubtless took their name of *hawk-moths*. **1824** FORSYTH *Fruit Trees* xxvii. 396 The Sphinges appear either early in the morning, or after sunset. **1868** *Rep. U.S. Commissioner Agric.* (1869) 310 This order [*sc.* Lepidoptera] has been divided into three groups, called.. butterflies, sphinges, and moths. **1882** *Cassell's Nat. Hist.* VI. 25 The larvæ of many Sphinges, etc., construct a cell in the ground.

5. a. *attrib.*, as ***sphinx-enigma, -face, -figure, -form, -look, -question, -riddle.***

1832 [G. LONG] *Egypt. Antiq.* I. x. 218 So great is the variety of forms in which sphinx-figures occur. *Ibid.* 225 Some light on the origin of the sphinx-form. **1837** CARLYLE *Fr. Rev.* I. VI. i, What Sphinx-questions; which the distracted world.. must answer or die! **1862** —— *Fredk. Gt.* XIII. i, One must act, and act at once; but it is a perfect sphinx-enigma to say How. **1886** W. GRAHAM *Social Probl.* 41 The veritable sphinx-riddle which not to solve is to be destroyed. **1900** *Cent. Mag.* Feb. 510/2 You still might see .. the sphinx face of the old West, smiling, mysterious, alluring. **1923** D. H. LAWRENCE *Ladybird* 230 The queer, blank, sphinx-look with which he gazed out beyond himself.

b. *Comb.*, as ***sphinx-faced, -guarded, -lined.***

1856 KANE *Arct. Expl.* I. vii. 69, I have.. heard that the close approach to land of these sphinx-faced monsters [*sc.* walrus] portends a storm. **1857** J. HAMILTON *Less. fr. Gt. Biogr.* 88 The Pharaohs sleep grandly in their sphinx-guarded sepulchres. **1865** J. H. INGRAHAM *Pillar of Fire* III. viii. 383 [Pharaoh] proceeded.. along the sphinx-lined avenue to the terrace of the Nile.

c. Special combs.: **sphinx-baboon**, the Guinea Baboon (*Cynocephalus* or *Papio sphinx*); **sphinx moth**, = sense 4.

1839 DARWIN *Surv. Voy. Nat.* III. ii. 37 Whenever I saw these little creatures.. I was reminded of the sphinx moths. **1871** *Cassell's Nat. Hist.* 149 The Sphinx Baboon.. is commonly seen in menageries, and stuffed in museums. **1939** DUNCAN & PICKWELL *World of Insects* x. 168 The caterpillars of the family of sphinx moths.. have earned their name of 'sphinx' by their habit of rearing up their front ends, drawing in their heads, and thus assuming a threatening attitude. **1972** *Sci. Amer.* June 73/1 The larger sphinx moths weigh from two to six grams.

Hence **ˈsphinxian** *a.*, of or pertaining to the Sphinx; sphinx-like. **ˈsphinxily** *adv.*, in a sphinx-like manner. **ˈsphinxine** *a.*, characteristic of the Sphinx; enigmatical, mysterious. **ˈsphinxineness**, sphinx-like obscurity.

1598 MARSTON *Pygmal., Sat.* ii. 142 And in such pitchy clouds enwrapped beene His *Sphinxian riddles, that old Oedipus Would be amaz'd. **1746** *Brit. Mag.* 53 Like the Monster represented in the Sphinxian Riddle. **1889** *Jrnl. Educ.* 1 Nov. 575/1 The Œdipus to this sphinxian enigma seems unlikely to make his appearance. **1889** *Pall Mall G.* 25 Nov. 4 Mr. Marston smiled *sphinxily. **1845** MRS. BROWNING in *Lett. R. Browning & E. B. Barrett* (1899) I. 53 People say of you and of me.. that we love the darkness and use a *sphinxine idiom in our talk. **1845** —— *Lett.* (1897) I. 254 The sin of Sphinxine literature I admit. Have I not struggled hard to renounce it? *Ibid.*, Tell me honestly.. if anything like the *Sphinxineness of Browning, you discover in me.

ˈsphinx-like, *a.* [f. prec.] Resembling (that of) the Sphinx; *esp.* enigmatical, mysterious, inscrutable, insoluble.

1837 [MISS MAITLAND] *Lett. Madras* (1843) 136 She was an immense creature, but young, and rather a good sphinx-like face. **1839** BAILEY *Festus* 137 The sphinx-like heart.. Loathes life the moment that life's riddle is read. **1885** 'MRS. ALEXANDER' *At Bay* iv, 'I know nothing. I have seen very little. I suspect every thing.' 'What a sphinx-like reply.'

sphondyle, variant of SPONDYLE.

ˈsphondyloid, *sb.* and *a.* [f. Gr. *σφόνδυλος*, var. of *σπόνδυλος*: see SPONDYLE.]

a. A solenoid. **b.** Solenoidal.

1852 FARADAY *Exper. Res. Electr.* (1855) III. 424 The magnet, with its surrounding sphondyloid of power. *Ibid.* 428 When.. a magnet.. is made into a horseshoe form, we see at once that the lines of force and the sphondyloids are greatly distorted. *Ibid.* 422 *note*, The sphondyloid body.

ˈsphragid(e. *rare*⁻⁰. [ad. L. *sphrāgīd-*, *sphrāgis* or Gr. *σφραγῖδ-*, *σφραγίς* seal, sealing earth.] Lemnian earth, sigillated earth.

1828–32 WEBSTER, *Sphragid* (**1847** *Sphragide*).

‖**sphragistes** (sfrəˈdʒɪstiːz). [a. Gr. *σφραγιστής* sealer: cf. next.] An Egyptian priest who kept and used the temple seal.

1847 LEITCH tr. *C. O. Müller's Anc. Art* §230. 201 The Egyptians used many signet rings. Even sacrifices were sealed by the sphragistes. **1858** BIRCH *Anc. Pottery* I. 28 One of whom was also a sphragistes or sealer.

sphragistic (sfrəˈdʒɪstɪk), *sb.* and *a.* [ad. F. *sphragistique* or Gr. *σφραγιστικ-ός*, f. *σφραγίς* seal.]

A. *sb. pl.* The scientific study or knowledge of seals or signet rings.

1836 *Partington's Brit. Cycl., Lit.*, etc. III. 837/1 *Sphragistics*, a branch of diplomatics which teaches the history of seals and the means which they afford of determining the genuineness of the documents to which they are attached.

B. *adj.* Of or pertaining to, relating to or dealing with, seals or signet rings.

1884 *Athenæum* 10 May 602 His unrivalled knowledge of sphragistic archæology. **1887** WYON *Gt. Seals Eng.* p. xvii, The seals follow and illustrate the.. successive styles of English sphragistic art.

sphragitid, *a. rare*⁻¹. [ad. F. *sphragitide*, ad. Gr. *σφραγῖτις*, f. *σφραγίς* seal.] = SIGILLATED *ppl. a.*

1694 MOTTEUX *Rabelais* IV. liv. (1737) 224 The Sphragitid Earth [is produced] at Lemnos.

ˈsphygmic, *a.* and *sb. rare.* Also 8 **sphugmick**. [ad. mod.L. *sphygmicus*, Gr. *σφυγμικός*, f. *σφυγμός*: see next.] **a.** *sb. pl.* The study of the pulse. **b.** *adj.* 'Pertaining to the pulse, or to the knowledge or doctrine of the pulse' (Craig, 1849).

1707 FLOYER *Physic. Pulse-Watch* 336 The Ignorance of the Europeans in the Sphugmicks Science.

sphygmo- (ˈsfɪgməʊ), a. Gr. *σφυγμο-*, combining form of *σφυγμός* pulse (f. *σφύζειν* to beat or throb), used in various scientific terms: **sphygmodyˈnameter** (see quot.); **ˈsphygmogram**, a diagram of pulse-beats as traced by the sphygmograph; **ˈsphygmograph**, an instrument which records the movements of the pulse by means of tracings; hence **ˈ*sphygmograph*** vb.; **sphygmoˈgraphic** *a.*, of or pertaining to, effected or produced by, the sphygmograph; **sphygmoˈgraphically** *adv.*; **sphygˈmography**, scientific description of the pulse or registration of pulse-beats; **sphygmomaˈnometer**, an instrument for measuring the force of the pulse; **ˌsphygmomanoˈmetric** *a.*; **ˌsphygmomaˈnometry**, the use of a sphygmomanometer; **sphygˈmometer**, an instrument for exhibiting or measuring the force or rate of the pulse; **sphygmoˈmetric** *a.*, relating to measurement of the pulse; **sphygˈmometry**; **ˈsphygmophone**, an instrument by which pulsations are rendered audible; **sphygmoˈphonic** *a.*, pertaining to the sound of pulsations; **ˈsphygmoscope**, an instrument for examining the pulse.

1876 *Catal. Sci. App. S. Kens.* 521 **Sphygmodynameter*, an apparatus for estimating the pressure of the blood [etc.]. **1887** *Brit. Med. Jrnl.* 14 May 1045/1 Dr. Suckling also showed a number of *sphygmograms. **1898** *Allbutt's Syst. Med.* V. 815 A pamphlet.. giving descriptions and sphygmograms of such pulses in hysterical cases. **1860** *Illustr. Lond. News* 14 Apr. 362/3 A new *sphygmograph or pulse register. **1875** PAYNE *Jones & Siev. Pathol. Anat.* 259 That there is an increased arterial tension.. is also demonstrated by the sphygmograph. **1897** *Allbutt's Syst. Med.* IV. 389 The educated finger, or I should say fingers, are as instructive as the sphygmograph. **1870** *Gentl. Mag.* Aug. 378 The doctors.. measuring, *sphygmographing, and generally making a tool of experiment of him. **1867** *Brit. Med. Jrnl.* 20 July 40/1, I refer to pulse No. 10 principally for the purpose of shewing how completely the *sphygmographic form may be modified by merely functional, that is to say nervous, disorder. **1879** H. C. WOOD *Therap.* (ed. 2) 38 Sphygmographic studies made of it.. have been thought to indicate a condition of general arterial spasm. **1895** tr. *Ferri's Crim. Sociol.* 167 The sphygmographic data on the circulation of the blood. **1867** *Brit. Med. Jrnl.* 13 July 20/1 The full pulse (*sphygmographically, that in which the second event is well marked or developed). **1885** J. B. YEO tr. *M. J. Oertel's Respiratory Therapeutics* II. 472 When.. inspiration is slow and cautious,.. sphygmographically the pulse waves altered by the rise of blood pressure immediately succeed to the average normal ones. **1859** MAYNE *Expos. Lex.* 1185 *Sphygmographia*,.. a description of the pulse, its nature and causes: *sphygmography. **1864** *Reader* Mar. 365/3 A memoir upon the value of Sphygmography in diagnosis. **1891** *Cent. Dict.*, *Sphygmomanometer. **1898** *Daily News* 12 May 6/3 Simple forms of sphygmomanometers. **1902** *Amer. Jrnl. Physiol.* V. 205 For *sphygmomanometric work it was found necessary to pack the small space between this collar and the forearm with soft muslin to prevent a distention of the reflected bands when the pressure within was raised. **1905** *Johns Hopkins Hosp. Rep.* XII. 69 Points of interest in *sphygmomanometry. **1962** *Lancet* 15 Dec. 1225/2 Many of the difficulties inherent in clinical sphygmomanometry of the newborn infant have been overcome by the latest development in photoelectric methods. **1834** *Lancet* 20 Sept. 936/2 At the meeting of the French Academy of Sciences on the 1st inst, M. Magendie read a report on an instrument invented by a Dr. Herisson, called the '*sphygmometer', and intended to measure the state of the pulse... The bottom of the instrument is placed over the radial artery, each pulsation of which elevates the mercury, and thus discloses to the eye the minutest variation of the circulation. **1842** BRANDE *Dict. Sci.*, etc. 1138 *Sphigmometer*,.. an instrument for counting the arterial pulsations. **1872** O. W. HOLMES *Poet Breakf.-t.* iii. (1885) 63 There were.. Sphygmometers and Pleximeters. **1890** *Practitioner* June 421 (*caption*) Upper curve, radial pulse obtained from healthy adult male by air modified sphygmograph (sphygmometer). **1899** *Allbutt's Syst. Med.* VII. 257 In states of over-fatigue.. the arterial blood is, according to sphygmometer readings, run at high pressure. **1898** *Ibid.* V. 673 Here *sphygmometric observations are wanting, though much to be desired. **1867** *Med. Rec.* (N.Y.) 15 July 243/2 Herrison's and Blundell's ideas on *sphygmometry were sunk in oblivion. **1908** G. OLIVER *Studies in Blood-Pressure* (ed. 2) ii. 42 Writers on sphygmometry have always grouped together all the instruments which derive their readings of the arterial pressure from a single artery. **1879** B. W. RICHARDSON in *Proc. R. Soc.* May 70 The *Sphygmophone. **1889** HANDERSON tr. *Baas' Outl. Hist. Med.* 1016 It has been combined with an electric chime of bells (sphygmophone) of Upham. **1881** *Med. Temp. Jrnl.* XIII. 75 The pulse is sixty-eight, and the three *sphygmophonic indications are present. **1856** *Lancet* 8 Nov. 510/1 The numerous cases of disease of the heart which have come under the care of Dr. Scott Alison.. have afforded abundant means of applying.. the new *sphygmoscope, or cardioscope, (contrived by that physician). **1859** MAYNE *Expos. Lex.* 1185/2 *Sphygmoscopium*,.. a sphygmoscope. **1862** *Catal. Internat. Exhib.*, *Brit.* II. No. 2849, Sphygmoscopes; stethogoniometer; and hydrophone, used in chest diseases.

sphygmology (sfɪg'mɒlədʒɪ). *Med.* [See SPHYGMO- and -LOGY.] The study of the pulse. Hence **sphygmo'logical** *a.*

1890 BILLINGS *Med. Dict.* II. 570/1 Sphygmology. **1931** G. SARTON *Introd. Hist. Sci.* II. 75 Sphygmology is even older than urology and more universal. *Ibid.* 87 The Shang-han-lun is divided into ten books of which the first is a sort of scientific (sphygmological) introduction to the others. **1941** *Bull. Hist. Med.* X. 210 It seems probable that some Aegimius may be credited with being the founder of sphygmology. **1973** C. R. S. HARRIS *Heart & Vascular System Anc. Greek Med.* v. 255 The supposed perception of fullness is a typical feature of post-Herophilian sphygmology from which only the Empirics apparently dissented. *Ibid.* vii. 409 But enough of these sphygmological conundrums.

‖**sphyræna** (sfaɪ'riːnə). *Zool.* [mod.L., a. L. *sphȳræna*, ad. Gr. σφύραινα, f. σφῦρα hammer.] A pike-like fish belonging to the genus *Sphyræna* or the family represented by this; one of the common species is the barracuda.

1849–52 OWEN in *Todd's Cycl. Anat.* IV. II. 876/1 The teeth of the *Sphyræna* are examples of the ordinary implantation in sockets. *Ibid.* 880/2 The most formidable dentition.. in the order of osseous fishes is that which characterizes the *Sphyræna*.

sphyrænoid (sfaɪ'riːnɔɪd), *a.* and *sb.* *Zool.* [f. prec. + -OID.] **a.** *adj.* Related to or resembling the genus *Sphyræna*. **b.** *sb.* A fish of this kind.

1849–52 OWEN in *Todd's Cycl. Anat.* IV. II. 881/1 It is in this position of the germs of the teeth that the Sphyrænoid fishes.. mainly differ. **1851** MANTELL *Petrifact.* v. §1. 416 Cycloid Order:.. Sphyrænoids.

sphyre, obs. form of SPHERE.

‖**sphyrelaton** (sfaɪ'riːlətɒn). [a. Gr. σφυρήλατον, f. σφῦρα hammer + ἐλατός, f. ἐλαύνειν to beat out.] Metal-work done with the hammer.

1855 tr. *Labarte's Arts Mid. Ages* i. 47 Sphyrelaton,.. hammer or repoussé work. **1878** DENNIS *Cities & Cemet. Etruria* II. 313 A canopus of this metal in a curule chair of the same, all in *sphyrelaton* or hammered work.

†**spi**, *int.* *Obs.*[−1] [a. MDu. *spi* (also *tspi*), a natural expression of disgust.] = FIE *int.*

a **1225** *Ancr. R.* 310 Alle þet him luueden, ȝeiden spi him on, and hatieð him alle.

spial ('spaɪəl). Forms: 5 *Sc.* **spyale**, 6 **-alle**, *Sc.* **spyell**, 6–7 **spyal**, **-all**, **spiall**, 6– **spial**. [Aphetic f. ESPIAL. Cf. SPY *sb.* and *v.*]

†**1.** Espial, spying; observation, watch. *Obs.*

c **1375** *Sc. Leg. Saints* xl. (*Ninian*) 831 þai.. spyale gat to se quhen he fra strinth of men mycht fundyn be. **1525** LD. BERNERS *Froiss.* II. xxix. 35/1 I caused by spyall the towne & castell of Thury in Albygois to be well aviewed. **1577–87** HOLINSHED *Chron.* III. 1097/1 Vpon such aduertisement as he receiued by spiall, of the queens being in the Guildhall. **1601** MOUNTJOY in Moryson *Itin.* (1617) II. 152, I.. since that time kept very good spiall upon him, and have had the sight of all his papers. **1611** B. JONSON *Catiline* IV. ii, I haue those eyes and eares, shall still keepe guard And spiall on thee.

2. A spy; a scout. Now *arch.* or *Obs.*

Very common *c* 1550–1600, especially in plural.

1548 UDALL, etc. *Erasm. Par. Matt.* i. 22 Because she preserued the spyalles sent from Jesu. **1605** BACON *Adv. Learn.* II. To King §10 As Secretaries, and Spyalls of Princes and States bring in Bills for Intelligence; so you must allowe the Spyalls and Intelligencers of Nature to bring in their Billes. *a* **1656** USSHER *Ann.* VI. (1658) 319 Understanding by his spialls, that Cilles with his army lay at Myus carelessely. **1678** SPELMAN *Life Alfred* (1709) 63 Others Eyes and Ears were not always sufficient Spyals. **1813** SCOTT *Rokeby* III. xxvii, Now, could a spial of our train On fair pretext admittance gain, That sally-port might be unbarr'd. **1837** CARLYLE *Fr. Rev.* II. I. iii, Roaming far out, obscure, as King's spial,.. the man has come thus far.

transf. **1605** SYLVESTER *Du Bartas* II. iii. IV. *Captaines* 549 Spiall of Nature, O all-seeing Sun.

3. *attrib.*, as ***spial-eye***, ***money***, ***ship***.

1520 *Lett. & Papers Hen. VIII*, III. I. 393 [For John Bourgchier.., deputy of Calais.., with 100*l.* a year for himself and 104*l.* a year for] spiall money. **1565** COOPER *Thesaurus*, *Catascopium*,.. a spiall shippe: a brigantine or pinneise. **1609** HEYWOOD *Brit. Troy* 129 When lustful Men aime at suche horride use, They watch all Spyal-eyes and listning Eares.

spiare, obs. form of SPIER.

spic (spɪk), *sb.* and *a.* *U.S. slang.* Also **spick**, **spig**, **spik**, and with capital initial. [Shortened f. SPIGGOTY *sb.* (and *a.*)] **A.** *sb.* **a.** A contemptuous and offensive name for a Spanish-speaking native of Central or South America or the Caribbean; a spiggoty.

1913 H. A. FRANCK *Zone Policeman 88* i. 10 It was my first entrance into the land of the *panameños*, technically known on the Zone as 'Spigoties', and familiarly, with a tinge of despite, as 'Spigs'. **1916** E. PEIXOTTO *Our Hispanic Southwest* 102 The Mexican men they despise and call 'spicks'. **1928** S. LEWIS *Man who knew Coolidge* II. 116 We need a supply of cheap labour, and where get it better than by encouraging these Wops and Hunks and Spigs and so on to raise as many brats as they can? **1936** *Opportunity* Aug. 239/1 Frank was just a 'huerco' to his mother, 'spick' to his white schoolmates in Queensville, Texas. **1949** W. FAULKNER *Knight's Gambit* 137, I don't intend that a fortune-hunting Spick shall marry my mother. **1953** F. SCOTT FITZGERALD *Tender is Night* ix. 275 'He's a spic!' he said. He was frantic with jealousy. **1964** E. LACY *Pity Honest* iii. 48 This is becoming a tough neighbourhood, full of Spics. **1977** D. E. WESTLAKE *Nobody's Perfect* (1978) 39 You'd put your kid in a school with a lotta niggers and kikes and wops and spics?

b. The Spanish language; *spec.* Spanish-American.

1933 E. HEMINGWAY *Winner take Nothing* (1934) 200, I wish I could talk spik... I don't get any fun out of asking that spik questions. **1977** *Amer. Speech 1975* L. 67 *Spic n*, 1: Spanish language 2: course in the Spanish language 'I've had two years of Spic.'

B. *adj.* = SPIGGOTY *sb.* (and *a.*) 3. *derog.*

1919 *Ladies' Home Jrnl.* Sept. 27 The Marines had been.. silencing the elusive 'spick' bandit in Santo Domingo. **1950** R. MOORE *Candlemas Bay* 29 Jerry Canneri. Or Carnoodle. Some such damn spik name. **1976** N. THORNBURG *Cutter & Bone* iii. 74 A nigger fag and two spic girls with a pet monkey.

spic, variant of SPICK *sb.*[1] *Obs.*

‖**spica** ('spaɪkə). [L. *spīca* ear of grain, etc.: see SPIKE *sb.*[1] In senses 3 and 4 after Gr. στάχυς.]

†**1.** ***oil of spica***, oil of spike. *Obs.*

c **1400** *Lanfranc's Cirurg.* 226 It is good.. to comforte þe place wiþ oile of mastic, & oile of spica.

2. *Bot.* A flower-spike.

1693 tr. *Blancard's Phys. Dict.* (ed. 2), *Spica*, the long Tops of Herbs, as of Lavender, &c. **1728** CHAMBERS *Cycl.* s.v. *Spica-Nardi*, The Ear or *Spica*, is about the Length and Thickness of a Finger. **1760** J. LEE *Introd. Bot.* III. iv. (1765) 173 *Spica, a Spike*, has sessile Flowers that are alternate and dispersed about a common Peduncle that is simple. **1793** MARTYN *Lang. Bot.* s.v. **1856** HENSLOW *Dict. Bot. Terms* 177.

3. *Astr.* A bright star in the constellation Virgo.

1728 CHAMBERS *Cycl.* s.v. *Virgo*, First of three [stars] under *Spica*. *Ibid.*, Last, and North of 3 under *Spica*. **1843** *Penny Cycl.* XXVI. 373/1 Spica (α Virginis), a star of the first magnitude, is in the hand, which holds ears of corn, typical of the harvest. **1886** SIR R. BALL *Story of Heavens* xviii. (1897) 380 There is a fine equilateral triangle, whereof Arcturus and Spica form two of the corners.

4. *Surg.* A form of bandage, the arrangement of which is suggestive of an ear of wheat or barley. Also *attrib.*

1731 BAILEY (vol. II), *Spica* (with Surgeons), a band used in Hernias. **1758** J. S. *Le Dran's Observ. Surg.* (1771) 193 Covering the Wound with a proper Dressing, sustained by the *Spica*. **1846** BRITTAN tr. *Malgaigne's Man. Oper. Surg.* 420 A compress [was] laid on the course of the canal, with a spica bandage. **1875** KNIGHT *Dict. Mech.* 2265/2 *Spica*,.. a form of bandage resembling a spike of barley. The turns of the bandage cross like the letter V, each leaving a portion uncovered.

spi'caceous, *a.* *Bot.* *rare*[−1]. [f. prec.: see -ACEOUS.] Having the form of a spike.

1755 *Phil. Trans.* XLIX. 253 It is a gramineous plant, of which some bear spicaceous flowers.

spicant, *a.* *rare*[−1]. [f. L. *spīca* or *spīcāre*, after heraldic terms in -ANT.] Spiky.

1867 *Gd. Words* 325/2 The many windings of Stert Valley, spicant with bulrushes.

spicat, obs. form of SPICKET, spigot.

spicate ('spaɪkət), *a.* Also 9 **spikate**. [ad. L. *spīcāt-us*, pa. pple. of *spīcāre* to furnish with spikes, to make pointed, f. *spīca* SPIKE *sb.*[1]]

1. *Bot.* **a.** Of plants: Having an efflorescence in the form of a spike. **b.** Of flowers: Arranged in a spike.

α. **1668** WILKINS *Real. Char.* II. iv. §4. 93 Spicate flowers. *Ibid.* 94 Spicate herbs. **1760** J. LEE *Introd. Bot.* III. xxi. (1765) 217 *Spicate*, with the Flowers in Spikes. **1857** A. GRAY *First Less. Bot.* 231 *Spicate*, belonging to or disposed in a spike. **1872** OLIVER *Elem. Bot.* II. 173 A perennial erect herb, with.. terminal spicate rose or purple flowers. **1876** HARLEY *Royle's Mat. Med.* 780 The flowers whitish, in long branched spicate racemes.

β. **1847** W. E. STEELE *Field Bot.* 192 Infl. capitate, spikate, unilateral, recurved. **1896** G. HENSLOW *Wild Fl.* 113 The terminal portion of the spikate inflorescence.

2. *Zool.* Having the form of a spike; pointed.

1856 W. CLARK *Van der Hoeven's Zool.* I. 314 *Athericera*. Antennæ.. presenting the form of a patella or capitulum, and in most supplied with a seta or spicate appendage.

spicated ('spaɪkeɪtɪd), *a.* Now *rare.* [See prec. and -ED[1].]

1. *Bot.* Having the form of a spike.

1661 BLOUNT *Glossogr.*, *Spicated*, eared, or in an ear, as corn is. **1712** *Phil. Trans.* XXVII. 422 The Flowers grow spicated in a loose tuft. **1750** G. HUGHES *Barbados* 254 The top of the stalk terminates in a spicated tuft.

2. Furnished with spikelets; bristly.

1702 *Phil. Trans.* XXIII. 1359, I plainly saw that all the bristles on the body of one of them.. were.. spicated (if I may make a word) or bearded like the Ear on the Seed head of some Grasses. **1742** H. BAKER *Microsc.* II. xxiii. 189 Those Hairs were spicated, or had other little Hairs issuing from their Sides. **1791** W. GILPIN *Forest Scenery* I. 51 The catkins of both are round, spicated balls. **1859** SALA *Gaslight & D.* xxv. 285 This big, barbated, spicated basso, with the beard of a sapeur.

‖**spiccato** (spik'kato), *a.* (*adv.*, *sb.*) *Mus.* [It., detached, distinct.] Of a style of staccato bowing, esp. on the violin: detached, *i.e.* with short breaks between notes caused by controlled bouncing of the bow; of music played in this manner. Also used *advb.*, as a direction to the performer and as *sb.*, an instance of spiccato playing; a passage in this style.

1724 [see STACCATO *a.* (*adv.*, *sb.*)]. **1740** J. GRASSINEAU *Mus. Dict.*, *Spiccato*, signifies to separate, divide, part,.. that is, to give every note its distinct sound, and is the contrary of what we call slurring. **1883** GROVE *Dict. Mus.* III. 650/2 *Spicato* [sic].., a term applied in violin-playing to a particular vibratory style of bowing. *Ibid.* 682/2 The Spicato [sic] is marked by dots over the notes. **1938** *Oxf. Compan. Mus.* 891/2 *Spiccato*,.. in music.. implying staccato effect. **1955** *Times* 12 May 5/6 The scherzo, which incidentally allowed Mr. Campoli to unfold long stretches of the most prodigious *spiccato* bowing. **1964** *Listener* 25 June 1043/1 Paganini's innovations in violin technique—the big bouncing *spiccato*, for instance. **1978** *Gramophone* Aug. 355/3 The lyrical grace of Norbert Brainin's playing in the Adagio and his *spiccato* triplets in the finale.

spice (spaɪs), *sb.* Forms: 3 **spis**, 4, 6 **spise**, **spyse**, 4–6 **spyce**, 3– **spice**. [ad. OF. *espice* (mod.F. *épice*), ad. L. *speciēs* SPECIES. Cf. SPECE.]

1. a. One or other of various strongly flavoured or aromatic substances of vegetable origin, obtained from tropical plants, commonly used as condiments or employment for other purposes on account of their fragrance and preservative qualities.

a **1225** *Ancr. R.* 370 þe on was iwuned, uor his kolde mawe uorto nutten hote spices. *c* **1250** *Gen. & Ex.* 2247 Fruit and spices of dere pris, Bereð ðat man ðat is so wis. *a* **1272** *Luue Ron* 168 in *O.E. Misc.*, þu ert swetture þan eny spis. **13..** *K. Alis.* 5651 (Laud MS.), þer ne groweþ no whete, Ne oþer corne, bot spyces swete, þerof hij maken her breed. **1382** WYCLIF *Luke* xxiii. 56 And thei turnynge aȝen, maden redy swete spices, and oynementis. *c* **1420** *Liber Cocorum* (1862) 11 Do þer to pynys and saunders,.. And oþer goode spyces þou take. **1450–80** tr. *Secreta Secret.* 33 Lete him haue savor of encence and othir good spicis among. *a* **1533** LD. BERNERS *Huon* lxxxi. 243 It is not possyble to gyue ony trewe Iugemente when you and we are full of wyne and spyces. **1553** EDEN *Treat. New Ind.* (Arb.) 27 Pouderinge with spyces the bodye therein inclosed, that no euyll sauoure maye passe foorth. **1625** N. CARPENTER *Geogr. Del.* II. iii. (1635) 53 Let our Merchants answer, which owe their Spices to Arabia. **1692** TRYON *Good Housew. made Doctor* xvii. 143 Such a prodigious encrease of sugars, Spanish Fruits, Wines and Spices. **1725** SLOANE *Jamaica* II. 77 It may deservedly be counted one of the best spices in common use, having a very fine relish of many, from thence call'd All-Spice. **1770** LANGHORNE *Plutarch* (1851) II. 816/2 The spices and rich robes that were burned with him were very expensive. **1842** LOUDON *Suburban Hort.* 646 Baked in pies with spices, they have an excellent flavour. **1891** FARRAR *Darkn. & Dawn* lix, Nero had so many spices burnt at her funeral that the learned doubted whether Arabia could furnish more in a single summer.

b. *fig.* (In ME. sometimes applied to persons.)

a **1225** *Ancr. R.* 78 Hope is a swete spice wiðinne þe heorte. **13..** *E.E. Allit. P.* A. 235 Ho profered me speche þat special spyce. *Ibid.* 938 þat specyal spyce þen to me spakk. *a* **1400** *Minor Poems fr. Vernon MS.* xxviii. 21 Heil spice sprong þat neuer was spent. *c* **1450** *Godstow Reg.* 21 That heuenly spyce hit is ful swete. **1605** BACON *Adv. Learn.* I. i. §3 This correctiue spice, the mixture whereof maketh knowledge so soueraigne, is Charitie. **1652** BENLOWES *Theoph.* x. iii. 179 No Grandee Patron court I, nor entice Love-glances from enchanting Eyes, Nor Blandishments from lisping Wantons vocall Spice. **1784** COWPER *Task* II. 606 Variety's the very spice of life, That gives it all its flavour. **1859** *Habits Gd. Society* xii. 323 The gentlemen of the bar.. make a charming spice to a dinner. **1874** L. STEPHEN *Hours in Library* (1892) I. x. 358 He meant something more, which gives the real spice to his writings.

c. An odour or perfume arising from, or resembling that of, spices. (Cf. 2 c.)

1560 BIBLE (Geneva) *Song Sol.* iv. 16 Blowe on my garden, that the spices thereof may flowe out. **1855** TENNYSON *Maud* I. XXII. i, The woodbine spices are wafted abroad.

2. a. Without article, as a substance or in collective sense. (In Sc. use freq. = pepper.)

a **1300** *Cursor M.* 2103 Asie.. es þe best, for þar in es.. Precius stans and spice of prise. *c* **1400** MAUNDEV. (1839) vi. 67 Thei ete it in stede of Spice. **1474** CAXTON *Chesse* 101 Medecynes maad wyth precious spyce. *a* **1548** HALL *Chron.*, *Hen. VIII*, 217 To whom the Erle of Sussex.. brought a voyde of spice and comfettes. **1611** SHAKS. *Wint. T.* IV. iii. 128 Your purse is not hot enough to purchase your Spice. **1694** CROWNE *Regulus* II. 12 A man all vertue, like a pye all spice, will not please. **1717** LADY M. W. MONTAGU *Let. to C'tess Mar* 18 Apr., They use a great deal of rich spice. **1805** SOUTHEY *Madoc in W.* xv, The dead,.. with precious gums and spice Fragrant, and incorruptibly preserved. **1842** LONGF. *Quadroon Girl* iii, Odours of orange-flowers and spice Reached them.

b. *dial.* (See quots.)

1674 RAY *N.C. Words* 44 *Spice*: Raisins, plums, figs and such like fruit. York-sh. [Hence in Bailey and Grose.] **1788** W. H. MARSHALL *Yorksh.* II. 354 *Spice*, dried fruit, as raisins, currants, etc. **1828** CARR *Craven Gloss.*, *Spice*, sweet meats of any kind. **1855** [ROBINSON] *Whitby Gloss.*, *Spice*, the common term here for sweetmeats and confectionery of all sorts, but especially for gingerbread articles.

c. Spicy fragrance. (Cf. 1 c.)

1833 TENNYSON *Pal. Art* 116, A summer fann'd with spice. **1850** —— *In Mem.* ci, And many a rose-carnation [shall] feed With summer spice the humming air.

d. *techn.* (See quot.)

1858 SIMMONDS *Dict. Trade, Spice*,..a technical name among sugar-refiners for bullocks'-blood.

e. A medicated preparation added to cattle or horse feed. ? Now only *Hist.*

1707 J. MORTIMER *Whole Art of Husbandry* 157 Take a quart of Ale, half an ounce of Diapente.., Horse-spice two Ounces. 1928 E. P. OPPENHEIM *Chron. Melhampton* 143 A retired dealer in cattle spices. 1961 M. W. BARLEY *Eng. Farmhouse & Cottage* v. i. 253 Thomas Morrison kept a much more interesting shop, in the last years of the seventeenth century... There was ironmongery..'horse spice and jollop' for the farmer.

†**3. a.** A sort, kind, or species. *Obs.*

1303 R. BRUNNE *Handl. Synne* 7585 Ȝyt þyr ys a-noþer spyce þat cumþ of þe fendes malyce. c1386 CHAUCER *Pars. T.* ¶102 The spices of penitence ben thre. c1449 PECOCK *Repr.* II. xiii. 228 Ech spice of moral yuel is moral yuel, and is a morali yuel spice. 1483 CAXTON *Cato* 3 b, Of the seuen spyces of ydolatrye. 1528 PAYNELL *Salerne's Regim.* bj b, There is an other spice of fleure, which is swete and some what warme. 1587 GOLDING *De Mornay* xiv. (1596) 211 For alterations or chaunges, are spices, or rather consequents of moouing.

†**b.** In the phr. *a spice of*, a kind of. *Obs.*

Freq. not clearly distinguishable from sense 5.

c1380 WYCLIF *Sel. Wks.* I. 27 For þis is a spise of pride that men clepen ypocrisie. c1400 *Lanfranc's Cirurg.* 180 Allopucia is a maner spice of lepre þat comeþ of rotid fleume. c1460 FORTESCUE *Abs. & Lim. Mon.* (1885) 144 Such givinge were no vertu, but a spice of prodigalite. 1520 WHITINTON *Vulg.* (1527) 3 b, It is a spyce of peuysshe pryde ..whan a man wyll take a singuler waye by hymselfe. 1538 ELYOT Addit., *Cachexia*, a spyce of a consumption, which procedeth of an yll disposition of the body. 1601 B. JONSON *Poetaster* IV. vi, Bountie is A spice of vertue.

†**4. a.** Appearance, semblance. *Obs.*

1382 WYCLIF *1 Thess.* v. 22 Absteyne ȝou fro al yuel spice, or liknesse. 1382 —— *2 Tim.* iii. 5 Hauynge sothli the spice, or licnesse, of pite, forsothe denyinge the vertu of it.

†**b.** = SPECIES 2. *Obs.*[−1]

c1425 *Orolog. Sapient.* vi. in *Anglia* X. 377 So longe tyme dwellith goddis body as ben hole þe spices of þe sacramente.

†**c.** = SPECIES 6. *Obs.*[−1]

1547 BALDWIN *Mor. Philos.* (1564) 106 Plato affirmeth that there is set in the soule of man..certaine spices, or as it were seedes of things.

5. a. A slight touch or trace *of* some physical disorder or malady. Now *dial.*

a1479 HARDING *Chron.* Pref. xxv, Though this werke haue some spice of blindnesse, Yet is the autoure not to bee blamed muche. 1530 PALSGR. 274/1 Spyce of the axes. 1579–80 NORTH *Plutarch, Sylla* (1895) III. 304 A paine and numnesse in his legges;..Strabo calleth it a spice of the gowte. 1635 BRATHWAIT *Arcadian Princ.* 44 Sure I am, their whole family seemes to have a spice of the same malady. 1719 DE FOE *Crusoe* I. (Globe) 96, I had a little Spice of the cold Fit, but it was not much. 1733 SWIFT *Let. to Sheridan* 27 Mar., Wks. 1841 II. 700/2, I have been much out of order with a spice of my giddiness. 1838 HOLLOWAY *Prov. Dict.* s.v., I have a spice of the rheumatism.

b. A slight touch, trace, or share, a dash or flavour, *of* some thing or quality.

In later use frequently with suggestion of sense 1.

1531 ELYOT *Gov.* I. xix, Daunsis whiche..contained in them a spice of idolatrie. 1564 *Brief Exam.* B ij, Those..do go about with these reliques to maynteyne at least a little spyse of Masse. 1611 MIDDLETON & DEKKER *Roaring Girl* II. i, I had my Latin tongue, and a spice of the French. a1677 BARROW *Serm.* Wks. 1716 I. 169 The contrary practice hath indeed within it a spice of slander. 1709 STEELE *Tatler* No. 39 ¶42 There must be a Spice of Romantick Gallantry in the composition of that very Pretty Fellow. 1790 GOUV. MORRIS in Sparks *Life & Writ.* (1832) III. 16 The Flemings have a spice of obstinacy in their character. 1835 W. IRVING *Tour Prairies* 280 The horse..had a considerable spice of devil in his composition. 1887 JESSOPP *Arcady* ii. 49 A certain gentle rebuke at your negligence and a spice of jealousy too.

c. A specimen or sample. *rare.*

1790 GROSE *Prov. Gloss.* (ed. 2) Suppl., *Spice*, a sample. I gave him a spice of his behaviour. c1816 MRS. SHERWOOD *Stories Ch. Catech.* xi. 91 He would often give the company a spice of what he had learned at school.

†**6.** *Cant.* (See quot.) *Obs.*

1812 J. H. VAUX *Flash Dict.* s.v., The spice is the *game* of footpad robbery... A spice is a footpad robber.

7. a. *attrib.* in combinations denoting receptacles or places for holding spice, as ***spice-bag***, ***-bowl***, †***bust***, ***-cabinet***, ***-dish***, ***-house***, ***jar***, etc., or preparations in which spice is an ingredient, as ***spice-ball***, ***-bread***, ***-broth***, ***-bun***, etc.; also misc., as ***spice-bazaar***, ***-blossom***, ***-merchant***, ***-plant***, ***-shop***, ***-trade***. Also SPICE-BOX, etc.

1591 PERCIVALL *Sp. Dict.*, *Alcartaz para especias*, a *spice bag, a coffin for spice. 1879 MISS JACKSON *Shropsh. Word-bk.*, **Spice-balls*, same as Faggits [a kind of sausages made of the liver and lights of a pig, boiled with sweet herbs, and finely chopped]. 1879 MRS. A. E. JAMES *Ind. Househ. Managem.* 71 There are very likely other ingredients..in the proper spice-balls, and a native 'vet'..will withhold some principal ingredient while pretending to give you the whole recipe. 1924 R. GRAVES *Mock Beggar Hall* 6 Scepticos heard this popular Figment in the *spice-bazaar. 1819 KEATS *Fall Hyperion* I. 21 Where trees of every clime,..With plantain, and *spice-blossoms, made a screen. 1665 WOOD *Life* (O.H.S.) II. 50 W., at Jeanses with *spice-bolls, 7*d.* 1727 SOMERVILLE *Fables* Wks. 1790 II. 106 In cradles, whittles, spice-bowls, sack, Whate'er the wanton gossips lack. 1555 MACHYN *Diary* (Camden) 91 After durge *speysse-bred and wine. 1579 W. FULKE *Refut. Rastel* 728 His comparing of the sacrament with spicebread and cake-bread sauoureth of a mynde that..derideth all religion. 1897 R. M. GILCHRIST *Peakland* 69 The landlady was busily kneading spice-bread. 1777 BRAND *Pop. Antiq.* App. 336 A smoking Prize of *Spice-Broth. 1857 *Household Words* XVI. 201 They all.. sat down to regale on the tea and *spice-buns we had provided. 1489 *Acta Dom. Concil.* (1839) 131 þe dosane of siluer spvnis, siluer salt-fat, & *spice bust. 1893–4 *T. Eaton & Co. Catal.* Fall & Winter 120/3 *Spice cabinets, 90c. 1420 *E.E. Wills* (1882) 46 Also a *spyce disshe of seluer. 1863 in Robson *Bards of Tyne* 22 There will be pies and *spice dumplings. 1468–9 *Durham Acc. Rolls* (Surtees) 92 Pro nova construccione unius *spyce-house ad exitum Coquine, xxxs. 1591 *Exch. Rolls Scotl.* XXII. 121 Andro Quhyte, maister in the spicehous. 1908 *Sears, Roebuck Catal.* 359/3 German china cereal and *spice jars..with names of spices or cereals on each jar. 1977 C. WATSON *One Man's Meat* iii. 25 The dining enclosure..was screened from cook top and sluice unit by rubber plants and rows of spice jars. 1588 *Exch. Rolls Scotl.* XXI. 368 David Manteithe, maister in the *spyce lardner. 1611 BIBLE *1 Kings* x. 15 The traffique of the *spice-merchants. 1862 *Catal. Internat. Exhib., Brit.* II. No. 5383, Examples of the most useful *spice plants. 1824 PIPER *Dial. Sheffield* 22 (E.D.D.), *Spice-pudding. c1475 *Cath. Angl.* 355/1 A *Spice schope, *apotheca vel ipotheca.* 1647 HEXHAM I, A spice shop, *een specerye winckel.* 1860 INGLEDEW *Ballads Yks.* 278 This wor a spice shop, where t' lads met. 1885 *Broad Yks.* 25 Temptin' *spice-stalls rang'd i' rows. 1670 R. COKE *Disc. Trade* 39 If the French King can establish a *Spice Trade, wherein he is wonderously industruous. 1796 MORSE *Amer. Geog.* II. 331 The good fortune of the Dutch, is rendering themselves masters of the spice-trade. 1590 in *Archaeol.* XL. 333 Item, iij *spice treyes, xvjd. 1848 tr. *Hoffmeister's Trav. Ceylon*, etc. iv. 171 It is the Bazaar, in which..the *spice-warehouses predominate.

b. *Comb.*, as ***spice-bearer***, ***-seller***, ***-vendor***; ***spice-bearing***, ***-breathing***, ***-burnt***, ***-enrichened***, ***-fraught***, ***-sweet***, ***-warmed*** adjs.

1845 KITTO *Cycl. Bibl. Lit.* sv. *Burial*, In the splendid funeral procession of Herod, 500 of his servants attended as *spice-bearers. 1796 H. HUNTER tr. *St. Pierre's Stud. Nat.* (1799) III. 647 The *spice-bearing trees of the Moluccas. 1648 J. BEAUMONT *Psyche* III. ccxiv, As one..doth wondring go Through those *spice-breathing paths. 1858 *Brit. Q. Rev.* LVI. 344 Raleigh's search after spice-breathing islands and gold-paved cities. 1589 WARNER *Alb. Eng.* v. xxvi, Rarer then the onely Fowle of *Spice-burnt Ashes bread. 1940 C. DAY LEWIS tr. *Virgil's Georgics* II. 39 Nor all Arabia's acres of *spice-enrichened soil. 1868 J. H. NEWMAN *Verses Var. Occas.* 42 Transport fresh as *spice-fraught gale. 1647 HEXHAM I, A *spice seller, *een specerye verkooper.* 1953 W. DE LA MARE *O Lovely England* 51 The *spice-sweet gorse. 1890 P. H. HUNTER *After the Exile* II. vi. 133 The goldsmiths and *spice-vendors voluntarily contracted for particular..portions of wall. a1847 ELIZA COOK *Sunshine* iv. 3 The winter hours were long to him who had no *spice-warmed cup.

8. Special Combs.: **spice apple**, a variety of the ordinary apple; **spice-berry** *N. Amer.*, wintergreen (*Gaultheria procumbens*); **spice-bush** *U.S.*, wild allspice, fever-bush (*Benzoin odoriferum*); also, an aromatic Californian tree of the laurel family; †**spice-conscience** (*attrib.*), **-conscienced** *a.*, having a delicate or tender conscience; **spice-islands**, the islands in the East from which spices were imported; **spice-isle**, one of the spice-islands (*poet. rare*); **spice-land**, a country which produces spices (in quots. *fig.*); **spice mill**, a small hand-machine for grinding spices; †**spice mortar**, a mortar used for braying or pounding spices in; **spice-nut**, a gingerbread nut; **spice-tea** *U.S.* (see quot.); **spice-tree**, a spice-bearing tree; **spice-wood**, (*a*) *U.S.*, the spice-bush; (*b*) wood of spice-bearing shrubs.

1611 COTGR., *Espice*,..the *Spice apple (whereof excellent Cyder is made). 1860 HOGG *Fruit Man.* 1 Aromatic Russet (Brown Spice,..Spice Apple). 1792 G. IMLAY *Topogr. Descr. N. Amer.* 216 There is a variety of shrubs in every part of the country, the principal of which are the myrtle and *spice berry. 1852 MRS. TRAILL *Canadian Crusoes* vi. 177 The little creeping wintergreen,.. which the Canadians call spice-berry. 1872 DE VERE *Americanisms* 404 The queen..is said to be the lovely, creeping snowberry..,among the young people who give the prize to the spice-berry. 1770 G. WASHINGTON *Jrnl.* 15 Oct. (1925) I. 409 The Soil..being as black as Coal and the Growth, Walnut, Cherry, *Spice Bushes. 1845–50 MRS. LINCOLN *Lect. Bot.* 161 The *Laurus benzoin*, called Spice-bush, has scarlet berries, and is an aromatic plant. 1856 BRYANT *Fountain* ii, There the spice-bush lifts Her leafy lances. 1866 *Treas. Bot.* 821/2 *Oreodaphne californica* is a common tree in the mountainous parts of California, where it goes by a variety of names, such as Mountain Laurel, Spice-bush, Balm of Heaven. c1613 ROWLAND *Four Knaves* (Percy Soc.) 97 Let *spice-conscience fellows talke their fill, Mine owne's mine owne. 1600 HOLLAND *Livy* VI. xxvii. 236 To chuse a third time they made a scruple, so *spice conscienced were they. 1711 ADDISON *Spect.* No. 69 ¶5 My Friend Sir Andrew calls..the *Spice-Islands our Hot-beds. 1776 MICKLE tr. *Camoens' Lusiad* Introd. xxxiv. *note*, To find the spice islands of the East was his [Columbus's] proposal at the court of Spain. 1834 COLERIDGE *Table Talk* 10 July, Like breezes blown from spice-islands of Youth and Hope. 1890 *Cassell's Pop. Educ.* IV. 156/2 Malaysia..includes.. Sumatra, Java, Borneo, and Celebes, and the Moluccas or Spice Islands. 1885 W. B. YEATS in *Dublin Univ. Rev.* Sept. 121 Where *spice-isles nestle on the star-trod seas. 1864 LOWELL *Fireside Trav.* 153 Those *spice-lands of character which we..must reach..by weary voyages. 1897 P. WARUNG *Tales Old Régime* 192 The honeyed sweetness of the spice-land. 1862 *Catal. Internat. Exhib., Brit.* II. No. 6141, Pepper and *spice mills. 1562 J. HEYWOOD *Prov. & Epigr.* (1867) 195 That *spice mortar to sell it be you willyng? 1628 R. NORTON *Gunner* 62 A Grocers or Apothecaryes spice Morter. 1829 T. HOOK *Bank to Barnes* 120 I passed a few minutes and a bad shilling in bargaining for some *spice-nuts. 1836–7 DICKENS *Sk. Boz, Scenes* xii. 107 To induce you to purchase half a pound of the real spice nuts. 1872 DE VERE *Americanisms* 395 *Spice-tea is..made from another laurel common at the South, the spice-bush. 1796 H. HUNTER tr. *St. Pierre's Stud. Nat.* (1799) II. 249 The laurel which bears it is, as well as *spice-trees, a plant of no great elevation. 1868 MORRIS *Earthly Par.* (1870) I. II. 510 As though in some Arabian plain he stood, Anigh the border of a spice-tree wood. 1756 P. KALM *Resa til N. Amer.* II. 204 *Spicewood. (Laurus æstivalis. *Spec.* 370). 1760 J. LEE *Introd. Bot.* App. 327 Spice Wood, *Laurus.* 1792 J. BELKNAP *Hist. New-Hampsh.* III. 97 The Spice-wood (*Laurus Benzoin*) or..Feverbush. a1813 A. WILSON *Amer. Blue Bird* Poet. Wks. (Belfast ed.) 278 Spicewood and sassafras budding together. 1819 KEATS *Fall Hyperion* I. 236 Many heaps Of other crisped spice-wood. 1846–50 A. WOOD *Class-bk. Bot.* 478 *Benzoin odoriferum*... Spice Wood.

spice (spaɪs), *v.* Also 6 **spise**, **spyce**. [ad. OF. *espicer* (mod.F. *épicer*), f. *espice* SPICE *sb.*; or directly from the sb.]

1. a. *trans.* To prepare or season (food, etc.) with a spice or spices. Also allusively (quot. 1821).

1377 LANGL. *P. Pl.* B. XIX. 283 Shulde no curyous clothe comen on hys rugge, Ne no mete in his mouth þat maister Iohan spiced. 1570 LEVINS *Manip.* 114 To spice, *condire.* 1611 BIBLE *Ezek.* xxiv. 10 Consume the flesh, and spice it well, and let the bones be burnt. 1658 ROWLAND tr. *Moufet's Theat. Ins.* 912 It is spiced at pleasure with Ginger, Saffron [etc.]. 1821 SCOTT *Kenilw.* xx, 'Fetch him wine,'..said the alchemist. 'Aha! and thou wouldst spice it for me,..wouldst thou not?' 1822 —— *Nigel* iii, She..spiced the toast with her own hands. 1885 LADY BRASSEY *The Trades* 291 Anciently ambergris was much used for spicing wines.

transf. 1600 DELONEY *Strange Hist.* Wks. (1912) 405 Yet his faire bodie was full sore infected, So ill they spiced both his fleshe and fishe.

b. *fig.* To season, to affect the character or quality of, by means of some addition or modification; usu. const. *with*. Also (*colloq.*) with *up*, to enliven, to make more interesting or racy.

1529 MORE *Dyalogue* IV. Wks. 257/2 One special thing, with which he spised al the poison. 1564 BULLEIN *Dial. agst. Pest* (1888) 27 Me think your conscience is to much spiced with sodaine deuotion. 1634 W. WOOD *New Eng. Prosp.* To Rdr., I have inserted many passages of mirth concerning them, to spice the rest of my more serious discourse. 1684 BUNYAN *Adv. to Sufferers* Wks. 1885 II. 728 His holy harmless and profitable notions, because they are spiced with grace, yield to him comfort, joy, and peace. 1837 W. IRVING *Capt. Bonneville* III. 103 Hardship and hard work, spiced with the stimulants of wild adventure. 1855 TENNYSON *Maud* I. XVIII. vii, O, why should Love..Spice his fair banquet with the dust of death? 1891 BARING-GOULD *In Troubadour-Land* iii. 39 The reader will think I have given him a dull chapter,..so I will..add an anecdote, to spice it. 1927 *Scribner's Mag.* Apr. 390/1 The brazen forgery in *The Gentlemen's Magazine* seems to have been a facetious attempt to spice up a sober-toned, political newsletter. 1979 *Arizona Daily Star* 8 Apr. (Wedding Suppl.) 15/2 One Tucson couple spiced up a wedding with circus performances, complete with a juggler and unicyclist.

absol. 1822 SCOTT *Nigel* xxvii, Mind to spice high with Latin.

c. *slang.* To adulterate (soot).

1798 J. MIDDLETON *View Agric. M'sex* 302 The chimney-sweepers who sell soot in London, mix with it ashes and earth, sifted very small and fine: this they term *Spicing the soot.*

2. †**a.** To embalm, to preserve with spices. *Obs.*

1432–50 tr. *Higden* (Rolls) V. 287 The body of this holy man spicede with mony spices was sende to his churche. 1555 EDEN *Decades* (Arb.) 160 Sumwhere also, they drye them, spyce them,..and so reuerently place them in certeyne tabernacles. 1598 W. PHILLIP tr. *Linschoten* 3/1 His body beeing seared and spiced was conuaied into his countrie of Alua.

†**b.** To perfume with or as with spices.

1648 HERRICK *Hesper.*, *Nupt. Song* ii, Treading upon Vermilion And Amber; Spiceing the Chaf't-Aire with fumes of Paradise.

c. *Cant.* To rob; to deprive *of* by robbery.

1812 J. H. VAUX *Flash Dict.* s.v., A rogue will say, I *spiced* the *swell* of so much, naming the booty obtained.

d. To dose (a horse) with spice in order to mislead the buyer.

1841 J. T. HEWLETT *Parish Clerk* I. vii. 111 [He] knew nothing of spicing a horse, or giving him a ball.

†**3.** In pa. pple.: Slightly affected *with* a physical disorder. *Obs.*[−1]

1576 FLEMING *Panopl. Epist.* 382 From drunkennesse proceedeth trembling handes, spiced with the Palsie.

†**4.** *intr.* Of a bird: To mute. *Obs.*[−1]

1682 N. O. *Boileau's Lutrin* III. 183 Dar'st thou presume (profane!) to spice i' th' Quire?

Hence ˈ**spicing** *vbl. sb.* (also with *up*); also **spicing apple**, a variety of apple (cf. *spice apple* SPICE *sb.* 8).

1664 EVELYN *Kal. Hort.* 72 The Kirkham Apple,.. Cushion Apple, Spicing, May-flower. 1707 MORTIMER *Husb.* (1721) II. 291 The Spicing Apple, of all Apples that are marked Red, is the meanest. 1844 M. STUART *O.T. Canon* §viii. (1849) 185 The story..although mixed with a spicing of fable in all probability has some truth for its basis. 1896 MRS. CAFFYN *Quaker Grandmother* 133 Boredom sharpened by a spicing of mischief. 1934 C. LAMBERT *Music Ho!* II. 127 There is no instance..of the spicing up of a simple harmonic basis.

spice-box. Also 6 **spys box**. [SPICE *sb.*]

1. A box, usually having several compartments, to keep spices in.

1527 *Test. Ebor.* (Surtees) V. 244 Le spicebox de every. 1533–4 *Rutland MSS.* (Hist. MSS. Comm.) IV. 348, j spys box with a little spone to the same. *a* **1625** FLETCHER *Bloody Brother* II. ii, Here stands a bak'd meat, he wants a little seasoning;.. my Spice-box, Gentlemen. **1858** SIMMONDS *Dict. Trade*, *Spice-box*, a kitchen-box with several divisions for holding different spices. **1874** H. H. COLE *Catal. Ind. Art S. Kens. Mus.* App. 288 Centre Piece, silver, consisting of a plateau fitted with spice boxes and receptacles for flowers.

2. A small decorated box, usually of Oriental workmanship.

1880 BIRDWOOD *Ind. Art* I. 160 Small boxes of very graceful form, covered with the most delicate tracery, and known to Europeans as spice-boxes.

spice-cake. Also 6 **spyce-, spise-**. [SPICE *sb.*] A cake seasoned with spice; *dial.*, a rich currant-cake. Also *Comb.*

1530 PALSGR. 274/1 Spycecake, *gasteau*. **1561** AWDELAY *Frat. Vacab.* 12 Such knaves commonly vse to buy Spice-cakes, Apples, or other trifles. **1605** *London Prodigal* V. i, I haue liued since yesterday two a clocke of a spice-cake I had at a buriall. **1648** HEXHAM II. s.v. *Kruydt*, A Spice-cake-baker. **1790** GROSE *Prov. Gloss.* (ed. 2) Suppl., *Spice-cake*, plumb-cake. **1825** BROCKETT *N.C. Gloss.*, *Spice-cake*, a cake full of currants. **1862** C. C. ROBINSON *Dial. Leeds* 417 *Spice-cake*, Christmas fare. Currants, candied lemon, and raisins, hold a conspicuous part in the manufacture of this article [etc.].

spiced (spaɪst), *ppl. a.* Also 4 **spisid**, 5 **spicid**, 6 **spised, spyced, spicte**. [f. SPICE *sb.* or *v.*]

1. Seasoned or flavoured with spice or spices; cured with spices.

c **1325** *Gloss. W. de Bibbesw.* in Wright *Voc.* 157 *Brakole*, a spiced cake. *c* **1380** WYCLIF *Wks.* (1880) 13 3if þei.. drynkyn dilicious ale and spisid and heiȝe wynes. **1479** in *Eng. Gilds* (1870) 421 To haue..their drynkyngs with spiced Cakebrede. **1487–8** *Rec. St. Mary at Hill* 139 To Milton for spicid Bunnes, xiiij d. **1529** *Cov. Leet Bk.* 697 That no persone..shall bake or make eny spised Caks with butter..but onelie suche persones as shal-be therunto assigned. **1589** GREENE *Menaphon* (Arb.) 34 Carmela seeing her brother refuse his spicte drinke, thought all was not well. **1611** BIBLE *Song Sol.* viii. 2, I would cause thee to drinke of spiced wine. **1681** *Manch. Crt. Leet Rec.* (1888) VI. 126 Joan Liegh for spiced bread. **1708** SEWEL I, Spiced sauce, *kruydige saus.* **1777** COWPER *Let. to Hill* Wks. 1837 XV. 37, I am much obliged to you for a tub of very fine spiced salmon which arrived yesterday. **1816** TUCKEY *Narrative Exped. R. Zaire* iii. (1818) 103 The keg of spiced rum which I had brought..was now produced. *a* **1848** in Bartlett *Dict. Amer.* s.v. *Liquor*, Spiced punch. **1896** *Allbutt's Syst. Med.* I. 404 Avoidance of seasoned and spiced food.

b. Impregnated with hot spices.

1666 H. STUBBE *Mirac. Conform.* 29 No Clothes could possibly warme him: he wore upon his head many spiced Caps.

†**2.** Of conscience, etc.: Nice, dainty, delicate, tender; over particular or scrupulous. *Obs.*

c **1386** CHAUCER *Prol.* 526 He waytud after no pompe ne reverence, Ne maked him a spiced conscience. *c* **1386** —— *Wife's Prol.* 435 Ye schulde be al pacient and meke, And have a swete spiced consciens. *c* **1550** MEDWALL *Nature* 509 (Brandl), Haue ye suche a spyced conscyence That wyll be entryked wyth euery mery thought? **1594** O. B. *Quest. Prof. & Pleas. Concern.* E ij, I remember how they dallied out the matter like Chaucers Frier at the first, vnder pretence of spiced holinesse. **1617** FLETCHER *Mad Lover* III. i, Take it; it is yours; Be not so spiced; 'tis good gold. **1631** MASSINGER *Emperor East* I. ii, Fool that I was, to offer such a bargain To a spiced-conscience chapman!

b. Accustomed to spices; blunted, jaded.

1771 MRS. GRIFFITH *Hist. Lady Barton* II. 268 As tasteless and insipid, as..the sweetest viand to the spiced palate.

3. Fragrant, aromatic; spice-laden.

1590 SHAKS. *Mids. N.* II. i. 124 In the spiced Indian aire, by night Full often hath she gossipt by my side. **1881** MRS. R. T. COOKE *Somebody's Neighbors* 39 Spiced carnations of rose and garnet crowned their bed in July and August. **1882** B. HARTE *Flip* i, The spiced thicket stretched between him and the summit.

†**spiceful,** *a. Obs.*$^{-1}$ [f. SPICE *sb.*] Full of spices; spicy.

1612 DRAYTON *Poly-olb.* v. 312 The sandie wyldes of spicefull Barbarie.

spice-like, *adv.* and *a.* [f. SPICE *sb.*]

A. *adv.* So as to smell like spices.

c **1250** *Gen. & Ex.* 2443 Iosep dede hise lich..riche-like smeren, And spice-like swete smaken. *Ibid.* 2515 Hise liche was spice-like maked.

B. *adj.* Resembling that of spice.

1578 LYTE *Dodoens* 519 The sayde leaues be of an aromaticall or spicelyke taste.

spice-plate. Now *Hist.* [SPICE *sb.*] A small plate or dish formerly used for holding spice.

1391 *Earl Derby's Exp.* (Camden) 100 Pro ij^{bus} spyceplates argenteis. *Ibid.*, Pro factura de les spyceplates. **1415** in *Kal. & Inv. Treas.* (1836) III. 367 .ii. spiceplates d'argent. **1459** *Paston Lett.* I. 469 Item, j. spice plate, well gilt like a double rose. **1537** *N. Co. Wills* (Surtees) 146 A spice plate of Spanysshe worke. **1568** GRAFTON *Chron.* II. 385 The Frenche king gaue to him an Owche and spice Plate of Golde of a great weight. **1778** WARTON *Hist. Eng. Poetry* II. xv. 346 *note*, The spice, for this mixture, was served, often separately, in what they called a spice-plate. **1884** *Leisure Hour* June 374/1 The marshal of the hall..bearing the grace-cup and spice-plate of his lord.

†'**spicer**[1]. *Obs.* Also 4 **spiser**, 4–5 **spyser**; 4 **spycier**, 4–6 **spycer**. [ad. OF. *espicier* (mod.F. *épicier*), f. *espice* SPICE *sb.* Cf. MDu. and MHG. *specier* (G. dial. *spezier*).] A dealer in spices; an apothecary or druggist.

1297 R. GLOUC. (Rolls) 11204 Willam þe spicer & geffray of hencsei. *a* **1340** HAMPOLE *Psalter* xliv. 10 Goed odurs of vertus ere takynd bi þere spiseres. **1362** LANGL. *P. Pl.* A. x. 121 Out of a Ragged Roote..Springeþ and spredeþ þat spicers desyreþ. *c* **1400** *Lanfranc's Cirurg.* 67 þanne I sente to þe spiceris schoppe þat was a greet weye fro me. **1474** CAXTON *Chesse* III. iv. (1883) 118 The pawon that is sette to fore the quene signefyeth the phisicyen Spicer and Apotyquaire. *a* **1513** FABYAN *Chron.* VII. (1811) 512 A spycer or grocer namyd Petyr Gylle, of Paris. **1566** SECURIS *Detect.* D v, Certayne, which are called spicers, or Poticaries. **1609** D. ROGERS in *Digby Myst.* (1882) p. xxi, Mercers, Spicers, bringe forthe y^e 3. kinges of Collen.

attrib. **14..** *Nom.* in Wr.-Wülcker 692 *Hec apoticaria*, a spyser wyfe. *Ibid.* 730 *Hec apoteca*, a spycerschope.

spicer[2] ('spaɪsə(r)). *rare*$^{-0}$. [f. SPICE *v.*] 'One that seasons with spice' (Webster, 1828–32).

†**spicerer.** *Obs.*$^{-1}$ [Cf. SPICER[1].] One skilled in the nature of spices or drugs.

1665 G. HAVERS *P. della Vallis Trav. E. India* 82 In the Colledge of Fryer Joseph Masagna, a famous Spicerer.

spicery ('spaɪsərɪ). Forms: 3–7 **spicerie** (4 **-eri**, 5 **-ere**, 6 **-eree**), 3– **spicery** (4–5 **-erye**); 4–6 **spycerie** (5 **-irie**, 6 **-arie**), **spy(e)cery(e**; 4 **spisorie**, 5 **spysory(e, spiserie**. [ad. OF. *espicerie* (mod.F. *épicerie*), f. *espice* SPICE *sb.* Cf. OF. *especerie* (= Sp. *especeria*, It. *spezeria*) SPECERY, which is also the source of MDu. *spec-*, *speserie* (Du. *specerij*), MLG. *specerie* (*spisserie*), MHG. *specierie*, *spezerie* (G. *spezerei*).]

1. *collect.* or in *pl.* Spices.

sing. **1297** R. GLOUC. (Rolls) 3162 He..Nom wiþ him spicerie þat to fysike drou. **13..** *Sir Beues* 3188 Wiþ pyment and wiþ spisorie. *c* **1380** WYCLIF *Sel. Wks.* I. 89 For Goddis lawe savouriþ wele whan it is defoulid, as spicerye ȝyveþ smell whan it is powned. *c* **1420** *Liber Cocorum* (1862) 42 Fore pore menne þys crafte is tolde þat mowon not have spysory, as þay wolde. **1470–85** MALORY *Arthur* XI. ii. 573 There with alle there was suche a sauour as alle the spyecery of the world had ben there. **1567** DRANT *Horace, Ep.* II. i. Hj, Wher francke incence is soulde And what soeuer spycerie in waste paper is roulde. **1593** ROYDON in *Spenser's Astrophel* S.'s Wks. 1910 I. 358 The Phœnix..Built vp her tombe of spicerie. **1652** EARL MONM. tr. *Bentivoglio's Hist. Relat.* 14 Having brought by many Voyages an inestimable Treasure of Spicery into Holland. **1689** BURNET *Tracts* I. 96 It tasted high of Spicery, though she assured me there was not one grain of Spice in it. **1776** MICKLE tr. *Camoens' Lusiad* 464 The richest gust of spicery's fragrant fire. **1819** CRABBE *T. of Hall* xxi. 169 And the good ladies whom at church he saw,..Could,..whispering, deal for spicery and lace. **1847** H. MILLER *First Impr. Eng.* v. (1857) 69 Several glasses of Sampson, a palatable Dudley beverage, compounded of eggs, milk and spicery. **1877** MORRIS *Jason* XI. 361 While on the veined pavement lie The honied things and spicery.

pl. *c* **1400** MAUNDEV. (Roxb.) vii. 26 Sum distilles gariofles, spikenarde, and oþer spiceries. **1527** R. THORNE in *Hakluyt* (1589) 254 Many Islandes which be Islandes of the Spiceries of the Emperor. **1591** SAVILE *Tacitus* Annot. 2, Windowes & doores..wherein the herse was placed, and all kinde of spiceries and odours..heaped therein. **1610** HOLLAND *Camden's Brit.* I. 71 There is a mighty heape of the said spiceries gotten together. **1630** *R. Johnson's Kingd. & Commw.* 552 All sorts of Trees, wilde Beasts, and Spiceries. **1777** ROBERTSON *Hist. Amer.* I. (1778) I. 34 He traded in many of the islands from which Europe had long received spiceries and other commodities. **1834** H. MILLER *Scenes & Leg.* xvii. (1857) 258 He supplied the proprietors with teas, wines, and spiceries. **1893** A. H. SAYCE *Higher Crit.* (1894) 133 Dedan was the leading tribe..which carried the spiceries of the southern coast to the populations of Palestine.

b. *fig.* in various applications.

1377 LANGL. *P. Pl.* B. IX. 100 (Trin. Coll. Cambr. MS.), And siththe to spille speche That spicerie [*v.r.* spyre] is of grace. **1576** GASCOIGNE *Steel Glas* Ep. Ded., Wks. 1910 II. 135 Were not the cordial of these two pretious Spiceries, the corrosyve of care woulde quickely confounde me. **1594** NASHE *Unfort. Trav.* Wks. (Grosart) V. 62 Arabian spiceries of sweete passions and praises. **1652** BENLOWES *Theoph.* IV. xcvii, All virtues fir'd in her pure breast their spicery. **1679** J. GOODMAN *Penit. Pard.* I. iv. (1713) 123 The name of the wicked shall rot, in despite of all the spicery of flatterers and parasites. **1828** LANDOR *Imag. Conv.* Wks. 1853 I. 340/2 After his hot and stimulating spicery, we now are running to ..sager poets. *a* **1881** RIPLEY in Frothingham *Rec. & Impr.* 266 The affluence of his [Emerson's] illustrations diffuses a flavor of oriental spicery over his pages.

2. †**a.** A spice-shop or spice-store, or a set of these; a source or supply of spices. *Obs.*

1297 R. GLOUC. (Rolls) 11224 þe bowiares ssoppe hii breke,..& suþþe þe spicerie Hii breke fram ende to oþer, & dude al to robberie. **1527** R. THORNE in *Hakluyt* (1589) 254 A head land called Malaca, where is the principal spicery.

b. The department of the royal household connected with the keeping of spices; esp. in ***Clerk of the Spicery***. Now only *Hist.*

1418–9 in *Cal. Proc. Chanc. Q. Eliz.* (1827) I. Introd. 16 Roger Wodehill,..som tyme clerc of ȝoure faders Spicerie. **1513** *Bk. Keruynge* in *Babees Bk.* (1868) 272 Speke with the panter and offycers of ye spycery for fruytes that shall be eten fastynge. *a* **1548** HALL *Chron., Hen. VIII*, 58 The kyng sent William Blacknall esquyer, Clerck of hys Spycery, with silver vessell, plate and other thynges. **1601** F. TATE *Househ. Ord. Edw. II*, § 11 (1876) 11 Al thinges touching th' office of the spicerie. *Ibid.* § 17. 14 Two towels of the clarke of the spicery. **1654** H. L'ESTRANGE *Chas. I* (1655) 63 They.. divested him of his place in the spicery. **1707** CHAMBERLAYNE *Pres. St. Gt. Brit.* (1710) 535 Her Majesty's Houshold Officers and Servants... Spicery: Richard D'Avenant, Esq., Clerk. **1780** BURKE *Corr.* (1844) II. 327, I propose..to abolish..all the offices of the kitchen, cellar, spicery, &c.

c. A room or part of a house set apart for the keeping of spices. Now only *Hist.*

1536 *MS. Rawl. D. 780* fol. 57 b, A new key for the stew howse Dore in the spycery. **1605** ARMIN *Foole upon F.* (1880) 10 The Pie was drawne,..but wanting Suger, stept aside to the spicerie to fetch it. **1705** ADDISON *Italy, Pesaro* 148 The Spicery, the Cellar and its Furniture,..are too well known to need a Description. **1883** *Eng. Illustr. Mag.* Nov. 81 Kitchens, cellars, pastries, spiceries,..and the like.

fig. **1638** BRATHWAIT (*title*), A Spiritual Spicerie, containing sundrie sweet Tractates of Devotion and Piety.

spice-wood: see SPICE *sb.* 8.

spici- ('spaɪsɪ), combining form of L. *spīca* ear of corn, SPIKE *sb.*[1], occurring in a few words, as **spi'ciferous** *a.* [L. *spīcifer*] (see quot.). '**spiciform** *a.*, having the form of a (flower-) spike. '**spicilege,** ‖**spici'legium,** †**spicilegy** [L. *spīcilegium*], a gleaning; a collection or anthology.

Mayne *Expos. Lex.* (1859) also gives ***spiciferous***, ***-florous***, ***-gerous*** as renderings of mod.L. formations.

1656 BLOUNT *Glossogr.*, **Spiciferous*, that beareth ears of corn. [Hence in Phillips and Bailey.] **1836** *Penny Cycl.* VI. 401/1 Verticillated either round some foreign body or under the form of *spiciform branches. **1870** HOOKER *Stud. Flora* 194 Heads purplish or white,..in a spiciform panicle. **1837** LANDOR *Pentameron* ii. Wks. 1853 II. 322/2 Yet we may almost make out in quantity, and quite in quality, our *spicilege from Virgil himself. **1846** G. S. FABER *Lett. Tractar. Secess.* 91, I shall exhibit some specimens of the process,..a *spicilegium only. **1859** *Archaeol. Cant.* II. 221 Which shall be, as it were, a 'Spicilegium', a gathering up of fragments. **1656** BLOUNT *Glossogr.*, **Spicilegy*, gathering ears of corn, gleaning or leising corn.

spicily ('spaɪsɪlɪ), *adv.* [f. SPICY *a.* + -LY[2].] In a spicy manner; pungently.

1855 in HYDE CLARKE *Dict.* **1896** J. K. BANGS *House-boat on Styx* xi. 142 The conversation had opened a trifle spicily.

spiciness ('spaɪsɪnɪs). [f. SPICY *a.* + -NESS.] The quality of being spicy (esp. in fig. senses).

1633 HERBERT *Temple, Odour* iii, That these two words might creep and grow To some degree of spicinesse to thee! **1655** VAUGHAN *Silex Scint.* (1858) 81 Cold showers nipt and wrung Their spiciness and bloud. **1730** BAILEY (fol.), *Aromaticalness*, Spiciness. **1876** *World* V. 11 Our English language does not lend itself so easily as the French to meretricious spiciness of phrase. **1895** *Outing* XXVII. 38 There is a spiciness in the fact.

†**spick,** *sb.*[1] *Obs.* Forms: α. 1, 3 **spic**, 4–5 **spyk** (5 **spike**), 6 **spycke**. β. 3 **spiche**. [OE. *spic* (= ON. and MSw. *spik*), var. of *spec* (once): see SPECK *sb.*[4]] Fat meat or bacon; fat, grease, lard.

α. *c* **832** *Charter* in *O.E. Texts* 446, ii weȝa spices & ceses. **835** *Ibid.* 449 An weȝ spices & ceses. *a* **1000** *Sax. Leechd.* II. 92 ðenim þa readen netlan..& spices. *c* **1205** LAY. 24437 þer com spic and water and aten vnimete. *c* **1330** R. BRUNNE *Chron. Wace* (Rolls) 12345 Dynabrok..[was] Rostyng a swyn,..his berd þer-wiþ al lothen, & al to-soilled wyþ þe spyk. *c* **1440** *Promp. Parv.* 469/1 Spyk, or fet flesche (*K.* spike of fleshe), *popa*. *a* **1529** SKELTON *E. Rummyng* 335 Another brought a spycke Of a bacon flycke.

β. *c* **1275** *XI Pains of Hell* 134 in *O.E. Misc.*, Heom me drepeþ myd þe piche As we brede wiþ þe spiche.

spick, *sb.*[2] Now *dial.* Also 6, 9 **spik**, 7 **spicke**. [ad. OF. *spic*, *espic* (Cotgr. *spique*): see ASPIC[2] and SPIKE *sb.*[1]] Lavender.

1558 WARDE tr. *Alexis' Secr.* 19 Take first..the oyle of Violettes,..oyle of Spick,..of eche of them a pound. **1559** MORWYNG *Evonym.* 232 Oyl of Spick... Set the herb (the flowers rather) of Spik or Lavendar a whyle in the sun. **1639** O. WOOD *Alph. Bk. Secrets* 121 Mixe therewith liquid Storax and oyle of Spicke. **1656** RIDGLEY *Pract. Physick* 85 Take..Spick, six grains, with Honey of Roses. **1844** W. BARNES *Poems Rural Life* 234 The lilies white's her maiden frocks, The spik to put 'ithin her box. **1885**– in s.w. dial. glossaries (Somerset, Wilts., etc.).

†**spick,** *sb.*[3] *Obs. rare.* [var. SPIKE *sb.*[2] or SPEEK *sb.*] A spike-nail.

1611 FLORIO, *Chiodo*, a naile, a spicke. **1628** in Foster *Eng. Factories India* (1909) III. 251 Spicks and nailes of all sorts.

spick, *sb.*[4] *dial.* Also **spic**. [Var. of dial. *speak*: see *E.D.D.*] A withy or rod, usu. pointed and doubled, used to secure thatch; a spar (SPAR *sb.*[4]).

1890 J. D. ROBERTSON *Gloss. Words County of Gloucester* 147 *Speeks* or *spicks*, the pieces of wood used for holding together the thatch on a rick. **1893** DARTNELL & GODDARD *Gloss. Words Wiltshire* 152 *Spick*.., in thatching, the same as *spar*. **1934** *Times Lit. Suppl.* 1 Feb. 71/3 The thatcher's tackle of 'spicks' or 'spars' (pointed hazelrods) which fix the bands to hold down the thatch. **1939** D. HARTLEY *Made in England* ii. 57 A bundle of the double withies split and bent into a twisted hook or double prong... These, when used in stack work, are called 'spics' or 'speks'. **1949** K. S. WOODS *Rural Crafts Eng.* III. vii. 109 *Thatching Spics.* The riving, or rending of the wood, which is the basis of a number of crafts, is illustrated.

†**spick,** *v. Obs.*$^{-1}$ [f. SPICK *sb.*[3]] = SPIKE *v.*[2] I.

1623 in Foster *Eng. Factories Ind.* (1908) II. 230 Our people..came theather..and spicked upp their ordinance.

spick, *a.* Short for SPICK AND SPAN *a.*

1882 GOSSE *Gray* vi. 127 His servant..had to keep the room as bright and spick as an old lady's bandbox. **1920** D. H. LAWRENCE *Lost Girl* vi. 99 He liked to have his clothes neat and spick.

spick, var. SPIC *sb.* and *a.*

spick and span, *a.*, *sb.*, and *adv.* Also **spick-and-span** (occas. **spic**). [Shortening of next. See also SPECK AND SPAN.]

A. *adj.* **1.** = next.

1665 PEPYS *Diary* 15 Nov., My Lady Batten walking through the dirty lane with new spicke and span white shoes. **1731** SWIFT *On Death Dr. Swift* xxv, His way of writing now is past;.. I keep no antiquated stuff; But spick and span I have enough. **1793** COWPER *Let.* Wks. 1836 VII. 214, I have built one summer-house already, with the boards of my old study, and am building another spick and span, as they say. **1809** *European Mag.* LV. 21 The great number of spick and span articles that have been received into our catalogue. **1849** H. MAYO *Pop. Superst.* (1851) 51 Fresh from the mint, and spic and span. **1877** SPURGEON *Serm.* XXIII. 442 Their shifting gospel changes about every ten years, and comes out spick and span as a new theology.

2. Particularly neat, trim, or smart; suggestive of something quite new or unaffected by wear: **a.** Of persons in respect of dress.

1846 THACKERAY *Crit. Rev.* Wks. 1886 XXIII. 159 Benvenuto, spick and span in his very best clothes. **1863** W. W. STORY *Roba di R.* I. iv. 64 The shopkeepers.. looking spick-and-span, as if they had just come out of a bandbox. **1886** 'MAXWELL GRAY' *Silence Dean Maitland* I. i. 9 A dog-cart,.. driven by a spick-and-span groom.

b. Of things.

1857 DUFFERIN *Lett. High Lat.* (ed. 2) 87 You must not suppose.. that the.. land-slip of Thingvalla took place quite in the spick and span manner the section might lead you to imagine. **1882** MRS. RIDDELL *Daisies & Butterc.* I. 121 This spick and span old house. **1888** W. E. NORRIS *Rogue* xxxi, A spick-and-span victoria, with a lady seated in it.

B. *sb.* That which is quite new or particularly trim and smart.

1758 H. WALPOLE *Let. to H. S. Conway* 21 July, I repeat what has been printed in every newspaper of the week, and then finish with one paragraph of spick and span. **1888** B. W. RICHARDSON *Son of Star* III. iii. 41 A Jewish legion of the spick and span of Jewish youth.

C. *adv.* In a spick and span manner.

1815 LAMB *Let. to Manning* in *Final Mem.* x. 99 Mary reserves a portion of your silk.. to make up spick and span into a bran-new gown. **1821** *Blackw. Mag.* IX. 134 Caparison'd all spick and span.

Hence **spick-and-spanness**.

1911 MRS. H. WARD *Case of Richard Meynell* II. viii. 174 [He] was himself a model of spick-and-span-ness. **1931** *Times Lit. Suppl.* 21 May 407/1 The ancient houses.. had a touch of mysterious romance that the bright spick-and-spanness of the new architecture misses. **1975** *New Yorker* 28 Apr. 52/2 A life that, in spite of its inferior neatness and spick-and-spanness, was essentially more serious and finer than our own.

spick and span new, *a.* Also **spick-and-span new**. (For other variations see quots.) [Emphatic extension of SPAN-NEW *a.* The same first element appears in the synonymous Du. and Flem. *spikspeldernieuw*, *-splinternieuw* (WFlem. *-spankelnieuw*).] Absolutely or perfectly new; brand-new; perfectly fresh or unworn.

The *β*-quots. show the more unusual spellings.

α. **1579–80** NORTH *Plutarch* (1895) II. 217 They were all in goodly gilt armours, and brave purple cassocks apon them, spicke, and spanne newe. *c* **1590** *Forewords to Stubbes' Anat.* (1877) 38 A spicke and spanne new Geneua Bible. **1614** B. JONSON *Barth. Fair* III. v. (1904) 66 Sir, this is a spell against 'hem, spicke and span new. **1659** FULLER *App. Inj. Innoc.* II. 31 The Animadvertor will not wear words at the second hand of my using, but will have them spick and span new of his own making. *a* **1668** DAVENANT *Jeffereidos* I. Wks. (1673) 225 They found him close, beneath a spick And almost span-new-peuter-Candlestick. **1742** *Lond. Mag.* 611 A spick and span new French or Dutch Habit. **1771** WESLEY *Wks.* (1872) IX. 181 This discovery is spick and span new; I never heard of it before. **1818** LADY MORGAN *Autobiog.* (1859) 165 These façades.. with spick-and-span-new plaster of Paris and patent cement. **1879** SALA *Paris Herself Again* (1880) II. xvii. 270 Its gilt railings.. looked spick-and-span new. **1893** VIZETELLY *Glances Back* I. i. 22 The handsome horses in spick-and-span new harness.

Comb. **1607** MIDDLETON *Fam. Love* IV. iii, I am.. of the spick and span new-set-up company of porters.

β. **1583** GOLDING *Calvin on Deut.* clxxxii. 1130/1 They [Papists] make men beleeue that the breade is no more a materiall thing... And that is spycke and spawne newe. **1598** FLORIO s.v. *Trinca, Nuoua di trinca*, as we vse to say spike and span new. **1653** GATAKER *Vind. Annot. Jer.* 73 In his Preface to his spik and span New Ephemeris. **1663** KILLEGREW *Parson's Wed.* II. vii, Spik and span new arguments. *c* **1789** MRS. UNWIN *Let.* in Burgon *Twelve Good Men* (1888) II. 351 Two spic and span new pieces. **1855** *Whitby Gloss.* s.v., Spic-and-span New. See *Brandnew*.

Hence **spick-and-span newness**. *rare.*

1640 BP. HALL *Episc.* III. vii. 36 The most manifestly spick-and-span-newnesse of this devised Discipline.

'spicket[1]. Now chiefly *dial.* and *U.S.* Also 5 **spyket**, **spykkett**, 6 **spicat**, 7, *Sc.* 8–9 **spiket**. [Alteration of SPIGOT *sb.*]

1. A spigot.

14.. *Lat.-Eng. Voc.* in Wr.-Wülcker 573 *Clipsedra*, a spyket. **14..** *Metr. Voc.* Ibid. 626 *Clepsidra*, spykkett. **1591** HARSEY *Trav.* (Hakl.) 252 [There were] som wines and spicats in their bellies to draw at. **1619** *Pasquil's Palm* (1877) 148 Into the vault the Iaylor down doth creep, Where how he deals with bung-holes and with spickets I cannot tell. *a* **1635** RANDOLPH *Poems* (1652) 16 His Eyes look like two Tunnels, his Nose like a Fausset with the Spicket out. **1739** BROME in *Lett. Eminent Persons* (1813) II. 119 He.. ran his fingers into the orifices, like spickets, of the arteries, and then knockt for his surgeon. **1747–96** MRS. GLASSE *Cookery* xxii. 343 Put them into a large vessel of wood or stone, with a spicket in it. **1804** A. DUNCAN *Marin. Chron.* IV. 72 The spicket I perceived out of the cask, and the liquor running about. **1836** HALIBURTON *Clockm.* Ser. I. xxxi, I guess I'll whip out of the bung while he's a lookin arter the spicket. **1893** LELAND *Mem.* II. 169 The Indian.. took a glass and turned on the spicket.

attrib. **1654** GAYTON *Pleas. Notes* IV. xvi. 256 Where his miscarriage is the more.. scandalous; insomuch, as that he is chiaus'd by two spicket-wenches.

b. In allusive use.

1615 DAY *Festivals* iv. 94 They.. spend their Birthright and Patrimonies upon the Spicket. **1654** GAYTON *Pleas. Notes* III. vi. 102 The Brethren of the Spicket.. lay downe for a fundamentall, that there is no living without Liquids.

2. A water-tap.

1888 J. & E. R. PENNELL *Sent. Journ.* 60 The waiter pointed to a small spicket and a handkerchief of a towel.

†**spicket**[2]. *dial. Obs.*$^{-1}$ Also **spickard**. [perh. a transferred use of prec.] (See quot.)

1728 *Phil. Trans.* XXXV. 573 The Owners [in Essex] are sure to choose for their own Use the.. fattest [crocus] Roots, but above all, they reject the longish pointed ones, which they call *Spickets* or *Spickards*.

spicknard, obs. form of SPIKENARD.

spicknel(l, obs. forms of SPIGNEL.

spick-span *a.*, abbrev. of SPICK AND SPAN *a.*

1815 W. H. IRELAND *Scribbleomania* 40 A wish Spick span from the press on wove foolscap to issue. **1888** *Public Opinion* (N.Y.) 15 Dec. 197 Their visits to a State's prison have been under the guidance of officials, before whom all is made spick-span. **1894** A. ST. AUBYN *Orchard Damerel* III. ii. 48 It could never have been.. clear like spic-span modern glass.

So **spick-span new** *a.*

1880 TENNYSON *Northern Cobbler* xix.

†**'spickwort**. *Obs.*$^{-1}$ = SPEARWORT 3 b.

1561 AWDELAY *Frat. Vacab.* (1869) 5 They [*sc.* palliards] be bitten with Spickworts, & somtime with rats bane.

spicose, *a.* *rare*$^{-0}$. [f. L. *spīca*.] (See quot.) Also **spi'cosity**.

1721 BAILEY, *Spicosity*, a being spiked or pricked like an Ear of Corn. **1775** ASH, *Spicose*, full of ears, having many ears like corn. [Hence in later Dicts.]

'spicous, *a.* *Bot.* ? *Obs.* [f. L. *spīca* spike.] Spicate; spiky, pointed.

1658 SIR T. BROWNE *Gard. Cyrus* iii. 46 The seeds about the spicous head or torch of *Tapsus Barbatus*. **1694** WESTMACOTT *Script. Herb.* (1695) 8 The Fruit or Apples.. are.. coated and armed with many spicous Pricks. [**1775** in ASH. Hence in later Dicts.]

Hence **'spicousness**. *rare*$^{-0}$.

1730 BAILEY (fol.), *Spicousness*, a being spiked like Ears of Corn; also Fulness of Ears.

‖**spicula** ('spɪkjʊlə). Pl. **spiculæ** (-juːliː). [mod.L., dim. of L. *spīca*, = L. *spīculum* SPICULUM.]

1. A sharp-pointed or acicular crystal or similar formation.

1747 tr. *Astruc's Fevers* 83 Whose stomach is lined with a sort of pituita, whereby the spiculæ of this poison are blunted. **1794** R. J. SULIVAN *View Nat.* I. 426 We have.. only to suppose, the particles which are employed in crystallization, to be endowed with a tendency to form spiculæ; and these spiculæ with a tendency to arrange themselves at equal angles of inclination. **1802** PLAYFAIR *Illustr. Huttonian Th.* 85 Where there is any admixture of that substance [*sc.* felspar], whether in slender spiculæ or in larger masses. **1825** FARADAY *Exp. Res.* xxx. 167 A substance comes over in small quantity,.. crystallizing in spiculæ in the receiver.

b. *esp.* A formation of this nature caused by the action of frost.

1783 *Phil. Trans.* LXXIII. 310 On dropping in a bit of ice,.. spiculæ of ice shoot suddenly through the water. **1792** BELKNAP *Hist. New Hampsh.* III. 20 The spiculæ [of hoar frost] were of all lengths, from an inch downward. **1854** BREWSTER *More Worlds* iii. 54 The frozen moisture may fall in spiculæ or crystals of ice. **1888** *Athenæum* 6 Oct. 451/3 It was argued that the vapour was changed into ice, and that the higher atmosphere was charged with spiculæ.

2. A small sharp-pointed process on some part of a plant or animal; a prickle.

1753 *Chambers' Cycl.* Suppl. s.v. *Spider*, They all have weapons issuing out of the mouth... They consist, in some, of two spiculæ, in the manner of a forked hook. **1792** BELKNAP *Hist. New Hampsh.* III. 125 It [the prickly ash] is armed with *spiculæ*, like the locust. **1800** *Phil. Trans.* XC. 370 The spiculæ on the shark's skin were also separated. **1815** KIRBY & SP. *Entomol.* iv. (1818) I. 114 Others are barbed like the spicula of a bee's sting. **1866** *Treas. Bot.* 1082/2 *Spicula*, a fine fleshy erect point.

b. In fungi: = SPICULE 2.

1866 *Treas. Bot.* 1082/2.

3. *Bot.* A floral spikelet. *rare.*

1760 J. LEE *Introd. Bot.* III. xxii. (1765) 227 *Spicula*, a little spike. **1793** MARTYN *Lang. Bot.*, *Spicula*, a Spicule or Spikelet. A partial spike, or a subdivision of it: as in some Grasses. **1830** LINDLEY *Nat. Syst. Bot.* 293 In certain genera with a simple spike.. this is clearly proved by the structure of the terminal flower or spicula.

4. A slender pointed fragment *of* bone, etc.

1835–6 *Todd's Cycl. Anat.* I. 237/1 A spicula of a fractured bone. **1870** H. LONSDALE *Life R. Knox* xii. 249 My finger was caught by a sharp spicula of bone.

5. = SPICULUM 3.

1845 GOSSE *Ocean* i. (1849) 53 In the substance of many species [of sponge].. are found *spiculæ*, or needle-like crystals, of pure flint. **1859** R. HUNT *Guide Mus. Pract. Geol.* (ed. 2) 252 Silicious spiculæ or the minute bones of sponges.

6. *Comb.*, as *spicula-like*; **spicula-forceps** (see quot. 1875).

1857 DANA *Min.* (1862) 124 The fine spicula-like crystalline grains of Epsom salt. **1875** KNIGHT *Dict. Mech.* 2265/2 *Spicula-forceps*, a dentist's long-nosed forceps for removing small fragments of bone, etc.

spicular ('spɪkjʊlə(r)), *a.* [f. SPICUL-A, SPICUL-E, or SPICUL-UM + -AR. Cf. F. *spiculaire*.]

1. Of the nature of a spicule or spicula; slender and sharp-pointed; also, characterized by the presence of spicules: **a.** In *Min.*, *Zool.*, etc.

1794 R. J. SULIVAN *View Nat.* I. 308 Spicular poisons, antimony and sublimate, may be rendered inoffensive by sheathing their points in oil or in wax. **1796** KIRWAN *Elem. Min.* (ed. 2) II. 197 [Tin stone] found massive,.. or in blunt, or spicular fragments. **1832** BREWSTER *Nat. Magic* xiii. 340 In several cavities in minerals I have found.. black spicular crystals. **1861** J. R. GREENE *Man. Anim. Kingd.*, *Cœlent.* 160 We find, in the genus *Zoanthus*, a spicular corallum. *Ibid.* 161 The spicular stage permanently exemplified in *Alcyonium*. **1872** H. A. NICHOLSON *Palæont.* 72 A peculiar tubular or spicular skeleton.

b. In general use.

1822–7 GOOD *Study Med.* (1829) I. 614 Calcareous or other spicular materials, inhaled while working on stones or metals. *Ibid.* IV. 556 Some spicular node within the cranium. **1844** H. STEPHENS *Bk. Farm* I. 298 Should the flakes be spicular and fall very thick and fast, then a heavy fall.. may be expected.

2. Characteristic of a spicule or spicules.

1813 *Edinb. Rev.* XXI. 55 The castellated and spicular appearance of the ruins of the sandstone.

†**'spiculate**, *v.* *Obs.* [In sense 1 f. L. *spīculāt-*, ppl. stem of *spīculāre* to point; in sense 2 f. L. *spīculum* sharp point, arrow, ray, etc.]

1. *trans.* To sharpen to a point. *rare*$^{-0}$.

1623 COCKERAM II, To make a sharp Point to a thing, *spiculate*.

2. To pierce or transfix. *rare*$^{-1}$.

1834 SOUTHEY *Doctor* lxxxvii. (1848) 191 In those representations [in old almanacks] man.. stood erect and naked, spiculated by emitted influences from the said signs.

spiculate ('spɪkjʊlət), *a.* *Bot.* [ad. L. *spīculāt-us*, pa. pple. of *spīculāre* to point.] (See quot.)

1832 LINDLEY *Introd. Bot.* 395. **1856** HENSLOW *Dict. Bot. Terms* 178 *Spiculate*,.. where a surface is covered with fine pointed fleshy appendages. Also.. when a spike is composed of several smaller spikes (or rather spikelets) crowded together.

'spiculated, *a.* [f. as prec. + -ED[1].]

†**1.** Containing spiculæ. *Obs.*$^{-1}$

1738 D. BAYNE *Gout* 105 Acrimony arises from the different modifications of spiculated salts. **1794** R. J. SULIVAN *View Nat.* I. 308 Blood and oil are globular; corrosive sublimate spiculated; and antimony is in small filaments, like needles.

2. Having the form of a spicula; slender and sharp-pointed.

1744 *Phil. Trans.* XLIII. 186 From its upper End arise five spiculated *Aristæ*. **1768** *Elaboratory* 218 The spiculated or needle-like form of the saline concretions.

3. Furnished with sharp points or spikelets.

1762 tr. *Büsching's Syst. Geog.* I. 236 Some whales have *Spicula* in their jaws... Of the spiculated kind with a flat back, the chief is the real Greenland Whale. **1777** MASON *Eng. Garden* II. 16 Extend a rail of elm, securely arm'd With spiculated paling. **1836–9** *Todd's Cycl. Anat.* II. 803 The spiculated edges of the cavity protruded into the pelvis.

spicu'lation. [f. SPICULA, etc.: see -ATION.] Formation into a spicule or spicules.

1868 G. M. HOPKINS *Jrnls. & Papers* (1959) 185 Spiculation in a dry blot in a smooth inkstand. **1880** *Jrnl. Linn. Soc.* XV. 150 Sketches of the spiculation of another sponge. **1900** B. D. JACKSON *Gloss. Bot. Terms* 247 *Spiculation*, Nylander's term for a hyphal constriction in spore-formation, the extremity being left as a spicule.

spicule ('spɪkjuːl). [a. F. *spicule*, or anglicizing of SPICULA, SPICULUM.]

1. *Bot.* **a.** A floral spikelet (cf. SPICULA 3). **b.** (See quot. 1855.)

1785 MARTYN *Lett. Bot.* xiii. (1794) 136 Spicules triangular. [*Note*] These are the little assemblages of flowers, or ultimate subdivisions of the panicle or whole. *Ibid.* 137 The spicules are ovate, and on short foot-stalks. **1855** MISS PRATT *Flower. Pl.* I. 5 *Spicules*, two little wing-like pieces often seen at the base of the leafstalk, as in the Rose.

2. One or other of the points of the basidia or sporophores in fungals.

1843 *Penny Cycl.* XXV. 183/1 The hymenium [of *Exidia glandulosa*] is covered with spicules. **1866** *Treas. Bot.* 1088/2 In such *Fungi* as agarics the sporophores.. bear generally four little points called spicules,.. on which the spores are seated. In *Tremella* the sporophores are globular or quadripartite, the spicules being drawn out into long threads. **1875** COOKE *Fungi* 22 With which also their structure agrees, excepting in the development of spicules.

3. In sponges: = SPICULUM 3.

1846 DANA *Zooph.* (1848) 645 The cortex.. shows numerous minute granules or spicules of lime, disseminated through it. **1860** MAURY *Phys. Geog.* xiv. 616 *note*, A considerable number of silicious spicules of sponges. **1885** J. E. TAYLOR *Brit. Fossils* i. 9 When alive the outer layer of 'sponge-flesh' is usually permeated with myriads of exceedingly small solid bodies, called fibres and *spicules*.

attrib. **1887** Sollas in *Encycl. Brit.* XXII. 416/1 A thin layer of organic matter, known as the *spicule sheath*, forms an outer investment to the spicule.

4. *Zool.* A needle-like or sharp-pointed process or part.

1861 J. R. Greene *Anim. Kingd., Cœlent.* 160 In some species of *Alcyonidæ* proper, the spicules attain a comparatively large size. **1872** H. A. Nicholson *Palæont.* 66 All the Radiolaria possess hard structures in the form of siliceous spicules or a siliceous test. **1890** *Science-Gossip* XXVI. 198 The ovate individuals..showed the mouth or osculum fringed with spicules standing erect.

5. A fine-pointed piece, splinter, or fragment of some hard substance; a spicula or spiculum.

1835 J. Paget *Let.* 16 Apr. in S. Paget *Mem. & Lett. Sir J. Paget* (1901) 57 The same appearances have been noticed in our dissecting-rooms, where they have been attributed to the deposition of small spicules of bone (which, indeed, they somewhat resemble). **1865** Milton & Cheadle *N.-W. Passage by Land* xv. 301 The fallen timber lay as thickly and entangled as the spiculæ in the children's game of spelicans. **1878** Huxley *Physiogr.* 62 A nucleus from which six little spicules or rods of ice are shot forth. **1879** Khory *Digest Med.* 37 Under the microscope granular matter, and spheres with spicules sticking on them, are seen. **1895** Hoffman *Beginnings of Writing* 37 A small bundle of needles, spicules of bone, or fish spines.

6. *Astr.* Any of numerous short-lived, relatively small radial jets of gas observed to occur in the sun's atmosphere in the chromosphere and lower corona.

1945 W. O. Roberts in *Astrophysical Jrnl.* CI. 136 Small spikes of chromospheric material, observed in Hα with the coronagraph and quartz-polaroid monochromator are described. These spicules, seen in polar regions of the sun, have very brief lifetimes, amounting on the average to 4 or 5 minutes. **1948**, etc. [see jet *sb.*[3] 4 c (ii)]. **1974** Bray & Loughhead *Solar Chromosphere* ii. 60 Spicules in the polar regions of the sun tend to follow the direction of the overlying coronal rays. **1978** Pasachoff & Kutner *University Astron.* viii. 191 Spicules are best seen when we are looking off the edge of the sun, beyond the limb.

spiculi- (ˈspɪkjʊlɪ), combining form, after L. models, of spicula, spicule, and spiculum, occurring in a few *Zool.* terms, as **spicuˈliferous** *a.*, bearing spicules. **ˈspiculiform** *a.*, formed like a spicule; sharp-pointed. **spicuˈligenous** *a.*, 'containing spicules' (Webster, 1847). **spicuˈligerous** *a.*, spiculiferous.

1836–9 *Todd's Cycl. Anat.* II. 866/1 In the fourth section, *Tubulifera*,..the abdomen is furnished..with a *spiculiferous ovipositor. **1841** *Penny Cycl.* XX. 423/2 Many hook-formed spiculiferous lobes. **1846** Dana *Zooph.* iv. (1848) 36 These *spiculiform organs..are of three kinds. **1852** —— *Crust.* II. 708 A slender spiculiform process. **1877** Huxley *Anat. Inv. Anim.* iii. 118 The inner cells..in the meanwhile have become *spiculigerous.

†**spiculine,** *a. Obs. rare.* [f. spicul-a or spicul-um + -ine[2].] = spiculated *ppl. a.* 2.

1754 *Phil. Trans.* XLVIII. 836 It seems to be from this spiculine or needle-like form..that antimonial preparations have their emetic quality. **1775** *Ibid.* LXV. 92 The first solution..deposits some of its colour in the form of minute spiculine crystals.

spiculo- (ˈspɪkjʊləʊ), combining form of spiculum (cf. sense 3), occurring in a few terms, as ***spiculo-fibre, -fibrous***.

1900 *Proc. Zool. Soc.* 137 Skeleton [of the sponge] forming a rectangular network, the meshes being..with a few slender primary lines of spiculo-fibre 2–4 spicules thick. *Ibid.* 138 Skeleton consisting of an axial or central open spiculo-fibrous network.

‖**spiculum** (ˈspɪkjʊləm). Pl. spicula. [a. L. *spiculum* sharp point, sting, dart, etc., dim. of *spica* spike *sb.*]

1. = spicula 1 and 1 b.

1746 R. James *Moufet's Health Improv.* 32 Another Class of Medicines.. consists of such Substances as sheath the Spicula, or sharp Points of the Acid. **1839** Darwin *Voy. Nat.* xvii. 398 We were enveloped in a cloud which was falling under the form of minute frozen spicula. **1863** Baring-Gould *Iceland* 119 Composed of minute spicula of ice.

transf. and *fig.* **1840** Fraser *Koordistan*, etc. II. vi. 146 The wind was..loaded with spicula of cold, which penetrated every limb and joint. **1847** Emerson *Repr. Men, Swedenborg* Wks. (Bohn) I. 317 His style lustrous with points and shooting spicula of thought.

2. *Zool.* A sharp-pointed process or formation.

1762 tr. *Büsching's Syst. Geog.* I. 236 Some whales have *Spicula* in their jaws, as those of Greenland, the Nordcaper, the Fin Fish. **1844** Emerson *Ess., Nature* (1901) 313 It publishes itself in creatures, reaching from particles and spicula..to the highest symmetries. **1856–8** W. Clark *Van der Hoeven's Zool.* I. 78 Crowded with microscopic calcareous spicula. **1859** J. Tomes *Dental Surg.* (1873) 5 Projecting inwards from the free edge of the outer and inner alveolar walls, we observe small spicula.

b. The excitatory dart in snails.

1838 *Penny Cycl.* XII. 105/2 Dr. Maton often observed these *spicula*, but never saw them actually projected from one to the other. **1856–8** W. Clark *Van der Hoeven's Zool.* I. 190 Male genital organ a double spiculum. **1866** R. Tate *Brit. Mollusks* iv. 119 The snails are furnished with spicula—crystalline darts, which they eject at each other.

3. One of the calcareous or siliceous needles found in sponges. Usu. in pl.

1842 *Penny Cycl.* XXII. 376/1 The calcareous and silicious spicula, and the formation and distribution of the pores and orifices of sponges. **1865** Gosse *Land & Sea* (1874) 266 These spicula or needles..make up the firm portion of the Sponge. **1877** Huxley *Anat. Inv. Anim.* iii. 114 A multitude of separate spicula, composed of an animal substance..impregnated with carbonate of lime.

attrib. **1883** Saville-Kent *Fisheries Bahamas* 33 In a third group, that of the *Calcispongiæ*, a spicula skeleton is likewise developed.

4. = spicula 4.

1872 Mivart *Anat.* 116 The malar bone may be merely a delicate spiculum of bone. **1874** G. Lawson *Dis. Eye* (ed. 2) 68 To detect a fine spiculum of steel, or a fragment of glass, ..which may have been impacted on the cornea.

spicy (ˈspaɪsɪ), *a.* Also 6 spycye, 8–9 spicey. [f. spice *sb.*]

1. Having the characteristic qualities of spice; of the nature of spice.

1562 Turner *Herbal* II. (1568) 50 The shel smelleth well, and is spycye, not onely in smell, but also in taste. **1626** Bacon *Sylva* §464 So Fennell-seeds are sweet before they ripen, and after grow spicy. **1667** Milton *P.L.* II. 640 Whence Merchants bring Thir spicie Drugs. **1725** De Foe *Voy. round World* (1840) 112 The herbs were of a spicy kind, and had a most pleasant agreeable taste. **1789** W. Buchan *Dom. Med.* (1790) 431 The diet must be..seasoned with spicy and aromatic vegetables. **1806** A. Hunter *Culina* (ed. 3) 125 The French Cooks make a spicey mixture that does not discover a predominancy of any one of the spices over the others. **1833** Ht. Martineau *Cinnamon & Pearls* iii. 54 The sun could penetrate to the pure white sand from which the spicy stems sprang.

fig. **1646** J. Hall *Poems* 37 When age shall..all that Red remove That on thy spicy lip now ly's. **1847** Emerson *Poems, Monadnoc* Wks. (Bohn) I. 438 Fountain-drop of spicier worth Than all the vintage of the earth.

b. Flavoured or mixed with spice.

1632 Milton *L'Allegro* 100 The Spicy Nut-brown Ale. **1807** Crabbe *Par. Reg.* I. 259 Here his poor bird th'inhuman cocker brings,.. With spicy food th'impatient spirit feeds.

2. Having the fragrance of spice; sweet-scented, aromatic: **a.** Of flowers.

1765 Cath. Talbot *Lett.* (1808) II. 21 Here [there is] a gale of spicy pinks, here the breath of lillies. **1797** Mrs. Radcliffe *Italian* xiii, The spicy myrtle sent forth all its fragrance. **1830** Tennyson *Poet's Mind* 13 Holy water will I pour Into every spicy flower Of the laurel-shrubs. **1845–50** Mrs. Lincoln *Lect. Bot.* 105/2 *Gaultheria procumbens* (spicy wintergreen). **1867** Augusta Wilson *Vashti* xxiv, An exquisitely beautiful and fragrant bouquet..fringed daintily with spicy geranium leaves.

b. Of air, breezes, etc.

1650 Vaughan *Silex Scint.* (1885) 51 Calm streams; Joyes full, and true; Fresh, spicie mornings. **1712** Pope *Messiah* 27 See spicy clouds from lowly Saron rise. **1713** —— *Windsor For.* 392 Led by new stars, and borne by spicy gales! **1820** Keats *Hyperion* I. 186 When he would taste the spicy wreaths Of incense. **1855** Browning *Fra Lippo* 340 Tasting the air this spicy night which turns The unaccustomed head like Chianti wine!

3. Containing or producing, abounding in, spices.

1648 Crashaw *Poems* (1904) 144 A fragrant Breath suckt from the spicy nest O' th' precious Phœnix. **1667** Milton *P.L.* IV. 162 As when..North-East windes blow Sabean Odours from the spicie shoare Of Arabie the blest. **1746** Hervey *Refl. Flower-Garden* 43 All the Odours of the spicy East. **1781** Cowper *Charity* 442 The stores [which] The sun matures on India's spicy shores. **1813** Shelley *Q. Mab* VIII. 64 Fragrant zephyrs there from spicy isles Ruffle the placid ocean-deep.

b. Consisting of spice; conveying spice.

1712 W. King *Brit. Pallad.* 39 Restore the spicy traffick of the East. **1840** Hood *Up Rhine* 31 Masts of spicy vessels From distant Surinam.

4. Of qualities: Appropriate to, or characteristic of, spices.

1652 Crashaw *Carmen Deo Nostro* Poems (1904) 197 O dissipate thy spicy Powres. **1728** Chambers *Cycl., Zeodary* ..for its spicy Warmth is commended in Cholics. **1732** Arbuthnot *Rules of Diet* in *Aliments*, etc. I. 244 Burnet, astringent, with a gentle spicy Quality. **1821** Clare *Vill. Minstr.* I. 115 Spikenard's spicy smell. **1883** *Cent. Mag.* Oct. 814/2 The great variety of flowers and their spicy flavour.

†**5.** *Sc.* (See quots.) *Obs.*

1768 [Sir D. Dalrymple] *Bannatyne Poems* 276 Thus a *spicy man* is still used for one self-conceited and proud. **1808** Jamieson, *Spicy*, proud, testy.

6. *slang.* **a.** Full of spirit, smartness, or 'go'.

1828 *Sporting Mag.* (N.S.) XXI. 324 We had a remarkably spicy team out of town. **1829** *Ibid.* XXIII. 291 Four little spicy devils, it would be difficult for anything I should think to catch. **1858–61** E. B. Ramsay *Remin.* vi. (1870) 238 It..requires to be performed with a particular and *spicy* dexterity of hand. **1898** Wollocombe *From Morn till Eve* viii. 196 A well-appointed drag appeared with its spicy team stepping well together.

b. Smart-looking; neat. Also as *adv.*

1846 Huxley in L. Huxley *Life* (1900) I. ii. 28 The spicy oilcloth..on the floor looks most respectable. **1854** F. E. Smedley *H. Coverdale's Courtsh.* i, The fortunate possessor of a spicy dog-cart, a blood mare to run in it. **1859** Meredith *R. Feveral* xxix, That young Tom! He've come to town dressed that spicy.

7. Of writing or discourse: Smart and pointed; pungent; having a flavour of the sensational or scandalous; somewhat improper.

1844 J. T. Hewlett *Parsons & W.* li, The articles were so clever, and so very 'spicy'. **1848** *Punch* XV. 62, I wish you would say something spicy about the new regulation. **1891** Farrar *Darkn. & Dawn* xxvi, It is composed of the spiciest libels against every senator of note whom he ventures to attack.

8. Exciting, exhilarating.

1853 Kane *Grinnell Exped.* xxxvii. (1854) 335 The spicy tingling of a crisis.

9. *Comb.*, as ***spicy-looking, -smelling***.

1819 Scott *Ivanhoe* xxxvii, A warming and spicy-smelling balsam. **1850** F. E. Smedley *F. Fairlegh* (1894) 4 A spicy-looking nag. **1901** *Wide World Mag.* VI. 469/2 It is planted thick with spicy-smelling pines and firs.

ˈspiddock. *north. dial.* Also 7 spidick, 9 spiddick. [Alteration of spigot *sb.*] A spigot.

1629 *Vestry Bks.* (Surtees) 298 For a spidick and a cannell, 1d. **1685** G. M[eriton] *Praise of Yorksh. Ale* 15 Then out they pulled the Tapps, And stuck the Spiddocks finely in their Hats. **1825** Brockett *N.C. Gloss.*, *Spiddick-and-fawcet*, a wooden instrument used as a substitute for a cock to let out liquors. **1849–** in dial. glossaries (Durh., Lanc., Yks., Cumbld.).

spider (ˈspaɪdə(r)), *sb.* Forms: 1 spiþra, 4 spiþre, 5 spiþer(e, spither, spyther; 5–7 spyder, 6– spider (7 spidar). [OE. *spiþra* (Saxon Leechd. II. 142):—**spinþra*, f. *spinnan* spin *v.*

In the obscure passage in *Saxon Leechd.* III. 42 the reading of the MS. is *spiden* (not *spider*) *wiht.*]

1. a. One or other of the arachnids belonging to the insectivorous order *Araneidæ*, many species of which possess the power of spinning webs in which their prey is caught.

The cunning, skill, and industry of the spider, as well as its power of secreting or emitting poison, are frequently alluded to in literature. The various species or groups of spiders are freq. denoted by some distinguishing word, as *bird-catching, crab-, cross-, diadem-, garden-, house-, jumping-, mason-, sedentary, spinning, trap-door-, wall-, wandering spider*, etc.: see these words.

1340 *Ayenb.* 164 And þe greate niedes of þe wordle him þingþ ase naȝt, and þeruore hise ne prayzeþ naȝt bote ase þe web of þe spiþre. **1398** Trevisa *Barth. De. P.R.* xviii. liv. (Bodl. MS.), þis formicalion..is a manere kinde of spiþeres. *c* **1440** *Wycliffite Bible* Job viii. 14 His trist schal be as a web of spiþers [*v.rr.* yreyns, areyns; *earlier version* attercoppis]. *c* **1440** *Promp. Parv.* 140/2 Eranye, or spyder, or spynnare. **1480** Caxton *Myrr.* II. xv. 101 The spyther or spyncop. **1526** *Pilgr. Perf.* (W. de W. 1531) 54 How the vyne of grace ..shold be kepte,..that neyther beestes, wormes, ne spiders come therto. **1592** Greene *Repent. R. Greene* Wks. (Grosart) XII. 180 They with the spider sucke poison out of the most pretious flowers. **1665** in *Verney Mem.* (1907) II. 244 The house..being horidly nasty,..the spiders are redy to drope into my mouthe. **1697** Dryden *Virg. Georg.* IV. 361 Or Secret Moaths are there in Silence fed; Or Spiders in the Vault their snary Webs have spred. **1727–46** Thomson *Summer* 269 The window..where, gloomily retir'd, The villain spider lives, cunning, and fierce, Mixture abhorr'd! **1782** Priestley *Corrupt. Chr.* II. vi. 51 In case..any fly or spider should fall into the wine. **1828** Lytton *Pelham* xx, Because rogues are like spiders, and eat each other, when there is nothing else to catch. **1861** Hulme tr. *Moquin-Tandon* II. v. ii. 262 In hot climates, Spiders are able to produce..a certain amount of local pain. **1896** tr. *Boas' Text Bk. Zool.* 283 The Spiders may be distinguished from other Arachnida by the separation of the cephalothorax from the abdomen by a deep constriction.

b. In allusive use.

1596 Shaks. *Merch. V.* III. ii. 121 Here in her haires The Painter plaies the Spider, and hath wouen A golden mesh t'intrap the hearts of men. **1894** Mrs. Dyan *Man's Keeping* (1899) 310 There was too much of the alluring spider and giddy fly business in the arrangement.

c. Applied to persons as an opprobrious or vituperative term.

1568 T. Howell *Arb. Amitie* (1879) 58 For spightfull spiders spare not, For curious carpers care not. **1579** Lodge *Reply Gosson* 35 From the same flower..whence the Spyder (I mean the ignorant) take their poison. **1594** Shaks. *Rich. III*, I. iii. 242 Why strew'st thou Sugar on that Bottel'd Spider, Whose deadly Web ensnareth thee about? **1602** *Narcissus* 1893 577 Dare you vse mee thus to my face, spidar? **1638** Chillingw. *Relig. Prot.* I. Concl. 410 If you were ten times more a spider then you are, you could suck no poyson from them. **1798** Southey *To a Spider* iii. Poet. Wks. 1837 II. 180 Hell's huge black Spider, for mankind he lays His toils, as thou for flies. **1821–2** Shelley *Chas. I*, IV. 16 Realms..beyond the shot of tyranny, Beyond the webs of that swoln spider. **1898** 'Merriman' *Roden's Corner* i. 3 In such a shop..there is always a human spider lurking in the background, who steals out upon any human fly that may pause to look at the wares.

†**d.** ***to swallow a spider***, to go bankrupt. *Obs.*

1670 Ray *Prov.* 194 He hath swallowed a spider, *i.e.* plaid the bankrupt.

e. ***electrical spider*** (see quot.).

1842 Francis *Dict. Arts, Sci.*, etc. s.v., *Electrical Spider*, a small ball of pith, cut of the size, and into the form of a spider, suspended by a long filament of silk, and with eight linen thread legs.

2. a. Applied, usually with distinguishing term, to other allied species of *Arachnida* resembling spiders in appearance; esp. the harvest-spider; a spider-mite. See also red spider, sea spider.

1665 Hooke *Microgr.* 198 The Carter, Shepherd Spider, or long-legg'd spider. **1688** Holme *Armoury* II. x. 215/2 The long legged Spider of the Garden, or Field. **1806** Shaw *Gen. Zool.* VI. II. 473 To this genus [*Phalangium*] belong those well known insects called long-legged, shepherd, or harvest Spiders. **1818** Kirby & Sp. *Entomol.* xxiii. (ed. 2) II. 307 Octopods..including the tribes of mites (*Acaridæ*); spiders (*Araneidæ*); long-legged spiders (*Phalangidæ*); and scorpions. **1848** [see long-legged *a.*].

b. (See quot.)

1863 Couch *Brit. Fishes* II. 43 The fishes of the genus *Trachinus*..have from an early date obtained for themselves a formidable reputation under the names of Spiders and Sea Dragons.

c. A spider-crab.

1853 T. Bell *Brit. Stalk-eyed Crustacea* 42 Like all the other triangular Crustacea, the fishermen inveterately term it [*sc.* the spinous spider-crab] 'spider'.

d. A species of artificial fly used in angling; a hackle-fly.

1857 W. C. STEWART *Pract. Angler* v. 81 Spiders dressed of very soft feathers are more suitable for fishing up than for fishing down.

3. a. A kind of frying-pan having legs and a long handle; also loosely, a frying-pan. Orig. *U.S.*

1807 in *Austin Papers* (1924) I. I. 132, 2 Spiders with Covers. **1830** GALT *Lawrie T.* III. xii. (1849) 125 A judicious selection of spiders and frying-pans. **1842** WHITTIER in Pickard *Life* (1895) I. 278 Like fishes dreaming of the sea, And waking in the spider. **1869** MRS. WHITNEY *We Girls* vi, It is slopping and burning, and putting away with a rinse, that makes kettles and spiders untouchable.

b. *U.S.* A trivet or tripod; a griddle.

1875 in KNIGHT *Dict. Mech.*

4. *Austr. slang.* A drink consisting of lemonade and brandy or similar ingredients, mixed; a soft drink with ice-cream floating in it.

1854 *Argus* (Melb.), They asked us what we would have to drink; we had a spider each. **1859** K. CORNWALLIS *New World* I. 300 Shandy-gaff, or spiders,—the latter to clear their throats of flies as they said. **1859** FOWLER *Southern Lights* 52. **1861** H. EARLE *Ups & Downs* 283 They are.. up to unlimited 'spiders', or lemonade and sherry. **1888** E. FINN *Chron. Early Melbourne* ii. 548 The favourite tipple of the bushman was mixed brandy and ginger beer—a 'spider', as it was called. **1941** *Coast to Coast* 229 'You've had your drink, so now you've got to buy us all a spider at Smith's'. .. I didn't want to go back and sit in Smith's and drink silly coloured muck with ice-cream floating in it. **1965** G. MCINNES *Road to Gundagai* 14 She reached for a thick yellow glass and poured in the ginger beer.. an enormous dollop of ice-cream which she dropped into the ginger beer. 'There's your spider.' **1974** BUCKLEY & HAMILTON *Festival* 127 You used to strut into the milk bar as though you owned the place. 'A lime spider, Harry.'

5. *Naut.* (See quots. and *spider-hoop*.)

1860 NARES *Naval Cadet's Guide* 5 *Spiders*, an iron outrigger to keep blocks clear of the ship's side. *c* **1860** H. STUART *Seaman's Catech.* 71 What are spiders? They are somewhat similar to goose necks, only they are supported by three legs, to enable them to resist strain in different directions; they are used for the after main brace and main sheet. **1874** THEARLE *Naval Archit.* 66 An iron forging termed a 'spider', with a square hole or a socket in the top, .. is let down over the top of the rudder. **1875** KNIGHT *Dict. Mech.* 2265/2 *Spider*,.. a hoop around a mast provided with belaying-pins.

6. a. *techn.* One or other of various parts or pieces of machinery, or of instruments and other apparatus, *esp.* one consisting of a framework or metal casting with radiating arms or spokes suggestive of the legs of a spider.

1860 CLARK & COLBURN *Recent Practice Locomotive Engine* 52/1 In driving wheels, the centre, or 'spider', for a 5-feet wheel to carry 4½ tons, will weigh 1800 pounds and upwards. **1875** KNIGHT *Dict. Mech.* 2265/2 *Spider*, a skeleton of radiating spokes; as a sprocket-wheel consisting of spokes on a rotating shaft. **1888** BOTTONE *Electr. Instrum. Making* (ed. 2) 109 Which pins.. serve to bolt the armature firmly to the brass star-wheel, or 'spider', by means of which it is affixed to the shaft. **1935** A. G. INGALLS *Amateur Telescope Making* (ed. 4) 371 Another interesting diffraction phenomena [*sic*].. known to most able telescope designers, is the fact that there will be fewer diffraction lines from a four-legged diagonal support spider than from one having only three legs. **1961** MICZAIKA & SINTON *Tools of Astronomer* iii. 75 Diffraction of light by the spider supporting the secondary mirror is a frequent complaint. **1966** L. A. H. EASTMAN tr. *Schenkel's Plastics Extrusion Technol. & Theory* xi. 326 The melt is.. fed via a 90° bend into a distributor spider, which may have four to eight symmetrically arranged radial channels.

b. (See quot.)

1875 KNIGHT *Dict. Mech.* 2265/2 *Spider*,.. the solid interior portion of a piston to which the packing is attached and to whose axis the piston-rod is secured.

c. *U.S. Coal mining.* (See quot.)

1883 GRESLEY *Gloss. Coal-m.* 230 *Spiders*,.. see Drum rings. [*Ibid.* 91 *Drum-rings*, cast iron wheels, with projections, to which are bolted the staves or laggings forming the surface for the ropes to lap upon.]

d. *Austral. Opal-mining.* (See quot. 1912.)

1912 *Empire Mag.* Nov. 281/2 *Spider*, a small iron instrument which serves the double purpose of holding the candle, and 'lifting' the seam of opal. **1940** I. L. IDRIESS *Lightning Ridge* xxiii. 158, I gouged around and under, then pryed it out with the spider point. **1958** M. D. BERRINGTON *Stones of Fire* iii. 33 A candle in a 'spider' that queer, spiked holder that is used below ground. **1967** *Sunday Mail Mag.* (Brisbane) 10 Dec. 3/5 The candle in its spider dropped to the floor and went out.

e. *Engin.* A metal sleeve within which an object may be gripped by screws or wedges.

1920 *Bull. U.S. Bureau of Mines* No. 182. 7 *Spider*, tool that encircles and holds the pipe by means of steel wedges. *Ibid.* 17 The swinging spider.. is probably one of the most useful inventions.. for the handling of casing in drilling oil wells. **1940** [see CAT-HEAD *sb.* 3 c]. **1950** A. W. JUDGE *Centre, Capstan & Automatic Lathes* II. iii. 135 The short end of the hub faces outwards, and the spider is gripped between the arms by three chuck jaws. **1977** R. D. LANGENKAMP *Handbk. Oil Industry Terms & Phrases* (ed. 2) 159 The spider is manually locked around a length of tubing just below the tool joint. Some advanced types of elevator spiders are air operated.

f. *Electronics.* A flexible linkage formerly placed between the moving cone and the fixed magnet assembly of a loudspeaker.

1928 *Wireless World* 6 June 608/1 A centring device in the form of a brass spider attached to the pin is supplied. **1948** G. A. BRIGGS *Loudspeakers* vi. 20 The bakelised spider gives a sharply defined bass response to the cone, resulting in a crispness in the tone. **1959** N. H. CROWHURST *Basic Audio* I. 49 To prevent the coil rubbing against the magnet poles, a centering 'spider' or suspension is used, which allows free movement in the direction of vibration, while preventing the coil from moving against the pole faces.

7. a. A lightly-built cart, trap, or phaeton with a high body and disproportionately large and slender wheels. Orig. *S. African.* Also (*Austral.*), a trotting gig.

1879 *Daily News* 21 Aug. 5/4, I don't know how often that 'spider' and I rolled over together into the mud. **1882** MRS. HECKFORD *Lady Trader* 241 A spanking pair of horses in a spider, brought the sheriff from Pretoria. **1895** *Outing* XXVII. 186 A few days later he journeyed again to Brooklyn .. and found her spider standing in front of the door. **1945** S. J. BAKER *Austral. Lang.* ix. 175 *Spider* or *junker*, a trotting gig. **1955** A. ROSS *Australia 55* 34 The drivers, dressed in silks like jockeys, sit behind their animals in tiny carriages known as spiders. **1969** *West Australian* 5 July 32/5 Causing Pyraket to strike and badly buckle the inside wheel of Master Flame's spider.

b. An early bicycle with the benefit of steel wheels, as opp. to those of wood. Cf. *spider-wheel*, sense 11 a below. Now only *Hist.*

1874 *Bicycling* 4 Had he lived in the days of the 'Coventry Spiders'. **1908** E. M. SNEYD-KYNNERSLEY *H.M.I.* ix. 82 Safety bicycles were not yet: the Boneshaker was not tempting, and the Spider was perilous.

8. In various elliptical uses (see sense 11): **a.** A spider-table. **b.** A spider-rest. **c.** A spider-cell. **d.** A spider-nævus.

(*a*) **1848** [M. W. SAVAGE] *Bachelor of the Albany* 70 A nest of spiders for embroidery or chess, an oblong table,.. and a round table.

(*b*) **1887** in *Cassell's Encycl. Dict.* **1896** W. J. FORD in Broadfoot *Billiards* 392 Beginners should be cautioned to watch carefully for foul strokes, especially when the rest or spider is being used.

(*c*) **1893** *Brit. Med. Jrnl.* 26 Aug. 462 Contemporaneously the nerve-cells shewed signs of degeneration, amongst them were seen the proliferating spiders.

(*d*) **1942** *Amer. Jrnl. Med. Sci.* CCIV. 251 The well known increase in excretion of estrogenic substances in pregnancy coincides with the period during which vascular spiders and palmar erythema tend to appear. **1948** D. BALLANTYNE *Cunninghams* iii. 15 Winter weather gave her the blue spiders. **1969** *Daily Colonist* (Victoria, B.C.) 9 Jan. 2/3 Does wearing a 'pants-type' girdle cause broken blood vessels in the thighs?.. These little vessels are called 'spiders'... These spiders are commonest in women; hence the hormone (estrogen) level is thought to have a bearing. **1974** R. M. KIRK et al. *Surgery* vi. 107 Hepatic failure causes weakness, .. vascular spiders (named from the spider-like appearance of dilated arterioles), palmar erythema.. and encephalopathy.

9. *Cards.* A variety of patience played with two packs.

1890 'CAVENDISH' *Patience Games* 186 The Spider.. requires quite sufficient exercise of thought to render it very interesting. **1901** 'TARBART' *Patience* 49 Spider. Played with two full packs of cards. **1930** W. S. MAUGHAM *Gent. in Parlour* xv. 78, I knew seventeen varieties of patience. I tried the Spider and never by any chance got it out.

10. *attrib.* and *Comb.* **a.** Simple attrib., as ***spider-cloth, -cord, -film, floss, -form, -kind, -silk, -snare, -sting, -thread, tribe.***

1916 D. H. LAWRENCE *Amores* 86 Great grey *spider-cloths hanging Low from the roof. **1863** GROSART *Small Sins* (ed. 2) 35 A scratch like the slenderest *spider-cord. **1835** BROWNING *Paracelsus* III. 76 Despising youth's allurements, and rejecting As *spider-films the shackles I endure. **1978** C. TOMLINSON *Shaft* 13 Finer than the lines Of *spider floss. **1954** J. R. R. TOLKIEN *Two Towers* 332 There agelong she had dwelt, an evil thing in *spider-form. **1753** *Chambers' Cycl.* Suppl., *Solipuga*,.. a small venomous insect of the *spider-kind. **1861** *Med. Times* 20 Apr. 421/1 A large black monkey of the spider kind. **1728** CHAMBERS *Cycl.* s.v. *Silk*, *Spider-Silk. Within a few Years the Secret has been found in France, of procuring and preparing Silk of the Webs of Spiders. **1875** *Encycl. Brit.* II. 295/2 With respect to the economic or mercantile value of spider silk. **1796** BURNS *Poem on Life* v, To put us daft; Syne weave, unseen, thy *spider snare, O' hell's damned waft. **1852** MUNDY *Antipodes* (1857) 179 Thanks to the *spider-sting, I felt too feverish to leave the ship. **1541** R. COPLAND *Galyen's Terap.* 2 A iij b, A *spyder threde. **1848** MRS. CARLYLE *Lett.* (1883) II. 31 His dislike to be connected in people's minds, by even the slightest spider-thread, with what he calls 'George Sandism'. **1868** WATTS *Dict. Chem.* V. 399 Spider-threads appear to consist essentially of.. sericin. **1894** BARING-GOULD *Deserts S. France* I. 1 The traveller.. having crossed that spider-thread viaduct of Garabit. **1805** BINGLEY *Anim. Biog.* III. 603 *Spider Tribe.

b. Passing into adj., with the sense 'like that of a spider; *esp.* slender, thin; spider-like, spidery'.

1632 MASSINGER *Maid of Hon.* I. ii, Be not taken with My pretty spider-fingers. **1723** FENTON *Mariamne* IV. v, His spider-constitution wou'd dissolve In its own venom. **1840** THACKERAY *Shabby-genteel Story* viii, A brown cut-away coat.. that fitted tight round a spider waist.

c. Appositive, chiefly in allusion to the cunning or wily nature of the spider, as ***spider-farmer, -saint, -siren.***

1678 BUTLER *Hud.* III. i. 1461 Those Spider-Saints, that hang by Threads Spun out o' th' Entrals of their Heads. **1899** *Daily News* 9 May 8 The toils set for him by the treacherous spider-farmer. *Ibid.* 12 July 8/2 An Indian opium den, and its spider-siren, inveigling poor flies of men to destruction.

d. With adjs. forming similative combs., as ***spider-legged, -limbed, -shanked, -tongued.*** Also ***spider-spruce, -thin; spider-leggy*** adjs.

1787 'G. GAMBADO' *Acad. Horsem.* (1809) 21 The pitiful *spider-legged things of this age fly into a ditch with you, at the sight of a pocket-handkerchief. **1871** KINGSLEY *At Last* i, Sand-brush,.. through which the spider-legged mangroves rose on stilted roots. **1894** W. S. SIMPSON *Mem.* (1899) 146 Not an angular spider-legged Frenchified hand, but a clear round legible hand. **1881** FREEMAN in W. R. W. Stephens *Life & Lett.* (1895) II. 216 First, W. makes a bold broad cross, somewhat as I might make; M. a *spider-leggy kind of one. **1855** R. R. MADDEN *Life C'tess Blessington* I. 367 The.. height of its slim, *spider-limbed, powdered footman. **1785** GROSE *Dict. Vulgar T.*, **Spider-shanked*, thin legged. **1948** C. DAY LEWIS *Poems 1943–47* 82 But look at her parlour, all lighted and *spider-spruce! **1928** V. WOOLF *Orlando* vi. 257 The Serpentine.. was a bronze colour; *spider-thin boats were skimming from side to side. **1939** G. GREENE *Confidential Agent* I. ii. 48 A.. cotton bedspread, clean and faded and spider-thin. **1934** DYLAN THOMAS *18 Poems* 24 Some let me make you of autumnal spells, The *spider-tongued, and the loud hill of Wales.

e. Instrumental, as ***spider-curtained*** adj.

1925 BLUNDEN *English Poems* 40 The *spider-curtained darkness in the attic of black Jacob's farm.

11. a. Special combs.: **spider angioma** *Path.*, a spider-nævus; †**spider-bag**, the cocoon spun by the spider for the protection of its eggs; **spider-band** *Naut.*, a spider-hoop (*U.S.*); **spider-brusher** *slang*, a domestic servant; **spider-cake** *U.S.*, a cake cooked in a spider pan; **spider cancer** *Path.*, spider-nævus; †**spider-cap**, a cap of a spider-like appearance formerly worn by women; **spider-cart**, = sense 7; †**spider-caul**, a spider's web (cf. CAUL *sb.*[1] 3); in quot. *fig.*, a male flirt; **spider-cell**, (*a*) *Biol.*, a bacillus having the appearance of a small spider; (*b*) *Anat.*, one of the characteristic cells of the neuroglia, having numerous delicate processes resembling the legs of a spider; †**spider's cloth**, †**spider cob**, a spider's web, a cobweb; **spider couching** *Needlewk.*, **spider-hoop** *Naut.* (see quots.); **spider-man**, one employed to work on high structures; a steeple-jack; **spider-nævus** *Path.* (see quots.); **spider-rest**, a billiard rest with legs of sufficient length to allow of its being placed over a ball without touching it; **spider-shanks** *dial.*, a person having long, thin legs; **spider-sheave**, a form of sheave or pulley-block somewhat resembling a spider in construction; **spider-stitch** *Needlewk.* (see quots.); **spider-table**, a slightly-constructed occasional table with spider-like legs; **spiderveil**, a kind of veil; **spider veins**, small dilated superficial veins around varicosities on a leg; †**spider-wevet**, a cobweb (in quot. *fig.*); **spider-wheel**, (*a*) a form of water-wheel; (*b*) *Needlewk.* (see *spider-stitch*); (*c*) a metal wheel with wire spokes (formerly applied *spec.* to a bicycle-wheel); hence **spider-wheeled**, *a.*, fitted with spider-wheels; **spider-work**, work having the characteristics or appearance of a spider's web; *spec.* in *Needlewk.* = OPUS ARANEUM.

A few other special terms, which appear to have little or no currency, are given in recent Dicts.

1956 *New Gould Med. Dict.* (ed. 2) 77/1 *Spider angioma. **1961** R. D. BAKER *Essent. Path.* xvi. 412 At autopsy one notes ascites and subcutaneous edema of the legs, often with hydrothorax. Spider angiomata are frequently observed on the skin. **1728** CHAMBERS *Cycl.* s.v. *Silk*, The *Spider-Bags are of a Grey Colour when new. **1833** T. HOOK *Love & Pride, Widow* iii, Carefully folded according to the suggestion of the venerable *spider-brusher. **1841** W. H. MAXWELL *Scotland* (1855) 11 The English spider-brusher is a gem beyond value. **1869** MRS. WHITNEY *We Girls* v, The flaky *spider-cake, turned just as it blushed golden-tawny over the coals. **1898** *Syd. Soc. Lex.*, *Spider-cancer, *Acne rosacea*. **1790** WESLEY *Wks.* (1872) VII. 360 Your needless ornaments..—ruffles, necklaces, *spider-caps, ugly, unbecoming bonnets. **1900** TREVES *Tale Field Hosp.* xxvii. 97 Left by the roadside.. were carts, light *spider-carts,.. and.. cumbrous impedimenta. **1641** BRATHWAIT *Eng. Gentlw.* 322 Let not then these *Spidercauls delude you, discretion will laugh at them, modesty loath them. **1888** ROLLESTON & JACKSON *Anim. Life* 433 Spherical '*spider' cells with clear contents. **1899** *Allbutt's Syst. Med.* VII. 715 At a later stage the spider-cells are transformed into a fibrillar meshwork. **1638** W. M. *Garcia's Sonne Rogue* 38 The hangings of their chambers are all mourning, with some borders of *spiders-cloth (cobwebs). *a* **1571** JEWEL *Serm.* (1609) 231 What profit had ye in your dreames, in your *spider cobbes, in your drosse, in your chaffe? **1882** CAULFEILD & SAWARD *Dict. Needlework* 92/9 **Spider couching*, a Raised Couching. Upon a linen foundation fasten down short pieces of whip-cord. Cut these of equal length, and arrange them like the spokes of a wheel or the chief threads of a spider's web. **1846** A. YOUNG *Naut. Dict.* 291 **Spider-hoop*, the hoop going round a mast to secure the shackles to which the futtock-shrouds are attached. **1863** *Ibid.* 362 The name of spider hoop is also given to a hoop of iron with belaying pins attached to it, or an iron hoop encircling a wooden rim, into which such pins are inserted for belaying brails or braces to. **1868** NARES *Seamanship* (ed. 4) 57 The spider hoop for the topgallant shrouds. **1955** *Britannica Bk. of Year* 489/2 **Spiderman*, an erector of building structures. **1958** *Radio Times* 25 July 3/1 These spider-men and steel-erectors work at great heights, often where there are no means of protection. They walk along girders at dizzy heights as though they were strolling along Piccadilly. **1962** *B.S.I. News* July 11/1 Safety harness worn by window-cleaners and spidermen. **1972** J. WAINWRIGHT *Night is Time to Die* 8 They used an expression familiar to all working policemen. 'Sudden Death.' It covers everything; from.. the spiderman who takes that one chance too many.. to the hippy who spins into permanent orbit. **1898** *Syd. Soc. Lex.*, *Spider-nævus. **1899** *Allbutt's Syst. Med.* VIII. 826 A common variety [of nævus] found on the face of children, is a small central red spot with a leash of vessels running to it (spider nævus). **1873** BENNETT & CAVENDISH *Billiards* 28 The heads of cushion and *spider-rests, are generally made of wood. **1828** LYTTON *Pelham* lxxxi, The tallest of the set, who bore the euphonious appellation of *Spider-shanks, politely asked me [etc.]. **1903** *Sci. Amer.* 31 Jan. 80/1 A couple of *spider-sheaves were sent ashore. **1882** CAULFEILD & SAWARD *Dict. Needlework* 62/2 Catherine Wheel..is also known by the name of Spider Wheel or *Spider Stitch, and is chiefly employed to fill up round holes in embroidery on muslin. *Ibid.* 242/2 Roue, also called Wheel and Spider Stitch, and made either with Point Croisé and Point de Toile, or of Point d'Esprit. **1844** W. H. MAXWELL *Scotland* xiv. (1855) 128 Mrs. C—— was seated in her easy-chair with a *spider table before her. **1861** LEVER *One of them* lii. 402 As they placed a little spider-table between them. **1922** JOYCE *Ulysses* 441 In smart Saxe tailormade, white velours hat and *spiderveil. **1976** *Vogue* Jan. 20/4 The treatment of broken and *spider veins on legs. **1581** J. BELL *Haddon's Answ. Osor.* III. 420 b, When you sate knittyng such fleying moats, and *spyderweuett and such stubble. **1868** *Chambers's Encycl.* X. 95/2 The latter are more often made of wrought-iron rods, with a slight axle. This wheel is much lighter.., and is called a suspension or *spider wheel. **1875** *Eng. Mechanic* 23 Apr. 146/2 With the spider-wheels I found that there was rather a tendency to get loose. **1882** *Bicycle* 15 The Spider-Wheel, invented by the Coventry Machinists Company and now almost universal. **1906** *Chambers's Jrnl.* Oct. 735/1 The introduction of the free spider-wheel, pneumatic-tired cycle. **1969** *West Australian* 5 July 32/5 On the turn out of the back straight in the last lap Majestic Scott's spider wheel was badly buckled. **1977** *Weekly Times* (Melbourne) 19 Jan. 57/4 (Advt.), Semitipper, 10–1 spread bogey... Hercules body and hoists..900 × 20 tyres, spider wheels. **1886** *Century Mag.* July 338/2 There may be a crowd of onlookers in every kind of trap, from a four-in-hand drag to a *spider-wheeled buggy drawn by a pair of long-tailed trotters. **1943** J. W. DAY *Farming Adventure* iii. 40 A high spider-wheeled dogcart. *c* **1812** BYRON in Peel *Luddites* (1880) vii. 35 By the adoption of one species of frame in particular, one man performed the work of many... Yet it is to [be] observed that the work thus executed was inferior in quality... It was called, in the cant of the trade, by the name of '*Spider work'. **1865** Spider-work [see OPUS ARANEUM]. **1874** *Queen Lace Bk.* I. 5 Darned Netting (Opus araneum; Spiderwork; Point conté). **1883** *Gd. Words* Dec. 791/2 This orchid is seldom seen without some gossamery spiderwork surrounding it.

b. In the names of animals, insects, birds, etc., which bear some resemblance to, or are associated in some way with, spiders, as **spider-ant, -diver, -eater, † -fish, -fly, -hunter, -mite, -shell, -tortoise, -wasp, -whelk** (see quots.); **spider beetle**, a long-legged beetle of the family Ptinidæ. Also SPIDER-CATCHER, -CRAB, -MONKEY.

1881 *Cassell's Nat. Hist.* V. 377 The females of this and other species have an aspect intermediate between that of a Spider and that of an Ant, whence the German entomologists give them the very characteristic name of '*Spider Ants'. *Ibid.* 381 The Spider Ants (*Mutillæ*). **1954** BORROR & DELONG *Introd. Study of Insects* xxii. 379 The Ptinidae, or *spider beetles, are small long-legged beetles.. somewhat spiderlike in appearance. **1979** P. L. G. BATEMAN *Household Pests* II. 106 Spider beetles are basically scavengers and infestations often originate in old birds' nests. **1827** *Sporting Mag.* (N.S.) XX. 39 These birds (*colymbus minutus*) are very common in the fleets, and are called by the Marshmen *Spider Divers. **1885** SWAINSON *Prov. Names Birds* 216 *Little Grebe*,..Spider diver. **1885** H. O. FORBES *Nat. Wand. E. Archip.* III. viii. 233, I obtained an interesting bird, a green species of *Spider-eater. **1608** TOPSELL *Serpents* 233 Yet these Serpents are thought to be none other then the Fishes called *Aranei*, or *Spyder-fishes. **1787** BEST *Angling* (ed. 2) 112 The *Spider-Fly. Comes on about the twentieth of April,..and continues on about a fortnight. **1813** BINGLEY *Anim. Biog.* III. 331 The Hippoboscæ form a connecting link betwixt the two-winged and the apterous insects. By some authors they have been denominated *mouches araignées*, or spider-flies. **1868** *Rep. U.S. Commissioner Agric.* (1869) 317 The *Hippoboscidæ*, or spider-flies, are found upon birds and animals. **1856–8** HORSFIELD & MOORE *Catal. Birds E. India Co.* II. 727 *Arachnothera magna*, the Great *Spider-hunter (Hodgson). **1862** JERDON *Birds India* I. 361 *Arachnothera pusilla*, the Little Spider-hunter. **1876–80** SHELLEY *Monograph Nectariniidæ* 358, I retain the Spider-hunters in the present family [*Arachnotherinæ*]. **1870** H. A. NICHOLSON *Man. Zool.* xxxvii. 269 The Garden-mites (*Trombidiidæ*) and *Spider-mites (*Ganasidæ*) live upon plants. **1879** E. P. WRIGHT *Anim. Life* 525 The Spider Mites are small eyeless creatures, parasitical on bats, birds, reptiles, and insects. **1752** J. HILL *Hist. Anim.* 144 The tuberculose Murex, the Scorpion shell, commonly called the *Spider-shell. **1896** LYDEKKER *Roy. Nat. Hist.* VI. 385 The spider-shells (*Pteroceras*), with the claw-like projections from the outer lip. *Ibid.* V. 64 The last member of this section of the family is the *spider-tortoise (*Pyxis arachnoides*) of Madagascar. **1816** KIRBY & SP. *Entomol.* xxiii. (1818) II. 309 The *spider-wasps (*Pompilus*, F.) walk by starts, as it were, vibrating their wings, at the same time. **1713** PETIVER *Aquat. Anim. Amboinæ* Tab. vi, *Tribulus*,..*Spider Welk.

c. In the names of plants, grasses, etc., as **spider flower**, an annual herb of the genus *Cleome* of the family Capparaceæ, esp. *C. hasslerana*, which has clusters of pink or white flowers with long stamens (cf. CLEOME); **spider grass**, (see quots.); **spider lily**, a bulbous plant belonging to the genus *Hymenocallis*, native to North and South America, or *Crinum*, native to tropical regions, both of the family Amaryllidaceæ, and bearing clusters of white or pink flowers, often fragrant; **spider ophrys, orchid, orchis**, (see quots.); **spider plant**, (*a*) (see quots. 1852, 1882); (*b*) a perennial herb, *Chlorophytum comosum*, of the family Liliaceæ, native to South Africa, of which forms bearing variegated linear leaves and clusters of white flowers are much cultivated as house plants. Also SPIDERWORT.

1861 A. WOOD *Class-Bk. Bot.* (ed. 10) 240 *Spider Flower... Herbs or shrubs. **1909** A. E. MACK *Bush Calendar* 4 Faded by the excessive rain were the red spider-flowers. **1931** W. N. CLUTE *Common Names Plants* 101 The spiderflower (*Cleome*) named from the long and sprawling stamens like spider's legs. **1968** PETERSON & MCKENNY *Field Guide Wildflowers* 230 Spider-flower... Note the extraordinarily long stamens projecting beyond the 4 narrow-stalked pink or white petals. **1889** MAIDEN *Usef. Pl.* 98 *Panicum divaricatissimum*, *Spider Grass. **1887** *Harper's Mag.* Feb. 351/1 The exquisite white *spider-lily, nodding in clusters on long stalks. **1908** E. J. BANFIELD *Confessions of Beachcomber* I. i. 21 Along the deltas of the creeks are fragrant, gigantic 'spider lilies' (*Crinum*). **1946** D. C. PEATTIE *Road of Naturalist* v. 58 The cypress woods around Charleston with sudden spider lilies. **1980** A. DESAI *Clear Light of Day* i. 7 They went slowly up the wide stairs between the massed pots of spider lilies and asparagus fern. **1796** WITHERING *Brit. Pl.* (ed. 3) II. 39 *Ophrys aranifera*, *Spider ophrys. **1889** MAIDEN *Usef. Pl.* 11 *Caladenia*, *Spider Orchids. **1785** MARTYN *Lett. Bot.* xxvii. (1794) 421 *Spider Orchis is a lower plant. **1839** LINDLEY *Sch. Bot.* 177 *Ophrys araneifera* (Spider Orchis). **1882** *Garden* 11 Feb. 89/1 The requirements of such fastidious plants as..the Bee, the Fly, the Spider Orchis..are seldom found in gardens. **1898** MORRIS *Austral Eng.* 429 Spider-Orchis, name given in Tasmania to the Orchid *Caladenia pulcherrima*, F. v. M. **1852** P. C. SUTHERLAND *Jrnl. Voy. Baffin's Bay* xix. II. 236 The most beautiful plant that one could see in a whole day's walking around Assistance Bay, was the *spider plant (*Saxifraga flagellaris*). **1882** FRIEND *Dev. Plant-n.*, Spider-plant, *Saxifraga sarmentosa*. **1946** M. FREE *All about House Plants* xv. 126 That plant with striped leaves known to many as spider-plant..increases by means of plantlets produced on the ends of its flower stalks. **1979** S. RIFKIN *McQuaid in August* vii. 48 Three enormous spider plants hung..in front of the window.

Hence **'spiderdom**, the world of spiders; **'spiderhood**, the existence of spiders; **'spiderish** *a.*, resembling a spider; hence **'spiderishness**.

1892 *Longman's Mag.* Aug. 367 The prime blame of spiderhood rests with Nature. **1897** *Strand Mag.* Feb. 287/2 The principles of Malthus are unknown in Spiderdom. **1935** O. STAPLEDON *Odd John* i. 3 Strangers were often revolted by his uncouth proportions. They called him spiderish. **1944** G. B. SHAW *Everybody's Political What's What?* xxxvi. 320 Commercial ability is often really mere spiderishness.

'spider, *v.* [f. prec.] **1.** *trans.* To catch or entrap after the manner of the spider.

1891 *Standard* 5 Oct. 2/2 Mr. Gladstone has fooled these people..to the very top of their bent. He has spidered them once more.

2. a. *intr.* To move in a manner suggestive of a spider. **b.** *trans.* To cause to move or appear thus.

1938 G. GREENE *Brighton Rock* VI. i. 236 Ida Arnold had been trained by the Board. Queerer things than that had spidered out under her fingers and old Crow's. **1975** *New Yorker* 26 May 39/3 It is impossible to resist a postscript at the bottom of that august form, though no doubt it would have to be spidered up the margin. **1976** 'F. CLIFFORD' *Drummer in Dark* vi. 27 His fingers spidered over the map, stressing a detail here, a field of fire there.

Hence **'spidering** *ppl. a.* and *vbl. sb.*

1973 T. PYNCHON *Gravity's Rainbow* I. 55 His little bureau is dominated now by a glimmering map,..written names and spidering streets. **1975** *New Yorker* 12 May 141/1 He wishes only, with his nimble, sinister spidering amid the complexities of our cultural situation, to give us —one of his favorite words—*frissons*.

spider-catcher. [SPIDER *sb.*]

1. One who catches spiders. Chiefly *fig.*, and freq. as a vague term of abuse (*obs.*).

1579 W. WILKINSON *Confut. Fam. Love* Brief Descr. p. iii, Not only in the priuate assemblies..did these spidercatchers swarme together. **1599** PEELE *Sir Clyom.* vii. 64 Charm, enchant, make a spider-catcher of me, if I be false to you ever. **1620** BP. HALL *Hon. Marr. Clergy* III. ii. (1628) 793 He that would doubt whether such an Epistle were written..may doubt whether spider-catcher, corner-creeper C.E....wrote a scurrilous letter. **1625** SHIRLEY *Love-Tricks* I. i, If I fail, call me spider-catcher. **1711** ADDISON *Spect.* No. 21 ⁋7 Innumerable Retainers to Physick..: Not to mention the Cockleshell-Merchants and Spider-catchers.

b. A monkey (Halliwell, 1847).

2. One or other of certain birds which catch or eat spiders, as: (*a*) The wall-creeper, *Tichodroma muraria*. (*b*) One or other of the East Indian sunbirds belonging to the genus *Arachnothera*; a spider-hunter. (*c*) *local.* (See quot. 1854.)

1668 CHARLETON *Onomast.* 86 *Picus Murarius*,..the Creeper, or Spider-catcher. **1678** RAY *Willughby's Ornith.* II. vi. §2. 143 The Wall-creeper, or Spider catcher. *Picus murarius*... It is somewhat bigger than a House-Sparrow. **1764** G. EDWARDS *Glean. Nat. Hist.* III. 320. **1840** tr. *Cuvier's Anim. Kingd.* 207 The Spider-Catchers (*Arachnotheres*) have the same long, arcuated beak, as the Sun-birds. **1854** MISS BAKER *Northampt. Gloss.*, *Spider-catcher*, the spotted Fly-catcher or Beam-bird, *Muscicapa grisola*.

†**3.** (See quot.) *Obs.*$^{-0}$

a **1700** B. E. *Dict. Cant. Crew*, *Spider-catcher*, a Spindle for a Man.

spider-crab. [SPIDER *sb.* 11 b.] One or other of several crabs belonging to the group *Oxyrhyncha*, esp. to the family *Maioidea*, and characterized by their long slender legs and spider-like appearance; a maia or maioid crab.

1710 SIBBALD *Hist. Fife* 55 *Cancer Araneus Johnstoni*, the Spider Crab. **1756** P. BROWNE *Jamaica* (1779) 421 The Spider-Crab... All the limbs are slender and delicate, in proportion to the size of the body. **1848** JOHNS *Week at Lizard* 229 A few spider-crabs..were also stored away. **1865** GOSSE *Land & Sea* (1874) 81 The spider-crab, or maia, of little value as food, though occasionally eaten. **1883** *Science* I. 466/2 The enormous spider-crabs of the Straits of Magellan.

'spidered, *a. rare.* [f. SPIDER *sb.*] †**a.** Like a spider in disposition or nature. *Obs.*$^{-1}$ **b.** Infested by spiders; cob-webbed.

1659 W. BROUGH *Sacr. Princ.* 477 Be not such a spider'd spirit, to suck poyson out of sacred flowers. **1787** WOLCOT (P. Pindar) *Lousiad* II. Wks. 1794 I. 251 Content can visit the poor spider'd room.

'spiderine, *a. nonce-wd.* [f. SPIDER *sb.*, after *feline*, etc.] Of the nature of a spider.

1887 BLACKMORE *Springhaven* xxviii. (ed. 3) II. 25 The human race happily is not spiderine.

spider-leg. Also spider leg. [SPIDER *sb.* 9 b.]

1. A thin, long leg like those of a spider.

Also *dial.* (in *pl.*), a spider-legged or lanky person.

1760 STERNE *Tr. Shandy* VII. i, Whilst..these two spider legs of mine..are able to support me. **1833** NYREN *Yng. Cricketer's Tutor* (1902) 107 He was..remarkably broad in the chest, with large hips and spider legs. **1859** GEO. ELIOT *A. Bede* xxi, In that period of spider-legs and inlaid cupids. **1861** *Romance of Dull Life* xxi. 154 How ridiculously slim the spider-legs of the dining-room sideboard!

2. *transf.* A long irregular marking, crack, wrinkle, etc., resembling in shape the leg of a spider. Also *attrib.* in ***spider-leg gold***.

1873 E. SPON *Workshop Rec.* Ser. I. 303/1 The breaking of the gold into irregular fractures called spider-legs. **1889** BINNS *Wilsden Orig.* No. 1. 1 (E.D.D.), Thi forheead's a big un, No line o' care, No 'student's spider-legs', Can be seen there. **1898** *Daily News* 28 Jan. 5/7 The nuggets there all have the 'spider-leg' gold adhering.

'spiderless, *a.* [f. SPIDER *sb.*] Destitute of, free from, spiders.

1892 W. H. HUDSON *La Plata* 178, It was nearly forgetting that England is not a spiderless country.

'spider-like, *adv.* and *a.* [f. SPIDER *sb.*]

A. *adv.* In or after the manner of a spider; with the power of faculty (real or supposed) of a spider.

Freq. in the 17th cent.

1604 HIERON *Wks.* I. 497 Mans corrupt nature, spider-like, turneth the wholesome doctrine into poison. **1673** DRYDEN *Marr. à la Mode* II. i, And when our eyes meet far off, our sense is such, That, spider-like, we feel the tenderest touch. **1700** C. NESSE *Antid. Armin.* (1827) 117 If man (spider-like) could spin a thread out of his own bowels. **1783** WOLCOT (P. Pindar) *Lyric Odes* I. vi, Like him, in holes too, spider-like, I mope. **1839** BAILEY *Festus* 128, I have that within me I can live upon: Spider-like, spin my place out anywhere. **1869** LD. LYTTON *Orval* II. vii. 69, I cannot pass Where pathway none can be. Nor from myself Spin, spiderlike, a passage through the vast And vacant air.

B. *adj.* Like or resembling a spider or that of a spider; having the characteristic appearance or qualities of a spider; spidery.

a **1653** GOUGE *Comm. Heb.* vi. 16 Some men have such a spider-like disposition, as they will suck poison out of the sweetest flowers. **1754** HAY *Ess. Deformity* 18, I..often restrain my inclination to perform those little Services, rather than expose my Spider like Shape. **1806** SHAW *Gen. Zool.* VI. II. 472 The present genus [*sc.* Phalangium], which, exclusive of its spider-like shape, is..armed with weapons resembling those of the genus Aranea. **1841** DICKENS *Barn. Rudge* (1849) 235/1 Struggling to free himself from her chaste, but spider like embrace.

spider-line. Also spider's line. [SPIDER *sb.*] One of the threads or filaments of spider-web used to form the reticle of various optical instruments, esp. of micrometers, and serving to obtain minute measurements; also loosely, any slender thread or wire used for this purpose.

1829 W. PEARSON *Pract. Astron.* II. 323 The spider's lines, or wires, are usually paid parallel to one another on a circular plate of brass. **1866** PARKINSON *Optics* (ed. 2) 209 Such a set of threads are commonly called cross-wires or spider lines. **1888** RUTLEY *Rock-Forming Min.* 14 Within the focus of the eye-glass, two fine wires or spider-lines are inserted.

attrib. **1829** W. PEARSON *Pract. Astron.* II. 245 Binocular Spider's-line and Glass-disc Micrometers. **1875** KNIGHT *Dict. Mech.* 1431/1 A substitute for the spider-line micrometer.

'spiderling. [-LING.] A little spider.

1885 H. C. MCCOOK *Tenants of Old Farm* 30 Thus the young spiderlings are snugly blanketed and tucked away. **1897** *Strand Mag.* Sept. 288/1 The spiderlings [when touched] disperse like the nations at Babel.

'spiderly, *a. rare.* [-LY[1].] Like a spider.

1891 C. MACEWEN *Three Women in Boat* xv. 113 The Grand Duke was..looking spiderly, ugly, but [etc.].

spider monkey. Also spider-monkey. [SPIDER *sb.* 11 b.] One or other of the monkeys belonging to the South and Central American genus

Ateles, characterized by their long spider-like limbs and prehensile tail.

1764 G. EDWARDS *Glean. Nat. Hist.* III. 222, I lately.. saw .. a Black Monkey something like the above-described: they called him a Spider Monkey, from his thinness and the length of his limbs and tail. **1813** BINGLEY *Anim. Biog.* (ed. 4) I. 89 The Four-fingered Monkey... The legs and arms are so long that the animal has hence obtained the name of Spider Monkey. **1836** MARRYAT *Pirate* iv, I always think of two spider-monkeys nursing two kittens. **1871** KINGSLEY *At Last* xvii, The Spider Monkeys are instinctively gentle and fond of man.

†'**spiderous**, *a. Obs.* [-OUS.] Spider-like.

1533 FRITH *Judgem. Tracy* Wks. (1572) 78/1 There is no man that can receiue venome by those wordes, except hee haue such a spyderous nature that he can turne an hony combe into perilous poyson. **1648** SYMMONS *Vindic.* 319 In which they speak truth, and had not themselves been of too spiderous a nature they might have made much good vse of them.

spider-web, *sb.* Also spider's web.

1. A cobweb. Freq. *fig.* or in fig. context.

α. **1535** COVERDALE *Job* viii. 14 His confidence shalbe destroyed, for he trusteth in a spyders webbe. **1611** BIBLE *Isaiah* lix. 5 They hatch cockatrice egges, and weaue the spiders web. **1725** *Fam. Dict.* s.v. *Spider*, Some in France have made a sort of Silk of Spiders Webs. **1728** CHAMBERS *Cycl.* s.v. *Web*, Spider's-Web, or Cob-Web. **1745** *Transl. & Paraph. Sc. Ch.* XXIV. ii, As the spider's web, when try'd it yieldeth, breaks and flies.

β. *a* **1649** DRUMM. OF HAWTH. *Hist. Jas. II*, Wks. (1711) 28 Wise princes suffered houses to grow as men do spider-webs, not taking heed of them so long as they were small. **1822** BYRON *Werner* IV. i. 308 My destiny has so involved about me Her spider web. **1889** *Spectator* 9 Nov., These spider-webs of fashion appear to confine the freedom of those who suffer under them more effectually than brick walls.

2. *transf.* and *fig.* Something resembling a cobweb in nature or appearance.

a **1700** B. E. *Dict. Cant. Crew*, *Spider's-web*, the subtilties of Logic. **1864** BROWNING *Caliban upon Setebos* 13 He looks out o'er yon sea which sunbeams cross And recross till they weave a spider-web. **1923** G. H. MCKNIGHT *English Words* iv. 53 The early years of the war were productive in slang language among the British troops... Wire entanglements were *fly traps* and *spider webs*. **1957** O. NASH *You can't get there from Here* 61 This is the most enticing spiderweb of a tarradiddle ever spun. **1978** J. CARROLL *Mortal Friends* II. v. 187 He was running his finger along the cold pane of the window, making spiderwebs in the fog.

b. A variety of turquoise characterized by a network of fine dark lines running through it. Also ***spider-web turquoise***.

1936 M. BEDINGER *Navajo Indian Silver Work* 18 There is another famous variety, of exceptionally good quality... It is a dark blue with black tracery all through it, which gives it the name of 'Spider Web' turquoise. **1968** J. SINKANKAS *Van Nostrand's Standard Catalog Gems* iv. 202 Persian spiderweb is similar except that a network of fine black lines divides the surface of the gem into a mosaic of even patches. **1975** R. WEBSTER *Gems in Jewellery* xiv. 79 The turquoise and the matrix of dark brown limonite or fawn-coloured sandstone are then cut together to give stones known as turquoise matrix or, if the veins are fine, spider web turquoise.

3. *attrib.* and *Comb.*, as ***spider-web bridge***, ***scales***, etc. Also ***spider('s)-web-like***.

1885 J. E. TAYLOR *Brit. Fossils* i. 28 For the passage of spider's-web-like threads of protoplasm. **1891** H. HERMAN *His Angel* 33 The spider-web-like chaos of jagged beams. **1897** *Outing* XXIX. 347/1 His father was old, and soon must cross the spider-web bridge, and leave his son to rule. **1898** *Weekly Reg.* 10 Sept. 328 Away, then, Messieurs Rigourists, with your spider-web scales.

Hence **spider-web** *v.*, (*a*) *trans.* to cover with a network resembling a spider-web; (*b*) *intr.* in various fig. uses (see quots.); **spider-webby** *a.*, resembling a spider-web.

1823 L. HUNT in *Liberal* II. 369 'What the devil's here? To bring my stockings home at last undone?'.. 'Undone... They so spider-web, it's a despair.' **1864** *Builder* 16 Apr. 274/2 The doors became dingier, the areas and lobbies more spider-webby. **1884** 'MARK TWAIN' *Huck. Finn* ix. 74 The rain would thrash along by so thick that the trees off a little ways looked dim and spider-webby. **1894** W. T. STEAD *If Christ came to Chicago* IV. iii. 286 The town was being spider-webbed with wires. **1936** I. L. IDRIESS *Cattle King* iv. 34 He and others have spider-webbed from around the Australian coasts far into the inland. **1974** M. HOYT *Thirty Miles for Ice Cream* x. 110 The deciduous trees, without their leaves, show at that distance as gray or a spider-webby black.

spiderwort. *Bot.* Also spider-wort.

†**1.** One or other plant of the liliaceous genus *Anthericum* (earlier *Phalangium*). *Obs.*

1597 GERARDE *Herbal* I. xxxiii. 45 The first [branched spiderwort] is called of the Latines.. *Phalangium*,.. in English it is called Spiderwoort... The leaues.. stand vpon the ground with long legs and the knees bowing vp like the spiders legs when he creepeth. **1629** PARKINSON *Parad.* xv. 152 The vnbranched Spiderwort most commonly flowereth before all the other. **1671** SALMON *Syn. Med.* III. xxii. 418 Spiderwort.. is Alexipharmick and cures the biting of all venomous beasts. **1705** MRS. BEHN tr. *Cowley's Plants* C.'s Wks. 1711 III. 379 Thou Spider-Wort dost with the Monster strive And from the conquer'd Foe thy Name derive. **1731** MILLER *Gard. Dict.* s.v. *Phalangium*, Branched Spider-wort... Unbranched Spider-wort... African Spider-wort [etc.]. **1751** J. HILL *Nat. Hist.* 375 The plane-leaved and simple-stalked Anthericum, single-stalked spiderwort. **1763** MILLS *Pract. Husb.* III. 312 The spiderwort,.. the lesser spearwort, the butterwort, have evidently suspicious marks.

b. ***mountain*** or ***saffron spiderwort*** (see quots.).

1796 WITHERING *Brit. Plants* (ed. 3) II. 339 *Anthericum serotinum*, Mountain Saffron. Saffron Spiderwort. **1866** *Treas. Bot.* 1083 Spiderwort,.. Mountain, *Lloydia serotina*.

2. One or other of the plants belonging to the genus *Tradescantia*; esp. *T. virginica*, Virginian spiderwort.

Parkinson states that he originated this use.

1629 PARKINSON *Parad.* xv. 152 Phalangium Ephemerum virginianum Ioannis Tradescant,.. Tradescant his Spider-wort. **1688** HOLME *Armoury* II. 109/2 The Virginia Spider-Wort, or Day Flower,.. is.. on the back of a sullen yellowish hue. **1731** MILLER *Gard. Dict.* s.v. *Ephemeron*, Virginian Spider-wort, with a small blue Flower, commonly call'd John Tradescant's Spider-wort. **1741** *Compl. Fam.-Piece* II. iii. 385 You have besides the scarlet Lichnis, Virginian Spiderwort. **1829** LOUDON *Encycl. Pl.* (1836) 260 *Tradescantia*. Spiderwort.. common,.. rose-flowered,.. thick-leaved [etc.]. **1831** AUDUBON *Ornith.* I. 154 The Virginian Spider-wort.. is distinguished by its erect, succulent stem. **1866** *Treas. Bot.* 1159/2 *Tradescantia virginica* is the Common Spiderwort of gardens. **1882** *Garden* 1 Apr. 212/2 This rare and beautiful Spiderwort is now finely in flower.

3. ***Savoy spiderwort***, the hemerocallis or day-lily; also, †a variety of *Tradescantia*.

1629 PARKINSON *Parad.* 150 *Phalangium Allobrogicum*, the Sauoye Spiderwort. **1688** HOLME *Armoury* II. 99/2 Savoy Spider-wort hath thin small sedgy leaves of a whitish green. **1721** MORTIMER *Husb.* II. 236 *Spider Wort*. The Italian and the Savoy are the only ones fit for your choice. **1731** MILLER *Gard. Dict.* s.v. *Ephemeron*, Virginian Spider-wort, with a large azure Flower, commonly call'd the Savoy Spider-wort. **1760** J. LEE *Introd. Bot.* App. 327 Spider-wort, Great Savoy, *Hemerocallis*. **1829** LOUDON *Encycl. Pl.* (1836) 260 *Hemerocallis Liliastrum*. Savoy-Spiderwort.

4. Any plant belonging to the order *Commelynaceæ*, which includes the genus *Tradescantia*.

1846 LINDLEY *Veget. Kingd.* 188 The Spiderworts are plants which exhibit a transition from the first remove out of the regions of sedge-like plants to the true Lilies. **1866** *Treas. Bot.* 228/1 *Cartonema*, the generic name of one of the Spiderworts.

attrib. **1856** A. GRAY *Man. Bot.* 485 *Commelynaceæ* (Spiderwort Family). **1861** BENTLEY *Man. Bot.* 680 *Commelynaceæ*, the Spider-Wort Order.

5. *U.S.* A plant of the genus *Cleome*, belonging to the caper family.

1846-50 A. WOOD *Class-bk. Bot.* 172 *Cleome pungens*, Spiderwort... A common garden plant, with curious purple flowers.

spidery ('spaɪdərɪ), *a.* [f. SPIDER *sb.* + -Y.]

Cotgrave (1611) has '*Araignier*, spiderie', but the word otherwise belongs to the 19th century.

1. a. Like a spider in appearance or form.

1837 *New Monthly Mag.* LI. 365 That grotesque race, the Sapajous,.. are slender,.. long in tail, and *spidery* in general appearance. **1859** LD. LYTTON *Wanderer* (ed. 2) 21 Spidery Saturn in his webs of fire. **1881** J. W. OGLE *Harveian Orat.* 93 That hideous spidery crustacean, the crab.

Comb. **1882** *Garden* 25 Mar. 194/3 A bright spidery-looking flower.

b. *fig.* Entangling like a spider.

1825 COLERIDGE *Let.* 21 Feb. (1971) V. 414 As we advance in years, the World, that spidery Witch, spins it's threads narrower and narrower, still closing in on us. **1875** M. COLLINS *Sweet & Twenty* III. II. vii. 19 Lest he should be picked up by the wily widow or spidery spinster.

2. a. Of legs or arms: Resembling those of a spider; long and thin.

c **1845** DE QUINCEY *Fatal Marksman* Wks. 1859 XII. 228 The old woman, stretching her withered spidery arms after the flying girl. **1880** MISS BROUGHTON *Second Thoughts* I. i, He is a.. fragile young man, slender as any reed, and with legs even more spidery than Jane's. **1896** CROCKETT *Cleg Kelly* vi. 47 Delicate little keys with spidery legs.

b. Suggestive of the appearance of a spider with long and thin legs.

1862 H. AÏDÉ *Carr of Carrl.* II. 228 The marchesa wrote, with characteristic effusion, in her long spidery characters. **1879** STEVENSON *Trav. Cevennes* 82 A spidery cross on every hill-top. **1894** A. SPINNER *Study in Colour* 132 The writing was quite legible, although rather crooked and spidery in places.

c. Like a spider-web in formation; suggestive of a cobweb or cobwebs.

Not always clearly separable from prec.

1860 *Ecclesiologist* XXI. 284 An ornate kind of German Late-Pointed, very spidery in detail. *a* **1893** SYMONDS in H. F. Brown *Biogr.* (1895) I. ii. 53, I hauled some spidery black weed out of a pool. **1909** BOND & CAMM *Roodlofts* 172 The tracery is spidery.

3. Suggestive of that of a spider, in respect of entanglement, cunning, etc.

1843 LYTTON *Last Bar.* VI. i, I have of late narrowly and keenly watched that spidery web which ye call a Court. **1875** BESANT & RICE *Harp & Cr.* xviii, He had the spidery look as his flabby face shone through the panes.

4. Of the nature of spiders.

1871 MISS BRADDON *Lovels of Arden* xi, There was a particular race of spiders, the biggest specimens of the spidery species it had ever been her horror to encounter.

5. Full of or infested by spiders.

1889 MARCHIONESS OF STAFFORD *How I Spent my Twentieth Year* 260 A gabled cottage.. in reality rather uncomfortable—stuffy and spidery. **1894** D. C. MURRAY *Making of Novelist* 15, I shall never forget the spidery black-painted galleries and staircases.

spidy, obs. form of SPEEDY *a.*

spie, obs. form of SPY *sb.* and *v.*

spied (spaɪd), *ppl. a. rare.* [f. SPY *v.* + -ED.] Of a spy: Discovered, found out.

c **1597** DONNE *Sat.* iv. 237, I shooke like a spyed Spie. **1637** B. JONSON *Sad Sheph.* I. ii, You are.. the spied spy that watch upon my walks. **1829** SCOTT *Anne of G.* xxvii, The very horse-boys know him.. and sutler women give him the name of the spied spy.

spiegel ('spi:g(ə)l). [Short for SPIEGELEISEN or SPIEGEL IRON.] = next. Also *Comb.*

1881 *Instr. Census Clerks* (1885) 93 Bessemer Steel Manufacture:.. Spiegel Cupola Man. **1884** in KNIGHT *Dict. Mech.* Suppl. 839/2.

‖**spiegeleisen** ('spi:g(ə)l,aɪz(ə)n). [G., f. *spiegel* mirror + *eisen* iron.] A crystalline and lustrous variety of white manganiferous cast-iron much used in the Bessemer process for the manufacture of steel.

1868 JOYNSON *Metals* 53 A much higher.. quality of iron is required to make steel by the Bessemer process, and, generally, a quantity of Spiegeleisen is required to be added to it. **1890** W. J. GORDON *Foundry* 102 Spiegeleisen is pig-iron's most highly carburized and crystalline form.

So **spiegel iron**.

1883 *Harper's Mag.* Aug. 334/1 A rill of spiegel-iron is let in. **1884** KNIGHT *Dict. Mech.* Suppl. 839/2 We have a spiegel iron in this country; it is made from the New Jersey Franklinite ore, and was at first called Franklinite iron.

spiel (spi:l), *sb.*[1] *Sc.* [See BONSPIEL.] A match at curling.

1824 MACTAGGART *Gallovid. Encycl.* 333 Then curling, and hurling, The channelstane at spiels. **1830** M'DIARMID *Sk. Nat.* 252, I know nothing more exhilarating than a *spiel* on the ice. **1901** R. M. F. WATSON *Closeburn* xiv. 232 In 1838 a spiel had not then been played in the memory of man in Aberdeenshire.

spiel (spi:l, ʃpi:l), *sb.*[2] *slang* (orig. *U.S.*). [a. G. *spiel* play, game; see also SPIEL *v.*]

1. Talk, a story; a speech intended to persuade or advertise, patter. Also *transf.*

1896 ADE *Artie* xi. 100 There was a long spiel by the high guy in the pulpit. **1906** *Daily Colonist* (Victoria, B.C.) 25 Jan. 6/1 We appointed him mayor at five minutes' notice and gave him the job of giving the Chinks the right kind of a spiel. **1925** WODEHOUSE *Sam the Sudden* xiii. 92 He pulled this long spiel about having had a letter from a guy he used to know named Finglass. **1926** J. BLACK *You can't Win* ii. 9 Your capable beggar on the street does not say 'please'. He rips off his spiel in such exact and precise language that you get your dime without it. **1931** 'D. STIFF' *Milk & Honey Route* 189 In the missions, to make him lonely and the more susceptible to the 'righteous spiel', they sometimes sing *Where is my wandering Boy Tonight?* **1937** *Printers' Ink Monthly* May 42/2 *Spiel*, the advertising copy. **1944** D. BURLEY *Orig. Handbk. Harlem Jive* 59, I latched on to this hard, mad spiel. **1953** H. MILLER *Plexus* I. iii. 137 Flatter the pants off him! Then go into a little spiel—you know what I mean. Give him some pointers on how to launch the magazine. **1959** *New Statesman* 19 Sept. 344/1 At the end of these flights the poor bored hostess is still compelled to repeat her antique *spiel*; 'We hope you have enjoyed your flight.' **1962** J. WAIN *Strike Father Dead* 59, I gave her just the Christian name, and she gave me the spiel about never having met anybody called that before, and its being a nice name, and so forth. *a* **1974** R. CROSSMAN *Diaries* (1975) I. 82 Then Callaghan started off with a long spiel which he read aloud from a Treasury brief on pale blue paper, describing the extreme gravity of the economic situation. **1980** *Listener* 13 Nov. 665/3 A long spiel.. from a tart about how much horrider Soho has become.

2. A swindle, a dishonest line of business.

1901 'J. FLYNT' *World of Graft* IV. 169 I've been shut up a number of years.. but I didn't mind them as much as you would; I took them as part of the spiel. **1921** P. & T. CASEY *Gay Cat* 303/1 'What's your spiel?' asks one hobo of another. **1932** W. HATFIELD *Ginger Murdoch* 175, I reckon you were thinking you had shaken me off, and could go about your spiel, whatever it is. **1954** T. A. G. HUNGERFORD *Sowers of Wind* 174 This isn't a spiel, Colonel... I know this bloke, and he's on the level.

spiel (spi:l, ʃpi:l), *v. slang* (orig. *U.S.*). Also †speel, speil. [ad. G. *spielen* to play, gamble.]

1. a. *intr.* To gamble. Also rarely *trans.*

1859 [implied at SPIELING *vbl. sb.*]. **1882** *Sydney Slang Dict.* 8/1 *Speel*, to gamble. **1892** I. ZANGWILL *Childr. Ghetto* I. iv. 124 They played loo, 'klobbiyos', napoleon... Old Hyams did not *spiel*, because he could not afford to. **1931** [see HALF *sb.* 6 i]. **1953** W. MANKOWITZ *Bespoke Overcoat* xiv. 21 You go to the dog tracks in the evening? Not for me. .. Horses? No horses, neither. You must spiel something. Poker, shemmy?

b. To play music.

1870 *Territorial Enterprise* (Virginia City, Nevada) 16 July 3/1 The new 'circus' is to be seen at the corner of D street and Sutton avenue—down var der orkan goes a spielin'. **1871** *Nassau Lit. Mag.* Feb. 179 Come now, old fellow, 'speil'. **1947** G. S. PERRY *Cities of Amer.* 187 Denver's Symphony chooses to spiel only when winter's winds doth blow.

2. To talk, esp. volubly or glibly; to patter. Also with *away*.

1894 *Mid-Winter Appeal* (San Francisco) 10 Mar. 1/3 Tell [the barker] to stop spieling now and then. **1904** 'O. HENRY' *Cabbages & Kings* xiii. 220 If you can borrow some gent's hat in the audience, and make a lot of customers for an idle stock of shoes come out of it, you'd better spiel. **1914** [see BALLYHOO *sb.*]. **1920** WODEHOUSE *Coming of Bill* I. v. 60 Spiel away, ma'am... The floor's yours. **1946** MEZZROW & WOLFE *Really Blues* (1957) vi. 70 One of the funniest things I ever heard was Mac spieling in Yiddish. **1966** R. SHECKLEY *Mindswap* vii. 49 Silent and disdainful, scorning to spiel, the little man stood with arms folded as Flynn walked up to the booth.

3. *trans.* To tell, to reel *off*; to announce; to perform.

1904 'O. HENRY' *Cabbages & Kings* iii. 58 I'll come right back and hear you spiel the rest before bedtime. **1936** W. A. GAPE *Half a Million Tramps* v. 139 When my turn came I was not ready to 'spiel' off the answers. **1962** *Coast to Coast 1961–62* 81 Garish neons had spieled, in Latin letters, the delights of innumerable honkeytonks. **1970** A. TOFFLER *Future Shock* xviii. 378 Each participant spieled off his reason for attending. **1977** *Time* 28 Nov. 64/1 In a few hours he would be on a.. stage singing his songs and spieling his narrative jazz poetry to an audience of college kids.

Hence '**spieling** *vbl. sb.*

1859 G. MATSELL *Vocabulum* 84 *Speiling*, gambling. **1898** A. M. BINSTEAD *Pink 'Un & Pelican* ix. 190 A raid upon a 'spieling' club by the police. **1904** 'O. HENRY' in *McClure's Mag.* July 353/2 It was just what Buck wanted—a regular business at a permanent stand, with no open air spieling.. on the street corners every evening. **1937** G. FRANKAU *More of Us* vii. 78 Nor think this spieling shames our British blood. **1959** T. H. WHITE *Godstone & Blackymor* 47 There was no patter now, no fair ground spieling. **1981** *Observer* 9 Aug. 3/2 'Pitching', or spieling, is how traders sell by a kind of inverted auction: prices start out sky-high, and buyers leap into the breach as the pitcher brings them tumbling down.

spiel, variant of SPEEL *sb.* and *v.*[1], [2].

spiel bone, variant of SPEAL BONE.

spieler ('spiːlə(r)). *slang* (orig. *U.S.*) Also speeler, †speiler. [a. G. *spieler* player, gambler, gamester.]

1. A gambler; a card-sharper or professional swindler. Now chiefly *Austral.*

1859 G. MATSELL *Vocabulum* 83 *Speiler*, a gambler. **1885** [see MURRUMBIDGEE]. **1886** *N. Zealand Herald* 1 June 4/7 It is stated that a fresh gang of 'speelers' are operating in the town. **1893** J. A. BARRY *S. Brown's Bunyip*, etc. 21 You want to get away amongst the spielers and forties of the big smoke? **1911** W. H. KOEBEL *In Maoriland Bush* xxii. 283 The professional sharper or 'spieler'.. wings his periodical flights from Sydney or Melbourne. **1929** *Detective Fiction Weekly* 13 July 731/2 Hard on their trail would come all the 'magsmen', the 'spielers', the dips, the 'broadsmen', and the 'pickers up'. **1935** H. R. WILLIAMS *Comrades of Great Adventure* 234 The spielers worked the three-card trick on the 'mugs'. **1957** J. WATEN *Shares in Murder* 156 You could match your wits against smart con-men and spielers.

2. One who spiels (SPIEL *v.* 2); a 'barker'; a voluble speaker.

1894 *Mid-Winter Appeal* (San Francisco) 19 May 15/1 Some spielers for the Midway who attempted to lick the Camp gate keeper were sent up for 24 hours. **1901** [see BALLYHOOER]. **1936** J. L. HODSON *Our Two Englands* vi. 109 The public.. are as fascinated by a good spieler or barker on the show front as they were then. **1937** *Printer's Ink Monthly* May 42/3 *Spieler*, a radio commentator. **1956** *Time* 11 June 42 Mary Costa.. agrees that a girl spieler should be 'good-looking but not too flashy to detract from the product'. **1976** *National Observer* (U.S.) 8 May 16/1 His style is all style, a curious amalgam that incorporates at its corniest Dare to Be Great spieler Glenn Turner.

3. A gambling club.

1931 *Police Jrnl.* IV. 502 A cardsharper (broadsman) met a confidence trickster (con-head) and a thief (tealeaf) in a gaming house (speiler). **1945** P. CHEYNEY *I'll say she Does* iii. 57 It's a gamblin' *spieler*... There's big play there every night. **1955** D. WEBB *Deadline for Crime* iv. 88 Throughout Soho and Mayfair there are a number of what are known as speilers, illicit gambling dens run by the underworld mainly for the underworld, or wealthier mugs of the racecourses. **1962** [see KITE *sb.* 4c]. **1976** J. O'CONNOR *Eleventh Commandment* iv. 62 A well-known boxing referee who used to run a dirty low-down dive of a spieler.

‖**Spielraum** ('ʃpiːlraʊm). *Philos.* Pl. Spielräume. [Ger. (J. von Kries *Die Principien der Wahrscheinlichkeitsrechnung*, 1886), f. *spiel* play + *raum* room.] The range of possibilities (orig. in probability theory) within which the probability of an outcome or likelihood of a hypothesis is to be assessed.

1921 J. M. KEYNES *Treat. Probability* vii. 88 Briefly.. he [*sc.* von Kries] may be said to hold that the hypotheses for the probabilities of which we wish to obtain a numerical comparison, must refer to 'fields' (Spielräume). **1937** *Mind* XLVI. 486 In this connexion he criticises von Kries's '*Spielraum*'-theory of probability. **1944** *Horizon* IX. 235, I propose to borrow from a theory of probability the concept of a *spielraum*. In connection with the judgments we make about freedom, this metaphor of a playing-space can be applied in three ways. **1961** J. N. FINDLAY *Values & Intentions* iii. 111 The image of a *Spielraum* or space of possibilities seems.. indispensable to the full development of partial belief. **1969** P. GEACH *God & Soul* vii. 97 There has to be this element of chance in things if human choices are to have any *Spielraum*.

spier ('spaɪə(r)). Forms: 3 spiare, 4 spiere, 4–7, 9 spier; 4 spyere, 5 spyar, -our, 5, 9 spyer. [f. SPY *v.* + -ER, or ad. OF. *espierre*, *espieur* (mod.F. *épieur*), whence also MDu. *spierre*, *spiere*, *spier* (later *spieder*).] One who spies or spies out; an espier; a spy.

c **1275** LAY. 1488 Spiares he sende to þis kinges ferde, to witen of his farecostes, ware he wolden fihte. þeos spiares verden, & sone aȝein comen. *c* **1380** WYCLIF *Sel. Wks.* III. 150 For prest is a spyere in his castel, to loke ofer perels of schepe. **1382** —— *1 Esdr.* viii. 31 The hond of oure God.. deliuerede vs fro the hond of the enemy and of the spiere in the weie. **1398** TREVISA *Barth. De P.R.* XI. xii. (Tollem. MS.), Myste is frende to þeuis and euel doares, for he hideþ here spieris and waytynges. *c* **1440** *Gesta Rom.* xxvii. 102 (Harl. MS.), He sente wacchemen & spyeris to fecche him. **1490** *Acc. Ld. High Treas. Scot.* I. 173 Johne Hammilton callit Master Spyar. **1496** *Ibid.* 305 Giffin to the Maister Spyour. **1589** PUTTENHAM *Eng. Poesie* I. xiii. (Arb.) 46 These terrene and base gods [Satyrs] being conuersant with mans affaires, and spiers out of all their secret faults. **1621** R. BOLTON *Stat. Irel.* 70 Upon paine of forfeiture of the said wares,.. halfe to the King, and the other halfe to the spier and finder of the same. **1850** A. H. CLOUGH *Dipsychus* IV. (1871) 110, I let them slip, Like an unpractised spyer through a glass.

spier, var. SPEER *sb.*[3] and *v.*[1]; obs. f. SPIRE *sb.*

spier-hawk, later f. *spere-hawk* SPARHAWK.

? *c* **1810** in Child *Ball.* IV. 484/2 Lord William.. spyed his bonnie spier-hawk, Was fleein aboon his head.

spierre, obs. form of SPIRE *sb.*[2]

†**spiery.** *Obs.* [f. SPY *sb.* or *v.* + -ERY. Cf. ESPIERY.] The fact or condition of being a spy; the action of spying; espionage.

c **1588** PARSONS in Morris *Troub. Cath. Forefathers* 2nd Ser. (1875) 312 After I had read over the whole story.. of his living in England,.. his examinations, confessions, fictions, accusations, slanders, spiery, recantation and the like. **1600** W. WATSON *Decacordon* (1602) 132 This good Cardinall [was] most spitefully infamed by these three Priests (though al in one predicament of spierie if any were).

†**spie-woman**, variant of SPAE-WOMAN. *Obs.*

1744 in D. M'Naught *Kilmaurs* (1912) xiv. 189 [Going to Glasgow to consult] a spie woman anent some beese that somebody had stolen from him.

spiff, *sb. slang.* [Of obscure origin. Cf. next.] *pl.* (See quots.) Also *attrib.*, as ***spiff stores, system.***

1859 *Slang Dict.* 98 *Spiffs*, the percentage allowed by drapers to their young men when they effect sale of old fashioned or undesirable stock. **1890** *Pall Mall G.* 2 April 3/2 To balance this network of penalties a 'spiff' system is usually adopted, spiffs being premiums placed on certain articles, *not* of the last fashion.

Hence **spiff** *v.*[1] *trans.*, to allow a certain sum as commission on (an article).

1891 *Ironmonger* 19 Sept. 387 A 'job' chandelier, not very unsaleable, may be 'spiffed', say 1*s.*, but a more unsaleable one should bear a higher sum.

spiff, *v.*[2] *slang.* [Cf. next and SPIFFY *a.*] In *pa. pple.* Made neat, spruce, or fine; smartly dressed or tricked *out.* Also with *up.*

1877 W. S. GILBERT *Foggerty's Fairy* ii, We flatter ourselves that we are spiffed out; at all events we've got our best dresses on. **1979** *Arizona Daily Star* 22 July J 3/2 The man doing it was an interior decorator, not an art conservator, and he did what he felt was best—he went in and spiffed up the church.

spiffing ('spɪfɪŋ), *a. colloq.* and *dial.* Also spiffin, *dial.* spiving. [Cf. next and such forms as *rattling*, *ripping*, *topping*, etc.] Excellent, first-rate, very good, etc.; fine or smart in, or with regard to, dress or appearance. Also as *adv.*

Sleigh *Derby. Gloss.* (1865) has *Spiffyn*, work well done. **1872** *Routledge's Ev. Boy's Ann.* 287/2 The vulgar Pupkins said,.. 'It was spiffing!' **1879–** in general dial. use (*Eng. Dial. Dict.*). **1884** G. MOORE *Mummer's Wife* (1887) 145 'Have you got good places for your posters?' 'Spiffing,' answered the man.

spiffy ('spɪfɪ), *a. colloq.* and *dial.* [Of obscure origin; the shorter form *spiff* is recorded in dialect use from 1862; also *spiff* 'a well-dressed man, a swell' (*Slang Dict.* 1874).] Smart, spruce.

1853 D. G. ROSSETTI *Let.* 2 Nov. (1965) I. 161 The frame for my water-colour has just come in and is spiffy cheesy jammy nobby [etc.]. **1860** *Slang Dict.* 223 *Spiffy*, spruce, well-dressed. **1881–** in dial. glossaries (Leicester, Warwick, Cornwall). **1896** MRS. LYNN LINTON in *Chambers's Jrnl.* 25 Jan. 50, I, in my older clothes, and by no means 'spiffy' in my get up. **1958** T. STANWELL-FLETCHER *Clear Lands* 24 This was with the comparatively new, very spiffy Canadian government's *C. D. Howe*. **1978** H. WOUK *War & Remembrance* viii. 86 She's turned into quite the spiffy New York gal.

spiflicate ('spɪflɪkeɪt), *v. humorous* or *colloq.* Also **spifflicate, spefflicate.** [Prob. a purely fanciful formation. Cf. SMIFLIGATE *v.*] *trans.* To deal with in such a way as to confound or overcome completely; to treat or handle roughly or severely; to crush, destroy.

Common in the 19th century.

α. **1785** GROSE *Dict. Vulgar T.*, To *spiflicate*, to confound, silence, or dumbfound. **1796** *New Brighton Guide* 39 Come, spificate that scoundrel Care, Gruel him, bruise him, never fear. **1818** MOORE *Fudge Fam. Paris* ix. 223 Alas, alas, our ruin's fated; All done up, and spiflicated! **1824** —— *Mem.* (1853) IV. 258 Asked him about Pendeli, which is long, as I feared, and my song, accordingly, spiflicated. **1842** BARHAM *Ingol. Leg.* Ser. II. *Babes in Wood* xi, So out with your whinger at once, and scrag Jane, while I spiflicate Johnny! **1873** *Brit. Q. Rev.* LVII. 276 The way in which the learned, racy old Hector smashes and spiflicates scientific idiots.. is delicious.

β. **1749** *Gentl. Mag.* Dec. 563 Whence the term *spifflicated*? **1841** HARTSHORNE *Salop. Ant.* Gloss., *Spifflicate*, to do some bodily injury. **1857** DUFFERIN *Lett. High Lat.* (ed. 3) 200 The best mode of spifflicating the white bears. **1894** STEVENSON & L. OSBOURNE *Ebb-tide* 221, I on'y ast you to stand by and spifflicate the niggers.

Hence '**spiflicating** *ppl. a.*

1852 [see ROWDY-DOW *sb.*]. **1891** MEREDITH *One of our Conq.* x, You've got a spiflicating style of talk about you.

spiflicated ('spɪflɪkeɪtɪd), *ppl. a. slang* (orig. *U.S.*). Also **spifflicated.** [f. prec. + -ED[1].] Intoxicated, drunk.

1906 'O. HENRY' *Four Million* 114 He uses Nature's Own Remedy. He gets spifflicated. **1910** [see PIE-EYED *a.*]. **1927** *New Republic* 9 Mar. 71/2 The following is a partial list of words denoting drunkenness now in common use in the United States.. spifflicated. **1931** *Sun* (Baltimore) 6 Jan. 6/7 Almost every name you could think of to describe the state of being drunk was given, but one splendid one that I know of was omitted—'spifflicated'. *a* **1966** 'M. NA GOPALEEN' *Best of Myles* (1968) 338 Drunk; jarred;.. spiflicated. **1971** H. A. SMITH *View from Chivo* i. 5, I do not believe.. that I was spifflicated last night.

spiflication (spɪflɪ'keɪʃən). *humorous* or *colloq.* [f. SPIFLICATE *v.*] The action of spiflicating; the fact or condition of being spiflicated; complete destruction.

1855 R. F. BURTON *El-Medinah* I. 204 Whose blood he vowed to drink—the Oriental form of threatening spiflication. **1859** MEREDITH *R. Feverel* xxi, You had better not mention anything.. of Benson's spiflication. **1887** *Pall Mall G.* 26 Sept. 3/1 The metaphysical spiflication of rash members of the bourgeoisie.

spig, var. SPIC *sb.* and *a.*

‖**Spigelia** (spaɪ'dʒiːlɪə). *Bot.* [mod.L. (Linnæus, 1737), f. the name of the Belgian physician and anatomist, Adrian *Spigelius* (1578–1625).] A genus of plants belonging to the order *Loganiaceæ* or worm-grass; a plant of this genus, esp. *Spigelia marilandica*, the pink-root of the Southern U.S., the roots and leaves of which are used medicinally. Also *attrib.*

1822–7 GOOD *Study Med.* (1829) I. 364 In the latter we may place.. the *spigelias*, and *scabiosa Indica*. **1847** DARLINGTON *Amer. Weeds*, etc. (1860) 165 Maryland Spigelia. Carolina or Indian Pink. **1861** BENTLEY *Man. Bot.* 591 *Loganiaceæ*. The Spigelia or Strychnos Order. **1875** H. C. WOOD *Therap.* (1879) 600 Spigelia is a most efficient remedy in cases of the roundworm.

spigelian (spaɪ'dʒiːlɪən). *Anat.* [f. *Spigeli-us* (see prec. and def.) + -AN.] ***spigelian lobe***, a term for the middle lobe of the liver, first particularized by Spigelius (Mayne).

1811 in R. HOOPER *Med. Dict.* s.v. **1905** H. ROLLESTON *Dis. Liver* 4 Davy described a pedunculated Spigelian lobe. *Ibid.* 200 One of the smaller lobes, such as the spigelian or caudate, may be enlarged.

spiggoty ('spɪgɒtɪ), *sb.* (and *a.*) *U.S. slang.* Also spiggity, spigotti, spigoty. [Orig. uncertain: prob. repr. broken English (see sense 1, quot. 1938): now generally superseded by SPIC *sb.* and *a.*] **1.** A contemptuous name for a Spanish-speaking native of Central or South America.

1910 'W. LAWTON' *Boy Aviators in Nicaragua* 331 Ring.. steamed down here on his gunboat just in time to fire that shell and throw a scare into the spiggotys at the very physicky moment. **1913** H. A. FRANCK *Zone Policeman 88* 10 It was my first entrance into the land of the panameños, technically known on the Zone as 'spigoties'. **1916** *Recruiter's Bull.* (U.S. Marine Corps, N.Y.) Jan. 10/1 Well, we did not get to Haut de Cap—we ran into a 'nest' of Spiggoties and things were pretty warm for about three hours. **1934** R. STOUT *Fer-de-Lance* xv. 248 'He's a dirty spiggoty.' 'No, Archie, Mr Manuel Kimball is an Argentine.' **1938** *Amer. Speech* XIII. 311/1 'Spiggoty' originated in Panama during Construction Days, and is assumed to be a corruption of 'spikee de' in the sentence 'No spikee de English', which was then the most common response of Panamanians to any question in English. **1959** R. CAMPBELL *I would do it Again* xxvi. 196, I learned that the young ladies were mostly Spigoties, a name applied to those of mixed Spanish and Indian blood.

2. Spanish-American; more generally, a foreign language.

1914 E. O'NEILL *Movie Man* in *Lost Plays* (1950) 37 Say, you're getting to be a regular talker of spigoty! Slip me the answer to that word 'basta', will you? **1922** H. L. FOSTER *Adventures Trop. Tramp* ix. 132 Just stood around the dock and jabbered a lot of spiggoty talk at me, like I could understand spiggoty! I don't know a word of this damned Spanish, and I'm glad of it! **1923** *Amer. Legion Weekly* 27 Apr. 12 Yer S.O.L. kid!! All I can dope out is the date—I can't get this frog spiggity a 'tall!!

3. *attrib.* passing into *adj.* Central or South American; foreign.

1918 W. S. POAGUE *Diary* 1 Feb. (? 1919) 28 We repaired to the town and had a white man's dinner with some spigotti liquor. **1937** H. KLEMMER *Harbor Nights* 197 *Marijuana* is a popular spiggoty drug which has spread rapidly into the North during recent years.

†**spight**, *pa. t.* and *pa. pple. Obs.* [prob. from an inf. **spicchen*, = G. dial. *spicken* to prick, push.] *trans.* Instigated, urged, stirred up.

1387 TREVISA *Higden* (Rolls) I. 7 By þe worþynesse and ensaumple of so worþy writeris i-spiȝt and i-egged [L. *provocatus*]. *Ibid.* VII. 429 Robert.. made [*v.r.* spiȝte; L. *excitavit*] meny Walsche men to rise aȝenst þe kyng.

spight, obs. f. SPEIGHT (woodpecker), SPITE *sb.* and *v.*

spightful, etc., obs. f. SPITEFUL, etc.

†**spig-nail**, obs. variant of SPIKE-NAIL.

a **1600** *Stat. Streets* xix. in Stow *Surv. Lond.* (1633) 666 No Carts that shall be shod with Spig naile, that shall come upon the streets of this City. **1755** STRYPE *Stow's Surv.* (ed. 6) II. 715/2 That no..Cart shod with Iron, or Spignails, or having more Horses than is allowed,..shall take up any Goods within this City.

spignel (ˈspɪgnəl). Forms: α. 6 **spignale**, 6–7 **spignell**, 7 **spygnal**, 6–7, 9 **spignel**. β. 6 **speknel**, **specknell**, **spiknel**, 6–7 **spicknell**, 6–9 **spicknel**, 9 **spikenel**. [Of obscure origin; perh. a later form of SPIGURNEL[1].]

†**1.** The aromatic root of the umbelliferous plant *Meum athamanticum*, used, when dried and ground, in medicine as a carminative or stimulant, or as a spice in cookery. *Obs.*

1502 ARNOLDE *Chron.* (1811) 188 Take cloues and gelofre, ..gynger and spignale,..and temper hem with good wyne. **1577** *Richmond Wills* (Surtees) 269 For arseneck xij[d]. Spicknell, turmirick, and galingall ij[s]. **1592** *Wills & Inv. N.C.* (Surtees, 1860) 212 One pound and a half specknell, 2s. **1610** MARKHAM *Masterp.* I. xl. 82 A penny worth of Galingal, two peniworth of spygnal of Spaine. **1718** QUINCY *Compl. Disp.* 169 Spignel..has an aromatick Pungency in its Scent, but also somewhat fetid.

2. The plant itself; meum; baldmoney.

α. **1579** LANGHAM *Gard. Health* 390 Meu, Meon, or Spignel, boyle or soke the roots in water, and drinke it to open mightely the stoppings of the kidneys and bladder. **1668** WILKINS *Real Char.* II. iv. 90 Umbelliferous herbs whose Leaves are more Finely cut into narrow segments..: Spignel. Bishopsweed. **1712** tr. *Pomet's Hist. Drugs* I. 43 Which has made some believe that Spignel was a species of Fennil or Dill. **1760** J. LEE *Introd. Bot.* App. 327 Spignel, *Athamanta*. **1822–7** GOOD *Study Med.* (1829) V. 53 The *athamanta meum*, or spignel, which once rivalled the reputation of madder, seems to have a peculiar influence in stimulating the lower viscera. **1861** S. THOMSON *Wild Fl.* (ed. 4) III. 296 The root[s]..of the meum or spignel..have ..been held in esteem.

β. **1548** TURNER *Names Herbes* 53 Meum..I neuer sawe thys herbe in Englande sauynge once at saynte Oswarldes where as the inhabiters called it Speknel. **1562** —— *Herbal* II. (1568) 56 Y[e] Spiknel of England (which peraduenture was ones called Spiknard). **1601** HOLLAND *Pliny* II. 77 Meu or Spicknell is not found in Italy, vnlesse it be in some Physitians garden. **1706** PHILLIPS (ed. Kersey) s.v., Spicknel or Spignel. **1866** *Treas. Bot.* 1083/2 Spikenel, or Spicknel, *Meum Athamanticum*.

b. Applied, with distinguishing terms, to other plants allied to or resembling this, as ***bastard, mountain, parsley, wild spignel*** (see quots.).

1597 GERARDE *Herbal* II. ccccix. 895 It is called..in English Spignell, or Spicknell... The second may be called bastard Baldmony, or bastard Spicknell. **1713** *Phil. Trans.* XXVIII. 190 Parsley Spignel. **1760** J. LEE *Introd. Bot.* App. 327 Spignel, Wild, *Seseli*. **1796** WITHERING *Brit. Plants* (ed. 3) II. 294 *Athamanta Libanotis*,..Mountain Spignel or Stone Parsley.

spigot (ˈspɪgət), *sb.* Forms: α. 4, 6 **spigote**, 5 **speget**, 5–6 **spygott(e**, **spygot**, 6–7 **spigott**, 4– **spigot**. β. 7 **spigget**, **spiggott**, 7–9 **spiggot**. See also SPICKET[1] and SPIDDOCK. [Of obscure history, but probably ad. early Prov. **espigot*, f. *espiga* SPIKE *sb.*[1]

For the formation cf. mod.Prov. *espigot* (F. dial. *épigot*; OF. *espigeot*, F. dial. *épigeot*) a badly-threshed ear of grain. Some approximation in sense appears in Prov. *espigoun*, *espigou* (= Sp. *espigon*, Pg. *espigão*, It. *spigone*), rung of a ladder, bar of a chair, bung of a cask. Pg. *espicho* (:—L. *spiculum*) has the sense of 'spigot'. Florio (1611) also gives It. *spigo* as 'spigot', but for this there appears to be no other evidence.]

1. A small wooden peg or pin used to stop the vent-hole of a barrel or cask; a vent-peg; a similar peg inserted into and controlling the opening or tube of a faucet and used to regulate the flow of liquor.

α. **1383–4** *Durham Acc. Rolls* (Surtees) 593 In iij duodenis de Spigotes empt. pro butelaria,..iijs. iiijd. **1388** WYCLIF *Job* xxxii. 19 Lo! my wombe is as must with out spigot, ether a ventyng. **14..** *Nom.* in Wr.-Wülcker 724 *Hec clipsidra*, a spygotte. *c* **1440** *Promp. Parv.* 469/1 Spygot, *clipsidra, ducillus, ductileum*. **1531–2** *Durham Househ. Bk.* (Surtees) 74, 2 dd. spigotts et cannells. **1590** *Shuttleworths' Acc.* (Chetham Soc.) 63 Spigotes and facetes, ij[d]. **1598** SHAKS. *Merry W.* I. iii. 24 O base hungarian wight: wilt thou the spigot wield? **1674** GREW *Anat. Pl., Disc. Mixture* (1682) 226 When one Atome is admitted into the..hole of another; as a Spigot is into a Fosset. **1768–74** TUCKER *Lt. Nat.* (1834) I. 568 If a careless servant does not mind to thrust the spigot fast into the barrel, the beer must necessarily run all away. **1809** MALKIN *Gil Blas* IX. ix. ¶5 We have..wherewithal to keep the spit and the spigot in exercise. **1843** JAMES *Forest Days* ix, A man with a mallet was busily engaged in driving a spigot and faucet to give discreet vent to the liquor within. **1896** CROCKETT *Cleg Kelly* viii. 61 Cleg went to the back of the door, where there was a keg with a spigot.

β. **1570** LEVINS *Manip.* 177/11 A spiggotte, *epistomium*. **1594** NASHE *Unfort. Trav.* Wks. (Grosart) V. 23 Nothing but spiggots and faussets of discarded emptie barrels. **1658** tr. *Porta's Nat. Magic.* x. ii. 256 Pull out the Spigget, that the hot Water may run out. **1673** RAY *Journ. Low Co.* 462 They gather it [petroleum] up,..and put it in a barrel set on one end, which hath a spiggot just at the bottom. **1743** *Lond. & Country Brew.* III. (ed. 2) 185 Sometimes the Weight of the Wort forces out the Spiggot. **1823** P. NICHOLSON *Pract. Build.* 340 A small barrel of water at the top, furnished with a spiggot.

b. *fig.* That which controls, lets out, or restrains.

Freq. used with reference to speech or language.

1780 WARNER in Jesse *Selwyn & Contemp.* (1844) IV. 402 You must be very serious in what you say about a speech. Do but pull out the spigot and let it run, and nobody can sport a clearer or a sweeter stream. **1830** CARLYLE *Misc.* (1857) II. 174 Something which he called the rudder of Government, but which was rather the spigot of Taxation. **1834** MEDWIN *Angler in Wales* I. 224 I should find such enemies in the preachers, that I might bung up my spigot. **1900** LAPSLEY *Co. Pal. Durham* 127 Having but a limited control of the spigot of taxation.

†**2.** A hollow wooden peg or tube used in drawing off liquor; a faucet. *Obs.*

Not always clearly distinguishable from sense 1.

1530 PALSGR. 693/2 I ronne, as lycour dothe out of a vessell by a spigot or faulset, whan it ronneth styll after a stynte. **1644** DIGBY *Nat. Bodies* xx. §3. 177 [To have] a little spigott, or quile att the outside of the hole, that by the narrow length of it helpeth in some sort (as it were) to sucke it. **1675** J. ROSE *Eng. Vineyard Vind.* 43 Drawing out your must by a spigot at the bottom of your vessel. **1725** *Fam. Dict.* s.v. *Birch-Wine*, [It] will need neither Stone nor Chip to keep it open, nor Spiggot to direct it to the Recipient.

3. In figurative or allusive use: **a.** In various proverbial phrases (see quots.).

1562 J. HEYWOOD *Prov. & Epigr.* (1867) 194 We apply the spigot, till tubbe stande a tilte. **1591** GREENE *Farewell to Follie* Wks. (Grosart) IX. 249 The foole was a fidler, and knewe scarse a speare from a spigot. **1594** LYLY *Mother Bombie* II. v, *Memp.* Ile teach my wag-halter to know grapes from barley. *Pris.* And I mine to discerne a spigot from a faucet. **1677** MIÉGE *Fr. Dict.* II. s.v. *Spare*, To spare at the spiggot, and let it run out at the bung-hole.

b. ***brother, knight, man, son of the spigot***, a tapster; a seller of liquor; an alehouse-keeper; ***hero, imp of the spigot***, one who indulges in liquor.

1821 SCOTT *Kenilw.* i, 'What, ho! John Tapster.' 'At hand, Will Hostler,' replied the man of the spigot. *Ibid.* viii, When an old song comes across us merry old knights of the spigot, it runs away with our discretion. **1828** MISS MITFORD *Village* Ser. III. (1863) 42 Like that renowned hero of the spiggot [Boniface]. **1839** SIR J. STEPHEN *Eccl. Biog.* (1850) 309 Under the guidance..of the imp of the spigot, Martin Luther.

4. A plain end of a pipe entering an enlargement (a 'socket' or 'faucet') of another as a means of forming a joint. Chiefly in attrib. phrases, as ***spigot and faucet joint, spigot and socket piece***.

1797 J. CURR *Coal Viewer* 55 The joints [of jack-head pumps] may be either spigot and faucet, or hoboy joints run with lead and regulus. **1840** *Civil Eng. & Arch. Jrnl.* III. 121/1 Some cocks of the smaller sizes have heretofore been cast with spigot and socket instead of flange outlets. *Ibid.*, The outlets are generally made with flanges, to which a socket and spigot piece with corresponding flanges are bolted. **1849** GREENWELL *Coal-trade Terms, Northumb. & Durh.* s.v., *Spigot and Faucit*, a description of pump joint, in which each pump is cast with a cup or faucit end; the other, or spigot end, being plain, for the purpose of insertion into the cup.

b. An annular projection (as on a cylinder cover or a flange) entering a corresponding depression in the adjacent piece.

1900 HASLUCK *Mod. Eng. Handybk.* 84 The spigots of the cylinder-covers are also chipped away the same width as the ports.

5. *attrib.*, as ***spigot-end, -hole***; also **spigot-joint**, a spigot and faucet joint; † **spigot-sucker**, one given to drinking or tippling.

1611 COTGR., *Pinteur*, a tippler, pot-companion, spiggot-sucker. **1849** Spigot end [see 4 above]. **1875** KNIGHT *Dict. Mech.* 2266/1 Spigot (or Faucet) Joint. **1879** MISS JACKSON *Shropsh. Word-bk.* 33 The..strainer placed over the spigot-hole within the mash-tub, to prevent the grains passing through into the wort. **1884** *Harper's Mag.* Sept. 608/2 The ..creatures made their escape through the spigot-hole.

Hence **ˈspigot** *v. trans.*, (*a*) to thrust a spigot into (in quots. *a* 1809, 1824 *fig.*); (*b*) to insert in the manner of a spigot.

a **1809** J. PALMER *Like Master* (1811) II. xiv. 211 But I must obey orders, or he might spigot me, mayhap, as they do in the foot-cavalry. **1824** LANDOR *Imag. Conv.* Wks. 1853 I. 173/2 Did not you or your father flay the devil alive? Did not you spigot him nor singe him? **1910** *Automobile Engineering 1911* 19/3 Single separate cylinders..are spiggotted deeply into the crankcase. **1954** *Automobile Engineer* XLIV. 507/2 This cover is spigoted into the housing and bolted to the front wall of the box.

†**spigurnel**[1]. *Obs. rare.* [ad. med.L. *spigurnella*, of obscure origin and meaning. Cf. SPIGNEL.] Some plant.

a **1400** *Stockholm Med. MS.* 95 Spyggurnell mal and refamall. *c* **1450** *Alphita* (Anecd. Oxon.) 174 *Spigurnella*, g. et ang. spigurnele uel freydele; mirabiliter ualet contra squinanciam;..angl. spinagre.

†**spigurnel**[2]. *Obs. rare.* Also 7 **spigurnell**. [ad. Anglo-L. *spigurnellus* (1314), *spigornellus* (1275), of obscure origin. 'Godefridus Spigurnell' was in the service of King John in 1207, and the office of *espicurnantia* is mentioned in a document, dated 1299, cited by Kennett.] (See quots.)

It is evident that the word had no real currency in English, and its appearance is due to Camden and Holland, copied by Phillips, Blount, Harris, Bailey, etc.

1610 HOLLAND *Camden's Brit.* I. 312 These Bohuns (to note so much by the way for the antiquity of a word now growne out of use) were by inheritance for a good while the Kings Spigurnells, that is, the Sealeres of his writs. **1679** BLOUNT *Anc. Tenures* 72 The Office of Spigurnel, or Sealer of the Kings Writs in Chancery. **1754** POCOCKE *Trav.* (Camden) II. 112 The Bohuns, who were the spigurnels or sealers of the king's writs.

spik, spikate, varr. SPICK *sb.*[2], SPICATE *a.*

spik, var. SPIC *sb.* and *a.*

spike (spaɪk), *sb.*[1] Also 4 **spik**, 6 **spyke**. [ad. L. *spīca* fem. (rarely *spīcum* neut. and *spīcus* masc.) ear of corn, plant-spike. In branch I corresponding to It. *spiga*, Prov., Sp. *espiga* fem., OF. *espi* (*espic*), F. *épi* masc.; in sense 4 to OF. *espic*, F. *spic* and *aspic* (see SPICK *sb.*[2], ASPIC[2]), It. *spigo*, Sp. *espliego* masc., also MDu. *spike*, *spijc*, Du. *spijk*, G. *spieke* fem. (also masc. in variant forms).]

I. 1. An ear of grain. Chiefly *poet.*

1393 LANGL. *P. Pl.* C. XIII. 180 Bote yf þe sed þat sowen is in þe sloh sterue, Shal neuere spir springen vp ne spik on strawe curne. **1601** HOLLAND *Pliny* XVIII. vii. I. 557 All kind of corne carrying spike or eare, called Frumenta. **1648** DENHAM *Cato Major Old Age* iii. (1669) 33 Drawn up in rancks, and files, the bearded spikes Guard it from birds as with a stand of pikes. **1700** DRYDEN tr. *Ovid's Meleager & Atalanta* 33 Suff'ring not their yellow Beards to rear, He [*sc.* the wild boar] tramples down the Spikes, and intercepts the Year. **1730–46** THOMSON *Autumn* 166 The gleaners spread around, and here and there, Spike after spike, their scanty harvest pick. **1796** WITHERING *Brit. Plants* (ed. 3) I. 83 Take a spike (or as it is frequently called, an ear) of wheat. **1798** COLERIDGE *Three Graves* III. ii, On the hedge-elms in the narrow lane Still swung the spikes of corn. **1860** ADLER *Prov. Poet.* xvi. 359 A man without love is worth no more than the spike without grain. **1875** [see SPICA 4].

b. *Astr.* ***the virgin's spike*** [tr. L. *spica Virginis*], = SPICA 3.

1559 W. CUNNINGHAM *Cosmogr. Glasse* 104 A fixed sterre, called the virgins spike. **1764** MASKELYNE in *Phil. Trans.* LIV. 359 The virgin's spike, and a small star preceding it. **1802** O. G. GREGORY *Treat. Astron.* vi. 109 On the 8th of April, 1801, at what hour will the star called *virgin's spike* be on the meridian of London?

c. The receptacle in which the grains of maize are fixed.

1800 *Med. Jrnl.* IV. 249 From the young fresh stalks, as well as from the spikes of India corn, a true sugar can be extracted. **1809** A. HENRY *Trav.* 134 I was requested not to break the spikes. *Ibid.*, The grains of maize..grow in compact cells, round a spike.

2. *Bot.* A form of inflorescence consisting of sessile flowers borne on an elongated simple axis.

1578 LYTE *Dodoens* 103 Long purple, spykie knoppes like to the eares or spikes of Bistorte. **1601** HOLLAND *Pliny* I. 364 The head of Nardus spreadeth into certaine spikes or eares, whereby it hath a twofold use, both of spike and also of leafe. **1668** WILKINS *Real Char.* 78 Naked stalks; and flowers in a spike. *Ibid.*, Whose leaves are of a dark green above,.. bearing a spike of flowers. **1676** M. LISTER in *Ray's Corresp.* (1848) 124 The fulminating powder, which the spikes of *Muscus Lycopod.* yield. **1726** *Flower Garden Displ.* (ed. 2) Introd., *Spikes*, Trusses or Bunches, when the Flowers grow in such a manner as to form an Acute Cone. **1753** *Chambers' Cycl.* Suppl. s.v. *Lychnis*, The wild white lychnis with a bending spike of flowers. **1784** COWPER *Task* VI. 159 Her beauteous head now set With purple spikes pyramidal. **1851** GLENNY *Handbk. Fl. Gard.* 158 The blossoms are purple, and grow in spikes at the ends of the branches. **1889** *Science-Gossip* XXV. 122 They were beautiful trees, with their leaves..growing in thickly-set spikes.

3. *attrib.* and *Comb.*, as ***spike-corn, -stalk***; ***spike-flowered, -like*** adjs; ***spike-wise*** adv.

1601 HOLLAND *Pliny* I. 559 White Amel-corn, called Olyra, which is among them holden for the third sort of *Spike-corne. **1833** *Penny Cycl.* I. 77/1 *Acer spicatum*, the *spike-flowered maple. **1857** HENFREY *Bot.* §126 The term catkin..is applied to the..*spike-like inflorescence of the Willow, Poplar, Birch. **1880** JEFFERIES *Gt. Estate* 136 Beside them a rolled spike-like bloom not yet unfolded. **1796** WITHERING *Brit. Plants* (ed. 3) I. 83 **Spike-stalk*,..a long, rough, slender receptacle, upon which the flowers composing a spike are placed. **1601** HOLLAND *Pliny* I. 559 The graines arranged *spike-wise.

b. In some specific names of plants, as **spike-cudweed, -grass, -mint, -rush** (see quots. and SPIKED *a.*[1] 2).

1715 *Phil. Trans.* XXIX. 355 Welted Antego *Spike-Cudweed. **1760** J. LEE *Introd. Bot.* App. 327 *Spike-grass, Winged, *Stipa*. **1771** R. F. FORSTER *Flora Amer. Sept.* 4 Spike-grass, *Uniola paniculata*. **1856** A. GRAY *Man. Bot.* 567 *Uniola*,..Spike-Grass. **1731** MILLER *Gard. Dict.* Index, *Spike-mint, Spear-mint. **1829** LOUDON *Encycl. Pl.* (1836) 48 *Eleocharis*,..*Spike-Rush. Spike oval naked. **1859** MISS PRATT *Brit. Grasses* 11 Spike-rush. Spikelet many-flowered, solitary, terminal.

II. †**4.** French lavender (*Lavandula Spica*); = SPICK *sb.*[2] *Obs.*

1539 ELYOT *Cast. Helthe* (1541) 11 Thinges good for a colde head: Cububes: Galingale:..Pionye: Hyssope: Spyke: Yreos. **1578** LYTE *Dodoens* 265 It is called..in English Spike and Lauender. **1591** SYLVESTER *Du Bartas* I. vi. 729 Here bitter Worm-wood, there sweet-smelling Spike. **1611** COTGR., *Spicaire*, Roman Spike, or Lauender. **1621** BURTON *Anat. Mel.* III. iv. I. i, Sweet sents of saffron, spike, calamus and cynamon. **1712** tr. *Pomet's Hist. Drugs* I. 26 Of a strong smell, very much like Spike or Lavender.

b. ***oil of spike***, an essential oil obtained by distillation from *Lavendula Spica* (and *L. Stœchas*), employed in painting and in veterinary medicine. (Cf. *spike-oil* in 7.)

1577 HARRISON *England* III. ix. (1878) II. 65 A most delectable and sweet oile, comparable to..oile of spike in smell, was found naturallie included in a stone. **1594** PLAT *Jewell-ho.* II. 9, I speak not here of the oile of spike which will extende very farre this way. **1669** STURMY *Mariner's Mag.* VII. xxxiv. 49 Yellow Oker, well ground Oyle of Spike or Turpentine. **1686** PLOT *Staffordsh.* 379 They use Litharge pounded and searced fine, mixt with oyle of Spike. **1753** J. BARTLET *Gentl. Farriery* 231 The hot oils, as spike, turpentine and origanum. **1815** J. SMITH *Panorama Sci. & Art* II. 755 They are then mixed with oil of spike, and applied to the glass with camel-hair pencils. **1861** BENTLEY *Man. Bot.* 610 Oil of Spike or Foreign Oil of Lavender. *Ibid.*, *L. Stœchas* also yields..an essential oil, which is commonly distinguished as the True Oil of Spike.

attrib. **1703** *Art's Improv.* I. 48 You need not fear much the laying on of the Varnish the second time, provided..it be Oil of Spike Varnish.

†**5.** *spike celtic*, a species of valerian. *Obs.*

1540 R. JONAS *Byrth Mankynde* 70 For this take spyke celtyke, whiche some call mary mawdelyne flower,..& sethe it in the oyle of sesamum,..& laye it on the place. **1579** LANGHAM *Gard. Health* (1633) 16 Seethe Spike celtike in oyle of Almonds, and a little Turpentine and dip well therein and apply it.

†**6.** Spikenard. *Obs.*[−1]

1540 HYRDE tr. *Vives' Instr. Chr. Wom.* (1592) F vj, Mary Magdalene poured upon the head of our Lorde, oyntment of pretious Spike.

7. *attrib.* (in sense 4), as *spike-flower*, *-lavender*, *-leaf*, *-oil* [cf. Du. *spijkolie*, G. *spieköl*], †*-water*.

1588 L. M. tr. *Bk. Dyeing* 12 Take 2 pound of *spike flowers, one pound of rose marie. **1741** *Compl. Fam.-piece* I. iv. 252 Then put to them Balm, Spike-flowers,..of each 1 Ounce. **1607** TOPSELL *Four-f. Beasts* 444 With the decoction or liquor which commeth from *Spike-Lauender. **1799** G. SMITH *Laboratory* I. 114 Temper..with oil of spike, i.e. spike-lavender. **1879** *Cassell's Techn. Educ.* III. 247/1 Oil of spike lavender, or..turpentine, may be used instead of the coal-naphtha. **1750** W. ELLIS *Mod. Husbandm.* III. I. 178 Boil some Lavender and *Spike-leaves. **1611** COTGR., *Huile nardin*, *spike oyle. **1685** BAXTER *Paraphr. N.T.* Mark xiii. 3 It was a Cruise of precious Spike-oil shaken and poured out. **1868** WATTS *Dict. Chem.* V. 399 According to Gastell, spike-oil is obtained from the leaves and stalks, true lavender-oil from the flowers, of several species of *Lavendula*. **1558** WARDE tr. *Alexis' Secr.* 46 b, Take..Lauender water, *Spike water, of eche of them thre vnces. **1572** in Feuillerat *Rev. Q. Eliz.* (1908) 175, i pynte of spike water.

spike (spaɪk), *sb.*[2] Also 4 **spyk**, 5 **spyke**. [Of doubtful origin: agrees in form and meaning with MSw. *spīk*, *spijk*, Sw. and Norw. *spik* nail, which may be a shortened form of MLG. *spīker* (LG. *spiker*, *spieker*; hence G. *spiker*, Da. *spiger*, Norw. *spikar*), = MDu. *spīker*, *spijcker* (Du. *spijker*), Fris. *spiker*, *spikker* (perh. from Du. and LG.), MHG. *spîcher* (G. dial. *speicher-*): see SPIKER[1]. It is possible that these may in some way be derived from L. *spīca* SPIKE *sb.*[1], as OF. *espi*, F. *épi*, Sp. and Pg. *espiga* have senses nearly or altogether coincident with those of 'spike'.

The evidence for a MDu. *spike* sb. or *spiken* v. is very slender: see Verdam, s.vv. The Swed. and Norw. words differ in gender from Norw. *spik*, Icel. *spík* fem., 'splinter, thin wornout scythe', and are prob. unconnected with this.]

1. a. A sharp-pointed piece of metal (esp. iron) or wood used for fastening things securely together; a large and strong kind of nail.

Cf. the earlier SPIKE-NAIL and SPIKING *sb.*

1345-6 in Nicholas *Hist. Royal Navy* (1847) II. 477 [Nails, called] glots, midelglots, spikes, rundnails, cloutnails [and] lednails. **1390** *Earl Derby's Exp.* (Camden) 26 Pro $M^{l}cc$ spyks, vj s. **1486** *Naval Acc. Hen. VII* (1896) 15, c lb of spykes..xxv^{s} ij^{d}; also for xl lb spikes. *a* **1616** BACON *Adv. Villiers* Wks. 1778 II. 270 We need not borrow of any other iron for spikes, or nails to fasten them together. **1627** CAPT. SMITH *Seaman's Gram.* xi. 53 It is strongly nailed with Spikes. **1706** PHILLIPS (ed. Kersey), *Speeks* or *Spikes*,..great and long Iron-nails with flat Heads and of divers Lengths. **1719** DE FOE *Crusoe* II. (Globe) 411 In this Manner he made many Things, but especially Hooks, Staples, and Spikes. **1753** HANWAY *Trav.* II. xvi. (1762) I. 69 Instead of iron bolts, they have spikes of deal. **1825** J. NICHOLSON *Operat. Mechanic* 565 Fasten them together by pins, spikes, or bolts, as the case may require. **1884** KNIGHT *Dict. Mech.* Suppl. 839/2 The following table shows the amount of spikes to a mile of railroad.

b. A pointed piece of steel used for driving into the touch-hole of a cannon in order to render it unserviceable.

1617 MORYSON *Itin.* II. 166 Some were found having spikes and hammers to cloy the cannon. **1828** SPEARMAN *Brit. Gunner* (ed. 2) 385 There are two descriptions of spikes in the service. The common conical spike, which serves for all natures of ordnance, is 4 inches long. **1859** GRIFFITHS *Artill. Man.* (1862) 60 For Spiking Ordnance, two kinds of spikes are used:..The Common Spike... The Spring, or temporary spike. **1876** VOYLE & STEVENSON *Milit. Dict.* 395/1 Spikes form a portion of the stores of a battery.

2. a. A sharp-pointed piece of metal (or other hard material) which is, or may be, so fixed in something that the point is turned outwards; a stout sharp-pointed projecting part of a metal object.

c **1470** HENRY *Wallace* x. 42 Sa tha sam folk he send to the dep furd, Gert set the ground with scharp spykis off burd. **1532-3** in E. Law *Hampton Crt. Pal.* (1885) 347 Item 11 spikes of Irne to stand uppon the sayd typys. **1676** WISEMAN *Surg. Treat.* v. iii. 359 In his falling he was catcht by one of those Spikes in the middle of his Wrist. **1728** CHAMBERS *Cycl.* s.v. *Movement*, The gutter'd Wheel, with Iron Spikes at bottom, wherein the Line of ordinary Clocks runs. **1791** BENTHAM *Panopt.* I. Postscr. 137 But a person cannot press against the point of a spike as he could against a bar. **1820** SHELLEY *Let. M. Gisborne* 35 Spain..grew dim with Empire:—With thumbscrews, wheels, with tooth and spike and jag. **1846** HOLTZAPFFEL *Turning* II. 818 The length of files is always measured exclusively of the tang or spike, by which the file is fixed in its handle. **1860** TYNDALL *Glac.* I. xi. 83 The iron spike at the end of the baton made a hole sufficiently deep [etc.].

b. *transf.* A stiff sharp-pointed object or part.

1718 LADY M. W. MONTAGU *Let. to Abbé Conti* 31 July, The spikes or thorns are as long and sharp as bodkins. **1756-7** tr. *Keysler's Trav.* (1760) I. 38 Shoes with long points or spikes..were worn. Some of these spikes were an ell long. **1850** DICKENS *T. Two Cities* II. i, His son was garnished with tenderer spikes [of hair]. **1868** MORRIS *Earthly Par.* II. 261 Then shot up on high A steady spike of light.

c. A young mackerel.

1884 GOODE *Nat. Hist. Aquat. Anim.* 298 Mackerel..six and a half or seven inches in length;..fish of this size are sometimes called 'Spikes'.

d. Usu. in *pl.* One of a number of sharp-pointed metal studs driven into the sole of a cricket boot, running shoe, etc., to give a surer foothold. Also (*pl.*) by metonymy, a pair of spiked shoes.

1832 P. EGAN *Bk. Sports* 348/2 And all in spikes and jackets clad, Elate for vict'ry came. **1898** *N.Y. Tribune* 23 Apr. 9/3 He was in collision with Jennings and McGann and his foot and legs were injured with their spikes. **1955** R. BANNISTER *First Four Minutes* ii. 16, I suddenly noticed that my best pair of spikes had split along the side. **1976** J. WAINWRIGHT *Who goes Next?* 29 'Footprints..Spiked. Now *he* isn't wearing spikes.' Enfield nodded towards the corpse. 'The two Herberts who found him—I doubt if *they'll* have spiked shoes.'

e. *fig.* A prickly resentment; anger, venom. Freq. in phr. *to have* (or *get*) *the spike*, to be (or become) angry or offended.

1890 J. D. ROBERTSON *Gloss. Words County of Gloucester* 147 'To have the *spike*' is to be out of temper, or offended. **1895** *Daily News* 4 Jan. 3/7 Of course Chris gets the spike (in a temper) because Sullivan had shopped him. **1922** JOYCE *Ulysses* 388 He had in his bosom a spike named Bitterness. **1960** N. HILLIARD *Maori Girl* II. xi. 141 But you don't have to get the spike with me just for that. **1978** *Chicago* June 166/3, I had located the spike inside him, the one that Arabs get hooked on when they detect a Jewish émigré.

f. (*a*) A quantity of alcohol, esp. spirits, added to a drink. *U.S. slang.*

1906 *Dialect Notes* III. 157 *Spike*, *n.*, alcohol, an alcoholic beverage. 'This punch has a good big spike in it.' **1969** J. CHEEVER *Bullet Park* xiv. 189 She..returned with a bottle of whiskey and spiked her coffee... The spike steadied her hand. **1974** *Times-Picayune* (New Orleans) 14 Aug. III. 2 It's like chips without dips, or punch without the spike.

(*b*) A small quantity *of* a radioisotope or other substance added to a material in order to act as a tracer, reference, etc.

1959 R. E. TATE in Hausner & Schumar *Nucl. Fuel Elements* viii. 110 Spike enrichment, in which some of the fuel elements..contain plutonium dispersed in an inert matrix, requires a high through-put of the enriched elements. **1962** *Analytical Chem.* XXXIV. 709/2 The U^{233} plus U^{236} isotopic dilution spike is added to an unknown uranium sample. **1965** *Jrnl. Geophysical Res.* LXX. 1844/1 Five to twenty grams of sample was dissolved in 1 *N* HCl, TH^{234} and U^{232} spike added, and the solution evaporated to dryness. **1976** *Nature* 24 June 685/2 After ensuring that the spike and sample were well mixed, the cadmium was chemically extracted by ion exchange.

g. A bayonet. *Mil. slang.*

1928 E. BLUNDEN *Undertones of War* 270 The cowman now turned warrior measured out His up-and-down *sans* fierce 'bundook and spike'.

h. A hypodermic needle or syringe used for the injection of an intoxicating drug; hence, the drug itself or an injection of this. *slang* (orig. *U.S.*).

[**1923** J. MANCHON *Le Slang* 285 *Spike*, *s...* 30 *V[ulgaire]* une aiguille.] **1934** *Detective Fiction Weekly* 21 Apr. 107/2 Both me and the twist was on junk and when they fanned us they found a spike on me but no stuff. **1953** ANSLINGER & TOMPKINS *Traffic in Narcotics* 315 *Spike*, a drug. *Also* a hypodermic needle, an injection of a drug. **1959** 'E. MCBAIN' *Pusher* viii. 383 'You say you shot up together? Did you both use the same syringe?' 'No, Annabelle had his spike, and I had mine.' **1964** *Daily Tel.* 25 Nov. 22/6 Among the terms used by addicts are..'blast parties', for groups of marijuana smokers, and 'spikes' for hypodermic needles. **1974** J. WAINWRIGHT *Evidence I shall Give* xxxvii. 211 It was a mounting yearning. A craving... He needed a spike—badly! **1979** P. DRISCOLL *Pangolin* xvii. 139 This punk kid, shooting amphetamines, can't find enough spikes.

i. (*a*) *Electr.* A pulse of very short duration in which a rapid increase in voltage is followed immediately by a rapid decrease; (*b*) a burst of electromagnetic radiation marked by short duration or great intensity, esp. one from space.

1935 *Arch. Neurol. & Psychiatry* XXXIV. 1140 Sharp negative spikes in the record often seem to be associated with motor movements of a clonic sort. **1957** *Wireless World* Jan. 10/2 Some of the output-signals have the form of sharp spikes, each pulse of ignition interference producing two spikes of the same polarity. **1969** J. J. SPARKES *Transistor Switching* iv. 109 Noise-voltage spikes in the earth line or at the input have to exceed about 600 mV before significant signals appear at the output. **1973** T. PYNCHON *Gravity's Rainbow* I. 146 He's been under Rollo Groast's EEG countless times since first he came to 'The White Visitation', and all's normal-adult except for, oh once or twice perhaps a stray 50-millivolt spike off a temporal lobe.

1969 *Astrophysical Jrnl. Lett.* CLVII. L73 Four out of five consecutive optical spikes, each reaching in some 10 days a peak of luminosity that is a factor of 2–3 above a varying background level,..have been observed for the single QSS 3C 345. **1974** *Nature* 8 Nov. 113/1 Well known transient phenomena such as supernovae, galactic radio noise spikes. **1975** D. G. FINK *Electronics Engineers' Handbk.* XI. 13 The typical output of an optical laser consists of a series of spikes. **1977** *Sci. Amer.* Oct. 53/2 Grindlay and Gursky suggested that the X-ray photons of a burst are released in a two-second 'spike'. **1980** *Nature* 7 Feb. 551/1 There are no clear spikes in the Kavalur bursts.

j. *Journalism.* A spindle on which recent newspaper stories are filed, *spec.* when rejected for publication.

1936 B. BROOKER *Think of Earth* II. iii. 141 The editor picked up a spike-file from the top of the desk. **1942** W. FAULKNER *Go down, Moses* 374 He took the press association flimsy from its spike and handed it to Stevens. **1962** [see *copy-taster* s.v. COPY *sb.* C]. **1974** D. SEAMAN *Bomb that could Lip-Read* vii. 58 The P.A. copy was neatly pierced by a spike, Fleet Street's time-honoured way of giving the thumbs-down to a story.

†**3.** A handspike. *Obs.*[−1]

1771 *Act 11 Geo. III*, c. 45 §7 To purchase or make.. Winches, Spikes, Dams, Flood Gates and Engines for the completing and carrying on the said Navigation. **1802** JAMES *Mil. Dict.*, *Spikes*, in gunnery. See *Hand-Spikes*.

4. *slang.* The workhouse. Also *spec.* the casual ward of a workhouse (see CASUAL *a.* 9); an institution affording more or less temporary accommodation for the homeless.

1866 *Temple Bar* XVII. 184 Let the 'spikes' be what they may they are a great deal better than the 'paddingkens'. **1894** D. C. MURRAY *Making Novelist* 107 To sleep in the workhouse is to go 'on the spike'. **1900** FLYNT *Tramps* 260 The next two nights of our stay..were spent in the Notting Hill casual ward, or 'spike', as it is called in tramp parlance. **1903** J. LONDON *People of Abyss* viii. 78 On asking him what the 'spike' was, he answered, 'The casual ward. It's a cant word.' **1933** 'G. ORWELL' *Down & Out* xxvi. 189 D'you come out o' one o' de London spikes (casual wards), eh? **1949** C. GRAVES *Ireland Revisited* viii. 125 At first we did not understand thieves' slang, or that a 'spike' meant a workhouse. (We were told to avoid the Portsmouth 'spike'.) **1972** *Times* 27 Dec. 2/8 'If this place was not here,' a proud articulate Glaswegian 'dosser' said, 'we'd be on the road or in the reception centre, the spike. I have been in the spike for the past 11 months.' **1980** *Guardian* 2 Oct. 18/1 A generation ago there were half a dozen lodging houses in the town..as well as the 'spike' or casual ward of the workhouse.

5. *attrib.* and *Comb.* **a.** Attrib., in the sense 'resembling or formed like a spike', as *spike bit*, *bowsprit*, *gimlet*, *rod*.

1766 *Museum Rust.* VI. 392 A hole made with a spike gimblet. **1815** *Hist. J. Decastro* I. 109 The man who had a spike bit in his hand, and would have forced the door. **1856** MORTON *Cycl. Agric.* II. 721/2 Rods of hazel, &c., split and twisted for use by the thatcher (spike rods). **1895** *Daily News* 19 June 3/2 With nothing standing but her spike bowsprit, which was painted white.

b. In the sense 'provided or furnished with spikes', as *spike-roller*, *-wheel*.

1799 A. YOUNG *Agric. Linc.* 74 A capital spike-roller, which cost £40. **1805** R. W. DICKSON *Pract. Agric.* I. 27 It is, perhaps, a more efficient implement than the spike-roller. **1875** KNIGHT *Dict. Mech.* 2267/2 Spike-wheel Propeller.

c. Misc., as *spike-hole*; *spike-heeled*, *-helmeted*, *-horned*, *-leaved*, *-like*, *-tailed* adjs.; *spike-wise* adv.

Also *spike-drawer*, *-extractor* (Knight, 1875).

1953 D. DODGE *To catch Thief* i. 11 She was dressed for the evening; a long gown, fragile, *spike-heeled slippers, a fur wrap. **1981** A. LURIE *Language of Clothes* iv. 106 French-speaking Canadians..negotiating the icy snow-heaped streets..in nyloned legs and spike-heeled boots. **1916** R. GRAVES *Goliath & David* 6 And look, *spike-helmeted, grey, grim, Goliath straddles over him. **1691** T. H[ALE] *Acc. New Invent.* 45 They were forced to..spile the *Spike-holes. **1890** W. P. LETT in Shields *Big Game N. Amer.* 84 There is a difference..between the branching and *spike-horned Deer. **1864** G. P. MARSH *Man & Nat.* 109 Dead trees, especially of the *spikeleaved kinds,..are often allowed to stand until they fall of themselves. **1896** *Pop. Sci. Jrnl.* L. 207 It was chipped..with a *spike-like stone implement. **1870** *North Alabamian* (Tuscaloosa, Ala.) 12 Jan. 1/2 'Who's that gentleman, my little man?' was asked of an urchin. 'That one with the *spike-tailed coat?' **1884** *Harper's Mag.* Sept. 514/2 You needn't worry about any spike-tailed coat or clerical tie. **1891** *Cent. Dict.* s.v., *Spike-tailed grouse*, the sharp-tailed..or pin-tailed grouse. **1850** BROWNING *Christmas Eve* ii, I sent my elbow *spike-wise At the shutting door, and entered likewise. **1865** G. MACDONALD *A. Forbes* xxxviii, They were kept upright..by the constant application, 'spikewise', of the paternal elbow.

6. Special Combs.: **spike-buck** *U.S.*, a buck in its first year; **spike-disease**, a disease affecting the leaves of certain plants and trees; **spike-fiddle** *Mus.* = REBAB; **spike-fish** *U.S.*, the sailfish (*Histiophorus americanus*); **spike heel**, a fashionable narrow high heel of a woman's shoe, tapering towards a point (cf. *stiletto heel* s.v. STILETTO *sb.* 5); hence, a spike-heeled shoe; **spike-horn**, (*a*) a deer's horn in the form of a spike; (*b*) a spike-buck (so *spike-horn buck*); **spike-machine** (see quot.); **spike-maul**, a mallet for driving in spikes; **spike microphone**, (*colloq.*) **mike** (see quot. 1962); **spike-nose** *U.S.* (see quot.); † **spike-park** *slang*, the grounds of a prison; **spike-pole** *dial.* (see quot. 1841); also, a pole fitted with a spike; † **spike-ring** (?); † **spike-shot**, cannon-shot having projecting spikes; **spike-tail** *U.S.*, a dress-coat; **spike-team** *U.S.* (see quots.).

1860 MAYNE REID *Hunters' Feast* xxiii, In the first year they grow in the shape of two short straight spikes; hence the name '*spike-bucks' given to the animals of that age. **1897** *Outing* XXX. 330 A tidy spike-buck splashed through a shallow. **1906** *Athenæum* 24 Nov. 661/3 A suitable reward to any one who can discover the cause of *spike disease in sandal trees. 1940 C. Sachs *Hist. Mus. Instruments* (1942) xii. 242 Most Islamic instruments..have no place in art music, with the exception of the Persian **spike fiddle* (called *rabâb* or *kamânga a'gûz* in the Near East)... Malay fiddles, which have preserved the old Persian name in the form *rebab*, are much simpler. 1974 Schacht & Bosworth *Legacy of Islam* (ed. 2) x. 500 Al-Fārābī also provides the first description of a bowed instrument, the *rabāb*. This was later known in two forms, one with a separate neck, the other a spike-fiddle with a hemispherical sound-chest. 1929 D. L. Moore *Pandora's Letter Box* xi. 205 The '*spike' heel now popular is disgustingly difficult to balance on. 1950 'S. Ransome' *Deadly Miss Ashley* xi. 136 A pair of sandals.. featured spike heels decorated with brilliants. 1971 D. C. Brown *Yukon Trophy Trails* ii. 31, I wanted to live in a log cabin, shoot my own steaks and never wear another pair of spike heels. 1869 *Amer. Nat.* Dec. 552 The *spike-horn differs greatly from the common antler of the *Cervus Virginianus*. *Ibid.* 553 The first spike-horn buck was merely an accidental freak of nature. 1897 *Outing* XXIX. 439 So the gamey spikehorn turned to bay. 1851 *Catal. Gt. Exhib.* I. 1468 2 A *spike machine. This machine is for the purpose of making wrought spikes. 1886 *Pall Mall G.* 16 June 14/1 Two squads, the one armed with claw bars, the other with *spike mauls. 1962 *Symposia of Zool. Soc.* VII. 8 There is also the '*spike' microphone, which is extremely small, and can be driven through hard material to record sounds in an inner chamber. 1966 *Economist* 3 Dec. 1029/2 Though there is no federal law against bugging or wire-tapping *per se*, the Supreme Court held that the spike microphone driven through the wall of Mr Black's hotel room constituted physical trespass. 1950 *Washington Post* 20 Mar. D1/4 Police had slipped the '*spike mike' into a wall common to the adjoining premises. 1973 'D. Halliday' *Dolly & Starry Bird* xvi. 248 *No one* in sneakers with spike mikes and tapes and transmitters? 1891 *Cent. Dict.*, **Spike-nose*, the pike-perch, or wall-eyed pike, *Stizostedion vitreum*. 1837 Dickens *Pickw.* xlii, No danger of overwalking yourself here—*spike park—grounds pretty—romantic but not extensive. 1841 Hartshorne *Salop. Ant.* Gloss., **Spike-pole*, a rafter eight feet long, bound with iron at its end,.. used in 'tying' dangerous places in the roof of a pit. 1848 Thoreau *Maine W.* (1894) 57 He uses..a long spike-pole, with a screw at the end of the spike to make it hold. 1597 *Wills & Inv. N.C.* (Surtees, 1860) 267 One *spike-ringe, j paire of goulde weights, and an oulde halbarte. *a* 1661 Fuller *Worthies, Kent* II. (1662) 61 They have Round-double- head- Bur- *spike- Crow- Bar- Case- Chain shot. 1894 Howells *Trav. fr. Altruria* 139 He says he isn't dressed for dinner; left his *spike-tail in the city. 1848 Bartlett *Dict. Amer.* 324 **Spike team*, a waggon drawn by three horses, or by two oxen and a horse, the latter leading the oxen or span of horses. 1890 L. C. D'Oyle *Notches* 178, I got there with a loaded waggon, and a 'spike' team—three mules.

†**spike**, *sb.*[3] *Obs.* = spike-hole.

1586 J. Hooker *Hist. Irel.* in *Holinshed* II. 93/2 He perceived one of the enemies leveling at the window or spike at which he stood. 1633 T. Stafford *Pac. Hib.* I. ix. 64 Where from out of a Spike, they slewe foure of our men. *Ibid.* III. viii. 317 A spike or window that..commands that part of the barbicon of the Castle.

spike, *sb.*[4] *slang.* [Back-formation f. spiky *a.*[2] 4: a use of spike *sb.*[2]] An Anglican who advocates or practises Anglo-Catholic ritual and observances.

1902 *Church Times* 14 Mar. 320/2 A priest is wanted for this parish. A hard-working Catholic. Not a 'spike'. 1914 J. W. Legg *Eng. Church Life* 159 It would seem that there were spikes (as Dr. Bright of Christ-church used to call them) in 1768. 1922 E. Raymond *Tell England* II. iii. 204 My altar has generally been two ration boxes, marked 'Unsweetened Milk', but the spike has surrounded it. And look here.., the spike knows how to die. He just asks for his absolution and his last sacrament, and—and dies. 1930 Sayers & 'Eustace' *Docs. in Case* i. 37 He turned out to be an earnest and cultivated middle-aged spike from Keble. 1952 R. Macaulay *Let.* 23 May (1961) 318 Is she one who would be shocked at seeing communicants at High Mass? There have always been those there, I gather; and 'spikes' don't like it. 1963 C. Mackenzie *My Life & Times* II. 203 In that summer of 1897 Sandys Wason was still a deacon... It was he who started using 'spike' for an extremist... One can still be spiked up; one can still talk of spikiness, and in Anglican circles be understood. 1980 A. N. Wilson *Healing Art* iv. 47 There were several other effigies of famous spikes, including the legendary Father Tooth.

Hence as *v.*[2] *trans.* with *up*: to make (more) 'spiky' or High Church; to enliven with ritual; also '**spikery**, 'spiky' character or behaviour.

1923 C. Mackenzie *Parson's Progress* xvi. 214 Was it really worth while trying to spike up the Rector and his services and his flock? 1958 B. Pym *Glass of Blessings* iii. 48 A new vicar trying to spike things up a bit. 1965 C. E. Pocknee *Parson's Handbk.* (ed. 13) vii. 85 There is no ancient authority for the custom of sitting for the psalms. This is a slovenly piece of modern 'spikery'. 1972 C. Stephenson *Merrily on High* ii. 35, I was encouraged by the high church ladies who would listen with amusement and interest to my plans for 'spiking' up the church. 1980 A. N. Wilson *Healing Art* ix. 110 For all her spikery, there would always be a part of herself which found it impossible to shake off the freedoms of scepticism.

spike (spaɪk), *v.*[1] [f. spike *sb.*[2] Cf. MSw. and Sw. *spika* to nail; also LG. *spikern*, Du. *spijkeren*.]

1. *trans.* With *up*: **a.** To fasten or close firmly with spikes or strong nails.

1624 Capt. Smith *Virginia* v. 198 He went to seeke for a wracke they reported lay vnder water with her hatches spiked vp.

†**b.** *spec.* = sense 2. *Obs.*

1644 Prynne & Walker *Fiennes' Trial* App. 34 Whereupon himselfe, and one Harris,..did spike up the touch-holes of their Canons to make them unservisable to the enemy. 1672 J. Lacey tr. *Tacquet's Milit. Archit.* 50 If they cannot carry away their Guns, they must spike them up, by driving Nails in their Touch-holes. 1747 *Gentl. Mag.* XVII. 308 We spiked up 15 field pieces, which we could not get off. 1799 *Hull Advertiser* 7 Sept. 1/4 Helder Point was last night evacuated and the guns in it spiked up.

†**c.** *spec.* (See quot.) *Obs.*[−0]

1704 J. Harris *Lex. Techn.* I, *Spiking up the Ordnance*, is fastning a Coin or Quoin with Spikes to the Deck, close to the Breech of the Carriages of the Great Guns, that they may keep close and firm to the Ship-sides and not break loose when the Ship Rolls.

d. To set up as on a spike.

1742 Young *Nt. Th.* IV. 771 They..Spike up their inch of reason, on the point Of philosophic wit, call'd argument.

2. To render (a gun) unserviceable by driving a spike into the touch-hole; also, to block or fill up (the touch-hole) with a spike. (Cf. 1 b.) Also *fig.*, esp. in phr. ***to spike* (*some*)*one's guns***.

1687 *Lond. Gaz.* No. 2270/5 Captain Archburnett..made himself Master of their Guns, which he ordered to be dismounted and spiked. 1700 Rycaut *Hist. Turks* v. iii. 150 In one of which [sallies] they spiked or nailed three Pieces of Cannon. 1706 Phillips (ed. Kersey) s.v., Among Mariners, the Touch-hole of a Gun is said *To be spiked*, when Nails are purposely driven into it, so that no Use can be made of that Gun by an Enemy. 1778 Orme *Milit. Trans. Ind.* II. I. 62 Ensign Pischard..seized and spike the four pieces of cannon. 1811 Wellington in Gurw. *Desp.* (1837) VII. 269 Unfortunately the guns in the battery were not spiked, or otherwise destroyed or injured. 1848 *Exchequer Rep.* II. 174 The defendant.. spiked the guns, and placed sentinels at the doors.

fig. 1823 T. Creevey *Let.* 11 Mar. in *Creevey Papers* (1903) II. iii. 66 He has himself entirely spiked his guns in the House of Commons. 1862 E. Hall *Jrnl.* 9 Mar. in O. A. Sherrard *Two Victorian Girls* (1966) II. 291 He proceeded to kiss her forehead... She should have spiked the first gun instead of leaving it to clear the way for the advance of others. 1871 Lowell *Study Wind.* (1886) 37 All the batteries of noise are spiked. 1927 *New Republic* 21 Sept. 122/2 They have flitted from one foolish suggestion to the other. The silliest of these was that, to spike the third-term objection, Mr. Coolidge would agree, if elected in 1928, to resign at the expiration of his eighth year of continued occupancy. 1953 L. P. Hartley *Go-Between* 16 My enemies would be off their guard, they would never suspect danger from a gun they had so thoroughly spiked. 1971 S. E. Morison *European Discovery Amer.: Northern Voy.* xiv. 469 It remained for Samuel de Champlain to spike the legend of a City of Norumbega, storied like a New Jerusalem.

3. To fix or secure by means of long nails or spikes. Chiefly with preps., as *on*, *to*.

1703 Moxon *Mech. Exerc.* 255 Pin'd or spiked down to the pieces of Oak on which they lye. *Ibid.*, [To] spike or pin the Planks to them. 1776 G. Semple *Building in Water* 102 Scantling of the same Size..will answer effectually, by pinning and spiking the Grooves on the corner Pile. 1823 P. Nicholson *Pract. Build.* 120 By spiking or bolting each piece [of timber] on both sides of the joint. 1833 Loudon *Encycl. Archit.* §83 Ceiling joists, joggled on,..and spiked.. at each end, to the top of the plate. 1875 Martin *Winding Mach.* 6 Four vertical 3-in. planks are spiked into the joints of the lining of the pit.

4. a. To make sharp like a spike. *rare*[−0].

1687 Miége *Gt. Fr. Dict.* II, To Spike, *faire pointu*; *enclouër*. 1736 Ainsworth I, To spike, or make sharp at the end, *spico, spiculo*.

b. To provide, fit, or stud with spikes.

1716 M. Davies *Athen. Brit.* II. 139 Too much also of our English Prose is spik'd over with keen Cynicks. 1777 Sir A. Campbell in C. H. Walcott *Life* (1898) 32, I am lodged in a dungeon..doubly planked and spiked on every side. 1847 Tennyson *Princ.* iv. 188 His brows Had sprouted, and the branches..grimly spiked the gates. 1850 'Bat' *Cricket Man.* 50 It is a good plan to have those shoes spiked which have been worn.

5. a. To pierce with, or as with, a spike. Also *refl.*

1687 Miége *Gt. Fr. Dict.* II, To spike himself, or fall upon spikes, *tomber sur des pointes de fer*. 1837 Barham *Ingol. Leg.* Ser. I. *Spectre Tappington*, Charles drank his coffee and spiked some half-dozen eggs. 1884 Browning *Ferishtah* 122 When cold from over-mounts spikes through and through Blood, bone and marrow.

b. *spec.* In certain sports, to injure (another player or competitor) by means of spiked shoes.

1867 *Athlete for 1866*, 13 Lord Jersey, a good third, notwithstanding having been accidentally spiked by one of the competitors. 1886 Shaw *Cash. Byron's Prof.* (1901) 197 'What does spiking mean?' said Lydia. 'Treading on a man's foot with spiked boots,' replied Lord Worthington.

c. To lace (a drink) with alcohol; to fortify (beer, etc.) by the addition of spirits. Also *transf. slang* (orig. *U.S.*).

1889 L. Pendleton *In Wiregrass* xviii. 201 Water from biled hops an' poke root, an' 's sweetened wi' 'lasses and spiked wi' good strong whiskey. 1900 *Dialect Notes* II. 63 *Spike*, to fortify a drink by adding wine or spirits. 1915 *Ibid.* IV. 229 *Spike*, to flavor with wine or whiskey, as 'She spikes her cakes.' 1941 J. Smiley *Hash House Lingo* 52 *Spike*, (bar) add liquor to a drink. 1952 B. Malamud *Natural* 24 A crushed cocoanut [*sic*] drink which he privately spiked with a shot from a new bottle. 1962 *Sunday Times* (Colour Suppl.) 14 Oct. 24/1 Spike a *béchamel* sauce with Parmesan cheese. 1980 G. Thompson *Murder Mystery* (1981) xxii. 175 She made tea, which he spiked with bourbon.

d. Of a newspaper editor: to reject (a story or part of one) as by filing it on a spike (spike *sb.*[2] 2 j).

1908 A. S. M. Hutchinson *Once aboard Lugger* v. vii. 263 Tiny little scrap of news..copied out a dozen times by Mr. Issy Jago and left..at the offices of as many newspapers. Seven sub-editors 'spiked' it, [etc.]. 1940 W. P. Crozier *Jrnl.* 9 Dec. in D. Ayerst *Guardian* (1971) xxxiv. 539 E.A.M. disgruntled because I spiked pars (for London letter) on last night's bombing. 1950 C. M. Kornbluth in *Astounding Science Fiction* July 150/2 The M[anaging] E[ditor].. decided nobody would believe it. He spiked the story on the 'dead' hook. 1961 B. Wells *Day Earth caught Fire* vii. 115 This is the newsroom, the place where all the best stories are spiked. 1978 L. Heren *Growing up on The Times* viii. 283, I discovered that my story had been spiked. It was the first and only time the paper had questioned my judgment, and I felt badly about it.

e. *intr.* To inject another or (for *refl.*) oneself with an intoxicating drug. Also *trans.* and *fig.*

1935 N. Ersine *Underworld & Prison Slang* 69 *Spike*, to take a shot of dope. 'He spiked about an hour ago.' 1971 J. Mandelkau *Buttons* v. 68 Almost immediately I was spiked with wine and acid. 1973 T. Pynchon *Gravity's Rainbow* I. 47 Kevin Spectro will take his syringe and spike away a dozen times tonight..to sedate Fox (his generic term for any patient). 1974 *Guardian* 28 Jan. 11/5 The addicts..'ll sometime try and spike you, try and get you mainlining too. 1977 'J. le Carré' *Honourable Schoolboy* ii. 46 The girl.. alone and spiked with tiredness.

f. To enrich (a nuclear reactor or its fuel) *with* a particular isotope; to add a small proportion of some distinctive material to.

1956 *Ann. Rev. Nucl. Sci.* VI. 330 A natural uranium power reactor of this size might not become critical, so that the reactor will be 'spiked' with a few enriched elements. 1959 F. G. Foote in Hausner & Schumar *Nucl. Fuel Elements* v. 78 The uranium can be spiked with either plutonium or U^{233}. 1971 *New Scientist* 13 May 386/2 Early work in Britain on spiking enriched uranium with plutonium as a possible fuel for Advanced Gas-cooled Reactors. 1974 *Nature* 1 Feb. 310/2 The homogenised mixture was spiked with a known volume of a solution containing 1 $\mu g\ ml^{-1}$ of the N-nitroso compound. 1976 *Lancet* 4 Dec. 1223/1 Concentrations were measured against cadmium standards..prepared from blood spiked with cadmium chloride standard solution. 1977 *Rolling Stone* 13 Jan. 31/2 Silkwood had slipped a vial of plutonium into her vagina or rectum, then used a syringe to spike her samples at home.

6. To drive *away* with or as with spikes.

1879 Geo. Eliot *Theo. Such* xviii. 346 To urge on that account that we should spike away the peaceful foreigner.

7. *intr.* To rise in a spike; to protrude angularly.

1958 *Listener* 18 Sept. 418/2 High mounds of rubble and tangled, bombed machinery which spiked into the air like the legs of dead animals. 1975 N. Nicholson *Wednesday Early Closing* i. 21 St. George's steeple spikes up against the sky, graceful as a larch tree and bold as Blackpool Tower.

spike (spaɪk), *v.*[2] [f. spike *sb.*[1] 2.] *intr.* Of plants: To form a spike or spikes of flowers. Also with *up*.

1711 *Phil. Trans.* XXVII. 377 The last and the preceding Summer it spiked very plentifully in Chelsea Garden. 1852 *Beck's Florist* 234 If a Hollyhock do not 'spike up' well..it cannot be called 'first rate'.

spike-bozzle (spaɪk'bɒz(ə)l), *v. slang* (orig. *Mil.*). Now *rare*. Also **spike-boozle**. [f. spike *v.*[1] 2: the second element is obscure (but see quot. 1962).] To render (an enemy plane, etc.) unserviceable; to destroy; to upset. Also *transf.*

1915 H. Rosher *In R. Naval Air Service* (1916) 123 Last night 'old man Zepp' came over here... Two machines went up to spike-bozzle him, but..never even saw him. 1923 *Blackw. Mag.* July 5/1 Piffers used to wear them..until the clothing department spike-bozzled them. 1942 Berrey & Van den Bark *Amer. Thes. Slang* §759/10 Spike bozzle, to chase an enemy plane. 1962 W. Granville *Dict. Sailors' Slang* 110/2 *Spike bozzle*, render ineffective; sabotage, blow up or otherwise destroy a ship or upset a plan. A merging of *spike*, a gun and bam-*boozle*, cheat, mystify, bemuse.

spiked (spaɪkt), *a.*[1] [f. spike *sb.*[1]]

1. Of plants: Having an inflorescence in the form of a spike; bearing ears, as grain.

1601 Holland *Pliny* II. 559 Wheat and such like spiked corne withstand the winter cold better than Pulse. 1640 Parkinson *Theat. Bot.* 1169 This greatest sort groweth up with..stalkes two foot high, on which stand long round spiked heads. 1712 *Phil. Trans.* XXVII. 416 Neither grows it upright and spiked, but procumbent and racemose. 1777 Potter *Æschylus, Supplicants* 114 Dogs..yield to the mast'ring wolves; And the soft reed to the firm spiked corn. 1830 Lindley *Nat. Syst. Bot.* 172 Herbaceous dicotyledons, with..opposite leaves, spiked flowers. 1870 Hooker *Stud. Flora* 315 Clusters of flowers spiked.

2. In specific names, as ***spiked brome-grass, clover, liatris, loosestrife, mint***, etc.

1597 Gerarde *Herbal* I. xcii. 339 The spiked Rose Plantaine hath very few leaues. 1731 Miller *Gard. Dict.* s.v. *Mentha*, Common Spik'd-Mint, usually call'd Spear-Mint. *Ibid.* s.v. *Veronica*, Narrow-leav'd spik'd Speedwell. *Ibid.*, Welsh spiked Speedwell. 1771 *Encycl. Brit.* I. 681 The pinnatus or spiked brome-grass. 1796 Withering *Brit. Plants* (ed. 3) II. 350 *Spiked Rush*. Near the summits of the Highland mountains. 1822 *Hortus Anglicus* II. 351 Spiked Liatris;..spike leafy, dense above. 1828 J. E. Smith *Engl. Flora* II. 343 Spiked Purple-Loosestrife... Flowers in whorled leafy spikes. 1851 Wilson *Rur. Cycl.* IV. 15/2 The spiked rampion, *Phyteuma spicatum*, has sometimes been used as an article of food. 1855 Miss Pratt *Flower. Pl.* III. 345 Spiked Rampion... This rare species has been found only in Sussex. 1888 *Boston* (Mass.) *Jrnl.* 6 Dec. 2/3 A native forage plant, called 'spiked clover', is attracting attention in California. The plant puts out white blossoms on slender spikes.

Hence †**spikedness**, 'likeness to an ear of corn' (Bailey, vol. II, 1727). *Obs.*[−0]

spiked (spaɪkt), *a.*[2] [f. spike *sb.*[2]]

1. Provided with spikes or sharp points.

1681 Grew *Musæum* I. vi. i. 125 The Spiked-Wilk. Murex Aculeatus. *a* 1727 Newton *Chronol. Amended* (1728) 319

An archer..crowned with a spiked crown. **1763** *Brit. Mag.* IV. 206 Shot, of all sizes, from 28 pounders to four ounces. .. Grape ditto... Spiked [ditto]. **1830** SKELTON *Meyrick's Arms & Armour* II. Pl. 80 The long spiked-rowel spur of Edward IV's time, of iron. **1850** 'BAT' *Cricket Man.* 104 Spiked Soles for Cricket Shoes. **1884** W. S. B. MCLAREN *Spinning* (ed. 2) 182 The three spiked workers..revolve above it in the opposite direction.

transf. **1876** GEO. ELIOT *Dan. Deronda* III. xlii. 242 The yoke of oppression was a spiked torture. **1897** *Allbutt's Syst. Med.* II. 157 [The temperature] is of a strikingly 'spiked' character when charted.

2. ***spiked buck***, a spike-buck. *U.S.*

1897 *Outing* XXIX. 439/1 A strong, young, spiked buck.

3. a. Laced or fortified with alcohol. Also *transf.* and *fig.*

In some examples parsable as pa. pple. of the verb.

1909 *Dialect Notes* III. 374 *Spike, v.tr.* 1. To mix an alcoholic with a non-alcoholic beverage. Chiefly in the *pp.* 'This lemonade is heavily spiked.' **1929** *Detective Fiction Weekly* 23 Mar. 161/2 'I can ditch a drink that I suspect of being spiked.' This word 'spiked' was that year [*sc. c* 1899] the very newest slang, signifying 'doped'. **1942** E. PAUL *Narrow St.* i. 2 Some of the early risers huddled round the counter to swallow their coffee, often spiked with cheap, watered rum or cognac. **1960** J. MCNAMEE *Florencia Bay* 52 Then the promoter who, on the strength of spiked assays, had floated a company. **1974** P. CAVE *Mama* (new ed.) xi. 95 The babble of conversation was liberally spiked with laughter, merriment and enthusiasm.

b. *transf.* Containing a small addition of a radioactive or otherwise distinctive material; enriched.

1959 F. G. FOOTE in Hausner & Schumar *Nucl. Fuel Elem.* v. 78 The best use of plutonium-spiked uranium fuels would be in fast neutron reactors. **1962** *Analytical Chem.* XXXIV. 709/2 Separate spiked and unspiked analyses must be made of the unknown uranium sample. **1975** *Sci. Amer.* Oct. 27/2 The idea is to add about half a gram of plutonium 239 to each kilogram of uranium. Since a kilogram of natural uranium contains 7·2 grams of U-235, the 'spiked' fuel would contain a total of 7·7 grams of fissionable material.

†**spike-hole.** *Obs.* [perh. f. SPIKE *sb.*^{2}, but the simple word in this sense (SPIKE *sb.*^{3}) occurs earlier than the compound.] A loop-hole or small opening in a wall.

1598 FLORIO, *Balestriera*, a spike hole or loope hole, to shoote out at. **1629** J. M. tr. *Fonseca's Dev. Contempl.* 90 Of all those Kingdomes..he hath not so much as one poore spike-hole in a wall. **1642** in *Lismore Papers* Ser. II. (1888) V. 47[They] played theire spicke holes and the tope of the Castle with small shott. **1690** *Lond. Gaz.* No. 2560/2 These ..beat the Enemy out of a Ravelin..and fired upon them through their own Spikeholes. **1742** JARVIS *Quix.* Pref. (1749) p. xviii, The dungeon is one of those strong stone towers..with small spike-holes high in the walls.

spikelet^1 ('spaɪklɪt). *Bot.* [f. SPIKE *sb.*^{1}]

1. A small group of florets in grasses, forming part of the spike.

1793 MARTYN *Lang. Bot.*, *Spicula*, a Spicule or Spikelet; a partial spike, or a subdivision of it: as in some Grasses. **1835** LINDLEY *Introd. Bot.* (ed. 2) 125 A locusta or spikelet, as the partial inflorescence of Grasses is denominated. **1850** TYAS *Fav. Field Fl.* Ser. II. 37 The common Quaking Grass, with its broadly egg-shaped spikelets, is indeed one of the most beautiful of the grasses. **1872** OLIVER *Elem. Bot.* I. v. 52 The flowers are arranged in short, broad spikelets, which spikelets are disposed alternately in two rows along the top of the stem.

2. A subdivision of an ear of grain.

1860 PIESSE *Lab. Chem. Wonders* 145 An individuality as definite as an ear of corn or a spikelet of barley. **1868** DARWIN *Anim. & Pl.* I. ix. 318 The ear is thus much narrower, and the spikelets stand out more horizontally, than in our present forms. **1893** *Jrnl. R. Agric. Soc.* Dec. 696 The spikelets of the ear are borne in groups of three.

spikelet^2 ('spaɪklɪt). [f. SPIKE *sb.*^{2}] A small spike or spike-shaped object; a prickle or thorn.

1851 MAYNE REID *Scalp Hunt.* xxvii. 203 We carefully pare off the volutes and spikelets [of the cacti]. **1876** tr. *Wagner's Gen. Pathol.* 121 The surface of the body is covered with little spikelets.

spike-nail. [SPIKE *sb.*^{2} Cf. MDu. and LG. *spikernagel*, MHG. *spîchernagel* (G. dial. *speichernagel*).] A large and strong nail, now *spec.* one upwards of three (or four) inches in length, with a small head.

1314-5 *MS. Acc. Exch. K.R.* Bdle. 492 No. 19 (P.R.O.), Item in C spiknail emptis, v d. **1562** *Ludlow Churchw. Acc.* (Camden) 109 For spyke nayles to make the pewe. *c* **1608** in Swayne *Sarum Churchw. Acc.* (1896) 160, viij long spike nayles for the Refters, 12 d. **1769** FALCONER *Dict. Marine* s.v. *Kelson*, It [the kelson] is secured by spike-nails [to the floor-timbers and crotches]. **1782** *Phil. Trans.* LXXII. 367 The spike-nail which had fastened the lead to it appeared perfectly sound. **1807** W. IRVING *Salmag.* (1824) 198 He put a good store of beads, spike-nails and looking-glasses in his trunk. **1866** *Harvard Mem. Biogr.*, *F. C. Hopkinson* II. 21 The method..was..to strike them alternately with a large Spike-nail.

spikenard ('spaɪknɑːd). Forms: α. 4- **spikenard** (4 **speke-**, **spyknard**), 5-6 **spikenarde**, **spyk(e)narde** (5 **spykenard**), 6 **spignard**, **spiknarde**, 7 **spick-**, 7-8 **spiknard**. β. 4 **spikanard**. γ. 6 **spekenardy**, 7 **spyke nardy**. [ad. late or med.L. *spīca nardī* (see SPIKE *sb.*^{1} and NARD *sb.*), rendering Gr. νάρδου στάχυς (also ναρδόσταχυς); perhaps partly after OF. *spicanarde* fem., *spica-*, *spice-*, *spiquenard* masc., = It. *spiganardi*, *-nardo*, Sp. *espicanardi*, *-nardo*. Cf. also MDu. *spikenaerde*, *-naert* (Du. *spijknardus*), MLG. *spikenardi* *-nard(us)*, MHG. *spîcanarde* (G. *spikenarde*, with many older variants), MSw. *spikinardus*, etc.]

1. An aromatic substance (employed in ancient times in the preparation of a costly ointment or oil) obtained from an Eastern plant, now identified as the *Nardostachys Jatamansi* of Northern India.

α. *c* **1350** *Leben Jesu* (1873) 63 Þat oygnement was of spikenard þat mani may do bote. **1382** WYCLIF *John* xii. 3 Therfore Marie took a pound of oynement spikenard [*v.r.* speke-nard], or trewe narde. *c* **1400** MAUNDEV. (Roxb.) vii. 26 Sum distilles gariofles, spikenarde, and oþer spiceries. **1465** *Mann. & Househ. Exp.* (Roxb.) 305 Item, for a unce of spykenarde, viij. d. **1545** RAYNALD *Byrth Mankynde* 84 Take of cupresse nuttes, spikenard, balaustium, acorne cuppes, of eche an ounce. **1599** B. JONSON *Cynthia's Rev.* v. iv, The decoction of turmericke, sesama, nard, spikenard. **1671** SALMON *Syn. Med.* III. xxii. 401 Indian-leaf; its virtues are the same with Mace and Spicknard. **1712** tr. *Pomet's Hist. Drugs* I. 50 Chuse the true Spiknard from the Levant. **1841** ELPHINSTONE *Hist. India* I. 11 A highly scented grass, the essential oil of which is supposed by some to have been the spikenard of the ancients. **1850** TENNYSON *In Mem.* xxxii. 12 She bathes the Saviour's feet With costly spikenard and with tears. **1872** OLIVER *Elem. Bot.* II. 192 Spikenard is the root of *Nardostachys jatamansi*, a North Indian plant. It has been highly valued as a perfume from early antiquity.

β. **1382** WYCLIF *Mark* xiv. 3 A womman..hauynge a box of precious oynement spikanard.

γ. **1545** RAYNALD *Byrth Mankynde* 83 Dyp wool in yͤ oyle of masticke or of spekenardy [**1613** spyke Nardy], and laye it vnto the place.

2. The plant yielding this substance; now *spec.* the North Indian *Nardostachys Jatamansi*, a plant of the Valerian order.

1548 TURNER *Names Herbes* (E.D.S.) 55 Nardus is named in greeke Nardos, in englishe Spyknarde. **1671** PHILLIPS, Spikenard, (*Nardus Indica*,) an Odoriferous Plant, the Oil whereof is much used in Medicine. **1714** *Steele's Poet. Misc.*, *Solomon's Song* 242 Spikenard and Cinnamon, that loves the Vale. **1830** LINDLEY *Nat. Syst. Bot.* 197 Valerian Jatamansi, or true Spikenard of the ancients, is valued in India..as a remedy in hysteria and epilepsy. **1858** SIMMONDS *Dict. Trade*, *Spikenard*, the *Nardostachys Jatamansi*, a dwarf herbaceous plant,..a native of the Himalayas. **1897** G. O. MORGAN *Ecl. Virgil* iv. 15 Ivy that every-where roves with the spikenard's growth interwoven.

fig. **1692** W. MARSHALL *Gosp. Myst. Sanct.* xiii. 298 Thus your Spikenards will yield their Smell, as godly sorrow.. peace,..joy.

3. †**a.** Lavender. *Obs.* (Cf. SPIKE *sb.*^{1} 4.)

1563 HYLL *Art Garden.* (1593) 94 Lauender is an hearbe sweet in smelling;..[and] for that it giueth no lesse sauor than the Spike, is of the same named Spikenard. **1579** LANGHAM *Gard. Health* (1633) 622 Spikenard (see Lauender). **1736** N. BAILEY *Household Dict.* s.v., Spikenard or Lavender Spike.

b. Valerian. *rare.* (Cf. SPIKE *sb.*^{1} 5.)

1688 HOLME *Armoury* II. 89 Spicknard, or Valerian, hath leaves like the Primrose, growing in bunches, out of which comes a stalk set with jagged leaves. **1864** J. GILBERT & G. C. CHURCHILL *Dolomite Mountains* 325 The Speik (*Valeriana celtica*) is a very small plant... You will be familiar with it as *spikenard*.

c. *Amer.* (See quots.)

1845-50 MRS. LINCOLN *Lect. Bot.* App. 75/2 *Aralia.. racemosa* (spikenard). **1864** GRISEBACH *Flora Brit. W. Ind.* 787/2 Spikenard, *Hyptis suaveolens*.

4. ***ploughman's spikenard***, the wild plant *Inula Conyza* (formerly assigned to the genera *Baccharis* and *Conyza*).

1597 GERARDE *Herbal* II. cclxv. 648 This plant *Baccharis* ..in English..may be called the Cinamom roote, or Plowmans Spiknarde. **1671** PHILLIPS, *Plowmans Spiknard*, a sort of plant called in Latin *Baccharis*. **1753** *Chambers' Cycl.* Suppl., *Baccharis*,..commonly called *plowman's spikenard*, a sweet scented shrubby plant. *Ibid.* s.v. *Flea Bane*, The common great *conyza*, called Plowman's spikenard. **1777** JACOB *Catal. Plants* 11 *Conyza squarrosa*, Plowman's Spikenard. **1821** CLARE *Vill. Minstr.* I. 115 Thy horehound tufts I love them well, And ploughman's spikenard's spicy smell. **1901** *Pall Mall Mag.* Sept. 105/1 Fragrant ploughman's spikenard now rises.

5. With various specific adjectives, as ***American***, ***bastard***, ***Celtic***, ***Cretan***, ***false***, ***French***, ***Indian***, ***mountain***, ***small***, ***Syrian***, ***West Indian***, ***wild spikenard*** (see quots.).

1866 *Treas. Bot.* 1083/2 *American Spikenard, *Aralia racemosa*. **1760** J. LEE *Introd. Bot.* App. 327 *Bastard French Spikenard, *Nardus*. **1693** tr. *Blancard's Phys. Dict.* (ed. 2), *Spica celtica*, or *Nardus celtica*, *celtic Spikenard. **1718** QUINCY *Compl. Disp.* 169 Celtick Spikenard.—This is reckon'd of kin to our Lavender, both by Family..and Virtues. **1760** J. LEE *Introd. Bot.* App. 328 Celtic Spikenard, *Valeriana*. **1891** *Cent. Dict.* s.v., *Cretan spikenard, *Valeriana Phu*. **1760** J. LEE *Introd. Bot.* 328 *False Spikenard, *Lavandula*. **1856** A. GRAY *Man. Bot.* (1860) 467 *Smilacina racemosa*. False Spikenard. **1857** —— *First Less. Bot.* (1866) 81 A compound raceme, as in the Goat's-beard and the False Spikenard. **1597** GERARDE *Herbal* II. ccccxxv. 921 *Nardus Narbonensis*, *French Spikenard. *Ibid.*, *Nardus Indica*, *Indian Spikenard. **1693** tr. *Blancard's Phys. Dict.* (ed. 2), *Nardus indica*, *Spica Indica*, Indian Spikenard, great quantities of it grow in Java. **1760** J. LEE *Introd. Bot.* App. 327 Indian or True Spikenard. **1597** GERARDE *Herbal* II. ccccxxv. 919 *Nardus Celtica*, *Mountaine Spikenard. *Ibid.*, Creeping mountaine Spikenard. **1831** DAVIES *Mat. Med.* 206 *Small Spikenard. False Sarsaparilla Root. *Aralia nudicaulis*. **1611** COTGR., *Nard Syriaque*, *Syrian Spikenard, Indian Spikenard. **1866** *Treas. Bot.* 1083/2 *West Indian Spikenard, *Hyptis suaveolens*. **1611** COTGR., *Nard rustique*, *Wild Spikenard, Valerian. **1647** HEXHAM I. (Herbs), Assarabacke or wilde Spiknard, *Hasel-wortel*. **1760** J. LEE *Introd. Bot.* App. 328 Wild Spikenard, *Asarum*. **1866** *Treas. Bot.* 1083/2 Wild Spikenard, *Aralia nudicaulis*.

6. ***oil of spikenard*** (see quots.).

1565 COOPER *Thesaurus*, *Vnguentum nardinum*, oyle of spikenarde. **1648** HEXHAM II, *Spijck-olie*, Oyle of Spike, or of Spike-nard. **1725** *Fam. Dict.* s.v., The Oil of Spikenard is a Sovereign Remedy for Sheep..incommoded with Obstructions. **1847** ROYLE *Mat. Med.* 621 A Volatile Oil [is secreted] by *Andropogon Calamus aromaticus*,..and several other species [of grasses]. This oil, often called *Oil of Spikenard*, is extremely grateful for its fragrance [etc.]. **1861** BENTLEY *Man. Bot.* 699 The oil known in India as Roshé or Rosé Oil, and in London as Turkish Essence of Geranium, ..is also sometimes termed *oil of spikenard*.

7. *attrib.*, as ***spikenard garden***, ***oil***.

1806 T. MAURICE *Fall Mogul* II. iv, Mild, as soft whispers of the vernal breeze That sweeps the spikenard gardens of the South. **1861** BENTLEY *Man. Bot.* 699 The precious Spikenard Oil of Scripture is supposed by some to have been derived from *A*[*ndropogon*] *Iwarancusa*.

†**spiker**^{1}. *Obs.* Also 6 **spyker**. [a. MDu. or MLG. *spīker*: see SPIKE *sb.*^{2}] A spike-nail.

1574 in Feuillerat *Revels Q. Eliz.* (1908) 237 Small spykers .j. dozen. **1576** *Ibid.* 263 Dimid. C of spykers, xvjᵈ. **1658** tr. *Porta's Nat. Magic* VII. i. 191 They have ships made fast.. by great spikers of wood.

spiker^2 ('spaɪkə(r)). [f. SPIKE *v.*^{1}]

1. A device for spiking a cannon.

1868 *Rep. to Govt. U.S. Munitions War* 112 Figures 2 and 3 represent a spiker for guns of large calibre.

2. One who spikes a gun; one who drives or hammers in a spike.

1884 'H. COLLINGWOOD' (W. J. C. Lancaster) *Under Meteor Flag* 290, I immediately withdrew the spikers, and.. we silently made the best of our way to the beach. **1887** *Sci. Amer.* 18 Jan. 389 There are 32 'spikers' to every five miles of track, each man of whom drives 840 spikes a day.

†'**spiket.** *Obs.* [f. SPIKE *sb.*^{1}] = SPIKELET^1.

1796 WITHERING *Brit. Plants* (ed. 3) I. 83 *Spiket* (*spicula*) or *Little Spike*, constituting a part of a larger composition of florets. *Ibid.* II. 149 The number of florets in each spiket very uncertain. **1817** *Blackw. Mag.* II. 235 The spikets on an ear of wheat are in two rows.

spike-tackle, -tub: see SPECK *sb.*^{4} 2.

1867 SMYTH *Sailor's Word-bk.* 642.

spikey, var. of SPIKY *a.*^{2}

'**spikily**, *adv.* [f. SPIKY *a.*^{2}] In a spiky manner; like spikes.

1893 'MAXWELL GRAY' *Last Sentence* I. I. vii. 135 [Hair] which..stood spikily out in every direction. **1959** *Times* 18 June 15/4 Higo Harada's Music for Piano and Violin, Op. 12,..was spikily intellectual music, rarely visited by any spirit of delight. **1976** J. COOPER *Harriet* (1977) xiii. 81 Her spikily mascara'd eyes softened.

'**spikiness.** [f. SPIKY *a.*^{2}] The quality of being spiky or sharp-pointed.

a **1722** LISLE *Husb.* (1757) 141 The spikiness and speariness of the tops. **1865** *Examiner* 4 Nov. 697/3 A real Christmas fire..reflected itself in the..tiles and the fantastic spikiness of the steel fender. **1962** *Listener* 3 May 788/3 The curious spikiness of the quartet writing. **1977** D. BAGLEY *Enemy* i. 10 Her comments were acute... I found her spikiness of mind very agreeable. **1979** E. H. GOMBRICH *Sense of Order* viii. 200 Does it make sense, therefore, to diagnose the spikiness of Gothic shapes by the same standards we might adopt when seeing such spiky forms in a contemporary hand?

'**spiking**, *sb.* *Obs.* exc. *dial.* Forms: 3-5 **spikyng(e**, 4-6 **spykyng(e** (5 **spykhyng**), 4-6, 9 **spiking**, 5-7, 9 **spikin**, 6 **spikene**, 9 **spiken**, **speken**, **-in**, **specking**. [prob. a MDu. *spiking*, synonymous with *spiker* (see SPIKE *sb.*^{2}) or denoting some variety of this.] A spike-nail.

1261 in *Rep. Comm. Pub. Rec. Irel.* (1815) Pl. ii, In fabricacione..ij malliorum et xx. spikyngorum, de mediocri forma. **1307-8** *MS. Acc. Exch. K.R.* Bdle. 14 No. 14 (P.R.O.), In .iij. C. de magnis Spykinges emptis,..iiij.s. **1354** *Mem. Ripon* (Surtees) III. 96 Et de Mˡ DC de spykinges grossis emp. ut infra pro coopertura ejusdem domus. **1399** *Ibid.* 133 Et in j mille de midelspykyng, iis. iid. **1408** *Ibid.* 139 Item et in iij mˡ dubylspykyng. **1484** *Churchw. Acc. Wigtoft, Linc.* (Nichols, 1797) 80 Paid for grete spikyngs to all the trestles of all the Belles. **1527-8** *Rec. St. Mary at Hill* (1905) 344 Paid for a hillett & a plate & spikinges for the Southe churchdur. **1586** *Shuttleworths' Acc.* (Chetham Soc.) 27 For dubblye and singley spikenes, ijᵈ. **1603** *Ibid.* 151 Duble spykinges,..iijˢ;..single spykinges,..xijᵈ. **1647** J. CARTER *Nail & Wheel* 27 There are a sort of nails (spikins I think they call them) they want heads: and so whatsoever is hang'd upon them slips of. *a* **1825** FORBY *Voc. E. Anglia*, *Spikin*, *Spekin*, a large nail with a round flat head. **1828** CARR *Craven Gloss.*, *Spiking*, a long nail without a head.

So †**spiking-nail.** *Obs.*

1311-2 in J. R. Boyle *Hedon* (1895) App. 13 Spyky[n]gnayl et lignis pro barris. *c* **1440** *Promp. Parv.* 469/1 Spykynge nayle. **1497** *Acc. Ld. High Treas. Scot.* I. 350 For ijᶜ spikin nalis.

'**spiking**, *vbl. sb.* [f. SPIKE *v.*^{1}]

1. The action of fastening or piercing with a spike or spikes.

1775 in ASH. **1887** *19th Cent.* Aug. 176 The spiking and subsequent death of John M.

2. ***spiking crib*** or ***curb***: (see later quots.).

1839 URE *Dict. Arts* 972 In this operation, three kinds of cribs are employed; called wedging, spiking, and main cribs. *Ibid.* 973 The next operation is to fix spiking cribs..to the rock. **1867** W. W. SMYTH *Coal & Coal-mining* 114 Lighter rings of wood, the spiking curbs, were then placed at intervals of 18 inches to 3 feet, according to the pressure. **1883** GRESLEY *Gloss. Coal-m.* 230 *Spiking Curbs*, light rings of wood to which planks are spiked... when plank tubbing is used in sinking through water-bearing ground.

3. The action of adding a spike (SPIKE *sb.*^{2} 2 f(*b*)).

1962 *Newnes Conc. Encycl. Nucl. Energy* 772/2 Spiking was first carried out in the NRX reactor in 1951. **1974** *Sci. Amer.* Feb. 121/1 The use of isotope-spiking and mass spectrometry. **1979** *Liquefied Petroleum Gas* (Shell Internat. Petroleum Co.) 4 In some instances LPG can also be transported by 'spiking'—that is, enriching crude oil with small quantities of LPG.

ˈspiking, *ppl. a.* [f. SPIKE *v.*^{1}]

1. ***spiking party***, a small body of men told off, or sent out, to spike guns.

1884 *Milit. Engineer.* I. II. 111 The artillery or spiking party will be from 4 or 5 to 40 or 50 men. **1891** *Pall Mall G.* 22 Oct. 6/2 General Davis, when a captain, headed the spiking party in the attack on the Redan.

2. Presenting the appearance of spikes; suddenly rising and falling.

1897 *Allbutt's Syst. Med.* II. 360 The range of temperature may be moderate—not exceeding 103°—or irregular with 'spiking' readings.

spiknard, -nel, obs. ff. SPIKENARD, SPIGNEL.

spiky (ˈspaɪkɪ), *a.*^{1} Also 6 **spikie, spykie.** [f. SPIKE *sb.*^{1}] Having the form of a flower-spike; characterized by the production of spikes or ears.

In some contexts not clearly distinct from SPIKY *a.*^{2}

1578 LYTE *Dodoens* 105 The floures grow..upon long purple, spykie, knoppes like to the eares or spikes of Bistorte. **1656** CULPEPPER *Eng. Physic. Enl.* 162 The stalk riseth above this Leaf..like the spiky head of the Adders-Tongue. **1778** J. SCOTT *Mor. Eclogues* iii. 9 Spiky mint rich fragrance breathing round. **1828** *Blackw. Mag.* Dec. 711/2 The tall harvest of spiky wheat. **1883** *Knowledge* 8 June 336/2 Rye-grass,..a common roadside weed..with a number of spiky flower-heads. **1884** *Pall Mall G.* 10 June 4/1 Sweet-vernal-grass..the peculiar spiky plant to which new-mown hay owes with us the whole of its delicious fragrance.

spiky (ˈspaɪkɪ), *a.*^{2} Also 8- **spikey.** [f. SPIKE *sb.*^{2}]

1. Fitted with a spike or spikes; having sharp projecting points.

1720 POPE *Iliad* xx. 585 The spiky Wheels thro' Heaps of Carnage tore; And thick the groaning Axles dropp'd with Gore. **1764** RANDALL *Semi-Virgilian Husb.* App. 1 Mr. Ellis, in one of his eight volumes on Husbandry, made mention of a spiky roller. **1767** R. JAGO *Edge-hill* III. 120 By gainful Commerce of her woolly Vests, Wrought by the spiky Comb. **1866** *Daily Tel.* 20 Jan. 3/6 His martial cloak.. around him, and the usual spiky helmet on his head. **1893** G. ALLEN *Scallywag* I. 97 A couple of large spiky shells.

Comb. **1778** [W. MARSHALL] *Minutes Agric., Observ.* 18 The latter has scarcely ten vigorous plants in the whole field; — though spikey-rolled, and repeatedly harrowed.

2. Having the form of a spike or spikes; stiff and sharp-pointed.

1742 BLAIR *Grave* 191 The tapering Pyramid!.. Whose spiky Top Has wounded the thick Cloud. **1796** KIRWAN *Elem. Min.* (ed. 2) I. 298 [Calcedony] filiform, tubular, or spiky. **1810** WORDSW. *Prose Wks.* (1876) II. 282 If ten thousand of this spiky tree, the larch, are stuck in at once upon the side of a hill, they can grow up into nothing but deformity. **1859** DICKENS *T. Two Cities* II. i, With his spiky hair looking as if it must tear the sheet to ribbons. **1894** W. BESANT *Equal Woman* 126 A dozen spiky thorns sticking into him in the most cruel manner.

Comb. **1849** CUPPLES *Green Hand* xvi. (1856) 158 The high bundles of knotted and jointed bamboo, with their spiky-tufted crowns.

3. *fig.* Suggestive of spikes; sharp.

1881 MRS. LYNN LINTON *My Love!* I. 94 To oppose smoothness to her spiky irritability. **1930** M. KENNEDY *Fool of Family* xv. 147 'How spikey you are!' protested Fenella mildly. 'Oh, yes. Keep your temper when I'm rude. You would.' **1955** *Times* 4 Aug. 10/5 What matter that the melodic line is as seductively curved as that of any of the great operatic romanticists of the near past, instead of being spiky and angular in the contemporary fashion? **1964** CRYSTAL & QUIRK *Prosodic & Paralinguist. Features in Eng.* iv. 47 Pitch variation, with extremes in a 'spiky' movement on the one hand..and in a 'glissando' movement..on the other. **1981** N. J. CRISP *Festival* vii. 176 He seemed more relaxed..not as spiky and difficult as he had been.

4. Of a particularly ritualistic or High-Church Anglican character. *slang.*

1893 W. BRIGHT *Let.* 20 Oct. (1903) 348 The ultras, as they might be called, on the Catholic side, present Church ideas, too often, in a form altogether too hard to be attractive; I believe I am said to have called it 'spiky', in a letter to my friend the Principal of Ely College. **1921** *Church Times* 12 Aug. 147/3 We wonder what would be thought of some of his sayings if they were uttered by a spiky young curate to-day. **1950** A. WILSON *Such Darling Dodos* 34 She became a daily communicant and delighted the more 'spikey' of her neighbours. **1962** *Times Lit. Suppl.* 13 July 505/1 Her story is of the American priest, Charles Phillips, whose churchmanship would in England be rated high-to-spiky. **1977** B. PYM *Quartet in Autumn* xxiv. 212 He had been a server at the spikiest Anglo-Catholic church.

spilakee, obs. variant of SPILLIKIN.

spilching. (See quot.)

1892 *Labour Comm.* Gloss. No. 9, *Spilching*, a trade term applied usually to a brick..which on being exposed to the weather becomes dry, crusts, and gradually falls away.

†**spilcock.** *Obs.*$^{-0}$ In 5 **spylkok.** [Of doubtful origin: cf. SPILQUERN.] A form of top.

c **1440** *Promp. Parv.* 469 Spylkok, or whyrlegygge, chylderys pley,..*giraculum*.

†**spilder.** *Obs.*$^{-1}$ In 5 **spildur.** [Of Scand. origin: cf. Norw. *spildra*, Sw. *spillra*, *spiller-*, in the same sense, and SPELDER *sb.*] A splinter.

c **1420** *Avow. Arth.* xiii, The grete schafte that was longe, Alle to spildurs hit spronge.

†**spile**, *sb.*^{1} *Obs. rare.* [Related to SPILE *v.*^{1} Cf. OFris., OS., OHG. *spil* (G. *spiel*, dial. *spil*, Du. *spel*, etc.).] Sport, play. (In fig. senses: cf. SPILE *v.*^{1} 1 b.)

c **1250** *Gen. & Ex.* 2977 Polheuedes, and froskes, & podes spile Bond harde egipte folc in sile [? *read* file = filth]. *Ibid.* 3462 Ðe ðridde daiȝes morȝe quile, ðunder and leuene made spile.

spile (spaɪl), *sb.*^{2} Also 7 **spyle.** [a. MDu. or MLG. *spīle* (Du. dial., WFris., and LG. *spile*; Du. *spijl*, NFris. *spīl*, G. *speil*), splinter, wooden pin or peg, skewer, etc.]

1. *north. dial.* and †*Sc.* A splinter, chip, or narrow strip, of wood; a spill.

1513 DOUGLAS *Æneid* IX. ix. 42 Sum stekyt throu the cost with spilis of tre Lay gaspand. **1540** *Acc. Ld. High Treas. Scot.* VII. 486 For glew, to glew on the spilis upoun ane patrown of ane gun. **1634** *Lowe's Chirurg.* (ed. 3) 111 The tumor being opened,..you must separate the [membrane]..gently from the flesh, either with your Spyle or other fit instrument proper to pull it out. **1671** SKINNER *Etymol. Ling. Angl.* s.v., A Spile or Spill. **1838** *Civil Eng. & Arch. Jrnl.* I. 242/2 Two wedges made out of one piece, and two spiles. *Ibid.*, He..drives in a wooden spile, which immediately stops the leak. **1869** PEACOCK *Lonsdale Gloss.* 79/1 *Spile*, a splinter. **1894** HESLOP *Northumbld. Gloss.* 677 Thor's a spile run into ma finger.

2. a. A small plug of wood for stopping the vent of a cask; a vent-peg; a spigot. Chiefly *dial.*

1707 MORTIMER *Husb.* 573 Have near the Bung-hole a little Vent-hole stopp'd with a Spile. **1796-** in many dial. glossaries. **1832** MARRYAT *N. Forster* v, He knelt to pull out the spile. **1896** *Sun* 11 Dec. 3/2 A number of spiles for extracting spirit from casks.

fig. **1836** HALIBURTON *Clockm.* Ser. I. xvi, This Province is like that are tree;..and if they don't drive in a spile and stop the everlastin flow of the sap, it will perish altogether.

b. *N.Amer.* A small wooden or metal spout for conducting sap from the sugar-maple.

1844 *Knickerbocker* XXIII. 444 The spiles you see sticking from sugar-holes in every maple. **1868** *Amer. Naturalist* Mar. 39 He remembers very distinctly making 'spiles' of its [*sc.* elder] stems when tapping sugar-trees. **1875** KNIGHT *Dict. Mech.* 2268/1 A notch is cut by an axe in the tree above the spile. **1879** BURROUGHS *Locusts & Wild Honey* 9 The bees get their first taste of sweet from the sap as it flows from the spiles. **1947** K. M. WELLS *Owl Pen* 89 It is time..to get the rusty spiles and sap buckets down from the beams in the woodshed. It is maple syrup time. **1973** L. RUSSELL *Everyday Life Colonial Canada* xi. 144 The operator drilled a hole into the side of the [maple tree] trunk..and set into this a small wooden spout called a spile.

3. *techn.* (See quot. and cf. SPILL *sb.*^{1} 3.)

1750 BLANCKLEY *Nav. Expos.* 156 *Spiles* are small Wood Pins, which are drove into the Nail-holes, when a Ship's Sheathing is taken off. [Hence in some later nautical Dicts.]

4. *attrib.* and *Comb.*, as ***spile-borer, -hole, -peg, -tap.***

a **1825** FORBY *Voc. E. Anglia*, *Spile-hole*, the air-hole in a cask. *Spile-peg*, the wooden peg closing the hole for the admission of air into a cask when it is tapped. **1875** KNIGHT *Dict. Mech.* 2268/1 *Spile-borer*, an auger-bit to bore out stuff for spiles. **1885** *Whitby Times* 31 July 2/6 Bar, &c.—Trays, waiters,..screws, spring spile taps, crushers.

spile (spaɪl), *sb.*^{3} Also 6 *Sc.* **spyl-.** [app. an alteration of PILE *sb.*^{1} after prec. or by wrong analysis of combs.]

1. a. = PILE *sb.*^{1} 3.

1513 DOUGLAS *Æneid* IX. x. 20 Aschame ȝe nocht..To be inclosit amyd a fald of stakis, And be assegit..With akyn spyllis and dikis on syk wys? **1614** in *Trans. Cumbld. & Westmoreld. Antiq. & Archæol. Soc.* (1912) 244 [Some of the] spiles [which had been placed at the king's charges for defence of the sea]. **1829** [see SPILE *v.*^{3}]. **1851** H. MELVILLE *Whale* ix, Another runs to read the bill that's stuck against the spile on the wharf. **1856** OLMSTED *Slave States* 351 A spile, pointed with iron, six inches in diameter, and twenty feet long, is set upon the stump by a diver. *Ibid.*, In very large stumps, the spile is often driven till its top reaches the water. **1878** N. H. BISHOP *Voy. Paper Canoe* 115 The government is building a remarkable pier of solid iron spiles, three abreast.

b. (See quot.)

a **1825** FORBY *Voc. E. Anglia*, *Spile*, a wedge of wood stoutly pointed with iron, used in clay or gravel pits, limestone quarries, etc., to let down large quantities at once.

c. *Mining.* A sharp-pointed post used in sinking by means of cribs.

1841 *Civil Eng. & Arch. Jrnl.* IV. 293/1 Supposing..the sand five fathoms..in depth,..and the length of the spiles six feet. *Ibid.*, The five rounds of spiles and cribs..will take up 10 feet of the diameter of the pit. **1883** GRESLEY *Gloss. Coal-m.* 231 *Spiles*, narrow-pointed tubbing wedges.

d. *attrib.* and *Comb.*, as ***spile-driver, -pier, -worm.***

1865 *Atlantic Monthly* Apr. 393/1 By means of a spiledriver, an iron pipe..is driven down until it rests upon the solid rock. **1894** *Harper's Mag.* Jan. 422 The operation of a spile-driver at Plymouth docks. **1895** *Funk's Stand. Dict.*, *Spile-worm*, a ship-worm; teredo. **1898** KIPLING *Day's Work* 2 An overhead-crane travelled..along its spile-pier.

†**2.** = PILE *sb.*^{1} 2 b. *Obs.*$^{-1}$

1649 J. ELLISTONE tr. *Boehme's Ep.* xv. 133 Yet what God will, be done; as many a spile of grass perisheth when the Heaven giveth not its raine.

†**spile**, *v.*^{1} *Obs.* In 1 **spilian,** 3 **spilien, spelien, spilen,** 4 **spyle-.** [OE. *spilian*, = OFris. *spilia* (WFris. *spylje*), OS. *spilôn* (MLG. and MDu., LG. and Du. *spelen*), OHG. *spilôn*, *spilên* (MHG. *spilen*, *spiln*, G. *spielen*); Icel. *spila*, Norw. and Sw. *spela*, Da. *spille*, are from LG.]

1. *intr.* To sport or play; to rejoice.

a **1000** *Institutes of Polity* in Thorpe *Laws* (1840) II. 322 [Hi] lufiað..idele blisse..& ealne dæȝ fleardiað, spelliað & spiliað, & nænige note dreoȝað. *a* **1023** WULFSTAN *Hom.* (1883) 45 Eowra leoda, þe spiliað and pleȝað and rædes ne hedað. *c* **1205** LAY. 13816 Þer he mid his hirede hæhliche spilede. *c* **1250** *Gen. & Ex.* 2532 God leue hem in his blisse spilen Among engeles & seli men. *c* **1315** SHOREHAM v. 89 Elizbeth wel þat aspyde, Hou a spylede onder hyre syde, And made hys reioyynge.

b. To play havoc, do damage. (Cf. SPILE *sb.*^{1})

c **1250** *Gen. & Ex.* 3183 Oc ðe [h]ail haueð so wide spiled, ðat his graue is ðor-vnder hiled.

¶**2.** *trans.* and *intr.* To say; to speak.

Freq. in Layamon, through confusion with *spellien* SPELL *v.*^{1} (cf. the first quot. in sense 1 above).

c **1205** LAY. 14102 Ofte heo stilledliche spækeð, & spilieð mid runen, of twam ȝunge monnen. *Ibid.* 14316 What weoren þat speche þe þat maide spilede.

spile (spaɪl), *v.*^{2} [f. SPILE *sb.*^{2} Cf. NFris. *spīle*, G. *speilen*, to fix or fit with spiles.]

1. *trans.* To stop up (a hole) by means of a spile. Also with *up*.

1691 T. H[ALE] *Account New Invent.* p. xxii, Nail-holes, which they use to spile up at stripping. *Ibid.* 45 They were forced to..spile the Spike-holes. **1837** in *Civil. Eng. & Arch. Jrnl.* I. 242/1 If there should be a defect in the joint it must be made afresh, as it can neither be spiled as a wooden joint, nor set up as a lead joint.

2. To draw (liquid) from a cask by spiling or broaching. Now *dial.*

1772 in J. Tomlinson *Doncaster* (1887) 237 Going to Rossington to Spile the Court Ale. *a* **1904** in *Eng. Dial. Dict.* s.v., I never spiled the beer.

3. To provide (a cask, tree, etc.) with a spile, in order to draw off liquid. Now *dial.* or *U.S.*

1832 MARRYAT *N. Forster* v, I've spiled them, and they prove to be puncheons of rum. **1836** —— *Midsh. Easy* xiv, Then one of the casks of wine was spiled. **1879-** in dial. glossaries (e. Anglia, s.w. Lincs., Cumbld., etc.). **1904** MRS. ATHERTON *Rulers of Kings* ix. 33 Of course the trees have to be spiled.

spile (spaɪl), *v.*^{3} [f. SPILE *sb.*^{3}] *trans.* To furnish, secure, or strengthen with timber or iron piles; = PILE *v.*^{1} 1.

1829 BROCKETT *N.C. Gloss.* (ed. 2), *Spile*, to make a foundation in soft or boggy ground by driving in spiles; i.e. piles or pieces of timber. **1869-** in dial. glossaries, etc.

spile-bon, obs. form of SPEEL-BONE *dial.*

spilikin, var. SPILLIKIN, SPELLICAN.

spiling (ˈspaɪlɪŋ), *vbl. sb.*^{1} [f. SPILE *v.*^{3}] The action of driving in spiles; also, spiles collectively.

1841 *Civil Eng. & Arch. Jrnl.* IV. 293 The spiling and cribs averaging each six inches thick. *Ibid.*, A..general idea of the mode of spiling and cribbing through the sand.

spiling (ˈspaɪlɪŋ), *vbl. sb.*^{2} [Origin obscure; found earlier as SPOILING *vbl. sb.*^{2}] (See quots.)

1846 A. YOUNG *Naut. Dict.* 291 *Spilings*, in shipbuilding, the dimensions of the curve or sny of a plank's edge. They are commonly measured by means of a rule-staff fastened for this purpose on the ship's timbers. *c* **1850** *Rudim. Navig.* (Weale) 150 *Spilings*, the dimensions taken from a straight line, a mould's edge, or rule-staff, to any given line or edge. **1894** *Outing* XXIV. 21/2 To take the spiling for shaping the planks, care and patience are required.

attrib. **1869** SIR E. REED *Shipbuild.* xx. 457 The edges of plating..are marked upon these moulds, and spiling lines.. are given out with them. **1894** *Outing* XXIV. 21/2 The spiling staff or batten is cut..the length of the gunwale line and four or five inches wide.

spilite (ˈspaɪlaɪt, ˈspɪlaɪt). *Min.* [orig. formed as F. *spillite* (Al. Brongniart: see A. H. de Bonnard in *Nouveau Dict. d'Hist. nat. appliquée aux Arts* (rev. ed.) (1819) XXIX. 371), f. Gr. σπίλος spot, stain.] An altered basalt, commonly amygdaloidal in structure, which is characterized by the albitization of its constituent feldspars and the presence of numerous secondary minerals, and is exemplified by many pillow-lavas.

Brongniart did not use *spilite* in its usual modern sense, applying it to amygdaloidal diabase, and much variation in usage has occurred subsequently. There is a comprehensive review by T. G. Vallance in *Proc. Linnean Soc. New South Wales* (1960) LXXXV. 8-52.

1834 *Jrnl. Geol. Soc. Dublin* I. 119 In adopting the term spilites in preference to that of amygdaloid,..I have been induced to do so because the English names were.. irrelevant to the variable nature of the mineral substances. **1879** RUTLEY *Stud. Rocks* xiii. 247 To some of these rocks occurring..in France, the name spilite has been applied. **1893** *Geol. Mag.* Decade III. X. 59 Prof. de Lapparent.. refers to these 'spilites' as amydaloidal melaphyres. **1895** L. FLETCHER *Introd. Study Rocks* (1898) Index 118/1. **1911** *Geol. Mag.* Decade V. VIII. 203 In addition to the pillow-structure there are certain characteristics that mark the spilites of Great Britain. The first of these is that they are as a rule very completely decomposed, and the second that their felspars are always rich in soda. **1937** A. Johannsen *Descriptive Petrogr. Igneous Rocks* III. 300 The British Geological Survey uses spilite 'to designate the Carboniferous, Devonian, and Ordovician pillow-lavas of Devon and Cornwall...' This variation from the original usage apparently still persists, for Holmes in 1920, defined them as basaltic rocks whose feldspars have been albitized. The term should be dropped. **1960** *Proc. Linnean Soc. New South Wales* LXXXV. 10 English-speaking geologists made little or no use of the term during the 19th century. Rocks which would have been called spilites by the French were usually known as greenstones. *Ibid.* 12 There appear to be four main criteria used in the recognition of spilites, namely, fabric, mineralogy, chemical composition and geological occurrence. Much of the confusion associated with the name spilite derives from the fact that various workers have emphasized different features. **1974** F. Fiala in G. C. Amstutz *Spilites & Spilitic Rocks* 18 Spilites are abundant in pillow lavas. Nevertheless, both terms are not synonymous, as has been assumed by many workers. **1981** F. J. Turner *Metamorphic Petrol.* (ed. 2) 223 (*heading*) Spilites as metamorphic rocks.

Hence **spiliti'zation**, alteration into spilite; **'spilitized** *a.*

1946 *Amer. Jrnl. Sci.* CCXLIV. 313 During spilitization the ferro-magnesian minerals were broken down, and.. the manganese, with other constituents, migrated to the tops of the flows. **1960** *Q. Jrnl. Geol. Soc.* CXVI. 388 Dewey and Flett.. came to the right conclusion in attributing a large proportion of spilitization of pillow-lavas to reactions quickly achieved under submarine volcanic conditions. **1962** E. A. Vincent tr. *Rittmann's Volcanoes & their Activity* viii. 225 In thick submarine basalt flows.. it is often to be observed that only their upper layers consist of spilitized pillow lavas. **1974** F. Fiala in G. C. Amstutz *Spilites & Spilitic Rocks* 19 The association of spilitized diabases and spilites with keratophyres is.. marked in the initial Devonian volcanism of northern Moravia. **1978** *Nature* 8 June 459/1 Due to the vitric nature and widespread secondary alteration (incipient spilitisation and weathering) the exact petrologic character and petrogenetic affinity of these rocks have not been clearly defined.

spilitic (spaɪl-, spɪ'lɪtɪk), *a. Geol.* [f. spilite + -ic.] Of, pertaining to, or of the nature of spilite; characterized by the presence of spilite.

1911 *Geol. Mag.* Decade V. VIII. 205 The basic felspar can be traced in every stage of development as we follow the spilitic lavas from the outer precincts of the aureoles to the actual contacts with the granite. *Ibid.* 243 The spilitic suite of igneous rocks. **1965** A. Holmes *Princ. Physical Geol.* (ed. 2) xxx. 1126 The volcanic rocks interbedded with eugeosynclinal sediments are characteristically submarine lavas of the spilitic suite.., including pillow lavas. **1974** D. S. Coombs in G. C. Amstutz *Spilites & Spilitic Rocks* 377 Augite was thus *unstable* relative to chlorite.. during the production of the diagnostic spilitic mineralogy. **1977** A. Hallam *Planet Earth* 201 The geosynclinal belt across Europe, with its associated zones of spilitic volcanics and serpentines, has been interpreted as site of an old ocean.

spill (spɪl), *sb.*[1] Forms: 4 spille, 5-6 spyll(e, 6-7 spil, 7- spill. [Of doubtful origin; app. in some way related to spile *sb.*[2]]

1. a. A splinter; a sharp-pointed fragment of wood, bone, etc.; a slip or sliver.

c **1300** *Beket* 850 We suspendieth such consail, for hit his noȝt worth a Spille. *c* **1400** *Destr. Troy* 11119 Pirrus with payn puld of his brest The spyll of his speire. **1550** T. Lever *Serm.* (Arb.) 135 Beware.. that ye staye not your selfe vnto a bryttell staffe, for it wyll brast in spylles and perce thorowe your handes. **1598** Hall *Sat.* iv. iii, What boots it.. to reserve their relics many years, Their silver spurs, or spils of broken spears. **1601** Holland *Pliny* II. 283 This herb.. draweth forth of the body any spils whatsoeuer. **1658** J. Jones *Ovid's Ibis* 43 Divine justice.. maketh.. the spils of the staff on which he leaned to run into his hands. **1748** in *6th Rep. Dep. Kpr.* App. ii. 123 Taking out all such lints, spills, and other things which will not receive the dye. **1846** Holtzapffel *Turning* II. 527 To preserve the edge of the tool, thin spills of hard wood are sometimes placed between the cutter and the bar. **1863** *Gd. Words* Apr. 282/1 Like what are called spills in the game of spillikins.

fig. **1600** Holland *Livy* vii. xxi. 263 This matter of usurie, the onely spill or bone (as it were) between, that seemed to hinder the uniting of their hearts.

b. *techn.* (See quots.)

1843 Holtzapffel *Turning* I. 197 The scrap-iron is sometimes twisted during the process of manufacture, to lay all the filaments like a rope, and prevent the formation of spills, or the longitudinal dirty seams found on the surface of inferior iron. **1904** *Kynoch Jrnl.* Oct.-Dec. 204 The reader will observe.. a flaw technically termed a 'spill', the result of a small hollow or depression near the surface of the ingot, which, in the process of rolling has been closed, but which, in the extending process of pressing the metal into a case has again been opened & made manifest. **1954** A. R. Bailey *Text-bk. Metallurgy* xi. 377 Cavities near the surface.. are likely to become opened up during working, become oxidised and fail to weld up, thus forming surface oxide laminations, sometimes known as spills.

2. a. A thin slip of wood, a folded or twisted piece of paper, used for lighting a candle, pipe, etc.

1821 M. Edgeworth *Let.* 14 Nov. (1971) 268 Harriet performed to admiration as Fire eater—I held lamp.. and lighted *spills* which she seemed to devour. **1839** Sir G. C. Lewis *Gloss. Heref.* s.v., Long thin splinters of wood used in farm houses for lighting candles are called spills. **1849** C. Brontë *Shirley* xxxvi, She had separated a slip of paper for lighting tapers—a spill, as it is called—into fragments. **1871** Tylor *Prim. Cult.* I. 68 The children stand in a ring; one lights a spill of paper and passes it on.

b. *attrib.* and *Comb.*, as *spill-box, -case, cup, -holder, -jar, pot, vase.*

1847 Alb. Smith *Stuck-up People* 84 It was termed a spill-case, to be sold, with similar ones, at a guinea the pair. **1851** *Parker's Jrnl.* 5 Apr. 185/2 The mantelpiece is probably painted to imitate marble, and on it are placed two 'spill-holders' of perforated card, with bouquets worked in silk on each. **1859** F. S. Cooper *Ironmongers' Catal.* 181 Spill Cups. **1860** Miss Yonge *Hopes & Fears* I. x. 362 The.. well-filled spill-holder and match-box on the mantel-shelf. **1862** *Catal. Internat. Exhib., Brit.* II. No. 6860, Several pairs of spill pots, various designs. **1866** Mrs. Riddell *Race for Wealth* xix, He has got a clock on the mantel-shelf,.. and spill-boxes,.. and cigar-cases. **1868** C. L. Eastlake *Hints on Household Taste* v. 134 Chimneypiece spill-vases, made of brass,.. decorated with a pattern in encaustic colour. **1903** A. Bennett *Leonora* x. 282 Reaching a second spill from the spill-jar on the mantlepiece. **1978** *Country Life* 13 Apr. (Suppl.) 38/1 (*caption*) A Pair of English Porcelain Spill Vases.

c. *ellipt.* A spill-holder in the form of a cylindrical jar; also, an umbrella-holder of similar form.

1895 *Army & Navy Soc. Price List* 15 Sept. 318 Oriental Goods:.. Spills: 6 in., pair 1/8. *Ibid.*, Umbrella Spills, 25 in. high, 9 in. diameter.

3. *techn.* (See quot. and cf. spile *sb.*[2] 3.)

1875 Knight *Dict. Mech.*, *Spill* (Shipwrighting), a small peg used to stop the hole left by a spike when drawn out.

4. *Mining.* (See quot.)

1881 Raymond *Mining Gloss.*, *Spills*, Corn[wall], long thick laths or poles driven ahead horizontally around the door-frames, in running levels in loose ground.

spill (spɪl), *sb.*[2] Also 7 spil. [app. a. Du. *spil* (MDu. *spille*) or LG. (MLG.) *spille*, G. *spille* (OHG. *spilla*), spindle, axis, pin, stalk, etc., app. for original **spinla*, f. *spin-* spin *v.* In some senses perh. associated with prec.]

†**1.** A small cylinder upon which yarn is wound; a spool. *Obs.*

1594 H. Willobie *Avisa* 38 Her Spill was neuer fully spone, For night vndid that day had done. *Ibid.* 39 The Spindle that you see me driue, Hath fyld the spill so often trend. **1615** Hieron *Wks.* I. 604 I will, now (as the vse in spinning is) that I haue.. twisted this threed, briefly wind it vpon the spill.

2. A rod or stalk of wood, metal, etc.

1594 Carew *Tasso* (1881) 71 A sepulchre of Cipresse sweete they stall Their Barricados neere, and highest spill Of Palme tree with his boughs orespreads it all. **1602** —— *Cornwall* 30 b, The Oysters.. haue a peculiar dredge, which is a thicke strong net, fastned to three spils of yron, and drawne at the boates sterne. *Ibid.* 124 b, One of the boyes conuerted the spill of an old candlesticke to a gunne. **1807** Vancouver *Agric. Devon* (1813) 118 A bridle.. should be fixed on the beam by a nut and screw, and passed down the spill with a lip, to grasp the head end of the sole. **1844** *Civil Eng. & Arch. Jrnl.* VII. 190/2 The 'button clack.. was a disc of metal with a central spill or stalk, which rose and fell in a guide. **1881** Greener *Gun* 236 By using more packing, or a larger spill, the same bit may be used to bore several sizes out of a barrel.

†**b.** A stem-like root. Also *spill-root. Obs.*

1766 *Museum Rust.* VI. 29 Mr. Lewis says it [*sc.* burnet-haulm] runs down in a spill six or eight inches. **1796** *Trans. Soc. Arts* XIV. 260, I do not suppose the transplanted ones will answer, having but one spill-root.

c. Of a gun: = nipple *sb.* 3.

1823 *Specif. J. Day's Patent* No. 4861, Nipple or spill to receive the copper percussion caps.

3. A pin or slender rod upon which anything turns; a spindle.

1730 *Phil. Trans.* XXXVI. 337 This is to be kept in Motion by a Gut-string (as the Spill of a Spinning-Turn is moved). **1762** *Ibid.* LII. 510 A large spill of iron, on which there is a brass weather-cock. **1770** *Ibid.* LXI. 74 It is remarkable that the spill was found in the bell-chamber, and the weather-cock in the battlements. **1881** Young *Ev. Man his own Mech.* §1486. 671 The spill that connects the handles and keys with the lever that acts on the catch [of the lock]. **1888-** in s.w. dial. glossaries.

†**spill**, *sb.*[3] *slang. Obs.* [Of doubtful origin: perh. from spill *v.*] A small gift of money; a tip.

1675 Crowne *Country Wit* ii. i, Give a spill to my watch, and my Grace shall drink your health in claret. *Ibid.* iv, Never make a bustle on your wedding-day! give the constable a spill. **1726** Ayliffe *Parergon* 173 The Bishops who consecrated this Ground, were wont to have a Spill or Sportule from the credulous Laity. **1774** Foote *Cozeners* i. Wks. 1799 II. 151, I will.. give him a good spill for his resignation into the bargain.

b. Const. *of* (money).

1707 J. Stevens tr. *Quevedo's Com. Wks.* (1709) T iij, For a small Spill of Money, he was.. my Friend. **1778** Foote *Trip Calais* ii. Wks. 1799 II. 347 For a little spill of money, he may put us in a way to get our daughter out. **1815** Scott *Guy M.* xxxiv, All dead but Gipsy Gab, and he would go off the country for a spill of money.

spill (spɪl), *sb.*[4] [f. spill *v.*]

1. A throw from a horse or vehicle; a fall or tumble; an upset.

a **1845** Barham *Ingol. Leg.* Ser. iii. *Blasphemer's Warn.* 355 Cursing his fill At his courser because he had given him a 'spill'. **1876** *Chambers' Jrnl.* 29 July 493/1 During the struggle [in polo].. mishaps now and then occur—happy if only a spill. **1895** Meredith *Amazing Marriage* xv, The coach rocked, they were sharp on a spill midway of the last descent.

2. a. A downpouring or dropping of liquid; a quantity spilled; *spec.* = *oil spill* s.v. oil *sb.*[1] 6 e.

c **1848** J. Keegan *Leg. & Poems* (1907) 482 If a spill of my heart's blood could be of any comfort to the poor creature, he should be welcome to it. **1888** *Harper's Mag.* Dec. 87 Soon the rain left off for a moment, gathering itself together again for another spill. **1972** L. M. Harris *Introd. Deepwater Floating Drilling Operations* xvii. 178 Equipment and practices designed for safety and reliability are the first line of defense against oil spills and pollution. Should a spill occur, however, advance planning can reduce its severity. **1975** *Petroleum Rev.* XXIX. 237/3 The ability of present-day booms to contain a spill is limited to good weather conditions.

b. A channel or passage for the escape of surplus water; a 'spill-way'.

1900 *Westm. Gaz.* 10 July 2/1 The waters flow down many spills and channels, though at present there are two main branches.

3. *Naut.* A slight breeze.

1899 *Daily News* 20 July 8/3 They found a spill from the stern again taking the ships on the starboard aft.

4. A diffusion of light, esp. beyond the area intended to be illuminated.

1952 [see baffle *sb.*[1] 5]. **1972** T. Coe *Don't lie to Me* (1974) i. 4 Her features.. hard to read in the dim spill from a nearby streetlight. **1977** P. Scupham *Hinterland* 9 A spill Of light poured off rough drapery As blacks and whites and ochre tones Work shifts about the curtain wall.

5. *Austral. Pol.* A vacating of other posts after one important change of office.

1956 J. T. Lang *I Remember* 311 There had to be an annual election of leader. That made it inevitable that some members would intrigue against the leader hoping for a Cabinet spill. **1974** *Courier-Mail* (Brisbane) 6 July 3/1 After Mr. Tucker's election as new party leader, Mr. Dean (Sandgate) moved for a 'spill' of all other Opposition front bench positions. **1975** *Australian* 18 Mar. 1 It will be left to Mr Fraser's supporters to force the issue and move against Mr Snedden through either a spill of leadership positions or a motion of no confidence.

6. *attrib.* and *Comb.*, as *spill-proof* adj.; **spill burner**, a form of burner used in some gas turbines which allows excess fuel to be recirculated; **spill valve**, a valve which serves to allow the escape of surplus fluid.

1945 *Proc. Inst. Mech. Engineers* CLIII. 464/2 (*caption*) o Indicates the condition giving a mean particle size of 200μ: On the *spill burner this limit is not attained. **1972** H. Cohen et al. *Gas Turbine Theory* (ed. 2) vi. 177 A second practical method of obtaining good atomization over a wide range of fuel flow: the spill burner. It is virtually a simplex burner with a passage from the vortex chamber through which excess fuel can be spilled off. **1920** E. Butler *Internal Combustion Engine Design & Pract.* (ed. 2) viii. 138 When used on an automobile, owing to vibration, they [*sc.* accumulator cells] should be occasionally examined for scaling or other damage, and also for loss of solution, if not *spill proof. **1944** W. A. Koehler *Princ. & Applications Electrochem.* (ed. 2) II. iv. 69 A portable radio battery with a transparent plastic case and spill-proof cover. **1963** *Glamour* Oct. 12/1 (Advt.), New spray mist! Unbreakable. Spill-proof... Intimate by Revlon. **1922** *Trans. Inst. Engineers & Shipbuilders Scotland* LXV. 421 This *spill valve opens from the discharge chamber of the pump and is worked by the same lever as actuates the pump plunger. **1959** *Motor Manual* (ed. 36) ii. 30 At a predetermined moment, this outlet is closed and fuel is then forced to the engine cylinder until a second outlet (commonly called a spill valve) is opened so as to release the pressure and return the surplus oil to the supply side of the system. **1975** T. D. Morton *Reed's Motor Engin. Knowledge for Marine Engineers* iii. 77 A fuel spill valve (pneumatically loaded) maintains rail pressure as decided at the controls.

spill (spɪl), *v.* Pa. t. and pa. pple. **spilled, spilt.** Forms: *Inf.* 1-2 spillan, 2-5 -en, 5 spyllyn; 3-6 spille, 4-6 spylle, 4-8 spil, 6 spyl(l; 4- spill. *Pa. t.* 1-4 spilde (4 spild), 4 spilede, 5 spillide, spyllede, 5, 7- spilled; 4 spilte, 4-5 spylt, 5-6 spylte, 4- spilt. *Pa. pple.* 1 ȝespilled, -od, 2 i-spilled, 5-6 spylled, 5- spilled (7 spill'd); 1, 5-6 spild (6 spilde), 3-5 i-spild (4 i-spilde, i-spyld, y-spild, 5 y-spyld); 1, 4- spilt (4, 6 spilte), 4 y-spilt(e, y-spylt, 5-6 spylt(e. [OE. *spillan*, = MDu. and Du. *spillen*, MLG. and LG. *spillen*, G. (*ver*)*spillen*, NFris. *spille*, *spilj*, obscurely related to the synonymous OE. *spildan*, = OS. *spildian* (MLG. and MDu. *spilden*), OHG. (obs. G.) *spilden*. It is not clear which of the two forms is represented by ON. *spilla* (Icel., Norw., Sw. *spilla*, Da. *spilde*), which may partly have contributed to the ME. uses of the word.]

I. 1. a. *trans.* To destroy by depriving of life; to put (or bring) to death; to slay or kill.

Common *c* 1300-1600. Now *Obs.* exc. *arch.*

c **950** *Lindisf. Gosp.* Luke xx. 16 [He] cymeð & spilleð buendo ðas. *Ibid.* John xi. 53 Of ðæm dæȝe.. ȝeðohton [hia] þætte hine spildon *uel* acuoeldon. *a* **1122** *O.E. Chron.* (Laud MS.) an. 1096, Ðær wearð eac Eoda.. þæs cynges aðum.. & sumne man to Lundene lædde, & þær spilde. *c* **1175** *Lamb. Hom.* 17 ȝif heo nulluð nefre.. gan to bote, hit is riht þet me hem spille. *c* **1205** Lay 16870 Let heom alle for-don, spillen & æc an-hon. *c* **1290** *S. Eng. Leg.* I. 348 With þis Askebert heo spac, þis child to slen and spille. *c* **1330** R. Brunne *Chron. Wace* (Rolls) 4806 Androcheus saw his felon wille, þat þe kyng þoughte hym to spille. **1387** Trevisa *Higden* (Rolls) II. 253 [þey] hadde leuere be lost and i-spilde þan be vnderlynges and seruauntes. **1418-20** in *Archaeol.* (1827) XXI. 72 Whan thay had hym so gretly agylte, And of hys men meny one spylte. *c* **1489** Skelton *Death Earl Northumbld.* 106 Alas for pite! that Percy thus was spylt, The famous Erle of Northumberland. *a* **1529** —— '*Now synge we*' 14 Thus was I spylt, Man, for thy gylte, And not for myne. **1573** L. Lloyd *Marrow of Hist.* (1653) 94 O Greece thou spillest more men with civil wars.., then would defend thy state against all the world. **1612** T. Taylor *Comm. Titus* i. 7 Caring no more in their fury to spill a man, then to kill a dogge. **1868** Morris *Earthly Par.* (1890) 44/2 Then if mine old line he must spill There let God save him if He will. **1887** —— *Odyss.* XI. 438 How many for Helen death did spill!

b. Contrasted with *save*.

13.. *K. Alis.* 3997 (Laud. MS.), þe kyng may don his will Sauen þat Percien oiþer hym spille. *c* **1385** CHAUCER *L.G.W.* 1917 *Ariadne*, So that the site was al at his wille To sauyn hem hym leste or ellis spille. **1430–40** LYDG. *Bochas* I. viii. (1544) 13 b, Ye may me saue and spill with a woord. **1526** SKELTON *Magnyf.* 1496 Surely it is I that all may saue and spyll. **1567** *Gude & Godlie B.* (S.T.S.) 170 Thow may me saif, thow may me spill, Baith lyfe and deide lyis in thy will. **1620–16** QUARLES *Feast for Worms* 631 Wks. (Grosart) II. 14 Loue cry'd out, Hold; for better sau'd, then spill'd; But Feare cry'd, Kill.

c. *refl.* To destroy or kill (oneself).

c **1375** *Sc. Leg. Saints* xxix. (*Placidas*) 435 He..oft-tyme wes in to wil hyme-self in-to þe flud to spil. **1390** GOWER *Conf.* I. 328 In this wise himself he spilte With his folhaste and deth he nam. **1412–20** LYDG. *Chron. Troy* II. 4368 For into teris þouȝ þou al distille, And rende þi silfe, as þou woldest þe spille. **1480** *Robt. Devyll* 68 in Hazl. *E.P.P.* I. 221 My wyfe soroweth in her partye, I feare that she wyll her selfe spyll. **1513** DOUGLAS *Æneid* II. x. 203 Gif thou list pas, quod scho, thi self to spill. *c* **1550** ROLLAND *Crt. Venus* III. 39 Quhilk spilt hir self for luif of Pyramus. **1609** DANIEL *Civ. Wars* VIII. xvii. Wks. (Grosart) II. 304 Thou first didst conquer vs; then rays'd our skill To vanquish others; here our selues to spill.

†**d.** *absol.* To cause death or slaughter. Freq. contrasted with *save, spare*, etc. *Obs.*

a **1300** *Cursor M.* 16330 Ne wat þou þat þe pouste es min to spill or latte ga? **1390** GOWER *Conf.* II. 114 For he to spille and noght to save Is schape, as thogh he were ded. *a* **1400–50** *Alexander* 1318 With þat Bucifalon..he brased in þe side, Springis out with a spere, spillis at þe gaynest. **1412–20** LYDG. *Chron. Troy* IV. 3317 Vn-to þe tyme þei haue of þe toun..ful possessioun, At her fre wil to spillen and to saue. *c* **1485** *Digby Myst.* (1882) II. 233 For he hath the pour of the princes alle, To saue or spylle. **1576** PETTIE *Petite Pallace* 78 Women ought to..spyll with Camma, to kyll with Lucrece. **1580** LYLY *Euphues* (Arb.) 452 Thinking no reuenge more princely, then to spare when she might spill. *a* **1618** SYLVESTER *Panaretus* 1546, I know it far more honourable To save then spill (in Cases tolerable). **1627** E. F. *Hist. Edw. II* (1680) 72 To save where you may spill proclaims your Goodness.

2. To destroy or put an end to (life). Now *arch.*

In later use perh. associated with sense 9.

c **950** *Lindisf. Gosp.* Luke xvii. 33 Seðe suahuelc soecað sauel his hal ȝewyrca spilleð hia. **13..** *K. Alis.* 1062 (Laud MS.), Miȝth she haue yfounde a knijf, She had yspilt sone her lijf. *c* **1430** *Sir Gener.* (Roxb.) 9738 Thogh my life in erth be spilt, Gladly I wold my soul saue. **1549–62** STERNHOLD & H. *Ps.* xxxv. 4 Confound them with rebuke and blame that seeke my soule to spill. **1590** SPENSER *F.Q.* III. vii. 54, I..Bad her commaund my life to saue, or spill. **1642** H. MORE *Song of Soul* II. ii. III. viii, Ay me! that dreary death such lovely life should spill. **1650** FULLER *Pisgah* II. xii. 249 Behold his life spilled, whilest wicked Balaams was spared in journey. *a* **1668** LASSELS *Voy. Italy* (1698) I. 4 You must carry your body steadily, or else spill your life. **1813** SCOTT *Trierm.* II. xxii, But trust me, that, if life be spilt,..in Arthur's grace Gyneth shall lose a daughter's place.

†**3. a.** To destroy, ruin, or overthrow (a person); to bring to ruin or misery. *Obs.*

c **950** *Lindisf. Gosp.* John vi. 39 þætte all þæt salde me ne ic losiȝe *uel* þætte ic ne spillo. *c* **1205** LAY. 28863 Ah he nes noht iseli; þat wes for unleoden spilden al his þeoden. *c* **1275** in *O.E. Misc.* 144 þat folk worþ eft wroþe i-spild þe nule to hire turne. *c* **1330** R. BRUNNE *Chron. Wace* (Rolls) 13624 þer hardinesse þem seluen spild! *c* **1386** CHAUCER *Manciple's T.* 326 Ful ofte for to muche speche Hath many a man been spilt as clerkes teche. *c* **1425** *MS. Digby 233* fol. 224 b/1 Necligence & mysavisement spilleth, perscheth, & leseth hem þat ben vnkunnynge. **1526** TINDALE *Heb.* ii. 1 We ought moche more to attende vnto tho thynges which we have herde, lest we be spilt. **1583** BABINGTON *Commandm.* viii. (1590) 344 This spoyle to speede our selues, and spill our Brethren in this lamentable and vnmercifull manner. **1615** T. ADAMS *Black Devil* 25 Hee walkes any way, to spill any man by any meanes. **1642** H. MORE *Song of Soul* II. iii. IV. xxx, Why had the first-made man such a loose will, That his innumerous of-spring he should fouly spill.

refl. *a* **1300** *Cursor M.* 17226 But i þat es sa dedli dill, Me spedis ai me-self to spill, Wit my flexsli lust to fill. *c* **1375** *Sc. Leg. Saints* xxix. (*Placidas*) 148 Quhen man for his gylt brekand my byding hymself spilt. *c* **1460** *Vrbanitatis* 82 in *Babees Bk.* 15 With fayr speche þou may haue þy wylle, And with þy speche þou may þe spylle. **1526** SKELTON *Magnyf.* 2165 Some fall to foly them selfe for to spyll. **1584–7** GREENE *Carde of Fancie* Wks. (Grosart) IV. 134, I will either spoile him, or spill my selfe. **1602** SHAKS. *Ham.* IV. v. 20 So full of Artlesse iealousie is guilt, It spill's it selfe, in fearing to be spilt.

†**b.** To destroy or ruin (the soul) by offending, or causing to offend, against moral laws. *Obs.*

c **1290** *S. Eng. Leg.* I. 131 þe honour of holi churche he lore, and is soule he miȝte so spille. *c* **1340** HAMPOLE *Pr. Consc.* 1320 And welthes..þe saul of man may lightly spille. *c* **1375** *Cursor M.* 2902 (Fairf.), Mony mon for þaire awen wil þaire body and þaire saule wil spil. **1509** HAWES *Conv. Swearers* 29 Wo worthe couetyse that dothe your soules spyll. **1556** in W. H. Turner *Select. Rec. Oxford* (1880) 246 Other..lamented, to see him spill his soul, wretchedly. **1623** R. CARPENTER *Consc. Chr.* 110 So the least sinne..vncontrolled [is sufficient] to spill the soule.

†**c.** To injure in respect of character; to spoil morally. *Obs.*

1377 LANGL. *P. Pl.* B. v. 41 Who-so spareth þe sprynge, spilleth his children. **1393** [see SPARE *v.*[1] 6 a. *a*]. *c* **1500** *Lancelot* 1990 It stant apone thi will For to omend thi puple, or to spill; Or have thi court of vertewis folk, or fullis. **1551** ROBINSON tr. *More's Utopia* (1895) 50 Gentlemen vouchesauffe to corrupte and spill none but picked and chosen men. **1637** RUTHERFORD *Lett.* (1862) I. xcix. 254 Verily, we know not what an evil it is to spill and indulge ourselves and to make an idol of our will. **1657** R. AUSTEN *Fruit-trees* II. 84 The common saying is: Spare the rod and spill the child. **1664** [see SPARE *v.*[1] 6 a. *a*].

†**4. a.** To wreck, destroy, or devastate; to spoil or ruin by demolition, etc. *Obs.*

Freq. from *c* 1400 to *c* 1620. In first quot. *absol.*

c **950** *Lindisf. Gosp.* John x. 10 Ðeaf ne cymes buta þætte ȝestele & eteð & losað *uel* spilleð. *c* **1125** *O.E. Chron.* (Laud MS.) an. 1125, On ðes ilces ȝeares wearð swa micel flod..þet feola tunes & men weorðan adrencte,..& corn & mædwe spilt mid ealle. *c* **1225** in *Rel. Antiq.* I. 48 The strong fend..Godes hondiwerc he spilde, For on appel of the tree. *a* **1300** *Cursor M.* 720 A-ganis godd wex he sa gril þat al his werk he wend to spil. **1340** *Ayenb.* 129 Vor þou art ase þe ilke þet slepþ ine þe ssipe þet is yspild. **1412–20** LYDG. *Chron. Troy* I. 3904 Her behestes manly to fulfille, Towardis Troye, þe cite for to spille. *c* **1470** HENRY *Wallace* VIII. 731 Palyce thai spylt, gret towris can confound. **1532** HERVET *Xenoph. Househ.* 16 b, The dogges kepe away wylde beastis, that they spille not the frute. **1573** TUSSER *Husb.* (1878) 109 Let Iuie be killed, else tree will be spilled. **1608** TOPSELL *Serpents* 39 Conyza strewed, the haunt of serpents spills. **1623** C. BUTLER *Fem. Mon.* vii. Q 2, The Mother-Waspes were many at first; yet the Rainie Spring and Summer did so spill their nests, that there were no small Waspes seene till Libra.

†**b.** With immaterial object. *Obs.*

Not always clearly distinguishable from 5 d.

1382 WYCLIF *Pref. Ep. Jerome* v, Verreye wisdom shal spil the fals wisdom. **1382** —— *Gen.* xli. 31 The greetnes of myseys is to spille the greetnes of plentithe. *a* **1400** *Sir Perc.* 1336 A sadde stroke I salle one hym sett His pride for to spylle! *c* **1420** *Chron. Vilod.* 2150 þat feyndus powere y dude þo spylle By help of þo angels, þat comen me to. **1567** *Gude & Godlie B.* (S.T.S.) 134 Man, I gaif the nocht fre will, That thow suld my Gospell spill. **1602** J. DAVIES (Heref.) *Mirum in Modum* Wks. (Grosart) I. 25/2 Naturally Contraries spill each other.

5. †**a.** To despoil or deprive *of* something. *Obs.*

c **1124** *O.E. Chron.* (Laud MS.) an. 1124, Six men [wæron] spilde of here æȝon & of here stanes.

†**b.** To deprive of chastity; to violate. *Obs.*

13.. *Sir Beues* (A.) 3256 Doþ be me al ȝoure wille, Schel he neuer eft wimman spille! *c* **1375** *Sc. Leg. Saints* xi. (*Simon & Judas*) 350 [She] sad, þat he agane hir will hyre difforsit, & sa cane spill. *c* **1470** HENRY *Wallace* I. 164 Both wiffis, wedowis, thai tuk all at thair will, Nonnys, madyns, quham thai likit to spill.

c. To spoil by injuring or damaging in some way; to render imperfect or useless; to destroy the goodness or value of (a thing). Now only *dial.*

a **1300** *Cursor M.* 6774 If i lent þe suilkin beist, þat ded be or spilt at leist. **1377** LANGL. *P. Pl.* B. v. 442, [I have] yspilte many a tyme Bothe flesche & fissche and many other vitailles. *c* **1420** *Avow. Arth.* iii, On him spild I my spere, And mycule of my nothir gere. **1532–3** *Acc. Ld. High Treas. Scot.* VI. 151 Item, to him for hors spilt in the Kingis service,..xl li. **1589** PUTTENHAM *Eng. Poesie* III. i. (Arb.) 150 They not onely guie it no maner of grace at all, but rather do disfigure the stuffe and spill the whole workmanship. **1643** TRAPP *Comm. Gen.* xxxiv. 8 Too much severity overthroweth, and quite spilleth a tender minde. **1703** BRAND *Descr. Orkney, Zetland*, etc. 112 When he Brewed, he would not suffer any Sacrifice to be given to Brouny, whereupon the..Brewings were spilt and for no use. **1773** FERGUSSON *Poems* (1789) II. 43 Ae scabbit yew spills twenty flocks. **1861** GEO. ELIOT *Silas Marner* xiv, If you've got anything as can be spilt or broke,..she'll be at it. **1875–87** in dial. glossaries (Sussex, Surrey, Kent).

d. With immaterial object. *Obs.* or *dial.*

a **1300** *Cursor M.* 26841 Qua all fulfilles þe laght, and in a point it spilles, He sal be plighti for þis an. *c* **1375** *Sc. Leg. Saints* iii. (*Andrew*) 926 þat oþir worthit me do his will, or halely my purpos spill. *c* **1400** *Destr. Troy* 12736 Whille he faryn was to fight in a fer lond, Sho spilt hade hir spousaile. **1483** CAXTON *G. de la Tour* K viij b, Of her..that of her falshede..breketh and spylleth her holy sacrement of maryage. **1500–20** DUNBAR *Poems* xv. 22 He that dois all his best servyiss May spill it all..Be fowll inoportunitie. **1568** T. HOWELL *Newe Sonets* (1879) 148 She geues him leaue to range his fill, Full loth she is his sporte to spill. **1590** GREENE *Mourn. Garm.* (1616) 14 For cares cause Kings full oft their sleepe to spill. *c* **1620** HUME *Orthogr. Brit. Tongue* (1865) 22 In al quhilk, if a man change the accent, he sall spill the sound of the word. **1632** RUTHERFORD *Lett.* (1862) I. xxii. 87 If ye mar or spill that business, ye cannot come back to mend that piece of work again. **1728** RAMSAY *Robt., Richy, & Sandy* 115 These to repeat braid spoken I wad spill, Altho' I should employ my utmost skill. **1790** SHIRREFS *Poems* 92 Tak' tent..the sport ye dinna spill.

†**6. a.** To waste by scattering, squandering, or misusing; to employ or expend wastefully. *Obs.*

a **1000** *Rituale Eccl. Dunelm.* 55 Ic ȝisette ðec ofer cynno & ofer rico þæte..[ðv] to worpa & ðv spilla [L. *disperdas et dissipes*]. *c* **1200** *Trin. Coll. Hom.* 213 He..spilleð on him þat he sholde spelien wrecche men. **1308** in Ritson *Songs & Ball.* (1877) 63/96 Throgh ham this lond is ilor To spille ale ant bred. **1377** LANGL. *P. Pl.* B. v. 380 I..spilte þat myȝte be spared, and spended on somme hungrie. *c* **1460** J. RUSSELL *Bk. Nurture* 47 And to þy mastir be trew, his goodes þat þow not spille. **1533** MORE *Debell. Salem* Wks. 959/2 Euery fond piece of his diuises, wherein this good man is content to leese tyme & spyll paper. **1551** CROWLEY *Pleas. & Pain* 117 When any pore men..were so bolde to calle it yll, My landis and goodis in waste to spyll, You shet them vp in prisone strong. **1579** LYLY *Euphues* (Arb.) 109 All my treasure spente on Iewells, and spylte in iolytye. **1633** P. FLETCHER *Purple Isl.* VIII. xxix, His spear a spit, a pot-lid broad his shield..: his word, 'Much better sav'd, then spill'd'. **1728** YOUNG *Love Fame* I. 186 Men, overloaded with a large estate, May spill their treasure in a nice conceit. **1786** *Har'st Rig* 51 Nae gude I e'er kent come o' them Gude food that spill.

†**b.** To spend (time, speech, labour) fruitlessly or unprofitably; to waste. *Obs.*

(*a*) *a* **1250** *Owl & Night.* 1020 He myhte bet sytte stylle, Vor al his hwile he scolde spille. *c* **1290** *S. Eng. Leg.* I. 97 For þov nast non more ȝwile to spille, þane speke embe nouȝt. *c* **1330** R. BRUNNE *Chron. Wace* (Rolls) 9354 Al a wyke þe kyng þer lay, He spilte his tyme, sped of no pray. **1393** LANGL. *P. Pl.* C. IV. 466 Ech man to..Spynnen, and spek of god, and spille no tyme. *c* **1450** LOVELICH *Merlin* 12462 ȝe don but spillen ȝoure tyme jn veyn.

(*b*) *a* **1225** *Juliana* 24 Speche þu maht spillen ant ne speden nawiht. *a* **1250** *Owl & Night.* 1027 Ne sunge ich hom neuer so longe, Mi song were i-spild ech del. *c* **1290** *S. Eng. Leg.* I. 69 þar-aboute þou spillest þi brethþ. **1377** LANGL. *P. Pl.* B. IX. 97 He doth best, þat with-draweth hym..To spille any speche. **1390** GOWER *Conf.* I. 82 He spilleth many a word in wast That schal with such a poeple trete. **1445** in *Anglia* XXVIII. 273 Ner thou spekist not sternely to hem,..ne spillest no wynde for pride. *a* **1536** *Songs, Carols*, etc. (E.E.T.S.) 43 Leve þi sweryng, & spill not þi wynde. *a* **1586** SIDNEY *Ps.* XI. i, Since I do trust Iehoua still, Your fearfull wordes why do you spill?

(*c*) *c* **1386** CHAUCER *Manciple's T.* 153 This holde I for a verray nycetee To spille labour for to kepe wyues. *c* **1425** *Craft of Nombrynge* (E.E.T.S.) 14 Ellis þou mayst spyl alle þi laber þere aboute.

†**7. a.** *intr.* To perish; to be destroyed or lost. *Obs.*

Freq. from *c* 1300 to *c* 1550.

a **1300** *K. Horn* 194 Nu þu miȝt us slen,..Bute ȝef hit beo þi wille Helpe þat we ne spille. **1340** *Ayenb.* 182 Spilþ ofte þet ssip þet geþ zikerliche ine þe heȝe ze. *c* **1350** *Will. Palerne* 1535 Mi perles paramours, my pleye & my ioye, spek to me spakli, or i spille sone. **1414** BRAMPTON *Penit. Ps.* (Percy Soc.) 11 But, Lord! late nevere mannes soule spylle. *c* **1450** *Mirk's Festial* 13 Suche a derth and hongyr..þat all negh spylleden for defawte. *a* **1536** *Songs, Carols*, etc. (E.E.T.S.) 8 Yff thy syn be never so yll, Yet for no syn thou shalt spyll. **1592** DANIEL *Sonnets Delia* xxxvi. Wks. (Grosart) I. 61 Her sight consented thus to see me spill.

†**b.** To go to ruin. *Obs.*

a **1300** *Cursor M.* 516 Adam..was wroght þan þe tent ordir for to fullfill, þat lucifer did for to spill. **1535** STEWART *Cron. Scot.* II. 532 Seand the realme in sic ane poynt to spill. **1567** *Satir. Poems Reform.* v. 48 Bot now..Sho moste be keipit or all will spill.

†**c.** To meet with bad fortune. *Obs.*[−1]

1390 GOWER *Conf.* II. 88 And natheles gret diligence Thei setten vpon thilke dede, And spille more than thei spede.

8. To fall off or decline in respect of good qualities; to degenerate or deteriorate, to spoil. *Obs.* exc. *dial.*

? *a* **1300** *Salomon & Sat.* (1848) 271 Mote hit al habben is wille Woltou, nultou, hit wol spille, Ant bicome a fule. **13..** *K. Alis.* 1719 (Laud MS.), Alisaunder! þou conion wood, In þe spilleþ þi faye blood. **1340** *Ayenb.* 232 þet þe guodnesse of maydenhod ne spille ine þe. **1387–8** T. USK *Test. Love* I. i. (Skeat) I. 7 Thus from my comfort I ginne to spille, sith she that shulde me solace is fer fro my presence. *a* **1450** *Le Morte Arth.* 23 How your courte by-gynnyth to spill off dughty knightis all by-dene. **1540** HYRDE tr. *Vives' Instr. Chr. Wom.* (1592) Dd vj, My goods spil daily, the heritage of mine ancestry perisheth. **1574–5** *Reg. Privy Council Scot.* II. 432 That the tymmer of the Frater of the said Abbay, quhilk consumis and spillis,..be tane doun. **1808** JAMIESON s.v., Meat is said to *spill*, when it begins to become putrid.

II. 9. *trans.* To shed (blood).

a **1125** *Gosp. Nicodemus* (Cott. Vesp. D xiv) 91 b, Seo ȝebletsod se þe nolde þæt min bold wære ȝespillod [*earlier text* min blod nolde aȝeotan]. *a* **1300** *Cursor M.* 2958 þai reft þam aght and spilt þair blode. *a* **1340** HAMPOLE *Psalter* xiii. 6 Swift ere þaire fete to spill blode. *c* **1400** *Rowland & O.* 816 His hert blode he gan þer spill. **1474** CAXTON *Chesse* 41 To shede and spylle blood is the condicion of a wylde beste. **1526** *Pilgr. Perf.* (W. de W. 1531) 205 His bolde spylled and shedde on the grounde. **1595–7** DANIEL *Civ. Wars* IV. xliv. Wks. (Grosart) II. 151, I constrayned am this bloud to spill. **1638** JUNIUS *Paint. Ancients* 131 A great deal of blood would have been spilled that day between them two. *c* **1680** BEVERIDGE *Serm.* (1729) I. 506 That very blood which was spilt upon the cross. **1761** HUME *Hist. Eng.* (1806) III. 790 After spilling an ocean of blood in those theological quarrels. **1829** HOOD *Eugene Aram* xiii, Woe, woe, unutterable woe, —Who spill life's sacred stream! **1848** GALLENGA *Italy* (1851) 279 To account for the blood thus wantonly spilt. **1855** TENNYSON *Maud* II. v. x, The red life spilt for a private blow.

10. a. To allow or cause (a liquid) to fall, pour, or run out (esp. over the edge of the containing vessel), usually in an accidental or wasteful manner; to lose or waste in this way.

a **1340** HAMPOLE *Psalter* xxi. 13 þai roght na mare to sla me þan to spill watere. *c* **1340** *Nominale* (Skeat) 356 [Mau] of chirne mylke spilluth. *c* **1440** *Promp. Parv.* 469 Spyllyn, or puttyn owte (*K.* powryn owte), *effundo*. **1489** CAXTON *Faytes of A.* II. xxxvii. 155 They shall lightly spylle the watre castyng the tubbes and other vesselles dounward. **1530** PALSGR. 728/2 Who hath spylled his potage upon the boorde clothe on this facyon? **1602** MARSTON *Ant. & Mel.* v. Wks. 1856 I. 56 Holde my dish, whilst I spill my pottage. **1636** JONSON *Discov.* Wks. (Rtldg.) 750 Their arguments are as fluxive as liquor spilt upon a table. **1779** *Mirror* No. 64, Like claret spilt on a smooth table. **1794** MRS. RADCLIFFE *Myst. Udolpho* li, Emily's hand trembled, and she spilt the wine as she withdrew it from her lips. **1827** FARADAY *Chem. Manip.* i. (1842) 17 Any of the metal [*sc.* mercury] which may be spilled is swept or wiped into the groove. **1859** DICKENS *T. Two Cities* I. v, The wine had stained the ground of the narrow street..where it was spilled. **1885–94** R. BRIDGES *Eros & Psyche* July xxvi, The lamp..One drop of burning oil spill'd from its side On Eros' naked shoulder.

transf. **1818** BYRON *Ch. Har.* IV. clxxiii, The..wind..which spills The ocean o'er its boundary. **1847** TENNYSON *Princ.* VII. 197 Leave The monstrous ledges there to slope, and spill Their thousand wreaths of dangling water-smoke.

absol. **1820** SCOTT *Monast* Introd. Ep., It is difficult, saith the proverb, to carry a full cup without spilling. **1887** J. DICKIE *Wds. Faith, Hope, & Love* (1891) 197 My cup runneth over. It cannot be moved without spilling.

b. *fig.* and in fig. context.

In quot. 1574 = 'to divulge, let out'; (see sense 16 a for 20th-c. use).

1574 HELLOWES tr. *Gueuara's Fam. Ep.* (1577) 257 Although it be a shame to spill it, I will not leaue to say that which..his friends haue said vnto me. **1583** GREENE *Mamillia* Wks. (Grosart) II. 55 He doubted if he should be ouer bold, he might spill his pottage. **1650** T. B[AYLEY] *Worcester's Apoph.* Ep. Ded., That the favours which were conferr'd upon me, were not spilt, but powred into a Violl. **1701** STANHOPE *Pious Breath.* IV. xiii. 276 The love of Sin pollutes, the love of Vanity spills the Wine. **1821** SHELLEY *Adonais* xxxvii, Be thou free To spill the venom when thy fangs o'erflow. **1894** *Harper's Mag.* Feb. 380 The fat's in the fire, the milk's spilt.

c. *transf.* (See quot.)

1870 MEDBERY *Men & Myst. Wall Str.* 137 *Spilling stock*, when great quantities of a stock are thrown upon the market, sometimes from necessity, often in order to 'break' the price.

11. To scatter, esp. by emptying from some receptacle or the like; to disperse.

a **1300** *Cursor M.* 14733 Þe moneurs for þair misgilt, þair bordes [Jesus] ouerkest, þair penis spilt. *a* **1400-50** *Alexander* 1419 Spedely with spry[n]galdis [they] spilt þaire braynes. *a* **1425** tr. *Arderne's Treat. Fistula* 35 Be þe tonges warly drawen out þat þai spill noȝt þe poudre. *c* **1440** *Pallad. on Husb.* IV. 402 Or in a seriol half water fild..let hem suspende, And close hit fast, in wynde lest they be spild. **1710** PHILIPS *Pastorals* IV. 72 As ruthless Winds the tender Blossoms spill. **1825** T. HOOK *Sayings* Ser. II. *Man of Many Fr.* I. 189 She is spilling all the sugar all over the table. **1847** TENNYSON *Princ.* IV. 511 Better have died and spilt our bones in the flood.

transf. **1854** MRS. BROWNING *Ragged Sch. Lond.* xii, But these others—children small, Spilt like blots about the city.

12. a. To cover or overlay *with* something by (or as by) spilling. *rare.*

1596 SPENSER *F.Q.* IV. x. 5 Though..all the others pauement were with yuory spilt. **1895** BARING-GOULD *Noémi* xxiv. (ed. 2) 336 The clouds were dispersing..; the floor of heaven was, as it were, spilt over with curds. **1918** D. H. LAWRENCE *New Poems* 30 In the street spilled over splendidly With wet, flat lights.

b. To empty (a cup, etc.) by spilling. *rare.*

1886 J. DICKIE *Wds. Faith, Hope, & Love* (1891) 147 'Twas anguish when earth's cup was spill'd.

13. *Naut.* **a.** To empty (a sail) of wind.

a **1625** *Nomenclator Nav.* (Harl. MS. 2301), When a sail hath much winde in it..we saie Spill the saile, which is done by letting goe the sheats and bowlings, &c. **1633** T. JAMES *Voy.* 95 The rest stood to spill and fill the sayle. *a* **1691** SIR D. NORTH in North *Lives* (1744) 15 He was sure to be duck'd that was at the Yard-arm spilling the Sail. **1769** FALCONER *Dict. Marine* (1780), *To Spill*, to discharge the wind out of the cavity or belly of a sail when it is drawn up in the brails in order to furl or reef it. **1867** SMYTH *Sailor's Word-bk.* 565 When the wind was going free, and the sail could not be 'spilled'. **1899** F. T. BULLEN *Log Sea-waif* 190 She.. rounded-to under our stern and 'spilled' her sail.

b. To discharge (wind) from the belly of a sail, or air from a parachute.

1875 KNIGHT *Dict. Mech.* 2268/1 *Spilling-line*, a line to spill the wind out of a sail, by keeping it from bellying out when clewed up. **1899** *Daily News* 20 Oct. 5/7 His club-topsail began to spill wind badly, and he gained nothing. **1925** *Literary Digest* 11 July 25/1 Used as a dividing mark in folding the parachute, and also to 'spill' the wind out of it after a landing. **1942** A. M. LOW *Parachutes in Peace & War* iii. 48 The parachute might 'spill air' & drop faster. **1976** A. WHITE *Long Silence* vii. 59 Spill air, ride the motion down as rapidly as is safe. Look around..trying to make out the other parachutes.

14. *colloq.* **a.** To cause to fall from a horse or vehicle; to throw or throw out.

1731-8 SWIFT *Polite Conv.* 70 The road was so bad that I ..call'd to the Coachman, Pray, Friend, don't spill us. **1785** GROSE *Dict. Vulgar T.*, *Spilt*, thrown from a horse, or over-turned in a carriage; pray coachee don't spill us. **1809** *European Mag.* LV. 20 The parson..met with a serious accident in being spilt from his horse. **1821** BYRON *Lett.* Wks. 1833 III. 301 Riding pretty sharply.., in turning the corner of a lane.., he was spilt. **1887** H. SMART *Cleverly Won* iii, It was a trick that might have spilled a practised horseman.

b. Similarly in other contexts. Also with *out.*

1850 SCORESBY *Cheever's Whalem. Adv.* vi. 82 He..spills us all at once into the sea. **1861** S. BROOKS *Silver Cord* xxvii, 'Mop, you old fool, will you come down?' said the manager, spilling out the reluctant animal [from the chair] to the ground. **1881** *Scribner's Monthly* XXII. 536/1 She [the ice-yacht] slows up and heels over,..and she quietly spills the crew out of the box.

fig. **1888** *Pall Mall G.* 29 Nov. 1/1 An intrigue..to spill Sir Charles and then to secure Mr. Monro's appointment to the vacant post.

15. a. *intr.* To flow or run over the brim or side; to escape or be wasted in this manner. Freq. with preps. and advs. Also *fig.*

1655 VAUGHAN *Silex Scint.* II. 174 Life without thee is loose and spills. **1683** MOXON *Mech. Exerc., Printing* xix. ¶ 1 The Mettal may spill or slabber over the Mouth of..the Mold. **1741** WATTS *Improv. Mind* I. ix. Wks. 1753 V. 238 He was so top-full of himself, that he let it spill on all the company;..he spoke too long. **1771** *Phil. Trans.* LXI. 496 To prevent the liquor from spilling when poured out. **1875** KNIGHT *Dict. Mech.* 2268/1 Any metal which dribbles or spills is caught into the spill trough. **1899** F. H. KING *Irrigation & Drainage* vi. 246 A long, sharp lip, over which the water may spill back into the canal.

transf. **1884** BURROUGHS *Pepacton* 217 Its body slumps off, and rolls and spills down the hill. **1900** *Cent. Mag.* Feb. 510/1 The reaches of this majestic range run south..until they spill out in the far Southwest. **1920** H. CRANE *Let.* 14 Apr. (1965) 37 A mood which rose and spilled over in a slightly cruder form than what you see. **1962** *Amer. Speech* XXXVII. 17 The metropolitan area of New York City..has spilled into the surrounding countryside, engulfing cities and communities which had their own economic and cultural centers. **1962** A. NISBETT *Technique of Sound Studio* iv. 84 Where a tape has spilled and wound round the spindle and become crumpled, speech recordings are often still playable. **1972** B. MOORE *Catholics* i. 17 An anchor spilled like entrails from its bow, falling deep into the sea. **1976** *Times* 10 Sept. 1/6 Cape riots spill into white zones. The anti-apartheid rioting spilled out of Cape Town and spread into white areas of Cape Province. **1976** P. & W. PROCTOR *Women in Pulpit* vii. 124 Although Connie Parvey is primarily a campus chaplain, her work in this case spilled over into the role of hospital chaplain.

b. *Naut.* To empty or become void of wind.

1762 FALCONER *Shipwr.* II. 139 Till close embrail'd, and squar'd, the belly spills. **1833** MARRYAT *P. Simple* xv. (1863) 103 The ship turned slowly to the wind, pitching and chopping as the sails were spilling.

16. a. *trans.* To utter (words); to confess or divulge (facts). *slang* (orig. *U.S.*).

[**1574**: see sense 10b.] **1917** R. W. LARDNER *Gullible's Travels* 213 'Go ahead and spill it,' I says. **1920** C. SANDBURG *Smoke & Steel* 44 Men at tables spill Peloponnesian syllables. **1923** 'B. M. BOWER' *Parowan Bonanza* iv. 47 Maybe he taught the parrot that lingo just to have her spill it in town and start a rush. **1925** E. WALLACE *King by Night* xxxi. 143 Spill it quick, Goldy. **1944** [see OIL *sb.*[1] 3j]. **1953** K. TENNANT *Joyful Condemned* xxiv. 233 She was going to spill everything to him..She would have pooled you, too. **1973** 'B. MATHER' *Snowline* vi. 70 You didn't come down here.. just to tempt me..with a beer. Spill it. **1977** I. SHAW *Beggarman, Thief* II. i. 119 He picked up the phone to call the Colonel, spill everything.

b. *to spill the beans*: to reveal a secret. *slang* (orig. *U.S.*).

1919 T. K. HOLMES *Man from Tall Timber* xxviii. 355 'Mother certainly has spilled the beans!' thought Stafford in vast amusement. **1921** R. D. PAINE *Comr. Rolling Ocean* viii. 136 The beans are spilled, and that is what Maddigan guessed the moment he set eyes on you. **1928** [see CLEAN *a.* 3g]. **1929** E. LINKLATER *Poet's Pub* vii. 91 'Tell me the truth,' she says. 'Spill the beans, Holly, old man!' **1945** *Sun* (Baltimore) 28 Nov. 1/1 A Government publication in this country spilled the beans concerning our urgent interest in experiments with uranium. **1958** E. DUNDY *Dud Avocado* I. vi. 93 Spilling beans of shattering truths or equally shattering lies. **1966** D. VARADAY *Gara-Yaka's Domain* vii. 82 Wilson in an indulgent moment of weakness 'spilt the beans'. **1979** G. HAMMOND *Dead Game* vii. 83 You asked me to trust you... So now I think you'd better spill the beans. **1982** *Listener* 23-30 Dec. 3/1 Julian Critchley spills the beans about El Vino and says why he likes it.

c. *to spill one's guts* (*out*): to divulge as much as one can, to confess. *slang* (chiefly *U.S.*).

1927 C. F. COE *Me—Gangster* iv. 78 'Throw him out, eh?' the old man snarled... 'Throw him out an' have him spill his guts about the whole gang?' **1945** S. J. BAKER *Austral. Lang.* vii. 140 *To hold one's guts*, to be silent, and *to spill one's guts*, to talk, reveal a secret. **1973** *Black Panther* 8 Sept. 10/3 Mistakenly believing that Haldeman and another assistant had told the truth during previous questioning, Butterfield spilled his guts out. **1979** 'A. HAILEY' *Overload* III. viii. 226 The kid—he was eighteen, by the way, and not long out of trade school—broke down and spilled his guts.

spill- (spɪl), the stem of SPILL *v.* in combination.

†**1.** In the sense 'that spoils, mars, destroys, or wastes', as ***spill-berry***, ***-bread***, ***-cause***, ***-good***, ***-love***, ***-pain*** (= bread), ***-soul***, ***-time***. *Obs.*

c **1563** *Thersites* in *Four Old Pl.* (1848) 82 The spere of spanysshe *spylbery sprente wt spiteful spottes. *c* **1320** in *Rel. Antiq.* I. 122 My wyf that shulde be;..Hue clepeth me *spille-bred. **1566** *Pasquine in Traunce* 64 Doe they use Bartolus, and Baldus, and such other *spill causes to set men togither by the eares? **1626** MINSHEU 683/1 *Spill-good, *vi[de]* Spend-thrift. **1377** LANGL. *P. Pl.* B. XIX. 336 [Pride] sente forth..his spye *spille-loue, one speke-yuel-byhynde. *c* **1460** *Towneley Myst.* xxiv. 124 *Secundus tortor.* *Spyll-payn in fayth I hight. **1591** FRAUNCE *C'tess Pembroke's Yuychurch* I. Cj, So sore inchaunted with *spill-soule spells. **1393** LANGL. *P. Pl.* C. VI. 28 An ydel man þow semest,.. oþer a *spille-tyme.

2. *dial.* In the sense 'spoilt', as *spill-wood.*

1847 HALLIWELL, *Spilwood*, refuse of wood, or wood *spilt* by the sawyers. *South.* **1852-83** in Hampshire and Sussex glossaries.

3. In the sense 'constructed for (or by) the passage of surplus water, for receiving overflow liquid, etc.', as ***spill-back***, ***-box***, ***channel***, ***stream***, ***-trough***, ***-water***; **spillbank** (see quot. 1961). See also SPILLWAY.

1899 F. H. KING *Irrigation & Drainage* vi. 247 The depth of the water over the lip of the *spill-back. **1909** H. M. WILSON *Irrigation Engin.* (ed. 6) xix. 560 The material brought up by these [buckets] is deposited on one of two endless belt-carriers running on booms which dump it on either *spillbank. **1961** L. D. STAMP *Gloss. Geogr. Terms* 427/2 Spill-bank is the term used by British and Indian engineers engaged in river training for the bank of coarse alluvium spilled over by a river in flood (C. C. Inglis). **1899** F. H. KING *Irrigation & Drainage* vi. 245 The *spill-box.. is, perhaps, as satisfactory a means for maintaining a nearly uniform head against..an opening as has yet been devised. **1888** *19th Cent.* Jan. 43 The Bhagirathi,..for centuries a mere *spill-stream from the parent Ganges. **1843** HOLTZAPFFEL *Turning* I. 327 The flask..is put on the surface of the pouring or *spill-trough. **1875** KNIGHT *Dict. Mech.* 2268/1 *Spill-trough*, (Brass-founding), the trough against which the inclined flask rests while the metal is being poured from the crucible. **1852** BURN *Techn. Dict.* II. s.v., *Spill-water, *réservoir, excavation pour recevoir les inondations d'une rivière.* **1875** ALEX. SMITH *New Hist. Aberdeen* I. 75 The Commissioners resolved to make..a spill-water to the south of the harbour.

4. In the sense 'that empties by spilling', as ***spillbucket.***

1938 L. MACNEICE *Earth Compels* 20 Bric-a-brac Pick-a-back *Spillbucket Splits.

spillage (ˈspɪlɪdʒ). [f. SPILL *v.* + -AGE.] The action or fact of spilling; that which spills or is spilt. Also *attrib.*

1934 WEBSTER, *Spillage*.., the act of spilling; that which spills or is spilled over; as, a trough to divert any *spillage.* **1937** *Times* 9 Oct. 9/6 A miner..was trapped underground by a fall of rock and completely buried. Dr. Saunders arrived at 3.15 p.m., by which time the rescue party had removed most of the spillage from the imprisoned man's body. **1947** *Sun* (Baltimore) 26 June 8/1 Recent oil spillages in and near Baltimore harbor have resulted in great annoyance to bathers. **1962** A. NISBETT *Technique of Sound Studio* vii. 128 Remember also when handling music tapes that any damage due to spillage or stretching, etc., will be more noticeable than on speech tapes. **1963** *Daily Mail* 15 May 4/4 On every bottle of brandy sold in the Hilton, two and two-thirds ounces are written off for 'spillage'. **1969** *Gloss. Aeronaut. & Astronaut. Terms (B.S.I.)* IV. 3 *Spillage drag*, the difference beween the drag at a given intake flow and the drag at some specified intake flow. *Ibid.* 4 *Spillage*, the amount by which the intake flow is less than some specified intake flow. **1969** *Daily Tel.* 30 Aug. 12/6 A pesticide spillage has killed 11,000 fish in the South Holland Drain. **1972** *Ibid.* 14 Apr. 19/3 A glass is often placed beneath the tap as a substitute for the drip tray and used for topping up... The patron should ensure that he rejects any beer which contains a mixture of this spillage. **1973** *Times* 30 July 11/2 If you spill anything you simply move your saucepan to another burner, lift off the support, and underneath there is a spillage bowl which has collected what has boiled over and which has only to be taken out and rinsed. **1976** *Washington Post* 23 Jan. A 14/4 Accidents are caused by drivers trying to avoid rock spillage..on the Beltway. **1976** *Offshore Platforms & Pipelining* 222/1 The utmost attention was given to reducing the risk of oil spillage during operations. **1976** *Cambridge Independent Press* 16 Dec. II. 7 (Advt.), Family-size oven with 'Cook Clean' panels... Hob light, auto-timer, slide-out spillage trays. **1977** *R.A.F. News* 27 Apr.-10 May 3/4 Allegations that excessive 'spillage' drag from the engine intakes will seriously impair Tornado's performance, particularly at high angles of incidence in the transonic speed range, were refuted.

spillard: see SPILLER *sb.*[3] and *v.*

spilled (spɪld), *ppl. a.* [f. SPILL *v.* + -ED[1].] = SPILT *ppl. a.*

1574 HELLOWES tr. *Gueuara's Fam. Ep.* (1577) 24 If they by chaunce found spild bread, rotten wheat..and such other things spoyled. **1865** DICKENS *Mut. Fr.* III. xii, If we could have packed the brute off with Georgiana;—but however; that's spilled milk. **1880** CABLE *Grandissimes* xiii, She had begun to sweep up some spilled buttons.

spiller (ˈspɪlə(r)), *sb.*[1] [f. SPILL *v.* + -ER[1].] One who sheds or spills; *esp.* a shedder of blood.

1530 PALSGR. 266/2 Schedar, a spyller, *respandevr.* **1592** WYRLEY *Armorie* 137 Blouds wilfull spiller seld doth mercie finde. **1611** COTGR., *Respandeur*, a shedder, a spiller. **1647** HEXHAM I. s.v. *Blood*, A spiller of Bloud, *een bloed-storter.* **1755** JOHNSON, *Shedder*, a spiller; one who sheds. **1775-** in ASH and later Dicts. **1899** *Westm. Gaz.* 9 Feb. 2/1 A mighty hunter, a spiller of life-blood.

spiller, *sb.*[2] *Obs.* exc. *arch.* [Alteration of SPELLER[3].] A branchlet on a deer's horn.

1590 COKAINE *Treat. Hunting* Dj, Some [bucks]..are plaine palmed without any aduauncers, with long spillers out behinde. **1660** HOWELL *Parly of Beasts* 62 Such silly coxcombs..deserve to wear such branch'd horns, such spilters [*sic*] and trochings on their heads, as that goodly Stagg bears. **1727** BAILEY (vol. II), *Spillers*, the small Branches shooting out from the flat Parts of a Buck's Horn at the Top. **1827** GRIFFITH tr. *Cuvier* IV. 85 Additional advancers and spillers, or snags on the anterior or posterior parts of the palm. **1864** *Reader* 23 Jan. 112/3 The spillers into which the palm divides were directed exteriorly, as in the reindeer and the fallow-deer.

spiller (ˈspɪlə(r)), *sb.*[3] Chiefly *Cornish dial.*, *Ir.*, and *Amer.* Also 9 **spillard** (**spilliard**). [Of obscure origin.]

1. A long fishing-line provided with a number of hooks; a trawl-line.

1602 CAREW *Cornwall* 31 b, In Harbor Eeles are taken mostly by Spillers made of a Cord..to which diuers lesser and shorter are tyed at a little distance, and to each of these a hooke is fastened with a bayt. *Ibid.*, This Spiller they sincke in the Sea. **1836** *1st Rep. Irish Fisheries* 151 The line and spillards are the modes of fishing chiefly practised. **1851** *Voy. Mauritius* iv. 160 A line some hundred yards in length, from which depend shorter lines, like an Irish 'spiller'. **1875** *Zoologist* 2nd Ser. X. 4500 A specimen of the torpedo.. caught on spillers (hook and line)..near Lamorna [in Cornwall].

attrib. **1836** *1st Rep. Irish Fisheries* 151 The long line, hand line, and spillard fishing grounds. **1900** C. LEE *Cynthia* 81 A group of men..baiting spiller-hooks with cuttle.

2. 'In the mackerel-fishery, a seine inserted into a larger seine to take out the fish.' Also *attrib.*

1884 *Bull. U.S. Nat. Museum* No. 27. 998 Mackerel pocket or spiller... The pocket was introduced into the mackerel-seine fishery in 1878 for holding the surplus catch which would otherwise spoil before being cleaned and salted. *a* **1891** in Nova Scotian use (*Cent. Dict.*). **1891** *Pall Mall G.* 10 Sept. 4/1 Supplementing the spring and autumn mackerel fishery by line and spiller seine and trammel with ordinary trawlings.

Hence **spiller** *v. intr.*, to fish with spillers.

1836 *1st Rep. Irish Fisheries* 151 Long line fishing, which is a kind of spillarding, is generally practised in hookers.

spiller (ˈspɪlə(r)), *sb.*[4] [f. SPILL *sb.*[1] + -ER[1].] = SPILL *sb.*[1] 2 a.

1936 M. MITCHELL *Gone with Wind* 71 Pork took a long spiller from the mantelpiece, lit it from the lamp flame and went into the hall.

spillet (ˈspɪlɪt). *Ir.* (and *Sc.*). [var. of SPILLER *sb.*[3]] = SPILLER *sb.*[3] 1. Also *Comb.*

1832 W. H. MAXWELL *Wild Sp. West* I. 262 If you shoot in foul ground, you will probably lose the spillet. **1858** SIMMONDS *Dict. Trade*, *Spillet-fishing*,..a name on the west coast of Ireland for a system of fishing [etc.]. **1875** *Zoologist*

2nd Ser. X. 4502 Having shot their spillets (or long lines) in the morning.

Hence **spille'teer**, one who spillers.

1832 W. H. MAXWELL *Wild Sp. West* I. 263 An indistinct glance of a dark object..brings the assistant spilleteer, gaff in hand, to the quarter.

† **spill-house.** *Obs.*$^{-1}$ [ad. Du. *speelhuis* or G. *spielhaus*.] A gaming house.

1778 EARL MALMESBURY *Diaries & Corr.* I. 181 All the French in London were sent to the..coffee-houses, ale-houses, and spill-houses to publish the intelligence.

spillikin (ˈspɪlɪkɪn), **spellican** (ˈspɛlɪkən). Forms: α. 8 **spilakee**, 9 **spilleken**, **-ekin**, **-acan**, 8– **spillikin**, 9 **-iken**, **spilikin**. β. 9 **spel(l)ican**, **spelekin**. [app. a diminutive of SPILL *sb.*[1]]

1. a. *pl.* A game played with a heap of slips or small rods of wood, bone, or the like, the object being to pull off each by means of a hook without disturbing the rest.

α. **1734** MRS. DELANY *Life & Corr.* (1861) III. 211 Your busyness done, and you at ease To take your game at spilakees. **1800** MAR. EDGEWORTH *Belinda* xix, Belinda was playing with little Charles Percival at spillikins. **1864** MISS YONGE *Trial* I. 173 In the nursery he was, playing at spillekens with his left hand. **1884** *Punch* 16 Feb. 73/2, I have heard that the Bishops play Spilikins for cups of tea. β. **1869** MISS MONTGOMERY *Misunderstood* xi. 211 Eagerly waiting for his game of 'Spelicans'. **1896** BEARDSLEY *Under the Hill* (1904) 17 Spiridion..looked up from his game of Spellicans and trembled.

b. One of the slips with which this is played.

1883 MRS. R. T. RITCHIE *Bk. Sibyls* iv. 220 The spillikens lie in an even ring where she had thrown them. **1890** HALLETT *Thousand Miles on Elephant* 251 Dead bamboos lay like spellicans cast about in every direction.

2. (See quot.)

1858 SIMMONDS *Dict. Trade, Spillikins*, pegs of wood bone or ivory, for marking the score of cribbage or other games.

3. *fig.* In *pl.*, Splinters; fragments. Also in sing.

1857 READE *White Lies* III. ix. 127 The shot..knocked him into spillekins. **1886** *Illustr. Lond. News* 3 July 2/1, I do not want to see the British empire split into spillikins. **1907** E. GOSSE *Father & Son* ii. 50 My nerves were a packet of spilikins. **1940** W. DE LA MARE *Pleasures & Speculations* 71 No fine shades of psychology, or ethical spellicans are here. **1945** —— *Burning-Glass* 44 To ponder upon a moth..A spelican from his palm.

4. *attrib.*, as ***spillikin-heap***, ***twig***, etc.

1860 *Zoologist* XVIII. 7060 Stepping cautiously and delicately over the spillacan twigs, like a Catholic priest in a crowded thoroughfare. **1891** V. C. COTES *Two Girls on Barge* 119 Not frivolous tea in a Sévres eggshell with a spellican development of spoon. **1900** *Blackw. Mag.* July 57/1 We became involved in a spillikin-heap of cross-purposes.

'spilling, *vbl. sb.*[1] [f. SPILL *v.* + -ING[1].]

† **1.** The action of destroying, spoiling, or marring.

a **1122** *O.E. Chron.* (Laud MS.) an. 999, Ne beheold hit nan þing..buton folces ʒeswinc & feos spilling. *c* **1440** *Promp. Parv.* 469 Spyllynge, or lesynge or schendynge, *confusio, deperdicio*. **1496** *Acc. Ld. High Treas. Scot.* I. 270 For spilling of his hous in Striuiling be the Abbot of Vnresoun. **1600** *Gowrie Consp.* A iv, Commanding him.. that hee should not spare for spilling of his horse. **1647** HEXHAM I, A spilling, spoiling, or marring.

† **2.** Wasting; wasteful employment. *Obs.*

c **1380** *Sir Ferumb.* 5425 Wan þay were to-gadre y-met, Spillyng of speche þar was gret y-mad bytwene hem þanne.

3. a. The action of causing to flow or run out wastefully; shedding; effusion.

a **1340** HAMPOLE *Psalter* xxix. 11 What profit is in spillynge of my blode? **1375** BARBOUR *Bruce* XIII. 19 The battale thair so felloune was, And sua richt gret spilling of blud. *c* **1440** CAPGRAVE *Life St. Kath.* v. 1631 He is cause of spillyng of mekel gentel blood. **1483** *Cath. Angl.* 355/1 A Spyllynge, *perfusio*. **1593** SHAKS. *Lucr.* 1236 One justly weeps; the other takes in hand No cause, but company, of her drops spilling. **1623** COCKERAM II, A Spilling commonly of blood, *effusion*. **1844** TUPPER *Crock of G.* xlviii. 314 About a thimbleful of water, after fifty spillings, arrived safely in a tumbler.

b. With advs., as *out*, *over*. Also *transf.*

1883 E. H. ROLLINS *New Eng. Bygones* 36 The daily spilling-out from the doors of family life. **1909** J. STUART *Burma thro' Cent.* i. 9 The spilling over from the kingdom.. of Yunnan probably began fully two thousand years ago.

c. The action of causing air to escape from a parachute; also such an escape of air.

1930 *Flight* 11 July 784/2 As usual, he judged his distance perfectly, and by judicious 'spilling' landed right in front of the club enclosure. **1951** *Gloss. Aeronaut. Terms (B.S.I.)* III. 15 *Spilling*, the escape of air, with local partial collapse, at the periphery of a parachute canopy, caused either by the instability of the parachute or by side-slipping.

4. *pl.* That which is spilt.

1772–3 *Act 13 Geo. III*, c. 52 §6 The other four grains shall be allowed him towards his waste and spillings in making the said assays. **1800** COLQUHOUN *Comm. Thames* iii. 99 The evil practice of staving Casks..to enlarge the quantity of spillings of Sugar, Coffee, &c. **1825** T. HOOK *Sayings* Ser. II. *Passion & Princ.* vi, Sundry circular deposits of ale and porter, the accidental spillings of last night's carouse. **1841** DICKENS *Barn. Rudge* xv, They trace the spillings of full pitchers on the heated ground.

5. *attrib.* and *Comb.*, as ***spilling-place***; **spilling-line**, *Naut.* (see quots. 1769, 1882); **spilling-staysail**, a sail controlled by a spilling-line.

1706 STEVENS *Span. Dict.* I, *Derramadero*, a scattering, or spilling place. **1762** FALCONER *Shipwr.* II. 314 High o'er the lee yard-arm the canvas swell'd; By spilling lines embraced, with brails confined. **1769** —— *Dict. Marine* (1780), *Spilling-lines*,..ropes fixed occasionally to the main-sail and fore-sail of a ship,..for reefing or furling them more conveniently. **1840** R. H. DANA *Bef. Mast.* xxxi, Reef-tackles were rove to the courses, and spilling lines to the topsails. **1851** KIPPING *Sailmaking* (ed. 2) 5 There are.. sometimes a mizen-royal-staysail, and main-spilling-staysail. **1882** NARES *Seamanship* (ed. 6) 125 The spilling lines..are small pieces of rope fitted on the fore side of the sail for picking up the reef line in reefing topsails.

'spilling, *vbl. sb.*[2] *Min.* [f. SPILL *sb.*[1] 4.] (See quot.)

1881 RAYMOND *Mining Gloss.*, *Spilling*, Corn[wall], a process of driving or sinking through very loose ground.

spillover (ˈspɪləʊvə(r)), *sb.* and *a.* Also **spill-over**. [f. SPILL- + OVER *adv.*] **A.** *sb.* That which spills over; the process of spilling over; (an) incidental development; a consequence, a repercussion, a by-product.

1940 [see KAROK]. **1949** *Richmond* (Va.) *Times-Dispatch* 6 Oct. 26/1 A rush to buy got under way as soon as the opening bell sounded. This was evidently a spillover from yesterday when the market established a new high for the year. **1957** J. I. M. STEWART *James Joyce* 10 This has no relevance to the action, and is a spill-over from Joyce's more openly autobiographical writing in the history of Dedalus. **1957** P. WORSLEY *Trumpet shall Sound* 269 Weber..looks for the source of change in social tensions..; the danger of resentment of disciplinary authority..; or the spill-over into irrational channels of affect which is not absorbed by the rational order. **1962** *Lancet* 12 May 1009/1, 32 patients had pulmonary disease preoperatively, presumably owing to 'spill-over', and only in those with chronic pulmonary suppuration did this fail to clear up. **1970** *Daily Colonist* (Victoria, B.C.) 11 Nov. 3/5 The threat to Canadian security possibly being greater from a spillover of violence and the potential of anarchy in the streets. **1971** *Gloss. Electrotechnical, Power Terms (B.S.I.)* III. ii. 27 *Spill-over*, in a.c. signalling on multi-link connections, that part of a signal which passes from one section to another before the connection between the sections is split. **1973** 'D. HALLIDAY' *Dolly & Starry Bird* vii. 97 The revolver was pointed straight at my head... I wasn't keen on the spillover into small arms. **1977** *New Yorker* 26 Sept. 66/3 The continuing rise in crime, its increasing spillover into the white community, and the failure of our criminal justice system..have created apprehension. **1979** *United States 1980/81* (Penguin Travel Guides) 309 Soho is a very livable combination of 19th-century cast-iron buildings, spillovers from Little Italy. **1980** *Times Lit. Suppl.* 5 Sept. 965/5 What economists call 'spillovers'—those unwanted side-effects, incidental to the legitimate production and use of man-made goods, that are familiar to the public as pollution, noise, congestion and other pervasive hazards and disadvantages.

B. *attrib.* or as *adj.* That results from spilling over; incidentally developed.

1953 J. S. HUXLEY *Evolution in Action* iv. 96 The nervous excitation spills over and is discharged into another channel, that of digging a nest hole. Such irrelevant spill-over activities are called displacement activities. **1961** *Listener* 2 Nov. 692/2 It is always experimental (and exciting) to work on the basis of 'spillover' audiences, and place a known 'difficult' programme immediately after a known winner. **1967** *Spectator* 14 July 44/1 With the postwar growth of technology and population these disservices or 'spillover effects'..have become too conspicuous to be ignored. **1971** *Physics Bull.* Nov. 654/2 The tilting of the subreflection of a Cassegrain antenna with the object of redirecting spillover radiation away from warm earth regions, has considerable geometric optical consequences. **1981** *Times* 31 July 19/1 If the United States slips into recession the spill-over effect could hamper what appears to be a slow recovery in the world chemical industry.

spillspilling (ˈspɪlspɪlɪŋ), *ppl. a.* *nonce-wd.* [Redupl. f. SPILL *v.*: see -ING[2].] Repeatedly spilling.

1922 JOYCE *Ulysses* 439 Advances with a tilted dish of spillspilling gravy.

spillway (ˈspɪlweɪ). Also **spill-way**. [f. SPILL- + WAY *sb.*[1]] **1. a.** A channel or slope built to carry away surplus water from a reservoir.

1889 *Pall Mall G.* 26 June 1/3 The by-wash, or, as the Americans term it, the spill-way was utterly insufficient. **1892** *Trans. Amer. Soc. Civil Eng.* XXVI. 640 The weir.. consisted partly of *stortebed* or spillway. **1943** J. S. HUXLEY *TVA* xi. 83 The road bridge across the spillway..became part of a bold composition finishing on a strong horizontal line and broken only by the small scale tower of the lift shaft. **1962** R. B. FULLER *Epic Poem on Industrialization* 133 It was but a warning trickle down the spillway Of the cosmic power dam. **1979** *United States 1980/81* (Penguin Travel Guides) 611 The world's largest concrete dam..has a spillway twice as high as Niagara Falls.

b. *Physical Geogr.* A natural feature providing a channel for the overflow or escape of water from a lake.

1914 DAVID & PRIESTLEY *Brit. Antarctic Exped. 1907–9 Rep. on Sci. Investigations* I. i. 5 At intervals the horst is breached by valleys..which form outlets, 'by-washes', or 'spillways' for the surplus inland ice and snow. **1929** C. R. LONGWELL *Pirsson's Textbk. Geol.* (ed. 3) I. vii. 156 Each of the lakes..has streams or springs flowing into it, and an outlet or spillway determined by the lowest point in the rim of the containing basin. **1957** G. E. HUTCHINSON *Treat. Limnol.* I. i. 80 When the ice had fully retreated, spillways to the west were established. **1971** *Nature* 3 Sept. 34/2 The latter [*sc.* a gorge] may have operated for a time as a spillway from a glacial lake covering the upper part of the Chew valley.

2. *attrib.*, as ***spillway dam***.

1913 P. A. M. PARKER *Control of Water* vii. 415 We find in spillway dams, that such damage as occurs is apparently due to a partial vacuum induced by the flowing water. **1951** W. F. HEALD *Scenic Guide Oregon* 11 The spillway dam, 1450 feet long crosses the north channel.

'spilly, *a.* *techn.* [f. SPILL *sb.*[1] 1 b.] Of iron: Exhibiting spills or dirty seams.

1843 HOLTZAPFFEL *Turning* I. 207 Some..twist the iron before the hammering to prevent it from becoming 'spilly'.

'spilosite. *Min.* [f. Gr. σπίλος spot, speck + -ITE[1] 2 b.] (See quot. 1885).

1882 GEIKIE *Text-Bk. Geol.* IV. viii. 578 Fleckschiefer, Bandschiefer,..the spilosite and desmosite of Zincken. **1885** *Ibid.* (ed. 2) II. ii. 127 Spilosite is a greenish, schistose rock, composed of finely granular or compact felspathic material, with small chlorite concretions or scales. **1895** L. FLETCHER *Introd. Study Rocks* (1898) Index 118/1.

† **spilquern.** *Obs.*$^{-0}$ In 4 **-querene**. [Cf. SPILCOCK.] A whirligig or top.

c **1375** *Gloss.* in *Rel. Antiq.* I. 9 *Giraculum, quidam ludus puerorum*, a spilquerene.

† **spilt,** *sb.* *Obs.*$^{-1}$ [Cf. SPILL *sb.*[1]] A splinter.

1577–87 HOLINSHED *Chron.* III. 1185/1 He was striken on the viser with a lance,..the spilts entring by the sight of his headpeece.

spilt, obs. form of SPELT *sb.*[1]

spilt (spɪlt), *ppl. a.* [f. SPILL *v.* Cf. SPILLED *ppl. a.*]

† **1. a.** Spoiled, ruined; destroyed. *Obs.*

c **1400** *Destr. Troy* 4060 Menelay the mighty..sped hym fro Spart his awne spilte rewme. *Ibid.* 10131 A space for his spilt men spedely to graue.

b. *Sc.* Rendered unwholesome or unfit for food through being kept too long.

1595 DUNCAN *App. Etym.* (E.D.S.), *Rancida caro*, spilt flesh. *Ibid.*, *Vappa*, spilt wine. **1887** *Scott. Leader* 11 Oct. 5/1 Selling 'Spilt' Pears. *Ibid.*, Dr. Anderson stated that ..'spilt' pears were unwholesome.

2. a. Of a liquid: That has been allowed to flow over or run out, *esp.* in an accidental or wasteful manner. Also with *out*, and in fig. context.

1483 *Cath. Angl.* 355/1 Spyllt, *butus*, *perfusus*. **1636** B. JONSON *Discov.* Wks. (Rtldg.) 743 Of this spilt water, there is a little to be gathered up: it is a desperate debt. **1683** MOXON *Mech. Exerc.*, *Printing* xix. ¶ 1 The spilt Mettal sticking about the out-sides of the Mouth. **1718** RAMSAY *Christ's Kirk Gr.* III. xiii, Boord, and floor, and a' did sail, Wi' spilt ale i' the dark. **1837** CARLYLE *Fr. Rev.* I. I. x, His words are like spilt water. **1859** DICKENS *T. Two Cities* I. v, Is all the spilt wine swallowed? **1881** O. WILDE *Poems* 149 The heart of the lotus drenched..With the spilt-out blood of the rose-red wine. **1939** DYLAN THOMAS *Map of Love* 11 Carved birds blunt their striking throats on the salt gravel, Pierce the spilt sky with diving wing in weed and heel An inch in froth.

b. ***to cry over spilt milk*** (or †***water***), or variants of this: To fret about some loss, mistake, etc., which cannot be remedied.

1738 SWIFT *Polite Conv.* I. 27 'Tis a Folly to cry for spilt Milk. **1828** J. NEAL *Rachel Dyer* xx. 248, I pity you both, but there's no help for you now—never cry for spilt milk. **1836** HALIBURTON *Clockm.* Ser. I. xxx, What's done, Sam, can't be helped, there is no use in cryin over spilt milk. **1849** ROBERTSON *Serm.* Ser. I. iv. (1866) 76 Not stop..to weep over spilt water. **1860** TROLLOPE *Castle Richmond* I. vi. 113 It's no use sighing after spilt milk.

† **spilter.** *Obs.*$^{-1}$ [Cf. SPILT *sb.*] A splinter or fragment.

? **1646** EARL MONM. tr. *Biondi's Civil Wars* v. 171 A peece of Ordnance bursting in two, a spilter thereof slew him.

spilter, error for SPILLER *sb.*[2]

spilth (spɪlθ). [f. SPILL *v.* + -TH[1] a.] That which is spilled; the action or fact of spilling.

1607 SHAKS. *Timon* II. ii. 169 Our Vaults haue wept With drunken spilth of Wine. **1812** W. TENNANT *Anster F.* II. xxxvi, Both chin and nose bedaub'd with spilth of snuff. **1830** W. TAYLOR *Hist. Surv. Germ. Poetry* I. 324 To avenge ..The spilth of brother's blood. **1865** CARLYLE *Fredk. Gt.* v. vii. II. 117 Grumkow..sent it spinning..through the bottles and glasses; reckless what dangerous breakage and spilth it may occasion.

fig. **1852** T. AIRD *Mem. Moir* M.'s Poet. Wks. I. v. p. cxxxii, Such things are not made by the brain; they are the spilth of the human heart. **1892** SYMONDS *Life in Swiss Highl.* iv. 116 A ruin of old granitic rocks around you, the spilth and waste of mountains.

‖ **spilus** (ˈspaɪləs). *Path.* [mod.L., ad. Gr. σπίλος spot, speck.] A spot or mark on the skin.

1822–7 GOOD *Study Med.* (1829) V. 696 It is this occasional dash that constitutes a spilus or mole. **1849** CRAIG, *Spilus*,..a congenital spot, appearing to consist of a partial thickening of the rete mucosum.

spin (spɪn), *sb.*[1] [f. the vb.]

1. a. An act or spell of spinning; also *techn.*, capacity for being twisted or spun; the product resulting from spinning.

1853 *Househ. Words* VII. 131/1 The apparatus for testing what is termed the 'spin' of the silk;—its capability of being twisted round with great velocity without..being damaged. **1884** W. S. B. MCLAREN *Spinning* (ed. 2) 62 As it is to be spun into worsted,..the longer the fibres remain the better will be the spin.

b. The product of a machine which rotates and twists toffee.

1913 D. H. LAWRENCE *Sons & Lovers* i. 4 She..went to get Annie a spin of toffee.

2. a. An act or spell of revolving or whirling round; a circular or rotatory movement; *spec.* a spell of spin-drying.

1831 MOORE *Summer Fête* Poet. Wks. (Oxf. ed.) 275 Teetotums we've for patriots got,..A glorious spin, and then—a tumble. **1864** DASENT *Jest & Earnest* (1873) I. 194 The circular motion imparted to the new matter by the original twist or spin which the sun gave to the mass. **1966** D. V. DAVIS *New Domestic Encycl.* (ed. 2) iii. 127 Each spin should be restricted to about 15 seconds. **1969** K. J. MILLS *Washing Wisdom* vi. 97 If a spin has been selected, then this will happen for the required time.

b. A head-over-heels movement; a somersault.

1842 LOVER *Handy Andy* i, Surprising was the spin the young equestrians took over the ears of the horse.

c. *Cricket.* A twisting motion given to the ball when bowled or thrown. Also, the ability to impart such a motion to the ball; spin-bowling.

Also in combs. *off-, over-, side-, underspin.*

1851 J. PYCROFT *Cricket Field* ix. 174 The more spin you give the ball, the better the delivery; because then the ball will twist, rise quickly, or cut variously, the instant it touches the ground. **1855** *F. Lillywhite's Guide to Cricketers* 81 A bowler with a great spin. **1861** *Bell's Life* 10 Nov. 6/3 But however good their trundling, pitch or pace, or break or spin, Still the monarch of all bowlers, to my mind was Alfred Mynn. **1862** PYCROFT *Cricket Tutor* 34 When there is no spin upon the ball, a batsman will risk a kind of guess-hit. **1884** *Lillywhite's Cricket Ann.* 25 Not able to get quite the same amount of spin on the ball. **1951** *Sport* 27 Apr.–3 May 12/1 Wardle's left-arm slows and the rapid advance of Eddie Leadbetter, the 23-year-old leg-break and googly bowler, offer spin enough to check the best opponents. **1955** *Times* 5 July 4/1 Silk was probably right in thinking that his seamers would get more out of it than his spinners, but what he did not know was that Oxford were likely to lose their composure against spin. **1958** *Times* 19 July 3/5 Even if we are to be short of spin in Australia our pace attack will be as formidable as it was four years ago. **1977** *World of Cricket Monthly* June 32/3 It was left to the spin of Holford to separate the dangerous pair.

d. *Aeronaut.* A steep descent in which an aircraft describes a helix at an angle of attack greater than the stalling angle; ***flat spin***: see s.v. FLAT *a.* 15.

1915 *Aeroplane* 10 Nov. 578/2 Several times their aeroplane got into a 'spin'. **1930** NAYLER & OWER *Aviation To-Day* 324 To come out of the spin the pilot pushes his stick forward so as to unstall the wings. **1939** [see SPIRAL *a.*[1] 1 b]. **1953** *Aeroplane* 30 Jan. 140/2 Apart from spins that resulted in fatal accidents, there were also quite a number before 1914 which had less drastic consequences. **1977** *New Yorker* 27 June 62/1 The Liberator..went into a spin, dived toward the earth.

e. The continued revolving of the clutch of a motor after being disengaged.

1919 B. H. DAVIES *Motor Driving* 129 The disc A is pressed against the disc B, which damps out the 'spin'. **1948** A. W. JUDGE *Mod. Motor Engineer* (ed. 4) II. 305 If the car is fitted with a clutch stop, or brake, this will effectively obviate clutch spin on disengagement. **1977** J. H. HAYNES *Ford Fiesta Owners Workshop Man.* v. 95/2 Clutch spin is a condition that occurs when there is an obstruction in the clutch.

f. *colloq.* The act of playing a gramophone record, esp. on the air; a session of playing gramophone records.

1977 *Broadcast* 28 Nov. 10/1 Records not receiving maxiplay but likely to get at least one daytime spin. **1977** *R.A.F. News* 11–24 May 20/6 Disc jockey SAC 'Duke' Bedford set off on a record non-stop spin of 72½ hours.

3. a. The act of causing something to spin.

1840 *P. Parley's Ann.* I. 85 Peter..changed tops with Thorp; and after having a few spins, ran home. **1856** 'STONEHENGE' *Brit. Rural Sports* 254/1 It is obvious that for this purpose a long rod is required to command a greater extent of water, and a more numerous series of spins.

b. The act of tossing a coin in the air as a means of deciding something.

1882 *Daily Tel.* 27 May, The Oxonians being fortunate in the spin of the coin.

4. a. A spell of continuous movement by way of exercise or pastime; a fairly rapid ride or run of some duration, now freq. in a motor vehicle or aircraft.

1856 'STONEHENGE' *Brit. Rur. Sports* 336/2 Shorter spins of three-quarters of a mile..will be adopted as often as the trainer sees fit. **1884** *Boston* (Mass.) *Jrnl.* 15 Sept., The bicyclist now..takes long spins from one end of the State to the other. **1890** 'R. BOLDREWOOD' *Col. Reformer* (1891) 319 He..was in much the same bodily..condition as if he had taken a ten-mile spin with a greatcoat on. **1907** G. MEREDITH *Let.* 7 Sept. (1970) III. 1606 To vary my growls ..I hire a motor and have a spin of 100 miles, a way of ensuring appetite and prolonged sleep. **1942** A. CHRISTIE *Body in Library* xi. 102 He took his car and went for a spin down to the front. **1960** M. SPARK *Ballad of Peckham Rye* vii. 164 'I called for you last Saturday,' Mr. Druce said. 'I thought you would care for a spin.' **1976** *Southern Even. Echo* (Southampton) 12 Nov. 14/5 A 15-year-old boy..took his father's car, and went in it for a spin around Basingstoke. **1978** G. VIDAL *Kalki* iii. 59 'We'll go for a spin,' said Kalki. .. First we had to get through to the Katmandu airport. That took an hour... It was five o'clock before we were able to take off.

b. A spell of quick rowing or sailing.

1875 SCUDAMORE *Day Dreams* 14 [They] would willingly have hired a boat for the purpose of having a spin with the Frenchmen. **1895** *Times* (weekly ed.) 30 Aug. 683/1 The Valkyrie went out for another spin on Wednesday.

c. *Austral.* and *N.Z. slang.* A (good, bad, etc.) experience or piece of luck.

1919 in W. H. DOWNING *Digger Dialects* 47. **1929** K. S. PRICHARD *Coonardoo* xix. 188 Mollie had had a crook spin when the children were little. **1934** T. WOOD *Cobbers* xi. 134 People generally said they were having a bad spin. **1948** D. BALLANTYNE *Cunninghams* 132 What a miserable bloody spin he was having. **1960** N. HILLIARD *Maori Girl* IV. iii. 261 Give her a decent spin now and she'll turn out all right. **1964** H. P. TRITTON *Time means Tucker* 113 When I remarked that he'd had a tough spin he grinned, 'Served me right for being such a blanky fool.'

5. Rapid or lively movement.

1891 MEREDITH *One of our Conq.* xix, Like the men who escape colds by wrapping in comforters instead of trusting to the spin of the blood.

6. *Math.* The local rotation of a continuous medium, as expressed by the curl of the local velocity; vorticity.

1878 W. K. CLIFFORD *Elements of Dynamic* I. II. ii. 123 The velocity-system due to a definite angular velocity about a definite axis is spoken of as the rotation-velocity. To specify it completely we must assign its magnitude and the position of the axis... A rotation-velocity, so denoted, shall be called a spin. **1878** W. K. CLIFFORD *Dynamic* 133 Hence every twist may be resolved into two spins, the axis of one of which is any arbitrary straight line. **1937** S. L. GREEN *Hydro- & Aero-Dynamics* ii. 14 There is an essential difference between motions with and without spin, i.e. between rotational and irrotational motion. **1958** *Science* 4 Apr. 731/3 The arrow, which points along the axis of spin and has length equal to the angular speed, is the 'vorticity'. .. The case of no spin is appropriate to some applications, particularly for waves on water and for aeronautics.

7. *Physics.* An intrinsic property of certain elementary particles which is a form of angular momentum and is usu. pictured as a rotation (it is distinct from angular momentum possessed by virtue of occupation of an orbital); a vector representing this in the case of a particular particle.

1926 UHLENBECK & GOUDSMIT in *Nature* 20 Feb. 264/1 To start with, we shall consider the effect of the spin on the manifold of stationary states which corresponds to motion of an electron round a nucleus. **1938** R. W. LAWSON tr. *Hevesy & Paneth's Man. Radioactivity* (ed. 2) viii. 83 The electrons exhibit a rotation proper to themselves and generally referred to as 'spin', and this confers upon them the property of small magnets. **1943** *Ann. Reg. 1942* II. 365 Mesons are of two types—the more usual with the longer life and zero spin and another of shorter life having a spin 1*h*. **1955** *Sci. News Let.* 19 Feb. 117/3 They have passed proton beams through two hydrogen filled chambers to get atoms whose spins are all in the same direction. **1966** C. R. TOTTLE *Sci. Engin. Materials* i. 13 Beryllium..can have two electrons in the 2*s* state, since they can have opposite spin. **1974** P. W. ATKINS *Quanta* 223/1 The spin is the intrinsic, characteristic, and irremovable angular momentum of a particle. A convenient fiction is to suppose that the spin is the angular momentum arising from the rotation of a body about its own axis.

8. *Austral. slang.* [Perhaps a different word.] Five pounds in money.

1941 *Coast to Coast 1941* 225 'How'd you go at the two-up?' I asked. 'Aw, I got a spin,' said Tom. **1949** L. GLASSOP *Lucky Palmer* 15 'Not five bob. A spin,' said the carpenter, fishing a five pound note out. **1962** S. GORE *Down Golden Mile* 261 Backed Sweet Friday for a spin... But it never run a drum.

9. *attrib.* and *Comb.*, as *spin axis*; (sense 7) ***spin angular momentum, multiplicity*** (= MULTIPLICITY 1 e (*a*)), ***quantum number, state***; **spin-allowed** *a.* *Physics*, consistent with the selection rules describing changes in spin quantum number; **spin bowler** *Cricket*, a slow bowler who imparts spin to the ball on delivery; also **spin-bowling**; **spin-dye** *v. trans. Textiles*, to dye (textiles) by a process which incorporates the colouring matter before the filament is formed; so **spin-dyed** *ppl. a.*, **spin-dyeing** *vbl. sb.*; **spin echo** *Physics*, a radio-frequency signal induced in a coil surrounding a system of (esp. nuclear) spins in a static magnetic field in the plane of the coil following the application of two radio-frequency pulses to the coil; freq. *attrib.*; **spin flip** *Physics*, the quantum jump of a particle from one spin state to another; **spin glass**, a dilute solid solution of a magnetic substance in a non-magnetic host; **spin-labelling** *Chem.*, the technique of labelling (LABEL *v.* 2) with stable paramagnetic radicals which can be studied using electron spin resonance techniques; so **spin-label** *v. trans.*; also as *sb.*, a radical or compound used in spin-labelling; **spin-labelled** *a.*; **spin-lattice** *Physics*, used *attrib.* with reference to the interaction between a crystal lattice and a particle possessing spin; **spin-orbit** *Physics*, used *attrib.* with reference to the interaction between spin and orbital motion, esp. of an electron in an atom; **spin polarization** *Physics* = POLARIZATION 2; so **spin-polarized** *a.*; **spin-spin** *Physics*, used *attrib.* with reference to the interaction between two or more particles possessing spin; **spin-stabilized** *a. Astr.*, (of a rocket, spacecraft, etc.) stabilized in a desired orientation by being made to rotate about an axis; so **spin-stabilization**; **'spin tunnel** *Aeronaut.* = *spinning tunnel* s.v. SPINNING *vbl. sb.* 8 c; **spin vector** *Math.* and *Physics*, a vector representing rotation; *spec.* one which by its magnitude and direction represents the intrinsic angular momentum of a particle; **spin wave** *Physics*, a cooperative oscillation in the alignment of electron spins, propagated through a magnetic material in the form of a wave.

1972 DEPUY & CHAPMAN *Molec. Reactions & Photochem.* iii. 34 Electronic transitions between states of the same multiplicity, i.e., singlet-singlet and triplet-triplet transitions, are *spin-allowed. **1973** Spin-allowed [see PHOSPHORESCENCE]. **1928** *Proc. R. Soc.* A. CXVII. 610 Goudsmit and Uhleenbeck have introduced the idea of an electron with a *spin angular momentum of half a quantum and a magnetic moment of one Bohr magneton. **1977** *Dædalus* Summer 27 Some quantum numbers, such as electric charge and spin angular momentum, refer to physical, measurable attributes of the particle. **1922** GLAZEBROOK *Dict. Appl. Physics* I. 421/2 A true circular disc, mounted eccentrically on a *spin-axis normal to its plane, illustrates the state of bad static balance. **1926** *Nature* 20 Feb. 264/1 This couple will cause a slow precession of the spin axis. **1977** *Dædalus* Fall 48 The spin axis of this satellite could be oriented at will by command from the Earth. **1920** D. J. KNIGHT in P. F. Warner *Cricket* 42 Let any player who does not believe in this dictum go and face such *spin bowlers as Barnes, Hearne, [etc.]..on a sticky wicket. **1955** *Times* 14 July 3/5 One has doubts as to just how much the spin bowlers approve of these pitches. **1976** DEXTER & MAKINS *Testkill* 90 A book he was planning on the history of the great spin bowlers. **1955** *Times* 5 July 4/6 They are clearly a useful team, well equipped with stroke-players but perhaps a little short of *spin bowling. **1963** *Times* 7 June 4/3 Mushtaq Mohammad, Pakistan's Test batsman, amply confirmed his ability against spin bowling. **1975** *Cricketer* May 20/1 Critics of the English cricket scene often bemoan the lack of spin bowling. **1948** *Jrnl. Soc. Dyers & Colourists* LXIV. 291/2 Dyes suitable for *spin-dyeing..are those of nitrodiarylamine, azo, and anthraquinone types. **1961** F. D. LEWIS *Chem. & Technol. Rayon Manufacture* xii. 148 Lack of space precludes more than a cursory consideration here of the spindyeing of viscose rayon yarns. *Ibid.* 149 It would not seem possible to spindye thread with a single organic pigment. **1963** A. J. HALL *Textile Sci.* iii. 132 Generally, by this use of pigments instead of dyes it is possible to produce coloured fibres and yarns having the maximum fastness properties; they are often designated 'spin-dyed' yarns. **1949** *Bull. Amer. Physical Soc.* XXIV. VII. 13/2 *Spin Echoes. E. L. Hahn, University of Illinois. **1963** *Times* 8 May 2/7 (Advt.), Post-Doctoral Research Fellowship..for work on relaxation time measurements by spin-echo techniques. **1979** *Nature* 22 Nov. 367/1 Experiments using the weakly inelastic scattering of neutrons have also become feasible; they give similar information [about the motion of polymer chains in a liquid], but for higher frequencies: from $10^{11}s^{-1}$ with 'back scattering spectrometers' down to $2 \times 10^{8}s^{-1}$ with the most recent 'spin echo' method. **1955** *Physical Rev.* C. 1505/1 The special form of the dispersion relations depends on the high-frequency behavior of the *spin-flip amplitude. **1971** *New Scientist* 1 Apr. 6/2 Light.. from a Q-switched carbon-dioxide laser is the 'pumping' source for the spin-flip laser. **1975** *Sci. Amer.* May 89/2 Units of time and distance are specified in terms of the frequency of the hydrogen spin-flip at 1,420 megahertz. **1970** P. W. ANDERSON in *Materials Res. Bull.* V. 549 (*heading*) Localisation theory and the Cu-Mn problem: *spin glasses. **1976** *New Scientist* 2 Dec. 533/1 The essential feature of the spin glass transition is that below some critical temperature, the magnetic atoms are locked or frozen into random orientations (hence the analogy with a glass). **1979** *McGraw-Hill Yearbk. Sci. & Technol.* 247/2 The transition from the paramagnetic to spin glass phase occurs as the material is cooled through a certain temperature point. **1965** T. J. STONE et al. in *Proc. Nat. Acad. Sci.* LIV. 1010 (*heading*) *Spin-labeled biomolecules. *Ibid.* 1785 Stone.. obtained a measure of the rotational mobility of the region of the macromolecule to which the spin labels were bonded. *Ibid.* 1791 It appears likely that the spin-labeling method will be useful in studies of the interaction of haptens, coenzymes, inhibitors, and substrates with proteins and other macromolecules. **1969** *New Scientist* 30 Oct. 224/2 The use of spin-labelled substrate analogues shows clearly ..the subtle changes in protein conformation that occur during the enzymic process. **1974** *Nature* 12 Apr. (verso rear cover), The most commonly used spin labels are molecules which contain a nitroxide moiety. **1975** D. H. BURRIN in Williams & Wilson *Biologist's Guide to Princ. & Techniques Pract. Biochem.* v. 161 By spin labelling glycerophosphatides with a stable nitroxide free radical, the lateral diffusion of the labelled molecules in a membrane ..may be studied. **1976** *Tetrahedron Lett.* June 2180 Spin labelling with carbonyl compounds was carried out for 1–2 days in pH 7·5 aqueous phosphate buffer. **1938** *Physica* V. 502 The period of the alternating field must be of the order of magnitude of the relaxation time τ of the *spin-lattice equilibrium. **1978** P. W. ATKINS *Physical Chem.* xix. 629 The motion of nuclei can affect the shapes and widths of lines in n.m.r. just as it does in e.s.r., and the spin-lattice and spin-spin relaxation times can be discussed in precisely the same way. **1956** *Nature* 18 Feb. 306/1 The 'electronegativity' of all the cations is not that of their ground states, for several of them are in states of lower *spin-multiplicity. **1977** I. M. CAMPBELL *Energy & Atmosphere* viii. 219 Radiative transitions between states of the same spin multiplicity are easy in the absence of contravention of other selection rules. **1932** BACHER & GOUDSMIT *Atomic Energy States* 14 The interaction between the two electrons is smaller than the *spin-orbit interaction of the 3_p electron. **1963** G. TROUP *Masers & Lasers* (ed. 2) 185 Because of spin-orbit coupling..the 'spin' S in the Hamiltonian is not necessarily equal to the true spin of the ion, but is rather an 'effective spin' related to the multiplicity of levels actually found. **1978** W. J. KAUFMANN *Exploration of Solar System* xi. 396 This means that Mercury rotates three times about its axis while circling the sun twice. This phenomenon is known as spin-orbit coupling. **1966** *Proc. Physical Soc.* LXXXIX. 587 The fundamental *spin polarization (**P**) is typically represented by **P**(x) = $P_0\hat{\epsilon}$ cos Qx where Q is the spin-density wave vector and ϵ is a unit vector along the direction of polarization. **1970** I. E. MCCARTHY *Nuclear Reactions* I. i. 7 They [*sc.* the proton and the neutron] may be identified separately by measuring the spin polarization of the beams. **1977** *New Scientist* 24 Feb. 455/2 The process is called 'spin polarisation by optical pumping'. **1968** M. S. LIVINGSTON *Particle Physics* vii. 138 If parity is not conserved in other weak interactions, it could lead to an asymmetry in the direction of emission of β rays from *spin-polarized radioactive nuclei. **1980** *Nature* 17 Jan. 248/1 One way of producing spin-polarised electrons is to take a storage ring, fill it with electrons or positrons, and leave for an hour or so. **1930** PAULING & GOUDSMIT *Struct. Line Spectra* iv. 53 It seems to be sufficient to give all electrons the same rotation, so that they have the angular momentum $sh/2\pi$, with s, the *spin quantum number, always 1/2. **1964** J. W. LINNETT *Electronic Struct. Molecules* i. 9 Since each spatial orbital is defined by the three quantum numbers n, l and m, this is equivalent to saying that each orbital can accommodate two electrons, and these only if they have different spin quantum numbers. **1934** H. E. WHITE *Introd. Atomic Spectra* xii. 186 (*heading*) *Spin-spin-, or ss-coupling. **1936** *Proc. R. Soc.* A. CLV. 641 This degeneracy can only be removed by an external magnetic field or by the spin-spin interaction between the ions. **1978** Spin-spin [see *spin-lattice* above]. **1961** *Planetary & Space Sci.* IV. 262/2 *Spin stabilization turned out to be one of the more difficult design problems encountered in the program. **1976** M. H. KAPLAN *Mod. Spacecraft Dynamics & Control* iv. 124 The use of spin stabilization in this orbit..was seen as a means of achieving the..mission at an early date. **1956** *Spaceflight* I. 19/1 The satellite..was intended to be *spin-stabilized so that one hemisphere..always faced the Sun. **1976** M. H. KAPLAN *Mod. Spacecraft Dynamics & Control* iv. 124 The concept of a spin-stabilized, 24-hour satellite was first proposed by the Hughes Aircraft Company in the fall of 1959. **1956** *Physical Rev.* CIV. 488/1 If the two *spin states are equally abundant, this indication implies that the average neutron width is not the same in each state. **1947** A. POPE *Wind-Tunnel Testing* i. 11 The vertical tunnels for testing parachutes differ from the *spin tunnels in that they require an even velocity front instead of the dish-shaped front required for the spin tunnel. **1959** F. D. ADAMS *Aeronaut. Dict.* 158/1 The air speed in the spin tunnel may be kept equal to the rate of descent of a tested model, causing the model, while spinning, to remain at a given height relative to the observer. **1882** MINCHIN *Unipl. Kinemat.* 260, θ is what we have called the expansion, while ω is the *spin-vector at *P*. **1899** C. J. JOLY in W. R. Hamilton *Elem. Quaternions* (ed. 2) I. III. ii. 492 This vector γ has been called the spin-vector of the function ϕ. **1948** *Physical Rev.* LXXIII. 415/1 The integral Lorentz transformations are represented by exactly those spin transformations which, together with their inverse, map integral spinvectors into integral spinvectors. **1981** *Sci. Amer.* Apr. 47/3 A particle with one-half quantum of intrinsic spin can have only two possible orientations; in the simplest case, where the particle is in motion, the spin vector can point either in the same direction the particle is moving or in the opposite direction. **1936** *Proc. R. Soc.* A. CLV. 644 For long waves one can carry out the transition to a continuum in the same way as Bloch did in his theory of '*spin waves'. **1953** *Rev. Mod. Physics* XXV. 235/2 The rf magnetic field excites spin waves with wave numbers in the range 1 to 10^5 cm^{-1}. **1973** *Sci. Amer.* Jan. 88/3 Waves produced by oscillations of magnetic moment in ferromagnetic and antiferromagnetic materials (spin waves) generate quasiparticles called magnons.

spin (spɪn), *sb.*² *Anglo-Indian.* [Abbreviation of SPINSTER.] An unmarried lady.

1842 C. RIDLEY *Let.* Mar. in *Cecilia* (1958) vii. 90 Mrs. Dixon, a good lady..who was sitting in a very tidy, very hot room with two old spins as companions. **1872** 'ALIPH CHEEM' (Yeldham) *Lays of Ind* (1876) 193 I'm going to rhyme about A most unhappy spin. *Ibid.* 200 O spins.! be warned ere yet too late. **1888** MRS. CROKER *Diana Barrington* xxiii, There were all the Gurrumpore spins in their beautiful new frocks!

†**spin**, *sb.*³ *Obs.*$^{-1}$ In 6 spynne. [a. G. *spinne*, *spünne*, related to SPEAN *sb.*] A teat.

1525 ANDREW tr. *Brunswyke's Surg.* iii. Bij/2 Vuula, yᵉ whiche is a lytell deme hangynge in yᵉ throte lyke the spynne.

spin (spɪn), *v.* Pa. t. **spun, span.** Pa. pple. **spun.** Forms: *Inf.* 1 spinnan, 3–7 spinne, 4–6 spynne (4 -en, 5 -yn), 5–6 spyn (7 spyne), 6– spin. *Pa. t.* 1 spann, 4–6 spanne (4–5 spane), 5– span; 1 *pl.* spunnon, -un, 4 *pl.*, 6 sponne, 5 *pl.* spon, 6 spunne, 6– spun. *Pa. pple.* 1 ȝespunnen, 3 i-, 4, 6 y-sponne, 7 *arch.* y-spunne; 4–5 sponnen, 4–6 sponne, 5–6 spon(e, 6 spoon(ne, 5–7 spunne (6 spune), 6– spun. Also 5 spynned, 6 (9 *dial.*) spinned. [Common Teut.: OE. *spinnan*, = OFris. **spinna* (WFris. *spinne*, EFris. *spinne*, *spin*, NFris. *spen*, *span*), MDu. and Du., MLG. and LG. *spinnen*, OHG. *spinnan* (MHG. and G. *spinnen*), ON. and Icel., Norw. and Sw. *spinna* (Da. *spinde*), Goth. *spinnan*; the stem is perhaps related to that of SPAN *v.*² and to Balto-Slavic forms (with initial *sp-* or *p-*) of similar meaning (Schade *Altd. Wbch.* 852/2).]

I. * **1. a.** *intr.* To draw out and twist the fibres of some suitable material, such as wool or flax, so as to form a continuous thread; to be engaged in or to follow this occupation.

c **725** *Corpus Gloss.* R 148 *Reuerant* [read *neuerant*], spunnun. *c* **975** *Rushw. Gosp.* Matt. vi. 28 Sceawiȝaþ lilia londes hu hie waexaþ, ne winnaþ, ne spinnaþ. *c* **1000** *Sax. Leechd.* II. 310 Nim þone hweorfan þe wif mid spinnað. *c* **1290** *St. Clement* 156 in *S. Eng. Leg.* I. 327 Nouþe mine hondene me beoth bi-nome, þat Ine may sevwy ne spinne. **1390** GOWER *Conf.* II. 170 Hire moder..Bad that sche scholde..lerne forto weve and spinne, And duelle at hom and kepe hire inne. *a* **1400** *Minor Poems fr. Vernon MS.* 707/99, I wolde wite, whon þat Eue gon spinne, Bi whom þat ȝoure gentrie stod? **1467** in *Eng. Gilds* (1870) 383 To dye, carde, or spynne, weve, or cloth-walke. **1530** PALSGR. 728 And you wyll speake with my mother she spynneth nowe at home. **1560** PILKINGTON *Expos. Aggeus* (1562) 217 When Adam dalve, and Eve span, Who was than a gentle-man? *c* **1655** MILTON *Sonn.* xx. 8 The Lillie and Rose, that neither sow'd nor spun. **1756–7** tr. *Keysler's Trav.* (1760) I. 388 The entrances are crouded with old women spinning. **1825** J. NICHOLSON *Operat. Mechanic* 422 The short interval when splicing the yarn, and preparing to set on to spin. **1882** 'OUIDA' *Maremma* I. 37 In bad weather she sat at home and span.

Phr. **1542** UDALL *Erasm. Apoph.* 342b, We saye in Englyshe to teache our dame to spynne.

fig. **1768–74** TUCKER *Lt. Nat.* (1834) I. 293 If you go to spin finer than they have been accustomed to, [they] cry out against it as an inconceivable absurdity. **1857** EMERSON *Poems* 171 The storm-wind wove, the torrent span, Where they were bid the rivers ran. **1876** SPURGEON *Commenting* 122 This author..is good but verbose. Some authors toil not, but they spin; Macculloch both toils and spins.

b. Of insects: To produce glutinous threads from the body by means of special organs.

c **1511** [see 3 d]. **1728** CHAMBERS *Cycl.* s.v. *Silk*, Before they begin to Spin, they always apply..these..Nipples against the Body whence the Web is begun. **1815** KIRBY & SP. *Entomol.* (1818) I. 408 You will find that precisely the same takes place in the minutest species that spins. **1833** TENNYSON *Two Voices* 180 For every worm..Draws different threads, and..Spins, toiling out his own cocoon. **1841** T. R. JONES *Anim. Kingd.* 297 When about to spin, the larva..allows a minute drop of the glutinous secretion to exude.

c. To make a noise like that of spinning.

1851 MEREDITH *Love in the Valley* v, Lone on the fir-branch, his rattle-note unvaried,..spins the brown eve-jar.

2. a. *trans.* To draw out (wool, flax, man-made fibre, or other material) and convert into threads either by the hand or by machinery.

c **1000** ÆLFRIC *Gram.* xv. 97 Hiȝ spinnað wulle. **13..** *K. Alis.* 6806 (W.), They haveth no wolle to spynne. **1399** GOWER *Praise Peace* 299 Men sein the wolle, whanne it is wel sponne, Doth that the cloth is strong and profitable. *a* **1450** *Knt. de la Tour* (1868) 79 She..came afore hym with a rocke under a gerdelle spynning black wolle. **1523** FITZHERB. *Husb.* § 146 Flaxe..tawed, hecheled, spon. **1577** B. GOOGE *Heresbach's Husb.* 39 The Towe is seuered from the Flaxe, and appoynted for his vse, so are they seuerally spon vpon the Distaffe. **1688** HOLME *Armoury* III. 286/2 Woll is principally, nay only spun at it, and at none of the other sorts of Wheels. **1796** H. HUNTER tr. *St.-Pierre's Stud. Nat.* (1799) III. 78 As for the two friends, they spun cotton from morning till night. **1835** URE *Philos. Manuf.* 222 The flax formerly spun to twelve pounds a bundle, is with hot water spun to six. **1874** GREEN *Short Hist.* vii. § 5. 386 The farmers' wives began everywhere to spin their wool from their own sheeps' backs. **1899** *Jrnl. Soc. Arts* 8 Dec. 62/2 The solution of gelatine must be coloured to the required shade before being spun. **1921** T. WOODHOUSE tr. *Foltzer's Artif. Silk* 23 This solution..is conducted or spun through special capillary tubes. **1974** *Encycl. Brit. Macropædia* VII. 258/2 Acetate is dry spun by extruding acetone solutions of cellulose acetate into hot air.

fig. *c* **1315** SHOREHAM III. 150 For wel to conne, and nauȝt to don, Nys naþer rawe ne y-sponne. *a* **1420** [see DISTAFF 1 b]. *c* **1440** *Cast. Persev.* 2618 in *Macro Plays*, For no man can be war be oþer tyl he hathe al ful spunne. **1525–46** [see DISTAFF 1 b]. **1633** G. HERBERT *Temple, Glimpse* vi, If I have more to spinne, The wheel shall go, so that thy stay be short.

b. = To spin off (see 5 a). Also with *up*.

a **1553** UDALL *Royster D.* I. iii, If thys distaffe were spoonne Margerie Mumblecrust..will drinke no water. **1593** G. HARVEY *Pierce's Super.* 163, I must spin-vp my taske.

c. To convert (or *intr.*, to admit of being converted) *into* thread, etc., by spinning. Also *transf.*

1669 STILLINGFL. *Serm.* iv. 151 For plain truths lose much ..and their strength is impaired when they are spun into too fine a thread. *a* **1676** HALE *Prim. Orig. Man.* (1677) 306 To spin some prepared Matter into vital and sentient *Semina* for those insect Animals. **1780** A. YOUNG *Tour Irel.* I. 166 The 8 lb. [of flax] will spin into..20 hanks or 5 spangles fit for a ten hundred cloth. **1842** OASTLER *Fleet Papers* II. 26 It will not spin into good yarn, nor weave into wearable cloths. **1883** HALDANE *Workshop Rec.* Ser. II. 320 The number of strands of gut spun into a cord varies with the thickness of catgut required. **1899** *Jrnl. Soc. Arts* 8 Dec. 63/2 If too much water is present the collodion will not be tenacious and therefore will not spin. **1963** A. J. HALL *Textile Sci.* ii. 50 If a suitable proportion of opaque white titanium dioxide pigment is added to the viscose solution just before it is spun into filaments, these can be produced with a lower lustre or even be matt.

refl. **1867** AUGUSTA WILSON *Vashti* xvii, Your mind.. exhausts and consumes itself, like fabled Arachne, spinning itself into filmy nothings.

d. (See quot.)

1802 JAMES *Milit. Dict.* s.v., *To spin hay*, is to twist it up in ropes, very hard, for an expedition... An expert horseman can spin five days forage into a very narrow compass.

e. To deposit (liquid sugar) on cakes, etc., in a thread-like form.

1883 HALDANE *Worksh. Rec.* Ser. II. 166 Sugar may be spun over the inside of the basket.

3. a. To form or fabricate (a thread, etc.) by the process of drawing out (and twisting) some suitable material; to prepare the material for (a fabric or garment) by this process.

c **1290** *St. Edmund* 167 in *S. Eng. Leg.* I. 436 Heo [*sc.* a hair-coat] nas i-sponne ne i-weoue, ake i-broide [of] strengus longue. **1362** LANGL. *P. Pl.* A. v. 130 My wyf..þat wollene cloþ made, Spak to þe spinsters for to spinne hit softe. **1382** WYCLIF *Judg.* xvi. 9 The threed of a top of flexe, that is sponnen with spotel. **1513** DOUGLAS *Æneid* x. xiii. 141 His coyte of goldin thredis brycht Quhilk his moder hym span. **1562** HEYWOOD *Prov. & Epigr.* (1867) 163 Which showth in deede That a fowle spinner may spin a fayre threede. **1607** SHAKS. *Cor.* I. iii. 93 All the yearne she spun in Vlisses absence. **1634** MILTON *Comus* 83 First I must put off These my skie robes spun out of Iris Wooff. **1735** JOHNSON *Lobo's Abyssinia, Voy.* iv. 25 They..Sew them together with Thread which they spin out of the Bark. **1805** *Act 45 Geo. III*, c. 30 Sched., Every pound..of gold thread, gold lace, or gold fringe, made of plate wire spun upon silk. **1832** HT. MARTINEAU *Life in Wilds* iv. 51 The lace-makers and jewellers and glass-cutters, and even those who spin glass for the amusement of the wealthy. **1874** H. H. COLE *Catal. Ind. Art S. Kens. Mus.* 137 The filigree..is like a fine web spun over the surface of the bottle. **1891** *Jrnl. Soc. Chem. Industry* 30 Apr. 359/1 This invention relates to the process and apparatus for spinning artificial silk from nitro-cellulose. **1973** *Materials & Technol.* VI. iv. 292 Dry spinning. This method is used to spin filaments from syrups which can be prepared by dissolving the fibre-forming materials in a suitable solvent.

transf. **1769** MRS. RAFFALD *Eng. Housekpr.* (1778) 186 When you spin a silver web, or a desert, always take particular care your fire is clear. *Ibid.*, You must not spin it before a kitchen fire.

b. In figurative contexts.

to spin street-thread, etc.: see STREET *sb.* *to spin a yarn* (to tell a story): see YARN *sb.*

13.. *K. Alis.* 7251 (W.), He hath y-sponne a threde, That is y-come of eovel rede. *c* **1450** *Pol. Poems* (Rolls) II. 231 Let theym [wear] suche clothis as they spane. *a* **1568** A. SCOTT *Poems* (S.T.S.) xxx. 7 Than is his weid of vertew spune. **1586** KYD *Verses Praise & Joy* 31 My thred is cut, and yet it is not spunne; And now I liue, and now my life is done. **1697** DRYDEN *Virg. Past.* IV. 57 The Fates, when they this happy web have spun. **1757** GRAY *Bard* 98 Weave we the woof. The thread is spun. **1820** SHELLEY *M. Gisborne* 154 How we spun A shroud of talk to hide us from the sun Of this familiar life. **1852** THACKERAY *Esmond* II. xiii, [A grave] so fresh made that the spring had scarce had time to spin a coverlet for it.

†**c.** In the ironical phrase ***to spin a fair thread.***

1554 LATIMER in Strype *Mem.* (1721) III. 93 If you tarry with them, you have sponne a fayre Threde. **1562** J. HEYWOOD *Prov. & Epigr.* (1867) 56 In beyng your owne foe, you spin a fayre threede. **1656** HOBBES *Liberty, Necessity, & Chance* (1841) 31 If it be so, he hath spun a fair thread, to make all this stir. [**1818** SCOTT *Rob Roy* xxiii, Spinners! ye'll spin and wind yoursell a bonny pirn.]

d. *transf.* Of insects. (Cf. 1 b.)

c **1511** *1st Eng. Bk. Amer.* (Arb.) p. xxxv/1 This wormes.. goo in too that fyre, and there they spynne lyke the wormes yat the sylke spynneth. **1660** tr. *Amyraldus' Treat. conc. Relig.* II. vi. 234 Insects spin silk for his service. **1700** C. NESSE *Antid. Armin.* (1827) 117 If man (spider-like) could spin a thread out of his own bowels. **1728** CHAMBERS *Cycl.* s.v. *Silk*, The Silk-Spider makes a Silk, every whit as beautiful..as the Silk-worm: It spins it out of the Anus. **1815** KIRBY & SP. *Entomol.* (1818) I. 406 All spiders do not spin webs. *Ibid.*, The thread spun by spiders. **1861** P. P. CARPENTER in *Rep. Smithsonian Instit. 1860*, 265 The animal [*Crenella*] spins for itself a silky nest.

fig. **1841** DE QUINCEY *Style* iv. in *Blackw. Mag.* Feb. 215/2 Those accidents of time and place which obliged Greece to spin most of her speculations, like a spider, out of her own bowels. **1850** TENNYSON *In Mem.* cxxiv, I found Him not.. thro' the questions men may try, The petty cobwebs we have spun.

4. *fig.* **a.** Of the Fates or other powers: To devise or appoint (one's destiny or fortune).

c **1374** CHAUCER *Troylus* III. 734 O fatal sustren, which, er any clooth Me shapen was, my destene me sponne. **1430–40** LYDG. *Bochas* VIII. xxv, The parchas susterne spon so hys fate. **1606** SYLVESTER *Du Bartas* II. iv. I. *Tropheis* 932 On David's head, God doth not spin good hap. **1649** G. DANIEL *Trinarch., Hen. V*, ccxxiii, To Spin his Fate To an ignobler End, then one soe Bold Had merited. **1726** POPE *Odyss.* xx. 250 May fate..spin thy future with a whiter clue! **1840** *Penny Cycl.* XVII. 242/2 The Fates are usually spoken of by the Greek and Roman poets as spinning the destinies of men.

b. To evolve, produce, contrive, or devise, in a manner suggestive of spinning.

c **1555** HARPSFIELD *Divorce Hen. VIII* (Camden) 227 This interpretation is finely spinned..out of the lawyer's fantastical head. **1633** G. HERBERT *Temple, Praise* i, Lord, I will..speak thy praise... My busie heart shall spin it all my dayes. **1664** COTTON *Scarron.* 56 Should I begin my story spinning, From the first end to th' last beginning. **1746** FRANCIS tr. *Horace, Sat.* II. i. 4 My Lines are weak, unsinew'd, others say—A Man might spin a thousand such a Day. **1791–1823** D'ISRAELI *Cur. Lit.* (1866) 509 Many secret agents..were spinning their dark intrigues. **1850** ROBERTSON *Serm.* Ser. II. ii. (1864) 24 A system of wild fancies spun out of the brain. **1870** MAX MÜLLER *Sci. Relig.* (1873) 60, I cannot help suspecting that language has been at work spinning mythology.

c. To draw out, prolong. (Cf. 6.)

1629 J. MAXWELL tr. *Herodian* (1635) 214 Which being no small detriment to the Romans, did spinne the Warre to a great length. **1713** SWIFT *Cadenus & Vanessa* Wks. 1755 III. II. 7 For sixteen years the cause was spun, And then stood, where it first begun. **1789** JEFFERSON *Writ.* (1859) III. 58 If the fear of the former alternative prevails they will spin the matter into negotiation. **1792** MME. D'ARBLAY *Diary* V. VII. 323 The little novel..would not have gone on improving, as the latter part begins already to seem spun.

** With adverbs.

5. spin off: a. To finish or clear *off* (a distaff, etc.) by spinning. (Cf. 2 b.)

1601 HOLLAND *Pliny* II. 549 One would imagine he saw every woman making hast to spin off her distaffe, striving avie who shall have done her taske first. **1601** SHAKS. *Twel. N.* I. iii. 110 It hangs like flax on a distaffe: & I hope to see a huswife take thee between her legs, & spin it off. **1690** TEMPLE *Ess., Poet.* Wks. 1720 I. 249 To spin off this Thread, which is already grown too long. **1735–1894** [see ROCK *sb.*² 2].

b. To throw or cast *off* (a composition) in a continuous or easy manner.

1895 *Daily News* 24 Apr. 7/4 He..used to spin off novels in the intervals between signing piles of papers.

6. spin out: a. To render lengthy or protracted; to protract, prolong.

Used with a variety of objects, the commonest types of which are illustrated by the separate groups of quotations. Cooper (1565, s.v. *Parcæ*) has 'to spynne out the threade of mans lyfe', and an early example of the literal use occurs s.v. SPINNER 2 (quot. 1393).

(*a*) **1603** in Moryson *Itin.* (1617) II. 282 Shee was still apt to beleeve that hee .. would spin out all things further then were requisite, with delayes and shifts. **1646** J. HALL *Horæ Vac.* 154 Neither is any warre so long spun out. **1670** G. H. *Hist. Cardinals* III. II. 282 It was done more to procrastinate, and spin out the Conclave. **1759** ROBERTSON *Hist. Scot.* II. Wks. 1813 I. 106 Under his management the negociations were spun out to a great length. **1770** LANGHORNE *Plutarch* (1879) II. 764/1 He spun out the debate till it was too late to conclude upon anything that day. **1865** CARLYLE *Fredk. Gt.* XXI. iv. VI. 476 Kaunitz .. span out the Turk pacification in a wretched manner for years coming. **1885** *Law Times* 30 May 74/1 That arbitration .. was spun out for forty-four days.

(*b*) **1607** TOPSELL *Four-f. Beasts* 574 Therefore they spin out their liues to the length of the thread. **1663** BP. PATRICK *Parab. Pilgr.* xxiv, They would fain spin out the most miserable life to the greatest length. **1734** WATTS *Reliq. Juv.* (1789) 130 Thus he spun out his supple soul, and drew A length of life amidst a vicious crew. **1872** *Punch* 19 Oct. 163/1 If I were condemned to execution, I should perhaps be inclined to spin out my time by talking till they took me off by force.

(*c*) **1633** FORD *Broken H.* I. i, You spin out your discourse. **1673** *Lady's Call.* I. v. §75 This section is spun out to a length very unproportionable to the former. **1710** STEELE *Tatler* No. 132 ¶10 Our innocent Conversation, which we spun out till about Ten of the Clock. **1787** MME. D'ARBLAY *Diary* 16 Feb., I .. spun out into an hour's discourse what might have been said in three minutes. **1813** PRICHARD *Phys. Hist. Man.* vii. §4. 357 This sort of argument has been .. so spun out by antiquaries of late times.

(*d*) **1644** PRYNNE & WALKER *Fiennes's Trial* 46 In this his defence (to spin out time) he led us in perambulation through all the Works, Forts, Dikes, Rampires [etc.]. **1673** *S'too him Bayes* 129 No body that hop'd to have a reprieve ever spun out time at last as thou hast done. **1761** HUME *Hist. Eng.* lxvi. (1806) V. 45 The French ambassadors spun out the time till the morning of the critical day. **1817** JAS. MILL *Brit. India* II. v. iv. 439 The distance of Madras would aid the Rajah in spinning out the time till the commencement of the rains.

b. To spend or occupy (time) in inactivity or without effect.

1608–14 in Leadam *Crt. Requests* (Selden) Introd. 96 Counsell .. doe .. Spyne and Trifle out one or two termes about the exceptions. **1646** H. P. *Medit. Seige* 42 Although I die at twenty, I have lived more then he that hath spunne out a hundred uselesse yeares. **1712** J. JAMES tr. *Le Blond's Gardening* 108 Those People are .. lazy, and have no Concern but to spin out the Day. **1789** in *Nairne Peerage Evid.* (1874) 127, I shall endeavour to spin out the remainder of my days as comfortably as my situation can permit.

c. To evolve or devise by mental effort; to express at length.

1652 N. CULVERWEL *Lt. Nature* xi. (1654) 97 Mans reason is fain to spend time .. in spinning out a Syllogisme. **1663** MARVELL *Corr.* Wks. (Grosart) II. 97, I have no more time left to spin out in words the kindnes which I acknowledge from you and beare to you. **1736** *Gentl. Mag.* VI. 466/2 How many hundred Declarations has Caleb D'Anvers spun out from a Thread of this Clue. **1828** SCOTT *Aunt Marg. Mirror* Introd., The sort of waking dreams which my imagination spins out. **1864** THACKERAY *D. Duval* viii. (1869) 107 He could spin out sentences by the yard. **1875** JOWETT *Plato* (ed. 2) IV. 426 To be spinning out a long soliloquy or address, as if I wanted to show off.

d. To draw out, extend, prolong, in length or duration.

1655 GURNALL *Chr. in Arm.* verse 14. ii. (1669) 13/2 He who is spun out at length, but not thicken'd suitable to his height. **1663** BP. PATRICK *Parab. Pilgr.* xxxix, The Paracelsian promise of spinning out the life of man to a length equal with the clew of time. **1717** PRIOR *Alma* III. 539 Would she, in friendship, peace, and plenty Spin out our years to four times twenty. **1865** CARLYLE *Fredk. Gt.* XX. i. VI. 5 Prince Henri and Fouquet have spun themselves out into a long chain of posts.

e. To bring to an end; to consume or exhaust. Chiefly *refl.* or in *pass.*

1718 *Entertainer* No. 35. 236 To beat the wind, and spider-like, to spin out ones self for those who will not thank him for it. **1728** RAMSAY *Fables, Fox turned Preacher* 51 His glass spun out, he ceast. **1809** MALKIN *Gil Blas* XI. vii. ¶3 My brain is fairly spun out.

f. To cause to last out; to use sparingly.

1726 SHELVOCKE *Voy. round World* 328 We might have spun out what we had by good husbandry. **1862** MRS. H. WOOD *Mrs. Halliburton's Troubles* I. xvi. 195 We must spin the money out .. until something comes in.

g. *intr.* To run out; to extend; to last out.

1724 DE FOE *Mem. Cavalier* (1840) 258 The time spinning out, [they] demanded longer time. **1758** J. BURTON *Monast. Ebor.* Pref. p. xi, This preface has spun out to a greater length than I expected. **1891** C. ROBERTS *Adrift Amer.* 51 In my .. state of ignorance with regard to making money spin out.

II. * 7. *intr.* To shoot or spring *up*; to grow or rise rapidly. *rare.*

13.. *E.E. Allit. P.* A. 35 So semly a sede moȝt fayly not, Þat spryngande spycez vp ne sponne. **1641** MILTON *Animadv.* Wks. 1851 III. 229 Their unquestionable charity, which .. like a working flame, had spun up to such a height of pure desire.

8. a. Of blood, etc.: To issue in a rapid stream; to gush or spurt. Freq. with *out*.

c **1400** *Laud Troy Bk.* 8942 Depe in-to his fflesch it ran, That the blod fast out span. *c* **1560** INGELEND *Disobed. Child* A iv, Shoulde I be content then thyther to runne, Where the bloude from my breeche thus shoulde spunne. **1573** L. LLOYD *Marrow of Hist.* (1653) 289 Alexander the great being wounded, and his blood spinning out. **1627** DRAYTON *Agincourt* 131 The blood out of their Helmets span. **1684** R. WALLER *Nat. Exper.* 155 That thin Spirit .. which in a small Thread spins out of the same Peel when it is squeezed. **1720** POPE *Iliad* XXI. 184 One raz'd Achilles' hand; the spouting blood Spun forth. **1881** MRS. R. T. COOKE *Somebody's Neighbors* 84 The sharp streams of milk spun and foamed into the pail below.

b. *trans.* To send *forth* in a stream. *rare*$^{-1}$.

1610 HOLLAND *Camden's Brit.* I. 279 Spatious pastures, and flockes of cattell spinning forth milke abundantly.

9. a. To move rapidly; to run quickly; now *esp.* to ride or drive at a rapid and even rate.

a **1400–50** *Alexander* 3033 He spynnes [*v.r.* spedes] him out a grete space fra hes peris all. *c* **1430** *Chev. Assigne* 331 An edder spronge out of his shelde & in his body spynethe. *c* **1450** *Cast. Persev.* 1400 With spete of spere to þee I spynne. **1556** J. HEYWOOD *Spider & Fly* lxiii. 45 Streight from that place they are speedilie spinning, To an other host. **1581** A. HALL *Iliad* v. 79 The which the heardman when he sees, for feare begins to spin.

1842 TENNYSON *Sir Galahad* v, The tempest crackles on the leads, And, ringing, spins from brand and mail. **1850** SCORESBY *Cheever's Whalem. Adv.* iii. (1859) 36 The boat spun after him with singular swiftness. **1883** F. M. CRAWFORD *Dr. Claudius* 200 There was a cab at the door, .. and in a minute more he was spinning along Fifth Avenue.

b. To pass or be spent quickly.

1850 THACKERAY *Pendennis* x, The young one is making the money spin. **1868** DICKENS *Lett.* (1880) II. 362, I hope that the time will soon begin to spin away.

c. *trans.* To cause to pass *away*; to carry *away* or convey rapidly.

1696 PHILLIPS, *Amusement*, any idle Employment to spin away time. **1877** MRS. OLIPHANT *Young Musgrave* I. xii. 205 Lovely horses who could spin her away over the broad country. **1880** MISS BRADDON *Just as I am* vi, I shall soon spin him over to Highclere.

10. a. To revolve or gyrate; to whirl *round*.

1667 MILTON *P. Pl.* VIII. 164 The Earth .. With inoffensive pace that spinning sleeps On her soft Axle. **1700** DRYDEN *Ovid's Met.* VIII. 112 Quick, and more quick he spins in giddy Gires, Then falls. **1784** COWPER *Task* III. 491 Thrice must the voluble and restless earth Spin round upon her axle, ere the warmth .. attain the surface. **1825** SCOTT *Talism.* xx, Dance, or we will scourge thee with our bowstrings, till thou spin as never top did under schoo'boy's lash. **1846** GREENER *Sci. Gunnery* 352 Do not require a bullet to spin twice on its axis, if once is sufficient. **1888** J. INGLIS *Tent Life in Tigerland* 260 Sometimes we spinned round and round like a teetotum.

fig. **1805** WORDSW. *Prelude* II. 47 We ran a boisterous course; the year span round With giddy motion. **1893** *Times* 15 June 9/6 The mind accustomed to spin upon the poles of Greek and pure mathematics.

b. Of the brain or head: To whirl; to be giddy or dazed.

1819 BYRON *Juan* II. cx, And as he gazed, his dizzy brain spun fast, And down he sunk. **1886** BARING-GOULD *Crt. Royal* III. xlvi. 93 My head spins. I cannot think. **1894** STEVENSON *Lett.* (1899) II. 327 My head is simply spinning with a multitude of affairs.

c. *Cricket.* Of a ball: to travel through the air with spin (SPIN *sb.*[1] 2 c).

1851 J. PYCROFT *Cricket Field* ix. 174 Clarke is not conscious of any attempt to make his ball spin or twist: a certain action has become habitual to him. **1970** N. CARDUS *Full Score* 120 Mailey would tell me how much he revelled in the 'feel' of a ball spinning from his fingers. **1980** *Cricketer International* Apr. 83/3 Hollies .. came up to bowl the next ball. It neither spun nor twisted in the air but drifted up and then down in a graceful parabola.

d. *Aeronaut.* Of an aircraft or its pilot: to perform or undergo a spin (SPIN *sb.* 2 d).

1914 *Aeroplane* 1 July 17/2 If a 'scout' started to spin round its own nose it would never come into control again. **1918** J. M. GRIDER *War Birds* (1927) 66, I am going up to ten thousand [feet] and shut off and spin down and see what happens. **1931** C. D. BARNARD *Learning to Fly* 151 Only a stalled aeroplane will spin—in other words when the machine is no longer airborne. **1952** *Technical Rep. Aeronaut. Res. Committee 1943* II. 755 The model usually spins more steeply and recovers from the spin more easily than the aeroplane.

e. Of a motor clutch: to continue to revolve after being disengaged.

1918 *Dyke's Automobile Encycl.* (ed. 7) 662/1 When a clutch spins, when thrown out of engagement, it is difficult to shift gears. **1928** *Motor Man.* (ed. 27) 57 The flange .. is brought into contact with the stop, which acts as a brake and prevents the cone or plate spinning. **1965** D. KABERRY *Ford Corsair* viii. 53/1 If the clutch is spinning, difficulty will be experienced in engaging gear, particularly from a standstill.

11. a. *trans.* To cause to turn or revolve rapidly; to twirl or whirl. Fig. phr. ***to spin one's wheels*** (U.S. colloq.), to mark time, to do nothing productive.

1612 DEKKER *If it be not Good* Wks. 1873 III. 296 Ile turne the wheeles: and spin the howers vp faster. **1830** GALT *Lawrie T.* II. i. I. 90 There be you spinning your thumbs with a small child that ha'n't got no mother. **1842** BROWNING *Spanish Cloister* vii, Spin him round and send him flying Off to Hell. **1870** EMERSON *Soc. & Solit.* vii. 138 When you spun tops and snapped marbles. **1960** *Wall St. Jrnl.* 15 Mar. 1 'We're just sitting here spinning our wheels,' says a disgruntled Naval aviator in California. **1974** *Evening Herald* (Rock Hill, S. Carolina) 19 Apr. 4/1 The Selective Service System has, in fact, done little but spin its wheels for the past 14 months.

b. To cause (a chafer) to fly while secured by a thread passed through its tail.

1801 STRUTT *Sports & Past.* IV. iv. 291 *note*, When a child I was caught by my mother .. in the act of spinning a chafer. **1844** J. T. J. HEWLETT *Parsons & W.* iii, To spear trout, spin cockchafers, bait cats.

c. With cognate object.

1828 LYTTON *Pelham* xl, They just walk a quadrille or spin a waltz.

d. *techn.* To shape (articles of sheet-metal) by pressure applied during rotation on a lathe.

1853 URE *Dict. Arts* (ed. 4) II. 865 'Raising' by means of 'spinning' and stamping has to a great extent superseded the older methods of tin plate working. **1884** *B'ham Daily Post* 24 Jan. 3/3 Britannia-metal Spinners.—Wanted a Man, who can Spin and Make Up.

e. *Cricket.* Of a bowler: to impart spin to (a ball) on delivery; to cause (the ball) to break after pitching.

1904 *Westm. Gaz.* 21 May 3/1 He can spin the ordinary left-hander's break-back. **1920** D. J. KNIGHT in P. F. Warner *Cricket* 49 Rhodes and Woolley .. seem to spin the ball in such a way that it gets straight up from the pitch in quite a different manner. **1960** [see CUT *v.* 31 a].

f. To make (an aircraft) perform a spin (SPIN *sb.* 2 d).

1918 J. M. GRIDER *War Birds* (1927) 87 Then Ortmeyer .. spun a Camel into the ground and killed himself. **1928** O. STEWART *Aerobatics* 13 Machines fitted with Handley-Page automatic slots are extremely difficult to spin. **1952** *Technical Rep. Aeronaut. Res. Committee 1943* II. 766 The aircraft was spun from 28,000 ft., one 2½-turn spin to the left being carried out and two 2½-turn spins to the right.

g. = SPIN-DRY *v.* Also *absol.*

1959 *Which?* Aug. 92/1 Tumbler driers are intended to take washing that has either been wrung or spun to a half-dry state. **1966** D. V. DAVIS *New Domestic Encycl.* (ed. 2) iii. 127 If you spin a minimum-iron fabric while it is hot you are much more likely to press in creases. **1969** K. J. MILLS *Washing Wisdom* vi. 98 Hook the outlet pipe over the sink. Spin for 15–20 seconds.

h. To play (a gramophone record).

1965 *Listener* 23 Dec. 1036/3 If he will dust off his old Plum Label HMV 78 .. and spin it, he will hear Gertrude Lawrence very distinctly saying to Noël Coward: 'Strange how potent cheap music is!' **1966** T. PYNCHON *Crying of Lot 49* v. 140 She sat alone .. listening to Mucho's colleague Rabbit Warren spin records.

12. *Angling.* **a.** *trans.* To cause (a minnow or other bait) to revolve in the water by fastening it on the hook in a particular manner.

1814–24 COL. HAWKER *Instructions Yng. Sportsm.* 173 Trolling, or spinning a minnow, is the other most general mode of trout fishing. *Ibid.* 175 A new gut seldom spins the minnow so well as one that is half worn out. **1856** 'STONEHENGE' *Brit. Rural Sports* 254/2 In dead water a well mounted minnow or gudgeon may be spun with great effect.

b. *intr.* To fish with a spinning bait.

1863 'OUIDA' *Held in Bondage* (1870) 7 De Vigne stopped to have a glance across country as he stood trolling and spinning. **1867** F. FRANCIS *Angling* i. 30 *note*, When spinning for trout.

c. *trans.* To fish (a pool, etc.), to rouse *up* (a fish), by means of a spinning bait.

1886 *Field* 30 Jan. 133/3 He was to be occasionally seen spinning the weir pool and scours below Marsh Lock. **1895** *Baily's Mag.* May 357/2 If he does not 'spin up' a fish, he brings his minnow in as short as he can.

13. *slang.* To reject (a candidate) at an examination; to pluck or plough. Usu. in *pass.*

1860 in *Slang Dict.* 223. **1865** *Pall Mall G.* 4 Aug. 9/2 The historical test is, we imagine, the one which will 'spin' most applicants. **1897** *Brit. Weekly* 7 Jan. 214/5 'How far through did you say he was with his medical course?' 'He was spun in the final,' I answered.

b. *intr.* To fail in an examination.

1869 *Pall Mall G.* 24 Nov. 3/2 If an ensign passes his regimental, and 'spins' in his special examination.

**** With adverbs.**

14. spin down: a. *trans. Biol.* To centrifuge so as to cause the separation of components.

1947 ACKERMAN & REGATO *Cancer* xiv. 817 The fluid is spun down and sectioned. **1965** *Proc. Nat. Acad. Sci.* LIV. 400 A unit of blood was drawn into a heparin receiving pack and spun down slowly for 15–20 min. **1978** *Sci. Amer.* Dec. 30/2 If the unbonded cells are then spun down into a mixed-up mass and given fluid containing antibiotics and the right salts, new hydras form in a few days.

b. *intr. Astr.* Of a rotating body, esp. a star: to rotate more slowly, usu. because of decreasing angular momentum. Also *trans.*

1967 *Nature* 24 June 1297/2 The boundary layer suction causes a slow internal motion which stretches vortex lines and spins down the solar interior. *Ibid.* 1299/1 The region itself spins down quickly. **1976** *Sci. News* 30 Oct. 280 This pulsar is spinning down so slowly that when the effects of its motion across the sky on its apparent (to us) spin rate are considered, it may actually be spinning up from the point of view of someone riding along with it. **1979** *Nature* 29 Feb. 602/2 Any loss of radiation from the region will transport vast quantities of angular momentum away from the rotating body. The reaction back on the body itself will cause it to spin down.

15. spin off: a. *trans.* To throw off by or as if by centrifugal force in spinning; freq. *fig.*, esp. (*a*) *U.S. Comm.*, to distribute (stock of a new company) to shareholders of a parent company; to create (a company) in this way; (*b*) to produce as a by-product, side-effect, or indirect benefit.

1957 *N.Y. Times* 9 June F1/3 Right now, there is considerable speculation that du Pont will 'spin off' its G.M. stock—that is, give it to its own stockholders in the form of a dividend. **1959** *Wall St. Jrnl.* 20 May 1/5 A subsidiary set up in early 1950 to rent out space in an engineering firm's new building was spun off in December, 1954. **1964** *Science* 29 May 1113 The Systems Development Corporation (SDC) was 'spun off' by RAND in 1956 to help specifically with design and programming for the first computerized air defense system. **1969** *Physics Bull.* June 215/2 If .. pulsars are neutron stars, .. then these could rotate at up to 10^3 Hz; they would 'spin off' electrons (or plasma) which would be accelerated in the star's magnetic field. **1969** *Wall St. Jrnl.* 3 July 4/2 The publicly owned company then 'spins off' those shares to its holders, who, in turn, often sell the shares to other traders. **1972** *Real Estate Rev.* Winter 5/2 A black who has invested his savings in a commercial or residential venture is not permitted.. to parlay small investments into big ones by spinning them off through refinancing vehicles. **1972** *Publishers Weekly* 4 Dec. 35/1 From the file, the publisher can now produce updated editions with minimum effort, and can spin off subsidiary products as well. **1974** *Nature* 29 Mar. 459/2 Several papers have already been spun off from discussions and presentations at the CETI conference. **1977** *Time* 10 Jan. 47/3 Tandy Corp. has spun off most of its other businesses into separate companies chaired by Charles Tandy. **1979** *Daily Tel.* 15 Jan. 5/6 'Softly, Softly' was spun off 'Z Cars' and no one complained about that.

b. *intr.* To be thrown or move off by or as if by centrifugal force in spinning; usu. *fig.*

1969 *N.Y. Rev. Books* 16 Jan. 33/2 (Advt.), More interesting, however, is the way in which the material is organized to allow the class or individuals to spin-off into the study of related problems. **1969** *Sci. Jrnl.* Nov. 74 People have claimed.. that space is a great thing because all the technology evolved will ultimately spin-off to the commercial market place. **1971** *New Scientist* 4 Mar. 488/1 These small companies specialising in technologically advanced products have 'spun off' largely from powerful local universities. **1971** *Daily Tel.* (Colour Suppl.) 6 Aug. 12/4 This prestige spins off to make Europeans more and more rail conscious.

16. spin out: *intr.* Of a vehicle: to skid round out of control. *N. Amer. slang.*

1954 *Amer. Speech* XXIX. 102 Last Sunday some car spun out and hit five parked cars. **1971** M. Tak *Truck Talk* 150 *Spin out*, to lose traction on a slippery road.

17. spin up: *Astr.* Of a rotating body, esp. a star: to rotate more quickly because of a gain in angular momentum or a redistribution of matter. Also *trans.*

1967 *Nature* 24 June 1299/1 If the interior were rotating at the rapid rate suggested by Dicke, the convective envelope would be spun up to this rate in a very short time. **1974** *Ibid.* 29 Nov. 366/1 As the Sun evolves, its rotating core gets smaller while its outer part spins up. **1976** [see sense 14 b above]. **1978** *Nature* 16 Feb. 635/1 Before the neutron star starts to accrete and spin up.. it spends a comparatively long time being spun down through the weak stellar wind of its companion. **1979** *Ibid.* 11 Jan. 116/1 The neutron star would be spun up in the process.

***18.* In combs., as **spin-'em-round**, a game of chance (see quot. 1859); also *dial.*, a merry-go-round; **spin-heat**, the rotatory form of heat-energy.

1851 Mayhew *Lond. Lab.* I. 4 The Proprietors of Street Games, as swings,.. down the dolly, spin-'em-rounds, prick the garter, thimble-rig, etc. **1859** *Slang Dict.* 98 *Spin-em-rounds*, a street game consisting of a piece of brass, wood, or iron, balanced on a pin and turned quickly around on a board, when the point, arrow shaped, stops at a number and decides the bet one way or the other. **1899** Lockyer in *Nature* 20 Apr. 585/2 To get concrete images of these effects we spoke of path-heat, spin-heat, and wobble-heat.

‖**spina** (ˈspaɪnə). [L. *spīna* SPINE *sb.*[1]]

1. The backbone. Now only *Path.* in ***spina bifida***, a congenital malformation of widely varying severity in which there is a failure of one or more vertebræ to surround completely the meninges and spinal cord, usu. with effects on spinal cord function. [mod.L. (N. Tulpius *Observationes Medicæ* (1641) III. 233, 235).]

c **1400** *Lanfranc's Cirurg.* 167 þese boones bineþe þe necke is clepid þe rigge ouþer spina. **1674** Grew *Anat. Pl., Disc. Mixture* (1682) 249 The Spina of a Fish (that which I used was of a cod-fish) maketh a Bullition one degree higher. **1720** *Phil. Trans.* XXXI. 100 These Tumours constantly attend the *Spina Bifida.* **1740** *Ibid.* XLIII. 11 A perfect *Spina bifida* must suppose the very canal and *Medulla spinalis* to divide into Two Branches. **1800** T. V. Okes (*title*), An Account of Spina Bifida. **1829** Cooper *Good's Study Med.* (ed. 3) V. 412 In spina bifida, the fluid is always within the dura mater of the cord. **1853** J. Erichsen *Science & Art of Surgery* xliv. 631 Spina bifida may be met with in any part of the vertebral column. **1878** T. Bryant *Pract. Surg.* I. 256 A spina bifida is essentially a hernia of the membranes of the cord through an opening in the spine. **1885** *Trans. Clin. Soc. London* XVIII. 361 Lastly, this examination serves to complete the refutation of the view.. that spina bifida in the great majority of cases is due to a dropsy of the central canal of the cord. **1887** *Lancet* 2 July 4/2 The term 'spina bifida occulta' is applied to a defect in the arches of the vertebræ such as occurs in the commoner forms of spina bifida, but no tumour or cyst appears externally. The deformity is, however, accompanied by some remarkable external conditions. **1965** E. D. Smith *Spina Bifida* i. 5/1 In 1875, Virchow, who introduced the term 'spina bifida occulta', used it to describe a spina bifida in association with lumbosacral hypertrichosis. **1966** [see *meningo-myelocele* s.v. MENINGO-]. **1974** Passmore & Robson *Compan. Med. Stud.* III. xxxvi. 9/1 Spina bifida is an incomplete vertebral arch. When this bony defect is covered with skin and fascia it is usually symptomless, and is called spina bifida occulta.

†**2.** *spina ventosa*: (see quots.). *Obs.*

1693 tr. *Blancard's Phys. Dict.* (ed. 2), *Spina Ventosa*, an Ulceration in which the Bones are eaten by a malignant Humour without any Pain. **1746** *Phil. Trans.* XLIV. 199 This Distemper was found to be a *Spina ventosa*, or Cariosity in the Body of the *Os Humeri*, whereby about four Inches of the solid Bone had been destroyed. **1753** *Chambers' Cycl.* Suppl. s.v., In the *spina ventosa* the caries, or erosion of the bone, is occasioned by a depravity of the contained fluids.

3. *Rom. Antiq.* The barrier running up the middle of a Roman circus.

1766 Smollett *Trav.* xxxii. II. 131 A good part of this was taken up by the spina, or middle space, adorned with temples, statues, and two great obelisks. **1832** W. Gell *Pompeiana* I. vi. 103 The *spina* or perhaps the goal is also visible. **1842** *Smith's Dict. Gr. & Rom. Antiq.* 230/1 At each extremity of the spina were placed.. three wooden cylinders.

†**spinace.** *Obs.* Also **spynas, spyn(n)es.** Earlier form of PINNACE.

1442 *Rolls of Parlt.* V. 59/2 There most be awaytyng and attendaunt opon hem IIII Spynes, in eche Spynes xxv men. *Ibid.* 60/1 The Shippes, Barges, Balingers and Spinaces. **1458** *Paston Lett.* I. 429 Then my Lord.. manned fyve schippis of forecastell, and iij. carvells, and iiij. spynnes. **1466** *Mann. & Househ. Exp.* (Roxb.) 205 My mastyr paid.. for a pompe, v. polyves, and odre aparaylle for the spynas.

spinaceous (spɪˈneɪʃəs), *a.*[1] [f. mod.L. *Spinacia* spinach.] Belonging to the spinach family.

1822 Loudon *Encycl. Gard.* 711 Spinaceous Plants. The excellence of this class consisting in the succulency of the leaves [etc.]. **1842** —— *Suburban Hort.* 659 Substitutes for spinaceous esculents are to be found in chenopodiaceous plants generally.

spinaceous (spaɪˈneɪʃəs), *a.*[2] [f. L. *spīna* spine + -ACEOUS.] Furnished with spines.

1875 Knight *Dict. Mech.* 2621/1 The tangles are used to catch small, delicate, or spinaceous forms of marine life.

spinach (ˈspɪnɪdʒ, -ɪtʃ). Forms: α. 6 **spynnage, spenege,** 7–9 **spinnage,** 6–9 **spinage.** β. 6 **spynache, spinech,** 6–7 **spinache,** 6– **spinach.** [ad. OF. *espinage*, (*e*)*spinache* (also *-ace*), = Catal. *espinach*, Sp. *espinaca*, It. *spinace*, Roum. *spenac*, med.L. *spinachia* (*-achium*), *spinacia* (*-acium*), of doubtful origin. Cf. MDu. *spinage*, *-agie*, *-aetse* (Du. *spinazie*, Flem. *spinagie*), LG. *spinase*, *-axe*, obs. G. *spinacie*, *-asche*, G. dial. *spinaz*, MHG. and G. *spinat* (whence Da. *spinat*, Sw. *spenat*).

The difficult problem of the ultimate origin of the word is complicated by variation of the ending in the Romanic languages. In addition to *espinache*, *-age*, OF. had also *espinoche* (still in dial. use), *-oce*, = med.L. *spinochia*, and *espinarde*, *espinar* (F. *épinard*), = Prov. *espinarc*, med.L. *spinarium*, *-argium*. Pg. exhibits the further variant *espinafre*. By older writers the stem of these forms was supposed to be L. *spīna*, in allusion to the prickly seeds of a common species. De Vic considers the various forms to be adoption of Arab *isfināj*, Pers. *isfānāj*, *ispānāk*, *aspanākh* (Richardson), but it is doubtful whether these are really native words. It is difficult to explain either the Romanic or the Oriental forms from the synonymous *Hispanicum olus* recorded from the 16th cent. and represented by older F. *herbe d'Espaigne* (Cotgrave).]

1. a. A plant (*Spinacia oleracea*) belonging to the N.O. *Chenopodiaceæ*, extensively cultivated for culinary purposes; the succulent leaves of this plant used as a vegetable.

α. **1530** Palsgr. 274 Spynnage an herbe, *espinars*. **1568** Turner *Herbal* III. 71 Spinage or spinech is an herbe lately found and not long in use. **1656** Earl Monm. tr. *Boccalini's Advts. fr. Parnass.* I. xvi. (1674) 18 Gardners might know Nettles and Henbane, from Spinnage and Lettice. **1732** Arbuthnot *Rules of Diet* in *Aliments*, etc. I. 249 Spinage emollient, but not very nourishing. **1774** Goldsmith *Nat. Hist.* (1776) III. 4 The grass has the appearance of boiled spinage. **1808** *Med. Jrnl.* XIX. 38 Neither boiled spinage, nor succory, possess this quality. **1861** Bentley *Man. Bot.* 623 Some are used as pot-herbs, as Spinage.

β. **1538** Turner *Libellus*, Seutlomalochon,.. a nostris spynache nominatur. **1568** [see above]. **1578** Lyte *Dodoens* 556 This pot-herbe, or rather Salet herbe, is called.. Spinache. **1671** Salmon *Syn. Med.* III. xxii. 433 Spinach.. is used in sallads,.. and helps inflamations.. of the Stomach. **1747** Wesley *Prim. Physick* (1762) 71 Eat largely of Spinach. **1791** Boswell *Johnson* 11 Apr. 1773, We had a very good soup, a boiled leg of lamb and spinach. **1839** Barham *Ingol. Leg.* Ser. I. *Lay St. Dunstan*, St. Dunstan himself sits there.. eating poach'd eggs with spinach and toast. **1883** *Cassell's Fam. Mag.* Sept. 593 The winter spinach must next be thinned out.

b. With distinguishing epithets denoting varieties of the common garden spinach.

1600 Surflet *Countrie Farme* II. xix. 226 Spinage (so called bicause his seede is prickly) is of two sorts, the male and the female. **1731** Miller *Gard. Dict.* s.v. *Spinachia*, The common prickly or narrow-leav'd Spinach. *Ibid.*, Common smooth-seeded Spinach. *Ibid.*, These Male Plants are by the Gardeners commonly called She Spinach. **1763** Mills *Syst. Pract. Husb.* IV. 89 The oblong oval leaved spinage, commonly called plantain spinage. **1842** Loudon *Suburban Hort.* 656 There are three varieties, the round-seeded,.. the Flanders spinach,.. and the prickly-seeded, or common winter spinach.

c. Applied (with distinguishing terms) to other species of *Spinacia*, or to plants in some way resembling or taking the place of this, as ***Australian***, †***Cretic***, ***French***, ***mountain***, ***New Zealand***, ***perennial***, ***strawberry***, ***wild spinach*** (see quots.).

1866 *Treas. Bot.* 267/2 *Australian spinach (*Chenopodium erosum*). **1874** *Ibid.* Suppl. 1343/2 Spinach, Australian, *Chenopodium auricomum*. **1889** Maiden *Usef. Pl.* 16 *Chenopodium murale*,.. Australian Spinach. **1753** *Chambers' Cycl.* Suppl. s.v. *Spinachia*, The procumbent *Cretic spinach. **1842** Loudon *Suburban Hort.* 657 The orache, or *French spinach.. is a chenopodiaceous polygamous annual. **1822** Loudon *Encycl. Gard.* 714 The Orach, or *Mountain Spinach, *Atriplex hortensis*. **1866** *Treas. Bot.* 108/2 The Garden Orache, or Mountain Spinach,.. [is] a native of Tartary. **1824** Loudon *Encycl. Gard.* (ed. 2) 637 *New Zealand Spinach, *Tetragonia expansa*. **1849** Balfour *Man. Bot.* §881 Some of them [ficoids] are used as articles of diet, as the leaves of.. New Zealand Spinach. **1842** Loudon *Suburban Hort.* 657 The *perennial spinach.. is a chenopodiaceous perennial, a native of Britain. **1760** J. Lee *Introd. Bot.* App. 328 *Strawberry Spinach, *Blitum*. *c* **1710** Petiver *Cat. Ray's Eng. Herbal* Tab. vii, *Wild Spinage. **1790** W. H. Marshall *Rur. Econ. Midl.* II. 443 *Spinage, wild*,.. goosefoot. **1867** Baker *Nile Trib.* viii, There are several varieties of wild spinach.

2. *ellipt.* As a moth-name.

1832 J. Rennie *Consp. Butterfl. & Moths* 123 The Spinach (*E. Spinachiata*, Stephens) appears in July. **1896** Lydekker *Roy. Nat. Hist.* VI. 117 The little moth.. known as the dark spinach (*Larentia chenopodiata*).

3. a. In allusive use (cf. GAMMON *sb.*[4] 3).

The words *gammon and spinage* are part of the refrain to the song 'A frog he would a-wooing go'.

1850 Dickens *Dav. Copp.* xxii, 'What a world of gammon and spinnage it is, though, ain't it!'

b. Nonsense, rubbish. *U.S. colloq.* (now *rare*).

[**1928** C. Rose in *New Yorker* 8 Dec. 27/2 (*caption*) 'It's broccoli dear.' 'I say it's spinach, and I say the hell with it.'] **1929** J. P. McEvoy *Hollywood Girl* xiii. 205 It's a flop and then I says to him, in other words I say it's spinach and I say to hell with it. **1933** E. Hawes (*title*) Fashion is spinach. **1934** A. Woollcott *While Rome Burns* 304 This.. reticence.. will.. be described by certain temperaments as.. good taste... I say it's spinach. **1950** R. Bissell *Stretch on River* xxi. 207 'It's a transferral of intent. It's a result of childhood trauma. It's Oedipus denial,' said my sister-in-law, who was beautiful, thank god, so you could put up with this spinach.

4. *attrib.* and *Comb.*, as ***spinach-coloured***, ***-like*** adjs., ***-plant***, ***-seed***; **spinach beet** (see quots.); = *silver beet* s.v. SILVER *sb.* and *a.* 21 e; **spinach-green**, (*a*) a dark green vegetable dye made from spinach; (*b*) a dark green colour; also *attrib.* or as *adj.*; **spinach jade** (see quot. 1964); also *attrib.*; **spinach moth** (see quot.); **spinach-stool**, an evacuation of the colour of spinach.

1842 Loudon *Suburban Hort.* 658 The *spinach beet, leaf beet, or white beet, *Beta cicla*,.. a native of the sea-shores of Spain and Portugal. **1885** W. Robinson tr. *Vilmorin-Andrieux's Veg. Garden* 279 The leaves of the Common White Leaf-Beet, or Spinach Beet, may be cut for use even earlier. **1978** *Times* 17 July 14/3 The experts recommend growing Swiss chard, otherwise known as spinach beet. **1843** Thackeray *Jerome Paturat* Wks. 1900 XIII. 393 A certain Oscar,.. who paints *spinach-coloured landscapes. **1845** E. Acton *Mod. Cookery* xx. 508 (*heading*) *Spinach green, for colouring sweet dishes. **1861** Mrs. Beeton *Bk. Househ. Managem.* 250 (*heading*) Spinach green for colouring various dishes... Pick and wash the spinach free from dirt, and pound the leaves in a mortar to extract the juice; [etc.]. **1896** *Westm. Gaz.* 7 May 3/1 A neckband of rich bright colour, cerise velvet or perhaps orange or spinach green. **1937** *Burlington Mag.* June 300/2 A fine example of the bold relief of the K'ang-hsi period is a bowl of spinach-green nephrite. **1943** R. Godden *Rungli-Rungliot* 4 The engine.. was painted a spinach-green. **1968** 'J. Ross' *Diminished by Death* xvii. 163 A figured silk confection in spinach green. **1975** *Times* 31 May 7/2 His former employers ought to be spinach-green with envy. **1980** *Catal. Fine Chinese Ceramics* (Sotheby, Hong Kong) 210 A spinach-green jade covered censer, raised on tripod supports. **1958** W. Willetts *Chinese Art* I. ii. 61 Siberian jade has a rather distinctive appearance owing to the presence of small particles of black graphite embedded in the stone, which leads the Chinese to call it '*spinach jade'. **1964** M. Medley *Handbk. Chinese Art* 108/2 *Spinach jade*, in Chinese *po-ts'ai-yü*; a nephrite from Siberia characterised by black flecks of graphite. **1976** 'M. Delving' *China Expert* xii. 158 Mei was wearing a *ch'i pao* of dark grey silk.. fastened up to the neck with spinach jade buttons. **1886** P. Robinson *Teetotum Trees* 123, I suddenly became aware of a peculiar circular movement in one of the *spinach-like plants. **1887** *Cassell's Encycl. Dict.* s.v., Northern *spinach-moth,.. *Cidaria populata*, a British geometer-moth. **1842** Loudon *Suburban Hort.* 657 It has been more or less in culture as a *spinach plant since the beginning of the present century. **1763** Mills *Syst. Pract. Husb.* IV. 89 The best way for those who have ground enough, is to sow their *spinage seeds alone. **1888** Goodhart *Dis. Children* (ed. 3) iv. 74 The *spinach stool has commonly been said to be due to altered blood.

spinachy (ˈspɪnɪdʒɪ, -ɪtʃɪ), *a.* [f. SPINACH + -Y[1].] Characteristic or suggestive of spinach.

1950 O. Nash *Family Reunion* (1951) 18 So spinach was too spinachy For Leonardo da Vinaci. **1981** P. Theroux *Mosquito Coast* xv. 191 Tiptoeing through this spinachy swamp on duckboards.

spinagre: see SPIGURNEL[1] (quot. *c* 1450).

spinal, *sb.* Also 4, 7 **spinall**, 5 **spynal**, 7 **spinnall, spinnel**, 9 **spinel.** [Of obscure origin; in sense 2 app. a. G. *spinal* (Du. *spinaal*), thread or yarn of various kinds.]

†**1.** Some textile fabric. *Obs.*

1399–40 *Compotus frat. orat. dominice in civitate Ebor.* (MS.), Et de xiiij d. pro iiij ulnis et dimidio et j quart. de spinall pro corpore dicti Richardi involvendo. **1431** *Maldon Crt. Rolls* Bundle 18 No. 6, j pese de spynal contin. xii ellys, prec. le elle iii d. obol.

2. A kind of yarn (see later quots.).

16.. *Advt. of M. Gregory, Haberdasher, at the Raven and Sun, Drury Lane*, Inkle and Spinnel, and Scotch Yarn. **1692** *Patent Office* No. 286. 1 The Makeing of Spinall Yarne is a new Invention never practiced before. *Ibid.*, Severall workmen out of Germany.. skilled in makeing the said spinnall. **1858** Simmonds *Dict. Trade* 203/2 Unwrought inkle, or short spinel, is bleached yarn. *Ibid.* 355/1 *Spinal*, a kind of unwrought inkle.

spinal, obs. form of SPINEL (ruby).

spinal ('spaɪnəl), *a.* Also 6–7 **spinall.** [ad. late L. *spīnālis*, f. *spīna* SPINE *sb.*[1] So F. *spinal*, It. *spinale*, Sp. *espinal.*]

1. Of or pertaining to, forming part of or located in, the spine or backbone: **a.** In ***spinal marrow*** or ***cord.***

(*a*) **1578** BANISTER *Hist. Man* I. 6 Cerebellum..lyeth vnder the brayne, and the spinall marey thence slydeth from the head. **1615** CROOKE *Body of Man* 875 Some Nerues.. doe arise from the brayne,..others from the Spinall marrow. **1646** SIR T. BROWNE *Pseud. Ep.* 189 The spinall marrow, which is but the braine prolonged. **1767** GOOCH *Treat. Wounds* I. 341 Wounds in any part of the spinal-marrow require no peculiar treatment. **1830** HERSCHEL *Study Nat. Phil.* 87 The seat of the exertion..is demonstrably..either in the brain or in the spinal marrow. **1881** MIVART *Cat* 15 If the skull and backbone be cut through, the white substance of the brain and spinal marrow will be found within them.

(*b*) **1836** *Penny Cycl.* V. 330/1 A long cord of nervous matter filling the cavity of the vertebral or spinal column, called the spinal cord. **1851** CARPENTER *Man. Phys.* (ed. 2) 417 Convulsive actions, which are dependent upon the medulla oblongata and spinal cord, may continue for a minute or two longer. **1899** *Allbutt's Syst. Med.* VI. 478 [Certain cases] were confused by him with cases of spinal cord origin.

b. With other sbs., as *artery*, *bone*, *canal*, etc. ***spinal puncture*** or ***tap***: the insertion of a needle into the subarachnoid space of the spine, usu. in the lumbar region, so that cerebrospinal fluid may be withdrawn or something introduced.

1725 POPE *Odyss.* x. 668 Full endlong from the roof the sleeper fell, And snapped the spinal joint and waked in hell. **1726** MONRO *Anat.* 181 That Protuberance..is called the Spinal Process, from which this whole Series of Bones has got its Name. **1760–72** H. BROOKE *Fool of Qual.* (1809) III. 99 The stake..they run up withinside the spinal bone. **1771** *Encycl. Brit.* I. 219 [It] is fixed..to the last spinal apophysis of the back. *c* **1793** *Ibid.* (1797) I. 759 A thin transparent substance, which from its indentations between the spinal nerves has obtained the name of *ligamentum denticulatum.* **1799** *Med. Jrnl.* II. 461 The spinal artery..had been noticed by Berengar, as a white shining line. **1826** KIRBY & SP. *Entomol.* xxxvii. IV. 18 Those remarkable nerves described by Lyonnet under the name of *spinal bridle* (*bride épinière*). **1845** BUDD *Dis. Liver* 360 They [hydatid tumors] have been met with, but in comparatively very few instances,..in the spinal canal. **1881** MIVART *Cat* 275 The 11th, or Spinal Accessory Nerve, is a comparatively insignificant one. **1896** *Brit. Med. Jrnl.* Suppl. 4 Jan. 1/3 Only a few drops of fluid could be obtained by spinal puncture. **1919** A. LEVINSON *Cerebrospinal Fluid* i. 25 Corning, who was the first to use spinal puncture, employed an operation that was fraught with danger to the cord. **1972** NOBACK & DEMAREST *Nervous System* iv. 35 Some CSF is withdrawn and replaced by air which acts as a contrast medium. The air is introduced by passing a needle either directly into the ventricle or between the lower two lumbar vertebrae (spinal tap) into the lumbar cistern. **1979** *Sci. Amer.* Aug. 66/3 He underwent at least 48 spinal taps, three air encephalograms and numerous myelograms. **1980** K. E. MOYER *Neuroanatomy* XII. 36/2 In a spinal tap, or spinal puncture, the needle is always introduced into the subarachnoid space below the termination of the spinal cord itself.

c. *absol.* With ellipse of *artery* or *nerve.*

1888 W. R. GOWERS *Man. Dis. Nervous System* II. 406 It usually supplies the 'bulbar' nuclei,..in part directly, and in part by the anterior spinal. **1899** *Allbutt's Syst. Med.* VIII. 33 If all are not directly innervated by the spinal accessory, division..may not be completely successful.

2. (See quot.) *rare*⁻¹.

1646 SIR T. BROWNE *Pseud. Ep.* 203 All spinall [fishes], or such as have no ribs, but only a back bone, or somewhat analogous thereto, as Eeles, Congers, Lampries.

3. Of diseased conditions: Affecting the spine.

1838 DICKENS *Nickleby* xxx, Letters inflicted with every possible variation of spinal deformity. **1878** A. M. HAMILTON *Nerv. Dis.* 219 Spinal hemorrhage is usually the result of a transmutism. **1878** R. BRAITHWAITE *Life & Lett. W. Pennefather* ii. 22 The memoranda..tell of such..suffering and debility, from spinal irritation. **1884** *Queen* 9 Feb. 132/2 (Advt.), Partial paralysis. Spinal curvature,.. constipation, corpulence, &c. **1976** J. BLACKBURN *Face of Lion* viii. 54 A cripple with one leg longer than the other and a pronounced spinal curvature.

Comb. **1875** KNIGHT *Dict. Mech.* 2268/1 *Spinal-Distortion Apparatus*, an apparatus designed to gradually restore the spine to its normal condition when it has become curved.

4. Resembling a spine or backbone in form or function.

1841 *Florist's Jrnl.* (1846) II. 301 There may be rain on the central, or spinal, mountains and hills. **1856** KANE *Arct. Expl.* I. xxiii. 301 Everywhere else the spinal ridge seemed unbroken. **1903** *Westm. Gaz.* 20 May 12/1 If water does not fall on his acres, he will bring it to them from his long spinal mountain range if necessary.

5. a. Of qualities: Arising from, seated in, the spine. Also *fig.*

1855 BAIN *Senses & Int.* I. ii. §18 The permanent tension of the muscle is in part due to spinal influence. **1890** *Pall Mall G.* 5 Sept. 1/2 The news will give a spice to sport, a spinal strength to the desultory conversation of the rambler.

b. ***spinal reflex***, a reflex involving the spinal cord but not the brain.

1898 *Phil. Trans. R. Soc.* B. CXC. 141 In the Dog and Cat the spinal reflex movements are more forcible. **1924** *Jrnl. Physiol.* LVIII. 411 Shivering to cold cannot be produced as a spinal reflex. **1978** *Brain Res.* CXLII. 431 Stimulation of all three segmental nerves simultaneously produced up to a 100% increase in size of the spinal reflex.

6. Of appliances: Adapted to, intended for, application to the spine. Of a seat or carriage: designed to support the spine. Now *Hist.*

1864–8 J. CHAPMAN (title-p.), Sea-Sickness, and how to prevent it..by Means of the Spinal Ice Bag. **1875** KNIGHT *Dict. Mech.* 2268/1 *Spinal Brace*,..a brace for remedying posterior curvature of the spine. **1884** *Queen* 16 Feb. 189/2 (Advt.), Leveson's Improved Invalid's Carriage... Adjustable Spinal Couches. **1895** *Arnold & Sons' Catal. Surg. Instrum.* 782 Spinal Support,..for double lateral curvature. **1900** *Illustr. London News* 25 Aug. 291/2 (Advt.), Adjustable Bath Chair or Spinal Carriage. **1917** *Harrods Gen. Catal.* 1038 A very easy and comfortable Bath Chair and Spinal Carriage Combined, enabling a person to take outdoor exercise in a sitting, reclining, or horizontal position. **1973** *Times* 7 May 17/7 Many years ago I travelled in a spinal carriage every few weeks from Selby to Leeds and back in the guard's van.

7. *Physiol.* **a.** Involving the spine as containing a major part of the central nervous system: ***spinal anæsthesia***, ***analgesia***, anæsthesia, analgesia induced by an injection into the spine (see quot. 1938); ***spinal block***, (*a*) an obstruction to the flow of the cerebro-spinal fluid; (*b*) spinal anæsthesia or analgesia; ***spinal shock***, a temporary flaccid paralysis and loss of reflexes in some muscles that may follow an injury to the spine, the ones affected being those whose nerves come from a point in the spinal cord below the site of the injury.

1885 *N.Y. Med. Jrnl.* XLII. 483/2 (*heading*) *Spinal anaesthesia and local medication of the cord. **1912** *Jrnl. Amer. Med. Assoc.* 23 Nov. 1859/1 There are practically no contraindications to the employment of spinal *analgesia. **1938** MAXSON & BABCOCK *Spinal Anesthesia* i. 1 Spinal anesthesia is the term most commonly used... It is technically correct when all the sensory faculties—touch, temperature and muscle sense, as well as pain—are abolished in the affected region. Spinal analgesia is the correct technical term when pain sense alone is abolished without the loss of the epicritical faculties. The distinction between the two terms, however, is rarely made. **1974** LICHTIGER & MOYA *Introd. Pract. Anesthesia* xv. 152 Tetracaine is the most commonly used drug for spinal anesthesia. **1976** D. D. MOIR *Obstetric Anaesthesia & Analgesia* vii. 209 Low spinal analgesia is eminently suited to the performance of forceps delivery. **1928** *Arch. Neurol. & Psychiatry* XIX. 613 The compression of the veins of the neck..is used most often in spinal lesions with level symptoms in order to determine whether a '*spinal block' is present. **1976** D. D. MOIR *Obstetric Anaesthesia & Analgesia* vii. 215 A low spinal block creates a tranquil patient, free of all pain and operating conditions are excellent. **1898** *Phil. Trans. R. Soc.* B. CXC. 134 Goltz's descriptions of *spinal shock are masterly, but they refer entirely to the Dog, and to transection below the middle of the back. **1962** D. D. BONNYCASTLE in Keele & Smith *Assessment of Pain in Man & Animals* 235 It was felt that these animals might still be exhibiting some degree of spinal shock, and therefore we prepared a colony of chronic spinal rats. **1978** *Exper. Neurol.* IX. 16 Spinal shock is caused by the lack of excitatory input from the brain.

b. Used to describe an animal whose spine has been severed from its brain.

1900 C. S. SHERRINGTON in E. A. Schäfer *Text-bk. Physiol.* II. 818 The spinal frog, when placed on its back, does not, as a rule, right itself. **1917** *Brain* XL. 230 'Spinal man' cannot stand, and shows no primary extensor activity. **1962** [see prec. sense]. **1971** *Sci. Amer.* Aug. 75/2 Sherrington found for example, that a spinal dog would withdraw a leg that received a sharp poke and would simultaneously brace the opposite leg to assume the weight removed from the withdrawn leg.

8. *Comb.*, as ***spinal-depressant***, ***-stimulant.***

1874 GARROD & BAXTER *Mat. Med.* 263 Commercial conia was found to exhibit spinal-stimulant and spinal-depressant actions.

Hence **'spinally** *adv.*

1885 MEREDITH *Diana* II. viii. 191 Spinally prepared..to repay dignity of mien with a similar erectness of dignity.

spinar ('spɪnɑː(r)). *Astr.* [f. *spin*(*ning st*)*ar*, after QUASAR, PULSAR.] A hypothetical, supermassive, rapidly rotating celestial object which may be located in the nuclei of some active galaxies and quasars, and which could help to account for the huge energy output of quasars.

1971 MORRISON & CAVALIERE in D. J. K. O'Connell *Nuclei of Galaxies* 487 By spinars we mean a class of bodies storing a considerable fraction of their total energy in a single, continuous degree of freedom—rotation... Pulsars are a very special subclass of spinars. **1977** *Astron. & Astrophysics* LVI. 166/2 We will consider..a supermassive oblique rotator (SOR) having solid-body rotation and quasi-dipole magnetic field. In the 'cold' version such a rotator coincides with a 'spinar' or a 'giant pulsar' proposed by Morrison. **1978** *Nature* 28 Sept. 282/1 The nonthermal radiation of a spinar can in some circumstances far exceed the thermal (Eddington-limited) component.

spinaret, variant of SPINNERET.

spination (spaɪ'neɪʃən). [f. L. *spīna* SPINE *sb.*[1]] The condition of having spines; the manner in which spines are formed or arranged.

1866 BOWERBANK *Brit. Spongiadæ* II. 199 The internal defensive spicula..are readily to be distinguished from the skeleton ones, by..their entire spination.

†**spin-coal.** *Obs.* (See quot.)

1712 *Phil. Trans.* XXVII. 541, XI. Coal, more black and shining, called Spin-Coal. [Hence in some later works.]

†**spincop.** *Obs.* In 5 **spyn-**. [a. older Flem. *spinnekoppe* (Kilian), Du. and Flem. *spinnekop*, f. *spinne* spider, or *spinnen* to spin: cf. COP *sb.*[3]] A spider.

1474 CAXTON *Chesse* II. iii, The lawes of somme ben like vnto the nettis of spyncoppis. **1480** —— *Myrr.* II. xv. 101 The spyther or spyncop. **1483** —— *Gold. Leg.* 114/1 By the wylle of god cam spyncoppes and made their werke and nettes afore him.

spind, variant of SPINE *sb.*[2], sward.

†**spinde.** *Obs.*⁻¹ In 5 **spynde.** [a. MDu. *spynde*, *spinde*, var. *spende*, = med.L. *spenda* (:—**expenda*): cf. SPENCE[1].] A larder, pantry.

1481 CAXTON *Reynard* (Arb.) 26 This preest had a spynde wherin henge many a good flitche of bacon.

'spindlage. Also **spindleage.** [f. SPINDLE *sb.*] The number of spindles employed in a particular mill, district, trade, etc.

1908 *Westm. Gaz.* 24 Jan. 4/1 During the last three years Lancashire has increased her cotton spindleage to the extent of about 11,000,000.

spindle ('spɪnd(ə)l), *sb.* Forms: α. 1 **spinil, spinel, spinl,** 5 *Sc.* **spyn(y)le,** 7 *Sc.* **spynell,** 6, 8 **spinnel,** 9 *dial.* **spin(n)el, -al, spin(n)le.** β. 4–6 **spindel** (4 **-elle,** 6 **-ell**), 5–6 **spyndel, -ell** (5 **-ill, -yl, -yll, -ylle, -ulle**), 6, *Sc.* 8–9 **spyndle,** (2) 6– **spindle.** [OE. *spinel* fem., = OHG. *spinela*, *-ala* (MHG. *spinele*, *-el*, *spinle*) and *spinnila*, *-ela*, *-ala* (MHG. *spinnile*, *-ele*, *-el*), f. the stem of *spinnan* SPIN *v.* The intrusive *d* of the later forms appears also in MDu. and Du., MHG. and G., OFris. *spindel* (NFris. *spandel*); cf. also Sw. *spindel* (MSw. *spinnil*) spider.

Early assimilation of *nl* gave rise to the MDu., MLG., and MHG. *spille* (Du. *spil*, LG. and G. *spille*): cf. SPILL *sb.*[2]]

I. 1. a. A simple instrument employed in spinning by hand, consisting of a slender rounded rod (usually of wood), tapering towards each end, which is made to revolve and twist into thread the fibres drawn out from a bunch of wool, flax, or other material.

c **725** *Corpus Gloss.* (Hessels) F 378 *Fusum*, spinel. *Ibid.* N 108 *Nitorium*, spinil. *a* **1100** *Gerefa* in *Anglia* IX. 263 He sceal fela towtola, flexlinan, spinle, reol, ȝearnwindan, stodlan..habban. *c* **1150** *Voc.* in Wr.-Wülcker 547 *Fusus*, spindle. *c* **1325** *Gloss. W. de Bibbesw.* in Wright *Voc.* 157 *Le fusil*, spindel. *c* **1350** *Geburt Jesu* in Horstm. *Altengl. Leg.* (1875) 105 Bot mid spindle and with nelde, his moder him bi wan. **1410** *Nottingham Rec.* II. 70, j spyndel, pretii ijd. **1470–85** MALORY *Arthur* XVII. vi. 698 Carue me oute of this tree as moche woode as wylle make me a spyndyl. *a* **1529** SKELTON *E. Rummyng* 299 They layde to pledge theyr wharrowe, Theyr rybskyn and theyr spyndell. **1577** B. GOOGE tr. *Heresbach's Husb.* 11 b, The smaller sort [of necessaries] be these,..Distaues, Spindelles, Wharles. **1615** CHAPMAN *Odyss.* x. 151 As she some web wrought; or her spindles twine She cherisht with her song. **1631** ANCHORAN *Comenius' Gate Tongues* 98 [They] draw their threads, whether it be with a reele, or with a spindle, and a wherne. **1720** POPE *Iliad* XXIII. 890 As closely following as the running Thread The Spindle follows. **1758** JOHNSON *Idler* No. 5 ¶8 The prejudices and pride of man have long presumed the sword and spindle made for different hands. **1816** SCOTT *Antiq.* xxvi, The younger children..watched the progress of grannie's spindle. **1863** TREVELYAN *Compet. Wallah* (1866) 335 Along the whole course of the Ganges the women flung their spindles into the river.

b. In a spinning frame, one of many steel rods, by each of which a thread is twisted and wound on a bobbin.

c **1790** *Encycl. Brit.* (ed. 3) V. 488/2 Large buildings.., many of which contain several thousands of spindles. **1831** G. R. PORTER *Silk Manuf.* 201 Upon each spindle, just above the bobbin, a piece of hard wood is so fixed by a pin as to cause the wood to revolve with the spindle. **1845** DISRAELI *Sybil* (1863) 155 After a day of labour passed.. amid the ceaseless and monotonous clang of the spindle and the loom. **1846** MCCULLOCH *Acc. Brit. Empire* (1854) I. 677 At first the mule carried only 144 spindles; but, by successive improvements, it was rendered capable..of working 300 or 400 spindles.

c. A spool or bobbin.

1837 HEBERT *Eng. & Mech. Encycl.* I. 320 The workman having placed his spindles of thread near him, begins to work on the first horizontal line of one of the squares. **1837** WHITTOCK *Bk. Trades* (1842) 113 (Carpet-weaver), Before the Weaver commences he prepares a number of small 'spindles' which hold the woollen yarn of the different colours required in the carpet.

2. a. *fig.* In allusions to the Fates imagined as spinning the thread of life or destiny, or in similar contexts.

1577 GRANGE *Golden Aphrod.* F ij, What tyme soeuer the turnyng spindle had thorowly twyned his fatall threede. **1608** DEKKER *Lanth. & Candle Lt.* Wks. (Grosart) III. 300 Shall I shew you what other bottomes of mischiefe, Plutos Beadle saw wound vpon the blacke spindels of the Night? *a* **1645** MILTON *Arcades* 66 To those that..turn the Adamantine spindle round, On which the fate of gods and men is wound. **1847** EMERSON *Repr. Men, Plato* Wks. (Bohn) I. 297 He beholds..the Fates, with the rock and shears; and hears the intoxicating hum of their spindle.

b. As a type of something slender.

a **1625** FLETCHER *Wom. Pleas'd* IV. iii, I am fall'n away to nothing, to a spindle.

c. *ellipt.* = SPINDLE-SIDE. *rare*⁻¹.

1877 BLACKMORE *Erema* li, The barony,..upon default of male heirs, devolved upon the spindle.

3. Such an amount of thread or yarn as can be prepared on a spindle at one time; hence, a certain quantity or measure of yarn, varying according to the material.

1452 *Cov. Leet Bk.* II. 271 The seid shirrifs to sesse & take the spyndels to ther owne behofe, & to paye þe spynner for hir labour. 1610 WEDDERBURNE *Compt Bk.* (S.H.S.) 79, 19 spynellis of yarn lyning, Ilk spynell cost me 28s. 1717 *Forfeited Estates Papers* (S.H.S.) Introd. p. xxvi, Yarn, 20 Spindles, 1 Hasp, and 3 Heer, at 2s. per Spindle. 1766 W. GORDON *Gen. Counting-ho.* 197, 3 bales linen yarn containing 1500 spindles. 1794 *Statist. Acc. Scot.* XI. 114 It is.. an easy task, for one of these two-handed females, to spin 3 spindles in the week. 1858 SIMMONDS *Dict. Trade* s.v., In cotton-yarn a spindle of 18 hanks is 15,120 yards; in linen yarn a spindle of 24 heers, is 14,400 yards. 1878 BARLOW *Weaving* 330, 4 Hasps = 1 spyndle = 60,000 yards.

4. a. A figure having the form of an elongated lozenge; *esp.* as a charge in Heraldry, = FUSIL[1].

1486 *Bk. St. Albans, Her.* F ij b, Off armys fusyllit in english spyndyllis now I will speke. 1589 PUTTENHAM *Eng. Poesie* II. xi. (Arb.) 105 The Fuzie or spindle, called Romboides. 1765 PORNY *Elem. Her.* iv. (1777) 123 The Fusil, called also a Spindle, is longer than the Lozenge. 1886 SYMONDS *B. Jonson* 2 In which shape they assume the semblance of the heraldic fusil, spindle, or rhombus.

b. *Med.* A dilatation of the fœtal aorta resembling a spindle in shape.

1898 *Allbutt's Syst. Med.* V. 707 This constriction or isthmus is succeeded by a fusiform dilatation, the aortic spindle of His.

c. *Cytology.* A bipolar configuration of fibres to which the chromosomes become attached by their centromeres at metaphase of mitosis before being pulled towards its poles; cf. *spindle fibre*, sense 17 below.

1878 *Q. Jrnl. Microsc. Sci.* XVIII. 114 The portion of the spindle which remains in the egg after the formation of the second polar cell reconstitutes itself into a nucleus. 1927 HALDANE & HUXLEY *Animal Biol.* ii. 58 A star-shaped figure of radiating fibres is seen in the cell. This divides into two, forming a spindle-shaped set of fibres with a radiating 'star' at each end, and the chromosomes arrange themselves where the fibres from the two stars meet, in the centre of the spindle. 1971 *Sci. Amer.* Oct. 77/3 The action of the mitotic spindle in pulling the chromosomes apart when a cell divides.

d. *Anat.* [tr. G. *spindel* (W. Kühne 1863, in *Arch. f. path. Anat. u. Physiol.* XXVII. 520).] = *muscle spindle* s.v. MUSCLE *sb.* 3 d.

1894 *Jrnl. Physiol.* XVII. 238 The spindles have been studied by Golgi (1880); Golgi's definition of them is 'bundles of incompletely developed muscle-fibres, surrounded by a special sheath, and to be found in muscles at every period of growth'. 1899 *Allbutt's Syst. Med.* VI. 711 Disease of sensory muscle nerves and their end organs, the 'muscle spindles'. 1930 MAXIMOW & BLOOM *Text-bk. Histol.* xiv. 276 The muscle fibers of the spindle are approximately half as thick as the ordinary muscle fibers. 1962 *Phil. Trans. R. Soc.* B. CCXLV. 82 All spindles contain two distinct types of intrafusal muscle fibre, 'nuclear bag fibres' and 'nuclear chain fibres', which differ in structure and innervation. 1974 [see *muscle spindle*].

e. *Anat.* Any of numerous small sensory organs within tendons and aponeuroses which consist of a spindle-shaped bundle of tendon fibres containing the branching endings of a nerve and enclosed in a capsule; a neurotendinous spindle; = *tendon organ, spindle* s.v. TENDON d.

1896 E. L. BILSTEIN tr. *Stöhr's Text-bk. Histol.* II. 115 The medullated nerves of tendons terminate in part in a close plexus of gray nerve-fibers, and in part in tendon-spindles. 1901, etc. [see *neurotendinous* adj. s.v. NEURO-]. 1905 J. S. FERGUSON *Normal Histol.* ix. 138 Nerve fibres enter the spindle and give off several medullated branches which run between the tendon bundles near the axis of the spindle. 1954 T. L. PEELE *Neuroanat. Basis Clinical Neurol.* xix. 420/1 Neurotendinous spindles are usually present near the musculotendinous junction. 1966 T. S. & C. R. LEESON *Histology* xx. 440/2 Neuromuscular spindles lie in muscle... Neurotendinous spindles are similar and are located in tendons and aponeuroses near their junctions with muscle.

f. *Med.* A configuration seen in an electroencephalogram (see quot. 1935).

1935 A. L. LOOMIS et al. in *Science* 14 June 597/2 The amplitude [of the waves] builds regularly to a maximum and then falls regularly so that we have designated these 'spindles', because of their appearance in the record. 1952 *Confinia Neurologica* XII. 73 Spindles are most prominent in the thalamus of cats under barbiturates. 1965 *Math. in Biol. & Med.* (Med. Res. Council) IV. 171 Often exact identification of the maxima and minima of the spindles can be difficult. 1983 *Brit. Med. Jrnl.* 12 Nov. 1401/1 A slowing of the alpha, concurrent alpha and theta, and beta spindles are found during relaxation and on the borders of sleep.

5. *ellipt.* **a.** = SPINDLE-TREE.

With quot. 1712 cf. SPINDLEKIN.

1712 *Phil. Trans.* XXVII. 421 Cape Spindle with a shining notch'd Leaf. 1891 *Daily News* 11 Nov. 5/2 The spindle is not a striking shrub, and its sober flowers are small and inconspicuous.

b. = Spindle-shell, -stromb (see 17).

1842 *Penny Cycl.* XXIII. 124/2 *Rostellaria curvirostris* (*Strombus fusus*, Linn.), the Spindle of collectors, is by far the most common of the Asiatic species.

II. 6. A rod, usually of iron or other metal, serving as an axis upon which, or by means of which, something revolves or is turned round.

In technical use this sense has developed into many special applications, esp. from the 17th cent. onwards. The earliest examples refer to the rod of the mill-stone (cf. *mill-* and *rind-spindle*).

c1343 *Durham Acc. Rolls* (Surtees) 543 In.. ij Spindels. 1345–6 *Ely Sacr. Rolls* II. 133 In j pari de Spyndel et cogg. pro molendino equino. 1458 in *Brit. Mag.* XXXI. 249 Item, to hym for makyng of the Spendel for the fane, xd. 1507–8 *Fabric Rolls York Minster* (Surtees) 94 Pro faccione j spyndill for remevyng of ye hamers of ye chyme. 1533 J. HEYWOOD *Play Wether* B iv, Our mylstons, our whele with her kogges & our trindill,.. Our hopper, our extre, our yren spyndyll. 1625–6 in Swayne *Sarum Churchw. Acc.* (1896) 310 Mending of the spindle of the clocke. 1627 CAPT. SMITH *Seaman's Gram.* ii. 8 Capstaine. The maine body of it is called the Spindle. 1687 A. LOVELL tr. *Thevenot's Trav.* I. 54 They fall a turning round with their naked feet, the left foot serving for a Pivot or Spindle to turn upon. 1719 DE FOE *Crusoe* I. (Globe) 74, I had no possible way to make the Iron Gudgeons for the Spindle or Axis of the Wheel to run in. 1764 J. FERGUSON *Lect.* 46 The trundle [of a water-mill] is fixt upon a strong iron axis called the spindle. 1788 *Massachusetts Spy* 25 Dec. 3/3 An apprentice.. being under the spindle of a grindstone, that was going by water, had the hair of his head caught by the spindle. 1815 J. SMITH *Panorama Sci. & Art* I. 20 The drill [of a lathe] is screwed, or otherwise fastened, upon the spindle. 1824 R. STUART *Hist. Steam Engine* 157 The tail or spindle of the valve *k*, being pressed upwards, opens the valve. 1862 *Catal. Internat. Exhib., Brit.* II. No. 6332, A spindle, which is to act on the bolt for shutting and opening the lock. 1900 HASLUCK *Mod. Eng. Handybk.* 98 When the engine is moving with great velocity,.. the weights or balls attached to the arms will fly further from the spindle, moving the ring on the spindle.

fig. 1869 J. MARTINEAU *Ess.* II. 175 The universe revolving round the spindle of necessity.

7. a. A cylindrical rod or bar provided with grooves so as to act as a screw; *spec.* that by which the platen of a hand printing-press is lowered and raised.

1398 TREVISA *Barth. De P.R.* v. xii. (1495) 117 The holes that ben the propre instrumentes of herynge ben wrapped and wounde as a spyndle of a presse. 1585 HIGINS tr. *Junius' Nomencl.* 217 *Cochlea*, the vice or spindle of a presse: the winding peece. 1677 MOXON *Mech. Exerc.* II. 31 The length of a Worm begins at the one end of the Spindle and ends at the other... The depth of the Worm is cut into the diameter of the Spindle. 1683 *Ibid., Printing* x. ¶ 12 The Spindle.. is sixteen Inches and a half, the length of the Cilinder the Worms are cut upon is three Inches and a quarter. 1825 J. NICHOLSON *Operat. Mechanic* 295 When the workman pulls this handle, he turns round the spindle *l*,.. and causes the platen to descend and produce the pressure. 1829 *Chapters Phys. Sci.* viii, When the spiral is formed upon a cylinder, it is called the spindle, or interior screw, and by some a male screw.

b. A revolving frame used for stirring a mixture.

c1793 *Encycl. Brit.* (ed. 3) XI. 422/2 The spindle is of light wood, and moves on a brass pivot in the bottom. It has four wooden wings. *Ibid.* 443/1 The.. stirring of the mixture with the spindle.

c. A spindle moulder (see sense 17).

1920 F. T. HILL *Pract. Aeroplane Constr.* 108 This is known as a French spindle, and its cutting action, in order to form the recesses, is shown in the enlarged view on the right. 1925 W. J. BLACKMUR *How to work Spindle Moulder* iii. 29 In working a spindle there are three kinds of cutters —those used on the square block, those used with the slotted cutters, and those used on the French spindle.

8. †**a.** The newel of a winding stair. *Obs. rare.*

1585 HIGINS tr. *Junius' Nomencl.* 215 *Scapus*,.. the spindle or maine peece of worke whereabout the winding staires doe run. 1611 COTGR., *Noyau*,.. the Nuell, or spindle of a winding staire.

b. *Geom.* (See quots.) *rare*$^{-0}$.

1706 [see PARABOLIC *a.* 2]. 1801 *Encycl. Brit.* (ed. 3) Suppl. II. 516/2 *Spindle*, in geometry, a solid body generated by the revolution of some curve line about its base or double ordinate. 1842 FRANCIS *Dict. Arts, Spindle*,.. as a solid, is a circular body, tapering towards both ends; as a superficies, it is flat, tapering also at both ends.

c. A rod upon which the core of a gun-shell is moulded.

1842 in BURN *Naval & Mil. Techn. Dict.* s.v. *Arbre.* 1889 *Pall Mall G.* 24 Jan. 7/2 By introducing dynamite into the spindle of the grape with a time fuse, much more execution will be done.

9. a. A stalk, stem, or shoot of a plant, esp. of cereals. ? *Obs.*

G. *spindel* has also this sense: cf. SPINDLE *v.* 1.

1577 B. GOOGE tr. *Heresbach's Husb.* 27 b, The blade of wheate is.. narrower than the Barley, the Spindel, Stalke, or Strawe thereof, is smoother and gentler. 1608 WILLET *Hexapla Exod.* 178 *Abib* signifieth the spindle with the eare. 1660 SHARROCK *Vegetables* 118 The Gardiner.. not suffering above one, two, or three spindles upon such roots or stools. 1707 MORTIMER *Husb.* (1721) II. 121 The Spindles must be often tyed up,.. lest by their bending they should break, and their Flowers be lost. 1750 W. ELLIS *Mod. Husb.* III. i. 28 Hail-Stones.. beat down and hurt the spindle of the Wheat. 1824 'A. SINGLETON' *Lett. from South & West* 82 They [*sc.* Virginians] also call, what we [*sc.* New Englanders] call the spindle, the tassel. 1871 *Amer. Naturalist* V. 245 The corn.. sent forth a new tassel or spindle.

b. In prepositional phrases, denoting a stage or manner of growth.

1686 PLOT *Staffordsh.* 23 Another storme of Hail.. cut the stalks of the Wheat and Barley (then in spindle) quite asunder. a1722 LISLE *Husb.* (1757) 116 The juices stagnate in the plants, and are not pushed on to tillow, but run to spindle. 1750 W. ELLIS *Mod. Husb.* III. xi. 153 The wheat was upon the spindle, and had not shot into Ear. 1764 *Museum Rust.* II. 21 When the corn is shot into spindle, and the ears begin to appear. 1896 *Midland Herald* 4 June (E.D.D.), Forward crops [of wheat] are in full spindle and give promise of being in full ear by the 14th inst.

†**10.** A rod or bar forming part of a plough or harrow. *Obs.*

1616 SURFL. & MARKH. *Country Farme* v. v. 532 The composition of plows.. consisteth vpon the beame, the skeath, the head, the hales, the spindles, the rest [etc.]. 1641 BEST *Farm. Bks.* (Surtees) 120 Att Martynmasse.. wee sette our foreman to cuttinge of.. saughs for hecke-stowers and harrowe-spindles. 1736 J. LEWIS *Hist. Antiq.* 15 Next the Handle of the Plough is this Wreest, supported by a Piece of Iron which they call a Spindle.

11. *Naut.* The upper part or section of a made wooden mast.

1597 VERE *Comm.* 48 My mainmast being in the partners rent to the very spindell which was eleven inches deep. 1670 COVEL in *Early Voy. Levant* (Hakluyt Soc.) 128 There appear'd a very bright Helena at the very spindle of the main top mast. 1697 DAMPIER *Voy.* (1699) 414 We saw a *Corpus Sant* at our Main-top-mast head, on the very top of the truck of the Spindle. 1794 *Rigging & Seamanship* 13 The spindle, or upper tree, of large masts is made of two pieces. c1860 H. STUART *Seaman's Catech.* 73 Two spindle pieces dowelled and bolted to each other... Two side trees.. dowelled and bolted to the spindle.

12. a. *U.S.* A stout iron rod or pole fixed on a rock as a guide to shipping.

1819 *Stat. at L.* (U.S.) III. 535 A spindle on the rock off the point of Fairweather Island. 1829 *Ibid.* IV. 345. 1843 *Amer. Jrnl. in Civ. Eng. & Arch. Jrnl.* (1844) VII. 68/1 Upon many of the reefs in Long Island Sound.. it has been the practice.. to erect wrought iron spindles of about 4 in. diameter, and from 15 to 25 ft. in height. 1904 *Hartford* (Connecticut) *Courant* 19 Aug. 13 What this man was really doing was simply placing a spindle on Magazine Rock.

b. A slender cylindrical rod (esp. of metal) or other object of this shape.

1829 *Nat. Philos., Mechanics* II. 30 (L.U.K.), The teeth of the wheel.. are made to act upon a form of wheel called a lantern... The cylindrical teeth or bars of the lantern are called trundles or spindles. 1902 ELIZ. BANKS *Newspaper Girl* 187 If he wants the article he puts it on a spindle or in a pigeon-hole.

transf. 1870 EMERSON *Soc. & Solit., Farming* Wks. (Bohn) III. 60 Set out a pine-tree, and it dies in the first year, or lives a poor spindle.

13. *Midl. dial.* The third swarm of bees from a hive in one year.

1825 HONE *Every-day Bk.* I. 647 A Warwickshire correspondent says, that in that county.. 'the second [swarm] from the same hive is called a *cast*, and the third.. a *spindle*'. 1853 *N. & Q.* 1st Ser. VIII. 575/2 In the midland counties the first migration of the season is *a swarm*,.. the third *a spindle*.

III. *attrib.* and *Comb.* **14. a.** In sense 1 (in later use especially in combs. relating to machine-spinning), as ***spindle-band, -box, -carriage, -hook, -maker, -production, -work.***

1483 *Cath. Angl.* 355/1 A Spyndelle maker, *fusarius*. 1598 FLORIO, *Fusaro*, a spindle maker. 1638 JUNIUS *Paint. Ancients* 298 He is likewise commended for a picture of spindle worke, wherein the threads of every spinning woman seem to make very great haste. 1770 in *Abridgm. Specif. Patents, Spinning* (1866) 18 [Two grooves, into which the] spindle-box [is fixed]. 1825 J. NICHOLSON *Operat. Mechanic* 422 One of the spindle-hooks of the spinning-machine. 1835 URE *Philos. Manuf.* 178 The part of the billy which contains the spindle-carriage is movable.. through what is called the billy-gate. *Ibid.* 274 These two bars together are called by workmen the spindle-box. 1892 J. NASMITH *Students' Cotton Spinning* ix. (1893) 357 It does not pay to use spindle bands made of inferior material. 1892 *Daily News* 1 Oct. 2/5 The demand for yarns is regular, and about equal to spindle production.

b. With numerals, as ***two-spindle***, etc.

1835 URE *Philos. Manuf.* 159 Some of them are two spindle,.. others six spindle-frames. 1884 W. S. B. McLAREN *Spinning* (ed. 2) 128, 2nd, two two-spindle gill boxes; 3rd, four-spindle drawing box.

c. In sense 6, as ***spindle-end, -gearing, -lathe, -screw, -valve.***

1869 RANKINE *Machine & Hand-tools* Pl. H 8, The pinion, *a*, keyed on the spindle end, takes into an intermediate wheel, *b*. *Ibid.*, The back shaft, E, being arranged to throw out of gear with the spindle gearing. 1875 KNIGHT *Dict. Mech.* 1262/2 The spindle-lathe has a rotating axis in the head-stock, to which the work is attached. *Ibid.* 2269/2 *Spindle-valve*, a valve having an axial guide-stem. 1895 *Model Steam Engine* 88 As the spindle-screws are of the same fineness, and with right and left threads.

15. a. Of the limbs (or person), in the sense, 'thin, slender, lacking in robustness'. See also SPINDLE-SHANK.

a1586 in Pinkerton *Anc. Sc. Poems* (1786) 201 To the rude scho maid ane vow, 'For I sall hit thy spindill schyn'. 1648 HEXHAM II, *Spille-been*,.. Spindle leggs, or leane Shankes. 1681 ? D'URFEY *Progr. Honesty* iv. 4 One that could flatter every Golden Clod, And call my Spindle Lord.. his God. 1688 HOLME *Armoury* II. 401/2 The slender Legs, such as have no Calf: Spindle Legs. 1828 LYTTON *Pelham* II. xxvi, You have thrust those spindle legs of yours into your coat-sleeves instead of your breeches! 1843 CARLYLE *Past & Pr.* II. x, The burden their poor spindle-limbs totter and stagger under.

b. Of things, in the sense 'having the form of a spindle; cylindrical with a taper towards either end'.

1708 *Phil. Trans.* XXVI. 79 *Turbinites*, The Spindle Periwinkle. c1711 PETIVER *Gazophyl.* VIII. lxxiii, Limington Spindle Fossil... A very rare Shell. 1765 *Treat. Dom. Pigeons* 55 It is a very small Pigeon, with a.. very short and spindle beak, and a round button head. 1840 J. BUEL *Farmer's Companion* 156 A spindle root may be able to draw an abundance of nourishment from land.. exhausted by short or creeping roots. 1903 AGNES CLERKE *Astrophysics* 443 All spindle-nebulæ were resolved into spirals viewed aslant.

16. In parasynthetic adjs., as ***spindle-celled, -formed, -pointed, -rooted***, etc. Also, ***spindle-like*** adj.; ***spindle-wise*** adv.

1871 T. H. GREEN *Introd. Pathol.* 117 The soft round-celled varieties are.. much more malignant than the firmer *spindle-celled growths. 1899 *Allbutt's Syst. Med.* VIII. 846 The treatment of spindle-celled sarcoma of the skin is not easy to formulate. *Ibid.* 600 Long, *spindle-formed, partially pigmented cells appear round the vessels. **1831** J. F. SOUTH tr. *Otto's Comp. Pathol. Anat.* 485 A whole row of *spindle-like swellings. **1884** BOWER & SCOTT tr. *De Bary's Phanerogr. & Ferns* 27 Their obliquely tapered or *spindle-pointed ends. **1796** C. MARSHALL *Gardening* xviii. (1813) 298 *Spindle rooted plants should be set where they are to blow, quite young. **1846** J. BAXTER *Libr. Pract. Agric.* (ed. 4) II. 226 The early short-topped and salmon among the spindle-rooted [radishes], and the small white and red among the turnip-rooted, may be sown for succession crops every fortnight. **1775** ASH, *Spindleshin[n]ed, having small legs. **1591** PERCIVALL *Sp. Dict.*, *Ahusada figura*, shaped *spindle wise.

17. Special Combs.: **spindle-back**, used *attrib.* to designate a chair with a back consisting of framed cylindrical bars; **spindle-berry**, the bright red fruit of the spindle-tree, *Euonymus europæus*; † **spindle bud**, ? a bud giving rise to a shoot or stem; **spindle cell** *Med.* and *Biol.*, a narrow, elongated cell; *spec.* one in the blood of some lower vertebrates analogous to the platelet in mammals; freq. *attrib.* (cf. *spindle-celled*, sense 16); **spindle cross** *Her.*, a cross having arms shaped somewhat like a spindle; **spindle fibre** *Cytology*, any of the microtubular strands which form the visible structure of a spindle (sense 4 c above); **spindle hour**, an hour during which a spindle is involved in spinning, used as a unit of measurement; **spindle machine, moulder**, a woodworking machine used to shape mouldings, in which one or more cutters are carried on a spindle; so **spindle moulding**; **spindle oil**, a light distillation product of petroleum, used for lubrication esp. of high-speed machinery; † **spindle-pear**, a pear having the elongated form of a spindle; **spindle-shell, -stromb** (see quots.); **spindle-twirl**, † **-whirl, -whorl**, a whorl used for weighting a spindle; **spindle-wood**, the spindle-tree, or the wood of this; **spindle-worm** *U.S.*, the maize eating larva of a noctuid moth (*Achatodes zeæ*).

1896 *Heal & Son Catal.: Bedroom Furnit.* 156 Solid Oak *Spindleback Rush-Seat Chair..£0 19 6. **1918** *Ibid.: Cottage Furnit.* 18 'Spindle Back' Arm Chair, stained oak colour..28/-. **1937** *Times* 15 Nov. 19/4 One could repeat this story in respect of the spindleback chairs made in the West of England from the Solway Firth to Herefordshire. **1959** G. SAVAGE *Antique Collector's Handbk.* 126 The Lancashire spindle-back chair is similar in many ways to the ladder-back. **1921** *19th Cent.* June 1039 The dying glory of bracken, oak, birch, mountain-ash and *spindle-berry. **1923** *Daily Mail* 12 Sept. 15/4 Pink spindle berries are lovely in a pewter mug. **1950** J. BROOKE *Goose Cathedral* viii. 167 The hedges were hung with a multitude of spindleberries—lurid purple bursting into fiery orange. **1657** AUSTEN *Fruit Trees* III. 16 They will become much larger than if all the *spindle buds were suffered to grow. **1878** T. BRYANT *Pract. Surg.* I. 135 Some *spindle-cell sarcomas will recur often after removal. **1901** A. P. OHLMACHER in Hektoen & Riesman *Text-bk. Path.* I. 200 It [*sc.* round-celled sarcoma] grows more rapidly, and is generally softer and more malignant than the spindle-cell sarcoma. **1905** J. S. FERGUSON *Normal Histol.* iii. 34 In the denser forms of mature connective tissue..the connective tissue cells lose their typical embryonal stellate form and become somewhat fusiform; they are then known as the spindle cells of connective tissue. *Ibid.* vi. 81 Confusion..has arisen from the supposed analogy of the true blood platelets of human blood with certain other structures found in the blood of the lower vertebrates, especially the 'spindle-cells' of amphibians. **1949** A. S. ROMER *Vertebrate Body* xiii. 427 In most nonmammalian vertebrates the thrombocytes take the form of spindle cells—small, oval, pointed structures with a central nucleus. **1959** W. ANDREW *Textbk. Compar. Histol.* ix. 371 Spindle cells are conspicuous and probably should be thought of as fusiform lymphocytoid cells rather than platelet-forming elements. **1971** T. J. HARA in Hoar & Randall *Fish Physiol.* V. iv. 88 Aside from the taste buds, specialized epidermal 'spindle' cells were found on the head and body of minnows and various teleost fishes. **1976** *Path. Ann.* XI. 214 (*caption*) Spindle cell variant of thymic carcinoid tumor. **1828** BERRY *Encycl. Her.*, *Pandall*, Pendall, or *Spindle Cross. **1878** *Q. Jrnl. Microsc. Sci.* XVIII. 229 The *spindle-fibres are identical with the stellate rays. **1974** *Encycl. Brit. Micropædia* VI. 946/1 In anaphase the chromatid pairs separate and are pulled to opposite ends of the cell by the spindle fibres. **1930** *Times* 24 Mar. 23/5 Mill activity in the cotton growing states, measured by *spindle hours, established a high record. **1970** P. R. LORD *Spinning in '70's* 11 Production per spindle hour has been increased by raising spindle speeds. **1902** G. ELLIS *Mod. Pract. Joinery* xxiii. 364 **Spindle machine*, an irregular moulding machine in which the cutters are fixed at the end of a vertical spindle which projects through the table. **1915** *Machine Woodworker* 15 Nov. 15/2 Running moulds from thickness boards on spindle machine may do if it is a special type of mould. **1912** *Ibid.* 15 July 17/2 A *spindle moulder being a machine that has to do a large variety of work, the stock of cutters should be large. **1925** W. J. BLACKMUR *How to work Spindle Moulder* i. 11 As the spindle moulder is used for working regular sections upon edges of various shaped pieces of wood it is best to place it close to the band saw. **1965** F. L. DUNSMORE *Technique Woodworking Machinery* II. i. 14 No machine has a greater selection of cutter heads than the spindle moulder. **1979** *Building* Dec. 105/3 Planing, thicknessing, sawing, routing and *spindle moulding. **1887** B. J. CREW *Pract. Treat. Petroleum* ix. 316 *Spindle oils. Distillers of residuum usually divide their products into three classes... The third..product constitutes the stock for spindle and machinery oils. **1931** *Engineering* 2 Jan. 1/2 Oil PL will be recognised as a 'spindle oil', used only for lightly loaded high speed journals. **1977** *Lubricants Business* (Shell Internat. Petroleum Co.) 1 Refining of the distillates, which removes unsuitable components, produces lubricating oil fractions of the desired properties ranging from thin spindle oil to heavy cylinder oil. **1664** EVELYN *Kal. Hort.* Dec. 80 The Squib-pear, *Spindle-pear, Virgin. *c* **1711** PETIVER *Gazophyl.* VI. lvi, Knotty chained Indian *Spindle Shell. **1775** *Phil. Trans.* LXV. 238 These anemonies had been found on old volutes, called spindle-shells (*fucus brevis*). **1861** P. P. CARPENTER in *Rep. Smithsonian Instit. 1860*, 175 Another group, of which the Spindle-shells are the type, have no varices at all. **1881** *Cassell's Nat. Hist.* V. 193 The 'Spindle-shell', *Fusus*.., is extensively dredged for the markets. **1861** P. P. CARPENTER in *Rep. Smithsonian Instit. 1860*, 198 These creatures may be regarded as *Spindle-strombs. **1881** *Cassell's Nat. Hist.* V. 192 The genus Rostellaria, or the 'Spindle-stromb', is marked by having a very much elongated spire. **1855** *Archaeol.* XXXVI. 135 About the middle of the body was a bronze finger ring, and a stone *spindle-twirl. **1648** HEXHAM II, *Een Spillewervel*, a Whirle for a Spindle, or a *Spindle-whirle. **1874** DAWKINS *Cave Hunt.* iii. 103 The number of personal ornaments and the *spindle-whorls imply the presence of the female sex. **1712** tr. *Pomet's Hist. Drugs* I. 129 The Tree is like *Spindle-Wood, or Priests-Cap. **1885** *St. James's Gaz.* 2 Jan. 6/1 Spindle-wood, which is nowhere plentiful, is reserved for skewers. **1839** T. W. HARRIS *Treat. Insects Injurious Veget.* (1862) 438 Indian corn..often suffers severely from the depredations of one of these Nonagrians, known to our farmers by the name of *spindle-worm.

Hence **'spindleless** *a.*, having no spindle or spindles.

1964 *Gloss. Letterpress Rotary Printing Terms* (*B.S.I.*) 7 *Spindleless reel stand*, a reel stand supporting the reel on free-running cones at each side of the reel. **1967** *Economist* 29 Apr. 459/3 There [*sc.* in Czechoslovakia] the BD 200 spindleless spinning unit has been developed; by next year it will be modified to run at 40,000 rpm as against the conventional spindle's 10,000.

spindle ('spɪnd(ə)l), *v.* Also 6 **spindel**. [f. the sb. (esp. in sense 9).]

1. a. *intr.* Of cereals: To shoot up into the slender stalks on which the ear is formed.

So G. *spindeln* in dialect use.

1577 B. GOOGE *Heresbach's Husb.* 27 When the Spring draweth on, it [*sc.* wheat] beginneth to spindle. *Ibid.* 32 When it beginnes to spindel, it must be well weeded. **1616** SURFL. & MARKH. *Country Farme* v. vi. 534, I must needs discommend that manner of weeding..which is used after the corn is spindled. **1651** R. CHILD in Hartlib *Legacy* (1655) 139 Corn sown in July,..if it should begin to spindle, (as the Husbandmen call it) it is very easy..to prevent it. *a* **1722** LISLE *Husb.* (1757) 127 In the hot countries it is a frequent calamity, that the corn will not spindle, that is, will not come out of the hose. **1763** MILLS *Pract. Husb.* II. 201 The whole had already spindled, which made me sorry I had sowed so early. **1805** DICKSON *Pract. Agric.* I. 550 Great care is necessary to see that the whole is completed before the crop begins to spindle. **1846** *Jrnl. R. Agric. Soc.* VII. II. 344 The author has never once seen a single plant of the..rye to spindle before the following spring.

b. Of flowering plants: To form the stalk or stem on which the flowers are produced.

1601 HOLLAND *Pliny* II. 253 Even so doth the decoction of Lonchitis, if it bee taken before it spindle and run vp to seed. **1665** REA *Flora* 163 When they begin to rise to spindle, nip of such as are smallest. **1725** *Fam. Dict.* s.v. *Pink*, When the Pinks begin to Spindle, they will then require a little more Care. **1821** CLARE *Vill. Minstr.* II. 173 Feather-headed grasses, spindling rank. **1824** T. HOGG *Carnation* 35 When the plants begin to spindle, or shoot up for bloom, they require to be supported by sticks.

c. With *up* or *upward(s)*. In later use sometimes implying too slender a growth.

1601 HOLLAND *Pliny* I. 558 No sooner commeth the spring, but they begin to grow up into straw, and to spindle upward pointwise. *a* **1722** LISLE *Husb.* (1757) 142 The blade, after it is come up, will die away, and then spindle up again. **1796** *Hist. Ned Evans* I. 282 He resembled those exotic plants which spindle up in our hot-houses. **1810** WORDSW. *Scenery Lakes* (1823) 61 The whole island planted anew with Scotch firs, left to spindle up by each other's side—a melancholy phalanx. **1841** *Florist's Jrnl.* (1846) II. 197 Too much water..makes them spindle up and flower prematurely. **1881** *Daily News* 4 June 5/6 Wheat is very thin,..the plant not stooling satisfactorily, but spindling up. *fig.* *a* **1864** HAWTHORNE *Dr. Grimshawe* i. (1891) 3 The cemetery..might probably have nourished..whatever else is of English growth, without that tendency to spindle upwards and lose their sturdy breadth.

2. a. To shoot out or up, to develop by rapid growth or attenuation, *into* something thin or unsubstantial.

1784 COWPER *Task* v. 11 From ev'ry herb..Stretches a length of shadow o'er the field. Mine, spindling into longitude immense,..Provokes me to a smile. **1833** M. SCOTT *Tom Cringle* xii, Here Sir, squealed Timothy, his usual gruff voice spindling into a small cheep. **1854** LOWELL *Jrnl. Italy* Wks. 1890 I. 203 That fairest variety of mortal grass which with us is apt to spindle so soon into a somewhat sapless womanhood. **1860** EMERSON *Cond. Life* ii. (1861) 46 The gardener, by severe pruning, forces the sap of the tree into one or two vigorous limbs, instead of suffering it to spindle into a sheaf of twigs.

b. To become spindly or weak.

1863 THORNBURY *True as Steel* I. 210, I will..betake myself to the service of the Elector.., where I can win a place for myself in the van, and not spindle and pine as I do here.

c. To rise in a slender form.

1897 *Catholic News* 6 Nov. 5/3 If one or two prayer-towers spindled above Ballydehob it would be a perfect Turkish village.

3. *trans.* To fit with, fix upon, a spindle or axis.

1833 LOUDON *Encycl. Archit.* §1301 An oak curb to be made to go all round the mill and the millwright [to be] assisted in rimming it, and spindling the stone.

4. To spin (a garment). *rare*$^{-1}$.

1887 AUSTIN *Pr. Lucifer* IV. ii, I will..clip the July fleeces for your hands To spindle me a jacket.

5. To recess and taper (a spar for an aeroplane's wing); to cut *out* (a recess) in a spar.

1918 *Aeronaut. Jrnl.* Feb. 44 Jigs for small parts should be so constructed that several pieces may be spindled at the same time. **1919** PIPPARD & PRITCHARD *Aeroplane Struct.* 201 Questions of strength determine the amount which can safely be spindled out. **1920** F. T. HILL *Pract. Aeroplane Constr.* v. 106 Having drilled the spar, the next operation will be to spindle out the recess. **1928** *Technical Rep. Aeronaut. Res. Committee 1926–7* 466 These specimens were first formed..with a length of 2 inches spindled to give a cross section geometrically similar to the fractured portion of the spar.

spindleage ('spɪnd(ə)lɪdʒ). [f. SPINDLE *sb.* + -AGE.] The total number of cotton spindles in use at a given time and in a specified area.

1921 A. S. WADE *Cotton Spinning* 15 The loss o[f] spindleage due to the reduction of the working week. **1954** R. ROBSON et al. in A. F. W. Coulson *Man. Cotton Spinning* I. i. 6 By 1928 the number of spindles had risen to just over 165 million but this was to represent the peak world spindleage. **1972** C. H. LEE *Cotton Enterprise* ii. 16 The spindleage of the trade grew from 1·7 million to four or five million between the early 1780's and 1812.

'spindled, *ppl. a.* [f. SPINDLE *sb.* or *v.*]

1. a. Of corn: Shot up into the slender pointed stalks which afterwards bear the ear.

1604 E. G[RIMSTONE] *D'Acosta's Hist. Indies* IV. xvii. 258 Of the seede sowen, at one instant, some is spindled, some is in the eare, and some doth but bud. **1608** WILLET *Hexapla Exod.* 178 Then the corne was spindled and began to be eared. **1764** *Museum Rust.* II. 253 He must then..go among the spindled corn.

b. With *up*: Overgrown in height or length in proportion to strength or stoutness.

1855 CHAMIER *My Travels* I. x. 167 A tall, thin king, spindled up like a weak geranium. **1885** *Bazaar* 30 Mar. 1255/3 These are fine compact bushy plants and not spindled up rubbish.

2. Attenuated, thin, slender.

1584 B. R. tr. *Herodotus* II. 76 There be two mountaines ..arising into sharpe and spindled tops. **1630** J. TAYLOR (Water P.) *Praise Clean Linen* Ded., Wks. II. 165 A good Legge is a great grace if it be discreetly essex'd in the calfe, and not too much spindled in the small.

3. a. Spindle-shaped; slightly bulging.

1844 H. STEPHENS *Bk. Farm* II. 460 In the former state, teats are very apt to become corded or *spindled*.

b. Of a spar or strut for an aeroplane wing: having been recessed and tapered. Also with *out*.

1919 S. CAMM *Aeroplane Construction* iii. 23 This [steel] strut..is superior to the solid spindled strut..which possesses a tendency to buckle laterally. **1928** *Technical Rep. Aeronaut. Res. Committee 1926–7* 467 The fracture ran through part of the bolt hole and tended to follow a 'zig-zag' course on its way into the spindled portion. **1930** *Flight* 17 Jan. 119/1 The wing is of equally simple construction with two spindled-out spruce spars and light girder ribs.

4. Twisted or wound on the spindle.

1866 J. B. ROSE tr. *Ovid's Met.* 93 The Minyeides..With rosy fingers twirl the spindled wool.

'spindleful. [f. SPINDLE *sb.* + -FUL 2.] As much (yarn or thread) as fills a spindle.

1611 COTGR., *Fusée*, a spoole-full, or spindle-full, of thread, yarne, &c. **1913** MACLAGAN *Our Ancest.* xiii. 131 The moon representing the ball or spindleful of thread.

† **spindlekin.** *Obs.*$^{-1}$ (Cf. SPINDLE *sb.* 5.)

1713 *Phil. Trans.* XXVIII. 64 Steerbecks Cape Spindlekin.

spindle-legged, *a.* [f. SPINDLE *sb.* 16.] = SPINDLE-SHANKED *a.*

1710 STEELE *Tatler* No. 148 ¶2 Many great families..are dwindled away into a pale, sickly, spindle-legged generation of valetudinarians. **1860** WORCESTER, *Spindle-legs*,..a spindle-legged person. **1863** MISS BRADDON *J. Marchmont's Legacy* i, It seemed as if the spindle-legged chairs and tables had grown attenuated..by much service.

† **spindler(s)-boat.** *Obs. rare.* In 3 **spindelerbote**, 4 **spindlerebote**, **spindeleresbot**, **spinleresbot**. [Of obscure origin.] Some kind of fishing-boat.

1243 *Munim. Gildh. Lond.* (Rolls) III. 449 Major et cives ..dicunt quod omnes naves extraneorum cum omnibus piscibus salsatis exceptis spindelerbotes [*v.r.* spindlerebotes] applicuerunt ad prædictam hetham. *c* **1365** *Liber Albus* Ibid. I. 374 Spindeleresbot [*v.r.* spinleresbot] qui ducit mulvellum recentem vel rayum.

spindle-shank. Also **spindleshank**, **spindle shank**. [SPINDLE *sb.* 15 a. Cf. G. *spindelbein* LG. *spil-*, *spillenbên*, Du. *spillebeen*.]

1. A long and slender leg. (Chiefly with contemptuous force and usu. in pl.) **a.** Of persons.

1570 ? REDFORD *Marr. Wit. & Sci.* II. i, But what if she finde fault with these spindle shankes? **1581** MULCASTER *Positions* xxiv. (1887) 98 Quicke riding,..which so helped his spindle shankes. **1674** tr. *Scheffer's Lapland* 12 Slender wasts, spindle shanks, and swift of foot. **1700** LOCKE in Fox Bourne *Life* (1876) II. 480, I hope in my next, I shall be able to give a better account of my spindle-shanks. **1709** STEELE & ADDISON *Tatler* No. 75. ¶8 The Marriage of one of our Heiresses with an eminent Courtier, who gave us Spindle-Shanks, and Cramps in our Bones. **1786** BURNS *To a Haggis* vi, His spindle shank a guid whip-lash. **1840** THACKERAY *George Cruikshank* Wks. 1899 XIII. 293 He will find them [Frenchmen] almost invariably thin, with ludicrous spindle-shanks. **1898** STEEVENS *With Kitchener to Khartoum* 89 They..are willowy in figure, and their legs run to spindle-shanks, almost ridiculously.

b. Of articles of furniture.

1841 DICKENS *Barn. Rudge* vi, A lonely bedchamber, garnished..with chairs whose spindle-shanks bespoke their age.

2. *trans.* A spindle-legged person.

1602 *How Chuse Good Wife* II. iii, When didst thou see the starveling school-master?..that shrimp, that spindle-shank. **1828–32** WEBSTER, *Spindle-shanks*, a tall slender person; in contempt. **1865** *Slang Dict.* 241 *Spindle-shanks*, a nickname for any one who has thin legs.

3. *attrib.* in the sense 'having spindle-legs'.

1604 T. M. *Black Bk.* in *Middleton's Wks.* (Bullen) VIII. 25 The spindle-shank spiders, which show like great lechers with little-legs.

spindle-shanked, *a.* [Cf. prec.]

1. Having long and slender legs; spindle-legged. (Usu. with contemptuous force.) **a.** Of persons or animals.

c **1600** *Timon* II. i. (1842) 25, I did reject..Demetrius Cause he was spindleshankt. **1692** *Lond. Gaz.* No. 2787/4 Went away from his Master.., one Cæsar Rammer,..aged about 14,..small of growth, and spindle-shank'd. **1713** STEELE *Guardian* No. 97, Her lawyer..is a little, rivelled, spindle-shanked gentleman. **1754** ? FIELDING *Fathers* II. i, I will neither marry my daughter to a spindle shanked beau, nor my son to a rampant woman of quality. **1800** *Sporting Mag.* XV. 107 The poor, slight, weedy, spindle-shanked stock of brood mares. **1837** CREEVEY in *C. Papers* (1904) II. 326 A chattering, capering, spindle-shanked gaby. **1863** *Blackw. Mag.* Sept. 276 The spindleshanked son of the notary Arouet.

b. Of articles of furniture.

1853 R. S. SURTEES *Sponge's Sp. Tour* (1893) 135 An old spindle-shanked sideboard, with very little middle.

2. Of legs: Long and thin.

1664 POWER *Exp. Philos.* I. 17 Such prodigiously little spindle-shank'd leggs.

spindle-shaped, *ppl. a.* [SPINDLE *sb.* 16.] Having the form of a spindle; fusiform.

Chiefly *Bot.*, *Zool.*, and *Anat.*; common in 19th c.

1776 J. LEE *Introd. Bot.* Explan. Terms 377 *Fusiformis*, spindle-shaped, simple, and gradually lessening downwards. **1796** WITHERING *Brit. Plants* (ed. 3) IV. 220 Stem..gradually increasing in thickness to the ground, and then tapering to a spindle-shaped root. **1834** MRS. SOMERVILLE *Connex. Phys. Sci.* 401 Not unfrequently they are long and narrow, like a spindle-shaped ray. **1859** D. BUNCE *Travels with Dr. Leichhardt* 15 Blue spindle-shaped fruits or berries. **1863** TYNDALL *Heat* viii. App. §5 (1870) 263 The flame longer, narrower, and nearly spindle-shaped. **1875** COOKE *Fungi* 84 It is..easily recognized by the spindle-shaped stem. **1927** [see SPINDLE *sb.* 4c]. **1966** J. S. COX *Illustr. Dict. Hairdressing & Wigmaking* 141/2 Spindle-shaped curler, a rounded rod, tapering towards each end.

'spindle-side. [f. SPINDLE *sb.*, after older Teutonic combs. Cf. OFris. *spindelsida*, MLG. *spinelside*, G. *spindelseite*; MDu. and MLG. *spille(n)-*, *spilside* (Du. *spillezijde*, G. *spillseite*); also OE. *spinlhealf*, MLG. *spillhalbe*, MDu. and OFris. *spindelhant*.] The female line of descent.

1851 SIR F. PALGRAVE *Norm. & Eng.* I. 526 When.. traditions of royalty are deduced through the spindleside, marriages accomplish the most radical of revolutions. **1868** FREEMAN *Norm. Conq.* viii. II. 243 One whose connexion with Normandy was only by the spindle-side. **1870** LOWELL *Study Wind.* 246 Such and such qualities he got from..a great-uncle on the spindle side.

'spindle-tree. [f. SPINDLE *sb.*, after G. *spindelbaum* (OHG. *spindel-*, *spinelpaum*, *spinnilapoum*), = MDu. *spindelboom*; cf. also G. *spillbaum*, Du. *spilboom*, MLG. *spillebôm*.]

1. An ornamental European shrub (*Euonymus Europæus*), furnishing a hard fine-grained yellowish wood formerly much used for spindles.

1548 TURNER *Names Herbes* (E.D.S.) 36 Euonymus.. maye be called in englishe Spyndle tree or square tree. **1578** LYTE *Dodoens* 760 Some call it..in Englishe Spindel tree, and Pricke timber: bycause the timber..serveth very well to the making both of Prickes and Spindelles. **1607** TOPSELL *Four-f. Beasts* 240 The prickle or spindle tree (called also Euonimus) which groweth in the Mount Occynius. **1668** WILKINS *Real Char.* 108 Spindle Tree. Not purgative; having slender flexile twigs. **1734** *Phil. Trans.* XXXVIII. 234 On the Twigs it is more even and greener, resembling that of the Evonymus, or Spindle-Tree. **1769** *Ibid.* LIX. 38, I have likewise my suspicions with regard to the Privet and Spindle tree. **1841** *Penny Cycl.* XXI. 184/1 It is also well seen in the Euonymus, or common spindle-tree, where it forms a beautiful orange-coloured mantle around the seed. **1872** OLIVER *Elem. Bot.* II. 159 Charcoal is prepared from the wood of the Spindle-tree, for the use of artists. **1884** *Longman's Mag.* June 191 Willows, laurels, figs, and spindle-trees grew side by side.

attrib. **1857** HENFREY *Bot.* 271 *Celastraceæ*. The Spindle-tree Order. **1866** *Treas. Bot.* 233/2 *Cassine*, a genus of South African plants belonging to the Spindle-tree family, *Celastraceæ*. **1868** WATTS *Dict. Chem.* s.v., Spindle-tree oil is prepared chiefly in Switzerland.

b. Applied, with distinguishing epithets, to other species of *Euonymus*, or to plants of different genera (see quots.).

1713 *Phil. Trans.* XXVIII. 64 Virginia Spindle-tree with rough Fruit. **1731** MILLER *Gard. Dict.* s.v. *Euonymus*, Ever-green African Spindle-Tree. *Ibid.*, Ever-green Ethiopian Spindle-Tree. **1760** J. LEE *Introd. Bot.* App. 328 Spindle-tree, Bastard, *Celastrus*. *Ibid.*, Spindle-tree, Bastard, *Kiggellaria*. *Ibid.*, Spindle-tree, Climbing, *Celastrus*. **1771** J. R. FORSTER *Flora Amer. Septentr.* 11 *Evonymus Americanus*. Spindle tree, American. **1829** T. CASTLE *Introd. Bot.* 52 Studded over with small warts,..as in warty spindle-tree.

2. *pl.* The natural order *Celastraceæ*, to which the genus *Euonymus* belongs.

1846 LINDLEY *Veget. Kingd.* 586 *Celastraceæ*, Spindle-trees. *Ibid.* 587 The radicle of Spindle-trees is inferior. **1866** *Treas. Bot.* 243/2 The Spindle-trees have a beautiful scarlet aril.

'spindling, (*vbl.*) *sb.* [f. SPINDLE *sb.* or *v.*]

1. a. The action of providing with a spindle or spindles. *rare*$^{-1}$. **b.** (See quot. 1611.)

1441–2 *Durham Acc. Rolls* (Surtees) 185 In reparacione molendini.., viz. in spyndillyng et factura unius novi saylyerde, iiis. viiid. **1611** FLORIO, *Fusarie*, trifles, toyes, spindlings.

2. The formation of a stem, stalk, or shoot, in plants.

1626 BACON *Sylva* §669 Another ill accident is drouth at the Spindling of the Corn, which with us is rare. **1707** MORTIMER *Husb.* (1721) II. 145 Their Leaves..may be tied in knots, which will prevent their spindling. **1726** *Dict. Rust.* (ed. 3), *Spindling*, a term which Gardiners use, to signify the first Appearance or putting forth of Flowers, Stems, or their running up in Length.

3. A spindly plant, animal, etc.

1842 TENNYSON *Amphion* xii, Half-conscious of the garden-squirt, The spindlings look unhappy. **1852** *P. Parley's Ann.* 330 Black sheep, or white sheep,..fat tails, or spindlings.

4. The process of recessing and tapering a spar for an aeroplane wing. Also *attrib.*, as ***spindling jig, machine.***

1918 *Aeronaut. Jrnl.* Feb. 40 In the spindling of spars the job should be placed in a jig having stops upon it. **1920** F. T. HILL *Pract. Aeroplane Constr.* v. 108 The base of the spindling jig. *Ibid.* 110 The only marking out required for spindling is the end of the recess. *Ibid.* 116 Flanges are grooved on the spindling machine with a jig.

5. *Med.* The occurrence of fairly regular alternating increases and decreases of amplitude in an electroencephalogram.

1963 *Electroencephalogr. & Clin. Neurophysiol.* XV. 766/2 The randomness can account for such characteristics as spindling without involving concepts of beating between alpha patterns. **1968** *Brit. Med. Bull.* XXIV. 257/1 Barnet and Lodge (1966) have averaged responses to 100 clicks or pure-tone bursts during deep sleep (high-voltage spindling in the EEG) in 22 infants.

'spindling, *ppl. a.* [f. SPINDLE *v.*]

1. Of plants: Growing or shooting out into (long) stalks or stems, esp. of a slender or weakly kind.

1750 G. HUGHES *Barbados* 217 Its numerous branches are spindling and weak. **1767** FAWKES *Theocr.* iv. 65 How high these thorns, and spindling brambles grow! **1805** R. W. DICKSON *Pract. Agric.* I. 546 Such warm sorts of land..are apt..to push the plants forward in such a rapid manner, that they become weak and spindling. **1851** *B'ham & Midl. Gardener's Mag.* Apr. 42 If they [*sc.* cuttings] are neglected in this particular they will grow spindling. **1885** *Athenæum* 23 May 669/1 Five spindling pines stand in the midst of a sandy waste.

fig. **1871** MRS. STOWE *My Wife* ix, Doubt..breaks a fellow up, and makes him morally spindling and sickly.

2. Of things: Slender, spindly.

1858 HOLLAND *Titcomb's Lett.* vi. 59 There are others who are coming up delicately with spindling shanks, and narrow shoulders. **1861** *Athenæum* 29 June 867 The spindling piers of stone are not grave enough in character.

spindly ('spɪndlɪ), *a.* Also 8 *Sc.* spinly. [f. SPINDLE *sb.*]

1. a. Of plants: Of a slender and weakly growth.

1651 in Hartlib *Legacy* (1655) 106 No more then a strong and fairly spread root could have a small and spindly head. **1743** MAXWELL *Sel. Trans. Agric. Scot.* 80 Where it.. continues as Quagmire, it is all Fog at Top, with a short spinly thin Grass. **1805** R. W. DICKSON *Pract. Agric.* I. 550 On such lands the growth of the crop may be so retarded as to become weak and spindly. **1855** *Jrnl. R. Agric. Soc.* XVI. I. 131 The corn turns yellow and spindly. **1880** MISS BIRD *Japan* I. 242 Sandy ridges with nothing on them but spindly Scotch firs and fir scrub.

b. Of growth: Characterized by slimness or attenuation and weakness.

1856 GLENNY *Everyday Bk.* 121/1 Cramped into a weakly spindly growth, a temporary bloom, and a premature decay. **1887** *Sat. Rev.* 1 Oct. 444 They [*sc.* trees] developed an abnormal spindly habit in their struggles upwards.

2. In general use: Having a slender elongated form implying, or suggestive of, weakness.

1827 *Sporting Mag.* (N.S.) XX. 170 A late writer.. complains of our present breed of racers as weak and spindly. **1871** B. TAYLOR *Faust* (1875) I. 108 Therefore I've worn, like many a spindly youth, False calves these many years upon me. **1883** MRS. G. L. BANKS *Forbidden to Marry* I. vi. 102 Spindly fire-irons. **1892** SLADEN *Japs at Home* xvi, The spindly little lacquer tables,..with bowed legs.

3. *Comb.*, as ***spindly-legged, -stemmed*** adjs.

1951 J. CLEARY in Murdoch & Drake-Brockman *Austral. Short Stories* 434 The other boy and the two girls, the freckle-faced, *spindly-legged..girls, are all working now. **1971** *Flying* Apr. 71/2 It was a big, spindly-legged beast. **1897** MARY KINGSLEY *W. Africa* 262 Some stretches of this forest were made up of thin, *spindly stemmed trees of great height.

spin-down ('spɪndaʊn), *sb.* [f. SPIN *v.* + DOWN *adv.*] A decrease in the speed of rotation of something.

1963 *Jrnl. Fluid Mechanics* XVII. 402 The initial angular velocity $\Omega_0 = 3{\cdot}668$ sec^{-1}, and the final angular velocity $\Omega_1 = 3{\cdot}033$ sec^{-1}. (This was a case of 'spin-down'.) **1967** *Astrophysical Jrnl. Lett.* CXLIX. L121 The 'spin-down' time of a cup of tea is approximately $(R^2/\nu\Omega)^{\frac{1}{2}}$, where R is the radius of the cup and Ω is the angular velocity of the tea. **1971** *New Scientist* 26 Aug. 452/2 The favourite explanation that decreases in period, or 'spin-ups', occur when starquakes take place in the deformed crust of the star seems to fall flat on its face when confronted with the discovery that the Crab pulsar, at least, also undergoes 'spin-downs'. **1977** *Astron. & Astrophysics* LX. 85/1 Braking by tidal torques and possibly magnetospheric friction can account for a spin-down of Venus within some 10^9 years.

spin-down (spɪn'daʊn), *a. Physics.* [f. SPIN *sb.*[1] + DOWN *a.*] Being or pertaining to a particle whose spin points downwards.

1965, etc. [see SPIN-UP *a.*].

spin-drier, -dryer (spɪn'draɪə(r)). Also without hyphen and as two words. [f. SPIN-DRY *v.*: cf. DRIER, DRYER.] A machine which removes excess water from washing by spinning it rapidly in a rotating perforated drum.

1939 *Archit. Rev.* LXXXV. 76/3 The laundry is all electric, and is equipped with a Rotary Washer and Spin Dryer, and Rotary Ironer, in which all the laundry of the house can be done without resort to clothes lines. **1948** *Sun* (Baltimore) 15 July 8 (Advt.), Be among the first to see the amazing new easy spindrier with automatic spin-rinse! **1958** *Observer* 2 Mar. 10/3 Spin-driers liberate housewives from the effort of wringing and pegging out clothes. **1959** G. FREEMAN *Jack would be Gentleman* vi. 114 We didn't have a spin dryer like you've got, only racks in the kitchen. **1967** *Spectator* 30 June 758/1 A canny Scot who salvaged Vat 69 filter pads and extracted whisky from them in his spin-drier was found to have done nothing illegal. **1972** J. AIKEN *Died on Rainy Sunday* 12 The spin-dryer whirred to a halt.

'spindrift. Orig. *Sc.* Also 7 spene-, 8 speendrift. [var. of SPOONDRIFT, app. due to local Sc. pronunciations of *spoon*; the form *speen-* is north-eastern, *spin-* south-western.]

a. Continuous driving of spray; spoondrift. Also *fig.* (example *attrib.*).

Common in English writers from *c* 1880, probably at first under the influence of W. Black's novels.

1600 MELVILL *Diary* (1842) 169 A how wa and spenedrift. **1755** R. FORBES *Ajax' Speech* 31 Twa-three swankies riding at the hand-gallop, garring the dubs flee about them like speen-drift. **1823** GALT *Entail* II. i. 9 Like the blast that brushes the waves of the ocean into spindrift. **1866** MACLEOD in *Gd. Words* Feb. 109 It..began to blow with furious gusts which angrily tore the small waves of the inland sea into spindrift. **1879** BLACK *Macleod of D.* xxix, Brief gleams of stormy sunlight lighting up the grey spindrift. **1883** G. C. DAVIES *Norfolk Broads* xxvii, The spindrift hid them every minute, and it appeared impossible they could live in such a boil.

fig. **1946** DYLAN THOMAS *Deaths & Entrances* 36 Not for the proud man apart From the raging moon I write On these spindrift pages.

b. *transf.* Driving snow, sand, etc. Also *attrib.*

1961 WEBSTER, *Spindrift*,..sand, dust, or snow driven before the wind like sea spray. **1971** C. BONINGTON *Annapurna South Face* xii. 147 At Camp V, the spindrift avalanches swished down all night, filling the platform, burying the tent. *Ibid.*, Cataracts of spindrift kept pouring over the cliffs above. **1972** D. HASTON *In High Places* vii. 90 A spindrift avalanche had come right down the chute, filling up the tent sack and covering everything... This wasn't the first time we'd been buried in spindrift.

c. *Comb.*, as ***spindrift-laden, -streaming*** adjs.

1971 D. HASTON in C. Bonington *Annapurna South Face* xvii. 214 Once again it was cold with snapping *spindrift-laden wind. **1916** BLUNDEN *Harbingers* 7 Or green and *spindrift-streaming shelf of stone.

spin-dry (spɪn'draɪ), *v.* Also spin dry. Inflected both as for SPIN *v.* (*dry* taken as adj.) and DRY *v.* [f. SPIN *v.* + DRY *v.* or DRY *a.*] *trans.* To remove excess water from (washing) by spinning it rapidly in a rotating perforated drum; to dry partially in a spin-drier. Also *absol.*

1927 *Sat. Even. Post* 19 Mar. 135 It takes the Savage [Washer & Dryer] just one-tenth the time to *spin-dry* the entire load *in its own tub.* **1951** *Good Housek. Home Encycl.* 304/1 The automatic type..will..spin-dry the clothes at a turn of the switch. **1958** *Observer* 2 Mar. 10/3 If clothes are spin-dried after soaking, much of their dirt goes out with the water. **1958** *Times* 2 June p. ix/5 Thus clothes can be boiled and then spun-dry ready for ironing. **1960** *Guardian* 15 Feb. 4/4 Finally, it [*sc.* a washing-machine] spins-dry. **1976** *Country Life* 22 Jan. 211/2 Give it a cool wash, however and spin dry if you like.

So **'spin-dry** *sb.*; **spin-'drying** *vbl. sb.*

1932 *House Beautiful* Jan. 50/2 The newest models [of washing machines] include a drying feature known as the 'spin dry' or 'extractor'. *Ibid.* 51/1 If the 'spin dry' is to work efficiently, it must not be overloaded, and clothes should be evenly distributed. **1956** *Archit. Rev.* CXX. 346/1 Spin-drying considerably reduces the line-drying time as opposed to wringing. **1962** *Which?* Aug. 238/1 Too much spin drying can set creases in drip dry cottons. **1978** P. PORTER *Cost of Seriousness* 36 When I start an allegro It's planned like those washing programmes Right through to the spin-dry.

spine (spaɪn), *sb.*[1] Also 5 spyne, spin. [ad. OF. *espine* (mod.F. *épine*, = Prov. *espina*, Sp. *espina*,

Pg. *espinha*, It. *spina*), or directly ad. L. *spīna* thorn, prickle, backbone, etc.]

I. 1. a. *Bot.* A stiff, sharp-pointed process produced or growing from the wood of a plant, consisting of a hardened or irregularly developed branch, petiole, stipule, or other part; a thorn; a similar process developed on fruits or leaves.

Botanically distinguished from a PRICKLE (q.v.), and sometimes also from a *thorn*, the latter being then restricted to processes originating from the epidermis only.

1430–40 LYDG. *Bochas* II. xxxi. (1554) 67 Serue the Lorde .. Which for thy sake was crouned with a spine, His heart eke perced to saue thee fro ruine. **1601** DENT *Pathw. Heaven* (1617) 36 The crab-stock spines, which grow out of the root of the very best apple tree. **1612** *Two Noble K.* I. i, Roses, their sharpe spines being gon. **1656** in BLOUNT. *a* **1722** LISLE *Husb.* (1757) 449 The spine, to which the pea adheres by a thread, is preserved entire. **1813** SIR H. DAVY *Agric. Chem.* (1814) 63 The tendrils, the spines, and other similar parts of plants. **1839** DARWIN *Voy. Nat.* xiv. 318 [A cactus] which, including the spines, was six feet and four inches in circumference. **1860** RUSKIN *Mod. Paint.* V. VI. viii. §14. 75 *note*, A branch of blackthorn with its spines. **1867** H. MACMILLAN *Bible Teach.* vii. (1870) 145 In the holly .. the leaves which grow nearest the ground are thickly furnished with spines.

b. *transf.* = NEEDLE *sb.* 11.

1859 BOYD *Recreat. Country Parson* ii. 28 There was not a breath of air through the spines of the firs. **1869** *Chambers's Jrnl.* Sept. 623 A few years ago, no one imagined that the spines (foliage) of pine-trees could be converted into wool.

†2. The sting of a bee. *Obs.*⁻⁰

1656 in BLOUNT *Glossogr.*

3. *Anat.* One or other of several sharp-pointed slender processes of various bones.

1706 PHILLIPS (ed. Kersey) s.v. *Pectinis Os*, The upper Part of this Bone is call'd its Spine. **1726** MONRO *Anat.* 107 Thro' the Middle of the Two Arches a small sharp Ridge runs, which has the Name of *Spine* bestowed on it by some, as indeed Anatomists commonly do apply this Name to all the long narrow-edged Protuberances of Bones. **1808** *Med. Jrnl.* XIX. 212 A very troublesome sensation near the spine of the left ilium. **1831** R. KNOX *Cloquet's Anat.* 99 At the middle part it is much diminished, and is limited by the two nasal spines. **1870** ROLLESTON *Animal Life* 7 The spines of the dorsal vertebræ.

4. *Zool.* A stiff, pointed, thorn-like process or appendage developed on the integument of certain fishes, insects, or lower forms of animal life.

1721 BRADLEY *Philos. Acc. Wks. Nat.* 148 On the forepart of its [an insect's] Body, near the Head, are placed two Branches .. from which proceed several capillary Spines. **1748** J. HILL *Hist. Fossils* 652 The various species of bodies allow'd to have been spines of the Echini. **1815** STEPHENS in *Shaw's Gen. Zool.* IX. I. 42 At the bend of the wing, just within, is a horn-coloured spine, about one-eighth of an inch long, and blunt at the end. **1835** J. DUNCAN *Beetles* 110 The tibiæ .. are frequently beset with stiff bristles, and armed more or less with spines or spurs. **1888** ROLLESTON & JACKSON *Anim. Life* 190 [In star-fish] the edges of a groove are bordered immediately by a series of fine moveable spines.

b. One of the prickles of a hedgehog, the quills of a porcupine, or similar growth on other animals.

1753 *Chambers' Cycl.* Suppl., *Erinaceus*, .. the common hedgehog... Its head, back, and sides, are covered with sharp spines. **1770** G. WHITE *Selborne* xxvii, No doubt their spines are soft and flexible at the time of their birth. **1774** GOLDSM. *Nat. Hist.* (1824) II. 104 In the one [species of porcupine], the spines are about an inch long; in the other, a foot. **1828** STARK *Elem. Nat. Hist.* I. 128 Crested Porcupine. With very long spines on the back. **1840** *Cuvier's Anim. Kingd.* 113 Some [rats] have spines mingled with their fur, as the Cairo Mouse .., which has spines on the back in place of hairs. **1870** YEATS *Nat. Hist. Comm.* 298 Bristles, hedgehog spines, and porcupine quills, are all modifications of hair.

c. *Ichth.* A spinous or spiny fin-ray; a fin-spine.

1774 GOLDSM. *Nat. Hist.* (1776) VI. 189 These fins differ very much from those of other fishes, which are formed of straight spines. **1828** STARK *Elem. Nat. Hist.* I. 476 Banstickle or Stickleback. Three spines on the back. **1867** F. FRANCIS *Angling* iii. (1880) 98 Master Perch has sharp spines.

d. *Conch.* A sharp projection of a shell.

1822 J. PARKINSON *Outl. Oryctol.* 156 A subfusiform univalve; .. the spine longish. *Ibid.* 203 Lip alæform; bent upwards on the spine.

5. a. Any natural formation having a slender sharp-pointed form.

1750 tr. *Leonardus' Mirr. Stones* 89 Its broad head .. being put before the light, the Spine appears within. **1899** *Allbutt's Syst. Med.* VI. 490 The dendrons are possessed of numerous minute lateral projections, gemmules, spines, or 'thorns', as they have been variously called.

b. *Needlework.* (See quot.)

1882 CAULFEILD & SAWARD *Dict. Needlework* 458/1 Spines .. are also called Pinworks, and are used to trim the raised Cordonnets that surround Spanish and Venetian Point Lace, and also other kinds of Point Lace. The Spines are long straight points that stick out from the edge of the Cordonnet.

c. A tall mass of lava projecting upwards from the mouth of a volcano.

1903 *Amer. Jrnl. Sci.* CLXVI. 270 The ancient summit of the mountain [*sc.* Mont Pelée] has lost most of its former prominence above the rim of the crater, but within the old Caldera a cone has risen which overtops the surrounding walls and terminates in a spine rising hundreds of feet above the main mass of the new cone. **1954** W. D. THORNBURY *Princ. Geomorphol.* xix. 500 The rapid growth of plug domes is further illustrated by one on Santa Maria volcano on Guatemala... It had a spine which attained a height of 66 meters. **1976** P. FRANCIS *Volcanoes* iii. 124 Evidence of just how viscous the lavas are, .. was provided by the great spine which was pushed up out of the vent of Mt Pelée, reaching over 300 metres in height.

II. 6. a. The spinal or vertebral column in man and vertebrates; the backbone. Also ***spine of the back***; now *dial.*

(*a*) *c* **1400** *Lanfranc's Cirurg.* 358 Of curis of woundis of þe spine ouþir spondilium.

1615 CROOKE *Body of Man* XIII. xx. (1631) 974 Vnder the name of the Spine we comprehend all that which is extended from the first Racke bone of the Necke vnto the Coccyx or Rumpe. **1646** SIR T. BROWNE *Pseud. Ep.* IV. i. 180 So cannot other animals lye upon their backs; though the spine lye parallell with the Horizon, yet will their legs incline, and lye at angles unto it. **1661** LOVELL *Hist. Anim. & Min.* Isagoge v, Amongst Fishes .. The *Psettaceous*, or plain and spinose, have a spine that seemeth to be divided in the midd'st. **1794** COWPER *Needless Alarm* 7 Many a neighb'ring squire .. Contusion hazarding of neck or spine. **1827** N. ARNOTT *Physics* I. 223 The head rests on the elastic column of the spine. **1834** MᶜMURTRIE *Cuvier's Anim. Kingd.* 27 The spine, most commonly, is continued into a tail. **1866** G. MACDONALD *Ann. Q. Neighb.* i. (1878) 5 The horses stand .. with their spines in a straight line.

(*b*) **1651** *Sir W. Raleigh's Ghost* 87 From the head, it .. is extended through the spine of the back. **1815** J. SMITH *Panorama Sci. & Art* II. 272 Having suspended some frogs .. by means of metallic hooks fixed in the spines of their backs. **1884–** in dial. glossaries and texts (Worcs., Glouc., Oxf., Berks., Herts., Cornw.).

b. *transf.* and *fig.* A part or formation having the function of a backbone.

1665 HOOKE *Microgr.* 117 The leaf being .. set into the *Pedunculus*, .. receiveth from that not onely a *Spine*, as I may call it, which, passing through the leaf, divides its [etc.]. **1807** J. BARLOW *Columb.* IX. 96 Yet what an age her shell-rock ribs attest! Her sparry spines, her coal-encumber'd breast! **1855** TENNYSON *Maud* II. II. iv, The shock Of cataract seas that snap The three decker's oaken spine. **1889** *Pall Mall G.* 23 Apr. 2/1 The span is the great arch that supports the first floor. The spine is the iron upright which runs outside the Tower from the second floor to the summit. **1912** GALSWORTHY *Inn of Tranquility* 189 The vice of drawing these distorted morals has permeated the Drama to its spine. **1977** *New Yorker* 9 May 126/2 A beauty called Laura .. who is the spine of the place. **1977** P. SCUPHAM *Hinterland* 44 Doors shake on their jambs: the spine of the house Thrills as the sprung wood quivers, and goes still. **1979** *Tucson Mag.* Mar. 8/2 No one cares or has the spine to sound off. **1981** F. INGLIS *Promise of Happiness* i. 3 We try to say what some of the best books are like, so that we can hand them on... This expression of the gift relationship .. gives spine and structure to this study.

c. A line or mark along the back.

1791 W. H. MARSHALL *W. England* (1796) II. 243 The Cattle .. chiefly of a dark red color; a few of them with white Glocestershire spines.

7. The heart-wood or duramen of a tree.

1630–1 [implied in *spine-lath*: see 11]. **1703** R. NEVE *City & C. Purchaser* 261 If the Elm be fell'd between November and February, it will be all Spine, or Heart. **1825–63** [see *spine-oak* in 11]. **1883** M. P. BALE *Saw-Mills* 336 *Spine*, is the name given to the mature wood of a tree, the outer layer being called alburnum or sapwood.

8. A ridge or elevated stretch of ground, rock, etc., having a position analogous to that of the backbone, or resembling it in some way.

1796 MORSE *Amer. Geog.* I. 567 The spine, or highest ridge of the peninsula. **1852** MUNDAY *Antipodes* (1857) 4 These spines of land, or rather rock, subdivide the south shore of Port Jackson. **1860** TYNDALL *Glac.* I. xxi. 148 These blocks ride upon a spine of ice, and form a moraine. **1895** MEREDITH *Amazing Marriage* xxxiv, Mickleham, where the Surrey chalk runs its final turfy spine North-Eastward.

9. a. *techn.* A longitudinal ridge; a fin; a longitudinal slat of a riddle.

1875 in KNIGHT *Dict. Mech.* 2269/2.

b. The back of a book, that is, the part bearing the title, etc., which is visible when the book is standing on a shelf; also, the corresponding part of a dust-jacket or a slide-box.

1922 M. SADLEIR *Vict. Bibliogr.* 14 Be wary of books in cloth which bear no publisher's imprint on the spine. **1931** *Publisher & Bookseller* 20 Feb. 345/2 The utility of having the selling price printed on the spine of a book jacket. **1952** V. CANNING *House of Seven Flies* i. 24 He stared at the coloured spines of the books in the rack. **1962** A. NISBETT *Technique Sound Studio* vi. 113 Programme details are written .. on the spine of the box in which it [*sc.* a tape] is kept. **1976** S. BRETT *So much Blood* i. 16 Brown velvet upholstery and the leather spines of books gave the quality of an old sepia photograph.

III. *attrib.* and *Comb.* **10. a.** In sense 6, as ***spine-ache***, ***-case***, ***-chisel***, ***-pad***, etc.; ***spinebreaker***; ***spine-breaking***, ***-broken*** adjs.; ***spine-wise*** advb.

1822–7 GOOD *Study Med.* (1829) III. 221 In no instance do I find the back-bone ache, or spine-ache, from which rhachialgia derives its name. *Ibid.* IV. 682 Baron Larrey speaks in terms of high commendation of the first, and especially in spine-cases, or paraplegia. **1823** CAMPBELL *Sp. Patriots* iii, Smile o'er the gaspings of spine-broken men. **1851** H. MELVILLE *Moby Dick* III. xlviii. 281 Launch me, spine-wise, on the sea. **1882** FLOYER *Unexpl. Baluchistan* 120 We bumped, stumbled, and jolted in a most horribly spine-breaking, bone-dislocating manner. **1895** *Arnold & Sons' Catal. Surg. Instrum.* 93 Spine Chisel. *Ibid.* 96 Spine Saw. *Ibid.* 513 Spine Hook. **1900** ISABEL SAVORY *Sportsw. India* viii. 256 Not only [to] wear a large *solá topi*, but have a spine pad sewn inside the coat. **1947** DYLAN THOMAS *Let.* 11 June (1966) 314 The hill to the nearest village is a spinebreaker.

b. In senses 1 and 4, as ***spine-clad***, ***-covered***, ***-finned***, ***-headed***, ***-like***, ***-pointed***, ***-tailed***, adjs.; ***spine-cushion***.

1846 PATTERSON *Zool.* 43 In the harder, or *spine-clad species [of Echinodermata]. **1849** *Sk. Nat. Hist., Mammalia* IV. 115 The Common Porcupine... This *spine-covered animal is found in Italy [etc.]. **1884** BOWER & SCOTT *De Bary's Phaner.* 310 The leaf-bundles run .. almost horizontally upwards towards the lower margin of the *spine-cushion. **1896** LYDEKKER *Roy. Nat. Hist.* V. 335 The *spine-finned fishes .. are distinguished .. by some of the anterior rays of the dorsal, anal, and pelvic fins usually taking the form of strong, unjointed, bony spines. *Ibid.* 547 The extinct Spine-finned Sharks,—order Acanthodii. **1804** SHAW *Gen. Zool.* V. II. 396 *Spine-headed Sucker, *Cyclopterus Bispinosus*. *c* **1880** *Cassell's Nat. Hist.* IV. 301 All the species of the Snake family .. have minute vestiges of hind limbs, scale-like or *spine-like. **1882** VINES tr. *Sach's Bot.* 457 The four cells are attached to each other by means of rigid spine-like projections. **1829** T. CASTLE *Introd. Bot.* 63 The apex of a leaf may .. be .. *spine-pointed or cuspidate. **1866** *Treas. Bot.* 1062/2 A Peruvian shrub, with elliptic spine-pointed leaves. **1802** SHAW *Gen. Zool.* III. I. 216 *Spine-tailed Lizard, *Lacerta Acanthura*. **1860** G. BENNETT *Gatherings Naturalist* 180 That remarkable little bird, the .. Spine-tailed Orthonyx. **1872** COUES *N. Amer. Birds* 183 *Chæturinæ*. Spine-tailed Swifts.

11. Special Combs.: **spine-basher** *Austral. slang*, a loafer; so **spine-bashing** *vbl. sb.* (and *pres. pple.*); **spine-bill**, one or other of two species of Australian honey-eaters of the genus *Acanthorhynchus*, characterized by their long spine-like bills; **spine-bone**, the spine; also *transf.*; **spine-chiller**, something (*rarely* someone) that inspires excitement and terror; *esp.* a horror or suspense story, film, etc.; **spine-chilling** *ppl. a.* and *vbl. sb.*, inspiring excitement and terror, horrifying; **spine-eel**, a spiny eel; **spine-fish**, a fish having sharp spines; **spine-freezer**, **-freezing** *ppl. a.*, = *spine-chiller*, *-chilling ppl. a.* above; † **spine-lath**, a heart-lath; **spine-machine**, a device for supporting or strengthening the human spine; **spine-oak**, the heart-wood of an oak (cf. 7); **spine road**, a major road linking other important routes or points; **spine-thriller**, **-tingler**, something pleasurably frightening; *esp.* an exciting story, etc.; **spine-tingling** *ppl. a.*, pleasurably frightening or disturbing; spine-chilling; **spine wall** *Building* (see quot. 1963). See also SPINE-TAIL.

1946 R. RIVETT *Behind Bamboo* 399 **Spinebasher*, one always on his back, always resting. **1976** *Sydney Morning Herald* 20 Mar. 14 The elbow-benders, spine-bashers, eternal babblers keep one ear to the loudspeakers, an ear to the ground. **1941** *Argus* (Melbourne) *Week-End Mag.* 15 Nov. 1/4 **Spine bashing*, having a rest; loafing. **1944** L. GLASSOP *We were Rats* 208 'She's sweet,' I said. 'Go and do some spine bashing.' **1966** G. W. TURNER *Eng. Lang. in Austral. & N.Z.* vi. 135 Lying down and doing nothing, what the Australian calls *spinebashing*. **1848** GOULD *Birds Australia* IV. Pl. 61 *Acanthorhynchus tenuirostris*. Slender-billed *Spine-bill. *Ibid.* Pl. 62 *A. superciliosus*. White-eyebrowed Spine-bill. **1911** A. E. MACK *Bush Days* 52 Spine-bills flashed by. **1977** *Daily News* (Perth, Austral.) 19 Jan. 11/2 Weighing only 10 grams the spinebill can put on an extra 10 per cent body weight in one day. *c* **1400** *Lanfranc's Cirurg.* 148 þei strecchen doun to þe eeris [*v.r.* ers] in lenkþe biside þe *spin boon [*v.r.* spyne bon]. **1621** LODGE *Summary of Du Bartas* I. 273 The marrow of the Spine-bone. *a* **1892** TENNYSON in *Mem.* (1897) I. 20, I used to stand on this sand-built ridge, .. and think that it was the spine-bone of the world. **1940** *Amer. Speech* XV. 205/1 **Spine-chiller*, a mystery film or play. **1942** BERREY & VAN DEN BARK *Amer. Thes. Slang* §202/4 *Sensational story or book*, .. spine chiller or tingler. **1957** *London Mag.* Aug. 59 *Elective Affinities* is a far more important novel than Walpole's *Castle of Otranto*, and yet there has only been one edition of it in the past hundred years, compared to the dozen or so of Walpole's unreadable spine-chiller. **1969** E. LEMARCHAND *Alibi for Corpse* xv. 189 Even now the idea of her .. gives me the willies. And Twentyman was a spine-chiller. **1976** *Listener* 21 Oct. 509/2 The arrival of a mysterious stranger, murder, a dumb-struck child, suicide. This was a spine-chiller, and no mistake. **1946** 'M. INNES' *From London Far* I. ii. 20 A sweet and—as he hoped—wholly *spine-chilling smile. **1958** *New Statesman* 25 Jan. 103/1 With unerring instinct H. G. Clouzot, the spine-chilling specialist of *The Wages of Fear* and *The Fiends*, has sought a new tension in Picasso. **1958** *Times Lit. Suppl.* 11 July 389/3 As an exercise in spine-chilling and blood-curdling, *Caves of Night* is masterly. **1960** H. AGAR *Saving Remnant* v. 127 'What, still so many Jews?'—that spine-chilling comment. **1983** *Listener* 10 Feb. 16/3 She realised that I was retailing an antiquarian donnish history instead of the mildly spine-chilling ghost story she expected. **1883** DAY *Indian Fish* 30 Few are of much economic importance, if we except the common goby, *spine-eels (*Mastacembelidæ*). **1827** HOOD *Hero & Leander* xxvi, Let no fierce sharks destroy him with their teeth, Nor *spine-fish wound him with their venom'd thorns. **1960** WODEHOUSE *Jeeves in Offing* iii. 41 Mrs. Cream .. worked in her room every afternoon on her new *spine-freezer. **1961** —— *Ice in Bedroom* i. 9, I dipped into one of her products once, misled by the title into supposing it to be a spine-freezer. **1937** *Discovery* Dec. 373/1 The *spine-freezing howl of the *kiret*. **1961** *Guardian* 3 Apr. 5/4 The spine-freezing wail of sirens. **1630–1** in Swayne *Sarum Churchw. Acc.* (1896) 192 Three hundred of *spind lathes, 2s. 6d. **1635–6** *Ibid.* 204, ij hundred of spine lathes to mend ouer the North dore of the Ch. **1803** HEY *Pract. Obs. Surg.* Pref. p. vii, Mr. E. makes excellent *Spine-machines, upon the true principle of supporting the weak part from the ground. **1825** COBBETT *Rur. Rides* (1885) II. 31 The best of *spine oak is generally chosen for these pins. **1863** WISE *New Forest* Gloss., *Spine-oak*, the heart of oak. **1961** *New Left Rev.* July/Aug. 56/1 A *spine road runs east-west between these blocks. **1971** *Guardian* 12 Oct. 28/4 Oxford city's consultants drew up an alternative for a spine road feeding into large car parks. **1912** *Maclean's Mag.* Nov. 135 (*heading*) Producing *spine thrillers. How successful melodramas are furnished—some confessions about art of capitalizing spines. **1962** *Listener* 21 June 1085/3 It ranges over the whole field of spine-thrillers, from puppets to poisons. **1942** *Spine tingler [see *spine-chiller* above]. **1978** *TV Times* 28 Jan.–3 Feb. 19/1 This week's *The South Bank Show* homes in on..the best Shakespearian actor alive today. Also on view: little spine-tinglers from his *Henry V*, *Henry VI* and *Coriolanus*. **1955** E. CALDWELL *Love & Money* 206 A *spine-tingling historical romance. **1968** *Blues Unlimited* Dec. 4 John Lee's spine-tingling guitar. **1978** J. B. HILTON *Some run Crooked* xi. 118 He spoke the words quietly..and there was something spine-tingling about them. **1949** *Archit. Rev.* CV. 236 Construction is box-frame with continuous reinforced concrete slabs, and with load-bearing *spine walls of reinforced concrete. **1963** *Gloss. Gen. Building Terms* (*B.S.I.*) 22 *Spine wall*, an internal loadbearing wall running in the direction of the main axis of a building or structure.

spine (spaɪn), *sb.*[2] *s.w. dial.* Also 7–8 **spind**. [OE. *spind* fat, = WFris. *spyn*, OS. *spind* (MLG. *spint*), MDu. and Du. *spint*, OHG. and G. dial. *spind*, *spint*, fat, sapwood. In Devon and Cornw. the forms *spend*, *spen* are also in use.]

1. Greensward, sward; turf. Also *attrib.*

1786 *Young's Annals Agric.* VII. 60, I would recommend some heaps to be made of the sward or spind, in the nature of denshiring or burnbaiting. **1791** W. H. MARSHALL *W. England* (1796) II. 264 Paring off and subverting, apparently with a Breast Plow, the 'spine' or rough sod of an orchard. **1807** VANCOUVER *Agric. Devon* (1813) 116 Cutting..the spine or green sward to a feather-edge. **1823** J. BADCOCK *Dom. Amusem.* 29 These planks subsequently covered with the spine of earth well kept. **1889** *Reports Provinces, Devon.* (E.D.D.), You can't grow a good spine under those trees.

2. The rind of pork or other meat; the layer of fat or meat adhering to the skin. Also *attrib.* in *spine-pork*, (see quot. 1886).

1847 HALLIWELL, *Spine*, the hide of an animal; the fat on the surface of a joint of meat. **1886** ELWORTHY *W. Somerset Word-bk.*, *Spine-pork*, the meat of small pigs, on which the bacon is left with the skin; hence the 'crackling'.

spine (spaɪn), *v. rare.* [f. SPINE *sb.*[1]]

†**1.** *intr.* To grow or develop like a spine. *Obs.*⁻¹

1621 G. SANDYS *Ovid's Met.* v. (1626) 101 A taile withall Spines from his changed shape.

2. *trans.* To shoot or hit in the spine.

1888 J. INGLIS *Tent Life Tigerland* 340 It was 'spined' (the shot had been a lucky one).

†**spineal**, *a. Obs.*⁻¹ [f. L. *spīne-us*, f. *spīna* thorn.] Made of thorns.

1688 HOLME *Armoury* III. 7/2 The Crown Spineal, or Crown of Thorns,..was made of sharp thorns.

spined (spaɪnd), *a.* [f. SPINE *sb.*[1]]

1. Having, provided or covered with, spines; spinous, spiny.

1777 PENNANT *Brit. Zool.* (ed. 4) IV. 4 Claws angulated; second joint spined. **1819** SAMOUELLE *Entomol. Compend.* 274 Feet..not strongly ciliated or spined. **1856** A. R. WALLACE in *Ann. Nat. Hist.* July 27 A female Mias, on a durian tree, kept up..a continuous shower of branches and of the heavy, spined fruits. **1882** P. M. DUNCAN *Transf. Insects* 91 Their legs are well developed; the hind ones are particularly strong, and the others are spined.

b. In the specific names of various animals, fishes, etc., as ***spined caterpillar***, ***cicada***, ***loach***, ***rat***, ***sea-screw***, ***shark***, ***sparus*** (see quots.).

1803 SHAW *Gen. Zool.* IV. II. 416 Spined Sparus, *Sparus Spinifer*. **1836** YARRELL *Brit. Fishes* I. 381 The Spined Loche Groundling. *Botia tænia*. **1839** *Penny Cycl.* XV. 496/2 *Echimys*, Geoff. (Spined Rats). **1840** SWAINSON & SHUCKARD *Insects* 64 One of the spined caterpillars of Brazil. *Ibid.* 130 The *Centronotidæ*, or spined cicadas, remarkable for..the spines upon their bodies. **1850** A. WHITE *List Specim. Crustacea Brit. Mus.* 49 *Dexamine spinosa*. Spined Sea-Screw. **1879** E. P. WRIGHT *Anim. Life* 464 Of the Spined Sharks, or *Spinacidæ*, there are a good many species.

2. Having a spine or spinal column.

1891 in *Cent. Dict.*

†**spinee.** *Obs.* In 4 spynee, spine, 5 spyneye. [ad. OF. *espinee* (not recorded in this sense), f. *espine* SPINE *sb.*[1]] A dish or confection flavoured with hawthorn flowers.

1381 in *Forme of Cury* (1780) 107 For to make spine. Nym the flowrys of the haw thorn clene gaderyd and bray hem al to dust [etc.]. *c* **1430** *Two Cookery-bks.* 20 Spyneye. [Receipt follows.]

spinel (ˈspɪnəl). Forms: 6 spynel, 7 spinnell, 7–9 spinell, 8–9 spinal, 7– spinel. [ad. older F. *espinelle* (mod.F. *spinelle*, It. *spinella*, Sp. *espinela*). See also ESPINEL and SPINELLE.]

1. a. A gem or precious stone of a red or scarlet colour, closely resembling the true ruby, now classed as belonging to the typical species of the spinel group of minerals (see sense 2).

1528 *MS. List of Jewelry* (P.R.O.), xiij rynges,..iij with Spynels,..oon with a crapawd. **1599** HAKLUYT *Voy.* II. 236 Rubies, Safires & Spinels. **1620** in Rymer *Foedera* (1710) XVII. 196 Two greate Stones called Spinnells. **1665** SIR T. HERBERT *Trav.* (1677) 88 Translucent stones which want neither beauty nor esteem; namely, Topazes, Amethysts, Spinels [etc.]. **1698** FRYER *Acc. E. India & P.* 214 The third sort of Ruby is called a Spinell. **1801** T. THOMSON in *Encycl. Brit.* Suppl. II. 203/2 If deep [red], the ruby is usually called balass; if pale rosy, spinell. **1892** *Daily News* 23 Mar. 5/4 The Spinel and the Balas, the one a lively poppy-red, the other a violet-rose, frequently usurp the dignity of a true ruby.

b. More fully in ***spinel ruby***.

1668 CHARLETON *Onomast.* 277 *Rubinus Spinellus*, the Spinel Ruby. **1753** *Chambers' Cycl.* Suppl. s.v. *Ruby*, The second is the spinal ruby. Under this name they [jewellers] know those rubies, which are of a somewhat less deep.. colour, than what they call the true ruby. **1796** KIRWAN *Elem. Min.* (ed. 2) I. 253 Spinell and Balass Rubies. **1815** J. SMITH *Panorama Sci. & Art* II. 411 In the emerald it [chromium] exists in the state of green oxide, and the spinal ruby contains it in the state of an acid. **1839** URE *Dict. Arts* 391 If..we make the edges of a spinel ruby..curvilinear. **1883** *Encycl. Brit.* XVI. 386/2 Varieties are—Spinel ruby when scarlet, Balas Ruby when rose-red.

2. *Min.* The typical species of a group of minerals (the ***spinel group***), which are compounds of sesquioxides with protoxides, and crystallize in the isometric system. The formula of the typical species is $MgAl_2O_4$.

1807 T. THOMSON *Chem.* (ed. 3) II. 482 This mineral, which has some resemblance to the spinel, was found composed of 60 parts alumina [etc.]. **1817** R. JAMESON *Char. Min.* (ed. 3) 132 Triple crystals occur in spinel and calcareous-spar. **1842** *Penny Cycl.* XXII. 348/2 Spinell is found in Ceylon and Siam in isolated and rolled crystals in the beds of rivers. **1888** RUTLEY *Rock-Forming Min.* 108 Ordinary spinel appears reddish, or colourless by transmitted light. **1953** F. H. POUGH *Field Guide Rocks & Minerals* II. 141 Spinel, like corundum, is a mineral of metamorphosed limestones and low-silica pegmatites, and consequently it is commonly associated with corundum. **1977** A. HALLAM *Planet Earth* 137 The name spinel broadly refers to a group which includes the minerals magnetite and chromite. In a narrower sense, spinel is the magnesium aluminum oxide member of the group.

b. One or other of the various minerals belonging to this group. The general formula of the minerals is $A^{2+}B_2{}^{3+}O_4$, *spec.* where *B* is Al. The name is also applied to any of a large number of artificial minerals having similar structures.

See also *chloro-spinel* (CHLORO-[1]) and *water-spinel*.

1837 DANA *Min.* 328 The fine colored spinels, when of large size, are highly esteemed as gems. **1863** —— *Man. Geol.* 139 The soft spinels of St. Lawrence co., called houghite. **1880** CLEMINSHAW *Wurtz' Atom. The.* 144 The spinels form a very natural isomorphous group. **1944** C. PALACHE et al. *Dana's Syst. Min.* (ed. 7) I. 688 In addition to the natural spinels a considerable number of artificial spinels have been described, where A = Co, Cd, Cu and B = Co, Ti, Sn, V, Ga, In, Mn. One of the further complexities of composition in the artificial spinels is a tendency for substitution of A atoms for part of the B atoms of the formula, i.e., the formula may be written $BABX_4$ (as in the compounds $GaMgGaO_4$, etc.). **1967** D. H. MARTIN *Magnetism in Solids* i. 39 The two crystal types to which the most fully investigated ferrimagnetics belong are those known as 'spinels' and 'garnets'. **1974** D. M. ADAMS *Inorg. Solids* iii. 69 The structure of a spinel is conveniently described by a parameter γ which equals the fraction of A^{2+} in octahedral sites. Thus, for a 'normal' spinel, $\gamma = 0$, for an 'inverse' spinel, $\gamma = 1$. A random distribution of A^{2+} amongst the two groups of sites gives $\gamma = 2/3$.

c. *attrib.*, as ***spinel-crystal***, ***structure***.

1851 *Amer. Jrnl. Sci.* Ser. II. XII. 210 Some of his specimens are spinel crystals..in one part, and true Houghite in another. **1944** C. PALACHE et al. *Dana's Syst. Min.* (ed. 7) I. 688 Another chemical feature of interest is the ability of artificial Mg, Al spinel to contain considerable excess of Al_2O_3 without impairment of the spinel structure. **1967** M. CHANDLER *Ceramics in Mod. World* vi. 178 Today most ferrites have spinel structures.

spinel, var. SPINAL *sb.*; obs. or dial. f. SPINDLE.

spineless (ˈspaɪnlɪs), *a.* [f. SPINE *sb.*[1]]

1. Of animals, plants, etc.: Having no spines or sharp-pointed processes; not spinous.

1827 GRIFFITH tr. *Cuvier* V. 223 Spineless Rats of the Old Continent. **1832** LINDLEY *Introd. Bot.* 49 In domesticated plants they [spines] often entirely disappear, as in the Apple and Pear, the wild varieties of which are spiny, and the cultivated ones spineless. **1840** *Penny Cycl.* XVIII. 170/2 Scales of Cones [of a pine] spineless at apex. **1890** *Cent. Dict.* s.v. *Perch*, *Spineless perch*, a pirate-perch.

2. a. Having a weak or diseased spine; deprived or destitute of the natural strength or support of the spine; exhausted, limp.

1860 DICKENS *Uncomm. Trav.* iv, A whole family of Sprites, consisting of a remarkably stout father and three spineless sons. **1876** BOTHMER *Germ. Home Life* 237 The sole heir to a vast property was a delicate spineless boy. **1877** W. S. GILBERT *Foggerty's Fairy* (1892) 97 He found Mrs. Pintle reclining in a spineless way on a comfortable sofa.

b. Lacking moral force, resolution, or vigour; marked by weakness or instability of character; feeble, flabby, irresolute.

1885 *The Voice* (N.Y.) 17 Dec. 2 We are sick of this spineless way of treating violators of law. **1891** MISS DOWIE *Girl in Karp.* 209 She had married this spineless person, broken him of his drinking habits. **1892** KIPLING in *Pall Mall G.* 24 Mar. 3/1 Clamouring for the aid of a spineless Government.

Hence **ˈspinelessly** *adv.*, **ˈspinelessness**.

1920 *Chambers's Jrnl.* 18 Dec. 35/2 His spinelessness and low tastes. **1948** A. L. ROWSE *End of Epoch* 186 The spinelessness, the disastrous disunity of the liberal elements in Germany. **1960** *Middlesex Hospital Jrnl.* Jan.–Feb. 12/1 At interviews, the salesman applicant has to steer a course between spinelessness and cockiness. **1977** J. PORTER *Who the Heck is Sylvia?* xii. 110 Capitulating as spinelessly as usual, Miss Jones..unfastened her seat belt. **1981** CRAIG & CADOGAN *Lady Investigates* xi. 214 Gregory's vacillation.. seems to be an example of the kind of spinelessness that he usually condemns in others.

ˈspinelet. [dim. of SPINE *sb.*[1]] A small spine or spiny process.

1901 *Proc. Zool. Soc.* 273 It is quite likely..that these horny spinelets are equally characteristic of *Galago garnetti*.

spinellane (spɪˈnɛleɪn). *Min.* [ad. G. *spinellan*, so named (1808) by the German geologist K. W. Nose, from its resemblance to SPINEL.] = NOSEAN, or a blue variety of this.

1815 AIKIN *Min.* (ed. 2) 208 Spinellane occurs in small crystals. **1842** *Penny Cycl.* XXII. 348/2 Spinellane..is found on the borders of Lake Laach, near Andernach on the Rhine. **1850** ANSTED *Elem. Geol.*, *Min.*, etc. 200 Hauyne, with a nearly allied mineral, Spinellane, also called Nosean, cannot with propriety be separated [from Lapis-lazuli].

spinelle (spɪˈnɛl). [ad. older F. *espinelle*, mod.F. *spinelle*: see SPINEL.]

1. = SPINEL 1.

1555 EDEN *Decades* (Arb.) 264 There is also..an other kynde of Rubies which wee caule Spinelle. **1599** HAKLUYT *Voy.* II. I. 264 There is great store of rubies, saphires, and spinelles in this Iland. **1600** in Nichols *Progr. Q. Eliz.* (1823) III. 454 One jewell of golde, garnished with two spynnelles and sparkes of dyamondes about yt. **1684** R. WALLER *Nat. Exper.* 128 The Spinelle, and the Ruby Baleis. **1796** KIRWAN *Elem. Min.* (ed. 2) I. 253 By Mr. Klaproth the spinelle which he analyzed..contained, 0,7635 argill, 0,1568 silex, 0,0263 of iron, and 0,0128 calx. **1802** [see 1 b]. **1876** *Encycl. Brit.* IV. 552/2 [In Burmah are] found..different varieties of chrysoberyl and spinelle.

b. ***spinelle ruby***, = SPINEL 1 b and 2 (cf. next).

1802 *Phil. Trans.* XCII. 305 The first of these substances ..is the spinelle ruby, now generally known by the name of spinelle. **1829** CRAWFURD *Jrnl. Emb. to Crt. of Ava* (1834) II. 201 The precious stones ascertained to exist in the Burmese territory are chiefly those of the sapphire family and the spinelle ruby. **1855** J. SCOFFERN in *Orr's Circ. Sci.*, *Chem.* 448 Chromate of iron..occurs crystallized in regular octahedrons, being..the analogue of magnetic oxide of iron, and the spinelle ruby.

2. *Min.* = SPINEL 2.

1804 R. JAMESON *Min.* I. 78 Spinelle... Its principal colour is red. **1823** H. J. BROOKE *Introd. Crystallogr.* 82 The octahedron will therefore..be adopted as the primary form of spinelle and red oxide of copper. **1876** PAGE *Adv. Text-bk. Geol.* vii. 146 Many of the older lavas yield agates, chalcedony, leucite, spinelle, olivine, and other precious minerals.

spinescence (spaɪˈnɛsəns). *Bot.* and *Zool.* [See next and -ENCE. So F. *spinescence*.] Spinescent character, condition, or formation.

1859 MAYNE *Expos. Lex.*, *Spinescentia*,..spinescence. **1894** *Nat. Sci.* Oct. 263 It is not altogether strange to find spinescent processes away from deserts; but I do maintain that spinescence is an important element in the facies of hot and arid deserts in a barren soil. **1908** *Smithsonian Misc. Coll.* v. 104 The differences are mainly in the spinescence or smoothness of the skin.

spinescent (spaɪˈnɛsənt), *a.* [ad. mod.L. *spinescent-*, *-ens*, pres. pple. of L. *spīnescere* to grow thorny, f. *spīna* SPINE *sb.*[1] So F. *spinescent*.]

1. *Bot.* Developing into, or terminating in, a spine or thorn; also, bearing or covered with spines; spiniferous.

1793 MARTYN *Lang. Bot.*, *Spinescens*, spinescent, becoming hard and thorny. **1841** *Florist's Jrnl.* (1846) II. 213 The calyx is small and entire, with five spinescent teeth. **1876** HARLEY *Royle's Mat. Med.* 666 A shrub with squamose spinescent branches.

2. *Zool.* Tending to become a spine or spinous process; spinous, spinulous.

1856–8 W. CLARK *Van der Hoeven's Zool.* II. 526 Feathers of back and rump rigid, often spinescent. **1894** [see SPINESCENCE].

spinet[1] (ˈspɪnɪt, spɪˈnɛt). Forms: α. 7– spinette, 8 spinnette. β. 7–9 spinnet. γ. 8 spinett, 8– spinet. [ad. older F. *espinette* (1522; mod.F. *épinette*), = It. *spinetta*, *-etto*. Sp., Pg. *espineta*, mod.L. *spineta* (*a* 1558 Scaliger *Poet.* I. xlviii). Cf. ESPINETTE.

Acc. to Scaliger *spineta* was formed on L. *spīna*, with reference to the crow-quills which had been introduced into the mechanism. This, however, would be an unusual application of *spīna*, and greater probability attaches to the explanation given by A. Banchieri in 1608, that the name was derived from the inventor of the instrument, Giovanni Spinetti of Venice, whose name Banchieri had seen on a spinet dated 1503. See *Grove's Dict. Mus.* s.v.]

1. A keyed musical instrument, common in England in the 18th century, closely resembling the harpsichord, but smaller and having only one string to each note.

A full description of the various kinds of spinet is given in *Grove's Dict. Mus.* s.v.

α. **1664** PEPYS *Diary* 1 July, One Cheswicke, a master who plays very well upon the Spinette. **1686** tr. *Chardin's Trav. Persia* 229 When the Spinette came they set it upon the Table in the midst of the Room. **1761** *Ann. Reg., Chron.* 128 Father de la Borde, the inventor of the electrical spinette. **1763** JEFFERSON *Writ.* (1892) I. 352, I am vastly pleased with her playing on the spinnette and singing. **1874** T. ARCHER *Sword & Shuttle* i. in *Casquet Lit.* 2nd Ser. I. 250/1 A spinette in the corner of the room was open. **1886** MRS. MARSHALL *Tower of Cliff* iv. 52 It is not every woman can.. play on the spinette.

β. **1696** H. PURCELL (*title*), A choice Collection of Lessons for the Harpsichord or Spinnet. **1713** SWIFT *Cadenus &*

Vanessa Wks. 1751 III. II. 27 When miss delights in her spinnet, A fiddler may a fortune get. **1786** *Ann. Reg., Chron.* 207/2 The strings of a spinnet were heard to vibrate. **1821** GALT *Ann. Parish* xii. 118 An old woman, sitting whole hours jingling with that paralytic chattel a spinnet. **1881** BESANT & RICE *Chapl. of Fleet* I. viii. (1883) 61 [She] had once been a proficient on the spinnet, but there was no spinnet to be had.

γ. **1702** STEELE *Funeral* II, There's the Spinet Mr. Campley, I know you're Musical. **1773** J. ADAMS *Wks.* (1850) II. 323 The young ladies..entertained us upon the spinet, &c. **1810** A. BOSWELL *Edinburgh* Poet. Wks. (1871) 51 While 'Nancy Dawson', 'Sandie o'er the lee',..Ring on the jingling spinet or guitar. **1847** H. MILLER *First Impr. Eng.* v. 74 He had fitted up an old spinet, until it awoke into life, in these latter days of Collards and Broadwoods. **1889** BRINSMEAD *Hist. Pianoforte* 94 The English spinet was similar to the virginal except in its shape.

attrib. and *Comb.* **1703** STEELE *Tender Husb.* III. ii, Madam, your Spinet Master is come. **1883** *Grove's Dict. Mus.* III. 656/1 Stephen Keene was a well-known spinet-maker. *Ibid.*, His spinets..reached the highest perfection of spinet tone possible.

2. *U.S.* In full ***spinet piano***. A type of small piano.

1936 *Arts & Decoration* Jan. 30/1 The spinet pianos are inviting musical instruments. Their design, suitable to the modern apartment or small house, delights the decorator and the owner. **1937** *Étude* Dec. 803/3 In a few months manufacturers had worked out many refinements in the popular vertical pianos, which came to be known under the generic terms of 'consoles' or 'spinets'. **1970** W. APEL *Harvard Dict. Mus.* (ed. 2) 804/2 *Spinet*,..a piano with strings perpendicular to the keyboard (as in an upright piano) but with an indirect action. **1977** J. PHILIPS *Five Roads to Death* (1978) I. ii. 31 There was a little spinet piano in one corner.

'spinet². *Obs.* exc. *arch.* [ad. L. *spīnēt-um* (f. *spīna* thorn) or It. *spineto*.] A thicket; a spinney.

1603 B. JONSON *Entertainm. at Althorpe* I The invention was, to have a Satyre lodged in a little Spinet by which her Majestie and the Prince were to come. **1635** BRATHWAIT *Arcadian Princess* II. 179 Walking one day in a delightfull spinet, beautified with shady poplars. **1848** TYAS *Fav. Field Fl.* Ser. I. 17 We came near a spinet, consisting chiefly of lofty well-grown ash trees.

†**'spinet³**. *Obs.*⁻¹ [dim. of SPINE *sb.*¹] A small spine or thorn.

1671 GREW *Anat. Pl.* I. iv. (1682) 33 Of affinity with these are the Spinets or Thorny Prickles upon the Edges and Tops of divers Leaves.

spine-tail. [SPINE *sb.*¹]

1. *Ornith.* One or other of several birds of unrelated genera characterized by their stiff, spine-like or mucronate tail-feathers.

1839 AUDUBON *Syn. Birds N. Amer.* 33 *Chætura*, Spine-tail. *Ibid.*, *Chætura pelasgia*, American Spine-tail. *c* **1880** *Cassell's Nat. Hist.* IV. 111 The third family of the Mesomyodi, or Songless Birds, the Spine-tails (*Dendrocolaptidæ*). **1890** *Cent. Dict.*, *Orthonyx*, a remarkable Australian genus of passerine birds; the spinetails. **1891** *Ibid.*, *Spine-tail*, the ruddy duck, *Erismatura rubida*. **1893** W. H. HUDSON *La Plata* 371 Small Spine-tail [*Synallaxis phryganophila*] and Nest.

b. *attrib.* in ***spine-tail grouse***, ***swift***.

1884 COUES *N. Amer. Birds* 457 *Chæturinæ*, Spine-tail Swifts. *Ibid.* 580 *Centrocercus*,..Spine-tail Grouse.

2. *Ichth.* (See quots.)

1851 GOSSE *Nat. Hist., Fishes* 147 *Teuthididæ*. (Spine-tails.) *Ibid.* 148 In form and general appearance the Spine-tails resemble the Chætodons.

spine-tailed: see SPINE *sb.*¹ 10 b.

†**spiney, spiny.** *Obs. rare.* [Of obscure origin.] A shoot or sucker of a plant or tree.

1649 BLITHE *Eng. Improver* xxii. 130 Every Root may send forth twentie or fortie Spineyes, and yet all nourished from the Earth, and these Stooles they grow upon also. **1652** —— *Eng. Improv. Impr.* 232 Every set having some suckors or spinies of root going out from them.

†**'spingard.** *Obs.*⁻⁰ [ad. med.L. *spingarda* (It. *spingarda*, Sp., Pg. *espingarda*, OF. **espingarde*): cf. ESPRINGAL, SPRINGAL(D.] (See quot.)

1671 PHILLIPS, *Spingard*, a kind of Chamber-gun, but now out of use.

†**'spinger.** *Obs. rare.* [? ad. It. *spingere* to push, thrust.] (See quots.)

1659 C. SIMPSON *Division-Violist* I. 9 There is yet another plain or smooth Grace, called a Spinger, which concludeth the sound of a Note more acute, by clapping down another Finger just at the expiring of it. **1676** MACE *Musicks Mon.* 109 The Spinger, is a Grace, very Neat, and Curious, for some sort of Notes.

spin-house. Now *Hist.* Also 8 spinn-. [ad. Du. *spinhuis* (MDu. *spinhuys*), G. *spinnhaus*. Cf. SPINNING-HOUSE.] A house or building in which persons are employed in spinning. **a.** In reference to Continental usage: A house of correction or penitentiary for women. **b.** A workhouse.

a. *a* **1700** EVELYN *Diary* 19 Aug. 1641, [At Amsterdam] we stepp'd in to see the *Spin-house*, a kind of Bridewell, where incorrigible and lewd women are kept in discipline and labour. **1703** tr. *Nieuhoff's Voy. to E. Indies* 306 For the Encouraging of Virtue and Suppressing of Debauchery in lewd Women, a Spin-House has been erected here. **1777** J. HOWARD *State of Prisons* 121 The States do not transport criminals: but men are put to labour in the Rasp-houses, and women do proper work in the Spin-Houses.

b. **1702** in Brand *Newcastle* (1789) I. 327 *note*, Work-house, alias spinn-house.

spini- ('spaɪnɪ), combining form of L. *spīna* spine, thorn (cf. SPINO-), used in various scientific terms, as ***spini-acute***, ***-dentate***, ***-tuberculate*** adjs.

Mayne *Expos. Lex.* (1859) employs ***spinicerebral***, ***-folious***, ***-pede*** to translate corresponding Latin formations; recent Dicts. give a number of other combs., as ***spinicerebrate***, ***-deltoid***, ***-spirular***, ***-spirulate***, esp. anatomical terms relating to the spinal cord and some other part or organ, as ***spinibulbar***, ***-cerebellar***, ***-muscular***, ***-peripheral***, etc.

1852 DANA *Crust.* I. 323 Hand..spini-dentate on the lower margin. *Ibid.* 463 The carpus spini-tuberculate above and pilose. *Ibid.* 479 Anterior angles spini-acute.

spiniferite (spaɪ'nɪfəraɪt). *Palæont.* [f. L. *spīnifer* (see next) + -ITE.] (See quot.)

1872 H. A. NICHOLSON *Palæont.* 69 In some sections of flint are found minute 'spherical bodies, covered with radiating and multicuspid spines', which have been termed *Spiniferites* or *Xanthidia*, and are probably the 'gemmules' of sponges.

spiniferous (spaɪ'nɪfərəs), *a.* [f. L. *spīnifer*, f. *spīna* SPINE *sb.*¹ Cf. F. *spinifère*.] Bearing, covered with, or having spines; spinose. Chiefly *Zool.* or *Bot.*

1656 BLOUNT *Glossogr.*, *Spiniferous*, that beareth prickles or thorns, thorney. **1851** G. F. RICHARDSON *Geol.* viii. 276 The Rajacidæ..have the body depressed in the form of a disc, and covered with spiniferous plates. **1867** J. HOGG *Microsc.* II. ii. 391 Small spicula, slightly curved, thickly spiniferous.

‖**spinifex** ('spaɪnɪfɛks). *Bot.* [mod.L. (Linnæus *Mantissa Plantarum* (1771) II. 163), f. *spīna* SPINE *sb.*¹ + *-fex* maker, f. *facere* to make.]

1. One or other of a number of coarse grasses (now classed in the genus *Triodia* or *Plectrachne*) which grow in dense masses on the sand-hills of the Australian deserts, and are characterized by their sharp-pointed, spiny leaves; esp. the porcupine-grass, *Triodia irritans*.

1846 J. L. STOKES *Discov. Australia* II. 209 In the valleys was a little sandy soil, nourishing the spinifex. **1847** CAPT. C. STURT *Narr. Exped. C. Australia* (1849) I. 405 The spinifex was close and matted, and the horses were obliged to lift their feet straight up to avoid its sharp points. **1890** LUMHOLTZ *Cannibals* 43 On the broad sandy heights in the vicinity the so-called spinifex is found in great abundance.

attrib. **1895** W. G. W. MARTIN *Pagan Irel.* 389 An interchange..of flint and basalt, or spinifex gum.

2. A genus of grasses common on Australasian sea-shores and characterized by the elastic spines of the seeds; a plant belonging to this genus, esp. *Spinifex hirsutus*.

1877 BAR. F. v. MÜLLER *Bot. Teach.* 126 The Desert Spinifex of our colonists is a Fescue, but a true Spinifex occupies our sand-shores.

spiniform ('spaɪnɪfɔːm), *a.* *Bot.* and *Zool.* [ad. mod.L. *spīniformis*: see SPINE *sb.*¹ and -FORM. So F. *spiniforme*.] Having the form of a spine or spinous process.

1833 HOOKER in *J. E. Smith's Eng. Flora* V. I. 108 Leaves smaller fewer with 3 sharp spiniform teeth at the extremity. **1852** DANA *Crust.* I. 470 Large hand with short and small but spiniform tubercles. **1868** tr. *Figuier's Ocean World* vii. 151 The axis..presents on its surface small spiniform projections.

spi'nigenous, *a.* *rare*⁻⁰. [f. L. type **spīnigena*.] 'Sprung up of a thorn' (Bailey, 1727).

spinigerous (spaɪ'nɪdʒərəs), *a.* [f. L. *spīniger* spine-bearing.]

1. *Ent.* (See quot.)

1826 KIRBY & SP. *Entomol.* IV. xlvi. 333 *Spinigerous*,.. when the Coleoptra have a spine common to them both.

2. *Bot.* and *Zool.* = SPINIFEROUS *a.*

1852 DANA *Crust.* I. 371 Front above obliquely subcristate, not spinigerous. **1888** ROLLESTON & JACKSON *Anim. Life* 311 Down the centre of each ray the spinigerous tubercles are in this species arranged with considerable regularity.

spinigrade ('spaɪnɪgreɪd), *a.* and *sb.* [f. mod.L. *spīnigrad-us*.] **a.** *adj.* Of or belonging to the *Spinigrada*, a class of echinoderms which move by means of spines or spinous processes. **b.** *sb.* An echinoderm of this class.

1841 E. FORBES *Brit. Starfishes* 19 *Ophiuridæ*, or Spinigrade Echinodermata. *Ibid.*, They are *Spinigrade* animals,..their progression being effected..by means of five long flexible-jointed processes..furnished with spines. **1864** *Intell. Observ.* IV. 251 The Star-fishes are divided according to their mode of locomotion into Spinigrades, moving by means of spines—Cirrhigrades, by suckers—and Pinigrades, by fins.

'spiniken. *Cant.* Also spinikin, spinniken. [f. SPIN *v.* + KEN *sb.*² Cf. SPIN-HOUSE b.] A workhouse.

1859 *Slang Dict.*, *Spinikin*, a workhouse. **1864** *Ibid.*, *Spiniken*, St. Giles's workhouse [etc.].

spininess ('spaɪnɪnɪs). [f. SPINY *a.* + -NESS.] The quality or state of being spiny.

c **1611** CHAPMAN *Iliad* III. Comment. 48 To make the old men resemble Grasshoppers for their cold, and bloodlesse spininesse. **1902** *Q. Rev.* July 125 A certain spininess which has developed even amongst genera that are elsewhere smooth. **1907** G. F. SCOTT-ELLIOT *Romance Plant Life* 181 The common Whin..is very nearly as perfect an example of thorniness and spininess.

‖**spinitis** (spaɪ'naɪtɪs). *Path.* [mod.L., f. *spīna* SPINE *sb.*¹ + -ITIS.] = MYELITIS.

1859 in Mayne *Expos. Lex.*, and in recent Dicts.

spink (spɪŋk), *sb.*¹ Now *dial.* Forms: 5–7 **spynke**, 6 **spynk**, 6–7 **spinke**, 6– **spink**. [prob. imitative of the note of the bird: cf. PINK *sb.*⁶]

1. One or other of the finches; esp. the chaffinch.

Also, in Lancs., Westm., Cumbld., the yellow-hammer.

c **1425** *Voc.* in Wr.-Wülcker 640 *Hic rostellus*, spynke. **1483** *Cath. Angl.* 355/2 A Spynke.., *spinx*. *a* **1529** SKELTON *P. Sparowe* 407 The larke with his longe to; The spynke, and the martynet also. **1591** SYLVESTER *Du Bartas* I. v, The Spink, the Linot, and the Gold Finch fill All the fresh Aire with their sweet warbles shrill. **1600** SURFLET *Countrie Farme* VII. lv. 886 The spinke is a very beautifull and melodious birde, but all spinkes haue not one and the same tunes. **1653** URQUHART *Rabelais* II. xiv, The little bird called a spink or chaffinch. **1767** W. HARTE *Amaranth*, *Eulogius* Poems (1810) 385 The spink chants sweetest in a hedge of thorns. **1787** LATHAM *Gen. Syn. Birds* Suppl. I. 165 The Chaffinch..called by some..Spink, from its cry. **1811–** in various dial. glossaries, chiefly northern, midland, and E. Anglian. **1875** BROWNING *Aristoph. Apol.* 341 Collops of hare, with roast spinks rare.

†**b.** *Sc.* Used as an abusive epithet. *Obs.*⁻¹

1508 KENNEDIE *Flyting w. Dunbar* 552 Spynk, sink with stynk ad Tertara Termagorum.

2. With distinguishing prefix, as ***herring spink***, the golden-crested wren; †***mountain spink***, the mountain finch or brambling. Also GOLDSPINK.

1611 COTGR., *Passe de bois*, the little brambling, or mountaine Spinke. **1906** *Westm. Gaz.* 21 July 13/1 By the fisher-men of the North Sea these little birds are known as 'herring spinks'.

3. Used to imitate or represent the characteristic note or cry of certain birds. (Usually with repetition.)

1898 R. KEARTON *Wild Life at Home* 82 Some tantalising accident scared her off with an angry 'spink, spink, spink'. **1899** CROCKETT *Kit Kennedy* 195 Here..the stone-chats cried 'Spink! spink! spink!'

Hence **spink** *v. intr.*, to utter the note 'spink'.

1892 *Blackw. Mag.* July 103 He spinks, and chatters, and vibrates his little quill. **1898** R. KEARTON *Wild Life at Home* 54 [The young blackbirds] 'spink, spink, spinked' as loudly and angrily as if a cat had intruded itself upon them.

spink, *sb.*² *north. dial.* [Related to LG. *spinke*, *spinkel* freckle, *spinkel* a speckled cow, *spinkelt* speckled, *spinkeln* to glitter.]

†**1.** A spot or marking of a different colour on cattle. *Obs.*⁻¹

1550–1 *York Wills* (Surtees) VI. 306 Too blake whies, one with a whyte spynke of the backe.

2. (See quot. 1829.)

1829 BROCKETT *N.C. Gloss.* (ed. 2), *Spink*, a spark of fire or light. **1870** GIBSON *Up-Weardale Gloss.* (E.D.D.), Not a spink of light.

spink, *sb.*³ *Sc.* and *north.* [Of obscure origin.] The cuckoo-flower or lady-smock, *Cardamine pratensis*.

Freq. erroneously defined as 'a pink' (Jamieson, 1808), or confused with other plants, as the primrose or polyanthus.

1773 FERGUSSON *Poems* (1785) 139 Or can our flow'rs, at ten hours bell The Gowan or the Spink excell? **1806** A. DOUGLAS *Poems* 99 Countless spinks an' daisies springin, Gaily deckt ilk vale an' hill. **1819** W. TENNANT *Papistry Storm'd* (1827) 9 Dear daffodillies, Kingcups and spinks, and livelie lillies.

†**spink**, *a.* *Obs.* [Cf. SPINK *sb.*²] = next.

1558 in *Archæol. Jrnl.* V. 316, I gyve to Isabell Carter one spynke oxe. **1618–9** *Knaresb. Wills* (Surtees) II. 54 A brandid spink cow.

spinked, *a.* *north. dial.* [See SPINK *sb.*²] Flecked, speckled, spotted. Usually of cattle.

1588 *Knaresb. Wills* (Surtees) I. 163 A tagged cowe spinked. **1591** *Ibid.* 176 A whye stirke spinked. **1828** CARR *Craven Gloss.*, *Spinked*, spotted.

spinkie ('spɪŋkɪ). *dial.* [f. SPINK *sb.*¹ + -IE.] = SPINK *sb.*¹ 1.

1911 D. H. LAWRENCE *White Peacock* II. vii. 316 There are two or three robins' nests, and a spinkie's.

spinks (spɪŋks). *Austral.* [f. SPINK *sb.*¹ + -S².] = *Jacky Winter* s.v. JACKY 3.

1945 BAKER *Austral. Lang.* xii. 211 The Brown Flycatcher is called..spinks. **1969** [see *Jacky Winter* s.v. JACKY 3].

spinless ('spɪnlɪs), *a.* [f. SPIN *sb.*¹ + -LESS.] Having no spin, or no tendency to spin.

1936 *Aeroplane* 22 Jan. 116/2 The plane must be totally different from anything on the market to-day. It must..be spinless and viceless. **1951** *Physical Rev.* LXXXI. 282/2 (*heading*) On the Lamb shift for spinless electrons. **1966** *Nucl. Sci. Abstr.* XX. 1931/1 (*heading*) A fortran code for computing angular distributions, polarizations and transport cross sections of neutrons scattered by spinless targets. **1981** M. GELL-MANN in J. H. Mulvey *Nature of*

Matter viii. 184 That theory should include..the spinless particles we believe we need for spontaneous symmetry breaking.

spinnable ('spɪnəb(ə)l), *a.* [f. SPIN *v.* + -ABLE.] Capable of spinning or of being spun.

1882 RUSKIN *Bible of Amiens* iii. 92 The British pride of wealth..may assuredly..possess itself of penny universes, conveniently spinnable on their axes. **1926** *Chambers's Jrnl.* 16 Oct. 726/1 The cotton fibres of spinnable length are removed..by machines called 'gins'. **1927** M. H. AVRAM *Rayon Industry* 186 Not every solution which possesses sufficient viscosity and is capable of being drawn into filaments is spinnable. **1967** A. ZIABICKI in H. F. Mark et al. *Man-Made Fibers* 16 There are known many spinnable liquids, such as honey and high-mineral oils, which nobody would consider fiber-forming.

Hence **spinna'bility**, the capacity for being spun; applied esp. to a solution from which a synthetic fibre may be drawn.

1939 *Chem. Abstr.* XXXIII. 4493 (*heading*) The relation between elasticity, streaming anomalies and spinability of solutions with particular reference to fibrinogen. **1953** R. J. W. REYNOLDS in R. Hill *Fibres from Synthetic Polymers* v. 91 Spinnability occurs at only a moderately high molecular weight. **1979** TADMOR & GOGOS *Princ. Polymer Processing* xv. 637 The problems of draw resonance and spinnability are not fully understood.

spinnaker ('spɪnəkə(r)). Also spinniker. [Said to have been a fanciful formation on *spinx*, mispronunciation of *Sphinx*, the name of the first yacht which commonly carried the sail.] A large three-cornered sail carried by racing-yachts, boomed out at right angles to the vessel's side, opposite to the mainsail, and used in running before the wind. Also carried on other sailing vessels. Also *attrib.*

1866 *Yachting Cal. & Rev.* Aug. 84 The Sphinx [set] a 'spinniker', a kind of large balloon jib extending from the topmast head to the deck, and before the wind a most powerful drawing sail. **1869** *Hunt's Yachting Mag.* June 266 Eva sent up her spinnaker boom in lieu of a topmast. *Ibid.* Oct. 450 Rosebud's crew especially deserve great credit for their smartness in handling their troublesome customer, i.e. the spinnaker. **1886** R. C. LESLIE *Sea Painter's Log* 89 The rig of the sailing-boats looks like a conglomeration of spinnakers. **1912** E. K. CHATTERTON *Fore & Aft* vii. 233 She [*sc.* a Thames barge] has all her canvas tanned with the exception of her jib staysail, which her skipper calls a 'spinnaker'. **1925** H. W. SMYTH *Sea-Wake* 179 The spinnaker hand, young and unspoiled in eye or thought, kept looking round him. *Ibid.* 191 'Hooroo,' began the spinnaker man, and no one interrupted him now; he had done the best day's spinnaker work of his life. **1927** G. BRADFORD *Gloss. Sea Terms* 168/1 Large jibs on English coast craft are sometimes called spinnakers. **1949** *Sun* (Baltimore) 9 Aug. 8/5 The big China-built cutter..carried a huge sky-blue Nylon spinnaker across the finish line. **1959** *Yachting World Annual* 9/2 *Columbia's* combination of a small, flat spinnaker and small short-luffed spinnaker staysail seemed to be pulling more effectively. **1963** G. MILLAR *Oyster River* 60 We put the nine-foot dinghy in the river (easily done with a short boom fitted into a spinnaker cup set low on the aft side of the mainmast). **1967** J. HOWARD-WILLIAMS *Sails* xii. 164 The spinnaker-staysail..sets under the spinnaker on a reach, in order to fill a slight gap forward. **1972** *Sail* May 100 A typical low aspect ratio spinnaker staysail.

fig. **1957** R. CAMPBELL *Coll. Poems* II. 253 The spring with rosy spinnaker outfanned Comes curling silver fleeces through the land.

spinnall, spinnel, obs. ff. SPINAL *sb.*

‖**spinnbar** ('ʃpɪnbɑː(r)), *a.* [Ger.] Of a viscous liquid: capable of being drawn into strands; spinnable.

1944 G. W. S. BLAIR *Survey Gen. & Appl. Rheol.* v. 68 Many spinnbar materials show flow-elasticity. **1945** *Proc. R. Soc. Med.* XXXIX. 8 Curves cannot be directly obtained for spinnbar materials because the ratio of pressure (stress) to rate of flow not only falls with rising stress but increases with increasing deformation (work-hardening).

‖**spinnbarkeit** ('ʃpɪnbɑːkaɪt). Also Spinnbarkeit. [a. G. *spinnbarkeit* (H. Erbring 1936, in *Kolloid-Beihefte* XLIV. 173), f. *spinnbar* (see prec.).] The capacity of a viscous liquid, esp. the cervical mucus, for being drawn into strands; spinnability.

[**1938** G. W. S. BLAIR *Introd. Industr. Rheol.* x. 108 Erbring, studying this property in detail, calls it 'Spinnbarkeit', which perhaps is best translated as 'fibrosity'.] **1944** —— *Survey Gen. & Appl. Rheol.* v. 69 Both tack and 'Spinnbarkeit' are often associated with adhesive properties. **1954** G. I. M. SWYER *Reproduction & Sex* iv. 47 During the two or three days immediately prior to ovulation, the healthy cervix pours forth a copious flow of clear, almost watery mucus which flows out over the vaginal surface of the cervix... At this time it possesses in marked degree the rheological property variously called 'spinnbarkeit', 'fibrosity' or, perhaps better, 'ductility', that is, the ability to be drawn out into a fine thread (or to be blown up into a sizeable bubble). **1975** *Acta Endocrinologia Suppl.* CXCIX. 242 The amount, spinnbarkeit and ferning of the cervical mucus correlated well with the estradiol concentration.

spinnel, north. f. SPINDLE *sb.*

spinnell, obs. f. SPINEL.

spinner ('spɪnə(r)). Forms: 3-4 spinnere, 4-6 spynner, 5 -ere, spynnare, 6 -ar, 5- spinner. [f. SPIN *v.* + -ER[1]. Cf. MDu. *spinnere* (Du. *spinner*), MHG. *spinre* (G. *spinner*).]

I. 1. a. A spider, esp. one which spins a web. Freq. *c* 1530-1615; now *dial.* or *rhet.*

c **1220** *Bestiary* 462 *Natura aranee*... Ðe spinnere on hire swid ȝe [? *read* spindle] weveð. *c* **1440** *Promp. Parv.* 469 Spynnare, or erany, *aranea*. **1495** *Trevisa's Barth. De P.R.* XVIII. ix. (W. de W.) 763 A serpent..sucketh gladly the moysture therof as the spynner suckyth flies. **1527** ANDREW *Brunswyke's Distyll. Waters* B j b, Whan a persone is stynged of a spynner. **1574** HYLL *Bees* 10 The spinner through her web hanging downe before the hiue..doth much molest and trouble them. **1601** HOLLAND *Pliny* II. 360 These be our common spiders or spinners which against wals vse to stretch out their large webs. **1682** H. MORE *Annot. Glanvill's Lux O.* 220 A Spinner hanging by its weak thread from the brim of ones Hat. **1706** PHILLIPS (ed. Kersey), *Spinner*,..a small sort of harmless Spider. **1768-74** TUCKER *Lt. Nat.* (1834) II. 654 The spinner's web hangs in the yielding air incapable of molesting it. **1838** *Murray's Handbk. N. Germ.* 19 The forlorn attempt of a solitary spinner to establish himself in the corner of a window. **1842** *Dumfries Herald* Oct., Earwigs, beetles, and long-legged spinners, the living ..residuum of the last cart-load of peas. **1876** ROBINSON *Whitby Gloss.*, *Spinner*, a spider.

attrib. *c* **1475** *Promp. Parv.* 469 (K.), Spinnar webbe, *tela aranee*. **1855** [ROBINSON] *Whitby Gloss.*, *Spinner-web* or *Spinner-mesh*, the spider's web.

b. A caterpillar which spins a web or cocoon; a silkworm. *rare.*

1598 FLORIO, *Cauagliere*,..a silke worme or spinner. **1841** HARRIS *Insects Massachusetts* 239 Their caterpillars..are generally spinners, and, with few exceptions, make cocoons in which they are transformed.

c. *dial.* A daddy-longlegs, = JENNY-SPINNER 1. Also *spinner-fly*.

1848 *Proc. Berw. Nat. Club* II. 330 The larva of the long-legged spinner fly (*Tipula oleracea*, &c.).

2. a. One who spins cotton, wool, yarn, etc.; *esp.* one whose occupation it is to do this; a workman or workwoman engaged in spinning; one who attends to or works a spinning-machine.

1393 LANGL. *P. Pl.* C. VII. 222 Hue spak to þe spynnesters [*v.r.* spinnere] to spynnen hit oute. *c* **1400** *Destr. Troy* 1595 Sporiors, Spicers, Spynners of clothe. **1450** *Rolls of Parlt.* V. 201/2 Many Cloth makers, that is to wite, men, Wevers, Fullers, Diers; and women, Kempers, Carders and Spynners. **1536** *Act 28 Hen. VIII*, c. 4 ¶ 1 Weauers, tuckers, spinners, diers, and wulpikers. **1573-80** TUSSER *Husb.* (1878) 122 Drie flax get in, for spinners to spin. **1610-11** *Shuttleworths' Acc.* (Chetham Soc.) 193 To a spinner, for spinning xvj days flaxe,..xvj[d]. **1679** T. JORDAN *Lond. in Luster* 17 Carders, Spinners, Dyers, Wool-combers, Sheerers, Dressers, Fullers. **1744** H. BROOKE *Love & Vanity* 211 Trust me from titled dames to spinners, 'Tis I make saints, whoe'er makes sinners. **1776** ADAM SMITH *W.N.* I. i. (1904) I. 8 The spinner is almost always a distinct person from the weaver. **1833** HT. MARTINEAU *Manch. Strike* 9 All present were spinners and power-loom weavers. **1875** KNIGHT *Dict. Mech.* 1494/2 Previous to the invention of the mule few spinners could make yarn of 200 hanks to the pound.

fig. **1881** MISS BRADDON *Asphodel* III. 175 My mother..was one of the lilies of the field,..my father..belonged to the toilers and spinners.

b. A manufacturer or merchant engaged in spinning, esp. cotton-spinning; a master-spinner.

1834 *Penny Cycl.* II. 346/1 For several years, the market prices of cotton twist were fixed by Arkwright, all other spinners conforming to his scale. **1863** BRIGHT *Sp., Amer.* 16 June (1876) 131 The wants of the spinners and the manufacturers of the world. **1881** H. SMART *Race for Wife* ii, The old county families are swept away by these spinners, brewers, solicitors, and such-like.

c. *transf.* The nightjar, *Caprimulgus europæus*.

1885 SWAINSON *Bird Names* 97.

3. *fig.* One who spins, tells, or relates (a story, yarn, etc.).

[**1621** BP. MOUNTAGU *Diatribæ* 134 You were ἀμάχιτος, not to be dealt withall by any Postillating Breuiarist, or Polyanthean spinner up of Sermon webs.]

1770 *Monthly Rev.* 72 Those mushroom romances, which our expert Novel spinners will manufacture in a Week. **1851** HAWTHORNE *Twice-told T.* II. vi. 97, I am a spinner of long yarns. **1874** GEO. ELIOT *Coll. Breakf.-P.* 31 Osric, spinner of fine sentences. **1898** L. STEPHEN *Stud. Biogr.* II. i. 5 Already an accomplished spinner of boyish stories.

4. a. = SPINNERET.

1815 KIRBY & SP. *Entomol.* (1818) I. 406 If you examine a spider, you will perceive in this part [of the abdomen] four little teat-like protuberances or spinners. **1839** DARWIN *Voy. Nat.* ix. 188 A spider..darted forth four or five threads from its spinners. **1875** *Encycl. Brit.* II. 292/1 The spinners consist of from one to three joints..; in *Tetrablemma* (Cambr.) they are enclosed in a kind of corneous sheath.

b. *techn.* A spinning-machine.

1875 KNIGHT *Dict. Mech.* 2269/2 *Spinner*, a general term for a spinning-machine... Specifically applied to a form of drawing and twisting device. **1879** *Cassell's Techn. Educ.* II. 107/1 This gigantic spinner and weaver needs very little assistance from man.

5. One of the principal supporting threads of the spider's web.

1861 *Sat. Rev.* 25 May 525 Long dark cables..looking like the first radial 'spinners' constructed by the spider to carry the finer and continuous tissue of his web.

II. 6. *Angling.* **a.** One or other of several flies, or artificial imitations of these, used esp. in trout-fishing.

1787 BEST *Angling* (ed. 2) 104 June. The Palmers 5. The Great Red Spinner 5. **1799-** [see *red spinner* RED *a.* 19]. **1867** F. FRANCIS *Angling* vi. 172 The spinners are only second in the estimation of the trout to the duns. *Ibid.* 181 The Brown Spinner..is another capital fly. **1898** *Westm. Gaz.* 5 May 4/2 He was using a small gilt spinner on fine tackle.

b. An angler who uses spinning-tackle.

1836 F. SYKES *Scraps fr. Jrnl.* 70 A great advantage for the spinner, as a quantity of baits are always to be had. **1867** F. FRANCIS *Angling* viii. 246 The very best spinners for large trout in the world are Thames fishermen.

c. (See quots.) Also *attrib.*

1884 KNIGHT *Dict. Mech.* Suppl. 840 *Spinner*, a trawling spoon-bait which revolves as it tows abaft the boat. *Ibid.*, *Spinner*, a flanged attachment in connection with a fish-hook to cause a lively motion of the hook and bait. **1895** *Outing* XXVI. 358 A 6-0 hook with a lively smelt wired to it spinner fashion.

7. a. A device which spins round or revolves; a teetotum, a top.

1794 G. ADAMS *Nat. & Exp. Philos.* IV. l. 383 Here is a small spinner with an iron axis: I spin the spinner, and then take it up by a magnet. **1895** *Westm. Gaz.* 25 July 3/3 His favourite game was the *Erratic Spinner*... These [i.e. ninepins] had to be knocked over with a top or spinner of polished steel.

b. A cricket-ball bowled with a spin.

1895 *Westm. Gaz.* 2 Mar. 5/2 [He] got an undeniable spinner past the stubborn bat of the Lancashire man.

c. The person who tosses the coins in the game of two-up; *come in spinner*: the cry commonly used to start the game. Chiefly *Austral.*

1911 L. STONE *Jonah* II. vi. 215 The spinner placed the two pennies face down on the kip, and then, with a turn of the wrist, the coins flew twenty feet into the air. **1945** T. RONAN *Strangers on Ophir* 119 Cries of 'Another quid to see him go. Get set on the side. All set, come in Spinner.' **1948** V. PALMER *Golconda* iv. 25 Step in, spinner... I'm backing heads... They're up. Fair go. **1958** 'N. CULOTTA' *They're a Weird Mob* viii. 117 He began to play... 'Come in, spinner' ..I sang softly. **1964** [see KIP *sb.*[6]]. **1975** L. RYAN *Shearers* 97 'All set?' Lofty asked. 'Set!' Sandy said. 'Come in, spinner!'

d. *Agric.* A rotating device for lifting potatoes out of the ground.

1923 J. R. BOND *Farm Implements & Machinery* xi. 164 The old high-speed spinner did considerable damage to the tubers. **1943** J. W. DAY *Farming Adventure* xvii. 197 Another machine with a great future is the potato digger or spinner. **1960** *Times* 5 July (Agric. Suppl.) p. viii/2 Spinners are still by far the most universal lifting appliances. **1973** M. PARTRIDGE *Farm Tools through Ages* v. 154/2 An iron share ..preceded the spinner as the machine was hauled forward, serving to break down the soil.

e. *Cricket.* A spin bowler.

1951 *People* 3 June 7/5 Jim Sims, Middlesex spinner, tells me that he's never felt fitter than he does this season. **1963** A. ROSS *Australia 63* 13 Since the departure of Laker and Wardle no class spinner of any kind had emerged. **1976** DEXTER & MAKINS *Testkill* 78 The spinner, Flinders,..hit Ackroyd for two staggering sixes into the Mound Stand.

f. *Surfing.* (See quot. 1970.)

1962 *Surfer* (1962-3) Dec.-Jan. 52/2 (Advt.), One beautiful turn can't make a good movie, but...1286 beautiful turns, nose rides, spinners..can. **1968** *Surfer Mag.* Jan. 73/2 He showed them skeg-first takeoffs, spinners. **1970** *Studies in English* (Univ. of Cape Town) I. 31 Another popular hot dogging stunt is the *spinner*, in which the surfer turns himself in a full circle on the board, preferably while he is on the nose.

8. Something which moves rapidly.

1881 *Daily Tel.* 5 July 2/1 These crank and nimble spinners [i.e. racing yachts] give you no chance of looking about.

9. A workman who 'spins' metal plate.

1884 [see SPIN *v.* 11 d].

10. *Aeronaut.* A metal fairing that is attached to and revolves with the propeller boss of an aircraft in order to streamline it.

1918 *Flight* 11 July 767/2 The airscrew..had its boss enclosed in the usual 'spinner'. **1944** *R.A.F. Jrnl.* Aug. 287 Peter looked at..the starboard engine cowling, and the spinner revolving at high speed, yet so perfectly made that it seemed to be a motionless dome. **1969** K. MUNSON *Pioneer Aircraft 1903-14* 159/1 The 2-blade propeller had a shallow, bowl-shaped spinner similar to that fitted to the Bristol M.1C.

11. Comb.: **spinner magnetometer**, a magnetometer used to measure the remanent magnetism of rocks, baked clay, etc., in which a sample is spun between coils and induces in them a current dependent on the strength and direction of the magnetic field; see also *spinning magnetometer* s.v. SPINNING *vbl. sb.* 8 d.

1955 *Jrnl. Geophysical Res.* LX. 332 Spinner magnetometer. This magnetometer is a further development of the type first pioneered by Johnson. **1963** *Jrnl. Sci. Instruments* XL. 162/1 The sensitivity of the spinner magnetometer is proportional to the speed at which the specimen is rotated. **1973** *Nature* 4 May 28/2 The remanent magnetizations were measured with a spinner magnetometer.

‖**spinner** (a ship): see SPINACE.

spinneret ('spɪnərɛt). Also spin(n)aret, spinnerette. [dim. of SPINNER: see -ET[1].]

1. An organ or process by which the silk, gossamer, or thread of certain insects, esp. silkworms and spiders, is produced; a spinning-organ; spec. (*a*) one of the pores or tubules on the lower lip of a silkworm or caterpillar; (*b*) one of the nipple-like mammillæ on the abdomen of a spider.

(*a*) **1826** KIRBY & SP. *Entomol.* III. xxx. 124 On each side of the apex of the under-lip is a minute feeler, and in the middle..is a filiform organ, which I shall call the *spinneret*

(*Fusulus*), through which the larva draws the silken thread employed in fabricating its cocoon. **1863** Spencer *Ess.* II. 336 It appears that the ultimate fibre of silk is coated, in issuing from the spinneret of the silk-worm, with a film of varnish. **1888** Rolleston & Jackson *Anim. Life* 148 The median lobe..carries.. a central tubular projection, the spinneret, upon which opens the common duct of the two silk glands.

(*b*) **1835–6** *Todd's Cycl. Anat.* I. 209/1 The surface of each of the spinnarets [of the spider] is pierced by an infinite number of minute holes. **1841** T. R. Jones *Anim. Kingd.* 317 The fluid silk,..when it is drawn through the microscopic apertures of the spinneret, affords the material whereof the web is constructed. **1849** *Proc. Berw. Nat. Club* II. 371 A minutely bituberculated wart, somewhat like the spinnerets of the spider. **1926** T. H. Savory *Brit. Spiders* 8 Now it raises its abdomen..and secretes a drop of silk from its spinnerettes.

fig. **1877** *Athenæum* 1 Dec. 701/2 The web is now before us, but the spinnerets used in the elaboration of most of it have been the scissors, and the gossamer, paste.

(*c*) **1835** Kirby *Hab. & Inst. Anim.* I. viii. 254 The spinnerets..of various shell fish [are] in their foot.

2. A cap or plate having a number of small holes through which a spinnable solution is forced in the production of man-made fibres; an individual hole or channel in such a plate.

1894 *Work* 7 July 391/2 The resultant..substance..is next forced..through minute holes in a glass spinneret. **1927** M. H. Avram *Rayon Indusry* viii. 197 Glass spinnerettes are now produced with 66 holes. **1957** D. C. Hague *Economics of Man-Made Fibres* iii. 93 Nylon is a truly synthetic fibre... In fact, it is a plastic which has been forced through a spinnerette to form a textile fibre. **1973** *Materials & Technology* VI. iv. 291 The number of holes in a spinneret will determine the number of filaments which will be present in the yarns; this usually varies between 15 and 100.

spinnerule (ˈspɪnər(j)uːl). *rare.* [f. as prec.: see -ule.] One of the minute tubules forming the spinneret of a spider.

1830 *Insect Archit.* (L.E.K.) 337 These are minute tubes which we may appropriately term *spinnerules*, as each.. emits a thread of inconceivable fineness. *Ibid.*, Spinnerets of a Spider magnified to show the Spinnerules.

spinnery (ˈspɪnərɪ). [f. spin *v.* + -ery 2. Cf. Du. *spinnerij*, G. *spinnerei*.] A spinning factory or establishment.

1837 *Blackw. Mag.* XLI. 854 In country districts, and about isolated spinneries. **1856** W. White *On Foot thro' Tyrol* ii. 40 The small stream..drives a spinnery on its way. **1893** *Month* July 329 The cotton spinnery at Pesth.

spinnet, obs. form of spinet[1].

spinney (ˈspɪnɪ). Forms: α. 4 **spenné**, 6 **spinnie**, 7 **spennie**, 8– **spinny**. β. 7 **spynney**, 7– **spinney**, 9 **spenney**. [ad. OF. *espinei*, *espinoi*, *-oy* masc., *espinoie*, *espinaye* (mod.F. *épinaie*) fem., a place full of thorns or brambles, f. *espine* spine *sb.*[1] Cf. spinet[2].]

†**1.** ? A thorn-hedge. *Obs. rare.*

13.. *Gaw. & Gr. Knt.* 1709 At þe last bi a littel dich he lepez ouer a spenné, Stelez out ful stilly bi a strothe rande. *Ibid.* 1896 As he sprent ouer a spenné, to spye þe schrewe.

2. A small wood or copse, esp. one planted or preserved for sheltering game-birds; a small clump or plantation of trees.

α. **1597** Gerarde *Herbal* ci. 353, I found this strange kinde of Gentian in a small groue of wood called the Spinnie. *c***1600** in J. H. Glover *Kingsthorpiana* (1883) 114 For Hantorne's Spennie, xii *d.* **1750** W. Ellis *Mod. Husb.* IV. iv. 18 When a Field is under such a fertile growth of this Grain, it appears somewhat like a Spinny, or Spring of Underwood. **1826** *Sporting Mag.* XVII. 331 The carriage not being able to get up to the spinny. **1857** Kingsley *Two Y. Ago* I. p. x, The downs..crowned with black fir spinnies, and dotted with dark box and juniper. **1876** *Fraser's Mag.* 470 Woods and spinnies of old trees are scattered about the rich corn-lands.

β. **1625** *Althorp MS.* in Simpkinson *Washingtons* (1860) p. lx, To Butlin 5 daies paling about the new spinney. *Ibid.*, One daie setting up stiles in the spynney. **1785** Cowper *Wks.* (1837) XV. 177, I told you..that the spinney has been cut down. **1814** *Ann. Reg., Chron.* 84/2 A small wood called Holyoak Spenney. **1840** Hood *Kilmansegg, Accident* iv, Had her horse but been fed upon English grass And sheltered in Yorkshire spinneys. **1883** Pennell-Elmhirst *Cream Leicestersh.* 43 The fox..had turned into the little spinneys bordering the hill.

attrib. **1821** Clare *Vill. Minstr.* II. 133 Ragged-robins by the spinney lake.

transf. **1905** Sir F. Treves *Other Side Lant.* i. i, A spinney of cranes and derricks.

spinning (ˈspɪnɪŋ), *vbl. sb.* [f. spin *v.* + -ing[1].]

I. 1. a. The action or operation of converting fibres into thread or yarn by hand-labour or by machinery.

Freq. also in combs., as *cotton-*, *flax-spinning*.

*c***1290** *S. Eng. Leg.* I. 261/18 With spinningue and with seuwingue. *c***1386** Chaucer *Wife's Prol.* 401 Deceite, weping, spinning god hath yive To wommen kindely. **1393** Langl. *P. Pl.* C. x. 74 That þei wiþ spynnynge may spare [they] spenen hit in hous-hyre. **1440** *York Mem. Bk.* (Surtees) I. 78 That noon..make no capez nother of meld woll nor meld garn, nother of thair awne spynnyng nor bought spon. **1523** Fitzherb. *Husb.* 49 b, A woman can nat get her lyuynge honestly wᵗ spynnynge on the dystaffe. **1573** Tusser *Husb.* (1878) 109 Sowe hemp and flacks, that spinning lacks. **1685** Baxter *Paraphr. N.T.* Matt. vi. 28 Christ here neither blameth Sowing, Spinning, or other meer labour. **1756** Dyer *Fleece* iii. 59 A diff'rent spinning every diff'rent web Asks from your glowing fingers. **1770** Langhorne *Plutarch* (1851) 29/1 She was not to be employed in any other labour but that of spinning. **1825** J. Nicholson *Operat. Mechanic* 404 The various modes of preparing flax for the operation of spinning. **1875** Knight *Dict. Mech.* 2272/2 The spinning of flax resembles the throstle-spinning of cotton.

fig. **1818** Byron *Juan* i. vii, I shall open with a line (Although it cost me half an hour in spinning).

b. The operation of producing a thread of some viscid material.

1753 *Chambers' Cycl.* Suppl. s.v., By making the viscous liquor..pass through a fine perforation in the organ appointed for this spinning. **1815** Kirby & Sp. *Entomol.* (1818) I. 408 The same preliminary step which the spider adopts in spinning.

c. The process or action of drawing into a thread; *spec.* the process of forming a man-made fibre by drawing or extruding a melt or viscous solution of a polymer through a spinneret; ***dry*, *melt*, *wet spinning***: (see quots. 1974).

1883 Haldane *Workshop Rec.* Ser. ii. 165/2 *Spinning.*—Proficiency in this requires much practice... Dip a tablespoon in the sugar [etc.]. **1896** *Jrnl. Soc. Chem. Industry* 30 May 317/2 The production of a lustrous thread of cellulose in continuous length, by the process of drawing or 'spinning' is..an accomplished fact. **1910** A. F. Barker *Textiles* iii. 59 Vanduara silk is obtained by using gelatine as a basis, the threads, after spinning, being treated with formaldehyde to render them insoluble in water. **1927** T. Woodhouse *Artificial Silk* v. 37 Coagulation may be effected in warm air by so called 'dry-spinning', when the solvents can be vaporized by such air. **1963** A. J. Hall *Textile Sci.* ii. 75 With the introduction of nylon an entirely new method of fibre spinning was established—so-called melt-spinning in which the polymer..is melted in a novel device above the spinneret so that it can..be extruded through the multi-holed spinneret into cold air. **1974** *Encycl. Brit. Macropædia* VII. 258/2 In wet spinning, the solution of fibre-forming material is extruded into a coagulating bath that causes the jets to harden. *Ibid.*, In dry spinning the fibre-forming substance is dissolved in a solvent before the solution is extruded. As the jets of solution emerge from the spinneret, a stream of hot air causes the solvent to evaporate from the spinning solution, leaving solid filaments. *Ibid.*, In melt spinning the fibre-forming material is melted and extruded through spinnerets, and the jets harden into solid filaments as they cool on emerging from the spinneret.

2. The product of this operation; the thread or yarn spun.

*c***1511** *1st Eng. Bk. Amer.* (Arb.) Introd. p. xxxv/1 Of that same spynnyng we make our clothynge. **1711** *Lond. Gaz.* No. 4850/3, 30 Pound weight of Legois Spinnings. **1887** *Daily News* 5 Nov. 2/5 In higher numbers and best spinnings there is a moderate amount of business. **1892** *Ibid.* 3 Aug. 2/6 Most spinnings were quoted at a slight advance.

3. The action of protracting or drawing *out* to undue length; an instance of this.

1644 D. P. P. (*title*), The Six Secondary Causes of the Spinning out of this Unnaturall Warre. **1736** Fielding *Pasquin* iv. i, The practical rules of writing,..the first and greatest of which is protraction, or the art of spinning. **1780** Wesley *Wks.* (1872) XIV. 295, I was indeed a little disgusted with the spinning out of the story. **1830** H. N. Coleridge *Grk. Poets* (1834) 268 The injudicious spinnings out of a shorter primitive text.

4. a. The action of turning or whirling round; rapid revolution.

1814–24 Col. Hawker *Instr. Yng. Sportsm.* 175 To prevent a counteraction to the spinning of the minnow. **1858** Greener *Gunnery* 278 Unscientifically formed projectiles.. have to receive a counteracting agency in the shape of additional spinning. **1866** Airy *Pop. Astron.* v. (1868) 184 In consequence of its spinning, the inclination of CP to CQ does not sensibly alter.

b. Of a motor clutch: the fault of continuing to revolve after being disengaged.

1913 W. E. Dommett *Motor Car Mech.* 125 The clutch shaft has a coned brake which prevents 'spinning' when gear changing. **1948** A. W. Judge *Mod. Motor Engineer* (ed. 4) II. 305 In some cases the use of a thicker lubricant in the gear-box will prevent clutch spinning.

c. *Aeronaut.* The action of an aircraft when in a spin (spin *sb.*[1] 2 d).

1915 *Aeroplane* 10 Nov. 578/2 It is always possible to avoid spinning or side-slipping in fog or cloud. **1930** Nayler & Ower *Aviation To-day* 324 Spinning..was first started in the War as a means to bewilder, or escape from, the enemy. **1977** *R.A.F. News* 27 Apr.–10 May 11/4 The Phantom pilots go up with an instructor for a twice-yearly check-out in the trials and tribulations of spinning.

5. The action of angling with a spinning bait.

1855 Kingsley *Glaucus* (1878) 22 There is good spinning with a brass minnow round the angles of the rocks. **1856** 'Stonehenge' *Brit. Rural Sports* 254/1 Spinning for perch is practised as follows. **1870** Pennell *Mod. Pract. Angler* 123 In all sorts of spinning..a good breeze is usually an advantage.

6. The operation of shaping metallic substances by means of a turning-lathe. Also *concr.*

1857 R. Hunt *Guide Mus. Pract. Geol.* (1859) 188 Sheet metal prepared for the process of 'spinning'. **1884** Knight *Dict. Mech.* Suppl. 840/1 *Spinning*, a mode of forming silver and other ductile metal into shapes. **1927** *Daily Tel.* 11 May 18/6 To place orders for general metal spinnings. **1964** H. Hodges *Artifacts* iv. 74 The method of shaping bronze vessels known as spinning is virtually a mechanical form of raising. **1973** J. G. Tweeddale *Materials Technol.* II. iv. 86 Spinning has certain similarities to panel-beating.

II. *attrib.* 7. (In sense 1.) **a.** Misc., as ***spinning-mistress*, *-process*, *-time*, *-work***.

1608 Willet *Hexapla Exod.* Ded. 2, The women..vse euery yeere to shew publikely their spinning work. **1677** Yarranton *Eng. Improv.* 159 Send for a Spinning Mistriss out of Germany, to..govern the little Maids, and instruct them in the Art of Spinning. **1707** Mortimer *Husb.* (1721) II. 37 The top Leaves..being most proper to feed the Worms towards their Spinning time. **1835** Ure *Philos. Manuf.* 14 The carding, drawing, roving, and spinning processes of a cotton-mill. **1899** *Daily News* 16 Jan. 9/4 The spinning end of the trade has been characterised by a fair amount of briskness.

b. In terms denoting appliances or machinery, or parts of these, employed in spinning, as ***spinning-engine*, *-frame*, *-hook*, *-machine*, *nozzle***, etc.; also in terms denoting substances that are spun to form man-made fibres, as ***spinning dope*, *solution*, *syrup***.

1959 *Times Rev. Industry* Sept. 5/3 There has been an expansion in the production of man-made fibres, already coloured during their spinning by the addition of pigments to the *spinning dope. **1678** *Patent Office* No. 202. 1 A new *Spining Engin whereby Six to an hundred Spinners and vpwards may be imployed by the Strength of one or two Persons. **1825** J. Nicholson *Operat. Mechanic* 387 The cotton..is carried to the *spinning-frame. **1879** *Cassell's Techn. Educ.* II. 337/2 The transition from Arkwright's spinning-frame..to the throstle-frame was easy enough. **1788** ? Burns *D. Davison* 15 Then Meg took up her *spinnin'-graith, And flang them a' out o'er the burn. **1750** Blanckley *Nav. Expos.* 80 *Spinning hooks are drove into the Rails for the Ropemakers to hang their threads on, as they spin them. *c***1790** *Encycl. Brit.* (ed. 3) V. 488 The rapid operations of the new *spinning machines. **1879** *Cassell's Techn. Educ.* II. 43/1 Paul's spinning-machine patent..is dated 1738. **1899** *Jrnl. Soc. Arts* 8 Dec. 63/2 The filtering is to eliminate every particle of suspended matter which may exist in the collodion before it arrives at the spinning machines. **1975** J. Kasparek in E. Dyson *Rotor Spinning* x. 161 (*heading*) Processing of man-made staple fibres on the.. rotor spinning machine. **1807** Vancouver *Agric. Devon* (1813) 446 It is not meant..to condemn the introduction of *spinning-machinery. **1835** Ure *Philos. Manuf.* 273 The machine for twisting the single threads of silk..is called the *spinning-mill. **1844** G. Dodd *Textile Manuf.* i. 18 Crompton, of Bolton, who invented the '*spinning-mule'. **1914** *Chem. Abstr.* VIII. 258 A process and device for perforating and cleaning the capillary tube of *spinning nozzles for artificial silk manufacture. **1921** T. Woodhouse tr. *J. Foltzer's Artificial Silk* xix. 192 The spinning nozzles or spinnerets, from which separate threads..issue. **1931** S. E. & E. R. Trotman *Artificial Silks* 49 The spinning nozzle consists of a head or rose containing a number of capillary apertures through which the spinning solution enters the coagulating bath or evaporating chamber. *a***1693** *Urquhart's Rabelais* iii. xxviii. (1737) III. 395 Wouldst thou..slander the *spinning-quills..of the weird sisters, Parcæ. **1921** T. Woodhouse tr. *J. Foltzer's Artificial Silk* vi. 40 When the solution of the cotton is complete, the *spinning solution begins to decompose, unless it is kept at a low temperature. **1973** O. Steinerová tr. *B. Piller's Bulked Yarns* xi. 434 The latter [*sc.* viscose staple fibres] were made dyeable by acid wool dyes due to addition of protein particles to the spinning solution. **1973** *Materials & Technology* VI. iv. 290 The *spinning syrup has to be extruded through very tiny holes in the spinneret. **1730** *Phil. Trans.* XXXVI. 337 As the Spill of a *Spinning-Turn is moved. **1865** Lubbock *Preh. Times* 163 Earthenware *spinning-weights. **1895** A. C. Haddon *Evol. Art* 177 These patterns are delineated on masks, posts, *spinning-whorls, and other objects.

c. In terms denoting places where spinning is carried on, as ***spinning-factory*, *-floor*, *gallery*, *-ground*, *-mill*, *-place***, etc.

1835 Ure *Philos. Manuf.* 351 At the elegant *spinning-factory of Egerton, near Bolton. **1890** W. J. Gordon *Foundry* 164 Finally it reaches the *spinning-floor. **1956** R. W. McDowell in W. A. Singleton *Stud. Archit. History* II. 133 Reference must be made to the '*spinning galleries'..an attractive feature of some.... Lakeland villages. **1976** G. Moffat *Short Time to Live* xi. 115 'What's brought you to Sandale?'.. 'Vernacular architecture, sir... Interiors too: spice cupboards, stone stairways, spinning galleries.' **1825** J. Nicholson *Operat. Mechanic* 419 There are two railways.. fixed along the *spinning-ground or rope-walk. **1835** Ure *Philos. Manuf.* 334 The better wages and steadier employment of their great *spinning-mills. **1689** in Picton *L'pool Munic. Rec.* (1883) I. 312 A *spinning place at yᵉ entrance into yᵉ town field. **1692** *Ibid.*, A spinning place.. for making cables. **1835** Ure *Philos. Manuf.* 400 That the *spinning-rooms in a cotton factory can be crowded is utterly impossible. **1677** Yarranton *Eng. Improv.* 47 After a young Maid hath been three years in the *Spinning School ..she will get eight pence the day. **1799** [A. Young] *Agric. Linc.* 441, I made many inquiries concerning the present state of the spinning schools.

d. In terms relating to the spinneret of spiders, etc., as ***spinning gland*, *organ*, *-tube*, *tubuli*, *-wart***.

1841 T. R. Jones *Anim. Kingd.* 317 At the base of the external spinning tubuli. **1878** F. J. Bell *Gegenbaur's Comp. Anat.* 250 The spinning glands of Spiders are further differentiations of dermal glands. *Ibid.* 291 In others this pair of stigmata is fused, and lies in front of the spinning-warts. **1885** McCook *Tenants Old Farm* 136 The spinning-tubes at the end of the abdomen. **1890** *Science-Gossip* XXVI. 130 The spinning organs of various kinds of spiders.

8. a. ***spinning-top***, = top *sb.*[2] 1.

1821 Clare *Vill. Minstr.* I. 5 The spinning-top whirl'd from the twitching string. **1862** *Gifts & Graces* xviii. 177 Many..a spinning-top, or popgun, had reached him from the hand of the kind squire. **1879** [see peery *sb.*].

b. ***spinning-rod*, *-tackle***, etc. (see spin *v.* 12).

1856 'Stonehenge' *Brit. Rural Sports* 263/2 The Spinning-Tackle for salmon. **1870** Pennell *Mod. Pract. Angler* 52 A trolling and spinning rod of about the stiffness I find preferable.

c. ***spinning tunnel***, a wind tunnel with a vertical air flow for testing the behaviour of model aircraft in simulated spins. Also ***free-spinning tunnel***.

1934 *Rep. & Mem. Aeronaut. Res. Committee* No. 1578. 2 Tests in the Free Spinning Tunnel were accordingly projected as a check upon the validity of the results which could be obtained with small dynamical models. *Ibid.* 12 In the spinning tunnel the models are usually about 1/25 scale, and thus the rate of rotation is about five times that of the full scale spin. **1937** *Technical Rep. Aeronaut. Res. Committee 1936* I. 452 The R.A.E. Free Spinning Tunnel was brought into use in 1932 to examine the spinning properties of various existing and projected designs of aeroplanes. **1939** *Ibid. 1937* I. 552 The effect of mass distribution has been explored as a matter of routine on all designs tested in the spinning tunnel. **1947** A. POPE *Wind-Tunnel Testing* i. 10 The NACA has two free-spinning tunnels, one 15 ft in diameter, the other 20 ft.

d. ***spinning magnetometer*** = *spinner magnetometer* s.v. SPINNER 1 I.

1960 *Archaeometry* III. 47 The great advantage that a spinning magnetometer has over the astatic type is that it can be used in a normal laboratory in the presence of a relatively large amount of local magnetic interference. **1963** R. M. COOK in Brothwell & Briggs *Science in Archaeol.* I. v. 64 In the spinning magnetometer the sample is rotated continuously to produce an alternating current.

'spinning, *ppl. a.* [f. SPIN *v.*]

1. That spins or produces thread.

1634 MILTON *Comus* 715 Millions of spinning Worms, That..weave the smooth-hair'd silk. **1708** SEWEL II, *Spinster*, a Spinning-woman. **1736** *Gentl. Mag.* VI. 681 You May, like Arachne, dare to vie, With any spinning Deity. **1840** tr. *Cuvier's Anim. Kingd.* 460 The second section of the sedentary and rectigrade Spiders—that of the *Inequitelæ* or Spinning Spiders. **1891** *Cent. Dict.*, *Spinning-mite*, any mite or acarid of the family *Tetraonychidæ*; a red-spider.

2. That spouts or gushes. *rare.*

1577 B. GOOGE *Heresbach's Husb.* III. (1586) 143 It easeth straight the flaming feuers paine, If in the foote you strike the spinning vaine.

3. That revolves, gyrates, or turns round. ***spinning reserve*** (Electr. Engin.), reserve power-generating capacity which is available to meet sudden increases in load.

1854 CT. E. DE WARREN tr. *De Sauley's Journ. Dead Sea* II. 273 A spinning dervise usually resides in the Grotto of Jeremiah. **1867** F. FRANCIS *Angling* i. 30 The chub..will run equally at a spinning-bait, or a live minnow. **1869** RUSKIN *Q. of Air* Pref. p. vii, A newly-constructed artificial rockery, with a fountain twisted through a spinning spout. **1883** *Fisheries Exhib. Catal.* 56 Artificial Spinning Baits, Flies and Insects. **1932** *Rep. Proposed Amer. Stand. Defs. Electr. Terms* (Amer. Inst. Electr. Engineers) 62/2 Spinning reserve is that reserve generating capacity connected to the bus and ready to take load. **1974** *Times* 21 Jan. 15/6 These 'spinning reserves' are carried on plant which is generating power, but not fully loaded. **1979** 'A. HAILEY' *Overload* I. i. 5 GSP & L's last spinning reserve had been brought to full load.

transf. **1862** PYCROFT *Cricket Tutor* 35 Spinning bowling is always liable to turn in or to break away contrary to all expectation.

4. *colloq.* Rapid, fast.

1882 *Society* 16 Dec. 4/2 The Cambridgeshire enjoyed a spinning run.

Hence **'spinningly** *adv.*

1923 *Daily Mail* 19 May 6 The ball is cracked spinningly through the gap between point and third man.

'spinning-house. [SPINNING *vbl. sb.*]

1. A room or building set apart for the purpose of spinning.

1463 *Bury Wills* (Camden) 20 Ye dore yt is out of ye parlour into ye spynnyng hous. *Ibid.*, The drawt chambyr above ye spynnyng hous. **1756** NUGENT *Gr. Tour, Italy* III. 113 The most remarkable thing..is its spinning-house for a manufacture of silk. **1772** *Hartford Merc. Suppl.* 18 Sept. 4/3 A Dressing Shop, a long spinning and Weaving House.

2. (See quots. and cf. SPIN-HOUSE.)

1803 *Gradus ad Cantabrigiam* 126 *Spinning House*, an ergastulum; a house of labour and correction; a prison for prostitutes under the jurisdiction of the Vice-Chancellor and Proctors. **1840** *Life J. Howard* in *Chivalry & Charity* 150 A spinning house, or Bridewell for women, at Amsterdam. **1874** *Slang Dict.* 304 *Spinning-house*, the place in Cambridge where street-walkers are locked up, if found out after a certain time at night. **1897** T. D. ATKINSON *Cambridge* 94 In 1790..the Gaol was removed to a new building at the back of the Spinning House.

spinning-jenny. [f. SPINNING *vbl. sb.* or *ppl. a.* + JENNY. The reason for this use of the personal name is uncertain.]

1. An early form of spinning-machine (introduced by James Hargreaves about 1764–7 and patented in 1770) in which several spindles were set in motion by a band from one wheel.

1783 *Trans. Soc. Arts* I. 34 The construction of this kind of Machine, called a Spinning Jenny, has since been improved. **1792** A. YOUNG *Trav. France* 269 So many spinning jennies have been destroyed by the people..that the trade is in a deplorable situation. **1816** *Ann. Reg., Chron.* 70/1 Demanding that he should give up a machine called a spinning jenny by the use of which they imagined themselves aggrieved. **1856** BRYANT *Rhode Isl. Coal* xiv, Thou..shalt be The moving soul of many a spinning-jenny.

attrib. **1826** COBBETT *Weekly Reg.* LVIII. 79 The unhappy creatures who have sweated out their lives in the spinning-jenny regions. **1834** *Tait's Mag.* I. 383 One Peel, a spinning-jenny fellow.

fig. **1831** CARLYLE *Sart. Res.* II. x, The basest of created animalcules, the Spider itself, has a spinning-jenny..within its head.

2. (Part of) a gambling apparatus.

1879 H. A. SIMMONS *Ernest Struggles* iv. 72 To the ceiling of the taproom was fixed what the men called a 'spinning jenny', which was a revolving hand, like that on a clock, with a number of figures round it. It was with this that the customers won and lost pots of beer. **1897** *Daily News* 9 June 3/3 Charged with gambling with a 'spinning jenny' at Hurst Park Racecourse... He had a table coloured red, white, and black, and was turning a rod or 'spinning jenny'.

Hence **spinning-jennyish** *a.*

1841 HOOD *Tale Trumpet* 157 Thoughts in the process of fabrication, By a Spinning-Jennyish operation.

'spinning-wheel. [f. SPINNING *vbl. sb.* Cf. Du. *spinnewiel*, WFris. *spinwiele*, NFris. *spenweel.*] A simple apparatus for spinning, formerly in common use, in which the formation of the thread is carried out by the help of a wheel worked either by the hand or foot.

1404 *Nottingham Rec.* II. 22, j. spynyng wheel. **1475** *Maldon Crt. Rolls* Bundle 49 No. 8, 1 saucer, 1 spynnyng-whele in manu servientis. *a* **1529** SKELTON *E. Rummyng* 296 Some layde to pledge..Theyr rocke, theyr spynnyng whele. **1542** *Richmond Wills* (Surtees) 30 Item, a spynnyng qweyll. **1617** *Shuttleworths' Acc.* (Chetham Soc.) 220 To the cookes wiffe, for a spinninge wheele, ijs iiijd. **1714** GAY *Sheph. Week* v. 123 My Spinning-Wheel and Rake, Let Susan keep for her dear Sister's sake. **1790** MME. D'ARBLAY *Diary* July, We had begun some intercourse..through an application I made to her for a spinning-wheel. **1859** JEPHSON *Brittany* vi. 67, I found the good-wife sitting at her spinning-wheel, and in the recess I observed two looms. **1882** CAULFEILD & SAWARD *Dict. Needlework* 458 Spinning wheels were universally employed on the Continent of Europe and in this country until the year 1764.

attrib. and *Comb.* **1801** *Encycl. Brit.* Suppl. II. 520/1 The upper pivot (which resembles the fore pivot or eye of a spinning wheel fly). **1876** SMILES *Sc. Natur.* vi. 101 The night-jar..was still out with his spinning-wheel-like *birr, birr.* **1884** LITTELL *Living Age* 691 The spinning-wheel sound which betrays the bear sucking his paws at his ease.

spinny, var. form of SPINNEY.

spino- ('spaɪnəʊ), used as comb. form of L. *spīna* spine, in a few terms of *Anat.*, *Bot.*, etc., as **spino-'bulbar, -'carpous, -cere'bellar, -'scapulen, -sympa'thetic, -'thalamic, -tu'berculous** *adjs.*

1808 BARCLAY *Muscular Motions* 383 The spino-scapulen portion of the deltoides is a flexor. **1846** DANA *Zooph.* (1848) 572 Small glomerate species, having a spino-tuberculous surface. **1859** MAYNE *Expos. Lex.* 1188/1 *Spinocarpus*,..having spinous fruit,..spinocarpous. **1869** G. LAWSON *Dis. Eye* 75 Some affection of the spino-sympathetic filaments. **1876** *Dunglison's Dict. Med. Sci.*, *Spinobulbar*, relating to the spinal cord and the medulla oblongata, as the spino-bulbar neuroses. **1900** E. A. SCHÄFER *Text-bk. Physiol.* II. 806 Another spino-cerebellar system, mainly crossed (heteromeric), lies in the ventro-lateral edge of the lateral column. *Ibid.* 807 Others [*sc.* spinal cells], it is said..enter the diencephalon, ending in the ventro-lateral nucleus of the optic thalamus, forming a spino-thalamic system. **1974** D. & M. WEBSTER *Compar. Vertebr. Morphol.* xii. 278 Like the ventral spinothalamic tract, with which it is confluent, the lateral spinothalamic tract joins the medial lemniscus in the brainstem. **1975** *Sci. Amer.* Jan. 71/2 They found that one of the main afferent tracts leading to the cerebellum, the ventral spinocerebellar tract, conveys information not about the state of the body or the external environment but about the activity of inhibitory interneurons in the spinal cord.

Spinocism, obs. form of SPINOZISM.

spinodal (spaɪ'nəʊdəl), *a.* and *sb. Physical Chem.* [f. SPINOD(E + -AL.] **A.** *adj.* Being or pertaining to a spinodal; involving a metastable condition described by such a curve. **B.** *sb.* A curve which is the locus of stationary points in a system of curves; *spec.* such a curve in a pressure-volume diagram or the like which delimits a region of thermodynamic metastability from one of instability.

1956 *Nature* 3 Mar. 419/2 A single kinetic law did not apply at all temperatures, which suggests that the spinodal curve may have some influence. **1961** *Acta Metallurgica* IX. 536/2 The spinodal is the locus of points within a miscibility gap where $\delta^2 F/\delta x^2 = 0$. F is the free energy of mixing and x the composition. *Ibid.* 801/2 Au-Ni thin foils decompose by what is almost certainly a spinodal mechanism. **1969** *Trans. Metallurg. Soc. AIME* CCXLV. 1707 Just above and just below the spinodal, we expect the reaction to proceed along a path which is not necessarily the energetically most favorable one. **1973** *Physics Bull.* Apr. 230 Spinodal decomposition of equimolar NaCl-KCl mixed crystals. **1974** *Nature* 29 Nov. 381/2 The locus of all the tangent points *c* defines a metastability limit (spinodal).

spinode ('spaɪnəʊd). *Geom.* [Irreg. f. L. *spīna* spine + NODE *sb.*] A stationary point on a curve; a cusp.

1852 CAYLEY *Math. Papers* (1889) II. 28, I shall, with reference to plane curves,..use the term 'node' as synonymous with double point, and the term 'spinode' as synonymous with cusp. **1852** G. SALMON *Higher Plane Curves* ii. (1879) 25 Such points are called cusps or spinodes. They are also called stationary points.

attrib. **1852** CAYLEY *Math. Papers* (1889) II. 29 The spinode-planes give rise to a developable which may be termed the 'spinode-develope'. Also the 'spinode-tangent' is the tangent to the curve of intersection at the spinode. **1869** *Ibid.* (1893) VI. 450 The spinode curve of the cubic surface. *Ibid.* 584 The spinode torse is the envelope of the parabolic planes of the surface.

spin-off ('spɪnɒf, -ɔ:-), *sb.* and *a.* orig. *U.S.* Also **spinoff.** [f. vbl. phr. *to spin off*: see SPIN *v.* 15.]

A. *sb.* **1.** *Comm.* A distribution of stock of a new company to shareholders of a parent company; a company so created.

1951 STANLEY & KILCULLEN *Federal Income Tax* 182 Sec. 112 (*b*) (11), added by the 1951 Act, permits the distribution of stock in a spin-off without recognition of gain to the stock-holders, subject to certain restrictions designed to prevent the use of spin-offs to distribute earnings and profits. **1956** *Sun* (Baltimore) 30 May 15/1 The proposed 'spin-off' was to be on the basis of three shares of Bestwall Gypsum for each share of Certain-Teed. **1969** *Daily Tel.* 4 June 3 Many had been anticipating a complete spin-off by B P of its United States subsidiary with a United States quotation and a chance of more direct public participation in the group's Alaskan activities. **1974** *Telegraph* (Brisbane) 8 May 46/4 Spea is a subsidiary of the Italstrade Company. Italstrade, in turn, is a subsidiary, or spin-off, of Italstat. **1981** *Observer* 4 Oct. 21/1 A growing phenomenon in British business life: the hive-off, spin-off or demerger—the management buy-out, in fact. **1981** *Times* 28 Oct. 19/5 Even split into four separate companies, the spin-offs would be equal fifteenth in the league table.

2. A by-product, an incidental development, side-effect, or benefit; the production or accrual of side-effects or indirect benefits; *spec.* (*a*) a business, organization, etc., developed out of or by (former) members of another larger business, etc.; (*b*) a show, television programme, etc., developed from an idea or character in another.

1959 *Wall St. Jrnl.* 12 May 1/4 Numerous firms have been organized by M.I.T. scientists who decided to strike out on their own—'spin-offs from M.I.T.', one research official terms them. **1961** *Guardian* 10 Oct. 6/6 'Technological fall-out' or 'technological spin-off'..are the terms used to denote the desirable social byproducts of the plan to send men to the moon. **1963** *Listener* 7 Nov. 735/2 The development out of (or 'spin off', as the Americans call it) magazines [*sc.* magazine programmes] must not be interpreted as any lack of conviction in their continuing role. **1967** *Technology Week* 23 Jan. 75/2 There were to be spin-offs in the form of a series of assist devices for emergency, temporary or permanent assistance to cardiac function. **1967** *Daily Tel.* 15 May 9/8 The close season is also the signal for another series of BBC Comedy Playhouse 'try-outs'. It produced 'Steptoe'; and last season, to use the current jargon, the 'spin-offs' in series form were 'The Whitehall Worrier', [etc.]. **1968** *Economist* 13 Jan. 55/2 It was flatly denied that the huge military and space programmes had been of any advantage, in terms of technological spin-off, to industry. **1968** P. MCKELLAR *Experience & Behav.* xv. 398 In this connexion we encounter the notion of 'spin off', the term used for other applications of findings that have emerged from space research. **1969** *Daily Tel.* (Colour Suppl.) 28 Mar. 7/3 A car..is a means of transport with a horrifying spin-off of death and injury. **1975** *Lady* 17 July 97/1 One of the spin-offs of our affluent society is that more people can afford to keep dogs. **1976** *TV Times* (Brisbane) 22 May 7/2 There is a tradition in American TV—if a show is a success, do a spin-off. In other words, take one or two characters from the parent series and build another series around them. **1977** SACHS & JAHN *Celestial Passengers* xxxii. 198 Space spinoffs have resulted in many new products to improve the quality of our recreational activities. *Ibid.* 193 Probably the best-known space spinoff to health is the cardiac pacemaker. **1979** *Jrnl. R. Soc. Arts* CXXVII. 626/1 If we can improve our productivity..then there will be all sorts of spin-offs from this in the way of leisure industries and service industries.

B. *attrib.* or as *adj.* That develops or is created as a spin-off.

1966 *National Observer* (U.S.) 18 July 7 Although the column hasn't been as successful churning up front-page news stories as some editors had hoped, it does develop an occasional 'spin-off' story. **1967** *Boston Globe* 18 May 35/6 Shares of the spin-off company will be distributed tax free to United Fruit stockholders. **1969** *Physics Bull.* July 268/2 Many of the successful 'spin-off' firms in the United States were based on a transfer of technology by individuals from large and continuing programmes in government and university laboratories. **1974** *Financial Times* 8 Apr. 23/7 Hardly anyone earns less than the proposed new minima, which would therefore raise only a few earnings and so would hit employers' wage bills and eat into Stage Three allowances only through the spin-off effect on holiday and sick pay. **1979** *Amer. Jrnl. Trop. Med. & Hygiene* XXVIII. 1043/2 No attempt was made to document 'spinoff' costs, notably losses of tourism revenue. **1980** J. WAINWRIGHT *Man of Law* xi. 64 With hindsight..I *knew*... But honesty demands that I ask spin-off questions. How much did I know?

† **spinogre,** obs. variant of SPINACH.

a **1400** *Sloane MS. No.* 5 fol. 12/1 *Spinatea*... G[allice] spinache, A[nglice] Spinogre.

spinoid ('spaɪnɔɪd), *a.* [f. L. *spīna* spine + -OID.] Resembling a spine; spine-shaped.

1882 *Gardeners' Chron.* XVII. 44 The small white petals have three teeth at the top, a callus inside in the middle, and a spinoid tooth on their base.

spinone (spɪ'nəʊni:). [It.] A wire-haired gundog of an Italian breed, usually white with tan or brown markings, drooping ears, and a docked tail.

1945 C. L. B. HUBBARD *Observer's Bk. Dogs* 188 The Spinone..has for centuries been the Italian all-purpose shooting dog. **1964** E. F. DALGLISH tr. *Schneider-Leyer's Dogs of World* xvi. 219 Spinone... A big, squarely built, rough-coated dog with long ears and docked tail. **1972** *Daily Tel.* 5 Dec. 7/7 Breeds of dog whose docking is permitted by the Kennel Club are: sporting spaniels,..Italian spinones,..Weimaraners, [etc.].

spinor ('spɪnə(r)). *Physics.* [a. G. *spinor* (B. L. van der Waerden 1929, in *Nachr. von d. Ges. d. Wissensch. zu Göttingen* 100), f. SPIN *v.* + *-or*, after TENSOR, VECTOR.] Any quantity existing in a space and having the property that rotation through 360° reverses its sign and leaves it otherwise unchanged; also, applied to quantities constructed from two or more of these in the way that tensors may be constructed from vectors.

1931 *Physical Rev.* XXXVII. 1022 With the spinor analysis developed by B. Van der Waerden.., which comprises all representations of the Lorentz group, even those not contained in ordinary tensor calculus, one is able to write all derivations and equations in an automatically covariant form. **1952** *Amer. Jrnl. Physics* XX. 253/2 The available literature on spinors is exceedingly hard to understand. **1974** P. A. M. DIRAC *Spinors in Hilbert Space* ii. 4 Spinors, like tensors, are geometrical objects embedded in a space and have components that transform linearly under transformations of the coordinates of the space. Spinors differ from tensors in that they change sign when one applies a complete revolution about an axis, while tensors are unchanged. **1974** G. REECE tr. *Hund's Hist. Quantum Theory* xv. 200 It was soon seen that the four-component Dirac ψ was a particular kind of entity... It was called a spinor. **1977** K. O. MAY tr. *Iyanaga & Kawada's Encycl. Dict. Math.* I. 216/2 Although $SO(n)$ ($n \geq 3$) is connected Lie group, it is not simply connected. The simply connected Lie group which is locally isomorphic to $SO(n)$ is called the spinor group and is denoted by $Spin(n)$.

Hence **spi'norial** *a.*, involving spinors, decribed by means of spinors.

1968 *Physics Bull.* Nov. 381/1 The wavefunction must have four components which transform according to the 'spinorial' transformation encountered by Pauli. **1978** *McGraw-Hill Yearbk. Sci. & Technol.* 356/1 A spinorial gauge field with spin 3/2.

spinose (spaɪ'nəʊs), *a.* [ad. L. *spīnōs-us* (whence also It. *spinoso*, Sp. *espinoso*, Pg. *espinhoso*, OF. *espinous, -eus*, F. *épineux*), f. *spīna* thorn.]

†**1.** = SPINOUS *a.* 1. *Obs.*

1660 H. MORE *Myst. Godl.* VIII. iii. 369 If this Childe of God prove something spinose and harsh in opposing, rebuking [etc.]. **1665** GLANVILL *Def. Van. Dogm.* 89 A spurious medley of nice, spinose, and useless notions. **1677** GALE *Crt. Gentiles* III. 20 Of spinose, frivolous questions, such as assume the name of Science but deserve not the same.

2. *Zool.* = SPINOUS *a.* 3.

1661 LOVELL *Hist. Anim. & Min.* Isagoge A vj b, Oxyrinchus, stellarie oculate and clavate, spinose, rough. *c* **1711** PETIVER *Gazophyl.* IV. xl, I have observed one or two of this Genus of Insects in England, tho not Spinose. **1742** *Phil. Trans.* XLII. 28 The Cartilaginous and Spinose kinds of Fishes. **1835** KIRBY *Hab. & Inst. Anim.* I. x. 307 The hard and often spinose crust of crabs or lobsters. **1852** DANA *Crust.* II. 1530 The tendency to spinose forms among the species of the colder temperate regions. **1896** LYDEKKER *Roy. Nat. Hist.* V. 65 The spinose land-terrapin (*Geoëmyda spinosa*).

3. *Bot.* = SPINOUS *a.* 2.

1693 *Phil. Trans.* XVII. 687 'Tis spinose, and trifoliate, the Flower and Seed of a coccineous Colour. **1753** *Chambers' Cycl.* Suppl. s.v. *Leaf, Spinose Leaf*, that whose disk or edge is armed with cartilaginous points..firmly affixed. **1772** J. R. FORSTER *Kalm's Trav.* I. 130 When the hedges consist of spinose bushes, the cattle will hardly attempt to get through them. **1870** HOOKER *Stud. Flora* 8 Achenes tubercled or spinose. **1872** OLIVER *Elem. Bot.* I. vii. 8 In Whin or Furze, both the leaves..and the branches are spinose.

Comb. **1857** T. MOORE *Handbk. Brit. Ferns* (ed. 3) 41 Serratures spinose-mucronate. **1857** HENFREY *Bot.* 56 These teeth..may be tipped with spines when they are termed spinose-serrate.

Hence **spi'nosely** *adv.*

1847 W. E. STEELE *Field Bot.* 84 Leaves minutely spinosely ciliated on edge. *Ibid.* 163 Leaves..spinosely serrate.

Spinosism, -ist, obs. ff. SPINOZISM, -IST.

spinosity (spaɪ'nɒsɪtɪ). [ad. late L. *spīnōsitās* (cf. It. *spinosità*): see SPINOSE *a.* and -ITY.]

1. The quality of being spinose or thorny. Chiefly *fig.*

1605 BACON *Adv. Learn.* II. 47 The part of Humane Philosophie..seemeth but a Net of subtiltie and spinositie. **1660** H. MORE *Myst. Godl.* VI. xviii. 275 The acuteness and spinosity of harsh and dry Opinions.

2. A rude or disagreeable remark; an argument or theory of a difficult and unprofitable character.

1653 H. MORE *Conject. Cabbal.* Wks. (1713) 105 Many spinosities and cutting passages that often happen unawares in..conversation. **1691** WOOD *Ath. Oxon.* II. 283 He..was not unseen in their subtilties and spinosities. **1701** NORRIS *Ideal World* I. vi. 330 Without running through all the scholastic spinosities upon this occasion. **1836** HOR. SMITH *Tin Trump.* (1876) 311 Amid the dry spinosities and tortuous labyrinths of theology.

spinoso- (spaɪ'nəʊsəʊ), used as comb. form of SPINOSE *a.*, as ***spinoso-dentate, -denticulate***, etc.

1848 DANA *Zooph.* 187 Lamellæ unequal, spinoso-dentate. *Ibid.* 229 Lamellæ..at apex spinoso-denticulate. **1852** —— *Crust.* I. 101 Arm and carpus..spinoso-tubercular. *Ibid.* 114 Third and fourth joints spinoso-tuberculate.

spinous ('spaɪnəs), *a.* [f. SPINE *sb.*[1] + -OUS, or ad. L. *spīnōs-us* SPINOSE *a.*]

1. *fig.* Resembling or suggestive of a thorn or thorns in respect of sharpness and aridity; unpleasant and difficult or unprofitable to handle or deal with. (Cf. SPINOSE *a.* 1.)

a **1638** MEDE *Disc. Script.* (1642) 92 This I take to be the true and genuine meaning of this passage,..nor needeth it any spinous Criticisms for its explication. **1660** tr. *Amyraldus' Treat. Relig.* III. xi. 535 They would not judge Religion a thing full of spinous questions and irresolvable difficulties. **1694** STRYPE *Mem. Cranmer* II. xiii. 196 Who had himself..vindicated the truth from the spinous and confused cavils of Sophisters. **1821** LAMB *Elia* I, *Old Benchers Inner T.*, Many a sarcastic growl did the latter cast out—for Coventry had a rough spinous humour.

2. *Bot.* Furnished with spines or thorns; thorn-bearing, thorny.

1668 WILKINS *Real Char.* 109 Larger leaves; not spinous. **1694** WESTMACOTT *Script. Herb.* 199 The Spinous tribe of herbs are many. **1776** J. LEE *Introd. Bot.* Explan. Terms 380 *Spinosus*, spinous, armed with Thorns. **1815** KIRBY & SP. *Entomol.* (1818) I. 288 Insects, which it first impales alive on the thorns of the sloe and other spinous plants. **1854** HOOKER *Himal. Jrnls.* I. vi. 157 With spinous involucres inclosing an eatable sweet nut. **1887** J. BALL *Nat. S. Amer.* 32 One of the spinous species of Solanum.

3. Armed or covered with spines or slender sharp-pointed excrescences; spinigerous. Chiefly *Zool.*

1774 GOLDSM. *Nat. Hist.* (1824) III. I. i. 13 Thus there are three grand divisions in the fish kind; the cetaceous, the cartilaginous, and the spinous. **1822** J. PARKINSON *Outl. Oryctol.* 147 The corselet..is sometimes spinous,..but it is generally smooth. **1834** McMURTRIE *Cuvier's Anim. Kingd.* 192 Fishes..whose operculum or preoperculum..[has] dentated or spinous edges. **1897** *Allbutt's Syst. Med.* IV. 271 Their surface [is] smooth, rough, or spinous.

b. In specific names, as ***spinous loach, shark, spider-crab, tortoise.***

1769 PENNANT *Brit. Zool.* III. 1 The Spinous Tortoise.. seems common to the Mediterranean. **1839** YARRELL *Brit. Fishes* Suppl. II. 54 The Spinous Shark. *Echinorhinus spinosus.* **1862** COUCH *Brit. Fishes* I. 54 The Spinous Shark was not known to naturalists before the latter part of the last ..century. **1881** *Cassell's Nat. Hist.* V. 133 The Spinous Loach (*Cobitis tænia*) is a rarer fish in this country. **1882** *Ibid.* VI. 198 The Spinous Spider Crab (*Maia squinado*).

4. Having the form of a spine or thorn; slender and sharp-pointed.

1758 MONRO *Anat. Bones* (ed. 6) 121 The fifteenth is the *spinous* [suture]; which is in the middle of the lower part of the nostrils. **1807** J. E. SMITH *Phys. Bot.* 414 Four naked seeds, with always more or less of spinous bristles..on their foliage. **1828** STARK *Elem. Nat. Hist.* I. 409 Tail forked, with a spinous ray on each side. **1854** *Proc. Berw. Nat. Club* III. 164 The scales on the back were..raised to a sharp edge, but not spinous nor curved backwards.

b. ***spinous process***, a process or apophysis of a spine-like form, esp. one of those on the vertebræ.

1732 MONRO *Anat.* (ed. 2) 201 The spinous Processes of the *Vertebræ* of the Back become gradually longer. **1797** ABERNETHY *Surg. Ess.* III. 28, I could..touch the transverse spinous process of the sphenoid bone. **1831** R. KNOX *Cloquet's Anat.* 115 The Anterior and Inferior spinous process of the ilium. **1843** R. J. GRAVES *Syst. Clin. Med.* xxx. 416 There was no tenderness over the spinous processes of the vertebræ. **1873** MIVART *Elem. Anat.* 179 Separated by a small notch from a strongly marked prominence called the posterior inferior spinous process.

5. Composed of spines.

1790 BEWICK *Hist. Quadrup.* 423 The Hedge-Hog..is provided by Nature with a spinous armour.

6. *Anat.* Of or belonging to the spine.

1826 S. COOPER *First Lines Surg.* 216 A rupture of the spinous, or some other artery of the dura mater.

7. *Comb.*, as ***spinous-finned, -pointed, -serrate, -tailed, -tipped, -toothed.***

1785 LATHAM *Gen. Synop. Birds* III. II. 555 Spinous-tailed Teal..inhabits Cayenne and Guiana. **1828** J. E. SMITH *Eng. Flora* II. 18 Leaves awl-shaped, spinous-pointed, rough. **1851** GOSSE *Nat. Hist., Fishes* 200 The Soft-finned Fishes are, in general, inferior to the Spinous-finned in [etc.]. **1870** HOOKER *Stud. Flora* 185 Leaves alternate, usually spinous-toothed. *Ibid.* 191 Bracts..acuminate or spinous-tipped.

Hence **'spinousness.**

1846 PATTERSON *Zool.* 48 It varies also in the length of the ray-spines, the spinousness of the disc and the relative proportions of rays and discs.

spin-out ('spɪnaʊt). *N. Amer. slang.* [f. vbl. phr. *to spin out*: see SPIN *v.* 16.] A skidding spin by a vehicle out of control.

1957 *Daily Progress* (Charlottesville, Va.) 28 Oct. 14/6 A spin-out in the last 10 minutes of the race may have cost Tony Briggs of Charlottesville top honors in the first preliminary race before the President's Cup automobile race. **1971** *Maclean's Mag.* Oct. 39/3 He had trouble eliminating his spin-outs, those heart-stopping moments when the car slithers in circles and semi-circles on the track.

Spi'nozan, *a.* [f. as next + -AN.] Of or pertaining to, originating with, Spinoza.

1879 *Expositor* X. 436 God, in Spinozan phrase, is simply *Natura naturans.*

Spinozism (spɪ'nəʊzɪz(ə)m). Also 8 **Spinocism, -osaism,** 8–9 **Spinosism,** 20 **Spinozaism.** [f. the name of the philosopher Baruch or Benedict de *Spinoza* (1632–77). So F. *spinosisme.*] The philosophical doctrines of Spinoza, or the general principle underlying these; pantheism as represented by Spinoza.

1728 CHAMBERS *Cycl.* s.v., The great Principle of Spinosism is, That there is nothing properly and absolutely existing, but Matter, and the Modifications of Matter. **1740** WARBURTON *Vind. Pope's Ess. Man* 24 Spinozism is the Destruction of an Universe, where every Thing tends..to the Perfection of the Whole. **1757** LAW *Lett. Import. Subj.* 177 As Spinocism is nothing else but a gross confounding of God and nature. *a* **1765** STUKELEY *Mem.* (Surtees). I. 127 He wrote a treatise against Mr. Pope's essay on man, to prove it to be atheism, spinosaism, deism,.. & what not. **1821** COLERIDGE *Lett., Convers.*, etc. I. 25 To guard my own character from the suspicions of pantheistic opinions, or Spinosism. **1881** ADAMSON *Fichte* 130 The theoretical part ..is nothing but an inverted or idealistic Spinozism. **1912** *Q. Rev.* Oct. 393 Modern Spinozaism is inclined to identify ethics with religion.

Spinozist (spɪ'nəʊzɪst). Also 7–9 **Spinosist,** 9– **Spi'nozaist.** [f. as prec. + -IST. So F. *spinosiste.*] One who accepts or advocates the philosophical doctrines of Spinoza.

1728 CHAMBERS *Cycl., Spinosism*, the Doctrine of Spinosa; ..the Retainers whereto, are called Spinosists. **1740** WARBURTON *Vind. Pope's Ess. Man* 24 The Spinozists..to hide the Impiety..are used to express the Omnipresence of God in Terms that any religious Theist might employ. **1814** W. WILSON *Hist. Dissent. Ch.* IV. 78 He was generally esteemed to be a Spinozist. **1852** H. MELVILLE *Pierre* XX. ii. 381 Why, lad, I have received propositions from the Editors of the Spinozaist to contribute a weekly column to their paper, and you know how very few can understand the Spinozaist. **1882–3** SCHAFF *Encycl. Relig. Knowl.* 309 The conversation [with Jacobi] shows that Lessing ended a confirmed Spinozist. **1912** *Q. Rev.* Oct. 398 He no longer speaks as a Spinozaist.

attrib. **1878** MORLEY *Diderot* I. 224 The true line of cleavage that would have enabled him..to shatter the Spinosist system.

So **Spinozite.** *rare.*

1690 in Maidment *Bk. Sc. Pasquils* (1868) 186 The Spinosit to his own interest true, Swears if a Trinitie, they have theirs too. **1946** *Mind* LV. 101 Some of these assumptions..are often confidently made by others than professed Spinozites.

Spinozistic (spɪnəʊ'zɪstɪk), *a.* Also **-osistic.** [f. prec. + -IC.] Of, pertaining to, or characteristic of Spinoza or his philosophical views.

1832 COLERIDGE *Table-t.* 4 April, I prefer the Spinozistic scheme infinitely. **1839** HALLAM *Hist. Lit.* IV. iii. §79 It has sometimes been doubted whether the Spinosistic philosophy excludes altogether an infinite intelligence. **1877** E. CAIRD *Philos. Kant* II. xv. 540 The Spinozistic conception of a unity of all affirmative predicates.

spin-rinse ('spɪnrɪns). [f. SPIN *v.* + RINSE *sb.*] A rinsing of washing in a rotating perforated drum which draws off water; a combined rinse and partial spin-dry.

1948 [see SPIN-DRIER, -DRYER]. **1961** *Guardian* 22 Mar. 8/3 A powerful spin-dryer.., to which a crafty bit of design has given a built-in spin-rinse percolating downwards through the clothes to give an effective rinse, hitherto lacking in the conventional spinner.

†**spin-rock.** *Obs. rare.* Also 5 **spynroke.** [ad. MDu. *spinrocke, -roc* (WFlem. *-rokke, -rok*), *-rocken* (Du. *-rokken*), = G. *spinnrocken*, †*-rocke, -rock*: see SPIN *v.* and ROCK *sb.*[2]] A distaff.

A variant of the Fr. phrase translated in quot. 1623 is similarly rendered in Dutch of the 16th cent.

1483 CAXTON *G. de la Tour* F j, She tooke in her handes a spynroke with blacke wolle and beganne to spynne. **1623** WODROEPHE *Marrow Fr. Tongue* 515/2 Those be old Wiues Tales, That is written in the Booke of Spin-Rockes [= F. *livre des quenouilles*]. **1648** HEXHAM II, *Een Wocke*, a Spin-rocke, or a Distaffe.

spin-scan ('spɪnskæn), *a.* and *sb.* [f. SPIN *v.* + SCAN *sb.*] **A.** *adj.* Applied to devices whose scanning motion is provided by the rotation of the craft carrying them.

1967 *Electronics* 6 Mar. 73 (Advt.), SB RC also built the spin-scan camera that has been sending back high-resolution black-and-white photos of the earth's cloud cover. **1979** *Sci. Amer.* Nov. 21 (Advt.), The satellite's 'camera' is a visible-infrared spin-scan radiometer.

B. *sb.* A scan performed or produced by such a device. Also *attrib.*

1972 *Space Research* XII. 1768 Television would have taken a shorter exposure (a fraction of a second, compared with several minutes for a spin scan). **1974** *Science* 25 Jan. 318/2 A 2·5 centimeter telescope aboard Pioneer 10 is capable of making two-dimensional spin-scan maps..at high resolution. **1974** *Nature* 6 Sept. 18/1 The most striking early results were the hundreds of photographs that resulted from the spin-scans of the planet, giving higher resolution pictures of the planet than had previously been possible.

So **'spin-scanning** *a.*

1972 *Space Research* XII. 1765 A summary description is made of spin-scanning devices for various space missions.

†**spinsers,** *sb. pl. Obs.*[−1] In 6 **spynsars.** [f. OF. *espince* 'pince, tenailles'.] = PINCERS 1.

1539 in *Victoria Hist. Sussex* II. 246/1 Reparacions..in Bellowes, Hamors,..sundry great Spynsars and Skepes.

spinster ('spɪnstə(r)). Also 4–5 **spynnester(e,** 5–6 **spynster** (6 **-starre**). [f. SPIN *v.* + -STER. Cf. MDu., Du., and WFris. *spinster*, NFris. *spen-, spanster.*]

1. a. A woman (or, rarely, a man) who spins, *esp.* one who practises spinning as a regular occupation.

1362 LANGL. *P. Pl.* A. v. 130 And my wyf at Westmunstre þat wollene cloþ made, Spak to þe spinsters for to spinne hit softe. **14..** *Lat.-Eng. Voc.* in Wr.-Wülcker 583 *Filatrix*, a spynnester. **1543** *Star Chamber Cases* (Selden) II. 254 Ther were..ther dwelling..dyuers good spynsters & carders. **1578** LYTE *Dodoens* 617 Spinsters use the stemmes..to winde yarne upon. **1600** PORY tr. *Leo's Africa* II. 103 Their women are excellent spinsters, whereby they are saide to gaine more then the men of the towne. **1647** R. STAPYLTON *Juvenal* 231 Destinies that spin the thred of life; Juvenal calls them spinsters. The distaffe bearer is Clotho, the spinster Lachesis. **1704** HEARNE *Duct. Hist.* (1714) I. 243 This monstrous Sight..that Soldiers that bore Arms should be commanded by a Spinster. **1758** JOHNSON *Idler* No. 2 ¶7, I should be, indeed, unwilling to find that, for the sake of corresponding with the Idler, the smith's iron had cooled on the anvil, or the spinster's distaff stood unemployed. **1836** [MRS. TRAILL] *Backw. Canada* 47 The spinster does not sit, but walks to and fro. **1910** *Contemp. Rev.* July 31 She would be a famous spinster and needlewoman.

fig. **1609** DEKKER *Gull's Horn-bk.* 16 Let the three huswifely spinsters of Destiny rather curtail the threed of thy life. **1698** FARQUHAR *Love & Bottle* III. i, Are my clothes so coarse, as if they were spun by those lazy spinsters the Muses?

b. A spider, or other insect that spins. *rare.*

1636 BRIDEOAKE *Poem* (MS. Bodl. 22 fol. 10), The little Spinster's Lawne [*sc.* web]. **1706** J. GARDINER tr. *Rapin's Gardens* (1728) 197 The gnat, the buzzing drone, the Palmer-worm, The wily Spinster, and the creeping snail.

2. a. Appended to names of women, originally in order to denote their occupation, but subsequently (from the 17th century) as the proper legal designation of one still unmarried.

1380 in T. Rogers *Oxf. City Docum.* (1891) 10 De Alicia Moris Spynnestere, vjd. **1496** *Nottingham Rec.* III. 48 Johanna Hunt,..spynster. **1545** *Knaresb. Wills* (Surtees) I. 49 Elizabeth Lethom, spynstarre. **1564-5** in *10th Rep. Hist. MSS. Comm.* (1885) 27 Joan Lambe, widow of London, spynster. **1580-1** *Ibid.*, Margaretta Tirrell spinster, alias dicta Margaretta Tirrell uxor Thome Tirrell. **1617** MINSHEU *Ductor*, A *Spinster*, a terme, or an addition in our Common Law, onely added in Obligations, Euidences, and Writings, vnto maids vnmarried. **1656** BLOUNT *Glossogr.*, *Spinster*;..this is the onely addition for all unmarried women, from the Viscounts Daughter downward. **1711** *Lond. Gaz.* No. 4865/4 Elizabeth Harris of London, Spinster. **1719** J. ROBERTS *Spinster* 135, I write myself spinster, because the laws of my country call me so. **1773** GOLDSM. *Stoops to Conq.* v. i, Constantia Neville, spinster, of no place at all. **1818** SCOTT *Rob Roy* xxxix, Diana Vernon, Spinster.

b. A woman still unmarried; *esp.* one beyond the usual age for marriage, an old maid.

1719 J. ROBERTS *Spinster* 349 As for us poor Spinsters, we must certainly go away to France also. **1832** W. IRVING *Alhambra* II. 140 The vigilant Fredegonda was one of the most wary of ancient spinsters. **1859** THACKERAY *Virgin.* xxii, Your sweet mistress, your spotless spinster, your blank maiden just out of the school-room. **1882** MISS BRADDON *Mt. Royal* I. vi. 183 Providence is wonderfully kind to plain little spinsters with a knack of making themselves useful.

3. *attrib.* and *Comb.*, as (sense 1, 1 b) ***spinster-caterpillar, -slave***; (sense 2 b) ***spinster aunt, -baiting, -like*** adj., ***sex***.

1743 FRANCIS tr. *Horace, Odes* III. xxvii. 64 A spinster-slave, Some rude barbarian's concubine. **1800** HURDIS *Fav. Village* 169 The spinster caterpillar ties aloft, Fine as the gossamer, his slender cord. **1828** LYTTON *Pelham* II. xii, A solitary candle, whose long, spinster-like wick was flirting away with an east wind. **1837** DICKENS *Pickw.* vi, Tupman and the spinster aunt established a joint-stock company of fish and flattery. **1891** MEREDITH *One of our Conq.* xxiii, The little dog had qualities to entrance the spinster sex. **1938** L. MACNEICE *Mod. Poetry* 191 Merely a piece of rather cruel spinster-baiting.

Hence **'spinsterdom, -ism, -ship**, = SPINSTERHOOD; **spin'sterial, -ian, 'spinsterish, -ous** *adjs.*, having the characteristics of a spinster; old-maidish; **'spinsterishness**.

1879 T. H. S. ESCOTT *England* I. vii. 178 Where there is enough of leisure, idleness, and *spinsterdom. **1883** *Sat. Rev.* 21 July 82 A single..thunder-shower may..doom maidens by the dozen to the sorrows of spinsterdom. **1849** ALB. SMITH *Pottleton Legacy* (1854) 415 His sisters..annoyed him with their *spinsterial propensities. **1874** J. HATTON *Clytie* xiii, The landlord's sister, a spinsterial Scotchwoman. **1819** *Sporting Mag.* V. 60 With all the finicality of *spinsterian consequence. **1881** *Graphic* XXIII. 146/3 The naval, military, clerical, or spinsterian would-be-investor. **1892** *Academy* 5 Mar. 237/3 His little *spinsterish ways at times grew rather tiresome. **1913** R. WEST *Let.* June in G. N. Ray *H. G. Wells & Rebecca West* (1974) 23 Your *spinsterishness makes you feel that a woman desperately and hopelessly in love with a man is an indecent spectacle. **1930** R. MACAULAY *Staying with Relations* iii. 44 The elegant spinsterishness of Claudia and Benet had turned, in Julia,.. to something more sensuous. **1818** *La Belle Assemblée* XVII. 75 The full terrors of *spinsterism took hold of all her faculties. **1874** in J. W. Howe *Sex & Educ.* 52 The respectable ranks of spinsterism. **1899** *Illustr. Lond. News* 11 Mar. 328, I take the liberty of calling them maiden ladies because their style is, so to speak, *spinsterous. **1816** SOUTHEY in *Q. Rev.* XV. 8 If the bride has an elder sister still in her state of *spinstership.

'spinsterhood. [f. SPINSTER 2 b.]

1. The condition of being an unmarried woman or old maid.

1823 LOCKHART *Reg. Dalton* I. vi, It must have required the tact of a very Beau Nash to detect in her appearance the very smallest symptom of spinsterhood. **1863** B. TAYLOR *H. Thurston* ii. 28 He married..a tall, staid, self-reliant creature, verging on spinsterhood. **1879** H. PHILLIPS *Notes Coins* 6 In antiquity these coins were known as *Maidens*, referring to the spinsterhood of the goddess represented upon them.

2. The collective body of unmarried women.

1844 *Blackw. Mag.* LV. 201 Is this a reason..for leaving, like an uncultivated waste,..the spinsterhood of Great Britain?

'spinsterly, *a.* and *adv.* [f. SPINSTER.]

A. *adj.* **1.** Appertaining to a spinner.

1827 LAMB *Let. to B. Barton* in *Final Mem.* xvi. 151, I feel most thankful for the spinsterly attentions of your sister. Thank the kind knitter in the sun!

2. Old-maidish.

1902 *Daily Chron.* 17 Nov. 5/2 New England..is not really spinsterly, but only so by comparison.

B. *adv.* In the manner of a spinster.

1894 *Sketch* 4 July 522/1 Miss Wilkins is handling the life too delicately, too spinsterly, too much, in fact, as a New England Nun.

spinstress ('spɪnstrɪs). [f. SPINSTER + -ESS.]

1. A female spinner.

1643 HOWELL *Twelve Treat.* (1661) 206 Spinstresses are become States-women, and every peasan turned politician. **1664** POWER *Exp. Philos.* I. 11 Ovid's Lydian-Spinstresse, that proud Madam which Pallas..transform'd into the Spider. *a* **1704** T. BROWN *Odes of Horace* Wks. 1711 IV. 359 Let meaner Souls by Virtue be cajol'd, As the good Grecian Spinstress was of old. **1713** *Gentleman Instructed* I. Suppl. p. lv, You are a kind of Mulatoe,..a compound of Gentleman and Spinstress. **1841** *Penny Cycl.* XX. 139/2 Lady Hamilton ..was painted in various characters, as..Sensibility, a Bacchante,..the Spinstress.

2. A maiden lady; a spinster.

1716 in Payne *Eng. Cath.* (1889) 11 Gertrude Beveridge, ..spinstress. **1821** SCOTT *Pirate* xii, He actually ventured to salute the withered cheek of the spinstress.

spinstrian: see SPINTRIAN *a.*

'spinstry. [f. SPINSTER + -Y (cf. -RY).]

1. The art or occupation of spinning; the product of spinning.

1611 COTGR., *Filandrerie*, spinstrie, spinning. **1652** CHARLETON *Darkn. Atheism* x. 353 The spinstry of Silk-worms. **1660** tr. *Amyraldus' Treat. conc. Relig.* II. iii. 193 The combates of the Gods one against another,..their imployments of the Forge and Spinstry. **1859** *Jrnl. Brit. Archæol. Assoc.* Dec. 309 The instruments of spinstry were borne in procession before a newly married bride.

transf. **1653** HEMINGS *Fatal Contract* II. ii, Come along, Or by the curious spinstrie of thy head, Which natures cunnin'st finger twisted out, I'l drag thee to my couch.

†2. Spinsterhood. *rare.*

1784 R. BAGE *Barham Downs* II. 242 It has come to pass very unnaturally, that I have lived to a very respectable age of Spinstry, without falling in love. **1894** *Wales* Aug. 192/1 The local gossips..watched the progress of events from the heights of maternity and spinstry.

spin-text. Also spintext. [f. SPIN *v.* + TEXT *sb.*, originally as a suggestive surname.] A clergyman or parson, *esp.* one who preaches long or weak sermons.

1693 CONGREVE *Old Bachelor* I. i, Talks of sending for Mr. Spintext to keep me Company... Spintext! Oh, the fanatick one-eyed parson! *c* **1700** T. BROWN *Lett. fr. Dead* Wks. II. 236 Representing Mr. Spin-text the Preacher, or Mr. Love-Lady the Chaplain, after a ridiculous manner. **1712** WARD *Yng. Libertine's Answ.* Wks. III. II. 33 Imploying some superannuated Spintext, to rattle off your poor Nephew. **1788** V. KNOX *Winter Even.* I. III. ii. 243 The race of formal spintexts and solemn saygraces is nearly extinct. **1834** SOUTHEY in *Corr. C. Bowles* (1881) 313 Poor Newton seems to have sat down to them as..a sorry spin-text to his sermon at the latter end of the week. **1889** *Antiquary* Nov. 194 Barrow was of the obsolete family of the Spintexts.

spin'thariscope. [Irreg. f. Gr. σπινθαρίς spark: see -SCOPE.] An instrument in which the rays emitted from the metal radium are evidenced by the production of tiny sparks.

1903 SIR W. CROOKES in *Science* 26 June 1002, I propose to call this little instrument the 'spinthariscope'. **1904** *Longm. Mag.* Dec. 126 He was as full of vivacity as a spinthariscope.

†'spinther. *Obs.*[−1] [a. Gr. σπινθήρ.] A scintillation.

1641 TRAPP *Theol. Theol.* 7 Small sparkes and spinthers of divine light.

†spinthere. *Min. Obs.* [a. F. *spinthère*, f. Gr. σπινθήρ spark.] = SPHENE.

1805 R. JAMESON *Char. Min.* II. 568 Spinthere... Its colour is greenish. **1821** URE *Dict. Chem.*, *Spinthere*..occurs in the department of Isere in France, incrusting calcareous spar crystals. **1836** T. THOMSON *Min., Geol.*, etc. I. 151 Sphene,..semelin, spinellane, spinthere.

†'spintle, obs. variant of SPINDLE *sb.*

1749 *Phil. Trans.* XLVI. 111 Sundry very large Comazants.., some of which settled on the Spintles at the Top-mast Heads.

'spintrian, *a. rare.* [f. L. *spintria*: see next. So F. *spinthrien.*] (See quot. 1656.)

1656 BLOUNT *Glossogr.*, *Spintrian*, pertaining to those that seek out, or invent new and monstruous actions of lust. *a* **1678** MARVELL *State Poems* Wks. 1726 II. 46 The poor Priapus,..in the mimicks of the spinstrian [*sic*] sport, Out-does Tiberius, and his goatish Court. **1887** L. C. SMITHERS tr. *Forberg's Man. Class. Erotol.* viii. 166 More than three may enjoy themselves together; this is what we call after Tiberius, the spintrian kind. **1913** C. MACKENZIE *Sinister St.* I. II. ix. 287 My library..holds as many secrets as the Spintrian books of Elephantis, long ago lost and purified by the sea.

†'spintry. *Obs. rare.* [ad. L. *spintria.*]

1. A species of male prostitute.

The L. form is used as a pl. by Goldsm. *Cit. World* xxxiv.

1598 GRENEWEY *Tacitus, Ann.* VI. i. (1622) 121 Then first of all were those vnknowen words of Sellaries and Spintries found out of the filthines of the place. **1603** B. JONSON *Sejanus* IV. v, [Some] are ravish'd hence, like captives, and.. dealt away, Unto his spintries, sellaries, and slaves.

2. A place used for unnatural practices.

1649 C. WALKER *Relat. & Observ.* II. 257 Their New erected Sodomes and Spintries at the Mulbury-garden.

‖**spinula** ('spaɪnjʊlə). *rare.* = SPINULE.

1826 KIRBY & SP. *Entomol.* xlvii. IV. 386 Certain intestinal worms,..some of which are furnished with lateral spinulæ.

spinulate ('spaɪnjʊlət), *a.* [See SPINULE and -ATE.] Furnished with spinules or small spines.

1866 BOWERBANK *Monogr. Brit. Spongiadæ* II. 66 *Polymastia spinula*,..Sponge... External defensive spicula of..fistulæ spinulate. *Ibid.* 69 There are numerous small spinulate spicula.

So **'spinulated** *a.*

1900 J. T. CUNNINGHAM *Sexual Dimorphism* 8 The presence of well-developed ctenoid or spinulated scales all over both sides of the body.

spinulation (spaɪnjʊ'leɪʃən). [See next and -ATION.] The form or arrangement of spinules.

1884 *Proc. Zool. Soc.* 83 The investigation of the spinulation of Starfishes.

spinule ('spaɪnjʊl). [ad. L. *spīnula*, dim. of *spīna* SPINE *sb.*[1] So F. *spinule.*]

1. A small or minute spine or thorn-like formation, esp. in lower forms of animal life.

1752 J. HILL *Hist. Anim.* 226 The Pleuronectes, with.. the lateral line rough, and spinules at the fins. **1819** SAMOUELLE *Entomol. Compend.* 233 Antennæ lamelliform, small, ciliated with spinules. **1846** DANA *Zooph.* (1848) 498 Slender spinules scarcely a line long. **1878** F. J. BELL *Gegenbaur's Comp. Anat.* 206 The tuft of spinules on the latter.

2. A particular kind of larva.

1857 GOSSE *Omphalos* 223 A tiny egg was discharged from a parent *Botryllus*, which presently produced a little active tadpole-like larva, called a 'spinule'.

Hence **'spinuled** *a.*, spinulate. **spinu'lescent** *a.*, having a tendency to produce small spines.

1829 LOUDON *Encycl. Plants* 448 *Mesembryanthemum spinuliferum*; spinulescent. **1880** *Linn. Soc. Jrnl.* XV. 143 Delicately spinuled teeth of such forms as Ophioscolex.

'spinuli-, comb. form of L. *spīnula* spinule, used in a few compounds, as ***spinu'liferous, 'spinuliform, spinuli-scabrous*** adjs.

1846 DANA *Zooph.* (1848) 495 A few minute spinuliform papillæ. **1852** —— *Crust.* I. 527 Lower margin..spinuli-scabrous. **1859** MAYNE *Expos. Lex.* 1188/2 *Spinuliferus*,.. having very small spines..: spinuliferous. **1900** *Proc. Zool. Soc.* 519 The spinuliferous..margins of the carapace.

'spinulo-, variant of prec.

1852 DANA *Crust.* I. 188 Hand externally spinulous..or spinulo-tuberculous.

spinulose (spaɪnjʊ'ləʊs), *a. Zool.* and *Bot.* [ad. mod.L. *spīnulōs-us*, f. *spinula* SPINULE.]

1. Furnished or covered with spinules.

a. *Zool.* **1819** SAMOUELLE *Entomol. Compend.* 221 Tibiæ spinulose. **1859** DANA *Crust.* II. 871 This part..excavate and minutely spinulose. **1877** HUXLEY *Anat. Inv. Anim.* vi. 278 Twenty-six spinulose thoracico-abdominal segments.

b. *Bot.* **1829** LOUDON *Encycl. Plants* 505 Stems and spinulose calyxes covered with wool. **1847** W. E. STEELE *Field Bot.* 14 Bracts spinulose at base with a long, terminal, slender spine. **1870** HOOKER *Stud. Flora* 183 Teasel..; hairy or spinulose herbs with angular stems.

2. Having the form of spinules.

1848 *Proc. Berw. Nat. Club* II. 288 The spinulose serratures begin..about the middle of the leaf. **1859** T. MOORE *Brit. Ferns* 46 Broad rounded segments..notched into a varying number of pointed but not spinulose teeth.

Comb. **1870** HOOKER *Stud. Flora* 466 Lobes oblong spinulose-toothed.

Hence **spinu'losely** *adv.*

1857 T. MOORE *Handbk. Brit. Ferns* (ed. 3) 123 Upper pinnules inciso-lobate with spinulosely serrate lobes.

spinulosin (spaɪnjʊ'ləʊsɪn). *Biochem.* [f. mod.L. *spīnulōs-us*, specific epithet of the fungus from which it was first isolated (see SPINULOSE *a.*): see IN[1].] A purple-black crystalline benzoquinone derivative, $C_8H_8O_5$, which is produced in cultures of the moulds *Penicillium spinulosum* and *Aspergillus fumigatus*.

1938 ANSLOW & RAISTRICK in *Biochem. Jrnl.* XXXII. 689 Birkinshaw & Raistrick (1931) reported the isolation from cultures of strains in the *Penicillium spinulosum* Thom series of a new mould metabolic product which was unnamed at that time, but for which the name *spinulosin* is now proposed. **1946** [see FUMIGATIN]. **1950** L. F. & M. FIESER *Org. Chem.* (ed. 2) xxxii. 770 Spinulosin..has been prepared from fumigatin by Thiele addition of acetic anhydride, hydrolysis of the resulting tetraacetate, and oxidation. **1979** *Biol. Abstr.* LXVII. 6332/2 A strain of *A. fumigatus* (Fresenius)..was grown on a culture medium with added saccharose. The synthesis of..spinulosin was studied under many different temperature, pH and inoculum conditions.

spinuloso- (spaɪnjʊ'ləʊsəʊ), combining form of SPINULOSE *a.*, as ***spinuloso-ciliate, -dentate, -denticulate, -granulate, -serrate.***

1833 HOOKER in *Smith's Eng. Flora* V. I. 121 The margins ..more or less spinuloso-dentate. *Ibid.* 124 The upper lobes ..spinuloso serrate. **1846** DANA *Zooph.* (1848) 162 Corallum having a subelliptical aperture, sides..spinuloso-denticulate. **1852** —— *Crust.* I. 186 Fourth, fifth and especially sixth joint spinuloso-granulate above. **1866** *Treas. Bot.* 1084/2 *Spinuloso-ciliate*, ciliated with fine spines.

spinulous ('spaɪnjʊləs), *a.* [f. SPINULE + -OUS.] = SPINULOSE *a.*

1846 DANA *Zooph.* (1848) 155 A few of the foliaceous Astræidæ..have the surface simply striated and spinulous. **1870** H. A. NICHOLSON *Man. Zool.* 108 The sclerobasis..in the latter..is always either smooth or spinulous.

spin-up ('spɪnʌp), *sb.* [f. SPIN *v.* + UP *adv.*[1]] An increase in the speed of rotation.

1960 *Jrnl. Geophysical Res.* LXV. 2994 (*caption*) Increased stability of both the theoretical and observed motion is seen after spinup. **1968** *New Scientist* 3 Oct. 8/2 The particular merit of the autogyro is that its rotor does not depend on engine power, except for the spin-up before take-off. **1969** *Nature* 29 Nov. 873/1 The time scale for the cracking and initial spin up is of the order of 0·01 to 0·1 s, the time for a shear wave in the crust to propagate a stellar radius. **1971** [see SPIN-DOWN *sb.*] **1977** *Astron. & Astrophysics* LX. 85/1 Subsequent retrograde spinup via thermally driven atmospheric tides can explain the present slow retrograde motion of the planet.

spin-up (spɪ'nʌp), *a. Physics.* [f. SPIN *sb.*[1] + UP *adv.*[2]] Being or pertaining to a particle with a spin pointing upwards.

1965 *Sci. Amer.* Jan. 106/3 The electrons' magnetic field at the nucleus is produced by..the net spin density, or the 'spin up' density minus the 'spin down' density. **1970** *Nature* 25 July 372/2 Four spin-up electrons at the corners of a tetrahedron and four spin-down electrons at the corners of an interpenetrating tetrahedron pointing the opposite way are arranged around each oxygen centre. **1973** *McGraw-Hill Yearbk. Sci. & Technol.* 287/1 With this technique, it is possible to calculate the difference between the spin-up and the spin-down populations in each electron shell. **1980** RUDDEN & WILSON *Elem. Solid State Physics* ii. 41 The first available electron is placed in the 1s spin-up state, the second in the 1s spin-down state.

spinx, rare variant of SPINK *sb.*[1]

1628 BURTON *Anat. Mel.* III. ii. III. i. (ed. 3) 468 Like a summer flye or Spinxes winges, or a raigne bow of all colours. **1823** E. MOOR *Suffolk Words, Spinx*, the chaffinch.

spiny ('spaɪnɪ), *a.* Also 6 spyny, 6–7 spinie, 7 spynie, 7–9 spiney. [f. SPINE *sb.*[1] + -Y.]

1. a. Having the characteristics of a thorn or thorns; resembling a thorn in form or qualities.

1586 KYD *Verses Praise & Joy* 1 Mongst spyny cares sprong vp now at the last. **1615** G. SANDYS *Trav.* 223 Psiloriti: from whose lofty and spiny top both seas may be discerned. **1663** COWLEY *Cutter Coleman St.* Pref., And so much for this little spiny objection which a man cannot see without a Magnifying Glass.

b. Thin and hard or dry; spare, lean.

Common in the first half of the 17th cent.

1598 FLORIO, *Smilzo*, bare, spinie, gant, leane, lanke. **1608** MIDDLETON *Mad World* III. ii, A little, short, old spiny gentleman. **1621** G. SANDYS *Ovid's Met.* VI. (1626) 111 Her thighs and legs to spiny fingers grow. **1650** BULWER *Anthropomet.* 232 The French commonly have more spinie and slender Legs then the Italian Gentleman. *a* **1722** [cf. *spiny-legged* in 5].

†**c.** Of turf or grass. *Obs.*

1607 J. CARPENTER *Plaine Mans Plough* 139 That which was old must be renewed, and the spinie turfe changed into a gentle soyle. **1615** G. SANDYS *Trav.* 198 The valley.. producing but a spiny grasse.

2. Abounding in, furnished or thickly set with, thorns. In early quots. *fig.*

1604 T. WRIGHT *Passions* I. iii. 11 Wee..touched the roote from whence did spring those spinie braunches of briarie passions. **1635** A. STAFFORD *Fem. Glory* (1860) 43 Bee constant, most pious Lordes, in the vertuous, though rough and spiny course you are to runne. **1644** DIGBY *Nat. Bodies* A iv b, So difficult and spiny an affaire, as the writing vpon such a nice and copious subiect. **1727** WARBURTON *Prodigies* 61 The spiney Desarts of Scholastic Philosophy. **1798** CHARLOTTE SMITH *Yng. Philos.* II. 164 The holly, whose shining thorny and spiny head..shadowed the whole eminence. **1830** LINDLEY *Nat. Syst. Bot.* 54 Shrubs, either unarmed or spiny. **1870** HOOKER *Stud. Flora* 127 Shrubs or small trees, often spiny.

3. a. Furnished or set with spines; covered with slender sharp-pointed processes.

1615 G. SANDYS *Trav.* 249 The body light, the taile spiny, and the colour dun. **1728** CHAMBERS *Cycl.* s.v. *Spine*, The hind Part thereof is Edg'd, or Spiny. **1778** *Encycl. Brit.* (ed. 2) III. 1610/1 The strigosus, or plated lobster, with a pyramidal spiny snout. **1804** CHARLOTTE SMITH *Conversations* II. 153 What endless swarms of creatures.. Of burnish'd scale and spiny fin! **1843** *Penny Cycl.* XXVI. 444 Shell oval, spiny or tuberculous. **1883** *Standard* 3 Aug. 5/7 Two..lizards with remarkable spiney skins.

Comb. **1857** T. MOORE *Handbk. Brit. Ferns* (ed. 3) 39 Pinnæ spiny-serrate.

b. In specific names of animals or fishes, as ***spiny ant-eater, dog fish, eel, globe-fish***, etc. **spiny rat**, a rodent of the family Echimyidæ, found in tropical South and Central America and distinguished by bristly fur.

1827 GRIFFITH tr. *Cuvier* III. 263 The Echidnes,..otherwise *Spiny Ant-eaters. **1894–5** LYDEKKER *Roy. Nat. Hist.* III. 286 The echidnas, or spiny anteaters, of which there are two species. **1896** *Ibid.* V. 533 The *spiny dog-fishes, rays, saw-fishes, and their kindred. **1882** JORDAN & GILBERT *Syn. Fishes N. Amer.* 368 *Mastacembelidæ.* (The *Spiny Eels.) **1896** LYDEKKER *Roy. Nat. Hist.* V. 395 The so-called spiny eels of the Oriental region and West Africa. **1834** GRIFFITH tr. *Cuvier* X. 566 Diodon, (Vulg. *Spiny globe-fish.) **1853** in Morris *Austral Eng.* (1898) 304/2 The *Spiny Lizard (*Moloch horridus*) of Western Australia. **1898** MORRIS *Austral Eng.* 430 *Spiny Lizard*, i.q. Mountain Devil. **1819** *Spiny lobster [see LOBSTER[1] 1 b]. **1862** ANSTED *Channel Isl.* II. ix. 233 The spiny lobster, locally called cray-fish.., is also very common. **1884** GOODE *Nat. Hist. Aquat. Anim.* 780 The Spiny Lobster or Rock Lobster, *Panulirus interruptus.* **1804** SHAW *Gen. Zool.* V. I. 4 *Spiny Loche... This is distinguished by a double spine situated on each side the head. **1884** *Encycl. Brit.* XVII. 6 *Acanthomys...* *Spiny-mice. **1894–5** LYDEKKER *Roy. Nat. Hist.* III. 119 The pretty little murine known as the Malabar spiny-mouse. **1876** A. R. WALLACE *Geogr. Distrib. Animals* II. xvii. 238 The Echimyidæ, or *spiny rats, are a family, chiefly South American. **1924** W. B. SCOTT *Hist. Land Mammals Western Hemisphere* v. 184 The spiny rats (*Echimys* and *Loncheres*) are so called from their appearance, not because they are related to the true rats. **1974** H. MACINNES *Climb to Lost World* ix. 147 A spiny rat, a rare creature: Mike Atherley and I both saw it more than once and thought that it had no tail. **1804** SHAW *Gen. Zool.* V. II. 342 *Spiny Shark. *Squalus Spinosus.* **1896** LYDEKKER *Roy. Nat. Hist.* V. 535 The spiny shark (*Echinorhinus spinosus*) of the Mediterranean and Atlantic. **1894–5** *Ibid.* III. 71 The Ethiopian *spiny squirrels are characterized by their coarse and spiny hair. **1879** E. P. WRIGHT *Anim. Life* 69 The *Spiny Tanrec (*Ericulus spinosus*). *c* **1880** *Cassell's Nat. Hist.* IV. 256 The *Spiny Trionyx, or Gymnopus.

4. Having the form of a spine; stiff and sharp-pointed.

1828 STARK *Elem. Nat. Hist.* I. 121 Fur ash gray,.. composed of rough spiny hairs. **1871** HUXLEY *Anat. Vert.* 318 The inner surface is often armed with spiny developments of the epidermis.

5. *Comb.*, as ***spiny-backed, -finned, -footed, -haired, -leaved***, etc. (Freq. in specific names.)

1885 HORNADAY *Two Years in Jungle* xxvi. 310 The fishermen catch and eat a good many *spiny-backed rays (*Urogymnus asperrimus*). **1881** *Cassell's Nat. Hist.* V. 78 Acanthopterygii, or *Spiny-finned fishes. **1802** SHAW *Gen. Zool.* III. I. 112 *Spiny-footed Frog. *Rana Spinipes.* **1829** GRIFFITH tr. *Cuvier* VI. 321 Spiny-footed Tyrant, *Tyrannus Calcaratus.* **1891** T. HARDY *Tess* (1900) 67 The pollard willows..became *spiny-haired monsters. **1847** DARLINGTON *Amer. Weeds*, etc. (1860) 206 The *Spiny-leaved Sow-thistle (*Sonchus Asper*). *a* **1722** LISLE *Husb.* (1757) 226 A *spiny legged beast never pays the grazier so well. **1866** *Treas. Bot.* 515/1 The leaves are pinnatifid with *spiny-pointed segments. **1880** GÜNTHER *Fishes* 41 The dorsal fin..is either *spiny-rayed, or soft-rayed. **1882** JORDAN & GILBERT *Syn. Fishes N. Amer.* 397 *Acanthopteri.* (The Spiny-rayed Fishes.) **1831** GRIFFITH tr. *Cuvier* IX. Syn. 38 *Spiny Tailed Guana. **1877** NEWTON in *Encycl. Brit.* VII. 505 The *Erismaturinæ* or Spiny-tailed Ducks.

†**spion.** *Obs.*$^{-1}$ In 7 spyon. [ad. F. *espion*, Sp. *espion*, or It. *spione.*] A spy or scout.

1615 HEYWOOD *Four Prentices* K j b, As assistants you haue vnder you The Serieant Maior, Quarter-maister, Prouost, And Captaine of the Spyons.

Spion Kop: see KOP 2.

spir, obs. form of SPEER *v.*[1], SPHERE *sb.*

†**spirable**, *a. Obs.* [ad. L. *spīrābilis*, f. *spīrāre* SPIRE *v.*[2] So It. *spirabile* Sp. *espirable.*]

1. Connected with breathing; having the power of breathing; respiratory.

1562 BULLEIN *Bulwarke, Bk. Simples* 25 It also is good.. for shorte windes in the spirable partes. **1576** NEWTON *Lemnie's Complex.* (1633) 215 It [death] is an abolishment and destruction of life and nature spirable. **1698** FRYER *Acc. E. India & P.* 311 We are followed by..continued Fevers, as well as those that accompany Catarrhs, from the Intemperament of the Spirable Parts.

2. Capable of being breathed; respirable.

1599 NASHE *Lenten Stuffe* 56 The spirable odor & pestilent steame ascending from it, put him out of his bias of congruity. **1610** HEALEY *St. Aug. Citie of God* XII. xiii. (1620) 723 The visible light, the spirable ayre, the potable water. **1715** tr. *Cicero's Tusculan Disp.* I. 20 That fortuitous jumbling together of light and round atoms, which Democritus, however, maintains to be warm and spirable. **1728** CHAMBERS *Cycl.* s.v. *Platonism*, The Starry Heaven, which he [Plato] teaches is not adamantine or solid, but liquid and spirable.

spiracle[1] ('spaɪərək(ə)l). Also 4 spyrakle, 5 -acle. [ad. L. *spīrācul-um* SPIRACULUM. So older F. *spiracle*, F. *spiracule*, It. *spiracolo, -aculo*, Sp. and Pg. *espiraculo.*]

†**1.** Breath, spirit. *Obs.*

Orig. after L. *spiraculum vitae* in Gen. ii. 7, vii. 22.

13.. *E.E. Allit. P.* B. 408 þenne mourkne in þe mudde most ful nede Alle þat spyrakle in-spranc. **1398** TREVISA *Barth. De P.R.* III. iii. (1495) 50 A soule is lyke to god a spiracle of lyfe. *Ibid.* 51 Oraclīphīcus [*sic*] callyth the soule lyghte other a spyrancle [*sic*] of beynge. **1607** B. BARNES *Devil's Charter* IV. ii, A bastard of our house,..In whom no sparke or spiracle of honor Appear'd. **1640** G. WATS *Bacon's Adv. Learn.* IV. iii. 207 We will stile that part of the generall knowledge concerning mans soule, the knowledge of the spiracle, or inspired substance. **1654** VILVAIN *Theorem. Theol.* Suppl. 261 Into which [body] he breathed the Spiracle or Spirit of Life.

2. A small opening by which a confined space has communication with the outer air; *esp.* an air-hole or air-shaft.

1620 tr. *Boccaccio's Decam.* 126 A cave..which received no light into it, but by a small spiracle or ventloope made out ingeniously on the hills side. **1661** EVELYN *Fumifugium* Misc. Writ. (1825) I. 220 Salt and sope boylers,..one of whose Spiracles does manifestly infect the aer more than all the chimnies of London. **1760–72** tr. *Juan & Ulloa's Voy.* (ed. 3) I. 472 There must have been here and there vent-holes, or spiracles. **1851** HAWTHORNE *Ho. Sev. Gables* i, The seven gables..presented the aspect of a whole sisterhood of edifices, breathing through the spiracles of one great chimney. **1856** J. STEVENSON *Ch. Historians Eng.* IV. II. 437 On splitting a vast rock..there appeared two dogs, but without any spiracle whatever.

fig. **1827** SCOTT *Napoleon* Misc. Wks. 1870 XIV. 326 The least spiracle, by which the voice of France could find its way to the ears of her sovereign.

b. *spec.* An opening in the ground affording egress to subterranean vapours or fiery matter; a volcanic vent-hole.

1671 R. BOHUN *Wind* 27 Wind, out of some cavityes and spiracles of the Earth. **1695** WOODWARD *Nat. Hist. Earth* III. (1723) 151 The *Camini* or Spiracles of Ætna. **1751** LAVINGTON *Enthus. Meth. & Papists* III. (1754) 120 Some Spiracles, or breathing Holes, in many Parts of the Earth, which scatter a pestilential Infection upon all that come near. **1762** tr. *Busching's Syst. Geog.* I. 216 The clefts and chasms which were the spiracles or outlets to those dreadful eructations. **1828** H. D. BESTE *Italy* 399 Other spiracles of mephitic might probably be found here. **1833** HERSCHEL *Astron.* v. 209 Powerful upward currents of the [sun's] atmosphere, arising, perhaps, from spiracles in the body. **1869** J. PHILLIPS *Vesuv.* viii. 209 A level place surrounded by fiery heights, having numerous chimney-like spiracles.

fig. **1833** CARLYLE *Misc. Ess., Diderot*, The subterranean fire..was here, we can say, forming itself a decided spiracle.

3. a. A pore *of* the skin. *rare.*

1650 H. BROOKE *Conserv. Health* 143 It [exercise] discusses Vapors and fuliginous excrements by the pores or Spiracles of the skin. **1837** MORIER *Abel Allnutt* xxxii. 188 The steam and fumes of the dinner..acting violently upon the spiracles of the skin belonging to the attendants.

b. A breathing-pore in the epidermis of plants; a stoma. *rare.*

a **1774** GOLDSM. *Surv. Exp. Philos.* (1776) II. 108 This undulation is very manifest in the spiracles of many plants viewed with the microscope. **1867** H. MACMILLAN *Bible Teach.* iii. (1870) 56 The whole stem being succulent and covered with spiracles or air-holes, thus acting as lungs along with the leaves.

c. *Zool.* A special aperture, orifice, or pore, chiefly in lower forms of animal life, by which respiration is effected.

1775 *Phil. Trans.* LXVI. 214 The torpedo..loosens the sands by flapping its fins, till its whole body, except the spiracles, is buried. **1797** *Encycl. Brit.* (ed. 3) XVII. 716/1 The teeth [of the saw-fish] are granulated;..and the spiracles five. **1816** KIRBY & SP. *Entomol.* xxi. (1818) II. 251 From a small hole just above each spiracle, [the insect] syringes a similar fluid in horizontal jets. **1847** *Proc. Berw. Nat. Club* II. 234 Prothoracic spiracle in most cases free and uncovered. **1882** *Entomol. Mag.* Mar. 220 A broad..stripe runs just above the spiracles, which are black.

transf. **1854** DE QUINCEY *War* Wks. 1862 IV. 286 The great phenomenon of war..keeps open in man a spiracle—an organ of respiration.

d. The blow-hole of a whale or other cetacean (and of certain sharks).

1796 BURKE *Let. to Noble Lord* Wks. VIII. 35 His whalebone, his blubber, the very spiracles through which he spouts a torrent of brine against his origin. **1849** *Sk. Nat. Hist., Mammalia* III. 146 The spiracle, or blow-hole, is a single orifice of a semicircular form, on the top of the head, directly over the eyes. **1898** F. T. BULLEN *Cruise 'Cachalot'* 192 A whale can no more force water through its spiracle or blow-hole than you or I through our nostrils.

'spiracle[2]. *rare*$^{-1}$. [f. SPIRE *sb.*[1] 8.] A little spire; a pinnacle.

1842 *Tait's Mag.* IX. 636/1 The fine old cathedral, with its eager crowds bending over buttress and spiracle.

spiracular (spaɪ'rækjʊlə(r)), *a. Zool.* [f. SPIRACUL-UM + -AR.] Of or pertaining to, serving as, a spiracle or spiracles.

1840 F. D. BENNETT *Whaling Voy.* II. 151 The spiracular canals of spouting-whales. **1848** *Proc. Berw. Nat. Club* II. 339 Spiracular lines not very distinct. **1880** GÜNTHER *Fishes* 80 They form a valve for the protection of the spiracular orifice of these fishes.

spi'raculiform, *a. Ent.* [f. next: see -FORM.] Having the form of a spiracle.

1826 KIRBY & SP. *Entomol.* III. 16 The openings for the entrance of the air spiraculiform. *Ibid.* IV. 128 The spiraculiform pores that mark the sides of the animal.

‖**spiraculum** (spaɪ'rækjʊləm). Pl. **-acula**. [L. *spīrāculum*, f. *spīrāre* to breathe.]

1. = SPIRACLE[1] 2 b.

a **1668** LASSELS *Voy. Italy* (1670) II. 295 There are divers *spiracula*, or Vents round about it, out of which the thick smoke presseth furiously. *a* **1705** RAY *Disc.* II. (1713) 13 The enclosed Fire was not of Force sufficient to make its way out, or found not *Spiracula* to vent itself. **1789** E. DARWIN *Bot. Gard.* I. (1791) Notes 12 The volcanos themselves appear to be spiracula or chimneys belonging to great central fires. **1820** T. S. HUGHES *Trav. Sicily* I. iv. 115 It contains two principal spiracula, or vents, from whence..huge stones and rocks are precipitated.

2. = SPIRACLE[1] 2.

a **1734** NORTH *Examen* II. v. §74 (1740) 360 Like a Chymist's Fire,..upon opening the Spiracula of the Furnace..the Flame broke out.

3. *Zool.* = SPIRACLE[1] 3 c.

1768 G. WHITE *Selborne* xiv, If some curious gentleman would procure the head of a fallow deer..he would find it furnished with two spiracula, or breathing places, besides the nostrils. **1797** *Encycl. Brit.* (ed. 3) VI. 676/2 All insects ..respire through pores..which are termed *spiracula.* **1816** KIRBY & SP. *Entomol.* (1818) II. 425 The remarkably large spiracula in glow-worms. **1878** F. J. BELL *Gegenbaur's Comp. Anat.* 396 Peripheral nerves pass out from the anterior ganglion... Others pass backwards to the spiracula.

‖**spiræa** (spaɪ'riːə). *Bot.* Also **spirea**. [L. *spīræa*, ad. Gr. σπειραία, app. f. σπεῖρα SPIRE *sb.*[3] Cf. F. *spirée*, Sp. *espirea*, and SPIREY.]

1. One or other species of an extensive genus of rosaceous plants or shrubs, many of which are largely cultivated for their handsome foliage and flowers.

The cultivated species are of foreign origin; but *Spiræa Ulmaria*, meadow-sweet, and *S. filipendula*, dropwort, are common wild plants in Britain.

1669 EVELYN *Kal. Hort.* (ed. 3) 90 Flowers in Prime,.. Pome-granads double, and single Flowers, Shrub *Spiræa, Agnus Castus.* *c* **1711** PETIVER *Gazophyl.* IX. lxxxix, Cape Spirea with white loose Flowers. **1731** P. MILLER *Gard. Dict.* s.v. *Spiræa frutex*, Spiræa with a Marsh-Elder Leaf. *Ibid.*, Sweet-scented African Spiræa with hairy Leaves. **1753** *Chambers' Cycl.* Suppl. s.v., 1. The willow-leaved *spiræa*. 2. The opulus-leaved *spiræa* [etc.]. **1760** J. LEE *Introd. Bot.* App. 328 Spiræa, African, *Diosma*. **1888** MISS BRADDON *Fatal Three* I. ii, Half hidden amidst the bank of feathery white spirea. **1894** *Daily News* 17 July 6/5 The leafy spiræa is much used for such decorations.

b. With *a* and pl. A single plant or shrub, or one particular species, of this genus.

1731 *Gentl. Mag.* I. 40 All sorts of flowering Shrubs which bear the Weather, as Roses,.. Lilac, Spireas, Altheas. **1846** LINDLEY *Veget. Kingd.* 563 Section of the flower of a Spiræa. **1868** *Rep. U.S. Commissioner Agric.* (1869) 85 The beetle frequents flowers; a great number were taken..on the flowers of a spiræa. **1886** *Pall Mall G.* 24 Apr. 7/2 Spireas, gardenias, narcissi, and lilies of the valley.

2. The genus composed of these plants.

1753 *Chambers' Cycl.* Suppl. s.v., The species of *spiræa*, enumerated by Mr. Tournefort, are these. **1797** *Encycl. Brit.* (ed. 3) XVII 697/2 *Spiræa*, in botany: A genus of plants .. in the natural system arranged under the 26th order. **1866** *Treas. Bot.* 1084/2 Of the foreign shrubby kinds of *Spiræa* some are very handsome.

3. *oil of spiræa*: (see quot. 1857).

1842 [see SALICYLOUS *a.*]. **1857** MILLER *Elem. Chem. Org.* vii. 479 Oil of Spiræa,.. Hydride of Salicyl; Salicylous Acid. **1866** ODLING *Anim. Chem.* 58 He might produce..oil of spiræa, for instance, from salicin.

spi'ræin. *Chem.* [f. prec. So F. *spiréine.*] A yellow crystalline powder obtained from the flowers of meadow-sweet (*Spiræa ulmaria*).

1868 WATTS *Dict. Chem.* s.v. *Spiræa*, When the dried flowers of meadow-sweet are exhausted with ether, a colouring-matter called spiræin is dissolved out.

†**spirage**, variant of SPERAGE *Obs.*

1647 HEXHAM I. (*Herbs*), Spirage, *Spergel-kruydt.* Wild Spirage, *Wildt Spergel-kruydt.*

spiral ('spaɪərəl), *sb.* [Subst. use of next. Cf. F. *spirale* fem. (also *spiral* masc., spiral spring), It. *spirale.*]

1. *Geom.* A continuous curve traced by a point moving round a fixed point in the same plane while steadily increasing (or diminishing) its distance from this.

spiral of Archimedes, a curve traced by a point moving uniformly along a line which at the same time revolves uniformly round a fixed point in itself. ***equiangular, hyperbolic, logarithmic, loxodromic, parabolic spiral***: see these words.

1656 tr. *Hobbes' Elem. Philos.* xvii. 194 The description of Archimedes his Spiral, which is done by the continual diminution of the Semidiameter of a Circle in the same proportion in which the Circumference is diminished. **1697** DRYDEN *Virg. Georg.* Ded. (1721) I. 179 At that time the Diurnal Motion of the Sun partakes more of a Right Line than of a Spiral. **1728** CHAMBERS *Cycl.* s.v., Then will the Points *M m, m*, &c. be Points in the Spiral, which connected, will give the Spiral itself. **1816** C. BABBAGE tr. *Lacroix' Different. & Integr. Calculus* 128 The spirals compose another class of transcendental curves. **1869** RANKINE *Machinery & Millwork* 54 Each point in the secondary piece ..describes a plane spiral about the fixed axis. **1882** MINCHIN *Umplanar Kinematics* 50 Prove that the Space Centrode is a parabola and the Body Centrode a spiral of Archimedes.

fig. **1845–6** TRENCH *Huls. Lect.* Ser. I. iv. 57 The advance may sometimes be rather in a spiral than in a straight line. **1848** H. ROGERS *Ess.* (1874) I. vi. 319 Other questions succeed,.. gradually approaching in one long spiral of interrogations the central position.

2. a. A curve traced by a point moving round, and simultaneously advancing along, a cylinder or cone; a helix or screw-line.

The *spiral* has sometimes been distinguished from the *helix*: see quot. 1728.

1670 COLLINS in Rigaud *Corr. Sci. Men* (1841) I. 147 The spiral described by the compound motion of a heavy body falling to the centre of the earth. **1681** tr. *Willis' Rem. Med. Wks.* Vocab., *Spiral*, a turning about, and as it were ascending. **1728** CHAMBERS *Cycl.*, *Spiral*, in Architecture, Sculpture, &c. is a Curve that ascends, winding about a Cone... By this it is distinguished from the Helix, which winds..around a Cylinder. **1788** *New Lond. Mag.* 44 The length of the Spiral described by the fly in passing from one pole to the other. **1835** MRS. SOMERVILLE *Connex. Phys. Sci.* (ed. 2) xvii. 172 By thus tracing these nodal lines he discovered that they twist in a spiral or corkscrew round rods and cylinders. **1876** VOYLE & STEVENSON *Milit. Dict.* 198/2 *Increasing Spiral*, a term applied to the twist or the spiral inclination of the grooves of rifled arms.

b. The degree in which the successive circles of such a curve approach each other.

1846 GREENER *Sci. Gunnery* 348 From the peculiar nature of the powder..the extreme spiral given to their grooves was required. **1864** *Daily Tel.* 1 Aug., Making the arm shoot well, is simply matter of detail, involving considerations of length of barrel, character and spiral of rifling.

c. *U.S. Football.* A kick or pass in which the ball in flight spins round its long axis.

1896 CAMP & DELAND *Football* vi. 61 *Spiral*, a kick similar to the twister, in which the ball maintains a true course while revolving on its long axis. **1910** W. CAMP *Book of Foot-Ball* viii. 308 Long passes are best made by holding the ball like a spear and sending a spiral. **1972** J. MOSEDALE *Football* v. 69 Fourteen times his soft spirals connected, for 216 yards.

d. *fig.* A progressive movement in one direction (esp. upwards or downwards, and marking a relentlessly deteriorating state of affairs), considered to take the form of a spiral; *spec.* one caused by the interaction or alternate overtaking of interdependent quantities; ***vicious spiral***: see VICIOUS *a.* 9.

1897 P. GEDDES *Let.* 10 Feb. in P. Boardman *Worlds of P. Geddes* (1978) vi. 155 New money = new crime = new report.. = new police and so on, in downward spiral. **1931**, etc. [see INFLATIONARY *a.*]. **1939** *Economist* 16 Dec. 405 The fear of an accelerating spiral of wages and prices. **1958** *Spectator* 15 Aug. 211/1 Steps to avoid a new arms race spiral. **1965** *Listener* 23 Sept. 439/2 We have got to get rid of the endless spiral, price increases and pay claims. **1975** *Physics Bull.* Aug. 345/1 The tendency for departments with the highest demand for undergraduate places to take the largest slice of the UGC cake has meant that engineering and physical science departments have fallen into a spiral of fewer students resulting in lower grants. **1980** *Times* 15 Jan. 14 Price of antique silver follows the gold spiral.

e. *Aeronaut.* A descent (or, rarely, a climb) made by an aircraft in the form of a helix; a continuous banking turn accompanying a descent or ascent.

1910 *Sphere* 30 July 103/2 This descent..was composed of several high-speed dives and short spirals. **1918** E. M. ROBERTS *Flying Fighter* 272 When I came out of my spiral, ..my engine would not start again. *Ibid.* 301 The Hun machine started upward in a spiral. **1941** POPE & OTIS *Elements of Aeronaut.* ix. 85 The spiral, usually done with power off, is merely a gliding turn, continued to make several complete turns, gradually descending. **1975** G. H. SAUNDERS *Dynamics of Helicopter Flight* v. 178 A neutrally stable spiral would require the pilot to take back out his cyclic input once his desired bank angle has been achieved.

3. a. A piece of wire coiled into a spiral form.

1825 *Annals Philosophy* X. 52 After which the extremity of the spiral being tied hard,.. I put the covered wire in a vice. **1881** J. HATTON *New Ceylon* vi. 154 Men and women alike wear the neck spiral, and the former also a closely-fitting spiral around their biceps. **1885** C. G. W. LOCK *Workshop Rec.* Ser. IV. 298/2 The spirals of the key-board must be bent their right shape.

b. *Bot.* A spiral vessel in plants.

1837 P. KEITH *Bot. Lex.* 241 According to Raspail it is composed of cells, tubes, and spirals yet visible. *Ibid.* 288 They have neither stomata nor spirals: hence they can neither form the green chromule, nor exhale moisture.

c. *Astr.* A spiral nebula.

1850 LD. ROSSE in *Phil. Trans. R. Soc.* CXL. 511 Night excellent, a spiral seen in an oblique direction, resolved well, particularly towards the centre, where it is very bright. **1866** LOCKYER *Guillemin's Heavens* 400 Brilliant spirals, unequally luminous,..diverge from the centre, and become separated..as they recede from it. **1881** G. F. CHAMBERS *Smyth's Celestial Cycle* 38 One of Lord Rosse's 'spirals'.

d. In general use: Any object having a spiral form.

1853 JAMES *Agnes Sorel* i, The stair-case was one of those narrow, twisting spirals. **1858** LARDNER *Handbk. Nat. Phil.* 119 In practice, the spiral through which the water is carried is not in the form of a tube. **1883** *Harper's Mag.* Aug. 375/2 Misfortune awaits the boat that ventures into this watery spiral. **1890** J. GAGNEY tr. *Jaksch's Clin. Diagnosis* iv. 70 The spirals are often overlaid with epithelium.

4. One of the separate circles or coils of a spiral or helical object. Cf. SPIRE *sb.*³ 1.

1728 CHAMBERS *Cycl.* s.v. *Screw*, The said Distance between the Spirals..of the Screw. *c* **1790** IMISON *Sch. Arts* I. 23 Supposing the distance of the spirals to be half an inch. **1825** J. NICHOLSON *Operat. Mechanic* 240 If, there-fore, a pipe of uniform bore be wrapped round a conic frustrum,.. the spirals will be very nearly such as will answer the purpose. **1891** KIPLING *Light that Failed* (1900) 272 He stroked the creaseless spirals of his leggings.

spiral ('spaɪərəl), *a.*¹ and *adv.* [ad. med.L. *spīrāl-is* (Albertus Magnus, *a* 1255), whence also F. *spiral*, It. *spirale*, Sp. *espiral.*]

1. Forming a succession of curves arranged like the thread of a screw; coiled in a cylindrical or conical manner; helical: **a.** In general use.

1551 RECORDE *Castle Knowl.* (1556) 249 In going betweene the firste degree of Capricorne, and the fyrste of Cancer, he..maketh aboue 182 reuolutions lyke spiral circles. **1668** WILKINS *Real Char.* 129 [Shells] more short in the spiral production, considerable for having a Purple juice. **1693** BENTLEY *Atheism* v. 17 The Spiral, and not Annulary, Fibres of the Intestines. **1712** tr. *Pomet's Hist. Drugs* I. 38 Little, thin, black Seeds, each one having a spiral head. **1781** COWPER *Retirem.* 231 As woodbine..In spiral rings ascends the trunk. **1805** SOUTHEY *Madoc in Azt.* x. 217 Then louder from the spiral sea-shell's depth Swell'd the full roar. **1825** J. NICHOLSON *Operat. Mechanic* 246 The spiral tubes in that axle take up the water. *a* **1878** SIR G. SCOTT *Lect. Archit.* (1879) II. 125 The intermediate pier is a round column,..with spiral flutings.

b. Of an ascending or descending course or path.

See also *spiral stair* in 3.

1794 R. J. SULIVAN *View Nat.* II. 46 Local lower heat, and proportionate superior cold, causes the rarefaction, which gives the spiral ascent. **1825** LONGF. *Sunrise on Hills* 18 Where upward.. The noisy bittern wheeled his spiral way. **1841** *Penny Cycl.* XXI. 173/2 An almost circular mountain of considerable height, which is ascended by a spiral road. **1876** T. HARDY *Ethelberta* (1890) 264 They paced the remainder of their spiral pathway in silence. **1908** F. W. LANCHESTER *Aerodonetics* vii. 180 The aerodrone..loses its equilibrium and comes rapidly to earth with a kind of spiral dive. **1912** *Flight* 31 Aug. 787/1 The machine at once started a spiral nose-dive. **1939** *Aircraft Engin.* XI. 40/3 There are many references to spiral or corkscrew descent in the literature..but this always implies a fully controllable motion at an angle of incidence below the critical angle; very different to the spin proper. **1961** C. B. SMITH *Testing Time* 53 To their horror, the men on the ground saw the aircraft drop out of control into a whirling dive, the 'spiral dive' which they knew meant almost certain death.

c. With abstract sbs.

1829 T. CASTLE *Introd. Bot.* 234 Losing the spiral character. **1831** SIR J. SINCLAIR *Corr.* II. 264 They have.. a species of the pigeon, which fly in a spiral or circular manner, upon one wing. **1860** EMERSON *Cond. Life, Beauty* Wks. (Bohn) II. 428 The spiral tendency of vegetation infects education also. **1880** BESSEY *Botany* 29 Good examples of ringed, spiral, and reticulated thickening.

fig. **1878** O. W. HOLMES *Motley* xvii. 115 That progress is by a spiral movement seems to be a law of Providence.

d. *Surg.* Of a fracture: curving round a long bone lengthwise.

1897 *Lippincott's Med. Dict.* 955/2 Spiral fracture. **1934** *Practitioners Library Med. & Surg.* V. ii. 301 Fractures of the Shaft of the Femur... Nonunion may occur... This is likely to happen in the oblique or spiral types. **1950** *Brit. Encycl. Med. Pract.* (ed. 2) IV. 369 (*caption*) Spiral fracture of tibia in boy aged 8 years, three weeks after accident; no clinical signs or symptoms except his refusal to use his leg. **1976** M. MACHLIN *Pipeline* xlii. 455 At the Medical Center Hospitals in Houston they had told him that the spiral break would take at least six months to heal to the point where the cast could be removed.

2. Curving continuously round a fixed point in the same plane at a steadily increasing (or diminishing) distance from it.

a **1639** WOTTON *Reliq.* (1651) 231 The Capitall..in a spirall wreathing, which they call the Ionian Voluta. **1656** tr. *Hobbes' Elem. Philos.* xvii. 194 That space in the Circle.. without the Spiral Line. **1728** CHAMBERS *Cycl.* s.v., The curve B..is called a Spiral Line, and the plain Space contained between the Spiral Line, and the Right Line BA, is called the Spiral Space. **1796** H. HUNTER tr. *St.-Pierre's Stud. Nat.* (1799) I. 562 They are disposed in the direction of a spiral line winding from East to West. **1833** SIR C. BELL *Hand* (1834) 204 Wherever the sense of feeling is most exquisite, there are minute spiral ridges of cuticle. **1870** F. R. WILSON *Ch. Lindisf.* 90 Among some bold spiral curves ..a hound-like quadruped is represented. **1895** W. MACPHERSON *Monymusk* I. 4 The tracings of the characteristic spiral ornaments..are still visible.

3. a. In various special collocations (chiefly in sense 1), as ***spiral bit, cam, pump, spring, stair***, etc. ***spiral bevel gear***, a bevel gear that is also a spiral gear; ***spiral binding***, a book binding in which a helical wire passes through a closely spaced row of holes near the inside edge of each leaf; so ***spiral-bound*** adj.; ***spiral divergence*** (Aeronaut.) = *spiral instability* below; ***spiral gear***, a gear wheel whose teeth are cut obliquely to the axis of the wheel and are curved to form part of what is approximately a spiral or helix; *esp.* a skew gear of this kind; so ***spiral gearing***; ***spiral instability*** (Aeronaut.), an instability in which an aeroplane undergoing a banked turn tends to enter a descending spiral as a result of sideslipping and reduction of the radius of turn; ***spiral stability*** (Aeronaut.), the capactiy of an aeroplane not to enter a spiral while executing a banked turn, or to recover from a steeply-banked spiral path.

spiral auger, battery, punch, screw, etc., are described by Knight *Dict. Mech.* (1875–84).

1915 V. W. PAGÉ *Automobile Repairing* ix. 767 The advantages of the *spiral bevel gear are mainly due to the shape of the teeth which roll into engagement more smoothly than the ordinary form of bevel gears. **1973** *Transmission & Rear Axle—Bedford Trucks & Coaches* (Vauxhall Motors) 168 The differential, spiral bevel gear and pinion can be serviced without removing axle from vehicle. **1949** MELCHER & LARRICK *Printing & Promotion Handbk.* 280/2 *Spiral binding, see *mechanical bindings*. **1968** F. H. HOLLIDAY *Man. Stationery, Office Machines & Equipment* II. viii. 440 The sheets..are fed on to a conveyor to be trimmed, knocked up and punched to receive the spiral binding. **1876** VOYLE & STEVENSON *Milit. Dict.* 40/2 **Spiral Bit*, a gun implement used for clearing the vents of ordnance when choked. **1961** *Lebende Sprachen* VI. 104/1 *Spiral-bound stenographer's notebook. **1969** D. FRANCIS *Enquiry* iii. 37 He stood..holding a spiral bound notebook. **1976** E. WARD *Hanged Man* xxxi. 200 A thick spiral-bound document. **1855** OGILVIE *Suppl.*, **Spiral Cam*,..the solid cam.., when the ridge is formed spirally on the cone. **1949** *Jrnl. R. Aeronaut. Soc.* LIII. 541/1 There are two common kinds of aircraft instability which usually would be judged tolerable according to the above criterion. These are the phugoid oscillation (longitudinal-symmetric motion) and the *spiral divergence (lateral-antisymmetric motion). **1970** T. HACKER *Flight Stability & Control* vii. 159 The possibility of eliminating spiral divergence by design can be made to stand out by means of stability diagrams. **1888** J. G. HORNER *Lockwood's Dict. Mech. Engin.* 338 **Spiral gear*, includes helical, stepped, and worm gearing. **1914** —— *Gear Cutting* v. 48 Since the special gear-cutting machines have come into general use, the manufacture of spiral gears has been established on a better commercial basis than hitherto. **1971** B. SCHARF *Engin. & its Lang.* xii. 155 In some types of multiple gear train, the same gear drives a helical gear (with parallel axis) as well as a spiral gear (with skew axis). *a* **1877** KNIGHT *Dict. Mech.* III. 2275/1 **Spiral gearing*, a gear-wheel having meshing spiral ribs and grooves. The teeth run around the periphery of the gear-wheel, and meet in an angle on a line midway from either edge of the wheel. **1930** *Engineering* 2 May 559/2 Spiral gearing has been found to have many valuable applications. **1914** L. BAIRSTOW et al. *Rep. & Mem. Advisory Comm. for Aeronautics* No. 77. 168 A machine which is liable to *spiral instability when gyroscopic actions are eliminated, cannot become stable owing to gyroscopic action of the propeller and engine. **1970** T. HACKER *Flight Stability & Control* vii. 162 The elimination of spiral instability..is achieved by the constraint of the angle of bank ϕ, obviously in addition to correcting the heading. **1728** CHAMBERS *Cycl.* s.v. *Screw*, Archimedes's Screw, or the *Spiral Pump, a Machine for the Raising of Water. **1815** J. SMITH *Panorama Sci. & Art* II. 120 If we wind a pipe round a cylinder, of which the axis is horizontal, and connect one end with a vertical tube, while the other..is at liberty to turn round.., the machine is called a spiral pump. **1884** KNIGHT *Dict. Mech.* Suppl. 842/1 *Spiral Pump*, a pump that raises its water by a spiral flange or screw, on the principle of the Archimedean screw. **1690** LOCKE *Hum. Und.* III. vi. §38 Some [watches] have the Balance loose, and others regulated by a *spiral Spring. **1869** RANKINE *Machine & Hand-tools* Pl. H9, The projecting piece, *a*, is kept up to the slide, *b*,..by means of the spiral spring and die, *h*. **1947** C. F. TOMS *Introd. Aeronautics* v. 222 The use of a certain amount of dihedral ..is essential for both directional and *spiral stability. **1978** M. SIMONS *Model Aircraft Aerodynamics* xi. 126 If the model is primarily a thermal soarer..effort should be concentrated on spiral stability. **1624** WOTTON *Archit.* (1672) 37 *Spiral, or Cockle Stairs. **1728** CHAMBERS *Cycl.* s.v., Spiral Stairs, in Building. **1839** W. CHAMBERS *Tour Holland* 40/1 We were conducted by a spiral stair to the higher part of the tower. **1756–7** tr. *Keysler's Trav.* (1760) II. 457 This column, with its *spiral stair-case,..was restored to its former beauty by Pope Sixtus V. **1840** LARDNER *Geom.* 245 Such a spiral surface is the form of spiral staircases, sometimes called geometrical staircases. **1850** OGILVIE, **Spiral-Wheels*, in mill work, a species of gearing much used in the textile manufactures. **1883** GRESLEY *Gloss. Coal-m.* 231 **Spiral worm*, a tool for extricating broken boring rods.

b. *Bot.* in ***spiral cell, thickening, tube, vessel.***

1832 LINDLEY *Introd. Bot.* 17 Spiral vessels..are membranous tubes with conical extremities; their inside being occupied by a fibre twisted spirally. **1837** P. KEITH *Bot. Lex.* 10 A revival of Grew's first opinion with regard to the function of the spiral tubes. **1861** BENTLEY *Man. Bot.* 15 In some cells the fibre forms are uninterrupted spiral from one end to the other: such are termed spiral cells. **1884** BOWER & SCOTT *De Bary's Phaner.* 157 This is the case in the closely-wound spiral tubes, which show transitional forms to the reticulate. **1933** *Trop. Woods* XXXVI. 4 Spiral Thickenings.—Helical ridges on the inner face of, and a part of, the secondary wall. **1953** K. ESAU *Plant Anat.* xi. 228 Such secondary thickenings [of the xylem] are called, respectively, annular, spiral or helical, and reticulate.

c. *Zool.* in specific names (see quots.). Also ***spiral cleavage***, a pattern of embryogenesis characteristic of certain invertebrate groups, in which the third cell division is asymmetrical and destroys all but four-fold rotational symmetry.

1802 SHAW *Gen. Zool.* III. II. 564 Spiral Hydrus... Yellowish Hydrus with..spirally contorted body. **1861** P. P. CARPENTER in *Rep. Smithsonian Instit. 1860*, 244 Family *Limacinidæ*. (Spiral Pteropods.) **1892** E. B. WILSON in *Jrnl. Morphol.* VI. 377 The events of the cleavage fall into three very marked periods which I shall designate respectively as the (1) spiral, (2) transitional, and (3) bilateral periods. *Ibid.* 441 The third spiral cleavage of the primary micromeres gives rise to four apical cells. **1948** *New Biol.* V. 113 The same fundamental pattern (called spiral cleavage because of the oblique direction of many of the divisions; the actual pattern of cells resulting is not a spiral) is found also in other groups, such as the flatworms. **1967** L. A. BORRADAILE et al. *Invertebrata* i. 2 The annelid superphylum has eggs that develop by means of spiral cleavage. When the blastula divides from the four-cell stage to the eight-cell stage the second quartet lie on top of and between the cells of the first quartet.

d. In attributive combs. (see quots.).

1846 JOYCE *Sci. Dial.* viii. 18 By means of one of those steel spiral-spring instruments..the fact might be ascertained. **1862** *Catal. Internat. Exhib., Brit.* II. No. 3500, Patent spiral-spring trusses. **1875** KNIGHT *Dict. Mech.* 2276 Spiral-vane Steam-engine. **1884** *Ibid.* Suppl. 842/1 Spiral Tube Boiler.

e. *Astr.* Special collocations in sense 2, as: ***spiral arm***, an arm of a spiral galaxy; ***spiral galaxy***, a galaxy in which bright stars and gas clouds tend to be located along arms that appear to spiral from a central nucleus; ***spiral nebula***, a spiral galaxy (now chiefly *Hist.*)

1914 A. S. EDDINGTON *Stellar Movements & Struct. of Universe* xi. 243 The star clouds of the Milky Way form its [*sc.* our galaxy's] *spiral arms. **1978** PASACHOFF & KUTNER *University Astron.* xxiii. 582 The interstellar extinction prevents us from studying parts of the spiral arms farther away from the sun. **1913** *Astrophysical Jrnl.* XXXVII. 112 The stellar accumulations might be arranged so as to produce the phenomenon of the Milky Way—on the supposition of a *spiral galaxy. **1944** H. SHAPLEY *Galaxies* i. 26 The subclassifications of bright spheroidal and spiral galaxies..are possible only for those systems near enough for large-scale photography. **1980** *Sky & Telescope* July 25 By studying star formation in spiral galaxies, we can do more than test theories of spiral structure. **1850** LD. ROSSE in *Phil. Trans. R. Soc.* CXL. 505 The other *spiral nebulæ discovered up to the present time are comparatively difficult to be seen. **1920** A. S. EDDINGTON *Space, Time & Gravitation* x. 160 The most remote objects known are the spiral nebulae, whose distances may perhaps be of the order a million light years. **1978** PASACHOFF & KUTNER *University Astron.* xxiii. 572 Another class of objects was once known as 'spiral nebulae'... However, these spiral nebulae are now known to be galaxies in their own right.

4. As *adv.* = SPIRALLY *adv.*[1]

1726 LEONI *Alberti's Archit.* II. 36/1 Those chanels that run spiral about the shaft. **1884** KNIGHT *Dict. Mech.* Suppl. 842/1 Plates laid together with something to maintain their distance and then rolled together spiral.

5. = *spiral-bound* adj., sense 3 a above.

1977 H. GREENE *FSO-1* ix. 83 [He] whipped out large black reading glasses, and peered downward at a spiral pad. **1978** R. THOMAS *Chinaman's Chance* xiii. 135 Durant was seated on the couch..a secretary's spiral notebook in his lap.

6. *Comb.*, as ***spiral-coated, -grooved, -horned, -pointed*** adjs.; ***spiral-wise*** adv.

1728 CHAMBERS *Cycl.*, The *Screw*..is a right Cylinder.. furrow'd Spiral-wise. **1807** J. E. SMITH *Phys. Bot.* 200 The sap must soon flow out of those spiral-coated tubes. **1827** G. HIGGINS *Celtic Druids* xlvi, A low spiral-pointed roof of stone. **1864** *Athenæum* 5 Mar. 342/2 Mr. Cuming also exhibited two [pins],..the heads of which are spiral-wise. **1884** KNIGHT *Dict. Mech.* Suppl. 842/1 The spiral grooved guide is a wrought-iron tube. **1894** LYDEKKER *Roy. Nat. Hist.* II. 250 The Himalayan markhor..or spiral-horned goat.

spiral (ˈspaɪərəl), *a.*[2] [f. SPIRE *sb.*[1] + -AL[1].] Rising like a spire; tall and tapering or pointed:

a. Of rocks, edifices, etc.

1658 PHILLIPS, *Spiral*, belonging to a pyramid or spire-steeple. **1665** J. WEBB *Stone-Heng* (1725) 181 Trophies.. were evermore made of high and spiral Stones: And they will have these..which are high and spiral, to be, not a Trophy, but a place for electing of Kings. **1740** DYER *Ruins Rome* 138 The spiral tomb Of ancient Chammos. **1772–84** *Cook's Voy.* (1790) V. 1675 The various summits which are spiral cannot be viewed without exciting the most awful ideas.

b. Of trees.

1729 SAVAGE *Wanderer* IV. 15 Turning, with sighs, far spiral firs he sees. *c* **1750** SHENSTONE *Elegies* xxiii. 91 Cheer'd by the verdure of my spiral wood. **1827** STEUART *Planter's G.* (1828) 338 It is indispensably necessary..that the standard or grove Trees should be kept spiral, and the underwood subordinate in its character. **1842** J. WILSON *Chr. North* I. 365 The sweet Furness Fells,..among its spiral larches showing..groves and copses of the old unviolated woods.

spiral (ˈspaɪrəl), *v.* [f. SPIRAL *sb.*]

1. a. *intr.* To wind or move in a spiral manner; to form spiral curves.

1834 M. SCOTT *Cruise Midge* xx, We began to ascend the narrow corkscrew path that spiralled through the rocky grass-piece. **1851** H. MELVILLE *Whale* III. 117 The.. curling line buoyantly rising and spiralling towards the air. **1904** E. ROBINS *Magnetic North* vii. 124 It curled and spiralled, and described..involved and long-looped flourishes.

b. To fly an aircraft in a spiral path. Also with *down, downwards.*

1916 E. C. MIDDLETON *Aircraft* iii. 33 The pilot either 'spirals' or glides down, until he is able to ascertain the direction of the prevailing wind. **1922** H. L. FOSTER *Adventures of Tropical Tramp* xi. 173 The aviator spiraled downwards towards his landing place. **1941** POPE & OTIS *Elements of Aeronautics* ix. 85 Practice is required..to spiral over a fixed spot when the wind is blowing. **1978** M. SIMONS *Model Aircraft Aerodynamics* iv. 37 Even better rates of climb would result if the model did not have to spiral.

c. *fig.* To move rapidly in one direction (usu. upwards), in a manner considered to resemble a spiral; to increase or decrease in response to the same movement of another quantity or other quantities. Cf. sense 2 d of the sb. above.

1922 H. CRANE *Let.* c 18 June (1965) 91 Under the influence of aether and *amnesia* my mind spiraled to a kind of seventh heaven of consciousness. **1941** *Time* 20 Oct. 35/1 Even if import and farm prices resist all controls, processors' and retailers' prices will rise but not spiral with them. **1942** E. W. KEMMERER *ABC of Inflation* 156 If wages and the prices of farm products are not adequately restricted but are permitted to spiral upward..the whole price situation will get out of control. **1959** *Listener* 18 June 1052/1 The cost of living has spiralled. **1977** *Milestones* Summer 19/1 A similar table published in the Autumn 1974 issue of *Milestones* shows how much the cost of spare parts has spiralled. **1979** *Tucson* (Arizona) *Citizen* 20 Sept. 1A/4 The dollar spiraled downward on European money markets today. **1979** *Daily Tel.* 5 Dec. 21 The..risks of sending demand, output and tax revenue spiralling down again while the cost of spending programmes such as unemployment benefit..spiral up.

2. *trans.* To twist or coil spirally.

1867 F. FRANCIS *Angling* vi. (1880) 226 Spiral it round to lash it on to the hook.

Hence ˈ**spiralling** *ppl. a.* and *vbl. sb.*

1944 AUDEN *For Time Being* (1945) 90 Even the problems of Trade Cycles And Spiralling Prices are regarded by the experts As practically solved. **1958** *Spectator* 18 July 92/3 The twin threat of a renewed world currency crisis and a spiralling of trade restriction. **1965** [see OH-SO *adv.*]. **1969** H. PERKIN *Key Profession* iv. 138 The post-war situation of spiralling prices and incomes. **1979** E. H. GOMBRICH *Sense of Order* vi. 160 Spiralling terminations suggest the curling of elastic matter. **1979** *Nature* 14 June 622/1 Viscous drag on the planet's orbital motion would then lead to a spiralling into the stellar core. **1980** *Oxf. Diocesan Mag.* June 7/2 The failure of extrinsic motivation to fill the need is evident from the spiralling demands of frustrated materialists.

spiˈraliform, *a.* [f. SPIRAL *sb.*: see -FORM.] Having or taking the form of spiral lines.

1895 *Jrnl. Hellenic Stud.* XIV. 329 In the wake of early commerce the same spiraliform motives were to spread still further afield to the Danubian basin. **1900** *Nature* 27 Sept. 527/1 The spiraliform system of design re-entered the British Isles in another form.

spiralism (ˈspaɪərəlɪz(ə)m). *Sociol.* [f. SPIRAL *sb.* + -ISM.] A term for mobility in career and place of residence as part of individual success in an industrial economy. So ˈ**spiralist** *sb.* and *a.*

1957 W. WATSON in M. Gluckman *Closed Systems & Open Minds* (1964) vi. 147 The progressive ascent of the specialists of different skills..forms a characteristic combination of social and spatial mobility which may be called 'spiralism'. *Ibid.* 148 A spiralist's possible range of activity is the total number of fields within which his education qualifies him to compete. *Ibid.* 149 The generic spiralist culture. **1962** A. SAMPSON *Anat. of Britain* xxviii. 461 The career of a corporation manager cuts across traditional societies and local communities; he is a 'spiralist' —moving towards the top in narrowing circles, from one community or country to another, gathering local experience before he settles in the head office as a senior executive. **1969** C. BELL *Middle Class Families* ii. 40 There were 13 'blocked' spiralists who admitted they were not at the top. **1971** —— & NEWBY *Community Stud.* v. 158 Social mobility in Franza proceeds by a kind of spiralism. Individuals must 'get out' in order to 'get on'.

spiˈrality. [f. SPIRAL *a.*[1] + -ITY.] Spiral character; the degree of a spiral curve.

a **1858** in Greener *Gunnery* 407 The tendency of a bullet to twist the rifle on one side is now avoided by reducing the spirality of the grooves. **1884** *Science* III. 583/2 The better the [cotton] fibre, the more perfect its spirality.

spiralization (ˌspaɪərəlaɪˈzeɪʃən). [f. SPIRALIZE *v.* + -ATION.] The acquisition of spiral form; (in quot. 1851, a spiral coil).

1851 H. MELVILLE *Moby Dick* II. xviii. 141 The whaleline ..is spirally coiled away in the tub..so as to form..layers of concentric spiralizations. **1910** J. A. FLEMING *Princ. Electr. Wave Telegr.* (ed. 2) 127 The increase in resistance of a solenoid due to the spiralization. **1928** T. C. CHAMBERLIN *Two Solar Families* xvii. 159 The propulsion of solar bolts into planetary space and the drawing of these into orbits by the joint action of the sun and the passing star (the spiralization) was only the beginning of the process of.. nebularization. **1941** *Cold Spring Harbor Symp. Quantitative Biol.* IX. 15/2 The outstanding question is whether or not this amount of 'contraction' can all be accounted for by spiralization. **1969** I. B. RAIKOV in T. T. Chen *Res. in Protozool.* III. 75 Shortly before nuclear division, the chromosomes undergo spiralization and become longitudinally split. **1980** *Macromolecules* XIII. 799/2 Since..spiralization of the chain cannot be invoked for steric control, the stereo-regularity can only result from the asymmetric spatial arrangement around the metal atom of the catalytic complexes.

ˈ**spiralize**, *v.* [f. SPIRAL *sb.* or *a.*[1]] *trans.* To cut spirally. *intr.* To move in a spiral. Hence ˈ**spiralized** *ppl. a.*, formed into a spiral shape; ˈ**spiralizing** *ppl. a.*

1851 H. MELVILLE *Moby Dick* I. xxxv. 265 Drink and pass!.. Short draughts—long swallows, men; 'tis hot as Satan's hoof. So, so; it goes round excellently. It spiralizes in ye. *Ibid.* II. lxvii. 180 Precisely as an orange is sometimes stripped by spiralizing it. **1928** T. C. CHAMBERLIN *Two Solar Families* 145 A group of bodies already separated may respond to the spiralizing whirl of two centers of gravity even more freely than an eruptive body from which the spiralized matter must be shot forth. **1940** *Jrnl. Genetics* XL. 67 The suggestion has been made..that whereas all non-heteropycnotic regions have a spiral structure the heteropycnotic regions are not spiralized at all. **1977** *Nucl. Instruments & Methods* CXLV. 258/2 A new extrapolation is computed to associate track segments. In this way a spiralizing track can be followed. **1980** *Macromolecules* XIII. 798 Neither a chiral carbon nor a spiralized chain participates in the first two addition steps.

ˈ**spiralled**, *ppl. a.* [f. SPIRAL *sb.*] Shaped spirally.

1665 HOOKE *Microgr.* 111 These Shells which are thus spirallied [*sic*] and separated with Diaphragmes, were some kind of Nautili or Porcelane shells. **1881** *Linn. Soc. Jrnl.* XV. 440 Shell, high and narrow, rather strong, white, spiralled.

spirally (ˈspaɪərəlɪ), *adv.*[1] [f. SPIRAL *a.*[1]]

1. In a spiral manner; in spiral lines or curves.

a **1608** DEE *Relat. Spir.* I. (1659) 52 The bonds seem of a smoky ashy colour, spirally going about the cloud. **1691** RAY *Creation* II. (1692) 48 The Heart..being a Muscular Part, the sides of it are composed of two orders of Fibres running circularly or spirally from Base to Tip. **1769** FALCONER *Dict. Marine* s.v. *Engagement*, The barrel..is rifled spirally. **1799** G. SMITH *Laboratory* 312 Let pieces of milled lead be rolled spirally. **1822** J. PARKINSON *Outl. Oryctol.* 210 A canal passing spirally up its sides. **1845** J. COULTER *Adv. in Pacific* vii. 75 They..cut the blubber the proper breadth spirally from the base of the head to the flukes. **1885** *Mag. of Art* Sept. 458/1 The coils all joined together and running parallel to each other, instead of spirally.

2. *Comb.*, as ***spirally-arranged, -coiled***, etc.

1815 KIRBY & SP. *Entomol.* (1818) I. 62 Two spirally-convoluted tubes were filled with a silky gum. **1816** *Ibid.* II. 423 Two minute oval sacs formed of an elastic spirally-wound fibre. **1822** J. PARKINSON *Outl. Oryctol.* 198 Two spirally-coiled tubular appendages nearly filling the shell. **1870** ROLLESTON *Anim. Life* 131 The mucous membrane.. is prolonged into spirally-arranged valvular folds. **1882** VINES tr. *Sachs' Bot.* 639 The concave side of the long spirally-curved vegetative cone.

ˈ**spirally**, *adv.*[2] *rare*$^{-1}$. [f. SPIRAL *a.*[2]] After the manner of a spire; high in air.

1806 A. DUNCAN *Nelson* 13 The..flags rising spirally above them afforded a..relief to the glare.

ˈ**spiraloid**, *a.* [f. SPIRAL *sb.* + -OID.] Resembling that of a spiral; approximating to a spiral form.

1866 LOCKYER *Guillemin's Heavens* 402 The spiraloid form is not confined to the nebula we have described. **1875** MARTIN *Machinery* p. iv, New system of spiraloid drum shown in section.

†**spirament.** *Obs.* [ad. L. *spīrāment-um*, f. *spīrāre* to breathe. So It. *spiramento*.]

1. A spiracle in an animal body; a pore.

1608 TOPSELL *Serpents* 124 Almighty God hath so ordained, that it should haue spiraments and breathing places in euery part of the body, to vent away the heate. **1657**

TOMLINSON *Renou's Disp.* 215 The fume..doth transmit itself through the spiraments of the skin.

2. An air-hole or vent-hole.

1654 R. CODRINGTON tr. *Iustine* III. 73 The winds do work more strong through the spiraments of the Caves. **1657** TOMLINSON *Renou's Disp.* 429 The vessel's spirament daubed with a singular cement.

So ‖**spiramentum**. *Obs.*⁻¹

1706 BAYNARD *Cold Baths* II. 238 The Pores are the Spiramenta through which it passes.

spiramycin (spaɪrə'maɪsɪn). *Pharm.* [ad. F. *spiramycine*, f. *spira-* (of unkn. origin): see -MYCIN.] A mixture of macrolide antibiotics obtained from the fungus *Streptomyces ambofaciens*.

1955 *Antibiotics Ann. 1954–5* 724 A new antibiotic, spiramycin, has been extracted from the culture filtrates of a previously undescribed species of streptomyces. **1974** *New England Jrnl. Med.* CCXC. 1110/2 Treatment with spiramycin during pregnancy reduced the overall frequency of the fetal infections.

spirane ('spaɪəreɪn). *Chem.* Also **spiran** (-æn). [ad. G. *spiran*: see SPIRO- 2 and -ANE.] Any organic compound having two rings in the molecule with a single atom (usu. of carbon or nitrogen) common to both; a spiro-compound.

In quot. 1919 used *attrib.* of the shared atom.

1911 *Jrnl. Chem. Soc.* C. I. 497 Spirans or dispirans are homo- or hetero-cyclic compounds containing two rings with a carbon atom common to both. **1919** *Ibid.* CXV. I. 323 Strains existing in one ring of a *spiro*-compound could not possibly make themselves felt in the second ring unless communicated by a spirane carbon atom, which itself is in a state of strain. **1950** E. DE B. BARNETT *Stereochem.* iv. 55 Any spirane in which the rings are identical but unsymmetrical should be enantiomorphic. **1972** NATTA & FARINE *Stereochem.* iv. 113 A class very similar to the allenes consists of the spirans—bicyclic compounds whose rings are attached to only one atom. **1978** R. L. BAUMGARTEN *Org. Chem.* xvii. 289 Biphenyls substituted with bulky ortho substituents, substituted allenes, and spiranes are among the classes of compounds that exhibit optical although there is no asymmetric carbon atom present.

spirant ('spaɪərənt), *sb.* and *a.* [a. L. *spīrant-*, *spīrans*, pres. pple. of *spīrāre* to breathe. So F. *spirant*, It. *spirante*, Sp. and Pg. *espirante*.] **a.** *sb.* A consonant which admits of a continued emission of some amount of breath, so that the sound is capable of being prolonged. **b.** *adj.* Pronounced with an accompanying emission of breath.

1862 W. D. WHITNEY in *Jrnl. Amer. Oriental Soc.* VII. VII. 319 The labial series has no sibilants; for its pair of fricatives, surd and sonant..so lack the hissing quality which distinguishes the..sibilants, that it seems preferable to put them in another class; which..we will call the spirants. **1866** WHITNEY in *Jrnl. Amer. Oriental Soc.* VIII. 348 If..any one of them..has passed over into a spirant, it can never recover an explosive character. **1882–3** SCHAFF *Encycl. Relig. Knowl.* III. 2155 The Semitic alphabet is.. characterized by fulness of guttural, uvular, and spirant consonants. **1894** LINDSAY *Latin Lang.* 51 The change from the bilabial to the labiodental spirant.

Hence **spi'rantic** *a.*

1896 *Classical Rev.* X. 59 In support of the spirantic theory, we have the difference of phonetic law in Sanskrit and Greek. **1896** *Academy* 21 Mar. 243/1 The author might safely have claimed the spirantic pronunciation as existent in Athens in the fourth century B.C.

spirantal (spaɪ'ræntəl), *a.* [f. SPIRANT *sb.* + -AL.] = SPIRANT *a.*

1893 J. CLARK *Man. Linguistics* iii. 41, kj, ghj, kᵘj, ghᵘj give for result a sort of geminated spirantal sound. **1928** J. & E. M. WRIGHT *Elem. Middle English Gram.* (ed. 2) vi. 131 The palatal spirantal element began to disappear in pronunciation from about the end of the fourteenth century in the south Midland and southern dialects. **1965** [see CHIPEWYAN].

spi'ranthy. *Bot.* [f. σπεῖρα SPIRE *sb.*³ + ἄνθος flower.] 'The occasional twisted growth of the parts of a flower' (Webster *Suppl.* 1879).

spirantization (ˌspaɪərəntaɪ'zeɪʃən). [f. next: see -IZATION.] Making into a spirant; development of a spirantal pronunciation. Also *attrib.*

1911 *Amer. Jrnl. Philol.* XXXII. 37 Breath stress was weaker here than in Germanic, where spirantization took place in spite of the escape of breath in a preceding nasal. **1939** *Language* XV. 64 The second point..is the problem of the spirantization of ungeminated non-emphatic stopped consonants. **1973** J. M. ANDERSON *Structural Aspects Lang. Change* 209 A second spirantization rule converted [ǧ] → [ž] through loss of occlusion. **1977** *Trans. Philol. Soc. 1975* 11 There is no principled way to separate a rule like the spirantization of intervocalic /b d g/ in Spanish from German obstruent devoicing or OE verbal ablaut.

spirantize, *v.* [f. SPIRANT *sb.* and *a.* + -IZE.] *trans.* To pronounce as a spirant, to make into a spirant. So '**spirantizing** *ppl. a.* and *vbl. sb.*

1896 *Academy* 21 Mar. 243/2 This was the point in the language at which the spirantising tendency would first attack the χ and the ϕ. **1911** *Amer. Jrnl. Philol.* XXXII. 36 The former [*sc.* Iranian] is spirantizing language, like the old Germanic. *Ibid.*, The spirantizing of voiceless aspirates in Iranian. **1936** *Language* XII. 247 If with the vowels we may include the semivowels, we note here the Balto-Slavonic palatalizations,..[and] the spirantizing of Latin *c* (that is, [k]) as it develops into the Romance languages. **1964** S. K. CHATTERJI in D. Abercrombie et al. *Daniel Jones* 411 In Bengali, the aspirates *ph*, *bh*, are normally spirantized to [ϕ, β]. **1977** *Word 1972* XXVIII. 252 It cannot be argued that early Guarani might have had an occlusive [d] in initial position and that it would have been a simple matter to spirantize it.

†**spirarck.** *Obs.*⁻⁰ [ad. Gr. σπειράρχης, f. σπεῖρα band, company.] (See quot.)

1656 BLOUNT *Glossogr.*, *Spirarck* (*spirarchus*), a Captain, in a foreward.

†**spirate,** *v.* *Obs. rare.* [f. L. *spīrāt-*, ppl. stem of *spīrāre* to breathe.] *trans.* To breathe out.

1649 J. ELLISTONE tr. *Behmen's Epist.* (1886) vi. 79 The one doth unfold and spirate or breathe itself forth out of another. **1765** LAW tr. *Behmen's Myst. Magn.* I. vii, That which is spirated or spoken forth is the Wisdom..of the Will.

'**spirated,** *ppl. a.* [f. L. *spīra* SPIRE *sb.*³] Spirally twisted.

1871 DARWIN *Desc. Man* II. xvii. 246 The males of this species have long straight spirated horns, nearly parallel to each other. **1890** *Cornh. Mag.* Sept. 230 [Their] tall, spirated horns and jet-black sides are indicative of their age.

spiration¹ (spaɪ'reɪʃən). Also 6 **spiracyon, -atione.** [ad. L. *spīrātiōn-*, *spīrātio*, n. of action f. *spīrāre* to breathe. So OF. (*e*)*spiracion*, F. *spiration*, It. *spirazione*, Sp. *espiracion*.]

1. *Theol.* †**a.** The action of breathing as a creative or life-giving function of the Deity. *Obs.*

1526 *Pilgr. Perf.* (W. de W. 1531) 217b, Job sayth, the spiryt of god hath made me & the spiracyon of the almyghty hath gyuen me lyfe. **1649** J. ELLISTONE tr. *Behmen's Epist.* 84 Man, who with his soule..is couched in the eternall Spiration (or generation) of the Divine power. *a* **1677** BARROW *Serm.* (1686) II. 490 To other substances of this kind it seemeth also assigned,..because God did by a kind of spiration produce them. **1708** DODWELL *Nat. Mort. Hum. Souls* 23 As the πνοή, or Flatus, is by the Fathers supposed to continue so long, and no longer, than the Act of Spiration, or Flation, lasts. **1765** LAW tr. *Behmen's Myst. Magn.* I. vii, This Egress from the Will in the Speaking or Spiration is the Spirit of the Deity.

b. The special action to which the origin of the Holy Ghost is assigned.

1602 J. DAVIES (Heref.) *Mirum in Modum* (Grosart) 17/1 Fatherhood, breathing, or Spiration, Son-hood, Procession. **1656** BLOUNT *Glossogr.* s.v., The Holy Ghost proceeds from the Father, and the Son,..produced through the will by an ineffable way, and this Divines term *Spiration.* **1699** BURNET *39 Art.* v. 69 The Word Procession, or as the School-men term it, Spiration, is only made use of in order to the naming this relation of the Spirit to the Father and Son. **1829** J. DONOVAN tr. *Catech. Counc. Trent* (1855) 83 As on the production of the third Person is imposed no proper name, but it is called spiration and procession. **1898** W. ADAMSON *J. Morison* 42 The doctrines of the eternal generation of the Son and the eternal spiration of the Spirit.

†**2.** The action of breathing or drawing breath in man and animals. *Obs.*

1568 SKEYNE *The Pest* (1860) 28 Cohibite also spiratione, to eschew occasioun of new corruptioun. **1594** R. ASHLEY tr. *Loys de Roy* 57b, The variable aire, sustayning with spiration and respiration all liuing creatures. **1615** CROOKE *Body of Man* 421 The spiration or breathing of colde is verie necessary for the preseruation of naturall heate. **1673–4** GREW *Anat. Pl., Anat. Trunks* (1684) 117 Even as in Animals, there are divers Kinds of Organs for Spiration.

†**3.** An inspiration; a spiritual influence. *Obs.*

1628 JACKSON *Creed* VI. xi. Wks. 1844 V. 131 Such as.. boisterously counterblast the sweet and placid spirations of celestial influence. **1686** HORNECK *Crucif. Jesus* xxvi. 846 Some other spirations, and breathings of the soul after God.

†**spi'ration**². *Obs. rare.* [f. L. *spīra* SPIRE *sb.*³] Spiral conformation.

1672–3 GREW *Anat. Pl., Anat. Roots* (1684) 73 The Spiration of the Fibres of these Vessels, may more easily be observed in the Trunk, than in the Root.

spi'rator. *rare.* [f. L. *spīrāre* to breathe.]

†**1.** A breathing passage or tube. *Obs.*⁻¹

1657 TOMLINSON *Renou's Disp.* 550 Eclegms..potently incide..humours, impacted in the spirators.

2. (See quot. 1876.)

1875 *Ure's Dict. Arts* (ed. 7) III. 877. **1876** *Catal. Sci. App. S. Kens.* 90 *Spirator*, an instrument designed to get a constant current and measureable volume of air driven or drawn over a body.

spire (spaɪə(r)), *sb.*¹ Forms: 1, 4–5 **spir**, 3– **spire**, 4, 6–7 **spier** (7 **spiere**), 5–6 **spyre**. [OE. *spír*, = WFris. *spier*, NFris. *spîr*, MDu. and Du. *spier*, MLG. *spîr*, *spyer*, *spyr*, MHG. *spîr* (G. *spier*, *spiere*), Da. *spire*, MSw. and Sw. *spira*, sprout, shoot, sprig, etc. Cf. SPEAR *sb.*²]

1. a. A stalk or stem of a plant, esp. one of a tall and slender growth. Now *rare*.

a **1000** *Sax. Leechd.* II. 266 Wiþ lungen adle, hindbergean leaf & hreodes spir. **1513** BRADSHAW *St. Werburge* I. 1603 There was in pycture..Our lorde apperynge in busshe flammynge as fyre, And nothynge therof brent, lefe, tree, nor spyre. **1523** FITZHERB. *Husb.* §20 Dockes have a brode lefe, and diuers high spyres, and very small sede in the toppe. **1601** HOLLAND *Pliny* II. 23 Raddishes eat the more pleasantly, if their leaues be cropt off before the master stem or spire be growne big. *a* **1722** LISLE *Husb.* (1757) 136, I observed the wheat on the ground, and that the first, or capital branch, consisted of an upright spire, between two leaves. **1768–74** TUCKER *Lt. Nat.* (1834) II. 414 The green leaves of corn, which protect and assist to draw up nourishment into the spire. **1815** SHELLEY *Alastor* 528 Tall spires of windlestrae Threw their thin shadows down the rugged slope.

fig. **1865** RUSKIN *Sesame* ii. 194 Among those sweet living things, whose new courage..is starting up in strength of goodly spire.

b. The tapering top of a tree; the portion of the main stem which shoots up above the branches.

1657 THORNLEY *Daphnis & Chloe* 162 One Apple hang'd upon the very top of the Spire of the Tree. **1820** SHELLEY *Orpheus* 27 There stands a group of cypresses; not such As, with a graceful spire and stirring life, Pierce the pure heaven. **1875** LASLETT *Timber* 72 No tops to be received, except the spire and such other top or limb as may be grown on the main piece.

c. A flower-spike.

1850 TENNYSON *In Mem.* lxxxiii, Bring orchis, bring the foxglove spire. **1852** M. ARNOLD *Empedocles* I. ii. 4 The giant spires of yellow bloom Of the sun-loving gentian. **1874** SYMONDS *Sk. Italy & Greece* (1898) I. viii. 169 Meadows, where..asphodel is pale with spires of faintest rose.

2. (Now *south* or *s.w. dial.*) **a.** *collect.* Reeds; reed-like coarse tall-growing plants or sedges (see later quots.).

a **1250** *Owl & Night.* 18 In ore waste þicke hegge, Imeind mid spire & grene segge. **1388** WYCLIF *Exod.* ii. 3 [She] puttide hym forth in a place of spier of the brenke of the flood. —— *Isaiah* xviii. 1 *margin*, Papirus is a kynde of spier. **1578** LYTE *Dodoens* 514 The common Reede or spier groweth in standing waters... This plante is called in.. English Common Pole Reede, Spier, or Cane Reede. **1796** W. H. MARSHALL *Rur. Econ. W. Eng.* I. 330 *Spire* (*Arundo*), reed. **1856** BROMEFIELD *Flora Vect.* 583 Common Sea-reed ..is known only as Spire, a term applied by the islanders to all the larger-spiked and close-panicled grasses, Carices and Typhæ. **1865** R. HUNT *Pop. Rom. W. Eng.* (1871) Ser. I. 201 Before the reed-like plant called by the present inhabitants the spire was planted.

b. A single plant of this; a reed.

1388 WYCLIF *Job* viii. 11 Whether a rusche may lyue with out moysture? ethir a spier [*v.r.* reed] may wexe with out watir? **1847** HALLIW., *Spires*, is chiefly applied to the tall species of sedge..; it is likewise used of the tall leaves of the common yellow iris... *Isle of Wight.* **1863** WISE *New Forest* 287 The phrase 'spire-bed'..is very common, meaning a particular field, near where the 'spires' grow.

c. *Mining.* (See quot.)

1875 KNIGHT *Dict. Mech.* 2276/2 *Spire*, the tube carrying the train to the charge in the blast-hole. Also called the *reed* or *rush*, as the spires of grass or rushes are used for the purpose.

3. a. A young or tender shoot or sprout; *esp.* the rudimentary shoot of a seed; the acrospire of grain; = SPEAR *sb.*² 2.

13.. in *Archiv Stud. neu. Spr.* LXXXI. 83/18 Whon greyne of whete is cast in grounde..þerof springeþ spires I-nowe. *c* **1374** CHAUCER *Troylus* II. 1335 As an oke comyth of a littil spire. **1398** TREVISA *Barth. De P.R.* XVII. xi. (Bodl. MS.), þe spire of þe lely springeþ oute of the side of þe cloue and nouȝt oute of þee ende. *c* **1440** *Pallad. on Husb.* III. 1034 When their spir up goon is,.. Let plaunte hem ther. **1604** POWER *Exp. Philos.* I. 65 The Grains of Barly being moistned with water,..the fermentation and heat presently appears,..and therefore it shoots forth into Spires. **1670** EVELYN *Sylva* (ed. 2) 83 [They] place the ends of them in water 'till towards the Spring, by which season they will have contracted a swelling spire or knurr. **1766** *Compl. Farmer* s.v. *Malt*, At this time, the spire should be near piercing through the outer skin of the barley. **1826** *Art of Brewing* (ed. 2) 7 Nature intended this for the future support of the spire.

fig. **1377** LANGL. *P. Pl.* B. IX. 100 Sitthe to spille speche þat spyre is of grace.

b. A blade or shoot *of* grass, etc.; = SPEAR *sb.*² 2b. (Freq. *c* 1660–1720; now *rare.*)

1646 BP. HALL *Balm Gilead* (1650) 372 What if there were as many Devils in the air, as there are spires of grasse on the earth? **1675** TRAHERNE *Chr. Ethics* 60 Every grain of dust,.. every spire of grass is wholly illuminated thereby. **1701** STANHOPE *Pious Breath.* III. v. (1704) 182 [Thy hand] only could produce the least spire of grass. **1724** WELTON *Disc.* 433 Look but upon a spire of grass. *a* **1729** CONGREVE *Ovid's Art Love* Wks. 1730 III. 320 Pointed Spires of Flax, when green, will Ink supply. **1849** BROWNSON *Wks.* VII. 18 We know that a spire of grass grows, but how it grows we know not. **1867** F. FRANCIS *Angling* vi. 204 The Wren-tail..may be seen in the fine sunny weather sunning itself on the long spires of grass.

c. *U.S.* Similarly of hair; = SPEAR *sb.*² 2c.

1868 MISS ALCOTT *Lit. Women* xv, I'd do as much for our Jimmy any day if I had a spire of hair worth selling.

4. A long slender and tapering growth in a plant:

a. The awn or beard of grain.

1530 PALSGR. 274 Spyre of corne, *barbe du ble.* **1877** *N.W. Linc. Gloss.* 234 *Spires*, the horns of barley.

†**b.** The stigma of the crocus, from which saffron is obtained. *Obs.*⁻¹

1633 BP. HALL *Occas. Medit.* 319 The saffron yields an odoriferous and cordial spire, whiles both the flower and the root are unpleasing.

5. An elongated or pointed shoot or tongue of fire or flame.

c **1450** *Mirk's Festial* 102 And when he come done to þe pepull,..two spyres of fyre stoden out of hys hed lyke two hornes. **1621** G. SANDYS *Ovid* II. (1626) 27 Parnassus grones beneath two flaming spires. **1667** MILTON *P.L.* I. 223 On each hand the flames Drivn backward slope their pointing spires. **1812** *Examiner* 21 Sept. 597/1 Spires of smoking flame. **1839** URE *Dict. Arts* 993 If the gas be copious, the flame elongates into a sharp spire. **1877** E. R. CONDER *Basis Faith* ix. 383 An immense instinct in his nature points upward, like a spire of flame.

6. a. A conical, tapering, pointed body or part of something; a sharp point.

1551 RECORDE *Pathw. Knowl.* I. Defin., They are lyke in forme to two such cantles ioyned togither..: or els it is called a rounde spire, or stiple fourme. *Ibid.*, A square spire. **1589** PUTTENHAM *Eng. Poesie* II. (Arb.) 108 Of the Spire or Taper called Pyramis. **1632** G. SANDYS *Ovid* I. 22 The whole skie being all the night long in the beames of the Sun (that little spire, the shadowe of the Earth excepted). **1658** tr. *Porta's Nat. Magic* 393 Make.. [a] vessel in the fashion of a Tunnel, or a round Pyramis;..let the spire of it..be open. **1725** POPE *Odyss.* IX. 386 The narrow'r end I sharpen'd to a spire. **1813** SHELLEY *Q. Mab* IV. 11 Icicles.. So stainless, that their white and glittering spires Tinge not the moon's pure beam. **1885** *Harper's Mag.* Apr. 703 She.. directed the capping of her hemp-stacks till the spires were ..symmetric.

b. A branch or prong of a deer's horn. (Cf. SPEER *sb.*[2]) Also *fig.*

1607 TOPSELL *Four-f. Beasts* 119, I haue seene the hornes to haue seauen spires or braunches. *Ibid.* 124 At one yeare old they haue nothing but small bunches..; at three yeares they grow forked into two spieres. **1641** MILTON *Church Govt.* I. vi, Haughty prelates..with their forked mitres,.. instead of healing up the gashes of the Church,..fall to gore one another with their sharp spires.

c. A metal spike or rod. *rare.*

*c*1710 CELIA FIENNES *Diary* (1888) 52 A little wall of a yard High of free Stone very ffine wrought, on which are to be Iron railes and spires. **1750** in D. Gilbert *Paroch. Hist. Cornwall* (1838) III. 430 One of those rocks..with an iron spire at the top thereof.

7. a. A tall, slender, sharp-pointed summit, peak, rock, or column.

1586 WHITNEY *Choice Emblems* I A mightie Spyre, whose toppe dothe pierce the skie. **1599** HAKLUYT *Voy.* II. 202 About an Harquebuz-shotte from Matarea is a spire of great height like to that at Rome. **1601** HOLLAND *Pliny* II. 577 The Ægyptians..speake much of these two Pyramides, the mighty spires and steeples whereof..do arise out of the very water. **1634** SIR T. HERBERT *Trav.* 22 Mæollis rises very high with a Peake or Pyramidall Spire. **1749** *Phil. Trans.* XLVI. 269 The whole Surface of the Rock shall rise into Points or Spires. **1833** TENNYSON *Dream Fair Wom.* xlvii, All night the splinter'd crags that wall the dell With spires of silver shine. **1847** —— *Princ.* IV. 262 Like a spire of land that stands apart Cleft from the main. **1855** *Orr's Circ. Sci., Inorg. Nat.* 143 The spires, or needle-shaped detached rocks, called in Switzerland *aiguilles.*

b. *poet.* A pyramidal heap or pile *of* something.

1818 KEATS *Endym.* I. 222 On the shrine he heaped a spire Of teeming sweets, enkindling sacred fire.

8. A tall structure rising from a tower, roof, etc., and terminating in a slender point; *esp.* the tapering portion of the steeple of a cathedral or church, usually carried to a great height and constituting one of the chief architectural features of the building. (Cf. SPEAR *sb.*[2] I.)

So MLG. *spyre* (1392), Sw. *spira*, Da. and Norw. *spir*.

1596 LODGE *Wits Miserie* B iij b, His beard is cut like the spier of Grantham steeple. **1610** HOLLAND *Camden's Brit.* 739 An high Towre in the middest and two Spires at the West end. **1643** BAKER *Chron., Eliz.* 117 The Spire of the Cathedrall Church of Pauls being..two hundred and sixty [feet] from the Square Steeple where it was placed. **1700** DRYDEN *Pal. & Arc.* I. 215 The Temples crown'd With golden Spires. **1727** SWIFT *Baucis & Philemon* Wks. 1755 III. II. 33 The chimney widen'd, and grew higher, Became a steeple with a spire. **1765** STERNE *Tr. Shandy* VII. v, The steeple, which has a spire to it, is placed in the middle of the church. **1815** SCOTT *Guy M.* iv, The spire of a church.. indicated the situation of a village. **1866** M. ARNOLD *Thyrsis* iii, And that sweet city with her dreaming spires,..Lovely all times she lies, lovely to-night. **1867** FREEMAN *Norm. Conq.* v. I. 310 Queenly Lübeck had not yet begun to cover her peninsula with her stately spires, her soaring gateways.

transf. **1878** STEVENSON *Inland Voy.* 77 My consciousness should be diffused abroad in all the forest, and give a common heart to that assembly of green spires.

9. *fig.* The highest point, summit, or top *of* something.

1600 J. DOWLAND *2nd Bk. Songs* ii. B ij b, From the highest spire of contentment, my fortune is throwne. **1607** SHAKS. *Cor.* I. ix. 24 To silence that, Which to the spire, and top of prayses vouch'd, Would seeme but modest. **1611** SPEED *Hist. Gt. Brit.* V. vi. §17. 36 The Romanes that stroue to mount hie on the spires of their intended glory.

10. *attrib.* and *Comb.* **a.** In senses 1–3, as *spire-end*; **spire-bed, mint, reed,** *dial.* (see quots.). Also SPIRE-GRASS.

*a*1722 LISLE *Husb.* (1757) 207 The germen, or the spire-end of the barley. **1863** PRIOR *Plant-n., Spear-mint* or *Spire-mint*, from its spiry, not capitate inflorescence. *Ibid., Spires*, or *Spire-reed*, the pool reed, *Arundo phragmites*. **1863** WISE *New Forest* Gloss., *Spire-bed*, a place where the 'spires', that is, the reed-canary grass (*Phalaris arundinacea*), grow.

b. In sense 8, as *spire-growth, -passion, -top*; **spire-light,** a window in a spire; **spire-roof,** a steeply sloping roof rising up into a spire. See also SPIRE-STEEPLE.

1842 *Penny Cycl.* XXII. 356 The cathedrals of Worms and Gelnhausen..exhibit many varieties of spires, or rather spire-roofs, springing up from gables at their base. **1846** *Archaeol. Jrnl.* II. 3 The spire itself, at about half its height, is encircled by spire-lights. **1853** C. WICKES *Illustr. Spires & Towers Eng.* (title-p.), The Architecture of the Middle Ages, and its Spire-Growth. **1882** STEVENSON *New Arab. Nts.* II. 144 The flag of England, fluttering on the spire-top, grew ever fainter and fainter. **1944** BLUNDEN *Cricket Country* v. 64 There is only one person known to me who quite equals my spire-passion.

c. With past pples. or adjs. (chiefly instrumental and similative), as *spire-adorned, -crowned, -shaped, -topped* adjs.; *spire-like, -straight* adjs.

1804 J. GRAHAME *Sabbath* (1808) 32 He toiled up the spire-topt hill. **1840** *Civil Eng. & Arch. Jrnl.* III. 32/1 This ..is covered by a very steep, or spire-shaped roof. **1879** WILL CARLETON *Farm Ballads* 87 The turreted, spire-adorned city. **1885** F. P. WARREN & CLEVERLY *Wand. Beetle* 56 The famous Roche à Bayard, rising almost sheer from the river, soars to its spire-like peak. **1893** *Daily News* 27 Apr. 5/5 Each corner is adorned with a spire-crowned pavilion. **1933** C. DAY LEWIS *Magnetic Mountain* 26 There, as a candle's beam Stands firm and will not waver Spire-straight in a close chamber.

spire, *sb.*[2] Chiefly *Sc.* and *north. dial.* Forms: 4–6 spyre, 5 spyr, spyer, spierre, 7 spier, 5, 7– spire. [app. of Continental origin, corresponding in sense 1 to ON. *spíra* (Norw. and Sw. *spira*, Da. *spire*), LG. *spiere, spier*, MDu. *spier* (rare), NFris. *spîr*, WFris. *spier, spjirre.* The original locality of the word, and its relation to SPIRE *sb.*[1], are not clear.]

†**1.** A spar or pole of timber; a bar or moderately long piece of wood. *Obs.* (Cf. SPAR *sb.*[1] 1–3.)

1392 *Mem. Ripon* (Surtees) III. 115 In iij spyres emp. de Joh. de Morpath pro skaffald, 15*d.* *c*1400 *Gamelyn* 503 Gamelyn spreyniþ holi water with an oken spire. *c*1400 *Laud Troy Bk.* 17170 [They] spered the ȝates wel and faste With many a spire that wel wolde laste. **1419** *Mem. Ripon* (Surtees) III. 144 Et in ij spyrys de esch emt. pro reparacione unius domus,..5*d.* **1470** *Cal. Anc. Rec. Dublin* (1889) 339 Noo freman [shall] goo without the citte to by hides, tallow, spirys, bordes. **1609** HOLLAND *Amm. Marcell.* 221 There lyeth foorth farther out a fouresquare beame or spire.

†**b.** The pole or shaft of a chariot. Also *attrib.*

1609 HOLLAND *Amm. Marcell.* 222 From the very midst of these ropes there riseth forth a beame of wood overthwart, and after the fashion of a yoke spire or tiller erected. **1610** —— *Camden's Brit.* (1637) 29 They were wont to..runne along the spire-pole and beame of the chariot.

2. A young tree suitable for making into a spar; a sapling. Also *attrib.*

1392 *Mem. Ripon* (Surtees) III. 116 In xxxij spyres emp. de Will. Mayllour, 16*s.* 4*d.* Et in eisdem prosternandis, 7*d.* **1543** *Mem. Fountains* (Surtees) 413 [Survey of woods], Young oke spyres,..small ashe spyres. **1620** *N. Riding Rec.* II. 234 For cutting and stealing in Watlas Springe, two ash-spires. **1634** BP. HALL *Contempl., N.T.* IV. xi, Like a wood new felled, that hath some few spires left for standers. **1703** *Lond. Gaz.* No. 3975/4 Persons having any small young Spire Elm Timber to dispose of. **1707** MORTIMER *Husb.* 394 Many times a Spire Elm will begin to grow hollow at the bottom when any of its Roots happen to perish. **1788** W. H. MARSHALL *Yorksh.* II. 355 *Spires*, timber stands (not common). **1828** in CARR *Craven Gloss.* **1854** MISS BAKER *Northampt. Gloss., Spires*, young trees that shoot up a considerable height before they branch out and form a head. **1876** *Davidson's Precedents* V. I. 225 All timber and other trees, pollards, spires, and saplings.

spire (spaɪə(r)), *sb.*[3] Also 6 spyre. [a. F. *spire* (= It. *spira*, Sp. and Pg. *espira*), or ad. L. *spīra*, ad. Gr. σπεῖρα coil, twist, winding.]

1. One of the series of complete convolutions forming a coil or spiral. **a.** One of the sinuous folds or windings of a serpent, etc.; a coil. Chiefly in pl.

1572 J. JONES *Bathes Ayde* II. 14 Y^{e} pypes did resemble the Spyres of a Dragon. **1608** TOPSELL *Serpents* 236 Some-times also they [i.e. serpents] sette vp such a Spire aboue the water, that a boate or little Barke without sayles may pass thorow the same. **1667** MILTON *P.L.* IX. 502 [The Serpent] erect Amidst his circling Spires, that on the grass Floted redundant. **1700** DRYDEN *Fables, Alexander's Feast* 29 A dragon's fiery form bely'd the god: Sublime on radiant spires he rode. **1712–4** POPE *Rape Lock* IV. 43 Now glaring fiends, and snakes on rolling spires. **1820** L. HUNT *Indicator* No. 22 (1822) I. 175 Tired out at length, they trail their spires, and gasp. **1868** BROWNING *Ring & Bk.* v. 1959 There was the reptile,..Renewing its detested spire and spire Around me.

b. In general or technical use.

1608 TOPSELL *Serpents* 150 The humour about the vitall spire [*sc.* the bowels]. **1634** T. JOHNSON *Parey's Wks.* XIV. v. (1678) 325 If on the third day..the spires or windings [of the bandage] be found more loose. *a*1661 FULLER *Worthies, Lond.* II. (1662) 194 With anfractuous spires, and cocleary turnings about it. **1774** PENNANT *Tour Scotl. in 1772*, 295 A great ox-horn,—the arm was twisted round its spires. **1822** SHELLEY *Fragm. Unf. Drama* 196 The plant..trailing its quaint spires Along the garden and across the lawn. **1839** URE *Dict. Arts* 473 Rifles should not be too deeply indented; ..and the spires should be truly parallel. **1870** *Rep. Smithson. Instit. 1869*, 8 The center of a coil of many spires of fine wire forming part of the galvanic circuit.

2. A spiral; a series of spiral curves or coils.

1611 B. JONSON *Catiline's Consp.* II. i, *Ful.* Binde my hair vp.. *Gal.* Will you ha't i' the globe, or spire? **1728** CHAMBERS *Cycl.* s.v. *Spiral*, 'Tis called from its Inventor, Archimedes's Spire, or Helix. **1761** *Brit. Mag.* II. 642 Of those perfect spires which lie in the same plane, there are two sorts. The first contains those curves whose spaces, or the distances between each circumvolution, are equal, commonly called Archimedes' spire. **1801** SHAW *Gen. Zool.* II. II. 391 The principal distinction of the Spanish Sheep is the fineness of the fleece, and the horizontally extended spire of the horns. **1887** D. MAGUIRE *Massage* (ed. 4) 114 These frictions are applied in every possible direction, now in a rectangular way, now obliquely describing spires and concentric..curves.

3. A curl or wreath of smoke, etc.

1699 GARTH *Dispens.* 7 Aromatick Clouds in Spires ascend. **1716** CHEYNE *Philos. Princ. Nat. Relig.* I. 65 Air seems to consist of Spires contorted into small Spheres. **1769** *Phil. Trans.* LIX. 334 There was not a spire of smoke to be perceived.

†**4.** As the name of a shell. *Obs.*$^{-1}$

1681 GREW *Musæum* I. vi. i. 132 The Level-Whirle, or the Spire.

5. *Conch.* The upper convoluted portion of a spiral shell, consisting of all the whorls except the body-whorl.

1822 J. PARKINSON *Outl. Oryctol.* 150 A shield-formed, subconical univalve; no spire. **1851** G. F. RICHARDSON *Geol.* (1855) 240 The spire forms a very important feature in the univalves, and on its being raised, flattened, concealed, or reversed, depend many of the generic and specific distinctions of the shells. **1870** ROLLESTON *Anim. Life* 51 The greater part of the shell has been removed, but a part of the spire has been left.

6. *attrib.* and *Comb.*, as *spire-shell, -ward* adj.; **spire-bearer** *Conch.*, a spirifer.

1713 PETIVER *Aquat. Anim. Amboinæ* ix, Thread listed Spire-shell. **1880** *Linn. Soc. Jrnl.* XV. 104 A broader furrow, in the bottom of which runs the suture on the spire-ward side of a fine rounded thread. **1881** *Cassell's Nat. Hist.* V. 265 The Spire-Bearers. The name..is derived from the spiral shape assumed by the calcareous labial appendages which nearly fill the interior of the dorsal valve.

†**spire,** *sb.*[4] *Sc. Obs.* = SPEER *sb.*[1]

1768 ROSS *Helenore* 136 I's no seek near the fire,—Let me but rest my weary banes, Behind backs at the spire. **1806** R. JAMIESON *Pop. Ballads* II. 406 The spire in a cottage, is properly the stem or leg of an earth-fast couple, reaching from the floor to the top of the wall.

spire, *sb.*[5] *rare.* Var. of SPAYARD.

The form may be due to SPIRE *sb.*[1] 6 b.

1856 'STONEHENGE' *Brit. Rur. Sports* I. x. 82 The Brocket has only small projections, called knobbers, with small brow antlers; the Spire a brow antler [etc.]. **1886** ELWORTHY *W. Som. Word-bk.* 700 *Spire*,..a male deer of three years old.

spire, *sb.*[6] *Coal-mining.* (See quot.)

1883 GRESLEY *Gloss. Coal-m.* 231 *Spires*, coal of a hard, dull, slaty nature, and difficult to break up.

spire, Sc. variant of SPEER *sb.*[4] (spray).

spire (spaɪə(r)), *v.*[1] Also 5–6 spyre, 6 spyer. [f. SPIRE *sb.*[1] Cf. Norw. and Sw. *spira*, Du. *spire*, in sense 1.]

1. *intr.* Of seeds, grain, etc.: To send forth or develop shoots, esp. the first shoot or acrospire; to germinate, sprout. Also with *out.* Now *rare* or *Obs.* (Cf. SPEAR *v.*[2])

*c*1325 *Gloss. W. de Bibbesw.* in Wright *Voc.* 158 *Ben germée*, [wel atome (? acome); *v.r.*] spired. **1398** TREVISA *Barth. De P.R.* XVII. xliii. (Tollem. MS.), Many men hangen oynones and garlek in þe smoke ouer þe fyre,..for þey schulde nouȝt spire and growe. Ofte oynones and garlek spireþ, þouȝe þey be nouȝt in erþe. *c*1440 *Pallad. on Husb.* III. 1034 Now curneles of mixe hit is to keste In molde in sum vessell, so fele attonys As wel may spire. **1471** RIPLEY *Comp. Alch.* III. xvii. in Ashm. (1652) 143 Then shall thy seeds both roote and spyre. **1577** HARRISON *England* II. vi. 95 b/2 The workeman not suffring it [malting barley]..to take any heate, whereby the bud ende shoulde spire. **1679** EVELYN *Sylva* (ed. 3) 8 If they [i.e. seeds] spire out before you sow them, be sure you commit them to the earth before the Sprout grows dry. **1728** *Phil. Trans.* XXXV. 569 As they [crocus roots] then begin to spire, and are ready to shew themselves above Ground. **1765** *Museum Rust.* III. 223 There is a sure disappointment in buying such grain, as the kerns will spire at different times.

transf. **1582** STANYHURST *Æneis* I. (Arb.) 27 Thee Troian Cæsar shal spire fro this auncetrye regal.

†**b.** *trans.* To produce; to put *forth. Obs. rare.*

1590 SPENSER *F.Q.* III. v. 52 In..race Of woman kind it fairest flowre doth spyre, And beareth fruit of honour and all chast desire. **1591** —— *Ruins Time* Ded., The seede of most entire loue..; which taking roote..would in their riper strength..[have] spired forth fruit of more perfection.

2. *intr.* Of plants, corn, etc.: To run up into a tall stem, stalk, or spike; to grow upwards instead of developing laterally. Now *dial.*

1398 TREVISA *Barth. De P.R.* XVII. lxxvi. (Bodl. MS.), ȝif þei beþ i-suffred in þe bigynnynge to growe to swiþe þan þei spireþ & sedeþ to sone & leseþ to sone here fairenes & grene coloure. *c*1440 *Promp. Parv.* 469 Spyryn, as corne and oþer lyke, *spico.* **1530** PALSGR. 728, I spyer, as corne dothe whan it begynneth to waxe rype, *je espie.* *a*1618 SYLVESTER *New Jerusalem* 31 Wks. (Grosart) II. 258 There, Mead and Field, spring, spire, and yeeld. **1669** WORLIDGE *Syst. Agric.* (1681) 163 As often as they spire, crop them. **1706** PHILLIPS (ed. Kersey), To *Spire*, to grow up into an Ear, as Corn does. **1828** CARR *Craven Gloss., Spire*, to shoot up luxuriantly. **1841** HARTSHORNE *Salop. Ant.* Gloss., *Spire*, to grow rapidly, shoot upwards quickly. **1894** HESLOP *Northumbld. Gloss.* s.v., A tree or plant which shoots out in length and not proportionately in breadth is said to *spire.*

3. To rise or shoot up into a spire or spire-shaped form; to rise or extend to a height in the manner of a spire; to mount or soar aloft. Also with *up.*

a. Of flames or fire.

1591 SPENSER *Ruins Rome* 220 As ye see huge flames spred diuerslie, Gathered in one vp to the heauens to spyre. **1652** CULVERWEL *Lt. Nat.* I. xviii. (1661) 163 The Candle of the Lord;..'tis fain to spire up, and climbe up..in a Pyramidal form. **1816** J. HODGSON in J. Raine *Mem.* (1857) I. 181 The flame of its wick spired slightly into length. **1839** URE *Dict. Arts* 993 If the tip begins to spire, he drops down on one knee, and holding the candle near the pavement, gradually raises it up. **1867** G. MACDONALD *Disciple*, etc. 53 Each ripple waves a flickering fire..; They laugh and flash, and leap and spire.

b. Of edifices, rocks, etc.

1687 A. LOVELL tr. *Thevenot's Trav.* II. 60 A square Minaret that spires into a Pyramid. **1748** *Anson's Voy.* I. vii. 74 These rocks terminate in a vast number of ragged points, which spire up to a prodigious height. **1790** PENNANT *London* (1813) 581 They spire into very elegant pinnacles. **1818** MILMAN *Samor* 308 Sudden around 'gan spire the mountain tops. **1872** TENNYSON *Gareth & Lynette* 302 A city.. Which Merlin's hand.. had touch'd, and everywhere .. tipt with lessening peak And pinnacle, and had made it spire to heaven.

c. Of leaves, branches, or trees.

1707 MORTIMER *Husb.* 330 It will be convenient.. to leave a leading Branch near the top to spire up and cover the wound. **1712** tr. *Pomet's Hist. Drugs* I. 136 The leaves only grow at the Top longwise, pointed as those of the Flower-de-lis, spiring, and opposite one to the other. **1798** COLERIDGE *Picture* 115 The crowded firs Spire from thy shores, and stretch across thy bed. **1870** BARING-GOULD *In Exitu Israel* I. i. 1 The upstart poplars.. spire above the venerable trees.

d. In fig. use.

1672 TEMPLE *Ess., Govt.* Wks. 1720 I. 105 A Common-wealth, the more it takes in of the general Humour and Bent of the People, and the more it spires up to a Head by the Authority of some one Person. **1857** EMERSON *Poems, Sphinx* xvi. Wks. (Bohn) I. 398 Uprose the merry Sphinx, And crouched no more in stone;.. She spired into a yellow flame; She flowered in blossoms red.

4. *trans.* **a.** To build *up* in the form of a spire. **b.** To direct or point upwards. **c.** To pierce with a sharp and lofty peak.

1750 WREN *Parentalia* 307 The Ground-work being settled, they had nothing else to do but to spire all up as they could. **1839** BAILEY *Festus* 53 Nay, I love Death. But Immortality, with finger spired, Points to a distant, giant world. **1874** LANIER *In Absence* iii. Poems (1892) 75 An Alp sublime.. Spiring the world's prismatic atmosphere.

†**spire**, *v.*[2] *Obs.* Also 5–6 spyre. [ad. OF. *spirer*, *espirer* (= Sp. and Pg. *espirar*, It. *spirare*), or L. *spīrāre* to breathe.]

1. *intr.* or *absol.* To breathe; to blow gently; to come *forth* or *out* as breath. Also *fig.*

1382 WYCLIF *Ecclus.* xliii. 17 In his wil shal spiren, or brethen, out the south. *a* **1395** HYLTON *Scala Perf.* II. xli. (MS. Bodl. 592), þe hooli goost spireþ where he wole & þou heerist his voice, but þou woost not fro whennes he comeþ or whidir he goiþ. **1526** *Pilgr. Perf.* (1531) 59b, Let the swete odour of deuocyon and prayer spyre out and ascende vp to thy lorde and spouse. **1535** JOYE *Apol. Tindale* (Arb.) 24 Here may ye smel out of what stynkyng breste and poysoned virulent throte thys peivisshe Pystle spyrethe and breathed forthe.

2. *trans.* To breathe (air, etc.). Const. *into*.

1382 WYCLIF *Gen.* ii. 7 The Lord God thanne fourmede man of the slyme of the erthe, and spiride in to the face of hym an entre of breth of lijf.

3. To breathe forth or out, to create or produce by the agency of the breath.

Used in the pa. pple. of the Holy Spirit in relation to the other Persons of the Trinity.

1435 MISYN *Fire of Love* 16 þe sone is cald, be-caus of þe fadyr he is gottyn; þe holy goste, be-caus of both þe holy fader & holy sone he is spiryd. **1613** DAY *Dyall* iii. (1614) 49 He is tearmed a Spirit,.. because he is spired or breathed from the Father and the Sonne. **1645** USSHER *Body Div.* (1647) 86.

b. To pour out by or as by breathing; to emit or give *forth* (odour).

1649 LOVELACE *Poems* 77 The rosin-lightning [should] flash, and Monster spire Squibs, and words hotter then his fire. **1657** W. MORICE *Coena quasi Κοινὴ* Def. xviii. 321 The leaves.. gently toucht do spire forth an excellent odour.

spire (spaɪə(r)), *v.*[3] [f. SPIRE *sb.*[3]] *intr.* To curl, twist, or wind spirally; to make a spiral curve; *esp.* to mount or soar with spiral movement.

Sometimes difficult to distinguish from SPIRE *v.*[1]

1607 TOPSELL *Four-f. Beasts* 54 The hornes [of the Bonasus] are recurued,.. so that they do not spire directly downeward but rather forward. **1718** *Entertainer* No. 41. 280 It is a Pitchy-smoak, and wheresoever it curls and spires, there we may.. find the.. Fire of Virtue. **1824** MISS L. M. HAWKINS *Annaline* II. 232 The whirlwind came spiring upwards. *a* **1850** BEDDOES *Poems* (1851) 214 The amazed circle of scared eagles Spire to the clouds. **1895** YEATS *Poems* 225 The worms that spired about his bones.

spire, obs. form of SPEER *v.*[1]

†**spire-alum.** *Obs.*$^{-1}$ Some variety of alum.

c **1375** *Litt. Red Bk. Bristol* (1900) II. 6 Qe nul alym soit vsee nule part en la ville en oueraigne forsqe Spyralym, Glasalym, et Bokkau.

†**spired**, *ppl. a.*[1] *Obs.* [f. SPIRE *v.*[1] 1.] Of barley: Sprouted; spoilt on this account for brewing purposes.

1548 *Act 2–3 Edw. VI*, c. 10 §2 Any Malte not beinge well and sufficiently made, or beinge made of mowburnte or spired Barley. **1649** THORPE *Charge at York Assizes* 28 If any Malt-maker do not make his Malt of good and sweet Barley, not Mow-burnt or Spired Barley. **1702** *Guide Constables* 46 Malt.. made of.. spired barly.

spired (spaɪəd), (*ppl.*) *a.*[2] [f. SPIRE *sb.*[2]]

1. Having a tapering, sharp-pointed top; peaked.

1611 SPEED *Theatr. Gt. Brit.* (1614) 115 The Severne,.. whose head rising from the spired mountaine Plymllimon [etc.]. **1650** in *Archaeol.* (1779) V. 434 There is one piramide in spired pinacle of marble. **1797** *Encycl. Brit.* (ed. 3) I. 501 Black, rocky, and marked with rugged spired tops.

b. Of a steeple, tower, etc.: Provided with or carrying a spire.

Also as the second element in combs.

1610 HOLLAND *Camden's Brit.* 248 An exceeding high spired steeple. **1681** W. ROBERTSON *Phraseol. Gen.* (1693) 334 Huge spired steeples, with a gallant ring of Bells. **1682** WHELER *Journ. Greece* II. 202 On the top of the Hill is a round spired Tower. **1779** MASON *Eng. Gard.* III. 173 Of some old Fane, whose steeple's Gothic pride Or pinnacled, or spir'd, would bolder rise. **1888** W. E. HENLEY *Bk. Verses* 157 Like rampired walls the houses lean, All spired and domed and turreted.

fig. **1851** WHITTIER *Chapel Hermits* xix, The breaking day, which tips The golden-spired Apocalypse! **1865** E. BURRITT *Walk to Land's End* 430 A great human prayer spired with faith and towering heavenward.

2. Sharply-pointed; tapering. *rare.*

1670–1 NARBOROUGH *Jrnl.* in *Acc. Sev. Late Voy.* I. (1694) 16 Three Tropick Birds.. with a long spired Tail as big as Pigeons.

3. Of plants: Stemmed, spiked. In combs., as *high-*, *sharp-spired*.

1780 BECKFORD *Italy* (1834) I. 263 Above the hut, their appearance was truly formidable, bristled over with sharp-spired dwarf aloes. **1838** MARY HOWITT *Birds & Fl.* 65, I love sweet flowers of every sort, High-spired or trailing low.

spired, (*ppl.*) *a.*[3] *rare.* [f. SPIRE *sb.*[3] or *v.*[3]]

†**1.** Spiral in appearance or form. *Obs.*$^{-1}$

c **1623** LODGE *Poor Mans Talent* (Hunter. Cl.) 75 Yf it [sediment of urine] be white, equall, and spired, it signifieth that the patientt is of a good Constitution of boddie.

2. *Conch.* Having a spire.

1891 in *Cent. Dict.*

spire-grass. [SPIRE *sb.*[1] Cf. SPEAR-GRASS.]

†**a.** = SPEAR-GRASS 1, SPEARWORT 3. *Obs.* **b.** One or other of various reeds or sedges. Cf. SPEAR-GRASS 2. Now *dial.*

1626 BACON *Sylva* §565 Where Alleyes are close Gravelled, the Earth putteth forth, the first yeare, Knot-grasse and after Spire-grasse. **1629** *Drayner Conf.* (1647) A iv b, There are many watry plashes, and much rotten Spire-grasse in it. **1851** STERNBERG *Northampt. Dial.*, *Spire-grass*, a tall species of sedge, growing on fenny land. **1851** MEREDITH *Flower of Ruins* Poems 33 The little harebell leans On the spire-grass that it queens, With bonnet blue.

spireless (ˈspaɪəlɪs), *a.* [f. SPIRE *sb.*[1]] Destitute of a spire or spires.

1833 CHALMERS in Hanna *Mem.* (1851) III. xix. 421 Re-entered the town near its singular and spireless church. **1894** *Outing* XXIV. 317/1 At early dawn when the huge spireless towers were becoming gradually distinct.

spirelet (ˈspaɪəlɪt). [f. SPIRE *sb.*[1] + -LET.] A small spire, esp. one erected on a church tower or turret. (Freq. from *c* 1850.)

1848 B. WEBB *Cont. Ecclesiol.* 257 The tower is square of brick, with an octagonal lantern, and above all a tall spirelet. **1867** BARING-GOULD *Path Just* 120 A small religious house hard by, with a spirelet and bell. **1894** *Ch. Q. Rev.* Apr. 52 In most cases the central tower of their churches becomes a mere spirelet.

attrib. **1900** *Jrnl. R. Archæol. Inst.* LVII. 3 It had a plain spirelet top with a finial.

†**spireme.** *Cytology. Obs.* Also **spirem.** [ad. G. *spirem* (W. Flemming *Zellsubstanz, Kern und Zelltheilung* (1882) xx. 195), f. Ionic Gr. σπείρημ-α coil, convolution.] The tangled strands of chromosomal material seen in the early stages of cell division, formerly believed to be a single continuous strand (or two in a diploid cell, etc.); = SKEIN *sb.*[1] 2 c.

1889 *Q. Jrnl. Microsc. Sci.* XXX. 171 We call this stage, with Flemming, the 'Knäuel-Stadium' (skein stage), or 'spirem', or 'mother-skein'. **1905** *Amer. Naturalist* XXXIX. 484 During synapsis the reticulum becomes transformed into a definite spirem. **1910** *Encycl. Brit.* VII. 714/1 As the spireme thread contracts, it segments into a number of short, and usually U-shaped, segments—the 'chromosomes'. **1936** *Discovery* May 161/1 The hypothesis of the continuous spireme, long given up by cytologists, is resurrected, and entirely inaccurate statements are made.

†**spire-steeple.** *Obs.* Also **spire steeple.** [SPIRE *sb.*[1]] A steeple surmounted by a spire; a church spire; = SPIRE *sb.*[1] 8. (Common from *c* 1610 to *c* 1725.)

1559 MORWYNG *Evonym.* 78 Upon this necke standeth the head of brasse with a top like a spire steple. **1610** HOLLAND *Camden's Brit.* 700 A very faire Church [at Ripon],.. with three high spire-steeples. **1635–56** COWLEY *Davideis* Notes 59 A Pyramide is a Figure broad beneath, and smaller and sharper by degrees upward, 'till it end in a Point, like our Spire-Steeples. **1725** in Picton *L'pool Munic. Rec.* (1886) II. 70 This Councill.. being very desirous.. to erect a convenient church, with a proper spire steeple. **1784** R. BAGE *Barham Downs* I. 7 From the window of the parlour.. I have a view of a tall spire-steeple. **1809** COLERIDGE *Friend* 23 Nov. 223 An instinctive taste teaches men to build their churches in flat countries with spire-steeples.

spirewise, *adv.* ? *Obs.* [f. SPIRE *sb.*[1] + -WISE.] In the manner of a tapering spire; pyramidally.

1610 GUILLIM *Heraldry* II. vi. (1611) 56 A Cheveron is an ordinary formed of a two fold line spirewise or pyramidall. **1658** ROWLAND tr. *Moufet's Theat. Ins.* 930 Some of them build their nests spire wise out of clay. **1683** LORRAIN tr. *Muret's Rites Funeral* 38 A kind of Square Tower,.. and on the top of it were four little Towers made Taper or Spire-wise.

†**spirey.** *Obs.*$^{-1}$ [? ad. F. *spirée.*] = SPIRÆA.

1713 *Phil. Trans.* XXVIII. 220 Curran leaved Spirey.. grows wild in Canada and Virginia.

spirey, obs. form of SPIRY *a.*

†**spirget.** *Obs.* Also 7 spurget. [Of obscure origin: cf. SPIRKET *sb.*[1]] A pin or peg for hanging things on.

1567 GOLDING *Ovid's Met.* VIII. 830 There hung a Boawle of Beeche upon a spirget by a ring. **1691** RAY *S. & E. Co. Words* 114 A *Spurget*, a Tagge or piece of Wood to hang any thing upon.

spiric (ˈspaɪərɪk), *a.* and *sb. Geom. rare.* [ad. Gr. σπειρικ-ός, f. σπεῖρα SPIRE *sb.*[3] Cf. F. *spirique.*]

a. *adj.* Of or pertaining to, having the form of, a tore or torus. **b.** *sb.* A plane section of a torus.

1788 T. TAYLOR *Proclus* I. 134 But, with respect to these sections, the conic were invented by Menæchmus,.. But the spiric by Perseus. **1891** in *Cent. Dict.*

So †**ˈspirical** *a. Obs.*$^{-1}$

1788 T. TAYLOR *Proclus* I. 134 Conic, or spirical sections are generated from a particular section of solids.

spiricle (ˈspaɪərɪk(ə)l). *Bot.* [dim. of SPIRE *sb.*[3]] A minute coiled thread in the coating of certain seeds and achenes, which uncoils when moistened.

1891 in *Cent. Dict.*

Spirifer (ˈspaɪərɪfə(r)). *Palæont.* [mod.L. *spirifer* (Sowerby, 1816), f. L. *spīra* SPIRE *sb.*[3] + *-fer* bearing.] A genus of fossil brachiopods, found abundantly in the Silurian, Devonian, and Carboniferous formations, characterized by long highly-developed spiral appendages; a member or species of this genus, or of the family *Spiriferidæ* of which it is the type. Also *attrib.*

1835 *Penny Cycl.* III. 125/1 A particular kind of fossil-shell, named a *spirifer*, has indeed been detected in it. **1839** DE LA BECHE *Rep. Geol. Cornwall*, etc. iii. 47 Those seams which contain casts of broken vertebral columns of.. spirifers, and corals. **1872** H. A. NICHOLSON *Palæontol.* 205 The true Spirifers are mainly Silurian and Devonian. **1890** GEIKIE *Class-Bk. Geol.* (ed. 2) xix. 266 The Devonian system [contains].. Cypridina-shales, Spirifer sandstone.

spiˈriferous (spaɪəˈrɪfərəs), *a.*[1] [ad. mod.L. *spirifer(us)* or F. *spirifère*: cf. prec.]

1. *Conch.* Having a spire.

1859 in MAYNE *Med. Lex.*

2. *Palæont.* Of a brachiopod: Having spiral appendages.

1891 in *Cent. Dict.*

spiˈriferous, *a.*[2] *Geol.* [f. SPIRIFER + -OUS.] Containing or yielding spirifers.

1888 *Encycl. Brit.* XXIV. 507/2 The spiriferous sandstone on the Denison Plains.. is doubtless Palæozoic.

spiriform (ˈspaɪərɪfɔːm), *a.* [ad. mod.L. *spiriformis* or F. *spiriforme.*] Having the form of a spire or spiral.

1841 T. R. JONES *Anim. Kingd.* 450 In all essential particulars this spiriform viscus is precisely analogous to the laminated cavity of the *Nautilus.* **1861** HULME tr. *Moquin-Tandon* II. VII. iii. 349 The females [of the *Trichocephalus*] are always straight; never spiriform, like the males. **1892** F. GALTON *Finger Prints* v. 77 A series of rings, spirals, and plaits.. breaking away into a.. spiriform arrangement.

spirillar (spaɪəˈrɪlə(r)), *a.* [f. SPIRILL-UM + -AR.] Of or belonging to the bacterial genus *Spirillum*; resembling a spirillum; characterized by the presence of spirilla.

1891 in *Cent. Dict.* **1896** *Allbutt's Syst. Med.* I. 510 We should find that some of its descendants are spirillar. *Ibid.* 952 Blood.. containing the spirillar organisms. **1904** *Brit. Med. Jrnl.* 17 Sept. 654 The pseudo-leucocytes that are present in the blood in.. spirillar fever.

spirillosis (spaɪərɪˈləʊsɪs). *Path.* [See next and -OSIS.] A disease or affection characterized by the presence of spirilla.

1904 *Jrnl. Microsc. Soc.* Feb. 100 Spirillosis of Fowls.—In the blood they found a spirillum and this blood produced the disease in other fowls.

‖**Spirillum** (spaɪəˈrɪləm). *Bacteriol.* Pl. **spirilla.** [mod.L., dim. of L. *spīra* SPIRE *sb.*[3]] A genus or group of bacteria characterized by a spiral structure; any member of this genus, esp. the species found in the blood in relapsing fever.

1875 HUXLEY & MARTIN *Elem. Biol.* 28 *Spirillum.* Elongated unjointed threads rolled up into a more or less perfect spiral: frequently two spirals intertwine. **1878** BRISTOWE *Th. & Pract. Med.* (ed. 2) 134 Spirilla are moving spiral filaments of extreme tenuity. **1895** *Westm. Gaz.* 8 Nov. 8/1 The water used in making the creams teemed with micrococci, bacilli, and spirilla.

b. *spirillum fever*, relapsing fever.

1886 PYE-SMITH *Fagge's Princ. & Pract. Med.* I. 201 With the analogy of spirillum fever to guide us. **1897** *Allbutt's Syst. Med.* II. 368 In spirillum fever there is no rash.

†**spirinche.** *Obs.*$^{-1}$ [ad. med.L. *spirinchus*, *spiringus*: see SPIRLING.] A smelt.

a **1682** SIR T. BROWNE *Acc. Fishes Norfolk* Wks. 1835 IV. 331 *Spirinches*, or smelt, in great plenty about Lynn.

spiring (ˈspaɪərɪŋ), *vbl. sb.*[1] [f. SPIRE *v.*[1]] The action of the verb in various senses; also *concr.*, a shoot or sprout.

c **1400** tr. *Secreta Secret., Gov. Lordsh.* 73 Trees er cled with newe leuys, þe erthe ys fair wyth spiringes. **1707** MORTIMER *Husb.* 376 They will be the taller and streighter by being forced up by the Wood that grows about them; tho' a deep Soil.. contributes much to their spiring. **1733** W. ELLIS *Chiltern & Vale Farm.* 158 It is freed from the risque of Spiring before the Nut is put into the Ground.

†**'spiring**, *vbl. sb.*² *Obs.*⁻¹ [f. SPIRE *v.*²] A breathing; a blowing.

1534 MORE *Answ. Poysoned Bk.* Wks. 1061/1 Christ.. bode him meruayl not therof, no more then of yᵉ spiring or mouing of the spirite or of yᵉ wind.

spiring ('spaɪərɪŋ), *ppl. a.*¹ [f. SPIRE *v.*¹]

1. That spires or rises up taperingly to a point; freq. *poet.* or *rhet.*, soaring aloft or reaching to a great height: **a.** Of edifices, rocks, etc.

1538 LELAND *Itin.* VIII. (1909) III. 59 The old building of the church of the abbay remayneth having ii. goodly spiring steples. **1613-6** W. BROWNE *Brit. Past.* I. iv, Carved Monuments, Spiring Colosses and high raised rents. **1738** [G. SMITH] *Cur. Relat.* II. 275 Surrounded.. by spiring Rocks, some eight, some sixteen, and others thirty Foot high. **1774** PENNANT *Tour Scotl. in 1772*, 343 Spiring summits of vast Mountains. **1800** BENTHAM in *Ess. Goth. Archit.* 85 This chapel.. is supported by strong spiring buttresses. **1825** *Stranger's Comp. Cambr.* 53 From its roof rises a spiring and airy lantern. **1906** CORNFORD *Defenceless Isl.* 30 The graceful lines, the spiring masts,.. suggest swift motion.

b. *fig.* Of the spirit.

1618 LITHGOW *Pilgr. Farewell* A iij, Prayse-worthie Pilgrime, whose so spiring Sprite Restes not content, incentred in one Soyle.

c. Of trees. (Cf. SPIRAL *a.*² b.)

1707 MORTIMER *Husb.* 390 If each other of these Trees be a spiring Tree, and the odd one between, a Fruit-tree to spread. **1801** SOUTHEY *Thalaba* I. xxiii, All trees that bend with luscious fruit,.. Or point their spiring heads to heaven. **1857** THOREAU *Maine W.* ii. (1867) 102 The lofty, spiring tops of the spruce and fir. **1886** MRS. CADDY *Footsteps J. D'Arc* 12 The spiring groves of distant elm and poplar are thrown out by the white clouds.

2. Of grass or plants: Shooting, sprouting; running up into a spire or stem.

1612 DRAYTON *Poly-olb.* xvi. 48 Where now the sharp-edg'd scythe shears up the spiring grass. **1677** PLOT *Oxfordsh.* 241 They.. plough it early in the year as soon as their clay is fallowed, and then there will spring some spiring-grass that will keep it from scorching. **1863** W. W. STORY *Roba di R.* II. iv. 115 Their spiring weeds that grow out of the eaves of the.. moss-stained tiles.

†**'spiring**, *ppl. a.*² *Obs.*⁻¹ [f. SPIRE *v.*²] Respiring.

1577 GRANGE *Gold. Aphrod.*, etc. Q iv b, Yet I forlorne a dolefull wight,.. Doe wishe me set farre from the light: And ridde of this my spyring breath.

'spiring, *ppl. a.*³ *rare*⁻¹. [f. SPIRE *v.*³] Spiral; winding spirally.

1872 TENNYSON *Last Tourn.* 510 She heard the feet of Tristram grind The spiring stone that scaled about her tower.

spirit ('spɪrɪt), *sb.* Forms: α. 3- spirit, 4-6 -ite, 4-5 -itt, 4, 6 spiryte, 5 spiryt, 9 *dial.* spirut; 4-6 spyrite, 5 -itte, -id, -ut, -ete, 5-6 -it, 4-5 spyryt, 5-6 -yte. β. 5 sperete, -ite, 5-6 speryt, 5, 7, 9 sperit, 9 sperrit. See also SPIRT, SPRIGHT, and SPRITE. [a. AF. *spirit* (*espirit*), *spirite*, = OF. *esperit*, *-ite*, *esprit* (mod.F. *esprit*), or ad. L. *spiritus* (It. *spirito*, Pg. *espirito*, Sp. *espiritu*) breathing, breath, air, etc., related to *spīrāre* to breathe.

Mod.F. has also *spirite* in the sense of 'spiritualist'. In G., Da., and Sw. the L. form *spiritus* occurs, chiefly in sense 21.

The earlier English uses of the word are mainly derived from passages in the Vulgate, in which *spiritus* is employed to render Gr. πνεῦμα PNEUMA and Heb. *rūaḥ*. The translation of these words by *spirit* (or one of its variant forms) is common to all versions of the Bible from Wyclif onwards.]

I. 1. a. The animating or vital principle in man (and animals); that which gives life to the physical organism, in contrast to its purely material elements; the breath of life.

In some examples with implication of other senses.

c **1250** *Gen. & Ex.* 203 God made Adam, and his licham of erðe he nam, And blew ðor-in a liues blast,.. A spirit ful of wit and sckil. **1340** *Ayenb.* 92 Þet body of man is.. þe vileste þet is, and þe spirit of man is þe zaule, and ys þe nobleste þing an þe heȝeste sseppe þet may by. **1382** WYCLIF *Eccl.* iii. 21 Who kneȝ, if the spirit of the sonus of Adam steȝe vp aboue, and if the spirit of bestis go doun bynethe? **1582** N. T. (Rhem.) *Jas.* ii. 26 For euen as the bodie without the spirit is dead: so also faith without workes is dead. **1611** BIBLE *Wisd.* xvi. 14 The spirit when it is gone foorth returneth not; neither the soule receiued vp, commeth againe. **1667** MILTON *P.L.* x. 784 Least that pure breath of Life, the Spirit of Man,.. cannot together perish With this corporeal Clod. **1728** CHAMBERS *Cycl.* s.v. *Person*, Thus, a Man, tho' consisting of two very different Things, *viz.* Body and Spirit, is not two Persons. **1850** TENNYSON *In Mem.* lvi, The spirit does but mean the breath. **1853** ABP. THOMSON *Laws Th.* (ed. 3) 61 When the breath is exhaled the spirit remains immortal.

transf. **1382** WYCLIF *John* vi. 64 The wordis that I haue spokun to ȝou, ben spirit and lyf. **1712** J. JAMES tr. *Le Blond's Gardening* 201 Water-Works are the Life of a Garden; 'tis these.. which animate and invigorate it, and, if I may so say, give it new Life and Spirit.

b. In phrases denoting or implying diminution or cessation of the vital power, or the recovery of this. Also *transf.*, life-blood.

In various Biblical passages used with reference to profound discouragement, or recovery from this: cf. sense 13.

a **1300** *Cursor M.* 12075 And sone þe spirit þat was fledd Again come in þat ilk stede. **1382** WYCLIF *Luke* viii. 55 And her spirit turnyde aȝeyn, and sche roos anon. *Ibid.* xxiii. 46 And he seyinge thes things, sente out the spirit [*v.r.* ȝaf vp the goost], ether diede. *a* **1425** tr. *Arderne's Treat. Fistula*, etc. 38 Neþerlesse þai may.. moue almost to þe breþing out of þe spirit. **1606** SHAKS. *Ant. & Cl.* IV. xv. 58 Now my Spirit is going, I can no more. **1611** BIBLE *Judg.* xv. 19 When he had drunke, his spirit came againe, and he reuiued. **1720** POPE *Iliad* XVIII. 120 Let me revenge it on proud Hector's heart, Let his last spirit smoke upon my dart.

transf. **1595** SHAKS. *John* IV. i. 110 There is no malice in this burning cole, The breath of heauen, hath blowne his spirit out.

c. In contexts relating to temporary separation of the immaterial from the material part of man's being, or to perception of a purely intellectual character. Chiefly in phr. ***in spirit***.

1382 WYCLIF *Rev.* iv. 2 Anoon I was in spirit, and lo! a seete was put in heuen, and on the seete oon sittinge. *c* **1400** MAUNDEV. (Roxb.) xiv. 61 In spirit he was rauischt intill heuen, whare he sawe heuenly priuetez. *c* **1440** *Alph. Tales* 451 He was ravisshid his spyrid fro his body vnto Pasch day. **1582** N.T. (Rhem.) *Rev.* i. 10, I was in spirit on the Dominical day. **1667** MILTON *P.L.* XI. 406 In Spirit perhaps he also saw Rich Mexico.., And Cusco in Peru. **1850** TENNYSON *In Mem.* xvii, For I in spirit saw thee move Thro' circles of the bounding sky.

d. Incorporeal or immaterial being, as opposed to *body* or *matter*; being or intelligence conceived as distinct from, or independent of, anything physical or material. (Cf. MIND *sb.*¹ 17 f.)

1382 WYCLIF *John* iii. 6 That that is born of spirit, is spirit. **1611** BIBLE *Isaiah* xxxi. 3 Now the Egyptians are men and not God, and their horses flesh and not spirit. **1690** LOCKE *Hum. Und.* II. xxiii. (1695) 164 The primary Ideas we have peculiar to Body, as contradistinguished to Spirit. *Ibid.*, The Ideas we have belonging, and peculiar to Spirit, are Thinking, and Will. **1725** WATTS *Logic* (1736) 23 Modes belong either to Body or to Spirit, or to both... Modes of Spirit belong only to Minds. **1832** BREWSTER *Nat. Magic* ii. 10 The sentinel which guards the pass between the worlds of matter and of spirit. **1845** BAILEY *Festus* (ed. 2) 39 Spirit is soul Deified. **1898** ILLINGWORTH *Div. Immanence* i. 5 If matter and spirit are thus only known in combination, it follows that neither can be completely known.

2. a. The soul of a person, as commended to God, or passing out of the body, in the moment of death.

c **1375** *Sc. Leg. Saints* i. (*Peter*) 730 And þis he ȝalde þe spyrit, of god in-to þe halde. **1382** WYCLIF *Luke* xxiii. 46 Fadir, in to thi hondis I bitake my spirit. **1509** FISHER *Funeral Serm. C'tess Richmond* Wks. (1876) 309 Sone after .. she departed & yelded vp her spyryte in to the handes of our lorde. **1582** N. T. (Rhem.) *Acts* vii. 59 They stoned Steuen.. saying: Lord Iesus, receiue my spirit. **1611** BIBLE *Luke* xxiii. 46 Father, into thy hands I commend my spirit. **1825** SCOTT *Betrothed* Concl., If you come to announce the doom of this poor frame, may God be gracious to the spirit which must be violently dismissed from it!

b. The disembodied soul of a (deceased) person, regarded as a separate entity; = SOUL *sb.* 12.

1375 BARBOUR *Bruce* IV. 757 The Pithones.. Rasit, throu hyr mekill slycht, samuell['s] sperit. **1426** LYDGATE *De Guil. Pilgr.* 11960 To the body a spyryt spak,.. The spyryt in the weye stood; The body.. hong on a tre. **1526** *Pilgr. Perf.* (W. de W. 1531) 7 All the holy sayntes that ben saued, and also the damned spirytes in hell. **1560** DAUS tr. *Sleidane's Comm.* 115 There by a signe made, he sheweth that he is the spirite of her. **1611** BIBLE *Heb.* xii. 23 To the generall assembly,.. and to the spirits of iust men made perfect. **1632** MILTON *Penseroso* 88 Where I may.. unsphear The spirit of Plato. **1741-2** GRAY *Agrippina* 14 'Twould dash his joy To hear the spirit of Britannicus Yet walks on earth. **1790** COWPER *Mother's Picture* 23 Hover'd thy spirit o'er thy sorrowing son, Wretch even then, life's journey just begun? **1819** SHELLEY *Cenci* IV. i. 93 Her spirit shall approach the throne of God Plague-spotted with my curses. **1840** HOOD *Open Question* 145 Spirit of Kant! have we not had enough To make Religion sad, and sour, and snubbish.

fig. **1742** YOUNG *Nt. Th.* II. 180 The spirit walks of ev'ry day deceas'd.

3. a. A supernatural, incorporeal, rational being or personality, usually regarded as imperceptible at ordinary times to the human senses, but capable of becoming visible at pleasure, and freq. conceived as troublesome, terrifying, or hostile to mankind.

a **1300** *Cursor M.* 17288 + 449 Spirit has nauther flesch ne bone, as I now haf sothtly. *c* **1330** R. BRUNNE *Chron. Wace* (Rolls) 8072 We fynde writen.. Of swylk manere of spyrites; Bytwyxte þe mone & þe erþe þei wone. **1387** TREVISA *Higden* (Rolls) III. 279 We haveþ i-lerned of Socrates, þat he was alway tendaunt to a spirit þat was i-cleped demon. **1422** tr. *Secreta Secret., Priv. Priv.* 143 This Spyritte that al thy workys seyth ande parcewyth. **1483** CAXTON *G. de la Tour* F j, His wyf.. sayd it was the fende or elles the goblyn or somme spyryte. **1560** DAUS tr. *Sleidane's Comm.* 116 After that Luthers doctrine was spred abroad and knowen, those spirites.. vanyshed cleane out of syght. **1596** SHAKS. *1 Hen. IV*, III. i. 52, I can call Spirits from the vastie Deepe. **1610** —— *Temp.* I. ii. 409 What, is't a Spirit?.. Beleeue me sir, It carries a braue forme. But 'tis a spirit. **1646** SIR T. BROWNE *Pseud. Ep.* 76 The conceit is excellent, and if the effect would follow somwhat divine, whereby we might communicate like spirits. **1667** MILTON *P.L.* I. 423 For Spirits when they please Can either Sex assume, or both. **1721** YOUNG *Revenge* III. i, Shut close the doors, That not a spirit find an entrance here. **1731-8** SWIFT *Polite Conv.* 110, I saw some thing in black, I thought it was a Spirit. **1799** WORDSW. *Nutting* 54 With gentle hand Touch—for there is a spirit in the woods. **1841** BROWNING *Pippa Passes* Poems (1905) 175 As if God bade some spirit plague a world. **1897** MARY KINGSLEY *W. Africa* 479 The spirit is malevolent: all native-made spirits are. **1902** J. M. ROBERTSON *Hist. Christianity* 71 Mithra.. being the first of the seven planetary spirits on whose names the week was based.

fig. **1850** TENNYSON *In Mem.* cii, As down the garden-walks I move, Two spirits of a diverse love Contend for loving masterdom.

transf. **1860** TYNDALL *Glac.* I. ii. 22 We had, in fact, the Spirit of the Brocken before us.

b. With qualifying terms, as *evil*, *familiar*, *guardian*, *wicked*, etc.

c **1340** HAMPOLE *Prose Treat.* 5 For thare may na wykked spyrite noye þare Ihesu es mekyll in mynde. *c* **1380** WYCLIF *Last Age Ch.* (1840) 34 Alas, þat no good spiryt dwellid wiþ me at my comynge into Goddis Chirche. **1382** —— *1 Sam.* xxviii. 7 There is a womman hauynge a dyuynynge spirite in Endore. **1508-** [see DAMNED *ppl. a.* 2]. *a* **1536** *Songs, Carols*, etc. 69 þe speryt infernall, all þe hole rowte. **1555-** [see EVIL *a.* 3 b]. **1565-** [see FAMILIAR *a.* 2 d]. **1582** N.T. (Rhem.) *Heb.* i. 14 Are they not al ministring spirits? **1611** BIBLE *1 Tim.* iv. 1 Giuing heed to seducing spirits. **1676** *Charge in Office of Clerk of Assize* 101 If any person have.. employed any wicked spirit, to any intent or purpose whatsoever. **1711** [see GUARDIAN 6 b]. **1785** C. WILKINS tr. *Bhaguat-Gheeta* 68 The evil spirits are terrified. **1827** SCOTT *Highl. Widow* v, The days and hours when the wicked spirits were supposed to have especial power over man and beast. **1860** PUSEY *Min. Proph.* 30 It has been thought that the evil spirits assault mankind in a sort of order or method.

transf. **1581** PETTIE *Guazzo's Civ. Conv.* I. (1586) 38 The more they are in prosperitie, the more they are beset with Flatterers,.. whereof it commeth that Princes are euer besieged by these euill spirites.

c. A being of this nature imagined as possessing and actuating a person.

1382 WYCLIF *Matt.* viii. 16 Thei brouȝte to hym many hauynge deuelys, and he castide out spiritis by word. **1382** —— *Acts* xvi. 16 Sum wench hauynge a spirit of dyuynacioun. **1546** LANGLEY *Pol. Verg. de Invent.* I. xviii. 33 To banish the Spirit out of yᵉ Demoniake. **1651** [see POSSESS *v.* 5 b]. **1711** SHAFTESB. *Charac.* (1737) III. 117 He had been seiz'd with this prophesying spirit-errant, processional, and saltant. **1728** CHAMBERS *Cycl.*, *Demoniac*,.. a Person possess'd with a Spirit, or Demon. **1850** [see POSSESS *v.* 5].

d. In generalized sense: A being essentially incorporeal or immaterial.

c **1340** HAMPOLE *Pr. Consc.* 3022 Bot now may som.. aske how þe saul may fele payne, þat es noght elles bot a spirit. *c* **1380** WYCLIF *Sel. Wks.* III. 502 Hit is heresye to trowe þat Crist is a spiryt and no body. **1382** —— *John* iv. 24 God is a spirit. **1653** BINNING *Serm.* 9 Angels and men next to God, are spirits, as He is a Spirit. *a* **1703** BURKITT *On N.T., John* iv. 24 God.. is not a bare spiritual substance, but a pure and perfect Spirit. **1710** BERKELEY *Princ. Hum. Knowl.* I. §6 In my mind, or in that of some other created spirit.. or of some eternal spirit. **1876** J. PARKER *Paracl.* I. i. 9 Man *has* a body, but he *is* a spirit.

4. With *the* and qualifying term, denoting some particular being of the above nature.

1375 BARBOUR *Bruce* IV. 758 [She raised] in his sted þe euill spirit þat gaf grath ansueir hir to. *a* **1425** *Cursor M.* 170 (Trin.), Iesu.. Was temptide with þe spirit of wronge. *c* **1440** *Alph. Tales* 281 Þer was ane hermett þat was tempid with þe spiritt of blasfemyng.

1797 COLERIDGE *This Lime-tree Bower my Prison* 42 Such hues As veil the Almighty Spirit, when He makes Spirits perceive his presence. **1836** *Penny Cycl.* VI. 208/2 The Indians.. consider it as the dwelling of the Great Spirit, or 'Manitou'. **1842** LYTTON *Zicci* 2 The Evil Spirit is pulling you towards him by the hair.

5. †**a.** One who kidnaps; an abductor. *Obs.*

1645 WHITELOCKE *Mem.* (1682) 140/1 An Ordinance agains such who are called Spirits, and use to steal away, and take up children. **1686** *Lond. Gaz.* No. 2532/1 The frequent Abuses of a lewd sort of People, called spirits, in Seducing many of His Majesties Subjects to go on Shipboard [etc.]. **1690** J. CHILD *Disc. Trade* x. 170 A sort of loose vagrant People,.. which Merchants and Masters of Ships, by their Agents (or Spirits, as they were called) gathered up about the Streets of London, and other places.

b. *Printing.* (See quots.)

1683 MOXON *Mech. Exerc., Printing* 373 The Press-man sometimes has a Week-Boy to take Sheets, as they are Printed off the Tympan. These Boys do.. black and dawb themselves; whence the Workmen do jocosely call them Devils; and sometimes Spirits, and sometimes Flies. **1888** JACOBI *Printers' Vocab.* 129 *Spirit*, the evil genius of a chapel.

c. (See quot.)

1825 in Drewitt *Bombay in Days Geo. IV* (1907) 176, I shall gain the character here of a 'spirit',.. having met several times at his house ladies of spotted reputation, and who are not visited by any one.

d. *ellipt.* The spirit duck.

1784 PENNANT *Arct. Zool.* II. 558 Called sometimes the Spirit, as is supposed, from its suddenly appearing again at a distance, after diving.

II. 6. a. ***the Spirit of God*** (or ***the Lord***), the active essence or essential power of the Deity, conceived as a creative, animating, or inspiring influence.

13.. *Cursor M.* 7106 (Gott.), Sampson slou þat leon kene, þe spirit of godd in him was sene. **1382** WYCLIF *Isaiah* lxi. 1 The spirit of the Lord [is] vp on me. —— *1 Cor.* ii. 11 What thingis ben of God, no man knowith, no but the spirit of God. **1582** N.T. (Rhem.) *Eph.* iv. 30 And contristate not the holy Spirit of God. **1604** HIERON *Wks.* I. 480 Were these inuented by Gods Spirit Or found you them in holy writ? **1667** in *Cath. Rec. Soc. Publ.* III. 70 One of those.. happy trees vnto which the spirit of God compares a iust man. **1841** TRENCH *Parab.* xiii. 220 The informing Spirit of God which prompts the works and quickens the faith. **1875** MANNING *Mission H. Ghost* i. 1 The Spirit of the Lord is God the Holy Ghost.

b. ***the Holy Spirit***, = HOLY GHOST 1.

a **1300** *Cursor M.* 19415 (Edinb.), þe hali spirite oute of him spac. *c* **1375** *Sc. Leg. Saints* x. (*Matthew*) 130 Eftyre cristis ascencione, þe haly spyrit of criste come done. *c* **1420** *Prymer* 40 Take þou not fro me þin hooli spirit. **1549** *Bk. Com. Prayer, Ord. Priests*, Laude and praise be to the father, .. And to the holy spirite. **1639**, etc. [see PROCESSION *sb.* 4]. **1709** WATTS *Hymn*, *'Come, Holy Spirit'* i, Come, Holy

Spirit, heavenly Dove. **1881** N.T. (R.V.) *Matt.* i. 18 The Holy Ghost. *marg.* Or, Holy Spirit: and so throughout this book. **1898** CHAVASSE *Litton's Ch. Christ* 18 Those who by the Holy Spirit have been convinced of sin.

c. ***the Spirit,*** = prec. In Christian charismatic groups: ***baptism in (of, etc.) the Spirit*** (and similar phrases), an experience subsequent to conversion and water-baptism, usually evidenced by speaking in tongues (see quot. 1972[2]): in allusion to Mark i. 8 and parallel passages; ***to receive the Spirit,*** to experience conversion, evidenced by speaking in tongues; ***to sing in the Spirit,*** to sing in a language apparently unknown to the singer (cf. I Cor. xiv. 15); so ***song in the Spirit; the Spirit moves me:*** see MOVE *v.* 11.

1382 WYCLIF *Mark* i. 12 Anon the Spirit puttide [Vulg. *expulit*] hym in to desert. *a* **1400** N.T. (Paues) *Rom.* viii. 26 þe Spirit also helpeþ oure infirmyte. *c* **1520** M. NISBET *John* i. 32, I saw the spirit cummande doun as a dow fra heuen. **1546** GARDINER *Declar. Joye* 88 Baptisme yᵉ sacrament of birth of yᵉ spirite, as ye speake, in newe englyssh, and of the holly goost as the olde english turned it. *a* **1619** FOTHERBY *Atheom.* II. xii. §2 (1622) 337 With diuine accents, tuning rarely right, Vnto the rapting Spirit, the rapted spright. **1679** *Establ. Test* 24 If the Spirit moves, he can disgorge himself against the Priests of Baal, the Hirelings. **1822** SHELLEY *Chas. I,* II. 223 The apostolic power with which the Spirit Has filled its elect vessels. **1865** T. T. CARTER in *Oxford Lent Sermons* xiii. 198 Within this new dispensation of the Spirit there is a specially sacred Presence of our Lord. **1896** R. A. TORREY *Baptism with Holy Spirit* i. 20 The Baptism with the Holy Spirit is the Spirit of God coming upon the believer,.. imparting to him gifts not naturally his own, but which qualify him for the service to which God has called him. **1902** *Christian* 11 Dec. 13/1 If we are born again, we have received the Spirit once for all. **1903** R. C. MORGAN *Outpoured Spirit* viii. 53 By coming unto Jesus.. as members of the Spirit-baptized Church. **1909** T. B. BARRATT *In Days of Latter Rain* 98 One who is filled with the Spirit.. gets visions, prophesies, sings in the Spirit, staggers under the overwhelming weight of the Glory. **1932** C. E. RAVEN *Creator Spirit* iv. 113 It is just as much within this one order that the Spirit works in creation as in those fuller manifestations which we call the Incarnation and Atonement. **1941** D. GEE *Pentecostal Movement* i. 7 For the individual recipient of the baptism in the Spirit it is subsequent to.. regeneration. **1948** L. W. BROWN in M. Warren *Triumph of God* vi. 154 There are.. those who maintain that no man has truly received the Spirit unless he has spoken with tongues. **1964** N. BLOCH-HOELL *Pentecostal Movement* ii. 28 Mrs. Arthur.. gives a striking account of angel visions and singing in the Spirit in perfect Latin followed by correct translation into English. *Ibid.,* With regard to the 'song in the Spirit' and the testimony of the nuns it must be remembered that the latter was no first-hand evidence. **1972** S. TUGWELL (*title*) Did you receive the Spirit? **1972** R. A. WILSON tr. *Hollenweger's Pentecostals* ii. 22 In a Bible school in Topeka, Kansas, run by Charles Parham, speaking in tongues was recognized as a distinguishing characteristic of the baptism of the Spirit. **1977** G. W. H. LAMPE *God as Spirit* iii. 91 Perhaps the most original and significant insights of Paul are that the Spirit's inspiration makes men Christlike and, ideally, makes the community a visible re-embodiment of Christ.

d. So ***the Spirit of truth*** or †***verity,*** etc.

1382 WYCLIF *John* xiv. 17 He schal ȝyue to ȝou another coumfortour, the spirit of treuthe. ? *a* **1533** FRITH *Answ. More* L ij b, That spiryte of veryte whiche is sent from God our Father through our sauyour.., to lyghten our darke ignoraunce. **1551** BIBLE *John* xv. 26 When the comforter is come,.. whiche is the spirite of truthe. **1819** J. MONTGOMERY *Hymn, 'Lord God the Holy Ghost'* iii, Spirit of Light, explore And chase our gloom away.

7. a. The active or essential principle or power *of* some emotion, frame of mind, etc., as operating on or in persons.

1382 WYCLIF *2 Tim.* i. 7 God ȝaf not to vs the spirit of drede, but of vertu, and of loue, and sobrenesse. *c* **1400** LOVE *Bonavent. Mirr.* (1908) 61 Knowynge hym by the spirit of prophecie. **1551** BIBLE *Isaiah* xix. 14 The Lorde hathe made Egypte droncken wyth the spirite of erroure, and they shall vse it. **1560** DAUS tr. *Sleidane's Comm.* 129 One of them, as though he were moved with the spirite of prophecie, runeth up and downe the citie. **1591** SHAKS. *Two Gent.* v. iv. 55 The gentle spirit of mouing words. **1601** —— *Twel. N.* I. i. 9 O spirit of Loue, how quicke and fresh art thou. **1675** OWEN *Indwelling Sin* (1732) i. 3 The effectual Power of the Spirit of Grace. **1705** in *Buccleuch Pap.* (Mont. Ho.) I. 354 The spirit of lying runs away with more torrys than ever I had the honour to know. **1779** *Mirror* No. 18, The dark and gloomy spirit of fanaticism, which prevailed so universally.. during the last century. **1820** BELZONI *Egypt & Nubia* III. 326 The spirit of contradiction excited by the illiberality of travellers. **1855** PRESCOTT *Philip II,* II. v. (1857) 247 The spirit of independence was fostered by the institutions of the country. **1872** MORLEY *Voltaire* (1886) 250 A momentary self-indulgence in the spirit of party.

b. With *a*: A tendency, inclination, impulse, etc., *of* a specified kind.

1388 WYCLIF *Isaiah* xix. 14 The Lord meddlid a spirit of errour in the myddis therof. *c* **1430** LYDG. *Min. Poems* (Percy Soc.) 9 God the ffulfylle withe intelligence, And withe a spyrut of goostly sapience. *Ibid.,* God send [thee] also.. A spiryt.. Of connyng. **1596** SHAKS. *1 Hen. IV,* v. ii. 64 A double spirit Of teaching, and of learning. **1765** *Museum Rust.* IV. 56 A certain spirit of improvement.. has been promoted and carried on. **1774** GOLDSM. *Nat. Hist.* (1776) I. 18 If possest with a spirit of theory, his imagination will supply the rest. **1833** HT. MARTINEAU *Vanderput & S.* ix. 133 The old woman had infused a further spirit of thankfulness into the suffering boy. **1844** DISRAELI *Coningsby* III. i, A slight spirit of mockery played over his speech. **1859** C. BARKER *Assoc. Princ.* iii. 62 To foster a spirit of comprehensive patriotism.

8. a. A particular character, disposition, or temper existing in, pervading, or animating, a person or set of persons; a special attitude or bent of mind characterizing men individually or collectively.

1561 RASTELL *Confut. M. Ivelles Serm.* 137 Not onlye Moyses had the grace of gouerning.., but seuentie elders.. had imparted vnto them of his spirite and dignitie. **1588** KYD *Househ. Phil.* Wks. (1901) 242 There mette vs another youth of lesse yeeres, but no lesse gentle spirit. **1611** SHAKS. *Wint. T.* II. iii. 127 Ioue send her A better guiding Spirit. **1665** SIR T. HERBERT *Trav.* (1677) 62 Observing in his pupil a Spirit fitted for the Government of that Monarchy. **1682** FLAVEL *Fear* Ded., A dear friend from whom I have often had the fair idea and character of your excellent spirit. **1712** ADDISON *Spect.* No. 363 ¶8 His Person, his Port, and Behaviour, are suitable to a Spirit of the highest Rank. **1754** GRAY *Progr. Poesy* 81 Latium had her lofty spirit lost. **1856** FROUDE *Hist. Eng.* (1858) I. i. 34 By these measures the money-making spirit was for a time driven back. **1897** *Cavalry Tactics* 5 Like the quality of tact, the cavalry spirit is perceptible only by its results.

b. The disposition, feeling, or frame of mind with which something is done, considered, or viewed. ***that's the spirit:*** exclamatory phr. used in commendation of someone's courage, determination, etc.

1601 BP. W. BARLOW *Serm. Paules Crosse* Pref. 10 But from what spirit these objections proceede, may soone be gessed at. *c* **1680** AUBREY in Ingleby *Shaks. Cent. Praise* (1880) 383 It seemed to him that he writt with the very spirit that Shakespear [did]. **1837** CARLYLE *Fr. Rev.* I. I. iv, It is not thy works,.. but only the Spirit thou workest in, that can have worth or continuance. **1861** M. PATTISON *Ess.* (1889) I. 31 Such is the spirit in which the history of our ancestors is ordinarily propounded to us. **1864** BRYCE *Holy Rom. Emp.* ix. (1875) 147 Otto laboured on his great project in a spirit almost mystic. **1923** *Spectator* 21 Apr. 657/2 'That's the spirit!' has been the immediate comment of the country. **1930** M. ALLINGHAM *Mystery Mile* xxvii. 272 'I was ashamed that he should be.. in my service.' 'That's the spirit,' said Campion. **1963** *Mad Mag.* July 47/1 Good! Good! *That's* the spirit! **1974** G. F. NEWMAN *Price* ii. 70 'I'm absolutely certain I'll be completely vindicated.' 'That's the spirit.'

9. A person considered in relation to his character or disposition; one who has a spirit of a specified nature: **a.** With preceding adjs. ***moving spirit*** (MOVING *ppl. a.* 2 b).

1591- [see CHOICE *a.* 1 b]. **1598** E. GUILPIN *Skial.* v, Here I converse with those diviner spirits Whose knowledge and admire the world inherits. **1601**- [see MASTER *sb.*[1] 25 a]. **1638** JUNIUS *Paint. Ancients* 10 Many lively spirits at length are most pittifully turned away from their forward course. **1655** FULLER *Ch. Hist.* IX. 194 Thus impossible it is to please froward spirits. **1718** *Free-thinker* No. 56. 8 The Brave Spirits of France now strive to vindicate their Liberty in Religious Matters. **1746** FRANCIS tr. *Horace, Epist.* I. xix. 11 Let thirsty Spirits make the Bar their Choice. **1808** SCOTT in *Lockhart* I. i. 27 He is.. led to be the associate and companion of those inferior spirits with whom he is placed. **1849** MACAULAY *Hist. Eng.* i. I. 34 A few regiments of household troops are sufficient to overawe all the discontented spirits of a large capital. **1883** *Manch. Guard.* 29 Oct. 5/2 That the army, at least the more active spirits within it, were discontented was notorious. **1902** [see MOVING *ppl. a.* 2 b]. **1926** S. BALDWIN *On England* 66 In a city like this, where the intelligence and the moving spirits of industry meet round this table, what an opportunity you have! **1954** N. MITFORD *Madame de Pompadour* xix. 242 The state papers still passed through her hands and the work was done in her room, but she ceased to be the moving spirit.

b. With other forms of qualification. *rare.*

1603 DANIEL *Def. Rhime* Wks. (1717) 21 Being.. in all Ages furnish'd with Spirits fit to maintain the Majesty of her own Greatness. *a* **1648** LD. HERBERT *Hen. VIII* (1683) 93 So haughty were the major part of the spirits in this assembly, that.. they condemned Luther's Books to the Fire. **1760–72** H. BROOKE *Fool of Qual.* (1809) III. 82 Our ship.. was full manned, with about two hundred and seventy spirits,.. ready, and desirous to go and meet death.

10. a. The essential character, nature, or qualities *of* something; that which constitutes the pervading or tempering principle of anything. (Common after 1800.) ***spirit of place*** [tr. L. *genius loci*], the characteristic atmosphere and influence of a particular place.

1690 TEMPLE *Ess., Poetry* Wks. 1720 I. 241 The true Spirit or Vein of ancient Poetry. **1721** BRADLEY *Philos. Acc. Wks. Nat.* 189 Which is enough to support the Spirit of Botany. **1746** FRANCIS tr. *Horace, Epist.* II. i. 224 It breathes the Spirit of the tragic Scene. **1843** RUSKIN *Mod. Paint.* I. II. iv. §3 The spirit of the hills is action, that of the lowlands repose. **1888** BRYCE *Amer. Commw.* v. xciii. III. 298 To do so would be alien to the whole spirit of American legislation. **1918** D. H. LAWRENCE in *Eng. Rev.* Nov. 319 All art partakes of the Spirit of Place in which it is produced. **1955** G. MURCHIE (*title*) The Spirit of Place in Keats. **1980** P. LIVELY *Judgement Day* iii. 26 It was as though the spirit of place, nowadays, exerted its power only over the young. **1981** *Sunday Tel.* 25 Jan. 30/2 Of even the great cathedral of Canterbury Hilaire Belloc wrote with deep sadness for a spirit of place sought but not found.

b. The prevailing tone or tendency *of* a particular period of time.

1820 SHELLEY *Lett.* Wks. 1880 IV. 166 It is the spirit of the age, and we are all infected with it. **1824** LANDOR *Imag. Conv.* Wks. 1846 I. 144 The spirit of the times is only to be made useful by catching it as it rises. **1884** GLADSTONE in *Western Daily Press* 22 Sept. 3/3 This legitimate process.. conducted in the spirit of the present day. **1891** *Pall Mall G.* 6 Aug. 3/1 The Spirit of the Age is against those who put party or programme before human needs.

c. The broad or general intent or meaning *of* a statement, enactment, etc. Used in contrast to LETTER *sb.*[1] 5.

Suggested by the use of the words in *2 Cor.* iii. 6.

1802 *Med. Jrnl.* VIII. 288 Knowing.. that Magistrates are generally obliged to inflict penalties according to the Letter and not according to the Spirit of an Act. **1850** ROBERTSON *Serm.* Ser. III. vi. (1857) 84 His faith appears to have consisted in disbelieving the letter, almost as much as in believing the spirit of the promise. **1880** *Church Times* 7 May 295/1 Anything in more flagrant violation of the spirit and letter of the Prayer Book can hardly be conceived than to send the Elect out of the choir to put on 'the rest of the Episcopal habit'. **1926** G. M. TREVELYAN *History of England* II. iii. 172 Radicals appealed to the letter and the spirit of 'Magna Charta' against gagging acts, packed juries and restrictions of the franchise. **1961** [see *protectorate law* s.v. PROTECTORATE *sb.* 4]. **1982** *Church Times* 15 Jan. 20/2 It is.. neither in the letter nor spirit of these resolutions for anyone .. to act in a way which has the effect of forcing one view upon those who hold the other.

III. 11. a. The immaterial intelligent or sentient element or part of a person, freq. in implied or expressed contrast to the body.

1382 WYCLIF *Ps.* l. 19 Sacrifise to God [is] a spiritt holly trublid. *c* **1386** CHAUCER *Knt.'s T.* 1907 Naught may the woful spirit in myn herte Declare a poynt of my sorwes smerte. *a* **1420** *Aunters of Arth.* xx, The holy goste, That enspyres alle sperites.. to come to that blysse. **1551** BIBLE *Luke* i. 47 My spirite reioyseth in god my sauiour. **1585** T. WASHINGTON tr. *Nicholay's Voy.* III. i. 69 b, [They] teach them to learne some art or occupation, according to the capacitie of their spirit. **1604** E. G[RIMSTONE] *D'Acosta's Hist. Indies* II. iv. 88 As well in the fruites of the earth, as in the bodies and spirits of men. *c* **1665** MRS. HUTCHINSON *Mem. Col. Hutchinson* (1846) 5 But these things bounded not their great spirits. **1743** FRANCIS tr. *Horace, Odes* II. iii. 2 In arduous Hours an equal Mind maintain, Nor let your Spirit rise too high. **1789** COWPER *Queen's Visit Lond.* 65 That cordial thought her spirit cheer'd. **1827** HALLAM *Const. Hist.* iii. (1876) I. 162 They stood the trial of their spirits without swerving from their allegiance. **1842** TENNYSON *Sir Galahad* iv, My spirit beats her mortal bars. **1872** MORLEY *Voltaire* 7 Many new things, after which the spirits of others were unconsciously groping and dumbly yearning.

b. In generalized sense, with *the.*

Freq. with reference to Matt. xxvi. 41.

1382 WYCLIF *Baruch* iii. 1 The soule in anguysshes, and the spirit tormentid crieth to thee. *c* **1440** *Gesta Rom.* i. 4 (Harl. MS.), þi flesch, þat dispisith all werkis that þe spirite lovith. *a* **1450** tr. *De Imitatione* II. viii. 48 Blesful is þat man whom.. he calliþ fro teres to þe ioy of þe spirit. **1560** DAUS tr. *Sleidane's Comm.* 55 Luther hath offended.. in.. not teaching those thinges, that are of the spirite. **1614** C. BROOKE *Ghost Rich. III,* E iv, As the Catholick Spirit in Man applyes Each Sence and Organ, to their proper Ends. **1665** R. HOWARD *Four Plays, Committee* III. 99 Saffron-posset-drink is very good against The heaviness of the Spirit. **1666** G. TORRIANO *Piazza Universale di Proverbi Italiani* 268/2 The *spirit* is ready, but the body is lame. **1781** COWPER *Hope* 299 Hopes.. that cannot.. cheer the spirit, nor refresh the sight. **1875** E. WHITE *Life in Christ* III. xx. (1878) 298 In such cases the spiritual action must at first be directly on the spirit and not at all on the mind. **1925** A. HUXLEY *Those Barren Leaves* III. xiii. 269 The spirit is willing, but the flesh is weak. Weak in pain, but weaker still.., more inexcusably weak, in pleasure. **1935** C. ISHERWOOD *Mr. Norris changes Trains* ix. 138, I really must apologize for my shortcomings as a correspondent... The spirit was willing, dear boy. I hope you'll believe that. **1938** W. S. MAUGHAM *Summing Up* x. 30 Though ceasing my methodical study of the old masters (for though the spirit is willing, the flesh is weak), I have continued with increasing assiduity to try to write better.

c. Without article; freq. in phr. ***in spirit.*** Also (with reference to John iv. 23), ***in spirit and in truth,*** spiritually and sincerely.

1382 WYCLIF *Rom.* xii. 11 Not slow in bisynesse, feruent .. in spirit. *Ibid. 1 Cor.* vii. 34 And a.. mayden thenkith what thingis ben of the Lord, that sche be hooly in body and spirit. *c* **1430** LYDG. *Min. Poems* (Percy Soc.) 48 This rose of Jericho,.. Pore in spirit, parfit in pacyence. **1582** N.T. (Rhem.) *Luke* x. 21 In that very houre he reioyced in spirit. **1582** N. LICHEFIELD tr. *Castanheda's Conq. E. Ind.* 143 The Captaine Generall was inwardly moued in spirit. **1663** BP. PATRICK *Parab. Pilgr.* xix, Losing more time by these dejections of spirit. **1670** CLARENDON *Hist. Reb.* XVI. §10 The poor man had not spirit enough to discern what was best for him. **1779** *Mirror* No. 10, Mr. Fleetwood felt an unusual elevation of spirit. **1859** THACKERAY *Virgin.* vi, Saddened and humbled in spirit, the young officer presented himself after a while to his old friends. **1860** RUSKIN *Mod. Paint.* V. VIII. i. 167 *note,* This being the true distinction between flesh and spirit. **1920** GALSWORTHY *In Chancery* III. xiv. 328 At this moment he knew with certainty that he would never be near to her in spirit and in truth, nor she to him. **1953** A. J. TOYNBEE *World & West* vi. 96 Our hearts are hungry for a divinity that we can worship in spirit and in truth.

12. The emotional part of man as the seat of hostile or angry feeling.

1382 WYCLIF *2 Chron.* xxi. 16 Thanne the Lord rerede aȝeinus Joram the spirite of the Philisteis, and of Arabes. **1607** SHAKS. *Timon* III. v. 104 And not to swell our Spirit, He shall be executed presently. **1611** BIBLE *Eccl.* x. 4 If the spirit of the ruler rise vp against thee, leaue not thy place. *a* **1715** BURNET *Own Time* (1724) I. 467 The carelessness and luxury of the court came to be so much exposed that the King's spirit was much sharpened upon it. **1862** TROLLOPE *Orley F.* xiv, She was prepared for war and her spirit was hot within her.

13. a. Mettle; vigour of mind; ardour; courage; disposition or readiness to assert oneself or to hold one's own.

1596 SHAKS. *1 Hen. IV,* IV. i. 101 All furnisht, all in Armes,.. As full of spirit as the Moneth of May. **1603** —— *Meas. for M.* III. i. 212 I haue spirit to do any thing that appeares not fowle. **1643** in Clarendon *Hist. Reb.* VI. §338 They have of late taken spirit, and begun to speak big words. *a* **1715** BURNET *Own Time* (1734) II. 427 A man of more spirit than discretion. **1749** FIELDING *Tom Jones* IV. viii, Molly had too much spirit to bear this treatment tamely.

1809 BYRON *Bards & Rev.* (ed. 2) Postscr., 'The age of chivalry is over,' or, in the vulgar tongue, there is no spirit now-a-days. **1862** STANLEY *Jew. Ch.* (1877) I. xv. 296 They replied with all the spirit of Arab chiefs. **1890** 'L. FALCONER' *Mlle. Ixe* i. 33 She consoled herself by describing what other people called disobedience as spirit.

b. In the phr. ***with* (..) *spirit*.**

1748 GRAY *Alliance* 95 What wonder if.. They guard with spirit what by strength they gain'd? **1799** NELSON 7 June in Nicolas *Disp.* (1846) VII. p. clxxxiv, Don Jose..has on several occasions conducted himself with spirit. **1816** SCOTT *Old Mort.* xxxii, Ere Morton or Burley had reached the post to be defended, the enemy had commenced an attack upon it with great spirit. **1830** MARRYAT *King's Own* xiii, The action was now maintained with spirit, but much to the disadvantage of the cutter.

c. Freq. in ***a man of spirit*.**

1747 HOADLY *Suspicious Husband* I. i, We Men of Spirit, Sir, are above it. **1780** *Mirror* No. 102, Youths entering on the stage of life are catched with the engaging appellation, 'a man of spirit'. **1812** *Lex. Bal.* Pref. p. vi, They may be initiated into all the peculiarities of language by which a man of spirit is distinguished from a man of worth.

14. a. A brisk or lively quality in things.

1588 KYD *Househ. Phil.* Wks. (1901) 272 The small wynes, and those of little spirite that quickly lose their strength. **1638** JUNIUS *Paint. Ancients* 229 Seeing..that nothing marreth the life and spirit of the invented things so much, as to force and strain them to a fore-determined purpose. **1686** HORNECK *Crucif. Jesus* (1716) 190 Wine hath Briskness and Spirit in it. **1852** MRS. STOWE *Uncle Tom's C.* xiv, So much motherliness and full-heartedness..seemed to put a spirit into the food and drink she offered. **1874** H. H. COLE *Catal. Ind. Art S. Kens. Mus.* App. 281 The action and modelling of the conventional griffin has some spirit about it.

b. Liveliness, vivacity, or animation in persons, their actions, discourse, etc. (Cf. 17 c.)

a **1700** EVELYN *Diary* 16 Aug. 1691, An honest discourse, but read without any spirit or seeming concern. **1750** GRAY *Long Story* 30 Arm'd with spirit, wit, and satire. **1783** MME. D'ARBLAY *Diary* 20 June, The absence of Dr. Johnson.. took off the spirit of the evening. **1867** RUSKIN *Time & Tide* v. §24 She danced her joyful dance with perfect grace, spirit, sweetness, and self-forgetfulness. **1886** *Athenæum* 30 Oct. 559/2 The twenty-second chapter..relates with some spirit the disputes between England and the United States.

IV. 15. a. A movement of the air; a wind; a breath (of wind or air).

In later use *poet.* and associated with other senses.

1382 WYCLIF *Gen.* viii. 1 The Lord..brouȝte to a spirit [**1388** wynd] vpon the erthe. And the watris ben lessid. *Ibid. Ps.* x. 7 Fyr, brunston, and the spiritis [**1388** spirit] of tempestis. **1561** DAUS tr. *Bullinger on Apoc.* (1573) 158 Fyre, brimstone, and spirite of tempest. **1601** HOLLAND *Pliny* I. 37 All the spirit and winde which should beare them [*sc.* birds] vp is withdrawne from them. **1626** BACON *Sylva* §39 All Purgers haue in them a raw Spirit, or Wind; which is the Principall Cause of Tortion in the Stomach. **1725** POPE *Odyssey* VII. 152 The balmy spirit of the western gale. **1820** SHELLEY *Witch Atlas* lx, With motion like the spirit of that wind Whose soft step deepens slumber.

†b. The act of breathing; (a) breath. *Obs.*

1382 WYCLIF *2 Thess.* ii. 8 The ilke wickid man..whom the Lord Jhesu schal sle with the spirit of his mouth. **1481** CAXTON tr. *Cicero, Old Age*, Their wisedom ascendyd in encreasing and contynued unto the last spirite of their lives. **1483** —— *Gold. Leg.* 129/2 For all her body bycam cold and she felte that her spirite helde her in her brest. **1581** MARBECK *Bk. Notes* 55 Him shall God destroie with yᵉ spirit of his mouth. **1678** WANLEY *Wond. Lit. World* 293 Forasmuch as the force of the words was sharp and that there was a succession of spirits.

c. *Gram.* An aspirate or breathing; a conventional mark indicating this; *spec.* in the writing or printing of Greek.

1555 EDEN *Decades* (Arb.) 169 Ye, all suche woordes as in their tonge are aspirate, are pronounced with lyke breath and spirite as is .f. **1612** BRINSLEY *Lud. Lit.* 232 Call vpon them oft to marke carefully the accents of each word, with the spirits. *a* **1653** GOUGE *Comm. Heb.* i. 3 The Greek makes an apparent distinction by a different spirit over the head of the first letter. **1680** DALGARNO *Deaf & Dumb Man's Tutor* 126 The unnecessary and troublesome luggage of Spirits and Accents. **1751** WESLEY *Wks.* (1872) XIV. 79 Every initial vowel has a spirit prefixed. **1827** FABER *Sacr. Cal. Prophecy* (1844) III. 163 The inscription in the Greek cursive character, even with the accompanying accents and spirits. **1861** SCRIVENER *N.T. Critic.* 39 The book has neither spirits..nor accents.

†d. *Mus.* An air; a melody. *Obs.*⁻¹

1608 WEELKES (*title*), Ayeres or Phantasticke Spirites for three voices.

16. a. One or other of certain subtle highly-refined substances or fluids (distinguished as *natural*, *animal*, and *vital*) formerly supposed to permeate the blood and chief organs of the body. In later use only *pl.*

See also ANIMAL SPIRITS 1, NATURAL *a.* 12 a, and VITAL *a.*

1387 TREVISA *Higden* (Rolls) I. 53 For þe son beme.. draweþ oute þe humours,..and by drawing oute of spirites makeþ hem coward of herte. *c* **1400** *Lanfranc's Cirurg.* 26 Þe toþer arterie..haþ two cootis, bi cause þat oon myȝt not aȝenstonde þe strenkþe of þe spiritis. *Ibid.* 162 Of þis clene blood þe spirit is engendrid; which spirit is..more sutil þan ony bodi. **1477** NORTON *Ord. Alch.* v. in Ashm. (1652) 82 The Spirit Vitall in the Hert doth dwell, The Spirit Naturall ..in the Liver.., But Spirit Animall dwelleth in the Braine. **1539** ELYOT *Cast. Helthe* (1541) 12 b, Spirite is an ayry substance subtyll, styrynge the powers of the body to perfourme theyr operations. **1587** GOLDING *De Mornay* xiv. (1592) 206 A mans..eyes faile because the Spirites of them fayle. **1615** CROOKE *Body of Man* 61 The reason is, because all the spirits are immured. *a* **1646** BURROUGHES *Exp. Hosea* vi. (1652) 266 The fatter mens bodies are, the lesse blood and the fewer spirits they have. **1697** DRYDEN *Virg. Georg.* III. 155 When his Blood no Youthful Spirits move, He languishes and labours in his Love. **1725** N. ROBINSON *Th. Physick* 250 What Remedies will be properest to repress the Disorders of the Spirits. **1791** *Pop. Tales Germ.* I. 190 Her spirits retired inward, her cheeks grew pale, and down she sank.

transf. **1719** W. WOOD *Surv. Trade* 3 It disperses that blood and Spirits throughout the Members, by which the Body Politick subsists. **1812** CARY *Dante, Parad.* XXVI. 70 With the eye's spirit running forth to meet The ray.

b. *pl.* Vital power or energy; the normal operation of the vital functions.

c **1386** CHAUCER *Knt.'s T.* 514 So feble eek were hise spiritz and so lowe,..that no man koude knowe His speche ne his voys. *c* **1450** *St. Cuthbert* (Surtees) 6065 Fra he was vp ryght sett, he began his spirits to gett with in a litil stounde. **1617** MORYSON *Itin.* I. 118 At last feeling my spirits begin to faile me, I was glad to returne. **1670** WALTON *Lives* III. 228 More he would have spoken, but his spirits failed him. **1700** ROWE *Amb. Step-Moth.* I. i, That ever will remain, And in my latest Spirits still survive. **1793** COWPER *To Mary* ii, Thy spirits have a fainter flow, I see thee daily weaker grow.

17. a. *pl.* The mind or faculties as the seat of action and feeling, esp. as liable to be depressed or exalted by events or circumstances.

1375 BARBOUR *Bruce* VI. 223 He..sumdeill affrayit wes; But in schort tym he till him tais His spiritis richt full hardely. *a* **1548** HALL *Chron., Rich. III*, 49 To visite his familie, and to recreate and refreshe his spirites (as he openly saide). **1592** *Arden of Feversham* I. 1 Arden, cheere vp thy spirits and droup no more. **1608** CHAPMAN *Dk. Byron* v. i. 133 For we shall never brag That we have made his spirits check at death. **1719** DE FOE *Crusoe* I. (Globe) 199 Dangers, the Sight of which, if discover'd to him, would..sink his Spirits. **1771** SMOLLETT *Humph. Cl.* (1815) 184, I find my spirits and my health affect each other reciprocally. **1825** SCOTT *Betrothed* xxii, The spirits of Eveline in particular felt a depression. **1845** J. COULTER *Adv. in Pacific* xi. 135 It is one of the means of keeping up the spirits of the men on long voyages. **1893** *Law Times* XCIV. 603/2 For the last three or four days he appears to have been depressed in spirits.

b. With adjs., as *good*, *great*, *high*, *low*, etc. Freq. ***in..spirits*.**

1737 GRAY *Lett.* (1900) I. 6 Low spirits are my true and faithful companions. **1743** BULKELEY & CUMMINS *Voy. S. Seas* 169 So that we are in pretty good Spirits. **1744** [see LOW *a.* 8 b]. **1780** *Mirror* No. 98, I walked home in great spirits. **1802** MAR. EDGEWORTH *Moral T.* (1816) I. vii. 41 She had a constant flow of good spirits. **1820** IRVING *Sketch Bk.* I. 49 She seems in better spirits than I have ever known her. **1884** *Daily News* 21 Feb. 5/3 The men are in high spirits at the prospect of a fight.

c. Vigour or animation of mind; cheerfulness, vivacity, liveliness. (Cf. 14 b.)

1716 LADY M. W. MONTAGU *Let. to Lady Rich* 16 Aug., I found myself perfectly recovered, and have had spirits enough to go and see all that is curious in the town. **1780** *Mirror* No. 81, I lost all my former spirits, as well as my former bloom. **1803** *Med. Jrnl.* IX. 211 Loss of appetite and spirits, succeeded with thirst. **1852** MRS. STOWE *Uncle Tom's C.* xxi, The horse would roll when he was bringing him up from the stable; he's so full of spirits.

d. ***in spirits***, in a cheerful mood; animated, elated, happy. ***out of spirits***, low-spirited.

1766 GOLDSM. *Vicar* xxxii, His time is pretty much taken up in keeping his relation..in spirits. **1779** in Jesse *Selwyn & Contemp.* (1844) IV. 259 [She] is..so out of spirits, that she is cruelly afraid she shall never live till her dear master's return. **1826** DISRAELI *V. Grey* IV. ii, I suppose he is quite in spirits at your success? **1838** LYTTON *Alice* I. i, Who can be out of spirits in such weather? **1907** G. B. SHAW *John Bull's Other Island* IV. 94 You seem rather out of spirits... You havnt got neuralgia, have you? **1966** G. GREENE *Comedians* I. v. 140 He seemed tired and out of spirits.

†18. *pl.* **a.** The faculties of perception or reflection; the senses or intellect; mental powers. *Obs.*

1526 *Pilgr. Perf.* (W. de W. 1531) 57 b, That..thou gather to the thy spirytes, & be..quyet. **1604** SHAKS. *Oth.* III. iv. 63 His Spirits should hunt After new Fancies. *c* **1645** HOWELL *Lett.* (1650) II. 115 Truly the more I scrue up my spirits to reach it, the more I am swallowed in a gulf of admiration. **1697** DRYDEN *Virg. Past.* IV. 66 To sing thy Praise, wou'd Heav'n my Breath prolong, Infusing Spirits worthy such a Song.

†b. Disposition, character. *Obs.*

1602 SHAKS. *Ham.* III. ii. 63 For what aduancement may I hope from thee, That no Reuennew hast, but thy good spirits To feed & cloath thee?

19. †a. A subtle or intangible element or principle in material things. *Obs.*

1626 BACON *Sylva* §98 The Spirits or Pneumaticalls, that are in all Tangible Bodies are scarce known. **1638** RAWLEY tr. *Bacon's Life & Death* (1650) 57 There is in every Tangible Body a Spirit, covered and encompassed with the Grosser Parts of the Body. **1661** SOUTH *Serm.* Wks. 1823 II. 328 In the rain, it is not the bare water that fructifies, but a secret spirit or nitre descending with it. *a* **1722** LISLE *Husb.* (1757) 218 The spirit of the straw is washed out by the rain. **1725** *Fam. Dict.* s.v. *Cider*, The Spirits of Cider being exceedingly apt to evaporate.

b. (See quot.)

1829 *Chapters Phys. Sci.* 235 The oxygenous gas..is a kind of vivifying spirit or quality, which is necessary to continue the lives of animals.

V. †20. a. One or other of four substances so named by the mediaeval alchemists. *Obs.*

c **1386** CHAUCER *Can. Yeom. Prol. & T.* 60 Ne eek oure spirites Ascencioun..Mowe in oure werkyng no thyng vs auaille. *Ibid.* 103 The firste spirit quyk siluer called is, The seconde Orpyment, the thridde ywis Sal Armonyak, and the ferthe Brymstoon. **1390** GOWER *Conf.* II. 84 Of bodies sevene..With foure spiritz joynt withal Stant the substance of this matiere.

†b. ***spirit of the world***: (see quot.).

1651 FRENCH *Distill.* v. 107 In the element of Water there is a great plenty of the Spirit of the world,..and..this Spirit hath three distinct substances, *viz.* Salt, Sulphur, and Mercury.

†c. *spec.* Mercury. *Obs.*

1704 J. HARRIS *Lex. Techn.* I, *Spirit*, which the Chymists call Mercury, is one of the 5 Principles separable from a Mixt, by Fire. **1725** WATTS *Logic* I. ii. §2 The chemist makes spirit, salt, sulphur, water, and earth, to be their five elements. **1728** CHAMBERS *Cycl.* s.v. *Element*, Mercury, which they [*sc.* chemists] also call *Spirit*.

†d. (See quot.) *Obs.*⁻¹

1733 W. ELLIS *Chiltern & Vale Farm.* 200 The Exhalations of the Sun that draws up a moist Vapour from the Earth, by some, called the Spirit, by others, the Salt of the Earth.

21. a. A liquid of the nature of an essence or extract from some substance, esp. one obtained by distillation; a solution in alcohol of some essential or volatile principle.

1610 JONSON *Alch.* II. vi, H'is busie with his spirits, but wee'll vpon him. **1651** FRENCH *Distill.* v. 139 Dissolve any sulphurous..metall..in *Aqua fortis*, or any other acid Spirit. **1728** CHAMBERS *Cycl.* s.v., The Chymists are said to draw a Spirit from Sulphur, Salt and other Bodies, when they extract the Essence..by Distillation or otherwise. **1813** SIR H. DAVY *Agric. Chem.* (1814) 136 All the common spirits may, I find, be deprived of their peculiar flavour by repeatedly digesting them with..charcoal and quicklime. **1831** J. DAVIES *Mat. Med.* 36 The spirits have a weaker odour than the distilled waters. **1875** H. C. WOOD *Therap.* (1879) 18 Spirits are alcoholic solutions of volatile principles made by direct solution or by distillation from the crude drugs.

fig. **1613** SYLVESTER (*title*), Lachrymæ Lachrymarum: or the Spirit of Teares, distilled for the vntymely Death of the incomparable Prince of Wales. **1639** FULLER *Holy War* II. xxxiv. (1840) 94 These Assassins..had in them the very spirits of that poisonous superstition. **1742** YOUNG *Nt. Th.* IV. 144 To drink the spirit of the golden day, And triumph in existence.

b. Without article: Liquid such as is obtained by distillation, *spec.* that which is of an alcoholic nature. Also *pl.*

sing. **1610** JONSON *Alch.* I. i, Have I..Wrought thee to spirit, to quintessence, with paines Would twise haue won me the philosophers worke? **1688** HOLME *Armoury* III. xx. (Roxb.) 250/2 Wine coopers termes:..Spiritt, wine double distilled. **1726** *Dict. Rust.*, *Spirit dulcified*, a choice Remedy for the Cholick in Horses. *a* **1774** GOLDSM. *Surv. Exp. Philos.* (1776) I. 380 A solid that will swim in water, will sink in spirit. **1799** G. SMITH *Laboratory* I. 334 In this manner are extracted from roses the three principles, spirit, oil, and salt. **1815** J. SMITH *Panorama Sci. & Art* II. 576 The substances from which spirit is obtained are usually barley, wheat, oats, rye, sugar, or molasses. **1854** RONALDS & RICHARDSON *Chem. Technol.* (ed. 2) I. 289 In this manner, by one operation, spirit containing about 60 per cent. of alcohol is obtained. **1863** HUXLEY *Man's Place in Nat.* I. 16 M. Palm..shot one, and forwarded it to Batavia in spirit.

pl. **1800** SOUTHEY in C. C. Southey *Life* (1850) II. 91 The head and hands were sent here; I have seen them in the Museum, in spirits.

c. orig. *pl.* Strong alcoholic liquor for drinking, obtained from various substances by distillation; *sing.* any particular kind of this.

1684 BUNYAN *Pilgr.* II. 67 He gave me also a piece of an Honey-comb, and a little Bottle of Spirits. **1742–3** HERVEY in *Johnson's Deb.* (1787) II. 409 It is not to be doubted, my Lords, but that spirits will, by this additional duty, be made one third part dearer. **1833** HT. MARTINEAU *Vanderput & S.* vi. 95 Every body agreed that spirits were the only safeguard against the perils of ditch water. **1884** *Graphic* 29 Nov. 562/2 An exuberance of animal spirits occasionally increased by spirits of another character.

sing. **1840** DICKENS *Old C. Shop* xxi, Quilp..drank three small glass-fulls of the raw spirit. **1848** THACKERAY *Van. Fair* lxvii, When she was prevailed on..to take a little spirit-and-water. **1884** J. P. QUINCY *Figures of Past* 265 The use of wine and spirit was practically universal at the time of which I am speaking.

d. With *of* (the name of the liquor). *rare.*

1700 T. BROWN tr. *Fresny's Amusem.* viii. Wks. 1709 III. I. 77 To the Charms of Coffee the wiser sort joyn'd Spirit of Clary, Usquebaugh, and Brandy. **1831** SCOTT *Cast. Dang.* xiii, Wilt thou take some refreshment?—or shall we go on without the spirit of muscadel?

22. a. An essence, distilled extract, or alcoholic solution, *of* a specified substance. Freq. *pl.*, esp. in later use.

Only the earlier or more important of these special designations are illustrated here: see also TURPENTINE, VITRIOL, and WINE.

a **1700** EVELYN *Diary* 27 Oct. 1675, By applying hot fire-pans and *spirit of amber to his head. **1737** [see AMBER *sb.*¹ 3 b]. **1839** URE *Dict. Arts* 1158 **Spirit of Ammonia* is, properly speaking, alcohol combined with ammonia gas; but the term is often applied to water of ammonia. **1871** GARROD *Mat. Med.* (ed. 3) 47 Aromatic Spirit of Ammonia... Often called Sal Volatile. **1853** ROYLE *Mat. Med.* (ed. 2) 599 *Spirit of Camphor... Dissolve Camphor..in Rectified Spirit. *Ibid* 701 *Spirit of Ether..Mix Sulphuric Ether.. with Rectified Spirit. *Ibid.*, Compound Spirit of Ether. **1871** GARROD *Mat. Med.* (ed. 3) 149 Spirit of ether is employed in making the ethereal tincture of lobelia. **1683–4** BOYLE *Mem. Nat. Hist. Hum. Blood* 122 The *Sp. of Harts-horn. **1685** [see HARTSHORN 2]. **1826** HENRY *Elem. Chem.* II. 609 Spirit of Hartshorn. This may be counterfeited by mixing the *aqua ammoniæ puræ* with the distilled spirit of hartshorn. **1666** BOYLE *Orig. Forms & Qual.* 337, I did.. make a red *spirit of Nitre, by the help onely of Oyl of Vitriol. **1710** J. CLARKE tr. *Rohault's Nat. Philos.* (1729) I. 113 A few Drops of Spirit of Nitre or of Oil of Vitriol. **1823** J. BADCOCK *Dom. Amusem.* 45 A strong solution of mercury, made with spirit of nitre. **1853** ROYLE *Mat. Med.* (ed. 2) 702 *Spirit of Nitric Ether. Hyponitrous Ether dissolved in Rectified Spirit. Sweet Spirits of Nitre. **1859** MAYNE *Expos. Lex.* 1189/2 *Spirit of nitrous ether. **1871** GARROD *Mat. Med.* (ed. 3) 151 Spirit of nitrous ether..is popularly known by the name of Sweet Spirits of Nitre. **1779** *Phil. Trans.*

LXX. 40 Apply to the precipitate solution of volatile alkali, sold by the name of *spirit of sal ammoniac. **1651** FRENCH *Distill.* i. 36 The *Spirit of salt being rectified may serve again. **1779** *Phil. Trans.* LXX. 30 Half an ounce of muriatic acid sold by the name of spirit of salt. **1807** T. THOMSON *Chem.* (ed. 3) II. 611 This residuum is usually called bittern, and sometimes in Scotland spirit of salt. **1860** *Ure's Dict. Arts* (ed. 5) II. 481 The solution of hydrochloric acid in water is the muriatic acid and spirit of salt of commerce. **1753** *Chambers' Cycl.* Suppl. s.v. *Silk*, If spirit of wine be poured upon spirit of sal armoniac, or *spirit of silk. **1704** J. HARRIS *Lex. Techn.* I, **Spirit of Sulphur*, commonly call'd Oil of Sulphur, .. is only the acid Part of Sulphur turned into a Liquor by the means of Fire. **1651** FRENCH *Distill.* iii. 66 Dissolve Salt-Armoniack in.. *spirit of Urine. **1710** J. CLARKE tr. *Rohault's Nat. Philos.* (1729) I. 129 An equal Quantity of Spirits of Wine and Spirits of Urine. **1797** *Encycl. Brit.* (ed. 3) IV. 598 (Plate), Pyroligneous acid. *Spirit of wood.

b. *Dyeing.* (See quots.)

1875 KNIGHT *Dict. Mech.* 428/1 [In] spirit-color printing, the colors are produced by a mixture of dye extracts and solution of tin, called by the dyers *spirits of tin.* **1877** *Encycl. Brit.* VII. 574/2 The so-called nitrate of tin (sometimes called 'bowl spirits', from being prepared in an earthenware bowl). **1880** D. SMITH *Pract. Dyer's Guide* (title-p.), Receipts for making all the Dye Spirits with which to dye every colour in the work.

VI. *attrib.* and *Comb.*

23. In senses 1–14: **a.** Simple attrib., in various applications, as ***spirit-blow, -body, -book, -call, -child, -communication, -doctor, -harmony, -house, -land, -medium, -mischief, -nature, -possession, -stream, thing, tower, -visit, -voice, -wall, -world***, etc.

Some of these are used in sense 23 g but now have a wider use in Anthropology.

1818 KEATS *Endym.* IV. 899 But the *spirit-blow Was struck, and all were dreamers. **1848** KINGSLEY *Saint's Trag.* II. ii, Spirit-love in *spirit-bodies. **1852** BAILEY *Festus* (ed. 5) 500 To.. strict collation of the *Spirit-book With the pretemporal volume, writ of God. **1949** BLUNDEN *After Bombing* 17 For young, for old, a *spirit-call Even now, bright music, stirs the air. **1845** S. JUDD *Margaret* I. xii, Call me your child,.. your *spirit-child, and so love me. **1869** GEO. ELIOT *Let.* 11 July (1956) V. 48 'Spiritualism' (by which I mean, of course, *spirit-communications). **1960** W. NAYLOR *Silver Birch Anthol.* 7 The uncertain art of continuous spirit communication. **1936** *Discovery* June 187/1 The would-be *spirit-doctor, who must have what the African regards as a faculty for 'seeing spirits'—we might term it clairvoyancy. **1874** GEO. ELIOT *Coll. Breakf.-P.* 278 The Church as.. fount of *spirit force. **1865** MISS BRADDON *Sir Jasper's Tenant* iii, Shadowy as those *spirit-hands of which we hear so much nowadays. **1928** BLUNDEN *Undertones of War* xvii. 177 The flush and abundance of antique life and memorial and achievement, such as blend into the great *spirit-harmony of the cities in that part of Europe. **1831** CARLYLE *Sart. Res.* III. viii, Like a God-created, fire-breathing *Spirit-host. **1856** *Spirit-house [see CIRCLE *sb.* 21 b]. **1966** MRS. L. B. JOHNSON *White House Diary* 27 Oct. (1970) 437 There were 'spirit houses' everywhere—brightly decorated little houses.. about the size of a bird house, standing on stilts—one beside almost every residence. These houses are to entice the spirits so they will leave *your* house to you. **1973** P. BERTON *Drifting Home* vi. 89 In Little Salmon, the graves are as numerous as the houses. Indeed they are like small cabins—a village of spirit houses with sloping roofs, glass windows and curtains, containing dead flowers and teapots and plates for the use of the deceased. **1841** E. A. POE in *Graham's Mag.* May 241/2 A traveller from the *spirit-land. **1845** HIRST *Poems* 157 Beyond the Vale of Shadows, lie dispread The spirit-lands. **1859** BARTLETT *Dict. Amer.* (ed. 2) 434 *Spirit-land*, an expression which, in the cant of the rappers, means the abode of departed spirits, the other world. **1869** RUSKIN *Q. of Air* iii. §157 The *spirit-life of art. **1662** HIBBERT *Body Divinity* I. 127 Soul-light is not enough to make us truly wise, but there must also be *spirit-light. **1830** MRS. HEMANS *Indian w. Dead Child* ix, I saw the spirit-light From his young eyes fade away. *a* **1835** —— *Song of Rose* Poems (1875) 550 Shall we not behold thee.. In *spirit lustre clothed? **1853** *Theatr. Jrnl.* 22 June 190/1 A celebrated '*spirit-medium'.. advertises a *seance* for the demonstration of spiritual communications. **1979** P. NIESEWAND *Member of Club* vii. 50 We've.. got.. to enlist the support of spirit mediums. The ancestral spirits are supposed to speak through them. **1915** W. B. YEATS *Reveries over Childhood & Youth* xiv. 70 Somnambulistic country girls.. become mediums for some genuine *spirit-mischief, surrendering to their desire for the marvellous. **1877** E. CAIRD *Philos. Kant* Introd v. 79 The *spirit-monad—the monad that has consciousness of itself. **1962** AUDEN *Dyer's Hand* (1963) 135 The greatest of *spirit-nature pairs and the most orthodox is, of course, Don Quixote-Sancho Panza. **1909** W. JAMES in *Proc. Soc. Psychical Research* XXIII. LVIII. 35 The whole record of *spirit-possession in human history. **1950** BLESH & JANIS *They all played Ragtime* x. 188 The incalculable power generated by the ring-shout rhythms brings about 'spirit-possession', referred to in jazz as being 'sent out of this world'. **1964** GOULD & KOLB *Dict. Soc. Sci.* 638/2 *Spirit possession* seems too broad a term to specify the social functions and active controlling role characteristic of the shaman. **1844** MRS BROWNING *Lady Geraldine's Courtsh.* liii, No new *spirit-power comprising. *a* **1835** MRS. HEMANS *Painter's last Wk.* Poems (1875) 596 Purified To *spirit radiance from all earthly stain. **1858** SEARS *Athan.* III. x. 333 This tide of humanity sweeps on into the *spirit-realm. **1852** BAILEY *Festus* (ed. 5) 529 So every bodily organ shall be changed Into a *spirit-sense. **1925** BLUNDEN *English Poems* 93 The time will come when, at the point to die I'll wish a *spirit-stream as cool and clear. **1886** W. B. YEATS in *Dublin Univ. Rev.* Jan. 75 Two *spirit things a man hath for his friends: Sorrow that gives for guerdon liberty, And joy. *a* **1957** Spirit-thing [see *root-sensation* s.v. ROOT *sb.*[1] 21]. **1657** J. WATTS *Vind. Ch. Eng.* 115 Refuse the Mother-tongue Translation, and call for the *Spirit-tongue Original. **1955** E. POUND *Classic Anthol.* III. 158 When he planned to begin a *spirit tower Folk rushed to the work-camp and overran All the leisure of King Wen's plan. **1936** E. SITWELL *Victoria of England* i. 20 According to Mr Owen's account, the Duke returned.., after death,.. in order to confide matters of importance to him... These *spirit-visits must, one imagines, have been the result of the Duke's interest in minor details. **1655** VAUGHAN *Silex Scint.* 40 Prayer is a *spirit-voyce. **1844** E. A. POE in *Graham's Mag.* Mar. 142/1 During the swell of the organ, the spirit-voice of the deceased addresses itself to the murderer. **1852** MRS. STOWE *Uncle Tom's C.* xxiv, The voice came over him as a spirit-voice. **1937** *Burlington Mag.* Oct. 162/1 These walls are now generally called *ying pi*—shadow- or *spirit-walls... They are often found in front of the street-door, but sometimes also inside the enclosure behind the entrance in order to shut out a view of the interior. They served too as a protection against demons. The idea is current that demons are stupid and therefore only walk straight forward. **1948** G. H. JOHNSTON *Death takes Small Bites* ii. 47 Alongside the road, protecting the big houses from wandering devils, were spirit-walls, blank and forbidding. **1847** MARY HOWITT *Ballads* 266, I see on *spirit-wings, How thou hast set them high. *Ibid.* 323 My *spirit-words were all too faint. **1855** BROWNING *In a Balcony* Wks. 1863 II. 494 The success And consummation of the *spirit-work. **1847** W. SMITH tr. *Fichte's Present Age* 62 So does the *Spirit-World not indeed *flow* together at the breath of Love, for in it there is no Winter, but there all *is* and *abides* in eternal communion with the mighty Whole. *a* **1853** ROBERTSON *Serm.* Ser. III. v. 62 The reality of the spirit-world. **1871** TYLOR *Prim. Cult.* I. 131 Two of the most popular means of communicating with the spirit-world. **1878** MACLEAR *Celts* ii. 28 *Spirit-worship, which peopled all the objects of nature with malignant beings.

b. Appositive, as ***spirit-bride, -chieftain, -enemy, -friend, -guardian, -lady, -wind***, etc.

1904 W. H. HUDSON *Green Mansions* xxi. 306 Nor did my mournful *spirit-bride come to me. **1917** G. FRANKAU *City of Fear* 26 My Soul would bide with its spirit-bride At the Inn of a Thousand Dreams. **1841** MRS. S. C. HALL *Ireland* I. 192 A belief in the existence of the *spirit-chieftain. **1900** *Month* Jan. 96 For ages.. these wild people had believed in spirit-guardians, and also in *spirit-enemies. **1839** BAILEY *Festus* 50 Have I not heard thee hint of *spirit-friends? Where are they now? **1845** G. MURRAY *Islaford*, etc. 186 The *spirit-lady soars away. **1845** BAILEY *Festus* (ed. 2) 119 There are *spirit-rulers of all worlds. **1848** *Ibid.* (ed. 3) 336 It will bear the gaze Of all the star souls and the *spirit stars Which will the living land of light indwell. **1838** MRS. BROWNING *Seraphim* II. Poems (1904) 87/2 Doth the *Spirit-wind Blow white those waters? **1894** *Wales* May 38/2 Lord, round me then with weeping clouds, And let my mind In quick blasts sigh beneath those shrouds, A spirit-wind. **1934** BLUNDEN *Choice or Chance* 3 (*heading*) Spirit-Wind.

c. With agent-nouns, as ***spirit-charmer, -hunter, -monger, -ridder, -seer, -wrestler***.

As the specific name of a religious sect, *Spirit-wrestlers* is a rendering of Russ. *Dukhobortsi*, f. *dukh'* spirit + *borets'* wrestler.

1711 SHAFTESB. *Charac.* (1737) II. 330 In ghostly company of spirit-hunters, witch-finders [etc.]. **1832** HOOD *Ode Ld. Gambier* iii, Consider The sorry figure of a spirit-ridder. **1862** S. LUCAS *Secularia* 91 'How,' exclaims the spirit-seer,..'do I envy you a sight of Bristow, in the year 1480'. **1877** J. E. CARPENTER tr. *Tiele's Hist. Relig.* 29 The magicians, soothsayers, and spirit-charmers. **1881** *Dr. Gheist, an Autobiogr.* 43 All the spirit-mongers are either old women or curates. **1897** (*title*), Christian Martyrdom in Russia. Persecution of the spirit-wrestlers (or Doukhobortsi) in the Caucasus. **1899** R. WHITEING *5 John St.* 329 The real spirit-wrestlers who struggle for a new blessing with the God within.

d. With vbl. sbs. and ppl. adjs., as ***spirit-cheering, -chilling, -crushing, -dazzling, -freeing, -giving, -healing, -lifting, quelling, -quenching, -strangling, -uplifting***, etc.

1838 MARY HOWITT *Birds & Fl.* 52 Raven, thou art *spirit-cheering. **1825** D. L. RICHARDSON *Sonets* 15 This sad heart By *spirit-chilling Sorrow unrepressed. **1858** HAWTHORNE *Fr. & It. Jrnls.* II. 221 It is extremely *spirit-crushing, this remorseless gray. **1946** R. S. THOMAS *Stones of Field* 12 Deadly as a falcon brooding over its prey In a tower of *spirit-dazzling and splendid light. **1858** T. GUTHRIE *Christ & Inheritance Saints* (1859) 20 The same *spirit-freeing words. **1946** BLUNDEN *Shelley* xvi. 199 The *spirit-giving blue sky of spring. **1798** COLERIDGE *Fears in Solitude* 12 O! 'tis a quiet *spirit-healing nook. **1605** SYLVESTER *Du Bartas* II. iii. III. *Law* 26 It is the *spirit-inspiring Spirit. **1841** E. A. POE in *Gift 1842* 161 *Spirit-lifting ecstasy of adoration. **1818** SHELLEY *Rosal. & Helen* 1156 His countenance.. burned with radiance Of *spirit-piercing joy. **1812** *Spirit quelling [see *nerve-racking* s.v. NERVE *sb.* 11 b]. **1817** SHELLEY *Rev. Islam* XI. xiv, On each unwilling heart Unusual awe did fall—a spirit-quelling dart. **1601** DONNE *Progresse of Soule* in *Poems* (1633) 3 *Spirit-quenching sicknesse, dull captivitie. **1948** F. R. LEAVIS *Great Tradition* v. 232 Coketown (the spirit-quenching hideousness of which is hauntingly evoked). *c* **1611** CHAPMAN *Iliad* III. 265 Two lambs, and *spirit-refreshing wine.. they bring. **1814** SCOTT *Lord of Isles* VI. i, The emotions of the *spirit-rousing time. **1777** POTTER *Æschylus, Choephoræ* 323 Bitter constraint, and *spirit-sinking fear. *a* **1822** SHELLEY '*She was an aged woman*' vii, The spirit-sinking noise Of heartless mirth. **1817** —— *Rev. Islam* IV. xxviii, The love that lies Hovering within those *spirit-soothing eyes. **1799** CAMPBELL *Pleas. Hope* I. 98 The dauntless brow, and *spirit-speaking eye. **1930** BLUNDEN *Summer's Fancy* 49 Of sloughs, of sleepless pangs, of Golgothas, of *spirit-strangling. **1817** SHELLEY *Rev. Islam* VII. iv, A wild, and sad, and *spirit-thrilling lay. **1830** TENNYSON *Ode to Mem.* 39 Those spirit-thrilling eyes. **1951** L. MACNEICE tr. *Goethe's Faust* 299 Here is the prospect free, *Spirit-uplifting. **1777** BRAND *Pop. Antiq.* 71 Mr. Bourne might have stiled this Chapter, A Sermon on *Spirit-walking. *Ibid.* 235 The Spirit-walking Time of Popery! **1809** MALKIN *Gil Blas* IX. i. ¶6 Six merchants.., all plodding *spirit-wearing personages.

e. With pa. pples., denoting either (*a*) 'of or by the spirit', 'by spirits', as ***spirit-baptized, -born, -filled, -guided, -haunted***, etc., or (*b*) 'in spirit', as ***spirit-broken, -crushed, -fallen, -froze, -rotten***, etc.

(*a*) **1602** FULBECKE *Pandects* Introd., The valiant Persians, the spirit-guided Hebrews, the prudent Grecians. **1645** QUARLES *Sol. Recant.* XII. 59 And what his spirit-prompted pen did write Was truth it self, and most exact upright. **1850** ROBERTSON *Serm.* Ser. III. ii. (1857) 23 Those called the Spirit-born, and those called the world. **1855** BAILEY *Mystic* 70 The spirit-haunted Kâf. **1895** J. MACNEIL (*title*) Spirit-filled life. **1897** MARY KINGSLEY *W. Africa* 417 Sending out long white arms.. and then drawing them back as if it were some spirit-possessed thing. **1903** R. C. MORGAN *Outpoured Spirit & Pentecost* 53 How are we to be filled with the Spirit? By drinking; by coming unto Jesus, and as members of the Spirit-baptized Church. **1936** J. BRICE *Pentecost* xiii. 226 The prayer-life of the Spirit-filled believer is transformed through his new apprehension of the Father. **1974** Spirit-baptized [see PENTECOSTAL *sb.* b]. **1977** *Belfast Tel.* 17 Jan. 2/8 (Advt.), Full Gospel Bible College at Millmount, Randalstown... We can promise you dynamic spirit-filled Ministry with David Hathaway.

(*b*) *a* **1628** F. GREVIL *Life Sidney* (1652) 60 If not with abrupt, and spirit-fall'n tolleration, yet with that invisible web of connivencie. **1649** G. DANIEL *Trinarch., Hen. V*, ccxxxvii, Stung with the Aspiche of invadeing feare, Or Spirit-froze, bound vp in bloodlesse veines. **1839** BAILEY *Festus* 268 See where she flies, spirit-torn, round the heavens. **1845** *Encycl. Metrop.* XI. 375/1 The injured but spirit-broken progeny of Ali and Fatima wanted resolution or ability to assert their cause. **1865** J. H. INGRAHAM *Pillar of Fire* I. xxv. (1872) 423 The queen.. seems heart-broken, spirit-crushed! **1880** SWINBURNE *Songs of Spring-t., Thalassius* 30 Death spirit-stricken of soul-sick days. **1922** D. H. LAWRENCE *Fantasia of Unconscious* v. 75 We are sympathy-rotten, and spirit-rotten, and idea-rotten.

f. Similative, as ***spirit-pure, -small, -wise; spirit-tongued, -winged***.

1817 SHELLEY *Rev. Islam* XII. xxxviii, The stream.. faster bare The spirit-winged boat. **1820** —— *Prometh. Unb.* II. i. 164 The crags.. mock our voices As they were spirit-tongued. **1842** BROWNING *By the Fireside* xxiii, The spirit-small hand propping it. **1845** —— *Statue & Bust* vii, A pale brow spirit-pure. **1848** BAILEY *Festus* (ed. 3) 309 Thou shalt perceive earth spirit-wise.

g. In expressions relating to the phenomena or doctrines of spiritualism, as ***spirit-circle, guide, healer, healing, photograph, photography, -writing***.

1856 *Spiritual Herald* Feb. 3 Spirit hands, spirit voices, spirit healing. **1858** W. M. WILKINSON (*title*), Spirit Drawings; a Personal Narrative. **1864** BROWNING *Dram. Pers.* 179 David.. peeps in the glass ball, Sets to the spirit-writing, hears the raps. **1865** MASSON *Rec. Brit. Philos.* 295 The heterodox science of the Swedenborgians and the spirit-manifestationists. **1867** J. H. POWELL (*title*), Mediumship:.. with brief instructions for the formation of Spirit-Circles. **1871** TYLOR *Prim. Cult.* I. 135 The Baron.. publishes a mass of fac-similes of spirit-writings thus obtained. **1872** *Spiritualist* 15 Apr. 25/1 Within the last six weeks in London, spirit photography has set in like a flood. **1877** H. P. BLAVATSKY *Isis Unveiled* II. ii. 118 A medium must be *passive*; and if a firm believer in his 'spirit-guide' he will allow himself to be ruled by the latter. **1887** *Encycl. Brit.* XXII. 405/2 'Spirit-photography,' or photographing of human and other forms invisible to all but specially endowed seers. **1893** *Fortn. Rev.* Jan. 125 Can a ghost be photographed? Are all the spirit-photos frauds? **1909** W. JAMES in *Amer. Mag.* Oct. 585/2 Rappings, apparitions, poltergeists, spirit-photographs, and materializations. **1956** R. M. LESTER *Towards Hereafter* x. 124 My husband and I visited a trance medium, and a spirit healer we now know as Dr Light spoke through her. **1960** *Spectator* 28 Oct. 649 One of their [*sc.* Spiritualists'] chief interests is 'spirit healing'; that is, any healing that is brought about by a non-human agency. **1982** E. JENKINS *Shadow & Light* xxii. 172 A matter between him and his spirit-guides, not one with which human beings had anything to do.

h. In specific names, as **spirit-butterfly, duck, -leaf, -weed, -wood** (see quots.).

1891 *Cent. Dict.*, **Spirit-butterfly*, a tropical American butterfly of the genus *Ithomia*. **1784** PENNANT *Arct. Zool.* II. 558 *Spirit Duck... Inhabits North America, from Hudson's Bay to Carolina. **1829** GRIFFITH tr. *Cuvier* VIII. 611 Spirit Duck, *Anas Albeola*. **1872** COUES *N. Amer. Birds* 290 Buffle-headed Duck. Butter-ball. Spirit Duck. Dipper. **1696** SLOANE *Cat. Plantarum Jamaica* 52 *Spirit leaf. **1864** GRISEBACH *Flora Brit. W. Ind.* 787/2 Spirit-leaf, *Ruellia tuberosa*. **1866** *Treas. Bot.* 1085/1 Spirit-leaf, or Spirit-weed, *Ruellia tuberosa*, now called *Cryphiacanthus barbadensis*. **1699** SLOANE in *Phil. Trans.* XXI. 119 None is more surprizing then one in Jamaica, called *Spirit-weed. **1866** [see above]. **1716** *Petiveriana* I. 259 *Spirit-wood, ..*Pneumatoxylum*.

i. Special *Comb.*: **Spirit baptism** = *baptism in the Spirit*, sense 6 c above.

1964 N. BLOCH-HOELL *Pentecostal Movement* vii. 142 Glossolalia, in connection with the Spirit baptism, was generally believed to be a permanent Gift of Grace. **1977** G. W. H. LAMPE *God as Spirit* vii. 199 It [*sc.* Pentecostalism] is very emphatic in its assertion of a two-stage relationship to God, reception of the Spirit, or Spirit-baptism, being sharply differentiated from the state of being a Christian without any added gift of God.

24. In sense 21 (freq. 21 c): **a.** Simple attrib., as ***spirit bubble, -extract, -flame, -licence, -trade***, etc.

1796 BURKE *Regic. Peace* Wks. VIII. 406 The spirit licences kept nearly the same level till the stoppage of the distilleries in 1795. **1842** *Penny Cycl.* XXII. 360/1 Spirit-trade. **1846** G. E. DAY tr. *Simon's Anim. Chem.* II. 186 Spirit-extract with chloride of sodium. **1862** *Catal. Internat. Exhib., Brit.* II. No. 2947, When the instrument is turned in any direction, the spirit bubble will be kept in the centre of its run. **1866** ODLING *Anim. Chem.* 68 The heat of the spirit-flame.. passing into the water.

b. In the sense 'used for holding, storing, or selling alcoholic spirits', as ***spirit-back, -beck***,

-bottle, -case, -cellar, -flask, -jar, -room, -shop, vault, etc.

1839 Ure *Dict. Arts* 402 The middle portion..are received into the *spirit-back. **1894** *Funk's Stand. Dict.*, **Spirit-beck*, a beck or vat for containing the spirit in a distillery. **1786** G. Frazer *Dove's Flight* 76 They have recourse to the *spirit-bottle..for consolation. **1849** R. G. Cumming *Hunter's Life S. Afr.* (1902) 78 They were both very drunk, having broken into my wine-cask and *spirit-case. **1833** Loudon *Encycl. Archit.* §916 The *spirit cellar is to have two tiers of catacombs (bins). **1829** G. Griffin *Collegians* II. xxix. 302 The assault made by Danny on her *spirit flask, which she now..discovered to be empty. **1834** Marryat *P. Simple* (1863) 161 He put the spirit-flask to his mouth. **1961** L. G. G. Ramsey *Connoisseur New Guide to Antique English Pott., Porc. & Glass* 73 Other manifestations of Early Victorian work..were the..spirit flasks formed into the shapes of human figures. **1858** Simmonds *Dict. Trade*, **Spirit-jar*, an earthenware jar.., for sending out spirits. **1797** *Encycl. Brit.* (ed. 3) XVII. 404/2 That part of the orlop which is over the after magazine, *spirit room, and fish room. *c* **1850** *Rudim. Navig.* (Weale) 143 The spirit-room is built in the hold, next before the fish-room, to contain the spirituous liquors for the use of the ship's company. **1835** *Mirror of Parliament* 20 May 983/2, I would willingly, if there was any chance of succeeding, include *spirit-shops. **1837** Ht. Martineau *Soc. Amer.* III. 202 Spirit-shops have been shut up by hundreds. **1858** Simmonds *Dict. Trade*, **Spirit-store*, a shop where spirits are kept for sale, wholesale and retail. **1848** Mrs. Gaskell *Mary Barton* II. iv. 57 The rest was taken in a *spirit vault, and the refreshment was a glass of gin. **1863** Hawthorne *Our Old Home* (1883) I. 327 Gin-shops, or what the English call spirit-vaults.

c. With agent-nouns, as ***spirit-dealer, -drinker, -grocer, -merchant***, etc.

1826 *Art of Brewing* (ed. 2) 44 It would be a matter of great convenience if one instrument only were adopted by the trade, as is the case with *spirit-dealers. **1864** A. McKay *Hist. Kilmarnock* 190 He spent a social hour in the house of a spirit-dealer. **1827** *Edin. Rev.* XLVI. 69 The *spirit-drinkers..never can agree in one party. **1899** *Allbutt's Syst. Med.* VI. 685 A man, aged 41, a spirit drinker. **1872** *Act 35 & 36 Vict.* c. 94 §81 The term '*spirit grocer'..means any person..having an excise licence to sell spirits by retail. **1841** Dickens *Barn. Rudge* xiii, To be looked upon as a common *spirit-guzzler. **1822** *Sunday Times* 20 Oct. 3/4 *Bankrupts*... James Cayne, jun. and Thomas Bullock Watts, of Yeovil, Somersetshire, *spirit-merchants. **1858** Simmonds *Dict. Trade*, *Spirit-merchant*, a vender of spirits. **1896** *Daily News* 4 Mar. 8/5 Her greatest danger came from the *spirit-sellers.

d. With vbl. sbs. and ppl. adjs., as ***spirit-bibing, -boiling, -drinking***, etc.

1827 *Edin. Rev.* XLVI. 69 The spirit-bibing party began to indulge in foolish..conversation. **1834** Marryat *P. Simple* (1863) 234 Mr. Apollo, who was above spirit-boiling heat with jealousy. **1897** *Daily News* 11 Feb. 5/5 Mr. Sharpe ..observed that the Celtic population are a spirit-drinking people.

e. In the sense 'that works, acts, etc., by means of spirit or spirits', as ***spirit blow-pipe, duplicator, -engine, kettle, -standard, -stove, thermometer, tube, weather-glass***.

1842 Francis *Dict. Arts, Alcoholic*, or **Spirit Blow-pipe*, a blow-pipe which acts by the inflammation of a stream of the vapor of spirits of wine. **1958** *Daily Mail* 24 July 6/6 We came to the *spirit duplicators... These machines *were* rather magical. They duplicated in seven different colours. **1858** Simmonds *Dict. Trade*, **Spirit-engine maker*, a manufacturer of the tavern, or bar, engines for drawing spirits for retail sale. **1890** *Girl's Own Paper* 4 Jan. 213/3 An Etna or small *spirit kettle, and a bottle of spirits; some tea and a little sugar. **1923** M. Beerbohm *Peep into Past* 10 His portly form..may be seen bending over the little spirit-kettle. **1960** C. Day Lewis *Buried Day* vii. 137 Cake-stand, ..heavy silver teapot, spirit-kettle and all. **1856** Kane *Arct. Expl.* I. xiv. 154 The reduced mean of our best *spirit-standards gave −67°. **1895** *Army & Navy Price List*, Kettle and *Spirit Stove. **1902** Eliz. Banks *Newspaper Girl* 170 One day I thought I'd cook some over my spirit-stove. **1827** Faraday *Chem. Manip.* iv. (1842) 139 A large and a small bulb, or a mercury and *spirit thermometer, will take different periods to heat and cool. **1842** *Penny Cycl.* XXII. 359/1 The *spirit-tube is used in determining the relative heights of ground at two or more stations. **1704** *Dict. Rust.* s.v., *Spirit Weather-Glass.

f. Applied to various dye-colours obtained from a mixture of dye extracts and solution of tin, as ***spirit black, blue, brown***, etc. Also ***spirit-colour***.

1836 *Penny Cycl.* VI. 157/1 Spirit-Colours are brilliant, but fugitive; they consist generally of decoctions of dye-woods, mixed with nitro-muriate or muriate of tin. **1867** *Ure's Dict. Arts* (ed. 6) I. 589, 2 quarts spirit pink. *Ibid.*, 1 gallon spirit yellow. *Ibid.* 590 Spirit black. **1875** Knight *Dict. Mech.* 428/1 Spirit-color printing.

g. Special combs.: **spirit fresco**, a method of fresco-painting, in which the colours are ground in a medium of wax, elemi resin, artist's copal, oil of spike or spirits of turpentine; **spirit-gum** (see quot.); **spirit-liver**, a liver affected by the drinking of spirits; **spirit varnish**, a varnish prepared by dissolving a resin in spirit; hence ***spirit-varnish*** vb.

1880 Gambier Parry (*title*), Spirit Fresco Painting. *Ibid.* 4 Wash over the part for the morning's work with pure spike oil, to refresh the surface (hence the name *Spirit Fresco). **1909** J. Ward *Fresco Painting* 38 The method of painting followed out in the spirit-fresco system..is almost precisely the same as that of the lime or buon-fresco process. **1891** *Cent. Dict.*, **Spirit-gum*, a quick-drying preparation used by actors and others to fasten false hair on the face. **1905** Rolleston *Dis. Liver* 197 The *spirit livers appeared to be more frequently fatty [than the beer livers]. **1850** Holtzapffel *Turning* III. 1375 These resins constitute the basis of what are called *spirit varnishes. **1887** *Pall Mall G.* 7 Mar. 6/1 The miserable, hungry appearance of the wood in all old violins known to be spirit varnished.

spirit ('spɪrɪt), *v.* [f. spirit *sb.*]

I. 1. *trans.* To make (the blood, a liquor) of a more active or lively character.

1599 Shaks. *Hen. V*, iii. v. 21 And shall our quick blood, spirited with Wine, Seeme frostie? **1644** in Hartlib *Legacy* (1655) 221 The blood being..spirited with subtle Nitre or Gunpowder, it..is distributed through the body. **1670** Evelyn *Pomona* (ed. 2) 55 Mustard made with Sack preserves boild Cider, and spirits it egregiously. **1822–7** Good *Study Med.* (1829) I. 511 We find it [*sc.* the blood] return from the lungs spirited with newness of life.

2. To infuse spirit, life, ardour, or energy into (a person); to inspirit, animate, encourage. Also const. *for* or *to*.

1608 Chapman *Dk. Byron* iii. i, Like men, that, spirited with wine, Pass dangerous places safe. **1682** N. O. *Boileau's Lutrin* iii. 28 Thy Valour firm d the wavering Troops that day, And spirited their Files with fresh array! **1698** Fryer *Acc. E. India & P.* 14 May had now began, when..we were once more spirited with milder Weather. **1719** De Foe *Crusoe* i. (Globe) 48, I also found some Rum.., which I had indeed need enough of to spirit me for what was before me. **1736** Lediard *Life Marlborough* II. 235 The small Advantages they had obtained..spirited them to entertain several towering Projects. **1758** *Ann. Reg.* 16 Spirited with this advantage, he pushed onwards. **1844** H. Rogers *Ess.* (1874) I. ii. 69 He was further spirited to it by an anonymous letter. **1851** *Chr. Spect.* I. 100 Let the song of faith spirit thee for the fight of faith.

b. With impersonal object.

a **1652** J. Smith *Sel. Disc.* ix. (1821) 423 There is a living soul of religion in good men which..spirits all the wheels of motion. **1679** J. Goodman *Penit. Pard.* ii. ii. (1713) 194 Hope and apprehension of feasibleness spirits all industry, actuates all faculties, raises the spirits.

c. To lead or urge *on* by encouragement.

1682 *New News fr. Bedlam* 30 Give Nature a Phillip with two or three quarts of Mum, to spirit them on for any Attempt. **1792** Mme. D'Arblay *Lett.* 2 Oct., I wish to spirit him on to collect them [*sc.* notes] into a pamphlet. **1840** Lady C. Bury *Hist. of Flirt* xv, What was labour to me when my cousin James was at hand to spirit me on?

d. To excite, instigate, or stir up.

a **1680** Charnock *Attrib. God* (1834) II. 686 It is not to spirit rebellion, but to give a merciful stop to it. **1701** Swift *Contests Nobles & Comm.* Wks. 1755 II. i. 36 Civil dissentions never fail of introducing and spiriting the ambition of private men.

3. To invest with a spirit or animating principle.

1629 T. Adams *Rage Oppression* Wks. 608 God hath.. tempered all our bodies of one clay, and spirited our soules of one breath. **1642** Cudworth *Disc. Lord's Supper* Introd. 2 There is ever some Soule of Truth, which doth secretly Spirit and Enliven the dead and unweildy Lump of all Errours, without which it could not move or stirre. **1650** R. Stapylton *Strada's Low C. Wars* i. 1 A Prince (the great body of whose Empire must be spirited with a great soul). **1717** Pope *Iliad* ix. 98 Thy high commands must spirit all our wars.

b. To invest with a particular spirit, disposition, or character.

Not always clearly distinguishable from 2 and 2 b.

1654 Owen *Saints' Persev.* v. 113 The first great Promise of Christ..is that which Spirits and principles all other promises whatsoever. **1662** R. Mathew *Unl. Alch.* 63 Your rash and hasty zeal, running upon Ordinances not spirited from on high. **1685** W. Adams *Dedham Pulpit* 108 This will spirit and dispose you to practise all those counsels. **1721** R. Keith tr. *T. à Kempis, Valley of Lillies* xxxiii. 105 The holy Spirit, who..taught him, and spirited him, and adorned his whole Life with Virtues. **1728** P. Walker *Life Peden* To Rdr. (1827) p. xxviii, They were some Way fitted and spirited for Trials.

c. Const. *by* or *with* (some principle, etc.). Chiefly in passive.

1646 J. Gregory *Notes & Obs.* (1650) 33 Thus spirited with this secret power, it [the Palladium] was dispos'd of in some eminent..place of the City. **1654** Owen *Saints' Persev.* v. 112 The generall intention of God in all Gospel Promises, whereby they being equally Spirited, become as one. **1671** Temple *Ess., Constit. & Int. Emp.* Wks. 1731 I. 107 In all these Wars the People were both united and spirited by the common Love of their Country. **1704** Swift *Mech. Operat. Spirit* Misc. (1711) 300 Spirited by a noble Zeal. **1741** Betterton *Hist. Eng. Stage* i. 21 They had warm Disputes behind the Scenes, which spirited the Rivals with ..a natural Resentment to each other.

d. To lead or win *over* by persuasion.

1656 Hammond *Leah & Rachel* (1844) 10, I shall abhor to spirit over any; but go along with such as are voluntarily desirous to go thither.

4. With *up*: To stimulate, animate, encourage, stir up, or excite (a person).

1712 Addison *Spect.* No. 482 ¶2 She is forced..to spirit him up now and then, that he may not grow musty, and unfit for Conversation. **1743** Bulkeley & Cummins *Voy. S. Seas* 11 Not knowing..by whom the Fellow might be spirited up, I acquainted the Captain with the Affair. **1760–72** H. Brooke *Fool of Qual.* (1809) I. 70 Being encouraged and spirited up..they became, by degrees, quite happy and jovial. **1797** Jane Austen *Sense & Sens.* xxx, Well, I shall spirit up the Colonel as soon as I can. **1847** Mrs. Gore *Castles in Air* xix, 'You might live at a worse place, Charley!' said I, spirited up for Yorkshire. **1871** Browning *Balaust.* 106 We want no colony from Athens here, With memories of Salamis,..To spirit up our captives.

b. Const. *against, into*, or *to*.

1716 Pope *Lett.* (1735) I. 288 Such a Mind as your's has no need of being spirited up into Honour. **1721** Amherst *Terræ Fil.* No. 8 (1726) 38 They made it their business to.. spirit up their neighbours to rebellion. **1728** H. Herbert tr. *Fleury's Eccl. Hist.* I. 328 The powerful party that had been spirited up against him. **1764** Goldsm. *Hist. Eng. in Lett.* (1772) II. 220 The French..continually spirited up the Indians to repel the new comers. **1809** W. Irving *Knickerb.*, vi. vii. (1849) 355 Spiriting them up to heroic deeds. **1841** W. Duncan *Cicero's Sel. Orat.* ii. 32 Many very powerful nations were spirited up against us. **1857** Trollope *Barchester T.* (1861) 130 Expecting that he should find his lordship..spirited up by his wife to repeat the rebuke.

c. To instigate or promote (rebellion, etc.).

1715 in *Westm. Gaz.* (1907) 14 May 2/3 Those Incendiaries who came hither on Purpose to spirit up a Rebellion. **1751** Smollett *Per. Pic.* (1779) IV. xcvii. 258 Attempts..to spirit up suits against him. **1770** *Langhorne Plutarch* (1879) I. 255/1 He determined to spirit up a cruel war.

II. 5. To carry off or away, to make away with or remove in a mysterious or dexterous manner: †**a.** To kidnap, in order to transport to the plantations in America. *Obs.* (Cf. 6 a.)

1666 *Lond. Gaz.* No. 107/1 Several persons escaped from the Vessel, who pretend they were spirited (as they term it) and invited upon several pretences aboard them, and then.. carried away. *a* **1683** Oldham *Wks* (1686) 85 These serve for Baits the simple to ensnare, Like Children spirited with Toys at Fair. **1693** I. Mather *Cases Consc.* (1862) 241 A Servant, who was Spirited or Kidnapt (as they call it) into America.

b. In general use.

1670 *Caveat to Conventiclers* 4 They do in a manner acknowledge, that they were Spirited out of their Bogs and Woods, and transported hither with vain hopes of preferment. **1678** *Strange News fr. Wicklow* 3 Mr. Uniack demanded if she could give them any account of a Gentleman..that had been Spirited out of their Company [by fairies] about an hour before. **1837** Carlyle *Fr. Rev.* i. v. i, Leading men from all the Three Orders are nightly spirited thither. *Ibid.* ii. v. v, Deserters are spirited over by assiduous crimps. **1858** R. S. Surtees *Ask Mamma* xlv. 199 [He] seemed to spirit the things off the table without sound or effort. **1889** Stevenson *Edinburgh* 46 Many a solid bulk of masonry has been likewise spirited into the air.

6. With *away* (cf. 5): **a.** To kidnap, carry off, or abduct (a person).

Freq. *c* 1670–*c* 1690, with reference to transporting boys to the West Indian plantations: cf. 5 a.

1670 Marvell *Corr.* Wks (Grosart) II. 323 An Act.. against spiriting away Children beyond Sea. **1682** *Lond. Gaz.* 1723/4 For Spiriting or Stealing away a Young Boy, and sending him to Jamaica. **1697** Dampier *Voy.* (1729) I. 178 We anchor'd, and sent..to treat about an Exchange for our Man they had spirited away. **1749** Fielding *Tom Jones* i. ix, Some..intimated, that she was spirited away with a design too black to be mentioned. **1769** Blackstone *Comm.* IV. 219 In the civil law, the offence of spiriting away and stealing men and children..was punished with death. **1820** Scott *Monast.* iv, She was sensible that he would have neither scruple nor difficulty in spiriting away the child. **1858** Froude *Hist. Eng.* III. xvii. 449 The archbishop spirited away the preacher into Kent. **1883** *Law Rep. 11 Q.B.D.* 592 The prosecutor had spirited away..the sister of the accused person, and had shut her up in a convent.

fig. **1688** Crowne *Darius* v. Wks. 1874 III. 449 What is it spirits me away to fear?

b. To take away, carry off, by some mysterious means or power; to transport with speed.

1696 C. Leslie *Snake in Grass* (1697) 97 Their Spiriting away the Letter of the Promised Seed. **1726** Penn *No Cross* xiii. §14 An Enemy to the State, for he [the miser] spirits their Money away. **1775** R. Chandler *Trav. Asia M.* (1825) I. Introd. p. xi, The jealousy of the papal court..spirited away these inestimable treasures. **1794** Godwin *Caleb Williams* 69 There is no Mrs. Jakeman now to spirit you away. **1861** Hughes *Tom Brown at Oxf.* xxxii, One shake of the hand, and she was spirited away in a moment.

c. Said of the action of spirits.

1825 J. Neal *Bro. Jonathan* I. 253 Peters had been.. spirited away in a thunderstorm. **1855** W. Irving *Chron. Wolfert's Roost* 179 Others jocosely hinted that old Pluto.. had spirited away the boy to the nether regions. **1889** Barrie *Window in Thrums* 102 It was thocht next mornin' 'at the ghost had spirited them awa.

III. †**7.** To extract spirit from; to distil. In quot. *fig.* *Obs.*$^{-1}$

1677 *Cleveland's Poems* Ded., Yet how many such Authors must be creamed and spirited to make up his *Fuscara*?

8. To treat with a solution of spirits.

1883 Haldane *Workshop Rec.* Ser. ii. 145 Worsted-and-Cotton Damasks,..after being spirited and rinsed,..must have a water starch to make them look strong and well when finished.

†**'spirital**, *a. Obs.* Also 7 -all. [a. OF. (*e*)*spirital*, or ad. L. *spīritālis*: see spirit *sb.*]

1. Pertaining to sacred concerns; = spiritual *a.* 2. Also *absol.*

1390 Gower *Conf.* I. 32 Wher sche cometh overal, Noght only of the temporal Bot of the spirital also. *Ibid.* 259 That the Papacie Thei wolde honoure and magnefie In al that evere is spirital.

2. Of the nature of spirit; of or pertaining to the spirit in contrast to the body or matter.

1598 Haydocke tr. *Lomazzo* ii. 193 Spirital and incorporal things. **1642** H. More *Song of Soul* ii. ii. ii. xi, This is a substance truly spiritall, That reason by her glistring lamp hath shown. *Ibid.* ii. ii. iii. xvii, That truths spiritall we may with ease Find out. *a* **1676** Hale *Prim. Orig. Man.* iii. vi. (1677) 277 When the Matter is fitly prepared, there is an illapse of this Vital, Formative, Spiritual Principle into it. **1707** J. Stevens tr. *Quevedo's Com. Wks.* (1709) 48 There being no likelihood that human Weakness could prevail against a spirital Power.

†**spiri'tality.** *Obs.*$^{-1}$ [f. prec. + -ITY, or ad. late L. *spīritālitas*. Cf. OF. *esperitalité*.] Spiritual nature or quality.

1677 GALE *Crt. Gentiles* IV. II. iii. 307 That al Spirits have, according to the degree of Spiritalitie, an amplitude of Essence.

†'**spiritally**, *adv. Obs. rare.* [f. prec. + -LY².]

1. In a spiritual manner.

1598 HAYDOCKE tr. *Lomazzo* II. 194 The body without the spirit cannot draw any thing vnto it; For whatsoever it would draw, it must draw it by the helpe of the spirit, that is spiritally. For a spirit cannot drawe a body vnto it bodily, but spiritally.

2. *Gram.* With breathing or aspiration.

1669 HOLDER *Elem. Speech* 58 We may conceive one of each pronounced Spiritally, the other vocally. But in attempting to pronounce these two Consonants.. and some of the vowels Spiritally, the Throat is brought to labour.

†**spiritalty.** *Obs.*$^{-1}$ = SPIRITALITY.

c **1400** tr. *Secreta Secret., Gov. Lordsh.* 97 Wete þat vche voys yn his ordre ys al hool whenne it ys stiryd yn þe Eyre þat berys it, & þat self noble spiritalte stirrys þerwith.

‖**spiritato.** *Obs. rare.* In 7 *pl.* **-ati, -aties.** [It. *spiritato*, pa. pple. of *spiritare*, f. *spirito* SPIRIT *sb.*] A religious enthusiast.

1659 GAUDEN *Tears Ch.* 195 Before these new Illuminates and Spiritaties rose up. **1678** CUDWORTH *Intell. Syst.* I. iii. §29. 134 A kind of Bewitched Enthusiasts and Blind *Spiritati*, that are wholly.. acted by a dark, narrow and captivated Principle of Life.

'**spiritdom.** [f. SPIRIT *sb.* + -DOM.] The domain of disembodied spirits.

1864 TYNDALL *Fragm. Sci.* (1879) I. 499 These [sounds of music] were acknowledged to be as great marvels as any of those of spiritdom.

'**spirited**, *a.* [f. SPIRIT *sb.*]

In addition to its uses as a simple word, *spirited* also occurs as the second element in a large number of combs., as *bold-, cold-, high-, humble-, low-, mean-, meek-, narrow-, poor-, public-spirited*, etc., which are dealt with under the first element or as main words.

†**1.** Impregnated with spirit or active properties.

1599 B. JONSON *Cynthia's Rev.* v. iv, Pure benjamin, the onely spirited sent, that ever awak'd a neapolitane nostrill. **1646** SIR T. BROWNE *Pseud. Ep.* 50 Which perhaps must not be taken strictly, but in the germe and spirited particles. **1677** MIÉGE *Fr. Dict.* II. s.v. *Sparkle*, To Sparkle as spirited wine nimbly filled out.

2. Of persons: Full of spirit or animation; of a lively and energetic disposition; prompt to act, or to assert oneself, in a worthy manner.

1599 B. JONSON *Cynthia's Rev.* IV. i, This tire (me thinkes) makes me looke very ingeniously, quick, and spirited. *Ibid.* v. iv, O brave and spirited! Hee's a right Jovialist. **1725** DE FOE *Voy. round World* (1840) 294 So generous, spirited, and grateful a person. **1748** *Anson's Voy.* II. vi. 193 The shouts ..of threescore sailors.., joyous as they always are, when they land..; the huzza's, I say, of this spirited detachment. **1780** *Mirror* No. 102, Nor is the ambition of those spirited ladies satisfied with speaking in public. **1828** D'ISRAELI *Chas. I*, II. x. 245 The spirited servant on whom the hope of his glory rested. **1852** MISS YONGE *Cameos* II. viii. 101 The French.. had always been forced back by the spirited little garrison. **1895** MEREDITH *Amazing Marriage* I. i. 4 He wealthy and rather handsome, and she quite lovely and spirited.

b. Energetic or enterprising in the pursuit of some study or business.

1769 *Junius Lett.* ii. (1788) 41 A most spirited as well as excellent scholar. **1799** A. YOUNG *Agric. Linc.* 74 A very spirited and active farmer. **1847** W. C. L. MARTIN *Ox* 82/1 The improvement in the short-horns.. under the superintendence of spirited individuals.

c. Of animals, esp. horses: Full of animation and vigour; mettlesome.

1774 GOLDSM. *Nat. Hist.* II. 362 The Persian horses.. are docile, spirited, nimble, hardy, courageous [etc.]. **1828** LYTTON *Pelham* II. viii, I saw a groom managing, with difficulty, a remarkably fine and spirited horse. **1846** J. BAXTER *Libr. Pract. Agric.* (ed. 4) II. 217 The cock.. should be brisk, spirited, and attentive.. in defending the hens. **1869** TOZER *Highl. Turkey* II. 319 A man.. seated on a spirited charger. **1871** BLACKIE *Four Phases Morals* i. 7 Men who wish to learn to ride do not choose the meekest and most docile beast.. but the most spirited.

3. Of things: Characterized by, displaying, or suggestive of spirit, animation, vigour, or energy:

a. Of literary work, speech, etc.

1715 POPE *Iliad* Pref. ¶35 The most noble and spirited translation I know in any language. **1768** in *Priv. Lett. Ld. Malmesbury* (1870) I. 166 Some very spirited expressions flung out in our King's speech. **1797** JANE AUSTEN *Sense & Sens.* xxxvii, A very spirited critique upon the party. **1835** T. MITCHELL *Acharn. of Aristoph.* 463 *note*, A spirited version of this chorus.. appeared in an early number of a monthly publication. **1867** FREEMAN *Norm. Conq.* I. v. 378 To which summons the Earl returns a spirited reply.

b. Of action, conduct, etc.

1765 in *Priv. Lett. Ld. Malmesbury* (1870) I. 132 Had the Governor acted a becoming or spirited part at first, matters had not risen into this confusion. **1796** SCOTT *Let.* in *Lockhart* (1837) I. vii. 238 By the wise precautions of the magistrates,.. and the spirited conduct of the gentlemen, I hope their designs will be frustrated. **1815** —— *Guy M.* xxx, A few such instances of spirited resistance would greatly check the presumption of these lawless men. **1841** *Excheq. Rep.* ii. 178 Her Majesty's government entertain a high sense of the very spirited and able conduct of Commander Denman. **1860** TYNDALL *Glac.* I. xxiii. 161 The thing was accomplished in a very spirited way. **1897** MARY KINGSLEY *W. Africa* 339 It was a spirited performance I assure you.

c. Of business or other enterprises.

1771 *Ann. Reg.* II. 109/2 Amongst the rarest instances of spirited husbandry ever met with among the common farmers of England. **1842** LANCE *Cottage Farmer* 26 To whose spirited exertions we are mainly indebted for the annual cattle-show. **1849** MACAULAY *Hist. Eng.* iii. I. 378 It was announced that a vehicle.. would perform the whole journey between sunrise and sunset. This spirited undertaking was solemnly.. sanctioned by the Heads of the University. **1879** *Cassell's Techn. Educ.* I. 225/2 A gradual and spirited revival of the Gothic style.

d. Of attitudes, features, etc., or artistic representations of objects.

1781 SIR J. REYNOLDS *Journ. Flanders & Holland* Wks. 1797 II. 57 Some horsemen are seen at a distance in very spirited attitudes. **1832** BREWSTER *Nat. Magic* iv. 78 The expence of exceedingly minute and spirited drawings. **1849** C. BRONTE *Shirley* vii, What clearly cut, spirited features! **1879** H. PHILLIPS *Notes Coins* 11 The action is spirited and by no means so stiff as the low state of the arts would have warranted us in expecting.

4. Of persons: Occupied or possessed by a (good or evil) spirit.

1667 MILTON *P.L.* IX. 613 So talk'd the spirited sly Snake. **1861** J. A. ALEXANDER *Gosp. Christ* iii. 47 A voice both of kindness and of authority, stole in upon your spirited senses.

5. *Gr. Gram.* Provided with a breathing.

1668 M. CASAUBON *Credulity* (1670) 98 As for example, αγνος: Accented and Spirited ἅγνος, it signifies.. a willow.

6. Impregnated with alcoholic spirit.

1822-7 GOOD *Study Med.* (1829) II. 693 The mischief produced by highly-spirited malt liquors.

'**spiritedly**, *adv.* [f. prec. + -LY².] In a spirited or lively manner; with spirit, animation, or vivacity.

1785 J. PHILLIPS *Treat. Inland Nav.* p. x, The horses.. contribute more spiritedly to the sport or pleasure of their possessors. **1799** COLERIDGE *Lett.* (1895) I. 313 'Christabel,' were it.. finished as spiritedly as it commences [etc.]. **1813** T. FAULKNER *Fulham* 88 This monument is very spiritedly executed. **1832** *Blackwood's Mag.* XXXI. 374 Henry.. spiritedly refused his brother's counsel. **1861** L. L. NOBLE *Icebergs* 31 We were moving spiritedly forward over a bright and lively sea.

b. Qualifying adjs. and ppl. adjs.

1780 YOUNG *Tour Irel.* II. xvii. 75 Lazy to an excess at work, but so spiritedly active at play. **1812** *Examiner* 25 May 328/1 A very spiritedly drawn and classical background. **1886** RUSKIN *Præterita* I. xii. 425 Spiritedly curling and projecting dark hair.

'**spiritedness.** [f. as prec. + -NESS.]

The formation is more common as a second element in combs., as *base-, high-, low-, mean-, narrow-, poor-, public-spiritedness.*

†**1.** Spiritual state or condition. *Obs.*$^{-1}$

1681 C. TAYLOR *Ep. Caution to Friends* 11 The ruin.. of his Soul forever, and the Souls of all, who in this Spiritedness adhere to him.

2. The character or quality of being spirited, lively, or animated; liveliness, vivacity.

1704 PENN in *Pennsylv. Hist. Soc. Mem.* IX. 356, I desire ..my officers will take a little more spiritedness and quickness upon them. **1834** *New Monthly Mag.* XLI. 318 The unostentatious spiritedness, the tranquil but forcible truth of their character. **1853** BAGEHOT *Lit. Stud.* (1911) I. 131 In spiritedness, the style of Shakespeare is very like to that of Scott. **1880** MEREDITH *Tragic Com.* (1881) 215 Her natural spiritedness detested the monotony.

'**spiriter.** *rare*$^{-1}$. [f. SPIRIT *v.* + -ER.] An abductor or kidnapper.

1675 COTTON *Burlesque upon B.* 146 Whilst the poor Boy, half dead with fear, Writh'd back to view his Spiriter.

'**spiritful**, *a. Obs.* or *dial.* [f. SPIRIT *sb.*]

1. Having a spiritual or refined character.

1546 BOLTON *Arraignm. Errour* 43 Others againe of finer tempers and spirits, that must be undone a finer way, a more spiritfull way, the grosse way is too low for them. **1643** MILTON *Divorce* Introd. Wks. 1851 IV. 10 The spiritfull and orderly life of our grown men. *a* **1665** J. GOODWIN *Filled w. the Spirit* (1867) 387 That such a doctrine or ministry, which some count legal and low is far more spiritful and raised than [etc.].

2. Of persons: Full of spirit or animation; spirited, vigorous, energetic. (Freq. *c* 1610-70.)

1598 DRAYTON *Heroical Ep.* (1619) Catal., Couragious Poole and that brave spiritfull Queene. **1650** HOWELL *Giraffi's Revolution Naples* I. 76 Naples,.. the Nurse of so many valiant Champions, and spiritfull Cavaliers. **1673** O. WALKER *Educ.* 192 Making us stand upon our guard, which renders the mind more diligent, vigorous, brisk, and spiritfull. **1748** RICHARDSON *Clarissa* (1811) III. 63 Miss Howe is a charming creature too; but confoundedly smart and spiritful. **1851** MAYHEW *Lond. Labour* I. 386/2 He was always a spiritful man, and it hurted him sorely that he should come to this at last. **1886** *Cheshire Gloss.* 332.

b. Of horses: Mettlesome.

1644 DIGBY *Nat. Bodies & Soul* 458 The spiritfull horse dutyfully beareth the soldier.

3. Of actions, etc.: Performed with, characterized by, spirit or vigour.

1614 LATHAM *Falconry* (1633) 87 All which.. tempteth the Hawke to flye couragiously with more eagernesse and spiritfull assurance to enioy him. **1643** MILTON *Divorce* xi. Wks. 1851 IV. 50 And what is life without the vigor and spiritfull exercise of life?

4. Of liquor: Impregnated with some active or lively principle; spirituous.

1608 SYLVESTER *Du Bartas* II. iv. IV. *Decay* 1155 The spirit-full bloud spins in his Father's face. **1644** DIGBY *Nat. Bodies* xvii. 145 Wine, or other spiritfull liquors. **1662** HIBBERT *Body Divinity* I. 312 Poyson.. is subtle and spiritful, and therefore incorporates with that which is most subtle in man, his spirits. **1675** BAXTER *Cath. Theol.* II. II. 36 To know that the Drink is pleasant to the tast, exhilerating, spiritful.

transf. **1643** T. GOODWIN *Child of Light* 97 That word is inspired with a principle, most quick, spiritfull, and active.

Hence †'**spiritfully** *adv.*; †'**spiritfulness.**

1644 DIGBY *Nat. Bodies* xxviii. 254 The exceeding life and spiritefulnesse of his eyes. **1655** tr. *Sorel's Com. Hist. Francion* IX. 10 Sir, said Nays, very spiritfully unto him, I plainly perceive [etc.]. *a* **1665** J. GOODWIN *Filled w. the Spirit* (1867) 464 This same activeness and spiritfulness in the service of God.

'**spirithood.** *rare.* [f. SPIRIT *sb.* + -HOOD.] The state of being a spirit.

1852 BAILEY *Festus* (ed. 5) 494 Day by day Grew spirithood to deathless angel kind.

'**spiriting**, *vbl. sb.* [f. SPIRIT *sb.* or *v.*]

1. The action or work of a spirit or sprite; the ministering of spirits. Also *fig.*

In mod. use only in echoes of the Shaksperian passage.

1768 *Shakspere's Temp.* I. ii. 298 (Capell), I will be correspondent to command, And do my spiriting [*fol.* spryting] gently. **1841** MOORE *Lalla Rookh* Poet. Wks. VI. Pref. p. xvii, Quick as Fancy required the aid of fact, in her spiritings. **1860** GEN. P. THOMPSON *Audi Alt.* cvi. III. 16 Like lawyers, they are ready to do their spiritings with as little of personal bitterness as human nature will admit. **1880** BROWNING *Dram. Idyls* Ser. II. 120 As I am free to do my spiriting.

2. Inspiration.

1845 MRS. BROWNING in *Lett. Browning & E. B. Barrett* (1899) I. 37 We turn to you.. for comfort and gentle spiriting.

3. *techn.* **a.** A solution of spirits with which carpets, lace, etc., are treated in their manufacture.

1883 HALDANE *Workshop Rec.* Ser. II. 146 When it [*sc.* a curtain] has been well worked in this [soap liquor], handle it directly out of the soap into the spiriting.

b. The application of a spirit, as a finishing process in french polishing. Also with *off*.

1933 C. CRAMPTON *Canework* (ed. 6) iii. 36 The last operation in french polishing, which gives the final gloss, is known as 'spiriting off'. **1960** C. H. HAYWARD *Staining & Polishing* ix. 55 Purpose of spiriting. The idea of this process is gradually to burnish the surface of semi-soft shellac.

†**spiritish**, *a. Obs.*$^{-1}$ [f. SPIRIT *sb.* + -ISH.] Dealing with spirits.

1588 J. HARVEY *Disc. Probl.* 32 Which neither.. cosening oraclers could euer insinuate:..or the superstitious inuocations of spiritish exorcistes discouer.

spiritism ('spɪrɪtɪz(ə)m). [f. SPIRIT *sb.* + -ISM. So F. *spiritisme.*] = SPIRITUALISM 3.

This form has to some extent been preferred by those specially interested in the subject, as being more distinctive than *spiritualism.*

1856 *Spiritual Herald* July 203 Witchcraft was an unfriendly form of spiritism, and calculated to produce fear. **1864** *Reader* 542/1 Spiritism (spirit-rapping, as commonly understood). **1865** *Cornh. Mag.* Oct. 504 The Maories seem to be in advance of us, if not of our French and American cousins, in spiritism. **1876** M. DAVIES *Unorthodox Lond.* 98 The line of demarcation between Swedenborgianism and modern Spiritualism—or Spiritism, as it is now called. **1880** HOWELLS *Undiscov. Country* iv. 69 In the development of the phenomena which now agitate the world, mesmerism came first, and spiritism came second.

'**spiritist.** [f. SPIRIT *sb.* + -IST.]

1. One who believes in spiritism; a spiritualist.

1858 *Brownson's Q. Rev.* Apr. 180 Mormons, Swedenborgians, and Spiritists, &c. **1867** CHRISTIE in Manning *Ess. Relig. & Lit.* Ser. II. 310 These remarks apply to such pretenders to Divine communications as.. the Jansenists, and modern Spiritists. **1896** *Pop. Sci. Jrnl.* L. 229 This condition finds its ideal fulfillment in the 'developing séance' of the spiritists.

b. *attrib.* as *adj.* = SPIRITISTIC *a.*

1865 *Cornh. Mag.* Apr. 481 Those who believe in spiritist and other marvels. **1877** J. E. CARPENTER tr. *Tiele's Hist. Relig.* 35 The spiritist side of Animism. **1887** *Amer. Nat.* XXI. 497 The spiritist practices of Chinese women.

2. = SPIRITUALIST 3.

1878 T. SINCLAIR *Mount* 39 Spiritists, or Comtists, let them keep to the moorlands of life. **1883** L. OLIPHANT *Altiora Peto* II. 16 Why he should shrink from this hypothesis for fear of becoming a materialist, as much as the scientific man does from it for fear of becoming a spiritist.

spiri'tistic, *a.* [f. SPIRIT *sb.* + -ISTIC.] Of or pertaining to, dealing or concerned with, spiritism; = SPIRITUALISTIC *a.* 2.

1867 *Eng. Leader* 15 June 333/1 That spiritistic 'literature' which has led astray.. so many weak and impressionable minds. **1880** HOWELLS *Undiscov. Country* iv. 70 The only perfectly ascertained fact of spiritistic science is the rap. **1898** *Pop. Sci. Monthly* LII. 493 New support for unfounded spiritualistic and spiritistic chimeras.

'**spiritize**, *v. rare.* [SPIRIT *sb.* + -IZE.] *trans.* To imbue with spirit or spiritual power.

1654 GAYTON *Pleas. Notes* III. vii. 111 The nimble Mercurie.. hath so spiritiz'd their whole Oeconomie, that they are Quick-silver to their finger ends. **1893** J. H. BARROWS *World's Parlt. Relig.* I. 617 To spiritize a stone, a block of wood, one must first have believed in a spirit.

ˈspirit-lamp. Also spirit lamp. [SPIRIT *sb.*] A lamp fed by methylated or other spirits, and used esp. for heating, boiling, or cooking.

1767 J. PRIESTLEY *Hist. & Present State of Electricity* VIII. xii. 700 The bar was heated by a spirit lamp placed underneath it. **1802** *Phil. Trans.* XCIII. 14 The.. solution, gently exhaled to dryness, and kept over a spirit-lamp. **1838** T. THOMSON *Chem. Org. Bodies* 372 Having put on the cover, the flame of a spirit-lamp was applied beneath the indigo. **1893** LADY I. BURTON *Life R. F. Burton* II. 8 Our hosts are astir, and already.. drinking tea made over a spirit-lamp.

attrib. **1827** FARADAY *Chem. Manip.* vi. (1842) 186 In operations of this kind, heat is applied.. by a small spirit lamp flame.

ˈspiritless, *a.* [f. SPIRIT *sb.* + -LESS.]

1. Deprived of the spirit or animating principle; having or possessing no spirit; lifeless.

1570 T. NORTON tr. *Nowel's Catech.* (1853) 160 His dead and spiritless body was laid in the grave. *c* **1611** CHAPMAN *Iliad* XII. 163 The man.. Fell now quite-spiritlesse to earth. *a* **1616** BEAUM. & FL. *Bonduca* V. i, 'Tis the Body Of the great Captain Penyus, by himself Made cold and spiritless. **1705** GREENHILL *Embalming* 5 Nature admonishes us that the spiritless Body should be restored to the Earth. **1852** BAILEY *Festus* (ed. 5) 346 A work or thought.. may Be.. like the air,.. Sweeping miles broad o'er far western woods,.. Or may be, nothing—bodiless, spiritless.

2. Devoid of lively or cheerful spirits; depressed, dejected, downcast, dull or melancholy.

1597 SHAKS. *2 Hen. IV*, I. i. 70 Euen such a man, so faint, so spiritlesse, So dull. *c* **1620** FLETCHER & MASS. *Double Marriage* II. i, Why are you still so sad?.. You make us dull, and spiritless. **1643** MILTON *Divorce* iv. Wks. 1851 IV. 29 Whereof who misses by chancing on a mute and spiritlesse mate, remaines more alone then before. **1726** LEONI *Alberti's Architecture* III. 18/1 Those that grieve.. seem fatigued and spiritless. **1778** MISS BURNEY *Evelina* lxxvi, I was totally spiritless and dejected. **1816** C. HUTTON *Concl. Life W. Hutton* 92, I.. found my father thinner, weaker, and more spiritless than I left him. **1826** *Literary Souvenir* 326 He sank spiritless, and almost lifeless, upon the gunwale of the vessel. **1876** *Trans. Clinical Soc.* IX. 189 The child, ceasing to play about, became spiritless.

transf. **1778** [W. H. MARSHALL] *Minutes Agric., Observ.* 67 The countenance of the Soil.. is pallid and spiritless.

3. Destitute or devoid of spirit, animation, or courage; lacking ardour or boldness.

1628 FELTHAM *Resolves* II. 5, I wish no man so spiritlesse, as to let all abuses presse the dulnesse of a willing shoulder. **1651** BIGGS *New Disp.* ¶ 100 We are uselesse and spiritlesse to our selves and the Common-Wealth. **1702** DENNIS *Monument* xiii, Their Soldiers and Commanders all grown faint, Dejected, spiritless with frequent Routs. **1776** GIBBON *Decl. & F.* viii. I. 214 The infantry was a half-armed spiritless crowd of peasants. **1839** DICKENS *Nickleby* xxxi, You are a base and spiritless scoundrel! **1850** MERIVALE *Rom. Emp.* xi. (1865) II. 21 Spiritless himself, he was incapable of infusing spirit. **1884** SWINBURNE *Midsummer Holiday*, etc. 169 As a swordless and spiritless nation.

b. Destitute of energy or enterprise.

1799 J. ROBERTSON *Agric. Perth* 71 About half a century ago,.. the fields [were] uncultivated and the farmers spiritless and poor. *c* **1825** LD. COCKBURN *Mem.* (1856) 168 The publishers we had were too spiritless even for their position. **1861** SMILES *Engineers* II. 49 The country was too poor or too spiritless to undertake their improvement on any comprehensive scale.

4. Marked or characterized by lack of animation, vivacity, or energy.

1651 N. BACON *Disc. Govt. Eng.* II. (1739) p. ix, Both the Election of a King, and the Solemnization of such Election, .. are spiritless motions without the presence of the people. **1712** STEELE *Spect.* No. 484 ¶5 Men have indulged themselves in a spiritless Sheepishness. **1753** RICHARDSON *Grandison* (1766) V. 269 What a spiritless figure does he make! **1796** MME. D'ARBLAY *Camilla* II. 38 The evening was passed in spiritless conversation. **1841** W. SPALDING *Italy & It. Isl.* II. 133 That spiritless apathy with which the subjects of the Italian principalities submitted to the rule of their despotic masters. **1878** T. HARDY *Ret. Native* IV. iv, The spiritless stir of the summer wind.

b. Of literary or artistic productions.

1737 *Gentl. Mag.* VII. 12/2 A literal Translation of the Hebrew Code.. must necessarily be,.. at best, but flat, insipid, and spiritless. **1797** T. HOLCROFT tr. *Stolberg's Trav.* II. xlvi, These colours, when singly laid on, are entirely spiritless. **1802** MAR. EDGEWORTH *Moral T.* (1816) I. 198 It was her business to sketch designs,.. but.. the figures were awkward and spiritless.

†**5.** Lacking spiritual zeal; cold. *Obs.*⁻¹

1680 H. MORE *Apocal. Apoc.* 37 And buy of Me white rayment, O Spiritless Laodicea, and desire to be cloathed with thy Spiritual Tabernacle from Heaven.

Hence **ˈspiritlessly** *adv.*

1669 H. MORE *Exp. 7 Epist.* ix. 142 The same [formal profession] will this Church of Laodicea hold on spiritlessly and lazily, with little life or zeal. **1873** MISS BROUGHTON *Nancy* III. 30 We part without a word, and I, spiritlessly, mount the staircase alone. **1879** W. COLLINS *Rogue's Life* i, Her son.. spiritlessly availed himself of the oleaginous refuse of the soap and candle trade.

ˈspiritlessness. [f. prec. + -NESS.] The quality or fact of being spiritless.

1669 H. MORE *Exp. 7 Epist.* ix. 150 This is one reason of the Spiritlesnesse and Inactivity of the Laodicean Church. *a* **1684** LEIGHTON *Comm. 1 Pet.* Wks. 1805 I. 442 This is not a loving agreement, arising from oneness of spirit, but a dead stupidity, arguing a total spiritlessness. **1840** *New Monthly Mag.* LIX. 386 The fair liquid amber.. subsided into spiritlessness. **1870** *Echo* 23 Sept., In view of the spiritlessness of the mass of the people.

spirit-level. Also spirit level. [f. SPIRIT *sb.* + LEVEL *sb.* 1.] A kind of levelling instrument for determining a horizontal line or surface, usually consisting of a hermetically-sealed glass tube filled with spirit and an air-bubble, which, when the tube lies exactly horizontal, occupies a position midway in its length.

1768 *Phil. Trans.* LVIII. 286 The spirit level shewing the axis of the telescope to be horizontal. **1793** SMEATON *Edystone L.* §97 It could be brought justly horizontal by means of a pocket Spirit-Level being placed upon it. **1805** R. W. DICKSON *Pract. Agric.* I. 292 This is to be done by means of levelling, in which the instrument called the spirit-level may be thus employed. **1834** *Brit. Husb.* I. 534 The instrument called a spirit or water level is the most proper for ascertaining the inclination of the ground with certainty. **1881** YOUNG *Ev. Man his own Mechanic* §282. 111 In bringing horizontal bars, shelves, etc., to a true level the spirit level must be used.

attrib. **1868** in *Rep. to Govt. U.S. Munitions War* 135 Two degrees of elevation taken with a spirit-level quadrant.

Hence **spirit-levelling** *vbl. sb.*

1861 SIR H. JAMES (*title*), Abstract of the Principal Lines of Spirit Levelling in England and Wales.

spirit-like, *a.* [f. SPIRIT *sb.* + -LIKE.] Like a spirit; resembling that of a spirit.

1644 DIGBY *Nat. Bodies* xxvii. 244 Those masters.. teach vs that the impressions vpon sense are made by spirituall or spiritelike things or qualities. **1839** LOWELL *Lett.* (1894) I. 41 Eyes the largest.. and most spirit-like I ever dreamed of. **1843** RUSKIN *Mod. Paint.* I. II. III. iii. §5 There is added to this [cloud-range] a spirit-like feeling. **1852** BAILEY *Festus* (ed. 5) 494 The souls of all things.. ripening fast To spirit-like perfection.

†**ˈspiritly,** *a.* *obs.*⁻¹ [f. SPIRIT *sb.* + -LY¹.] Of horses: Spirited, mettlesome.

1629 T. ADAMS *Love's Copy* Wks. 815 Pride.. comes out like a Spanyard.. mounted on a spiritley lennet named Insolence.

ˈspiritous, *a.* ? *Obs.* Also 8 *poet.* spir'tous. [f. SPIRIT *sb.* + -OUS. Cf. It. *spiritoso*, Sp. *espiritoso*.]

1. Of the nature of spirit; having the qualities of an essence or distilled product; highly refined or dematerialized.

1605 TIMME *Quersit.* III. 149 The two volatile salts.. wil be best mingled by reason of their subtilty and spiritous substance. **1653** H. MORE *Antid. Ath.* III. ix. §12 The blood was found so pure and spiritous, that it spurted into his face as he cut him. **1667** MILTON *P.L.* VI. 479 Materials dark and crude, Of spiritous and fierie spume. **1733** TULL *Horse-hoeing Husb.* xiv. 83 When it [hay] stands 'till full Blown, the most spiritous, volatile, and nourishing Parts of its Juices is spent on the next Generation. **1766** *Phil. Trans.* LVI. 96 The heat used in making the spiritous extract.

fig. **1641** MILTON *Ch. Govt.* II. iii, Such the most covert and spiritous vices as would slip easily between the wider and more material grasp of Law. **1651** H. MORE *Enthus. Tri.* (1712) 14 That Melancholy partakes much of the nature of Wine, he evinces from that it is so spiritous. *Ibid.*, And that Melancholy is flatuous or spiritous [etc.].

b. Of liquors: Alcoholic; = SPIRITUOUS *a.* 3 b.

1799 DUNDAS in Owen *Wellesley's Desp.* (1877) 642 The encreasing produce of the revenue on salt, opium and spiritous liquors. **1801** CHARLOTTE SMITH *Lett. Solit. Wand.* I. 322 Not allowing me to take any thing spiritous. **1836** MACGILLIVRAY *Trav. Humboldt* xxv. 381 From the fermented juice a spiritous liquor.. is procured.

2. Exhilarating, enlivening. *rare*⁻¹.

1624 WOTTON *Archit.* 68 The second point is Vsefulnesse, which will consist in a sufficient Number of Roomes, of all sorts, and in their apt Coherence,.. without confusion;.. that it may appear airie and spiritous, and fit for the welcome of cheerefull Guests.

†**3.** Of persons: Lively, vivacious, high-spirited.

1629 WALTON in Wotton *Reliq.* (1672) 445, I writ by him to the Queen.. about your Spiritous nephew. **1737** *Gentl. Mag.* VII. 373/1 A gay companion,.. Fond without folly, spir'tous without rage. **1746** W. HORSLEY *Fool* (1748) I. 49 The spiritous Mrs. Frolic.

transf. **1763** *Brit. Mag.* IV. 468 Her eyes darted the most spiritous rays.

†**4.** *Gram.* Of consonants: Pronounced with breathing or aspiration. *Obs.*

1668 WILKINS *Real Char.* 367 The Spiritous Consonants to be breathed through the Mouth. *Ibid.* 375 The Spiritous Consonants that are Mutes.

Hence **ˈspiritousness.** *rare*⁻¹.

a **1691** BOYLE (J.), Not withstanding the great thinness and spiritousness of the liquor.

†**spirit-plate.** *Obs.* The blast-wall or mouth-screen of a smelting-furnace.

1686 PLOT *Staffordsh.* 162 That next the bellows, [is] the tuarn or tuiron wall; that against it, the wind-wall or spirit-plate.

spirit-rapper. [Back-formation from next.] One who professes that he can induce spirits to communicate with him by means of rapping.

1853 H. PAUL *Rappings & Table Movings* 9 A rival spirit rapper! A genuine Medium. **1854** O. A. BROWNSON (*title*), The Spirit-Rapper; an autobiography. **1860** JEAFFRESON *Bk. Doct.* II. 38 To electro-biologists, spirit-rappers, and table-turners the same arguments must be used. **1881** FROUDE *Short Stud.* IV. II. 165 Their pretensions deserve essentially no more respect than those of spirit-rappers.

spirit-rapping. [f. SPIRIT *sb.* + RAPPING *vbl. sb.*¹]

1. *pl.* Rappings alleged to be made by spirits in answer to questions addressed to them.

1852 *Harper's Mag.* Dec. 129/1 The spirit-rappings are again engrossing a lion's share of the talk. **1853** H. SPICER *Sights & Sounds* 88 This lady was a medium, and as the subject of 'spirit rappings' was already [etc.]. **1859** in BARTLETT *Dict. Amer.* (ed. 2) 434.

2. Professed communication from or with spirits by means of raps or knockings made by these.

1853 H. MATTISON (*title*) Spirit rapping unveiled! **1854** N. S. GODFREY (*title*), The Theology of Table-Turning, Spirit-Rapping, and Clairvoyance, in connection with the Antichrist. **1862** G. H. TOWNSEND *Man. Dates* s.v. The modern spirit-rapping originated in America, in the family of John D. Fox, in March, 1848. **1867** AUGUSTA WILSON *Vashti* x, I don't believe in spirit-rapping, and such stuff as dancing tables, and spinning chairs.

spiritrump. *Ent.* [ad. F. *spiritrompe*.] = ANTLIA.

a **1843** *Encycl. Metrop.* (1845) VII. 280/1 The Antlia of Kirby and Spence, or Spiritrump of Latreille, is a most remarkable character of the Lepidopterous Order.

ˈspiritsome, *a.* [f. SPIRIT *sb.* + -SOME¹.] Of the nature of spirit; spirit-like.

1876 MRS. WHITNEY *Sights & Ins.* vi. 81 Faint points and shapes, looming larger, bluer, surer,—but always so soft, so spiritsome!

spirit-stirring, *a.* [SPIRIT *sb.*] That stirs or animates the spirits; spirit-rousing.

1604 SHAKS. *Oth.* III. iii. 352 The Spirit-stirring Drum, th' Eare-piercing Fife. **1740** DYER *Ruins Rome* 102 The spirit-stirring form Of Caesar, raptur'd with the charm of rule. **1741–2** GRAY *Agrippina* 124 There will not want.. ears to own Her spirit-stirring voice. **1794** GODWIN *Caleb Williams* 158 The haziness of the morning was followed by a spirit-stirring and beautiful day. **1807** *Edin. Rev.* X. 385 All spirit-stirring topics will surely fail. **1861** G. F. BERKELEY *Eng. Sportsman* xiv. 241 Conveying to me a spirit-stirring information. **1886** T. MICHELL *Scot. Exped. to Norway* I. i. 12 The spirit-stirring poem by Edvard Storm.

spiritual (ˈspɪrɪtjuːəl), *a.* and *sb.* Forms: 4–5 spirituel(l, 4–6 -elle, 4 spyrytuele, 5 spyryt-, spyrit-, spirytuel(l; 4– spiritual, 4–5 -ale, 6–7 -all, 5 spirytuall, spyrytual(e, 5–6 -all, speritual (5 -ale), 6 spyritualle. [a. OF. *spirituel* (12th c., = It. *spirituale*, Sp. and Pg. *espiritual*), or ad. L. *spīrituāl-is*, f. *spīritus* SPIRIT *sb.* Cf. ESPIRITUAL, SPRITUAL, and SPIRITAL.]

A. *adj.*

I. **1. a.** Of or pertaining to, affecting or concerning, the spirit or higher moral qualities, esp. as regarded in a religious aspect. (Freq. in express or implied distinction to *bodily*, *corporal*, or *temporal*.)

1377 LANGL. *P. Pl.* B. XIV. 284 So pouerte propreliche, penaunce, and ioye, Is to þe body pure spiritual helthe. *c* **1400** *Anturs of Arth.* xx, Of thies speritual thynges spyre me na mare. *c* **1430** LYDG. *Min. Poems* (Percy Soc.) 97 Spiritual gladnesse most for to habounde, This day mynistred til oure refeccioune. **1474** CAXTON *Chesse* (1883) 42 For they doo spirytuell and also corporall werkis. **1529** MORE *Dyaloge* I. Wks. 157/1 It then bycame to be the spirituall busynesse and occupacion of man. **1563** FOXE *A. & M.* 1111 In the sacrament.. there is not the very substaunce.. but a spirituall partaking of the bodye and blood of Christ. **1592** in J. Morris *Troubles Cath. Foref.* (1877) 38 A man.. much given to meditation, and receiving thereby many spiritual consolations. **1630** B. JONSON *New Inn* III. ii, Love is a spiritual coupling of two souls. **1663** BP. PATRICK *Parab. Pilgr.* xxvii, Since they are most proper to Beginners, and.. those who enter upon the Spiritual Race. **1753** CHALLONER *Cath. Chr. Instr.* 20 The spiritual Kindred which is contracted between the Gossips and the Child. **1784** P. WRIGHT *New Bk. Martyrs* 798/1 To administer those spiritual helps that were suitable to men in their circumstances. **1835** I. TAYLOR *Spirit Despot.* vii. 289 The spiritual essence of popery has outlived the over-throw of the papal domination. **1883** J. PARKER *Apost. Life* II. 327 The thing I aim at is spiritual restoration, spiritual completeness, spiritual immortality.

Comb. **1872** HOWELLS *Wedding Journ.* (1892) 269 A spiritual-worldliness which was the clarified likeness of this-worldliness. **1916** JOYCE *Portrait of Artist* (1969) v. 252 Turned off that valve at once and opened the spiritual-heroic refrigerating apparatus, invented and patented in all countries by Dante Alighieri. **1929** D. H. LAWRENCE *Paintings of D. H. Lawrence* A4ᵛ This no doubt is all in the course of the growth of the 'spiritual-mental' consciousness.

b. Applied to material things, substances, etc., in a figurative or symbolical sense.

1387–8 T. USK *Test. Love* III. ix. (Skeat) I. 98 How was it, that sightful manna in deserte to children of Israel was spirituel mete? **1550** COVERDALE (*title*), A Spyrytuall and most Precyouse Pearle teaching all men to love and imbrace the Crosse. **1576** G. TYRRELL in J. Morris *Troubles Cath. Foref.* Ser. II. (1875) 30 Abundance of spiritual riches far passingly supplieth the lack of the other [i.e. corporal]. **1611** BIBLE *Transl. Pref.* ¶1 The Spirituall and sincere milke of the word. **1667** MILTON *P.L.* XII. 491 His Spirit.. shall write To guide them in all truth, and also arme With spiritual Armour. *a* **1729** J. ROGERS *Nineteen Serm.* vi. (1735) 117 All eat of the same spiritual Bread, and drank of the same spiritual Cup. **1820** SOUTHEY *Wesley* II. 331 With regard to the bodily effects that ensued, whenever the spiritual influenza began. **1871** MORLEY *Carlyle* in *Crit. Misc.* Ser. I. (1878) 173 A cloud of sedulous ephemera still suck a little spiritual moisture. 1889 STEVENSON *Edinburgh* 168 Every kind of spiritual disinfectant.

c. Of songs, etc.: Devotional, sacred; *spec.* in sense 5 of the sb.

1382 WYCLIF *Eph.* v. 19 Spekinge to ȝou silf in psalmes, and ymnes, and spiritual songis. 1567 *Gude & Godlie B.* (S.T.S.) 1 Singing of the Psalmes, and spiritual sangis. 1611 BIBLE *Eph.* v. 19; *Colos.* iii. 16. 1660 F. BROOKE tr. *Le Blanc's Trav.* 364 Dancings in stately rooms, or gardens, with spirituall songs, rather a sort of adoration than a dance. 1905 [see *gospel song* s.v. GOSPEL *sb.* 9]. 1964 *Amer. Folk Music Occasional* I. 15 Q. What kind of music did you like best at this time, spiritual music or blues or what? R. I always liked the spiritual music the best.

†**d.** Of transcendent beauty or charm. *Obs.*[−1]

1480 CAXTON *Myrr.* II. iv. 69 Ther ben yet plente of other places so delectable, so swete, and so spyrytuel that yf a man were therin, he shold saye, that it were a very paradys.

e. ***spiritual home*** (with no religious connotation), a place or milieu, other than one's home, which seems especially congenial or in harmony with one's nature, or to which one feels a sense of belonging or indebtedness.

1932 *Week-End Rev.* 7 May 586/1 If they write about it at all they make it clear that Europe is their spiritual home. 1941 A. CHRISTIE *Evil under Sun* iii. 52 A man like you would be at Deauville or Le Touquet... That's your—what's the phrase?—spiritual home. 1962 WODEHOUSE *Service with Smile* xi. 164 He disliked Lord Ickenham, considering him a potty sort of feller whose spiritual home was a padded cell in some not too choosy lunatic asylum. 1967 [see PAPER *sb.* 8 b]. 1977 [see RASTAFARIAN *a.* and *sb.*].

2. a. Of, belonging or relating to, concerned with, sacred or ecclesiastical things or matters, as distinguished from secular affairs; pertaining to the church or the clergy; ecclesiastical.

1338 R. BRUNNE *Chron.* (1810) 283 He sent to þe kyng tuo bisshops of renoun, & schewed þat spiritualle þing þorgh pouert ȝede alle doun. c 1380 WYCLIF *Sel. Wks.* III. 305 þei meyntenen þis cursed þefte boþe bi seculer power and spiritual swerd. a 1440 *Found. St. Bartholomew's* (E.E.T.S.) 5 Thou shalte founde a Chirche... This spirituall howse, almyghty God shalle ynhabite and halowe yt. 1467 in *Eng. Gilds* (1870) 390 In eny cymitory or londe spirituelle. 1500–20 DUNBAR *Poems* lxxi. 25 Couatyce ringis into the spirituall state, ȝarnand banifice the quhilk ar now vacand. a 1548 HALL *Chron., Hen. V,* 37 We have in our spirituall conuocacion graunted to your highnes..a some of money. 1570–6 LAMBARDE *Peramb. Kent* (1826) 249 If any Clerke gave to a layman..any spirituall goodes he should stand excommunicate. 1654 WHITLOCK *Zootomia* 362 The Scabberd of Power (if not of Justice,) seemeth to have Locks on them, that only the spirituall Keyes can open. a 1700 EVELYN *Diary* 26 Apr. 1689, The penalty is to be the losse of their dignitie and spiritual preferment. 1727 DE FOE *Eng. Tradesm.* v. (1841) I. 33 The duties of life, which are either spiritual or secular. 1844 LINGARD *Anglo-Sax. Ch.* (1858) I. ii. 78 The prelate watched over the spiritual interests. 1863 MRS. OLIPHANT *Salem Chapel* i. 6 The young man knew very little of the community which he had assumed the spiritual charge of.

†**b.** Of law: Canon, canonical. *Obs.*

1474 CAXTON *Chesse* III. iii. (1883) 95 As well in the spirituell lawe as in the temporall. 1642 tr. *Perkins Prof. Bk.* i. §49. 22 If a bastard eigne (who is *mulier* in the spirituall law,) continueth possession in lands [etc.].

†**c.** Of a day: Devoted to or set apart for special religious or sacred observances; holy. *Obs.*

1490 CAXTON *Rule St. Benet* 134 The souereyn may breke his mele for a stranger, wythout it be a spirytuel fastynge daye. 1526 *Pilgr. Perf.* (W. de W. 1531) 1 b, Whiche..in maner declareth the hole mater of these vij spirituall dayes.

d. ***spiritual court***, a court having jurisdiction in matters of religion or ecclesiastical affairs.

1498–9 *Plumpton Corr.* (Camden) 133 A spoliacion in the spirituall court. 1538 STARKEY *England* 139 In theyr spiritual courtys, they haue no punnyschement.. conuenyent to such fautys. 1681 H. NEVILE *Plato Rediv.* 131 Neither the Chancery,..nor the Spiritual Courts, nor the Cheats in trade. 1758 in Blackstone *Comm.* (1765) I. 20 This appears in a particular manner from the spiritual courts of all denominations. 1809–10 COLERIDGE *Friend* (1865) 55 A ..period during which the powers and the aims of law were usurped..by the clergy and the courts spiritual. 1845 MRS. S. AUSTIN *Ranke's Hist. Ref.* I. 111 The confusion arising from the jurisdiction of the spiritual and temporal courts.

3. Of persons: **a.** Standing to another, or to others, in a spiritual relationship.

c 1386 CHAUCER *Pars. T.* ⁋516 Alle we haue o fader flesshly & o moder, that is to seyn Adam and Eue & eek o fader spirituel, that is god of heuene. c 1440 *Alph. Tales* 189, I had iij spirituall maisters, and þe furste was drede, & the secunde was shame, and þe iij was luff. 1483 CAXTON *Cato* A vij, For herto ben bounden of ryght not onely the carnal faders but also the spyrituel. 1555 EDEN *Decades* To Rdr. (Arb.) 51 Thincrease of this spirituall Israell vnto whome.. he was the father of fayth. 1562 WINȜET *Wks.* (S.T.S.) II. 23 Be thame he wald..quikin his spirituale pepil afoir slane. 1567 ALLEN *Def. Priesthood* 226 We call them Confessours, & of olde in Greece, they were named Spirituall maisters or Fathers. 1697 BURGHOPE *Disc. Relig. Assemb.* 122 He preferrs his own parish priest..as being his spiritual father. 1769 H. VENN in *Life* (1835) 152 A lady said to me, 'You, sir, are my spiritual father'. 1820 MILNER *Suppl. Mem. Eng. Cath.* 66 *note,* The distinguished Professor of Divinity and Spiritual Director of the Pontifical Seminary of Douay. 1843 *Quincy* (Illinois) *Herald* 15 Dec. 3/1 Hyram Smith has had a revelation confirming the spiritual wife system. 1859 BARTLETT *Dict. Amer.* (ed. 2) 434 *Spiritual wife,*..a Mormon extra wife or concubine. 1901 KIPLING *Kim* v. 111 The comfort..of being properly..respected as her spiritual adviser by a well-born woman. 1925 *Ladies' Home Jrnl.* Apr. 38/1 It is considered by the elderly women of Utah a great and sacred privilege to be the spiritual wife of Brigham Young or the Prophet Joseph Smith in the world to come. 1951 J. T. MCNEILL *History of Cure of Souls* iii. 42 Among ancient civilizations, that of India seems to have given the greatest prominence to the spiritual director. 1980 *Tablet* 26 Jan. 8/2 He..cited..divorced Catholics in second marriages who, after prayer and consultation with a spiritual director, have returned to the sacraments. *Ibid.* 95/3 A letter I wrote in reply to my spiritual children was produced.

b. Ecclesiastical, religious. Freq. in ***spiritual lords*** and ***spiritual man*** (or ***person***).

(*a*) 1399 *Rolls of Parlt.* III. 451 The Kyng comond with his Spirituel Lordes. c 1460 FORTESCUE *Abs. & Lim. Mon.* xv. (1885) 145 The gretteste lordes off þe lande, both spirituelles and temporellis. 1516 *Sc. Acts, Jas. V* (1875) XII. 36/1 We prelatis spirituall, Barouns Temporall, and Commouns of..Scottlaund. 1625 in Ellis *Orig. Lett.* Ser. I. III. 203 When he had consulted with the Lords spirituall and Temporall. 1661 *Reflex. upon the Oaths Suprem. & Alleg.* 50 Ecclesiastical Courts, which we call the Spiritual Courts, and Spiritual Judges, and Spiritual Authority. 1727 SWIFT *Poison. E. Curll* Wks. 1755 III. I. 150 I do also heartily beg pardon of all persons of honour, lords spiritual and temporal, gentry, burgesses, and commonalty. 1824 in *Nairne Peerage Evid.* (1874) 73 With the advice and consent of the lords spiritual and temporal and commons in this present Parliament assembled. 1863 H. COX *Instit.* I. vii. 62 The Lords Spiritual and Temporal form one legislative assembly.

(*b*) c 1460 FORTESCUE *Abs. & Lim. Mon.* xv. (1885) 146 Ther were chosen xij spirituell men, and xij temporell men. 1480 in *10th Rep. Hist. MSS. Comm.* App. V. 316 What ever condicion or degree he be of, spirituell or temporell. 1530 *Act 22 Hen. VIII,* c. 15, Spyrituall persones of the prouynce of the archebyshopryche of Canturburye. 1582 in *Cath. Rec. Soc. Publ.* V. 32 Being examined whether he be a spirituall or a temporall man, answereth that he is a Spirituall man and a Priest. 1642 BIRD *Mag. Honour* 146 The brethren and sonnes..of every Knight, being spirituall men, may.. purchase lycense and dispensation. 1726 AYLIFFE *Parergon* 129 All Bishops and Abbots sat in State-Councils by Reason of their Office, as they were spiritual Persons. 1848 STEPHEN *Laws Eng.* (ed. 2) II. 39 *note,* Any sale or assignment by any spiritual person of any patronage belonging to him in virtue of his office.

c. Devout, holy, pious; morally good; having spiritual tendencies or instincts.

1382 WYCLIF *Gal.* vi. 1 Ȝe that ben spiritual, teche siche a maner man in spirit of softenesse. c 1400 *St. Alexius* (Laud MS. 622) 842 þere is a Man of dedes gode, Spirituel, & mylde of mode. c 1450 HOLLAND *Howlat* 166 Thir ar fowlis of effect,..Spirituale in all thing, Leile in thar leving. 1674 MARVELL *Corr.* Wks. (Grosart) II. 423 The good acquaintance you have among those spirituall people. c 1791 *Encycl. Brit.* (ed. 3) VII. 447/1 These milder alterations were zealously opposed by a branch of the Franciscans called the *spiritual.* 1836 *Going to Service* xii. 140, I have a spiritual lady to serve. 1883 [see SPIRITUALITY 3].

4. a. Of or pertaining to, consisting of, spirit, regarded in either a religious or intellectual aspect; of the nature of a spirit or incorporeal supernatural essence; immaterial.

In early use not always distinct from sense 1.

1303 R. BRUNNE *Handl. Synne* 12170 He myȝt se weyl þyng þat was spyrytuele. 1382 WYCLIF *1 Cor.* xv. 44 It is sowun a beestly body, it schal ryse a spiritual body. c 1400 MAUNDEV. (Roxb.) xvi. 74, I am noȝt erthely, bot spirituall. c 1475 *Partenay* 5291 When to ende nyhed he, That the soule moste yelde being spirituall. 1557 N.T. (Genev.) *Eph.* vi. 12 For we wrestle not against fleshe and bloud: but.. against spiritual wickednesses. 1662 STILLINGFL. *Orig. Sacræ* III. i. §17 If there be then such things in the World which matter and motion cannot be the causes of then there are certainly spiritual and immaterial Beings. 1667 MILTON *P.L.* IV. 677 Millions of spiritual Creatures walk the Earth Unseen. 1696 PHILLIPS (ed. 5), *Spiritual,* said of a Being that has no Body, that falls not under the Senses. 1825 COLERIDGE *Aids Refl.* 67 The Will is pre-eminently the spiritual Constituent of our Being. 1846 RUSKIN *Mod. Paint* II. III. ii. §17 It is degrading to the spiritual creature to suppose it operative through impulse of bone and sinew. 1875 J. P. HOPPS *Princ. Relig.* ii. 9 The real man is the spiritual being who controls and uses all the faculties and organs of the body.

b. Appropriate or natural to a spirit.

1667 MILTON *P.L.* VIII. 110 His Omnipotence, That to corporeal substances could adde Speed almost Spiritual.

c. ***spiritual healing***, cure or healing attributed to the agency of (a) spirit; faith-healing.

1899 H. W. DRESSER *Spiritual Healing* vi. 54 How can I live according to the principles of spiritual healing among people who have no sympathy with the new principles. 1926 W. T. WALSH *Sci. Spiritual Healing* iii. 30, I announced a service of spiritual healing to be held in the church every Thursday morning after the celebration of the Holy Communion. 1980 *Spiritual Healer* XXVIII. 131 We have known many instances of migraine..being overcome through spiritual healing.

5. Consisting of pure essence or spirit; volatile; spirituous, alcoholic. Now *rare* or *Obs.*

1477 NORTON *Ord. Alch.* vi. in Ashm. (1652) 95 All other Vessells be made of Glasse, That spirituall matters should not out-passe. 1626 BACON *Sylva* §387 All Sweet Smells have joyned with them, some Earthy or crude Odours; And at some distance the Sweet, which is the more Spiritual, is perceived. a 1648 DIGBY *Closet Opened* (1677) 125 Thus you have only the spiritual parts of the Tea. 1826 *Art of Brewing* (ed. 2) 69 Stout ales..labour under one material want—that of spiritual vigour.

6. Of or pertaining to, emanating from, the intellect or higher faculties of the mind; intellectual.

1725 WATTS *Logic* I. iii. §1 Spiritual or intellectual Ideas are those which we gain by reflecting on the Nature and Actions of our own Souls. 1749 FIELDING *Tom Jones* XVI. v, That refined degree of Platonic affection which is..entirely and purely spiritual. 1813 SHELLEY *Q. Mab* v. 162 Blunting the keenness of his spiritual sense With narrow schemings and unworthy cares. 1853 LYTTON *My Novel* VIII. xi, Whatever she gained in the graver kinds of information, became transmuted, through her heart and her fancy, into spiritual golden stores. 1873 HAMERTON *Intell. Life* XI. iv. 417 The great spiritual function of the intellectual class.

7. Characterized by or exhibiting a high degree of refinement of thought or feeling. (Cf. SPIRITUEL *a.*)

1784 J. BARRY *Lect. Paint.* vi. (1848) 227 The harmony resulting from all those variegating masses of colour, together with the light, easy, graceful, spiritual manner in which the whole [picture] is conducted. 1820 KEATS *St. Agnes* xxxv, Those sad eyes were spiritual and clear. 1840 DICKENS *Old C. Shop* xliii, The delicate face,..the too bright eye, the spiritual head,..told their silent tale.

8. Clever, smart, witty. (Cf. SPIRITUEL *a.*)

1791–1823 D'ISRAELI *Cur. Lit.* (1834) I. 228 It may not here be improper to take notice of a wise and spiritual saying of this young prince. 1837 CARLYLE *Fr. Rev.* II. I. x, Of all this the spiritual biographies of that period say nothing. 1872 *Routledge's Ev. Boy's Ann.* July 493/1 We French are extremely spiritual, and..are never at a loss for an answer.

9. a. Concerned with spirits or supernatural beings.

1841 LANE *Arab. Nts.* I. 69 Who acquired a very great and extensive celebrity for his attainments in spiritual and natural magic. 1855–7 (*title*), Yorkshire Spiritual Telegraph, containing a number of extraordinary communications from the Spiritual World. 1860–1877 (*title*), The Spiritual Magazine.

b. = SPIRITUALISTIC *a.* 2.

spiritual funeral, one conducted after the fashion of the believers in Spiritualism (Bartlett).

1858 in Bartlett *Dict. Amer.* (1859) 434 A spiritual funeral was held at Lowell lately.

II. †**10.** Of or pertaining to breathing; respiratory. *Obs.*

1398 TREVISA *Barth. De P.R.* v. xxvi. (Bodl. MS.), þe schuldres ben nedeful to defende þe spiritualle membres. c 1460 J. METHAM *Wks.* (E.E.T.S.) 89 It signifieth good dysposicion of the hert and of the spirituall membris in a man. 1576 G. BAKER tr. *Gesner's Jewell of Health* 169 Briefly, all matters found in the Lungs, and spirituall members, this singularly purgeth.

B. *sb.* **I.** †**1. a.** *collect.* The spirituality; the clergy. *Obs.*

? a 1400 *Morte Arth.* 2414 It es a foly to offende oure fadyr vndire Gode... Ȝif we spare the spirituelle, we spede bot the bettire.

†**b.** An ecclesiastic or cleric. *Obs.*[−1]

c 1450 HOLLAND *Howlat* 733 Haile speciose, most specifyit with the spiritualis! 1682 WHELER *Journ. Greece* v. 356 There are but few among them [Greeks], who have where-withal to live, but will learn, while they are young, to write and read, whether Spirituals, or Seculars.

2. a. A spiritual or spiritually-minded person.

1532 MORE *Confut. Tindale* Wks. 365/2 He sayth himselfe that yᵉ spirituals do searche the bottome of gods commaundementes and fulfyll them gladly. *Ibid.* 715/1 The very Isaackes, the very Iacobs, and the very spiritualles, & the verye apostles.

b. *Eccl. Hist.* (With initial capital.) A member of the Congregation of Narbonne, a branch of Franciscans which advocated a stricter observance of the rule of poverty and simplicity of dress.

The branch was pronounced schismatic by Pope John XXII in 1318.

c 1791 *Encycl. Brit.* (ed. 3) VII. 447/2 The one [party], embracing the severe discipline and absolute poverty of St. Francis, were called spirituals. 1855 MILMAN *Lat. Chr.* XII. vi. V. 419 The Spirituals, the Fraticelli,..openly avowed their belief. *Ibid.* 420 The sudden election to the Popedom of Cœlestine V,..a new St. Francis, to the Spiritualists a true Spiritual. 1862 G. H. TOWNSEND *Man. Dates, Spiritualists,* called also the Zealous, or the Spirituals.

c. An inhabitant of the 'spiritual kingdom'.

1807 SOUTHEY *Lett. fr. Eng.* (1814) III. 158 The celestials chiefly using the vowels U and O, the spirituals preferring E and I.

d. *U.S.* A spiritual wife (see prec. 3 a).

1855 *Putnam's Monthly Mag.* VI. 147/1 These extra wives [of the Mormons] are known by sundry designations—some call them 'spirituals', others, 'sealed ones'.

3. a. *pl.* Spiritual matters, affairs, or ideas.

1582 N.T. (Rhem.) *Eph.* vi. 12 Our wrestling is not against flesh and bloud: but..against the spirituals of wickednes in the celestials. 1607 [see CARNAL *a.* 4 b]. 1625 BURGES *Tithes* 14 Why he should pay so much of his Carnals for Spirituals. 1649 F. ROBERTS *Clavis Bibl.* Introd. ii. 32 He condemns the contrary unskilfulnesse in the Scriptures, as the..root of all errour in spirituals. 1665 BOYLE *Occas. Refl.* I. v. (1848) 86 Translate now (O my Soul) all this unto Spirituals. 1716 M. DAVIES *Athen. Brit.* I. 170 Twas no great piece of News to hear of Laymen's ministring in Spirituals to Church-People. 1774 MME. D'ARBLAY *Early Diary* (1889) I. 303 I have found much pleasure in Madame de Maintenon's Letters (except in Theologicals and Spirituals). 1840 MILL *Diss. & Disc.* (1875) I. 433 Such was the prevailing tone of English belief in temporals; what was it in spirituals? 1893 *Pall Mall G.* 9 Jan. 3/2 Spirits and spirituals taken in excess..work the same effect with weak and over-excited brains.

b. Matters which specially or primarily concern the church or religion.

1647 N. BACON *Disc. Govt. Eng.* I. vii. 25 There was but one Metropolitan.., so as his power was in spirituals over many Kingdoms. 1689 POPPLE tr. *Locke's 1st Let. Toleration* L.'s Wks. 1727 II. 246 If..such a Power be granted unto the Civil Magistrate in Spirituals. 1794 tr. *Barruel's Clergy during Fr. Rev.* 98 That it did not belong to the secular power to meddle in spirituals. 1853 M. KELLY tr. *Gosselin's Power Pope Mid. Ages* II. 360 That the Church and the pope have received..full power to govern the world, both in spirituals and temporals. 1873 MORLEY *Rousseau* xii. II. 178 The civil power does best absolutely and unreservedly to ignore spirituals.

c. Spiritual or ecclesiastical goods or possessions; spiritualities.

1827 *Gentl. Mag.* XCVII. II. 536 Forming part of their spirituals (because such their spirituals always include an absolute right over other people's temporals). **1863** BLYTH *Hist. Notices & Rec. Fincham* 39 The spirituals were such revenue as was connected with spiritual duties and the cure of souls, and consisted almost entirely of tithes, glebe lands, and house.

4. a. A spiritual counterpart or analogue.

1650 T. VAUGHAN *Anima Magica* 52 Learn to refer all Naturals to their Spirituals, per viam Secretioris Analogiæ.

b. A spiritual (as opposed to a material) thing.

1661 GLANVILL *Van. Dogm.* 97 In our notion of spirituals, we, as much as we can, denudate them of all material Phantasmes. **1708** H. DODWELL *Nat. Mort. Hum. Souls* 127 It does now affect us to think of Spirituals, whilst we have no sensible Impression made upon us by Things purely Spiritual, but by those only which are only Corporeal.

c. Spiritual quality or power; *pl.* spiritual faculties.

1649 F. ROBERTS *Clavis Bibl.* 239 The Succession of Elisha as Prophet in stead of Elijah; a double portion of his spirituall resting upon him. **1652** BENLOWES *Theoph.* IV. xix, Spiritual light spirituals clears.

5. = *Negro spiritual* s.v. NEGRO 7.

1866 *Harper's Mag.* May 775/1 Maum Rina flavored all her dishes with these 'spirituals', as they are called among the negroes. **1870** T. W. HIGGINSON *Army Life* 197, I had for many years heard of this class of songs under the name of 'Negro Spirituals'. *Ibid.* 199 This seemed the simplest primitive type of 'spiritual'. **1926** A. NILES in W. C. Handy *Blues* 9 These songs [*sc.* the blues] were woven of the same stuff as the other overlapping items in the long list,—the work-songs, love-songs..; yes, and decidedly the spirituals. **1947** S. BELLOW *Victim* iv. 39 Harkavy and a girl he had brought to the party were singing spirituals and old ballads. **1981** M. DOODY in Martin & Mullen *No Alternative* iv. 53 'Oh! Sometimes it causes me to tremble, tremble, tremble' as the spiritual goes.

II. †6. *pl.* The respiratory organs. *Obs.*

c **1400** *Lanfranc's Cirurg.* 161 Þis diafragma departiþ þe spirituals from þe guttis, & in þe holownes þat is aboue liggiþ þe herte & þe lungis. **1610** HEALEY *St. Aug. Citie of God* XXII. xxiv. (1620) 848 The courses of the veines, sinewes and arteries, and the secrets of the spirituals.

spiritualism ('spɪrɪtju:əlɪz(ə)m). [f. SPIRITUAL *a.* + -ISM. Cf. F. *spiritualisme*, It. *spiritualismo.*]

1. The exercise of the mental or intellectual faculties, or their predominance over body. *rare.*

1831 CARLYLE *Sart. Res.* II. viii, Savage Animalism is nothing, inventive Spiritualism is all.

2. a. Tendency towards, or advocacy of, a spiritual view or estimate of things, esp. as a leading principle in philosophy or religion.

1796 [see IDEAL *sb.* 1]. **1836** LYTTON *Athens* (1837) II. 408 The serene and lofty spiritualism of Anaxagoras. **1857** ROBERTSON *Serm.* Ser. III. i. (1857) 6 We find the Unitarian of the old school denouncing the spiritualism of the new and rising school. **1869** SEELEY *Ess. & Lect.* v. 133 Religion re-assumed its ancient Judaic form of austere and ardent spiritualism. **1884** *Contemp. Rev.* Feb. 264 The very source of [Dante's] inspiration is the austere spiritualism of the Catholic creed.

b. A spiritual view or aspiration.

1850 CARLYLE *Latter-d. Pamph.* vii. (1872) 224 Like a set of grisly undertakers come to bury the dead spiritualisms of mankind.

c. Spiritual nature or quality.

1855 MILMAN *Lat. Chr.* XIV. ii. (1864) IX. 96 Dante [could] represent such things with the most objective truth, yet without disturbing their fine spiritualism.

3. The belief that the spirits of the dead can hold communication with the living, or make their presence known to them in some way, esp. through a 'medium'; the system of doctrines or practices founded on this belief. Cf. SPIRITISM.

Also specifically called ***modern spiritualism*** by way of distinction from sense 2.

1853 J. DIX *Transatlantic Tracings* xiv. 244 Every two or three years the Americans have a paroxysm of humbug—.. at the present time it is Spiritual-ism. **1855** E. W. CAPRON (*title*), Modern Spiritualism, its Facts and Fanaticisms, its Consistencies and Contradictions. **1860** *All Year Round* No. 66. 370 Witchcraft, demonology, possession, and the like, revived in the modest phrase of Spiritualism. **1878** T. H. SINCLAIR *Mount* 37 Spiritualism, or, as its advocates name it now on both sides of the Atlantic, Spiritism. **1886** MYERS *Phant. Living* I. Introd. p. lix, On this basis the creed of 'Modern Spiritualism' has been upbuilt.

4. Belief in the existence and influence of spiritual beings.

1850 J. R. LOGAN in *Jrnl. Indian Archipelago* IV. 552, I would proceed at once to facts illustrative of the different forms of spiritualism which prevail in Eastern Asia and Asianesia. **1867** E. B. TYLOR in *Proc. R. Inst.* V. 90 A slight acquaintance with the spiritualism of the savage has sometimes led to its being considered as the result of a degeneration from the opinions of more cultured races. **1871** TYLOR *Prim. Cult.* I. 385 The sense of Spiritualism in its wider acceptation, the general doctrine of spiritual beings, is here given to Animism.

spiritualist ('spɪrɪtju:əlɪst). [f. as prec. + -IST. Cf. F. *spiritualiste*, Sp. and Pg. *espiritualista.*]

1. a. One who regards things from a spiritual point of view or interprets them in a spiritual sense; one whose ideas or doctrines have a purely spiritual basis or tendency.

In early use sometimes with depreciatory force.

1649 H. LAWRENCE *Some Consid. Vind. Scriptures* 37 Certaine demands, which these pretended spiritualists will be sure to make to me. **1673** H. HALLYWELL *Acc. Familism* 19 Those high-flown Spiritualists the Quakers are of the same mind. **1716** M. DAVIES *Athen. Brit.* II. 42 This is the great Rule the reform'd Order of Protestant Spiritualists, call'd Quakers and others, seem to walk by. **1800** C. BUTLER *Life A. Butler* xii, Approved of by St. Francis of Sales and other spiritualists. **1845** G. OLIVER *Coll. Biogr. Soc. Jes.* 50 As a Spiritualist also, he must have been pre-eminent, judging from many of his letters now before me. **1865** MILL *Exam. Hamilton* 492 Proofs that the most sincere Spiritualists may consistently hold the doctrine of so-called necessity.

b. *spec.* (See quots. and cf. SPIRITUAL *sb.* 2 b.)

1716 M. DAVIES *Athen. Brit.* II. 225 Those Montanists were call'd also Cataphrygians, Spiritualists, Apostolicks, [etc.]. **1862** G. H. TOWNSEND *Man. Dates* s.v., Spiritualists, called also the Zealous,..formed a portion of the great order of Franciscans, who, about 1245, under the name of Spiritualists, advocated the strict observance of the rule and vow of poverty, which had been one of their fundamental laws. **1882–3** SCHAFF *Encycl. Relig. Knowl.* 832 The Spiritualists, as the severer party [of Franciscans] was called, were cruelly persecuted.

†2. One who supports the spiritual or ecclesiastical authority as against the secular or temporal.

1651 HOBBES *Leviath.* III. xxxix. 248* That Governor must be one; or else there must needs follow Faction, and Civil war in the Common-wealth, between the Church and State; between Spiritualists, and Temporalists.

3. A believer in, or adherent of, spiritualism as a philosophical doctrine.

1796 F. A. NITSCH *Kant's Princ. concerning Man* 153 The Spiritualists having discovered immaterial objects convert the mind into a spirit, and so on. **1836** I. TAYLOR *Phys. The. Anoth. Life* i. 15 The spiritualist will retain the advantage he has gained over his opponent [the materialist]. **1876** P. G. TAIT *Rec. Adv. Phys. Sci.* i. (ed. 2) 25 Whether it show itself in the comparatively harmless folly of the spiritualist or in the pernicious nonsense of the materialist.

4. A believer in modern spiritualism or spiritism; a spiritist.

1852 E. B. BROWNING *Let.* 13–14 May in *Lett. Brownings to George Barrett* (1958) 181 Lady Elgin is a great spiritualist with a leaning to Irvingism & a belief in every sort of incredible thing. **1859** BARTLETT *Dict. Amer.* (ed. 2) 435 *Spiritualist*, a believer in the doctrine of spiritualism. **1860** O. W. HOLMES *Prof. Breakf.-t.* i. 13 The Spiritualists have some pretty strong instincts to pry over. **1881** FROUDE *Short Stud.* IV. II. 227 A spiritualist assured me that I could work a miracle myself if I had but faith.

5. *attrib.* or as *adj.* Spiritualistic.

1837 J. S. MILL in *Westm. Rev.* XXVII. 17 Many sterling thoughts are..disguised in phraseology borrowed from the spiritualist school of German poets and metaphysicians. **1860** FARRAR *Orig. Lang.* i. 20 The spiritualist school of the nineteenth century. **1898** WATTS-DUNTON *Aylwin* x. i, The studio of the famous spiritualist-painter.

spiritualistic (ˌspɪrɪtju:əˈlɪstɪk), *a.* (and *sb.*) [f. prec. + -IC.]

1. Of or pertaining to, characterized by, philosophical or theological spiritualism; of the nature of spiritualism.

1852 A. P. FORBES *Explan. Nicene Creed* 47 Spiritualistic Pantheism, introduced by Hegel, has still many followers. **1871** ALABASTER *Wheel of Law* p. lvi, The Malays, being Mahometans, ought..to have shown the superior civilisation due to spiritualistic belief. **1881** HUXLEY in *Nature* XXIV. 344 The subtle thinker, to whom we owe both the spiritualistic and the materialistic philosophies of modern times.

2. Of or pertaining to, associated or connected with, modern spiritualism; spiritistic.

1865 *Athenæum* 18 Nov. 684/3 In his restlessness and perplexity he has recourse to a spiritualistic medium. **1875** E. WHITE *Life in Christ* III. xxi. (1878) 300 If this was true under the Mosaic Law how much more emphatically must spiritualistic 'seeking to the dead' be an abomination now! **1882** HINSDALE *Garfield & Educ.* I. 79 An itinerant spiritualistic and scientific lecturer and debater.

b. *sb. pl.* Matters pertaining to spiritualism.

1886 TUPPER *My Life as Author* 387 If we dare to do this, higher interests are endangered than spiritualistics.

Hence **spiritua'listically** *adv.*, by a spiritualist or by means of spiritualism; towards spiritualism.

1880 *Times* 27 Sept. 12/2 Professing the same [pills] to be spiritualistically prescribed for the cure of..neuralgia. **1891** *Sat. Rev.* 28 Feb. 272/1 The cupidity and credulity of a spiritualistically minded valet.

spirituality (ˌspɪrɪtju:ˈælɪtɪ). Also 5 spiritualite(e, 5–7 -alitie, 6 -allitie, -elity; 6 spyrytualite, 7 spirittuality. [a. OF. (*e*)*spiritualité*, *-alleté* (mod.F. *spiritualité*, = It. *spiritualità*, Sp. *espiritualidad*, Pg. *-idade*), or ad. late L. *spīrituālitās*, f. *spīrituālis* SPIRITUAL *a.*: see -ITY, and cf. SPIRITUALTY.]

1. The body of spiritual or ecclesiastical persons; = SPIRITUALTY 3. Now *Hist.*

c **1441** *Pol. Poems* (Rolls) II. 207, I come before the spiritualte; Two cardynals, and byshoppis fyve [etc.]. **1513** *Life Henry V* (1911) 23 Intendinge to oppresse the church, the spirituallitie, the Kinge and the realme. **1583** STUBBES *Anat. Abus.* II. (1882) 67 The corruptions and abuses of the spiritualitie, or (as some call it) of the ecclesiasticall hierarchie. **1625** PURCHAS *Pilgrims* II. 1753 This exchange commeth most commonly from the Spiritualitie, who doe secretly use it. **1709** STRYPE *Ann. Ref.* I. xxvi. 255 He blamed both spirituality and laity. **1825** SCOTT *Betrothed* xviii, You of the spirituality make us laymen the pack-horses of your own concerns. **1900** GASQUET *Eve Ref.* iii. (1905) 58 According to the lawyer, it should be the owner of the soil who should apportion the payment, and failing him, the Parliament, and not the spirituality.

b. A spiritual society.

1854 T. C. UPHAM *Life Mme. Guyon* xxxiv. 293 She was considered the head of the new spirituality.

2. That which has a spiritual character; ecclesiastical property or revenue held or received in return for spiritual services. Now *arch.*

1456 SIR G. HAYE *Law Arms* (S.T.S.) 105 All the grettest thingis that ar belangand the governance of bathe temporalitee and spiritualitee ar to be knawin and kend be the pape. **1468–9** *Inchaffray Charters* (S.H.S.) 159 Quhat tym we the saide georg Abbat beis admittit be our Juge ordinare to the spiritualite ande be our souerane lord the king to the temporalite of the said Abbisse. **1651** [see TEMPORALTY 1]. **1709** STRYPE *Ann. Ref.* I. xxvi. 270 In the First Year of the Queen, the Supreme Government over her Spirituality and Temporality, was given to her. **1818** SCOTT *Hrt. Midl.* xliii, The said incumbent might lawfully enjoy the spirituality and temporality of the cure of souls at Knocktarlitie.

b. *pl.* Spiritual or ecclesiastical things; ecclesiastical possessions, rights, etc., of a purely spiritual character; = SPIRITUALTY 2 b. Now *Hist.*

1417 in Ellis *Orig. Lett.* Ser. II. I. 61 The Gardeins of the spirituallities of Ardmaghe. **1570** *Act 13 Eliz.* c. 12 §1 Parlyament..shall bryng from such Bysshop or Gardyan of Spyrituallties [*v.r.* Spyrytualtyes]..a testimoniall of such Assent. **1635** PAGITT *Christianogr.* I. iii. (1636) 187 Who doe extoll the Pope..not onely..in spiritualities, but also in Temporalities. **1664** H. MORE *Myst. Iniq.* 433 So these pretended Successours of Peter..have notoriously imitated that example of Simon in buying and selling Spiritualities. **1726** AYLIFFE *Parergon* 200 They are Guardians of the Spiritualities during the Vacancy of the Bishoprick. **1727** WILLIS *Surv. Cathedr., Durham* 232 The Temporalities of Durham are valued at 1233*l.* 4*s.* 2*d.* and the Spiritualities at 494*l.* 19*s.* 3*d.* **1809** BAWDWEN *Domesday Bk.* 7 The King [has no right] in the manors of the Earl, excepting what relates to Spiritualities which belong to the Archbishop, in all the land of St. Peter of York. **1874** STUBBS *Const. Hist.* I. xiv. 140 Their spiritualities, the tithes and oblations, were not to be taxed.

3. The quality or condition of being spiritual; attachment to or regard for things of the spirit as opposed to material or worldly interests.

1500–20 DUNBAR *Poems* lxxxiv. 45 Sum spark of licht and spiritualitie Walkins my witt, and ressoun bidis me rys. **1641** R. BROOKE *Eng. Episc.* 7 If you then consider the quantity, the variety, the spirituality, of the Ministeriall worke under the Gospell. **1675** OWEN *Indwelling Sin* iv. (1732) 35 The more of Spirituality and Holiness is in any Thing, the greater is its Enmity. **1753** CHALLONER *Cath. Chr. Instr.* 177 His Life is written by the great St. Athanasius, and is full of excellent Lessons of Spirituality. **1787** COWPER *Lett.* Wks. 1837 XV. 194 That spirituality which once enlivened all our intercourse. **1808** JEBB *Corr. w. Knox* (1834) I. 403 Prayer is, undoubtedly, the life and soul of spirituality. **1852** MISS YONGE *Cameos* (1877) III. xxxiii. 340 Painting, which had hitherto aimed chiefly at spirituality,..now made nature and beauty its primary object. **1883** H. DRUMMOND *Nat. Law in Spir. W.* ii. (1884) 89 No spiritual man ever claims that his spirituality is his own.

b. Spiritual character or function.

1661 R. BURNEY *Κέρδιστον Δῶρον* 15 A King for his spirituality is properly and Hieroglyphically to be pourtrayed half in Heaven..and part on the Earth.

c. With *a* and pl. A spiritual thing or quality as distinct from a material or worldly one; †a pious remark or saying.

1676 *Life Father Sarpi* in *Brent's Counc. Trent* 73 He was never known to use any hypocritical actions,..not to speak with affected Spiritualities. **1840** CARLYLE *Heroes* iii. (1904) 114 Apart from spiritualities; and considering him [Shakspere] merely as a real, marketable..possession. **1855** W. H. MILL *Applic. Panth. Princ.* (1861) 46 If..the so-called spiritualities which he alleges be the main inducement offered to the Christian.

†4. An immaterial or incorporeal thing or substance; a spirit. Also *fig. Obs.*

1628 T. SPENCER *Logick* 207 That includeth a corporall substance, and a spiritualitie, called life. **1664** POWER *Exp. Philos.* III. 155 Might not such Microscopes hazard the discovery of the Aerial Genii, and present even Spiritualities to our view? **1825** J. NEAL *Bro. Jonathan* III. 428 The very dogs were lying about..as if they were..a species of new, four-footed spirituality.

†5. The fact or state of being spirituous or of consisting of pure spirit; volatile state or quality.

1644 DIGBY *Nat. Bodies* xxvi. 240 The heate and spirituality of the bloud. **1660** tr. *Paracelsus' Archidoxis* I. I. 8 Medicine doth mundifie bodies, in whom is a spirituality. **1678** R. R[USSELL] tr. *Geber* I. x. 17 Luna or Silver is subtiliated and attenuated and reduced to Spirituality as above said.

6. The fact or condition of being spirit or of consisting of an incorporeal essence.

1681–6 J. SCOTT *Chr. Life* II. vii. (1718) 543 They who are to be judged being, by reason of their spirituality, in a Condition to attend to every one's Trial while they are undergoing their own. *a* **1708** BEVERIDGE *Thes. Theol.* (1711) II. 336 We must celebrate..God's spirituality..by serving Him in spirit. **1871** TYLOR *Prim. Cult.* II. 372 Such morbid disturbances are explained as symptoms of divine visitation, or at least of superhuman spirituality. **1884** J. TAIT *Mind in Matter* Introd. 5 That He is invisible is accounted for by His spirituality.

†spiritualizate, *pa. pple. Obs.*[−1] [Cf. next.] Changed into or impregnated with spirit.

1471 RIPLEY *Comp. Alch.* Ep., in Ashm. (1652) 116 Which oftentimes must againe be Spiritualizate.

spiritualization (ˌspɪrɪtjuːəlaɪˈzeɪʃən). [f. next + -ATION. Cf. F. *spiritualisation*, Sp. *espiritualizacion*.] The action of the verb SPIRITUALIZE.

1. The action of changing into spirit; conversion or transformation of a corporeal or material substance into a spiritual condition.

1665 NEEDHAM *Med. Medicinæ* 285 The Fifth Concoction is in the Arteries, where its [the blood's] Spiritualisation and vitality is perfected. **1674** BLOUNT *Glossogr.* (ed. 4), *Spiritualization*, is the changing the whole body into spirit; a Chymical term. **1824** *Monthly Mag.* LVIII. 38 That spiritualization..which must take place previous to the admission of any bodies into that region of spirits. **1891** [F. C. S. SCHILLER] *Riddles Sphinx* 397 Matter also undergoes a process of spiritualization.

transf. **1863** COWDEN CLARKE *Shaks. Char.* iv. 104 That spiritualisation of fun, frolic, and mischief—immortal Puck.

2. The action of spiritualizing or making spiritual; the state of being spiritualized.

1809 *Crit. Rev.* Ser. III. XVI. 464 This spiritualization of the old faith. **1851** RUSKIN *Stones Ven.* I. i. §29 The history of Gothic architecture is the history of the refinement and spiritualisation of Northern work under its influence. **1879** FARRAR *St. Paul* I. 144 Nor had they seen that His fulfilment of the Law had consisted in its spiritualisation.

b. Interpretation in a spiritual sense.

1820 SOUTHEY *Wesley* I. 204 Madness never gave birth to combinations of more..blasphemous obscenity, than they did in their fantastic allegories and spiritualizations.

spiritualize (ˈspɪrɪtjuːəlaɪz), *v.* [f. SPIRITUAL *a.* + -IZE, or ad. F. *spiritualiser* (16th c.). Cf. It. *spiritualizzare*, Sp. and Pg. *espiritualizar*.]

1. *trans.* To render spiritual; to invest with a spiritual character; to raise or change to a spiritual (or more spiritual) condition.

Freq. in the 17th c.

1631 R. H. *Arraignm. Whole Creature* xiii. §1. 173 The Soules food, if I may so say, is spiritualized to the sustentation of the spirit. **1655** FULLER *Ch. Hist.* II. 57 Christ more spirituallized their Joy, rather to rejoyce that their Names were written in Heaven. **1696** STANHOPE *Chr. Pattern* (1711) 81 This man is as it were spiritualized, can have recourse to God without distraction. **1801** B. MAXWELL *Let.* in *Mem. B. Ewing* (1829) 37 That any thing I should write should be helpful in spiritualising another. **1882** MISS BRADDON *Mt. Royal* II. xii. 279 Illness and solitude had done much to exalt and spiritualize Angus Hamleigh's mind.

b. To convert into, invest with, a spiritual sense or meaning; to expound or understand in a spiritual sense; to explain *away* in this manner. Also *absol.*

1645 CALAMY *Indict. agst. Eng.* 26 Oh that God would give us hearts to spiritualize these stories! **1663** BOYLE *Usef. Exp. Nat. Philos.* I. v. 115 Beasts inhabit and enjoy the world: man, if he will do more, must study, and (if I may so speak) spiritualize it. **1696** C. LESLIE *Snake in Grass* 166 They have Spiritualiz'd away all the Letter of the Scripture, the Sacraments, and Christ's Humanity. **1734** WATTS *Relig. Juv.* (1789) 221 Must we spiritualize the affairs of larks, and worms, and squirrels, and learn religion from all the trifles in nature? **1798** GRAVES *Charac. Apos.* 126 Nothing is attributed to natural causes; every thing is spiritualized and magnified. **1833** *Fraser's Mag.* VIII. 47 There is an increasing tendency to spiritualise away the pains of what is technically called Hell. **1845** KITTO *Cycl. Bibl. Lit.* s.v. *Commentary*, Pious reflections, and multitudinous inferences enter largely into our popular books of exposition. They Spiritualise, but they do not expound.

c. To render spiritual in appearance; to refine in a high degree.

1889 HISSEY *Tour in Phaeton* 101 The softened light spiritualises the landscape. **1898** WATTS-DUNTON *Aylwin* III. vi, Sinfi's noble features, illumined and spiritualized by a light that seemed more than earthly.

†**2.** To invest with full spiritual or ecclesiastical status or rights. *Obs.*⁻¹

1641 *Termes de la Ley* 126 If Chappels founded by Lay men were not approved of by the Diocesan, and as they terme it, spiritualized, they are not accounted Benefices.

3. †**a.** To change, convert into, or reduce to spirit; to render volatile or spirituous. *Obs.*

1644 DIGBY *Nat. Bodies* xxvi. 238 This motion of the hart driueth the bloud (which is warmed and spiritualised, by being boyled in this furnace) through due passages into the arteries. **1694** SALMON *Bate's Dispens.* (1713) 347/2 From what has been said it appears, first, that the Gold ought to be spiritualized or subtilized. **1721** BAILEY, *Spiritualize* (in Chymistry) is to reduce a compact mixt Body into the Principle call'd Spirit. **1741** *Phil. Trans.* LV. 242 It seems fitted,..by its expansive quality, to rarify and as it were spiritualize the blood.

b. To invest with the immaterial qualities or nature of a spirit.

1659 H. MORE *Immort. Soul* (1662) 154 This body is far more active then ours, being more spiritualized, that is to say, having greater degrees of motion communicated unto it. **1818** KEATS *Endym.* IV. 993 Then 'twas fit that from this mortal state Thou shouldst, my love, by some unlook'd for change Be spiritualis'd.

†**4.** *absol.* To inform with spirit. *Obs.*⁻¹

1713 DERHAM *Phys.-Theol.* 4 A Mass of Air, of subtile penetrating Matter, fit..to excite, animate, and spiritualize; and in short, to be the very Soul of this lower World.

Hence **ˈspiritualizing** *ppl. a.*

1845 KITTO *Cycl. Bibl. Lit.* s.v. *Commentary*, A preaching, spiritualising commentary does not deserve the appellation of commentary at all. **1853** DE QUINCEY *Autob. Sk.* Wks. I. 27 That softening and spiritualising haze which belongs..to the action of dreams. **1899** W. R. INGE *Chr. Myst.* viii. 317 The spiritualising power of human love.

spiritualized (ˈspɪrɪtjuːəlaɪzd), *ppl. a.* [Cf. SPIRITUALIZE *v.*]

†**1.** Containing an infusion of spirits. *Obs.*⁻¹

1593 NASHE *Christ's T.* 70 b, Why ensparkle they theyr eyes with spiritualiz'd distillations? Why tippe they theyr tongues with *Aurum potabile*?

2. Rendered spiritual; characterized by spirituality.

1651 N. BACON *Disc. Govt. Eng.* II. vi. 50 The persons of these Spiritualized men were of so aiery constitution, as they could not be holden by hands made out of the Clay. **1720** WELTON *Suffer. Son of God* II. xiv. 373 He alone is the True spiritualized Soul, who only aims at God's Glory. **1826** SCOTT *Woodst.* i, Dry bran and sapless pottage, unfitted for the spiritualized palates of the saints. **1860** *Smith's Dict. Bible* I. s.v. *Ark*, The climax of spiritualised religion.

3. Changed from a bodily or material condition to a spiritual one; converted into spirit.

1799 GILPIN *Serm.* xxii. 269 Whatever may be the immediate state of our souls, our bodies, in some spiritualized form which we understand not, shall be again united to them. **1857** KEBLE *Eucharist. Ador.* 52 The..contemplation of a certain presence of His now spiritualized Body among them. **1873** L. FERGUSON *Disc.* 71 His body..was immediately after death brought to life again in a spiritualised and incorruptible form.

spiritualizer (ˈspɪrɪtjuːəlaɪzə(r)). [f. SPIRITUALIZE *v.*]

1. One who gives a spiritual sense to a Scriptural statement, etc.; one who interprets spiritually.

1698 tr. *Abp. Fenelon's Maxims Saints* 202 Altho' the said Book doth..make an enumeration of false spiritualizers. *a* **1779** WARBURTON *Div. Legat.* IX. ii. Wks. 1788 III. 655 The Socinians, who boast to have interpreted Scripture on the severest and justest Laws of Logic and Criticism, have, in this instance,..deviated more from these Laws than the most licentious of the Allegorists, or the wildest of the Spiritualizers. **1828** E. IRVING *Last Days* 362 O ye niggard spiritualizers of God's universal promise! **1842** FABER *Prov. Lett.* (1844) II. 35 A thorough-going spiritualiser will tell you the covert meaning of every dish and spoon in Solomon's temple.

2. A spiritualizing agency or quality.

1822 WHEWELL in S. Douglas *Life* (1881) 73 It..is something of the same kind of consoler and spiritualiser in small matters that religion is in great ones. **1867** H. BUSHNELL *Mor. Uses Dark Th.* 21 Sleep is a spiritualizer.

spiritualizing (ˈspɪrɪtjuːəlaɪzɪŋ), *vbl. sb.* [f. as prec.] The action of the verb SPIRITUALIZE; a spiritual interpretation.

1649 F. ROBERTS *Clavis Bibl.* Introd. ii. 16 Man ascending unto God, by the Spiritualizing of his Nature. **1696** C. LESLIE *Snake in Grass* 166 Their [*sc.* Quakers'] Principle is Spiritualizing. **1842** *Penny Cycl.* XXIV. 247/2 His kingdom was not so much a new one, as a fulfilling and spiritualizing of the former dispensation. **1864** *Macm. Mag.* Oct. 469 The mystic spiritualizings of an Irving.

b. In attributive use.

1842 A. R. C. DALLAS *Look to Jerus.* (ed. 2) 49 The spiritualizing system of interpretation. **1856** R. A. VAUGHAN *Mystics* (1860) I. 52 If this spiritualizing mania be Philo's great claim to distinction. **1873** SYMONDS *Grk. Poets* x. 339 The spiritualizing tendency of modern genius, symbolical in Shelley's 'Adonais'.

spiritually (ˈspɪrɪtjuːəlɪ), *adv.* Also 4 **spirituellyche**, 5 **spirytuelly.** [f. SPIRITUAL *a.*]

1. In a spiritual manner; in or as to the spirit; as regards or in respect of spiritual things; in accordance with spiritual principles.

1340 *Ayenb.* 84 Hi zet man spirituellyche ine his riȝte stat huerinne he wes uerst ymad. **1398** TREVISA *Barth. De P.R.* I. (1495) 3 By the..simylitude of thynges visible our wit or our vnderstondynge, spirytuelly,..may be so well ordred [etc.]. *c* **1440** *Alph. Tales* 194 Our Ladie..enoyntid þis seke man..& curid hym bothe spirituallie & bodelie. **1456** SIR G. HAYE *Law Arms* (S.T.S.) 20 As evill bitter wateris gerris mony folk dee temporaly, sa dois..heresy and lollardry the saule dee spiritualy. *a* **1513** FABYAN *Chron.* v. cxiii. (1516) G iij/1 Yᵉ Quene..brought in hir armes the yonge Baby, to the which she was moder bothe naturally, and spiritually. **1560** DAUS tr. *Sleidane's Comm.* 66 The body and blud of Christ is received spiritually. **1650** JER. TAYLOR *Holy Living* ii. §3. 90 In the same degree that Virgins live more spiritually then other persons. **1755** YOUNG *Centaur* ii. Wks. IV. 145 Spiritually blind, deaf, and stupid, they see not the great Omnipresent walking in the garden. **1828** LYTTON *Pelham* I. xx, Mr. Howard de Howard is too unsubstantial not to be spiritually inclined. **1893** *Bookman* June 86/1 This Russian baroness..spiritually directing the Czar of all the Russias.

b. *Comb.* in ***spiritually-minded.***

1526 TINDALE *Rom.* viii. 6 To be carnally mynded is deeth, and to be spiritually mynded is lyfe, and peace. **1564-78** BULLEIN *Dial. agst. Pest.* (1888) 122 He is so spiritually mynded that he forgetteth poore Roger. **1681** OWEN (*title*), Grace and Duty of being Spiritually-Minded. **1831** SCOTT *Cast. Dang.* v, Methinks thou art more spiritually-minded than can always be predicated of a wandering minstrel. **1844** tr. *M. T. Asmar's Mem. Babylonian Princ.* II. 57 Being..a spiritually-minded woman, she yielded her consent.

†**2.** In or according to a spiritual sense. (Opposed to *literally*.) *Obs.*

13.. *E.E. Allit. P.* B. 1492 Bifore þe sancta sanctorum soþefast dryȝtyn Expouned his speche spiritually to special prophetes. *c* **1400** MAUNDEV. (Roxb.) xv. 68 Þai vnderstand noȝt haly writte spiritually, bot after þe letter. **1550** SENONOYS *Godly Sayings* (1846) 74 Understand ye spiritually that whiche I have spoken unto you. **1559** W. CUNNINGHAM *Cosmogr. Glasse* Pref. 2 All they agree in this poynt,..but yet as touchinge the situation, some vnderstand it spiritually.

†**3.** In a spiritual or ecclesiastical capacity.

c **1511** *1st Eng. Bk. Amer.* Introd. (Arb.) p. xxx/2 The Grekes haue spyrytually the Patriarcke of Constantynnoplen, and many Archebysshops, bysshops, and abbottes.

4. As a spirit or spiritual being; with supernatural beauty, radiance, etc.

1816 BYRON *Siege Corinth* xi, Bespangled with those isles of light, So wildly, spiritually bright. *a* **1850** ROSSETTI *Dante & Circle* I. (1874) 95 She..Grew perfectly and spiritually fair.

5. In respect of distilled spirit or alcohol. *rare.*

1866 *Athenæum* 12 May 634/1 French wine being spiritually weaker, than either port or sherry.

spiritual-mindedness. [Cf. *spiritually-minded* SPIRITUALLY *adv.* 1 b.] The quality or state of being spiritually-minded or of having the mind set upon spiritual things.

1647 N. WARD *Simp. Cobler* 43, I have..seen so much..spirituall mindednesse in..Christians. **1688** OWEN *Dominion of Sin & Grace* Wks. 1852 VII. 524 This case of the affections I have handled..at large in my discourse of Spiritual-mindedness. **1791** BOSWELL *Johnson* 22 Mar. 1776, I have always loved the simplicity of manners, and the spiritual-mindedness of the Quakers. **1863** GROSART *Small Sins* (ed. 2) 82 No lamentation over want of spiritual-mindedness.

ˈspiritualness. [f. SPIRITUAL *a.* + -NESS.] The fact, quality, or state of being spiritual in origin, character, or nature; spirituality.

Very common in the 17th c.; now *rare.*

1561 DAUS tr. *Bullinger on Apoc.* (1573) 149 b, Otherwyse there is no spiritualnesse at all: for they be altogether fleshe. **1579** W. WILKINSON *Confut. Fam. Love* B ij, Out of your spiritualnes judge all things according to the ballance of equitye. *a* **1603** T. CARTWRIGHT *Confut. Rhem. N.T.* (1618) 438 The spiritualnesse of our bodies doth not take away their naturall and essentiall properties. **1642** D. ROGERS *Naaman* 108 The spiritualnesse and precisenesse of Christ is a burthen to them. **1693** FIRMIN *Rev. Vind.* i. 6 It was the Law opened in the Spiritualness of it, that took of Paul from his own Righteousness. **1721** BAILEY, *Spirituality*, Spiritualness, Devotion. **1889** *Pall Mall G.* 15 June 6/1 A pseudo spiritualness which makes small account of the daily behaviour and moral stamina of our teachers and preachers.

b. A spiritual condition or state. *rare*⁻¹.

a **1658** DURHAM *Comm. Revelation* I. (1660) 29 To be in the spirit is..to be in a spiritualnesse abstracted from carnalnesse.

†**ˈspiritualship.** *Obs.* [f. SPIRITUAL *a.*: see -SHIP 3.] The personality of an ecclesiastic. (Used as a mock title.)

1670 EACHARD *Cont. Clergy* 90 A sober and temperate clergy, that will not eat so much as the laity, but that..the least of every thing may satisfie their spiritualship. **1680** HICKERINGILL *Narr. Tryal* Wks. 1716 II. 206 If the Judge had the keeping of his Spiritualship, Mr. H. should neither be so rich, nor so fat.

spiritualty (ˈspɪrɪtjuːəltɪ). Forms: 4–6 **spiritualte(e**, 5 **-allte, speritwalte, spyryt-**, 6 **spyritualte**; 5 **spyryt-, spirituelte(e**; 4–7 **spiritualtie**, 5– **spiritualty** (6 **-tye**). [ad. OF. *espirit-, esperituaulté, spiritualté*, etc.: see SPIRITUAL *a.* and cf. SPIRITUALITY.]

†**1.** The quality or state of being spiritual; spiritual character; = SPIRITUALITY 3. *Obs.*

1377 LANGL. *P. Pl.* B. v. 148 Þus þei speken of spiritualte Þat eyther despiseth other, Til þei be bothe beggers and by my spiritualte libben. *a* **1420** *Aunters of Arth.* xx, These ar the gracius giftus of the Holi Gost, That enspires iche sprete...Off this spiritualIte speke we no more. **1421** *26 Pol. Poems* xviii. 8 In brennyng contemplacion, þe hiȝest lyf of spiritualte. ? *a* **1500** *Chester Pl.* IX. 166 In tokening of thy dignitie and that office of Spiritualty, receave..deuoutly myne offring.

†**b.** = HOLINESS *sb.* 2. *Obs.*⁻¹

1613-8 DANIEL *Coll. Hist. Eng.* Wks. V. 168 The King of France whom he had excommunicated.., shortly after so wrought, as his Spiritualty was surprized at Anagne.

2. †**a.** = SPIRITUALITY 2. *Obs.*

c **1380** WYCLIF *Wks.* (1880) 276 So þat alle clerkis lyue clenly on spiritualte, as crist & his apostlis deden. **1387** TREVISA *Higden* (Rolls) VII. 335 Kyng William..ruled boþe temperalte and spiritualte [L. *secularia et ecclesiastica*] at his owne wille. *c* **1400** MAUNDEV. (Roxb.) iii. 10 He es þare lorde bathe of temperaltee and of spiritualtee. **1700** [see TEMPORALTY 1]. **1709** STRYPE *Ann. Ref.* I. xxv. 245 Keeper of the spiritualty of the city and diocese of Bristol.

b. *pl.* = SPIRITUALITY 2 b. Now *Hist.*

c **1380** WYCLIF *Wks.* (1830) 369 Siþ þai han now þe more part of þe temporal lordeschips, and wiþ þat þe spiritualtees and þe greete mouable tresouris of þe rewme. **1531-2** *Act 23 Hen. VIII*, c. 20 §2 Bysshopes..shall..entyerly have and enjoye all the spiritualties and temporalties..in..beneficiall maner. **1570** *Act 13 Eliz.* c. 12 §1 The Bysshop or Gardian of the Spyritualties of some one Diocesse where he hath..Ecclesiastical Lyving. **1607** COWELL *Interpr.* s.v. *Gardeyn*, The guardeyn of the spiritualties, may be either Guardeyn in lawe,..or guardian by delegation. **1726** AYLIFFE *Parergon* 125 Of Common Right, the Dean and Chapter are Guardians of the Spiritualties, during the Vacancy of a Bishoprick. **1763** BURN *Eccles. Law* (1767) I. 202 Spiritualties of bishopricks in the time of vacation. **1835** TOMLINS *Law Dict.* s.v. *Guardian*. **1912** *Eng. Hist. Rev.* Oct. 768 A complete list of the..temporalties and spiritualties belonging to a parish church.

3. The body of spiritual or ecclesiastical persons; the spiritual estate of the realm; the clergy; = SPIRITUALITY 1.

c **1400** *Destr. Troy* 3100 Ho tentit not in Tempull to no tall prayers,..Ne speche of no spiritualtie, with speciall ne other. *c* **1450** LOVELICH *Grail* xlviii. 218 Axeth hem..what maner of men that they welen be, Owther wedded men, owther speritwalte. **1482** CAXTON *Polychronicon* VIII. xi. 405 As for the temporaltyees beynge in the handes of the spiritueltc. **1529** MORE *Dyaloge* III. Wks. 225/1 So dare I boldly say that the spiritualtie of Englande..is in learning and honest liuing well able to matche..the spiritualtie of anye nacion christen. **1579** FENTON *Guicciard.* III. (1599) 143 The diuision being no lesse amongst the spiritualtie then the layetie. **1641** MILTON *Ch. Discipl.* II. 86 The boistrous and contradictional hand of a temporall, earthly and corporeal Spiritualty. **1699** BURNET *39 Art.* xxxvii. 384 The Synods..were for the greatest part mixed Assemblies in which the Temporalty and the Spiritualty sate together. **1849** W. FITZGERALD tr. *Whitaker's Disput.* 248 He says *all*, not merely the learned, or the bishops, or the spiritualty. **1856** FROUDE *Hist. Eng.* (1858) I. iii. 248 The spiritualty defended themselves by prescription and usage. **1878** STUBBS *Const. Hist.* III. xix. 290 We may regard the spiritualty of England, the clergy or clerical estate, as a body completely organised.

†**b.** A body or set of ecclesiastics or clergy. *Obs.*

1513 *Life Hen. V* (1911) 184 And all the saide spiritualtie, singinge the offices accustomed in like case, conueyed the saide corps [etc.]. **1545** JOYE *Exp. Dan.* V. I v, Then the kynge cried commanding his spiritualtye, his wyse men, enchaunters,..to be brought unto him. **1624** BEDELL *Lett.* iii. 68 We learne that no earthly power, no Magistrate is a spirituall man, vnlesse hee bee one of the Popes spiritualtie. **1653** MILTON *Hirelings* Pref., A spiritualtie of men devoted to their temporal gain.

†**4.** *pl.* Ecclesiastical ground or precincts. *Obs.*

1470–85 MALORY *Arthur* XVII. xxiii. 724 Bors lete bery hym by his syster and by Galahad in the spyrytueltees.

†**spiritu'ascence, -'ascency.** *Obs. rare.* [f. L. *spīritus* SPIRIT *sb.*] Spirituosity.

1662 H. STUBBE *Indian Nectar* vii. 137 The spirituascency of the seed little. *Ibid.* 139 A..resemblance, in its colour, consistence, and spirituascency, to the white of an Egg. **1684** tr. *Bonet's Merc. Compit.* XIX. 831 Aromaticks..correct that dulness and deficient spirituascence..of the Stomach.

†**'spirituated,** *a.* *Obs.*$^{-1}$ [f. as prec.] Impregnated with, or converted into, spirit.

1657 G. STARKEY *Helmont's Vind.* 292 The glorified, spirituated and perfected Sulphurs,..by their fermentall irradiation, at once mortifie whatever is malignant in the body.

‖**spiritu'el, -'elle,** *a.* [F. *spirituel* masc., *-elle* fem.: see SPIRITUAL *a.*] Of a highly refined character or nature, esp. in conjunction with liveliness or quickness of mind.

The distinction between the masc. and fem. forms has not always been observed in English.

α. **1673** DRYDEN *Marr. à la Mode* III. i, Do not call it my service, that's too vulgar; but do my *baise-mains* to the princess Amalthea; that is *spirituelle*! **1738** MRS. DELANY *Life & Corr.* (1861) II. 20 She has such a flow of spirits and of wit;..she is by much the most spirituelle creature I ever met with. **1867** AUGUSTA WILSON *Vashti* xvii, To-day there was a *spirituelle* beauty in the white face that he had never seen before. **1886** *Illustr. Lond. News* 9 Jan. 45/1 The expression of her countenance..was *spirituelle* in a high degree. **1895** *Q. Rev.* Oct. 467 She was as delightful, racy, *spirituelle* a companion after as before her religious change.

β. **1709** MRS. MANLEY *Secret Mem.* (1720) III. 120 She was very Beautiful, and more *Eveliez* and *Spirituel* than any I had met. *Ibid.* 146 Gay Conversation of the Modish, most *Spirituel*. **1833** LYTTON *Godolphin* lxiv, The admired—the cultivated—*spirituel*—the splendid Godolphin.

Hence **spiritu'elly** *adv.*

1825 *New Monthly Mag.* XV. 367 It tells them some very disagreeable truths, and..tells them so *spirituel*-ly, that..the castigation..is sport to all the rest of the world.

†**spirituose,** *a.* *Obs. rare.* = SPIRITUAL *a.* 4.

1677 GALE *Crt. Gentiles* IV. v. §1. 305 Al life consisting in a spirituose actuositie. *Ibid.* 306 The Angelic life is of al creatid lifes the most actuose, spirituose, and noble.

spirituosity (spɪrɪtjuːˈɒsɪtɪ). [f. next + -ITY. So F. *spirituosité*.]

1. The state or quality of being spirituous or of containing spirit, esp. through distillation.

1669 W. SIMPSON *Hydrol. Chym.* 31 Which digestion of the spleen so promoting the blood in its tincture, and height of spirituosity [etc.]. **1674** PETTY *Disc. Dupl. Proportion* 93 The measuring of the Spirituosity of Liquors, or in what proportions several Liquors contein more or less of inflameable or ardent parts. **1778** *Phil. Trans.* LXVIII. 500 The spirituosity of different liquors distilled from wine. **1826** *Art of Brewing* (ed. 2) 102 A flavour partaking of the spirituosity of wine. **1880** *Libr. Univ. Knowl.* VI. 281 The wines in this part are rich in color, and distinguished by much body and spirituosity.

†**2.** Spiritual nature or quality; animating force or energy. *Obs. rare.*

1677 GALE *Crt. Gentiles* IV. v. §1. 306 Whatever Spirituositie or Actuositie there is in any created life. *Ibid.* 307 The Life of God carries in it the most perfect Spirituositie, as he is the most simple pure Spirit.

spirituous (ˈspɪrɪtjuəs), *a.* [f. L. *spīritu-s* + -OUS, or ad. F. *spiritueux* (16th c.), Sp. and Pg. *espirituoso*.]

1. Spirited, animated, lively, vivacious. Now *rare.*

1599 B. JONSON *Cynthia's Rev.* III. ii, Well, I am resolv'd what Ile doe.—What my good spirituous sparke? **1703** J. SAVAGE *Lett. Antients* xlv. 109 The Greeks, who are a spirituous and wise People, not to be us'd as the barbarous Nations are by their Tyrants. **1709** *Phil. Trans.* XXVII. 74 A very Vivacious and Spirituous Animal. **1751** ELIZA HEYWOOD *Betsy Thoughtless* II. 10 Her once gay and spirituous behaviour..was now become all dull and gloomy. **1888** DOUGHTY *Arab. Des.* I. 593 The Emir in his spirituous humour, and haughty familiar manners.

2. Of the nature of, having the properties of, spirit; containing spirit or volatile principle in a natural state. (Freq. in 17th cent.)

1605 TIMME *Quersit.* I. vii. 30 Vineger,..in regard of..that most thin, spirituous, sower essence of salt, doe pierce into the most inward parts. **1646** SIR T. BROWNE *Pseud. Ep.* 88 If the matter be spirituous, and the cloud compact, the noise is great and terrible. **1694** W. WOTTON *Anc. & Mod. Learn.* (1697) 239 The Fæculencies are separated from the more spirituous Parts, and by their Weight sink to the Bottom. *a* **1722** LISLE *Husb.* (1757) 302 Though the grounds are very rich, the juices of the grass are from thence less spirituous. **1737** BRACKEN *Farriery Impr.* (1757) II. 185 Oats and Beans is a more warm and spirituous Feed than Hay. **1794** G. ADAMS *Nat. & Exp. Philos.* II. xvii. 264 It is thin and clear like water, though somewhat more spirituous and viscous. **1837** P. KEITH *Bot. Lex.* 306 Vegetable substances are always resinous, or oily, or spirituous, when the oxygen which they contain is to the hydrogren in a smaller proportion than in water.

fig. **1673** DRYDEN *Marr. à la Mode* II. i, Fancy will every touch and glance improve, And draw the most spirituous parts of love. **1705** J. DUNTON *Life & Err.* vii. (1818) I. 275 My happiness was too spirituous and fine to continue long. **1709** MRS. MANLEY *Secret Mem.* (1720) III. 29 That little valuable spirituous Particle [*sc.* sincerity], that animated the Whole!

3. Containing or impregnated with spirit or alcohol obtained by distillation; containing an infusion of alcohol; alcoholic; ardent.

1681 tr. *Belon's New Myst. Physick* Introd. 10 Medicine must be invited.., by refined and spirituous Medicaments, to procure Preservation. **1694** SALMON *Bate's Dispens.* (1713) 46/2 Cover and lute it, and distil S.A. so will you have a spirituous Water. **1742** tr. *Algarotti's Newton's The.* II. 194 They were obliged to cut the most spirituous Wine with a Hatchet. **1767** GOOCH *Treat. Wounds* I. 246 Spirituous, warm, subtile medicines are to be used. **1813** T. THOMSON *Lect. Inflam.* 605 Spirituous and resinous substances have long been in repute for the cure of burns. **1857** MILLER *Elem. Chem., Org.* vii. §2. 503 The spirituous varnishes dry the most rapidly. **1867** J. HOGG *Microsc.* I. ii. 142 Dropping into it carefully..a spirituous solution of iodine.

b. Freq. in *spirituous liquor*(*s*).

1732 ARBUTHNOT *Rules of Diet* in *Aliments*, etc. I. 245 Strong Waters or Spirituous Liquors contract and harden the solid Parts most of all. **1764** BURN *Poor Laws* 242 As the laws stand, a licence from the officers of excise alone, for retailing spirituous liquors, is not sufficient. **1815** J. SMITH *Panorama Science & Art* II. 88 When the instrument is immersed in spirituous liquor. **1836** THIRLWALL *Greece* xiv. II. 197 The modern Tartars extract a spirituous liquor from the milk of their mares. **1862** TROLLOPE *N. Amer.* I. xvii. 377 No wine or spirituous liquors may be used.

4. Of or belonging to spirit or alcohol; like or resembling that of spirit.

1667 *Phil. Trans.* II. 496 The Thames-water..in eight months time..acquires a Spirituous quality, so as to burn like Spirit of Wine. **1699** EVELYN *Acetaria* (1729) 167 Spirituous and active Force to animate and revive every Faculty and Part. **1838** T. THOMSON *Chem. Org. Bodies* 789 When this sap was left exposed to the air..it became milky [and]..acquired a spirituous smell and taste. **1862** MILLER *Elem. Chem., Org.* (ed. 2) 155 Wood spirit is a limpid, inflammable, colourless liquid, of a penetrating spirituous odour. **1867** F. H. LUDLOW *Little Briggs* 218 The spirituous soupçon which tingles through the siropy flavors of an arrack punch.

b. Accomplished or carried out by means of spirit or alcohol.

1800 tr. *Lagrange's Chem.* II. 167 There are reckoned to be three kinds of fermentation: spirituous, acetous, and putrid.

†**5.** = SPIRITUAL *a.* 4. *Obs.*

1662 R. MATHEW *Unl. Alch.* 60 When thy now rotting body is destroyed, thou again shalt receive a spirituous body. **1678** CUDWORTH *Intell. Syst.* 785 The Irrational Part or Life thereof, is Separable only from this Gross Body..; but hath (after Death) a Spirituous or Aiery Body. **1727** DE FOE *Hist. Appar.* iv. (1840) 30 Such inhabitants as are spirituous, and invisible. **1745** ELIZA HEYWOOD *Female Spect.* No. 15 (1748) III. 120 As great an enemy as indolence is to our spirituous part, activity in things unfit is yet much more so.

†**6.** Spiritual, in various senses. *Obs.*

a **1631** DONNE *Serm.* (1634) IV. 7 God gives not his people ..valour, and then leaves them to a spirituous quarrelsomenesse. **1712** W. KING *Joan of Hedington* Pref., Wks. 1776 III. 11 She seems spirituous, and..not disinclinable to virtuous courses. **1727** WARBURTON *Prodigies & Miracles* I. 54 What then must we expect from this spirituous Imposture; which persuades the credulous Reader that the Soul of History is here disingaged from the unweildy..Carcasses of Chronicle and Annal?

Hence **'spirituously** *adv.*, †in a spirited manner.

1751 ELIZA HEYWOOD *Betsy Thoughtless* IV. 52 'Bless me, madam!' cried Mrs. Munden, spirituously, 'would your ladyship have me give up..that slender pittance?'

'spirituousness. [f. SPIRITUOUS *a.*]

1. = SPIRITUOSITY I.

1660 BOYLE *New Exp. Phys. Mech.* xxiv. 193 The great thinness and spirituousness of the Liquor. **1670** H. STUBBE *Plus Ultra* 106 He plants a kind of..fire in the heart, which ..imprints a spirituousness in the blood that issueth out into the Arteries. **1725** *Fam. Dict.* s.v. *Wine*, These [i.e. strong wines] by their Spirituousness, wonderfully conduce to the Digestion of the gross Food of our Country.

2. = SPIRITUOSITY 2.

1727 BAILEY (vol. II), *Spirituousness*, Fulness of Spirits, Liveliness. **1740** *Phil. Trans.* XLI. 301 How can one believe, that..a little more Activity, a little more Spirituousness, should compose..any Organization?

spiritus (ˈspɪrɪtʊs). [L., = breath, aspiration, spirit.] **1.** *Gr. Gram.* = BREATHING *vbl. sb.* 9; ***spiritus asper***: see ASPER *sb.*[1]; ***spiritus lenis*** (ˈliːnɪs), smooth breathing; the sign (ʼ) placed over an initial vowel to show that it is not aspirated.

[**1470** PRISCIANUS *Grammatici* (1855) I. II. 51 In dictione tenor certus, absque ea incertus, non potest tamen sine eo esse. Similiter spiritus asper vel lenis.] **1867** MAX MÜLLER *Chips from German Workshop* II. 87 Sanskrit v is generally represented in Greek by the Digamma, or the spiritus lenis. **1878** W. G. RUTHERFORD *First Gr. Gram.* 3 This sign (ʽ) is called *spiritus asper*, or rough breathing. **1888** KING & COOKSON *Princ. Sound & Inflexion Gr. & Latin* viii. 171 An initial *j* becomes the spiritus asper, sometimes changed to spiritus lenis. **1936** G. K. ZIPF *Psycho-Biol. of Lang.* iii. 84 In Greek..the aspiration of the first aspirate was lost, even though the first aspirate was only an *h* (spiritus asper), that is, a phoneme which consisted exclusively of the aspiration. **1948** D. DIRINGER *Alphabet* viii. 458 By adopting this system of rough and smooth breathing (*spiritus asper* and *spiritus lenis*) for the vowel sounds,..the Greek alphabet helped to preserve flexibility in the Greek speech. **1976** *Archivum Linguisticum* VII. 170 Thus Schmalstieg does not give a clear explanation of..other initial aspirations like the *spiritus asper* in Greek.

2. ***spiritus rector*** (ˈrɛktɔː(r)), a ruling or directing spirit.

1911 W. JAMES *Some Probl. Philos.* i. 16 Thus a '*spiritus rector*' would be a metaphysical,—a 'principle of attraction' a theological,—and a 'law of the squares' would be a positive theory of the planetary movements. **1935** A. REVUSKY *Jews in Palestine* xii. 202 The leader and *spiritus rector* of this movement, Vladimir Jabotinsky. **1942** D. D. RUNES *Dict. Philos.* 300/1 *Spiritus rector*,..some sort of subtle natural force in corporeal beings. The alchemists applied the expression to some substance..said to be capable of transmuting metals into gold, and also an elixir which was supposed to prolong life indefinitely. **1959** R. F. C. HULL tr. *Jung's Aion* in *Coll. Wks.* IX. 167 It [*sc.* the self]..is older than the ego, and..is the *spiritus rector* of our fate. **1977** *Times* 20 Dec. 13/6 It has often been reported that the international oil companies were the real *spiritus rector* for the explosion of oil prices during the winter of 1973–74. **1980** *Encounter* May 35/1 More than fifteen years ago he was the *spiritus rector* of the *European Journal of Sociology*.

spirity (ˈspɪrɪtɪ), *a.* (and *adv.*). Chiefly *dial.* or *colloq.* Also 9 *dial.* **spirrit(t)y, sperrity, spe(e)rity,** etc. [f. SPIRIT *sb.* + -Y.]

1. Full of or characterized by spirit, animation, energy, or vivacity; spirited.

1633 STRUTHER in Spurgeon *Treas. Dav.* Ps. xxxvi. 4 To make them more spirity [Satan] can horse them on restless contention. **1765** in *Priv. Lett. Ld. Malmesbury* (1870) I. 136 He is a most active, spirity man, and by his great mental exercises keeps himself from anything like a lethargy. **1808** E. SLEATH *Bristol Heiress* I. 65 That was spoken like a young woman of sense!—A fine spirity lass. **1830** GALT *Lawrie T.* VIII. v. (1849) 376 Semple is a spirity man.

b. As *adv.* Spiritedly; with spirit.

1894 BLACKMORE *Perlycross* 64, I answered him quite spirity.

2. Of the nature of spirit; spirituous. *rare.*

a **1722** LISLE *Husb.* (1757) 421 The dews soke into the broad-clover, and thin the spirity juice. *Ibid.*, The spirity juice..is..thinned by the water getting into it. **1899** DOYLE *Duet* (1909) 126/1 Do you notice a sort of low, sweetish, spirity kind of scent?

'spirivalve, *a. Zool.* [a. F. *spirivalve*, f. L. *spīra* SPIRE *sb.*[3]] **a.** Of shells: Univalve and spiral. **b.** Having a spiral univalve shell.

1835 KIRBY *Hab. & Inst. Anim.* I. ix. 267 Trachelipods..; greatest part of the body spirally convolved,..inhabiting a spirivalve shell. **1836–9** *Todd's Cycl. Anat.* II. 384/1 Many of the spirivalve Gasteropoda..are provided with a calcareous plate, which..closes accurately the mouth of the shell.

†**spirk.** *Obs.*$^{-1}$ [prob. related to E. Anglian *spurk* to spring or shoot up.] A sprout or shoot.

1565 GOLDING *Ovid's Met.* IV. (1567) 46 b, By little and by little did with growing top begin A pretie spirke of Frankinsence aboue the Tumbe to win.

'spirket[1]. *E. Angl. dial.* Also 7 spirkit, 9 sper-, spurket. [Of obscure origin: cf. prec. and SPIRGET.] A stout peg or hook on which to hang things.

1644 J. CARTER *Nail & Wheel* (1647) 14 The use of such a nail, or peg, or spirkit is to hang things out of hand. **1787** MARSHALL *Norfolk* Gloss., *Spirket*, a hook to hang things on. **1806** BLOOMFIELD *Wild Flowers* 44 She passed a clean white hog..They'd kilt the day before. High on the spirket there it hung. **1823** E. MOOR *Suffolk Words*, *Sperket*, wooden, hooked, large peg, not much curved, to hang saddles, harness, etc. on. **1899** MISS BETHAM-EDWARDS *Lord of Harvest* ii. 22 The big boiler hanging from the spirket now contained a bit of beef and a plum pudding.

†**'spirket**[2]. *Naut. Obs.* In 8 spirkit. [Cf. next and SPURKET.] ***spirket risings***, = next 1.

1711 W. SUTHERLAND *Shipbuild. Assist.* 44 The Spirkit Risings..are placed under the Lower Gun-deck Ports. *Ibid.*, The Spirkit Risings under the Middle Deck Ports.

spirketting (ˈspɜːkɪtɪŋ). *Naut.* Also 8 spirkit-, 9 **spirkitting, sparketting.** [app. f. *spirket* (cf. prec.), var. of SPURKET.]

1. Inside planking between the waterways and the ports of a vessel. (See quots. 1750, 1769.)

1748 *Anson's Voy.* II. iv. 158 Her spirkiting and timbers were very rotten. **1750** BLANCKLEY *Nav. Expos.* 156 Spirketing are Strakes of thick Plank wrought from the lower Edge of each Port to each Deck respectively within Side of the Ship. **1769** FALCONER *Dict. Marine* (1780), *Spirketing*, that range of planks which lies between the waterways and the lower edge of the gun-ports within the side of a ship of war. **1801** *Naval Chron.* VI. 202 Carlings, and sparketting, much damaged by shot. **1805** *Shipwright's Vade-M.* 202 All clamps and spirkittings above the lower gun-deck should have three port shifts in midships. *c* **1860** H. STUART *Seaman's Catech.* 69 The spirketting works up so as to form the lower sills of the ports. **1874** THEARLE *Naval Archit.* 43 The butts of shelf, spirketting, clamps, and waterway should all be carefully disposed with reference to each other.

attrib. **1869** SIR E. REED *Shipbuild.* xvii. 368 The preceding method..is also applicable to deck tie-plates, clamp or spirketing plates.

2. (See quot. 1846.)

1846 A. YOUNG *Naut. Dict.* 291 In merchant vessels, when there is a strake of ceiling wrought between the upper-deck and the plank-sheer, it is called the spirketting, or quick-work. **1850** WEALE *Dict. Terms* 246 *Kevels*..are some-times fixed to the spirketing on the quarter-deck, when the timber-heads are deficient.

spirling (ˈspɜːlɪŋ). Now only *Sc.* Also 5–6 **spyrlyng(e**. [a. MLG. *spirling* or MDu. *spierling*: cf. SPARLING and SPURLING.] The smelt, *Osmerus eperlanus*.

c **1425** *Voc.* in Wr.-Wülcker 641 *Hic gamerus*, spyrlyng. *c* **1440** *Promp. Parv.* 52/2 Broche for spyrlynge or herynge, *spiculum*. **1500–20** DUNBAR *Poems* xxv. 95 Quhair fische to sell is non bot spirling. **1526** *Househ. Exp. Sir T. Lestrange* (B.M. Add. MS. 27448) fol. 38 Item, in playce, vj d. Item, in Spyrlyngs, j d. **1655** MOUFET & BENNET *Health's Improv.* xvii. 143 Sticklebacks and minoes, and spirlings, and anchovaes. **1668** CHARLETON *Onomast.* 143 *Apua*,..the Spirling, Smy, or Sea-Dace. **1769** *De Foe's Tour Gt. Brit.* (ed. 7) IV. 19 Trouts, Perch, Pike, Scate,..Lyths, Spirlings..are also caught on the Scottish coasts in great plenty. **1830** M. DONOVAN *Dom. Econ.* II. 187 The Smelt or Spirling is remarkable for two qualities, the transparency of its body, and its odoriferous smell. **1870** P. H. MACKERLIE *Lands & Owners Galloway* I. 35 This river has salmon and that delicate fish the spirling.

attrib. **1887** *Scottish Leader* 20 Sept. 4 Salmon..illegally caught in the spirling nets. *Ibid.*, The interdict..would not interfere with spirling fishing.

spiro- (ˈspaɪrəʊ). **1.** Combining form of L. *spīra*, Gr. σπεῖρα, SPIRE *sb.*[3], used in a number of scientific terms, as **spirobacˈteria**, bacteria with spirally twisted cells; **Spirochæte** (ˈspaɪrəʊkiːt) (also **-chet-** in this word and its derivatives): a genus of bacteria having a highly twisted spiral form; in mod. use, any bacterium of the order Spirochætales, comprising actively motile non-spore-forming organisms having a helical form; hence **spiroˈchætal** *a.*, that is a spirochæte; caused by spirochætes; **ˌspirochætiˈcidal** *a.*, lethal to spirochætes; **spiroˈchæticide** a spirochæticidal substance; **spirochæˈtosis**, infection with or a disease caused by spirochætes.

1876 tr. *Wagner's Gen. Pathol.* 93 *Spirobacteria are distinguished from vibrio, by the closer and narrower, regular, permanent spiral of the filament. **1916** *Jrnl. Exper. Med.* XXIII. 377 We discovered a *spirochætal microorganism which is now believed to be the cause [of Weil's disease]. **1922** *Encycl. Brit.* XXXI. 906/1 It is best described as spirochætal jaundice rather than by the older name of Weil's disease. **1969** EDINGTON & GILLES *Path. in Tropics* vii. 298 Leptospirosis is caused by infection with spirochaetal organisms. **1877** HUXLEY & MARTIN *Elem. Biol.* 29 **Spirochæte*. Much like spirillum, but longer and with a much more closely rolled spiral. **1899** tr. *Jaksch's Clin. Diagnosis* vi. 206 Mobile swarms are seen in the centre of the mass, while at its circumference appear the spirochæte-like bodies. **1908** *Practitioner* Oct. 549 The treponema, or, as they are usually designated in this country, the spirochaetes. **1919** *Chambers's Jrnl.* June 415/2 This organism belongs to the class known as spirochaetes, of which the spirochaete of syphilis and that of relapsing fever are other members. **1939** R. CAMPBELL *Flowering Rifle* II. 47 The fierce spirochete. **1973** R. G. KRUEGER et al. *Introd. Microbiol.* iii. 59/1 The order is subdivided into two families: Spirochaetaceae for the larger..spirochaetes, which are free-living or parasitic in shellfish; and Treponemataceae for spirochetes that are only about 0·2–0·3 μm in diameter and do not exceed 16 μm in length. **1913** *Jrnl. Exper. Med.* XVIII. 435 (*heading*) A study of the *spirochæticidal action of the serum of patients treated with Salvarsan. **1949** M. A. JENNINGS in H. W. Florey et al. *Antibiotics* II. xxxi. 1037 Penicillin possessed some spirocheticidal activity. **1920** *Jrnl. Amer. Med. Assoc.* 25 Dec. 1768/1 The efficacy of..*spirocheticides in the so-called chemical prophylaxis of syphilis is limited to a period of not more than eight hours after the spirochete has had the opportunity of invading the healthy person. **1906** *Jrnl. Hygiene* VI. 580 (*heading*) *Spirochaetosis of mice due to *Spirochaeta muris* n.sp. in the blood. **1951** WHITBY & HYNES *Med. Bacteriol.* (ed. 5) xxi. 350 Spirochætes and fusiform bacilli of Vincent's type may be found in large numbers in various conditions, particularly of the lung, known as spirochætosis. **1981** *Brit. Med. Jrnl.* 21 Nov. 1362/1 A review of 100 consecutive rectal biopsy specimens obtained from patients with rectal bleeding or diarrhoea showed that 10 had spirochaetosis.

2. *Chem.* Formative element used in the names of organic compounds whose molecular structure includes two rings with a single atom (usu. of carbon or nitrogen) common to both. Also in *Comb.* or as quasi-*adj.*, as ***spiro-compound***. [Introduced in Ger. (A. Baeyer 1900, in *Ber. d. Deut. Chem. Ges.* XXXIII. 3771).]

1908 *Chem. Abstr.* II. 75 (*heading*) Spirocyclane. *Ibid.*, The term 'spiro' is applied by the author to systems of two cycloids, having only one carbon atom in common. **1909** *Jrnl. Chem. Soc.* XCVI. I. 652 The product, decomposed by cold water, yields the spirocyclane derivative. **1915** *Ibid.* CVII. II 1080 (*heading*) The formation and stability of *spiro*-compounds. **1932** *Proc. R. Soc.* A. CXXXIV. 359 The anhydrous crystals of racemic *spiro*-dihydantoin have a density of 1·94. **1960** *Jrnl. Amer. Chem. Soc.* LXXXII. 5560/1 According to the number of spiro atoms present, the compounds are distinguished as monospiro, dispiro, trispiro compounds *etc.* **1976** A. L. TERNAY *Contemp. Org. Chem.* vii. 185 A spiro compound results when two rings share one atom. **1978** *Nature* 5 Jan. 44/2 During irradiation of spiropyrans, in non-polar solvents dimer and charge-transfer complexes are formed. **1978** *Further Perspectives Org. Chem.* (CIBA) 40 Evidence for the possible spiro intermediate would give enormous support and we are seeking it.

spirograph (ˈspaɪərəʊgrɑːf, -æ-). *Med.* [f. SPIRO- + -GRAPH.] An instrument which provides a continous tracing of the movements of the lungs during respiration.

1890 in GOULD *New Med. Dict.* **1934** *Publ. Mod. Lang. Assoc. Amer.* XLIX. 1168 The air pressure and vibrations taken back of the point of contact with the spirograph. **1977** *Bull. Exper. Biol. & Med.* LXIV. 1662 The investigation is stopped when changes in the helium concentration in the spirograph decrease to a certain small value.

Hence **ˈspirogram**, the tracing produced by a spirograph; **spirographic** *a.*, pertaining to or observed by means of a spirograph; **spiroˈgraphically** *adv.*; **spiˈrography**, the study of respiration by means of a spirograph.

1946 L. N. GAY *Bronchial Asthma* i. 7 (*caption*) Spirographic tracings of Hofbauer. **1956** HINSHAW & GARLAND *Dis. of Chest* vi. 89 Tracings of respiration, sometimes called spirograms, are readily made by means of a calibrated spirometer equipped with a writing device. **1959** *Presse Médicale* No. 47. Suppl. 2/1 Having studied clinically and spirographically a population of 232 patients, authors make first a distinction between three groups according to the intensity of dyspnea. *Ibid.*, Spirography allows effectively to make a distinction between three groups of patients. **1977** *Lancet* 22 Jan. 156/1 (*caption*) Spirogram of habitual hyperventilator showing irregular amplitude and frequency of respiration and sighing tendency. *Ibid.* 26 Mar. 709/1 Their diagnosis of hyperventilation is based on ..a spirographic pattern for which criteria of abnormality are lacking. **1977** *Bull. Exper. Biol. & Med.* LXXXIII. 3 On the basis of indices obtained by the motion-picture spirography method, a definite idea can thus be obtained of the functional state of the apparatus for controlling respiration under different conditions.

spirogyra (spaɪrəʊˈdʒaɪərə). Also **Spiro-**. [mod.L. (H. F. Link in C. G. D. Nees von Esenbeck *Horæ Physicæ Berolinensis* (1820) i. 5), f. SPIRO- + Gr. γῦρός, γῦρά round.] A green filamentous fresh-water alga of the genus of this name.

1875 BENNETT & DYER tr. *Sach's Text-bk. Bot.* II. 220 Each single cell of Spirogyra, like an isolated cell of Closterium, &c., constitutes an individual. **1906** G. F. S. ELLIOT *First Course Pract. Bot.* 57 The joint protoplasm, called the 'zygospore',..begins to divide and form a new Spirogyra. **1937** E. E. STANFORD *Gen. & Econ. Bot.* xiii. 346 Spirogyra..is so abundant, so characteristic, and so readily studied that it commonly passes as a 'characteristic' chlorophyte, which decidedly it is not. **1962** *Listener* 16 Aug. 240/1 There are many other kinds of microscopic organisms,..the desmids, the green strands of Spirogyra, and the rest. **1971** P. CRAMPTON tr. *Heyerdahl's Ra Expeditions* iii. 50 A shallow pool about as big as a washbasin, but completely covered with green spirogyra.

spiroid (ˈspaɪrɔɪd), *a.* [ad. mod.L. *spīroīdēs* (cf. Gr. σπειροειδῶς spirally), f. *spīra* SPIRE *sb.*[3]: see -OID. So F. *spiroide*.] Tending to a spiral form.

1849 HERSCHEL *Outl. Astron.* 468 It would be easy..to trace..the form of the spiroid curve. **1859** MAYNE *Expos. Lex.* 1190/1 *Spiroides*,..resembling a screw: spiroid.

spiroidal (spaɪˈrɔɪdəl), *a.* [f. SPIROID *a.* + -AL.] = SPIROID *a.*

1928 T. C. CHAMBERLIN *Two Solar Families* xiv. 143 If a series of projected bolts were shot forth from a sun in succession toward the star while all were being pulled forward by the star but in different degrees, the train they formed would obviously be curved in a spiroidal manner. **1972** *Nature: Physical Sci.* 6 Nov. 22/1 The majority of the crystals were acicular or whisker-like although a few were spiroidal.

spiroil (ˈspaɪrəʊɪl). *Chem.* Also **spiroile, spiroyl**. [ad. F. *spiroyle*, irreg. f. mod.L. *Spiræa* SPIRÆA: see -YL.] (See quots.)

1838 T. THOMSON *Chem. Org. Bodies* 614 This is what has induced M. Löwig to consider the acid or oil as a compound of 1 atom hydrogen with the compound base $C^{12} H^{5} O^{4}$, to which he has given the name of spiroil. **1841** BRANDE *Chem.* (ed. 5) 1251 Chloride of spiroile... Iodide of spiroile. **1868** WATTS *Dict. Chem.*, *Spiroyl*, Löwig's name for the radicle $C^{7} H^{5} O^{2}$ (more generally called *salicyl*, or *salicosyl*), which may be supposed to exist in oil of spiræa.

Hence **ˈspiroilate, spiˈroilic** *a.*, **ˈspiroilide, ˈspiroilous** *a.*

1849 CRAIG, **Spiroilate*, a compound of spiroilic acid and a base. **1837** R. D. THOMSON in *Brit. Annual* 346 *Spiroilic acid. **1841** BRANDE *Chem.* (ed. 5) 1251 A crystallized product ..which Löwig terms spiroilic acid. **1868** WATTS *Dict. Chem.*, *Spiroylic acid*, syn. with Salicylic Acid. **1838** T. THOMSON *Chem. Org. Bodies* 615 A *spiroilide of potassium was formed. When this spiroilide is treated with muriatic acid [etc.]. **1841** BRANDE *Chem.* (ed. 5) 1251 Evolving hydrogen and producing a spiroilide of potassium. **1868** WATTS *Dict. Chem.*, **Spiroylous acid*, syn. with *Salicylol*.

† **spirol**[1]. *Obs.*$^{-1}$ [ad. obs. F. *spirole*.] A kind of cannon (see quot.).

1653 URQUHART *Rabelais* I. xlvii. 209 Long pieces of Artillery called Basilisks, and smaller sized ones, known by the name of spirols.

ˈspirol[2]. *Chem.* (See quot. and SPIROIL.)

1868 WATTS *Dict. Chem.*, *Spirol*, a name applied to phenylic alcohol, because it may be obtained from spiroylic (salicylic) acid, in the same way as benzol from benzoic acid.

spirolactone (spaɪrəʊˈlæktəʊn). *Chem.* and *Pharm.* [f. SPIRO- 2 + LACTONE 2.] Any spirane in which one of the rings is a lactone; *spec.* any of the series of steroid derivatives to which spironolactone belongs.

1958 *Canad. Med. Assoc. Jrnl.* LXXIX. 883/1 The administration of Spirolactone results in a persistent and significant increase in sodium excretion. **1959** *Jrnl. Org. Chem.* XXIV. 743/1 The spirolactone side chain was built onto a steriod nucleus containing an aromatic A ring. **1961** *Lancet* 16 Sept. 618/2 With the development of the 17-spirolactones, which are aldosterone antagonists, a new method has become available for investigating possible cases of primary aldosteronism. **1970** PASSMORE & ROBSON *Compan. Med. Stud.* II. xi. 10/1 The main reason for believing that spirolactones are aldosterone antagonists is that they reverse all the renal effects of aldosterone.

spirometer (spaɪˈrɒmɪtə(r)). [Irreg. f. L. *spīrāre* to breathe: see -OMETER.] An instrument for measuring the breathing power of the lungs.

1846 HUTCHINSON in *Medico-Chirurg. Trans.* XXIX. 146 General and practical deductions, to detect disease by the spirometer, with the method of its application. **1858** O. W. HOLMES *Aut. Breakf.-t.* (1883) 206 Estimating height, weight, force by the dynamometer and the spirometer. **1877** M. FOSTER *Physiol.* II. ii. (1878) 255 It may be measured by a modification of a gas meter called a spirometer.

Hence **spiroˈmetric, spiroˈmetrical** *adjs.*

1887 *Jrnl. Education* No. 210. 29 The distance naturally separating them..on the spirometric register. **1887** C. DENISON *Pref. Climate Consumption* 9 The large spiro-metrical records of those who live at great elevations. **1896** *Allbutt's Syst. Med.* I. 310 (a) Increase of chest circumference, (b) increase of spirometric capacity.

spirometry (spaɪˈrɒmɪtrɪ). [See prec. and -METRY.] Measurement of breathing-power or lung-capacity; the use of the spirometer.

1859 in MAYNE *Expos. Lex.* 1190/1. **1862** H. W. FULLER *Dis. Chest* 25 Spirometry, which has received its fullest development from Dr. Hutchinson. **1890** *Lancet* 9 Aug. 294/2 A number of observations in spirometry.

spironolactone (ˌspaɪərənəʊˈlæktəʊn). *Pharm.* [f. SPIROLACTONE.] A steroid spirolactone derivative, $C_{24}H_{32}O_4S$, which is an aldosterone antagonist, increasing sodium excretion, and is used esp. in the treatment of œdema and hypertension associated with hyperaldosteronism.

1960 *Austral. Ann. Med.* IX. 188/1 In the present paper we describe the use of a similar drug, spironolactone ('SC 9420', 'Aldactone', Searle). **1961** *Lancet* 2 Sept. 528/2 Spironolactone 100 mg. four times daily definitely improved six out of seven myasthenic patients. **1974** R. M. KIRK et al. *Surgery* vii. 146 Treatment with diuretics or spironolactone, and dietary salt restriction, help to reduce the accumulation of fluid. **1977** *Lancet* 17 Sept. 600/2 Spironolactone relieved muscle fatigue in paramyotonia congenita—an effect possibly mediated by the accompanying hyperkalæmia.

spiroplasma (ˈspaɪərəʊplæzmə). *Biol.* [mod.L., f. SPIRO + PLASMA.] Any of a group of pathogenic prokaryotes lacking a cell wall and related to the mycoplasmas, but characterized by their helical structure and rotatory movement.

1973 DAVIS & WORLEY in *Phytopathology* LXIII. 407/1 In order to distinguish the organism from previously described species and to avoid possible inappropriate use of the term 'mycoplasmalike',..we are coining the term spiroplasma. **1976** *Ann. Rev. Microbiol.* XXX. 181 More recently, spiroplasmas have been cultivated from corn plants infected with corn stunt disease.

spirous (ˈspaɪərəs), *a. rare.* [f. SPIRE *sb.*[1]] Spire-shaped; spiry.

1841 *Florist's Jrnl.* (1846) II. 278 *Epidendrum selligerum* (side-saddle)... The flowers spirous, upright.

spirr, obs. form of SPEER *v.*[1]

† **spirt**, *sb.*[1] *Obs.* Also 5 **spyrt**, 6 **spert(e**. [Reduced form of SPIRIT.] = SPIRIT *sb.*, in various senses.

1447 BOKENHAM *Seyntys* (Roxb.) 9 The margaryte if of blood descende,..many spyrtys it counfortyth souvereynly. **1541** R. COPLAND *Galyen's Terap.* 2 H ij b, Yf some thing passe in the myddes of the way of the spert, y[t] is the ayre, forth w[t] it bredeth the coughe. **1607** HIERON *Wks.* I. 569 That item which the Spirt of God giueth by the prophet. *a* **1619** FOTHERBY *Atheom.* II. xiv. §4 (1622) 357 Euery Poet is inspired, with a kind of heauenly spirt. **1782** ELPHINSTON *Martial* XII. ccxi. [= III. xcvii.] 465 Let not Snow..chill this bundle of spirt [L. *hunc libellum*].

spirt (spɜːt), *sb.*^{2} Also 6 spyrt. [Of obscure origin: cf. SPURT *sb.*^{1}]
†**1. a.** A brief period of time; a short space. *Obs.*
c1550 WEVER *Lusty Juv.* D iij, I wil play a spyrt, why should I not? 1582 STANYHURST *Æneis* III. (Arb.) 85 Heere for a spirt [they] linger, no good opportunitye scaping. 1612 SHELTON *Quix.* I. i. (1620) I. 2 The Spirts that he was idle (which was the longer part of the Year).
†**b.** A short distance. *Obs.*$^{-1}$
a1668 LASSELS *Voy. Italy* I. 85, I must except the Strada Noua here, which for a spirt surpasseth all the streets I ever saw any where else.
2. *Naut.* A short or slight spell *of* wind.
1726 SHELVOCKE *Voy. round World* 5 A small spirt of wind would now run us into fair weather. 1799 *Naval Chron.* I. 440 Orders came down.. to sail from Cawsand Bay the first spirt of wind. 1805 *Ibid.* XIII. 243 She sails the first spirit of Wind. 1837 T. HOOK *Jack Brag* xx, I think we shall have a spirit of wind presently.
3. A sudden outbreak or brief spell of activity or exertion; a spurt.
1829 GEN. P. THOMSON *Exerc.* (1842) I. 55 It would undoubtedly cause a spirt of employment and felicity in Ireland. But as soon as this spirt was over [etc.]. 1844 DICKENS *Mart. Chuz.* iv, The strife,.. after breaking out afresh some twice or thrice in certain inconsiderable spirts and dashes, died away in silence. 1856 'STONEHENGE' *Brit. Rural Sports* II. II. ii. 386/1 On the days intervening between the gallops a very short and quick spirt will serve to freshen the horse's wind. 1883 'ANNIE THOMAS' *Mod. Housewife* 142 That dinner's only a spirt, you know.

spirt, *sb.*^{3} Now *dial.* [Metathetic form of SPRIT *sb.* Cf. SPURT *sb.*^{2}] A sprout or shoot.
1634 HOLLAND *Pliny* I. 446 These Filberds.. within their belly.. haue in the mids a little chit or spirt [1601 spurt] as if it were a nauill. 1882- in western dial. glossaries (Warw., Worc., Heref.).

spirt (spɜːt), *sb.*^{4} [f. SPIRT *v.*^{1} Cf. SPURT *sb.*^{3}]
1. A jet or slender spout of water or other liquid.
1716 GAY *Trivia* III. 106 Water, dash'd from fishy Stalls, shall stain His hapless Coat with Spirts of scaly Rain. 1840 BROWNING *Sordello* IV. 135 In the centre spreads.. A laver, broad and shallow, one bright spirt Of water bubbles in. 1865 DICKENS *Mut. Fr.* IV. i, A small spirt of blood burst from his nose. 1879 J. BURROUGHS *Locusts* 120 There was a spirt or two of rain.
b. The sound made by a jet of liquid.
1874 T. HARDY *Far fr. Mad. Crowd* iii. I. 26 Soon a soft spirt, alternating with a loud spirt, came in regular succession from within the shed.
2. A sudden jet of fire, or puff of smoke.
1851 HAWTHORNE *Snow Image* (1879) 111 Looking at the little spirts of fire. 1871 MEREDITH *H. Richmond* xxix, He sent out quick spirts of smoke rolling into big volumes. 1878 BROWNING *Poets Croisic* 21 Spirt and spirt Of fire from our brave billet's either edge.
fig. 1879 BROWNING *Ivan Ivanovitch* 23 Man's inch of masterdom,—spot of life, spirt of fire,—To star the dark and dread.

spirt (spɜːt), *v.*^{1} [Of obscure origin: cf. MHG. and G. dial. *spirzen* to spit, Icel. (17th c.) *spirta* (fig.) to utter. The form SPURT *v.*^{1} is recorded a little earlier.]
1. *intr.* Of liquids (or small objects): To spring or burst out in a small quantity but with some force; to issue in a jet.
1582 STANYHURST *Æneis* III. (Arb.) 71 From that stub lyke-wise foorth spirt drops bluddelye stilling. 1626 BACON *Sylva* §314 Beer or ale while it is new and full of Spirit (so that it Spirteth when the Stopple is taken forth). 1668 WILKINS *Real Char.* 105 That whose seed when ripe will spirt out of the cod. 1692 RAY *Disc.* I. iii. (1693) 42 The water breaks forth with great force,.. spirting several fathoms high. 1728 POPE *Dunc.* II. 178 Thus the small jett.. Spirts in the gardner's eyes who turns the cock. 1758 REID tr. *Macquer's Chym.* I. 136 This spirts out in fine small jets. 1827 SCOTT *Surg. Dau.* xiv, Upon whose muslin robe a part of the victim's blood had spirted. 1844 THACKERAY *Contrib. to Punch* Wks. 1898 VI. 74 His coat and waistcoat buttons spirt violently off his garments. 1905 J. B. FIRTH *Highways Derbyshire* xxv. 369 Through the sluices at the sides the water was spirting gaily.
fig. c1826 LANDOR *Imag. Conv.* Wks. 1846 I. 190 Wit vibrates and spirts.
2. *trans.* To send out in a jet or slender rapid stream; to squirt.
1582 STANYHURST *Æneis* II. (Arb.) 59 [The adder] with toonge three forcked furth spirts fyre freshlye regendred. 1625 PURCHAS *Pilgrims* II. 1827 The Rose water that was spirted by little young Jewes. 1635 J. HAYWARD tr. *Biondi's Banish'd Virg.* 203 Others were busied in spirting and sprinkling water in her face. 1697 DRYDEN *Virg. Georg.* IV. 622 His finny Flocks.. rowling round him, spirt the bitter Sea. 1796 MME. D'ARBLAY *Camilla* I. 149 The same gentleman.. was now spirting lavender water all about him. 1817 KIRBY & SP. *Entomol.* xvii. (1818) II. 73 A pair [of ants] .. rearing upon their hind-legs mutually spirt their acid. 1843 THACKERAY *Irish Sk. Bk.* ii, A tablecloth, over which a waiter has just spirted a pint of obstreperous cider. 1895 SIR H. MAXWELL *Duke Britain* v. 72 Fill your mouth with water and spirt it into the opening.
fig. 1582 STANYHURST *Æneis* I. (Arb.) 35 In that od Isle raigneth, from Troyblud spirted, Acestes. 1628 WITHER *Brit. Rememb.* II. 2115 Lest I should spirt a blot So black, as that it would not be forgot In future Ages. a1661 FULLER *Worthies, Linc.* II. (1662) 158, I find one Pen spirting ink upon him. 1860 THACKERAY *Round. Papers* iii. *Ribbons*, Our fountain of Honour.. has spirted a baronetcy upon two, and bestowed a coronet upon one noble man of letters.
transf. 1857 DICKENS *Dorrit* II. xxx, He spirted it [the hotel-bill] into Mr. Flintwinch's face, when the old man advanced to take it.
b. Const. *forth, out, up.*
1646 SIR T. BROWNE *Pseud. Ep.* 137 Toades are sometimes observed to exclude or spirt out a dark and liquid matter behinde. 1664 POWER *Exp. Philos.* I. 39 The Lamprey hath a fistula.. at the back part of the head, whereat they spirt out water. 1716 GAY *Trivia* II. 144 Oft' the loose Stone spirts up a muddy tide Beneath thy Foot. 1817 KIRBY & SP. *Entomol.* xxi. (1818) II. 239 Sometimes they will even spirt out that liquor. 1826 *Ibid.* III. xxx. 150 Perforated tubercles, which when the animal is molested spirt forth a transparent fluid. 1840 DICKENS *Old C. Shop* xlv, When every chimney spirted up its flame.
3. To knock *out* with something spirted.
1642 FULLER *Holy & Prof. St.* III. v. 162 He that eats cherries with Noblemen shall have his eyes spirted out with the stones.
Hence '**spirted** *ppl. a.*; '**spirting** *vbl. sb.*
1834-6 P. BARLOW in *Encycl. Metrop.* (1845) VIII. 415 Some inconvenience is caused by the spirting. 1847 TENNYSON *Princ.* VII. 187 Red with spirted purple of the vats. 1860 O. W. HOLMES *Prof. Breakf. T.* xii, We all like the spirting up of a fountain.

spirt, *v.*^{2} Now *dial.* [Metathetic form of SPRIT *v.* Cf. SPURT *v.*^{2}] *intr.* To sprout or germinate, esp. abnormally or unseasonably; †to shoot *up* in growth.
1584-5 in Miss Jackson *Shropshire Word-bk.* (1879) 403 Their corne.. was layd flat to the grownde, and so by meanes spirtid. 1599 SHAKS. *Hen. V*, III. v. 8 Shall a few Sprayes of vs,.. Our Syens, put in wilde and sauage Stock, Spirt vp so suddenly into the Clouds, And ouer looke their Grafters? 1764 *Warwicksh. Letter* in *Museum Rust.* III. 136 The ears.., in a wet time, will spirt, and so spoil the whole. 1863 in BARNES *Dorset Gloss.* 1879- in western dial. glossaries (Shropsh., Worc., Warw., Glouc.).

spirt (spɜːt), *v.*^{3} [f. SPIRT *sb.*^{2} Cf. SPURT *v.*^{3}] *intr.* To make a spurt; to turn or dart *about* quickly; to exert oneself for a short time.
1599 NASHE *Lenten Stuffe* 53 Our Herring smoker.. spirted ouer seas to Rome with a Pedlers packe of them. 1856 'STONEHENGE' *Brit. Rural Sports* I. III. ix. 216 The short running and quick turning of the rabbits, which spirt about even more sharply than hares. 1857 HUGHES *Tom Brown* I. iv, They comes out about twice or three times a week, and spirts a mile alongside of us.

spirting ('spɜːtɪŋ), *ppl. a.* [f. SPIRT *v.*^{1}]
1. That spirts (in *trans.* or *intr.* senses).
1583 MELBANCKE *Philotimus* N iv, All beuenimd is her spirting tongue. 1648 HERRICK *Hesper., Country-life* I. 48 Making thy peace with Heav'n.., With holy-meale and spirting salt. 1656 W. DU GARD tr. *Comenius' Gate Lat. Unl.* 137 With a spirting quill. 1792 A. YOUNG *Trav. France* 274 With the addition of some spirting *jets d'eau.* 1865 DICKENS *Mut. Fr.* I. x, The lady has prodded little spirting holes in the damp sand before her with her parasol.
b. *spirting cucumber*: see CUCUMBER 3.
1578 LYTE *Dodoens* III. xl. 372 Of the wilde spirting Cucumbre. 1611 COTGR., *Concombre sauvage*, the wild Cowcumber, Spirting Cowcumber, Touch-me-not. 1741 *Compl. Fam.-Piece* II. iii. 362 You may now sow, in natural Ground, the wild spirting Cucumber. 1760 J. LEE *Introd. Bot.* App. 328 Spirting Cucumber, *Momordica.* 1830 LINDLEY *Nat. Syst. Bot.* 193 The perennial roots of all the order appear to contain similar bitter drastic virtues, especially that of the.. Spirting Cucumber.
2. Resembling that made by spirts of liquid.
1594 NASHE *Unfort. Trav.* Wks. (Grosart) V. 121 Inchained chirping birds, whose throates.. made a spirting sound.

spirtle ('spɜːt(ə)l), *sb.* [Cf. next.] A small spirt or jet; a sprinkle.
1881 in EVANS *Leic. Gloss.* 251. 1892 KIPLING *Barrack-r. Ballads* 115 Out of the grass, on a sudden, broke A spirtle of fire, a whorl of smoke.

spirtle ('spɜːt(ə)l), *v.* Now *dial.* Also 7 spertle. [f. SPIRT *v.*^{1} + -LE.]
1. *trans.* To sprinkle, spatter, or splash *with* something. Also *fig.*
1603 DRAYTON *Odes* (1619) xi. 28, I creepe behind the Time From spertling [= being spirtled] with their Crime. 1610-1 J. DAVIES (Heref.) *Paper's Compl.* Wks. (Grosart) II. 76/1 He scraped mee With Pens that spirtled me with Villany. 1854- in midland and western glossaries.
2. To cause to spatter or splash; to disperse in small particles.
1612 DRAYTON *Poly-olb.* ii. 283 The braines and mingled blood were spertled on the wall. 1704 *Phil. Trans.* XXV. 1786, I suppose from some of the fouled Oyl of the Pump spirtled on the Wheels. 1713 DERHAM *Phys.-Theol.* I. iv. 34 The Terraqueous Globe.. would by the centrifugal force of that Motion, be soon dissipated, and spirtled into the circumambient Space. 1749 W. ELLIS *Sheph. Guide* 117 A sharp rain that so bashes the earth and spirtles it upon the grass as to cause a rot on.. sheep.
3. *intr.* To become dispersed or scattered.
1725 N. ROBINSON *Th. Physick* 7 Without which Power this Globe of ours would spirtle into ten thousand Millions of Pieces.

spirt-net. Now *dial.* [? f. SPERT I.] (See quots.)
1686 BLOME *Gentl. Recreat.* II. 200/2 Fishing with a Spirt-Net,.. being a common sort of Net, generally made with indifferent Meshes, and so it may do well for small Fish as well as for great. 1886 ELWORTHY *W. Somerset Word-bk.* 700 *Spirt-net*, a kind of fishing net... It is a shallow bag in shape, tapering off to what is called a 'purse', made with a much finer mesh.

‖**Spirula** ('spaɪrjʊlə). *Zool.* [mod.L., dim. of L. *spīra* SPIRE *sb.*^{3}] A genus of cephalopods having a flat spiral shell in the hinder part of the body; an animal of this genus, or one of the shells.
1835-6 *Todd's Cycl. Anat.* I. 546/2 The shell of the Spirula is.. convoluted on one plane, with the whorls disjoined. 1851 WOODWARD *Mollusca* I. 13 The argonaut, with his relative the spirula, both carnivorous. 1881 *Cassell's Nat. Hist.* V. 181 The beautiful pearly-white shell known as Spirula.
So '**spirule.** [Cf. F. *spirule.*]
1851 MARY ROBERTS *Mollusca* 57 The Spirule, like the Nautilus, has a chambered, siphonated shell.

spiry ('spaɪərɪ), *a.*^{1} Also 7 spirie. [f. SPIRE *sb.*^{1}]
1. Of grass or other plants, stems, etc.: Forming slender pointed shoots.
1602 CAREW *Cornwall* 56 The middle part of the Shire.. beareth Heath and Spirie Grasse. 1626 BACON *Sylva* §592 As for the Leaues, their Density appeareth, in that, either they are Smooth and Shining,.. Or in that they are Hard and Spiry. 1703 ROWE *Ulyss.* II. i, When ev'ry spiry Grass, and painted Flow'r, Is hung with pearly Drops of Heav'nly Rain. 1764 *Museum Rust.* I. 453 The oat-stubble, the sedge, or long lowland spiry grass. 1794 GISBORNE *Walks in Forest* vi. (1796) 101 Spiry rushes in divergent files Rise fledged with rime. 1805-6 CARY *Dante, Inf.* II. 129 As florets.. Rise all unfolded on their spiry stems. 1834 PRINGLE *Afr. Sk.* vii. 232 Waving with a crop of long spiry grass. 1865 *Cornh. Mag.* May 629 The spiry reed, that bare.. The sponge of vinegar and gall.
b. Of trees: Rising in a slender tapering form without much branching.
1664 EVELYN *Pomona* viii. 20 If the top prove spiry, or the fruit unkind, then the due remedy must be in re-graffing. 1712 POPE *Messiah* 74 Waste sandy Vallies.. The spiry Fir and shapely Box adorn. 1740 DYER *Ruins Rome* 54 Thro' spiry cypress groves, and tow'ring pine. 1784 COWPER *Task* III. 570 The spiry myrtle.. Shines there, and flourishes. 1814 WORDSW. *Laodamia* 169 A knot of spiry trees for ages grew From out the tomb. 1843 tr. *Custine's Empire of Czar* II. 279 The marshes with their spiry pines and stunted birches. 1879 STEVENSON *Trav. Cevennes* 125 A range of meadows, set with spiry poplars.
Comb. 1833 LOUDON *Encycl. Archit.* §105 Firs, or pines, or other spiry topped trees.
2. Having the characteristic form of a spire; tapering up to a point: **a.** Of parts of buildings.
1664 EVELYN tr. *Freart's Archit.* 140 Pinnæ and Battlements were made sometimes more Sharp, Towring or Spiry. 1703 [R. NEVE] *City & C. Purchaser* 2 Sharp and spiry Battlements, or Pinacles. a1748 THOMSON *Hymn Solitude* vii, I just may cast my careless eyes Where London's spiry turrets rise. 1803 JANE PORTER *Thaddeus* (1826) III. xi. 244 The spiry aisles of Harrowby-Abbey were discernible through the mist. 1823 GIFFORD in *Q. Rev.* XXIX. 369 The village church, with its spiry steeple.
b. Of hills, rocks, etc.
1694 E. CHAMBERLAYNE *Pres. St. Eng.* (ed. 18) I. 35 Carnarvanshire.., with spiry Hills, the highest in all Wales. 1786 W. GILPIN *Mount. & Lakes Cumberland* II. 229 A solitary rock, tho spiry, has often a good effect. 1811 PINKERTON *Mod. Geogr.* (ed. 3) 281 The spiry pinnacles of rock that rear themselves from among the perpetual snows .. of the higher Alps. 1840 F. D. BENNETT *Whaling Voy.* II. 45 Two spiry cliffs.. bound the lake on opposite sides. 1889 *Science-Gossip* XXV. 205/1 The sea.. leaving on the outskirts.. numerous stacks, islets, and spiry rocks.
c. In miscellaneous applications.
1716 GAY *Trivia* III. 358 The spiry Flames now lift aloft their Heads. 1725 POPE *Odyss.* x. 175 A stream of curling smoke, ascending blue, And spiry tops. 1789 E. DARWIN *Bot. Gard.* (1791) I. 99 Loud o'er the camp the Fiend of Famine shrieks,.. High-poised in air her spiry neck she bends. 1805 J. LUCCOCK *Nature Wool* 306 Some samples.. were very kempy, with coarse and spiry tops to the staple. 1819 H. BUSK *Vestriad* v. 468 Spiry lance of dark and polish'd wood. 1871 B. TAYLOR *Faust* (1875) II. v. 283 Soon the climbing spiry flashes Set the tree-tops in a glow.
3. Of form: Resembling that of a spire.
1777 G. FORSTER *Voy. round World* I. 253 The mountains, clothed with forests, rose majestic in various spiry forms. 1789 CHARLOTTE SMITH *Ethelinde* (1814) V. 214 A group of yew and cypress relieved, by their spiry form, the more solid and regular mass of stone. 1842 SELBY *Brit. Forest Trees* 521 When young, the Cedar presents a pyramidal or spiry form. 1865 GEIKIE *Scen. & Geol. Scotl.* viii. 219 The height and the angular spiry forms of the mountain ridges.
4. Of places: Full of spires; spire-crowned.
1728-46 THOMSON *Spring* 952 Spiry towns by surging columns mark'd Of household smoke. 1756 DYER *Fleece* I. 50 The leas And ruddy tilth which spiry Ross beholds. 1843 RUSKIN *Mod. Paint.* (1860) V. VIII. iv. §10. 189 The group of spires, without it, would not.. give a proper impression of Lausanne, as a spiry place. 1889 STEVENSON *Edinburgh* 180 The spiry habitable city.
5. *slang.* Highly distinguished.
1825 T. HOOK *Sayings* Ser. II. I. 229 Mr. Abberly used to think it quite spiry to wear a white hat and sit upon the coach-box and drive them himself on Sundays.
6. Characterized by slenderness or slimness of growth or form.
1853 R. S. SURTEES *Sponge's Sp. Tour* xx. 99 The light spiry ease of an animal full of strength and running. 1856 'STONEHENGE' *Brit. Rural Sports* I. XI. i. 97/1 It would be impossible.. to distinguish a large spiry foxhound from one of the smallest and lightest of her Majesty's beautiful pack [of staghounds].

spiry ('spaɪrɪ), *a.*^{2} [f. SPIRE *sb.*^{3}] Curving or coiling in spirals.
1676 DRYDEN *State Innoc.* IV. i, Hid in the spiry volumes of the snake, I lurked within the covert of a brake. 1697 —— *Virg. Georg.* I. 334 Around our Pole the spiry Dragon glides. 1725 POPE *Odyss.* IV. 619 On spiry volumes there a Dragon rides. 1798 SOTHEBY tr. *Wieland's Oberon* (1826) I. 157 Soft

through the ivory flows his gentle breath, And from its spiry folds sweet fairy tones ascend.

† **spiscious**, *a. Obs.*$^{-1}$ [For *spissous*: see SPISS *a.*] Of a thick consistency.

1655 tr. *Sorel's Com. Hist. Francion* III. 54 It could not properly be called a liquor, but rather a certain concreted mist or spiscious Froath.

spise, obs. form of SPICE *sb.* and *v.*

† **spise**, *v. Obs. rare.* Also spyse. [Aphetic form of DESPISE *v.*] *trans.* To despise.

13.. *Seuen Sages* 2311 (W.), Al the werld [will] the spise, Yif thou do bi here [= by her], and lete the wise. *c* **1400** *Destr. Troy* 3889 He spake neuer dispituosly, ne spiset no man. **1435** MISYN *Fire of Love* 44 Þat, vanite spisyd & spurnyd, to trewth vnpartyngly we draw.

spiserie, -orie, obs. forms of SPICERY.

† **spiss**, *a. Obs.* Also 6 spysse, 6–7 spisse. [ad. L. *spiss-us* (whence It. *spesso*, Pg. *espesso*, Sp. *espeso*, OF. *espes*, *espeis*, *espais*, F. *épais*).] Thick, dense, compact, close.

c **1530** *Judic. Urines* I. iii. 9 b, Spisse is thycke. *Ibid.* II. vii. 28 b, And in these maner wyse maye vryne be spysse. **1567** MAPLET *Gr. Forest* 67 The male [plant] is of more spisse or tough branches. **1614** BREREWOOD *Lang. & Relig.* To Rdr., This spisse and dense, yet polished, this copious, yet concise .. Treatise of the variety of Languages. **1658** A. FOX *Würtz' Surg.* III. xvii. 275 Boil these to a spisse Cataplasme. **1670** *Phil. Trans.* V. 1028 This little Chrystalline being of a more spiss consistence then the great one, its refraction is also more strong. **1711** *Ibid.* XXVII. 274, I saw a Spot arise.., and again nearly disappear; and then again appear strong and spiss. **1784** J. KEEBLE *Harmonics* 29 The number of spiss or small intervals.

Hence † **'spissly** *adv.*; † **'spissness**. *Obs.*

1598 FLORIO, *Condensità*, a thicknes, a densitie, a spisnes. *Ibid.*, *Spessezza*, thicknes, spissenes. **1611** COTGR., *Espessement* thickly, spissely, close together. *Ibid.*, *Espesseur*, thicknesse, densitie, spissenesse, closenesse.

† **'spissament.** *Obs. rare*$^{-1}$. [ad. L. *spissāmentum*, f. *spissāre* (see next). Cf. It. *spessamento*, Sp. *espesamiento*.] A thickening substance.

1652 FRENCH *Yorksh. Spa* iv. 46 The body is to be anointed with oyle, with spissaments or thickeners that the quality onely of the cooler be received, and not the substance.

'spissated, *ppl. a. rare.* [f. *spissāt-us*, pa. pple. of L. *spissāre*, f. *spiss-us* SPISS *a.*] Thickened.

1727 BAILEY (vol. II), *Spissated*,.. thickened. *a* **1779** WARBURTON *Div. Legation* II. iv. Wks. 1788 I. 266 The images, which the spiscated [*sic*] juice of poppy presents to the fancy. **1859** MAYNE *Expos. Lex.* 1190 *Spissatus*,.. thickened: spissated.

So **'spissating** *ppl. a.*, thickening. *rare.*

1657 *Physical Dict.* s.v.

† **spi'ssation.** *Obs.*$^{-0}$ [ad. L. *spissātio*.] A thickening (1727 in BAILEY, vol. II).

† **spissative**, *a. Obs.*$^{-1}$ [Cf. prec. and -IVE. So Sp. *espesativo*.] Serving to thicken.

1678 R. R[USSELL] tr. *Geber* II. I. II. i. 38 For Temperate Heat only is Spissative of Humidity.

† **spissed**, *a. Obs. rare.* [f. SPISS *a.*] Thickened, condensed.

1635 HEYWOOD *Hierarchy* III. Comm. 161 The Spissed Fire turnes into thickned Aire; The Aire condenst, to Water makes repaire. *Ibid.* IV. 214 Of such a spissed Substance there's no need.

† **'spissid**, *a. Obs.*$^{-1}$ [f. L. *spiss-us* SPISS *a.* + -ID[1].] Thick.

1781 *Phil. Trans.* LXXI. 375 Around their edges they are environed with a spissid sub-pellucid liquid, which seems to glue them to the branch.

spissitude ('spɪsɪtju:d). [ad. L. *spissitūdo*, f. *spissus* SPISS *a.* Cf. It. *spessitudine*.] Density, thickness, compactness.

c **1440** *Pallad. on Husb.* XII. 479 With walkers cley is salt so doon therto, The spissitude of hit to ha fordone. **1601** HOLLAND *Pliny* I. 611 For all the spissitude and thicknesse that they seeme to haue, they admit gently our sight to pierce into their bottome. **1658** A. FOX *Würtz' Surg.* II. xiv. 103 In the Joynt must not remain any spissitude or grossness when it is almost healed. **1682** H. MORE *Annot. Glanvill's Lux O.* 213 Spirits may have a contracted spissitude which is not Penetrable. **1720** HALLEY in *Phil. Trans.* XXXI. 3 The great strength of their native Light, forming the resemblance of a Body, when it is nothing else but the spissitude of their Rays. **1756** P. BROWNE *Jamaica* 235 It may be given with success in most diseases arising from a lentor or spissitude of the juices. **1822–7** GOOD *Study Med.* (1829) II. 17 The relative spissitude.. ascribed to the elastic and muscular arterial coats. **1839** URE *Dict. Arts* 927 To produce a proper spissitude of stuff for making paper.

So † **'spissity** [ad. L. *spissitās*]. *Obs.*$^{-0}$

1623 COCKERAM i, *Spissitie*, thicknesse. [Also in Blount, Phillips, etc.]

† **'spissy**, *a. Obs. rare.* [f. L. *spiss-us* SPISS *a.*] Dense, compact.

1570 LEVINS *Manip.* 108 Spissy, massy, *spissus*. **1637** N. WHITING *Albino & Bellama, Vind. Poesy* H 7 The spissye aire.. Turnes into sea, earth's made a thickned water. **1683** PETTUS *Fleta Min.* I. (1686) 101 Sometimes with the digg'd Gold.. there breaks a small grey spissy Oar.

spit, *sb.*[1] Forms: α. 1 spitu, 2–4 (6 *Sc.*) spite, 3, 5 spyte. β. 4–6 spete, 5 speete, 6 speet; *Sc.* 5–7 speit (6 speite, speitt), 6 speat (9 speate), 8–9 speet. γ. 4–6 spet, 5 spette. δ. 4–6 spitte, 6–8 spitt, 5– spit; 5–6 spytt(e, 6 spyt. [OE. *spitu*, = MDu. *spit*, *spet* (Flem., Du., WFris. *spit*), MLG. *spit* (*spyt*), *spet* (LG. *spit*, *spet*, *speet*, etc.), OHG. and MHG. *spiz* (obs. G. *spisz*, *spiss*, etc.; G. *spiess*); MSw. *spit* (Sw. *spett*) and Da. *spid* are from LG. By adoption into Romanic the word appears as It. (Naples dial.) *spito*, Sp. and Pg. *espeto* spit, F. *épois* (pl.) the points of a deer's horn.]

1. a. A cooking implement consisting of a slender sharp-pointed rod of metal or wood, used for thrusting into or through meat which is to be roasted at a fire; a broach.

α. *c* **1000** ÆLFRIC *Gram.* xi. (Z.) 80 *Ueru*, spitu. *Ibid.* xiv. 89 *Ueribus*, spitum. *a* **1100** in Assmann *Ags. Hom.* xv. 39 Sumne [heo] mid spiten betweon felle & flæsce þurhwræcon. **11..** *Voc.* in Wr.-Wülcker 548 *Ueru*, spite. *c* **1290** *S. Eng. Leg.* I. 208 Some op-on grediles of Ire i-rostede weren also, Some ase gyes, þe spites of Ire þoruȝ-out heom i-do. **1297** R. GLOUC. (Rolls) 4213 [He had] yspited him þoru out mid an yrene spite & rostede in þis grete fur. *c* **1340** *Nominale* (Skeat) 491 *Broche, luche et esquele*, Spite, ladul and dissch. *a* **1400** *Octouian* 122 The kokes knaue, that turneth the spyte. *c* **1440** *Promp. Parv.* 469 Spyte, for rostynge,.. *veru.* **1480** CAXTON *Chron. Eng.* ccxv. 202 They toke a spyte of coper brennyng and put it in to his body. **1596** DALRYMPLE tr. *Leslie's Hist. Scot.* I. 287 Rosting at the fyre, vpon a spite of trie.

β. *a* **1300** *Body & Soul* in *Map's Poems* (Camden) 334 Thine cokes snelle, that scholden.. greithe thi mete, With spetes. *c* **1400** *Brut* (1906) 253 [They] toke a spete of Copur brennyng, & put hit.. into his body. *c* **1430** *Two Cookery-bks.* 8 Put þe porke on a fayre spete, an rost it half y-now. **1513** DOUGLAS *Æneid* V. ii. 117 Sum vthir.. the colis hett Wndir the speitis swakkis. **1538** in *Lett. Suppress. Monast.* (Camden) 194, ij gret brasse pottys,.. spetys, pannys. **1676** in Macintosh *Anc. Rec. Kirkwall* (1892) 78 Ane pair of long caces [*read* raxes] and ane speit. **1679** J. SOMERVILLE *Mem. Somervilles* (1815) I. 240 When any persones of qualitie wer to be with him, he used to wryte in the postscript of his letters, Speates and Raxes. **1747** in *Nairne Peerage Evid.* (1874) 80 Three speets one shilling sixpence. **1824** SCOTT *Ep. to J. G. Lockhart* 42 *Speates and raxes* ere five [o'clock] for a famishing guest, sir.

γ. **1392** *Earl Derby's Exp.* (Camden) 205, vj spets et meremris pro rakks. **1483** *Cath. Angl.* 355/2 A Spette of flesche, *verutum.* **1559** *Bury Wills* (Camden) 153 A skommer, a spet, a gredyron. **1564** *Wills & Inv. N.C.* (Surtees, 1835) 219 Tongs, poore, shouell, spet, and that belongs thervnto.

δ. **1391** *Earl Derby's Exp.* (Camden) 102 Pro iiij magnis spittes longis, et ij paruis spittes. *c* **1420** *Liber Cocorum* (1862) 13 Rost hit afterwarde.., then serve thou may Hit forthe with spit. **1495** *Nottingham Rec.* III. 38 Unum spytte cum uno cobberd. **1540** *Test. Ebor.* (Surtees) VI. 119 The gretest yron spit that I have. **1553** EDEN *Treat. New Ind.* (Arb.) 30 They rosted also mans fleshe vpon spyttes. **1607** SHAKS. *Cor.* IV. iv. 5 Least that thy Wiues with Spits, and Boyes with stones In puny Battell slay me. **1671** MILTON *P.R.* II. 343 Fowl of game, In pastry built, or from the spit. **1710** PALMER *Proverbs* 107 It ends with poison in the cup, or with the spit in his guts. **1740** SOMERVILLE *Hobbinol.* II. 131 A Spit he seiz'd, Just reeking from the fat Surloyn. **1809** MALKIN *Gil Blas* IX. ix. ¶5 We have.. wherewithal to keep the spit and the spigot in exercise. **1848** LYTTON *Harold* II. i, The meats were not placed on the table, but served upon small spits. **1870** BRYANT *Iliad* I. I. 25 Transfixed with spits, And roasted with nice care.

fig. **1607** HIERON *Wks.* I. 413 Thrust through with a spit of reproch.

Comb. **1617** MINSHEU *Ductor*, A Spitter, a yong male Deere, that beginnes to haue his hornes grow vp sharpe spitwise.

b. *to beat* (etc.)..*with the spit*, to treat with unexpected harshness (following upon kindly usage or hospitality). Now only *dial.* (in *transf.* use).

1553 T. WILSON *Rhet.* 72 b, Suche are not to be lyked that geue a man a shoulder of mutton, and breake his heade with the spitte when thei haue doen. **1584** GREENE *Arbasto* Wks. (Grosart) III. 214 Thou art bidden to the feast by loue, and art beaten with the spit by beauty. **1674-** [see ROAST MEAT 2 c]. **1686** WOOD *Life* (O.H.S.) III. 186 Din'd at the College. [*note*] 'Gave me roast-meat and beat me with the spit.' **1690** W. WALKER *Idiomat. Anglo-Lat.* 43 To bid one to roast and beat him with the spit. **1876** ROBINSON *Whitby Gloss.* 182/1 'Nevver invite a friend to a roast and then beat him with the spit,' do not confer a favor and then make the obligation felt.

c. The contents of a spit. *rare*$^{-1}$.

1634 SIR T. HERBERT *Trav.* 150 They have Camell or Mutton cut in mammocks or small bits put vpon scuers.. rosted in the fire; of this they sell three or foure spits for two pence.

† **2. a.** A fin-spine of a fish. *Obs.*$^{-1}$

c **1205** LAY. 21329 He.. bihaldeð hu ligeð i þan stræme stelene fisces;.. þer fleoteð heore spiten swulc hit spæren weoren.

† **b.** The point *of* a spear. *Obs.*

c **1450** *Cast. Persev.* 1400 in *Macro Plays.* With spete of spere to þee I spynne; Goddis lawys to þee I lerne.

† **3.** A straight horizontal stroke used as a mark in books; = OBELISK *sb.* 2. *Obs.*

1388 WYCLIF *Esth.* x. 3 Which chapitre we bi oure custom han bifor markid with a spite. **1583** [see OBELISK *sb.* 2]. **1610** HEALEY *St. Aug. Citie of God* 733 The booke is not corrected but rather corrupted by those asteriskes, and spits. **1627** BP. HALL *Epist.* II. v. 303 Either your stars or your spits shall be welcome to my margent.

4. † **a.** A slender or sharp-pointed rod. *Obs.*

1485 *Naval Acc. Hen. VII* (1896) 51 Merlyng Irenes, iiij, Spyttes of Iron, j, Canne hokes, ij. **1577** HARRISON *England* 91 b/1 In sundry parts of Lancasshyre.. the people go.. into their Fennes and Marises with long spittes, which they dashe here and there.. into the grounde.

b. *Printing.* An iron rod carrying the wheel by which the carriage of a hand-press is run out or in.

1728 CHAMBERS *Cycl.* s.v. *Printing*, Under the Carriage is fix'd a small piece of Iron call'd the Spit, with a double Wheel in the middle. **1808** STOWER *Printer's Gram.* 323 The axis, or spit, is a straight bar of iron,.. about three inches longer than the whole breadth of the carriage. **1833** J. HOLLAND *Manuf. Metal* II. 210 The handle [of the rounce] .. was attached to a rod which crossed the platten; this rod was connected with the spit by means of machinery.

c. A thatching-peg. (Cf. BROACH *sb.*[1] 5.)

1833 LOUDON *Encycl. Archit* §122 These are fastened to the thatch, by staples, or spits, or broaches. **1901** *N. & Q.* 9th Ser. VIII. 178 The owner thought I meant the thatch-pegs, which held the thatch down, so he said, 'Speets'.

d. A rod or skewer on which fish are strung and hung up to dry. (Cf. BROACH *sb.*[1] 2 b.)

1833 LOUDON *Encycl. Archit.* §739 In the neighbourhood of Aberdeen, and in various places in the north of Scotland, haddocks are strung up on rods called spits. **1865** W. WHITE *E. Eng.* I. 146 These open partitions or racks are called 'loves'. They support the speets, which are sticks or laths, long enough to lie across from one to the other. **1883** R. HALDANE *Workshop Rec.* Ser. II. 443 Each fish (herring) is then threaded through the gills, on long thin spits holding 25 each.

e. A shuttle-pin.

1875 KNIGHT *Dict. Mech.* 2279.

f. An instrument used by Customs officers for probing and examining cargo.

1925 *Chambers's Jrnl.* 19 Sept. 668/1 A barbed 'spit' is used for examining cotton, wool, and various coarse goods, so that a portion of the interior may be drawn out. A flat, wooden 'spit' is used in the examination of rolls of carpet, cloth, linoleum... A short, fine 'spit' is used for probing the stuffing and packing in and around furniture. **1970** M. GREENER *Penguin Dict. Commerce* 310 *Spit*, a weapon used by Customs authorities to discover whether dutiable goods are hidden in other cargo.

5. A sword. (Chiefly contemptuous.)

1642 in Hazl. *E.P.P.* IV. 316 So that the vapour is all frenchified, With out-stucke bomm, straight breech, and spit at side. **1681** OTWAY *Soldier's Fort.* II. i, I know five or six more of the same stamp; that never came abroad without terrible long Spits by their sides. **1733** FIELDING *Don Quix. in Eng.* II. v, Throw by your spit, sir; throw by your spit, and I don't fear you. **1749** —— *Tom Jones* XV. v, Don't think I am afraid of such a fellow as thee art! because [thou] hast got a spit there dangling at thy side. **1785** GROSE *Dict. Vulgar T.*, *Spit*, a sword. **1871** B. TAYLOR *Faust* (1875) I. XIX. 171 Out with your spit without delay! You've but to lunge and I will parry.

6. a. A small, low point or tongue of land, projecting into the water; a long narrow reef, shoal, or sandbank extending from the shore.

1673 HICKERINGILL *G. Father Greybeard* 138 That sand with the two horns is the spits. **1764** J. BYRON *Voy.* (1773) I. 27 They drew up upon a stoney spit, which ran a good way into the sea. **1775** ROMANS *Florida* App. 72 Off of the Look-out on St. Rosa Island lies a spit, which you must avoid. **1802** *Naval Chron.* VIII. 211 Above the third buoy.. lies a dangerous spit. **1859** in *Merc. Marine Mag.* (1860) VII. 110 The spit or horn.. extends $1\frac{1}{2}$ miles. **1871** B. TAYLOR *Faust* (1875) II. II. 154 Around yon narrow spit the waves are rippling.

b. Const. *of* (land, sand, etc.).

1697 DAMPIER *Voy.* (1699) II. 461 It is a small spit of sand, just appearing above the Waters edge. **1727** A. HAMILTON *New Acc. E. Ind.* I. xxvii. 343 There are.. several Spits of Sand jetting a pretty Way into the Sea from Points of Land. **1836** W. IRVING *Astoria* I. 132 The entrance from the sea.. is bounded on the south side by a flat sandy spit of land, stretching into the ocean. **1863** BARING-GOULD *Iceland* 112 A long spit of black rubble round which the lake curls. **1884** *Contemp. Rev.* Aug. 325 The old town.. stood on an insulated spit of shore.

7. Special Combs.: **spit-boot**, a boot or gaiter fastening by means of an iron spike (*obs. dial.*); † **spit-file** (see quot.); † **spit-fish** [cf. MSw. *spitfisk*, G. *spiessfisch*], the sea-pike; **spit-jack**, a spit with a turning mechanism (see quot. 1967); † **spit-nose**, a species of *Oxyrhynchus*; **spit-point**, a sharp slender point; **spit-pointed** *a.*, having a point like a spit; † **spit-rack**, a rack used for supporting a spit or spits; † **spit-staff** (?); † **spit-turner**, a device for turning a spit; † **spit-wheel**, a wheel serving to turn a spit.

1707 N. BLUNDELL *Diary* (1895) 55 A pair of *Spit-Boots. **1729** WALKDEN *Diary* (1866) 43 Bought a pair of bellows and spit boot spurs. **1828** CARR *Craven Gloss.*, *Spit-boots*, a species of boot, now very rarely in use. They opened on the outside of the leg. When put on, they were secured at the bottom by a sharp iron spit or spike, which passed into an iron socket. **1851** *Cumbld. Gloss.*, *Spit-boots*, heavy leather gaiters with iron fastenings. **1688** HOLME *Armoury* III. xxii. (Roxb.) 272/1 A *Spit file.. is an Iron rod thicker then a good wyer; it is bent a little from the handle to a square and then runs out streight. **1601** CHESTER *Love's Mart.* lxxxii, There swimmes the Shad, the *Spit-fish, and the Spurling. **1611** COTGR., *Spet*,.. a slender, long,.. blackish-backt sea-fish, called by some the Spit-fish, and by others.. the sea-Pike. **1668** CHARLETON *Onomast.* 136 *Lucius Marinus*, the Sea-Pike, or Spitt-Fish. **1967** *Antique Finder* Aug. 11/3 **Spit jacks*... These mechanisms were fitted on the wall at the side of the fireplace in order to rotate the carcass in front of the fire. A heavy weight was suspended from a cord and wound over the cylinder. The power was conveyed by a series of cogged wheels to another cylinder connected by a cord with a grooved disc on the end of the spit itself, which it slowly turned. **1971** R. HOWE *Mrs. Groundes-Peace's Old Cookery Notebk.* 65 There was the 'spit-jack', a weight-driven spit, considered in the sixteenth century as a labour-saving device. **1668** CHARLETON *Onomast.* 156 *Oxyrincus Rondeletii*, ..the *Spitnose. **1796** WITHERING *Brit. Plants* (ed. 3) III. 609 Leaves..ending in *spit-points. *Ibid.* 855 Leaves..narrow, *spit-pointed. *a* **1693** *Urquhart's Rabelais* III. xxxviii. 318 *Spitrack fool. **1828** TYTLER *Hist. Scotland* I. 399 About a thousand spit racks, with meat on them. **1608** WEDDERBURNE *Compt Bk.* (S.H.S.) 113 A *speit staf and carvit wark thairon. *c* **1475** *Pict. Voc.* in Wr.-Wülcker 770 *Hic veruvertor*, a *spete-turnere. **1703** MOXON *Mech. Exerc.* 51 The Wood-work belonging to the Jack, is a Barrel, a *Spit-wheel and a Handing of the Winch. **1776** HAWKINS *Hist. Mus.* I. 335 The dog who treads the spit-wheel.

spit (spɪt), *sb.*[2] Also 5 spyt. [f. SPIT *v.*[2] Cf. SPET *sb.*[1] and Da. *spyt* (NFris. *spiit*).]

1. a. The fluid secreted by the glands of the mouth, esp. when ejected; saliva, spittle; a clot of this.

See also CUCKOO-SPIT, *frog-spit*.

a **1300** *Cursor M.* 24085 þai sputt on him þair spit. *c* **1440** *Promp. Parv.* 469 Spyt, or spotle, *sputum, screa, saliva*. *c* **1530** *Hours of Blessed Virgin* 78 His face wth spit defil'd. **1611** COTGR., *Crachat*, spittle, or spit; also, a spitting. **1633** P. FLETCHER *Poet. Misc.* Wks. 1909 II. 256 See how with streams of spit th' are drencht. **1700** FLOYER *Cold Baths* I. 47 Temperate Bathing..ripens the Spit, and helps it up. **1747** tr. *Astruc's Fevers* 291 The yellow spits generally expectorated in a peripneumony. **1865** *Morning Star* 7 Jan., The presence of 'stour', or dust,..the particles of which.. manifest themselves in what is called the 'black spit'. **1904** *Brit. Med. Jrnl.* 10 Sept. 35 The spit ceased to be fetid.

b. *Path.* Spitting due to morbid condition.

1897 *Allbutt's Syst. Med.* II. 967 The men become prematurely old; they suffer from cough and spit.

c. ***spit and sawdust***: the floor covering (esp. formerly) typical of the general bar of a public house (see quot. 1937); hence, the bar itself. Freq. *attrib.* (also *transf.*). Cf. SAWDUST *sb.* 3 b.

1937 PARTRIDGE *Dict. Slang* Add. 995/1 *Spit and sawdust*, a general saloon in a public-house: C. 20. Ex the sawdust sprinkled on the floor and the spitting on to the sawdust. **1969** D. CLARK *Death after Evensong* ii. 40 Where shall I start? In the spit and sawdust? I take it you'll do the saloon bar yourself. **1971** R. BUSBY *Deadock* x. 158 The Porter's Arms, a spit and sawdust public house near the markets. **1972** *Guardian* 24 Feb. 10/2 Pub styles polarize into 'Spit and Sawdust'..and 'Architects' Fanciful'. **1976** *Rhyl Jrnl. & Advertiser* 9 Dec. 1/1 He thought that a 'rough and ready, spit and sawdust affair' could be produced and made available for consideration at the council's estimates meetings. **1977** *Lancashire Life* Mar. 58/2 They also convert buildings into billiard clubs, where the decor is attractive and the spit-and-sawdust era is just a memory.

2. a. The act of spitting; an instance of this.

a **1658** LOVELACE *Lucasta, Toad & Spider* 13 The speckl'd Toad..Defies his foe with a fell Spit. **1700** C. NESSE *Antid. Armin.* (1827) 30 Fortune is but the devil's blasphemous spit upon divine providence. **1763** C. JOHNSTON *Reverie* I. 143, I began to hope that I should come off with a spit in the face, or a kick on the breech at worst. **1853** E. FITZ-GERALD *Lett.* (1889) I. 224 The Athenaeum in which you will see a more determined spit at me. **1896** *Daily News* 19 May 8/1 Whenever Masai retire from a conference without spitting the spit of peace, squalls may be expected.

transf. **1882** *Proc. R. Geogr. Soc.* IV. 471 [There was] a little spit from a Mahratta musket.

b. ***a spit and a stride***, a very short distance.

1676 COTTON *Walton's Angler* II. 23 You are now..within a spit, and a stride of the peak. **1676** *Poor Robin's Intell.* 4–11 Apr. 1/1 He had not gone above a spit and a stride but he meets another arch Wag. **1677** W. HUGHES *Man of Sin* I. x. 44 They, I think, out-spake him, a spit and stride, who prayed unto the Pope [etc.]. **1828** in CARR *Craven Gloss.*

c. ***to go for the big spit***: to vomit. *Austral. slang.*

1967 F. HARDY *Billy Borker yarns Again* 40 Don't tell me the Gargler went for the big spit. **1970** *Private Eye* 10 Apr. 16 He goes for the big spit and accidentally entombs a nice old lady and her dog in tepid chuck. **1975** R. BEILBY *Brown Land Crying* 225 Goin' for the big spit, was I? I don't remember.

3. ***the very spit of***, the exact image, likeness, or counterpart of (a person, etc.). Also, ***the (dead) spit of***. *colloq.*

1825 KNAPP & BALDWIN *Newgate Cal.* III. 497/2 A daughter,..the very spit of the old captain. **1836** T. HOOK *G. Gurney* I. 202 You are a queer fellow—the very spit of your father. **1885** HALL CAINE *Shadow of Crime* II. xxvi. 129 A brother..the spit of hissel'. **1886** MACQUOID *Sir J. Appleby* III. x. 143 This young chap has got his dear grandmother's eyes, why, he's the very spit of her. **1901** E. W. HORNUNG *Black Mask* 37 I'll chance you having another ring..the dead spit of mine. **1921** 'K. MANSFIELD' *Let.* Sept. (1977) 232 One of his [*sc.* Cézanne's] men gave me quite a shock. He's the *spit* of a man I've just written about, one Jonathan Trout. **1936** M. DE LA ROCHE *Whiteoak Harvest* v. 98 Easy for a boy to look like his grandmother. There was Renny—the spit of old Gran! **1953** A. UPFIELD *Murder must Wait* xvii. 154 The son's the dead spit of the old man. **1966** [see GRAMP].

b. With addition of *fetch, image, picture*. ***spit and image***: see also IMAGE *sb.* 4 b. Also ***spit image*** and absol. *spit*. Cf. the (later) forms *spitten image, spitting image* s.v. SPITTEN *a.*, SPITTING *ppl. a.* 3 respectively.

1859 SALA *Gas-light & D.* xxix. 334 He would be the very spit and fetch of Queen Cleopatra. **1869-** in dialect use (*Eng. Dial. Dict.*). **1895** E. CASTLE *Lt. of Searthey* vi. 71 She's like the poor lady that's dead and gone, the spit an' image she is. **1929** J. B. PRIESTLEY *Good Companions* I. v. 166 That's theirs... It's the spit image o' yours, too. **1949** *Penguin New Writing* XXXVI. 35 My husband saw a man that was the spit-image of King no further away than Jackson. **1966** *New Statesman* 18 Feb. 235/1 For most of the last two acts he's catapulted in and out of doors, changing on the way into the cheerfully sodden porter of the bordel who happens to be his spit.

4. A slight sprinkle or shower of rain or snow.

1849 CUPPLES *Green Hand* x. (1856) 90 The night was quite dark, the rain coming in sudden spits out of the wind. **1851** T. J. TAYLOR *Operat. Running Streams* 33 On the occurrence of a thunder spit. **1889** F. M. PEARD *Paul's Sister* III. xxvi. 138 The day was mild,..with occasional spit of rain.

5. *attrib.*, as ***spit-venom***; also **spit-box**, a spittoon; **spit-curl** orig. *U.S.*, (see quots.); **spit-insect**, † (*a*) (see quot. 1755); (*b*) the cuckoo-spit insect, *Philænus spumarius*; cf. *spittle-bug* s.v. SPITTLE *sb.*[2] 4; **spit-kid** *Naut.*, a receptacle for spit.

1833 M. SCOTT *Tom Cringle* xviii, There was no paucity of silver dishes, basins, *spitboxes, censers, and utensils of all shapes..and sizes. **1840** R. H. DANA *Bef. Mast* xxii, Having a large spit-box always under the steps. **1890** J. CAGNEY tr. *Jaksch's Clin. Diagnosis* iv. 88 The sputum has a rusty tinge .., and adheres firmly to the spit-box. **1831** *Boston* (Mass.) *Transcript* 9 Sept. 2/1 What would the reverend Doctor say of the '*spit curls', and Chinese precision of a modern dandyzette's head gear? **1857** [see *beau-catcher* s.v. BEAU *sb.* 3]. **1859** BARTLETT *Dict. Amer.* (ed. 2) 435 *Spit-curl*, a detached lock of hair curled upon the temple; probably from having been at first plastered into shape by the saliva. **1872** DE VERE *Americanisms* 324 The female ornament..is the spit-curl. **1903** FARMER & HENLEY *Slang* VI. 314/1 *Spit-curl, subs. phr.* (costers').—A curl lying flat on the temple; a *soap-curl*. **1957** L. DURRELL *Justine* I. 37 A spitcurl at each temple. **1968** J. IRONSIDE *Fashion Alphabet* 198 *Spit curls*, small curls brought forward on to the cheek, often moistened with 'spit'. **1755** *Dict. Arts & Sci.* IV., **Spit-insect*, in zoology, the cicada with brown wings, and two white spots on them, and a double white line. **1950** J. BROOKE *Goose Cathedral* iv. 82 Little green spit-insects dropped out of the tamarisks into one's cup. **1891** *Cent. Dict.* s.v., *Spitkid. **1898** KIPLING *Fleet in Being* 13 After dinner, as they were smoking above the spit-kids. **1597** HOOKER *Eccl. Pol.* v. ii. §2 The *spit-venome of their poisoned hearts breaketh out to the annoyance of others.

spit, *sb.*[3] Also 9 *dial.* **speet.** [a. MDu. or MLG. *spit* (Du., LG., WFris. *spit*, NFris. *spet, spatt*; also MDu. *speet*, MLG. *spêdt*): see SPIT *v.*[3]]

1. Such a depth of earth as is pierced by the full length of a spade-blade; a spade-graft: **a.** Followed by adjs., esp. *deep*.

The sing. is sometimes used after numerals instead of the pl.

1507–8 in Gage *Hist. Suffolk* (1838) 145 For making of a diche..ij spitte depper then the cast of the cawsy now is. **1645–50** BOATE *Ireland's Nat. Hist.* (1860) 128 A good clay (which commonly lyeth one or two spits deep). **1670** J. SMITH *Eng. Improv. Reviv'd* 36 The ground is delved two spit deep. **1691** RAY *Coll. Eng. Wds.* (ed. 2) Pref., We say a Spade-graft or a Spit deep. *a* **1722** LISLE *Husb.* (1757) 25 Whole beds of chalk, an half spit thick. **1763** *Museum Rust.* I. 254, I make my labourers dig up the intervals one spit deep. **1807** VANCOUVER *Agric. Devon* (1813) 285 These drains..should be made one foot (or spit) wide, and one spit deep. **1882** *Gard. Chron.* XVII. 84 The best method of preparing the soil for the reception of young trees is to dig or trench it at least two spits deep.

b. In other contexts.

1677 PLOT *Oxfordsh.* 66 At Teynton also, within a spit of the surface, they dig a sort of earth they there call Lam. *a* **1679** SIR J. MOORE *Eng. Interest* (1703) 47, I..digg my hole 4 Foot square, but no deeper than one Spit, or thereabout. **1792** *Trans. Soc. Encour. Arts* X. 4 The soil was dug one full spit, and the turf inverted. **1842** LANCE *Cottage Farmer* 11 Digging one acre of Wheat Land, twelve inches deep, by two 6-inch spits. **1862** O'CURRY *Lect. Anc. Irish* xxxiii. (1873) III. 291 It [a curious harp] was raised by labourers at the depth of twelve spits or spadings under the earth in Coolness Moss.

c. A thrust *of* the spade in digging.

1844 H. STEPHENS *Bk. Farm* II. 552 Manure, which should either be dug down 18 inches deep with a double spit of the spade, or ploughed down with a double furrow.

2. A layer of earth of a spade's depth: **a.** With adjs. denoting the relative position of the layer.

1663 GERBIER *Counsel* 53 Brickmakers are accustomed to dig the top spit..and to throw it with the other clay. **1670** J. SMITH *Eng. Improv. Reviv'd* 36 The second spit or undermost earth is laid upon the first spit or spadeful of earth. **1706** LONDON & WISE *Retir'd Gard.* I. ii, The first Spit, or Top Earth is always allow'd to be better than that which lyes under it. **1757** MRS. GRIFFITH *Lett. Hen. & Frances* (1767) III. 217 The Difference..may be compared to [that between] the upper Sod, and the under Spit, of the Earth. **1824** T. HOGG *Carnation* 23 Loam..should consist of the top spit and crumbs only. **1851** GLENNY *Handbk. Fl. Gard.* 9 Use a compost of two-thirds loam, from the upper spit of a pasture, and one-third sand. **1882** *Garden* 28 Jan. 54/1 The soil..is entirely composed of the top spit of a neighbouring meadow.

b. In other contexts.

1780 YOUNG *Tour Irel.* I. 63 He dug it over, levelled it, and burnt the spit in great heaps. **1791** *Trans. Soc. Encour. Arts* IX. 42 Covering them [potatoes] with straw and a spit of earth. **1805** DICKSON *Pract. Agric.* I. 323 He only digs one spit fourteen inches deep with the bottom land-ditching spade. **1844** *Jrnl. R. Agric. Soc.* V. I. 9 He returns and with another spade longer and narrower than the last cuts out the next spit or lower part of the drain.

3. The quantity of earth taken up by a spade at a time; a spadeful.

1675 *Lond. Gaz.* No. 1031/4 The River side,..where the Lord Bishop diggeth the first Spit. **1733** TULL *Horse-Hoeing Husb.* xx. 292 You will find..most of the Pieces or Spits, which are dug out of your Sight, to be of twice that Thickness. **1792** BELKNAP *Hist. New Hampsh.* III. 119 This being dug in spits of a proper size, and dried, becomes valuable fewel. **1837** *Flemish Husb.* 20 in *Husb.* (L.U.K.) III, Digging out spits of earth with the spade.., and setting them up on the surface already ploughed. **1881** WHITEHEAD *Hops* 43 The modern diggers..do not lift each 'spit' up on their spuds and throw it over, as the old-fashioned workmen did in other days.

b. A series of spadefuls taken in a line.

a **1722** LISLE *Husb.* (1757) 21 Farmer Bond..carried a spit [of dung] all along from the heap, and spread it near to the brink of the furrows. **1765** *Museum Rust.* IV. 374 A spit of earth out of the trenches is..to be cast amongst the plants of coleseed in the rows.

4. *dial.* A special form of spade (see quots.).

1828 CARR *Craven Gloss.*, *Spit*, a spade with a mouth almost semicircular. **1830** *Cumb. Farm Rep.* 65 in *Husb.* (L.U.K.) III, A narrow-mouthed spade (technically called a spit) corresponding to the breadth of the tile to be used. **1866-** in dial. glossaries (Lanc., Yks., Linc., Glouc.),

5. *attrib.* and *Comb.*, as ***spit-deep*** adv., ***-dung, -shovel***.

1693 *Phil. Trans.* XVII. 826 Some of these *Tubera*, which lay *Spit deep under ground. **1765** *Museum Rust.* IV. 311 Digging, spit-deep, sixteen rods, at three-pence per rod. *a* **1800** PEGGE *Suppl. Grose*, *Spit-deep*, the depth of a spade only. **1672** F. DROPE *Fruit-Trees* 3 Upon this Bed must be laid some *spit-dung (*i.e.* such horse-dung as is rotted in the heap, and may be digged with a spade). **1778** [W. H. MARSHALL] *Minutes Agric., Observ.* 111 *note*, The ordinary distinction of Long-Dung and Short or Spit-Dung. **1825** *Greenhouse Comp.* I. 115 Loam with..vegetable mould, or mould of spit dung. **1864** *Jrnl. R. Agric. Soc.* XXV. II. 329, I..buy good spit-dung, ready for use, as I want it. **1678** *Phil. Trans.* XII. 946 The *Spit-shovel is to be made of a thin streight Iron ten Inches long, and five Inches broad, with a Socket in the side of it to put a staff or handle. **1728** *Ibid.* XXXV. 568 A narrow Spade, commonly termed a Spit-shovel.

Spit, *sb.*[4] Colloq. abbrev. of *Spitfire* (in full *Supermarine Spitfire*), a British fighter aeroplane produced between 1936 and 1947.

1941 *Saturday Rev. Lit.* (U.S.) 4 Oct. 9/3 A pilot 'aviates' ..a Wimpy or Spit (Spitfire). **1948** G. V. GALWEY *Lift & Drop* ii. 25 From time to time Miss Procter..said 'Here come the jet jobs,' or 'The Spits are lovely.' **1965** *New Statesman* 7 May 718/2 'Look, Ron,' he cried, 'my old Spit!' **1980** J. MCCLURE *Blood of an Englishman* vi. 64, I was flying Spits, Hurricanes, while Bonzo..was in Bomber Command.

spit, *v.*[1] Forms: *α.* 3 spit(i)en (*pa. t.* spitede, *pa. pple.* i-spited, y-spited, -spyted), 5 spite, spyte. *β.* *Sc.* and *dial.* 6 spete, 6, 8–9 speet. *γ.* 5–6 spytte, 6 spyt, 6– spit (*pa. t.* and *pa. pple.* spitted), 7 spitt. [f. SPIT *sb.*[1] Cf. MDu. (Du.) and MLG. *speten*, MDu. and LG. *spitten*, older G. (now dial.) *spissen* (G. *spiessen*).]

1. *trans.* To put on a spit; to thrust through with a spit.

c **1205** LAY. 26522 He..smat hine þurh mid þan spere swa he ispited weore. **1297** R. GLOUC. (Rolls) 4213 Þis grisliche geant adde..yspited him þoru out mid an yrene spite. *c* **1440** *Promp. Parv.* 469 Spyte mete on a spete, *veruo*. **1483** *Cath. Angl.* 356/1 To Spytte..flesche, *verutare*. **1530** PALSGR. 729, I wyll spytte my meate or ever I wyl set my pyes in the oven. **1581** A. HALL *Iliad* II. 31 The gigots and the other flesh in peeces they did spit. *c* **1611** CHAPMAN *Iliad* IX. 209 Then of a well-fed swine A huge fat shoulder he cuts out, and spits it wondrous fine. **1699** DAMPIER *Voy.* II. I. 31 Little bits of Pork, spitted 5 or 6 of them at once, on a small skiver, and roasted. **1749** SMOLLETT *Gil Blas* x. x, He lighted a fire, spitted a leg of mutton. **1787** FARLEY *Lond. Art Cookery* (ed. 4) 35 Having spitted your pig,..lay it down to a brisk clear fire. **1833** LOUDON *Encycl. Archit.* §1515 The operation, when the meat is once spitted,..goes on of itself. **1879** BEERBOHM *Patagonia* xi. 171, I lost no time in spitting some meat and setting it to roast.

b. *transf.* To pierce, transfix, or stab with a sharp weapon, etc.; to fix or impale *on* or *upon* something sharp.

α, *γ*. *c* **1430** *Pilgr. Lyf Manhode* II. cxxviii. (1869) 124 A spere, that was al ful of eren of men perced, whiche weren spited ther on. **1599** SHAKS. *Hen. V*, III. iii. 38 Your naked Infants spitted vpon Pykes. **1607** R. C[AREW] tr. *Estienne's World Wond.* 144 Two brethren..who were spitted vpon a stake some fifteene yeares ago. *a* **1643** W. CARTWRIGHT *Ordinary* IV. i, Hee'l spit you If he but know you are a usurer. **1781** COWPER *Charity* 354 Whether he measure earth,..Weigh sun-beams, carve a fly, or spit a flea. **1847** E. BRONTE *Wuthering Heights* vi. I. 106 If she had been spitted on the horns of a mad cow. **1870** THORNBURY *Tour rd. Eng.* I. ii. 51 They were found, side by side, each having spitted the other with his rapier.

fig. **1589** R. HARVEY *Pl. Perc.* 11 Heresay is too slender an euidence to spit a mans credit vpon.

refl. **1818** SCOTT *Rob Roy* x, My falcon Cheviot, who spitted himself on a heron's bill.

β. **1513** DOUGLAS *Æneid* IX. xii. 90 And Phegeas [he] doun brytnys in the feyld, Spetit throw owt the body and his scheyld. **1575** *Gamm. Gurton* v. ii. 181 If he came, [he] bad me not sticke to speet hym. **1785** BURNS *Jolly Beggars* xxxix, He swore by a' was swearing worth, To speet him like a pliver.

c. Of a Customs officer: to examine with a 'spit' (SPIT *sb.*[1] 4 f).

1925 *Chambers's Jrnl.* 19 Sept. 668/1 The officer..selects a number of bales for inspection. These he 'spits'—that is, he inserts a special iron instrument, which is capable of penetrating to the interior of a large bale and extracting a small piece of the commodity.

2. To pierce or stud (a thing) *with* spikes.

a **1225** *Juliana* 57 [He] lette..a swiðe wunderlich hweol meten & makien & þurh spitien [*v.r.* spiten] hit al..wið irnene gadien.

3. a. To fix (herrings or other fish) on a spit or rod for drying or smoking.

1617 *Minutes Archd. Colchester* (MS.), Allegauit that his servant dyd spitt herrings vpon the saboth day,..for otherwise the herrings had bene all lost. 1865 W. WHITE *E. Eng.* II. 140 The fish are washed and speeted by gangs of women, who with nimble fingers hang them one by one through gills and mouth upon speets.

b. To string (needles) together by passing a wire through the eyes.

1862 *Catal. Internat. Exhib., Brit.* II. No. 6449, These little labourers take the needles when they have been 'eyed' and proceed to 'spit' them, that is, to pass a wire through the eye of every needle.

spit, *v.*[2] Forms: *Inf.* 1 spittan, 3–4 spitten, 5 spyttyn; 4–6 spitte, spytte, spyt (5–6 spytt), 6– spit (6–7 spitt). *Pa. t.* α. 3–7 spitted (6 *Sc.* -it), 4–6 spytted. β. 4–6 spitte, spytte, 4– spit (4 spitt, spyt, 5 spytt); 6 spett(e, 6–7 spet; 6 spatt(e, 6– spat; 6–9 spate, 7 spot, 4, 9 *dial.*, sput. *Pa. pple.* α. 1 ȝispitted, 4–6 spytted, 6–7 (9 *dial.*) spitted (6 *Sc.* -it). β. 6–7 spet (6 spette), 5– spit (6–7 spitte, 6 spytte), 9– spat, *dial.* sput. γ. 6 spetten, 7–8 (9 *dial.*) spitten, 9 *dial.* spatten, sputten. [Northern OE. *spittan* (also *ȝespittan*), = G. dial. *spitzen*, of imitative origin; cf. MSw. *spytta*, *spotta* (Sw. *spotta*), Norw. dial. *spytta* (*sputta*), Da. *spytte*, NFris. *spütte*, older G. (now dial.) *sputzen*, also ON. and Icel. *spýta* (Norw. dial. *spyte*) and OE. *spǣtan* SPETE *v.*

OE. instances are rare, the common words being *spǣtan*, *spǣtlan*, and *spīwan*. From the 15th cent. the conjugation has included forms properly belonging to the obsolete SPETE, together with new formations on the analogy of strong vbs. See also SPET *v.*]

I. *trans.* † **1.** To eject saliva on (a person) as a sign of contempt. *Obs.*

c950 *Lindisf. Gosp.* Mark x. 34 Hia spittes hine & hia suingeð hine. c975 *Rushw. Gosp.* Luke xviii. 32 Swungen [he] bið & ȝispitted bið. a1225 *Ancr. R.* 290 Spit him amidde þe bearde to hoker & to schom, þet flikereð so mit þe. c1230 *Hali Meid.* 17 þenne spit leccherie, to schome & to bismere, meidenhad o þe nebbe.

2. To eject from the mouth by the special effort involved in expelling saliva.

to spit sixpences: see SIXPENCE 2 d.

c975 *Rushw. Gosp.* Matt. xxvii. 30 þa spittende on him heor spaðl, ȝenoman þæt hreod & sloȝun his heafud. a1225 *Juliana* 49 Hare ahne blod ich habbe ofte imaket ham to spitten & to speowen. a1300 *Cursor M.* 24085 Þai sput on him þair spit. c1385 CHAUCER *L. G. W.* 1433 *Hypsiphyle*, Two bolys makyd al of bras That spittyn fer. c1440 *Alph. Tales* 180 He strake hym opon þe breste, at he spytt blude with iij dayes. 1481 CAXTON *Reynard* (Arb.) 111 The wulf had so moche payne and anguyssh..that he spytte blood. 1509 HAWES *Past. Pleas.* XXXIII. (Percy Soc.) 166 With his thre hedes he spytte all his venum. 1590 *Pasquil's Apol.* I. B iij, Hath the Toade no poyson before he spits it? 1600 SURFLET *Countrie Farme* I. xii. 65 That cluttered blood which the sicke partie shall haue spet. 1697 DRYDEN *Virg. Georg.* IV. 148 A thirsty Train That..spit from their dry Chaps the gather'd Dust again. 1711 ADDISON *Spect.* No. 117 ¶7 Sir Roger told me, that old Moll had been often brought before him for making Children spit Pins. 1789 *Med. Comm.* II. 297 He..spate a vast quantity of tough white froth. 1803 *Med. Jrnl.* IX. 430 He..began to spit thick matter of a greenish colour. 1821 SCOTT *Kenilw.* xxiv, This master-fiend shall spit a few flashes of fire..on the spot, if it will do you pleasure. 1897 *Allbutt's Syst. Med.* IV. 162 Recovery may ensue after the patient has been spitting muco-pus for weeks.

fig. a1568 ASCHAM *Scholem.* II. Wks. (1904) 239 Their whole knowledge..was tied onely to their tong & lips,..and therfore was sone spitte out of the mouth againe. 1608 SHAKS. *Per.* III. i. 8 Thou stormest venomously; Wilt thou spit all thyself? 1777 BRAND *Pop. Antiq.* 101 *note*, Boys have a Custom (*inter se*) of spitting their Faith, or as they also call it here, their Saul (Soul), when required to make Asseverations in a Matter of Consequence.

b. With *forth*, *out*, *up*.

c1386 [see c]. c1450 *St. Cuthbert* (Surtees) 6353 He wald þe penys oute haue spit, he moght noght opyn his mouth ȝit. 1509 HAWES *Past. Pleas.* XXXVII. (Percy Soc.) 192 Toward me he came,..Spyttyng out fyre. 1530 PALSGR. 729 The adder dyd spytte forthe her venyme by and by. 1558 WARDE tr. *Alexis' Secr.* 21 b, He turned..vpon the beddes side, and spitte out a great parte of the matter. 1663 BP. PATRICK *Parab. Pilgr.* ix, As men do with bitter Pills which..if they chaw them, prove so distastful, that they are ready to spit them out again. 1745 tr. *Columella's Husb.* VIII. xvi, When he..had tasted of a pike.. and had spitten it out, he followed the impudent action with a jest. 1779 in Jesse *Selwyn & Contemp.* (1844) IV. 258 Those rascals we have seen take so much snuff and spit it up again. 1842 LOVER *Handy Andy* xviii, He..saw the trumpeter spitting out a mouthful of beer. 1898 *Allbutt's Syst. Med.* V. 55 Since then he had spat up thick phlegm.

fig. 1598 CHAPMAN *Hero & Leander* 111, Takes news as if it were too hot to eat, And spits it slavering forth for dog-fees meat. 1613 SHAKS. *Hen. VIII*, I. ii. 61 This makes.. Tongues spit their duties out. 1915 T. S. ELIOT *Love Song J. Alfred Prufrock* in *Poetry* (Chicago) June 132 How should I begin to spit out all the butt-ends of my days and ways.

c. With various fig. objects (as *venom*, *poison*, *fire*, etc.) denoting the utterance or expression of malice, hatred, anger, or other violent feeling. *to spit blood*, (*a*) to express vehement anger, to rage (*colloq.*); (*b*) *slang*, of a spy, etc.: to fear exposure; *to spit chips* (Austral. slang), (*a*) to feel extreme thirst; (*b*) to manifest acute anger or vexation.

c1386 CHAUCER *Pard. T.* Prol. 135 Thus spitte I out my venym vnder hewe Of hoolynesse, to semen hooly. 1560 DAUS tr. *Sleidane's Comm.* 20 Herein they..spitte oute the poyson of theyr hatred. 1583 BABINGTON *Commandm.* (1590) 364 When hee woulde haue euen spit fire in Anthonies face and galled him as greatly as hee could. 1621 in Kempe *Losely MSS.* (1836) 454 Y[e] Spaniards, against whom they are apt..to spitt theyr spleens. a1656 BP. HALL *Rem. Wks.* (1660) 161 One spits his poyson upon the blessed Trinity. 1701 FARQUHAR *Sir H. Wildair* I. i, Let 'em spit their venom among themselves, and it hurts nobody. 1759 DILWORTH *Pope* 16 When the venom you spit falls short of your aim. 1863 HOLLAND *Lett. Joneses* vi. 98 There be women..who can scold or cry or howl or spit fire. 1901 *Bulletin Reciter* (Sydney) 108 While you're spitting chips like thunder... And the streams of sweat near blind you. 1946 A. MARSHALL *Tell us about the Turkey, Jo* 142, I was spitting chips. God, I was dry! 1947 J. MORRISON *Sailors belong Ships* 189 Old Mick Doyle's with them. He's spitting chips because they're not using sea water. 1954 P. GLADWIN *Long Beat Home* 17 It's enough to make you spit chips when you think of Sydney—movies and vaudeville comedies and a decent musician once in two years. 1963 J. JOESTEN *They call it Intelligence* I. iv. 45 When a resident agent is forced to lie low, because counter-espionage is on his trail, it is said of him that he is 'spitting blood'. 1963 WODEHOUSE *Stiff Upper Lip, Jeeves* ix. 72 If there's one thing that makes a collector spit blood, it's hearing about another collector getting a bargain. 1965 I. SOUTHALL *Ash Road* 77 Not when I saw Mr Fairhall last. He was spittin' chips because Peter had gone away. 1966 L. DEIGHTON *Billion-Dollar Brain* x. 90 A man tailed or suspected is said to be 'spitting blood'. 1966 'L. LANE' *ABZ of Scouse* 102 When I think of it I could spit blood.

refl. 1735 POPE *Prol. Sat.* 320 Or at the ear of Eve, familiar Toad, Half froth, half venom, [he] spits himself abroad, In puns, or politics, or tales, or lies.

d. With compl. *in one's face*, *teeth*, etc. Chiefly in fig. use.

1526 *Pilgr. Perf.* (W. de W. 1531) 97 Euer spyttynge thy offences in thy tethe. 1593 SHAKS. *Rich. II*, I. i. 194 My teeth shall teare The slauish motiue..And spit it..euen in Mowbrayes face. 1636 BRATHWAIT *Rom. Emp.* 94 He bit off his tongue and spit it in her face. a1711 KEN *Urania* Poet. Wks. 1721 IV. 475 Sweet Poetry has suffer'd most, By Bards ..Who in her beauteous Visage spit The Putrefaction of their Wit. 1781 COWPER *Hope* 662 While bigotry..spits abhorrence in the Christian's face.

e. In phrases denoting great or exact likeness or resemblance. (Cf. SPIT *sb.*[2] 3.)

F. *craché* is similarly used.

1602 BRETON *Wonders worth Hear.* (1879) 8/1 Twoo girles,..the one as like an Owle, the other as like an Urchin, as if they had beene spitte out of the mouthes of them. 1664 COTTON *Scarron.* 106 Hee's e'en as like thee as th' adst spit him. 1690 C. NESSE *Hist. O. & N.T.* I. 159 We are of our father the devil,..as like him as if spit out of his mouth. 1788 GROSE *Dict. Vulgar T.* (ed. 2) s.v., He is as like his father as if he was spit out of his mouth; said of a child much resembling his father. 1825– in *Eng. Dial. Dict.*

3. a. To emit, cast, throw, in a manner similar to the ejection of saliva.

13.. *E.E. Allit. P.* C. 338 Oure fader to þe fysch ferslych biddez, þat he hym sput spakly vpon spare drye. 1595 SHAKS. *John* II. 211 The Canons..ready mounted..to spit forth Their Iron indignation gainst your walles. c1611 CHAPMAN *Iliad* IV. 452 The sea thrusts vp her waues;..she rores, And..spits euerie way her fome. 1773 *Let.* 26 Aug. in *Maryland Hist. Mag.* (1920) XV. 280 The wind is strong at N:E. & it spits Rain. 1803 B. HUNT *Diary* 16 Apr. in *Chester Co.* (Pa.) *Hist. Soc. Bull.* (1898) 7 Continues cold and Spiting snow. 1835 N. WYETH *Jrnl.* 12 Jan. in F. G. Young *Sources Hist. Oregon* (1899) I. 243 Spit snow all day at night set in to snow. 1837 CARLYLE *Fr. Rev.* II. I. iii, Sulphur-cloud spitting streaks of fire? 1863 HAWTHORNE *Our Old Home* (1879) 94 The clouds now spat down a few spiteful drops upon us. 1911 *Daily Mail* 1 Nov. 7/2 The bullets came crashing through the cactus leaves, spitting up sand all around us.

†**b.** To cause to be expelled in spittle. *Obs.*

1608 TOPSELL *Serpents* 45 The roote of Teasill young, for Fullers yet vnfit, Drunke in warme water, venome out doth spit.

c. *colloq.* To leave (visiting-cards).

1782 MME. D'ARBLAY *Diary* 24 Dec., As I had the coach, I then *spit* cards at Mrs. Chapone's, who has sent me an invitation.

d. To extrude or lay (eggs or spawn).

1847 HALLIWELL, *Spit*, to lay eggs, said of insects. 1909 *Toilers of Deep* Sept. 225/1 The adult oyster 'spits' its many thousands of eggs into the water.

4. With *out* (or †*forth*): To utter in a proud, spiteful, plain, or unreserved manner. Also without adv.: To speak (a language). Freq. in phr. *to spit it out*: to reveal, confess, disclose something.

1595 SHAKS. *John* II. i. 458 A large mouth indeede, That spits forth death, and mountaines. 1639 S. DU VERGER tr. *Camus' Admir. Events* 310 Those students, who returning from the Universities, spit out at their mouth the superfluities of their memory. 1657 J. SMITH *Myst. Rhet.* 80 Thus Michael spits out bitter reproaches against David. 1701 CIBBER *Love makes Man* II. i, *Car.* Does my younger Brother speak any Greek yet, Sancho? *Sanc.* No, Sir, but he spits French like a Magpy. 1855 MRS. GASKELL *North & South* I. xxv. 313 I'm easier in my mind for having spit it out. 1876 T. HARDY *Ethelberta* (1890) 5 A good saying well spit out is a Christmas fire to my withered heart. 1904 A. GRIFFITHS *Fifty Yrs. Publ. Serv.* 11 Now Sir, speak up... Don't be afraid, spit it out. 1920 GALSWORTHY *Skin Game* I. 31 Don't be so mysterious, mother. If you know something, do spit it out! 1935 AUDEN & ISHERWOOD *Dog beneath Skin* II. v. 115 Go on, then, spit it aht! 1950 J. CANNAN *Murder Included* vi. 123 'I've gotta clue.'..'Spit it out, for mercy's sake, boy.' 1981 A. PRICE *Soldier No More* 43 'Well—spit it out, man! Don't just stand there,' Willis exhorted him.

5. To put *out* by means of spitting.

1681 COTTON *Wond. Peak* 62 The water breaks on Rocks in such a showr..as made us doubt 'Twould hazard spitting all our Candles out.

II. *intr.* **6.** To eject saliva (at or on a person or thing) as a means of expressing hatred or contempt. Usually with preps., as *against*, *at*, *in*, *on*, etc.

c975 *Rushw. Gosp.* Matt. xxvi. 67 Þa spittadun [hiæ] on his ondwliotu & mid hondum hine sloȝun. a1240 *Wohunge* in *O.E. Hom.* I. 279 Hwen þat te sunefule men i þi neb spitted. a1300 *Cursor M.* 16635 Þai spitted on his lueli face. 13.. *K. Alis.* 891 (Linc.), 'Fy on þe!' quoþ Nycolas: And spitte amydde his face. c1400 *Laud Troy-B.* 18577 [She] tare here clothes & on hem spit. c1440 *Jacob's Well* 193 He spytted on þe cros, he dyspysed oure lady. 1483 CAXTON *Gold. Leg.* 231/2 They..spytten ayenste the fals ydollys and Statues. 1508 DUNBAR *Tua Mariit Wemen* 396, I spittit quhen I saw That super spendit euill spreit. 1542 UDALL *Erasm. Apoph.* 56 Aristippus spitted on the evill favoured face of Simus. 1608–9 MIDDLETON *Widow* V. i, Spit at me, gentlemen, If ever I'd such a thought. 1630 LENNARD tr. *Charron's Wisd.* II. iv. (1670) 256 For to go against his own nature, is to tempt God, to spit against the heavens. 1732 BERKELEY *Alciphr.* v. §13 A determined purpose to murder any man who shall but spit in his face. 1797 *Monthly Mag.* XLVIII. 114 Equal to being tweaked by the nose, spitten upon and buffeted. 1825 SCOTT *Talism.* viii, 'Out upon the hound!' said Richard, spitting in contempt, by way of interjection. 1852 MRS. STOWE *Uncle Tom's C.* xxxviii, 'The more fool you!' said Legree, spitting scornfully at him. 1891 FARRAR *Darkn. & Dawn* li, They spit when they pass a temple; they turn away with horror from sacrifices.

b. In fig. use; freq. with *in one's face*.

(*a*) 1562 WINȜET *Wks.* (S.T.S.) I. 108 Think ȝe nocht that this maist barber ruidnes..wald be spittit at be a Iow or an Ethnik? 1579 TOMSON *Calvin's Serm. Tim.* 327/2 Therefore they are so much the more to be accursed and to be spette at. 1612 BP. HALL *Contempl.*, *O.T.* II. iv, How shall not all the world spit at this holy cruelty. 1663 BP. PATRICK *Parab. Pilgr.* xx, They will strain themselves to spit upon their sins. 1716 M. DAVIES *Athen. Brit.* II. 220 Simon Magus was betimes spit upon by the Primitive Bishop Irenæus. 1831 SCOTT *Ct. Rob.* xiii, I am a Christian man, spitting at, and bidding defiance to, Apollo, Bacchus, Comus, and all other heathen deities. 1851 MRS. BROWNING *Casa Guidi Wind.* I. 288 If we turned and spat Upon our antecedents, we were vile. 1868 TENNYSON *Lucretius* 196, I hate, abhor, spit, sicken at him.

(*b*) 1639 S. DU VERGER tr. *Camus' Admir. Events* 286 You spit upon your owne face. a1715 BURNET *Own Time* (1766) II. 143 He said the petitioners for a Parliament spit in the king's face. 1761 HUME *Hist. Eng.* (1806) IV. 637 They could get no other answer than that God had spitten in his face. 1810 W. WILSON *Hist. Dissent. Ch.* III. 86 Say he died spitting in the devil's face, contemning him and his doctrine.

7. To eject saliva from the mouth; to expectorate.

a1300 *Cursor M.* 13544 Wit þis vn-to þe erth he spitt. 1377 LANGL. *P. Pl.* B. x. 40 But þo þat feynen hem folis.. Spitten and spewen and speke foule wordes. c1440 *Promp. Parv.* 469 Spyttyn, *screo, spuo, exspuo*. a1450 MYRC *Par. Pr.* 890 Kepe þe welle þat þou ne spytte. 1530 PALSGR. 728 It is a foule thyng at a sermonde to here people spytte and retche or rough as they do. 1599 B. JONSON *Ev. Man out of Hum.* III. i, I haue beene taking an ounce of tabacco hard by here, ..and I am come to Spit priuate in Paules. 1609 HOLLAND *Amm. Marcell.* 186 Hee was never seene abroad and out of his house to have snit his nose, or spit. 1674 R. GODFREY *Inj. & Ab. Physic* 131 He almost continually spitted, and daily grew worse. c1720 PRIOR *Conversat.* 67 Out of breath, he turn'd to spit. 1778 in Jesse *Selwyn & Contemp.* (1844) III. 295 She spits and coughs much. 1841 LANE *Arab. Nts.* I. 68 When any of you has a bad dream, spit three times over your left shoulder. 1892 T. HARDY *Well-Beloved* III. i, Men drank, smoked, and spat in the inns.

b. With preps., as *about*, *against*, *at*, *in*, *into*, *on*, *upon*. Also *spec.* with *out*, of ceramic glazes: to form blisters which burst during firing.

1382 WYCLIF *Ecclus.* xxviii. 14 If thou shul spitten vpon it, it shal ben queynt. 14.. *Rule Syon Monast.* liii. in *Collect. Topogr.* (1834) I. 31 None schal..spyt up on the stayres.. but yf they trede it oute forthewythe. 1526 TINDALE *John* ix. 6 As sone as he had thus spoken, he spate on the grounde. 1596 SHAKS. *Tam. Shr.* III. i. 40 Spit in the hole man, and tune againe. 1605 DANIEL *Queen's Arcadia* 125 Wks. (Grosart) III. 221 If she meet but with my dog, she..playes with his eares, Spits in his mouth. 1633 G. HERBERT *Temple, Unkindness* iii, My friend may spit upon my curious floore. 1668 H. MORE *Div. Dial.* II. xviii. (1713) 146 To spit in the Mouth of a Dog..is not indecorous for the Man, and grateful also to the Dog. 1714 ADDISON *Lover* No. 39, Sitting at table, he spits full upon the servants who waited there. 1777 BRAND *Pop. Antiq.* 101 *note*, In Combinations of the Colliers, &c. in the North, for the Purpose of raising their Wages, they are said to spit upon a Stone together, by Way of cementing their Confederacy. 1824 LANDOR *Imag. Conv.* Wks. 1853 I. 45/1 Nick gave unto him a shilling, having first spatten thereon, as he, according to his superstition, said, for luck. 1861 PETHERICK *Egypt*, etc. 424 Then rising and spitting in my face in token of amity, he said he was happy that I had sent for him. 1883 STEVENSON *Silverado Sq.* 146, I could not continue to give him a salary for spitting on the floor. 1904 *Trans. Eng. Ceramic Soc.* IV. 30 The china vase..with the Seger porcelain glaze..has no sign of blister..., and does not spit out in the kiln. *Ibid.* 32 The earthenware trials that have spit out are not verified by the china trials.

c. *to spit in* or *on one's hands*, in fig. use.

1577 GRANGE *Gold. Aphrod.* Hj b, If I haue anoynted your palmes with hope, spitte on your handes and take good holde. 1590 GREENE *Neuer too Late* Wks. (Grosart) VIII. 85 What Francesco? spit on thy hand, and lay holde on thy hart. 1834 [S. SMITH] *Lett. J. Downing* xxvii. (1835) 185 Afore I had time to spit in my hands, the Gineral finished the war. 1949 H. L. MENCKEN *Mencken Chrestomathy* xxx. 626 Is it hot in the rolling-mill? Are the hours long? Is $15 a day not enough? Then escape is very easy. Simply throw up your job, spit on your hands, and write another 'Rosenkavalier'. a1975 WODEHOUSE *Sunset at Blandings* (1977) ii. 20 There was a time when you had to employ wild horses to drag me from London, and they had to spit on their hands and make a special effort.

d. Of certain animals when angry.

a1668 LASSELS *Voy. Italy* (1698) II. 199 The Lion and the Leopard fighting together, spit angrily in one anothers faces. **1774** GOLDSM. *Nat. Hist.* (1776) IV. 314 A whole day is often passed.. which is spent in growling, quarrelling, and spitting at each other. **1844** HOOD *Tale of Temper* 52 No household cat that ever lapp'd To swear and spit was half so apt. **1872** 'A. MERION' *Odd Echoes Oxf.* 3 Reproving My grimalkin for the dreadful way in which she spat and swore.

†**e.** *Phr.* (See quot., and cf. 7 b, quot. 1777.) *Obs.*

1777 BRAND *Pop. Antiq.* 101 *note*, We have too a kind of popular Saying, when Persons are of the same Party, or agree in Sentiment, 'they spit upon the same Stone'.

8. To sputter.

1611 COTGR., *La lumiere petille*, the candle sparkles, or spits. **1671** GREW *Anat. Pl., Idea* (1684) 17 So Fenil-Seeds, held in the flame of a Candle, will spit and spurtle. **1773** GOLDSM. *Stoops to Conq.* III, Zounds; how she fidgets and spits about like a catherine wheel. **1852** READE *Peg Woff.* (1889) 6 The sausage began to 'spit'. **1866** WATTS *Dict. Chem.* IV. 326 If exposed to the air in the melted state it [*sc.* palladium] absorbs oxygen and spits like silver. **1871** *Archaeol.* XLIII. 101 Vegner's paper was bad, his ink worse, his pen 'worser' still, spitting strangely.

9. a. Of rain or snow: To fall in scattered drops or flakes. (Usually with *it* as subject.)

1567 [see SPITTING *ppl. a.* I]. **1778** [W. H. MARSHALL] *Minutes Agric.* Observ. 129 To *sprinkle* (or *spit*), to rain slow in largish drops. **1818** MISS FERRIER *Marriage* vii, 'And'—putting her hand out at the window—'I think it's spitting already'. **1836–7** DICKENS *Sk. Boz, Tales* vii, It had been 'spitting' with rain for the last half-hour. **1860** TYNDALL *Glac.* I. xxv. 189 The fine snow.. was caught by the wind and spit bitterly against us. **1887** SERVICE *Life Dr. Duguid* 171 Feeling that it was spittin' through the win', I quickened my step.

b. To penetrate as if sent by spitting.

1850 *Blackw. Mag.* May 554/1 A bullet whizzed by my head, and spat into the opposite bank.

10. ***spit and polish***, the occupation of cleaning up or furbishing, as part of the work of a sailor or soldier; also in extended use, precise correctness, smartness; freq. as a derogatory expression in contrast with purposeful work or utility. Also *attrib.*, smart in appearance; hence ***spit-and-polished*** adj.

1895 *Westm. Gaz.* 13 Nov. 3/2 After all his energies had been expended on what in old days was termed 'spit and polish', he took the cow-pen in hand. **1898** *United Service Mag.* Dec. 277 To lessen the time spent in spit and polish to the detriment of real cavalry work. **1914** C. BERESFORD *Mem.* I. 120 From that day onwards I set myself steadily against bright-work and spit-and-polish. **1920** *Q. Rev.* Jan. 196 Gunnery had been neglected in pursuit of 'spit and polish'. **1949** 'J. TEY' *Brat Farrar* xiii. 116 He had understood Brat's distrust of the [stables'] spit and polish. **1950** *Daily Progress* (Charlottesville, Va.) 23 Sept. 1/7 Officially Pretzer was.. part of the spit and polish First Infantry Division. **1958** *Times* 12 Nov. 3/3 Holst's suite, 'The Planets', was very, very much better.. thanks to.. the orchestra's ever-increasing spit-and-polish. **1977** L. MEYNELL *Hooky gets Wooden Spoon* xiii. 172 Some nice chubby-faced spit and polish Sandhurst type. **1977** *Times* 8 Nov. 4/3 The spit-and-polished toecaps of his boots. **1979** *United States 1980/81* (Penguin Travel Guides) 614 The 4,300 spit-and-polished midshipmen have a 3:45 PM dress parade on Warden Field.

III. 11. The vb. stem in combination as **spit-cat, kitten** *colloq.* = SPITFIRE *sb.* 3.

1898 A. OLLIVANT *Owd Bob* v. 51 Eh, but art' a tearin' spit-cat surely! **1912** KIPLING *Divers. Creatures* (1917) 9 There's a nice little spit-kitten for you!

spit, *v.*[3] Now *dial.* Also 7 spitt. [OE. *spittan*, = MDu. and MLG. *spitten* (Flem., Du., LG. *spitten*, WFris. *spitte*, NFris. *spat*; also MDu. *spetten*, MLG. *speten*), perh. related to SPIT *sb.*[1]]

1. *intr.* To dig with a spade; to delve.

1393 LANGL. *P. Pl.* C. IX. 184 An hep of eremites henten hem spades, Spitten and spradde donge in despit of hunger. **1648** HEXHAM II, *Spaden*, to Delve, or to Spit.

2. *trans.* To plant with a spade.

1610 HOLLAND *Camden's Brit.* 453 When the heads thereof [*sc.* saffron] have been plucked up and after twenty daies spitted or set againe under mould. **1728** *Phil. Trans.* XXXV. 573 Spitting and setting the Heads, *1l. 12s. od.*

b. *intr.* To admit of being dug in.

a **1722** LISLE *Husb.* (1757) 19 If dung was.. short, such as ox-dung and horse-dung that would spit.

3. *trans.* To dig (*up*) with a spade; also, to turn up with a plough.

So OE. *wád spittan*, to dig up woad.

1648 HEXHAM II, *Spitten*, to Spitt, as, to Spitt turfe. **1725** *Phil. Trans.* XXXIII. 397 Oftentimes the Tenants spit up as much as will serve their Turn for a Winter's burning. **1764** RANDALL in *Museum Rust.* III. 95 He must remember to go twice in a place with his plough, to keep the ground double spitted. **1843** *Jrnl. R. Agric. Soc.* IV. I. 41 Cross furrows.. afterwards dug or 'spitted' by the spade. **1889** *Trans. Dev. Assoc.* XXI. 102 He sometimes comes up to spit the ground.

spital ('spɪtəl). Also 7 spitall, 8 spittal. [Late respelling of SPITTLE *sb.*[1] after HOSPITAL.]

1. = SPITTLE *sb.*[1] I. Also in phr. ***to rob the spital***.

1634 *Younger Brother's Apol.* 50 Bryand Lyle,.. hauing two sonnes, both leprous, built for them a Lazaretto or Spitall. **1648** HEXHAM II. App., *Spitael*, a Spitall, or Hospitall. **1737** J. CHAMBERLAYNE *St. Gt. Brit.* (ed. 12) I. III. x. 226 This house has been a Religious house, time out of mind, sometimes under the Denomination of a Priory or College, sometimes under that of a Spittal [*earlier edd.* Spittle] or Hospital. **1749** FIELDING *Tom Jones* XII. i, Defrauding the Poor,.. or, to seie it under the most opprobrious Colours, robbing the Spittal. **1764** CHURCHILL *Poems, Independence* 19 They rob the very Spital, and make free With those alas who've least to spare. **1830** SCOTT *Demonol.* iv. 132 A witch from the spital or almshouse. **1865** *Daily Tel.* 26 Oct. 5/2 'Every inch a Queen' was Eugénie when she drove from cholera-infected spital to spital. **1884** TENNYSON *Becket* I. iv, I ha' nine darters i' the spital.

b. ***spital sermon***: see SPITTLE *sb.*[1] 5 c.

1755 JOHNSON, *Spittal*... In use only in the phrases, *a spittal sermon*, and *rob not the spittal*. **1827** DE QUINCEY *Murder* Wks. 1862 IV. 25 One good horse-shoe is worth about two and a quarter Spital sermons. **1863** *Macm. Mag.* Mar. 412 When Barrow preached a spital-sermon before the Lord Mayor and Corporation of London.

2. *fig.* A foul or loathsome place.

1771 SMOLLETT *Humph. Cl.* To Sir W. Phillips 10 May, He declares he will sooner visit a house infected with the plague, than trust himself in such a nauseous spital for the future.

3. A shelter for travellers.

1794 WORDSW. *Guilt & Sorrow* xvii, Kind pious hands did to the Virgin build A lonely Spital, the belated swain From the night terrors of that waste to shield.

'Spitalfield(s), The name of a district in the east of London (so called from St. Mary Spital), used *attrib.*: (*a*) in ***Spitalfield(s) breakfast, weaver*** (see quots.); (*b*) applied to silk and velvet made up there into furnishings, etc., or to the weavers (orig. Huguenot refugees) involved in this trade. Occas. *absol.*

1812 H. & J. SMITH *Rejected Addresses* 120 Spital-fields with real India vies... Old calico, torn silk, and muslin new. **1819** M. EDGEWORTH *Let.* 24 Mar. (1971) 185 Mr. Buxton very plain sense and admirable facts about Newgate and Spitalfield weavers and all that. **1861** C. M. YONGE *Young Step-Mother* iii. 26 He was.. of the Protestant French sort, that.. ran away from the Sicilian vespers, or the Edict of Nantes, I don't remember which; only the Spitalfields weavers have something to do with it. **1865** *Slang Dict.* 242 Spitalfield's breakfast, at the East end of London this is understood as consisting of a tight necktie and a short pipe. **1880** DAY *Fishes Gt. Brit.* I. 81 This for [i.e. *Trachinus draco*], not *T. vipera*, are sold in Whitechapel as food, and are said to be known as Spitalfield weavers. **1894** *Country Gentleman's Catal.* 155/2 Umbrellas.. very best Spitalfields twill silk. **1952** M. COST *Hour Awaits* 89 The small red drawing-room, its damask hangings of Spitalfields silk. **1955** R. FASTNEDGE *Eng. Furniture Styles* iii. 86 Queen Anne's state bed, at Hampton Court, is hung, with Spitalfields velvet, patterned in rich colours on a cream ground. **1972** P. ROGERS *Grub Street* ii. 115 Such persistant troublemakers as the Spitalfields weavers. **1976** T. JEAL *Until Colours Fade* ii. 30 The Red Drawing Room.. its walls were lined with faded crimson Spitalfield's silk. **1980** J. ROSE *Elizabeth Fry* iv. 68 The Spitalfields weavers, thrown out of work by the powerlooms.

'spitball. *N. Amer.* Also spit-ball, spit ball. [f. SPIT *sb.*[2] + BALL *sb.*[1]] **1.** A spittle-ball (see SPITTLE *sb.*[2] 4), esp. one thrown as a missile by a schoolchild.

1846 *Knickerbocker* XXVII. 410 They.. crooked pins, made pop-guns, ejected spit-balls. **1899** W. JAMES *Talks to Teachers* 92 The spitballs that Tommy is ready to throw. **1939** L. M. MONTGOMERY *Anne of Ingleside* xi. 71 Bertie Shakespeare Drew threw a spit-ball at her. **1956** M. STEARNS *Story of Jazz* (1957) xix. 252 Gillespie was also perfecting his spitball-throwing technique while in the Calloway band. **1977** I. SHAW *Beggarman, Thief* II. iii. 143 They [*sc.* the teachers] spend most of the time trying to keep the kids from.. throwing spitballs.

2. *Baseball.* A ball moistened on one side with saliva or sweat before pitching, so that it acquires a swerve. (Illegal in the official game.)

1905 J. J. MCGRAW *Official Baseball Guide* 13 The perfect 'spit' ball drops from a batter's hips to his knees or below in perhaps two feet of forward motion. **1912** C. MATHEWSON *Pitching in Pinch* 20 Some spit-ball pitchers announce when they are going to throw a moist one by looking at the ball as they dampen it. **1928** G. H. RUTH *Baseball* vi. 75 All spit balls break down, but by turning the wet spot one way or the other the pitcher can make the ball break in or out as he desires. **1946** MEZZROW & WOLFE *Really the Blues* (1957) viii. 125 His arms [were] pumping like he was a pitcher winding up to shoot a spitball over the plate. **1976** *Billings* (Montana) *Gaz.* 7 July 4-A/2 That's what I can do for the Cubs. I guarantee that they will be snarling and swearing, gouging, spiking, mauling. They'll be throwing beanballs and spitballs.

3. *transf.* and *fig.*

1888 *Judge* 10 Nov. 68/1 All statements to the opposite effect are spit-balls at the moon. **1925** FRASER & GIBBONS *Soldier & Sailor Words* 266 *Spit ball*, hand-grenade. (U.S. Army.) **1931** W. G. MCADOO *Crowded Years* xv. 225 Their vitriolic comments.. consisted chiefly of mere verbal spitballs thrown in a.. mood of.. sabotage. **1933** E. O'NEILL *Days without End* i. 33 They'd turned naughty schoolboys and were throwing spitballs at Almighty God. **1960** I. WALLACH *Absence of Cello* 58 She also thought that their impulse to outrage was over-developed. 'You all sit around and throw spitballs at the world,' she said. **1981** T. BARLING *Bikini Red North* xii. 263 It doesn't make a spitball of difference. The deadline stands.

Hence **'spitball** *v. intr.*, to throw out suggestions for discussion; **'spitballer**, one who throws spitballs.

1928 *Chicago Tribune* 7 June 19/4 The Giants.. made only three hits off.. Clarence Mitchell, the southpaw spitballer. **1955** H. KURNITZ *Invasion of Privacy* (1956) viii. 64 I'm just thinking out loud... Spitballing we call it in the movie business. **1961** J. B. PRIESTLY *Saturn over Water* iv. 52 No, don't tell me we're not talking about painting. I'm only spitballing while I try to think. **1976** C. LARSON *Muir's Blood* xvii. 98 'Are you serious?' Blixen asked. 'I'm spitballing,' Schreiber replied. **1977** *New Yorker* 2 May 100/3 The spitballer won't grow into His father's jacket.

spit-boot: see SPIT *sb.*[1] 7.

spitchcock ('spɪtʃkɒk), *sb.* Forms: 6 **spechcock**, 7 **spitchcoke, -cocke,** 7– **spitchcock.** [Of obscure origin.]

†**1.** A method of preparing an eel for the table (see sense 2). Also in advb. use. *Obs.*

1597 BRETON *Wit's Trenchmour* Wks. (Grosart) II. 10/1 The Cunger must be sowst, and the Eele in a Spechcock, or els they are not in their kind. **1771** MRS. HAYWOOD *New Present for Maid* 70 To broil an Eel Spitchcock.

2. An eel cut into short pieces, dressed with bread-crumbs and chopped herbs, and broiled or fried. Also *transf.*

1601 CHESTER *Love's Martyr, Dial.* lxxxi, A Spitchcoke, Stocke-fish, and the litle Pilcher. *a* **1643** W. CARTWRIGHT *Ordinary* II. i, Then a fresh turbot brought in for a buckler, With a long spitchcock for the sword adjoin'd. **1672** R. WILD *Let.* 9 He hath released more souls.. than all the Popes since Cerberus the first have saved from being made Spitchcocks in that Kitchin of his Holiness. **1844** J. T. J. HEWLETT *Parsons & W.* v, How he will enjoy a spitchcock. *attrib.* **1687** MIÉGE *Gt. Fr. Dict.* II, A Spitchcock Eel, *sorte de grosse Anguille (qu'on rôtit ordinairement)*.

¶**3.** = SPATCHCOCK *sb.* I. (In quot. *attrib.*)

1834 M. SCOTT *Cruise Midge* (1836) I. v. 132 Give me another cup of coffee.. and the wing of that spitchcock chicken, if you please.

spitchcock ('spɪtʃkɒk), *v.* Also 8 **spitscock.** [f. prec.]

1. *trans.* To prepare (*esp.* an eel) for the table as, or after the manner of, a spitchcock.

1675 COTTON *Burlesque upon B.* 98 Sing'd like a Hog And spitch-cock't like a salted Eele. *c* **1700** T. BROWN *Lett. fr. Dead* (1707) II. 124 The first Course consisted of a huge Platterful of Scorpions Spitscock'd [etc.]. **1736** BAILEY *Household Dict.* s.v. *Eel*, To spitchcock eels. Having cleans'd a large eel with salt and water,.. then draw off the skin [etc.]. **1791** G. HUDDESFORD in *Salmagundi* 144 Raw sprats he swore were worth all fish beside, Fresh, stale, stew'd, spitchcock'd, fricassee'd or fried. *a* **1845** BARHAM *Ingol. Leg.* Ser. III. *Knt. & Lady*, If you chance to be partial to eels,.. Have them spitch-cock'd—or stew'd.

2. To deal with (a person) in a similar manner; *fig.* to handle severely.

1674 P. WHALLEY *Established Relig.* 18 Had the Emperor given according to his quality.. the Dr. had escaped Spitch-cocking. **1694** ECHARD *Plautus* 14 He designs to Spitch-cock me, I believe. Wou'd Old Nick had these bloody-minded Fellows. **1721** MRS. CENTLIVRE *Artifice* IV. i, Oh! that I had her in Spain! I'd spitch-cock her like an Eel. **1814** LAMB *Corr.* 264 But if they catch me in their camps again let them spitchcock me!

spitchcocked ('spɪtʃkɒkt), *ppl. a.* [f. as prec.]

1. Of eels, etc.: Prepared as, made into, a spitchcock. Also *transf.* and *fig.*

a **1643** W. CARTWRIGHT *Ordinary* II. i, No mild words shall bury My spitted, spitchcock'd.. Rost'd fury. *a* **1683** OLDHAM *Wks.* (1686) 77, I.. drip like any Spitch-cock'd Huguenot. **1708** W. KING *Cookery* 55 No Man lards salt Pork with Orange Peel, Or garnishes his Lamb with Spitchcockt Eel. **1799** *Monthly Mag.* VII. 140 This spitchcock'd rattle-snake, And toasted toad. **1821** SCOTT *Kenilw.* i, Though there were as good spitchcock'd eels on the board as ever were ta'en out of the Isis. **1840** J. T. J. HEWLETT *P. Priggins* xvi, A dinner of Spitchcock'd eels and underdone beefsteaks was ordered.

¶**2.** = SPATCHCOCKED *ppl. a.*

1861 HUGHES *Tom Brown at Oxf.* iii, The college kitchen furnished a spitchcocked chicken, or grilled turkey's leg.

spitchered ('spɪtʃəd), *a. slang* (orig. *Naut.*). [f. Maltese *spicca* finished, ended, perh. ult. f. It. *spezzare* to break into pieces, fragment.] Rendered inoperative, ruined.

1920 *Blackw. Mag.* Mar. 340/2 'Cease firing!' screamed the C.O. 'He's spitchered.' **1946** J. IRVING *Royal Navalese* 163 *Spitcher'd*, finished, done. **1970** P. DICKINSON *Seals* i. 14 That damned gadget might.. be functioning right as rain in thirty seconds, or it might be spitchered for ever.

spit-dung: see SPIT *sb.*[3] 5.

spite (spaɪt), *sb.* Forms: α. 4, 6 **spyt,** 4–6 (8) **spyte** (5 **spyyte, spytte**); 4– **spite** (4 **spitt,** 5 **spit,** 6 **spiet**). β. 6–9 **spight** (6 **spighte**). [Aphetic form of DESPITE *sb.* (OF. *despit*), corresponding to MDu. (and Du.) *spijt* (WFris. *spyt*), MLG. *spyt, spît* (LG. *spit*, NFris. *spit, spid*), MSw. *spit*. The spelling *spight*, on the analogy of native words in *-ight*, was common from *c* 1575 to 1700 both in the simple word and derivatives.]

†**1.** Action arising from, or displaying, hostile or malignant feeling; outrage, injury, harm; insult, reproach. *Obs.* (Cf. DESPITE *sb.* 2 and 3.)

a. In the phr. *to do* (one) *spite* or *a spite*.

a **1300** *Cursor M.* 15568 Þou sal þam se yeitt to night do me ful gret spite. **13..** *Ibid.* 7725 (Gött.), Godd it forbede, þat þu.. euer him do spitt or schame. *c* **1380** *Sir Ferumb.* 686 Þou hast y-lyued þy lif to longe, to do me such a spyte. *a* **1533** LD. BERNERS *Huon* l. 169 To do hym the more spyte I shall make lyes ynowe. **1589** R. ROBINSON *Gold. Mirr.* (1851) 18 He piteis poore that weepe, When wrong hath done them spite. **1636** JONSON *Discov.* Wks. (1692) 694 It is as great a spite to be praised in the wrong place,.. as can be done to a noble nature. **1658** *Whole Duty of Man* XI. §7. 231 Men will make.. spoile of the goods of one, to whom they bear a grudg, though they never designe to get any thing to themselves by it, but only the pleasure of doing a spight to the other.

b. In other contexts.

13.. *Gaw & Gr. Knt.* 1444 þere at þe fyrst þrast he þryȝt to þe erþe, & sped hym forth good sped, boute spyt more. a1400 *Amis & Amil.* 1594 It is gret spite to al mi kende. c1440 *Promp. Parv.* 469 Spyyte, repref or schame, ..*obprobrium.* 1449 *Rolls of Parlt.* V. 148/1 Not oonly..to the irreparable hurt,..but also a everlastyng spite, and perpetuell denigration in the fame..of this noble Reme. 1549 Coverdale, etc. *Erasm. Par. Gal.* 21, I carie about in my bodye all the spite, that I haue for Christe sustayned, as emprisonmentes, scourgynges [etc.]. 1596 Drayton *Legends* i. 653 To make Time worke him everlasting spight. 1615 Chapman *Odyss.* x. 181 Two days, two nights, We lay here pining in the fatal spights Of toil and sorrow. 1633 P. Fletcher *Purple Isl.* vii. lviii, His Will his Law, he weigh'd not wrong or right; Much scorn'd to bear, much more forgive a spight.

2. a. A strong feeling of (†contempt,) hatred or ill-will; intense grudge or desire to injure; rancorous or envious malice. (Cf. despite *sb.* 4.)

α. c1330 *Arth. & Merl.* 3135 (Kölbing), King Lot..& oþer of priss Of his ȝiftes spite hadden. 13.. *E.E. Allit. P.* B. 755, I schal my þro steke, & spare spakly of spyt..& my rankor refrayne. c1400 *Destr. Troy* 12093 He besit hym..þe burde for to seche,.. Till he aspiet hir with spit..Doune in a dungion. a1425 *Cursor M.* 2610 (Trin.), Greet spit she leteþ bi me. *Ibid.* 4619 Nay sir he seide take not to spit. 1526 *Pilgr. Perf.* (W. de W. 1531) 301 b, With all spyte & disdayne, cryenge moost outrageously Crucifigatur. 1585 T. Washington tr. *Nicholay's Voy.* ii. viii. 42 This Poet being full of poeticall spyte and indignation. 1633 P. Fletcher *Purple Isl.* i. vi, Sing what thou list, be it of Cupids spite (Ah lovely spite, and spitefull lovelinesse!) 1667 Milton *P. L.* ix. 178 Whom us the more to spite his Maker rais'd From dust: spite then with spite is best repaid. 1746 Francis tr. *Horace, Epist.* i. xiv. 54 None there with Eye askance my Pleasures views, With Hatred dark, or poison'd Spite pursues. 1765 Gray *Shaks.* 5 Much have I borne from canker'd critic's spite. 1849 Macaulay *Hist. Eng.* vi. II. 79 He knew..what all this liberality meant. It was mere Whiggish spite to himself and his religion. 1868 Freeman *Norm. Conq.* (1876) II. App. 677 He at least has no spite against Harold.

Comb. 1592 Nashe *P. Penilesse* 14 b, Assemble the famous men of all ages, and tel me which of them all sate in the sunshine of his soueraignes grace..but he was spiteblasted, heaued at, & ill spoken of.

β. 1577 *St. Aug. Manual* (Longman) 45 Let the devils then doe their spight. 1598 Sylvester *Du Bartas* ii. i. ii. *Imposture* 54 Hate, Pride, and Envious spight, His hellish life do torture day and night. 1642–4 Vicars *God in Mount* 64 The poysonous malice and incorrigible spight and splene of the malignant partie. 1672 Marvell *Reh. Transp.* i. 234 Nothing but his spight against the Nonconformists. 1729 Law *Serious C.* 396 They are no foundation for envy or spight or hatred. 1774 Goldsm. *Nat. Hist.* IV. 198 An ape ..stamping with its feet..to show its spight.

b. In the phrases *for* (also †*of*) or *in spite*.

(*a*) ?a1400 *Morte Arth.* 270, I myght noghte speke for spytte, so my herte trymblyde! a1400–50 *Alexander* 745 Quen he had spokin so, for spyte he spittis in his face. 1559 *Mirr. Mag., Salisbury* xxiii, To take his towne of Yvery, which of spight Did to vs dayly al the harme they might. 1570 *Satir. Poems Reform.* xiii. 64 [They] hangit vp for spyte twa theuis besyde him. 1652 Culpepper *Eng. Physic.* 75 The Root was longer until the D—l (as the Fryars say) bit away the rest for spight envying its usefulness unto mankinde. 1663 Butler *Hud.* i. i. 216 Still so perverse and opposite, As if they worshipp'd God for spight. 1865 M. Arnold *Ess. Crit.* vi. 194 Anything to quarrel with one! anything for spite!

(*b*) 1565 J. Hall *Crt. Virtue* 30 Why should they saye to vs in spighte, Where is their God? 1597 Hooker *Eccl. Pol.* v. lxxii. (1611) 390 Some in disdaine and spite termed grace drunkennesse. 1657 Trapp *Comm. Ezra* i. 5 Julian the Apostate once did [encourage the Jews] in spight to the Christians, but it came to nothing. 1680 Morden *Geog. Rect., France* (1685) 161 Arlet the Skinners Daughter, of whom Duke Robert begat William the Conqueror; in spight to whom, and disgrace to his Mother, the English call Whores, Harlots. 1842 Tennyson *Dora* 37 And half in love, half spite, he..wed A labourer's daughter.

c. *fig.* Of fortune, nature, the elements, etc.

1562 Bullein *Bulwarke, Bk. Sicke Men* 77 b, With a lustie manly courage he defied the spight of Fortune. 1595 T. P. Goodwine *Blanchardyn* I iv b, Since..fortune hath spit her deadly spight. 1610 Holland *Camden's Brit.* 466 A certaine peculiar spite and envie of Nature. 1616 B. Jonson *Forest* xi. 830 To know vice well, And her blacke Spight expell. 1627 May *Lucan* ii. 264 Windes rage, and Thunders spight, Plaine grounds must suffer. 1708 Ozell tr. *Boileau's Lutrin* 54 The wormy boards, by Time's corroding Spight disjoin'd. 1814 Scott *Lord of Isles* vi. xxxvii, Ourself the cause, through fortune's spite, That once broke short that spousal rite.

d. *spite fence*, a wall, fence, etc., erected with the intention of causing annoyance. orig. and chiefly *U.S.*

1899 *Everybody's Mag.* I. 70/2 Meanwhile an ordinance was passed making the building of spite fences illegal. 1928 *Hearst's Internat.* Aug. 89/2 For the full depth of the boundary ran a tall fence of unpainted boards set upright. This fence was fully eighteen feet high. It was what is known as a spite-fence. 1957 R. V. Heuston *Salmond on Torts* (ed. 12) v. 201 An occupier of land is free to erect a wall or fence with the sole object of blocking his neighbour's view, or preventing him from acquiring an easement of light —a 'spite-fence' as it is sometimes called. 1977 *New Yorker* 23 May 50/3 To gain privacy from the street, he put up a nine-foot wall, which one of his neighbors, interpreting it as a spite fence, sued unsuccessfully to have removed.

3. a. With *a* and pl. A particular instance of malignant or rancorous feeling directed towards a special object. Freq. in phr. *to have a spite at.*

a1400 *Sir Degrev.* 101 There wonede an eorl.., a lord of mochelle pryd,..He hade a grete spyt of the knyght. a1568 Ascham *Scholem.* i. (Arb.) 78 This is not the opinion of one, for some priuate spite, but the iudgement of all. 1573 Tusser *Husb.* (1878) 204 But where a spight Of force must bee, What is that wight May disagree? 1612 T. Taylor *Comm. Titus* i. 12 Oh, saith one, this Preacher..hath some spight at me. 1663 Bp. Patrick *Parab. Pilgr.* xxiv, He bears an ill will to us, and owes us a spite. 1726 Swift *Gulliver* ii. i, Being afraid the boy might owe me a spite. 1849 Cupples *Green Hand* vi. (1856) 63 The mystery to her always is *why* the neighbours had a spite at me. 1890 *Spectator* 11 Jan., In a battle of sterile spites with the French people.

b. A mood or humour. *rare*$^{-1}$.

1723 Swift *Stella at Wood Park* 1 Don Carlos, in a merry Spight, Did Stella to his House invite.

†4. a. Matter for regret. *Obs.*$^{-1}$

c1400 *Rom. Rose* 7254 It is gret pite, out of drede, For they wole be noon ypocritis. Of hem me thynketh (it) gret spite is.

†b. An annoying matter, affair, or thing. *Obs.*

1577–82 Breton *Toyes Idle Head* Wks. (Grosart) I. 54/2 My Lady lawght: Is loue, quod she, A spight and sporte, to both at ones? 1598 B. Jonson *Ev. Man in Hum.* i. iii, I ha' no bootes, that's the spight on't. 1606 *Choice, Chance*, etc. (1881) 48 What a spight it was to see a horse of service drawe in a doung-carte. 1655 Fuller *Ch. Hist.* i. 34 But now the Spight is, that an unparallel'd Critick in Antiquity, leaves this Patrick at this time sweating in the Irish Harvest.

†c. A feeling of annoyance or irritation. *Obs.*

a1586 Sidney *Arcadia* v. (1598) 443 She ioyned the vexation for her friend, with the spite to see her selfe as she thought rebelliously detained. 1670 Temple *Let. Sir J. Trevor* Wks. 1720 II. 233 After this I waited with great Spight and Impatience..about five Hours.

5. a. *Phrase.* **in spite of**, in defiance (†scorn or contempt) of; in the face of; notwithstanding. (Cf. despite *sb.* 5.)

α. c1400 *Destr. Troy* 1968 But for noy of my nobilte & my nome gret, I shuld..spede the to spille in spite of þi kynge. 1563 *Mirr. Mag., Blacke Smyth & Ld. Awdeley* lx, He dyed, Clad in his cote armor paynted all in paper, Al torne and reversed in spyte of his behaver. 1568 Grafton *Chron.* II. 113 In spite both of him and his Legate, they kept company with them that were excommunicate. 1617 Moryson *Itin.* i. 232 They..said, that the Scripture must be beleeved, in spite of all Cosmographers and Philosophers. 1687 A. Lovell tr. *Thevenot's Trav.* i. 36 He told us that the arrows would fight together in spite of us. 1711 Steele *Spect.* No. 79 ¶1 The Heart of Man deceives him in spite of the Lectures of half a Life. 1765 *Museum Rust.* IV. 266 They grow poor, in spite of all possible industry. 1818 Scott *Br. Lamm.* xx, The tears, in spite of her, forced their way between her fingers. c1853 Kingsley *Misc.* (1859) I. 15 The English are attacked treacherously in spite of solemn compacts. 1881 Walford *Dick Netherby* xxi, I'll go on my own way in spite of you all.

β. 1576 Gascoigne *Steele Gl.* (Arb.) 49 This worthy bird hath taught my weary Muze To sing a song, in spight of their despight. 1581 Pettie tr. *Guazzo's Civ. Conv.* iii. (1586) 129 b, The wife in spight of the husband, gave halfe the meate..to a poore bodie. 1627 Drayton *Agincourt*, etc. 89 In spight of Fate they'll giue their Foe the worse. 1666 Boyle *Orig. Forms & Qual.* 165 The Water will, in spight of the Form, continue far lesse cold, then..its nature requires. 1702 Rowe *Tamerl.* Prol., In spight of Time, the Sacred Story lives. 1762 *Gentl. Mag.* XXXII. 217/2 The benefits of innoculation have established the practice in spight of all opposition. 1816 F. H. Naylor *Hist. Germany* I. i. i. 16 In spight of their efforts.

b. In phrases with †*face*, †*heart*, †*nose*, *teeth*. (Cf. 6 b.)

14.. in *Tundale's Vis.* (1843) 108 They schall askape in spyte of thi face. 1549 [see tooth *sb.* 5]. 1570– [see nose *sb.* 6 b]. 1574 tr. *Marlorat's Apocalips* 13 Euen in spight of their harts they saw Christ sitting at the right hand of God. 1622 Gataker *Spir. Watch* (ed. 2) 73 It would euen enforce them to looke about them in spight of their teeth. 1689–1835 [see tooth *sb.* 5].

c. In the phr. *in spite of spite.* Now *arch.*

1592 Warner *Alb. Eng.* vii. xxxvi. (1612) 172 In spight of Spight in Hespera I golden fruit would pull. 1622 Wither *Philarete* N vij, Those that sleight thee now, shall loue thee, And, in spight of spight, approue thee. 1855 Tennyson *Maud* i. xiii. i, His face, as I grant, in spite of spite, Has a broad-blown comeliness.

†d. *in (one's) spite*, = in spite of (one). *Obs.*

1615 Chapman *Odyss.* x. 382 Ile guard thee free, And saue thee in her spite. 1709 Pope *Ess. Crit.* 34 Mævius scribbles in Apollo's spight. 1732 —— *Ess. Man* i. 285 In erring reason's spight One truth is clear; Whatever Is, is Right. 1765 Goldsm. *New Simile* 4 The modern scribbling kind, who write In wit, and sense, and nature's spite.

†e. *in the spite of*, in spite of. *Obs.*

1632 Sanderson *Serm.* 546 In the spight of so many enemies. 1716 M. Davies *Athen. Brit.* III. 92 In the sight and spight of the Scotch Forces, under Cardinal Beton.

6. a. spite of, = prec. (Cf. despite *sb.* 6.)

1509 Hawes *Past. Pleas.* xix. (Percy Soc.) 96 Spyte of your enemyes, I shal me so spede, That in short tyme ye may rewarde my mede. c1600 Shaks. *Sonn.* cvii, Death to me subscribes; Since spight of him Ile liue in this poore rime. 1681 Dryden *Abs. & Achit.* i. 565 For, spight of him, the weight of Business fell On Absalom, and wise Achitophel. 1761 Mrs. F. Sheridan *Sidney Biddulph* II. 167 Her surprize, spite of her assumed airs of grandeur, was not to be concealed. 1823 Bentham *Not Paul* 168 Spite of reason, religion, and Jesus, the victory is, in this account, given to James. a1873 Deutsch *Lit. Rem.* (1874) 366 That stamp of unity which it now possesses, spite of the occasional difference of style.

†b. In phrases (cf. 5 b and 5 c). *Obs.*

1526 Rastell in *Shaks. Jest Bk.* (1866) 45 He agayn said he wold bryng them ouer spyte of his teth. 1532 Tindale *Expos. v–vii. Matt.* (1550) 39 b, To obeye theyr cruelnesse and tyrannye spite of their heades. 1573 Tusser *Husb.* (1878) 130 Least..it noieth or perisheth, spight of thy hart. 1600 W. Watson *Decacordon* (1602) 10 Satisfaction and restitution will be demaunded,..spite of their teeths. *Ibid.* 341 [The Jesuits] shall be lanced into the quicke, spite of spite it selfe. 1618 Brathwait *Rem. after Death* E vij, To such an one as sole executour, Spite of our nose playes Executioner. 1664–75 [see nose *sb.* 6 b].

c. With *of* omitted. (Cf. despite *sb.* 6.)

1878 S. Phillips *On Seaboard* 62 Spite dark Torquemada and his hecatombs of slain, Spite Te Deums sung by Tiber side for murder on the Seine.

spite (spaɪt), *v.* Also 6 spyte, 6–8 spight. [Aphetic form of despite *v.* (OF. *despiter*): cf. prec. and MDu. *spîten* (Du. *spijten*, WFris. *spite*), MLG. *spîten.*]

†1. *trans.* To regard with contempt or spite.

a1400–50 *Alexander* 2346 þire athils of Atenes..kest vp a crie,..Sum in comending of his carpe & on [*read* oþer] clene it spitid. 1483 *Cath. Angl.* 355/2 To spite, *despicere.* 1541 Paynell *Catiline* v. 9 It doth not a lyttel helpe.., that the ryches of these men is spyted amonge strange nations. 1567 Drant *Horace, Ep.* i. xiv. E v, Not any there with waywarde eyes for my good lucke shal spyte me. 1601 B. Jonson *Poetaster* v. iii. (1905) 121 While these..applaud my poemes; I would not wish but such as you should spight them. 1659 N. R. *Prov., Eng. Fr.*, etc. 64 It is better to be spited then pitied. 1690 Norris *Beatitudes* (1694) I. 185 Envy, which, indeed, spites every thing that is excellent.

2. To treat spitefully or maliciously; to annoy or thwart in a spiteful manner.

It is doubtful whether the pa. pple. *spit* in the *Destr. Troy* 2114 belongs here.

1592 Shaks. *Rom. & Jul.* iv. v. 55 Beguild, diuorced, wronged, spighted, slaine, Most detestable death, by thee beguil'd. 1598 R. Bernard tr. *Terence* (1607) 139 They spighted me miserably. 1658 *Whole Duty of Man* xvi. 133 Not caring what they suffer themselves, so they may spite their enemy. 1833 Ht. Martineau *Loom & Lugger* ii. i. 7, I should be sorry to say anything about spiting the Spitalfields weavers. 1864 Dasent *Jest & Earnest* (1873) I. 161 You have been spited by the Kellner, whom you have perhaps not saluted that day... You have been spited, and only had a little piece. 1885 *Manch. Exam.* 26 June 5/3 The double object of gratifying themselves and spiting the English.

b. In the phr. *to spite (one)*, in order to vent spite or spleen upon (another); with the object or intention of vexing or annoying.

c1555 Harpsfield *Divorce Hen. VIII* (Camden) 209 For nothing else but to spight the Pope. 1605 Shaks. *Macb.* iii. i. 111, I am recklesse what I doe, To spight the World. 1683 Wood *Life* (O.H.S.) III. 72 Thanksgiving day: appointed I presume on that day to spite the Presbyterians. 1880 'Ouida' *Moths* I. 31 I'll keep the child to spite her. 1885 'Mrs. Alexander' *At Bay* xi, I don't fancy Deering will cut off his nose to spite his face.

3. To fill with spite or vexation; to annoy, offend, irritate.

c1563 *Jack Juggler* C iv b, It spiteth my hart to haue lost it by suche open negligence. 1581 Pettie tr. *Guazzo's Civ. Conv.* i. (1586) 41 b, There is nothing spites us more, than to heare a man commend himselfe. 1627 *Lisander & Cal.* ii. 26 He..was justly spighted to see as well his brother as all the rest take them to their advantage. 1686 F. Spence tr. *Varilla's Ho. Medicis* 293 It spighted him infinitely, when people discoursed him upon the modesty of his ancestors. 1701 Swift *Contests Nobles & Comm.* Wks. 1755 II. i. 27 The nobles, spighted at this indignity done them by the commons, firmly united in a body. 1756 Home *Douglas* iii. i, One whom distress has spited at the world. 1816 Scott *Bl. Dwarf* xvi, The danger of intrusting thyself..in the power of one so spited against humanity. 1865 Le Fanu *Guy Dev.* III. v. 50 She was spited with it, as so many others are, because it won't do for us what we must do for ourselves.

†4. *intr.* To be angry or annoyed; to cherish spite. *Obs.*

c1560 Ingelend *Disobed. Child* D j b, Wherfore let my father spyte and spurne, My fantasye wyll neuer turne. 1577 Tusser *Husb.* (1878) 188 Let fortune spight, and boldly take thine ease. 1579–80 North *Plutarch, Fabius Max.* (1895) II. 80 This Livius spighted to see suche honour done to Fabius, so that one day..he burst out and said [etc.].

†b. With *at* (a person or thing). *Obs.*

1567–8 *Gismond of Salerne* i. iii. 16 It was my cruel fate that spited at my pleasant life forepast. 1581 A. Hall *Iliad* ix. 164 Wherat my mother spited much, and eke did iealous grow. 1616 Breton *Good & Badde, An Atheist* Wks. (Grosart) II. 10/2 He spightes at the gracious, and spurnes the godly. 1641 Prynne *Antipathie* 42 In this Bishops time, the Italians had gotten many Benefices in England, who being much spited at [etc.].

Hence **'spited** *ppl. a.*, **'spiting** *vbl. sb.*

c1460 *Towneley Myst.* xxiv. 286 Wyst I that he spake it in spytyng of me Tytt shuld I spede forto spyll hym. 1573–80 Tusser *Husb.* (1878) 159 Not minding by writing to kindle a spiting. 1705 Stanhope *Paraphr.* II. 423 A Pattern of reproached and spighted Innocence.

spiteful ('spaɪtfʊl), *a.* and *adv.* Forms: α. 5–6 spyteful, -full (5 -fulle), 6–7 spytfull; 5– spiteful, 5–7 -full (7 spitfull). β. 6 spyght-, 6–8 spightfull, -ful. [f. spite *sb.* + -ful.]

†1. Expressive of, characterized by, contempt or disdain; contemptuous, disdainful, opprobrious.

c1440 *Pol., Rel., & L. Poems* (1903) 227 With wordis greete and spiteful ooþ þou defendist pee of þi foule folie. c1450 *Myrr. our Ladye* 243 She knew before that he shulde be greatly payned wyth spyteful repreues and harde tormentes. 1533 More *Debell. Salem* v. Wks. 939/1 When he called the chief priest a whyted wal, whiche was a spyghtfull word among them. a1548 Hall *Chron., Hen. VI*, 130 b, The Parisians..taunted the Englishmen with the most spitefull wordes, and shamefull termes. 1639 S. Du Verger tr. *Camus' Admir. Events* 115 He returned her answeres..full of reproaches, and spitfull termes. a1700 Evelyn *Diary* 25 Dec. 1657, These were men of high flight and above ordinances, and spake spiteful things of our Lord's Nativity.

†b. Bringing contempt or opprobrium; disgraceful, shameful. *Obs.*

1550 Becon *Jewel of Joy* Wks. 1564 II. 40 b, Jesus Chryst ..suffred the moste spitefull death of the crosse. 1577–82

BRETON *Toyes Idle Head* Wks. (Grosart) I. 54/2 Dame Venus game. Which spightfull sporte for to attaine Some so doo dull their sences all. *c* **1586** C'TESS PEMBROKE *Ps.* XCII. iv, Mine eye shall spy My spies in spightfull case.

2. Full of, possessed or animated by, spite; malicious, malevolent. Also *fig.* of things.

1490 CAXTON *Eneydos* xii. 46 The influences of the heuens so spytefull. **1561** T. NORTON *Calvin's Inst.* I. (1634) 70 He is of nature froward, spitefull, and malicious. **1591** LYLY *Endym.* IV. iii, Belike you cannot speake except you bee spightfull. **1663** BUTLER *Hud.* I. iii. 362 The distress He suffer'd from his spightful Mistress. **1699** GARTH *Dispens.* I. 5 A spightful noise his downy Chains unties, Hastes forward, and encreases as it flies. **1820** KEATS *Lamia* II. 228 Let..the spiteful thistle wage War on his temples. **1841** BROWNING *Pippa Passes* Poems (1905) 166 She'll still face down The spitefullest of talkers in our town. **1874** HOLLAND *Mistr. Manse* 73 And in the midnight came the rain; In spiteful needles at the first.

b. Of the tongue, words, etc.

1557 *Tottell's Misc.* (Arb.) 212 Of wicked wiues this is the lot, To kill with spitefull tong. **1576** GASCOIGNE *Steele Glas* (Arb.) 47 For spyteful tongs.. Deeme worst of things, which best..deserued. **1640** BP. HALL *Episc.* II. xvii, Pamphlets with spightfull invectives. *a* **1656** —— *Rem. Wks.* (1660) 102 Bitter or spightfull words against his Brethren. **1711** ADDISON *Spect.* No. 169 ¶ 11 A spiteful Saying gratifies so many little Passions. **1868** TENNYSON *Spiteful Let.* i, It is here, the close of the year, And with it a spiteful letter. **1884** F. M. CRAWFORD *Rom. Singer* I. 16 People are saying many spiteful things about him.

c. Of feelings, actions, etc.

1560 DAUS tr. *Sleidane's Comm.* 356 b, Whan they uttered their malice and spitefull hatred against us. **1582** STANYHURST *Æneis* II. (Arb.) 61 In father his presence with spightful villenye cancred. **1662** EVELYN *Chalcogr.* 54 The famous S. Roch and the spitefull coronation with thornes. **1730** BAILEY (fol.), *Spitefulness*, a spiteful Temper. **1821** SCOTT *Kenilw.* xxii, The old man was muttering, with spiteful impatience, 'Am I for ever to be recalled to the affairs of earth from those of heaven?' **1862** BURTON *Bk. Hunter* (1863) 285 Having torn through a life of spiteful controversy with his fellow-men.

†**3.** Distressing, annoying, vexing. *Obs.*

a **1548** HALL *Chron., Hen. VI*, 84 His name and fame was spitefull and dreadfull to the common people. **1606** G. WOODCOCK *Hist. Ivstine* XII. 53 Afterwardes that all thinges might seeme more spightfull, he gaue generall commaundement to his company, that they should..adore him. **1633** G. HERBERT *Temple, Assurance* i, O spiteful bitter thought! Bitterly spiteful thought! Couldst thou invent So high a torture!

†**4.** As *adv.* Excessively, extremely. *Obs.*

c **1440** *Alph. Tales* 306 It was spitefull dere. *c* **1548** in Hazl. *E.P.P.* IV. 12 A spightfull gay thynge, of all that ever I wyst.

spitefully (ˈspaɪtfʊlɪ), *adv.* [f. prec.]

1. In a spiteful manner; with spite.

1532 MORE *Confut. Tindale* 45 If the deuyll sholde hym self syt & deuise to speke spyghtfully. **1560** DAUS tr. *Sleidane's Comm.* 433 Marques Albert had written certen thinges spitefully and bitterly. **1635** R. N. tr. *Camden's Hist. Eliz.* I. 30 Having been spightfully used with unworthy reproaches. **1646** CRASHAW *Poems* (1904) 139 Cruel Auster ..Sham'd not spitefully to wast All his leaves. *a* **1704** T. BROWN *Let. M. Burghope* Wks. 1711 IV. 255, I could dwell spightfully upon this Subject for an hour or two. **1714** SWIFT *Imit. Hor.* I. vii, The farmers, spitefully combin'd, Force him to take his tithes in kind. **1855** *Poultry Chron.* III. 388 A basket coop placed over a spitefully disposed hen. **1878** BROWNING *Poets Croisic* 11 The spit of sandy rock which juts Spitefully northward.

†**2.** Excessively, extremely. *Obs.*⁻¹

1567 *Trial Treas.* (Percy Soc.) 38 My littell finger is spitefully sore: You will not beleue how my hele doth ake.

spitefulness (ˈspaɪtfʊlnɪs). [f. as prec.] The quality, character, or fact of being spiteful.

1530 PALSGR. 274 Spytefulnesse, *despitevseté*. **1576** FLEMING *Panopl. Epist.* 197 You abhorre that principalitie, with equall proportion of spightfulnesse. **1628** WITHER *Brit. Rememb.* III. 1119 With spightfulnesse, that scarce can matched be. **1648–9** *Eikon Bas.* 124 The spightfulness of a few. **1711** W. KING tr. *Naude's Ref. Politics* iv. 133 The spightfulness of two Monks, who had no other weapons but their pens and their tongues. **1741** RICHARDSON *Pamela* (1824) IV. 69 As to the Accusation of Spitefulness. **1841** DICKENS *Barn. Rudge* vii, Every little bone in Miggs's throat and neck developed itself with a spitefulness quite alarming. **1884** *Fortn. Rev.* June 813 That small spitefulness which is sometimes the concomitant of weak or effeminate natures.

spite-king. *rare*⁻¹. [f. SPITE *sb.* or *v.*] One who has a spite at kings.

1614 CAMDEN *Rem.* 155, I know not why that Spite-king Buchanan should enuie lesser titles to Princes.

spitel: see SPITTLE.

spiteless (ˈspaɪtlɪs), *a.* [f. SPITE *sb.* + -LESS.] Devoid of or free from spite.

1875 BROWNING *Aristoph. Apol.* 111 Innocuous anger, spiteless rustic mirth.

†**spitemouse.** *Obs. rare.* (See quot.)

1668 CHARLETON *Onomast.* 22 *Mus Araneus*, the Hardshrew, or Spitemouse, or Erdshrew.

spiteousely, etc., varr. SPITOUSLY *adv. Obs.*

†**spite-wed**, *a. Obs.*⁻⁰ (See quot.)

1589 PUTTENHAM *Eng. Poesie* (1869) 236 Sir Thomas Smith.., seeking to geue an English word to this Greeke word ἄγαμος, called it Spitewed, or wedspite.

spitfire (ˈspɪtfaɪə(r)), *a.* and *sb.* Also 6–7 **spitfier**, 7 **spetfire**, 6–9 **spit-fire**. [f. SPIT *v.*²]

A. *adj.* **1. a.** That spits fire; fire-spitting; *fig.* irascible, displaying anger or hot temper.

1600 ROWLANDS *Lett. Humours Blood* ix. 15 That with a spit-fier Serpent so durst fight. **1791** NAIRNE *Poems* 103 Where..spit-fire cats their midnight revels keep. **1850** WHIPPLE *Ess. & Rev.* II. 306 A spitfire satirist, or moody misanthrope. **1866** CHAMBERS *Ess.* Ser. II. 90 A venerable spitfire terrier,..mentally engaged in the business of rat-catching. **1894** MRS. H. WARD *Marcella* I. 10 A little spitfire outsider.

b. Heated, angry.

1894 *Tablet* 20 Jan. 86 The lurid vapours of spit-fire controversies.

2. ***spitfire-jib***: (see quot.). *Naut.*

1858 MAYNE REID *Ran away to Sea* (1859) xii. 93 Even under such a wind she still continued to carry most of her sail..while her storm, spit-fire, and third jibs were still kept bent to the breeze. **1867** SMYTH *Sailor's Word-bk.* 643 *Spitfire-Jib*, in cutters, a small storm-jib of very heavy canvas. **1894** *Outing* XXIV. 193/1, I advise that a 'spit-fire' or storm jib be carried whenever a sail of any distance is contemplated.

B. *sb.* **1. a.** A thing which emits or vomits fire; *esp.* a cannon.

1611 COTGR., *Bouches à feu*, Spit-fires; Artillerie, Ordnance. **1614** ROWLANDS *Fooles Bolt* (Hunterian Cl.) 19 Spaines Hell spawne of fleete,..With all their brasen Spit-fiers. **1680** C. NESSE *Ch. Hist.* 423 Those two monstrous spet-fires, call'd the Earth-quake and Grand-Diabolo,.. planted against Rhodes and Constantinople. **1785** *Span. Rivals* 5 Yes, that spitfire, the Rock of Gibraltar will bear us witness. **1842** F. TROLLOPE *Vis. Italy* II. 199 Vesuvius..is the most renowned of all accessible spit-fires. **1901** 'LINESMAN' *Words by Eye-witness* v. (1902) 113 The 3-inch spitfire on the lower slopes of Spion Kop.

b. A slight eruption or explosion.

1887 RUSKIN *Præterita* II. 61 Firing up under their feet in little splutters and spit-fires of the most appalling heresy.

2. One whose temper is fiery; an irascible, passionate, or quick-tempered person.

1680 BAXTER *Cath. Commun.* (1684) 38 Malignant Spit-fires do already write books full of palpable Lies against other men. **1687** T. BROWN *Saints in Uproar* Wks. 1730 I. 77 'Tis some comfort to me however, Bully Spit-fire, that thou canst not abuse me, without falling foul upon my Country. **1721** AMHERST *Terræ Fil.* No. 32 (1726) 169 Not so fast, (I beg of you) my dear little spit-fire. *c* **1750** *Devon. Dial.* (1837) 7 Thecca spitfire woud a fitted en to a T. **1831** CARLYLE *Sart. Res.* II. viii, Deuce on it,..the little spit-fires! **1881** BESANT & RICE *Chapl. of Fleet* II. iv, What a little spitfire was this Nancy of mine!

3. A cat in an angry state.

1825 SCOTT *Fam. Lett.* (1894) II. xxiv. 395 We thought we should have to have opened the wall to get out the little spit-fire alive. **1878** BROWNING *Poets Croisic* 131 If she missed Priority of stroking, soon were stirred The dormant spit-fire.

†**spit-frog.** *Obs. rare.* [f. SPIT *v.*¹] In contemptuous use: A sword.

1615 FENNOR *Defence* in J. Taylor (Water P.) *Wks.* (1630) II. 152/2, I would not see thy spightfull Spit-frog drawne. **1658** HARRINGTON *Oceana* 6 What pastures you have will come unto the ballance of propriety, without which the publick sword is but a name or meer spit-frog.

ˈspitful. [f. SPIT *sb.*³] A spadeful.

1842 LOUDON *Suburban Hort.* 129 Without the cross-piece or perforated handle of the spade, the operator could not easily lift a spitful or turn it over. **1855** DELAMER *Kitchen Garden* (1861) 165 When..I have taken out a spitful of mould, and put in its place a spitful of loam.

ˈSpithead. The name of an anchorage and a strait which lie off Portsmouth, used *attrib.* in ***Spithead nightingale*** (see quots.) and ***Spithead pheasant*** (*a*) a bloater; (*b*) a kipper. *Naut. slang.*

1890 BARRÈRE & LELAND *Dict. Slang* II. 283/1 *Spithead nightingales* (naval), boatswains, and boatswains' mates, on account of their calls. **1948** PARTRIDGE *Dict. Forces' Slang* 177 *Spithead pheasant, a*, a bloater. (Navy.) **1954** *News Chron.* 4 Nov. 1/4 He had to produce: 1. a cat; 2. a Spithead Pheasant (a kipper); 3. a Sick Bay Shackle (a safety-pin). **1963** *Times* 26 Feb. 12/6 Spithead pheasant—slang for a kipper—still appears on the Navy's menu, but Spithead nightingales—bo'sun's mates and call boys are 'off'.

spither, obs. form of SPIDER *sb.*

spitish (ˈspaɪtɪʃ), *a.* Also 7 **spightish**. [f. SPITE *sb.* + -ISH.] Spiteful, snappish.

1627 W. SCLATER *Exp. 2 Thess.* (1629) 301 Spightishest insidiations of Satan. **1667** in *Cath. Rec. Soc. Publ.* III. 71 Herevppon that churl became spightish and furious. **1848** BARNES *Poems* (ed. 2) Gloss., *Spitish*, spiteful; snappish. **1891** T. HARDY in *Harper's Mag.* April 700/2 This answer made Pa'son Billy..rather spitish, not to say hot. **1909** *Westm. Gaz.* 5 June 2/2 From it..came spitish puffs of wind.

†**spitling.** *Obs. rare.* Also **spyt(e)ling, spiteling**. [? f. SPITTLE *sb.*³] Refuse, rubbish.

1620 MARKHAM *Farew. Husb.* iii. 27 Meanure it either with Oxe dung,..the spyteling [**1649** spiteling] of House-floores, or sweepings of Channels and Streets. **1638** *Ibid.* xiii. 72, I would have every Husband-man to make much of the rubbish, sweepings, parings, and spytlings of his house and yard.

spit-locking, *vbl. sb. Mil.* [? f. SPIT *sb.*³] (See quots.) Also **spit-lock** *v.*

1834 J. S. MACAULAY *Field Fortif.* iii. 49 Having set up the profiles, trace with a pick-axe (*note* Termed 'spit-locking') the escarp and counterscarp lines. **1892** G. PHILIPS *Text Bk. Fortif.* (ed. 5) 153 Cutting a groove along the surface of the ground with the point of a pick (*spit-locking*). *Ibid.* 154 The bounding lines of the parapet..may be spit-locked.

†**spitous**, *a.* and *adv. Obs.* Forms: *α.* 4–5 **spitus**, **-ous**, 5 **-ouse**, **-uose**; 5 **spytus**, **-ous**, **-ows**. *β.* 4 **spetos**, 5 **-ous(e**, **-ows**. [Aphetic ad. AF. *despitous*, f. *despit*: see SPITE *sb.*]

1. = DESPITOUS *a.*

α. a **1300** *Cursor M.* 14097 Martha thoght sco helpe ne wald, A spitus plaint to crist sco tald. **13..** *E.E. Allit. P.* B. 845 Whatt! þay sputen & speken of so spitous fylþe. ? *a* **1366** CHAUCER *Rom. Rose* 979 That arowe was as with felonye Envenymed, and with spitous blame. *c* **1400** LOVE *Bonavent. Mirr.* (1908) 256 Was there euere eny theef or worse odyus man so sone dampned and putte to so spitouse deth? *c* **1450** LOVELICH *Merlin* 2830 More feers he was & more hydows, also more egre, & mochel more spytows, thanne the whyte [dragon] was. **1481** CAXTON *Reynard* (Arb.) 106 Isegrym wende wyth thyse mockyng and spytous wordes to haue goon out of his wytte.

β. **13..** *Gaw. & Gr. Knt.* 209 A spetos sparþe to expoun in spelle que-so myȝt. *a* **1400–50** *Alexander* 2458 Sparrethis spetous to spend & speris in handis. *Ibid.* 4567 He was spetous of speche & spised his driȝtins. *c* **1450** LOVELICH *Merlin* 2850 So spetows was þe bataylle betwixen hem.

2. As *adv.* = next.

c **1400** *Laud Troy Bk.* 7480 Then was wroth Episcropus That Ector spake to him so spitous; Dispitusly Ector he myssayde.

†**spitously**, *adv. Obs.* Forms: *α.* 4 **spitusli** (5 **-ly**), **spytously**, 4–5 **spitously** (4 **-liche**, 5 **-lich**); 5 **spetously**, **-owsle**. *β.* 5 **spiteouseley**, **-iously**. *γ.* 5 **spet-**, **spytuously**, **spytt-**, **spituosly**, **spiteuoseli**, **spytwysly**. [f. prec.] = DESPITOUSLY *adv.*

α. **13..** *Cursor M.* 5082 (Gott.), Þe coupe into ȝour seck put i, And presuned ȝou ful spitusli. **13..** *E.E. Allit. P.* B. 1285 Alle he spoyled spitously in a sped whyle. **1387** TREVISA *Higden* (Rolls) II. 321 Þe childe anon þrewe doun þe crowne, and tradde þeron spitousliche wiþ his feet. *c* **1440** *Cast. Persev.* 27 Spylt is man spetously, whanne he to synne asent. *a* **1450** *Knt. de la Tour* (1868) 43 The houndes.. chaced and bote hem spitously bi the eeres and thies.

β. c **1400** *Destr. Troy* 3698 Hit spirit vp spitiously fyue speire lenght. *c* **1460** *Pol., Rel., & L. Poems* (1903) 204 Whan I smote so spiteousely.

γ. c **1440** *Partonope* 2003 A stroke smote he Vpon Sornogour[s] helme so gay, So spetuously that he gan affray. *c* **1450** in Aungier *Hist. Syon Monast.* (1840) 261 If any ley vyolente hande upon her souereyne or spituosly smyte or wownde her. **1495** *Trevisa's Barth. De P.R.* XVIII. vii. 753 A boore resyth full spytuously ayenste the poynt of a spere of the hunter.

ˈspit-out. *Ceramics.* [f. vbl. phr. *to spit out*: see SPIT *v.*² 7 b.] Accidental blistering of a glaze when fired, caused by air or gas bubbles; the blisters so caused.

1909 *Trans. Engl. Ceramic Soc.* VII. 1 'Spit-out' is one of a number of 'mysterious' faults which occur in the manufacture of pottery. **1930** A. B. SEARLE *Encycl. Ceramic Industries* III. 199/1 'Spit-out' is most abundant when the atmosphere in the kiln is alternately reducing and oxidising. **1964** H. HODGES *Artifacts* ii. 52 Pin-holes..and spit-out (fine, broken blisters) are most commonly due to the evolution of gases from the body during firing puncturing the molten glaze. *a* **1977** *Harrison Mayer Ltd. Catal.* 19/2 Spit-out. This is a common fault which occurs during the decorating fire and consists of the formation of minute blisters or bubbles in the glaze... Spit-out occurs at the higher enamel kiln temperature.

spit-poison. *rare*⁻¹. [f. SPIT *v.*²] A venomous or malicious person.

a **1716** SOUTH *Serm.* (1744) X. 290 There goes a person for whom no one breathing was ever the better,..the scourge of society, a spit-poison, a viper.

ˈspit-roast, *v.* [f. SPIT *sb.*¹ + ROAST *v.*] *trans.* To cook (meat or fish) on a spit, either over a fire or in an oven. Freq. as *vbl. sb.* and *ppl. a.*

1954 J. A. BEARD *Compl. Bk. Barbecue & Rotisserie Cooking* 39 (*heading*) Rotisserie & spit roasting. **1959** *Good Food Guide* 27 The new landlord has already succeeded in astonishing the locality by spit-roasting a whole calf in the open for a Church festival. **1961** *House & Garden* Feb. 45 A spit-roasted chicken bought from the supermarket. **1961** S. BECK et al. *Mastering Art French Cooking* vi. 240 Spit roasting, when the chicken is wrapped in fat and continually rotated, is far less exacting than oven roasting. **1973** *Country Life* 13 Dec. 2024/2 Pike is particularly delicious when spit-roasted whole. **1976** *Times* 14 Feb. 11/5 Spit roasted is how these birds are served... Baste them frequently while spit roasting..you can check whether your spit roasted chicken is ready. **1978** *Lancashire Life* Nov. 150/2 John explains how the spring chicken will be spit roasted.

‖**spitskop** (ˈspɪtskɒp). *S. Afr.* Also **spitzkop**, and in dim. forms **spitzkopje**, **-koppie**. [Afrikaans *spitskop*, f. Du. *spits* pointed + *kop* KOP.] A sharp-pointed hill; also (with capital initial) used as a proper name.

1872 C. A. PAYTON *Diamond-Diggings S. Afr.* 3 He has the tabular mountains and 'spitzkops' (sharp pointed hills and peaks)..till he arrives within a few hours' distance of the Vaal. **1889** [see RANDJIE]. **1905** G. W. STOW *Native Races S. Afr.* xx. 396 The headquarters of 'Kousopp were at the two spitzkopjes to the left of the 'Gumaap. **1937** A. J. H. GOODWIN in I. Schapera *Bantu-Speaking Tribes S. Afr.* ii. 33 The flat-topped and 'spitzkop' hills so typical of the Karroo country and other parts. **1974** *Standard Encycl. S. Afr.* X. 221/2 The Spitskoppies group is a collection of gigantic granite rocks or 'island' mountains rising out of the Namib plain... It is a broken range dominated by the Great Spitskop (..1742 metres).

spit-sticker. *techn.* Also in shortened form spit-stick. [ad. Flem. *spitsteker*, = G. *spitzstichel.*] (See quots.)

1837 WHITTOCK *Bk. Trades* (1842) 304 The Jeweller requires, for finishing his work,..certain gravers,.. scrapers, 'spit-stickers', &c. **1875** KNIGHT *Dict. Mech.* 2279/1 *Spit-sticker*, a graver or sculper, with convex faces. **1909** WEBSTER, Spit-stick. **1920** R. J. BEEDHAM *Wood Engraving* 3 The spit-sticks..are tools by which the cut can be easily broadened by gradually pressing the point deeper into the wood. **1960** G. LEWIS *Handbk. of Crafts* 187 The Spitstick, like the graver, is made in several thicknesses. Its section is triangular, with sides tapering gently down to a point.

†**spittard.** *Obs.* [app. f. SPIT *sb.*[1]; see -ARD, and cf. G. *spiessert.*] = SPITTER[1].

There is prob. some connexion with SPYCCARD, but the exact nature of this is not clear.

1538 ELYOT, *Subulo*, an harte hauynge hornes without tynes, callyd as I suppose a spyttarde. **1607** TOPSELL *Four-f. Beasts* 122 Of the Hart and Hinde..When they begin to haue hornes, which appeare in the second yeare of their age, like Bodkins without braunches,..the Germans cal such an one Spitzhirtz, which in English is called a Spittard.

'**spitted,** *a. rare*[−1]. [f. SPIT *sb.*[1]] Prolonged into a single point or spike.

1626 BACON *Sylva* §757 Whether the Head of a Deer, that by age is more Spitted, may bee brought againe to be more Branched.

spitten ('spɪt(ə)n), *a. dial.* Repr. corrupted pronunc. *spit and (image, picture)* s.v. SPIT *sb.*[2] 3 b. Cf. *spitting image* s.v. SPITTING *ppl. a.* 3; *splitting image* s.v. SPLITTING *ppl. a.* 5.

1878 W. DICKINSON *Gloss. Dial. Cumberland* (ed. 2) 92/1 *Spitten picter*.., a strong likeness. **1887** HALL CAINE *Deemster* II. xxvi. 233 He looked the spitten picture of my ould father. **1910** A. BENNETT *Clayhanger* I. ii. 17 A nice-behaved young gentleman, and the spitten image of his poor mother. **1928** *Eng. Jrnl.* Dec. 819 Hit's the spitten image of you, Jilson. Your likeness, pint blank... Thar you are a-settin' in your cheer, a-holdin' your fiddle; thar's your basket. **1936** W. HOLTBY *South Riding* v. iv. 313 Spitten image of his dad, little Alf is, isn't he, Reg? **1941** J. FAULKNER *Men Working* vi. 105 Ifen hit ain't the spitten image of that church acrost the street.

†'**spitter**[1]. *Obs.* [See SPITTARD above. The form corresponds to G. *spiesser* (also *spiesshirsch*, *spitzhirsch*, = older Flem. *spieshert*, Du. *spithert*).] A young deer with simple unbranched horns; a brocket or pricket; = SPITTARD.

1565 COOPER *Thesaurus*, *Subulo*, an harte hauynge hornes without tines, called a Spitter. **1565** GOLDING *Ovid's Met.* x. (1593) 238 This goodlie spitter being void of dread..did haunt mens houses. **1601** HOLLAND *Pliny* I. 336 The lungs of a red Deer, especially the Spitter of that kind. **1610** GUILLIM *Heraldry* III. xiv. 128 In others [*sc.* beasts] plaine and uniforme, without Tines, as in Spitters. **1661** LOVELL *Hist. Anim. & Min.* Isagoge Bj, The hornes, in the stagge are ramous, simple in the spitter, palmate in others, ramous, and little in roes.

spitter[2] ('spɪtə(r)). [f. SPIT *v.*[2]]

1. One who spits or ejects saliva. Also *fig.*

1382 WYCLIF *Isaiah* l. 6 My face I turnede not awei fro the blameres, and the spitteres in me. **1615** CROOKE *Body of Man* 186 Melancholy men are all of them..great Spitters. **1707** FLOYER *Physic. Pulse-Watch* 239 The Splenetics are great Spitters. **1750** H. WALPOLE *Lett. to Mann* (1833) II. 344 He would not see them, but wrote to the Spitter (or as he is now called, Lord Gob'em,) to say, that he had affronted him very grossly before company. **1869** J. G. WOOD *Bible Anim.* 554 Buxtorf, however, explains the word ['*akshûb*, adder] as the Spitter.

†**2.** A pea-shooter. *Obs.*[−1]

1688 HOLME *Armoury* III. xvi. (Roxb.) 82/1 Shooting in [= with] a trunk staffer [*sic*] or spitter.

3. *U.S. Baseball.* = SPITBALL 2.

1908 *Baseball Mag.* July 7/2, I found by holding the ball with my finger tips and steadying it with my thumb alone I could get a peculiar break to it... It is not a 'spitter'. **1975** *New Yorker* 14 Apr. 98/2 The next pitch broke down sharply over the plate, and everyone cried, 'Spitter! Hey, a spitter!'

'**spitter**[3]. Now *dial.* [f. SPIT *v.*[3]]

1. A spade or spud.

1600 F. WALKER tr. *Span. Mandeville* 69 Commaunding certaine men to digge with spytters, they found..vnder the grounde a graue. **1706** PHILLIPS (ed. Kersey), *Spade* or *Spitter*, (among Husband-men) a Tool to dig the Ground with. **1825** JENNINGS *Obs. Dial. W. Eng.* 71 *Spitter*, a small tool with a long handle, used for cutting up weeds, thistles, &c. *Ibid.* 72 To move the earth lightly with a spade or spitter.

2. A spademan; a delver or digger.

1648 HEXHAM II, *Een Kley-steker*, a digger or spitter of Clay. *Ibid.*, *Een Spader*, a Delver, a Spademan, a Spitter. **1728** *Phil. Trans.* XXXV. 568 As soon as the Digger or Spitter has gone once the Breadth of the Ridge, he begins again at the other Side.

'**spitter**[4]. *rare*[−0]. [f. SPIT *v.*[1]] 'One who puts meat on a spit' (Johnson, 1755).

spitter-spatter. *rare*[−1]. [f. SPATTER *v.*] Trifling talk.

1619 J. TAYLOR (Water P.) *Kicksey Winsey* Wks. 1630 I. 39/1 With such fine scimble, scemble, spitter spattar, As puts me cleane besides the money-matter.

†**spittery.** *Obs.*[−1] [f. SPIT *v.*[2], after F. *crachoir.*] A spittoon.

a **1693** *Urquhart's Rabelais* III. xv. 127 They..spit in the Spitteries.

'**spitting,** *vbl. sb.*[1] [f. SPIT *v.*[1]] The action of piercing with, or fixing on, a spit. Also *attrib.*

1613 SHAKS. *Hen. VIII*, II. iv. 183 This respite..enter'd me..with a spitting power and made to tremble The region of my Breast. **1631** MABBE *Celestina* xv. 164 Shee used such diligence..that shee drew water at the second spitting. **1648** HEXHAM II, *Aen't Spit-stekinge*, a Spitting, or a Broaching of meate.

'**spitting,** *vbl. sb.*[2] [f. SPIT *v.*[2]]

1. a. The action of ejecting saliva from the mouth; expectoration.

13.. *K. Alis.* 898 (Linc.), Hadde he biden ony þing, Abouȝt he hadde his spittyng. *a* **1340** HAMPOLE *Psalter* xxi. 5, I am reproue of men, in spittynge, buffetynge, and pungynge with þe thornes. *c* **1430** *Freemasonry* (Halliw. 1840) 711 From spyttynge and snyftynge kepe the also. **1526** *Pilgr. Perf.* (W. de W. 1531) 250b, His betynges & buffetynges.., with spyttynges, bobbynges & other turmentes. **1565** COOPER *Thesaurus, Excreatio*, a spittyng out with retchynge. **1609** B. JONSON *Silent Woman* IV. i, The spitting, the coughing, the laughter, the neesing. **1648** SANDERSON *Serm.* II. 235 Clamours and outcries, railing, and spitting, and buffeting. **1733** CHEYNE *Eng. Malady* II. ix. §5 (1734) 212 The Spitting or Salivation, so common in Nervous Distempers. **1786** J. HUNTER *Treat. Vener. Dis.* VI. i. (1810) 456 He rubbed in..mercurial ointment, and had a slight spitting. **1808** *Med. Jrnl.* XIX. 506, I looked..for a return of his consumptive symptoms after the spitting had ceased. **1872** DARWIN *Emotions* xi. 260 Spitting seems an almost universal sign of contempt or disgust.

b. Const. *of* (blood, fire, etc.).

1565 COOPER *Thesaurus* s.v. *Excreatio*, It is bruysed.. against spittyng of bludde. **1634** MASSINGER *Very Woman* III. v, Here will be spitting of fire o' both sides presently! **1725** *Fam. Dict.* s.v., When this Spitting of Blood comes from the Stomach. **1789** W. BUCHAN *Dom. Med.* (1790) 339 Spitting of blood is generally preceded by a sense of weight. **1843** R. J. GRAVES *Syst. Clin. Med.* xxii. 261 We are surprised to find that cases of spitting of blood are not much more frequent.

2. Saliva ejected from the mouth; spittle.

a **1300** *Cursor M.* 25489 Iesus, þat wald..þi suete face.. With Iuus spitting file. *c* **1340** HAMPOLE *Pr. Consc.* 655 Of þe comes mykel foul thyng, Als fen, and uryn and spyttyng. **1483** *Cath. Angl.* 355/2 To cast Spyttynge, *desputare, exscreare.* **1639** S. DU VERGER tr. *Camus' Admir. Events* 210 All Berards brags were as so many spittings vomited up against heaven. **1691** tr. *Emiliane's Observ. Journ. Naples* 114 So that the Precious Blood..is spilt upon the Ground, amongst the Filth and Spittings of the People. **1701** STANHOPE *Pious Breathings* VII. ix. 333 That adorable face.. was then defiled..with the spittings of unhallowed lips. **1837** CARLYLE *Fr. Rev.* II. v. v, In descending, he received a spitting (*crachat*) on the head, and some others on his clothes.

3. a. Sputtering; *spec.* of molten silver.

1611 COTGR., *Petillement*,..the spitting of a candle. **1866** *Chambers' Encycl.* VIII. 729/2 Silver,..when..it is fused,..absorbs a considerable quantity of oxygen, which it expels in the act of solidification with a peculiar sound, technically known as spitting. **1887** *Encycl. Brit.* XXII. 71/1 The presence of even very little base metal in the silver prevents this 'spitting'.

b. A slight sprinkle or shower of rain.

1707 in R. M. F. Watson *Closeburn* (1901) App. 274 All.. shall be reckoned but as spittings before the great shower. **1869-** in dial. glossaries.

c. *techn.* (See quot.)

1879 *Cassell's Techn. Educ.* I. 271/1 In the needle-gun.. the 'spitting' of fire at the breech is inconveniently great.

4. *attrib.* **a.** In sense 'for spitting in or on', as *spitting-box*, *-cup*, *-dish*, *-kettle*, *-mug*, *-pan*, etc.

1687 MIÈGE *Gt. Fr. Dict.* II, A *spitting Box, *un Crachoir.* **1794** PARR *Let. Maltby* Wks. 1828 VIII. 336 Is there a smoking room, an arm-chair, a spitting-box, a wax-candle? **1834** MARRYAT *P. Simple* (1863) 88 A large tin spitting-box [was] fixed to his chest by a strap over the shoulders. **1684** HEDGES *Diary* (Hakl. Soc.) I. 149 A Beetle Box, Plate, Arrack Bowl, *Spitting Cup, and Silver handle for a Fan. **1706** STEVENS *Span. Dict.* I, *Escupidero*, a *spitting Dish. **1815** *Hist. J. Decastro* III. 339 Let's have..pipes and tobacco, some sawdust and a *spitting kettle. **1895** *Army & Navy Price List* 15 Sept. 1316/1 *Spitting Mugs. **1834** MARRYAT *P. Simple* (1863) 88 There were *spitting-pans placed in different parts of the decks for the use of the men. **1731-8** SWIFT *Polite Conv.* 39 Come, pray, stand out of my *spitting place. **1727** POPE, etc. *Art of Sinking* 125 Paint, diet-drinks, *spitting-pots, and all other necessaries of life. **1776** *Pennsylv. Even. Post* 27 Apr. 212/1 Blue and white artichoke cups and spitting pots. **1836** J. M. GULLY *Magendie's Formul.* 127 The water used in washing the spitting-pots. **1662** PEPYS *Diary* 21 Nov., To bed this night, having first put up a *spitting-sheet, which I find very convenient. **1684** A. HALL *Will* (Somerset Ho.), One paire of spitting sheetes now used upon my bed. **1707** J. STEVENS tr. *Quevedo's Com. Wks.* (1709) 164 They left me, looking all over like an old Man's Spitting-sheet. **1831** J. JEKYLL *Corr.* (1894) 286 The cigar-smokers of Dublin use *spitting vases in the shape of mitres.

b. In sense of 'facilitating or inducing spitting', as *spitting-drop*, *-pill.*

1629 MASSINGER *Picture* IV. ii, He's acquainted With the green water, and the spitting-pill's Familiar to him. **1692** *Poor Robin's Alm.* Advt., Spitting-Drops, that any one may safely take.

c. Misc., as *spitting distance*, *exordium*, *range*, *sickness.*

1599 NASHE *Lenten Stuffe* Wks. (Grosart) V. 245 This counterpoyson of the spitting sickenesse. **1600** SIR W. CORNWALLIS *Ess.* I. xii. H iv, He [Montaigne]..forceth you not to attention with a hem, and a spitting Exordium. **1774** J. EDWARDS *Hist. Redemp.* II. ii. (1788) 226 He did not think it too much..to become the laughing-stock and spitting-stock of the vilest of men. **1895** SIR H. MAXWELL *Dk. Brit.* xix. 280 You had him almost within spitting range. **1959** P. BULL *I know Face, but*..iv. 70 One of the reasons I had closed with the Chatham offer was that it was within spitting distance of London. **1965** *Listener* 3 June 841/3 All this the spectators can see at spitting distance. **1977** *Western Mail* (Cardiff) 5 Mar. 6/1 More than doubled pre-tax profits has taken the Midland Bank to within spitting distance of its two giant High Street rivals—National Westminster and Barclays.

'**spitting,** *vbl. sb.*[3] Now *dial.* [f. SPIT *v.*[3]] The action of digging, or of ploughing to a spade-depth; a small trench made with a spade.

1594 *Min. Archd. Colch.* (MS.) fol. 25b, Frauncis Fromont, the sonne, of Lytleburye, dyd work all daye vppon St. James daye at spitting of saffron ground in Walden. **1648** HEXHAM II, *Een spadinge, ofte spittinge*, a Spading, or a Spitting. **1764** RANDALL *Semi-Virgilian Husb.* Introd. lv, This action of the Sun is most considerable in Ridge work, especially in the Double Spitting, in the destruction of Weeds. **1892** in *Eng. Dial. Dict.*

'**spitting,** *ppl. a.* [f. SPIT *v.*[2]]

1. That spits, in various (chiefly *transf.*) senses of the verb.

1567 DRANT *Horace, Ep.* E ij, A linnine slop in spitting snowe. **1687** MIÈGE *Gt. Fr. Dict.* I, *Cracheur*, a spitting (or spawling) man. **1860** TYNDALL *Glac.* I. xxvii. 211 The spitting snow-dust raised by the wind. **1888** CHURCHWARD *Blackbirding* 81, I saw the spitting flashes and heard the bangs. **1901** 'LINESMAN' *Words by Eye-witness* xii. (1902) 252 There is a roar from the razor-back, an angry spitting reply from the donga. **1910** W. B. YEATS *Green Helmet* 33 With my spitting-cat heads, my frenzied moon-bred band. **1953** DYLAN THOMAS *Under Milk Wood* (1954) 48 And in Willy Nilly the Postman's dark and sizzling damp tea-coated misty pygmy kitchen where the spittingcat kettles throb and hop on the range.

2. In specific names of reptiles, etc., as **spitting asp, click-beetle, gecko, snake; spitting cobra,** the African black-necked cobra, *Naja nigricollis.*

1653 ROWLAND *Topsell's Serpents* 653 The *Ptyas* or spitting [**1608** spetting] Asp resembleth an Ash colour. **1802** SHAW *Gen. Zool.* III. I. 279 Spitting Gecko. *Lacerta Sputator.* **1855** MORTON *Cycl. Agric.* I. 47 *A[griotes] sputator.*—The pasture or spitting click-beetle is much smaller than *A. obscurus.* **1887** *Encycl. Brit.* XXII. 197/1 One [genus], *Sepedon hæmachates*,..or 'Ring-Neck Snake,' ..shares with the cobra a third Dutch name, that of 'spuw slang' (Spitting Snake). **1931** R. L. DITMARS *Snakes of World* xiii. 167 The Spitting Cobra or Black-necked Cobra ..comes close to being the most dangerous snake of Africa. **1976** G. DURRELL *Stationary Ark* ii. 28 This [word] was expectorated with a venom that would have done credit to a spitting cobra.

3. *spitting image*, alteration of *spitten image* (see SPITTEN *a.*). Cf. *splitting image* s.v. SPLITTING *ppl. a.* 5.

1901 A. H. RICE *Mrs. Wiggs* vii. 94 He's jes' like his pa —the very spittin' image of him! **1917** A. W. BLUE *Quay Head Tryst* 70 He's the spittin image o' a thrawn fechter. **1929** H. S. WALPOLE *Hans Frost* III. v. 370 In another twenty years..she would be her mother's spitting image. **1938** N. COWARD *Operette* I. vii. 58 Believe it or not, she was the spitting image of Princess Ena! **1960** H. PINTER *Caretaker* II. 33 Your spitting image he was. *a* **1974** R. CROSSMAN *Diaries* (1975) I. 243 Far from adapting himself to his new position he is adapting his new position to himself (No. 10, as I saw the other day, is the spitting image of his little house in Hampstead).

†**spittle,** *sb.*[1] *Obs.* Forms: α. 3–4, 6 **spitel** (5 **-ele**), 4–6 **-ell**; 4 **spytel**, 5 **-elle**, **spytyl**, 5–6 **-ylle**; 5 **spetel**, 6 **-yle**; 5–6 **spittell**, 6 **-el**, *Sc.* **spittaill, spyttell, -yll(e, spettell, -ylle.** β. 6 **spyttle**, 6–7 **spitle**, 6–9 **spittle.** γ. 7 **spitol, -oll.** See also SPITAL. [ME. *spitel*, *spittel*, etc., = MLG. *spittel*, *spettel*, MHG. *spittel*, *spittol* (G. *spittel*), ultimately representing an aphetic form of HOSPITAL, modified on the analogy of native words in *-el.* Forms with more original ending appear in OHG. *spitâl* (*spitaul*; G. *spital*), MLG. *spittâl*, *spettâl*, MDu. *spit(t)-*, *spetael*, MDa. *spital*, *spedal*, MSw. *spital(e*, *spetal(e*, Icel. *spítal*, *-ali.* The common source of these is app. Italian or Levantine: cf. It. *spedale*, dial. *spitale*, mod.Gr. σπιτάλι; also med.L. *spitalerius* (1342 in Du Cange), med.Gr. σπιταλιώτης (*c* 1350).]

1. A house or place for the reception of the indigent or diseased; a charitable foundation for this purpose, *esp.* one chiefly occupied by persons of a low class or afflicted with foul diseases; a lazar-house. (Now written SPITAL.)

α. *a* **1225** [see 4]. *c* **1315** [see 5 a]. **1388** WYCLIF *1 Kings* ii. 34 *marg.*, Rabi Salomon seith, that he made in desert a spitele for pore men. *c* **1400** *Rom. Rose* 6505 Whanne I see beggers quakyng,..Lete bere hem to the spitel anoon. *c* **1425** *St. Mary of Oignies* II. ii. in *Anglia* VIII. 152 Houses of mesels, þat are callid spitellis. *a* **1529** SKELTON *Col. Cloute* 1186 At..Saynt Mary Spyttell, They set not by vs a whystell. **1556** *Chron. Gr. Friars* (Camden) 43 At sent Mary spettell, the iij. dayes in Ester weke, preched the vicar of Stepney one Jerome.

β. **1571–92** [see b]. **1601** B. JONSON *Ev. Man in Hum.* II. iii, May they lie and starue in some miserable spittle. **1698** FRYER *Acc. E. India & P.* 150 We descended from this..to the Spittle, where we found the Poor faring well from their Benefactors. **1748** THOMSON *Cast. Indol.* I. lxxvi, She felt, or fancy'd..All the diseases which the spittles know. **1839**

STONEHOUSE *Isle of Axholme* 129 Burton Lazars..being the chief of all the spittles and lazar houses in England.

b. Distinguished from *hospital*, as being of a lower class than this.

1571 GRINDAL *Articles* B iv b, Whether your Hospitals, Spittles, and almose houses be well and godly vsed according to the foundation and auncient ordinances of the same. **1577** tr. *Bullinger's Decades* (1592) 156 There is mention made..of Hospitals for olde men, or spittles for beggars. **1592** *Nobody & Someb.* in Simpson *Sch. Shaks.* (1878) I. 289 He..for widdowes buildes Almes-houses, Spittles, and large Hospitals. **1621** BURTON *Anat. Mel.* III. i. III. i. 524 Put vp a supplication to him in the name of..an hospitall, a spittle, a prison. *a* **1641** BP. MOUNTAGU *Acts & Mon.* (1642) 385 They were fitter, if any were alive, for some Spittle or Hospitall, then for any service that they were able to do for Herod. **1702** *Guide for Constables* 98 Alms-houses, hospital, school or spittle.

c. *transf.* (See quot.)

1665 *Voy. E. India* 437 The Banians..have Spittles (as they say) on purpose to recover lame Birds and Beasts.

2. Phr. ***to rob the spittle***, to make gain or profit in a particularly mean or dastardly manner.

1632 QUARLES *Div. Fancies* I. xciv, Of all men, Vs'rers are not least accurst; They robb the Spittle; pinch th' Afflicted worst. **1679** ALSOP *Melius Inq.* I. ii. 100 To what end steal from the Reformed Churches? which had been merely to rob the Spittle. **1708** O. DYKES *Mor. Refl. Eng. Prov.* xix. 79, I am not to..ruin a Family, or rob the Spittle, to redress his Grievances.

3. *fig.* A foul receptacle or collection. Const. *of*.

1624 HEYWOOD *Gunaik.* IX. 438 Making their corrupt bodies no better than sinkes of sinnes, and spittles of diseases. **1642** FULLER *Holy & Prof. St.* III. xv. 192 Their souls have been the Chappells of sanctity, whose bodies have been the Spitolls of deformity. **1652** BENLOWES *Theoph.* X. x, Gluttons who make themselves spittles of each disease.

4. *attrib.* and *Comb.*, as ***spittle-beggar***, ***-door***, ***-evil*** (= leprosy), ***-founder***, ***-holiness***, ***-luck***, ***-mare***, etc.

1611 COTGR., *Vn gueux de l'ostiere*, a rogue, vagabond, or *Spittle begger. **1647** N. WARD *Simp. Cobler* 20 The least Error, if grown sturdy and pressed, shall set open the *Spittle-door of all the squint-ey'd, wry-necked, and brasen-faced Errors that are or ever were of that litter. *a* **1225** *Ancr. R.* 148 Moiseses hond,..so sone he hefde wiðdrawen hire ut of his boseme, bisemede oðe *spitel-vuel, & þuhte leprus. **1599** CHAPMAN *Hum. dayes Myrth* Plays 1873 I. 76 Yron and steele, vncharitable stuffe, good *spittle-founders, enemies to whole skinnes. *c* **1548** in Hazl. *E.P.P.* IV. 13 Ye are much bounde to God for suche a *spittell holines. **1545** ASCHAM *Toxoph.* (Arb.) 53 Blynde Fortune, stumbling chaunce, *spittle lucke. **1650** B. *Discollim.* 44 He gives me a leane lame *spittle Mare. **1612** DABORNE *Chr. turn'd Turke* 933 Insatiat goat, thou thinkst our wiues are such, As are your holy sisters,..Your *spittle nuns. **1599** NASHE *Lenten Stuffe* Wks. (Grosart) V. 247 They woulde not moue or stir one foote till they had disclaimd and abiurd their bedred *spittle-positions. **1599** B. JONSON *Cynthia's Rev.* II. v, Bawds and blinde Doctors, Paritors, and *spittle Proctors. **1632** MASSINGER & FIELD *Fatal Dowry* III. 1, I will rather choose a *spittle sinner Carted an age before. **1542** UDALL *Erasm. Apoph.* 96 b, All yᵉ rable of other like *spittle vilaines. **1596** LODGE *Wits Miserie* N j b, He is secretary to the *spittle whores.

5. Special Combs.: **a.** **spittle-house**, = sense 1.

c **1315** SHOREHAM I. 1828 Bote þe syke in-to a spytel hous Entry, þer beþ museles. **14..** *Lat.-Eng. Voc.* in Wr.-Wülcker 596 *Misothonium*, a Spytylhous. *c* **1440** *Promp. Parv.* 469 Spytylle howse, *leprosorium*. *c* **1480** HENRYSON *Test. Cres.* 391 He..Delyuerit hir in at the Spittaill hous. **1530** PALSGR. 274 Spytle house, *laderye*. **1558** *Act 1 Eliz.* c. 21 §30 Any Hospitall, Measondue or Spittel House..for the Sustentacion and Relief of pore People. **1600** NASHE *Summer's Last Will* G ij, As it is the Spittle-houses guise, Ouer the gate to write their founders names. **1607** SHAKS. *Timon* IV. iii. 39 Shee, whom the Spittle-house..Would cast the gorge at.

b. **spittle-man**, an inmate of a spital.

1593 G. HARVEY *Pierce's Super.* 185 Is it not impossible, for Humanity to be a spittle-man,..History a bankrowt? **1607** J. DAVIES (Heref.) *Summa Totalis* (Grosart) 26/1 Good Preachers, that liue ill (like Spittlemen) Are perfect in the way they neuer went. **1653** H. COGAN tr. *Pinto's Trav.* xxxi. 122 They..go up and down the streets with certain Clappers, like our Spittle men.

c. **spittle sermon**, one of the sermons preached on Easter Monday and Tuesday from a special pulpit at St. Mary Spital outside of Bishopsgate (afterwards at St. Bride's and finally at Christ Church in the City).

For later references see SPITAL 1 b.

a **1596** *Sir T. More* I. i. 113 You knowe the spittle sermons begin the next weeke. *a* **1637** B. JONSON *Underwoods* lx, The lady may'ress pass'd in through the town, Unto the Spittle sermon.

spittle (ˈspɪt(ə)l), *sb.*² Forms: 5 spyttle, 6 spyttel, -ell, spitell, 6– spittle. [Modification of SPATTLE *sb.*¹ or SPETTLE, after SPIT *v.*²]

1. a. Saliva, spit.

to lick, swallow, (one's) spittle: see LICK *v.* 1 b, and SWALLOW *v.*

1480 CAXTON *Myrr.* II. xv. 100 The spyttle of a man fastyng sleeth comynly the spyncoppe & the tode yf it touche them. **1530** PALSGR. 274 Spyttell that cometh out of the mouthe, *crachat, saliue.* **1594** T. B. *La Primaud. Fr. Acad.* II. 97 Although spittle be but an excrement and superfluitie, ..yet it is not vnprofitable, because it wetteth and moysteneth the tongue. **1650** BULWER *Anthropomet.* ix. 103 Their gums are seen with their teeth, their spittle slavering forth. **1673** *Phil. Trans.* VIII. 6152 When he treats of the Tast, he well considers..the nature of the Spittle. **1710** J. CLARKE tr. *Rohault's Nat. Philos.* (1729) I. 169 Those [bodies] that are perfectly dry or hard, have no Taste 'till they are mixed with our Spittle. **1782** PRIESTLEY *Corrupt. Chr.* II. VII. 84 The priest touched his mouth and ears with spittle. **1841** LANE *Arab. Nts.* I. 96 He put his finger to his mouth, and moistened it with his spittle. **1862** J. F. CAMPBELL *Tales W. Highl.* III. 270 Under cats, and dogs, and men's spittle.

b. *Sc.* A quantity of saliva ejected at one time.

1722 RAMSAY *Three Bonnets* III. 20 His floor was a' tobacco spittles. **179.** W. SIMSON in *Poets of Ayr.* (1910) 34 Scots rhyme then, though prime then, Will no' be worth a spittle. **1822** GALT *Sir A. Wylie* xxi, A gauze gown..spoilt with a spittle, or ony other foul thing out of the mouth of man.

†**2. a.** ***spittle of the sun***, gossamer. *Obs.*⁻¹

1574 HYLL *Weather* viii, Many long webbes (which some call the spittle of the Sun) driving in the aire, declare winde, or a tempest to folow.

†**b.** ***spittle of the stars***, honey-dew; nostoc. *Obs.*

1577 B. GOOGE *Heresbach's Husb.* IV. (1586) 180 b, Hony dewe,..a certaine spittle of the starres. **1656** T. WHITE *Peripatet. Instit.* 148 When any such matter is found in the Fields, the very Countrey-men cry it fell from Heav'n and the Starres, and, as I remember, call it the Spittle of the Starres. **1657** S. PURCHAS *Pol. Flying-Ins.* 133 Pliny affirmed the Hony-dew to bee either the sweat of the heaven, or the slaver or spittle of the stars.

3. The frothy secretion of an insect. Cf. CUCKOO-SPIT, -SPITTLE.

1821 CLARE *Vill. Minstr.* I. 135 Insects of mysterious birth..Hid in knots of spittle white.

4. Special Combs.: **spittle-ball**, a ball of chewed paper wet with saliva; †**spittle-bishop**, a Roman Catholic bishop (in allusion to the use of spittle in baptism); **spittle bug** *U.S.* = *froghopper* s.v. FROG¹ 8; cf. CUCKOO-SPIT² 1; **spittle-fly**, **-insect**, *U.S.* an insect forming, or bred in, a frothy secretion; †**spittle-wort**, pellitory, *Anacyclus Pyrethrum*.

1555 PHILPOT in Strype *Eccl. Mem.* (1721) III. App. 159, I have ben six tymes in examination, twice before the spitell bishopes. **1580** BLUNDEVIL *Horsemanship* IV. 43 b, Pirethum, otherwise called of some Spittlewort. **1882** *Vermont Agric. Rep.* VII. 77 Dr. Cutting spoke of the frog hopper, usually known as the spittle bug on grass. **1885** LELAND *Brand-new Ballads* (ed. 2) 4 As in country schools the urchins cast each one a spittle-ball. **1948** *Sun* (Baltimore) 9 June 26/8 Spittle-bug infection has damaged alfalfa fields. **1972** SWAN & PAPP *Common Insects N. Amer.* xiii. 136 Spittlebugs are named for the sticky, bubbly mass of froth with which the nymphs surround themselves.

ˈspittle, *sb.*³ Now *dial.* Forms: 1, 3–4 spitel (3 sputel), 5 spytelle, -yll, 6 spitil, 6–7 spittell; 4 spitle, 7– spittle. [OE. *spitel* (in the combs. *hand-*, *wád-spitel*), related to SPIT *sb.*³ and *v.*³]

1. A spade or small spade; a spud.

a **1100** *Gerefa* in *Anglia* IX. 263 Spade, scofle, wadspitel. **12..** [implied in SPITTLE-STAFF]. **133.** in *Cal. Inq. post Mortem* (1909) VII. 422 [Thirty] spitles [for digging turfs in the marsh]. **1334–5** *Ely Sacr. Rolls* II. 69 In iij ferr. emp. pro spitel, 6ᵈ. **1483** *Cath. Angl.* 356/1 A Spytelle, *spata.* **1514** *Hist. Monast. St. Peter, Glouc.* (Rolls) III. Introd. p. xl, Staves and knives, shovils, spitils, and mattockes. **1570** *Richmond. Wills* (Surtees) 228 One spittell, ij prig-netts, xijᵈ. **1617** *Shuttleworths' Acc.* (Chetham Soc.) 226 Hen. Grymshaye, for a spittle of iron and steele, xiiijᵈ. **1675** *Hereford Dioc. Reg.* (MS.), Digging with a small spade or spittle in his Garden. **1788** W. H. MARSHALL *Yorksh.* II. 355 *Spittle*, a spaddle, or little spade. **1828–** in many dial. glossaries.

2. A hoe or scraper.

1832 *Scoreby Farm Rep.* 21 in *Husb.* (L.U.K.) III, The ground..was kept tolerably clean by the spittle and hand hoe. *Ibid.*, This plantation has been kept perfectly clean with the spittle or Dutch hoe. **1855** [ROBINSON] *Whitby Gloss.*, *Spittle*, an iron blade fixed across the end of a staff for scraping a shop floor in muddy weather.

3. A baking implement; a shovel or peel.

1838 HOLLOWAY *Prov. Dict.*, *Spittle*, a board used in turning oat cakes. **1876–83** in Yks. and Lanc. glossaries.

4. *attrib.* and *Comb.*, as ***spittle fork***, ***-maker***, ***-spade***. See also SPITTLE-STAFF.

14.. *Tundale's Vis.* 724 Summe had..nawg[er]es, Cultorus, syþus kene wytall, Spytyll-forkus þe sowlys to fall. **1601** HOLLAND *Pliny* I. 608 Let there bee then either a small furrow rased along just through the middest of the shaddow with a spittle spade, or the point of some hooke. **1881** *Instr. Census Clerks* (1885) 43 Spittle Maker (Spade Handle).

spittle (ˈspɪt(ə)l), *v.*¹ *rare.* Also 4 spitel. [In early use f. SPIT *v.*² + -LE; later f. SPITTLE *sb.*²]

1. *intr.* To eject spittle; to spit.

c **1340** *Nominale* (Skeat) 154 *F[emme] coupe pur vn muche*, W[oman] spitelith for a flie. **1876** ROBINSON *Whitby Gloss.* 182 It was once the custom 'to spittle' at the name of the Devil in church.

2. *trans.* To make foul with spittle.

1596 NASHE *Saffron Walden* Wks. (Grosart) III. 51 To helpe his bedred stuffe to limpe out of Powles Churchyard, that else would haue laine vnreprivably spittled at the Chandlers.

ˈspittle, *v.*² *rare.* [f. SPITTLE *sb.*³] *trans.* To dig (*in*), to pare, etc., with a spittle. Hence **ˈspittling** *vbl. sb.*

1727 S. SWITZER *Pract. Gard.* 158 Dig it into the ground, but not deep, only just spittle it in, as gardiners term it. **1807** T. RUDGE *View Agric. Glouc.* 155 About the beginning of June,..they [*sc.* plants] are 'spittled', that is, the work-man, with a..small spade, turns over the surface mould carefully between every plant. *Ibid.* 156 Spittling generally costs a guinea and a half an acre. **1828** CARR *Craven Gloss.*, *Spittle*, to pare off the surface of the ground.

ˈspittled, *a.* [f. SPITTLE *sb.*² + -ED²: cf. SPITTLE *v.*¹] Covered with spittle.

1926 *Scots Observer* 1 Jan. 5/1 The tangled, insect-spittled vetches. **1939** DYLAN THOMAS *Map of Love* 12 The spittled eyes, the salt ponds in the sleeves.

spittle-house, -man: see SPITTLE *sb.*¹ 5.

†**ˈspittler.** *Obs.*⁻¹ [f. SPITTLE *sb.*¹] = HOSPITALLER 2 or 3.

a **1550** *Image Hypocr.* IV. 209 in *Skelton's Wks.* (1843) II. 441/2 Some be Templers And Exemplers, Some be Spitlers, And some be Vitlers.

ˈspittle-staff. Now *dial.* [f. SPITTLE *sb.*³] A kind of spade or digging implement.

12.. *Ancr. R.* 384 ȝif eax ne kurue, ne þe spade [*v.rr.* spitel staf, sputel stef] ne dulue. **1605** *Knaresb. Wills* (Surtees) I. 252 To Marmaduke Coghill one spitbell [*sic*] staffe and one iron appell craddell. **1676** *Hatton Corr.* (Camden) I. 133 One came behind Mr. Downs and with a spittle staff cleft his scull. **1866** BROGDEN *Prov. Lincs.*, *Spittle-staff*, a spud, used for stubbing thistles. **1877–** in Linc. and Durh. glossaries.

spittly, *a.* Also **spittley**. [f. SPITTLE *sb.*²] Marked by the presence of spittle.

1611 COTGR., *Salival*, spittlie, slimie. *Ibid.*, *Saliveux*, spittlie, slauering. *a* **1861** [see BOXY *a.*² 1]. **1935** E. R. EDDISON *Mistress* xxi. 434 Spittly and slimy..from the beast's mouth I plucked it out. **1949** L. A. G. STRONG *Maud Cherrill* ix. 47 Once again would come the sly leer and the spittly whisper. **1980** J. O'FAOLAIN *No Country for Young Men* iv. 71 'God blosht the wet turf,' she whispered and blasted it herself with spittly breath.

spittoon (spɪˈtuːn). Also **spitoon**. [f. SPIT *v.*² + -OON.] A receptacle for spittle, usually a round flat vessel of earthenware or metal, sometimes having a cover in the form of a shallow funnel with an opening in the middle.

1840 in Thornton *Amer. Gloss.* s.v., A well-dressed gentle-man picked up a China spittoon. **1841** DICKENS *Barn. Rudge* x, Not at all particular on the subject of spittoons. **1851** N. HAWTHORNE in J. Hawthorne *Hawthorne & his Wife* (1885) I. 420 There were spittoons..at equal distances up and down the broad entries. **1888** W. R. CARLES *Life in Korea* ii. 21 One or two small brass spittoons were on the floor.

spitty (ˈspɪtɪ), *a.* [f. SPIT *sb.*² and *v.*² + -Y¹.] Resembling spit; spitting or inclined to spit. Also *fig.*

1742 W. ELLIS *Mod. Husb.* June x. 73 They believe the Grass-hopper will breed from this spitty Matter. **1865** H. J. DANIEL *Muse in Motley* 43 He wud spet, Iss, spetty like a toad. **1909** *Chambers's Jrnl.* June 388/1 It took longer to get acquainted with the Major, who..spoke in such a spitty, hissy, foreign kind of way. **1945** B. MACDONALD *Egg & I* vi. 99 Great winds came bounding down..; blew rain at us in spitty gusts. **1950** *Audio Engin.* Sept. 32/2 The program material sounds *ragged* and *spitty*, and the *whisker* at the main peak can sometimes be detected. **1976** U. HOLDEN *String Horses* ii. 26 Lavender..smiled her spitty smile.

spituose, spitus, varr. SPITOUS *a. Obs.*

†**ˈspity**, *a. Obs.*⁻¹ In 5 spyty. [ad. MDu. *spītich* (Du. *spijtig*), f. *spīt* SPITE *sb.*] Spiteful.

1481 CAXTON *Reynard* (Arb.) 101 What many a spyty worde haue ye brought forth wyth false lesyngis.

Spitz (spɪts). [G. (also *spitzhund*), special use of *spitz* pointed, peaked.] A dog belonging to one of a group of northern breeds distinguished by thick fur, a pointed muzzle, pricked ears, and a tail curled over the back. Also *attrib.*, as ***Spitz dog***.

1842 H. STANLEY *Let.* 18 July in N. Mitford *Ladies of Alderley* (1938) 38 In this town [*sc.* Ems] wherever you go you see a white Spitz dog with a curly tail & black eyes. **1845** *Zoologist* III. 1104 The prevalence of the Spitz in Europe would readily account for such a combination. **1883** *Cent. Mag.* Apr. 911/1 Madonna was occupied with a spitz, holding it at one minute and pulling it by the tail the next. **1897** *Private Life of Queen* xviii. 147 The perky little tan-coloured German Spitz-dog, 'Marco'. *a* **1910** 'O. HENRY' *Rolling Stones* (1912) 181 Six burglars..bore away..a five-hundred-dollar prize Spitz dog. **1948** [see LAIKA]. **1978** *Times* 11 Feb. 2/4 The Japanese spitz, a small, white prick-eared creature like an undernourished Samoyed, appeared at Crufts for the first time.

spitz-devil. [f. SPIT *sb.*² or *v.*² Cf. the variant *spitting-devil.*] A small sputtering fire-ball made from wetted gunpowder. Also ellipt. ***spitz***.

1880 CARNEGIE *Pract. Trap.* 15 Light it, and place it in the hole instead of the spitz. *Ibid.* 16 After having made a 'spitz devil', as we called it at school, light it in the hole.

Spitzenberg (ˈspɪtsənbɜːg). Also **spitzenberg**, **Spitzenbergh**, **Spitzenburg**. [Origin unkn.; cf. quot. 1795.] An apple with a red and yellow skin, belonging to the North American variety so called, developed from a seedling first found at Esopus, N.Y.; also, the tree bearing this fruit.

1795 J. JAY *Let.* 12 Dec. in *Columbia Library Columns* (1970) XIX. 43 Ten are what we call Spitzenberghs, from the Name of the Man in whose orchard the first tree of the kind was found. **1809** 'D. KNICKERBOCKER' *Hist. N.Y.* I. III. i. 122 Mottled and streaked with dusty red, like a spitzenberg apple. *a* **1817** T. DWIGHT *Trav. New-Eng.* (1821) I. 45 The varieties of apple-trees are:..Spitzenberg, Holden Sweeting, Fall pippin. **1869** *Rep. Comm. Agric. 1868* (U.S. Dept. Agric.) 482 [He] names the Baldwin for dessert and cooking, the Spitzenburg for cooking. **1894** H.

FREDERIC *Copperhead* 71 He..picked out another apple—a spitzenberg this time. **1921** *Daily Colonist* (Victoria, B.C.) 8 Oct. 19/1 (Advt.), 320 Boxes of Apples..from our own ranch..Spitzenberg at $3.23. **1949** J. B. HERRICK *Memories* 5 Father laid in..a barrel each of Spitzenburgs and Baldwins.

Spitzflöte ('spɪtsflɜːtə). Also with small initial and anglicized **Spitz-flute, spitz flute**, etc. [Ger., f. *spitz* pointed, acute + *flöte* flute.] An organ stop of the type of the gemshorn, yielding a tone resembling that of the flute.

1855 E. J. HOPKINS *Organ* 118 The pipes of the Spitzflute are slightly conical. **1884** *Encycl. Brit.* XVII. 831/1 The 8 spitzflöte may be regarded as a variety of open diapason. **1894** T. ELLISTON *Organs* 119 *Spitz flute*, 8 ft. pitch. **1923** N. A. BONAVIA-HUNT *Mod. Organ Stops* 31 The spitzflöte differs in having a more graduated taper. **1925** W. L. SUMNER *Organ* x. 301 In British organs the stop is usually called spitzflöte or spitz flute... The spitzflöte has an interesting..and attractive tone with more harmonic development than the usual English gemshorn. **1966** H. & J. NORMAN *Organ Today* xi. 120 The Spitzflute (or more accurately Spitzflöte) is a large-scale open flute, the taper giving it blending qualities that would otherwise be lacking.

spitzkop, var. SPITSKOP.

spitzy ('spɪtsɪ), *a.* [f. SPITZ + -Y[1].] Resembling or pertaining to a Spitz dog. Also *fig.*, pointed.

1937 AUDEN & MACNEICE *Lett. from Iceland* xii. 185 A sort of little sheepdog, black and white with a thick but not very long coat, a broad forehead and a spitzy foreface. **1952** C. L. B. HUBBARD *Pembrokeshire Corgi Handbk.* i. 14 The extremely sharp-pointed tips to the ears prevalent in the more Spitzy Pembrokeshires. **1968** *Sunday Truth* (Brisbane) 3 Nov. 58/4 He had a 'spitzy nose'—a sharp nose—a scar on his left arm where he had been hurt by machinery.

spiv (spɪv), *sb. slang.* [Origin obscure: perh. from SPIFF *v.*[2], SPIFFY *a.*] A man who lives by his wits and has no regular employment; one engaging in petty blackmarket dealings and freq. characterized by flashy dress.

1934 A. BRACEY *School for Scoundrels* 336 *Spiv*, petty crook who will turn his hand to anything so long as it does not involve honest work. **1937** *Even. News* 12 Mar. 15/6 (Advt.), With the Lincoln and the Grand National in the offing, the twisters, the welshers, the 'spivs' and the 'boys' are getting ready for a profitable session of the gentle sport of rooking the racegoer. **1939** [see BARROW *sb.*[3] 4]. **1945** [see LAIRY *a.*[2] 1]. **1947** *Times* 13 Aug. 6/1 If spivs meant men living by their wits, the nets could be thrown very wide indeed. **1948** I. BROWN *No Idle Words* 107 It is queer that its opposite [of *deep*], wide, should have replaced it in Spiv-English. **1952** 'J. HENRY' *Who lie in Gaol* viii. 123 In appearance, he resembled the typical spiv; with coat-hanger shoulders, and pointed shoes, and a smile that would have been an asset to any confidence man. **1958** *People* 4 May 1/4 Who was responsible for letting the spivs hi-jack the crowds at Wembley? **1965** *New Statesman* 26 Nov. 851/1 The emergence of Robert Stephens, once a type-cast West End performer of small, seedy spiv-roles, as a major heroic actor in the making. **1978** *Cornish Guardian* 27 Apr. 3 Metrication will be an open invitation for every spiv and racketeer to cheat the British public.

Hence as *vb.*, (*a*) *intr.*, to make one's living as a spiv; (*b*) *trans.*, to spiff, to spruce (oneself) *up*; **spivved** (spɪvd), *ppl. a.*; **'spiv(v)ery**, behaviour characteristic of a spiv or the state of being a spiv; **'spivvish, 'spiv(v)y** *adjs.*, characteristic of a spiv; **'spivishly** *adv.*

1945 B. NAUGHTON in C. Madge *Pilot Papers* 99 See his Spivy coat—the width of the lapels, the padded-out shoulders? **1947** *Times* 18 Nov. 2/4 Instead of that brave new Britain all they had left was a land fit for bookies to spiv in. **1948** *Chambers's Jrnl.* Oct. 547/1 That is their focus, their touchstone—recognition of a unique quality in him, not to be obliterated by the sordid elements in his story, his obvious shiftiness of character, his spivery attributes or his too frequent lapses. **1948** C. DAY LEWIS *Otterbury Incident* ii. 18 Tilting his hat at an even more spivvish angle. **1951** KOESTLER *Age of Longing* I. i. 7 Surrounded by relatives and friends, a spivvy son and an insipid daughter,..he would have to meet the ultimate ordeal. **1952** A. WILSON *Hemlock & After* I. v. 96 I've spivved along on my own steam as far as I can go. **1956** D. M. DAVIN *Sullen Bell* 87 There were few people in the restaurant, spivvish-looking and absorbed. **1957** R. HOGGART *Uses of Literacy* ix. 225 Where domestic or personal roots are weak or have been forcibly broken, these attitudes can quickly lead to an extensive moral 'spivvery'. **1959** I. JEFFERIES *Thirteen Days* iii. 37 Scruffy lot. They'll get spivved up quick enough for a Naafi girl. **1965** *New Statesman* 19 Mar. 463/1 The spivvish businessman. **1966** J. GLOAG *Sentence of Life* ii. 30 The inspector's jacket was sharply, spivishly waisted. **1971** B. W. ALDISS *Soldier Erect* 177 We spivved ourselves up, put on clean shirts, and strolled out of camp. **1976** *Times* 5 Feb. 21/5 Willott..has no time for spivvery within or without the law. **1976** *Listener* 26 Feb. 245/4 The pelvic lead singer, spivved, moustached, sharp. **1978** *Time Out* 18 Aug. 55/5 Hoffman, spivvy and moustached for maximum seediness, is an ex-con on parole who can't go straight.

spla-board. [? f. SPLAY *a.* or *v.*[1]] (See quot.)

c **1850** *Rudim. Navig.* (Weale) 151 *Spla-boards*, boards or planks fixed to an obtuse angle, to throw the light into the filling-room of a magazine.

'splachnoid, *a. Bot.* [f. mod.L. *Splachn-um* (Linnæus), ad. Gr. σπλάγχνον (Dioscorides), some moss or lichen.] Characteristic of, related to, *Splachnum*, a genus of mosses of elegant form and colour.

1833 HOOKER in *J. E. Smith's Eng. Flora* V. I. 6 So remarkable a plant as this [*Œdipodium*], with a splachnoid habit. *Ibid.* 17 As in all the splachnoid family. **1866** *Treas. Bot.*, *Tayloria*, a remarkable genus of splachnoid mosses.

splack, *adv. rare*[−1]. [Echoic.] With a sound suggestive of splashing and smacking.

a **1960** E. M. FORSTER *Maurice* (1971) xxxviii. 182 Mr London and Mr Featherstonhaugh dived splack into the water lilies.

'splacknuck. Also splacnunc. [Invented by Swift.] An imaginary animal of Brobdingnag; a strange animal or person.

1726 SWIFT *Gulliver* II. ii, That my master had found a strange animal in the field, about the bigness of a splacknuck. **1807** W. IRVING *Salmag.* (1811) I. 68 Philadelphians gave the preference to racoon and splacnuncs. **1820** *Examiner* 626/1 In the grip of the farmer at Botley we accordingly leave this reverend splacknuck. **1842** TENNYSON in H. Tennyson *Mem.* (1897) I. vii. 180 Your modern ladies shriek at a pipe as if they saw a 'splacknuck'.

† **'splaiting**, *vbl. sb. Obs.* [Of obscure origin: cf. SPLAT *v.*[1] 2, and *shoulder-splate*.] (See quot.)

1580 BLUNDEVIL *Horsemanship* v. 52 Of splaiting of the shoulder. This commeth by some dangerous sliding or slipping, whereby the shoulder parteth from the breast, and so leaves an open rift..in the flesh and film next under the skin. [Hence in Topsell (1607) and Phillips (1658-96), as *Splayting*; Kersey (1706), etc., as *Splaying*.]

splake (spleɪk). *N. Amer.* [f. SP(ECKLED (*ppl.*) *a.* + LAKE *sb.*[4]] A trout produced by crossing the lake trout, *Salvelinus namaycush*, and the speckled trout, *S. fontinalis*.

1954 *Sun* (Baltimore) 27 May 2/7 Biologists of the Ontario Department of Lands and Forests have completed the first step of an experiment in producing a new variety of game fish. The 'splake' has resulted. It is a hybrid, the result of crossing speckled and lake trout. **1968** *Globe & Mail* (Toronto) 5 Feb. 6/4 A hardier type of trout called splake.. is being introduced. **1979** *Whig-Standard* (Kingston, Ontario) 9 Feb. 26/1 Splake from inland waters are highly colored compared to those from the great lakes which are usually silvery.

† **splanade**, obs. form of ESPLANADE.

Cf. obs. G. *splanade*, WFlem. *splenade*.

1682 [see ESPLANADE 2]. **1737** [S. BERINGTON] *Mem. G. de Lucca* (1738) 82 Where the break of the Hill made that agreeable Splanade, there stood an ancient Pyramid.

splanchnic ('splæŋknɪk), *a.* and *sb. Anat.* Also 7 -nick, **splancknick**. [ad. med. or mod.L. *splanchnic-us*, ad. Gr. σπλαγχνικός, f. σπλάγχνον, usu. pl. σπλάγχνα, the inward parts, esp. the heart, lungs, liver, and kidneys. So F. *splanchnique*.]

A. *adj.* **1. a.** Situated in, connected with, the viscera or intestines. Freq. in ***splanchnic nerve(s***.

1694 WESTMACOTT *Script. Herb.* 49 It most sharply irritating the Splancknick fibres..compels..serosities to be cast out. **1831** R. KNOX *Cloquet's Anat.* 536 Of the splanchnic nerves. These nerves are two in number, and distinguished into great and small. **1832** OWEN *Mem. Pearly Nautilus* 63 The splanchnic veins from the liver, ovary, gizzard, &c. **1845** TODD & BOWMAN *Phys. Anat.* II. 137 The great splanchnic nerve arises by separate roots. **1870** FLOWER *Osteol. Mamm.* ii. 9 There are also certain bones called *splanchnic*, being developed within the substance of some of the viscera.

b. Occupied by the viscera (esp. in ***splanchnic cavity***); of a visceral character.

1830 R. KNOX *Béclard's Anat.* 39 The splanchnic cavity of the trunk is divided into two by..the diaphragm. **1851** *Rep. Brit. Assoc.* XX. 219 A space intervenes,..to designate which the term 'peritoneal', or 'splanchnic', may be used with perfect anatomical propriety. **1881** *Jrnl. Microsc. Sci.* Jan. 73 The two layers of the mesoblast, somatic and splanchnic. **1898** *Allbutt's Syst. Med.* V. 394 This appears to take place chiefly in the splanchnic area.

2. Affecting, pertaining or relating to, the viscera.

1681 WILLIS *Operat. Med.* II. ii. 89 Splanchnick remedies or those which respect the bowels of the lower Belly. **1822-7** GOOD *Study Med.* (1829) V. 307 In Splanchnic Obesity, the encumbered viscera are more or less buried in beds of fat. **1874** COUES *Birds N.W.* 592 Other minor points of splanchnic details.

B. *sb.* A splanchnic nerve. Chiefly in *pl.*

1840 G. V. ELLIS *Anat.* 360 The great splanchnic..is a large white nerve,..which descends to the diaphragm. **1877** DICKINSON *Diabetes* 17 After division of the splanchnics which are in the direct line of hepatic innervation.

So † **'splanchnical** *a. Obs. rare.*

1681 tr. *Willis' Rem. Med. Wks.* Vocab., *Splanchnical*, belonging to the spleen. **1702** *Phil. Trans.* XXIII. 1582 Those generated in the..Guts, beget Cholical, Splanchnical, Hypocondriacal Pains.

splanchno- ('splæŋknəʊ), combining form of Gr. σπλάγχνον (see SPLANCHNIC *a.*), occurring in a few terms of *Anat.* and *Path.* relating to the viscera, as **splanchno'cranium**, those lower and anterior bones and cartilages of the head and face that are derived from visceral arch elements; opp. *neurocranium* s.v. NEURO-; hence **splanchno'cranial** *a.* **splanch'nography** (see quot.). **splanchno'megaly** [Gr. μεγαλ-, μέγας large], an enlarged condition of the viscera. **splanchno'pleural** *a.*, pertaining to the splanchnopleure. **'splanchnopleure**, one of the two layers or divisions of the mesoblast. **splanchno'pleuric** *a.*, = *splanchnopleural*. **splanchnop'tosis**, a downward displacement of the viscera. **splanchno'skeletal** *a.*, relating or belonging to the visceral skeleton. **splanchno-'skeleton**, the visceral skeleton, consisting of hard or bony parts developed in the viscera or sense-organs. **splanch'notomy** (see quot.).

1974 D. & M. WEBSTER *Compar. Vertebr. Morphol.* iv. 58 Of the *splanchnocranial cartilages, the most anterior pair is the mandibular arch. **1907** W. N. PARKER tr. *Wiedersheim's Compar. Anat. Vertebrates* (ed. 3) 75 A series of cartilaginous arches arise in serial order on the ventral side of the brain-case; these encircle the anterior part of the alimentary tract like hoops, incomplete dorsally, and are distinguished as the visceral portion of the skull (*splanchnocranium). **1931** SAUNDERS & MANTON *Man. Pract. Vertebr. Morphol.* xii. 121 The brain-box and sense capsules form the neurocranium, while the jaws and visceral arches form the splanchnocranium. **1974** D. & M. WEBSTER *Compar. Vertebr. Morphol.* iv. 59 (*caption*) Lateral view of the splanchnocranium of an acanthodian. **1849** CRAIG, **Splanchnography*, an anatomical description of the viscera. [**1900** DORLAND *Med. Dict.*, Splanchnomegalia.] **1910** *Practitioner* Jan. 34 There is sometimes also a general increase in the size of the various internal organs, a condition of *splanchnomegaly. **1970** N. G. SCHNEEBERG *Clin. Endocrinol.* v. 70/2 Generalized marked splanchnomegaly occurs, though enlargement of the liver is most common. **1888** ROLLESTON & JACKSON *Anim. Life* 614 Testes and ovaries are formed by the growth of *splanchno-pleural coelomic-epithelium. **1875** HUXLEY in *Encycl. Brit.* II. 53/2 The splitting of the mesoblast into two layers, a *splanchnopleure and a somatopleure. **1888** *Jrnl. Microsc. Sci.* XXVIII. 111 The lower end lies..between the somatopleure and splanchnopleure. **1900** *Nature* 12 Apr. 560 The appearance, in the development in the vascular system, of a *splanchnopleuric subintestinal vein. **1898** *Allbutt's Syst. Med.* V. 486 These practices, as he alleges, lead in a considerable percentage of women to *splanchnoptosis. **1848** OWEN *Homologies Vert. Skeleton* 111 The bones..are..entitled to rank..in the category of sense-capsules or '*splanchno-skeletal' pieces. *Ibid.* 114 The bones or parts of the *splanchno-skeleton. **1875** *Encycl. Brit.* I. 820/1 In man, the teeth being excluded, there is neither exo- nor splanchno-skeleton, but only an endo-skeleton. **1851** DUNGLISON *Med. Lex.*, **Splanchnotomy*, dissection or anatomy of the viscera.

splanchnology (splæŋk'nɒlədʒɪ). [See prec. and -LOGY. So F. *splanchnologie*.]

1. The scientific study of the viscera.

1706 PHILLIPS (ed. Kersey), *Splanchnology*, a Discourse, Treatise, or Description of the Entrails of a Humane Body. **1796** SOUTHEY *Lett. fr. Spain* (1799) 477 The three exercises ..shall be upon Myology, Neurology, and Splanchnology. **1831** R. KNOX *Cloquet's Anat.* 8 Angiology... Adenology... Splanchnology. **1897** *Catal. Yale Univ.* 293 Examinations at the end..of the second year upon Angeiology, Neurology and Splanchnology.

2. The visceral system.

1842 *Penny Cycl.* XXII. 57/1 His personal observations made on the osteology and splanchnology of the animal. **1854** BADHAM *Halieut.* 162 His luxurious ancestors..had beaked and clawed at pleasure the whole splanchnology of the giant Tityus. **1874** COUES *Birds N.W.* 592 The splanchnology of the four differs more extensively.

Hence **splanchnological** *a.*; **splanchnologist**.

1727 BAILEY (vol. II), *Splanchnologist*, a Describer or Treater of the Bowels. **1886** *Encycl. Brit.* XX. 436/1 Three orders, distinguished chiefly by osteological and splanchnological characters.

splash (splæʃ), *sb.*[1] [f. SPLASH *v.*[1]]

1. a. A quantity of some fluid or semi-liquid substance dashed or dropped upon a surface.

1736 AINSWORTH I, A splash, or splatch of dirt. **1818** TODD, *Splash*, wet or dirt thrown up from a puddle [etc.]. **1833** LOUDON *Encycl. Archit.* §542 The shapes of the patches will be further altered by the addition of each splash of colour. **1863** BARING-GOULD *Iceland* 120 The snow was blotched with large splashes of blood. **1879** 'E. GARRETT' *House by Works* I. 185 A Turkey rug..lay on the stone floor, ..befouled with splashes of grease and dirty water.

b. *spec.* (See quot.)

1813 MONTAGU *Suppl. Ornith. Dict.* A a 3 b, Where the fowler perceives perforations made by the bill of a Woodcock,..or the mutings, called the splash.

c. The fragmentary metal resulting from the shattering of bullets upon impact.

1865 *Pall Mall G.* 22 Sept. 5/2 Several sheep..had been poisoned by swallowing minute portions of bullets—the 'splash'—which lay scattered on the grass. **1887** *Daily News* 25 Oct. 4/7 He granted an injunction..to use the other target in a way that would cause bullets or splashes of bullets to fall upon the plaintiff's land.

d. *Amer.* A body of water suddenly released in order to carry down logs.

1879 *Lumberman's Gaz.* 23 Aug., Some of these..logs may possibly be moved by a splash to have been made at Little Falls dam.

e. A small quantity of liquid, *spec.* a dash of soda-water or tonic, etc., added to spirits as a drink.

1922 JOYCE *Ulysses* 551 Here, to buy yourself a gin and splash. **1935** G. GREENE *England made Me* v. 243 The atmosphere of..the week-end jaunt, the whisky and splash. **1965** 'J. LE CARRÉ' *Looking-Glass War* xv. 173 Woodford's wife added a little soda to her Scotch, a splash: it was habit rather than taste. **1977** *Rolling Stone* 30 June 81/3, I walked to the bar, ordered a double vodka with a splash of tonic no fruit.

2. *colloq.* A striking or ostentatious display, appearance, or effect; something in the nature of a sensation or excitement; a dash: **a.** In the phrases ***to make***, or ***cut, a splash***.

1804 G. COLMAN *Let.* 9 Jan. in A. Mathews *Mem. Charles Mathews* (1838) I. xx. 434 A vile part, surely, for the *début* of a man who is to make a *splash*. **1806** SURR *Winter in Lond.* II. 91 Three of my old school-fellows at Eton, who were very clever, and cut a splash in the 'Microcosm'. **1824** LADY GRANVILLE *Lett.* (1894) I. 287, I expect our drum to make a great splash. **1842** LOVER *Handy Andy* xvii, A band is all very well for making a splash in the first procession. **1890** *Spect.* 14 June 829/1 Distinction shows itself without making a splash, without calling attention to itself.

b. In other contexts. Also *attrib.*

1810 *Splendid Follies* III. 188 Many a demirep lounges in Tom's curricle for a splash through the city. **1832** J. ROMILLY *Diary* 6 May (1967) 12 Missed Hearing Roze's Sermon..:—hear it was poor: tho with a splash passage against the wickedness of manufactures. **1863** FONBLANQUE *Tangled Skein* II. 33 What a grand splash you had on the 31st! We saw it all in the 'Illustrated'. **1885** *Daily Tel.* 28 Dec. (Encycl. Dict.), Enable him to have a rattling good splash for it somehow—break or make.

c. Without article: Sensation, excitement.

1899 *Westm. Gaz.* 5 Dec. 3/1 That last speech of his caused enough splash for some time to come.

d. *colloq.* The prominent display in a newspaper of an advertisement, headline, or story; the material so displayed, usu. of a dramatic or sensational character. Freq. *attrib.*

1922 JOYCE *Ulysses* 638 The usual splash page of letterpress about the same old matrimonial tangle. **1932** H. NICOLSON *Public Faces* xi. 288 We must get the news back here before to-night—time for full splash in tomorrow's papers. **1933** W. MOSS *Polit. Parties Irish Free State* iii. 127 'Splashes', i.e. full-page advertisements using the most effective appeals and backed with extensive and detailed argument. **1948** *Manch. Guardian Weekly* 1 July 2 The perfect 'splash' story in the lull after the Republican Convention. **1960** J. ROBB *Front Page Story* 46 Percy tossed the latest copy over to Bert, the 'Splash' sub. 'Splash' sub was the title given to the man who normally handled only the page-one lead. He was usually..the best sub-editor in the office. **1966** *New Statesman* 13 May 680/3 The paper had reverted to its old jittery habit of lifting other people's splashes and exclusives. **1974** *Globe & Mail* (Toronto) 23 Oct. 12/7 'Anything could happen,' said..Michael Wilson after the London papers gave splash play to his announcement. **1977** *New Yorker* 24 Oct. 55/2 The violent crimes.., if they occur in New York City, get a one-day splash in the *News*. **1979** P. NIESEWAND *Member of Club* iv. 31 Courtney turned back to the paper..to look at the front page. The splash story was the row over the death of a young South African commando. **1982** *Chicago Sun-Times* 2 Dec. 67 Speakes gave a thorough briefing on the Cabinet Council study, providing the rest of the nation a Page 1 splash the next day.

3. a. The act or result of suddenly and forcibly striking or dashing water or other fluid; the sound produced by this.

1819 SHELLEY *Cyclops* 19 All my boys..with splash and strain Made white with foam the green and purple sea. **1842** LOVER *Handy Andy* xi, Billy made all the splash he could in the water as Murphy lifted the fish to the surface. **1898** WATTS-DUNTON *Aylwin* xiv. iv, And hark! that pebble which falls into the water with a splash.

fig. **1834** SOUTHEY *Doctor* xii. (1864) II. 213 Popularity [is] a splash in the great pool of oblivion.

b. *ellipt.* A splash-net.

1855 'C. IDLE' *Hints Shooting & Fishing* [232 The Splash Net. *Ibid.*] 235 To use the splash advantageously at night, the tide and weather must both be in your favour.

4. a. The act, result, or sound of water falling or dashing forcibly upon something.

1832 DE LA BECHE *Geol. Man.* (ed. 2) 83 This water being apparently derived from the drain of the mountains behind, and the splash of the sea. **1847** TENNYSON *Princ.* I. 214 The splash and stir Of fountains spouted up and showering down. **1885** *L'pool Daily Post* 1 May 4/9 What if days of foggy drizzle alternate with days of steady splash?

b. *Med.* Also ***splash sound***. A sound produced by a mixture of air and liquid in the stomach or other cavity when it is sharply disturbed. Cf. SPLASHING *vbl. sb.*[1] 1 b.

1890 F. TAYLOR *Pract. Med.* 435 The presence of air and liquid together in the pleural cavity may be demonstrated by the test known as Hippocratic succession, or splash sound. **1908** HUTCHISON & RAINY *Clin. Methods* (ed. 4) 66 It should be remembered..that a splash may be elicited over even a normal stomach shortly after a meal containing much fluid, ..and care should also be taken not to mistake a splash produced in the transverse colon for a stomach splash. **1938** N. L. ECKHOFF in H. Rolleston *Brit. Encycl. Med. Pract.* VII. 226 A splash may be heard in cases of pyloric obstruction, and in some cases of obstruction in the colon. **1971** [see SPLASHING *vbl. sb.*[1] 1 b].

5. a. A large or irregular patch of colour or light.

1832 T. BROWN *Bk. Butterfl. & M.* (1834) I. 197 In *Papilio agala* this silver is disposed in distinct splashes, or spots. **1856** in A. J. C. Hare *Two Noble Lives* (1893) II. 88 C. wore his..uniform, which made such a splash of gold that we were quite fine enough. **1883** STEVENSON *Silverado Sq.* 253 [The light] fell in a great splash upon the thicket. **1897** LD. E. HAMILTON *Outlaws of Marches* iii. 24 A bright bay..with a great white splash on its forehead.

b. A variety of the domestic pigeon. Also *attrib.*, as ***splash bird, cock, tumbler***.

1854 *Poultry Chron.* I. 332/1 For the best pair of Almond, or Splash Tumblers. *Ibid.*, What is a Splash, but an Almond-bred bird? **1867** TEGETMEIER *Pigeons* 120 It is no easy matter to lay down certain rules for matching Splashes, or indeed any other coloured birds. **1879** L. WRIGHT *Pigeon Keeper* 112 These..included Almonds, Splashes,..black Splash cock, and red cock.

6. *slang.* **a.** (See quot.)

1865 *Slang Dict.* 242 *Splash*, complexion powder used by ladies to whiten their necks and faces.

b. Amphetamines. *U.S.*

1969 J. GARDNER *Complete State of Death* ix. 166 The American..addicts..call most of the amphetamines 'speed', in the same way as they talk of others as 'bennies', 'splash', 'cartwheels'. **1974** M. C. GERALD *Pharmacol.* xvii. 332 Amphetamines (Benzedrine),..*Bennies, Peaches, Splash.*

splash (splæʃ), *sb.*[2] [Alteration of PLASH *sb.*[1], probably by association with prec. and next.] A shallow pool.

1760 HUTTON *Dial. Storth & Arnside* l. 37 (E.D.D.), A lile splash o' water o'th bare sand. **1802** MONTAGU *Ornith. Dict.* N 3, The nest..is placed on a tump or dry spot, near a splash or swampy place. **1823** E. MOOR *Suffolk Words, Splashes*, shallow accumulations of water from wintry wet, in the low parts of meadows or marshes. **1893** 'SON OF THE MARSHES' (D. Jordan) *Forest Tithes* 194 The beautiful grey and white gulls, resting in and around the clear shallow splashes.

splash (splæʃ), *v.*[1] [Alteration of PLASH *v.*[2]]

I. *trans.* **1. a.** To bespatter, to wet or soil, by dashing water, mud, etc.

1722–7 BOYER *Dict. Royal* I. s.v. *Rejaillir*, He splashed his Face with Dirt. **1755** JOHNSON, *Splash*, to daub with dirt in great quantities. **1798** W. HUTTON *Family of Hutton* 98 Our trooper dismounted, and cast a large stone with design to splash her. **1818** J. W. CROKER in *C. Papers* 8 Dec. (1884) I. 121 We ride together, and in the dirty roads splash one another. **1861** GEO. ELIOT *Silas M.* iii, You'll..get back home at eight o'clock, splashed up to the chin. **1891** FARRAR *Darkn. & Dawn* iv, The slaves..were splashing his face with the water of the fountain.

b. To stain, mark, or mottle with irregular patches of colour or light. Chiefly in *pa. pple.*

1833 LOUDON *Encycl. Archit.* §542 The surface of the wall to be splashed must be well seasoned, and perfectly dry. **1865** GOSSE *Land & Sea* (1874) 32 Two eggs of a dirty white, mottled and splashed with brown. **1890** E. H. BARKER *Wayfaring in France* 191 Where the sunny grass was splashed by the dark shadows of cypresses.

2. a. To cause (a liquid or semi-liquid substance) to fly about; to scatter, throw up or about, with some force or commotion. Also, to pour *out* with a splash.

1762 LLOYD *Ep. Churchill* Poems 191 Where the mock female shrew and hen-peck'd male Scoop'd rich contents from either copious pail,..And dash'd and splash'd the filthy grains about. **1848** THACKERAY *Van. Fair* xxii, The few children made a dismal cheer, as the carriage, splashing mud, drove away. **1859** *Habits of Gd. Society* v. 224 You must carefully turn the joint so as not to splash the gravy. **1878** HUXLEY *Physiogr.* 191 The liquid is..so splashed about that it falls in drops. **1908** E. F. BENSON *Blotting Bk.* ii. 51 Mills..splashed himself out a liberal allowance of brandy into his glass.

fig. **1824** LANDOR *Imag. Conv.* Wks. 1846 I. 189 Juvenal.. stamps too often, and splashes up too much filth.

b. *fig.* To write *down* carelessly or quickly.

1897 *Daily News* 2 Mar. 3/5, I witnessed many other scenes like the ones which I have rapidly splashed down for you upon paper.

c. *colloq.* To present (news, etc.) ostentatiously, or as a 'splash' (SPLASH *sb.*[1] 2 d).

1930 *London Mercury* Feb. 317 All the evening papers have 'splashed' the story. **1934** A. P. HERBERT *Holy Deadlock* 210 She was 'splashed' in the newspapers as a sort of modern St. Joan. **1946** J. W. DAY *Harvest Adventure* xvi. 272 London and provincial newspapers 'splashed' this first organized revolt against a tyranny and waste of public money. **1958** *Punch* 1 Jan. 59/3 The story was splashed over the front page. **1969** [see PAR *sb.*[4]]. **1979** A. BRINK *Dry White Season* II. vi. 138 The photograph of Emily embracing Ben was splashed on the front page of an English newspaper.

d. *colloq.* To spend (money) extravagantly or ostentatiously. Freq. const. advbs., esp. in phr. ***to splash*** (money) ***out on*** (something). Also *absol.*

1934 *Times* 7 Mar. 7/5 Public money ought not to be splashed about in this manner without grave and searching examination by the House of Commons. **1938** S. BECKETT *Murphy* 79 He thought for a second of splashing the fourpence. **1946** F. SARGESON *That Summer* 82 After we'd splashed on a talkie we went home. **1960** S. BARSTOW *Kind of Loving* II. ii. 170, I splash eight-and-six on a pound box of chocolates and send them with a little note. **1973** *Courier & Advertiser* (Dundee) 1 Mar. 2/2 Allied now plan to splash out an extra £150,000 on advertising. **1973** E. LEMARCHAND *Let or Hindrance* xiv. 170 They..splashed the lolly around when the pay packets came in. **1978** *Morecambe Guardian* 14 Mar. 17/2 Splash out on something new to wear; the result will be worthwhile.

3. To cause (something) to dash or agitate a liquid, esp. so as to produce a sound.

1879 FROUDE *Cæsar* xix. 319 Splashing their oars, and making as much noise as possible. **1889** MRS. LYNN LINTON *Thro' Long Night* I. I. ii. 20 Sly may..splash his spatulous fingers in rose-water.

4. To make (one's way) with splashing.

?*c* **1830** W. IRVING *Knickerbocker* III. v. §5 The..little vessel ploughed and splashed its way up the Hudson. **1890** DOYLE *White Company* xxviii, Through this the horses splashed their way.

II. *intr.* **5. a.** To cause dashing or noisy agitation of a liquid; to move or fall with a splash or splashes.

1715 PRIOR *Down-Hall* 47 Pray get a Calesch, That in Summer may Burn, and in Winter may Splash. **1818** SCOTT *Rob Roy* xxxi, The heavy burden splashed in the dark-blue waters. **1843** LE FEVRE *Life Trav. Phys.* III. III. ix. 194 In order to reward myself..I splashed away in a bath. **1884** *Marshall's Tennis Cuts* 271 Where the startled wild fowl splash in Sludgeboro's lagoons and marshes.

b. With preps. or advs. implying movement.

1818 SCOTT *Br. Lamm.* xxiv, In to the water we behoved a' to splash, heels ower head. **1837** CARLYLE *Fr. Rev.* I. VII. xi, Poor Weber went splashing along, close by the Royal carriage. **1862** MRS. H. WOOD *Mrs. Hallib. Troub.* I. i, To splash through the wet streets..was an expedition rather agreeable to Francis. **1902** BELLOC *Path to Rome* 300 Through the..rain I splashed up the main street.

c. To use a splash-net.

1855 'C. IDLE' *Hints Shooting & Fishing* 234 When it is intended to continue splashing during the night, the net must be taken in carefully.

d. Const. *down.* Of a spacecraft: to alight on the sea after a space flight. Also *transf.* Cf. SPLASHDOWN.

1962 *Daily Tel.* 4 Oct. 1/7 Cdr. Walter Schirra..'splashed down' safely in the Pacific at 10.28 (BST) last night. **1965** *Economist* 4 Sept. 873/1 By the time they splashed down on Sunday Lieutenant-Colonel Cooper and Lieutenant-Commander Conrad had completed the longest-ever manned flight in space. **1969** *Times* 3 June (Suppl.) p. iii/4 Apollo 11 is due to splash down at 5.52 on July 24. **1978** *Times* 1 Aug. 2/1 The ill-fated [balloon] Zanussi in which they splashed down.

6. a. Of liquids: To dash or fly in some quantity and with some degree of force.

1755 *Dict. Arts & Sci.* II. s.v. *Foliating*, So that the amalgam, when you pour it in, may not splash. **1827** FARADAY *Chem. Manip.* vii. (1842) 218 A few particles may splash upon the hotter parts of the retort. **1871** R. ELLIS tr. *Catullus* lxiv. 185 Nowhere open way, seas splash in circle around me. **1880** *Trans. Seismol. Soc. Japan* I. II. 22 The manner in which water was observed to splash out of wash-hand basins.

b. Const. *up.*

1837 CARLYLE *Fr. Rev.* III. I. viii, Redhot balls..'filled internally with oil of turpentine which splashes up in flame'. **1851** MRS. BROWNING *Casa Guidi Wind.* II. 539 Heroes' blood Splashed up against thy noble brow in Rome.

7. Of bullets: To throw off fragments on striking an object.

1894 *Westm. Gaz.* 1 June 4/2 The bullet struck just slightly above the place and then 'splashed', as it is generally called.

splash, *v.*[2] *dial.* [Alteration of PLASH *v.*[1]] *trans.* To pleach (a hedge).

1828 CARR *Craven Gloss.*, *Splash*, to cut and trim hedges. **1854** MISS BAKER *Northampt. Gloss.*, To splash a hedge, is to cut away the rough wood..and lay in the smooth, trimming it up on the ditch side. **1899** *Jrnl. R. Agric. Soc.* 1 Mar. 93 On well managed farms most hedges are splashed about the month of August.

†**splash**, obs. dial. var. of SPLICE *v.*

1672 *Vestry Bks.* (Surtees) 338 For splashing the bell-ropes, 4 d. [Cf. SPLICING *vbl. sb.*[1], quot. 1524–5.]

splash (splæʃ), *adv.* [The stem of SPLASH *v.*[1]] In a splashing manner; with a splash or splashing sound.

1795 SCOTT *William & Helen* xlvii, Tramp! tramp! along the land they rode, Splash! splash! along the sea. **1841** LYTTON *Nt. & Morn.* v. i, The full flood of sound..came splash upon him. **1895** *Outing* XXVI. 30/2 Spat-spat, splash! they fell.

splash-, the stem of SPLASH *v.*[1], occurring in some combs., as **splash-and-dash** *a.*, making much fuss and show; **splashback**, a panel fastened to and protecting the wall behind a sink, cooker, etc., from splashes; **splash cymbal**, a small, light cymbal; **splash-dash** *adv.*, in a headlong manner; **splashguard**, a guard fitted to an object to prevent splashing; **splash-net**, a small fishing-net; hence ***splash-netting*** vbl. sb.; **splash-paper**, paper coloured in irregular patches; **splash party** *U.S.*, a party at which the guests engage in swimming and other water sports; **splashplate**, a metal splashback on a cooker; **splash pool**, a shallow paddling pool for children; **splash-proof**, *a.*, impermeable to splashes; **splash-work**, spatter-work; **splash zone**, that area adjacent to the sea, a waterfall, etc., that is continually splashed by water.

1830 GALT *Laurie T.* II. vii. (1849) 63 Very unlike the ordinary *splash and dash ways of young men in a hurry to be rich. **1926–7** *Army & Navy Stores Catal.* 295/3 *Bathroom accessories...* White opal *Splash Back with fitted 5-in. shelf. **1961** *Which?* Dec. 317/1 Oven, grill and hotplate controls were either on the front of the cooker or on the splash-back. **1971** *Ideal Home* Apr. 52/1 Plain blue tiles form a splashback panel round the back. **1982** *Daily Tel.* 3 Aug. 9/1 Cast iron washstand.., with tiled splashback and mirror, is rare and costly at £1,000. **1961** *Splash cymbal [see *crash cymbal* s.v. CRASH *sb.*[1] 7]. **1964** Splash cymbal [see CHOKE *v.* 10 b]. **1807** W. IRVING *Salmag.* (1824) 74 On they push, *splash-dash, mud or no mud. **1917** *Harrods Gen. Catal.* 516/1 The 'Reliance' *Splash Guard. Solid Red Rubber... When ordering please state outside diameter of tap. **1962** *Which?* Mar. 87/1 All the continuous feed models [of waste-disposers]..had a splashguard, a slotted rubber cover across the entrance to the grinding chamber which allows you to push waste through but prevents water and scraps from being flung out. **1855** 'C. IDLE' *Hints Shooting & Fishing* 232 The *Splash Net. **1893** *Daily Tel.* 14 Dec. 3/1 Preparations for splash-net fishing. **1901** *Scotsman* 4 Mar. 10/1 The *splash-netting is carried on in shallow water. **1811** *Art Bookbinding* 50 It will..have a fine effect when colouring *splash paper, marbling edges, etc. **1930** *Amer. Speech* VI. 121 *Splash*.., swimming: *Splash Party of Girls' Club Lively Affair. **1956** W. H. WHYTE *Organization Man* xxii. 291 'Splash' parties (all you can eat for a dollar). **1967** *Gloss. Terms Gas Industry* (*B.S.I.*) 89 *Splashplate, a panel above and behind a hotplate. **1970** *Which?* June 175/1 Many of the stoves had splash plates—usually of painted metal. **1971** *Sunday Express* (Johannesburg) 28 Mar. 16/3 (Advt.), Beautiful 3 bedroomed home with really lovely garden... *Splash pool for children. **1976** *Billings* (Montana) *Gaz.* 16 June 5-D/4 (Advt.), Keep kids cool all summer. 8′ × 18″ splash pool with vinyl liner. **1929** *Radio Times* 8 Nov. 451/2 A 20 amp-hour accumulator... Vent is large, *splash-proof and spray-tight and screws in. **1965** *Wireless World* July 36 (Advt.), Dustproof and splashproof. **1797** Mrs. A. M. Bennett *Beggar Girl* (1813) II. 28 Miss could play a few marches,..make fillagree and *splash-work. **1891** *Melbourne Argus* 16 May 13/5 The picture seems to have been made in the way splashwork is done. **1933** *Jrnl. Marine Biol. Assoc.* XVIII. 453 During the winter, continued storms will keep the height of the *splash zone at five feet or more. **1956** F. W. Adams in D. L. Linton *Sheffield* 330 [*Scapania undulata*.] Common in waterfalls, 'splash zones', reservoir-overflows, and just below the water line on stones in non-calcareous streams. **1976** *Offshore Platforms & Pipelining* 30/1 A central shaft..will permit divers to go 50 m below sea level when there is rough water in the splash zone.

2. Used (usu. without following hyphen) with reference to a system of lubrication in which oil is distributed throughout an engine in the form of drops initially splashed from a reservoir by the working of certain moving parts. So ***splash lubrication***.

1906 *Evening Express* (Liverpool) 9 Mar. 7/4 If the splash system of lubrication were more generally adopted by the makers there would be no trouble on this score. **1907** F. Strickland *Man. Petrol Motors & Motor Cars* xvi. 247 The difficulty in splash lubrication is to provide enough oil for the various parts, without having so much in the crank chamber that it works up into the cylinder and produces smoke. **1924** A. W. Judge *Mod. Motor Cars* I. iv. 119 A low speed engine, an over-cooled one, or a splash-lubricated one would require a low-viscosity or 'thin' grade [of oil]. **1939** J. I. Clower *Lubricants & Lubrication* xiv. 358 Splash oiling is widely used on small, vertical and horizontal single-acting machines [*sc.* compressors]. **1963** [see fly-wheel]. **1966** *McGraw-Hill Encycl. Sci. & Technol.* VII. 607/1 In splash lubrication, the oil entering the engine flows to troughs into which extensions of the connecting rods dip.

splash-board. Also **splashboard.** [f. prec.]

1. A guard or screen in front of the driver's seat on a vehicle, serving to protect him, or others sitting beside him, from being splashed with mud from the horse's hoofs. Also in fig. context.

1826 Disraeli *Vivian Grey* II. iii. viii. 121 By dint of rattling the whip against the splash-board. **1842** Dickens *Amer. Notes* (1850) 91/2 He takes a rein in each hand;..and dances on the splashboard with both feet. **1860** Thackeray *Round. Papers, Late Gt. Vict.*, I was his conscience, and stood on the splash-board of his triumph-car.

1861 G. M. Musgrave *By-Roads* 75 Our fast mare..had nearly pitched me on to the splashboard. **1894** Baring-Gould *Kitty Alone* II. 102 Pepperill fastened it to the splashboard, and drove on.

2. A board fixed over or beside a wheel to intercept splashings.

1850 Holtzapffel *Turning* III. 1297 A splash-board is fixed behind the wheel, to catch the water thrown off, by centrifugal force. **1902** *Brit. Med. Jrnl.* 31 May 1341/2 It is further recommended that for the wet spinning rooms.. modified splashboards should be obligatory.

3. *Naut.* A screen above the deck-line.

1907 C. D. Stewart *Partners of Providence* vi, The splash-board stood up in front of the wheel like a back-yard fence. **1912** J. Masefield *Dauber* v, A sea Washed them both in, over the splashboard.

4. A splashback; a protective panel attached to a wall.

1868 C. L. Eastlake *Hints on Household Taste* viii. 183 The common bed-room wash-stand..has a splash-board to protect the wall against which it is placed. **1976** *Billings* (Montana) *Gaz.* 16 June 11-A/4 Even a minimal remodeling job can cost $2,500 before the flower-print wallpaper is stuck on the splashboard.

splashdown ('splæʃdaʊn). Also **splash-down.** [f. splash- + down *adv.*] The alighting of a spacecraft on the sea. Also *transf.*

1961 *Washington Post* 5 May B2 They [*sc.* several warships] are strung out about 60 miles apart, and their mission is to retrieve Shepard after 'splashdown'. *Ibid.* 6 May A1 The perfect flight, from lift-off to splash-down, lasted only 15 minutes. **1968** [see *recovery fleet* s.v. recovery 10]. **1968** *Guardian* 28 Dec. 8/2 From launch to splashdown the Apollo-8 mission went entirely without hitch. **1970** N. Armstrong et al. *First on Moon* xiv. 347 The Navy's weathermen had predicted acceptable splash-down conditions. **1978** *Times* 1 Aug. 2/2 (*caption*) He [*sc.* a member of the crew of a balloon] hears the recording of their splashdown transmission.

splashed (splæʃt), *ppl. a.*[1] [f. splash *v.*[1]]

1. Marked with splashes or irregular patches of colour.

1765 *Treat. Dom. Pigeons* 56 In decline of life they as gradually decrease, till they become sometimes a mottled, splashed, or whole colour. **1854** *Poultry Chron.* I. 124 Only tipped with black, or with splashed and smudgy feathers. **1858** Skyring *Builder's Prices* 95 Imitation granite, or splashed work. **1882** *Pall Mall G.* 21 June 10/1 A globular vase of splashed crimson and purple crackle.

2. Wet, soiled, or stained with splashes of water, mud, or the like.

1837 Carlyle *Fr. Rev.* iii. i. vii, O ye hapless dulled-bright Seigneurs, and hydrophobic splashed Nankeens. **1858** Froude *Hist. Eng.* III. 126 As the multitude rocked to and fro, a splashed rider spurred through the streets. **1891** C. James *Rom. Rigmarole* 167 Two or three splashed and booted men stood round about, staring at me.

splashed (splæʃt), *ppl. a.*[2] [f. splash *v.*[2]] Pleached; secured or strengthened by pleaching.

1886 *Field* 23 Jan. 96/1 A high splashed fence on a bank, reminding one more of Dorsetshire than Wilts, emptied no less than four saddles. **1890** *Blackw. Mag.* Oct. 459 No cattle can storm a moorland splashed bank.

splasher[1] ('splæʃə(r)). [f. splash *v.*[1]]

1. a. A guard placed over or beside a wheel to prevent splashing or accidental contact.

1848 *Q. Rev.* Dec. 50 Cylinders, connecting-rods, splashers, leading and trailing wheels, &c.,..of which a locomotive engine is composed. **1875** in Knight *Dict. Mech.* 2279.

b. A splash-board.

1887 *United Service Gaz.* 25 June, A semi-state landau, with..splasher in front, in place of the Salisbury boot or hammer cloth.

2. A flat board strapped to the foot for walking on soft ground or mud.

1859 H. C. Folkard *Wild-Fowler* 99 Immediately after the gun was fired, the fowler or his assistant had to put on splashers and proceed over the ooze. **1887** *Chambers's Jrnl.* IV. 2 Boys and girls..went out on them with 'splashers' on their feet to gather shellfish.

3. A piece of cloth or the like hung behind a washstand to protect the wall from splashes. *U.S. Obs.* exc. *Hist.*

1895 *Montgomery Ward Catal.* Spring & Summer 123/1 Stamped Splashers, white cotton duck; size, 18 × 28 inches. *Ibid.* 577/2 Toilet Splasher for protecting wall above washstand, etc., waterproof, made of sewed wood splints, to roll up. **1905** D. Belasco in M. J. Moses *Representative Amer. Dramas* (1925) ii. 73/1 A washstand, backed by a 'splasher' of white oilcloth, is near the bed. **1945** *Sun* (Baltimore) 20 June 4-0/3 The furnishings of the Victorian style bedroom were simple linen scarfs... They were used on the flat surfaces, and 'splashers' of linen were fastened to the wall back of the washstand.

'splasher[2]. *dial.* [f. splash *v.*[2]] An implement used in pleaching; a splashing-bill.

1868 *Daily News* 26 Dec., She laid hold of a hedge splasher,..and M'Quade got hold of an old cavalry sword. **1881** in Evans *Leic. Gloss.*

'splashet. *rare*[−1]. = plashet.

1896 *Q. Rev.* Apr. 435 Many a meadow formerly..full of soft splashets, is now, through subsoil drainage, sound and dry.

'splashily, *adv.* [f. splashy *a.*[2]] In a splashy manner.

1891 *Blackw. Mag.* CL. 626/2 It was a fruit-piece splashily painted. **1978** D. Francis *Trial Run* vi. 87, I watched some horses..their feet plopping splashily in the wet.

'splashiness. *rare.* [f. splashy *a.*[1]] 'Wateriness' (Bailey, 1727, vol. II). Also, the quality of being splashy.

1978 *Listener* 30 Mar. 412/4 There is a certain wayward splashiness about some of its more 'texturising' sections—all bells, string glissandi and chattering winds.

splashing ('splæʃɪŋ), *vbl. sb.*[1] [f. splash *v.*[1]]

1. a. The action of the verb, in various senses.

1722-7 Boyer *Dict. Royal*, Splashing, *l'Action d'éclabousser.* **1775** Ash, *Splashing*,..the act of daubing with wet and dirt. **1837** Carlyle *Fr. Rev.* iii. i. vii, There are marchings and wet splashings by steep paths. **1845** J. Coulter *Adv. in Pacific* ix. 114 A whole shoal of them [sharks] were moving about, I suppose attracted by my splashing in the water. **1886** W. J. Tucker *E. Europe* 14 Centring all was a fountain at play, intermingling its musical splashings with the..song of birds.

b. *Med.* Noisy motion of air and liquid inside the body.

1890 F. Taylor *Pract. Med.* 344 In cases of hydro- or pyo-pneumothorax, shaking the patient will elicit a splashing sound. **1897** Hutchison & Rainy *Clin. Methods* 62 If 'splashing' be elicited it will be partly heard and partly felt. Distinct splashing elicited three hours after a meal..is very suggestive of a dilated stomach. **1971** R. B. Cole *Essent. Respiratory Dis.* iii. 29 The presence of air and fluid in the pleural space (hydro-pneumothorax) is indicated if a splash can be heard on auscultation when the thoracic cage is gently shaken. It should not be confused with the splashing of gastric contents.

2. *techn.* (See quots.)

1833 Loudon *Encycl. Archit.* §542 Splashing is a mode of colouring walls, which may be performed..in water, in glutinous, or in oil, colours. *Ibid.*, The object of splashing is either to imitate the lichens and weather stains of an old wall, or some particular kind of stone.

3. *attrib.* in ***splashing leather.*** **splashing-board** = splash-board 1.

1809 *Sporting Mag.* XXXIV. 200 The pole came out of the splashing leather. **a1817** Jane Austen *Northanger Abbey* (1818) I. vii. 87 Seat, trunk, sword-case, splashing-board, lamps, silver moulding, all you see complete; the iron work as good as new, or better. He asked fifty guineas.

'splashing, *vbl. sb.*[2] *dial.* [f. splash *v.*[2]] Pleaching. Also ***splashing-bill***, a pleaching-bill.

1869 Blackmore *Lorna D.* xxxviii, The ramparts of ash, which is made by what we call 'splashing'. **1899** *Jrnl. R. Agric. Soc.* Mar. 104 The work on well-established hedges is most quickly performed by a long-handled splashing-bill.

'splashing, *ppl. a.* [f. splash *v.*[1]]

1. Causing some stir or sensation; making something of a display.

1820 Creevey in *C. Papers* (1904) I. 326 We are now evidently going to have a splashing debate. **1850** W. P. Scargill *Eng. Sk.-Bk.* 4 The roystering,..splashing, dashing accomplishments of the country gentleman. **1898** *Westm. Gaz.* 24 Jan. 1/3 The fact does not..diminish the danger of a splashing intervention in foreign affairs.

2. Making or causing a splash or splashes.

1837 Ht. Martineau *Soc. Amer.* III. 25 A splashing rain drove us down into the cabin. **1883** Stevenson *Silverado Sq.* 1 It feeds in the springtime many splashing brooks. **1889** *Science-Gossip* XXV. 224, I unwittingly entered the drowsily splashing ferry-boat and leaped upon the quay.

3. Of the nature of, suggestive of, a splash.

1897 *Allbutt's Syst. Med.* IV. 661 Mention must be made of the splashing sounds which may be produced by shaking the patient.

Hence **'splashingly** *adv.*

1831 Trelawny *Adv. Younger Son* lxxv, I heard something fall splashingly into the boat. **1882** E. O'Donovan *Merv Oasis* II. 107 Some heavy rain-drops fell splashingly.

'splashy, *a.*[1] [Alteration of plashy *a.*[1] Cf. splash *sb.*[2]] Full of shallow pools or puddles; wet and soft.

1727 Bailey (vol. II.), *Splashy*, washy, wet, watery. **1742** Richardson *De Foe's Tour Gt. Brit.* II. 34 Not far from hence is Sedgmore, a watry, splashy Place. **1821** Clare *Vill. Minstr.* II. 185 Winter leaves her splashy slough. **1847** C. Brontë *Jane Eyre* xxviii, [A light] led me..through a wide bog; which..was splashy and shaking even now, in the height of summer. **1890** Baker *Wild Beasts* I. 195 Even at this season the ground was splashy beneath the heavy weight of our advancing line.

splashy ('splæʃɪ), *a.*[2] [f. splash *sb.*[1] or *v.*[1]]

1. Of a splashing character; falling, etc., with a splash or in splashes.

1856 Dickens *Lett. to W. Collins* (1892) 56 We wallowed in an odd sort of dinner, which would have been splashy if it hadn't been too sticky. **1864** Carlyle *Fredk. Gt.* xvi. xi. IV. 431 Brown leaves, splashy rains, and winds moaning. **1878** H. S. Wilson *Alpine Ascents* ii. 28 Rain dimpling with a thousand splashy drops the pools of water.

2. Of sounds: Such as are made by a splash.

1834 M. Scott *Cruise Midge* xx, One or two cranes,.. taking wing with a rustling splashy flaff, glided silently past us. **1885** Warren & Cleverly *Wand. Beetle* 34 How inseparable an association of these foreign rivers is the splashy whack of the battoir.

3. Making a show or stir; attracting attention; sensational. Cf. splash *sb.*[1] 2 d.

1836 Marryat *Midsh. Easy* xxv, It's the yellow carriage of that old lady with her..two splashy footmen! **1848** *Punch* 27 May 226/2 It is perfectly fair that this gentleman..should be enabled to make what is termed a 'splashy' effect in civilised society. **1972** 'T. Coe' *Don't lie to Me* ix. 87 The killing had originally gotten a pretty splashy play in the newspapers. **1976** *Scotsman* 25 Nov. 14/2 A preposterous miracle has rescued the 'Observer'. It was the sort of last-minute, cliff-hanging rescue which the 'Observer' would hesitate to make a big, splashy story out of.

4. Done in splashes; not even or regular.

1880 *Academy* 11 Dec. 430/3 The fine, but splashy, sketches..will rightly attract many admirers. **1884** *Brit. Alm. & Comp.* 167 His manner of handling is rather sketchy and splashy. **1887** *Ch. Times* 7 Oct. 785/2 The organ accompaniment..they complained of as being splashy and spasmodic.

splat, *sb.*[1] [f. splat *v.*[1]] A flat piece of wood, a flat bar or rail, *esp.* one forming the central part of a chair-back.

1833 Loudon *Encycl. Archit.* §2108 The splats (the middle part of the back, which either connects the top and bottom rails, or the two side styles) are carved. **1854** Miss Baker *Northampt. Gloss.*, *Splat*, the rails or staves used for the framing of a chair. The flat steps of a ladder bear the same name. **1904** *Burlington Mag.* V. 382/1 The carving.. is peculiarly good, both in the splats and the front leg.

splat, *sb.*[2] [f. splat *v.*[2]] **1.** *colloq.* A slapping and splashing sound; a smack.

1958 S. A. Grau *Hard Blue Sky* vi. 375 Annie was throwing the mud by handfuls and listening to the splat and sizzle. **1974** *Publishers Weekly* 11 Nov. 48/1 She tosses her head as she thinks how superior she'll be and, of course, the basket of eggs falls with a 'Splatt!' [*sic*]. **1976** 'Trevanian' *Main* (1977) iv. 72 A spoiled child dangles from her free hand... She gives it a good shake and a splat on the bottom. **1979** D. Gurr *Troika* xxiv. 176 The dough hit him across the face with a vicious slapping *splat*.

2. *Metallurgy.* **a.** Used *attrib.* and in *Comb.* with reference to a method of cooling hot liquid metal extremely rapidly by causing droplets of the metal, propelled by a shock wave, to strike and spread out upon a (usu. rotating) metal surface; so ***splat-cool*** vb., ***-cooled*** ppl. adj., ***-cooling*** vbl. sb., ***splat-quench*** vb., etc.

1960 *New Scientist* 28 July 286/2 Known as 'splat cooling', it consists in melting about 25 mg of metal in a shock tube by inductive heating. The resultant liquid drops are shot out of the tube by the shock wave and, travelling at high speed, impinge on the inside rim of a fast-revolving copper wheel. Because the splattering drops spread into a very thin film and the centrifugal force imparted by the spinning wheel ensures good thermal contact, the metal or alloy cools at something like a million degrees a second. **1965** *Trans. Metall. Soc. AIME* CCXXXIII. 1584/1 Heat-transfer coefficients..for aluminum and silver splat cooled essentially on a nickel substrate. **1968** *Acta Metallurgica* XVI. 1204/2 Alloys from 5 to 95% Sn in approximately 5% steps were splat cooled. **1968** *Jrnl. Chem. Physics* XLVIII. 1911/1 No stacking disorder was observed in splat-quenched two-phase alloys between α-Pb and ε [*sc.* a Pb-Bi alloy]. **1972** *Materials Sci. & Engin.* X. 343/1 Small pieces of the homogenized ingots were splat quenched at a rate of approximately 10^6 deg per sec. **1974** *Nature* 8 Nov. 100/2 He [*sc.* Pol Duwez] conceived the idea of blasting a small molten drop of alloy by means of a gaseous shock wave against a sloping piece of copper: the technique soon acquired..the onomatopoeic designation 'splat-cooling'. **1976** *Ibid.* 29 Jan. 271/3 A technique for splat-quenching and compaction of Al-Fe alloys.

b. A thin, localized film of metal produced in splat-cooling.

1965 *Trans. Metall. Soc. AIME* CCXXXIII. 1581/1 Upon impact the metal spread into a thin nonuniform film called a splat, about 10^{-4} cm thick. **1976** *Materials Sci. & Engin.* XXIII. 101/2 Chemical analyses of splats..indicated that some Cr was lost.

†**splat**, *v.*[1] *Obs.* Also 5 splatt, 5–6 splatte, 5 (8–9) splate; *pa. pple.* 5, 7 splat. [Obscurely related to SPLET *v.* and SPLIT *v.* Cf. also SPLATE *v.*]

1. *trans.* To cut up, to split open; *esp.* to dress (a pike) in this manner for cooking.

In later use only as a traditional entry from lists of 'proper' terms.

c **1400** *Laud Troy Bk.* 14008 He layde him as brod & flat As is a pike when he is splat. *a* **1440** *Sir Eglam.* 490 To splatt the bore they wente fulle tyte, Ther was no knyfe that wolde hym byte. *c* **1450** *Two Cookery-bks.* 101 Take the pike, and roste him splat on a gredire. *Ibid.* 105 Take a tenche, and splat him, and roste him on a gredire. **1495** *Act 11 Hen. VII*, c. 23 §1 Every suche fisshe shuld be splatted downe to a handfull of the taille. **1513** *Bk. Keruynge* in *Babees Bk.* (1868) 265 Splatte that pyke. **1615** MARKHAM *Eng. Housew.* II. ii. 57 A Gigget of Mutton which is the legge splatted and halfe part of the loine together. [**1688** HOLME *Armoury* III. 78 Splat that Pike. (Also in Phillips, Bailey, etc.) **1787** BEST *Angling* (ed. 2) 169 *Splate a pike*, cut him up. **1853** *Fraser's Mag.* XLVIII. 694 The reader will remember..that he gobbets trout,..splates pike,..and sides haddock.]

2. Of a horse: To strain (the shoulder).

Cf. SPLAITING *vbl. sb.*

1614 MARKHAM *Cheap Husb.* I. 30 There be many infirmities which make a Horse halt, as..splatting the shoulder, shoulder pight, straines in ioynts, and such like.

3. To spread out flat.

1615 W. LAWSON *Orch. & Gard.* iii. (1623) 8 And where, or when, did you euer see a great tree packt on a wall? Nay, who did euer know a tree so vnkindly splat, come to age?

splat, *v.*[2] (*int.* and *adv.*) *colloq.* [Shortening of SPLATTER *v.*]

1. *intr.* To land with a sharp smacking sound, or with a sound as of slapping and splashing. Also as *adv.*, as *to go splat*, and *int.*

1897 'H. S. MERRIMAN' *In Kedar's Tents* v. 55 A bullet went 'splat' against a rock. **1922** J. A. DUNN *Man Trap* xvi. 226 A bullet whistled by Jimmy's head, *splatting* on the lava crust. **1937** J. STEINBECK in *Esquire* Sept. 200/3 His fist splatted into Johnny Bear's smiling mouth. **1970** R. D. ABRAHAMS *Positively Black* iv. 101 This here bird flies over head and really lets go, right splat on her head. **1976** J. GRADY *Great Pebble Affair* (1977) 96 I'll jump out of the window... I hope I splat and spoil all the upholstery on those goddamn jalopies. **1977** *Undercurrents* June–July 34/3 Picked up the tap and splat! It leapt across the room.

2. *trans. Metallurgy.* To cause droplets of (a metal) to strike a surface and form a film in the process of splat-cooling.

1965 *Trans. Metall. Soc. AIME* CCXXXIII. 1583/1 Two metals, aluminum and silver, were selected to be splatted because of their high thermal conductivities and lack of oxidation problems.

Hence **'splatted** *ppl. a.*, **'splatting** *vbl. sb.*

1976 *Phil. Mag.* XXXIV. 236 The average energy loss.. was determined..from specimens immediately after splatting. *Ibid.*, Prior to performing microanalysis it was necessary to calibrate the variation of energy loss E_p with copper concentration for splatted material.

splatch (splætʃ), *sb.* Now *Sc.* and *U.S.* [app. of imitative origin: cf. SPLOTCH and Sc. *sclatch.*] A large or solid splash or spatter of mud, etc.; a large or glaring patch of colour.

1665 HOOKE *Microgr.* 3 A great splatch of London dirt. **1671** SKINNER *Etymol. Ling. Angl.* s.v., A splatch of dirt. **1825** JAMIESON *Suppl.*, *A splatch o' dirt*, a clot of mud thrown up in walking or otherwise. **1872** BLACK *Adv. Phaeton* xiii. 186 Behind us Kidderminster looked like a dusky red splatch in a plain of green. **1891** *Columbus* (Ohio) *Disp.* 20 Aug., Masses of ancient trees, through which splatches of color from thatch, tile or gable, hint of quiet village homes.

splatch, *v. Sc.* and *U.S.* [Cf. prec.] *trans.* To mark or diversify with, or as with, large splashes.

1825 JAMIESON *Suppl.*, *To splatch*,..to bedaub, to splash. **1893** *Columbus* (Ohio) *Disp.* 17 Aug., It is a mass of hills.. splatched with knots of noble trees.

'splatchy, *a.* [f. SPLATCH *sb.*] Marked or coloured in a splashy manner.

1708 SEWEL I, Splatchy, *geblanket.* **1722–7** BOYER *Dict. Royal* II, Splatchy, (painted, counterfeit,) *fardé.* **1910** *Daily Chron.* 26 Feb. 6/2 It is often supposed to imply something in the nature of a daub, vivid but splatchy.

†**splate**, *v. Obs.*[−1] [Of obscure origin: cf. SPLAT *v.*[1] and SPLAITING *vbl. sb.*] *intr.* To extend.

c **1440** *Pallad. on Husb.* II. 123 Thy vynys soil be not to molsh or hard,..Ne splate [*v.r.* splatte] hit not to flat, but sumwhat lene.

splather ('splæðə(r)), *v. dial.* [Perh. var. of SPLATTER *v.*] *intr.* To splash; to sprawl.

1877 F. ROSS et al. *Gloss. Words Holderness* 134/2 *Splather*,..to splash water or mud. **1886** R. HOLLAND *Gloss. County of Chester* 333 A procumbent plant which spreads over the ground would be said to 'splather about'. **1887** T. DARLINGTON *Folk-Speech S. Cheshire* 365 *Splather*,..to sprawl. 'He had bu' just spokken th' word, an' o'er he went *splatherin'* i' th' middle o' th' bruk.' **1936** F. CLUNE *Roaming round Darling* xiv. 118 The closed Experiment Farm, now profusely splathered with flora and fauna animate and inanimate.

Also as *sb.* (see quot. 1877); hence **'splathering** *ppl. a.*

1877 E. PEACOCK *Gloss. Words Manley & Corringham, Lincolnshire* 235/1 *Splather*, (1) a splash. (2) Noisy talk. **1879** *Dewsbre Olmenac* in *Eng. Dial. Dict.* (1904) V. 673/2 Matters hev gotten squared up efter a deeal o' conflab an splather. **1929** J. B. PRIESTLEY *Good Companions* I. v. 188 She sends a long splathering telegram and never puts her address in it. **1937** PARTRIDGE *Dict. Slang* 811/2 *Hold your splathers!* be silent!

†**'splatter**, *sb.*[1] *Obs.* [Irreg. f. SPATULE or SPATULA.] A spatula.

1539 in *Vicary's Anat.* (1888) App. iii. 173 The surgeons ..in whyte cotes, with their bendes of whyte & Grene bawdryke-wyse, & their splatters ouer the bende. **1563** T. GALE *Antidot.* II. 27 Continuallye styrrynge it wyth a splatter vntyll it bee colde. **1612** WOODALL *Surg. Mate* Wks. (1653) 9 Spatulaes or splatters..are most needful instruments to spread unguent, and emplaisters withal. **1639** T. DE GRAY *Compl. Horsem.* 77 With your splatter spread it upon the place. **1656** BLOUNT *Glossogr.* (1660), *Spat*,..a little slice or Splatter, wherewith Surgeons and Apothecaries use to spread their plaisters and salves.

'splatter, *sb.*[2] *Sc.* and *U.S.* [f. SPLATTER *v.*]

1. A heavy or loud splash or spatter.

1819 W. TENNANT *Papistry Storm'd* (1827) 56 Chariots and horse-hoofs round did scatter Scamander's sand wi' spairge and splatter. **1894** CROCKETT *Raiders* xiii. (ed. 3) 122 Then came a splatter of musketry up the passage.

2. An irregular assemblage.

1895 *Advance* (Chicago) 8 Aug. 192/2 [Boston] is a splatter of houses with lanes among them.

'splatter, *v.* Chiefly *dial.* and *U.S.* [Imitative.]

1. *intr.* To splash continuously or noisily:

a. Of persons, etc., in water or mud.

1784–5 *Ann. Reg.* 324/2 We..were, God knows how, but as merry as grigs, to think how we should splatter in the water. **1826** J. WILSON *Noct. Ambr.* Wks. 1855 I. 239 How engagingly delicate the virgin splattering along,..draggle-tailed and with left leg bared to the knee-pan! **1854** MISS BAKER *Northampt. Gloss.*, *Splattering*, splashing about in water so as to make a noise. **1896** CROCKETT *Grey Man* xii. 85 A good many Craufords were already splattering like wounded waterfowl in the moss.

b. Of water or other liquid.

1884 *Kendal Mercury & Times* 26 Sept. 2/6 The water comes gurgling, then splattering down betwixt great masses of rock. **1897** *Outing* XXX. 381/1 To one side a stream tumbled over it the whole ten feet, and splattered into a little pool below.

c. Of objects.

1931 W. G. CARR *By Guess & by God* 91 A salvo of shells splattered around the periscope. **1976** 'E. MCBAIN' *Guns* (1977) iii. 66 It had certainly been traumatic pulling the trigger of the .38 and watching the back of that cop's head come off and splatter onto the Seagrim's poster. **1978** *Amer. Poetry Rev.* July/Aug. 4/1 His deep brown feces splatter over Queen Anne's Lace and the waving sedge Of the pond.

2. a. *trans.* To spatter or sputter (something); to cause to spatter.

1785 BURNS *To W. Simpson* Postscr. xiii, Tho' dull prose-folk latin splatter In logic tulzie. **1831** *Blackw. Mag.* XXIX. 708 Baser Helot still who ate up that loathsome lie, and splattered it out again! **1897** *Outing* XXX. 132/2 It was a grateful summer shower that splattered the dust on the road.

b. To beat or batter.

1881 J. SARGISSON *Joe Scoap's Jurneh through Three Wardles* 31 If it wasn't for that oald grey heid o' thine Ah wud splatter thee. **1897** W. BEATTY *Secretar* xiv. 110, I would have splattered his harns on the causey. **1959** I. & P. OPIE *Lore & Lang. Schoolch.* x. 198 Recommendations by boys in East and South-East London: 'Bash him up.' 'Beat him up.'.. 'Splatter him.'

3. To bespatter or splash *with* something.

1888 in *Berkshire Gloss.* 152. **1894** R. H. DAVIS *Eng. Cousins* 83 Their wives splattered with the mud of the Mile-End Road.

4. *Comb.* in **splatter-work** (see quot.).

1897 SINGER & STRANG *Etching, Engraving*, etc. 124 Splatter work, very customary in poster designing and other large lithographic pictures, is made by filling a short bristle brush with lithographic ink, and drawing a knife or other edge across.

Hence **'splattered** *ppl. a.*

1805 A. WILSON *Poems & Lit. Prose* (1876) II. 145 Through this deep swamp in splattered plight..we laboured on. **1882** *Philadelphia Even. Star* 2 May, There is a masculine run upon fancifully splattered shirtings. **1979** E. NEWMAN *Sunday Punch* i. 1 The prize being, for some of the fighters, fame and fortune, often accompanied by splattered noses.

'splatterdash. *rare.* [See SPATTERDASH.] A long gaiter or legging; a spatterdash.

1772 NUGENT *Hist. Fr. Gerund* II. 261 White linen splatter-dashes with blue stripes beautiful to behold. **1881** A. M'LACHLAN in Edwards *Mod. Sc. Poets* Ser. II. 261 His legs they were..button'd upward to the knee Wi' great drab splatter-dashes.

'splatterdock. *U.S.* [f. SPLATTER *v.* Cf. *spatter-dock.*] The yellow pond-lily.

1832 J. P. KENNEDY *Swallow B.* xxv. (1872) 223 He does not fling away five hundred pounds..to maintain his title to a bed of splatterdocks. **188.** HARRIS in Goode *Amer. Fishes* (1888) 37 Large individuals are caught on the edges of the splatterdocks.

†**'splatter-face.** *Obs.*[−1] [Alteration of *platter-face*: see PLATTER[1] b.] A broad flat face.

1707 J. STEVENS tr. *Quevedo's Com. Wks.* (1709) 304 Good Mrs. Abigail..said of me, That I had a splatter Face, like an over grown School-boy.

'splatter-faced, *a.* Now *dial.* [Cf. prec.] Having a broad flat face.

1707 J. STEVENS tr. *Quevedo's Com. Wks.* (1709) 346 You splatter-fac'd Cully! **1785** G. A. BELLAMY *Apology* (ed. 3) I. 26 This goggle-eyed, splatter-faced, gabbart-mouthed wretch, is not my child! **1861** HUGHES *Tom Brown at Oxf.* vi, A splatter-faced wench neither civil nor nimble! **1894** in HESLOP *Northumbld. Gloss.*

†**splatter-footed**, *a. Obs.*[−1] [Cf. prec. and *platter-foot.*] Having broad flat feet.

1649 QUARLES *Virgin Widow* II, Go, ye weasel-snouted, addle-pated, buzzle-headed, splatter-footed Mooncalf.

splaw, *a. rare.* Now *dial.* Also 9 **splaa.** [Cf. SPLAY FOOT.] Of feet: Splay; clumsy.

1767 *Woman of Fashion* I. 112 [She] sat with her splaw Feet at a convenient Distance from each other; the Toes turned in. **1881** *Isle of Wight Gloss.* s.v. *Splaa*, I can't get a shoe to fit your splaa foot.

splay (spleɪ), *sb.* Also 6–7 *pl.* **splaies**; 6 **spleigh.** [f. SPLAY *v.*[1]]

1. a. *Arch.* 'A return of work deviating from a right angle, generally applied to the bevelled jambs of windows and doors' (Loudon).

1507–8 in Gage *Hist. Suffolk*: *Thingoe* (1838) 147 Plasteryng the beystales and the splaies. **1587** FLEMING *Contn. Holinshed* III. 1545/2 This sluse was composed with two arches, in length sixtie foot (besides the splaies). **1604** in Willis & Clark *Cambr.* (1886) II. 492 For altering certenne pannelles of his worke for the splaies of yᵉ greate wyndoes. **1708** *Phil. Trans.* XXVI. 37 Part of the Copeing of the Splay of the Gabel-end it self was broken down. **1725** W. HALFPENNY *Sound Building* 13 How to find the inward Edge AFB, so that it shall diminish gradually from nothing at the Crown F, to the Splay of the Jaums at the Springing AC and DB. **1833** LOUDON *Encycl. Archit.* §849 To cut all the rakes and splays, and all the chasings required for the lead flashings. **1855** W. CORY *Lett. & Jrnls.* (1897) 65, I would carve the name of a man on each stone in the splays and lintels. **1876** T. HARDY *Ethelberta* xxxviii, The day-light.. scarcely reached further into Lord Mountclere's entrance-hall than to the splays of the windows.

attrib. **1669** in Willis & Clark *Cambr.* (1886) II. 558 There shalbe sufficient vpright iron barrs in all the lights of all the lower windowes,..to be sufficient iron splay barrs.

b. The degree of bevel or slant given to the sides of an opening, etc.

1860 W. L. COLLINS *Luck of Ladysmede* (1862) I. 95 The bold splay of the window-sides, contrived so as to throw as much light as possible within. **1893** *Reliquary* Jan. 13 The inner head stones are by far the larger, as the splay is considerable.

c. The outward spread of a bowl or cup.

1874 H. H. COLE *Catal. Ind. Art S. Kens. Mus.* 138 The bowl has a good splay and a curved rim.

d. A tapered widening of the carriageway at a road intersection or corner provided in order to increase visibility for motorists.

1956 *Proc. Inst. Civil Engineers* V. II. 356 The splay provided in the boundary line of the minor road approaching the intersection should remove any possible restriction on vision at the point where the vehicle turning right-in has to cross the right-out stream from the minor road. **1963** W. F. CASSIE in E. Davies *Traffic Engin. Practice* x. 280 A minor road intersecting a major road. There are three possibilities..: (*a*) right-angled intersection; (*b*) right-hand splay; and (*c*) left-hand splay. **1968** J. L. PAISLEY in *Ibid.* (ed. 2) iv. 99 At uncontrolled junctions visibility splays should be provided to give full visibility to right and left. **1977** *Cornish Times* 19 Aug. 5/2 The Cornwall Surveyor.. offered no objections subject to the formation of a suitable access with visibility splays of 30 by 500 feet in each direction along the adjoining highway.

†**2.** A spread or expanse *of* boughs. *Obs.*

1594 O. B. *Quest. Prof. Concern.* 7 b, You have spoken so darkely, that for the thick spleigh of boughes and broad leaues of this tree, I cannot discerne your meaning.

splay, *adv.* and *a.* [f. prec., or after SPLAY-FOOT, -FOOTED.]

A. *adv.* **1. a.** = SPLAY-FOOT 3. **b.** In an oblique manner; slantingly. Also ellipt. *cut splay*, bricks cut with a slope or slant.

a **1734** NORTH *Lives* (1826) I. 144 He walked splay, stooping and noddling. **1825** J. NICHOLSON *Operat. Mechanic* 554 The sloping of the bricks thus, is called *cut splay.* Plain tile creasing and cut splay are charged by the foot run.

B. *adj.* **1.** Oblique; awry; off the straight.

1876 M. ARNOLD *Lit. & Dogma* Pref. p. xxv, In the German mind, as in the German language, there does seem to be something splay. **1895** R. L. STEVENSON *Amateur Emigrant* 38 We had a fellow on board, an Irish-American, for all the world like a beggar in a print by Callot; one-eyed, with great, splay crow's-feet round the sockets. **1952** DYLAN THOMAS *Coll. Poems* p. viii, Though song Is a burning and crested act, The fire of birds in The world's turning wood, For my sawn, splay sounds.

2. *Comb.*, as *splay-kneed*, *-toed.* **splay fault** *Geol.*, a subsidiary fault diverging at an acute angle from a larger dislocation.

1896 'H. SETON MERRIMAN' *Flotsam* iv, The waiter, in his rusty black and splay-toed shuffling boots. **1899** *Westm. Gaz.* 2 Feb. 2/3, I see you..The slave of some splay-kneed mechanic. **1942** E. M. ANDERSON *Dynamics of Faulting* vii. 150 Splay faults may..be expected to diverge from the main fracture at about this angle [*sc.* 22½°]. **1969** BENNISON &

WRIGHT *Geol. Hist. Brit. Isles* vii. 147 These structures continue across into Northern Ireland but are much less strongly developed there and are replaced by series of en-echelon and splay faults. **1971** *Nature* 19 Feb. 538/1 North and south of the Gregory rift..the periclinal ends of the uplifted area are broad transverse depressions traversed by splay-faults.

splay (spleɪ), *v.*[1] Also 6 **spley(gh, spleigh;** *pa. pple.* 5 **splaid,** 6 **splaied, splaide, spleyde, spleade, spled.** [Aphetic form of DISPLAY *v.*]

†**1.** *trans.* To unfold, unfurl, or expand (a banner); = DISPLAY *v.* 1. *Obs.*

c **1330** R. BRUNNE *Chron. Wace* (Rolls) 9918 Bot horn ne trompe dide non blowe.. Til alle were splayed ilka banere. *c* **1400** *Song Roland* 452 They splayd baners, for men se it shold. **1430–40** LYDG. *Bochas* VIII. xiii. (1558) 8/2 Swerd or septer.. There was none nor baners splayde wyde. *a* **1529** SKELTON *Agst. Garnesche* ii. 30 Ye grounde yow vpon Godfrey.. Your stondarde, Syr Olifranke, agenst me for to splay. **1555** EDEN *Decades* I. iii. (Arb.) 83 They assayled the one the other as fiersely, as if mortal ennemies, with theyr baners spleade, shulde fight for theyr goodes. **1594** R. C[AREW] *Godfrey of B.* (1881) 21 He saw the loftie Standard splayd, With Peters Diademe and with his keyes.

†**b.** To display *in* a banner. *Obs.*[−1]

c **1430** LYDG. *Min. Poems* (Percy Soc.) 26 The fyve rosis portraid in the shelde, Splaid in the baner at Jherusalem.

†**c.** To adorn *with* displayed banners. *Obs.*[−1]

1533 *Coronation Q. Anne* A j, All the worshypfull Craftes and Occupacyons.. toke theyr barges which were splayed with goodly baners.

2. To spread out, expand, extend; to open out in a spreading manner. Also with *out*.

In mod. use suggested by SPLAY *sb.* 1.

c **1402** LYDG. *Compl. Bl. Knt.* 33 The floures.. gunne for to sprede, And for to splay out her leves on brede Ageyn the sunne. **1530** *Hickscorner* 19 She sawe her sone, all deed, Splayed on a crosse with the fyve welles of pyte. **1548** UDALL, etc. *Erasmus Par. Luke* Pref. 11 b, The grayne of mustard-sede.. dyd ferre and wyde spleigh his boughes abrode. **1567** GOLDING *Ovid's Met.* VI. (1593) 130 And over Leda she had made a swan his wings to splay.

1879 J. GILBURT in *Lett. to Clergy* 191 Their portals large splayed out embracingly. **1881** *Nature* XXIV. 571 If the tube be touched.. the shadow will be splayed out in a striking manner. **1893** 'Q' (QUILLER COUCH) *Delect. Duchy* 127 The.. table.. collapsed flat.., with its four legs splayed under the circular cover.

transf. *c* **1557** ABP. PARKER *Ps.* xxxiv. 81 Upon the iust and godly men, the Lorde hys eyes doth splay.

†**b.** To spread or open out so as to exhibit fully; = DISPLAY *v.* 3. *Obs.*

c **1440** *Pallad. on Husb.* I. 625 The cok confesseth emyne[n]t Cupide When he is gemmy tayl bygynnyth splay About hymself. **1513** in Glover *Hist. Derby* (1829) I. App. 61 Sir John Sowch.. bayryth goulls, a Faucon splay'd syttyng upon a stok. *a* **1548** HALL *Chron., Hen. VIII*, 72 The clothe of his estate of the blacke Egle all splaied on riche clothe of golde. **1575** LANEHAM *Let.* (1871) 40 A gray Mare, ..her pannell on her bak,.. her tail splayd at most eaz.

†**c.** To cut up or carve. *Obs.* (Cf. DISPLAY *v.* 2 b.)

In some late works miscopied as SOLAY.

1486 *Bk. St. Albans* F vij b, A Breme splayed. **1513** *Bk. Keruynge* in *Babees Bk.* (1868) 265 Splaye that breme. [Hence in Holme (1688), etc.]

†**d.** (See quot. and cf. SPLAITING *vbl. sb.*) *Obs.*

1463 *Paston Lett.* II. 143 The ferror.. seyth he [a horse] was splayyd, and hys shulder rent from the body.

†**3.** *absol.* **a.** To come into view; to display or show oneself. *Obs.*

a **1400** *Stockholm Medical MS.* ii. 186 in *Anglia* XVIII. 312 On lammesse-day Erly on morw, or sonne splay. *a* **1513** FABYAN *Chron.* VI. (1811) 236 Thilfer, a Norman, splayed before the hoost of Normans, and slewe an Englysshe man, or knyght, that came agayne hym.

†**b.** Of wings: To spread *out*; to be extended.

1426 LYDG. *De Guil. Pilgr.* 697 Ther kam a dowe whyt as snowh, With hys wynges splayng oute. *Ibid.* 18521 On the pomel.. Wonder hygh ther sate a krowe, His whynges splayynge to and ffro.

4. *trans.* To bevel or make slanting; to construct with a splay.

1598 in Willis & Clark *Cambr.* (1886) II. 252 The windoes ..shalbe well splayed on the inside. **1823** P. NICHOLSON *Pract. Build.* 310 In working the cornice, the top or upper side should be splayed away towards its front edge. **1851** RUSKIN *Stones Ven.* I. xvi. §4 These angles.. should at once be bevelled off, or, as it is called, splayed. *a* **1878** SIR G. SCOTT *Lect. Archit.* (1879) I. 278 The simplest method.. is to splay the jambs and arch of the window.

b. To take *off* by splaying.

1879 *Cassell's Techn. Educ.* I. 297/2 The upper surface.. becomes an octagon when the angles at the corners are splayed off.

5. *intr.* **a.** To have, take, or lie in, an oblique or slanting direction.

1725 W. HALFPENNY *Sound Building* 13 A.. Door, or Window, whose Jaums.. splays more or less. *Ibid.* 14 The Arch.. will splay gradually to AC and DB. **1875** MARTIN *Winding Machinery* 45 It is not impossible to build them with sides which splay more and more. **1875** SIR T. SEATON *Fret-Cutting* 151 The little side ornaments splay outwards and incline downwards.

b. To spread out in an awkward manner.

1848 THACKERAY *Bk. Snobs* xxxii, It was a finger, as knotted as a turkey's drumstick, and splaying all over the piano.

splay, *v.*[2] Now *dial.* [Alteration of SPAY *v.*] *trans.* To spay (female animals). Also *fig.*

1601 HOLLAND *Pliny* I. 230 Sowes also are splaied as well as camels. **1651** CLEVELAND *Poems* 4 Geld the loose wits, and let the Muse be splaid. **1663** BOYLE *Usef. Exp. Nat. Philos.* II. v. 234 The well-known practice of splaying swine and bitches. **1794** BISHTON *View Agric. Salop* 10 The bull calves are cut, and many heifers splayed. **1841** HARTSHORNE *Salop. Ant.* Gloss., *Splay*, to castrate an heifer.

splayed (spleɪd), *ppl. a.*[1] [f. SPLAY *v.*[1]]

†**1.** *Her.* = DISPLAYED *ppl. a.* 2. *Obs.*

a **1513** FABYAN *Chron.* VII. (1811) 288 Y[e] Emperoure was fled, leuynge his baner of the splayed egle behynde hym. **1562** J. SHUTE tr. *Cambini's Turk. Wars* 3 b, Scanderbeg caused to take downe the Turckes enseigne and to set up his with the splayed egle of Sable in a feelde of Gules. **1631** WEEVER *Anc. Funeral Mon.* 825 A Vulture splaied, which is the Crest of the Shernborns. **1659** in *Rep. Hist. MSS. Comm.* Var. Coll. (1907) IV. 242 To adde on the same stampe on the other side the splayed eagle.

2. Expanded, extended, spread (*out*).

a **1547** SURREY *Æneid* IV. 787 The Quene the peping day Espyed, and nauie with splaid sailes depart The shore. **1565** GOLDING *Ovid's Met.* II. (1593) 27 Doris with her daughters all, of which some cut the wals [= waves] With splaied arms. **1583** MELBANCKE *Philotimus* A iij, They girde it out with splayed wynges, and ouer-stripp the Easterne wynds.

1770 G. WHITE *Selborne* xxxii, The fore-hoofs were upright and shapely, the hind flat and splayed. **1863** *Reader* 31 Oct. 502 The splayed vertebræ are grimly distinct—along yards on yards of spine. **1901** 'LINESMAN' *Words by Eyewitness* iii. (1902) 40 Spion Kop itself,.. the thumb of the vast splayed-out hand.

3. Made or cut with a splay; slanting, bevelled: **a.** Of masonry.

1823 RUTTER *Fonthill* 9 The splayed jambs of the northern doorway are large. **1837** *Civil Eng. & Arch. Jrnl.* I. 34/1 The bricks in the angles of the splayed work are to be neatly cut. **1865** BELLEW *Blount Tempest* I. 68 The Keep presents ..the same massive walls.. and the same splayed windows. **1883** *Specif. Alnwick & Cornh. Rlwy.* 3 The bricks for the splayed corners of the piers.

b. Of boards, metal plates, etc.

1858 SKYRING *Builder's Prices* 22 Floors:.. straight joints, splayed headings, 42*s.* **1883** *Specif. Alnwick & Cornh. Rlwy.* 20 The hinges.. made of wrought-iron;.. the hooks to have wrought-iron plates with splayed edge.

splayed, *ppl. a.*[2] Now *dial.* [f. SPLAY *v.*[2]] Spayed; having the ovaries excised.

c **1611** CHAPMAN *Iliad* XIX. Comment., Vnlesse you will take it for a splayed or gelded Sow. **1614** MARKHAM *Cheap Husb.* V. i. (1668) 101 The males will make.. excellent Bacon or Pork, and the females which are called splayd-guelts, will do the like. **1768** PENNANT *Brit. Zool.* I. 31 The meat of a splayed goat. **1847** HALLIW. s.v., Nothing could have any chance of running against them but a splayed bitch.

fig. **1698** [R. FERGUSON] *View. Eccles.* 49 The Report has wretchedly clipt what the Display had coyned, and the Display is now splay'd.

splayer. [? f. SPLAY *v.*[1]] (See quot.)

1875 KNIGHT *Dict. Mech.* 2279/2 *Splayer*,.. a segment of a cylinder on which a molded tile is pressed to give it a curved shape, for a pantile,.. gutter or drain tile.

splay foot, splay-foot. [f. SPLAY *v.*[1]]

1. a. A flat, spread out, clumsy foot, esp. one which turns outwards.

1548 ELYOT, *Plancus*, he that hath a splaie foote. **1586** SIDNEY *Arcadia* I. iii. (1912) 21 Only her face and her splayfoote have made her accused for a witch. **1611** MIDDLETON & DEKKER *Roaring Girl* IV. ii, Have not many handsome legs in silk stockings villanous splay feet? **1816** SCOTT *Old Mort.* vi, Splay feet of unusual size, long thin hands [etc.]. **1862** MERIVALE *Rom. Emp.* lxiv. (1865) VIII. 81 The splay foot of the mountain peasant girl. **1877** MISS A. B. EDWARDS *Up Nile* x. 283 The camels planted their splay feet obstinately in the sand.

fig. **1838** LYTTON *Alice* VII. iii, To have his gentle tenor crushed.. by the heavy splay foot of Mr. Tiddy's manly bars ..was insufferable.

b. Used as a term of abuse.

1612 SHELTON *Quix.* I. IV. vi. 45 Good man Splay-foot, unmannerly Clown.

2. *attrib.* = SPLAY-FOOTED *a.* *Obs.* or *rare.*

1631 DEKKER *Match Mee* II. 25 Th'art a damn'd Bawd: A soaking, sodden, splay-foot, ill-fac'd Bawd. **1690** D'URFEY *Collin's Walk thro' Lond.* 53 Thou Splay-foot blind phanatick Rogue. **1719** —— *Pills* (1872) I. 144 He sent a splayfoot Taylor. **1922** JOYCE *Ulysses* 690 A slender splayfoot chair of glossy cane curves.

fig. **1622** MASSINGER & DEKKER *Virg. Martyr* IV. ii, I would not give up the cloak of your service to meet the splayfoot estate of any left-eyed Knight. **1663** BUTLER *Hud.* I. iii. 192 In small Poets splay-foot Rhimes. **1766** [ANSTEY] *Bath Guide* Epil. 244 Oft have I read the.. Splay-foot Measures of thy Simkin's Lays.

3. As *adv.* In a splay-footed manner.

1626 MIDDLETON *Women Beware Women* II. ii, She must be neither slut nor drab, Nor go too splay-foot with her shoes.

Hence **splayfooting** *vbl. sb.* (In quot. *fig.*)

1675 WOOLLEY *Gentlew. Comp.* 31 Fops will venture the spraining of their tongues, and splayfooting their own mouths if they can.

splay-footed, *a.* Also 6 **splaie-.** *β.* 6–7 **spla-,** 7 **splea-.** [f. as prec.] Having splay feet.

α. **1545** ELYOT, *Planci*, they whiche be splay footed. **1577** HELLOWES *Gueuara's Chron.* 403 He was splay footed, and also poare blind. **1594** NASHE *Terrors of Night* To Rdr., Martin Momus, and splaie footed Zoylus,.. are now reuiu'd againe. **1652** GAULE *Magastrom.* 186 The long-footed are fraudulent; and short-footed, sudden; and splay-footed, silly. **1695** *Lond. Gaz.* No. 3057/4 A splay footed and down look'd man. **1809** W. IRVING *Knickerb.* (1861) 186 A gigantic Swede, who, had he not been.. splay-footed, might have served for the model of a Samson. **1892** J. LUMSDEN *Sheephead & Trotters* 233 This long-limbed and somewhat splay-footed genius.

β. **1593** *Passionate Morrice* (1876) 82 Other [suitors], which were well legde, shaled with their feete, or were splafooted. **1608** MACHIN *Dumb Knt.* IV, Sure I met no splea-footed baker, No hare did crosse me. **1647** LILLY *Chr. Astrol.* clxxxv. 788 All Clowns, crump-shouldered or splea-footed. **1688** *Lond. Gaz.* No. 2392/4 A bandy-leged splafooted.. Man.

b. *fig.* Clumsy, awkward; sprawling.

1716 M. DAVIES *Athen. Brit.* II. 139 The rest moulded upon Lucretius's Splay-footed numbers. **1756** FRANCIS tr. *Horace, Epist.* (ed. 7) II. i. 183 Nor wish [I] to stand expos'd to public Shame,.. Nor in splay-footed Rhimes to shew my Face. **1765** FALCONER *Demagogue* 380 Splay-footed words, that hector, bounce, and swagger.

'splaying, *vbl. sb.*[1] [f. SPLAY *v.*[1]]

1. The action of extending; extension.

For *Splaying* in Kersey (1706) see SPLAITING *vbl. sb.*

1530 TINDALE *Answ. More* Wks. (1573) 277/2 The casting abroad of his hands [is] the splaying of Christ vpon the crosse.

2. The action of making with a splay; the manner or extent of this.

1725 W. HALFPENNY *Sound Building* 13 A.. Door, or Window.., whose Crown lies level without splaying. **1844** *Civil Eng. & Arch. Jrnl.* VII. 247/1 The splaying of the arches.. was neither justified by science nor practice. **1851** RUSKIN *Stones Ven.* I. xvi. §9 The splaying or chamfering of the jamb of the larger door will be deepened. **1881** *Athenæum* 4 June 756/3 The Interior of the New Church.. is.. noteworthy on account of the bold splaying of the clearstory.

3. The fact of spreading outwards.

1881 *Nature* XXIV. 571 This splaying or bulging of the shadow is due to the interference of the molecular streams.

'splaying, *vbl. sb.*[2] [f. SPLAY *v.*[2]] Spaying.

1607 TOPSELL *Four-f. Beasts* 673 Another part of a good Swinehard is, to looke to the gelding of his Swyne, and splaying of the females. **1611** COTGR., *Chastrement*, a gelding, libbing, speying, splaying.

'splaying, *ppl. a.* [f. SPLAY *v.*[1]] Sloping or spreading outwards.

1874 H. H. COLE *Catal. Ind. Art S. Kens. Mus.* 143 The body of the vessel is like an ordinary lota.., with a long and broad splaying neck. *Ibid.* App. 273 A thin bowl-shaped cup with splaying rim.

splay-legged, *a. rare*[−1]. [Cf. SPLAY-FOOTED *a.*] Having straddling legs.

1638 COWLEY *Love's Riddle* I. i. 269 Although splay-leg'd, crooked, deform'd in all parts.

splay-mouth. *rare*[−1]. [Cf. next.] A distorted or wry mouth.

1693 DRYDEN *Persius* I. (1697) 410 Hadst thou but.. a Face behind, To see the People, what splay-Mouths they make.

splay-mouthed, *a.* ? *Obs.* [f. SPLAY *v.*[1]] Having a wide or wry mouth. Also *transf.*

1651 CLEVELAND *Poems* 41 Had I but Elsing's gift (that splay-mouth'd brother). **1687** T. BROWN *Alsop's State Conform.* Wks. 1711 IV. 119 This is a happiness, crys our splay-mouth'd Tallow-Chandler. **1718** *Entertainer* No. 30. 202 The Splay-Mouth'd Covenanters, that Sanctified Crew of Hypocrites. **1812** *Examiner* 14 Sept. 590/1 His vulgar volubility and splay-mouthed pronunciation.

splea-footed, obs. f. SPLAY-FOOTED.

spleageant: see SPLEDGET.

spleat, obs. f. SPLEET *sb.*

†**speck.** *Obs. rare.* In 4–5 **splek(ke,** 5 **spleke.** [Cf. next and PLECK 2.] A speck, a spot.

1398 TREVISA *Barth. De P.R.* VIII. xviii. (Bodl. MS.), þe mone.. takeþ a foule splekke and vnsemely. *Ibid.* VIII. xxix. (Tollem. MS.), þe schadow of þe erþe, of þe whiche is reboundid a maner dym splek [**1495** spleke] in þe body of þe mone.

†**splecked,** *a. Obs. rare.* In 4 **spleckid, splekked,** 5 **spleket.** [Cf. MDu. *gesplect* (Verdam s.v. *gespekelt*) and PLECKED *a.*] Specked, spotted.

1382 NICHOLAS OF HEREFORD *Bible* Pref. Ep. vii. (MS. Bodl. 959), þe reed horssez spleckid whyt. **1387** TREVISA *Higden* (Rolls) I. 429 In þe welmes.. Is y-founde reed splekked stones. *Ibid.* II. 303 Alle þe splekked lamberne and kedes.. schulde be Iacob his mede. **1422** tr. *Secreta Secret., Priv. Priv.* 230 Spleket eyen and whyte eyen tokenyth dredfulnesse.

†**splecky,** *a. Obs.*[−1] [f. SPLECK.] Spotty.

1398 TREVISA *Barth. De P.R.* VIII. xxviii. (Tollem. MS.), Yf þe sonne is splekky,.. it bodeþ a rayny day.

†**spledget.** *Obs. rare.* Also 6 **spleageant,** 7 **spleget.** [Alteration of (*plegent*) PLEDGET.] A pledget.

1563 T. GALE *Antidot.* II. 66 This Trochisse made in pouder and tempered.. and layed on spleageants, doeth put away inflammations. **1639** O. WOOD *Alph. Bk. Secrets* 28 Take honey of Roses, dip Spledgets therein. *Ibid.* 205 Lay it on with a Spledget of Lint. **1656** BLOUNT *Glossogr.*, *Pleget* or *Spleget*, a long plaister of cloth or leather [etc.].

spleen (spliːn), *sb.* Forms: 4 (6–7) **splen;** 4–7 **splene;** 5–7 **spleene,** 6– **spleen.** [ad. OF. *esplen* (*esplien, esplene*, etc.), or L. *splēn*, a. Gr. σπλήν, related to Skr. *plīhan*, L. *liēn*. In Romanic the word has survived in many Italian dialects, and in Romanian *splină*, but It. *splene* is of learned origin, while mod.F. *spleen* (†*spline*) and Sp.

esplin have been adopted from English in sense 8 c.]

1. a. *Anat.* An abdominal organ consisting of a ductless gland of irregular form, which in mammals is situated at the cardiac end of the stomach and serves to produce certain changes in the blood; the milt or melt.

α. a 1300 *Vox & Wolf* in *MS. Digby 86* lf. 138 b/1 þou hauest þat ilke ounder þe splen, þou nestes neuere daies ten. 1390 GOWER *Conf.* III. 100 As it is in Phisique write Of livere, of lunge, of galle, of splen, Thei alle unto the herte ben Servantz. 1577 B. GOOGE *Heresbach's Husb.* III. (1586) 151 Swine..do woonderously labor with the abundance of the splen. 1650 B. *Discolliminium* 46 A..lumpe, compounded of..Satyres Splens, Polcatts Lites.

β. c 1400 *Lanfranc's Cirurg.* 80 If þe lyuere eiþer þe splene ben I-greued,..þou muste rectifien hem. 1460–70 *Book of Quintessence* 18 Brennynge watir in þe which gold is fixid.. heliþ þe splene. 1530 PALSGR. 274 The splene in a man, in a beest the melte. 1578 LYTE *Dodoens* 25 It is good against.. the stopping of the Milte or Splene. 1601 HOLLAND *Pliny* I. 343 Vnto this Cawle, is fastned the Splene on the left side of the belly just over-against the liver. 1619 [see SPLENIC *a.* 1].

γ. ?a 1400 *Morte Arth.* 2061 The comlyche kynge.. cowpez fulle evene..emange the schortte rybbys, That the splent and the spleene on the spere lengez! c 1623 LODGE *Poor Mans Talent* G iij, The spleene is a member longe, softe, and rare, like vnto a spounge, and is scituated on the lefte side. 1661 LOVELL *Hist. Anim. & Min.* 37 The Spleen [of a cow] eaten with honey..helpeth the paine of the spleen. 1707 FLOYER *Physic. Pulse-Watch* 116 In this Fever the Spleen is affected. 1767 GOOCH *Treat. Wounds* I. 411 The Spleen is an oblong, flat body of a livid color; its substance is soft, and texture very loose. 1802 *Med. Jrnl.* VIII. 277 A propulsion of blood from the exterior parts to some of the viscera, particularly the spleen and liver. 1851 CARPENTER *Man. Phys.* (ed. 2) 300 The structure and functions of the Spleen..have been among the most obscure subjects in Anatomy and Physiology. 1884 DAY *Fishes Gt. Brit.* I. p. lvi, The spleen among fishes is found..as a dull reddish body of a rounded form.

†b. Regarded as the seat of melancholy or morose feelings. *Obs.*

1390 GOWER *Conf.* III. 99 The Splen is to Malencolie Assigned for herbergerie. c 1425 tr. *Arderne's Treat. Fistula*, etc. 60 Bot þe splene haþ no vertu of gendryng anyþing, siþe it is noþing bot a receptakle of malencolie. c 1430 LYDG. *Min. Poems* (Percy Soc.) 201 Wheer ovir many an hed hath ake, In skorn whan she lyth on the splene. 1539 ELYOT *Cast. Helthe* (1541) 22 The splene or mylte is of yl juice, for it is the chamber of melancholy. 1605 *1st Pt. Ieronimo* III. i, Not one little thought..But should raise spleens big as a cannon bullet Within your bosomes. *Ibid.* III. ii, Why, this would vex The resolution of a suffering spleene. 1665 BOYLE *Occas. Refl.* II. xiv. (1848) 142 Those petty Chilnesses that formerly I..was apt to impute to nothing but Fumes of the Spleen, or Melancholy Vapours.

†c. Regarded as the seat of laughter or mirth. *Obs.* (Freq. c 1600.)

1390 GOWER *Conf.* III. 100 The galle serveth to do wreche, The Splen doth him to lawhe and pleie, Whan al unclennesse is aweie. 1398 TREVISA *Barth. De P.R.* v. xli. (Bodl. MS.), Some men menyn þat þe melte is cause of laugȝhing, for by þe splene we laugȝhen. 14.. *Pol., Rel., & L. Poems* (1866) 37 The mynde is in the Brayne... Gladnes in the splene. 1547 BOORDE *Brev. Health* ccvii. 71 A splene, the whiche..doth make a manne to laughe. 1598 BP. HALL *Sat.* IV. i. 74 Now laugh I loud, and breake my splene to see This pleasing pastime of my poesie. 1610 HOLLAND *Camden's Brit.* (1637) 464 Such matter as will make you laugh your fill, if you have a laughing spleene. 1635 QUARLES *Embl.* II. iv. (1718) 77 Come burst your spleens with laughter to behold A new found vanity. 1681 COLVIL *Whigs Supplic.* (1751) 91 Some for laughter burst their reins, And other some did split their spleens.

†2. In various phrases: **†a.** *of* or *on the spleen*, in jest or play. *Obs.*

c 1460 SIR R. ROS *La Belle Dame* 327 For wordes which said ben of þe splene, In fayr langage, paynted ful plesantlye. a 1500 *Nut-brown Maid* in *Arnolde's Chron.* (1811) 203 When men wyl breke promyse, they speke the wordis on the splene.

†b. *from the spleen*, from the heart. *Sc. Obs.*

c 1480 HENRYSON *Poems* (S.T.S.) III. 148 This prayer fra my splene is. 1500–20 DUNBAR *Poems* xlvi. 70 God bad eik lufe thy nychtbour fro the splene. 1571 *Satir. Poems Reform.* xxv. 79 When synneris repentis from þe splene.

†c. *to the spleen*, to the heart. *Sc. Obs.*

a 1568 A. SCOTT *Poems* (S.T.S.) xiii. 17, I thoill rycht grit distress, Bayth nycht & day, hard persit to þe splene.

†3. Merriment, gaiety, sport. *Obs.*

1588 SHAKS. *L.L.L.* v. ii. 117 With such a zelous laughter so profound, That in this spleene ridiculous appeares, To checke their folly, passions solemne teares. 1596 —— *Tam. Shr.* Induct. i. 137 Haply my presence May well abate the ouer-merrie spleene, Which otherwise would grow into extreames.

†4. a. A sudden impulse; a whim or caprice.

1592 SHAKS. *Ven. & Ad.* 907 A thousand spleens bear her a thousand ways. 1596 —— *1 Hen. IV*, v. ii. 19 A haire-brain'd Hotspurre, gouern'd by a Spleene. a 1625 FLETCHER *Wom. Pleas'd* I. ii, Not wandring after every toy comes cross ye, Nor struck with every spleen.

†b. Caprice; changeable temper. *Obs.*

1596 SHAKS. *Tam. Shr.* III. ii. 10, I must forsooth be forst To giue my hand..Vnto a mad-braine rudesby, full of spleene. 1596 —— *1 Hen. IV*, II. iii. 81 Out you mad-headed Ape, a Weazell hath not such a deale of Spleene, as you are tost with.

†5. a. Hot or proud temper; high spirit, courage, resolute mind. *Obs.*

1592 SHAKS. *Rom. & Jul.* III. i. 163 All this..Could not take truce with the vnruly spleene Of Tybalt deafe to peace. 1598 B. JONSON *Ev. Man in Hum.* III. i, She [= beauty] will infuse true motion in a stone,..Stuffe peasants bosoms with proud Cæsars spleene. 1600 HEYWOOD *1st Pt. Edw. IV*, Wks. 1874 I. 34 That I shrunk back, that I was neuer seene To show my manly spleen but with a whip. 1605 *Play of Stucley* in Simpson *Sch. Shaks.* (1878) I. 213 Your kind submission might have wrought What your high spleen and courage cannot do.

†b. Impetuosity, eagerness. *Obs.*

1595 SHAKS. *John* II. i. 448 With swifter spleene then powder can enforce The mouth of passage shall we fling wide ope. *Ibid.* v. vii. 50 Oh, I am scalded with my violent motion And spleene of speede, to see your Maiesty.

6. Violent ill-nature or ill-humour; irritable or peevish temper: **a.** With possessive pronouns, etc.

1594 SHAKS. *Rich. III*, II. iv. 64 O prepostorous And franticke outrage, end thy damned spleene. 1608 CHAPMAN *Dk. of Byron* v. i. 136 Let others learn by him to curb their spleens, Before they be curb'd, and to cease their grudges. 1642–4 VICARS *God in Mount* (1844) 64 The poysonous malice and incorrigible spight and spleene of the malignant partie. 1710 STEELE *Tatler* No. 4 ¶3 His spleen is so extremely moved on this Occasion that he is going to publish a Treatise against Opera's. 1781 WESLEY *Wks.* (1872) XIII. 462, I impute this to his violent spleen against logic. 1824 DIBDIN *Libr. Comp.* 745 The spleen and sophistry that marked the notes of the earlier cantos of Child Harold. 1885 RAWLINSON *Egypt & Bab.* II. xii. 425 This time he..vented his spleen on the Jews by renewed attacks and oppressions.

b. Without limiting word.

1604 DEKKER *King's Entertainm.* H iv b, Iustice in causes, Fortitude gainst foes, Temprance in spleene. 1662 PLAYFORD *Skill Mus.* Pref. (1674) 5 It abateth Spleen and Hatred. 1728 YOUNG *Love of Fame* IV. 16 Vex'd at a public fame, so justly won, The jealous Chremes is with spleen undone. 1752 HUME *Pol. Disc.* v. 81 An author, who has.. more spleen, prejudice and passion than any of these qualities. 1822 HAZLITT *Table-t.* Ser. II. xviii. (1869) 381 This may be very well as an ebullition of spleen or vanity. 1859 TENNYSON *Marriage of Geraint* 273 Whereat Geraint flash'd into sudden spleen.

7. With *a*: **a.** A fit of temper; a passion. Also *transf. Obs.* exc. *arch.*

1589 R. HARVEY *Pl. Perc.* (1860) 13 Fie, fie, will you vpon a spleen run vpon a Christen body with full cry and open mouth? 1590 SHAKS. *Mids. N.* I. i. 146 Briefe as the lightning in the collied night, That (in a spleene) vnfolds both heauen and earth. 1609 R. BARNERD *Faithf. Shepheard* 74 Neuer speake with partiall affection against any in a spleene, euill will seldome speaks well. [1814 CARY *Dante, Par.* XXX. 47 As when the lightning, in a sudden spleen Unfolded, dashes from the blinding eyes The visive spirits.]

†b. A grudge; a spite or ill-will. *Obs.*

1616 *Min. Archd. Colchester* (MS.) fol. 110 There is a spleene betwixt one of the Churchwardens..and this partie. 1665 MANLEY *Grotius' Low C. Wars* 825 The Duke having a spleen to the City. 1692 R. L. ESTRANGE *Josephus, Wars Jews* VII. xxx. (1733) 802 Onias did not do all this..for God's sake,..but out of a Spleen he bore to the Jerusalem Jews. 1722 DE FOE *Col. Jack* (1840) 201 The devil owing me a spleen ever since I refused being a thief.

8. With *the*: **†a.** Amusement, delight. *Obs.*$^{-1}$

1601 SHAKS. *Twel. N.* III. ii. 72 If you desire the spleene, and will laughe your selues into stitches, follow me.

†b. Indignation, ill-humour. *to bear* (one) *upon the spleen*, to bear resentment against. *Obs.*

1600 W. WATSON *Decacordon* (1602) 101 Howsoeuer vpon the spleene they sought for it at that time: he acquainted the Pope Clement with it. 1623 BINGHAM *Xenophon* 36 The Ægyptians, whom you principally beare vpon the spleen. 1629 J. MAXWELL tr. *Herodian* (1635) 38 Divers that..bore Perennius upon the spleene, for his intolerable haughty and disdainefull carriage.

c. Excessive dejection or depression of spirits; gloominess and irritability; moroseness; melancholia. Now *arch.*

1664 KILLIGREW *Pandora* II, Onely some fumes from his heart, Madam, makes his head addle. 'Tis call'd the spleen of late, and much in fashion. 1673 TEMPLE *Obs. on United Prov.* Wks. 1720 I. 54 Strangers among them are apt to complain of the Spleen, but those of the Country seldom or never. 1711 SHAFTESB. *Charac.* (1737) II. I. 199 At first, I look'd on you as deeply in the Spleen. 1726 SWIFT *Gulliver* IV. vii, Yet here I could discover the true seeds of the spleen, which only seizeth on the lazy, the luxurious, and the rich. 1838 LYTTON *Alice* 66 This quiet room gives me the spleen.

d. Without article in the same sense.

1690 TEMPLE *Ess., Poetry* Wks. 1720 I. 248 Our Country must be confess'd to be what a great foreign Physician called it, the Region of Spleen. 1718 LADY M. W. MONTAGU *Let. to Mrs. Thistlethwayte* 25 Sept., [I have] a mind weakened by sickness, [and] a head muddled with spleen. a 1763 SHENSTONE *Ess.* Wks. 1765 II. 205 Spleen is often little else than obstructed perspiration. 1811 MISS L. M. HAWKINS *C'tess & Gertr.* I. 25 Professing that he knew not now in whom to place confidence, he gave himself up to spleen and seclusion. 1860 W. COLLINS *Wom. in White* II. ii. 179 He is the victim of English spleen.

personif. 1712–4 POPE *Rape Lock* IV. 16 The gloomy Cave of Spleen.

9. *attrib.* **a.** In sense 1, as ***spleen artery, blood, -lymph, -mixture, -powder, -pulp, side, vein,*** etc.

1601 HOLLAND *Pliny* II. 146 When hee hath drunke it, [let him] lie vpon the spleene side. 1611 COTGR., *Artere splenitique*, the spleene arterie. *Ibid.* s.v. *Veine*, *La petite gastrique*..is the first branch of the spleene veine. 1834 *Good's Study Med.* (ed. 4) I. 367 The spleen-powder and spleen-mixture of Bengal. 1847–9 *Todd's Cycl. Anat.* IV. 778/2 He [Gerlach] altogether denies the existence of these granule-cells..in the spleen-pulp. *Ibid.* 796/2 In calves and sheep a reddish spleen-lymph is often found. 1897 *Allbutt's Syst. Med.* IV. 536 Caseous masses..loosely embedded in the spleen substance.

b. In transf. senses, as ***spleen-fit, -fog,*** etc.

a 1653 G. DANIEL *Idyll* iii. 75 All the world Trades in this magicke; though the foole be hurl'd Spleen-Shittle-Cocke. 1737 M. GREEN *Spleen* 8 If spleen-fogs rise at close of day, I clear my ev'ning with a play. 1878 BROWNING *Poets Croisic* 28 Song's remedies for spleen-fits.

c. spleen index, rate, the proportion of the population having enlarged spleens (as determined by palpation), useful as indicating the incidence of malaria.

1969 EDINGTON & GILLES *Path. in Tropics* ii. 13 The former [methods] determine parasite rates in random blood samples and *spleen indices... A close correlation exists between parasite and spleen rates. 1903 STEPHENS & CHRISTOPHERS *Pract. Study Malaria* xxiii. 261 Above ten years, the *spleen rate is usually considerably in excess of the parasite rate. 1935 *Discovery* Jan. 11/1 In these districts today the spleen rate, indicating the incidence of malaria amongst the inhabitants, is very low. 1963 E. PAMPANA *Textbk. Malaria Eradication* iv. 72 The spleen rate underestimates the true percentage of enlarged spleens.

10. *Comb.*, as ***spleen-born, -devoured, -pained, -piercing, -shaped, -sick, -struck, -swollen*** adjs.

1570 LEVINS *Manip.* 121 Splensicke, *spleneticus*. 1601 HOLLAND *Pliny* II. Index s.v., For the Spleene pained, swelled, hard, obstructed, or otherwise diseased. 1609 *Ev. Woman in Hum.* I. i. in Bullen *O. Pl.* IV, Another, with a spleene-devoured face, Her eies as hollow as Anatomy. 1649 G. DANIEL *Trinarch.* To Rdr., A fine Spleen-peirceing Witt. 1677 MIÉGE *Fr. Dict.* II, Splenetick, Spleen-sick, or troubled with the Spleen. 1763–5 CHURCHILL *Gotham* I. 14 A gloom thro' which to spleen-struck minds, Religion, horror-stamp'd, a passage finds. 1775 SHERIDAN *Rivals* Pref., They are usually spleen-swoln from a vain idea of increasing their consequence. 1859 TENNYSON *Merlin & V.* 552 You breathe but accusation vast and vague, Spleen-born, I think, and proofless. 1888 ROLLESTON & JACKSON *Anim. Life* 113 A spleen-shaped body, the albuminiparous gland.

spleen (spliːn), *v.* Also 7 splene. [f. the sb.]

1. †a. *trans.* To regard with spleen or ill-humour; to have a grudge at. *Obs.*

a 1629 HINDE *J. Bruen* li. (1641) 168 Is it then your antipathy against goodnesse..that provokes you to swell against them, and so much to splene and spite them? 1675 J. SMITH *Chr. Relig. App.* II. 18 A man so vitious as his hatred to Vertue made him spleen Nicæus,..and all good men.

†b. To fill with spleen; to make angry or ill-tempered. *Obs.*

1689 N. LEE *P'cess Cleves* IV. i, Such Love as mine, and injur'd as I thought, Wou'd spleen the Gaul-less Turtle, wou'd it not? a 1734 NORTH *Examen* (1740) 326 The author ..is manifestly spleened at the force with which they wrote and preached in the controversy. 1801 S. & HT. LEE *Canterb. T.* V. 258 Stanhope, too much spleen'd for conversation, withdrew.

c. *intr. U.S.* To feel spleen or deep anger.

1885 *Congregationalist* 1 Jan. (Cent.), It is fairly sickenin'; I spleen at it. 1889 R. T. COOKE *Steadfast* xviii. 198 [It] makes me spleen to think on't! 1902 H. L. WILSON *Spenders* x. 110 Well, I knew Dan'l J. purty well, and I spleened against some of his ways, but that's done fur.

2. *trans.* To deprive of the spleen.

a 1735 ARBUTHNOT (J.), Animals spleened grow salacious.

spleenatick, -ive, -etic: see SPLENATIC, etc.

spleenful (ˈspliːnfʊl), *a.* [f. SPLEEN *sb.*] Full of spleen; passionate, irritable, peevishly angry:

a. Of persons (or animals).

1588 SHAKS. *Tit. A.* II. iii. 191 Now will I..let my spleenefull Sonnes this Trull defloure. 1631 HEYWOOD *Eng. Elizab.* (1641) 90 Thus she remained a sorrowfull and dejected prisoner, in the hands of spleenfull and potent adversaries. 1687 DRYDEN *Hind & P.* III. 1196 The spleenful Pigeons never could create A Prince more proper to revenge their hate. 1795 WOLCOT (P. Pindar) *Pindariana* Wks. 1812 IV. 225 'Twas thus I spleenful cried. 1818 KEATS *Endym.* IV. 256 About the wilds they hunt with spear and horn, On spleenful unicorn. 1859 TENNYSON *Marriage of Geraint* 293 Then rode Geraint, a little spleenful yet, Across the bridge.

b. Of actions, feelings, etc.

1593 SHAKS. *2 Hen. VI*, III. ii. 128 My selfe haue calm'd their spleenfull mutinie. 1616 R. C. *Times Whistle* (1871) 97 These, these they be, on which I doe engage My vexed Muse to wreck her spleenfull rage. a 1645 HEYWOOD *Fortune by Land & Sea* I. i, You speak out of some spleenful rashness, And no deliberate malice. 1718 POPE *Iliad* XV. 111 Smiles on her lips a spleenful joy express'd. 1827 HOOD *Mids. Fairies* lxxii, With more spleenful speeches and some tears. 1893 *Temple Bar* XCVII. 61 The spleenful emphasis with which the Squire puffed out the last word.

Hence **ˈspleenfully** *adv.*, in a spleenful manner.

1882 in *Imperial Dict.*

spleenical (ˈspliːnɪkəl), *a. rare*$^{-1}$. [f. SPLEEN *sb.* + -ICAL.] Spleenful.

1818 KEATS *Let.* Oct. (1931) I. 262 You see there is nothing spleenical in all this. The only thing that can ever affect me personally..is any doubt about my powers for poetry.

ˈspleenish, *a.* Now *rare.* Also 6–7 splenish. [f. SPLEEN *sb.*]

†1. Apt to disorder the spleen. *Obs.*$^{-1}$

1598 BP. HALL *Sat.* IV. iv. 20 When splenish morsels cram the gaping maw.

2. Somewhat spleenful or splenetic.

1610 BP. HALL *Apol. Brownists* 3 [They] are often times moued to shoote..the bitter arrowes of spightfull and splenish discourses. 1649 J. ARNWAY *Tablet* (1661) 8 The common and known fruits of fiery and spleenish tempers. 1651 BAXTER *Let. to Ch. Kederminster* 5 They will..think them spleenish or ungodly that will not offer a sacrifice to Mars. 1890 H. M. STANLEY *Darkest Africa* I. xii. 321 They ..sought by other means to gratify their spleenish hate.

Hence **'spleenishly** *adv.*; **'spleenishness**.
1775 S. J. PRATT *Liberal Opin.* lxxxiv. (1783) III. 116 To shut the book in a passion, or spleenishly tear out the leaf. **1847** WEBSTER, *Spleenishness*, state of being spleenish.

spleenless ('spli:nlɪs), *a. rare.* [f. SPLEEN *sb.*]
1. Destitute of a spleen.
1398 TREVISA *Barth. De P.R.* XVIII. xx. (Bodl. MS.), Camelion is..spleneles and woneþ in dennes as an ewte. **1899** *Brit. Med. Jrnl.* 2 Dec. 1567 Max Malener may claim, it appears, the first operation on a spleenless patient.
2. *fig.* Mild, gentle.
1615 CHAPMAN *Odyss.* XII. 347 A spleenelesse wind so stretcht Her wings to waft vs, and so vrg'd our keele.

†**spleen-stone**. *Obs.* [f. SPLEEN *sb.*] A stone supposed to cure disorders of the spleen.
1595 RALEIGH *Discov. Guiana* (1596) 24 A kinde of greene stones, which the Spaniards call *Piedras Hijadas*, and we vse for spleene stones. **1613** R. HARCOURT *Voy. Guiana* 36 There are diuers kinds of Stone of great vse, and good price, as Jasper, Purphery, and the Spleene-stone. **1666** in Myddelton *Chirk Castle Acc.* (1908) 131 Paid the man that came with the spleene stone from Dolgrog. **1691** *Lond. Gaz.* No. 2680/4 Lost.., a Green Spleen Stone cut Triangular. **1775** MOTHERBY *Med. Dict.*, *Ophites*, called also serpentinus, ophite, or spleen-stone.

spleenwort ('spli:nwɜ:t). Also 6 **splen(e)-, spleenewort, spleen-,** 6–7 **spleenewoort**. [f. SPLEEN *sb.*, after L. *splēnion* or *asplēnon*, a. Gr. σπληνίον, ἄσπληνον (also ἀσπλήνιος, -ον adj.), f. σπλήν spleen.]
1. a. One or other of various ferns belonging to the genus *Asplenium*; also, the genus itself.
1578 LYTE *Dodoens* III. lxv. 406 Of brode or large Splenewort or Miltwast. **1597** GERARDE *Herbal* II. ccccluv. 979 Called..in English Spleenwoort, Miltwaste, Scale Ferne, and Stone Ferne. **1607** TOPSELL *Four-f. Beasts* 616 Spleenwort giuen vnto sheep..is the best remedy for this Malady. **1688** HOLME *Armoury* II. 97/2 *Spleenwort*, hath divers stalks of leaves. **1711** POPE *Rape Lock* IV. 56 Safe past the Gnome thro' this fantastic band, A branch of healing Spleenwort in his hand. **1753** *Chambers's Cycl.* Suppl. *App.*, *Spleen-wort*, ..called..in English more commonly milt-waste. **1862** ANSTED *Channel Isl.* 183 The varieties of Asplenium or spleenwort are very numerous and beautiful. **1885** GERARD *Waters of Hercules* viii, Between the stones..the maidenhair and spleenwort were beginning to peep.
pl. **1859** T. MOORE *Brit. Ferns* (1864) 59 The Spleenworts are called *Asplenium* by botanists.
†**b.** Hart's-tongue; scolopendrium. *Obs.*
1725 *Fam. Dict.* s.v. *Jaundice*, Boil therein an Handful of the Roots of Smallage..and wild Succory, with as much Harts-tongue or Spleenwort. **1796** WITHERING *Brit. Pl.* (ed. 3) III. 766 *Asplenium scolopendrium*. Spleenwort or Harts-tongue.
c. With various distinguishing terms.
The number of varieties thus distinguished is very large: see also MAIDENHAIR 6 and SEA 23 f.
1796 WITHERING *Brit. Pl.* (ed. 3) III. 768 *Asplenium viride*. Green-ribbed Spleenwort. *Ibid.* 770 *A. lanceolatum*. Spear-shaped Spleenwort. **1801** CHARLOTTE SMITH *Lett. Solit. Wand.* II. 92 Having found here the white spleenwort in fructification. **1845–50** MRS. LINCOLN *Lect. Bot.* App. 78/2 *Asplenium ebenum* (ebony spleen-wort). **1846–50** A. WOOD *Class-bk. Bot.* 630 Swamp Spleenwort... Dwarf Spleenwort. *Ibid.* 631 Silvery Spleenwort. **1847** H. MILLER *Test. Rocks* (1857) 30 The minute forked spleenwort of Arthur Seat. **1862** ANSTED *Channel Isl.* II. viii. 183 Black spleenwort is as common in the islands as in England. **1865** GOSSE *Land & Sea* (1874) 333 Here the Marine Spleenwort grows out of the vertical fissures.
†**2.** ***rough spleenwort***, a former name for various ferns (see quots.). *Obs.*
1597 GERARDE *Herbal* II. ccccluv. 978 *Lonchitis aspera*, Rough Spleenewort. **1600** SURFLET *Countrie Farme* II. xlii. 262 *Scolopendrium*, or rough spleene-woort, called also harts-toongue. **1633** *Gerarde's Herbal* II. ccccIxxi. 1140 *Lonchitis aspera maior*. Great rough Spleene-woort. **1760** J. LEE *Introd. Bot.* App. 328 Spleen-wort, Rough, *Lonchitis*. *Ibid.*, Spleenwort, Rough, *Polypodium*. **1777** JACOB *Catal. Plants* 61 *Osmunda Spicant*, Rough Spleenwort. **1785** MARTYN *Lett. Bot.* xxxii. (1794) 489 Rough Spleenwort [*note*, Osmunda Spicant] has lanceolate, pinnatifid fronds.
†**3.** A pteroid fern, *Lonchitis*. *Obs.*
By some early botanists confused with *Asplenium*.
1579 LANGHAM *Gard. Health* 616 Splenwort, or Lonchitis, is very good against the hardnes, stopping, and swelling of the milt. **1597** GERARDE *Herbal* 979 *Lonchitis Maranthæ*, Bastard Spleenewort. **1753** *Chambers's Cycl.* Suppl., *Lonchitis*, spleenwort,..the name of a genus of plants.
4. *U.S.* A species of cactus.
1846–50 A. WOOD *Class-bk. Bot.* 275 *Cereus Phyllanthus*. ..Spleenwort... Flowers white.
5. *Comb.*, as ***spleenwort-leaved***, ***-like*** adjs.
1753 *Chambers's Cycl.* Suppl. s.v. *Filix*, The spleenwort leaved..Portugal fern. *Ibid.*, The spleenwort like..African fern. **1786** ABERCROMBIE *Arr.* in *Gard. Assist.* 30 *Liquidambar*,..Spleenwort-leaved. **1841** *Penny Cycl.* XXI. 229/2 *Senecio hastatus*, the spleenwort-leaved groundsel.

spleeny ('spli:nɪ), *a.* [f. SPLEEN *sb.*] Spleenful; splenetic.
1604 MARSTON & WEBSTER *Malcontent* v. ii, You were to boisterous, spleeny. **1607** MARKHAM *Cavel.* VIII. Ded. A ij b, That I with a more spleeny spirit do condemne you, then all other trades whatsoeuer. **1689** G. HARVEY *Curing Dis. by Expect.* iv. 18 A Man or Woman afflicted with any hypochondriac spleeny Distemper. **1793** BURNS *Impromptu on Mrs. Riddel's Birth-day* 8 My dismal months no joys are crowning, But spleeny English, hanging, drowning. **1867** in J. Brown *Life Sc. Probationer* (1877) 260 Don't argue that I am envious, or *spleeny*, or much filled with animosity towards the Kirk.

spleet, *sb.* Now *dial.* and *rare*. [a. MDu. *splete* (WFlem. *splete*), *spleet* (Du. *spleet*) or MLG. (and LG.) *splete*, NFris. *splēt*, related to SPLIT *v.*] A small strip of split wood or willow.
1609 C. BUTLER *Fem. Mon.* iii. §9 If the hiue be then fourteene inches ouer within, it may wel receiue foure spleets. **1657** S. PURCHAS *Pol. Flying-Ins.* 60 Mr. Southern and others..advise, that if Bees finde fault with a Hive, and will not continue in it, to pull out the spleats. *a* **1679** SIR J. MOORE *Eng. Interest* (1703) 104 Your Hive being pruned put in your spleets. **1704** *Dict. Rust.* (1726) s.v. *Bee-hives*, Either Wicker-Hives made with Spleets of Wood,..or Straw-Hives. **1766** *Museum Rust.* VI. 2 Bind their stems together with a spleet of willow, or some tough wood. *Ibid.* 3 A small wreath, made of spleet, is slipped on the upper end of the staff. **1899–** in *Eng. Dial. Dict.*
Hence †**spleet** *v.*[1] *trans.*, to fit (a bee-hive) with slips of wood. *Obs.*
1609 C. BUTLER *Fem. Mon.* iii. §9 This is the easiest & quickest way of spleeting a hiue. **1661** WORLIDGE *Syst. Agric.* (1681) 186 The way they usually Spleet the ordinary Strawn and Daubed Hives, every Countrey Coridon understands.

spleet, *v.*[2] Chiefly *Sc.* [Obscurely related to SPLIT *v.* Cf. SPLEET *sb.* and LG. *spleeten* (rare).] *trans.* and *intr.* To split.
1585 HIGINS tr. *Junius' Nomencl.* 62/2 *Piscem exdorsuare*, ..to spleete out, or part alongest the ridge bone iust in the midst. **1606** SHAKS. *Ant. & Cl.* II. vii. 131 Mine owne tongue Spleet's what it speakes. **1647** HEXHAM I, To Spleet a fish, *een visch splyten.* **1701** J. BRAND *Orkney* ii. (1703) 25 At all times it is highly dangerous..to pass through between the Isles, do with small Boats, because of the many blind Rocks lying there, upon which sometimes the Inhabitants do spleet. *c* **1730** W. STARRAT in Ramsay *Poems* (1760) 222 We'll to the harning drive, When in fresh lizar they get spleet and rive. **1828** MOIR *Mansie Wauch* xii, Men.. holding their sides, laughing like to spleet them. **1866** in EDMONDSTON *Gloss. Shetl. & Orkney* 115. **1900** *Shetl. News* 22 Sept. (E.D.D.), Da auld axe ta spleet da lamb's head wi'.

'spleeted, *ppl. a.* [f. SPLEET *v.*[1] or *v.*[2]] Made with, or consisting of, split rods.
1681 WORLIDGE *Syst. Agric.* (ed. 3) 327 *Hurdles*. made.. either of spleeted Timber or of Hazle Rods. *Ibid.* 334 *Wattels* also signify spleeted Gates or Hurdles.

spleet-new, *a. Sc.* [app. f. SPLEET *v.*[2] Cf. SPLIT-NEW *a.*] Perfectly new.
1815 G. BEATTIE *John o'Arnha* (1826) 15 It was baith sleekit an' spleet new. **1835** J. BROWN *Lett.* (1907) 33, I have got the beautiful edition of Byron in 6 volumes, spleet new.

spleget, var. SPLEDGET *Obs.*

spleigh, obs. f. SPLAY.

splek(ked: see SPLECK(ED.

splen, obs. f. SPLEEN *sb.*

splen-, var. of SPLENO- before vowels, occurring in a few medical terms, as **'splenæmia, -'algia** [cf. F. *splénalgie*], **-'algic** *a.*
1822–7 GOOD *Study Med.* (1829) II. 529 The Splenalgia, or pain in the spleen.., is for the most part a slight attack of this disease [splenitis]. **1850** OGILVIE, *Splenalgy*, a pain in the spleen or its region. **1858** AITKEN *Pract. Med.* 417 This form of the disease [leucocythæmia] has been named *splenæmia* by Virchow.

†**splenatic**, *a. Obs.* Also 7–8 **-ick**; 7 **spleenatick**. [ad. med.L. *splēnaticus* (OF. *splenatique*, Roum. *splinatic*), var. of *splēnēticus* SPLENETIC *a.*]
1. Affected with disease of the spleen. *rare*⁻¹.
1607 TOPSELL *Four-f. Beasts* 189 The Spleene drunke in vrine, cureth the spleenatick.
2. Seated in, arising from, the spleen.
1621 BURTON *Anat. Mel.* I. i. III. v, Windy melancholy, which Laurentius subdivides into three parts,..Hepaticke, Splenaticke, Mesariacke. **1628** *Ibid.* (ed. 3) II. v. III. i. 371, I finde those that commend vse of apples, in Splenaticke.. melancholy.
3. Of persons: Spleenful.
1663 BUTLER *Hud.* I. i. 209 More peevish, cross, and spleenatick, Then Dog distract, or Monky sick. **1664** *Ibid.* II. i. 237 King Pyrrhus cur'd his Splenatick And testy Courtiers with a kick. **1721** AMHERST *Terræ Fil.* Pref. p. xxi, The splenatick man delights in satire.
4. Caused by, due to, spleen.
a **1661** FULLER *Worthies*, *Warwick* III. (1662) 121 Queen Mary..understanding it a Splenatick design against Cardinal Poole. **1707** FREIND *Peterborow's Cond. Sp.* 219 The first Line dispers'd all those splenatick Fumes.

†**splenative**, *a. Obs.* Also 6 **spleanatiue**, 7 **spleen-**. [ad. L. type **splēnatīvus* (cf. prec.), or independently f. SPLEEN *sb.*]
1. Acting on the spleen.
1592 NASHE *P. Penilesse* 32 b, My two cunning Philosophers were driuen to..seeke out splenatiue simples, to purge their popular Patients of the Opinion of their old Traditions.
2. Spleenful; of a hot or hasty temper.
1593 NASHE *Christ's T.* To Rdr., Into some spleanatiue vaines of wantonnesse..haue I foolishlie relapsed. **1602** SHAKS. *Ham.* v. i. 284 Though I am not Spleenatiue, and rash, Yet haue I something in me dangerous. **1630** DAVENANT *Cruel Brother* II, Even so the mighty Nations of the Earth Change..Their Battailes fierce to Duells spleenatiue, Or witty quarrels of the Penne. **1660** tr. *Wishart's Hist. Warrs Scot.* xii. 104 The two spleenative Armies.

splendacious (splɛn'deɪʃəs), *a.* Also **-atious, -aceous.** [Fancifully f. SPLEND-ID *a.*: see -ACIOUS.] Very splendid; gorgeous, magnificent.
1843 *Blackw. Mag.* LIII. 379 The room is papered with some splendacious pattern in blue and gold. **1848** THACKERAY *Trav. Lond.* Wks. 1886 XXIV. 349 The silver dish-covers are splendaceous. **1872** [EARL PEMBROKE & G. H. KINGSLEY] *S. Sea Bubbles* ix. 241 Loney..made a splendacious bedstead to sling his mat to.
Hence **splen'daciously; splen'daciousness.**
1853 THACKERAY *Lett.* 14 Feb., On my first arrival, I was annoyed at the uncommon splendatiousness. **1872** 'ALIPH CHEEM' (Yeldham) *Lays of Ind* (1876) 6 One of them..more splendaciously dressed..than the rest.

†**'splendancy.** *Obs.*⁻¹ [See next and -ANCY.] = SPLENDENCY.
1591 HORSEY *Trav.* (Hakl. Soc.) 234 The representacion of the sun shining in his full splendancie.

†**'splendant**, *a. Obs.* [f. L. *splend-ēre* + -ANT[1]. Cf. OF. *(e)splendiant*.]
1. = SPLENDENT *a.* 1 and 1 b.
1578 BANISTER *Hist. Man* I. 1 The splendant sparke of reason, which shall light ech mans iudgement. **1598** ROWLANDS *Betraying of Christ* (Hunterian Cl.) 51 Heav'ns glorious lampe..Turning his splendant beames of gold, to drosse. **1616** R. C. *Times Whistle* (1871) 90 When brighter starres Darken their splendant beauty. **1635** HEYWOOD *Hierarchy* III. Comm. 171 It is still seene to shine with many splendant stars.
2. = SPLENDENT *a.* 3.
1590 *Serpent of Division* A iij, When the noble and famous citie of Rome was most shining in her felicity, and splendant in her glorye. **1598–9** E. FORDE *Parismus* I. (1661) 1 The splendant fame of his renowne. **1610** MARCELLINE *Tri. Jas. I*, 46 Neither could I receive a Princesse more splendant in Beauty, and all good Graces. **1631** R. H. *Arraignm. Whole Creature* xii. §1. 112 Whose wisedome was so glorious and splendant, as a Beacon on a Mount, a Citty on a Hill.

splendar, obs. f. SPLINDER *sb.*

†**'splendence.** *Obs.*⁻¹ [Cf. late L. *splendentia*, It. *splendenza*.] Splendour.
1604 PRICKET *Hon. Fame* (1881) 32 More, then if Ten hundred thousand sunnes at once all shinde, and clearly should their radiant splendence guise.

†**'splendency.** *Obs.* [See prec. and -ENCY.] Splendour.
a **1591** H. SMITH *Arrow agst. Ath.* v. (1593) K iij b *marg.* Visibility or splendencie of the church in outward shew. **1607** *Schol. Disc. agst. Antichr.* II. vi. 75 Men..are delighted with the magnificence and with the splendencie of rites and ceremonies.

splendent ('splɛndənt), *a.* [a. L. *splendent-*, *splendens*, pres. pple. of *splendēre* to be bright or shining. So It. *splendente*, *-iente*, Sp. and Pg. *esplendente*, OF. *esplendent*.]
1. Shining brightly by virtue of inherent light.
1474 in *Coventry Leet Book* (1908) 393 O splendent Creator!..More bryghter then Phebus, excedent all lyght! **1503** HAWES *Examp. Virt.* I. 6 Whan the golden sterres clere were splendent. **1583** MELBANCKE *Philotimus* X ij b, The same Ioue whiche giues the Sun his splendent globe, hath giuen the Moone..her horned head. **1605** *Tryall Chev.* III. iii. in Bullen *O. Pl.* III. 314 Like the Sunne in his Meridian Throne, Too splendent for weake eyes to gaze upon. **1646** SIR T. BROWNE *Pseud. Ep.* 233 As is very observable in their red and splendent Planets, that is of Mars and Venus. **1686** GOAD *Celest. Bodies* III. ii. 437 Kepler has noted a Splendent Air in the day-time. **1812** CARY *Dante, Parad.* IX. 14 Another of those splendent forms approach'd. **1876** J. ELLIS *Caesar in Egypt* 120 Their splendent world of light they permeate.
fig. **1609** *Ev. Woman in Hum.* v. i. in Bullen *O. Pl.* IV, Be stars to Firmaments, and, as you are Splendent, so be fixed, not wandering.
b. Of rays, light, etc.
1509 *Parl. Deuylles* B iv b, With aungelles to synge in lyght splendent. *c* **1605** ROWLEY *Birth Merlin* IV. v, Again, behold from the igniferous body Seven splendent and illustrious rays are spread. **1676** *Phil. Trans.* XI. 744 It will for all this resume a splendent brightness even in the cold water itself. **1758** *Ibid.* LI. 253 Its light was most surprisingly splendent.
fig. **1614** JACKSON *Creed* III. 179 Though cloudes of enuy now may seeme, thy splendent rayes to choake. **1636** FITZ-GEFFREY *Holy Transp.* (1881) 185 A Starre which though his Orbe be earth,..Yet doth from heauen deriue his splendent light. *a* **1666** WHARTON *Poems* Wks. (1683) 355 Religion's outward worth and splendent Rays.
2. Reflecting light with great brilliancy; bright, gleaming, resplendent.
1578 BANISTER *Hist. Man* v. 81 This bowell..in a dogge hath for the most part a more splendent red. **1607** TOPSELL *Four-f. Beasts* 86 He had on his right side an exceeding splendent white spot. *Ibid.* 148 The best Grey-hound hath ..a neate sharpe head, and splendent eyes. *a* **1635** RANDOLPH *Poems* (1638) 30 A splendent buckle in the maiden zone. **1671** J. WEBSTER *Metallogr.* iv. 28 It is..most dense, uniform, splendent, yellow, and is a most pretious thing. **1814** H. BUSK *Fugitive Pieces* 7 Maria..seiz'd the splendent shears. **1826** FARADAY *Exp. Res.* (1859) 193 By evaporation it gave a splendent white crystalline salt. **1859** THACKERAY *Virgin.* II. 179 Her complexion really was as pure as splendent Parian marble.
b. Extremely brilliant, gorgeous, or magnificent.
1567 DRANT *Horace, Ep.* A vij, Both godds, and noblemen in splendent vestures gay. **1583** STUBBES *Anat. Abus.* I. (1879) 39 To think that the Lorde our God is delighted in the splendente shewe of outward apparell. **1635** A. STAFFORD *Fem. Glory* (1860) 7 If the Inne was so splendent, so sumptuous, what may we thinke of the amiable Guest,

that lodg'd in it? **1646** G. DANIEL *Poems* Wks. (Grosart) I. 66 Now the Horses proud Breath fire, and trample with a furious heat, To hurrie in the Splendent Chariot. **1817** STEPHENS in *Shaw's Gen. Zool.* X. I. 246 Splendent Thrush. .. This most splendid bird is generally admitted to be distinct from the Shining Thrush. **1858** CARLYLE *Fredk. Gt.* v. v. I. 575 Long Files of Giants, splendent in gold-lace and grenadier-caps, have succeeded.

3. *fig.* Having qualities comparable to material brightness or brilliancy; pre-eminently beautiful, grand, or great.

1509 HAWES *Past. Pleas.* I. (Percy Soc.) 5 The fayre lady excellent, Above all other in cleare beauty splendent. **1649** G. DANIEL *Trinarch.*, *Hen. V*, xxiv, And lead vs on Tryvmphant through the Port Of Victorye, to Honour's Splendent Court. *a* **1763** SHENSTONE *Love & Honour* 17 Th' Iberian realm Could boast.. No race more splendent, and no form so fair. **1837** CARLYLE *Fr. Rev.* I. II. i, Book-paper, splendent with Theories, Philosophies, Sensibilities.

b. Of qualities, actions, etc.

The first quotation is from a letter given as a ridiculous example of the use of 'ink-horn terms'.

1553 T. WILSON *Rhet.* (1580) 165 Beeyng accersited to suche splendente renowme, and dignitie splendidious. **1599** *Broughton's Let.* vii. 22 The splendent brightnes of the Trueth, which burnes.. so gloriously. **1615** DANIEL *Hymen's Tri.* Ded., By your splendent worthiness Your name shall longer live than shall your walls. **1654** GATAKER *Disc. Apol.* 97 The splendent lustre of Calvins repute. **1873** M. COLLINS *Squire Silchester* II. xiii. 158 The splendent genius of.. Christopher North.

Hence † **'splendently** *adv. Obs.*

1576 PETTIE *Petite Pallace* 12 b, Did it not make her glory & virtue shew more splendently to the whole world? **1601** BP. W. BARLOW *Defence* 30 So splendently appearing these 60. yeares together. **1613** JACKSON *Creed* II. 352 Scripture.. shines most splendently, most clearly, like a light.

splender, obs. or dial. var. SPLINDER.

splendescent (splɛn'dɛsənt), *a.* [a. L. *splendescent-*, *splendescens*, pres. pple. of *splendes-cĕre* to become bright.] Splendid, gorgeous.

1848 CLOUGH *Bothie* i, Splendescent as a god of Olympus. **1850** *Brit. Museum* (Chambers) 225 Some of these little creatures, with their inimitable plumage of splendescent purple.

‖**splendeurs et misères** (splɑ̃dœrz e mizɛr). [Fr., lit. 'splendours and miseries', from the title of Balzac's novel sequence *Splendeurs et Misères des Courtisanes* (1839–47).] The glories and degradation of life set side by side; hence, applied to other co-existent extremes of conditions. Cf. *splendours and miseries* s.v. SPLENDOUR *sb.* 5.

1952 *Observer* 13 Jan. 7/5, I don't seem to have read any piece of criticism in the past month that doesn't speak of *splendeurs et misères*, so I'd better jump on the band-waggon. **1977** *N.Y. Rev. Bks.* 15 Sept. 42/4 *Mario Puzo Inside Las Vegas*.. seems to me one of the liveliest testimonials to the *splendeurs et misères* of gaming fever I've read.

† **'splendicant**, *a. Obs.*—[1] [a. pres. pple. of L. *splendicāre* to shine.] Resplendent, brilliant.

1592 R. D. *Hypnerotomachia* 99 And by what industrie in her starrie forehead.. she had infixed the fairest part of the heavens, or the splendycant Heraclea.

splendid ('splɛndɪd), *a.* [ad. L. *splendid-us*, f. *splendēre* to be bright. So F. *splendide*, It. *splendido*, Sp. and Pg. *esplendido*.]

1. a. Marked by much grandeur or display; sumptuous, grand, gorgeous.

1624 in Ellis *Orig. Lett.* Ser. I. II. 172 His enterteynment .. was as splendid as that country could afford. **1647** CLARENDON *Hist. Reb.* I. §167 All cost was employed to make their Entertainments splendid. **1717** LADY M. W. MONTAGU *Let. to Lady Rich* 1 Jan., It is not very expensive to keep a splendid table. **1752** YOUNG *Brothers* I. i, I know this splendid court of Macedon, And haughty Philip, well. **1797** S. & HT. LEE *Canterb. T.* I. 367 Accommodation so splendid I know not that I should desire were I a prince. **1818** SCOTT *Br. Lamm.* xxii, The entertainment was splendid to profusion. **1849** MACAULAY *Hist. Eng.* ii. I. 175 The capital was excited by preparations for the most splendid coronation that had ever been known. **1856** FROUDE *Hist. Eng.* (1858) I. ii. 176 He had the splendid tastes in which the English people most delighted.

b. Of persons: Maintaining, or living in, great style or grandeur.

1658 SIR T. BROWNE *Hydriot.* v. 80 But man is a Noble Animal, splendid in ashes, and pompous in the grave. *a* **1687** PETTY *Pol. Arith.* (1690) 86 The King and some great Men of France appear more Rich and Splendid than those of the like Quality in England. **1779** JOHNSON *L. P.*, *Pope* Wks. IV. 7 Pope was, through his whole life, ambitious of splendid acquaintance.

2. a. Resplendent, brilliant, extremely bright, in respect of light or colour. *rare.*

1634 SIR T. HERBERT *Trav.* 193 In the night, during which the streets are splendide with glistering Lights and Torches. **1750** tr. *Leonardus' Mirr. Stones* 154 The topaz is a most splendid and famous stone of those they call burning gems. **1774** GOLDSM. *Nat. Hist.* (1824) II. 424 These splendid inhabitants of the air [*sc.* kingfishers] possess.. the brightest colours, the roundest forms [etc.]. **1820** KEATS *Hyperion* II. 353 In each face he saw a gleam of light, But splendider in Saturn's. **1829** *Chapters Phys. Sci.* 319 These colours, already so splendid and various when seen in one aspect, are still more diversified [etc.].

b. Magnificent in material respects; made or adorned in a grand or sumptuous manner.

1685 BAXTER *Paraphr. N.T.* Matt. vi. 28 A more beautiful flower than Solomon's most splendid Ornaments could match. **1699** C. HOPKINS *Court-Prosp.*, *Peace* i, All [rooms] she keeps Silent, but Splendider than that of Sleeps. **1802** in *Nairne Peerage Evid.* (1874) 165 We arrived in this great and splendid capital. **1863** LYELL *Antiq. Man* 46 A splendid Hindoo temple has lately been discovered. **1891** FARRAR *Darkn. & Dawn* lxv, Almost mad with misery, he returned to his splendid chamber in the Golden House.

c. Having or embodying some element of material grandeur or beauty.

1815 J. SMITH *Panorama Sci. & Art* II. 150 A splendid machine was constructed for this purpose [*sc.* ballooning].. by the younger Montgolfier. **1851** THACKERAY in *Scribner's Mag.* II. 142/2 The splendider scenery of the Alps. **1860** TYNDALL *Glac.* II. i. 238 All these splendid phenomena are, I believe, produced by diffraction.

Comb. **1819** LADY MORGAN *Autobiog.* (1859) 320 A most picturesque and splendid-looking stranger in Greek costume.

d. In specific names of birds or insects.

1811 SHAW *Gen. Zool.* VIII. I. 191 Splendid Creeper... Steel-blue and gold-green Creeper, with black wings and tail [etc.]. **1832** J. RENNIE *Butterfl. & Moths* 168 The Splendid Codling (*Semasia Splendana*, Stephens).

3. a. Imposing or impressive by greatness, grandeur, or some similar excellence.

1653 GAUDEN *Hierasp.* Pref. 34 Persons of more ample conditions, splendider fortunes, and higher quality. **1750** JOHNSON *Rambler* No. 68 ¶1 Of actions that deserve our attention, the most splendid are not always the greatest. **1784** COWPER *Task* v. 320 That thus he may procure His thousands, weary of penurious life, A splendid opportunity to die. **1819** SCOTT *Ivanhoe* xlii, For this service a splendid *soul-scat* was paid to the convent of Saint Edmund's. **1849** MACAULAY *Hist. Eng.* vii. II. 191 If a design was splendid, Mordaunt seldom inquired whether it were practicable. **1872** MORLEY *Voltaire* (1886) 3 Luther and Calvin in their separate ways brought into splendid prominence their new ideas of moral order.

b. Dignified, haughty, lordly.

1833 T. HOOK *Parson's Dau.* I. v, A splendid contempt for female intellect.

4. Of persons: Illustrious, distinguished.

1647 CLARENDON *Hist. Reb.* I. §196 He intended the Discipline of the Church.. should be applied to the greatest and most splendid Transgressors. **1660** *Guillim's Heraldry* (ed. 4) III. iii. 115 Which Family is not a little splendid by the actions of two persons of it.

5. Excellent; very good or fine.

1644 R. BAILLIE *Lett. & Jrnls.* (1841) II. 215 Mr. Edwards hes written a splendid confutation of all Independents' Apologie. **1849–50** ALISON *Hist. Europe* XIV. xciv. §4. 4 The summit of these ridges afforded a splendid position for the French artillery to fire upon the English guns. **1882** *Proc. R. Geog. Soc.* IV. 460 He was taught to be a splendid shot with the gun and with the bow.

6. Used, by way of contrast, to qualify nouns having an opposite or different connotation. ***splendid isolation***, phr. used with reference to the political and commercial uniqueness or isolation of Great Britain; also *transf.* Cf. ISOLATION 1 a (quots. 1896[1,2]).

1667 MILTON *P.L.* II. 252 Our state Of splendid vassalage. **1714** R. FIDDES *Pract. Disc.* II. 15 Even their best actions [are] no better than splendid sins. **1756** BURKE *Subl. & B.* Wks. 1842 I. 44 In many cases this splendid confusion would destroy all use. **1848** H. ROGERS *Ess.* (1874) I. vi. 294 Even the most successful crime is but a splendid misery. [**1896** G. E. FOSTER in *Official Rep. Deb. H. Com. Canada* 16 Jan. 176 The great mother Empire stands splendidly isolated in Europe.] **1896** *Times* 22 Jan. 10/1 Splendid isolation... A few weeks ago England appeared to stand alone in the world, surrounded by jealous competitors and .. unexpected hostility. **1898** *19th Cent.* Apr. 524 When she gives, proudly, notice to the whole world of her *splendid isolation*. **1902** J. CHAMBERLAIN in *Times* 7 Jan. 4/4 It is the duty of the British people to count upon themselves alone. .. I say alone, yes, in a splendid isolation, surrounded and supported by our kinsfolk. **1912** *Review of Reviews* July 63/1 The abandonment by Great Britain of her splendid isolation. **1933** *Times* 21 Feb. 12/3 A Nazi band played in splendid isolation in the square. **1976** *National Observer* (U.S.) 13 Nov. 1/2 In a little while Williams and his bodyguard will be leaving this splendid isolation (we are in a hotel suite 30-odd floors above Central Park South) and going to the Ambassador Theatre.

† **splen'didious**, *a. Obs.* [f. L. *splendid-us* + -IOUS.] Splendid, magnificent, brilliant.

1432–50 tr. *Higden* (Rolls) I. 11 Seenge the poverte and insufficience of my connynge after so splendidious laboures. **1553** [see SPLENDENT *a.* 3 b]. **1599** B. JONSON *Ev. Man out of Hum.* II. ii, His lady? what, is shee faire? splendidious? and amiable? *a* **1630** J. TAYLOR (Water P.) *Wks.* II. 256/1 Vnhappy Phaetons Splendidious Sire. **1653** H. COGAN tr. *Pinto's Trav.* xxiii. 85 All which became more splendidious by the Trumpets, Cornets, Hoboys,.. that were heard in every corner.

Hence † **splen'didiously** *adv. Obs.*—[1]

1432–50 tr. *Higden* (Rolls) I. 39 Whose booke Roberte Byschoppe of Herefforde onornede splendidiously.

splendidly ('splɛndɪdlɪ), *adv.* [f. SPLENDID *a.* + -LY[2].] In a splendid manner.

1. With much grandeur or display; sumptuously, grandly, gorgeously: **a.** In respect of living, state or ceremony, etc.

1651 HOBBES *Leviath.* III. xlii. 294 The Bishops of those times.. lived splendidly. **1682** WOOD *Life* 22 Jan., The old lady Sanderson.. was buried verie splendidly in Westminster Abbey Church. **1693** DRYDEN *Juvenal* III. 238 How he lives and eats; How largely gives; how splendidly he treats. **1703** *Lond. Gaz.* No. 3919/2 His Grace was splendidly treated by the Corporation in the Town Hall. **1839** THIRLWALL *Hist. Greece* VI. 185 The burial of the dead.. was splendidly solemnised. **1841** THACKERAY *Drum* I. xxviii, Dukes.. were splendidly served at her feasts. **1863** GEO. ELIOT *Romola* II. vii. (1880) II. 68 The Rucellai.. kept a great table and lived splendidly.

b. In respect of appearance, adornment, etc.

1675 OGILBY *Britannia* Introd. E, The old or Royal Exchange.. more splendidly Re-built by the City and Company of Mercers. **1772–84** *Cook's Voy.* III. 220 All the women appeared very splendidly dressed, after the Kamtschadale fashion. **1823** SCOTT *Quentin D.* xiii, The apartments.. were far more splendidly furnished than any which Quentin had yet seen in the royal palace. **1837** P. KEITH *Bot. Lex.* 374 A plumage that is most splendidly brilliant. **1847** C. BRONTË *Jane Eyre* vii, They were splendidly attired in velvet, silk and furs.

2. In a manner or style compelling admiration; magnificently, gloriously.

1774 GOLDSM. *Nat. Hist.* I. iii. I. 19 These have been the enquiries that have splendidly employed many.. philosophers. **1859** HELPS *Friends in C.* Ser. II. I. To Rdr., Not prone in the first instance to war, though splendidly tenacious in battle when it does come. **1880** MEREDITH *Tragic Com.* (1881) 132 To break conventional laws, and be splendidly irrational.

3. Excellently, finely.

1883 *Harper's Mag.* Feb. 393/1 We were steaming along splendidly now. **1912** *Throne* 7 Aug. 222/1 A set of chambers.. which he said would suit us splendidly.

4. *Comb.*, as ***splendidly-bound***, etc.

1648 J. BEAUMONT *Psyche* XI. liii, Six yellow springs.. Disgorge their splendidly-contagious flood. **1818** LADY MORGAN *Autobiography* (1859) 215 With splendidly-bound 'Heures' and magnificent reticules. **1886** C. E. PASCOE *London of To-day* v. (ed. 3) 71 The gay throng of splendidly-uniformed military and naval officers. **1890** 'R. BOLDREWOOD' *Col. Reformer* (1891) 222 Well mounted.. on splendidly-conditioned animals.

'splendidness. [f. as prec. + -NESS.] The quality or state of being splendid; magnificence, grandeur.

1648 J. BEAUMONT *Psyche* VIII. lxiii, Resolv'd to try his eyes Upon that Infant-face of Splendidness. *a* **1657** W. BURTON *Itin. Anton.* 251 The splendidness of the Buildings, and the magnificence of the Churches. **1674** BP. CROFT *Fast Serm.* 14 Their splendidness and voluptuousness of living. **1728** MORGAN *Algiers* I. iii. 44 He drew the Eyes of all the Spectators by the Splendidness of his purple Robe. **1980** *N.Y. Times* 5 Oct. VII. 33/5 Miss Leffland at her best is extraordinarily good; indeed, there is not a contemporary writer of short stories from whom truth of feeling, splendidness of insight, and a human beauty both aching and real can more confidently be expected.

† **'splendidous**, *a. Obs.* [f. L. *splendid-us* + -OUS.] = SPLENDIDIOUS *a.*

1605 B. JONSON *Volpone* II. ii, Who, euer since my arriuall, have detayned me to their vses, by their splendidous liberalities. **1640** G. ABBOTT *Job Paraphr.* 138 Where is this man's princely pompe, that but even now was so splendidous?

Hence † **'splendidously** *adv. Obs.*

1640 G. ABBOTT *Job Paraphr.* 126 Neither shall the place where he lived so splendidously ever enjoy him so any more.

splendiferous (splɛn'dɪfərəs), *a.* [In early use f. med.L. **splendifer* (for late L. *splendōrifer*): cf. OF. *splendifere*. In mod. use jocular (cf. SPLENDACIOUS *a.*) and orig. *U.S.*]

† **1.** Full of, abounding in, splendour. *Obs.*

c **1460** G. ASHBY *Dicta Philos.* 1031 Who that is wele cherisshed with a king And is with hym grete & splendiferous. **1538** BALE *Br. Com. J. Bapt.* in *Harl. Misc.* (Malh.) I. 215 O tyme most ioyfull, daye most splendiferus. **1546** COVERDALE *Calvin's Treat. Sacram.* D j, Seyng that y[e] bryght and splendiferouse veritie is of it selfe able to confute so absurde a vanitie.

2. *colloq.* Remarkably fine; magnificent.

1843 HALIBURTON *Sam Slick in Eng.* xiii, A splendiferous white hoss, with long tail and flowin' mane. **1854** P. B. ST. JOHN *Amy Moss* 283, I only escaped.. by means of a splendiferous girl call'd Kate. **1863** C. READE *Hard Cash* xxviii. II. 188, I see the splendiferous articles arrive, and then they vanish for ever.

splen'diferously, *adv. joc.* [f. SPLENDIFEROUS *a.* + -LY[2].] Splendidly; magnificently.

1900 J. VAIZEY *About Peggy Saville* viii. 57 If you weren't so fat, you would do splendiferously for Ophelia. **1930** D. H. LAWRENCE *Apocalypse* (1932) i. 22 And nowhere does this happen so splendiferously as in Revelation. **1959** *Good Food Guide* 292 This splendiferously-named hotel. **1982** *Country Life* 28 Jan. 251/4 It is almost impossible to use *Brewer* to look up what you want to find.. and this goes as splendiferously for the new edition as ever in the past.

splen'diferousness. *joc.* [f. SPLENDIFEROUS *a.* + -NESS.] Splendour; magnificence.

1934 in WEBSTER. **1971** J. H. GRAY *Red Lights on Prairies* v. 103 The splendiferousness of the new schools, warehouses.

† **'splendious**, *a. Obs.* [Cf. It. *splendioso.*] Splendid.

1609 ARMIN *Maids of More-Cl.* (1880) 116 Which are as sun-shine, sometimes splendious. **1644** NYE *Gunnery* I. (1647) 48 By that splendious light you shall see every flaw, crack or honycomb. **1654** FLECKNOE *Ten Years Trav.* 10 In so noble Company, so splendious Entertainment, and so magnificent Equipage.

splendir, dial. variant of SPLINDER.

† **'splendish**, *v. Obs. rare.* [Cf. RESPLENDISH *v.*] **a.** *intr.* To shine. **b.** *trans.* To make splendid.

1565 J. PHILLIP *Patient Grissell* 1235 Of Pango I the Countis am, my praise doth splendish bright. **1583** STUBBES

Anat. Abus. I. (1879) 18 To splendish, beautifie and set forthe the maiestie and glorie of this his earthly kyngdome.

splendorous ('splɛndərəs), *a.* Also 7 **splend'rous, splendrous,** 8–9 **splendourous.** [f. *splendor* SPLENDOUR *sb.*] Full of splendour; resplendent, bright.

1591 DRAYTON *Moyses Map Miracle* (1604) 70 Himselfe inuested in a splendorous flame. **1594** —— *Idea* 215 Your Beautie is the hot and splend rous Sunne. **1627** —— *Agincourt* 35 In Warlike state the Royall Standard borne Before him, as in splendrous Armes he road. **1639** G. DANIEL *Ecclus.* xxv. 31 Splendrous, and in a height Transcending all bright Iustice. **1796** P. L. COURTIER *Pleas. Solitude* (1802) 85 In Corydon's splendourous Ball. **1871** G. MACDONALD *Wks. Fancy & Imag.* III. 215 A light that.. spreads a finer joy, Than cloudless noon-tide splendorous o'er the world.

splendour ('splɛndə(r)), *sb.* Also 5–6 **splendure,** 7 **-eur;** 6– **splendor.** [ad. AF. *(e)splendur, -our* (OF. *esplendor,* etc.), or L. *splendor,* f. *splendēre* to shine. So F. *splendeur,* It. *splendore,* Sp. and Pg. *esplendor.*]

1. a. Great brightness; brilliant light or lustre.

α. *c* **1450** *Cov. Myst.* (Shaks. Soc.) 191 In the sunne consydyr ȝe thynges thre, The splendure, the hete, and the lyght. **1600** FAIRFAX *Tasso* VII. xliv, When.. The shining fort his goodly splendure losed. **1603** HOLLAND *Plutarch's Mor.* 1188 Mixing splendeur and light together with the said deepe azure.

β. **1526** *Pilgr. Perf.* (W. de W. 1531) 30 Lyke as the beame of the materyall sonne.. causeth a splendour or bryghtnes. **1626** BACON *Sylva* §8 It may be, Percolation doth not only cause Clearness and Splendour, but Sweetness of Savour. **1698** FRYER *Acc. E. India & P.* 128 The splendour of the Moon being shaded by the sides of the Mountains. **1782** *Phil. Trans.* LXXII. 427 The wax tapers took flame immediately with an uncommon splendour. **1825** SCOTT *Talism.* vi, His bright blue eye, which at all times shone with uncommon keenness and splendour. **1897** F. T. BULLEN *Cruise 'Cachalot'* 104 Slowly.. the intruding gloom overspread the sweet splendour of the shining sky.

Comb. **1821** SHELLEY *Epipsych.* 81 The splendour-winged stars. **1836** BROWNING *J. Agricola in Medit.* 4 Splendour-proof I keep the broods of stars aloof.

γ. **1596** DRAYTON *Leg., Matilda* xxxv. Poems (1605) Ff vij b, Such bountie Nature did to them impart, Those lampes two planets, clearer then the seauen, That with their splendor light the world to heauen. **1597** J. PAYNE *Royal Exch.* 47 He neyther saw that splendor and glory.., nor the heavens open. **1630** J. TAYLOR (Water P.) *Praise Clean Linen* Wks. II. 169/2 Till Tytans glory from the burnish'd East.. the rotundious Globe with splendor filles. **1684** *Contempl. St. Man* II. ix. (1699) 232 A Wheel of Squibs and Fire-Works.. casts forth a thousand lights and splendors. **1732** ARBUTHNOT *Rules of Diet* in *Aliments,* etc. I. 414 A certain Splendor or Shining in the Eyes, with a little Moisture. **1782** *Phil. Trans.* LXXII. 199 Inflammable air is also the principle which.. gives them their metallic splendor. **1871** B. TAYLOR *Faust* Prol. (1875) I. 11 And swift and swift beyond conceiving The splendor of the world goes round.

b. *Her.* (See quots.)

1766 PORNY *Heraldry* (1777) Dict., The Sun is said to be in Splendor when it is represented with the lineaments of a human face, and environed with raies. **1868** CUSSANS *Her.* (1893) 102 The Sun is always supposed to be Proper, or In his Glory, or Splendour,.. unless otherwise specified.

2. Magnificence; great show of riches or costly things; pomp, parade.

β. **1616** *Fortescue Papers* (Camden) 15 Whome the splendour of fortune hath not beene able to make.. lesse vertuous. **1664** H. MORE *Myst. Iniq.* 280 His purple Cardinals are so Emperor like and of such a senatorious splendour. **1732** LEDIARD *Sethos* II. VII. 48 Their ambassy appear'd in splendour before your haven. **1770** GOLDSM. *Des. Village* 286 While thus the land adorned for pleasure all In barren splendour feebly waits the fall. **1837** LOCKHART *Scott* I. ii. 63 The antique splendour of the ducal house. **1863** MISS BRADDON *J. Marchmont's Legacy* III. i. 8 Paul Marchmont was fond of splendour, and meant to have as much of it as money could buy. **1886** C. E. PASCOE *Lond. of To-day* xxxi. (ed. 3) 286 One of the most splendid streets in London, deriving its splendour from its club-houses.

personif. **1731** POPE *Ep. Burlington* 180 'Tis Use alone that sanctifies Expense, And Splendour borrows all her rays from Sense.

γ. **1680** BURNET *Rochester* 91 A people naturally fond of a visible splendor in Religious Worship. **1713** STEELE *Guardian* No. 19 ⁋3 Riches and outward splendor have taken up the place of it. **1756–7** tr. *Keysler's Trav.* (1760) II. 103 With regard to external splendor,.. I am inclined to think that modern Rome is superior to the ancient. **1824** W. IRVING *T. Trav.* II. 104 Its faded embellishments spoke of former splendor. **1858** HAWTHORNE *Fr. & It. Jrnls.* II. 98 Gold-laced cocked hats and other splendors.

3. Brilliant distinction, eminence, or glory; impressive or imposing character.

1604 E. G[RIMSTONE] *D'Acosta's Hist. Indies* VI. xxvi. 487 Monteçuma set Knighthood in his highest splendor. **1647** CLARENDON *Hist. Reb.* I. §145 Without any other Friendship or Support, than what the splendour of a Pious life.. would reconcile to him. **1750** JOHNSON *Rambler* No. 72 ⁋10 Excellencies of higher reputation and brighter splendour. **1830** D'ISRAELI *Chas. I,* III. ix. 196 The splendour of the present progress had not hitherto been equalled in our annals. **1873** HAMERTON *Intell. Life* II. ii. 62 The splendor of the intellectual life.

4. Brilliant or ornate appearance or colouring. Also *Comb.*

1774 GOLDSM. *Nat. Hist.* (1824) II. 349 A very extensive tribe, remarkable for the splendour and the variety of their plumage. **1820** SHELLEY *Witch Atl.* iii, Like splendour-winged moths. **1854** tr. *Hettner's Athens* 18 The Attic plain lies before us in a splendour and beauty, to describe which the forms and colours of the painter are powerless.

5. ***splendours and miseries*** = SPLENDEURS ET MISÈRES.

1943 S. SITWELL (*title*) Splendours and miseries. **1971** A. MORICE *Death of Gay Dog* iv. 44, I took in a survey of the room, to see what further splendours and miseries were in store for us. **1981** *Times* 1 Apr. 11/2 *Omnibus* looked at the splendours and miseries of acting.

'splendour, *v.* [f. prec.]

1. *intr.* To move with splendour.

1853 T. PARKER *Theism* (1865) 116 When a star with fiery hair came splendouring through the night, it filled mediæval astronomers with amazement. **1887** SERVICE *Life Dr. Duguid* 272 The golden language of a priceless love Went splendouring like a song of heav'n down.

2. *trans.* To invest with splendour.

a **1867** A. SMITH *Life Drama* I. 49 Poems (1901) 3 'Tis not for me To fling a Poem, like a comet, out, Far-splendouring the sleepy realms of night.

splendrous, obs. variant of SPLENDOROUS *a.*

†**'splendy,** *a.* *Obs.*$^{-1}$ [f. L. *splend-ēre.*] Lustrous, glittering.

1683 PETTUS *Fleta Min.* I. (1686) 230 There appertains to the harsh flowing Copper Oars.. what is splendy, mispickly, glimery or spady.

sple'nectomy. *Surg.* [ad. mod.L. *splēnectomia,* f. Gr. σπλήν SPLEEN *sb.* + ἐκτομή excision. So F. *splénectomie.*] Excision or removal of the spleen. Also **sple'nectomist,** one who removes the spleen (*Cent. Dict.* 1891); **sple'nectomize** *v. trans.,* to excise the spleen of (an animal or person).

1859 MAYNE *Expos. Lex.* 1192/1 *Splenectomia,*.. old term for excision of the spleen;.. splenectomy. **1897** *Allbutt's Syst. Med.* IV. 516 Effects of splenectomy in man. *Ibid.* 522 Experiments on rabbits that had been splenectomised. *Ibid.* 528 Laudenbach found them in a splenectomised dog.

splenetic (splɪ'nɛtɪk), *a.* and *sb.* Forms: 5–6 **splenetyk(e,** 6 **-ike, -ique,** 7–8 **-ick,** 7– **splenetic;** 7 **spleenetick.** [ad. late L. *splēnētic-us,* f. *splēn* SPLEEN. So F. *splénétique,* It. *splenetico,* Sp. and Pg. *esplenetico.* See also SPLENATIC *a.* and SPLENITIC *a.*

Metrical examples show that down to the beginning of the 19th cent. the stress was on the first syllable, as given by Bailey, Johnson, and early 19th cent. Dicts.]

A. *adj.* **1.** Of or pertaining to, connected with, the spleen; splenic. Also *fig.*

1544 PHAER *Regim. Lyfe* (1553) G iv, The passion splenetyke commeth by a colde humoure melancolyke. **1628** BURTON *Anat. Mel.* Democr. to Rdr. (ed. 3) 75 That Spleneticke Hypocondriacall winde.. which proceeds from the spleen and short ribbes. **1722–7** BOYER *Dict. Royal* II, The Splenetick Vein, or Artery. **1758** J. S. tr. *Le Dran's Observ. Surg.* (1771) Dict., *Vas Breve,* a Vein passing.. to the Splenetick Vein. **1818** KEATS *Endym.* IV. 399 These raven horses, though they foster'd are Of earth's splenetic fire, dully drop Their full-vein'd ears. **1897** *Allbutt's Syst. Med.* IV. 527 Microscopically they were composed of splenetic tissue much pigmented.

†**2.** Affected with, or suffering from, disease or disorder of the spleen; in later use, affected with melancholia or hypochondria. *Obs.*

1544 PHAER *Regim. Lyfe* (1546) H v, The pacient is called splenetike, whiche ye maye knowe by that, that after meate they have payne in theyr left syde. *c* **1550** H. LLOYD *Treas. Health* M viij, For them that be splenetike. **1656** RIDGLEY *Pract. Physick* 105 They that have a weak Spleen are properly called spleenetick. **1697** J. SERGEANT *Solid Philos.* 200 Splenetick or Maniacal Men can fancy they are made of Glass. **1733** CHEYNE *Eng. Malady* II. viii. 193 All the Symptoms and Disorders of a splenetick Person will be naturally and readily deduced from too thick and glewy or sharp Juices. **1766** GOLDSM. *Ess.* i. ⁋1 If he be splenetic, he may every day meet companions.. with whose groans he may mix his own.

absol. **1658** ROWLAND *Topsell's Four-f. Beasts* 149 The Spleen [of a dog] drunk in Urine, cureth the Spleenetick [1607 spleenatick]. **1750** tr. *Leonardus' Mirr. Stones* 72 It cures the splenetick, being bound to the spleen.

†**b.** Characterized by, tending to produce, melancholy or depression of spirits. *Obs.*

a **1700** EVELYN *Diary* 20 Dec. 1673, They spake of the excellent aire and climate in respect of our cloudy and splenetic country. *a* **1704** T. BROWN *Walk round Lond.* Wks. 1709 III. III. 41 To contribute your Assistance in order to expel these Splenetick Vapours. **1759** GOLDSM. *Polite Learn.* xi, They should be made up in our splenetic climate to be taken as physic. **1781** COWPER *Conversat.* 582 The friend.. Whose wit can brighten up a wintry day, And chase the splenetic dull hours away.

3. Having an irritably morose or peevish disposition or temperament; given or liable to fits of angry impatience or irritability; ill-humoured, testy, irascible. (Freq. in the 18th c.)

1592 G. HARVEY *Pierce's Super.* 158, I was never so splenetique when I was most dumpish but I could smile at a frise jest. **1693** CONGREVE *Double-Dealer* IV. vi, I don't know whether to be splenetic or airy upon't. **1702** POPE *Wife of Bath* 90 Now gayly mad, now sourly splenetick, Freakish when well, and fretful when she's sick. **1748** RICHARDSON *Clarissa* (1811) I. 189 A splenetic woman, who must have somebody to find fault with. **1780** BENTHAM *Princ. Legisl.* ii. §5 The fear of future punishment at the hands of a splenetic and revengeful Deity. **1841** DICKENS *Barn. Rudge* xli, Neighbours who had got up splenetic that morning, felt good-humour stealing on them as they heard it. **1876** GEO. ELIOT *Dan. Der.* I. v, Her hostess who, though not a splenetic or vindictive woman, had her susceptibilities.

absol. **1756** C. SMART tr. *Horace, Sat.* II. v. (1826) II. 147 By voluntary garrulity you will offend the splenetic and morose. **1829** I. TAYLOR *Enthus.* viii. 207 The disappointed, the splenetic, and the fanatical.

b. Of humour, temper, etc.

1712 STEELE *Spect.* No. 392 ⁋3 Tho' his splenetick contracted Temper made him take fire immediately. **1759** DILWORTH *Pope* 115 His splenetic turn of mind adapted him for the sequestered life he was so fond of. *c* **1820** S. ROGERS *Italy, Foreign Trav.* (1836) 169 It was in a splenetic humour that I sat me down. **1865** DICKENS *Mut. Fr.* I. iv, She had an amazing power of gratifying her splenetic or worldly-minded humours by extolling her own family.

4. Characterized by, arising from, displaying or exhibiting, spleen or ill-humour.

1693 DRYDEN *Juvenal* Ded. (1726) p. xliv, Horace seems to have purg'd himself from those splenetick Reflections in those Odes and Epodes. **1749** FIELDING *Tom Jones* XI. i, To write within such severe rules as these, is as impossible as to live up to some splenetic opinions. **1775** in Jesse *Selwyn & Contemp.* (1844) III. 118 Forget what I lately wrote to you: it was the overflowing of a splenetic moment. **1806** SURR *Winter in Lond.* II. 159 In a moment of splenetic pride the jewels were dispatched. **1862** CARLYLE *Fredk. Gt.* XI. iii. III. 77 His envies, deep-hidden splenetic discontents and rages. **1899** E. GOSSE *Life J. Donne* I. 44 The poem closes with an outburst of splenetic raillery.

†**5.** Of medicines: Acting on, good for, the spleen. *Obs.*

1658 SIR T. BROWNE *Gard. Cyrus* iv, The Splenetick medicine of Galen. **1684** tr. *Bonet's Merc. Compit.* III. 92 If the Spleen be affected, spleneticke Medicines must be added. **1728** CHAMBERS *Cycl.* s.v. *Water,* Splenetic Waters, are those proper against Diseases of the Spleen.

B. *sb.* **1.** †**a.** One who suffers from disease or disorder of the spleen. *Obs.*

1398 TREVISA *Barth. De P.R.* v. xlv. (Bodl. MS.), In drinke it [urine] halpeþ splenetikes & clenseþ roted woundes. *c* **1440** *Pallad. on Husb.* VIII. 125 This wyn.. soloueth fleume and helpith splenetyk. **1728** in CHAMBERS *Cycl.*

b. One who has a splenetic disposition; a splenetic, peevish, or ill-humoured person.

1703 STEELE *Tender Husb.* III. ii, The Spleneticks Speak just as the Weather lets 'em. **1779** ALEXANDER *Hist. Women* Introd. (1782) I. p. viii, The subject upon which satirists had discharged their wit, and splenetics their ill-humour. **1784** *Unfortunate Sensibility* I. 144, I cannot see why any poor splenetic should interfere.

†**2.** A splenetic medicine or remedy. *Obs.*

c **1643** LD. HERBERT *Autobiog.* (1824) 38 They that are subject to the Spleen from their ancestors ought to use those herbs that are splenetics. **1718** QUINCY *Compl. Disp.* 121 It is commended.. for a most noble Epatick, Splenetick, and Vulnerary.

Hence **sple'neticness,** the fact or condition of being splenetic. *rare*$^{-0}$.

1727 in Bailey (vol. II).

†**sple'netical,** *a.* and *sb.* *Obs.* [f. prec.]

A. *adj.* **1.** = SPLENETIC *a.* 1.

1599 A. M. tr. *Gabelhouer's Bk. Physicke* 162/1 [A prescription] For Spleneticalle dolour. *a* **1639** WOTTON *Reliq.* (1651) 488, I have received much benefit.. touching my spleneticall Infirmity. **1694** WESTMACOTT *Script. Herb.* 13 Wild-Ash.. will yield a Liquor highly commended in Scorbutical and Splenetical Affects. **1708** *Brit. Apollo* No. 72. 2/1 Splenetical and Hypocondriacal Distempers.

2. Disposed to mirth. (Cf. SPLEEN *sb.* 1 c.)

a **1661** HOLYDAY *Juvenal* (1673) 185 Splenetical Democritus did make His lungs with a perpetual laughter shake.

B. *sb.* = SPLENETIC *sb.* 2.

1671 SALMON *Syn. Med.* III. xv. 358 Splenetical are such things as are appropriated to the Spleen, the seat of Melancholly.

splenetically (splɪ'nɛtɪkəlɪ), *adv.* [f. as prec.] In a splenetic manner; with spleen.

1779 ALEXANDER *Hist. Women* Introd. (1782) I. p. v, We laugh at their credulity, and splenetically satirise.. all their faults and follies. **1816** SCOTT *Bl. Dwarf* v, More splenetically than became a philosopher or hermit. **1856** MASSON *Ess. Biog. & Crit.* 193 Whether the above was splenetically sent to Calcott.. is not certain. **1873** MRS. WHITNEY *Other Girls* x, 'I guess you'll find it so,' said Eliza Mokey, splenetically.

'splenetive, *a. rare.* [Cf. SPLENATIVE *a.*]

1. = SPLENETIC *a.* 3.

1679 *Fletcher's Elder Brother* IV. i. (Fol.[2]), Some splenetive [Q.[1] spleenative] Youths now, that had never seen more than thy Country smoak, will grow in choler.

2. = SPLENETIC *a.* 4.

1829 *Examiner* 421/1 The *Quarterly*.. pours forth splenetive sophisms. **1839** JAMES *Gentlem. Old School* i, With a sharp splenetive oath the horseman tore the gate open.

†**'splenetize,** *v.* *Obs.*$^{-1}$ [f. SPLENET-IC *a.* + -IZE.] *trans.* To render splenetic or ill-humoured.

1700 S. PARKER *Philos. Ess.* 39 These violent and frequent Alterations in the Weather serve for a perpetual Monitor by discomposing their Constitutions,.. and splenetizing the poor Gentlemen all-over.

splenial ('spliːnɪəl), *a.*[1] and *sb.* *Zool.* and *Anat.* [f. L. *splēni-um* (Pliny), ad. Gr. σπληνίον bandage or compress.]

A. *adj.* **1.** ***splenial bone*** or ***piece,*** a splint-like bone or process applied to the inner side of the lower mandible in certain classes of vertebrates below Mammalia.

1848 OWEN *Homologies* 15 As it is always applied like a surgeon's splint or plaster to the inner side of most of the other pieces,.. 'splenial'.. suggested itself to me as the most appropriate name. **1849–52** —— in *Todd's Cycl. Anat.* IV. II. 882/2 The alveolar border of the splenial element of the mandible. **1875** HUXLEY in *Encycl. Brit.* I. 755/1 It obviously represents the angular, coronary, and splenial elements, and may be termed the *angulo-splenial*.

2. ***splenial border***, the posterior border of the corpus callosum; hence ***splenial sulcus***, etc.

1891 *Cent. Dict.* s.v., The splenial border of the corpus callosum. **1904** DUCKWORTH *Study Anthrop. Lab.* 67 On the mesial aspect of the hemisphere [of the brain] the pars genualis of the splenial sulcus is not visible.

B. *sb.* The splenial bone or process.

1854 OWEN in *Orr's Circ. Sci., Org. Nat.* I. 195 The coronoid is a short compressed plate; the splenial is a longer, slender plate, applied to the inner side of the articular and dentary, and closing the groove on the inner side of the latter. **1888** ROLLESTON & JACKSON *Anim. Life* 402 In *Urodela* teeth occur..in the lower jaw on the dentary and splenial.

†**splenial**, *a.*^{2} *Obs.*$^{-1}$ [f. *splen* SPLEEN *sb.*] Splenetic, ill-natured, spiteful.

1641 *Apprehend. Capt. Butler* 1 The Papists have often made bould adventures to shew their malicious and spleniall intents, towards the Protestants.

†**'spleniatic**, *a. Obs.*$^{-0}$ [f. L. *splēn* SPLEEN *sb.*]

1704 J. HARRIS *Lex. Techn.* I, *Spleniatick Artery*, is said by some to be the greatest branch of the *Cæliaca*, whence it goes to the Spleen, and therein ends.

splenic ('splɛnɪk), *a. Anat.* and *Path.* Also 7 splenike, 7–8 -ick. [ad. L. *splēnic-us*, ad. Gr. σπληνικός, f. σπλήν SPLEEN *sb.* Cf. F. *splénique* (Paré), It. *splenico*, Sp. *esplenico*.]

1. *Anat.* Of, pertaining to, connected with, or situated in the spleen.

Freq. in ***splenic artery, plexus, vein, vessel***.

1619 PURCHAS *Microcosmus* v. 40 The Liuer by the splenike branch, transferreth them to the Serjeant of the scullery the Splene. **1666** G. HARVEY *Morb. Angl.* xxvi. (1672) 64 Wee'l suppose the Spleen..principally obstructed in its lower parts and Splenick branch. **1667** *Phil. Trans.* II. 578 The Gastrick and Splenick Arteries. **1702** *Ibid.* XXIII. 1186 The Splenick Vein has divers Cells opening into it near its Extremities in Human Bodies. **1728** CHAMBERS *Cycl.* s.v. *Plexus*, The Splenic Plexus sends out Branches to the left Part of the Ventricle and Panchreas. **1758** J. S. tr. *Le Dran's Observ. Surg.* (1771) 284 The Passage of the Sword was near the splenick Vessels. **1851** CARPENTER *Man. Phys.* (ed. 2) 301 The areolæ formed by the trabecular tissue, commonly known as the splenic follicles. **1872** HUXLEY *Physiol.* v. 126 An artery called the splenic artery which proceeds almost directly from the aorta.

b. ***splenic flexure***, the bend of the colon near the spleen.

1808 J. BARCLAY *Musc. Motions* 545 At the liver it exhibits the hepatic flexure; at the spleen the splenic flexure. **1879** *St. George's Hosp. Rep.* 270 A stricture was found situated in the descending colon, about two inches from the splenic flexure.

2. = SPLENETIC *a.* 5. *rare*$^{-0}$.

1730 in BAILEY (fol.).

3. *Path.* Of diseases, etc.: Of or affecting the spleen; esp. ***splenic fever***, malignant anthrax.

1867 J. HOGG *Microsc.* II. i. 296 Splenic diseases in sheep. **1868** *Rep. U.S. Commissioner Agric.* (1869) 5 On the breaking out of the splenic fever at the halting places of Texas cattle. **1876** BRISTOWE *Th. & Pract. Med.* 578 The hepatic lesion which so commonly goes along with splenic enlargement. *Ibid.*, The presence of splenic hypertrophy. **1884** *Chr. Commw.* 11 Dec. 120/1 The cause of splenic fever, the terrible 'Woolsorters' Disease'.

Hence †**'splenical** *a. Obs.*$^{-1}$ **'splenicness**, splenetic condition or state (Bailey, vol. II, 1727).

1693 tr. *Blancard's Phys. Dict.* (ed. 2), *Splenica*, Splenical Medicines, are such as by attenuating and volatilizing the grosser parts, remove the Distempers and Obstructions of the Spleen. [Hence in Phillips (1696).]

'splenico-, comb. form of L. *splēnicus* SPLENIC *a.*, used occas. as in ***splenico-phrenic*** (see quot.).

1835–6 *Todd's Cycl. Anat.* I. 14/1 The peritoneum..in passing from the spleen to that muscle [the diaphragm] forms the fold called *splenico-phrenic*.

spleniculus (splɪ'nɪkju:ləs). *Med.* [mod.L., f. L. *splen* SPLEEN *sb.* + *-iculus*, diminutive ending.] A detached portion of the spleen, a small accessory spleen.

[**1848** QUAIN & SHARPEY *Elem. Anat.* (ed. 5) II. 1089 These are commonly named accessory or supplementary spleens (splenculi [*sic, bis*], lienculi).] **1897** *Brit. Med. Jrnl.* 16 Jan. 145/2 A spleniculus was left [after splenectomy], and that patient did not suffer from any of these symptoms. **1939** MCNEE & MCMICHAEL in H. Rolleston *Brit. Encycl. Med. Pract.* XI. 402 In the neighbourhood of the spleen there are usually some small haemolymph glands or spleniculi... Their enlargement may cause persistence of clinical symptoms after splenectomy. **1973** A. I. S. MACPHERSON et al. *Spleen* iii. 97 Spleniculi or accessory spleens are found in 10 to 20 percent of all post-mortem examinations.

splenification (splɛnɪfɪ'keɪʃən). *Path.* [a. F. *splénification*, or ad. mod.L. *splēnificātio*, f. *splēn* SPLEEN *sb.*] = SPLENIZATION.

1859 in MAYNE *Expos. Lex.* 1192. **1876** F. T. ROBERTS *Handbk. Med.* (ed. 2) 352 This condition of the lung being termed splenification.

'splenify, *v. Path.* [Cf. prec. and -FY.] In *passive*: To undergo splenization.

1873 F. T. ROBERTS *Handbk. Med.* 448 In extreme cases, the vesicular structure is scarcely apparent, and the tissue breaks down very readily, when the lung is said to be 'splenified'.

splenish, obs. form of SPLEENISH *a.*

†**splenitic**, *a. Obs.* In 6 -ike, -ique, 7 -ick(e, -ic. [var. of SPLENETIC *a.* So obs. F. *splenitique*.] Splenetic, splenic, in various senses.

1578 LYTE *Dodoens* 6 The same..helpeth such as are splenitike. *Ibid.* 555 The young leaues..are very good also to be eaten of suche as be splenitique. **1661** J. CHILDREY *Brit. Bacon* 60 The Waters are so good for Splenitick Diseases. **1671** SALMON *Syn. Med.* III. xxii. 434 It attenuates, opens, cleanses, is Diuretick and Splenitick. **1684** tr. *Bonet's Merc. Compit.* VIII. 297 Bleeding must frequently be repeated in the splenitick Vein.

‖**splenitis** (splɪ'naɪtɪs). *Path.* [a. Gr. σπληνῖτις, f. σπλήν SPLEEN *sb.*: see -ITIS.] Inflammation of the spleen, or a particular form of this.

1753 *Chambers' Cycl.* Suppl. s.v., Splenitis is also used by some authors to express a tumor or inflammation of the spleen. **1776–84** CULLEN *First Lines Physic.* Wks. 1827 II. 81, I might here consider the Splenitis, or inflammation of the Spleen. **1835** *Cycl. Pract. Med.* IV. 55/2 The symptoms of acute splenitis..are..a feeling of weight, fulness, and pain in the left side. **1897** *Allbutt's Syst. Med.* IV. 534 The softened and often diffluent condition of the spleen seen in cases of bacterial infection may be described as a splenitis.

†**'splenitive**, *a. Obs. rare.* [Cf. SPLENATIVE *a.*, -ETIVE *a.*] Splenetic.

1633 P. FLETCHER *Purple Isl.* III. xix. *note*, Hence Stratonicus merrily said, that in Crete dead men walked, because they were so splenitive, and pale-coloured. **1815** *Monthly Mag.* XXXVIII. 111 He was however too splenitive, austere, impatient,..to reach the abacus of excellence in the science of lexicography.

splenium ('spli:nɪəm). *Anat.* [a. L. *splēnium* (see SPLENIAL *a.*^{1} and *sb.*).] The thick posterior part of the corpus callosum of the brain.

1845 W. J. E. WILSON *Anatomist's Vade Mecum* (ed. 3) viii. 411 Posteriorly [the corpus callosum]..forms a thick rounded fold (splenium), which is continuous with the fornix. **1902** D. J. CUNNINGHAM *Text-Bk. Anat.* 529 The massive posterior end [of the corpus callosum]..lies over the mesencephalon... It is called the splenium, and it consists of an upper and a lower part. **1968** PASSMORE & ROBSON *Compan. Med. Stud.* I. xxiv. 44/2 The corpus callosum forms a prominent feature and its divisions into the rostrum, genu, body and splenium can be readily recognized. **1977** *Neurology* XXVII. 688/2 If we infer that inferior splenium has a significant functional role in relaying visual verbal codes from the right to left cerebral hemisphere, a plausible corollary may be that color-valuing tends to use superior or dorsal splenium.

‖**splenius** ('spli:nɪəs). *Anat.* [mod.L., f. Gr. σπληνίον: cf. SPLENIAL *a.*^{1}] A broad muscle, or either of the two portions (the *splenius capitis* and *colli*) composing it, which occupies the upper part of the back of the neck and is attached to the occipital bone.

1732 A. MONRO *Anat.* (ed. 2) 111 Some tendinous Fibres of the Complexi and Splenii. *Ibid.*, In the Depression on each side..the Splenius is inserted. **1831** R. KNOX *Cloquet's Anat.* 249 The splenius extends the head, inclining it laterally, and impresses upon it a rotatory motion which turns the face to one side. **1873** MIVART *Elem. Anat.* 290 The splenius is placed obliquely in the neck.

attrib. **1835–6** *Todd's Cycl. Anat.* I. 748/1 The sterno-mastoid and splenius muscles.

splenization (splɛnɪ'zeɪʃən). *Path.* [a. F. *splénisation* or ad. mod.L. *splēnisātio*, f. *splēn* SPLEEN *sb.*] The conversion of substance into tissue resembling that of the spleen; *esp.* the diseased condition of the lungs when this has taken place; splenification.

1849 in CRAIG. **1862** H. W. FULLER *Dis. Chest* 220 The first [condition of the lungs] is that of engorgement or splenization. **1901** OSLER *Princ. & Pract. Med.* 11 Hypostatic congestion and the condition of the lung spoken of as splenization, are very common.

spleno- ('spli:nəʊ), a. Gr. σπληνο-, combining form of σπλήν SPLEEN *sb.*, employed in a number of pathological and anatomical terms, as **sp'lenocele**, (see quot.); **'splenocyte** [-CYTE], one of the mononuclear leucocytes formerly thought to be characteristic of the spleen; **sple'nography, sple'nology, sple'norrhagy, sple'notomy** (Craig, 1849; cf. F. *spléno-cèle, -graphie*, etc.); **,splenohepato'megaly** [HEPATO-; cf. *splenomegaly*] = *hepatosplenomegaly* s.v. HEPATO-; **spleno-lymphatic, -medullary, -myelogenic**, etc.; **splenome'galia, -'megaly** [Gr. μεγάλ-, μέγας large], enlargement of the spleen; hence **spleno'megalic** *a.*; **'splenopexy** [-PEXY], surgical fixation of a wandering spleen; **,splenopor'tography** [ad. F. *splénoportographie* (G. Sotgiu et al. 1952, in *La Presse Médicale* LX. 1295/1)], radiography of the hepatic portal system following the introduction of a contrast medium into the spleen to make the system detectable; so **spleno'portogram**, a radiograph obtained in this way; **spleno'renal** *a.*, connecting the spleen and a kidney; **spleno-typhoid**, typhoid fever complicated with disorder of the spleen.

The number of such compounds has been greatly increased by recent medical writers.

1799 HOOPER *Med. Dict.*, **Splenocele*, a rupture of the spleen. **1900** DORLAND *Med. Dict.* 621/1 *Splenocyte. **1925** STRONG & ELWYN *Bailey's Text-bk. Histol.* (ed. 7) iv. 82 They are..free mesenchymal elements..aggregated in enormous numbers in the mammalian splenic pulp (splenocytes). **1979** *Nature* 18 Jan. 218/2 Some of these IFC were..cultured..in the presence of irradiated syngeneic splenocytes or thymocytes as feeder layer. **1900** DORLAND *Med. Dict.* 621/1 *Splenohepatomegaly. **1936** Splenohepatomegaly [see LIPOIDOSIS]. **1879** REYNOLDS *Syst. Med.* V. 221 In the '*spleno-lymphatic' form [of leucocythæmia] an initial splenic enlargement is associated with glandular swellings, and in the 'spleno-myelogenic' form, with changes in the marrow. **1897** *Allbutt's Syst. Med.* IV. 591 Splenic or *spleno-medullary leuchæmia. [**1898** *Allbutt's Syst. Med.* V. 539 Splenic anæmia is the name by which the disease is best known in this country; but it has also been called..*spleno-megalie primitive*; under the last name chiefly it is described in French literature.] **1900** DORLAND *Med. Dict.* 621/2 **Splenomegalia, splenomegaly*, enlargement of the spleen. **1952** COLE & ELMAN *Textbk. Gen. Surg.* (ed. 6) xxiv. 679 The typical case of hemolytic jaundice or anemia is diagnosed without difficulty. Cardinal manifestations are slight to moderate jaundice, splenomegalia, and anemia of the spherocytic, reticulocytic type. **1900** *Guy's Hosp. Rep.* LIV. 1 *Splenomegalic cirrhosis of the liver. **1900** *Splenomegaly [see *splenomegalia* above]. **1903** T. K. MONRO *Man. Med.* 316 (*heading*) Splenic anæmia (primary splenomegaly). **1974** *Trypanosomiasis & Leishmaniasis* (Ciba Foundation) 207 Symptoms like marked general lymphadenopathy and splenomegaly should be considered as signs of activation of the immune apparatus. *Spleno-myelogenic [see *spleno-lymphatic* above]. **1897** *Brit. Med. Jrnl.* 16 Jan. 133/2 The great difference between splenectomy and *splenopexy is that in the former case the individual is deprived of an organ, and, although we do not know with any degree of precision what its real use is, we are nevertheless bound to display caution in dealing with it. **1923** POOL & STILLMAN *Surg. Spleen* v. 88 Although the immediate results of splenopexy are claimed to be favorable, the late results are uncertain. **1955** R. T. SHACKELFORD *Surg. Alimentary Tract* II. vi. 996 The fixation (splenopexy) of a 'wandering spleen'..has been abandoned. Splenectomy rather than splenopexy is indicated. **1953** *Ann. Surg.* CXXXVIII. 583/2 The *splenoportogram for this patient..demonstrated a well functioning portacaval shunt in the three-second film which was taken during the injection of the last 5 cc. of the opaque media. **1969** S. I. SCHWARTZ *Princ. Surg.* xxix. 1052/1 (*caption*) Normal splenoportogram. Note site of injection in spleen and diffusion of radiopaque material through organ. **1953** *Ann. Surg.* CXXXVIII. 582/2 It employs the visualization of the splenic and portal veins by roentgenographic examination. This is accomplished by injecting contrast media directly into the spleen... Sotgiu, Cacciari and Frassineti, working in Bologne, reported favorable results in four patients. It is from these authors that we have borrowed the term '*Splenoportography'. **1980** *Rec. Adv. Surg.* X. 5 Pre-operative determination by means of..splenoportography..and selective arteriography ..are important. **1945** *Ann. Surg.* CXXII. 479 It is undesirable..to resort to the use of a vein graft in the performance of a *splenorenal anastomosis. **1974** R. M. KIRK et al. *Surgery* vi. 108/1 (*caption*) Portal venous hypertension is reduced by portacaval or splenorenal shunt. **1976** *Lancet* 11 Dec. 1300/2 Our results suggest that hypergastrinæmia is more likely to follow portacaval than splenorenal anastomosis. **1868** *Guy's Hosp. Rep.* XIII. 416 The operation of *splenotomy as a means of cure [for leucocythæmia] is physiologically unsound. **1883** *Science* I. 66/2 This diminution is most marked from a hundred and fifty to two hundred days after the splenotomy. **1896** *Allbutt's Syst. Med.* I. 833 *Spleno-typhoid occupies a somewhat different position.

'splenoid, *a. rare*$^{-0}$. [f. L. *splēn* SPLEEN *sb.*] 'Spleen-like; having the appearance of the spleen.'

1882 in *Imperial Dict.*

splenosis (splɪ'nəʊsɪs). *Med.* [f. SPLEN(O- + -OSIS.] The presence in the body of numerous separate pieces of living splenic tissue.

1939 BUCHBINDER & LIPKOFF in *Surgery* VI. 933 A case is reported of autotransplantation of splenic tissue throughout the abdominal cavity following trauma of the spleen... We offer the term splenosis to describe this condition. **1947** *Canad. Med. Assoc. Jrnl.* LVI. 376/2 A case of splenosis is reported, in which seeding occurred after splenectomy for non-traumatic reasons. **1973** A. I. S. MACPHERSON et al. *Spleen* ix. 224 The seeding of viable cells from the ruptured spleen throughout the peritoneal cavity and their subsequent growth to form numerous tiny nodules of histologically normal splenic tissue has been described and has been given the name 'Splenosis'.

†**'splenous**, *a. Obs.*$^{-1}$ [f. *splene* SPLEEN *sb.*] Splenetic, spleenful. Hence †**'splenously** *adv.*

1606 WARNER *Alb. Eng.* XV. xcix. 390 There is an Academie, which I reuerence so much, As gessed against it splenous thoughts me splenously would touch.

splent(e, obs. or dial. varr. SPLINT *sb.* and *v.*

splenter, obs. f. SPLINTER *sb.*

splenty, obs. f. SPLINTY *a.*

splenunculus (splɪ'nʌŋkjʊləs). *Med.* [mod.L., f. L. *splēn* SPLEEN *sb.* + *-unculus*, diminutive ending.] = SPLENICULUS.

[**1848**: see SPLENICULUS.] **1897** [see LIENCULUS]. **1909** ADAMI & NICHOLLS *Princ. Path.* II. x. 222 Nearly 400 of these splenunculi were found scattered throughout the abdominal cavity. **1962** *Lancet* 26 May 1104/1 After the removal of the splenunculus there was remission. **1974** W. A. SODEMAN *Pathologic Physiol.* (ed. 5) xxiii. 680/2 Such a hemolytic relapse has been documented..in a splenectomized patient with hereditary spherocytosis; at surgery a splenunculus was found to weigh 217 grams.

splenwort, obs. f. SPLEENWORT.

†**splet**, *sb. Obs.*$^{-1}$ (Meaning obscure.)
1552-3 in Swayne *Sarum Churchw. Acc.* (1896) 97 A bottell of glasse wt splettes.

splet, *v.* Now *dial.* Also 6 splette. [ad. Flem. or LG. *spletten*, obscurely related to SPLIT *v.* and SPLEET *v.*[2]]

1. *trans.* To split.
1530 PALSGR. 729, I splette a fysshe a sonder,..*je ouuers.* Some splet their pyckes whan they broyle them, but I wolde broyle them hole. **1545** ASCHAM *Toxoph.* II. (Arb.) 109 To haue a goose quyll spletted and sewed againste the nockynge. **1746** *Exmoor Scolding* (E.D.S.) 174 Oh the Dowl splet tha! who told theckee Strammer? **1871-76** in *Eng. Dial. Dict.*

†**2.** To spread, smear. *Obs.*
1530 PALSGR. 729, I splette a saulve abrode upon a clothe, *je placque.* Splette this dyaculome upon a lynen clothe.

†**splet-bone.** *Obs.* App. = spauld-bone.
c **1400** *Lanfranc's Cirurg.* 357 Woundis of þe splet boonys of þe arme & of þe hondis, & anothami.

†**splete.** *Obs.*$^{-0}$ (Meaning obscure.)
1483 *Cath. Angl.* 356/1 Splete, *rignum.*

†**spleter.** *Obs.* [?f. SPLET *v.*, or var. of SPLITTER *sb.*[1]] A splinter.
a **1548** HALL *Chron., Hen. VIII*, 123 When they saw the spleters of the dukes spere strike on the kynges hed piece. *Ibid.*, All the kynges head pece was full of spleters.

spleuchan (ˈspluxən). *Sc.* (and *Ir.*). Also 8-9 spluchan, 9 spleughan. [a. Gael. *spliùchan*, Ir. *spliuchán.*] A tobacco pouch, freq. used as a purse.
1785 BURNS *Death & Dr. Hornbook* xiv, Deil mak his king's-hood in a spleuchan! **1815** SCOTT *Guy M.* I, There's some siller in the spleuchan that's like the Captain's ain. **1865** ALEX. SMITH *Summer in Skye* II. 135 'Do you smoke?' 'Oh, yes, but I have forgot my spleuchan.'

spley, obs. or dial. f. SPLAY *v.*[1]

†**spleyer.** *Obs.* (Meaning obscure.)
1486 *Bk. St. Albans, Her.* B iv, Fesy bagy is whan tokenys of armys be disseiuered from the cheef of the cotearmure to the right spleyer in the feelde. *Ibid.*, From the laste poynt of the cootarmure to the spleyer.

splib. *U.S. Blacks.* [Origin obscure.] A Black person; a Negro.
1964 *N.Y. Times Mag.* 23 Aug. 62/2 *Soul brother*, Negro; also referred to as *scobe, blue, splib.* **1969** A. YOUNG *Dancing* 5 Nobody want no nice nigger no more... They want an angry splib A furious nigrah. **1970** *Atlantic Monthly* Jan. 38 Any other terms such as 'boy', 'spook', 'splib',..or 'colored' carry connotations of prejudice. **1976** *Amer. Speech 1974* XLIX. 184 *Splib*,..liberal black who looks angry but will not upset the status quo.

splice (splaɪs), *sb.* [f. the vb. Cf. Sw. *spliss, splits.*]

1. a. A joining or union of two portions of rope, cable, cord, etc., effected by untwisting and interweaving the strands at the point of junction. Chiefly *Naut.*
The various kinds of splices are freq. denoted by some distinguishing term, as *cut, drawing, eye* or *ring, long, round, short* (etc.) *splice.*
1627 CAPT. SMITH *Seaman's Gram.* v. 26 Splicing is so to let one ropes end into another they shall be as firme as if they were but one rope, and this is called a round Splice; but the cut Splice is to let one into another with as much distance as you will. *c* **1635** CAPT. BOTELER *Dial. Sea Services* (1685) 192 When an Eye is to be made at the end of a Rope, the ends of the Strands..are with a Fidd drawn into the ends of the other Ropes Strands and this is called a Splice. **1711** *Milit. & Sea Dict.*, Make a Splice, and seaze the Ends down with some Sinnet. **1769** FALCONER *Dict. Marine* s.v., The long splice..is much neater and smoother than the short-splice. **1846** A. YOUNG *Naut. Dict.* 291 Explanations of various kinds of splices..are given in Dana's Seaman's Manual. **1866** *Even. Standard* 13 July 3 The Atlantic Cable... The Great Eastern..will leave Berehaven this afternoon, arriving at the buoys..to-morrow morning, when the splice will be made. **1867** F. FRANCIS *Angling* ix. (1880) 316 Where you have to tie and untie your own splices.
transf. **1833** M. SCOTT *Tom Cringle* xv, The Vice-Admiral has got a hint from Sir —, to kick that wild splice, young Cringle, about a bit.

b. *techn.* A joining of two pieces of wood, metal girders or rails, concrete beams, etc., formed by overlapping and securing the ends; a scarf-joint.
1875 in KNIGHT *Dict. Mech.* 2280/1. **1877** *Rep. & Awards Group XVIII U.S. Centennial Comm. Internat. Exhib. 1876* 66 (*caption*) Rails and splices used on Pennsylvania Railroad and branches. **1892** L. DE C. BERG *Safe Building* II. x. 113 In locating the rivets of a splice care should be taken not to weaken the original plate. **1934** RELF & JOHANSEN *Handbk. Aerodynamics* (ed. 2) I. ix. 638 In splicing built-up or box spars the splices in the flanges should come at the points of inflection. **1951** R. D. CHELLIS *Pile Foundations* xi. 271 If piles are restrained throughout their full length in firm soil ..a splice consisting of a full butt weld or single web and flange plates welded on in the field suffices. **1977** J. P. COOK *Composite Construction Methods* x. 209 In the usual steel frame, column sizes are normally kept constant for a height of two stories, with the column splice about 3 or 4 ft above the floor level.

c. *Cricket.* The v-shaped tang of a bat-handle, which forms a joint with the blade; the joint itself. Also in slang phr. ***to sit on*** (or ***upon***) ***the splice***, to play a cautious defensive game.
1906 A. E. KNIGHT *Compl. Cricketer* 44 The spliced handle was a later development, and some of the earliest splices were of ash. *Ibid.* 352 To sit upon the splice.—To play with too much caution, to deliberately refrain from scoring. **1912** *Daily Mirror* 9 July 14/2 Vidler sat icily on the splice, playing the right game and keeping up an end while Crutchley got runs. **1927** *Punch* 26 Jan. 108/1 'I don't think you're helping the score at all,' I protested. 'You're just sitting on your splice and leaving it all to me.' **1935** *Encycl. Sports* 195/1 Cricketers who bought a new bat treated it almost with reverence... They oiled every part of it, except the handle and splice. **1963** A. ROSS *Australia 63* iii. 79 Dexter, hooking at him, nearly returned a gentle catch off the splice. **1968** L. FREWIN *Best of Cricket's Fiction* II. 267 There was a business-like look about him, the air of one who without being the least downhearted or inclined to sit upon the splice, was yet determined to take no foolish risks.

d. A joint made in editing or repairing film or magnetic or paper tape.
1923 F. A. TALBOT *Moving Pictures* (ed. 3) viii. 100 In making the splice care has to be observed to introduce the two pieces true to frame-line, gauge and marginal perforations. **1931**, **1936** [see BLOOP *v.*]. **1949** FRAYNE & WOLFE *Elem. Sound Recording* xxix. 603 A program can be edited in advance by cutting out portions or inserting other portions, since splices in the tape cannot be heard. **1973** *Screen* Spring/Summer 43 Montage in the narrow sense (ie as an editing splice) has a diminishing importance in certain modern films.

2. *slang.* Union by marriage; a marriage; a wedding.
1830 GALT *Lawrie T.* II. i. (1849) 43 She ben't five-and-twenty—she'll make a heavenly splice! **1862** *Cornh. Mag.* Jan. 54 Till the splice is made she's a right to please herself. **1876** HOLLAND *Seven Oaks* xxi. 303 I'm a little interested in her myself and I'm going to pay for the splice.

3. *attrib.* and *Comb.*, as ***splice manner, -work***, etc.; **splice-bar**, = *splice-piece*; **splice-grafting**, a method of grafting in which the scion and stock are cut obliquely and bound firmly together; whip- or tongue-grafting; hence ***splice-graft*** vb.; **splice-joint, -piece** (see quots.).
1815 *Trans. Horticultural Soc.* I. 239 The amputated parts [of the pear-stocks] were then accurately fitted and bound, as in splice, or whip-grafting, to scions of Pear Trees. **1830** W. TAYLOR *Hist. Surv. Germ. Poetry* II. 397 [Dryden's style is] never approached by a German splice-work of anapaests and iambics. **1842** LOUDON *Suburban Hort.* 288 Splice-grafting, tongue-grafting, or whip-grafting, is the mode most commonly adopted in all gardens where the stocks are not much larger in diameter than the scion. *Ibid.* 289 In splice-grafting the shoots of peaches, nectarines, and apricots. **1875** KNIGHT *Dict. Mech.* 2280/1 *Splice-piece*,..a fish-plate or break-joint piece at the junction of two rails. **1884** *Ibid.* Suppl. 842/2 *Splice joint*, the connecting joints between rails on railways. **1894** *Times* 16 Aug. 6/4 Railway fish plates or splice bars.

splice (splaɪs), *v.* Also 6-7 splise. [ad. MDu. *splissen*, of doubtful origin, but perh. related to SPLIT *v.*; in the Continental languages now represented by Du. dial., LG. and G. *splissen*, WFris. *splisse*, NFris. *splesse, splasse*, Sw. *splissa*; also G. *spleissen, splitsen*, Du. *splitsen*, Sw. *splitsa*, Da. *splidse*. The Du. word is also the source of F. *épisser* (†*épicer*), whence *épissoir* splicing-iron, and *épissure* a splice.]

I. 1. a. *trans.* To join (ropes, cables, lines, etc.) by untwisting and interweaving the strands of the ends so as to form one continuous length; to unite (two parts of the same rope) by interweaving the strands of one end into those of another part so as to form an eye or loop; to repair (rigging) in this way. Chiefly *Naut.*
Also const. with preps. and advs., as *into, round, together.*
1524-5 [see SPLICING *vbl. sb.* 1]. *a* **1625** *Nomenclator Navalis* (Harl. MS. 2301), To splice is to make fast the ends of Roapes one into the other by joining the strands at the ends of both the Roapes. **1633** T. JAMES *Voy.* 23 We went to worke..to splise our Cables. **1675** COCKER *Morals* 15 All the Lines, made since Sol's Race began, Spliced into one, would prove too short to sound this bottomless..Sea. **1709** *Lond. Gaz.* No. 4547/2 He spliced his Rigging, and repaired the Damages as fast as he could. **1795** NELSON in Nicolas *Disp.* (1845) II. 14 Employed shifting our topsails and splicing our rigging. **1825** J. NICHOLSON *Operat. Mechanic* 422 The two ends of these yarns he splices together. **1864** *Soc. Sci. Rev.* I. 266 As the sailor wants to be taught how to splice a rope or rove his tackle. **1891** C. ROBERTS *Adrift Amer.* 213, I very soon ingratiated myself with the other men by teaching them to splice rope.
absol. **1706** E. WARD *Wooden World Diss.* (1708) 80 Shew me the Gentleman, crys he, that can knot or splice, or make Pudding as it should be? **1891** C. ROBERTS *Adrift Amer.* 213, I was rather surprised to find that they could not splice.

b. To form (an eye or knot) in a rope by splicing.
1773 *Life N. Frowde* 24, I could not only go to any Part of the Vessel that I was bid, but splice a Knot and go aloft. **1845** J. COULTER *Adv. in Pacific* vii. 72 One end [of the line] is bent on to the harpoon; the other (with an eye spliced in it) is left hanging out of the sternpost tub.

c. ***to splice the main-brace***: see MAIN-BRACE[1] b.

2. a. To join (two pieces of timber, etc.) by overlapping or scarfing the two ends together in such a way as to form one continuous length; to fasten *together* in this way; to graft by a similar process. Also, to fasten together (metal girders and rails, concrete beams, etc.) similarly.
1626 CAPT. SMITH *Accid. Yng. Seamen* 3 The Carpenter is to..[be] euer ready for calking, breaming,..fishing or spliceing the Masts or Yards. *Ibid.* 13 A Iury-mast; which is made with yards, rouftrees, or what they can, splised or fished together. **1728** CHAMBERS *Cycl.*, To *Splice* among Gardeners, is to graft the Top of one Tree into the Stock of another, by cutting them sloping, and fastening them together. **1763** MILLS *Syst. Pract. Husb.* IV. 408 The branches of the old tree thus spliced in the rind yield an uncommon quantity of fruit. **1791** W. GILPIN *Forest Scenery* I. 128 A very noble fir.., which was not spliced in the common mode, but was converted in it's full dimensions, into the bowsprit of the Britannia. **1857** HUGHES *Tom Brown* I. ix, East and Tom were..splicing a favourite old fives'-bat. **1860** MAYNE REID *Hunters' Feast* xvii, The breaking of our waggon-tongue..delayed our journey. There was plenty of good hickory-wood,..and Jake..soon spliced it again. **1875** [see SPLINT *sb.* 4 b]. **1892** L. DE C. BERG *Safe Building* II. x. 113 If any part of a girder ..is spliced, made of two parts, the number of rivets each side of splice..should be made sufficient to transfer the full strength of original plate across the joint. **1913** W. H. SELLEW *Steel Rails* iv. 263 The stiffness of the rail that is to be spliced. **1951** R. D. CHELLIS *Pile Foundations* ix. 201 (*caption*) Exposing reinforcing preparatory to splicing a large precast concrete pile. **1976** R. CHUDLEY *Construction Technol.* III. vii. 75 Where members of the frame are joined or spliced together the connections are generally mechanical (nut and bolt).

b. *transf.* To unite in this manner by means of surgery or natural healing.
1755 J. SHEBBEARE *Lydia* (1769) I. 178 Surgeon Macpherson..having thus spliced the fox's tail to the little skill he had in surgery. **1867** LATHAM *Black & White* 87 The glass cases of broken bones,..as poor mother nature had tried to glue them together and splice them again, gave some idea of the horrors of war.

c. In various transferred and figurative uses: To unite, combine, join, mend. Also *spec.* in *Biol.*, to join or insert (a gene or gene fragment).
1803 *Spirit Public Jrnls.* VII. 68 And when they would buy, a whole company splice Their pence.., to make up the price. **1809** MALKIN *Gil Blas* V. i. ¶63 My legacy consisted of a broken fortune to splice. **1810** CRABBE *Borough* x. 245 The long tale, renew'd when last they met, Is spliced anew, and is unfinish'd yet. **1828** CREEVEY in *C. Papers* (1904) II. 154 He splices so many subjects upon one another, it is difficult to make a selection. **1890** D. G. MITCHELL *Eng. Lands* ii. 74 We know..that he takes to the work of mending plays, and splicing good parts together. **1975** *Nature* 18 Dec. 563/1 The genes to be cloned would first be spliced on to either a bacterial plasmid..or on to the DNA of bacteriophage lambda which would then infect the bacterium. **1977** *Sci. News* 29 Jan. 70 The controversial research in question is a class of experiments that..include splicing the genes of a virus or bacteria to partially purified DNA from mammals or birds..known to produce potent toxins or pathogens. **1979** *Newsweek* 4 June 64 One valuable product has already resulted from the work: human insulin, manufactured by splicing fragments of DNA that manufacture the hormone in humans into an intestinal bacterium.

d. To bind, fasten, fix firmly or securely.
1847 DISRAELI *Tancred* III. iii, If you were in the middle of the desert and the least grumbling, you would be spliced on a camel.

e. To make a splice or joint in (a length of film or magnetic or paper tape); to join (film or tape) *in, on* or *up*. Occas. *intr.* (or *absol.*).
1912 F. A. TALBOT *Moving Pictures* xii. 137 Occasionally when a film is being run through the projector it becomes severed by some means or other. Before it can be used again the break must be repaired by splicing the two parts together. **1931** WILKINSON & REIS in L. Cowan *Recording Sound for Motion Pictures* xiv. 200 When film is spliced on a standard splicing machine, the splice crosses the sound track at right angles to its length. **1958** W. E. STEWART *Magn. Recording Techn.* ii. 42 The wire, still useful in some applications, cannot be spliced so easily as tape. **1962** L. DEIGHTON *Ipcress File* xxiv. 156 The film lab had been very thorough, they had spliced on to the end of the film the incident of my arrest. **1973** A. BROINOWSKI *Take One Ambassador* x. 140 The odd *faux pas*..would have to be cut; splice in a bedroom scene there. **1974** N. FREELING *Dressing of Diamond* 174 Snip a bit off this [tape] and splice it up. **1978** L. DAVIDSON *Chelsea Murders* xxiii. 141 He put in six solid hours at the editing... He compared and cut and spliced till two in the morning. **1978** [see SPLICER 2 b]. **1980** S. HOCKEY *Guide Computer Applic. Humanities* ii. 25 Sections of corrected [paper] tape can be spliced or glued into the original.

f. *Cricket.* To strike (the ball) with the splice of the bat, as a mishit.
1982 *Guardian* 19 Feb. 22/2 Botham went for a swinging pull shot, and spliced it tamely but safely to mid-wicket.

3. *slang.* **a.** To join in matrimony; to marry. Chiefly in *passive.*
1751 SMOLLETT *Per. Pic.* vii, Trunnion! Trunnion! turn out and be spliced, or lie still and be damned. **1788** in GROSE *Dict. Vulg. T.* (ed. 2). **1834** MARRYAT *P. Simple* (1863) 295 My two sisters are both to be spliced to young squireens in the neighbourhood. **1853** C. BRONTE *Villette* xlii, Alfred and I intended to be married in this way almost from the first; we never meant to be spliced in the hum-drum way of other people. **1873** MRS. R. T. RITCHIE *Wks.* (1891) I. 148 There goes a parson... Shall I run after him and get him to splice us off-hand?

b. *intr.* To get married. Also const. *with.*
1874 E. EGGLESTON *Circuit Rider* xxiii. 216, I heerd say as he was goin' to splice with a gal that could pray like a angel afire. **1875** J. G. HOLLAND *Sevenoaks* xii. 155, Jim, be ye goin' to splice? **1981** T. HEALD *Murder at Moose Jaw* xii. 144

If the old flapper spliced with the colonel she stood to lose a million dollars.

4. *intr.* To fit *into* something with a splice.

1882 NARES *Seamanship* (ed. 6) 125 The end [of the spilling line] splicing into the head of the sail.

II. †**5.** *trans.* and *intr.* To split. *Obs. rare.*

1664 EVELYN *Sylva* 74 Making the stroke upward, and with a sharp Bill, so as the weight of an untractable bough do not splice and carry the bark with it. *Ibid.* 92 In arms of Timber which are very great, chop a nick under it close to the Boal, so meeting it with the down-right strokes, it will be cut without splicing.

Hence **spliced** (splaɪst) *ppl. a.*, formed, joined, repaired, or reinforced by splicing.

1859 T. P. SHAFFNER *Telegraph Man.* xli. 597 Fig. 13 is the two ends spliced, having first been cleaned. **1867** G. H. SELKIRK *Guide to Cricket Ground* iii. 44 A new handle can be inserted..and the 'spliced bat' will be quite as good as before—indeed, many players have their bats spliced at first, thinking it a great improvement. **1870** MORRIS *Earthly Par.* III. IV. 250 Though a spliced staff e'en as strong may be As one ne'er broken. **1870** *Routledge's Ev. Boy's Ann.* Suppl. 7/2 A spliced Cricket Bat. **1875** KNIGHT *Dict. Mech.* 2280/1 *Spliced Eye*, the rope is bent around a thimble, and the end spliced into the standing part. **1891** W. G. GRACE *Cricket* ii. 42 This one [*sc.* a bat] had a spliced handle with a strip of whalebone down the centre of it, and was very much prized. **1897** *Sears, Roebuck & Co. Catal.* 243/3 Men's Seamless Cotton Half Hose... Spliced heels and toes. **1931** WILKINSON & REIS in L. Cowan *Recording Sound for Motion Pictures* xiv. 201 A similar section of silent track, matching the average density of the spliced tracks, is..cemented into the hole. **1968** J. IRONSIDE *Fashion Alphabet* 69 *Spliced heel*, heel reinforced with the same fabric as the stocking. **1970** E.-O. LIBUDA tr. *Heinhold's Power Cables & Application* xlvi. 457 Brazing is necessary for spliced connections [in copper conductors].

splicer ('splaɪsə(r)). [f. SPLICE *v.* + -ER.]

1. One who splices ropes, etc.

1840 R. H. DANA *Bef. Mast* xxv, There was only one 'splicer' on board, a fine-looking old tar. **1881** *Instr. Census Clerks* (1885) 64 Woollen Cloth Manufacture:..Spinner... Splicer. **1889** CLARK RUSSELL *Marooned* (1890) 32 A real splicer in aspect.

2. a. A tool or implement used in splicing.

1923 J. H. COOK *Fifty Years on Old Frontier* 114 A wire cutter, splicer, and staple-puller combined.

b. A mechanical device used to splice film or tape.

1927 E. G. LUTZ *Motion-Picture Cameraman* xi. 243 (*caption*) B. & H. 16 mm. rewinder and splicer. **1931** WILKINSON & REIS in L. Cowan *Recording Sound for Motion Pictures* xiv. 202 A diagonal splicer has been evolved to produce a silent splice. **1953** K. REISZ *Technique Film Editing* 274 The two reels, one of sound track, one of picture, both provisionally held together by paper clips, are joined on a splicer. **1978** G. MCDONALD *Fletch's Fortune* xxx. 201 'I need one of those cassette tape recorders. You know, with a tape splicer. I need to splice some tape.' 'Mine doesn't have a splicer.'

splicing ('splaɪsɪŋ), *vbl. sb.* [f. SPLICE *v.* Cf. Du. *splitsing*, G. *splissung*, *splitsung*, NFris. *splessing*, Da. *splidsning*, Sw. *splissning*.]

I. 1. a. The action or operation of making a splice or splices.

1524–5 *Rec. St. Mary at Hill* (1905) 327 Paid for Splisyng of y bell Ropis, v d. **1627** [see SPLICE *sb.* 1]. *a* **1642** SIR W. MONSON *Naval Tracts* III. (1704) 339/2 The Splicing and Bending of Cables. **1758** J. BLAKE *Plan Mar. Syst.* 7 Exercising those who are received into the service, in knotting and splicing. **1772–84** *Cook's Voy.* (1790) V. 1929 Our spare hands were employed incessantly, in knotting and splicing. **1912** F. A. TALBOT *Moving Pictures* xii. 138 To facilitate..splicing a small clamping device is used. **1931** L. E. CLARK in L. Cowan *Recording Sound for Motion Pictures* ix. 144 In splicing a certain amount is lost at each end. **1973** *Screen* Spring/Summer 42 The montage in question is not ..necessarily montage in the narrow sense (ie splicing). **1980** *Daily Tel.* 18 Jan. 14/6 The scientists..have modified common laboratory bacteria by 'gene splicing' to produce human interferon.

fig. **1829** BENTHAM *Justice & Cod. Petit.* Wks. 1843 V. 485 Now as to Court Christian... Nothing requisite to be done otherwise than in the quiet way, by splicing; by splicing performed imperceptibly.

b. *attrib.*, chiefly in the names of tools used in splicing, as ***splicing-block***, ***-clamp***, ***fid***, ***-hammer***, ***machine***, ***-piece***, ***-shackle***, ***-tape***; also ***splicing process***.

1750 BLANCKLEY *Nav. Expos.* 55 Spliceing fidds are used to splice or fasten Ropes together, and are made tapering at one End. **1858** H. BUSHNELL *Serm. New Life* 129 He was not obliged to accommodate his ignorance..by any such splicing process in words. *c* **1860** H. STUART *Seaman's Catech.* 55 The ends are joined together by a splicing-piece or shackle. **1875** KNIGHT *Dict. Mech.* 2280/1 Splicing-hammer, -shackle. **1884** *Ibid.* Suppl. 842/2 Splicing Clamp. **1927** E. G. LUTZ *Motion-Picture Cameraman* xi. 241 Joining films is made with the aid of a splicing-block which has as its main feature series of teeth over which the film-perforations fit. **1931** Splicing machine [see SPLICE *v.* 2 e]. **1958** J. TALL *Techniques of Magnetic Recording* x. 161 The splicing tape should be laid down..at an angle. **1974** H. BURSTEN *Questions & Answers about Tape Recording* xviii. 246 The leading edge of the splicing tape presents a resistance.

2. = *splice-grafting* (see SPLICE *sb.* 3).

1653 BELLINGHAM *Plat's Gard. Eden* 118 Grafting whip-stock wise, and letting the cions into the stock by a slit... Some call this the Splicing way. **1672** DROPE *Fruit Trees* iii. 40 Whip-grafting (otherwise called Backing, Packing, or Splicing).

3. The spliced part of a rope, etc.; a splice.

1892 *Law Times* XCIV. 79/2 The covering of the splicing of the rope had become frayed. **1895** R. B. C. GRAHAM *Notes Menteith* v. 72 A rod with as many splicings as Petrucchio's bridle.

II. †**4.** A piece split off; a slender slip of wood. *Obs.*⁻¹

1725 *Family Dict.* s.v. *Ozier*, The Peelings or Splicings of the former [osier] are used by Gardeners and Coopers.

spliff (splɪf). *slang* (orig. *W. Indies*). Also splif. [Origin unknown.] A cannabis cigarette, *spec.* one rolled in a conical form; a smoke of cannabis.

1936 *Daily Gleaner* (Kingston, Jamaica) 3 Oct. 35 Here is the hot-bed of ganja smoking..and even the children may be seen at times taking what is better known as their 'spliff'. **1953** R. MAIS *Hills were Joyful Together* I. xi. 111 He took the spliff and lit up, dragged long at it, drawing the smoke deep down into his lungs. **1959** C. MACINNES *Absolute Beginners* 76 A third just said, 'Great', with a soft dream in his eyes—but that may have been because he'd just been dragging on a splif inside the toilet. **1969** FABIAN & BYRNE *Groupie* (1970) i. 9 He showed me how to roll spliffs—as he called them—so that I could roll for him. **1972** J. BROWN *Chancer* ii. 30 They might be going..to meet a pusher or they might be going just for a few spliffs and to catch the party feeling. **1975** *High Times* Dec. 137/1 Like Marley, he's a spliff-toking Rastafarian. **1977** *Transatlantic Rev.* LX. 192 Coon rolled a massive splif and blew clouds of ganja gremlins through the hatch.

'splinder, *sb.* Chiefly *Sc.* Forms: 5 splyndre, 9 splinder; 5 splendre, 5–6, 9 splender (6 -ar, 9 -ir). [Related to SPLINTER *sb.* Cf. SPLINE *sb.* and NFris. *splüner-nii* quite new.] A splinter. Chiefly in phr. ***in*** or ***into splinders***.

c **1440** *Wycliffite Bible* 2 Kings xviii. 21 (MS. Bodl. 277), þe splyndre or speele þerof schal entre into hys hoond. *c* **1470** HENRY *Wallace* IX. 921 Speris full sone all in to splendrys sprang. **1535** STEWART *Cron. Scot.* I. 381 The speiris lang..In splendaris sprang aboue thame in the air. **1562** WINȜET *Wks.* (S.T.S.) I. 3 To brek in splenderis the schip on the feirful rokis. **1819** W. TENNANT *Papistry Storm'd* (1827) 93 In splendirs flew the stane about. *Ibid.* 201 Ilk ane upon its marble crown Smashin' itsel' to splinders. **1880** W. T. DENNISON *Orcadian Sketch-bk.* 133 He dang hid's bothom [= its bottom] clean i' splender.

So **'splinder** *v. intr.*, to splinter. *rare.*

c **1450** *Merlin* x. 155 [They] mette so sore to-geder..that her speres splyndered in peces. **1731** MESTON *Mob contra Mob* v. (1738) 27 Thrawn Trees do always splinder Best with a Wedge of their own Timber.

spline (splaɪn), *sb.* [Orig. E. Anglian dial.: perh. for *splind* (cf. older Da. *splind*, NFris. *splinj*) and related to SPLINDER *sb.*]

1. a. A long, narrow, and relatively thin piece or strip of wood, metal, etc.; a slat.

1756 S. WHITE *Collat. Bee-Boxes* (1759) 26, *c. c.* are two Splines of Deal to keep the Boards even and strengthen them. **1806** W. TAYLOR in *Ann. Rev.* IV. 772 The heavel, which is a row of loops fastened to a spline. **1866** *Spectator* 13 Jan. 30/1 She slept on the splines of the bed, having no bedding. **1886** *Shoolbred's Catal. Furniture*, etc. 177 The ends [of a garden chair] are wrought iron, the splines wood. **1905** RIDER HAGGARD *Gardener's Year* 218 He sent me a score [of orchids], tied on to a spline with string.

fig. **1805** W. TAYLOR in Robberds *Mem.* (1843) II. 106 My chief complacency in the poem results from the art..with which the new splines are fitted in.

attrib. **1883** *Daily News* 5 July 3/1 Spars were fixed across, and the spline frames of the seats laid down length-ways as flooring.

b. *spec.* (See quot. 1891.)

1891 *Cent. Dict.*, *Spline*, a flexible strip of wood or hard rubber used by draftsmen in laying out broad sweeping curves, especially in railroad work. **1904** *Drapers' Co. Res. Memoirs* XIII. 12 The curves..were plotted with our coordinatograph for a series of values of *k* or *r* on a large scale, drawn in with a spline and integrated with a Coradi compensating planimeter. **1953** A. H. ROBINSON *Elements Cartogr.* v. 83/1 For larger curves, the defining points of which are far apart, a flexible curve or a spline with weights is more satisfactory.

c. *dial.* (See quot.)

1892 P. H. EMERSON *Son of Fens* 204 A spline is a ten and a half foot measure.

2. *techn.* A rectangular key fitting into grooves in a shaft and wheel or other attachment so as to allow longitudinal movement of the latter. Now *esp.* such a key that is formed integrally with the shaft; also, a corresponding recess in a hub along which the key may slide.

1864 in WEBSTER. **1875** KNIGHT *Dict. Mech.* 339/1 The cutter-block..traverses as a slide on a spline down a huge boring-bar. **1909** KIMBALL & BARR *Elements Machine Design* viii. 196 Sometimes it is desirable to have the hub free to slide axially along the shaft, but constrained to rotate with it. In such cases a feather or spline is used. **1932** R. C. H. HECK in C. E. O'Rourke *Gen. Engin. Handbk.* xviii. 532 Often a gear has to slide along its shaft. The key in this service is called a spline or feather. **1952** F. J. CAMM *Newnes Engineer's Ref. Bk.* (ed. 5) 854 The efficiency of a spline for driving purposes is measured by the amount of contact made by the male and female splines. **1966** G. W. MICHALEC *Precision Gearing* vii. 324 Generally, involute internal and external teeth are mated, but non-involute splines are also suitable. **1979** *Industrial Fasteners Handbk.* I. 318 There are two basic forms of spline—straight-sided splines which may number 4, 6, 10 or up to 16 splines equally distributed around the circumference of a shaft, and serrated splines which are in the form of adjacent triangular teeth.

3. *Math.* Also ***spline curve***. A continuous curve constructed so as to pass through a given set of points and have continuous first and second derivatives.

1946 I. J. SCHOENBERG in *Q. Appl. Math.* IV. 48 For $k = 4$ they represent approximately the curves drawn by means of a spline and for this reason we propose to call them spline curves of order *k*. **1966** *Notices Amer. Math. Soc.* XIII. 140 This paper extends and strengthens convergence properties previously published..for periodic splines and for nonperiodic splines satisfying general end conditions. **1978** *Nature* 1 June 407/2 Cubic spline interpolation was applied at standard depths to 800 m.

Hence **spline** *v. trans.*, to fit with a spline; to secure (a part) by means of a spline; **splined** *ppl. a.*, provided with a spline or splines; **'splining** *vbl. sb.*; ***splining machine***, one for cutting key-seats and grooves (Webster, 1864).

1891 *Cent. Dict.*, *Spline* v. **1901** *Shop & Foundry Practice* II. §15. 14 Fig. 13 shows a jig designed for holding shafts for key-seating or splining, plain cutters being used for the purpose. *Ibid.* 15 The shafts..which are to be splined or key-seated, are laid into these grooves and are clamped. **1909** N. HAWKINS *Mech. Dict.* 529/2 *Splined shaft*, a shaft provided with a long feather way; as a splined feed rod on a lathe. **1920** *Autocar Handbk.* (ed. 10) x. 125 In order to allow the gear wheels to drive the shaft on which they are placed, or vice versa, the latter is often grooved or 'splined'. **1926** *Motor Man.* (ed. 26) v. 82 The worm-wheel spindle emerges from the off side of the steering box, and splined thereto is a short lever, generally known as the drop arm. **1952** P. S. HOUGHTON *Gears* ix. 156 The length of bearing in an involute splined hub will depend upon the chosen materials. **1953** *Straight-Sided Splines & Serrations* (*B.S.I.*) 5/2 If two shafts are splined to different fits by the same cutter..the radius of the arc at the root..will vary slightly from the designed arc. **1967** [see KNOCK-OFF *a.* 2 b]. **1979** *Industrial Fasteners Handbk.* I. 318 British Standard 3550:1963 specifies dimensions of involuted splined shafts and splined holes with a 30° pressure angle.

splint (splɪnt), *sb.* Forms: α. 4–6 **splente**, 4–9 **splent** (5 splentt, 6 splenntt, spleynt). β. 5–6 **splynt(e**, **splinte**, 6– **splint**. [a. MDu. *splinte* (Du. *splint*), or MLG. *splinte*, *splente* (LG. *splinte*, *splente*, and *splint*, whence G., Da., Sw., Norw. *splint*) metal plate or pin, = OHG. *splinza* 'repagulum, pessulus', of doubtful etymology: cf. SPLINE *sb.* and SPLINTER *sb.*]

1. a. One of the plates or strips of overlapping metal of which certain portions of mediæval armour were sometimes composed; *esp.* one of a pair of pieces of this nature used for protecting the arms at the elbows.

α. **13..** *Coer de L.* 4979 He was armyd in splentes off steel. **1374** *Acc. John de Sleford* in *For. Acc. 49 Edw. III* B, In.. xj paribus splentes, ij paribus tibialium. ? *a* **1400** *Morte Arth.* 2061 The splent and the spleene on the spere lengez! **1474** *Rental-bk. Cupar-Angus* (1879) I. 194 Tha sal be.. welbeseyn with Jakkis, hattis, and splentis. **1530** PALSGR. 274 Splent, harnesse for the arme, *garde de bras*. **1561** *Wills & Inv. N.C.* (Surtees, 1835) 193 A stuffed Jacke, a payre of splents. *a* **1578** LINDESAY (Pitscottie) *Chron. Scot.* (S.T.S.) I. 281 The number of iiijᵉ speiris weill arrayit in jake and splent and wther airmor. *a* **1802** *Kinmont Willie* xvii. in Scott *Minstrelsy*, He has calld him forty marchmen bauld,.. With spur on heel, and splent on spauld. **1819** SCOTT *Leg. Montrose* viii, Such force, as to drive the iron splents of the gauntlet into the hand of the wearer.

fig. *c* **1450** *St. Cuthbert* (Surtees) 6320 When he forthe went, Aboute his nek agayne sho [a snake] cleuyd. Shame mare þan him greuyd Of þat sary splent.

β. **1499** *Crt. Rolls Maldon, Essex* Bundle 58 No. 5, Unum par brygonders, 1 par splynts. **1517** in *Archaeol.* XLVII. 310, dcxl splyntes, and dcccviij salettes. **1555** EDEN *Decades* (Arb.) 237 They carye..certeyne armure of golde: especially great and rounde pieces on theyr brestes, and splintes on there armes. **1819** SCOTT *Ivanhoe* ii, The knees and feet were defended by splints, or thin plates of steel, ingeniously jointed upon each other. **1824** MEYRICK *Armour* III. 27 Having not only splints at the elbows, but the breast and back-plates made flexible in the same manner.

b. *Zool.* (See quot.)

1896 tr. *Boas' Zool.* 408 True scales; if these are much broader than they are long, as on the ventral side of the body in Snakes, they are termed splints.

2. a. A slender, moderately long and freq. flexible, rod or slip of wood cut or cleft off and serving for some particular purpose, esp. as a lath or wattle, or prepared for use in some manufacture.

The exact meaning in the first two quotations is uncertain.

α. *c* **1325** *Gloss. W. de Bibbesw.* in *Reliq. Antiq.* II. 84 Splentes, *trenchons*. *c* **1340** *Nominale* (Skeat) 449 *Traches et trenchous*, Sulle-trees and splentes. **1348** in *1st Rep. Hist. MSS. Comm.* (1874) 65/1 For splentes for the vineyard, 7*d.* For hordlis, 4*s.* 6*d.* **1410** *Crt.-roll Gt. Waltham Manor* (MS.), Defrondaverunt salices..ad valenciam ii carectat. Splents, pretium viiiᵈ. *c* **1450** *Two Cookery-bks.* 73 Ley splentes vnderneth and al abouȝt the sides, that the Capon touche no thinge of the potte. **1523** FITZHERB. *Husb.* §122 Whan the swarme is knytte, take a hyue, and splente it within with thre or foure splentes. **1530** PALSGR. 274 Splent for an house, *laite*. **1594** BARNFIELD *Affect. Sheph.* (Arb.) 13 Or wilt thou in a yellow Boxen bole, Taste with a woodden splent the sweet lythe honey? **1601** HOLLAND *Pliny* I. 459 When the wood is cut into many clefts & splents, fresh and green, they are heaped vp on high [etc.]. **1847** HALLIW., *Splent*, a lath... The term is still in use in Suffolk. Splents are parts of sticks or poles, either whole or split, placed upright in forming walls, and supported by rizzers [= poles] for receiving the clay daubing.

β. **1398** TREVISA *Barth. De P.R.* XIX. cxxviii. (1495) 933 Calathus is a baskette made of splyntes to beere fygges therin. **1463** *Crt.-roll Gt. Waltham Manor* (MS.), Pro splintes inde habend. pro camera ad finem orientalem ejusdem domus. **1483** *Ibid.*, Reparabunt..dictam domum et cameram in daubitura, videlicet cum Splynts et Cley mixt. cum stramine. **1577** HARRISON *England* II. xii. 84 b/2 An ouerthwart post in their walles, wherevnto they fasten their Splintes or radles. **1598** FLORIO, *Assicella*, a little board or a planke or splint of thin boords. **1633** QUARLES in P. Fletcher *Purple Isl.* Commend. Verses, Mans Bodie's like a house: his greater bones Are the main timber; and the lesser ones Are smaller splints. **1707** MORTIMER *Husb.* 215 The Hive being taken and housed,..loosen the ends of the splints with your Finger. **1751** J. BARTRAM *Observ.* 48 The 2 splints of wood spreading each side, directs the point into the fish. **1809** A. HENRY *Trav.* 14 The bark is lined with small splints of cedar-wood. **1864** STRAUSS, etc. *Eng. Worksh.* 231 The paraffin dipped splints are taken to the woodmatch-framing department. **1885** *Harper's Mag.* Mar. 559/1 We take a broom splint sometimes, or a penknife, or a pin.

b. *Mil.* (See quot.)

1875 KNIGHT *Dict. Mech.*, *Splint*, a tapering strip of wood, used to adjust a shell centrally in the bore of a mortar.

3. a. A splinter of wood or stone; a chip or fragment. Now chiefly *north. dial.*

a. c **1400** *Laud Troy Bk.* 7397 Here speres brast In splentes. **1495** [see *β*]. **1574** HYLL *Bees* xxxvii, Of it selfe this draweth forth thornes or splents of wood runne deepe into the fleshe. **1612** *North's Plutarch* 1126 So soone as ever they pulled out the head and splent of the dart. **1849-** in dial. glossaries (Durh., Cheshire, Northumbld.).

β. **1398** TREVISA *Barth. De P.R.* XI. ii. (Tollem. MS.), þe mater [of snow] is broke in brode parties, as it were splyntes [**1495** splentes] of shellis. **1578** T. PROCTER *Gorg. Gallery* H iij b, My Hart like Ware so lightly did not brooke More then one stroke, ere Cupid brought to passe One splint of skale therof to take away. **1599** A. M. tr. *Gabelhouer's Bk. Physicke* 312/2 To extracte a Thorne or Splinte out of anye wounde without payne. *a* **1604** HANMER *Chron. Ireland* (1809) 301 The splints of broken staves fly about their ears. **1638** A. READ *Chirurg.* xxii. 163 These things are to bee done when splints of the scull doe pricke the menings. **1708** J. C. *Compl. Collier* (1845) 22 If he haue not Judgment, the Shivers or Splints of the Whin or hard Stone..will Wound him severely. **1865-** in Yks. and Lancs. dial. glossaries. **1868** WHITMAN *Chants Democratic* Poems 147, I see the savage types, the bow and arrow, the poisoned splint [etc.].

b. *S. Afr.* A fragment or broken piece of diamond.

1872 C. RHODES *Let.* in B. Williams *Cecil Rhodes* (1921) iv. 29 You must not however think that every diamond one finds is a beauty, the great proportion are nothing but splints. **1887** J. W. MATTHEWS *Incwadi Yami* xxvii. 415 Faithfully carrying out their master's behests, and never robbing him of a single splint. **1903** W. R. CATTELLE *Precious Stones* 79 Beyond the small pieces resulting from cleavages, other fragments are saved which cannot be cut to jewels. Some of these are called 'splints', and are used for mechanical purposes or ground to powder.

4. a. *Surg.* A thin piece of wood or other more or less rigid material used to hold a fractured or dislocated bone in position during the process of reunion; by extension, any appliance or apparatus serving this purpose. Also, an object used to fasten or immobilize teeth or the jaws.

'Splints vary almost infinitely in form and size, according to the part to which they have to be adapted, and the position in which it is to be held' (*Penny Cycl.* XXII. 368/1). 'A number of these are specially described in recent Medical Dicts.' (*N.E.D.*).

a. c **1400** *Lanfranc's Cirurg.* 63 If þat þe prickynge eiþer þe dislocacioun nediþ splentis [*v.r.* splyntes], make þat þe splentis & byndynge faile aboue þe wounde. **1565** COOPER *Thesaurus*, *Canalis*, a splent for a broken limme. **1594** O. B. *Quest. Profit. Concern.* 32* b, I had rather be packing while my bones be whole, then to be promised golden splents when they are broken. **1634** *Lowe's Chirurg.* 359 Then it must be banded more slacke, using more bands and no splents. **1748** tr. *Vegetius' Distempers Horses* 181 Afterwards you shall put square Olive Splents upon it not less than four Fingers broad. **1836-8** B. D. WALSH *Aristoph.*, *Acharnians* v. i, Prepare lint, plaister, greasy wool, and splents To bind his ancle up!

β. c **1410** *Master of Game* (MS. Digby 182) xii, Bynde it with flexe above..with iiii. splyntes wele ybounde þerto one agaynn an other because þat þe bones shuld not remewe. **1580** HOLLYBAND *Treas. Fr. Tong*, *Attelles*, little splintes which Surgeons set about ones legge or broken arme. **1643** J. STEER tr. *Exp. Chyrurg.* xv. 63 *A* is a splint of the breadth of three fingers. **1656** RIDGLEY *Pract. Physick* 162 Splints.. are made of much paper and then Chips of Wood. c **1720** W. GIBSON *Farrier's Guide* I. vi. (1723) 93 To each Side of this Bone is fastned a Splint, in Shape like a Bodkin. **1826** S. COOPER *First Lines Surg.* (ed. 5) 278 Splints ought to be made of strong materials, and of a sufficient length to reach beyond the two joints nearest the fracture. **1849** H. MILLER *Footpr. Creat.* iv. (1874) 41 A splint of wood or whalebone fastened over a fractured toe or finger. **1876** C. GIBBON *Robin Gray* viii, His arm was still in splints. **1948** *Brit. Dental Jrnl.* LXXXV. 223/1 Removable acrylic bite blocks or splints with clasps were constructed.., so that the bite was opened..and the mandible moved forward. **1962** BLAKE & TROTT *Periodontology* xiv. 144 The main object of periodontal splint design is to make use of sound teeth to give stability to mobile teeth.

b. *transf.* (See quot.)

1875 KNIGHT *Dict. Mech.* 2280/2 *Splint*, a wooden strip for splicing and stiffening a fractured bar or beam.

5. *Farriery.* **a.** A callous tumour developing into a bony excrescence formed on the metacarpal bones of a horse's or mule's leg, occurring usually on the inside of the leg along the line of union of the splint-bones with the cannon-bone.

through-splint: see THROUGH- 2.

a. **1523** FITZHERB. *Husb.* §97 A splent is the leaste soraunce that is, that alwaye contynueth, excepte lampas. **1562** TURNER *Baths* (1568) 2, I thinke verely that the bath of brimstone..will heale splentes, spavines, and all knobbes. **1609** DEKKER *Lanth. & Candle Lt.* Wks. (Grosart) III. 280 A Horse cannot be lustie at legges, by reason that either his hoofes bee not good, or that there be Splents, or any other Eyesore about the nether Ioynt. **1688** HOLME *Armoury* II. 152/1 The Splent..is a spungy hard gristly bone..which by making the Horse stark, causeth him to stumble. **1721** W. GIBSON *Farrier's Dispens.* III. xvi. 305 Bladders, Wind-galls, Splents, and other Swellings in the Legs and Joints. **1737** BRACKEN *Farriery Impr.* (1757) II. 67 If there be large Splents, they may truly be called Blemishes. **1830** HINDS *Osmer's Treat. Horse* 267 Splents cause lameness. **1859** *Blackw. Mag.* LXXXV. 455 The animal's legs were so enlarged by splents that they were literally cylindrical.

β. **1599** PORTER *Angry Wom. Abingt.* I. ii. B ij, A leg both straight and cleane, That hath nor spauen, splint nor flawe. **1677** *Lond. Gaz.* No. 1183/4 An Iron gray Gelding, having on each Leg a Splint. **1690** DRYDEN *Don Sebastian* I. i, Feel his legs master; neither splint, spavin, nor windgall. **1724** *Lond. Gaz.* No. 6266/4 Two large Splints on his two fore Legs. **1741** *Compl. Fam.-Piece* III. 435 The Splint is a fixed callous Excrescence..growing on the Flat of the Inside or Outside, and sometimes on both, of the Shank Bone. **1831** YOUATT *Horse* 244 The splint is invariably found on the outside of the small bone, and generally on the inside of the leg. **1856** LEVER *Martins of Cro' M.* 312 There's a splint on the off-leg!

b. The growth of this, as a specific malady in horses.

1594 GREENE & LODGE *Looking-Gl. Lond.* 266 G.'s Wks. (Grosart) XIV. 18 If he haue outward diseases, as the spavin, splent, ring-bone, wind-gall. **1639** T. DE GRAY *Compl. Horsem.* 38 Mallenders, splent, serewe, ring-bone, and such like infirmities in the fore-feet. **1704** *Dict. Rust.* (1726), *Splint*, a Disease in an Horse. **1831** YOUATT *Horse* 365 *Splent.*—It depends entirely on the situation of the bony tumour.., whether it is to be considered as unsoundness. **1847** T. BROWN *Modern Farriery* 114 It is difficult to conceive how splent should appear on the outside of the small bones.

†**6.** = TENT *sb.*³ 2. *Obs.*⁻¹

1607 TOPSELL *Four-f. Beasts* 187 When the vineger is consumed, then put in the Opponax, and of both together make like taynters or splints and thurst them into the wound.

†**7.** A separate turn or coil in a spiral. *Obs.*

1607 TOPSELL *Four-f. Beasts* 717 The splents of the spire are smooth and not deep, being for the most part like vnto the wreathing turnings of Snails.

8. (See quot. 1883 and SPLINT COAL.)

1789 T. WILLIAMS *Min. Kingd.* I. 218 Sometimes masses of splent or parrot..will be found upon the side or at the bottom of a ravine. **1793** EARL DUNDONALD *Descr. Estate Culross* 4 The Coals are partly Smithy Coals, and partly Rich Caking Splents. *Ibid.*, There are several Seams of Dry Splents. **1849** GREENWELL *Coal-trade Terms, Northumb. & Durh.* (1851) 49 *Splint.*—Coarse grey-looking coal... Suitable for burning lime, and the better sorts for steam purposes. **1883** GRESLEY *Gloss. Coal-m.* 231 *Splint* or *Splent*, a laminated, coarse, inferior, dull-looking, hard coal, producing much white ash; intermediate between cannel and common pit coal. **1889** *Pall Mall G.* 1 Oct. 6/3 The prices fixed for splint are 2*s.* higher.

attrib. **1887** P. M'NEILL *Blawearie* 57 Where the men had first to descend one of these stairs..to the splint seam.

9. a. *attrib.* and *Comb.*, chiefly in sense 2, as ***splint-cutter***, ***-cutting***, ***-machine***, ***-plane***; ***splint-like*** adj.; **splint-boot**, a special boot for a horse suffering from a splint. See also SPLINT-BONE.

1858 SIMMONDS *Dict. Trade*, *Splint-cutter*, a shaper and maker of splints. **1862** *Catal. Internat. Exhib., Brit.* II. No. 4693, Web, Fetlock, Speedy, Splint,..and Strengthening Boots. **1862** HUXLEY *Lect. Working Men* 141 The splint-like bones in the leg of the horse. **1875** KNIGHT *Dict. Mech.* 2281 *Splint-machine*, a machine for riving or planing small slats or splints for use in making woven-slat blinds, baskets [etc.]. *Ibid.*, *Splint-plane*, one for riving splints from a block or board. **1889** A. R. WALLACE *Darwinism* 385 We find in the places of the second and fourth digits only two slender splintlike bones.

b. In the sense 'made or formed of splints', as (in sense 1) ***splint-armour***, (in sense 2) ***splint-basket***, ***-bottom***, ***-chair***, ***letter-case***; ***splint-bottomed*** adj.

(*a*) **1842** BURN *Nav. & Milit. Dict.*, *Écrevisse*, splint-armour. **1885** DILLON *Fairholt's Costume Eng.* II. 376 Splint armour for the legs..is common in German effigies.

(*b*) **1850** *Knickerbocker* XXXVI. 73 She wiped out the seats of some splint-bottomed chairs with her calico apron. **1867** *Summer in L. Goldthwaite's Life* 175 The finest and whitest and most graceful of all possible little splint baskets. **1871** B. TAYLOR in Hansen-Taylor & Scudder *Life & Lett.* (1884) II. xxiii. 564 An old-fashioned, high-backed splint-chair. **1876** 'MARK TWAIN' *Tom Sawyer* vi. 68 The master, throned on high in his great splint-bottom armchair, was dozing. **1889** MARY E. WILKINS *Mor. Exigency* (1891) 28 There were a few poor attempts at adornment on the walls; a splint letter-case, a motto worked in worsteds [etc.]. **1919** T. K. HOLMES *Man from Tall Timber* iv. 36 A comfortable armchair with splint-bottom. *Ibid.* v. 46 Their splint-bottomed armchairs.

splint (splɪnt), *v.* Forms: *a.* 5–7 **splent**, 6 **splente**. *β.* 7- **splint**. [f. the sb. Cf. Sw. *splinta* to split or splinter.]

†**1.** *trans.* To cover, furnish, or construct with splints or thin strips of wood, etc. *Obs.*

? *a* **1400** *Morte Arth.* 3264 A-bowte cho whirllide a whele with hir whitte hondez... The spekes..was splentide alle with speltis of siluer. **1523** FITZHERB. *Husb.* §122 Whan the swarme is knytte, take a hyue, and splente it within with thre or foure splentes. **1613** MARKHAM *Eng. Husbandman* I. II. xv. 110 Then you shall make a studde wall, which shall be splinted. **1632-3** in Willis & Clark *Cambr.* (1886) II. 697 The Particions and studyes, to be splented and Clayed betweene the Studds. **1639** HORN & ROB. *Gate Lang. Unl.* xlviii. §527 The partition wall he buildeth up even, being splented and dawbed with clay-mortar.

2. To adjust, bind, or fit a surgical splint to (a fractured bone, etc.); to put into splints; to hold firmly in position, to secure, by means of a splint or splints.

a. **1543** TRAHERON tr. *Vigo's Chirurg.* VI. i. 181 b, Yf the dislocation be with a fracture,..after restauracion ye shall bynde it & splent it. **1577** B. GOOGE *Heresbach's Husb.* III. (1586) 143 b, Their legges, if they happen to be broken,.. being wrapped first in wooll..and afterward splented. **1610** MARKHAM *Masterp.* II. cxxxix. 442 Then splent it [a broken bone] with three broad, smooth, & strong splents. **1639** T. DE GRAY *Expert Farrier* 243 Clap..over that a peece of leather cut and shaped for the purpose, and so splent it to keepe it fast on. **1648** HEXHAM II. s.v. *Spalcken*.

β. **1606** BP. W. BARLOW *Serm. 21 Sept.* B ij, To heale the infected, to splint the spreined, to reduce the wandring. **1612** WOODALL *Surg. Mate* Wks. (1653) 152 The member being onely artificially bound, and splinted orderly. **1725** *Fam. Dict.* s.v. *Surbating*, Stop up his Foot therewith,.. covering it with a Piece of an old Shoe, and splint it. **1842** BURN *Nav. & Milit. Dict.* I. s.v. *Attelle*, To splint, to put on a splint. **1875** BEDFORD *Sailor's Pocket Bk.* viii. (ed. 2) 303 If a broken limb be not splinted the ends may be forced through the skin.

†**b.** To secure or keep *in* (a dressing, etc.) with a splint or splints. *Obs. rare.*

1610 MARKHAM *Masterp.* II. ci. 385 With a little tow stoppe all the foote, and especially the frush, and splent it in so as it may not fall out.

c. *fig.* and *transf.* To strengthen or support as if with splints.

a **1634** CHAPMAN *Bussy d' Ambois* v. iv. (1641) 70 An Emperour might die standing, why not I? Nay without help, in which I will exceed him; For he died splinted with his chamber Groomes. **1832** *Examiner* 721/2 He wants strength of character;—but authority will come in aid of his peculiar deficiency, and splint him up. **1877** *Encycl. Brit.* VI. 108/2 Inner and outer layers of epithelial tissue, splinted by connective tissue.., are always developed.

†**d.** To stop with a splint. *Obs.*⁻⁰

1648 HEXHAM II, *Spalcken den mondt*, to Gagge or Splent the mouth.

†**3.** To cut or split (wood, etc.) into splints or splinters; to cleave or slit apart or *in two*. *Obs.*

1591 PERCIVALL *Sp. Dict.*, *Desgajar*, to cleaue a sunder, to slit, to splent. **1598** FLORIO, *Schiantare*,..to riue, to splint, to shiuer. **1600** ABBOT *Exp. Jonah* iv. 68 He looketh whether any planke were rift or splint in two.

†**b.** (See quot.) *Obs.*⁻¹

1737 BRACKEN *Farriery Impr.* (1757) II. 167 Where the Horse is young and fond of running, it would splint him, or knock him up (as we say) if the Rider were to make his Flourishes upon his Back like a Rope-dancer.

†**4.** *intr.* Of the heart: To burst or split. *Obs.*⁻¹

1594 CAREW *Tasso* (1881) 55 Hard heart of mine why splintst? why breakst not thou?

splintage (ˈsplɪntɪdʒ). [f. SPLINT *sb.*] The application or use of surgical or dental splints.

1891 in *Cent. Dict.* **1956** H. & A. J. KAZIS *Complete Mouth Rehabilitation* vii. 88 As a result of splintage there is a reduction of the stress load on the supporting bone. **1970** R. D. MUCKART in G. Murdoch *Prosthetic & Orthotic Pract.* xi. 471 Maintenance of mobility and the prevention of deformity or contracture is by far the most important function of upper-limb splintage. **1978** *Jrnl. R. Soc. Med.* LXXI. 186 The wrist fixation device is designed to control Colles' fracture by internal splintage.

splint-bone. Also **splint bone**, 9 **splent bone.** [SPLINT *sb.* 5, 10.]

1. *Farriery.* †**a.** = SPLINT *sb.* 5. *Obs.* **b.** One or other of the two small metacarpal bones of the foreleg of a horse, lying behind and in close contact with the cannon-bone or shank.

1704 *Lond. Gaz.* No. 4027/4 A Splint Bone in the inside of her near fore Leg. **1831** YOUATT *Horse* 64 The larger metacarpal or cannon or shank in front, the smaller metacarpal or splent bone behind. **1854** OWEN in *Orr's Circ. Sci., Org. Nat.* I. 244 The small bone called 'splint-bone', by veterinarians, articulated to the 'mesocuneiform', is the stunted metatarsal of the second toe..; the outer 'splint-bone', articulated to the 'cuboides', is the similarly stunted metatarsal of the fourth toe. **1881** *Fortn. Rev.* Dec. 751 But on each side of this enlarged toe there are, beneath the skin, rudimentary bones of two other toes, the so-called splint-bones.

2. *Anat.* = FIBULA 2.

1859 in MAYNE *Expos. Lex.*

splint coal. [Cf. SPLINT *sb.* 8.] Coal with a more or less splintery fracture; orig. a less bituminous variety of Scotch cannel coal; now chiefly, a hard and highly bituminous coal burning with great heat.

a. **1789** T. WILLIAMS *Min. Kingd.* I. 109 In this line the splent coal, etc. has been worked. **1801** *Encycl. Brit.* (ed. 3) Suppl. II. 231/2 A specimen of the slaty kind [of cannel coal] from Airshire, called *splent coal.* **1815** AIKIN *Min.* (ed. 2) 61 Candle Coal. Cannel Coal. Splent Coal.

β. **1839** URE *Dict. Arts* 963, I found good splint coal of the Glasgow field to have a specific gravity of 1·266. **1861** SIR W. FAIRBAIRN *Iron* 75 It is well known that the anthracite and splint coal can be used most effectively and economically with the hot-blast.

attrib. **1887** P. M'NEILL *Blawearie* 92 We remember.. traversing one [mine] in the splint coal seam barely two and a half feet wide.

'splinted, (*ppl.*) *a.* Also 6–7 **splented.** [f. SPLINT *sb.* or *v.*]

†**1.** Formed or made of, built with, splints or thin strips of wood. *Obs.*

1538 in *East Anglian* (1910) 227 At the backe side of a splented wall where the cley was broken away. **1703** [R. NEVE] *City & C. Purchaser* 207 Sifted through a fine Splinted-sieve.

†**2.** Cut into splints; split. *Obs.*

1616 SURFL. & MARKH. *Country Farme* II. lxii. 318 There are also other hiues which are made of splinted wands of hassell or such like pliant wood. **1624** CAPT. SMITH *Virginia* II. 34 To scarrifie a swelling, or make incision, their best instruments are some splinted stone.

3. Of a horse: Affected with the splint; having a splint or splints. *rare.*

1697 *Lond. Gaz.* No. 3323/4 Stolen.., a brown bay Gelding.., splinted under both his Knees.

4. Bound or held in a surgical splint or splints.

1888 W. E. HENLEY *Bk. Verses* 28 Stumps are shaking, crutch-supported; Splinted fingers tap the rhythm.

†**'splinten,** *a. Obs.*—[0] [f. SPLINT *sb.*] Made of splints (see quot.).

1688 HOLME *Armoury* III. xiv. (Roxb.) 17/1 The second [sort of basket] is made of more finer stuffe, the Rime and handles platted with shaved wood, the round bottome the like, woven very strongly togather... These are termed splenten Basketts.

splinter ('splɪntə(r)), *sb.* Forms: 5 **splynter,** 6– **splinter,** 7 **splenter.** [a. MDu. *splinter* (Du. and WFris. *splinter*), *splenter* (WFlem. *splenter*), = LG. *splinter* (hence in G.), *splenter*, related to SPLINT *sb.* Cf. SPLINDER *sb.*]

1. a. A rough (usually a comparatively long, thin, and sharp-edged) piece of wood, bone, stone, etc., split or broken off, esp. as the result of violent impact; a chip, fragment, or shiver.

1398 TREVISA *Barth. De P.R.* XVII. vii. (Bodl. MS.), A reod.. hurteþ þe hande sone wiþ splynters. *a* **1450** *Knt. de la Tour* (1868) 9 The staf brake,.. and the pece and the splinter therof lepte, and smote oute the ladies eye. **1578** LYTE *Dodoens* 56 It draweth forth thornes and Splinters or shivers. **1624** CAPT. SMITH *Virginia* II. 25 His arrowes were fiue quarters long, headed with the splinters of a white christall-like stone. **1657** TRAPP *Comm. Ps.* xxix. 6 God.. maketh those huge trees, the splinters of them, to flie up into the air. **1711** in *10th Rep. Hist. MSS. Comm.* App. V. 161 The bomb,..a splinter of which struck the lady. **1770** LANGHORNE *Plutarch* (Rtldg.) 478/1 An arrow shattered the bone in such a manner, that splinters were taken out. **1801** COL. STEWART in Nicolas *Disp. Nelson* (1845) IV. 308 A shot through the mainmast knocked a few splinters about us. **1841** H. MILLER *O.R. Sandst.* vi. 116 Almost..every splinter of sandstone, every limestone nodule, contained its organism. **1873** SPON *Workshop Rec.* Ser. I. 59 The best means of drilling holes in glass is by using a splinter of a diamond.

b. *fig.* and in fig. context.

1589 *Pappe w. Hatchet* To Father & Sons, Ile make such a splinter runne into your wits, as shal make them rankle till you become fooles. **1642** FULLER *Holy & Prof. St.* III. xx. 207 He fears not to have the splinters of his party (when it breaks) flie into his eyes. **1690** TEMPLE *Ess., Poetry* Wks. 1720 I. 245 This Vein of Conceit seemed proper for such Scraps or Splinters into which Poetry was broken. **1730** YOUNG *Ep. fr. Oxf.* 184 Satire recoils whenever charg'd too high, Round your own fame the fatal splinters fly. **1856** W. E. AYTOUN *Bothwell* (1857) 95 The splinters and the accidents That flash from every deed of crime.

c. Used (chiefly with negatives) to denote a very small piece or amount, or something of little or no value.

1606 SHAKS. *Tr. & Cr.* I. iii. 283 Hee'l say..The Grecian Dames are sun-burnt, and not worth The splinter of a Lance. **1658** OSBORNE *Mem. Jas. I*, 56 It is..the..Custome and pure Nature of Humanity to venerate the least splinter of Antiquity. **1728** MORGAN *Algiers* II. v. 320 As for the Ship he talked of, they were resolutely bent not to part with the least Splinter of it. **1769** HOME *Fatal Discov.* II, She is not worth the splinter of a spear.

d. In phr. *in* or *into splinters.* Also *all to splinters*, completely, thoroughly.

1612 DRAYTON *Poly-olb.* xii. 486 With the fearful shock, Their spears in splinters flew. **1656** RIDGLEY *Pract. Physick* 172 When the bone broken into Splinters, is thrust inward. **1711** STEELE *Spect.* No. 32 ¶2 Looking-Glasses.. sometimes shivered into ten thousand Splinters. **1757** W. WILKIE *Epigoniad* VIII. 258 Short from the steel, the staff in splinters broke. **1847** TENNYSON *Princ.* v. 483 Into fiery splinters leapt the lance. **1884** 'H. COLLINGWOOD' (W. Lancaster) *Under Meteor Flag* 159 We beat Flinn all to splinters.

e. A sharp piece of rock projecting from the main body.

1860 TYNDALL *Glac.* I. xiv. 94 A cliff, which afforded us.. some protruding splinters to lay hold of by the hands.

f. A splinter group (see sense 7 b below). orig. and chiefly *U.S.*

1948 *Sun* (Baltimore) 20 Aug. 1/2 The Republican party and its Dewey-Warren ticket, without 'leftist or extreme right splinters', is the nation's only hope 'to put an end to disunity'. **1972** D. E. WESTLAKE *Bank Shot* viii. 56 Probably a new splinter... They keep fractionalizing, makes it extremely difficult to keep proper surveillance. **1977** *New Yorker* 9 May 67/2 The old-guard splinter of the Congress which Mrs. Gandhi had routed in 1969. **1981** *Listener* 1 Jan. 24/1 A newly imaginative use of a Red Brigade splinter.

2. A surgical splint. *Obs.* or *dial.*

1597 A. M. tr. *Guillemeau's Fr. Chirurg.* 46 The splinter must be made of stiffe paper, of latinn, or of any other substance. **1658** A. FOX *Wurtz' Surg.* II. xvi. 122 These splinters were like such, as I used to Bone-fractures. **1820** A. COOPER, etc. *Surg. Ess.* (ed. 2) 165 The under splinter was a firm excavated piece of deal.

3. a. A comparatively thin piece or slender strip of wood prepared or used for some particular purpose. Cf. SPLINT *sb.* 2.

1648 HEXHAM II, *Een Schindel*, a Shingle, or a Splenter. **1673–4** GREW *Anat. Pl., Anat. Trunks* (1682) 121 The Perpendicular Splinters or Twigs of a Basket. **1723** *Pres. State Russia* I. 307 The Roofs are made of thin Splinters of Fir. **1842** LOUDON *Suburban Hort.* 271 Piercing the stems or roots by a longitudinal cut through a joint, and keeping the wound open with a wedge or splinter.

b. Used as a torch, or dipped in tallow and used as a candle.

1751 *England's Gaz.* s.v. *Macclesfield*, Fir-trees..which are dug up for various uses, but chiefly for splinters, that serve the poor for candles. **1791** W. BARTRAM *Carolina* 470 Some take with them little fascines of fat Pine splinters for torches. **1828** CROKER *Leg. S. Irel.* II. 155 While his rosy daughter held a splinter to her mother. **1851** T. H. TURNER *Dom. Archit.* I. ii. 68 It was therefore lit up with splinters and flambeaux. **1862** T. W. HIGGINSON *Army Life* (1870) 24 Perusing a hymn-book by the light of a pine splinter.

†**4.** A fibre or filament of undressed hemp. Cf. SHIVER *sb.*[1] 2. *Obs.*—[1]

1673 BOYLE *Ess. Effluviums* II. 15 The thrids or splinters of Hemp the Rope was made up of.

†**5.** = SPLINT *sb.* 5. *Obs.*—[1]

1704 *Dict. Rust.* (1726) s.v. *Rules buying Horses*, If there be hard knots on the inside of the Leg, they are Splinters.

6. *ellipt.* = SPLINTER-BAR 2. *rare.*

1794 FELTON *Carriages* (1801) I. 62 The front bar to a single-horse carriage is what the draught is mostly taken from, by means of a splinter hung thereto. **1801** tr. *Gabrielli's Myst. Husb.* II. 68 The driver..appeared to have his doubts whether he should not object to my getting into the elegant vehicle, the splinter being certainly, in his opinion, more calculated for a person in my station.

7. a. *attrib.* and *Comb.*, as ***splinter forceps, -hoop, wound***; **splinter bid** *Bridge*, an unusual jump bid showing a singleton or void in the suit bid; **splinter-deck**, an armour-plated deck on a ship (see also quot. 1909); **splinter hæmorrhage**, a narrow, elongated hæmorrhage resembling one produced by a splinter; **splinter net, -netting** *Naut.*, a net or netting of small rope spread on board a warship during action to protect the men from falling splinters; **splinter-new** *a. dial.* [cf. G. *splinterneu*, Du. *splinternieuw*, etc.], quite new. See also SPLINTER-BAR, -PROOF.

1977 *Oxf. Times* 11 Feb. 8/7 The bidding went: One Heart —pass—Three Spades (*splinter bid showing a singleton or void together with a heart fit). **1978** *N.Y. Times* 29 Mar. C 25/2 For slam purposes, the splinter bid, or unusual jump to show a singleton or a void, solves many problems. **1909** *Cent. Dict.* Suppl. 346/2 A deck worked for protective purposes below a protective deck is called the *splinter-deck. **1933** *Jane's Fighting Ships* 171 Above again is a 1$\frac{1}{16}$" splinter deck against aerial attack. **1973** J. QUICK *Dict. Weapons & Mil. Terms* 416/3 *Splinter deck*, a deck fitted with armor. **1895** *Arnold & Sons' Catal. Surg. Instrum.* 82 *Splinter Forceps. **1931** W. BOYD *Path. Internal Dis.* i. 40 There may be small '*splinter hemorrhages' under the nail —a linear track as if a sliver had been run in. **1971** ROBBINS & ANGELL *Basic Path.* ix. 274/2 Seeding of the nail beds and of the skin produces small petechial hemorrhages known as 'splinter hemorrhages' or microabscesses. **1681** GREW *Musæum* IV. iii. 374 A plain Indian Fan,..Made of the small stringy parts of Roots,..bound together with a *Splinter-Hoop. **1894** *Daily News* 21 Mar. 5/2 Bulkheads, boats, *splinter nets. **1799** *Hull Advertiser* 17 Aug. 4/2 The flames coming up the companion and setting fire to the *splinter netting. **1830** MARRYAT *King's Own* xvii, The hatchways being covered over with a strong splinter-netting. **1824–** *Splinter-new (in Sc., Cumbld., Yks. dial. glossaries and texts). **1833** M. SCOTT *Tom Cringle* ix, The *splinter wound in his head burst afresh.

b. *attrib.* or as *adj.* Of or pertaining to a group, party, etc., which splits itself off as an independent entity from a larger political or social group, esp. as ***splinter group***. orig. *N. Amer.*

1935 *Economist* 19 Oct. 742/2 The new 'splinter parties', it will be observed—the Co-operative Commonwealth Federation (farmer-labour), Mr. H. H. Stevens's 'Reconstructionists', and the Social Credit League—have hardly succeeded in making a scratch on the traditional surface of Canadian politics. **1948** *Manch. Guardian Weekly* 15 Jan. 5/2 He challenges the Republicans to dodge the stigma of reaction and encourages the Wallace 'splinter groups' to hold firm. **1948** *Sun* (Baltimore) 23 Feb. 8/3 While splinter minorities may have a voice in the legislature, they cannot extend that voice beyond their own minority base. **1950** *Times* 27 Feb. 5/3 The Cabinet is made up of an uneasy coalition of splinter parties. **1958** *Spectator* 17 Jan. 73/2 The formation of superior-minded splinter groups which have no wish to become part of the main body of the Church. **1898** MIDDLETON & TAIT *Tribes without Rulers* 209 Splinter-segments of a clan do not form cores of tribes. **1964** R. BRADDON *Year Angry Rabbit* v. 43 The fourteen new splinter nations now beginning to flake off the edges of a ripely rich Soviet Russia. **1968** *Guardian* 17 June 8/1 The ineffective splinter-group politics of the Fourth Republic. **1975** *N.Y. Times* 8 Nov. 26/2 The women's movement has increasingly allowed itself to be dominated..by radical splinter groups and issues which lack support among the majority of women. **1978** L. HEREN *Growing up on The Times* ix. 293 Malcolm X formed a splinter movement, the organization of Afro-American unity. **1979** D. SANDERS *Queen sends for Mrs Chadwick* 82 Supposing..the two main parties are dead-locked... They would have to turn to whatever splinter party happened to be closest to their own line.

splinter ('splɪntə(r)), *v.* [f. the sb. Cf. Du. *splinteren*, WFris. *splinterje*, LG. and G. *splintern*; WFlem. *splenteren.*]

1. a. *trans.* To break or split into splinters or long narrow pieces, or in such a way as to leave a rough jagged end or projections.

1582 STANYHURST *Æneis* I. (Arb.) 21 The oars are cleene splintred. **1593** NASHE *Christ's T.* Wks. (Grosart) IV. 53 My leane withered hands..are all to shiuered and splinterd in their wide cases of skinne. **1769** FALCONER *Dict. Marine* (1780) s.v. *Engagement*, This mutual assault..: battering, penetrating, and splintering the sides and decks. **1806** *Monthly Mag.* XXI. 403 A strong bull..splintered with his horns the upper post. **1867** TROLLOPE *Chron. Barset* II. lxxvii. 325 The trees that the storms have splintered are never of use. **1898** WOLLOCOMBE *Fr. Morn till Eve* v. 48 The top of the pole..had been splintered, and was held together by a very thin shred.

b. *fig.* and in fig. context.

1603 SHAKS. *Ham.* III. i. 159 (Q.[1]), The Courtier, Scholler, Souldier, all in him, All dasht and splinterd thence. **1849** M. ARNOLD *Mycerinus* 99 While the deep-burnish'd foliage overhead Splinter'd the silver arrows of the moon. **1859** TENNYSON *Guinev.* 18 [He] sought To make disruption in the Table Round Of Arthur, and to splinter it into feuds.

c. To bring or cause to fall *down*, to break off or rend *from*, in splinters.

1807 J. BARLOW *Columb.* VII. 230 High from the decks the mortar's bursting fires Sweep the full streets, and splinter down the spires. **1871** L. STEPHEN *Playgr. Eur.* (1894) xiii. 320 Long lines of the débris that have been splintered by frost from the higher wall [of rock].

d. To form by shivering or splitting.

1878 BROWNING *La Saisiaz* 7 Five short days, sufficient hardly to entice, from out its den Splintered in the slab, this pink perfection of the cyclamen.

†**2.** To bind, fix, or secure by means of a splint or splints; = SPLINT *v.* 2. Freq. *fig.* Also with *up. Obs.*

1594 SHAKS. *Rich. III*, II. ii. 118 The broken rancour of your high-swolne hates, But lately splinter'd, knit, and ioyn'd together. **1623** FLETCHER & ROWLEY *Maid in Mill* I. iii, Those men have broken credits, Loose and dismembred faiths..That splinter 'em with vows. **1659** BP. WREN *Monarchy Asserted* 148 That Place, which I find..so strangely shattered, that it will be very hard for Me to Splinter up the broken confused Pieces of it. **1720** DE FOE *Capt. Singleton* iv. (1840) 73 As to his arm, he found one of the bones broken;..and this he set, and splintered it up, and bound his arm in a sling.

3. a. *intr.* To split; to break, burst, or fly *into* or *to* splinters or fragments; to come *away* in splinters.

1625 J. GLANVILLE *Voy. Cadiz* (Camden) 48 This forte was built of a kinde of stone not apt to splinter. **1802** AIKIN *Woodl. Comp.* (1815) 5 Oak-timber is fitted for this purpose [i.e. shipbuilding],..by the property of not readily splintering. *a* **1832** CRABBE *Posth. Tales* x. 97 The dry boughs splinter in the windy gale. **1857** MILLER *Elem. Chem., Org.* ii. 99 When heated, it [i.e. anthracite] splinters into small fragments. **1886** G. R. SIMS *Ring o' Bells* I. i. 42 The boy..tugged at the iron ring till the rotten woodwork splintered away from the bolt.

b. *poet.* To pierce *through* in the form of, or after the manner of, splinters.

1821 CLARE *Vill. Minstr.* I. 80 Stronger lightnings splinter through the cloud. *Ibid.* 213 The moon..Splinters through the broken glass.

c. *fig.* To break off to form a splinter group or groups; *loosely*, to divide or split. Also with *off.*

1967 M. L. KING *Trumpet of Conscience* iii. 49 Under the impact of social forces unique to their times, young people have splintered into three principal groups, though of course there is some overlap among the three. **1972** *Guardian* 11 Jan. 9/1 Later Frank Ashbourn joined them.. and in May 1970 he and Mersh splintered off to form South Sea Bubble. **1976** *Oxford Diocesan Mag.* July 11/1 But the village's young people, distressed at seeing the parishioners splinter off to other towns for church, asked to hold the new prayer assembly in place of Mass.

splinter-bar. Also **splinter bar.** [f. SPLINTER *sb.*]

1. A swingle-tree or whipple-tree.

1765 *Museum Rust.* IV. 78 A two-wheeled plough complete, with draught-chain, and splinter-bars, or whipple-trees. **1767** S. PATERSON *Anoth. Trav.* I. 104 A splinter-bar at the end of the traces, to which a small cord leading from the mast is fastened. **1793** W. H. MARSHALL *Rur. Econ. W. Eng.* (1796) II. 350 The yoke and single chain ..are..much preferable to collars, traces, and splinter bars. **1855** RUFFINI *Dr. Antonio* i, The rearing of the leader was caused by the knocking of the splinter bar against his legs. **1893** *Spectator* 23 Dec. 909 The plough-teams with looped-up splinter-bars banging against the trace-chains.

2. A cross-bar in a carriage, coach, or other vehicle, which is fixed across the head of the shafts, and to which the traces are attached.

The definition in Webster (1847), 'A cross-bar in a coach, which supports the springs', is repeated by later Dicts.

1794 W. FELTON *Carriages* (1801) I. 59 The draught is much preferable when taken from a splinter-bar, which yields to the motion and pull of the horse. **1837** W. B. ADAMS *Carriages* 145 The distance of the splintre [*sic*] bar from the central pin or perch bolt is regulated by the size of the wheels. **1859** F. A. GRIFFITHS *Artill. Man.* (1862) 167, 4 Spare Splinter Bars,..4 pair of Shafts, per Battery, are distributed among the Waggons. **1877** THRUPP *Hist. Coaches* ii. 33 The horses are harnessed to splinter or drawing bars.

transf. **1890** D. K. CLARK *Steam Engine* II. 408 The splinter-bar is formed of 3-inch angle-iron, ½ inch thick, and is connected to the axle by two wrought-iron arms.

b. With distinguishing terms.

1802 *Sporting Mag.* XX. 308 Affixed to the usual or main splinter-bar. **1852** BURN *Nav. & Milit. Dict.* II. 280 Swing splinter-bar, or rear master-bar, *volée mobile de derrière.*

splintered (ˈsplɪntəd), *ppl. a.* [f. SPLINTER *v.*] Broken into splinters; split off as a splinter; shattered, shivered.

1718 *Free-thinker* No. 95. 283 A Seamstress has been.. sadly wounded by the splintered Glass. **1791** COWPER *Yardley Oak* 128 A splinter'd stump bleach'd to a snowy white. **1804** ABERNETHY *Surg. Obs.* 183 It would be right.. to take away the splintered portions of bone. **1842** TENNYSON *Sir Galahad* i, The splinter'd spear-shafts crack and fly. **1871** L. STEPHEN *Playgr. Eur.* (1894) xiii. 333 The occasional fall of a splintered fragment of rock.

b. Of rocks, etc.: Ragged or jagged through splintering.

1833 TENNYSON *Dream Fair Wom.* xlvii, The splinter'd crags that wall the dell With spires of silver shine. **1850** B. TAYLOR *Eldorado* v. (1862) 42 A chain of splintered peaks in the distance. **1867** MORRIS *Jason* XIV. 38 A little bay Walled from the sea by splintered cliffs and grey.

ˈsplintering (ˈsplɪntərɪŋ), *vbl. sb.* [f. as prec.] The action or process of breaking into splinters. Also *fig.*

1815 SCOTT *Guy M.* x, A large fragment of the rock.. had fallen without any great diminution by splintering. **1865** KINGSLEY *Herew.* xv, What splintering of lances there will be about her! **1889** WELCH *Text Bk. Naval Archit.* vi. 89 On account of the splintering which would ensue should the unarmoured side be struck by shot. **1958** *Listener* 11 Sept. 366/2 He [*sc.* Ben-Gurion] is.. haunted by a well-nigh perverse splintering of political parties at home. **1968** P. OLIVER *Screening Blues* ii. 62 The distinctions in the names [of Negro Churches] were indicative of the splintering of the churches into separate factions.

attrib. **1846** GREENER *Sci. Gunnery* 59 Their splintering powers are certainly very extensive indeed.

So **ˈsplintering** *ppl. a.*, that splinters; also of sound.

1828 SPEARMAN *Brit. Gunner* (ed. 2) 323 To produce the greatest damage to any splintering object. **1889** DOYLE *Micah Clarke* 292 A splintering crash from inside the Cathedral announced some fresh outrage.

splinterless (ˈsplɪntəlɪs), *a.* [f. SPLINTER *v.* + -LESS.] Of glass: guaranteed not to break into splinters; = SPLINTER-PROOF *a.* 2 (now the more usual term).

1928 *Sunday Express* 15 Jan. 6 The manufacture of splinterless glass. **1928** *Daily Express* 19 June 3 A splinterless shock-proof safety glass.

splinter-proof, *sb.* and *a.* [See PROOF *a.* 1 b.]

A. *sb. Mil.* A structure serving for protection from the splinters of bursting shells.

1805 JAMES *Milit. Dict.* (ed. 2), *Splinter-proof*, a fence or guard... It consists of a shelving sort of frame.. of.. timber. **1832** SOUTHEY *Hist. Penins. War* III. 705 There were no Barracks, nor any covering for the troops except holes,.. to serve for them as splinter-proofs. **1863** P. BARRY *Dockyard Econ.* 15 From the security of the splinter-proofs at Shoeburyness. **1884** *Milit. Engin.* I. II. 41 The splinter-proofs which form the roof of this cover must be laid in position.. before the construction of the battery is commenced.

B. *adj.* **1.** *Mil.* Of sufficient strength to ward off the splinters of bursting shells.

1834 J. S. MACAULAY *Field Fortification* 71 The best description of field powder-magazine, is constructed of splinter-proof timbers of about 10 inches by 8. **1884** *Milit. Engin.* I. II. 38 Gun-pits and epaulments,.. screened and provided with splinter-proof cover for the gun detachments.

2. That does not break into splinters; designed so as not to splinter.

1941 *AWA Techn. Rev.* V. 214 The control panel is mounted.. below a re-entrant window of splinter-proof glass. **1964** *Economist* 19 Sept. 1124/3 A perfect mirror. It is unbreakable, splinterproof, lightweight.

splintery (ˈsplɪntərɪ), *a.* (and *adv.*) Also 8–9 splintry. [f. SPLINTER *sb.* and *v.* + -Y. Cf. Du. *splinterig*, WFris. *splinterich.*]

1. *Min.* Of fracture: Characterized by the production of small splinters.

1796 KIRWAN *Elem. Min.* (ed. 2) I. 34 Of this [i.e. compact] fracture there are six sorts, the uneven, even, conchoidal, splintery, earthy, and hackly. **1799** —— *Geol. Ess.* 215 Primitive limestone.. is said sometimes to discover a splintry fracture. **1804** *Edin. Rev.* III. 301 Let its fracture be splintery, and it becomes hornstein. **1884** J. E. LEE tr. *Römer's Bone Caves of Ojcow* 2 A compact white oolitic limestone with a splintery or flatly conchoidal fracture.

2. Of stone, minerals, etc.: Liable to split into splinters; breaking or separating easily into splinters; *spec.* having a splintery fracture.

1807 VANCOUVER *Agric. Devon* (1813) 11 In those places where the upper parts of the rock are of a splintry texture. **1823** W. SCORESBY *Jrnl.* 405 Common calcedony, inclining to splintery quartz. **1886** FENN *Patience Wins* 50 The stone we found here and there was slaty and splintery.

b. Of rocks, etc.: Marked by splintering; rough or jagged.

1829 SCOTT *Anne of G.* i, The ridgy precipices.. showed their splintery and rugged edges over the vapour. **1843** RUSKIN *Mod. Paint.* I. II I. vii. §5. 76 Salvator bids him stand under some contemptible fragment of splintery crag. **1876** PAGE *Adv. Text-bk. Geol.* xi. 194 Abounding in steep precipices and splintery peaks.

3. Of the nature of a splinter; resembling a splinter in shape or form.

1839 URE *Dict. Arts* 978 To prevent the seam, which forms the ceiling over the workmen's heads, from falling down and killing them by its splintery fragments. **1880** BLACKMORE *Mary Anerley* III. 24 There was no severe cold yet;.. no splintery needles of sparkling drift.

fig. **1836** LANDOR *Min. Pr. Pieces* Wks. 1853 II. 457/1, I was never an admirer.. of those abrupt and splintery sentences, which.. sparkle only when they are broken.

Comb. **1888** RUTLEY *Rock-Forming Min.* 192 The laths do not show splintery-looking ends.

4. Abounding in or full of splinters.

1857 DICKENS *Dorrit* xi, It was a large room, with a rough, splintery floor.

5. As *adv.* In a splintering manner. *rare*$^{-1}$.

1784 *Phil. Trans.* LXXIV. 453 It.. breaks more woody and splintery.

splinting (ˈsplɪntɪŋ), *vbl. sb.* Also 6 splyntyng, splentynge, 7 splenting. [f. SPLINT *v.*]

†**1.** The action of constructing or providing with splints or laths; the material used in this. *Obs.*

1527 *Luton Trin. Guild* (1906) 190 Payd to Thomas Long for vnderpynnynge, splentynge, & davbing & for Roddis, vs. jd. **1622** CALLIS *Stat. Sewers* (1647) 110 If a house be decayed in splinting, thack, walling, or in such petty matters.

2. a. The action of putting into surgical or dental splints; binding or securing by means of a splint or splints.

1548 ELYOT, *Mora*,.. a staye that surgions vse in splyntyng of sore legges. **1611** COTGR., *Esclisser*, to bind vp in splents, or keepe straight by splenting. **1648** HEXHAM II, *Een Spalckinge*, a Splenting of broken bones. **1897** *Trans. Amer. Pediatric Soc.* IX. 168 b, His mother having learned of the splinting of his arms and hands at night. **1960** W. L. MCCRACKEN *Partial Denture Construction* xiv. 270 Splinting should not be used for the purpose of retaining a tooth that would otherwise be condemned for periodontal reasons.

b. *concr.* Material for a splint or splints.

1895 *Arnold & Sons' Catal. Surg. Instrum.* 671 Splinting (Gooch's),.. per piece 18 × 22.

†**3.** Splintering, splitting. *Obs.*$^{-0}$

1598 FLORIO, *Schiantatura*, a riuing, a splinting, a shiuering.

ˈsplinty, *a.* Now *rare.* Also 8 splenty. [f. SPLINT *sb.* + -Y.] Of a splintery nature or texture; of the nature of splint or splint coal.

1611 COTGR., *Esquilleux*, splintie, scalie; full of little splints, or scales. **1725** *Phil. Trans.* XXXIII. 397 The undermost [vein] is about eighteen Fathoms from the Surface, call'd the Splenty Coal..; it's a hard but not large Coal. **1789** J. WILLIAMS *Min. Kingd.* I. 109 Splenty coals and others.. are wrought to the south-west of Dalkeith. **1840** *Civil Eng. & Arch. Jrnl.* III. 414/2 This ore is generally found.. in caverns or churns of the mountain limestone in large masses, splinty and globulated. **1881** in *Eng. Dial. Dict.*

splirt, *v. Sc.* and *dial.* [Cf. SPLURT *v.*] *intr.* To spirt or spout.

1791 LEARMONT *Poems* 79 E'en thy ga' Splirts on law stations frae thy sting. **1825-** in some northern and midland dial. glossaries.

splish-splash, *v. rare.* [f. SPLASH *v.*[1], with usual variation of vowel.] *intr.* To splash repeatedly.

1720 SWIFT *Irish Feast* 44 The Floor is all wet,.. While the Water and Sweat, Splish, splash in their Pumps. **1834** MEDWIN *Angler in Wales* I. 160 They went splish-splashing through an almost interminable inundation.

So **splishy-splashy** *a.*, sloppy, slushy. *rare*$^{-1}$.

c **1850** *Denham Tracts* (1895) II. 72 A cold, comfortless (splishy-splashy) Sabbath morning.

split (splɪt), *sb.*[1] Also 6 splitte, 7 splitt. [f. SPLIT *v.* and *ppl. a.* Cf. LG. *splitt*, G. *spliss*, NFris. *spledd.*]

1. a. A narrow break or opening made by splitting; a cleft, crack, rent, or chink; a fissure.

1597 A. M. tr. *Guillemeau's Fr. Chirurg.* lf. xiv b/2 That which must entre into the splitte, or els betweene the depressed bones. *Ibid.* lf. xvii b/2 In the which is a splitte, throughe the which the blade passeth. **1648** HEXHAM II, *Een Splete*, a Split, or a Cleft. **1849** CUPPLES *Green Hand* iv. (1856) 50 The long ragged split to westward was opened up, and a clear glaring glance of the sky.. shot through it. **1855** RUFFINI *Dr. Antonio* ii, I see a split in that door behind your bed. **1888** RUTLEY *Rock-Forming Min.* 171 The cleavage planes.. give rise to striations or fine splits.

b. *techn.* An angular groove cut on glass vessels.

1850 HOLTZAPFFEL *Turning* III. 1299 For angular grooves, or splits, up the side of a decanter, or similar object, a mill with an angular edge is employed. **1891** *Sale Catal. Glass Wks. Stourbridge*, Twenty clarets, cut splits.

c. A division formed by splitting.

1875 BUCKLAND *Log-Bk.* 227 A horn on one side branching into splits, the other being perfect in form.

2. a. A piece of wood separated or formed by splitting. Now *U.S.*

1617 MINSHEU *Ductor* 462/2 Splits, or splents of wood. **1633** FORD *'Tis Pity* v. iii, Some under-shrubs shall in my weighty fall Be crush'd to splits; with me they all shall perish! **1664** *Min. Bk. Coopers Glasgow* in Jamieson *Suppl.* (1887) 321 That.. nane of thame.. sal buy any runges, stinges, splittis, or stappis, from the saidis four persounes. **1725** *Family Dict.* s.v. *Bee-Hive*, And these are either Wicker-Hives, made with Splits of Wood,.. or Straw-Hives. **1778** PRYCE *Min. Cornub.* 151 To each crank is fixed a straight half split of balk timber. **1837** HEBERT *Engin. & Mech. Encycl.* I. 154 The osiers are divided into four parts, lengthways, which are called splits. **1864** LOWELL *Fireside Trav.* 151 Making our bed of some 'splits' which we poked from the roof. **1875** KNIGHT *Dict. Mech.* 2281/2 *Split*, a ribbon of wood rived from a rough piece of green timber.

Comb. **1872** DE VERE *Americanisms* 58 Hickory and oak both yield the necessary wood, and chairs of this kind are known, especially in the South, as split-bottom chairs. **1893** T. N. PAGE *Ole Virginia* 204 He was plumped down in his great split-bottomed chair.

b. *Weaving.* A dent (orig. a piece of split reed or cane) in the reed of a loom. *Sc.*

1748 *Rec. Elgin* (1903) I. 188 The web of 1200 wrought two's in a reed containing 1200 splits upon 40½in. **1839** URE *Dict. Arts* 1056 In Scotland, the splits of cane which pass between the.. ribs of the reed, are expressed by hundreds, porters, and splits. The porter is 20 splits. **1875** KNIGHT *Dict. Mech.* 1903/2 Two warp-threads count for 1 split.

c. *techn.* (See quot. 1858.)

1858 SIMMONDS *Dict. Trade*, *Splits*, a term, in the leather trade, for divided skins which have been separated into two sections by the cutting machine; there being tanned splits and salted splits. **1875** KNIGHT *Dict. Mech.* 2281/2 Splits of the smaller skins, such as goat and sheep, are made into wash or glove leather. **1882** *Encycl. Brit.* XIV. 386 In the case of a single split the portions form a grain and flesh side.

d. *Canad.* (chiefly *Newfoundland*). A piece of kindling-wood. Usu. in *pl.*

1858 R. T. S. LOWELL *New Priest in Conception Bay* I. 74 The fire, where the round bake-pot stood, covered with its blazing 'splits'. **1919** W. T. GRENFELL *Labrador Days* 198 'Get a few more splits, then, boy,' she replied, 'and I'll be cutting t' pork t' while.' **1976** TAYLOR & HORWOOD *Beyond Road* 55 Well, one time I was only a small boy gettin' in the splits—that's kindling.

e. *Anglo-Irish.* A piece of bogwood burned for illumination.

1892 *Ballymena Observer* 29 Apr. 6/1 *Splits*, long thin pieces of bogwood used for giving light. **1957** E. E. EVANS *Irish Folk Ways* xiv. 185 Considerable use was made of buried timber dug from the bogs, of oak for roofing beams and.. resinous 'splits' to give light.

3. a. A rupture, breach, division, or dissension in a party or sect, or between friends.

1729 WODROW *Corr.* (1843) III. 439 The brethren.. might meet together,.. and consider what was to be done.. to guard against a split among ourselves. **1826** SCOTT *Diary* 21 Jan., I fear the split betwixt Constable and Cadell will render impossible what might otherwise be hopeful enough. **1852** DISRAELI *Ld. G. Bentinck* xxv. 520 He felt.. that there would be a 'split' in the ranks. **1886** DK. DEVONSHIRE in B. Holland *Life* (1911) II. xxi. 127 The responsibility of provoking an open split in the party.. was too great.

b. A body or party formed by a rupture or schism.

1883 *Standard* 22 Mar. 2/1 The Patriotic Brotherhood.. consisted of part of the 'splits' of the Old Ribbon Society combined. **1891** *Newcastle Daily Jrnl.* 9 Mar. 8/2 'Do you belong to the split?' asked one Scotchman of another.

4. a. (*at*) *full split*, or *like split*, at full speed; as fast as possible. *U.S.*

1836 HALIBURTON *Clockm.* Ser. I. xxx, Most on 'em, arter the second shot, cut and run full split. *a* **1848** MAJ. DOWNING *May-day in N.Y.* 64 (Bartlett), There was no end to the one-hoss teams, goin' like split all over the city. **1867** *Routledge's Ev. Boy's Ann.* 665 [To] drive by so close, at full split, as to just turn the fly round. **1890** 'R. BOLDREWOOD' *Robbery under Arms* 145 Out of the house in one minute, and in saddle and off full-split the next.

b. *the splits*, in acrobatics or stage-dancing: (see quot. 1883). Also in sing.

1861 MAYHEW *Lond. Labour* III. 90, I had to do the splits and strides. *Ibid.* 99/2, I had learnt to do a split, holding a half-hundred in my teeth. **1883** *Chambers's Jrnl.* 130 Doing the splits is.. separating the legs until they extend at right angles to the body, which is thus lowered to the ground. **1895** *Pall Mall G.* 1 Feb. 4/2 The average music-hall audience.. demanding extravagant high-kicking, splits, and cart-wheels.

c. The act or process of splitting; an instance of this.

1898 *Allbutt's Syst. Med.* V. 914 Blows or crushes resulting in the split of a vessel.. have produced aortic aneurism. **1902** *N. & Q.* 9th Ser. IX. 172/1 One of the most striking 'splits' [of an infinitive].

d. *U.S.* = *split-up* s.v. SPLIT-.

1972 *N.Y. Law Jrnl.* 10 Oct. 3/2 Tacking is permitted for stock dividends and splits, recapitalizations, [etc.]. **1976** [see *split-down* s.v. SPLIT-].

5. *Mining.* **a.** (See quot. 1881.)

1877 RAYMOND *Statist. Mines & Mining* 316 The ore in the western branches of the two splits is decidedy softer than that in the eastern ones. **1881** —— *Mining Gloss.* s.v., When a parting in a coal-seam becomes so thick that the two portions of the seam must be worked separately, each is called a *split*.

b. A division of a ventilating air-current.

1883 GRESLEY *Gloss. Coal-m.* 231 Each separate district should have its own split of fresh air. **1892** *Labour Comm. Gloss.* No. 3, *Splits*, the radiating passages through which the main current of air ventilating a mine is subdivided or *split* up for circulation.

c. (See quot.)

1886 J. BARROWMAN *Sc. Mining Terms* 63 *Split*, a room or end driven through a pillar.

6. *slang.* An informer; a detective; a policeman.

1812 J. H. VAUX *Flash Dict.*, To *split upon* a person, or *turn split*, is synonymous with *nosing*,.. or *turning nose.* **1857** *Slang Dict.* 19. **1891** M. WILLIAMS *Later Leaves* xxvii. 326 A man came into one of the other compartments, and.. said: 'You are talking to a split'. **1932** 'G. ORWELL' *Coll. Essays* (1968) I. 89 He would.. exclaim 'Fucking toe-rag!'..

meaning the 'split' who had arrested him. **1935** G. Ingram *Cockney Cavalcade* xiii. 202 'Here's the 'splits', boys!' A young lad who had been at the entrance with some others, had seen a police-car draw up and risked his liberty by dashing in to warn the hall occupants. **1966** W. Merrilees *Short Arm of Law* 140 At this point a destination board attendant asked another railway employee what the splits were after.

7. *colloq.* **a.** A drink composed of two liquors.
1882 *Society* 11 Nov. 22/2 The 'nips', the 'stims', the 'sherries and Angosturas', the 'splits' of young Contango. **1892** *Nation* 28 July 66/1 One of the principal of the illicit beverages is a deadly compound called 'split', composed of alcohol and water.

b. A split soda; a bottle of mineral water half the usual size; a half-bottle of champagne.
1884 G. Moore *Mummer's Wife* (1887) 168 When she had finished Montgomery tried to persuade her to try a 'split' with him. **1896** *Bradford Observer* 5 Oct., Apollinaris [table water]. Now supplied in splits. **1973** T. Pynchon *Gravity's Rainbow* i. 5 All that's keeping him up there is an empty champagne split in his hip pocket, that's got hooked somehow. **1980** *N.Y. Times* 6 Nov. c2/3 To uncork a split of Champagne, some of which froths to the ground.

c. A split roll or bun.
1905 *Westm. Gaz.* 29 Dec. 2/1 We..were dried and warmed and given hot tea, splits and butter, and cakes.

d. A split vote.
1894 *Westm. Gaz.* 28 Aug. 7/1 If Mr. Burgess got Conservative splits, as well as split votes between himself and Mr. Broadhurst.

e. A sweet dish consisting of sliced fruit (esp. banana, split open lengthways), with ice-cream, syrup, etc. orig. *U.S.*
1920, etc. [see *banana split* s.v. banana 4]. **1936** [see parfait]. **1938** G. Greene *Brighton Rock* i. i. 17 That's what I want, a sundae. Delia likes splits best. **1939** A. Huxley *After Many a Summer* i. x. 135 Virginia was at the soda-counter, pensively eating a chocolate-and-banana split. **1979** M. Denny *Fruit in Season* 33 Banana splits... Place one banana per person in a dish with a portion of ice-cream in the centre... Pour a little chocolate sauce over.

f. *N. Amer.* A split-level house.
1970 *Toronto Daily Star* 24 Sept. 28/7 Back splits, side splits, bungalows. **1976** *Billings* (Montana) *Gaz.* 6 July 5-d/7 (Advt.), This gorgeously decorated 4 level split. **1980** *Times* 7 Apr. 5/6 French-speakers [in Montreal] would buy 'side halls, split levels, back splits'.

g. A split shift (see split *ppl. a.* 3 a).
1973 R. Busby *Pattern of Violence* iii. 41 I'm working the split today. Get that boss of yours to give you a couple of hours off. **1977** P. Carter *Under Goliath* xxvi. 145 She.. went moaning on... They were still at it at nine o'clock when Mr Black came back from his split.

8. *slang.* **a.** A division or share of the proceeds of a legal or illegal undertaking.
1889 Clarkson & Richardson *Police!* xxiii. 321 A share. .. Regular, split, drop. **1916** *Variety* 27 Oct. 12/1 W. S. Campbell..would not accept the 55–45 division of the receipts offered by the management, Campbell wanting a 50–50 split. **1934** J. T. Farrell *Young Manhood of Studs Lonigan* xiii. 206, I wasn't working for a long time, and then I got me this job, and now I'm also lined up with a can-house, and get my split on anybody I bring there. **1964** J. P. Clark *Three Plays* 121 Both thieves Will certainly be content to settle For an even split. **1973** J. Leasor *Host of Extras* i. 24 'I'll give you five thousand cash, the pair.' I must know *someone* who could advance this on the promise of a fifty per cent split down the middle of the selling price?

b. *N. Amer.* A girl, a woman.
1935 A. J. Pollock *Underworld Speaks* 111/2 *Split*, a girl. **1975** *Globe & Mail* (Toronto) 16 Dec. 9/5 An announcement was posted that the force's first female officer Constable Jacqueline Hall, had been hired. 'He's gone and hired another split, as if we don't have enough whores and splits in the department already,' Mrs. Nesbitt quoted the sergeant as saying.

9. *Croquet.* (See quot. 1961.)
1896 *Cassell's Bk. Sports & Pastimes* 305 The Split is a stroke used when you desire in taking croquet to move both balls some distance. **1961** *Croquet* ('Know the Game' Ser.) 36/1 *Split*, a croquet stroke in which the balls go in different directions.

10. *U.S. Sports.* A draw; a drawn series of matches.
1967 [see double-header c]. **1974** *Cleveland* (Ohio) *Plain Dealer* 13 Oct. c1/1 The loss evened the C's exhibition slate to 2–2 and gave them a split in the two-game series with the Toros. **1976** *Springfield* (Mass.) *Daily News* 22 Apr. 40/2 With the VL getting only a split in six battles.

†**split**, *sb.*[2] *Obs. rare.* [Given by earlier Continental writers (16–17th cent.) as an Alpine or 'Illyrian' name.] (See quots.)
1713 Petiver in *Phil. Trans.* XXVIII. 212 Yellow Fumitory or Split. *Ibid.* 213 Its glaucous Leaves and pale Flowers, differ it from the yellow Split.

split (splɪt), *v.* Pa. t. and pa. pple. **split** (also 6– **splitted**, 9 **splitten**). [ad. MDu. *splitten* (Du. *splitten*, WFris. *splitte*), obscurely related to *spletten* splet *v.* and *splīten* (Du. *splijten*), MLG. and LG. *splīten*, MHG. *splīzen* (G. *spleissen*), etc. Cf. also spleet *v.*[2] The earlier examples and senses indicate a nautical origin for the use of the word in English.]
It is doubtful whether the following early example is a figurative use of sense 1 b, or of sense 2:—
1576 Gascoigne *Steele Gl.* E iij b, Great Alexander, drounde in drunkennesse, Cæsar and Pompey, split with priuy grudge.

I. *trans.* **1.** Of storms, rocks, etc.: To break up (a ship); to cause to part asunder. Chiefly in *pass.*
1590 Shaks. *Com. Err.* i. i. 104 Our helpefull ship was splitted in the midst. **1597** J. King *On Jonas* (1618) 53 It fell not vpon rocks or shelues, but by the power of the onely winde was almost splitted. **1604** E. G[rimstone] *D'Acosta's Hist. Indies* iii. xvi. 170 The first shippe was split with a tempest that did rise in the Lake. *c* **1643** Ld. Herbert *Autobiog.* (1824) 100 We coming..straight upon the Pier of Dover,..our ship was unfortunately split against it. **1680** C. Nesse *Ch. Hist.* 345 By swallowing up the ship in the midst of the sea, or by splitting her upon the rocks. **1708** *Constit. Watermen's Co.* lii, If any Waterman..happen to have his Boat..split, staved, or any ways damnified.
fig. **1642** D. Rogers *Naaman* To Rdr., [A rock which] unhappily split their hopes, and made shipwracke of all.

b. Of persons: In *pass.*, to suffer shipwreck. Also in fig. contexts, and *fig.*
1602 Marston *Ant. & Mel.* iii. E j b, That when a soule is splitted, sunke with griefe, He might fall thus, vpon the breast of earth. **1621** Brathwait *Nat. Embassie* 9 He who Vlisses-like stands firme..shall be a spectator of his Companions misery, in himselfe secured while they are splitted. **1640** in *Lett. Lit. Men* (Camden) 165 That I should sitt a Judge ther, wheere I was latelie in possibilitie to have been splitt & ruined. *a* **1704** T. Brown *Sat. agst. Wom.* Wks. 1730 I. 54, I shun the rock where Strephon has been split. **1772–84** *Cook's Voy.* (1790) II. 445 We were surrounded with innumerable quantities of ice, and were in constant danger of being split by them.
transf. *c* **1611** Chapman *Iliad* xxiii. 386 We ride A way most dangerous; turn head, betime take larger field, We shall be splitted.

c. To have (one's vessel) wrecked.
a **1700** Evelyn *Diary* 12 Sept. 1641, Here we split our skiff.

2. To divide longitudinally by a sharp stroke or blow; to cause to burst or give way along the grain or length; to cleave or rend.
1593 Shaks. *3 Hen. VI*, ii. vi. 30 Come Yorke and Richard,..I stab'd your Fathers bosomes; Split my brest. **1603** —— *Meas. for M.* ii. ii. 116 Thou..with thy sharpe and sulpherous bolt Splits the vn-wedgable and gnarled Oke. *a* **1625** *Nomencl. Nav.* (Harl. MS. 2301) s.v., If a Shot come and break a carriage of a Peece, wee saye it hath split the Carriage. **1680** Moxon *Mech. Exerc.* xii. §13. 207 With the Cleaving-knife and the Mawl, split it into a square piece near the size. **1774** Goldsmith *Nat. Hist.* (1776) I. 157 At Cajeta, in Italy, a mountain was split in this manner by an earthquake. **1827** Faraday *Chem. Manip.* v. (1842) 151 It must be either broken in the hand, or split or crushed by a hammer on the anvil. **1849** James *Woodman* xviii, I care not much whose head I split, if it comes in my way. **1878** Browning *Poets Croisic* 32 Quick on flash Followed the thunder, splitting earth downright.
fig. **1590** Shaks. *Com. Err.* v. i. 308 Oh times extremity Hast thou so crack'd and splitted my poore tongue [etc.]? **1606** —— *Per.* iii. i. 44 Blow, and split thyself.

b. *Naut.* Of wind: To rend or tear (a sail). Also of persons or a vessel: To have (a sail) rent or torn by the wind.
a **1625** *Nomencl. Nav.* (Harl. MS. 2301) s.v., When the winde hath blowne a Saile to peeces, wee saie the Saile is split. **1669** Sturmy *Mariner's Mag.* i. 17 It is more Wind, come, hawl down both Top-sails close... The Sail is split. **1745** P. Thomas *Jrnl. Anson's Voy.* 26 We split both our Main and Fore-top-sails. **1748** *Anson's Voy.* ii. v. 170 The weather proved squally, and we split our maintop-sail. **1800** Nelson 26 Feb. in Nicolas *Disp.* (1845) IV. 200 Ordered the Foudroyant to be anchored,..she having split her main topsail and foresail. **1901** D. B. Hall & Ld. A. Osborne *Sunshine & Surf* ii. 17 The whole of our top-gallant square sail was split to ribbons.

c. *Agric.* To plough (a ridge) so as to throw the furrow-slice outward.
1807 Vancouver *Agric. Devon* (1813) 116 The work is performed by what is called splitting; that is, the plough always turns upon the left to the first furrow, and the coulter is held close all the way to the lifted slice previously turned over. **1844** H. Stephens *Bk. Farm* I. 470 A ridge that has been ploughed the reverse to gathering up from the flat is said to be *split*, which is the short phrase for crown-and-furrow ploughing. **1891** W. J. Malden *Tillage* 106 This is known as splitting the ridge, and is the best form.

d. *Mining.* (See quot.)
1883 Gresley *Gloss. Coal-m.* 231 *Split*, to divide a pillar or post by driving through it one or more roads.

e. To separate or take apart longitudinally.
1875 Knight *Dict. Mech.* 2279/2 The ends of the two others [*sc.* rope-strands] are united by splitting and interlacing in the same manner.

3. In various fig. uses: **a.** Of violent grief or pain.
1594 Shaks. *Rich. III*, i. iii. 300 O but remember this another day: When he shall split thy very heart with sorrow. **1605** —— *Lear* v. iii. 177 Let sorrow split my heart, if euer I Did hate thee. **1813** *Examiner* 19 Apr. 242/2 Absolute happiness is in the power of no one, who has got..a head to be split with aching. **1829** Scott *Anne of G.* xvii, In parting from thee I am splitting mine own heart in twain.

b. Of loud noise.
1602 Shaks. *Ham.* iii. ii. 12 [To] teare a Passion to tatters, ..to split the eares of the Groundlings. **1607** —— *Cor.* v. vi. 52 You..had no welcomes home, but he returnes Splitting the Ayre with noyse. **1837** Carlyle *Fr. Rev.* ii. i. xii, The King swears; and now *be* the welkin split with vivats. **1865** Parkman *Champlain* (1875) 327 The air was split with shrill outcries.

c. Of excessive laughter. (Cf. side *sb.*[1] 1 c.)
1687 Miège *Gt. Fr. Dict.* ii. s.v., To split himself with laughter. **1704** Cibber *Careless Husb.* iii, Seeing us ready to split our sides in laughing at nothing. **1809** Malkin *Gil Blas* x. x. ⁋39 He laughed ready to split his sides. **1839** Hood *Nocturnal Sk.* i, In the small Olympic pit, [to] sit split Laughing at Liston. **1852** Mrs. Stowe *Uncle Tom's C.* iv, Lor! I was fit to split myself.

4. a. To divide or apportion to, or between, two or more persons.
1670 Cotton *Gamester* x. (1680) 83 If the Honours are equally divided among the Gamesters of each side, then they say Honours are split. **1719** Swift *Stella's Birthday* 9 O, would it please the gods to split Thy beauty, size, and years, and wit! No age could furnish out a pair Of nymphs [etc.]. **1824** Han. More in W. Roberts *Life* (1835) IV. 243 When I am obliged to split my attentions, it is a little fatiguing. **1837** Dickens *Pickw.* ii, Not worth splitting a guinea;..toss who shall pay for both. **1864** Lowell *Fireside Trav.* 225 They were just alike,..and you could not split an epithet between them. **1889** Doyle *Micah Clarke* 220, I have been splitting a flask with our gallant Colonel.
absol. **1866** Geo. Eliot *F. Holt* xi, I'll plump or I'll split for them as treat me the handsomest.

b. To divide or break up into separate parts or portions.
1706 E. Ward *Wooden World Diss.* (1708) 38 Standing upon the firm Deck, he..falls to splitting his Text most methodically. **1777** Burke *Let. to Sheriffs of Bristol* Wks. 1842 I. 217 There are people, who have split and anatomised the doctrine of free government, as if it were an abstract question. **1785** Paley *Mor. Philos.* iii. ii. v. §2 The proprietors..have it in their power to facilitate the maintenance..of families..by building cottages [and] splitting farms. **1813** *Ann. Reg.*, *Gen. Hist.* 49 The thing complained of was a novel practice of splitting votes by will. **1849** Macaulay *Hist. Eng.* ii. I. 236 The practice of splitting freeholds for the purpose of multiplying votes dates from this memorable struggle. **1868** *Rules Stock Exch.* no. 85, A Member splitting a ticket shall pay any increased expense caused by such splitting.

c. To divide or separate (persons) into parties, factions, groups, etc.
1712 Steele *Spect.* No. 461 ⁋ 2 We are..split into so many different Sects and Parties. **1784** Cowper *Task* v. 195 When Babel was confounded, and the great Confed'racy of projectors..Was split into diversity of tongues. **1861** Ld. Brougham *Brit. Const.* iv. 63 They are easily split into parties by intrigue. **1885** Gladstone in B. Holland *Life Dk. Devonsh.* (1911) II. xxi. 91 The question of the House of Lords, of the Church, or both, will probably split the Liberal Party.
refl. **1885** *Manch. Exam.* June 165/2 The enemy split themselves into two parties.

d. To divide or separate by the interposition of something.
1824 L. Murray *Eng. Gram.* (ed. 5) I. 463 What is called splitting particles, or separating a preposition from the noun which it governs, is to be avoided. **1841** Lytton *Night & Morning* ii. v, The man..said..'Pawdon me, and split legs!' therewith stretching himself between Philip's limbs, in the approved fashion of inside passengers! **1894** *Field* 9 June 835/1 Mr. Marshall split Messrs Taylor's pair with Orphan, a good-looking grey. **1895** *Daily News* 6 July 8/1 Mrs. Williamson splits her infinitives; hers is not a dandy way of writing.

e. *Mining.* (See later quots.)
1850 Ansted *Elem. Geol., Min.*, etc. 490 This whole current is divided by splitting into sixteen currents of above 11,000 cubit feet per minute. **1860** *Mining Gloss.*, *Newcastle Terms* 63 *Splitting the air*, dividing the air into different portions, each ventilating a separate district of the mine. **1883** Gresley *Gloss. Coal-m.* 231 *Split*, to divide the ventilative current after it reaches the pit bottom.

f. *Croquet.* To drive (a ball) with a 'splitting' stroke.
1877 *Encycl. Brit.* VI. 610 Make that hoop, and split, roll, or rush the ball placed there to help to hoop second back.

5. In various phrases: **a.** ***split me*** (or ***my windpipe***), used as an imprecation.
1700 T. Brown tr. *Fresny's Amusem.* viii. Wks. 1709 III. i. 72 A Bully of the Blade came strutting up,..crying out, Split my Wind-pipe, Sir, you are a Fool. **1701** Cibber *Love makes Man* ii. ii, I never fenc'd so ill in all my Life—never in my Life, split me! **1811** *Sporting Mag.* XXXVII. 10 Split me if ever I sell it for less. **1840** Thackeray *Catherine* ix, I had you here to amuse me—split me!

b. ***to split a hair*** or ***hairs***, ***straws***, ***words***, to make fine or subtle distinctions, esp. in argument or controversy; to be over-subtle or captious.
(*a*) **1674** Boyle *Excell. Theol.* Pref. 10 The great difficulty ..so to behave oneself, as to split a hair between them, and never offend either of them. **1691** tr. *Emiliane's Observ. Journ. Naples* 55 Shewing himself very inventive and dexterous at splitting a Hair in his way of handling Scholastick matters. **1742** [see hair *sb.* 8 j]. **1768–74** Tucker *Lt. Nat.* (1834) I. 23 Though we are obliged sometimes to split the hair we need not quarter it. **1780** M. Madan *Thelyphthora* II. 4 They splitted the hair..by condemning those who say 'the church may err in teaching otherwise'. **1809** Malkin *Gil Blas* ii. v. ⁋5 They would not split a hair about the loss of a wife or two. **1866** Bright *Sp.*, *Reform* 13 Mar. (1876) 346 It never entered into my mind the Government would split hairs in this fashion.
(*b*) **1845** Disraeli *Sybil* v. iii, I am no changeling, nor can I refine and split straws, like your philosophers. **1905** E. Glyn *Viciss. Evangeline* 225 He does not split straws, or bandy words.
(*c*) **1875** Jowett *Plato* (ed. 2) II. 286 Why will you continue splitting words?

c. ***to split the difference***, to halve an amount in dispute between two parties; to take the mean between two sums or quantities; to compromise on this basis. Also *fig.* (Cf. difference 2 d.)
1715 M. Davies *Athen. Brit.* I. Pref. 28 The Arian Pamphlets are not half so diverting as the Popish Libels; tho' as to their Idolatry, the difference may be split. **1771** *Ann. Reg.*, *Chron.* 145/1 The disagreement..is now amicably settled, by the splitting the difference between his surveyor's estimate and that taken by the surveyor for the executors. **1855** *Poultry Chron.* III. 66/2 As £7 had been named [in place of £13], perhaps if they 'split' the difference, and said £10, that would settle the matter. [**1893**

Daily News 13 Mar. 2/7 They refuse to 'split' the half-crown per ton which represented the difference between buyer and seller.]

d. *Naut.* (See quot.)

1867 SMYTH *Sailor's Word-bk.* 644 *Splitting the books*, the making of a new complete-book after payment, in which the dead, run, or discharged men are omitted; but the numbers . . against the men's names . . must be continued.

e. ***to split one's*** (or ***the***) ***ticket*** or ***ballot***: to vote for candidates of more than one party in an election. Also *ellipt. U.S.*

1842 *Spirit of Times* (Philadelphia) 14 July 2/1 The cry is raised of 'Vote the whole ticket! Don't split your ticket!' **1848** J. J. HOOPER *Widow Rugby's Husb.* (1851) 23 Never split in my life. **1905** *N.Y. Even. Post* 17 Oct. 1 Plenty of talk is heard about intentions to split ballots. **1946** *Chicago Daily News* 20 Nov. 18/5 Democrats . . decided the country did need a change, and split their ticket. **1975** R. STOUT *Family Affair* (1976) xiii. 141 He asked if I had split the ticket, and I said yes, I had voted for Carey but not for Clark. **1980** *Times* 8 Oct. 8/4 To persuade electors to 'split the ticket'—to vote for a Republican President and for a Democratic senator.

f. ***to split the atom***, to cause atomic nuclei to undergo fission. Also *fig.*

1909 *Busy Man's Mag.* Oct. 44/2 He [*sc.* Professor J. J. Thomson] is known both as 'The Man of Ion', and as the man 'who split the atom'. **1930** SAYERS & 'EUSTACE' *Documents in Case* II. 262 If anyone goes quietly away into a corner to experiment with high-voltage electric currents, they start a lot of ill-informed rubbish about splitting the atom. **1932** *Discovery* Mar. 69/2 The problem of splitting the atom is briefly this: given . . that at the centre of every atom there is a minute nucleus whose electrical charge fixes the elementary nature of the atom, can we by any agency detach a part of this charge? **1935** J. GUTHRIE *Little Country* xxi. 335 With the blast of his cornet, Archibald Packer had split the Temmian atom. **1964** M. GOWING *Britain & Atomic Energy 1939–1945* 18 They bombarded a foil of the metal lithium, disrupting the lithium nuclei which, after combining with incident protons, split into two alpha particles. The experimenters had 'split' atoms by artificial means. **1981** *Daily Tel.* 24 Sept. 16/4 The first scientists to work on 'splitting the atom'.

6. *slang.* To disclose, reveal, let out. (Cf. 13.)

1850 THACKERAY *Pendennis* xliii, Did I split anything? **1902** *Munsey's Mag.* XXVI. 501/1 We can't have him splitting that Mr. Lemp's in the wood.

7. *slang* (orig. *U.S.*). To depart from, to leave. Freq. in phr. ***to split the scene***: cf. SCENE 8 e.

1956 O. DUKE *Sideman* III. vii. 272 Naw, man—I split that scene. **1963** *Freedomways* III. 522 Evil Indians sink feathered arrows into the good guys, who kicked a couple of times and then split the scene. **1968** BUSBY & HOLTHAM *Main Line Kill* vi. 66 Where you bin? We thought you split the scene without giving us the word. **1971** *Sunday Sun* (Brisbane) 26 Sept. 3/3 When he split the Brisbane scene he left behind documents that could be incriminating to the drug gangsters. **1973** *Black Panther* 27 Oct. 17/2 We'll be splitting this place soon and once the book is written we won't have to come back. **1978** S. WILSON *Dealer's Move* i. 12 He and Miranda split Scotland for good and came down to London.

II. *intr.* † **8.** As predicate to *all*: To go to pieces. *Obs.*

1590 GREENE *Never too Late* (1600) 47 With that he set downe his period with such a sigh, that as the Marriners say, a man would haue thought all would haue split again. **1590** SHAKS. *Mids. N.* I. ii. 32. **1610** BEAUM. & FL. *Scornf. Lady* II. iii, Two roaring Boys of Rome, that made all split. **1611** MIDDLETON & DEKKER *Roaring Girl* IV. ii, If I sail not with you both till all split, hang me up at the mainyard.

9. Of a ship: To part or break by striking on a rock or shoal, or by the violence of a storm.

1593 SHAKS. *3 Hen. VI*, v. iv. 10 Whiles . . the Ship splits on the Rock, Which Industrie and Courage might haue sau'd. **1613** PURCHAS *Pilgrimage* (1614) 730 Their Admirall here splitteth on a Rocke, but the men are saved by the helpe of the other shippes. **1645** HARWOOD *Loyal Subj. Retiring-room* 15 A wise Pilot will not run his ship wilfully on a rock, but if a tempest drive it, he will shew his skill and courage to save it from splitting. **1718** OZELL tr. *Tournefort's Voy.* I. 112 This is the most dangerous Rock to split upon, in all the Archipelago. **1735** JOHNSON *Lobo's Abyssinia, Voy.* iv. 24 These [ships] are the more convenient, because they will not Split, if thrown upon Banks, or against Rocks. **1820** SHELLEY *Vision Sea* 26 The great ship seems splitting! it cracks as a tree.

b. Of persons: To suffer shipwreck in this manner. Freq. in fig. context and *fig.*

1610 SHAKS. *Temp.* I. i. 65 Mercy on vs. We split, we split. **1657** BENLOWES *Wisdom* I. (1905) 474 While sinners split on shelves, saints to Heav'n's harbour steer. **1678** DRYDEN *All for Love* Pref., And this is the rock on which they are daily splitting. **1726** SWIFT *Gulliver* I. i, The wind was so strong, that we were driven directly upon it, and immediately split. **1754** SHERLOCK *Disc.* (1759) I. 113 There is no Danger of their splitting upon these insuperable Difficulties. **1764** G. PSALMANAZAR *Mem.* 283, I know but too well how many excellent critics had already split upon that fatal rock.

10. To part asunder, to burst, to form a fissure or fissures, esp. in a longitudinal direction.

a **1625** *Nomencl. Nav.* (Harl. MS. 2301) s.v., When Sheeuers breake wee say they split. *a* **1661** FULLER *Worthies* (1840) I. 110 The oak . . may be called cowardly, as riving and splitting round about the passage of the bullet. *a* **1728** WOODWARD *Fossils* I. 17 All the Stone that is Slaty . . will split only lengthways or horizontally. **1796** WITHERING *Brit. Plants* (ed. 3) III. 831 Veil splitting at the side. **1820** SHELLEY *Prometh. Unb.* I. i. 40 When the rocks split and close again behind. **1855** *Orr's Circ. Sci., Inorg. Nat.* 173 The clay . . assumes a tendency to split in certain directions much more readily than in others. **1882** VINES tr. *Sachs' Bot.* 806 It is evident that before the bark splits . . the transverse tension must attain a certain intensity.

b. Used hyperbolically to denote the effect of excessive laughter, pain, or repletion.

(*a*) **1677** MIÈGE *Fr. Dict.* II, To split with laughter. **1693** DRYDEN *Juv.* (1697) 333 Shou'd such a Fight appear to view, All Men wou'd split, the Sight wou'd please whilst new. **1729** SWIFT *Grand Quest.* 175 Madam, I laugh'd till I thought I should split. **1840** THACKERAY *Barber Cox* Feb., One or two men, who roared with laughter ready to split. **1862** J. MEREDITH *Old Chartist* ix, I'm nearly splitting.

(*b*) **1722–7** BOYER *Dict. Royal* I. s.v. *Fendre*, My Head is ready to split in two, I have a violent Head-ake. **1756** MRS. CALDERWOOD in *Coltness Coll.* (Maitl. Club) 194 By the time we arrived, my head was like to split with perfect fear. **1849** CUPPLES *Green Hand* xvii. (1856) 168, I lay on my back, . . my head aching like to split.

(*c*) **1771** GOLDSM. *Haunch Venison* 104 'A pasty!' re-echo'd the Scot; 'Tho' splitting, I'll still keep a corner for that'. **1783** WOLCOT (P. Pindar) *Ode to R.A.'s* Wks. 1812 I. 49 The Poet might have guttled till he split.

c. To admit of being cleft.

1846 J. BAXTER *Libr. Pract. Agric.* (ed. 4) II. 169 The wood splits clean and easy, and is best adapted for split-paling and laths.

11. To part, divide, or separate in some way.

1712 ADDISON *Spect.* No. 415 ¶ 10 As in such Bodies the Sight must split upon several Angles, it does not take in one uniform Idea. **1856** STANLEY *Sinai & Pal.* ii. (1858) 111 The . . river, which rises at the point where Hermon splits into its two parallel ranges. **1862** MILLER *Elem. Chem., Org.* (ed. 2) 94 If boiled for some hours with hydrochloric acid glycyrrhizin splits into a brownish resin and glucose. **1898** *Allbutt's Syst. Med.* V. 956 There is an element of caprice in murmurs, which may rise, fall, split, or perhaps vanish for a time.

b. To break up into separate groups or parties.

1824 SCOTT *Redgauntlet* ch. xii, The land-sharks were on them, . . and so they were obliged to split and squander. **1871** L. STEPHEN *Playgr. Eur.* (1894) v. 137 We somehow contrived to split into three parties. **1871** M. LEGRAND *Cambr. Freshm.* 299 This ceremony over, the party split of its own accord into two sections.

c. *U.S. Sports.* To draw, to tie; *spec.* in *Baseball*, to win one game of a double-header, or to win half of the games in a series. Also *trans.*

1975 *Cleveland* (Ohio) *Plain Dealer* 31 Mar. 1-D/5 If Houston loses both of its remaining games and the Cavs split, the Cavs . . have a better record against other division teams than Houston does. **1979** *Tucson* (Arizona) *Citizen* 20 Sept. 10D/1 He split two decisions this season in hookups with Gaylord Perry.

12. To break up *into* factions, sects, or similar divisions; to separate through disagreement or difference of opinion; to fall out or disagree.

1730 T. BOSTON *Mem.* ix. 264 The parties were at the very point of splitting. **1732** BERKELEY *Alciphr.* VI. §29 What or where is the profession of men, who never split into schisms? **1845** S. AUSTIN *Ranke's Hist. Ref.* I. 379 He had not the power of keeping the princes of the empire together; . . on the contrary, every thing about him split into parties. **1890** W. A. WALLACE *Only a Sister?* 120 'Well, don't let us split on a small point of detail,' he began.

b. *slang.* To break or quarrel *with* a person.

1835 JAMES *Gipsy* xi, I don't want to split with Pharold. **1859** *Slang Dict.* 99 *To split with a person*, to cease acquaintanceship, to quarrel.

c. *slang* (orig. and chiefly *U.S.*). Of a couple: to become divorced; to separate.

1942 BERREY & VAN DEN BARK *Amer. Thes. Slang* §360/2 *Divorce* . . split. **1951** E. COXHEAD *One Green Bottle* x. 267 'Why did Chris go off early? Is anything wrong?' 'We've split,' Cathy answered. **1976** *National Observer* (U.S.) 14 Aug. 1/4 They had to split. If they don't love each other, what else can they do? **1978** *Detroit Free Press* 2 Apr. 19A/2 The [divorce] suit ended months of speculation that the TV sportscaster and film producer were splitting. **1982** 'J. GASH' *Firefly Gadroon* i. 13 Women are always unreasonable. . . We split after a terrible fight.

13. *slang.* To turn evidence or informer; to peach; to give information detrimental to others; to betray confidence.

1795 POTTER *Dict. Cant* (ed. 2), *Split*, turning evidence. **1824** *Compl. Hist. Murder Mr. Weare* 242 Such was the intense anxiety of some parties . . to hear whether Thurtell had split. **1840** DICKENS *Old C. Shop* lxvi, If anybody is to split, I had better be the person. **1876** BESANT & RICE *Gold. Butterfly* xvi, Janet would not split even when she was dying. And then there was very little to split about when she died.

b. Const. *on* or *upon* (a person).

1812 in J. H. VAUX *Flash Dict.* **1838** DICKENS *O. Twist* xxv, I might have got clear off, if I'd split upon her. **1875** 'A. R. HOPE' *My Schoolboy Fr.* 78 Of course you won't split on us. **1891** V. L. CAMERON *Log Jack Tar* 208 When he investigated the matter some among them split upon the ringleaders.

c. Const. *about* (a matter).

1836 *Ann. Reg., Chron.* 23 Feb. 34/1, I will split about the murder, and get you scragged. **1876** [see 12].

14. *colloq.* To run, walk, etc., at great speed.

1790 R. TYLER *Contrast* II. ii. (1887) 39, I was glad to take to my heels and split home, right off. **1848** BARTLETT *Dict. Amer.* 324. **1868** DICKENS *Lett.* (1880) II. 361 The spectacle of our splitting up the fashionable avenue . . excited the greatest amazement. **1872** *Routledge's Ev. Boy's Ann.* 30 Over him she [*sc.* the mare] goes, and down the hill as hard as she can split.

b. To do anything with great vigour.

a **1848** *Maj. Jones's Courtship* (Bartlett), I set the niggers a drummin' and fifin' as hard as they could split.

15. *slang* (orig. *U.S.*). To depart, to take one's leave.

1954 *Time* 8 Nov. 42 *Split*, . . depart. **1956** O. DUKE *Sideman* III. ix. 294 But that's why the cat split. **1956** B. HOLIDAY *Lady sings Blues* (1973) iii. 38, I grabbed him and told him to do something because I had to split for the bathroom again. **1962** *Radio Times* 17 May 43 After the gig, dad, let's split to your pad for some suds. **1967** W. MURRAY *Sweet Ride* viii. 128 Since nobody asked you over, why don't you just split so we can finish our lunch? **1977** *Sounds* 1 Jan. 21/4 In the main hall Roger Scott from London's Capital Radio arrived, took one look at the wasteland and split.

III. 16. With advs., as *away*, *down*, *off*, *out*, *up*:

a. In transitive senses. With *out*: also *slang* (now *Obs.* or *rare*), to separate or disentangle from another.

1648 HEXHAM II, *Opsplijten*, to Split up, or to Rive open. ? *a* **1735** M. CLERK in *Dict. Nat. Biogr.* (1887) XI. 44/1 He only cut off a chiel's lug, and he ought to ha' split doun his heid. **1799** [A. YOUNG] *View Agric. Lincoln.* 72 A wheel plough . . for crossing broad high lands at an equal pitch; which is liked better . . than either gathering up, or splitting down. **1807** PIKE *Sources Mississ.* (1810) II. App. 25 We cut down a small green cotton-wood tree, and with much labor split out a canoe. **1846** A. YOUNG *Naut. Dict.* 291 *Splitting out blocks*, a process sometimes resorted to when it is necessary to remove the blocks on which a vessel rests on a slip or in a dock [etc.]. **1855** *Orr's Circ. Sci., Inorg. Nat.* 39 These, which are often of vast dimensions, are split off from the peaks of the higher mountains. **1883** *Manch. Guard.* 22 Oct. 5/2 To split up Manchester into half a dozen distinct constituencies. **1924** G. C. HENDERSON *Keys to Crookdom* 419 *Splitting out*, separating pickpocket from his victim in case of trouble. The stall splits out the wire. **1931** *Collier's* 16 May 66/2 Everybody else is busy trying to split out Regret and the bloodhounds.

b. In intransitive senses. With *out*: also *slang*, to quarrel; to part company; to take one's leave (cf. sense 15 above). With *up*: also *colloq.*, to break up a relationship (esp. of a couple); *spec.* to become divorced.

1843 *Penny Cycl.* XXV. 204/2 The outer layer of which splits up into star-like expanding rays. **1850** G. W. MATSELL *Vocabulum* 84 *Split out*, no longer friends; quarrelled; dissolved partnership. **1852** MISS YONGE *Cameos* I. i. 4 Soon the kingdom of France split away from the Empire. **1852** MRS. STOWE *Uncle Tom's C.* vii, Sam . . dexterously contriving to tickle Andy . . , which occasioned Andy to split out into a laugh. **1865** KINGSLEY *Herew.* i, A Roman camp, guarding the King Street, or Roman road, which splits off from the Ermine Street. **1867** FREEMAN *Norm. Conq.* (1877) I. 160 The Empire did not at once split up into national kingdoms. **1879** *Macmillan's Mag.* Oct. 505/2 There is a reeler over there which knows me, we had better split out. **1903** G. H. LORIMER *Lett. from Self-Made Merchant to his Son* viii. 104 He and his father split up, temporarily, over it, and, of course, it cost me the old man's trade and friendship. **1927** J. BLACK *You can't Win* x. 132 'Where are you going, kid?' . . 'If you are going to split out, I'll go to San Francisco for a while.' **1942** BERREY & VAN DEN BARK *Amer. Thes. Slang* §360/2 *Divorce* . . . split up. **1956** B. HOLIDAY *Lady sings Blues* (1973) xxii. 176 Even if I could have split out I'd have been in a snowstorm of lawsuits. **1959** 'E. PETERS' *Death Mask* i. 15 When we split up . . I felt it was all my fault. I had to be free of him. **1976** M. MACHLIN *Pipeline* xlvii. 491 You just split out like a streak of blue lightning, without saying nothing to nobody. **1976** W. CORLETT *Dark Side of Moon* I. i. 29 'He thought his parents were . . splitting up?' 'Divorce?' . . he thought it was on the cards.'

split (splɪt), *ppl. a.* [f. SPLIT *v.*]

1. a. That has undergone the process of splitting; divided in this manner; riven, cleft.

1648 HEXHAM, *Gespleten klauwen*, Split or Cloven Clawes. **1673** HICKERINGILL *Greg. Father Greyb.* 314 Wry faces, mops, mows, split jaws. **1748** *Anson's Voy.* II. x. 241 A large split bamboe . . as a trough. **1825** JENNINGS *Obs. Dial. W. Eng.* 71 *Spars* . . are commonly made of split willow rods. **1849** NOAD *Electricity* (ed. 3) 379 To insulate the wire from the hook, a split quill is slipped over the wire, on which it rests. **1899** *Allbutt's Syst. Med.* VIII. 468 Tender nodosities or nodes on the shins, from a pea to a split walnut in size.

b. Of a surface: Exposed by splitting.

1715 LEONI *Palladio's Archit.* (1742) I. 8 River-pebbles split in the middle, . . laid with the split-side outwards. **1837** P. KEITH *Bot. Lex.* 121 If a thin slice of one of them is taken from the split surface of the trunk of an Oak or Elm. **1851–4** TOMLINSON *Cycl. Arts & Manuf.* (1867) II. 34 As the hide is split, one half, which is the split flesh side, passes over the knife; the other half, or the split grain side, continues to adhere to the drum. **1891** MALDEN *Tillage* 106 It is not uncommon to throw the split-furrows on to the unploughed land, so that the ridges are not too high.

c. *Bot.* (See quot.)

1832 LINDLEY *Introd. Bot.* 388 Split (*fissus*); divided nearly to the base into a determinate number of segments.

2. In various special collocations: **a.** In designations of apparatus, implements, parts of machinery, or similar objects, as ***split bandage***, ***cane***, ***chuck***, ***-ring***, etc.; ***split bearing*** (Mech.), a bearing for a shaft in which the housing and bush are each split laterally into two parts for ease of assembly; ***split flap*** (Aeronaut.), a flap occupying only the lower part of the wing thickness.

1846 BRITTAN tr. *Malgaigne's Man. Oper. Surg.* 202 The soft parts being divided, the utility of a *split bandage in keeping them back is generally allowed. **1902** R. GRIMSHAW *Mod. Workshop Hints* xiv. 268 (*heading*) Filling *split bearings with babbitt. **1973** O. S. NOCK *Gresley Pacifics* I. vii. 91/2 The inside big end . . necessarily had split bearings. **1843** HOLTZAPFFEL *Turning* I. 217 The *split bolster is employed for cutting out long rectangular holes or mortices. **1890** L. C. D'OYLE *Notches* 143 Taking my rod (a light *split-cane) in his hands, he shook it—and grinned. **1892** *Photogr. Ann.* II. 385 A stand upon the split cane principle. When the ring and bottom fittings are removed, the stick opens out into three pieces. **1830** *Mechanic's Mag.* XIII. 50, I call it the *split-chuck, for want of a more appropriate name. **1884** F. J. BRITTEN *Watch & Clockm.* 237 Split chucks were made here many years ago. **1849** CRAIG, In Surgery, **split-cloth*, a bandage for the head, consisting of a central part, and six or eight tails. **1929** *Techn. Notes U.S. Nat. Advisory Comm. Aeronaut.* No. 324. 1 It is known that . . a suction exists between the parts of a *split flap located at the trailing edge. **1968** MILLER & SAWERS *Technical Devel. Mod. Aviation* iii. 84 The adoption of retractable undercarriages, which increased drag when they were lowered for landing, made it less important to use flaps which increased drag as greatly as the split flap. **1882** SOUTHWARD *Pract. Printing* (1884) 6 Certain fractions are cast in one piece... If other fractions are needed, they require to be made up with small types, called *split fractions. **1878** BARLOW *Weaving* 168 The second [contrivance] is generally used in weaving the richest silks .., and is termed the *split harness. **1843** HOLTZAPFFEL *Turning* I. 221 The two parts are previously prepared either to the form of the tongue or *split joint. **1869** RANKINE *Machine & Hand-tools* Pl. H 4, A leading screw working in a *split nut beneath the slide rest. **1875** KNIGHT *Dict. Mech.* 2281/2 **Split-pin*, a pin or cotter with a head at one end and a split at the other. **1879** *Man. Artill. Exerc.* 171 Take out split-pin and unscrew steel pivot out of metal plate. **1884** F. J. BRITTEN *Watch & Clockm.* 237 Separate *split plugs for different sized objects are provided. **1888** JACOBI *Printers' Vocab.* 129 **Split rigger*, riggers made in two equal portions and screwed together in order to facilitate shifting or changing. **1853** C. M. YONGE *Heir of Redclyffe* II. xxi. 340 It was locked, but the key was on her own *split-ring. **1858** GREENER *Gunnery* 316 A novel safety guard;.. swivel double like a split ring. **1875** KNIGHT *Dict. Mech.* 2281/2 A split-ring has an opening by which keys may be introduced to be strung upon it.

b. In miscellaneous uses, as ***split brilliant, crow, eagle, -face, leather, pea(se, skirt, stitch***, etc.; ***split baluster*** (see quot. 1969); ***split end*** (Amer. and Canad. Football), an end (END *sb.* 3 g) positioned at some distance from the rest of the formation; ***split falls*** (see quot. 1960); ***split graft*** (Med.) = *split-skin graft*, sense 5 a below; ***split jump*** (Figure-skating), a jump during which the legs are momentarily kicked out into the splits position; ***split pea***, rhyming slang for 'tea' (*obs.*); cf. ROSY LEE; ***split shot, stroke*** (Croquet) = SPLIT *sb.*[1] 9; ***split-turn***, a sharp turn.

1904 P. MACQUOID *Hist. Eng. Furnit.* ix. 228 The *split baluster ornament.. has been variously named split baluser, cannon, or mace decoration. **1934** *Burlington Mag.* Sept. 125/1 An extensive use of relief decoration in the form of turned 'split balusters' is also rather characteristic of many of these pieces. **1969** J. GLOAG *Short Dict. Furnit.* 635 *Split baluster*, a turned baluster split centrally, and applied ornamentally to a surface. **1850** HOLTZAPFFEL *Turning* III. 1332 The *split brilliant.. only differs from the full brilliant .. in the foundation squares being divided horizontally into two triangular facets. **1785** GROSE *Dict. Vulgar T.*, **Split crow*, the sign of the spread eagle. **1889** F. E. GRETTON *Memory's Harkback* 224 The sign of the church might well have been the spread or *split eagle. **1955** C. V. MATHER *Winning High School Football* vii. 187 (caption) The halfback splits half the distance with the *split end. **1968** *Globe & Mail* (Toronto) 10 July 27/5 Adkins will be the split end with underrated Jay Roberts, a tough blocker, remaining at tight end. **1977** *New Yorker* 10 Oct. 177/2 Using only two backs.. and sending four split ends.. downfield, Restic had Harvard throw fifty-seven passes that afternoon, thirty-one of them valid. **1923** D. H. LAWRENCE *Birds, Beasts & Flowers* 182 And white teeth showing in your dragon-grin as you race, you *split-face. **1939** *Country Life* 11 Feb. p. xxxiii/1 (Advt.), Made in Cavalry Twills.. Sheppards Checks, *Split falls or fly front. **1960** C. W. CUNNINGTON et al. *Dict. Eng. Costume* 75/2 *Falls*, a buttoned flap to the front of breeches and.. of pantaloons and trousers... 'Small' or 'Split Falls' was a narrow central flap. **1929** *Surg., Gynecol. & Obstetrics* XLIX. 96/2 In lining a contractile cavity with a *split graft allowance should always be made for contraction. **1958** *New Biol.* XXVII. 40 Split-grafts are prepared by enzyme digestion of the fibres joining the epidermis to the dermis, which frees the epidermis for use as the graft. **1961** J. S. SALAK *Dict. Amer. Sports* 416 **Split jump*,.. a variation of the jump from the back edge with the free toe assisting. **1968** Split jump [see LAYBACK 2 b]. **1875** KNIGHT *Dict. Mech.* 2281/2 *Split-leather is an inferior article, and is used for light boots and shoes [etc.]. **1854** MISS BAKER *Northampt. Gloss.*, **Split-lift*, a narrow strip of leather split in two, which forms the lift, or seat of a shoe. **1846** LINDLEY *Veg. Kingd.* 63 *Andræaceæ.* — *Splitmosses. **1846** *Split-paling [see SPLIT *v.* 9 c]. **1736** BAILEY *Household Dict.* s.v. *Pease*, The *split pease do not need it. **1806** A. HUNTER *Culina* (ed. 3) 39 One pint of split pease. **1857** 'DUCANGE ANGLICUS' *Vulgar Tongue* 20 *Split-Pea*, tea. **1858** SIMMONDS *Dict. Trade, Split-pease*, husked peas, split for making pease-soup or pease-puddings. **1894** A. ROBERTSON *Nuggets*, etc. 191 He was as like Pat Kineen .. as two split peas are like each other. **1931** S. KAYE-SMITH *Hist. Susan Spray* III. 296 I'll make you a nice cup of split pea. **1975** *Oxf. Compan. Sports & Games* 218/2 When the balls travel in different directions the stroke is also known as a *split shot. **1976** *Scotsman* 20 Nov. (Weekend Suppl.) 4/1 The look of clothes today suggests country more than town. .. Capes and ponchos, loose knits and *split skirts, are more at home on town birds than country cousins. **1814** W. BROWN *Hist. Propag. Chr.* (1823) I. 620 *note*, The name of *split-snake.. we considered as descriptive not so much of its split appearance as of the singular sensation occasioned by its bite. **1880** L. HIGGIN *Handbk. Embroidery* iii. 22 **Split Stitch* is worked like ordinary 'stem', except that the needle is always brought up *through* the crewel or silk, which it splits. **1882** CAULFEILD & SAWARD *Dict. Needlew.* 194/2 *Split stitch*, a stitch much used in ancient Church Embroidery.. to work the faces and hands of figures. **1897** *Encycl. Sport* I. 254/1 **Split stroke*, taking croquet so as to drive the balls on courses nearly at right angles to one another. **1852** MRS. MEREDITH *My Home in Tasmania* I. 159 '*Split stuff,' by which is meant timber.. split into 'posts and rails', slabs, or paling. **1852** MUNDY *Antipodes* (1857) 29 A mile or so of road lined with pretty cottages—pretty although formed only of 'split stuff'. **1882** JORDAN & GILBERT *Syn. Fishes N. Amer.* 223 *Pogonichthys macrolepidotus*, *Split-tail. **1887** J. G. FRAZER *Totemism* 10 A remarkable feature of some of these Oraon totems is, that they are not whole animals, but parts of animals... Such totems may be distinguished as **split totems.* **1932** W. FAULKNER *Sartoris* III. 252 The damn thing zoomed past and did a *split-turn and came back at me again. **1898** *Year-bk. U.S. Dept. Agric.* 122 Another new insect.. is the so-called tobacco leaf-miner, or '*split worm'.

c. Phr. ***to keep on a split yarn*** and varr.: to keep in a state of alert. *Naut. slang.*

1929 *Papers Mich. Acad. Sci., Arts & Lett.* X. 298/2 *Having everything on a split yarn*, ready to start at once. **1958** W. KING *Stick & Stars* 73 All submariners had to be kept on a split yarn in case England was invaded.

3. a. Separated, divided, parted, or apportioned in some way. In special collocations, as ***split draught, duty***, etc.; ***split beam***, a beam (of radiation, etc.) that has been split into two or more components, *spec.* as used in a radar technique in which a single aerial transmits alternately two beams slightly displaced from each other in order accurately to obtain the direction of a target; freq. *attrib.*; ***split beaver*** (slang) (see quots.); ***split decision*** (Boxing), a decision made on points in which the judges and referee are not unanimous in their choice of a winner; ***split entrance, entry*** adj. (N. Amer.), designating a house in which the entrance is half-way between the levels of the two floors; also *absol.* as *sb.*; cf. SPLIT-LEVEL *a.*; ***split-field*** = next; usu. *attrib.*; ***split-image***, (*a*) an image in a rangefinder or focusing system that has been bisected by optical means, the halves of which are displaced when the system is out of focus, used esp. in various types of camera; usu. *attrib.*; (*b*) = *splitting image* s.v. SPLITTING *ppl. a.* 5; ***split instant, minute, moment***, an extremely small space of time; cf. SPLIT-SECOND *a.* and *sb.*; ***split page*** (U.S. Journalism) (see quot. 1970); ***split-phase*** (Electr.), used *attrib.* with reference to devices, esp. induction motors, that utilize two or more voltages at different phases produced from a single-phase supply; also *transf.*; ***split rail*** (orig. U.S.), a fence rail split from a log; freq. *attrib.*, as ***split-rail fence***; ***split run***, a press run of a newspaper in which some portions contain certain copy, advertisements, etc., not carried by other portions; ***split screen*** (Cinemat., Television, and Computing), a screen on which are projected simultaneously two or more images; ***split shift***, (*a*) a working shift split into two or more periods separated by an interval or intervals of several hours; (*b*) a shift overlapping the times of two other shifts; ***split ticket*** (see quots.); ***split trial*** (U.S. Law), a trial conducted in two stages of which the first will establish facts necessary to the impartial or swift conducting of the second; ***split week***, (*a*) *Theatr.* (see quot. 1948); (*b*) a working week in which days off occur other than at the weekend.

1947 CROWTHER & WHIDDINGTON *Science at War* 25 This '*split-beam' method of direction-finding gives very accurate results. **1966** D. TAYLOR *Radar* ii. 24 Special stations.. with facilities for 'split-beam' d.f. [*sc.* direction finding] were provided for accurate tracking of ships and fire-control purposes. **1966** [see SPECTROPHOTOMETER]. **1978** R. V. JONES *Most Secret War* xlii. 397 The method was to set a Freya station on the coast of France so that its split-beam pointed over the target in London. **1972** *New Society* 7 Dec. 591/1 The business has evolved its own jargon; full frontals are 'beavers', becoming '*split-beavers' if the legs are parted. **1976** LIEBERMAN & RHODES *Compl. CB Handbk.* vi. 137 *Split beaver*, stripper. **1977** E. J. TRIMMER et al. *Visual Dict. Sex* (1978) xxiv. 270 In the further stages of frankness 'beaver' and 'split beaver' shots show the hairy vulva. **1978** J. IRVING *World according to Garp* xiii. 241 Pictures of naked women... If you could see the sex parts.. that was a beaver. .. If the parts were *open*, that was called a *split* beaver. **1970** *Times* 28 Sept. 13/4 Buchanan, the British lightweight champion, gained a 15 round *split points decision over Ismael Laguna of Panama. **1976** *Daily Times* (Lagos) 8 Oct. 30/3 The 29-year-old Panther.. then said he had already petitioned the Nigerian Boxing Board of Control over the decision which gave Billy Savage the title by a split decision on September 24. **1871** *Routledge's Ev. Boy's Ann.* 530 The other flues may be arranged either as a wheel-draught or a *split-draught. **1875** KNIGHT *Dict. Mech.* 2281/2 *Split-draft*, (Furnace,) in steam-boilers, when the current of smoke and hot air is divided into two or more flues. **1895** *Daily News* 25 June 6/3 *Split duty, dividing the day's work into two or more portions, had been a sore point among the London sorters for many years. **1968** *Globe & Mail* (Toronto) 13 Feb. 31/2 (Advt.), Beautiful *split entrance bungalow. **1967** *Boston Sunday Globe* 23 Apr. B42/5 (Advt.), Keep that city job and enjoy country living in these unusually attractive *split entry ranches. **1976** *Laurel* (Montana) *Outlook* 23 June 19/1 (Advt.), You will never regret buying this new 4 bdrm split entry. **1941** *Amateur Photographer's Handbk.* (ed. 2) vi. 121 Some people find this *split-field type of range finder difficult to use. **1976** C. REYNOLDS *Photoguide to Filters* 156 One special accessory is the split-field lens. **1839** URE *Dict. Arts* 327 Whenever the metal is run off by the tap-hole into the two basins,.. called *Split-Hearths. **1950** R. A. MCCOY *Pract. Photogr.* ii. 15 To operate the *split image type [of rangefinder] it is necessary to look through the finder and observe that the image seems to be broken in the center and offset. **1960** *Focal Encycl. Photogr.* (rev. ed.) 946/2 The parallax effect appears as a split image which joins up across a dividing line when the lens is set to maximum sharpness. **1977** J. HEDGECOE *Photographer's Handbk.* 15 As a focusing aid a 'split image' or focusing screen rangefinder may be sunk into the center of the underside of the screen. **1981** 'M. INNES' *Lord Mullion's Secret* 179 He was by a strange freak of heredity the split image of one commemorated by Nicholas Hilliard some centuries ago. **1936** M. MITCHELL *Gone with Wind* xx. 348 'Rain,' she thought... But, in a *split instant: 'Rain? No!... Cannon!' **1839** DE LA BECHE *Rep. Geol. Cornw.*, etc. x. 308 Some good examples of *split lodes are to be seen in the Marazion and Breague districts. **1931** W. G. CARR *By Guess & by God* 27 Using his one periscope for *split-minute looks. **1957** I. ASIMOV *Naked Sun* ii. 31 For one fleeting *split moment he bent his head back and stared directly at Solaria's sun. **1953** B. WESTLEY *News Editing* 419/1 **Split page*, same as 'second front page'. **1957** J. STEINBECK *Pippin IV* 58 Colour photographs filled the split-page of every newspaper. **1970** R. K. KENT *Lang. Journalism* 26 *Split page*, the front page of a newspaper's second section; second front page. **1895** S. P. THOMPSON *Polyphase Electric Currents* ix. 175 This is a form of *split-phase motor having two or more sets of coils placed at different angles. **1921** W. S. IBBETSON *Motor & Dynamo Control* vi. 174 This split-phase winding has a very high resistance and induction, so that the current in it lays nearly 90° behind that in the running coils. **1953** *Pedestrian* Summer 26 Sometimes the policeman is operating what is known as a split phase; pedestrians may cross half the road in front of halted traffic and not realize that the traffic on the other half has the right of way. **1976** C. G. GROLLE *Compl. Guide Electr. Repairs* viii. 120 All split-phase motors have a centrifugal switch that drops out the contacts on the start winding after full speed is attained. **1826** T. FLINT *Recollections of Last Ten Years* 206 Scarcely has a family fixed itself, and enclosed a plantation with the universal fence,—*split rails [etc.]. **1897** *Essex Antiq.* (Salem, Mass.) Feb. 27/2 The split-rail fence is also old. Logs, generally of ash, about nine feet in length, and a foot or more in diameter, split the entire length into about sixteen equal parts, formed the rails, which were chamfered at each end. Of such split sections posts were also made, having holes cut in them in the proper places to receive the ends of the rails. **1934** *Bulletin* (Sydney) 14 Feb. 30/2 A new post or a new set of rails has to be put in a split-rail fence. **1976** SCOTT & KOSKI *Walk-In* (1977) xxx. 216 A weathered split-rail fence.. announced the boundary. **1961** WEBSTER, *Split run. **1963** D. OGILVY *Confessions Advert. Man* (1964) vi. 110 In split-run tests, long copy invariably outsells short copy. **1977** D. GROSSMAN *Samson Management Lexicon* ii. 19 Split-run copy testing. **1979** *Austral. Financial Rev.* 15 Aug. 22/6 The commission's investigations cover practices known in some sectors of the trade as 'split runs' and 'blowing'. A split run involves several print runs of the same editorial content, but with different advertising content. **1953** R. BRETZ *Techniques Television Production* xi. 206 In the case of the phone conversation the *split screen might appear in a direct cut after a single shot of the person making the call. **1958** *Times* 20 Jan. 3/2 Attempts to quicken the action [of a film] by a split screen device fail lamentably in their object. **1970** W. WAGER *Sledgehammer* (1971) xv. 91 As if in some film.. Williston's neatly typed dossiers.. jumped into focus... Actually they appeared side by side in a split-screen effect, hung there for a long moment and vanished. **1977** *Time* 26 Sept. 42/2 Alvy and Annie, on a split screen, talking to their shrinks about the frequency with which they have sex. **1955** M. REIFER *Dict. New Words* 196/1 **Split shift*,.. a work schedule or shift in which there is a break in the working hours. **1960** *Guardian* 30 June 10/4 Split shifts (e.g. 4–9 a.m. and 5–8 p.m.) and split days off. **1964** G. L. COHEN *What's Wrong with Hospitals?* ii. 39 Wards operating a three-shift system, instead of the generally abhorred 'split shift' which gave nurses a useless afternoon break. **1970** F. MCKENNA *Gloss. Railwaymen's Talk* p. v, The footplate crew has an even worse cycle—what is called the 'split shift' system. **1978** *Detroit Free Press* 16 Apr. F5/3 (Advt.), We have psychiatric nursing positions available on all shifts. No split shifts. **1876** BESANT & RICE *Gold. Butterfly* iv. 32 The twins were taking their third *split soda—it was brotherly to divide a bottle. **1836** J. HOYT *Let.* 21 Nov. in W. L. Mackenzie *Life M. Van Buren* (1846) 262, I was reproached by you for having voted a '*split ticket'. **1848** BARTLETT *Dict. Amer.* 410 It sometimes happens.. that individuals.. erase one or more of the names and substitute others more to their liking. This is called a split-ticket [**1859** also a scratch ticket]. **1872** DE VERE *Americanisms* 270 At times the party itself is divided into fractions,.. and the result of such a split in their own ranks, is a split ticket. **1964** *Economist* 31 Oct. 482/2 A 'split-ticket' group.. to urge voters to support Mr Johnson and Mr Keating, the Republican senatorial candidate. **1960** *Annals Amer. Acad. Pol. & Soc. Sci.* CCCXXVIII. 52/1 Of all the time-saving remedies, the *split trial should prove the most powerful. **1967** *North-Western Reporter* 2nd. Ser. CL. 323/1 In that year [*sc.* 1878] secs. 4697–98–99, R.S. 1878, were enacted and provided a split trial in which the insanity issue was tried first and if the accused was found sane he was then tried on his plea of not guilty before the same jury. **1926** *Split week [see HAM *sb.*[1] 5]. **1948** H. L. MENCKEN *Amer. Lang.* Suppl. II. 691 *Split week*, a week on the road divided between two or more towns. **1974** P. WRIGHT *Lang. Brit. Industry* ix. 81 *Split weeks* have also become fashionable instead of unvarying Saturday-to-Saturday weeks.

b. ***split infinitive***: see INFINITIVE *sb.* 1.

c. *fig.* With reference to division or dissociation affecting a person's mental life or the self. In special collocations, as ***split consciousness, man, mind, -mindedness, personality***; ***split-minded*** adj.

1958 R. F. C. HULL tr. *Jung's Undiscovered Self* v. 74 The rupture between faith and knowledge is a symptom of the *split consciousness which is so characteristic of the mental disorder of the day. **1944** H. READ *Educ. Free Men* x. 32 We divide the intelligence from the sensibility of our children, create *split-men (schizophrenics, to give them a psychological name), and then discover that we have no social unity. **1962** M. MCLUHAN *Gutenberg Galaxy* 51 (*heading*) The Homeric hero becomes a split-man as he assumes an individual ego. **1938** *Split mind [see SCHIZOID *a.* a]. **1945** KOESTLER *Yogi & Commissar* III. i. 121 Typical examples of socially approved split-mind patterns are the Astronomer who believes both in his instruments and in Christian dogma [etc.]. *a* **1974** R. CROSSMAN *Diaries* (1977) III. 372 The fact is that Jim is absolutely *split-minded.

1976 *Jrnl. R. Soc. Arts* CXXIV. 630/2, I must admit to being rather split-minded on this subject. **1947** S. O'Faolain *Irish* i. 23 A delightful dualism—the moderns would call it *splitmindedness. **1963** R. F. C. Hull tr. *Jung's Mysterium Coniunctionis* in *Coll. Wks.* XIV. iii. 248 The surprisingly common phenomenon of masculine split-mindedness, when the right hand mustn't know what the left is doing. **1919** M. K. Bradby *Psycho-Anal.* x. 129 The *split personalities of hysterics and mediums..have a subjective meaning. **1931** E. Wilson *Axel's Castle* ii. 40 A theory which makes one's poetic self figure as one of the halves of a split personality. **1966** 'H. MacDiarmid' *Company I've Kept* xiii. 259 In my view, he [*sc.* Walter Elliott] was a split personality. **1974** *Listener* 31 Jan. 131/1 Every nation becomes a bundle of contradictions and paradoxes—practically a split personality.

4. a. With advs., as ***split-off***, ***-up***.

1856 Kane *Arct. Expl.* II. xiv. 148 These split-off lines of ice were evidently in motion. **1880** Miss Giberne *Sun, Moon, & Stars* 294 The split-up rays tell us much more than the kinds of metals in different stars.

b. ***split-up***, long-legged. *slang.*

1874 *Slang. Dict.* 304 *Split up*, long in the legs. Among athletes, a man with good length of limb is said to be 'well split up'. **1891** *Field* 7 Mar. 334/3 The winner, Grand Fashion, is a leggy, split-up black, but decidedly the best mover of the lot.

5. a. In attrib. combs., as ***split-mouth sucker***, ***split-oak railing***, ***split-site comprehensive*** (***school***), ***split-site school***, ***split-timber house***. ***split-brain***, used with reference to a person or animal whose corpus callosum has been severed or is lacking, so that there is no direct connection between the two halves of the brain; ***split-dose*** (Med.), applied to the technique of administering a given quantity of ionizing radiation in several exposures so as to reduce its harmful effects in relation to its therapeutic ones; ***split-half*** (Statistics), used *attrib.* with reference to the technique of splitting a body of supposedly homogeneous data into two halves and calculating the results separately from each to assess their reliability; also *absol.*; ***split-skin graft*** (Med.), a skin graft which involves only the superficial portion of the thickness of the skin; cf. *split graft*, sense 2 b above.

1958 R. W. Sperry in Harlow & Woolsey *Biol. & Biochem. Bases Behavior* 418 In recent efforts to learn more about connectivity principles in perceptual integration, we have been putting to use the demonstrated functional independence of the two hemispheres in what we have come to call the '*split-brain' preparation... In these split-brain animals one can leave intact a whole hemisphere to maintain generalized background function. **1968** Passmore & Robson *Compan. Med. Stud.* I. xxiv. 94/2 At times, the non-dominant hand may 'go off on its own' and have to be restricted by the dominant hand. One begins to doubt whether a split brain man is singular or plural. But in no sense does he resemble a schizophrenic, in spite of the layman's interpretation of that word. **1972** R. E. Ornstein *Psychol. of Consciousness* ii. 55 In day-to-day living, these 'split-brain' people exhibit almost no abnormality. **1947** *Radiology* XLIX. 321/1 In this study the *split-dose technic was applied to recovery as tested by lethal effects. **1968** *Brit. Med. Bull.* XXIV. 246/2 Young..has written a program to synthesize the results of split-dose experiments from survival curves at various phases of the cycle. **1935** *Psychol. Rev.* XLII. 158 This conception of *split-half or comparable-form reliability as simply inter-item correlation can and should be brought into relationship with Kelley's concept or reliability as adequacy of sampling. **1946** *Jrnl. Educational Psychol.* XXXVII. 473 Since any test may be split in a large number of ways, the split-half method of estimating test reliability fails to give a unique result. **1971** *Computers & Humanities* V. 260 Because 0101 and 0410 had high internal reliability (split half), we did not cut, Xerox, and translate further samples from these books. **1882** Jordan & Gilbert *Syn. Fishes N. Amer.* 144 *Quassilabia lacera*,..*Split-mouth Sucker. **1895** Cornish *Wild Eng.* 121 The ordinary high *split-oak railing. **1972** *Guardian* 8 Mar. 12/6 Since they are..formed from a merger of two or three existing schools, the *split-site comprehensive schools have some attraction for local educational authorities. **1973** *Times* 11 Apr. 8/6 A minibus is used in one of our split-site comprehensives. **1975** *Times* 30 Dec. 3/2 The survey of 18 split-site schools, most of them divided by one or two miles across cities and industrial roads, concludes that they are 'the unfortunate by-products of imposing a comprehensive system too quickly'. **1981** *West Lancs. Evening Gaz.* 11 Nov. 9/8 But in 24 of the 63 cases, the authority would have to create either a split-site school, or a school with more than 490 pupils. **1929** *Surg., Gynecol. & Obstetrics* XLIX. 82 (*heading*) The use and uses of large *split skin grafts of intermediate thickness. **1977** *Proc. R. Soc. Med.* LXX. 480/1 Excision and split-skin graft undertaken in 5 patients was successful in the 3 who were traced. **1827** P. Cunningham *N.S. Wales* II. 170 In the *split-timber houses, a frame is first put up.

b. *Comb.*, as ***split-eared***, ***-nosed***, ***-tongued*** adjs.

c **1880** *Cassell's Nat. Hist.* IV. 272 The sub-order Fissilingues, the Split-tongued Lizards. **1894** *Outing* XXIV. 173/2, I hunted on many horses.., but never on a better than my shaggy, split-eared, one-eyed Whitey. **1900** *Westm. Gaz.* 12 Mar. 7/1 An abundance of explosive soft-nosed and split-nosed ammunition.

split-, the verbal stem in combs., as **split-down** *U.S. Stock Exchange* (see quot. 1976); cf. *split-up* below; **split-farthing** *a.*, mean, miserly; **split-fig** (see quots.); **split-off**, an act of splitting off; something that splits off or that has become split off; **split-plough**, a plough used for splitting ridges; **split-up**, an act of splitting up; *spec.* in the U.S. Stock Exchange: the division of a stock into two or more stocks of the same total value; cf. *split-down* above.

1932 *Sun* (Baltimore) 16 Apr. 15/8 The whys and wherefores of the '*split-down' movement in the capital structures of various corporations, in contrast with the stock 'split-ups' popular in the boom days of 1928–29 are now being explained in Wall Street. **1976** D. W. Moffat *Econ. Dict.* 257/2 The reverse split, or split-down in which a corporation reduces the number of shares into which its ownership is divided. The single word split usually refers to a split-up. **1787** W. H. Marshall *E. Norfolk* (1795) II. 384 *Nip*, a near, *split-farthing house-wife. *a* **1700** B. E. *Dict. Cant. Crew*, **Split-fig*, a Grocer. **1882** Jago *Cornwall Gloss.* 274 *Split-fig*, a very stingy person. Nickname for a grocer who would cut a raisin in two, rather than give overweight. **1935** Z. N. Hurston *Mules & Men* I. ii. 40 Ah knowed one preacher dat was called to preach at one of dese *split-off churches. De members had done split off from a big church. .. He come and preached at dis split-off for two whole weeks. **1964** *New Statesman* 14 Feb. 248/1 The split-off of science into a separate culture. **1840** J. Buel *Farmer's Comp.* 118 These high furrows are separated in the spring with the four-horse *split-plough. **1878** H. Sweet tr. H. Paul in *Trans. Philol. Soc.* (1879) 390 Even in the parent Indogermanic language long before its *split-up, there were no longer any roots, stems and suffixes, but only ready-made *words.* **1908** G. H. Lorimer *Jack Spurlock* iv. 76, I should have told her then about my split-up with the Governor. **1928** E. S. Mead *Corporation Finance* (ed. 6) I. xxx. 358 We may note finally the difference between a stock 'split-up' and a stock dividend. In the first case two or three shares are issued for one share of existing stock, and when this is par-value stock the par value is reduced. **1944** *Sun* (Baltimore) 9 Sept. 11/1 Pepsi-Cola added ⅞ to its brisk upturn of the previous day in response to the three-for-one splitup proposal. **1975** *High Times* Dec. 51/2 Last year I was still spinning from my split-up with a man. **1976** Split-up [see *split-down* above].

split-arse, -ass, *a. slang.* [f. split *ppl. a.* + arse *sb.*] **1.** ***split-arse mechanic*** (see quot.).

1903 Farmer & Henley *Slang* VI. 317/1 *Split-arse mechanic*,..a harlot.

2. *Forces' Slang* (orig. *Air Force*).

a. Classy, showy; (of an airman) reckless, that performs stunts; (of aircraft) having good manœuvrability.

1917 F. T. Nettleingham *Tommy's Tunes* 49 The expression 'a splitass merchant' is applied indiscriminately to a reckless individual or to a really good flyer capable of executing stunts with a modicum of safety. **1919** W. H. Downing *Digger Dialects* 47 *Split-ass*, unusual. **1934** V. M. Yeates *Winged Victory* II. xii. 288 They were sufficiently splitarse and did all the stunts, but there was nothing like a Camel for lightness of touch. **1946** J. Irving *Royal Navalese* 163 Split-ass, showy. **1966** A. La Bern *Goodbye Piccadilly* vi. 67 The Royal Air Force and the Fleet Air Arm used to describe certain flyers as 'split-arse types'. This coarse expression was reserved for outstandingly reckless airmen.

b. ***split-arse cap*** (see quots.).

1931 Brophy & Partridge *Songs & Slang Brit. Soldier* (ed. 3) 360 *Split-arse cap*, the old R.F.C. cap, rather like a Glengarry. **1945** C. H. Ward-Jackson *It's a Piece of Cake* (ed. 2) 56 *Split-arse cap*, the field service cap as distinct from the peaked dress service cap.

Hence as *sb.*, a flying stunt (see also quot. 1919); as *v. intr.*, to make a sudden turn in an aircraft; to perform stunt flying; **'split-arsing** *vbl. sb.* and *ppl. a.*

1917 F. T. Nettleingham *Tommy's Tunes* 49 So won't you splitass back Along the track To my dear old Omer Town. **1919** W. H. Downing *Digger Dialects* 47 *Split-ass*, an aeroplane on its side in banking for a sharp turn. **1929** *Papers Mich. Acad. Sci., Arts & Lett.* X. 325/2 *Splitass*, to do stunt flying, or to fly in a reckless manner. **1931** Brophy & Partridge *Songs & Slang Brit. Soldier* (ed. 3) 360 *Split-arsing*,..stunting low and flying near the roofs of..huts. **1934** V. M. Yeates *Winged Victory* III. iv. 326 The triplanes had come down..and did some diving at the splitarsing Camels but didn't hit anyone. *Ibid.* vi. 347 Something fired at him. He splitarsed and nearly hit an SE. **1945** C. H. Ward-Jackson *It's a Piece of Cake* (ed. 2) 56 *Split-arse*, stunt.

†splite. *Obs.*⁻¹ In 5 splyte. [? a. LG. *splîte*, related to *splîten* to split.] A narrow opening.

1489 Caxton *Faytes of A.* II. xiv. H iij, The walles must be ..soo thykke and so brode that aleyes may be there made wyth holes and splytes that archers be sette for to shutte.

'splitful. *Weaving.* [f. split *sb.*[1] 2 b.] A division of the warp, consisting of the threads passing between each pair of dents or splits.

1834–6 P. Barlow in *Encycl. Metrop.* (1845) VIII. 734/2 There is likewise a third rod which divides the warp into what is usually called *splitfuls*, for two threads alternately pass over and under it.

'split-level, *a.* [f. split *ppl. a.* + level *sb.*]

1. a. Designating a house or other building which has a floor between the floor-levels of two adjoining storeys (see quot. 1957); applied to this type of design. Also, designating a room having a floor on two levels. Also *absol.* orig. *U.S.*

1952 *N.Y. Times* 7 Sept. VIII. 1/1 A community of 129 split-level houses. **1955** *New Yorker* 1 Oct. 102/2 In the majority of the ads for new houses, 'split-level' is the big word, the selling word. There are, it appears, a good many kinds of split-levels. **1957** *Times* 12 Nov. (Canada Suppl.) p. xv/2 A visit to one of the new planned communities will convince the stranger that Canada has gone split-level mad, provided he knows what split-level means. This is the house originally designed for a sloping site, with entrance midway between upper and lower floors. **1958** *Spectator* 18 July 116/2 It is the first split-level church building in America. **1959** [see multilevel *a.*]. **1960** *Guardian* 3 Feb. 6/6 The split-level £2,000 room. *Ibid.* 24 Feb. 12/5 The house is on a sloping site, so this split-level treatment makes sense. **1963** J. N. Harris *Weird World Wes Beattie* (1964) ii. 20 One split level was much like another to him, but the general arrangements of Mrs. Ledley's house showed quiet good taste. **1968** P. Ableman *Vac* xvii. 91 There was a spiral staircase leading to split-level bedrooms. **1980** *Times* 29 Feb. 23 (Advt.), Luxury individually designed modern split level detached house.

b. Of a cooker: having the oven and hob in separately installed units.

1960 *Times* 4 Jan. 13/1 British manufacturers are at last taking advantage of the experience of the Americans... Now, in England, a number of manufacturers are producing standard units incorporating split level cookers with the oven at waist level, the hob fixed into the working surface, [etc.]. **1976** *S. Wales Echo* 25 Nov. 27/4 (Advt.), Extended kitchen, including Creda split-level oven and hob. **1978** *Cornish Guardian* 27 Apr. 16/3 (Advt.), Large kitchen, split level cooker etc.

2. *transf.* and *fig.*

1955 *N.Y. Times Mag.* 30 Oct. 4/4 Mr. Spectorsky has looked on a community..and seen only what he planned to see—the fieldstone houses and the split-level personalities, the couples who cannot make ends meet on forty or fifty thousand a year. **1959** *N.Y. Times* 23 Aug. I. 66/4 (Advt.), Urban and suburban fashion-seekers find the split-level dress a good investment. **1960** *Washington Post* 14 Jan. D 1/2 The migrant worker leads a split-level life... One state may provide adequate housing and other services. But as soon as he steps across a state line he may find himself in an area with no program to meet his needs. **1965** *New Statesman* 19 Mar. 456/3 George is the natural man drawn to pubs and barmaids, Arbuthnott the conscience that natters at him. This sort of split-level Englishman seems to belong with Mr Pooter. **1968** *Language* XLIV. 501 Morphologically conditioned sound change (analogical change) is normally of such a nature that no new phoneme arises in a 'split-level' analysis. **1973** *Irish Times* 2 Mar. 13/4 We Irish are now inured to a split-level morality: we react in low key and circumspection when one of 'our own people' murder or maim; but vehemently when the slayer is 'one of them'.

split-new, *a.* [app. f. split *sb.*[1] or *v.* Cf. Sc. spleet-new.] Perfectly new, brand-new.

1695 Bp. Sage *Presbytery* (1697) 246 A split new Democratical Systeme; a very Farce of Novelties. **1800** *Monthly Mag.* April 239/2 'The coat is split new.' This no doubt is a Scotticism. **1849** Cupples *Green Hand* xi. (1856) 115, I 'scribes the whole o' my togs as if I'd made 'em,—'split new,' says I.

split-second, *a.* and *sb.* Also **split second(s)**. [Abbrev. of *split second(s) hands*: see split *ppl. a.* 2 a and second *sb.*[1] 3.] **A.** *adj.* **1.** Designating a stop-watch having two seconds hands, one underneath the other and one of which may be stopped independently of the other. Also *absol.*

1884 F. J. Britten *Watch & Clockm.* 245 The Split Seconds..is a form of chronograph in which there are two centre seconds hands, one under the other. **1888** *Encycl. Brit.* XXIV. 398/1 Watches are also made with what are called *split seconds*-hands. **1897** *Sears, Roebuck Catal.* 377/2 This is the best cheap Split Second Horse Timer made. **1916** H. L. Wilson *Somewhere in Red Gap* ix. 379 When I left 'em Jake was holding a split-second watch on the waiter he'd just given an order to. **1971** T. C. Collocott *Dict. Sci. & Technol.* 1106/1 *Split-seconds chronograph*,..a chronograph with two independent centre seconds hands, one underneath the other.

2. Occurring, executed in, or lasting a fraction of a second; timed or calculated to a fraction of a second; sudden, instantaneous.

1946 'M. Innes' *From London Far* III. v. 206 The issue of modern naval conflicts depends upon split-second decisions. **1951** *People* 3 June 2/4 Watch for the two split-second appearances of twenty-one-years-old Audrey Hepburn. **1957** *New Yorker* 2 Nov. 68/2 He pictures himself as being locked in a death struggle with ringing telephones, split-second appointments, and traffic jams. **1959** W. Golding *Free Fall* iv. 82, I was..sitting my bike, willing them to die..because this demanded split-second timing. **1975** R. L. Duncan *Dragons at Gate* iv. 125 An instant pressure on the trigger, sound dispersed by a silencer, split-second work. **1978** *Poland* May 50/2 A player who cannot report punctually..cannot be counted on to carry out complex tactical maneuvers requiring split-second decisions when he is under a great mental strain.

B. *sb.* A fraction of a second.

1912 Chesterton *Manalive* I. iv. 97 Mr. Moon stood for one split second astonished. **1935** S. Lewis *It can't happen Here* iv. 40 Typed revelations timed to the split-second. **1940** [see receiver[1] 1 c]. **1950** *Sport* 22–28 Sept. 12/1 (*caption*) Racing in, a split second too late for the tackle, is home centre-half, Tommy Cummings. **1978** J. Wainwright *Jury People* xl. 141 For a split second, she'd known pain she'd never dreamed existed..then she'd passed out.

†'splitted, *ppl. a. Obs.* [f. split *v.*] = split *ppl. a.*

1593 Shaks. *2 Hen. VI*, III. ii. 411 Euen as a splitted Barke, so sunder we. **1597** A. M. *Guillemeau's Fr. Chirurg.* 23/1 Of the haremouthe, or splitted and cloven lippes. **1602** Marston *Antonio's Rev.* IV. iv, I am a poore, poore orphant .., The wrack of splitted fortune. **1635** J. Johnson *Hist. Tom a Lincolne* (1828) 87 Like to a splitted ship torne by the tempest of the sea. **1695** Bp. Sage *Presbytery* (1697) 407 Why may not the two parts of the splitted Estate join together?

So **'splitten** *ppl. a. rare.*

1832 Motherwell *Poems* 17 Alack! What gain they but a splitten skull. **1896** Kipling *Seven Seas* 68 Like a splitten sail, to left and right she tore.

†**'splitter**, *sb.*[1] *Obs.* [a. LG. *splitter* (G. *splitter*, Sw. *splittra*), related to *spliten* to split.] A splinter. (Cf. SPLETER.)

1546 LANGLEY tr. *Pol. Verg. de Invent.* II. xi. 54 b, The winter garlandes..which are made of wode splitters or Iuerie died with many colores began to be had in quotidian usage. **1602** SEGAR *Honor, Milit. & Civ.* 168 The seuenth encounter was between John Marshal and Bouciquaut, who was somewhat hurt with a splitter. **1616** J. LANE *Contn. Sqr.'s T.* XII. 120 Theie meete amidd:..so that bothe brokenn splitters flewe in th' aier.

splitter ('splɪtə(r)), *sb.*[2] [f. SPLIT *v.* + -ER[1].]

1. a. One who, or that which, splits or cleaves, in various senses.

1648 HEXHAM II, *Een Kliever*, a Cleaver, or a Splitter. **1706** STEVENS *Span. Dict.*, *Rajador*, a Hewer, a Cleaver, a Splitter. **1731** SWIFT *Div. Ch. Livings* Misc. (1735) V. 127 How shou'd we rejoice, if..Those Splitters of Parsons in sunder shou'd burst. **1839** URE *Dict. Arts* 1141 The splitter begins by dividing the block [of slate]..to a proper size. **1889** WELCH *Text Bk. Naval Archit.* iv. 77 For lap-work, a tool called a splitter is employed to make a split in one of the edges. **1890** W. J. GORDON *Foundry* 144 It is taken from the annealing-kiln..to be cut up by the 'splitter' to the best advantage.

b. *spec.* One employed in splitting fish.

1623 WHITBOURNE *Newfoundland* 82 Seuen are to be skilfull headders, and splitters of fish. *c* **1682** J. COLLINS *Salt & Fishery* 91 The Splitters immediately split them, beginning at the Tail, and so continue to the Head, close by the back Fin. **1761** *Ann. Reg., Chron.* 188/2 Every boat-master, splitter, and master voyage [*sic*], who are the chief people among the fishermen. **1822** HIBBERT *Descr. Shetl. Isl.* 519 A splitter, as he is called, then, with a large knife, cuts a fish open from the head to the tail. **1883** L. Z. JONCAS *Fisheries Canada* 16 The splitter now seizes the fish, and with a single stroke of his knife he removes the back bone.

c. *Austr.* A wood-cutter.

1841 in Lang *Phillipsland* (1847) 133 Mokitte shot near Mount Cole; it is said by a (timber) Splitter. **1858** SIMMONDS *Dict. Trade*, *Splitter*, a name in Tasmania for a wood-cutter. **1870** A. L. GORDON *Bush Ballads* 32 At the splitter's tent I had seen the track of horse-hoofs.

d. An auxiliary set of gears that provides a set of ratios between those of the main gearbox. Freq. *attrib.*

1963 *Automobile Engineer* LIII. 228/2 An overdrive in front of the gearbox can be used as a splitter gear..to provide intermediate ratios between any two of the gearbox. These can be engaged without operating the clutch. **1967** *Economist* 8 July (Commercial Vehicles Suppl.) p. xxx/1, Even when there are enough speeds in the splitter box (which may be either in front or behind the normal box) rear axles are getting more complicated. **1977** *Belfast Tel.* 27 Jan. 21/8 (Advt.), 1969 Leyland Super Commet, 6-wheel Tipper, fitted with p.a.s., splitter box, 401 engine. **1977** 'D. RUTHERFORD' *Return Load* ii. 32 'How many gears have you got?' 'Thirteen forward and two reverse.'..'It's got a splitter.' Sally said..'You don't have to move the gear lever thirteen times.'

2. *fig.* **a.** In phrases: One who makes fine or subtle distinctions.

a **1700** B. E. *Dict. Cant. Crew*, *Splitter-of-Causes*, a Lawyer. **1771** *Ann. Reg., Hist. Europe* 32/1 Of which they were as well qualified to judge as the most acute and subtil splitter of cases in all the courts. **1863** MISS BRADDON *Aurora Floyd* vi, The splitter of metaphysical straws and chopper of logic.

b. One who favours minute subdivision in scientific classification.

1887 *Darwin's Life & Lett.* II. 105 *note*, Those who make many species are the 'splitters', and those who make few are the 'lumpers'. **1898** *Athenæum* 22 Jan. 123/1 Babington belonged to that category of botanists..denominated 'splitters'.

3. A splitting headache.

1860 THACKERAY *Lovel* v. (1869) 224, I have got such a splitter of a headache. **1886** *Punch* 27 Nov. 263 Next morning Mr. Dumpkin has a headache, such a Splitter!!

4. One who causes splitting of votes.

1895 *Westm. Gaz.* 4 Mar. 2/2 The figure cut by the splitters themselves has in all cases been very poor.

5. *Hunting slang.* A first-rate hunt.

1843 *Ainsworth's Mag.* III. 219 'What a fine country before us!' observes a third; 'what a splitter we shall have!' says a fourth. **1976** *Shooting Times & Country Mag.* 16–22 Dec. 25/2 There was more than a holding scent and..we were in for a splitter.

'splitter, *v. rare.* [f. SPLIT *v.* + -ER[5], or ad. G. *splittern*.] *intr.* To break into fragments.

1860 THACKERAY *Round. Papers, Week's Holiday*, Atlas..would drop the moon..on to the white marble floor, and it would splitter into perdition. **1896** *Daily News* 29 Apr. 7/3 Called of God to save Russia from the 'splittering' which has filled Europe with rival creeds.

†**splittern.** *Obs.*[−0] (See quot.)

1598 FLORIO, *Galette delle gambe dietro del cauallo*, the ioint of the hinder legs of a horse, called the hought or the spliterne [**1611** splitterne] of a horse.

splitting ('splɪtɪŋ), *vbl. sb.* [f. SPLIT *v.* + -ING[1].]

1. The action of the vb.; cleaving or rending: **a.** In intransitive uses. Also with *asunder*.

c **1595** CAPT. WYATT *Dudley's Voy.* (Hakl. Soc.) 54 When wee expected nothing less then splittinge of sailes, breakinge of shroudes [etc.]. **1597** A. M. tr. *Guillemeau's Fr. Chirurg.* 23/1 The cleavinge or splittinge in the lippes,..and in the nose. **1611** COTGR., *Debris*,..a breaking, or splitting asunder, as of a ship against a rocke. **1722–7** BOYER *Dict. Royal* I, *Eclat de rire*, a splitting with Laughing. **1798** HUTTON *Course Math.* (1807) II. 335 It is to be suspected that the great penetration..was owing to the splitting of his timber in some degree. **1838** *Civil Eng. & Arch. Jrnl.* I. 330/1 The failure of the wall, by its separating into two thicknesses along the middle,..is called splitting. **1882** VINES tr. *Sachs' Bot.* 734 The splitting asunder of whole masses of tissue during freezing.

b. In transitive uses. Also with *out*.

1872 HOLLAND *Marble Proph.* 102 When the chopping and splitting were done. **1890** 'R. BOLDREWOOD' *Col. Reformer* (1891) 131 A long spell of bush work—splitting, fencing,..what not. **1899** *Westm. Gaz.* 5 May 1/2 The Chief Constructor..will personally direct the splitting out of the only twelve blocks remaining under the vessel.

2. a. The action of dividing, separating, or parting.

1737 *Gentl. Mag.* VII. 34/1 Lest the Managers, by Splitting of Votes, should escape the Prosecution commenced against them. **1765** BLACKSTONE *Comm.* I. 173 To prevent the splitting of freeholds. **1766** *Ibid.* II. 215 The inconveniences that attended the splitting of estates. **1833** HT. MARTINEAU *Loom & Lugger* I. i. 3 Such a splitting into two parties. **1885** *Athenæum* 12 Sept. 333/1 It is equally difficult to escape the charge of tedious and needless splittings.

b. Similarly with *up*.

1847 tr. *Bunsen's Ch. Future* 10 Along with the splitting up of the divine idea in man, the human race also was split up out of unity into plurality. **1862** MILLER *Elem. Chem., Org.* (ed. 2) 288 The formation and the splitting up of these saccharides. **1895** *Knowledge* July 149 The splitting up of the rays which occurs on the transmission of light through a prism.

c. *spec.* in *Psychol.* The process of division or dissociation affecting the mind or self. Also with *off*.

1890 W. JAMES *Princ. Psychol.* I. ix. 227 According to M. Janet these secondary personalities are always abnormal, and result from the splitting of what ought to be a single complete self into two parts. **1910** tr. *Freud's Orig. & Devel. Psycho-Anal.* in *Amer. Jrnl. Psychol.* XXI. 191 We followed his [*sc.* Janet's] example when we made the mental splitting and the dissociation of personality the central points of our theory. *Ibid.*, I soon came to another view of the origin of hysterical dissociation (or splitting of consciousness). **1927** HENDERSON & GILLESPIE *Text-Bk. Psychiatry* v. 101 The most extensive, and at the same time the most profound, of all personality changes is the 'splitting of the personality' that occurs in advanced schizophrenia. **1945** M. KLEIN *Contributions to Psycho-Analysis* (1948) 346 The early splitting of the mother figure into a good and bad 'breast mother' as a way of dealing with ambivalence had been very marked. **1967** J. A. HADFIELD *Introd. Psychotherapy* xviii. 134 A severe shock such as a car accident or even a severe illness can result in a splitting off of some part of consciousness.

3. *pl.* That which is split, cleft, or chopped.

1867 *Morn. Star* 8 Oct., A Salisbury butcher announces..meat at the following prices:..Beef—brisket, 7d.; splittings, 7½d.; rumps, 8d. **1887** D. C. MURRAY & HERMAN *Traveller Returns* vi. 78 Upon this small logs and splittings, dry and green alike, were thrown.

4. *Mining.* (See quot.)

1883 GRESLEY *Gloss. Coal-m.* 231 *Splittings*, two horizontal level headings driven through a pillar in pillar workings, in order to work away the coal.

5. *attrib.*, chiefly in the sense of 'used or adapted for splitting', as ***splitting-knife***, ***-machine***, ***-mill***, ***-tool***; **splitting-block** (see quot. 1711); **splitting-board** (see quot. 1875); **splitting field** *Math.*, the least field which includes all roots of a specified polynomial.

1711 W. SUTHERLAND *Shipbuild. Assist.* 25 Blocks of hard knotty Stuff..upon which you lay other Blocks, called Splitting-blocks, of the freest Timber that can be got, for the Conveniency of cleaving out again, when you are ready to launch. **1802** A. YOUNG *Autobiog.* (1898) 383, I have fixed straw work here,..and my splitting machines are all distributed. **1841** H. SCRIVENOR *Hist. Iron Trade* vi. 120 All below that size were cut in the splitting-mill. **1846** HOLTZAPFFEL *Turning* II. 459 Paring or splitting tools, with thin edges. **1875** KNIGHT *Dict. Mech.* 2162/2 The blocks are fed to the splitting-knives by fluted rollers. *Ibid.* 2281/2 *Splitting-board* (Mining),..a dividing board used in mine ventilation to divide the incoming air. **1886** A. WEIR *Hist. Basis Mod. Europe* (1889) 377 The rollers..saved the smaller gauges from being consigned to the splitting mill. **1942** E. ARTIN *Galois Theory* ii. 22 A splitting field is of finite degree since it is constructed by a finite number of adjunctions of algebraic elements, each defining a field of finite degree. **1971** E. C. DADE in Powell & Higman *Finite Simple Groups* viii. 256 If F is algebraically closed, then it is a splitting field for any simple F-algebra.

'splitting, *ppl. a.* [f. SPLIT *v.*]

1. a. Causing to split or rend.

1593 SHAKS. *2 Hen. VI*, III. ii. 97 The splitting Rockes cowr'd in the sinking sands. **1606** —— *Tr. & Cr.* I. iii. 49 When the splitting winde Makes flexible the knees of knotted Oakes. **1624** CAPT. SMITH *Virginia* III. 64 The flashes of fire from heaven, by which light onely we kept from the splitting shore.

b. Ear-splitting; deafening.

1821 BYRON *Sardanap.* I. ii, Worse than the rabble's shout, or splitting trumpet. **1891** FARRAR *Darkn. & Dawn* lv, Splitting outbursts settled into a long continued roar.

c. *Croquet.* Of a stroke: Causing the balls to go in divergent directions.

1874 HEATH *Croquet Player* 37 The Splitting Stroke. In this stroke, the two balls..fly off from each other at an angle. It is the most important of the croquet-strokes.

2. Parting asunder; separating by cleavage.

1725 POPE *Odyss.* VII. 358 The splitting Raft the furious tempest tore. **1883** *Gd. Words* Nov. 732/1 Besides the very small disease germs, there are many 'splitting-fungi'. **1891** T. HARDY *Tess* (1900) 24/1 The aspect of the straight road enlarged,..the two banks dividing like a splitting stick.

3. Extremely fast; very rapid.

1829 in *Standard* 6 Apr. (1908) 8/2 On the pistol being fired, the boats went off at a splitting rate. **1865** DICKENS *Mut. Fr.* III. xv, A weak-spirited, improvident idiot..racing off at a splitting pace for the workhouse. **1873** *Routledge's Young Gentl. Mag.* 270/2 At a splitting gallop.

4. Of a headache: Violent, severe. Also *fig.* of the head.

1828 *Oscotian* I. 461 Felt a splitting head-ache under my night-cap. **1835** DICKENS *Let.* 18 Dec. (1965) I. 109 The noise and confusion here..is so great that my head is actually splitting. **1847** MRS. GORE *Castles in Air* xxviii. III. 49, I woke next morning..with a splitting head-ache. **1857** G. A. LAWRENCE *Guy Livingstone* iii. 23 Pale men with splitting heads..after a heavy drink. **1884** *Punch* 15 Nov. 230/2 Head split open; splitting headache as result. **1893** EARL DUNMORE *Pamirs* II. 191, I had a splitting headache in consequence of my fall.

5. ***splitting image***, an exact likeness. Also (*dial.*) ***splitten image***. Cf. *spitting image* s.v. SPITTING *ppl. a.* 3.

1880 T. CLARKE *Specimens Westmoreland Dial.* II. 36 Soa t'kersmas up i't'fells Et just be t'splitten image Ov a kersmas 'mang yersells. **1939** D. HARTLEY *Made in England* i. 3 Evenness and symmetry are got by pairing the two split halves of the same tree, or branch. (Hence the country saying: he's the 'splitting image'—an exact likeness.)

splittism ('splɪtɪz(ə)m). [tr. Chinese *fēnliè zhǔyì*: see SPLIT *v.* and -ISM.] In Communist use: the pursuance of factional interests in opposition to official party policy. Also *transf.* Hence **'splittist**, one who practises splittism; also as *adj.*

1962 *Guardian* 15 Dec. 7/1 That dread word, 'Splittism', which has never before darkened a page of the Sino-Soviet polemic, broke through to the surface of the Peking 'People's Daily' yesterday in the first open discussion of the possibility of a split. This term, taken from the translation of the Chinese document into English by the official New China News Agency, appears from the context to be identical with the Russian Communist concept of 'fractionalism'. **1964** *Economist* 8 Feb. 490/3 In Peking's view splittism means opposing and betraying Marxism-Leninism, usually in the interests of the bourgeoisie. **1968** *Ibid.* 5 Oct. 22/3 It is no longer the 'splittists' in Peking who are on trial before the majority of the world's communist parties, but the hard-liners in the Kremlin. **1969** *Daily Tel.* 11 Feb. 19/7 Frelimo and the Organisation of African Unity Liberation Committee are aware of the dangers of 'splittist'—as Peking calls it—tendencies. **1976** *Times* 20 Oct. 10 We must..repudiate all those who betray Marxist-Leninist-Mao Tse-tung thought, tamper with Chairman Mao's directives, practise revisionism and splittism, [etc.]. **1978** *Peking Rev.* 10 Mar. 9/2 The 'gang of four'..once again indulged in splittist activities and devised all kinds of schemes and plots. **1980** *Economist* 31 May 9/1 One challenge to western unity..had been compounded by another..and the danger of splittism was evident.

'splitty, *a.* [f. SPLIT *v.* Cf. WFris. *splittich.*] Liable to split.

1875 SIR T. SEATON *Fret-Cutting* 114 If the wood should be unusually 'splitty', the notch can be cut little by little.

sploach, sploch, obs. forms of SPLOTCH.

splodge (splɒdʒ), *sb.* [Cf. next and SPLOTCH *sb.*] A thick, heavy, or clumsy splotch.

1854 *Househ. Words* IX. 74/1 She was a dollop of dripping, a splodge of grease. **1862** SALA *Accepted Addr.* 275 The monstrous splodges of colour the marvellous man sent of late years to the..exhibitions. **1880** MRS. PARR *Adam & Eve* xxviii. 388 To..display the two splodges of red sealing-wax.

splodge (splɒdʒ), *v.* [Imitative of the sound.]

1. *intr.* To trudge or plod splashily through mud or water.

1859 A. WHITEHEAD *Leg.* (1896) 56 (E.D.D.), Away he splodg'd in pensive mood, Towards the temple in the wood. **1899** F. V. KIRBY *Sport E.C. Africa* ix. 106 As I had braved the first [muddy channel] and got wet through, I 'splodged' through them all in succession.

2. Used adverbially: With a heavy splash.

1898 H. KIRKE *25 Yrs. Brit. Guiana* 180, I had hardly spoken when splodge! splodge! came the rain in my face.

Hence **'splodger**. (See quot.)

1860 *Slang Dict.* 224 *Splodger*, a lout, an awkward countryman.

splodgily ('splɒdʒɪlɪ), *adv.* [f. SPLODGY *a.* + -LY[2].] In a splodgy manner. Also *fig.*

1963 *Times* 16 Feb. 4/1 This matches the dancing not wisely but too well, and her imaginative splodgily-splashed costumes looked ill-cut. **1978** R. HILL *Pinch of Snuff* xiv. 141 'Your girl's got two minutes, missus,' he said splodgily.

splodgy ('splɒdʒɪ), *a.* [f. SPLODGE *sb.*] Full of splodges; showing coarse splotches of colour.

1882 *Contemp. Rev.* June 952 The large splodgy canvases with which the Academy is so full.

splore (splɔə(r)), *sb. Sc.* [Of obscure origin.]

1. A frolic, merrymaking, revel, carousal.

1785 BURNS *Jolly Beggars* 1st Recit., A merry core..In Poosie Nancy's held the splore. **1816** SCOTT *Bl. Dwarf* vii, You that like to hear o' splores, heard ye ever o' a better ane than I hae had this morning? **1873** C. GIBBON *Lack of Gold* xxviii, Like enough the folk have kept him to join in some splore.

2. A commotion or disturbance; a skirmish or encounter; a scrape.

1785 BURNS *Holy Willie* xiii, An' when we chasten'd him therefor, Thou kens how he bred sic a splore. **1818** SCOTT *Rob Roy* xxxv, Then came the splore about the surrendering your papers. **1843** *Cracks about Kirk* I. 16 Mony a splore you and me hae had; but we can shake hands yet. **1879** 'S.

Tytler' *Bride's Pass* v, He has not the ability to run wild and get into splores.

Hence **splore** *v. intr.*, to revel or riot; to make a commotion or show; to brag or boast, etc.

1796 Burness *Thrummy Cap* (1893) 7 I'm a Christian man, Wha never lik'd to curse nor ban, Nor steal nor lie, nor drink nor splore. **1825** Jamieson *Suppl., To splore, v.n.*, to show off, to make a great show. **1862-** in *Eng. Dial. Dict.*

splosh (splɒʃ), *sb. colloq.* and *dial.* [Echoic: cf. splash *sb.*[1] and slosh *sb.*] **1.** The dull, splashing sound of the impact of a hard object striking or struck by something wet and soft; the impact itself. Also, a quantity of liquid suddenly dashed or dropped.

1857 C. E. DeLong in *Calif. Hist. Soc. Q.* (1930) IX. 133 Storming like fury..a mixture of snow and rain..splosh almost knee deep. **1895** E. M. Stooke *Not Exactly* xi. 280 Arter all 'tis but dree minutes or zo of acoot zufferin' in th' grip o' Bill Brooks, then a bit of a splosh, an' hout the beggur comes. **1916** J. K. Bangs *From Pillar to Post* xii. 235 The committee hustled me into the hall with no more damage than one rather slush splosh of snow. **1919** W. Deeping *Second Youth* xii. 112 The roof had dropped a splosh of water on Uncle Reginald's new hat. **1936** A. G. Street *Gentleman of Party* i. 11 An hour of steady splosh, splosh, splosh, of their horses' feet in thick batter of mud which creamed over the road. **1954** L. M. Boston *Children of Green Knowe* 64 A [snow]flake landed on his cheek... He felt the splosh. **1983** 'F. Parrish' *Bait on Hook* ii. 35 'At splosh o' paint on the mudguard. Got reason to remember 'at, I 'ave.

2. *slang.* Money.

1893 G. Elen *'E dunno where 'e Are (song)* Since Jack Jones come into that little bit o' splosh. **1916** 'Taffrail' *Pincher Martin* vi. 100 The show's orf 'less I kin raise some splosh some'ow. **1924** *Westm. Gaz.* (weekly ed.) 30 Aug. 526/3 The gentleman in the Old Kent Road who came into a little bit of splosh. **1950** Wodehouse *Nothing Serious* 216 The jolliness of having all that splosh in the old sock. **1967** A. Wilson *No Laughing Matter* ii. 82 Intentions need a bit of splosh to back em up.

splosh, *v.* (*int.* and *adv.*) *colloq.* and *dial.* [f. prec.] **a.** *trans.* To splash (something); to cause (something) to move with a splashing sound. **b.** *intr.* To move with a splash. Also *int.* and as *adv.*

1890 *Harry Fludyer* 47 Such larks when you heard the ball go splosh on a man's hat. **1901** J. Prior *Forest Folk* xi. 111 Nell continued to turn the handle of her old barrel churn. Splash! splosh! went the cream. **1904** *Eng. Dial. Dict.* V. 678/2 (S. Not.), What are yer sploshin the watter about for? **1923** Wodehouse *Inimit. Jeeves* iii. 30, I began to sing like a bally nightingale as I sploshed the sponge away. **1924** Galsworthy *White Monkey* ii. ix. 194 Down came death —splosh!—and a creature wiped out, like a fly on a wall. **1926** *Somerset Year Bk.* 54 She brought down th' liddle shutter again splosh-bang. **1930** R. Campbell *Poems* 10 Jack Squire through his own teardrops sploshes. **1931** W. Faulkner in *Amer. Mercury* Mar. 261/2 She made the sound into the cup and the coffee sploshed out on to her hands and her dress. **1941** W. Fortescue *Trampled Lilies* v. 61, I sploshed through the morass of mud and manure. **1966** M. Woodhouse *Tree Frog* iii. 24 He was sploshing around in a quicksand. **1978** S. Radley *Death & Maiden* i. 6 He sploshed on down the muddy track.

Hence **'sploshing** *vbl. sb.*

1929 W. Deeping *Roper's Row* xxx. 334 The sound of debate would cease suddenly. Boards creaked. Sploshings and sandpaperings recommenced. **1974** P. Dickinson *Poison Oracle* v. 115 The awkward sploshings of his paddle ..had been the loudest sounds in the marsh.

sploshy ('splɒʃɪ), *a.* [Imitative.]

a. Sloppy. Also, characterized by splashing or sploshing.

1838 *N.Y. Advertiser & Express* 28 Mar. 1/4 On Tuesday it was muggy and sploshy. **1881** *Harper's Mag.* Aug. 391 On horseback Rachel looks,—excuse the word but it expresses it,—sploshy. **1905** *Sat. Rev.* 29 July 133/1 Mr. Redmond, in rather a sploshy way, threatened dire obstruction. **1972** [see plasticized *ppl. a.* 2].

b. = splotchy *a.*

1942 E. Waugh *Put out More Flags* iii. 199 Cedric turned from the portrait of Angela... 'Is it finished?' 'Yes. It was very hard to make the man finish it, though.' 'It hardly looks finished now, does it Daddy? It's all sploshy.'

c. = splashy *a.*[2] 3.

1966 [see *coffee-table book* s.v. coffee *sb.* 5 b].

splotch (splɒtʃ), *sb.* Also 7 **sploch, sploach.** [Of obscure origin; perh. merely imitative.] A large irregular spot or patch of light, colour, or the like; a blot, smear, or stain. Also *fig.*

1601 Holland *Pliny* II. 266 Betonie is a soueraigne herbe ..for the blacke sploches that haue continued a long time vpon the skin. **1673** Wycherley *Gentl. Dancing-Master* v. i, Thou spot, sploach of my family and blood! **1683** Moxon *Mech. Exerc., Printing* xxiv. ¶10 If..the Leather..be Black and White in Splotches. **1755** *Gentl. Mag.* XXV. 373 See, from thy bite rise blister'd blotches, And from thy ordure filthy splotches. **1812** Sir R. Wilson *Priv. Diary* (1862) I. 247 During my progress, the carter's nose twice froze in splotches as big as half-a-crown. **1863** Miss Braddon *Eleanor's Victory* I. v. 111 The leaves were crumpled, and smeared with stains and splotches of grease. **1885** Lady Brassey *The Trades* 145 Their dark-brown leaves, covered with bright splotches of red and yellow.

splotch (splɒtʃ), *v.* [f. prec.] *trans.* To cover with splotches; to splash or stain in patches.

1654 Gayton *Pleas. Notes* iii. ii. 71 The bumps in his flesh, which was like a bruised Pig (but not so white), splotch'd all over. **1863** Trevelyan *Compet. Wallah* (1866) 219 He splotches his turban with pink paint. **1880** L. Wallace *Ben-Hur* iv. iii. 176 In places black moss splotched the otherwise bald stones.

splotchy ('splɒtʃɪ), *a.* [f. splotch *sb.*] Covered with splotches or stains; having the appearance of splotches.

1863 Miss Braddon *Eleanor's Victory* v, There were splotchy engravings scattered here and there through the pages of Monsieur Féval's romance. **1874** Helps *Ivan de Biron* vii. xii. 448 The splotchy aspect of the painted scenery.

†**'splotty,** *a. Obs. rare.* [f. OE. *splott* spot; cf. *ȝesplottud* spotted.] Spotted, speckled.

1382 Nicholas of Hereford *Gen.* xxx. 35 (MS. Bodl. 959), þe schepe..& þe weþeres, dyuers & splotty. *Ibid.* xxxi. 10 Males steying up upon femalez, vary & splotty.

spludge (splʌdʒ). *U.S. dial.* [Echoic: cf. splurge *sb.*] A 'splurge' or ostentatious display; *to cut a spludge* = *to cut a splurge* s.v. splurge *sb.* 1 a.

1831 *Essayist* II. 80/2, I was naturally anxious to see a little more of Tennessee life, and inasmuch as it was said there was to be a great *spludge* at the shooting, I went with him. **1856** F. M. Whitcher *Widow Bedott Papers* ix. 89 She tries to cut a spludge and make folk think she's a lady. **1913** *Dialect Notes* IV. 113 [Kansas words] *Spludge*, splurge.

splunge (splʌndʒ), *v.* *dial.* and *U.S.* [Imitative.] *intr.* To plunge.

1839 Marryat *Diary Amer.* Ser. i. II. 232 Here are two real American words:—'Sloping'—for slinking away; 'Splunging', like a porpoise. **1844** Carlyle in Froude *Life* (1884) I. 335 After a certain period of splunging and splashing. **1897** R. M. Johnston *Old Times Mid. Georgia* 68, I had no more ideas of getting married again than I had of splunging head foremost into the very bottom o' Rudisill's mill-pond.

splurge (splɜːdʒ), *sb.* orig. *U.S.* [Imitative.]

1. a. An ostentatious display or effort. Also in phr. *to cut a splurge*, to make an ostentatious display.

1828 'F. Herbert' *Talisman for 1829* ii. 107 'What a splurge' (said a Kentucky representative, in one of the favorite and most expressive words of Western invention) —'what a splurge she makes'. **1860** Bartlett *Dict. Amer.* (ed. 3) 112 *Cut a splurge*,..to make a show or display in dress. **1864** *Boston* (Mass.) *Commw.* 3 June, Manton Marble ..has just made a splurge in a letter addressed to the President. **1886** C. D. Warner *Summer in Garden* 152 They make a great deal of ostentatious splurge; and many of them come to no result at last. **1895** *Punch* 1 June 258/2 My anti-gambling old Gaffer 'as spiled the whole splurge. **1897** *Chicago Tribune* 19 Sept. 37/1 Two shrewd young Hoosiers ..came to Chicago in 1891 and cut a big splurge in monetary and real estate circles. **1977** *Daily Tel.* 19 Jan. 4/3 Presidential inauguration ceremonies..will go on for the rest of the week in a $3 million (about £1,700,000) splurge of dances, parties and celebrations.

b. A sudden extravagant indulgence, esp. in spending.

1928 *Publishers' Weekly* 16 June 2429 The Sales Force hadn't the courage to urge big splurges. **1929** W. Deeping *Roper's Row* xxx. 342 He was not to be the slave of other people's animal appetites, their sex splurges. **1937** M. Hillis *Orchids on your Budget* iv. 74 For years she has been putting something aside—not for a rainy day, but for a splurge. **1957** M. Millar *Soft Talkers* 193 A chicken salad which she looked at ravenously but barely touched, as if she knew too well the penalties of such a splurge. **1976** *National Observer* (U.S.) 27 Mar. 12/6 The Air Transport Association predicts a 6 per cent increase in air travel this year. 'We don't see any tremendous splurge,' a spokesman said.

c. *spec.* in *Journalism*, a large or showy advertisement, feature, etc.

1960 E. Partridge *Charm of Words* 31 A full-page advertisement..is usually called either a *splash* or, if showy, a *splurge*. **1971** 'L. Black' *Death has Green Fingers* x. 109 We've got..quite a splurge about the rose industry generally.

2. A heavy splash or downpour.

1879 Sala *Paris Herself Again* II. xvii. 270 The rain came down..in brief but uncomfortable 'splurges'.

splurge (splɜːdʒ), *v.* orig. *U.S.* [Imitative.]

1. a. *intr.* To make an ostentatious display; to show off.

a **1848** *Maj. Jones's Courtship* 101 (Bartlett), Cousin Pete was thar splurgin about in the biggest, with his dandy-cut trowsers and big whiskers. **1888** C. D. Warner *Their Pilgr.* iv. 114 People who..buy or build expensive villas, splurge out for a year or two, then fail.., and disappear.

b. To spend money extravagantly. Freq. const. *on*. Also *trans.*

1934 in Webster. **1947** *Chicago Sun* 28 Jan. 17/2 When I got around to furnishing my office, I thought I'd splurge on a good 18th Century English armchair. **1961** *Observer* 19 Mar. 3/3 The cigarette manufacturers splurged [on advertising], in spite of or because of cancer fears. **1975** *High Times* Dec. 130/1 If you really get into omelettes, you should splurge and procure a good copper or stainless steel omelette pan. **1977** *Spare Rib* June 6 So what does Bhagwan offer which is so compelling that feminists will splurge this sort of money? **1979** R. Jaffe *Class Reunion* (1980) ii. v. 229 You don't have to splurge on Maxim's now—we can go somewhere simple.

2. To splash heavily. (Cf. splodge *v.* 1.)

1887 T. Stevens *Around World on Bicycle* i. viii. 189, I don my gossamers as soon as the rain slacks up a little, and splurge ahead through the mud.

Hence **'splurging** *ppl. a.*

1884 L. Oliphant *Altiora Peto* 90 The..American heiress and her friend—two of my splurging young countrywomen.

splurgy ('splɜːdʒɪ), *a.* orig. *U.S.* [f. splurge *sb.* + -y.] Showy, ostentatious.

1852 *Yale Tomahawk* May 4/3 They even pronounce his speeches splurgy. **1871** H. Bushnell in M. B. Cheney *Life* (1880) 524 Great care to be had of language—no hollow generalities, no splurgy matter, nothing fine. **1884** *Harper's Mag.* Oct. 701/1 If one is..indifferent to the splendid but splurgy meerschaum. **1937** *Sunday Times* 20 Feb. 6/1 Diana is equally obviously one of those big splurgy actresses who have been successes up to the word Gone.

Hence **'splurgily** *adv. U.S.*

1887 *Atlantic Monthly* LX. 279 Living freely, generously, and, if one may say so, splurgily.

splurt (splɜːt), *v.* [Imitative: cf. splirt *v.*]

1. *trans.* To squirt or spirt out (liquid). *dial.*

1825-54 in N. Cy. and Northampt. glossaries (s.v. *Splirt*).

2. *intr.* To sputter or splash.

1845 J. Keegan *Leg. & Poems* (1907) 259 When the fire-canoe of the pale-face first hissed and splurted in the great waters of the mighty Missouri.

splutter ('splʌtə(r)), *sb.* [Imitative: cf. sputter *sb.* Noted by Johnson as 'a low word'.]

1. A noise or fuss.

1677 Miége *Fr. Dict.* ii, To keep a great splutter,..*faire grand bruit*. **1711** Swift *Jrnl. to Stella* 8 Sept., What a splutter you keep, to convince me that Walls has no taste! **1735** Burdon *Pocket-Farrier* 70 What a splutter has Mr. Solleysell made in his Works. **1809** T. Donaldson *Poems* 33 Your comrades, Davie, when you're dead, May raise an unco' splutter. **1893** in *S.E. Worcester Gloss.* 37.

b. Violent and confused declamation, discourse, or talk; an instance of this.

1688 *Vox Cleri Pro Rege* 6 After all this Splutter at the Churchmen and Clergy of England, he falls next to shoot his angry Bolts at the Collection. **1791** A. Wilson in *Poems & Lit. Prose* (1876) II. 35 For gudesake whist!.. Its nonsense a' this splutter. **1868** Swinburne *Blake* 15 The only original work of its author..consisting mainly of mere wind and splutter. **1881** Huxley in L. Huxley *Life* II. 33 Dinner.. with a confused splutter of German to the neighbours on my right.

c. A controversy or dispute.

1838 Mrs. Carlyle *Lett.* I. 109 He has had a splutter with Leigh Hunt.

2. A loud or violent sputter or splash.

1815 Scott *Guy M.* i, About a rood of the simple masonry giving way in the splutter with which he passed. **1841** Dickens *Barn. Rudge* iv, Until, with great foam and froth and splutter, it would force a vent, and carry all before it. **1873** G. C. Davies *Mount. & Mere* ix. 68 A couple of ducks ..made away with a great splutter.

fig. **1821** Lamb *Elia* i. *Old Benchers Inn. Temple*, Is the splutter of their hot rhetoric one half so refreshing and innocent as the little cool playful streams [etc.]? **1887** [see spitfire *sb.* 1 b].

splutter ('splʌtə(r)), *v.* [f. prec.]

1. *trans.* To utter hastily and indistinctly. Also const. *out*.

1729 T. Cooke *Tales*, etc. 119 Call them, without Reserve, Dog, Monkey, Owl, And splutter out at once Fish, Flesh, and Fowl. **1826** Lamb *Pop. Fallacies* vii, When he has been spluttering excellent broken sense for an hour together. **1850** Boker *Anne Boleyn* i. iii, And then shake heaven with angel merriment To hear you splutter—'Lord, all this is ours!' **1879** Thornbury *Tour rd. Eng.* II. xx. 62 King James spluttered out his alarm at Jesuit plots in clumsy Latin.

2. a. To scatter in small splashes.

1835 *Politen. & Gd.-breed.* 66 If you are eating soup, take care not to splutter it about. **1853** R. S. Surtees *Sponge's Sp. Tour* xlii. 232 Twirling the pen between his fingers, and spluttering the ink over the paper.

b. To bespatter (a person). Also *fig.*

a **1869** C. Spence *Fr. Braes Carse* Poems (1898) 196 Ae jaw-hole [will] splutter fifty folk. **1901** *N. & Q.* 9th Ser. VIII. 401/1 His pen was busy spluttering detractors.

3. *intr.* To talk or speak hastily and confusedly.

1728 De Foe *Mem. Capt. Carleton* 64 There came in a Dutchman, spluttering and making a great Noise, that he was sure he could discover one of the Conspirators. **1828** Carr *Craven Gloss.*, *Splutter*, to speak fast and inarticulately. **1881** Besant & Rice *Chapl. of Fleet* ii. xx. (1883) 279 He could not even swear. He could only splutter.

4. To make a sputtering sound or sounds.

1818 Scott *Rob Roy* vii, You may see Jobson on such occasions..puffing, strutting, and spluttering, to get the Justice put in motion. **1860** Thackeray *Round. Papers, Autour de mon Chapeau*, Dawn, it may be, rises unheeded;.. while waning candles splutter in the sockets. **1878** Lady Brassey *Voy. Sunbeam* 17 A dozen of them spluttering and fighting for the coin in the water at the same time.

b. To go *out* with a sputter.

1906 Treves *Highways Dorset* xii. 183 The attempt spluttered out like an over-fed candle.

5. Of a pen: To scatter ink in writing.

1837 Dickens *Pickw.* xxxiii, A hard-nibbed pen which could be warranted not to splutter. **1863** Miss Braddon *J. Marchmont's Legacy* II. iv. 90 You see if my pen doesn't splutter, the moment I address Richard Paulette.

6. To fly in small splashes or pieces.

1849 Lytton *Caxtons* 17 The fragments spluttered up round my father's legs. **1862** *Gifts & Graces* xv. 156 She dropped her fat round cake..right into her cup of tea, the contents of which spluttered all over her bonnet-ribbons.

†**splutter,** *int. Obs.* [Perversion of *God's blood*: see god *sb.* 14 a and Cuts[1].] A form of oath,

usually attributed to Welshmen. Also ***Splutterdenails*** (= blood and nails).

1719 D'URFEY *Pills* (1872) V. 7 Welch Taffy he raves and crys Splutterdenails. **1731** FIELDING *Grub St. Op.* III. xiv, Mr. Puzzletext, you are not mad, I hope? *Puz.* Splutter! my lady, but I am. **1748** SMOLLETT *R. Random* xxv, Splutter and oons! you lousy tog, who do you call my master?

splutterer ('splʌtərə(r)). [f. SPLUTTER *v.*] One who splutters.

1840 in SMART. **1882** *Daily News* 21 Feb. 4/5 Referring to the plaintiff as a 'cross-grained and ill-conditioned splutterer'.

'spluttering, *vbl. sb.* [f. as prec.] The action of the verb in various senses.

1739 *J. Miller's Jests* No. 167, But all his spluttering was in vain. **1840** THACKERAY *Catherine* vi, He emptied, with much spluttering and grimaces,..the beer into the fire. **1856** MRS. CARLYLE *Lett.* II. 299 What galloping and spluttering over the paper.

'spluttering, *ppl. a.* [f. as prec.] That splutters or sputters.

1706 E. WARD *Wooden World Diss.* (1708) 28 The End of War-ships is Fighting; but this spluttering Manager seems to believe them built..purely for Sailing. **1846** HAWTHORNE *Mosses* I. i, By the hissing and spluttering rain. **1852** MOTLEY *Corr.* (1889) I. v. 141 The noisy spluttering politics which constitute our vital elements. **1882** MISS BRADDON *Mt. Royal* III. viii. 164 Dopsy exploded in a little spluttering laugh behind her napkin.

splutteringly ('splʌtərɪŋlɪ), *adv.* [f. SPLUTTERING *ppl. a.* + -LY².] In a spluttering manner.

1941 *Penguin New Writing* X. 21 The rifles volleyed splutteringly three times and the funeral was over. **1969** *Listener* 16 Jan. 85/3 This is often a splutteringly funny book, but the humour seems to me to spring from an underlying sadness and spiritual discomfort. **1978** P. MASON *Shaft of Sunlight* iii. 47 He..made me try—splutteringly—to explain why the whole of the Rhondda valley could not be sentenced to transportation for life without having even poached a hare.

spluttery ('splʌtərɪ), *a.* [f. as SPLUTTERING *ppl. a.*] Suggestive of spluttering.

1866 *Spectator* 10 Nov. 1261/2 The gilding on it [a new book] has a spluttery effect.

spoak(e, obs. ff. pa. t. and pa. pple. SPEAK *v.*; obs. ff. SPOKE *sb.*

spoal, obs. form of SPOOL *sb.*¹

spoalty, var. SPAULTY *a.*

†**spoch-dog.** *Obs.*⁻¹ Some kind of dog.

1684 CREECH *Virg. Ecl.* III. 25 His Spoch-Dog [L. *Lycisca*] barkt, I cry'd, the Robber, see.

Spock-marked ('spɒkmɑːkt), *a. joc.* [f. the name of Benjamin McLane *Spock* (b. 1903), U.S. physician and specialist in child care + MARKED *ppl. a.*, after *pock-marked*.] (Adversely) affected by an upbringing held to be in accordance with the principles of Dr. Spock, esp. as set forth in his *Common Sense Book of Baby and Child Care* (1946).

1967 A. COMFORT *Anxiety Makers* vi. 186 Liberal and sane advice can still leave the children of anxious parents permanently Spock-marked. **1974** J. COOPER *Women & Super Women* 10 Permanently Spock-marked, they believe the world owes them a living.

spode¹. *rare.* [a. F. *spode*, or ad. L. *spodos* (Pliny), Gr. σποδός ashes, dross, dust.]

= SPODIUM.

1611 COTGR., *Spodizateur*, one that maketh Spode, or getteth soot, &c., from Brasse, by trying, or melting it. *Ibid.*, *Spodon de canne*, artificiall, or counterfeit Spode, made of the rootes of reedes, and Ox bones burned. [**1861** HULME tr. *Moquin-Tandon* II. iii. 81 Ivory calcined until it becomes white has been regarded as absorbent:..some therapeutists have termed it Spode or Spodium.]

Spode² (spəʊd). [See def.] The surname of a maker of china, Josiah Spode (1754–1827), used *attrib.* to designate ware manufactured by him. Also *ellipt.*, = Spode-ware.

1869 C. SCHREIBER *Jrnl.* 16 Sept. (1911) I. 37 The only thing the small shops at Exeter presented was a little Spode basket. **1875** L. TROUBRIDGE *Life amongst Troubridges* (1966) 106 We fished out several things—a blue Spode plate, for which we gave a shilling, [etc.]. **1893** *Auction Catal. Porcelain W. P. Hamond* 4 Two Spode cups. *Ibid.* 5 A Spode Dessert Service. **1899** M. COBBETT *Bottled Holidays* 149 A big, long-lipped, spode-ware jug, capable of holding a gallon. **1908** *Daily Rep.* 25 Aug. 8/3 Very little Spode has been for sale.

spodic ('spɒdɪk), *a. Soil Science.* [f. Gr. σποδ-ός wood ashes, embers + -IC.] Of a soil horizon: that is an illuvial deposit rich in aluminium oxide and organic matter and usu. also contains iron oxide.

1960 *Soil Classification* (*7th Approximation*) (U.S. Dept. Agric., Soil Survey Staff) v. 46/2 The spodic horizon is an illuvial accumulation of free sesquioxides accompanied by appreciable amounts of organic carbon, an illuvial accumulation of free iron not accompanied by roughly equivalent amounts of illuvial crystalline clay, or an illuvial accumulation of organic carbon usually if not always accompanied by an accumulation of aluminum combined in some form other than that of the crystalline silicate clays. **1972** J. G. CRUICKSHANK *Soil Geogr.* iii. 91 Podsolisation involves the translocation downward or laterally of iron and aluminium compounds from silicate clays, and their concentration in a specific lower horizon (B_2, B_f, or spodic horizon). **1979** *Nature* 4 Oct. 366/2 Soils in this forest are histosols (peat soils) with some spodic (podzolic) characteristics.

spodiosite ('spɒd-, 'spəʊdɪəsaɪt). *Min.* [ad. Sw. *spodiosit* (H. V. Tiberg 1872, in *Geol. Förening. Stockholm Förhandl.* I. 84), f. Gr. σπόδιος ash-grey: see -ITE¹.] A phosphate and fluoride of calcium, Ca_2PO_4F, found as orthorhombic crystals; also, any of a series of artificial minerals having similar crystal structures but containing other elements.

1887 *Jrnl. Chem. Soc.* LII. I. 346 In consequence of the chemical and crystallographical resemblance between spodiosite and kjerulfine, the author suggests that the two minerals may be isomorphous compounds. **1911** *Jrnl. Physical Chem.* XV. 469 The spodiosite found at Nordmark in Sweden occurs in orthorhombic crystals. **1953** *Mineral. Mag.* XXX. 167 These orthorhombic cell dimensions provide some justification for the inclusion by Dana of spodiosite in the wagnerite group. **1970** *Inorg. Chem.* IX. 2264/2 Spodiosites with the general formula Ca_2XO_4Cl, with X = P, V, Cr, and As have been prepared. **1974** *Jrnl. Amer. Ceramic Soc.* LVII. 102/1 Spodiosite analogs, a class of compounds related to apatites, are used in phosphors and have possible future industrial applications as laser hosts and bioceramic materials.

‖**spodium** ('spəʊdɪəm). Now *rare.* Also 6 **spodiom.** [L. *spodium* (Pliny), ad. Gr. σπόδιον, = σποδός SPODE¹. Cf. It. *spodio*, Sp., Pg. *espodio.*] A fine powder obtained from various substances by calcination. (See quots. and cf. NILL *sb.*¹)

a **1425** tr. *Arderne's Treat. Fistula*, etc. 63 Medicynez restrictyuez bene þise; Camphore, accacia, spodium [*text* spodin], coriandre. **1528** PAYNELL *Salerne's Regim.* (1535) 71 As spodium doth helpe and comforte the liuer. **1588** T. HICKOCK tr. *C. Frederick's Voy.* 38b, The Spodiom conieaIeth in certaine canes. **1601** HOLLAND *Pliny* II. 520 There is a kind of Spodium also made of lead in the furnace. **1661** LOVELL *Hist. Anim. & Min.* 216 The ashes of their bones if salted, serve in stead of spodium. **1662** J. DAVIES tr. *Mandelso's Trav.* II. 152 Spodium is the ashes of a tree growing near Sunda. **1671** PHILLIPS, *Spodium*, a sort of soot which rising from the trying of Brass, falls down at length to the bottom. **1728** CHAMBERS *Cycl.* s.v., The Moderns make their Spodium of Ivory burnt and calcined to a Whiteness. **1861** [see SPODE¹].

'spodizator. *rare.* [ad. F. *spodizateur* (Rabelais), f. *spode* SPODE¹.] One who makes spodium.

1694 MOTTEUX *Rabelais* v. xx, Her Abstractors, Spodizators, Masticators, Prægustics..and other Officers, for whom I want Names. [**1840** *Fraser's Mag.* XXI. 8 Like the young spodizator in the court of that royal lady to whom we have just referred.]

spodo- ('spɒdəʊ), *a.* Gr. σποδο-, combining stem of σποδός SPODE¹, as in **spodo'genic** *a.*, **spo'dogenous** *a.*, *Path.* characterized by the production of waste organic matter. **'spodomancy**, divination by means of ashes (Smart, 1836). **spodo'mantic** *a.*, divining by ashes.

1857 KINGSLEY *Two Y. Ago* I. vii. 186 [He] stared fiercely into the fire, as if to draw from thence omens of his love, by the spodomantic augury of the ancient Greeks. **1897** *Allbutt's Syst. Med.* IV. 525 This process may lead to what is called a spodogenous enlargement of the organ. **19..** *Buck's Med. Handbk.* VI. 413 (Cent. Suppl.), Spodogenic.

Spodosol ('spɒdəʊsɒl). *Soil Science.* [f. Gr. σποδός wood ashes, embers + -SOL.] Any soil belonging to an order characterized by the presence of a spodic horizon and including most podzols and podzolic soils.

1960 *Soil Classification* (*7th Approximation*) (U.S. Dept. Agric., Soil Survey Staff) xii. 192/1 The Spodosols include primarily the soils that have been called Podzols, Brown Podzolic soils, and Ground-Water Podzols. Not all soils called Podzols, however, are in this order. **1969** BUCKMAN & BRADY *Nature & Properties of Soils* (ed. 7) xii. 317 The low native fertility of most Spodosols makes them uncompetitive for tilled crops. **1978** R. W. SIMONSON in W. C. Mahaney *Quaternary Soils* 15 Direct evidence for transfers of organic matter within profiles has been obtained by measuring amounts moving down from A horizons of Spodosols.

spodumene ('spɒdjuːmiːn). *Min.* Also **spodumen.** [a. F. *spodumène*, G. *spodumen* (B. J. d'Andrada, 1800), ad. Gr. σποδούμενος, pple. of σποδοῦσθαι to be burnt to ashes, f. σποδός SPODE¹.] A silicate of aluminium and lithium, of varying colour, found both in crystals and massive.

α. **1805** R. JAMESON *Min.* II. 563 Spodumene... Colour greenish-white, which passes into apple-green. **1837** DANA *Min.* 305 Spodumene..was so called because it assumes a form like ashes before the blowpipe. **1897** *Edin. Rev.* Oct. 353 The Hiddenite, or green spodumene, is an extremely rare and very pretty stone.

β. **1822** *Imison's Sci. & Art* II. 84 It..has been met with in the petalite, spodumen, and lepidolite. **1851** MANTELL *Petrifactions* iv. §1. 364 Felspathic substances. Triphane; spodumen; petalite.

spoewslang, var. SPUUGSLANG.

spoffish ('spɒfɪʃ), *a. slang.* [Of obscure origin.] Bustling, fussy, officious.

1836–7 DICKENS *Sk. Boz, Tales* v, As a little spoffish man ..entered the room. *Ibid.* vii, He..was smart, spoffish, and eight-and-twenty. **1884** E. YATES *Recoll.* II. 244 A little spoffish American gentleman..had regarded me with great curiosity.

So **'spoffy** *a.*

1860 *Slang. Dict.*, *Spoffy*, a bustling busy-body is said to be spoffy.

spogeour, obs. form of SPOUCHER (scoop).

spoil (spɔɪl), *sb.* Forms: 4, 6–7 **spoyle**, 4, 6–8 **spoile**, 4, 6– **spoil**, 6 **spoylle**, 7–8 **spoyl**; 4–5 **spuyle**, 5 **spuyl**. See also SPULYIE. [ad. OF. *espoille*, *espuille*, f. *espoillier* (see next); or directly f. SPOIL *v.*¹ In senses 5–6 after L. *spolium*, pl. *spolia*.

As in the verb, there are notable gaps in the continuity of the older senses.]

I. 1. Goods, esp. such as are valuable, taken from an enemy or captured city in time of war; the possessions of which a defeated enemy is deprived or stripped by the victor; in more general sense, any goods, property, territory, etc., seized by force, acquired by confiscation, or obtained by similar means; booty, loot, plunder.

a. In collective sing.

13.. *K. Alis.* 986 (Laud MS.), Alisaundre took þe spoyle of þe cite. *Ibid.* 2555 After þat was parted þe spoyle. **1382** WYCLIF *Jer.* xxi. 9 Who forsothe shul..flee to the Caldeis that besegen ȝou, shal lyue, and be shal to hym his soule as spoile. **1530** PALSGR. 274 Spoyle that is gotten in warfare, *despoille.* **1568** GRAFTON *Chron.* II. 300 All suche as were at this battayle, were all made riche..by wynning of Golde, Siluer, plate, and Jewels, that was there found in the spoyle. **1582** N. LICHEFIELD tr. *Castanheda's Conq. E. Ind.* 163 With this spoyle the king of Calicut remained..ill contented. **1607** SHAKS. *Cor.* v. vi. 44 That we look'd For no lesse Spoile, then Glory. **1671** MILTON *Samson* 1203 As on my enemies, where ever chanc'd, I us'd hostility, and took thir spoil. **1774** GOLDSM. *Nat. Hist.* (1776) VIII. 122 If they meet with an insect,..several of them will fall upon it at once, and having mangled it, each will carry off a part of the spoil. **1781** GIBBON *Decl. & F.* (1787) III. 467 They were more ambitious of spoil than of glory. **1821** SCOTT *Pirate* vii, Several of the people..of Jarlshof were now hastening along the beach, to have their share in the spoil. **1838** THIRLWALL *Greece* xliii. V. 270 He led his army back..laden with the spoil of Locris. **1876** MATHEWS *Coinage of World* xiv. 123 Prussia and Austria then attacked Denmark and took Holstein and Schleswig from it, finally quarrelling over the spoil.

fig. **1697** DRYDEN *Virg. Georg.* I. 411 To gather Laurel-berries, and the Spoil Of bloody Myrtles. **1816** BYRON *Prisoner of Chillon* i, My limbs are..rusted with a vile repose, For they have been a dungeon's spoil.

b. In pl. Also more fully in ***the spoils of war***.

(*a*) *a* **1340** HAMPOLE *Psalter* cxviii. 162, I sall be glad on þi wordis as he þat fyndis spoils many. **1382** WYCLIF *Gen.* xlix. 27 The morwen tide he shall eete a pray, and the euen-tide he shal dyuyde spoylis. —— *Luke* xi. 22 Sothli if a strongere comynge aboue ouercome him, he..schal dele abrood his spuylis. **1535** COVERDALE *2 Macc.* viii. 27 So they toke their weapens and spoyles & kepte the Sabbath, geuynge, thankes vnto the Lorde. **1591** SHAKS. *1 Hen. VI*, II. i. 80, I haue loaden me with many Spoyles, Vsing no other Weapon but his Name. **1601** R. JOHNSON *Kingd. & Commw.* (1603) 167 The Tartars choosing this for their seate and countrie, beautified it with the spoiles of Asia. **1654** BRAMHALL *Just Vind.* iii. (1661) 37 Why did they not..preserve the spoiles of the cloisters for publick and charitable uses? **1712** HEARNE *Collect.* (O.H.S.) III. 311 Offering to him the Spoyls of the Enemy. **1746** FRANCIS tr. *Horace, Epist.* II. ii. 36 A common Soldier, who by various Toils And Perils gain'd a Competence in Spoils. **1790** BURKE *Fr. Rev.* Wks. 1907 IV. 59 Are the curates to be seduced from their bishops, by holding out to them the delusive hope of a dole out of the spoils of their own order? **1823** SCOTT *Quentin D.* xiii, A rich Turkey carpet, the spoils of the tent of a Pacha after the great battle of Jaiza. **1868** J. H. BLUNT *Ref. Ch. Eng.* I. 325 The great spoils of which the king had possessed himself. **1891** FARRAR *Darkn. & Dawn* lxi, Informers who had recently been enriched with the spoils of the innocent.

fig. **1667** MILTON *P.L.* IV. 159 Now gentle gales..dispense Native perfumes, and whisper whence they stole Those balmie spoiles. **1774** GOLDSM. *Nat. Hist.* (1776) I. 133 The new islands which are sometimes formed from the spoils of the continent.

(*b*) **1697** DRYDEN *Virg. Georg.* IV. 810 Mighty Cæsar, thund'ring from afar, Seeks on Euphrates' Banks the Spoils of War. **1865** C. STANFORD *Symb. Christ* i. (1878) 6 Who after a long pursuit recovered the prisoners with all the spoils of war. **1892** tr. *Villari's Machiavelli* II. iv. II. 184 Only of the spoils of war has the prince the right to be lavish.

c. *transf.* That which is or has been acquired by special effort or endeavour; esp. objects of art, books, etc., collected in this way.

Sometimes with slight suggestion of the primitive sense.

1750 GRAY *Elegy* 50 But Knowledge to their eyes her ample page Rich with the spoils of time did ne'er unroll. **1751** H. WALPOLE *Lett.* (1846) II. 390, I had just seen her collection,..composed of the spoils of her father's and the Arundel collections. **1820** HAZLITT *Table-T.* xvii. (1911) 252 The Louvre is stripped of its triumphant spoils. **1868** G. DUFF *Pol. Surv.* 7, I found him surrounded by the literary spoils which he had brought across the Alps. **1892** *Daily News* 23 Dec. 6/4 The plates represent the spoil of all the great galleries of Europe.

†**d.** *pl.* (See quots.) *Obs.* [F. *dépouilles.*]

1725 tr. *Dupin's Eccl. Hist. 17th Cent.* I. II. iii. 48 The Name of Spoils was given to the Goods the Clergy left at their Demise. **1772** tr. *J. F. de Isla's Friar Gerund* IV. ii. 21 His spoils (so it is usual in communities to call the effects left by the deceased Religious) consisted almost intirely of his manuscript sermons.

e. The public offices, or positions of emolument, distributed among the supporters of a successful political party on its accession to power. Chiefly *U.S.* and in pl.

sing. **1770** *Junius Lett.* xli. (1788) 232 Who is there so senseless as to renounce his share in a common benefit, unless he hopes to profit by a new division of the spoil? *c* **1789** GIBBON *Mem.* Misc. Wks. 1796 I. 164 From a principle of gratitude I adhered to the coalition: my vote was counted in the day of battle, but I was overlooked in the division of the spoil. **1812** *Massachusetts Ho. Repres. to Governor*, The weaker members of the party..would be overlooked..; whilst the more powerful would disagree in the division of the spoil.

pl. **1830** J. S. JOHNSON in *Congressional Deb.* 2 Apr. 299 The country is treated as a conquered province, and the offices distributed among the victors, as the spoils of the war. **1843** WHITTIER *What is Slavery?* Wks. 1889 III. 107 Leave these to parties contending for office, as the 'spoils of victory'. **1888** BRYCE *Amer. Commw.* II. 271 The post of policeman is 'spoils' of the humbler order, but spoils equally divided between the parties.

2. a. The action or practice of pillaging or plundering; the carrying off or taking away of goods as plunder; rapine, spoliation. Now *Obs.* or *arch.*

Freq. *c* 1550–1625, esp. without article.

1532 CROMWELL in Merriman *Life & Lett.* (1902) I. 348 The hole spoyle and eloyning of the sayd goods & plate was made onely by the sayd Edmond Knyghtley. **1550** T. LEVER *Serm.* (Arb.) 94 Suche Scottes or Frenchemen, as makyng spoyle for theyr owne profit, would not spare to dystroye thys realme. **1592** in J. Morris *Troubles Cath. Forefathers* (1877) 19 He..had a bag of money..which..he had before gotten by the spoil of Catholics. **1603** KNOLLES *Hist. Turks* (1621) 79 So was the citie of Constantinople..for that time saued from saccage and spoile. **1648** GAGE *West. Ind.* 49 The City was yeelded to the spoil, and the Spaniards took the gold, plate and feathers. **1710** O. SANSOM *Acc. Life* 334 The continued cruelty, violence and spoil, that was made upon our Friends. **1823** SCOTT *Quentin D.* xix, Well were the Liegois then assured, that..this Charles..would have given their town up to spoil. **1829** —— *Rob Roy* Introd., The alleged acts of spoil and violence on the MacLarens cattle.

personif. **1589** R. ROBINSON *Gold. Mirr.* (1851) 25 And greedy spoile spares not to spill, to pray on others good.

b. ***to make spoil of***, to pillage or plunder; to extort or collect goods, provisions, etc., from.

1613–8 DANIEL *Coll. Eng. Hist.* Wks. (Grosart) IV. 164 [He] enters France in the chiefest time of their fruits, making spoil of all in his way. **1643** R. BAKER *Chron.* (1653) 229 The Welchmen..break into the borders of Herefordshire, making spoil and prey of the Country as freely as if they had leave to do it. **1891** FARRAR *Darkn. & Dawn* xxxii, In this way they made spoil of all the country side.

†3. An act or occasion of pillaging or plundering; an incursion for the sake of booty or plunder; a marauding expedition or raid. *Obs.*

1543–4 *Act 35 Hen. VIII*, c. 12, The same Scottes..make ..inuasions, spoyles, burnynges,..and depopulations in this his realme. **1585** T. WASHINGTON tr. *Nicholay's Voy.* II. ix. 43 The Turkes haue made dyuers rodes & spoiles into the same. *a* **1586** SIDNEY *Arcadia* (1622) 323 Lycurgus..went toward her, rather as to a spoile then to a fight. **1603** KNOLLES *Hist. Turks* (1621) 1314 The fregats of Russia,.. the which had continually made inroads and spoyles vpon his lands. **1646** J. TEMPLE *Irish Reb.* (1746) 214 The being found upon Examination guilty of the late Spoils committed most barbarously on the English.

4. An object or article of pillage, plunder, or spoliation; a prey.

1594 KYD *Cornelia* I. 90 The Rocks..if thou sholdst but touch, thou straight becomst A spoyle to Neptune. **1596** SHAKS. *1 Hen. IV*, I. i. 74 And is not this an honourable spoyle? A gallant prize? **1791** COWPER *Iliad* I. 24 So may the Gods who in Olympus dwell Give Priam's treasures to you for a spoil. **1808** W. WILSON *Hist. Dissent. Ch.* I. 251 The Priory of the Holy Trinity..was fixed upon as an early spoil. **1821** BRYANT *Ages* xvi, Oh, Greece! thy flourishing cities were a spoil Unto each other.

II. 5. a. The arms and armour of a slain or defeated enemy as stripped off and taken by the victor; a set or suit of these. ***opime spoils*** [L. *spolia opima*]: (see quot. 1770 and OPIME *a.*).

a **1547** SURREY *Æneid* II. 352 Ay me, what one? that Hector how vnlike, Which erst returnd clad with Achilles spoiles. **1601** HOLLAND *Pliny* I. 170 Before he was full 17 yeres of age, hee had gained already two complete spoiles of his enemies. **1611** SIR W. MURE *Mes Amours* Wks. (S.T.S.) I. 10 Ye goddesse airmed With proud, presuming Cupid's conquered spoyle. **1697** DRYDEN *Æneid* II. 359 Hector, who return'd, from toils Of war, triumphant in Æacian spoils. **1718** POPE *Iliad* XVI. 808 The radiant arms are by Patroclus borne; Patroclus' ships the glorious spoils adorn. **1770** LANGHORNE *Plutarch* II. 366 What they take from the enemy in the field, they call by the general name of spoils, but these which a Roman general takes from the general of the enemy, they call opime spoils. **1810** DAVIDSON tr. *Virgil* (1843) 286, I vow that you..shall be clad in the spoils torn from the pirate's body.

transf. *a* **1586** SIDNEY *Arcadia* II. xxviii, Thou God, whose youth was deckt with spoiles of Pythons skin.

fig. **1768–74** TUCKER *Lt. Nat.* (1834) II. 659 Our abhorrences and tormenting passions,..were designed for our benefit, that in struggling with them we..gain the *spolia opima*, the richest spoils.

b. A single article acquired in this way.

1697 DRYDEN *Æneid* XII. 149 O pon'drous spoil [*sc.* a lance] of Actor slain. *a* **1700** EVELYN *Diary* Apr. 1646, A Turkish bridle..taken from a basshaw whom he had slain. With this glorious spoile I rid the rest of my journey as far as Paris.

6. a. The skin of a snake stripped or cast off, *esp.* that cast off naturally; the slough. Also *pl.* Now *Obs.* or *arch.*

1601 HOLLAND *Pliny* II. 363 As for the skinne or spoile of a snake, if it be put alone in a chist..it wil kil the moth. **1626** BACON *Sylva* §969 The Wearing of the Spoil of a Snake, for preserving of Health,..is but a Conceit: For that the Snake is thought to renew her Youth, by Casting her Spoil. **1638** RAWLEY tr. *Bacon's Life & Death* (1650) 51 Like the old Skin, or Spoile of Serpents. **1742** tr. *Algarotti's Newton's Theory* II. 200 Laying aside it's old Spoils like the Snake, it may again grow young.

b. The cast or stripped-off skin of any animal.

1664 POWER *Exp. Philos.* I. 12 House spiders have..a sleek thin skin: which they change once a moneth, sayes Muffet; though I hardly believe they cast their spoils so often. **1697** DRYDEN *Virg. Georg.* III. 589 Skins of Beasts, the rude Barbarians wear; The Spoils of Foxes, and the furry Bear. **1725** POPE *Odyss.* IV. 593 She..from her azure car, the finny spoils Of four vast phocæ takes. **1906** C. M. DOUGHTY *Dawn in Britain* III. 42 With buskins of the spoil Of mountain broc.

c. *pl.* The remains of an animal body; the parts left intact or uneaten.

1695 WOODWARD *Nat. Hist. Earth* I. (1723) 16 A Dissertation concerning Shells,..proving..that they are the real Spoils of once living Animals. *Ibid.* 26 These are the real Spoils and Remains of Sea-Animals. **1704** SWIFT *Batt. Bks.* Wks. 1768 I. 177 Numbers of flies, whose spoils lay scattered before the gates of his [the spider's] palace. **1865** G. F. BERKELEY *Life & Recoll.* II. 313, I never found the remains of a tench..where were what we denominate the 'Spoils' of an otter.

III. 7. The action or fact of spoiling or damaging; damage, harm, impairment, or injury, esp. of a serious or complete kind. Now *rare.*

a. With *of* (= inflicted on) or possessive pron.

1572 in Feuillerat *Rev. Q. Eliz.* (1908) 409 To the grett hurt, spoylle, & dyscredyt of the same. **1592** KYD *Murther J. Brewen* Wks. (1901) 292 It is thou and no man else that can triumph in my spoyle. **1600** SURFLET *Countrie Farme* II. lxvi. 414 They rotte and destroy the honie,..and the spoile of the honie causeth the bees to die. **1677** GILPIN *Demonol.* (1867) 118 The like spoil of duty is made when we adventure upon it in our own strength. **1691** T. H[ALE] *Acc. New Invent.* 22 Were this Spoil of Iron-work chargeable with nothing but what is contained in the Lead and Nails.

b. With *of* (= caused by).

1575–85 ABP. SANDYS *Serm.* (1841) 69 Although God hitherto hath preserved his vineyard from the spoil of these foxes. **1682** PENN *No Cross* xi. (ed. 2) 229 Poor Mortals!.. who with all their Pride cannot secure themselves from the Spoil of Sickness. **1691** RAY *Creation* (1714) 162 Guard them from the invasions and spoil of Beasts. **1820** SHELLEY *Sensit. Pl.* III. 25 The noonday sun..Mocking the spoil of the secret night.

c. Without const., or with *upon*; chiefly in phr. ***to do, make***, etc. (***great, much***) ***spoil***.

1575 TURBERV. *Faulconrie* 358 They will haue a disease in the backe,..and moreouer they shall be in daunger of vtter spoyle. **1596** DRAYTON *Legends* II. 549 Ruing the spoile done by his fatall hand. **1609** C. BUTLER *Fem. Mon.* (1634) 43 Mice..which in Winter are wont to make much spoil. *a* **1648** LD. HERBERT *Hen. VIII* (1683) 562 Sir John Wallop ..landed at Calais, and from thence..did much spoil upon the French. **1722** DE FOE *Plague* (1754) 154 Our three Travellers were obliged to keep the Road, or else they must commit Spoil, and do the Country a great deal of Damage in breaking down Fences and Gates. **1760** *Patrington Haven Act* 23 To make such recompence..for any damage or spoil that may be done. **1888** *Pall Mall G.* 28 Sept. 10/2 He was entitled..to raise minerals from the land, and to commit the necessary damage and spoil without making any compensation.

d. ***on spoil***, spoiling. *rare*$^{-1}$.

1750 in Temple & Sheldon *Hist. Northfield, Mass.* (1875) 378 Thus poorly have our Garrisons been stored; whilst many Hundred Pair of Snow Shoes lie on Spoil some where or other.

†8. a. An act or instance of spoiling, damaging, injuring, etc.; a damage, impairment, or injury; a piece or work of destruction. *Obs.*

1550 T. LEVER *Serm.* (Arb.) 95 In theyr doynges appeareth..a procedyng from euyl vnto worse, by an vncharitable spoyle, and deuyllyshe destruccion. **1581** MULCASTER *Positions* xl. (1887) 225 At home spoiles, soilthes, twentie things, are nothing in the parentes homely eye. **1598** MANWOOD *Lawes Forest* viii. (1615) 66 A wast of the forest is as much by common intendment, as to say, a spoile of the couerts or pasture of the forest. **1607** COWELL *Interpr.*, *Waste*..signifieth..a spoile made, either in houses, woods, gardens, orchards, &c. by the tenent for terme of life. **1660** F. BROOKE tr. *Le Blanc's Trav.* 19 They creepe up the trees, shake down the fruit, and make a great spoyle. *a* **1722** LISLE *Husb.* (1757) 442, I observed in the barley several full-grown ears withered lying along in a track of the field, which seemed to be a great spoil.

†b. A spoiler or destroyer *of* something. *Obs.*$^{-1}$

c **1611** CHAPMAN *Iliad* V. 331 Away flew Venus then, And after her cried Diomed: 'Away, thou spoil of men'.

9. †a. A spoiled or waste part of a timber-tree; wood of this kind. *Obs.*

1567 in F. J. Baigent *Crondal Rec.* (1891) 167 The same tenauntes maye lawfully haue..all the loppes, toppes, barkes, spoyles, and offalles of all..tymbre..trees. **1609** [see next].

†b. ? A piece of ground spoiled or rendered unserviceable in some way. *Obs.*$^{-1}$

1609 *Mem. Ripon* (Surtees) III. 334 Commons, Wastes, Spoils, Heaths, Moors, Fishings, Woods, Underwoods and Trees and the Spoil of the same woods.

c. Some thing spoiled or imperfectly executed, esp. in the process of manufacture.

1892 *Pall Mall G.* 29 Dec. 3/1 At the termination of the printing the notes are finally counted and packed up for delivery. If there are any 'spoils' they are burned. **1898** *Westm. Gaz.* 7 Mar. 7/1 The Progressives had already given way to the Moderates on two points, but the latter party now declared that this paper was a 'spoil'.

d. In spoil-five: A drawn game.

1891 in *Cent. Dict.*

10. *techn.* Earth or refuse material thrown or brought up in excavating, mining, dredging, etc.

1838 F. W. SIMMS *Publ. Wks. Gt. Brit.* i. 62 About three hundred thousand yards will be taken from this cutting to the embankment north of New Cross, and the remaining quantity will be placed in spoil. The deposit of the spoil and the formation of the embankment are both proceeding rapidly. **1863** *Edin. Rev.* Apr. 409 Countless mounds,.. which have been gradually formed round the pits, by the accumulation of 'spoil', or rubbish which has been brought up from below. **1894** *Times* 29 Jan. 14/2 The dredged material will be delivered by the buckets..into steel hoppers on either side of the vessel, each of which is capable of containing 7,000 cubic feet of spoil.

11. a. *attrib.* and *Comb.*, chiefly in sense 10, as ***spoil-earth, -ground, -heap, tip***, etc.; also, in sense 1, ***spoil-hunting*** adj., ***-taker***. See also SPOIL BANK.

1609 HOLLAND *Amm. Marcell.* XXV. viii. 274 The Romans ..when they had..driven away the Saracen spoyle-takers [etc.]. **1848** BUCKLEY *Iliad* 67 The spoil-hunting daughter of Jove averted the deadly weapon. **1883** GRESLEY *Gloss. Coal-m.* 232 *Spoil-bank* or *Spoil-heap*, the place on the surface where spoil is deposited. **1891** S. C. SCRIVENER *Our Fields & Cities* 36 A quarry—a very old one, judging by the many large heaps of spoil-earth..over which grass had grown. **1927** F. B. YOUNG *Portrait of Clare* I. iii. 34 The black dome of the Mawne Road spoil-heap fell away on her left into the tree-softened contours of Mawne Bank. **1967** *Times Rev. Industry* May 58/1 Around it [*sc.* Doncaster] stretches a flat, ill-drained corner of Yorkshire's West Riding, pockmarked with colliery spoil tips. **1972** *Times* 4 July 3/2 A devastated landscape of abandoned slurry ponds and spoil tips. **1973** *Times* 18 May 4/5 Above them towered the 300ft Eppleston spoilheap, started in the 1820s and at its peak containing well over 1,500,000 tons of red shale, dwarfing the houses.

b. In sense 1 e (*pl.*); esp. **spoils system**, the system or practice of a successful political party giving government or public offices, etc., to its supporters. See also SPOILSMAN.

1833 WHITTIER in Pickard *Life & Lett.* (1895) I. 170 To fall down and do homage to Andrew Jackson with the idolatrous 'spoils party' of the day. **1839** R. MAYO *Political Sk. Eight Years in Washington* 40 Mr. Jefferson.. authorized a friend to compromise with the federalists for.. a guarantee against the spoils system. **1883** *Nation* XXXVI. 539 According to the old ways of the spoilsmonger. **1888** BRYCE *Amer. Commw.* I. xxxiv. I. 521 The practice of dismissing Federal officials belonging to the opposite party, and appointing none but adherents of their own party to the vacant places,..is the so-called Spoils System.

spoil (spɔɪl), *v.*[1] Pa. t. and pa. pple. **spoiled, spoilt.** Forms: 4 **spoili,** 4– **spoil,** 4–6 **spoyll, spoill** (5 **spoillen**), 4–7 **spoyle** (5 **-yn**), **spoile,** 4–8 **spoyl,** 9 *dial.* **spile, spwile;** 4–5 **spuyl(e,** 5 **spulen, spole.** See also SPULYIE *v.* [ad. OF. *espoillier* (*espollier*), = It. *spogliare*:—L. *spoliāre*, f. *spolium*: see SPOIL *sb.* 5, 6. Perh. also to some extent an aphetic form of DESPOIL *v.*

There are striking gaps in the continuity of some of the earlier senses (cf. the sb.), and in senses 10–14 *spoil* has taken the place of the earlier SPILL *v.* The use of *spoilt* as well as *spoiled* for the pa. t. and pa. pple., dating from the 17th cent., is restricted to senses 11–14.]

I. 1. a. *trans.* To strip or despoil (a dead or helpless person); *esp.* to strip (a defeated or slain enemy) of arms and armour. (Cf. 6.) Now *arch.*

13.. *Coer de L.* 2058 The Griffons..Grete slaughter of our English maked, And spoiled the quick all naked. *c* **1330** R. BRUNNE *Chron. Wace* (Rolls) 5432 (P.), Þat ylke noble Hamon Romayn Spoiled a Breton þat was slayn. *c* **1400** *Destr. Troy* 6416 To spoile that spilt kyng he sped ferr. **1450** *Rolls of Parlt.* V. 212/2 The same mysdoers..murdred and slough the seid William Tresham and spoiled him and robbed hym. *a* **1513** FABYAN *Chron.* VI. (1811) 160 The prysoners..were so nere spoylyd, that they were fayne to take vyne leuys to couer with theyr secret membrys. **1600** HOLLAND *Livy* LXXIX. 1249 When the conquerour was in disarming and spoiling him when he had slaine. **1715** POPE *Iliad* IV. 584 The Greeks with shouts press on, and spoil the dead. **1757** W. WILKIE *Epigoniad* II. 46 To spoil the slain the ardent victor flew. **1870** BRYANT *Iliad* IV. I. 129 So did the high-born Ajax spoil the corpse of Simoïsus.

†b. To disrobe, unclothe (a person); to divest of clothes. *Obs.*

c **1375** *Sc. Leg. Saints* xlvi. (*Anastasia*) 216 Þare-for he spoylit þaim in hy, þat he mycht nakit se þare flesch. *c* **1386** CHAUCER *Clerk's T.* 318 (Petworth MS.), He bade þat wommen shulden spulen hir riȝt þere. **1388** WYCLIF *2 Cor.* v. 4 For that we wolen not be spuylid, but be clothid aboue.

†c. *refl.* To unclothe, undress, or disarm (oneself). Also with double object. *Obs. rare.*

1382 WYCLIF *Song Sol.* v. 3, I spoilede me my coote. *a* **1400–50** *Alexander* 4962 Þe kyng at his comaundment with his kniȝtis him spoilis, Puttis of to þe selfe serke.

†d. To strip or take off (arms). *Obs.*$^{-1}$

c **1611** CHAPMAN *Iliad* XV. 492 While these made-in to spoil his arms.

2. a. To strip (persons) of goods or possessions by violence or force; to plunder, rob, despoil. Also *fig.* Now *rare* or *arch.*

a **1340** HAMPOLE *Psalter* ii. 9 Þou sall noght be tyraunt til þaim, to pil þaim & spoile þaim. **13..** *E.E. Allit. P.* B. 1774 With mony a legioun ful large, with ledes of armes, þat now has spyed a space to spoyle Caldeez. 1382 WYCLIF *Exod.* xii. 36 The Lord ȝaf grace to the puple before the Egipciens, that thei wolden leene hem; and thei spuyleden the Egipciens. c1400 *Pilgr. Sowle* (Caxton, 1483) III. vii. 54 By fals menes and subtyll extorcion they haue spoyled the pore peple. 1526 TYNDALE *Acts* ix. 21 Ys nott this he that spoylled them which called on this name? 1585 T. WASHINGTON tr. *Nicholay's Voy.* I. v. 4 [They] had robbed & spoyled him. but..had restored vnto him that which was taken from him. 1624 QUARLES *Job Milit.* xiii. 55 Thy hands ..have spoyl'd The hopeless Widdow, with her helplesse Child. 1651 HOBBES *Leviath.* II. xvii. 85 To robbe and spoyle one another, has been a Trade. 1692 WASHINGTON tr. *Milton's Def. People Eng.* M.'s Wks. 1738 I. 491 We ought to pray for Highway-men, and for our Enemies... Not that they may plunder, spoil and murder us; but that they may repent. 1851 D. WILSON *Preh. Ann.* IV. i. 490 The native chiefs of the [Orkney] islands and neighbouring coasts who had been spoiled and driven from their possessions by the Vikings. 1884 RIDER HAGGARD *Dawn* xxviii, He might even be able to spoil that Egyptian George.

transf. 1697 DRYDEN *Virg. Georg.* IV. 268 He spoils the Saffron Flow'rs, he sips the Blues Of Vi'lets.

†b. In *pass.* with objective complement. *Obs.*

1432–50 tr. *Higden* (Rolls) IV. 443 Symple men were spoylede theire goodes.

3. a. To pillage or plunder (a country, city, house, ship, etc.); to clear of goods or valuables by the exercise of superior force; to ravage or sack.

Common in the 17th c.; now *arch.*

1382 WYCLIF *Exod.* iii. 22 Whanne ȝe gon out, ȝe shulen not goon out voyd;..and ȝe shulen spoyle Egipte. 1387 TREVISA *Higden* (Rolls) VI. 327 After þat þe Danes hadde i-spoylled Londoun and Kent. *Ibid.* VIII. 107 Tweyne of þe kynges schippes were..i-spoyled by men of Cipres. 1412–20 LYDG. *Chron. Troy* II. 3873 Þei..cruelly begonne In al hast to spoillen þe castel. 1442 *Rolls of Parlt.* V. 61/1 The Janueyes..semed..to make the said Sarazynes have good knowledge of the entrees into the said Ile, and there sodenly spoiled ii. Shippes. 1535 COVERDALE *1 Macc.* i. 31 When he had spoyled the cite, he set fyre on it. 1597 BEARD *Theatre God's Judgem.* (1612) 269 With an armie of fiue hundred thousand men he wasted and spoyled all fields, cities, and villages that he passed by. 1639 FULLER *Holy War* II. iii. 46 Their rich tents, which seemed to be the exchequer of the East-country, spoiled. 1678 WANLEY *Wond. Lit. World* V. ii. §25. 470/1 In which Tumult the City was sack'd and spoiled. a1727 NEWTON *Chronol. Amended* (1728) 20 Sesac spoils the Temple, and invades Syria. 1765 LYTTLETON *Hist. Hen. II* (1769) II. 339 The enemy.. entered triumphant into Hereford, spoiled and fired the city, razed the walls to the ground [etc.]. 1858 G. MACDONALD *Phantastes* (1878) II. 124 They proceeded, by spoiling the country houses around them, to make a quite luxurious provision. 1859 TENNYSON *Guinev.* 136 To slay the folk, and spoil the land.

transf. 1526 *Pilgr. Perf.* (W. de W. 1531) 23 He spoyleth his barnes for the sede, and spendeth his goodes to sowe his grounde. 1577 B. GOOGE *Heresbach's Husb.* IV. (1586) 183 b, When you have thus spoyled your Hiues, you shall carry all your Coames into some handsome place. 1601 DONNE *Progr. Soule* xxix, Foules they [i.e. fish] pursue not, nor do under-take To spoile the nests industrious birds do make.

†b. = HARRY *v.* 2 b. *Obs.*

c1400 MAUNDEV. (Roxb.) xiii. 57 Þe same tyme þat he went till hell and heried it, þe same tyme sall he spoile þe werld. a1450 MYRC *Par. Pr.* 509 The eleuenþe [article of the creed] ys for to telle How he wente to spoyle helle. 1563 *Homilies* II. *Resurrection*, Thus is death swalowed vp, by Christes victory, thus is hell spoyled for euer. 1659 PEARSON *Creed* V. 507 Thus still the Fathers which speak of [Christ's] spoiling hell, of leading captivity captive.

4. a. To seize (goods) by force or violence; to carry off as spoil; to rob or steal; to take *out of* or away improperly. *Obs.* or *arch.*

13.. *E.E. Allit. P.* B. 1285 Alle he spoyled spitously in a sped whyle, þat Salomon so mony a sadde ȝer soȝt to make. c1380 WYCLIF *Sel. Wks.* I. 21 Þei han more bisynes to spuyle fro men þer worldely goodis. 1529–30 *Rec. St. Mary at Hill* 353 To arrest Fold..for dyuers thinges spoillid out of our said house contrary to the Custom of the Cittie. 1560 DAUS tr. *Sleidane's Comm.* 400 b, What thinge soever was founde there,..it was spoyled. 1585 T. WASHINGTON tr. *Nicholay's Voy.* I. xv. 15 b, [He] put his men there on land to ouerrun, rauish & spoile, all whatsoeuer they shuld find for their aduantage. 1611 BIBLE *Mark* iii. 27 No man can.. spoile his goods, except he will first bind the strong man. 1781 COWPER *Expost.* 62 Jerusalem a prey, her glory soil'd, Her princes captive, and her treasures spoil'd. 1819 SHELLEY '*Men of England*' iii, That these stingless drones may spoil The forced produce of your toil?

transf. 1549–62 STERNHOLD & H. *Ps.* xlix. 5 Orels my foes which at my heeles are prest my life to spoyle? 1560 BIBLE (Geneva) *Prov.* xxii. 23 For the Lord wil..spoile the soule of those that spoile them.

†b. To detract *from*. *Obs.*⁻¹

1553 EDEN *Treat. New Ind.* (Arb.) 5 Wherfore if honest commendacions be a iust reward dew to noble enterprises, so much do they robbe and spoyle from ye dignitie therof, which in any poynt diminishe the same.

5. *absol.* To commit or practise spoil or pillage; to plunder, ravage.

c1400 *Siege Melayne* 986 Þou bygynnes sone for to spoyle, ..Thou settis more by a littill golde..þan to fighte one goddes foo. 1535 COVERDALE *Job* xxiv. 5 The wilde asses in yᵉ deserte go by tymes (as their maner is) to spoyle. 1597 BEARD *Theatre God's Judgem.* (1612) 269 On this manner he went spoyling through Fraunce. 1610 HOLLAND *Camden's Brit.* 719 The Danes robbing and spoiling wherever they came. 1816 SCOTT *Antiq.* xxviii, A soldier! then you have slain and burnt, and sacked and spoiled? 1867 TENNYSON *Victim* ii, But still the foeman spoil'd and burn'd.

II. (Const. *of*.) **6. a.** To strip (a person, body, etc.) *of* arms, clothes, or the like. (Cf. 1.) Also *refl.* Now *arch.*

13.. *Seuyn Sages* 500 (W.), He het his sone take, And spoili him of clothes nake. c1375 *Sc. Leg. Saints* xlix. (*Thecla*) 204 Son ves tecla..spoylit of hir clathis. 1388 WYCLIF *Lev.* vi. 11 He schal be spuylid of the formere clothis. c1440 *Gesta Rom.* iv. 9 (Harl. MS.), Iff ony man weere so hardy for to spoyle him of his armys, after þat he were y-buried, he shuld lese his life. 1497 BP. ALCOCK *Mons Perfect.* C iij, He wol spoyll hymself of all his garmentes to the entent that his adversary sholde haue noo holde of hym. 1514 BARCLAY *Cyt. & Uplondyshman* (Percy Soc.) 6 They spoyle the lambes and foxys of the skynne. 1590 SPENSER *F.Q.* II. ii. 33 Where they are well receiu'd, and made to spoile Themselues of soiled armes. c1611 CHAPMAN *Iliad* XVI. 462 If I be taken hence Spoiled of mine arms. 1720 STRYPE *Stow's Surv.* (1754) I. III. i. 529/2 The parson.. caused his Monument to be broken, his Body to be spoiled of his leaden sheet. 1734 tr. *Rollin's Anc. Hist.* (1827) I. 151 Cleonnis killed eight Spartans..and spoiled them of their arms. 1870 BRYANT *Iliad* XV. II. 102 See'st thou not how eagerly the Greeks Are spoiling Dolops of his arms?

†b. To strip (a tree) *of* bark. *Obs. rare.*

Cf. SPOILED *ppl. a.* 2.

1578 LYTE *Dodoens* VI. lxxv. 756 The timber waxeth red, assoone as it is spoyled of his rinde. 1653 BLITHE *Eng. Improver Impr.* 166 And if you spoil them [beech trees] of their Barque they die.

†7. *refl.* To divest or rid (oneself) *of* sins, etc.

a1395 HYLTON *Scala Perf.* II. xxxi. (W. de W. 1494), Spoyle yourself of the olde man with all his dedes. c1440 *Mor. Wisdom* 1140 in *Macro Plays* 73 Spoyll yow of yowur olde synnys & foly. 1582 N.T. (Rhem.) *Col.* iii. 9 Spoiling your selues of the old man.

8. a. To deprive, despoil, pillage, or rob *of* something. †Also const. *from* (= of).

Very common in the 16th cent.; now *arch.*

a1400–50 *Alexander* 4419 Ȝe lett men of þar libertes.., Thryngis þam in-to thraldom & of thaire þede spoiles. 1461 *Rolls of Parlt.* V. 478/2 To have spoiled the Coroune of Englond therof, as they didde of the seid Toune. 1526 SKELTON *Magnyf.* 1876 Here Magnyfycence is beten downe and spoylyd from all his goodys and rayment. 1570–6 LAMBARDE *Peramb. Kent* (1826) 145 He overruled the Nobility and outfaced the Clergie, spoiling both the one and the other of their livings. 1613 PURCHAS *Pilgrimage* (1614) 60 The King..banished him into the vtmost bounds of Chanaan, hauing first spoiled him of all his goods. 1621 BURTON *Anat. Mel.* I. ii. III. xv. (1651) 137 Others..spoile Parsons of their revenews. 1703 POPE *Thebais* 104 My sons their old, unhappy sire despise, Spoil'd of his Kingdom, and depriv'd of eyes. 1838 ARNOLD *Hist. Rome* I. 44 Many were they whom he spoiled of their goods. 1871 FREEMAN *Norm. Conq.* (1876) IV. 706 He had spoiled many men wrongfully of their inheritance.

b. To deprive or despoil *of* some quality, distinction, etc.

c1430 LYDG. *Min. Poems* (Percy Soc.) 195 Wyntir.. Spoleth tre and herbe of al ther fresshe bewte. 1495 *Trevisa's Barth. De P.R.* II. xx. (W. de W.) 47 Though fendes ben obstynate in euyll yet they arn not spoyllid of sharpe wytte. 1558 KNOX *First Blast* (Arb.) 11 God by the order of his creation hath spoiled woman of authoritie and dominion. 1586 T. ROGERS *39 Art.* i. (1633) 7 Spoyling so both the Son, and holy Ghost of their deity, and the whole Trinity of their properties. 1630 PRYNNE *Anti-Armin.* 117 It spoils the Lord of the very glory of his grace. 1691 T. H[ALE] *Acc. New Invent.* p. xiii, The 'Constant Warwick'.. was in its repairing spoiled of the excellency of its sailing. 1712 STEELE *Spect.* No. 263 ¶4 Anger spoils the Person against whom it is moved of something laudable in him. 1756 BURKE *Subl. & B.* Wks. 1842 I. 40 When you do this, you spoil it of every thing sublime. 1833 MRS. BROWNING *Prometh. Bound* Poems 1850 I. 143 Having spoiled the gods Of honours, crown withal thy mortal men. 1858 G. MACDONALD *Phantastes* vi. 76 She was giving me, spoiled of my only availing defence, into the hands of my awful foe.

III. †9. To carve or cut up (a hen). *Obs.*

c1440 *Promp. Parv.* 470 Sp[o]ylyn, or dysmembryn as menn don caponys or other fowlys,..*artuo*. 1486 *Bk. St. Albans* F vij b, An Hen spoylede. 1508–13 *Bk. Keruynge* a j b, Spoyle that henne, frusshe that chekyn. a1661 HOLYDAY *Juvenal* (1673) 78 'Tis no small difference, with what gesture men Of Art Vnlace a Hare and Spoil a Hen. 1739 R. BULL tr. *Dedekindus' Grobianus* 228 To spoil the fattest Hen our Youth was bid, And this man he literally did.

†10. a. To destroy, bring to an end. *Obs.*

1579 LYLY *Euphues* (Arb.) 44 The birde *Trochilus* lyueth by the mouth of the Crocodile and is not spoyled. 1581 STUDLEY tr. *Seneca's Trag., Hercules Œtæus* 111, I spoylde thy father Hercules; this hand, this hand aleare Hath murdred him. 1590 SHAKS. *Com. Err.* v. 37 For Gods sake take a house, This is some Priorie, in, or we are spoyl'd. 1640 tr. *Verdere's Rom. of Rom.* II. 123, I was ready to have spoiled you, if you had persisted in your malice. 1724 *Lond. Gaz.* No. 6305/1 The Horse..ran down a Precipice and was spoil'd. 1726 SHELVOCKE *Voy. round World* 241 Our launch being with the head towards the sea, I thought we were irretrievably spoil'd now.

refl. 1616 *Pasquil & Kath.* v. 47 [*Stage direction.* He drawes his Rapier.] *Winif.* Heele spoile himselfe: Let's run and call for helpe!

†b. To inflict serious bodily injury upon (an animal or person). *Obs.* (merged in 11).

1577 B. GOOGE *Heresbach's Husb.* 119 It must be sene to, that they be euen matched, least the stronger [horse] spoyle the weaker. 1597 VERE *Comm.* 28 The Cap-stain being too strong for my men, cast them against the ships side and spoiled many of them. 1653 H. COGAN *Diodorus Siculus* 176 In closing with the Beast he should be sure to hold him so fast as he should not be able to spoile him with his teeth. 1665 *Voy. E. Ind.* 381 If they strike an Horse, or Camel,.. they will so break their bones, as that they will spoil, nay kill them at one blow.

†c. In *pass.* Of troops: To suffer severely; to be incapacitated for warfare. *Obs.*

1665 MANLEY *Grotius' Low C. Wars* 155 While they were thus valiantly fighting, they were cut off by the Guns, at a great distance, and so spoiled with shot, that they were glad at last again to quit the place. 1690 LUTTRELL *Brief Rel.* (1857) II. 101 If our forces had continued longer before it, they had been spoiled [by excessive rain].

d. *slang.* To damage seriously in boxing. Also *transf.*

1811 *Sporting Mag.* XXXVIII. 8 There is not a pugilist on the list whom Belcher could not *spoil* by a sort of *gifted* science. 1847 *Sporting Life* 16 Oct. 106/2 Hudson returned some heavy hitting; but Cannon would not be denied, although he met with a stopper that would have spoiled the upper works of the best chancery lawyer in the kingdom. 1866 *Chambers's Jrnl.* 20 Jan. 33/1 Come on, you beggar!.. I'll spile your pretty face for you.

11. a. To damage, impair, or injure, esp. to such an extent as to render unfit or useless; to destroy (entirely or partially) the good, valuable, or effective properties or qualities of; to mar or vitiate completely or seriously.

1563 ABP. PARKER *Articles* A ij b, Whether any man..haue felled or spoiled any woode or timber in any Churche yarde. 1577 B. GOOGE *Heresbach's Husb.* 44 Take heede of Swyne, that spoyle..the grounde ilfauoredly. 1602 MARSTON *Ant. & Mel.* III. Wks. 1856 I. 37 O, you spoyle my ruffe, unset my haire. 1692 WOOD *Life* (O.H.S.) III. 391 A great flood, all grass spoyl'd. 1717 LADY M. W. MONTAGU *Let. to C'tess Mar* 10 Mar., These costly napkins..were entirely spoiled before dinner was over. 1767 T. HUTCHINSON *Hist. Mass. Bay* II. 162 The harbours this year were much spoiled. 1798 S. & HT. LEE *Canterb. T.* II. 415 Supper had been waiting till quite spoiled. 1826 *Art of Brewing* (ed. 2) 181 Of all sorts of old casks, beer vessels are the worst—as they always spoil cider. 1888 *Law Times* LXXXV. 132/2 The tenant for life.. is at liberty to fell such trees as are spoiling each other.

b. To ruin in respect of commerce or trade.

1618 in Foster *Eng. Factories India* (1906) I. 14 The Dutch have spoyled the Moluccoes which they fought for, and spent more then they will yeild them, if quiett, in seaven yeares.

†c. To ravish or violate (a woman). *Obs.*

1678 COTTON *Scarron.* IV. Wks. (1715) 67, I am half afraid lest he Should chance to spoil her Majesty. 1694 MOTTEUX *Rabelais* IV. xlvii, He has spoiled me. I am undone.

d. In *pass.* Of persons: To have the clothes damaged with mud. *rare*⁻¹.

1697 *C'tess D'Aunoy's Trav.* (1706) 132 The Coaches [go] up to the middle, so that it [*sc.* mud] dashes all upon you, and you are spoyled unless you either pull up the Glasses, or draw the Curtains.

e. To render (a ballot paper) invalid, as by improper marking, deliberate defacement, etc.; to invalidate (a vote) in this manner.

1872 *Act 35 & 36 Vict.* §33 If the voter inadvertently spoils a ballot paper, he can return it to the officer, who will, if satisfied of such inadvertence, give him another paper. ?1886 *Truth About Irish Election 1885* (Irish Loyal & Patriotic Union) 24 He clearly informed him that he would *spoil his vote*. 1953 *Ann. Reg. 1952* 235 The pro-Germans had been urged to abstain or to spoil their ballot papers. 1978 G. HERMET et al. *Elections without Choice* i. 3 The difference between free and controlled elections is indicated by the opportunity a voter has..to have his franchise recognised through registration..to decide how to vote, even to spoil his ballot, without external pressure.

12. With immaterial object: To affect injuriously or detrimentally, esp. to an irretrievable extent; to destroy or prevent the full exercise, development, or enjoyment of:

a. Of things or actions.

1578 LYTE *Dodoens* 420 Al the Crowfootes are dangerous and hurtful,..especially the..*Apium risus*, the whiche taken inwardly spoyleth the senses and understanding. a1586 SIDNEY *Astr. & Stella* Sonn. xviii, My wit doth striue those passions to defende, Which, for reward, spoile it with vaine annoyes. 1652–62 HEYLIN *Cosmogr.* III. (1673) 213/1 He was likely to have made himself a good bargain by it; if the sudden coming of the King of Barma, had not spoiled his markets. 1662 STILLINGFL. *Orig. Sacræ* III. iii. §2 The least thought of business would quite spoile his happiness. 1687 A. LOVELL tr. *Thevenot's Trav.* III. 96 It is surrounded with ugly shops made of Wood,..which spoils the prospect of it. 1709 *Tatler* No. 136 ¶13 The Sale of the said Clothes is spoiled by your Worship's said Prohibition. 1752 J. GILL *Trinity* vii. 144 That beautiful antithesis between Moses and Christ is spoiled. 1812 *New Bot. Gard.* I. 59 It will spoil their flowering. 1866 J. MARTINEAU *Ess.* II. 208 A mistake in arithmetic spoils our accounts. 1885 'MRS. ALEXANDER' *Valerie's Fate* ii, The notion worried and distracted her and spoiled the rest of her evening.

b. Of persons.

1626 *Haughton's Wom. will have her Will* IV. ii. G iij b, The Rogue is waking yet to spoyle [1616 marre] your sport. 1753 MISS COLLIER *Art Torment., Gen. Rules* (1811) 197 But if she should object to these things, you may accuse her of affectation, and a design of spoiling company. 1775 SHERIDAN *Rivals* v. iii, I hope..you won't be so cantankerous as to spoil the party by sitting out. 1801 tr. *Gabrielli's Myst. Husb.* III. 197, 'I caught him just as he was ..going out a pleasuring for the day.' 'Then facks, you spoiled his sport.' 1859 TENNYSON *Guinev.* 450 Thou hast spoilt the purpose of my life. 1885 'MRS. ALEXANDER' *At Bay* ix, I never heard of such madness. Why, you will spoil your life.

c. In the phrase ***to spoil all*** or ***everything***.

1653 WALTON *Angler* xxi, Be sure that your riches be justly got, or you spoil all. 1686 tr. *Chardin's Trav. Persia* 180 The Queen was a very beautiful Person,..but her demeanor spoil'd all. 1756 A. MURPHY *Apprentice* II. ii, Nay, but prithee now—I tell you you'll spoil all—what made you stay so long? 1871 FREEMAN *Norm. Conq.* (1876) IV. 144 As usual, local and internal dissensions spoiled everything.

13. a. To injure in respect of character, esp. by over-indulgence or undue lenience. Also, in weakened sense, to treat with excessive consideration or kindness.

1694 CONGREVE *Double-Dealer* III. iii, I swear, my dear, you'll spoil that child. 1749 FIELDING *Tom Jones* XIV. viii, One daughter, whom in vulgar language, he and his wife had spoiled; that is, had educated with the utmost tenderness and fondness. **1796** MRS. INCHBALD *Nature & Art* I. ix. 47 Considering the labour that was taken to spoil him, he was rather a commendable youth. **1826** DISRAELI *V. Grey* I. i, It was discovered that he had been spoiled, and it was determined that he should be sent to school. **1838** LYTTON *Alice* 14 My dear Evelyn, you are born to spoil every one. **1861** in Mrs. G. Porter *Ann. Publishing Ho.* (1898) III. 60 With every respect and admiration for Tennyson, I think he is childish about criticisms. His adulators spoil him. **1888** J. PAYN *Myst. Mirbridge* v, She does not spoil her eldest born. *absol.* **1895** *Daily News* 19 Apr. 4/7 It must be owned that even when she does spoil she spoils very nicely.

b. *Cant* and *slang*. (See quots.)

1812 J. H. VAUX *Flash Dict.* s.v., To prevent another person from succeeding in his object, .. subjects you to the charge of having spoiled him. **1884** R. C. LESLIE *Sea Paint. Log* (1886) 76 Well, it's a pity spoiling a nice gent like 'im. [*Note.*] The expression 'spoil a gent' is used by such men in the sense of disgusting him with the sea and so losing a good customer.

14. a. *intr.* To lose the valuable properties or qualities; to become unfit for use; to deteriorate; to go bad, decay. Also *transf.*

1692 *Laws Nevis* xv. (1740) 14 The Lesses were not able .. to grind off what Canes lay spoiling in the Ground. **1726** LEONI *Alberti's Archit.* II. 109/1 Rain water .. soon spoyls if it is kept in any vessel made of wood. **1774** GOLDSM. *Nat. Hist.* (1776) V. 4 Lest the feathers should spoil by their violent attrition against the air. **1796** SOUTHEY *Lett. fr. Spain* (1799) 457 Cargoes that are liable to spoil, such as all kinds of grain. **1828–32** WEBSTER s.v., Fruit will soon spoil in warm weather. **1857** HUGHES *Tom Brown* II. ii, 'That sort of boy's no use here,' said East, 'he'll only spoil'.

b. ***to be spoiling for*** (a fight, etc.), to long for, to desire ardently or earnestly. Also const. *inf.* Orig. *U.S.*

1865 *Sk. fr. Cambr.* 67 We are in the condition which the Yankees call 'spoiling for a fight'. **1890** STEVENSON *Lett.* (1899) II. 191 The native population .. chronically spoiling for a fight. **1893** *Nation* (N.Y.) 16 Nov. 368/2 Dr. James Martineau, who, in spite of his eighty-nine years, seemed still to be 'spoiling for an argument'. *a* **1960** E. M. FORSTER *Maurice* (1971) vii. 42 Durham .. would be found at all hours curled up in his room and spoiling to argue.

15. *techn.* (See quots. and SPOIL *sb.* 10.)

1847 DWYER *Hydraulic Engineer.* 129 The most rapid method of executing the earthwork of Railways, when the excavation exceeds the embankment, is to throw part of the excavation from the side slope to spoil. **1862** *Rep. E. Ind. Rly. Co.* 30 As the cuttings are comparatively few, it is intended to throw the stuff from them to spoil on either side of the line.

†**spoil,** *v.*[2] *Obs.*$^{-1}$ In 5 spoylle. [a. MDu. *spoelen* (G. *spülen*).] *trans.* To rinse or wash out.

c **1481** CAXTON *Dialogues* 26 Respaulme la hanap, Spoylle the cuppe.

†**spoil,** *v.*[3] *Naut. Obs.*$^{-1}$ [See SPOILING *vbl. sb.*[2]] *trans.* To measure or adjust.

1794 *Rigging & Seamanship* 22 The other half is then canted on and spoiled for faying.

spoil-, the stem of SPOIL *v.*[1] in comb. with sbs., as **spoil-five**, a round game of cards which is said to be 'spoiled' if no player wins three out of a possible five tricks; †**spoil-paper**, a petty author or scribbler; **spoil-pudding** *slang* (see quot.); **spoil-trade**, one who spoils trade. Also SPOIL-SPORT.

1839 CARLETON *Fardorougha* xvi, Busy at the game of '*spoil five'. **1841** LEVER *C. O'Malley* lxxv, What do you say to a little spoil five, or beggar my neighbour? **1610–11** in J. Davies (Heref.) *Paper's Compl.* Wks. (Grosart) II. 81/2 Nor list I purchase penance at that rate, As some *Spoile-Papers haue deerely done of late. **1788** GROSE *Dict. Vulgar T.* (ed. 2), **Spoil Pudding*, a parson who preaches long sermons, keeping his congregation in church till the puddings are over done. **1705** HICKERINGILL *Priest-cr.* II. viii. 77 Go on, I'll be no *Spoil-Trade, go Cheat and be Cheated, to the end of your Lives. **1854** *Poultry Chron.* I. 222/1 Thinking it best in such barefaced cases to become a 'spoil-trade', I have forwarded you the particulars. **1885** A. DALE *Jonathan's Home* 100 Their American brothers look upon them .. as spoil-trades and unscrupulous bargainers.

spoilable ('spɔɪləb(ə)l), *a.* [f. SPOIL *v.*[1]] That can be spoiled; capable of spoiling.

1648 HEXHAM II, *Schendelick*, Deflowrable, Spoilable. **1815** L. HUNT *Feast Poets* 124 These are not the persons in question,—they are not the spoilable men. **1849** LD. COCKBURN *Jrnl.* (1874) II. 321 This place is not exempted from the doom which makes everything spoilable. **1890** C. SMITH *Riddle L. Haviland* II. ii. I. 99 That is the only spoilable thing about me.

spoilage ('spɔɪlɪdʒ). [f. SPOIL *v.*[1] + -AGE.]

†**1.** The action or fact of plundering or robbing.

1597 BEARD *Theatre God's Judgem.* (1612) 249 Not satisfied with the pillage and spoilage of their houses. **1611** COTGR. s.v. *Tirer*, What hath beene got by miserie and pillage, comes to be subiect to vnthriftie spoylage.

2. a. The action of spoiling; the fact of being spoilt.

1816 BENTHAM *Chrestom.* Wks. 1843 VIII. 51 The expence produced by spoilage, during the teaching, is a counter-consideration, which must not be neglected.

b. The deterioration or decay of foodstuffs and perishable goods. orig. *U.S.*

1928 *Mineral Water Trade Rev.* 18 Jan. 16/1 The question of spoilage is not thoroughly dealt with in this country. Spoilage is an American term denoting any kind of deterioration found in a bottled carbonated beverage. **1958** *New Scientist* 24 July 481/1 The time that elapses between the killing of a whale and its arrival at the processing plant is often long enough for serious bacterial spoilage to develop, impairing both the yield and quality of the oil and the flesh itself. **1976** *National Observer* (U.S.) 27 Mar. 3/1 Israel has relied on subtler tactics to control the West Bankers. These have included detaining farmers' produce trucks to cause spoilage.

3. That which is or has been spoilt; *spec.* in printing (see quot. 1888).

1888 JACOBI *Printer's Vocab.* 130 *Spoilage*, applied to the sheets spoilt in printing, sometimes called 'waste'. **1892** —— in *Athenæum* 27 Aug. 289/2 A very small percentage [of extra sheets] to cover waste and spoilage.

spoil bank. Also **spoil-bank**. [f. SPOIL *sb.* 7 c or 10.] A bank or large mound consisting of refuse earth or similar waste material.

1830 BOOTH *L'pool & Manch. Rly.* 55 The remainder, deposited as spoil banks, may be seen heaped up like Pelion upon Ossa. **1854** *Hull Improv. Act* 9 The piece of land .. on the foreshore of the river Humber, near to a spoil bank. **1888** LEES & CLUTTERBUCK *B.C. 1877* xiii. (1892) 126 It was nearly all loose red shale, very much like the burnt spoil-banks common in colliery districts.

spoiled (spɔɪld, -lt), *ppl. a.* [f. SPOIL *v.*[1]]

1. a. Pillaged, plundered; ravaged. *Obs.* or *arch.*

c **1440** *Promp. Parv.* 470 Spoylyd, or spolyyd, *spoliatus.* **1550** T. LEVER *Serm.* (Arb.) 94 For your charitable pytye of myserable spoiled people. **1598** W. PHILLIP tr. *Linschoten* 191/2 For that a whole day we could see nothing els, but spoyled men set on shore. **1624** *3rd Rep. Hist. MSS. Comm.* 32/2 Theophilus, the poor Bishop of miserable spoiled Llandaff. **1637** MARMION *Cupid & Psyche* II. iii, There's not a man forsaken, Or god, for my sake, that bewayles his deare, Or bathes his spoyled bosome with a teare. *absol.* **1611** BIBLE *Amos* v. 9 The Lord .. strengtheneth the spoiled against the strong: so that the spoiled shall come against the fortresse.

b. Taken as spoil. *rare*$^{-1}$.

1718 POPE *Iliad* XVI. 612 What grief .. must Glaucus undergo, If these spoil'd arms adorn a Grecian foe!

†**2.** Of wood: Stripped of bark. *Obs.*$^{-1}$

c **1515** *King's Coll. Cambr., Estimate*, Tymbre: Remayneth in store of former provision ynowgh redy spoyled to perfourme all the saide Stalles and Rodelofte.

3. a. Deprived of good or effective qualities or properties by injury, disease, etc.; damaged, impaired, injured; defective.

1597 A. M. tr. *Guillemeau's Fr. Chirurg.* 33 How we ought to extirpate the spoylede & superfluouse fingers. **1837** CARLYLE *Fr. Rev.* I. III. iii, Our new Duke d'Orléans... Never yet made Admiral, and now turning the corner of his fortieth year, with spoiled blood and prospects. **1856** *Brit. Alm.* 94 Spoiled stamps. **1879** *St. George's Hosp. Rep.* IX. 527 The 6 spoiled eyes were found in 3 males and 3 females.

b. ***spoiled five***, = ***spoil-five*** s.v. SPOIL-.

1842 LEVER *J. Hinton* xix, The worthy priest .. was deep in a game of spoiled five with the farmer.

c. Of a vote or ballot paper: rendered invalid.

1944 *Federal Reporter* (U.S.) CXXXVIII. 248/1 In the election .. 201 [employees] cast ballots, with the result 39 unchallenged votes for United, 51 for International .. 7 votes were challenged spoiled, or blank. **1958** W. MACKENZIE *Free Elections* xv. 131 Even if there is compulsory voting, this general dissent may express itself through the proportion of 'spoiled papers' handed in. *Ibid.* 136 Administrative difficulties arise not over papers that are clearly 'spoiled' but over marginal cases. **1973** *Irish Times* 2 Mar. 8/1 Electorate, 37,299... Spoiled votes, 488. **1976** *Guardian* 17 Apr. 24/3 There was only one spoiled paper in the 94 per cent poll.

d. ***spoiled nun, priest***, a nun or priest who has repudiated her or his vocation.

1904 S. JOYCE *Dublin Diary* (1962) 26 He is the spoiled priest to his finger tips. **1916** J. JOYCE *Portrait of Artist* (1969) i. 35 He had heard his father say that she was a spoiled nun. *c* **1932** F. SCOTT FITZGERALD in A. Mizener *Far Side of Paradise* (1951) 307 The novel should do this. Show a man who is a natural idealist, a spoiled priest. **1977** *Times Lit. Suppl.* 13 May 593/1 Romantic wickedness (or, in O'Flaherty's own spoiled-priest phrase, 'romantic sin').

4. Of persons, esp. children: Injured in character by excessive indulgence, lenience, or deference.

1648 HEXHAM II. s.v. *Bedorven*, A spoiled child, by giving it his will too much, or by cockering him. *c* **1779** *Whitefoord Papers* (1898) 166 He was .. a kind of spoil'd child whom you must humour in all his ways. **1825** SCOTT *Betrothed* iii, Some of the petty resentment of a spoiled domestic. **1849** MACAULAY *Hist. Eng.* v. I. 619 The spoiled darling of the court and of the populace. **1884** *St. James's Gaz.* 9 July 6/2 Prince Victor Napoleon is, in almost every sense of the term, a spoiled child.

spoiler ('spɔɪlə(r)). [f. SPOIL *v.*[1] + -ER.]

1. a. One who pillages, plunders, or robs; a ravager, spoliator, despoiler.

1535 COVERDALE *2 Kings* xvii. 20 Therfore dyd yᵉ Lorde cast awaye all yᵉ sede of Israel, .. and delyuered them in to the handes of the spoylers. **1598** BARRET *Theor. Warres* I. ii. 11 Many disorders doe happen by the disorder of couetous spoilers. **1611** BIBLE *Isaiah* xxi. 2 The treacherous dealer dealeth treacherously, and the spoiler spoileth. **1680** OTWAY *Orphan* IV. vii, A cruel Spoiler came, Cropt this fair Rose, and rifled all it's Sweetness. **1760–72** H. BROOKE *Fool of Qual.* (1809) III. 65 One tenth for the use of the society .., and the other nine for the benefit of the spoilers. **1790** BURKE *Fr. Rev.* Sel. Wks. 1898 II. 192 Can any philosophic spoiler undertake to demonstrate .. the comparative evil of having a .. portion of landed property. **1844** H. H. WILSON *Brit. India* II. 81 Driving them into the interior, .. leaving their fields and homes to the spoiler. **1877** MISS A. B. EDWARDS *Up Nile* vii. 181 One can easily imagine how these spoilers sacked and ravaged all before them. *fig.* **1821** LAMB *Elia* I. *My Relations*, I hate people who meet Time half-way. I am for no compromise with that inevitable spoiler. **1824** PRAED *Athens* 199 If the flush of youth .. Could bid the spoiler turn his scythe away, Or snatch one flower from darkness and decay.

b. Said of animals, insects, etc.

1774 GOLDSM. *Nat. Hist.* (1776) IV. 225 One of them stands centinel upon a tree, while the rest are plundering .. : in the mean time, the rest of the spoilers pursue their work with great silence and assiduity. **1779** COWPER *Pine-apple & Bee* 5 On eager wing the spoiler came, And search'd for crannies in the frame.

2. a. One who or that which spoils, destroys, injures, mars, etc.

1577 B. GOOGE *Heresbach's Husb.* 35 Chyche .. is a great spoyler of land. **1648** HEXHAM II, *Brodder*, .. a Marrer, or a Spoiler of worke. **1694** MOTTEUX *Rabelais* v. (1737) 215 Wheadling Gablers, .. Spoilers of Paper. **1733** W. ELLIS *Chiltern & Vale Farm.* 297 Camock .. is a greater Spoiler of the Corn. **1766** GOLDSM. *Vicar* x, The sun was dreaded as an enemy to the skin without doors, and the fire as a spoiler of the complexion within. **1900** *Westm. Gaz.* 28 Nov. 2/1 The sun is a spoiler of intrinsic colour.

b. *Boxing.* An inferior fighter who sets out to disrupt his opponent's style.

1948 *Sun* (Baltimore) 29 June 15/2 Walcot is only a timid defensive heavyweight to whom the words 'offense' and 'attack' are abhorrent. In the language of the ring he is known as a 'spoiler', the type of fighter who can make an opponent look bad but who can never look good himself. **1959** *Times* 14 Oct. 16/5 Carroll, a 'spoiler' when at close quarters, has a good left jab.

c. *U.S.* One who mars the chance of victory for an opponent, while not being a potential winner. Also, applied to a thing. Esp. in *Sport* and *Pol.*

1950 *Sun* (Baltimore) 9 June 20/4 In meeting San Francisco here .. the Colts will get a crack at their biggest 'spoiler' of the past two seasons. **1965** *N.Y. Times* 1 Nov. 40 It seems clear that William Buckley will poll enough votes to be a 'spoiler', though it is not yet certain for whom. **1967** CONNABLE & SILBERFARB *Tigers of Tammany* iv. 117 Van Buren was the 'spoiler' in a three-way race. **1968** *N.Y. Times* 25 Jan. 19 Mr. Javits .. described the six-year-old Conservative party as 'a faction' that had been set up as 'a spoiler' party. **1971** *Ibid.* 22 Aug. IV. 3/4 What he [*sc.* George Wallace] is doing these days is laying the premise for another 'spoiler' campaign in 1972. **1976** J. V. O'BRIEN *William O'Brien* viii. 194 It was felt that the Protestant vote had gone not to O'Brien but to the spoiler candidate and ex-Lord Mayor. **1979** *N.Y. Post* 20 Aug. 44 It looks like we're out of it now, so we'll just have to be spoilers from here on. *Ibid.* 46, I suppose you can't have a 'spoiler' in soccer. **1980** *Washington Post* 11 Sept. 1/1 Not that Anderson is yet seen as a serious challenger for the presidency... But he is now perceived as a genuine factor in the presidential election, a certified political spoiler.

3. a. *Aeronaut.* A flap or the like that can be made to project from the upper surface of an aircraft wing to break up a smooth air-flow and so increase drag.

1928 DE PORT & BORDEN *Rep. U.S. Air Corps Materiel Div. Airplane Branch* No. 2878. 2 The 'spoiler' or 'lift destroyer' described in this report causes a decrease in lift by a 'burbling' action. **1932** *Rep. U.S. Nat. Advisory Comm. for Aeronautics* No. 439. 3/1 When ailerons and spoilers are used together the full effect of both is not obtained if the spoilers are located directly in front of the ailerons. **1947** A. C. DOUGLAS *Gliding & Advanced Soaring* iii. 84 When the spoilers are raised a certain amount of the lift of the wing is destroyed and the machine must glide at a steeper angle in order to keep the speed constant. **1978** R. JANSSON *News Caper* xiii. 115 Thackaray trimmed once more, and briefly pulled on the spoilers to reduce our air speed.

b. A structure on a motor vehicle intended to reduce lift and so increase the pressure on the wheels at high speed; also, one located so as to reduce the drag caused by components on the underside of a car.

1963 *Times* 8 Mar. 3/7 A special feature .. is the tail, which is sharply cut-back in Ferrari style, the roof sweeping down to end in a 'spoiler' or raised lip. This treatment eliminates turbulence and wind drag by killing low-pressure over the tail, and keeping weights on the rear wheels at high speed. **1965** *Observer* 10 Oct. 5/1 It has retractable spoilers which can be pushed up to increase high-speed stability. **1974** L. DEIGHTON *Spy Story* i. 10 His car .. was .. all dressed up in black vinyl, Lamborghini-style rear-window slats, and even a spoiler. **1979** *Time* 2 Apr. 6 (Advt.), The front spoiler is there to give you increased tyre adhesion at high speeds.

spoil-five: see SPOIL-.

†'**spoilful,** *a. Obs.* Also 6 spoylefull. [f. SPOIL *sb.* + -FUL.] Causing or characterized by destruction or pillage; plundering, spoliatory.

1590 SPENSER *F.Q.* II. x. 63 Having oft in batteill vanquished Those spoylefull Picts, and swarming Easterlings. *c* **1611** CHAPMAN *Iliad* VIII. 180 And he with spoilful fire had burn'd the fleet, if [etc.]. **1615** —— *Odyss.* III. 437 But thou .. too long .. Thy goods left free for many a spoilfull guest. **1670** MILTON *Hist. Eng.* IV. Wks. 1851 V. 179 As if thir landing had bin at the mouth of Humber, and thir spoilfull march far into the Country.

spoilȝie, obs. f. SPULYIE *sb.* and *v.*

spoiling ('spɔɪlɪŋ), *vbl. sb.*[1] [f. SPOIL *v.*[1]]

1. a. The action of pillaging, plundering, or robbing; spoliation.

c **1380** WYCLIF *Wks.* (1880) 425 þey ben not in þis þer vikeris, but in bodily trauel & spuyling of men. **1395** PURVEY *Remonstr.* (1851) 155 The spoilinge of the rewme bi beringe out of the tresore to straungeris. *c* **1400** *Apol. Loll.* 7 Feipful curats owen to sorowe .. of þe spoling of þer sogetis. *c* **1440** *Promp. Parv.* 470 Spoylynge, or spolyynge, *spoliacio, depredacio.* *a* **1548** HALL *Chron., Edw. IV*, 20 The Esterlinges .. had done yᵉ last yeres past much preiudice &

domage to the Englishe marchantes, both in takyng and spoyling of shippes. **1590** SPENSER *F.Q.* II. x. 7 A saluage nation..That..By hunting and by spoiling liued then. **1612** T. TAYLOR *Comm. Titus* iii. 2 Yet this sinne is a greater breach of loue then theft, or spoyling of the goods. **1647** SPRIGGE *Anglia Rediv.* II. iv. (1854) 109 If..you shall surrender it, and save the loss of blood, or hazard the spoiling of such a city. **1726** LEONI *Alberti's Archit.* I. 15/2 After the plunder and spoiling of the Temple. **1829** SCOTT *Anne of G.* xxxii, So I got into Charles's own pavilion, where Rudolph and some of his people were trying to keep out every one, that he might have the spoiling of it himself. **1869** BOUTELL *Arms & Armour* vi. 89 The results..of the spoiling of some dead Roman soldier.

b. An instance or occasion of this.

c **1380** WYCLIF *Sel. Wks.* III. 348 Bi þis spuylyng þei bilden Caymes castelis, to harme of cuntreis. *c* **1400** *Apol. Loll.* 76 Wat aȝen batails, aȝen reseruacouns, aȝen furst frutis, & oþer spolingis of goodis of þe kirk. *a* **1513** FABYAN *Chron.* VI. clx. (1811) 151 He in wrath..entryd the countrey of Burgoyne,..and executyd therin many spolynges and other inordynate dedys. **1560** DAUS tr. *Sleidane's Comm.* 405 Spoylynges & robbinges of townes. **1601** J. WHEELER *Treat. Comm.* 87 Manifold robberies, & spoilings at sea. **1692** WASHINGTON tr. *Milton's Def. People Eng.* ii. M.'s Wks. 1851 VIII. 67 The Wars that he rais'd, the Spoilings and Plunderings and Conflagrations that he occasioned. **1819** SCOTT *Ivanhoe* xxxiii, Easing a world of such mis-proud priests as thou art of their jewels..is a lawful spoiling of the Egyptians. **1886** MRS. LYNN LINTON *Paston Carew* xix, It would be a spoiling of the Egyptians perfectly justifiable.

2. The action of destroying, injuring, marring, etc.; an instance or occasion of this.

1479 in *Eng. Gilds* (1870) 321 So..Edmond complayned of spoyllyng of hys gowne and lackyng of his cloth. **1564–78** BULLEIN *Dial. agst. Pest.* (1888) 17 Euen so in tragedie he bewailed the sodaine resurrection of many a noble man before their time, in spoylyng of Epitaphes. **1573** TUSSER *Husb.* (1878) 105 Make riddance of carriage, er yeere go about, for spoiling of plant that is newlie come out. **1632** SANDERSON *Serm.* 14 Euil manners haue bin the spoyling of many good words. **1695** CONGREVE *Love for L.* II. x, They're all so, Sister, these Men—they love to have the spoiling of a Young Thing. **1712** SWIFT *Let. Eng. Tongue* Wks. 1755 II. II. 188 There is another sett of men, who have contributed very much to the spoiling of the English tongue. **1836** E. HOWARD *R. Reefer* lx, D——n his smooth face!—I should like to have the spoiling of it. **1875** J. C. COX *Ch. Derbysh.* I. 374 At that time..the spoiling of church bells was considered a necessary adjunct to a reformation in religion.

3. *Rugby Football.* The act or process of disrupting the opposing side's play; usu. *attrib.* Also *transf.*

1937 C. W. JONES *Rugby Football* i. 1 Experiments are being made with a new rule affecting the spoiling around the scrummages. **1959** *Times* 19 Oct. 14/2 Some dazzling moves started by breaks by Mulligan, who throughout found Jeeps in fine spoiling form. **1967** J. POTTER *Foul Play* ix. 111 A finer display of spoiling tactics and spectacular bouleversements had probably never disgraced a hockey field. **1978** *Rugby World* Apr. 43/3 It was a very interesting game, but I thought the criticism by the Barbarians of spoiling tactics after the game was unjustified.

†ˈ**spoiling**, *vbl. sb.*[2] *Naut.* [Of obscure origin.] = SPILING *vbl. sb.*[2]

1794 *Rigging & Seamanship* 5 Let that distance, or spoiling, be set off from the surface. *Ibid.* 10 *Spoiling* is taking the greatest distance of the inequalities between any two pieces to be fayed together.

ˈ**spoiling**, *ppl. a.* [f. SPOIL *v.*[1]] Despoiling, ravaging; doing damage.

1565 SHACKLOCK *Hatchet of Heresyes* 87 b, A spoyling tyrant. **1607** TOPSELL *Four-f. Beasts* 741 It had beene a shameful misery to indure the tyranny of such spoiling beastes. **1610** HOLLAND *Camden's Brit.* (1637) 199 The Danes in their spoyling rage burnt it to the ground. **1611** COTGR., *Spoliatrice*, a spoyling, or despoyling woman.

ˈ**spoilless**, *a.* [f. SPOIL *sb.* 1.] Unaccompanied by spoil or plunder.

1818 HERVÉ *Beauties Paris* I. 30 To the great spoiler of the continent these bloodless victories and spoilless ravages would have proved as profitable..as have his real conquests.

ˈ**spoilsman.** *U.S.* [f. SPOIL *sb.* 1 e.] One who obtains, or seeks to obtain, a share of political spoils.

1850 in T. H. Benton *Thirty Years* (1856) II. 784 The spoils-man that would sell his country for a mess of pottage. **1860** MOTLEY *Netherl.* (1868) I. 38 The spoilsmen, whose purpose was to rob the exchequer and enrich themselves. **1888** BRYCE *Amer. Commw.* III. lxv. II. 487 The extension of examinations will tend more and more to exclude mere spoilsmen from the public service.

spoil-sport. [f. SPOIL-.] One who acts so as to spoil the sport or plans of others.

1801 M. EDGEWORTH *Belinda* I. iii. 97 Harriot swore at the colonel, for the veriest *spoil-sport* she had ever seen. **1821** SCOTT *Kenilw.* xxviii, Mike Lambourne was never a make-bate, or a spoil-sport, or the like. **1855** KINGSLEY *Westw. Ho!* xxx, Spoil-sports! The father of all manner of troubles on earth, be they noxious trade of croakers! **1886** G. ALLEN *Maimie's Sake* xi, Before that spoil-sport Hetty came in and so rudely interrupted us.

attrib. **1886** *Pall Mall G.* 5 Nov. 4/2 He..was prevented ..by a spoil-sport Adelaide merchant.

Hence **spoil sport** *v. intr.*, to behave as a spoil-sport.

1869 TAYLOR & DUBOURG *New Men & Old Acres* III. 72 *Brown.* I'm locked in... Let me out. *Lilian.* (Unlocking door...) What was that for? *Brown.* (*Laughing.*) For fear I might spoil sport. **1946** K. TENNANT *Lost Haven* (1947) xvii. 285 He did not want to spoil sport; he wanted the whole gang.

spoilt (spɔɪlt), *ppl. a.* [f. SPOIL *v.*[1]] = SPOILED *ppl. a.* in various senses.

1816 JANE AUSTEN *Emma* III. xvii. 312, I am losing all my bitterness against spoilt children. **1841** BROWNING *Pippa Passes* Poems (1905) 182 The wry spoilt branch 's a natural perfect bow! **1875** JOWETT *Plato* (ed. 2) I. 264 He is a Thessalian Alcibiades, rich and luxurious—a spoilt child of fortune. **1890** *Science-Gossip* XXVI. 21 The egg had a very patchy and spoilt appearance. **1935** W. G. GILLINGS *Handbk. for Presiding Officers* 25 The spoilt ballot paper shall be at once cancelled by the presiding officer. **1983** *Times* 5 July 10/7 *We* are not protesting like spoilt children.

Comb. **1833** HOOD *Publ. Dinner* 174 Wet-footed—spoilt-beaver'd,..You haste home to supper.

spoilure (ˈspɔɪljʊə(r)). *rare.* [f. SPOIL *v.*[1], after *failure.*] The act of plundering or despoiling.

a **1918** W. OWEN *Poems* (1931) 77 Be slowly lifted up.. Great gun..about to curse... Be not withdrawn, dark arm, thy spoilure done. **1928** *Daily Sketch* 7 Aug. 19/2 Lion, my Lord, this camp was left in your charge. You made a big spoilure of it, so I am taking your work away.

spoilyie, obs. f. SPULYIE *sb.* and *v.*

spoine, obs. form of SPOON *sb.*

spojour, obs. variant of SPOUCHER (scoop).

Spokane (spəʊˈkæn), *sb.* (and *a.*) Also 9 **Spokan, Spokein.** [Native name.] A North American Indian people of the Salish group; the language of this people. Also *attrib.* or as *adj.*

1831 R. COX *Adventures on Columbia River* I. ix. 197 The Spokans we found to be a quiet, honest, inoffensive tribe. **1838** S. PARKER *Jrnl. Exploring Tour beyond Rocky Mts.* 284 We passed to-day several small villages of the Nez Percé and Spokein nations. **1875** H. H. BANCROFT *Native Races Pacific States* III. iii. 615 The northernmost Salish language is the Shushwap.., then there are the..Pend d'Oreille, the Spokane, the Soaiatlpi, and the Okanagan, which with others spoken on the Columbia show close affinities. **1894** *Messenger Sacred Heart Jesus* Apr. 273 Colonel George Wright gained a general victory over the..Spokanes. **1933** V. F. RAY *Sanpoil & Nespelem* 9 The Sanpoil spoke a dialect of Interior Salish and were surrounded by other Salish speaking peoples. All of the neighboring dialects were intelligible to them except Columbia and Spokane. **1944** N. W. ROSS *Westward Women* 71 She had to learn the Spokane language... This was a difficult task, as the sounds the Spokanes made in speech were like nothing so much as the sounds of husking corn. **1965** *Canad. Jrnl. Linguistics* Spring 78 Languages of sure affiliation..Spokan. *Ibid.* 159 In Spokane, one of the Interior Salish languages showing the greatest contrast, there are four terms that are generation-reciprocal. **1974** J. FAHEY *Flathead Indians* ii. 22 Flatheads married freely among contiguous Pend Oreilles, Nez Percés, and Spokanes.

spoke (spəʊk), *sb.* Forms: α. 1 **spaca**, 3, *north.* and *Sc.* 4– **spake**, 4–5 **spak**, 6–7, 9 **spaik** (7 **spauk**). β. 3– **spoke**, 5 **spook-**. γ. 6–7 **spoak**(**e**. [OE. *spáca* masc., = OFris. *spêke* (WFris. *speake, speak*), MDu. *speke, speec* (Du. *speek*), OS. *spêca* (MLG. and LG. *spêke*), OHG. *speicha* (MHG. and G. *speiche*) fem.; the ultimate etym. is uncertain.

The MDu. or MLG. *speke* was adopted in ME.: see SPEKE[2]. Du. *spaak*, LG. *spake*, etc., represent a different word (see sense 4 a).]

1. a. One of the set of staves, bars, or rods radiating from the hub or nave of a wheel and supporting the felloes or rim.

α. *c* **888** K. ÆLFRED *Boeth.* xxxix. §7 Swa swa þa spacan sticiað oðer ende on þære felȝe oþer on þære nafe. *Ibid.*, þa felȝa..hongiað on þæm spacan. *c* **1000** ÆLFRIC *Gloss.* in Wr.-Wülcker 106 *Cantus*, felȝa... *Radii*, spacan. *a* **1225** *Leg. Kath.* 1921 Hat..ȝarkin fowr hweoles, & let þurh-driuen..þe spaken & te felien mid irnene gadien. **1334–5** *Durh. Acc. Rolls* (Surtees) 525 In ij felys, ij spakes positis in rotis longe carecte. *c* **1375** *Sc. Leg. Saints* l. (*Catherine*) 853 All þe spakis..sall be fichit with hukis sere. *c* **1425** *Voc.* in Wr.-Wülcker 665 *Hic radius*, spake. **1513** DOUGLAS *Æneid* VI. ix. 185 On quhelis spakis speldit vtheris hingis. **1582** *Wills & Inv. N.C.* (Surtees, 1860) 45 In the hen house. Certaine spaikes, j swall, j lose bord [etc.]. **1614** in D. Wedderburne *Compt-bk.* (S.H.S.) 248 Fyve faldomis of burnewod with sum filleis and spaukis. **1815** G. BEATTIE *J. o' Arnha* (1826) 16 The spaiks were like to lift their linen.

fig. **1737** RAMSAY *Sc. Prov.* (1750) 61 It is the best spake in your wheel.

β. *c* **1275** *XI Pains of Hell* 69 in *O.E. Misc.*, A þusend spoken beoþ þer-on. *c* **1290** *S. Eng. Leg.* I. 208/278 A grislich ȝweol with spokene longe i-nowe. *c* **1340** *Nominale* (Skeat) 324 M[an] in the nathe doth spokes. *c* **1386** CHAUCER *Sompn. T.* 549 Twelf spokes hath a cart whel comunly. **1426** LYDG. *De Guil. Pilgr.* 12642 Fyrst off alle, the[e] avyse How thys whel hath...iiij. spokys strechchyd oute. **1523** FITZHERB. *Husb.* §5 The wheles..be made of nathes, spokes, fellyes, and dowles. **1627** CAPT. SMITH *Seaman's Gram.* xiv. 64 They haue wheeles made with spokes like coach wheeles and..strongly shod with iron. **1717** ADDISON tr. *Ovid's Met.* Wks. 1758 I. 162 Here fell a wheel, and here a silver spoke, Here were the beam and axle torn away. **1799** G. SMITH *Laboratory* I. 27 Ten or twelve inches will be enough for the diameter of wheels with six spokes. **1873** RICHARDS *Operat. Handbk.* 165 The Blanchard lathe..may turn from five to seven hundred small spokes a day.

γ. **1577** B. GOOGE *Heresbach's Husb.* 11 b, The smaller sort [of husbandry necessaries] be these,..Strikes, Spoakes [etc.]. **1594** *Shuttleworths' Acc.* (Chetham Soc.) 89 For setting on towe felkes and towe spoakes in a wheele, v[d]. *c* **1620** Z. BOYD *Zion's Flowers* (1855) 58 The spoakes..still neerer..gather, Till in the Nave in their points hard meete together. **1687** *Lond. Gaz.* No. 2272/4 The Good-speed,.. loaden with Iron, Spoaks for Carts, &c.

b. In fig. contexts, esp. in reference to the wheel of Fortune.

1412–20 LYDG. *Chron. Troy* IV. 1757 While she is benygne, By influence graciously tassygne Hir spokes meue vn-to ȝoure plesaunce. **1535** LYNDESAY *Satyre* 1139, I dreid ȝe spaiks of Spritualitie Sall rew that ever I came in this cuntrie. **1602** SHAKS. *Ham.* II. ii. 517 Breake all the Spokes and Fallies from her wheele. *Ibid.* III. iii. 19 Maiestie..is a massie wheele,..To whose huge Spoakes, ten thousand lesser things Are mortiz'd and adioyn'd. **1644** in Hartlib *Legacy* (1655) 278 If all such dispersed spoaks and vallies were fixed in one Centre (viz. a faithfull, carefull, skilfull Steward). **1813** SHELLEY *Q. Mab.* IX. 153 The restless wheels of being,..Whose flashing spokes..Bicker and burn to gain their destined goal. **1834** MARRYAT *P. Simple* (1863) 69 The wheel of fortune keeps turning for the comfort of those who are at the lowest spoke.

c. One of a set of radial handles projecting from a cylinder or wheel (esp. a steering-wheel).

1648 WILKINS *Math. Magic* I. vi. 37 An axis or cylinder, having a rundle about it, wherin there are fastned divers spokes, by which the whole may bee turned round. [**1769** FALCONER *Dict. Marine* s.v. *Helm*, The spokes of the wheel generally reach about eight inches beyond the rim or circumference, serving as handles to the person who steers the vessel.] **1841** R. H. DANA *Seaman's Man.* 181 In relieving the wheel, the man should..go to the wheel behind the helmsman and take hold of the spokes. **1867** SMYTH *Sailor's Word-bk.* 729 The helm..has a barrel,..and a wheel with spokes to assist in moving it.

d. *Basket-Making.* = STAKE *sb.*[1] 5 d.

1897 A. FIRTH *Cane Basket Work* ii. 17 *Spokes*, the coarser canes used as the foundation, and round which the weavers are placed. **1925** A. A. GILL *Practical Basketry* 39 After the spokes are arranged for weaving, take a short strand. **1958** O. R. SCOTT *Basketry Step by Step* 8 The uprights of a basket are called stakes or spokes.

2. a. A bar or rod of wood, esp. one used or shaped for a particular purpose; a stake or pole; a hand-spike; a weaver's beam.

1467 *Sc. Acts, Jas. III* (1814) II. 87 And at na merchandis gudis be revin nor spilt with vnresonable stollin as with spakis. **1496** *Acc. Ld. High Treas. Scot.* I. 289 To cary a laid of spakis fra the Castel to the Abbay, to mak pailȝoune pynnys. **1513** *Ibid.* IV. 508 Ane dusan akyn sperris to mak wyndes spakis. **1681** W. ROBERTSON *Phraseol. Gen.* (1693) 1162 A weavers spoke, *panus, jugum.* **1869** MCLENNAN *Peasant Life* 1st Ser. 260 She brought him to the weaver's cottage, and pointed out 'the spaik'.

b. A round or rung of a ladder, etc. Also *fig.*

a **1658** LOVELACE *Posth. Poems* (1659) 71 Yet the Spoaks by which they scal'd so high, Gamble hath wisely laid of *Vt Re Mi.* **1833** LOUDON *Encycl. Archit.* §990 The hay-racks to be made 2 feet and a half wide; the rungs (spokes) of 1 inch and a half deal. **1892** STEVENSON *Across the Plains* 197 Except for the weekly spokes and shafts of the ladder.

c. *Sc.* One of a set of poles adapted for carrying a coffin to the graveside.

a **1670** SPALDING *Troub. Chas. I* (1850) I. 74 Sum..liftis the Marquess corpis vpon litter:..the Marques sone..wes at his heid, the Erll of Morray on the right spaik, the Erll of Seafort on the left spaik [etc.]. **1822** GALT *Sir A. Wylie* civ, When the coffin was borne to the entrance of the sepulchre, the spakes were drawn out. **1861** E. B. RAMSAY *Sc. Life & Char.* Ser. II. vi. 120 It was the old fashion, still practised in some districts, to carry the coffin to the grave on long poles or 'spokes', as they were commonly termed. **1887** P. M'NEILL *Blawearie* 12 It's a gey queer funeral this,.. neither a hearse to draw, nor a spake to carry the deid on.

d. (See quots. and cf. 4 a.)

1858 SIMMONDS *Dict. Trade, Spoke*,.. contrivance for skidding the wheels of a vehicle. **1875** KNIGHT *Dict. Mech.*, *Spoke*, a fastening for a wheel to lock it in descending a hill.

3. *fig.* **a.** In phrases denoting an attempt to give advice, or have some say, in a matter. Still in colloq. use in ***to put in one's spoke*** (cf. OAR *sb.* 5 a).

1580 LYLY *Euphues* (Arb.) 291 With that Philautus came in with his spoake, saying [etc.]. *Ibid.* 413 Camilla not thinking to be silent, put in her spoke as she thought into the best wheele. **1601** B. JONSON *Poetaster* II. i. (1905) 28 You would seeme to be master? You would haue your spoke in my cart? you would aduise me to entertaine ladies?

†**b.** In uses suggestive of association with SPEAK *v.*: A saying, maxim, remark. *Obs.*

It is doubtful whether mod. dial. *spoke* in the sense of 'speech', 'story', is a survival of this usage.

1594 NASHE *Unfort. Trav.* Wks. (Grosart) V. 108 The spoke was this, *Frustra pius*, as much as to say, as fruitles seruice. **1599** PORTER *Angry Wom. Abingt.* (Percy Soc.) 40 Hee'l answere With some rime rotten sentence or olde saying, Such spokes as the ancient of the parish vse. **1615** *Curry-combe for Coxcombe* iii. 135 Had we a good Towne-stocke, thou shouldest haue a pension, for thy good spoake.

c. Denoting speech or action intended to advance a person's interests. *rare.*

1867 SMYTH *Sailor's Word-bk.* s.v., To put a spoke in a man's wheel, is to say something of him to his advantage. **1884** 'H. COLLINGWOOD' (W. J. C. Lancaster) *Under Meteor Flag* 50, I shall perhaps be seeing..your new captain..this evening, and, if so, I will put a spoke in your wheel for you.

4. *fig.* **a.** In phrases denoting action which is intended or likely to thwart, obstruct, or impede some person or proceeding; esp. ***to put a spoke in one's wheel.***

Possibly a mistranslation of Du. *een spaak* (= bar, stave) *in 't wiel steeken.*

(*a*) **1583** MELBANCKE *Philotimus* G j b, If you haue learnd the eight liberall science, I mean cogging, I will sett a spoke to your cogge. **1661** *Merry Drollery* II. 37 He..look'd to be made an emperor for't, But the Devel did set a spoke in his Cart. *c* **1681** HICKERINGILL *Trimmer* iv. Wks. 1716 I. 377 The reason why I have not been prefer'd, and advanc't according to my merits, is the whispers, and sly insinuations of such Trimmers suggestions, as this is, which has put a spoke in my Ladder.

(*b*) **1617** FLETCHER *Mad Lover* III. vi, I'le put a spoak among your wheels. **1656** LD. BROGHILL in *Thurloe's St. Papers* (1742) V. 295 Argile has been very industryous to be chosen, but we have put a spoke in his wheel. **1712** STEELE *Spect.* No. 498 ⁋2 They had clapt such a Spoke in his Wheel, as had disabled him from being a Coachman for that Day. **1801** tr. *Gabrielli's Myst. Husb.* III. 164 If you was to attempt to make your escape, I should be obligated to put a spoke in your wheel. **1853** E. FORBES in Geikie *Mem.* xiv. (1861) 527, I trust in you..to put a spoke in the wheels of my opponents if you find them going too fast. **1885** *Manch. Exam.* July 135/1 Capitalists..were trying to put a spoke in the wheel of Socialism.

(*c*) **1607** HIERON *Wks.* I. 411 Shee should not put in her spoke to withstand the motion, but should rather further her husband in such an honest businesse. *a* **1677** BARROW *Serm.* (1687) I. 149 He letteth them proceed on in a full carriere: ..then instantly he checketh, putteth in a spoak, he stoppeth, or turneth them backward. **1840** HOOD *Up Rhine* 8, I did hope the policy would haue put a spoke in our tour, but, unluckily, it gives me latitude to travel all over Europe.

b. Some thing, action, or fact which prevents, impedes, or obstructs; an impediment or obstacle.

Usually with *in the* (or *one's*) *wheel*: cf. above.

1689 *Mem. God's last 29 Yrs. Wond. Eng.* 64 Both which Bills were such Spokes in their Chariot-wheels, that made them drive much heavier. **1748** FOOTE *Knights* I. Wks. 1799 I. 69 So, Jack, here's a fresh spoke in your wheel... This is a cursed cross incident! **1755** KIDGELL *Card* II. 179 Here Mrs. Walker thought it would be no small Spoke in the Wheel of her present Design, to take up her Residence herself. **1845** DISRAELI *Sybil* (1863) 212 Rely upon it a bold united front at this moment would be a spoke in the wheel. **1855** THACKERAY *Newcomes* ix, And thinks I there's a spoke in your wheel, you stuck-up little old Duchess.

5. *transf.* †**a.** *Bot.* A pedicel or peduncle of an umbel; a radius or ray. *Obs.*

1578 LYTE *Dodoens* 614 The spokes [of *Ammi visnaga*].. the Italians and Spaniardes doo use as tooth-picks. **1796** WITHERING *Brit. Plants* (ed. 3) I. 83 *Spokes* (radii), the fruit-stalks of flowers collected into Umbels or Umbellules. *Ibid.* II. 79 Fruit-stalks..forming a sort of umbel, the outer spokes of which are gradually shorter and shorter.

b. A ray or beam of light, sunshine, etc.

1849 CUPPLES *Green Hand* xiv. (1856) 138 The sun had got low, and he shivered his dazzling spokes of light behind one edge of it [a bank of vapour]. *Ibid.* 152 While here and there a broad bright hazy spoke off the sun came cutting down into the forest.

6. *attrib.* and *Comb.*, as ***spoke-flange***; **spoke-bone** *Anat.*, = RADIUS *sb.* 1 c; **spoke-brush, -river, -wood** (see quots.). Also SPOKE-SHAVE.

A number of technical uses are given and defined in Knight *Dict. Mech.* (1875) and Suppl. (1884), as *spoke-auger, -clamp, -gage, -groove, -lathe, -wheel; spoke-pointer, -setter, -trimmer; spoke driving, -facing, -inserting*, etc.

a **1843** *Encycl. Metrop.* (1845) VII. 303 [In fishes] there is usually an aperture between the lower edge of the spoke-bone and the upper edge of the ulna. *Ibid.* 326 The Fore-Arm [in birds] consists of two bones, the cubit and spoke-bone, of which the latter is always in a state of semipronation. **1851** MAYHEW *Lond. Labour* I. 362/1 The street-vendors sell wash-leathers,..spoke-brushes (to clean carriage-wheels), and coach-mops. **1851** J. BROWN *Forester* (ed. 2) iv. 362 Young oaks, of the size generally termed spoke-wood, sell well. **1858** SIMMONDS *Dict. Trade, Spoke-river*, a wheelwright, or shaper of spokes or rounds for ladders. **1869** *Archaeol.* XLII. 126 Skewerwood..is also called spoke-wood. **1876** J. GREENWOOD *Low-life Deeps* 218 The sand-paperer..had caught up a spoke-brush, and was poising it for a throw. **1898** *Cycling* 48 The hub should not measure less than 2 in. between the spoke-flanges.

spoke (spəʊk), *v.* [f. the sb.]

1. *trans.* To furnish or provide with spokes or bars; to mark *with* spoke-like lines or rays.

1720 POPE *Iliad* XXI. 45 As from a sycamore, his sounding steel Lopp'd the green arms to spoke a chariot-wheel. **1756** MRS. CALDERWOOD in *Coltness Coll.* (Maitl. Club) 122 Just by the water-pump there was a crib [for chickens] fixt about a yard from the ground; it was spoked in the bottom, so that the filth fell through. **1839** HAWTHORNE *Transform.* xlix, A triumphal car,..its slow-moving wheels encircled and spoked with foliage. **1890** R. BRIDGES *Shorter Poems* II. 5 The white water-lily spoked with gold.

2. To thrust a spoke into (a wheel, etc.) in order to check movement; *fig.* to block, impede, or obstruct.

1854 MISS BAKER *Northampt. Gloss.* s.v., 'Spoke your cart' is a phrase of similar significancy. **1896** *Daily News* 4 June 5/4 Six pages of amendments skilfully handled are sufficient to spoke the wheels of any private Bill.

3. To drive or force (a wheel or vehicle) *forward* by pushing the spokes.

1860 *Chambers's Jrnl.* XIV. 236 Those under the vehicle can 'spoke' the wheels forward. **1882** E. O'DONOVAN *Merv Oasis* I. iii. 54 The waggons, often down to the axle, had to be forcibly spoked forward by the men.

spoked (spəʊkt), *a.* [f. SPOKE *sb.*]

†**1.** Arranged radially; radiate, radiated. *Obs.*

1597 GERARDE *Herbal* 914 There stande at the top tufts or spoked rundles, the flowers whereof are either white or purple. **1652** CULPEPPER *Eng. Physic.* 55 It riseth a little above a foot high, bearing white flowers in spoked tufts.

2. Made or provided with spokes.

1890 H. S. HALLETT *1000 Miles on Eleph. in Shan States* 437 Carts..remarkable for the size of their spoked wheels.

'spokeless, *a.* [f. SPOKE *sb.*] Destitute of spokes; made without spokes.

c **1449** *Pol. Poems* (Rolls) II. 222 The Carte nathe [i.e. the Duke of Buckingham] is spokeles, For the counseille that he gaffe. **1842** *P. Parley's Ann.* III. 236 Its wheel tireless and nearly spokeless. **1891** *Bicycling News* 4 Apr. 198 The latest departure in the field of cycling inventions is a spokeless wheel.

'spoken, *a. rare.* [f. SPOKE *sb.*] Pertaining to or connected with a spoke or spokes (see quot.).

1790 W. H. MARSHALL *Rur. Econ. Midl.* II. 443 *Spoken chain*, an appendage of a waggon, peculiar to this district; a long strong chain, to be fixed to the spoke of the wheel, when the team is 'stalled' or set fast in a slough.

spoken ('spəʊk(ə)n), *ppl. a.* [Pa. pple. of SPEAK *v.*]

As the second element in combs., *spoken* is used in the sense of 'speaking' or 'given to speaking' in a specified way, as in *blunt-, broad-, civil-, fine-, out-, plain-spoken*, etc. Most of these date from the 17th cent. or later, but *fair-spoken* is found in 1460. ON. and Icel. *talaðr* (pa. pple. of *tala* to speak) is similarly used, even without a qualifying term.

1. With preps.: That is or has been spoken *about, of, to*, etc.

1595 *Drake's Voy.* (Hakl. Soc.) 24 The..adventure she had been at in the glorious spoken-of jorney. **1865** 'ANNIE THOMAS' *On Guard* xxi, She may not only speak, but may think, with affection..of the spoken about. **1875** WHITNEY *Life Lang.* x. 207 The speaker and the spoken-to.

2. a. Of language, words, etc.: Uttered in speech; oral. Also, colloquial as distinguished from *literary*.

1837 P. KEITH *Bot. Lex.* 370 To enable us to appreciate the value of tones, whether they be the modulations of music, or the articulation of a spoken language. **1867** *Trans. Philol. Soc.* Suppl. I On Palaeotype, or the representation of spoken sounds..by means of the ancient types. **1885** GLADSTONE in *Westm. Gaz.* 8 June 4/2 Reminding me that spoken words may fulfil a purpose higher than we mostly dream of.

b. Expressed, declared, made known by speech or utterance.

1851 BRIMLEY *Ess., Wordsw.* 164 We should like to have had some record of spoken feelings. **1879** B. TAYLOR *Germ. Lit.* 204 There is a vast difference between the silent and the spoken protest.

c. *ellipt.* Words which are spoken (in place of being sung) in connexion with a song or other musical performance; a part of this nature.

1865 DICKENS *Mut. Fr.* IV. xvi, A comic song..with 'Spoken' in it. **1900** H. LAWSON *On Track* 10 Thus warmed up, Pinter starts with an explanatory 'spoken' to the effect that the song he is about to sing illustrates some of the little ways of woman.

d. ***the spoken word***, speech (as opp. to written language, etc.), esp. in the context of radio broadcasting.

1832 CARLYLE in *Fraser's Mag.* Apr. 257/1 Whether man *can* any longer be so interested by the spoken Word, as he often was in those primeval days. **1929** *Radio Times* 29 Nov. 432 Poetry..has its roots in the spoken word: the written word is only a means of saving poetry from the oblivion of time. **1940** R. S. LAMBERT *Ariel & All his Quality* iii. 60 The 'spoken word' is the most contentious and most closely scrutinised part of the broadcast programme. **1944** *Ann. Reg. 1943* 62 Training..in understanding of the written and spoken word. **1961** *Listener* 28 Sept. 456/1 One criticism that has been made of spoken-word material in the Third is that it has sometimes been too esoteric. **1972** *Ibid.* 2 Nov. 574/2 It was the treatment of the spoken word that seemed to fox the early fathers of broadcasting.

Hence **'spokenness**, the fact or quality of having been spoken or uttered.

1805 *Monthly Mag.* XX. 513 The idea of spokenness has been progressively detached from the word 'language'. **1947** L. MACNEICE *Dark Tower* 10 But when no character can be presented except through spoken words, whether in dialogue or soliloquy, that very *spokenness* makes this distinction between subjective and objective futile.

spokeshave ('spəʊkʃeɪv), *sb.* Also 7- spoke-shave. [f. SPOKE *sb.* + SHAVE *sb.*[1] Hence WFlem. *spokschaaf.*] A form of drawing-knife or shave used for shaping and finishing spokes; a carpenter's tool having the blade or plane-bit set between two handles placed lengthwise and used for planing curved work; a transverse plane.

1510 STANBRIDGE *Vocabula* (W. de W.) Cj, *Radula*, a spokeshaue or a playne. **1572** in *Midl. Co. Hist. Coll.* (1856) II. 363 A spokeshaue, a wimble, a hammer. **1688** HOLME *Armoury* III. 317/2 A Spoke-shave, is an Iron with a sharp edge set in a piece of Wood with two handles after the manner of a Plain. **1794** *Rigging & Seamanship* 152 *Spoke-shave*,..is a piece of steel, 4 or more inches long, and one inch ½ broad; sharp at one edge as a knife. **1837** W. B. ADAMS *Carriages* 152 The ends being tapered down one after the other with a spoke-shave till the whole amalgamate neatly. **1881** YOUNG *Ev. Man his own Mechanic* §250. 93 The spokeshave and the drawing-knife are the tools that are comprised in the second division of paring tools.

fig. **1602** MARSTON *Ant. & Mel.* II. Wks. 1856 I. 129 Are you all like the spoke-shaves of the church? Have you no mawe to restitution?

attrib. **1846** HOLTZAPFFEL *Turning* II. 491 This theoretical cutter would present all the difficulties of the spoke-shave iron.

Hence **'spokeshave** *v. intr.*, to use a spokeshave.

1887 T. HARDY *Woodlanders* II. viii. 139 The one or two woodmen who sawed, shaped, spokeshaved on her father's premises.

spokeslady ('spəʊksleɪdɪ). [Cf. SPOKESWOMAN.] = SPOKESWOMAN.

1936 *Richmond* (Va.) *Times-Dispatch* 23 June 7/4 'Don't you quote us, though,' the spokeslady hastened. **1969** *Guardian* 31 July 9/5 'It came out like that, and they decided to leave it like that,' a spokeslady said. **1972** *Daily Tel.* 25 Sept. 7/1 Our most clamorous spokeslady for censorious opinion.

spokesman ('spəʊksmən). Also 6 spokisman, 7 spoksman, spookesman, spoaksman, spoakesman. [Irreg. f. *spoke*, pa. pple. of SPEAK *v.*, on analogy of *craftsman*, etc. Cf. the earlier SPEAKMAN.]

†**1.** An interpreter. *Obs. rare.*

1519 HORMAN *Vulg.* 43 b, Mythrydate spake..to men of xxii rymes, euery man in his owne langage, without any spokisman. **1556** T. HOBY tr. *Castiglione's Courtyer* Transl. Ep. A ij, Themistocles..entertayned most honorably with the King of Persia, willed vpon a time to tell his cause by a spokesman.

2. a. One who speaks for or on behalf of another or others; esp. in later use, one who is chosen or deputed to voice the opinions or represent the views of a body, party, etc.; a mouthpiece.

Freq. from *c* 1550 to *c* 1650 and in recent use.

a **1540** BARNES *Wks.* (1573) 354 Vnto God..wee neede no spokesman nor no mediatour but alonely a deuoute mynde. *c* **1585** *Faire Em* III. 734 He hath been an earnest spokesman in your cause. **1610** J. DOVE *Advt. Seminaries* 22 He would be for him instead of an interpreter, and a spokesman for him with God. **1651** FULLER *Abel Rediv.* 540 This our Robert, whose zeale for the truth..preferred him without any other friend or spokesman. **1705** HICKERINGILL *Priest-cr.* I. (1721) 28 People cannot join in publick Prayers, except they have a Spokesman or Speaker. **1761** HUME *Hist. Eng.* (1806) IV. lx. 521 The spokesman of the committee, one Duglass, began with a severe aspect [etc.]. **1849** MACAULAY *Hist. Eng.* ix. II. 462 The king gave an audience to all the bishops who were then in London... The primate was spokesman. **1869** FREEMAN *Norm. Conq.* (1875) III. 297 The Barons prayed him to be their spokesman with the Duke. **1976** *Times* 21 May 2/4 Mary Whitehouse, spokesman for the campaign. **1976** *Daily Tel.* 30 June 2/1 A spokesman for the British Medical Association.

b. *transf.* The chief representative or exponent *of* a movement, period, etc.

1828 CARLYLE in *Foreign Rev.* II. 95 [Goethe] made himself the spokesman of his generation. **1840** —— *Heroes* iii. (1904) 98 Dante is the spokesman of the Middle Ages. **1867** FREEMAN *Norm. Conq.* (1877) I. 9 The romantic narrative of which Geoffrey of Monmouth is the chief spokesman.

3. †**a.** The speaker or chairman of a legislative or administrative body. *Obs. rare.*

1607 in M. H. Peacock *Hist. Wakefield Gram. Sch.* (1892) 55 Of the Spokesman or President Governour:..the Governours beinge come together, the Spokesman..shall delyver up the keyes of his office.

b. A public speaker, esp. one who formally addresses a deliberative or legislative assembly.

Not always clearly distinct from sense 2.

1663 BOYLE *Usef. Exp. Nat. Philos.* I. iii. 58 The Master, or that other person of the Society, who is most capable and the best spoakesman, is by a kind of natural right engag'd to the duty of returning praise. **1693** FREKE *Ess., Apology* 4 There is many an excellent Spokesman that makes a bad Writer. *a* **1704** T. BROWN *Dial. Dead* Wks. 1711 IV. 38, I was long of the Court of Aldermen, and one of the chief Spoaks-men of the Common-Council. **1835** LYTTON *Rienzi* I. ix, A rough table, from which they besought Pandulpho to address the people. The pale citizen, with some pain and shame, for he was no practised spokesman, was obliged to assent. **1863** GEO. ELIOT *Romola* xxii, Some were in close.. discussion; others were listening with keen interest to a single spokesman.

transf. **1885** *Encycl. Brit.* XVIII. 323 *Psittacus erithacus*.. is the most accomplished spokesman of the whole group [of parrots].

Hence **'spokesmanship**, (*a*) the office or position of spokesman; (*b*) [cf. -MANSHIP] skilful use of the position of spokesman.

1870 *Athenæum* 26 Nov. 686 Then had Guðmund Thorgeirsson the spokesmanship-at-law for twelve years. **1889** *Daily News* 25 Jan. 6/4 He felt there was some fitness in his spokesmanship that evening, for he was the representative of an institution [etc.]. **1960** *Encounter* May 27 Such spokesmanship underplays the potential excitement of the work itself. **1963** *Times* 19 Apr. 8/5 Official explanations about why there is no such sign at the chief bookshop of all in Kingsway are simply an exercise in spokesmanship.

†**spokesmate.** *Obs. rare.* [f. as SPOKESMAN + MATE *sb.*[2]] A spokesman and friend.

1583 STANYHURST *Æneis* III. 52 O sacred Troyan,..Of Gods thee spoaks mate [**1582** spooks make], thee truchman of hallo'd Apollo. **1640** H. MILL *Nights Search* 162 His spokesmate, or the pander doth finde out Where's money to be lent.

spokespeople ('spəʊks,piːp(ə)l). [Cf. SPOKESMAN.] Two or more 'spokespersons'.

1974 *Black Panther* 27 Apr. 8/4 Spokespeople for several leftist groups feel the murders are being carried out by a terrorist organization called 'The Black Hand'. **1977** *Undercurrents* June–July 5/2 Each group of ten or twenty had elected a 'spokesperson' who met in plenary with other 'spokespeople'. **1983** *Listener* 18 Aug. 27/2 The BBC spokespeople were obliged to come back with efforts to explain that the comparison..was not as clear as it might seem.

spokesperson ('spəʊks,pɜːs(ə)n). [f. SPOKESMAN, after *chairperson* (see PERSON *sb.* 2 f).] A manufactured substitute for 'spokes-woman' or 'spokesman'.

One of numerous words formed to avoid alleged sexual discrimination in terminology.

1972 *Guardian* 18 Feb. 11/3 The spokesperson (non-sexist term) for UCWR complained that she had been 'physically assaulted by a university administrator'. **1976** *New Yorker* 29 Nov. 172/2 One's heart and imagination .. were repelled by the ascetic, sexual, Christian woman who recurs in Mrs. Spark's novels so often as to suggest, if not an alter ego, a spokesperson. **1978** J. IRVING *World according to Garp* xviii. 402 A 'spokesperson' for the Ellen Jamesians. **1981** *Economist* 28 Nov. 30/1 As a feminist fillip Miss Joan Lestor .. has been made spokesperson for women's rights and welfare.

spokester ('spəʊkstə(r)). *rare*⁻¹. [f. as SPOKESMATE + -STER.] A female speaker; a spokeswoman.

1850 THACKERAY *Sk. & Trav. Lond.* Wks. 1898 VI. 699 One of the ladies .. begged her companion .. to show me in to lunch. The spokester was a stout and tall woman.

spokeswoman ('spəʊks,wʊmən). [Cf. SPOKESMAN.] A woman who speaks for another or others; a female advocate or representative; a woman speaker.

1654 GAYTON *Pleas. Notes* IV. i. 173, I know not how he had wonne upon my wenches, They were his spokeswomen, and high Abetters. **1656** W. DU GARD tr. *Comenius' Gate Lat. Unl.* 229 After hee hath set his affection upon som woman (either by himself, or by a spokesman, or spokeswoman) hee is called a Wooer. **1818** SCOTT *Br. Lamm.* xxiii, 'Did ye ever see the foul thief?' asked her neighbour. 'Na!' replied the other spokeswoman. **1840** P. D. HARDY *Holy Wells Irel.* 25 A most unexpected proposal, which the spokeswoman .. undertook to make. **1890** *Athenæum* 11 Oct. 476/3 She [Mrs. Henry Wood] is emphatically the spokes-woman of the middle class. **1974** *Sunday* (Charleston, S. Carolina) 28 Apr. 5-A/8 A hospital spokeswoman said Mrs. Agnew had scheduled her visit and was receiving routine care. **1976** *Film & Television Technician* Nov. 7/4 'The arguments against racism have to take place at a local level, they can't be imposed from above,' said a spokeswoman from Transport House. **1979** *Guardian* 23 Jan. 1/8 A spokeswoman .. said the response from members yesterday was 'phenomenal'.

Hence **'spokes,womanship**.

1894 SAINTSBURY in *Sat. Rev.* 3 Mar. 230 The spokeswomanship of the *Flower and the Leaf* can no more decide the point than any other dramatic or poetic assumption of character by this or another bard.

spokewise ('spəʊkwaɪz), *adv.* [f. SPOKE *sb.* + -WISE.] After the manner of the spokes of a wheel.

1844 KINGLAKE *Eothen* xii, My quilt, and my pelisse, and my cloak were spread out so that I might lie spokewise. **1911** J. WARD *Roman Era Brit.* vii. 115 Six internal walls radiating spoke-wise from a small central hexagonal cell.

spoking ('spəʊkɪŋ), *vbl. sb.* [f. SPOKE *v.*] The action of fitting with spokes; used *attrib.* in *spoking-machine* (see quot.).

1875 KNIGHT *Dict. Mech.* 2285/1 *Spoking-machine*, one for setting spokes in the hub with a uniform dish.

spoky ('spəʊkɪ), *a.* Now *rare.* Also 6-7 **spokie** (6 -ye), 9 **spokey**; 7 **spoaky**, 8 **-ey**. [f. SPOKE *sb.* + -Y.]

†**1.** *Bot.* **a.** Having or consisting of parts arranged radially like the spokes of a wheel; radiate, radiated. *Obs.*

1551 TURNER *Herbal* I. C vj, Dyll .. hath many smal braunches comming furth of a great stalke, .. wyth a spokye top as fenell hath. **1578** LYTE *Dodoens* 270 The floures .. grow in round spokie tuffets or rundels, at the toppe of the stalkes. **1597** GERARDE *Herbal* I. xix. 24 With a spokie pannicle, somwhat thicker and greater than the common Couch Grasse. **1657** W. COLES *Adam in Eden* l, The white Flowers grow in spoaky roundels. **1672** JOSSELYN *New Eng. Rarities* 70 The Flowers are Blew, small, and many, growing in spoky tufts at the top. **1713** *Phil. Trans.* XXVIII. 183 Its Leaves very like the Jagged Sow-Thistles, with Spoakey Tufts of Purple Flowers.

†**b.** Resembling wheel-spokes in form and arrangement. *Obs.*

1601 HOLLAND *Pliny* II. 274 In the top thereof it beareth certaine little heads inuironed with spokie leaues, and those disposed round in manner of a starre.

2. Of a wheel: Having or provided with spokes.

1832 WILSON in *Blackw. Mag.* XXXII. 178 That small, spokey, but rimless wheel.

†**spold.** *Obs. rare.* In 1, 3 **spald**, 5 **spolde**. [OE. *spáld*, var. of *spádl*, *spátl* SPATTLE *sb.*¹] Spittle.

*a***900** CYNEWULF *Elene* 300 ðe mid horu speowdon on þæs andwlitan, þe eow eaʒena leoht fram blindnesse bote ʒefremede .. þurh þæt æðele spald. *c***1260** in Napier *Hist. Holy Rood Tree* 78/1 Þat leueli leor wid spald ischent. *c***1450** *Mirk's Festial* 83 For þe spolde of a fasting man may sle any eddyr bodyly.

†**spole**, obs. variant of SPAULD, shoulder.

*a***1723** in Child *Ballads* III. 342/1 Vnder the spole of his right arme Hee smote Sir Andrew quite throw the hart.

spole, obs. or dial. f. SPOOL *sb.* and *v.*

†**spole-worm.** *Obs. rare.* Also **spoul-**. [ad. older Flem. *spoel-worm* (Kilian), G. *spulwurm.*] A tapeworm infesting the human body.

1527 ANDREW *Brunswyke's Distyll. Waters* D j b, The same water dronke .. is good for the worme in the body named the spole worme. *Ibid.* E j b, Two ounces dronke fastynge in the mornynge is good for the evyll worme called the spoul worme.

spolʒie, obs. var. SPULYIE.

'spoliage. *rare*⁻¹. = SPOLIATION 1.

1806 in Owen *Wellesley's Desp.* (1877) 799 The awful instance before us .. shows whither an unbridled system of military government .. may lead, if founded in the love of war, and military spoliage.

'spoliary. *rare*⁻¹. [ad. L. *spoliārium*, f. *spolium* SPOIL *sb.*] A place in the Roman amphitheatre where the slain gladiators were stripped.

1692 WASHINGTON tr. *Milton's Def. People* v. Wks. 1851 VIII. 154 An Act of the Senate made upon that occasion is extant in Lampridius: .. 'let the Parricide be drawn, let him be torn in pieces in the Spoliary'.

†**'spoliate,** *pa. pple. Obs.*⁻¹ [ad. L. *spoliātus*, pa. pple. of *spoliāre*: see next.] Destitute, devoid.

*c***1470** HENRYSON *Mor. Fab., Preach. Swallow* xl, This carle and bond of gentrice spoliate.

spoliate ('spəʊlɪeɪt), *v.* [f. L. *spoliāt-*, ppl. stem of *spoliāre* to spoil, f. *spolium* SPOIL *sb.* Cf. F. *spolier*, Prov. and Pg. *espoliar*, It. *spogliare.*] *trans.* To spoil or despoil; to rob or deprive *of* something.

1722-7 BOYER *Dict. Royal* I, *Spolier*, to spoliate, spoil. **1839** *John Bull* 15 Apr., After having violated and spoliated every other corporation in the country. **1853** *Fraser's Mag.* XLVIII. 710 Spoliating the land of our trees. **1876** *Contemp. Rev.* Jan. 304 Bonaparte was spoliating the Pope.

absol. **1835** *Tait's Mag.* II. 520 The exactions of an alien church, which insults while it spoliates.

Hence **'spoliating** *ppl. a.*

1840 *Penny Cycl.* XVIII. 321/1 The spoliating parties called a diet to sanction this iniquitous transaction. **1895** *Daily News* 6 Nov. 8/3 The scheme of spoliation which was partially successful under a spoliating Government.

'spoliated, *ppl. a.* [f. L. *spoliāt-us*: cf. SPOLIATE *ppl. a.*] Despoiled; taken as spoil or booty.

1815 MME. D'ARBLAY *Let.* 2 May, In this starved, spoliated, and sleepless condition, he arrived. **1866** *Pall Mall G.* 18 July 7 The spoliated volumes turned out to be the indexes for those years.

spoliation (spəʊlɪ'eɪʃən). Also 5 **-acioune**, 5-6 **-acio(u)n**, 6 **-atioun**. [ad. L. *spoliātio*, n. of action from *spoliāre* (see SPOLIATE *v.*), or a. F. *spoliation* (16th cent.).]

1. The action of spoliating, despoiling, pillaging, or plundering; seizure of goods or property by violent means; depredation, robbery. Also, the condition of being despoiled or pillaged.

*c***1400** *Beryn* 1600 Þere nys within our shippis no þing of spoliacioun, But all trewe marchaundise. *Ibid.* 2979 What nedith .. to make such aray? Sith wee been pese-marchantis, & vse no spoliacioune. **1478** *Acta Domin. Conc.* 3/1 Þe accioun .. anent þe spoliacioun of certane gudes pundit and takin be þaim. **1503** in Littlejohn *Aberd. Sheriff Crt.* (1904) 47 Patrick .. persewit thir persones .. for the Spoliacioun of xviiiˣˣ bollis of atis. **1566** *Reg. Privy Council Scot.* I. 481 The manifest piracie and depredatioun committit be certane Scottismen in the pilleing and spoliatioun of thair schippis and gudis. **1800** COLQUHOUN *Comm. Thames* viii. 267 These guards secure the Revenue of the State from waste and spoliation. **1832** tr. *Sismondi's Ital. Rep.* xii. 277 He brought Rome into a state of poverty and spoliation hitherto unexampled. **1889** JESSOPP *Coming of Friars* vi. 285 A very large proportion of the endowments .. came from the spoliation of the parochial clergy.

b. *transf.* (See quot.)

1767 GOOCH *Treat. Wounds* I. 233 Robbing the blood too much of its density or red globules, .. by some Physicians, is very significantly called, *spoliation.*

c. An act or instance of despoiling or plundering; a robbery; an exaction of a spoliatory nature.

1800 WEEMS *Life Washington* (1877) 178 But [they] still continued their spoliations. **1843** J. W. CROKER in *C. Papers* (1884) II. 421, I believe that there was a more extensive spoliation of papers than we imagined. **1853** KINGSLEY *Hypatia* Pref. p. ix, It substituted a fixed and regular spoliation for the fortuitous and arbitrary miseries of savage warfare.

2. *Eccl.* A writ or suit brought by one incumbent against another holding the same benefice by an illegal or questionable title (see later quots.).

1498-9 *Plumpton Corr.* (Camden) 133 The best remedy for your incumbent was .. to have a spoliacion in the spirituall court agaynst the preyst that now occupyeth, because he is one disturber. **1607** COWELL *Interpr.*, *Spoliation* .. is a writ, that lyeth for an incumbent, against another incumbent, in case where the right of patronage commeth not in debate. **1767** BURN *Eccl. Law* III. 342 The same law is, where one telleth the patron that his clerk is dead; whereupon he presents another; there the first incumbent .. may have a spoliation against the other.

b. The action on the part of one incumbent of depriving another of the emoluments of a benefice.

1726 AYLIFFE *Parergon* 117 A Benefice is said to be vacant de Facto, and not de Jure, when the Possession thereof is lost by Spoliation or Intrusion. **1768** BLACKSTONE *Comm.* III. iii. vii. 91 Spoliation is an injury done by one clerk or incumbent to another, in taking the fruits of his benefice without any right thereunto, but under a pretended title.

3. *Law.* The action of destroying a document, or of injuring or tampering with it in such a way as to destroy its value as evidence.

1752 MRS. DELANY *Autobiogr. & Corr.* (1861) III. 188 My Lord Chancellor .. has acquitted D.D. of all guilt of spoliation, but not of the consequences that may attend the destroying or loss of the deed. **1867** SMYTH *Sailor's Wordbk.* 644 Spoliation of a Ship's Papers. An act which, by the maritime law of every court in Europe, not only excludes further proof, but does, *per se*, infer condemnation.

4. The action of spoiling, damaging, or injuring.

1867 J. HOGG *Microsc.* (ed. 6) I. iii. 220 The structure of many creatures is so delicate, as to require the very greatest care to prevent mutilation, and the consequent spoliation of the specimen.

spoliative ('spəʊlɪətɪv), *a.* [f. L. *spoliāt-*, ppl. stem of *spoliāre* to spoil, or a. F. *spoliative*: see SPOLIATE *v.* and -IVE.]

1. Spoliatory. *rare*⁻¹.

1875 *Contemp. Rev.* XXV. 190 Political economists .. have met all practical inferences of a subversive or spoliative tendency by [etc.].

2. *Med.* Having the effect of seriously diminishing the amount of the blood.

1876 BARTHOLOW *Mat. Med.* (1879) 466 This is a powerfully spoliative and depressing emetic. **1898** P. MANSON *Trop. Diseases* x. 293 There was a time when, under a spoliative treatment, by bleeding and calomel, dysentery proved a very fatal disease indeed.

spoliator ('spəʊlɪeɪtə(r)). [a. L. *spoliātor*, agent-n. from *spoliāre* (see SPOLIATE *v.*), or ad. F. *spoliateur* (16th c.).] One who commits spoliation or robbery; a pillager, plunderer, a spoiler.

1831 *Examiner* 695/2 The spoliators were gaining admittance to the house. **1845** PETRIE *Eccl. Archit. Irel.* 370 It might be, that a successful spoliator thus deprived the possessors of the means of future defence. **1875** HELPS *Soc. Press.* iv. 61 The spoliators (such I must call them) would probably be deficient in those powers of imagination which .. would teach men that [etc.].

spoliatory ('spəʊlɪətərɪ), *a.* [f. L. *spoliāt-*, ppl. stem of *spoliāre* (see SPOLIATE *v.*) + -ORY².] Of the nature of, characterized by, spoliation or robbery; pillaging, plundering.

1790 BURKE *Corr.* (1844) III. 143 If I were to adopt the plan of a spoliatory reformation. **1813** J. C. HOBHOUSE *Journey* (ed. 2) 290 The spoliatory taste of some amateurs. **1857** J. RAINE *Mem. J. Hodgson* I. 60 It was dissolved by the first spoliatory statute. **1895** *Daily Tel.* 6 Mar. 7/1 To defend themselves .. against spoliatory attack.

spolt, dial. var. SPALT *a.*, brittle.

spome, obs. var. SPUME *sb.*

spon, obs. form of SPOON *sb.*

†**spon**, *v. Obs. rare.* In 6 **spone**, **spoyn**. [f. *spon* SPOON *sb.* or MLG. *spôn*: cf. G. *spänen* in the same sense.] *trans.* To secure (wine) from waste by tightening the cask with chips of wood.

1541 *Rutland MSS.* (Hist. MSS. Comm.) IV. 312 Gaskyn wyne: .. for spoynyng the same wine jd. **1574** in *Rep. MSS. Ld. Middleton* (Hist. MSS. Comm.) 448 For iij. hh. [= hogsheads] of clarred wyne, xij *li.* xv *s.*; .. sponenge the wyne, vj *d.*

†**sponage.** *Obs. rare.* [Cf. prec.] The operation of tightening a wine-cask with chips.

1526 in *Househ. Ord.* (1790) 195 Item, Cellaridge, Cranage, Sponage, Romage, and Carriage of Wine, £100 0s. 0*d.* **1576** in Nichols *Progr. Jas. I* (1828) II. 48 In cellaring, carriage, cowperage, cranage and sponage of wine.

sponcing, variant of SPONSON.

†**spond**, *sb. Obs.*⁻¹ [ad. L. *sponda.*] A bed or couch.

1763 *Brit. Mag.* IV. 196 She lay upon a spond covered with gold tissue, under a canopy of state.

†**spond**, *v. Obs.*⁻¹ [f. L. *spond-ēre* to bind or promise.] *trans.* To promise or pledge.

1698 FRYER *Acc. E. India & P.* 369 A time .. of Labour and Travel, whereby they approve themselves what their Parents only Sponded for them.

spondaic (spɒn'deɪɪk), *a.* and *sb.* Also 8 **-aick**. [ad. F. *spondaïque* (16th c.; = It. *spondaico*, Sp. and Pg. *espondaico*), or L. *spondaic-us* (see SPONDIAC *a.*). Cf. G. *spondäisch.*]

A. *adj.* **1.** Of verses (or parts of these): **a.** Composed of spondees. **b.** Having a spondee in positions where a different foot is normal; *esp.* of hexameters, having a spondee in the fifth foot.

1722-7 BOYER *Dict. Royal* I, *Spondaïque*, .. a spondaick Verse. **1728** CHAMBERS *Cycl.* s.v. *Spondee*, There are also Spondee or Spondaic Verses; that is, Verses composed wholly of Spondees, or at least that end with Two Spondees. **1789** M. MADAN tr. *Persius* (1795) 34 *note*, The end of this verse is spondaic. **1797** *Encycl. Brit.* (ed. 3) XV. 254/2 An hexameter line .. when regular and not spondaic .. never has fewer than thirteen [syllables]. **1847** *Proc. Philol. Soc.* III. 105 The same argument may be drawn from the construction of spondaic anapæstic verses. **1861** PALEY *Aeschylus* (ed. 2) *Persians* 32 *note*, On the spondaic termination see Suppl. 7.

2. Characterized by a spondee or spondees.

1751 JOHNSON *Rambler* No. 94 ¶ 10 This at least was the power of the spondaick and dactylick harmony. **1773** MELMOTH tr. *Cicero, Old Age* 193 A certain piece of musick composed in solemn spondaic measures. **1824** L. MURRAY

Eng. Gram. (ed. 5) I. 385 The Trochaic, Iambic, or Spondaic [movement]. **1869** FREEMAN *Norm. Conq.* (1875) III. 225, I do not know the meaning of this strange epithet and spondaic cadence.

3. Of words: Consisting of two long syllables.

a **1849** POE *Longf.*, etc. Wks. 1864 III. 364 Our spondees, or, we should say, our spondaic words are rare.

B. *sb.* A spondaic foot or line.

1839 T. MITCHELL *Aristoph., Frogs* 357 *note*, On the anapæstic spondaics which follow, see Hermann.

†**spondaical**, *a. Obs.*⁻¹ [f. as prec. + -AL[1].] = next.

1603 FLORIO *Montaigne* I. xlvi. 149 A solemne, grave, severe, and spondaicall kinde of musike.

spon'dean, *a. rare.* [f. L. *spondē-us* (see next) + -AN.] Of music: Characterized by or consisting of spondees.

1776 BURNEY *Hist. Mus.* I. 35 The first of these [enharmonic melodies] they reckon to have been the nome or melody called Spondean. *c* **1800** R. CUMBERLAND *J. De Lancaster* (1809) I. 287 By the simple recitation of the spondean hymn.

spondee ('spɒndiː). Also 4, 6–7 sponde, 6 -ie, spondæ, 7 -æe. [ad. L. *spondē-us*, incorrectly *spondæ-us* (sc. *pes*), ad. Gr. σπονδεῖος, f. σπονδή solemn drink-offering; or a. F. *spondée* (= It. *spondeo*, Sp. and Pg. *espondeo*).]

1. *Pros.* A metrical foot consisting of two long syllables. Also *attrib.*

α. *a* **1390** *Wycliffite Bible, Job* Prol., Vers of sixe feet, rennende with dactile and sponde feet. **1567** DRANT *Horace, Ep.* A viij, In the fourth roume and seconde roume Iambus still hath bene. In Ennius or Accius, Spondie is seldom seene. **1596** J. DAVIES *Orchestra* lxvi, Yet all the feete .. Are onely Spondeis, solemne, graue, and sloe. **1670** EACHARD *Cont. Clergy* 13 Upon the first scanning, he knows a sponde from a dactyl. **1746** FRANCIS tr. *Horace, Art of Poetry* 259 *note*, Horace blames Ennius and Accius .. for making their Verses hard and heavy by ill-placing the Spondees. **1771** MACKENZIE *Man Feel.* xx, It is a spondee, and I will maintain it! **1835** T. MITCHELL *Aristoph., Acharn.* 571 *note*, Originally, this kind of address was composed in pure anapæsts, without any mixture of spondees or dactyls. **1888** *Cent. Mag.* Mar. 671/2 Jerry made a spondee of Frank's name [*sc.* Mallard].

β. **1586** W. WEBBE *Eng. Poetrie* (Arb.) 81 Thys verse consisteth of these fiue feete, one Chore, one spondæ, one dactyl, and two Choreis. **1603** HOLLAND *Plutarch's Mor.* 1253 Those which were endited to the praise of Mars and Minerva, and with Spondæes. **1666** DRYDEN *Ann. Mirab., Let. Howard*, The quantity of every syllable, which they might vary with Spondæes or Dactiles.

2. *Mus.* (See quots.)

1861 J. S. ADAMS *5000 Mus. Terms* 94 *Spondee*, a musical foot consisting of two long notes, accented thus - -. **1875** STAINER & BARRETT *Dict. Mus. Terms, Spondee*, a musical foot consisting of two long syllables.

†**spondence**. *Obs.*⁻¹ [f. L. *spond-ēre* to promise: see -ENCE.] A pledge or promise.

1657 *Burton's Diary* (1828) I. 412 These are the spondences and undertakings of the Parliament.

‖**spon'deus**. *Obs.* Also -æus. Pl. spondei, -æi. [L.] = SPONDEE. Also *attrib.*

1567 DRANT *Horace, Art Poet.* A viij b, The stade Spondeus foote. **1586** W. WEBBE *Eng. Poetrie* (Arb.) 80 The two first feete, eyther *Dactyli* or *Spondæi* indifferent. **1589** PUTTENHAM *Eng. Poesie* (Arb.) 129 This makes a good Dactill and a good spondeus. **1603** HOLLAND *Plutarch's Morals* 1252 These were the beginnings of the enharmonique Musicke: For first of them they put a Spondæus. **1704** J. HARRIS *Lex. Techn.* I, *Spondæus*, is the Foot of a Latin Verse, consisting of two Syllables, and both of 'em long, as *Ingens.*

†**spondiac**, *a. Obs. rare.* Also 7 spondeiak. [ad. L. *spondīac-us* (less correctly *spondaic-us*), ad. Gr. σπονδειακός.] = SPONDAIC *a.*

1589 PUTTENHAM *Eng. Poesie* (Arb.) 129 Which words serue well to make the verse all spondiacke or iambicke. **1603** HOLLAND *Plutarch's Morals* 1254 In song they seemed not .. proper and fit for the Spondeiak kinde.

†**spondiasm**. *Obs. rare.* [ad. Gr. σπονδειασμ-ός, f. σπονδεῖος SPONDEE.] In ancient Greek music: (see quot. 1801).

1603 HOLLAND *Plutarch's Morals* 1252 Unlesse a man having an eie unto a vehement Spondiasme, will conjecture .. the same to be a kinde of Diatonos. **1801** BUSBY *Dict. Mus., Spondiasm*, an alteration in the harmonic genus by which a chord was elevated three dieses above its ordinary pitch, so that the *spondiasm* was precisely the opposite of the eclysis.

spondulicks (spɒn'djuːlɪks). *slang.* Orig. *U.S.* Also -ics, -ix; spondoolic(k)s, -ix. Also as quasi-*sing.* spondoolick, spondulick, etc. [Of fanciful formation.] Money, cash. Also, a piece of money, a coin.

1857 in R. H. Thornton *Amer. Gloss.* (1912), He lost .. All the brass and all the needful, All the spondulix and buttons. **1863** *Ibid.*, Those ordering job work should come down with the spondulicks as soon as the work is done. **1864** [see DINGBAT 1]. **1868** *All Year Round* 19 Sept. 354/1 A restaurant .. where the tallest sort of feeding may be had at all hours at the lowest possible cost to the spondoolics. **1889** E. SAMPSON *Tales of Fancy* 36, I was instructed to allow my opponent to gain a lap in advance .. in order to draw out the spondoolicks. **1896** J. H. BLOOMFIELD *Cuban Exped.* 20 As long as the Cubans can raise the spondulix, they'll get plenty of people to fit out expeditions for them. **1899** T. M. ELLIS *3 Cat's-eye Rings* 32 Oh, I shall pull in the spondulicks, .. I tell you. **1902** W. N. HARBEN *Abner Daniel* 58 The one with the spondoolix wonders harder than the one who has none. **1912** W. OWEN *Let.* 23 Apr. (1967) 131, I shall do nothing until Father brings me some 'spondoolick'. **1923** E. P. OPPENHEIM *Inevitable Millionaires* xi. 121 'Do I understand that the young man .. has dissipated the whole of his patrimony, in twelve months?' he inquired. 'Every bean,' Harold assented. 'Not a spondulik left.' **1966** *Courier-Mail* (Brisbane) 9 Aug. 1/10 (Advt.), *Spondooliks.* Dollars, pounds or call it what you like, you'll save plenty at Direct Disposals. **1980** *Private Eye* 29 Feb. 13/1 No one seemed very anxious to come up with the spondulicks.

'**spondyl(e**. Now *rare.* Forms: α. 5– spondyle, 5–7 -dile, 8–9 sphondyle. β. 6– spondyl, 6–7 -dyll, 6 -dylle, 6–7 -dille, 7 -dil(l. γ. 5–7 spondel, 6 -dele, -delle, 7 spondle. [a. F. *spondyle*, †*spondile, -ille* (= Sp. *espondil*, Pg. *espondyl*, It. *spondillo*), or ad. L. *spondylus, sphondylus*, ad. Gr. σπ-, σφόνδυλος. Cf. SPONDYLUS.]

†**1.** One or other of the joints of the spine; a vertebra. *Obs.*

α. *c* **1400** *Lanfranc's Cirurg.* 146 Bitwene þe firste spondile & þe secunde. *Ibid.* (Addit. MS. 12056), The firste spondyle ys y-bounden to þe secunde. **1541** R. COPLAND *Guydon's Quest. Chirurg.* E ij, It descendeth by the spondyles vnto the ende of the backe. **1601** HOLLAND *Pliny* II. 257 The first spondyle or turning joint in the chine of a Dragon. **1653** URQUHART *Rabelais* I. xxvii, To others again he unjoynted the spondyles or knuckles of the neck.

β. **1541** R. COPLAND *Guydon's Quest. Chirurg.* D iv b, Through the myddes of the spondylles or rydge bones tyll vnto the ende of the backe. **1547** BOORDE *Brev. Health* x. 10 b, A senowe the whyche doth growe out of the myddle of the spondyls. **1590** BARROUGH *Meth. Physick* I. xvii. (1639) 28 It is good also to annoint the first and second Spondill in the neck. **1637** B. JONSON *Sad Shepherd* II. vii, A kind of rack Runs downe along the Spondylls of his back. **1667** *Lond. Gaz.* No. 159/4 A great shot .. entring the spondilles of his back.

γ. *c* **1400** *Lanfranc's Cirurg.* 146 In þe necke þer ben .vij. spondelis, þat is to seie whirlboonys. **1548–77** VICARY *Anat.* vi. (1888) 45 The Spondelles of the necke be seuen. **1607** WALKINGTON *Opt. Glass* 120 The spondles or ioynts of the backe-bone. **1615** CROOKE *Body of Man* 113 It hath his beginning at the first spondle of the loynes. **1650** BULWER *Anthropomet.* 194 Being pliant, [it] easily permits the Spondels to slip awry inwards.

†**b.** *transf.* A formation like a vertebra. *Obs.*

1658 ROWLAND tr. *Moufet's Theat. Ins.* 937 The third species hath four wings; .. in the tail there are five red spondils.

†**2.** A joint *of* a wheel, vessel, etc. *Obs.*

1650 CHARLETON *Paradoxes* 40 You may rejoyne, that .. there succeeds a participation of the substance of the Load-stone in the porosities .. of the steel, or spondils of the glasse. **1660** JER. TAYLOR *Ductor* Ep. Ded., That every spondyl of the wheels may mark out those vertues which we are then to exercise. **1662** J. CHANDLER *Van Helmont's Oriat.* 217 The Sea salt .. doth stick fast to the spondils or chinks of the vessels.

3. *Zool.* = SPONDYLUS.

1668 WILKINS *Real Char.* 130 Exanguious Testaceous Animals... 4. Oyster. Spondyl. **1776** MENDES DA COSTA *Elem. Conch.* 248 The spondyles are most generally eared shells with unequal valves, rude or uncouth in shape. **1835** KIRBY *Hab. & Inst. Anim.* I. viii. 256 Lamarck .. observes that the Spondyls have the margin of the mantle furnished with two rows of tentacular threads. **1854** BADHAM *Halieut.* 42 Such a pond, too, is the best nidus for .. balani, and sphondyles.

†**4.** Some kind of fossil. *Obs.*⁻¹

1708 *Phil. Trans.* XXVI. 78 *Ichthyospondylus*, The Spondyl, or Fairy Salt-seller.

spondylitic (spɒndɪ'lɪtɪk), *sb.* and *a. Path.* [f. SPONDYLIT(IS + -IC.] **A.** *sb.* A person suffering from spondylitis.

1898 *N.Y. Med. Jrnl.* 8 Oct. 510/1 A comparison shows that the spondylitics are far below the average height for age. **1973** *Nature* 9 Feb. 367/2 Such people are the ankylosing spondylitics and the children originally irradiated *in utero.*

B. *adj.* Of spondylitis; caused by or associated with spondylitis.

1900 in DORLAND *Med. Dict.* **1949** F. HERNAMAN-JOHNSON et al. *Ankylosing Spondylitis* I. ii. 16 Russian surgeons, and later, American surgeons, began to operate on spondylitic cases. *Ibid.* iii. 26 The patient with a commencing spondylitic arthritis of the hip may show some of the classical early signs of tuberculosis. **1977** *Lancet* 17 Sept. 591/2 Clinical investigation of first-degree relatives of patients with classic ankylosing spondylitis will reveal spondylitic symptoms in approximately 15%. **1980** *Jrnl. R. Soc. Med.* LXXIII. 65 Views of the cervical spine showed minor spondylitic changes.

spondy'litis. *Path.* Also -ilitis. [mod.L., f. L. *spondyl-us* SPONDYL(E + -ITIS. So F. *spondylite.*] Inflammation of the vertebral column.

1849 CRAIG, *Spondilitis.* **1859** in MAYNE *Expos. Lex.* **1897** *Allbutt's Syst. Med.* III. 63 Stiff neck due to diseases of the cervical spine, such as caries and .. rheumatoid spondylitis.

spondylo- ('spɒndɪləʊ), comb. form of Gr. σπόνδυλο-ς or L. *spondyl-us* vertebra, occurring in a few recent terms, chiefly *Path.*, in the sense 'of or pertaining to, connected with, the spine', as *spondylocace, -dynia, -pyosis, -tomy.*

1859 MAYNE *Expos. Lex.* 1194/1.

spondylolisthesis (ˌspɒndɪləʊlɪs'θiːsɪs). *Path.* [mod.L. (H. F. Kilian *Spondylolisthesi* (1853) 33), f. Gr. σπόνδυλ-ος, var. σφόνδυλος vertebra + ὀλίσθησις dislocation, slipping.] The forward displacement of the body of the lowest lumbar vertebra (but not the posterior lamina and spine) relative to the bones of the pelvis, or of any other lumbar vertebra relative to the one below it.

1858 *Brit. & Foreign Med.-Chir. Rev.* XXII. 177 (*heading*) The nature and origin of spondylolisthesis. **1885** *Trans. Obstetr. Soc.* XXVI. 187 Neugebauer considers that the predisposing cause of spondylolisthesis is either a congenital deficiency between the superior and inferior articular process on both sides, or a fracture of the same parts. **1932** *Brit. Jrnl. Surg.* XIX. 374 There are two types of spondylolisthesis... In [the first] .. the entire 5th lumbar vertebra slips forwards upon the sacrum and carries the rest of the spine with it. The second type .. consists in the separation (or spondylolysis) of the 5th lumbar vertebra into two portions .., in such a way that the part bearing the spinous process and inferior articular surfaces moves backwards and the rest of the vertebra slips forwards upon the sacrum. **1977** *Proc. R. Soc. Med.* LXX. 421/1 In a proportion of patients the spondylolysis progresses to spondylolisthesis and may then cause symptoms and signs. **1981** *Church Times* 4 Sept. 12/4 As one born with congenital spondylolisthesis (a dangerous defect of the spine linkage requiring bone grafts chiselled off my hip), I am delighted with my restricted life.

Hence ˌ**spondylolis'thetic** *a.*

1884 *Amer. Jrnl. Med. Sci.* LXXXVIII. 600 Neugebauer's description of spondylolisthetic subjects applied exactly to this case. **1932** *Brit. Jrnl. Surg.* XIX. 380 That the supports of the spondylolisthetic 5th lumbar vertebra are very insecure is obvious.

spondylolysis (spɒndɪ'lɒlɪsɪs). *Path.* [f. as prec. + -LYSIS.] The splitting or partial disintegration of a vertebra.

1885 *Trans. Obstetr. Soc.* XXVI. 188 A specimen of spondylolisthesis upon one side, a hemiolisthesis of the fourth lumbar vertebra caused by a similar spondylolysis. **1932** [see SPONDYLOLISTHESIS]. **1959** *Jrnl. Bone & Joint Surg.* XLI. A. 311 A preceding bone abnormality or defect of the isthmus need not be necessarily present for the development of spondylolysis. **1977** [see SPONDYLOLISTHESIS].

Hence **spondylo'lytic** *a.*

1959 *Jrnl. Bone & Joint Surg.* XLI. A. 312 In the spondylolytic cases .. the articular processes above and below the affected vertebra were free to reach and compress the isthmus.

spondylosis (spɒndɪ'ləʊsɪs). *Path.* [ad. F. *spondylose* (P. Marie 1898, in *Bull. de la Soc. Méd. des Hôp.* 11 Feb. 121), f. as prec.: see -OSIS.] Ankylosis of the spine, or of a vertebral joint.

1900 *Jrnl. Nerv. & Mental Dis.* XXVII. 558 (*heading*) A case of rhizomelic spondylosis. **1942** *Jrnl. Bone & Joint Surg.* XXIV. 827 The apparatus and routine used in twenty-two cases of rhizomelic spondylosis treated by roentgenotherapy combined with well-established orthopaedic measures. **1949** F. HERNAMAN-JOHNSON et al. *Ankylosing Spondylitis* I. iv. 40 (*heading*) 'Old man's spine' (spondylosis). *Ibid.*, The radiograph of a case of spondylosis shows a general curvature of the spine. **1977** *Brit. Med. Jrnl.* 26 Mar. 822/1 The local and root symptoms of cervical spondylosis are usually well controlled by non-operative methods.

Hence **spondy'lotic** *a.*

1964 *Amer. Jrnl. Roentgenol.* XCII. 1268/1 Spondylotic changes in the cervical and lower thoracic spinal column sometimes affect the spinal cord. **1972** *Lancet* 8 July 71/2 Patients with spondylotic myelopathy.

‖**spondylus** ('spɒndɪləs). *Zool.* Pl. **spondyli.** [L.: see SPONDYL(E).] One or other of the species of bivalves belonging to the genus *Spondylus*, characterized by foliaceous spines. Also *attrib.*, as ***spondylus shell.***

1601 HOLLAND *Pliny* II. 446 The fish likewise called Spondylus, is said to rid away the tertian ague. **1753** *Chambers' Cycl.* Suppl., *Spondylus*, .. a kind of oister of an oblong and umbonated form, of which there are several species. **1777** PENNANT *Brit. Zool.* (ed. 4) IV. 58 *Spondyli*, a sort of Bivalve, with strong hinges, found in the Mediterranean sea. **1835–6** *Todd's Cycl. Anat.* I. 112/2 The annexed figure of the organs of the *spondylus.* **1840** *Cuvier's Anim. Kingd.* 372 The Spondyli are eaten like Oysters. **1885** LADY BRASSEY *The Trades* 160 One large cabinet .. includes many interesting specimens, especially of the various kinds of spondylus. **1932** R. F. FORTUNE *Sorcerers of Dobu* v. 189 The groom and his kin .. must accumulate .. a spondylus shell necklace or two. **1979** *Archaeology* July 11/2 Many Precolumbian ornaments and beads were manufactured from the rosy-colored rims of spondylus shells.

spone, obs. pa. pple. SPIN *v.*; obs. f. SPOON *sb.*

†**spone**, *v. Sc. Obs.*⁻¹ [Aphetic form of DISPONE *v.*] *trans.* To spend.

1456 *Burgh Rec. Peebles* (1872) 116 To geyf hym a sufiand lewyn, and the layf be sponyt on the plas qwar mast ned is.

spong. Now *dial.* [var. of SPANG *sb.*[3]]

1. A long narrow piece or strip (*of* ground or land).

1650 FULLER *Pisgah* II. ix. 185 Shiloh succeeds (in a narrow southern spong of this Tribe). *Ibid.* IV. ii. 22 A spong of ground somewhat nigh a thousand miles, .. and not bearing a proportionable breadth. *a* **1800**– in dialect glossaries (E. Anglia, Leic., Northampt.).

†**2.** (See quot.) *Obs.*⁻¹

1811 MISS L. M. HAWKINS *C'tess & Gertr.* II. 103 A laboring man gave notice that he was going to drive the *tumbril* (two-wheeled cart) to the *spong* (drift-way for cattle).

sponge (spʌndʒ), *sb.*[1] Forms: α. 1– sponge (2 spunge). β. (Chiefly *north.* and *Sc.*) 4–7 **sponge,**

5 spoungge, spwnge, 5–6 spownge, 6 spoung, 6, 9 spoonge. γ. 6–9 spunge, 7 spundge. [OE. *sponge* (acc. -*ean*) and *spunge* (*spiunge*), ad. L. *spongia*, *spongea*, a. Gr. σπογγιά, later derivative form of σπόγγος sponge. In other Teutonic languages the word appears as OS. *spunsia*, MDu. *spongie*, *sponge*, *sponse* (WFlem. *sponsie*, Du. *spons*, WFris. *spons*, *spouns*), and in the Romanic group as OF. *esponge* (16th cent. in Littré), F. *éponge*, Sp. and Pg. *esponja*, It. *spugna*.

OE. had also the more popular and older form *spynge*, *spinge*.]

I. 1. a. The soft, light, porous, and easily compressible framework which remains after the living matter has been removed from various species of porifers (see 3), characterized by readily absorbing fluids and yielding them on pressure, and much used in bathing, cleansing surfaces, etc.

In older Sc. use (see β) app. also 'a brush'.

α. **c 1000** *Ags. Gosp.* Matt. xxvii. 48 Ða hrædlice arn an heora & ʒenam ane spongean [*c* **1160** ænne spongen], & fylde hiȝ mid ecede. *c* **1160** *Hatton Gosp.* Mk. xv. 36 þa arn hyre an & fylde ane spunge mid eisile. *a* **1225** *Ancr. R.* 262 Nes his pitaunce o rode bute a sponge of galle. **1387** Trevisa *Higden* (Rolls) I. 185 Sponges i-watred and i-holde at hir nostrilles. *a* **1425** tr. *Arderne's Treat. Fistula*, etc. 26 In þe mornyng be it clensed with hote watre and a sponge. **1497** *Naval Acc. Hen. VII* (1896) 88 Sponges grete ij and small xxvj. **1523** Fitzherb. *Husb.* §44 Than washe your shepe there-with, with a sponge or a pece of an olde mantell. **1560** Daus tr. *Sleidane's Comm.* 204 b, The Crosse,.. Nayles, Sponge, launce, Crowne of thorne. **1625** N. Carpenter *Geogr. Del.* II. v. (1635) 68 Others againe.. suppose the earth to bee like a sponge to drinke vp the water. **1676** L'Estrange *Seneca's Mor., Anger* xii. (1696) 423 He.. caus'd their Mouths to be stopt with Sponges. **1800** *Med. Jrnl.* III. 556, I have constantly recommended cold vinegar .. to be applied.. by means of a sponge. **1863** Ansted *Ionian Isl.* 255 A considerable fishery for fine sponges, of which many, fully equal to fine Turkey sponges, come into the market. **1876** Harley *Royle's Mat. Med.* 783 The Sponge is imported from the Mediterranean and the Red Sea.

β. **1388** Wyclif *Mark* xv. 36 And oon ranne, and fillide a spounge with vynegre. *c* **1400** Maundev. (Roxb.) iii. 9 [þai] held to þaire noses spoungez moisted with water. **1483** *Cath. Angl.* 356/1 A Spoungge.., *spongia*. **1491** *Acc. Ld. High Treas. Scot.* I. 188 For a spwnge to the Kingis claythis, ij s. **1501** *Ibid.* II. 27 Byrs spowngis for the Kingis bonatis, vj d. **1549** *Ibid.* IX. 353 Item, ane spoung send to Dunfermeling to his graces sone, iiij s. **1612** *Halyburton's Ledger* (1867) 329 Spounges or brushes.

γ. **1572** in Feuillerat *Revels Q. Eliz.* (1908) 180 For spunges for snoballs. **1580** Lyly *Euphues* (Arb.) 425 The Spunge is full of water, yet is it not seene. **1661** J. Childrey *Brit. Bacon.* 41 An earth porous like a spunge. **1726** Pope *Odyss.* xx. 189 And let the abstersive spunge the board renew. **1767** Gooch *Treat. Wounds* I. 259 To wipe it dry with a spunge.

fig. **1602** *How Chuse Good Wife* v. ii, For her death The spunge of either eye Shall weep red tears. **1622** Donne *Serm.* xvi. 159 Every man is but a spunge, and but a spunge filled with teares. **1726** Bolingbroke *Study Hist.* vii. (1752) I. 265 Colbert made the most of all these advantageous circumstances, and whilst he filled the national spunge, he taught his successors how to squeeze it.

transf. **1607** Topsell *Four-f. Beasts* 271 With flew or wooll of Hares.. the Grecians made spunges.. to clense the eies of men. **1728** Chambers *Cycl.* s.v., Pyrotechnical Spunges are made of the large Mushrooms or fungous Excrescences growing on old Oaks, Ashes, Firs, &c.

b. As a type of something of small value.

1671 Milton *P.R.* IV. 329 Collecting toys, And trifles for choice matters, worth a spunge.

c. *to throw* (or *chuck*) *up the sponge*, to abandon a contest or struggle; to submit, give in. *colloq.*

1860 *Slang Dict.* 224 'To throw up the sponge,' to submit, give over the struggle,—from the practice of throwing up the sponge used to cleanse the combatants' faces, at a prize-fight, as a signal that the 'mill' is concluded. **1872** 'Mark Twain' *Roughing It* xlvii. 333 One of the boys has gone up the flume.. throwed up the sponge.. kicked the bucket.. he's dead! **1874** Trollope *Phineas Redux* I. xxxix. 325 When.. Thursday afternoon came, Mr. Daubeny 'threw up the sponge'. **1877** T. A. Trollope *Life Pius IX*, II. 130 This tranquil confidence.. degenerated.. into inertness, acquiescence in evil, and.. throwing up the sponge. **1889** 'R. Boldrewood' *Robbery under Arms* xxiv, If Tim had got this letter.. he'd have chucked up the sponge and cleared out for good and all.

2. Without article: The material of which this is composed.

1398 Trevisa *Barth. De P.R.* XIII. xxviii. (Tollem. MS.), It is made harde and turneþ in to sponge. **1683** Salmon *Doron Med.* I. 110 If for Application by Spunge, Cloath, or Stuph. **1753** *Chambers' Cycl.* Suppl. s.v., A pound of spunge .., on drying carefully.., will be reduced to eleven ounces. *Ibid.*, Burnt spunge is much recommended as a sweetner of the blood. **1813** T. Thomson *Lect. Inflam.* 345 The tent was formed of prepared sponge. **1879** *Cassell's Techn. Educ.* I. 382/2 Inferior sponge, with a large-holed texture, called horse sponge.

transf. **1875** Knight *Dict. Mech.* 2286/1 Artificial sponge is made of caoutchouc [etc.].

3. a. *Zool.* One or other of various species of aquatic (chiefly marine) animals (or colony of animals) of a low order belonging to the group *Porifera*, characterized by a tough elastic skeleton of interlaced fibres.

1538 Elyot, *Achilleum*, a sponge, whiche is verye softe, and hath smalle holes. **1552** *Ibid.*, *Cystiolithi*, certayne stones, whiche growe in spunges, holsome against diseases of the bladder. **1633** G. Herbert *Temple, Providence* xxxiv, Frogs marry fish and flesh; bats, bird and beast; Sponges, non-sense and sense. **1651** Jer. Taylor *Course Serm.* I. 4 We are no more such really, then Mandrakes are Men, or Spunges are living creatures. **1725** *Family Dict.* s.v., The Ancients would have a Spunge to be Zoophite. *Ibid.*, There are two sorts of Spunges, the Male.. and the Female. **1774** Goldsm. *Nat. Hist.* (1776) I. 289 Here are seen the madrepores, the sponges, mosses, sea mushrooms, and other marine productions. **1834** McMurtrie *Cuvier's Anim. Kingd.* 11 It is a kind of sponge, which has the same form as the body. **1857** Livingstone *Trav.* xiv. 249 Around the reeds.. we see fresh-water sponges. **1884** Goode *Nat. Hist. Aquat. Anim.* 843 Nearly all Sponges possess a skeleton or the rudiments of one.

b. With distinguishing terms, denoting various species of these.

glass-rope sponge, glass-sponge: see glass *sb.*[1] 16.

1681 Grew *Musæum* II. v. ii. 251 The Hollow Cylindrick or Pipe-Sponge. **1753** *Chambers' Cycl.* Suppl. s.v., 9. The branched river-spunge. 10. The hairy spunge. 11. The sail spunge [etc.] **1797** *Encycl. Brit.* (ed. 3) XVII. 708 Branched sponge;.. cock's comb sponge;.. tow-sponge [etc.]. **1861** Hulme tr. *Moquin-Tandon* II. III. ii. 89 Fine Syrian Sponge. .. Fine Archipelago Sponge... White Sponge of Syria, called also Venetian Sponge. **1883** Adderley *Fisheries Bahamas* 49 The finest type of all, the Levant toilet or Turkish cup-sponge (*Spongia officinalis*).

†c. ***sponge of the river***: (see quot.). *Obs.*

1611 Cotgr., *Esponge d'eau douce*, a certaine hearbe, that flotes on riuers, and is called, Spunge of the riuer.

4. a. A moistened piece of the above substance (sense 1) as used for wiping a surface in order to obliterate writing, etc. Also in fig. context.

1555 Eden *Decades* (Arb.) 196 The leaues, wheron they wryte with any sharpe instrument, and blotte the same againe with a spunge or sum suche other thynge. **1591** Spenser *Ruins Time* 361 Great ones.., Of whome no word we heare, nor signe now see, But as things wipt out with a sponge to perishe. **1644** Sir E. Dering *Prop. Sacr.* c iiij b, *Clavis Mystica* under-went a great deal of Spunge. **1768–74** Tucker *Lt. Nat.* (1834) II. 216 The hand-writing against us is not blotted out, yet.. we have a sponge given us to wipe it away ourselves. **1865** Miss Braddon *Only a Clod* iv, Do you think two years' absence won't act as a sponge, and wipe my image out of her thoughts. **1867** Goldw. Smith *3 Eng. Statesm.* (1882) 212 No great nature ever passes a sponge over its former self.

b. *fig.* That which blots out of existence, wipes out of memory, effaces, etc.

1558 Bp. Watson *Sev. Sacram.* xviii. 117 Daylye confession.. is.. a sponge to wype awaye the fylthynesse of oure synnes. **1657** Trapp *Comm. Ezra* ix. 7 Confession.. is that happy Spunge, that wipeth out all the blottes and blurres of our lives. **1748** Geddes *Composit. Antients* 268 Fear, grief, pain, and desire, are the most effectual spunges. **1799** Han. More *Fem. Educ.* (ed. 4) I. 36 Which fits of charity are made the sponge of every sin, and the substitute of every virtue.

c. A method of cancelling or wiping off debts without payment.

1717 (*title*), Fair Payment no Spunge: or, some Considerations on the Unreasonableness of Refusing to Receive back Money Lent on Publick Securities. **1753** Hanway *Trav.* I. vii. (1762) II. 40 We have an example in France.. of a large national debt being paid with a sponge. **1787** Bentham *Def. Usury* xii. 124 A sponge.. is the only needful and only availing remedy. **1803** Cobbett in *Pol. Reg.* (1817) 8 Feb. 176 Your tax upon the funds, or.. that admirable sponge which you are now about to apply to one twentieth part of the debt.

5. A kind of mop or swab for cleansing a cannon-bore after firing.

a **1625** *Nomencl. Navalis* (MS. Harl. 2301) s.v., The spunge of a peece of Ordnaunce is that which makes it cleane; they are comonlie Sheepeskins putt at the ende of a Staffe. **1627** Capt. Smith *Seaman's Gram.* xiv. 66 A Spunge is such another staffe, with a peece of a Lambe skin at the end.., to thrust vp and downe the Peece. **1669** Sturmy *Mariner's Mag.* v. xii. 45 A Gunner.. ought to have in readiness.. Sheep-skins to make Spunges. **1769** Falconer *Dict. Marine* s.v. *Cannon*, In the land-service, the handle of the spunge is nothing else than a long wooden staff. **1846** A. Young *Naut. Dict.* 292 For a long gun, the sponge and rammer are fixed each on a separate staff. **1884** 'H. Collingwood' (W. J. C. Lancaster) *Under Meteor Flag* 40 A sponge was thrust out of one of the upper deck ports, catching him in the face.

II. 6. † a. The fibrous matted root of asparagus shoots. *Obs.*

c **1440** *Pallad. on Husb.* IV. 233 This seedis [of asparagus] wol connect intil oon roote, This calle a sponge. **1563** Hyll *Art Garden.* (1593) 58 The small rootes will be so folded and tyed one to an other, that they will seeme to be fastned and ioyned togither in one, and this is named of the ancient Gardner, a Spunge. **1577** B. Googe *Heresbach's Husb.* II. (1586) 54 The rootes haue sundry long threeds, which they call the Spoonge.

b. A spongy gall or excrescence on rose-bushes; = bedeguar 2.

1608 Topsell *Serpents* 97 A certaine little Worme which is found in the sponge of the Dogge-bryer (called of the Physitions Bedeguar). **1698** *Phil. Trans.* XX. 464 In brief, it is nothing else but the Sponge of the Dogs Rose, called by some Bedeguar. **1861** Hulme tr. *Moquin-Tandon* II. III. v. 153 Bedeguars—commonly called 'Soft Apples' or 'Vegetable Sponges'.

c. Something having the appearance or consistency of a sponge.

1683 K. Digby *Chym. Secr.* 12 The ☉ and ☿ will be precipitated indistinguishible, in the form of a black Spunge. **1893** F. F. Moore *Gray Eye or So* xxvii, Sitting for five or six hours on gigantic sponges (damp) of heather.

d. The soft fermenting dough of which bread is made. Freq. in the phr. *to set* (or *lay*) *the sponge*.

1747 H. Glasse *Art of Cookery* (ed. 2) xvii. 297 To make White Bread.. when your Spunge has stood its proper Time clear the Oven, and begin to make your Bread. **1796** A. Simmons *Amer. Cookery* 38 *Butter biscuit.* One pint each milk and emptins, laid into flour, in sponge. **1822** *Imison's Sci. & Art* II. 152 This is called *setting the sponge.* **1830** M. Donovan *Dom. Econ.* I. 355 To this strained matter, one half of the whole quantity of flour is to be added, and well worked up with the hands so as to form sponge. **1857** Miller *Elem. Chem., Org.* 113 The mass swells up, or, as the baker terms it, the sponge rises. **1896** T. Hardy *Jude* v. iii, He was obliged to go to bed at night immediately after laying the sponge.

e. A stretch of ground of a swampy nature.

1856 Olmsted *Slave States* 157, I am aware of but a single attempt, as yet, to cultivate the sponge or true swamp soil. **1890** *Contemp. Rev.* Jan. 137 The 'great sponge', from which the Zambesi and the Congo draw their remote supplies. **1901** *Q. Rev.* July 22 It has been conjectured that some of these sponges may be fed by the waters of the Victoria Nyanza.

f. *techn.* Metal in a porous or sponge-like form, usu. obtained by reduction without fusion.

1861 Sir W. Fairbairn *Iron* 176 M. Chenot makes steel direct from the ore by converting it into a substance he calls *sponge*, in a peculiarly constructed furnace. **1877** Raymond *Statist. Mines & Mining* 389 To remove the silver sponge, which falls to the bottom and is taken out. This sponge is very light. **1884** Knight *Dict. Mech.* Suppl. 844 The sponge .. is plunged in a bath of resin, tar, or some fatty matter.

g. With defining word: a type of thick jelly eaten as a dessert.

1859 J. H. Walsh *Eng. Cookery Bk.* 275 Lemon sponge. .. Take half an ounce of isinglass.. the juice of eight lemons. **1907** *Yesterday's Shopping* (1969) 55/1 Sweets.. Lemon Sponge, Raspberry Sponge (in copper moulds, 10/0 extra, returnable). **1978** E. Lothian *Country House Cookery from West* 19 Orange sponge. 1 oz (30 g) gelatine. 4 oranges.

h. A sponge-cake; the mixture from which such a cake is made.

1877 *Cassell's Dict. Cookery* 920/1 *Sponge, Savoy*,.. pour the batter gently into a mould. **1907** *Yesterday's Shopping* (1969) 55/2 Golf Sponge, iced chocolate, coffee, pink or white.. each of 0/11. **1917** *Harrods Gen. Catal.* 1269/2 Sponge Swiss Roll.. per lb. 1/8... Caracas Roll (Rich Chocolate Sponge).. per lb. 1/10. **1948** *Good Housek. Cookery Bk.* II. 447 Steamed sponge puddings. *Ibid.* 579 Genoese Sponge (basic recipe) 3 oz. butter 2½ oz. flour ½ oz. cornflour 3 large eggs 4 oz. caster sugar. **1960** R. Daniel *Death by Drowning* v. 54 A jam sponge, please. **1975** *Times* 10 May 13/4 The mixture can be baked.. as a sponge flan.

† 7. An open-work coat of mail. *Obs.*$^{-1}$

1600 Holland *Livy* IX. xl. 344 Their brest and stomack was fenced with spounges, the left leg armed with a good greeue.

III. *fig.* **8.** An immoderate drinker; a soaker.

1596 Shaks. *Merch. V.* I. ii. 108, I will doe any thing Nerrissa ere I will be married to a spunge. **1693** Bowles in *Dryden's Juvenal* v. 34 For him is kept a Liquor more Divine, You Spunges must be drunk with Lees of Wine. **1708** *Brit. Apollo* No. 73. 2/2 For ever too th' Amphibious Spunge does drink. **1785** Grose *Dict. Vulgar T.*, *Spunge*, a thirsty fellow, a great drinker. **1887** Henley *Villon's Good-night* 3 You spunges miking round the pubs.

9. a. One who or that which absorbs, drains, or sucks up, in a sponge-like manner.

In various passages of Elizabethan writers the exact sense of the word is not quite clear.

1603 J. Davies (Heref.) *Microcosmos* Wks. (Grosart) I. 63/1 These senslesse spunges of Improbity Are full of pleasure, but it is vnright. **1607** Walkington *Opt. Glass* xii. (1664) 130 We count a Melancholick man the very Spunge of all sad Humors. **1677** Otway *Cheats of Scapin* II. i, Do ye not see every Day how the Spunges [*sc.* the lawyers] suck poor Clients. **1755** Young *Centaur* iii. Wks. 1757 IV. 168 Our thirsty spunges of sensuality, who suck up every drop of it. **1891** O. W. Holmes *Over Teacups* viii. 181 The muscles are great sponges that suck up and make use of large quantities of blood. **1893** Saltus *Madam Sapphira* 219 After hours of that sponge for thought [*sc.* fatigue] which the saddle alone supplies.

b. *spec.* One who or that which appropriates or absorbs material or other advantages, wealth, etc.

1601 Sir W. Cornwallis *Ess.* xl. Cc iv, This spunge sucketh dry the commerce of societies. **1602** Shaks. *Ham.* IV. ii. 12 *Rosin.* Take you me for a Spundge, my Lord? *Ham.* I sir, that sokes vp the Kings Countenances, his Rewards, his Authorities. **1647** Clarendon *Hist. Reb.* I. §162 Ireland, which had been a Spunge to draw.. all that could be got from England.

c. A person, etc., of this kind as a source from which something may be recovered or extracted.

1602 Shaks. *Ham.* IV. ii. 22 It is but squeezing you, and Spundge you shall be dry againe. *a* **1618** Raleigh *Prerog. Parl.* 9 The people,.. when they saw hee had squeased those spunges of the Common-wealth,.. willingly yeelded to giue him satisfaction. *c* **1670** Hobbes *Dial. Com. Laws* (1681) 156 Empson and Dudley were no Favourites of Hen. the 7th, but Spunges, which King Hen. the 8th did well squeeze. **1722–7** Boyer *Dict. Royal* I, *Presser l'éponge*,.. to squeeze the Spunge, to make one refund. **1779** Earl Carlisle in Jesse *Selwyn & Contemp.* (1844) IV. 256 He is a sponge full of knowledge, which you may squeeze at your leisure.

d. An object of extortion; a source of profit or pecuniary advantage.

1625 Purchas *Pilgrims* II. 1480 Which make Merchants to conceale their Riches lest they should be made Spunges. **1630** Brathwait *Eng. Gentlem.* (1641) 31 Another not so proud as covetous:.. such an one makes all his inferiours his sponges. **1781** Cowper *Expost.* 531 Thy monarchs.. in distress Found thee a goodly sponge for Power to press. **1821** *Examiner* 744/1 Ireland has been made all along a sponge for sinecurists, a field for jobbers. **1835** James *Gipsy* ii, I will be no sponge to be squeezed for any man's pleasure.

10. One who meanly lives at the expense of others; a parasite, a sponger.

1838 Stephens *Trav. Turkey* 36 As I could only contribute [to the meal] a couple of rolls of bread, .. I am inclined to think that he considered me rather a sponge. **1866** Whipple *Character & Charact. Men* 22 That large .. class of our fellow-citizens who are commonly included in the genus 'sponge'. **1883** H. Drummond *Nat. Law in Spir. W.* 350 All social sponges; all satellites of the court; all beggars of the market-place.

IV. *attrib.* and *Comb.* **11. a.** Attrib. in various uses, as ***sponge-bag***, ***-bank***, ***-basin***, ***-bath***, ***-bed***, ***box***, etc.

The number of such combs. in recent use is very large, chiefly in the senses 'forming part of, found in, sponges', 'producing or yielding sponges', 'used in fishing for sponges', 'used or intended for holding a sponge'.

1858 Simmonds *Dict. Trade*, **Sponge-bag*, an oil-skin case for a toilet sponge. **1885** Lady Brassey *The Trades* 333 Then we went .. to see the *sponge-bank, where some of the finest specimens of sponge are procured. **1862** *Catal. Internat. Exhib., Brit.* II. No. 5825, *Sponge basin, soap box. **1859** *Habits of Gd. Society* i. (new ed.) 106 The best bath for general purposes .. is a *sponge bath. **1883** in Adderley *Fisheries Bahamas* 55 The complete exhaustion of the *sponge beds. **1885** Lady Brassey *The Trades* 310 It is through this strait that many if not most of the *sponge-boats go. **1895** *Army & Navy Co-op. Soc. Price List* 191/2 *Sponge box for travelling, patent aluminium. **1970** *Canadian Antiques Collector* Oct. 18/2 Similar trifles for feminine use included snuff boxes, sponge boxes and bodkin cases. **1849** *Ann. Nat. Hist.* IV. 87 When living and isolated the *sponge-cell is polymorphous. **1883** Adderley *Fisheries Bahamas* 7 A new *sponge-field was discovered last year. **1867** *Chambers's Encycl.* IX. 57/2 The number of men employed in the Ottoman *sponge-fishery is between 4000 and 5000. **1855** T. R. Jones *Anim. Kingd.* (ed. 2) 28 To this contractile substance .. he [M. Dujardin] proposed to give provisionally the name of *Halisarca* (*sponge-flesh). **1883** Adderley *Fisheries Bahamas* 53 To .. protect the selected *sponge grounds from robbery. **1674** N. Fairfax *Bulk & Selv.* 128 Drilling through their pores or *spung-holes. *Ibid.* 185 Any little spungholes or crannies. **1883** Adderley *Fisheries Bahamas* 6 They are taken to Nassau to be sold in the *sponge-market. **1870** H. A. Nicholson *Man. Zool.* v. 70 The so-called '*sponge-particles' or 'sarcoids'. **1889** *Science-Gossip* XXV. 230 Sometimes casts of the exhalant *sponge pores were made in chalcedony overlaid with quartz. **1899** *Allbutt's Syst. Med.* VIII. 821 The free bleeding will be staunched by *sponge-pressure. **1878** Huxley *Physiogr.* xvi. 271 A highly fossiliferous limestone with .. *sponge spicules. **1885** J. E. Taylor *Brit. Fossils* i. 17 The various appearances of *sponge structure under the microscope. **1887** *Encycl. Brit.* XXII. 429/2 Recent statistics as to the extent of the *sponge trade. **1862** *Catal. Internat. Exhib., Brit.* II. No. 6130, *Sponge tray, soap boxes. **1848** Carpenter *Anim. Phys.* ii. 113 The class of *Porifera*, or the *Sponge tribe. **1883** *Encycl. Brit.* XVI. 689/1 Within the trabeculæ of the *sponge-work blood circulates. **1899** *Allbutt's Syst. Med.* VII. 266 The blood-vessels form an expressible sponge-work. **1885** Lady Brassey *The Trades* 310 Many *sponge-yards, where the process of cleaning and drying sponges is carried on.

b. In the sense 'made of sponge'.

1859 Semple *Diphtheria* 248 The *sponge-brush is moistened with the caustic liquid. **1849** Noad *Electricity* (ed. 3) 490 A rapid series of shocks may thus be communicated .. by means of the *sponge directors. **1837** *Penny Cycl.* IX. 27/1 Its interior may be .. cleaned by .. running *sponge-rammers through the .. straight pipes. **1739** S. Sharp *Treat. Surgery* p. xxi, A piece of *Sponge-Tent, which is made by dipping a dry bit of Sponge in melted Wax [etc.]. **1803** *Med. Jrnl.* X. 490 Keeping the abscess open by means of a sponge tent. **1876** *Trans. Clinical Soc.* IX. 106 Sponge-tents are to be used to dilate the wound.

12. *Comb.* **a.** Parasynthetic, as ***sponge-coloured***, ***-footed***, ***-leaved***, etc. **b.** With agent-nouns, as ***sponge-diver***, ***-fisher***, ***-maker***, etc. **c.** With vbl. sbs. and ppl. adjs., as ***sponge-bearing***, ***-farming***, ***-fishing***, etc.

a. **1753** *Chambers' Cycl.* Suppl. s.v. *Pine*, Spunge-leaved Pine. **1826–7** *Encycl. Metrop.* (1845) XVIII. 580 Fluviatile, sponge-shaped. **1845** G. Dodd *Brit. Manuf.* IV. 33 A very curious sponge-coloured slab of stalagmitic marble. **1896** *Westm. Gaz.* 26 Apr. 1/3 The silent sponge-footed camels.

b. **1788** *6th Rep. Dep. Kpr. Pub. Rec.* II. 179 Henry Cook, .. Spunge Maker. **1858** Homans *Cycl. Comm.* 1751 The principal sponge-fishers of the Archipelago and Levant. **1879** *Cassell's Techn. Educ.* II. 238 The sponge-divers in the Archipelago. **1887** *Pall Mall G.* 23 Feb. 9/1 The prisoner .. was a sponge trimmer.

c. **1861** Miss Beaufort *Egypt. Sepulchres* II. 334 The sponge-gathering is a very lucrative business. **1875** Knight *Dict. Mech.* 2286/1 On the Barbary coast sponge-fishing is .. actively prosecuted. **1885** J. E. Taylor *Brit. Fossils* i. 16 Fossil sponge-hunting. *Ibid.* 23 Sponge-bearing chalk-flints. **1887** *Encycl. Brit.* XXII. 428/2 The method of sponge-farming.

13. a. Special Combs.: **sponge-bag trousers**, a pair of men's checked trousers, patterned in the style of many sponge-bags; **sponge biscuit**, a flour-biscuit of a similar composition to sponge-cake; **sponge cloth**, (*a*) (see quots.); (*b*) a thin piece of spongy material used for cleaning; (*c*) a type of cotton fabric (see quot. 1957); **sponge-finger**, an elongated form of sponge-biscuit; **sponge-glass**, a device for discovering sponges at the bottom of the sea; **sponge-gold**, gold as it remains after the silver has been removed in the process of 'parting'; **sponge-head**, the top of an artillery sponge-staff; **sponge-hook**, a hook with which sponges are pulled up from the sea-bottom; **sponge-iron**, iron ore rendered light and porous by the removal of foreign matter; **sponge mixture**, (*a*) a packet of prepared dry ingredients for making a sponge-cake; (*b*) the ingredients of a sponge-cake mixed together ready for baking; **sponge-pole**, = *sponge-staff* (*b*); **sponge rubber**, liquid rubber latex processed into a sponge-like substance; freq. *attrib.*; **sponge sandwich**, a sponge-cake consisting of two halves sandwiched together with a filling; in earlier use, covered with custard and eaten as a pudding; **sponge-staff**, (*a*) the staff of an artillery sponge; (*b*) the staff of a sponge-hook; †**sponge-stone** (see quots.); **sponge-swamp** (see sense 6 e).

1915 V. Woolf *Voyage Out* xxiii. 376 Can't you imagine him—bald as a coot with a pair of *sponge-bag trousers? **1977** A. J. Ayer *Part of My Life* ii. 35 The members of Pop also had the privileges .. of wearing coloured waistcoats, sponge-bag trousers, braid on their tail-coats, flowers in their button-holes and sealing wax on their top-hats. **1736** Bailey *Househ. Dict.* s.v. *Biscuit*, To make *Spunge Biscuit. **1837** Mrs. Gaskell *Let.* 18 Mar. (1966) 10 Aunt L. has .. expressed a strong wish to hear 'her dear little voice once again' and has a spunge biscuit behind her pillow this 4 days to give her. **1892** T. F. Garrett *Encycl. Pract. Cookery* 147/1 *Sponge Biscuit.*—Beat ten eggs very thick and smooth. **1954** D. Hartley *Food in England* vii. 218 (*heading*) Egg and lemon jelly (using sponge biscuits). **1862** *Catal. Internat. Exhib., Brit.* II. No. 3643, Patent *sponge cloths for cleaning machinery and fire-arms. **1876** Voyle & Stevenson *Milit. Dict.* 397/1 *Sponge Cloth*, a peculiar kind of cloth, moist with oil; it is used to clean the screws of Armstrong guns. **1902** D. Salomons in A. C. Harmsworth *Motors & Motor Driving* vi. 93 Sponge cloths are a desirable accessory for cleaning and for polishing up. **1919** *Queen* 26 July 138 White sponge cloth is the thing for this new coat and skirt. **1957** M. B. Picken *Fashion Dict.* 318/2 *Sponge cloth...* Cotton fabric of coarse yarn woven in honeycomb weave to produce open spongy effect. **1976** W. Trevor *Children of Dynmouth* iii. 58 Timothy rinsed the sponge-cloth he was using, squeezing it out in his bowl of dirty water. He wiped the inside of the oven .. and closed the door. **1906** *Westm. Gaz.* 11 Sept. 10/2 The biscuits, *sponge-fingers, sultana-cakes [etc.]. **1885** Lady Brassey *The Trades* 301 Their *sponge-glasses .. may perhaps be best described as square buckets with a glass bottom to them. **1887** Goode *Fisheries U.S.* 823 The sponge-glass as originally constructed consisted of a small, square, wooden box having a glass bottom. **1882** *U.S. Rep. Prec. Met.* 648 Pouring melted phosphorus upon hot *sponge-gold. **1828** Spearman *Brit. Gunner* (ed. 2) 177 Number 2 passes his sponge .. to 4, who straps on the *sponge-head. **1840** Gen. Mercer in R. J. Macdonald *Hist. Dress R.A.* (1899) 56 Mine [*i.e.* a hat] was one of the low fans, with the spunge-head feather. **1881** Ingersoll *Oyster-Industr.* (Hist. Fish. Industr. U.S.) 248 **Sponge-hook.*—The bent, two-pronged iron tool at the end of a pole, with which sponges are gathered from the bottom. **1887** Goode *Fisheries U.S.* 823 The sponge-hooks are made of iron, with three curved prongs, measuring in total width about 5 or 6 inches. **1874** J. A. Phillips *Elem. Metall.* 434 The precipitation of copper is very rapidly effected by the use of *sponge-iron. **1926–7** *Army & Navy Stores Catal.* 50/1 *Sponge mixture .. pkt. -/5½. **1962** 'O. Mills' *Headlines make Murder* x. 119 She .. poured boiling water on her sponge mixture. **1975** *Times* 10 May 13/4 A sponge mixture that you bake yourself tastes very much nicer than a shop bought one. **1881** Ingersoll *Oyster-Industr.* (Hist. Fish. Industr. U.S.) 248 **Sponge-pole.*—The pole by which the hook is operated in gathering sponges. **1932** *New Yorker* 9 Apr. 56/3 A luxurious soft pile combined with a *sponge rubber back. **1934** G. F. Charnock *Mech. Technol.* (ed. 2) xxii. 278 Sponge rubber, such as is sometimes used for upholstery, and in which the pores are many times larger than the cells of expanded rubber, is not such an effective insulator. **1951** *Archit. Rev.* CIX. 164 (*caption*) A sponge rubber overlay is fitted over the springs. **1967** N. Freeling *Strike out where not Applicable* 20 Metal furniture, upholstered in sponge rubber, covered with grey plastic. **1884** *Myra's Cookery Bk.* xiv. 309 *Sponge sandwiches... Sponge cakes 6—cut in half lengthways. **1917** *Harrods Gen. Catal.* 1269/2 Sponge Sandwiches .. each 1/6. **1967** A. Laski *Seven Other Years* iii. 30, I want you to go .. and get a sponge sandwich for tomorrow. A chocolate sponge with cream. **1772** *Phil. Trans.* LXII. 90, I took .. sheet lead .. and beat it on a *sponge staff to make it round. **1883** *Fisheries Exhib. Catal.* (ed. 4) 160 Sponge Staffs, with Hook attached, used in obtaining .. sponge. **1668** Charleton *Onomast.* 253 *Lapis Spongiæ*, .. the *Sponge-stone. **1712** tr. *Pomet's Hist. Drugs* I. 100 The Spunge-Stone .. is made of the Matter of Spunges petrified. **1753** *Chambers' Cycl.* Suppl. s.v., The spunge-stone, or tartarous incrustation on this plant. **1901** *Q. Rev.* July 22 There is a '*sponge' swamp, or stream-head.

b. In names of crustacea, insects, etc., as **sponge centre-shell, crab, moth, shrimp**.

1591 Sylvester *Du Bartas* I. v. 378 And so the Sponge-Spy warily awakes The Sponge's dull sense, when repast it takes. **1681** Grew *Musæum* I. vi. ii. 148 The Spung-Centre-Shell. *Balanus Spongiarum*. **1848** Maunder *Treas. Nat. Hist.* 197/1 Sponge Crab.—*Dromia vulgaris*. **1888** *Amer. Naturalist* Mar. 256 The Sponge Shrimp. *Alpheus*. **1891** *Cent. Dict.*, *Sponge-moth*, the gipsy-moth.

c. In names of plants, etc., as **sponge-cucumber, gourd, -leather, mushroom, -tree, -wood**.

1891 *Cent. Dict.*, **Sponge-cucumber*, same as *sponge-gourd*. **1861** Bentley *Man. Bot.* 548 The fruit of *Luffa fœtida* is termed the *Sponge Gourd, as it consists of a mass of fibres entangled together, and is used for cleaning guns, &c. **1887** *Cassell's Encycl. Dict.*, *Sponge-leather, .. *Polytrichum commune*. **1681** Grew *Musæum* II. iii. iv. 239 The *Sponge Mushroom .. hath the substance of a Tree-Mushroom. **1760** J. Lee *Introd. Bot.* App. 328 *Spunge-tree, *Mimosa*. **1829** Loudon *Encycl. Plants* 858 *Acacia farnesiana*, Sponge Tree... [Native of] St. Domin[go]. **1828** *Encycl. Metrop.* (1845) XIX. 487/2 One species, *Gastonia spongiosa*, native of the Island of Bourbon; a tree with bark similar to sponge, it is called by the natives *Sponge wood. **1866** *Treas. Bot.* 1086/2 Spongewood, *Æschynomene aspera*.

sponge, *sb.*[2] Also 7–8 **spunge**. [f. the vb.]

1. The act of living parasitically on others.

1693 *Humours Town* 37 Another .. is faine to live upon the Spunge the rest of his days. **1716** C'tess Cowper *Diary* (1864) 105 Lady W. Powlett complains of Mademoiselle Schutz, and says she is so importunate and troublesome, and always upon the Spunge.

2. An act of wetting or wiping (off) with or as by means of a sponge. Also with advs.

1720 A. Hutcheson *Collect. Calcul. S. Sea Scheme* 138 Whether the Parliament .. shall now take the Benefit of such a Spunge made by the Directors of the South-Sea Company. **1873** Tristram *Moab* xv. 285 For myself a sponge at that heat was quite enough. **1905** *Daily Chron.* 21 Apr. 4/5 The mildest form of the cold bath is the cold sponge down. **1954** M. Stewart *Madam, will you Talk?* vii. 60, I hadn't time for a bath, but I took a quick cool sponge down. **1960** *House & Garden* Mar. 63/1 All the paper will need will be a sponge down. **1977** W. Golding *Moving Target* (1982) 66 Ann has just had a sponge-down in the beastly bath.

†**sponge**, *sb.*[3] *Obs.* Also **spunge**. [ad. older F. *esponge* (mod.F. *éponge*), alteration of OF. *esponde*:—L. *sponda* frame (of a bed, etc.).] A heel of a horse-shoe.

1580 Blundevil *Horsemanship* IV. 62 b, The Grauelling .. commeth by meanes of little grauell stones getting betwixt the hooue, or calking, or sponge of the [horse's] shooe. **1596** Mascall *Cattle* 156 In shooing the fore feete, make your shooes with a broade webbe and with thick sponges. **1607** Markham *Cavel.* VI. (1617) 64 The heeles shal be made with extraordinary long spunges, & those spunges more broad and flat then commonly is vsed. **1726** *Dict. Rust.* s.v., Those who make the spunges of their Horses Shoes too long .. spoil their Feet.

sponge (spʌndʒ), *v.* Also 6–9 **spunge** (7–8 **spung**), 6 **spundge**; *Sc.* 6, 9 **spounge**, 9 **spoonge**. [f. sponge *sb.*[1], or ad. OF. *esponger* (mod.F. *éponger*), late L. *spongiāre* (rare).]

I. 1. a. *trans.* To wipe or rub with a wet sponge for the purpose of cleaning. Also with advs., as *down*, *over*, *up*.

1392 *Earl Derby's Exp.* (Camden) 178 Et per manus eiusdem pro spongyng j last barello. **1530** Palsgr. 729, I sponge a gowne or any other garment to scoure the fylthe out of it, *je esponge*. **1550** H. Rhodes *Bk. Nurture* in *Babees Bk.* 73 Brush thou, and spunge thy cloaths to, that thou that day shalt weare. **1609** T. Cocks *Diary* (1901) 81 Given to nursse for spunginge my jerkyn ijd. **1612** Drayton *Poly-olb.* ii. 440 In their sight to spunge his foame-bespawled beard. **1687** Miége *Gt. Fr. Dict.* II, To spunge a Thing over. **1848** Mrs. Gaskell *M. Barton* vi, Too busy planning how her .. gown .. might be sponged, and turned. **1889** Gunter *That Frenchman* viii. 89 It [the dress-suit] looks very nice now, and Gretchen can sponge it up to-morrow.

absol. **1853** Kane *Grinnell Exp.* 326 Another .. sponged freely and regularly .. in water colored brown by coffee.

fig. **1842** Tennyson *St. Simon Stylites* 156 God hath now Sponged and made blank of crimeful record all My mortal archives.

b. To swab the bore of (a cannon), esp. after a discharge. Also *absol.*

a **1625** *Nomencl. Navalis* (MS. Harl. 2301) s.v., Wee have it also fitted to the ends of a stiff roape .. to spunge and lade within Board. We over spung a Peece [etc.]. **1669** Sturmy *Mariner's Mag.* To Rdr., To spunge, lade, and fire a Gun. **1769** Falconer *Dict. Marine* (1780) s.v. *Cannon*, To spunge a piece therefore is to introduce this instrument into the bore, and thrusting it home .., to clean the whole cavity. **1828** Spearman *Brit. Gunner* (ed. 2) 175 Number 1, points and commands; 2, sponges; 3, loads. **1863** Kinglake *Crimea* (1877) III. i. 119 In less time than it took the Russian artillerymen to sponge and load their guns.

c. *spec.* (See quot.)

1775 Ash, *Sponge* (v.t.), .. to take off the gloss of new cloth with a sponge.

d. To wipe, wet, or moisten, *with* some liquid applied by means of a sponge.

1800 *Med. Jrnl.* III. 557, I then directed .. the whole surface of his body to be sponged with cold vinegar. **1815** J. Smith *Panorama Sci. & Art* II. 742 To make the colour of the sky spread more evenly, it is a frequent practice to sponge the paper with clean water. **1876** Bristowe *Th. & Pract. Med.* (1878) 174 The patient should be .. frequently sponged with tepid water. **1899** *Allbutt's Syst. Med.* VIII. 780 The best treatment would be to sponge the parts with a one in two thousand perchloride of mercury.

†**2. a.** With *up*: To make spruce, smart, or trim.

1588 Greene *Pandosto* Wks. (Grosart) IV. 296 His Wife, a good cleanly wenche, brought him all things fitte, and spunged him vp very handsomelie. **1590** Tarlton *News Purgat.* (1844) 83 On goes she with her holiday partlet & spundging herself up went with her husband to church. **1605** Chapman *All Fools* I. i. 73 Undressed, sluttish, nasty, to their husbands; Spung'd up, adorn'd, and painted to their lovers. **1626** Middleton *Women Beware Women* II. ii, When she was invited to an early wedding; She'ld dress her head o'r night, spunge up herself, And give her neck three lathers.

†**b.** Similarly without *up*. *Obs.*

1592 Greene *Upst. Courtier* Wks. (Grosart) XI. 239 He as neatly spunged as if he had been a bridegrome. **1594** Nashe *Terrors of Night* To Rdr., You shal haue them .. spend a whole twelue month in spunging & sprucing them.

3. a. To apply with a sponge. *rare*$^{-1}$.

1607 Topsell *Four-f. Beasts* 184 Diuers Authors haue also prescribed these outward medicines against the bitinges of Dogs in generall, namely Vinegar spunged, the lees of vineger [etc.].

b. To remove, wipe *away*, *off*, or *up*, by means of a sponge. Also in fig. context.

1624 QUARLES *Job Militant* xii, O! bathe me in his Blood, spunge euery Staine, That I may boldly sue my Counterpaine. **1767** GOOCH *Treat. Wounds* I. 258 After the bone is laid sufficiently bare, and the blood well spunged up. **1846** BRITTAN tr. *Malgaigne's Man. Oper. Surg.* 10 Carefully sponge away the blood or serum which exudes during the application of the caustic. **1906** F. S. OLIVER *A. Hamilton* IV. iv. 309 All the old accounts were sponged off the slate.

c. To take *out*, extract, by means of a sponge or in a similar manner.

1686 tr. *Chardin's Trav. Persia* 91 Golden-sand which the People spong'd out of the Water with their sheep-skins. **1894** *Daily News* 17 July 6/3 The collector would not fairly be stigmatised as a Vandal if he sponged out the plate. *Ibid.*, These [book-]plates, containing the names.. of the owners from whose books they have been 'sponged'.

4. To convert (flour or dough) into 'sponge'. Also *intr.*

1772 *Ann. Reg.* II. 109/2 So will a thimble-full of barm, by adding of warm water, raise or spunge any body of flour. **1876** *Mid-Yorks. Gloss.* 134/2. **1962** M. E. MURIE *Two in Far North* II. vii. 171 The [bread] sponge didn't sponge in spite of red damask tablecloth and fur parka I had lovingly wrapped it in.

5. *intr.* To issue or rise in a spongy form; to foam; to drip as from a sponge.

1790 J. FISHER *Poems* 93 Sips o' it seem to come spunging Out frae your mouth. **1867** *Stamford Mercury* 20 Sept., She did not even sponge at her mouth. **1880** LOMAS *Alkali Trade* iii. 73 The cast-iron burner pipe.. should project some 6 or 9 in. into the interior, to prevent any sponging back of the acid. **1884** BURROUGHS *Locusts & Wild H.* 112 Rain.. sponging off every leaf of every tree in the forest and every growth in the fields.

6. *trans.* To throw up the sponge on behalf of (one who is beaten in a fight). *slang.*

1851 MAYHEW *Lond. Labour* II. 56 They'll fight on till they go down together, and then if one [dog] leave hold, he's sponged.

II. *fig.* **7.** To rub or wipe out, to efface or obliterate: **a.** With *out* or *out of.*

a **1548** HALL *Chron., Hen. VIII*, 200 b, Which spot no wayes can be sponged out nor recompenced, for shame in a kynred can by no treasure be redemed. **1570** FOXE *A. & M.* 688/1, I trust.. y^t your dyrtie pen.. hath not so bedaubed and bespotted me.. but I hope to spunge it out. **1629** LYNDE *Via Tuta* 285 After I.. had noted six hundred seuerall passages to be spunged and blotted out. **1654** WHITLOCK *Zootomia* 258 To spunge out prejudicate Notions or Opinions. **1838** ELIZA COOK *Lines written at Midn.* vi, Time .. That sponges out all trace of truth. **1887** D. C. MURRAY & HERMAN *Traveller Returns* v. 69 Its gloom saturated the forest rim, and then sponged it out of sight. **1888** W. RICHMOND *Chr. Econ.* 232 The difficulty is one to be met in detail. It cannot be sponged out by any general statement.

b. Without adv.

a **1636** LYNDE *Case for Spectacles* (1638) 103 Or must we beleeve, that your Inquisitors would take such infinite care and paines to review all Authours for 1600. yeares, and spunge them onely in the Index? **1819** KEATS *Otho* I. iii. 44 No, not a thousand foughten fields could sponge Those days paternal from my memory. **1866** CRUMP *Banking* ii. 70 It would remain in the power of the tribunal.. to sponge from their name the least suspicion.

c. With *off.* (Chiefly of debts.)

1720 A. HUTCHESON *Collect. Calcul. S. Sea Scheme* 138 Whether the Parliament had, by an express Law, Spunged off Seven Millions of this Debt. **1803** COBBETT in *Pol. Reg.* (1817) 8 Feb. 177 There is none of the debt sponged off by this tax. **1824** *Examiner* 817/2 The debt would be spunged off.

8. a. To divest *of* something. *rare*$^{-1}$.

1594 KYD *Cornelia* II. 7 O eyes,.. make the blood.. trickle by your vaults; And spunge my bodies heate of moisture so, As my displeased soule may shunne my hart.

b. To drain or empty; to clear out. *rare.*

1610 GUILLIM *Heraldry* III. xvi. 147 When they haue done, and their Clients purses well spunged, they are better friends then euer they were. **1814** SCOTT *Wav.* xlvi, This the young Highlander performed, not without examining the pockets of the defunct, which, however, he remarked, had been pretty well spunged.

c. To deprive (one) *of* something by sponging; to press (one) *for* money; to squeeze.

1631 R. H. *Arraignm. Whole Creature* i. 11 Those Hogs hee must feed, till they spunge him of all his substance. **1677** MIÈGE *Fr. Dict.* II, To spunge one, to get what one can of him. **1692** SOUTH *Serm.* (1697) I. 538 How came such multitudes.. to be spunged of their Plate and Money. **1716** *Wodrow's Corr.* (1843) II. 132 Yea, taking the clothes off the people's very backs,.. and always spunged them for money. **1724** RAMSAY *Vision* xii, By rundging, and spunging, The leil laborious pure [= poor].

9. † **a.** To obtain by pressure or extortion. *Obs.*

1686 tr. *Chardin's Trav. Persia* 95 Their Principal Revenue arising from what they spunge from their Vassals. **1691** T. H[ALE] *Acc. New Invent.* p. lxxiv, To spunge Composition out of such as are willing to buy their Peace.

b. To get from another in a mean or parasitic manner. Also with *up.*

1676 WYCHERLEY *Pl. Dealer* Prol., If y'ave any wit, 'Tis but what here you spunge and daily get. **1707** J. STEVENS tr. *Quevedo's Com. Wks.* (1709) 369 Any that would spunge a Dinner. **1735** SWIFT in *Portland Papers* VI. 61 (Hist. MSS. Comm.), I spend six hogsheads every year, which some of my Prebendaries.. sponge from me at noon or evening. **1760–2** GOLDSM. *Cit. W.* xxvii, They spunged up my money whilst it lasted. **1871** B. TAYLOR *Faust* (1875) I. 201 Once many a bit we sponged; but now, God help us, that is done with.

10. a. *intr.* To live on others in a parasitic manner; to obtain assistance or maintenance by mean arts.

1673 R. HEAD *Canting Acad.* 103 He may Spunge, and have his Leachery for nothing. *a* **1700** B. E. *Dict. Cant. Crew, Spunge*, to drink at others Cost. **1785** GROSE *Dict. Vulgar T., To spunge*, to eat and drink at another's cost. **1849** W. IRVING *Goldsm.* xxv. 222 An Irishman.. who lived nobody knew how nor where; sponging wherever he had a chance. **1884** G. MOORE *Mummer's Wife* (1887) 203 Fearing to look as if she were sponging, Kate insisted on.. standing treat.

b. Const. *on* or *upon* (a person, etc.).

(*a*) **1677** MIÈGE *Fr. Dict.*, To spunge upon one, *écornifler.* **1693** *Humours Town* 101 The poor Curate is fain to Spunge upon the Wealthier Sinners of his Parish. **1706–7** FARQUHAR *Beaux' Strat.* IV. iii, I had rather spunge upon Morris, and sup upon a Dish of Bohee scor'd behind the Door. **1730** FIELDING *Tom Thumb* II. i, There when I have him, I will spunge upon him. **1824** *Hist. Gaming* 41 Frequenting shabby ale-houses, sponging upon credulous persons. **1857** RUSKIN *Pol. Econ. Art* 198 They will cheat the public at their shops or sponge on their friends at their houses. **1887** MISS BRADDON *Like & Unlike* x, I hope I shall never be obliged to sponge upon you.

(*b*) **1681–6** J. SCOTT *Chr. Life* iii. Mortification iii, What man in his Wits would keep such a Company of devouring Lusts about him, that are perpetually spungeing upon his Estate. *a* **1692** POLLEXFEN *Disc. Trade* (1697) 155 [They] must live by preying, pilfering or spunging upon other Mens Labours. **1855** TROLLOPE *Warden* xx, It was an easy matter to abandon his own income, as he was able to sponge on that of another person. **1902** L. STEPHEN *Stud. Biogr.* III. iii. 114 Humbugs, ready to.. spunge upon his benevolence.

c. With *for* (something).

1719 D'URFEY *Pills* (1872) I. 200 That all Bullies should pay; And sponge no more for recreation. **1735** SHERIDAN *Let. to Swift* 5 Oct., Do not think to sponge upon me for anything but meat, drink, and lodging. **1837** LYTTON *E. Maltrav.* I. xvii, A doubt lest I should some day or other sponge upon his lordship for a place. **1883** STEVENSON *Treas. Isl.* I. v, I'm to be a poor, crawling beggar, sponging for rum, when I might be rolling in a coach!

11. To go about in a sneaking or loafing fashion, esp. in order to obtain something.

1825 JAMIESON *Suppl.* s.v. **1866** *Lond. Rev.* 3 Mar. 245/2 Soldiers.. loafing and spunging from tavern to tavern during the entire day.

III. 12. *intr.* (See quot.)

1881 INGERSOLL *Oyster-Industr.* (Hist. Fish. Industr. U.S.) 248 *Sponge*, or *To go Sponging.*—To go on a cruise for gathering sponges.

Hence **'spongeable** *a.*, able to be wiped with a sponge.

1971 *Ideal Home* Apr. 75/2 Spongeable wallpaper. **1976** *Milton Keynes Express* 23 July 22/5 (Advt.), Roller blind kits and dozens of fabulous spongeable fabrics at Bedford Wednesday Market behind statue.

sponge-cake. [SPONGE *sb.*^{1}] A very light sweet cake made with flour, eggs, and sugar. Also *fig.*

1808 JANE AUSTEN *Let.* 15 June (1952) 191 You know how interesting the purchase of a sponge-cake is to me. **1843** MRS. CARLYLE *Lett.* I. 269 A hot jelly, and one modest sponge cake. **1860** *All Year Round* No. 48. 514, I cannot dine on stale sponge-cakes that turn to sand in the mouth. **1874** BURNAND *My Time* 97 He returned.. with a bottle of lemonade.. and two sponge-cakes in a bag. **1902** W. JAMES *Var. Relig. Exper.* xiv. 364 Naturalistic optimism is mere syllabub and flattery and sponge-cake in comparison. **1909** W. S. CHURCHILL *Let.* 15 Sept. in R. S. Churchill *Winston S. Churchill* (1969) II. *Compan.* II. xii. 911 It appears to me to belong to the whipped cream and sponge cake style of painting.

attrib. **1846** SOYER *Cookery* 565 Have buttered a large sponge-cake mould. **1883** 'ANNIE THOMAS' *Mod. Housewife* 9 Some nice soup and a spongecake-pudding.

Hence **'sponge-cakey** *a.*

1858 MRS. GASKELL *Let.* 1 Oct. (1966) 896 Some little sponge cakey puddings. **1971** B. W. ALDISS *Soldier Erect* 15, I flung my sexual emotions into gear by imagining sponge-cakey vulvas.

sponged (spʌndʒd), *ppl. a.* Also 5 spounged, 7 spunged. [f. SPONGE *sb.*^{1} or *v.*]

† **1.** Of a spongy texture; porous. *Obs.*$^{-1}$

1398 TREVISA *Barth. De P.R.* XIV. xxxii. (Bodl. MS.), þouȝ cragges be neuer so hard and rouȝe and scharpe wiþ-oute, ȝitte wiþin þei beþ somdele sponged [**1495** spounged] and holowȝe.

2. Saturated with moisture like a sponge.

1628 FELTHAM *Resolves* II. xii. 31 Who can but thinke what a nastie Beast he is in his drunkennesse,.. how like a nated Sop spunged, euen to the cracking of a skinne?

3. a. Wiped or cleansed with a sponge.

1871 BROWNING *Pr. Hohenst.* Poet. Wks. 1897 II. 296/1 The old plan saved, instead of a sponged slate And fresh-drawn figure?

b. Of colour, paint, design, etc.: applied with a sponge. Hence *sponged ware*, pottery decorated by being dabbed with a sponge impregnated with colour. Cf. *spatterware* s.v. SPATTER *v.* 7.

1925 *Heal & Son catal.: Table Wares* (1972), A sponged design in clear blue under-glaze on white ground. **1957** MANKOWITZ & HAGGAR *Conc. Encycl. Eng. Pott. & Porc.* 101/1 Mocha was made here [at Greens] as well as sponged and lined wares. **1971** L. A. BOGER *Dict. World Pott. & Porcelain* 323/1 *Sponged Ware.* In American ceramics; decorating the surface of pottery by dabbing with a sponge or something of the sort.

spongeful ('spʌndʒfʊl). [f. SPONGE *sb.*^{1} + -FUL 2.] As much as fills a sponge.

1867 MACGREGOR *Rob Roy on Baltic* 243 We ran the canoe into a mass of tall reeds, to see if she had got any water. There were only three spongefuls. **1871** NAPHEYS *Prev. & Cure Dis.* II. iv. 537 A spongeful of warm water.

'spongeless, *a.* [-LESS.] Having no sponge.

1868 DICKENS *Uncomm. Trav.* xxv. 149 My sponge being left behind at the last Hotel,.. I went spongeless.

spongelet ('spʌndʒlɪt). [f. SPONGE *sb.*^{1} + -LET.]

1. *Bot.* = SPONGIOLE I.

1835 LINDLEY *Introd. Bot.* (ed. 2) 36 The stigma and the spongelets of the roots. **1841** *Florist's Jrnl.* (1846) II. 210 They will push forth sponglets into the moss. **1870** *Academy* 12 Mar. 155 In the very first phases of vegetation where the primary spongelet.. is clearly the absorbent of moisture.

2. A small sponge.

1887 in *Cassell's Encycl. Dict.*

sponge-like, *a.* [f. SPONGE *sb.*^{1} + -LIKE.] Like or resembling a sponge; spongy.

1594 T. B. *La Primaud. Fr. Acad.* II. 49 The matter of Kernels is more Sponge-like. **1642** H. MORE *Song of Soul* III. App. xxxix, Wherein they bathe Themselves, and sponge-like suck that vitall flood. **1798** *Hull Advertiser* 1 Sept. 3/3 Plumb-stones had an incrustation attached to them of a sponge-like substance. **1837** P. KEITH *Bot. Lex.* 402 The *cutis vera*.. is itself chiefly cellular and sponge-like in its structure. **1866** *Treas. Bot.* 513/2 The sponge-like masses in which the capsules of *Polyides* are immersed.

spongeoid, *a. rare*$^{-1}$. [f. SPONGE *sb.*^{1} + -OID.] = SPONGOID *a.* 2.

1822 J. PARKINSON *Outl. Oryctol.* 61 The fructiform figures which the spongeoid fossils so frequently possess.

spongeol, anglicized form of SPONGIOLE.

1832 *Planting* 16 (L.U.K.) III, The fibres of the root, with the minute spongeols. *Ibid.* 32.

spongeo-piline: see SPONGIOPILINE.

† **spongeosity,** obs. variant of SPONGIOSITY.

1541 R. COPLAND *Guydon's Quest. Chirurg.* E j, This bone is perced and hath great spongeosyte to purge the grosse superfluytees.

spongeous ('spʌndʒəs), *a.* Also 6 spoungeous, 6–7 spungeous. [ad. L. *spongeōs-us*, f. *spongea* SPONGE *sb.*^{1} Cf. SPONGIOUS *a.*]

1. Of the nature or character of a sponge; porous, spongy.

α. **1398** TREVISA *Barth De P.R.* XIV. xxxii. (Tollem. MS.), Thouȝe cragges be neuer so harde and rouȝe and scharp withoute, ȝit within þey ben sumdel spongeous. **1541** R. COPLAND *Guydon's Quest. Chirurg.* E iv, Fro the vaynes and arteres and the spongeous fleesshe. **1548–77** VICARY *Anat.* v. (1888) 43 The Uuila is a member made of a spongeous fleshe. **1610** W. FOLKINGHAM *Art of Survey* I. viii. 19 A Wood-like rottennesse, viz. drie, spongeous, full of holes. **1698** A. BRAND *Emb. fr. Muscovy into China* 21 The Agarius Tree, whose spongeous substance is.. carried to Archangel. **1758** J. S. tr. *Le Dran's Observ. Surg.* (1771) 227, I.. found a *Caries*.. penetrating into their spongeous Texture. **1847** ANSTED *Anc. World* x. 233 In the sand associated with the chalk.. spongeous bodies.. are also met with in a perfect state. **1889** Z. A. RAGOZIN *Media, Babylon, & Persia* 35 Many are the rivulets.. that dribble and trickle through spongeous stone and rocky rifts.

β. **1601** HOLLAND *Pliny* II. 514 It is spungeous and brittle, apt to break or resolue into flakes. **1658** FRANCK *North. Mem.* (1821) 350 A marly spungeous clay. **1683** K. DIGBY *Chym. Secr.* 96 To render it more Spungeous. **1728** CHAMBERS *Cycl.* s.v. *Disease*, Spungeous Membranes of the Head.

b. Soft and yielding as a sponge. *rare*$^{-1}$.

1607 BREWER *Lingua* IV. iv, I lay my head between two spungeous pillowes.

2. Characterized by porousness or sponginess.

c **1600** T. PONT *Topogr. Acc. Cunningham* (Maitl. Club) 6 The surface of the soyle.. being of it selve of a spongeous nature, sucking the humiditie. **1822** J. PARKINSON *Outl. Oryctol.* 22 That spongeous state which accompanies bituminization.

sponger ('spʌndʒə(r)). Also 7–9 spunger. [f. SPONGE *v.* or *sb.*^{1} + -ER^1.]

1. One who lives meanly at another's expense; a parasite, a sponge.

1677 MIÈGE *Fr. Dict.* I, *Ecornifleur*,.. a Spunger, a smell feast. **1681** T. FLATMAN *Heraclitus Ridens* No. 74 (1713) II. 203 A Detachment of sorry Spungers from the Suburb Shovel-board Tables and Nine-pin Alleys. **1710** SWIFT *Lett.* (1767) III. 19, I dined with some friends that board hereabout, as a spunger. **1731** MEDLEY *Kolben's Cape G. Hope* I. 109 My company.. only listen'd as Spongers, in order to be treated with the other bottle. **1866** *Cornh. Mag.* Sept. 287 Shameless and impudent spungers. **1888** *Pall Mall G.* 3 Sept. 3/2 The spongers for free hospitality at scientific and other annual congresses.

b. Const. *on.*

a **1732** GAY *Fables* II. viii, Crush'd in his luxury and pride, The spunger on the public dy'd. **1860** THACKERAY *Lovel* i, An old sponger on other people's kindness. **1890** *N. Lindsey Star* 9 Aug. 5/3 Those spongers on the nation's earnings are quite happy without work.

2. One who uses a sponge, esp. in order to cleanse the bore of a cannon.

1828–32 WEBSTER, *Spunger*, one who uses a sponge. **1859** GRIFFITHS *Artill. Man.* (1862) 228, 4. The sponger. 3. The loader. **1886** *Cent. Mag.* Apr. 909/1, I was serving on one of the thirty-two pounders, and my sponger was an old man-o'-war's man.

b. One who transfers designs to pottery by means of a piece of sponge.

1881 *Instr. Census Clerks* (1885) 88 Earthenware, China, Porcelain, Manufacture:.. Sponger,.. Stamper.

3. A gatherer of, a diver or fisher for, sponges.

1880 N. H. BISHOP *Sneak-Box* 289 An almost uninhabited region, where only an occasional fisherman or sponger is met. **1887** GOODE *Fisheries U.S.* 826 To allow the slimy matter, called 'gurry' by the spongers, to run off easily.

b. A vessel engaged in sponge-fishing.

1885 *Harper's Mag.* Jan. 217/1 We cast longing glances at certain Nassau spongers, trim, shapely cock-boats.

spongi- (ˈspʌndʒɪ), combining form, after L. types, of SPONGE *sb.*^{1}, occurring in a few terms, as **ˈspongiculture, sponˈgiferous** *a.*

1833–4 J. PHILLIPS *Geol.* in *Encycl. Metrop.* (1845) VI. 656 Traces of spongiferous bodies. **1876** PAGE *Adv. Text-bk. Geol.* xviii. 353 The spongiferous cherts of the Portland and coralline oolites. **1902** *Encycl. Brit.* (ed. 10) XXXII. 813/2 Sponges in Commerce, Spongiculture.

ˈspongiary. *Zool.* [ad. mod.L. *Spongiaria* (pl.), f. L. *spongia* SPONGE *sb.*^{1}] A sponge.

1860 *Edinb. New Philos. Jrnl.* XII. 223 The spongiaries.., or skeletons, or remains of the sponge after the death and decomposition of the live jelly, or living being. *Ibid.*, A great many spongiaries are not amorphous, but have very distinct forms.

spongiform (ˈspʌndʒɪfɔːm), *a.* [f. SPONGI-.]

1. Resembling a sponge in structure; light and porous.

1805–17 R. JAMESON *Char. Min.* (ed. 3) 97 *Spongiform.* In this figure the cells are cylindrical. **1841** *Penny Cycl.* XIX. 199/2 Cavernous quartz is termed Spongiform quartz or Swimming stone. **1875** *Encycl. Brit.* III. 251/2 An infinite number of minute cavities, which render the product light and spongiform.

2. Zoologically resembling a sponge.

1839 DE LA BECHE *Rep. Geol. Cornwall*, etc. ix. 264 This view seems borne out by the alcyonic and other spongiform remains. **1876** PAGE *Adv. Text-bk. Geol.* xv. 280 Of spongiform organisms we may mention mammillopora.

ˈspongily, *adv.* [f. SPONGY *a.*] In a spongy manner.

1882 *Nature* XXV. 363 Increase of storage capacity can be given to corrugated or to spongily and otherwise roughened lead elements.

spongin (ˈspʌndʒɪn). [f. SPONGE *sb.*^{1} + -IN.] The horny or fibrous substance found in the skeleton of sponges: = KERATOSE *sb.*

1868 WATTS *Dict. Chem.* V. 404 *Spongin*, Städeler's name for the organic matter of sponge. **1887** SOLLAS in *Encycl. Brit.* XXII. 416 An axial fibre of organic matter,—probably of the same nature as spongiolin or spongin, the chief constituent of the fibres of horny sponges. **1888** ROLLESTON & JACKSON *Anim. Life* 252 Lamellae of Keratin or Spongin, a substance near akin chemically to silk.

sponginess (ˈspʌndʒɪnɪs). Also 7–8 **spunginess.** [f. SPONGY *a.* + -NESS.]

1. Spongy or porous character, nature, or quality.

α. **1610** MARKHAM *Masterp.* I. lxiv. 134 It through the sponginesse is apt to sucke in all manner of filth. **1659** H. MORE *Immort. Soul* II. ix. 214 The sponginess & laxness of the Brain. **1815** J. SMITH *Panorama Sci. & Art* II. 603 In what the soil extracts from the stream by its sponginess. **1836–41** BRANDE *Chem.* (ed. 5) 512 Animal Charcoal.. often has a peculiar lustre and sponginess. **1883** J. MILLINGTON *Are we to read backwards?* 76 The paper should be.. free from sponginess.

β. **1611** FLORIO, *Móllo*,.. the soft or spunginesse of any thing, as of crummes of bread. **1707** MORTIMER *Husbandry* (1721) II. 20 Because of its spunginess the Rain easily penetrates. **1788** *Med. Comm.* II. 209 A spunginess.. of the membrane.

b. *fig.* and *transf.*

a **1631** DONNE *Serm.* cii. Wks. 1839 IV. 370 For this plurality.. of Sin hath first found a Sponginesse in the Soule. **1670** CLARENDON *Contempl. Ps.* Tracts (1727) 666 We must have all that looseness and sponginess of our hearts removed. **1852** MUNDY *Antipodes* (1857) 29 The size and sponginess of the two Sydney butchers.

2. *Path.* The characteristic soft fungous condition of the gums in scurvy.

1873 F. T. ROBERTS *Handbk. Med.* 824 Sponginess of the gums with tendency to bleed, and rapid destruction of the teeth are frequently noticed. **1897** *Allbutt's Syst. Med.* II. 158 It.. frequently begins with a simple sponginess of gums.

sponging (ˈspʌndʒɪŋ), *vbl. sb.* [f. SPONGE *v.* or *sb.*^{1}]

1. The action of washing or wiping with a sponge.

1575 in Feuillerat *Revels Q. Eliz.* (1908) 254 The Charges of this Office grew by meanes of.. Brusshing, Spunging,.. putting in order.. of the garmentes, Vestures [etc.]. **1593** NASHE *Christ's T.* Wks. (Grosart) IV. 208 To see how you torture poore old Time with sponging, pynning and pounsing. **1704** J. HARRIS *Lex. Techn.* I, *Spunging* of a great Gun, is clearing of her Inside, after she hath been discharged, with a Wad of Sheep-skins, or the like. **1775** ASH, *Sponging*,.. the act of wiping away as with a sponge. **1875** B. MEADOWS *Clin. Observ.* 65 Prescribed animal diet; regular exercise; cold sponging. **1898** *Allbutt's Syst. Med.* V. 1031 There should be spongings, first with warm and afterwards with cool water.

attrib. **1859** *Habits of Gd. Society* ii. (new ed.) 122 The hip-bath.. or the sponging-bath.

2. The action of living parasitically on others.

1677 MIÈGE *Fr. Dict.* I, *Ecornifierie*,.. spunging, or feast smelling. **1693** *Humours Town* 37 There are others whose youthful Extravagancies have driven 'em to the wretched fate of Spunging. **1731** SWIFT *Let. to Gay* 29 June, This will maintain you, with the perquisite of sponging while you are young. **1838** LONGF. in *Life* (1891) I. 300, I have almost given up the Portland plan. It.. would look like sponging, in these hard times. **1849** *Knife & Fork* 32 Sponging is a subtle art—so subtle, that few out of its many thousand votaries have attained to any great eminence in it.

attrib. **1707** J. STEVENS tr. *Quevedo's Com. Wks.* (1709) 225 Encouraging me to follow the spunging Course of Life.

3. The practice or occupation of gathering sponges. Also *attrib.*

1868 H. D. GRANT *Rep. Wrecking in Bahamas* 72 A large number of boats and men are employed in sponging. **1887** GOODE *Fisheries U.S.* 823 The Key West sponging-fleet consisted in 1879 of 86 vessels. *Ibid.* 826 When on the sponging-grounds the men breakfast at daylight.

4. *Cookery.* The action or process of setting a sponge of flour, yeast, water, and salt.

1895 J. GOODFELLOW *Elem. Princ. Breadmaking* xiv. 93 The golden rules to follow in sponging are.. Work at as low a temperature as possible... Use as little yeast as possible. **1929** E. B. BENNION *Breadmaking* 250 Sponging and doughing. **1949** A. R. DANIEL *Baker's Dict.*, *Sponging*, the baker's term for setting a sponge of flour, yeast, or barm, water, and salt.

ˈsponging, *ppl. a.* [f. SPONGE *v.* + -ING^2.] That sponges on others; parasitic.

a **1700** B. E. *Dict. Cant. Crew*, *A Spunging Fellow*, one that lives upon the rest and Pays nothing. **1707** J. STEVENS tr. *Quevedo's Com. Wks.* (1709) 353 There is a sort of Spunging, elemosinary Travellers. **1859** GEO. ELIOT *A. Bede* iii, To some of my readers Methodism may mean nothing more than.. sponging preachers, and hypocritical jargon. **1889** *Times* 7 Oct. 8/3 The daughter of a 'sponging' drunkard.

sponging-house. Also 7–9 **spunging-.** [f. SPONGING *vbl. sb.* (in the sense of SPONGE *v.* 8 c).] A house kept by a bailiff or sheriff's officer, formerly in regular use as a place of preliminary confinement for debtors.

α. *a* **1700** B. E. *Dict. Cant. Crew*, *Spunging-house*, a By-prison. **1722** DE FOE *Moll Flanders* 60 In about two Years and a Quarter he Broke, got into a Spunging-House. **1765** *Ann. Reg.* I. 134 It was again debated by several eminent lawyers, whether spunging-houses were to be deemed prisons, and finally determined in the negative. **1802–12** BENTHAM *Ration. Judic. Evid.* (1827) IV. 636 In jail, or in a spunging-house, his effects.. are as much in his power as if he were at home. **1871** M. COLLINS *Marq. & Merch.* I. ix. 283 [We] have been in a spunging-house together.

fig. **1827** HOOD *Whims & Oddities, Bianca's Dream* xii, In Death's most dreary spunging-house to lie.

β. **1838** JAS. GRANT *Sk. Lond.* 21, I have been arrested, and now locked up in a sponging-house for a debt I am wholly unable to pay. **1855** THACKERAY *Newcomes* I. 251 He had made himself much liked in the sponging-house. **1874** L. STEPHEN *Hours in Library* (1892) II. iv. 135 His creditors.. become more pressing, and at last he gets into a sponging-house.

spongio- (ˈspɒndʒɪəʊ), combining form, on Greek analogies, of Gr. σπογγιά, L. *spongia*, SPONGE *sb.*^{1}, as in **ˈspongioblast** *Biol.*, one of the embryonic cells of the brain and spinal cord from which the neuroglia is formed; **spongio-ˈfibrous** *a.*, provided with sponge-like fibres; **spongiˈologist, -logy,** = SPONGOLOGIST, -LOGY; †**ˈspongioplasm** *Biol.* [ad. G. *spongioplasma* (F. Leydig *Zelle und Gewebe* (1885) vii. 173)], a fibrillar or protoplasmic network pervading the cell-substance and forming the reticulum of the cell (*Obs.*); hence **spongioˈplasmic** *a.*

1902 *Science* 17 Jan. 103 Mitotic figures are occasionally found in multipolar nerve cells and in *spongioblasts. **1822** J. PARKINSON *Outl. Oryctol.* 56 *Alcyonium incrustans*.—Lobated; *spongio-fibrous within. **1873** *Ann. Nat. Hist.* XI. 245 *note*, The later *spongiologists.. almost unanimously refer the sponges to a place among the Protozoa. **1892** *Athenæum* 13 Aug. 228/1 The arguments of other spongiologists. **1895** *Funk's Stand. Dict.*, *Spongiology. **1886** NANSEN *Histol. Elem. Nervous Syst.* 38 The contents of the cells consists, also, of the same two substances of *spongioplasm and hyaloplasm. **1891** [see RETICULUM 4 b]. **1896** [see ENCHYLEMA]. **1933** M. FERNÁN-NÚÑEZ tr. *Ramón-Cajal's Histology* xvii. 299 The chromatic granules offer in their interior a vacuolated spongioplasm. **1936** W. SEIFRIZ *Protoplasm* xv. 266 The older workers in cytology held similar opinions, expressed in the 'spongioplasm' (framework) and 'hyaloplasm' (intervening fluid) of Leydig and the 'ground substance' and 'reticulum' of Carnoy and others. **1886** NANSEN *Histol. Elem. Nervous Syst.* 56 What he called fibrillæ, are the *spongioplasmic walls between the real 'primitive fibrillæ'.

spongioblastoma (ˌspʌndʒɪəʊblæˈstəʊmə). *Path.* [ad. G. *spongioblastom*: see *spongioblast* s.v. SPONGIO- and -OMA.] A malignant tumour, usu. of the brain or optic nerve, believed to be derived from spongioblasts.

1918 *Neurol. Bull.* I. 276/2 He [*sc.* Kaufmann] suggests the name *columnar cell glioma* and provisionally the term *spongioblastoma*. **1925** *Arch. Neurol. & Psychiatry* XIV. 145 They are both—neuroblastomas and spongioblastomas—richly cellular, very proliferative and rapidly growing. **1967** *Nursing Times* 27 Jan. 108/2 The highly malignant spongioblastoma multiforme which can kill within a month or two of its first symptom.

ˈspongioid, *a.* [f. L. *spongi-a* sponge. Cf. SPONGEOID *a.*, SPONGOID *a.*] Like that of a sponge.

1884 *Proc. Zool. Soc.* 178 The curious translucent gelatinous substance known as spongioid tissue so eminently characteristic of rickets.

spongiole (ˈspʌndʒ-, ˈspɒndʒɪəʊl). [a. F. *spongiole* (De Candolle), ad. L. *spongiola* asparagus-root (Columella), rose-gall (Pliny), dim. of *spongia* SPONGE *sb.*^{1}]

1. *Bot.* The tender extremity of the radicle of a plant, characterized by loose sponge-like cellular tissue; a spongelet.

1832 LINDLEY *Introd. Bot.* 77 In Pandanus the spongioles of the aerial roots consist of numerous very thin exfoliations of the epidermis. **1850** DAUBENY *Atomic The.* viii. (ed. 2) 244 The spongioles of the roots always contain an azotized material, which is from them transmitted to all the other parts of the plant. **1870** tr. *Pouchet's Universe* (1871) 264 The water-lentil, which spreads its carpet of verdure on the surface of our pools, possesses nothing but spongioles.

2. = SPONGE *sb.*^{1} 6 b. *rare*$^{-1}$.

1884 *Evang. Mag.* June 252 There are often seen in rose-bushes, small green mossy-looking tufts called 'spongioles', .. produced by a small insect.

spongiolin: (see SPONGIN, quot. 1887).

spongiopiline (ˌspʌndʒɪəʊˈpaɪlaɪn, -ɪn). Also **spongio-pilene, -pyline, spongeo-piline.** [f. SPONGIO- + Gr. πῖλ-ος felt + -INE.] (See quot. 1858.)

1851 *Catal. Gt. Exhib.* I. 263 Impermeable Spongio-pilene. **1858** SIMMONDS *Dict. Trade*, *Spongiopiline*, a substitute for the ordinary poultice, made of small pieces of sponge and wool or cloth felted together, on an impermeable back. **1862** *Catal. Internat. Exhib.*, *Brit.* II. No. 3578, Electro conducting spongeo-piline. **1876** HARLEY *Royle's Mat. Med.* 250 Soft linen, or spongiopiline, may be saturated with the warm solution and worn as a poultice.

‖**spongiosa** (spʌndʒɪˈəʊzə). *Anat.* [L. *spongiōsa* (sc. *substantia*): see SPONGIOSE *a.*]

a. The tissue constituting the bulk of the posterior grey column of the spinal cord. Now *rare*. **b.** Cancellous or spongy bone tissue, such as that found within the ends of the long bones.

1947 H. C. ELLIOTT *Textbk. Nerv. System* xiii. 157/1 Like the dorsal gray column, the spinal V nucleus has a dorsolateral substantia gelatinosa, the relay nucleus for pain fibers, and a more central spongiosa for touch fibers. **1949** *New Biol.* VI. 73 If we take a bone such as the thigh-bone (femur) and saw it in two lengthways, we find that the two ends near the joints consist of a spongy lattice (spongiosa) while the shaft is a hollow tube of dense bone (compacta). **1954** T. L. PEELE *Neuroanat. Basis Clinica Neurol.* v. 79/1 The 'body', or spongiosa, is subdivided into a ventrally placed basal part adjoining the intermediate gray columns, a dorsally placed 'cervix' or neck, and a 'caput' or head. **1966** *Lancet* 31 Dec. 1430/1 Histological sections.. confirmed the increase in trabecular bone in experiment 11. The increase was striking in both primary spongiosa.. and secondary spongiosa. **1982** *Calcified Tissue Internat.* XXXIV. 425/2 Osteoclasts in the primary spongiosa near the growth plate were the first to incorporate ^{3}H-TdR.

spongiose (spʌndʒɪˈəʊs), *a.* [ad. L. *spongiōs-us* spongy, f. *spongia* SPONGE *sb.*^{1}] Of a spongy texture; porous.

1755 *Dict. Arts & Sci.* IV. s.v., The spongiose or ethmoide bone of the nose. *Ibid.*, The spongiose bodies of the penis. **1826** KIRBY & SP. *Entomol.* IV. xlvi. 259 *Spongiose*... A soft elastic substance resembling sponge. **1859** W. H. RUSSELL in *Times* 24 Mar. 9/4 Mango, peepul, and other spongiose and heartless timbers are of no good.

spongiosis (spʌndʒɪˈəʊsɪs). *Path.* [f. SPONGIO- + -OSIS.] †**a.** (See quot. 1907.) *Obs.* **b.** Accumulation of fluid between the cells of the epidermis.

1907 A. WHITFIELD *Skin Dis. & their Treatm.* xi. 172 Some of the epithelial cells become swollen from the imbibition of the plasma, and the condition thus produced is known as spongiosis. **1932** R. L. SUTTON *Introd. Dermatol.* iv. 30 Intercellular edema, or spongiosis, is shown by widening of intercellular spaces. **1966** WRIGHT & SYMMERS *Systemic Path.* II. xxxix. 1461/2 Spongiosis, separation of cells of the prickle cell layer by an accumulation of fluid between them—in other words, oedema of the epidermis. Sometimes referred to tautologically as 'intercellular oedema' to distinguish it from so-called 'intracellular oedema' (which is hydropic degeneration of the cytoplasm of epidermal cells, as seen, for example, in certain viral infections). **1976** *Lancet* 27 Nov. 1168/2 The epidermis showed several areas of basal vacuolation and spongiosis with many eosiniphilic bodies.

†**spongiˈosity.** *Obs.* Also **-iosite(e.** [ad. F. *spongiosité* (14th cent.), ad. med.L. *spongiositas* (13th cent.), f. L. *spongiōsus*: see SPONGIOSE *a.*]

1. Spongy or porous nature; = SPONGINESS 1.

1543 TRAHERON *Vigo's Chirurg.* 65 b/1 It is conuenient, to applie a mollifycatiue.. playster,.. bycause of the Spongiosite of the dugge. **1678** R. RUSSELL tr. *Geber* II. I. 68 Flowing through the Bowels of the Minera and Spongiosity of the Earth.

2. A sponge-like part.

1543 TRAHERON *Vigo's Chirurg.* I. iii. 4 Thys bone hathe manye holes and spongiositees whych serve to purge the superfluities of the brayne.

spongious (ˈspʌndʒɪəs), *a.* Now *rare*. Also 5 **spongyouse,** 6 **-yous, -ius, -iouse,** 7–8 **spungious.** [ad. L. *spongiōsus* (see SPONGIOSE *a.*). Cf. F. *spongieux*, †*espongieux*, It. *spugnoso*, Sp. *esponjoso*.]

1. Of the nature of a sponge; spongy.

Very common *c* 1550–1700.

a. *c* **1400** *Lanfranc's Cirurg.* 108 þei [bones] ben sumwhat spongious [*v.r.* spongyouse] in þe myddis. **1543** TRAHERON *Vigo's Chirurg.* II. xv. 60 Uvula (as the Anatomystes say) is a spongyous membre. **1597** GERARDE *Herbal* I. xxiv. 35 They are full stuft with a spongious substance. **1652** FRENCH *Yorksh. Spa* vii. 70 The ground.. is spongious, and drinks in water apace. **1678** R. RUSSELL tr. *Geber* II. I. 98 Solid Woods give a strong Fire, spongious a weak. **1709** *Phil. Trans.* XXVII. 121 There are several spongious *Laminæ* which arise from its lower part. **1778** *Ibid.* LXVIII. 672 In the spongious bones of the upper jaw. **1825** *Examiner*

732/2 Soft, fluid, porous, spongious, but withal tenacious matter. **1869** BLACKMORE *Lorna D.* ii, He came up to me.. with a piece of spongious coralline.

β. **1604** E. G[RIMSTONE] *D'Acosta's Hist. Indies* IV. xii. 245 In weight it is diminished five partes of that it was, and is spungious. **1657** HEYLIN *Ecclesia Vind.* 177 An oake.. which was of an hollow or spungious body. **1758** J. S. *Le Dran's Observ. Surg.* (1771) 236 This *Caries* more commonly attacks those Bones that are Spungious.

2. Of or pertaining to a sponge.

1846 *Proc. Berw. Nat. Club* II. 196 Of a..spongious texture. **1851** G. F. RICHARDSON *Geol.* 214 Many of the moss agates are of spongious origin.

Hence †**'spongiousness**, sponginess. *Obs.*

1597 A. M. tr. *Guillemeau's Fr. Chirurg.* 37 b/1 The fleshe in that place is not of such a crassitude and spongiousnes as in the ioyncte. **1611** COTGR., *Spongiosité*, spunginesse, or spungiousnesse; a spungie lightnesse. **1727** BAILEY (vol. II), *Spongiousness*, Spunginess.

'spongite. [a. F. *spongite*: see SPONGE *sb.*[1] and -ITE[1] 2.] 'A fossil apparently identical in structure with sponge' (*Imp. Dict.* 1882).

spongo- ('spɒŋgəʊ), *a.* Gr. σπογγο-, combining form of σπόγγος sponge, as in **'spongoblast, -clast** *Biol.* (see quots.); **'spongolite** *Geol.* [ad. F. *spongolithe* (L. Cayeux 1897, in *Mém. Soc. géol. du Nord* IV. 99)], a rock formed almost entirely of sponge spicules; **'spongolith**, a fossil sponge; **spon'gologist**, an authority on sponges; a spongiologist; **spon'gology**, the science or knowledge of sponges; **'spongotype** (see quot.).

1888 ROLLESTON & JACKSON *Anim. Life* 252 The hyaline lamellae [in sponges] are secreted by pear-shaped cells or **spongoblasts*.., which are probably modified connective tissue or mesodermic cells. *Ibid.* 798 *note*, According to von Lendenfeld,..these cells..are destructive in nature,—hence *spongoclasts. **1945** M. F. GLAESSNER *Princ. Micropalaeont.* ii. 23 Some rocks known as *spongolites are largely formed of siliceous sponge spicules. **1963** *Geol. Mag.* C. 296 The Ardagh spongolites appear to have been laid down as a biohermal deposit. **1968** R. W. FAIRBRIDGE *Encycl. Geomorphol.* 780 In rare cases, sponge banks accumulate quite extensive deposits of siliceous spicules (spongolite or sometimes 'spiculite'). **1860** MAURY *Phys. Geog. Sea* xiv. §614 *note*, It would not be strange if these fifty-two forms were *spongoliths. **1883** in Adderley *Fisheries Bahamas* 43 Three distinct.. Mediterranean forms are usually recognised, both by the trade and scientific *spongologists. **1889** *Athenæum* 13 July 67/3 No more fascinating branch of natural history exists than the new *spongology. **1892** HERKOMER *Etching* 104 A '*Spongotype'. Enough can be seen in this imperfect illustration to gauge the possibilities of the process. It is printed from the untouched (steel-surfaced) electrotype.

spongoid ('spɒŋgɔɪd), *a.* Also **spungoid**. [f. Gr. σπόγγ-ος SPONGE *sb.*[1] + -OID. Cf. Gr. σπογγοειδής, σπογγώδης, and SPONGEOID *a.*]

1. *spongoid inflammation*, a kind of soft cancer or morbid growth. (Cf. FUNGUS *sb.* 2.)

1808 *Med. Jrnl.* XIX. 431 A disease totally different from that affection named by them Fungus Hæmatodes, or Spongoid Inflammation. **1834** COOPER *Good's Study Med.* (ed. 4) II. 579 *note*, The medullary sarcoma of Abernethy,.. the spongoid inflammation of John Burns, and the soft cancer of several other writers.

2. Having the form or structure of a sponge.

1833-4 J. PHILLIPS *Geol.* in *Encycl. Metrop.* (1845) VI. 659 The abundance of spungoid fossils is a very remarkable character of the English and Westphalian chalk. **1843** *Penny Cycl.* XXVI. 245/1 *Ventriculites*, a genus of spongoid Zoophyta.

3. Resembling that of a sponge.

1847-9 *Todd's Cycl. Anat.* IV. I. 29/2 Its thickness becomes considerably augmented, its texture spongoid.

spongy ('spʌndʒɪ), *a.* Forms: *α.* 6-9 spungy, 6 -ye, 6-7 -ie. *β.* 6-7 spongie, 7-9 spongey, 7- spongy. [f. SPONGE *sb.*[1] + -Y.]

1. Having a soft elastic or porous texture resembling that of a sponge; deficient in solidity or firmness, so as to be readily compressible:

a. Of flesh, animal tissue, etc., sometimes with special reference to morbid conditions.

α. **1539** ELYOT *Cast. Helthe* 31 b, The tounge is of a spungy & sanguine substance. **1545** RAYNALD *Byrth Mankynde* 45 Leuing al the grosser part in yͤ spungye body of the houpe-call. **1612** WOODALL *Surg. Mate* Wks. (1653) 15 If the disease be a Kinde of spungie flesh. **1695** J. EDWARDS *Perfect. Script.* 245 The lower part of the ear..is spungy and flexible. **1712** S. SEWALL *Diary* 4 Jan., Major Walley's Left foot is opened underneath, and found to be very hollow, and spungy.

fig. *a* **1628** F. GREVIL *Alaham* II. iii, The spungie hearts of men Their hollowes gladly fill with women's love.

β. **1646** SIR T. BROWNE *Pseud. Ep.* (1658) 158 It hath in the tongue a spongy and mucous extremity. **1774** GOLDSM. *Nat. Hist.* (1776) V. 250 The muscular, spongy flesh of the tongue. **1809** *Med. Jrnl.* XXI. 339 The other parts..were very pulpy, soft, spongy, and broken down. **1843** R. J. GRAVES *Syst. Clin. Med.* xvi. 192 His mouth became very sore,..his gums spongy. **1898** *Allbutt's Syst. Med.* V. 204 Islets of spongy tissue separate the individual nodules.

b. Of parts of plants, timber, etc.

α. **1589** *Pappe w. Hatchet* C iv, Elders..being fullest of spungie pith, proue euer the driest kixes. **1613** PURCHAS *Pilgrimage* (1614) 506 The wood is of a spungie substance. **1710** WHITWORTH *Acc. Russia* (1758) 135 Timber..cut in the spring after the sap is run up, which makes the wood spungy. **1769** E. BANCROFT *Guiana* 47 Their internal substance is white, spungy, and saponaceous. **1807** CRABBE *Birth Flattery* 301 Where spungy rushes hide the plashy green.

β. **1578** LYTE *Dodoens* 181 The roote is white and of a spongie substance. **1671** GREW *Anat. Pl.* (1682) 47 This Inner Coat..is a very Spongy and Sappy body. **1784** COWPER *Task* III. 522 Then rise the tender germs, upstarting quick, And spreading wide their spongy lobes. **1842** LOUDON *Suburban Hort.* 182 The shoots there are generally more luxuriant and spongy. **1860** RUSKIN *Mod. Paint.* V. VI. vi. §4. 43 A root [of a tree], properly so called, is a fibre, spongy or absorbent at the extremity. **1884** BOWER & SCOTT *De Bary's Phaner.* 410 Lamellar cavernous parenchyma.., which from this spongy character has also been called 'spongy parenchyma'.

c. Of ground or soil, esp. through excess of moisture.

α. **1652** EARL MONM. tr. *Bentivoglio's Hist. Relat.* 10 The scituation of all the other Provinces is low and spungie. **1677** *Lond. Gaz.* No. 1224/3 The ground about the place being very spungy in wet weather. **1708** J. C. *Compl. Collier* (1845) 25 It must of necessity rise through the Spungy Earth. **1799** *Scotland Descr.* (ed. 2) 16 The morasses, of which the soil is either a spungy turf, or a black consistent peat-earth. *c* **1853** KINGSLEY *Misc.* (1859) I. 151 The soft tread of..horse-hoofs upon the spungy vegetable soil.

β. **1732** *Ray's Disc.* (ed. 4) 12 A spongey kind of Earth. **1796** WITHERING *Brit. Plants* (ed. 3) III. 793 Rotten spongy ground. **1818** SHELLEY *Marenghi* xxiv, The coarse bulbs of iris-flowers he found Knotted in clumps under the spongy ground. **1844** H. STEPHENS *Bk. Farm* I. 507 Where clay is.. very spongy, tough, and wet. **1889** F. COWPER *Capt. of Wight* 259 There is not a hole or a spongy place anywhere.

d. In miscellaneous applications.

1616 SURFL. & MARKH. *Country Farme* v. xx. 577 Neither must it [manchet bread] be made too light or spungie. **1672** PETTY *Pol. Anat.* 375 The art of making the excellent, thick, spungy, warm coverlets, seems to be lost. **1713** GAY *Rur. Sports* 135 When floating Clouds their spongy Fleeces drain. **1716** —— *Trivia* I. 45 The Frieze's Spongy Nap is soaked with Rain. **1753** HANWAY *Trav.* v. lxix. (1762) I. 314 Their cloths are spungy, but they are thin, light, and soft. **1834** *Brit. Husb.* I. 340 The ashes..produced from soft soap ..will be found light and spongy. **1836-41** BRANDE *Chem.* (ed. 5) 109 The rising of fluids in porous and spongy bodies.

e. Of suspension and braking systems in motor vehicles: deficient in firmness.

1952 FRADZEE & BEDELL *Automotive Maintenance & Trouble Shooting* x. 396 A spongy pedal on hydraulic brake systems may be due to excessive clearance between the shoes and the drum. **1954** I. FLEMING *Live & let Die* xiii. 134 All the fun of driving had been taken out of them..with hydraulic-assisted steering and spongy suspension. **1962** *Which? Car Suppl.* Oct. 123/1 The Fiat 1500..had one disconcerting point [*sc.* in its braking system]—the long pedal travel necessary, which always felt 'spongy' and gave the impression that there was less power available in the brakes than in fact was the case. **1967** B. C. MACDONALD *Car Doctor A to Z* iii. 19 (*heading*) Pedal has 'spongy' feel.

2. Of hard substances: Having an open porous structure resembling that of a sponge:

a. Of bones, *spec.* of certain bones of the skull.

1591 SYLVESTER *Du Bartas* I. vi. 573 Whereby the moist Brain's spongy boan doth sup Sweet-smelling fumes. **1594** T. B. *La Primaud. Fr. Acad.* II. 123 It is called by the phisicions the siue-bone, or otherwise (& that more properly) the spungy bone. **1607** TOPSELL *Four-f. Beasts* 401 A Splent is a spungy harde grissell or bone, growing fast on the inside of the shin-bone of a Horse. **1753** *Chambers' Cycl.* Suppl. s.v. *Bone*, Bones..which have thin solid sides, and a thick intermediate spongy part. **1854** OWEN in *Orr's Circ. Sci.*, *Org. Nat.* I. 166 Most of the bones of fishes are solid or spongy in their interior. **1876** *Quain's Anat.* (ed. 8) I. 53 The inferior turbinated, *maxillo-turbinal*, or spongy bone, is a slender lamina, attached [etc.].

b. Of stone, ice, minerals, etc.

1615 G. SANDYS *Trav.* 22 The walls..consisting of great square stone, hard, blacke, and spongie. **1694** *Marten's Voy. Spitzbergen* in *Acc. Sev. Voy.* II. 44 This Ice becometh very spungy by the dashing of the Sea. **1796** KIRWAN *Elem. Min.* (ed. 2) I. 13 When it [silex] is exceedingly comminuted,..it is light and spungy. **1800** tr. *Lagrange's Chem.* I. 333 Hence those tender calcareous, cellular stones, and perhaps also the spungy tufs. **1834** L. RITCHIE *Wand. by Seine* 74 Such stones as were most spungy and defective, and, of course, most easily cut. **1856** KANE *Arct. Expl.* II. xxiii. 231 The falling of some of the party through the spongy ice.

c. Of metals, esp. platinum.

1807 T. THOMSON *Chem.* (ed. 3) II. 64 Spongy alumina; when exposed to a red heat, loses 0·58 parts of its weight. **1827** FARADAY *Chem. Manip.* xiv. (1842) 314 Spongy platina ..causes the union of oxygen and oxide of carbon at common temperatures. **1849** D. CAMPBELL *Inorg. Chem.* 246 [This] leaves the metal, in a highly divided state, as a greyish-black powder, and known as spongy platinum. **1884** KNIGHT *Dict. Mech.* Suppl. 845/2 The production of spongy platinum..is a task more easy in appearance than in reality.

3. a. Resembling a sponge in respect of moisture or capacity for containing this.

1598 SYLVESTER *Du Bartas* II. i. IV. *Handicrafts* 759 With th' other hand he gripes and wringeth forth The spungy Globe of th' execrable Earth. **1602** MARSTON *Ant. & Mel.* IV, Even this brinish marsh Shall squeeze out teares from out his spungy cheekes. **1611** SHAKS. *Cymb.* IV. ii. 349, I saw ..the Roman Eagle wing'd From the spungy South, to this part of the West. **1659** S. TITUS *Killing no Murder* 5 Had not his Highnes had a faculty to be fluent in his teares..: Had he not had spungie eyes [etc.]. **1872** *Echo* 10 Aug., After plenty of rain, with leaden water and a dismal, spongy look everywhere.

fig. **1599** B. JONSON *Ev. Man out of Hum.* Prol., With a gripe, [to] Crush out the humour of such spongie soules. **1611** COTGR. s.v. *Mer*, When Princes doe squeeze out of their spungie Officers the moisture which they haue purloyned from them.

b. Resembling a sponge in absorptive qualities; absorbent. Chiefly *fig.*

1605 SHAKS. *Macb.* I. vii. 71 What [can we] not put vpon His spungie Officers? **1606** —— *Tr. & Cr.* II. ii. 12 There is no Lady..More spungie, to sucke in the sense of Feare. **1697** DRYDEN *Virg. Georg.* I. 438 Oft whole sheets descend of slucy Rain, Suck'd by the spongy Clouds from off the Main.

c. Of the nature or character of a sponger or parasite; = SPONGING *ppl. a.*

1602 MARSTON *Ant. & Mel.* IV, Blowne up with the flattering puffes Of spungy sycophants.

4. *fig.* Deficient in substance or solidity.

1603 FLORIO *Montaigne* III. v. 524 The wordes: no longer windie or spungie, but of fleshe and bone. **1665** J. WEBB *Stone-Heng* (1725) 82 To set a petty Gloss upon a spungy Conjecture. **1680** H. MORE *Apocal. Apoc.* 273 R. H. in his answer..is plainly not so much copious as loose and spungy, and not at all solid. **1829** BEST *Pers. & Lit. Mem.* 171 The puffy, spungy,..washy, style that prevails at the present day. **1896** *St. James's Gaz.* 6 Jan. 4/2 Mr. Olney's English is, as usual, rather spongy.

5. Of texture or other qualities: Resembling that of a sponge.

1611 COTGR., *Spongiosité*,..a spungie lightnesse. **1633** P. FLETCHER *Purple Isl.* IV. xxvii, [The lungs] Built of a lighter frame, and spungie mold. **1733** W. ELLIS *Chiltern & Vale Farm.* 84 Hollow, spungy Texture of Parts. **1765** A. DICKSON *Treat. Agric.* (ed. 2) 69 The soil may be of a spungy nature. **1800** *Med. Jrnl.* III. 199 The sore had an ugly, spungy aspect. **1827** FARADAY *Chem. Manip.* xiv. (1842) 315 The platina in the spongy state. **1860** TYNDALL *Glac.* II. xxvi. 372 The ice on which the dirt-bands rest..appears to be of a spongier character.

fig. **1865** GEO. ELIOT *Ess.* (1884) 202 A spongy texture of mind that gravitates strongly to nothing.

6. Resembling that pressed from a sponge.

1605 G. ELLIS *Lament. Lost Sheep* lxxvii, That spungy moysture, that in deadly thrall For thy pale lips the sonnes of men thought meete. *a* **1864** HAWTHORNE *Amer. Note-bks.* (1879) II. 191 With a spongy moisture diffused through the atmosphere.

7. *Comb.*, as *spongy-flowered*, *-footed*, *-looking*, *-wet*, *-wooded* adjs.

1825 *Greenhouse Comp.* II. 26 A spongy-wooded greenhouse shrub. **1829** LOUDON *Encycl. Plants* (1836) 600 *Adlumia cirrhosa*; spongy-flower'd. **1835** WILLIS *Pencillings* II. lv. 130 The small donkey..pricking back his long ears as if he were counting his spongy-footed followers. **1855** TENNYSON *To Rev. F. D. Maurice* xi, The lawn as yet Is hoar with rime, or spongy-wet. **1870** H. A. NICHOLSON *Man. Zool.* xiv. (1875) 143 It forms spongy-looking, orange-coloured crusts.

sponk, obs. form of SPUNK.

†**spon-new**, *a. Obs. rare.* [Southern form of SPAN-NEW *a.*] Perfectly new.

13.. *K. Alis.* 4055 Richeliche he doþ him schrede, In spon neowe knytis wede. *a* **1400** *Minor Poems fr. Vernon MS.* 75/586 Heil whos sone has wrouht Al vr hele sponnewe.

sponsal ('spɒnsəl), *a.* [ad. L. *sponsāl-is*, f. *sponsus*, *-a*, spouse.] Of or pertaining to marriage; spousal; wedded, wedding.

1656 BLOUNT *Glossogr.*, *Sponsal*, belonging to betrothing or mariage. [Hence in Bailey, etc.] **1840** *Penny Cycl.* XVIII. 197/1 A vase, executed for her majesty, as a sponsal present by her. **1866** J. B. ROSE tr. *Ovid's Fasti* II. 595 O maidens fair, Choose not a sponsal day. *Ibid.* IV. 1097 Tithonia thrice must leave the sponsal bed.

‖**sponsalia** (spɒn'seɪlɪə). [L., neut. pl. of *sponsālis*: see prec.] Espousals, marriage.

1535 STEWART *Cron. Scot.* III. 390 That quietlie..Betuix thame selffis *sponsalia* tha maid, Syne in his place ressauit hir as wyfe. **178.** R. WATSON *Chem. Ess.* V. 376 (Jod.), An order, equally determined, is observable in the times of accomplishing the sponsalia of plants.

†**sponsa'litious**, *a. Obs.*$^{-0}$ [ad. late L. *sponsālītius*, *-īcius*, f. *sponsālia*: see prec.] = SPONSAL *a.*

1656 in BLOUNT *Glossogr.*

sponsi'bility. *rare*$^{-1}$. [f. next: see -ITY.] Responsibility, respectability.

1767 COWPER *Let. to Mrs. C.* 3 Apr., Though my friend, ..before I was admitted an inmate here, was satisfied that I was not a mere vagabond, and has since that time received more convincing proofs of my sponsibility, yet [etc.].

sponsible ('spɒnsɪb(ə)l), *a.* Now only *dial.* [Aphetic f. RESPONSIBLE *a.*: cf. next.] Responsible, reliable, respectable.

1721 WODROW *Hist. Suff. Ch. Scot.* (1830) III. 439/1 Till caution was found, by two sponsible persons, [that] she should present herself to the sheriff when called. **1765** COWPER *Let.* 3 July, My woollen-draper, a very healthy, wealthy, sensible, sponsible man. **1810** S. GREEN *Reformist* I. 120 'My Lord,' replied the creditor, 'I am an honest, sponsible shoemaker'. **1836-8** HALIBURTON *Clockm.* Ser. II. xxii. (1839) 276 But John Bull is like all other sponsible folks; he thinks 'cause he is rich he is wise too. **1856** G. HENDERSON *Pop. Rhymes* 97 One of the decent neighbours, and most sponsible man in the company.

sponsion ('spɒnʃən). [ad. L. *sponsio*, noun of action f. *spondēre* to promise solemnly, give assurance, etc.]

1. A solemn or formal engagement, promise, or pledge, freq. one entered into or made on behalf of another person.

1677 OWEN *Justif.* vii. Wks. 1850 III. 170 The apostle interposeth himself by a voluntary sponsion to undertake for Onesimus. **1692** BURNET *Disc. Pastoral Care* vi. 54 No Church before ours..took a formal Sponsion at the Altar from such as were ordained Deacons and Priests. **1709** STRYPE *Ann. Ref.* I. xxxiv. 345 Because in the Initiation of Baptism we stuck not to the Abrenuntiations and Sponsions made for us. **1737** WATERLAND *Eucharist* 16 A kind of

Sponsion and Security for the present and future Performance of the whole Duty of Man. **1801** NAPLETON *Advice Minister Gosp.* 35 This is a great and weighty sponsion. **1850** R. D. HAMPDEN *Charge Visit. Diocese Heref.* 39 Many children have not been baptized in the Church —have never had those sponsions made for them, which the instructions of the Church Catechism presuppose.

b. *spec.* (See quot. 1853.)

1776 in Sparks *Corr. Amer. Rev.* (1853) I. 258 The agreement entered into by Gen. Arnold was a mere sponsion on his part, he not being invested with powers for the disposal of prisoners not in his possession. **1853** WHEWELL *Grotius* II. 130 *Sponsions* is the term we may use when any persons not having a commission from the Supreme Authority make any engagement which properly touches that authority.

2. *Rom. Law.* An engagement to pay a certain sum to the other party in a suit, in the event of not proving one's case.

1632 SANDERSON *Serm.* 207 The Defendant also making the like sponsion and entring the like bond, in case he should be cast. **1880** MUIRHEAD *Gaius* IV. §13 In the same way as.. the action for a definite sum of money due is perilous for a defender rashly denying his liability, on account of his sponsion.

Hence †**'sponsional** *a.*, entering into an engagement or pledge. *Obs.*

a **1684** LEIGHTON *Serm.* Wks. (1859) 526 It is evident that he is righteous, even in that representative and sponsional person he put on.

sponson ('spɒnsən), *sb.* Also 9 **sponsing**, **sponcing**. [Of obscure origin.]

1. One or other of the triangular platforms before and abaft the paddle-boxes of a steamer.

α. **1835** *Naut. Mag.* IV. 154 The 'Lightning' was ran into by a collier, which struck her just abaft her paddle-box... Her sponcings and sponcing-timbers were broken. **1846** A. YOUNG *Naut. Dict.* 292 *Sponsings*, or *Sponcings*, in a steam-ship, the curve of the timbers and planking towards the outer part of the wing before and abaft each of the paddle-boxes.

β. **1838** *Civil Eng. & Arch. Jrnl.* I. 384/2 Breadth over the sponsons, 43 ft. Ditto over the paddle boxes, 48 ft. **1871** KINGSLEY *At Last* i, Then had come.. a day of.. watching.. the water from the sponson behind the paddle-boxes.

attrib. **1835** [see above]. **1867** SMYTH *Sailor's Word-bk.* 644 *Sponson-Rim*, the same as *wing-wale*. **1875** KNIGHT *Dict. Mech.* 2287 *Sponson-beam*, one of the two projecting beams uniting the paddle-box beam with the ship's side.

2. A gun platform, standing out from the side of a vessel. Also *attrib.*

1862 W. H. RUSSELL *Diary North & S.* I. 291 The ship.. is armed.. with rifled field-pieces and howitzers on the sponsons. **1887** *Daily News* 24 Oct. 5/5 The system.. of carrying heavy guns.. in sponson ports so high on the poop and forecastle. **1897** *Ibid.* 28 July 8/5 Their construction (five sponsons on each side of the upper deck) causes them to roll heavily.

3. a. *Canad.* An air-filled buoyancy chamber in a canoe, intended to reduce the risk of sinking even if the canoe becomes filled with water; so ***sponson canoe***.

1911 *Daily Colonist* (Victoria, B.C.) 14 Apr. 19/1 (Advt.), Don't fail to see the safety sponson canoes that cannot sink. **1917** P. L. HAWORTH *On Headwaters of Peace River* i. 6 The craft in question were really Chestnut sponson canoes, seventeen feet long... It had never been my intention to take a sponson canoe on the trip. **1968** R. M. PATTERSON *Finlay's River* 109 This proved to be a seventeen-foot Chestnut 'Pleasure Model' canoe fitted with sponsons—that is, with air-chambers along the gunwales so designed that the canoe, with an average load in it, would float even when swamped and full of water.

b. A projection from the hull or body of some kinds of aircraft, intended to increase its lateral stability in the water; also, a stabilizer in the form of a float at the end of a wing.

1928 V. W. PAGÉ *Mod. Aircraft* xvi. 668 It is a braced monoplane type, the hull being supplemented by sponsons of aerofoil section at each side. **1930** *Flight* 31 Oct. (Aircraft Engineer Suppl.) 1192b/2 Design of wing-tip floats or sponsons. **1935** [see AERODYNAMICS]. **1965** [see HYDROPLANE *sb.* 2]. **1971** *Maclean's Mag.* Oct. 70/2 Only part of the propeller, some of the rudder, and pieces of the sponsons at the front actually cut into the water. **1983** *Times* 5 Aug. 2/8 The helicopter hit the sea... The impact ripped open the bottom of the fuselage and removed the sponsons containing emergency flotation gear.

Hence **'sponson** *v. trans.*, to support, or set *out*, on a sponson. Also **'sponsoned** *ppl. a.*

1895 *Morn. Post* 10 Aug. 4/5 The same may be said of cruisers, part of whose most important armament is sponsoned out on the broadside. **1897** *River & Coast* 4 Sept. 13/1 The sponsoned deck acts as a guard to the hull.

sponsor ('spɒnsə(r)), *sb.* [a. L. *sponsor*, agent-noun f. *spondēre*: cf. SPONSION.]

1. *Eccl.* One who answers for an infant at baptism; a godfather or godmother.

1651 BAXTER *Inf. Bapt.* 153 How could the Sponsors be indangered while there were Parents? *a* **1700** EVELYN *Diary* 6 Oct. 1687, I was godfather to Sir John Chardin's sonn... The Earle of Bath and Countesse of Carlisle, the other Sponsors. **1737** *Gentl. Mag.* VII. 21/1 It is well known, that the Business of Sponsors at Baptism is in general brought to a very scandalous Pass. **1807** CRABBE *Par. Reg.* III. 959 Here, with an infant, joyful sponsors come. **1850** R. I. WILBERFORCE *Holy Baptism* 103 The practice of requiring sponsors at Baptism is of ancient date. **1907** *Verney Mem.* II. 237 When her daughter was born nothing would satisfy Lady Abdy but that Sir Ralph should stand sponsor.

fig. **1848** THACKERAY *Van. Fair* xxxiii, His Lordship.. was a credit to his political sponsor.

2. a. One who enters into an engagement, makes a formal promise or pledge, on behalf of another; a surety.

1677 MIÉGE *Fr. Dict.* II, Sponsor, or surety that undertaketh for another. **1681** J. SCOTT *Chr. Life* I. iv. (1684) 207 Our Mediator is called the *Sponsor*, or Surety of a better Covenant. **1741** C. MIDDLETON *Cicero* VIII. II. 197 Magius, oppressed with debts,.. had been urging Marcellus, who was his sponsor for some part of them, to furnish him with money to pay the whole. **1800** *Asiat. Ann. Reg.* V. 58/1 Sponsors also are of two kinds, one for appearance, the other for payment. **1864** D. G. MITCHELL *Sev. Stor.* 107, I found it requisite.. to become sponsor for his good conduct. **1880** MUIRHEAD *Gaius* III. §118 The positions of sponsor and fidepromissor are much the same. *Ibid.* Dig. 535 All.. who failed.. to relieve sponsors (sureties) who had paid for them.

b. One who stood surety for the appearance and good faith of either party in a trial by combat.

1825 SCOTT *Talism.* xxviii, The sponsors of both champions went, as was their duty, to see that they were duly armed, and prepared for combat. *Ibid.*, The sponsors, heralds, and squires now retired to the barriers.

3. *transf.* Of things (after sense 1 or 2).

1846 LANDOR *Hellenics* Wks. II. 486 We are what suns and winds and waters make us; The mountains are our sponsors. **1870** EMERSON *Soc. & Solit.* Wks. (Bohn) III. 134 All the good days behind him are sponsors, who speak for him. **1889** GRETTON *Memory's Harkback* 233 In Essex, especially, the aguish climate stood sponsor for the absence of clerics as a rule.

4. One who pays, or contributes towards, the cost of a broadcast programme or other spectacle, *spec.* in return for commercial advertisement.

1931 P. DIXON *Radio Writing* 18 The sponsor wants a dramatic type of program and is willing to spend one thousand dollars a week for the program. **1953** *Manch. Guardian Weekly* 2 July 15/2 United States broadcasting started as a service of information and entertainment for the family accompanied by restrained acknowledgements to the sponsor before and after each programme. **1956** AUDEN & KALLMAN *Magic Flute* (1957) 57 To name a sponsor or to praise a brand. **1972** 'E. LATHEN' *Murder without Icing* (1973) vii. 67 It is axiomatic in all sports coverage that the sponsor's time should never intrude on the action.

'sponsor, *v.* [f. prec.] **1.** *trans.* **a.** To be surety for, to favour or support strongly.

1884 *L'pool Mercury* 6 June 5/8 The eldest daughter, who has ever sponsored her father's cause. **1888** *Standard* 24 Feb. 5/1 The Company is to be most powerfully sponsored.

b. To promote and support (a resolution, bill, etc.), esp. in a legislative assembly.

1961 *Time* 14 July 25/3 The U.A.R. forthwith sponsored a Security Council resolution. **1964** *Ann. Reg. 1963* III. ii. 152 Virtually the same resolution as had been vetoed in the Security Council was sponsored in the General Assembly by 44 nations. **1973** *Daily Tel.* 19 Nov. 3/3 Sir Gerald Nabarro .. successfully sponsored legislation on clean air, coroners, oil burners, and thermal insulation.

2. To pay, or contribute towards, the expenses of a radio or television programme, a performance or other event or work, *spec.* in return for advertising space or rights.

1931 F. A. ARNOLD *Fourth Dimension* x. 78 The travelogue type of program, sponsored by a tourist agency or a steamship company. **1931** P. DIXON *Radio Writing* 25 When an advertiser decides that the program's worth sponsoring. **1963** *Amer. N. & Q.* I. 67/1 Ohio State University and its Press deserve great credit for sponsoring the work through the English Department, the University Libraries, and the Graduate School. **1976** *Jrnl. R. Soc. Arts* June 364/2 But a lot of them are sponsoring these concerts now, which are being broadcast regularly with the names of the sponsors.

3. To support (someone) in a fund-raising activity by pledging a certain sum for each unit completed. Cf. SPONSORED *ppl. a.* 2.

1967 *Oxfam News* Jan. 2/3 Over £35,000 was raised by young people.. sponsored by friends at a penny a mile or more. *Ibid.* June 6/2 Marathon marches.. are a big money-spinner... Everyone who walks collects threepence per completed mile from a friend who has sponsored them.

'sponsored, *ppl. a.* [f. SPONSOR *v.* + -ED[1].]

1. Financially supported or promoted; freq. of radio or television programmes, etc., having (a portion of) their expenses paid by a commercial interest in return for granting advertising space or rights.

1931 F. A. ARNOLD *Fourth Dimension* 31 Sponsored programs are those that are prepared for advertisers or organizations that pay for their time on the air and also pay for the program that is broadcast. **1932** *B.B.C. Yearbk. 1933* 35 The danger to Press interests that would be involved in changing over from public-service to sponsored broadcasting. **1953** O. LANCASTER in *Daily Express* 28 Nov. 1/4 (*caption*) Will sponsored TV help Miss Cheesecake in her career? **1973** *Ann. Rep. Curators Bodl. Libr. 1971–2* 54 The OSTI-sponsored experiment with MARC tapes was completed in 1971.

2. Of a fund-raising activity (orig. a walk), usu. organized on behalf of a charity, in which each participant obtains pledges from sponsors to donate a certain sum for each unit completed.

[**1966** *Oxfam News* Apr. 1/4 There were Oxfam-sponsored walkers.. in the.. annual Margate to Maidstone 50-mile walk. Sponsors paid 3d. for each completed mile.] **1967** *Ibid.* Jan. 2/3 Teenage support for Oxfam increased... The 'sponsored walk' caught on. **1970** *Times* 11 May 10/4 (*caption*) People taking part in a sponsored walk along the Grand Union Canal.. to raise funds for the British Council for Rehabilitation of the Disabled. **1973** [see SLIM-IN]. **1977** *R.A.F. News* 11–24 May 8/4 Flt Lt O'Doherty.. organised a sponsored team ride from Lands End to John O'Groats.

'sponsoress. [f. SPONSOR *sb.* + -ESS.] A female sponsor.

1871 G. A. LAWRENCE *Anteros* xxi, Lady Montfort, another relative,.. offered to be the bride's sponsoress at St. James'.

sponsorial (spɒn'sɔərɪəl), *sb.* and *a.* [f. SPONSOR: see -ORIAL.]

A. *sb.* A baptismal sponsor or name-father.

1836 MARRYAT *Pirate* vii, You will now on the coast meet with a Blucher, a Wellington, a Nelson, &c., who will wring swabs.. without feeling that it is discreditable to sponsorials so grand.

B. *adj.* Of or pertaining to a sponsor.

1847 in WEBSTER. **1853** *Chr. Rememb.* No. 79. 62 The clause just quoted of the sponsorial exhortation. **1862** WILBERFORCE in Hopkins *Hawaii* Pref., She.. sends out sponsorial gifts befitting England's Queen. **1897** *Daily News* 12 May 4/4 He would rather regard the former in their sponsorial function.

sponsorship ('spɒnsəʃɪp). [f. SPONSOR *sb.* + -SHIP.] The state of being a sponsor; the office of a sponsor.

1809 MALKIN *Gil Blas* XI. i, The governor's lady, wishing to draw the bonds of sponsorship still closer in this friendly party, stood for Scipio's daughter. **1848** KINGSLEY *Saint's Trag.* II. v, It knits them unto me, and me to them, That bond of sponsorship. **1895** *Daily News* 16 Feb. 2/4 To undertake the sponsorship of a resolution which asks the House to put aside this measure. **1931** P. DIXON *Radio Writing* 25 The sponsorship of the Philadelphia Symphony Orchestra by Philco. *Ibid.* 26 The men who do 'Amos 'n' Andy'.. worked for years without sponsorship and at very small salaries. **1955** *Bull. Atomic Sci.* Mar. 104/3 Will sponsorship, however, be forthcoming soon enough and on a sufficient scale? **1966** *Oxfam News* Oct. 4/1 A contingent .. from Oxfam House took part in the walk and faces.. became.. winning and chatty as sponsorships were sought. **1978** 'D. RUTHERFORD' *Collision Course* 20 Regent have decided to put some sponsorship money into motor racing.

†**'spontal,** *a.* *Obs.*[−0] [ad. L. *spontāl-is.*] (See quot.) Also †**'spontane** *a.* *Obs.*[−0] (Cf. next.)

1656 BLOUNT *Glossogr.*, *Spontal, Spontane*,.. that doth or is done willingly, naturally, without help or constraint, voluntary.

†**spontaneal,** *a.* *Obs.* [f. L. *spontāne-us* + -AL[1].] Spontaneous, in various senses.

1602 FULBECKE *1st Pt. Parall.* 58 But curtesie is a free, spontaneal and ingenious quality, to which no inforcement can be used. **1653** R. G. tr. *Bacon's Hist. Winds* 361 Let the seventeenth Motion be the Spontaneall or Willing Motion of Rotation or wheeling. **1669** W. SIMPSON *Hydrol. Chym.* 82 The occasional and spontaneal depravations of their ferments.

spontaneity (spɒntə'niːɪtɪ, -'neɪɪtɪ). [ad. L. type **spontāneitas*, f. *spontāne-us*. So F. *spontanéité*, It. *spontaneità*, Sp. *espontaneidad*, Pg. *-idade*.]

1. Spontaneous, or voluntary and unconstrained, action on the part of persons; the fact of possessing this character or quality.

1651 C. CARTWRIGHT *Cert. Relig.* I. 181 Thus we see how Bernard doth agree with Calvin in making the freedome of mans will to consist in a spontaneity, and a freedom from coaction. **1681** FLAVEL *Meth. Grace* xxix. 504 He laid down his life with the greatest chearfulness and spontaneity that could be. **1702** tr. *Le Clerc's Prim. Fathers* 348 Freedom, in his Opinion, is only a meer Spontaneity, and doth not imply a Power of not doing what one doth. **1789** BELSHAM *Ess.* I. ix. 171 Physical liberty; by which he means the principle of spontaneity. **1804–6** SYD. SMITH *Mor. Philos.* xvii. (1850) 251 Actions performed without the spontaneity of the agent, are automatic. **1851** CARLYLE *Sterling* III. vii, The general aspect of him indicated freedom, perfect spontaneity, with a certain careless natural grace. **1899** *Allbutt's Syst. Med.* VIII. 302 There is less energy and less spontaneity and originality.

2. Spontaneous or voluntary action or movement on the part of animals (or plants); activity of physical organs in the absence of any obvious external stimulus.

1721 J. CLARKE *Orig. Mor. Evil* 113 Because they [animals] have not the Power of abstract Reasoning.. we call it generally Spontaneity. **1789** E. DARWIN *Bot. Gard.* II. (1791) 153 See note on Collinsonia for other instances of vegetable spontaneity. **1793** COWPER *Let.* 23 Feb., Considering more nearly, I found it [a minnow] alive, and endued with spontaneity. **1837** P. KEITH *Bot. Lex.* 340 We regard the term Spontaneity as being less exceptionable than that of Instinct; but still it is a spontaneity that feeling has nothing to do with. **1866** J. MARTINEAU *Ess.* I. 168 The instincts and spontaneities of animals. **1877** M. FOSTER *Physiol.* III. v. (1878) 472 How absolutely devoid of spontaneity or irregular automatism is the spinal cord of the frog.

3. a. The fact or quality in things of being spontaneous in respect of production, occurrence, etc.

1751 JOHNSON *Rambler* No. 131 ¶12 Community of possession must include spontaneity of production. **1794** MRS. PIOZZI *Synon.* II. 361 We cannot commend the opulence of the ground, but its richness and spontaneity. **1823** CHALMERS *Serm.* I. 129 Every constitutional desire would run out in the unchecked spontaneity of its own movements. **1899** *Allbutt's Syst. Med.* VI. 546 The most conspicuous feature of these [tabetic] fractures is their spontaneity.

b. The fact or quality of coming without deep thought or premeditation.

1826 J. Gilchrist *Lect.* 35 *note*, Many remarks..to which we had given some credit for originality and spontaneity. **1839** Hallam *Hist. Lit.* III. v. §7 Poets who, delighted with the spontaneity of their ideas, never reject any that arise. **1873** Symonds *Grk. Poets* i. 2 Those poems of nascent nations,..marvellous in their infantine spontaneity.

spontaneous (spɒnˈteɪnɪəs), *a.* [f. L. *spontāne-us*, f. *sponte* of one's own accord, freely, willingly. So F. *spontané(e*, It. *spontaneo*, Sp. and Pg. *espontaneo*.]

1. Of personal actions: Arising or proceeding entirely from natural impulse, without any external stimulus or constraint; voluntary and of one's own accord.

1656 Hobbes *Liberty*, etc. (1841) 79 That all voluntary actions, where the thing that induceth the will is not fear, are called also spontaneous, and said to be done by a man's own accord. **1690** C. Nesse *Hist. & Myst. Test.* I. 43 Her eating therefore was a spontaneous act. **1727** De Foe *Hist. Appar.* i. (1840) 16 By apparition also I am to understand such appearances of these superior beings, as are spontaneous and voluntary. **1781** J. Moore *View Soc. It.* (1790) I. ix. 91 The spontaneous respect paid to the antiquity of their families. **1839** Hallam *Hist. Lit.* II. i. §29 The resemblance of natural disposition made it a spontaneous act of Muretus to fall into the footsteps of Cicero. **1868** M. Pattison *Academ. Org.* 6 The movement was by no means a spontaneous one on the part of the House.

b. Of persons: Acting voluntarily and from natural prompting.

1732 Berkeley *Alciphr.* II. §21 It was needless to establish professors..while there are so many spontaneous lecturers in every corner of the streets. **1829** I. Taylor *Enthus.* iv. 79 The ranks of a numerous body of men can never be filled up by spontaneous labourers of this sort.

c. Of utterances, etc.: Coming freely and without premeditation or effort.

1856 *N. Brit. Rev.* XXVI. 52 The privileged visitor.. would..have heard from him..similar spontaneous expositions of Scripture. **1870** Burton *Hist. Scot.* lxxii. (1873) VI. 265 A spontaneous thought which he could not help uttering. **1885** *Manch. Exam.* 9 Sept. 3/1 The fun is never strained or beaten out, but is always fresh, spontaneous, and luxuriant.

2. Of motion: Arising purely from, entirely determined by, the internal operative or directive forces of the organism.

1659 H. More *Immort. Soul* II. ii. 126 Sense..must like-wise Imagine, Remember, Reason, and be the fountain of spontaneous Motion. **1695** J. Edwards *Perfect. Script.* 334 Things that had sense and spontaneous motion. **1750** G. Hughes *Barbados* III. 61 Animals are sensitive organic Bodies, endued with spontaneous Motion. **1807** J. E. Smith *Phys. Bot.* 2 Vegetables..have in some instances spontaneous, though we know not that they have voluntary, motion. **1848** Carpenter *Anim. Phys.* 17 These two functions,—sensibility and the power of spontaneous motion,—being peculiar to animals, are called the functions of animal life. **1880** Bessey *Botany* 196 Living protoplasm has everywhere, under proper conditions, the power of spontaneous movement. **1882** Vines tr. *Sachs' Bot.* 871 These movements were termed 'spontaneous nutations'.

3. Of natural processes: Occurring without apparent external cause; having a self-contained cause or origin.

In 19th cent. use esp. of chemical or physical changes: see quots. under (*b*).

(*a*) **1664** Power *Exp. Philos.* II. 117 The Spontaneous Dilatation and Elastick Rarefaction of that little remnant of Ayr. **1692** Bentley *Boyle Lect.* iv. 114 A spontaneous production of Mankind may not possibly have been true. **1751** Johnson *Rambler* No. 163 ¶3 He expects every moment to be placed in regions of spontaneous fertility. **1765** *Museum Rust.* IV. 200, I suppose there was no corn on it of spontaneous growth. **1831** Scott *Cast. Dang.* v, The old man looked with horror at the spontaneous motion of the book. **1859** Mill *Liberty* iv. (1865) 45/2 He suffers these penalties only in so far as they are..the spontaneous consequences of the faults themselves. **1860** Tyndall *Glac.* II. 292 The spontaneous falling of the stones appeared more frequent this morning.

(*b*) **1805** Saunders *Min. Waters* 338 The spontaneous changes which this water undergoes. **1813** J. Thomson *Lect. Inflam.* 51 When inflammation occurs..without our being able to trace its production to the action of any obvious cause, it is termed spontaneous inflammation. **1836-41** Brande *Chem.* (ed. 5) 561 The aqueous solution..is subject to spontaneous decomposition. **1861** J. R. Greene *Man. Anim. Kingd., Cœlent.* 182 The mode in which spontaneous fission occurs among many other forms of *Actinozoa*.

†**b.** *spec.* Of lassitude. *Obs.*

1675 Owen *Indwelling Sin* ix. (1732) 105 A spontaneous Lassitude, or a causeless Weariness and Indisposition of the Body. **1732** Arbuthnot *Rules of Diet* in *Aliments*, etc. 378 Its Symptoms are a spontaneous Lassitude or Sensation of Weariness.

4. a. ***spontaneous generation***, the development of living organisms without the agency of pre-existing living matter, usually considered as resulting from changes taking place in some inorganic substance. (Cf. equivocal *a.* 3.)

The possibility of such development, once generally accepted as a fact and subsequently rejected, has been a subject of debate in more recent times.

1656 Cowley *Pindar. Odes, Notes* Wks. 1710 I. 278 The Generation of Serpents, which is Spontaneous sometimes. **1665** Hooke *Microgr.* 141 For the Sea..affords as many Instances of spontaneous generations as either the Air or Earth. **1728** Chambers *Cycl.* s.v. *Equivocation*, Equivocal Generation,..which we also call spontaneous, was commonly asserted and believed among the antient Philosophers. **1835** J. Duncan *Beetles* 194 Admitting the doctrine of spontaneous generation, it was necessary [etc.]. **1857** Henfrey *Bot.* 543 The idea of a spontaneous generation of organic bodies is now exploded. **1882** Vines tr. *Sachs' Bot.* 944 The first and simplest plants had no ancestors; they arose by spontaneous generation.

fig. **1870** Max Müller *Sci. Relig.* (1873) 377 You see the spontaneous generation of mythology with every new name that is formed.

b. ***spontaneous combustion***, the fact of taking fire, or burning away, through conditions produced within the substance itself; *spec.* the alleged occurrence of this fact in persons addicted to the excessive use of alcohol.

(*a*) **1809** *W. Nicholson's Jrnl. Nat. Philos.* XXIII. 278 The spontaneous combustion of a large quantity of charcoal. **1863** Watts *Dict. Chem.* I. 1093 The spontaneous combustion..of masses of tow, cotton, or rags saturated with oil. **1876** Voyle & Stevenson *Milit. Dict.* 397/1 New-burnt charcoal, and particularly new ground charcoal, is very liable to spontaneous combustion.

(*b*) **1795** *Repertory of Arts* II. 424, I shall not pass over in silence the spontaneous combustions of human bodies. **1799** *W. Nicholson's Jrnl. Nat. Philos.* III. 305 The apparently spontaneous Combustion of living Individuals of the human Species. **1832** Brewster *Natural Magic* xiii. 321 The extraordinary phenomenon of the spontaneous combustion of living bodies. **1853** Dickens *Bleak Ho.* Pref., It was shewn upon the evidence that she had died the death to which this name of spontaneous combustion has been given. **1882** *Syd. Soc. Lex.* s.v. *Combustion, Spontaneous combustion*... In most of the cases recorded,..either they have been near a fire, or some suspicious circumstances suggestive of murder have been present.

5. Growing or produced naturally without cultivation or labour.

1665 Hooke *Microgr.* 214 Spontaneous Vegetables seeming a food proper enough for spontaneous Animals. **1684** Penn in *Academy* (1896) 11 Jan. 37/1, I have observed three sorts [of vines]... Thes are spontaneous. **1705** R. Beverly *Virginia* II. iv. (1722) 127 Whence they had their Indian Corn, I can give no Account; for I don't believe that it was spontaneous in those Parts. **1725** Pope *Odyss.* IX. 125 Spontaneous wines from weighty clusters pour. **1760-2** Goldsm. *Cit. W.* xxxi, Spontaneous flowers take place of the finished parterre. **1805** Saunders *Min. Waters* 333 Except the turf, and some scanty heath, no spontaneous vegetation is to be seen. **1837** Ht. Martineau *Soc. Amer.* II. 49 We passed 'a spontaneous rye-field'. **1883** Day *Indian Fish* 8 Fish cured with salt-earth, or spontaneous but untaxed salt.

b. Freq. with *fruits, products, productions.*

a **1727** Newton *Chronol. Amended* i. (1728) 183 These several colonies..fed on the spontaneous fruits of the earth. **1751** Johnson *Rambler* No. 169 ¶4 There are regions of which the spontaneous products cannot be equalled in other soils by care and culture. **1826** Syd. Smith *Wks.* (1859) II. 67/2 If the English were in a paradise of spontaneous productions, they would continue to dig and plough. **1839** Hallam *Hist. Lit.* III. iv. §96 When men lived on the spontaneous fruits of the earth. **1872** Morley *Voltaire* 6 The self-raised spontaneous products of some miraculous soil.

c. Produced, developed, coming into existence, by natural processes or changes.

1732 Arbuthnot *Rules of Diet* in *Aliments*, etc. 290 Constitutions abounding with a spontaneous alkali, ought to avoid alkaline Substances. **1779** *Encycl. Brit.* (ed. 2) IV. 2671/2 Mr. Wilcke..distinguishes it by the name of spontaneous electricity. **1826** *Art of Brewing* (ed. 2) 28 Leaving a portion of matter unattenuated, to produce briskness, and, consequently, spontaneous fineness and flavour. **1846** G. E. Day tr. *Simon's Anim. Chem.* II. 249 The urine which threw down a spontaneous sediment. **1862** Marsh *Eng. Lang.* iii. 59 All the gorgeous spontaneous hues of sun-lit cloud.

6. Quasi-*adv.* = next.

1667 Milton *P.L.* VII. 203 Chariots wing'd..now came forth Spontaneous. **1720** Pope *Iliad* XVII. 248 The stubborn arms..Conform'd spontaneous, and around him closed. **1780** Cowper *Progr. Error* 364 But we, as if good qualities would grow Spontaneous, take but little pains to sow. **1810** Scott *Lady of L.* I. xxxii, Till to her lips in measured frame The minstrel verse spontaneous came.

spontaneously (spɒnˈteɪnɪəslɪ), *adv.* [f. prec. + -ly.] In a spontaneous manner.

1. By natural impulse; of a free and unconstrained will; of one's own accord.

1660 R. Coke *Justice Vind.* 7 Therefore Children..have will, and do things spontaneously. **1670** G. H. *Hist. Cardinals* III. II. 266 Considering the offers many had spontaniously made him. **1751** Johnson *Rambler* No. 175 ¶10 He who is spontaneously suspicious, may be justly charged with radical corruption. **1794** R. J. Sulivan *View Nat.* I. 130 For what is power or energy? Is it not a disposition to act, either spontaneously, or in consequence of some impression? **1809** Syd. Smith *Wks.* (1859) I. 161/2 Monk spontaneously sent down some confidential letters, which turned the scale of evidence. **1856** Dove *Logic Chr. Faith* I. §2. 37 This is correct so long as the mind acts.. spontaneously. **1877** Brockett *Cross & Crescent* 456 The Sublime Porte spontaneously informed the prince..that it would spare no effort [etc.].

b. Without thought or premeditation.

1800 S. & Ht. Lee *Canterb. T.* (ed. 2) III. 167 [The apology] sprang spontaneously to his lips. **1831** D. E. Williams *Life & Corr. Sir T. Lawrence* II. 383 In his letters, his opinions and sentiments are poured forth warmly and spontaneously as they arose. **1870** J. H. Newman *Gram. Assent* II. viii. 331 Taste, skill, invention in the fine arts..are exerted spontaneously, when once acquired.

2. By natural action; without apparent or obvious external cause or influence.

1658 Evelyn *Fr. Gard.* (1675) 85 The unripe figs,..if they stay till they spontaneously quit the trees [etc.]. **1664** Power *Exp. Philos.* II. 143 You shall see the water spontaneously arise..in the Tube. **1764** Reid *Inquiry* vi. §24 Truth goes forth spontaneously if not held back. **1776** Adam Smith *W.N.* II. v. (1869) I. 364 If [the capital] was produced spontaneously, it would be of no value in exchange. *a* **1806** Horsley *Serm.* xvii. (1816) II. 68 As the inquiry is of the highest importance, and spontaneously presents itself, it is to this that I shall devote the remainder of the present discourse. **1825** J. Neal *Bro. Jonathan* III. 188 A great bell ..far below me, rang out, spontaneously, of itself. **1875** Jowett *Plato* (ed. 2) I. 206 If only wisdom can be taught, and does not come to man spontaneously.

b. *spec.* By natural chemical or physical change or development.

1771 *Encycl. Brit.* II. 120/1 Some earths and stones abound so with nitre, that it effloresces spontaneously. **1794** G. Adams *Nat. & Exp. Philos.* I. xii. 501 It takes fire spontaneously by the contact of air. **1804** Abernethy *Surg. Obs.* 91 It is no uncommon circumstance to meet with wens, that have burst spontaneously. **1837** P. Keith *Bot. Lex.* 35 The nascent bulbs, which..spontaneously detach themselves from the parent plant. **1878** Huxley *Physiogr.* xv. 251 In other cases the coral animal spontaneously splits in two halves. **1892** *Photogr. Ann.* II. 517 This remarkable group of crystals was produced..quite spontaneously.

3. By natural growth; without being specially planted or cultivated.

a **1682** Sir T. Browne *Tracts* (1683) 52 This same plant may grow naturally and spontaneously in several countries. **1733** W. Ellis *Chiltern & Vale Farm.* 84 Young Oaks..that spontaneously grow up from the Acorns. **1765** *Museum Rust.* IV. 242 Common hay which is mixed with burnet growing spontaneously. **1836** Macgillivray *Trav. Humboldt* xxv. 384 It is supposed by botanists that it grows spontaneously in the mountainous regions.

b. By natural production; without tillage.

1700 Evelyn *Diary* 13 July, Some foreign country which would produce spontaneously pines, firs,..yew, holly, and juniper. **1748** *Anson's Voy.* I. v. (ed. 4) 61 The soil of the Island is truly luxuriant, producing fruits of most kinds spontaneously. **1830** Herschel *Study Nat. Philos.* 2 The coarse aliments which the earth affords spontaneously.

spontaneousness (spɒnˈteɪnɪəsnɪs). [f. as prec.] The state or quality of being spontaneous.

a **1649** in *N. & Q.* Ser. I. X. 357 Spontaniousnes, and readines to helpe those who are in distress or suffer injury. *a* **1676** Hale *Prim. Orig. Man.* I. ii. (1677) 49 It is impossible to resolve the spontaneousness of many of their animal motions into those Principles. **1837** Ht. Martineau *Soc. Amer.* III. 267 This can only be done by those who do approve and reverence spontaneousness. **1872** Spurgeon *Treas. Dav.* Ps. liv. 6 The spontaneousness of our gifts is a great element in their acceptance.

†**spontany**, *a.* *Obs.*$^{-1}$ [ad. L. *spontāne-us.*] Spontaneous.

1387-8 T. Usk *Test. Love* III. iv. (Skeat) l. 33 Voluntarie or spontanye it is; for by spontanye wil it is do, that is to saye, with good wil not constrayned.

spontoon (spɒnˈtuːn). Now only *Hist.* [a. F. *sponton* (also *esponton* espontoon), = Sp. *esponton* (Pg. *espontão*), ad. It. *spontone*, *spuntone*, f. *puntone*, *punto* point.] A species of half-pike or halberd carried by infantry officers in the 18th century (from about 1740).

The It. form *spontone* is used as a foreign word by Barret *Theor. Warres* (1598) IV. iv. 113.

1746 Dk. Cumb'ld in *10th Rep. Hist. MSS. Comm.* App. I. 443, I dare say there was neither Soldier nor Officer..who did not kill their one or two Men with their Bayonets & Spontoons. **1746** *Lond. Mag.* 242 The Spontoon..is a Weapon used of late Years by the Officers of Foot instead of the Half-Pike. **1769** Pennant *Brit. Zool.* III. 64 The nose was very long, narrow, and sharp-pointed, not unlike the end of a spontoon. **1786** *Gentl. Mag.* Apr. 350/1 The officers who mounted guard..were paraded with their swords drawn instead of spontoons, for the first time since the regulation took place. **1802** James *Milit. Dict.* s.v., When the spontoon was planted, the regiment halted; when pointed forwards, the regiment marched; and when pointed backwards, the regiment retreated. **1819** Scott *Leg. Montrose* xxi, I am just now like the half-pike or spontoon of Achilles, one end of which could wound, and the other cure. **1841** Emerson *Ess.* Ser. I. xii. (1876) 284 Like the spontoons and standards of the militia, which play such pranks in the eyes and imaginations of school-boys.

transf. **1785** Burns *Jolly Beggars* xiii, From the gilded spontoon to the fife I was ready; I asked no more but a sodger laddie.

spoof (spuːf), *sb.* (and *a.*) *slang.* [Invented by A. Roberts (b. 1852), comedian.]

1. A game of a hoaxing and nonsensical character. Also, a trivial round game of cards in which certain cards when occurring together are denominated 'spoof'.

1884 *Topical Times* 13 Dec. 3/2 The revival of Spoof in Great Britain and America is..wholly due to private enterprise, and..Monsieur Arthur Roberts. **1889** *Pall Mall G.* 14 May 5/1 'The Adelphi Club was the birthplace of the mysterious game called "Spoof", was it not?'—'Yes, I invented the pastime.' **1894** D. C. Murray *Rising Star* II. 235 There is in theatrical circles an amusement which is known as the game of spoof. **1895** Mrs. Croker *Village Tales* 89 We..were sitting in our dining-room tent fanning ourselves vigorously and playing 'spoof'.

2. a. Hoax, humbug; an instance of this.

1889 E. Dowson *Let.* 19 May (1967) 80 We sat dejectedly in the office but were obliged to admit finally that it was a case of 'spoof'. **1897** *Westm. Gaz.* 23 Apr. 2/1 There seems just a little too much 'spoof' about the long-talked-of Trickoli. **1905** *Sat. Rev.* 16 Sept. 370 One sees that the whole thing is a clumsy spoof.

b. A skit or 'send-up'; *spec.* a film, play, or other work that satirizes a particular genre.

1958 *Oxf. Mag.* 13 Mar. 374/2 This..programme.. proved to be an experimental double-dose of theatrical spoof. **1958** *Films in Review* May 254/1 There had been a few films which foreshadowed the screwball pattern, particularly the hilarious Hollywood spoof *Bombshell*. **1975** D. Lodge *Changing Places* ii. 61 Even the weather forecast seemed to be some kind of spoof. **1977** *Time* 3 Jan. 71/1 The prolific Gardner sets a spoof of pulp fiction inside a philosophical monologue on good and evil.

3. *attrib.* and as *adj.* Hoaxing, humbugging.

1884 *Topical Times* 13 Dec. 3/2 At Byzantium many Spouf Courts were; but when it became the capital of the Greek empire the game fell into disuse. **1895** A. Roberts in *Daily News* 26 Aug. 6/3 My 'spoof French' has often been the subject of amusement. **1899** *Westm. Gaz.* 27 June 7/2 Asking him to..send a 'spoof wire'—meaning any sort of nonsense. **1914** G. B. Shaw *Fanny's First Play* 229 How am I to know how to take it? Is it serious, or is it spoof? If the author knows what his play is, let him tell us what it is. **1927** [see spoof *v.* b]. **1946** V. Tempest *Near Sun* iii. 27 The spoof-feint raid that has been put on to make Jerry think that we are going to central Germany. **1978** K. Gregory *First Cuckoo* 25 [Readers] are invited to spot the 'spoof' letter whose apparent erudition hoaxed the editor into printing it.

spoof, *v. colloq.* and *slang.* [f. the sb.] **a.** *trans.* To hoax or humbug; †to avoid by means of a ruse. Also *absol.*

1889 E. Dowson *Let.* 10 Mar. (1967) 48 It is the 'après' wh. spoofs us. *Ibid.* 11 Nov. 115 The Lord Mayorlet's Tom Foolery was a nuisance. I spoofed it successfully by going from Limehouse to Bloomsbury by tram. **1895** *Punch* 28 Dec. 301/1, I 'spoof' him—to use a latter-day term. **1901** *Daily Mail* 2 Apr. 5/7 The House gave the willing tribute of laughter to the fact that it had been 'spoofed'. **1933** *Sun* (Baltimore) 8 July 6/7 It will be found necessary to handle our Doctor with much circumspection if he is not spoofing. **1977** 'J. le Carré' *Honourable Schoolboy* i. 31 The story had everything... It spoofed the British.

b. To make (something) appear foolish by means of parody; to 'send up'. Also *absol.*

1927 *Observer* 20 Nov. 20/5 This is a spoof piece which fails, through sheer clumsiness, to spoof. **1953** [see googol]. **1981** W. Safire in *N.Y. Times Mag.* 29 Mar. 10/3 'Urbababble'..spoofs the lingo of those urbane people in the city business.

c. To render (a radar system, etc.) useless by providing it with false information.

1972 *Sci. Amer.* July 18/3 The opposition need not even destroy the installation; by sampling the pulses emitted by the system it can contrive to 'spoof' or jam it. **1977** *R.A.F. News* 27 Apr.–10 May 20/4 They were, however, 'soft spots' in a defensive system. They would have to be attacked again and again and they would have to be spoofed by the considerable number of methods now available.

Hence **spoofed** (spu:ft) *ppl. a.*; **'spoofer**, one who spoofs; **'spoofery**, †(*a*) *pl.*, a low sporting club; also *spec.* the Adelphi (cf. spoof *sb.*, quot. 1889) (*obs. slang*); (*b*) trickery, hoaxing; **'spoofing** *vbl. sb.* and *ppl. a.*

1895 *People* 6 Jan. 13/4 About half-past one this morning I was in the 'Spooferies'—Where? In the 'Spooferies'—the Trafalgar Club they call it now—in Maiden-Lane. **1903** A. M. Binstead *Pitcher in Paradise* x. 227 'And when it comes to comparing the Spooferies with the House of Lords,' the missive concluded, 'it is a million to one on the Spooferies.' The other name of the Spooferies was the Adelphi Club. **1914** *Conc. Oxf. Dict.* Addenda, *Spoofer.* **1920** *Quill* Dec. 9 The after-dinner speeches..were brilliant impromptu spoofings directed at the guest of honor. **1926** A. H. Godwin *Gilbert & Sullivan* 219 Bunthorne..is, in common language, a spoofer. **1926** K. Grahame in G. Sanger *Seventy Years a Showman* 20 The whole thing was unabashed 'spoofery'—clumsy fakes, dried fish, abortions in bottles,..and so on. *a* **1936** Kipling *Something of Myself* (1937) iii. 48 There were..'spoofing'-letters from subalterns to be guarded against. **1958** P. Scott *Mark of Warrior* ii. 176 He's got me spoofed in terms of the exercise. **1965** H. Kahn *On Escalation* v. 86 If the super-ready status is accompanied by limited 'spoofing' or 'jamming' or other hostile acts. **1975** *New Yorker* 19 May 22/3 It's an atrocity, of course, and one of the most spoofed of all the Jeanette MacDonald-Nelson Eddy operettas. **1976** *Time* 20 Dec. 53/3 Gardner has set himself two roles..: the hilarious spoofer of pulp fiction [etc.]. **1978** G. Mitchell *Wraiths & Changelings* xv. 147 Ghosts are part of my stock-in-trade.. so..I'm up to most of the dodges... The plainsong..was the only artistic effort..attempted in any of the spoofery.

spoogslang, var. spuugslang.

spook (spu:k), *sb.* [ad. Du. *spook*, G. *spuk* (also †*spuch*), app. of LG. origin, appearing first in MLG. *spôk*, *spoek*, *spouk*, *spûk* (whence MSw. *spook*, Da. *spøg*), and older Du. *spoocke* (Kilian); other modern forms are LG. *spôk*, *spok*, WFris. *spoek*, NFris. *spook*, *spuk*, Sw. *spöke*. No certain cognates have been traced.] **1.** A spectre, apparition, ghost. Often somewhat *joc.* or *colloq.*

First in American usage, which is illustrated separately in the first set of quotations.

(*a*) **1801** *Mass. Spy* 15 July (Thornton), By mine dunder I fly so swift as any spook. **1833** Paulding *Banks Ohio* III. iii. 40 Who ever heard of a spook eating? *a* **1853** 'Dow, Jr.' *Patent Serm.* iii. 158 (Thornton), There did I see a Spook, sure enough,—milk-white, and moving round. **1878** W. H. Daniels *That Boy* i, The corners of New England which spooks and spirits were the last to leave.

(*b*) **1859** Aytoun & Martin tr. *Goethe's Poems and Ball.*, *Magician's Apprentice* 102 Broom, avaunt thee! To thy nook there! Lie, thou spook, there! **1873** Stephens *Black Gin*, etc. 11, I am haunted by a spook with oblique eyes and a pigtail. **1891** *Tablet* 19 Sept. 446 To what particular order of spook or spectre may he be assigned?

attrib. **1842** *Spirit of Times* (Philad.) 7 Mar. (Thornton), A-clatterin' the ghosts of dishes..as tho' he was bringin' in a spook-dinner. **1878** Aylward *Transvaal To-day* 213, I became acquainted with a 'spooke story,'..which [etc.]. **1896** *Westm. Gaz.* 10 Jan. 3/3 An alleged spook-photo.

2. *slang* (orig. and chiefly *U.S.*). An undercover agent; a spy.

1942 Berrey & Van den Bark *Amer. Thes. Slang* §458/16 'Spotter.' (One who spys upon employees.).. *Silent eye, spook, spotter. Ibid.* §765/7 *Rat, rubber heel, spook, spotter,* a person employed to detect irregularities. **1954** *People* (Austral.) 3 Nov. 24/1 The *spooks* were senior constables who wore no uniform, worked in pairs and followed constables about the city and suburbs to see if they did their work properly. **1961** *John o' London's* 20 Apr. 434/1 The idea of making a living as a spy—'spook' in current Washington slang—is repugnant to most of us. **1966** R. Thomas *Spy in Vodka* (1967) vi. 50 I'd like him to get out of the spook business. **1979** L. Pryor *Viper* i. 9 'My training was also in espionage at the CIA farm.'.. 'A spook,' I said in wonder.

3. *slang* (orig. and chiefly *U.S.*). A derogatory term for a Black person.

1945 L. Shelly *Hepcats Jive Talk Dict.* 17/2 *Spook* (n), frightened negro. **1953** K. Tennant *Joyful Condemned* xxvii. 262 The boss of the ward..was doing time for going with 'spooks'—negroes. **1966** *New Statesman* 25 Nov. 778/1, I find a disturbing minority of my English contemporaries..pointedly tossing off inconsequential remarks about spades and spooks in my company. **1977** E. Leonard *Unknown Man, No. 89* xxiii. 235 We almost had another riot... The bar-owner..shoots a spook in his parking lot.

Hence (as more or less colloquial or nonce-formations) **'spookic(al** *a.*, **'spookish** *a.*, **'spookism, spooko'logical** *a.*, **spoo'kology.**

1887 *Sat. Rev.* 11 June 823/2 The new *spookic studies have come to stay. **1886** *Ibid.* 11 Dec. 773/2 Those who have watched..the recent outburst of *spookical activity. **1886** *Athenæum* 25 Dec. 858/2 The great thing in the book is the creation of the 'spookical' uncle. **1893** *Athenæum* 18 Mar. 343/2 There is some *spookish mystery about a reappearance. **1886** *Ibid.* 25 Dec. 858/2 By his own rash act he resolved himself into *spookism. **1897** *Westm. Gaz.* 6 July 2/3 Everything happened in the most orthodox *spookological manner. **1893** *Ibid.* 15 July 5 *Spookology in Vienna.

spook (spu:k), *v.* [f. spook *sb.* Cf. MLG. *spôken*, Du. *spoken*, G. *spuken* (dial. *spuchen*); also WFris. *spoekje*, NFris. *spooke*, Sw. *spöka*, Da. *spøge*.]

1. a. *trans.* To haunt (a person or place).

1883 Olive Schreiner *Afr. Farm* i. ii, She heard a rustling,..and knew it was your father coming to 'spook' her. **1976** *Publishers Weekly* 21 June 88/1 The ghost of the highwayman Black Charlie who spooks Flora with regular visitations.

b. To frighten or unnerve; *spec.* (of a hunter, etc.) to alarm (a wild animal). *slang* (chiefly *N. Amer.*).

1935 E. Hemingway *Green Hills Afr.* i. i. 13 We spooked one [kudu]... No chance of a shot. **1944** *Nat. Geogr. Mag.* June 669/1 To get photographs of the herds Williams took to the saddle, since a man on foot is liable to 'spook', or stampede them. **1959** W. Faulkner *Mansion* ix. 222 Pupils and teacher both who were already spooked..by the sudden presence of the unexplained white woman. **1973** A. Garner *Red Shift* 12 You're spooking me. You're too quiet. **1980** M. Gordon *Company of Women* (1981) ii. 187 You always act like you're waiting for something... It spooks me.

2. *intr.* **a.** To play the spook; to 'walk' as a ghost. Also with *it* and *fig.*

1871 *N.Y. Tribune* 24 Feb. 1/5 Once he saw Toussaint L'Ouverture spooking about with an air of mournful majesty. **1886** [see astrally *adv.*]. **1890** Lowell *Fitz Adam's Story* Poems IV. 206 Yet still the New World spooked it in his veins, A ghost he could not lay with all his pains. **1893** Leland *Mem.* I. 10 The ghost went with them, and there it still 'spooks' about as of yore. **1973** E.-J. Bahr *Nice Neighbourhood* xviii. 190 A free-wheeling teen-ager ..[who] seems to be spooking around half-shot all the time.

b. To take fright; to become alarmed. *N. Amer. slang.*

1928 R. Santee *Cowboy* xvii. 250 As luck would have it I got a throw, for the cattle spooked an' run. **1941** E. Hemingway *For whom Bell Tolls* xxii. 272 He'll probably leave tracks like an old bull elk spooking out of the country. **1957** W. Faulkner *Town* i. 14 The old dug-in city fathers.. spooked to the desperate expedient of..exhuming..the story of the Cuban dice game. **1974** R. M. Pirsig *Zen & Art of Motorcycle Maintenance* iii. xx. 245, I spook very easily these days... *He* never spooked at anything.

spooked, *ppl. a. U.S. slang.* [f. spook *v.* + -ed[1].] **a.** Frightened; nervy; dogged by ill-fortune.

1937 E. Hemingway *To have & have Not* i. iii. 50 He would get to worrying and get so spooked he wouldn't be any use. **1952** B. Harwin *Home is Upriver* xiii. 128 The cattle backed away to the far side, a skittish, spooked mass of bristling horns and rolling eyes. **1969** L. Sanders *Anderson Tapes* (1970) li. 137 Don't get spooked when something comes up you didn't figure on. **1970** E. Tidyman *Shaft* (1971) x. 132 There were still some people..staring into the night. The spooked, the stoned and the sleepless. **1977** E. Leonard *Unknown Man, No. 89* xxi. 214 He was running for town, spooked good now, in a panic.

b. *spooked up*, excited, pepped up.

1939 Wodehouse *Uncle Fred in Springtime* iii. 43, I saw one of those Western pictures at our local cinema last night, in which a character described himself as being all spooked up with zip and vinegar. That is precisely how I feel. The yeast of spring is fermenting in my veins, and I am ready for anything. **1969** C. Burke *God is Beautiful, Man* (1970) 85 Well this makes her pretty happy and she gets so spooked up about it that she ran into the city and forgot her jar of water.

'spookery. *colloq.* [f. spook *sb.* + -ery.] Spookiness, eeriness; also, something spooky.

1893 *Athenæum* 18 Feb. 214/1 The writer drags in sundry 'hauntings' and 'spookeries' of a mild nature. **1894** *Contemp. Rev.* LXVI. 651 The spookery business could not have saved him. **1927** [see psych *sb.* 2 a]. **1935** *Times Lit. Suppl.* 3 Jan. 10/4 The author does not exclude provincial and foreign spookeries. **1960** *Times* 20 Aug. 3/7 *Der Freischütz* ..the quintessence of early romanticism with its naive spookery. **1973** E. Pace *Any War will Do* (1974) i. 23 Taking corners too quickly seemed to be another sign of the immaturity..that makes a man opt for the profitless thrills of 'spookery' in the first place.

'spooking, *vbl. sb.* [f. spook *v.* + -ing[1].]

1. a. The action of calling spirits; a séance.

1919 E. H. Jones *Road to En-Dor* i. 2 'What's the suggestion?' Alec asked. 'Spooking,' said I. 'Cripes!' said Alec... Matthews brought in the..table... Little wrote a letter of the alphabet on [squares] and arranged them in a circle... I polished the tumbler... We had constructed our first 'Ouija'. **1930** H. G. Wells *Autocracy of Mr. Parham* ii. iv. 135, I will not relax one jot or one tittle in these precautions until I have demonstrated forever the farcical fraudulence of all this solemn spooking.

b. Haunting, frightening.

1961 *Amer. Speech* XXXVI. 224 The use of *spook* can extend to the frightening of people; it is not limited to physical *spooking* but can indicate mental frightening. **1966** T. Pynchon *Crying of Lot 49* v. 106 Oedipa wondered what hangups, crises, spookings in the middle of the night might be developed from the shadowed subtleties of his mouth, hidden under a full beard. **1979** *Angling* July 19/3 The spooking of fish by striking at line bites.

2. The action of spying.

1977 M. Herr *Dispatches* (1978) 51 The romance of spooking started to fall away..leaving the spooks on the beach.

'spookist. [f. spook *sb.* + -ist.] A spiritualist or medium.

1902 G. W. E. Russell *For Better? For Worse?* xi. 171 A man whom I knew well was taken suddenly and seriously ill, and his relations, who were enthusiastic spookists, telegraphed for the celebrated clairvoyante Mrs Endor. **1920** M. Asquith *Autobiogr.* I. v. 72 If he could 'get through'—to use the orthodox expression of the spookists —he would find all his opinions on this subject more than justified. **1959** *Listener* 9 Apr. 645/1 This eminent spookist had such a look of the slim operator.

'spooky, *a.* [f. spook *sb.* + -y[1].]

1. a. Of, pertaining to, or characteristic of spirits or the supernatural; frightening, eerie. *colloq.*

1854 *Wide West* (San Francisco) 16 July 1/5 After treading many dark passages, the guide, having unlocked all sorts of 'spooky' looking iron doors,..ushered us before the tomb. **1883** *Harper's Mag.* Nov. 929/1 'Tis a spooky place, that grave-yard. **1906** E. Dyson *Fact'ry 'Ands* xviii. 239 There was somethin' spooky 'n' soopernatural erbout er pertickler weird 'n' unaccountable erfluvium. **1929** T. Wolfe *Look Homeward, Angel* xxvii. 378 Don't start that.. spooky stuff! It makes my flesh crawl. **1948** *Time* 1 Nov. 90/2 Shakespeare's *Macbeth* is a turbulent melodrama, full of spooky claptrap. **1960** R. Dahl *Kiss, Kiss* 187 This..is really beginning to get interesting—a trifle spooky, too. **1977** J. F. Fixx *Compl. Bk. Running* viii. 104, I had the spooky feeling that I was dressed up in somebody else's body. **1980** G. Mitchell *Whispering Knights* ix. 98 'It's a spooky-looking place,' said Capella nervously.

b. *Surfing. slang.* Of a wave: dangerous or frightening.

1966 *Surfer* VII. iv. 48 Morne Plage features a left breaking over a coral reef and tapering into a big black deep spooky pass a half a mile from the coast. **1970** *Studies in English* (Univ. Cape Town) I. 34 Waves, especially the bigger and more powerful ones, are often dangerous and frightening, and can sometimes be referred to as *spooky*... *Spooky* might indicate the difficult or the unpredictable, as in: 'Things get a little spooky when you're faced with fifteen feet of soup.'

2. Of a person (or animal): nervous; easily frightened; superstitious. *N. Amer. slang.*

1926 D. Branch *Cowboy & his Interpreters* 12 There were times when the steer would get spooky and mad. **1932** L. Golding *Magnolia St.* ii. v. 354 I'm not a spooky person but I sometimes think he was the Devil. **1947** *Westerners Brand Bk.* (Denver Posse) 51 Range cattle..were too 'spooky' in those days for man-made bridges. **1962** G. MacEwan *Blazing Old Cattle Trails* i. 4 Attendants knew that the nervous and spooky longhorns were easily alarmed and would stampede at the slightest provocation. **1979** *Fortune* 26 Mar. 24/2 Even those spooky about coping with Italian traffic can easily find the well-marked way to Monza, about ten miles northeast of Milan.

3. Of or pertaining to spies or espionage. *U.S. slang.*

1975 *Times* 12 June 18/4 The Central Intelligence Agency spooks are the most spooky spooks. **1979** L. Pryor *Viper* iv. 79 They're tough, crusading terrorists... That isn't going to make your job..any easier... Keep your spooky friends out of my life. **1980** J. Melville *Chrysanthemum Chain* 120 Somebody on the spooky side of the Embassy might have a view.

Hence **'spookily** *adv.*, in a spooky manner; **'spookiness.**

1890 *Critic* 4 Jan. 3/2 An air of spookiness pervades the volume. **1955** R. Hobson *Nothing too Good for Cowboy* xviii. 186 These wild ones [*sc.* steers] were held in one bunch and slithered spookily along immediately behind my saddle horse. **1959** 'P. Quentin' *Shadow of Guilt* xiv. 126 We both stood looking at the shirt... It had a spookily human quality.

spool (spu:l), *sb.*[1] Forms: α. 4–7 spole, 7 spoole, spowle, 7– spool. β. *north.* and *Sc.* 5– spule (6 spwle). γ. 8- 9 spole (8 spoal). δ. 6 spoyle, 8-9 *dial.* spoil. [ad. ONF. *espole* (13th cent.) or the source of this, MDu. **spole, spoele, spuele* (Du. *spoel*), MLG. and LG. *spôle* (hence Da. and Sw. *spole*), OHG. *spuola* fem. (G. *spule*) and *spuolo, spuol* masc. (obs. or dial. G. *spul*). In Romanic now represented by F. *espoule*, F. and Sp. *espolin*, It. *spola, spuola*.

The appearance of *spole* beside *spool* in the 18th cent. seems to indicate a second adoption of the word from some Continental source.]

1. a. A small cylindrical piece of wood or other material on which thread is wound as it is spun, esp. for use in weaving; a bobbin.

α. *c* **1325** *Gloss. W. de Bibbesw.* in Wright *Voc.* 157 *Les tremes*, the spoles. **14..** *Lat.-Eng. Voc.* in Wr.-Wülcker 613 *Spola*, a Quyl, or a Spole. *c* **1440** *Promp. Parv.* 470 Spole, or scytyl, webstarys instrument,..*spolia, panulea.* **1530** Palsgr. 274 *Spole*, a wevers instrument. **1620** Shelton *Quix.* IV. xxix. 228 She is skilful in such Works,..never ceasing to handle small Spindles or Spooles. **1681** O. Heywood *Diaries* (1881) II. 173 She..rose up, went to the wheel.., winded half-a-score spooles. **1783** *Specif. Oldham & Prestwidge's Patent* No. 1368, A sliding frame which moves the bobbins..upon the spindles to distribute the yarn equally upon the spools. **1802** Mar. Edgeworth *Dun* Tales 1848 IV. 416 He continued to throw the shuttle, whilst his little boy and his wife by turns wound spools for him. **1842** *Encycl. Brit.* (ed. 7) XXI. 825/1 The yarn destined for the warp is wound off upon little spools of wood called bobbins. **1879** *Cassell's Techn. Educ.* IV. 274/2 Here the slivers are run side by side upon a wooden spool or bobbin.

β. **1483** *Cath. Angl.* 357/1 A Spule, *panus.* **1509** *Burgh Rec. Edin.* (1869) I. 122 The armes of the webstaris, viz. thair signe of the spule to be vmaist in ilk baner. *a* **1568** R. Semple in *Bannatyne MS.* (Hunter. Club) 356 Weill wrocht in the lwmis with wobster gwmis, Bayth thik and nymmill gais the spwle. **1842** *Whistle-binkie* Ser. III. 40 Curlers, gae hame..To your pens, to your spules, or your thummills. **1887** *Jamieson's Sc. Dict.* Suppl. 226/2 A *spule* is a pirn for yarn or a pirn of yarn. Besides, the copes of yarn used in thread-making are called *spules.*

γ. **1757** Dyer *Fleece* III. 82 Patient art..has a spiral engine form'd, Which on an hundred spoles, an hundred threads..twines,..easy-tended work. **1772** in *6th Rep. Dep. Kpr. Pub. Rec.* App. II. 161 A Machine..by which..a great number of Threads may be spun at one and the same time on a number of Spoals. **1789** E. Darwin *Bot. Gard.* II. ii. 103 Then fly the spoles, the rapid axles glow. **1837** Whittock *Bk. Trades* (1842) 412 (*Spinner*), As the threads become twisted by..a tall wheel which carries round the 'spole'. **1877-** in dial. glossaries (W.Yks., Linc., Leic., etc.).

δ. **1796** W. H. Marshall *Rur. Econ. Yorksh.* (ed. 2) II. 346 *Spoil*, the weaver's quill.

b. In fig. uses.

1611 J. Davies (Heref.) *Wit's Pilgr.* xxvii, The wheeling of the Spheares..Winde vp thy lifes-Threed on the Spowle of yeares. **1821** Clare *Vill. Minstr.* I. 170 Short is the thread on life's spool that is mine. **1866** Geo. Eliot *F. Holt* ii, That's a spool to wind a speech on. Abuses is the very word. **1896** C. K. Paul tr. *Huysmans' En Route* v. 65 The first comer who will wind about me his spool of commonplaces.

c. A small shaped cylinder of wood on which sewing-thread is wound; a reel.

1852 Mrs. Stowe *Uncle Tom's Cabin* xx, She tangled, broke, or dirtied her thread, or, with a sly movement, would throw a spool away altogether. **1861** Wynter *Soc. Bees* 260 The needle..carries a continuous thread wound off a reel or spool. **1890** W. J. Gordon *Foundry* 160 The spool..holds 400 yards of good cotton. It is a good article, and people can pay for it.

d. Any cylinder on which cord, wire, tape, etc., is wound for convenience or for a special purpose.

1864 *Reader* 5 Oct. 483/2 It also actuates the break-piece,..thereby producing electric induction in the outer coils of the two pairs of spools alternately. **1883** *Cent. Mag.* July 381 Reeling up his line to the snell of the hook, and with his thumb on the spool of the reel. **1889** *Anthony's Photogr. Bull.* II. 76 We want a film thin enough to be used on spools. **1936** *Discovery* Aug. 238/2 The film..is mounted in a supply spool on the top part of the camera. It is carried around guide spools and across the focal plane to the take-up spool. **1955** R. Hobson *Nothing Too Good for Cowboy* xviii. 186 Two spools are attached in a light-tight box to the top of the instrument. **1967** *Tape Recording Mag.* July 260/1 The..conventional, spool-to-spool machines. **1977** W. Marshall *Thin Air* v. 58 Feiffer watched the twin spools on the tape recorder winding in Number Two's words.

2. A mesh-pin used in net-making.

1838 C. Bathurst *Notes on Nets* 17 Large meshes may be made on small spools, by giving the twine two or more turns round them. **1844** H. Stephens *Bk. Farm* II. 72 Spools, being made as broad as the length of the side of the mesh, are of different breadths.

3. The sliding member of a spool valve.

1960 Lee & Blackburn in J. F. Blackburn et al. *Fluid Power Control* ix. 239 The spool valve must be very accurately made since it depends upon closeness of fit between spool and sleeve to hold the leakage down. **1974** *Encycl. Brit. Micropædia* X. 344/3 In the mid or neutral position of the spool, ports A and B are blocked. The movement of the spool may be manually or electrically controlled.

4. *attrib.*, as *spool-cotton, -frame, -pin, -stand, -ticket, -wheel*; † **spool-knave** (see quot. 1688); **spool valve**, a valve in which a shaft with channels in its surface slides inside a sleeve with ports in it, the flow between which depends on the position of the shaft in the sleeve; **spool-wood**, wood for making spools.

1538 *Nottingham Rec.* III. 200 Unum wollenlome cum ryngrathes, warpbarres et spoyle whele. **1688** Holme *Armoury* III. 288/2 There is another sort of Spool Knave made of Wood..in which there is holes made..for two, three, four, or more Spools to be wound off into Clews. *Ibid.*, He beareth Argent, a Spool Knave, with the Spool Pin therein. **1845** *Glance Interior China* 81 The spool-frame..is provided with two long posts, each two feet high, on the top of which is a transverse beam. **1851-4** Tomlinson *Cycl. Arts* (1867) II. 470/1 As it is usual to form a rope of three strands, three spole-frames are combined together in this laying machine. **1858** Simmonds *Dict. Trade, Spool-stand*, a rest or support for bobbins. **1862** *Catal. Internat. Exhib., Brit.* II. No. 3677, Spool cotton, enamelled and six-cord. *Ibid.* No. 5136, Spooltickets. **1895** *N.B. Daily Mail* 4 Oct. 5/2 The barque Assyria, laden with spoolwood and deals. **1908** R. Peele *Compressed Air Plant for Mines* xx. 248 The throw of the spool valve..is produced indirectly by the introduction of a system of small, auxiliary ports, connecting the ends of the valve chest with the cylinder. **1926** R. M. Evans in J. Roberts *Mining Educator* I. 618/2 There are two forms..: the air-thrown or spool-valve drill for use with compressed air, and the tappet drill for use with steam. **1971** *Farmers Weekly* 19 Mar. 82/4 Three hydraulic spool valves were fitted on the side of the trailer. One lifted and lowered the trailer. **1976** D. E. Turnbull *Fluid Power Engin.* vi. 172 The spool valve was originally developed..more than a century ago when it was used for controlling the flow of steam to steam engine cylinders at the famous Gorton locomotive works in Manchester.

b. Designating (an article of) furniture popular in N. Amer. during the second half of the 19th cent. and decorated with spool-shaped turnery.

1928 Johnson & Sironen *Man. Furnit. Arts & Crafts* I. xiii. 79 The first and most noticeable product of the [powered wood-working] machine was a type [of furniture made up almost entirely of turned posts, frames, legs and arms and became known as spool furniture. **1931** S. Glaspell *Ambrose Holt & Family* xxvii. 263 She went up to the bed, a walnut spool bed. **1946** *Sun* (Baltimore) 16 July 10/3 The spool rack..had nice roomy shelves, which were used to store many back copies of the *Sun-papers.* **1969** J. Gloag *Short Dict. Furnit.* 636 *Spool Furniture*, an American style, introduced in the 1850s, and based on the use of spool turning on the members of chairs, beds, tables, and wash stands. This form of decoration with its string of spools was an attenuated variation of the more robust bobbin turning..of the mid- and late 17th century. **1974** R. B. Parker *God save Child* (1975) xxii. 153 There was a spool bed with a gold-patterned spread. **1981** *Times Lit. Suppl.* 20 Feb. 210/1 Jane Carlyle sitting in her spool chair.

Hence **spoolful.** *rare*$^{-0}$.

1611 Cotgr., *Fusée*, a spoole-full, or spindle-full, of thread, yarne, &c.

† **spool**, *sb.*^{2} *Sc. Obs.* In 5 spule. [app. an alteration of *spune* spoon *sb.* 1 b.] *collect.* Wooden roofing-shingles. Also *attrib.*

1496 *Acc. Ld. High Treas. Scot.* I. 279 Item,..in part payment of theking of the chapell..with spule, iiij li. xij d. *Ibid.* 302 For theking of a rude of spule thak. *Ibid.* 307 Item, giffin to Johne Lam of Leith, in part of payment of nalis to the spule thak of the werkhous and chapel in the Castel of Edinburgh,..iij li. xij s.

spool (spuːl), *v.* [f. spool *sb.*^{1} Cf. Du. *spoelen*, LG. *spôlen*, G. *spulen.*] **a.** *intr.* To wind spools. Also with advbs. and *transf.* **b.** *trans.* To wind (thread, film, etc.) on (to) a spool. Also *transf.*

1603 Holland *Plutarch's Mor.* 337 A weaver will say that his worke is to make a web.., and not to spoole, winde quils,..or raise and let fall the weights. **1623** in *Hist. MSS. Comm., Var. Coll.* I. 94 Some of them make..their workfolkes..spoole their chaines, twist their list. **1845** S. Judd *Margaret* II. ix. (1871) 271, I spooled on the doorstone for ma. **1976** S. Brett *So Much Blood* x. 126 'I'll spool through and see if there's anything relevant.'.. Gerald busied himself spooling on and playing snatches of the tape. **1976** B. Lecomber *Dead Weight* iii. 46 The Boeing's engines spooled up to a keening howl. **1977** *Time* 10 Jan. 6/1 Poised at the gate. Once more the course spools through the mind. Now the Starter's signal. **1978** J. Carroll *Mortal Friends* IV. iv. 433 His fear unraveled itself and then spooled quickly around his winch of a throat. **1979** G. Scott *Hot Pursuit* ix. 80, I began to spool the film of what had happened through my mind. **1980** S. Brett *Dead Side of Mike* x. 116 Shall I spool it [*sc.* a cassette] back and see if there's something we missed?

Hence **spooled** *ppl. a.*

1862 *Catal. Internat. Exhib., Brit.* II. No. 3885, Thrown silks, gum and soft-dyed and spooled. **1897** *Sears, Roebuck Catal.* 333/1 Spooled Wire for Tissue Paper Work.

ˈ**spooler.** Also 6 spullar, 7 -er. [Cf. prec.] One engaged in winding thread on spools.

1554 *Act 1 Mary* III. c. 7 §1 Spinners, Carders, and Spullars of Yarne. [**1678** Phillips, *Spullers*, of Yarn, those that try if it be well spun and fit for the Loom.] **1764** Burn *Poor Laws* 156 The weavers supply the office of spooler and warper. **1797** *Encycl. Brit.* (ed. 3) XVII. 341/2 Every lock of wool..becomes the means of support to..spinners, spoolers, warpers. **1877** *Ibid.* (ed. 9) VI. 502/1 It is given..to the hank-winder, who winds it on a large bobbin, and that in its turn is handed to the spooler. **1893** *Congregationalist* Sept. 14 A spooler from the thread mill and a 'hand' from the laundry.

ˈ**spooling,** *vbl. sb.* Also 6 spoul-, 6-7 spol-, 7 spoyl-. [f. spool *v.*] The action or employment of winding spools.

c **1640** J. Smyth *Lives Berkeleys* (1883) I. 167 The Accompts whereof declare the charges in the..spoolinge, warpinge, quillinge,..and the like. **1738** *Gentl. Mag.* VIII. 658 They..demanded a Note..that they would for ever forward give 15*d.* a Yard for Weaving and 1*s.* for Spooling. **1891** Miss Dowie *Girl in Karp.* 232 All the..shearing, washing, carding, spinning and spooling. **1969** *Listener* 13 Feb. 193/3 There is no lacing or spooling. The films in the cassette are sealed. **1976** *Offshore Platforms & Pipelining* 209/1 Studies show that this method of spooling between flanges can be used on lines and risers.

b. *attrib.*, as *spooling-machine*, † *-turn*, *-wheel.*

c **1564** in Noake *Worcest. Relics* (1877) 10 A spynynge turne and a spolynge turne xij d. *Ibid.* 12, ij spyninge tournes, a spoulinge tourne. **1598** Florio, *Spola*,..a weauers role, spoling wheele or quill turne. **1617** Minsheu *Ductor*, A Quil-turne, that turnes the quilles, or spoyling Wheele. **1648** Hexham II, *Een Garen-kroone*,..a Spoling-wheele. **1841** *Civil Eng. & Arch. Jrnl.* IV. 62 The spooling machine is cited as superior to that used in England. **1862** *Times* 27 Mar., A beautiful automatic spooling machine by Brookes.

† **spoom,** *v. Obs.* [Alteration of spoon *v.*^{1}] *intr.* To run *before* the sea, wind, etc.; to scud. Also *fig.*

c **1620** Fletcher & Mass. *Double Marr.* II. i, We'll spare her our main top-sail... Down with the foresail too, we'll spoom before her. **1628** F. Fletcher *World Encomp. by Sir F. Drake* 40 By no means that we could conceiue could helpe themselues, but by spooming along before the sea. **1653** Urquhart *Rabelais* II. i. 4 If it happened the foresaid members to be..spooming with a full saile bunt faire before the winde. **1687** Dryden *Hind & P.* III. 96 When vertue spooms before a prosperous gale, My heaving wishes help to fill the sail. **1830** Moriarty *Husband Hunter* II. 119 As he skims the broad surface of the vast Atlantic, or spooms along the mighty Southern Ocean.

ˈ**spooming,** *ppl. a.* [f. prec.]

† **1.** Running before the wind. *Obs.*$^{-1}$

1741 H. Brooke *Constantia* Poems (1810) 391 The wind fresh blowing from the Syrian shore, Swift through the floods her spooming vessel bore.

2. [By association with *spume.*] Foaming.

1818 Keats *Endym.* III. 70 O Moon! far-spooming Ocean bows to thee. **1865** *Reader* 4 Nov. 509/3 With a spooming plunge..He wrestles shoreward, paddling piteously.

spoon (spuːn), *sb.* Forms: α. 1 spoon, 1, 4-5 spon, 3-6 spone (5-6 sponne). β. 5 spoune, 6-7 spoun- (6 spown); 5- spoon, 6-7 spoone. γ. 5-6 *north.* and *Sc.* spoyn; *north.* 6 spoine, 9 spooin. δ. *Sc.* 5-6 spwne, 5-6, 9 spune, 9 speen; *north.* 5 spvne, 7, 9 speaun, 9 speun, speean, etc. [Common Teutonic: OE. *spón*, = OFris. *spôn* (WFris. *spoen, spoan*, EFris. *spōn*, NFris. *spōn, spön, spūn*), MLG. and LG. *spôn*, ON. and Icel. *spónn* (Norw. *spōn*); the original stem **spǣnu-* is differently (but normally) represented in ON. *spánn* (MSw. *spān*, Sw. *spån*, Da. *spaan*), OHG. and MHG. *spân* (G. *span*), MDu. *spaen* (Du. *spaan*). In OE., as in most of the Continental languages, the word has only the general sense of 'chip'; sense 2 is specifically Scandinavian (Norwegian and Icelandic), but MLG. *spôn* had also the meaning of 'wooden spatula' as in *botter-spôn*.]

† **1. a.** A thin piece of wood; a chip, splinter, or shiver. *Obs.*

c **725** *Corpus Gloss.* G 100, *Gingria*, spon. *c* **900** tr. *Baeda's Hist.* III. II. (1890) 156 Moniȝe ȝen to-dæȝe of þæm treo þæs halȝan Cristes mæles sponas & scefþon neomað. *a* **1000** *Sax. Leechd.* II. 292 ðenim þone neowran wyrttruman, delf up, þwit niȝon sponas on þa winstran hand. *c* **1320** *Sir Tristr.* 2039 Bi water he sent adoun Liȝt linden spon. **1387** Trevisa *Higden* (Rolls) V. 455 Of þe spones of þis croys beeþ i-doo meny vertues and wondres. *Ibid.* VI. 297 þere was nouȝt oon spone þerof i-seie flete uppon þe water. *c* **1400** *Beryn* 3430 And wee hewe a-mys eny maner spone, We knowe wele..what pardon wee shull have. *a* **1513** Fabyan *Chron.* v. cxxx. (1811) 113 Of the spones of y^t crosse ar tolde manye wounders, the which I ouer passe.

† **b.** A roofing-shingle. Also *collect. Obs.*

1316-7 *Durham Acc. Rolls* (Surtees) 514 In v^c. Bord. et Spone colpand., xxvj s. viij d. **1357** *Ibid.* 560 Et in ij mill. Spons faciend. ibidem. **1414-5** *Ibid.* 611 Item in j M^l del spone empt. ad dictam Cameram (Prioris). **1475-6** in Swayne *Sarum Church-w. Acc.* (1896) 361 Of William Edyngdon for spones of j elme, ix d.

2. a. A utensil consisting essentially of a straight handle with an enlarged and hollowed end-piece (the bowl), used for conveying soft or liquid food to the mouth, or employed in the culinary preparation or other handling of this.

Spoons are frequently distinguished according to the material of which they are made, as *horn, silver, wooden spoon*, or the special use for which they are adapted, as *dessert-, marrow-, mustard-, salt-, soup-, table-, tea spoon.*

α. *c* **1340** *Nominale* (Skeat) 501 *Cotel, saler et culier*, Knyf, saler and spon. *c* **1380** Wyclif *Sel. Wks.* I. 299 þei bringen her cuppe and her spone, in tokene þat to drynke and pulment þei ben oblishid bifore oþer. *a* **1400-50** *Bk. Curtasye* 674 in *Babees Bk.*, Two keruyng knyfes,..þe thrydde to þo lorde, and als a spone. *c* **1420** *Liber Cocorum* (1862) 51 Breke ten egges in cup fulle fayre,..And swyng þy 3olkes with spone. *a* **1529** Skelton *Bouge of Court* 436 In his other sleue, me thought, I sawe A spone of golde, full of hony swete. **1553** Eden *Treat. New Ind.* (Arb.) 18 In the stede of spones, they vse leaues of trees.

β. **1426** Lydg. *De Guil. Pilgr.* 23678 And the fatte away thei pulle with the spoon of cruelte ycalled Syngularyte. **1531** *Rec. St. Mary at Hill* (1905) 47, x spowns with dyomond Cnops. **1582** *Wills & Inv. N.C.* (Surtees, 1835) 104 One dossen of silver spoones. **1605** H. Plat *Delightes for Ladies* II. x, This you must now and then taste in a spoone. **1651** in *10th Rep. Hist. MSS. Comm.* App. I. 38 A dissoun of spounis of mother of perill. **1681** Bellon *New Myst. Physick* Introd. 57 This Extract is to be given of it self, in a Spoon. **1756-7** tr. *Keysler's Trav.* (1760) II. 174 Utensils, as spoons, knives, writing instruments, &c. of foreign and distant nations. **1796** H. Hunter tr. *St.-Pierre's Stud. Nat.* (1799) II. 191 The leaf of the first is rounded in form of a spoon. *c* **1850** *Arab. Nts.* (Rtldg.) 605, I began with some rice, which I took in the common way with a spoon. **1853** Soyer *Pantroph.* 263 The Roman spoons..end on one side by a point, to pick shell-fish from their shell. **1875** Knight *Dict. Mech.* 2288/1 Ancient Egyptian spoons were made shell-shaped.

transf. **1706** Stevens *Span. Dict.* s.v. *Cuchara*, When a Man makes a Spoon of a Crust, as soon as he has supp'd his Broath, he eats his Spoon.

γ. *c* **1470** Henry *Wallace* ii. 272 His fostyr modyr..with a spoyn gret kyndnes to him kyth. **1483** *Cath. Angl.* 357/1 A spoyn, *cocliar.* **1527** *Knaresb. Wills* (Surtees) I. 21 A sylver spoyn. **1561** *Wills & Inv. N.C.* (Surtees, 1835) 193 A pistola of gold & a syluer spoine.

δ. *c* **1475** *Cath. Angl.* (A) 357/1 A Spvne, *cocliar.* **1492** *Acc. Ld. High Treas. Scot.* I. 200 To the Dwke of Ross, to bordour a spwne obowte, iij vnicornis. **1543** *Aberd. Reg.* (1844) I. 187 Ane masar of siluer, ane spwne of syluer. **1549** *Compl. Scot.* vi. (1873) 43 Euyrie scheiphird hed ane horne spune. **1684, 1818** [see 3 a]. **18..** *Ballad, The Ram of Diram* iv, The horns that war on the ram's head, Were fifty packs o' speens.

b. In allusion to the gift of a spoon to a child at its christening. *Obs.*

1613 Shaks. *Hen. VIII*, v. iii. 168 Come, come my Lord, you'd spare your spoones.

c. A spoonful of sugar or other substance.

1922 Joyce *Ulysses* 69 He scalded and rinsed out the teapot and put in four full spoons of tea. **1944** C. Himes *Black on Black* (1973) 200 By the time I find they was gettin' up for breakfast all the breakfast was gone but a spoon of grits. **1968** P. Dickinson *Skin Deep* vii. 142 How many spoons shall I put in?.. Bob likes six. **1980** R. Hill *Spy's Wife* iv. 22 Aspinall came in with a tea tray. 'Three spoons for me,' said Monk.

d. A dose or measure of an intoxicating drug, *spec.* two grammes of heroin. *U.S.*

1968–70 *Current Slang* (Univ. S. Dakota) III–IV. 118 *Spoon*, a level teaspoon of heroin. (Drug users' jargon). **1977** J. Cheever *Falconer* 46 Two spoons had been found, hidden in Farragut's toilet bowl.

e. *pl.* A pair of spoons held in the hand and beaten together as a simple percussion instrument.

1972 *Jazz & Blues* Nov. 27/1 'Main line' has added interest in that Shorty accompanies himself on spoons. **1977** P. Carter *Under Goliath* xxvii. 147 It was a terrific party... Mr Mitchell played the spoons and Mr Gannon brought out his accordion and we had a singsong.

3. In proverbial and other phrases:

a. In the proverb ***he should have a long spoon that sups with the Devil***, or variations of this.

c **1386** Chaucer *Sqr.'s T.* 594 Therfore bihoueth hire a ful long spoon That shal ete with a feend. **1539** Taverner *Erasm. Prov.* (1552) 9 He had nede to haue a longe spone that shulde eate with the deuyl. **1597** Jas. I. *Dæmonol.* i. v. 16 They that suppe keile with the Deuill, haue neede of long spoons. **1610** Shaks. *Temp.* ii. ii. 103 This is a diuell, and no Monster: I will leaue him, I haue no long Spoone. **1623** Webster *Devil's Law-Case* iv. ii, Here's a latten spoon, and a long one, to feed with the devil! **1684** *Yorkshire Dial.* 55 (E.D.S.), He mun heve a lang-Shafted speaun that sups kail with the Devil. **1818** Scott *Hrt. Midl.* xlv, He suld hae a lang-shankit spune that wad sup kale wi' the deil. **1838** Barham *Ingol. Leg.* Ser. i. *Lay St. Nicholas*, Who suppes with the Deville sholde have a long spoone! **1886** Mrs. Lynn Linton *Paston Carew* xxxvii, He had voluntarily supped with the devil, and his spoon had been too short.

b. In miscellaneous uses (see quots.).

1634 Rowley *Noble Soldier* iii. iii. in Bullen *Old Pl.* (1882) I, Now! what hot poyson'd Custard must I put my Spoone into? *a* **1635** Corbet *Poet. Strom.* (1648) 69 When private Men gett sonnes they get a spoone, Without Ecclypse, or any Starr at noone. **1722–7** Boyer *Dict. Royal* ii. s.v., To be past the Spoon, (to be beyond the State of Infancy). **1825** Knapp & Baldwin *Newgate Cal.* IV. 283/2 Throws out with a shovel what he brings in with a spoon. **1859** Bartlett *Dict. Amer.* (ed. 2) 437 'To do business with a big spoon,' is the same as to cut a big swathe. **1863** Trafford *World in Ch.* I. 296 Miss Sarah has always fond of putting her spoon into other people's broth.

c. ***to be born with a silver spoon in one's mouth***, to be born in affluence or under lucky auspices.

1801 *Deb. U.S. Congress* 9 Jan. (1851) 905 It was a common proverb that few lawyers were born with silver spoons in their mouths. **1849** Lytton *Caxtons* ii. iii, I think he is born with a silver spoon in his mouth. **1885** E. Gosse *Shaks. to Pope* 50 There never was a child so plainly born with the traditional silver-spoon in his mouth as Waller.

d. ***to make a spoon or spoil a horn***, to make a determined effort to achieve something, whether ending in success or failure. orig. *Sc.*

The making of spoons out of the horns of cattle or sheep was common in Scotland till late in the 19th cent.

1818 Scott *Rob Roy* xxii, I aye said he was ane o' them wad make a spune or spoil a horn. **1820** Hogg *Tales* (1866) 262 Cliffy Mackay will either mak a speen or spill a guid horn. **1860** Trollope *Castle Richmond* xv, It's better to make the spoon at once, even if we do run some small chance of spoiling the horn. **1892** *Boy's Own Paper* Dec. 87/1 Your son..will turn out something some day. He'll make a spoon or spoil a horn.

4. An implement of the form described above (sense 2), or something similar to this, used for various purposes: **a.** As a surgical instrument.

a **1425** *Arderne's Treat. Fistula*, etc. 24 Take þe instrument þat is called coclear—a spone. **1895** *Arnold & Sons' Catal. Surg. Instrum.* Index, Spoons, Cataract. Spoons, Enucleation. Spoons, Erasion. **1899** *Allbutt's Syst. Med.* VI. 293 The pus and decomposing clot are scraped away with a sharp spoon.

b. In melting, heating, or assaying substances. †Also, the bowl *of* a ladle.

1496 *Acc. Ld. High Treas. Scot.* I. 296 For a ladil of irne, for the plumbis ȝetting, and a spune of irne. **1692** *Capt. Smith's Seaman's Gram.* ii. vii. 95 Eight, Is the Length of the Spoon of the Ladle. **1827** Faraday *Chem. Manip.* xxiii. (1842) 577 The wires of deflagrating spoons may be passed through them. **1838** T. Thomson *Chem. Org. Bodies* 742 It does not burn by itself when heated in an open spoon. **1881** Raymond *Mining Gloss.*, *Spoon*, an instrument made of an ox or buffalo horn, in which earth or pulp may be delicately tested by washing to detect gold, amalgam, etc.

c. A wooden golfing-club having a slightly concave head. Also, a lofted stroke played with this club.

1790 C. Jones *Hoyle's Games Impr.* 288 The Spoon..[is used] when in a Hollow. **1858** [see gutta[2] 1 b]. **1878** 'Capt. Crawley' *Football*, etc. 80 (*Golf*), A variety of clubs, known as the long spoon, short spoon, putter, &c. **1897** *Encycl. Sport* I. 459 Spoons, or wooden clubs of different lengths, with their faces hollowed out at various angles, are now almost obsolete. **1927** *Daily Mail* 8 July 14/4 The 3 at the difficult twelfth, where he was five yards from the pin with a drive and a spoon and holed the putt, would have shaken any youthful rival. **1962** *Times* 9 June 3/2 He struck a spoon, which ran pleasingly up on to the ninth green. **1971** L. Koppett *N.Y. Times Guide Spectator Sports* vi. 128 The No. 3 wood, or the 'spoon', provides distance with more loft.

d. A kind of artificial bait having the form of the bowl of a spoon, used in spinning or trolling.

1851 G. H. Kingsley *Sp. & Trav.* (1900) 449 In the broken water above I spun my spoon. **1867** F. Francis *Angling* iv. 113 The spoon is an excellent lure; they may be had of all sorts, sizes, fashions, and colours. **1897** *Encycl. Sport* I. 14 There is probably no better all-round artificial spinning-bait for salmon and pike than the spoon.

e. A part of a cotton drawing-frame.

1853 Ure *Dict. Arts* (ed. 4) II. 830 The slivers from these pass over a series of conductors, termed 'spoons'... These instruments are weighted guide levers, mounted so as to be capable of turning upon centres.

f. *Cricket.* A ball lofted by a soft or weak shot; a stroke which 'spoons' the ball. Cf. spoon *v.*[2] 2 b.

1871 'Thomsonby' *Cricketers in Council* 3 A ball hit into the air is a 'spoon', unless it goes a long way, when it becomes a 'skyer'. **1906** A. E. Knight *Compl. Cricketer* 353 *Spoon*, a badly mistimed hit.

g. *Surfing.* = rocker[1] 5 e.

1963 *Pix* 28 Sept. 62/4 *Spoon*, the slight upward slope in a surfboard. **1970** *Studies in English* (Univ. Cape Town) I. 28 *Rocker*, or *banana*,..indicates the curvature of the surfboard along its length; in other words, the surfboard, when viewed from the side, is higher at both ends than in the centre. More specific is the word *spoon*, which applies to the upturn of the nose of the surfboard.

5. †**a.** ***spoon of the brisket***, the hollow at the lower end of the breast-bone. *Obs.*

1576 Turberv. *Venerie* 129 The rauens morsell (which is the gryssell at the spoone of the brisket). *Ibid.* 135 There is a little gristle which is vpon the spoone of the brysket, which we cal the Rauens bone. **1637** B. Jonson *Sad Shepherd* i. vi, He that undoes him; Doth cleave the brisket-bone, upon the spoone Of which, a little gristle growes. [**1863** Thornbury *True as Steel* III. 3 He scooped out the gristle from the spoon of the brisket.]

†**b.** ***spoon of the stomach***, the pit of the stomach. *Obs.*[−1]

c **1550** H. Lloyd *Treas. Health* I v, Boyle Frankensence.. and make a plaster thereof and bynd it to the spone of the stomake.

c. *Zool.* A spoon-shaped part or process.

1725 Sloane *Jamaica* II. 317 Its [a spoonbill's] Head.. ended in a round Spoon of two Inches Diameter. **1861** in *Rep. Smithsonian Instit. 1860* 251 Anatina has the spoon [*supra* a spoon-shaped plate] supported by a clavicle at the umbos.

6. The student last in each class in the list of mathematical honours at Cambridge; *spec.* the 'wooden spoon' (see wooden *a.*).

1824 *Gradus ad Cantabr.* s.v., The last of each class of the honours is denominated *The Spoon...* The Wooden Spoon, however, is κατ' ἐξοχὴν The Spoon. **1852** C. A. Bristed *Five Yrs. Eng. Univ.* 125 There was more numerical difference between them than between the Second Wrangler and the spoon. *Ibid.* 225 The Senior Wrangler having perhaps 3,000 or 3,500 marks to the Spoon's 200.

7. *slang* or *colloq.* A shallow, simple, or foolish person; a simpleton, ninny, goose.

1799 *Carlton Ho. Mag.* 217 The spoons or novices are permitted from prudential motives to be successful at the commencement. **1812** J. H. Vaux *Flash Dict.* s.v. *Spoony*, It is usual to call a very prating shallow fellow, a *rank spoon.* **1837** Morier *Abel Allnutt* xxii. 130 'None but a spoon would ever think so,' said the stranger. **1882** Mrs. Houstoun *Recomm. to Mercy* ii, There now, you are going to cry!.. Now, that is being a spoon.

8. a. ***to be spoons with, about,*** or ***on***, to be sentimentally in love with (a girl). *slang.*

c **1859** J. S. Coyne *Everybody's Friend* i. i. 7 It was one of my nonsensical effusions, when I was spoons about you... Mrs. F. Spoons! Feath. Well, when I was dying in love with you, my dear. **1860** *Slang Dict.* 224 'When I was spoons with you,' i.e., when young, and in our courting days before marriage. **1863** *E. Arden* (parody) in *Melbourne Punch*, Philip Ray and Enoch Arden, Both were 'Spoons' on Annie Lee. **1883** D. C. Murray *Gate of the Sea* I. i. 7 Tregarthen ..has gone spoons on the Churchill.

b. *pl.* Without const.: Sentimental or silly fondness. Also applied to persons: Sweethearts. *Rarely* in *sing.*, an instance of sentimental love-play; a fond lover.

1846 *Spirit of Times* 18 Apr. 92/2 The girls are beautiful, with a very liberal allowance of 'the spoons', as our friend Smith would say. **1868** E. Yates *Rocks Ahead* ii. ii, This time it's an awful case of spoons. **1882** H. C. Merivale *Faucit of B.* III. ii. xii. 42 They were old spoons too when they were young. **1888** Gunter *Mr. Potter* x. 127 The moment he saw Ethel it became a wonderful case of 'spoons' upon his part. *c* **1921** D. H. Lawrence *Mod. Lover* (1934) 188 A young chap goes out on Sunday night for a bit of a spoon. What is it but natural? *Ibid.* 195 Yes, his reputation as a spoon would not belie him. He had lovely lips for kissing. **1939** Joyce *Finnegans Wake* 115 Some softnosed peruser might mayhem take it up erogenously as the usual case of spoons, *prostituta in herba.*

9. *attrib.* **a.** In general use, as ***spoon-case, -diet, -food***, † ***-stele***, etc.

1483 *Cath. Angl.* 357/1 A *Spoyn case, *cocliarium.* **1534** *Wells Wills* (1890) 91, ix coclearia argentea, que continentur in quodam loculo vocato 'a spone case'. **1922** Joyce *Ulysses* 30 And snug in their spooncase of purple plush, faded, the twelve apostles. **1826** in A. C. Hutchison *Pract. Obs. Surg.* (ed. 2) 161 The rigid adherence to *spoon diet. **1799** J. Robertson *Agric. Perth* 185 The meal of it is seldom made into bread;..they use it mostly in *spoon-food. **1896** *Allbutt's Syst. Med.* I. 393 In case of mumps spoon-food only is to be given. **1601** Holland *Pliny* II. 296 It is an usuall thing..to bore the same through with a *spoon stele or bodkin. **1765** J. Wedgwood *Let.* 17 June (1965) 34 The articles are..teapot and stand, *spoon-tray, Coffeepot, [etc.]. **1977** Fleming & Honour *Penguin Dict. Decorative Arts* 751/1 *Spoon tray*, a small oval or oblong dish used in mid-c18 England to hold tea-spoons. **1777** *Pennsylvania Even. Post* 11 Feb. 73/2 Philip Clark..has a remarkable way of throwing his head back when he eats *spoon victuals. **1877** G. Box *Eng. Game Cricket* 461 *Spooning*, getting under the ball. In derision, it is called 'spoon victuals', especially at Cambridge. **1880** Spurgeon *Serm.* XXVI. 590 Spoon victuals and milk must always be in the house.

b. In the sense 'resembling a spoon in shape', as ***spoon-apparatus, -bonnet, -chisel***, etc.

1846 Holtzapffel *Turning* II. 539 The *spoon-bit, is generally bent up at the end to make a taper point. **1863** Kingsley *Water-Bab.* iii. 90 People must always follow the fashion, even if it be *spoon bonnets. **1902** *Westm. Gaz.* 2 Dec. 9/1 She will have the same *spoon bow and a long overhang aft and a modified fin keel. **1875** Knight *Dict. Mech.* 2288/1 **Spoon-chisel*, a bent chisel with the basil on both sides, used by sculptors. **1833** J. Holland *Manuf. Metal* II. 23 *Spoon-forks, as those articles,..furnished with four or five prongs, are denominated. **1875** Knight *Dict. Mech.* 2288/1 **Spoon-gouge*, a gouge with a crooked end, used in hollowing out deep parts of wood. **1799** G. Smith *Laboratory* I. 139 Melt them together in a silver or brass *spoon ladle. **1851** Kingsley *Yeast* iii, We show them where the fish lie, and then..they can't get them out without us and the *spoon-net. **1922** Joyce *Ulysses* 653 He..drew two *spoonseat deal chairs to the hearthstone. **1758** *Elaboratory* 45 *Spoon stoppers must be fitted to these necks. **1858** Lardner *Hand-bk. Nat. Phil.* 139 A horizontal wheel which has been much used in France, called *roue à cuiller*, or *spoon wheel.

10. *Comb.* **a.** In parasynthetic adjs., as ***spoon-beaked, -billed, -fashioned, -formed.***

1597 A. M. tr. *Guillemeau's Fr. Chirurg.* 6 b/2 That instrumente which we call the spoonewyse or spoonefashoned bullet-drawer. **1822** J. Parkinson *Outl. Oryctol.* 178 *Myariæ*—Bivalves;..a spoon-formed tooth on one or both valves. **1896** Lydekker *Roy. Nat. Hist.* V. 513 The spoon-beaked sturgeon (*Polyodon folius*) of the Mississippi.

b. Miscell., as ***spoon-maker, -manufacturer, -warmer; spoon-like, -wise*** adjs.

a **1686** Sir T. Browne *Norf. Birds* Wks. 1852 III. 314 They..are..remarkable in their white colour, copped crown, and *spoon or spatule-like bill. **1708** Sewell ii, *Lepelswyze*, spoon-like. **1837** *Penny Cycl.* VII. 430/1 On each side of this spoon-like process..is seen in each valve a large thick tooth. **1881** *Encycl. Brit.* XII. 300/1 Its own point falls into a spoon-like indent. **1490** *Canterb. City Rec.*, Stephanus Rycards, *spoonemaker. **1647** Hexham i, A spoone-maker, *een lepel-maker.* **1881** *Instr. Census Clerks* (1885) 46 Domestic Implement Maker:..Spoon Maker. **1835** *Statist. Acc. Scot.* (1845) III. 166 The *spoon-manufacturer, who must remain stationary to fabricate his wares. **1885** *Catal. Service of Plate* 4 A *spoon warmer. **1597** A. M. tr. *Guillemeau's Fr. Chirurg.* 7 b/2 With the little *spoonewyse bullet-drawer, we shalbe able to drawe forth the bullets.

11. a. Special Combs.: **spoon-back**, the back of a chair (of a type esp. popular in the late-18th and 19th cent.) curved concavely to fit the shape of the occupant; a chair of this style; hence *attrib.*, as ***spoon-back chair***; also **spoon-backed** *a.*; **spoon-bait**, = sense 4 d; also *fig.*; **spoon-bending**, the distortion of a spoon-handle by apparently psychokinetic means; also **spoon-bend** *v. intr.* and **spoon-bender**; **spoon bow**, a ship's bow having full round sections reminiscent of the bowl of a spoon; so **spoon-bowed** *a.*; **spoon bread** *U.S.* (chiefly *Southern*) = *egg bread* s.v. egg *sb.* 7 (of such a consistency that it is usu. served with a spoon); †**spoon-brod**, brads for nailing roof-shingles; **spoon canoe** *Canad.*, a spoon-bowed canoe; **spoon-child**, a child which has to be fed with a spoon; **spoon drain** *Austral.*, a shallow drain across a street; **spoon-fashion** *adv.*, fitting into each other after the manner of spoons; †**spoon-feather, -feathered** *a.* (?); †**spoon-hammer, -hand** (see quots.); **spoon-hook**, a spoon-bait; **spoon-nail**, †(*a*) shingle-nails; (*b*) an irregular form of the human nail; †**spoon-tree** (see quot.); **spoonways** *adv.*, = *spoon-fashion*; **spoon-wood** (see quots.).

1909 G. O. Wheeler *Old Eng. Furnit.* (ed. 2) v. 167 In our illustration..we see one of those transitional specimens with cane-panels and *spoon-back. *Ibid.* v. 156 (*caption*) Queen Anne cabinet, and spoon-backed chair showing early cabriole legs. **1936** *Burlington Mag.* July 42/2 Half-way between the spoon-back chair and the strapwork back of the

George II period. **1969** J. Gloag *Short Dict. Furnit.* (ed. 2) 636 *Spoon back*, sometimes used in America for the banded back chair, of the Queen Anne period, the term may have been suggested because the profile of the back resembles the curve of a spoon. In England a comparatively rare early 19th century chair with an open concave back and semi-circular top rail is called a spoon-back... Mid-Victorian single chairs with oval, waisted backs are also described as spoon-backed. **1979** A. Scholefield *Point of Honour* 40 We sat down in two Victorian spoon-back chairs. *c* **1878** J. Albery *Crisis* in *Dram. Works* (1939) II. 321 She has thrown away her heart..on..young Denham. Any cold, glittering thing does for *spoon-bait. **1883** *Fisheries Exhib. Catal.* 195 Spoon-baits, trolling-spoons,..and insects for salmon.. and pickerel fishing. **1888** Goode *Amer. Fishes* 61 Uncultured brethren who prefer the ignominious method of trolling with hand-line and spoon-bait. **1975** *Nature* 2 Oct. 354/3 Some of the children still claimed they could *spoon-bend without cheating. **1977** *Times* 3 Nov. 6/1 Britain and Japan have a higher proportion of *spoon-benders a head than any other country..people who can distort cutlery simply by thinking about it. *Ibid.* 6/4 The military implications of spoon-bending. **1979** J. Wainwright *Duty Elsewhere* i. 7 He was ready to give E.S.P. the benefit of a man-sized doubt. He even claimed to have an open mind concerning the spoon-bending gag. **1909** *Cent. Dict.* Suppl., *Spoon-bow. **1927** [see *bulb-keel* s.v. bulb *sb.* 5]. **1969** *Islander* (Victoria, B.C.) 23 Nov. 11/2 She is still under construction, a 54-foot fishing schooner with the same spoon bow as the famous Bluenose and the Lunenburg schooners. **1900** *Westm. Gaz.* 18 Aug. 6/3 It is so rarely that the..*spoon-bowed cruiser of modern build is seen with such a name at her stern. **1932** *Scribner's Mag.* June 364/3 It was time for me to speed back to the *spoon bread and young broiled turkey that were being prepared for me now in Edith's kitchen. **1941** W. A. Percy *Lanterns on Levee* i. 11 Oh, the poor little boys..never put a lump of butter into steaming batter-bread (spoon-bread is the same thing). **1960** J. J. Rowlands *Spindrift* iii. 176 Spoon-bread made from coarse water-ground corn-meal. **1979** M. G. Eberhart *Bayou Rd.* i. 17 We can have some flour and spoon bread and chicken. **1361-2** *Durham Acc. Rolls* (Surtees) 127 In cc *Sponbrod empt,..xij d. **1907** T. Crosby *Among An-ko-me-nums of Pacific Coast* 141 The canoes of the Pacific coast are of the type usually called 'dugouts'..[including] a '*spoon canoe', flat-bottomed and nearly straight with hardly any bow or stern. **1976** *Islander* (Victoria, B.C.) 13 June 5/3 Their graceful spoon canoes, hand hewn, 30 feet long, 3 feet 6 inches wide..were only used on the shallow draft, northern rivers. **1868** W. Cory *Lett. & Jrnls.* (1897) 244 The waiter almost feeds one like a *spoon-child. **1934** *Bulletin* (Sydney) 7 Mar. 21/1, I saw your ropes fly off when you went over the *spoon drain. **1972** *Advertiser* (Adelaide) 13 June 5/8 To lessen level crossing accidents, a double spoon drain at the approaches to all level crossings may help. **1856** Kane *Arct. Expl.* II. xxii. 222 Petersen and myself, reclining '*spoon-fashion', cowered among them. **1879** Atcherley *Trip Boërland* 162 All five were fast asleep 'spoon fashion' on the ground. **1648** Hexham II, *Een duyfken*,..a young Dove, or a Pigeon with *spoone feathers. *c* **1340** *Nominale* (Skeat) 852 *Poucynes enbrauncheez*, *Spon-fytherede chykenes. **1657** Reeve *God's Plea* 189 When your prosperity crept out of the nest, and first cast the shell from her spoonfeathered head. **1688** Holme *Armoury* III. 309 The *Spoon hammer..hath round Buttons at both ends. **1785** Grose *Dict. Vulgar T.*, **Spoon hand*, the right hand. **1888** Goode *Amer. Fishes* 465 The latter is taken by trolling with a..minnow bait, or a *spoon-hook. **1894** *Outing* XXIV. 227/1 A swivel and a fluted or kidney-shaped spoon-hook. *c* **1310** *Durham Acc. Rolls* (Surtees) 511 In cccc de *Sponayl empt. pro camera Prioris, xij d. **1899** *Hutchinson's Arch. Surg.* X. 148 The nail, instead of presenting a convex surface, is depressed into a slight hollow—'the *spoon nail'. **1772** J. R. Forster *Kalm's Trav.* I. 262 The *Spoon-tree never grows to a great height... The Indians..used to make their spoons and trowels of the wood of this tree. **1789** Trotter *Dis. Seamen* 54 They are stowed *spoonways, and so closely locked into one another's arms, that it is difficult to move without treading upon them. **1814** Pursh *Flora Amer. Septentr.* II. 362 *Tilia glabra*... This tree is known by the name of Lime- or Line-tree; Basswood; *Spoonwood. **1847** Darlington *Amer. Weeds*, etc. (1860) 214 *Kalmia latifolia*. Mountain Laurel. Calico Bush. Spoon-wood.

b. In the names of animals, birds, etc., as **spoon-beak, -egg, -goose, -hinge, -muscle, -shell, -worm** (see quots.).

1893 Cozens-Hardy *Birds Norf.* 49 **Spoonbeak*, Shoveller duck. *c* **1711** Petiver *Gazophyl.* x. xciv, Many girdled *Spoon-egg. **1782** P. H. Bruce *Mem.* VIII. 259 There is another kind called *spoon-geese; their beaks..at the extremity are flat like the mouth of a spoon beaten out. *c* **1711** Petiver *Gazophyl.* x. xciv, Small, white, thin *Spoon-hinge. *Ibid.*, Small, white, thin, *Spoon-Muscle. **1867** Lovell *Edible Mollusks* 155 On some parts of the Devonshire coast it [truncated mya] is known as the *spoon-shell. **1841** E. Forbes *Brit. Star-fishes* 259 Gaertner's *Spoon-worm. *Thalassema Neptuni*. *Ibid.* 263 Common Spoon-worm. *Echiurus vulgaris*. **1855** Kingsley *Glaucus* 83 That curious and rare radiate animal, the Spoonworm. **1879** E. P. Wright *Anim. Life* 580 One..is known on the coast of the South of England as Neptune's Spoon-worm.

spoon, *v.*[1] *Naut. Obs.* (exc. *arch.*). Also 6 spone, 7 spoone, spoune. [Of obscure origin. See also spoom *v.*]

1. *intr.* In sailing, to run *before* the wind or sea; to scud. Also with *away*. (Common in 17th cent.)

1576 in *Hakluyt's Voy.* (1904) VII. 206 We had so much wind that we sponed after the sea. **1588** Parke tr. *Mendoza's Hist. China* 301 They sponed before the winde with their foresayle halfe mast hie. **1627** Capt. Smith *Seaman's Gram.* ix. 40 If she will neither Try nor Hull, Then Spoone, that is, put her right before the wind. **1669** Sturmy *Mariner's Mag.* I. ii. 17 The Ship lies very broad off; it is better spooning before the Sea, than trying or hulling. **1694** Motteux *Rabelais* IV. xviii. (1737) 75 The next day we spied nine Sail that came spooning before the Wind. **1722** De Foe *Col. Jack* xviii. (1840) 298 We went spooning away large with the wind for one of the islands. **1726** Swift *Gulliver* II. i. [copying quot. 1669], The ship lay very broad off, so we thought it better spooning before the sea, than trying or hulling. **1769** Falconer *Dict. Marine* (1780), *Spooning*. By the explanation of this term in our dictionaries, it seems formerly to have signified that movement in navigation, which is now called scudding. Be that as it may, there is at present no such phrase in our sea-language. [**1886** R. F. Burton *Arab. Nts.* (abr. ed.) I. 151 We ceased not spooning before a fair wind till we had exchanged the sea of peril for the seas of safety.]

fig. **1671** Crowne *Juliana* v, Whilst you set sail..And leave this floating world behind. Till spooning gently on,.. You turn an angel unaware.

2. To move rapidly *on* or *upon* another vessel.

1608 *Admiralty Crt. Exam.* 40, 20 Dec., The sea going high forced the Scottishe shipp to Spoone on borde the Elizabeth. *Ibid.*, [It] came spooning uppon the Elizabeth.

3. *trans.* (See quot.)

c **1635** Capt. N. Boteler *Dial. Sea Services* (1685) 293 They use to set the Fore sail to make her the steddier, and this is called spooning the Fore-sail.

spoon (spu:n), *v.*[2] [f. spoon *sb.*]

I. 1. *trans.* To lift or transfer by means of a spoon. Chiefly with preps. and advs., as *into*, *off*, *out*, *up*.

1715 *Disc. Death* 75 How must his meat be chewed for him, and Papp spooned into his Mouth. **1826** Disraeli *V. Grey* II. v, She negligently spooned her soup, and then, after much parade, sent it away untouched. **1845** Alb. Smith *Fort. Scattergood Fam.* xxii, Mr. Bam at the sideboard.. spooning up the [salad-]dressing. **1860** Dickens *Uncomm. Trav.* xix, He..spooned his soup into himself with a malignancy of hand and eye that blighted the amiable questioner. **1905** *Rec. St. Mary at Hill* p. lxvii, The spoons were used to spoon out the incense.

fig. and *transf.* **1840** M. Edgeworth *Let.* 30 Dec. (1971) 574 At Coffee time she spooned out a fine compliment to Miss E about Frank and Rosamond. **1856** Mrs. Browning *Aur. Leigh* v. 161 A pewter age,..An age of scum, spooned off the richer past. **1870** H. A. Nicholson *Man. Zool.* xxxiv. 193 The expanded epipodite of the second pair of maxillæ, which constantly spoons out the water from..the branchial chamber.

2. In games: **a.** *Croquet*. (See quot. 1896.)

1865 F. Locker *Lond. Lyrics, Mr. Placid's Flirtation* vii, Belabour thy neighbour, and spoon through thy hoops. **1872** R. C. A. Prior *Notes Croquet* 56 *Spoon* is a term that could hardly have been suggested by any application of a mallet to a ball. **1896** *Encycl. Sport* I. 254 The following are foul strokes..: To spoon *i.e.* to push a ball without an audible knock.

b. *Cricket*. To hit or lift (the ball) up in the air with a soft or weak stroke. Also, to hit (a simple catch).

1836 E. Jesse *Angler's Rambles* 296 She had a perfect knowledge of what was a *bad hit*; and when her lover *spooned* a ball up into the air, which was of course caught, he generally walked off to a distant part of the field. **1879** *Boy's Own Paper* 13 Dec. 168/2 To the younger boys he gave slow balls, which they were induced to 'spoon', and were caught out in consequence. **1882** *Daily Tel.* 17 May, Having made five he spooned one to long off. **1912** A. Brazil *New Girl at St. Chad's* vii. 115 She played too soon at a short-pitched ball, and spooned a catch to mid-on. **1976** J. Snow *Cricket Rebel* 113 Soon afterwards he spooned a simple catch from a stroke ringsiders described as a 'protective jab'.

c. *Golf*. To hit (a ball) in putting so as to lift it.

1896 W. Park *Game of Golf* 217 The ball must be fairly struck at, and not pushed, scraped, or spooned.

3. To catch (fish) by means of a spoon-bait.

1888 Mrs. H. Ward *R. Elsmere* 346 He had with him all the tackle necessary for spooning pike.

4. a. *intr.* To lie close together, to fit into each other, in the manner of spoons.

1887 *Harper's Mag.* Apr. 781/2 Two persons in each bunk, the sleepers 'spooning' together, packed like sardines. **1894** *Outing* XXIV. 343/2 The precision with which we could 'spoon' that sad night was truly beautiful to behold.

b. *trans.* To lie with (a person) spoon-fashion.

1887 *Harper's Mag.* Dec. 49/2 'Now spoon me.' Sterling stretched himself out on the warm flag-stone, and the boy nestled up against him.

5. To hollow out, make concave, after the fashion of a spoon.

1897 *Encycl. Sport* I. 459 (*Golf*), The face of the brassy is often 'spooned' or sloped backward, so as to raise the ball in the air.

II. 6. *intr.* **a.** To make love, esp. in a sentimental or silly fashion. *colloq.*

1831 Lady Granville *Lett.* (1894) II. 77 The billiard room, in which they spooned. **1864** Meredith *Emilia* xxxvi, You might have—pardon the slang—*spooned*, who knows? **1872** Lever *Ld. Kilgobbin* lxxix, So long as a man spoons, he can talk of his affection. **1898** Wollocombe *Fr. Morn till Eve* vii. 84 Many danced, while others spooned under the influence of the summer moonlight.

b. Const. *on* (a person).

1882 A. Edwardes *Ballroom Repentance* I. 68 The young woman with ribbons, you know, that you were spooning on.

7. *trans.* To court or pay addresses to (a person), esp. in a sentimental manner.

1877 Mrs. Forrester *Mignon* I. 252 It was pleasant to spoon her when there was nothing else to do. **1894** K. Grahame *Pagan Papers* 148 When a Fellow was spooning his sister once, they used to employ him to carry notes.

†**'spoonage.** *Obs.*[−1] [f. spoon *sb.* + -age.] The practice of feeding with a spoon.

1586 Warner *Alb. Eng.* II. x. 48 Sucke she might a Teat for teeth, And spoonage too did faile.

spoonbill ('spu:nbɪl). [f. spoon *sb.* + bill *sb.*[2], after Du. *lepelaar* (in Kilian *lepeler*, *lepel-gans*), f. *lepel* spoon.]

1. *Ornith.* One or other of various species of birds belonging to the widely distributed genus *Platalea*, characterized by having a long spatulate or spoon-shaped bill; esp. the common white species, *P. leucorodia*.

1678 Ray *Willughby's Ornith.* III. 288 The Spoon-bill. *Platea sive Pelecanus*... The Bill is..of the likeness of a Spoon, whence also the Bird it self is called by the Low Dutch, *Lepelaer*, that is, Spoon-bill. **1681** Grew *Musæum* I. iv. 66 The Head of the Shovler or Spoonbill. **1774** Goldsm. *Nat. Hist.* (1776) VI. 6 The Spoonbill..differs a good deal from the crane, yet approaches this class more than any other. **1828** Lytton *Pelham* II. iii, What,..that one foot square of mortality, with an aquatic-volucrine face, like a spoonbill? **1862** J. G. Wood *Illustr. Nat. Hist.* II. 670 The beak of an adult Spoonbill is about eight inches in length, very much flattened. *c* **1880** *Cassell's Nat. Hist.* IV. 188 Only half a dozen species of Spoonbills are known.

b. With distinguishing terms.

1678 Ray *Willughby's Ornith.* III. 289 *Tlauhquechul*, or the Mexican Spoon-bill,..feeds only on living fish. *Ibid.*, The Brasilian Spoon-bill... In figure..agrees with the European *Platea*, differing only in colour. **1725** Sloane *Jamaica* II. 317 *Platea incarnata*. The American Scarlet-Pelican, or, Spoon-Bill. **1785** Latham *Gen. Synop. Birds* III. I. 13 White Spoonbill, *Platalea leucorodia*. *Ibid.* 16 Roseate Spoonbill, *Platalea Ajaja*. *Ibid.* V. I. 17 Dwarf Spoon-bill, *Platalea pygmea*. *c* **1835** *Encycl. Metrop.* (1845) XXIII. 409/1 *Platalea Tenuirostris*,..Slender-beaked Spoonbill. **1836** *Asiatic Researches* I. I. 71 The Pigmy Spoonbill is ash grey above, and white beneath. **1898** Morris *Austral Eng.* 430 The Australian species are—Royal Spoonbill, *Platalea regia*; Yellow-billed S., *P. flavipes*.

c. *pl.* The genus *Platalea*, to which these species belong.

1819 Stephens *Shaw's Zool.* XI. II. 641 The Spoonbills live in society in the maritime marshes, or near the mouths of great rivers. **1834** McMurtrie *Cuvier's Anim. Kingd.* 150 The Spoonbills approximate to the storks in the whole of their structure. **1879** E. P. Wright *Anim. Life* 328 The Spoonbills and Ibises form the family called *Plataleidæ*.

2. A spatulate or spoon-shaped bill.

1802 Paley *Nat. Theol.* xv, In the swan, the web-foot, the spoon-bill, the long neck,..bear all a relation to one another.

3. *Ichth.* (See quots.)

1882 *Imperial Dict.* IV. 168/1 *Spoon-bill*,..a name given to a kind of sturgeon (*Polyodon spatula*) found in the Ohio, Mississippi, &c. **1892** J. A. Thomson *Outl. Zool.* 430 The paddle-fish or spoon bill of the Mississippi.

4. *attrib.* and *Comb.*, as ***spoonbill bonnet, fashion, -like***; **spoonbill cat, duck, snipe** (see quots.).

1881 *Daily News* 10 Mar. 5/1 When the *spoonbill bonnet was abruptly cast aside for the bonnet no bigger than a cheese plate. **1882** Jordan & Gilbert *Syn. Fishes N. Amer.* 83 *Polyodon spathula*, Paddle-fish; *Spoon-bill Cat. **1813** Montagu *Ornith.* Suppl., *Scaup-Duck*... Provincial [name]. *Spoon-bill Duck. **1874** Coues *Birds N.W.* 570 *Spatula clypeata*... Shoveller; Spoonbill Duck. **1883** *Pall Mall G.* Suppl. 2 June, The extraordinarily rare *spoonbill snipe.

spoon-billed, *a.* [Cf. prec.] Having a spoon-shaped bill. Used in specific names (see quots.).

Also *spoon-billed butterball, heron, teal* or *widgeon*, etc.

1668 Charleton *Onomast.* 99 *Anas Platyrinchos Gesneri*, ..the spoon-bill'd Duck. **1844** *Ann. Nat. Hist.* XIII. 178 This curious bird (a spoon-billed Tringa) described by Dr. Pearson. **1869** *Ibis* V. 430 A full description of the spoon-billed Sandpiper. **1886** Newton in *Encycl. Brit.* XXI. 261/1 The marvellous Spoon-billed Sandpiper, *Eurinorhynchus pygmæus*, whose true home has still to be discovered.

spoondrift ('spu:ndrɪft). [f. spoon *v.*[1] + drift *sb.*] Spray swept from the tops of waves by a violent wind and driven continuously along the surface of the sea. Now commonly spindrift.

1769 Falconer *Dict. Marine* (1780), *Spoon-Drift*, a sort of showery sprinkling of the sea-water, swept from the surface of the waves in a tempest, and flying according to the direction of the wind like a vapour. **1791** Nairne *Poems* 109 When the bold seaman can no longer brave The dreadful spoondrift of the foaming wave. **1840** *Civil Eng. & Arch. Jrnl.* III. 181/2 A light-vessel..ever and anon submerged in the trough of sea, spray, and spoon-drift. **1847** Sir J. C. Ross *Voy. Antarct. Reg.* I. 51 The violent gusts that rushed along the almost perpendicular coast line, raising the spoon-drift in clouds over us. **1886** R. C. Leslie *Sea Painter's Log* 108 The hard black hills of water..being almost hidden a few hundred yards from the ship by this driving spoondrift.

transf. **1867** Smyth *Sailor's Word-bk.* 644 Driving snow is also sometimes termed spoon-drift.

spooned, *a.* [f. spoon *sb.* + -ed.] Having the shape of, hollowed out like, a spoon.

1890 *Daily News* 14 June 5/1 Why is the 'baffed' or spooned bonnet of one year given up next year in favour of a bird of paradise? **1904** *Westm. Gaz.* 1 Jan. 3/2 It is a confession of inability to get a ball..into the air without the use of a spooned club.

'spooner[1]. [f. spoon *sb.* + -er[1].]

†**1.** One who makes spoons. *Obs.*[−1]

c **1515** *Cocke Lorell's B.* 9 Sponers, torners, and hatters.

2. A spoon-holder.

1896 *Advance* (Chicago) 10 Sept., Tea Pot, Sugar-bowl, Creamer and Spooner.

'spooner[2]. [f. spoon *v.* 5 + -er[1].] One who spoons or makes love sentimentally.

1887 Black *Sabina Zembra* xi, 'Spooners are not very interesting—.' 'I beg your pardon?' said she innocently.

'Lovers, I should say.' *c* **1921** D. H. LAWRENCE *Mod. Lover* (1934) 195 Emmie..cuddled into his arms. He was famous as a spooner, and she was famous as a sport. **1976** *Times* 24 Mar. 13/3 A wilderness of forms for the convenience of spooners.

'spoonerism. [f. the name of the Rev. W. A. *Spooner* (b. 1844).] An accidental transposition of the initial sounds, or other parts, of two or more words.

Known in colloquial use in Oxford from about 1885.

1900 *Globe* 5 Feb., To one unacquainted with technical terms it sounds as if the speaker were guilty of a spoonerism. **1923** [see MARROWSKY b]. **1976** *Oxford Diocesan Mag.* July 15/1, I am *not* going to put on any weight until I'm fifty, when I shall allow myself to become matronly, ready to be a follower of 'soda and gobbly matrons', as enjoined by the marriage service. (A good Spoonerism that, created quite involuntarily by my mother some years ago.)

Hence **Spoone'rismus** [nonce mock-German], a spoonerism; **'spoonerize** *v. trans.*, to alter (a word or phrase) by a spoonerism; **'spoonerized** *ppl. a.*

1923 A. HUXLEY *Antic Hay* xx. 284 When pain and anguish wring the brow, an interesting mangle thou, as we used to say in the good old days when the pun and the Spoonerismus were in fashion. **1927** *Daily Express* 22 July 7 Zoojolical Gardens... But why not let the misprint stick? The Zoo gardens are 'jolical' gardens, and probably the London Zoological Society would have no objection to them being spoonerised as such. **1972** D. W. BAHLMAN in E. W. Hamilton *Diary* p. xxv, The Herbert family, Hamilton, and other friends..called themselves the Bilton Waggers, a Spoonerized version of Wilton Baggers. **1974** V. NABOKOV *Look at Harlequins* (1975) II. v. 101 Only a lunatic would have chosen a pair of third-rate publicists to write about—spoonerizing their names in addition!

'spoonery. *nonce-word.* [f. SPOON *sb.* 7 + -ERY.] Foolishness, silliness.

1824 *Blackw. Mag.* XV. 558 Your lads pretended to respect the constitution—they are not guilty of such spoonery.

spoon-feed ('spu:nfi:d), *v.* [f. SPOON *sb.* + FEED *v.*] *trans.* To feed with a spoon. Chiefly *fig.*

1615 ROWLANDS *Mel. Knight* (Hunterian Cl.) 20 Taught by the prating Nurse which did spoon-feed him. **1864** BROWNING *Dram. Pers., Death in Desert* 109 So, minds at first must be spoon-fed with truth. **1890** *19th Cent.* Nov. 855 They are anxious to more than spoon-feed the people of Ireland with self-government. **1900** *Athenæum* 28 Apr. 520/3 To urge men to learn is a far higher profession than to spoon-feed them with learning.

Hence **spoon-fed** *ppl. a.*, **spoon-feeding** *vbl. sb.* (both *fig.* in quots.).

1901 *Daily Chron.* 21 May 6 (Encycl. D.), The Conservative papers claim..that spoonfed undertakings have no solid commercial basis. **1905** M. F. REANY *Medical Profession* i. 21 'Spoon-feeding'..is excellent for obtaining good examination results, but is it quite so productive of good practioners? **1978** *Listener* 19 Jan. 87/2 The mixture of spoonfeeding and stimulation is..the essential quality of the lectures on scientific themes given..to an audience of children.

spoonful ('spu:nfʊl). [f. SPOON *sb.* + -FUL.] As much as fills a spoon; such an amount as can be lifted in a spoon.

α. *c* **1290** *S. Eng. Leg.* I. 193 He nadde nouȝt a spone-ful ale. *c* **1380** in *Rel. Ant.* I. 52 Pouder of seede of lanett a sponfull, and of love-ache a sponfull. *a* **1425** tr. *Arderne's Treat. Fistula*, etc. 75 Putte perin a sponful of comon salt. *c* **1475** HENRYSON *Poems* (S.T.S.) III. 152 Thre sponfull of þe blak spyce. **1547** BOORDE *Brev. Health* §207 Drynke halfe a sponeful mornyng and euenynge. **1599** B. JONSON *Ev. Man out of Hum.* IV. i, How cleanly he wipes his spoon at euery spoonfull of any whit-meat he eats. **1625** *Laws Stannaries* iii. (1808) 17 A true note in writing..certifying the just number of pieces, slabs, or spoonfuls of tin above a pound weight. **1669** W. SIMPSON *Hydrol. Chym.* 328 It gives help..being taken to the quantity of three or four spoonfulls. **1738** *Gentl. Mag.* VIII. 661/1 Sometimes a Spoonful, and sometimes but some few Drops. **1800** tr. *Lagrange's Chem.* I. 430 Throw this mixture by spoonfuls into a crucible. **1890** *Science-Gossip* XXVI. 263 When a spoonful of food is dropped in, the water seems in a moment to be alive with fish.

β. **1527** ANDREW *Brunswyke's Distyll. Waters* D j, Dronke of the same water foure spones full at nyght is good agaynste the hote cowgh. **1599** A. M. tr. *Gabelhouer's Bk. Physicke* 145/2 Administre of this water thre spoonesfulle. **1863** BATES *Nat. Amazon* v. (1864) 125 We had brought with us a bag of farinha,..and a few spoonsful of salt. **1897** 'OUIDA' *Massarenes* xiii, Two spoonsful of Cognac in it.

b. *transf.* A very small quantity or number.

1531 ELYOT *Gov.* I. xv, If he haue a spone full of latine, he wyll shewe forth a hoggeshede withoute any lernyng. **1551** T. WILSON *Logike* (1580) 79 One that hath but a spone-full of witte, maie answere to this question. **1652** N. CULVERWEL *Lt. Nature* I. xv. (1661) 127 Babes in Intellectuals must take in..those spoonfuls of Knowledge. **1894** *Advance* (Chicago) 9 Aug., Those who come [to a service] find only 'a spoonful' present, and no leader.

'spoonified, *ppl. a.* [f. SPOON *sb.* 7.] Converted into a 'spoon' or silly fellow.

1838 'QUIZ JR.' *Char. Sk. Young G.* 35 The 'Spoonified Young Gentleman' has a puffy, potatoe-looking phiz.

'spoonily, *adv. rare.* [f. SPOONY *a.* 1.] In a foolish or silly manner.

1861 WHYTE MELVILLE *Tilbury Nogo* 52 Little did I think how spoonily I had managed my good fortune.

'spooniness. Also spoony-. [f. SPOONY *a.*]

1. Foolishness, silliness.

1824 *Blackw. Mag.* XVI. 273 Abating a little spooniness about respect due to the audience,..it appears to us to be a most sensible piece of criticism.

2. The condition of being sentimentally in love.

1856 D. G. ROSSETTI *Let.* June (1965) I. 303, I fear tin is out of question, as I think *all* contributors write for love or spooniness. **1864** E. YATES *Broken to Harness* I. v. 80 A sharp attack of what is commonly known as 'spooniness'. **1882** MISS BRADDON *Mt. Royal* II. ix. 185 A man in the last stage of spooniness will stand anything.

'spooning, *vbl. sb.* [f. SPOON *v.*[2] 6.] Courting or love-making of a sentimental kind.

1872 LEVER *Ld. Kilgobbin* lxx, That coquetry of admiration and flattery which, in the language of slang, is called spooning. **1891** BARING-GOULD *In Troubadour Land* ix, Raymond,..not seeing the fun of this romantic spooning of his wife, waylaid and slew him.

attrib. **1880** MISS BRADDON *Just as I am* vii, Did the spooning process seem a little flat this evening?

'spoonish, *a.* [f. SPOON *sb.* 7.] Foolish.

1833 *Fraser's Mag.* VIII. 627 A more boobyish, spoonish specimen of slip-slop was never submitted.

'spoonism. [f. SPOON *sb.* 7.] Foolish conduct or behaviour; silliness.

1839 *Fraser's Mag.* XX. 152 Spoonism and spunging-houses are not usually selected and approved as the main-springs of romantic story.

'spoonless, *a.* [f. SPOON *sb.* + -LESS.] Lacking a spoon.

1837 CAMPBELL in *Athenæum* 11 Mar. 174/1 My spoonless fingers whipped considerable portions into my mouth.

'spoon-meat. [f. SPOON *sb.* + MEAT *sb.*] Soft or liquid food for taking with a spoon, esp. by infants or invalids.

1555 WATREMAN *Fardle of Facions* II. x. 225 Thei are ware, not to spill any spone meate. **1573** TUSSER *Husb.* (1878) 101 No spoone meat no bellifull, labourers thinke. **1639** O. WOOD *Alph. Bk. Secrets* 195 Eate neither Milke, Broath, nor spoone meat, salt meats, nor fried. **1675** H. WOOLLEY *Gentlew. Comp.* 71 Do not venture to eat Spoon-meat so hot, that the tears stand in your eyes. **1740** CIBBER *Apol.* (1756) II. 114 To shew that he was a child, they fed him on the stage with spoon-meat. **1831** CARLYLE *Sart. Res.* I. xi, Did he, at one time, wear drivel-bibs, and live on spoon-meat? **1884** HUXLEY in L. Huxley *Life* (1900) II. 70 A fortnight's spoon-meat reduced me to inanity.

b. With *a* and pl. A kind of this.

1611 COTGR., *Ioncade*, a certaine spoone-meat made of creame, Rose-water, and Sugar. **1684** tr. *Bonet's Merc. Compit.* VI. 217 To refresh the Patient with Broths and comfortable Spoon-meats. **1705** tr. *Bosman's Guinea* 106 The best..that the poor Sick can get here, are Culinary Vegetables and Spoon-Meats. **1783** *Med. Comm.* I. 238 It allowed spoon-meats to pass.

c. *fig.* and *transf.*

1589 R. HARVEY *Pl. Perc.* (1860) 9 Martin cald his Arguments Spoon Meat in his protest. **1608** DEKKER *Belman of London* Wks. (Grosart) III. 166 The fift Iump, is called Spoone-meate, and that is a messe of knauerie serued in about Supper time. **1649** G. DANIEL *Trinarch, Hen. IV*, lxxxviii, Aldermen are still Caudle and Custard, Spoon-meat to the Mouth Of present Power. **1879** GEO. ELIOT *Theo. Such* v. 113 All human achievement must be wrought down to this spoon-meat.

spoon-shaped, *ppl. a.* [SPOON *sb.*] Having the shape of a spoon; cochleariform.

1817 KIRBY & SP. *Entomol.* xxiii. II. 331 At the extremity of each tarsal joint these animals are furnished with a spoon-shaped sucker. **1822** *Hortus Anglicus* II. 14 Leaves spoon-shaped. **1884** F. J. BRITTEN *Watch & Clockm.* 94 Drills for tempered steel..are generally rounded, or spoon-shaped, as it is called.

†**'spoonwort.** *Bot. Obs.* [f. SPOON *sb.*, after the Latin name or Du. *lepelblad*, G. *löffelkraut*.] The common scurvy-grass, *Cochlearia officinalis.*

1578 LYTE *Dodoens* 117 Spooneworte, at the first his leaves be broade and thicke. **1597** GERARDE *Herbal* II. lxxxii. 323 The common Scuruie grasse or spoonewoort, hath leaues somwhat like a spoone. **1657** S. PURCHAS *Pol. Flying-Ins.* 94 Bees gather of these flowers following... In March. .. Spoonwort. **1725** *Fam. Dict.* s.v. *Scurvy-Grass*, Hence it is that they have had the Latin Name as also that of Spoon-wort in English. **1760** J. LEE *Introd. Bot.* App. 328 Spoon-wort, *Cochlearia.*

spoony ('spu:nɪ), *sb.* Also 9 **spooney, spoonie.** [f. SPOON *sb.* 7.]

1. A simple, silly, or foolish person; a noodle.

1795 POTTER *Dict. Cant* (ed. 2), *Spoony*, a foolish pretending fellow. **1818** *Sporting Mag.* III. 51 He must still race on..and his owner must find spooneys to keep him company at this sport. **1848** THACKERAY *Van. Fair* xxxiv, What the deuce can she find in that spooney of a Pitt Crawley. **1865** LE FANU *Guy Dev.* III. xxv. 264 Time.., if he makes us sages in some particulars, in others, makes us spoonies.

2. One who spoons or is foolishly amorous.

1857 'C. BEDE' *Verdant Green* III. iv, You don't mean to say you've been doing the spooney—what you call making love? **1878** MARY C. JACKSON *Chaperon's Cares* I. v. 57 Pen calls him a spoony, and ridicules him unmercifully.

spoony ('spu:nɪ), *a.* Also **spooney.** [f. SPOON *sb.* 7, 8, or *v.* 6, 7.]

1. a. Of persons, etc.: Foolish, soft, silly.

1812 J. H. VAUX *Flash Dict.*, *Spoony*, foolish, half-witted, nonsensical. **1813** COL. HAWKER *Diary* (1893) I. 68 We had some prime slang on the road and, of course, blew up every spoony fellow we could meet. **1835** JAMES *Gipsy* xiv, I was spooney enough to let him get off. **1876** *Mod. Christianity* 60 Then you think that Priests are bound to be mild and spoony?

Comb. **1812** J. H. VAUX *Flash Dict.* s.v., A man who has been drinking till he becomes disgusting..is said to be spoony drunk. **1841** LEVER *C. O'Malley* lxxxviii, 'Very singular style of person'—lisped a spooney-looking cornet.

b. Of things: Characterized by foolishness or silliness.

1834 C. MATHEWS *Let.* 13 Mar. in A. Mathews *Mem. Charles Mathews* (1839) IV. xiii. 280 It [*sc.* misreporting a speech] has such a *spoony* appearance, breaking out in a fresh place with such a phrase. **1843** E. FITZGERALD *Lett.* (1889) I. 115, I am really at last going to settle in some spooney quarters in the country. **1846** THACKERAY *Crit. Rev.* Wks. 1886 XXIII. 236 That picture is more decidedly spoony than, perhaps, any other of this present season. **1850** —— *Pendennis* xiii, They [letters] are too spooney and mild.

2. a. Sentimentally or foolishly amorous.

1836 MARRYAT *Midsh. Easy* xxii, I never was in love myself, but I've seen many others spooney. **1859** LEVER *D. Dunn* lxvi, The man who is not actually in love with you, but only 'spooney'. **1882** B. M. CROKER *Proper Pride* I. iii. 52 They are not a bit a spooney couple; at least I never see any billing or cooing.

b. Const. *on* or *upon.*

1828 *Sporting Mag.* XXII. 23, I must confess, I felt rather spoony upon that vixen. **1861** HUGHES *Tom Brown at Oxf.* vi, Blake got spooney on a gipsy girl. **1891** NAT GOULD *Double Event* 60 Marston's awfully spoony on Kingdon's lass.

c. Expressive of sentimental fondness.

1882 B. M. CROKER *Proper Pride* I. v. 85 Not a spooney, love-lorn effusion, but a good, rational, amusing letter. **1884** *Cent. Mag.* Dec. 191/2 The little sighs I sigh, and all the spooney ways and looks I can't help treating them to.

Hence **'spooneyship.** *nonce-word.*

1838 *New Monthly Mag.* LIII. 453 To be thrown over.. is such evidence of spooneyship as a man of sense or spirit can never willingly submit to.

'spoonyism. Also **spooneyism.** [f. prec. + -ISM.] Spoony or foolish state or quality; silliness, spooniness.

1852 *Tait's Mag.* XIX. 340, I discovered her alone,..and ..insensibly found myself reduced to the most absurd state of spooneyism. **1863** MISS BRADDON *Aurora Floyd* xiii, His innate manliness of character preserved him from any taint of that quality our argot has christened spooneyism. **1889** *Illustr. Lond. News* 12 Oct. 454/3 No one since Younge has so understood the 'spoonyism' of the young soldier, his sheep-faced manner in the presence of his adored one.

spoor (spʊə(r)), *sb.*[1] Also 9 **spore.** [a. Du. *spoor* (in South African use), repr. MDu. *spoor*, *spor*, = OE., MLG., OHG. and MHG., ON. *spor* (ME. *-spore*, *-spurre*, WFlem. *speur*, WFris. *spoar*, G. dial. *spor*, Da., Norw., Icel. *spor*, Sw. *spår*), related to MHG. *spür(e*, *spur*, G. *spur*. The stem is also represented in OE. *spyrian* SPEER *v.*[1]]

1. The trace, track, or trail of a person or animal, esp. of wild animals pursued as game.

α. **1823** in Pringle *Eng. Settlers Albany, S. Afr.* (1824) 84 Soon afterwards the *spoor* (foot-prints) of three Caffers was discovered, and of course we then knew where they went. **1849** E. E. NAPIER *Excurs. S. Afr.* I. 197 Following the 'spoor', or tracking the footmarks of man, or beast, is considered quite a science amongst the border Colonists. **1850** R. G. CUMMING *Hunter's Life S. Afr.* xii, At one stream the fresh spoor of a troop of lions was deeply imprinted in the wet sand. **1863** BARING-GOULD *Iceland* 103, I rode on ahead, following the spoor of other horses. **1880** R. S. WATSON *Visit to Wazan* vii. 120 We several times passed the recent spoor of wild boars.

β. **1852** THOREAU *Lett.* (1865) 66 The vast valley-like 'spore'..of some celestial beast.

b. *transf.* and *fig.*

1865 [W. F. CAMPBELL] *Short Amer. Tramp* 5 Icebergs were seen, and a spoor was followed to St. Louis, on the Mississippi. *Ibid.* 84 Surely the spoor of the Arctic Current was under foot. **1870** HUXLEY *Lay Serm.* ix. (1874) 179 It is the spoor of the game we are tracking. **1873** J. GEIKIE *Gt. Ice Age* vi. 78 When we..follow the spoor of those [glaciers] that crept down from the Southern Uplands.

c. *collect.* (without article).

1850 R. G. CUMMING *Hunter's Life S. Afr.* xxi, I walked to the fountain to seek for elephants' spoor. **1873** *Routledge's Yng. Gentl. Mag.* May 351, I left my skärm and looked for spoor. **1879** ATCHERLEY *Trip Boërland* 153 They had discovered a water-hole, surrounded with numerous spoor.

2. The track of a vehicle.

Cf. ME. *cart-spore*, *-spurre*, and *whele-spore*.

1850 R. G. CUMMING *Hunter's Life S. Afr.* xiii, Eventually..we discovered the spoor of the waggons. **1861** C. J. ANDERSON *Okavango* iv. 46 During the first day's march..we followed the spoor of our waggon.

spoor, *sb.*[2] ? *dial.* (See quot.)

1837 in *Archaeol.* (1838) XXVII. 299 In this drift the shield was found, being forced to the surface by the spoor (the implement used in ballasting).

spoor (spʊə(r)), *v.* [f. SPOOR *sb.*[1] or ad. Du. *sporen.*]

1. *trans.* To trace (an animal) by the spoor.

1850 R. G. CUMMING *Hunter's Life S. Afr.* xxi, He could not see those [elephants] we were spooring. **1863** W. C. BALDWIN *Afr. Hunting* 122 We spoored them beautifully into a dense thicket. **1899** F. V. KIRBY *Sport E.C. Afr.* xvi. 173 An hour later we spoored our rhino into a thick bamboo jungle.

2. *intr.* To follow a spoor or trail.

1865 [W. F. CAMPBELL] *Short Amer. Tramp* i. 5 While thus spooring for some thousands of miles, other things were noticed. **1896** BADEN-POWELL *Matabele Campaign* iv, One nigger-boy, who can ride and spoor and can take charge of the horses.

Hence **'spooring** *vbl. sb.*

1850 R. G. CUMMING *Hunter's Life S. Afr.* xv, I had great faith in the spooring powers of the Bamangwato men. **1863** W. C. BALDWIN *Afr. Hunting* 392 Though we..had the benefit of January's spooring, we could never find him. **1895** *Longm. Mag.* July 265 Preparing a fresh supply of snuff against his coming spooring operations.

spoor(e, obs. forms of SPUR *sb.*

spoorer ('spʊərə(r)). [f. SPOOR *v.*] One who follows an animal, etc., by the trace or trail; a tracker.

1850 R. G. CUMMING *Hunter's Life S. Afr.* xv, Several of the spoorers affirmed that they had heard the elephants break a tree in advance. **1863** W. C. BALDWIN *Afr. Hunting* 259, I followed silently in the rear of the spoorers. **1899** F. V. KIRBY *Sport E.C. Afr.* x. 112 As a spoorer I have never known a better.

†**spoorn.** *Obs. rare.* Also 6 sporne. [Of obscure origin.] A special kind of spectre or phantom.

1584 R. SCOT *Discov. Witchcr.* VII. xv. (1886) 155 They have so fraied us with..Robin goodfellow, the spoorne, the mare, the man in the oke,..and such other bugs, that we are afraid of our own shadowes. **1587** GOLDING *De Mornay* xxxiv. (1592) 546 Thereupon also did some of the Gentiles surmise, that they had crucified a Ghost or Sporne in steade of him. [*a* **1627** MIDDLETON, etc. *Witch* I. ii, Dwarfs, Imps, the Spoorn, the Mare, the Man i' th' Oak.]

spor, obs. form of SPUR *sb.* and *v.*

spo'radial, *a. rare*⁻⁰. [Cf. next and -IAL.] Sporadic. (Worcester, 1846, citing *Phil. Mag.*)

sporadic (spɒ'rædɪk), *a.* Also 7 -ick. [ad. med.L. *sporadic-us* (13th c.), a. Gr. σποραδικός, f. σποραδ-, σποράς scattered, dispersed, f. the stem of σπορά, σπόρος sowing: cf. σπείρειν to sow, scatter. So F. *sporadique* (1690), It. *sporadico*, Sp. *esporadico*.]

1. *Path.* Of diseases: Occurring in isolated instances, or in a few cases only; not epidemic.

a **1689** SYDENHAM *Wks.* (1788) I. i. 6 These I call intercurrent or sporadic acute diseases, because they happen at all times, when epidemics rage. **1728** CHAMBERS *Cycl.*, *Sporadic*, in Medicine, an Epithet given to such Diseases as have some special or particular Cause, and are dispersed here and there. **1752** *Phil. Trans.* XLVII. 385 The plague.. has been mostly sporadic, seldom epidemical. **1843** R. J. GRAVES *Syst. Clin. Med.* xiv. 152 Other sporadic and epidemic fevers. **1845** G. E. DAY tr. *Simon's Anim. Chem.* I. 326 A man who died of sporadic cholera. **1884** *Manch. Exam.* 25 June 5/2 The disease is distinctly sporadic, or due to local causes, and therefore unlikely to spread.

2. a. Scattered or dispersed, occurring singly or in very small numbers, in respect of locality or local distribution.

1813 T. YOUNG in *Quarterly Rev.* Oct. 255 All the Asiatic and European languages..which may be subdivided into five orders, Sporadic, Caucasian, Tartarian, Siberian, and Insular. **1830** LINDLEY *Nat. Syst. Bot.* 90 About 92 genera ..are what are called sporadic, or dispersed over different and widely separated regions. **1856** S. P. WOODWARD *Mollusca* III. 350 Those species which characterise particular regions are called 'endemic'... The others, sometimes called 'sporadic', possess great facilities for diffusion. **1865** FARRAR *Chapt. Lang.* 29 In various sporadic families, which some would call Turanian. **1877** M. FOSTER *Physiol.* I. iii. (1878) 89 In the sporadic ganglia the evidence of automatic action seems more clear.

b. Appearing, happening, etc., now and again or at intervals; occasional.

1847 H. BUSHNELL *Chr. Nurture* viii. (1861) 206 Sporadic cases of sanctification. **1864** R. F. BURTON *Mission to Gelele* II. 71 Sporadic heroines..are found in every clime and in all ages. **1877** OWEN *Desp. Wellesley* p. xix, A series of sporadic encounters of a petty and inglorious..character. **1882** *Times* 7 Feb., The continuance of sporadic troubles in Basutoland.

c. Of single persons or things: Accidental; isolated.

1821 SYD. SMITH *Wks.* (1850) 316 Has any sporadic squire the right to say, that it shall be punished with death? **1875** H. JAMES *R. Hudson* iv. 129 Rowland began to think of the Baden episode as a mere sporadic piece of disorder. **1878** STEWART & TAIT *Unseen Univ.* vii. §217. 215 This production was..a sporadic or abrupt act.

d. *Astr.* Applied to a meteor that is isolated and does not appear to belong to a shower. Also *absol.*, a sporadic meteor.

1929 C. HOFFMEISTER in *Astrophysical Jrnl.* LXIX. 167, I have developed some methods..to find out..which portion of meteors..may be regarded as 'sporadic', i.e., the directions of motions being distributed in an irregular way without indication of radiation in currents... Meteors emanating from a real radiant are mostly of cometary character and sporadic meteors are mostly of interstellar origin. **1954** A. C. B. LOVELL *Meteor Astron.* xxi. 429 A good deal of attention has been given..to the problem of the velocity of sporadic meteors, and the conclusion now seems inescapable that they must be contained in the solar system as distinct from the interstellar view which has prevailed for so long. **1961** D. W. R. MCKINLEY *Meteor Sci. & Engin.* i. 3 The number of sporadics greatly outweighs the total number of meteors belonging to the well-known showers. **1978** V. F. BUCHWALD *Iron Meteorites* I. i. 11/1 It is commonly inferred that all meteors—including the sporadic—are fragments of comets.

3. a. Characterized by occasional or isolated occurrence, appearance, or manifestation.

1842 *Penny Cycl.* XXII. 378/1 The occasional occurrence of diseases..usually epidemic, in a sporadic form. **1852** H. ROGERS *Ecl. Faith* (1853) 146 Its manifestation will not be sporadic, but it will be in one race as in another. **1865** CARLYLE *Fredk. Gt.* XVIII. xiv. V. 368 Meanwhile, the Austrians on front do, in a sporadic way, attack..our batteries. **1881** WESTCOTT & HORT *Grk. N.T.* Introd. §113 All known MSS. shew..traces of sporadic and casual mixture.

b. *sporadic E-layer, -region*: a discontinuous region of ionization that occurs from time to time in the E-layer of the ionosphere and results in the anomalous reflection back to earth of VHF radio waves. Also *ellipt.* as *sporadic E*, *sporadic-E*, used *attrib.* and *absol.*

1937 *Terrestrial Magnetism* XLII. 76 No relation between the sporadic *E*-region ionizations and magnetic disturbances of widespread character is apparent so far. **1949** *Nature* 2 Apr. 528/2 The usual measure of sporadic *E*-layer ionization is the so-called 'critical frequency', that is, the highest reflected frequency for this layer. **1955** *Sci. Amer.* Sept. 129/1 One of the outstanding mysteries of the ionosphere is a type of irregularity called 'sporadic E'. **1967** *Economist* 22 July 280/1 UHF is virtually immune to sporadic-E problems which so beset VHF. **1974** E. HARNISCHMACHER in F. Verniani *Struct. & Dynamics of Upper Atmosphere* 272 The Sporadic E layer, Es, is the most irregular and the thinnest layer of the ionosphere.

4. *Math.* Being a finite simple group that does not fall into any of the infinite classes into which most finite simple groups fall. Also *absol.* as *sb.*

1968 *Proc. Nat. Acad. Sci.* LXI. 398 (*heading*) A perfect group of order 8,315,553,613,086,720,000 and the sporadic simple groups. **1968** *Manifold* I. 12 Apart from the Mathieu groups, no other sporadic simple groups were known until Zvonomir Janko discovered one in Australia..in 1965. **1973** *Amer. Math. Monthly* LXXX. 1028 Still, some hardy souls felt a thorn in their side. For the five groups of Mathieu all reason defied; Not A_n, not twisted, and not Chevalley, They called them sporadic and filed them away. **1980** *Sci. Amer.* May 68/1 There is good reason to believe the number of sporadic groups is finite, and indeed many mathematicians believe the sporadics that have already been identified, a total of 26, complete the list of finite simple groups.

spo'radical, *a.* Now *rare* or *Obs.* [See prec. and -ICAL.] = prec.

1654 VILVAIN *Theor. Theol.* vi. 142 Som sporadical excerptions shal be presented more plausible. **1665** NEEDHAM *Med. Medicinæ* 52 When they are sporadical, here and there sprinkled up and down among the people. **1829** COOPER *Good's Study Med.* (ed. 3) I. 410 It [jaundice] is generally a sporadical complaint.

spo'radically, *adv.* [f. prec. + -LY².]

1. In isolated cases or instances.

1763 *Phil. Trans.* LIV. 78 Some years it is felt sporadically all the winter. **1822-7** GOOD *Study Med.* (1829) II. 121 We find intermittents..existing..sporadically as well as epidemically. **1872** COHEN *Dis. Throat* 97 Although sometimes appearing sporadically, diphtheria is essentially an endemic disease. **1899** *Allbutt's Syst. Med.* VI. 909 Those cases [of meningitis] which though occurring sporadically, resemble the epidemic..form of the disease.

2. In a scattered or dispersed manner; at intervals; occasionally; here and there.

1852 TH. ROSS tr. *Humboldt's Trav.* III. xxxii. 352 No snow falls sporadically in any of the eastern systems. **1875** E. WHITE *Life in Christ* IV. xxvi. (1878) 425 That the belief.. lingered in the churches sporadically for several centuries. **1885** *Athenæum* 16 May 623/1 The Septuagint does not exist in a critical edition; its Hebrew original has only been sporadically restored.

spo'radicalness. *rare*⁻¹. [f. as prec. + -NESS.] The quality of being sporadic.

1884 WHITNEY in *Amer. Jour. Philol.* V. 287 The precative active..is rare even to sporadicalness, being..made from only about 60 roots in the whole language.

sporal ('spɔərəl), *a. Bot.* [f. SPORE + -AL¹.] Consisting of, relating to, spores.

1882 *Encycl. Brit.* XIV. 561/1 Apothecia at first nucleiform, becoming variously dehiscent, with sporal mass.

sporan, variant of SPORRAN.

sporange (spɒ'rændʒ). *Bot.* [Anglicized f. SPORANGIUM, or a. F. *sporange*.] = SPORANGIUM.

1857 HENFREY *Bot.* 153 Their spores are matured in special organs, called capsules or sporanges, formed from the foliar organs. **1872** OLIVER *Elem. Bot.* II. 285 Exposing the minute stalked sporanges of which each sorus is composed.

sporangial (spɒ'rændʒɪəl), *a. Bot.* [f. SPORANGI-UM.] Of or pertaining to a sporangium.

1848 *Annals Nat. Hist.* I. 165 The sporangial frustules of the Diatomaceous plant. **1857** M. J. BERKELEY *Crypt. Bot.* 488 The spore-sac is sometimes separated from the columella as well as from the sporangial wall. **1881** *Nature* XXIV. 559 In Equisetum the sporangial whorls are naked.

sporan'giferous, *a. Bot.* [f. as prec. + -FEROUS.] Bearing sporangia.

1866 J. SMITH *Ferns Brit. & Foreign* 105 Fertile fronds plain, the under side sporangiferous. **1875** BENNETT & DYER tr. *Sachs' Bot.* 375 The deciduous sporangiferous stems of the species just named. **1890** *Athenæum* 29 Nov. 743/1 Sporangiferous and plant-forming hairs.

sporangiole: see SPORANGIOLUM.

‖**sporangiolum** (spɒ'rændʒɪələm). *Bot.* Also (anglicized) **sporangiole**. [dim. of SPORANGIUM.] A small sporangium.

1824 R. K. GREVILLE *Flora Edin.* p. xxiv, When the sporangium contains distinct bodies inclosing *Sporidia*, the sporangium is said to contain Sporangiola. **1859** MAYNE *Expos. Lex.*, Sporangiole. **1875** COOKE *Fungi* 52 It is still more evident if we sow the spores of the sporangiolum. **1895** F. W. OLIVER tr. *Kerner's Nat. Hist. Plants* II. 673 In *Thamnidium* the sporangial branch ends in a large sporangium, and in addition bears laterally a number of tiny sporangia (sporangioles) containing four spores each. **1928** C. W. DODGE tr. *Gäuman's Compar. Morphol. Fungi* ix. 105 Under favorable conditions of nourishment, however, they are continued through several generations when the sporangioles become as large and multispored as the sporangia. **1953** J. RAMSBOTTOM *Mushrooms & Toadstools* xviii. 209 In this common form..the fungus usually shows finely-branched endings (arbuscules) with characteristic granular masses (sporangioles) when they are being absorbed by the host plant. **1969** F. E. ROUND *Introd. Lower Plants* iv. 67 No flagellate cells have ever been found in the class [*sc.* Zygomycetes]..; the spores germinate directly into a germ tube and are formed either in a large spherical sporangium or in various reduced few-spored 'sporangioles' or even singly.

spo'rangiophore. *Bot.* [See -PHORE.] A structure bearing sporangia.

1875 BENNETT & DYER tr. *Sachs' Bot.* 377 A ring of slender sporangiophores, around each of which were clustered three or four sporangia full of spores.

sporangiospore (spɒ'rændʒɪəspɔə(r)). *Bot.* [f. SPORANG(IUM + -O + SPORE.] A spore produced in a sporangium.

1889 in *Cent. Dict.* **1899** *Ann. Bot.* XIII. 477 Léger [in 1897] distinguishes three types of spores in the Mucorineae: sporangiospores, chlamydospores and zygospores. **1930** H. M. FITZPATRICK *Lower Fungi* vii. 149 In *Geolegnia* the encysted sporangiospores are thick-walled and remain quiescent in the sporangium until freed by the disintegration of its wall. **1974** *Encycl. Brit. Macropædia* XII. 761/2 The lower fungi (*i.e.*, more primitive) produce spores in sporangia, which are saclike sporophores whose entire cytoplasmic contents cleave into spores, called sporangiospores. Sporangiospores are either naked and flagellated (zoospores) or walled and nonmotile (aplanospores).

spo'rangite. *Geol.* [f. next: see -ITE.] A spore-case of various fossil plants.

1889 *Science-Gossip* XXV. 99 The sporangites are highly bituminous, and contain..nearly twice as much carbon as cellulose.

‖**sporangium** (spɒ'rændʒɪəm). *Bot.* [mod.L., f. Gr. σπορά SPORE + ἀγγεῖον vessel.] A receptacle containing spores; a spore-case or capsule.

1821 W. J. HOOKER *Flora Scotica* II. 78 Filaments gelatinous,..within filled with elliptical *sporangia*. **1839** LINDLEY *Introd. Bot.* (ed. 3) 266 If the interior of the sporangium be now investigated. *Ibid.* 267. **1863** M. J. BERKELEY *Brit. Mosses* i. 8 In many cases life ceases in the parent plant after the formation of the sporangia. **1881** *Nature* XXIV. 560 Another genus..is allied by the structure of its sporangium to Angiopteris.

attrib. **1875** COOKE *Fungi* 51 The sporangia-bearers are at first always branchless and without partitions.

spore (spɔə(r)). [ad. mod.L. *spora*, a. Gr. σπορά sowing, seed. So F. *spore*, It. *spora*.]

1. *Bot.* One of the minute reproductive bodies characteristic of flowerless plants.

1836 BERKELEY in Smith's *Eng. Flora* V. II. 341 Fertile branchlets..bearing quaternate spores. **1839** LINDLEY *Introd. Bot.* (ed. 3) 260 The sporangia burst..and emit minute particles named spores or sporules, from which new plants are produced. **1863** M. J. BERKELEY *Brit. Mosses* i. 2 The cellular product of the germinating spores..in Mosses consists of more or less branched threads. **1889** *Science-Gossip* XXV. 185 Causing the peristome..to open.., disclosing the interior of the capsule with its beautiful golden spores.

fig. **1862** O. W. HOLMES *Old Vol. of Life* (1891) 46 The spores of a great many ideas are floating about in the atmosphere.

2. *Zool.* and *Biol.* A very minute germ or organism.

1876 tr. *Wagner's Gen. Pathol.* 85 The latter represent the cells, which are the germs of new individuals (spores, etc.). **1888** ROLLESTON & JACKSON *Anim. Life* 859 The contained protoplasm gives origin to a single spore..or to a large number.

3. a. *attrib.*, as ***spore-capsule***, ***-cell***, ***-dot***, ***-fruit***, ***-germ***, ***-sac***, ***-theca***, ***-wall***; **spore print**, a permanent image of the spore-producing structures of a fungal fruiting body, made by allowing spores to fall a short distance on to a surface where they adhere.

Also *spore-bud*, *-cyst*, *-formation*, *-membrane*, etc.

1856 W. L. LINDSEY *Hist. Brit. Lichens* 69 The spore-wall varies in thickness. **1857** HENFREY *Bot.* 154 The fruits consist of capsules of globular or oval form (sporo-carps, or spore-fruits). *Ibid.* 168 The larger (spore-sacs), containing the spore-germs. **1866** *Treas. Bot.* 978/1 The spores are formed in a joint or joints of the spore-threads. **1882** VINES tr. *Sachs' Bot.* 233 The entire spore-capsule of a Moss. *Ibid.* 437 The mother-cell splitting up into four spore-cells. **1885** GOODALE *Physiol. Bot.* (1892) 164 The formation in ferns of the sori, or spore-dots. **1900** MCILVAINE & MACADAM *Thousand Amer. Fungi* p. xxx, When a spore-print is to be taken, select a fully-grown specimen, remove the stem, place the spore-bearing surface upon the gummed paper, cover tightly with an inverted bowl or saucer, and allow to stand undisturbed for eight or ten hours. **1969** F. E. ROUND *Introd. Lower Plants* vi. 85 Spore colour is a valuable aid to identification and is easily detected by placing a mature 'mushroom' head on a piece of white paper and leaving overnight to produce a 'spore print'.

b. *Comb.*, as *spore-bearing*, *-forming*, *-producing*.

1857 T. MOORE *Handbk. Brit. Ferns* (ed. 3) 10 The involute..segments of the spore-bearing leaf. **1880** BESSEY *Botany* 319 Little lateral branches budding out upon the spore-forming hyphæ. **1882** VINES tr. *Sachs' Bot.* 387 In many cases..the spore-producing generation attains great dimensions.

spore, obs. or dial. f. SPUR *sb.* and *v.*

spore-blind, variant of SPUR-BLIND *a. Obs.*

spore-case. *Bot.* [f. SPORE.] A receptacle containing spores; a sporangium.

1836 *Penny Cycl.* V. 75/1 These tubes are undivided, separable.., and bear asci (spore-cases) on their inside. **1857** T. MOORE *Handbk. Brit. Ferns* (ed. 3) 3 Ferns.. produce certain peculiar bodies called spore-cases, containing spores or germinating atoms. **1872** H. A. NICHOLSON *Palaeont.* 489 The fruit was a long cone or spike, bearing spore-cases under scales.

sporeling ('spɔəlɪŋ). [f. SPORE + -LING[1], after *seedling*.] A young plant (e.g. a fern) developed from a spore.

1910 C. T. DRUERY *Brit. Ferns* iv. 27 Given improved seedlings (we prefer seedling to sporeling, even in Ferns, since practically a seed precedes the young Fern) of this class, the probability is that their offspring will vary still more. **1914** *Plant World* Feb. 31 Both tetraspores and carpospores..were sown on oyster shells... In about twenty-four hours, when the resulting sporelings were firmly attached, the shells were clamped to boards. **1946** *Nature* 19 Oct. 536/1 Ontogeny was also illustrated by living sporelings and beautiful microscope preparations from fronds of different ages of the fern-royal. **1970** R. CARSON *Rocky Coast* i. 38 The algal spores swarming in the water, ready to settle down and become sporelings.

Spörer ('ʃpøːrə(r)). *Astr.* Also Spoerer, Sporer. The name of Gustav-Friedrich Wilhelm *Spörer* (1822–96), German astronomer, used *attrib.* and in the possessive, as **Spörer's law**, an empirical relationship noticed by Spörer according to which the mean latitude of sunspots tends to decrease as a sunspot cycle progresses; **Spörer minimum**, the interval between about A.D. 1400 and 1510 during which little activity is thought to have taken place on the sun.

1922 *Monthly Notices R. Astron. Soc.* LXXXII. 536 Each cycle begins with an activity in high latitude; each cycle ends with the last remnants of activity transferred to a low one. This is what is known as 'Spoerer's Law of Zones'. **1968** P. MOORE *Sun* v. 52 Spörer's law is undoubtedly significant, and if we could explain it we should obtain a valuable clue as to the cause of the solar cycle. **1976** J. A. EDDY in *Science* 18 June 1196/1 The earlier minimum, which we might call the Spörer Minimum, persisted by our 10-parts-per-mil criterion from about 1460 through 1550... We can presume that the Spörer Minimum was probably as pronounced as the Maunder Minimum and that during those years there were few sunspots indeed. *Ibid.* 1199/3 The Spörer Minimum of the 16th century is coincident with the other severe temperature dip of the Little Ice Age. **1978** *Daily Tel.* 8 May 11/8 The 15th century..marked the Sporer Minimum of sunspots..and was cold.

sporge, obs. form of SPURGE *sb.* and *v.*

sporid, anglicized f. SPORIDIUM. *rare.*

1847 WEBSTER (citing Lindley), *Sporid*, in botany, a naked corcle, destitute of radicle, cotyledon, and hilum. **1900** *Dundee Advertiser* 24 July 4 The great German botanist de Bary inoculated young barberry leaves with sporids from the black rust of old wheat straw.

sporidesmin (spɒrɪ'dɛzmɪn). *Biochem.* Also sporo-. [f. mod.L. *Sporidesmium*, generic name of the fungus from which the first such substance was isolated (H. F. Link 1825, in D. C. L. Willdenow *Linnæus' Species Plantarum* (ed. 4) VI. II. 120), f. SPORID(IUM (or *spori-*, comb. form of Gr. σπορά SPORE) + Gr. δεσμ-ός band, bundle: see -IN[1].] Any of a class of toxins that are produced by fungi and cause various diseases of animals, esp. sheep, when ingested.

1959 SYNGE & WHITE in *Chem. & Industry* 5 Dec. 1547/1 We propose the name 'sporidesmin' for the substance now described. **1963** *Jrnl. Chem. Soc.* 3172 On alkaline degradation ammonia, methylamine, and a red ketone were isolated from both sporidesmins. **1969** EDINGTON & GILLES *Path. in Tropics* xi. 486 Various toxic substances have been isolated from moulds contaminating animal foodstuffs during this century, sporodesmin isolated from *Pithymyces chartarum* and causing liver necrosis and cirrhosis in sheep being an example. **1975** *N.Z. Jrnl. Agric.* Sept. 17/1 Very high zinc intakes protected against sporidesmin, the fungal toxin causing facial eczema. **1981–2** *Deer Farmer* (N.Z.) Summer 11/1 The susceptibility of both Red and Fallow deer to sporidesmin, the facial eczema toxin.

sporidiiferous (spɒˌrɪdɪ'ɪfərəs), *a. Bot.* Also sporidiferous. [f. SPORIDI-UM + -(I)FEROUS.] Bearing sporidia.

α. **1836** BERKELEY in Smith's *Eng. Flora* V. II. 353 Sporidia ..naked (without any..asci, or true sporidiferous flocci). **1848** LINDLEY *Introd. Bot.* (ed. 4) II. 119 Cellular tissue, among which spores, or sporidiferous asci are generated. **1872** OLIVER *Elem. Bot.* II. 293 Those of the former Tribe being termed Sporiferous, those of the latter Sporidiferous.

β. **1866** *Treas. Bot.* 610/1 The transition into the sporidiiferous fungi is not so acutely marked. *Ibid.* 613/1 The sporidiiferous series. **1875** COOKE *Fungi* 49 Those ampulla cells are sporidiiferous asci.

spo'ridiole. *Bot.* = next.

1863 *N. Syd. Soc. Year-bk. Med. & Surg.* 176 It appears to consist of small globules perfectly round, diaphanous and without sporidioles internally. **1875** COOKE *Fungi* 27 There are to be found also in the species of this genus globose bodies, designated 'sporidioles'.

‖**spori'diolum.** *Bot.* [mod.L., dim. of next.] A sporule.

1832 LINDLEY *Introd. Bot.* 209 *Sporidiola* are sporules. **1836** BERKELEY in Smith's *Eng. Flora* V. II. 276 The *sporidia* oblong-elliptic, containing three or four round *sporidiola*. **1845** *Encycl. Metrop.* XXV. 836/1 Sporidia nearly globose, unequal, filled with sporidiola.

‖**sporidium** (spɒ'rɪdɪəm). *Bot.* [mod.L., dim. (after Gr. types) of σπορά SPORE.]

a. A case or cell containing sporules. **b.** A sporule.

1821 W. J. HOOKER *Flora Scotica* II. 16 Its sporules are included in a sort of capsule..which he [*sc.* Ditmar] calls *sporidium*. **1830** LINDLEY *Nat. Syst. Bot.* 334 Sporules lying either loose among the tissue, or enclosed in membranous cases called sporidia. **1867** J. HOGG *Microsc.* II. i. 272 A gelatinous or membranous pericarp or conceptacle, in which an indefinite number of sporidia are contained. **1887** W. PHILLIPS *Brit. Discomycetes* 444 A filiform sporidium removed from an ascus.

Comb. **1875** COOKE *Fungi* 64 The second section is termed Sporidiifera, or sporidia-bearing.

sporier, obs. form of SPURRIER.

spo'riferous, *a. Bot.* [f. mod.L. *spor-a* SPORE + -(I)FEROUS.] Bearing spores. Also **sporifi'cation**, the process of forming spores. **spo'rigenous** *a.*, producing spores. **spo'rigerous** *a.*, bearing spores.

1836 BERKELEY in Smith's *Eng. Flora* V. II. 341 Quaternate..*sporiferous branchlets. *Ibid.*, The sporiferous state. **1857** HENFREY *Bot.* 158 The fructification or sporiferous apparatus of the Ferns is produced upon the leaves. **1882** VINES tr. *Sachs' Bot.* 316 The distribution of the bands of sporiferous filaments in the colourless sterile tissue. **1887** *Challenger Rep.* XVIII. I. p. cxxxvii, *Sporification..has been hitherto observed only in a very small number of genera. **1867** J. HOGG *Microsc.* II. i. 303 Bringing the whole into contact with *sporigenous cells. **1866** *Treas. Bot.* 100/1 The distinction from *sporigerous *fungi* is not therefore as definite as might be wished. **1897** *Allbutt's Syst. Med.* II. 308 Germs or sporules..which.. rapidly develope into sporigerous bacilli.

Spork (spɔːk). Also spork. [Blend of SP(OON *sb.* + F)ORK *sb.*] A proprietary name for a piece of cutlery combining the features of a spoon, fork, (and sometimes, knife).

1909 in *Cent. Dict.* Suppl. **1970** *Official Gaz.* (U.S. Patent Office) 11 Aug. TM 65 Van Brode Milling Co., Inc., Clinton, Mass... *Spork* for Combination Plastic Spoon, Fork and Knife. **1971** P. J. R. NICHOLS *Rehabil. Severely Disabled* II. iii. 117 Spoons or spoons with fork ends (sporks), either fitted with a swivel or shaped to a child's needs, are the commonest aids supplied. **1975** *Equipment for Disabled: Home Managem.* (ed. 4) 50/1 The spork can be adapted by bending and/or lengthened by rivetting on an extension. **1976** *Trade Marks Jrnl.* 22 Dec. 2628/1 *Spork*... Cutlery, forks and spoons, all included in Class 8. D. Green and Company.., Sutton, Surrey..; manufacturers and merchants.

†**sporkenwood.** *Obs.*[−1] [ad. older Flem. *sporckenhout* (Kilian).] The black alder.

1599 A. M. tr. *Gabelhouer's Bk. Physicke* 258/1 The moone beinge in the signe Libra, cut then off the hayre, and burye the sayede hayre vnder a tree of Sporckenwoode.

sporles, obs. form of SPURLESS *a.*

sporn(e, obs. forms of SPURN *v.*

sporne, var. SPOORN *Obs.*

sporo- ('spɒrəʊ, 'spɔərəʊ), combining form of Gr. σπορά SPORE, employed in a considerable number of recent scientific terms relating to the spores of plants or elementary forms of animal life, as **sporoblast**, **-cyte**, **-derm**, **-duct**, **-genous** *a.*, **-gone**, **-gonic** *a.*, **-gonium**, **-gony**, **-phorous** *a.*, **-phyll**, **-phyllary** *a.*, **-phyte**, **-phytic** *a.* (also **-phytically** *adv.*), **-zoal** *a.*, **-zoan**, **-zoic** *a.*, **-zoid**, **-zoite**, **-zoon**; **sporo'genesis**, the formation of spores; **'sporoplasm**, the protoplasm of a spore.

1888 ROLLESTON & JACKSON *Anim. Life* 860 The protoplasm..segments..into a number of nucleated *sporoblasts. *Ibid.*, The sporoblast assumes by degrees its definitive shape, elliptical and pointed at the ends. **1891** *Cent. Dict.*, *Sporo-cyte. **1899** *Allbutt's Syst. Med.* VIII. 945 The sporocytes, when mature, divide into spores. **1866** *Treas. Bot.* 1088/2 **Sporoderm*, the skin of a spore. **1885** *Encycl. Brit.* XIX. 854/1 Sometimes the cyst is complicated by the formation of *sporoducts. **1888** ROLLESTON & JACKSON *Anim. Life* 861 The spores are discharged from the cyst by special tubular sporoducts. **1890** WEBSTER, **Sporogenesis*, reproduction by spores. **1905** *Bot. Gaz.* XL. 93 The events of sporogenesis in *Pallavincia Lyellii* present ..no fundamental differences from those of other liverworts and higher plants. **1969** A. M CAMPBELL *Episomes* xiv. 166 It was suggested..that activation of an episome might play a causative role in sporogenesis. **1888** *Encycl. Brit.* XXIV. 126/1 The *carpogonium* or *sporogenous portion. **1897** *Nature* LVII. 44/2 Sporogenous tissue, and its conversion into assimilatory tissue. **1881** *Ibid.* XXIV. 74 This so-called fruit is in reality a distinct plantlet, called a '*sporogone', which by..simple multiplication gives birth to the spores. **1902** *Encycl. Brit.* (ed. 10) XXXII. 816/1 There exists a whole group of Coccidiida,..of which only the *sporogonic cycle is known. **1875** BENNETT & DYER tr. *Sachs' Bot.* 295 The asexual generation or *sporogonium is only at first formed in the calyptra [of mosses]. **1882** VINES tr. *Sachs' Bot.* 226 The oosphere..finally developes into a capsule supported on a long stalk, the Sporogonium, in the interior of which are produced numbers of spores. **1888** ROLLESTON & JACKSON *Anim. Life* 749 '*Sporogony,' or development from a non-sexual spore, occurs in a few instances. **1859** MAYNE *Expos. Lex.* 1195/2 *Sporophorus*,..bearing or containing seed: *sporophorous. **1879** *Encycl. Brit.* IX. 828/2 The sporophorous hyphæ are branches of the mycelium. **1888** VINES in *Encycl. Brit.* XXIV. 129/2 The wall of the sporo-carp is formed by a portion of the *sporophyll. **1895** —— *Text-bk. Bot.* 70 A leaf bearing one or more sporangia is termed a sporophyll. **1897** *Nature* 11 Nov. 45/2 The transference of *sporophyllary organs to vegetative ones. **1886** *Athenæum* 25 Dec. 866/3 These take the form of buds similar to the *sporophyte which produced them. **1895** tr. *Kerner's Nat. Hist. Plants* II. 476 The fern-plant bears no sexual organs, and must be regarded as the asexual generation (or sporophyte). **1886** *Athenæum* 25 Dec. 866/3 These.. would be termed cases of '*sporophytic budding'. **1970** *Bot. Gaz.* CXXXI. 139/2 The incompatibility system of the family is of the homomorphic, *sporophytically controlled type. **1893** R. R. GURLEY in *Bull. U.S. Fish Comm.* 1891 413 *Cystodiscidae*... A bi-valve shell..: condition of *sporoplasm unknown. [*Note*] *Sporoplasm*. Protoplasm of the spore. **1947** *Ann. Rev. Microbiol.* I. 6 Typically each spore results from the cooperative activity of six cells, two giving rise to the valves of the sporocyst, two producing the polar capsules,..and two being sporoplasm cells each with a gamete nucleus. **1979** *Jrnl. Protozool.* XXVI. 448/2 Mature spores are short-lived and within 12–24 h begin to extrude their sporoplasms in all directions. **1899** *Allbutt's Syst. Med.* VIII. 946 The transmission of the *sporozoal parasite..of Texas cattle fever. **1888** ROLLESTON & JACKSON *Anim. Life* 862 There are three *Sporozoans included in this sub-class. **1894** *Lancet* 3 Nov. 1025 The shuttle-shaped spores..so frequent in *sporozoic infection of animals. **1882** OGILVIE, **Sporozoid*, ..a moving spore furnished with cilia or vibratile processes. **1888** ROLLESTON & JACKSON *Anim. Life* 861 The contents [of the sporocyst] are resolved into falciform bodies or *sporozoites. **1900** *Brit. Med. Jrnl.* 10 Feb. 301 The skin bitten by the proboscis through which the infected mosquito inoculates its sporozoites. **1885** *Encycl. Brit.* XIX. 855/2 An amœba-like organism,..either a *Sporozoon or referable to those parasitic spore-producing Proteomyxa.

'sporocarp. *Bot.* [f. prec. + Gr. καρπ-ός fruit. So F. *sporocarpe.*] A fructification containing sporangia; a spore-fruit or spore-case.

1849 BALFOUR *Man. Bot.* §1127 In the higher Algæ, the sporocarps..are united together in conceptacles. **1857** [see SPORE 3]. **1880** BESSEY *Bot.* 327 Upon the mycelium there arise..small rounded or oblong masses, the young sporocarps.

'sporocyst. [f. SPORO- + CYST *sb.* So F. *sporocyste.*]

1. *Zool.* A cyst or capsule containing spores, forming a stage in the development of Trematodes, etc.

1861 HULME tr. *Moquin-Tandon* II. VII. xiii. 392 The Echinococci are worms which are enclosed in very variable numbers in a membranous cyst (sporocyst). **1877** HUXLEY *Anat. Inv. Anim.* iv. 209 There is, therefore, a very close resemblance between this cestoid embryo and the sporocyst of a Trematode. **1888** ROLLESTON & JACKSON *Anim. Life* 651 The Sporocyst possesses the power..of multiplying either by transverse fission,..or by gemmation.

2. *Bot.* (See quot.)

1866 *Treas. Bot.* 1088/2 *Sporocyst*, the spore-case of algals.

sporodesmin, var. SPORIDESMIN.

sporodochium (-'dəʊkɪəm). *Bot.* Pl. **-dochia.** [ad. mod.L. *sporidochium* (H. F. Link 1824, in D. C. L. Willdenow *Linnæus' Species Plantarum* (ed. 4) VI. II. 1), f. Gr. σπορά SPORE + δοχή receptacle + L. *-ium*. neut. suffix.] A fungal fructification composed of an exposed mass of conidia overlying a cushion-like layer of short conidiophores.

1913 *Phytopathology* III. 24 The chief contrast to pionnotes lies in the Tubercularia-like hemispherical form of the sporodochia. **1947** *Ann. Rev. Microbiol.* I. 66 Miller ..presented good evidence that the sporodochia produced by isolates of *Fusarium* growing on agar media are in reality patch mutants. **1971** P. H. B. TALBOT *Princ. Fungal Taxonomy* x. 143 A sporodochium..is a compound sporophore of pulvinate (cushion-shaped) form, composed of a stromatic base giving rise to closely grouped erect conidiophores.

Hence **sporo'dochial** *a.*, of or pertaining to a sporodochium.

1913 *Phytopathology* III. 36, I find it very easy to produce cotton, tomato, and cowpea wilt with the young pionnotes and sporodochial stage of the 3-septate conidia which the vascular parasites freely form in pure culture. **1973** *Ibid.* LXIII. 831/1 Sporodochial development counts were made at full bloom.

sporonin ('spɒrənɪn). *Biochem.* [a. G. *sporonin* (Zetsche & Huggler 1928, in *Ann. der Chem.* CDLXI. 94): see SPORO- and -IN[1].] An inert substance forming the resistant outer covering of spores. Cf. SPOROPOLLENIN.

1928 *Chem. Abstr.* XXII. 2949 This, after prolonged digestion with HCl, followed by boiling with 5% alkali, affords a new brownish yellow substance, sporonin, $(C_{10}H_{16}O_3)x$. **1964** *Grana Palynologica* V. 247 According to Zetsche the membranes consisted of cellulose and a specific substance called sporonin, or pollenin if derived from pollen, which was responsible for the chemical stability of the membranes. **1974** STANLEY & LINSKENS *Pollen* ix. 138 Because of the similarity of spore wall sporonin to pollen wall pollenin they [*sc.* Zetsche et al.] subsequently used the word '*sporopollenin*'.

sporont ('spɒrɒnt, spə'rɒnt). *Zool.* [f. SPORO- + Gr. ὀντ-, ὤν, pres. pple. of εἶναι to be, exist.] A protozoan cell at a stage of the life cycle following syngenesis and preceding the formation of spores.

1885 [see CEPHALONT]. **1900** *Jrnl. R. Microsc. Soc.* 337 The macrogametes are fertilised by microgametes, and in each case an oocyst is formed round the conjugates. The new nucleus (sporont-nucleus) divides, the daughter-nuclei also divide, and later the protoplasm, so that four sporoblasts are formed within the oocyst. **1912** [see GAMONT]. **1947** *Ann. Rev. Microbiol.* I. 7 Fusion of these gametes in pairs produces eight zygotes which become sporonts. **1977** *Jrnl. Protozool.* XXIV. 55/1 Binucleate and quadrinucleate sporonts..were observed.

Hence **sporonti'cidal** *a.* [-CIDE], lethal to sporonts.

1970 W. PETERS *Chemotherapy & Drug Resistance in Malaria* iv. 123 Pyrimethamine alone at a dose of 0·078 mg/kg had no sporonticidal action. **1977** *Martindale's Extra Pharmacopoeia* (ed. 27) 343/2 The biguanides..have..a rapid sporonticidal action against some strains.

'sporophore. *Bot.* [f. SPORO- + -PHORE. So F. *sporophore.*]

1. A spore-bearing process or stalk.

1849 BALFOUR *Man. Bot.* §1122 The reproductive organs consist of spores or spherical cells..supported often on simple or branched filamentous processes..called sporophores..or basidia. **1861** BENTLEY *Man. Bot.* 387 Each basidium commonly bears four spores,..situated on stalks or branches proceeding from it. These stalks have been termed by some sporophores, a name which has been also used as synonymous with basidia. **1887** W. PHILLIPS *Brit. Discomycetes* 344 Stylospores..produced on the surface of the stroma in tufts between the cups on clavate sporophores.

2. The asexual generation of plants.

1875 DYER in *Encycl. Brit.* III. 692/1 It will be convenient to use the word *Sporophore* for the agamogenetic generation, in which special cells (*spores*) are detached from the parent to serve as a means of propagation. **1882** VINES tr. *Sachs' Bot.* 225 The second stage in the process of development of the plant, or the asexual generation (sporophore).

sporopollenin (-'pɒlənɪn). *Biochem.* [a. G. *sporopollenin* (Zetsche & Vicari 1931, in *Helv. Chim. Acta* XIV. 64): see SPORONIN and POLLENIN.] An inert substance, consisting largely of polysaccharides, that forms the resistant outer coating of spores and pollen grains.

1931 *Chem. Abstr.* XXV. 2455 The crude sporopollenin, *i.e.* mixt. of spore and pollen membranes, obtained was purified as previously described. **1966** *Jrnl. Chem. Soc.: C* 16/2 A major problem in the study of sporopollenins is their degradation by sufficiently mild methods to give relatively large molecular species. **1978** HOYLE & WICKRAMASINGHE *Life Cloud* x. 91 The first possibility..was that it might be a rather exotic material, sporopollenin. This substance forms a major component of the protective coatings in pollens and spores and is chemically and thermally extremely stable.

'sporosac. *Zool.* [f. SPORO- + SAC².] A simple form of gonophore.

1859 *Annals Nat. Hist.* IV. 140 These medusiform sporosacs. **1861** J. R. GREENE *Man. Anim. Kingd., Cœlent.* 40 The simplest kind of gonophore consists of a well-defined protuberance from the body-wall, the 'sporosac'. **1888** ROLLESTON & JACKSON *Anim. Life* 762 A sporosac..lodged in an ampulla or cavity of the coenosteum.

sporotrichosis (-trɪ'kəʊsɪs). *Med.* [f. mod.L. *Sporotrich-um* (orig. *Sporothricum*), former name of the genus *Sporothrix* (H. F. Link 1809, in *Mag. für die neuesten Entdeckungen in der ges. Naturkunde* III. 12), f. Gr. σπορά SPORE + τριχ-, θρίξ hair: see -OSIS.] A disease caused by the chronic presence in the tissues of the fungus *Sporothrix schenckii*, common in soil and wood and freq. introduced by a superficial scratch, typically producing nodules and ulcers in the lymph nodes and skin.

1908 *Brit. Jrnl. Dermatol.* XX. 301 Sporotrichosis is not incompatible with the presence of syphilis or tuberculosis. **1939** *Yearbk. Dermatol. & Syphilol. 1938* 57 The most common type of sporotrichosis reported is the cutaneous or localized form with secondary regional lymphangitis. **1976** EDINGTON & GILLES *Path. in Tropics* (ed. 2) v. 284 Sporotrichosis..assumed almost epidemic proportions in miners in South Africa due to splinters infecting the skin.

sporran ('spɒrən). Also **sporan.** [a. Sc. Gael. *sporan*, Ir. *sparán* purse.] A pouch or large purse made of skin, usually with the hair left on and with ornamental tassels, etc., worn in front of the kilt by Scottish Highlanders.

1818 SCOTT *Rob Roy* xxxiv, I advise no man to attempt opening this sporran till he has my secret. **1837** W. F. SKENE *Highlanders Scot.* I. ix. I. 227 The resemblance to the Highland dress is very striking, presenting also considerable indication of the sporran or purse. **1884** W. C. SMITH *Kildrostan* I. i. 170 His gillies..all in the brave tartan, with plaid and sporran. **1891** MRS. J. W. HARRISON *Life Mackay of Uganda* 14 The kilt and sporan and Glengarry bonnet.

sporring, variant of SPURRING *vbl. sb.*

sport (spɔət), *sb.*¹ Also 5 spoort, 5–6 sporte. [Aphetic form of DISPORT *sb.*]

I. 1. a. Pleasant pastime; entertainment or amusement; recreation, diversion.

c **1440** *Ipomydon* 601 Whan they had take hyr sporte in halle, The kynge to counselle gan hyr calle. **1472–5** *Rolls of Parlt.* VI. 156/1 Lordes,..Yomen, and other Comyners, have used the occupation of shotyng for their myrthes and sportes with Bowes of Ewe. *c* **1515** *Cocke Lorell's B.* 3 To searche theyr bodyes fayre and clere, Therof they had good sporte. *a* **1548** HALL *Chron., Hen. VIII*, 69 The Ladies had good sporte to se these auncient persones maskers. **1596** SHAKS. *Tam. Shrew* Induct. i. 91, I haue some sport in hand, Wherein your cunning can assist me much. **1606** —— *Tr. & Cr.* I. i. 116 But to the sport abroad, are you bound thither? **1648** GAGE *West Ind.* 193 The good Master thought it bad sport to see Swords at his breast. **1663** S. PATRICK *Parab. Pilgr.* xxii. (1687) 232 Let them see that you can rest from your labours, and yet not spend your whole time in sport and play. **1725** POPE *Odyss.* IV. 850 Aside, sequester'd from the vast resort, Antinous sate spectator of the sport. **1809** MALKIN *Gil Blas* V. i. ⁋28 If I come across them tomorrow..they shall see such sport as will be no sport to them. **1821** CLARE *Vill. Minstr.* (1823) I. 42 Great sport to them was jumping in a sack. **1848** THACKERAY *Van. Fair* xv, 'I'm glad you think it good sport, brother,' she continued.

personif. **1590** SPENSER *Muiopotmos* 290 Before the Bull she pictur'd winged Loue, with his yong brother Sport. **1632** MILTON *L'Allegro* 31 Sport that wrincled Care derides, And Laughter holding both his sides.

†**b.** Amorous dalliance or intercourse. *Obs.*

? *a* **1550** *Freiris Berwik* 170 in *Dunbar's Poems* (1893) 291 Than in hett luve thay talkit vderis till. Thus at thair sport now will I leif thame still. **1570** in Farmer & Henley *Dict. Slang.* **1604** SHAKS. *Oth.* II. i. 230 When the Blood is made dull with the Act of Sport. **1617** MORYSON *Itin.* III. 48 Italians love a fearefull wench, that often flies from Venus sport. **1697** DRYDEN *Virg. Georg.* III. 197 When now the Nuptial time Approaches for the stately Steed to climb; Distend his Chine, and pamper him for Sport. **1700–***c* **1796** in Farmer & Henley *Dict. Slang.*

c. *spec.* Pastime afforded by the endeavour to take or kill wild animals, game, or fish. Freq. with adjs. referring to the result achieved.

(*a*) **1653** WALTON *Angler* ii, I am..glad to have so fair an entrance to this day's sport. **1772–84** *Cook's Voy.* II. I. iv. (1842) 371 Some hours after we got on board, the other party returned, having had but indifferent sport. **1787** BEST *Angling* (ed. 2) 130 The higher an angler goes up the Thames,..the more sport, and the greater variety of fish he will meet with. **1838** JAMES *Robber* ii, Sir Walter desired me to compliment you, sir, and to wish good sport. **1875** HAYWARD *Love agst. World* 5 Smoking and discussing the probability of sport. **1885** 'MRS. ALEXANDER' *At Bay* IV, Pressing Glynn to come down..for the twelfth of August, promising him good sport.

transf. **1864** BURTON *Scot Abr.* I. iii. 114 The Scots lords were grieved..that these should return without having any sport..which the Border wars afforded.

(*b*) **1735** SOMERVILLE *Chase* III. 141 A chosen few Alone the Sport enjoy, nor droop beneath Their pleasing Toils. **1828** SCOTT *F.M. Perth* viii, I was thinking to see my hawks fly, and your company will make the sport more pleasant. **1860** MAYNE REID *Hunters' Feast* xxiii, The American deer is hunted for its flesh, its hide, and 'the sport'.

d. Participation in games or exercises, esp. those of an athletic character or pursued in the open air; such games or amusements collectively.

1863 *Meliora* Oct. 195 If recreation is found, or pastime is sought in activity or change,..it is called diversion; and if we set ourselves to take part in the amusement,..it constitutes sport. **1885** 'MRS. ALEXANDER' *At Bay* iii, I..found he was well up in sporting, or rather turf, matters. There is very little *sport* in them.

e. In proverbial phr. ***the sport of kings*** (latterly, influenced by sense 5), orig. applied to war-making, but later extended to hunting and horse-racing (also surf-riding).

[*a* **1668** DAVENANT *Soldier going to Field* in *Works* (1673) 322 For I must go where lazy Peace, Will hide her drouzy head; And, for the sport of Kings, encrease The number of the Dead. **1691** DRYDEN *King Arthur* II. 19, I count not War a Wrong: War is the Trade of Kings, that fight for Empire; And better be a Lyon, than a Sheep.] **1735** W. SOMERVILE *Chace* I. 14 My hoarse-sounding Horn Invites thee to the Chace, the Sport of Kings, Image of War, without its Guilt. **1843** R. S. SURTEES *Handley Cross* I. xiii. 253 'Untin', as I have often said, is the sport of kings—the image of war without its guilt, and only five-and-twenty per cent. of its danger. **1918** G. FRANKAU *Poet. Works* (1923) II. xxi. 130 Weep for the King of Sports, the Sport of Kings;..On thousand tracks, unridden, desolate, Hay waves from winning-post to starting-gate. **1935** T. BLAKE *Hawaiian Surfboard* iii. 66 News reels and still cameramen will be on hand to shoot the thrilling rides that always accompany big surf, so the rest of the world may see the 'sport of kings' by picture. **1961** L. MUMFORD *City in History* ii. 44 With concentration on war as the supreme 'sport of kings', an ever larger portion of the city's new resources..went into the manufacture of new weapons. **1968** W. WARWICK *Surfriding in N.Z.* 1 Surfriding was practised almost exclusively by members of Hawaiian royal families: hence surfriding's now anachronistic title, 'Sport of Kings'. **1978** *N.Y. Times* 29 Mar. B4/7 The track plans to feature rhinoceroses thundering down the homestretch in the next novelty of the sport of kings.

2. a. ***in sport***, in jest or joke; by way of fun or diversion; not seriously or in earnest.

c **1440** *Alph. Tales* 141 And he knew sho was bod a symple thyng & ansswerd halfe in sporte & said [etc.]. **1535** COVERDALE *Prov.* xxvi. 19, I dyd it but in sporte. **1576** FERRERS in Gascoigne *Kenelworth Castle* G.'s Wks. 1910 II. 94 And as my love to Arthure dyd appeere, so shal't to you in earnest and in sport. **1600** SHAKS. *A.Y.L.* I. ii. 30 Loue no man in good earnest, nor no further in sport neyther, then [etc.]. **1784** COWPER *Task* II. 369 He doubtless is in sport, and does but droll. **1829** *Chapters Phys. Sci.* 317 The inexhaustible variety of shades which nature, as in sport, has diffused over the surface of different bodies. **1879** FARRAR *St. Paul* (1883) 210, I have assumed that the name was given by Gentiles, and given more or less in sport.

b. Jest, jesting; mirth or merriment.

1671 MILTON *Samson* 396 Thrice I deluded her, and turn'd to sport Her importunity. **1778** MME. D'ARBLAY *Diary* 26 Aug., Dr. Johnson..in the evening..was as lively and full of wit and sport as I have ever seen him. **1827** CARLYLE *Misc.* (1840) I. 18 He thinks as a humorist, he feels, imagines, acts as a humorist; Sport is the element in which his nature lives and works.

3. ***to make sport***: **a.** To provide entertainment or diversion. (Chiefly with dat. of person.)

1481 *Cely Papers* (Camden) 74 ȝe have a fayre hawke... I trwste to God sche schall make yow and me ryught grehyt sporte. ? *a* **1500** *Chester Plays* I. 1 Interminglinge therewith, onely to make sporte, Some thinges not warranted by any writt. **1588** SHAKS. *L.L.L.* IV. i. 101 This Armado is..one that makes sport To the Prince and his Booke-mates. **1592** *Arden of Feversham* III. i. 85 He will murther me to make him sport. **1616** LANE *Contin. Sqr.'s T.* XI. 196 Hee that makes them sport shall have their hartes. **1663** COWLEY *Cutter Coleman St.* II. ii, 'Twill make us excellent sport at night. **1784** COWPER *Task* VI. 386 To make him sport..are causes good And just, in his account, why bird and beast Should suffer torture. **1909** MRS. H. WARD *Daphne* ii. 47 That little Yankee girl had really made good sport all the way home.

b. To engage in, furnish oneself with, or find, recreation or diversion. Chiefly with preps., as *at, of, with.*

1590 SHAKS. *Com. Err.* II. ii. 30 When the sunne shines, let foolish gnats make sport. **1598** —— *Merry W.* III. iii. 160 If I suspect without cause, Why then make sport at me, then let me be your iest. **1667** PEPYS *Diary* 28 June, How sad a thing it is, when we come to make sport of proclaiming men traitors. **1699** T. BROWN *Let. to Dr. Brown at Tunbridge* Wks. 1711 IV. 129, I..leave the Dr. and you to make what Sport you shall think fit with me. **1853** J. H. NEWMAN *Hist. Sk.* (1873) II. I. i. 28 The energy of these wild warriors made sport of walled cities.

c. ***to show sport***, to provide pastime by exhibiting spirit and courage in attack or defence.

1834 LYTTON *Pompeii* V. ii, Eumolpus is a good second-rate swordsman;..doubtless they will shew sport. But I have no heart for the game. **1846** JAMES *Heidelb.* i, This seems a wild boar of the forest. We must force him from his lair; and he will show sport, depend upon it.

II. 4. a. A matter affording entertainment, diversion, or mirth; a jest or joke.

1450 *Paston Lett.* Suppl. 31 If ther myt ben purveyd any mene that it myt ben dasched,..it wer a good sport; for than he wold ben wode. **1515** BARCLAY *Egloges* i. (1570) A vj, Lo here is a sport, our bottell is contrary To a Cowes vtter [etc.]. **1560** DAUS tr. *Sleidane's Comm.* 119 b, It is a sporte and a pleasaunt syght to see, howe the Ravens wyll stryve amonges them selves for the carion. **1596** SHAKS. *Merch. V.* I. iii. 146 In a merrie sport..let the forfeite Be nominated for an equall pound Of your faire flesh. **1625** BACON *Ess., Boldness* (Arb.) 519 Especially, it is a Sport to see, when a Bold Fellow is out of Countenance. **1671** MARVELL *Corr.* Wks. (Grosart) II. 391 On this they voted it a libel, and to be burned by the hangman. Which was done; but the sport was, the hangman burned the Lords order with it. **1818** SCOTT *Hrt. Midl.* xxxix, I was the same David Deans of whom there was a sport at the Revolution.

†**b.** ***to make a sport of***, to make a jest of. *Obs.*

1535 COVERDALE *Prov.* x. 23 A foole doth wickedly & maketh but a sporte of it. —— *1 Esdras* i. 51 Loke what God spake vnto them by his prophetes, they made but a sporte of it. **1599** SHAKS. *Much Ado* II. iii. 163 He would but make a sport of it, and torment the poore Lady worse.

5. a. An occupation or proceeding of the nature of a pastime or diversion.

1526 *Pilgr. Perf.* (W. de W. 1531) 88 Myrth and sportes maketh the soule remysse, slacke, and neglygent. **1608** SHAKS. *Per.* V. iii. 41 Your present kindness Makes my past miseries sports. **1678** *Yng. Man's Call.* 71 They are too commonly seeming sports, real vexations. **1780** JOHNSON *Lett.* (1892) II. 172 The high sport was to burn the jails. This was a good rabble trick. **1790** COWPER *Let. J. Hill* 2 May, I am still at the old sport—Homer all the morning, and Homer all the evening. **1831** SCOTT *Ct. Robt.* ii, But I will settle this sport presently.

b. *spec.* A game, or particular form of pastime, esp. one played or carried on in the open air and involving some amount of bodily exercise.

1523 FITZHERB. *Husb.* §153 If they played smalle games,.. than myght it be called a good game, a good playe, a good sporte, and a pastyme. **1590** SPENSER *F.Q.* I. xii. 7 The fry of children young Their wanton sports and childish mirth did play. **1604** E. G[RIMSTONE] *D'Acosta's Hist. Indies* VI. xxviii. 492 The Prelates have laboured to take from them these dances;..but yet they suffer them, for that part of them are but sportes of recreation. **1660** PEPYS *Diary* 18 Sept., Here some of us fell to handycapp, a sport that I never knew before. **1697** DRYDEN *Virg. Past.* x. 86, I..bend the Parthian Bow: As if with Sports my Sufferings I could ease. **1746** FRANCIS tr. *Horace, Art of Poetry* 546 Monarchs were courted in Pierian Strain, And comic Sports reliev'd the wearied Swain. **1764** GOLDSM. *Trav.* 154 The sports of children satisfy the child. **1800** WINDHAM *Sp.* (1812) I. 338

If we, who have every source of amusement open to us, and yet follow these cruel sports, become rigid censors of the sports of the poor. 1837 Dickens *Pickw.* vii, I am delighted to view any sports which may be safely indulged in. 1871 Freeman *Norm. Conq.* (1876) IV. xx. 606 In such a state of things hunting might be a sport, as war might be a sport.

c. *pl.* A series of athletic contests engaged in or held at one time and forming a spectacle or social event. (Cf. game *sb.* 4 b.)

1594 Kyd *Cornelia* iv. i. 134 Like them that (stryuing at th' Olympian sports To grace themselues with honor of the game) Annoynt theyr sinewes fit for wrestling. 1697 Dryden *Æneid* v. 84 That day with solemn sports I mean to grace. 1736 Gray *Statius* i. 35 Oft in Pisa's sports, his native land Admired that arm. 1860 *Chambers's Encycl.* I. 519 Athletic sports were first witnessed at Rome 186 B.C. 1892 *Isis* 27 Apr. 3/1 The Oxford and Cambridge Sports, which were kept at Kensington.

†**d.** A theatrical performance or show; a play.

1571 in Feuillerat *Revels Q. Eliz.* (1908) 129 In sundry Tragedies, Playes, Maskes and Sportes. 1590 Shaks. *Mids. N.* iii. ii. 14 The shallowest thick-skin of that barren sort, Who Piramus presented, in their sport, Forsooke his Scene. 1593 —— *Rich. II*, iv. i. 290 Marke..the Morall of this sport.

e. ***a sport of terms, wit, words***, a playing upon, trifling with, or fantastical use of terms, etc.; a passage or piece of writing characterized by this. ? *Obs.*

1685 Stillingfl. *Orig. Brit.* iv. 208, I cannot think Learned Men write these things any otherwise, than as Sports of Wit which are intended for the diversion..of the Reader. 1725 W. Broome *Notes Pope's Odyss.* ix. II. 329 An Author who should introduce such a sport of words upon the stage, even in the Comedy of our days, would meet with small applause. 1774 J. Bryant *Mythol.* II. 282 Clemens speaks of this Ogdoas, as the νοητος κοσμος: which is certainly a sport of terms. 1830 Sir J. Mackintosh *Life More* Wks. 1846 I. 423 Enabling the writer to call the whole a mere sport of wit.

6. a. ***sport of nature***, = lusus naturæ. ? *Obs.* (Cf. sporting *vbl. sb.* 2.)

1635 Hakewill *Apol.* (ed. 3) 230 Cockles, periwinkles and oysters of solid stone:..whither they have bin shell-fish and living creatures, or else the sports of nature in her works. 1668 Culpepper & Cole *Barthol. Anat.* i. xxvii. 64 Spigelius, because he could not somtimes find it, did count it a sport of Nature. 1756–9 A. Butler *Lives Saints, St. Keyna* (1821) X. 164 They seem either petrifactions or sports of nature in uncommon crystallizations in a mineral soil. 1773 Langhorne *Fables of Flora* ix. 9 Thus Nature with the fabled elves We rank, and these her Sports we call. 1804 Parkinson *Organic Rem.* i. 31 They described their peculiar forms as the sports of nature. 1822–7 Good *Study Med.* (1829) V. 241 It is in this organ more especially, that rudimental attempts at fetal organization, the mere sports of nature, are frequently found produced without impregnation.

b. A plant (or part of a plant), animal, etc., which exhibits abnormal variation or departure from the parent stock or type in some respect, esp. in form or colour; a spontaneous mutation; a new variety produced in this way.

(*a*) 1842 Loudon *Suburban Hort.* 405 Selecting from accidental variations, or as they are technically termed, sports. 1870 *Henfrey's Bot.* 620 What are termed 'sports' by gardeners, *i.e.* shoots differing in character from those on the other portions of the plant. 1890 *Science-Gossip* XXVI. 32 The nectarine, which is usually regarded as only a sport from the peach.

(*b*) 1854 *Poultry Chron.* I. 282 The common variety [of Pea fowl] and the white, which latter is, I presume, an *albino* 'sport' from the former. 1884 *Harper's Mag.* Aug. 465/1 Dinsmore, born of bony..New England, was yet like a 'sport' of some far-descending Visigoth strain.

fig. 1889 *Daily News* 14 Feb. 4/8 That grotesque 'sport' of scientific development, Professor Tyndall. 1893 *Nation* LVI. 66/1 They belong with Emily Dickinson's verses—the 'sports' of literary decadence. 1954 N. R. Ker in R. M. Wilson *Ancr. Riwle* p. xii, If the whole method of writing and the orthography of the Caius manuscript were typically English the aberrant *r* could be explained..as a 'sport' by an English scribe in a period of experiment and change. 1971 *Lancet* 9 Oct. 811/1, I found myself immersed in a tangle of phys- words... Except for a few sports like 'physbuttock' (from fizz) they all come from two roots.

7. That with which one plays or sports; that which forms the sport *of* some thing or person.

a. That which is driven or whirled about by the wind or waves as in sport.

1667 Milton *P.L.* ii. 181 While we..Caught in a fierie Tempest shall be hurl'd Each on his rock transfixt, the sport and prey Of racking whirlwinds. 1697 Dryden *Æneid* vi. 117 But, oh! commit not thy prophetic mind To flitting leaves, the sport of ev'ry wind. 1705 Addison *Italy* 7 When the Winds in Southern Quarters rise, Ships from their Anchors torn become their Sport. 1788 *Massachusetts Spy* 2 Oct. 3/3 For 24 hours she was the sport of the waves. 1837 Carlyle *Fr. Rev.* i. iii. viii, Blown, like a kindled rag, the sport of winds. 1887 Bowen *Æneid* i. 442 Long tossed on the waves, and a sport by the hurricanes made.

b. An object or subject of amusement, diversion, jesting, mirth, etc.; a laughing-stock, plaything, toy.

1693 *Humours Town* 80 They cannot see how they are the Sport and Laughter of ev'ry Company they come into. 1694 Southerne *Fatal Marr.* ii, Am I then the sport, The Game of Fortune, and her laughing Fools? 1709 Pope *Ess. Crit.* 517 And while self-love each jealous writer rules, Contending wits become the sport of fools. 1746 Francis tr. *Hor., Sat.* ii. v. 91 Thus foil'd, Nasica shall become the sport Of old Coranus, while he pays his court. 1796 Morse *Amer. Geog.* I. 330 Rhode Island was doomed to be the sport of a blind and singular policy. 1853 Maurice *Prophets & Kings* xii. 205 Those who treated the divine covenant as a fantasy and a fiction, became themselves the sports of every fantasy and fiction. 1898 Watts-Dunton *Aylwin* xi. iii, You, whom Destiny..has taken in hand as a special sport.

8. One concerned with or interested in sport:

a. *U.S.* (See first two quots. and sportsman 2.)

1861 W. H. Russell *My Diary North & South* (1863) I. 40 Some dozen of the most over-dressed men I ever saw were pointed out to me as 'sports'; that is, men who lived by gambling-houses and betting on races. 1874 *Slang Dict.* 305 *Sport*, an American term for a gambler or turfite—more akin to our sporting man than to our sportsman. 1892 *Welsh Rev.* I. 689 'Unhappy Mr. Collings, the victim of a thousand sports,' I murmured, americanising my language for the nonce.

b. One who follows or participates in sport or a particular sport; a sportsman.

1873 Leland *Egypt. Sketch-Bk.* 69 Such hardened sinners as old pigeon-shooting sports. 1890 *Pall Mall G.* 30 June 3/3 All modern sports will be delighted with the picture of the cosy parlour in which the ancient sports are enjoying themselves after the fatigues of the 'First.' 1894 Astley *50 Yrs. Life* II. 93 There was a houseful of 'sports' of both sexes.

c. *U.S.* A young man; a fellow.

1897 Flandrau *Harvard Episodes* 215 'I don't suppose they're "cheap" sports,..not the way you mean.' 'Expensive sports, then?' 1901 D. B. Hall & Ld. A. Osborne *Sunshine & Surf* i. 4 A small club, called the University, which is chiefly kept up by the young men—the 'sports', as they are called in this part of the world.

d. A good fellow, a lively, sociable person (applied to men or women); one who behaves in a 'sportsmanlike' fashion. Also ***good sport***; ***old sport*** (freq. as a familiar term of address, more usually of men than women); ***be a sport***, act in a generous and sportsmanlike spirit.

1881 Ld. Rhondda *Let.* 30 Oct. in *D. A. Thomas Viscount Rhondda* ii. 24 X—— didn't make herself particularly unpleasant to me, though no doubt she was annoyed about something. I think she is rather a sport because she is such a good type of a certain class of character. 1905 *Punch* 22 Mar. 199, I shouldn't mind, Old Sport. 1913 *Ibid.* 21 May 405, I say, old chap, I've not had a smoke for half-an-hour, so I think I'll go on top. Be a sport and go inside with the women, will you? 1915 R. H. Davis *With Allies* viii. 159 All that was asked of the stranded Americans was to keep cool and, like true sports, suffer inconvenience. 1917 M. B. Owen *Secret of Typewriting Speed* 85 It is better to be known by everyone as a 'fine girl' than a 'good sport'. 1918 C. Mackenzie *Sylvia Scarlett* i. ii. 64 You're no sport, Maudie. You've got the chance of your life and you're turning it down. 1920 W. J. Locke *House of Baltazar* xvii. 208 The old man must be a good sport. *a*1922 T. S. Eliot *Waste Land Drafts* (1971) 5 Myrtle was always a good sport. 1923 Galsworthy *Captures* 145 'Let me go, mister!' came the hoarse voice again. 'Be a sport!' 1925 F. Scott Fitzgerald *Great Gatsby* iii. 57 Want to go with me, old sport? 1931 W. Faulkner *Sanctuary* vi. 57 'Come on,' Temple said. 'Be a sport. It wont take you any time in that Packard.' 1932 J. Farrell *Young Lonigan* ii. 65 He told himself Bertha was a pretty good sport, all things considered. 1933 E. O'Neill *Ah, Wilderness!* iii. i. 83 He's a hot sport, can't you tell it? 1942 A. Christie *Body in Library* ix. 85, I did like her. I thought she was a good sport. 1952 M. Laski *Village* ii. 48 People turned to slap Roy on the back and say 'Well done, old sport.' 1973 *Guardian* 2 Mar. 15/8 The North Vietnamese..walked out of a drafting committee in protest against..one of Waldheim's men... Waldheim is being a good sport and going round explaining that he is not the least offended. 1982 P. McGinley *Goosefoot* viii. 114 Will you come out..this evening?.. Come on, be a sport.

e. Chiefly *Austral.* A familiar form of address, esp. used to a stranger. Occas. *sports.*

1935 [see jolt *sb.* 4 a]. 1943 K. Tennant *Ride on Stranger* v. 48 The small boy rose and said rapidly: 'Fair go, sports.' 1952 E. Lambert *Twenty Thousand Thieves* i. 29 'Have a swig, sport.' He took the bottle..and helped himself to a mouthful. 'Thanks, sport.' He handed the bottle back and idly he noted that he had never called a man 'sport' before. 1962 L. Davidson *Rose of Tibet* ii. 48 Houston introduced himself. 'Glad to know you, sport. You've caught me at a busy moment.' 1975 R. Beilby *Brown Land Crying* 80 'Come on, sport,' the doorman was saying patiently. 'You can't stop here. You've had a skinful.'

9. *colloq.* †**a.** A film about athletic sports (*obs.*). **b.** *ellipt.* or in *pl.* The sports section of a newspaper. *U.S.*

1913 [see *feature picture* s.v. feature *sb.* 4 c]. 1923 *Nation* (N.Y.) 17 Oct. 25/1 Crime and comic strips, sports and 'columns'—the *Leader* provides them all. 1955 W. Tucker *Wild Talent* v. 65 He asked, 'Can I have the sports?' Conklin pulled the section from the paper.

c. A sports car; a sports model of a motor car.

1948 M. Laski *Tory Heaven* ix. 123 Rupert..was driving her down in his own super-charged super-sports Bentley. 1952 A. R. D. Fairburn *Strange Rendezvous* 50 Epicene Sir Giles..plays at Walton Heath, and drives a sports. 1974 R. Rendell *Face of Trespass* xviii. 168 The powerful purr of a Jaguar sports.

III. 10. *attrib.* and *Comb.*, as ***sport breeder***, ***-lover***, ***-maker***, ***-meeting***; ***sport-affording***, ***-giving***, ***-hindering***, ***-loving***, ***-minded***, ***-starved*** adjs.

1582 Stanyhurst *Æneis* iv. (Arb.) 119 When she the weeds Troian dyd marck, and sporte breder old bed. *a*1586 Sidney *Arcadia* iii. (1622) 401 Such a sport-meeting, when rather some song of loue, or matter for ioyful melody was to be brought forth. 1611 Cotgr., *Badin*,..a Iugler, Tumbler, or any such sport-maker. *a*1625 Fletcher *Woman's Prize* i. ii, What a grief of heart is't?..to lie and tell The clock o'th lungs, to rise sport starv'd? 1631 Mabbe *Celestina* xii. 137 O troublesome and sport-hindring doores. 1860 G. H. Kingsley *Vac. Tour* 124 Two or three birds,..affording no sport themselves, and not permitting any sport-affording bird to approach their haunts. 1895 *Daily News* 21 Jan. 7/7 Five dozen..of these sport-giving fish [i.e. perch]. 1897 *Outing* XXIX. 343/2 Four sport-loving young women. 1929 *Daily Express* 12 Jan. 3 To-day the thoughts of sport-lovers will be spread over thirty-two battle-grounds, where the third round of the F.A. Cup competition will be fought. 1960 V. Jenkins *Lions down Under* vii. 103 The people of Christchurch are extremely sport-minded.

b. In plural, as ***sports centre***, ***club***, ***complex***, ***day***, ***deck***, ***department***, ***desk***, ***edition***, ***editor***, ***equipment***, ***field***, ***girl***, ***ground***, ***hall***, ***news***, ***outfitter***, ***page***, ***pavilion***, ***programme***, ***section***, ***shop***, ***stadium***, ***-writer***; ***sports-holding***, ***-mad***, ***-minded*** adjs.

1973 *Times* 27 July (Leisure Suppl.) p. i/2 The Sports Council..claimed that England and Wales need 842 indoor multi-purpose sports centres built by 1981 to supply the leisure demands of the public. 1965 'J. le Carré' *Looking-Glass War* xii. 145, I got the knife at cost..through the sports club. 1976 *Globe & Mail* (Toronto) 30 Jan. 4 (*caption*) Metro says university to pay 50%-plus to use sports complex. 1940 F. Sargeson *Man & his Wife* (1944) 54 When the last war ended I was at the High School. We got the news of the armistice on our annual sports day. *a*1936 Kipling *Something of Myself* (1937) viii. 229 The new three-deckers..hellishly noisy from the sports' deck to the barber's shop. 1981 J. M. Brinnin *Beau Voyage* (1982) 59 The sports deck echoing with the click of the discs used in shuffleboard. 1975 G. Howell *In Vogue* 80/1 Jean Patou's new sports department sells jersey and marocain bathing suits. 1968 D. Francis *Forfeit* viii. 101 The sports desk is a big asset to the paper. 1959 M. Shadbolt *New Zealanders* 75 Mr Jackson lay belly-upwards on an unshaded part of the baked-brittle back lawn. The Saturday sports edition covered his face. 1902 Eliz. Banks *Newspaper Girl* 237 The sports-editor devoted his hitherto undiscovered talents to evolving alliterative headlines. 1969 Sports editor [see *night-editor* s.v. night *sb.* 13 c]. 1969 H. MacInnes *Salzburg Connection* iv. 50 He had opened a sports-equipment shop in Salzburg. 1931 *What is Fascism & Why?* 174 You must give houses, schools, baths, gardens, and sports fields to the working Fascist people. 1938 J. Betjeman in *New Statesman* 12 Nov. 777/1, I adore you, Pam, you great big mountainous sports girl. 1933 J. Buchan *Prince of Captivity* iv. i. 325 The aeroplane..had landed in the sports ground of the factory. 1972 G. Bromley *In Absence of Body* ix. 119 'Where's the match played?' 'At their sports ground.' 1943 Sports hall [see Siporex]. 1976 *Dumfries & Galloway Standard* 25 Dec. 18/6 (Advt.), Sports Hall Area £3.00 per hour. 1895 *Westm. Gaz.* 29 Apr. 7/2 So now sixteen sports-holding clubs have resolved to form a Scottish Amateur Athletic Union. 1963 *Times Lit. Suppl.* 24 May 370/2 Australians..are sports-mad. 1960 I. Cross *Backward Sex* iii. 76 She was not exactly sports-minded. 1928 *Radio Times* 27 Apr. 149/2 (*caption*) Bert simply puts up with [the radio set]..for the sake of the sports news. 1967 Sports news [see *city page* s.v. city 9]. 1897 *Westm. Gaz.* 30 Apr. 5/2 An employé of [a] sports outfitter. 1930 J. B. Priestley *Angel Pavement* ii. 57 Mr. Smeeth..arrived at the sports page, where the prospects of certain women golfers were discussed at considerable length. 1976 L. Henderson *Major Enquiry* ii. 11 Milton glanced only briefly at the headlines of the newspaper before he turned to the sports pages. 1931 'G. Trevor' *Murder at School* ii. 42 The pair had reached the sports pavilion. 1938 J. Joyce *Let.* 6 June (1966) iii. 424 The director who has charge of the singing almost resents even a friendly introduction from the director, say, who controls the sports programme. 1973 J. Porter *It's Murder with Dover* vi. 60 He sat in front of the television watching that sports programme. 1940 G. Marx *Let.* in *Groucho Lett.* (1967) 46, I picked up the paper Tuesday morning, nervously turned to the sports section. 1926 S. Lewis *Mantrap* xxv. 288 Joe and he would..found a sports-shop of their own. 1971 C. Whitman *Death Suspended* iv. 80 Alec was at his sports shop. 1973 *Times* 5 Dec. 16/3 Those responsible for the conduct and management of any designated sports stadium. 1932 Sportswriter [see quarterback *sb.* 2 b]. 1972 J. Mosedale *Football* ii. 21 The principal address at the Philadelphia Sportswriters Association banquet.

c. Used (chiefly *pl.* in U.K. and *sing.* in U.S.) to designate articles of attire suitable for outdoor sports or for informal wear, as ***sport(s) clothes***, ***coat***, ***jacket***, ***shirt***, ***shoe***, ***skirt***, ***suit***, ***wear***, etc.; also ***sport(s)-coated***, ***-jacketed***, ***-shirted*** adjs.

(*a*) 1912 *Sphere* 17 Aug. p. ii/1 The shirts I can also specially commend for holiday as well as for..sports wear. 1914 *Queen* 4 July 15 (Advt.), Smart fitting mercerised Sports Coat. 1922 *Moving Picture Stories* 23 June 23/2 A great many of the new sports clothes are shown with the divided skirt and pantalette cuff. 1925 *Eaton's News Weekly* 2 May 10 The sports shirt above, of fine white Oxford material. 1927 'C. Barry' *Mouls House Mystery* xx. 178 In an hour, Gilmartin was at his home, clad in an old sports jacket. 1930 J. Buchan *Castle Gay* xii. 191 At a small draper's..a jacket of rough tweed was purchased—what is known in the trade as a 'sports' line. 1948 'J. Tey' *Franchise Affair* x. 110 The male with the sports jacket and the pin-striped trousers. 1952 B. Hamilton *So Sad, so Fresh* ii. 22 These sports-coated, bepiped, sophisticated young bloods. 1955 N. Fitzgerald *House is Falling* vii. 107 Brigadier Poodle Poole-Casey, hatless and sports-jacketed. 1962 J. D. Salinger *Franny & Zooey* 132 And there was old Dick.. Sitting at a table in blue jeans and a gruesome sports jacket. 1967 N. Freeling *Strike out where not Applicable* 70 She was the kind of woman that would not look her best in sports clothes. 1973 'S. Harvester' *Corner of Playground* iii. i. 173 The sports-shirted wrestler. 1975 G. V. Higgins *City on Hill* ii. 34 His silver-blue double-knit sportscoat was too large. 1982 'M. Innes' *Sheiks & Adders* vii. 61 An English youth..in a very commonplace sports-shirt and dark trousers.

(*b*) 1916 H. L. Wilson *Somewhere in Red Gap* v. 188 Beryl Mae Macomber in her sport shirt. 1925 *Eaton's News Weekly* 2 May 10 Sport shoes of smoked elk and tan calf, with crepe rubber sole and heel. 1927 P. Bottome *Belated Reckoning* iv. 57 The happy princess..beautiful in her English 'sport suit' and crushed felt hat. 1946 *Reader's Digest* July 85/1 Found in addition were an Army blouse.. and a sport jacket. 1946 *Chicago Daily News* 17 May 35/8

And to think I've been afraid to be seen outside in my new sport coat! **1950** M. HUXLEY *Let.* 21 June in A. Huxley *Lett.* (1969) 625 When you order shirts please ask whether they have an Airtex blue with sport collar, long sleeves; that is a collar which at will is worn with or without tie. **1966** H. KEMELMAN *Saturday Rabbi went Hungry* (1967) xiv. 89 The local chief of police was wearing a sport shirt and chinos. **1972** J. MOSEDALE *Football* ii. 21 He arrived resplendent in a new sport jacket. **1977** R. E. HARRINGTON *Quintain* xi. 120 Atlas had changed from his plaid dinner jacket into a sport coat.

d. *pl.* Applied to fast, low-built motor cars of a racing type. Freq. as ***sports car***. Also *transf.* and occas. in *sing.*

(*a*) **1925** *Correct Lubrication* 52 Lea-Francis (sports models). **1928** *Proc. Inst. Automobile Engineers* XXII. 316 With regard to the acceleration of 'sports' cars, I agree that rough running and noise are taken for power development. **1932** G. WINN *Unequal Conflict* xviii. 350 She nourished a wild hope that..she would find Derek's silver sports car standing outside. **1936** 'N. BLAKE' *Thou Shell of Death* iii. 46 A Lagonda sports-tourer. **1955** E. POUND *Classic Anthol.* I. 60 His sports-car leads with the iron-grays, Six reins are in his hand. **1963** BIRD & HUTTON-STOTT *Veteran Motor Car* 73 One of the pleasantest sports-touring cars of the pre-war era. **1967** N. FREELING *Strike out where not Applicable* 39 It is not far..especially for the fast sports coupé. **1971** 'D. SHANNON' *Murder with Love* iv. 68, I don't somehow think Mrs. Franks drives a Mercedes sports model. **1977** C. McCULLOUGH *Thorn Birds* xviii. 484 He pushed on, gunned the red sports car up..the Domokos Pass.

(*b*) **1927** U. SINCLAIR *Oil!* iv. 80 But that didn't trouble Mr. Bankside, who had already..bought himself..a big new limousine, also a 'sport-car'. **1927** *Scribner's Mag.* Feb. 159/1 Laban, furious, mounts his Sport-model Camel and takes after the elopers. **1955** *Amer. Speech* XXX. 238 The best known writer on the subject, Tom McCahill, calls his most recent book *The Modern Sports Car* (New York, 1954); but a volume by Raymond F. Yates and Brock W. Yates.. is named *Sport and Racing Cars* (New York, 1954). Of the two, *sports car* is unquestionably the more commonly used. **1978** J. IRVING *World according to Garp* xiv. 280 The man's sport car still chugged like an animal.

11. a. Special Combs., as **sportcast(er, sportcasting** = *sportscaster*, etc., sense 11 b below; †**sport-earnest**, something which partakes of the nature of both sport and earnest; **sportfest** [FEST], a festival of sport; a meeting for athletics or other competitive sports; **sport-fisherman**, a sea-going boat equipped for sportfishing; **sportfishery; sportfishing** orig. *U.S.*, fishing by rod and line for sport or recreation; hence (as a back-formation) **sportfish**, a fish caught thus for sport rather than (primarily) for eating; †**sport-staff** *Sc.*, a quarter-staff.

1939 *Amer. Speech* XIV. 6 Newspaper and magazine columns..'Sportorial', 'Sportcast', 'Sportlight'. **1938** *Variety* 28 Dec. 30/4 Jim Britt, WBEN sportcaster, promised a copy of a set of health rules to any listeners who would write in. **1941** *Time* 31 Mar. 50/1 Adam has sponsored the sportcasting of big-time bouts. **1615** T. ADAMS *Lycanthropy* Ep. Ded., I have put up the wolfe, tho' not hunted him, judging myselfe too weake for that sport-earnest. **1937** AUDEN & MacNeice *Lett. from Iceland* xi. 147 The sport-fest was a primitive affair. Some part singing..and a swimming race. **1950** E. BRADNER *Northwest Angling* III. i. 172 As a sport fish, the salmon is highly valued by the anglers of the Pacific Coast. **1971** *Nature* 18 June 422/3 The billfishes of the family Istiophoridae, which include several well known sportfish such as the sailfish, the marlins, and spearfishes. **1954** *Field & Stream* Jan. 72 (*caption*) *Miss Chevy IV*, unique 34-foot, V-bottom, twin-engine sport fisherman. **1967** *Jane's Surface Skimmer Systems 1967–68* 107/2 Sportfisherman is a luxury fishing yacht with living and sleeping accommodation for four. **1955** (*title*) Sport fishery abstracts. I. I. **1910** C. G. HOLDER in *Proc. 4th International Fishery Congress* I. 201 (*heading*) Sport fishing in California and Florida. **1926** *Daily Colonist* (Victoria, B.C.) 15 July 5/3 Something had to be done in order to save the sport fishing of Vancouver Island. **1978** A. GILCHRIST *Cod Wars* v. 36 The Icelandic government (well aware of the amount of money which sport-fishing brings into the country) takes care of the availability of salmon in two important ways. **1634** *Burgh Rec. Stirling* (1887) 172 In hambringing and taking agane to Edinburgh the sport stafes and gownes.

b. *pl.* **sportscaster** *N. Amer.* [after *broadcaster*: cf. *newscaster*, etc.], one who presents a sports broadcast on radio or television; a broadcasting sports commentator; hence **sportscasting**; also **sportscast**, a sports broadcast; **sportsfest** = *sportfest*, sense 11 a above; **sports finder** *Photogr.*, a direct-vision viewfinder usu. consisting of a simple frame which allows action outside the field of view of the camera to be seen, fitted esp. to twin-lens reflex cameras; **sports medicine**, the branch of medicine dealing especially with the consequences of engaging in sports.

1961 WEBSTER, Sportscast. **1976** N. NIELSEN *Brink of Murder* i. 11 The sportscast on the portable TV was in progress. **1938** *Amer. Speech* XIII. 239 Note that newscaster and sportscaster are now common terms in *Variety*. **1952** B. WOLFE *Limbo* xx. 323 With each passing day the sportscaster's voice lost a few more decibels of its professional bounce. **1964** M. McLUHAN *Understanding Media* xxx. 303 A sportscaster had just begun his fifteen-minute reading from a script. **1981** 'E. McBAIN' *Heat* iii. 51 The sportscaster read off the baseball scores. **1969** C. ARMSTRONG *Seven Seats to Moon* xii. 125 J sat all the way through the sportscasting. **1976** *Listener* 5 Aug. 151/1 Television caught both aspects of this mammoth *sports-fest* [sc. *The Olympic Games*] very well. **1953** A. MATHESON *Leica Way* 100 The sports finders are an earlier version of the brilliant finders. **1977** J. HEDGECOE *Photographer's Handbk.* 165 Most twin lens reflexes have a 'sports finder' which folds out of the hood. **1961** (*title*) Journal of sports medicine and physical fitness. **1973** *Times* 13 Dec. 7/2 Britain is far behind some European countries, America and Australia in her attitude to sports medicine, Dr Ian Adams, medical officer to Leeds United Football Club, said. **1977** J. F. FIXX *Compl. Bk. Running* xxii. 248 The general physician is not interested in sportsmedicine.

†**sport**, *sb.*[2] *Obs.*$^{-1}$ [ad. OF. *esporte, sporte* (= Sp. *espuerta*, Pg. *esporta*, It. *sporta*):—L. *sporta* basket. Cf. SPORTLET.] (See quot.)

1656 *Act Commw.* c. 20 Rates (1658) 459 Baskets called Hand-baskets or Sports the dozen, ..04[*s.*] 00.

sport (spɔət), *v.* Also 5–6 **sporte**. [Aphetic form of DISPORT *v.*, or f. SPORT *sb.*[1]]

I. †**1.** *refl.* **a.** To amuse, divert, recreate (oneself); to take one's pleasure. *Obs.*

Fairly common down to the end of the 17th c.

c **1400** *Destr. Troy* 7909 Ector..went Fro the burghe to þe batells of þe bold grekes, For to sport hym a space. **1483** *Pol., Rel., & L. Poems* (1903) p. xlvi, Rydyng a hontyng, hym silff to sporte & playe. **1530** PALSGR. 729, I wyll go sporte me in this gardayne for an houre or twayne. **1579** GOSSON *Sch. Abuse* (Arb.) 58 Many of you whiche were wont to sporte your selues at Theaters. **1638** JUNIUS *Paint. Ancients* 144 Bupalus and Anthermus, to sport themselves, ..made the statue of Hipponactes the Poet, who was halfe a Dwarfe. **1653** WALTON *Angler* iv. 63 Some [lambs] leaping securely in the cool shade, whilst others sported themselves in the cheerful sun. **1712** POPE *Ep. to Miss Blount* 14 Cheerful he play'd the trifle, Life, away; Till fate scarce felt his gentle breath suppress, As smiling Infants sport themselves to rest. **1779** *Mirror* No. 64, The gay, whose minds, unbent from serious and important occupations, had leisure to sport themselves in the regions of wit and humour.

†**b.** Const. *with* (= in the company of) some person, *by, in,* or *with* some action, proceeding, or thing. *Obs.*

(*a*) *c* **1400** *Destr. Troy* 9103 The grekes agayne [might] go to the toune, To sporte hom with speciall, & a space lenge. **1478** *Paston Lett.* III. 237 If it lyke yow that I may come.. and sporte me with yow at London a day or ij. *a* **1533** LD. BERNERS *Huon* liii. 180 Let youre doughter go in to her chambre & sporte her with her damselles. **1586** T. B. *La Primaud. Fr. Acad.* I. 490 Whereas he in the meane while skorned hir, sporting himselfe with Cleopatra in the sight and knowledge of all men.

(*b*) **1477** EARL RIVERS (Caxton) *Dictes* 69 Whan ye shal be wery of studyng, sporte you in redyng goode stories. **1547** BALDWIN *Mor. Philos.* 92 When thou art weary of study, sport thy selfe with reading of good stories. *c* **1590** GREENE *Fr. Bacon* vii, Seeing I have sported me with laughing at these mad and merry wags. **1611** SHAKS. *Wint. T.* II. i. 60 Let her sport her selfe With that shee's big with. **1624** CAPT. SMITH *Virginia* III. v. 59 Our Captaine sporting himselfe by nayling them [fish] to the grownd with his sword. **1670** COVEL in *Early Voy. Levant* (Hakluyt Soc.) 134 After we had sported our selves a while with shooting in these thickets and Plashes. **1733** NEAL *Hist. Purit.* II. 200 The ministers of state sported themselves in the most wanton acts of arbitrary power. **1756** W. LAW *Coll. Lett.* xi. (1760) 161 Pleasing himself with supposed deep Enquiries after strict Truth, whilst he is only sporting himself with lively, wandering Images of This and That. **1781** COWPER *Conversat.* 18 So language..Too often proves..A toy to sport with and pass time away.

c. *transf.* Of things.

1610 HOLLAND *Camden's Brit.* 203 Ex growing bigger, and sporting himselfe, as it were, with spreading into many streames. **1668** CULPEPPER & COLE tr. *Barthol. Anat.* III. ix. 149 Nature variously sporting her self in the Muscles of the Ear. **1720** *Lett. Lond. Jrnl.* (1721) 50 Imagination,.. roaming casually from Object to Object, and sporting it self with Phantoms and Non-entities. **1723** P. BLAIR *Pharmaco-Bot.* I. 16 These [varieties] may justly be called sporters.., so many *Lusus Naturæ* sporting themselves from more simple colours. **1746** HERVEY *Medit.* (1818) 127 Here, she [i.e. beauty] indulges a thousand freaks, and sports herself in the most charming diversity of colours.

2. a. *intr.* To amuse, entertain, or recreate oneself, *esp.* by active exercise in the open air; to take part in some game or play; to frolic or gambol.

c **1483** *Pol., Rel., & L. Poems* (1903) 290 When I wolde sporte with company also, I dare not out I am so sore agast. **1526** SKELTON *Magnyf.* 80 [If] you haue not your owne fre lyberte To sporte at your pleasure, to ryn and to ryde. *c* **1590** MARLOWE *Faustus* 3 Not marching now in fields of Thracimene,..Nor sporting in the dalliance of loue. **1645** HARWOOD *Loyal Subj. Retiring-room* 29 Doe you not see the Keeper sport with his Lion, when the Spectatour will scarce trust his chaine? **1662** J. DAVIES tr. *Olearius' Voy. Amb.* 54 Having sported two or three Hours, we were treated with a Collation. **1746** FRANCIS tr. *Horace, Epist.* II. i. 200 As the Year brought back the Jovial Day, Freely they sported, innocently gay. **1803–6** WORDSW. *Intimat. Immortality* ix, See the Children sport upon the shore. **1856** *N. Brit. Rev.* XXVI. 133 The Iobajjy..dance and sing and sport whenever they have a moment's leisure. **1882** OUIDA *Maremma* I. 147 Cupa and Horta sported amidst the flowers.

b. Of animals, insects, etc.

1667 MILTON *P.L.* IV. 343 Sporting the Lion rampd, and in his paw Dandl'd the Kid. *Ibid.* VII. 405 Of Fish that.. sporting with quick glance Show to the Sun thir wav'd coats dropt with Gold. **1735** SOMERVILLE *Chase* IV. 115 Alone to range the Woods, or haunt the Brakes where dodging Conies sport. **1774** GOLDSM. *Nat. Hist.* (1776) II. 20 These little animals, which thus appear swimming, and sporting, in almost every fluid we examine. **1826** SAMOUELLE *Direct. Collect. Insects & Crust.* 27 Numbers [of these insects] will be seen sporting in the noontide sun. **1889** *Science-Gossip* XXV. 197 The winged atoms sporting in the golden beams.

c. *transf.* and *fig.* Of things.

1593 SHAKS. *Lucr.* 907 Advice is sporting while infection breeds. **1641** SUCKLING *Poems* (1709) 24 Her Beams..Part with her Cheek, part with her Lips did sport. **1732** POPE *Ep. Cobham* 46 When Sense subsides, and Fancy sports in sleep. **1742** YOUNG *Nt. Th.* I. 105 For human weal, heav'n..Dull sleep instructs, nor sport vain dreams in vain. **1818** *La Belle Assemblée* XVII. 40/6 A few ringlets that are made to sport round the face. *a* **1864** HAWTHORNE *Amer. Note-bks.* (1879) II. 101 The wind sported with her gown. **1878** BROWNING *La Saisiaz* 39 Knowledge stands on my experience: all outside its narrow hem, Free surmise may sport and welcome!

d. With *it*.

1793 W. ROBERTS *Looker-on* No. 57 (1794) II. 355, I.. shall..study to surprise her in those moments when she is sporting it with Zephyr and Flora. **1837** *Tait's Mag.* IV. 492 I'll foot it and sport it by fountain and rill.

e. To engage in, follow, or practise sport, esp. field-sport; to hunt or shoot for sport or amusement.

1789 *Loiterer* 20 June 9 The Squire of the Parish..will.. give him unlimited leave to sport over his Manor. **1812** in Col. Hawker *Diary* (1893) I. 42 Any fellow who has sported on the estate at Bradford Wood. **1850** BIGSBY *Shoe & Canoe* II. 130 In summer my friends performed the functions of country gentlemen. They farmed, fished, and sported. ? **1860** DARWIN *More Lett.* (1903) I. 143, I should think no one beside yourself has ever sported in Spitzbergen and Southern Africa. **1890** *Spectator* 13 Dec., The 'sporting' section of society was anxious to be sure whether it could 'sport' in buildings of its own without interference from the police.

3. a. To indulge in sport, fun, or ridicule, *at, over,* or *upon* a person or thing. Also with *it.*

a **1533** LD. BERNERS *Gold. Bk. M. Aurel.* (1546) N iiij b, I find there simple folke, at whom I maie sport. **1623** BINGHAM *Xenophon, Lipsius' Compar. Wars* 4, I come to Darts, which they likewise sport at. **1684** WOOD *Life* 6 Aug., Dr. George Reynell..thrust in among them, upon whome some of the company sported. **1850** BLACKIE *Æschylus* II. 135 A barbarian truly Art thou, if o'er the Greek to sport it thus The fancy tempts thee.

b. To deal *with* in a light or trifling way; to trifle, dally, or play *with* something.

1630 PAGITT *Christianogr.* I. iii. (1636) 137 They sport after the same manner, with by-past offenses, forgiving the sinnes of dayes, monthes, or yeeres. **1663** S. PATRICK *Parab. Pilgrim* xxix. (1687) 349 You could not have well gratified me more than you do, in sporting with that which others more morose would have taken for a reproach. **1769** *Junius Lett.* xxix. (1788) 152 To sport with the reputation..of another, is something worse than weakness. **1796** HUNTER *St.-Pierre's Stud. Nat.* (1799) III. 678 The opinions of the People should not be sported with. **1831** SCOTT *Cast. Dang.* xiii, In irritating a madman you do but sport with your own life. **1850** MERIVALE *Rom. Emp.* xxxvii. (1865) IV. 267 Though he had sported with her feelings for the furtherance of his settled policy. **1861** READE *Cloister & H.* lxxx, My misery is too great to be sported with.

4. †**a.** Of Nature: To produce or develop abnormal or irregular forms or growths as if in sport.

1760 STERNE *Tr. Shandy* IV. (1903) 234 Nature, though she sported.—she sported within a certain circle. **1769** E. BANCROFT *Guiana* 23 The surrounding forests, where Nature sports in primaeval rudeness. *Ibid.* 227 It seems as if Nature sported in variety.

b. Of plants, animals, etc.: To deviate or vary abnormally from the parent stock or specific type; to exhibit or undergo spontaneous mutation.

Cf. the early reflexive use in 1 c, quot. 1723.

1768 R. DOSSIE *Mem. Agric.* I. 444 Seminal varieties [of cabbage] sport, to use the gardener's phrase. **1840** *Penny Cycl.* XVIII. 164/2 In the Malay Archipelago it acquires an enormous size, and sports into a variety called the double pine-apple. **1854** *Poultry Chron.* II. 23 The silver spangles 'sport' less frequently than any variety I have met with. **1882** GRANT ALLEN in *Nature* 27 July 302 All flowers, as we know, easily sport a little in colour.

c. *trans.* Of a plant: To produce (variations) by mutation. *rare*$^{-1}$.

1841 *Florist's Jrnl.* (1846) II. 89 Even in the garden, the Pansy retains its tendency to sport varieties of bloom.

†**5.** *trans.* To amuse or divert (a person); to provide with sport or amusement; to cheer, enliven. *Obs.*

1577 HANMER *Anc. Eccl. Hist., Euseb.* VIII. xxiv, He beeing brought out of prison, and linked with malefactors to pastime and sport the people. **1579** GOSSON *Sch. Abuse* (Arb.) 31 Yet will they seeke when they neede not, to bee sported abrode at playes and Pageauntes. **1612** J. DAVIES (Heref.) *Muse's Sacr.* Wks. (Grosart) II. 25/2 There's nought hath being got On, or in Earth, in Water, or in Aire, That eyther feedes, or heales, or sports me not. **1638** SIR T. HERBERT *Trav.* (ed. 2) 13 We..were sported all the way (till we dropt anchor) by Whales. *a* **1763** SHENSTONE *Economy* II. 4 Nor grove nor stream Invites thee forth to sport thy drooping Muse.

6. †**a.** To express or represent in music or poetry. *Obs.*$^{-1}$

1693 DRYDEN *Persius* VI. 9 Now, sporting on thy Lyre the Loves of Youth, Now Virtuous Age, and venerable Truth.

†**b.** To play or toy with (something). *Obs. rare.*

1709 MRS. MANLEY *Secr. Mem.* (1736) IV. 106 She would ..sport his Lips with her Fingers. **1807–10** TANNAHILL *Poems* (1846) 29 He baits the trap—catches a mouse—He sports it round the floor.

c. To pass, spend, or enjoy (time) in sport or amusement. Also with *away*.

1760 FAWKES, etc. *Anacreon. Odes* xlix. 6 First draw a Nation blithe and gay, Laughing and sporting Life away. **1793** BURNS '*When wild war's deadly blast was blawn*' iii At length I reach'd the bonie glen, Where early life I sported.

1871 R. Ellis *Catullus* lxviii. 16 Whiles in jollity life sported a spring holiday.

7. To take or cast *away* in or as in sport; to throw *away* wantonly or recklessly; to scatter or squander. Now *rare.*

1713 *Guardian* No. 72, Let him who wantonly sports away the peace of a poor lady, consider what discord he sows in families. **1763** Wilkes in *N. Briton* (1772) III. 17 The liberty of an English subject is not to be sported away with impunity. **1778** *Ann. Reg., Hist. Eur.* 136/1 He had sported away thirty thousand lives. **1798** *Geraldina* I. 76 Since we could find money to sport away at this rate, he would wait no longer. **1869** Freeman *Norm. Conq.* (1875) III. 39 The wealth of Eadward's shrine was borne away to be sported broadcast among the minions of Henry's court.

II. In slang or colloquial uses.

†**8.** To read (an author) for sport or amusement. *Obs. rare.*

1693 *Humours Town* 16 Then for Books, 'tis only to sport an Author in a Bookseller's Shop. *a* **1704** T. Brown *Lond. & Lacedem. Oracles* Wks. 1709 III. iii. 122 Last Night being very restless in my Bed, I thought fit to divert the Time with Sporting an Author.

†**9. a.** To invest or stake (money) in some sport or in a highly speculative undertaking; to bet or wager. Also, to lay or make a (bet). *Obs.*

1707 *Refl. upon Ridicule* 386 She mingles with the Rascality, to sport the little Money she has got. **1784** *New Spectator* No. 10. 2 The man who ventures to sport that money in a lottery which ought to be appropriated to other uses, is but too apt to fly to the private gaming table. **1802** *Spirit Publ. Jrnls.* VI. 333 During the time allowed before starting,..great clamour ensued, and much money was sported. **1806** *Ibid.* X. 60 Not a few bets were sported on the occasion. **1850** Thackeray *Pendennis* xix, The chaps will win your money as sure as you sport it.

fig. **1826** Hood *Backing the Favourite* ii, At dear O'Neil's first start, I sported all my heart.

†**b.** *absol.* To engage in betting; to speculate.

1760 C. Johnston *Chrysal* (1822) I. iv. 29 Sporting upon private adventures, taking in unwary confidence, flinging the fair trader,..were now too small a game for me. **1813** *Ann. Reg., Chron.* 44 He..for some years had sported considerably on the turf.

c. To spend (money) freely or extravagantly and with ostentation.

1859 H. Kingsley *G. Hamlyn* xxxi, I took him for a flash overseer, sporting his salary, and I was as thick as you like with him. **1896** Farjeon *J. Fordham* iii. 279 Louis had plenty of money to sport; e'd been backin' winners.

10. a. To display or exhibit, esp. in public or company. Freq. with implication of some degree of parade, ostentation, or show.

Very common from *c* 1770 to *c* 1830. The groups of quotations illustrate variation in the object.

(*a*) **1712** Steele *Spect.* No. 366 ¶3 The Numbers..are as loose and unequal, as those in which the British Ladies sport their Pindaricks. **1768** [W. Donaldson] *Life Sir B. Sapskull* I. iv. 31 My grandfather [might have] missed the opportunity of sporting his historical abilities. **1784** *New Spectator* No. 22. 3 The consequence of Miss Pedant's so universally sporting her knowledge is, that she is forsaken by all the world. **1800** Coleridge *Lett.* (1895) 323 He sported of his own account a theologico-astronomical hypothesis. **1844** E. FitzGerald *Lett.* (1889) I. 145 Don't suppose I think it good philosophy in myself to keep here out of the world, and sport a gentle Epicurism. **1867** Froude *Short Stud.* I. 138 If a man..sports loose views on morals at a decent dinner party,..he is not invited again.

(*b*) **1768** [W. Donaldson] *Life Sir B. Sapskull* II. xx. 158 [He] bought a set of horses..and sported the gayest equipage at all public places. **1785** Trusler *Mod. Times* I. 146 Here's Parson Rawbones... I shall sport him..at a day lecture, or an early sacrament. **1819** Crabbe *T. Hall* xv. 206 Then I shall hear what Envy will remark When I shall sport the ponies in the park. **1838** Dickens *Nickleby* xxiii, A pilot, who sported a boat-green door, with window frames of the same colour. **1868** Miss Braddon *Run to Earth* i, You sported your pocket-book too freely last night.

(*c*) **1784** *New Spectator* No. 22. 4 Mamma, and a Constant Admirer, sported their conspicuous..presence in the upper-boxes. **1819** *Metropolis* III. 132 She may be seen, when highly dressed, sporting her fine figure at her balcony.

b. To display on the person; to wear.

Very common from *c* 1780.

1778 *The Love Feast* 30 Some macaroni Barristers have presumed to sport Bags and Pig-Tails. **1786** Mrs. A. M. Bennett *Juvenile Indiscr.* I. 144 The regimentals,..stiff plaited chitterling, and silk stockings, were sported at church. **1805** T. Harral *Scenes of Life* III. 64 One of his fingers, however, sported a ring. **1849** Col. Hawker *Diary* (1893) Sported my Peninsular medal this day at the Queen's Levée. *a* **1868** M. J. Higgins *Ess.* (1875) 161 His ostensible luggage is small, yet he sports a wonderful variety of garments. **1893** Vizetelly *Glances Back* I. i. 6 A country gentleman, sporting the orthodox blue coat,..and top-boots.

c. To set up, go in for, keep, support, or use (a carriage, etc.).

1806 Surr *Winter in London* I. 24 To retain the coach and black geldings which old Sawyer had sported before him. **1813** Hor. Smith *Horace in London* 127 With a low bow I'll quit the stage, And sport a villa near Parnassus. **1819** *Metropolis* III. 124 She is not, however, the only one..who sports her wax-lights from the retrenchment in coals. **1858** E. B. Ramsay *Remin.* v. (1867) 119 We hope some day to sport buttons.

d. In other uses (see quots.).

1770 *Gentl. Mag.* XL. 560 It is said by the sons of science at Oxford, of a man in ebrious circumstances, That he cannot sport a right line. **1788** Grose *Dict. Vulgar T.* (ed. 2), *To sport or flash one's ivory*, to shew one's teeth. **1794** *Gentl. Mag.* LXIV. 1085/2 They sported knowing, and they sported ignorant; they sported an ægrotat... They sported an exeat, they sported a dormiat. **1877** *Five Years Penal Servitude* 82 If a man wishes to see the governor, the doctor, or the chaplain, he is to 'sport the broom', lay his little hairbroom on the floor at the door, directly the cell is opened in the morning.

11. (Chiefly *Univ. slang.*) **a.** *to sport* † *timber*, or (usu. *one's* or *the*) *oak*, to keep one's door shut. Also *fig.*

1785 Grose *Dict. Vulg. T.* s.v. *Oak.* **1788** *Ibid.* (ed. 2), *To sport timber*, to keep one's outside door shut: this term is used in the inns of courts to signify denying one's self. **1806** J. Beresford *Miseries Hum. Life* vi. xxxv, Seeing the sun quietly slink behind a mass of black clouds, where he *sports oak* for the rest of the day. **1828** [H. D. Beste] *Italy* 275 There was no need, in the college phrase, to *sport oak.* **1911** Beerbohm *Zuleika D.* xii. 187 The man who now occupied my room had sported his oak—my oak. **1932** R. Aldington *Soft Answers* 72 My bell rang again... Had they come back to make my flat the battleground for another Idiot scene? It was no use sporting the oak with the lights in my windows. **1951** S. Spender *World within World* ii. 50 If one arrived early one was liable to find the heavy outer door of his room, called 'the oak', sported as a sign that he was not to be disturbed. **1974** J. I. M. Stewart *Gaudy* viii. 145 The light on the little landing was extinguished, but Ivo Mumford's oak had not been sported.

b. To close or shut (a door), esp. from the inside and as a sign that one is engaged.

c **1803-** [see oak *sb.* 4 c]. **1824** *Blackw. Mag.* Oct. 460 *note*, The door being *sported*, simply means that it was *shut*. **1850** Kingsley *A. Locke* xiii, Stop that till I see whether the door is sported. **1889** Gretton *Memory's Harkback* 59 His door was always sported; he had but little intercourse with the other Fellows.

c. To shut (a person) *in* by closing the door.

1825 Hone *Every-day Bk.* I. 291 Shutting my room door, as if I was 'sported in'. **1852** Bristed *Five Yrs. Eng. Univ.* (ed. 2) 336 Generally..your Cantab takes care to guard against such a surprise by 'sporting' himself in.

†**12.** To open (a door) with some force or violence; to force open. *Obs.*

1806 J. Beresford *Miseries Hum. Life* xiv. vi, Your half-fastened door is unceremoniously sported by a billow, which completely swamps your dressing-room. **1815** Scott *Guy M.* xlviii, Gae down and let loose the dog;..they're sporting the door of the Custom-house.

13. To entertain or treat (a person) with food or drink by way of compliment or hospitality. Also with double object. *rare.*

1828 Lytton *Pelham* III. xvi. 277 He kept his horses, and sported the set to champagne and venison. **1830** —— *P. Clifford* iv, I doesn't care if I sports you a glass of port. **1894** A. Morrison *Tales of Mean Streets* 41 There was a milliner's window, with a show of..hats... 'Which d'yer like, Lizer?—.. I'll sport yer one.'

Hence **'sported** *ppl. a.* (in sense 11 b).

1872 'A. Merion' *Odd Echoes Oxf.* 38 No more buttery, beer, and grub, No more rows with sported oak! **1887** Jessopp *Arcady* 171 Outside the 'sported door' of some college magnate.

sporta'bility. [f. next + -ity.] Capacity for being sportive or playful.

1768 Sterne *Sent. Journ., Passport*, I have something within me which cannot bear the shock of the least indecent insinuation; in the sportability of chit-chat I have often endeavoured to conquer it. **1782** Eliz. Blower *Geo. Bateman* III. 105 Assuming an air of juvenile sportability. **1835** *Fraser's Mag.* XII. 235 We see the Greek girl preparing to sing with a languishing sportability of air.

†**'sportable,** *a. Obs.*$^{-1}$ [f. sport *v.* + -able.] Capable of being sportive.

1767 Sterne *Tr. Shandy* ix. vi, He had lost the sportable key of his voice, which gave sense and spirit to his tale.

'sportance. *rare.* [f. sport *v.* + -ance.] Sport, play; sportive or frolicsome activity.

c **1440** *Cast. Persev.* 141 in *Macro Plays*, Dere Frendys, we thanke ȝou of all good dalyaunce & of all ȝoure specyal sportaunce. **1584** Peele *Arraign. Paris* i. iii, The rounde in a circle our sportance must be; Holde handes in a hornepype, all gallant in glee. **1891** F. Thompson *Sister-Songs* (1895) 45 Where sprites of so essential kind Set their paces, Surely they shall leave behind The green traces Of their sportance in the mind.

†**sporteer.** *Obs.*$^{-1}$ [f. sport *sb.*^{1}] One who is given to sport.

1654 *Citie Matrons* 3 Renegado Wives, Ladies of Pleasure, Sporteers, and starch'd Exchangers.

sporter ('spɔətə(r)). Also 6 *Sc.* sportour. [f. sport *v.* + -er^2. Cf. disporter.]

†**1.** *Sc.* One who amuses or diverts others; a buffoon or jester. *Obs.*

1536 Bellenden *Cron. Scot.* (1821) I. 199 He tuk sic delite in singaris, sportouris, and menstralis. **1596** Dalrymple tr. *Leslie's Hist. Scot.* II. 14 To seik out..all persounis, minstrelis, gemsteris, sportouris, gyuen till ydlenes. *Ibid.* 30 Be a certane sportour [L. *morione*] he was spyet.

2. One who is given to, or takes part in, sport of any kind; a gamester; a sportsman or sporting man.

1611 Cotgr., *Ioueür*, a player, gamester; dallier, sporter. **1658** E. Phillips *Myst. Love* 89 There was a Gallant in the Town, a brave and jolly Sporter. **1684** D'Urfey *Races at New-market* in *Bagford Ball.* (1876) 80 Run and endeavour to bubble the sporters. **1709** *Brit. Apollo* No. 44. 2/2 The Sporters in Venus's Garden. **1751** Smollett *Per. Pickle* viii, The beast [a horse] was too keen a sporter to choose any other way than that which the stag followed. **1768** *Woman of Honor* III. 36 The great sporters at the races have no..idea of keeping up the breed of horses. **1810** *Splendid Follies* III. 192 This illustrious-hearted young sporter.

b. A sporting dog.

1825 Loudon *Encycl. Agric.* §6643 The trouble occasioned to the master will be trifling, because connected with a pleasing employ to him as a sportsman, and who will thus have his own sporters for nothing.

c. As a moth-name.

1832 J. Rennie *Consp. Butterfl. & Moths* 81 The Sporter (*Diphthera ludifica*).

†**3.** *transf.* = sport *sb.*^{1} 6 b. *Obs. rare.*

1723 P. Blair *Pharmaco-Bot.* i. 16 These [varieties] may justly be called Sporters or Strollers, so many *Lusus Naturæ* sporting themselves from more simple Colours [etc.].

4. One who trifles *with* something serious.

1834 J. Brown *Sanctification* vii. 330 A sporter with my misery, he would have but tormented me before the time.

5. *colloq.* One who sports or wears a garment.

1892 *Daily News* 6 July 3/6 The sporters of special blazers and dainty flannels look hardly less miserable.

sportful ('spɔətfʊl), *a.* [f. sport *sb.*^{1} Freq. in the 17th c.; in the 19th chiefly used by Carlyle.]

1. Yielding sport, diversion, or entertainment; having an element of recreation, play, or frolic.

c **1400** *Beryn* 294 Othir beddis [of herbs]..ful fressh i-dight For comers to the hoost, riȝte a sportful sight. **1436** *Pol. Poems* (Rolls) II. 155 Hyt was a sportfulle syghte, How hys darttes he did schak. **1591** Sylvester *Du Bartas* i. iii. 259 If neere unto the Eleusinian Spring, Som sport-full Jig som wanton Shepheard sing. **1611** Middleton & Dekker *Roaring Girle* D.'s Wks. 1873 III. 163 Lets away. Of all the yeare this is the sportfulst day. **1657** S. Purchas *Pol. Flying-Ins.* 289 The Drones are a lazie and carelesse generation, delighting themselves in sportfull recreations. **1700** Rowe *Amb. Step-Moth.* iii. i, Where the sportful Chace had call'd us forth. **1760** Home *Siege of Aquileia* v, If from Rome thou went'st A sportful journey to the Baian shore. **1798** Ferriar *Illustr. Sterne*, etc. 242 They tempt the reader..into pleasing and sportful fields of narration. **1830** Carlyle *Misc. Ess.* (1888) III. 25 A view of man and man's life not less cheerful, even sportful, than it is deep and calm. **1858** —— *Fredk. Gt.* x. ii. (1872) II. 580 A young fool, bent on sportful pursuits instead of serious.

b. Devised or carried on merely in sport; not earnest or serious.

1601 Shaks. *Twel. N.* v. i. 373 How with a sportfull malice it was follow'd, May rather plucke on laughter then reuenge. **1606** —— *Tr. & Cr.* i. iii. 335 Though't be a sportfull Combate, Yet in this triall much opinion dwels. **1651** H. More *Second Lash* in *Enthus. Tri.*, etc. (1656) 185, I shall now begin the game of my personated Enmitie, or sportfull Colluctation with him.

c. Of movements: Lively, frolicsome.

1691 Ray *Creation* (1714) 41 This sportful dance of atoms. **1713** *Guardian* No. 71, He couches and frisks about in a thousand sportful motions. **1848** *Fraser's Mag.* XXXVIII. 71 The sportful leap of a trout.

2. Of persons, their minds, etc.: Having an inclination or tendency to engage in sport or play; sportive, playful.

a **1593** Marlowe *Edw. II*, i. i. 64 Crownets of pearle about his naked armes, And in his sportfull hands an Oliue tree. **1593** Shaks. *3 Hen. VI*, v. i. 18 Oh vnbid spight, is sportfull Edward come? **1632** Massinger *Emperor of East* i. ii, There I am call'd The Squire of Dames,..And by the allowance of some sportful ladies, Honour'd with that title. **1671** Wood *Life* (O.H.S.) II. 238 She not pleasing him, being not sportfull enough. **1755** *Man* No. 23. 2 The powers of the imagination, and the sportful wits of men are rouzed..by..nature in the Spring. **1767** Sir W. Jones *Seven Fountains* Poems (1777) 37 But when the sportful train beheld from far The nymphs returning with the stately car. **1827** Carlyle *Germ. Rom.* II. 110 They who were then sportful on the green are now serious in the church. **1827** —— *Misc.* (1857) I. 332 With a heart at once of the most earnest and the most sportful cast.

transf. **1633** P. Fletcher *Purple Isl.* iv. xiii, Here sportfull Laughter dwells, here ever sitting, Defies all lumpish griefs, and wrinkled care. **1707** *Curiosities in Husb.* 41 Figures.. which we admire as the Work of sportful Nature.

b. Of animals, birds, fishes, etc.

1607 Topsell *Four-footed Beasts* 6 They [i.e. monkeys] are very sportful, and giuen to imitate the actions of men like apes. **1650** Fuller *Pisgah* ii. xiii. 271 And the most sportfull fishes dare not jest with the edged-tools of this Dead-Sea. **1697** Dryden *Virg. Georg.* i. 497 When sportful Coots run skimming o'er the Strand. **1768–74** Tucker *Lt. Nat.* (1834) I. 91 The poet beholds shady groves, sportful flocks, and verdant lawns. **1768** Sir W. Jones *Solima* 96 The camels bounded o'er the flowery lawn, Like the swift ostrich, or the sportful fawn. **1862** D. Campbell *Lang., Poet., & Music Highland Clans* 145 Sportful in his proud career, he [the salmon] springs at the midges.

'sportfully, *adv.* Now *rare.* [f. prec.] In a sportful manner; in sport; jestingly; sportively.

a **1568** Sidney *Arcadia* iii. xvii. (1912) 452 And [this] unfathered Lady could sportfully put on the Lions skin upon her owne fair shoulders. **1632** G. Herbert *Priest Temple* ix, He..talks..also in a serious manner, never jestingly, or sportfully. **1681–6** J. Scott *Chr. Life* ii. iii. 130 Now there is nothing more surprising..than to see or hear a serious thing sportfully represented. **1782** J. Brown *Nat. & Rev. Relig.* vi. i. (1796) 447 This commandment forbids..our profaning and abusing his name..in angrily or sportfully cursing. **1831** Carlyle *Misc. Ess.* (1888) III. 179 Nor in his satire does he ever lose pleasure but rebukes sportfully.

'sportfulness. Now *rare.* [f. as prec.] The quality or state of being sportful; sportiveness.

1581 Sidney *Apol. Poetrie* (Arb.) 65 So as neither the admiration and commiseration, nor the right sportfulnes, is by their mungrell Tragy-comedie obtained. *a* **1631** Donne *Let.* Wks. (1633) 371 When sadnesse dejects me,..I kindle squibs about mee againe, and flie into sportfulnesse and company. **1667** H. More *Div. Dial.* ii. xiii. (1713) 126 The birth of Monsters; which I look upon but as a piece of Sportfulness in the order of things. **1710** R. Ward *Life H. More* 48 It is hard to represent the Wit, Reason, Zeal, Phancy, Sportfulness, and Seriousness,..there is contain'd in this Writing. **1780** *Mirror* No. 100, A sportfulness of external behaviour. **1831** Carlyle *Misc. Ess.* (1888) III. 98

Majesty rather than grace, still more than lightness or sportfulness, characterises him. **1898** *Christian Herald* (N.Y.) 12 Jan. 24/1 That which opened in sportfulness ended in violence.

‖**sportif** (spɔrtif), *a.* (*sb.*) [Fr.] Of a sporting character, sportive; interested in or pursuing athletic sports. Also, of a garment: suitable for sporting or informal wear. Also *absol.* and as *sb.*

1934 C. LAMBERT *Music Ho!* IV. 242 The musical equivalent of this obsession with the mechanical, the *sportif* and the soi-disant contemporary, is provided by the naïvely realistic orchestral pieces of Honegger, such as *Pacific 231* and *Rugby*. **1938** E. HEMINGWAY *Fifth Column* (1939) 171 There were two kinds: the drunkards and the sportifs... The sportifs took it out in exercise. **1958** *Manch. Guardian* 4 Aug. 3/6 Last year it was..the man who played boogie-woogie on a gramophone all night in the next room and when I complained said I wasn't *sportif* and made a bigger row than ever. **1963** *Times* 1 May 9/6 Elegance is the word that immediately comes to mind—elegance with more than a touch of the *sportif*, for the performance is a good bit better than you might expect from a car of less than 1-litre capacity. **1966** *Listener* 30 June 939/1 All nations are now *sportif*, although they do not necessarily acclaim the same sports as we do. **1977** *Times* 30 July 10/1 The hooded sweat-shirt is..casual and sportif yet neat and warm.

'**sportiness.** *colloq.* [f. SPORTY *a.*] Sporty quality or tendency.

1896 *Daily Chron.* 31 Oct. 8/2 We should have ruthlessly stamped out the first symptom of 'sportiness' in our nursing staff.

sporting ('spɔətɪŋ), *vbl. sb.* [f. SPORT *v.*]

1. a. The action of the verb; engagement or participation in sport.

1483 *Vulgaria* 4 Thoos chylder..which are gouen so muche to play & sportyng. **1581** A. HALL *Iliad* II. 41 His mates..in diuers mirth the shore in sporting fil. **1582** T. WATSON *Centurie of Love* xcii, Hebe,..Goddesse of youth, and youthlie sporting. **1638** SIR T. HERBERT *Trav.* (ed. 2) 159 The higher roomes are garnisht with variety of landskips, and represents their way of sporting, hawking,.. and other fancies. **1662** J. CHANDLER *Van Helmont's Oriat.* 95 Let us feign by sporting, and grant a heat to be actually under the Earth and Water. **1796** WINDHAM *Speeches* (1812) I. 286 Dogs kept for sporting, were peculiar to the rich, and though he did not mean to arraign sporting, he thought it not the highest sort of amusement. **1827** D. JOHNSON *Ind. Field Sports* 178 From this time their sporting was conducted on a much more grand and formidable scale. **1838** LYTTON *Alice* II. v, Maltravers..had neither outshone the establishment, nor interfered with the sporting of his fellow-squires.

b. An instance or occasion of this; †a sport.

1490 CAXTON *Eneydos* xv. 59 Passynge the tyme in grete playsaunces, festes, playes & sportynges. **1598** MARSTON *Pygmal. Sat.* xxxv, Could he abstaine mid'st such a wanton sporting From doing that, which is not fit reporting? **1614** GORGES *Lucan* III. 86 The common sort to sportings bent. **1687** AYRES *The Swallow* Wks. (1906) 322 Dear Bird thy tunes and sportings here, Delight us all the day.

transf. **1666** BP. S. PARKER *Free & Impart. Censure* (1667) 76 The Quaintest plays and sportings of wit. *Ibid.* 79 Metaphors being only the sportings of Fancy.

2. †**a.** The action on the part of Nature of producing an abnormal form or variety; an instance or occasion of this. *Obs.* Cf. SPORT *sb.*[1] 6.

1695 WOODWARD *Nat. Hist. Earth* I. (1723) 40 They are no Shells, but meer Sportings of active Nature. **1696** WHISTON *Th. Earth* III. iv. 201 [To] ascribe the plainest remains of the Animal and Vegetable Kingdom to the sportings of Nature,..as some persons are inclinable to do. **1746** *Phil. Trans.* XLIV. 317 The *Lusus Naturæ* or sportings of Nature is a general solution too often brought in. **1756** C. LUCAS *Ess. Waters* III. 119 The infinite diversity..may be looked upon as so many sportings of nature.

†**b.** Irregular diffusion or deposition *of* pollen.

1763 *Ann. Reg., Nat. Hist.* VI. 73 Thus..amongst apple-trees, a mixture of fruit hath been observed on the same tree, supposed by the sporting of the farina.

c. The action on the part of plants, etc., of deviating or varying from the parent stock or type by spontaneous mutation; an abnormal form or variation so produced; a sport.

1841 *Florist's Jrnl.* (1846) II. 176 It is doubtful whether any of these sportings will produce a permanent variety. **1842** *Ibid.* III. 84 This is remarkably the case in the natural 'sporting of varieties', as it is called. **1865** GOSSE *Land & Sea* (1874) 371 That ferns are more liable to what is technically called 'sporting', than other plants. **1882** *Garden* 14 Jan. 32/3 The lecturer then alluded to sporting from seed as another method of raising new forms.

3. *attrib.* and *Comb.* **a.** In older usage, as ***sporting device, game, matter, place, time***, etc.

1480 *Coventry Leet-bk.* 458 þe people maken þe same seuerall grounde a sportyng place with shotyng & other games. **1565** COOPER *Thesaurus*, *Ludicrum certamen*, a sportyng game. **1579** L. TOMSON *Calvin's Serm. Tim.* 310/1 It is no sporting matter when the Lorde calleth vs to serue him in this office. **1587** GOLDING *De Mornay* xiv. (1592) 220 So the Soule which is in the Jaile of his souereine Lord God, hath no respit or sporting time to come tell vs what is done there. **1597** SHAKS. *2 Hen. IV*, IV. ii. 105 Like a Schoole broke vp, Each hurryes towards his home, and sporting place.

b. In later and mod. use, as ***sporting celebrity, party, purpose***; freq. in senses 'formed or undertaken for sport', 'concerned with or interested in sport', as ***sporting association, column, event, magazine, newspaper, page, paper, tour***, and 'used in or for sport', as ***sporting bullet, cartridge, dog, gear, goods, gun, jacket***.

1728 RAMSAY *Anacreontic on Love* 25 If that the rain Has wrang'd aught of my sporting-gear. **1789** WHITE *Selborne* cii, No sporting dogs will flush woodcocks till inured to the scent and trained to the sport. **1793-** (*title*), The Sporting Magazine; or Monthly Calendar of the Transactions of the Turf. **1815** *Ann. Reg., Chron.* 110 Several persons of fashion as well as sporting celebrity. **1818** SCOTT *Rob Roy* v, The uniform of a sporting association. **1820** W. TOOKE *Lucian* I. 109 My little sporting-dog..began to bark. **1825** T. HOOK *Sayings* Ser. II. *Man of Many Fr.* (Colburn) 87 Dyson could always make up a little sporting party. **1837** DICKENS *Sk. Boz* 2nd Ser. 53 A brown coat, something between a great-coat and a 'sporting' jacket, on his back. **1849** C. BRONTË *Shirley* III. iv. 75 He reads only a sporting paper. **1860** DICKENS *Uncomm. Trav.* x, If I cherished betting propensities, I should probably be found registered in sporting newspapers [etc.]. **1869** *Boyd's Business Directory* 500 John H. Mann, importer and dealer in guns, fishing tackle, gun powder, and all sporting goods. **1879** *Cassell's Techn. Educ.* I. 271/1 The stout pasteboard sporting cartridges. **1885** 'MRS. ALEXANDER' *At Bay* ii, A little further conversation on financial and sporting topics. **1901** *Bookman* Oct. 123/2 Americans..have noted the peculiarities of the diction of the writers of the sporting columns. **1907** M. E. BRADDON *Dead Love has Chains* vi. 130 Slang has to be forgiven in a man, like smoking, and sporting papers, and motors. **1915** *Lit. Digest* 21 Aug. 360/3 Bozeman Bulger..contributes to the sporting page of the New York *Evening World*. **1920** *Times* 14 June 15/3 Among the sporting events which follow each other in..June, Royal Ascot..is unique. **1961** P. WHITE *Riders in Chariot* ix. 259 He would..go away, or reach for the sporting page. **1978** R. B. PARKER *Judas Goat* xxii. 135 'Picked up a new shotgun at a sporting goods store,' he said.

c. Special Combs., as **sporting-box**, a small residence for use during the sporting season (see BOX *sb.*[2] 14); **sporting door** *Univ. slang* (see quot. and SPORT *v.* 11 b); **sporting editor** *U.S.*, a sports editor; **sporting-house**, a house, hotel, or inn frequented by sportsmen; *U.S.* a betting or gambling house; a brothel or disorderly house; †**sporting-piece**, a plaything; **sporting print**, a print of a scene taken from the field-sports; also *transf.*; †**sporting stock**, a laughing-stock; a butt.

1840 HOWITT *Visits Remark. Places* 1st Ser. 210 The Duke of Devonshire's house..serves for a *sporting-box, when his Grace comes hither in autumn to the moors. **1852** BRISTED *Five Yrs. in Eng. Univ.* (ed. 2) 58 Be it premised, for the benefit of the uninitiated, that Oxonians call the *sporting door 'the oak'. **1857** *Spirit of Times* 1 Aug. 340/2 We see exactly, where the '*sporting editor' of *The Times* has made his fatal mistake about handicaps and handicappers. **1899** T. HALL *Tales* 128 The somewhat intellectual-looking sporting editor of the aforesaid *Universe*. **1857** HUGHES *Tom Brown* I. iv, It is a well-known *sporting-house, and the breakfasts are famous. **1894** STEAD *If Christ came to Chicago* 5 The novice in the sporting house, as well as the hardened old harridan who drives the trade in human flesh, are herded together. **1740-1** RICHARDSON *Pamela* II. 36 Here I am again! a pure *Sporting-piece for the Great! a mere Tennis-ball of Fortune. **1849** THACKERAY *Pendennis* I. xviii. 168 Six *sporting prints, and four groups of opera-dancers..formed the late occupant's pictorial collection. **1964** R. JEFFRIES *Embarrassing Death* viii. 84 Two thousand men eager to pay five or ten shillings for a 'sporting print' every month. **1973** G. GREENE *Honorary Consul* II. iii. 81 A corridor hung with Victorian sporting prints: riders falling into a stream, checked at a bullfinch, rebuked by the master. *a* **1553** UDALL *Royster D.* III. iii, We do hym loute and flocke, And make him among vs, our common *sporting stocke.

sporting ('spɔətɪŋ), *ppl. a.* [f. SPORT *v.*]

1. a. Engaged in sport or play.

1653 HOLCROFT *Procopius, Vandal Wars* I. 22 It was then acounted as an idle riddle among sporting boys. **1725** POPE *Odyss.* VI. 112 O'er the green mead the sporting virgins play.

†**b.** Sportive; playful. *Obs. rare.*

1600 J. PORY tr. *Leo's Africa* I. 40 [An elephant] will in a sporting maner gently heave up with his snowte such persons as he meeteth. **1656** W. DU GARD tr. *Comenius' Gate Lat. Unl.* 311 They shall feed not upon Ambrosia and Nectar (as the sporting poets did fain) but on hidden.. sweets. **1712** SWIFT *Wonderful Prophecy* Wks. 1751 III. I. 173 Think not that this baleful dog-star only shaketh his tail at you in waggery... It is not a sporting tail, but a fiery tail.

c. Of plants, etc. (See SPORT *v.* 4 b.)

1850 *Beck's Florist* 211 We would recommend a trial of the seed from these sporting flowers. **1859** DARWIN *Orig. Spec.* i. (1860) 9 'Sporting plants'; by this term gardeners mean a single bud or offset, which suddenly assumes a new and sometimes very different character from that of the rest of the plant. **1886** *Field* 6 Mar. 303/2 The sporting character of roses was as much observed at that time as now.

2. a. Interested in, accustomed to take part in, field sports or similar amusements; *spec.* in phr. ***sporting parson***.

1748 C'TESS SHAFTESBURY in *Priv. Lett. Ld. Malmesbury* (1870) I. 71 There we met several sporting gentlemen. **1826** F. REYNOLDS *Life & Times* I. iii. 99 The family consisted of the Dowager Lady Grandison,..an old Irish Major—a sporting parson—the house apothecary—my father, my aunt, and myself. **1828** LYTTON *Pelham* II. xxiv, Sporting characters..were a species of bipeds that I would never recognise as belonging to the human race. **1859** THACKERAY *Virgin.* vi, Harry was away from home with some other sporting friends. **1885** MISS BRADDON *Wyllard's Weird* iv, 'I can't think what has come to Grahame,' muttered a sporting squire to his next neighbour. **1901** *Daily Tel.* 23 July 10/6 Those who imagined that the last 'sporting parson' had disappeared from the Church of England are quite mistaken. **1982** M. YOUNG *Elmhirsts of Dartington* ii. 21 His mother..meant him to be a priest, not a sporting parson.. but a proper God-fearing priest.

b. Esp. ***sporting man***; now used to denote a sportsman of an inferior type or one who is interested in sport from purely mercenary motives. Also used in other collocations referring to low gaming and betting.

1824 R. HUMPHREYS *Mem. J. Decastro* 206 Bob Todrington, a sporting man (caricatured by Old Dighton). **1840** BARHAM *Ingol. Leg.* Ser. I. *St. Odille* vi, Now I think I've been told,—for I'm no sporting man,—That the 'knowing-ones' call this by far the best plan. **1853** R. S. SURTEES *Sp. Tour* (1893) 235 'Is he inclined to go the pace?' 'Oh, quite,' replied Jack; 'his great desire is to be thought a sportsman.' 'A sportsman, or a sporting man?' asked Soapey. **1857** *Household Words* 12 Sept. 264/1 With its sparring snobs, and flashing satins, and sporting gents and painted cheeks. **1889** *Pall Mall G.* 21 Oct. 6/1 Every sporting man is flattered if termed a sportsman, but it would be almost an insult to speak to a sportsman as a sporting man. **1902** G. B. SHAW *Mrs Warren's Profession* p. xxix, Well, does anybody who knows the sporting world really believe that bookmakers are worse than their neighbors? **1946** K. TENNANT *Lost Haven* (1947) ii. 40 Her mother was entertaining some sporting friends who had dropped in to settle up certain transactions. **1967** S. BECKETT *Stories & Texts for Nothing* III. 84 Thronged already with sporting men fevering to get their bets out of harm's way before the bars open.

c. *N. Amer.* Used *spec.* to denote a prostitute or loose woman, as ***sporting girl, woman***. Cf. SPORTSWOMAN b.

1925 *Amer. Speech* I. 151/2 The woman of the underworld is spoken of as a 'sporting woman'. **1938** A. J. LIEBLING *Back where I came From* 152 Most of the women ..go out by the day as house-workers. There may be a few sporting girls, but if so they don't work their own block. **1951** E. PAUL *Springtime in Paris* iv. 89 The *place* Xavier Privas, where the former sporting girls and their male friends congregate. **1971** J. GRAY *Red Lights on Prairies* vi. 143 The existence of a colony of sporting women at Nose Creek was prejudicially affecting the morals and welfare of the Community.

3. a. Characterized by sport or sportsmanlike conduct; affording or producing sport. Also, of or characterized by conduct consonant with that of a sportsman or 'good sport'.

1799 *Times* 1 June 4/3 Hunting Box, pleasantly situate in a sporting part of the Country. **1867** F. FRANCIS *Angling* iv. (1880) 136 It is the most sporting way of fishing for them. **1893** *Times* 29 Apr. 11/4 The debate was naturally too one-sided to afford any sporting interest either to the combatants or to the spectators. **1897** MISS KINGSLEY *W. Africa* 617 Those very sporting vessels, the British and African, and the Royal African steamers. **1920** 'O. DOUGLAS' *Penny Plain* xi. 115 'Isn't it awful..about our minister marrying..a girl twenty years younger than himself.' 'But how sporting of him,' Pamela said. **1923** WODEHOUSE *Inimitable Jeeves* x. 112, I had.. got as far as the lift before I remembered what it was that I had meant to do to reward Jeeves for his really sporting behaviour in this matter of the chump Cyril. **1962** S. RAVEN *Close of Play* III. xv. 186 By declaring when they did, they left Baron's Lodge with three-hundred and twenty-two runs to make in two hours... It was, on the whole, a sporting declaration.

b. ***sporting chance***, a chance such as is met with or taken in sport; one of an uncertain or doubtful nature. Also, an opportunity that a sportsman might consider. *colloq.*

1897 MISS KINGSLEY *W. Africa* 252 One must diminish dead certainties to the level of sporting chances along here. **1913** *Granta* 7 Mar. 255/2 If bad shows are booked for this theatre the *actors* are not the people to be blamed; they are, naturally, trying to do their best—give them a sporting chance. **1977** M. ALLEN *Spence in Petal Park* xxxi. 146 All that rubbish they learnt on the rugger field about giving the other fellow a sporting chance... The world just doesn't work like that.

sportingly ('spɔətɪŋlɪ), *adv.* [f. prec.]

1. As a matter of amusement or diversion; in or with jesting words or speech; not earnestly or seriously. ? *Obs.*

1576 FLEMING *Panopl. Epist.* 211 Pythagoras..first toucheth the condition and estate of him, whether seriously or sportingly, it is vncertaine. **1581** SIDNEY *Apol. Poetrie* (Arb.) 44 The Satirick..Who sportingly neuer leaueth, vntil hee make a man laugh at folly. **1651** H. MORE *Second Lash* in *Enthus. Tri.*, etc. (1656) M j b, Thus Reader, is your argument against laughing as solidly argued as sportingly laughed out of countenance. **1674** BP. BROWNRIG *Serm.* II. 5 The mysteries of Religion are not slightly..or sportingly to be handled. **1768** STERNE *Sent. Journ.*, *Passport, Versailles*, Besides, continued I, a little sportingly—I have come laughing all the way from London to Paris. **1848** S. WARREN *Now & Then* iv. 173, I sportingly said 'No, come with us'.

2. With sportive, playful, frolicsome, or lively action or demeanour.

c **1630** RISDON *Surv. Devon* § 107 The river Ex sportingly disperseth itself into branches. *a* **1639** W. WHATELEY *Prototypes* II. xxvi. (1640) 22 Sports must be done sportingly, not with the like seriousnesse..as serious matters. **1776** S. J. PRATT *Pupil of Pleas.* (1777) I. 46 Catching up a myrtle-sprig, [I] kept it, sportingly, as if to conceal a new sigh. *c* **1789** *New Liverpool Songster* 337 How echoes the horn in the vale, Whose notes do so sportingly dance on the gale.

b. Towards sport or enjoyment.

a **1643** LD. FALKLAND, etc. *Infallibility* (1646) 156, I told you the applying of it to that place would have afforded some game if I had beene so sportingly disposed.

3. In or after the manner characteristic of sport; in sporting language or terms; like a sportsman.

1798 *Sporting Mag.* XI. 57 Fertile fabrications so sportingly portrayed. **1831** *Blackw. Mag.* XXIX. 872 He was beat by three good lengths... But to speak less sportingly [etc.]. **1844** W. H. MAXWELL *Sports & Adv. Scot.* iii. (1855) 38 No man rode more sportingly to hounds. *Ibid.* xx. 173 A salmon.. took the fly sportingly. **1883** *Pall Mall G.* 21 Dec. 4/2 Next to good sport, the honest English sportsman likes to dress sportingly.

† **sporting-wise**, *adv. Obs.*⁻¹ [f. SPORTING *ppl. a.* + -WISE.] In sport or jest; jestingly.

1579–80 NORTH *Plutarch* (1895) IV. 207 There were some which sporting-wise did openly call him Alexander.

sportive (ˈspɔətɪv), *a.* and *sb.* [f. SPORT *sb.*¹ or *v.* + -IVE.]

A. *adj.* **1. a.** Inclined to jesting or levity; disposed to a playful lightness of thought or expression.

1590 SHAKS. *Com. Err.* I. ii. 58, I am not in a sportiue humor now: Tell me, and dally not, where is the monie? **1593** NASHE *Christ's T.* Wks. (Grosart) IV. 260 They are nought els but cleanly coyned lyes, which some pleasant sportiue wittes haue deuised, to gull them most groselie. **1676** GLANVILL *Seasonable Refl.* 31 'Tis equally absurd to be sportive about affairs that are serious. **1778** MME. D'ARBLAY *Diary* 26 Aug., Two little productions.. full of a sportive humour. **1782** V. KNOX *Ess.* (1819) III. 238 With a rich and sportive fancy he combined a solid judgment. **1837** DISRAELI *Venetia* I. ii, A curious fountain carved.. in one of those capricious moods of sportive invention. **1855** MACAULAY *Hist. Eng.* III. 541 Three generations of serious and of sportive writers wept and laughed over the venality of the senate.

b. Characterized by lightness or levity; not earnest or serious.

1593 NASHE *Christ's T.* Wks. (Grosart) IV. 109 The younge men in their merry-running Madrigals, and sportiue Base-bidding Rundelayes. **1655** *Musarum Deliciæ* Title-p., Conteining severall select Pieces of sportive Wit. **1742** GRAY *Spring* 42 Methinks I hear in accents low The sportive kind reply. **1743** FRANCIS tr. *Hor., Odes* II. xii. 17 In raillery the sportive jest. **1813** HOR. SMITH *Horace in London* 46 Whom Echo.. Shall chaunt in sportive numbers? **1826** F. REYNOLDS *Life & Times* II. 166 The ensuing sportive anecdotes may appear frivolous. **1882** OUIDA *Maremma* I. 32 Of sportive love offered and returned.

2. Of the nature of, inclined to, amorous sport or wantonness. Now *arch.*

1594 SHAKS. *Rich. III*, I. i. 14, I, that am not shap'd for sportiue trickes, Nor made to court an amorous Looking-glasse. *c* **1600** —— *Sonn.* cxxi. 6 For why should others false adulterat eyes Giue salutation to my sportiue blood? **1855** BROWNING *Fra Lippo Lippi* 6 Where sportive ladies leave their doors ajar.

3. a. Disposed to be playful or frolicsome.

a **1637** B. JONSON *Horace, Art Poet.* 150 Stuff'd menacings [fit] The angry brow, the sportive, wanton things. **1651** JER. TAYLOR *Serm. for Year* II. x. 129 The bait is in their mouths, and they are sportive; but the hook hath strook their nostrils, and they shall never escape the ruine. *a* **1721** PRIOR *To Madam K.P.* 7 Lively the Nymphs and sportive are their Swains. **1762** FALCONER *Shipwr.* II. 70 Beneath the lofty stem A shoal of sportive dolphins they discern. **1807** CRABBE *Par. Reg.* II. 417 There, Werter sees the sportive children fed. **1819** SHELLEY *Cyclops* 92 This sportive band of Satyrs near the caves. **1865** ALEX. SMITH *Summer in Skye* I. 259 He cannot be sportive for the fear that is in his heart.

transf. **1697** POTTER *Antiq. Greece* (1715) II. xx. 401 Then tow'rds the Wind the sportive Ashes cast Upon the Sea. **1784** COWPER *Task* I. 346 So sportive is the light Shot through the boughs, it dances as they dance. *Ibid.* 567 The sportive wind blows wide Their flutt'ring rags. **1798** WORDSW. *'Five years have past'* 16 Little lines Of sportive wood run wild. **1827** R. POLLOCK *Course of Time* 111, Its breath was cold, and made the sportive blood Heavy and dull and stagnant.

b. Of qualities, etc.

1743 FRANCIS tr. *Hor., Odes* III. xviii. 13 See my flocks in sportive vein Frisk it o'er the verdant plain. **1812** J. WILSON *Isle of Palms* II. 450 A gaudy flag.. Hung up in sportive joy by those Whose sports and joys are past. **1815** J. SMITH *Panorama Sci. & Art* II. 222 Exhibiting a kind of dance, performed with the most sportive vivacity.

4. a. Of or pertaining to, marked or characterized by, sport; of the nature of sport or amusement; affording or providing sport or diversion.

1705 HICKERINGILL *Priest-cr.* I. (1721) 52 They go to Bowls, and other sportive Exercises every Sunday. **1774** GOLDSM. *Nat. Hist.* (1776) V. 358 He then placed them in a cage at his chamber window, to be amused by their sportive flutterings. **1810** SCOTT *Lady of Lake* I. xviii, The sportive toil.. Had dyed her glowing hue so bright. **1839** T. MITCHELL *Frogs of Aristoph.* 148 *note*, A die (the sportive instrument of playful youth). **1874** MAHAFFY *Social Life Greece* xi. 351 The Greeks made their serious pursuits, especially their religion, sportive.

b. Undertaken, given, etc., in (mere) sport.

1743 FRANCIS tr. *Hor., Odes* I. viii. 16 Where are now the livid scars Of sportive, nor inglorious, wars? **1794** MRS. RADCLIFFE *Myst. Udolpho* xlvii, The apparition of the dead comes not on light or sportive errands. **1837** W. IRVING *Capt. Bonneville* II. 105 Quickened by a sportive volley which the Indians rattled after him. **1849** MACAULAY *Hist. Eng.* iii. I. 400 It was now not a sportive combat, but a war to the death.

5. a. Produced in, or as in, sport; *spec.* of the nature of a sport or abnormal variation; anomalous. Now *rare* or *Obs.*

1796 H. HUNTER *St.-Pierre's Stud. Nat.* (1799) 277 Examine, on their gowns and handkerchiefs, the sportive productions of their imagination. **1799** *Med. Jrnl.* I. 73 The mineral kingdom, with all the riches, beauties, and sportive productions it contains. **1804** PARKINSON *Organic Remains* I. 24 The *vis plastica*, the *vis formativa*, and the sportive creations of nature, were terms yet in frequent use. **1822–7** GOOD *Study Med.* (1829) I. 458 By what means they are rendered subservient to such an infinite variety of sportive and anomalous effects.

b. Of plants, etc.: Liable to sport or vary from the true type; characterized by sporting.

(*a*) **1850** *Beck's Florist* 24 *Duchess of Sutherland*.. is a feathered rosy byblœmen, rather sportive. **1868** DARWIN *Anim. & Pl.* I. 315 [He] was forced to reject some of his new sub-varieties, which he suspected had been produced from a cross, as incorrigibly sportive. **1892** *Gardeners' Chron.* 27 Aug. 250/2 P. aculeatum, though far less sportive than P. angulare, afforded material for a fine selection.

(*b*) **1891** W. ALLAN *Dis. Skin* iv. (ed. 3) 52 It is this sportive tendency manifested by skin diseases which adds so much to the difficulty of their diagnosis.

6. a. Taking part in, following or interested in, sport or sports.

1893 C. G. LELAND *Mem.* I. 37 Uncle William was a kind-hearted 'sportive' man, who took *Bell's Life.* **1969** *Daily Tel.* 13 Mar. 18 Sportive readers of this paper's report yesterday on the pay talks of 90 Tonbridge cricket ball makers are puzzled.. that these craftsmen should be represented by the National Union of Furniture Trade Operatives.

b. Of clothes: suitable for sporting or informal wear. Cf. SPORTIF *a.*

1935 *Amer. Speech* X. 193/2 Combinations like *smoothly sportive, fetchingly feminine*.. are numberless. **1963** C. BEATON *Diary* 15 Feb. (1979) 358 In his yachting jacket and sportive shoes, he has something about his swash-buckling style that reminds me of Douglas Fairbanks, Senior.

† **B.** *sb.* A thing merely amusing or diverting and not of a serious character. *Obs.*⁻¹

1616 E. BOLTON *Hypercritica* (1722) 237 If they have seen that incomparable Earl of Surrey his English translation of Virgil's Æneids.., [they] will bear me witness that those others were Foils and Sportives.

ˈsportively, *adv.* [f. prec. + -LY².]

1. With the lively movements characteristic of sport; playfully.

1597 DRAYTON *Heroical Epistles* 68, I saw the soft ayre sportiuely to take it. **1794** MRS. RADCLIFFE *Myst. Udolpho* xxxvi, Now she moved with solemn steps,.. and now tripped sportively along the path. **1797** —— *Italian* xvii, As they sportively threw about their sugar-plums. **1807–8** W. IRVING *Salmag.* (1824) 340 The females that passed in review before me, tripping sportively along. **1812** CARY *Dante, Purg.* XVI. 88 Forth from his plastic hand.. the soul Comes like a babe, that wantons sportively.

2. In or with sportive or jesting words; jocosely, facetiously.

1631 HEYLIN *St. George* 90 Therefore sportively accoasting him,.. said [etc.]. **1762** STERNE *Tr. Shandy* v. xxxix, Well, my good Doctor, cried my father, sportively. **1780** MME. D'ARBLAY *Diary* June, A sportively complimentary conversation took place. **1807–8** W. IRVING *Salmag.* (1824) 217 In the play of his fancy [he] will sportively say Some delicate censure that pops in his way. **1842** BROWNING *Rudel to the Lady of Tripoli* I, Men call the Flower the Sunflower, sportively. **1871** FREEMAN in W. R. W. Stephens *Life* (1895) II. vii. 46 We were all much troubled to hear.. about your own accident. You were able to speak sportively about [etc.].

3. In sport or jest.

1793 MISS H. M. WILLIAMS *Lett. France* II. 43 One day Lewis XV. sportively created him governor of Lucienne.

ˈsportiveness. [f. as prec.] The fact, quality, or condition of being sportive.

1601 YARINGTON *Two Traj.* III. ii. in Bullen *O. Pl.* IV, Pick out mens eyes, and tell them thats the sport Of hood-man-blinde, without all sportiveness. **1653** WALTON *Angler* i, Shall I conclude her simple, that has her time to begin, or refuse sportiveness as freely as I myself have? **1756–7** tr. *Keysler's Trav.* (1760) III. 95 The virgin mother's looks most exquisitely express her sweet complacency at their innocent sportiveness. **1779** *Mirror* No. 2, In the first character I may sometimes indulge a sportiveness to which I am a stranger in the latter. **1838** DICKENS *Nickleby* xviii, Some very pretty sportiveness ensued. **1858** DORAN *Court Fools* 132 The warrant being drawn up in sportiveness, he signed the document. **1875** JOWETT *Plato* (ed. 2) V. 223 The young of all creatures.. are always.. overflowing with sportiveness and delight at something.

ˈsportless, *a.* [f. SPORT *sb.*¹ + -LESS.] Destitute or devoid of sport; marked by the absence of sport.

1621 G. SANDYS *Ovid's Met.* II. (1626) 28 The Fishes to the bottom diue: nor dare The sportlesse Dolphins tempt the sultrie Ayre. **1631** P. FLETCHER *Pisc. Ecl.* vii. 1 Her weeping eyes in pearled dew she steeps, Casting what sportlesse nights she ever led. **1895** *Baily's Mag.* May 356 The use of the minnow.. is a method of taking fish which is sportless, artless, and as bad as anything I know.

† **sportlet.** *Obs.*⁻¹ [Cf. SPORT *sb.*² and -LET.] A small basket or hand-basket.

1447 BOKENHAM *Seyntys* (Roxb.) 142 Wyth thre rosys and thre applys in hys hand he hade A sportelet, and doun up on hys kne He hym set and offryd it on to Dorothe.

ˈsportling. *rare.* [f. SPORT *sb.*¹ or *v.* + -LING.]

1. A small sportive or playful animal, bird, etc.

c **1720** A. PHILIPS *Odes, To Miss Carteret* 20 When again the lambkins play, Pretty sportlings full of May. *c* **1720** SWIFT *On Rover* [in ridicule of prec.] 34 Where the linnets sit and sing, Little sportlings of the spring.

† **2.** A sport or abnormal variation. *Obs.*⁻¹

1723 P. BLAIR *Pharmaco-Bot.* I. 16 All the other are only sportlings from them.

† **ˈsportly**, *a. Obs.* [f. SPORT *sb.*¹ + -LY¹.]

1. Of or pertaining to, connected with, sport; sporting; sportsmanlike.

1682 *Lond. Gaz.* No. 1741/3 As many as wish well to their Town, or are Incouragers of Sportly Meetings. **1711** SHAFTESB. *Charac.* (1737) III. 217 As little favourable.. as these sportly gentlemen are.. towards the care or culture of their own species. **1781** P. BECKFORD *Th. Hunting* (1802) 185 You also object to my saying *catch* a fox: you call it a bad expression, and say that it is not sportly.

2. Sportive, frolicsome, playful. *rare*⁻¹.

1696 A. DE LA PRYME *Diary* (Surtees) 78 Turneps.. make them so sportly, lively, and vigorous that they play and leap like young kidds.

sportsman (ˈspɔətsmən). [f. SPORT *sb.*¹]

1. A man who follows, engages in, or practises sport; esp. one who hunts or shoots wild animals or game for pleasure.

Also *transf.*, in recent use, one who in his conduct or dealings displays the typical good qualities of a sportsman.

1706–7 FARQUHAR *Beaux' Strat.* I. i, *Aim.* A sportsman, I suppose? *Bon.* Yes, sir, he's a man of pleasure; he plays at whisk and smokes his pipe eight-and-forty hours together sometimes. **1727** GAY *Begg. Op.* I. ii, A good sportsman always lets the hen-partridges fly. **1776** GIBBON *Decl. & F.* xi. (1782) I. 367 His nephew.. presumed to dart his javelin before that of his uncle... As a monarch and as a sportsman Odenathus was provoked. **1856** KANE *Arctic Explor.* II. xxviii. 277 Our sportsmen would clamber up the cliffs and come back laden with little auks. **1894** *Outing* XXIV. 476/1 Some have been true sportsmen—and as I take it, the phrase true sportsmen includes everything that is manly and gentlemanly.

transf. **1831–3** CAPT. B. HALL *Frag. Voy. & Trav.* Ser. II. I. 244 This skilful sea-sportsman [a dolphin] arranged all his springs.. [so] that he contrived to fall, at the end of each, just under the very spot on which the exhausted Flying-fish were about to drop!

b. *sportsman's companion, knife* (see quots.).

1863 *Athenæum* 19 Dec. 841/3 Mr. Baskcomb exhibited an ancient nut-cracker, and a sportsman's companion, found at Tutbury Castle. **1875** KNIGHT *Dict. Mech.* 2288/1 *Sportsman's Knife*, one containing a number of tools, to be used in emergencies.

c. *Electr.* (See quots.)

1842 FRANCIS *Dict. Arts & Sci.* s.v., *Electrical Sportsman*, an amusing and ingenious instrument, to illustrate the fact that a charged electrical jar will discharge itself if the outer and inner coating approach too closely. **1862** *Catal. Internat. Exhib., Brit.* II. No. 5598, Gas pistol, thunder house, sports-men, and other instrument[s] for showing the proportion of frictional electricity.

2. *U.S.* A gambler, betting-man.

1848 in BARTLETT.

sportsmanlike (ˈspɔətsmənlaɪk), *a.* Also **sportsman-like.** [f. prec. + -LIKE.] Resembling a sportsman; like that of a sportsman; consonant with the character or conduct of a sportsman.

1816 SCOTT *Antiq.* xxii, He indulges his sportsman-like propensities by shooting my pigeons. **1824** MISS MITFORD *Village* Ser. I. (1863) 240 Having something smart and sportsman-like in his appearance. **1853** KANE *Grinnell Exped.* I. (1856) 483 If he has with him the light javelin.. he may be tempted to use it now: but this, I believe, is not altogether sportsmanlike. **1889** RIDER HAGGARD *Allan's Wife* 296 The lion is a sportsmanlike animal, and.. prefers to kill his own dinner.

b. *colloq.* Honourable, straightforward.

1899 E. PHILLPOTTS *Human Boy* 119 Freckles, who was an awfully sportsmanlike chap really.

sportsmanly (ˈspɔətsmənlɪ), *a.* [f. as prec. + -LY¹.] Worthy of, becoming or befitting, a sportsman; sportsmanlike. So **ˈsportsmanliness.**

1778 [W. H. MARSHALL] *Minutes Agric.* 9 Sept. 1776, But the rules of Sportsmanliness are not so generally understood as those of Good-Breeding. *Ibid.*, It is sometimes sportsmanly to suffer the huntsman to pursue the hounds, where it would be unsportsmanly in any other horseman to follow. **1912** *Nation* 5 Oct. 9/1 My sportsmanly approval was misplaced.

sportsmanship (ˈspɔətsmənʃɪp). [f. as prec. + -SHIP.] The performance or practice of a sportsman; skill in, or knowledge of, sport; conduct characteristic or worthy of a sportsman.

1745 FIELDING *Tom Jones* III. x, He had.. greatly recommended himself.. by leaping over five barred gates, and by other acts of sportsmanship. **1826** MISS MITFORD *Village* II. 308 The boys showed great sportmanship [*sic*] on this occasion. **1841** *Edinb. Rev.* LXXIII. 382 He was not one of the Brummell set, or he would scarcely attribute the origin of Melton to their sportsmanship. **1897** *Outing* XXX. 239/2 If this advance.. in oarsmanship can be accompanied with an advance in sportsmanship.

† **ˈsportsome**, *a. Sc. Obs.* [f. SPORT *sb.*¹ + -SOME.] Amusing, diverting, sportive.

1533 BELLENDEN *Livy* I. ii. (S.T.S.) I. 19 Be þis evander was institute ane sportsum play, þat ȝoung men suld ryn nakit.. to wourschip pan Liceus. *Ibid.* I. xvi. 90 In þe mene tyme ane of þame begouth to schaw ane. sportsum fabil.

sportster (ˈspɔətstə(r)). [f. SPORT *sb.*¹ + -STER.] **a.** A sports coat. *rare.* **b.** A sports car. Cf. ROADSTER 2 d.

1963 *N.Y. Times* 20 Dec. 11 Sportster. Made of cotton Safari cloth, lined with wool alpaca. **1971** *New Scientist* 6 May 324/1 (*heading*) Spark speeds sportsters. **1974** P. J. FILBY *Specialist Sports Cars* 90/1 The 803, which was an open sportster with a ladder frame chassis bonded to its fibreglass body.

sportswoman (ˈspɔətswʊmən). [f. SPORT *sb.*¹]

a. A woman who follows or practises, is addicted to or interested in, sport, esp. field-sport. Also *transf.* in recent use, a woman who displays the typical good qualities of a sportswoman. Cf. note at SPORTSMAN 1 a.

1754 SHEBBEARE *Matrimony* (1766) II. 206 My good Dame is a very unfair Sportswoman. **1796** *Sporting Mag.* VII. 288 The celebrated Miss Barlow, well known as an accomplished sportswoman. **1810** LADY LYTTELTON *Corr.* iv. (1912) 93, I used to hate hunting talk; but..I grew a complete sport's-woman in theory before we left the country. **1865** *Sat. Rev.* 11 Mar. 281/2 A quarry worthy of the aim of an ambitious sportswoman. **1896** *Cath. News* 9 May 15/3 The dashing sportswoman who used to hunt like a man. **1906** KIPLING *Puck of Pook's Hill* 148 She'd say she'd get us whipped. She never did, though... Aglaia was a thorough sportswoman. **1925** F. SCOTT FITZGERALD *Great Gatsby* iv. 86 Miss Baker's a great sportswoman... She'd never do anything that wasn't all right. **1948** F. THOMPSON *Still glides Stream* ii. 42 If I can't bear a bit of pain at my time of life I'm no sportswoman.

†**b.** A loose woman or harlot. *Obs.*

1816 *Sporting Mag.* XLVIII. 161 A great bustle..has been made by the police among the sportswomen of the lowest rank.

'sportulary, *a.* *Obs.*⁻¹ [f. L. *sportula* little basket, dole, gift, dim. of *sporta* SPORT *sb.*²] Supported by, dependent or subsisting on, the doles or gifts of patrons.

1649 BP. HALL *Cases Consc.* III. vii. (1650) 231 Hereupon it is, that these sportulary preachers are faine to sooth up their many maisters.

†**'sportule.** *Obs.*⁻¹ [a. F. *sportule* or ad. L. *sportula* (see prec.).] A dole, gift, or present.

1726 AYLIFFE *Parergon* 173 The Bishops who consecrated this Ground, were wont to have a Spill or Sportule for the same from the credulous Laity.

sporty ('spɔətɪ), *a.* *colloq.* or *slang.* [f. SPORT *sb.*¹]

1. Sportsmanlike, sportsmanly; sporting.

1889 *Daily News* 11 Mar. 2/3 The very 'sporty' little venture was watched with much interest. **1893** *Weekly Express & Mail* (N.Y.) 28 June, This is the 'sporty' way to capture them, but the professional frog hunters go for their prey..with scoop nets and long poles. **1897** *Outing* XXX. 484/2 It's awfully sporty of them to lend fresh ponies to their opponents.

Comb. **1896** *Gody's Mag.* Feb. 152/1 A sporty-looking drummer.

2. Of a motor car: of a racing type; resembling a sports car in appearance or performance.

1962 A. LURIE *Love & Friendship* xii. 228 Traded in his Pontiac got him one of those new Valiants,..kind of sporty for a man his age. **1966** *Economist* 9 July p. xvii/2 Chevrolet's Corvair only began to sell when the Monza version was introduced after a few months, with bucket seats and a 'sporty' reputation, but precious little else for the extra $250. **1972** *Sunday Express* 9 Jan. 5/1 Performance is distinctly sporty. Its top gear acceleration of 40–60 in 9 seconds beats anything else in the class.

sporular ('spɒrjʊlə(r)), *a.* [f. SPORULE + -AR.] Having the character of, pertaining to, a sporule.

1819 LINDLEY tr. *Richard's Observ.* 42 If some part only have received the sporular matter. **1840** HARVEY *Brit. Algae* Introd. p. xxiii, I am more disposed to consider them viviparous capsules, in which the sporular map has been converted into minute filaments.

sporulate ('spɒrjʊleɪt), *v.* [f. as prec. + -ATE³.]

1. *trans.* To convert into spores.

1885 LANKESTER in *Encycl. Brit.* XIX. 854/1 A part of the protoplasm is not sporulated but forms a capillitium.

2. *intr.* To form spores or sporules.

1891 in *Cent. Dict.* **1897** *Nature* 21 Oct. 601/1 In a cell about to sporulate the nucleus is found in the centre of the cell. **1898** MANSON *Trop. Diseases* i. 16 The non-flagellated plasmodium..sporulates in the human blood-corpuscle.

Hence **'sporulated, 'sporulating** *ppl. adjs.*

1897 *Allbutt's Syst. Med.* II. 749 The breaking up of the sporulating parasite. **1898** P. MANSON *Trop. Diseases* iii. 79 The breaking down of the sporulated plasmodium.

sporulation (spɒrjʊ'leɪʃən). [f. as prec. + -ATION.] Conversion into spores; spore-formation.

1876 tr. *Schutzenberger's Fermentation* 55 The sporulation and budding differ in no respect from the analogous phenomena which are observed in yeast. **1896** *Allbutt's Syst. Med.* I. 761 As soon as sporulation commences the segments become more perfectly marked out.

sporule ('spɒrjuːl). *Bot.* and *Zool.* [a. F. *sporule* or ad. mod.L. *sporula* (Hedwig): see SPORE and -ULE.]

1. A spore or spore-granule.

a. *Bot.* **1819** LINDLEY tr. *Richard's Observ.* 42 Sporules differ from seeds,..above all, in their want of embryo. *Ibid.*, The rudiment of a sporule. **1845** DARWIN *Voy. Nat.* i. 5 After this fact one need not be surprised at the diffusion of the far lighter and smaller sporules of cryptogamic plants. **1875** *Zoologist* X. 4416 The matter contained in the sporules of the genus Fucus is of a glutinous nature.

attrib. and *Comb.* **1830** LINDLEY *Nat. Syst. Bot.* 313 Any sporule-case in Cellulares. *Ibid.*, A cluster of sporule-like areolæ.

b. *Zool.* **1836–9** *Todd's Cycl. Anat.* II. 433/2 In some animals these sporules are formed in all parts of the body indiscriminately. *Ibid.*, The sporules of some Zoophytes. **1846** J. D. DANA *Zooph.* v. (1848) 91 The sporules..which constitute the surface dots alluded to.

2. *fig.* A germ.

1861 *Q. Rev.* CX. 368 Mere words..necessarily contain the sporules of mighty principles.

Hence **sporu'liferous** *a.*, bearing sporules.

1824 R. K. GREVILLE *Flora Edin.* p. lxxiii, Sporuliferous pulp not spontaneously emitted. **1847** *Proc. Berw. Nat. Club* II. 214 The erect filaments are two lines in height,..with a hoary sporuliferous head.

sporyar(e, -er, obs. forms of SPURRIER.

‖**sposa** ('sposa). Now *rare.* [It.] A wife; a bride. Also as **cara sposa** ('cara), 'dear wife'; a devoted female companion. Cf. SPOSO.

1624 J. CHAMBERLAIN *Let.* 4 Dec. (1939) II. 589 Tom Cary a privado of the Princes bedchamber was dispatcht..into Fraunce with a love letter and some rich and rare jewell to the Sposa. **1781** N. MUNDY *Let.* 15 Oct. in A. E. Newdigate-Newdegate *Cheverels* (1898) iii. 48 Adieu my dear Sr Roger, may you and yr Cara Sposa meet in health & spirits. **1793** W. B. STEVENS *Jrnl.* 13 Mar. (1965) I. 72 His Wife..handsome enough for a Cara Sposa. **1797** E. WYNNE *Jrnl.* 22 Jan. in A. Fremantle *Wynne Diaries* (1952) xx. 265 The *sposa* received so many fine compliments of congratulation that she was quite at a loss. **1821** SHELLEY *Let.* 22 Oct. (1964) II. 363 La Guiccioli his [*sc.* Byron's] cara sposa who attends him impatiently.

sposage, -aile, obs. forms of SPOUSAGE, -AL.

†**spose**, obs. variant of SPOUSE *sb.*

App. intended to distinguish the masc. from the fem.

1604 T. WRIGHT *Passions Mind* I. vii. 29 The Spose sayd vnto his Spouse,..Thou hast wounded my heart with one of thine eyes.

spose, obs. form of SPOUSE *v.*

s'pose (spəʊz), *v.* Also **spose, 'spose, spoze.** Repr. an informal pronunc. of SUPPOSE *v.*

1852 R. S. SURTEES *Mr Sponge's Sporting Tour* xvii. 84 Law, ma! but you don't 'spose pa would ever allow such a thing. **1873** TROLLOPE *Harry Heathcote* (1874) i. 12 'I s'pose the poor must live somewheres,'..said Mrs. Growler, the old maid-servant. ?**1912** R. FRY *Let.* (1972) I. 358, I 'spose women weren't artists enough. **1936** L. DURRELL *Let.* in *Spirit of Place* (1969) 40, I no longer care. .. A new phase I spoze. **1945** A. KOBER *Parm Me* 44 If you're not enjoying yesself, Max, spose you sit with them. **1968** D. O'GRADY *Bottle of Sandwiches* (1969) i. 7 'And s'posin' it rains in the meantime?' 'See what you mean. Small marquee, eh?' **1971** *Black World* June 72/1, I paid them out of receipts I was sposed to turn in. **1980** H. R. F. KEATING *Murder of Maharajah* iii. 37, I s'pose we're not strictly his guests. We're the Maharajah's guests.

sposh (spɒʃ). *U.S.* [Imitative.] Slush, mud.

1845 in Bartlett *Dict. Amer.* (1848) 325 The streets were one shining level of black sposh. **1846** CHEEVER *Wand. Pilgrim* xxiv. (1848) 134 Making our way..in this penetrating *sposh.* **1884** BURROUGHS *Birds & Poets* 109 Yellow sposh and mud and water everywhere.

Hence **'sposhy** *a.*, soft and watery.

1842 *Yale Lit. Mag.* VIII. 96, I can't always decipher quail tracks—specially in *sposhy* weather. **1884** S. O. JEWETT *Country Doctor* iii. 22 The sposhy apples that grows in wet ground.

‖**sposo** ('sposo). Now *rare.* [It.] A husband. Also as **caro sposo** ('caro), 'dear husband'. Cf. SPOSA.

1778 F. BURNEY *Diary* Aug. (1940) I. 12 Hetty, who, with her *sposo*, was here to receive us. **1792** —— *Let.* 2 Oct. (1972) I. 229 Her caro sposo has continued very tolerably well. **1816** JANE AUSTEN *Emma* III. vi. 88 The thing would be for us all to come on donkies, Jane, Miss Bates, and me—and my caro sposo walking by. **1858** TROLLOPE *Three Clerks* III. xviii. 328 The gentleman who has the honour of being her intended sposo. **1887** *Athenæum* 21 May 670/2 Italian girlhood..has two sole points of interest, the *sposo* and the fashion plate. **1976** *Times Lit. Suppl.* 30 Jan. 103/1 Nor was her husband..a mere *caro sposo*: their devotion was total.

spot (spɒt), *sb.*¹ Also 3–7 **spotte**, 4–7 **spott**, 4–6 **spote**. [ME. *spot*, = MDu. *spotte, spot* (WFlem. *spotte*), LG. (EFris.) *spot*, MDa. **spot* (pl. *spottæ*), speck, spot, NFris. *spot, spōt*, Norw. *spott*, speck, spot, piece of ground; also ON. and Icel. *spotti* (*spottr*) small piece, bit. It is doubtful whether the word is original in all these languages.]

I. 1. *fig.* **a.** A moral stain, blot, or blemish; a stigma or disgrace.

a **1200** *Vices & Virtues* 95 Wepeð forð mid me..& waschen ðe spottes of ure euele ðeawes! *c* **1340** HAMPOLE *Pr. Consc.* 2646 He suld..Mak him redy and clense hym clene Of al spottes of syn þat mught be sene. **13..** *E.E. Allit. P.* A. 764 Cum hyder to me, my lemman swete, For mote ne spot is non in þe. *c* **1400** *Apol. Loll.* 53 He schal draw spott of good þing iuel tane. *c* **1450** tr. *De Imitatione* III. lxi. 144 Lete us putte no spotte in our glory in fleyng fro þe crosse. **1526** *Pilgr. Perf.* (W. de W. 1531) 185 b, This spot of synne god dothe away. **1560** DAUS tr. *Sleidane's Comm.* 129 To the intent they myght washe out this spotte, they invente an other waye more easye. **1639** S. DU VERGER tr. *Camus' Admir. Events* 45, I had rather dye a thousand deaths, then to set such a spot on my blood, and posterity. **1650** HUBBERT *Pill Formality* 104 Neither should their spot have been differenced or known from the spot of the wicked. **1784** COWPER *Tiroc.* 685 Safe under such a wing, the boy shall show No spots contracted among grooms below. **1837** CARLYLE *Fr. Rev.* III. II. i, The Gironde has touched, this day, on the foul black-spot of its fair Convention Domain.

b. Without article, esp. in ***without spot.***

a **1340** HAMPOLE *Psalter* xiv. 2 He þat ingase wiþouten spot. **1390** GOWER *Conf.* II. 22 Goodlihiede and innocence Withouten spot of eny blame. **1404–8** *26 Pol. Poems* vii. 54 [Let] No fende spot vppon the spyȝe. **1548–9** (Mar.) *Bk. Com. Prayer* 126 b, Without spot of sinne. **1580** *Reg. Privy Council Scot.* III. 281 His guidsire..and himself..hes faithfullie servit his Hienes..without spot or reproche. **1611** BIBLE *1 Tim.* vi. 14 Keepe this commandement without spot. **1781** COWPER *Expost.* 261 Thy services, once holy without spot, Mere shadows now. **1821** SHELLEY *Adonais* xlv, Sublimely mild, a Spirit without spot. **1844** DICKENS *Chimes* 11, As to character,..[they] will have it as free from spot and speck in us afore they'll help us.

†**c.** ***the spot of***, the stain or stigma of (something disgraceful). *Obs.*

a **1548** HALL *Chron., Edw. IV*, 49 Lest he..should be noted with the spot of Nygardshyp. **1567** in *6th Rep. Hist. MSS. Comm.* 642/1 Quhairin gif we failȝe, we ar content to vndirly the spot of vntrewth, ingraitnes and defamatioun. **1603** *Reg. Privy Council Scot.* VI. 524 The perpetuall spott of perjurie dew to thame for thair violatioun of the said assuirance. **1647** N. BACON *Disc. Govt. Eng.* I. xxxviii. (1739) 57 First Twelve men enquired of the fame and ground thereof; which if liked, rendred the party under the spot of delinquency.

d. Applied to persons.

1526 TINDALE *2 Pet.* ii. 13 Spottes they are and filthynes. —— *Jude* 12 These are spottes which..feast togedder. **1606** SHAKS. *Ant. & Cl.* IV. xii. 35 Follow his Chariot, like the greatest spot Of all thy Sex. **1616** R. C. *Times' Whistle* (1871) 79 By some devill got, For man could never, sure, beget a spot Of such vncleannesse. **1673** WYCHERLEY *Gentl. Dancing-Master* v. i, Thou spot, sploach of my family and blood!

2. a. A small discolouring or disfiguring mark; a speck or stain.

1340 *Ayenb.* 228 Þe huite robe huerinne þe spot is uouler and more yzyenne þanne in anoþer cloþ. **1377** LANGL. *P. Pl.* B. XIII. 315 Þi best cote..Hath many moles and spottes, it moste ben ywasshe. **1509** HAWES *Past. Pleas.* XXXVIII. (Percy Soc.) 196 Ful lyke the gold that is moost pure and fyne, Withouten spotte of blacke encombremente. **1591** HARINGTON *Orl. Fur.* XXXIII. lxx, The Moone was like a glasse all voyd of spot. **1617** MORYSON *Itin.* III. 174 They cannot bee more provoked, then by casting any spot upon their heads. **1698** FRYER *Acc. E. India & P.* 213 The Diamond..Without Spots or Foulness, is called a Paragon-stone, and in full Perfection. **1784** COWPER *Task* IV. 554 The stain Appears a spot upon a vestal's robe, The worse for what it soils. **1827** FARADAY *Chem. Manip.* vii. (1842) 200 All retorts with spots..in the part to be heated should be rejected.

b. Const. *of* the substance causing the stain or disfigurement. (Passing into sense 7.)

c **1400** MAUNDEV. (Roxb.) ix. 36 Ȝit þe spottes of þe qwhit mylk er sene apon þe stanes. *c* **1440** *Alph. Tales* 150 Onone as sho tuchid it þer apperid a dropp & a spott of blude. *Ibid.* 33 ; þer was not on all his clothis a drope of myre nor a spott of clay. **1595** SHAKS. *John* IV. ii. 253 An innocent hand, Not painted with the Crimson spots of blood. **1677** MIÈGE *Fr. Dict.* II, A spot of oyl on a sute of cloaths. **1736** BAILEY *Household Dict.* s.v., To take a Spot of Oil out of Sattin, &c. **1820** SHELLEY *Œd. Tyr.* II. ii. 77 A spot or two [of ditchwater] on me would do no harm. **1825** SCOTT *Talism.* xxviii, What signifies counting the spots of dirt that we are about to wash from our hands?

3. In special senses: †**a.** A mark or speck on the eye; also, a disease characterized by these.

a **1400** *Stockholm Med. MS.* fol. 98, For a spot in þe eye. **1483** *Cath. Angl.* 356/1 A Spotte jn ye eghe.., *glaucoma.* **1500** *Ortus Vocab.*, *Glaucoma*, a spott in the eye. *c* **1623** LODGE *Poor Mans Talent* C 2, The spotts in the eies may easily bee cured in the yonger sort. **1639** O. WOOD *Alph. Bk. Secrets* 59 This cureth Spot, Pearle, Web, or any thing else in the Eye.

b. An eruptive or other disfiguring mark on the skin.

a **1425** tr. *Arderne's Treat. Fistula*, etc. 50 Al spottez or filþez of þe skyn which giffeþ oute watre. *c* **1440** *Alph. Tales* 82 So þe pestelence come;..& when he had þe spottys þe fadur held hym vp in his armys. **1560** BIBLE (Geneva) *Lev.* xiii. 4 If the white spot be in ye skin of his flesh [etc.]. **1611** COTGR., *Rousseurs*, little, red, wan, or blackish pimples or spots in the face, &c. **1669** [see BLOTCH *sb.* 1]. **1725** N. ROBINSON *Th. Physick* 296 Scorbutic Spots and Blotches emboss the Legs, Arms, and Thighs. **1789** *Massachusetts Spy* 15 Jan. 1/4 For common spots, or bunched cancers, put some of the salts on lint. **1818–20** E. THOMPSON tr. *Cullen's Nosology* 319 *Spilosis*... Spots. **1843** ABDY *Water Cure* 53 A girl..had..several spots in the face.

fig. **1781** COWPER *Expost.* 105 His unsuspecting sheep.. Catch from each other a contagious spot, The foul forerunner of a gen'ral rot.

c. A dark mark on the face of the sun, moon, or a planet. (Cf. *sunspot.*)

1605 CAMDEN *Rem., Epigr.* 15 Of the fiery colour of the Planet Mars, And the spotts in the Moone he giueth this reason. *c* **1641** BP. MOUNTAGU *Acts & Mon.* (1642) 117 It is lately discovered that spots are in the Sun: and if our sight deceive us not, there be in the Moone. **1706** E. WARD *Wooden World Diss.* (1708) 48 You discover him by his Phrases, as apparently as you can the Spots of the Moon with a Telescope. **1784** COWPER *Task* I. 714 Where finds Philosophy her eagle eye, With which she gazes at yon burning disk Undazzled, and detects and counts his spots? **1854** TOMLINSON tr. *Arago's Astron.* 79 The spots, which have served for determining the period of the rotation of Mars. **1872** RUSKIN *Eagle's N.* §206 Science does its duty, not in telling us the causes of spots in the sun; but [etc.].

d. A discoloration produced upon the leaves or fruit of a plant by various fungi.

1852 *Beck's Florist* 140 How to prevent the 'spot', and some other diseases to which Pelargoniums are heir. **1905** *Daily News* 14 Apr. 4 That dread disease of cucumber and melon plants, known as 'spot'.

e. *colloq.* (See quot.)

1894 *Daily News* 1 Feb. 7/1 The eggs..are what we call 'spots', half good and half bad.

II. 4. a. A small, usually roundish, mark of a different colour from the main surface.

c **1220** *Bestiary* 736 in *O.E. Misc.*, He is blac so bro of qual, mið wite spottes sapen al. *c* **1400** MAUNDEV. (Roxb.) xxii. 101 Þai hafe on þaire heuedes a reed spotte. *c* **1480** HENRYSON *Test. Cres.* 260 Hir gyse was gray, and full of spottis blak. **1535** COVERDALE *Jer.* xiii. 23 Like as the man of

Inde maye chaunge his skynne, & the cat of the mountayne hir spottes. **1590** SHAKS. *Mids. N.* II. i. 11 The Cow-slips tall, her pensioners bee, In their gold coats, spots you see. **1638** JUNIUS *Paint. Ancients* 94, I shall but mention here.. the partie-coloured spots of pretious stones. **1736** GRAY *Statius* II. 25 A tiger's pride..With native spots and artful labour gay. **1774** GOLDSM. *Nat. Hist.* (1776) II. 151 While we distinctly behold the black spots that are to the right and left. **1844** MARDON *Billiards* 111 The marked ball should have but one spot, and that as small as possible. **1892** *Photogr. Ann.* II. 578 The usual series of masks, upon which are placed the two white spots.

transf. **1632** LITHGOW *Trav.* VI. 292 The Countrey..ouercled heere and there with spots of Sheepe and Goates. **1884** STABLES *Our Friend the Dog* vii. 61 *Spot*—A hollow between the eyes, marking the union of the frontal with the nasal bones.

fig. **1634** MILTON *Comus* 5 Above the smoak and stirr of this dim spot, Which men call Earth. **1781** COWPER *Expost.* 694 A world is up in arms, and thou, a spot, Not quickly found if negligently sought [etc.].

†**b.** A patch worn on the face; a beauty-spot.

1579 LYLY *Euphues* (Arb.) 116 Their shadowes, their spots, their lawnes,..their ruffes, their rings. **1592** —— *Midas* I. ii, Earerings, borders, crippins, shadowes, spots, and so many other trifles. **1665** PEPYS *Diary* 13 Jan., The first time that ever I saw her to wear spots. **1667** L. STUCLEY *Gospel Glass* xxi. (1670) 214 Are not some puff'd up with their fine Clothes,..Ribbons, Dressings, yea with their very Spots? **1735** POPE *Ep. Lady* 43 Ladies, like variegated Tulips, show;..Their happy Spots the nice admirer take.

c. Phr. ***to knock (the) spots off*** or ***out of***, to beat thoroughly, surpass, excel. orig. *U.S.*

1856 *Spirit of Times* 22 Nov. 196/1 Addison County leads the van (or 'knocks the spots off', as we say here) in Vermont, and is celebrated over the world for its fine horses. **1861** *Atlantic Monthly* June 747/1, I wish I had control of chain-lightning for a few minutes;..I'd make it come thick and heavy and knock spots out of Secession. **1867** LATHAM *Black & White* 125 We did knock the spots off them that time. **1887** F. FRANCIS *Saddle & Mocassin* 152 She can knock the spots out of these boys at that game. **1888** *Pall Mall G.* 24 Feb. 5/1 The breezes blowing..in a way which 'knocked spots'..out of the fragrance of the hayfields. **1903** A. BENNETT *Truth about Author* xiii. 171 'We will write a play together... We can do something that will knock spots off——' etc., etc. We determined upon a grand drawing-room melodrama which should unite style with those qualities which make for financial success on the British stage. **1943** A. L. ROWSE *Cornish Childhood* 186 They [*sc.* the Nazis]..have at any rate been intelligent, and knocked spots off those public-school gentlemen.

d. A pip on a playing-card. Also, a playing-card having a specified number of pips (cf. sense 5 d). In recent use *U.S.*

1578 J. STOCKWOOD *Sermon preached..24 Aug.* 142 They perfectlye can tell howe manye spottes there be in a payre of Cardes..when as they scarce reade a leafe of the Bible twice in a Moneth. **1844** 'J. SLICK' *High Life N.Y.* II. xxx. 215 'Jest so,' sez I, a fli[n]gin down the ten spot o' clubs and the ace-o' diamonds. **1873** J. H. BEADLE *Undevel. West* iv. 92 The ace is your winning card. The eight and ten spot win for me. **1976** *Washington Post* 19 Apr. B8/3 South won the opening trump lead with his ten-spot. **1977** D. ANTHONY *Stud Game* xix. 118, I had a poker game... I played mechanically, counting spots and backing the odds.

5. a. A variety of domestic pigeon, having white plumage with a spot of another colour above the beak.

a **1672** WILLUGHBY *Ornith.* (1676) 133 *Spots*, Anglicè, quoniam in fronte supra rostrum maculam habent singulæ. **1725** *Fam. Dict.* s.v. *Pigeon*, There are, indeed, many Sorts of Pigeons, such as..Barbs,..Owls, Spots, Trumpeters. **1765** *Treat. Dom. Pigeons* 132 The Spot..is about the size of a small runt, and was brought hither from Holland. **1834** MUDIE *Feathered Tribes* I. 74 The principal ones [*sc.* pigeons] are..the Smiter, the Spot, the Tumbler [etc.]. **1861** DARWIN *Orig. Spec.* (ed. 3) 26, I also crossed a barb with a spot, which is a white bird with a red tail and red spot on the forehead. **1881** LYELL *Pigeons* 73 The spot has been described by every English writer, including Willoughby, and is common on the Continent.

b. A spotted textile material.

1798 JANE AUSTEN *Lett.* (1884) I. 186 My coarse spot I shall turn..into a petticoat very soon. **1839** URE *Dict. Arts* 1232 The draught and cording of a spot whose two sides are similar, but reversed.

c. In moth-names (see quots.).

1832 J. RENNIE *Consp. Butterfl. & Moths* 94 The Gold Spot..appears the middle of August. *Ibid.* 97 The Marbled White Spot. *Ibid.* 153 The Diamond Spot.

d. *U.S.* With numbers: A dollar(-bill).

1846 DURIVAGE & BURNHAM *Stray Subjects* 135, I moved towards the money, but he prevented my raising it, by covering it with a *twenty*-spot. **1848** LOWELL *Biglow P.* Ser. I. ix. 176 He said He'd give a fifty spot right out, to git ye, 'live or dead. **1896** *J. Lillard's Poker Stories* 246 But one single dollar remained of that five spot.

e. *U.S.* Either of two marine food fishes of the family Sciænidæ, *Leiostomus xanthurus* or the channel bass, *Sciænops ocellata.*

1877 C. HALLOCK *Sportsman's Gazetteer* 396 Spot.—*Liostomus obliquus.* **1882** JORDAN & GILBERT *Syn. Fishes N. Amer.* 574 *Liostomus xanthurus*, Spot; Goody; Oldwife. **1885** *Harper's Mag.* Jan. 221/1 It might be a spot..or a tarpon. **1902** JORDAN & EVERMANN *Amer. Food & Game Fishes* 260 For bait use live mullet, spot, grunt, or other small fish. **1961** E. S. HERALD *Living Fishes of World* 192/1 The spot, *Leiostomus xanthurus*, found from Cape Cod to Texas, is easily recognized by the spot above the base of the pectoral fin.

f. = *spot board* in sense 15 below.

1922 E. J. EVANS *Building Contracts* xviii. 81 It is essential that all plant, such as Derby's sieves, cornice moulds.. spots, scaffolding, etc.,..be on site in readiness. **1927** A. H. TELLING *ABC of Plastering* 195 It is part of the labourer's business to see that the 'spot' is supplied with 'stuff' for the plasterer's use. **1964** [see *spot board*, sense 15 below].

6. *Billiards.* **a.** One or other of the three marked places on a billiard-table, esp. the one at the upper end of the table upon which the red ball is placed. Similarly in *Snooker*, etc. **b.** *ellipt.* The spot-ball, or the person who plays it; a spot stroke, or the score obtained by this.

18.. *Laws of Billiards* xiii. in Mardon *Billiards* (1844) 115 If the red ball has been put into a pocket, it must not be placed on the spot till the other balls have done rolling. **1856** CRAWLEY *Billiards* (1859) 5 Three spots will be found on all good tables;..the third a distance of thirteen inches from the Cushion. This is called *the spot.* **1857** 'C. BEDE' *Nearer & Dearer* i. 1 'How is the game?' 'Twenty spot; ten striker.' *Ibid.* ii. 14, I can't make out the red from the spot. **1880** *Times* 28 Sept. 11/5 He kept possession of the table until he had added up 151 (40 spots).

III. 7. a. A small piece, amount, or quantity; a particle, a drop. Usu. with *of* (cf. 2 b); now esp. *colloq.* with abstract nouns, as ***spot of bother***, ***trouble***, etc.

c **1400** *Laud Troy Bk.* 17137 For he leffte not of hir a spot That he ne hit hewe as flesch to pot. **1662** HIBBERT *Body Divinity* I. 284 The whole course of life is but..a little spot of time between two eternities. **1738** WESLEY *Ps.* CIII. iv, As high as Heaven its arch extends, Above this little Spot of Clay. **1799** WORDSW. *Ruth* 71 As quietly as spots of sky Among the evening clouds. **1840** *Florist's Jrnl.* (1846) I. 219 That most numerous class of growers, who grow but a little spot. **1849** CUPPLES *Green Hand* xvi. (1856) 157 'Twas no use looking as yet for a spot of room. **1881** JEFFERIES *Wood Magic* II. ii. 66 A few spots of rain came driving along. **1915** H. ROSHER *In R.N.A.S.* (1916) 117 Pity I'm not due for another spot of leave yet. **1924** D. B. W. LEWIS *At Sign of Blue Moon* 272 What about a spot of lunch? **1933** M. ALLINGHAM *Sweet Danger* ii. 21 Since the spot of bother last year, the tunnel is no longer a tunnel. **1951** *People* 3 June 5/6 A dead-broke barrister who turns burglar following a spot of light coaching from a retired cracksman. **1959** H. HAMILTON *Answer in Negative* iv. 52 The police will be coming..to deal with a spot of trouble. **1976** F. MUIR *Frank Muir Book* 43 The first major French ballet company visited New York in 1827. They had a spot of bother with their tights.

†**b.** A piece *of* work. *Obs.* (Cf. PIECE *sb.* 7.)

1689 *Andros Tracts* III. 203 Whether it would not be a fine spot of work..to restore them to their former places? **1723** MRS. CENTLIVRE *Wonder* III. 31 Zounds! she here! I have made a fine spot of work on't. **1777** DIBDIN *Quaker* I. i, A very pretty spot of work this! **1821** SCOTT *Nigel* xxvii, Here is a bonny spot of work, and me alone, and on foot too!

c. ***in spots***, occasionally, at intervals; to some extent. *U.S.*

1852 MRS STOWE *Uncle Tom's C.* xvi, Mammy has a kind of obstinacy about her, in spots, that everybody don't see as I do. **1859** BARTLETT *Dict. Amer.* (ed. 2) 437 A boatman on the Mississippi, being asked how he managed to secure sleeping time, answered, 'I sleep in spots'; that is, at intervals, by snatches. **1872** DE VERE *Americanisms* 636 The phrase 'He is clever in spots', gives a man credit for fragmentary ability.

d. *colloq.* A drop *of* liquor. Also preceded by a defining word and *absol.*

1885 D. C. MURRAY *Rainbow Gold* ii, A little spot of rum, William, with a squeeze of lemon in it. **1896** *Evesham Jrnl.* 11 Jan. (E.D.D.), Defendant..said he never had a spot of beer. **1924** LAWRENCE & SKINNER *Boy in Bush* vi. 85 Y' slog t' th' nearest pub t'cadge a beer spot. **1930** J. DEVANNY *Butcher Shop* 200 The 'spot' she craved, or failing that a cup of tea. **1936** WODEHOUSE *Laughing Gas* ix. 90 May I offer you a spot?.. I can recommend the Scotch. **1950** G. GREENE *Third Man* viii. 63 'Have another drink, Mr. Martins?' 'No, I don't think I will.' 'Well, I'd like another spot.'

e. *slang* (orig. and chiefly *U.S.*). A term of imprisonment. Usu. preceded by numeral, designating a term of the specified number of years. Cf. sense 5 d.

1901 'J. FLYNT' *World of Graft* 220/2 *Spot*, term in prison. A 'one spot' means a sentence of one year. **1907** J. LONDON *Road* 84 He had never been in the particular penitentiary to which we were going, but he had done 'one-', 'two-', and 'five-spots' in various other penitentiaries (a 'spot' is a year). **1966** M. BREWER *Man against Fear* x. 105 He was serving a three spot for cunning... He got into a row with one of the warders.

8. a. A particular place or locality of limited extent.

13.. *E.E. Allit P.* A. 13 Syþen in þat spote hit fro me sprange, Ofte haf I wayted [etc.]. *Ibid.*, To þat spot..I entred in þat erber grene. **1667** MILTON *P.L.* IX. 439 Spot more delicious then those Gardens..of reviv'd Adonis, or renownd Alcinous. *a* **1700** EVELYN *Diary* Apr. 1646, The most pleasant spot in Italy. **1743** BULKELEY & CUMMINS *Voy. S. Seas* 106 Having publickly declar'd, that he will never go off this Spot. **1857** LIVINGSTONE *Trav.* iii. 54 Our next station is a lovely spot in the otherwise dry region. **1891** FARRAR *Darkn. & Dawn* xlvii, There was one spot in Rome which was calm amid all tumults.

b. A small space or extent *of* ground, etc.

c **1440** *York Myst.* xxxii. 332 A spotte of erthe for to by, wayte nowe I will, To berie in pilgrimes. **1677** W. HUBBARD *Narrative* (1865) II. 70 Some Spots and Skirts of more desirable Land upon the Banks of some Rivers. **1697** DRYDEN *Virg., Georg.* IV. 191 Lab'ring well his little Spot of Ground. **1726** SWIFT *Gulliver* II. vii, Whoever could make ..two blades of grass to grow upon a spot of ground [etc.]. **1765** *Museum Rust.* IV. 259 You must not sow lucerne without corn, unless your spot of land is too small to use a harrow in. **1811** *Regul. & Orders Army* 137 A Tent.. pitched upon the best dry Spot of ground in the vicinity. **1845** J. COULTER *Adv. in Pacific* v. 42 Nearly at the summit ..there is a spot of excellent land, of four or five acres in extent. **1891** MARY E. WILKINS *Humble Romance* 53 The products of his garden spot were his staple articles of food.

transf. **1779** FORREST *Voy. N. Guinea* 122 Off the rock of Sipsipa, are three spots of breakers,..one without another.

c. *north. dial.* A place of employment; a situation.

1877- in northern glossaries, etc. **1892** M. C. F. MORRIS *Yorksh. Folk-talk* 206 Martinmas was the season for the lads and lasses to change their spots, as they call their situations.

d. = SLOT *sb.*[2] 6, esp. in a performance, show, or programme; *spec.* in *Broadcasting*, a short interval for an advertisement or announcement; an advertisement or announcement occupying such an interval. orig. *U.S.*

1923 *N.Y. Times* 7 Oct. IX. 2 *Spot*, an act's position on a bill. **1926** *Amer. Mercury* Dec. 465/1 Fields and Fink moved in to a homer in the next to closing spot. **1937** *Amer. Speech* XII. 101 *Spot* or *spot announcement* refers to a brief announcement, usually commercial, spotted at various times. **1950** *Sport* 22–28 Sept. 18/2 Jack..continued to fill the centre-half spot in the Celtic line-up. **1958** *Listener* 25 Sept. 462/2 Occasional spectacular successes may please advertisers who happen to have 'spots' next to them. **1958** *Manch. Guardian* 29 Sept. 4/4 Spots, unlike full-length programmes, would reach people not already prejudiced in favour of the candidate. **1960** *Twentieth Cent.* Apr. 357 Dons..will do anything for a television spot. **1962** H. E. BEECHENO *Introd. Business Stud.* ix. 81 They [*sc.* TAM ratings] also help to determine, on the commercial channel, the prices of advertising 'spots'. **1967** *Technology Week* XX. 95/2 (Advt.), Your spot? Perhaps operating a ground computer complex. **1972** *Newsweek* 10 Jan. 9/2 Among these super-rich, two families contend for the No. 1 spot in the financial pecking order. **1972** G. DURRELL *Catch me a Colobus* vii. 139 He appeared on the local television as 'Uncle Ambrose', doing a children's spot in which he always had an animal of some sort to show them and talk to them about. **1976** *Southern Even. Echo* (Southampton) 17 Nov. 21/3 The 125cc solo class provides a championship medal for yet another Italian, Pietro Bianchi, with Spain's Angel Nieto in second spot. **1977** J. WAINWRIGHT *Do Nothin' till you hear from Me* x. 177 Tricks to get the tempo moving... Tricks to introduce a solo spot. **1978** S. BRILL *Teamsters* iii. 98 What pervaded Fitzsimmons' union..was a generally low level of competence in the top-paying spots. **1980** *Times* 5 Feb. 19/4 At present rates £44,300 would buy 49 30-second spots on each [radio] station during day-time shows.

e. *colloq.* With preceding adj.: a situation of the (unpleasant or difficult) kind specified; ***in a spot***, in difficulties, in trouble.

1929 C. F. COE *Hooch* v. 103 Jimmie Daust is in a bad spot, too. **1932** WODEHOUSE *Hot Water* xvi. 257 If that guy's in a spot, I'm glad of it. **1940** A. CHRISTIE *One, Two, buckle my Shoe* 160 It's the sort of business that might land him in a tight spot. **1967** E. S. GARDNER *Case of Queenly Contestant* vii. 84 He was afraid his father would find out. He was in a spot. So he turned to the troubleshooter. **1978** A. PRICE *'44 Vintage* xviii. 200 She'd probably only been humouring him, like any nice girl in an awkward spot might do.

f. *colloq.* A place of entertainment; *spec.* = ***night spot*** s.v. NIGHT *sb.* 14.

1954 G. GREENE *Twenty-One Stories* 205 I should be taken to plenty of Spots if I wasn't with a husband. **1956** B. HOLIDAY *Lady sings Blues* (1973) iii. 32 It was jumping with after-hour spots, regular-hour joints, restaurants, cafés, a dozen to a block. **1970** C. MAJOR *Dict. Afro-Amer. Slang* 108 *Spot*, usually a nightclub but also any popular place.

9. ***on*** (or ***upon***) ***the spot***: **a.** Without having time to move from the place; straightway, at once.

1677 MIÉGE *Fr. Dict.* II, To die on the spot, *mourir sur la place.* **1686** tr. *Chardin's Trav. Persia* 229 Had I drank as much as my neighbours, I had dy'd upon the spot. **1709** STEELE *Tatler* No. 40 ¶ 10 In which Engagement there were Eighteen Hundred Men kill'd on the Spot. **1760-72** H. BROOKE *Fool of Qual.* (1809) II. 151, I shall..run mad on the very spot for joy. **1835** I. TAYLOR *Spir. Despot.* iii. 94 Punishing the refractory either on the spot or in the persons of their posterity. **1856** READE *Never too Late* xi, They had not yet..murdered a single one on the spot. **1885** 'MRS. ALEXANDER' *Valerie's Fate* iii, I invited them both on the spot to afternoon tea on Saturday.

b. At the very place or locality in question. In phr. ***the man on the spot.*** See also ON-THE-spot *a.*

1687 MIÉGE *Gt. Fr. Dict.* II, I was upon the spot, *j'ai ete sur les Lieux.* **1699** BENTLEY *Phal.* 209 The Prizes..for those that perform'd best, were ready upon the spot, and made part of the Procession. **1719** DE FOE *Crusoe* I. (Globe) 309 The two Merchants..who liv'd just upon the Spot, and who ..were very rich. **1740-1** CHALLONER *Mem. Missionary Priests* Pref., Grave contemporary writers, informed by such as were upon the spot, or themselves eye-witnesses of what they write. **1811** *Regul. & Orders Army* 80 Officers who may be ordered..to return Home from a Foreign Station, are to apply for a Passage to the principal Agent of the Transport Board, on the Spot. **1881** L. B. WALFORD *Dick Netherby* xxii, Mischief was brewing..and he ought to be on the spot to counteract it. **1897** I. MALCOLM in R. S. Churchill *W. S. Churchill* (1967) I. Compan. II. xii. 848, I write like the 'man on the spot' The most inconceivable rot. **1922** M. ASQUITH *Autobiogr.* II. i. 21, I took my host aside and asked him if 'the man on the spot'—generally a favourite with the stupid—had given him his views on South Africa. **1955** G. GREENE *Quiet American* I. ii. 21, I always like to know what the man on the spot has to say. **1978** *Listener* 26 Jan. 119/3 If the man on the spot senses paralysis on the field, he ought to be able to abdicate.

c. Doing exactly what is necessary; precise and accurate. Also ***off the spot***, inexact, irrelevant.

1884 *Daily News* 16 Feb. 5/2 His county..will miss Midwinter sorely next summer, especially as he appears to be well on the spot. **1884** *Lillywhite's Cricket Ann.* 6 Our ground fielding was well on the spot. **1886** *Athenæum* 27 Mar. 420/3 Mr. Lang's new book..is his..in its tendency to be 'off the spot' and to make mistakes.

d. ***to put*** (a person) ***on the spot***: (*a*) *colloq.* (orig. *U.S.*), to place (someone) in a particular location; to put in a difficult or embarrassing position; (*b*) *U.S. slang*, to arrange for the murder of (someone), to kill; also *fig.* Cf. sense 8 e above.

1928 *Detective Fiction Weekly* 11 Aug. 735/2 We learned that the State still had one reliable witness, who could 'put us on the spot'. **1929** *Amer. Speech* IV. 343 *Put-on-the-spot*, left waiting at an appointed meeting place. **1929** M. A. GILL *Underworld Slang* 9/2 *Put on the spot*, killed. **1930** *Punch* 16 Apr. 442 You get rid of inconvenient subordinates..by 'putting them on the spot'—that is deliberately sending them to their death. **1930** *Sun* (Baltimore) 31 Oct. 1/3 Confident that America's prohibition law is about to be 'put on the spot', enterprising English vintners are already preparing for a resumption of their happy relations with their American clientele. **1934** G. ADE *Let.* 24 June (1973) 184 The Democrats have put every independent voter on the spot by nominating [Sherman] Minton at the dictation of Paul McNutt. **1937** *Sunday Express* 21 Feb. 1/3 (*heading*) Englishman 'put on the spot'. **1951** M. LOWRY *Let.* 5 June (1967) 244 The last thing we'd want to do is to put you on the spot or embarrass you. **1960** H. INNES *Doomed Oasis* II. iii. 145, I couldn't exactly say it in my report of the search. It would have put the Company on the spot, if you see what I mean.

10. a. A particular small area, part, or definite point in any surface or body.

1827 FARADAY *Chem. Manip.* vii. (1842) 215 Delivering the products of the distillation through minute apertures, and upon particular spots. **1860** WRAXALL *Life in Sea* viii. 181 The Sea-snails have their gills at very different spots. **1884** tr. *Lotze's Metaph.* 498 The many stimuli which at one and the same time excite the spots *p q r*...of the retina.

b. *transf.* with adjs.

Also ellipt. *the spot*, the affected part or important point. **1859** *Habits of Gd. Society* (new ed.) 48 Those dreams which to some [people] are the only bright spots of their lives. **1887** H. S. CUNNINGHAM *Cæruleans* I. 165 Mr. Ambrose touched a very tender spot in Camilla's heart. **1902** *Westm. Gaz.* 12 July 10/1 Lord Kitchener has a particularly soft spot for pets.

c. *Cricket.* (*a*) The point at which a ball should pitch for optimum length and direction; (*b*) an irregular place on the pitch from which the ball, when bowled, may move in an unexpected direction.

1855 F. LILLYWHITE *Guide to Cricketers* 29 The second day, however, Dean and Nixon found out the 'spot', and seemingly deposited every ball..on the precise place. **1859** *All Year Round* 23 July 305/2 The wicket..had no dead spots, no lively ones; no chance for 'shooters', none for 'bumpers'. **1901** *Encycl. Sport* I. 247/1 To bowl 'on the spot' is to bowl a good 'length'. **1908** W. E. W. COLLINS *Leaves from Old Country Cricketer's Diary* ix. 145 Their fast bowler found a spot on which the ball shot dead instead of bumping. **1950** F. N. S. CREEK *Teach yourself Cricket* vi. 111 A mere mechanical ability to pitch the ball on some regular spot called a 'good length' is of little value. **1980** *Wisden Cricket Monthly* Apr. 31/1 He was heartened by the presence of an awkward spot—a pretty large one, right on his length—from which the ball flew viciously from the very start.

d. Phr. *to hit* (or *go to* or *touch*) *the spot*: to be exactly what is required, 'to fit the bill' (said esp. of food or drink). *colloq.* (chiefly *U.S.*).

1868 *Putnam's Mag.* I. 670/1 'I hope that last corjul set you up?' 'Yes, Mr. Plunkitt, it went right to the spot.' **1897** *Strand Mag.* May 500/2 Then percussion or detonation was tried, and that 'touched the spot'! **1908** 'O. HENRY' *Voice of City* 235 Oh, pass the bottle... That hits the spot... My first drink in three months. **1923** W. NUTTING *Massachusetts Beautiful* 241 Did ever a dish of apple dowdy go to the spot like that? **1949** F. P. KEYES *Dinner at Antoine's* xvii. 268 That hot chocolate and those big chunks of roast beef certainly hit the spot. **1974** P. DE VRIES *Glory of Hummingbird* xviii. 275 'They haven't got a name for it [*sc.* a pancake] yet.'.. 'Batter Up. It hits the spot.' **1976** 'E. MCBAIN' *Guns* (1977) vii. 194 Colley would love a drink... A gin and tonic would hit the spot.

e. *Stock Exch.* With preceding adj.: a share in which dealings are of the specified kind.

1928 *Daily Sketch* 10 Aug. 20/3 Courtaulds' shares remain a firm spot at 4½. **1981** *Times* 23 Apr. 18/3 Another dull spot was Danish Bacon, which gave up 2p to 104p after results.

f. *Assoc. Football.* With *the*: the penalty spot (see PENALTY 5).

1970 *Liverpool Daily Post* 26 Sept. 5/5 *Smith made no mistake from the spot*: Smith scored a penalty. **1976** *Ilkeston Advertiser* 10 Dec. 19/5 Penalty expert Alan Crisp gave the goalkeeper no chance from the spot. **1977** *Guardian* 9 Mar. 20/3 Amid strong protests from several Forest players, the referee pointed to the spot.

11. *Comm.* (From 9.) **a.** *ellipt.* as *adv.* At immediate cash rates; for cash payment.

The full phrase *on the spot* (or *on spot*) is also in use. **1884** *York Herald* 23 Aug. 7/2 Cottonseed steady, at £8 5s. od. to £9 on the spot... Linseed oil..spot and up to the end of the year 18s. 7½d. **1900** *Daily News* 13 June 2/3 Silver remained nominally at 27⅝d. per ounce spot, and 27 9–16d. forward.

b. *pl.* Goods at immediate cash rates. Also in *sing.*

1881 *Harper's Mag.* Apr. 734/2 'Spots', 'futures', 'longs' and 'shorts' were unknown terms. **1890** *Pall Mall G.* 3 Sept. 6/2 He was supposed to have held from 130,000 to 150,000 bales—spots and futures. **1930** *Sunday Times* 12 Oct. 2/4 Raw Rubber prices became easier, and spot was dealt in down to 3 11–16d. **1976** *Scotsman* 25 Nov. 2/8 Silver fluctuated with sterling and ended about 2p down at 262.50p for spot and 273p for three-month.

12. *ellipt.* for SPOTLIGHT *sb.* (*a*).

1920 WODEHOUSE *Jill the Reckless* xvi. 231 Another debate on the subject of blues, ambers, and the management of the 'spot'. **1930** [see FLOOD *sb.* 7]. **1960** J. SYMONS *Progress of Crime* xl. 218 We cut off our engines after putting the spots on first to make sure this was the right show. **1968** K. WEATHERLY *Roo Shooter* 40 While the kangaroo shooter swings the spot in wide-reaching sweeps, the rabbit shooter uses it at about thirty-five yards and shoots into the sidelight. **1977** *Times* 24 Sept. 22/4 Wall spots are just over £6, table and standard lamps at reasonable prices.

IV. *attrib.* and *Comb.*

13. Simple attrib. **a.** In terms relating to the weaving of spotted fabrics, as *spot-leaf*, *-thread*, *-treadle*.

1839 URE *Dict. Arts* 1233 The spot threads..[are represented] by marks in the intervals. *Ibid.*, The spot-treddles on the right hand work the row contained in the first six spot-leaves.

b. In sense 3 c, as *spot-cavity*, *-cycle*, *-display*, etc.

1867–77 G. F. CHAMBERS *Astron.* I. i. 30 At epochs of minimum spot-display. **1885** AGNES CLERKE *Hist. Astron.* 200 The absolute depth of spot-cavities..was determined by Father Secchi. **1903** —— *Astrophysics* 18 The mode of their conformity to the spot-cycle. *Ibid.* 92 It is commonly taken for granted that the widened lines constitute the spot-spectra. **1909** G. FORBES *Hist. Astron.* 105 During the sun-spot maximum the corona seems most developed over the spot-zones—*i.e.*, neither at the equator nor the poles. **1926** H. MACPHERSON *Mod. Astron.* iii. 41 The regions where the bombs are likely to appear are around and among active spot-groups. *Ibid.* 45 A relation between high-rotation speeds and spot-development.

c. In sense 6, as *spot-break*, *-hazard*, *-stroke*, etc.

1844 E. R. MARDON *Billiards* Pl. xxviii: The 'Spot' Stroke. **1869** ROBERTS *Billiards* 137 Spot hazard: When-ever the red is cut or driven off the spot into any pocket. **1873** BENNETT & CAVENDISH *Billiards* 12 His largest spot-break 57 hazards. *Ibid.* 25 One ball is coloured red; the other two are white, but one of the white balls has a black spot on it, and is called the Spot-white. **1875** *Encycl. Brit.* III. 676/2 The spot stroke is a winning hazard made by pocketing the red ball in one of the corners from the spot.

d. In sense 11, as *spot market*, *parcel*, *price*, *rate*, *sale*, etc.

1881 *Standard* 14 Sept. 4/7 The 'spot' transactions..form the smallest proportion of the operations of the market. **1882** *Times* 22 Feb., A similar succession of movements has taken place in the spot price of No. 2 Spring. **1887** *Pall Mall G.* 20 June 10/2 The spot sales at Liverpool on Saturday were only 5,000 bales. **1887** *Daily News* 16 July 6/8 Spot parcels continue in good demand, and prices steady. **1888** *Times* 26 June 12/1 There has been no alteration in the value of spot oil during the past week. **1933** Spot rate [see PREMIUM 3 c]. **1939** *Sun* (Baltimore) 12 Dec. 17/6 As the price of tin for future delivery advanced..local cash or spot market prices declined slightly. **1956** *Ann. Reg. 1955* 436 Dealings in lire were restricted to the spot market. The Bank of England began the publication of official spot T.T. rates for lire. **1971** Spot rate [see PREMIUM 3 c]. **1982** *Daily Tel.* 3 Aug. 13/2 Saudi oil is being traded on the spot market at up to $3 a barrel discount.

e. In sense 9: = 'made on the spot', as *spot decision*, *fine*, etc. See also *spot test* (*b*), sense 15 below, and SPOT CHECK *sb.*

1921 Z. COPE *Early Diagnosis Acute Abdomen* i. 3 Spot-diagnosis is impressive but unsafe. **1934** *Amer. Speech* IX. 113/1 One man may make a *spot count*, for eight or nine hours. **1953** *Times* 29 July 6/6 He said that the 'spot scrutiny' of vehicles such as has been carried out in Bedfordshire was one of the best ways of indentifying those which should not be on the roads. **1959** *Economist* 21 Mar. 1047/1 He may now be obliged to make spot decisions with inadequate notice in highly controversial circumstances. **1976** *Wymondham & Attleborough Express* 17 Dec. 2/1 Prosecution is a waste of time of already crowded courts, so what about spot fines for these moronic motor maniacs. **1979** H. S. KENT *In on Act* xxii. 247 Although..I would often be glad of a 'spot opinion' on one of my new problems, it was never quite the same again.

14. In parasynthetic adjs., as *spot-billed*, *-eared*, *-lipped*, *-winged*.

1713 PETIVER *Aquat. Anim. Amboinæ* Tab. iv, Smooth spot-lipt Casket. **1809** SHAW *Gen. Zool.* VII. II. 328 Spot-winged Shrike. **1811** *Ibid.* VIII. I. 244 Spot-eared Creeper. **1905** *Westm. Gaz.* 9 Oct. 6/3 The spot-billed toucanet (*Seleindera maculirostris*), now to be seen..at the 'Zoo'.

15. Special Combs.: **spot ad, advertisement** *Broadcasting*, an advertisement occupying a short break during or between programmes; so **spot advertising** *vbl. sb.*; **spot announcement** *Broadcasting*, an announcement occupying a short break during or between programmes; **spot-barred** *a.*, *Billiards* (see quot.); **spot board** *Plastering* (see quot. 1964); **spot cash** orig. *U.S.*, money paid on the spot; **spot commercial** = *spot advertisement*; **spot dance**, a competitive dance in which a spotlight plays on the dancers until the music stops, at which time the couple on whom the spotlight rests wins; † **spot-dial**, a sun-dial indicating the time by means of a spot; **spot effect** *Broadcasting*, a sound effect created in the studio (see quots. 1941 and 1976); also *attrib.* in *pl.*; **spot fairy**, a variety of domestic pigeon; **spot-fish** = sense 5 e; **spot height** *Surveying*, the height of a point above mean sea level, usu. as marked on a map; **spot kick** *Assoc. Football*, a penalty kick; also *attrib.*; **spot lamp** = SPOTLIGHT *sb.*; **spot-lens**, a lens having the central portion obstructed by a spot; **spot level** *Surveying* = *spot height*; also *fig.*; **spot-like** *a.*, resembling a spot; **spot-list** *v. trans.*, to place (a building) on a list (LIST *sb.* 6 a (*b*)) as the result of special consideration; so **spot-listing** *vbl. sb.*; **spot-made** *a.*, made on the spot, makeshift; **spot map**, a map in which spots or points indicate individual locations or occurrences of something; **spot meter**, a photometer that measures the intensity of light received within a cone of small angle, usu. 2° or less; **spot news** *Journalism* (orig. *U.S.*), news reported of events as they occur; also *attrib.*; **spot pigeon** = sense 5 a; **spot plate** *Chem.*, a plate having several small depressions in which spot tests can be performed; **spot-proof** *a.*, (of a fabric) that is not susceptible to small stains; **spot-reducing** *vbl. sb.*, reduction of fat in selected areas of the body; **spot-removing** *a.*, taking out stains; **spot-skin** *a.*, having spotted skins; **spot snapper**, an American fish (see quot.); **spot stitch** (see quot.); **spot test**, (*a*) a chemical test performed using a single drop of sample; (*b*) = SPOT CHECK *sb.*; also **spot-test** *v. trans.*, to subject to a spot test; **spot testing** *vbl. sb.*; **spot welding** *Engin.*, a form of resistance welding in which one or more small, localized welds are produced on the overlapping surfaces to be joined; so **spot weld** *sb.*, a weld of this kind; also (with hyphen) as *v. trans.*, to join by spot welding; **spot-welded** *ppl. a.*; **spot welder**, an apparatus that carries out spot welding; **spot wobble** *Television* (now *disused*), small periodic oscillation of the scanning spot, formerly used to render the scanning lines less noticeable; **spot zoning** *U.S.*, the special rezoning (see ZONING *vbl. sb.*) of an area to meet a particular interest.

1934 J. RORTY *Our Master's Voice Advertising* 269 Canada prohibits the broadcasting of '*spot ads'. **1962** *Rep. Comm. Broadcasting 1960* 82 in *Parl. Papers 1961–2* (Cmnd. 1753) IX. 259 The principle of the control of advertising time applied only to '*spot' advertisements, and not in any analogous way to advertising magazines. **1961** *Ann Reg. 1960* 452 The amount of '*spot' advertising in the clock hour was to be reduced to 7½ minutes. **1979** *Guardian* 4 Aug. 8/7 This danger [of competition] can..be avoided..if only a different kind of advertising is permitted on the new commercial channel: if it may show only *block* not *spot* advertising. **1937** *Spot announcement [see sense 8 d above]. **1949** *Consumer Reports* May 236/2 A 'spot announcement'..can..be inserted between the close of one commercial program and the opening of the next. **1976** *National Observer* (U.S.) 3 July 13 To defend his position, Mr. Reagan taped a 1½ minute 'spot' announcement. **1885** *Rules Billiards* §43 In a *spot-barred game only one winning hazard is allowed to be made in the top pockets. **1931** W. VERRALL in T. Corkhill *Brickwork, Concrete & Masonry* VIII. xxxi. 1940 The *spot board, as it is sometimes called, is made of floor boards, about 3 ft. long, nailed together with cleats at the back. **1939** *Archit. Rev.* LXXXV. 213 Where hand-mixing [of plaster] is carried out the mess and waste that are inevitable when plaster is mixed on 'banker-boards' and then transferred to 'spot-boards' should be avoided where possible. **1964** J. S. SCOTT *Dict. Building* 307 *Spot board or gauge board or spot*, a plasterer's board about 3 ft square on which he works up the plaster before he puts it on. It rests on a stand about 27 in. high. **1879** *Bradstreet's* 8 Oct. 4/3 A business Utopia where credit shall be unknown and '*spot cash' an unvarying rule. **1909** A. N. LYONS *Sixpenny Pieces* ii. 12 The spot-cash practitioners of Mile End Road are rather strange..to us. **1957** V. PACKARD *Hidden Persuaders* xii. 131 After the car went on sale reports from dealers stated that 90 per cent of the people buying paid spot cash. **1978** *Dumfries & Galloway Standard* 21 Oct. 21/3 (Advt.), Caravans wanted, spot cash, any size, any make. **1955** *Times* 28 July 9/7 Television uses many old pictures to fill less valuable time, mainly as vehicles for strings of '*spot' commercials that effectively break any thread they may possess. **1962** A. NISBETT *Technique Sound Studio* i. 18 He [*sc.* the announcer] also presents programme trailers and (in many countries outside Britain) spot commercials. **1976** *National Observer* (U.S.) 10 Apr. 2/5 The networks have said they will make regular prime-time spot-commercial time available. **1944** M. LASKI *Love on Supertax* iii. 40 Such refinements as '*spot-dances' and..jazz superbly played. **1947** *Daily Gleaner* (Kingston, Jamaica) 4 Nov. 15/1 Spot dances, raffles, games and a grand floor show. **1687** G. CLERKE *Spot-dial* 5 The *Spot-Dial is of two sorts; in the one the Lines go to a black Spot, in the other a bright Spot goes to the Lines. **1734** WATTS *Reliq. Juv.* lxvii. 295 On a Ceiling Dial, usually called a Spot-Dial. **1941** *B.B.C. Gloss. Broadcasting Terms* 31 **Spot effects*, effects created in a studio where the performance of which they form part is taking place. **1944** L. MACNEICE *Christopher Columbus* 17 'Effects'..are of two kinds—records on a gramophone or spot effects in the studio. **1961** G. MILLERSON *Telev. Production* i. 14 A spot-effects man sounds the horn of an 'approaching car'. **1976** B. ARMSTRONG *Gloss. TV terms* 84 *Spot effect*, a brief sound—door closing, bell ring—added during the dub. **1881** LYELL *Pigeons* 88 The stork..has been already described in a late publication, under the name of '*Spot Fairy'. **1875** *Fur, Fin & Feather* 122 You are always welcome to a seat in his boat, if disposed for snipe or duck, or *spot-fish. **1913** A. R. HINKS *Maps & Survey* i. 23 There is a strong tendency to give *spot heights for summits, and not for the bottoms of depressions. **1928** E. D. LABORDE *Pop. Map Reading* iii. 65 In actual practice, it is often difficult to find the exact height of ground: small areas of high ground are not always marked with spot heights. **1977** D. BEATY *Excellency* vi. 74 He drew his track on the maps and charts..and memorized the spot-heights over the Alps. **1950** *Sport* 22–28 Sept. 4/4 He has handed over the responsibility of taking penalty kicks to left-back 'Jock' Ferrier, who converted a *spot-kick last Saturday. **1971** *Post* (S. Afr., Cape ed.) 9 May 23/5 Dumile Melane never faltered with the spot-kick amid cheers from jubilant Cubs supporters. **1977** *Belfast Tel.* 22 Feb. 30/6 Magee remains the Blues' spot kick expert and, if a penalty is awarded.., he will be the man to take it. **1937** *Motor Catal.* (East London Rubber Co.) 151 'Raydyot' *Spot Lamp... Universal movement. **1962** H. C. WESTON *Sight, Light & Work* (ed. 2)

vi. 197 A low voltage 50 watt spot-lamp unit..can be mounted at a distance of 6 ft. from the work and yet provide an illumination upwards of 300 lm/f.[2] **1976** *Liverpool Echo* 22 Nov. 14/3 (Advt.), Daimler Sovereign 1973, automatic, power steering,..spotlamps, [etc.]. **1862** *Catal. Internat. Exhib., Brit.* II. No. 2948, That portion of the light of the ordinary *spot lens, which really tends to obliterate the shadows.., is stopped. **1908** N. F. MACKENZIE *Methods of Surveying* x. 118 From these '*spot levels' the actual contour lines are sketched in by interpolation. **1920** J. K. FINCH *Topographic Maps & Sketch Mapping* I. i. 19 The exact height of the ground is only shown at important points on hachure maps. This is done by means of 'spot levels' or 'spot heights' scattered over the map. **1958** *Listener* 20 Nov. 813/1 As the polls attempt a nation-wide cross-section one would expect them to reflect the gradual development and movement of political opinion..more steadily and consistently than the spot-levels, so to speak, which are taken at by-elections, with all their variations of locality, candidate, and so on. **1974** W. H. IRVINE *Surveying for Construction* iii. 12/1 At present spot levels are shown to the nearest foot but with metrication the levels will be to the nearest 100 mm. **1847–9** *Todd's Cycl. Anat.* IV. I. 69 The species begins as a *spot-like crust of uniform texture. **1887** W. PHILLIPS *Brit. Discomycetes* 360 Sporidia hyaline; cups seated on a spot-like crust. **1974** *Country Life* 31 Jan. 197/3 After representations by the Victorian Society, the building was recently *spot-listed. **1977** M. BINNEY in Binney & Burman *Change & Decay* 188/1 If a church is of any merit yet still not listed it is worth asking the Department of the Environment to consider spotlisting it. **1973** *Times* 8 Jan. 3/3 Widespread '*spot listing' to save buildings threatened by development may be counter-productive. **1894** *Outing* XXIV. 173/2 The bridles were mostly *spot-made with a bit of cord doing service as reins. **1901** PARKES & KENWOOD *Hygiene & Public Health* xi. 666 '*Spot maps'—maps of a district, on which the deaths or cases of various infectious diseases are spotted out—furnish valuable graphic expressions of any grouping. **1973** J. J. MCKELVEY *Man against Tsetse* ii. 81 In three months the commission acquired 460 collections of flies and made a spot map of tsetse locations. **1979** *Dictionaries* I. 36 The spot maps will be effectively utilized to show the distribution of a single [dialectal] term. **1955** J. LIPINSKI *Miniature & Precision Cameras* vi. 240 The incident light meter may measure the light incident upon the scene. Or the *spot meter may measure it from a white card. **1976** *Physics Bull.* Sept. 395/3 A range of luminance (brightness) spotmeters and illuminance meters will be displayed. **1912** S. WASHBURN *Cable Game* 9 The other type, the 'cable men', are collectors of what might be called '*spot' news. **1936** E. WAUGH *Waugh in Abyssinia* 82 There were demands from Fleet Street for daily items of 'spot news'. **1976** *National Observer* (U.S.) 15 May 2/3 Other Pulitzer winners were: Sydney Schanberg of the New York Times, international reporting; ..and the staff of the Chicago Tribune, spot-news reporting. **1783** LATHAM *Gen. Synop. Birds* II. II. 615 *Spot Pigeon. This is remarkable, from having on the forehead, above the bill, a spot, which is of the same colour as the tail. **1928** *Chemist-Analyst* XVII. I. 18/2 *Spot plate for outside indications. **1937** J. W. MATTHEWS tr. *Feigl's Spot Tests* ii. 5 Spot plates are made from glazed porcelain, and usually contain 6–12 adjacent depressions of equal size that hold 0·5–1 c.c. of liquid. **1981** *Sci. Amer.* Feb. 128/1 The aluminum compound responsible for the buffering effect of buffered aspirin can be detected with filter paper or a spot plate. **1950** *Spotproof [see HABUTAI]. **1958** *Times* 6 Oct. 13/1 Leather and suède jackets and coats many of which are treated to be spot-proof against rain. **1960** *Sunday Express* 27 Nov. 14/3 Gymnasia with *spot-reducing and general slimming equipment. **1970** *Harrod's Catal.* May 14/1 Spot reducing 'Faradic' and 'G.5' from £2. 2. 0. **1670** EACHARD *Cont. Clergy* 56 Many a good-wife..knows not any thing of the all-powerfulness of aqua-fortis, how that it is such a *spot-removing liquor. **1871** BROWNING *Balaust.* 1318 With them fed in fellowship..*spot-skin lynxes. **1876** GOODE *Fishes Bermudas* 55 The *Spot snapper and the Yellow-tail correspond doubtless to *Mesoprion uninotatus*..and to *Ocyurus chrysurus*. **1882** CAULFEILD & SAWARD *Dict. Needlework* 125/2 **Spot stitch*, a stitch made with a Foundation of Double Crochet with spots upon it in Treble Crochet. **1921** *Chem. Abstr.* XV. 2599 *Spot tests which depend upon the formation of $PbCrO_4$ or of $AgCrO_4$ are fairly sensitive. **1948** *Ann. N.Y. Acad. Sci.* XLIX. 268 Prior to quantitative analysis..the fractions are spot-tested on paper impregnated with ninhydrin. **1955** *Times* 16 June 9/3 'Spot tests' could be extended, and it would be well if the Minister were to declare his intention with regard to them. **1960** *Jrnl. Iron & Steel Inst.* CXCIV. 285/3 For Cu, a spot test is suggested which allows estimation in the range 0·1–0·5 p.p.m. **1942** *Industr. & Engin. Chem.* (Analytical Ed.) 15 Apr. 278/2 (*heading*) Application of infrared radiation to *spot-testing. **1969** *Listener* 28 Aug. 287/1 Miss Atwood's Toronto heroine works for Seymour Surveys, spot-testing consumer products. **1908** *Engineering* 9 Oct. 486/1 The pedal of one of the machines on view had been made..by attaching a piece of angle iron on each side of the lever by two '*spot welds'. **1951** *Ibid.* 13 Apr. 439/1 The shear strength of an individual spot weld was nearly twice that of a rivet. **1977** *Modern Railways* Dec. 488/1 The main handicap..was the high labour cost which resulted from the 50,000 rivets and 60,000 spot-welds involved in the construction of one vehicle. **1909** *Engineering* 15 Jan. 69/3 We have seen three thicknesses of 3/16-in. iron *spot-welded together, the spot being about ⅜ in. in diameter. **1958** *Ibid.* 14 Mar. 344/2 The panels are..automatically seam-welded before being spot-welded to the framing. **1973** A. PARRISH *Mech. Engineer's Ref. Bk.* VI. 34 Aluminium is readily spot welded but the welding parameters must be closely controlled because the metal has a short plastic temperature range. **1921** *Automobile Engineer* Mar. 106/3 (*caption*) A *spot welded bonnet. **1969** J. G. TWEEDDALE *Welding Fabrication* II. iii. 87 In a spot welded assembly the joint is comparatively rigid. **1914** *Proc. Inst. Mech. Engineers* 167 An attempt was made to put down one small machine, a *spot welder or a contact welder. **1963** H. R. CLAUSER *Encycl. Engin. Materials & Processes* 573/2 Semi-portable spot welders are..available for assemblies such as automotive structures, housings, and cases that cannot be handled by permanently placed..machines. **1976** Spot welder [see *seam welder* s.v. SEAM *sb.*[1] 10]. **1908** *Engineering* 9 Oct. 486/1 The method of *spot-welding appears cheaper, quicker, and as good as riveting. **1912** *Automobile Engineer* 30 Oct. 387/3 In the spot-welding machine the sheets are joined at spots instead of rivets. **1970** K. BALL *Fiat 600, 600 D Autobook* xii. 141/1 The body structure is made up from nine separate assemblies joined together by spot welding. **1951** *Sun* (Baltimore) 19 Oct. (B ed.) 5/7 First sets to incorporate '*spot wobble' are 15-inch home receivers. Focusing is by the normal line-pattern method, but the flick of a switch converts to 'spot wobble'. **1956** *B.B.C. Engin. Monogr.* No. 1. 5/2 The obliteration of the line structure by carefully adjusted spot wobble is of course essential in any telerecording system if beat patterns are to be avoided when the film is scanned. **1932** *Sun* (Baltimore) 6 May 14/2 All cities which have zoning laws go through a period of attacks that aim to break them down for private as opposed to public interests. The practice is called '*spot' zoning. **1933** *Ibid.* 16 Nov. 12/1 The Board of Zoning Appeals has disapproved a proposed 'spot-zoning' ordinance in the interest of the promoters of a distillery. **1946** *Amer. Home* Sept. 96/3 There is..one very deplorable habit among the creators and administrators of Zoning Laws which was, to permit what is known as 'spot zoning'. This may allow a small 'spot' of business to establish itself in an exclusively residential area. **1976** *Tulane Law Rev.* L. 357 The term 'spot zoning'..may mean rezoning not in accordance with a comprehensive plan, rezoning in the absence of a mistake or change, or rezoning which is arbitrary and improper.

spot, *sb.*[2] [f. SPOT *v.* 9.] A person employed by an omnibus company to keep secret watch on its employees.

1894 *Daily Graphic* 24 Mar. 11/2 The men were continually being harassed, and 'spots' were jumping on their 'buses at all times to spy on them.

spot (spɒt), *v.* Also 5–6 **spotte**, 6–7 **spott**. [f. SPOT *sb.*[1] Cf. WFlem. *spotten* to mark or stain, NFris. *spotte* to fix, settle.]

I. 1. a. *trans.* To stain, sully, or tarnish, in respect of moral character or qualities.

c **1412** HOCCLEVE *De Reg. Princ.* 3766 His disciples loued so clennesse..Hir eyen they out of hir heedes brente, Lest sighte of hem spotte myght her entente. *c* **1450** LYDG. *Secrees* 741 That ther Imperial magnanymyte Shulde nat be spottyd..Towchyng the vice of froward Coveityse. **1502** ATKYNSON tr. *De Imitatione* I. i. (1893) 154 For them that folowe sensuall pleasure,..they spot theyr conscience, & lese the grace of god. **1560** DAUS tr. *Sleidane's Comm.* 8 b, Neither to suffer so greate an evill to spot & blemishe that noble house of Saxonie. **1623** FLETCHER *Rule a Wife* v. Wks. 1906 III. 231 You rob two Temples,..You ruine hers, and spot her noble Husbands. **1669** DRYDEN *Tyrannic Love* v. i, Be all the Discords of our Bed forgot, Which, Virtue witness, I did never spot. **1855** MOTLEY *Dutch Rep.* I. iii. (1866) 113 Who might be spotted merely with the errors introduced by Luther. **1858** H. BUSHNELL *Nat. & Supernat.* xv. (1864) 498 He spots with blemish the religion that already has a right to his faith.

refl. **1577** tr. *Bullinger's Decades* (1592) 128 If..wee doe spot our-selues with a filthie and uncleane life. **1599** SANDYS *Europæ Spec.* (1632) 18 Some,..not content to spott themselves with all Italian impurities, proceed on to empoyson their country also.

†**b.** To stain with some accusation or reproach; to asperse or vilify. *Obs.*

a **1542** WYATT in *Tottell's Misc.* (Arb.) 58 Mistrust me not, though some there be, That faine would spot my stedfastnesse. **1623** T. SCOTT *Tongue-Combat* 9 Those of the Reformed Religion whom..you spot with three or foure crimes. **1652** BROUGH *Preserv. agst. Schism* 27 St. Jude spots them thus; There they feed themselves without feare. *a* **1718** PENN *Tracts* Wks. 1782 I. 492, I do not mention it to spot that Doctor.

2. a. To mark with spots of some defiling or discolouring substance; to stain in spots.

c **1440** *Promp. Parv.* 470 Spotton, *maculo*. **1530** PALSGR. 729 Who hath spotted your shyrte sleve with ynke? **1549** LATIMER *5th Serm. bef. Edw. VI* (Arb.) 151 He yat medleth wyth pitch is like to be spotted with it. **1600** SURFLET *Countrie Farme* 502 It spotteth and staineth the linnen so mightily, as that such staines will neuer be got out. **1675** HOBBES *Odyssey* VI. (1686) 71 Your Cloths..(Which in the house sulli'd and spotted lie). **1763** MILLS *Syst. Pract. Husb.* II. 415 Two..kinds of mildew, one of which spots the blades and stems of corn. **1798** COLERIDGE *France* 69 Ye that, fleeing, spot your mountain-snows With bleeding wounds. **1831** SCOTT *Ct. Rob.* xvii, The blood which we have shed may spot our hand,..but it shall scarce stain our forehead. **1870** MORRIS *Earthly Par.* III. 91 With rust his armour bright was spotted o'er.

b. *absol.* (in fig. use).

a **1743** SAVAGE *False Historians* Poems (1790) 292 Sure of all plagues with which dull prose is curst, Scandals, from false historians, spot the worst.

3. *intr.* To be subject or liable to spots; to become spotted.

1850 *Rep. Comm. Patents: Agric. 1849* (U.S.) 456 These varieties spot better, and produce a finer leaf than any I have ever seen. **1879** *Warehousemen & Drapers' Trade Jrnl.* 13 Dec. 594 Even those [gloves] which have been so treated continue to 'spot'. **1882** *Garden* 11 Mar. 168/2 A damp, cool atmosphere, with little artificial heat, causes the flowers to spot.

II. 4. *trans.* **a.** To mark, cover, or decorate, with spots.

1591 GREENE *Conny Catch.* (1592) II. 4 They will straight spot him by sundry pollicies, and in a blacke horse, marke saddle spots. **1687** MIÈGE *Gt. Fr. Dict.* II, To spot Gawze-Hoods, *broder des Coifes de Gaze*. [See also SPOTTER *sb.* 1.] **1713** *Guardian* No. 10 ⁋5 Sometimes I take a Needle, and spot a Piece of Muslin for pretty Patty Cross-stitch. **1720** *Lond. Gaz.* No. 5914/1 If any Person..shall file, square, or new spot any Dice. **1818** *Art Bookbinding* 51 This colour is for spotting the edges. **1864** *Athenæum* 854/2 He spots the other spear-bearers [with blood] in a similar manner. **1885** D. GLASGOW *Watch & Clock Making* 118 The art of spotting such small pieces by hand is not easily acquired.

b. To ornament (the face) with a patch or patches.

1666 M. M. *Solomon's Prescr.* 82 Go, Gallants, get to your Glass; Powder and Curle, Paint and Spot, Deck and Adorn you, as you were wont. **1711** ADDISON *Spect.* No. 81 ⁋1 The Faces on one Hand, being spotted on the right Side of the Forehead, and those upon the other on the left.

c. *U.S.* (See quots.)

1792 BELKNAP *Hist. New Hampsh.* III. 75 Where they find the land suitable for a road, the trees are spotted by cutting out a piece of the bark. **1828–32** in WEBSTER. **1859** BARTLETT *Dict. Amer.* (ed. 2), *Spot*, to mark a tree by cutting a chip from its side.

d. *N.Z.* To form by selecting the choicest spots or parts of a piece of land.

1856 E. M. CURR *Waste Lands of Province of Wellington* 30 The practice of which I speak is called in New Zealand '*spotting*' or '*spoiling*' country. **1864** E. MUTER *Trav. & Adv. Officer's Wife* II. xiii. 260 'Cockatoos', as the station-owners call the other [class of land-purchasers], who 'spotted' his run all over with fifty and one hundred acre sections. **1898** MORRIS *Austral Eng.* s.v. *Spotting*, The squatter spotted his run, purchasing choice spots.

e. To moisten *with* a drop of liquid; to place a drop of (liquid) *on* (*to*) a surface, etc.

1954 R. E. OESPER tr. *Feigl's Spot Tests* (ed. 3) II. iv. 158 The moist reagent paper is spotted with the test solution. **1972** *Sci. Amer.* June 34 (*caption*) The mixture is spotted at one corner (X) of a square of filter paper; the fragments are separated by chromatography in one direction and by electrophoresis in another. **1977** *Lancet* 26 Nov. 1140/2 Blood is spotted on to filterpaper. **1978** *Nature* 9 Feb. 577/2 Even concentrated lysates did not result in killing or lysogenisation when spotted on a lawn of Mu-sensitive bacteria.

5. a. Of things: To form, appear as, spots upon (a surface); to stud.

1801 SOUTHEY *Thalaba* I. xi, No palm-tree rose to spot the wilderness. **1817** SHELLEY *Rev. Islam* IX. iii, Many ships spotting the dark blue deep. **1822–7** GOOD *Study Med.* (1829) V. 568 Pimples very minute..; chiefly spotting the limbs. **1892** 'M. FIELD' *Sight & Song* 22 Pinks and gentians spot her robe.

b. *intr.* Of rain: To fall in large, scattered drops, esp. before a shower or storm.

1849– in dial. glossaries. **1909** *Westm. Gaz.* 21 Aug. 2/2 It began to spot with rain.

6. *Billiards.* To place (a ball) on some particular spot.

1844 E. R. MARDON *Billiards* 99 Missing the balls, the player must spot a ball. **1873** BENNETT & CAVENDISH *Billiards* 139 Spot the white just behind the left-hand corner of the D. **1899** *Allbutt's Syst. Med.* VIII. 258 If they play billiards, they let their adversary spot the red and take the balls out of the pockets.

7. To free from spots or small defects; to remove or efface (small marks). † Also with *out*.

1885 C. G. W. LOCK *Workshop Rec.* Ser. IV. 382/2 After the prints are mounted, dried, and spotted out, roll them upon a hot steel plate. **1896** *Kodak News* Sept. 87/1 Any little holes or scratches..should be carefully spotted out with a fine sable brush and stiff water colour. **1915** B. E. JONES *Cinematograph Bk.* 176 Having cleaned and spotted the film, attention may be given to any torn portions or broken perforations. **1937** *Discovery* Feb. p. xiv/1 This book [*sc.* J. Deschin *New Ways in Photography*]..contains many suggestions and practical methods for getting better results in..spotting prints. **1979** *Amateur Photographer* 7 Feb. 4 (Advt.), A custom hand print, cropped, hand printed, spotted, dry mounted and heat sealed.

8. *N. Amer.* To place (something) in a particular location; *esp.* to place (a railway car) in the proper place for loading or unloading.

1917 *Dial. Notes* IV. 329 *Spot*, to stop (a car) at the proper place on a railroad track. **1936** B. BROOKER *Think of Earth* I. iii. 38 It was a wilderness of rusting steel and rotten ties where old dump-cars were 'spotted' for repairs. **1937** *Liberty* 25 Dec. 20/1 Already strategically spotted throughout..our population are sergeants and lieutenants and chiefs of police of the new 'supertrained' school. **1947** *Sun* (Baltimore) 13 May 6/3 Passengers would walk..under cover to their planes spotted alongside the pier. **1956** T. RADDALL *Wings of Night* (1957) xii. 106 You might phone the railway people and tell 'em to spot four or five boxcars on the Hall's Creek siding not later than Tuesday. **1962** J. ONSLOW *Bowler-Hatted Cowboy* xiv. 136 When I arrived at the yards the cars were ready spotted opposite the loading-chutes. **1970** J. H. GRAY *Boy from Winnipeg* 55 The rest of us spotted our lunch kits, towels, and swimming things at a convenient table. **1979** *Arizona Daily Star* 22 July I. 6/4 If you're playing a Nevada audience, you can't give them all new stuff, and you have to be careful how you spot it.

III. 9. a. *Cant.* To mark or note as a criminal or suspected person.

1718 *Acc. Trial Isaac Rabbins* 1 Isaac, You have been spotted before, How came you to go so far from your own Home now? **1851** MAYHEW *Lond. Lab.* I. 484 At length he became 'spotted'. The police got to know him. **1859** *Slang Dict.* 99 *Spotted*, to be known or marked by the police.

b. To inform against, split upon (a person).

1865 DICKENS *Mut. Fr.* I. xii, This man had 'spotted' the other, to save himself and get the money.

10. *colloq.* **a.** To single out or guess beforehand (the winner in a horse race).

1857 *Morn. Chron.* 22 June (Encycl. Dict.), Having met with tolerable success in spotting the winners. **1866** G. A. LAWRENCE *Sans Merci* xix, It was quite a sight to see those two, conning over the handicaps, and 'spotting' probable 'good things'. **1888** E. J. GOODMAN *Too Curious* xi, I spotted a few winners.

b. To catch sight of; to mark or note; to recognize or detect.

1848 E. Z. C. JUDSON *Mysteries & Miseries of New York* I. 116 To spot is to recognize—to mark. **1849** G. G. FOSTER *New York in Slices* 15 The expertness acquired by the keepers of these shops in 'spotting' their man is truly wonderful. **1860** O. W. HOLMES *Elsie V.* xxi, The inside Widow having 'spotted' the outside one through the blinds.

1868 MISS BRADDON *Run to Earth* I. i. 17, I saw the landlord spot the notes and gold. **1880** J. PAYN *Confid. Agent* II. 271 Honest John had known him to be a policeman—'spotted him', as he had expressed it—at the first glance.

c. To hit in shooting.

1882 B. HARTE *Flip* ii, It's an even thing if she wouldn't spot me the first pop [i.e. with a revolver].

d. *Mil.* To locate (an enemy position). Also *intr.* and const. *for*.

1914 *Aeroplane* 11 Nov. 425/2 He poised..for a spell to spot the lurking place of the battery. **1915** D. O. BARNETT *Let.* 23–25 Jan. 51, I had a man with a periscope spotting for me, and he registered some near things for the Bosch's face. **1916** 'BOYD CABLE' *Action Front* 135 'Stand by for trouble. That brute is spotting for his gun.' The aeroplane dropped a light, turned, and circled round to the left. **1918** C. BRIGHT *Telegraphy, Aeronautics & War* 51 While he is spotting he is continually subjected to tremendous shelling. **1942** *Hutchinson's Pictorial Hist. War* 18 Mar.–9 June 62 (*caption*) Men of a Cypriot company..spotting for enemy aircraft. **1973** R. DENTRY *Encounter at Kharmel* ix. 152 I'll come in low. You spot. I'll be busy.

e. To watch out for and observe (a certain class of objects) as a hobby. See also TRAIN-SPOT *v.*

1919 G. B. SHAW *Inca of Perusalem* in *Heartbreak House* 212 Chips keeps owls and rabbits. Spots motor bicycles. **1957** *Times Lit. Suppl.* 8 Nov. 675/2 As other boys spot railway engines, Alan Villiers as a child in Melbourne spotted and studied the big sailing ships lying at anchor in Port Phillip bay.

spot check, *sb.* orig. *U.S.* Also hyphened. [f. SPOT *sb.*¹ + CHECK *sb.*] A check made on the spot; a quick check made on a random sample. Also *attrib.*

1933 *Sun* (Baltimore) 15 Aug. 8/1 The spot check made on bread prices from February 15 to August 2 in sixteen representative cities. **1946** *N.Y. Times* 30 June L-25/2 Spot checks are made but many of these slaughter houses go as long as five weeks without a check. **1947** *Sun* (Baltimore) 3 Apr. 5/1 Troops and police made a surprise spot-check of identities in the center of Jerusalem today, hastily erecting roadblocks while they examined the papers of pedestrians and persons in trucks and automobiles. **1963** *Language* XXXIX. 465 A survey of the vast..literature of ethology, supplemented by repeated spot checks of ongoing research projects, reveals that the study of signaling behavior in animals has, by and large, been taxonomically parochial. **1972** *Daily Tel.* 1 Mar. 2 A spot check by the Inner London Education Authority last autumn showed that 17,000 out of 165,000 secondary school pupils were absent that day. **1978** L. DEIGHTON *SS-GB* iv. 37 They saw the soldiers doing the spot-check. Parked across the roadway there were three Bedford lorries. **1980** *Sunday Times* 24 Aug. 1/1 Six French paratroopers have also been charged after spot-checks on kitbags revealed stolen electrical goods.

Hence **spot-'check** *v. trans.*, to subject to a spot check; also *absol.*; **spot-'checking** *vbl. sb.*

1944 U. SINCLAIR *Presidential Agent* I. ii. 43 Robbie Budd lived and breathed and ate and talked aeroplanes: cat-walks and bulkhead segments, stabilizers and de-icers, sub-assemblies and spot-checking—a whole new vocabulary. **1955** *Times* 5 July 10/7 They had decided..not to make vehicle tests compulsory and they were considering falling back on the proposal..to extend 'spot checking' to private vehicles. **1962** *Guardian* 15 Jan. 3/4, I recently saw vehicles being spot-checked by the Ministry of Transport. **1962** E. SNOW *Red China Today* (1963) xxxviii. 277 We spent another forty days spot-checking all over the county. **1972** *Accountant* 14 Sept. 314/1 He'd spot-checked them against actual orders. **1976** C. WESTON *Rouse Demon* (1977) xix. 90 By spot-checking instead of monitoring each complete tape, Adrian had managed to go through seven. **1980** P. MOYES *Angel Death* i. 9 Once in a while, a Customs Officer will..do a certain amount of spot-checking on visiting private yachts.

†spote. *Obs. rare.* [f. OE. *spát-, stem of *spátl* SPATTLE *sb.*¹, *spǽtan* SPETE *v.*] Spittle.

c **1315** SHOREHAM II. 142 As a mesel þer he lay, A-stouned, in spote and blode. *c* **1320** *Cast. Love* 1147 Al was his face bifoulet wᵗ spot, And eke grete boffetes among me him smot. *a* **1800** PEGGE *Suppl. Grose, Spote*, spittle. Lanc.

spotel, -il, spotle, obs. varr. SPATTLE *sb.*¹

spotless ('spɒtlɪs), *a.* Also 4 -lez, 6 -les, 6–7 -lesse. [f. SPOT *sb.*¹ Cf. WFlem. *spotteloos*.]

1. Free from spot or stain; not marked with, or disfigured by, spots; of a pure or uniform colour.

13.. *E.E. Allit. P.* A. 856 Of spotlez perlez þay beren þe creste. **1588** SHAKS. *Tit. A.* I. i. 182 The people of Rome..Send thee..This Palliament of white and spotlesse Hue. **1606** MARSTON *Parasitaster* IV. G 4, Vntrodden snow is not so spotless. **1653** R. SANDERS *Physiogn.* 157 The body being clear, fair, pure, neat, and spotless. **1726–46** THOMSON *Winter* 812 Fair ermines, spotless as the snows they press. **1853** C. BRONTE *Villette* xxiii, The bed seemed to me like snow-drift and mist—spotless, soft, and gauzy. **1876** MISS BRADDON *J. Haggard's Dau.* II. 15 The red-brick floor spotless as if it were a floor in a picture.

b. In specific names.

1827 GRIFFITH tr. *Cuvier* V. 274 The Ai seems to vary considerably as the Spotless Ai, the Yellow-faced Ai. **1832** J. RENNIE *Consp. Butterfl. & Moths* 19 The Spotless Brown (*Polyommatus Titus*). *Ibid.* 188 The Spotless Straw (*Depressaria immaculana*).

2. *fig.* Free from stain or blot; immaculate, pure.

1577 [see SPOTTINESS]. **1590** SPENSER *Tears Muses* 388 Sweete Loue deuoyd of villanie..But pure and spotles. **1634** W. TIRWHYT tr. *Balzac's Lett.* 318, I..do protest unto you..that my fidelity is spotless. **1667** MILTON *P.L.* IV. 318 How have ye..banisht from mans life..Simplicitie and spotless innocence. **1738** WESLEY *Ps.* CXXI. vi, Like thy spotless Master thou, Fill'd with Wisdom, Love and Power. **1781** GIBBON *Decl. & F.* xxxiii. III. 333 The people applauded his spotless integrity. **1836** THIRLWALL *Greece* xiv. II. 228 His mother's reputation was not deemed spotless. **1875** MANNING *Mission H. Ghost* xii. 331 So, I may say, all are bound to live a life that is spotless before God.

absol. **1850** THACKERAY *Pendennis* liv, O you spotless, who have the right of capital punishment vested in you.

b. Guiltless or innocent *of* something. *rare*⁻¹.

1619 FLETCHER, etc. *Knt. Malta* II. v, Ye fight for her, as spotless of these mischiefs, As heaven is of our sins.

spotlessly ('spɒtlɪslɪ), *a.* [f. prec. + -LY².] In a spotless manner; without spot or stain; immaculately.

1852 HAWTHORNE *Blithedale Rom.* xxiv. (1885) 236 Toadstools,..some spotlessly white. **1855** KINGSLEY *Westw. Ho!* ii, So Mr. Frank was arrayed spotlessly. **1888** MISS BRADDON *Fatal Three* I. ii, The room was spotlessly clean.

fig. **1887** *Pall Mall G.* 12 Oct. 4/1 The whole of Donegal, Fermanagh, and Monaghan, are as spotlessly Nationalist as any part of Connaught.

spotlessness ('spɒtlɪsnɪs). [f. as prec. + -NESS.] The quality or state of being spotless.

1624 DONNE *Devot.* 305 Lord, if thou looke for a spotlessnesse, whom wilt thou looke vpon? *a* **1684** LEIGHTON *Wks.* (1835) I. 116 As for this Blood, it is nothing but purity and Spotlessness. **1727** in BAILEY (vol. II). **1865** W. H. GILLESPIE *Arg. Being & Attrib. God* IV. ii. (1871) 142 Holiness is moral stainlessness, spotlessness, unsulliedness. **1888** HONNOR MORTEN *Hosp. Life* 16, I confess that a little less light and air and spotlessness, would have made me feel more at home.

'spotlight, *sb.* Also **spot light, spot-light.** [f. SPOT *sb.*¹ + LIGHT *sb.*] A source of artificial light casting a narrow and intense beam; *esp.* (*a*) *Theatr.*, a lamp used to cast intense illumination on a small area of a stage; also, the light cast by such a lamp; also *fig.* (cf. LIMELIGHT); (*b*) an auxiliary lamp on a motor vehicle.

1904 *Minneapolis Times* 1 Aug. 4 In the drama that was enacted Mr. Galvin was not in the spotlight at any time, but it cannot be denied that his was an important part. **1916** *Lit. Digest* (N.Y.) 8 Jan. 89/1 It will put the magnates and the self-styled fighters..into the back-ground and give the players the spot-light. **1920** *T. Eaton Catal.* Spring & Summer 395/5 Spotlights are very necessary accessories, especially in country driving. **1921** *Daily Colonist* (Victoria, B.C.) 11 Oct. 7/4 (Advt.), These new Spot Lights constitute the most remarkable improvement in the history of the flashlight business. This flash-light is capable of throwing a beam 300 feet or more. For motoring, picking out road signs, boating,..or for night flash signalling, nothing can equal them. **1922** C. AIKEN *Jig of Forslin* 25 While in the warm dark seats, we watch the spot-light Dazzle upon the singer's hair and eyes. **1922** M. B. HOUSTON *Witch Man* xiv. 193 He has a nice baritone, but he's the sort of man who gravitates to the centre of the floor and deliberately absorbs all the spot-light. **1928** *Daily Express* 7 July 5/2 Ahead of him was the professor's spot-light, making a little glow upon the ground... Charlie..dared not approach within serviceable distance of the professor's torch. **1930** J. B. PRIESTLEY *Good Companions* II. ii. 295 He comes to me and asks all about curtains and footlights and spot-lights and props, and he goes about looking so important when he's anything to do. **1931** H. F. PRINGLE *Theodore Roosevelt* I. xi. 135 The spotlight focused on Roosevelt, a spotlight so white and continuous that the other..commissioners found themselves in..shadow. **1937** *Motor Catal.* (East London Rubber Co.) 151/1 'Bosch' Spotlight... Gives a brilliant, long beam, which can be trained upon the kerb, on the road ahead, or signposts. **1946** D. C. PEATTIE *Road of Naturalist* ii. 24 Some sixty years ago the spot-light fell upon Pronuba. **1949** 'P. WENTWORTH' *Spotlight* xxviii. 175 He wanted the hall to be dark, with the single lamp on the mantelpiece arranged to be as much like a spotlight as possible. **1957** *Encycl. Brit.* XXI. 285/2 The spot-light—in contrast to the flood light—which can be controlled and focussed accurately upon one particular spot. **1964** L. DEIGHTON *Funeral in Berlin* xix. 113 A V.W. saloon with blue flasher and spotlight full on. **1967** N. FREELING *Strike out where not Applicable* 129 It was a kind of altar. No spotlights, thank heaven, but a decided feeling of stiffly-bunched-madonna-lilies. **1972** *Times* 30 Nov. 23/8 A strong consumer and governmental spotlight on food prices. **1973** 'R. MACLEOD' *Nest of Vultures* ii. 40 A half-dozen blinding spotlights were trained on a postage-stamp stage. **1978** R. LUDLUM *Holcroft Covenant* vi. 79 Several passengers were reading under the beams of tiny spotlights, but most were asleep. **1980** M. BOOTH *Bad Track* i. 18 On the front of the radiator grille was mounted a pair of very large Cibie spotlights that dwarfed the standard headlamps.

'spotlight, *v.* Also **spot-light.** [f. the sb.] *trans.*

a. To illuminate with a spotlight. Also *fig.*

1923 [implied at SPOTLIGHTED *ppl. a.*]. **1926** H. T. WILKINS *Marvels Mod. Mechanics* 234 These panorama lamps can be swung round in a circle, and, along with flood lights, be concentrated in a beam of rays to 'spot-light' the stage stars. **1935** *Amer. Speech* X. 192/2 A dress that scarfs and sleeves itself with stripes will *spotlight* her and *outsmart* her neighbors. **1942** *Sun* (Baltimore) 1 Jan. 22/8 He hoped that the publicity in connection with the measure has 'spotlighted' the abuse of charity racketeers. **1955** *Radio Times* 22 Apr. 15/3 Each programme in the series will spotlight a particular breed of dog. **1963** *Listener* 21 Feb. 353/3 His understanding of the jazz idiom spotlighted the 'bluesy' features of the Concerto beautifully. **1973** R. PERRY *Ticket to Ride* i. 11 The standard lamp..was softly spotlighting her from behind. **1975** J. CLEARY *Safe House* ii. 73 An elderly motorbike..the weak beam of its headlamp spotlighting them as they stood at the back of the truck. **1976** C. BLACKWOOD *Stepdaughter* i. 56, I feel that my future career as a painter stands spot-lit and exposed. **1977** F. YOUNG in J. Hick *Myth of God Incarnate* ii. 29 Too often the so-called out-dated substance-categories have been spotlighted and criticized.

b. Chiefly *U.S.* To hunt (game) by spotlight. Cf. JACK-LIGHT *v.*

1934 in WEBSTER. **1968** *Daily Progress* (Charlottesville, Va.) 26 Jan. 3/4 After illegally spotlighting and killing a deer [etc.].

So **'spotlighted, -lit** *ppl. a.*; **'spotlighter**, one who hunts by spotlight; **'spotlighting** *vbl. sb.*, (*a*) illumination by spotlight; (*b*) hunting by spotlight; also *attrib.*

1923 B. HECHT *Florentine Dagger* v. 72 A crowd..stood watching officials and the spotlighted figures of mystery enter. **1932** *Observer* 26 June 13/4 The spotlit nocturne that follows..is starred by Spessiva's solos. **1934** WEBSTER, Spotlighter, Spotlighting. **1952** *New Yorker* 4 Oct. 119/1 With insufficient spotlighting, the spectacle was like a succession of obscure museum paintings in need of cleaning. **1953** E. SIMON *Past Masters* II. 110 Everyone returning from the spotlighted centre was surrounded. **1961** *Daily Progress* (Charlottesville, Va.) 27 Jan. 3 (*heading*) Deer 'spotlighting' convictions hit 14. *Ibid.*, The deer 'spotlighters' were ordered to pay a total of $3,250 in fines. **1972** L. HANCOCK *There's a Seal in my Sleeping Bag* i. 13 He was surprised to learn in Australia that pit-lamping or spotlighting not only is legal but the accepted way of hunting.

spotlunge, obs. form of SPATTLING *vbl. sb.*¹

spot on, -on, *adv.* and *a.* (*phr.*) [f. SPOT *sb.*¹ + ON *adv.*] Completely accurate(ly), precise(ly), exactly right.

1920 E. H. YOUNG *By Sea & Land* i. 56 All these X-chasing instruments make my head go round. You can overdo all that, I say; shoot quick and spot on—that is the best way in the long run. **1956** C. WILLCOCK *Death at Flight* iii. 34 'What a spot for a front tyre to choose to burst,' he said. 'Funny thing, sir, the outer casing looks as though it was in spot-on condition.' **1961** *Punch* 18 Jan. 130/3 'Self-discipline and self-restraint', to use the P.M.'s spot-on terms, become minimal requirements in the ordinary citizen. **1962** L. DAVIDSON *Rose of Tibet* vii. 134 Our oracle here warned that you would be coming... The time was fixed fairly spot-on. **1966** M. WOODHOUSE *Tree Frog* xxv. 182 Neither the altimeter nor the compass is one hundred per cent spot on, because we didn't have time for an instrument check. **1969** W. GARNER *Us or Them War* i. 14 'I'm still getting things right?' The plain-clothes man said, 'Spot on, Mr Morton.' **1973** *Times* 14 May 9/1, I moved my run-up back from 109ft to 114ft and fitted in 18 strides so that I was hitting the board spot on. **1976** *Courier-Mail* (Brisbane) 2 June 4/5 It's about time somebody with influence said the sort of things Mr. Colin Lamont..said about education. He is spot on. **1977** *Sounds* 9 July 8/1 Pristine production and spot on playing, A.R.S. could be up there alongside the L.A. crowd if they concentrate more on albums full of songs of this quality. **1978** R. PERRY *Dutch Courage* vii. 82 Although the sarcasm was overdone, the cynicism was spot on. **1981** T. BARLING *Bikini Red North* ix. 194 Getting here..with a day to spare is spot-on timing. **1982** *N. & Q.* Oct. 472/2 His thesis is provocative, its evidences spot-on, and his conclusions pretty convincing.

'spotsman. [f. SPOT *v.*] A smuggler.

1895 'Q' (QUILLER COUCH) *Story of Sea* I. xxvii. 651 Our spotsman had employed a Mounts' Bay boat for his voyage; and one fine evening..he landed his cargo of kegs at the foot of the cliffs.

spotted ('spɒtɪd), *a.* and *ppl. a.* Also 5 **spottid, -yd,** 6, 9 *Sc.* **-it,** 7 **spotede.** [f. SPOT *sb.*¹ and *v.* Cf. NFris. *spŏted*.]

1. a. Marked or decorated with spots.

c **1250** *Gen & Ex.* 1721 And if of ðo spotted cumen, ðo sulen him ben for hire numen. **1388** WYCLIF *Gen.* xxx. 35 He departide..the geet and scheep geet buckis, and rammes, dyuerse and spottid. *c* **1400** MAUNDEV. (Roxb.) xxxi. 143 Þer er also wilde swyne,..dappeld and spotted, as it ware founez of daes. **1513** DOUGLAS *Æneid* I. vi. 32 [She was] cled into the spottit linx hyde. **1582** in Brown *Abstr. Somerset Wills* (1887) 93 Let my son Thomas have the spotted colt. *c* **1611** CHAPMAN *Iliad* XVII. 15 (1887) 223 Not any lion,..Nor spotted leopard, nor boar. **1648** HEXHAM II, *Gespickelt laken*, Speckled or Spotted cloath. **1697** DRYDEN *Virg. Georg.* III. 415, I pass the Wars that spotted Linx's make With their fierce Rivals. **1750** tr. *Leonardus' Mirr. Stones* 87 This sort is spotted and purple. **1799** [A. YOUNG] *Agric. Linc.* 148 Best eating potatoes are spotted lemons. **1854** *Poultry Chron.* II. 176 Their spotted plumage resembling the spotted markings on the neck and breast of a common cock pheasant. **1874** H. H. COLE *Catal. Ind. Art S. Kens. Mus.* 251 A very quaint flower pattern on a spotted white ground.

b. Const. *with* (some colour, etc.).

1555 EDEN *Decades* I. vii. (Arb.) 91 They were all paynted and spotted with sundry coloures. **1604** SHAKS. *Oth.* III. iii. 435 A Handkerchiefe Spotted with Strawberries. **1660** F. BROOKE tr. *Le Blanc's Trav.* 187 Girafes..are docile beasts, white and spotted with red. **1703** DAMPIER *Voy.* III. II. 32 Very remarkable Hills.., their sides all spotted with Woods and Savannahs. **1774** GOLDSM. *Nat. Hist.* (1776) VII. 224 This animal..is finely spotted with various colours. **1828** STARK *Elem. Nat. Hist.* I. 189 Plumage of a clear brown, spotted with deeper colour. **1855** WHITMAN *Leaves of Grass, Sea-Drift* (1884) 197 Four light-green eggs spotted with brown.

c. With adverbial or other addition.

1585 T. WASHINGTON tr. *Nicholay's Voy.* IV. xiii. 126 b, A Leopardes skynne well spotted. **1685** BURNET *Lett.* (1686) 240 Marble beautifully spotted. **1687** A. LOVELL tr. *Thevenot's Trav.* I. 237 No Lynx could be more exactly spotted, nor any Skin of a Tygre so pretty. **1774** GOLDSM. *Nat. Hist.* (1776) VII. 223 The skin..being rough, hard, and variously spotted. **1816** TUCKEY *Narr. Exped. R. Zaire* iii. (1818) 121 The domestic animals are sheep spotted black and white.

d. *Mining.* Having the ore irregularly distributed through the workings.

1874 RAYMOND *Statist. Mines & Mining* 365 The ground is spotted and very rich in places. **1895** *Times* 19 Feb. 3/6 This reef..appears to be what..is called 'spotted', the ore varying greatly in value in the distance of a few feet.

2. a. Disfigured or stained with spots.

1532 MORE *Confut. Tindale* Wks. 740/1 Syth that al the iustice of man is as the scripture sayeth like a fowle spotted clowte. **1619** WEST *Bk. Demeanor* 167 in *Babees Bk.*, Keep it neat and cleane, For spotted, dirty, or the like, is lothsome to be seene. **1649** E. REYNOLDS *Hosea* iii. 23 The Moon returnes but a faint and spotted light upon the world. **1765** *Museum Rust.* IV. 417 For every pound weight of Cocoons ..of a weaker, lighter, spotted, or bruised quality. **1903** *Smart Set* IX. 19/1 One spotted peach will contaminate a whole basket.

b. *fig.* Morally stained or blemished.

1522 MORE *De quat. Noviss.* Wks. 83/1 The perilous pride of them that for theyr few spotted vertues..take themself for quick saintes. **1560** BECON *New Catech.* v. Wks. 1564 I. 445 b, All creatures were founde spotted in the syght of God. **1637** R. ASHLEY tr. *Malvezzi's David Persecuted* 52 Always egged on by the bitter touches of their spotted beginning. **1691** HARTCLIFFE *Virtues* 67 Tho they are the most filthy and spotted Crimes. **1742** YOUNG *Nt. Th.* v. 50 The flow'rs of eloquence, profusely pour'd O'er spotted vice, fill half the letter'd world. **1817** COLERIDGE *Zapolya* Prel. 114 Do you press on, ye spotted parricides! **1891** H. LYNCH *Meredith* 68 Richard's undertaking in the reform of spotted woman.

absol. **1891** MEREDITH *One of our Conq.* xxxv, The white he was ready to take for silver,..the spotted had received corruption's label.

c. Const. *with* (something disgraceful).

a **1548** HALL *Chron., Rich. III*, 29 b, That note of infamie with the whiche his fame was iustely spotted and stayned. **1578** BANISTER *Hist. Man* VIII. 102 With no small negligence is he spotted in this point. *a* **1629** HINDE *J. Bruen* xxx. (1641) 95 Seldome any such meetings, but are either sprinkled with blood, or spotted with some grosse filthinesse. **1754** H. WALPOLE *Lett.* (1846) III. 76, I have scarce an idea left that is not spotted with clubs, hearts, spades, and diamonds. **1808** BENTHAM *Sc. Reform* 2 The abuses, with which the regular system of procedure is spotted.

d. Marked, suspected.

1864 *Daily Tel.* 17 May, Because the defaulter becomes a 'spotted' man, whose word can never more be trusted.

3. a. ***spotted fever***, a fever characterized by the appearance of spots on the skin; now *spec.* epidemic cerebro-spinal meningitis, and typhus or petechial fever. Also, = *Rocky Mountain (spotted) fever* s.v. ROCKY *a.*[1] 1 c.

1650 in *Verney Mem.* (1907) I. 474 S[r] Charles his sickness was a spotted feaver. **1671** SALMON *Syn. Med.* I. lv. 147 The Spotted Feaver, is a continual malignant burning Feaver [etc.]. **1747** tr. *Astruc's Fevers* 344 The first [class] comprehends those of a true spotted-fever, the second those of a spurious one. **1775** *Ann. Reg.* II. 4/1 Her Majesty's illness, which was a most malignant spotted fever, baffled every endeavour. **1822-7** GOOD *Study Med.* (1829) II. 239 While, from the purple or flea-bite spots,..this variety has been very generally treated of at home, under the name of Spotted Fever. **1842** [see PETECHIAL *a.*]. **1896** *Allbutt's Syst. Med.* I. 667 Petechiæ were so common and so abundant in the earlier American Epidemics that the name 'spotted fever' was applied to the disease. **1902** WILSON & CHOWNING in *First Biennial Rep. Montana State Board of Health* 27 Enough was accomplished to warrant the formation of a working hypothesis..that the so-called 'Spotted Fever' is due to the presence in the patient's blood of the above mentioned haematozoan..; and that the parasite is conveyed to man through the bite of a tick. **1903** *U.S. Hygienic Lab. Bull.* XIV. 7 (*heading*) Spotted fever (tick fever) of the Rocky Mountains. *Ibid.*, I have suggested as a name for the disease 'Tick Fever', as there are already two diseases sometimes called 'spotted fever'.

b. Similarly ***spotted death, pestilence, sickness.***

1666 DRYDEN *Ann. Mirab.* cclxvii, When spotted Deaths ran arm'd thro' every Street. **1783** WALDRON *Contn. B. Jonson's Sad Sheph.* III. 64 The spotted pestilence his bow'r surround! **1825** SCOTT *Talism.* iii, How few can they deliver From lingering pains,..Red Fever, spotted Pestilence! **1899** *Allbutt's Syst. Med.* VIII. 853 The 'spotted sickness' of tropical America.

4. In specific names: **a.** Of animals, as ***spotted axis, boa, cavy, cougar, deer***, etc.

Also in a number of moth-names given by Rennie *Consp. Butterfl. & Moths* (1832).

1781 PENNANT *Hist. Quadrup.* I. 105 The *Spotted Axis.. will bear our climate. *c* **1880** *Cassell's Nat. Hist.* III. 49 The Spotted Axis; the Hog Deer, and the Roebuck. **1802** SHAW *Gen. Zool.* III. II. 343 The *spotted Boa is sometimes scarcely inferior in size to the Constrictor. **1781** PENNANT *Hist. Quadrup.* II. 363 The *Spotted Cavy..inhabits Brazil, and Guiana. **1860** MAYNE REID *Hunter's Feast* vii, Some naturalists speak of *spotted cougars—that is, having spots that may be seen in a certain light. **1679** in Yule & Burnell *Hobson-Jobson* (1886) 651/2 There being conveniency in this place for ye breeding up of *Spotted Deer. **1698** FRYER *Acc. E. India & P.* 71 Being here presented with *Chitrels*, or Spotted Deer. **1894** LYDEKKER *Roy. Nat. Hist.* II. 353 The Indian Spotted Deer, or Chital (*Cervus axis*). **1754** CATESBY *Carolina* II. App. 110/1 The *Spotted Eft. **1797** *Encycl. Brit.* (ed. 3) IV. 149/1 The..harnessed antelope..is frequent at the Cape, where it is called the bonte-bok, or *spotted goat. **1818-22** *Encycl. Metrop.* (1845) XIV. 671/1 Spotted Goat of the Cape. *c* **1880** *Cassell's Nat. Hist.* III. 59 The *Spotted Hog Deer is a rare species. **1781** PENNANT *Hist. Quadrup.* I. 252 The *Spotted Hyæna..inhabits Guinea, Æthiopia, and the Cape. **1893** LYDEKKER *Roy. Nat. Hist.* I. 488 The Spotted Hyæna (*Hyæna crocuta*)..is by far the largest and most powerful of the three living species. **1751** *Spotted Lizard [see LIZARD 1 b]. **1831** GRIFFITH tr. *Cuvier* IX. Syn. 34 Spotted Lizard, *Lacerta Guttulata*. **1789** A. PHILLIP *Voy. Bot. Bay* 276 *Spotted Martin. The species is about the size of a large polecat. **1781** PENNANT *Hist. Quadrup.* I. 186 *Spotted Monkey. **1789** A. PHILLIP *Voy. Bot. Bay* 147 The *Spotted Opossum. **1879** E. P. WRIGHT *Anim. Life* 402 The pretty *Spotted Salamander..inhabits the greater part of Central and Southern Europe. *c* **1880** *Cassell's Nat. Hist.* IV. 371 The Spotted Salamander, ..*Salamandra maculosa*,..is the type of this genus. **1865** GOSSE *Land & Sea* (1874) 67 The common *spotted seal (*Phoca vitulina*). **1648** HEXHAM II, *Een Plack-slange*, a *spotted Snake or Adder. **1802** SHAW *Gen. Zool.* III. II. 446 Spotted Snake. *c* **1880** *Cassell's Nat. Hist.* IV. 301 Taking the Common English Spotted Snake as an example. **1802** SHAW *Gen. Zool.* III. I. 47 The Testudo guttata, or *Spotted Tortoise. **1884** GOODE *Nat. Hist. Aquat. Anim.* 158 The 'Spotted Tortoise' or 'Speckled Turtle', *Chelopus guttatus*. *c* **1880** *Cassell's Nat. Hist.* II. 59 The *Spotted Wild Cat.. is of a grey colour, spotted with black.

b. Of birds, as ***spotted bower-bird, crake, cuckoo, eagle, emu, falcon***, etc.

Many others occur in Latham's *Gen. Synop. Birds* (1781-85), as *spotted boat-bill, booby, bunting, buzzard*, etc.

1865 *Intell. Observ.* No. 38. 103 The *spotted Bower-bird. **1879** E. P. WRIGHT *Anim. Life* 254 Equally interesting are the habits of the Spotted Bower Bird (*Chlamydera maculata*). **1824** STEPHENS in Shaw's *Gen. Zool.* XII. I. 223 *Spotted Crake. **1879** E. P. WRIGHT *Anim. Life* 321 The Spotted Crake (*Porzana maruetta*) is another native species. **1782** LATHAM *Gen. Synop. Birds* I. II. 539 *Spotted Cuckow; ..inhabits Cayenne. **1895** LYDEKKER *Roy. Nat. Hist.* IV. 2 The great spotted cuckoo (*C. glandarius*) has twice occurred in England. **1781** LATHAM *Gen. Synop. Birds* I. I. 38 *Spotted Eagle... The length of this bird is two feet. **1845** YARRELL *Brit. Birds* 1st Suppl. 11 The Spotted Eagle, *Aquila nævia*. **1895** LYDEKKER *Roy. Nat. Hist.* IV. 230 The spotted eagle (*Aquila maculata*) of Central Europe. *c* **1880** *Cassell's Nat. Hist.* IV. 235 The *Spotted Emu (*Dromæus irroratus*) has often bred in captivity in this country. **1770** PENNANT *Brit. Zool.* IV. 8 *Spotted Falcon... Size of a buzzard. **1783** LATHAM *Gen. Synop. Birds* II. I. 323 *Spotted Flycatcher;..frequents the warmer parts of the European continent. **1879** E. P. WRIGHT *Anim. Life* 243 The Spotted Fly-catcher (*Muscicapa griseola*) can hardly be said to be a song-bird. **1772** *Phil. Trans.* LXII. 389 *Tetrao Grous*, *Spotted Grous. **1831** WILSON, etc. *Amer. Ornith.* IV. 193 The red grouse,..and *Tetrao canadensis*, or spotted grouse, have but sixteen [feathers in the tail]. **1768** PENNANT *Brit. Zool.* II. 357 The *Spotted Redshank..in size..is equal to the preceding [i.e. Green Shank]. **1829** GRIFFITH tr. *Cuvier* VIII. 78 *Spotted Ring Pigeon,..*Columba Arquatrix*. **1768** PENNANT *Brit. Zool.* II. 369 The *Spotted Sandpiper..is common to Europe and America. **1872** COUES *N. Amer. Birds* 260 *Tringoides*, Spotted Sandpiper. **1802** MONTAGU *Ornith.* s.v. *Snipe*, *Spotted Snipe, *Scolopax Totanus*. **1772** *Phil. Trans.* LXII. 410 *Scolopax*,..*Spotted Woodcock. **1782** LATHAM *Gen. Synop. Birds* I. II. 569 Canadian *Spotted Wood-pecker;..wing coverts and quills spotted with white. **1802** MONTAGU *Ornith.* s.v., The Spotted Woodpecker is less frequent in England than the Green. **1890** *Science-Gossip* XXVI. 47/1 The great spotted woodpecker (*Picus major*).

c. Of fishes, as ***spotted bass, blenny, cat, dog-fish, goby, grunt***, etc.

1876 GOODE *Anim. Resources U.S.* in *Smithsonian Coll.* XIII. VI. 62 Red fish or *spotted bass (*Sciænops ocellatus*). **1805** BARRY *Orkney* 292 The *Spotted Blenny..is found under stones among the sea-weed. **1881** DAY *Fishes Gt. Brit.* I. 208 *Centronotus Gunnellus*... Spotted blenny. **1796** *Spotted cat [see CAT *sb.*[1] 4 b]. **1861** *Spotted Dogfish [see DOGFISH 1]. **1883** DAY *Fishes Gt. Brit.* II. 309 *Scyllium canicula*,..Spotted dog-fish. *Ibid.* 310 Spotted, small-spotted, and lesser-spotted dog-fish. **1770** *Spotted Goby [see GOBY]. **1881** *Cassell's Nat. Hist.* V. 98 The Spotted Goby..differs from the other species in wanting the silk-like pectoral fins. **1876** GOODE *Fishes Bermudas* 54 The fishermen recognize several others, as the Yellow, Streaked, *Spotted, and Black Grunts. **1884** GOODE *Nat. Hist. Aquat. Anim.* 412 The *Spotted Hind, *Epinephelus Drummond-Hayi*,..has been but recently discovered. **1836** YARRELL *Brit. Fishes* II. 448 *Petromyzon marinus*, *Spotted Lamprey. **1881** DAY *Fishes Gt. Brit.* I. 306 *Spotted-ling, white-ling, and stake. **1804** SHAW *Gen. Zool.* V. II. 316 *Spotted Ray. **1881** *Cassell's Nat. Hist.* V. 42 This species..is sometimes known as the Spotted Ray and as the Painted Ray. **1884** GOODE *Nat. Hist. Aquat. Anim.* 266 *Spotted Black Rock-Fish (*Sebastichthys melanops*). *Ibid.* 267 *Spotted Rock Trout (*Hexagrammus decagrammus*). **1883** *Harper's Mag.* Dec. 101/1 The *spotted sunfish..is more democratic, affecting muddy streams. **1884** GOODE *Nat. Hist. Aquat. Anim.* 365 The Spotted Squeteague..is usually known on the Southern coast as the 'Salmon' or '*Spotted Trout'. *Ibid.* 177 *Lophopsetta maculata*, is sometimes called the *Spotted Turbot. **1881** *Cassell's Nat. Hist.* V. 75 The Cook Wrasse (*Labrus mixtus*)..is also known..as the Red Wrasse, Striped Wrasse, and *Spotted Wrasse.

d. Of plants, as ***spotted archangel, arse-smart, cat's-ear(s), cowbane***, etc.

1822 *Hortus Anglicus* II. 89 *L[amium] Maculatum*. *Spotted Archangel. **1731** MILLER *Gard. Dict.* s.v. *Persicaria*, Dead, or *Spotted Arsmart. **1753** *Chambers' Cycl.* Suppl. s.v. *Persicaria*, The common mild or spotted arsmart. **1796** WITHERING *Brit. Plants* (ed. 3) III. 691 *Hypochæris maculata*... *Spotted Cats-ears. **1848** [see CAT *sb.*[1] 19 b]. **1855** PRATT *Flower. Pl.* III. 193 Spotted Cat's-ear ..is a rare plant. **1846-50** A. WOOD *Class-bk. Bot.* 286 *Cicuta maculata*. Water Hemlock. *Spotted Cowbane. **1597** GERARDE *Herbal* I. xcviii. 157 *Spotted Dogs Stones bringeth foorth narrow leaues. **1847** *Spotted Gum [see GUM *sb.*[2] 5]. **1889** MAIDEN *Usef. Pl.* 242 *Eucalyptus hæmastoma*... Spotted Gum. **1731** MILLER *Gard. Dict.* s.v. *Pulmonaria*, Common *spotted Lungwort, by some call'd Sage of Jerusalem. **1829** T. CASTLE *Introd. Bot.* 68 As in the spotted and officinal lung-wort. **1796** WITHERING *Brit. Plants* (ed. 3) II. 28 *Orchis maculata*... Female-handed Orchis. *Spotted Orchis. **1898** MORRIS *Austral Eng.* 431 *Spotted-Orchis*, Tasmanian name for the Orchid *Dipodium punctatum*. **1855** PRATT *Flower. Pl.* V. 210 *Spotted Palmate Orchis. **1882** *Garden* 11 Feb. 89/1 The Spotted Palmate Orchis is found, I believe, in every part of the Kingdom. **1855** PRATT *Flower. Pl.* IV. 303 *Spotted Persicaria. **1796** WITHERING *Brit. Plants* (ed. 3) II. 381 *Persicaria*... *Spotted Snakeweed. **1874** *Treas. Bot.* Suppl. 1344/1 *Spotted Tree of the Queensland colonists. *Flindersia maculosa*, the trunk of which is remarkably spotted by the falling off of the outer bark in patches. **1889** MAIDEN *Usef. Pl.* 216 *Flindersia maculosa*... Spotted or Leopard Tree. **1846-50** A. WOOD *Class-bk. Bot.* 379 *Chimaphila maculata*, ..*Spotted Wintergreen.

5. *Comb.*, as ***spotted-beaked, -bellied, -billed***, etc. (in specific names).

1829 GRIFFITH tr. *Cuvier* VIII. 620 *Spotted-beaked Duck, *Anas Maculirostris*. **1782** LATHAM *Gen. Synop. Birds* I. II. 494 *Spotted-bellied Barbet;..the plumage beneath rufous white, spotted with black. **1829** GRIFFITH tr. *Cuvier* VII. 472 Spotted-bellied Tamatia, *Bucco Tamatia*. **1785** LATHAM *Gen. Synop. Birds* III. II. 487 *Spotted-billed Duck, *Anas poecilorhyncha*. **1824** STEPHENS in *Shaw's Gen. Zool.* XII. II. 134 Spotted-billed Wigeon. **1811** SHAW *Gen. Zool.* VIII. I. 223 *Spotted-breasted Creeper. **1829** GRIFFITH tr. *Cuvier* VI. 72 *Spotted-eared Owl, *Strix maculosa*. **1753** *Chambers' Cycl.* Suppl. s.v. *Orchis*, The white-flowered *spotted-leaved palmated meadow orchis. **1782** LATHAM *Gen. Synop. Birds* I. II. 772 *Spotted Necked Humming Bird. **1783** *Ibid.* II. II. 645 Spotted-necked Turtle. **1829** GRIFFITH tr. *Cuvier* VIII. 65 Spotted-necked Quail. **1894** LYDEKKER *Roy. Nat. Hist.* II. 97 The spotted-necked otter (*Lutra maculicollis*). **1781** LATHAM *Gen. Synop. Birds* I. I. 106 *Spotted-tailed Hawk;..on each tail-feather ..are three white spots. **1809** SHAW *Gen. Zool.* VII. I. 196 Spotted-Tailed Hobby. **1781** LATHAM *Gen. Synop. Birds* I. I. 68 *Spotted-winged Falcon. **1783** *Ibid.* II. I. 345 Spotted Winged Flycatcher.

6. Special collocations: **Spotted Dick**, a suet pudding made with currants or raisins; **spotted dog**, (*a*) a white or light-coloured dog with black or dark spots, esp. a Dalmatian; (*b*) *fig.* = *Spotted Dick*; also *attrib.*; **spotted metal, stems** (see quots.); **spotted wilt**, a virus disease of herbaceous plants, esp. tomatoes, in which it causes curling and necrotic spotting of the leaves.

1849 SOYER *Modern Housewife* 350 Plum Bolster, or *Spotted Dick.—Roll out two pounds of paste..., have some Smyrna raisins well washed [etc.]. **1892** *Pall Mall G.* 15 Dec. 2/3 The Kilburn Sisters..daily satisfy hundreds of dockers with soup and Spotted Dick. **1854** C. M. SMITH *Working-Men's Way in World* xii. 288 For supper come smoking sheep's-heads..and '*spotted dog', a very marly species of plum-pudding. **1910** F. W. HACKWOOD *Inns, Ales, & Drinking Customs* 288 The 'Talbot' readily became known among the vulgar as the 'Spotted Dog'. **1930** E. C. ASH *Pract. Dog Bk.* 47 The Spotted Dog [*sc.* the Dalmatian] became the dog of the Circus. *a* **1936** KIPLING *Something of Myself* (1937) i. 18 An enormous currant roly-poly—a 'spotted dog' a foot long. **1974** *Country Life* 25 Apr. 990/1 The other hound..reminded me of a spotted dog pudding at school. **1876** HILES *Catech. Organ* iv. (1878) 22 A mixture is often used [for organ pipes] called '*Spotted Metal', from the surface being covered with spots, or mottled. **1881** C. A. EDWARDS *Organs* 125 'Spotted metal' is the name given to a compound of tin and lead, in the proportion of one-third of the former to two-thirds of the latter. **1851** MANTELL *Petrifactions* i. 35 Specimens of certain fossil vegetables which are abundant in most coal fields, and are commonly known as *Spotted-stems, or Stigmariæ. **1919** C. C. BRITTLEBANK in *Jrnl. Dept. Agric. Victoria* XVII. 231 It is well to have a common name for every tomato disease, and I propose that of '*Spotted Wilt' for this latest one, from the spotting and subsequent wilting of the attacked plants. **1950** *N.Z. Jrnl. Agric.* June 587/1 Iceland poppies should be inspected regularly from now on for symptoms of the virus disease known as spotted wilt. **1979** *Ann. Appl. Biol.* XCIII. 173 Chlorotic ring-spots.., leaf specking, terminal bud necrosis,..and severe stunting of groundnut (*Arachis hypogaea*) were shown to be caused by tomato spotted wilt virus.

spottedness ('spɒtɪdnɪs). [f. prec. + -NESS.] The quality or state of being spotted.

1611 COTGR., *Mouscheture*, a spottednesse, or spotting. **1642** J. EATON *Honey-c. Free Justif.* 177 We see and feel nothing but fouleness and spottednesse. **1727** BAILEY (vol. II), *Speckledness*, Spottedness. **1881** C. A. YOUNG *Sun* 145 The state of the sun as to spottedness. **1883** *Science* II. 72/2 A maximum of solar spottedness seems to have passed.

spotter ('spɒtə(r)). [f. SPOT *v.* or *sb.*[1]]

1. a. One who makes spots.

1611 COTGR., *Barbouilleur*, ..a blotter, spotter, smutter, besmearer of. **1687** MIÈGE *Gt. Fr. Dict.* I, *Brodeuse de Gaze*, a Spotter of Hoods, a Woman that spots Hoods. **1755** JOHNSON, *Spotter*, one that spots; one that maculates. **1881** *Instr. Census Clerks* (1885) 70 [Persons employed in] Lace Finishing:.. Spotter, Stamper [etc.].

b. A device for making spots on watch-plates.

1884 F. J. BRITTEN *Watch & Clockm.* 245 This upright spindle carrying the spotter is kept constantly rotating by a band from a foot wheel.

2. a. *U.S.* A spy or detective, esp. one employed by a company to keep watch on employees, or one who watches for infringements of prohibition-laws.

1876 *Scribner's Monthly* Apr. 911/2 The stockholders and directors, the 'car-starters' and 'spotters'. **1878** O. W. HOLMES *Motley* 139 He was a paid 'spotter', sent by some jealous official to report on the foreign ministers. **1883** *American* VI. 333 A conductor..had a private detective arrested for following him about, and the 'spotter' was fined ten dollars by a magistrate.

b. In target practice, one who notes the point where a shot strikes; a marker.

1893 *Daily News* 21 July 5/6 Surridge got a bull 'just in at ten o'clock', to use the spotter's descriptive slang.

c. A look-out, an observer; a scout; one who identifies or looks out a target; *spec.* (Mil.), an aviator who locates enemy positions and directs fire.

1903 A. M. BINSTEAD *Pitcher in Paradise* v. 127 So vigilant and observant was that solitary optic that its owner was the chosen 'spotter' of a most relentless band of racecourse pickpockets. **1914** *Illustr. London News* 29 Aug. 320/3 Electric contrivances for communicating messages between the 'spotter' aloft and the gun-layer below. **1918** E. M. ROBERTS *Flying Fighter* 108 The fire was being directed from the ground from what the battery commander called the O.P., or observation post. He sent me up to that post with one of the spotters. **1925** J. C. GOODWIN *Queer Fish* xvi. 153, I surmise that they are 'spotters', posted where they are to warn the proprietor of the card-room should the police or their informers put in an appearance. **1935** A. J. CRONIN *Stars look Down* I. ix. 70, I heard the Tynecassel spotter was coming down to watch ye at the next Sleescale match. **1935** A. J. POLLOCK *Underworld Speaks* 112/1 *Spotter*, an accomplice who sizes up the victim and surroundings for the purpose of robbery, murder, kidnaping or a beating. **1939** *Illustrated* 16 Dec. 28 The 'spotter' sweeps the sky with his powerful telescope in search of aircraft. **1940** *Sun* (Baltimore) 13 Aug. 1/7 The Germans..have mounted long-range guns between Calais and Boulogne..but they will be simply shooting into the blue unless they have effective spotters aloft. **1940** *Times* 13 Nov. 3/1 Spotters with machine-guns man the roofs. **1943** *Times* 9 Oct. 2/5 The spotters 'tell' every outgoing or incoming aircraft by direct telephone line to the nearest R.O.C. centre. **1949** *Times* 5 Jan. 4/5 Aircraft from Kuala Lumpur carried spotters for the naval gunners. **1955** *Times* 21 June 9/4 One spotter aircraft to each forest operating company is the minimum requirement for efficiency. Such spotters can ask for..'bulldozer' rights for a patrol on a hot scent to pass through the areas of other units without being shot in error. **1959** I. & P. OPIE *Lore & Lang. Schoolch.* xvii. 373 The sentinel may..be called a guard, spotter, scout, [etc.]. **1963** T. & P. MORRIS *Pentonville* 353 Crime or crimes are to a great extent planned in gaol..then the necessary men (i.e. safe blower, drivers, spotters, con men, fence,) are found in here and given the word. **1976** *Globe & Mail* (Toronto) 11 June 9/8 Once Mr. Drmbie or his spotter sight a fire, they circle, swoop in at treetop level and note the size of the blaze. **1976** *Eastern Even. News* (Norwich) 13 Dec. 4/3 Chic is heavily involved in all forms of entertainment and is the local 'spotter' for television's 'New Faces'. **1977** 'O. JACKS' *Autumn Heroes* vii. 96 'Spotter plane, boss.'..'I don't like the idea of a spotter.' **1980** J. O'FAOLAIN *No Country for Young Men* i. 23 The Tans came in shooting... At the barracks, 'spotters' with bags over their heads and slits for their eyes identified known activists.

d. One who spots (SPOT *v.* 9 e) trains, etc. See also TRAIN-SPOTTER.

1950 *Oxf. Jun. Encycl.* IX. 400/1 The main activity of spotters' clubs is the collecting of locomotive numbers. **1957** *Railway Mag.* Dec. 887/2 (*heading*) Necktie for spotters. **1958** *Times* 6 Dec. 7/4 As a young 'spotter' [of car registration numbers in Egypt] I quickly noticed that the Arabic face was always legible at a considerably greater distance than the Western face. **1973** *Times* 27 July (Leisure Suppl.) p. iv/4 Steam railway enthusiasts seem to grow in number each year as spotters young and old rue the passing of steam.

3. *attrib.*, as (sense 2 c) ***spotter aircraft, pilot, plane.***

1942 *Daily Tel.* 1 Jan. 1/8 Three enemy fighters..and a 'spotter' aircraft were shot down. **1959** *Times* 18 May 6/1 From Marks Tey, Essex, on the main Colchester road, spotter aircraft yesterday radioed a report of a 20-mile queue of close-packed traffic. **1976** *Globe & Mail* (Toronto) 11 June 9/8 A second source of fire information—three Cessna spotter aircraft flying 3,000 feet overhead signalling radio reports into the fire control room. **1967** *Listener* 21 Sept. 355/3 The radio in the company HQ chatters with constant news from the ground control and the spotter pilots. **1958** *Observer* 3 Aug. 1/4 Floating 1,000 ft. over Southern England in the Automobile Association's spotter plane..I watched the holiday traffic streaming out of London yesterday. **1977** *Time* 22 Aug. 10/1 Israeli batteries—sometimes directed by observers in spotter planes—fired 16 times at Palestinian forces. **1981** E. CLARK *Send in Lions* v. 53 Spotter planes searched the vastness of the Sahara.

'spottily, *adv.* [f. SPOTTY *a.*] In a spotty manner; without uniformity.

1890 *Pall Mall G.* 16 Jan. 6 The missions work spottily. Many..are doing good work; but it is, as I say, only done ineffectively, in patches.

spottiness ('spɒtɪnɪs). [f. SPOTTY *a.* + -NESS.] The character or state of being spotty.

1577 *St. Aug. Manual* I vij, O light whiche hatest all spottinesse, in asmuch as thou art most cleane & spotlesse. **1611** COTGR., *Papillotage*, a spatling, or spottinesse. **1820** L. HUNT *Indicator* No. 37 (1822) I. 292 How we like to see a couple of legs..splashed unavoidably..till their horrid glare is subdued into spottiness. **1863** *Gd. Words* Apr. 281/1 Nine times in a century the sun passes through all its states of purity and spottiness. **1892** *Photogr. Ann.* II. 227 The evil of spottiness, patchyness, and confusion.

spotting ('spɒtɪŋ), *vbl. sb.* [f. SPOT *v.* + -ING[1].]

1. a. The action or process of making spots; the fact of becoming spotted.

c **1430** *Pilgr. Lyf Manhode* II. lxv. (1869) 100 That keepeth him from sinne, and from spottinge of rust. **1530** PALSGR. 274 Spottyng with colour, *taincture*. **1591** PERCIVALL *Sp. Dict.*, *Espanzimiento*, sprinckling or spotting. *a* **1610** HEALEY *Theophrastus* (1636) 43 To put in good store of Fullers earth, to keepe them from soile and spotting. **1711** ADDISON *Spect.* No. 81 ¶3 This artificial Spotting of the Face. **1838** *Penny Cycl.* XI. 358/1 To this disparity of temperature..may be certainly ascribed the bad setting, spotting, and shrivelling of grapes. **1846** J. BAXTER *Libr. Pract. Agric.* (ed. 4) II. 381 To prevent the spotting of the fruit produced by the action of the sun. **1879** *Cassell's Techn. Educ.* IV. 222/2 The defects [in varnishing coaches]..are those of 'spotting', 'blooming', 'pin-holing'.

b. *spec.* (See quot.)

1884 F. J. BRITTEN *Watch & Clockm.* 245 Spotting..[is] the process of finishing chronometer and occasionally watch plates by polishing thereon equidistant circular patches.

c. The removal of spots. † Also with *out.*

1892 *Photogr. Ann.* II. 877 A series of colours in tubes specially prepared for painting, spotting out, &c. **1940** *Amer. Speech* XV. 360/1 *Spotting*, eliminating spots from negatives. **1951** *Good Housek. Home Encycl.* 269/2 *Spotting*, ..the term applied to a process in the cleaning of a garment such as a suit. **1958** *Spectator* 4 July 15/3 The store or small cleaner will deal with finishing such as spotting and pressing. **1977** J. HEDGECOE *Photographer's Handbk.* 267 Spotting is the filling in of clear specks (which would otherwise print black) until they match the surrounding tone, and so vanish.

2. A set or number of spots; a marking composed of spots.

1600 SURFLET *Countrie Farme* III. xxviii. 486 The best of all the rest, is the short shanked apple, which is marked with spottings. **1649** OGILBY tr. *Virg. Georg.* III. (1684) 95 *note*, Of the Marks of a good Heifer..(that is, Sowrness of Look, ..Spotting of the Body) [etc.]. **1721** BRADLEY *Philos. Acc. Wks. Nat.* 57 The various Colouring and Spotting of their Eggs. **1841** *Florist's Jrnl.* (1846) II. 131 The spotting is smaller, but in every other particular they are very like. **1898** MEREDITH *Odes Fr. Hist.* 33 Along drear leagues of crimson spotting, white With mother's tears of France.

3. The action of placing on a spot.

1849 MARDON *Billiards* (ed. 2) Pl. 74 A break would have followed the spotting of the red ball that must have yielded the number of points required.

4. *U.S.* (See quot.)

1904 *Electr. World & Engin.* 24 Sept. 506 (Cent. Suppl.), This breaking up and switching of the trains into sections, which is called 'spotting'.

5. A slight discharge of blood via the vagina, *esp.* as a side-effect of oral contraceptives; light staining due to this.

1900 DORLAND *Med. Dict.* 624/2 *Spotting*, a slight menstrual show upon a woman's napkin. **1944** MILLER & BRYANT *Gynecol. & Gynecol. Nursing* iv. 57 A faint spotting noted on the underclothing or nightclothing may be the only symptom of an early carcinoma of the cervix. **1962** *Lancet* 22 Dec. 1315/2 The clinical criterion of adequate dosage most commonly used was absence of break-through bleeding and spotting. **1977** *Ibid.* 5 Nov. 947/1 According to Islamic precepts, intercourse is prohibited during menstruation, and spotting is interpreted as a prolonged menstrual period.

6. The action of observing, acting as a look-out; *spec.* (Mil.), the action of locating enemy positions from an aircraft and directing fire.

1914 A. HURD *Fleets at War* iv. 136 Jellicoe did all that was possible..to instal a fire-control set of instruments in each ship for 'spotting' and controlling at long-range shooting. **1918** W. H. BERRY *Aircraft in War & Commerce* vi. 77 At the Dardanelles..some of the 'spotting' [by seaplanes] for the battleship guns..was not beaten later. **1928** C. F. S. GAMBLE *Story of North Sea Air Station* viii. 113 The duties of this air station were:..(*f*) Spotting for coastal batteries.

7. *attrib.*, as ***spotting colour, machine, scope*** [SCOPE *sb.*[3] b], ***shuttle, woof.***

1805 *Trans. Soc. Arts* XXIII. 241 The spotting shuttles save clipping, and the waste of spotting yarn. **1839** URE *Dict. Arts* 1233 In working spots, one thread, or shot of spotting-woof, and two of plain, are successively inserted. **1884** C. G. W. LOCK *Workshop Rec.* Ser. III. 15/1 A mottled appearance is produced on brass by a 'spotting' machine. **1892** *Photogr. Ann.* II. 221 With the spotting colour we can carefully erase the other people's hands. **1960** C. E. CHAPEL *Art of Shooting* xv. 147 The shooter may have a spotting scope. This is a telescope of comparatively high power, which may be mounted on a tripod and placed near the shooter..and used to observe the location of shot holes on the target. **1970** R. A. STEINDLER *Firearms Dict.* 238/2 With the help of a spotting scope.., the spotter informs the shooter as to the exact point of bullet impact on the target. **1980** *Hunting Ann. 1981* 62/2 If you are serious about trying for a trophy, use a spotting scope.

'spotting, *ppl. a.* [f. SPOT *v.* + -ING[2].] Making or causing spots. Also *fig.*

1650 BULWER *Anthropomet.* 158 The discreeter sort of Ladies who are not guilty of this spotting vanity. **1827** CLARE *Sheph. Cal.* 56 The streaking sugar and the spotting plum.

spottle, obs. variant of SPATTLE *sb.*[1]

'spottle, *v. rare.* [f. SPOT *v.* + -LE.] *trans.* To spot or dot thickly; to bespatter.

1847- in midland dial. glossaries. **1859** F. E. PAGET *Curate Cumberworth* 15 He delighted in making maps of Asia Minor, and could spottle an impromptu Ægean with wriggling islands.

spotty ('spɒtɪ), *a.* and *sb.* Also 5 spotti, 6–7 spottie. [f. SPOT *sb.*[1] + -Y.]

A. *adj.* **1. a.** Full of, marked with, spots; spotted.

1340 *Ayenb.* 192 þou ne sselt naȝt maky none sacrefice to God of oxe ne of ssep þet by spotty. **1382** WYCLIF *Gen.* xxx. 35 He seuerde.. the wetheres, dyuerse and spotti. *c* **1400** *Pilgr. Sowle* (Caxton, 1483) IV. xxvi. 71 A clere myrroure wyll more playnly represente the fourmes..of thynges.. than wylle another that is fowle and spotty. *c* **1440** *Pallad. on Husb.* VIII. 74 Yf hit [*sc.* the ram's tongue] be spotty, that a man may write Yf he bigete hym spotty lombis yonge. **1513** *Act 5 Hen. VIII*, c. 4 §1 If the same Worsted..taketh any Wet, incontinent it will shew spotty and foul. **1587** MASCALL *Govt. Cattle, Sheep* (1627) 200 The spottie Rams will commonly be seene in the Lambes. **1620** VENNER *Via Recta* ii. 40 The colour of the face becommeth pale.., and the skin ..polluted with a white spotty deformity. **1667** MILTON *P.L.* I. 291 To descry new Lands, Rivers or Mountains in her spotty Globe. **1816** SINGER *Hist. Cards* 95 *note*, All the impressions are similar to that of the frontispiece, being spotty or greyish. **1822-7** GOOD *Study Med.* (1829) V. 567 The spotty and minutely tubercular lichens. **1874** RUSKIN *Fors Clav.* xlvi. 229 A dozen of the fattest, shiniest, spottiest trout I ever saw.

Comb. **1598** SYLVESTER *Du Bartas* II. i. III. *Furies* 391 He strangled His spightfull stepdam's Dragon spotty-spangled. **1884** COUES *N. Amer. Birds* 625 *Actodromas*,..Spotty-throat Sandpipers.

b. *fig.* or in fig. context.

a **1400** *Leg. Rood* (1871) 213 A white lambe, with senn blak Spotty myȝt he neuere bene. **1561** T. NORTON *Calvin's Inst.* IV. viii. (1634) 569 The Church,..whereof all the members are spotty and very uncleane. **1631** R. BYFIELD *Doctr. Sabb.* 112 You would prove of Christians, spotty feasters. **1675** N. LEE *Nero* II. ii, The Gods rain curses on me..If e're I harbour'd..a thought But what was Noble, of your spotty loves.

2. Patchy; lacking in uniformity or harmony:

a. Of painting.

1812 *Examiner* 25 May 329/1 The lights..are sometimes spotty. **1884** *Bazaar* 22 Dec. 664/1 Walters is showing a disposition for more lively colouring, but..this year's paintings..are hard and spotty.

b. Of literary work.

a **1849** POE *Lit. Crit., Mr. Ward* Wks. 1865 III. 160 In no other supposition can we reconcile the spotty appearance of the whole with a belief in the sanity of the author. **1870** LOWELL *Study Wind.* 261 The true artist in language is never spotty, and needs no guide-boards of admiring italics.

c. *gen.* Unsteady, uneven; patchy; sporadic, intermittent. orig. and chiefly *U.S.*

1932 *Sun* (Baltimore) 25 Feb. 19/6 The advance [of the curb market] was somewhat spotty, but on the whole, the list developed a firm tone. **1934** *Ibid.* 17 Sept. 8/1 Business conditions..are..'spotty'. One section may flourish,.. while another suffers. **1937** R. S. MORTON *Woman Surgeon* i. 21 My grown brothers played whist with my father before dinner... His luck was spotty. **1937** E. B. WHITE *Let.* 31 May (1976) 155 My attendance at meals may be a little spotty—for a twelvemonth I shall not adjust my steps to a soufflé. **1957** K. A. WITTFOGEL *Oriental Despotism* 55 The spotty distribution of his administrative centers. **1970** A. TOFFLER *Future Shock* v. 72 Available statistics, unfortunately, are spotty. **1977** H. FAST *Immigrants* I. 57 Clair's schooling was spotty, but she learned to read. **1979** *Dictionaries* I. 97 Philosophers' general interest in dictionaries has been spotty.

3. Occurring in spots; characterized by such occurrence.

1821 *Examiner* 284/2 Their spotty and crowded arrangement. **1892** STEVENSON *Across the Plains* 79 A rough, spotty undergrowth partially conceals the sand.

B. *sb.* A small wrasse of New Zealand, *Labrichthys bothryocosmus.*

1872 in Morris *Austral Eng.* s.v. *Poddly.* **1878** *Trans. New Zeal. Instit.* XI. 384 Wrasse, Parrot-fish, and Spotties were often in the market.

spotyl, obs. variant of SPATTLE *sb.*[1]

'spoucher. Now *Sc.* (and *Ir.*). Forms: 4 spojour, spogeour, 5 spougeour; 4 sp(o)uchour, 6 *Sc.* spowcheour, 9 spoucher, spoocher. [ad. ONF. *espuchoir* (= OF. *espusoir, espuisoir*), f. *espuchier, espuichier* (= OF. *espuicier, espuisier*, mod.F. *épuiser*) to drain, empty of water.] A wooden vessel for baling out or conveying water; a water-scoop. In early use *Naut.*

1336-7 *Acc. Exch. K.R.* 19/31 m. 5 In ij. spojours emptis ad eandem [galeam] ad aquam in dictis Wyndingbalies ponendam..viiij. d. **1338** *Roll 'T.G.' 11,097* in Nicolas *Hist. R. Navy* (1847) II. 475 Un ketill, un spogeour, ii. seilyngnedeles, un dyall. **1352** *Excheq. Acc. Q.R.* Bundle 20. no. 27, Pro quodam instrumento ligneo vocato 'spuchour' pro aqua fundanda et defendenda de nave. *Ibid.*, Pro quodam vase vocato 'spouchour'. **1420** *For. Acc. 3 Hen. VI*, F/2 b, ij lanternys, j spougeour, ij poleys pro le shroude et j sketfat.

1548 *Extr. Aberdeen Reg.* (1844) I. 259 Certane wther varklummes, sic as spowttis, spowcheouris [*printed* spowth-], and cruikis. **1890** in SIMMONS *Donegal Gloss.* (E.D.D.). **1898** *Proc. Philos. Soc. Glasgow* XXX. 45 Fire water—fire a spoucher full.

spouis(s, obs. Sc. ff. SPOUSE *sb.*

spoult, dial. var. SPALT *a.*

spoulty, var. SPAULTY *a.*

spoul worme, var. SPOLE-WORM *Obs.*

spoune, obs. f. SPOON *sb.* and *v.*

spounge, obs. f. SPONGE *sb.* and *v.*

spourge, obs. f. SPURGE *sb.* and *v.*

spourtlit, obs. Sc. f. SPURTLED *ppl. a.*

'spousage. *Obs.* exc. *arch.* Forms: 4 sposage, 5–6 spowsage, 5– spousage (6 spousag). [ad. AF. *esposage*, OF. *espousage* (cf. ESPOUSAGE), f. *espo(u)ser* SPOUSE *v.*]

1. Wedlock; = SPOUSAL *sb.* 1 and 1 b.

Freq. const. with preps., as *in, into, of,* or *out of*, with reference to the legitimacy of children.

13.. *Evang. Nicod.* 730 þat quest þat gan him deme Trew in sposage borne. **13..** *Cursor M.* 3043 (Gött.), þou[3] ismael be noght of sposage [*Trin.* Of Ismael out of spousage]. *a* **1395** HYLTON *Scala Perf.* II. xliv. (W. de W. 1494), That it myghte come to theffecte of true spousage. *c* **1400** MAUNDEV. (Roxb.) viii. 28 To proue þaire childer, wheder þai be geten in leel spousage or noght. *c* **1460** *Towneley Myst.* xxx. 277 An vsage, swilk..makys theym.. lif in syn for hir sake, And breke thare awne spowsage. *c* **1500** *Lancelot* 1331 For þow was not byget in to spousag. **1508** DUNBAR *Tua Mariit Wemen* 155 Or how ȝe like lif to leid in to leill spousage? *c* **1550** ROLLAND *Crt. Venus* III. 221 Quene Iocasta..Tuik hir awin sone of spowsage in the band.

2. = SPOUSAL *sb.* 2.

1338 R. BRUNNE *Chron.* (1810) 153 Whan þei were trouth plight, & purueied þe sposage, Helianore forth hir dight to Rouhan hir menage. **14..** *Sir Beues* (M) 277 Thou mvst kepe Vppon the ffeld all my shepe, Till the spousage be brought to end. *c* **1450** *Cov. Myst.* (Shaks. Soc.) 90 Every damesel..Xulde be browght in good degre Onto her spowsage. **1501** DOUGLAS *Pal. Hon.* III. xxxv, Of duke

Pirithous the spousage in that tide, Quhair the Centauris reft away the bride, Thair saw I. *a* **1548** HALL *Chron., Hen. VI*, 148 b, It should seme that God with this matrimony was not content. For after this spousage the Kynges frendes fell from hym. *c* **1555** HARPSFIELD *Divorce of Hen. VIII* (Camden) 248 The very true, perfect, and full marriage is the same company .. and living together which is consecrate by the league or bond of spousage or promise that one doth make to the other. **1656** BLOUNT *Glossogr., Spousage*, .. the contract or betrothing before full marriage. **1720** WHEATLY *Bk. Com. Prayer* (ed. 3) x. 407 In the old Manual for the use of Salisbury, before the Minister proceeds to the marriage, he is directed to ask the Woman's Dowry, *viz*. the Tokens of Spousage.

transf. and *fig*. **1497** BP. ALCOCK *Mons Perfect*. D iij, The weddynge and spousage of the lambe. **1513** BRADSHAW *St. Werburge* I. 1548 Kynge Vulfer, her father, at this ghostly spousage Prepared great tryumphes and solempnyte. **1550** BALE *Image Both Ch*. II. G ij, Not the spousage of their soules haue they broken by no fylthye traditions of men. **1888** *Ecclesiologist* 1 June 6 Spousage of a virgin to Christ.

b. Const. *of* (betrothal or matrimony). *rare*.

a **1591** R. GREENHAM *Wks*. (1599) 288 *note*, The spousage of betrothing before ful mariage. **1596** DALRYMPLE tr. *Leslie's Hist. Scot*. II. 392 The King hes obteinet her haly spousage of matrimonie.

3. A spouse, wife. *rare*$^{-1}$.

1513 DOUGLAS *Æneid* XI. vi. 109 The Goddis eik sa far dyd me invy, That in my natiue land neuer sall I spy My chaist spousage.

spousal ('spaʊzəl), *sb*. Forms: α. 4 **spusail(e, -eil, spusseayl; sposayle, -eyl, -eil,** 4–5 **-ail(e; spousaile,** 4–6 **-ayl(e,** 4–7 **-ail;** 4–5 **spousaille,** 5 **-ayll(e;** 4–5 **spowsail(e, -ayle,** etc. β. 5 **spousel(le,** *pl*. **spouselx,** 5– 6 **spousale,** 5– **spousal,** 6–7 **spousall.** [ad. OF. *espus-*, *espos-*, *espousaille* (freq. in pl.): see ESPOUSAL.]

†**1.** The condition of being espoused or married; the married state; wedlock. *Obs*.

a **1300** *Cursor M*. 13710 Þis womman þe band has broken of hir sposail. *c* **1375** *Sc. Leg. Saints* x. (*Matthew*) 333 For gud spousale is plesand thinge to god. *c* **1386** CHAUCER *Clerk's T*. 115 Boweth youre nekke vnder the blisful yok Of soueraynetee .. Which þat men clepeth spousaille or wedlok. *c* **1430** LYDG. *Min. Poems* (Percy Soc.) 31 Thou seist thou haddist in yong age wantonnesse, Therfore in olde age the nedithe have trewe spousaille. **1590** SPENSER *F.Q*. II. x. 75 Whose emptie place the mightie Oberon Doubly supplide, in spousall, and dominion.

fig. *c* **1450** *Myrr. our Ladye* 138 That speketh of the spousayle that ys betwene oure lorde Iesu cryste and holy chyrche. **1599** SHAKS. *Hen. V*, v. ii. 390 So be there 'twixt your Kingdomes such a Spousall, That neuer may ill Office or fell Iealousie .. Thrust in betweene the Pa[c]tion of these Kingdomes.

Comb. **1621** BRATHWAIT *Nat. Embassie* (1877) 280 One spousall-lothing, one her honour louing.

†**b.** In vbl. phrases, as ***to break*** or ***spill spousal***, to be unfaithful to the marriage vow, to commit adultery; ***to hold spousal***, to keep the marriage vow.

a **1300** *Cursor M*. 28486 Mi spuseil haf i broken rife, And ledd þe wers my spused wife. **1303** R. BRUNNE *Handl. Synne* 1622 Grete mede he getyþ with-oute fayle þat wele wyl holde hys spousayle. *c* **1400** *Destr. Troy* 12736 Whille he faryn was to fight in a fer lond, Sho spilt hade hir spousaile. **1430–40** LYDG. *Bochas* II. v. (MS. Bodl. 263), How trewe spousaile .. In your cite was broke.

2. The action of espousing or marrying; the celebration of a marriage or betrothal; an instance or occasion of this. Now *arch*.

a **1300** *Cursor M*. 10781 Thoru þe spusail þat was mad þar Was mani broght to ioi fra care. **1338** R. BRUNNE *Chron*. (1810) 308 As þe courte of Rome had ordeynd þat spousale, Right opon þat dome he weddid hir sanzfaile. **1390** GOWER *Conf*. I. 181 Envie tho began travaile In destourbance of this spousaile. **1447** BOKENHAM *Seyntys* (Roxb.) 51 And yf þe knot be now undo Of oure spousayle. **1458** *Paston Lett*. I. 425 The seyd Kyng ys decesed wythynne thys vj. wekes, or the spouselle was made. **1544** tr. *Littleton's Tenures* 85 Where .. after the spousayle he hath yssue by the same woman a sonne. **1590** SPENSER *F.Q*. I. ii. 23 My hoped day of spousall shone. **1667** MILTON *P.L*. VIII. 519 Till the amorous Bird of Night Sung Spousal, and bid haste the Evning Starr. **1833** MRS. BROWNING *Prometh. Bound* Poems 1850 I. 169 Why lengthen out thy maiden hours, when fate Permits the noblest spousal in the world? **1871** R. ELLIS tr. *Catullus* lxiv. 158 Hadst not a will with spousal an honour'd wife to receive me?

b. Freq. in pl. *spousals*.

a **1325** *MS. Rawl. B. 520* fol. 61 3if matrimonie or sposailes weren forth lad in assise. **1390** GOWER *Conf*. III. 308 Now have I told of the spousailes. *c* **1430** LYDG. *Min. Poems* (Percy Soc.) 40 Al that wedlock askethe and spowsayles, Al was redy to pleasaunt apparailes. **1492** *Rolls of Parlt*. VI. 450/1 After the Spouselx betwene him and the said Anne. **1531** ELYOT *Gov*. II. xii, Not withstandyng any ceremonye doone at the time of the spousayles, the mariage .. is not confirmed, vntyll at nyght. **1590** SWINBURNE *Testaments* 48 Al the goods and cattels personal that the wife had at the time of the spousals, or celebration of the mariage. **1613** PURCHAS *Pilgrimage* (1614) 649 You may feast with them at their spousals, and againe, after a view of their liues, at their funerals. **1669** DRYDEN *Tyrannic Love* v. i, Ethereal music did her death prepare, Like joyful sounds of spousals in the air. **1743** FRANCIS tr. *Hor., Odes* III. v. 9 Could they to foreign spousals meanly yield, Whom Crassus led with honor to the field? **1805** SOUTHEY *Madoc* II. 94 Four maids, the loveliest of the land, are given In spousals. **1832** LYTTON *Eugene A*. II. i, By the end of the ensuing month it was agreed that the spousals of the lovers should be held. **1874** SYMONDS *Sk. Italy & Greece* (1898) I. xiii. 279 With the morrow the Church blessed the spousals.

fig. **1857** EMERSON *Poems* 48 Knowing well to celebrate .. The spousals of the new-born year.

†**c.** Performance of the marriage ceremony. *Obs*.

a **1450** MYRC *Par. Pr*. 532 Þe .vij. sacramentes of holy chyrche, .. Ordere of prest, and spousayle, And þe laste elynge.

†**3.** A wedding gift or present; a dowry. *Obs*.

1382 WYCLIF *1 Kings* xviii. 25 The kyng nedith no sposeilis [L. *sponsalia*], but oonli an hundrid tersis of Philisteis. **14..** *Sir Beues* 4277 (M.), Vnto sir Myles was she wed. The kyng gaue Myles in spousayll The Erle-dome of Cornwayll.

spousal ('spaʊzəl), *a*. Also 6 *Sc*. **-ale,** 6–7 **-all.** [attrib. use of prec., or ad. L. *sponsāl-is* by assimilation to this.]

1. Of, pertaining or relating to, espousal or marriage; nuptial, matrimonial.

1513 DOUGLAS *Æneid* VII. x. 39 Lat thaim begyne Sik wedlok to contrak and spousale feyst. **1517** TORKINGTON *Pilgr*. (1884) 12 The spousall words be *In signum veri perpetuique Domini*. **1577–87** HOLINSHED *Chron*. III. 1097/2 When I was wedded to the realme .. (the spousall ring whereof I haue on my finger). **1588** SHAKS. *Tit. A*. I. i. 337 There shall we Consummate our Spousall rites. **1635** PAGITT *Christianogr*. III. (1636) 28 Concerning cases spousal and matrimonial. **1647** TRAPP *Comm. Rev*. ii. 4 That spousall-love that God so well remembreth. **1671** MILTON *Samson* 387 Spousal embraces, vitiated with Gold. **1725** POPE *Odyss*. VI. 31 Thy spousal ornament neglected lies. **1726** *Ibid*. XVIII. 334 Till Hymen lights the torch of spousal love. **1821** SOUTHEY *Exped. Orsua* 60 A large robe of rich silk .. was given her as the spousal present. **1877** BRYANT *Sella* 318 There already stood The priest prepared to say the spousal rite. **1888** DOUGHTY *Arabia Deserta* I. 471 The spousal money that the Moor had given to .. her half-brother.

2. Of a hymn, poem, etc.: Celebrating or commemorating an espousal or marriage.

1596 SPENSER (*title*), Prothalamion, or a Spousall Verse made .. in Honour of the Double marriage of .. the Ladie Elizabeth and the Ladie Katherine Somerset. *a* **1599** —— *F.Q*. VII. vii. 12 Where Phœbus self, .. They say, did sing the spousall hymne full cleere. **1761** J. SCOTT (*title*), A Spousal Hymn, or an Address to His Majesty on his Marriage. [**1841** D'ISRAELI *Amen. Lit*. (1867) 476 A spousal hymn on the double marriage of two ladies.]

Hence '**spousally** *adv*., by espousal or marriage; in the manner of a spouse; as a spouse. *rare*.

1501 in *Antiq. Rep*. (1808) II. 255 They now were in their either other presens spousally ensured. **1898** MEREDITH *Odes Fr. Hist*. 48 Not deigning spousally entreat, But harsh.

spouse (spaʊz, -s), *sb*. Forms: 3–4 **spus, spuse,** 3– **spouse,** 4 **spouce;** 4 **spows,** 5 **spowce,** 5–8 **spowse,** 6 **spowze;** also *Sc*. 5 **spoys,** 6 **spouis(s,** 6–7 **spous,** 8 **spuse.** [a. OF. *spus*, *spous* masc., *spuse* fem., varr. of *espus*, *espouse*, etc.: see ESPOUSE *sb*. In some early ME. instances (see 3) the masc. *spus* is distinct from the fem. *spuse*.]

1. A married woman in relation to her husband; a wife; †a bride. Usually with possessive pronouns, *of*, or *to*.

c **1200** *Trin. Coll. Hom*. 135 Elizabet þi spuse shal hauen a cnauechild. *c* **1250** *Owl & Night*. 1527 Þat were gulte þat leof is oþer wymmon to pulte .. & haueþ atom his rich[t]e spuse. *a* **1300** *Cursor M*. 3043 Þof ysmael be noght o spus, O him sal gret men cum and crus. **13..** *Sir Beues* 143 And þow schelt after her wedde to spouse, To þin amy. *a* **1400–50** *Alexander* 2677 Þare fand he .. þe trew spouse Of ser Dary. *c* **1430** LYDG. *Min. Poems* (Percy Soc.) 40 To you, dere herte, my veray trouthe I plihte As to my spouse. *a* **1553** UDALL *Royster D*. v. i, Sir, .. doe not ye therfore your faithfull spouse mystrust. **1596** SHAKS. *Tam. Shr*. IV. v. 67 So qualified, as may beseeme The Spouse of any noble Gentleman. *c* **1614** SIR W. MURE *Dido & Æneas* I. 200, I, .. Jove's spowse, and sister, heaven's arch-empresse great. **1667** MILTON *P.L*. IV. 169 The fishie fume, That drove him, though enamourd, from the Spouse Of Tobits Son. **1711** S. SEWALL *Diary* 1 Feb., He thanks me for my Respect to him and his Spouse. **1782** COWPER *Gilpin* ii, John Gilpin's spouse said to her dear [etc.]. **1833** TENNYSON *Dream Fair Wom*. xli, A name for ever!—lying robed and crown'd, Worthy a Roman spouse. **1870** BRYANT *Iliad* I. I. 30 Thou wilt find the task Too hard for thee, although thou be my spouse. **1877** MARY M. GRANT *Sun-Maid* i, He chose Lady Anna as a fitting spouse because he liked her rank.

fig. **1859** E. FITZGERALD *Omar* xl, [How I] Divorced old barren Reason from my Bed, And took the Daughter of the Vine to Spouse.

b. Used as a term of address. (Also in sense 2.)

c **1386** CHAUCER *Sec. Nun's T*. 144 O sweete and wel biloued spouse deere, .. Ther is a conseil Which that right fayn I wolde vn-to yow seye. **1706–7** FARQUHAR *Beaux' Strat*. v. iv, They tell me Spouse that you had like to have been rob'd. *Mrs. Sull*. Truly, Spouse, I was pretty near it. **1821** SHELLEY *Epipsych*. 130 Spouse! Sister! Angel .. O too soon adored, by me!

2. A married man in relation to his wife; a husband; †a bridegroom. Usually with possessive pronouns.

c **1200–** [see 3]. **13..** *Cursor M*. 10170 (Gött.), To samirtale widuten strijf, Be-tuix any spouse and his wijf. *a* **1340** HAMPOLE *Psalter* xviii. 5 As spouse cumand forth of his chawmbire. **1390** GOWER *Conf*. I. 301 This wif .. sih how that hire seli spouse Was sett. **1447** BOKENHAM *Seyntys* (Roxb.) 57 Thus she gan crye Welkecome dere spouse and god gramercy. *a* **1513** FABYAN *Chron*. (1811) 654 At whiche mariage was no persones present but the spowse, the spowsesse, the duches of Bedforde [etc.]. **1564–5** *Reg. Privy Council Scot*. I. 327 George Kennedie, hir pretendit spous. **1597** J. PAYNE *Royal Exch*. 43 So gloriouse and Princely a spowze to take .. so poore and meane an espowzes. **1608** [see SPOUSED *ppl. a*. b]. **1771** SMOLLETT *Humph. Cl*. (1815) 232 To fill the place of the deceased, not only as the son of the sachem, but as the spouse of a beautiful squaw. **1782** COWPER *Mut. Forbearance* 1 The lady thus address'd her spouse. **1844** WILLIS *Lady Jane* I. 82 Ours Are the best wives on earth. They love their spouses. **1856** MRS. BROWNING *Aur. Leigh* II. 412, I am scarcely meek enough To be the handmaid of a lawful spouse.

†**b.** An affianced suitor; one's fiancé. *Obs*.$^{-1}$

a **1553** UDALL *Royster D*. I. v, I am bespoken: And I thought verily thys had bene some token From my dear spouse Gawin Goodluck.

3. *fig*. In religious use: **a.** Applied to the Church, or to a woman who has taken religious vows, in relation to God or Christ.

(*a*) *c* **1200** *Trin. Coll. Hom*. 149 Swiche teares wiep þe holie spuse uppen hire spus. *a* **1225** *Ancr. R*. 2 Louerd! seið Godes Spuse to hire deorewurðe Spus [etc.]. *c* **1380** WYCLIF *Sel. Wks*. III. 339 Cristis Chirche is his Spouse. *a* **1536** *Songs, Carols*, etc. (1907) 69 The chirche is callid þe spowse of Jhesu Criste. **1570** B. GOOGE *Pop. Kingd*. IV. 51 b, How are the Idoles worshipped, if this religion here Be Catholike, and like the Spowse of Christ accounted dere? **1641** WITHER *Haleluiah* I. l, Thy God, is now thy Father dear; His holy Spouse, thy Mother too. **1782** J. FLETCHER *Lett*. Wks. 1795 VII. 239 The Church, the Spouse of the Son of God. **1827** POLLOK *Course T*. v, The Church, the holy spouse of God.

(*b*) *c* **1230** *Hali Meid*. 5 Swuch wurðschipe, as hit is to beo godes spuse, Ihesu cristes brude. *c* **1290** *S. Eng. Leg*. I. 52 Go .. to þe Abbesse of þe house, Dame Aldred þat clene Maide, þat is godes spouse. *c* **1430** *Life St. Kath*. (1884) 19 Now myn owne doughter be glad .. for now ȝe lak noo thyng þat longeth to an heuenly spouse. *c* **1440** *Gesta Rom*. v. 13 (Harl. MS.), Ony sowle, þe which is spouse of god. *c* **1610** *Women Saints* 83 Their no lesse religious sister Walburge, a moste chaste spouse of Christ. *a* **1700** in *Cath. Rel. Soc. Publ*. IX. 343 God .. had perticularly designed her for his especiall Elected and Beloved spowse. **1756–9** A. BUTLER *Lives of Saints, S. Catherine of Bologna*, She looked upon it as the greatest honour to be in any thing the servant of the spouses of Christ. **1886** MONAHAN *Rec. Ardagh & Clonmacnoise* 2 That youthful spouse of Christ [St. Bridget].

b. Applied to God or Christ in relation to the Church (or its members) or to women of religion.

c **1200** *Trin. Coll. Hom*. 149 Swiche teares wiep þe holie spuse uppen hire spus. *c* **1220** *Bestiary* 717 in *O.E. Misc*., He is ure soule spuse. *c* **1375** *Sc. Leg. Saints* xxxiv. (*Pelagia*) 102 We, þat suld god plese maste, oure verray spouse. *c* **1430** LYDG. *Min. Poems* (Percy Soc.) 178 Perpetuelly .. Knet to your spouse callid Crist Jhesu. **1526** *Pilgr. Perf*. (W. de W. 1531) G g b, Let the swete odour of deuocyon and prayer spyre out and ascende vp to thy lorde & spouse. **1657** *Penit. Conf*. vii. 117 That the Church would not have made so bold .. without express warranty from her Spouse? **1753** CHALLONER *Cath. Chr. Instr*. 207 Because the Church is then in Mourning for her Spouse.

†**4.** The married state; marriage, wedlock. *Obs*.

c **1250** *Owl & Night*. 1334 Þu .. me atwist þat ic singe bi manne huse & theche wyue breke spuse. *a* **1300** *Cursor M*. 3907 Quat of his wiues tuin in spus, And wat of hand wimmen in hus, Tuelue suns had he o þaa. *Ibid*. 11132 Als dos þe men þat liues in spus. **1340–70** *Alex. & Dind*. 393 Alle leccheries lust vs loþeth to founde, Or to bringe vs in brigge for to breke spouce.

5. *attrib*. and *Comb*., as ***spouse-bed***, ***-faith***, ***-feast***; ***spouse-lost*** adj.

1550 COVERDALE *Spir. Pride* vii. (1588) 80 Those .. matrones, which being sore tempted, .. do neuerthelesse kepe their spouse faith toward their husbandes vndefiled. **1591** SYLVESTER *Du Bartas* I. vii, Let her, that .. Dares spot the Spous-bed with unlawful kisses, Blush. **1598** *Ibid*. II. i, Sith spousebed spotless laws of God allow. **1601** *Downfall Earl Huntington* II. i. in Hazl. *Dodsley* VIII. 129 To this end came I to the mock spouse-feast. **1615** BRATHWAIT *Strappado* (1878) 320 Like spouse-lost Turtles, do we flocke together.

spouse (spaʊz), *v*. *Obs*. exc. *arch*. Forms: 3–4 **spuse** (4 **spusen, spus**); 3–4 **spose;** 3–4 **spousi, spousy,** 4–5 **spousen** (5 **spowsyn**), 4–6 **spowse,** 3– **spouse** (9 *Sc*. **spouss**). [ad. OF. *espuser*, *esposer*, *espouser*: see ESPOUSE *v*. In some early examples the pa. t. and pa. pple. are formed without *-d*.]

†**1.** *trans*. To join or unite in marriage or wedlock. Chiefly employed in the passive, and usu. const. *to*, *unto*, or *with* (a person). *Obs*.

c **1290** *S. Eng. Leg*. I. 110 So þat heo i-cristned was, .. and i-spouse in þe place. *a* **1300** *Floriz & Bl*. 788 He let hem to one Chirche bringe, And spusen hem wiþ one gold ringe. *c* **1300** *Havelok* 1175 He weren spused fayre and wel, þe messe he deden eueridel. *c* **1330** *Arth. & Merl*. 6566 After mete asked king Ban .. Whi Gvenour, his douhter precious, To sum gentil man nere yspouse. *c* **1386** CHAUCER *Clerk's T*. 3 Ye ryde as coy and stille as dooth a mayde were newe spoused. *c* **1460** *Brut* ccxxxix. 338 Yn þis same ȝere come Quene Anne yn-to Engelond, for to be spoused vnto King Richard. **1491** CAXTON *Vitas Patr*. (1495) I. xlviii. 93 b/2 He to whom I shold haue be spowsed and maryed wente his waye secretely. **1565** STAPLETON tr. *Bede's Hist. Ch. Eng*. 58 It was not lawfull for a Christian woman and virgin to be maried, or spoused to a paynime. **1595** *Locrine* I. i, Thou shalt be spoused to fair Guendolen. **1638** BRATHWAIT *Barnabees Jrnl*. II. (1818) 63 Her I sought, but she was spoused.

fig. *a* **1310** in Wright *Lyric P*. xxv. 72 Jesu, mi soule is spoused to the. *c* **1380** WYCLIF *Sel. Wks*. I. 142 Clerkis seien þat whan a man is brouȝt þus to Goddis chambre, þan he is fully spousid with God, and dowid [etc.]. **1471** RIPLEY *Comp. Alch*. in Ashm. (1652) 186 Spowsyd wyth the Spryts of lyfe to lyve in love and rest. **1526** *Pilgr. Perf*. (W. de W. 1531) 187 So the soule .. begynneth to be spoused & coupled to God. **1615** BRATHWAIT *Strappado* (1878) 89 The very hearts of her attendants .. Were spous'd to this pure virgin euerywhere. **1667** MILTON *P.L*. v. 216 They led the Vine To wed her Elm; she, spous'd, about him twines Her mariageable arms.

2. To give in marriage; to promote or procure the marriage of; to marry (*esp.* a woman *to* a man).

1297 R. GLOUC. (Rolls) 10839 Seint edmund þo at canterburi spousede to vr kinge þe erles doȝter of prouence elianore to wiue. **1305** in *E.P.P.* (1862) 66 To spouse hire & his sone to-gadere he hadde iþoȝt. **1388** WYCLIF *2 Cor.* xi. 2 Y haue spousid ȝou to oon hosebonde. **1509** BARCLAY *Shyp of Folys* (1570) 97 If that a man of hye or lowe degree Would spouse his daughter vnto a straunge man. **1565** STAPLETON *Fortr. Faith* 85, I haue spoused you to one husband.

refl. **1340** *Ayenb.* 225 Þaȝ hit by zuo þet ha zeneȝi dyadliche þet efter zuych ane beheste him spouseþ. *c* **1430** *Life St. Kath.* (1884) 83 And I haue spoused me to hym. **1528** ROY *Rede me* (Arb.) 91 Their vowes, Wherby theym selves they spowse To god.

†**b.** To betroth; = ESPOUSE *v.* 1. *Obs.*[−1]

1533 BELLENDEN *Livy* III. xvi. (S.T.S.) II. 9 O appius, I haue spousit my dochter to Icelius and nocht to þe. **1590** SPENSER *F.Q.* I. x. 4 The eldest two,..Fidelia and Speranza, virgins were; Though spousd, yet wanting wedlocks solemnize.

3. To take (a woman) as a wife; to marry, wed. Freq. from *c* 1300 to *c* 1450; now *arch.*

1297 R. GLOUC. (Rolls) 589 So þat king lotrin..spouse is doȝter. *c* **1300** *Havelok* 2875, I rede þat þu hire take, And spuse. *c* **1386** CHAUCER *Clerk's T.* 386 This Markys hath hire spoused with a ryng. *c* **1450** *Merlin* xxv. 450 He was gon in to Carmelide for to spouse his wif. **1475** *Bk. Noblesse* (Roxb.) 24 King Lowes of Fraunce in his yong age.. spoused the said Alienore. *a* **1513** FABYAN *Chron.* (1516) II. 129/2 In yᵉ moneth of Ianuary next ensuynge..kynge Philip spoused his seconde wyfe Blaunche. **1596** SPENSER *F.Q.* V. iii. 2 To Faerie land; Where he her spous'd, and made his ioyous bride. **1663** BUTLER *Hud.* I. ii. 283 He Spous'd in India, Of Noble House, a Lady gay. **1805** tr. *Lafontaine's Hermann & Emilia* II. 5, I will spouse Roslace; but Rolfs shall not possess Emilia.

fig. **1517** TORKINGTON *Pilgr.* (1884) 12 They..Spoused the see with a ryng.

b. *fig.* To devote oneself to, to try (one's fortune). *Sc.*

1822 GALT *Sir A. Wylie* xciii, Your old companion..they say has spoused his fortune and gone to Indy. **1870** CHAMBERS *Pop. Rhymes* 90 It was time for the wife that had twa sons to send them away to spouss their fortune.

†**4.** *absol.* To take a spouse. *Obs.*

a **1300** *Cursor M.* 2336 Wit þe lau þat þai liued in Men suld not spuse bot in þer kin. *Ibid.* 10653 Þen did þe biscop command þar, þat all þe maidens..Be send all to þair frendes dere, For to mari and forto spus. **1622** S. WARD *Christ All in All* (1627) 21 Spouse not but in the Lord.

†**spouse-breach**[1]. *Obs.* Forms: α. 3 spus-, spousbruche, 5 spousebriche, spowsebrige. β. 3 spus-, 4 spous-, 4–6 spouse-, 5 spowsebreche, 6 spous-, 6–7 spouse-breach. [f. SPOUSE *sb.* + BREACH *sb.*, after OE. *ǣwbryce*, ME. *ewe-*, *eu-*, EAUBRUCHE[1].] Adultery. Also *transf.* (*arch.* in quot. 1922).

α. *a* **1225** *Ancr. R.* 56 [David] forȝet him suluen, so þet he dude..one Bersabee spus bruche. **1297** R. GLOUC. (Rolls) 4504 He..huld hire in spousbruche in vyl flesses dede. **1422** tr. *Secreta Secret., Priv. Priv.* 128 Who so euer were atteyntid of Spowse-brige, he sholde lesse both his eighyn. *c* **1430** *Hymns Virgin* (1867) 47 Oonis he saued a weddid wijf, In spousebriche þat hadde doon mys.

β. *c* **1250** *Kent. Serm.* in *O.E. Misc.* 30 Lecherie, spusbreche, Roberie, Manslechtes. *c* **1315** SHOREHAM IV. 395 Of lecherye comeþ..Commune hordom, spousbreche. **1387** TREVISA *Higden* (Rolls) I. 89 No trespas among hem is i-punisched so grevousliche as spouse breche. *c* **1420** *Chron. Vilod.* 743 Þe furst day of his crownyng, In to spousebreche he fell anon. *a* **1476** H. PARKER *Dives & Pauper* (W. de W. 1496) III. x. 373/1 He forbydeth the wyll & the consent of herte to lecherye & to spousebreche. *c* **1550** R. BIESTON *Bayte Fortune* A vj b, Spousebreche with sume is counted not a myte. **1589** WARNER *Alb. Eng.* VI. xxx. (1597) 150 We seuerally are..arayned Of Cuckoldie, of Spous-breach, and of Bastardy. **1637** HEYWOOD *Royall King* IV. iii, Whence might this distaste arise? From any loose demeanor, wanton carriage, Spouse-breach, or disobedience in my daughter?

transf. **1398** TREVISA *Barth De P.R.* XVIII. xliii. (Bodl. MS.), þei [elephants] fight neuer for females noþer knoweþ spouse breche. *Ibid.* XVIII. lxvi, Leopardus is a cruel beeste and is gendred in spowsebreche of a parde and of a lionas. **1922** JOYCE *Ulysses* 47 He [*sc.* a dog] rooted in the sand,..a pard, a panther, got in spousebreach.

†**spouse-breach**[2]. *Obs. rare.* [Cf. prec. and EAUBRUCHE[2].] An adulterer.

c **1315** SHOREHAM I. 2001 Þat on may spousebreche bycome For defaute of þet oþer. *a* **1325** *Prose Psalter* xlix. 19 Ȝyf þou sest a þef, þou ran wyþ hym, and laid þy porcioun wyþ spouse-breches.

†**spouse-break**, *sb.* and *a.* *Obs. rare.* In 4 spus(e-, spows-, spouse-brek(e. [f. SPOUSE *sb.* + BREAK *sb.*[1]]

A. *sb.* Adultery. (Cf. SPOUSE-BREACH[1].)

a **1300** *Cursor M.* 27940 Spusbrek [*v.r.* spows-brek] es betuix tua, þat spused ar bath, or an o þaa. **1357** *Lay Folks Catech.* 551 An other [species of lechery] is auoutry, that is spouse-brek.

B. *adj.* Adulterous.

a **1300** *Cursor M.* 185 O spouse-brek womman þat þe Iuus dempt to stan. *Ibid.* 27322 Wijf spuse-brek sal dern penance Do.

†**spouse-breaker.** *Obs.* [f. SPOUSE *sb.* + BREAKER: cf. prec.] An adulterer.

a **1300** *Cursor M.* 25778 Spous-breker be þat womman þat juus dempt for to stan. **1387** TREVISA *Higden* (Rolls) III. 157 He made his felawe a spouse brekere. *c* **1400** *Apol. Loll.* 54 Fraudars, misdoars, sortylogers, spousbrekars. *c* **1425** AUDELAY *XI Pains of Hell* 62 in *O.E. Misc.*, Bynd spouse-brekers with awouters, And ranegates with raueners. **1548–77** VICARY *Anat.* i. (1888) 15 That he be no spousbreaker, nor no drunkarde. **1562** LEGH *Armory* 105 The Swanne pursueth the cockolde-maker.., & will not leaue the spouse breaker, tyll he kyll or bee killed.

†**spouse-breaking**, *vbl. sb.* *Obs.* [f. as prec. + BREAKING *vbl. sb.*] = SPOUSE-BREACH[1].

a **1300** *Cursor M.* 26231 Suilk sinnes..Als spousbrecking, and als hordom. *c* **1380** *Lay Folks Catech.* 1400 Anoþer [deadly sin] is avowtri, þat ys spowse-brekynge. *c* **1400** *Apol. Loll.* 89 If ani do mansleing, spowsbrekyng, or ani þing of wrong to man. *a* **1513** FABYAN *Chron.* (1811) 270 [He] sayd that hym had ben leuer to be syke & dye of Goddys honde, than to lyue in spouse brekyng.

†'**spoused,** *ppl. a.* *Obs.* [f. SPOUSE *v.*] Espoused, married, wedded.

a **1300** *Cursor M.* 10458 Quar-for suld i haue ioi and blis Quen i mi spused lauerd mis? *Ibid.* 28264 Mi spused wyfe i haue misledd Bath in burdyng and in bedde. *c* **1375** *Sc. Leg. Saints* vii. (*James Less*) 314 A voyce sal be hard wele rath one spowsit men & wemen bath. *c* **1425** *Eng. Conq. Ireland* (1896) 120 [They] mythten neuer haue chyldren of her spoused wyues. **1521** in *Acts Parlt. Scot.* (1875) XII. 39/1 To seperate himselff fra his avn spousit Wyff. **1588** A. KING tr. *Canisius' Catech.* 116 Vnto ye faithfull spoused persones is..giuen fruictfulnes. **1616** B. JONSON *Epigr.* I. v, The world the temple was,..The spoused pair two realms. **1654** GAYTON *Pleas. Notes* IV. xxiv. 280 Now all the plot and chiefe contrivance, Was how to get his spoused wife—hence.

b. Used *absol.* as quasi-*sb.*

a **1300** *Cursor M.* 2898 Sibbe ne spused tak yee nan. *Ibid.* 10170 Tuix ani spused and his wijf. **1608** B. JONSON *Masque Ld. Hadington's Marr.* Wks. (1616) 943 In the happy choyce, The spouse, and spoused haue the formost voyce!

†**spousehead.** *Obs.* Forms: 4 spous-, 5 spousehed, spous(e)ed, spowse-, 5–6 spousehede, 6 -hedde. [f. SPOUSE *sb.* + -HEAD.] = next.

c **1380** WYCLIF *Sel. Wks.* III. 162 þei synnen most grevousely in brekyng of Gods spousehed. **14..** *R. Glouc. Chron.* 3370 (MS. Digby 205) fol. 51 b, He founde Ioye for þe Countas of spousehed [*v.rr.* spoushed, spousehede] was vnbounde. *c* **1450** *Cov. Myst.* (Shaks. Soc.) 392 When oure Lord comyth in his spoused pure. **1493** *Festivall* (W. de W. 1515) 143 She was wedded to the kynge of heuen & myght not breke that spousehede. **1599** THYNNE *Animadv.* (1875) 68 Yf the storke by anye meanes perceve that his female hath brooked spouse-hedde, he will no moore dwell with her.

spousehood (ˈspaʊzhʊd, -s-). Now *arch.* Forms: 2 spushad, 3 -hod, 3–4 spoushod (4 -od), 5 -hode, spousehod, -hode (-ode), 5–6 -hoode, 9 spousehood. [f. SPOUSE *sb.* + -HOOD.] The marriage state; matrimony; wedlock.

In Shoreham's poems (I. 1609, 1623, etc.) the ending *-hop* (once *-op*) is more frequent than *-hod* (*-od*).

c **1175** *Lamb. Hom.* 143 Þe sunfulle men þet spushad brekeð. *c* **1200** *Trin. Coll. Hom.* 45 Ðo þre kinges bitocneð þre hodes of bilefulle men; on is meidhod, þat oðer spushod, þe þridde widewehod. **1297** R. GLOUC. (Rolls) 1507 He þe emperoures doȝter in spoushod nome. *c* **1315** SHOREHAM I. 1996 In spoushod beþ godnesse þre. **1398** TREVISA *Barth. De P.R.* VI. xiv. (Tollem. MS.), He likeneþ..þe synagogue to an euil wyf þat brekeþ spoushode. **1493** *Festivall* (W. de W. 1515) 167 b, In tyme of peryll of deth fader and moder may crysten theyr owne children without harmynge of theyr spouseholde [*sic*]. **1891** J. WINSOR *Columbus* viii. 166 Such an intimacy as spousehood only can sanction.

spouseless (ˈspaʊzlɪs, -s-), *a.* [f. SPOUSE *sb.*]

1. Of a person: Having no spouse; bereaved or deprived of a spouse.

1460 *Pol., Rel., & Love Poems* (1866) 207 Broþerles, Spouselees, ful wrecchid y-wis. **1610** HEALEY *St. Aug. Citie of God* III. 122 Here a husband fights, and there a father; Would you be spouselesse (wiues) or fatherlesse? **1725** POPE *Odyss.* I. 315 To tempt the spouseless queen with am'rous wiles, Resort the nobles from the neighb'ring isles. **1818** BYRON *Ch. Har.* IV. xi, The spouseless Adriatic mourns her lord. **1892** MEREDITH *Sage enamoured* ii. Poems 1898 I. 54 Across his path the spouseless Lady cast Her shadow.

2. Characterized by the absence of a spouse.

1812 W. TENNANT *Anster F.* (1838) I. 15 In spouseless solitude without a mate. **1876** SWINBURNE *Erechtheus* 583 She besought him by her spouseless fame.

†**spousess.** *Obs.* Forms: 4–7 spousesse, 5–7 spowsesse, 6 spouses. [f. SPOUSE *sb.* + -ESS[1].] A female spouse; a wife, bride. Also, a betrothed or affianced woman.

Chiefly *fig.* in religious use (cf. SPOUSE *sb.* 3).

1388 WYCLIF *Isaiah* lxi. 11 As a spouse made feir with a coroun, and as a spousesse ourned with her brochis. **1395** PURVEY *Remonstr.* (1851) 53 Bi sovereyn wisdom, goodnesse, and love to holi chirche his spousesse. *c* **1430** *Life St. Kath.* (1884) 21 The Spouse loueth the Spousesse, the Sauyour visiteth hir. *c* **1480** in *Lib. Pontif. Bainbridge* (Surtees) 238 To kepe us his true handmaydyns, virgins, and spousessis. **1513** BRADSHAW *St. Werburge* I. 3076 Her spouse Ihesus hauynge pyte and cure Vpon his spouses. **1547** tr. *Abp. Herman's Consultation* H h vj, They whiche haue mutually promised matrimonie betwene themselues shal go both the spouse and spousesse [etc.]. **1615** *Curry-Combe for Coxe-Combe* iv. 157 The Mother of Christians, the Spousesse of the Holy Ghost.

†'**spousing,** *vbl. sb.* *Obs.* [f. SPOUSE *v.*]

1. The action of the vb. in various senses; marriage, matrimony, wedlock; espousal, betrothal.

a **1250** *Owl & Night.* 1336 Þurh me nas neauer ischend spusing. *c* **1275** *Sinners Beware* 159 in *O.E. Misc.*, Þeos prude leuedies, þat luyeþ drywories, And brekeþ spusynge. *c* **1315** SHOREHAM I. 1727 Spousynge At seue ȝer me maky may, Ac none ryȝt weddynge. *c* **1430** *How Good Wife taught her Daughter* in *Babees Bk.* 46 Loke to þi douȝtren..& gadere faste towarde her mariage, And ȝeue hem to spowsynge as soone as þei ben ablee. *c* **1450** *Mirour Saluacioun* (Roxb.) 29 Thogh marie was joynte vnto man be spovsing.

b. With possessives.

a **1250** *Owl & Night.* 1553 He weneþ heo wile anon to-breke Hire spusyng. **1297** R. GLOUC. (Rolls) 8879 He sede þat heo ssolde is sone to hire spousinge auonge. **1388** WYCLIF *Song Sol.* iii. 11 The diademe, bi which his modir crownede hym, in the dai of his spousyng. **1435** MISYN *Fire of Love* 71 Qwhen þai to weddynge or þe fest of cristis spowsynge ar cald.

c. *attrib.* in ***spousing-band, chamber, cloth, garment, girdle, gown.***

a **1250** *Owl & Night.* 1472 Þauh spusyng-bendes byndeþ sore. **1495** *Acc. Ld. High Treas. Scot.* I. 263, xiiij ellis of quhite dammas, to be the Princis spousing goune. **1513** DOUGLAS *Æneid* X. xi. 113 Of Lavynya the spousyng chalmyr. *a* **1568** in *Bannatyne MS.* (Hunter. Cl.) 770 Thair is no differance Betuix the gallowis and the spowsing claith. *a* **1605** MONTGOMERIE *Devot. Poems, Poets Dreme* i, God give me grace for to begin My spousing garment for to spin. **1666** *Despauterii Gram. Instit.* D 5 b (Jam.), *Cestus*.., a spousing girdle.

2. An instance or occasion of this; an espousal or marriage.

1297 R. GLOUC. (Rolls) 9069 Mid nobleye & prute inou þis spousinge was ydo. *a* **1300** *Havelok* 2888 Þat spusinge was [in] god time maked. **13..** *Sir Beues* 4565 Þe feste was riale inow, Ase scholde be at swiche a spusinge And at þe kinges couroning.

†'**spousy.** *colloq.* *Obs.* [f. SPOUSE *sb.* + -Y[4].] A humorous diminutive of SPOUSE.

1797 MRS. M. ROBINSON *Walsingham* IV. 337 The joiner will fly off in a tangent, and you'll get no spousy after all. **1801** *Times* 11 Nov., The Peace is very unpopular with the Lawyers' and Citizens' wives, because spousy and footman must pull the cockades out of their hats. **1818** *Blackw. Mag.* III. 533 They made Braun's spousy..appear a perfect skeleton.

spout (spaʊt), *sb.* Forms: 4–6 spowte, 6–7 (9) spowt (6 *Sc.* spowtt-, spowit); 5–7 spoute (5 spute), 6–7 *Sc.* spoutt-, 6– spout. [ME. *spowte*, *spoute*, of doubtful origin, corresponding to older Flem. *spuyte* (also *spoyte*, *spoeyte*), Du. (and WFris.) *spuit*, NFris. *spütj*, spout, squirt, fire-engine; cf. MSw. *eldsputa* a fire-throwing war-engine, Norw. dial. *sputa* cuttle-fish. See SPOUT *v.*]

I. 1. a. A pipe by which rain-water is carried off or discharged from a roof.

1392 *Mem. Ripon* (Surtees) III. 113 In salario Ricardi de Bettes facientis guturas cum spowtis super quamdam novam cameram..cum plumbo de stauro ecclesiæ. **1412–20** LYDG. *Chron. Troy* II. 697 Gargoyl & many hidous hed, With spoutis þoruȝ, & pipes. *c* **1475** *Pict. Voc.* in Wr.-Wülcker 800 *Hoc stillicidium*, a spowte. **1538** in *Lett. Suppress. Monast.* (Camden) 198 Dyverse gutteres, spowtes, and condytes. *a* **1548** HALL *Chron., Hen. VIII*, 166 In the fyrst worke were gargylles of golde fiersly faced with spoutes runnyng. **1600** SURFLET *Countrie Farme* I. iv. 7 The cesterne shall be set in such a place, as that it may receiue all that commeth from such spouts as are belonging to roofes or lower lofts of the house. *c* **1720** PRIOR *Fatal Love* I Poor Hal caught his death standing under a spout,..And curs'd was the weather that quench'd the man's flame. **1788** GIBBON *Decl. & F.* l. V. 191 A spout (now of gold) discharges the rain-water, and the well Zemzem is protected by a dome. **1823** *Act 4 Geo. IV*, c. 3 §42 A Spout..from the Roof down to the Ground, to carry off..the Water. **1845** ALB. SMITH *Fort. Scattergood Fam.* xxxii, The splashing cataracts from the eaves and spouts of the dwellings.

b. A pipe or similar conduit through which water or other liquid flows and is discharged; that part of a fountain, pump, etc., from which the water issues.

1408 in *Eng. Hist. Rev.* (1899) XIV. 517 Les spowtes lignea ducentia aquam a dicto Watergate usque dictam rotam. **1474–5** *Durham Acc. Rolls* (Surtees) 95 Factura unius le Spowte inter pandoxatorium et ortum porcorum. **1548** *Extr. Aberdeen Reg.* (1844) I. 259 Certane wther varklummes, sic as spowttis, spowcheouris, and cruikis, worth xxx s. **1594** T. B. *La Primaud. Fr. Acad.* II. 122 The nose is giuen to man that it might serue the braine in stead of a pipe and spowt to purge it of flegmatike humours. **1601** SHAKS. *Jul. C.* II. ii. 77 She dreampt..she saw my Statue, Which like a Fountaine with an hundred spouts Did run pure blood. **1632** LITHGOW *Trav.* VII. 316 Betweene the Riuer and this pond, there are sixe passages or spouts digged through the Banke. **1705** ADDISON *Italy* 142 A beautiful Marble Fountain, where the Water runs continually thro' several little Spouts. **1747** WESLEY *Jrnl.* Feb. (1849) I. 444 They brought an hand-engine;..the constable came, seized upon the spout of the engine, and carried it off. **1774** GOLDSM. *Nat. Hist* (1824) I. xx. 144 A hollow copper ball, with a long pipe;..through this spout it is to be filled with water. **1815** J. SMITH *Panorama Sci. & Art* II. 117 The spout of the pump should be opposite the horizontal part of the pipe. **1833** LOUDON *Encycl. Archit.* §1020 The situation of the spout or trunk of wood..for supplying water to the cisterns. **1858** LARDNER *Hand-bk. Nat. Phil.* 113, G I is a short tube proceeding from the side of the barrel... K is the spout of discharge.

fig. **1592** TIMME *Ten Eng. Lepers* B iij, Some rashe heades being Conchæ, before they be Canales, that is to say, Spoutes, before they have filled their Cesterne. **1611** SHAKS. *Wint. T.* III. iii. 26 And (gasping to begin some speech) her eyes Became two spouts. **1885** *Sat. Rev.* 3 Jan. 2/1 Another type of Correspondent there is whose function is to serve as spout for this or that Continental statesman.

†**c.** A syringe. *Obs.*[−1]

1546 PHAER *Bk. Childr.* X ij, Iuyce of purcelane:..dryue it in wyth a spoute called of the surgions a syrynge.

†**d.** = SPOUT-HOLE 1. *Obs.*

1661 LOVELL *Hist. Anim. & Min.* 197 They have..sharp and little teeth: great eyes. A spout betwixt the eyes. **1681** GREW *Musæum* I. 38 He squirts the water out at his Nostrils, in the same manner as the Dolphin doth at his Spout. **1747** *Gentl. Mag.* 174/2 His spouts are in his forehead, and not on the hinder part of his head, as in other whales. **1774** GOLDSM. *Nat. Hist.* (1824) III. 27 The cachalot..with a spout in the neck; that with a spout in the snout.

e. *Mining.* A short passage connecting an air-head with a gate-road.

1839 URE *Dict. Arts* 990 Lateral openings, named spouts, are led from the air-head gallery into the side of work. **1853** *Ibid* (ed. 4) II. 225 A series of 'spouts' or openings are driven upwards from the gate-road. **1883** GRESLEY *Gloss. Coal-m.*, *Spout*, a short underground passage in the Thick-coal workings connecting a main road with an air-head.

2. a. A tubular or lip-like addition to, or projection from, a vessel to facilitate the pouring out of liquid from it.

1444 *Test. Ebor.* (Surtees) II. 101, j laver cum ij spowtes deaurat. pond. vij unc. et dim. **1591** SYLVESTER *Du Bartas* I. iv. 278 Mean-while the Skinker, from his starry spout, After the Goat, a silver stream pours out. **1650** BULWER *Anthropomet.* 113 They of Goa..drink out of a Copper-Can with a Spout. **1664** POWER *Exp. Philos.* II. 125 We took a Glass-Cruet, with a small Spout, and fill'd it with Water. **1755** JOHNSON, *Beak*,..the spout of a cup. **1790** *Act 30 Geo. III*, c. 31 §3 Spouts to China, Stone, or Earthen-ware Teapots. **1842** LOUDON *Suburban Hort.* 147 The larger rose, *e*, is used without the middle piece of the spout. **1846** DICKENS *Cricket on Hearth* i, The kettle..carrying its handle with an air of defiance, and cocking its spout pertly. **1866** R. M. BALLANTYNE *Shifting Winds* i, He..willed to screw off the spout of the family tea-pot,..and..he did it.

b. In pigeons: (see quots.).

1879 L. WRIGHT *Pigeon Keeper* 85 Carriers..are..peculiarly subject to 'spouts'. *Ibid.* 231 Spouts..consist of a folded corner in the lower eyelid, through which there is a constant gradual drain of fluid.

3. A contrivance having the form of a trough or box with open ends, by which flour, grain, coals, etc., are discharged from, or conveyed to, a receptacle; a shoot.

1557 in Hazl. *E.P.P.* III. 110 The one clarke stode at the spoute Thereas the meale shoulde come out. **1629** *Reg. Privy Council Scot.* III. 15 [They] hewed doun to the ground the spouttes of the compleaners said mylne. **1677** YARRANTON *Eng. Improv.* 136 There must be in each side of the Granaries, Three or Four long Troughs or Spouts fixt in the uppermost Loft. **1793** EARL DUNDONALD *Descr. Estate Culross* 55 Shipping the Coal, from an elevated Coal Steath and Spout, instead of by Hand-barrows. **1821** *Acc. Peculations in Coal Trade* 3 The Coals descending from a spout into the vessel. **1860** *Mining Gloss., Newcastle Terms* 64 *Spouts*, boxes down which the coals are run from the waggons into the ships. **1884** *Tyne Improv. Comm. Bye-Laws* 29 Pitch..shall not be boiled..within 40 feet of any staith, drop, spout, warehouse or other erection on or near to the dock.

4. a. A lift formerly in use in pawnbrokers' shops, up which the articles pawned were taken for storage. Also *transf.*, a pawnshop.

1834 W. H. AINSWORTH *Rookwood* II. III. v. 345 To the spout with the sneezers in grand array. **1837** DICKENS *Pickw.* xlii, Spout—dear relation—uncle Tom. **1855** *Gentl. Mag.* Oct. 446 Mr. Hull, pawnbroker,..committed suicide ..by hanging himself within his 'spout'. **1859** SALA *Tw. round Clock* (1861) 286 The half-pence rattle, shillings are tested, huge bundles rumble down the spout. **1866** HOWELLS *Venetian Life* 108 Instead of many pawnbrokers' shops there is one large municipal spout.

b. Hence *to put* (or *shove*) *up the spout*, to pawn. *up the spout*, pawned, pledged; also *fig.*, in a bad way, in a hopeless condition, out of the question.

1812 J. H. VAUX *Flash Dict.* s.v., To pledge any property at a pawnbroker's is termed..shoving it up the spout. **1848** THACKERAY *Van. Fair* xxx, Please to put *that* up the spout, ma'am, with my pins, and rings, and watch and chain, and things. **1886** D. C. MURRAY *Cynic Fortune* vii, I haven't a suit of clothes fit to go in; even my wig and gown are up the spout together.

fig. **1829** P. EGAN *Boxiana* 2nd Ser. II. 351 At the expiration of thirty-five minutes, and seventeen rounds, the *flue faker* acknowledged he was '*up the spout*'. **1846** *Swell's Night Guide* 64 And when she saw all hope was up the spout, She spouted everything a spout would take. **1853** DODS *Early Lett.* (1910) 35 The fact is, Germany is up the spout, and consequently a damper is thrown over my hopes for next summer. **1854** MISS BAKER *Northampt. Gloss.*, 'He's up the spout.' A phrase applied to a person in a state of bankruptcy. **1857** TROLLOPE *Three Clerks* xviii, I shall be up the spout altogether if you don't do something to help me. **1864** —— *Small Ho. at Allington* xxxvi, He was regularly up the spout with accommodation bills.

c. *to put* (someone) *up the spout*: to make pregnant (esp. out of wedlock); also simply *up the spout*, in the womb; pregnant. Cf. *up the pole* s.v. POLE *sb.*[1] 1 b. *slang.*

1937 PARTRIDGE *Dict. Slang* 815/2 *Spout, up the*,..pregnant with child... Often in form, *to have been put up the spout.* **1949** *Landfall* III. 234 Well, they say he put her up the spout. **1956** P. SCOTT *Male Child* II. i. 95 All these years taking every possible care and suddenly there's one up the spout. **1970** 'S. TROY' *Blind Man's Garden* viii. 100 Up the spout, isn't she? I thought Michel would have had more bloody savvy.

d. A gun barrel. Usu. in phr. *up the spout*, of a bullet or cartridge: in the barrel and ready to be fired. *slang.*

1943 C. H. WARD-JACKSON *Piece of Cake* 55 *Spout*, a gun barrel. **1943** *R.A.F. Jrnl.* Aug. 12 He'd a round up the spout from being on this guard..and when he pulled the trigger there was a bang and a flash. **1966** D. VARADAY *Gara-Yaka's Domain* xi. 128 The pin failed to fire the dud cartridge in the chamber. There was no time to pump another into the spout. **1969** M. GILBERT *Blood & Judgement* vii. 70, I can count six here in the clip... There's probably one up the spout. **1976** G. SEYMOUR *Glory Boys* xv. 191 The Uzi was concealed there. Wonder if he's put the catch off, thought Jimmy, put one up the spout.

II. 5. *Sc.* A razor-fish.

1525 in *Excerpta e Libr. Domicilii Jacobi Quinti* (Bann. Cl.) 7 Bukes, spouttis, grenbans, podlokis. **1710** SIBBALD *Hist. Fife* 55 The Sheath, or Razor Fish; our Fishers call them Spouts. **1742** RICHARDSON *De Foe's Tour Gt. Brit.* IV. 9 Scollops, and Spouts, are cast up by the Tide in such Numbers on the Isles, that the People cannot consume them. **1793** *Statist. Acc. Scot.* VII. 543 Lobsters, partens, cockles, muscles, and spouts or razor fish. **1806** NEILL *Tour* 93 Besides..rasor-fish or spouts, they have abundance of what are called *culleocks* and smurlins. **1837** R. DUNN *Ornith. Orkney & Shetl.* 8 Razor-fish, commonly called spouts.

6. a. A waterspout.

Common in 17th and 18th cent.; now *rare*.

1555 EDEN *Decades* (Arb.) 386 They sawe certeyne stremes of water which they caule spoutes faulynge owt of the ayer into the sea. **1570** DEE *Math. Pref.* d iv b, He ought to haue expert coniecture of Stormes, Tempestes, and Spoutes. **1606** SHAKS. *Tr. & Cr.* v. ii. 171 The dreadfull spout, Which Shipmen doe the Hurricano call. **1698** T. FROGER *Voy.* 90 There we saw two of those pillars of water that arise out of the Sea, and which are commonly call'd Spouts. **1719** *Phil. Trans.* XXX. 1097 A vast breach in the Ground, which was made by a Spout, which fell upon Emott-more. **1769** FALCONER *Dict. Marine* (1780) s.v. *Water-spout*, The whirlwinds and spouts are not always..in the day-time. **1819** KEATS *Song of Four Fairies* 82 To the torrid spouts and fountains, Underneath earth-quaked mountains. **1842** *Penny Cycl.* XXII. 382/2 Some spouts disappear almost as soon as they are formed, and others have been known to continue nearly an hour.

b. A heavy downpour or pelt (*of* rain).

1648 B. PLANTAGENET *Descr. New Albion* Pref. 3 The storm grew far more tempestuous with..terrible gusts and spouts, that made the rivers rise, and my friends to hide. **1692** RAY *Disc.* II. ii. (1693) 74 Of great Spouts of Rain..that set the whole Countrey in a Flood. **1851** MAYNE REID *Scalp Hunt.* xli. 319 The rain fell, not in drops, but in 'spouts'.

7. a. A discharge of water or other liquid, in some quantity and with some degree of force, from the mouth of a pipe or similar orifice.

1500–20 DUNBAR *Poems* xxxiii. 104 He maid a hundreth nolt all hawkit Beneth him with a spowt. **1617** MORYSON *Itin.* I. 153 With the turning of a cocke, spoutes of water rise up in great force. **1718** LADY M. W. MONTAGU *Let. to Mrs. Thistlethwayte* 1 Apr., Marble fountains in the lower part of the room, which throw up several spouts of water. **1793** SMEATON *Edystone L.* §317 *note*, This momentary Spout of the Edystone may perhaps be best compared with the momentary jet of boiling water..from the Fountain Geisser in Iceland! **1825** HONE *Every-day Bk.* I. 1044 The most usual form is a simple opening to throw the jet or spout upright. **1851** MAYNE REID *Scalp Hunt.* xxxii. 250 The red spout [of blood] gushed forth, and the victim fell forward. **1877** BLACK *Green Past.* xxxviii, These spouts and jets increased to a shower.

transf. **1771** *Encycl. Brit.* II. 124/2 The volatile phosphorus continues two hours; after which the little spout of light contracts to the length of a line or two.

b. Spouting power or force. *rare.*

a **1774** GOLDSM. *Surv. Exp. Philos.* (1776) I. 405 Thus at b, the water had no spout for want of height to drive it; at c, the water hath no spout for want of room to descend.

c. *Agric.* A spring of water forcing its way up through the soil.

1791 *Statist. Acc. Scotl.* I. 442 The land abounds with boggs and springs, or what husbandmen call *spouts*. **1801** *Farmer's Mag.* Nov. 414 The benefit arising from draining, whether by carrying away surface-water, or freeing the land from spouts, occasioned by water bursting out from higher grounds. **1840** J. BUEL *Farmer's Comp.* 96 When wetness is caused by spouts or springs, rising from below, the object is to prevent the water rising to or saturating the soil. **1844** H. STEPHENS *Bk. Farm* I. 505, 4-feet drains have completely removed the spouts.

d. The column of spray thrown into the air by a whale in the act of respiration.

1824 J. F. COOPER *Pilot* xvii, 'Tis a right whale,..I saw his spout. **1839** T. BEALE *Nat. Hist. Sperm Whale* 42 From the extremity of the nose the spout is thrown up. **1850** SCORESBY *Cheever's Whalem. Adv.* vi. (1858) 78 Its spout..flashes up from the ocean just like smoke. **1898** F. T. BULLEN *Cruise Cachalot* xviii. 217 We flew after a retreating spout to leeward.

8. a. An outpour or rush of water falling from a higher to a lower level, esp. in a detached stream; a waterfall or cascade of this kind.

a **1700** EVELYN *Diary* 27 Feb. 1644, Before this grotto is a long poole into which ran divers spouts of water. **1775** A. BURNABY *Trav.* 29 Coming to a ledge of rocks, which runs ..cross the river, it divides into two spouts... The spout on the Virginian side makes three falls. **1806** FORSYTH *Beauties Scotl.* III. 388 The river rushes over the Auchinlilie Lin or Spout, a tremendous cataract. **1836** G. BACK *Arctic Land Exped.* x. 334 The river, from an imposing width, now gradually contracted to about fifty yards... In the language of *voyageurs*, this form is denominated a spout. **1879** STEVENSON *Trav. Cevennes* (1886) 126 A streamlet made a little spout over some stones to serve me for a water-tap.

b. A similar fall of earth or rock.

1883 STEVENSON *Silverado Sq.* 234 The great spout of broken mineral, which had damned the canyon up. **1883** —— *Treas. Isl.* xv, From the side of the hill..a spout of gravel was dislodged.

9. a. *slang.* (See quot.)

1787 GROSE *Prov. Gloss.* s.v., He is in great spout, he is in high spirits. **1888** in *Berkshire Gloss.* 153.

b. A recitation or declamation. *rare*$^{-1}$.

1832 HOOD *Stage-Struck Hero* 59 If one should just break out, Perchance, into a little spout, A stick about the skull is.

10. A spurt; a sudden dart.

1787 BURNS *Petit. Bruar Water* ii, If, in their random, wanton spouts, They near the margin stray;..They're left ..In gasping death to wallow.

III. 11. *attrib.* and *Comb.*, as ***spout-kind***, ***-like*** adj.; **spout-bath** *N.Z.*, a natural douche-bath; **spout-coals**, coals loaded from a spout; **spout cup**, (*a*) a cup with a spout (now only *Hist.*); (*b*) the upper end of a rain-spout; **spout-fish**, a mollusc which spouts or squirts out water, *esp.* a razor-fish; **spout-head**, (*a*) a rose on a watering-can; (*b*) a spring or fountain; **spout-mouth**, (*a*) a mouth resembling the spout of a vessel; (*b*) *Mining* (see quot.); **spout-mouthed** *a.*, having a mouth shaped like a spout; † **spout-pen** (see quot.); † **spout-pitcher**, a pitcher with a spout; **spout-plane** (see quot.); † **spout-pot**, a pot with a spout; **spout-road** *Mining* (see quot.); **spout-shell** *Zool.* (see quots.); **spout-vessel**, a coal-boat loaded by means of a spout; **spout-well**, a well from which the water issues by a spout; **spout-whale**, [cf. older Flem. *spuyt-wal*], a spouting whale.

1929 C. C. MARTINDALE *Risen Sun* 164 There are things in New Zealand that they call '*spout-baths'. A solid shining stream thuds on to your back from a height, and you feel as strong as it does. **1977** *N.Z. Herald* 5 Jan. 2-20/11 (Advt.), Rotorua Boulevard Motel, New units, sleep 1–6, restaurant adj, TV, putting green, hot swimming pool, 6 pvte spa and spout baths. **1821** *Acc. Peculat. in Coal Trade* 5 Certificates ..whereby he may see which are *spout or keel coals. **1702** *Lond. Gaz.* No. 3806/8 An old fashioned *Spout Cup mark'd E.L. **1864** ATKINSON *Stanton Grange* 11 A starling built its nest in one of the spout-cups to the eaves-gutters of our house. **1956** G. TAYLOR *Silver* iv. 80 *Spout Cups.* Found also in faience, they are no more than a tankard or two-handled cup..ending in a curved spout. **1970** *Canadian Antiques Collector* June 28/2 What were spout cups? Used to feed invalids and children. Popular in the 18th century. Bulbous body, domed cover, duck-neck spout with handle generally at the right angle to the spout. **1805** BARRY *Orkney* 287 The Razor,..or, as we name it, the *spout-fish, is also found in sandy places. **1895** *Stand. Dict., Spout-fish*, a bivalve that squirts water from its siphons, as the soft clam. **1904** E. RICKERT *Reaper* 269 The Spanish treasure-ship.. poured her silver among the tang and spout-fish. **1733** W. ELLIS *Chiltern & Vale Farm.* 359 Pouring it through the streaming Holes of the *spout Head. **1818** KEATS *Endym.* II. 89 As if, athirst with so much toil, 'twould sip The crystal spout-head. **1699** EVELYN *Diary* 26 Mar., A larger [whale] of the *Spout kind, was killed there 40 years ago. **1829** HOOD in *The Gem* 182 That damsel thrusting out a pair of pouting lips, still more *spout-like, at a rusty ribbon. **1875** HUXLEY & MARTIN *Pract. Biol.* xi. 109 A short open spout-like tube. **1838** CARLYLE in Froude *Life in Lond.* (1884) I. 135 Radical Grote.., a man with strait upper lip, large chin, and open mouth (*spout mouth). **1886** J. BARROWMAN *Sc. Mining Terms* 63 *Spout-mouth*, a place on a level road where the material from a spout road is filled into the hutches. *c* **1711** PETIVER *Gazophyl.* VII. lxi, *Spout-mouth'd Condore Button-shell. **1891** MEREDITH *One of our Conq.* xiv, We have ..our spout-mouthed young man, our eminently silly woman. **1713** PETIVER *Aquat. Anim. Amboinæ* Tab. xiii, *Strombus tuberosus*..Knobbed *Spout-pen. **1648** HEXHAM II, *Een Bespruyt-kruycke*, a Sprinkling, or a *Spout-picher for gardens. **1875** KNIGHT *Dict. Mech.* 2288/2 **Spout-plane*, a round-soled plane used in hollowing out stuff for spouting and troughs. **1608** WILLET *Hexapla in Exod.* 590 Vessels to powre in wine with, like vnto our *spout pots. **1631** in *Wills Doctors' Comm.* (Camden) 93 The deepe silver bason, the spout pott and maudlyn cupp of silver. **1879** MISS JACKSON *Shropsh. Word-bk.* 404 **Spout-road*, same as *Cungit* [= 'a road in a mine driven out of the main road for the convenience of drawing the coals']. **1886** J. BARROWMAN *Sc. Mining Terms* 63 *Spout-road*,..a road so steep that the mineral slides down of itself to a level. **1861** P. P. CARPENTER in *Rep. Smithsonian Instit. 1860* 198 Family Aporrhaidæ. (*Spout Shells.) **1881** *Cassell's Nat. Hist.* V. 209 The genus Aporrhais, or the 'Spout-shell', is a shell with an elongated spire. **1821** *Acc. Peculations in Coal Trade* 3 This is the reason why a *spout vessel is preferred to a keel ship. **1875** W. McILWRAITH *Guide Wigtownshire* 118 The spring of water..has been diverted into tiles, and forms a *spout-well. **1701** BRAND *Descr. Orkney*, etc. iv. (1703) 48 There are likewise a great number of little Whales,..which they call *spout-Whales or Pellacks.

spout (spaʊt), *v.* Also 5–6 **spoute**, 5–7 **spowt**. [ME. *spouten*, corresponding to MDu. *spouten* (*spoyten*), older Flem. *spuyten*, Du. *spuiten* (WFris. *spuitsje*), NFris. *spūte*, *spūtji*, *spjūte*, MSwed. and Swed. dial. *spūta*: cf. SPOUT *sb.* (whence senses 7 and 8). The stem *spūt-* appears also in ON. and Icel. *spýta* (Norw. dial. *spyte*) to spit.]

I. *intr.* **1.** To discharge a liquid or other substance in a copious jet or stream; to gush with water, blood, etc. Also const. *with*.

c **1330** R. BRUNNE *Chron. Wace* (Rolls) 8196 When þey [the dragons] hadde longe to-gyder smyten, Spatled, spouted [*v.r.* spouted sperkes], belewed, & byten. *c* **1460** J. RUSSELL *Bk. Nurture* 293 With youre mouthe ye vse nowþer to squyrt nor spout. **1605** SHAKS. *Lear* III. ii. 2 Blow You Cataracts, and Hyrricanos, spout, Till you haue drench'd our Steeples, drown the Cockes. **1645** MILTON *Tetrach.* Wks. 1851 IV. 242 Is it now at last obscurely drawn forth, only to cure a scratch, and leave the main wound spouting? **1718** POPE *Iliad* XVI. 385 His arm falls spouting on the dust below. **1726** LEONI *Alberti's Archit.* I. 15/1 Coverings should be so disposed..that one may not spout upon the other. *c* **1812** MOORE '*Why is a Pump?*' 4 A pump..up and down its awkward arm doth sway, And coolly spout and spout and spout away. **1841** WHITTIER *St. John* 80 While the walls of thy castle Yet spouted with flame. **1848** THACKERAY

Van. Fair lxiii, There are some huge allegorical waterworks still, which spout and froth stupendously upon *fête* days.

b. *spec.* Of a whale: To throw up spray in the act of respiration; to blow.

1796 MORSE *Amer. Geog.* I. 223 When the seamen see a whale spout. **1840** R. H. DANA *Bef. Mast* xviii, He sheered off, and spouted at a good distance. **1861** HOLLAND *Less. in Life* x. 139 When the whales ceased spouting, the earth took up the business.

c. To emit a morbid discharge. (Cf. SPOUT *sb.* 2 b.)

1879 L. WRIGHT *Pigeon Keeper* 104 There are eye-wattles that develop quickly, as in Carriers, though they are apt to 'spout' at a later date.

2. Of liquids: To issue with some force and in some quantity from a narrow orifice; to spurt copiously.

1500–20 DUNBAR *Poems* lxiii. 86, I man..lat the venim ische all out,—Be war, anone, for it will spout. **1582** STANYHURST *Æneis* III. (Arb.) 90 Thee goare blood spowteth of eeche syde, And swyms in the thrashold. **1608** MIDDLETON *Trick to catch Old One* IV. v, One cup more... Is the sack spouting? **1662** J. DAVIES tr. *Olearius' Voy. Amb.* 191 At its breaking out of the Earth it spouts higher than the Sea it self. **1748** *Anson's Voy.* II. i. 123 If they are deeply wounded in a dozen places, there will instantly gush out as many fountains of blood, spouting to a considerable distance. *a* **1774** GOLDSM. *Surv. Exp. Philos.* (1776) I. 405 It will not spout at all, but drivel down the side of the vessel. **1800** VINCE *Hydrost.* i. (1806) 6 Whether the fluid spouts downwards, horizontally, upwards, or in any direction. **1874** T. TAYLOR *Leic. Sq.* xi. 272 A handsome basin..was planned for a jet d'eau, which..never spouted.

b. With *out* or *up*.

1687 A. LOVELL tr. *Thevenot's Trav.* II. 18 There is a Pipe, that throws up a great deal of Water..with so much force that it spouts up almost as high as the Dome. **1722–7** BOYER *Dict. Royal* I. s.v. *Rejaillir*, A Fountain that spouts or spurts out, or up. **1803** *Imison's Sci. & Art* I. 252 If a hole be made in the side of a vessel, the water will spout out [horizontally]. **1885** RIDER HAGGARD *K. Solomon's Mines* iii, A ribbon of white surf, which spouts up in pillars of foam.

c. To spring, bound. Now *dial.*

c **1650** in *Percy's Fol. MS.* (1867) I. 374 He spowted forward as he had beene a deere, till he was passed out of her sight. **1819–** in *Eng. Dial. Dict.*

3. *fig.* To engage in declamation or recitation; to make a speech or speeches, esp. at great length or without much matter.

In J. Heywood *Sp. & Flie* (1556) xxxix. 4, and R. Wilson *Coblers Prophesie* (1594) B 2 b, *spout* is used by ignorant speakers in place of *spute* or *dispute*.

1756 *Gentl. Mag.* XXVI. 36 A paltry, scribbling fool—to leave me out—He'll say perhaps—he thought I could not spout. **1780** MME. D'ARBLAY *Diary* May, I used to hear him spouting by the hour together. **1787** *Ibid.* 15 Aug., He began to spout, and act, and rattle away, with all his might. **1806** J. BERESFORD *Miseries Hum. Life* xv. Introd., What are you at now?..spouting to yourself like a mad stroller. **1837** CARLYLE *Fr. Rev.* II. iv. iv, The far-sounding Street-orators cease, or spout milder. **1878** E. JENKINS *Haverholme* 25 A practical man, spouting in the House about our national obligations to liberty.

II. *trans.* **4.** To discharge, cast out, or pour forth (water, etc.) in a stream of some force and volume.

13.. [see I]. *c* **1440** *Pallad. on Husb.* I. 1097 A condit coold into hit bringe aboute, Make pipis watir warm inward to spoute. *c* **1440** *Alph. Tales* 416 He consydurd þe depenes of þis pytt, & he saw þer-in ane vglie dragon spowtand fyre. **1509** HAWES *Past. Pleas.* XVIII. 79 A dragon..Havyng thre hedes divers in fygure, Whych in a bathe..Spouted the water. **1543** TRAHERON *Vigo's Chirurg.* III. i. x. 100 Let thys decoction be spouted into the wounde..wyth a syrynge. **1599** DALLAM in *Early Voy. Levant* (Hakluyt Soc.) 11 We saw 2 or 3 greate monstrus fishis or whales, the which did spoute water up into the eayere. **1635** HEYWOOD *Hierarchy* I. 6 From the dry stones he can water spout. *c* **1645** HOWELL *Lett.* (1650) II. 25 She took a mouthfull of claret, and spouted it into the poope of the hollow bird. **1739** R. BULL tr. *Dedekindus' Grobianus* 248 b, The Parish Engine spouts excessive Streams To quench the Blaze. **1835** HAWTHORNE *Tales & Sk.* (1879) 75 It was composed of large logs,.. blazing fiercely, spouting showers of sparks into the darkness. **1870** BRYANT *Iliad* IV. I. 126 The surge Tosses on high and spouts its foam afar.

fig. **1568** T. HOWELL *Arb. Amitie* (1879) 51 So where thou thoughtst to spoute thy spite, thou hast hir brought to blisse. **1599** NASHE *Lenten Stuffe* Wks. (Grosart) V. 232 Neuer since I spouted incke, was I of woorse aptitude [etc.]. **1671** BARROW *Duty & Reward Charity* 12 The good Man doth not plant his bounty in one small hole, or spout it on one narrow spot. **1853** KANE *Grinnell Exp.* xxxix. (1856) 359 A group of narwhals, imprisoned by the congelation,.. spouted their release. **1859** MEREDITH *R. Feverel* xl, Each one..laughed, and looked shocked afterwards, or looked shocked, and then spouted laughter.

b. With *out*.

1398 TREVISA *Barth. De P.R.* XVII. cxii. (Bodl. MS.), ȝif a man is vnder water with oile in his mouþe & spowteþ oute þe oile [etc.]. **1596** DALRYMPLE tr. *Leslie's Hist. Scot.* I. 44 Sche into the mane sey spoutis out thir v. fludes. **1667** MILTON *P.L.* VII. 416 Leviathan..at his Gilles Draws in, and at his Trunck spouts out a Sea. **1756–7** tr. *Keysler's Trav.* (1760) IV. 454 He observed two large holes.., which he imagines to have been the apertures through which the fish spouted out the water. **1839** DARWIN *Voy. Nat.* xv. 336 The volcano of Osorno was spouting out volumes of smoke.

fig. **1596** DALRYMPLE tr. *Leslie's Hist. Scot.* II. 401 Nouther left thair wod..barbaritie, quhil out tha spoutit it vpon the Carmelitis, dominicanis, and Franciscanis. **1820** HAZLITT *Table-T.* Ser. II. i. (1869) 4 Spouting out torrents of puddled politics from his mouth.

c. With *up*.

c **1386** CHAUCER *Man of Law's T.* 487 Who kepte Ionas in the fisshes mawe Til he was spouted vp at Nynyuee? *a* **1700** EVELYN *Diary* 5 May 1645, In one of these..is an Atlas spouting up the streame to a very great height. **1796** T. TWINING *Trav. India*, etc. (1894) 17, I distinctly saw and heard these fish spout up the sea to the height of several feet. **1837** CARLYLE *Fr. Rev.* I. v. vi, By a mixture of phosphorus and oil-of-turpentine spouted up through forcing pumps.

5. To wet or drench by a stream of liquid.

1575 TURBERV. *Faulconrie* 269 The bathing or spowting hir with water is a meane to make the powder to frette awaye, and containe the hawkes feathers. **1886** C. SCOTT *Sheep-farming* 135 After draining for a short time, they are passed down shoots to the men at the spouts, where..they are well spouted.

6. To utter readily or volubly; to talk (a language); to declaim or recite.

1612 BEAUM. & FL. *Coxcomb* IV. i, And can you these tongues perfectly?.. Pray spout some French. **1627** W. HAWKINS *Apollo Shroving* I. i. 7 I'de rather spinne at home, then heare these Barbarians spout Latine. **1667** DRYDEN *Sir Martin Mar-all* IV. i, I hope I am old enough to spout English with you, sir? **1771** MME. D'ARBLAY *Early Diary* (1889) I. 128 Dr. King has been with me all the afternoon, amusing himself with spouting Shakespeare, Pope, and others. **1784** COWPER *Tiroc.* 327 His skill..In bilking tavern bills, and spouting plays. **1808** SCOTT in *Lockhart* (1837) I. i. 35, I spouted the speech of Galgacus at the public examination. **1852** JERDAN *Autobiog.* I. xix. 144 Doing nothing but teach the wife of his lodging-house host to spout tragedy. **1889** RUSKIN *Præterita* III. 57, I heard Macaulay spout the first chapter of Isaiah.

7. [f. SPOUT *sb.*] *slang.* To pawn.

1811 *Lexicon Balatronicum*, *Spouted*, pawned. **1812** J. H. VAUX *Flash Dict.* s.v., To pledge any property at a pawnbroker's is termed spouting it. **1850** THACKERAY *Pendennis* lxi, He wouldn't spout the fenders and fire-irons —he ain't so bad as that. **1861** HUGHES *Tom Brown at Oxf.* xxiv, The dons are going to spout the college plate.

8. To fit or furnish with spouts.

1853 *Encycl. Brit.* (ed. 8) II. 268/2 To have the eaves of the whole building spouted. **1894** *Westm. Gaz.* 22 Jan. 6/3 Why should they not have houses properly built, properly spouted and roofed to keep out the wet.

'spoutage. *rare*⁻¹. [f. SPOUT *sb.* I.] Provision of spouts.

1612 STURTEVANT *Metallica* 93 Spouteage may more conueniently be made of pipes, brought downe within the middest of the Birch walls.

'spouted, (*ppl.*) *a.* [f. SPOUT *sb.* and *v.*]

1. Discharged in a spout or stream.

1833 TENNYSON *Pal. Art* vii, A row Of cloisters..Echoing all night to that sonorous flow Of spouted fountain-floods. **1867** MORRIS *Jason* VIII. 102 So to the cage he came, Whose bars now glowed red hot with spouted flame.

2. Provided with a spout or spouts.

1841 *Florist's Jrnl.* II. 34 Use a spouted pot on all necessary occasions. **1879** *Cassell's Techn. Educ.* IV. 107/2 Small, well-shedded and spouted (troughed) fold-yards. **1912** *Oxf. Excav. Nubia* (Exhib. Guide) 9 A great number of shallow cups, spouted vases for oil, saucepans and jugs.

spouter ('spaʊtə(r)). [f. SPOUT *v.*]

1. †**a.** = SPOUT-HOLE I. *Obs.*⁻¹

1622 R. HAWKINS *Voy. S. Sea* (1847) 75 The Indian.. thrusteth in a logg into one of his spowters, and..knocketh it in so fast that by no means the whale can get it out.

b. A spouting whale.

1830 N. S. WHEATON *Jrnl.* 519 In a calm to-day, we had a number of whales, and the whole tribe of spouters about the vessel. **1845** *Encycl. Metrop.* VII. 344/1 The Spouters are mostly characterized by width, flatness, shallowness, and equal extent of the jaws. **1867** SMYTH *Sailor's Word-bk.* 645 *Spouter*, a whaling term for a South Sea whale.

c. A whaling-vessel. Also *Comb.*

1840 R. H. DANA *Bef. Mast* v, The 'spouter', as the sailors call a whaleman, had sent up his main top-gallant mast and set the sail. *Ibid.* xxv, When we got on board, we found everything to correspond—spouter fashion. **1901** F. T. BULLEN *Sack of Shakings* 208 I've been fishing now a good many years in Yankee spouters.

2. †**a.** A reciter or amateur actor. *Obs.*

c **1760** (*title*), The Spouter's Companion; or Theatrical Remembrancer, containing..Prologues and Epilogues [etc.]. **1779** *Mirror* No. 54 ¶14 People may be spouters without culture; but laborious education alone can make perfect actors. **1788** GROSE *Dict. Vulgar T.* (ed. 2), *Spouters Club*, a meeting of apprentices and mechanics to rehearse different characters in plays. **1809** MALKIN *Gil Blas* x. x. (Rtldg.) 372 The major-domo, a great spouter, undertook to train me for the stage.

b. A fluent or voluble declaimer or speaker.

1782 V. KNOX *Ess.* clii. (1819) III. 170 The judicious observer..despises him..as the mere rival of the noisy spouters at the Forum. **1809** T. PICKERING in *M. Cutler's Life*, etc. (1888) II. 317 The other spouters, implicitly confiding in their leaders, are but parrots repeating the notes proceeding from the palace. **1850** THACKERAY *Pendennis* xl, Foker..voted Erith a prig and a dullard,..the dreariest of philanthropic spouters. **1884** SPURGEON in *Sword & Trowel* June 262 There's no stopping these foaming spouters—they must just run themselves dry.

3. a. One who, or that which, spouts *out* something.

1796 LAMB in *Final Mem.* (1848) I. i. 201 These mighty spouters out of panegyric waters have..scattered their spray even upon me.

b. A spouting oil-well.

1886 *Pall Mall G.* 13 Oct. 6/1 How long Tagieff's 'spouter' will last, and what its ultimate yield will be, will depend upon circumstances. **1901** *Daily Chron.* 31 May 7/1 There have been some honest companies.., and these have worked to pay dividends by securing a spouter.

4. *pl.* Coals loaded from a spout.

1821 *Acc. Peculat. Coal Trade* 3 Coal merchants..are always anxious to purchase spouters, as the coals are of a larger quality.

spout-hole. [f. SPOUT *v.*]

1. The blow-hole or spiracle of a whale or other cetacean.

1694 NARBOROUGH *Voy.* II. 126 He hath a Spouthole on his Head..like a Whale. **1725** *Phil. Trans.* XXXIII. 261 Their Way of Breathing is by two Spout-Holes in the Top of the Head. **1770** *Ibid.* LX. 322 The spout-hole..appeared to be provided with a sphincter. **1840** F. D. BENNETT *Narr. Whaling Voy.* II. 151 One of this species..expanded its spout-hole, and produced a sucking sound on inspiration. **1845** J. COULTER *Adv. in Pacific* ii. 12 Whales of every kind blowing the water from their spout-holes.

2. A natural opening in rocks through which the sea spouts.

1849 DANA *Geol.* 272 Some of the spout-holes of Koloa are unusually grand.

3. *Mining.* A short siding or narrow heading.

1883 GRESLEY *Gloss. Coal-m.* 232.

'spoutiness. *rare.* [f. SPOUTY *a.*] Tendency to discharge water.

1808 J. ROBERTSON *Agric. Inverness* 26 The extent of spouty land..must be very considerable, and this spoutiness..demonstrates the great extent of till in the county of Inverness.

'spouting, *sb.* [f. SPOUT *sb.*] Roof-spouts collectively; material for these.

1875 KNIGHT *Dict. Mech.* 2288/2 Hollowing out stuff for spouting and troughs. **1885** *Law Times* 23 May 65/1 It was necessary to put up a ladder to the roof for the purpose of priming some spouting. **1894** *Jrnl. R. Agric. Soc.* June 288 The spoutings of the farm buildings contribute a great deal to the contents of all such ponds.

'spouting, *vbl. sb.* [f. SPOUT *v.*]

1. The action of issuing or discharging in a spout or stream.

1611 COTGR., *Sourgeon*,..the rising, boyling, or spouting vp of water in a spring. **1665** GLANVILL *Def. Van. Dogm.* 34 No more difficulty in this Hypothesis, then in the direct spouting of water out of a pipe. **1796** T. TWINING *Trav. India*, etc. (1894) 17, I had once considered the spouting of whales as a fabulous exageration. **1839** BEALE *Sperm Whale* (ed. 2) 44 At the termination of this breathing time, or as whalers say, when he has his 'spoutings out', the head sinks slowly. **1889** *Nature* 21 Mar. 482 The waste occasioned by 'spouting' [of oil-wells] is at times enormous.

b. *attrib.*, as ***spouting-canal, -hole, -tube.***

1835–6 *Todd's Cycl. Anat.* I. 581/1 The orifice of the spouting hole..is situated towards the summit of the head. **1840** F. D. BENNETT *Narr. Whaling Voy.* II. 151 The spouting-canal [in the whale] may perform both the offices attributed to it. **1845** *Encycl. Metrop.* VII. 344/1 The Gangetic Dolphin is remarkable for..a roof over the spouting apparatus. *Ibid.*, The passage of the spouting tube.

2. Declamation or recitation; speech-making, speechifying.

1788 GROSE *Dict. Vulg. T.* (ed. 2), *Spouting*, theatrical declamation. **1805** M. CUTLER in *Life*, etc. (1888) II. 185 There was much spouting, and some handsome speaking. **1848** THACKERAY *Van. Fair* xxxiv, To be freed..from the dreary spouting of the Reverend Bartholomew Irons. **1893** VIZETELLY *Glances Back* I. xvii. 327 Spouting was a positive passion with Hannay.

attrib. **1802** MAR. EDGEWORTH *Moral T.* (1816) I. xiv. 110 The spouting action of a player. **1814** JANE AUSTEN *Mansf. Park* xiii, For anything of the acting, spouting, reciting kind, I think he has always a decided taste. **1884** E. YATES *Recoll.* iii, 'The Lays of Ancient Rome' had been favourite spouting-pieces at Highgate.

b. ***spouting club*** (or ***society***), a society meeting for the purpose of practising recitation, declamation, or oratory.

1756 A. MURPHY *Apprentice* I. i, A Spouting-Club, friend Gargle!—What's a Spouting-Club? *Ibid.* II. i, The Spouting-Club,..the Members..roaring out Bravo. **1781** V. KNOX *Lib. Educ.* §20 Neither is it desirable, that he should acquire that love..of declaiming, which may introduce him to spouting clubs, or disputing societies. **1806** H. SIDDONS *Maid, Wife & Widow* II. 146 He was a great orator at the spouting societies. **1850** THACKERAY *Pendennis* lxii, Many a Spouting-Club orator would turn the Bishops out of the House of Lords to-morrow.

'spouting, *ppl. a.* [f. SPOUT *v.*]

1. Issuing in a spout or stream.

1601 HOLLAND *Pliny* I. 91 The same is shadowie, full of woods, and watered with veines of spouting Springs. **1697** DRYDEN *Æneid* III. 822 With spouting blood the purple pavement swims. **1712** J. JAMES tr. *Le Blond's Gardening* 202 That is called spouting Water, which..forms single Jets, Sheafs, Bubblings of Water, &c. **1720** POPE *Iliad* XXI. 184 One [lance] raz'd Achilles' hand; the spouting blood Spun forth. **1839** tr. *Lamartine's Trav.* 127/1 Guards are placed.. to watch over the safety of the khan;..fountains of spouting water keep it always cool.

2. a. Discharging liquid in a copious stream.

1654 GAYTON *Pleas. Notes Quix.* I. 3 That other Knight .., whom I call the Knight of the high Scurrado, or Spouting Pestle. **1693** EVELYN *De la Quint. Compl. Gard.* II. 5, I will say in another place, what Water is in the Pipes of spouting Fountains. **1780** tr. *Von Troil's Iceland* 256 At Geyser is the largest of all the spouting-springs in Iceland. **1896** KIPLING *Seven Seas* 25 The wreck that lies on the spouting reef Where the ghastly blue-lights flare.

b. *spec.* Of whales: Throwing up spray in the act of respiration; blowing.

1648 HEXHAM II, *Een Spuyt-wal*, a Spouting whale. **1668** CHARLETON *Onomast.* 167 *Balæna Physeter*,..the puffing, or spouting Whale. **1835–6** *Todd's Cycl. Anat.* I. 576/1 The Spouting Whales always feed upon living food. **1843** *Penny Cycl.* XXVII. 287/2 The Zoophagous or Spouting Cetaceans. **1845** *Encycl. Metrop.* VII. 339/2 The Spouting Family, which includes the Porpesse-like and Whale-like Tribes.

c. ***spouting well*** = SPOUTER 3 b.

1861 *Chem. News* 28 Sept. 164/2 At about 325 feet in depth, there is about 40 feet of white sandstone, near the top of which 'spouting wells' are found. **1898** *Knowledge* 1 June 124/2 The 'spouting' wells of Russia entirely eclipse those of America in output. **1912** TOWER & ROBERTS *Petroleum* v. 83 On the basis of the general character of the yield wells are divided into two classes, the flowing, spouting, or gushing wells, and the pumping wells.

3. Given to speech-making; declamatory.

1796 REYNOLDS *Fortune's Fool* IV. i, In the garret is a spouting author. **1889** *John Bull* 2 Mar. 140 The spouting agitator whose speeches have incited to these criminal deeds.

'spoutless, *a.* [f. SPOUT *sb.*] Destitute or deprived of a spout.

1784 COWPER *Task* IV. 776 There the pitcher stands A fragment, and the spoutless tea-pot there. **1824** *Blackw. Mag.* XV. 152 An old squat spoutless china tea-pot. **1857** GEO. ELIOT *Ess.* (1884) 73 The spoutless tea-pot holding a bit of mignonette. **1897** MARY KINGSLEY *W. Africa* 209 These utensils are spoutless and round.

'spouty, *a.* [f. SPOUT *v.*] Given to spouting or discharging water.

1705 EARL HADDINGTON *Forest Trees* (1765) 6, I..find it thrive in rich, poor, middling, heathy, gravelly, spouty, clay and mossy ground. **1708** *Phil. Trans.* XXVI. 62 The place was cover'd with a Scurf of wet spouty Earth about a Foot thick. **1746** *Rep. Conduct Sir J. Cope* 139 A Column of them in Disorder were coming along westwards under a 'spouty' bank. **1844** H. STEPHENS *Bk. Farm* I. 505, I have frequently made lines of drains across the spouty sloping faces of fields. **1892** *Blackw. Mag.* Oct. 472/2 Oak would root itself firmly in the valleys,..alder in swamps and spouty land.

†spowe. *Obs.* [Of Scand. origin: cf. Icel. *spói*, Norw. *spoe*, *spue*, Da. *spove*, Sw. *spof.*] A curlew or whimbrel.

1519 in *Archaeol.* (1834) XXV. 422 Item..iij Plovers, iij Spowes, & iij Stynts. *Ibid.* 426 Item iij Spowes of Gist. **1526** T. L'ESTRANGE *Househ. Exp.* (Addit. MS. 27448) fol. 38 b, Item, a spowe, a radshanke, and a snype, ij d. *Ibid.*, viij redshancks viij d, vii spowes x d.

‖spoye. *Obs. rare.* [ad. MFlem. *spoye*: see SPAY *sb.*] A sluice or water-gate.

1528 *Lett. & Pap. Hen. VIII* (1872) IV. II. 2231 Wherfor ..ryvers and spoyes must be made [at Calais]. *Ibid.*, Eight gotes or spoyes of stone.

†spoyl, obs. variant of SPILE *sb.*[2]

1782 CREVECOEUR *Lett.* 196 Employ themselves..either in making bungs or spoyls for their oil casks.

spoyl(e, spoyll, obs. forms of SPOIL *sb.* and *v.*[1]

spoylle, variant of SPOIL *v.*[2] *Obs.*

spoze, var. S'POSE *v.*

‖Sprachgefühl ('ʃpraːxgəfyːl). [Ger., f. *sprache* speech + *gefühl* feeling.] The intuitive feeling of a speaker for the essential character of a language; linguistic instinct. Also *loosely*, the character or genius of a language.

1902 GREENOUGH & KITTREDGE *Worlds & their Ways* ix. 127 Men of genius may take great liberties with their mother tongue without offence; but..let them violate its *Sprachgefühl*, and their mannerism becomes, as it were, a foreign language. **1914** *Pedagogical Seminary* June 256 If there is to be instruction in modern foreign languages the age of about ten is for most children the best to begin it. If it comes before this the child has not developed sufficient *Sprachgefühl* for his *own* language, has not developed sufficient idiomatic sense of it to avoid the danger of interference. **1938** E. PARTRIDGE *World of Words* II. vi. 163 The *Sprachgefühl*, feeling for speech, exercises a pervasive influence in a language so long cultivated as English. **1953** K. JACKSON *Lang. & Hist. in Early Britain* 682 It may be thought that the language was in some way committed by its *Sprachgefühl* to a penultimate accent. **1976** *Amer. Speech 1973* XLVIII. 224 Whether this development is associated with the loss of sprachgefühl in a community where the use of a language is declining is a possibility to be considered.

sprack (spræk), *a.* Chiefly *dial.* Also **spract.** [Of obscure origin: current mainly in west midland and south-western counties. Cf. SPRACKLY *adv.* and SPRAG *a.*] Brisk, active; alert, smart; in good health and spirits.

1747 ASTON *Suppl. Cibber's Lives* 15 Mr. Dogget was a little, lively, spract Man. **1785** SARAH FIELDING *Ophelia* II. vi, He will be..glad to hear you set out..so *hoddy* and *sprack*! **1817** LADY GRANVILLE *Lett.* (1894) I. 92 She will not shrink from so sprack an adviser. *Ibid.* 111 She gives life to society, and everything is more sprack. **1856** MISS MULOCK *J. Halifax* vii, He observed that 'master looked sprack agin'. **1880** FREEMAN in W. R. W. Stephens *Life* (1895) II. 195, I am getting mighty sprack, and live as it were with clenched fists.

Hence **'sprackish** *a.*

1882 MRS. NATHAN *Langreath* I. 312 Your Ladyship looks quite sprackish this evening!

sprack-barley, obs. variant of SPRAT-BARLEY.

'sprackle, *v. Sc.* Also 9 **spraickle.** [Of obscure origin: forms with *ch* are frequent in later use.] *intr.* To clamber.

1786 BURNS *Dining w. Ld. Daer* i, Sae far I sprackled up the brae, I dinner'd wi' a Lord. **1822** SCOTT *Nigel* xxxi, Wad ye have naebody spraickle up the brae but yoursell, Geordie?

'sprackly, *adv. rare.* [Cf. SPRACK *a.*] Actively, smartly.

1393 LANGL. *P. Pl.* C. XXI. 10 Sprakliche [B. XVIII. 12 spakliche] he lokede, As is þe kynde of a knyght þat comeþ to be doubed. **1863** BARNES *Poems Dorset Dial.* 3rd Ser. 35 Two sleek-heäir'd meäres do sprackly pull My waggon vull.

sprad, obs. pa. pple. of SPREAD *v.*

'spraddle, *v.* Now chiefly *dial.* and *U.S.* [? f. *sprad*, pa. pple. of SPREAD *v.*] **1.** *intr.* To sprawl.

1632 QUARLES *Div. Fancies* I. iv, O! what a ravishment 't had beene..To see thy busie Fingers cloathe and wrappe His spradling Limbs in thy indulgent Lappe! **1864** BLACKMORE *Clara Vaughan* (1872) 76 So those two were allowed to spraddle on the floor. **1889** *Temple Bar* LXXXV. 2 About the floor..spraddled forms of deal.

2. *trans.* To spread or stretch (one's legs, etc.) wide apart. Also *transf.*

1913 J. LONDON *Son of Sun* vii. 241 He stood with legs spraddled over a large grass basket. **1928** 'BRENT OF BIN BIN' *Up Country* xv. 264 As she walked she spraddled the off hind hoof. **1929** 'SEAMARK' *Down River* i. 6 Let this decrepit tub of yours spraddle her old legs a little faster.

3. The vb.-stem in combination with ppl. adjs., to form adjs., as ***spraddle-footed***, ***-hipped***, ***-legged.*** *U.S.*

1935 Z. N. HURSTON *Mules & Men* I. viii. 177 Don't set there all spraddle-legged. **1974** D. SEARS *Lark in Clear Air* ii. 33 They were big, old, spraddle-hipped, spavined bays with a lot of Clyde in them. **1975** J. GORES *Hammett* (1976) xiv. 102 The boy stood spraddle-footed on the porch.

Hence **'spraddled** *ppl. a.* (also with *out*: see also quot. 1927); **'spraddling** *ppl. a.*

1632 Spradling [see sense 1 above]. **1898** H. S. CANFIELD *Maid of Frontier* 89 He rode with the spraddling seat of a man more accustomed to the plow than to the scout's saddle. **1926** E. HEMINGWAY *Sun also Rises* xviii. 230 They held him and lifted him. It was uncomfortable and his legs were spraddled. **1927** *Amer. Speech* Dec. 169 To put on airs or be dudishly dressed was to be 'all spraddled out'. **1930** D. RUNYON in *Collier's* 1 Feb. 46/2 Down he comes all spraddled out. **1935** L. A. G. STRONG *Tuesday Afternoon* 83 Between his spraddling knees he had spread a clean white napkin. **1940** *Harper's Mag.* Oct. 513/2 Every now and then a nigger would come flying out and go sailing through the air ..spraddled like a flying squirrel. **1975** J. GORES *Hammett* (1976) xxxii. 221 Laverty's right knee pumped, twice, up between Lynch's spraddled legs.

sprag, *sb.*[1] Now *dial.* [Of obscure origin: cf. Sw. dial. *sprag*, *spragg(e* in the same sense.] A slip; a twig or spray.

1676 NEWTON *Corr.* (1850) 260 We desire graffs rather then sprags. **1895** P. H. EMERSON *Birds Norfolk* 81 He alights on the familiar old hawthorn 'sprag', as the fenmen call a spray.

sprag, *sb.*[2] [Of obscure origin.]

†1. A lively young fellow. *Obs.*

1706 E. WARD *Wooden World Diss.* (1708) 52 He'll often tell ye what a Sprag he was in the Days of Yore.

2. a. A young salmon.

1790 GROSE *Prov. Gloss.* (ed. 2) Suppl., *Sprag*, a young salmon. **1882** DAY *Fishes Gt. Brit.* II. 68 Salmon;..from one to two years old..it is known as..sprag ..(Northumberland).

b. A young cod.

1875 F. T. BUCKLAND *Log-Bk.* 92 These sprags are a distinct species of Cod. **1886** *Field* 23 Jan. 106/3 Sprags (half-grown cod), 2s. 6d. to 3s. each.

sprag, *sb.*[3] [Of obscure origin.]

1. *Mining.* A prop used to support the coal or roof during the working of a seam.

1841 HARTSHORNE *Salop. Ant.* Gloss., *Sprags*, 'uprights,' or pieces of wood placed upright against the sides of a coal pit, to support the 'lids'. **1862** *Chambers's Jrnl.* Apr. 216 They are particularly enjoined..to support the roof..with props or sprags of larch or other wood. **1881** *B'ham Daily Post* 16 Feb. 7/2 The provision of the Mines Inspection Act, which requires that sprags in the workings shall be placed not farther than 5 ft. from each other.

2. a. A stout piece of wood used to check the revolution of a wheel (or roller), usually by inserting it between two of the spokes.

Also *U.S.*, a rod or bar which can be dropped so as to prevent a vehicle from running backwards. More widely, any of several devices formerly fitted to motor vehicles to prevent them from running backwards down a hill (see quots.).

1878 F. S. WILLIAMS *Midl. Railw.* 524 Having armed themselves with a piece of timber called a 'sprag' to be used if required as a brake, they set off. **1886** *Pall Mall G.* 13 Sept., Sprags and other articles were thrown under the wheels without effect. **1890** 'R. BOLDREWOOD' *Miner's Right* iii, A 'sprag', being a stout piece of hard wood, was inserted between the rope and the iron roller on which the rope ran. **1902** A. C. HARMSWORTH et al. *Motor & Motor-Driving* xv. 332 The Sprag..is an adjunct fitted to most cars... The sprag should be dropped before the car actually starts to run backwards. *c* **1915** *Autocar Handbk.* (ed. 6) xiv. 216 The sprag is normally held up clear of the ground by a cord, but when the car is likely to stop on a hill the driver should release the cord in good time, and let the 'devil' drag on the ground. Then directly the car stops, the pointed end of the bar digs into the ground. *Ibid.* 217 Another good form of sprag consists of a strong pawl, which is allowed to trip over ratchet teeth out on a revolving part of the gear... Even with good brakes the one great advantage of a sprag is that it permits the car to be restarted on the steepest hill with both brakes off. **1933** *Motoring Encycl.* 723/2 The sprags often fitted on horse-drawn vehicles..have been revived in a new form on motor vehicles. *Ibid.*, The sprag is arranged at the rear of the gear-box, and consists of a roller and wedge adapted to produce a gripping motion on a drum..which turns with the transmission shaft.

b. *fig.* Cf. SPOKE *sb.* 4 a.

1914 'HIGH JINKS, JR.' *Choice Slang* 21 A sprag in the wheel of progress. **1973** R. DENTRY *Encounter at Kharmel* vii. 111 If you were in the President's shoes, how would you put a sprag in Ziauddin's wheel?

sprag, *a. rare.* [app. a mispronunciation of SPRACK *a.*] Smart, clever.

The Shakspere passage is the source of later instances, and has app. led to the insertion of the form in some dialect glossaries.

1598 SHAKS. *Merry W.* IV. i. 84 *M. Pag.* He is a better scholler then I thought he was. *Eu.* He is a good sprag-memory. **1810** LAMB *Lett.* (1888) I. 263 But the epitaphs were trim, and sprag, and patent. **1830** SCOTT *Let.* in *Lockhart* (1838) VII. 229, I had, being, as Sir Hugh Evans says, a fine sprag boy, a shrewd idea that his magnetism was all humbug.

sprag, *v.* [f. SPRAG *sb.*[3]]

1. *trans.* To prop up or sustain (esp. coal in a mine) with a sprag or sprags.

1841 HARTSHORNE *Salop. Ant.* Gloss., *Sprag*, to support or prop up any thing that inclines. **1865** *Even. Stand.* 7 Feb., Several of the men as well as deceased neglected to sprag or spern their work. **1890** *Daily News* 31 May 6/7 As an effect of an overhanging piece of coal not being 'spragged', it might have fallen upon the defendant.

absol. **1894** *Times* 1 Mar. 10/2 Joseph Critchley said that there was plenty of timber for the men to have spragged if they thought proper.

2. To check or stop (a wheel) by inserting a sprag.

1878 F. S. WILLIAMS *Midl. Railw.* 525 Mr. Woodiwin.. seized the plank..and tried to sprag the wheel with it. **1892** *Pall Mall G.* 16 Mar. 5/2 The wheels were 'spragged', to prevent the men being lowered too rapidly.

fig. **1887** *Carlisle Jrnl.* 6 Dec. 3/5 The Tories..gave a Hares and Rabbits Bill, and then spragged the trap that was to catch the vermin.

3. To accost truculently. *Austral. slang.*

1916 C. J. DENNIS *Songs of Sentimental Bloke* 130 *Sprag*, to accost truculently. **1935** L. LUARD *Conquering Seas* iii. 41 'Twas only to save you from getting spragged. *a* **1938** C. J. DENNIS in *Penguin Bk. Austral. Ballads* (1964) 236 A tug named Tyball..Sprags 'em an' makes a start to sling off dirt.

Hence **'spragging** *vbl. sb.*; **'spragger.**

1865 *Pall Mall G.* 26 Sept. 7/2 Nearly fifty per cent. of the lives lost..proceeded from falls of roof.., a large proportion of which might have been avoided by a more..methodical system of 'propping' and 'spragging'. **1881** *Instr. Census Clerks* (1885) 84 Ironstone Miner... Token Lad. Pick Carrier. Spragger. **1884** *Times* 8 Jan. 2/6 A 'spragger' is to be found on all mineral railways and tramways, his business being to 'sprag' the wheels when going down an incline.

Sprague-Dawley (spreɪg'dɔːlɪ). The names of R. W. *Dawley* (1897–1949) U.S. physical chemist who established the strain, and of his wife, née *Sprague*, used *attrib.* to designate an inbred strain of rat much used in laboratories.

A proprietary name in the U.S.A.

1951 *Proc. Soc. Exper. Biol. & Med.* LXXVII. 635/2 Weanling rats of the Sprague-Dawley (SD) strain have a lower choline requirement..than was observed in rats of the Alabama Experiment Station (AES) strain. **1967** B. S. WOSTMANN et al. in M. L. Conalty *Husbandry Lab. Animals* 195 Germfree rats were of the Sprague-Dawley or Lobund Wistar strains. **1970** *Jrnl. Gen. Psychol.* LXXXIII. 88 The *Ss* were 70 male albino rats of the Sprague Dawley strain. **1978** *Official Gaz.* (U.S. Patent Office) 3 Jan. TM 67/1 Sprague-Dawley. The Mogul Corporation... Pub. 10-11-77. Filed 6-9-77.

spraich. *Sc.* Now *rare* or *Obs.* Also 6 **spreich,** 6–7 **sprache,** 6 **sprauch.** [Imitative.] A scream or outcry.

1513 DOUGLAS *Æneid* XI. i. 82 With hair down schaik, and petuus spraichis and cryis. **1533** BELLENDEN *Livy* III. xviii. (S.T.S.) II. 16 Cryand with lamentabill spraichis. **1596** DALRYMPLE tr. *Leslie's Hist. Scot.* I. 186 A spraich ryses from the nerrest, monie of the Scottis..spur with speid that iniure to reuenge. **1605** in Pitcairn *Crim. Trials* II. 463 Heiring hir and hir said servand gif þe sprache and cry.

sprain (spreɪn), *sb.* Also 7 **sprein.** [prob. f. SPRAIN *v.*]

1. A severe wrench or twist of the ligaments or muscles of a joint, causing pain and swelling of the part. Also *fig.*

1601 HOLLAND *Pliny* II. 334 The ioints if they haue gotten a sprein by any rush, find remedy by the dung of bore or sow, if it be laid to hot in a linnen cloth. **1603** —— *Plutarch's Mor.* 124 Anger..resembleth not..the sinewes of the soule, but is like rather to their stretching spreines and.. convulsions. **1677** TEMPLE *Cure of Gout* Misc. (1680) 202, I confess I was in pain, and thought it was with some sprain at Tennis. **1706** PHILLIPS (ed. Kersey), *Sprain*, a violent contortion or wrestling of the Tendons of the Muscles. **1762–71** H. WALPOLE *Vertues Anecd. Paint.* (1786) V. 219 He contracted a great lameness from a sprain. **1829** SCOTT *Anne of G.* ix, He still feels the sprain which he received in his spring after yonder chamois. **1842** *Penny Cycl.* XXII. 383/1 The treatment to be adopted for sprains is the immediate application of leeches. **1882** 'EDNA LYALL' *Donovan* xx, 'Only a sprain, I think,' he answered, faintly.

2. Without article: The condition of being sprained.

1805 *Med. Jrnl.* XIV. 459 Dr. Kinglake's last argument.. remains to be examined, the analogy of common sprain to gout. **1899** *Allbutt's Syst. Med.* VIII. 174 It is not easily met when it is present as the vague condition called sprain of the back.

sprain (sprein), *v.*[1] Also 7 sprein. [Of doubtful origin. Connexion with OF. *espreign-*, *espreindre* to squeeze out, is not clear.]

1. *trans.* To wrench or twist (a part of the body) so as to cause pain or difficulty in moving.

1622 MABBE tr. *Aleman's Guzman d'Alf.* II. 101, I was loath to kicke and fling against it, lest.. I might loosen my lading,.. if not spraine, and hurt my selfe. **1667** PEPYS *Diary* 14 July, I, by leaping down the little bank,.. did sprain my right foot, which brought me great present pain. **1673** COLES *God's Sov.* i. 24 By over-grasping we may sprain our Hands, and unfit 'em for Service otherwise within their compass. **1716** GAY *Trivia* I. 38 The sudden Turn may stretch the swelling Vein, The cracking Joint unhinge, or Ankle sprain. **1804** *Med. Jrnl.* XII. 503 The Rev. Mr. Smith.. sprained his ancle, and treated it as a sprain with cold applications. **1816** A. C. HUTCHISON *Pract. Obs. Surg.* (1826) 174 In this very dock-yard.. a man complained of having sprained his loins. **1861** READE *Cloister & H.* III. 134 He would see my leg. It was sprained sore, and swelled at the ankle.

fig. **1641** MILTON *Reform.* II. Wks. 1851 III. 51 These devout Prelates.. for these many years have not ceas't in their Pulpits wrinching, and spraining the text. **1642** FULLER *Holy & Prof. St.* III. xix. 204 And would it not have wrench'd and sprain'd his soul with short turning?

2. *to sprain one's ankle*: (of a woman) to be seduced (and become pregnant); to lose one's virginity. *euphem. Obs.* exc. *Hist.*

1785 F. GROSE *Classical Dict. Vulgar Tongue* s.v. *Ankle*, a girl who is got with child, is said to have sprained her ankle. **1940** M. SADLEIR *Fanny by Gaslight* I. 286 'I suppose you are still—still a ——.'.. 'I suppose you mean, have I sprained my ankle yet?'

Hence **sprained** *ppl. a.*; **'spraining** *vbl. sb.*[1]

1606 BP. W. BARLOW *Serm.* 21 Sept. B ij, To heale the infected, to splint the spreined. **1675** WOOLLEY *Gentlew. Comp.* 31 Fops will venture the spraining of their tongues. **1849** CLARIDGE *Cold Water Cure* 132 Sprained Shoulder.—A patient fell down an ice-berg and severely bruised his shoulder. **1875** W. S. HAYWARD *Love agst. World* 97 Who ever heard of any one going to bed for a sprained ankle.

sprain, *v.*[2] Now *rare* or *Obs.* Also 5 spreyne. [app. a back-formation from *spreynd(e*, *spreynt(e*, pa. t. and pa. pple. of SPRENGE *v.*] *trans.* †**a.** To sprinkle. **b.** *Agric.* To sow (seeds, etc.) with the hand. Hence **'spraining** *vbl. sb.*[2]

c **1440** *Palladius on Husb.* XI. 161 That spryngith soone yf aysel on hem reyne—I mene on hem al light yf hit me spreyne. **1750** W. ELLIS *Mod. Husb.* I. I. 51 The other had a Seedsman to sprain his pease in every Thorough or Furrow. **1763** *Museum Rust.* I. 261 A seeds-man carries them in a box, and sprains them thinly out of his hand. **1799** [A. YOUNG] *Agric. Linc.* 130 On other lands he sprains in the seed by hand, in every third furrow. **1847** *Jrnl. R. Agric. Soc.* VIII. I. 62 The seed is sown under the furrow in the 'spraining' method; one seedsman to two ploughs.

spraing (spreiŋ), *sb.* Also 6-7 sprayng, 6 sprang. [app. of Scand. origin; cf. MIcel. and Norw. *sprang* fringe, lace.] **1.** *Sc.* A glittering or brightly-coloured stripe, streak, or ray.

1513 DOUGLAS *Æneid* VII. iii. 82 Wyth fyry sparkis lyke to goldin bemys, Or twynkland sprayngis with thair giltin glemys. **1536** BELLENDEN *Cron. Scot.* (1821) I. p. xli, The thrid kind [of hounds] is.. reid hewit, or ellis blak, with small spraingis of spottis. **1597** SKENE *De Verb. Sign.* s.v. *Actilia*, Partial gilt, with spranges or streames of Gold fuilʒie. *a* **1670** SPALDING *Troub. Chas. I* (1850) I. 57 Thair wes sein.. ane gryt blaseing star like to ane comet,.. haueing lang broyndis or sprayngis spredding fra the samen. **1725** RAMSAY *Gentle Sheph.* I. i, A tartan plaid,.. the borders blue: With spraings like gowd, and siller, cross'd with black. **1808** MAYNE *Siller Gun* II. xiv, The mark.. Far glist'ning, circled white and red, Wi' spraings o' blue. **1813-24** in *Eng. Dial. Dict.*

2. Also †**sprain**. A disease of potatoes in which they appear sound on the outside but show curved lines of discoloration when cut.

1909 *Jrnl. Board Agric.* XVI. 33 Several complaints have reached the Board respecting the losses caused to potato growers from the ailment known as sprain in potatoes, and it is asserted that cases of it.. are causing some anxiety in Scotland and elsewhere. **1929** *Trans. Brit. Mycol. Soc.* XIV. 150 Spraing. (Sprain, Internal Rust Spot.)... Internal brown spot. **1980** F. HOPE in E. Gram et al. *Recognition & Control of Pests & Diseases of Farm Crops* (ed. 3) 155/1 Spraing is thought to be caused by a virus. **1980** *Amat. Gardening* 4 Oct. 12/1 The [potato] crop is affected with a physiological disorder known as spraing.

spraing, *v. Sc.* Also 6 spraying, sprang, 8 spring. [f. prec. Cf. MIcel., MSw., and Norw. *spranga* to ornament with fringes or lace.] *trans.* To variegate or diversify with coloured stripes or streaks. Hence **sprainged** *ppl. a.*

1532 *Acc. Ld. High Treas. Scot.* VI. 74 For xxiiij elnis reid and ʒallow bucram to spraying the said pailʒeoune. **1539** *Ibid.* VII. 270 Item, deliverit to him to be the uthir half of the saidis cotis and to sprang thair hois, iiij elnis dimmegrane. **1701** BRAND *Descr. Orkney*, etc. (1703) 54 One bird.. all stripped or sprainged on the back. **1742** R. FORBES *Jrnl.* in *Ajax' Sp.* (1755) 34, I hae nae mair claise but a spraing'd faikie, or a riach plaidie. **1773** FERGUSSON *Leith Races* xviii, Some liveries red or yellow wear, And some are tartan spraingit! **1846** *Whistle Binkie, Songs Nursery* 71 The window's spraing'd wi' icy stars.

sprain-legged, *a.* [f. SPRAIN *sb.* or *v.*] Having a sprained leg.

1721 D'URFEY *Operas*, etc. 224 The sprainleg'd-Gentleman, whom late I told ye down amongst 'em sate.

spraints, *sb. pl.* Forms: 5-6 sprayntes, 6-7 spraynts, 7 spraintes, 7- spraints. [ad. OF. *espraintes* (14th cent.; mod.F. *épreintes*), f. *espraindre* to squeeze out.] **a.** The excrement of the otter.

c **1410** *Master of Game* (MS. Digby 182) x, Men clepeth þat þe stepes or þe marches of þe Otyr... And his fumes tredeleth [*read* -es] oþer sprayntes. **1576** TURBERV. *Hunting* lxxiv. 201 An Otter.. must come forth in the night to make his spraynts. *Ibid.*, He may partly perceive it by ye sprayntes. [**1616** BULLOKAR *Eng. Expos.*, *Spraints*, dung of an Otter. **1630** J. TAYLOR (Water P.) *Navy Landsh.*, *Huntsm.* Wks. I. 93/1 It is called a Deeres Fewmets,.. a Foxe or a Badgers Feance, and an Otters Spraintes. **1688** HOLME *Armoury* II. 133/2 The Ordure.. of.. An Otter, its called the Spraynts. **1753** *Chambers' Cycl.* Suppl. *App.*, *Spraints*, among sportsmen, a term used for the dung of the otter.] **1801** W. B. DANIEL *Rur. Sports* I. 375 His landing place, which will be found.. either by his *spraints*, his seal, or the remains of fish. **1857** KINGSLEY *Two Y. Ago* xviii, Two or three more gentlemen.. are scrambling over the rocks above, in search of spraints. **1885** *Standard* Apr. 5/2 His 'spraints' tell their own tale.

b. In sing. form (also used *collect.*).

1834 MEDWIN *Angler in Wales* II. 159 R—— soon descried a spraint, that appeared fresh. **1851** KINGSLEY *Yeast* viii, I haven't seen the spraint of one here this two years. **1960** G. MAXWELL *Ring of Bright Water* xi. 155 There is a lavatory at every other holt, and the excrement (which is known as 'spraint', and has no offensive odour..) often forms a high pyramidal pile. **1979** *Guardian* 16 Mar. 11/3 A spraint is a blackish smear of digested fishbone and otter-lunch which the animal tends to leave.

So †**'sprainting**. *Obs. rare.*

c **1410** *Master of Game* (MS. Digby 182) xxiv, Of oþer stynkynge beestes he shall clepe it dyrtte, and þat of þe otyr he shall clepe sprayntynge.

†**sprainture**. *Obs.*[−1] [ad. OF. *esprainture*, f. as prec.] Sprinkling.

1481 CAXTON tr. *Cicero, Old Age* e viij, The seed is heeted by the naturell moisture of the erthe and thorough the heete of the sonne and also by the sprayinture of dewys.

sprait, var. SPREAT *Sc.*

sprakelynge, obs. var. SPARKLING *ppl. a.*[1]

sprale, sprall(e, obs. ff. SPRAWL *v.*

sprancle: see SPRANKLE *sb.*, *v.*

sprang. *rare.* [Cf. SPRONG, and WFlem. *sprange* the upper part of a popinjay-pole.]

†**1.** A rung or round of a ladder. *Obs.*[−1]

1527 *Churchw. Acc.*, *Yatton* (Somerset Rec. Soc.) 143 Payd for sprangs to church lader, ij[d].

2. A shoot or branch.

1847 ALB. SMITH *Chr. Tadpole* xlviii, The walks were choked up.. by the long sprangs of the vines and shoots of the standard fruit trees.

sprang, obs. form of SPRAING *sb.* and *v.*

sprangle ('spræŋg(ə)l), *sb. U.S.* [f. next.] A branching rootlet; a ramification, a sprawl.

1896 *Advance* (Chicago) 21 May 738/1 Skepticism has its roots and spreads its feeding sprangles chiefly in the affections and the will. **1898** *Ibid.* 19 May 662/1 This [Philippine] archipelago lies upon the map a great sprangle of intermingled land and water.

sprangle ('spræŋg(ə)l), *v.* Now *dial.* and *U.S.* [Of obscure origin: cf. SPRANTLE *v.*]

1. *intr.* Of persons or animals: To struggle; to spread out the limbs, to sprawl.

14.. *Sir Beues* (MS. O) 3878 Good game had Sabere to sene, How they lay spranglynge on the grene. **1566** J. PARTRIDGE *Plasidas* (Roxb.) 105 There he layde his sprangling corps, almost deuoyde of breath. **1825** JAMIESON *Suppl.*, *To Sprangle*, to struggle; including the idea of making a spring to get away; Roxb[urghshire].

2. To straggle; to spread out in branches or ramifications.

1881 *Oxfordsh. Gloss.* (E.D.S.) 98 A lot o' gret spranggelin' cabbage. **1882** *Cornh. Mag.* May 580 Over its fence sprangles a squash-vine in ungainly joy. **1896** *N. York Wkly. Witness* 18 Nov. 3/3 The Mississippi sprangles as it nears the Gulf, as the great volume of water empties through three outlets.

†**sprangle**, alteration of SPRANKLE *v. Obs.*

1495 *Trevisa's Barth. De P.R.* VII. lxiv. 279 In theym that haue the Lepra.. the syght spranglyth. *Ibid.*, Theyr eyen ben more spranglynge.

'sprangly, *a. U.S.* [f. SPRANGLE *v.*] Spreading, sprawling.

1840 C. F. HOFFMAN *Greyslaer* II. III. i. 103 His great sprangly beard. **1886** *Leslie's Pop. Monthly* XXII. 503/1 We can command a view through their sprangly branches. **1891** *Advance* (Chicago) 3 Dec., Far up into this whole section the ocean thrusts its crooked and sprangly fingers.

sprank[1]. In 6 spranck(e. [perh. f. PRANK *v.*[4], but mod. dial. *a good sprank* 'a fair quantity' is associated with *sprank* 'a sprinkling'.] A show or display.

1568 T. HOWELL *Arb. Amitie* (1879) 48 Where oft the flouds doe floe vpon the beaten banck; Their sandes debarre the grasse to groe, to spread his Aprill spranck. **1581** J. BELL *Haddon's Answ. Osor.* 416 b, Besides a number of old notable men and no small spranecke of the newer sort also.

†**sprank**[2]. *Obs.*[−1] [= MDu. *spranke* (Du. and WFris. *sprank*).] A spark.

1581 J. BELL *Haddon's Answ. Osor.* 326 b, The superstitions thereof [being] wholly rooted out, they would revive the lively sprankes [L. *lumen*] of the auncient Church being vtterly extinct.

†**sprankle**, *sb. Obs. rare.* [Cf. next and WFris. *sprankel.*] A spark or sparkle.

1398 TREVISA *Barth. De P.R.* XV. cxviii. (Bodl. MS.), Fuyre come downe fro heuen and brend þe countrey to asschen,.. and som liknes þerof is ʒitte iseen, in sprankles & iselen on treen. *c* **1475** *Partenay* 4016 With teres makyng sprancles manyon.

†**sprankle**, *v. Obs.* [= Du. *sprankelen*, WFris. *sprankelje*: cf. prec. and SPRANK[2].]

1. *intr.* To throw out sparks; to sparkle.

1387 TREVISA *Higden* (Rolls) II. 237 For the workes of mankynde defouled þe ayer so hiʒe,.. by worschippynge of fuyre þat smokede and spranclede vp so hiʒe. **1398** —— *Barth. De P.R.* VIII. xxix. (Tollem. MS.), In nyʒte rowynge, yf þe mone lyʒte sprankeleþ on þe oris, þan tempeste schal come in schorte tyme. *Ibid.* XVI. xxix, Crisolitus is a litel stone of Ethiopia schynynge as golde, and sprankelynge as fire.

2. To crackle.

1387 TREVISA *Higden* (Rolls) I. 319 Salt Agrigentinus.. melteþ in fuyre, and lepeþ and sprankeleþ [*v.r.* sprancleth] in water. **1398** —— *Barth. De P.R.* XVII. xxxi. (Bodl. MS.), þe gode [reed] sprankeleþ in þe mouþe and [is] ful swete.

Hence †**sprankling** *vbl. sb. Obs.*[−1]

1398 TREVISA *Barth. De P.R.* VIII. xxxiii. (Tollem. MS.) By chaungynge of coloure and sprankelynge of bemis.

sprant, *a.* ? Error for SPRUNT *a.*

1704 W. KING *Remarks Tale Tub* 16 At last there stood up a sprant Young Man that is Secretary to our Scavenger.

†**sprantle**, *v. Obs.*[−1] [Cf. SPRANGLE *v.*] *intr.* To struggle or sprawl.

1390 GOWER *Conf.* II. 5 [A swan] wher sche lay Sprantlende with hire wynges tweie, As sche which scholde thanne deie.

spraser, sprasy, varr. SPRAZER.

†**sprash.** *Obs.*[−1] [Meaning obscure.]

1775 S. J. PRATT *Liberal Opin.* lxiv. (1783) II. 232 A damned sprash, indeed, cries Nabal, wiping his face, but the man is gone the world over.

sprat (spræt), *sb.*[1] Also 7 spratt, sprate. [Later form of SPROT[1].]

1. A small sea-fish, *Clupea Sprattus*, common on the Atlantic coasts of Europe.

1597 DELONEY *Canaans Calamitie* Wks. (1912) 432 One sprat to us is sweeter gotten gaines, Then so much siluer, as this house can hold. *a* **1625** FLETCHER *Bloody Brother* II. ii, A plump Vintner Kneeling, and offring incense to his deitie, Which shall be only this, red Sprats and Pilchers. **1661** LOVELL *Hist. Anim. & Min.* 225 Sprats.. are squalid, leane, and not of copious aliment. **1727** SWIFT *City Shower* Wks. 1755 III. II. 40 Drown'd puppies, stinking sprats,.. and turnip tops, come tumbling down the flood. **1789** MRS. PIOZZI *France & Italy* I. 204 Fresh anchovies.. dressed like sprats in London. **1800** COLQUHOUN *Comm. Thames* XV. 436 Sprats and Herrings are caught only during a short season. **1870** YEATS *Nat. Hist. Comm.* 320 Forty bushels of sprats serve for an acre of land.

b. *collect.* Fish of this species.

1611 FLORIO, *Affumate*, blote hearings, dried sprate. **1856** *Farmer's Mag.* Jan. 37 In a condition more appropriate to the desired object than when the sprat and herring were thrown over arable land. **1881** *Cassell's Nat. Hist.* V. 13 Perch, Gurnards, Smelts, Pike, Herring, Sprat, and Eel.

c. As a specific name.

1769 PENNANT *Brit. Zool.* III. 295 The sprat grows to about the length of five inches. **1837** M. DONOVAN *Dom. Econ.* II. 195 The Sprat very much resembles the herring, except in size. **1865** COUCH *Brit. Fishes* IV. 109 The Sprat is known in the German Ocean and the Baltic, and from thence round the British Islands. **1896** LYDEKKER *Roy. Nat. Hist.* V. 489 The much smaller sprat.. differs by the absence of vomerine teeth.

2. One or other of various small fishes, usually one resembling a sprat.

1603 G. OWEN *Pembrokeshire* (1891) 123 Spratte or sand eele. **1871** KINGSLEY *At Last* vi, The yellow-billed sprat [*Alosa Bishopi*].. is usually so poisonous that 'death has occurred from eating it'. **1882** JORDAN & GILBERT *Syn. Fishes N. Amer.* 274 *Stolephorus compressus*, 'Sprat'. **1883** DAY *Fishes Gt. Brit.* II. 232 Sprat.. is in places erroneously employed for the young of the herring. **1884** GOODE *Nat. Hist. Aquat. Anim.* 277 *Rhacochilus toxotes*... This species is called 'Alfione' at Soquel, 'Sprat' at Santa Cruz.

3. *fig.* **a.** Applied to persons, usually as a term of contempt.

1601 SHAKS. *All's Well* III. vi. 113 When his disguise and he is parted, tell me what a sprat you shall finde him. **1605** *Tryall Chev.* II. i. in Bullen *Old Pl.* III. 289 Bowyer a Captayne? a Capon,.. a lame haberdine, a red beard Sprat, a Yellow-hammer. **1882** *Macm. Mag.* XLV. 394 Barelegged sprats of all shapes and sizes dance in the surf. **1901** G. DOUGLAS *House w. Green Shutters* 155 It was a downcome.. to pack in among a crowd of the Barbie sprats.

b. A small amount, a mere morsel.

1815 J. ADAMS *Wks.* (1856) X. 129 Five millions would be but a sprat for the nourishment of leviathans.

c. In phrases denoting the venturing of a small expenditure in the hope of a large gain.

1856 READE *Never too Late* lix, Did you never hear of the man that flung away a sprat to catch a whale? **1864** *N. & Q.* 3rd Ser. VI. 495/1 Give a Sprat to catch a Mackarel. **1876** *Chambers's Jrnl.* 1 Jan. 7/2 He is said to have actually sold certain classes of articles below prime cost. That, no doubt, was a little hazardous. It was safe only on the principle of throwing out a sprat to catch a herring.

4. *slang.* A sixpence.

It is doubtful if the application in quot. 1857 is correct.

1839 *Slang. Dict.* 34 *Sprat*, sixpence. **1857** *Morn. Chron.* 2 Dec. (Encycl. Dict.), Several Lascars were charged with passing sprats, the slang term applied to spurious fourpenny pieces, sixpences, and shillings. **1902** H. LAWSON *Childr. Bush* 6 The crown [of the hat] was worn as thin as paper by the quids,..bobs and tanners or sprats..that had been chucked into it.

5. *attrib.* and *Comb.*, as ***sprat-catcher, -fishery, -fishing, -gridiron, -net, -seine, -tinning***; **sprat-day** (see quot.); †**sprat-fare**, sprat-fishing; **sprat-herring, -weather** (see quots.).

1599 NASHE *Lenten Stuffe* Wks. (Grosart) V. 242 Those Colchester oyster-men, or whiting-mungers and *sprat-catchers. **1851** MAYHEW *Lond. Labour* I. 69 Sprats..are generally introduced about the 9th November. Indeed, 'Lord Mayor's day' is sometimes called '*sprat day'. *c* **1568** in *Rep. Hist. MSS. Comm.* Var. Coll. IV. 302 [300 mariners for the] *spratte fare [taking yearly 3,000 lasts of sprats]. **1883** F. A. SMITH *Swedish Fisheries* 9 The revenue of the herring and *sprat fisheries of the whole country may be estimated. **1837** *Penny Cycl.* VII. 277/1 *Sprat-fishing commences in the early part of November. **1858** SIMMONDS *Dict. Trade*, **Sprat-gridiron*, a gridiron made specially for broiling sprats. **1884** GOODE *Nat. Hist. Aquat. Anim.* 579 The '*Sprat' Herring of New York, *Clupea indigena.* **1862** *Catal. Internat. Exhib., Brit.* II. No. 3799, Mackerel, herring, pilchard, and *sprat nets. **1883** R. C. LESLIE *Sea-painter's Log* ix, From the small mesh required, a *sprat-seine of any size is costly. **1892** *Pall Mall G.* 8 Feb. 7/1 The opening of the *sprat-tinning industry at Deal..has greatly enhanced the value of these fish. **1847** HALLIW. s.v., The dark roky days of November and December are called **sprat weather*, from that being the most favorable season for catching sprats.

b. In names of birds, as **sprat-borer, -diver, -loon, -mowe** (see quots.).

1785 LATHAM *Gen. Synop. Birds* III. II. 342 This bird [Speckled Diver] is pretty frequent..on the river Thames, where it is called by the fishermen Sprat Loon, being often seen in vast numbers among the shoals of that fish. **1802** MONTAGU *Ornith.* s.v. *Diver*, Sprat Loon. Greatest Speckled Diver. Cobble. **1855** *Trans. Philol. Soc.* 37 (Norfolk words) *Sprat-mowe*, Herring-gull. **1864** ATKINSON *Prov. Names Birds, Sprat-borer*, Prov. (Essex) name for young of Red-throated Diver—*Colymbus septentrionalis.* **1892** 'SON OF MARSHES' *Lond. Town* ix. 153 To mention a few of the family of the divers, we have the sprat diver [etc.].

Hence **sprat** *v. intr.*, to fish for sprats. Also **'spratting** *vbl. sb.*

1883 R. C. LESLIE *Sea-painter's Log* ix, A seine is also used for spratting in bays where the shore is clean. **1893** *Daily News* 14 Jan. 3/4 The spratting season has been a complete failure as far as Essex fishermen are concerned. **1893** *Times* 20 Nov. 10/1 The Walmer lifeboat was also driven into Dover.., after rescuing the Steven and Sarah with two hands, who were out spratting.

†**sprat,** *sb.*[2] *Obs. rare.* [Of obscure origin: cf. SCRAT *sb.*[1]] An evil spirit.

1432 tr. *Higden* (Rolls) I. 419 Therefore there were ij. Merlynes; oon of them callede Ambrosius, geten of a spratte at Kaermerthyn. **1549** SIR T. SMITH *Exam. W. Wycherly* (MS. Lansd. 2) fol. 26, He..hath used the crystal to invocate the sprat called Scariot..; which sprat hath given him knowledge an hundred time.

sprat, *sb.*[3] *Sc.* [Cf. SPART[2] and SPROT[2].] A kind of rush or rush-like grass.

a **1578** LINDESAY (Pitscottie) *Chron. Scot.* (S.T.S.) I. 336 The fluir laid witht greine cherittis, witht sprattis, medwartis and flouris. **1780** YOUNG *Tour Irel.* 137 It kills all sprats (*juncus*) and produces a fine sweet herbage. **1792** *Statist. Acc. Scot.* IV. 518 That species of grass which grows on marshy ground, commonly called spratt, is much used for fodder. **1853** G. JOHNSTON *Bot. East. Borders* 199 There is not much danger of lairing where Sprats grow abundantly.

†**sprat,** *sb.*[4] *Obs. rare.* (See quot.)

1756 F. HOME *Exper. Bleaching* 211 Lime is by no means fit for discharging the oil in the cloth, but for cleaning it of the dead part, commonly called *sprat.*

sprat, *v.*: see SPRAT *sb.*[1]

sprat-barley. Also 6 sprot-, 8 sprack-. [? f. SPROT[1] and SPRAT *sb.*[1]] A species of barley, *Hordeum zeocriton*, with short broad ears and long awns.

1523 FITZHERB. *Husb.* § 13 There be thre maner of barleys, ..sprot-barleye, longe-eare, and beare-barley... Sprot-barley hath a flat eare most comonly [etc.]. **1651** R. CHILD in *Hartlib's Legacy* (1655) 78 There is not onely the ordinary Barley, but big sprat-Barley, which hath lately been sown in Kent with good profit. **1677** PLOT *Oxfordsh.* 240 If the Land be rank, [they sow it] with that they call sprat-Barly. **1707** MORTIMER *Husb.* (1721) I. 133 The common allowance of Seed is four Bushels to an Acre, though they say that three Bushels of Sprat Barley will do. **1736** LEWIS *Hist. Antiq.* 15 Sprack-Barley has formerly been pretty much sown in the rich Land in the Marshes. **1812** SIR J. SINCLAIR *Syst. Husb. Scot.* I. 314 Barley is apt to lodge, which ruins the seeds, except sprat or battle-dore barley is sown. **1846** J. BAXTER *Libr. Pract. Agric.* (ed. 4) I. 83 The sprat or battle-dore barley makes good malt. **1861** BENTLEY *Man. Bot.* 699 *H. zeocriton*, Sprat or Battledore Barley.

spratkin. [f. SPRAT *sb.*[1]] A little sprat.

1674 N. FAIRFAX *Bulk & Selv.* 180 He will have set before us such a Hoghen moghen Leviathan, that that of Holy Job would be but a kind of Spratkin to it ward.

'spratter. [f. SPRAT *sb.*[1]] **a.** *dial.* The guillemot. **b.** A vessel or man engaged in sprat-fishing.

1863 WISE *New Forest* Gloss., *Spratter*, the common guillemot (*Uria troile*). **1883** R. C. LESLIE *Sea-painter's Log* ix, She may have been a pleasure-yacht in her day, but can never be so again; for once a spratter, always a spratter. *Ibid.*, Strange to say, spratters, especially in rough weather, rather dread getting the net full of fish.

'spratle, *sb. Sc.* [f. SPRATTLE *v.*[2]] A struggle or scramble.

1824 SCOTT *Redgauntlet* ch. xii, We will suppose that any friend like yourself were in the deepest hole in the Nith, and making a sprattle for your life.

†**'sprattle,** *v.*[1] *Obs. rare.* [? Metathetic form of SPARTLE *v.*[1]] *intr.* and *trans.* To scatter, disperse.

1422 tr. *Secreta Secret., Priv. Priv.* 137 Kynge Richarde out of Irlande into Walis arryuet, ther anoone spratlit al his ryche retenue. *Ibid.* 233 Eyen that bene whit y-freklet, or I-sprotid,..or reede y-spratelid throgh the eyen, bene moste to blame amonge al otheris.

'sprattle, *v.*[2] *Sc. rare.* [Cf. Sw. *sprattla* in the same sense.] *intr.* To scramble, to struggle.

1786 BURNS *To a Louse* iii, There ye may creep, and sprawl, and sprattle. —— *A Winter Night* iii, Silly sheep, wha..thro' the drift, deep-lairing, sprattle.

'spratty, *a.*[1] *rare.* [f. SPRAT *sb.*[1]] Containing or consisting of sprats.

a **1880** F. T. BUCKLAND *Nat. Hist. Brit. Fishes* (1883) 282 Among the whitebait..there are a great many sprats. This is called 'spratty stuff'.

'spratty, *a.*[2] *Sc.* [f. SPRAT *sb.*[3]] Producing rushes; rush-like, rushy.

1808 J. VEITCH in *Edin. Encycl.* I. 253/1 A trial was made ..on a piece of exceeding stiff spratty lee, with two ploughs of Small's construction. **1886** J. RUSSELL *Remin. Yarrow* iv. (1894) 75 Where it [the soil] is wet and spongy, the grass is long, coarse, and spratty.

sprauchle, spraughle, later ff. SPRACKLE *v.*

spranucy ('sprɔːn(t)sɪ), *a. slang.* Also sprauntsy, sproncy. [Of uncertain origin: perh. related to dial. *sprouncey* cheerful (*Eng. Dial. Dict.*).] Smart or showy in appearance or sound of voice.

1957 L. P. HARTLEY *Hireling* xi. 90 She's bought new sprauncy clothes for the children. **1959** H. HOBSON *Mission House Murder* viii. 57 That sprauncy Girton voice of hers. **1969** *Guardian* 4 Feb. 7/2 The 'sprauntsy' (showy) antique dealers. **1971** G. EWART *Gavin Ewart Show* I. 21 Two sprauncy birds inhibit the parkway. **1976** 'P. B. YUILL' *Hazell & Menacing Jester* xiii. 142 They pay sixty grand to live in a sproncy little street like this.

sprawl (sprɔːl), *sb.* Also 8 *Sc.* spraul. [f. SPRAWL *v.*]

1. a. The, or an, act of sprawling; an awkward or clumsy spreading out of the limbs.

1719 OZELL tr. *Misson's Mem.* 25 When the Dog thinks he is sure of fixing his Teeth, a Turn of the [Bull's] Horn.. gives him a Sprawl thirty Foot high. **1820** KEATS *Eve of St. Agnes* xli, To the iron porch they glide, Where lay the Porter, in uneasy sprawl. *a* **1847** ELIZA COOK *Old Mill-Stream* xiii, And the running,..the pull and the haul, Had a glorious end in the slip and the sprawl. **1857** MRS. MATHEWS *Tea-Table T.* I. 188 The triumphant shout which accompanies his awkward sprawl on the carpet.

b. A straggling array or display *of* something.

1827 *Blackw. Mag.* XXII. 474 Through one long wide sprawl of men, women, and children, we wheeled past the Gothic front. **1858** HAWTHORNE *Fr. & It. Jrnls.* I. 217 The sprawl of nakedness with which Michael Angelo has filled his sky.

c. ***the sprawls***, a disease affecting the legs of young ducks. *dial.*

1880- in south-western glossaries.

d. The straggling expansion of an indeterminate urban or industrial environment into the adjoining countryside; the area of this advancement. Freq. with defining adj. (see *suburban* and *urban sprawl* at first element).

1955 *Times* 23 Aug. 10/2 It is sad to think that London's great sprawl will inevitably engulf us sooner or later, no matter how many 'green belts' are interposed in the meantime between the colossus and ourselves. **1958** *Listener* 23 Oct. 641/1 As the new industrial zones came to life on the edges of the built-up areas, they frequently appeared to be no more than an extension of the old industrial sprawl. **1967** *Ibid.* 3 Aug. 147/2 Planning so far has failed to contain sprawl. **1971** P. GRESSWELL *Environment* 122 Green Belt policy stopped sprawl in crucial places at a crucial time. **1977** *Listener* (N.Z.) 15 Jan. 9/2 It's a sad reflection on our society that 'suburban' has become a dirty word, synonymous with 'subtopia' and responsible for many urban problems from neurosis to sprawl.

2. A struggle. *rare*[−1].

1795 A. WILSON *Hollander* Poet. Wks. (1846) 193 Jock and him has aft a spraul Wha'll bring the biggest dark [= day's work] in.

3. *dial.* and *U.S.* Activity, energy, go.

1888- in south-western glossaries and texts. **1894** *Advance* (Chicago) 25 Oct. 124/1 Fact of it is neither of them had sprawl enough to disagree. **1896** T. HARDY *Jude* I. ii, Poor or'nary child—there never was any sprawl on thy side of the family.

sprawl (sprɔːl), *v.* Forms: α. 1 spreawlian, 2 spreulen; *north.* and *Sc.* 5-6, 8-9 sprewl, 8 sprowl, 9 spreul, sprule. β. 4-7 spraule, 5-7 spraul. γ. 4 sprawel, 5 sprawlyn, 6- sprawl. δ. 6 spralle (sprale), 6-7 sprall. [OE. *spreawlian*, = NFris. *spraweli* in the same sense.]

1. *intr.* To move the limbs in a convulsive effort or struggle; to toss about or spread oneself out; in later use, to be stretched out on the ground, etc., in an ungainly or awkward manner.

α. *c* **1000** *Prudentius Gloss.* in *Germania* XXIII. 392 *Palpitet*, spreawliȝe. *a* **1100** in Napier *O.E. Glosses* 216/1 *Palpitat, moritur*, spreulede. *c* **1425** WYNTOUN *Cron.* VIII. 1835 Þe kynge saw in to þat tyde A woman slayne, and of hir syde A barne he saw fal out sprewlande. *c* **1450** *St. Cuthbert* (Surtees) 1957 At þe last sho lay sprewland o brade, Lyke to dye. **1513** DOUGLAS *Æneid* v. viii. 115 Doun duschit the beist, deid on the land gan ly, Sprewland and flikkerand in the deid thrawis. **1722** RAMSAY *Three Bonnets* IV. 97 The Peterenians..That gar Fowk lik the Dowps of Priests, Else on a Brander like a Haddock, Be broolied, sprowling like a Paddock. **1781** J. HUTTON *Tour to Caves* (ed. 2) Gloss., *Sprewl*, to spurn and kick with both hands and feet when held down. **1825-** in JAMIESON, etc.

β. *a* **1300** *Havelok* 475 Þer was sorwe, wo so it sawe! Hwan þe children bi þe wawe Leyen and sprauleden in þe blod. **1388** WYCLIF *2 Sam.* xviii. 14 Whanne he spraulide, ȝit cleuynge in the ook. —— *Tobit* vi. 4 It [the fish] bigan to spraule bifor hise feet. *c* **1400** *Laud Troy Bk.* 16964 He.. sclow hem doun as he were wood; Thei lay & sprauled in her blood. **1530** PALSGR. 729 And you spraule on this facion you shall have the lesse favoure. **1542** BOORDE *Dyetary* xxviii. (1870) 292 And let euery man beware..to spraule with the legges out of the bed. **1602** MARSTON *Ant. & Mel.* I. Wks. 1856 I. 16 Senseless he sprauld, all notcht with gaping wounds. **1623** MARKHAM *Cheap Husb.* (ed. 3) I. ii. 20 If he spraule or paw forth with his feet, you shall..giue him..a good ierke or two. **1663** BUTLER *Hud.* I. iii. 731 Some lye sprauling on the ground With many a gash and bloudy wound.

γ. *c* **1340** HAMPOLE *Pr. Consc.* 475 For þan may he noght stande ne crepe Bot ligge and sprawel, and cry and wepe. *c* **1440** *Promp. Parv.* 470 Sprawlyn, *palpito.* **1581** A. HALL *Iliad* III. 54 Then with his knife the two yong lambs he slue, And weakly sprawling in their blood, on ground from him he threw. **1609** C. BUTLER *Fem. Mon.* (1634) 98 The better part of these brave Soldiers..lay, some dead, some half-dead, sprawling on the ground. **1687** A. LOVELL tr. *Thevenot's Trav.* I. 164, I saw one once give a great Dog such a blow with his foot, as left him sprawling with his four legs up in the Air. **1717** PRIOR *Alma* I. 275 Before the child can crawl, He learns to kick, and wince, and sprawl. **1753** MISS COLLIER *Art Torment.* I. iii. (1811) 79 If they..afterwards should choose to cool their limbs by sprawling about on the wet grass after the dew is fallen. **1824** W. IRVING *T. Trav.* I. 312, I rode over him one day as he and his horse lay sprawling in the dirt. **1870** ROCK *Text. Fabr.* Introd. p. cxxi, Rich barons and titled courtiers would sprawl amid the straw and rushes.

δ. **1530** PALSGR. 729, I spralle, as a yonge thing doth, that can nat well styrre, *je crosle.* *a* **1535** FISHER *Serm.* Wks. (1876) 421 The burninge wormes and serpents shal sprale aboue thee. **1567** DRANT *Horace, Ep.* xix. F vij, They.. practysde it full well, All night to sprall and stryue with wyne. **1614** GORGES *Lucan* III. 105 The bruised corpes to death doth sprall, And mingles bloud and ioynts withall. **1675** HOBBES *Odyss.* (1677) 232 A fawn, that sprall'd and labour'd to get free.

b. To crawl from one place to another in a struggling or ungraceful manner. Also *fig.*, to proceed, issue.

1582 STANYHURST *Æneis* II. (Arb.) 47 That this new practise from my old foes treacherye sprauleth. **1663** HEATH *Flagellum* To Rdr., All the different Sects and Schisms which He kept in perpetual separation..now run into a coalition; and like divided parcels of dying vipers, sprawl towards a union with this their Head. **1692** BENTLEY *Boyle Lect.* iii. 27 Who were there then in the world, to observe the Births of those First Men,..as they sprawl'd out of Ditches? **1851** THACKERAY *Eng. Hum.* v. (1853) 240 The sturdy little painter is seen sprawling over a plank to a boat.

c. With complement: ***to sprawl one's last***, to make a last convulsive struggle in death.

1837 CARLYLE *Fr. Rev.* III. VII. v, Sansculottism, once more flung resupine, lies sprawling; sprawling its last. **1863** *Reader* 7 Nov. 538 One of them..is sprawling his last as a Japanese..seems able to sprawl it.

2. Of things: To spread out, extend, climb, etc., in a straggling fashion.

1745 H. WALPOLE *Lett.* (1846) II. 55 Those hands that are always groping, and sprawling, and fluttering. **1815** SCOTT *Guy M.* ii, His long mis-shapen legs sprawling abroad. **1885** *Manch. Exam.* 17 Jan. 5/4 A great, awkward..goods train lies sprawling across the main artery of traffic. **1890** H. FREDERIC *Lawton Girl* 31 A broad rickety veranda sprawling its whole width. **1892** QUILLER-COUCH *Warwickshire Avon* 26 The jasmine and the ivy sprawl up its sad-colored walls.

b. In specific uses (see quots.).

1802 JAMES *Milit. Dict.*, *To sprawl*, to widen out in an irregular and unsoldier-like manner.—This term is chiefly applicable to the cavalry. **1875** *Chambers's Jrnl.* 80 Sportsmen who hope for success must beware of letting their shot sprawl.

c. Of handwriting or written matter.

1840 THACKERAY *Shabby-genteel Story* ii, Is it not a sweet name? It sprawls over half the paper. **1858** R. S. SURTEES *Ask Mamma* lxvii. 302 The description then sprawled over four sides of letter paper. **1883** F. M. PEARD *Contrad.* I. 33 The handwriting, as he noted, was large and rather inclined to sprawl.

3. *trans.* To spread or stretch out (something) in a wide or straggling manner. Usu. with *out.*

1541 PAYNELL *Catiline* xli. 61 This myschiefe is sprawled abrode further than you thynke; For it hath not onely ouerflowen Italy, but is also runne ouer the mountayns Alpes. **1768-74** TUCKER *Lt. Nat.* (1834) I. 438 Though I can sprawl out legs too, I feel neither ground to tread on, nor water to push against. **1815** SCOTT *Guy M.* xx, Sprawling out his leg, and bending his back like an automaton. **1837** CARLYLE *Fr. Rev.* II. I. xii, Speechless nurselings..sprawl out numb-plump little limbs. **1878** *Fraser's Mag.* XVIII. 385 Is our exuberance of military power so great that we can afford to sprawl our military stations all over the Mediterranean?

Hence **sprawled** *ppl. a.*

1884 STEVENSON *Lett.* (1899) I. 314 The blind man in these sprawled lines sends greeting.

sprawler ('sprɔːlə(r)). [f. prec.] One who or that which sprawls. Also *spec.* as a moth-name.

1832 J. RENNIE *Consp. Butterfl. & Moths* 35 The Sprawler (*Petasia Cassinea*..) appears in October. **1839** DICKENS *Nickleby* xxiii, Isn't it enough to make a man crusty to see that little sprawler put up in the best business every night. **1880** *New Virgin.* II. 105 Half-a-dozen black little shiny sprawlers.

sprawling ('sprɔːlɪŋ), *vbl. sb.* [f. as prec.] The action of the verb in various senses.

13.. *E.E. Allit. P.* B. 408 Þenne mourkne in þe mudde most ful nede Alle þat spyrakle in spranc, no sprawlyng awayled. *c* **1440** *Promp. Parv.* 470 Sprawlynge, *palpitacio.* **1556** PHAER *Æneid* IV. L iij b, The blade in fomy blood, and hands abrode in spraulíng thrown. *c* **1616** CHAPMAN *Batrachom.* 138 Who amids the Fenn Swumme with his brest vp; hands held vp in vaine,.. And often with his sprawlings, came aloft. **1822** *Monthly Mag.* LIII. 335 The fairest blossoms of Persian or Arabian poetry..degenerate into extravagant sprawlings.

'**sprawling**, *ppl. a.* [f. as prec.] That sprawls, in senses of the verb: **a.** Of animals or persons, their actions, etc.

1550 J. COKE *Eng. & Fr. Heralds* §29 The vyle blacke poysoned spralyng todes. **1577** STANYHURST *Descr. Irel.* ii. 9/1 If you put the heire of an horse taile in mire..for a certaine space, it will turne to a little thin spraulyng worme. **1598** MARSTON *Sco. Villanie* III. xi. 225 The whirle on toe, The turne about ground, Robrus sprauling kicks. **1693** CREECH in *Dryden's Juv.* (1697) 333 The Cranes descend, and bear The sprawling Warriors through the liquid Air. **1740** SOMERVILLE *Hobbinol.* I. 318 Whirl'd aloft High o'er his Head the sprawling Youth he flung. **1791** NAIRNE *Poems* 80 Both hands were necessary now, To drag it off to make a sprawling bow. **1802** JAMES *Milit. Dict.* s.v., *A sprawling charge*, a loose and irregular movement of cavalry, instead of a close, compact, forward attack. **1848** MRS. JAMIESON *Sacr. & Leg. Art* (1850) 50 Of the sprawling, fluttering, half naked angels..what shall be said? **1899** *Allbutt's Syst. Med.* VII. 363 Its gait is of a peculiar sprawling character.

transf. **1623** MIDDLETON *More Dissemblers* IV. ii, A pretty, womanish, faint, sprawling voice.

b. Of things.

a **1770** C. SMART *Hop Garden* II. 98 Oft I've seen..the mad pickers, tam'd to diligence, Cull from the bin the sprawling sprigs, and leaves That stain the sample. **1844** DICKENS *Mart. Chuz.* xxxix, A great black sprawling splash upon the floor. **1884** *Sat. Rev.* 5 July 12/2 The huge sprawling Archdeaconry of Richmond. **1885** RUNCIMAN *Skippers & Sh.* 268 Others strolled down the broad sprawling street of the village.

c. Of handwriting.

1826 DISRAELI *V. Grey* I. ii, Travelling cases, directed in a boy's sprawling hand. **1852** MRS. STOWE *Uncle Tom's C.* xxviii, He..signed his name to it in sprawling capitals. **1907** H. WYNDHAM *Flare of Footlights* xv, The writing seemed vaguely familiar, but for the moment he could not identify the sprawling feminine hand.

'**sprawlingly**, *adv.* [f. SPRAWLING *ppl. a.* + -LY[2].] In a sprawling manner.

1921 *Spectator* 7 May 585/2 Gauntly outlined, white and still, Three haystacks peer above the hill; Three agèd rakes thrust sprawlingly Fantastic tendons to the sky. **1980** *Economist* 15 Mar. 104/1 Several books of sociology, history, politics and literary criticism uneasily brought together into one weightily erudite but sprawlingly inconclusive survey.

sprawly ('sprɔːlɪ), *a.* [f. as SPRAWL *v.*] Of a sprawling character; straggly. Also *Comb.*

1798 JANE AUSTEN *Lett.* (1884) I. 160 Why is my alphabet so much more sprawly than yours? **1897** BLACKMORE *Dariel* xlix, I fell in with the rear of that sprawly-jointed troop. **1905** *Longman's Mag.* Mar. 443 A sprawly, squirmy, noisy kitten.

† **sprawne**, obs. variant of PRAWN *sb.*

1688 HOLME *Armoury* II. 338/1 A Prawne..is vulgarly called a Sprawne.

spray (spreɪ), *sb.*[1] Also 4–7 **spraye**, 4–6 **sprai**, 7 **sprey** (8 **spry**). [Of obscure origin. Connexion with SPRAG *sb.*[1] is uncertain.]

1. a. *collect.* Small or slender twigs of trees or shrubs, either as still growing or as cut off and used for fuel, etc.; fine brushwood.

1297 R. GLOUC. (Rolls) 11522 Gret fur he made þer aniȝt of wode & of sprai. *a* **1310** in Wright *Lyric P.* vi. 27 Bytuene Mershe ant Averil when spray biginneth to springe. **1615** W. LAWSON *Country Housew. Gard.* (1626) 31 If these two kindes thriue, they reforme but a spray, and an vndergrowth. **1652** WADSWORTH tr. *Sandoval's Civ. Wars Spain* 351 His souldiers..fetched a great quantitie of sprey, or bavins,..and set fire to them. **1707** *Clergyman's Vade-M.* (1709) 214 With old Stocks, or Trees of above 20 Years old, but some Spry or small Underwood. **1778** [W. H. MARSHALL] *Minutes Agric.* 7 Apr. 1775, As much prime wood as would, with a little spray, have made three bakers bavins. **1842** LOUDON *Suburban Hort.* 631 Pea sticks, which are branches of trees or shrubs well furnished with spray. **1852** MORFIT *Tanning & Currying* (1853) 96 Majestic trees ..with spreading tortuous branches and spray. **1887** T. HARDY *Woodlanders* I. vii. 134 All he had required had been a few bundles of spray for his man Robert.

b. With *the* (or *that*).

The sense in the first quot. is somewhat doubtful.

a **1300** *Floriz & Bl.* 275 Ho so wonede a moneþ in þat spray, Nolde him neure longen away. *c* **1425** *Thomas of Erceld.* 86 He knelyde downe appone his knee, Vndir-nethe þat grenwode spraye. **1513** DOUGLAS *Æneid* XII. Prol. 90 The spray bysprent with spryngand sproutis dispers. **1577** B. GOOGE *Heresbach's Husb.* II. (1586) 62 b, All the spraye that springeth aboue the flowre, is commonly cut off. **1707** MORTIMER *Husb.* (1721) II. 22 Being gathered Green..and the Spray stripped off in August. **1791** W. GILPIN *Forest Scenery* I. 106 The mode of growth in the spray, corresponds exactly with that of the larger branches, of which indeed the spray is the origin. **1823** SOUTHEY in *Q. Rev.* XXX. 3 The tree sheds its leaves not singly, but with the spray from which they spring. **1866** *Treas. Bot.* 141/1 The branches are used as fuel..; the spray for thatching.

fig. *a* **1677** HARRINGTON *Grounds & Reas. Mon.* Wks. (1700) 32 Certainly these People were strangely blind..to admit the spray of such a stock.

c. In the poetic phrase ***on*** or ***upon (the) spray.***

1375 BARBOUR *Bruce* XVI. 64 This wes in the moneth of May, Quhen byrdis syngis on the spray. *c* **1386** CHAUCER *Sir Thopas* 59 The wodedowue vp on the spray She sang ful loude & clere. **1508** DUNBAR *Gold. Targe* 51 A saill, als quhite as blossum vpon spray. **1523** SKELTON *Garl. Laurel* 1412 How her ble was bryght as blossom on the spray. **1870** HARDY *Satires of Circumstance* (1914) 20 When I set out for Lyonnesse, A hundred miles away, The rime was on the spray. **1893** F. THOMPSON *Poems* 66 Oh, there were flowers in Storrington On the turf and on the spray. **1921** W. DE LA MARE *Veil* 19 Thrush and robin perched mute on spray.

2. a. A slender shoot or twig.

1387 TREVISA *Higden* (Rolls) IV. 157 Þere herdes fond hym among mory flagges and sprayes, and sente hym to Silla. **1398** —— *Barth. De P.R.* XVII. viii. (Tollem. MS.), The beste [Amomum] is þat, þat is..sprad up on reed sprayes. **1503** HAWES *Examp. Virt.* xii. 236 Where byrdes sate on many a spray. **1567** FENTON *Trag. Disc.* v. (1898) I. 201 The pleasant apple, mustering..upon the heyght of the highest spraise. **1578** LYTE *Dodoens* VI. lxxxviii. 771 The branches be harde, and parted into other spraies. **1607** WALKINGTON *Opt. Glass* 115 Like spraies and branches from the stemme of a tree. **1630** DRAYTON *Muses Eliz.* Nymphal iv. 111 Amongst the liuely Birds melodious Layes, As they recording sit vpon the Sprayes. **1704** POPE *Pastorals, Winter* 56 No more the birds shall..hearken from the sprays. **1785** G. FORSTER tr. *Sparrman's Voy. Cape G. Hope* (1786) I. 196 The frame of this arched roof..is composed of slender rods or sprays of trees. **1833** HT. MARTINEAU *Brooke Farm* xii. 135 A few ears dangling from the sprays for gleaners. **1854** S. DOBELL *Balder* I. Poet. Wks. 1875 II. 12 Little window in the wall Eye-lashed with balmy sprays of honeysuckle.

fig. *c* **1400** *Pilgr. Sowle* (Caxton, 1483) v. ix. 100 A blessid floure out of this spray shall sprynge. **1563** *Mirr. Mag., Hastings* ix, None aryse To former type, but they catch vertues spraye, Which mounteth them that clyme by lawfull waye. **1593** SHAKS. *3 Hen. VI*, II. vi. 50 Who..set his murth'ring knife vnto the Roote, From whence that tender spray did sweetly spring, I meane our Princely Father. **1599** —— *Hen. V*, III. v. 5 Shall a few Sprayes of vs..Spirt vp so suddenly into the Clouds, And ouer looke their Grafters? **1781** COWPER *Charity* 629 Thus have I sought to grace a serious lay With many a wild, indeed, but flow'ry spray. **1873** EARLE *Philol. Eng. Tongue* (ed. 2) §593 The sprays of language are those phrasal forms which are produced by the combination of symbolic words.

b. *pl.* Hazel, birch, or other twigs used in thatching.

1520 *Churchw. Acc. St. Giles, Reading* (ed. Nash) 11 For Sprayes & thatchyng of the ij[c] tents at the gravell pytt, ij[s] xj[d]. **1677** PLOT *Oxfordsh.* 64 In some places Wood is so scarce, that they cannot get spraies to fasten on Thatch. **1733** W. ELLIS *Chiltern & Vale Farm.* 162 Great Plantations of Hazel, that..are also of vast Service to the Thatcher, by its Stretchers, Sprays, and Withs. **1854–** in midland dialect use.

c. A graceful shoot or twig of some flowering or fine-foliaged plant or tree, used for decoration or ornament; an artificial imitation of this.

1862 *Catal. Internat. Exhib., Brit.* II. No. 4848, Manufactured sprays, birds, leaves, seeds, and other artificial florists' materials. **1873** 'OUIDA' *Pascarel* I. 64 He would never meet me without some spray of roses, or some boughs of lemon. **1885** 'MRS. ALEXANDER' *At Bay* v, Her first ball-dress, a delicious combination of white silk *tulle* and lace, with sprays of wild roses.

d. A brooch or clip fashioned in imitation of a bouquet of flowers, or of a twig with fruit or foliage. In full, ***spray brooch.***

1803 C. WILMOT *Jrnl.* 6 Mar. in T. U. Sadleir *Irish Peer on Continent* (1920) 142 Necklaces, sprays of brilliants, towering on the head like feathers, diamond nets, combs. **1863** MRS. GASKELL *Dark Night's Work* v. 64 Your pearls.. were..handsome..but we must have them re-set; the sprays are old-fashioned. **1939** P. WENTWORTH *Lonesome Road* viii. 50, I should love to give her a diamond spray from Woolworth's. *Ibid.* xii. 73 The oak spray..two diamond oak-leaves and three acorns. **1951** *Catal. of Exhibits, South Bank Exhib., Festival of Britain* 39/1 Ruby and diamond spray brooch. **1966** *Harper's Bazaar* Sept. 76 A pair of Victorian diamond sprays in the hair..£900. **1979** *Country Life* 11 Oct. Suppl. p.v., Modern diamond and emerald spray brooch.

3. A metal casting resembling a set of twigs.

1831 J. HOLLAND *Manuf. Metal* I. 270 When the whole has become sufficiently cooled, the boxes are opened, the spray, as the cluster of castings is called, taken out. **1843** HOLTZAPFFEL *Turning* I. 332 The whole mass when poured has been compared to a great fern leaf with its leaflets, and is usually called a spray. **1879** *Cassell's Techn. Educ.* IV. 263/1 The pattern-maker connects a number of them in a 'spray', *i.e.*, a central stem, with branches springing out on either side.

4. *attrib.*, as ***spray-bavin***, ***-drain***, ***-faggot***, etc.

1778 [W. H. MARSHALL] *Minutes Agric.* 31 Dec. 1774, *Spray bavins..10s. a hundred. **1850** OGILVIE, **Spray drain*,..a drain formed by burying the spray of trees in the earth, which serves to keep open a channel. **1687** MIÈGE *Gt. Fr. Dict.* II, *Spray Fagots, *fagots de menu bois.* **1764** *Museum Rust.* II. 382 The small twigs, cut from the ends of spray faggots. **1793** YOUNG *View Agric. Sussex* 33 The spray-faggot of all his extensive woods being cut down as fuel for his kilns. **1898** W. T. GREENE *Cage-Birds* 59 White and *spray millet is the correct food for them [the chestnut-eared finches]. **1844** ALB. SMITH *Adv. Mr. Ledbury* (1856) I. xix. 147 He carried a long staff,..pulled from some *spray-pile. *a* **1728** WOODWARD *Fossils* II. 110 A Piece of *Spray Wood. *c* **1730** HAYNES *Voc.* in *N. & Q.* (1883) VIII. 45/1 Spray wood, brush wood. **1802** *Trans. Soc. Arts* XX. 170 Cut all the spray wood, and make the tree a perfect skeleton, leaving all the healthy limbs.

spray (spreɪ), *sb.*[2] Also 7–8 **spry(e.** [app. related to the forms cited under SPRAY *v.*[2] Cf. also SPREW[1].]

1. a. Water blown from, or thrown up by, the waves of the sea in the form of a fine shower or mist.

α. **1621** G. SANDYS *Ovid's Met.* II. (1626) 228 Now tossing Seas appeare to front the sky, And wrap their curles in clouds, frotht with their spry. **1719** DE FOE *Crusoe* I. (Globe) 42 We were immediately driven into our close Quarters to shelter us from the very Foam and Sprye of the Sea. **1750** G. HUGHES *Barbados* 178 These trees..are chiefly planted near the sea-side to shelter the neighbouring fields ..from being blasted by the salt spry of the sea. **1755** JOHNSON, *Spray*... 2. The foam of the sea, commonly written *spry*. **1818** KEATS *Endym.* IV. 157 The salt sea-spry.

fig. **1751** SMOLLETT *Per. Pic.* lxxiii, Swab the spry from your bowsprit, my good lad.

β. **1726** BAILEY (ed. 3), *Spray* (of the Sea), a sort of watery Mist like a small Rain, occasioned by the dashing of the Waves, which flies some Distance, and wets like a small Shower. **1789** TROTTER *Dis. Seamen* 54 The gratings are also half covered when it blows hard, to keep out the salt spray or rain. **1813** SIR H. DAVY *Agric. Chem.* (1814) 339 In great storms the spray of the sea has been carried more than 50 miles from the shore. **1887** FENN *Master of Ceremonies* i, There had been no windy nights when the spray was torn from the tops of waves to fly in showers over the houses.

b. Water or other liquid dispersed by impact or other means in fine mist-like particles.

1750 G. HUGHES *Barbados* 124 A large fire..to burn the bark and dry up the Spry and juices that fly from them in cutting. **1824** BYRON *Juan* XVI. ix, Like a soda bottle when its spray Has sparkled. **1837** W. IRVING *Capt. Bonneville* II. 131 Torrents came tumbling from crag to crag, dashing into foam and spray. **1852** MRS. STOWE *Uncle Tom's C.* xxviii, He almost fancied that that bright face and golden hair were looking upon him, out of the spray of the fountain. **1877** MISS A. B. EDWARDS *Up Nile* ix. 251 Still the boats chase each other along the dark river, scattering spray from their bows.

c. In fig. uses.

1796 [see SPOUTER 3 a]. **1837** CARLYLE *Fr. Rev.* I. IV. iv, One vast suspended-billow of Life,—with spray scattered even to the chimney-tops! **1889** *Spectator* 9 Nov. 630/1 It may even be that..the vanquishers..are sending out a thick spray of roving robbers westward.

2. orig. *Med.* **a.** A jet of medicated vapour or the like, used esp. as a disinfectant or a deodorizer. Hence also applied to any jet of (esp. liquid) particles emitted by an atomizer or similar device.

1870 *Brit. Med. Jrnl.* 2 July 21/1 The value of sprays in the treatment of affections of the throat and windpipe..is much hindered by the inconvenience attending the use of the apparatus... Clarke's [apparatus] produces a fine spray. **1875** KNIGHT *Dict. Mech.* 2288/2 *Spray*,..the vapor from an atomizer. **1880** W. MACCORMAC *Antisept. Surg.* 155 It may prove useful for dressing, and where a steam spray is not available. **1891** KIPLING *Light that Failed* viii. 146, I haven't any spray, and I never leave charcoal unfixed overnight. **1896** *Allbutt's Syst. Med.* I. 305 The free application of antiseptic sprays for purifying the atmosphere of sick chambers. **1963** R. CARSON *Silent Spring* iii. 23 There were cockroaches in the house..and..a spray containing endrin was used. **1974** A. J. HUXLEY *Plant & Planet* xxviii. 337 Temperate fruit growers may apply fifteen different sprays in a season.

b. An instrument used for applying such a jet.

1881 RICHARDSON in *Good Wds.* XXII. 52 Any servant can at any time use the spray. **1895** *Arnold & Sons' Catal. Surg. Instrum.* 161 Cocaine Spray, complete.

3. a. *attrib.* (in sense 1), as ***spray-drop***, ***-pearl***, ***-rainbow***, ***-smoke***.

1826 MRS. HEMANS *Forest Sanct.* I. lxv, Like spray-drops from the strife of torrents flung. **1860** NEALE in *St. Margaret's Mag.* (1895) Jan. 247 The spray-rainbow sometimes arching above my head. **1864** LOWELL *Fireside Trav.* 286 The white spray smoke of Tivoli that drove down the valley. **1883** A. I. MENKEN *Infelicia* 32 To lay my crown of spray-pearls at his feet.

b. *Comb.*, as ***spray-based***, ***-clouded***, ***-dabbled***, ***-decked***, ***-haired***, ***-spangled***, ***-topped***, ***-wet*** adjs.; ***spray-like*** adj. and adv.

1832 MOTHERWELL *Poems, Witches' Joys* iv, Every labouring wave..Gives them a ghastly lover To wring their white hands over, And tear their spray-wet hair In the madness of despair. **1839** BAILEY *Festus* 158 The failing of a fountain's spray-topt stream. **1843** RUSKIN *Mod. Paint.* I. II. III. iv. §6 The legitimate rain-cloud, with its ragged spray-like edges. **1849** LEVER *H. Templeton* xx, His fair brown hair spray-washed and floating back with the breeze. **1859** K. CORNWALLIS *New World* I. 7 The spray-decked waters of the Sound. **1861** E. T. HOLLAND in *Peaks, Passes, & Glac.* Ser. II. I. 21 The one [stream] was broken and feathered in many a spray-spangled fountain. **1895** W. B. YEATS *Poems* 210 With blown, spray-dabbled hair. **1930** R. CAMPBELL *Adamastor* 74 The rocks, spray-clouded, are your signal guns. **1939** DYLAN THOMAS *Map of Love* 4 Spray-based and rock-chested sea. **1956** P. LARKIN *Less Deceived* 38 Rain patters on a floor that tilts and sighs. Fast-running floors, collapsing into hollows, Tower suddenly, spray-haired.

c. *attrib.* in terms relating to artificial spraying or production of spray, as ***spray apparatus***,

booth, can, inhalation, instrument, job, nozzle, pipe, process, pump, etc.; **spray-gun**, an apparatus for applying a liquid substance in the form of spray; an atomizer; **spray irrigation**, a form of irrigation in which water is sprayed from pipes running along or above the ground and reaches the surface in the form of droplets; **spray line**, a perforated pipe used in spray irrigation; **spray pond**, a pool over which water is sprayed in a chamber through which air is passed, so as to cool the air or humidify it; **spray refining, steelmaking**, a continuous method of making steel in which molten iron falling in a stream is atomized by jets of oxygen and flux that combine with impurities in the droplets; hence **spray steelmaker**, an installation in which spray steelmaking is carried out; **spray tower**, a hollow tower in which a liquid is made to fall as a spray, e.g. to cool it or to bring it into contact with a gas.

1896 *Allbutt's Syst. Med.* I. 305 The method is the same, whether air be used, as in the well-known hand-ball spray apparatus, or steam. **1959** *Times* 17 Feb. 2/3 The manufacture of Industrial Equipment such as Ovens, Spraybooths. **1975** 'R. Butler' *Where all Girls are Sweeter* vi. 63 A man was spraying a car in a spray booth. **1972** *Times* 14 Dec. 9/5 A higgledy-piggledy mixture of colours..all laid on with spray cans and felt-tipped marker pens. **1980** *Times Lit. Suppl.* 5 Sept. 972/4 Not only are felt-pens and spray-cans rare in Africa, but so is literacy. **1920** *Brass World* Dec. 343 *(caption)* A new spray gun invention. **1944** R. Chandler *Five Murderers* 31 A woman..was popping at aphis [*sic*] with a spray-gun. **1956** 'B. Buckingham' *Three Bad Nights* xiv. 122 Battered old spray-guns with which they were sprinkling the plants. **1974** 'S. Woods' *Done to Death* 29 Mr Gillespie was pottering about in his garden with a green spray-gun in his hand. **1879** *St. George's Hosp. Rep.* IX. 600 She was ordered spray inhalation of lactic acid..every two hours. **1875** Knight *Dict. Mech.* 2288/2 *Spray-instrument*, ..one for the administration of an anæsthetic or refrigerant in a finely divided liquid form. **1931** *Circular U.S. Dept. Agric.* No. 195. 1 Recently spray-irrigation equipment, designed for the irrigation of general farm crops, has been developed in Germany. **1950** *N.Z. Jrnl. Agric.* LXXX. 520/1 Centrifugal pumps are most commonly used for spray irrigation. **1974** Withers & Vipond *Irrigation* ii. 55 Spray irrigation..is suitable for use in temperatures down to −9°C (16°F). **1963** L. Deighton *Horse under Water* xvii. 69 The last rays of the sun did a spray job on one side of da Cunha's bony head. **1971** *Engineering* Apr. 95/2 (Advt.), Your problem will be solved by an enthusiastic team well versed in the study of Spray Characteristics and Patterns for any particular Sprayjob. **1961** H. J. Hine *Dict. Agric. Engin.* 130 It is possible to divide up the methods of overhead application to field soil into spray lines, sprinklers and rainers. **1974** Withers & Vipond *Irrigation* ii. 54 A more elaborate spray line consists of a water pipe, about 30 mm diameter, perforated in one quadrant along its length, and mounted on light tressles. **1919** Fraser & Jones *Motor Vehicles & their Engines* viii. 65 The suction created by the rush of air past the spray nozzle causes the gasoline to be delivered to the mixing chamber in a fine spray. **1966** Gurney & Cotter *Cooling Towers* iii. 62 *(caption)* Typical sections of cooling tower timber distribution system showing header, lateral and porcelain spray nozzle. **1867–72** Burgh *Mod. Marine Engin.* 272/2 The spray pipes, in connection with the injection valves, are secured beyond them, within the condenser. **1924** L. C. Lichty *Measurement Natural Gas* III. iv. 349 Two general methods are used to cool the water, namely, the spray pond or cooling tower method. **1951** J. Jackson *Cooling Towers* ii. 7 Spray ponds are only suitable where a close approach to the wet-bulb temperature is not required; their main use lies in cooling water prior to discharge into a river. **1881** Richardson in *Gd. Words* XXII. 52 For practical purposes ..I think the simple spray process is the best. **1880** Miss Bird *Japan* I. 303 The odour of carbolic acid pervaded the whole hospital, and there were spray producers enough to satisfy Mr. Lister! **1913** *Chambers's Jrnl.* Jan. 61/2 The stamps are moistened within the machine by a tiny spray pump. **1950** *N.Z. Jrnl. Agric.* May 470/1 A spray pump [for a garden]..may be of bucket or knapsack type according to personal preference. **1967** A. H. Cottrell *Introd. Metallurgy* xi. 141 Very recently a new steel-making process, spray-refining, has been developed by the British Iron and Steel Research Association. A stream of molten iron from a blast furnace falls through a ring of jets, which breaks it up into droplets,..and a second ring of jets which inject powdered lime and other fluxes. **1975** *Steel USSR* V. 493 The optimum working pressure in the chamber for carrying out spray refining of pig iron in a vacuum is 150 mmHg. **1965** *Economist* 25 Dec. 1437/2 *(heading)* Spray steelmaking. **1966** *Ibid.* 15 Oct. 293/3 As operated at present, the spray steelmaker is far from continuous: it only runs during part of a blast furnace tap and its capacity is limited by the size of the ladle that is pushed underneath. **1966** *Observer* 16 Oct. 9/1 The revolutionary 'spray' steel-making process, developed by the British Iron and Steel Research Association in Sheffield,..has all the makings of a major technological advance. **1976** *Metals Abstr.* IX. 1750/2 *(heading)* An investigation into oxidation processes occurring during spray steelmaking using naturally alloyed pig iron. **1937** T. K. Sherwood *Absorption & Extraction* vi. 168 Spray towers are best suited to the absorption of very soluble gases. **1951** J. Jackson *Cooling Towers* ii. 7 Like the cooling pond and the spray pond, the spray tower is probably suitable only for easy cooling duties. **1979** A. L. Lydersen *Fluid Flow & Heat Transfer* vi. 155 Spray towers are the simplest type of gas scrubbers.

d. Special Comb. relating to natural spraying or the production of spray, as **spray region**, the region at the top of the atmosphere where molecules are so far apart that their paths are determined by gravity and upward moving ones are likely to escape into space; **spray zone**, that area near the sea or a waterfall that is often moistened by spray.

1949 *Jrnl. Brit. Interplanetary Soc.* VIII. 255A While it is generally believed that the Zodiacal Light is due to extra-terrestrial particles, it is possible that the scattering particles are molecules in the 'spray' region, very high up in the Earth's atmosphere. **1963** G. M. B. Dobson *Exploring Atmosphere* i. 8 The top of this spray region, which is the top of the atmosphere, is quite indefinite. **1946** *Ecology* XXVII. 321/1 These communities of the spray zone are present only in situations either exposed directly to spray or very well protected from desiccation. **1976** *New Phytologist* LXXVI. 361 Two contrasting coastal habitats which create salinity problems for species occupying them are the spray zone and the salt marsh.

†**spray**, *sb.*[3] *Obs. rare.* [Of obscure origin: cf. spraich *sb.*] Outcry.

13.. *K. Alis.* 2801 (Laud MS.), Spray, and grade, and dismayeyng; Wymmen shrikyng, gyrles gradyng. *Ibid.* 7882 Michel spray, mychel gradyng, Michel weep, mychel waylyng.

†**spray**, *sb.*[4] *Obs.* Also sprey. [var. of spree *sb.*] A spree or drinking-bout; frolic.

1813 *Ann. Reg., Chron.* 59/2 He said he had had a fine sprey, and was burnt to death in the inside. **1819** Scott *Leg. Montrose* Introd., The Sergeant was apt to tarry longer at the Wallace Arms..than was consistent with strict temperance... After such sprays, as he called them, were over [etc.]. **1826** J. Wilson *Noct. Ambr.* Wks. 1855 I. 206 A feather that's got rumpled by sport and spray.

†**spray**, *v.*[1] *Obs.* Also 5 spra. [? Related to spray *sb.*[1]] *intr.* To spring, take rise.

c **1425** *Thomas of Erceld.* 335 And mekill bale sall after spraye, Whare joye & blysse was wonte to bee. *c* **1460** *Towneley Myst.* xiv. 449 In bedlem, land of Iuda,..Out of it a duke shall spra. *Ibid.* xvi. 219 Of bedlem a gracyus lord shall spray.

†**spray**, *v.*[2] *Obs.*[−1] [ad. MDu. *sprayen, spraeyen*, = MHG. *spræjen, spreien*, in the same sense.] *trans.* To sprinkle.

1527 Andrew *Brunswyke's Distyll. Waters* L iv b, Flesshe or other thynges sprayed with the same water abydeth longe tyme good.

spray, *v.*[3] *rare.* [f. spray *sb.*[1]]

1. *trans.* To furnish with sprays or twigs.

1572 Bossewell *Armorie* II. 88 b, And the hande highte *Palma*, when the fingers benne streithte foorthe, as it were boughes, or braunches sprayed.

2. *intr.* To grow *out* into sprays or twigs; to ramify.

1872 C. King *Sierra Nevada* ii. 41 Hugh branches which quickly turn down, and spray out. **1891** J. Winsor *Columbus* vi. 131 It became clear that the currents of the Atlantic.. sprayed in a circling fringe in the North Atlantic.

spray (spreɪ), *v.*[4] [f. spray *sb.*[2]]

1. *trans.* **a.** To diffuse or send in the form of spray; to scatter in minute drops.

1829 Carlyle *Misc.* (1857) II. 91 A strong beam of light ..sprayed itself into innumerable sparks. **1852** M. Arnold *'Ye Storm-winds'* etc., 49 Where the nich'd snow-bed sprays down Its powdery fall. **1881** *Gd. Words* XXII. 51 The solution may be..sprayed freely into the safe. **1897** *Allbutt's Syst. Med.* IV. 685 A 5 per cent. solution of menthol should be sprayed up the nostril.

b. *fig.*

1923 H. G. Wells *Men Like Gods* III. iv. 284 From some slope above a lark had gone heavenward, spraying sweet notes. **1924** R. Campbell *Flaming Terrapin* ii. 23 The trees came crashing down lengthwise, And sprayed their flustered birds into the skies. **1976** E. Dunphy *Only a Game?* iv. 125 They were giving us space to come further forward, and giving us room to turn and spray it about.

2. a. To sprinkle with or as with spray; to wet with fine particles of water or other liquid, esp. by means of a special instrument or apparatus.

1861 Ld. Lytton & Fane *Tannhäuser* 57 While from beneath The creeping billow of calamity Sprays all his hair with cold. **1884** E. P. Roe *Nat. Ser. Story* ix, The foliage was ..sprayed by a garden syringe. **1897** *Allbutt's Syst. Med.* IV. 678 An excellent plan of treatment is..to spray the nose with one of the liquid paraffins.

b. *transf.* To subject to a rapid succession or shower of bullets, shot, etc.

1926 T. E. Lawrence *Seven Pillars* VI. lxxvii. 404 Wood ..got the Indians ready to spray the guard tent. **1977** C. Forbes *Avalanche Express* xv. 152 The man behind the gun ..sprayed the Wagon-Lit... A hail of bullets thudded into their compartment.

3. *absol.* **a.** To scatter or throw up spray.

1891 *Cent. Dict.* s.v., The instrument will either spout or spray. **1906** *Blackw. Mag.* Nov. 664/1 Below, the Porto, a fine trouting stream,..foams and sprays and chafes.

b. Of a male cat: to mark its environment with the smell of its urine, as an attractant to the female.

[**1949** M. C. Gay *How to live with a Cat* xi. 175 A tomcat sprays whiffs of cat smell about in the hope of luring a maiden feline to his moon-bespattered lair.] **1954** L. F. Whitney *Compl. Bk. Cat Care* xvi. 199 The males specifically lose their potent and..obnoxious odour, stop spraying and use their pans or boxes. **1967** A. Lewin *Unaltered Cat* II. iv. 117 If he's frustrated, he'll begin to spray. It's an unpleasant odour, except, of course to a female cat.

4. *intr.* To issue or rise as spray.

1895 *Funk's Stand. Dict.* s.v., He caused the perfume to spray.

Hence **sprayed** *ppl. a.*[1]

1892 *Pall Mall G.* 3 May 6/3 The argument that there is not the slightest danger of poisoning in using sprayed apples.

sprayable (ˈspreɪəb(ə)l), *a.* [f. spray *v.*[4] + -able.] Capable of being sprayed.

1957 B. A. Dombrow *Polyurethanes* iv. 67 Heaters..are necessary to reduce the initial viscosity of the prepolymer to a sprayable consistency. **1972** D. G. Shepherd *Aerospace Propulsion* iv. 108 Another possible fuel is powdered metal, for example magnesium or aluminium, mixed with a liquid hydrocarbon to form a pumpable and sprayable slurry.

spray drying (stress variable). Also **spray-drying.** [spray *sb.*[2] or *v.*[4]] A method of drying foodstuffs, ceramic materials, etc., by spraying finely-divided particles of the substance into a current of hot air or another gas, the water in the particles being rapidly evaporated.

1921 *Jrnl. Industr. & Engin. Chem.* May 448/2 Spray drying is comparatively expensive, mainly because it is impossible to utilize all the heat going through the drying chamber. **1946** [see *flash-drying* vbl. sb. s.v. flash *sb.*[2] 14 b]. **1968** *Economist* 15 June 64/3 The dried milk market, so far dominated by Cadbury's 'Marvel' which is the product of an improved spray drying technique, is worth around £3 million a year.

Hence (as a back-formation) **spray-dry** *v. trans.*; **spray-dried** *ppl. a.*; **spray drier**, a machine or installation that performs spray drying.

1921 *Jrnl. Industr. & Engin. Chem.* May 448/2 It is very difficult to give the cost of operating a spray dryer either in dollars or in heat units. **1932** *Bull. Hannah Dairy Res. Inst.* No. 3. 134 Rancidity appeared less frequently in roller-dried than in spray-dried powders. **1945** *Biochem. Jrnl.* XXXIX. p. xxvi, We have examined..the biological value of the proteins (nitrogen) of a sample of spray dried milk manufactured in 1939. **1950** *Thorpe's Dict. Applied Chem.* (ed. 4) x. 197/2 The essential features in spray-drying eggs are the avoidance of scorching..and the production of a powder containing not more, and preferably less, than 5% moisture. **1961** M. Hynes *Med. Bacteriol.* (ed. 7) xii. 196 More than 10 per cent of imported spray-dried egg contain live *Salmonellæ*. **1967** M. Chandler *Ceramics in Mod. World* ii. 62 The spray dryer consists of a cylindrical drum ..with a conical outlet at the bottom. **1971** *Sci. Amer.* Oct. 5/3 (Advt.), Our engineers solved the..problem..by spray-drying it [*sc.* powdered ceramic] in a blast of hot air. **1979** A. L. Lydersen *Fluid Flow & Heat Transfer* vi. 167 A spray dryer for detergent containing 45 weight% water.

sprayed, *ppl. a.*[1]: see spray *v.*[4]

sprayed, *ppl. a.*[2] [f. *spray* (also *spry, spreathe*, etc.), of obscure origin, common in south-western dialects, chiefly in the pa. pple.] Roughened or made sore by exposure to cold.

1869 Blackmore *Lorna D.* xxxi, It was much worse than Jamaica ginger grated into a poor sprayed finger. **1911** *Kingsbridge Gaz.* 26 May 3/2 For chapped and sprayed hands caused by wind and cold.

sprayer (ˈspreɪə(r)). [f. spray *v.*[4]] One who or that which sprays; *esp.* a machine for diffusing insecticides over plants and trees.

1891 in *Cent. Dict.* **1894** *Times* 19 Nov. 4/4 The machine used was Strawson's standard sprayer. **1900** *Trans. Highl. & Agric. Soc.* 302 The sprayer [of trees], therefore, should not be smoking.

sprayey (ˈspreɪɪ), *a.*[1] [f. spray *sb.*[1]] Having sprays or small twigs; spray-like.

1849 Lever *H. Templeton* xii, The candles were.. glittering like stars through the sprayey branches [of the larch-tree]. **1859** —— *Dav. Dunn* lviii, Ferns..mingled their sprayey leaves with the wild myrtle. **1882** *Garden* 14 Jan. 25/2 Soft packing..may consist of soft sprayey faggots.

sprayey (ˈspreɪɪ), *a.*[2] [f. spray *sb.*[2]] Casting or carrying spray; of the nature of spray.

1831 *Blackw. Mag.* XXX. 111 The dark-watered fountain shedding its gloomy, or rapid, or sprayey stream, down the cheek of a lofty rock. **1854** G. Greenwood *Haps & Mishaps* 69 The roll of heavy seas, the rush of sprayey winds. **1892** Miss Broughton *Mrs. Bligh* viii, A..dark rain-cloud sails up and shakes out three sprayey drops from its skirts upon them.

ˈ**spraying**, *vbl. sb.* [f. spray *v.*[4]] The action of dispersing as, or sprinkling with, spray; *concr.* a liquid used as a spray.

1891 *Jrnl. R. Agric. Soc.* 853 Paris green, used as a spraying for destruction of orchard caterpillars. **1894** *Board of Agric. Circular* No. 10. 3 The solution was made to penetrate the soil by frequent sprayings. **1896** E. G. Lodeman *(title)*, The Spraying of Plants..for..destroying Insects.

attrib. **1884** Knight *Dict. Mech.* Suppl. 846/2 *Spraying Machine*, a machine..to irrigate growing cotton plants with wet poison to destroy the cotton caterpillar.

ˈ**spraying**, *ppl. a.* [f. as prec.] Casting up or scattering spray.

1877 Talmage *Serm.* 49 With rolling rivers..and spraying fountains. **1879** H. Drummond in G. A. Smith *Life* (1899) 161 Green, foaming, spraying, roaring river.

ˈ**sprayless**, *a.* [f. spray *sb.*[2]] Having no spray.

1872 *Daily News* 21 Aug., The waves lie in great, green, heavy, almost sprayless masses.

sprayman (ˈspreɪmən). Also **spray-man.** [f. spray *v.*[4] + man *sb.*[1]] A person who sprays crops with insecticide or the like.

1959 *Bull. World Health Organization* XX. 23 No clinical symptoms of dieldrin poisoning have been observed among the teams of spray-men. **1969** W. F. DURHAM in Miller & Berg *Chem. Fallout* xxiii. 439 Both respiratory and dermal exposure of spraymen were greater for day than for nocturnal spraying. **1973** J. J. MCKELVEY *Man against Tsetse* iii. 190 The spraymen walked along the outer margins of the vegetation on each river bank.

spray-on (ˈspreɪɒn), *a.* [f. SPRAY *v.*⁴ + ON *adv.*] Of a liquid substance: that is applied in the form of spray. Also of the container.

1959 *Wall St. Jrnl.* 3 July (Eastern ed.) 13/4 The company also reports brisk sales of its new aerosol package spray-on cans of enamel. **1965** *Harper's Bazaar* Dec. 89/1 Spray-on fragance flacons combine luxury with efficiency of application. **1976** R. RENDELL *Demon in my View* ii. 19 Arthur still felt guilty about using spray-on polish instead of the old-fashioned wax kind.

spray-painting (stress variable). [SPRAY *sb.*² or *v.*⁴] The application of paint in the form of spray.

[**1902**: see *painting-machine* s.v. PAINTING *vbl. sb.* 6.] **1921** C. W. TERRY *Practical Motor Body Building* xliii. 310 Spray painting by compressed air is a system followed by many of the large modern motor car builders. **1934** *Archit. Rev.* LXXV. 12/2 As a constructivist painter Moholy-Nagy was the first to..employ spray-painting to secure more exact chromatic effects. **1968** J. IRONSIDE *Fashion Alphabet* 229 *Flocking*. This is a method of applying patterns or dots to fabric... The method is rather similar to spray-painting. **1978** *N.Y. Times* 30 Mar. C13/3 (Advt.), French polishing and spray painting for piano refinishing.

Hence (as a back-formation) **spray-paint** *v. trans.*, to paint (a surface) by means of a spray; also as *sb.*, paint that is applied thus; **spray-painted** *ppl. a.*

1928 *Daily Express* 5 Oct. 2/1 A new base-material with which the car is covered, and which can be spray-painted to any finish desired by the customer. **1973** 'E. MCBAIN' *Hail to Chief* iv. 51 The decrepit brick building..had been spray-painted with graffiti. **1975** B. GARFIELD *Hopscotch* x. 97 He spent the next hour buying..automobile spray-paint. **1975** *Listener* 16 Oct. 491/3 Political posters and spray-painted slogans on every square inch of stone.

sprazer (ˈsprɑːzə(r)). *slang.* Also **spraser, sprasy, sprazey**, etc. [ad. Shelta *sprazi.*] Sixpence; a sixpenny piece. Cf. SPROWSIE.

1931 [see HALF *sb.* 6 i]. **1934** [see HOLE *sb.* 2]. **1936** J. CURTIS *Gilt Kid* xvii. 175 I'll..let you have the odd twenty-seven [pounds] and a sprazer. **1939** J. B. PRIESTLEY *Let People Sing* x. 257 See if we can't take another spraser or two from the punters. **1961** *John o' London's* 30 Nov. 610/3 Sixpence—*tanner, spraf, sprarsy*.

spread (sprɛd), *sb.* Also 5 **spredd.** [f. the verb. Cf. LG. *spredde, spreide*, G. *spreite*.]

I. †**1.** ***a bitter spread***, a hard experience. *Obs.*

c **1440** *Bone Florence* 1843 The maryner set hur on hys bedd, Sche hadd soone aftur a byttur spredd.

2. a. The act of spreading in space; degree or extent of this.

1626 BACON *Sylva* §676 No Flower hath that kinde of Spread that the Woodbine hath. **1733** W. ELLIS *Chiltern & Vale Farm.* 129 Many and long Roots, which by their circular spread..are more than ordinarily capacitated to receive the fertile Benefits of the..Dung and Stale. **1784** COWPER *Task* VI. 145 These naked shoots..., more aspiring, and with ampler spread, Shall boast new charms. **1821** JOANNA BAILLIE *Metr. Leg., Wallace* xxxii, Broad grew his breast with ampler spread. **1858** W. ECCLES *Guide Blenheim Palace* (ed. 7) 13 Beeches, which have now attained a growth of such luxuriance and spread of branches. **1865** CAMERON *Malayan India* 171 The trees being of one age are of a uniform height, thickness of trunk, and spread of top.

b. With *the*: The extent, expanse, or superficial area *of* something.

1691 T. H[ALE] *Acc. New Invent.* 125 Determine the number of Men for sailing from the Spread of Canvas. *Ibid.* 127 Equations between the spread of Sails, and the Velocity of the Wind. *a* **1701** MAUNDRELL *Journ. Jerus.* (1749) 142, I measured one of the largest [trees], and found it..thirty seven yards in the spread of its boughs. **1733** W. ELLIS *Chiltern & Vale Farm.* 119 Raise a Border six or twelve Inches high, according to the spread thereof. **1840** DANA *Bef. Mast* xxiii, He knew..the spread of every sail..in feet and inches. **1856** OLMSTED *Slave States* 321, I found that the spread of its branches covered a circle of the diameter of forty-two paces. **1883** STEVENSON *Silverado Sq.* 254 Under the immense spread of the starry heavens.

c. Capacity for spreading or extending; tendency to spread or go apart.

1772 C. HUTTON *Bridges* 58 The..thickness of a pier.. shall just balance the spread or shoot of the arch. **1885** C. T. DAVIS *Manuf. Leather* 558 Skins dressed by this process,.. it is claimed, are made soft, pliable, and with elasticity or spread.

d. The point at which something spreads.

1896 *Westm. Gaz.* 25 July 3/1 A beautiful old orchard is full [of mud] to the spread of the trees' branches.

e. *Diamond-cutting.* The width of a stone considered in proportion to its depth.

1813 J. MAWE *Treat. Diamonds* i. 47 The artist..has to examine carefully, in what direction the stone may be cut, so as to afford the greatest breadth, or *spread* as it is technically termed. **1930** W. R. CATTELLE *Precious Stones* 62 Since the trade have found how important it is to have a proper 'spread' to the stone..there has been a tendency to demand stones too shallow for the best results.

†**f.** *Aeronaut.* = SPAN *sb.*¹ 5 d. *Obs.*

1894 *To-Day* II. 171/2 The wings have a spread of twenty yards square. **1909** A. BERGET *Conquest of Air* 188 The spread of the wings is 10·20 metres. **1912** C. B. HAYWARD *Pract. Aeronaut.* 262 The ratio of spread to depth (aspect ratio) of the monoplanes is usually less than that of biplanes.

g. *Econ.* The difference between two rates or prices.

1919 A. C. WHITAKER *Foreign Exchange* xii. 369 The spread between the local and the foreign money rates. **1928** *Britain's Industr. Future (Liberal Industr. Inquiry)* IV. xxiv. §7.331 The Linlithgow Committee..came to the conclusion that 'the spread between the producer's and the consumer's prices is unjustifiably wide'. **1938** *Sun* (Baltimore) 8 June 6/1 Charges of price-cutting came into the open at a hearing May 19 on distributors' request for a wider 'spread' between the prices they paid for milk and those for which they sold it. **1978** *N.Y. Times* 29 Mar. B2/1 But adding to the rise in farm beef prices is the widening spread between what a cattle raiser gets for a steer and what a roast costs in the supermarket.

h. The degree or manner of variation of a quantity among the members of a population or sample.

1929 *Jrnl. du Counseil* IV. 219 It has hitherto been the practice to employ such statistical methods as finding the mean length, median length, or semi-inter-quartile range in dealing with the 'spread' of length frequency groups. **1957** *Practical Wireless* XXXIII. 696/2 The current gain of the first stage transistor has been quoted as about 50 times, but it could be as low as 30 times, due to manufacturing spread. **1974** *Listener* 7 Nov. 595/2 Now there is a more even spread of intelligence and the skew in the graph is at both ends.

i. The expansion of a person's girth, esp. at middle age; paunchiness. Also, an example of this. Usu. in phr. ***middle-aged spread***: see MIDDLE-AGED *a.* 1 b. *colloq.*

1930 *Field* 29 Nov. 775/2 An older woman..middle-aged, with, possibly, a 'spread'. **1931**, etc. [see MIDDLE-AGED *a.* 1 b]. **1976** N. THORNBURG *Cutter & Bone* iv. 86 Swanson could have passed for a decade older, having already achieved a comfortable middle-aged spread.

3. a. With *a*: An expanse or stretch *of* something. Also, a spread-out layer or stream (quot. 1747).

1712 ADDISON *Spect.* No. 549 ¶3, I have got a fine Spread of improveable Lands. **1746** HERVEY *Medit.* (1818) 99 Nearer the houses we perceive an ample spread of branches. **1747** *Gentl. Mag.* 311 Which made the corn run in a thin even spread under it. **1824** *Examiner* 71/2 A dark spread of calm water. **1840** BARRET *Water Colour Paint.* 104 The sky at this time of the afternoon frequently exhibits a tender spread of yellow. **1880** BLACKMORE *Mary Anerley* II. 63 He struck into the gill from a trackless spread of moor.

b. *Naut.* A display *of* sails.

1849 CUPPLES *Green Hand* vii. (1856) 64 The whole spread of her mizen and main canvass shining like gold cloth against the fore. **1889** WELCH *Text Bk. Naval Archit.* ii. 40 A mastless ship requires less stability than one carrying a large spread of canvas.

c. A ranch, esp. for raising cattle; a large farm. Also *fig.* orig. and chiefly *U.S.*

1927 W. JAMES *Cow Country* 67 He'd paid a big price for the said spread, and he was lord and master there sure enough. **1947** *Trail Riders Bull.* Feb. 20/1, I wuz top bronc buster for the Tumblin' L spread. **1963** R. D. SYMONS *Many Trails* iii. 25 So he had a few dollars coming in, and could see his way, as he would have said, to running a 'spread'. **1966** G. DURRELL *Two in Bush* vi. 186 Harry, together with Bevan Bowan, took us out to a 'spread' not far from Canberra (a tiny little smallholding of some 200,000 acres) on which they were investigating another facet of the kangaroo's biology. **1973** J. WAINWRIGHT *Devil you Don't* 30 'The Ponderosa' was his spread and no cheap, jumped up, fiddle-foot was gonna muscle in. **1981** J. BEECHING *Death of Terrorist* iii. 34 He thought of his ranch up in Texas. 'Not a big spread,' he said modestly.

d. *Geol.* A relatively thin sedimentary deposit.

1956 A. L. ARMSTRONG in D. L. Linton *Sheffield* vi. 90 It is from these beds that the sands and gravels of the lower terraces and valley spreads were mainly derived. **1977** *Antiquaries Jrnl.* LVII. 187 Some sarsens..could be derived from chalk or Greensand as could the soliflucted spread in the Vale of Pewsey.

e. *Cytology.* A microscopic preparation (as a smear or a squash) in which material is spread for observation rather than thin-sectioned, esp. for the purpose of showing chromosomes at metaphase.

1963 *Stain Technol.* XXXVIII. 284 Heteroploidy was not observed in any of the spreads, unlike those observed in long term cultures of rabbit endothelial cells. **1968** *Brit. Med. Bull.* XXIV. 261/2 Typical spreads produced in her laboratory show metaphase material in about one of very 50 fields of 100 × 100 μ. **1978** *Nature* 23 Mar. 325/1 Figure 2 shows the distribution of silver grains in autoradiograms of human metaphase chromosome spreads.

4. The fact of being spread abroad, diffused or made known; diffusion, dispersion:

a. With *a*.

1675 R. BURTHOGGE *Causa Dei* 389 Of so large a spread then was the knowledge of God. **1732** NEAL *Hist. Purit.* (1822) I. 18 The translation of the New Testament by Tyndal..had a wonderful spread among the people. **1760–2** GOLDSM. *Cit. W.* lxiii, The period of renewed barbarity began to have an universal spread much about the same time. **1805** SOUTHEY in C. C. Southey *Life* (1850) II. 324 It would yield either to a general spread of knowledge..or to the unrestrained attacks of infidelity.

b. With *the* and *of*. (The common use.)

1750 ABP. HERRING in J. Duncombe *Lett.* (1773) II. 271, I cannot account for the large spread of the story. **1785** COWPER *Let. J. Newton* 24 Sept., While the spread of the gospel continues so limited as it is. —— *Let. W. Bagot* 9 Nov., [The Bishop's charge] deserves the most extensive spread. **1855** PRESCOTT *Philip II*, II. iii. I. 321 It may seem strange that the spread of the reformed religion should so long have escaped..the Holy Office. **1891** *Speaker* 2 May 534/1 The growth of education and the spread of scientific training.

c. Without article.

1864 E. A. PARKES *Pract. Hygiene* I. xvii. 429 The conditions of spread of [yellow fever in a ship] are probably as favourable as in the most crowded city. **1897** *Allbutt's Syst. Med.* II. 89 The disease disregards anatomical boundaries,..the direction of spread being determined..by contiguity.

d. *Billiards.* A rebound of a cue ball from the object ball at a considerable angle from its former course. *U.S.*

1858 M. PHELAN *Game of Billiards* (ed. 3) 102 To effect a 'spread' it is not necessary to hit the object-ball so far off from the centre as would appear at the first glance. **1913** M. DALY *Daly's Billiard Bk.* iii. 46 Try the same plan for the dead follow and the dead 'spread' (wide angle carom).

II. †**5.** ? A long oar or sweep. *Obs.*⁻¹

1698 FRYER *Acc. E. India & P.* 26 These Boats are as large as one of our Ware-Barges,..but padling with Paddles instead of Spreads, and carry a great Burthen with little trouble.

6. a. *slang.* Butter.

1812 J. H. VAUX *Flash Dict.*, *Spread*, butter. **1865** *Slang Dict.*, *Spread*, butter, a term with workmen and schoolboys.

b. Any substance suitable for spreading on bread to make it tasty, such as paste or jam. orig. *U.S.*

1866 *Hours at Home* III. 507/2 A late rebel told me that, while with Lee upon the Gettysburgh campaign, he went to a farm-house one day and demanded some 'spread', as they call marmalade in that matter-of-fact country. **1886** F. R. STOCKTON *Casting away of Mrs. Lecks* 40 There was some sort of jam left at the bottom, so that the one who gets the last biscuit will have some-thin' of a little spread on it. *c* **1938**, etc. [see *sandwich spread* s.v. SANDWICH *sb.*² 3]. **1962** M. DUFFY *That's how it Was* xiii. 107, I had to..mix up some chocolate spread from cocoa, sugar and a little milk. **1972** *Daily Tel.* 11 Nov. 2/7 There were increases of 3·41 per cent in the prices of jams, honey, and spreads.

7. *colloq.* A banquet, feast, meal.

Common from about 1825.

1822 *Gentl. Mag.* XCII. I. 31 Spreads on the grass for the better sort of people. **1844** J. T. J. HEWLETT *Parsons & W.* vi, I gave very correct feeds—spreads we used to call them. **1893** VIZETELLY *Glances Back* I. xv. 300 He..was a constant attendant as these little spreads.

8. a. A bed-cover, coverlet. orig. *U.S.*

Prob. after Du. *sprei* (†*sprey, spree*) or G. *spreite* (dial. *spreit, spreet*, LG. *spreed*). Kilian gives *spreeder* and *bed-spreeder* as current in Du. and Fris. of his time. The comb. *bed-spread*, given as local U.S. by Bartlett (1848), is now also common in English use.

1852 MRS. STOWE *Uncle Tom's C.* xx, [She would] flourish the sheets and spreads all over the apartment. **1888** *Pall Mall. G.* 1 Nov. 3/2 Each bed..was provided with a feather tick; but the night being warm these spreads were thrown off.

b. A shawl (*Slang Dict.* 1859).

9. An article or advertisement displayed prominently in a newspaper or periodical; *spec.* printed matter occupying two facing pages. Also *fig.* orig. *U.S.*

[**1858** O. W. HOLMES *Autocrat of Breakf.-Table* 131 One gives a 'spread' on lines, and the other on paper—that is all.] **1877** *Harper's Mag.* Dec. 50/1 His remarkable ability is best seen when occasion arises for a 'spread'. **1924** in WEBSTER. **1931** *Week-End Rev.* 7 Nov. 563/2 The inclusion of a four-page 'spread', printed in two colours. **1940** [see *centre spread* s.v. CENTRE *sb.* 19]. **1951** M. MCLUHAN *Mech. Bride* (1967) 61/1 Another full-page spread shows a threesome in a panic. **1956** H. KURNITZ *Invasion of Privacy* xviii. 117 The afternoon papers, and the late radio broadcasts..had given the Morley case a big spread. **1969** A. GLYN *Dragon Variation* viii. 238 You'll give the match a good spread in your papers, won't you, Paul? **1972** D. LEES *Zodiac* 7 Get a centre page spread with pictures.

10. *U.S. Stock Exchange.* A contract combining the option of buying shares of stock within a specified time, at a specified price above that prevailing when the contract is signed, and the option of selling shares of the same stock within the same time, at a specified price below that prevailing when the contract is signed. Cf. SPREAD EAGLE *sb.* 4 b, STRADDLE *sb.* 2 a.

1879 in WEBSTER. **1885** *Harper's Mag.* Nov. 844/1 A 'straddle'..differs from the 'spread' in that the market price at the time of purchase is filled into the latter, while in the 'straddle' the price may vary from that of the market, by agreement or otherwise. **1900** S. A. NELSON *ABC of Wall St.* 160 *Spread.* This is a double stock privilege which entitles the holder to the right to deliver or demand a certain amount of stock on specified terms, or grain price differences between different options, or between the same option in different cities, or between the put and call price. **1957** CLARK & GOTTFRIED *University Dict. Business & Finance* (1967) 332/1 If a stock is selling at 100, a speculator may buy a *spread* option for $5 per share, with a *spread* in the buying and selling prices of 5 points up or down. Thus, if the stock later goes below 90 (including the 5 point *spread* and the 5 point cost of the option), it can be sold at a profit. **1970** SLOAN & ZURCHER *Dict. Econ.* (ed. 5) 412 *Spread*, as applied to security trading, two separate options, a *put*.. specifying a price below the prevailing market, and a *call*.. specifying a price above the prevailing market, both options applying to the same security and expiring on the same date.

11. *Bridge.* (See quot. 1929.) Cf. SPREAD *v.* 17.

1929 M. C. WORK *Compl. Contract Bridge* 245 *Spread*, a hand which Declarer can show in proof of his ability to win all thirteen tricks. **1977** *Field* 13 Jan. 65/1 Only the duplication of values prevented the contract from being a spread.

12. a. *Geol.* An array of seismometers used simultaneously to detect and record disturbances resulting from a single shot in a geophysical survey.

1942 *Geophysics* VII. 138 The problem of the wide shot spread is much more complicated than that of the vertical shot. **1945** *Ibid.* X. 351 To correct for these weathering variations a series of short refraction shots was taken at each recording spread. **1962** *Jrnl. Geophysical Res.* LXVII. 2852/2 The method used was to keep the geophone spread fixed and to move the shot away from the spread. **1977** A. HALLAM *Planet Earth* 29/1 Large spreads of seismometers have recently been set up, one of the largest being in Norway.

b. *Oil Industry.* The total assemblage of men and equipment needed for a particular job, esp. laying a pipeline.

1974 *Petroleum Rev.* XXVIII. 765/1 The prospect of lay barge spreads capable of operating in depths of up to 1,000 feet certainly posed problems. **1975** *North Sea Background Notes* (Brit. Petroleum Co.) 32 The land line was laid in three spreads, two working between the Tay and Cruden Bay and the third from the Tay to Grangemouth. **1976** *Offshore Platforms & Pipelining* 175/3 Two of the pipeline spreads will use automatic welding.

spread (sprɛd), *v.* Forms: *Inf.* α. 3 **spræde**, 3–6 (9 *dial.*) **sprede** (3–4 **-en**, 5 **-yn**); 5 **spreede**, 7, 9 *dial.* **spreed**; 5 **spreyde**, 6 *Sc.*, 9 *dial.* **spreid**; 6 **spreade**, 6– **spread** (9 *dial.* **spreead**). β. 4 **spredd**, 4, 6 **spredde** (6 *arch.* **-en**), 4, 6–7 **spred**. γ. 4 **sprad**, 6 *Sc.* **spraid**, 9 *dial.* **sprade**. *3rd sing. pres.* 2–4 **spret** (2, 4 **sprat**). *Pa. t.* α. 3–5 **spradde**, 4–5 (9 *dial.*) **sprad**; 4, 6 (9 *dial.*) **sprade**. β. 3–6 **spredde**, 4 **spredd**, 4–7 (9 *dial.*) **spred**, 7– **spread**. γ. 7 **spreded**, 9 *dial.* **spreeded**, *Sc.* **spreidit**. *Pa. pple.* α. 2–4 **i-sprad**, 3–4 **y-sprad** (4 **-spradde**), 6 **i-sprode**; 3–6 (9 *dial.* and *arch.*) **sprad** (5 **spradde**). β. 2–4 **i-spred** (4 **hi-**), 4 **y-spred**, 5 **e-spred**; 3–4 **spredd**, 3–7 (9 *dial.*) **spred** (4 **sprid**), 4–7 **spredde**; 5 *Sc.* **spreid**, 6 (9 *dial.*) **spreed**, 7 **sprede**; 6 **spreade** (*Sc.* **spraid**), 7– **spread**. γ. 5 **spraden**, 9 **spreaden**, **spredden** (*dial.* **spreeden**, etc.). δ. 6 **spredded**, 8 **spreaded**. [OE. *sprǣdan* (in combs., esp. *tó-sprǣdan*, and *sprǣdung*), = OFris. **sprêda* (WFris. *spriede*, NFris. *spriad*, *spreer*), MDu. *spre(e)den* (WFlem. *spreeden*, *spreen*), *spreiden*, (Du. *spreiden*, *spreien*), MLG. and LG. *sprêden*, *spreiden* (LG. also *spreen*, *spreien*), OHG. *spreitan* (MHG. and G. *spreiten*, G. dial. *sprêten*); not native in Scand., Da. *sprede* (†*spree*) and Sw. *sprida* (MSw. *spridha*, *spredha*) being from LG. The ultimate etymology is uncertain.]

I. *trans.* **1. a.** To stretch or draw out (a cloth, etc.) so as to display more or less fully; to open out or lay out so as to cover or occupy some space.

c **1200** ORMIN 1015 Witt tu þatt an waȝheriftt Wass spredd fra wah to waȝhe. *c* **1205** LAY. 1215 Seoððen he nam þe hude ..of þare hinde, bi-foren þan wefede he heo spradde. *c* **1338** R. BRUNNE *Chron.* (1810) 117 Almerle his banere sprad, & oþer barons mo. **1387** TREVISA *Higden* (Rolls) III. 61 But þe Romayns wyfes..wente wiþ hir heer i-sprad. *c* **1400** *St. Alexius* (Trin. Coll. Oxf. 57) 460 þat writ anon he gan sprede, And by-fore hem alle rede. *c* **1450** *Mirk's Festial* 115 Wherfor mony..spradden cloþys in þe way. **1533** WRIOTHESLEY *Chron.* (Camden) I. 21 Their was a raye cloath, blew, spreed from the highe desses of the Kinges Benche unto the high alter of Westminster. **1594** KYD *Cornelia* I. 74 The golden Sunne, where ere he driue His glittring Chariot, findes our Ensignes spred. **1615** G. SANDYS *Trav.* 227 These two did spread a Turkie carpet on the rocke, and on that a table-cloth. **1652** NEEDHAM tr. *Selden's Mare Cl.* 97 To have..Nets spread between stakes driven into the Sea. **1697** DRYDEN *Virg. Georg.* IV. 361 Spiders in the Vault their snary Webs have spred. **1733** W. ELLIS *Chiltern & Vale Farm.* 111 Lay, chamber, and spread their Roots, so that the Fibres might not touch one another. **1823** F. CLISSOLD *Ascent Mt. Blanc* 22 A soft breath of wind spread its folds, and floated it gently in the air. **1848** DICKENS *Dombey* xxvi, The Major..sent the Native—who always rested on a mattress spread upon the ground..—to light him to his room. **1902** R. BAGOT *Donna Diana* xvii. 335 He spread the newspaper on the table before him.

transf. and *fig.* **1370–80** *Visions St. Paul* 242 in *O.E. Misc.*, His owne cha[r]tre haþ he rad, þat his synnes were inne isprad. *c* **1440** CAPGRAVE *Life St. Kath.* v. 1824 Spreede me in thi mercy, lete me neuere falle In to myn enemyes handes. **1526** *Pilgr. Perf.* (W. de W. 1531) 275 b, Holy charite.. dilateth & spredeth the herte of man or woman. **1638** *Penit. Conf.* vii. (1657) 128 All sins are not so necessarily to be spread before the Priest. **1671** MILTON *Samson* 1147 Invocate his aid.., spread before him How highly it concerns his glory now To [etc.]. **1715** POPE *Iliad* I. 65 A sudden night he spread, And gloomy darkness roll'd around his head. **1780** *Mirror* No. 101, The toils which her own imagination, and the art of Marlow, had spread for her. **1802–12** BENTHAM *Ration. Judic. Evid.* (1827) V. 123 It is not for the purpose of advocating, but of reprobating exclusion of testimony, that these remarkable cases are spread upon the carpet.

b. *spec.* To expand, unfurl, or set (sails).

1297 R. GLOUC. (Rolls) 2828 Hor seiles hii spredeþ in þe se & hider hii comeþ iwis. **1570–6** LAMBARDE *Peramb. Kent* (1826) 111 They shall spread their sailes to go towards those parts that the King intendeth. **1582** N. LICHEFIELD tr. *Castanheda's Conq. E. Ind.* I. xxviii, The whole Fleete hauing wayed, did then begin to cut and spread their sayles. **1611** BIBLE *Isaiah* xxxiii. 23 They could not well strengthen their mast, they could not spread the saile. **1697** DRYDEN *Æneid* VI. 418 He spreads his canvas; with his pole he steers. *a* **1721** PRIOR *Dial. betw. Charles & Clenard* 353 A large Ship going out of Port, Charles, with her Sails all spread. **1781** COWPER *Truth* 5 Man, on the dubious waves of error toss'd, ..Spreads all his canvass. **1823** SCOTT *Quentin D.* xxv, Not a French banner has been borne down, not a sail spread from England.

c. Const. *on*, *over*, *under*, *upon*.

1382 WYCLIF *2 Kings.* viii. 15 He toke an couerlyte,..and spradde vpon his face. **1535** COVERDALE *Numb.* iv. 13 They shal..sprede a clothe of scarlet ouer it. *Ibid.* 14 They shal sprede a couerynge of doo skynnes theron. **1596** DALRYMPLE tr. *Leslie's Hist. Scot.* I. 94 Thair heid thay laid vpon..a groffe seck spred vndir thame. **1611** BIBLE *Job* xxvi. 9 Hee..spreadeth his cloud vpon it. —— *Isaiah* xxv. 7 He wil destroy..the vaile that is spread ouer all nations. **1746** FRANCIS tr. *Hor., Sat.* II. iv. 102 What!..on foul couches Tyrian carpets spread? **1761** GRAY *Fatal Sisters* 31 Gondula, and Geira, spread O'er the youthful king your shield. **1820** SCOTT *Monast.* x, I should have spread my mantle over the frailties of my spiritual father. **1837** P. KEITH *Bot. Lex.* 399 Each membrane represents a bag or sac, without any opening, spread upon the organs.

d. To display in wide extension.

1600 FAIRFAX *Tasso* VI. xxii, A goodly plaine displayed wide and broad, Betweene the citie and the campe was sprad. **1764** GOLDSM. *Trav.* 411 Where wild Oswego spreads her swamps around. **1766** —— *Vicar* viii, Where wilds, immeasurably spread, Seem lengthening as I go. **1807** J. BARLOW *Columb.* I. 220 He saw, thro' central zones, the winding shore Spread the deep Gulph. **1838** THIRLWALL *Greece* xxxiv. IV. 345 The Euxine spread its waters before their eyes. **1889** S. LANGDON *Appeal to Serpent* i. 12 The magnificent vision which lay spread beneath when the great city came up close to the 'holy mountain' itself.

e. To flatten out; to make of a thin flat form.

Used *spec.* with ref. to diamonds: see quots. 1704–6 and 1850.

1704 *Lond. Gaz.* No. 4034/4 A seven Stone Diamond Ring,..the middle Stone weighing about 5 Grains spread. **1706** *Ibid.* 4200/4 The Diamond weighing near 11 Grains, well spread, and of a perfect Water. **1811** PINKERTON *Mod. Geog. Polynesia* (ed. 3) 522 The nose is always spread at the point, perhaps owing to the mode of salutation, in which they press their noses together. **1850** HOLTZAPFFEL *Turning* III. 1322 This cut is employed upon such stones as are thin, and large on the surface, or, as it is called, much spread. **1900** HASLUCK *Mod. Eng. Handy-bk.* 129 Small drills..are generally made by filing the round steel wire..and then spreading the small end with a single blow from a.. hammer.

f. To thrust (walls) out or apart.

1793 SMEATON *Edystone L.* §274 The whole would lie upon the ledges like a single stone, without any tendency to spread the walls.

g. *Mus.* To play (the notes of a chord or a chord itself) in rapid succession instead of simultaneously.

1873 H. C. BANISTER *Music* 17 The notes..are to be played..in Arpeggio,..or spread obliquely, as it is termed. **1938** *Oxf. Compan. Mus.* 48/1 *Arpeggiare* (It.), to play harpwise, i.e. (on the piano, etc.) to spread the notes of a chord, from the bottom up. **1953** W. EMERY *Bach's Ornaments* 102 On the harpsichord or clavichord, a chord is often very much more effective when spread than when played *sec*. **1977** *Gramophone* June 68/2 The violinist also spreads some of his two-note chords.

2. †**a.** To draw or stretch out (the limbs or a person) in some form of punishment or torture. *Obs.*

a **1225** *Ancr. R.* 390 His leoue licome þet was ispred o rode. *a* **1240** *Ureisun* in *O.E. Hom.* I. 185 Hwi nam ich in þin earmes..swa istrahte and isprad on rode. *a* **1300** *Cursor M.* 16668 þai..ledd him þan to þe rode tre, and þar-on þai him spred. *c* **1375** *Sc. Leg. Saints* iii. (*Andrew*) 410 Gyf þat I dred þe croice, quhare-in criste wes spred, þe Ioy of it I na prechit ȝow. *c* **1450** *Myrr. our Ladye* 249 The mother se her sonne cruelly spredde on the crosse. *c* **1475** HENRYSON *Orph. & Euridyce* 149 Turnand a quhele.., And on it spred a man hecht ixione. **1526** R. WHYTFORD *Martiloge* (1893) 100 So were they sprad vpon a gredyren wᵗ hote coles & broyled.

b. To lay down with the limbs relaxed.

1693 DRYDEN *Juv.* VI. 85 Many a fair Nymph has in a Cave been spread, And much good Love, without a Feather-Bed. **1697** —— *Virg. Past.* x. 21 Mænalian Pines the God-like Swain bemoan, When spread beneath a Rock he sigh'd alone.

3. a. To send out in various directions so as to cover or extend over a larger space. Also *fig.*

a **1200** *Vices & Virtues* 45 Carite sprat his bowes on bræde and on lengðe swiðe ferr. *a* **1225** *Ancr. R.* 400 þe soðe sunne ..was forði istien on heih..uorto spreden ouer al hote luue gleames. *c* **1400** *Cursor M.* 27877 (Cott. Galba), Glotony and dronkinhede, ful mani branches out þai sprede. **1526** *Pilgr. Perf.* (W. de W. 1531) 30 Than grace spredeth her beames, that all the soule of man is bryght as a lanterne. **1565** COOPER *Thesaurus* s.v. *Pando*, The elme spreadeth the branches or boughes. **1615** W. LAWSON *Country Housew. Gard.* (1626) 23 Looke how far a tree spreads his boughs aboue, so far doth he put his roots vnder the earth. **1667** MILTON *P.L.* IV. 643 Pleasant the Sun When first on this delightful Land he spreads His orient Beams.

b. To hold out, stretch out, extend (the hands or arms).

c **1250** *Kent. Serm.* in *O.E. Misc.* 31 Ure lord him.. spredde his hond, and tok his lepre. *a* **1300** *Havelok* 95 And oþer he refte him hors or wede, Or made him sone handes sprede. *a* **1340** HAMPOLE *Psalter* cxlii. 6, I spred my hend till þe. *c* **1450** *Mirk's Festial* 124 He..fell downe to þe grownd, wyth hys armes sprad abrod, as Crist sprad hys armes on þe cros. *a* **1529** SKELTON *'Now synge we'* 60, I hold my armes abrode, The to receyue redy isprode! **1628** MILTON *Vac. Exerc.* 93 Trent, who like some earth-born Giant spreads His thirsty Armes. **1781** COWPER *Charity* 596 Like him, the soul..Spread wide her arms of universal love. **1815** SHELLEY *Alastor* 183 He..spread his arms to meet Her panting bosom. **1842** TENNYSON *Talk. Oak* 225 Then close and dark my arms I spread, And shadow'd all her rest.

c. To extend, open out (the wings, etc.).

1390 GOWER *Conf.* I. 173 He sprat his wynge and up he fleth. *c* **1400** *Pilgr. Sowle* (Caxton) v. i. (1859) 69 They rysen, and mounten ferre fro the erthe, and spreydyn theyr wynges. **1663** BP. PATRICK *Parab. Pilgr.* xv, He rejoyced to spread his healing wings over every place. **1667** MILTON *P.L.* II. 928 At last his Sail-broad Vannes He spreads for flight. **1784** COWPER *Task* III. 135 The fly, That spreads his motley wings in th' eye of noon. **1817** SHELLEY *Rev. Islam* VI. xlv, When the earth..Shook with the sullen thunder, he would spread His nostrils to the blast. **1837** CARLYLE *Fr. Rev.* III. v. iii, Swift-rending is her stroke; look what a paw she spreads.

d. To extend, make larger or wider. *rare.*

1387 TREVISA *Higden* (Rolls) VI. 399 He bulde newe citees ..and sprad þe endes of his kyngdom wydder þan dede his fader. *c* **1400** BRAY *Conq. Irel.* (1871) 295 The Pope.. grauntyd the Kyng that he shuld ynto Irland wend for to.. spred the termys of holy Churche. **1596** DALRYMPLE tr. *Leslie's Hist. Scot.* I. 147 To spred the boundes of that Jmpire baith braid and wyde.

4. a. To distribute or disperse (a substance or a number of things) over a certain superficies or area; to scatter.

c **1250** *Gen. & Ex.* 490 Or or flum noe spredde his fen. *c* **1340** *Nominale* (Skeat) 118 W[oman] scheruth corne and muk spredith. *c* **1394** *P. Pl. Crede* 301 Nou han þei..spicerie sprad in her purse, to parten where hem lust. **1426** AUDELAY *Poems* 78 Fore blak blood he se e-spred Apon the aschelere even. *c* **1450** *Merlin* xv. 240 Ther sholde ye haue sein grete trouble of tables downcaste and the vitaile I-spredde wide. **1573** TUSSER *Husb.* (1878) 33 Sawe dust spred thick, makes alley trick. **1592** *Soliman & Pers.* v. ii, Spredding on the boord A huge heape of our imperiall coyne. **1667** MILTON *P.L.* IV. 255 The flourie lap Of som irriguous Valley spread her store. **1687** A. LOVELL tr. *Thevenot's Trav.* I. 36 There you see..men sitting upon a Carpet on the ground, with a great many Books spread round about them. **1727** *Philip Quarll* (1816) 42 He was busy..in turning and spreading the grass. **1742** *London & Country Brew.* I. (ed. 4) 7 When the Malt is dried it must not cool on the Kiln, but be..spreaded wide in an airy Place. **1815** J. SMITH *Panorama Sci. & Art* II. 611 For grass land..half as much [marl], thinly and evenly spread, will generally suffice. **1841** LANE *Arab. Nts.* I. 96 He poured out the powder into it, and spread it. **1895** R. W. FRAZER *Silent Gods, Pearl of Temple* (1896) 57 The ryots who spread the water in the fields..lay dead before the rice was ready for reaping.

b. To distribute in a thin layer; *esp.* to smear. Also *fig.* (quot. 1731–8).

1558 WARDE tr. *Alexis' Secr.* 28 Than hauyng put to it the Storax, spredde it vpon a linnen cloth. **1579** FULKE *Refut. Rastel* 783 The residue of the..bread..was giuen to.. children.., whether to spredde their butter,..or to eate it with cheese, I cannot saye. **1611** BIBLE *1 Kings* vi. 32 He.. ouer-layd them with gold, and spread gold vpon the Cherubims, and..the palme trees. **1731–8** SWIFT *Polite Conv.* Introd., They [polite speeches] ought to be husbanded better, and spread much thinner. **1815** J. SMITH *Panorama Sci. & Art* II. 207 A small quantity of the amalgam, spread upon another piece of leather. **1870** *Pall Mall G.* 23 Sept. 12/1 The unknown genius spreads butter upon his bread.

c. To place in an open or expanded manner; to distribute *over* a certain space, time, etc.

1592 KYD *Sp. Trag.* III. iii. 101 Ile spread the Watch,.. Strongly to guard the place where Pedringano [etc.]. *a* **1631** DONNE *Epithalam. Linc. Inn* 1 The Sun-beames in the East are spred. **1634** SIR T. HERBERT *Trav.* 209 In some places [a stream] spreads Meanders. **1743** FRANCIS tr. *Horace, Odes* II. i. 5 For whom the triumphs o'er Dalmatia spread Unfading honors round thy laurel'd head. **1748** *Anson's Voy.* II. v. 180 We spread our ships in such a manner, that it was not probable any vessel of the enemy could escape us. **1827** FARADAY *Chem. Manip.* i. (1842) 13 Sometimes it is easy to spread these [flues] over one side or wall of the room. **1855** *Orr's Circ. Sci.*, *Inorg. Nat.* 133 The knowledge needed by the artist..involves various inquiries, spread over many sciences. **1885** *Act 48–49 Vict.* c. 50 §11 The repayment of the money to be borrowed shall be spread over a series of years.

d. To lay out (a meal, banquet, etc.).

1784 COWPER *Task* I. 433 Beneath the open sky she spreads the feast. **1794** MRS. RADCLIFFE *Myst. Udolpho* xxxviii, At a banquet spread under a gay awning. **1828** DUPPA *Trav. Italy*, etc. 63 The table on which the last supper was spread is in the church of St. John Lateran. **1852** HAWTHORNE *Blithedale Rom.* xxiv, Some old-fashioned skinkers and drawers..were spreading a banquet. **1868** HOLME LEE *B. Godfrey* xlvii, Tea was spread on the round table.

e. To record or enter *on* a documentary record. *U.S.*

1845 J. F. COOPER *Chainbearer* II. iv. 44 It will greatly aid the reader..if I spread on the record the language that passed between my late agent and..his confidant. **1894** T. F. ROBLEY *Hist. Bourbon County, Kansas* 184 Councilmen Dimon, White and Drake caused the following order to be spread upon the minutes. **1910** *Atlantic Monthly* Feb. 231 Achievements in that field are naturally not spread on the record as are exploits in railway financiering. **1931** *Randolph Enterprise* (Elkins, W. Va.) 26 Mar. 1/5 Resolved that a copy of these resolutions be sent to the family, a copy spread on the minutes of the lodge, [etc.].

5. a. In *pass.* of persons, animals, etc.: To be scattered, dispersed, or distributed over or throughout some area.

c **1250** *Gen. & Ex.* 650 And or he was on werlde led, His kinde was wel wide spred. **1297** R. GLOUC. (Rolls) 3264 We ssolleþ hom abbe al uor noȝt..Vor hii beþ naked & onywar & yssprad wyde. *a* **1300** *Cursor M.* 6046 O þam it was sua mani bredd, Ouer all þe land þan ware þai spredd. **1387** TREVISA *Higden* (Rolls) II. 169 þerfore it is þat þey beeþ i-spred so wyde. *c* **1536** in Thynne *Animadv.* (1875) 80 Thes holy men beyn thus about sperd [*read* spred], thorow all this lond, in euery sled. *a* **1700** EVELYN *Diary* 3 Dec. 1657, This sect was now wonderfully spread. **1774** GOLDSM. *Nat. Hist.* (1776) IV. 302 The other [dromedary] is found spread over all the Desarts of Arabia. **1826** SAMOUELLE *Direct. Collect. Insects & Crust.* 44 He met with a certain species of Papilio in abundance and spread all over the island. **1841** *Penny*

Cycl. XX. 148/2 The Rook is spread over the greater part of Europe.

†**b.** To cause to increase or multiply; to beget.

a **1300** *Cursor M.* 10684 It was boden in þair ledd Wit mariage þe folk to sprede. **1624** Heywood *Gunaik.* I. 49 Young Epaphus.. To Phaeton objects that he was bred Of mortal straine, and not divinelie spred.

6. To disseminate or diffuse; to cause to become prevalent or (more) widely existent, present, known, felt, etc.

Various contexts are illustrated by the separate groups of quotations.

(*a*) *a* **1300** *Cursor M.* 6213 Son was in land þe tiþand spredd þe folk was turned again and fledd. *c* **1330** R. Brunne *Chron. Wace* (Rolls) 3111 Hym schamed sore of his chaunce þat hit was so wyde yspred þat his lemman was a-wey led. *c* **1386** Chaucer *Prioress' T.* Prol. 2 O lord our lord, thy name how merueillous Is in this large worlde ysprad. **1503** Hawes *Examp. Virt.* vii. 94 Of whose noble dedes the brute and sowne Was spred by euery straunge habytacyon. **1595** in *Cath. Rec. Soc. Publ.* V. 350 Yt was spread in the cuntry that he had convinced the minister in diverse pointes of religion. **1662** *Extr. St. Papers Friends* Ser. II. 151 Such base lyes.. are now dayly & hourely spread abroad against our present Gracious King. **1678** Sir G. Mackenzie *Crim. Laws Scot.* I. xxix. §6 (1699) 151 She having spread these Mis-reports before she was cited. **1725** Berkeley *Proposal Conv. Savage Amer.* Wks. 1871 III. 217 Missionaries for spreading the gospel among their countrymen. **1746** P. Francis tr. *Horace, Art Poet.* 469 [This] shall.. across the seas To distant nations spread the writer's fame. **1823** Scott *Quentin D.* xii, For this Louis promised to provide, by spreading a report that the Ladies of Croye had escaped. **1849** Ticknor *Span. Lit.* I. 33 His reputation was early spread throughout Europe, on account of his general science.

(*b*) *a* **1300** *Cursor M.* 12716 Quen drightin gan to sprad his grace Til his aun choslings treu. *c* **1380** Wyclif *Sel. Wks.* I. 246 þis wrong is brood sprad in Cristendom. **1422** tr. *Secreta Secret., Priv. Priv.* 208 The taste is a commyn witte, Spraden throgh the body. **1450–80** tr. *Secreta Secret.* 29 Nature spredith it through alle parties of the body, and therfore the stomak hath litille part of þe hete. **1538** Starkey *England* I. i. 7 So ys the mynd then most perfyt when hyt communyth & spredyth hys vertues abrode. *c* **1614** Sir W. Mure *Dido & Æneas* II. 106 O how quick doth love.. spread in every parte A furiows flame! **1668** Wilkins *Real Char.* I. i. 3 The present Coptic or Ægyptian.. was probably spred amongst that people in the days of Alexander the Great. **1720** Pope *Iliad* XVII. 770 Cheering his men, and spreading deaths around. **1768** Goldsm. *Good-n. Man* I, She could spread an horse-laugh through the pews of a tabernacle. **1831** Scott *Ct. Rob.* xxvi, Do thy gifts, accomplishments, and talents, spread hardness as well as polish over thy heart? **1854** *Poultry Chron.* II. 266 It seems likely that, by thus spreading the local interest, shows.. might become self-supporting. **1874** Green *Short Hist.* iii. §4. 128 Wandering teachers.. crossed sea and land to spread the new power of knowledge.

(*c*) **1743** Francis tr. *Horace, Odes* IV. iv. 27 The Rhætian bands.. Were wont to spread their baneful terrors far. **1794** Mrs. Radcliffe *Myst. Udolpho* xxxiv, It spread a general alarm among Montoni's people. **1831** Scott *Quentin D.* Introd., Numerous private emissaries of the restless Louis .. were every where spreading the discontent which it was his policy to maintain. **1849** Macaulay *Hist. Eng.* vi. II. 157 His arrival spread dismay through the whole English population.

7. *refl.* **a.** To extend, expand, etc., in various senses.

1340 *Ayenb.* 17 þis zenne him to-delþ and spret ine zuo uele deles þet onneaþ e me may hise telle. **1400** tr. *Secreta Secret., Gov. Lordsh.* 91 Also þare ys a tree þat hauys leuys of vygour, and his braunches spredyn hem on þe erthe. **1526** *Pilgr. Perf.* (W. de W. 1531) 25 b, Remember his extension ..on the crosse, and consyder how mekely he spred hym selfe on the same. **1590** Spenser *F.Q.* III. i. 20 Before the gate a spatious plaine, Mantled with greene, it selfe did spredden wyde. **1611** Tourneur *Ath. Trag.* I. i, Tis true. Had not my Body spredde it selfe Into posteritie; perhaps I should Desire no more increase of substance. **1649** G. Daniel *Trinarch., Rich. II*, cclxxx, The King now spreads himselfe; and, as a source, Issues in larger Streames, to take in more, Hee fills the Cisterns nere him. **1698** Fryer *Acc. E. India & P.* 141 The Clouds had spread themselves over the Tops of the Hills. **1711** Addison *Spect.* No. 120 ¶11 This natural Love is not observed in animals to ascend from the Young to the Parent;.. it spreads it self downwards. **1748** *Anson's Voy.* III. ii. 309 The mixture of these woods and lawns.. as they spread themselves differently through the vallies. **1821** Shelley *Adonais* xlii, He is a presence.., Spreading itself where'er that Power may move [etc.]. **1855** Kingsley *Westw. Ho!* xxv, They began to spread themselves along the stream. **1871** Freeman *Norm. Conq.* (1876) IV. 202 A city which in the tenth century.. had spread itself far beyond the Roman Walls.

b. *U.S.* To exert oneself; also, to make a display, to show off.

1857 S. H. Hammond *Wild North. Scenes* 266 (Bartlett), He had promised, to use his own expression, to spread himself in the preparation of this meal. **1891** E. Kinglake *Australian at Home* 58 The gentleman who had just 'spread himself' was very angry at having the effect of his speech thus spoiled. **1892** E. Reeves *Homeward Bound* 204, I must (to use your slang) be allowed 'to spread myself' a little, and give you a minute account of everything I see.

absol. **1860** J. G. Holland *Miss Gilbert's Career* x. 173 He sort o' stands round, and spreads, and lets off all the big talk he hears. **1884** 'Mark Twain' *Huck. Finn* xxi. 206 He howled, and spread around, and swelled up his chest. **1897** Howells *Landlord at Lion's Head* 376 One of the jays, who was spreading on rather a large scale, wanted Jeff to spread with him.

8. a. To cover, overlay, deck, or strew, *with* something. Also without const.

a **1300** *Leg. S. Gregory* (1876) 771 On bed he fel hir biside, Yspred it was wiþ grene palle. *a* **1300** *Cursor M.* 15027 þai spred þe strete wit cloth and flur. *a* **1400–50** *Alexander* (D.) 1514 He.. arayes all þe cyte, Spredes ouer with bawdkens all þe brode stretes. **1596** Spenser *F.Q.* VI. ii. 5 On his head [was] an hood with aglets sprad. **1611** Bible *Isaiah* xl. 19 The goldsmith spreadeth it ouer with golde. **1693** Dryden *Juvenal* xvi. 69 *note*, The Courts of Judicature were hung, and spread, as with us. **1697** —— *Æneid* XII. 174 The morn .. Had scarcely spread the skies with rosy light. **1718** Lady M. W. Montagu *Let. Mrs. Thistlethwayte* 1 Apr., The rooms are all spread with Persian carpets. **1812** Byron *Ch. Har.* II. vii, Silence spreads the couch of ever welcome rest. **1828** Lytton *Pelham* I. xxiii, Another table, still spread with the appliances of breakfast.

transf. *c* **1320** *Sir Tristr.* 442 þe forest was fair and wide, Wiþ wilde bestes y-sprad.

b. To lay (a table) for a meal or other purpose.

c **1460** Sir R. Ros *La Belle Dame* 101 The boordes wer spred in ryght lytell space. **1565** J. Phillip *Patient Grissell* (Malone Soc.) 7 She spread the table and made me good cheare. **1671** Milton *P.R.* II. 340 A Table richly spred, in regal mode, With dishes pil'd. **1697** Dryden *Æneid* III. 291 We spread the tables on the greensward ground. **1761** Gray *Desc. Odin* 41 Tell me.. For whom yon glitt'ring board is spread. **1859** *Habits of Gd. Society* 88 He must be there to talk to the chaperons,.. to spread the card-table and form the rubber. **1885** 'Mrs. Alexander' *Valerie's Fate* iv, Valerie spread her grand-uncle's little table and placed his food before him.

absol. **1590** Shaks. *Com. Err.* II. ii. 189 Dromio, goe bid the seruants spred for dinner.

c. To cover with a thin layer of some soft substance, esp. butter; to prepare in this way.

1579 Fulke *Refut. Rastel* 783 What so euer remained.. shoulde be giuen to.. children..(not spred.. with butter) but sprinkled with wine. **1621** T. Williamson tr. *Goulart's Wise Vieillard* 6 Contenting himselfe to eate.. a piece of bread spread with honey. **1707** in Hearne *Coll.* (O.H.S.) II. 43 He eats.. Bread and Butter, which he spreads with his Thumb. **1827** Scott *Surg. Dau.* i, Every old woman.. can prescribe a dose of salts, or spread a plaster. **1888** *Times* 3 Jan. 9/5 They spread their bread with ox-fat.

9. †**a.** To over-run or overspread (an area). *Obs.*

c **1400** *Brut* lxxxiii, þai.. wenten oute of here shippis, and spraden al þe contreye. **1633** T. Stafford *Pac. Hib.* I. ii. 22 MacGuire, who with some Horse (likewise dispersed) had spread a good circuit of ground, in hope.. to get some bootie. **1654** E. Johnson *Wonder-working Provid.* 1 The multitude of irreligious.. affected persons spred the whole land like Grasshoppers. **1720** De Foe *Capt. Singleton* vi. (1840) 109 Our negroes spread the banks of the lake.. for game. **1722** —— *Plague* (1884) 78 The Gangren.. had spread her whole Body.

b. *poet.* To cover; to extend over.

1700 Dryden *Pal. & Arc.* III. 104 Rich tapestry spread the streets. **1725** Pope *Odyss.* I. 173 A purple carpet spread the pavement wide. **1800** Moore *Anacreon* xvii. 24 Now from the sunny apple seek The velvet down that spreads his cheek! **1821** Clare *Vill. Minstr.* I. 130 Refreshing greenness spread the plain.

c. To extend or reach along.

1794 *Rigging & Seamanship* 127 The head spreads the topgallant yard.

10. With advs. (*abroad, forth, out, up*), in preceding senses.

a. **1382** Wyclif *Gen.* xxxii. 12 Thow hast spokun.. that thow shuldist sprede abrood my seed as the grauel of the see. *c* **1449** Pecock *Repr.* 213 A clooth steyned or ymagis sprad abrood in dyuerse placis of the chirche. *a* **1533** Ld. Berners *Huon* lii. 176, I spred abrode a towel on the grene grasse. **1594** Kyd *Cornelia* IV. i. 200 His glory, spred abroade by Fame. **1653** Ramesey *Astrol. Restored* 199 The credit or applause desired will be the more blazed and spread abroad. **1700** Dryden *Ovid's Met., Baucis & Philemon* 49 Baucis.. rakes the Load Of Ashes from the Hearth, and spreads abroad The living Coals. **1825** Scott *Betrothed* viii, The morning light was scarce fully spread abroad. **1842** Loudon *Suburb. Hort.* 392 Fermentation is always most rapid in summer; and if the materials are spread abroad during frost, it is totally impeded.

b. **1388** Wyclif *Deut.* xxxii. 11 He spredde forth his wyngis. *c* **1400** tr. *Secreta Secret., Gov. Lordsh.* 71 þe kendly hete ys y-drawe þerto and spred forth by al þe body to þe stomak. **1535** Coverdale *1 Kings* vi. 27 The Cherubins spred forth their wynges. **1611** Bible *Num.* xxiv. 6 As the valleyes are they spread forth, as gardens by the riuer side. *c* **1614** Sir W. Mure *Dido & Æneas* I. 1003 Now silent night spred foorth her sable wings. **1817** Shelley *Rev. Islam* X. xxxviii, Fix on high A net of iron, and spread forth below A couch of snakes and scorpions.

c. **1382** Wyclif *Deut.* xxxii. 11 He sprade out his weengis. **1483** *Cath. Angl.* 356/2 To Sprede oute, *dilatare, distendere.* **1571** Golding *Calvin on Ps.* lxxi. 19 Our mindes must be spredded out.. to conceive yᵉ largenes of it. **1611** Bible *Exod.* xxxvii. 9 And the Cherubims spread out their wings.. ouer the Mercie seat. **1719** De Foe *Crusoe* II. (Globe) 523 A third [ship] without any Colours spread out. **1865** Carlyle *Fredk. Gt.* XVIII. v. (1872) VII. 176, I spread-out to you, dear Sister, the detail of my sorrows. **1885** 'Mrs. Alexander' *Valerie's Fate* vi, The sky spread out a boundless space of deepest blue.

d. **1657** Austen *Fruit Trees* I. 58 The [fig] trees must be set against a South wall, and be spread up with nailes and Leathers.

II. *intr.* **11. a.** To receive extension or expansion; to cover or occupy a wider space by this means.

a **1300** *Cursor M.* 18113 A deu, al for to mak þam hale, On þam sal spred. **1338** R. Brunne *Chron.* (1810) 38 A rede cloude in þe skie about Ingland gan sprede. **1523** Fitzherb. *Husb.* §10 The hyer and farther that ye caste your corne, the better shall it sprede. **1583** Melbancke *Philotimus* Qj, A litle sparke spreading burnes a whole Cittie. **1663** Gerbier *Counsel* 10 Nature of Aire being to ascend, and when it meets with a sudden opposition it spreads. **1686** W. Harris tr. *Lemery's Course Chem.* (ed. 2) 49 Gold will spread under the hammer more than any other Metal. **1725** De Foe *Voy. round World* (1840) 332 The water began to spread over the flat ground. **1789** Mrs. Piozzi *Journ. France* I. 400 London spreads chiefly the Marybone way perhaps. **1860** Tyndall *Glac.* I. 124 The clouds spread more and more. **1885** *Manch. Exam.* 6 July 5/1 A fire broke out and spread with great rapidity.

transf. *c* **1330** *Amis & Amil.* 1317 So hard thai hewe on helme and side,.. That thai sprad al of blod.

b. With advs., as *about, abroad, forth, out.* Also *to spread off*, to withdraw from.

c **1400** *Laud Troy Bk.* 10940 Odemon saw Ector was dede, He saw his blod aboute sprede. **1530** Palsgr. 730, I spredde a brode, as a ryver that breaketh out of his channell or any suche lyke thyng. **1535** Coverdale *Joel* ii. 2 A stormy daye, like as the mornynge spredeth out vpon the hilles. **1711** Addison *Spect.* No. 159 ¶8, I saw the Valley opening at the farther End, and spreading forth into an immense Ocean. **1837** Carlyle *Fr. Rev.* I. VII. vi, Our straight frondent Avenue.. spreads out into Place Royal and Palace Forecourt. **1849** Cupples *Green Hand* xv. (1856) 151 The fog spread off the water near us.

c. Of conditions, qualities, etc.

1565 Cooper *Thesaurus* s.v. *Mano*, Runnyng sores: or sores that spread farther and farther. **1611** Donne *Anat. World* 357 Our blushing red, which us'd in cheekes to spred, Is inward sunke. **1720** De Foe *Capt. Singleton* xi. (1840) 197 The mortification seemed to spread. **1799** Underwood *Dis. Childhood* (ed. 4) II. 25 Should the shingles spread and become sore, it should be treated as directed below. **1815** Stephens in *Shaw's Gen. Zool.* IX. I. 60 The green becomes gradually more brilliant.. and spreads over the coverts of the wings and tail. **1864–8** Browning *J. Lee's Wife* III. iv, But why must cold spread? **1899** *Allbutt's Syst. Med.* VI. 106 The readiness with which it [*sc.* sarcoma] spreads in upon.. the pulmonary tissue.

d. To become larger; to increase in size.

1630 *R. Johnson's Kingd. & Commw.* 10 The more they decline from the Æquator, the more they spread in stature and tallnesse. **1756** J. Warton *Ess. Pope* I. vii. 407 The sybil .. is likewise represented as spreading.., and growing larger and larger. **1799** Underwood *Dis. Childhood* (ed. 4) I. 208 The gums swell, spread, and become hot.

e. To go apart; to separate.

1839 *Civil Eng. & Arch. Jrnl.* II. 146/1 The violent vicissitudes of the seasons soon deranged the foundation.., and caused the [railway] track to spread. **1847** Smeaton *Builder's Man.* 146 The walls of a public building in Paris had spread, or.. were thrown out of their perpendicular. **1890** Baker *Wild Beasts* II. 3 The toes spread widely upon soft ground.

12. a. Of immaterial things: To become diffused or disseminated.

a **1225** *Ancr. R.* 98 Vor ase holi writ seið, 'hore speche spret ase cauncre'. *a* **1240** *Ureisun* in *O.E. Hom.* I. 199 þuruh þine muchele milce þet spert [*read* spret] so swuðe wide. **1340** *Ayenb.* 29 Ouerweninge, þet makeþ to moche sprede þe merci of our lhorde. **13..** *E.E. Allit. P.* B. 1607 þurȝ þe sped of þe spyryt þat sprad hym with-inne. *c* **1410** Hoccleve *Mother of God* 81 Thy gracious bountee spredith al aboute. **1508** Kennedie *Flyting w. Dunbar* 348 It was the gud langage of this land, And Scota it causit to multiply and sprede. **1592** Shaks. *Ven. & Ad.* 903 A second fear through all her sinews spread. *a* **1656** Bp. Hall *Rem. Wks.* (1660) 189 Arianisme began in a family, spread over the World. **1697** Collier *Ess. Mor. Subj.* I. (1703) 139 The infection spreads like lightning; and 'tis a credit to live counter to reason. **1712** Addison *Spect.* No. 265 ¶6, I am informed that this Fashion spreads daily. **1782** Priestley *Corrupt. Chr.* I. I. 75 His opinions are acknowledged to have spread much. **1815** J. Smith *Panorama Sci. & Art* II. 293 This system of nomenclature.. spread with great rapidity to other countries. **1849** Macaulay *Hist. Eng.* iv. I. 457 Discontent and suspicion would spread fast through society. **1874** Green *Short Hist.* viii. §I (1882) 449 A new moral and religious impulse spread through every class.

b. Of tidings, rumour, fame, etc.

a **1300** *Cursor M.* 15062 On þin worthi werkes don Farr spredes þi fame. **13..** *E.E. Allit. P.* C. 365 þis speche sprang in þat space & spradde alle aboute. *c* **1400** *26 Pol. Poems* 129 That I dyd in pryuyte, There opynly hit owte shall sprede. **1475** *Bk. Noblesse* (Roxb.) 45 The renome of his noble astate and name sprad thoroughe alle cristyn roiaumes. **1523** Ld. Berners *Froiss.* I. ccccxcvii, It was sayd howe surly they were at Burdeaux,.. whiche wordes sprade abrode in the hoost. **1637** Milton *Lycidas* 81 Fame.. lives and spreds aloft by those pure eyes. **1662** J. Davies tr. *Mandelslo's Trav.* 96 Which increas'd as the noyse of the attempt spread more and more into the City. **1764** *Museum Rust.* IV. 10 The account of this, spreading into Holland, determined the Dutch to send colonies there. *c* **1807** Wordsw. *Somnambulist* 73 His fame may spread, but in the past Her spirit finds its centre. **1891** Farrar *Darkn. & Dawn* xlii, The city had hardly been more agitated when the news of Caligula's murder had spread among the citizens.

13. Of flowers, leaves, etc.: To unfold, expand.

a **1250** *Owl & Night.* 437 þe blostme gynneþ springe & sprede. **1375** Barbour *Bruce* XVI. 67 Lewis on the branchis spredis, And blomys bricht besyd thame bredis. *c* **1385** Chaucer *L.G.W.* 48 To sen these flouris agen the sunne to sprede. **1423** Jas. I *Kingis Q.* 21 The tender flouris opnyt thame and sprad. **1535** Stewart *Cron. Scot.* II. 530 Flouris spreidand.. Of diuers hew, with mony cullour cleir. **1662** J. Davies tr. *Olearius' Voy.* 323 As soon as it is put into warm water, it spreads and reassumes its former green Colour. **1686** W. Harris tr. *Lemery's Course Chem.* (ed. 3) 523 It is best gathering Roses newly spread a little after Sun-rising. **1765** *Museum Rust.* IV. 94 When the barley begins to spread, (or brewer).

14. To extend by growth; *spec.* of trees, to grow outwards.

c **1290** *S. Eng. Leg.* I. 348 Him þouȝte þat þare stod a treo ..þat a-non to þe steorrene it tilde and swyþe wide it spradde [*v.r.* spredde]. *a* **1300** *Cursor M.* 27877 O glotori and o drunkenhede Fele wick branches we sprede. **1340** *Ayenb.* 131 Vor uirtue wext an heȝ ase palme.. and þanne spret and keste his boȝes an ech half. **1559** *Mirr. Mag., Mowbray's Banishm.* xiv, The deper doth the sounde roote sprede abrode. **1573** Tusser *Husb.* (1878) 98 Good hop hath a pleasure to climbe and to spred. **1615** W. Lawson *Country Housew. Gard.* (1626) 24 The roots.. may not goe downeward, nor vpward out of the earth... Therefore they must needs spread far vnder the earth. **1676** Marvell *Mr. Smirke* 27 When it germinates, spreds, blossomes, and bears fruit. 1697 Dryden *Virg. Georg.* iv. 422 A Steer.. whose Head Now first with burnish'd Horns begins to spread. 1743 Francis tr. *Horace, Odes* iv. xi. 6 With living wreaths to crown our heads The parsley's vivid verdure spreads. 1796 Withering *Brit. Plants* (ed. 3) I. 83 Not rising high, but spreading wide upon the ground. 1802 *Barrington's Hist. N.S. Wales* viii. 283 The she oaks were more inclined to spread than grow tall. 1826 *Art Brewing* (ed. 2) 174 When the trees are full grown, they..injure the crop below; the roots, also, spread to a great distance. 1847 Tennyson *Princ.* iv. 188 The branches thereupon Spread out at top.

15. a. To extend over a larger area by increase or by separation; to disperse.

c 1250 *Gen. & Ex.* 2567 Ay wex ðat kinde, mor & mor, And ðhogen, & spredden in londe ðor. c 1290 *S. Eng. Leg.* I. 48 His Men pleiden and arnden bi þe weie, and spradden a-boute ful wide. a 1300 *Cursor M.* 3792 Wit þe i sal be in al þi nede And gar þin oxspring wide spred. c 1450 *Merlin* xvii. 272 As soone as the saisnes were logged thai spredde abrode in the contrey to forry. 1523 Ld. Berners *Froiss.* cccxxi. 498 So the men of armes sprad abrode. 1596 Dalrymple tr. *Leslie's Hist. Scot.* I. 45 Quhair ance it fixis the rute it spredis. 1605 Chapman *All Fools* v. ii. 372 Very well done; now take your severall wives, And spred like wilde-geese. 1667 Milton *P.L.* i. 354 Her barbarous Sons Came like a Deluge on the South, and spread Beneath Gibraltar to the Lybian sands. 1748 *Anson's Voy.* ii. v. 173 By spreading in their cruise, there might be less danger of any of the enemy's ships slipping by unobserved. 1853 J. H. Newman *Hist. Sk.* (1873) I. i. ii. 59 The Romans spread gradually from one central city. 1866 Darwin *Orig. Spec.* (ed. 4) iv. 152 That those species which spread widely tend generally to spread *very* widely.

b. To arise or spring. *rare*$^{-1}$.

1642 H. More *Song of Soul* ii. ii. i. 8 How the mixture of their rayes may breed Th' opinion of uncertain quality, When they from certain roots of life do spreed.

16. To stretch out, extend.

a 1300 *Cursor M.* 17196 Vnnethes dar i sceu mi nedes Bot wit þe hend to me þou spredis. a 1310 in Wright *Lyric P.* xxv. 70 Iesu, of love soth tocknynge, Thin armes spredeth to mankynde. a 1327 A. Davy *Five Dreams* 12/34 Out of boþe his eren [came] Foure bendes;..hij spredden fer & wyde in þe cuntre. c 1385 Chaucer *L.G.W.* Prol. 143 (Cambr.), Lo ȝond he comyth, I se hise wyngis sprede.

1748 Gray *Alliance* 100 In the sultry climes, that spread Where Nile redundant o'er his Summer-bed From his broad bosom life and verdure flings. 1798 Landor *Gebir* Wks. 1846 II. 490 There spreads a marble squared And smoothened. 1816 Shelley *Mont Blanc* 65 Broad vales.. that spread And wind among the accumulated steeps. 1854 *Poultry Chron.* II. 92 Thin, hackle-like feathers, spreading and drooping all round. 1898 R. Bridges *Hymn Nature* Poems (1912) 404 Below their breezy crowns..Spreadeth the infinite smile of the sunlit sea.

17. *Bridge.* (See quot. 1964.) Cf. spread *sb.* 11.

1929 M. C. Work *Compl. Contract Bridge* 245 *Spread*, to 'claim the rest'. 1964 Frey & Truscott *Official Encycl. Bridge* 520/1 *Spread*,..verb: to spread the hand, either as a claim or as a concession of the remaining tricks.

spread (sprɛd), *ppl. a.* Also 6–7 spred. [f. prec.]

1. a. Extended, expanded; displayed; diffused.

c 1511 *1st Eng. Bk. Amer.* (Arb.) Introd. p. xxxi/2 They seke the holy graue to Iherusalem with open or spred baners. 1609 Holland *Amm. Marcell.* 111 Antoninus..set his course against our State and Common-wealth..even with spred and full sail. 1611 Cotgr. s.v. *Penne*, The spread wings of a bird. 1667 Milton *P.L.* ii. 886 A Bannerd Host Under spread Ensigns marching. 1753 Richardson *Grandison* (1781) III. 7 No, Miss Grandison, said I, laying my spread hand upon the letter. 1771 *Encycl. Brit.* I. 204/2 The shape of a spread fan. 1854 *Poultry Chron.* II. 56 The cock, while playing, sweeps the ground with his spread tail. 1877 Raymond *Statist. Mines & Mining* 315 A diverging vein-system..something like the spread fingers of a hand held downward.

b. In predicative use, or with qualifying words.

1626 Bacon *Sylva* §421 How to make the trees themselves, more tall; more spread; than they use to be. 1691 Ray *Creation* (1714) 214 Lofty and towring Trees for Timber, lowly and more spread ones for shade and fruit. 1693 C. Mather *Wonders Invis. World* (1862) 16 In so spread a Business as this. 1847 Helps *Friends in C.* i. iv. 64, I think one of the causes sometimes given, that reading is more spread, is a true..one. 1855 *Orr's Circ. Sci., Inorg. Nat.* 162 Others..occupy evenly spread and little disturbed districts.

c. In comb. with *-out*.

1867 Morris *Jason* xvii. 520 Watching the spread-out linen slowly dry. 1877 Huxley & Martin *Elem. Biol.* 209 A V-shaped notch about the size of a spread-out frog's web.

d. *Phonetics.* Pronounced with the lips drawn out rather than rounded; unrounded.

1902 [see *fan consonant* s.v. fan *sb.*[1] 11]. 1965 *Language* XLI. 26 The spread phonemes /ī/ and /ēi/ are realized in the back allophones.

2. Laid out or prepared for a meal.

1891 T. Hardy *Tess* xxxvi, The spread supper-table, whereon stood the two full glasses of untasted wine.

3. a. Special collocations: **spread adder**, a blowing adder; **spread brilliant**, a brilliant cut in a thin flat form; **spread charge**, a gun-charge which scatters on being fired; **spread head** *U.S. Journalism*, a display heading; hence **spread-headed** *a.*

1750 D. Jeffries *Treat. Diamonds* (1751) 26 Of the method of manufacturing, and valuing, spread Brilliants. 1892 in Greener *Breech-Loader* 279, I have used the spread charge with good results in covert shooting. 1902 *Blackw. Mag.* Apr. 494/2 The spread-adder is one of the nastiest-looking customers. 1907 *Everybody's Mag.* XVI. 321 There is no such thing as fashion in dogs, despite the frequent 'spread heads'. 1923 O. G. Villard *Some Newspapers & Newspapermen* 152 It has not been able to rise without the vulgar comic section or the Sunday pictorial, and the usual spread-headed Sunday features.

b. spread (window) glass, sheet or cylinder glass.

1805 *Act 45 Geo. III*, c. 30 Sched., The making of spread window glass commonly called or known by the name of broad glass. 1839 Ure *Dict. Arts* 576 Next to it in cheapness of material may be ranked broad or spread window glass. *Ibid.* 578 A spread-glass work, where they make British sheet glass, upon the best principles.

4. In parasynthetic combinations, as ***spread-kneed, -legged, -lipped, -winged*** adjs.

1932 W. Faulkner *Light in August* vii. 140 McEachern lowered himself stiffly to the top of a feed box, spread-kneed, one hand on his knee and the silver watch in the other palm. 1969 L. Michaels *Going Places* 21, I stood spread-legged, bolt naked. 1973 G. W. Turner *Stylistics* ii. 63 If Australians tend to use spread-lipped vowels.., they perhaps seem matey fellows. 1936 R. Campbell *Mithraic Emblems* 89 A spread-winged phœnix from its ash The Cross remained against the sky. 1972 R. Adams *Watership Down* xlv. 375 Four partridges..sailed down, spread-winged, into the field.

Hence ˌ**spread'outness** *rare*, the quality or condition of being spread out.

1879 W. James in *Mind* IV. 339 Since the essences of things are as a matter of fact spread out and disseminated through the whole extent of time and space, it is in their spread-outness and alternation that he [*sc.* the entire man] will enjoy them. 1915 G. F. Stout *Man. Psychol.* (ed. 3) ii. i. 214 There is another inseparable character belonging to many kinds of sensation, though, probably, not to all, which may be called Extensity or extensiveness or diffusion or 'spreadoutness'.

spreadable ('sprɛdəb(ə)l), *a.* [f. spread *v.* + -able.] That can be easily spread: esp. of butter, etc. So **spreada'bility**.

1940 'Plastes' *Plastics in Industry* xi. 165 The easy spreadability of animal and vegetable glues is a very important property. 1962 P. Bracken *I hate to housekeep Bk.* vi. 65 The moisture in the onion turns this into a good spreadable spread for sandwiches or canapés. 1971 *Nature* 26 Nov. 238/1 The causes of cracks in cheese, poor spreadability in butter. 1979 J. Rathbone *Euro-Killers* i. 10 The butter was..cool but spreadable.

sprea'dation. *rare.* [irreg. f. spread *v.* 8 b.] = spread *sb.* 7.

1810 *Splendid Follies* III. 26 They returned to the Bear, where they found a spreadation of sandwiches, fruit, jelly and cyder. 1884 Jean Middlemass *Poisoned Arrows* III. xvii. 193 Have all that absurd spreadation taken away,..and a luncheon as like every day as possible, got ready at once.

spread-bat. *dial.* [f. spread *v.*] A stick serving to keep apart the traces or chains in ploughing or harrowing. (Cf. spreader 3 a.)

1778 [W. H. Marshall] *Minutes Agric.* 29 July 1775, One who has more spunk in him, shall attend to the spread-bats, and whippins in future. 1875– in Kent, Surrey, and Sussex glossaries.

spread eagle, *sb.* Also spread-eagle. [spread *ppl. a.*]

1. a. A representation of an eagle with body, legs, and both wings displayed, esp. as the emblem of various states or rulers, or as an inn-sign.

1570 Foxe *A. & M.* (ed. 2) 388/1 The emperour..caused other money to be made of leather, which on the one syde had his image, and on the other syde the spread egle. 1590 in *Archaeol.* (1884) XLVIII. 154 One dammaske table clothe wrought with ye Spreed Egle of vij yerdes long. 1602 J. Willis *Art Stenographie* E 5, This Character, bearing the similitude of a Spread Eagle, may signifie the Romaine Empire, being the Ensigne thereof. 1685 Wood *Life* (O.H.S.) III. 160 At the Spread Eagle (commonly called the Spread Crow). 1701 Luttrell *Brief Rel.* (1857) V. 81 Some flags are made here with a spread eagle upon them, the arms of his imperial majesty. 1723 *Pres. St. Russia* I. 115 Post-boys..have no Post-Horns, but only the Mark of the Spread-Eagle. 1854 *Poultry Chron.* II. 27 The annual dinner will take place at the Spread Eagle on Thursday.

Comb. 1663 Dryden *Wild Gallant* ii. i, I use to tell him of his two capon's tails about his hat, that are laid spread-eaglewise to make a feather.

b. A figure in fancy-skating.

1824 Miss Mitford *Village* Ser. i. (1863) 15 He admired, with an ardour and sincerity never excited by..the spread-eagles of the Seine and the Serpentine. 1868 *Hurst Johnian Mag.* X. 343 As I am writing for young skaters I may as well mention the 'spread eagle', a feat of not much value.

c. A boastful or self-assertive person.

1881 Blackmore *Christowell* i, It may be denied by young spread-eagles, of competitive and unruly mind, that this is the highest form of human life.

2. A person secured with the arms and legs stretched out, esp. in order to be flogged.

1785 Grose *Dict. Vulgar T.*, *Spread eagle*, a soldier tied to the halberts in order to be whipped, his attitude bearing some likeness to that figure, as painted on signs. 1792 *Grose's Olio* 228 Should you be caught, you know the consequence—That the spread eagle is your certain lot. 1834 Marryat *P. Simple* (1863) 38 Mr. Jenkins desired the other men to get half-a-dozen foxes and make a spread eagle of me. 1882 *Daily Tel.* 12 Sept. 2/2 The iron-hard pressure of it pins you against the shrouds as if you had been made a spread-eagle.

fig. 1871 Froude *Table-T. Shirley* 149, I suppose I shall as usual be made a spread-eagle by the *Saturday* [*Review*].

3. A fowl flattened out for broiling.

1854 'C. Bede' *Verdant Green* ii. vii, Spread-eagle is a barn-door fowl smashed out flat, and made jolly with mushroom sauce. 1865 Visc. Milton & W. B. Cheadle *N.W. Passage by Land* ii. (1867) 22 We manage at last to pluck and split open the ducks into 'spread-eagles', roasting them on sticks, Indian fashion.

4. *U.S. Stock Exchange* **a.** An operation by which a broker agrees to buy shares of stock within a specified time at a specified price, and sells the option of buying shares of the same stock within the same time at a higher price. **b.** = spread *sb.* 10. Cf. straddle *sb.* 2 a.

1857 *Merchants' Mag.* XXXVII. 136 The buyer can call when he pleases, which would compel the 'spread eagle' operator to deliver. 1870 J. K. Medbery *Men & Myst. Wall St.* 86 One modification of this is the Spread Eagle, formerly a highly popular style of speculation with capitalists who had plenty of money and a wide-awake broker. 1910 *Encycl. Brit.* V. 55/1 A combined option of either calling or putting is termed a 'straddle', and some-times on the American stock exchange a 'spread-eagle'.

5. *attrib.* **a.** High-sounding, grandiloquent.

1839 *Morn. Post* 21 Sept., The notion of lifting him with a spread-eagle title into the chief saloon.

b. *U.S.* Bombastic, extravagant, ridiculously boastful, esp. in laudation of the United States.

In allusion to the figure of the eagle on United States flags, etc.

1858 *Harper's Wkly.* 28 Aug. (Thornton), The sermon was a splendid failure,..and is yet laughed at as the 'Spread Eagle sermon'. 1858 *N. Amer. Rev.* Oct. 454 It pleases our English critics to charge upon American writers in the mass ..what has come to be designated as 'the spread-eagle style' —a compound of exaggeration, effrontery, bombast, and extravagance. 1894 H. Gardener *Unofficial Patr.* 125 You've read a lot of spread-eagle stuff, I don't doubt.

c. Aggressively assertive of United States interests or claims.

1885 *Pall Mall G.* 2 Jan. 2/1 The new form of spread-eagle policy which the past year had witnessed.

6. *attrib.* Suggestive of the form or appearance of a spread eagle.

spread-eagle orchid, a popular name (*U.S.*) for the orchid *Oncidium Carthaginense*.

1856 'Stonehenge' *Brit. Rur. Sports* 376 That 'spread-eagle' style of gallop which destroys a horse's chances at once. 1881 Mahaffy *Old Gk. Educ.* iii. 32 Wild swinging of their arms, in spread-eagle fashion. 1894 *Daily Tel.* 7 May 5/4 The 'spread-eagle' system adopted by cyclists, who straggle all over the road.

7. quasi-*adv.* Like a spread eagle, with arms and legs outstretched.

1922 Joyce *Ulysses* 492 A blond feeble goosefat whore.. lolls spreadeagle in the sofacorner. 1954 *Sun* (Baltimore) 16 Jan. 12/2 He told the two men to stand 'spread eagle' against the wall of a building while Joseph L. Klingenberg..frisked them. 1973 W. H. Hallahan *Ross Forgery* iv. 59 Ross stripped the klutz of all his clothes and staked him spread-eagle to the ground under a tropical sun.

spread-eagle, *v.* Also spreadeagle. [f. prec.]

1. *intr.* To cut spread eagles in skating.

1826 J. Wilson *Noct. Ambr.* Wks. 1855 I. 102 Mr. Tory, ..a handsome fallow, and as good a skater as ever spread-eagled. 1831 —— in *Blackw. Mag.* XXIX. 303 The grand simplicity of the masters that spread-eagled in the age of its perfection.

2. a. *trans.* To tie up (a person) for punishment. (Cf. prec. 2.) Also *fig.*

1829 Marryat *F. Mildmay* xvi, I saw a poor fellow spread-eagled up to the grating. 1891 in *Ch. Bells* (1892) 1 Jan. 93 Too many witnesses are spread-eagled that a court may laugh and cross-examiners be considered clever. 1894 Sala *Things I have Seen* I. 245, I have heard of offending soldiers being 'spread-eagled', that is to say, tied by the wrists and ankles to the wheel of a gun or an ammunition waggon.

b. To fasten, pin firmly, stretch out, etc., in the form of a spread eagle.

1887 *N. & Q.* 1 Oct. 278/2 Cod—as well as haddock and ling..may be seen spread-eagled across transverse sticks to dry. 1894 Rider Haggard *People of Mist* xxxix, On this surface of ice they were lying spread-eagled. 1895 Crockett *Cleg Kelly* xx, His elbows were spread-eagled over the table. 1955 J. P. Donleavy *Ginger Man* xxvi. 252 The kangaroo fell spread-eagled to the floor. 1976 'D. Halliday' *Dolly & Nanny Bird* v. 65 He spreadeagled a broad, powerful hand and clenched Johnson's in it.

c. To drive apart, scatter, esp. of the wicket in *Cricket*.

1887 *Cricket* 24 Nov. 460/2 A high one from Miss Tompkins spread-eagled Miss White's wicket. 1905 H. A. Vachell *Hill* xii. 266 It [i.e. the ball] shot under Scaife's bat, and spread-eagled his stumps. 1955 *Times* 15 June 6/3 McDonald added only 12 runs in 65 minutes before his stumps were spreadeagled by Worrell.

3. To beat completely, esp. in racing.

1864 *Daily Tel.* 18 July, When poor old Flash-in-the-Pan spread-eagled his field for the Chester Cup. 1883 *Ibid.* 1 Jan. 2/7 He..spread-eagled his opponents for the Hunters' Hurdle Plate. 1887 H. Smart *Cleverly Won* iv, You've heard how she spread-eagled the hunt a month ago?

4. *intr.* To speak or act in a spread-eagle fashion.

1866 *Sat. Rev.* 20 Jan. 77/1 If, when merely spread-eagling, she speaks on her own hook. 1892 *Ibid.* 23 Jan. 86/1 The extent to which President Harrison may 'spread-eagle' in the Chilian business.

Hence **spread-eagled** *ppl. a.*; **spread-eagling** *vbl. sb.*

1887 H. Smart *Cleverly Won* iii, Such a spread-eagling of a field had rarely been witnessed. 1940 L. MacNeice *Last Ditch* 21 Light on her feet and gentle with her fingers; Put on a little flesh, became an easy Spreadeagled beauty for Renaissance painters. 1982 B. Fantoni *Stickman* xxiii. 161 Stepping over Lonnie's spread-eagled body, I lit a cigarette.

spread-eagleism. [f. SPREAD EAGLE *sb.* 5 b.] Extravagant laudation of the United States or assertion of their political importance; tendency to bombast or grandiloquence in this connexion or in similar cases.

1859 G. F. TRAIN (*title*), Spread-Eagleism. *Ibid.* p. ix, We cannot fasten an ism on him (except Spread-Eagleism). **1864** *Realm* 6 July 3 Abuse of England is part of the platform of spread-eagleism: it pleases the Irish element, and produces votes. **1889** J. M. ROBERTSON *Ess. Crit. Method* 104 Napier's account of a Peninsular battle..with its *saugrenu* spread-eagleism.

So **spread-eagleist**, one who is characterized by spread-eagleism.

1885 *Pall Mall G.* 1 Dec. 5/2 He is little better than a brilliant failure, first among phrasemongers and the champion spread-eagleist of his time.

spread eaglet. *rare*$^{-1}$. = SPREAD EAGLE *sb.* 1.

1602 *Met. Tabacco* D iv b, Tabacco had been richer armorie, Then Lions, Crosses, or Spread Eaglets be.

'spreaded, *ppl. a.* [f. SPREAD *v.*] Stretched out, extended, expanded.

1565 GOLDING tr. *Ovid's Metam.* VII. (1567) 90 b, Hard by vs as it hapt that time, there was an Oken tree With spreaded armes. **1818** KEATS *Endym.* I. 867 With wings outraught, And spreaded tail. *Ibid.* III. 389 Like a new fledg'd bird that first doth show His spreaded feathers to the morrow chill.

†So **'spreaden** *ppl. a. Obs.*

1620 QUARLES *Feast Wormes* (1638) 2 Amongst the Hebrewes, where thy spredden fame Fore-runs the welcome of thine honoured name. **1629** —— *Argalus & Parthenia* III. Wks. (Grosart) III. 279/2 Her spredden traine did cover His crooper. **1642** H. MORE *Song of Soul* II. i. I. iii, So rais'd upon her spreaden wing, She softly playes, and warbles in the wind.

spreader ('sprɛdə(r)). [f. SPREAD *v.*]

I. 1. One who spreads, strews, or scatters.

1483 *Cath. Angl.* 356/2 A Spreder of gresse.., *herbarius.* **1641** BEST *Farm. Bks.* (Surtees) 33 One spreader will spreade as much in a day as sixe goode mowers will mowe. **1712** N. BLUNDELL *Diary* (1895) 105 All my Marlers, Spreaders,..and Carters din'd here. **1854** *Jrnl. R. Agric. Soc.* XV. I. 109 The spreaders carry the manure forward and deposit it in the bottoms of the drills. **1891** *Labour Comm.* Gloss., *Spreaders*, women who spread the softened jute on the card.

2. A diffuser, disseminator, or promulgator *of* something.

1551 CRANMER *Answ. Gardiner* 17 The Papistes..haue ben the chiefe spreaders abrode of it. **1562** *Act 5 Eliz.* c. 5 §40 Such Persons shall be punished as Spreaders of false News are and ought to be. **1641** PRYNNE *Discov. Prelates' Tyr.* II. 152 The spreaders abroad of false, seditious and scandalous newes. **1649** —— *Demurrer to Jews' Remitter* 83 The Jews..are the greatest venters, spreaders of abominable Blasphemies. **1710** STEELE *Tatler* No. 225 ¶4 He..would be considered as a Spreader of false News is in Business. **1787** BENTHAM *Def. Usury* xiii. 187 The spreaders of English arts in foreign climes.

3. A piece of wood, metal, or other material, by which things or parts are stretched out or kept asunder: **a.** (See quots. and cf. SPREAD-BAT.)

1839 SIR G. C. LEWIS *Gloss. Heref.*, *Spreader*, a cross-piece of wood, which prevents the traces of the fore-horses of a team from collapsing. **1852** C. W. HOSKYNS *Talpa* i. (1854) 3 Bang goes a trace or a spreader, and the plough comes to a standstill. **1875** KNIGHT *Dict. Mech.* 2288/2 *Spreader*,..a stick which stretches apart the ends of a chain to which the single-trees are attached.

attrib. **1871** in De Vere *Americanisms* 351 The captain.. was attacked with a spreaderstick (a piece of wood used as a swingle-tree on the tow-track).

b. In misc. uses (see quots.).

1875 KNIGHT *Dict. Mech.* 2004/1 *Runner*,..the slider of an umbrella to which the spreaders are pivoted. **1881** RAYMOND *Mining Gloss.*, *Spreaders*, pieces of timber stretched across a shaft as a temporary support of the walls. **1884** ERICHSEN *Surgery* (ed. 8) I. 68 A wide 'spreader' made of a piece of wood with a hole in it for the rope..to pass through. **1888** FENN *Dick o' the Fens* 88 The net, at whose two ends was fixed a pole as spreader.

c. *Naut.* A bar attached to the mast of a yacht in order to tighten the shrouds.

1895 *Daily News* 11 Sept. 5/5 In weathering it her gaff or spreaders struck Defender's shrouds. **1901** *Daily Chron.* 6 June 7/5 All her wire rigging except the masthead shrouds going over the spreader.

4. a. A machine by which heckled stricks of line are combined and drawn out into slivers.

1853 URE *Dict. Arts* (ed. 4) I. 758 In the preparation of line the first operation is called 'spreading', and the machine employed a 'spreader'. **1884** *Western Morn. News* 9 Aug. 1/5 Cards, spreaders, drawings, rovings.

b. A device for spreading the jet of water issuing from a hose.

1858 SIMMONDS *Dict. Trade*, *Spreader*, an attachment [to] the branch pipe of a fire-engine for scattering the water over a large surface. **1863** *Appleby's Handbk. Mach. & Iron Work* 59 Copper Branch-pipe... Brass Jet and Spreader extra, 7/6 each. **1894** *Westm. Gaz.* 3 May 3/3 The Spiral Spreaders, which can be..fixed in position as lawn sprinklers, are excellent.

c. An apparatus or device by which something is spread or scattered.

1864 *Jrnl. R. Agric. Soc.* XXV. II. 368 Each shaft or inlet should be provided with a louver or 'spreader' within the stable, to prevent occasional down-draughts. **1882** *Rep. Prec. Metals U.S.* 586 The pulp goes on to the distributing board, which is provided with spreaders.

d. = *lifting beam* s.v. LIFTING *vbl. sb.* 2 b. Also *spreader beam.*

1960 S. P. OPPENHEIMER *Erecting Structural Steel* vii. 88 Slings having a center ring and known as spreaders or bridle slings are used. *Ibid.*, When a long, thin piece, which might buckle under compression, is to be lifted, an additional heavy spreader beam is used above separate single slings placed at the ends. **1968** W. G. RAPP *Construction of Structural Steel Building Frames* vi. 175 To choke the load with a sling around it one eye is passed through the other, the free eye is then hooked or shackled into the hoisting spreaders on the main load hook. **1970** *Specification for Flat Lifting Slings* (*B.S.I.*) 20 Use a spreader beam or other suitable arrangement to ensure that the slings are as nearly as practicable vertical.

II. †**5.** *Cant.* Butter. *Obs.* (Cf. SPREAD *sb.* 6.)

1610 ROWLANDS *Martin Mark-all* E iv, *Spreader*, butter.

6. a. Something which spreads or grows outwards.

a **1639** WOTTON *Surv. Educ.* in *Reliq.* (1651) 321 If their Child be not such a speedy spreader, and brancher like the Vine. **1845** *Jrnl. R. Agric. Soc.* VI. I. 198 The oak is naturally a wide spreader.

b. A side-channel.

1845 COL. HAWKER *Diary* (1893) II. 252 We then poled up the 'spreader', but the water was too low to allow my gun to bear on the birds.

c. A catch which operates by spreading.

1884 KNIGHT *Dict. Mech.* Suppl. 827/1 *Socket*, a tool used in well boring.., screwing on to the top of the rod, attaching by gripers, hooks, shoulders, collars, spreaders, etc.

7. A surfactant.

1918 *Jrnl. Econ. Entomol.* XI. 67 The surface tension and specific gravity are probably factors of importance in determining the value of a spreader. **1941** *Nature* 12 Apr. 438/2 The efficiency of..'spreaders' in a given oil may be gauged by the direct measurement of their spreading power against surface contamination in the Adam-Langmuir surface pressure trough. **1963** H. MARTIN *Insecticide & Fungicide Handbk.* iii. 57 Where high or medium volume is used, the addition to the spray of surface-active 'wetters' or 'spreaders' may be recommended in order to increase the cover obtained.

III. 8. *Comb.*, as **spreader-bar** = SPREADER 3; **spreader light**, a light attached to the spreader of a yacht.

1927 C. A. LINDBERGH *We* iii. 44 The wheels touched earth..rolled.., sank into the spreader bar and we nosed over. **1954** W. FAULKNER *Fable* 222 When they sat up it was together as though a spreader bar connected them. **1968** J. ARNOLD *Shell Bk. Country Crafts* xi. 166 Between the two horses, the trace-chains were kept steady by a spreader-bar. **1947** *Sun* (Baltimore) 3 July 15/5 The practice of a flashlight on sails as something approaches in the darkness is a good one, the authorities say, and the spreader lights now carried by many sailing yachts is [*sic*] an even better idea. **1977** G. V. HIGGINS *Dreamland* ix. 96 With the spreader lights on the main-mast on, I took down the mizzen sail.

spreading ('sprɛdɪŋ), *vbl. sb.* [f. SPREAD *v.*]

1. The action of the verb in various senses: **a.** In transitive uses.

a **1000** *Rituale Eccl. Dunelm.* (Surtees) 109 Sprædvng [L. *propagationem*] mennisces cynnes. *a* **1240** *Ureisun* in *O.E. Hom.* I. 185 Wiþ þe ilke spredunge [of the arms]..as þe moder to hire child. *c* **1440** *Promp. Parv.* 470 Spredynge, *dilatacio, extencio.* *c* **1465** *Pol., Rel., & L. Poems* (1903) 3 Þe egile..Thorowe þe spredinge of his wengis þat neuer begane to flee. **1508** DUNBAR *Flyting* 206 Oft for ane causs thy burdclaith neidis no spredding. **1560** BIBLE (Geneva) *Ezek.* xxvi. 5 Thou shalt be for the spreading of nettes in the middes of the sea. **1601** HOLLAND *Pliny* I. 508 Touching the spreading of mucke, and mingling it with the mould of a land. **1657** *Attest Innoc. Z. Crofton* A iij, Many of his friends considering the spreading of this scandal,.. did see the necessity of speaking in his behalf. **1765** *Museum Rust.* IV. 123 The reward of manuring a cold clay with coal-ashes, even in the year immediately following the spreading of it. **1853** [see SPREADER 4 a]. **1900** *Westm. Gaz.* 11 Jan. 2/2 This is the doctrine of 'spreading', that we had over the Clerical Tithes Act.

b. In intransitive uses.

1382 WYCLIF *Ezek.* xxxi. 7 He was moost fayr in his greetnes, and in spredynge of tendre trees. *c* **1440** *Promp. Parv.* 470 Spredynge, or streykynge owte, *extencio, protencio.* **1538** STARKEY *England* I. ii. 63 Lyke as the cloudys let the schynyng and spredyng of the sone beamys downe to the erth. **1577** tr. *Bullinger's Decades* (1592) 678 Whose goinges foorth (or spreadinges abroade) haue beene..from euerlasting. **1617** MORYSON *Itin.* III. 144 Harts (notable for their greatnesse, and the spreading of their hornes). **1639** O. WOOD *Alph. Bk. Secrets* 134 The water thereof is perfect good to stay the spreading of the Canker. **1683** MOXON *Mech. Exerc., Printing* x. ¶4 The spreading of the ends of these two Tennants into the spreading of the Mortesses in the Cheeks. **1797** *Encycl. Brit.* (ed. 3) XVIII. 102/1 The patient may suffer from the spreading of the disease. **1832** H. MELVILL in *Preacher* III. 97/1 The creatures whom he hath sent forth to tenant the spreadings of immensity. **1899** *Allbutt's Syst. Med.* VII. 574 A spreading of the fluid into the retro-ocular tissue.

2. *attrib.*, as ***spreading commission, knife, place, sheet***; also in mod. technical usage, as ***spreading furnace, hammer, machine, room,*** etc.; **spreading-board,** (*a*) a board on which sheep are laid while being shorn (*rare*); (*b*) a setting-board for insect specimens; **spreading factor** *Biol.* = HYALURONIDASE.

c **1586** C'TESS PEMBROKE *Ps.* XCII. v, Where God doth dwell Shall be his spreading place. **1625** DONNE *Serm.* iii. 26 He hath given us that spreading commission to..preach to every creature. **1648** HEXHAM II, *Een Spreeder*, the Spreding-sheete of a bed. **1688** HOLME *Armoury* III. xiv. (Roxb.) 3/1 The second..which is called a chopping Knife, or a cookes chopper, or a spreading Knife. **1837** *Penny Cycl.* VIII. 95/1 The spreading-machine is not universally used; ..for fine yarns..machine-spreading does not answer so well as hand-spreading. **1839** URE *Dict. Arts* 578 The spreading furnace or oven is that in which cylinders are expanded into tables or plates. *Ibid.* 611 The French gold-beaters employ besides this hammer..the spreading hammer. **1874** HARDY *Far from Madding Crowd* I. xxii 247 The issue of their dialogue was the taking of her hand by the courteous farmer to help her over the spreading-board into the bright May sunlight outside. **1885** C. G. W. LOCK *Workshop Rec.* Ser. IV. 2/2 (Waterproofing), To make the thick paste into a sheet, what is termed a 'spreading machine' is used. *Ibid.* 5/1 The spreading-rooms of some of the largest establishments. **1909** in WEBSTER. [**1930** *Science* 14 Nov. 508/2 The ink particles were..spread through a wider area under the influence of the factor.] **1939** *Nature* 9 Dec. 978/2 The occurrence of spreading factor in bacterial filtrates has so far been found to go parallel with their mucinase content. **1963** V. NABOKOV *Gift* ii. 111 To drive a pin smoothly through the insect's thorax, stick it in the cork groove of the spreading board. **1978** *Exper. Cell Res.* CXV. 227 Techniques previously developed for the purification of the fetal calf adhesion and spreading factor were directly applied to human serum.

spreading ('sprɛdɪŋ), *ppl. a.* [f. SPREAD *v.*]

1. a. Extending or growing outwards; increasing in size or area.

a **1593** MARLOWE tr. *1st Bk. Lucan* 530 Fiery meteors,.. Now spearlike, long; now like a spreading torch. **1651** DAVENANT *Gondibert* I. i. 52 Her spreading stature talness was, not length. **1683** MOXON *Mech. Exerc., Printing* xxiv. ¶19 While he is taking the Sheet off the Tympan, he gives a quick spreading glance upon it. **1725** POPE *Odyss.* II. 404 Me from our coast shall spreading sails convey. **1746** HERVEY *Medit.* (1818) 127 Soon arises the anemone, encircled at the bottom with a spreading robe. **1794** MRS. RADCLIFFE *Myst. Udolpho* xxxvi, To see the dipping oars imprint the water, and to watch the spreading circles they left. **1827** KEBLE *Chr. Y., Ordin.*, Through the hallow'd air The spreading cloud of incense soar'd. **1851** RUSKIN *Stones Ven.* (1874) I. ix. 111 The eye always requires, on a slender shaft, a more spreading capital than it does on a massy one. **1897** W. ANDERSON *Surg. Treat. Lupus* 15 In large areas of lupus..the spreading edge may be excised.

fig. *a* **1647** HABINGTON *Surv. Worcs.* (Worcs. Hist. Soc.) III. 424 The worthy and large spreadinge family of the Throckmortons.

b. Of trees or plants.

1593 SHAKS. *3 Hen. VI*, v. ii. 14 Whose top-branch ouer-peer'd Ioves spreading Tree. **1611** BIBLE *Wisd.* xvii. 18 A melodious noise of birdes among the spreading branches. **1634** MILTON *Comus* 184 Here to lodge Under the spreading favour of these Pines. **1697** DRYDEN *Virg. Georg.* IV. 216 With spreading Planes he made a cool Retreat. **1720** PRIOR *Truth & Falsehood* 11 Under a spreading beach They sat. **1743** FRANCIS tr. *Horace, Odes* III. i. 14 Others..joy to plant the spreading grove. **1794** MRS. RADCLIFFE *Myst. Udolpho* xxxii, Beneath the dark and spreading branches. **1842** LOUDON *Suburban Hort.* 531 A good bearer, a spreading tree. **1869** TOZER *Highl. Turkey* I. 292 [We] lay down to rest under a spreading ash-tree.

c. *Bot.* Having a gradual outward tendency or direction.

1796 WITHERING *Brit. Plants* (ed. 3) II. 166 Calyx 5-flowered: panicle spreading. **1841** *Penny Cycl.* XXI. 182/2 Five petals, which are usually spreading. **1858** A. IRVINE *Handbk. Brit. Pl.* 753 Teeth with spreading or spreading-erect cartilaginous points. **1890** *Science-Gossip* XXVI. 275 Leaflets ovate, with long spreading hairs near the underside of the mid-rib.

Comb. **1840** *Penny Cycl.* XVIII. 171/2 The spreading-leaved Pine... A lofty tree, with leaves eight or nine inches long. **1846–50** A. WOOD *Class-bk. Bot.* 194 *Talinum patens*, Spreading-flowered Talinum.

2. a. In specific names of plants.

1548 TURNER *Names Herbes* 45 *Lactuca sessilis*, in englishe spredynge Lettis. **1823** CRABB *Techn. Dict.* II, *Scorzonera residifolia*,..Spreading Viper's-Grass. **1836** *Penny Cycl.* VI. 432/1 *Cerasus prostrata*, the spreading cherry. **1859** PRATT *Brit. Grasses* 65 Spreading Millet-grass. *Ibid.* 71 Spreading Silky Bent.

b. ***spreading adder*** *U.S.*, the hog-nosed snake, *Heterodon contortrix*, a harmless snake which characteristically inflates its body, flattens its head, and hisses loudly. Cf. HOG-NOSE.

1842 J. E. DEKAY *Zool. N.Y.* III. 52 The Hog-nosed Snake..is also called Dead Adder, Spreading Adder, Hog-nose and Buckwheat-nose. **1904** R. STUART *River's Children* 91 Rattlers and copperheads, spreading-adders, moccasins, and conger-eels come up to the island. **1931** W. FAULKNER in *Amer. Mercury* Mar. 261/2 Her mouth pursed out like a spreading adder's, like a rubber mouth. **1972** E. WIGGINTON *Foxfire Bk.* 295 Spreading adder. They tell me they're an awful poisonous snake.

3. Tending to become (more) widely diffused or prevalent.

1560 BIBLE *Lev.* xiii. 57 If it appeare stil in the garment, ..it is a spreading leprie. **1647** *Power of Keys* v. 119 By the spreading, leprous quality of their example. **1697** DRYDEN *Virg. Georg.* I. 182 Spreading Succ'ry choaks the rising Field. **1746** FRANCIS tr. *Horace, Sat.* II. viii. 98 From bed to bed the spreading whisper flies. **1843** R. J. GRAVES *Syst. Clin. Med.* xxv. 319 The disposition to fresh ulceration of a spreading and intractable character. **1899** *Allbutt's Syst. Med.* VIII. 712 'Spreading gangrene'..and pyæmia are natural consequences.

'spreadingly, *adv.* [f. prec.] In a spreading manner.

1600 THYNNE *Epigr.* (1876) 82 Thow Bacchus plant,.. Why dost thou clyme my howse so spreddinglie? **1602** —— in *Chaucer's Wks.* b j, What fame Arpinas spreadingly doth find By Tullies eloquence and oratorie. **1641** MILTON *Reform.* 6 The best times were spreadingly infected.

'spreadingness. *rare.* [f. as prec.] Tendency to spread.

1671 *Phil. Trans.* VI. 2211 As for the Spreadingness of the Plague, he esteems..that it is not so Contagious as is commonly believed. **1674** N. FAIRFAX *Bulk & Selv.* Ep.

Ded., Though I cannot raise nor greaten the height and spreadingness of your Worth.

† **spreadle(s.** *Obs. rare.* In 4 spredeles, spridels. [repr. OE. **sprǣdels*, f. *sprǣdan* SPREAD *v.* Cf. WFlem. *spreedsel* something spread.] A spreading-place (for nets).

1386 *Cart. Abb. Whiteby* (Surtees) II. 503 Item de spredeles de retez. **1387** *Ibid.* 505 Item quant as spridels, nul altre les doits avoir si non labbe.

† **spread-net.** *Obs.* [f. SPREAD *v.*] (See quot.)

1686 BLOME *Gentl. Recreat.* II. 130/2 Of the Spread-Net, or Drag-Net. There is another way to take Partridges with a Spread-Net, which is by some called a long Tramel-Net.

'spread-over. Also spreadover. [f. SPREAD *v.* 4 c + OVER *prep.*] A system of distributing work or holidays over a period of time; *spec.* an arrangement by which a fixed number of work-hours may be performed at varying times within a given period. Also *attrib.* Cf. *split shift* (*a*) s.v. SPLIT *ppl. a.* 3 a.

1923 *Westm. Gaz.* 14 Apr. 1/2 A 'spread-over' of 44 hours. **1924** *Ibid.* 7 Mar. 1/2 The 'spread-over' system—the performance of eight hours' work any time within twelve hours. **1930** *New Statesman* 27 Dec. 350/2 The Lancashire miners resolved..to work the spreadover. **1963** *Times* 1 June 12/2 There is in most Coventry factories no observance of the Whitsun holiday, the period having been moved to September to allow a better spread-over of holidays. **1976** P. R. WHITE *Planning for Public Transport.* v. 104 A substantial number of bus crews..work 'split' or 'spreadover' shifts, covering both morning and evening peaks. **1978** *Daily Tel.* 21 Mar. 2/8 Supplementary payments bus crews may qualify for, such as spread-over duties, unsocial hours, [etc.].

spreadsheet ('sprɛdʃiːt). *Computers.* [f. SPREAD *ppl. a.* + SHEET *sb.*[1]] A program that allows any part of a rectangular array of positions or cells to be displayed on a VDU screen, with the contents of any cell able to be specified either independently or in terms of the contents of other cells.

1982 *Micro Software Mag.* May–June 4/1 Software designers have used two distinct methods in their attempt to provide the perfect package for financial modelling on a microcomputer: dynamic on-screen spreadsheet calculations, and the more traditionally processed logic file. **1983** *Daily Tel.* 13 Aug. 18 A good spreadsheet will let you put in all your figures, then just press one specified key and do all the calculations at once producing your completed accounts.

'spready, *a. rare.* [f. SPREAD *v.*] **1.** Tending to spread; expansive.

1566 J. PARTRIDGE *Hist. Plasidas* Biij, The lusty fish.. fetching frischoes here and there, With spready finne at sea. **1924** R. HALL *Unlit Lamp* v. 30 She looks like a tree... A beech tree? No, that's too spready—a larch tree.

2. Of a meal: plenteous, lavish. Cf. SPREAD *sb.* 7.

1962 G. AVERY *Greatest Gresham* ix. 165 Nice to have a spready tea for once.

3. Spreadable, easily spread.

1974 J. E. UNDERHILL *Wild Berrries Pacific Northwest* 19 With a jelly..we..have a product that is very smooth and 'spready'.

spreagh (sprɛx). [Alteration of SPREATH *sb.*, prob. by association with CREAGH *sb.*] (See quots. and SPREATH *sb.*)

1809 SCOTT *Lett.* (1894) I. 146, I met an old follower of Rob Roy, who had been at many a spreagh (foray) with that redoubted freebooter. **1818** —— *Rob Roy* xxvi, Driving a spreagh (whilk is, in plain Scotch, stealing a herd of nowte). **1823** —— *Quentin D.* vii, 'You will not deny that they are cattle-lifters?' said Guthrie. 'To drive a spreagh, or so, is no thievery,' said Balafré.

Hence **'spreaghery** (also **sprechery**), cattle-raiding; plunder, booty.

1814 SCOTT *Wav.* xli, It is unspeakable the quantity of useless sprechery which they have collected on their march. **1818** —— *Rob Roy* xxvi, They lay by quiet eneugh, saving some spreagherie on the Lowlands.

spreame, error for *spearme* SPERM *sb.*

1576 TURBERV. *Venerie* 186 If you take a bytche Foxe.. and cut out hir gutte whiche holdeth hir spreame or nature.

spreat. *Sc.* Also sprait. Var. of SPRET.

a **1600** *Lindesay's* (Pitscottie) *Chron. Scot.* (1728) 146 The floors [were] laid with green scharets and spreats, medwarts and flowers. **1802** LEYDEN *Lord Soulis* lxvi, And on the spot, where they boil'd the pot, The spreat and the deer-hair ne'er shall grow. **1837** *Glasgow Courier* in *Boston Herald* 14 Feb. 4/2 The tenant of the farm..lately purchased a quantity of sprait, or coarse hay.

spreath (spriθ), *sb. Sc.* Now only *arch.* Forms: 5–6 spreith, 5 spreithe (6 spreicht), 6 spreth, 7, 9 spraith, 7– spreath. [ad. Gael. *spréidh* cattle. Cf. INSPREITH and SPREAGH.]

† **1.** Booty, plunder, spoil. *Obs.*

c **1425** WYNTOUN *Cron.* VIII. 6467 (Cott. MS.), Son eftyr þai Donwart in þe towne helde þar way, And tuk þar spreithe and presowneris. *Ibid.* 6473 Off þat sprethe mony richit war þar. **1513** DOUGLAS *Æneid* II. vii. 27 Our othir feris rubbis, tursing away, fute hait, The spreith of Troy. *Ibid.* xii. 6 Wardanes tway, For to observe and keip the spreith or pray.

† **b.** *spec.* Cattle taken as spoil. *Obs.*—[1]

1513 DOUGLAS *Æneid* I. viii. 62 We com nocht hidder.. To spuilȝe temples or riches of Libia, Nor by the coist na spreicht to drive awa.

2. A herd *of* cattle carried or driven off in a raiding expedition.

1665 J. FRASER *Polichron.* (S.H.S.) 85 He wasted and spulied the whole country, carrying away a vast spreath of their strongest cattle. **1794** *Statist. Acc. Scot.* XIII. 149 A party of the Camerons had come down to carry a spreath of cattle, as it was called, from Moray. **1874** HISLOP *Sc. Anecd.* 273 Taking 'spreaths' or herds of cattle from their hereditary enemies.

3. A cattle-raid.

1773 MRS. RADCLIFFE *Lett. fr. Mount.* (1813) I. 110 Those plunderers,..who used to consider making a spreath as a gallant exploit; now, a spreath was carrying away forcibly a herd of cattle, and fighting their way through all opposition. **1836** *Tait's Mag.* III. 426 It was..the scene of continual spreaths, liftings, reavings, and herriments.

So † **spreath** *v. intr.*, to pillage or plunder. *Obs.*

c **1425** WYNTOUN *Cron.* VIII. 6279 Scottismen wes all þat nycht sprethand, And maid all þairis þat euer þai fand.

sprechery: see SPREAGHERY.

‖ **Sprechgesang** ('ʃprɛçgəˌzaŋ). *Mus.* Also sprechgesang. [Ger., lit. 'speech song'.] A style of dramatic vocalization intermediate between speech and song. See next.

1925 W. H. KERRIDGE tr. *Wellesz' Arnold Schönberg* 138 The *Dreimal sieben Gedichte* (*Thrice seven songs*), from Albert Giraud's *Pierrot Lunaire*..are written for a *Sprechgesang* (song-speech), piano, flute.., clarinet.., violin.., and violoncello. **1938** *Oxf. Compan. Mus.* 883/1 'Sprechgesang', the older term, is properly singing tinged with a speaking quality, whereas 'Sprechstimme' is rather speech tinged with a singing quality. **1947** E. NEWMAN *Life Richard Wagner* IV. xxii. 437 There used to be much talk, a generation or so ago, about the so-called *Sprechgesang*—a term apparently designed to make more acceptable to us the canine sounds emitted by some Wagnerian singers. **1959** *Listener* 11 June 1039/3 The Stravinsky sounded tense and its Sprechgesang (or was it perhaps just ordinary muttering) very dramatic. **1978** P. GRIFFITHS *Conc. Hist. Mod. Music* iii. 36 *Pierrot lunaire* is an ambiguous work in many senses. The soloist is required to use Sprechgesang, a mode of vocalization lying between song and speech.

‖ **Sprechstimme** ('ʃprɛçʃˌtɪmə). *Mus.* Also sprechstimme. [Ger. (Grimm, 1871), lit. 'speech voice'.] A term used by Schoenberg to describe the voice of a performer singing according to the principles of *Sprechgesang*; also *loosely*, = prec.

1922 *Music & Lett.* III. 83 *Pierrot Lunaire*..represents the zenith of Schönberg's powers... In a foreword the composer explains that the voice part is to be what he calls a 'Sprechstimme', neither song nor speech, but something in between. **1938** [see SPRECHGESANG]. **1954** *Grove's Dict. Mus.* (ed. 5) VIII. 26/2 *Sprechstimme*.., a human voice written for by a composer who requires from the performer a delivery according to the principles of *Sprechgesang*. **1961** *Listener* 17 Aug. 257/3 The *Gurrelieder* provided Schönberg with the first occasion to make use of a speaking part that anticipates the *Sprechstimme* of *Pierrot Lunaire* in being in strict rhythms and with a fixed pitch. **1968** *Ibid.* 31 Oct. 591/2 Berg's strict distinction between Schoenbergian *sprechstimme* and half-sung phrases frequently receives cavalier treatment. **1982** *Times Lit. Suppl.* 25 June 693/2 His words are shared out among the whole company, cowled and carrying candles, like a coven going in for *sprechstimme*.

† **'Sprecious.** *Obs.* Also s'pretious, sprecious. [See GOD *sb.* 14 a and PRECIOUS *a.* 2 b.] Shortened form of *God's precious* used as an asseveration or oath.

1610 B. JONSON *Alch.* II. i, 'Sprecious!—What do you mean? **1614** —— *Barth. Fair* I. v, To seeke mee?.. S'pretious—to seeke me! **1632** BROME *Crt. Beggar* II. i, Sprecious! How now! my Fob has been fubd to-day of six pieces.

'spreckle. *Sc.* and *north.* Also 6 spraikle. [= MHG. *spreckel*, *sprekel*, obs. or dial. G. *spreckel*, *spräckel*, *sprackel*, Sw. *spräckla*, Norw. *sprekla*: cf. next.] A speck or speckle.

1513 DOUGLAS *Æneid* v. ii. 90 Of freklit spraiklis all hir bak schone, As golden mailȝeis hir scalis glitterand brycht. **1866–** in Sc. and north. dial. glossaries.

spreckled ('sprɛk(ə)ld), *ppl. a.* Now *dial.* Also 6 sprekled. [Cf. prec. and G. (obs. or dial.) *gespreckelt* (also *sprecklicht*, *-lig*, etc.), Da. *spraglet*, MSw. *spräklott*, Norw. *spreklutt*, Icel. *sprek͏lóttr*.] Speckled.

1535 COVERDALE *Jer.* xii. 8 As a spreckled byrde, a byrde of dyuerse coloures. —— *Zech.* i. 8 Behynde him were there reade, spreckled and whyte horses. **1786** BURNS *To Mount. Daisy* ii, The bonie Lark,..Wi's spreckl'd breast. **1825–** in dial. glossaries (N. Cy., Yks., Lancs., Linc., E. Ang., Nhp., Warw.). **1833** *Wauldby Farm Rep.* 109 in *Husb.* (L.U.K.) III, Three bushels of the spreckled or partridge peas. **1850** J. STRUTHERS *Poet. Wks.* I. p. cxxiv, The spreckled daisy and the pale primrose. *a* **1867** MRS. E. SMITH *Mem. Highl. Lady* x. (1898) 177 He was called the Spreckled Laird on account of being marked with the smallpox.

spred(e, obs. forms of SPREAD *sb.* and *v.*

spree (spriː), *sb.* Chiefly *colloq.* [A slang word of obscure origin: cf. SPRAY *sb.*[4]]

1. a. A lively or boisterous frolic; an occasion or spell of somewhat disorderly or noisy enjoyment (freq. accompanied by drinking). Also *transf.* and as *shopping*, *spending spree*, etc. (see under the first element).

1804 TARRAS *Poems* 73 I'm blythe to see a rantin spree. **1810** *Sporting Mag.* XXXV. 69 Wednesday —— wanted a spree. **1840** E. E. NAPIER *Scenes & Sports For. Lands* II. v. 145 A stanch sportsman, always foremost in a spree of this kind. **1856** B. TAYLOR *North. Trav.* 34 The little public square..was crowded with people, many of whom had already commenced their Christmas sprees. **1878** BESANT & RICE *Celia's Arb.* xxii, We went ashore, the men had a spree, and the officers made themselves agreeable to the young ladies.

transf. **1849** MRS. CARLYLE *New Lett. & Mem.* (1903) II. 4, I have taken a spree of Novel reading, too. **1955** *Times* 29 Aug. 11/1 What has been described as a profit boom and a dividend spree is being used to foster the idea that wage claims can be advanced one after the other without respite. **1976** J. SNOW *Cricket Rebel* 21 A six-hitting spree by Jim Pressdee who..made 115. **1983** *Times* 22 Feb. 17/2 (*heading*) Kellock joins own shares buying spree.

b. *spec.* A more or less prolonged bout or spell of drinking; a drunken carousal.

Not always clearly separable from prec.

1811 *Lexicon Balatronicum*, *Spree*,..a drinking bout. **1854** *Poultry Chron.* II. 381 The cock was half seas over, or in other words, drunk, and having a regular spree. **1890** 'R. BOLDREWOOD' *Col. Reformer* (1891) 132 A strong man gets over it..till the time of the next spree comes round.

c. In the phrases ***on a spree***, ***on*** or ***upon the spree***.

(*a*) **1847** *Illustr. Lond. News* 10 July 27/3 The balloon looked something like the dome of St. Paul's out on a spree. **1865** HOLLAND *Plain Talk* v. 168 It is further complained that operatives drink and go on sprees. **1880** WEBB *Goethe's Faust* II. vi. 144 She's out on a spree!

(*b*) **1851** MAYHEW *Lond. Labour* I. 446 We were too fond of what was called getting on the spree. **1859** *Slang Dict.* 99 'Going on the spree,' starting out with intent to have a frolic. **1892** STEVENSON *Across the Plains* 113 The cheap young gentleman upon the spree.

2. Rough amusement, merrymaking, or sport; prolonged drinking or carousing; indulgence or participation in this.

1808 JAMIESON, *Spree*, innocent merriment. **1828** *Sporting Mag.* XXIII. 34, I will give you a frequent line on the spree of the West. **1899** F. T. BULLEN *Log Sea-waif* 291 The captain..did not return for several days, being supposed..to have entered upon a steady course of spree.

Hence **spree** *v. intr.*, to have or take part in a spree; also with *it* and *trans.*, to spend (money) recklessly; **'spreeing** *vbl. sb.*, indulgence or participation in a spree or sprees; also *attrib.*; **'spreeish** *a.*, given to indulgence in sprees; slightly intoxicated; also *absol.*

1825 C. WESTMACOTT *Eng. Spy* I. 382 The spreeish or the sprightly. **1845** in N. E. Eliason *Tarheel Talk* (1956) iv. 137 They both had been spreeing it the evening before with some members of Congress. **1855** MRS. GASKELL *North & S.* xvii, I've longed for to be a man to go spreeing, even if it were only a tramp to some new place in search o' work. **1859** BARTLETT *Dict. Amer.* (ed. 2) 438 *To spree it*, to get intoxicated. **1860** Spreeing [see BUMMING *vbl. sb.*]. **1864** RAMSBOTTAM *Lanc. Rhymes* 38 While aw'd brass, aw'r sure to spree. **1874** ELMSLIE in *Brit. Wkly.* (1911) 2 Nov. 138/3 We generally 'spree together', whenever we can find time. **1885** 'MARK TWAIN' *Let.* 11 Sept. (1917) II. 457 The drunkenness (and sometimes pretty reckless spreeing) ceased before he came East. **1888** *Times* (weekly ed.) 16 Nov. 3/4 [She was] not drunk, but..a little spreeish. **1890** GUNTER *Miss Nobody* x, Paying their spreeing expenses when occasion offered. *Ibid.* xvii, After the wicked has been spreeing, gaming, and tooting all night. **1897** 'MARK TWAIN' *Following Equator* i. 33 It was the remittance-man's custom to..spree away the rest of his money in a single night. **1907** G. B. SHAW *Let.* 27 July (1972) II. 703 The guarantee fund shall not be drawn upon for current expenses at the Savoy (Barker would spree it on a single scene in Peer Gynt). **1928** —— *Intelligent Woman's Guide Socialism* lxiv. 296 They destroy the sense of security which induces the possessors of spare money to invest it instead of spreeing it.

spreed(e, obs. or dialect forms of SPREAD *v.*

spreet, variant of SPRIT *sb.*

spreet(e, obs. varr. SPRITE.

spreet-sail, obs. f. SPRIT-SAIL.

spreeu, var. SPREW[2].

sprein, obs. f. SPRAIN *sb.*

spreit, obs. var. SPRITE.

‖ **spreite** ('ʃpraɪtə). *Palæont.* Also Spreite. Pl. spreiten. [Ger., a layer of lamina, esp. something extending between two supports.] A banded pattern of uncertain origin found in the infill of the burrows of certain fossil invertebrates.

1962 W. HÄNTZSCHEL in R. C. Moore *Treat. Invertebrate Paleont.* W. 182/2 The vast majority of trace fossils remain unchanged through the geologic eras. This is true for nondescript, smooth furrow-like crawling trails and cylindrical burrows, as well as for more distinctive U-shaped burrows with *Spreite*. *Ibid.* 200/1 *Gyrophyllites*.., vertical shaft from which rosettes of short, simple (feeding) tunnels radiate at different levels, as in a mine; 'leaves' with sculpture of *Spreiten* burrows. **1976** *Nature* 17 June 576/2 The burrow walls are laminated parallel to the long axis of the burrow, and the infill exhibits a cuspate ('spreite') structure.., probably indicating active backfilling by the animal responsible.

spreitles, var. SPRITELESS *a. Obs.*

sprekelia (sprɛˈkiːlɪə). [mod.L. (L. Heister *Systema Plantarum Generale* (1748) 5), f. the name of J. H. von *Sprekelsen* (d. 1764) who sent bulbs of the plant to Linnæus + -IA[1].] A bulbous plant of the monotypic genus so called, belonging to the family Amaryllidaceæ, native to Mexico, and bearing linear leaves and large crimson flowers; = *Jacobæa lily* s.v. JACOBÆA 2.

1840 *Edwards's Bot. Reg.* XXVI. 33 (*heading*) The Tumbler Sprekelia, shorter-flowered variety. **1962** *Amateur Gardening* 10 Mar. 33/2 Sprekelia..takes us to..Mexico... The oddly shaped flowers with three erect and three drooping petals are deep crimson. **1975** *Country Life* 16 Jan. 158/3 Dormant sprekelia bulbs will be..replanted.

sprencle, obs. f. SPRINKLE *v.*

†ˈ**sprendle.** *Obs.*[−1] [Cf. WFlem. *sprendel* splinter.] ? A split piece of wood.

1465 *Mann. & Househ. Exp.* (Roxb.) 566 The said Barkere axsethe alowance for dawbynge, ij.s j.d. Item, for sprendeles, iij.d... Item, for splentes, viij.d.

†**sprenge**, *sb. Obs.*[−1] [f. next.] Sprinkling.

c **1380** WYCLIF *Serm.* Sel. Wks. II. 287 Sprenge [*v.r.* spryngyng] of salt on þis flour is wisdom þat man haþ to serve God in clennesse.

sprenge, *v. Obs.* exc. *arch.* in pa. t. and pa. pple. Pa. t. and pa. pple. **sprent.** Forms: *Inf.* 1 **sprengan, sprængan,** 3–5 **sprengen,** 4–5 **sprenge** (5 **spreinge**). *Pa. t.* 1 **sprengde,** 3 **spreinde,** 4 **sprende, spreynte,** 5, 7 **sprent.** *Pa. pple.* α. 3 **y-sprengd(e,** 3–4 **i-sprengde,** 4 **i-sprenged;** 4 **sprengde, sprengd,** 4–6 **sprenged,** 5 **sprengid(e, spreyngde.** β. 3 **i-spreind(e,** 4 **y-spreynd, y-spraind, spreind(e,** 4–5 **spreynd(e, spreyned,** 5 **spreined;** 4–5 **spreynt(e,** 5 **spreinte,** 5, 7 **spreint.** γ. 4 **sprende,** 5 **sprenct,** 5–7 **sprente,** 5–7, 9 **sprent,** 6 **sprant.** [OE. *spręngan* (:—**sprangjan*, f. the pret. stem of *springan* SPRING *v.*), = OFris. **sprenga* (EFris. *spræng*, NFris. *sprêng*), **sprenza* (WFris. *springzje*), MDu. and Du. *sprengen*, OHG. *sprengan* (MHG. and G. *sprengen*), ON. and Icel. *sprengja* (MSw. *sprängia*, Sw. *spränga*, Da. *sprænge*) to cause to spring, to sprinkle, etc. Cf. BESPRENGE *v.*]

1. *trans.* To sprinkle (a liquid, etc.). Also *absol.*

a **941** *Laws Athelstan* in Thorpe *Laws* I. 226 Spræncge se mæsse-preost haliȝ-wæter ofer hiȝ ealle. *c* **1000** ÆLFRIC *Lev.* iv. 17 Nime se sacerd his blod, and dyppe his finger þær on, and sprenge seofon siðon on þæt ryft. **1382** WYCLIF *Isaiah* lxiii. 3 Sprengd is the blod of hem vp on my clothis. *c* **1386** CHAUCER *Cook's T.* 503 Gamelyn sprengeth holy-water with an oken spire. **1412–20** LYDG. *Chron. Troy* IV. 3668 For she sawe blood spreint so cruelly On hir lordis dredful garnement. *a* **1536** *Songs, Carols*, etc. (1907) 69 The blode ..Was sprente on þe people. **1591** WILMOT *Tancred & Gismund* V. i, The bloud..Sprent on his corps, and on his paled face.

b. To scatter, disperse, distribute, spread abroad or about, etc. Also *absol.*

c **1000** *Ags. Gosp.* Matt. xxv. 24 Þu ripst þær ðu ne seowe & gaderast þær ðu ne sprengdest. *a* **1225** *Ancr. R.* 92 Wuteð to soðe þet euer so þe wittes beoð more ispreinde utwardes, se heo lesse wendet inwardes. **1297** R. GLOUC. (Rolls) 2542 Misbileue in to al þis lond among men was ysprengd. **1382** WYCLIF *Eccl.* iii. 5 Time of sprenging abrod stones, and time of gadering togidere. *c* **1386** CHAUCER *Knt.'s T.* 1311 A fewe freknes in his face y-spreynd. **1642** H. MORE *Song of Soul* II. App. xlviii, What then shall hinder but a roscid air With gentle heat eachwhere be 'sperst and sprent. **1834** LD. HOUGHTON *Mem. Many Scenes* (1844) 30 The diligent flock Tracks out the scant grass that is sprent on the rock. **1855** SINGLETON *Virgil* I. 316 Snowy Paros, and, sprent o'er the main, The Cyclades.

†**c.** To produce by sprinkling. *Obs.*[−1]

c **1290** *S. Eng. Leg.* I. 319 A swyþe foul þing is þat sed of ȝwan Man is i-spreind [*v.r.* þat man is mid i-sprenged].

2. To sprinkle (a person or thing) with some liquid. Also *fig.*

c **1000** ÆLFRIC *Exod.* xxiv. 8 He nam þæt blod and sprengde þæt folc. *Ibid.* xxix. 21 Þu sprengst Aaron and his reaf. *a* **1225** *Ancr. R.* 16 Hwon ȝe beoð al greiðe sprengeð ou mid hali water. *c* **1290** *S. Eng. Leg.* I. 202 Þe prior spreinde [*v.r.* sprende] him with holi water. *c* **1325** *Prose Psalter* l. 8 Þou sprengest me, Lord, wyþ þy mercy. **1382** WYCLIF *Ps.* l. 9 Thou shal sprenge me, Lord, with isope, and I shal ben clensid. **1470–85** MALORY *Arthur* XVII. vii. 699 A grete company of angels..took water whiche was broughte by an angel..and sprente alle the shyp. **1495** *Trevisa's Barth. De P.R.* IX. vi. 352 By nyghte somer bredyth dewe..and sprengyth [*Bodl. MS.* springeþ] therwyth grasse and herbes. **1578** T. PROCTER *Gorg. Gallery* in *Heliconia* (1815) I. 46 For fate..My youthly Yeares with tears hath sprent.

absol. *c* **1380** *Sir Ferumb.* 3291 Þer-wiþ sche mellede vynegre anon..þar þat fyr was setled on þe walle; oueral þer-with sche spreynte.

†**b.** To cleanse by or as by sprinkling. *rare.*

1382 WYCLIF *Heb.* x. 22 We, spreynt [*v.r.* sprengd] the hertis fro yuel conscience,..holde the confessioun of oure hope. [**1388** Be oure hertis spreined fro an yuel conscience.]

3. In *pa. pple.* and const. *with*: Besprinkled, besprent.

1382 WYCLIF *Numb.* vii. 19 A silueren fiole..ful of tryed flour spreynt with oyle. *c* **1400** N. LOVE *Bonavent. Mirr.* i. (1908) 265 The crosse of oure lorde that was than spreyned with his preciouse..blood. *c* **1489** CAXTON *Blanchardyn* vi. 25 The gentyl mayde..ful sprenct wyth grete teerys. **1540–54** CROKE *13 Ps.* (Percy Soc.) 6 My bed with tears is over sprent. **1596** SPENSER *F.Q.* IV. ii. 18 Streames of bloud did rayle Adowne,..That all the ground with purple bloud was sprent. **1600** HOLLAND *Livy* IV. xiv. 149 Being spreint with his blood thus slaine. *a* **1618** SYLVESTER *Maiden's Blush* 516 Hee teares his hoary haire, With Ashes sprent. [**1825** BROCKETT *N.C. Gloss.*, *Sprent*, bespattered, splashed with dirt.]

b. With reference to colour.

1382 WYCLIF *Gen.* xxx. 39 The sheep shulden..beere spotty, and speckid, and spreyned with dyuers colour. **1552** *Inv. Ch. Surrey* (1869) 88 A vestment of blewe velvyt with a crosse of redde velvyt sprenged with gold. *c* **1563** *Thersytes* in Hazl. *Dodsley* I. 425 The spere of spanysshe spylbery sprente wt spiteful spottes. **1590** SPENSER *F.Q.* II. xii. 45 Other where the snowy substaunce [was] sprent With vermell. **1867** M. ARNOLD *Thyrsis* Poems (1877) II. 216 The cheek grown thin, the brown hair sprent with grey. **1883** R. BRIDGES *Prometheus* 1146 Gay-spun garments sprent with gold.

c. In fig. use.

c **1374** CHAUCER *Boethius* (1868) 42 Þe swetnesse of mannes welefulnesse is yspranid [*sic*] wiþ manye bitternesses. *c* **1386** —— *Man of Law's T.* 422 To worldly blisse spreynd with bitternesse. ? *a* **1450** LYDG. *Ord. of Fools* (Cott.) 30 Tonge spreynte with suger, the galle kepte secrete. **1513** DOUGLAS *Æneid* IV. i. 43 Quhar that our hous with broderis deid wes sprent.

Hence †**sprenged** *ppl. a.*, †ˈ**sprenging** *vbl. sb.*

1382 WYCLIF *Exod.* xii. 34 Thanne the puple tok sprengid meel, or it were sowrid. —— *Num.* xix. 9 Thei ben to the multitude..into water of sprengynge. —— *1 Pet.* i. 2 In to halewinge of the spirit, in to obedience, and sprengynge of the blood of Jhesu Crist, grace and pees to ȝou be multiplied.

sprenge, obs. f. SPRING, SPRINGE *sb.*

Sprengel (ˈʃprɛŋ(ə)l). The name of Hermann Johannes Philip *Sprengel* (1834–1906), German-born English chemist, used *attrib.* and in the possessive to denote devices developed by him, as **Sprengel('s) (air, mercury) pump**, a vacuum pump in which exhaustion is produced by trapping bubbles of gas between short columns of mercury falling down a narrow vertical tube; also *absol.*; **Sprengel('s) tube**, a glass U-tube that narrows to a capillary at each end, used to determine the specific gravity of a liquid by weighing the tube when filled with the liquid and then with water at the same temperature.

1868 *Chem. News* 7 Feb. 73/2 Could any one give me information about the dimensions for a Sprengel air pump, and the quantity of mercury required. I wish to use it for exhausting vacuum tubes for a 4-inch spark induction coil. **1868** E. ATKINSON tr. *Ganot's Physics* (ed. 3) 144 Sprengel's air pump. **1879** *Jrnl. Chem. Soc.* XXXVI. 197 The use of Sprengel's tube..has given much better results [than a specific gravity bottle]. **1883** *Encycl. Brit.* XVI. 31/1 One [improvement]..is to pass the mercury, before it enters the 'falling' tube, through a bulb in which a good vacuum is maintained, by means of an ordinary air-pump or a second 'Sprengel'. **1890** *Rep. Brit. Assoc. Adv. Sci. 1889* 232 The density of ice and of water at various temperatures may then be determined, a Sprengel tube—which is easily made—being used for warm water. **1906** *Chem. News* 19 Jan. 28/2 It is by the well-known Sprengel mercury pump that his name will be best remembered. **1932** *Proc. R. Soc.* A. CXXXV. 514 A continuously operating Sprengel pump.. removed the gas from that part of the apparatus..and delivered it, without loss, into the Töpler pump. **1934** *Analyst* LIX. 172 The under-surface of the arms of the Sprengel tube is made of white enamel glass. **1962** J. THEWLIS *Encycl. Dict. Physics* V. 715/1 The Sprengel pump was used extensively in the early days of vacuum experimentation. It is now obsolete, because its rate of working is very low and the ultimate vacuum reached only of the order of 10^{-5} mm mercury.

†**sprenges.** *Obs.*[−1] [Of doubtful origin.] A disease of cattle.

The passage does not occur in the Latin original.

1577 B. GOOGE *Heresbach's Husb.* III. (1586) 134 There is a disease called the Sprenges, wherein he will smite his head backwarde to his Belly, and stampe with his Legges.

†**sprengles.** *Obs.*[−1] [app. repr. OE. **sprengels*, f. *sprengan* SPRENGE *v.* Cf. G. *sprengel* and SPRINGEL.] A sprinkler.

1395 *E. E. Wills* (1882) 5 An haliwater pot, with the sprengls.

sprenkle, sprenkyll(e, obs. ff. SPRINKLE.

†**sprent**, *sb.*[1] *Obs. rare.* [Of obscure origin.] ? A young turbot or other flat-fish.

1324–5 *Durh. Acc. Rolls* (Surtees) 14 In 12 Rayes, 9 Sprentes de t[r]botes;..3 Sprentes de t[r]botes, 6 kelinges. *Ibid.*, In..12 torbotes sprentes [*pr.* sprontes. Cf. **1531–2** *Durh. Househ.-bk.* (Surtees) 122, 5 lyngs, 1 but, et 1 butspreynte. **1532–3** *Ibid.*, 3 lyngs et 3 butsprents.].

sprent, *sb.*[2] *north.* and *Sc.* [f. SPRENT *v.* Cf. Icel. *sprettr* a short gallop, Norw. *sprett* a sprinkle, splash, etc.]

1. †**a.** A sprinkler. *Obs.*[−1]

14.. in J. R. Boyle *Hedon* (1875) App. 120 Pro factura.. iij. sprentes et j. kilpe pro le haliwater.

b. A sprinkle; a spot or stain caused by sprinkling. Chiefly *north. dial.*

1860 HOLME LEE *Leg. fr. Fairy Land* 1 This gossamer was finer than any spider's web, and all over it were sprents of dew. **1865–** in Yks. and Lancs. glossaries.

2. a. A spring, leap, bound.

1513 DOUGLAS *Æneid* XI. xiv. 68 The serpent..In lowpyt thrawis wrythis wyth mony a sprent. **1887** in DARLINGTON *S. Chesh. Gloss.*

b. A spring of a lock, etc. Also *fig.*

1621 LD. DUNFERMLINE in G. Seton *Mem.* (1882) 130, I find me now far remoued from the springs or sprentis that mouis all the resortis off our gouerment. **1645** RUTHERFORD *Tryal & Tri. Faith* (1845) 31 When there is a stone in the sprent and in-work of the lock, the key cannot open the door. **1808** JAMIESON s.v., The back sprent of a clasping knife.

c. (See quot.)

1710 RUDDIMAN *Gloss. Douglas' Æneis* s.v., We use the word *sprent*, for the spring, or elastick force of any thing.

3. The fastening or hasp of a chest, trunk, etc. Also *attrib.*

1511 *Acc. Ld. High Treas. Scot.* IV. 276 For expens maid ..one the said organis..in naillis and sprentis of irne. **1570** *Henry's Wallace* IV. 238 Wraithly till it [the door] he went; Be force of handis it raisit out of the sprent [*v.r.* stent]. **1644** in *Trans. Antiq. Soc. Scot.* (1792) I. 174 A key and sprent band. **1808** in JAMIESON. **1855–** in Yks. and Northumbld. glossaries. **1875** W. WELSH *Poet. & Prose Wks.* 67 Open that auld kist wi' the sprent.

4. A springe or snare.

1822 *Lonsdale Mag.* III. 13 (E.D.D.) Catching partridges and woodcocks in sprents. **1878–** in Cumberland glossaries.

sprent, *v.* Now only *north. dial.* and *Sc.* Also 9 Sc. **spraint.** [a. early Scand. **sprenta* (ON. and Icel. *spretta*, Norw. *spretta*, Sw. *sprätta*, Da. *sprætte*), the causal weak vb. corresponding to **sprinta* SPRINT *v.*, but in Eng. chiefly used intransitively.]

1. *intr.* Of persons, animals, etc.: To spring, spring forward, jump, leap; to move quickly or with agility.

Freq. in the 15th c.; usually in the past tense and const. with advs. and preps.

α. **13..** *Cursor M.* 12527 (Gött.), A nedder sprent vte of þe sand, And stanged iame. **13..** *Gaw. & Gr. Knt.* 1896 As he sprent ouer a spenné, to spye þe schrewe. **1375** BARBOUR *Bruce* XII. 49 Than sprent thai sammyn in-till a lyng. ? *a* **1400** *Morte Arth.* 3311 Bot ȝit he sprange and sprente, and spraddene his armes. *a* **1450** *Le Morte Arth.* 1846 To the chambyr dore he sprente. *Ibid.* 1892 The kynghtis sprent as they were wode. **1508** DUNBAR *Gold. Targe* 242 Wyth spirit affrayde apon my fete I sprent. **1513** DOUGLAS *Æneid* XI. xiii. 158 And furth scho sprent as spark of gleid or fyre. **1585–90** J. STEWART *Poems* (S.T.S.) II. 59 Quho mycht be formest, formest sprent away. *Ibid.* 65 Vith na les speid than this my pen may sprent.

β. **1804** TARRAS *Poems* 73 I'm content to see ye spraint, Right free o' dool an' care. **1897** LD. E. HAMILTON *Outlaws Marches* i. 3 Here am I sprainting after ye this mile past.

†**b.** Of things, esp. blood: To spring, fly, spurt *out* or *about*. *Obs.*

c **1325** *MS. Tiberius E. vii.* fol. 70 Þair mowthes er like a pot welland, Wharof hate dropes ay sprentes out. *c* **1340** HAMPOLE *Pr. Consc.* 6814 Thurgh sparkes of fire þat obout sal sprent. *c* **1400–50** *Alexander* 743 Als sprent of my spittyng a specke on þi chere, þou sall be diȝt to þe deth. *a* **1470** HARDING *Chron.* CXV. ix, The bloodde..sprent out, all hote and newe, Into his eyen.

†**c.** Of smell: To arise, issue; to be given out or forth. *Obs. rare.*

c **1480** WATTON *Spec. Chr.* 46 b, Their oyle was medled with swete oynement Out of whiche swete sauour sprent. **1513** DOUGLAS *Æneid* XII. Prol. 142 Redolent odour vp from rutis sprent.

†**d.** To sprout or shoot. *Obs. rare*[−0].

1647 HEXHAM I, To Sprout or sprent; *siet boven* to Spring.

†**2.** To spring by breaking or splitting; to shiver *in* or *into* splinters. *Obs.*

c **1400** *Destr. Troy* 7248 And aither lede full lyuely lachit vpon other, þat his speire alto sprottes sprent hom betwene. *c* **1470** HENRY *Wallace* x. 23 Than speris sone all in to splendrys sprent. *c* **1475** *Rauf Coilȝear* 819 Their speiris in splenders away Abufe thair heid sprent.

3. *trans.* To sprinkle, spatter, or splash.

1788 W. H. MARSHALL *Yorksh.* II. 355 To *Sprent*, to splash or smear with small spots. **1835** CLARE *Rural Muse* 36 What hour the dewy morning's infancy..sprents the red thighs of the humble bee. **1855** [ROBINSON] *Whitby Gloss.*, *To Sprint* or *Sprent*, to splash, to bespot, or squirt upon with a fluid. **1894** HESLOP *Northumbld. Gloss.* 680 Yo'r sprentin the watter aal ower the place.

Hence †ˈ**sprenting** *vbl. sb.*, a springing, a leap.

1432–50 tr. *Higden* (Rolls) I. 369 Also there be in Yrlonde iij. weres,..ouer whom salmones wylle passe þro a sprentenge.

sprent(e, pa. t. and pa. pple. SPRENGE *v.*

spreot, obs. form of SPRIT *sb.*[1]

spret. *Sc.* and *north. dial.* Also **sprett.** [Obscurely related to SPRAT *sb.*[3] See also SPREAT and SPRIT *sb.*[3]] A kind of rush, esp. the joint-leaved rush; coarse, reedy, or rush-like grass; a stalk or stem of this.

1397–8 *Durham Acc. Rolls* (Surtees) 215 Pro sprettis et stramine emp. pro tectura. **1777** LIGHTFOOT *Flora Scot.* II. 1131 *Juncus articulatus*,..Sprett. **1794** *Statist. Acc. Scot.* XIII. 583 On part of it grows a coarse kind of grass called sprett, which is cut by the farmers for hay. **1808** in JAMIESON. **1870** *United Presbyt. Mag.* 199 All the houses received a fresh covering of rushes or sprett every year. **1878** *Proc. Berw. Nat. Club* VIII. 452 The earliest plants that appear, which are known by the vernacular names of moss, ling, spret, &c. **1894** in HESLOP *Northumbld. Wds.*

Hence ˈ**spretty** *a.*, of the nature of spret; full of, producing or growing, spret.

1808 FORSYTH *Beauties Scotl.* V. 298 Spretty coarse grass is not easily killed by frost. **1878** *Proc. Berw. Nat. Club* VIII.

453 *Spretty-grasses*, a general term for the succulent products of meadow or bog-land, but chiefly for the different rushes (*Juncus*) which are cut for bog-hay. **1882** J. WALKER *Jaunt to Auld Reekie* 240 Our bard Through spretty fields his shining plough-shares drave.

spret, obs. var. SPRIT *sb.*[1], SPRITE *sb.*, obs. f. 3rd pers. sing. pres. indic. of SPREAD *v.*

sprete, obs. var. SPRITE *sb.*[1] and *v.*

sprete seyle, obs. f. SPRITSAIL.

†**spreth**, *a. Obs.*−[1] [prob. related to G. *spröde* (obs. and dial. *spröd, spred*, etc.), WFlem. *sprooi*, brittle, weak.] Frail, liable to sin.

c **1315** SHOREHAM IV. 50 þanne ich may wyssy ase ich can, Mi self þaȝ ich be spreþ, þat [etc.].

spretlesse, var. SPRITELESS *a. Obs.*

sprett(e, obs. varr. SPRIT *sb.*, SPRITE *sb.*

spretuall, var. SPRITUAL *a. Obs.*

sprety, obs. var. SPRITY *a.*

spreuere, var. of SPERVER *Obs.*

spreul, north. and Sc. var. SPRAWL *v.*

sprew, var. of SPRUE *sb.*[1]

†**sprew**[1]. *Obs.*−[1] [Of obscure origin: cf. MHG. *sprêwen, spreuwen*, G. *spreuen*, to sprinkle.] Spray.

1633 T. JAMES *Voy.* 117 The Cables began to freeze in the house and the Ship to be frozen over with the sprewe of the Sea.

sprew[2] (spru:). *S. African.* Also spreeu, spreo, spreuw. [ad. Du. *spreeuw* starling.] A bird belonging to the genus *Spreo* (of the family *Sturnidæ*), esp. *S. bicolor*, characterized by its iridescent plumage; a glossy starling.

1795 C. R. HOPSON tr. *C. P. Thunberg's Trav. Europe, Africa & Asia* (ed. 2) II. 48 A kind of *Corvus*, (or crow) called *Spreuw*, was found.. in great plenty. **1801** [see FISCAL *sb.* 3]. **1867** E. L. LAYARD *Birds S. Afr.* 173 The red-wing spreo, aided by finches,.. would soon pick the crop [of grapes]. **1897** ANNE PAGE *Afternoon Ride* 58 The golden-green gleam on the wing of a sprew. **1913** J. J. DOKE *Secret City* 229 'Jolly fine birds, spreeuws,' he said. **1939** S. CLOETE *Watch for Dawn* 106 A spreeu dug its beak into some half-dried dung for the fly-worms that were in it. **1961** B. C. TAIT *Durban Story* 69 Blue-black sprews flash above incredibly green lawns.

sprewce, sprews(e, obs. ff. SPRUCE, PRUSSIA(N.

sprewl, north. and Sc. var. SPRAWL *v.*

sprey, variant of SPRAY, spree.

spreynd(e, spreynt(e, obs. pa. t. or pa. pple. of SPRENGE *v.*

spreyt(e, obs. varr. SPRITE *sb.*

spreytles, var. SPRITELESS *a. Obs.*

‖**sprezzatura** (ˌsprɛttsaˈtura). [It.] Ease of manner, studied carelessness; the appearance of acting or being done without effort; *spec.* of literary style or performance.

1957 N. FRYE *Anat. Criticism* 93 The quality that the Italian critics called *sprezzatura*. **1960** E. H. GOMBRICH *Art & Illusion* III. vi. 193 *Sprezzatura*, the nonchalance which marks the perfect courtier and the perfect artist. **1960** *Spectator* 14 Oct. 569 The style governed by *sprezzatura*, dash and mandarin neoclassicism. **1973** *Times Lit. Suppl.* 14 Sept. 1063/2 Literary fashion and his own aristocratic *sprezzatura* demanded that he affect an unconcern.

sprig (sprɪg), *sb.*[1] Also 4-5 sprigge, 5-6 spryg(ge, 6 sprygg, 9 sprigg. [Of obscure origin.]

1. A small slender nail, either wedge-shaped and headless, or square-bodied with a slight head on one side. †Also *collect.*

In both senses, but now especially in the second, indentical with a *brad.*

1359 [see *transom-nail* s.v. TRANSOM 7]. **1426-7** *Rec. St. Mary at Hill* (1905) 65 Also for y^c^ sprygge þe same day, iiij d. **1480** *Wardr. Acc. Edw. IV* (1830) 122 To Piers Draper for M[l] sprigge price vj d. **1539-40** in *Archaeol. Cant.* (1893) XX. 243, 2 'some' of 'sprygg' 10s. **1552** *Churchw. Acc. St. Michaels, Cornhill* (MS.), For nayles and sprygs to the setting up of the new pewe. **1653** HOLCROFT *Procopius, Goth. Wars* III. 97 They fit to one another the blunt ends of foure Iron sprigs, of equall length. **1688** HOLME *Armoury* III. 51 Brad is a Nail without a head to floor Rooms withall; it is with us termed a Sprig, and is about the size of a ten penny Nail. **1713** J. WARDER *True Amazons* xiii. 117 Some two-penny Dove Nails, or small Hinges, with some Nails and three-penny Sprigs. **1796** STEDMAN *Surinam* I. 109 After having had iron sprigs driven home underneath every one of his nails on hands and feet. **1844** H. STEPHENS *Bk. Farm* I. 117 Battens.. fastened down to stout joists with Scotch flooring sprigs driven through the feather-edge. **1875** *Carpentry & Join.* 64 The bottom of the drawer is to be.. secured by a small brad or sprig to the back.

b. *Naut.* (See quot.)

1794 *Rigging & Seamanship* 10 *Sprig*, a small eye-bolt, ragged at the point.

c. A wedge-shaped piece of tin used to hold glass in a sash until the putty dries.

1823 P. NICHOLSON *Pract. Build.* 422 Large squares should be further secured by small sprigs being driven into the rebates of the sash. **1875** *Carpentry & Join.* 106 Let a sprig be put in under each as it is put in place—before it is puttied.

2. A small projecting part or point. Also *spec.* (chiefly *N.Z.*), a stud or spike attached to the sole of a boot, esp. in *Sport.*

1679 MOXON *Mech. Exerc.* VII. ¶3 Carpenters have their Shank made with an hollow Socket at its top, to receive a strong wooden Sprig made to fit into that Socket. **1683** *Ibid., Printing* xi. ¶21 An Iron Stud with a square Sprig under it, to be drove and fastned into a Wooden Horse. **1688** HOLME *Armoury* III. xxi. (Roxb.) 263/2 The Sprig or Pin of the handle is commonly set into the tip of an Harts Horn for its halve. **1847** HALLIW. s.v., A triangular piece of iron is screwed to their shoe-heels, having three points half an inch long projecting downwards. These are called sprigs. **1930** [implied at SPRIG *v.*[1] 1]. **1949** D. M. DAVIN *Roads from Home* I. ii. 27 John hammered the last tack into a sprig of his football boots. **1972** *Guardian* 11 Nov. 21/5 You look at Sid [Going] when we're changing, he's got sprig (stud) marks all over him. **1981** I. A. GORDON in *N.Z. Listener* 2-8 May, The *sprig* (though it has acquired a new meaning on the football field), was originally a short headless nail.

3. *attrib.* and *Comb.*, as ***sprig-box, maker, -nail***; **sprig-awl, -bit**, a bradawl.

1477-9 *Rec. St. Mary at Hill* (1905) 84 For iij quarters Sprygge nayle, iij d ob. *c* **1480** *Ibid.* 104 For m[l] di. Sprygge nayle. **1609-10** in Swayne *Sarum Churchw. Acc.* (1896) 306 Sprigge nayles for the stepps, 12 d. **1688** HOLME *Armoury* III. 298/1 A Nail, (of some termed a Sprig Nail, because without a Head). **1797** *J. Robinson's Directory Sheffield* 63 Dickinson, Enoch, sprig maker. **1798** W. HUTTON *Life* 17 A fork, with one limb, was made to act in the double capacity of sprig-awl and gimlet. **1815** J. SMITH *Panorama Sci. & Art* I. 116 The smallest sort of boring tool is a kind of bodkin, called the brad-awl, or sprig-bit. **1896** 'J. ACKWORTH' *Clog Shop Chron.* 34 As he bent over his work a great tear splashed down into the sprig-box before him.

sprig (sprɪg), *sb.*[2] Also 4, 6-7 sprigge (6 sprygge), 7 sprigg. [Of obscure origin; relationship to LG. *sprick*, dry twig, is doubtful.]

1. a. A shoot, twig, or spray of a plant, shrub, or tree; †a rod.

14.. *Langland's P. Pl.* C. VI. 139 Ho so spareþ þe spring [*v.r.* sprigge] spilleþ hus children. **1555** EDEN *Decades* (Arb.) 228 This.. sprygge whiche bryngeth foorth the sayde cluster is a hole yeare in growyng. **1578** LYTE *Dodoens* 681 The flowers grow amongst the leaues, uppon the young sprigges or sprayes. **1624** CAPT. SMITH *Virginia* II. 31 Their arrowes are made some of straight young sprigs, which they head with bone. **1676** GREW *Anat. Pl., Anat. Fl.* (1682) 152 Where there are several Sprigs upon one Stem, as in Fenil, Hemlock, and the like. **1728-46** THOMSON *Spring* 162 Herds and flocks Drop the dry sprig, and, mute imploring, eye The falling verdure. **1827** G. HIGGINS *Celtic Druids* 34 The Druids pretended to perform various operations by means of sticks, sprigs, or branches of trees. **1856** in Delamer *Fl. Garden* 122 This beautiful Jasmine is.. very useful for cutting for bouquets, and the sprigs will last in water a long time.

fig. **1580** T. M. *Pref. Verses* 40 in Baret *Alv.*, There grew the floures, that Tullie first did see, There sprang the sprigs on which he first did feed.

b. A small spray *of* a particular plant, etc.

1563 T. GALE *Antidot.* II. 41 You maie in the place hereof vse a sprigge of the Oke. **1599** *Warn. Faire Wom.* II. 1072 There came a sprigge of fearne, borne by the wind Into the roome. **1605** SHAKS. *Lear* II. iii. 16 Sprigs of Rosemarie. **1621** MIDDLETON *Sun in Aries* Wks. (Bullen) VII. 348 Peace [is represented] with a branch of laurel; Patience a sprig of palm [etc.]. *a* **1721** PRIOR *Charity never faileth* v, Then how short-liv'd will be thy Praise Like what thou labour'est for, a sprig of Bayes. **1736** BAILEY *Household Dict.* s.v. *Mint*, Two or three sprigs of this mint being drank with the juice of garden mint. **1837** DICKENS *Pickw.* xxviii, Sprigs of holly with red berries.. ornament the window. **1847** H. MILLER *Test. Rocks* (1857) 308 Agate, in some specimens, contains its apparent sprigs of moss.

transf. **1867** F. FRANCIS *Angling* xi. (1880) 411 A few sprigs of green peacock herl.

c. *collect.* (See quot.)

1832 *Planting* 91 in *Husb.* (L.U.K.) III, Sprig of wood.—In some instances understood as the branches of a tree.

2. *fig.* **a.** An offshoot, a minor development, part, or specimen, of something.

1576 FLEMING *Panopl. Epist.* 272 To weede out.. the bitter plant of couetousnesse,.. that of the same not.. one braunch, sprig, leafe nor seede be remaining. **1581** MULCASTER *Positions* xxxv. (1887) 131 Not bowghes and braunches, but euen the twigges and sprigges of the petiest circumstances. **1608** WILLET *Hexapla Exod.* 308 The sprigges and branches of vices. **1660** tr. *Amyraldus' Treat. conc. Relig.* III. iii. 347 So totally rooted out of all the Writings in the World,.. as not one slip or sprig to be left of it. **1815** SCOTT *Guy M.* xxxvii, The following sprig of sepulchral poetry. **1878** BROWNING *Poets Croisic* 139 Never hope to graff a second sprig of triumph there!

b. Applied to persons (usually with disparaging force): A scion *of* some person, class, institution, etc.

1601 CHESTER *Love's Mart.* cx, Yet Fortunes vnseene immortalitie Sometimes cuts downe sprigs of a Monarchie. **1646** QUARLES *Judgem. & Mercy* Wks. (Grosart) I. 76/1 A poore Sprig of disobedient Adam. **1721** AMHERST *Terræ Fil.* No. 36. 188 To hear a smart damsel reprimand a young sprig of learning for his rudeness. **1768** *Wom. of Hon.* II. 202 Are even some of the illustrious sprigs of our Nobility clear of that scoundrel-vice? **1810** *Sporting Mag.* XXXV. 28 Our sprigs of fashion are.. fond of driving the mail. **1847** H. MILLER *First Impr. Eng.* xx. (1857) 353 A zealous sprig of High-Churchism who preached to them. **1883** *Congregationalist* Sept. 731 The pretensions of a pert young sprig of divinity.

c. Without const.: A stripling; a young fellow.

1661 J. DAVIES *Civ. Warres* 365 A young sprig, who had never.. ventured to involve himself in bloud and murthers. **1766** [ANSTEY] *Bath Guide* xi. 127 Th' unfortunate Sprig Seems as if he was hunting all Night for his Wig. **1789** WOLCOT (P. Pindar) *Ep. falling Minister* Wks. 1812 II. 124 Yet was this Youth proclaim'd a pretty Sprig. **1815** SCOTT *Guy M.* liii, A sprig whom I remember with a whey face and a satchel not so very many years ago. **1879** F. W. ROBINSON *Coward Consc.* II. xvii, When.. we were a couple of city sprigs together.

3. †**a.** A branch of a nerve, vein, etc. *Obs.*

1638 A. READ *Chirurg.* xi. 80 If any severall part bee paralytik.. the cause is.. in the sprig of some nerve inserted in that part. **1684** BOYLE *Porousn. Anim. & Solid Bod.* vii. 61 A vein and artery to bring in and carry back Blood.. by distinct sprigs sent from the great branch. **1730** CHAMBERLAYNE *Relig. Philos.* I. ix. §8 This Nerve.. after having sent some Sprigs to the Plexus Nervosus.. ends there.

b. A piece of some substance or material resembling a sprig of a plant.

1660 BOYLE *New Exp. Phys. Mech.* xlii. 384 Half-a-score Sprigs of Coral. **1680** MOXON *Mech. Exerc.* XIII. 222 Some Turners to shew their Dexterity.. Turn long and slender Sprigs of Ivory, as small as an Hay-stalk, and perhaps a Foot or more long. **1758** BORLASE *Nat. Hist. Cornw.* 84 The coralline moss,.. sprig, and bunchy coral dispersed on the rocks. **1787** WOLCOT (P. Pindar) *Apol. Ode upon Ode* Wks. 1812 I. 456 Commanded of dead Hair the sprigs To do their duty upon Wigs. **1839** DE LA BECHE *Rep. Geol. Cornwall*, etc. ii. 31 A conglomerate with a calcareo-magnesian cement, containing sprigs of copper.

4. a. An ornament in the form of a sprig or spray; in later use esp. one made of diamonds.

1591 SYLVESTER *Du Bartas* I. v. 605 Upon her crown a crest Of starrie Sprigs. **1602** MARSTON *Ant. & Mel.* v. Wks. 1856 I. 58, I ha bought mee a newe greene feather with a red sprig. **1629** SHIRLEY *Wedding* II. i, When thou art at the Peacock, remember to call for the sprig. **1639** in *12th Rep. Hist. MSS. Comm.* App. IX. 7 One Great Salt with 4 Boxes, 4 Spriggs, and 1 cover. **1718** *Free-thinker* No. 57. 13 The rich Sprig of Diamonds that sparkles in your Hair. **1756-7** tr. *Keysler's Trav.* (1760) I. 259 The queen had a sprig of diamonds which she usually wore on her bosom. **1806** SURR *Winter in Lond.* II. 157 He, having.. the said family plate,.. lent me.. a sprig for my hair.

b. A design, imitative of a sprig, embroidered, woven, or stamped on a textile fabric, or applied to ceramic ware, etc.

1771 MRS. HARRIS in *Priv. Lett. Ld. Malmesbury* (1870) I. 214 The habit muslin with green and gold sprigs. **1844** G. DODD *Textile Manuf.* vii. 229 In 'sprigged net' the groundwork and a portion of every sprig are made at the machine, and the outline of every sprig is then worked by hand. **1858** LYTTON *What will He do?* I. xiv, What pretty sprigs! Where can such things be got? **1874** H. H. COLE *Catal. Ind. Art S. Kens. Mus.* 250 White ground covered by oval outlined red and green sprigs.

c. A small detached piece of pillow-lace, made separately for subsequent use in composite work.

1851 *Catal. Gt. Exhib.* 560 Brussels and Honiton sprigs, manufactured from cotton thread. **1882** CAULFEILD & SAWARD *Dict. Needlew.* 459/1.

5. *ellipt.* **a.** A silver-sprig rabbit. (See SILVER *sb.* 21 b.)

1859 J. C. ATKINSON *Walks & Talks* 30 The boys understood him to call rabbits of this variety.. by the name of 'sprigs' or 'silver-sprigs'.

b. *U.S.* The sprigtail duck, *Dafila acuta.*

1888 G. TRUMBULL *Names Birds* 38. **1895** *Outing* XXVI. 30/2 Making a blind good enough for any duck except sprig, which are as wary as wild geese.

6. *attrib.* and *Comb.* (chiefly in sense 4 b), as ***sprig-birch, -crystal, -formed, mould, -muslin, -pattern, -silk***, etc.

a **1728** WOODWARD *Fossils* I. 32 This kind the Lapidaries call Peble-Crystal. The Crystallin hexagonal Columns they call Sprig-Crystal. **1748** J. HILL *Hist. Fossils* 172 The common, hexangular, whitish, pellucid Ellipomacrostylum, or sprig Crystal. **1772** *Phil. Trans.* LXII. 399 They feed on grass-seeds, and buds of the sprig-birch. **1775** S. J. PRATT *Liberal Opin.* c. (1783) III. 219 She then mentioned something about sprig silks. **1806** J. GRAHAME *Birds of Scot.* 51 Her sprig-formed nest upon some hawthorn branch Is laid so thinly. **1841** THACKERAY *Gt. Hoggarty Diamond* iii, I recollect I had on.. a white sprig waistcoat. **1874** H. H. COLE *Catal. Ind. Art S. Kens. Mus.* 207 The silver pattern, applied in bands of leaves and in a small sprig diaper. *Ibid.* 262 The central portion of the scarf has a sprig pattern. **1922** HARDY *Late Lyrics & Earlier* 1 And maids come forth sprig-muslin drest. **1951** J. B. KENNY *Compl. Bk. Pottery Making* vii. 123 A sprig mold is a block of plaster with a depression shaped like the ornament in reverse. **1956** G. HEYER (*title*) Sprig muslin. **1976** *Canadian Antiques Collector* (Toronto) Mar.-Apr. 20/1 There were over 22 sprig moulds for making applied decorative relief to pots.

sprig, *a.* [Of obscure origin.] Spruce, smart.

App. still surviving in dialect use (E.D.D.).

1675 COTTON *Scoffer Scoft* 115 For all he wears his beard so sprig, And has a fine Gold Periwig.

sprig, *v.*[1] [f. SPRIG *sb.*[1]]

1. *trans.* To fasten with sprigs or brads. Also with *down, on*, etc., and *spec.* (*N.Z.*), to equip (a boot) with sprigs. Cf. SPRIG *sb.*[1] 2.

1713 J. WARDER *True Amazons* 120 Let all the Pieces and Frames be well sprig'd to this Head. **1840** *Civil Eng. & Arch. Jrnl.* III. 419/1 On the floor is sprigged down a rib of wood. **1871** *Routledge's Ev. Boy's Ann.* 59 The back may be glued and sprigged on to the frame. **1892** *Labour Comm. Gloss.* No. ix, Boys who cannot fit on the parts but can only sprig them together. **1930** C. V. Grimmett *Getting Wickets* v. 105 Had his boots been properly sprigged, it is probable that he would easily have taken the catch.

absol. **1902** *How to Make Things* 61/1 Glue and sprig on.

2. *intr.* To drive in sprigs.

1898 J. Macmanus *Bend of Road* 101 If you spake less an sprig more he'll have his boot the quicker.

Hence **sprigged** *ppl. a.*^{1}; **'sprigging** *vbl. sb.*^{1}

1883 *Goole Wkly. Times* 14 Sept. 4/5 Men's Sprigged Blucher Boots. **1899** *Daily News* 12 May 3/1 When the sprigging of boots, instead of hand-sewing them, came into operation.

sprig, *v.*^{2} [f. sprig *sb.*^{2}]

†**1. a.** *intr.* To form rootlets. *Obs.*$^{-0}$

1611 Cotgr., *Cheveler*, to sprig, or sprigle; to root, or put forth a hairie, or small root.

b. *trans.* To divide into branches.

1658 Bromhall *Treat. Specters* I. 68 Those nerves, which are sprigg'd from the back-bone into the joynts all about.

2. *trans.* To decorate or cover with designs representing sprigs. Also *absol.*

1731 Mrs. Delany *Life & Corr.* (1861) I. 284 A very fine blue satin, sprigged all over with white. **1745–6** *Ibid.* II. 414 Some are so silly, they tell me, as to have them sprigged with silver. **1761** Mrs. F. Sheridan *Sidney Biddulph* V. 237 Dolly was helping Cecilia to sprig some fine muslin that she is now working for an apron. **1850** Kingsley *A. Locke* ii, Wondering when I..should shine..in a blue satin tie sprigged with gold. **1895** *Daily News* 5 June 5/3 The fleur-de-lys..is used to sprig the wide expanse where there is no other decorative design. **1960** H. Powell *Beginner's Bk. Pottery* II. ii. 21 When sprigging, you may find that the small, thin sprigged shapes dry too quickly.

fig. **1830–6** O. W. Holmes *Evening* Poems 1892 I. 21, I can hail the flowers That sprig earth's mantle.

'spriggan. *Cornish dial.* [prob. Cornish.] A sprite, a goblin.

1865 R. Hunt *Pop. Rom. W. Eng.* Ser. I. 66 The Spriggans are found only about the cairns, coits or cromlechs, burrows, or detached stones. **1891** J. H. Pearce *Esther Pentreath* III. viii, She found Aichel watching her as closely as if he were some gruesome spriggan set to guard the old mill or herself.

sprigged, *ppl. a.*^{1}: see sprig *v.*^{1}

sprigged (sprɪgd), *ppl. a.*^{2} [f. sprig *sb.*^{2} or *v.*^{2}]

1. Adorned or ornamented with sprigs.

†**a.** Of feathers. (Cf. sprig *sb.*^{2} 4). *Obs.*

1613 Chapman *Maske Inns Crt.* A ij, On their heads high sprig'd-feathers, compast in Coronets, like the Virginian Princes they presented.

b. Of fabrics, etc.

Very common from *c* 1750.

1701 *Lond. Gaz.* No. 3705/4 Two Pieces of white Sprigg'd India Satin. **1724** S. Sewall *Diary* 5 Apr., My Wife wore her new Gown of Sprig'd Persian. **1775** *Pennsylv. Even. Post* 23 Dec. 592/2 A great variety of flowered, striped and sprigged muslin. **1815** *Zeluca* III. 307 To know if the rent in my sprigged dress is darned. **1874** Symonds *Sk. Italy & Greece* (1898) I. xiv. 296 Her bridal dress of sprigged grey silk. **1888** *Daily News* 5 Nov. 7/1 Silk sprigged nets continue to sell with some freedom.

c. Of ceramic ware: adorned with, or forming, sprigs or other ornaments in applied relief. Cf. sprig *sb.*^{2} 4 b.

1756 J. Bowcocke *Acct. Bk.* in L. Jewitt *Ceramic Art Gt. Brit.* (1878) I. vii. 209 Mr. White: 1 imag'd cup and 7 sprig'd chocolates. **1906** R. L. Hobson *Porcelain of All Countries* xx. 190 The 'sprigged' pattern..consists of sprays of Chinese plum. **1960** [see sprig *v.*^{2} 2]. **1971** L. A. Boger *Dict. World Pott. & Porc.* 323/2 *Sprigged ware*, in English ceramics; a contemporary English name given to 18th century wares decorated in applied reliefs principally of flowers, foliage, and stems.

2. Having the form of a sprig or sprigs; minutely branched.

1714 Gay *Sheph. Week* VI. 135 Sprigg'd rosemary the lads and lasses bore. **1847** *Jrnl. R. Agric. Soc.* VIII. II. 472 The [flax] stalk will abound in small branches, or become, as it is called, 'sprigged'.

'sprigger^1. [f. sprig *sb.*^{1} or *v.*^{1}] One who or that which drives in sprigs.

1881 *Instr. Census Clerks* (1885) 76 Boot and Shoe Making:..Pressman. Sprigger. Rivetter. Tacker. Nailer. **1892** *Labour Comm. Gloss.* No. ix, *Sprigger*, a machine used in the boot industry to make and drive rivets or sprigs into the goods to hold the parts together.

'sprigger^2. [f. sprig *sb.*^{2} or *v.*^{2}] One who ornaments a textile fabric or other material with sprigs.

1888 *Pall Mall G.* 11 July 7/2 Embroiderers, spriggers, and lacemakers.

'sprigging, *vbl. sb.*^{2} [f. sprig *v.*^{2}]

1. The action or occupation of making sprigs in or on textile fabrics. Also *attrib.*

1775 Ash, *Sprigging*, the act of adorning with sprigs. **1886** *Let. Donegal* 25 The collapse of the 'sprigging' business, by which at one time a good embroideress could earn 1*s.* 6*d.* a day. **1888** *Daily News* 2 June 6/1 The now flourishing industry known as sprigging. Six years ago sprigging as a calling was almost extinct.

2. Ornamentation or needlework consisting of sprigs.

1775 Ash, *Sprigging*,..an ornament of sprigs. **1888** *Daily News* 25 May 2/2 Large quantities of Irish-made lace, embroidery, sprigging, &c., are regularly sent to the Continent.

3. The process of decorating ceramic ware with sprigs or other ornaments in applied relief.

1928 W. B. Honey *Old Eng. Porc.* iii. 63 'Sprigging' is the Staffordshire name for the process of applying these reliefs. **1961** L. G. G. Ramsey *Connoisseur New Guide Antique Eng. Pott., Porc. & Glass* 35 The ornament was obtained by 'luting' to the surface of the pot previously moulded relief-motifs, and by connecting these with 'stems' formed of threads of clay rolled out thin between the hands. This whole process was known as 'sprigging'. **1969** G. Wills *Eng. Pott. & Porc.* 102 What is known to potters as 'sprigging'..was done by using a patterned mould made of plaster. The soft clay was pressed into it and the surplus scraped carefully away.

sprigging, *ppl. a.* [Cf. sprig *v.*^{2} 1.] Growing in the form of a sprig or young shoot.

1583 Melbancke *Philotimus* I iv, Sprigging flowers ar in their baine and tender groweth, better for poesies to delight then medicines for diseases.

spriggy ('sprɪgɪ), *a.* [f. sprig *sb.*^{2}] Abounding in sprigs or small branches; suggestive of a sprig or sprigs.

1597 Gerarde *Herbal* 610 The flowers stand at the top of the spriggie braunches. **1611** Cotgr., *Scionneux*,..twiggie, spriggie. **1669** W. Simpson *Hydrol. Chym.* 258 Plants.. begin..to shoot forth spriggy roots. *a* **1722** Lisle *Husb.* (1757) 334, I like not..when the ends of the wool on the backs of the sheep twist, and stand spriggy. *Ibid.* 365 When hazle grows spriggy in the body, and shoots forth from the sides of the bark. **1826** *Blackw. Mag.* XIX. 244 A vine-leaf pattern perhaps—or something spriggy. **1854** Meall *Moubray's Poultry* 71 The comb large with very deeply indented ridge, presenting almost a 'spriggy' appearance.

spright (spraɪt), *sb.*^{1} Also 6 spryght(e. [var. of sprite *sb.*, after native words in *-ight*.]

†**1.** = spirit *sb.* in various senses. *Obs.*

1536 *Primer Hen. VIII*, 2 Blessed be God,..Wch hath strengthened His feeble flock, Wth stedfast faith & bold spright. **1563** Googe *Eglogs* (Arb.) 54, I.. sought the chief[e]st means I could to helpe my weryed spryght. **1601** B. Jonson *Poetaster* III. i, I drinke, as I would wright, In flowing measure, fill'd with flame and spright. *a* **1649** Drumm. of Hawth. *Flowers Sion* v. Wks. (S.T.S.) II. 41 Of this Light, Eternall, double, kindled was thy Spright Eternallie. *c* **1700** Dryden *Cock & Fox* 104 You groan,..As something had disturb'd your noble Spright.

†**b.** *pl.* = spirit *sb.* 17. *Obs.*

1577 *St. Aug. Manual* (Longman) 33 Thou preparest a table..against I come to refresh my appalled sprights. **1596** Spenser *F.Q.* v. iii. 40 Turne we here to this faire furrowes end Our wearie yokes, to gather fresher sprights. **1605** Shaks. *Macb.* IV. i. 127 Come Sisters, cheere we vp his sprights, And shew the best of our delights.

2. A disembodied spirit, a ghost; a supernatural being, goblin, fairy, etc. (Cf. spirit *sb.* 2 b and 3.)

a **1533** Ld. Berners *Huon* cxxxii. 492 Glad was Huon when he had loste the syghte of the spryghte. **1590** Spenser *F.Q.* II. x. 8 Where companing with feends and filthy Sprights,..They brought forth Giants. **1610** Shaks. *Temp.* I. ii. 381 Foote it featly heere, and there, and sweete Sprights beare the burthen. **1687** A. Lovell tr. *Thevenot's Trav.* I. 176, I lay at the foot of that Eminence, and the Sprights did not at all disturb my rest. **1731–8** Swift *Polite Conv.* Introd. 33 Some scrupulous Persons,..who, by a prejudiced Education, are afraid of Sprights. **1813** Hogg *Queen's Wake* 19 Each glen was sought for tales..Of boding dreams, of wandering spright.

transf. **1570** Googe *Pop. Kingd.* I. 4 An Emprour great of might, Whose necke was stampt and trode vpon by this deformed spright [*sc.* the Pope].

†**spright,** *sb.*^{2} *Obs.*$^{-1}$ (See quot.)

1626 Bacon *Sylva* §704 It is certaine, that we had in use at one time, for Sea-Fight, short Arrowes, which they called Sprights, without any other Heads, save Wood sharpened; which were discharged out of Muskets.

†**spright,** *a. Obs.*$^{-1}$? Error for sprightly *a.*

1658 Earl Monm. tr. *Paruta's Wars Cyprus* 125 A spright youth, who..had carried himselfe gallantly in severall offices.

†**spright,** *v. Obs. rare.* [f. spright *sb.*^{1}]

1. *trans.* To haunt, as by a spright.

1611 Shaks. *Cymb.* II. iii. 144, I am sprighted with a Foole, Frighted, and angred worse.

2. To invest with spirit.

1611 J. Davies (Heref.) *Commend. Poems, Coryat* Wks. (Grosart) II. 13/2 To make Eyes delighted With that which by no Art can be more sprighted.

†**sprighted,** *a. Obs. rare.* [f. spright *sb.*^{1}] Having a spirit of a specified kind.

1599 Hakluyt *Voy.* II. 75 A well sprighted man and wise. **1600** Rowlands *Lett. Humours Blood* vii. 84 Enuie's the fourth: a Deuill, dogged sprighted.

sprightful ('spraɪtfʊl), *a.* Now *rare.* Also 5 spryght-. [f. spright *sb.*^{1} Cf. spiritful *a.*]

1. Of persons: Full of spirit; animated, lively.

1595 Shaks. *John* IV. ii. 177 Spoke like a sprightfull Noble Gentleman. **1607** Beaum. & Fl. *Woman Hater* IV. iii, I could be far more sprightful, had I eaten. **1658** Bromhall *Treat. Specters* I. 112 The servant..recovering life, and becoming as sprightful as ever he was. **1692** O. Walker *Grk. & Rom. Hist.* 253 Julia Mœsa,..a Subtil, Prudent, and Sprightful Woman. **1780** Mrs. H. Cowley *Belle's Strat.* 45 Parson Dobbins was the sprightfuller man of the two.

transf. **1591** Sylvester *Du Bartas* I. iii. 226 Our sprightfull Pulse the Tide doth well resemble.

†**b.** Of horses: Spirited. *Obs.*

a **1635** Randolph in R. Dover *Ann. Dubr.* (1636) C iv b, A noble Swayne, That spurr'd his spright-full Palfrey ore the playne. **1656** Cowley *Pindar. Odes, Extasie* ix, The Horses were..The noblest, sprightfulst breed. **1674** Flavel *Husb. Spiritualized* ix. 105 If one should give thee a handsom and sprightful horse.

2. Of actions, sounds, etc.: Marked by spirit, animation, or liveliness.

1628 Feltham *Resolves* II. xiv. 40 Light aires turne vs into sprightfull actions; which breathe away in a loose laughter. **1638** Mayne *Lucian* (1664) 238 Who..thinke they haue done nothing great or sprightfull. **1681–4** J. Scott *Chr. Life* 8 The constant, free, and sprightful Exercise of his Faculties. **1807–8** W. Irving *Salmag.* (1824) 321 Striking up the right jolly and sprightfull tune of *Ca Ira.* **1898** J. M. Cobban *Angel of Covenant* i. 3 'See, Alec!' she cried in that sweet, sprightful voice which always moved me.

†**3.** Of liquids, etc.: Impregnated with spirit; spirituous. *Obs.*

1615 Crooke *Body of Man* 238 These bodies..are full of blacke, thicke and sprightfull blood. **1630** J. Taylor (Water P.) *Farew. Tower Bottles* Wks. III. 125/1 Few Ships my visitation did escape, That brought the sprightfull liquor of the Grape. **1669** Worlidge *Syst. Agric.* (1681) 113 The Pear-tree bears almost its weight of Sprightful Winy Liquor.

Hence **'sprightfully** *adv.*; **'sprightfulness.**

1593 Shaks. *Rich. II*, I. iii. 3 The Duke of Norfolke, *sprightfully and bold, Stayes but the summons of the Appealants Trumpet. **1611** Cotgr., *Vivement*, liuelily, quickly, lightly, sprightfully. **1653** Urquhart *Rabelais* II. xxxix. 299 He so sprightfully carried himself. **1905** *Westm. Gaz.* 23 Sept. 12/1 The girl..who 'enjoys life sprightfully, daringly, and glowingly'. **1648** J. Beaumont *Psyche* XV. ci, He who our brave *sprightfulness could make Of dull and sleepy nothing. **1686** Goad *Celest. Bodies* I. ix. 35 In the Competitorship for Sprightfulness, we find one..surpassed by the other. **1708** *Brit. Apollo* No. 16. 1/2 That sprightfullness of Thought, he had been formerly Master of. **1898** J. M. Cobban *Angel of Covenant* p. xii, Ye knew not..the wit and sprightfulness of his speech.

sprightle ('spraɪt(ə)l), *v. Midland dial.* [Back-formation f. sprightly *a.*] *intr.* With *up*: to become lively or alert.

1896 G. F. Northall *Warwickshire Word-bk.* 224 *Sprightle up! excl.*, be lively, alert (sprightly). **1920** D. H. Lawrence *Lost Girl* ix. 206 Oh but she sprightles up a bit sometimes.

†**'sprightless,** *a. Obs.* [f. spright *sb.*^{1}] Spiritless; devoid of spirit or animation.

1591 Sylvester *Du Bartas* I. vi. 782 Whoso doth not admire His spirit, is sprightless. **1598** Marston *Sco. Villanie* II. vii. 203 Nay, he is sprightlesse, sense or soule hath none. **1635–56** Cowley *Davideis* I. 139 Are ye grown Benum'd with Fear, or Vertues sprightless cold? **1638** Quarles *Hieroglyphics* XIV. iv, Her sprightlesse flame grown great with snuff. **1710** Steele *Tatler* No. 197 ¶2 In pursuit of such cold and sprightless Endeavours to appear in Publick.

'sprightlily, *adv. rare*$^{-1}$. [f. sprightly *a.*] In a sprightly or lively manner.

1891 H. Lynch *Meredith* 103 Lively youths, maidens and matrons, who act chorus, wittily, epigrammatically, and sprightlily.

sprightliness ('spraɪtlɪnɪs). [f. next + -ness.] The character or state of being sprightly; liveliness, vivacity, animation.

1650 T. B[ayley] *Worcester's Apoph.* 105 With some sprightlinesse he spake aloud. **1684** Burnet *More's Utopia* 130 They think it a madness for a Man..to corrupt the sprightliness of his Body by Sloth. **1712** Addison *Spect.* No. 446 ¶8 The fine Woman is generally a Composition of Sprightliness and Falshood. **1781** Cowper *Conversat.* 635 Youth has a sprightliness and fire to boast, That in the valley of decline are lost. **1832** *Proc. Berw. Nat. Club* I. 5, I was struck with the cries of the birds we noticed: there was no sprightliness in them, nor melody. **1894** Jeaffreson *Bk. Recoll.* II. 237 A lady..delightful by force of her colloquial sprightliness.

sprightly ('spraɪtlɪ), *a.* and *adv.* [f. spright *sb.*^{1} + -ly.]

A. *adj.* **1.** Of persons: Full of vivacity or animation; cheerful, gay, brisk.

1596 Nashe *Saffron Walden* To Rdr., Frisking come aloft sprightly Mercury, that hath wings for his moustachies, wings for his ey-browes, [etc.]. **1602** Marston *Ant. & Mel.* IV. Wks. 1856 I. 52 Seest thou that sprightly youth? **1670** Cotton *Espernon* II. v. 208 Most sprightly and gay Nobility, and Gentry of the Court. **1740** Richardson *Pamela* Pref. (1824) I. 4 To engage the attention of the gay and more sprightly readers. **1766** Goldsm. *Vicar* xxiii, Nor was I displeased at seeing them once more sprightly and at ease. **1807** Crabbe *Birth Flattery* 15 Thee, sprightly siren, from this train I choose. **1874** L. Stephen *Hours in Library* (1892) I. ii. 88 The..old tradesman could be..as sprightly and audacious as the most profligate man about town.

absol. **1734** Watts *Reliq. Juv.* (1789) 18 There are both the sprightly and the stupid, the foolish and the wise. **1751** Johnson *Rambler* No. 174 ¶2 The error..is very frequently incident to the quick, the sprightly, the fearless, and the gay. **1825** C. Westmacott *Eng. Spy* I. 382 The spreeish or the sprightly.

b. Of animals: Lively, sportive.

1735 Somerville *Chase* I. 86 To train the sprightly Steed, more fleet than those Begot by Winds. **1742** Young *Nt. Th.* I. 437 The sprightly Lark's shrill Mattin wakes the Morn. **1830** J. Milne *Widow & Son* (1851) I. 141 The crowing of the sprightly cock. **1883** 'Annie Thomas' *Mod. Housewife* 24 The mare was as sprightly as a cat.

c. Of plants: Quick-growing. *rare*$^{-1}$.

1693 Evelyn *De la Quint. Compl. Gard.* 41 The principal Roots of..Raspish Bushes, and some other very sprightly Shrubs.

2. Characterized by animation or cheerful vivacity: **a.** Of actions, qualities, etc.

1606 Shaks. *Ant. & Cl.* IV. vii. 15, I will reward thee Once for thy sprightly comfort. **1646** Quarles *Judgem. & Mercy* Wks. (Grosart) I. 76/2 My bones are full of unctious marrow, and my blood, of sprightly Youth. *a* **1704** T. Brown *Charms of Bottle* Wks. 1711 IV. 160 Here the sprightly Repartees fly about with the Glass. **1788** Mme.

D'ARBLAY *Diary* 2 Aug., He was himself all ease and sprightly unconsciousness. **1831** SINCLAIR *Corr.* II. 89 The conversation was sprightly, and well calculated for the lively company. **1868** J. H. BLUNT *Ref. Ch. Eng.* I. 111 Her beauty had faded away, her sprightly buoyancy had gone.

b. Of personal bearing, looks, etc.

1606 SHAKS. *Ant. & Cl.* IV. xiv. 52 Wee'l hand in hand, And with out sprightly Port make the Ghostes gaze. **1635** QUARLES *Emblems* IV. iii. 193 The sprightly voice of sinew-strengthning Pleasure. **1672–5** COMBER *Comp. Temple* (1702) 157 Our looks were sprightly and chearfull. **1748** HERVEY *Medit.* (ed. 4) I. 33 How vain the Lustre of thy sprightly Eye! **1751** JOHNSON *Rambler* No. 179 ¶4 The sprightly trip, the stately walk, the formal strut. **1823** SCOTT *Quentin D.* ii, The combination of fearless frankness and good-humour, with sprightly looks. **1873** DIXON *Two Queens* XVI. v. III. 212 Her sprightly air..made her an attraction.

absol. **1784** COWPER *Tiroc.* 665 Behold that figure,..His sprightly mingled with a shade of sad.

c. Of mind, disposition, or character.

1673 [R. LEIGH] *Transp. Reh.* 12 One of those glorious enterprises..which the bishop's active and sprightly mind was busied in. **1719** DE FOE *Crusoe* II. (Globe) 330 The French, whose Temper is allow'd to be more volatile..and more sprightly. **1777** SHERIDAN *Sch. Scand.* Portr. 108 Such too her talents, and her bent of mind, As speak a sprightly heart by thought refined. **1878** BROWNING *Poets Croisic* 99 So did her sprightly nature nowise lack Lustre when draped.

d. Of places in respect of social life or gay appearance.

1764 GOLDSM. *Trav.* 241 Gay sprightly land of mirth and social ease. **1809** PINKNEY *Trav. France* 278 It is well paved, ..and the air being clear, it always looks clean and sprightly. **1832** G. DOWNES *Lett. Cont. Countries* I. 290 It is, altogether, a sprightly, lively place, garnished with pleasing environs. **1875** F. W. NEWMAN in I. G. Sieveking *Mem.* (1909) 315 The gardens are becoming sprightly.

3. Of things: Having lively qualities or properties; naturally brisk; suggestive of animation or gaiety: **a.** Of liquors.

1605 PLAT *Delightes for Ladies* III. xxvii, You shall finde the same most excellent and sprightly drinke. **1661** BOYLE *Scept. Chem.* VI. (1680) 418 These [crystals] I obtained not from Must, but True and sprightly Wine. **1709** PRIOR '*If Wine*' i, Let..Bacchus fill the sprightly Bowl. **1748** THOMSON *Cast. Indol.* I. xxxiv, Whatever sprightly juice or tasteful food On the green bosom of this earth are found. **1796** H. HUNTER tr. *St.-Pierre's Stud. Nat.* (1799) I. 297 In ours, which are sprightly [wines], nothing is at the bottom but mere dregs. **1830** M. DONOVAN *Dom. Econ.* I. 93 Oats make an excellent malt, which..affords an excellent, mantling, sprightly, sweet drink.

b. In miscellaneous uses.

1621 QUARLES *Esther* vii, Sooner shall the sprightly flames of fire Descend, and moysten. **1635–56** COWLEY *Davideis* II. 803 A silk Mantle.., Where the most sprightly Azure pleas'd the Eyes. **1665** BOYLE *Reflect.* (1848) 79 That pleasant and sprightly scent which makes the Rose so welcome to us. **1704** POPE *Windsor For.* 94 While youth ferments your blood, And purer spirits swell the sprightly flood. **1804** C. BROWN tr. *Volney's View Soil U.S.* 271 The winds between east and north are sprightly and cool. **1885–94** R. BRIDGES *Eros & Psyche* Mar. xvii, Naked he goeth, but with sprightly wings Red, iridescent, are his shoulders fledged. **1901** *Year-bk. U.S. Dep. Agric.* 388 Flesh [of grape] tender, breaking, juicy;..flavor mild, sweet and sprightly.

c. Of sounds.

1648 CRASHAW *Poems* (1904) 120 The sprightly notes Of sweet-lipp'd Angell-Imps. **1670** DRYDEN *Conq. Granada* I. III. i, Methinks it is a noble, sprightly Sound. The Trumpet's Clangor, and the Clash of Arms! **1725** POPE *Odyss.* I. 531 Mean time the Lyre rejoins the sprightly lay. **1752** YOUNG *Brothers* II. i, These sprightly tuneful airs but skim along The surface of my soul, not enter there. **1817** STEPHENS in *Shaw's Gen. Zool.* X. I. 90 Their song is a sprightly warble, and is sometimes continued for a length of time. **1882** J. F. S. GORDON *Hist. Moray* I. 282 There is a sprightly song and dance called 'Kinrara'.

d. Of musical instruments.

1697 DRYDEN *Virg. Georg.* III. 131 When he hears from far The sprightly Trumpets, and the Shouts of War. *a* **1721** PRIOR *Colin's Mistakes* ii, The sounding Clarion, and the sprightly Horn. **1757** W. WILKIE *Epigoniad* I. 9 While to the sprightly harp, the voice explains The loves of all the gods. **1791** COWPER *Odyss.* VIII. 127 The herald hanging high The sprightly lyre.

†**4.** Ghostly, spectral. *Obs.*⁻¹

1611 SHAKS. *Cymb.* V. v. 428 As I slept, me thought Great Iupiter vpon his Eagle back'd Appear'd to me, with other sprightly shewes Of mine owne Kindred.

B. *adv.* In a sprightly manner; with vigour and animation.

1604 DEKKER *Kings' Entertainm.* Wks. 1873 I. 295 Nine Trumpets and a Kettle Drum did very sprightly and actively sound the Danish March. **1642** H. MORE *Song of Soul* IV. 35 Her hid Centralitie So sprightly's quickned with near Union With God. **1654** WHITLOCK *Zootomia* 479 The Chevalry of Verse charges them more sprightly and Irresistibly. *a* **1895** PAGET *Autobiog.* (1896) 80 A vessel sprightly approached with an admiral's flag at the fore.

†'**sprightness.** *Obs.*⁻¹ Sprightliness.

1674 N. FAIRFAX *Bulk & Selv.* 136 A sort of mechanical ..twitchings and animal sprightnesses which are..set on foot.

†**sprighty,** *a. Obs. rare.* [f. SPRIGHT *sb.*[1]] = SPRIGHTLY *a.* (1 and 3 a).

1609 *Pimlyco* C iv b, Rosa Solis, Aqua Vitæ, And Nugs of Balme, so quicke, and sprighty. *a* **1625** FLETCHER *Love's Pilgr.* III. ii, A Son of his, a yong and hopeful gentleman,.. A sprighty man, of understanding excellent. **1641** J. JACKSON *True Evang. T.* I. 79 The spirit of the sprighty Ascanius in Virgil.

†**sprigle,** *v. Obs.* (See SPRIG *v.*[2] 1 a.)

'**spriglet.** [f. SPRIG *sb.*[2] + -LET.] A little sprig.

1892 E. CASTLE *Eng. Bk.-plates* 73 From the numerous nooks..sprout flowerets and spriglets.

sprig tail, sprigtail. [f. SPRIG *sb.*[1]]

1. A short pointed tail.

1676 *Lond. Gaz.* No. 1108/4 A Bay Mare above 14 hands, a Sprig Tail. **1690** *Ibid.* No. 2607/4 He had with him a white Mungrel crop-ear'd Dog, with a sprig Tail. **1721** *Ibid.* No. 6000/3 A black Gelding..with a Sprig Tail, a little Hair upon it. **1772** *Oxf. Jrnl.* 21 Nov. 1 A black horse with a sprig tail. **1853** R. S. SURTEES *Sponge's Sp. Tour* (1893) 16 There's the little Hirish 'oss with the sprig-tail.

2. *U.S.* A species of duck; = PINTAIL 2.

1782 T. JEFFERSON *Notes St. Virginia* (1787) 118 Ballcoot. Sprigtail. Didapper or Dopchick. **1814** A. WILSON *Amer. Ornith.* VIII. 73 The Sprigtail is an elegantly formed, long-bodied Duck, the neck longer and more slender than most others. **1874** J. W. LONG *Amer. Wild-fowl.* Introd. 16 In the shoal-water class are the mallard, sprigtail or pintail. *Ibid.* 166 Many shots will frequently be had at wood-duck, teal, and sprigtails in this sport.

sprig-tailed, *a.* [f. as prec.] Having a sharp-pointed tail.

1676 *Lond. Gaz.* No. 1141/4 The Horse is a sorrel Guelding, seven years old, sprig tail'd. **1698** *Ibid.* No. 3368/4 Lost.., a sorrel Mare.., mealy Nose,..and also Sprig Tailed. **1853** R. S. SURTEES *Sponge's Sp. Tour* (1893) 34, I was on my little handy, sprig-tailed bay. **1872** COUES *N. Amer. Birds* 39 A cuneate tail..is also called pointed, in contradistinction to rounded, as in the sprig-tailed duck.

sprincle, obs. form of SPRINKLE *v.*

†**sprind,** *a. Obs. rare.* [OE. *sprind*, of obscure origin.] Active, vigorous.

c **1000** *Salom. & Sat.* (Kemble) 150 His ȝeðoht he is springdra [*sic*] and swiftra ðonne xii. ðusendu haliȝra gasta. *a* **1100** in Napier *O.E. Gloss.* I. 3607 *Adultum*, i. *iuuenem*, ȝeþoȝenne, sprindne. *c* **1315** SHOREHAM I. 22 And be a man neuer so sprind, ȝef he schel libbe to elde, Be him wel siker, þer-to he schel.

sprindge, obs. form of SPRINGE.

spring (sprɪŋ), *sb.*[1] Forms: 1, 3– **spring**, 2, 4–7 **springe**; 1, 4–6 **spryng(e**, 3–4 **sprung**, 4 **sprenge**, 6 **spreng**. [OE. *spring* and *spryng* masc., formed respectively from the primary and weak grades of the stem *spring-*, *sprang-*, *sprung-*: see SPRING *v.*, from which a number of the later senses are directly derived.

In the OE. the simple word is comparatively rare, chiefly occurring in senses which have not survived. Sense 1 (more common in the combs. *æ-* and *wyllspring*, *-spryng*) is also that of OS. *aha-*, *gispring*, MDu. (Du.) and MLG. *spring* (MLG. and Du. dial. *spreng*), OHG. (MHG. and G. dial.) *spring*, *sprung*. In sense 13 the equivalent forms are MSw. and Da. *spring*, OHG. (MHG. and G.), MLG. and MSw. *sprung*, MDu. (Du. and WFris.), G. dial., *sprong*, MLG. (LG.), MSw. *sprang* (Sw. *språng*).]

I. 1. The place of rising or issuing from the ground, the source or head, *of* a well, stream, or river; the supply of water forming such a source. Now *rare.*

816 in Birch *Cartul. Saxon.* (1885) I. 495 Æt þæs bernes ende æt ðæs wæ teres sprynge. *a* **1300** *Cursor M.* 1314 In middes þe land he sagh a spring Of a well. **1398** TREVISA *Barth. De P.R.* XIV. xxxi. (Bodl. MS.), In þeese hiȝe mounteyns is snowe alwey,..and heedes and springes of welles and of greete ryuers. *c* **1440** *Promp. Parv.* 470 Sprynge, of a welle, *scaturigo*, *scatebra*. **1535** COVERDALE *2 Esdras* xiii. 47 Yᵉ Hyest shall holde styll the sprynges of the streame agayne. **1600** E. BLOUNT tr. *Conestaggio* 4 Great riuers, whose mouthes are knowne, but not their springs. **1604** E. G[RIMSTONE] *D'Acosta's Hist. Indies* II. iv. 88 At what time it is Summer in Egypt,..then is it winter at the springes of Nile. **1665** MANLEY *Grotius' Low C. Wars* 293 The Springs of the Well [might be] stopped, or at least intercepted. **1728** CHAMBERS *Cycl.* s.v. *Tides*, So that entering the Mouths of Rivers, it [*sc.* the sea] drives back the River-waters towards their Heads, or Springs. **1815** SHELLEY *Alastor* 478 The sound Of the sweet brook that from the secret springs Of that dark fountain rose.

2. a. A flow of water rising or issuing naturally out of the earth; a similar flow obtained by boring or other artificial means.

c **1250** *Gen. & Ex.* 581 Ilc wateres springe here strengðe undede. *a* **1300** *Cursor M.* 11699 Vnder þi rote þar es a spring, I wil þat vte þe water wring. *c* **1325** *Chron. Eng.* 191 in Ritson *Metr. Rom.* II. 278 In four sprunges the tonnes liggeth. *Ibid.* 195 The tuo sprunges urneth yfere. *c* **1420** *Contin. Brut* ccxxiv. 292 þere arose a suche a..wellinge op of wateres and floodes, bothe of þe see and also of fresshe ryvers & spryngez, þat [etc.]. **1483** *Cath. Angl.* 356 A Sprynge of water, *scatebra*, *scatirigo*. **1570** DEE *Math. Pref.* d j b, Being a Spring, standing, or running Water. **1585** T. WASHINGTON tr. *Nicholay's Voy.* II. xxi. 58 A faire fountain ..either of a natural spring or artificial. **1610** HOLLAND *Camden's Brit.* (1637) 497 There are two little Springs, the one fresh, the other somewhat brackish. **1665** SIR T. HERBERT *Trav.* (1677) 386 It has also some Springs of good Water. **1732** POPE *Ess. Man* I. 137 For me, Health gushes from a thousand springs. **1765** A. DICKSON *Treat. Agric.* (ed. 2) 150 If there are springs in all places,..it will be necessary to make drains at the sides. **1812** PLAYFAIR *Nat. Phil.* I. 285 Springs, in which the water does not considerably change its heat from one season of the year to another. **1855** *Orr's Circ. Sci., Inorg. Nat.* 200 At Vaucluse, there is a spring of water yielding from thirteen to forty thousand cubic feet..per minute. **1878** HUXLEY *Physiogr.* 25 Springs of this simple character, which issue at the junction of permeable and impermeable strata, are extremely common.

fig. *c* **1440** *Jacob's Well* 2 þanne delve doun..tyl þou fynde vij sprynges of watyr of grace. **1593** SHAKS. *2 Hen. VI*, IV. i. 72 Kennell,..whose filth and dirt Troubles the siluer Spring, where England drinkes. **1596** SPENSER *F.Q.* IV. ii. 18 Streames of bloud did rayle Adowne, as if their springs of life were spent. **1696** TATE & BRADY *Ps.* cxliii. 10 From Mercy's healing Spring Revive me. **1697** DRYDEN *Virg. Georg.* IV. 408 An ancient Legend I prepare to sing, And upward follow Fame's immortal Spring. **1751** CHATHAM *Lett. Nephew* ii. 7 Drink as deep as you can of these divine springs [*sc.* Homer and Virgil]. **1771** *Encycl. Brit.* I. 644 When old age approaches,..the springs of life dry up. **1818** KEATS *Endym.* II. 738 And then there ran Two bubbling springs of talk from their sweet lips. **1851** MAURICE *Patriarchs & Lawg.* vii. (1855) 145 That he should open springs in hearts hitherto ice-bound!

b. A flow of water possessing special properties, esp. of a medicinal or curative nature. Usually with various distinguishing adjs., as *chalybeate*, *hot*, *mineral*, *thermal*, *warm*, etc.

1787 *Phil. Trans.* LXXVIII. 187 About two leagues to the east of this mass I discovered a brackish mineral spring. **1800** [see THERMAL *a.* 1]. **1819** WARDEN *United States* II. 176 The sweet springs, another mineral water. *Ibid.*, At the distance of a mile are the red springs, which, like the former, have a tonic or bracing quality. **1839** DE LA BECHE *Rep. Geol. Cornwall*, etc. xv. 517 Chalybeate springs are very common. **1847** H. MILLER *First Impr. Eng.* xi. (1857) 189 The underground history of the mineral springs of Great Britain. **1850** *Johnston's Gen. Gazetteer, Bath*, The hot springs..are saline and chalybeate.

c. *pl.* A place or locality having such springs to which invalids or pleasure-seekers resort.

1849 MACAULAY *Hist. Eng.* iii. I. 347 In his younger days the gentlemen who visited the springs slept in rooms hardly as good as the garrets which he lived to see occupied by footmen. **1859** SAXE *Poems* (1872) 239 Pray, what do they do at the Springs?

d. *transf.* A jet or spray of water. *rare*⁻¹.

1818 LADY MORGAN *Autobiog.* (1859) 111 All appeared silence and desolation; neither the *grands* nor *petits eaux* threw up their diamond springs in the sunshine.

3. *fig.* A source or origin *of* something. Also occas. without const.

a. Predicated of persons or personifications.

a **1225** *Juliana* 50 Of al þat uuel iþe world..ich am an of þe sprunges, þat hit mest of springeð. *c* **1410** HOCCLEVE *Mother of God* 88 Of al vertu, thow art the spryng & welle! **1412–20** LYDG. *Chron. Troy* I. 1710 þouȝ he [Ovid] of poetis was þe spring & welle. **1509** HAWES *Past. Pleas.* XLIII. (Percy Soc.) 212 And thus I, Fame, am ever magnified,..The spryng of honour and of famous clarkes. **1605** SHAKS. *Macb.* II. iii. 103 *Macb.* The Spring, the Head, the Fountaine of your Blood Is stopt.. *Macd.* Your Royall Father's murther'd. **1685** BAXTER *Paraphr. N.T.* John i. 9 As the Lord and Spring of Nature, he giveth all men their Intellectual Natural Light. **1709** WATTS *Hymn* 1 My God, the Spring of all my Joys, The Life of my Delights. **1876** MORRIS *Æneid* XII. 166 Father Æneas, spring of the Roman weal.

b. In general use.

1523 CROMWELL in Merriman *Life & Lett.* (1902) I. 30 Suche yerely reuenues and wellyng spryngges as [*read* of] treasure as shuld..be browght into this Realme. **1550** W. LYNNE *Carion's Cron.* 1 That commaundement of God is the springe and beginninge of all lawes. **1582** STANYHURST *Æneis* III. (Arb.) 73 Theare mount Ide resteth, thee springe of progenye Troian. **1612** SYLVESTER *Tropheis Hen. Gt.* cv, This noble Spirit doth to his Spring re-mount, This Bounties Flood retireth to his Fount. **1719** W. WOOD *Surv. Trade* 193, I have discoursed on the African Trade, by reason it is the Spring and Parent whence the others flow. **1730** CHAMBERLAYNE *Relig. Philos.* Dedic., The Gothic, the common Spring of all the Western Languages of Europe. **1817** JAS. MILL *Brit. India* II. v. v. 516 It was not one spring alone of dissension which distracted the government of Madras. **1892** WESTCOTT *Gospel of Life* 106 Language reveals the deepest springs of thought.

4. *attrib.* and *Comb.*, as ***spring-level***, ***-nymph***, ***pond***, ***-vein***; ***spring-fed***, ***watered***, adjs.; **spring-branch** *U.S.*, a brook or stream fed by or flowing directly from a spring; **spring-hole** *N.Amer.*, = *spring-pit*; **spring-house** *N.Amer.*, an outhouse built over a spring or stream and used as a larder, dairy, etc.; **spring-keeper** *U.S.* (see quot.); **spring-pit**, a hole or cavity formed by a spring where it issues or rises; **spring-salt** (see quot.); **spring-teller**, one who finds springs by dowsing, etc.; **spring-tooth** (in allusion to *Judges* xv. 19).

1823 *Amer. State Papers: Public Lands* (U.S. Congr.) (1834) III. 811 One hundred [acres] on Sweet *spring branch, St. Mary's river. **1851** MAYNE REID *Scalp Hunt.* xxvi. 191 Deer and antelopes came to the spring-branch to drink. **1848** BUCKLEY *Iliad* 136 He came to *spring-fed Ida. **1883** *Cent. Mag.* Sept. 651 These ponds are, of course, spring-fed. **1868** *Rep. U.S. Commissioner Agric.* (1869) 329 Keep her a few days in a pool or *spring-hole. **1874** J. W. LONG *Amer. Wildfowl.* xi. 171 The mallards..roosting in the small spring-holes and creeks. **1956** K. M. WELLS *By Jumping Cat Bridge* xiv. 83 We followed it, up to the spring hole on the edge of the flat land, a no-good bit of bog hole on the edge of arable land. **1797** F. BAILY *Tour* (1856) 433 This subterraneous cavity would afford an excellent convenience for a *spring house. **1894** *Outing* XXIV. 382/2 To see her at her best was at the butter-making down at the old spring-house. **1933** H. ALLEN *Anthony Adverse* ii. 26 A fresh cheese cool from the spring house, and a firm, white loaf caught in a silver clamp provided with a small steel saw in the shape of a dragon's head with teeth amused Maria. **1972** E. WIGGINTON *Foxfire Bk.* 207 Roll the sausage into balls, pack them in a churn jar..and set in the water trough in your spring house. **1980** *Knoxville* (Tennessee) *News-Sentinel* 6 Apr. C4/5 He also said, 'Milk kept in the *springhouse* will blink and sometimes clabber during a severe thunderstorm or toad-strangler.' **1859** BARTLETT *Dict. Amer.* (ed. 2) 438 **Spring-keeper*, a salamander, or small lizard-shaped animal, found in springs and fresh water rivulets. **1895**

MRS. WILSON 5 *Yrs. India* 261 It costs a large sum to make a well where the *spring-level is so deep. **1897** *Edin. Rev.* Apr. 458 The Danaid *spring-nymphs had to carry water in a sieve to prove their virginity. **1862** A. NEWTON *Zool. Anc. Europe* 21 These [fresh-water tortoises] were found..in a peat bog, by the side of a *spring-pit, at East Wretham, about seven feet below the surface. **1711** *Lond. Gaz.* No. 4887/4 All well water'd with *Spring Ponds. **1799** J. GIRVIN *Impolicy prohib. Export. Rock Salt* 5 Salt is very properly distinguished by Mineralogists into Fossile-Salt, *Spring-Salt, and Sea-Salt. **1871** *Routledge's Ev. Boy's Ann.* 56 The method used by the '*spring-tellers' or 'water-finders' was simple enough. **1593** G. HARVEY *Pierce's Super.* 172, I barre the Cheeke-bone, for feare of Sampsons tune... But the *spring-tooth in the iawe, will do vs no harme. **1610** HOLLAND *Camden's Brit.* (1637) 402 As for *spring-veines there are none to bee found. **1884** *Mag. Art* March 215/2 The velvety green of *spring-watered field-plots.

II. 5. The action or time of rising or springing into being or existence: **a.** The appearing or coming on, the first sign, *of* day, morning, etc.; the dawn. Also, the beginning of a season.

Fairly common from *c* 1380 to *c* 1600; now *Obs.* exc. *poet.* Cf. DAY-SPRING and OE. *up-spring*.

13.. *K. Alis.* 3586 (Bodl. MS.), For riȝth in þe dayes sprynge Tolomeus on hem com fleiȝeynge. **1382** WYCLIF *1 Macc.* v. 30 It is maad in spryng of the day, whanne thei reysiden her eeȝen. *c* **1391** CHAUCER *Astrol.* II. §6 To knowe the spring of the dawing and the ende of the euenyng. **1483** CAXTON *G. de la Tour* I vj b, At the sprynge of the daye they were at the monument. *c* **1530** TINDALE *Jonas* iv. C viij, The lorde ordeyned a worme agenst the springe of yᵉ morow morninge. **1560** DAUS tr. *Sleidane's Comm.* 323 To the intent at the springe of the daye..they might invade the City. **1590** SHAKS. *Mids. N.* II. i. 82 Neuer since the middle Summers spring Met we. **1611** BIBLE *1 Sam.* ix. 26 It came to passe about the spring of the day. **1623** LISLE *Ælfric on O. & N. Test.* Ded., Thou..shalt..Extend thy fame from Set to Spring of day. **1842** TENNYSON *St. Sim. Styl.* 108, I, 'tween the spring and downfall of the light, Bow down one thousand and two hundred times.

†**b.** *spring of the leaf*, the time when trees begin to burst into leaf again. *Obs.*

1538 in Ellis *Orig. Lett.* Ser. I. II. 98 Whiche I thynke shalbe about the spryng of the lefe. **1670** J. SMITH *Eng. Improv. Reviv'd* 31 A good Labouring man may ditch and quick-set about the Spring or fall of the Leaf a ditch of six foot broad and five foot deep.

†**c.** The increase *of* the moon. *Obs.*⁻¹

1559 MORWYNG *Evonym.* 116 Gather the Plantes..in faire weather, in the spring of the mone.

d. An outburst or fresh development. *rare*⁻¹.

1604 BACON *Adv. Learn.* I. vi. §15 At one and the same time [the Reformation] it was ordayned by the Divine Providence, that there should attend withall a renovation and new spring of all other knowledges.

6. a. *the spring of the year*, = sense 6 b. ? *Obs.*

1530 PALSGR. 274 Spring of the yere, *printemps, prin.* **1548** TURNER *Names Herbes* (E.D.S.) 80 In the sprynge of the yere, it hath yealowe floures. **1551** RECORDE *Cast. Knowl.* (1556) 31 From thence ['the eleuenth daye of Marche'] they recken the Springe of the yeare thre monethes. **1665** BOYLE *Occas. Refl.* (1848) 58 If then, in the Spring of the Year, our Reflector see the Gardener pruning a Fruit-tree. **1731** MILLER *Gard. Dict.* s.v. *Brassica*, In the Spring of the Year these Cabbages will shoot out strongly. **1828** *Farmer's Jrnl.* 12 May.

b. The first season of the year, or that between winter and summer, reckoned astronomically from the vernal equinox to the summer solstice; in popular use in Great Britain comprising the months of February, March, and April, in U.S. March, April, and May. Also *transf.*, a season resembling this in some respect.

Used without article or with *the*, and in specialized cases with *a*, etc. Often with initial capital, and in poetry freq. personified.

(*a*) *a* **1547** SURREY in *Tottel's Misc.* (Arb.) 4 Description of Spring, wherin eche thing renewes, saue onelie the louer. **1573** TUSSER *Husb.* (1878) 100 At spring (for the sommer) sowe garden ye shall. **1596** SPENSER *F.Q.* VII. vii. 28 So, forth issew'd the Seasons of the yeare; First, lusty Spring, all dight in leaues of flowres. **1607** LEVER *Q. Eliz. Tears* li, Beauteous floures, (The pretty children of the Earth and Spring). **1697** DRYDEN *Virg. Georg.* IV. 751 Alone he tempts ..Th' unhappy Climes, where Spring was never known. **1733** TULL *Horse-hoeing Husb.* xi. 106 (Dubl.), If it be not sown before Spring, its Grain will be thin. **1779** *Mirror* No. 16, The effects of the return of Spring have been frequently remarked. **1819** SHELLEY *Ode West Wind* v, O, Wind, If Winter comes, can Spring be far behind? **1848** L. HUNT *Jar of Honey* vii. 84 Thou still..art the same blithe, sweet thing Thou ever wast, O Spring. **1885** J. ASHBY-STERRY *Lazy Minstrel* (1892) 6 Spring's Delights are now returning!

(*b*) *a* **1547** SURREY in *Tottle's Misc.* (Arb.) 15 Like as when, rough winter spent, The pleasant spring straight draweth in vre. **1577** GOOGE tr. *Heresbach's Husb.* 22 Touching the season of your plowing, it must be cheefely in the spring. **1609** DEKKER *Ravens Alm.* Wks. (Grosart) IV. 194 Let vs now try if the spring will prooue any more cheerefull. **1665** BOYLE *Occas. Refl.* (1848) Pref. p. xviii, A dozen ordinary Pictures of the Spring (which yet are wont to charm Vulgar eyes). **1733** TULL *Horse-hoeing Husb.* xi. 128 (Dubl.), The Wheat will have the Benefit of them earlier in the Spring. **1742** GRAY *Spring* 26 The insect-youth are on the wing, Eager to taste the honied spring. **1828** WORDSW. *Morn. Exerc.* 48 Yet might'st thou seem..to sing All independent of the leafy spring. **1842** TENNYSON *Locksley Hall* 20 In the Spring a young man's fancy lightly turns to thoughts of love.

(*c*) **1596** SHAKS. *2 Hen. IV*, I. iii. 38 As in an early Spring, We see th' appearing buds. **1596** —— *Rich. III*, III. i. 94. **1604** E. G[RIMSTONE] *D'Acosta's Hist. Indies* II. xiii. 111 Yet those which inhabite there, take it for a delightful spring. **1697** DRYDEN *Virg. Georg.* IV. 179 To sing The Pæstan Roses, and their double Spring. **1726-46** THOMSON *Winter* 1069 The storms of Wintry Time will quickly pass, And one unbounded Spring encircle all. **1742** GRAY *Eton Coll.* 20 The gales..seem..To breathe a second spring. **1830** TENNYSON *Nothing will die* ii, A spring rich and strange, Shall make the winds blow. **1859** —— *Merlin & V.* 407 My blood Hath earnest in it of far springs to be.

c. *fig.* The first or early stage or period *of* life, youth, etc.

1590 GREENE *Mourn. Garm.* (1616) B ij b, Sophonos.. carried graue thoughts, and in the spring of his youth such ripe fruits, as are found in the Autumne of age. **1591** SHAKS. *Two Gent.* I. iii. 84 Oh, how this spring of loue resembleth The vncertaine glory of an Aprill day. **1621** J. TAYLOR (Water P.) *Motto* D 3, Who in the Spring, or Summer of his Pride, Was worship'd, honor'd, almost deifi'd. **1742** GRAY *Spring* 49 On hasty wings thy youth is flown; Thy sun is set, thy spring is gone. **1781** BURKE *Correspondence* (1844) II. 437 A storm came upon us in the early spring of our toleration. **1826** DISRAELI *V. Grey* IV. iv, You are blighted for ever in the very spring of your life. **1834** LYTTON *Pompeii* I. vi, Apæcides was in the spring of his years.

d. Contrasted with *fall*, esp. in the phr. *spring and fall* (cf. FALL *sb.*¹ 2). Now *arch.*

1643 R. BAKER *Chron.* (1653) 183 So great oddes there is between the Spring and Fall of Fortune. *c* **1680** HICKERINGILL *Hist. Whiggism* Wks. 1716 I. II. 153 Parliaments are to sit frequently... I do not say, as often as you take Physick (Spring and Fall at least). **1754** J. BARTLET *Gentl. Farriery* (ed. 2) 173 This disease..in some horses shews itself spring and fall. **1764** WARBURTON *Lett.* (1809) 354, I do not wonder that any studious man should in England want physic at Spring and Fall. **1826** [see FALL *sb.*¹ 2].

e. This season in a particular year.

1621 LD. DUNFERMLINE in G. Seton *Mem.* (1882) 130, I haue bein twayis or thrise this spring ellis at Archerie. **1677** PRIDEAUX *Lett.* (1875) 59 We shall goe on buildeing to, as soon as spring begins. **1711** LADY M. W. MONTAGU *Let. to W. Montagu* 24 Mar., I am going to the same place I went last spring. ? *a* **1758** GRAY *Song* 2 Ere the spring he would return. **1801** *Farmer's Mag.* Nov. 465 There can be no scarcity of that grain before the Spring. **1849** MACAULAY *Hist. Eng.* v. I. 659 *note*, Ferguson..was excluded by name from the general pardon published in the following spring. **1855** *Ibid.* xvii. IV. 12 In the spring of 1691, the Waldensian shepherds..were surprised by glad tidings.

f. Used with numerals to mark a definite period, esp. in the age of a person or animal.

1697 DRYDEN *Virg. Georg.* III. 299 When to four full Springs his Years advance. **1820** BYRON *Mar. Fal.* II. i. 371 Were I still in my five and twentieth spring.

g. *ellipt.* Spring wheat.

1896 *Daily News* 30 Nov. 2/7 Wheat to-day is very firmly held... English reds, 36s.; American springs, 37s.

h. *ellipt.* A spring salmon (see sense 7 c below).

1913 *Chambers's Jrnl.* Oct. 729/2 Next in value comes the 'spring', the largest fish often weighing sixty-five pounds. **1921** *Daily Colonist* (Victoria, B.C.) 12 Mar. 9/4 In May it [*sc.* the largest cannery in the North] will commence to pack springs. **1975** H. WHITE *Raincoast Chron.* (1976) 222/1 Some men hand trolled springs during the winter.

7. *attrib.* and *Comb.* **a.** Attrib., passing into adj., in the sense 'of or pertaining to the spring'; 'appearing, happening, occurring, etc., in the spring', as ***spring-ague, -beam, -bird, -blood, -blossom***, etc.; **spring cabbage**, a variety of cabbage that matures in the spring; a cabbage of this variety; **spring greens**, the leaves of young cabbage plants, used as a vegetable; also, a cabbage of a variety that matures in spring; **spring juices** (see quot.); **spring-pottage, soup**, pottage or soup made of or from fresh green vegetables; **spring roll**, a Chinese snack consisting of a pancake filled with vegetables and fried in the shape of a roll; **spring training** *Baseball*, pre-season fitness and skills training taking place in spring.

1711 SHAFTESB. *Charac.* (1737) I. 14 They might, instead of making a cure,..turn a *spring-ague or an autumn-surfeit into an epidemical malignant fever. **1684** Z. CAWDREY *Certainty Salvation* 28 The first warm and invigorating *Spring-beam to the Frost-nipt Loyalty of the Nation. **1760** T. SMITH *Jrnl.* (1849) 273 The robin and *spring birds came a week or ten days sooner than usual. **1855** BROWNING *Old Pictures Florence* xxiii, I have loved the season Of Art's *spring-birth. **1825** J. WILSON *Poems* II. 96 Bright as *spring-blossoms after sunny showers. **1820** KEATS *Isabella* xiii, Even bees, the little almsmen of *spring-bowers. **1862** G. M. HOPKINS *Vision of Mermaids* (1929), Until it seem'd their father Sea Had gotten him a wreath of sweet *Spring-broidery. **1842** J. C. LOUDON *Suburban Horticulturist* III. v. 629 This [*sc.* tying up the leaves] may be usefully practised with the earliest *spring cabbages. **1900** W. D. DRURY *Bk. Gardening* 1196/1 (Index), Spring cabbages. **1979** P. J. SALTER et al. *Know & grow Veg.* iv. 104 Spring cabbage..may be short of nitrogen. **1837** CARLYLE *Fr. Rev.* III. II. vi, To be concerting measures for the *spring Campaign. **1834** *Chambers's Edin. Jrnl.* III. 255/1 The remainder may be ready for *spring crop with very little labour. **1962** E. SNOW *Red China Today* (1963) xxiii. 174 In July, on a visit to the Agricultural Exhibition Building, I was told by the director that, the spring crop having failed, only phenomenally good weather during August could save the autumn harvest. **1978** *Biol. Abstr.* LXVI. 2091/2 (*heading*) Effect of gibberellic acid..sprays on a spring crop of artichoke. **1817** LADY MORGAN *France* I. 52 The morning light of an early *spring day. **1601** HOLLAND *Pliny* I. 313 This Erithace commeth of the *Spring-dew. **1813** SCOTT *Trierm.* I. i, Generous as spring-dews that bless the glad ground. **1818-20** E. THOMPSON *Nosologia* (ed. 3) 321 Lichen; *Spring Eruption, Scorbutic Pimples. **1843** LYTTON *Last of Barons* II. vi. vii. 256 The love of Sibyll was no common girl's *spring-fever of sighs and blushes. **1859** BARTLETT *Dict. Amer.* (ed. 2) 438 *Spring fever*, the listless feeling caused by the first sudden increase of temperature in spring. It is often said of a lazy fellow, 'He has got the spring fever'. *a* **1586** SIDNEY *Arcadia* III. (1629) 387 Thus poesies of the *spring flowers were wrapt vp in a little greene silke, and dedicated to Kalas breasts. **1884** MRS. C. PRAED *Zero* iv, The floor was carpeted with moss and spring flowers. **1765** *Treat. Dom. Pigeons* 110 Their young ones..were as large as middling *spring fowls. **1897** KIPLING in *Scribner's Mag.* Dec. 679 'Send your road is clear before you when the old *Spring-fret comes o'er you. **1969** in *Current Trends in Linguistics* (1972) X. 155 *Spring fret*, animals' feeling of restlessness in the spring. (Ga.). **1615** A. NICCHOLS *Marr. & Wiving* x. 30 Lust,..the *Spring-frost of beauty. **1842** LOUDON *Suburban Hort.* 417 Retarding the blossoming of the trees, and lessening the risk of their being injured by spring frosts. **1919** C. S. PEEL *Daily Mail Cookery Bk.* (ed. 2) vii. 134 Vegetables which can be cooked in this manner —cauliflowers, brussels sprouts, *spring greens, broccoli tops, [etc.]. **1937** MIDDLETON & HEATH *From Garden to Kitchen* iii. 52 Every alternate one can be pulled out and used as spring greens. **1972** Y. LOVELOCK *Veg. Bk.* I. 69 Spring greens, either hearted or leafy, are gradually superseding the tougher British colewort. **1851** MRS. BROWNING *Casa Guidi Wind.* 129 Until it loose The clammy clods and let out the *spring-growth. **1868** *Rep. U.S. Commissioner Agric.* (1869) 255 As soon as the spring growth, sometimes called the midsummer shoot, is completed. **1824** LOUDON *Encycl. Gard.* (ed. 2) 662 The juice [of water-cress] is decocted with that of scurvy-grass and Seville oranges, and forms the popular remedy called *spring juices. **1831** W. PATRICK *Indigenous Pl. Lanark.* 46 Leaves [of Brooklime]..; generally gathered for medical purposes, and together with scurvy-grass, an ingredient in that nauseous composition called Spring juices. **1818** KEATS *Teignm.* ix, I've gather'd young *spring-leaves, and flowers gay Of periwinkles and wild strawberry. **1872** SYMONDS *Study Dante* 175 Like one of the white *spring-lilies of the Alps. **1765** *Museum Rust.* IV. 279 The *spring litters [of pigs] stand greatly in need of the milk and whey. **1870** H. SMART *Race for Wife* i, The first *spring meeting became his assizes. **1775** ASH, **Springmonths*, the months of the spring quarter. **1837** CARLYLE *Fr. Rev.* I. IV. ii, Through the spring months, as the Sower casts his corn abroad. **1818** SHELLEY *Marenghi* 124 Many a fresh *spring morn would he awaken. **1775** ASH, **Spring morning*, a mild growing morning. **1773** *Ann. Reg.* 87 After eating a hearty breakfast of *Spring-pottage. **1836-7** DICKENS *Sk. Boz, Scenes* xii, We wonder what Greenwich Fair is — a periodical breaking out, we suppose, a sort of *spring-rash. **1943** M. P. LEE *Chinese Cookery* i. 21 *Spring rolls... After having made all the rolls, fry them in..hot lard. **1972** D. BLOODWORTH *Any Number can Play* xxii. 219 Helping himself to a spring roll from a trolley of hot Chinese delicacies. *a* **1722** LISLE *Husb.* (1757) 299 Strike fresh sap-roots, or buds preparative to the ensuing spring, and which will the next year be the *spring-roots. **1731** MILLER *Gard. Dict.* s.v. *Melissa*, The variegated Sort makes a..pretty Appearance in the *Spring Season. **1789** T. WRIGHT *Watering Meadows* (1790) 8 Between March and May we are sure of *Spring-seed. **1733** TULL *Horse-hoeing Husb.* xi. 107 (Dubl.), That long Interval betwixt Autumn and *Spring Seed-times. *a* **1746** HOLDSWORTH *Virgil* (1768) 35 Scarce any tree growing faster than a young Alder,..especially in the *spring-shoot. **1763** *Museum Rust.* I. 141 When the ground is properly prepared, it should be planted with sets, being the spring shoots pulled up in a madder-plot. **1946** DYLAN THOMAS *Deaths & Entrances* 41 Tell his street on its back he stopped a sun And the craters of his eyes grew springshoots and fire. **1763** MILLS *Pract. Husb.* IV. 365 Immediately after a hasty *spring-shower. **1857** J. W. DAVIDSON *Mendelssohn's Six Bks. Songs without Words* p. ii/1 The *Allegretto Grazioso*, in A major..to which he is believed to have given the name of *Frühlingslied* (*Spring Song). **1889** O. WILDE in *Woman's World* II. 111/2 However, if the 'Songs of the Inner Life' are not very successful, the 'Spring Songs' are delightful. **1958** *Anglia* LXXVI. 55 The well-known Spring-song ..'Lencten is come wiþ love to toune'. **1836** FONBLANQUE *Eng. under Seven Administr.* (1837) III. 313 A *spring soup, a turbot, a few made dishes, a dessert, &c. **1859** SALA *Tw. round Clock* (1861) 195 He..had twice spring soup, and twice salmon and cucumber. *a* **1722** LISLE *Husb.* (1757) 138 The *spring-tillows..do arise from the foot of the root of the winter-stems or shoots. **1897** *Sporting News* 27 Mar. 5/3, I am on my way to join the Boston team at Savannah where the players have all been ordered to report for *spring training. **1928** G. H. RUTH *Babe Ruth's Own Book of Baseball* i. 17 In 1925 when I collapsed in Asheville, during the spring training trip, a lot of people figured I'd never put on a uniform again. **1976** *National Observer* (U.S.) 12 June 14/3 Randolph was hardly awed at becoming a Yankee... I came to spring training looking for a job. **1641** BROME *Joviall Crew* II. (1652) D iv b, For a *spring-trick of youth, now, in the season. **1837** LOCKHART *Scott* II. 243 As soon as the *spring vacation began. **1612** WEBSTER *White Devil* II. i. 166 Neglected cassia or the naturall sweetes Of the *Spring-violet. **1707** MORTIMER *Husb.* 233 The *Spring winds, which nips the young Buds. **1835** T. MITCHELL *Aristoph., Acharn.* 785 *note*, The ἄνεμοι ὀρνιθίαι, or spring-winds, which bring with them the birds of passage. **1844** H. STEPHENS *Bk. Farm* II. 482 There is found little or nothing to call forth the burst of *spring-work comes.

b. In the sense 'sown or suitable for sowing in the spring', as ***spring barley, corn, kale, onion, rye, wheat***, etc.

1861 BENTLEY *Man. Bot.* 699 *H*[*ordeum*] *vulgare*, Bere, Bigg, Four-rowed or *Spring Barley. **1733** TULL *Horse-hoeing Husb.* xi. 107 (Dubl.), Wheat..hence having about thrice the time to be maintain'd that *Spring Corn hath. **1763** MILLS *Pract. Husb.* III. 171 Turneps..occupying the whole ground when it should be sowed with spring-corn. **1812** *Examiner* 11 May 292/1 All the spring corn..in a very backward state. **1885** STALLYBRASS tr. *Hehn's Wand. Pl. & Anim.* 450 They, who probably planted only spring-corn. **1815** J. SMITH *Panorama Sci. & Art* II. 637 Of the various sorts of cabbage, fit for field culture, the Scotch gray, the open green or *spring kale, and the turnip-rooted, are the hardiest. **1786** ABERCROMBIE *Gard. Assist.* 252 More..on warm borders to stand for *spring lettuces. **1882** *Garden* 28 Jan. 65/3 This land we intend for *Spring Onions. **1765** *Museum Rust.* IV. 226 It seems adviseable to delay the sowing of *spring-rye as long as can be. **1766** *Compl. Farmer* 5 H, Having sown *spring wheat after a crop of madder. **1812** SIR J. SINCLAIR *Syst. Husb. Scot.* 244 A discrimination is highly necessary between winter wheat sown in the spring, and the Siberian, or real spring wheat. **1868** *Rep.*

U.S. Commissioner Agric. (1869) 417 They had been in the habit of using too much seed for spring wheat.

c. In the specific or popular names of plants, birds, fishes, insects, etc., as **spring-beauty, -bell, crocus, gentian, -grass; †spring-froth, herring, usher, wagtail**: (see quots.); **spring peeper**, a very small tree frog, *Hyla crucifer*, of eastern North America; **spring salmon** *N. Amer.*, a Pacific coast salmon that returns from the sea to the river in spring, esp. the chinook, *Oncorhynchus tshawytscha*.

(*a*) **1846–50** A. Wood *Class-bk. Bot.* 194 *Claytonia Caroliniana.* *Spring Beauty. *Ibid.*, *C. Virginica.* Virginian Spring Beauty. **1874** *Treas. Bot.* Suppl. 1344 *Springbell, *Sisyrinchium grandiflorum.* **1846–50** A. Wood *Class-bk. Bot.* 543 *Crocus vernus.* *Spring Crocus. **1829** Loudon *Encycl. Plants* 202 *Gentiana verna*, *spring gentian. **1713** *Phil. Trans.* XXVIII. 179 Soft Crested Grass..is thicker, softer, and more loose than our common Crested Grass, and in spike more nearly resembles our yellow *Spring Grass. **1771** *Encycl. Brit.* I. 327 *Anthoxanthum..odoratum*, or spring-grass, a native of Britain. **1845–50** Mrs. Lincoln *Lect. Bot.* 139 The sweet scented spring-grass (*Anthoxanthum odoratum*).

(*b*) *a* **1722** Lisle *Husb.* (1757) 449 An account of the cuckow-spit, or *spring-froth. **1868** *Chambers's Encycl.* X. 387/1 The Alewife is called *Spring Herring in some places, and *gasperau* by the French Canadians. **1884** Goode *Nat. Hist. Aquat. Anim.* 579 The 'Spring' Herring or 'Alewife', *Clupea vernalis.* **1906**, etc. *Spring peeper [see peeper[1] 2 b]. **1950** *Chicago Tribune* 28 Mar. 14/3 Then there are those who listen for choruses of spring peepers. **1977** *Globe & Mail* (Toronto) 11 Apr. 8/3, I don't know how many people other than those who live in the country are familiar with one of our prime sounds of spring: the spring peeper. **1850** G. Hines *Voy. round World* 331 In this country [*sc.* America] they are generally distinguished by the names of *spring-salmon and fall-salmon. **1905** D. S. Jordan *Introd. Study of Fishes* II. 80 The economic value of any species depends in great part on its being a 'spring salmon'. **1964** G. C. Carl *Some Common Fishes Brit. Columbia* 28 A few mature [Chinook salmon] may enter the larger rivers in late spring or early summer (hence the name 'spring salmon'). **1832** J. Rennie *Consp. Butterfl. & Moths* 102 The *Spring Usher (*Anisopteryx leucophearia*..) appears in oak woods the end of February and March. **1802** Montagu *Ornith.* s.v. *Wagtail*, *Spring, or Summer Wagtail.

8. *Comb.*, as *spring-budding, -digging, -dressing, flowering*, etc.; *spring-born, -gathered, -made, -planted*, etc.; **spring green** *a.*, light green.

(*a*) **1852** W. Wickenden *Hunchback's Chest* 281 In the *spring-budding meadows. **1763** Mills *Pract. Husb.* IV. 351 After each *spring digging,..the same care and management of the vines..must be continued. **1795** D. Walker *View Agric. Hertford* 39 The *spring or top dressings are the leading features of the Hertfordshire farming. **1842** Loudon *Suburban Hort.* 669 Excepting in the first spring after sowing, no spring dressing is required till May. **1932** W. Faulkner *Light in August* (1933) vii. 138 Into the bleak, clean room the *springfilled air blew in fainting gusts. **1731** Miller *Gard. Dict.* s.v. *Colchicum*, *Spring-flowering Meadow-Saffron. **1866** *Treas. Bot.* 110/1 A pretty spring-flowering plant. **1733** Tull *Horse-Hoeing Husb.* xi. 128 (Dubl.), This thus pulveriz'd Surface turn'd in, in the *Spring-Hoeing, enriches the Earth. **1881** O. Wilde *Poems* 178 Each *spring-impassioned tree Flames into green. **1817** Keats *Curious Shell* 14 What is it that hangs from thy shoulder, so brave, Embroider'd with many a *spring peering flower? **1782** *Encycl. Brit.* (ed. 2) IX. 6631 The *spring planting may be performed the end of January or beginning of February. **1765** *Museum Rust.* IV. 312 If the *spring-ploughing for barley or oats has been nine or ten inches deep. **1846** Keightley *Notes Virg., Georg.* i. 43 The poet commences his precepts with the spring-ploughing of the land. **1826** *Art of Brewing* (ed. 2) 164 Soon after the *spring racking,..the casks may be gradually stopped. **1925** G. Greene *Babbling April* 25 She waits without fear that *spring-scented day. **1765** *Museum Rust.* IV. 322 It is very common for grass-seeds to fail on such land, even from the *spring-sowing. **1883** F. A. Smith *Swedish Fisheries* 5 An essay on the cultivation of *spring-spawning fishes. **1842** Loudon *Suburban Hort.* 439 A top-dressing of putrescent manure may be..left on the surface till the *spring-stirring.

(*b*) **1868** Morris *Earthly Par.* (1890) 55/1 Unscared the *spring-born thrush did pass. **1857** Thornbury *Songs Cavaliers & Roundheads* 53 The sweet *spring-gather'd flowers fall before his feet in showers. *a* **1722** Lisle *Husb.* (1757) 304 The *spring-made cheese was tarter. **1812** *New Botanic Gard.* I. 32 These *spring-planted roots flower.. after those which were planted in autumn. **1786** Abercrombie *Gard. Assist.* 128 Plant out *spring-raised cabbages. *Ibid.* 137 Begin to weed the general *spring-sowed crops. **1801** *Farmer's Mag.* Nov. 473 The grain of *Spring sown fields. **1868** *Rep. U.S. Commissioner Agric.* (1869) 182 Indeed no grain will yield more than half a crop of poor quality, (on the Pacific slope,) when spring-sown. **1864** Swinburne *Atalanta* 2112 As winter's wan daughter Leaves lowland and lawn *Spring-stricken. **1649** G. Daniel *Trinarch., Hen. IV*, ccxlviii, Northumberland, who like a *Spring-taught Snayle Was crauling to haue Nibbled the fresh leafe. **1855** *Woman's Devot.* II. 299 The fair shadowing green of the *spring-touched larch.

(*c*) **1891** M. E. Wilkins *Humble Romance*, etc. 46 The cottages were painted uniformly white, and had blinds of a bright Spring-green colour!

III. †9. a. A young growth on a tree, plant, or root; a shoot, sprout, or sucker; a small branch, sprig, or twig; the rudimentary shoot of a seed. In early quots. *fig. Obs.* (Freq. *c* 1560–*c* 1650.)

a **1300** *Cursor M.* 27380 Quilk ar þaa sinnes þat scrift sal scau I sal þam recken siþen on rau, wit þair springes herefter neist. *Ibid.* 27737 Vnheind talking,..hurtes grett, and sclander and tene; þir ar þe springes o wreth fythtene. *c* **1440** *Promp. Parv.* 470 Sprynge, of a tre or plante,..*planta, plantula.* **1502** Arnolde *Chron.* 62 b/2 Yf thou wylt plante an Almaunde tree..putte many kyrnels togyder in the erth or seuerelly and whan the sprynge is growen oute [etc.]. **1559** Morwyng *Evonym.* 304 Wet the end of a fether or other lyke thing, as some yong and tender spring of a trie. **1578** Lyte *Dodoens* 4 The roote..putting foorth on every side much encrease of new springs. *Ibid.* 369 Thymelæa hath many smal springs or branches, of the length of a cubite. **1660** Sharrock *Vegetables* 117 A spring of scarce discernable growth may serve as a foundation to the pedal of the blossom.

†b. A growth of this nature cut or slipped off, esp. for planting; a rod or switch; a cutting, set, or slip. Also *fig. Obs.*

1377 Langl. *P. Pl.* B. v. 41 Who-so spareth þe sprynge spilleth his children. **1387–8** T. Usk *Test. Love* III. vi. (Skeat) l. 4 'That tree to sette, fayn wolde I lerne.'..'The first thing, thou muste sette thy werke on grounde siker and good, accordaunt to thy springes.' *c* **1485** *E.E. Misc.* (1855) 67 There is moste connabylle tyme for sedys, graynys, and pepyns, and Autumpe for spryngys, and plantys. **1563** Hyll *Art Garden.* (1593) 85 Between the old plants set yong springs, slipped off from the old. **1601** Holland *Pliny* II. 196 The same yong springs eaten alone by themselues in a salad, in maner of the tender crops and spurts of the Colewort,..do fasten the teeth. **1657** R. Austen *Fruit-trees* i. 60 After a yeare or two divers young springs may be drawne from the roots.

†c. A young tree, esp. one growing from a set or slip; a sapling. *Obs.*

1499 Pynson *Promp. Parv.* P iv/2 Springe or younge tre. **1545** in I. S. Leadam *Sel. Cas. Crt. Requests* (1898) 85 To fell & cutt down viij yong Sprynges abowte Allhaloutyd. **1552** Huloet, Arboure or place made with quicke springes. **1563** Hyll *Art Garden.* (1593) 6 That ground..which naturally bringeth forth of his own accord, both elms and wilde young springs.

fig. *c* **1535** Elyot *Educ.* B iv, Good aduertisements and preceptes, wherby the yonge spryng of vertuous maners shall growe streyghte.

†d. *transf.* A young man, a youth. *Obs.*

1559 *Mirr. Mag., Earl Northumbld.* iv, A sonne I had.. That being yong, and but a very spring [etc.]. *c* **1586** C'tess Pembroke *Ps.* cv. ix, Their eldest-borne, that countries hopefull spring. **1590** Spenser *Muiopot.* 292 Winged Loue, With his yong brother Sport;..The one his bowe and shafts, the other Spring A burning Teade about his head did moue.

10. a. A copse, grove, or wood consisting of young trees springing up naturally from the stools of old ones; a plantation of young trees, esp. one inclosed and used for rearing or harbouring game; a spinney. Now *dial.*

Freq. in the 16th and 17th c., often in local names.

1399 *Fabric Rolls York Minster* (Surtees Soc.) 132 Pro xxj rodis de hegyng circa le spring in Langwath. **1468–9** *Durham Acc. Rolls* (Surtees) 155 Pro factura liij rod. fossat. circa unam percellam terre juxta parcum de Shynkcley pro salvacione de le Spryng ibidem..xiij *s.* ix *d.* *c* **1490** *Plumpton Corr.* (Camden) 74 To cause suer search to be made, what horse & cattaille ther be, that goes in my spring within my parke at Spofford. **1523** Fitzherb. *Husb.* §135 So is a spryng beste kepte, where there is neyther manne nor foure-foted beastes within the hedge. **1576** Turberv. *Hunting* xxxi, In small groues or hewts,..priuily enclosed within the greater springs in the Forests and strong couerts. **1600** Fairfax *Tasso* xiii. xxxi, If his courage any champion moue To trie the hazard of this dreedfull spring, I giue him leaue..: This said, his Lords attempt the charmed groue. **1620–6** Quarles *Feast for Worms* 476 A Herd of Deere are browzing in a spring, With eager appetite. **1652** Blithe *Eng. Improver Impr.* (ed. 3) 157 Although much dry,..hungry land doth not many times afford a thick Coppice, or good Spring. *a* **1700** B. E. *Dict. Cant. Crew* s.v. *Ringwalks*, They go drawing in their Springs at Hart-Hunting. **1788–** in dialect glossaries (Yks., Lanc., Linc., Herts., Kent, etc.).

fig. **1591** Lyly *Endym.* v. ii, *Top.* Howe shall I bee troubled when this younge springe shall growe to a great wood! *Epi.* O, sir, your chinne is but a quyller yet.

b. Const. *of* (wood, oak, etc.).

1483 *Cath. Angl.* 356 A Sprynge of wodde, *virgultum.* **1614** *Minutes Archdeaconry Essex* (MS.), He had cattle broke into a yonge springe of wood. **1667** Milton *P.L.* ix. 218, I..In yonder Spring of Roses intermixt With Myrtle, find what to redress till Noon. **1690** in *Hunter MSS.* (Chapt. Durham) VII. 203 A parcell of ground whereon there is a new spring of Oakes growne 3 and 4 yards high. **1732** *N. Riding Rec.* IX. 120 All that spring of wood, adjoining to the last-mentioned close. **1750** W. Ellis *Mod. Husb.* IV. iv. 18 A Spinny, or Spring of Underwood. **1780** *Newcastle Courant* (E.D.D.), On the estate there are two fine springs of wood.

c. *collect.* Young growth, shoots, or sprouts, esp. the lower or under growth of trees or shrubs. Now *dial.*

1482 *Rolls of Parlt.* VI. 224/1 To save the spryng of their Wood so felled. *Ibid.* The same spryng hath be in tyme passed, and daily ys distroyed. **1523** Fitzherb. *Husb.* §126 Lay thy small trouse or thornes..ouer thy quickesettes, that shepe do not eate the sprynge nor buddes of thy settes. **1579** Spenser *Sheph. Cal.* June 53 The byrds, which in the lower spring Did shroude in shady leaues. **1601** Holland *Pliny* I. 514 The Pine tree also with her shaddow nippeth and killeth the yong spring of all plants within the reach thereof. **1670** Evelyn *Sylva* (ed. 2) xxxiv. 220 When the Spring is of two years growth, draw part of it for Quicksets. **1823, 1854**, in Suffolk and Northampt. glossaries.

d. *attrib.* and *Comb.*, as *spring-fall, -felling, -shaw.* Chiefly *dial.* Also spring-wood.

1800 Tuke *Agric. Yks.* 184 What is called 'spring-felling', that is, felling the whole growth of the trees and underwood.., but so as not to injure the crown of the roots. **1856** 'Stonehenge' *Brit. Rural Sports* 58 Pointers or setters which are broken to run in when ordered, may do in open spring-falls,..but they are too large for thick covert. **1887** Parish & Shaw *Dict. Kent. Dial.*, *Spring-shaw*, a strip of the young undergrowth of wood, from two to three rods wide.

11. A springing up, growing, or bursting forth of plants, vegetation, etc.; a growth or crop; also, a race or stock of persons. Now *rare.*

1624 Chapman *Homer's Hymn Apollo* 554 A most dreadful and pernicious thing, Call'd Typhon, who on all the human spring Conferr'd confusion. **1641** Best *Farm. Bks.* (Surtees) 10 Some fresh pasture wheare there is a good timely springe appearinge on the grownd. *a* **1652** Brome *Lovesick Crt.* iv. ii, By a perpetual spring of more procere And bigger bladed grass. **1822** W. J. Napier *Pract. Store-farm.* 58 Upon the part particularly alluded to, there appears to have arisen a great spring of natural fiorin.

IV. †12. a. Rise, beginning, first appearance, or birth (*of* something). *Obs.*

a **1225** *Leg. Kath.* 320 Ah we witen wel þet ure lahen, ure bileaue, & ure lei hefde lahe sprung [L. *primordia*].

1550 Bale *Unchaste Votaries* i. (1560) 17 Ye very spring or fyrst going forth of the Gospel. *a* **1568** Ascham *Scholem.* i. (Arb.) 141 The Latin tong,..from the spring, to the decay of the same. **1594** Hooker *Eccl. Pol.* i. vi. §1 Men, if we view them in their spring, are at the first without understanding or knowledge at all. **1682** Grew *Anat. Pl.* Introd. 3 Plants have their set and peculiar Seasons for their Spring or Birth.

b. In the phr. *to take* (..) *spring from* or *out of*, to have source or origin in, to rise or originate in.

1585 T. Washington tr. *Nicholay's Voy.* iv. xv. 129 The riuer of Salef, which takes her spring from the mount of Taur. **1605** B. Jonson *Queen's Masques, Blackness* A iij b, This riuer taketh spring out of a certain Lake, east-ward. **1835** I. Taylor *Spir. Despot.* v. 222 The spiritual power.. taking its spring from Christianity.

†c. ? The yolk *of* an egg. *Obs.*[−1]

1600 Surflet *Countrie Farme* i. xii. 54 Stampe them all togither with the spring of an egge.

13. †a. The rising *of* the sea (to an exceptional height) at particular times. (Cf. sense 13 b.) *Obs.*

1398 Trevisa *Barth. De P.R.* viii. xxix. (Tollem. MS.), Alwey in þe new mone þe sprynge of þe see is heyest, and also in þe ful mone. **1539** *Act. 31 Hen. VIII*, c. 4, Ouerflowyng..of..grounde lying by the said riuer, with the high springes of the sea. **1585** T. Washington tr. *Nicholay's Voy.* ii. xxiv. 65 All the whole length of the Citie is washed with the springs of the Sea.

b. = spring-tide 2. Chiefly *pl.* (So G. *spring.*)

1584 in J. J. Cartwright *Chapt. Hist. Yorks.* (1872) 268 We say that there ryseth at the sprynge 18 foott water, and at the nepe eleaven foot water. **1622** Hawkins *Voy. S. Sea* (1847) 180 It seemeth an iland, and in high springes I judge that the sea goeth round about it. **1641** J. Taylor (Water P.) *Last Voy.* B 6 b, The trade..is at the least two hundred Tunnes of all commodities, every spring, which is every fortnight or lesse. **1751** *Anc. & Pres. St. Navig. Lyn, Wisbeach*, etc. 25 The tides then generally run high, by Reason of the Springs putting in. **1779** Forrest *Voy. N. Guinea* 15 The tide rises six feet on the springs. **1820** Scoresby *Acc. Arctic Reg.* I. 147 The rise of tide may be stated at about six feet during the springs. **1858** *Merc. Marine Mag.* V. 366 The stream runs 5 knots at springs, and 3 knots at neaps. **1892** Lowndes *Camping Sk.* 211 Only the highest 'springs' could touch us.

transf. **1590** Spenser *F.Q.* i. i. 21 But when his [*sc.* the Nile's] later spring gins to auale, Huge heapes of mudd he leaues.

attrib. **1846** McCulloch *Acc. Brit. Empire* (1854) I. 59 There is a bar outside the entrance; but as it has about 13 feet water over it even at the lowest spring ebbs, it [etc.].

c. Without article.

1883 *Encycl. Brit.* XXIII. 353 The difference between the intervals is greater at spring than at neap.

14. a. An act of springing or leaping; a bound, jump, or leap.

c **1450** in *Rel. Ant.* I. 309 Thy spryngys, thy quarters, thy rabetis also. *c* **1450** *Merlin* i. 15 As she sodenly made a sprynge, the childe fill oute of hir arme. **1526** *Pilgr. Perf.* (W. de W. 1531) 20 b, An holy monke, whiche in the poynt of his dethe sodeynly gaue a great sprynge vpwarde. **1674** tr. *Martiniere's Voy. N.C.* 40 Upon which they [*sc.* reindeer] gave such a spring, we thought [etc.]. **1698** Fryer *Acc. E. India & P.* 111 They carry the Leopards on *Hackeries*,..to give them the advantage of their Spring. **1737** Bracken *Farriery Impr.* (1757) II. 167 Altho' his Adversary's Horse make a Spring, and run past him. **1820** Scoresby *Acc. Arctic Reg.* II. 294, I made a spring towards a boat..and caught hold of the gunwale. **1843** R. J. Graves *Syst. Clin. Med.* xxxi. 428 Taking two of the large stone stair-steps at each spring. **1869** Blackmore *Lorna D.* iii, John Fry..in the spring of fright had brought himself down from Smiler's side.

fig. **1878** Stewart & Tait *Unseen Univ.* i. §46. 63 When Science was pausing for the spring she has since made. **1889** *Spectator* 26 Oct., They must have..a certain largeness of view besides, shown in their repeated..springs at colonial empire.

b. A recoil or rebound of something after being bent or forced out of its normal position or form.

1680 Moxon *Mech. Exerc.* 184 Unless..with every Spring of the Pole they should lift their treading Leg so high as [etc.]. **1779** Cowper *Human Frailty* 5 The bow well bent, and smart the spring, Vice seems already slain. **1853** Kane *Grinnell Exp.* xxiii. (1856) 196 A startling sensation, resembling the spring of a well-drawn bow.

c. A quick, convulsive, or elastic movement made by certain plants or animals in dispersing or depositing seed, eggs, etc.

1801 *Farmer's Mag.* Nov. 451, I took some of the flies,.. and pressing them a little, they quitted several eggs, which they quit one by one, with a sudden spring. **1837** P. Keith *Bot. Lex* 112 The pericarp of many fruits, which open when ripe with a sort of sudden spring, ejecting the seed with violence. *Ibid.* 159 The elastic spring with which the anther flies open.

d. A distance capable of being covered by a spring or leap.

1817 Shelley *Rev. Islam* ii. xxix, Her spirit..far wandering, on the wing Of visions that were mine, beyond its utmost spring. **1831** Scott *Ct. Rob.* xvi, A tiger, chained within no distant spring of his bed.

e. An escape or rescue from prison. *slang* (orig. *U.S.*).

1901 'J. Flynt' *World of Graft* ii. 32 It is comparatively easy to make a 'spring' out of the clutches of the law when there is sufficient money to hand around to the various persons with 'pull'. **1923** A. Stringer *Diamond Thieves* xx. 385, I *did* wait. But his swell friends didn't come across wit' any spring. **1968** 'B. Mather' *Springers* xv. 161 We just.. waited for what we knew would eventually come. A spring. **1977** F. Ross *Dead Runner* i. 41 Springing some bugger from the Scrubs—O.K. Not easy... You can't pull a spring like that without help on the inside.

15. A flock *of* teal. Now *arch.*

c **1450** *Egerton MS. 1995* in *Philol. Soc. Trans.* (1909) 51 A sprynge of Telys. *c* **1470** *Hors, Shepe, & G.* (Roxb.) 30 A spryng of teeles. **1486** *Bk. St. Albans* f vj b. [Hence in later lists.] **1856** 'Stonehenge' *Brit. Rural Sports* 78 The following Terms are in Use among Wildfowl-shooters:—A flock..of teal, 'a spring'. **1892** *Cornh. Mag.* Aug. 152 Further out we notice a 'spring' of nine teal.

16. A cut or joint of pork consisting of the belly or lower part of the fore-quarter. *Obs.* exc. *dial.*

1598 Florio, *Bambetti*, that ioynt of meate we call a spring or pestle of porke. **1622** Fletcher *Prophetess* i. iii, Can you be such an Ass.. To think these springs of Pork will shoot up Cæsars? **1654** Gayton *Pleas. Notes* iii. 96 Pray hand the Spring of Porke to me. **1708** W. Wilson tr. *Petr. Arbiter* 97 He shall make you.. a Turtle of a Spring of Pork. **1771** Mrs. Haywood *New Present for Maid* 20 The fore-quarter [of a hog] contains the spring and the fore-loin. **1844** H. Stephens *Bk. Farm* II. 240 The belly or spring [of pork], also fit for pickling, or for rolling up,.. for brawn.

17. *Naut.* †**a.** A breach or opening in a vessel through the splitting or starting of a plank or seam. *Obs.*$^{-1}$

1611 B. Jonson *Catiline* iii. i, Each petty hand Can steer a ship becalmed; but he that will Govern and carry her to her ends must know.. Where her springs are, her leaks; and how to stop 'em.

b. A crack or split in a mast or spar, esp. one of such a size as to render it unsafe to carry the usual amount of sail.

G. *sprung* has the general sense of 'split, crack'.

1744 J. Philips *Jrnl. Exped. Anson* 157 We.. discover'd a great Spring in the Foremast. **1748** *Anson's Voy.* ii. ii. 135 The spring was two inches in depth. **1792** *Trans. Soc. Arts* X. 212 An accident by a shot, a spring, a rottenness. **1846** A. Young *Naut. Dict.* 292 A spar is said to be sprung, when it is cracked or split,.. and the crack is called a spring.

18. The quality or capacity of springing; the power inherent in, or possessed by, a thing of spontaneously resuming or returning to its normal state or bulk when pressure or other force is withdrawn; elastic energy or force; elasticity.

a. Of the air.

Freq. from *c* 1660 to *c* 1770; now *rare* or *Obs.*

1660 Boyle *New Exp. Phys. Mech.* i. 24 There is yet another way to explicate the Spring of the Air. **1687** D. Abercromby *Acad. Sci.* App. iv. 4 By the help whereof [*sc.* the air-pump] he proves the Elastic Power and Spring of the Air. **1719** Quincy *Phys. Dict.* (1722) 9 The Air.. hath been found.. by the Force of its own Spring, to possess 13000 times the space it does when pressed by the incumbent Atmosphere. *a* **1774** Goldsm. *Surv. Exp. Philos.* (1776) II. 84 This pressure is increased by another cause, I mean the air's spring or elasticity. **1815** J. Smith *Panorama Sci. & Art* II. 6 The operation is continued till the spring of the air in the receiver is no longer sufficient to lift the valves *a b*.

b. Of solids.

1674 N. Fairfax *Bulk & Selv.* 72 The spring of the earth over-ballancing the weight of it as to power. **1683** Moxon *Mech. Exerc., Printing* xxiv. ¶5 Pieces of Felt.. will Squeeze and retain their Spring for a considerable time. **1733** Cheyne *Eng. Malady* ii. x. §2 (1734) 219 There is in all Animal Fibres.. an original Mechanism of Elasticity or Spring. **1753** Hogarth *Anal. Beauty* x. 60 A small wire that has lost its spring, and so will retain every shape it is twisted into. **1789** *Trans. Soc. Arts* VII. 159 There is a spring in the whalebone, which prevents it turning steady. **1874** Pitt-Rivers *Evol. Culture, Princ. Classif.* (1906) 16 Yielding few .. woods that have sufficient spring for the construction of the bow. **1879** S. C. Bartlett *Egypt to Pal.* iv. 73 The knives and daggers had an elastic spring, which.. they retain to this day.

c. Elasticity or springiness as possessed by persons or the limbs; buoyancy and vigour in movement.

a **1700** Dryden (J.), Heav'ns! what a spring was in his arm, to throw! **1723** Steele *Consc. Lovers* iii. 48 What a Spring in her Step! **1784** Cowper *Task* i. 135 Th' elastic spring of an unwearied foot That mounts the stile with ease. **1820** Hazlitt *Table-T.* Ser. ii. xvi. (1869) 317 Do nothing to take away.. the spring and elasticity of your muscles. **1845** Bailey *Festus* (ed. 2) 235 It is sad To.. Know eyes are dimming, bosom shrivelling, feet Losing their spring. **1899** *Allbutt's Syst. Med.* VI. 678 At first the patient finds that he is losing his spring in walking.

19. *transf.* Buoyancy, activity, vigour *of* mind, temper, etc.; active power or faculty.

1682 Sir T. Browne *Chr. Mor.* iii. §20 Persons vitiously inclined.. having the Elater and Spring of their own Natures to facilitate their Iniquities. **1714** R. Fiddes *Pract. Disc.* ii. 116 If the mind be too long bent upon one thing, twill lose its spring and activity. **1752** Hume *Ess. & Treat.* (1777) I. 192 A selfish villain may possess a spring and alacrity of temper. **1831** Scott *Ct. Rob.* xxvii, Ere he has.. recovered, in some degree, the spring of his mind, and the powers of his body. **1887** Ruskin *Præterita* II. 41 Happy journey by the Eastern Riviera began to restore my spring of heart.

20. a. *Arch.* The point at which an arch or vault springs or rises from its abutment or impost; the commencement of curvature in an arch.

1726 Leoni *Alberti's Archit.* II. 38/2 Columns of height sufficient to reach to the spring of their Arches. **1772** C. Hutton *Bridges* 63 When the arch stones only are laid, and the pier built no higher than the spring. **1864** Boutell *Her. Hist. & Pop.* xix. (ed. 3) 317 The arches recede inwards from their spring from the Circlet. **1875** Merivale *Gen. Hist. Rome* lxxix. (1877) 670 There remain on the face of the Palatine some indications of what may have been the spring of the first arch.

attrib. **1735** J. Price *Stone-Br. Thames* 4 The Piers,.. under the Chaptrel, or Spring Stones, have a Square Course. **1825** J. Nicholson *Operat. Mechanic* 539 The supports of an arch are called the *spring walls*. **1859** T. H. Turner *Dom. Archit.* III. ii. vii. 312 But there are the spring-stones of a fan-tracery vault.

¶**b.** The rise of an arch; the ascent or slope *of* a bridge.

1753 *Scots Mag.* Aug. 422/1 The arch.. was fifty-five feet wide, and had but eight feet of spring. **1886** Stevenson *Kidnapped* xxvi, An old, hobbling woman.. set forth again up the steep spring of the bridge.

21. a. *techn.* (See quot. 1825.) Also *attrib.*

1825 J. Nicholson *Operat. Mechanic* 601 The bevel by which the edge of the plank is reduced from the right angle when the plank is sprung, is termed the spring of the plank. **1842** Gwilt *Archit.* Gloss., *Spring Bevel of a Rail*, the angle made by the top of the plank, with a vertical plane touching the ends of the railpiece, which terminates the concave side.

b. *Naut.* The sheer, the upward curvature or rise, of the deck planking of a vessel or boat.

So G. *spring* and *sprung*.

1838 *Civil Eng. & Arch. Jrnl.* I. 353/1 The reason why she has such an extraordinary sheer or spring in the fore part of her upper deck. **1881** *Standard* 9 Aug. 6/3 The boat is high at the bow and stern, being built with what is known as a good spring.

c. *Bootmaking.* The raising or rise of the toe of a last above the ground-line. Also, arch or curvature in the instep.

In quot. 1885 *spec.* applied to the steel support which gives the desired curvature to the boot or shoe.

1885 J. B. Leno *Art of Boot & Shoemaking* viii. 54 The patterns for the springs of large size boots should have a good quarter of an inch left on at sides and bottom. *Ibid.* xix. 145 The spring is attached to the inner sole... Care should be taken in.. fixing the metal shield... Instances have occurred in which the spring, through being inadequately shielded, has pierced through the inner sole to the foot. **1902** F. Y. Golding *Manuf. Boots & Shoes* 107 *Spring* is the term used to denote the elevation of the toe of the last... If the substance of the sole be light very little spring is required. *Ibid.*, Sometimes the term 'spring' is used to describe the hollowness or arch of the waist. **1905** E. J. C. Swaysland *Boot & Shoe Design* 20 For light dress work the spring of the toe should be half an inch. **1916** F. Plucknett *Boot & Shoe Manuf.* ii. 17 It is advisable to put spring into the forepart of the last, equal to the amount which the boot would probably acquire in wear. **1935** J. Ball in F. Y. Golding *Boots & Shoes* VI. xi. vi. 39 Spring is the amount of *curve* from the joint to the point of the toe, and whereas a light flexible shoe requires very little, the stouter and stiffer the sole the greater the amount of spring.

V. 22. An elastic contrivance or mechanical device, usually consisting of a strip or plate of steel (or a number of these) suitably shaped or adjusted, which, when compressed, bent, coiled, or otherwise forced out of its normal shape, possesses the property of returning to it.

Springs vary greatly in form, size, and use, but are used chiefly for imparting or communicating motion (either by gradual unwinding, as in the spring of a clock or watch, or by sudden release), for regulating or controlling movement, or for lessening or preventing concussion.

Cf. G. *springfeder*, Du. *-veer*, Da. *-fjær*, Sw. *-fjäder*.

a. In a clock, watch, etc., or in general use.

1428 *Acts Privy Council* (1834) III. 289 Item for amendyng of the spryng of the barell [of a clock] vs viij d. [**1472** in Rogers *Agric. & Prices* (1882) IV. 622 A spring to a clock is purchased by King's College, Cambridge, for 2*d*.] **1598** Florio, *Molla*, a wheele of a clocke that mooueth all the rest called the spring. **1599** T. M[oufet] *Silkwormes* 35 Ingenious Germane, how didst thou conuey Thy Springs, thy Scrues, thy rowells, and thy flie? **1611** Shaks. *Cymb.* ii. ii. 47 To th' Truncke againe, and shut the spring of it. **1677** Moxon *Mech. Exerc.* ii. 28 The Spring H forces the Bolt forwards when it is shot back with the Key. **1713** *Lond. Gaz.* No. 5155/4 A Gold Watch,.. going with a Spring, Without Fusey, Chain or String. **1771** *Encycl. Brit.* III. 936 The quickness or slowness of the vibrations of the balance depend not solely upon the action of the great spring, but chiefly upon the action of the spring *a, b, c*, called the spiral spring. **1825** Scott *Talism.* xii, At the same time was heard the sound of a spring or check, as when a crossbow is bent. **1860** Dickens *Uncomm. Trav.* xiv, One.. rap was rapped that might have been a spring in Mr. Testator's easy-chair to shoot him out of it. **1875** Knight *Dict. Mech.* 2275/2 A helical spring has coils of decreasing diameter as they approach the center.

b. In a carriage, coach, or other vehicle.

1665 Pepys *Diary* 5 Sept., After dinner comes Colonel Blunt in his new chariot made with springs. **1706** *Lond. Gaz.* No. 4235/3 The sole Benefit of making and vending certain Steel Springs he hath.. invented for ease of Persons riding in Coaches. **1794** W. Felton *Carriages* (1801) I. 72 Short light springs which contain but few plates, have frequently no hoops. **1837** W. B. Adams *Carriages* 117 What is technically understood in carriages by the term 'spring' is a plate or plates of tempered steel properly shaped to play in any required mode. **1876** *Encycl. Brit.* V. 137/1 The elliptic springs, upon which nearly all carriages are now mounted.

23. *fig.* **a.** That by which action is produced, inspired, or instigated; a moving, actuating, or impelling agency, cause, or force; a motive.

Frequent from *c* 1700, either with direct allusion to the literal sense (*a*), or in a more indefinite use (*b*) which is sometimes not clearly distinguishable from sense 3.

(*a*) *c* **1616** S. Ward *Coal fr. Altar* (1627) 41 They ascribe it either to vaine glory, or couetousnesse; the only springs that set their wheeles on going. **1681** Dryden *Abs. & Achit.* 499 By these the Springs of Property were bent, And wound so high, they Crack'd the Government. **1720** Ozell *Vertot's Rom. Rep.* II. xii. 214 The Springs Pompey set at work to deprive all the Commanders of the Commonwealth of their Posts. **1748** Geddes *Compos. Antients* 15 The spring, the just tone of the soul, is broke. **1767** A. Young *Farmer's Lett. to People* 61 These men are yet more able.. to put all the springs of a perfect culture in motion. **1815** J. Cormack *Abol. Fem. Infanticide Guzerat* xiv. 278 The springs of this mighty political engine, however, have, generally speaking, already lost their elasticity. **1863** Kinglake *Crimea* (1876) I. xiv. 255 Morny.. prepared to touch the springs of that wondrous machinery by which a clerk can dictate to a nation. **1872** Bagehot *Physics & Pol.* 162 At once the fatal clog is removed, and the ordinary springs of progress.. begin their elastic action.

(*b*) **1691** Ray *Creation* (1714) 47 What is the Spring and principal Efficient of this Reciprocation. **1717** J. Keill *Anim. Oeconomy* (1738) 150 Secretion is the Spring of all the animal Functions. **1719** De Foe *Crusoe* i. (Globe) 177 A strange Impression upon the Mind, from we know not what Springs, and by we know not what Power. **1774** Franklin *Ess.* Wks. 1840 II. 385 The spring or movement of such intercourse is.. gain, or the hopes of gain. **1810** S. Smith in *Edin. Rev.* XV. 309 Instead of hanging the understanding of a woman upon walls,.. we would make it the first spring and ornament of society. **1853** Merivale *Rom. Rep.* ii. (1867) 39 The love of gold was the sordid spring of the most brilliant enterprises of the republic. **1871** Lowell *Pope* Wks. 1890 IV. 31 The exposer of those motives.. whose spring is in institutions and habits of purely worldly origin.

b. Freq. const. *of* action (or conduct).

1722 Wollaston *Relig. Nat.* ix. 173 The springs of all human actions. **1779** Forrest *Voy. N. Guinea* 285 It is difficult.. to come at the true springs of action. **1806** Surr *Winter in Lond.* III. 174 Whether public zeal and patriotic motives, were the springs of his lordship's conduct. **1850** Merivale *Rom. Emp.* ii. (1865) I. 73 The real springs of human action were unknown to him, or disregarded by him. **1885** J. Martineau *Types Eth. Th.* II. ii. iii. §1. 518 Numerous springs of action and modes of feeling which neither interest nor reason could be shown to evolve.

c. In the phr. ***springs of life***.

1728–46 Thomson *Spring* 329 While sickly damps, and cold autumnal fogs, Hung not, relaxing, on the springs of life. **1819** Scott *Let.* in *Lockhart* (1837) IV. viii. 268 A grief of that calm and concentrated kind which.. gradually wastes the springs of life.

†**d.** A device; a trick or artifice. *Obs. rare.*

1753 Miss Collier *Art Torment.* ii. iii. (1811) 164 This method of granting favours in a disgustful manner, is one of our chief springs, and must be practised in as many connections as you possibly can introduce it.

24. *Naut.* **a.** A rope put out from the end or side of a vessel lying at anchor, and made fast to the cable. (So G. *spring*, *springtau*.)

1744 J. Philips *Jrnl. Exped. Anson* 156 We clapt a Spring on the Sheet-cable to prevent her from swinging. **1753** Hanway *Trav.* iii. xlviii. (1762) I. 219 We were obliged to put a spring on our cable, in order to bring our guns to bear on them. **1769** Falconer *Dict. Marine* (1780), *Spring* is.. a rope passed out of one extremity of a ship and attached to a cable proceeding from the other, when she lies at anchor. **1800** *Hull Advertiser* 16 Aug. 1/4 A gun-brig.. moored with springs on her cables. **1836** Marryat *Midsh. Easy* xxx, He had warped round with the springs on his cable, and had recommenced his fire upon the Aurora. **1882** Nares *Seamanship* (ed. 6) 202 Slip the cable, and then the spring.

attrib. **1806** A. Duncan *Nelson* 94 The French fleet.., moored on spring cables.

b. (See quots.)

1769 Falconer *Dict. Marine* (1780), *Spring* is likewise a rope reaching diagonally from the stern of a ship to the head of another which lies along-side or abreast of her, at a short distance. *Ibid.*, Springs of this sort are.. occasionally applied from a ship to a wharf or key. **1867** Smyth *Sailor's Word-bk.*, *Spring*, a hawser laid out to some fixed object to slue a vessel proceeding to sea.

attrib. **1875** Knight *Dict. Mech.*, *Spring-line*, in a ponton-bridge, a line passing diagonally from one ponton to another. **1916** *Daily Colonist* (Victoria, B.C.) 23 July 4/6 The mate was on the forecastle head, but outside the rail, when the spring line parted. One end of the big hawser flicked up and smashed the mate's leg. **1975** H. White *Raincoast Chron.* (1976) 156/1 A deck-hand expertly heaves a throwing-line ashore. Somebody catches it, pulls in the steel spring-line from amidships.

25. *attrib.* **a.** Simple attrib. in various senses, esp. 'fitted with a spring or springs', 'acting like a spring', 'of or pertaining to a spring', as ***spring-arbor***, ***-balance***, ***-bar***, ***-barrel***, ***-bed***, etc.

The number of these is very great, and only the more important are illustrated here. Others are recorded and explained by Knight *Dict. Mech.*, and in recent Dicts.

1696 W. Derham *Artific. Clock-m.* 2 Next for the Spring. That which the Spring.. laps about, in the middle of the Spring-box, is the *Spring-Arbor. *a* **1788** Imison *Sch. Arts* I. 273 At the top of the spring-arbor, is the endless-screw, and its wheel. **1842** *Penny Cycl.* XXII. 385 **Spring-balance*, a machine in which the elasticity of a spring of tempered steel is employed as a means of measuring weight or force. **1889** *Science-Gossip* XXV. 36 If a body were resting on a delicate spring balance. **1856** 'Stonehenge' *Brit. Rural Sports* 394 The *Spring-bar to which the stirrup-leather is attached, and which easily allows this part of the saddle.. to be set at liberty the moment the rider is hung by it. **1875** Knight *Dict. Mech.*, *Spring-bar*, a bar parallel with the axle and resting upon the middle of the elliptic spring. **1881** W. E. Dickson *Organ-Build.* v. 65 The spring-bar has a slip of wood.. glued or bradded to it. **1850** Denison *Clock & Watch-m.* 110 It is all wound off the *spring barrel on to a fusee. **1846** Holtzapffel *Turning* II. 913 The cloth.. passes from a roller over a round bar, and comes in contact with the *spring bed, which is a long elastic plate of steel, fixed to the framing of the machine. **1858** Simmonds *Dict. Trade*, *Spring-bed*, an elastic or air mattress. **1862** *Catal. Internat. Exhib.*, *Brit.* II. No. 3579, Russell's Camp Hospital Spring Bed or Dhoolee Stretcher. **1847** *Illustr.*

London News 13 Mar. 165/1 There is..a *spring-bell, which the Prisoner is to sound when he requires the attendance of an officer. 1882 Miss Braddon Mt. Royal III. vi. 102 Jessie Bridgeman touched a spring bell on the tea-table. 1835 Dickens in Evening Chron. 18 June 3/4 *Spring blinds were fitted to the windows. 1889 Cassell's Bk. Househ. I. 250/2 Spring blinds, though very nice when they work well, are subject, as an old housekeeper once said, to 'tempers'. 1934 Cassell's Home Encycl. 86/2 Automatic or spring blinds are made with a hollow roller. 1786 Jefferson Writ. (1859) II. 74 Your *spring-block for assisting a vessel in sailing cannot be tried here. 1875 Knight Dict. Mech., Spring-block, a common block..connected to a ring-bolt by a spiral spring. 1634 in Archaeol. (1853) XXXV. 199 One two-leaf wyndowe with longe boult, *springe boult, and staples. 1703 R. Neve City & C. Purchaser 33 Iron-mongers distinguish those for House-building, into..Plate, Round, and Spring Bolts. 1829 Scott Anne of G. xvi, 'Enter here then, gentlemen,' said the jailor, undoing the spring-bolt of a heavy door. 1892 Photogr. Ann. II. 289 These fit over spring bolts projecting on either side from a block. 1693 Lond. Gaz. No. 2896/4 Both wearing light bob Wigs, and..Camblet Coats,..with new *Spring Boots, and Spurs. 1776 R. Daniel in Abridgm. Specif. Patents, Wearing App. III. (1876) 1 New kind of boots called spring boots. 1696 W. Derham Artific. Clock-m. 2 That which the Spring lies in, is the *Spring-box. 1825 J. Nicholson Operat. Mechanic 500 The chain, which requires to be uncoiled from the spring-box. 1888 Jacobi Printers' Vocab. 130 Spring-box, the receptacle at the head of the press holding the spring which acts on the bar-handle. 1858 Simmonds Dict. Trade, *Spring-braces, elastic suspenders for men's trousers. 1888 Jacobi Printers' Vocab. 130 *Spring brass, rules cast in flexible brass—the reverse of 'soft' or 'bending' brass rule. 1838 Civil Eng. & Arch. Jrnl. I. 408/1, I claim, as my invention or improvement in carriages,..the peculiar adaptation of *spring buffers and spring fastenings. 1884 F. J. Britten Watch & Clockm. 46 *Spring callipers..are useful when it is desired to retain a measurement. 1844 H. Stephens Bk. Farm II. 595 It terminates in a handle furnished with a *spring-catch. 1892 Photogr. Ann. II. 273 The shutter..is held by a spring catch. 1843 Penny Cycl. XXV. 425/1 On the large plate P, is a *spring-click. 1871 *Spring clip [see release sb.[1] 6b]. 1888 Rutley Rock-Forming Min. 18 The most generally useful contrivances are spring clips. 1737 Gentl. Mag. VII. 67 There are some *Spring Clocks and Watches, so contriv'd by Art as to lose no Time in winding. 1829 Chapters Phys. Sci. 92 The wheels in the spring clocks and in watches are urged on by the force of a spiral spring. 1850 Denison Clock & Watch-m. 109 This inequality of force is removed in English spring clocks and watches. 1894 T. W. Fox Mech. Weaving ix. 259 *Spring cords..consist of two wooden end-pieces..into which two wires..are driven. 1780 Mirror No. 80, The Elastic Cushion and *Spring Curls, which..are as natural and becoming..[as] the natural hair itself. 1858 Greener Gunnery 323 Take a *spring cushion (something like the spring machine found at all fairs for testing the force of a man pressing against it). 1883 Gresley Gloss. Coal-m. 232 *Spring-dart, an arrow or fish-headed boring tool for extricating a lost implement, or for withdrawing lining tubes. 1873 Spon Workshop Receipts Ser. I. 3/1 The differences of the distances..may be measured by *spring dividers. 1875 Knight Dict. Mech. 2750 The *spring-dog is depressed by a lever. 1886 J. Barrowman Sc. Mining Terms 63 Spring-dog, a spring hook used on a winding or haulage rope. 1826 Scott Woodstock xiv, He would have Woodstock a trap,..you the *spring-fall which should bar their escape. 1838 *Spring fastening [see spring buffer]. 1812 Sporting Mag. XXXIX. 136 The danger attending the use of the *spring-flask in shooting. 1895 Strand Mag. 113 In the Hall a *spring floor has been laid over the ordinary hard oak boards. 1846 Brittan tr. Malgaigne's Man. Oper. Surg. 374 Place in the wound either a canula, or a *spring forceps whose branches hold its edges open. 1867 Smyth Sailor's Word-bk., *Spring-Forelock, one jagged or split at the point, thereby forming springs to prevent its drawing. 1797 J. Curr Coal Viewer 67, 2 of them [double spring beams] go 18 or 20 inches through the main wall for the convenience of fixing the outside *spring frame. 1780 Mirror No. 68, The last time I came from London I brought down a parcel of *spring garters. 1841 Civil Eng. & Arch. Jrnl. IV. 13/1 A full description of the four instruments employed..to determine the pressure of the steam,..namely, the barometer-gauge,..and the *spring-gauge. 1850 Holtzapffel Turning III. 1254 Long conical holes, such as axletree boxes, are sometimes ground upon the *spring grinder. 1897 Sears, Roebuck Catal. 194d/2 Chocolate Goat Button, made with *spring heel, new opera toe with tip. 1952 M. Allingham Tiger in Smoke viii. 140 'He's got nerve.'..'Likewise spring heels and rubber bones.' 1688 Holme Armoury III. xxii. (Roxb.) 277 The second is a *Spring Hooke, or Springer; it is a kind of double Hook with a spring,..which being strucken into the mouth of any fish, the 2 hooks fly asunder, and so keeps the fish mouth open. 1862 Catal. Internat. Exhib., Brit. II. No. 6089, Spring hooks, curb chains, pole chains. 1883 Gresley Gloss. Coal-m. 232 Spring hook, an iron hook attached to the end of a winding capstan, or crab rope, fitted with a spring for closing the opening, and thus preventing the kibble, &c., from falling off. 1835–6 Owen in Todd's Cycl. Anat. I. 287/2 It has been denied that the *spring-joint [of birds] ever exists at the knee. 1901 P. Marshall Metal-w. Tools 14 In this pattern the legs have a spring joint at the top which tends to keep them apart. 1815 J. Smith Panorama Sci. & Art II. 325 With the mortar and levigating stone, a *spring-knife is very useful. 1882 Encycl. Brit. XIV. 323 The turner giving the rotation by means of the treadle and *spring-lath attached to the ceiling. 1852 Seidel Organ 128 The palate, together with its spring, must be taken out. For this purpose an instrument called a *spring lever is used. 1858 *Spring machine [see spring cushion above]. 1850 *Spring mattress [see mattress[1] 1]. 1875 Knight Dict. Mech., Spring-mattress, one having metallic springs beneath the hair or moss filling. 1843 Holtzapffel Turning I. 135 When the elastic tool, or '*spring passer', has been compressed,..it is put in motion. 1831 J. Holland Manuf. Metal II. 16 The workman takes what he calls a *spring piercer, a tool..consisting of two somewhat elastic steel blades. 1875 Knight Dict. Mech., *Spring-pin, in the English practice, a rod between the springs and axle-boxes, to regulate the pressure on the axles. 1881 Greener Gun 263 It..may be removed by completely turning out the spring pin. 1837 W. B. Adams Carriages 123 The elasticity of a *spring plate somewhat resembles the elasticity of a common cane. 1888 Jacobi Printers' Vocab. 130 *Spring points, these are a special kind of press points which assist in throwing the sheet off the spur of the point as printed. 1831 J. Holland Manuf. Metal I. 87 The cumbersome wooden frame-work of the old forges, including the timber, *spring-pole and hammer beam. 1837 Hebert Engin. & Mech. Encycl. II. 814 The string is fastened to the end of the spring-pole in a similar manner. 1883 Gresley Gloss. Coal-m. 233 Spring pole, a fir pole having considerable elasticity, to which the boring rods are suspended. 1662 H. More Antid. Ath. II. ii. §10 Which Pressure (as in all flexible Bodies that have a *Spring-power in them) is perpetual. 1853 Ure Dict. Arts (ed. 4) II. 831 The action of the *spring-presser is to consolidate the roving. 1694 Phil. Trans. XVIII. 103 Its shape is not very unlike to a sort of *Spring-Purse (as they are called) which many People use. 1701 Lond. Gaz. No. 3739/4 A striped Silk Spring-Purse. 1860 All Year Round No. 57. 162 A hundred *spring rattles would not realise the noise. 1850 Denison Clock & Watch-m. 239, I have lately seen some small French clocks with a *spring remontoire on the second wheel. 1821 P. Egan Life in London (1822) II. iv. 266 A fine collection of maps, concealed by the cornices of the book-cases, on *spring rollers, can be referred to without the least trouble. 1971 Habitat Catal. 86/2 Roller blinds..come complete with spring roller and fixing brackets. 1687 Smith Art Painting (ed. 2) 11 With a fine *Spring-Saw, cut it into scantlings. 1778 Life T. Boulter 57 A certain sum to procure some spring saws. 1818 Scott Hrt. Midl. xxxiii, She had procured..a spring-saw for me. 1867 Smyth Sailor's Word-bk., *Spring-searcher, a steel-pronged tool to search for defects in the bore of a gun. 1853 Heal & Son Catal.: Bedsteads, Sofas and Couches..with squab or *spring seats. 1858 Simmonds Dict. Trade, Spring-seat, a chair or couch with a spring in it. 1862 Catal. Internat. Exhib., Brit. II. No. 4721, Elliptical spring-seat saddle, and tree showing action of spring. 1884 Knight Dict. Mech. Suppl., Spring Seat, the support for the lower part of a spring, shaped according to circumstances. 1839 T. C. Hofland Brit. Angler's Man. v. (1841) 124 The *spring-snap was formerly much in use. 1856 'Stonehenge' Brit. Rural Sports 256 The *Spring Snap-Bait is..composed of a case which connects and keeps in place the shanks of the hooks.., but which, when drawn out, expand by their own elasticity. Ibid., The snap-hook is either the plain or the *spring snap-hook. 1864 Athenæum 27 Feb. 294 Pulling the door quickly after them, so as to hasp the *spring-sneck in the brass lock. 1815 J. Smith Panorama Sci. & Art II. 266 Upon the glass arm is cemented a piece of brass r, containing a *spring socket. 1871 Voyle Milit. Dict. (ed. 2), *Spring spike, in artillery, a spike with a spring attached to it, used for rendering a gun temporarily unserviceable. 1745 in J. S. McLennan Louisbourg (1918) 177 Ye fore *Spring Stay was Shott away. 1837 W. B. Adams Carriages 126 Leathern braces..were supported by a bracket or buttress of iron called the 'Spring Stay'. 1841 R. H. Dana Seaman's Man. 125 Spring-stay, a preventer-stay, to assist the regular one. 1867 Smyth Sailor's Word-bk., Spring-Stays, are rather smaller than the stays, and are placed above them, being intended as substitutes should the main one be shot away. 1833 Loudon Encycl. Archit. §84 To put an oak solid two-light proper frame..with..*spring stay-irons (irons to keep the window open) to the back kitchen. 1837 W. B. Adams Carriages 135 For this reason it would be advantageous to use *spring-steel in lieu of iron. 1843 Holtzapffel Turning I. 192 Its superior elasticity also adapts it to the formation of springs; some kinds of steel are prepared expressly for the same under the name of spring-steel. 1868 Joynson Metals 78 When blistered steel has to be drawn out or reduced by the rolls, it forms 'spring steel'. 1880 W. Carnegie Pract. Trapping 50 Arrange the nooses in such a manner that if one of them or the crutched stick is touched the latter falls, and releasing the crosspiece, the *spring-stick flies up, and the bird with it. 1884 C. G. W. Lock Workshop Rec. Ser. III. 74/2 The *spring-studs must of course be insulated from the clock-plate. 1942 Rep. & Memoranda Aeronaut. Res. Committee No. 2029. 9 Notes on the *Spring Tab. R.A.E. Report No. B.A. 1665. (5058.) April, 1941. (Unpublished.) 1969 Gloss. Aeronaut. & Astronaut. Terms (B.S.I.) v. 10 Spring tab, a balance tab, the angular movement of which is geared to the compression or extension of a spring embedded in the main control circuit. 1778 Encycl. Brit. (ed. 2) III. 2171 To remove these inconveniencies, some needles are made of one piece of steel of a *spring temper. 1875 Knight Dict. Mech. 2061 They are polished, and then brought to 'spring temper' by heating. 1923 J. R. Bond Farm Implements & Machinery v. 49 The simple *spring tine as first introduced on the Canadian cultivator had not sufficient strength. 1971 Farmers Weekly 19 Mar. 84 The RCM firm offers a choice of tines to fit one basic frame—a normal spring tine..or subsoiler tines. 1839 Ure Dict. Arts 579 This opening is then enlarged, by introducing the blade of a pair of *spring-tongs. 1859 R. Hunt Guide Mus. Pract. Geol. (ed. 2) 103 Several of the tools [for glass-making] are exhibited,..the *spring tool, the shears, &c. 1875 Knight Dict. Mech., Spring-tool, the light tongs of the glass-blower whereby handles and light objects are grasped. 1616 Surfl. & Markh. Country Farme 648 Some *spring-trappes, to snickle or halter either bird or beast. 1800 Mar. Edgeworth Belinda xxii, A man whose leg had..been caught in the spring-trap. 1820 T. Mitchell Aristoph. I. 80 There is generally some covert meaning in the names of Aristophanes..; his readers' feet are always treading on spring-traps. 1710 Addison Tatler No. 224 ¶5 Little cuts and figures, the invention of which we must ascribe to the Author of *Spring-Trusses. 1790 Ann. Reg., Hist. 115/2 Among these arms were some walking sticks with *spring-tucks concealed within them. 1912 Motor Man. (ed. 14) 206 *Spring washers are less effective, but answer well enough for the less vital parts of the mechanism. 1929 Ibid. (ed. 26) 20 Spring washer, a tempered steel washer cut through at one place and given a 'set' to provide a certain amount of spring. Used under a nut to keep it secure. 1714 Mandeville Fab. Bees (1733) II. 177 If he was wholly unacquainted with the nature of a *spring-watch. a1825 in J. Nicholson Operat. Mechanic 523 This locking..has the advantage..of being firmer, and less liable to be out of repair, than any locking where *spring-work is used. 1879 Cassell's Techn. Educ. IV. 299 'Spring work,'..that is, any articles in which springs are introduced.

b. With the names of vehicles, in the sense 'having springs, hung or suspended on springs', as ***spring ambulance, -carriage, -cart, -van, -wagon***.

1864 Sala in Daily Tel. 6 April, A couple of *spring ambulances, drawn by four horses apiece. 1842 Penny Cycl. XXII. 386 C-springs..were formerly used for almost all kinds of *spring-carriages. 1848 Thackeray Van. Fair xxxix, You'll drive her over in the *spring-cart. 1860 Dickens Uncomm. Trav. v, She shall be fetched by niece in a spring-cart. 1900 H. Lawson On Track 86 It was her mother an' sister in the spring-cart,..the doctor in his buggy. 1836–7 Dickens Sk. Boz, Scenes xii, The charge of having once made the passage in a *spring-van. 1865 —— Mut. Fr. I. x, A spring van is delivering its load of greenhouse plants at the door. 1837 W. B. Adams Carriages 117 The tax to which *spring vehicles are subject. 1794 Gentl. Mag. LXIV. II. 1074 The best thing to be done generally..is to put the patient into a *spring-waggon. 1849 F. B. Head Stokers & Pokers viii, Each species of goods..is immediately unloaded and despatched by spring waggons to its destination. 1897 Miss B. Harraden H. Strafford 101 The spring-waggon had sunk up to the hubs.

c. In similar combs. used attributively or objectively, as ***spring-blade knife***, etc.

1875 Knight Dict. Mech., *Spring-blade knife, a pocket-knife whose blade is thrown out or held out by a spring. 1858 Simmonds Dict. Trade, *Spring-blind maker, a maker of window blinds working on springs. 1948 Penguin Music Mag. June 54 Sir Henry Wood..recommended the use of *spring-clip mutes which fastened on the music desks. 1972 Times 23 Sept. 9/1 These spring-clip pans..spring open when a clip at the side is released. 1897 Sears, Roebuck Catal. 192/1 The most handsome and up-to-date *spring heel shoe ever placed on the market. 1853 in Inquiry Yorksh. Deaf & Dumb (1870) 30 *Spring-knife manufacturer. 1870 Ibid. 34 A spring-knife cutler. 1934 Heal & Son Catal.: Better Furnit. 2 'Chassis'..(to fix to *spring-mattress frame). 1836–7 Dickens Sk. Boz., Tales i, There were meat-safe-looking blinds..and *spring-roller blinds. 1973 Sun 4 Sept. 20/2 (Advt.), Spring roller blinds from £2.94... Inc. all fittings, fringe and pull cords. 1907 *Spring-side safety iron [see iron sb.[1] 4i]. 1921 W. de la Mare Memoirs of Midget viii. 48 She, too, was in black, with a long, springside boot. 1874 Lawson Dis. Eye 94 A *spring-stop speculum..is to be introduced between the [eye-]lids, so as to keep them apart. 1805 Dickson Pract. Agric. I. 32 With these *Spring-teeth-Rakes one person is said to do considerably more work than with the common wood rakes. 1923 J. R. Bond Farm Implements & Machinery v. 54 (caption) Canadian *spring-tine cultivator with corn and grass seed boxes. 1960 Farmer & Stockbreeder 15 Mar. 98/3 The spring-tine rake to the rear..is provided to meet necessary safety regulations. Ibid. 134/1 It's a Spring-tine Cultivator—Spring-tine Harrow..all in one. 1890 W. J. Gordon Foundry 138 Another *spring tong arrangement, in which the legs are wood. 1867 J. Hogg Microsc. I. ii. 157 This consists of a *spring-wire coil acting on an inner tube.

26. *Comb.* **a.** With agent-nouns (denoting persons or implements), as ***spring-contractor, -forger, -maker***.

1843 Civil Eng. & Arch. Jrnl. VI. 245 Description of Lieutenant D. Rankine's [Railway] *Spring Contractor. 1858 Simmonds Dict. Trade, *Spring-forgers, workmen in the cutlery trade, who form the spring or piece of steel at the back of clasp and folding pocket-knives. 1837 W. B. Adams Carriages 81 The *spring-makers assert that steel of a finer quality would not answer so well. 1858 Simmonds Dict. Trade, Spring-maker, a manufacturer of steel compound springs for carriages, or of metal springs for easy chairs. 1896 Daily News 22 June 11/3 At West Bromwich there is a strike amongst the spring makers.

b. With vbl. sbs. and pres. pples., as ***spring-making, -shaping***.

1837 W. B. Adams Carriages 123 It is evident that the whole process of spring-making is defective. 1884 Knight Dict. Mech. Suppl. 848 Spring Shaping Machine. 1890 W. J. Gordon Foundry 151 Two smithies, with over 100 fires, and turning and spring-making shops.

c. With pa. pples. or adjs., as ***spring-framed, -jointed, -snecked, -tempered, -tight***, etc.

Spring-heeled Jack, a name given to a person who from his great activity in running or jumping, esp. in order to rob or frighten people, was supposed to have springs in the heels of his boots; *dial.* a highwayman.

1978 J. Irving World according to Garp xv. 311 In a Laundromat... They had opened one of the big *spring-doored dryers. 1928 J. E. Haswell Horology vii. 78 In the category '*spring-driven' clocks are placed the numerous types which derive their motive power from the energy of a coiled mainspring. 1899 Fortn. Rev. LXV. 113, I ought also to mention a *spring-framed machine, the Triumph. 1958 Times 20 Aug. 2/6 Zhukov, Pudov, and Ozog all flashed past the now weary Eldon in pursuit of the fleeing, *spring-heeled Pole. 1977 Vogue Dec. 11/2 'Colleagues' has something inert and passive about it, compared with the spring-heeled activity of 'work mates'. 1840 Hood Kilmansegg, Fancy Ball xi, Tom, and Jerry, and *Spring-heel'd Jack. 1855 Smedley Occult Sciences 76 Like the lately popular Spring-heeled Jack. 1887 S. Cheshire Gloss. 367 There are so many o' these Spring-heeled Jacks about. 1786 in 6th Rep. Dep. Kpr. Pub. Rec. II. 174 A Buckle..with a new-constructed *spring-jointed Plate. 1920 Galsworthy In Chancery II. xiv. 236 His *spring-mattressed bed. 1960 E. L. Delmar-Morgan Cruising Yacht Equipm. & Navigation 37 If the compass is of the *spring-mounted type [etc.]. 1853 R. S. Surtees Sponge's Sp. Tour (1893) 120 He had never been able to accomplish the art of opening a gate, especially one of those gingerly-balanced, *spring-snecked things. 1952 Dylan Thomas Coll. Poems 174 No *springtailed tom in the red hot town. a1788 Imison Sch. Arts II. 164 A piece of *spring-tempered steel will not retain as much magnetism as hard steel. 1876 Preece & Sivewright Telegraphy 82 This is effected by means of a carrier arm fixed '*spring-tight' on an axle. 1938 C. Culpin Farm Machinery vii. 95 The *spring-tined harrow is a really light cultivator that can be adjusted to produce very variable effects.

d. Special Combs.: **spring bows** = BOW-COMPASS 1; **spring collet** *Engin.*, a tapered collet that is slotted along much of its length, so that when moved in a similarly tapered seat the separate parts are pressed against the stock inside the collet; **spring line**, a line where the water table reaches the surface and along which springs are numerous; **spring-loaded** *a.*, containing a compressed or a stretched spring pressing one part against another; **spring rate** = RATE *sb.*[1] 8c; **spring sail** (see quot. 1931); **spring sweep** = prec.; **spring-tree**, a saddle-tree with two springs.

1895 *Army & Navy Co-op. Soc. Price List* 686 Spring Bows, set of three, Ink, Pencil, and Divider, in case. **1964** G. BAKER *Scale Drawing* 31 Spring-bows do not have knee-joints because the angle of working is so small as not to matter. **1932** W. P. TURNER *Machine Tool Work* xiii. 290 The clamping lever..is pushed back, which moves the hollow push sleeve..against the end of the spring collet, forcing it into the nose cap, thus closing the collet on the stock and holding it firmly. **1971** B. SCHARF *Engin. & its Lang.* viii. 61 The bore (internal diameter) of the spring collet matches the size and shape of the bar to be gripped. **1932** *Geol. Mag.* LXIX. 407 West of the spring line, thin outcrops of hard ferrugineous sandstone occur in the clays. **1963** L. F. CHITTY in Foster & Alcock *Culture & Environment* vii. 181 Other finds suggest an alternative route by the present hillside road over Clee Hill, with its far-extending outlook, keeping above the spring-line to Doddington. **1975** J. G. EVANS *Environment Early Man Brit. Isles* vii. 159 Stream courses have a similar effect.., and the well known phenomenon of 'spring-line settlement' is an extreme example of this form of geographical determinism. **1904** *Engin. Rev.* XI. 418/2 Delivery valves.. of the mushroom spring-loaded type. **1938** *Brit. Jrnl. Psychol.* XXIX. 40 A spring-loaded pencil..made record on a sheet of graph paper. **1979** J. WAINWRIGHT *Tension* v. 21 The door is spring-loaded. **1957, 1959** Spring rate [see RATE *sb.*[1] 8c]. **1931** S. P. B. MAIS *England of Windmills* p. xxiv, [Andrew] Meikle was..the inventor of the spring sail. *Ibid.*, The spring sail is made up of wooden shutters, or a canvas-covered wire frame, hinged at one edge and connected to a common sail-rod so that they all open or shut simultaneously. **1971** S. FREESE *Windmills & Millwrighting* iv. 58 The framework of spring sails consists of eight or ten sail bars, spaced 3 ft. apart and forming a series of bays, in each of which are three shutters 4 or 5 ft. by 11 in., wood or metal framed, and covered by wood or canvas. **1919** *Jrnl. Franklin Inst.* CLXXXVII. 178 In some cases these shutters worked against the tension of a spring instead of the pull of a weight, and such were known as Meikle's 'spring sweeps'. **1924** *Trans. Newcomen Soc. 1922–3* III. 50 It was desired to fit patent sail regulation instead of 'spring' or 'sail' sweeps. **1963** E. H. EDWARDS *Saddlery* xiv. 97 In the modern spring tree of correct design..the necessity for a cut-back head is largely obviated by the fact that the head itself is set back at an angle of 45 degrees. **1976** *Horse & Hound* 3 Dec. 31 (Advt.), Parzival all purpose/jumping [saddle]. Again built on the same spring tree, finished in Stubben's special dark brown Sella leather.

spring (sprɪŋ), *sb.*[2] Forms: 4–6 **spryng(e**, 6– **spring**. [Prob. related to OF. *espring(u)er, -ier*, etc., to dance: see SPRING *v.*[1] Cf. MHG. *sprung* dance.]

†**1.** Some kind of dance. *Obs.*⁻¹

*c*1384 CHAUCER *H. Fame* III. 145 Pipers of alle Duche tonge To lerne loue Daunces, sprynges, Reus, and these straunge thynges. *c*1460 *Wisdom* 750 in *Macro Plays* 60 Ye xall se a sprynge of Lechery, þat to me attende. [Cf. l. 688.]

2. A tune upon the bagpipes or other musical instrument, esp. a quick or lively tune; a dance-tune. Chiefly, and now only, *Sc.*

*c*1475 HENRYSON *Poems* (S.T.S.) III. 37 Him to reios ȝit playit he a spryng. **1508** DUNBAR *Poems* VI. 109 A bag pipe to play a spryng. *a*1536 *Songs, Carols*, etc. (1907) 125, I dide no-thyng to hym this day, But piped hym a sprynge. **1622** FLETCHER *Prophetess* v. iii, We will meet him, And strike him such new springs, and such free welcoms, Shall make him scorn an Empire [etc.]. **1725** RAMSAY *Gentle Sheph.* I. i, Gie's a bonny spring, For I'm in tift to hear you play and sing. **1757** SMOLLETT *Reprisal* I. ii, The commander has sent for her to play a spring to the sasenach damsel. *a*1835 HOGG *Tales & Sk.* (1837) II. 351 Let me strengthen my heart with ae spring on my pipes before I venture. **1886** STEVENSON *Kidnapped* xxv, Robin took the pipes, and played a little spring in a very ranting manner.

trans. **1788** PICKEN *Poems* 17 Frae the sprigs, the sylvan quire War liltan up their early spring.

prov. **1721** KELLY *Sc. Prov.* 20 Another would play a Spring, e're you tune your Pipes. **1737** RAMSAY *Sc. Prov.* (1750) 16 Auld springs gi'e nae price.

b. *fig.* or in fig. context. *Sc.*

1572 *Satir. Poems Reform.* xxxviii. 21 Bot now Prouest Marschell in playing this spring;..Beleuis thow this trumprie sall stablische thy style? *a*1585 MONTGOMERIE *Cherry & Slae* 919 Bot sen ȝe think it easy thing To mount aboif the mune, Of ȝour awin fidle tak a spring, And daunce quhen ȝe haif done. **1637** RUTHERFORD *Lett.* (1891) 350 Christ..will give you leave to sing as you please, but He will not dance to your daft spring. **1686** G. STUART *Joco-Ser. Disc.* ii. 27 Experience will this unriddle; Sae take a Spring of thine awn Fiddle. **1784** BURNS *Ep. J. R[ankine]* vi, I've play'd mysel a bonie spring, An' danc'd my fill! **1815** SCOTT *Guy M.* xxxvi, Ou, sir, if the gentleman likes he may play his ain spring first; it's a' ane to Dandie. **1887** *Jamieson's Sc. Dict.* Suppl. 226 'Tak a spring o' your ain fiddle', i.e., Follow your own plan and take the consequences.

spring, *sb.*[3] *Obs.* exc. *dial.* [Alteration of SPRINGE *sb.*] A snare or noose.

1604 BRETON *Grimello's Fortunes* Wks. (Grosart) II. 5/1 Why sir, I set no springs for Woodcocks. *Ibid.* 10/1 To make a meanes, by which to catch this Wood-cocke in a fine spring. **1621** QUARLES *Esther* xiv, The rau'ning Fox, that did annoyance bring Vnto thy Vineyard, 's taken in a Spring. **1648** C. WALKER *Hist. Independ.* 129 This engine..is set then any spring or trap to catch any active Presbyterian. **1725** *Fam. Dict.* s.v. *Lark*, Country People..make use of Springs..to take Larks with. **1771** SMOLLETT *Humph. Cl.* (1815) 224 My friend, Justice Buzzard, has set so many springs for my life. **1881–6** in Lanc. and Leic. glossaries.

spring (sprɪŋ), *v.*[1] Pa. t. **sprang, sprung.** Pa. pple. **sprung.** Forms: *Inf.* 1 **springan**, 3 (7) **springen**, 3–6 **springe** (3 **springue**, 4 **sprinke**, 5 **sprenge**), 4– **spring**; 4–6 **sprynge** (5 **-yn**), 4–5 **spryng.** *Pa. t.* 1– **sprang** (1 **spranc**, 5 **sprank**), 4–6 **sprange** (5 **spranke**); 1–7 **sprong** (4 **spronk**), 4–7 **spronge** (3 **sprongue**); 3–4 (*subj.*) **sprunge**, 6– **sprung**; *pl.* 1 **sprungon**, 2–4 **sprungen**, 3–4 **sprongen.** *Pa. pple.* 1–4 **sprungen** (6 *Sc.* **sprungin**); 3–5 **i-sprunge** (6 *arch.* **i-sprung**), 3, 6 **sprunge**, 6– **sprung**; 4 **y-sprongen, sprongun**, 4–6 **sprongen** (5–6 **-yn**); 3–4 **i-spronge**, 4 **(h)y-spronge, i-sprong**, 6, 8 *arch.* **y-sprong**; 3–6 **spronge**, 4–7 **sprong**, 6 *Sc.* **sproung**; 8 **sprang.** [Common Teutonic: OE. *springan* (more commonly *áspringan*), = OFris. *springa* (WFris. *springe*, NFris. *spring*), MDu. (and Du.) *springen*, OS. *springan* (MLG. *springen*, usually *sprengen*), OHG. *springan* (MHG. and G. *springen*), ON. (Icel., Norw., Sw.) *springa* (Da. *springe*). Hence OF. *espringuer* to dance, It. *springare* to wag the legs.]

I. *Intransitive senses.*

* **1.** Of things: To change place or position by sudden and rapid movement without contact; to move with a sudden jerk or bound (in later use esp. by resilient force); to dart or fly. Freq. with advs.

Beowulf 2582 Beorȝes weard..wearp wælfyre; wide sprungon hildeleoman. *c*888 K. ÆLFRED *Boeth.* xxv, þeah þu teo hwelcne boh ofdune to þære eorðan..swa sprincð he up & wrigað wið his ȝecyndes. **993** *Battle of Maldon* 137 He ..þæt spere sprengde, þæt hit sprang onȝean. *c*1205 LAY. 23924 Heo..fusden feondliche þat fur him sprong after. *c*1250 *Gen. & Ex.* 1804 Ðor wrestelede an engel wið, Senwe sprungen fro ðe lið. **13..** *E.E. Allit. P.* A. 13 Syþen in þat spote hit fro me sprange, Ofte haf I wayted. *c*1384 CHAUCER *H. Fame* III. 989 As fire ys wont to quyk and goo From a sparke spronge amys.

1669 WORLIDGE *Syst. Agric.* 193 A Hasel or other stick.. that being stuck into the ground may spring up like unto the springs they usually set for fowl. **1680** [see SPRINGING *vbl. sb.*[1] 5b]. **1728** CHAMBERS *Cycl.* s.v. *Elasticity*, The component Parts..must..spring back to their former natural State. **1829** *Chapters Phys. Sci.* 157 The elasticity of water is farther proved by its..springing upward..when poured upon any body. **1870** MORRIS *Earthly Par.* III. 20 He drew adown the wind-stirred bough, and took The apples thence; then let it spring away.

fig. **13..** *K. Alis.* 3070 (Laud MS.), þe folkes herte so gan sprynge Aȝeins Alisaunder þe kynge. **1508** DUNBAR *Tua Mariit Wemen* 160 With that sprang vp hir spreit be a span hecher. **1829** SCOTT *Anne of G.* xvii, Arthur Philipson's heart sprung high at the appearance of these strangers.

b. To be resilient or elastic; to shift or move on account of this.

1667– [see SPRINGING *ppl. a.* 4]. **1821** SCOTT *Nigel* i, A step that sprung like a buck's in Epping Forest. **1869** RANKINE *Machine & Hand-tools* Pl. M 2, It is impossible for the tables to spring in the least. **1881** A. A. KNOX *New Playground* 121 We delighted in our mule-carriage; if the springs did not spring very much, at any rate the mules were never tired. **1888** JACOBI *Printers' Vocab.* 130 A forme of type or plates is liable to 'spring', or go off its feet, if not properly locked up.

c. To rise suddenly *to*, come suddenly *into*, the eyes, face, etc.

1848 DICKENS *Dombey* iii, With tears springing to her eyes. **1873** BLACK *Pr. Thule* xxvi. 433 A flush of decision sprang into his face. **1885** 'MRS. ALEXANDER' *Valerie's Fate* iii, The quick color that sprang to her cheek at his words. **1891** FARRAR *Darkn. & Dawn* xxii, An indignant refusal sprang to his lips.

†**2.** Of fame, rumour, etc.: To spread, extend. Freq. with *wide*. *Obs.*

(*a*) *Beowulf* 18 Beowulf wæs breme, blæd wide sprang, Scyldes eafera, Scedelandum in. *c*1200 *Trin. Coll. Hom.* 127 Ðo sprong þe word of his holi liflode wide into þe londe. *c*1205 LAY. 6302 Of hire wisdome sprong þat word wide. *c*1290 *S. Eng. Leg.* I. 442 So wide sprong is guode los. *c*1320 *Sir Tristrem* 22 His name, it sprong wel wide. **1387** TREVISA *Higden* (Rolls) VI. 303 þis word..sprang wel wyde. **1458** in *Archaeol.* (1842) XXIX. 327 Hys worship sprygethe wyde.

(*b*) *c*950 *Lindisf. Gosp.* Matt. ix. 26 ðe-eade *vel* spranc mersung ðas..in alle eorðo. [*c*1000 þes hlisa sprang ofer eall þæt land.] *a*1300 *K. Horn* (Camb.) 211 So schal þi name springe Fram kynge to kynge. *c*1374 CHAUCER *Anel. & Arc.* 74 Thurgh oute the world..so gan her name spryng That her to seen had euery wight likyng. **1390** GOWER *Conf.* I. 343 Bot moerdre, which mai noght ben hedd, Sprong out to every mannes Ere. *c*1425 *Eng. Conq. Irel.* (1896) 40 Her-aftyr spronge tythyngges of the Erle..ynto englond. *c*1480 HENRYSON *Orph. & Euryd.* 73 His noble fame so far It sprang & grewe. *a*1548 HALL *Chron., Hen. IV*, 26 For sodainly sprange out a fame..that king Richard was yet livyng. *a*1578 LINDESAY (Pitscottie) *Chron. Scot.* (S.T.S.) I. 357 The word sprang throw the contrie that the king of Scotland was landit.

†**b.** Of a scent: To be diffused. *Obs.*⁻¹

?*a*1366 CHAUCER *Rom. Rose* 1704 The swote smelle spronge so wide, That it dide alle the place aboute [fill].

3. Of persons or animals: To bound or leap.

a. With advs. or preps.

*c*1205 LAY. 21481 Cador sprong to horse, swa spærc him doh of fure. *c*1300 *Havelok* 91 He..sprong forth so sparke of glede. *c*1330 R. BRUNNE *Chron. Wace* (Rolls) 12839 In to þe most pres Ider þen sprong. *a*1400–50 *Alexander* 1318 Alexander..Springis out with a spere. *a*1425 *Cursor M.* 12527 (Trin.) A nedder sprong out of þe sond. **1484** CAXTON *Fables of Æsop* I. x, [The serpent] sprange after his neck for to have strangled hym. **1579** SPENSER *Sheph. Cal.* Mar. 79 With that sprong forth a naked swayne. **1632** LITHGOW *Trav.* I. 37, I sprung forward through the throng. **1697** DRYDEN *Virg. Georg.* IV. 339 The pleasing Pleiades appear, And springing upwards spurn the briny Seas. **1788** COWPER *Mrs. Montagu* 26 Like Pallas springing arm'd from Jove. **1797** S. & HT. LEE *Canterb. T.* (1799) I. 205 [He] lightly sprung over the fence by which they were separated. **1855** MACAULAY *Hist. Eng.* xvi. III. 670 Some of the English sprang to their arms and made an attempt to resist. **1891** FARRAR *Darkn. & Dawn* xliii, His first impulse was to spring forward. *Ibid.* lx, His daughter sprang to his embrace.

fig. **1817** JAS. MILL *Brit. India* II. v. vii. 610 The whole of the district which owned the sway of the Rajah sprung to arms. **1878** BOSW. SMITH *Carthage* 220 Mago was young and adventurous and sprang at the task assigned him.

transf. *a*1822 SHELLEY *Triumph Life* 2 Swift as a spirit hastening to his task.., the Sun sprang forth Rejoicing in his splendour. **1871** L. STEPHEN *Playgr. Eur.* (1894) x. 228 The mighty peaks..spring at one bound to a height of some ten thousand feet.

b. Without const. Also *spec.* of partridges, to rise from cover.

*a*1300 *K. Horn* (Camb.) 593 þe fole bigan to springe, & horn murie to singe. *c*1440 *York Myst.* xxxvi. 224 Full faste schall I springe for to spede. **1474** CAXTON *Chesse* II. ii. (1883) 33 Octauian maad his sones to be taught..to swyme, to sprynge, and lepe. **1530** PALSGR. 730 Marke hym whan he daunseth, you shall se hym springe lyke a yonckher. **1589** R. ROBINSON *Gold. Mirr.* (1851) 51 The Partridge sprang, my hauke fled from my fist. **1667** MILTON *P.L.* VII. 465 The Tawnie Lion..then springs. **1709** O. DYKES *Eng. Prov. w. Mor. Refl.* (ed. 2) 148 The Partridge..always springs afterwards upon the first Sight of a Setter or a Dog in the Field. **1820** SHELLEY *Arethusa* i, Gliding and springing She went, ever singing, In murmurs as soft as sleep. **1847** C. BRONTË *Jane Eyre* xxvi, The lunatic sprang and grappled his throat viciously. **1891** FARRAR *Darkn. & Dawn* xxxiv, Nero persuaded himself that his mother was watching him like a tiger-cat in act to spring.

c. To rise quickly, or with a bound, from a sitting or recumbent posture. With advs. and preps.

1474 CAXTON *Chesse* III. vii. (1883) 141 Ye kynge..sprang out of his chare and resseyuyd them worshipfully. **1590** SPENSER *F.Q.* III. i. 62 The whole family..Rashly out of their rouzed couches sprong. **1667** MILTON *P.L.* VIII. 259 Till rais'd By quick instinctive motion up I sprung,..and upright Stood on my feet. **1757** W. WILKIE *Epigoniad* IX. 284 Springing from the ground, Both chiefs at once ascend the lofty mound. **1760–72** H. BROOKE *Fool of Qual.* (1809) IV. 72 The..monster sprung up and cast himself..upon our hero. **1819** SCOTT *Leg. Montrose* vi, At an early hour in the morning the guests of the castle sprung from their repose. **1841** LANE *Arab. Nts.* I. 104 When the Sultan heard this lamentation, he sprang upon his feet. **1860** TYNDALL *Glac.* I. xx. 137 Good news caused me to spring from my bed.

d. *slang.* To offer a higher price.

1851 MAYHEW *Lond. Lab.* II. 28 If the seller finds he can get him to 'spring' or advance no further.

e. Phr. ***where did you spring from?*** and varr., used when someone appears unexpectedly. *colloq.*

1853 DICKENS *Bleak Ho.* xx, Where have you sprung from? **1892** I. ZANGWILL *Childr. Ghetto* III. II. vi. 109 'Hullo! where did *you* spring from?' It was Raphael who had elicited the exclamation. He suddenly loomed upon the party. **1924** WODEHOUSE *Leave it to Psmith* ix. 181 'Wherever,' she inquired, 'did you spring from, Ed?' **1932** G. HEYER *Devil's Cub* ix. 141 Several persons hailed him, demanding to know whence he had sprung. **1971** 'S. WOODS' *Serpent's Tooth* 154 She was, perhaps, the last person he had expected... 'Where did you spring from?'

f. *U.S. slang.* To escape or be released from arrest or imprisonment.

1904 H. HAPGOOD *Autobiogr. of Thief* ix. 188 Soon after I was transferred from Sing Sing..a friend..said '..If you can get on Keeper Riley's gallery I think you can spring (escape).' **1926** *Clues* Nov. 162/2 *Spring*, to be released, as from jail or prison. **1955** *Publ. Amer. Dial. Soc.* XXIV. 184 You get snatched in the neck and it costs you twelve hundred to spring. **1962** 'K. ORVIS' *Damned & Destroyed* xii. 82 When I sprung..Moss was standing by the prison door.

g. *Austral.* and *U.S. slang.* To pay *for* a treat. Also without const.

1906 E. DYSON *Fact'ry 'Ands* xviii. 250 Feathers..said reproachfully to the Aberdeen engineer..whose turn it was to 'spring': 'Blime, cobber, er yer givin' ther barmaid er perpetual 'oliday 'r what?' **1973** W. MCCARTHY *Detail* iii. 163 I'm springing for chow tonight and charging it to the Service. **1976** M. MACHLIN *Pipeline* ix. 107 We'll spring for the booze.

4. To fly asunder or in pieces; to burst, break, crack, or split; to give way. Also *fig.* of the heart.

*c*1320 *Cast. Love* 593 Er him ouȝte þe herte to springe, þen he scholde him wraþþe for eny þinge. *c*1400 *Destr. Troy* 1195 Speires vnto sprottes sprongen ouer hedes. *c*1420 *Avow. Arth.* xiii, The grete schafte that was longe, Alle to spildurs hit spronge. *a*1450 *Le Morte Arth.* 3920 An C tymes hys herte nye sprange, By that bors had hym the tale tolde. **1623** in Foster *Eng. Factories Ind.* (1908) II. 345 By reason of a plancke that spronge in hir. **1627** CAPT. SMITH *Seaman's Gram.* ii. 4 If one of those ends should spring, or giue way, it would be a..troublesome danger. **1820** HENNEN *Princ. Milit. Surg.* (ed. 2) 217 At length an artery sprung, which, in the attempt to secure it, most probably burst under the ligature. **1857** HUGHES *Tom Brown* I. ix, Splicing a favourite old fives'-bat which had sprung. **1871** B. TAYLOR

Faust (1875) II. II. 153 At once a flood of light I'll fling, Yet softly lest the glass should spring.

b. In pa. pple. †(*a*) Of horses: Foundered. *Obs.* (*b*) Of planks, masts, etc.: Split, cracked, 'shaken'. (*c*) *slang.* Of persons: Intoxicated.

(*a*) *a* **1400** *King & Hermit* 68 The kyng had folowyd hym so long, Hys god sted was ne sprong. **1676** *Lond. Gaz.* No. 1120/4 The Gelding is sprang of the near leg before. **1696** AUBREY *Misc.* xiii. 110 To Cure a Beast that is Sprung, that is poysoned.

(*b*) **1704** J. HARRIS *Lex. Techn.* I, When a Mast is only crack'd..then they say, The Mast is Sprung. **1745** P. THOMAS *Jrnl. Anson's Voy.* 271 The Carpenters discovered the Fore Mast to be sprung. **1765** J. BYRON in Hawkesworth *Voy.* (1773) I. 59 Capt. Mouat, who commanded the Tamar, informed me that his rudder was sprung. **1834** MARRYAT *P. Simple* (1863) 128 To examine the main-topsail yard, which had been reported as sprung. **1863** W. C. BALDWIN *Afr. Hunting* vi. 222 The dissel-boom was sprung, and the hind axle also. **1894** *Times* 29 May 11/1 It will not be possible to race this cutter..owing to her mast being sprung.

(*c*) **1826** *Sporting Mag.* XVIII. 327 Both himself and his brother dragsman—in the language of the road—were sprung. **1856** MRS. STOWE *Dred.* I. vi. 86 He reckoned they was a little bit sprung. **1901** G. DOUGLAS *House w. Green Shutters* 227 [He] came staggering round the corner, 'a little sprung'.

c. Of mines: To go off, explode.

a **1658** CLEVELAND *Poor Cavalier* Wks. (1687) 328 At Langport..thy Rear miscarry'd too, And by a strong Intelligence the same time, Thy Hooks and Buttons sprung with Sherburns Mine. **1698** T. FROGER *Voy.* 30 On the 22nd the mines sprang, and took very good effect. **1747** *Gentl. Mag.* XVII. 437 The mine will spring by its gallery. **1829** *Encycl. Metrop.* (1845) VI. 303/1 If likewise it be wished that one mine shall spring before another, it is only necessary to shorten the hose.

5. To swell *with* milk; to give signs of foaling or calving.

1607 MARKHAM *Cavel.* I. (1617) 5 It must be good ground, because it may make your Mares spring with milke. **1714** *Lond. Gaz.* No. 5233/4 A brown Mare in Foal,..Springs for Foaling, and is 5 Years old. *a* **1722** LISLE *Husb.* (1757) 281 Two understanding farmers..observed a heifer's udder to spring much. *Ibid.* 317 The butcher..found their udders spring with milk. **1828** CARR *Craven Gloss.*, *Spring*,..to give symptoms of calving. **1868** ATKINSON *Cleveland Gloss.*, *Spring*, to relax or become flaccid in the parts about the Barren, or 'shape' when the time of calving is drawing close on; of a cow.

** **6.** To issue or come forth suddenly, to break out, esp. in a jet or stream. Freq. with *forth* or *out*.

Beowulf 2966 Him for swenge swat ædrum sprong forð under fexe. *a* **900** *O.E. Martyrol.* 25 Aug. 152 Him sprungon spearcan of þam muðe. *a* **1225** *Leg. Kath.* 2456 Þer sprong ut, mid te dunt, milc imenget wið blod. **1297** R. GLOUC. (Rolls) 6187 Of þe helmes þat fur sprong out, vor hii were stronge beye. *c* **1375** *Cursor M.* 9102 (Fairf.), His body [to] driue nakid wiþ skourges þorou þat prange; out of his bak þe blode sprange. *c* **1375** *Sc. Leg. Saints* xxvi. (*Nicholas*) 581 Of his body oyle cane spryng, þat helful wes til al sare thing. *c* **1480** HENRYSON *Orph. & Euryd.* 150 The bludy teres sprang out of his eyne.

1822 SHELLEY *Scenes fr. Faust* II. 110 And near us, see, sparks spring out of the ground. **1829** SCOTT *Anne of G.* xxxiv, The perspiration which sprung from his brow. **1857** ROBERTSON *Serm.* Ser. III. v. 69 From whose dissevered neck the blood sprung forth.

transf. *a* **1300** *Cursor M.* 1600 Þis word out of his hert sprang. *c* **1425** *Seven Sages* (P.) 299 Yf ony word hym hadde sprong, That men myght here of his tong. **1535** COVERDALE *2 Chron.* xxvi. 19 The leprosy spronge out of his foreheade in the presence of the prestes.

b. *esp.* Of water: To rise or flow in a stream out of the ground. Freq. with *out* or *up*.

(*a*) *c* **1175** *Lamb. Hom.* 141 Þe stan to-chan, and fouwer walmes of watere sprungen ut þer-of. **12..** *Song to Virgin* 26 in *O.E. Misc.* 194 Þe welle springet hut of þe, *uirtutis*. *c* **1290** *St. Brendan* in *S. Eng. Leg.* I. 237 Watur of þis harde stone ..þare sprong out eche daye. **1390** GOWER *Conf.* I. 293 Every thing which he can telle, It springeth up as doth a welle. *c* **1400** MAUNDEV. (Roxb.) xii. 51 It commez fra þa mount Liban of twa welles þat springes vp þare. **1611** BIBLE *Num.* xxi. 17 Israel sang..Spring vp O well. **1730** A. GORDON *Maffei's Amphith.* 168 Pipes, by which..they caused odoriferous Liquor to spring up from the bottom to the top of the Amphitheatre. **1765** A. DICKSON *Treat. Agric.* (ed. 2) 138 If..the land is wet, even at some distance above the place where the water springs out. **1832** R. & J. LANDER *Exped. Niger* II. xiv. 281 Our own [hut] had positively pools of water springing up out of the ground.

(*b*) *c* **1220** *Bestiary* 62 in *O.E. Misc.*, A welle he sekeð ðat springeð ai boðe bi niȝt and bi dai. *c* **1290** *S. Eng. Leg.* I. 318 For þare beoz ase it veynene weren onder eorþe.., and þarof springueth þis wellene ech-on. *c* **1320** *Cast. Love* 843 Þe welle springeþ of alle grace þat fulleþ þe diches in vche a place. **1390** GOWER *Conf.* I. 119 Beside a roche..He syh wher sprong a lusty welle. **1400** tr. *Secreta Secret.*, *Gov. Lordsh.* 79 Waters þat spryngyn yn stony lond..er heuy & noyant. **1470–85** MALORY *Arthur* XVIII. xxi. 764 There he wold lye doune and see the welle sprynge and burbyl. **1530** PALSGR. 730, I have sene the place where Temmes springeth. **1585** T. WASHINGTON tr. *Nicholay's Voy.* II. xi. 45 A very faire fountayne whiche springeth of very good waters through a conduit. **1610** HOLLAND *Camden's Brit.* (1637) 519 Of one hill spring three great Rivers. **1675** E. WILSON *Spadacrene Dunelm.* 17 Such a quantity of water.. as springs daily out of the Earth. **1706** PHILLIPS (ed. Kersey), To *Spring*, to rise, come, or spout out, as a River or Water does. **1781** COWPER *Charity* 366 How copious and how clear Th' o'erflowing well of Charity springs here! **1816** BYRON *Stanzas Augusta*, '*Through the day*' vi, In the desert a fountain is springing.

†**c.** To gush *with* blood. *Obs.*⁻¹

1533 BELLENDEN *Livy* I. xxii. (S.T.S.) I. 125 Þe wound þat was springand with huge stremes of blude.

7. Of morning, dawn, etc.: To come above the horizon; to begin to appear.

c **1250** *Gen. & Ex.* 60 Ðat was ðe firme morgen tid, ðat euere sprong in werlde wid. *Ibid.* 3264 Ðo sprong ðe daiening. *a* **1300** *K. Horn* (Camb.) 124 Al þe day & al þe niȝt, Til hit sprang dai liȝt. *c* **1380** *Sir Ferumb.* 5259 On þe morȝnyng wan þe day him sprong, Charlis ȝeode ys host among. *a* **1400–50** *Alexander* 2044 Begynnys sone in þe gray day as any gleme springis. *c* **1440** *Astron. Cal.* (MS. Ashm. 391), To wete euery day what houre & what mynute the day begynneþ to sprynge. **1513** DOUGLAS *Æneid* IV. iv. 1 Furth of the see, with this, the dawing springis. **1577–87** HOLINSHED *Chron.* I. 49/2 By the light of the daie that then began to spring. **1611** BIBLE *Judges* xix. 25 When the day began to spring. **1700** DRYDEN *Pal. & Arc.* III. 121 Phospher..Promis'd the Sun, ere Day began to spring. **1803** VISCT. STRANGFORD *Poems of Camoens* (1810) 54 Dear is the dawn, which springs at last. **1876** MORRIS *Sigurd* III. 182 But meseems that the earth is lovely and each day springeth anew.

b. In fig. contexts.

1382 WYCLIF *Isaiah* ix. 2 To the men dwellende in the regioun of the shadewe of deth, liȝt sprungen is to them. *c* **1400** *Pilgr. Sowle* I. xxii. (1859) 26 To whome is ysprunge veray sterre of trouth. *c* **1450** *Myrr. our Ladye* 255 Lyghte spryngeth in darkenesse, helle ys pryued of robry. *c* **1460** *Wisdom* 1163 in *Macro Plays*, The tru son of ryghtusnes.. Xall sprynge in hem þat drede hys meknes. **1535** COVERDALE *Isaiah* lx. 3 The Gentiles shal come to thy light, & kynges to the brightnes yᵗ springeth forth vpon yᵉ. **1579** W. WILKINSON *Confut. Fam. Love* A iv, The light of Gods truth might spryng foorth agayne. **1671** MILTON *Samson A.* 584 But God..can as easie Cause light again within thy eies to spring.

†**c.** To ascend in the sky. *Obs.*⁻¹

15.. in *Dunbar's Poems* (S.T.S.) 317 The mone sprang nevir abone his kne.

*** **8.** Of vegetation: To grow; to arise or develop by growth.

a. Const. *from*, *of*, *out of*.

c **1000** ÆLFRIC *Hom.* II. 314 Swa swa of anum treowe springað maneȝa boȝas, swa gað of anre lufe maneȝa oðre mihta. *c* **1290** *S. Eng. Leg.* I. 7 [He] bad him legge þulke kurneles onder is fader toungue 3wane he were ded, and burien him, and lokie ȝwat þarof sprongue. *a* **1300** *Cursor M.* 22878 (Edinb.), Þoru his wil dos þat mihti kinge Out of hard tre to spring First þe lef and þan þe flowr. **1387–8** T. USK *Test. Love* III. vii. (Skeat) l. 5 Thou desyrest to knowe the maner of braunches that out of the tree shulde springe. *c* **1400** MAUNDEV. (Roxb.) ii. 6 Of þase foure graynes schuld spring trees. **1560** BIBLE (Geneva) *1 Kings* iv. 33 From the cedar tre..euen vnto the hyssope that springeth out of the wall. **1593** SHAKS. *Rich. II*, I. ii. 13 Edwards seuen sonnes.. Were as..seuen faire branches springing from one roote. *a* **1689** MRS. BEHN tr. *Cowley's Plants* C.'s Wks. 1711 III. 391 The noble Flow'r that did from Ajax spring. **1815** J. SMITH *Panorama Sci. & Art* II. 661 Shoots of the same year's growth, springing from wood of the last year's growth. **1837** P. KEITH *Bot. Lex.* 186 It may be regarded as an indubitable fact that all plants spring from seed. **1845** GOSSE *Ocean* i. (1849) 35 From a number of little rootlets.. springs a straight olive-brown stem.

fig. *c* **1386** CHAUCER *Pars. T.* ¶388 Than is Pride þe generall rote of alle harmes, for of þis rote spryngen certein braunches, as Ire, Envye [etc.]. **1681–6** J. SCOTT *Chr. Life* (1747) III. 272 The primitive Root out of which the vast Stock of the Catholick Church sprung. **1813** SHELLEY *Q. Mab* v. 45 Commerce! beneath whose poison-breathing shade No solitary virtue dares to spring. **1872** MORLEY *Voltaire* 6 Some miraculous soil from which prodigies and portents spring.

b. Without const.

c **1055** *Byrhtferth's Handboc* in *Anglia* VIII. 312 On lengtentima springað oððe greniað wæstmas. *a* **1250** *Owl & Night.* 437 Þe blostme gynneþ springe & sprede. *Ibid.* 1042 For he is wod þat soweþ his sed þer neuer gras ne springeþ ne bled. *a* **1300** *Cursor M.* 4702 Na corn on erth, ne gress sprang. **1390** GOWER *Conf.* I. 53 He syh upon the grene gras The faire freisshe floures springe. *c* **1440** *Pallad. on Husb.* XI. 160 Basilicon..spryngith soone yf aysel on hem reyne. *c* **1480** HENRYSON *Orph. & Euryd.* 90 Lyke till a flour þat plesandly will spring. **1523** FITZHERB. *Husb.* §124 Make they settes..to stande halfe a foote and more aboue the erthe, that they may sprynge oute in many braunches. **1577** B. GOOGE *Heresbach's Husb.* 22 The weedes..plucked vp by the rootes before they haue seeded, wyll neuer spring agayne. **1653** RAMESEY *Astrol. Restored* 312 They begin to bud and shout forth, as the Vine, Fig-tree and others then springing. **1697** DRYDEN *Virg. Georg.* II. 450 The Grass securely springs above the Ground; The tender Twig shoots upward to the Skies. **1765** *Museum Rust.* IV. 455 It springs well, and its flax is sooner ripe than any other. **1830** TENNYSON *Poems* 44 For her the green grass shall not spring,..Till Love have his full revenge. **1883** *Specif. Alnwick & Cornhill Rlwy.* 21 In all cases where the seed does not spring, the Contractor is to re-sow the same.

fig. **1297** R. GLOUC. (Rolls) 5966 Here sprong lo þe uerste more [= stock] of hom of normandye.

c. With *up*.

a **1300** *Cursor M.* 20788 In þe toumb..Mai naman find na thing bot flur Springand up of suet sauur. **1382** WYCLIF *Matt.* xiii. 5 Anoon thei ben sprungen vp, for thei hadde nat depnesse of erthe. **1500–20** DUNBAR *Poems* x. 41 Now spring vp flouris fra the rute. **1565** COOPER *Thesaurus*, *Germinasco*, to shoote or sprynge vp. **1611** BIBLE *Isaiah* xliv. 4 And they shall spring vp as among the grasse, as willowes by the water courses. *a* **1770** JORTIN *Serm.* (1771) I. iii. 40 Among the good seed spring up Tares. **1796** H. HUNTER tr. *St.-Pierre's Stud. Nat.* (1799) II. 536 The olive-tree which Minerva had there caused to spring up. **1837** P. KEITH *Bot. Lex.* 158 At first a tuft of fungi sprung up accidentally on some particular spot. **1863** W. C. BALDWIN *Afr. Hunting* ix. 423, I hear that the young grass is fast springing up.

†**d.** In the pa. pple. used predicatively. *Obs.*

13.. *Minor Poems fr. Vernon MS.* xxviii. 21 Heil spice sprong, þat neuer was spent. **1390** GOWER *Conf.* III. 249 The lilie croppes on and on, Wher that thei weren sprongen oute, He smot of. *c* **1440** *Pallad. on Husb.* III. 377 Fertile, & fressh, ek knotty, sprongen newe Thy graffes be. **1530** PALSGR. 730 This yere is farre forthe, the hawthorne buddes be spronge forthe all redy. **1599** THYNNE *Animadv.* (1875) 50 The trompettes chapplettes were of oke serriall newly spronge, and not coome to perfectione. **1667** MILTON *P.L.* x. 548 There stood A Grove hard by, sprung up with this thir change.

9. Of conditions, qualities, etc.: To take rise, to originate or proceed.

a. Const. †*of* or *out of*; *from* or *whence*.

(*a*) *a* **1200** *Vices & Virtues* 63 Of ðesere godes dradnesse springþ ut an oðer godes ȝiue. *c* **1200** ORMIN 4936 Forr alle mahhtess springenn ut Off soþ meocnessess rote. *a* **1300** *Cursor M.* 27538 Vte o þir seuen [sins] all oþer springes, als of þe stouen þe branches hinges. **1377** LANGL. *P. Pl.* B. XI. 194 For on Caluarye of Crystes blode, Crystenedome gan sprynge. *c* **1440** *Jacob's Well* 283 It springeth out of compassioun, and of ruthe of an-oþeres synne. **1538** STARKEY *England* I. iv. 130 The chefe poynt that perteynyth to theyr honowre,..wych ys ryse and spronge of a long custume. **1578** in *Hakluyt's Voy.* (1904) VIII. 10, I am glad that it so increaseth, whereof soever it springeth. **1603** G. OWEN *Pembrokeshire* (1892) 261 Out of which knott hath spronge the peace of this lande. **1631** WIDDOWES *Nat. Philos.* 36 His oyle..helpeth diseases of the brest; and other springing of colde. **1651** HOBBES *Leviathan* I. xii. 58 New Religions may againe be made to spring out of them. **1772–84** *Cook's Voy.* (1790) V. 1625 Some good, however, generally springs up out of evil. **1818** CRUISE *Digest* (ed. 2) II. 343 Such a limitation being by way of use, springs out of the estate. **1875** JOWETT *Plato* (ed. 2) V. 69 Out of the union of wisdom and temperance with courage, springs justice.

(*b*) *c* **1386** CHAUCER *Pars. T.* ¶321 It is necessarie to vnderstonde whennes that synnes spryngen, and how they encreessen. **15..** in *Dunbar's Poems* (S.T.S.) 329 Beseiking him, fra quhome all mercy springis, Ws to ressaue. *a* **1586** SIDNEY *Ps.* x. iv, From his mouth doth spring Cursing and cosening. *a* **1601** ? MARSTON *Pasquil & Kath.* (1878) II. 374 From thee doth spring..her cause of sorrowing. **1630** PRYNNE *Anti-Armin.* 137 From whence then springs this inequality? **1718** *Free-thinker* No. 10. 68 Nothing but Confusion and Immorality can spring from Falsehood, in the End. **1790** MME. D'ARBLAY *Diary* Apr., Humour springing from mere dress, or habits,..is quickly obsolete. **1849** MACAULAY *Hist. Eng.* ii. I. 155 The coalition which had restored the king terminated with the danger from which it had sprung. **1874** GREEN *Short Hist.* iv. §4. 192 A yet more important result sprang from the increase of population.

b. Without const. In later use commonly with *up*.

(*a*) **1297** R. GLOUC. (Rolls) 5935 After hor daye sone þe sorwes spronge bliue. *Ibid.* 9819 After sein tomas deþe..þer sprong contek suiþe strong. *c* **1380** WYCLIF *Sel. Wks.* II. 338 Among al blasphemes þat ever sprongen, þis is þe moost cursid. **1387** TREVISA *Higden* (Rolls) V. 285 For Pelagius his heresye, þat gan among hem to springe. **1400** tr. *Secreta Secret.*, *Gov. Lordsh.* 73 Hete sprynges þanne yn alle kyngdomes. *c* **1425** *Cast. Persev.* 889 in *Macro Plays*, Sum Pryde I wolde spronge hyȝe in þi hert. **1508** DUNBAR *Gold. Targe* 158 Curage in thame was noucht begonne to spring. **1563** T. GALE *Antidot.* I. 1 The utilitie springinge by the right vse of these [medicines] is great. **1663** BP. PATRICK *Parab. Pilgr.* xiv, New pleasures will be springing forth unto us. **1669** MARVELL *Corr.* Wks. (Grosart) II. 292 We have other great matters spring daily upon us. **1711** in *10th Rep. Hist. MSS. Comm.* App. V. 163, I ask..whether such an intent ever sprung in the brains of the Irish Commissioners. **1783** JOHNSON *Lett.* (1788) II. 302, I read your last kind letter with great delight; but when I came to love and honour, what sprung in my mind? **1902** V. JACOB *Sheep-Stealers* xiv, A little rift had sprung between the two brothers.

(*b*) **1560** DAUS tr. *Sleidane's Comm.* 328 b, There sprang up many adversaries. **1610** HOLLAND *Camden's Brit.* 180 There have sprung up also in these later times, two other Courts. **1642** H. MORE *Song of Soul* I. ii. 99 Sense upon which holy Intelligence And heavenly Reason..Do springen up. **1663** BP. PATRICK *Parab. Pilgr.* xxv, The delight which he perceived began to spring up in him. **1822** LAMB *Elia* I. *Old Actors*, Thought springing up after thought, I would almost say, as they were watered by her tears. **1849** MACAULAY *Hist. Eng.* iii. I. 342 In a market town which had sprung up near the castle of the proprietor. **1874** GREEN *Short Hist.* iii. §4. 128 The scholastic philosophy sprung up in the schools of Paris.

†**c.** In pa. pple. used predicatively. Also with *up*. *Obs.*

(*a*) *c* **1327** in Wright *Pol. Songs* (Camden) 339 Falsnesse is so fer forth over al the londe i-sprunge. **1382** WYCLIF *Exod.* xii. 30 Ther was sprongun a greet crye in Egipte. **1452** in *Catal. Anc. Deeds* (1906) V. 350 The cause also of such dyvorce had and movet sprongen or comyn opon the party of the said Margarete. *c* **1460** *Reg. Oseney Abbey* (1913) 93 A thyng i-sprunge late, bitwene religiouse men..of the oone partie, and a worthy man..of þe oþer. **1502** ARNOLDE *Chron.* (1811) 138 Syth dyuers opynions and dyuers streyues hade ben sprongen betwene th' Aldermen and the Commounalte. **1545** *Act 37 Hen. VIII*, c. 17 Preamb., Heresies,..idolatrie, ipocrisies, and supersticions sprongen and growing within the same [church]. **1667** MILTON *P.L.* VI. 312 If Natures concord broke, Among the Constellations warr were sprung.

(*b*) **1529** *Supplic. to King* (E.E.T.S.) 44 Enormytyes and abuses sprongen vp in the Christen religion. **1556** OLDE *Antichrist* 14 The gospell, which was than but grene, & newly sprongen up. **1685** BAXTER *Paraphr. N.T.* John i. 1 Whereas there are of late many Heresies sprung up about the person..of Christ.

10. Of persons (or animals): To originate by birth or generation; to issue or descend. Usu. const. *from*, *of*, or *out of*.

a. In pa. pple.

c **1175** *Moral Ode* 175 (Lamb. MS.), Alle þo þat isprunge beð of adam and of eue. *c* **1250** *Gen. & Ex.* 4023 Ðis folc, sprungen of israel, Is vnder god timed wel. *c* **1275** LAY. 25082 Alle þeos weren min eldre, of wan we beoþ i-sprunge. *c* **1330** *Arth. & Merl.* 8024 (Kölbing), Þis deuelen felle þat ben ysprongen out of helle. **1377** LANGL. *P. Pl.* B. XVI. 196 God..Sent forth his sone..To occupien hym here til issue were spronge. **1382** WYCLIF *Gen.* xxv. 4 Forsothe of Madian was sprongun Epha. *a* **1440** *Found. St. Bartholomew's* (1895) 2 Thys manne, sprongyng or boryne of lowe lynage, .. beganne to haunte the housholdys of noble men. *c* **1450** *M.E. Med. Bk.* (Heinrich) 214 Item drynk aissches mad of ey schelles, þat bryddes were sprong, in whyt wyn. **1585** T. Washington tr. *Nicholay's Voy.* II. viii. 41 The Mahomies .. were the first gentlemen sprong out of the ancient stocke of Iustinian. **1586** Marlowe *1st Pt. Tamburl.* III. iii, Their lims more large .. Than all the brats ysprong from Typhon's loins. **1652** Benlowes *Theoph.* VII. xxxi, Sprung of Thyself, or rather no way sprung! Chief Good! *a* **1764** Lloyd *Progr. Envy* Poet Wks. 1774 I. 135 Fancy, her name, ysprong of race divine. **1791** Cowper *Iliad* XVI. 542 Under yon great city fight no few Sprung from Immortals whom thou shall provoke. **1835** T. Mitchell *Aristophanes, Acharn.* 558 *note*, Alcibiades, who, on the mother's side, was sprung from Cœsyra. **1865** Swinburne *Atalanta* 36 Thou, sprung of the seed of the seas As an ear from a seed of corn. **1871** Freeman *Norm. Conq.* (1876) IV. 229 Adeliza of Löwen, sprung from those lands kindred in blood and speech with England.

transf. *a* **1300** *K. Horn* 548 (Camb.), We beþ kniȝtes ȝonge Of o dai al isprunge [*Harl.* alle to day ysprونge].

b. In other uses.

1297 R. Glouc. (Rolls) 337 Þer ssolle kinges come and springe of þi blod. *a* **1300** *Cursor M.* 5599 Þe kinges kin i sal vn-do, O quam sprang of þe sauueur. *c* **1386** Chaucer *Pars. T.* ¶761 Of soch seed as cherles spryngen, of soch seed spryngen lordes. **1480** Caxton *Chron. Eng.* cii. 83 Moche peple sprong and come of hem. **1500–20** Dunbar *Poems* lxxxvi. 22 Our wicht invinsable Sampson sprang the fra. **1590** Spenser *F.Q.* II. x. 8 But whence they sprong, or how they were begot, Vneath is to assure. **1604** E. G[rimstone] *D'Acosta's Hist. Indies* I. xxv. 80 From him sprang two families or linages. **1665** Dryden & Howard *Ind. Queen* II. i, You grieve to see Your young Prince glorious, 'cause he sprang from me. **1720** Ozell *Vertot's Rom. Rep.* I. I. 3 He consecrated it to the God of War, from whom he would have it thought he sprung. **1752** Young *Brothers* I. i, From this Philip's bed Two Alexanders spring. **1779** *Mirror* No. 32, His father having sprung nobody knows whence. **1837** P. Keith *Bot. Lex.* 138 Enlarged vesicles that have sprung from a primitive molecule. *Ibid.* 225 Ovid replenishes his post-diluvian world with animals that sprang up out of the earth. **1850** Irving *Goldsmith* i. 18 He sprang from a respectable, but by no means a thrifty stock. **1891** Farrar *Darkn. & Dawn* ii, His face was stamped with all the nobility of the Domitian race from which he sprang.

c. To come into being. Also with additions as *forth*, *to life*.

1667 Milton *P.L.* III. 334 Mean while The World shall burn, and from her ashes spring New Heav'n and Earth. **1784** Cowper *Task* III. 769 Springs a palace in its stead, But in a distant spot. **1813** T. Busby *Lucretius* I. I. 1055 Nought that beneath the etherial concave grows, Had sprang to life, or to perfection rose. **1817** Shelley *Rev. Islam* X. xviii, The winds.., as before Those winged things sprang forth, were void of shade. **1820** Byron *Juan* III. lxxxvi. i, The isles of Greece! .. Where Delos rose, and Phœbus sprung!

d. To arise as an offshoot *from* a society.

1782 Priestley *Corrupt. Chr.* I. I. 114 The Monophysites [were] a sect which sprung from the Eutychians. **1847** Prandi tr. *Cesare Cantu, Reform. Eur.* I. 214 From the Order of the Benedictines there sprang the Maurines.

11. To grow (*up*); to increase or extend in height or length; to grow out *from* some thing or part.

1382 Wyclif *Dan* vii. 20 Of ten hornes whiche it hadde in the hed, and of the tother that was sprungen vp. ?*a* **1400** *Morte Arth.* 3265 The spekes .. The space of a spere lenghe springande fulle faire. *c* **1440** *Pallad on Husb.* XII. 572 Ley vnder laure, and flakis vp let springe [*glossed* exurgere]. **1486** *Bk. St. Albans, Hawking* cij, Yet have I sene sum fowkys take hem owte of mewe when the sarcell were bot halfe i-spronge. **1674** Ray *Coll. Words* 115 The cake of Silver after it grows cold springs or rises up into branches. **1882** Vines tr. *Sachs' Bot.* 544 Three or five large broad protuberances .. spring from the periphery of the floral axis.

b. To attain to a certain height or point by growth. Also *fig.*

c **1400** *Rom. Rose* 6954 Therof alle perseners be we, And tellen folk where so we go, That man thurgh us is sprongen so. **1530** Palsgr. 730 Howe you be spronge sythe I sawe you. **1577** B. Googe *Heresbach's Husb.* II. (1586) 51 According to the height that I would haue the Hedge to spring. **1627** May *Lucan* VI. 118 Corne as yet not sprong To the full height. **1651** J. Davies *Civ. Warres* 365 They could not digest to see a young sprig .. sprung up to be a commander. *a* **1861** T Woolner *My Beautiful Lady, Day Dream* 13 Beholdest thou Thy babe, now sprung a man?

c. Of arches, etc.: To take a curving or slanting upward course *from* some point of support. Also without const.

(*a*) **1739** C. Labelye *Piers Westm. Bridge* 8 Semi-circular Arches, springing from about 1 Foot higher than Low-water Mark. **1814** Scott *Diary* 12 Aug. in *Lockhart*, Doubtless an arched roof sprung from the side walls. **1825** J. Nicholson *Operat. Mechanic* 573 The inclined ridges, springing from the angles of the walls, are called hips. **1859** Jephson *Brittany* v. 54 A fine massive round tower with a turret springing from it about halfway up its height. **1881** Young *Ev. Man his own Mechanic* §962. 458 A wall plate is nailed to receive the rafters, one of which springs from each of the front posts.

(*b*) **1776** G. Semple *Building in Water* 14 The Arch .. springs at high Water Mark. **1875** Manning *Mission H. Ghost* xi. 308 The piers rise until the arch begins to spring.

d. In pa. pple.: Set out, extended.

1879 *Cassell's Techn. Educ.* IV. 351/1 The ribs must be well 'sprung' from the spine.

12. With *up*. Of a breeze: To begin to blow.

1719 De Foe *Crusoe* II. (Globe) 479 A Breeze of Wind springing up the same Evening, we weighed and set Sail for the Brasils. **1748** *Anson's Voy.* II. (ed. 4) 349 When a gale sprung up, it constantly blew off the land. **1805** Nelson 25 Spet. in Nicolas *Disp.* (1846) VII. 50 As the breeze is now springing up from the NW. **1877** Miss A. B. Edwards *Up Nile* v. 111 By and by a little breeze springs up.

II. *Transitive senses.*

**** **13.** †**a.** To sprinkle (a liquid, etc.); = sprenge *v.* 1. *Obs.*

1387 Trevisa *Higden* (Rolls) II. 23 Reyn is y-seie arered vppon þe hilles and anon i-spronge aboute in þe feeldes. *Ibid.* V. 7 He ordeyned holy water .. to be springe in Cristen mennis hous. *c* **1400** *Lanfranc's Cirurg.* 170 Whanne þou hast sewid þe wounde bineþe .. þanne springe þeron poudre consolidatif. *c* **1440** *Pallad. on Husb.* I. 907 Also the fleen wol sleen, on thy pament oildreggis ofte ysspronge. *c* **1485** *E.E. Misc.* (1855) 78 Sprynge of that water alle abowte. **1581** J. Bell *Haddon's Answ. Osor.* 416 Spryng holy water, sing Masses for the quicke and the dead.

b. To sprinkle (a person or thing); = sprenge *v.* 2. Usu. const. *with*. *Obs.* exc. *dial.*

WFlem. *springen* is similarly employed in place of *sprengen*. See also bespring *v.*

1382 Wyclif *Isaiah* lii. 15 He shal springe manye Jentiles. **1387** Trevisa *Higden* (Rolls) II. 331 Israel toke wiþ hem mele and floure i-spronge wiþ oyle. **1392** in Warner *Antiq. Culin.* (1791) 17 Set hem adoun and spryng hem with vynegar. *c* **1420** *Liber Cocorum* (1862) 7 Bray hit a lytelle, with water hit spryng. *c* **1440** *Pallad. on Husb.* XII. 569 Olyues that me fyndeth lying crispe, With rugis drawe, in salt it is to sprynge. **1519** Horman *Vulg.* 178 b, Take a lytell pece of erthe and spryng it with water. **1576** G. Baker tr. *Gesner's Jewell of Health* 239 A certaine vessell .. both sprowngen rounde about, and covered with Chimney soote. **1854** Miss Baker *Northampt. Gloss.* s.v., To spring clothes is to moisten them a little previous to ironing.

†**14. a.** To grow (a beard). *Obs.*$^{-1}$

a **1330** *Otuel* 1445 A yong knight, that sprong furst berd, Of no man he nas aferd.

†**b.** To produce, bring forth. *Obs.*

1525 Fitzherb. *Husb.* §130 There be trees wil .. growe well, and sprynge rotes of them-selfe. **1601** Holland *Pliny* I. 545 The same fig trees when they begin to spring leaf and look green. *a* **1648** Ld. Herbert *Hen. VIII* (1683) 84 A seed which will spring any thing in corrupt minds. **1692** Dryden *Cleomenes* III. ii, If, as we dream, Egyptian earth, impregnated with flame, Sprung the first man.

†**c.** In fig. use. Also with *up*. *Obs.*

(*a*) **1475** *Paston Lett.* III. 130 Iff Sporle woode sprynge any sylver or golde, it is my wyll that fyrst of alle ye [etc.]. **1593** Lodge *Phœnix Nest* Misc. Pieces A ij b, Striue no more, Forspoken ioyes to spring. **1598** B. Jonson *Ev. Man in Hum.* I. i, Their indulgence must not spring in me A fond opinion, that he cannot erre. *c* **1611** Chapman *Iliad* XXIV. 494 Thy tears can spring no deeds To help thee, nor recall thy son. **1649** Lovelace *Poems* 67 When Joy wip't it [*sc.* the tear] off, Laughter straight sprung 't agen. **1697** Collier *Ess. Mor. Subj.* II. (1709) 72 He that has Such a burning Zeal, and springs such mighty Discoveries, must needs be an admirable Patriot.

(*b*) **1624** Massinger *Parl. Love* v. i, The too much praise .. Could not but spring up blushes in my cheeks. **1639** —— *Unnat. Combat* III. iii, Nor shall the raine of your good counsell fall Upon the barren sands, but spring up fruit.

†**15.** To cast *out* or *in*; to drain *off*. *Obs.*

1398 Trevisa *Barth. De P.R.* XVIII. x. (Bodl. MS.), [The adder] biteþ and springeþ oute venym. *c* **1440** *Jacob's Well* 248 þat castyth out synne & springeth in vertewe. **1579** Langham *Gard. Health* 667 Steepe the leaues in cold water, & at night spring off the water.

†**16.** To cause to well up or flow out of the ground. *Obs.*

c **1440** *Jacob's Well* 2 þanne þi welle is depe ynow .. for to springe watyr of grace. *Ibid.* 275 þis grace in þe ground of equyte, þat spryngeth vp þise vij. stremys of vertuys. **1526** *Pilgr. Perf.* (W. de W. 1531) 112 A well whiche .. sholde sprynge fayre water & swete. **1667** *Phil. Trans.* II. 485 Lakes, some changing Copper into Iron, and causing storms, when any thing is cast into them; and others, sprung up by Earth-quakes.

†**17.** To cause to appear or rise to view. *Obs.*

c **1400** Love *Bonavent. Mirr.* (1908) 50 This day the sonne of riȝtwisnesse .. sprang openly his bemes of mercy. *c* **1646** Crashaw *Poems* (1904) 254 Thine was the Rosy Dawn that sprung the Day Which renders all the starres she stole away.

18. To cause (a bird, *esp.* a partridge) to rise from cover.

1531 Elyot *Gov.* (1580) 61 The men sprange the Birdes out of the bushes. **1575** Painter *Pal. Pleas.* ii. (1890) 4 His spaniells sprong a Partrich. **1592** Lyly *Midas* IV. iii, Thou shouldest say, start a hare, rowse the deer, spring the partridge. **1621** Burton *Anat. Mel.* II. ii. III. (1651) 240 A Hawk, .. when the game is sprung, comes down amain, and stoopes upon a sudden. **1682** Wheler *Journ. to Greece* VI. 260 We sprang Ducks and Snipes. **1711** Addison *Spect.* No. 108 ¶4 Honest Will began to tell me of a large Cock-Pheasant that he had sprung in one of the neighbouring Woods. *a* **1793** G. White *Observ. Birds* in *Selborne* (1833) 293 [The] land-rail .. flies in a very .. embarrassed manner .., and can hardly be sprung a second time. **1856** 'Stonehenge' *Brit. Rural Sports* 33/1 Before the birds are sprung, he should pat and encourage the dog. **1883** *Cent. Mag.* 487/2 In October and November, the sportsman often 'springs' coveys containing birds too small to be shot.

b. In fig. contexts.

1589 [? Lyly] *Pappe w. Hatchet* (1844) 39 That there is not a better Spanniell in England to spring a couie of queanes than Martin. *c* **1590** Greene *Fr. Bacon* (1630) 16 Here's good game for the hawke, .. a couie of Cockscombes, one wise man I think would spring you all. **1614** B. Jonson *Barth. Fair* v. iv. (1904) 130, I may perhaps spring a wife for you, anone. **1678** Butler *Hud.* III. ii. 1203 Your greedy slav'ring to devour .. sprung the Game .. Before y' had time to draw the Net. *a* **1721** Sheffield (Dk. Buckhm.) *Wks.* (1753) II. 162 Which can hardly fail of springing some game in such an ample field of fame and glory. **1774** Foote *Cozeners* I. Wks. 1799 II. 148 What new game have you sprung? **1812** [see plant *sb.*[1] 7].

c. To make (a horse) gallop.

1737 Bracken *Farriery Impr.* (1757) II. 165 A Horse happens to be sprung out at his full Speed. **1837** Apperley *Chase, Turf, & Road* (1845) 62 We always spring 'em over this stage. **1874** Reynardson *Down Road* (1887) 160, I must spring them a bit, .. or we shall never get up the Lodge Hill.

fig. **1849** De Quincey *Eng. Mail Coach* i. Misc. (1854) 302 He unloosed, or, to speak by a stronger word, he *sprang*, his known resources: he slipped our royal horses like cheetahs.

19. *Naut.* Of a vessel, or those on board: To have (a mast, yard, etc.) split, cracked, or started. †Also of the wind: To cause to split.

For the phrases *to spring a butt, one's luff*, see butt *sb.*[7] and luff *sb.*[1] 3.

1595 *Drake's Voy.* (Hakl. Soc.) 11 The Exchange, a small shippe, spronge her mast, and was sunke. *c* **1620** Z. Boyd *Zion's Flowers* (1855) 20 A boisterous wind .. Springs the .. mast. **1669** *Lond. Gaz.* No. 421/1 Off the Lizard she sprang her main Mast by the board. **1671** Clarendon *Hist. Reb.* XIV. §71 The Ship in which himself was, that sprung a plank in the Indies. **1745** P. Thomas *Jrnl. Anson's Voy.* 23 We sprung the Main-top-sail Yard. **1799** *Hull Advertiser* 13 July 1/4 St. Joaquim .. sprung her foremast; .. St. Paulo sprung her tiller. **1820** Scoresby *Acc. Arct. Reg.* I. 106 The ice which fell, struck the ship so high and so forcibly, that it .. sprung the bowsprit. **1840** R. H. Dana *Bef. Mast* xxxv, We snapped off three flying-jib booms .. ; sprung the spritsail yard.

b. To have or make (a leak) open or start.

1611 [see below.] **1624** [see leak *sb.* 1]. **1687** A. Lovell tr. *Thevenot's Trav.* I. 17 In an hours time, we were got off, without springing the least leak. *a* **1721** Prior *Vicar of Bray & Sir T. More* Wks. 1907 II. 252 You would not have stopped that part of the Ship where the Leak was sprung. **1782** [see leak *sb.* 1]. **1851** Dixon *W. Penn* xviii. (1872) 159 The vessel sprang a leak. **1894** *Times* (weekly ed.) 2 Feb. 91/3 After she left Swansea she sprang a leak.

fig. **1611** Beaum. & Fl. *Philaster* IV. i. (1620) 40 The wench has shot him betweene wind and water, and I hope sprung a lake. **1623** Massinger *Dk. Milan* III. ii, He hath sprung a leak too, Or I am cozened. *a* **1680** Butler *Rem.* (1759) I. 206 His Talent has but sprung the greater Leak.

20. a. *Mil.* To explode (a mine).

1637 in *Verney Mem.* (1907) I. 112 As thay had sprung there mine. **1677** *Lond. Gaz.* No. 1244/2 This morning we Sprung a Mine under a Ravelin .., which did considerable execution. **1712** J. James tr. *Le Blond's Gardening* 108 They .. blow them up, by placing .. Barrels of Powder at the Foot of them, to which they give Fire, .. and this they call Springing a Mine. **1744** M. Bishop *Life & Adv.* 187 They sprung several Mines and blew up a great Number of our Men. **1810** Wellington in Gurw. *Desp.* (1836) VI. 463 To be prepared to spring the mines in these bridges if the enemy should advance. **1894** Wolseley *Marlborough* I. 121 The enemy sprang two mines.

fig. **1679** Alsop *Mel. Inq.* II. vii. 346 When we are mounted he springs his Mine, and blows us all up with his Retractation. **1792** S. Rogers *Pleas. Mem.* II. 119 Go, spring the mine of elevating thought. **1816** Wordsw. *Sonn. Liberty* II. xlv. 93 He springs the hushed Volcano's mines. **1823** Scott *Quentin D.* xxxiv, I only grieve that I cannot spring it like a mine, to the destruction of them all!

b. To sound (a rattle).

Also in pres. pple. *springing* = being sprung.

1812 *Ann. Reg., Chron.* 26 Mr. Johnston sprung a rattle. **1840** R. H. Dana *Bef. Mast* xix, We made him [*sc.* the rattlesnake] spring his rattle again, and began another attack. **1842** C. Whitehead *R. Savage* (1845) III. 335 Men calling, rattles springing, .. doors unlocking and unbolting in every court. **1887** Stevenson *Misadv. J. Nicholson* ii. 4 He heard the alarm spring its rattle.

21. †**a.** To start (something); to set going. *Obs.*

1611 Speed *Hist. Gt. Brit.* IX. xvi. 50 The Yorkists .. thought it now a fit season to spring their practice. **1667** Pepys *Diary* 10 Nov., To spring nothing in the House, nor offer anything but just what is drawn out of a man. **1700** Dryden *Ovid's Met., Cinyras & Myrrha* 153 Surpriz'd with Fright, She starts, and leaves her Bed, and springs a Light.

†**b.** To utter or pass (bad coin); to let off (a joke). *Obs.*

a **1658** Cleveland *Lond. Lady* 80 Down Fleet-street next she rowls .. To spring clip'd-half-crowns in the Cuckow's Nest. **1686** F. Spence tr. *Varilla's Ho. Medicis* 234 They saw him .. not valuing to lose a Friend, rather than not have the Pleasure of springing a Witticism.

c. *colloq.* To give, pay, or disburse (a sum of money); to buy (a certain amount).

1851 Mayhew *Lond. Labour* I. 53 It's a feast at a poor country labourer's place, when he springs six-penn'orth of fresh herrings. **1883** J. Greenwood *Odd People in Odd Places* 244 In hope that he might spring a few shillings more than he had promised. **1904** Max Pemberton *Red Morn* xi, I'll spring one hundred pounds, sir, if you will tot it up.

d. To bring (an announcement, etc.) suddenly (*up*)*on* a person or persons. Also without following prep.

1876 'Mark Twain' *Tom Sawyer* xxxiv. 265 Old Mr. Jones is going to try to spring something on the people here to-night. **1884** *Manch. Exam.* 20 June 5/4 The hole-and-corner arrangement by which Sir Henry Peek's resignation was sprung upon the constituency. **1891** H. Herman *His Angel* 167 The threat of springing the naked facts upon the young lady. **1895** Roberts & Morton *Adventures of Arthur Roberts* xi. 145 'Dinner!' ejaculated Johnson. 'Yes, we shall have to spring the landlady for that at once. That's where she will want a bit of the ready money on account.' **1896** 'Merriman' *Sowers* xxvii, She was one of those mothers who rule their daughters by springing surprises upon them. **1922** *Ladies' Home Jrnl.* July 72/1 But one day she sprang a surprise; she sprinkled the salad with Dromedary [Shredded Coconut]—*father actually smiled.* **1943** K. Tennant *Ride on Stranger* i. 1 'One I didn't mind,' he admitted. 'Two's plenty. But to spring it on a man like this.' His tone was one of outrage. **1969** *Listener* 14 Aug. 204/1 The official French government spokesman sprang the wholly unexpected news: the franc was to be devalued. **1979** D. Eden *Storrington Papers* xiii. 149 She's a bit upset. I did rather spring it on her.

e. To cast or throw suddenly.

1884 E. Jenkins *Week of Passion* I. iv. 110 He must expect to be countermined, to have a thousand ingenious obstacles sprung in his way.

22. To cause (a thing) to spring, move suddenly, fly with a jerk, etc.

1665 HOOKE *Microgr.* 210 These six leggs he [a flea] clitches up altogether, and when he leaps, he springs them all out. **1821** CLARE *Vill. Minstr.* II. 102 If but the breezy wind their floats should spring. **1828** *Examiner* 436/1 The Page's cloak had 'sprung' its shoulder-button. **1831** *Ibid.* 675/2 It blows a gale enough..to spring the teeth from out your jaws. **1878** C. TUTTLE *Border Tales* 73 He mounts up on the platform, and begins to spring it up and down.

fig. **1865** MEREDITH *R. Fleming* xlvi, He uttered a threat that sprang an answer from her bosom in shrieks. **1880** —— *Trag. Com.* v, It sprang Clotilde a stride nearer to reality.

b. *Mil.* To shift (a weapon, etc.) smartly from one position to another.

1780 *Encycl. Brit.* VI. 4438 Make ready: i.e. Spring the firelock briskly to the recover. **1796** *Instr. & Reg. Cavalry* (1813) 232 Carbines sprung, and unstrapped. **1833** *Reg. Instr. Cavalry* I. 29 Each man springs his ramrod as the officer passes him, and then returns it. *Ibid.* 98 The carbine is 'sprung' by the right hand seizing the swivel, and securing it through the ring. **1859** F. A. GRIFFITHS *Artill. Man.* (1862) 46 Spring arms—Two. Load.

c. To cause (some mechanism, etc.) to work with a sudden movement; to force open by pressure. Also *fig.* and in fig. contexts.

1828 LYTTON *Pelham* III. xix, Until I had hit upon the method of springing the latch, and so winning my escape from the house. **1894** *Cornh. Mag.* Mar. 293 The inquiring bee, on his collecting rounds, can thus see at a glance whether any particular flower has been 'sprung' or not, as we technically call it. **1897** LD. H. TENNYSON *Mem. Tennyson* I. 19 He would spring all their traps. **1930** D. HAMMETT *Dain Curse* xv. 165 'All right, spring it,' I said, as we sat down in his..living room. 'Any trace of Gabrielle yet?' he asked. 'No. But spring the puzzle. Don't be literary with me, building up to climaxes and the like... Just spread it out for me.' **1980** J. BARNES *Metroland* III. iv. 161, I started again, more seriously this time, masochistically trying to spring that familiar trigger for panic and terror.

d. To apply or adjust by force applied to some elastic or resilient body.

1842 BROWNING *Gismond* xi, What says the body when they spring Some monstrous torture-engine's whole Strength on it? **1872** *Routledge's Ev. Boy's Ann.* Apr. 307/1 Pieces of brass tube, on which are 'sprung' lengths of flexible gas tubing.

e. To bend or deflect from a straight line.

1873 *Routledge's Yng. Gentl. Mag.* July 503/2 Don't drive it in too hard, as it will 'spring' the plane-iron, and make it concave. **1887** *Pall Mall G.* 28 May 8/1 It is so stiff that the utmost power of a man is required to spring it even very slightly.

23. To release (a person) from custody or imprisonment, esp. to contrive such a release by means of bail. Also, to contrive an unlawful escape from prison. *slang* (orig. *U.S.*).

1900 'FLYNT' & 'WALTON' *Powers that Prey* 62 It cost his push a thousand plunks to spring him from the coppers. **1911** C. B. CHRYSLER *White Slavery* ix. 70 If you get nicked ..you can 'raspberry' the 'bull' and get 'sprung'. **1929** *Sun* (Baltimore) 15 Nov. 1/6, I got sick of him [*sc.* the lawyer] and I started examining the jury myself. They sprung me in five minutes. **1936** J. STEINBECK *In Dubious Battle* iii. 24 They'll give him the works if George doesn't get busy. Tell George to try to spring him for a drunk... If a sanity board ever gets hold of that poor devil, he's in for life. **1963** *Security Gaz.* V. 187/3 Those who may be preparing to 'spring' an inmate. **1967** *Punch* 15 Mar. 375 In the main the British bail system works better than the American one. Over there a professional bondsman..'springs' the accused man for roughly ten per cent of the bail fixed. **1974** *Daily Tel.* 2 Sept. 3 Miss Mary Tyler, the English school-teacher who has spent more than four years in Indian jails awaiting trial, is to be returned to a high security prison this week in case militant Maoists try to 'spring' her. **1977** J. CHEEVER *Falconer* 13 I'm in cellblock F... Last Tuesday they forgot to spring us for supper. **1980** *Observer* 3 Apr. 9/5 What the Minister has in mind is the 'springing' of the dockers in 1972 following the intervention of that hitherto mysterious figure, the Official Solicitor.

24. *techn.* **a.** *Arch.* To commence the curve of (an arch).

1703 MOXON *Mech. Exerc.* 273 The level of the place, whence you begin to spring the Arch. **1807** R. C. HOARE *Tour Irel.* 198 The arches which were sprung to support it. **1823** P. NICHOLSON *Pract. Build.* 339 Impost or Springing —The upper part..of a wall employed for springing an arch.

b. *Shipbuilding.* (See quot.)

c **1850** *Rudim. Navig.* (Weale) 151 To *Spring*, is to quicken or raise the sheer.

c. *Naut.* To move, haul, or swing (a vessel) by means of a spring or cable. Cf. SPRING *sb.*[1] 24.

a **1865** W. H. SMYTH *Sailor's Word-bk.* (1867) 646 *Sprung* ..the ship slued round by means of guys. **1898** S. B. LUCE *Text-bk. Seamanship* 217 Ships may be sprung broadside to the wind..for the purpose of better ventilation; or in engagements at anchor, to bring the guns to bear on various points. **1922** C. C. SOULE *Naval Terms & Definitions* 69/2 *Spring*, to turn a vessel with a line.

d. *Bootmaking.* To raise (the toe or waist of a last) above the ground-line (see also quot. 1953).

1905 E. J. C. SWAYSLAND *Boot & Shoe Design* iii. 21 An upward curve in the waist of about an eighth of an inch... This is very much less than lasts are usually sprung in the waist. **1916** F. PLUCKNETT *Boot & Shoe Manuf.* ii. 16 Provision should be made for alteration in shape which would be likely to take place in wear.., *e.g.* springing the toe of the last. **1953** A. V. GOODFELLOW in J. H. Thornton *Textbk. Footwear Manuf.* II. vii. 89 The effect of springing a pattern, or changing the relationship between one part and another of the same pattern is to lengthen one line and shorten another.

***** †**25. a.** = LEAP *v.* 9. *Obs.*

1585 T. WASHINGTON tr. *Nicholay's Voy.* IV. xxxi. 154 [They] sought the fairest stoned horses to spring their mares.

b. To leap over; to cover with a spring.

1825 SCOTT *Talism.* xxvi, He that would climb so lofty a tree, Or spring such a gulf as divides her from thee. **1854** *Orr's Circ. Sci., Org. Nat.* I. 96 The grasshoppers..being capable, with ease, of springing some hundred times their own length. **1907** J. H. PATTERSON *Man-Eaters of Tsavo* viii. 89 If the lion could spring the twelve feet which separated me from the ground.

spring, *v.*[2] [f. SPRING *sb.*[1], in various senses.]

†**1.** *trans.* To allow (timber or ground) to send up shoots from the stools of felled trees. *Obs.*

1690 *Let.* in *Hunter MSS.* VII. No. 200, I have ordered the workmen to hedg in two Acres of Ground allready sprung 2 yards high... I shall spring more if you require it.

2. *intr.* To pass or spend the season of spring *at* a place. *rare*⁻¹.

1835 *Fraser's Mag.* XI. 507 Every third man has wintered at Naples, springed at Vienna.

3. *trans.* To give spring or elasticity to.

1843 E. JONES *Poems, Sens. & Event* 115 To measureless action spring'd by her in a moment. **1875** F. J. BIRD *Dyer's Hand-bk.* 54 The wool will come out of this bath rather dirty and grey-looking. In order to spring it [etc.].

4. To provide or fit with a spring or springs.

1884 [see SPRUNG *ppl. a.*[2] 1]. **1905** *Automobile Topics* 27 May 491 (Cent. Suppl.), Having learned to properly spring horse-drawn and railway carriages.

spring-, the verbal stem used in a few specific names, as **spring-beetle** (see quot.); **spring-hare,** the jumping hare of South Africa; **spring-jack, -lobster** (see quots.).

1835 J. DUNCAN *Beetles* (Nat. Lib.) 159 This operation is attended with a sharp snapping noise, which has caused these insects to be termed click-beetles, in addition to the names of skipjacks and *spring-beetles, by which they are likewise known in England. **1900** *Daily Express* 27 June 7/1 We could hear them probing a suspicious-looking *spring hare's burrow. **1848** *Proc. Berw. Nat. Club* II. 327 A mechanism..which..causes them to rise with a jerk, accompanied with a snapping noise, whence they have been named 'clicks' or '*spring-jacks'. **1879** E. P. WRIGHT *Anim. Life* 533 Here are to be placed the *Spring Lobsters (Palinuridæ), the Cray-fish (Astacidæ).

springal: see SPRINGLE *sb.*[1] and *sb.*[2]

'springal(d[1]. *Obs.* exc. *Hist.* Forms: α. 4, 6 **spryngalle** (5 **-al**), 4 **spryngelle, -ele,** 5 **-ell;** 4 **springal** (**-ol**), 4, 6 **-all.** β. 4–5 **spryngald(e** (5 **-olde**), 4–6 (9) **springald** (5 **-alt, -olt**). [ad. OF. *espringale, -alle* cf. ESPRINGAL), or a. AF. *springalde* (Anglo-Lat. *springaldum*), app. f. OF. *espringuer* SPRING *v.*[1] Hence also MDu. and MHG. *springale*, MLG. *springal.*] An engine of the nature of a bow or catapult, used in mediæval warfare for throwing heavy missiles; also, the missile thrown by an engine of this kind.

α. **13..** *Coer de L.* 4346 The Sarezynes..schotte with arweblaste and spryngalles. *c* **1380** *Sir Ferumb.* 3310 Summe springols stipe bente, & schute gleyues scherpe. *c* **1410** *Master of Game* (MS. Digby 182) ii, He smyteth as a stroke of a spryngell, for he hath gret strength in þe hed and in the Body. **1523** LD. BERNERS *Froissart* I. cxliv. 172 This castell ..was well fortyfied with springalles, bombardes, bowes, and other artillary.

β. **1305–6** in *Cat. Doc. rel. Scotl.* (1888) 392 Unum springald cum balistis et quarellis. **1375** BARBOUR *Bruce* XVII. 247 Spryngaldis and schotis..That till defend castell afferis, He purvait. *c* **1400** *Rom. Rose* 4191 And eke withynne the castelle were Spryngoldes, gunnes, bows, archers. **1422** in Ellis *Orig. Lett.* Ser. II. I. 95 Being at the Siege of Harflewe, there smyten with a Springolt through the hede. **1568** GRAFTON *Chron.* II. 281 This Castell..was well fortefied with Springaldes, Bombardes, Bowes, and other Artillery. **1909** W. DEEPING *Red Saint* xl. 340 The King's men who still held the castle, had thrown springalds of fire down upon the houses, setting the thatch ablaze.

'springal(d[2]. Now *arch.* Forms: α. 5 **sprynhold,** 6 **spryngolde,** 6–7 **springold(e,** 6 **-hold, -olte, -ol** (**springehole**). β. 6 **spryng-, springe-, -hald,** 6–7, 9 **springald** (9 **-alt**). γ. 6 **spryngall,** 6–9 **springal, -all;** 8 **springle.** [Of doubtful origin; perh. a formation from SPRING *v.*[1] suggested by prec. In very common use from *c* 1500 to 1650; in 19th cent. revived by Scott.]

1. A young man, a youth, a stripling.

α. *c* **1440** *Alph. Tales* 221 When he was a grete yong sprynhold, sho wold kys hym & halsse hym. **1518** WHITINTON *De Heteroclitis Nom.* A iv, *Pubes*, spryngolde. **1534** —— *Tullyes Offices* I. (1540) 48 Marcus Drusus, a yong springolte of synguler granyte. **1535** *Goodly Primer, Passion* III, A certain young springhold that followed Christ. *a* **1575** tr. *Pol. Verg. Eng. Hist.* (Camden No. 36) 186 He banished this springehole as relagate in Fraunce. **1664** COTTON *Scarron.* I. Wks. (1725) 46 Queen Dido ravish'd to behold The Carriage sweet of this Springold.

β. **1501** DOUGLAS *Pal. Hon.* I. xlv, Lustie Springaldis and mony gudlie lord. **1535** COVERDALE *Dan.* i. 17 God gaue now these foure spryngaldes connynge and lernynge. **1611** BEAUM. & FL. *Knt. Burning Pestle* II. ii, Sure the Devil, God bless us, is in this Springald. **1816** SCOTT *Old Mort.* xiii, 'A pretty springald this, upon my honour!' said Claverhouse. **1824** BYRON *Juan* XV. lxx, Also the younger men too: for a springald Can't, like ripe age, in gourmandise excel. **1892** GUNTER *Miss Dividends* (1893) 197 This will bring your young springald down here very suddenly, I imagine.

γ. **1542** UDALL *Erasm. Apoph.* 123 Beholdyng a certain young spryngall. **1589** [? LYLY] *Pappe w. Hatchet* D iij b, Springalls and vnripened youthes, whose wisedomes are yet in the blade. **1613** PURCHAS *Pilgrimage* (1614) 374 This was their education till 17. yeares of age: at which time they were of the second ranke of Springals and youths. **1693** DRYDEN, etc. *Juvenal* (1697) 269 Go, boast your Springal, by his Beauty curst To Ills. **1720** MRS. MANLEY *Power of Love* (1741) 242 The young Springle..promised her all she could ask. **1748–58** MENDEZ *Sqr. Dames* I. xv. in Dodsley *Coll. Poems* (1755) IV. 130 The springal was in wholesom lustihed. **1819** SCOTT *Ivanhoe* xii, This same springal, who conceals his name,..hath already gained one prize. **1890** F. W. ROBINSON *Strange Family* 68, I loved this..warm-hearted, hot-headed springall.

2. *attrib.* as *adj.* Youthful, adolescent.

Cf. Cheshire dial. *springow*, nimble, active.

a **1614** J. MELVILL *Diary* (Wodrow Soc.) 119 To be sa miserablie corrupted in the entress of his springall age. **1633** FORD *Broken Heart* III. ii, Your fiery metal, or your springal blaze Of huge renown.

†**'springant,** *a. Her. Obs.*⁻⁰ (See quot.)

1731 BAILEY (ed. 2), *Springant*,..a term apply'd to any beast in a posture ready to give a spring or leap.

‖**springar** ('sprɪŋgə(r)). [Norw.] A Norwegian country-dance in three-four time; also, the music for this dance.

1947 [see HALLING]. **1959** *Listener* 2 July 37/1 To achieve the truly national in Norwegian music they should not rest content to quote *springars* and *hallings*, and other dances. **1964** W. G. RAFFÉ *Dict. of Dance* 474/1 *Springar* has nine different steps, and is a dance in which partners show their individual qualities—the man his virility and accomplishment, the girl her skill and grace.

'spring-back. Also **spring back, springback.**

1. [f. SPRING *sb.*[1] 22.] **a.** A folder with a spring clip incorporated in the spine to hold the papers placed in it; also, the clip itself. **b.** = *loose back* s.v. LOOSE *a.* 9. Also *attrib.*

1895 *Montgomery Ward. Catal.* Spring & Summer 247/1 Music Folio, imitation leather, spring back. **1919** 'ETIENNE' *Strange Tales from Fleet* 64 The stupendous and well-filled 'spring-back', replete with bills, a few receipts, and reams of official correspondence. **1923**, etc. [see *loose back* s.v. LOOSE *a.* 9]. **1948** G. V. GALWEY *Lift & Drop* vi. 162 Bourne opened the spring-back correspondence file. **1982** P. D. JAMES *Skull beneath Skin* xli. 332 The archives were bound in springback folders.

2. [f. SPRING *v.*[1]] The capacity to spring flexibly back into position after subjection to pressure. Freq. *attrib.* or as *adj.* Also *fig.*

1945 *Richmond* (Va.) *Times-Dispatch* 2 Mar. 19/3 It [*sc.* a type of compressed wood] can be made.. with negligible springback tendencies. **1970** *Motoring Which?* July 116/1 All the arm-type mirrors we included were either spring-back or collapsible. **1972** A. AMIN tr. *Ahmad's No Harvest but Thorn* x. 98 She leapt over the spring-back wooden fence like a young mouse-deer startled by a *pulut* fox. **1973** J. G. TWEEDDALE *Materials Technol.* II. iv. 87 Whenever a material possesses significant elasticity, as in cold working, there is difficulty with spring back. **1975** *N.Z. Jrnl. Agric.* Sept. 55/2 The finished fence..has a feeling of controlled flexibility and springback to true that augurs well for its stock-holding qualities. **1977** *Time* 31 Jan. 40/1 Charles Schultze agrees that the first quarter 'will show a pretty good springback' from the recent economic pause.

spring-beam. [f. SPRING *sb.*[1] or *v.*[1]] The distinctive name of certain strong timbers forming part of the fittings of an engine or paddle-box.

Other senses are recorded by Knight *Dict. Mech.*

a. **1797** J. CURR *Coal Viewer* 61 Allow proper height for the inside spring beams..and about 6 inches for the springs. **1825** J. NICHOLSON *Operat. Mech.* 180 In engines used for this purpose there are two pieces of wood, called spring-beams, placed across each end of the beam. **1883** GRESLEY *Gloss. Coal-m.* 232 *Spring beams*, two stout parallel timber beams built into a Cornish pumping-engine-house, nearly on a level with the engine beam.

b. **1843** *Civil Eng. & Arch Jrnl.* VI. 70/1 They have no connexion with the spring-beam or frame of the paddle-boxes. **1846** A. YOUNG *Naut. Dict.* 310 The projecting ends of the paddle-beams with a fore and aft beam of wood fitted between them, called a spring beam.

spring-board. [f. SPRING *sb.*[1] or *v.*[1]]

1. A projecting board or plank, from the end of which a person jumps or dives. Also *fig.*

1866 *Routledge's Ev. Boy's Ann.* 659 A long swimming bath..with spring board to jump off. **1885** MRS. LYNN LINTON *Chr. Kirkland* III. 223 The spring-board whence she took her next leap into the arena of insolence. **1887** *Contemp. Rev.* May 717 He uses truth simply as a spring-board whence to jump into a region created by his own fancy.

attrib. **1898** *Daily News* 31 Mar. 8/6 The display concluded with an exhibition of springboard diving.

2. An elastic board used to assist in vaulting.

1799 *Times* 1 June 3/4 He positively leaps over a large tilted waggon and four horses..and does not make use of a spring board or trampoline. **1841** THOREAU *Jrnl.* 23 Jan. (1906) I. v. 174 Like the spring-board on which tumblers perform and develop their elasticity. **1900** *Daily News* 24 Sept. 6/3 With the aid of a spring-board he vaults with ease over nine men placed in a row.

3. *N.Amer.* and *Austral.* A board on which a wood-feller stands when working at some height from the ground.

1883 E. INGERSOLL in *Harper's Mag.* Jan. 200/2 These [holes] were intended for the insertion of their iron-shod 'spring boards'—pieces of flexible planking..upon which they were to stand while chopping at a height too great to reach from the ground. **1934** *Bulletin* (Sydney) 19 Sept. 20/1 Nerves of steel are needed day by day By those who on the springboard stand, while forest monarchs sway. **1972** *Daily Colonist* (Victoria, B.C.) 16 July 6/5 He captured first place in the springboard chop open competition to become Canadian champion. **1975** H. WHITE *Raincoast Chron.*

(1976) 102/2 Metal-tipped springboards set in notches were used by the early fallers to climb above the butt-swell [of a tree].

4. *U.S.* A light kind of vehicle.

1883 STEVENSON *Silverado Sq.* 174 A couple in a waggon, or a dusty farmer on a spring-board toiling over the 'grade' to..Calistoga.

‖**springbok** (sprɪŋbɒk). Also 8–9 -bock, 9 -boc. [Cape Du., f. *springen* to spring + *bok* goat, antelope.] **1.** A species of antelope, *Antilope euchore*, abounding in South Africa, characterized by a habit of springing almost directly upwards when excited or disturbed. Cf. SPRINGER[1] 3 b.

α. **1775** *Phil Trans.* LXVI. 283 We saw some herds of the spring-bocks, a species of antelope. **1777** FORSTER *Voy. round World* I. 84 The spring-bock..live in vast herds in the interior part of Africa. **1827** GRIFFITH tr. *Cuvier* IV. 17 The Springbock, or Pouched Gazelle. **1871** DARWIN *Desc. Man* II. xvii. (1890) 509 The spring-boc..has rather short upright horns.

β. **1785** G. FORSTER tr. *Sparrman's Voy. Cape G. Hope* (1786) II. 83 This animal, which is called by the colonists Spring-bok. **1834** PRINGLE *Afr. Sk.* 1 A tame springbok followed him. **1850** R. G. CUMMING *Hunter's Life S. Afr.* (1902) 18/1 The extraordinary manner in which springboks are capable of springing is best seen when they are chased by a dog. **1880** *Silver & Co.'s S. Africa* (ed. 3) 171 Immense migratory troops of the graceful spring-bok also cover these plains.

attrib. **1884** *Pall Mall G.* 8 Aug. 3/2 A most successful attempt to bring springbok venison fresh to England.

2. *pl.* (usu. with capital initial). **a.** A nickname for a South African national sporting team or touring party. Also *sing.*, one who represents South Africa in international sport.

1906 *S. African News Weekly* 3 Oct. 24/1 A crowd of 9,000 ..accorded the springboks a great reception as they walked on the field. **1932** *Grocott's Mail* (Grahamstown, S. Afr.) 2 Jan. 3 It cannot be said that many English rugby critics strongly favour England's chance against the Springboks on Saturday. **1959** *Cape Argus* 23 Jan. 19/6 (*heading*) Hockey Springboks train. **1970** *Times* 5 Feb. 9/3 Such an admission would be a natural sequel to our recent failure to protect our Springbok guests from repeated insult and persecution. **1975** *Country Life* 16 Jan. 137/3 The French, who lost both their matches against the Springboks..are often underestimated.

b. A nickname for a contingent of South African troops. Also *sing.*, a South African soldier.

1916 'CAPTAIN' (*title*) With the Springboks in Egypt. **1925** FRASER & GIBBONS *Soldier & Sailor Words* 267 *Springboks*.., the South African contingent in the war. From their badge, the Colonial emblem of a springbok antelope. **1943** J. BURGER *Black Man's Burden* 236 The Springboks (Union troops) are spoken of as the successors to the pioneer Voortrekkers. **1944** *Eastern Province Herald* 25 Aug. 1 The company is doing urgent tank maintenance and repair work for the Fifth and Eighth armies; and the Marshall said that he was impressed by the efficiency of the Springbok 'backroom boys'.

springbuck. Anglicized form of prec.

1775 *Phil. Trans.* LXVI. 311 They informed us, they had seen great flocks of the spring bucks. **1824** BURCHELL *Trav.* I. 290 Numbers of that beautiful antelope, the Spring-buck, ..were seen. **1857** LIVINGSTONE *Missionary Trav. S. Africa* v. 103 We saw the last portion of a migration of springbucks. **1887** R. HAGGARD *Jess* x, A couple of dozen or so of graceful yellow springbuck.

attrib. and *Comb.* **1895** J. G. MILLAIS *Breath fr. Veldt* 23 The most..successful springbuck shooter of Beaufort West. *Ibid.* 24 A springbuck hunt.

spring chicken. [f. SPRING *sb.*[1] 6 b.]

1. A small chicken (esp. a roasting bird); *spec.* one aged between eleven and fourteen weeks and weighing around one and a half kilograms (see also quot. 1958).

1780 J. WOODFORDE *Diary* 13 June (1924) I. 285 We had for dinner..three nice Spring Chicken rosted. **1849** D. J. BROWNE *Amer. Poultry Yd.* (1855) 107 Generally speaking, spring chickens are more desirable. **1892** [see ON *prep.* 20 f]. **1917** *Harrods Gen. Catal.* 1267 Poultry... Chickens (Spring). **1943** L. I. WILDER *These Happy Golden Years* xxi. 191 Ma finished frying a spring chicken while the new potatoes and the peas were cooked. **1958** *Times* 18 Aug. 11/2 The term 'spring chicken' has come to be something of a misnomer for the small bird now available at poulterers... all the year round. It is the product of a specialist industry which has developed this particular type of bird to come to maturity in about 10 weeks only. **1974** *Times* 7 Mar. 13/5 Spring chickens are also in the shops, these are a little older [than *poussins*]—from eight weeks to four months.

2. *fig.* A young person. Freq. in phr. ***to be no spring chicken*** and varr., to be no longer young. *colloq.* (orig. *U.S.*).

1910 *National Police Gaz.* (U.S.) 6 Aug. 3/1 She wasn't a Spring chicken, by any means, yet she wasn't old. *a* **1911** D. G. PHILLIPS *Susan Lenox* (1917) II. ii. 20 Miss Hinkle was showing her age—and she was 'no spring chicken'. **1964** 'E. MCBAIN' *Axe* vii. 125 I'm not a spring chicken any more... I'm fifty-two years old. **1973** G. BEARE *Snake on Grave* iv. 23 She was no spring chicken any more, she was pushing forty. **1977** *New Yorker* 10 Oct. 131/1 Americans were impressed by Dr. White's prescription whenever they saw a photo of President Eisenhower swinging a golf club or of Dr. White, no spring chicken himself, bent low over the handlebars of his bicycle. **1981** D. M. THOMAS *White Hotel* IV. i. 145 You're just a spring chicken, Lisa dear!

spring-cleaning. [f. SPRING *sb.*[1] 6 b.] The general cleaning of a house, etc., usually performed in the spring. Also *attrib.*

1857 E. M. STONE *Life J. Howland* i. 28 At the annual 'spring cleaning', they discovered a bundle of manuscripts. **1873** H. MARTINEAU *Let.* 6 Mar. in *Autobiogr.* (1897) III. 416 This will be a busy month, with the spring cleaning and whitewashing. **1887** J. ASHBY STERRY *Lazy Minstrel* (1892) 153 Spring Cleaning's a terrible bore! **1897** MARY KINGSLEY *W. Africa* 79 Things were in a spring-cleaning confusion.

Hence **spring-clean** *v. trans.* and *intr.* Also *transf.* and *fig.*, and as *sb.*, the act of spring-cleaning; **spring-cleaner**.

1849 C. BRONTË *Shirley* I. xi. 289 Very handsome..these shining brown panels are..but—if you know what a 'Spring-clean' is—very execrable and inhuman. **1889** *Pall Mall G.* 15 July 3/1 There are few points of mutual sympathy between the poet and the spring-cleaner. **1894** *Daily News* 21 Apr. 6/6 Houseboat-owners are at present busily engaged in painting and spring cleaning their craft. **1908** in *Englische Studien* (1935) Apr. 119 He was helping his wife to 'spring-clean'. **1926** *Socialist Rev.* Dec. 14 House to house inspections [should be] made in the worst areas; in fact, a regular spring-clean of the whole town organised. **1957** L. DURRELL *Justine* I. 23 It was thrown away by Hamid in the course of a spring-clean. **1961** *Countryman* Autumn 515 The exhausted hound awoke and started a relentless spring-clean of his dusty coat. **1978** N. MARSH *Grave Mistake* i. 36, I was helping springclean at the time. **1979** *Guardian* 19 July 14/5 If, early next week, the Carter White House has truly been spring-cleaned..then the Presidency will be much strengthened.

springe (sprɪndʒ), *sb.* Also 3, 6 sprenge, 5 sprynge, 7–8 sprindge. [app. repr. OE. **sprencg*, related to SPRENGE *v.* and SPRING *v.*[1] Cf. the later SPRING *sb.*[3]]

1. A snare for catching small game, esp. birds.

α. *c* **1250** *Owl & Night.* 1066 Þi song mai beo so longe genge, þat þu schalt hwippen on a sprenge. **1398** TREVISA *Barth. De P.R.* XIV. xliii, Þere beþ manye foulers þat leggeþ and setteþ nettes, springes, and grenes. **1594** BARNFIELD *Aff. Shepherd* II. ix. (Arb) 13 Wilt thou set springes in a frostie Night To catch the long-billd Woodcocke and the Snype? **1598** SYLVESTER *Du Bartas* II. ii. II. *Babylon* 93 He in former quests did use Cals, pit-fals, toyls, sprenges, and baits and glews. **1653** W. RAMESEY *Astrol. Restored* 187 It addeth vigour to the Springes, Nets, Dogs, &c. **1727** SWIFT *Gulliver* IV. ii, I sometimes made a shift to catch a rabbit, or bird, by springes made of Yahoos' hair. **1780** W. COXE *Russ. Disc.* 77 The skins of guillinot [*sic*] and puffin, which they catch with springes. **1815** *Sporting Mag.* XLV. 189 Springes are, I believe, always set in standing wood. **1841** MARRYAT *Poacher* ii, Joey could set a springe. **1908** SIR H. JOHNSTON *Grenfell & the Congo* II. xxvii. 762 They also make use of springes of raphia rind.

β. **1615** CHAPMAN *Odyss.* XXII. 570 A Mauis, or a Pygeon, ..caught with a Sprindge, or Net. **1697** DRYDEN *Virg. Past.* v. 94 Nor Birds the Sprindges fear, not Stags the Toils. **1712–4** POPE *Rape Lock* II. 25 With hairy Sprindges we the Birds betray.

2. *fig.* **a.** In allusions to the catching of woodcocks.

α. **1602** SHAKS. *Ham.* I. iii. 115, I, Springes to catch Woodcocks. **1613** H. PARROT (*title*), Laquei Ridiculosi, or Springes for Woodcocks. **1668** DRYDEN *Even. Love* II. i, So, there's one woodcock more in the springe. **1822** SHELLEY *Chas. I*, II. 39 An idiot in lawn sleeves and a rochet setting springes to catch woodcocks. **1877** TENNYSON *Harold* II. ii, We hold our Saxon woodcock in the springe, But he begins to flutter.

β. **1611** MIDDLETON & DEKKER *Roaring Girl* D.'s Wks. 1873 III. 188 Heere's the sprindge I ha set to catch this woodcocke in. **1663** DRYDEN *Wild Gallant* III, *Isa.* Alas, poor Woodcock, dost thou go a Birding! Thou hast e'en set a Sprindge to catch thy own Neck.

b. In other contexts.

1612 WEBSTER *White Devil* v. vi. 132 O I am caught with a springe. **1698** FARQUHAR *Love & a Bottle* I, And have your ladies no springes to catch 'em in? **1748** RICHARDSON *Clarissa* (1811) III. lvi. 309, I had not drawn my sprindges close about her. *a* **1797** H. WALPOLE *Mem. Reign Geo. III* (1845) I. xix. 276 The lawyers on either side were employed in discovering springes or loop-holes. **1856** MRS. BROWNING *Aur. Leigh* II. 1096 Shall I pardon you If thus you have caught me with a cruel springe? **1875** JOWETT *Plato* (ed. 2) I. 222 He wanted to catch me in his springes of words.

springe (sprɪndʒ), *a.* ? *dial.* Active, agile.

App. not recorded in actual dialect use.

1859 GEO. ELIOT *A. Bede* xxv, The lissom'st springest fellow i' the country. **1861** —— *Silas Marner* xi, The Squire's pretty springe, considering his weight.

springe (sprɪndʒ), *v.*[1] [f. SPRINGE *sb.*]

1. *trans.* To catch in a springe or snare. Also *refl.* Freq. *fig.*

? *a* **1616** BEAUM. & FL. *Q. of Corinth* IV. iii, We springe our selves, we sink in our own bogs. **1812** COMBE *Syntax, Picturesque* xv, And what's still worse, he'll springe a hare. **1856** MRS BROWNING *Aur. Leigh* VIII. 928 An active poacher ..tired of springeing game so long upon my acres. **1891** *Blackw. Mag.* CL. 243/1 Vast quantities of snipe..are netted or springed.

2. *intr.* To set snares.

1895 OWEN & BOULGER *The Country* Feb. 54 The poor people springe for him [the snipe] in the moister parts.

springe, *v.*[2] Now *dial.* [var. of SPRENGE *v.*] *intr.* To sprinkle water.

1599 NASHE *Lenten Stuff* Wks. (Grosart) V. 286 Our Norwich..was a poore fisher towne, and the sea spawled and springed vp to her common stayres. [Cf. Forby *Voc. E. Anglia* (*a* 1825) 321 *Springe*, to spread lightly; to sprinkle.]

springed (sprɪŋd), *ppl. a.* [f. SPRING *sb.*[1] or *v.*[2]] Provided with a spring or springs.

1892 E. REEVES *Homeward Bound* 44 First and second carriages,..both being swung on wheels at each end, and well cushioned and springed.

†**springel.** *Obs.* Also 5 springill, spryngil(l. [app. f. SPRING *v.*[1] The suffix may be after med.L. *aspergillum*.] A sprinkler for holy water. Also *Comb.* in ***springel-stick***.

13.. *Minor Poems fr. Vernon MS.* xxxvii. 730 Siþen he wole wiþ springel-stikke ȝiuen holy water abouten þikke. *c* **1400** *Beryn* 138 A monk, þat toke þe spryngill with a manly chere. *Ibid.* 142 The Frere feynyd fetously the spryngil for to hold To spryng oppon the remnaunt. **1494** *Will of Cumbe* (Somerset Ho.), My grete holy water stop & the springill therto.

springer[1] ('sprɪŋə(r)). [f. SPRING *v.*[1] So MDu. (and Du.), MLG., MHG. (and G.), Da. *springer*, MSw. (and Sw.) *springare*.]

I. † **1.** A source or origin. *Obs.*[−1]

c **1386** CHAUCER *Pars. T.* ¶ 387 Now ben thay cleped chiveteyns, for als moche as thay ben chief and springers of all othere synnes.

2. a. A growing tree or plant. *rare*[−1].

1706 EVELYN *Sylva* (ed. 4) IV. §4 The young men and maidens..go out into the woods and copp'ces, cut down and spoil young springers to dress up their May-booth.

b. A variety of mushroom.

1866 *Treas. Bot.* 1088 *Springers*, a local name applied to the variety of *Agaricus arvensis* figured by Bulliard, and distinguished by its elongated pileus, tall stem, and thinner ring.

3. a. A fish which springs or leaps; now *spec.* a newly-run salmon.

1727 J. G. SCHEUCHZER tr. *Kæmpfer's Hist. Japan* I. 137 Tobiwo is what the Dutch call a Springer (Flying-fish) because it leaps out of the water. **1753** *Chambers' Cycl.* Suppl., *Springer*, in ichthyology a name given by authors to the grampus, or arca. **1853** PAPPE *Edible Fishes C. Good Hope* 27 *Mugil Multilineatus*... Springer; Leaping Mullet. **1886** *Field* 23 Jan. 106/2 Only one succeeded in landing a fish, viz., Tom Murphy, who got a nice springer [*sc.* salmon], weighing 11½ lb. **1893** *Daily News* 23 Feb. 6/4 The newly run fish which the Irish fisherman calls a 'springer'.

b. *Zool.* The springbok. Also ***springer antelope***.

1781 PENNANT *Quad.* I. 82 The Springer Antelope.. weighs about fifty pounds, and is rather lesser than a roebuck. **1785** G. FORSTER tr. *Sparrman's Voy.* II. 139 This tract of country..harboured a considerable number of springers, quaggas, and hartbeests. **1827** GRIFFITH tr. *Cuvier* IV. 208 The Springer Antelope..is the largest of a small subordinate group. *Ibid.*, The Springer resembles the Dorcas of nomenclators, but is nearly a third larger in size.

4. a. One who springs or leaps. Also with advs.

1775 ASH, *Springer*,..one that leaps. **1796** MORSE *Amer. Geog.* II. 254 They are also called springers, or leapers, from the agility with which they leap, rather than walk. **1828** SOUTHEY *Lett.* (1856) IV. 89 Which is being interpreted, the Leaper, or the Springer. **1856** *N. & Q.* Ser. II. II. 36/1 'Springers' is the name given to the 62nd regiment.

fig. **1894** DRUMMOND *Ascent of Man* vii. 345 They were only offspring, springers off.

b. *dial.* A youth.

a **1825** in FORBY *Voc. E. Anglia*.

c. *Naut. slang.* A physical-training instructor in the navy.

1935 *N. & Q.* 29 June 465/1 The officer in charge of physical training was known in my ship..as 'Bunje'. The modern term is 'Springer', both words being descriptive of the acrobatic nature of these duties. **1964** J. HALE *Grudge Fight* vi. 93 The springers all fancy their chance in the training line.

5. *Arch.* The support from which an arch springs; the impost at each end of an arch.

1611 COTGR., *Imposte*,..the springer of an arched gate, the moulding that bears th' arch. **1751** LABELYE *Westm. Bridge* 75 The N.W. Springers of the middle Arch. **1772** C. HUTTON *Bridges* 60 The height of the pier to the springer 18 feet. **1838** *Civil Eng. & Arch. Jrnl.* I. 127/2 A string-course or springer of stone for the abutments of cast-iron ribs which are to carry the crown of the arch. *a* **1878** SIR G. SCOTT *Lect. Archit.* (1879) I. 60 The ribs, all meeting in a solid springer at the foot, brought down the pressure, and deposited it firmly upon the points of support.

6. a. A spring-hook.

1688 [see *spring-hook* s.v. SPRING *sb.*[1] 25 a].

b. A springe.

1813 MONTAGU *Suppl. Ornith. Dict.* s.v. *Woodcock*, Springes or springers are usually set in moist places on the verge of woods.

7. A cow or heifer near to calving.

1844 [see SPRINGING *vbl. sb.*[1] 8]. **1891** *Australasian* 15 Aug. 320/4 A full number of cattle yarded for the week's supply, comprising milkers, springers, and dry cows.

II. 8. a. 'One who rouses game' (J.).

b. A small variety of spaniel. Cf. SPRINGING *ppl. a.* 10.

1808 *Sporting Mag.* XXX. 41 A beautiful old English Springer. **1829** GLOVER *Hist. Derby* I. 136 The Springer is a lively animal, and very expert in raising woodcocks and snipes from their haunts. **1845** YOUATT *Dog* iii. 45 The largest and best breed of springers is said to be in Sussex. *c* **1880** *Cassell's Nat. Hist.* II. 132 The Springer is used for the same purpose as the Cocker, but is a larger, stronger, and steadier Dog.

attrib. **1886** *York Herald* 6 July 3/6 A springer puppy.. was playing near the house.

9. ***springer-up*** (see quot. 1859). *slang.*

1851 MAYHEW *Lond. Lab.* I. 51/2 One of these [tailors] is considered somewhat 'slop', or as a coster called him, a 'springer-up'. **1859** *Slang Dict.* 99 *Springer-up*, a tailor who sells low priced ready made clothing... The clothes are said to be 'sprung up', or 'blown together'.

10. One who fires or sets off a mine.

1861 MEREDITH *Evan Harrington* xxxi, The springers of the mine about to explode.

11. *slang.* A racehorse on which the betting odds suddenly shorten (see quot. 1961).

1922 E. WALLACE *Flying Fifty-Five* xi. 67 The 'springer' in the market, the horse that opened at ten to one and came rapidly to five to two. **1961** J. PRESCOT *Case for Hearing* iv. 61 Plenty of punters like to know how the market's moving so that they can go for the 'springer', the horse that suddenly shortens in price because someone in the know slaps a lot of money on at the last possible moment.

'springer[2]. [f. SPRING *sb.*[1] or *v.*[2]] (See quot.)

1858 SIMMONDS *Dict. Trade, Springer and Liner*, a workman who puts in watch springs.

†**springer**[3]. *Obs.*[−1] [f. SPRING *v.*[1] 13 or SPRINGE *v.*[2]] An instrument for sprinkling water.

1601 W. PARRY *Trav. Sir A. Shirley* 25 They have a spowte or springer to spirt some part of their water uppon their privy partes.

†**'springet.** *Obs.*[−1] [f. SPRING *sb.*[1] 9 + -ET[1].] A small or young shoot.

1659 GELL *Amendm. Eng. Tr. Bible* 236 In that springet, that sprout of righteousness, by whom .. he saveth us.

Springfield ('sprɪŋfiːld). The name of *Springfield*, Mass., used *attrib.* and *absol.* to designate firearms produced at the U.S. government armoury located there.

1813 *Niles' Reg.* IV. 87/2 [The] gun.. is but one pound and a half heavier than the common Springfield gun. **1849** *Knickerbocker* XXXIII. 3 They carried slung from their saddles the excellent Springfield carbines, loading at the breech. **1866** *Harper's Mag.* Aug. 407/1 'Puss' had been doing his best with his 'Springfield', but all at once he stopped firing. **1904** *Kynoch Jrnl.* Apr.-June 95 The Government of the United States had adopted in 1855 the Springfield rifle—a muzzle-loader, calibre .58 bore, with which a 500 grain bullet & 60 grains of powder were used. **1933** F. B. WILLOUGHBY *Alaskans All* 3 His flannel shirt, high laced boots, the hunting-knife in his belt, and the Springfield by his side, made it difficult for me to realize he was a priest. **1964** M. MCLUHAN *Understanding Media* xxxii. 341 The old-timers who backed the Springfield rifle against perimeter fire. **1976** 'O. JACKS' *Assassination Day* (1978) v. 81 The rifle.. was an old World War II American Springfield.

spring-flood. [f. SPRING *sb.*[1] + FLOOD *sb.* So Du. *springvloed*, WFris. *-floed*, G. *-flut*, Da. and Sw. *-flod.*]

†**1.** = SPRING-TIDE 2. Also in fig. context. *Obs.*

c **1386** CHAUCER *Frankl. T.* 342 Thanne shal she been euene atte fulle alway And spryng flood laste bothe nyght and day. *c* **1440** *Jacob's Well* 193 þat ȝe mowe flowe in sprynge-flood of vertuys, hye vp to þe hyll of heuen. **1648** HEXHAM II, *Een Springh, ofte Springh-vloedt*, a Spring-floud, or a Spring-tide.

2. A river-flood occurring in spring-time.

1823 JOANNA BAILLIE *Poems* 30 Then streams, like a spring-flood, her wealth without measure. **1853** MOODIE *Life in Clearings* 29 The spring-floods bring with them a great quantity of waste timber and fallen trees from the interior.

'springful, *a. rare*[−1]. [f. SPRING *sb.*[1] 2.] Abounding in, full of, springs.

1612 DRAYTON *Poly-olb.* xiv. 306 That most spring-full place Where out of Blockeley's bankes so many Fountaines flowe.

spring garden. [f. SPRING *sb.*[1] 2 and 9.]

†**a.** A nursery for young plants. In quot. *fig. Obs.* †**b.** A garden having concealed jets of water liable to be set in action by persons treading on the mechanism. *Obs.* †**c.** A pleasure-garden frequented by the public. *Obs.*

In later use chiefly as the special name of popular resorts in Hyde Park and at Vauxhall.

1603 FLORIO *Montaigne* II. xxxvi. 431 All.. haue made vse of.. his Bookes, as of a Seminarie, a Spring-garden or Storehouse of all kinds of sufficiency and learning. **1611** BEAUM. & FL. *Four Plays* I, Sophocles would.. Like a spring garden shoot his scornfull blood Into their eyes, durst come to tread on him. *a* **1664** KATH. PHILIPS *Country Life* Poems (1667) 90 To Hide-parke let them go, And hasting thence be full of fears, To lose Spring-Garden shew. **1685** (*title*), The Mysteries of Love and Eloquence,.. as they are managed in the Spring Garden, Hyde Park. *c* **1700** CELIA FIENNES *Diary* (1888) 181 Its a place that is used like our Spring Gardens, for the Company of the Town to walk in the Evening. **1751** (*title*), A Sketch of the Spring-Gardens, Vaux-hall. **1752** (*title*), The Spring-Garden Journal.

d. A garden containing many plants that bloom early in the year.

1883 W. ROBINSON *Eng. Flower Garden* I. p. l/1 What we should counsel those who care for their spring gardens is this: To begin and always to work with a series of nursery beds. **1914** E. A. BOWLES *My Garden in Spring* xvii. 295 If you have enjoyed strolling round the spring garden with me .. I hope later on you will accompany me on a second journey to review the summer aspect of the place and plants. **1947** H. NICOLSON *Diary* May (1968) 97 Sissinghurst is lovely. The spring-garden has lost its early bloom.

spring-gun. Also spring gun. [SPRING *sb.*[1]]

1. A gun capable of being discharged by one coming in contact with it, or with a wire or the like attached to the trigger; formerly used as a guard against trespassers or poachers, and placed in concealment for this purpose.

1775 SHERIDAN *Duenna* I. iii, Steel traps and spring guns seemed writ in every wrinkle. **1776** BOSWELL *Life Johnson* (Oxf. ed.) I. 659 He should have warned us of our danger.. by advertising, 'Spring-guns and men-traps set here'. **1816** *Sporting Mag.* XLVIII. 29 Till had been killed by a spring-gun on Lord Ducie's liberty. **1825** *Gentl. Mag.* XCV. I. 262 Lord Suffield moved the first reading of the Bill for prohibiting the use of Spring Guns as a means of protection for game. **1865** BARING-GOULD *Were-wolves* xv. 259 It was on the night of the 15th March that the spring-gun shot him.

2. A toy gun in which the missile is discharged by the release of a spring.

1837 W. B. ADAMS *Carriages* 127 The child's spiral spring-gun is a familiar illustration of the mode in which this spring can best act. **1905** A. R. WALLACE *My Life* I. 66 Among our favourite playthings were pop-guns and miniature spring-guns and pistols.

‖**springhaas** ('sprɪŋhɑːs). *S. Afr.* Also (with hyphen) **spring-haas.** [Afrikaans, f. Du. *spring* jump, leap + *haas* hare.] The jumping hare, *Pedetes capensis*, a nocturnal rodent with large and powerful hind legs and a hopping gait.

1785 G. FORSTER tr. *Sparrman's Voy. Cape Good Hope* II. 195 By the colonists it [*sc.* the *jerbua Capensis*] is called *berghaas*, or *spring-haas* (the mountain or bounding hare). **1837** J. E. ALEXANDER *Narr. Voy. W. Afr.* I. 347 One of the party shot a *spring-haas*, or jumping hare, formed like the kangaroo, with very short fore-legs and long hind ones. **1890** A. MARTIN *Home Life on Ostrich Farm* xi. 225 Most uncanny of all the hares is the spring-haas. This creature.. is never seen in the daytime, and can only be shot on moonlight nights. **1942** S. CLOETE *Hill of Doves* 145 His pulse.. is fast and jumping like a springhaas.

springhalt. Also 7 spring-halt, 8 -hault. [app. an alteration of STRINGHALT, through association with SPRING *v.*[1] Cf. WFlem. *springhielde* spavined.] = STRINGHALT. †Also as *adj.*, affected with stringhalt.

1613 SHAKS. *Hen. VIII*, I. iii. 13 They haue all new legs, And lame ones; one would take it.. the Spauen A[nd] Spring-halt rain'd among 'em. **1639** *Crabtree Lect.* 67 Thou [a farrier] art troubled.. with.. the Spring-halt in thy hippes,.. the Scratches in thy heels. **1718** HUTCHINSON *Witchcraft* ix. 128 Dost thou not.. twitch up thy Houghs just like a Springhault Tit? *a* **1843** SOUTHEY *Comm.-pl. Bk.* Ser. II. (1849) 535 Curious Cure for the Springhalt.

attrib. **1899** *Allbutt's Syst. Med.* VII. 871 Sudden flexion of the leg or thigh.. has been spoken of as 'Springhalt tic'. *Ibid.* 876 Sudden flexion of the leg or thigh may result in a spring-halt movement.

spring-hare ('sprɪŋhɛə(r)). Also **springhare, spring hare.** [Partial tr. Afrikaans *spring-haas*: see SPRINGHAAS.] = SPRINGHAAS.

1822 W. J. BURCHELL *Trav. Interior S. Afr.* I. 343 Besides the holes of the Aardvark, those of the Springhaas (Springhare).. were very frequent. **1853** F. GALTON *Trop. S. Afr.* ix. 281 The spring-hare.. is a creature about two feet long, shaped like a kangaroo in body and in tail, but with a different head; it burrows and lives in holes all day, but at night frisks about and grazes. **1912** J. STEVENSON-HAMILTON *Anim. Life Afr.* xvi. 253 The Spring Hare.. is found locally through Africa south of the Equator. **1937** K. BLIXEN *Out of Africa* ii. 96 The little spring-hares were out on the roads.. jumping along. **1966** E. PALMER *Plains of Camdeboo* x. 179 All around us in their roomy burrows were springhares, those kangaroo-like creatures with their enormous hind legs that go hoppity-hoppity over the veld at night.

spring-head. Also springhead. [f. SPRING *sb.*[1] 2 and 22. Cf. the earlier HEADSPRING.]

1. The source or fountain of a stream or river; a well-head; = SPRING *sb.*[1] 2.

1561 DAUS tr. *Bullinger on Apoc.* (1573) 303 b, Finally he sheweth also the originall or springe head of this riuer. **1570** T. NORTON *Nowell's Catech.* (1853) 181 Though dutiful works of godliness be derived from the Spirit of God, as little streams from the spring-head. **1605** BACON *Adv. Learn.* I. iv. §12 Water will not ascend higher than the levell of the first springhead from whence it descendeth. *a* **1691** BOYLE *Hist. Air* (1692) 140 The place where it works most, is about 40 or 50 yards from the spring-head. **1748** *Anson's Voy.* II. xii. 262 We found the water a little brackish, but.. the nearer we advanced towards the spring-head the softer and fresher it proved. **1787** BEST *Angling* (ed. 2) 127 He may with delight observe the spring head.. and confluxes of each particular river. **1825** *Beverley Lighting Act* ii. 11 Aqueduct, feeder, pond or spring-head. **1868** *Rep. U.S. Commissioner Agric.* (1869) 328 Close below a spring-head dig a trench,.. so that the whole water shall pass through it gently.

b. *fig.* and in fig. context.

1610 J. HEALEY *St. Aug. Citie of God* (1620) 549 We should go to drinke at truths spring-head. **1647** COWLEY *Mistress, The Wish* iii, Here's the Spring-head of Pleasures flood, Where all the Riches lie. **1718** BLACKMORE *Alfred* (1723) II. 38 At the Spring-Head to drink the purest Streams .. Of Truth Divine, I all my Hours apply'd. **1816** COLERIDGE *Lay Serm.* (Bohn) 377 Out of which.. all our other opinions flow, as from their spring-head and perpetual feeder. **1837** WHEWELL *Hist. Induct. Sci.* (1857) I. 14 When our speculations are duly fed from the spring-heads of Observation,.. we may have a living stream of.. Knowledge.

c. The source or fountain *of* some quality, the origin or cause *of* some action, etc.

1555 HARPSFELD in Bonner *Hom.* 9* He wayeth ryghtlye hys synnes, from the originall roote and sprynge heade. **1596** G. BABINGTON *Profit. Exp.* 150 God is the author and verie spring head of all good. **1642** *Answ. 'Plaine English'* 5, I can lead them backward to the spring-head of their calamity. **1669** GALE *Ct. Gentiles* I. Introd. 4 Touching the spring-head and Derivations of human Arts and Sciences. **1694** ATTERBURY *Serm.* (1726) I. ii. 63 Love (the Spring-Head of Charity) as it is the sweetest of All Passions, so it is one of the strongest too. **1868** STANLEY *Mem. Westm. Abbey* 140 Those famous 'seven sons' [of Edward III], the spring-heads of all the troubles of the next hundred years. **1896** *Sunday Mag.* Nov. 724 Who made London.. the springhead of the world's philanthropies?

2. *techn.* (See quot.)

1875 KNIGHT *Dict. Mech.* 2290/2 *Spring-head*, a box, clutch, or connection at the point of contact of the outer ends of an elliptic spring.

spring-headed, *a.* [f. SPRING *v.*[1]] Having heads which spring afresh.

1590 SPENSER *F.Q.* II. xii. 23 Spring-headed Hydraes, and sea-shouldring Whales.

'springily, *adv.* [f. SPRINGY *a.* + -LY[2].]

1. With an elastic or springy step.

1881 MRS. C. PRAED *Policy & P.* III. 44 She stepped springily on to the verandah. **1884** W. D. HOWELLS *Silas Lapham* (1891) I. 60 The mare was springily jolting over the snow.

2. After the manner of a spring.

1884 LATHROP *True & other Stories* II. 229 Were you to place your hand on her shoulder, she would resist springily. **1887** D. C. MURRAY & HERMAN *Traveller Returns* ii. 24 The mere ring of hair which fringed his head was grizzled, but it curled springily still like wire.

springiness ('sprɪŋɪnɪs). Also 7-8 **springy-.** [f. SPRINGY *a.* + -NESS.]

1. The quality of being springy or elastic.

1665 *Phil. Trans.* I. 29 Here are found inquiries concerning.. Springiness and Tenacity. **1692** BENTLEY *Boyle Lect.* viii. 283 The Air is a thin fluid Body, endued with Elasticity or Springiness. **1751** *Phil. Trans.* XLVII. 300 Their springiness makes them separate when the introductor is mounted on the canula. **1841** B. HALL *Patchwork* I. vi. 86 We passed.. along the turf, the springiness of which proved a vast relief. **1862** SMILES *Engineers* III. 229 There was, and still is, a sort of springiness in the road over the Moss.

transf. **1826** DISRAELI *V. Grey* v. vi, The springiness of my mind has gone.

b. Elasticity of movement in persons or animals.

1812 TENNANT *Anster Fair* IV. iii, Th' audacious men of boasted springiness. **1847** L. HUNT *Men, Women, & B.* I. iii. 43 With what a.. massy springiness they brush by you. **1869** *Daily News* 6 Nov., There was a cheeriness.. and a springiness in their movements that betokened first-rate condition. **1886** MISS BRADDON *One Thing Needful* v, The bays went with a certain springiness, which told Lashmar that they were very fresh.

2. a. Capacity for sprouting or growing. **b.** The characteristic features of spring-time.

1674 N. FAIRFAX *Bulk & Selv.* 129 The seeds of most or all growths, kept beyond their full time,.. loose their springinesses. **1824** MISS MITFORD *Village* Ser. I. (1863) 66 Even the early elder shoots, which do make an approach to springiness, look brown.

3. Wet, moist, or spongy condition in land.

1828-32 in WEBSTER.

springing ('sprɪŋɪŋ), *vbl. sb.*[1] [f. SPRING *v.*[1]]

I. 1. a. The action, on the part of seeds, plants, etc., of sprouting or growing.

a **1300** *Cursor M.* 9927 It castes lem ouer al sa bright.. Alsros þat es als in springing. **1387-8** T. USK *Test. Love* II. i. (Skeat) l. 89 The seed of suche springinge in al places.. shulde ben sowe. **1422** tr. *Secreta Secret., Priv. Priv.* 142 The wyntyr helpyth to the Sprynggynge and the bourgynge of naturall thyngis. **1568** WITHALS *Dict.* 2/1 The sprynggynge of the leafe, *germinatio.* **1597** GERARDE *Herbal* I. iii. 5 Their time of springing, flowring and fading. **1611** BIBLE *Ps.* lxv. 10 Thou makest it soft with showres, thou blessest the springing thereof. **1633** FLETCHER *Purple Isl.* XII. xiii, Successive storms.. The timely yeare in its first springings kill. **1730** BAILEY (fol.), *Germination*, a springing, sprouting, or budding forth. **1889** RUSKIN *Præterita* III. 41, I gathered what wild flowers were in their first springing.

transf. and *fig.* **1576** FLEMING *Panopl. Epist.* A ij, To nothing is graunted a perpetuall springing. **1653** BINNING *Serm.* (1845) 310 How many souls are choked.. in the very Springing, by the thorns of the Cares of this World.

b. With *up*, in fig. use.

1538 STARKEY *England* I. i. 15 Excepte ther be joynyd some gud prouysyon for theyr sprynggyng vp and gud culture, they schal neuer bryng forth theyr frute. **1587** GOLDING *De Mornay* xxxiii. (1592) 531 Eyther the springing vp of Religion is vpon some great Coniunction,.. or els at the springing vp therof [etc.]. **1620-51** I. JONES *Stone-Heng* (1725) 11 Upon the first springing up of Christian Religion here. **1653** H. MORE *Moral Cabbala* IV. ii. 29 The sundry Germinations and Springings up of the works of Righteousness in him are a delectable Paradise to him.

2. †**a.** The first appearance, the rise or dawn, *of* the day, etc. *Obs.*

c **1380** *Sir Ferumb.* 3562 Out ate ȝeate þey rydeþ ryȝt, In þe sprynggyng of þe day. **1382** WYCLIF *Job* iii. 9 The springing of the risende morwetid. *c* **1400** tr. *Secreta Secret., Gov. Lordsh.* 66 To knowe þe steryngge of þe firmament and þe firste risynge or sprynggynge of þe signes. **1495** *Act 11 Hen. VII*, c. 22, That.. every artificer and laborer be at ther werke in the springing of the day. **1705** STANHOPE *Paraphr.* I. 25 The Springing of the Morning.

b. The beginning, the early part, of the year, etc.; †the season of spring.

a **1513** FABYAN *Chron.* VII. ccxxiii. 248 In the sprynggynge of somer.., Odo, byssop of Bayou,.. was delyuered out of pryson by William Conquerour. *a* **1645** STRODE *Poet. Wks.* (1907) 123 Mourne, mourne, yee lovers: sadly singing Love hath his Winter, and no springing. **1889** BARING-GOULD & SHEPPARD *Songs West* 35 (E.D.D.), 'Twas in the springing of the year, In eighteen hundred two.

†**c.** The increase or waxing of the moon. *Obs.*

c **1440** *Pallad. on Husb.* I. 218 In sprynggynge of the mone [L. *crescente luna*] is best to sowe. *Ibid.* III. 375 While the mone is in sprynggyng.

d. With *up*: (see quot.).

1769 FALCONER *Dict. Marine* (1780), *Tete de vent*, the rising, or springing-up of a breeze.

†**3.** Origin, source. *Obs.*

1382 WYCLIF *Ecclus.* xlix. 19 Ouer alle lif in the springyng [L. *origine*] of Adam. *c* **1425** tr. *Arderne's Treat. Fistula*, etc. 60 Blode is norischyng of al membrez,..and al haþ bigynnyng or sprynggyng of blode.

4. The action of rising or flowing out of the ground.

c **1420** *Brut* ccxxiv. 292 In wynter þere arose suche a sprynggynge and wellinge op of wateres and floodes. *c* **1440** *Promp. Parv.* 471/1 Spryngynge, of a welle or oþer waxynge watyr. **1601** HOLLAND *Pliny* I. 46 There is a fountaine.. which, according to the springing and issuing forth out of this or that place, signifyeth the change in the price of corne. **1738** *De Foe's Tour Gt. Brit.* (ed. 2) III. 190 This Derwent is famous for its springing out of those Hills called Derwent Fells. **1817** SHELLEY *Rev. Islam* VI. xli, Knowledge, from its secret source enchants Young hearts with the fresh music of its springing.

5. a. The action of leaping or bounding.

c **1590** in Hazl. *E.P.P.* IV. 199 And after supper they did make good sporte With dauncing and springing. **1611** COTGR., *Grouillis*,..the springing of a child in the wombe. **1898** WATTS-DUNTON *Aylwin* XV. i, She recalled..my springing up and running to the mass of *débris* and looking round it.

b. Resilient or elastic movement or force.

1680 MOXON *Mech. Exerc.* x. 187 The springing up of the Pole makes an intermission in the running about of the work. **1831** J. HOLLAND *Manuf. Metal* I. 339 The springing of a saw is often regarded..as a certain proof of its quality. **1841** BROWNING *Pippa Passes* Poems (1905) 181 As I walk There's springing and melody and giddiness. **1889** *Science-Gossip* XXV. 271 There being no pressure there is no danger of 'springing' when the clips are removed.

6. The action of cracking or giving way.

c **1595** [see SPENDING *vbl. sb.* 4]. **1623** in Foster *Eng. Factories Ind.* (1908) II. 228 Some soddaine leake by the springing of a butt head. **1805** *Naval Chron.* XIII. 344 The springing of her mast.

7. a. *Arch.* = SPRING *sb.*[1] 20.

1703 [see SKEW *v.*[2] 5]. **1735** J. PRICE *Stone-Br. Thames* 7 Up to the springing of the Arches. **1776** G. SEMPLE *Building in Water* 16 The middle Arch is 26 Feet high from the springing. **1833** LOUDON *Encycl. Archit.* §1105 Elliptical arches to be put across.., with neat wood impost mouldings at the springings. *a* **1878** SIR G. SCOTT *Lect. Archit.* (1879) I. 54 The first idea for obviating it was to lower the springing of the vault.

b. The point of growth from the trunk.

1825 J. NICHOLSON *Operat. Mechanic* 571 The wood is stronger in the middle of the trunk than at the springing of the branches. **1843** HOLTZAPFFEL *Turning* I. 35 Those parts of wood described as curls, are the result of the confused filling in of the space between the forks, or the springings of the branches.

8. (See quot.)

1844 H. STEPHENS *Bk. Farm* II. 445 About a fortnight before the time of reckoning, symptoms of calving indicate themselves in the cow... These symptoms are called *springing* in England, and the heifers which exhibit them are *springers*.

II. †**9.** The action of sprinkling. *Obs.*

1388 WYCLIF *1 Pet.* i. 2 Bi obedience, and springyng of the blood of Jhesu Crist. *c* **1400** *Trevisa's Higden* (Rolls) VII. App. 522 There came a ȝonglinge with a golden chalys ful of water, and aqueynt the stronge heete wit springinge of water.

10. a. The action of causing a mine to explode.

1665 MANLEY *Grotius' Low C. Wars* 287 At the springing of that Mine, Bodies of Men might have been seen hovering piece-meal in the Air. **1709** *Lond. Gaz.* No. 4544/2 The Governor..is said to have been killed by the springing of the great Mine. **1785** BURKE *Sp. Nabob Arcot's Debts* Wks. 1842 I. 343 The assignees of his debt, who little expected the springing of this mine,..thought it best to take ground on the real state of the transaction. **1848** DICKENS *Dombey* lv, The springing of his mine upon himself. **1882** HAMLEY *Traseaden Hall* II. 166 An important step..was the springing some heavily charged mines.

b. The action of causing a rattle to sound.

1813 HOR. SMITH *Horace in London* 115 What a discord of bugles and bells, What whistling, and springing of rattles! **1845** *Ann. Reg.* 78/1 He heard the breaking of glass and the springing of the policeman's rattle.

11. The action of causing a bird to rise.

1711 ADDISON *Spect.* No. 108 ¶4 The springing of a Pheasant. **1883** *Cent. Mag.* Aug. 402 Often, the best of markers will be baffled in finding the birds..after the springing of the covey.

12. The action of bringing suddenly *on* one.

1888 SMALLEY *London Lett.* I. 227 The springing of the Home Rule Bill on the Liberal party by Mr. Gladstone.

III. 13. *attrib.* and *Comb.* †**a.** *springing-time*, = SPRING-TIME 1. *Obs.*

1387 TREVISA *Higden* (Rolls) I. 65 Þe ȝates of Caspij beeþ ..in springyng tyme faste i-barred for serpentes and addres. **1398** —— *Barth. De P.R.* XVII. ii. (Bodl. MS.), Treen þat nedeþ to be sette beþ moste in springinge tyme..for temporat heete and moisture. *c* **1440** *Pallad. on Husb.* III. 374 This eyther craft for spryngyng tyme is born. **1523** LD. BERNERS *Froiss.* I. xx. 29 Whan the Spryngyng tyme began. *a* **1533** —— *Gold. Bk. M. Aurel.* (1546) B, The fruites in the spryngyng tyme haue not the vertue to gyue sustenaunce.

b. In sense 7 a, as *springing course*, *-high* adj., *-line*, *plate*, *-point*, *stone*, *wall*.

1776 G. SEMPLE *Building in Water* 114 The..Piers..you may begin upon the Platform... But it would do best to begin them on the *springing Course. **1842** GWILT *Archit.* Gloss., *Springing Course*, the horizontal course of stones, from which an arch springs or rises. **1883** *Specif. Alnwick & Cornhill Rlwy.* 5 When stone imposts or springing courses are used, the stones are always to be equal to the full thickness of the arch. **1776** G. SEMPLE *Building in Water* 48 We compleatly finished the North Pier, *springing high. **1875** KNIGHT *Dict. Mech.*, **Springing-line*,..the line from which an arch rises. **1879** *Cassell's Techn. Educ.* II. 251 The boundary line or lines of the intrados..are called *springing lines* of an arch. **1853** *J. Nicholson's Operat. Mechanic* 801 The masonry of the North Abutment is fifteen feet thick at the *Springing Plate. **1879** *Cassell's Techn. Educ.* I. 297/2 This may be said to be the *springing-point of the arches. *Ibid.*, The pier..is surmounted by a cap, or *springing stone. **1838** *Civil Eng. & Arch. Jrnl.* I. 151/1 The thickness of the *springing walls is two bricks, the arch one and a half brick.

c. Misc., as *springing-board*, *faculty*, *power*, *tool*.

1846 GEO. ELIOT *Let.* 29 Oct. (1954) I. 224, I do not know whether I can get up any steam again in the subject... I must have the book as a *springing-board. **1859** *Habits of Gd. Society* (new ed.) 82 To whom a mere word serves as the springing-board from which to rise to new trains of thought. **1698** PETIVER in *Phil. Trans.* XX. 397 A peculiar species I.. call Snap-Beetles, from their elastick or *springing Faculty. **1839** DARWIN *Voy. Nat.* ii. (1879) 31, I amused myself one day by observing the *springing powers of this insect. **1846** HOLTZAPFFEL *Turning* II. 536 The finishing or hanging tools,..called also *springing tools, which are made of various curves and degrees of strength, yield to these small accidental motions.

'springing, *vbl. sb.*[2] [f. SPRING *sb.*[1] 22 or *v.*[2]] The process of providing with a spring or springs. Also, the state or quality of a set of springs; hence, the suspension of a vehicle.

1899 *N. & Q.* 17 June 479/2 A practical work on the springing and adjusting of watches. **1906** *Westm. Gaz.* 14 Nov. 9/2 Additional smoothness in running has been secured by certain modifications in the springing. **1952** *Times* 19 Aug. 11/6 The springing gives a comfortable ride for the passengers. **1978** *Lancashire Life* Apr. 141/1 The springing is quite soft, so it soaks up the bumps.

'springing, *ppl. a.* [f. SPRING *v.*[1]]

1. a. Of plants, etc.: Sprouting, growing. Also in fig. context.

13.. *E.E. Allit. P.* A. 35 So semly a sede moȝt fayly not, þat spryngande spycez vp ne sponne. **1513** DOUGLAS *Æneid* XII. Prol. 90 The spray bysprent with spryngand sproutis dispers. **1592** *Soliman & Pers.* v. iv, Ah, Perseda, how shall I mourne for thee? Faire springing Rose, ill pluckt before thy time. **1592** SHAKS. *Ven. & Ad.* 417 If springing things by anie iot diminisht, They wither in their prime. **1631** P. FLETCHER *Piscatory Eclog.* VII. xix, The starres [change] their courses, flowers their springing pride. **1694** PRIOR *Hymn to the Sun* ii, As His Infant Months bestow Springing Wreaths for William's Brow. **1707** *Curios. Husb.* 208 These springing Leaves require Nourishment. **1743** FRANCIS tr. *Hor., Odes* v. xvi. 62 Nor heats excessive burn the springing grain. **1829** LYTTON *Disowned* 17 A glimpse of the green sward, and springing flowers, of a small garden. **1891** *Science-Gossip* XXVII. 66 When the air grows soft on the springing corn we need no longer sigh over the hidden fate of Romulus.

b. *fig.* Coming into existence; beginning to develop; rising; just appearing or commencing.

1549 COVERDALE, etc. *Erasm. Par. 1 Tim.* 5, I persecuted the springing glory of the Gospel. **1605** BACON *Adv. Learn.* II. iii. §2 Prophecies..are not fulfilled punctually at once, but haue springing and germinant accomplishment. **1639** S. DU VERGER tr. *Camus' Admir. Events* 92 This little child.. had so many springing graces..that she promised ere long to be a Paragon of beauty. **1670** COTTON *Espernon* I. I. 12 Neither did he..cultivate his springing fortune with an assiduity and diligence unbecoming his Spirit, and Blood. **1725** POPE *Odyss.* IV. 796 These rites to piety and grief discharged, The friendly gods a springing gale enlarged. **1781** COWPER *Ep. Prot. Lady* 32 Sudden sorrow nips their springing joys. **1821** SHELLEY *Hellas* 56 Thermopylae and Marathon Caught..The springing Fire.

c. *fig.* Of youth, or of persons in respect of this.

1579 SPENSER *Sheph. Cal.* Feb. 52, I scorne thy skill, That wouldest me, my springing youngth to spil. **1592** G. HARVEY *Four Lett.* Wks. (Grosart) I. 219, I speake generally to euery springing wit. *a* **1604** HANMER *Chron. Irel.* (1633) 200 In his springing yeeres hee suckt the sweet milk of good learning. **1649** JER. TAYLOR *Gt. Exemp.* I. §1 Her person was young, her yeers florid and springing. **1822** LAMB *Elia* I. *Decay Beggars*, The Blind Beggar..seated..with his more fresh and springing daughter by his side.

d. Characterized by growth.

1634 W. TIRWHYT tr. *Balzac's Lett.* 108 You may spend here with us, one of these warm and Springing Winters, laden with Roses.

2. Rising or flowing out of the ground. Also in fig. context.

c **1375** *Sc. Leg. Saints* xxvii. (*Machor*) 528 Quhare a fare sted was, enhournyt with treis sere, & spryngand wellis. **1483** *Cath. Angl.* 356/2 Sprynygnge, *scaturiens*. *c* **1490** R. KEMERSTON in *Itin. W. de Worcester* (1778) 355 The water of Dee begynneth at a springynge welle in a hille side. **1535** COVERDALE *Lev.* xiv. 5 He shall take the lyuynge byrde with the Ceder wodd,..and dyppe them in the bloude of the slaine byrde vpon the sprengynge water. **1560** ROLLAND *Seven Sages* 97 Thow springand well of vice. **1635** SWAN *Spec. M.* vi. §2 (1643) 196 The differing qualitie of springing waters. **1704** TRAPP *Abra-Mulé* I. i, The springing Fountains of my Eyes. **1856** STANLEY *Sinai & Pal.* viii. (1858) 330 Pella, so called by the Macedonian Greeks from the springing fountain.

3. Coming into view; dawning.

1590 SPENSER *F.Q.* II. iii. 1 And Titan..Gan cleare the deawy ayre with springing light. **1648** CRASHAW *Poems* (1904) 144 Taint not the pure streames of the springing Day. **1665** BOYLE *Occas. Refl.* IV. ii. (1848) 174 Among all Birds.., scarce any give so early and so sweet a welcome to the Springing day.

4. Resilient, elastic.

1667 *Phil. Trans.* II. 440 A springing wire C, with a bended end F. **1728** CHAMBERS *Cycl.* s.v. *Sounding*, At a little Distance is a piece of Lead or Stone fix'd, by means of a springing Wire. **1743** FRANCIS tr. *Hor., Odes* v. ii. 35 He sets the springing snare, To catch the stranger crane, or timorous hare. **1894** J. BURROUGHS *Locusts & Wild H.* 128 A luxurious couch of boughs upon springing poles was prepared.

5. That springs, leaps, or bounds.

c **1760** SMOLLET *Ode Leven-Water* 13 The springing trout in speckled pride. **1803** SHAW *Gen. Zool.* IV. II. 623 Springing Gurnard, *Trigla Evolans*. **1836–9** *Todd's Cycl. Anat.* II. 861/2 *Elateridæ*, or springing-beetles, which are commonly known in their state of larvæ, as the *wire-worm*.

6. Of movement, etc.: Characterized by leaping or resilience.

1674 SIR W. PETTY (*title*), Discourse..concerning the use of duplicate proportion..with a new hypothesis of springing or elastique motions. **1810** SCOTT *Lady of L.* III. xiii, With short and springing footstep pass The trembling bog and false morass. **1893** SELOUS *Trav. S.E. Africa* 439 The bull..went off at once into a springing gallop. **1899** *Allbutt's Syst. Med.* VII. 901 A centre concerned with the co-ordination of springing movements in the legs.

7. Of cows or heifers: Near to calving.

1693 *Lond. Gaz.* No. 2898/4 The red was a Springing Cow, with a small star in the Forehead. **1856** MORTON *Cycl. Agric.* II. 726/1 *Springing* (Warwicks.), applied to heifers in calf; beginning to show signs of milk.

8. *Law.* = CONTINGENT *a.* 9.

1766 BLACKSTONE *Comm.* II. 334 Herein these, which are called contingent or springing, uses differ from an executory devise. **1818** CRUISE *Digest* (ed. 2) V. 274 A springing or shifting use cannot be defeated or destroyed by a fine levied of the estate out of which such springing or shifting use is to arise. *Ibid.* VI. 504 If this springing trust, to arise on the contingency of a marriage, was good, why should not the springing trust in the present case be equally good. **1845** WILLIAMS *Real Prop.* (1877) 290 Executory interests created under the Statute of Uses are called springing or shifting uses.

9. Rising in, or forming, a curve.

1799 [A. YOUNG] *Agric. Linc.* 358 The hind quarters so corresponding, with a springing rib, as to form an oval. **1825** J. NICHOLSON *Operat. Mechanic* 579 It is required to find the curvature of the springing ribs. **1872** SHIPLEY *Gloss. Eccl. Terms* 263 That stone in an arch which is equally distant from its springing extremities.

10. Causing game-birds to rise.

1725 D. EATON *Let.* 13 July (1971) 30 Mr. Joseph Lynwood..considering..that he had better mind other business than shooting (for they were all springing spaniels), hang'd three of them of his own accord. **1842** PRICHARD *Nat. Hist. Man* 72 Well-bred and well-taught springing spaniels were abundant.

Hence **'springingly** *adv.*

1837 VERLANDER *Vestal*, etc. 76 The barb steps not so springingly upon his native plain. **1891** MEREDITH *One of our Conq.* I. xiii. 251 The thought was tonic for an instant and illuminated him springingly.

†**'springish**, *a. Obs.*[−1] [f. SPRING *sb.*[1] 2 + -ISH.] Of ground: Somewhat wet through springs.

1663 GERBIER *Counsel* 55 Inconveniency of putting Chalk in walls of Houses on Springish ground.

springle ('sprɪŋ(ə)l), *sb.*[1] Also 7 **springal**. [? f. SPRING *sb.*[3]] A springe or snare. Also *fig.*

1602 CAREW *Cornwall* 24 They [woodcocks] arriue first on the North coast, where almost euerie hedge serveth for a Roade, and euerie plashoote for Springles to take them. **1654** VILVAIN *Theorem. Theol.* Supp. 230 Men may catch.. Woodcocks in Springals. *c* **1720** DE FOE *An Apparition* (1841) 259 In the springle their courtship had laid for me. **1869** BLACKMORE *Lorna D.* ix, The..netting of the wood-cocks, and the springles to be minded in the garden. **1880** CARNEGIE *Pract. Trap.* vii, The Springe or Springle—Its application in a variety of ways.

attrib. **1875** BLACKMORE *Alice Lorraine* I. xviii. 197 The rod bowed like a springle-bow.

'springle, *sb.*[2] [? f. SPRING *sb.*[1] 9.] A thatching rod.

1829 LOUDON *Encycl. Plants* 793 The plant [hazel] is of some value for hoops,..wattling-fences, and springles to fasten down thatch. **1841** HARTSHORNE *Salop. Ant.* Gloss., *Springle*, a rod four feet long, generally of hazle or the mountain ash, used in thatching. **1876–** in dial. use (Hereford, Essex, Shropsh., Herts.).

springle ('sprɪŋ(ə)l), *v.*[1] Now *rare* or *arch.* [f. SPRING *v.*[1] 13, or var. SPRINKLE *v.*[1] *Bespringle* occurs earlier.] *trans.* To sprinkle. Also *absol.*

1502 ARNOLDE *Chron.* (1811) 168 Than thou most moyst them twyes or thries in the day, not yeting but dewyng or springling. **1561** DAUS tr. *Bullinger on Apoc.* (1573) 100 The postes or dore cheekes of the Israelites were springled with the bloud of the lambe. **1648** HEXHAM II, *Versprengen*, to Strowe, or to Springle here and there. *Ibid.*, *Een verspreydinge*,..a Scattering, a Springling, or a Sheading abroad. **1799** J. ROBERTSON *Agric. Perth* 172 When the young shoots appear, another springling of earth is given from the trenches. **1910** G. K. CHESTERTON *Alarms & Discursions* 57 Some overflowings from such a fountain of information may therefore be permitted to springle these pages.

†**'springle**, *v.*[2] *Obs.*[−1] In 5 **spryngol-**. [var. of SPRINKLE *v.*[2]] *intr.* To sparkle.

c **1400** *Seven Deadly Sins* (MS. Laud 416 fol. 39 b), [They] sette this whele vppon her hede; As eny hote yron yt was spryngolyng rede.

springless ('sprɪŋlɪs), *a.* [f. SPRING *sb.*[1]]

1. a. Having no motive power. *rare*[−1].

1684 T. BURNET *Theory Earth* I. 213 Those were springless machines, that act only by some external cause.

b. Of persons: Spiritless; inert.

1885 STEVENSON *Prince Otto* I. i, A springless, putty-hearted, cowering coward!

2. Deprived of the power of springing.

1823 *Blackw. Mag.* XIV. 314 They remind me of a mutchkin of wasps in a bottle,..helpless, hopeless, stingless, wing-less, springless.

3. Of vehicles, etc.: Lacking springs; having no spring.

1837 *Fraser's Mag.* XV. 639 A long, narrow, and springless caravan. **1860** *All Year Round* No. 73. 550 The heavy vehicle..which..clatters by, as springless as an artillery tumbril. **1880** JEFFERIES *Greene Ferne Farm* 88 A sudden jolt of the springless waggon.

4. Devoid of a spring of water.

1876 RUSKIN *Fors Clav.* lxxii. 380 As the seed by the drought,..so the soul..athirst in the springless sand.

5. Having no spring season. Also *fig.*

1909 *Spectator* 5 June 396/2 Springless though my prospect lies, I see God's sunshine when your eyes Smile welcome. **1927** E. SITWELL *Rustic Elegies* 82 Delivered from that springless frost.

springlet ('sprɪŋlɪt). [f. SPRING *sb.*[1] + -LET.]

†**1.** A young sprout or shoot. In quot. *fig.* of children. *Obs.*[−1]

a **1750** A. HILL *Wks.* (1753) II. 355 How does the budding springlets of his lovely family?

2. A small spring or fountain.

1808 SCOTT *Marmion* VI. xxxvii, From out the little hill Oozes the slender springlet still. **1844** *Blackw. Mag.* LVI. 212 They shall drive nice and slowly round about the springlet. **1879** J. BURROUGHS *Locusts & Wild H.* 121 Every little rill and springlet.

fig. **1830** J. WRIGHT *Retrospect* I. 48 The soul's dried springlets that now bound along. **1865** A. W. BUCHAN *Song of Rest* v. 142 Its paltry springlets intervene To lure our vision from the heavenly scene.

spring-like, *adv.* and *a.* [f. SPRING *sb.*[1]]

A. *adv.* As in, like to, the season of spring.

1567 GOLDING *Ovid's Met.* VII. (1593) 160 The ground did spring-like florish there. **1905** *Westm. Gaz.* 2 Feb. 10/1 A new impulse of literary vitality seems to have swept spring-like over the American Continent.

B. *adj.* Resembling that of the spring season; like that prevalent during spring; vernal.

1729 SAVAGE *Wanderer* v, There the last blossoms spring-like pride unfold. **1848** *Hoffmeister's Trav. Ceylon*, etc. v. 195 The climate here is most agreeably temperate and spring-like. **1869** *Routledge's Ev. Boy's Ann.* 391 The weather was cool and springlike. **1885** 'MRS. ALEXANDER' *At Bay* iii, Miss Lambert..looked lovely in soft, clear white Indian muslin, over spring-like green.

'**springling.** *rare.* [-LING[1].] (See quots.)

1647 HEXHAM I, A Springling or a stripling, *een jongh gheselleken*. **1881** *Standard* 10 Sept. 2/1 A suite of ponds contains year-old salmon, talked of at the fishery as 'springlings'.

spring-lock. [f. SPRING *sb.*[1] 25 a.]

1. A common form of lock in which a spring presses the bolt outwards, thus rendering it self-locking except when secured by a catch.

1485 *Rec. St. Mary at Hill* (1905) 29 Also ther be xxx spryng lockes & keyes. **1602** MIDDLETON *Blurt, Master-Constable* II. ii, All the hinges, the spring-locks, and the ring, are worn to pieces. **1677** MOXON *Mech. Exerc.* 21 Chamber-door Locks, called Spring-Locks. **1722** DE FOE *Plague* (1884) 117 The Gate..having a Spring Lock fastened it self. **1821** SCOTT *Kenilw.* xli, He had fled to this place of concealment, forgetting the key of the spring-lock. **1862** *Catal. Internat. Exhib., Brit.* II. No. 6197, Spring lock for front doors.

2. A lock which opens on pressing a spring.

1820 KEATS *Cap & Bells* lvii, He..Touch'd a spring-lock, and there in wool, or snow,..lay an old And legend-leaved book.

spring-locked, *a.* [f. SPRING *sb.*[1]] Having the spring or source stopped.

1621 G. SANDYS *Ovid's Met.* XV. (1626) 311 Cool Amasenus, watering Sicily, Now flowes; now spring-lockt, leaues his channell dry.

springol(d, -olt, obs. forms of SPRINGAL(D.

spring-tail. *Zool.* Also **springtail, spring tail.** [f. SPRING *sb.*[1] or *v.*[1]] One or other of various species of insects which leap or spring by means of their tail.

1797 *Encycl. Brit.* (ed. 3) XV. 169/1 *Podura*, or spring-tail, ..a genus of insects of the order of aptera. **1854** *Orr's Circ. Sci., Org. Nat.* I. 96 The velvet spring-tail..leaps by jerking its tail downwards from under its body. **1879** E. P. WRIGHT *Anim. Life* 491 The springtails had, however, attracted the attention of naturalists long before that date.

spring tide, spring-tide. [SPRING *sb.*[1]]

1. The season of spring; spring-time.

1530 PALSGR. 306/1 Belongyng to the springe tyde, *vernal*. **1576** FLEMING *Panopl. Epist.* 352 What man is able to affirme, that he euer sawe the Spring tide without Marche Uiolettes? **1601** R. JOHNSON *Kingd. & Commw.* (1603) 13 It hapneth very often that the northren or western winde.. bringeth springtide before the winter season be fully expired. **1632** LITHGOW *Trav.* III. 85 There is no land more temperate for ayre, for it hath a double spring-tyde. **1795** *Gent. Mag.* July 539 The animalculæ that in spring-tide often almost obscure the sun itself. **1864** SKEAT tr. *Uhland's Poems* 251 Spring-tide reigns o'er stream and field. **1870** LOWELL *Study Wind.* 228 A breath of uncontaminate springtide seems to lift the hair upon my forehead.

b. *fig.* and *transf.*

1596 SPENSER *Astrophel* Epit. ii. 10 His life was my spring tide. **1602** FULBECKE *Pandects* Ded. p. i, Which in one and this very springtide haue in my selfe knowne the force of seasons. **1640** T. CAREW *Poems, To my Cousin* 2 Happy youth, that shalt possesse Such a spring-tyde of delight. **1879** GEO. ELIOT *Theo. Such* xiv. 249 He is no longer in his spring-tide. **1879** M. COLLINS *Pen Sketches* I. 213 The spring-tide of her youth.

2. A tide occurring on the days shortly after the new and full moon, in which the high-water level reaches its maximum.

Cf. Du. and WFris. *springtij*, NFris. *-tidj*, G. *-(ge)zeit*. In quots. 1689 and 1724 the reference is to the corresponding lowness of the ebb.

a **1548** HALL *Chron., Hen. VIII*, 209 b, At whiche season was suche a spryng tide, that it brake the walles of Hollande and Zelande. **1573** TUSSER *Husb.* (1878) 60 At full and at change, spring tides are strange. **1634–5** BRERETON *Trav.* (Chetham Soc.) 97 Here is an haven..whereinto at a spring-tide a ship of 100 ton may enter. **1689** *Lond. Gaz.* No. 2478/1 Whither he would march the next Spring-Tide, the Strand ..not being fordable for Foot till that time. **1724** in Picton *L'pool Munic. Rec.* (1886) II. 52 Which stones..are adry only on spring tydes. **1776** DALRYMPLE *Ann. Scotl.* I. 138 A sudden land-flood, met by a spring-tide, surrounded and overwhelmed the town. **1839** STONEHOUSE *Isle of Axholme* 49 The spring tides run at the rate of nine miles an hour. **1879** FROUDE *Cæsar* xvi. 265 When the full moon brought the spring tide.

b. *fig.* and in fig. context.

c **1620** Z. BOYD *Zion's Flowers* (1855) 42 In a Spring tide Sin doth overflowe. **1679** J. GOODMAN *Penit. Pard.* II. iv. (1713) 222 They [new converts] find they cannot maintain those spring-tides constantly at the same height. **1778** JOHNSON *Lett.* (1892) II. 72 You appear to me to be now floating on the springtide of prosperity; on a tide not governed by the moon. **1809** SCOTT *Let.* in *Lockhart* (1837) II. vii. 253 The spring-tide may for ought I know, break in this next session of Parliament. **1853** R. S. SURTEES *Sponge's Sp. Tour* xxxi. 188 He once did us the honour..of walking down Bond-street with us, in the spring-tide of fashion. **1890** *Spectator* 29 Mar., It should convince them that there is no spring tide flowing strongly towards Home-rule.

3. *transf.* A copious flow or large quantity *of* something.

1593 NASHE *Christ's T.* Wks. (Grosart) IV. 79 Heere ebbe the spring-tide of my Teares. **1645** QUARLES *Sol. Recant.* VI. 71 If spring tides of Gold should a degree Transcend thy wish, perchance it would want thee. **1660** SECKER *Nonsuch Prof.* Pref. 7 In the highest flood and spring-tides of outward mercies, its hard to keep our hearts within the channell. *a* **1704** T. BROWN *Dial. Dead* Wks. 1711 IV. 27 What of late Years brings daily such Gluts and Spring-Tides of Souls to our Infernal Mansions. **1753** H. WALPOLE *Lett.* (1846) II. 472 This has been quite a spring-tide of diversion. **1808** SCOTT *Marm.* I. Introd. 217 Woe, wonder, and sensation high, In one spring-tide of ecstasy! **1887** KNOX LITTLE *Broken Vow* 163 To check the springtide of my girlish joy.

4. *attrib.* and *Comb.*, as ***spring-tide flood, joy,*** etc.

1662 H. HIBBERT *Body Divinity* II. 32 An ebullition or a spring-tide-like overflow. **1748** THOMSON *Cast. Indol.* I. lxiii, When spring-tide joy pours in with copious flood, The higher still th' exulting billows flow. **1785** BURNS *Ep. W. Simpson* xi, At Wallace' name, what Scottish blood, But boils up in a spring-tide flood. **1808** SCOTT *Marm.* III. viii, No thrush Sings livelier from a spring-tide bush. **1819** KEATS *Eve of St. Mark* 10 The chilly sunset faintly told..Of rivers new with spring-tide sedge. **1866** S. B. JAMES *Duty & Doctrine* (1871) 62 That Heavenly spring-tide radiance which can never fade away.

spring-time. Also **springtime, spring time.** [SPRING *sb.*[1] 6 b.]

1. The season of spring; = SPRING-TIDE I.

1495 *Trevisa's Barth. De P.R.* (W. de W.) III. xxiv. 73 In the sprynge tyme the calde is temperat and in herueste also. **1538** ELYOT, *Vernus*, freshe, as the spring time. **1560** DAUS tr. *Sleidane's Comm.* 137 b, In the begynnyng of the spryng tyme. **1600** PORY tr. *Leo's Africa* III. 121 This towne is so durtie in the spring-time, that it would irke a man to walke the streetes. **1667** MILTON *P.L.* I. 769 As Bees In spring time..Poure forth thir populous youth about the Hive In clusters. **1710** ADDISON *Tatler* No. 218 ¶9, I look upon the whole Country in Spring-time as a spacious Garden. **1768** HOLDSWORTH *Virgil* 121 It is the custom..to hough the land in the spring-time. **1855** *Poultry Chron.* III. 422 This [illness in bees] appears most frequently in the spring time. **1864** BOWEN *Logic* ix. 300 How the green herb in the spring-time absorbs inorganic matter and assimilates it to itself.

2. a. The earlier period of a person's life; youth.

1593 SHAKS. 3 *Hen. VI*, II. iii. 47, I..now melt with wo, That Winter should cut off our Spring-time so.

1853 TALFOURD *Castilian* I. i, In this season, which renews their spring-time. **1866** S. B. JAMES *Duty & Doctrine* (1871) 65 So ill-advised as to grudge spring-time its rounded cheek and supple limb. **1877** BLACK *Green Past.* ii, She might have been taken for the very type of English girlhood in its sweetest springtime.

b. A time or period comparable in some way to spring. Usu. const. *of*.

a **1764** LLOYD *Song* Poet. Wks. 1774 II. 36 The spring-time of love then employ. **1784** COWPER *Task* II. 512 In vain they push'd inquiry to the birth And spring-time of the world. **1862** STANLEY *Jew. Ch.* (1877) I. vi. 118 With all its faults and shortcomings it was the spring-time of their national existence. **1897** JESSOPP *Donne* ii. 44 Notes.. addressed to the great lady in the..happy springtime of her married life.

3. *attrib.*, as ***spring-time call, day,*** etc.

1563 B. GOOGE *Eglogs* i. (Arb.) 35 My yeares be great, I wyl be gone, for spryngtyme nyghts be colde. **1842** LOVER *Handy Andy* xliv, The old lady..was hailed with a chorus of 'Cuckoo!' by the multitude, one half of which ran after the coach..shouting forth the spring-time call. **1838** MRS. BROWNING *To Miss Mitford* 6 Overleaning them this springtime day. **1886** WINCHELL *Walks Geol. Field* 280 It was during the spring-time empire of water that the Great Lakes stood at their highest levels.

†**spring-tree.** *Obs.* [f. SPRING *v.*[1]] A bar or cross-piece to which the ends of a horse's traces are attached; a swingle-tree. Also *attrib.*

1623 *Althorp MS.* in Simpkinson *Washingtons* (1860) p. xlii, To Butlin 6 daies paling, and making springtrees for the coach. **1648** WILKINS *Math. Magic* I. iv. 26 At each of its extremities there is a severall spring-tree..to which either horses or oxen may be fastned. *a* **1723** WREN *Disc. Archit.* in Phillimore *Times*, etc. (1881) 346 At the end of this Rope is a Spring-tree (as our Coachmen use for ye two fore Horses). **1766** *Compl. Farmer* s.v. *Madder* 5 I 1/1 The part where the links of the spring-tree bar are fastened. *Ibid.* s.v. *Potatoe* 6 E 3/2, I put a double spring-tree bar to the cultivator, to avoid the poaching of the horses.

spring-water. Also **spring water.** [SPRING *sb.*[1] 2. Cf. MDu. *sprincwater*, LG. *springwater*, G. *springwasser*.] Water issuing or obtained from a spring or fountain.

c **1440** *Jacob's Well* 238 Deluyth doun depe in lownesse, tyl ȝe fynde a springe watyr of grace. **1587** HARRISON *Descr. Eng.* II. vi, Bruers obserue..the nature of the water:..the fennie and morish is the worst, and the cleerest spring water next vnto it. **1634–5** BRERETON *Trav.* (Chetham Soc.) 82 Fair spring-water..is an excellent medicine. **1682** K. DIGBY *Chymical Secr.* II. 201 Pour upon them Spring-water. **1758** BORLASE *Nat. Hist. Cornw.* 25 Simple Spring-Water may be considered either as superficial or subterraneous. **1771** *Phil. Trans.* LXI. 510 The weight of spring-water contained in the cube of half that foot..is thus determined. **1849** NOAD *Electricity* (ed. 3) 370 Place on the top of the other binding screw a drop of spring-water. **1886** WINCHELL *Walks Geol. Field* 34 The supplies of spring-water are sometimes sufficient to meet the demands of towns and cities.

attrib. **1833** LOUDON *Encycl. Archit.* §150 At a short distance from the house, is shown the situation of the spring-water well.

spring-well. [f. SPRING *sb.*[1] 2 + WELL *sb.*] A spring or well of water; a spring-head or fountain. Also *fig.*

a **1300** in Birch *Cartul. Sax.* II. 473 So bi strete on hole-dene; endlang denes to springwellen. *c* **1450** *Myrr. Our Ladye* 280 All helthe cometh from god, that ys the sprynge welle of all goodnesse. **1535** COVERDALE *Isaiah* xlix. 10 He.. shal lede them, and geue them drinke of the springe welles. **1544** BETHAM *Precepts War* I. ii. B iij, When these two vyces be the spryngwel and heed of al myschefe. **1601** *Reg. Mag. Sig. Scot.* 391/2 The spring-well quhilk is the heid of the burne Tayok. *c* **1845** *Fullarton's Gazetteer Scot.* s.v. *Dornock*, A spring-well on the spot..is still called Sword-well. **1893** O'DONOGHUE *Brendaniana* 171, I discovered these two caves and this spring-well.

spring-wood. [f. SPRING *sb.*[1] 10 and 6 b.]

1. a. *collect.* Wood growing in a spring or copse of young saplings.

1523 FITZHERB. *Husb.* §135 To kepe sprynge-wodde. **1893** HEATH *Eng. Peas.* 92 He was employed in cutting down small, or 'spring-wood'..used for the purpose of making supports to the cuttings in the lead mines.

b. A copse or wood of springs or young trees.

1623 in *Fabric Rolls York Minster* (Surtees Soc.) Gloss., One springwood called Hagsett, lately bought of Robert Greaves. *a* **1722** LISLE *Husb.* (1757) 362 For a general rule, newly weaned calves are less hurtful to newly cut spring-woods than any other cattle. **1815** FAREY *Agric. Derbysh.* II. 219 Spring-woods, as those are here called, which bear underwood as well as timber, and are cut at stated periods. **1828** CARR *Craven Gloss.*, *Spring-woods*, young woods fenced off for cattle, and allowed to spring. **1881** *Leicester Gloss.* 252 *Spring-wood*, a wood of young trees.

2. A ring or layer of wood formed round a tree each spring.

1884 BOWER & SCOTT *De Bary's Phaner.* 475 It is..called an annual zone, annual layer, or annual ring, and its limiting layers just mentioned are called spring-wood and autumn-wood. **1885** GOODALE *Physiol. Bot.* (1892) 139 That [wood] which is produced earliest (spring wood) has somewhat larger ducts and wood-cells than that which is formed later (autumn wood).

'**springwort.** [ad. G. *springwurz, -wurzel*, f. *springen* SPRING *v.*[1]] A mysterious herb having magic powers.

1889 T. F. THISTLETON-DYER *Folk-lore Plants* 50 There is the magic springwort, around which have clustered so many curious lightning myths and talismanic properties. *Ibid.* 304 The magic springwort..has a mysterious connection with the woodpecker.

springy ('sprɪŋɪ), *a.* [f. SPRING *sb.*[1] and *v.*[1]]

1. †**a.** Growing in the season of spring. *Obs.*[−1]

1593 Q. ELIZ. *Boeth.* I. metr. vi. 16 Nor seake not thou with gredy hand The sprengy Palmes [L. *vernos palmites*] to weld. [Cf. SPRINGINESS 2 b.]

b. Characteristic of the season of spring; spring-like.

1860 S. WARNER *Say & Seal* II. xviii. 229 It was April now, and a soft springy day. **1936** N. COWARD *To-night at 8.30* III. 85 Quite Springy out, isn't it?

2. a. Characterized by the presence of springs of water.

1641 BEST *Farm Bks.* (Surtees) 4 Lowe, moist, and springy groundes are the best to increase milke in an ewe. **1733** W. ELLIS *Chiltern & Vale Farm.* 262 It will greatly improve springy, or over-wet Grounds, if we first drain them. **1799** [A. YOUNG] *Agric. Lincoln.* 245 Many similar springy sides of hills are to be met with all the way to Ranby. **1853** *Jrnl. R. Agric. Soc.* XIV. I. 36 Occasional parts of the field were found springy and full of water. **1865** MRS. WHITNEY *Gayworthys* xxvi. (1879) 250 A huge, dry slippery log that lay over a springy spot.

b. Coming from springs. *rare*[−1]

1653 BLITHE *Eng. Improver Impr.* 19 That thou maist goe under that..springie moysture that breeds and feeds the Rush.

3. a. Endowed with spring or elasticity.

1660 BOYLE *New Exp. Phys. Mech.* i. 27 Though the Air were granted to consist of Springy Particles. **1685** —— *Effects Motion* ii. 14 Which depends chiefly upon the Celerity of the springy Corpuscles of the Air. **1709** FLOYER *Cold Bathing* I. iv. 93 The Animal Spirits being compressed, are more lively, springy, and fitter for Motion. **1734** *Phil. Trans.* XXXVIII. 414 Her Hair was long and springy as that of a living Person. **1786** *Med. Comment.* II. 105 The tumor ..was a little springy. **1817** KEATS *Sleep & Poetry* 95 A laughing schoolboy..Riding the springy branches of an elm. **1839** FR. A. KEMBLE *Resid. in Georgia* (1863) 36 Moss ..as light as horse-hair, as springy, and elastic. **1887** RIDER HAGGARD *Allan Quatermain* 67 A light but exceedingly tough native wood, something like English ash, only more springy.

b. Of the muscles or body, or of persons, etc., with reference to these.

1776 MICKLE tr. *Camoens' Lusiad* 454 Their springy shoulders stretching to the blow. **1822** SCOTT *Peveril* ii, He satisfied himself..that though her little frame was slight, it was firm and springy. **1837** *Fraser's Mag.* XVI. 367 The prompt equerry had led the springy coursers to the gate. **1871** L. STEPHEN *Playgr. Eur.* (1894) xiii. 324 His muscles feel firm and springy.

c. Elastic to the tread.

1797 COLERIDGE *This lime-tree bower my prison* 7 Friends, whom I never more may meet again On springy heath. **1875** W. S. HAYWARD *Love agst. World* 13 Away they thundered over the springy turf. **1886** *Cornh. Mag.* July 58 The stage is..very 'springy', a condition designed to help acrobatic performances.

4. Marked or characterized by spring, elasticity, or resilience: **a.** In general use.

1669 W. SIMPSON *Hydrol. Chym.* 93 The springy motion of the animal spirits. **1672–3** GREW *Anat. Pl., Roots* II. (1682) 82 The Aer being of an Elastick or Springy Nature. **1710** T. FULLER *Pharm. Extemp.* 249 It..roborates the Springey Tone of the Lungs. **1741** A. MONRO *Anat. Bones* (ed. 3) 171 In raising the Trunk, these Cartilages will assist by their springy Force. **1837** JAMES *Phil. Augustus* I. ii, There was a springy vigour in the atmosphere, as if the wind itself were young. **1888** RUTLEY *Rock-Forming Min.* 193 Then drive a needle, by a sharp, springy tap.., into the mica. **1893** *Brit. Jrnl. Photogr.* XL. 745 Resisting with all its springy power.

b. *esp.* Of the bearing or movements of persons or animals.

1818 *Sporting Mag.* II. 166 His attitude was springy, and ready for quick action. **1820** SCOTT *Monast.* xxxii, The springy step..reminded Henry Warden of Halbert. **1889** 'R. BOLDREWOOD' *Robbery under Arms* xx, Rainbow [a horse] sailed off with his beautiful easy springy stride.

†**sprink**, *sb. Obs. rare.* [Cf. SPRINK *v.*, and G. (rare) *sprenke* freckle, NFris. *sprēnk* a sprinkle.]

1. A sprinkler or holy water brush.

1566 in Peacock *Eng. Ch. Furniture* (1866) 75 A water sprinkell for our holy water with sprinck.

2. A sprinkle.

1568 T. HOWELL *Arb. Amitie* A viij b, The Talbot true.. Lost neuer noblenesse, By sprinck of spot distayned.

†**sprink**, *a. Obs.*⁻¹ Smart, spruce.

1602 BRETON *Wonders Worth Hearing* Wks. (Grosart) II. 9/1 His apparell most Silke and Ueluet, his cloake and his hat well brushed, his ruffes well set,..a sprinke youth.

sprink, *v. Obs.* exc. *dial.* [Cf. SPRINKLE *v.*[1], and the synonymous G. (rare) *sprenken*, NFris. *sprēnk(e).*] *trans.* To sprinkle.

c **1400** in *Househ. Ord.* (1790) 469 With a feder sprinke and spot the congour. *c* **1440** *Psalmi Penit.* (1894) 28 With holi water thu schalt me sprinke. **1589** FLEMING *Virg. Georg.* III. 40 The adder woonted..to sprincke hir strong poison vpon cattell. **1596** WARNER *Alb. Eng.* XI. lxiv. (1602) 276 With yearely hallowed Mosca, which the Primate hauing blest, He thinks..him in Heauen already whom the primat sprinks with it. **1632** HEYWOOD *Iron Age* II. III. i, Fatall Pyrhus..That in the shadow of this sacred place Durst sprinke the childs blood in the fathers face. **1866–89** in Lincoln dial. glossaries.

Hence †'**sprinker**, a sprinkler. *Obs.*⁻⁰

1648 HEXHAM II, *Een Quispel*, a Sprincker, or a thing to cast water upon [*sic*].

sprinkle ('sprɪŋk(ə)l), *sb.*[1] Forms: 4 sprynkil, 6 -kill, sprinkil(l; 5–6 sprenkylle (5 sprenkle), 6 spryn-, 6–7 sprinkell(e; 5 spryncle, 6–7 sprinc(k)le, 6- sprinkle. [Related to SPRINKLE *v.*[1] Cf. MDu., MLG., obs. G. and Da. *sprinkel*, MDu. and Du., G. *sprenkel*, speckle, spot, freckle.]

†**1.** A sprinkler, *esp.* one for sprinkling holy water. *Obs.*

Also freq. in ***holy-water sprinkle***, for other senses of which see HOLY WATER 2.

1382 WYCLIF *Exod.* xii. 22 The litil sprynkil of ysop wetith in bloode. *c* **1475** *Pict. Voc.* in Wr.-Wülcker 756 *Hoc aspersorium*, a sprenkylle. **1483** CAXTON *Gold. Leg.* 34/1 Four crosses..besprent with Holy Water styck or spryncle. **1519** HORMAN *Vulg.* 16 b, Geue me holy water with the sprinkell. **1582** N. LICHEFIELD tr. *Castanheda's Conq. E. Ind.* I. xvi. 42 b, These men..in their Pagodes, who with a sprinkle tooke water out of a certaine fountaine. **1606** SYLVESTER *Du Bartas* II. iv. I. *Tropheis* 683 This black Sprinkle, tuft with Virgin's tress, Dipt, at your Altar, in my Kinsman's bloud. **1619** FLETCHER *Mons. Thomas* v. vi, Give me my holy sprinkle... Give me my holy water-pot. **1647** HEXHAM I, A Sprinkle, *een quispel.*

†**2.** A spot or speckle. *Obs. rare.*

1481 CAXTON *Reynard* xxxii. (Arb.) 82 The thirde colour was grene lyke glas, But ther were somme sprynklis therin lyke purpure. **1577** FRAMPTON *Joyful News* I. (1596) 18 The blood stone is a kinde of Iasper of diuers colours..full of sprincles like to blood.

3. An (or the) act of sprinkling; a quantity which is sprinkled.

1641 MILTON *Ch. Govt.* II. ii, Baptizing the Christian infant with a solemne sprinkle. **1665** LOCKE in Fox Bourne *Life* (1876) I. iii. 114, I had a good sprinkle of holy water. **1818** *Art Bookbinding* 53 They throw on a finer sprinkle, and save much colour. **1854** GREENWOOD *Haps & Mishaps* 122 Where,..for baptismal and holy waters, [were] the sprinkle and gush of their blood. **1888** STEVENSON *Black Arrow* 172 A thin sprinkle of snow and thin flakes of foam came flying.

fig. **1862** CARLYLE *Fredk. Gt.* XIV. iv. (1872) V. 188 Is it in a sprinkle of disconnected factions that you will wait Prince Karl?

b. A small number or quantity; a sprinkling.

1768 *Ann. Reg., Projects* 109/1 We had but a small sprinkle of the common turnip cabbage among the whole. **1825** E. HEWLETT *Cottage Comforts* vi. 43 The only tree..that had a good sprinkle of fruit. **1844** MAITLAND *Dark Ages* 126 A thicker and more extensive sprinkle of better-instructed persons. **1890** *Daily News* 2 Sept. 2/7 There has been a good sprinkle of the new growth on the market to-day.

4. *techn.* A colour effect produced by sprinkling; a mixture for producing this.

1835 HANNETT *Bibliopegia* 101 On the fancy colours and sprinkles it is usual to attach lettering pieces of morocco. **1885** W. J. E. CRANE *Bookbinding* iii. 27 Bole Armenian, for making sprinkle for edges.

'**sprinkle**, *sb.*[2] [Imitative.] A light, tinkling sound.

1846 LANDOR *Imag. Conv., Tasso & Cornelia* Wks. II. 183/1 At Sorrento you hear nothing but the light surges of the sea, and the sweet sprinkles of the guitar.

'**sprinkle**, ('sprɪŋk(ə)l), *v.*[1] Forms: *α.* 5–6 sprencle, 5–6 -kle, sprenkyll(e, 5 -kel. *β.* 5–6 sprynkil(l, 6 sprinkil(l, -kel; 5–6 sprycle, 6 -kle, sprincle, 6–7 sprinckle, 6- sprinkle. [Related to Du. *sprenkelen* (Kilian *sprenckelen*), G. *sprenkeln*, NFris. *sprēnkeli*, and to WFris. *sprinkelje*, LG. *sprinkeln* (MLG. in pa. pple. *sprinkelt*).]

1. *trans.* To scatter in drops; to let fall in small particles here and there; to strew thinly or lightly.

α. *c* **1400** MAUNDEV. (Roxb.) xviii. 85 Þai..takes þaire blude and sprenklez it apon þaire mawmets. *c* **1425** tr. *Arderne's Treat. Fistula*, etc. 74 After þe fomentyng be sprenkled aboue puluis of bole, of sanguis draconis,..and sich like. *c* **1440** *Promp. Parv.* 470/2 Sprenkelyn, or strenkelyn, *aspergo, conspergo.* **1509** FISHER 7 *Penit. Ps.* li. Wks. (1876) 110 He was made clene..with ysope dypped in the blode of certayne beestes and sprenceled vpon hym. **1535** COVERDALE *Exod.* ix. 8 Let Moses sprenkle it [*sc.* ashes] towarde heauen before Pharao.

β. **1526** *Pilgr. Perf.* (W. de W. 1531) 179 b, Some of her systers counseyled her to haue holy water euer redy at hande, & to spryncle it vpon hym whan he cometh. **1551** MORE *Utopia* II. v. (1895) 166 They burne swete gummes and speces for perfumes, and pleasaunt smelles, and sprincle about swete oyntmentes and waters. *c* **1613** MIDDLETON *No Wit like Woman's* IV. ii, If I sprinkled on the widow's cheeks A few cool drops. **1697** DRYDEN *Virg. Georg.* I. 118 Sprinkle sordid Ashes all around. **1736** BAILEY *Househ. Dict.* s.v. *Pork*, Sprinkle upon them a little common salt. **1765** *Museum Rust.* IV. 101 Afterwards let water be sprinkled over the shot. **1827** FARADAY *Chem. Manip.* xviii. (1842) 486 It is best mixed by..sprinkling the powder into it. **1891** FARRAR *Darkn. & Dawn* xxv, Some of the poison was sprinkled on a leaf of lettuce.

fig. **1602** SHAKS. *Ham.* III. iv. 124 Oh gentle Sonne, Vpon the heate and flame of thy distemper Sprinkle coole patience. **1706** E. WARD *Wooden World Diss.* (1708) 102 If he sprinkle any Grace over the Platter, it's a plain Symptom, that his Maw's out of order.

absol. **1611** BIBLE *Lev.* xiv. 7 He shall sprinckle vpon him ..seuen times.

b. *fig.* To disperse, distribute, or scatter here and there.

1514 BARCLAY *Cyt. & Uplondyshman* (Percy Soc.) 29 Now are they sprencled & sparcled abrode, Lyke wyse as shyppes be docked in a rode. **1530** PALSGR. 730/1 He sprenkylleth his monay abrode as thoughe he cared nat for it. **1591** HARINGTON *Orl. Fur.* Pref. ¶ vi b, Some things that Virgill could not haue,..you finde, in my author sprinckled ouer all his worke. **1650** FULLER *Pisgah* II. ix. 187 Besides cities, many private dwellings were sprinkled on mount Ephraim. **1686** SNAPE *Anat. Horse* II. vii. 82 Small branches do spring from this coronary vein, and are dispersed or sprinkled all down the surface or outside of the Heart. **1719** YOUNG *Busiris* v. i, Behold thy troops are thin, Thy men are rarely sprinkled o'er the field. **1827** KEBLE *Chr. Y.* 6 Sprinkled along the waste of years Full many a soft green isle appears. **1879** SPENCER *Data of Ethics* x. 184 There are sprinkled throughout society men to whom active occupation is a need.

2. To bedew, bespatter lightly, or powder (a thing or surface); to besprinkle. Usu. const. *with.*

14.. *R. Glouc. Chron.* 2761 (MS. Digby 205), þe werke with his blode..men schulde sprenkle. **1414** BRAMPTON *Penit. Ps.* (Percy Soc.) 23 Sprenkle me, Lord! with watyr of terys. **1495** *Trevisa's Barth. De P.R.* XVII. xcvii. 663 The threde is..wasshe and spryncled wyth water vntyll that it be whyte. **1544** *Supplic. Hen. VIII*, 41 Whom the blynde prestes doo bothe sence & spryncle with holy water. **1602** *Kyd's Sp. Trag.* III. xii a. 67 Duly twice a morning Would I be sprinkling it with fountaine water. **1613** PURCHAS *Pilgrimage* (1614) 588 There are diuerse which..sprinkle the streets twice a daie because of the heat and dust. **1697** DRYDEN *Virg. Georg.* IV. 553 She sprinkl'd thrice, with Wine, the Vestal Fire. **1727** SWIFT *Descr. Morning* Wks. 1755 III. II. 41 The slipshod 'prentice from his master's door Had par'd the dirt, and sprinkled round the floor. **1774** GOLDSM. *Nat. Hist.* (1776) VII. 311 Care should be used.. to sprinkle them with salt if they continue to adhere. **1825** J. NEAL *Bro. Jonathan* I. 307 She had sprinkled the face of her baby all over with large tears. **1853** SOYER *Pantroph.* 67 Let the whole stew, and then sprinkle it lightly with pepper. **1878** T. HARDY *Ret. Native* v. viii, The floor was merely sprinkled with rain, and not saturated.

refl. **1535** COVERDALE *Jer.* vi. 26 Gyrde a sacke cloth aboute the,..sprynkle thy self with aszshes. **1560** DAUS tr. *Sleidane's Comm.* 153 It is no newes to the Bishoppes..to sprincle, and defile them selves with innocent bloude. **1607** TOPSELL *Four-f. Beasts* 185 For remedy, they wash their hands and sprinckle themselues..with that water.

fig. **1576** FLEMING *Panopl. Epist.* 17 If so be my discredit ..had been equal..to theirs, which sprinckle us with these blottes of blame. **1581** G. PETTIE tr. *Guazzo's Civ. Conv.* I. (1586) 23, I meant those, who though sprinckled with some imperfections, yet wrie rather to the good, then the euill. **1614** B. JONSON *Barthol. Fair* I. i, Why! we were all a little stained last night, sprinkled with a cup or two. **1836** H. COLERIDGE *North. Worthies* (1852) I. 25 He takes care to sprinkle his letters with loyalty.

b. To dot, intersperse, or diversify *with* something. Usu. in *pass.*

1591 SYLVESTER *Du Bartas* I. iv. 208 The Firmament.. Spreads his blew curtain,..Sprinkled with eyes, speckled with Tapers bright. **1596** SPENSER *State Irel.* Wks. (Globe) 675/2 Wherby you wished the Irish to be sowed and sprinckled with the English. **1781** COWPER *Task* I. 164 A level plain Of spacious meads with cattle sprinkled o'er. **1804** C. B. BROWN tr. *Volney's View* 332 An irregular savannah..sprinkled with a few trees. **1859** JEPHSON *Brittany* vi. 67 A wide extent of country..sprinkled with farmhouses. **1892** MRS. R. T. RITCHIE *Rec. Tennyson* III. iv. 187 A road..ran across commons sprinkled with geese and with lively donkeys.

c. To colour with small specks or spots.

Chiefly in passive, or *techn.* in bookbinding.

1750 tr. *Leonardus' Mirr. Stones* 94 Dionysia has a brown or iron colour, sprinkled over with snow spots. **1818** *Art Bookbinding* 19 The edges may now be coloured, sprinkled, or marbled, to fancy. **1855** *Poultry Chron.* III. 374 He may perhaps observe it sprinkled over with black spots. **1885** C. G. W. LOCK *Worksh. Rec.* Ser. IV. 241/2 Books may be sprinkled so as to resemble a kind of marble by using 2 or 3 different colours.

absol. **1835** HANNETT *Bibliopegia* 90 Sprinkle very finely with black and then with brown. *Ibid.*, Put about a tea-spoonful of vitriol to a cup of the black, and sprinkle coarsely over.

†**3.** To cleanse or purify. *Obs. rare.*

1535 COVERDALE *Heb.* x. 22 Sprenkled in oure hertes from an euell conscience.

4. *intr.* **a.** To spring or fly *up* in fine drops.

1594 NASHE *Unfort. Trav.* Wks. (Grosart) V. 174 Bloud spilt on the ground sprinkles vp to the firmament. **1626** BACON *Sylva* §8 It will make the Water friske and sprinckle vp, in a fine Dew.

b. To rain or fall in fine or infrequent drops.

1778 W. H. MARSHALL *Minutes Agric.* Observations 129 It began..to sprinkle. [*Note*] To *sprinkle* (or *spit*), to rain slow in largish drops. **1828** in WEBSTER. **1858** HAWTHORNE *Fr. & It. Note-bks.* II. 249 The rain..continued to sprinkle.

†'**sprinkle**, *v.*[2] *Obs.* Also 5 sprenkle, 6 sprycle, sprinckle (*Sc.* sprink-, sprynkill), 7 sprinkel-. [app. related to SPRANKLE *v.*]

1. *intr.* To sparkle.

c **1400** MAUNDEV. (Roxb.) xxxi. 139 His eghen er so fast stirrand and sprenkland as fyre. **1535** *Trevisa's Barth. De P.R.* XVI. xxix, Crisolitus is a lityll stone of Ethiopia shyninge as golde, and sprinkling as fyre. **1542** BOORDE *Dyetary* x. (1870) 254 Wyne..must sprycle in the cup when it is drawne or put out of the pot. **1573** TWYNE *Æneid* XII. 26 From his face with rage that boyles The sparkles sprinckling flie. **1600** FAIRFAX *Tasso* XVIII. xvi. 318 The heau'nly dew was on his garments spred,..And sprinkled so, that all that palenesse fled. **1630** D. DYKE *Myst. Selfe-Deceiuing* 201 The wine sprinkling and leaping in the glasse.

2. *Sc.* To wriggle; to dart quickly.

1513 DOUGLAS *Æneid* XI. xiv. 71 Allthocht scho [a serpent] wreill, and sprynkill, bend, or skyp, Evir the sarar this ern strenis his gryp. *Ibid.* XII. Prol. 56 The syluer scalyt fyschis on the greit Ourthwort cleir stremis sprynkland for the heyt.

sprinkled ('sprɪŋk(ə)ld), *ppl. a.* [f. SPRINKLE *v.*[1]]

1. Besprinkled (with moisture, colour, etc.). Also *absol.*

1382 WYCLIF *Gen.* xxxi. 12 Se alle the malis,..varye, and sprynklid, and spottid. **1781** COWPER *Charity* 609 Relenting forms would lose their pow'r,..And ev'n the dipt and sprinkled live in peace. **1832** J. RENNIE *Consp. Butterfl. & Moths* 88 The Sprinkled Wainscot (*Leucania suffusa*) appears in June. **1888** JACOBI *Printer's Vocab.* 130 *Sprinkled edges*, cut edges of books are sometimes finely sprinkled with colour to prevent them getting soiled.

2. Dispersed by, or as by, sprinkling.

1590 SPENSER *F.Q.* I. vii. 32 With sprincled pearle, and gold full richly drest. **1647** H. MORE *Minor Poems, Cupid's Conflict* xlii, So Natures carelesse pencill..With sprinkled starres hath spattered the Night. **1697** DRYDEN *Virg. Georg.* IV. 335 With sprinkl'd Water first the City choak. **1700** —— *Pal. & Arc.* III. 76 Some sprinkled Freckles on his Face were seen. **1862** B. TAYLOR *Poet's Jrnl.* (1866) 31 The sprinkled drops of moonshine flashed.

sprinkler ('sprɪŋklə(r)). [f. SPRINKLE *v.*[1]]

1. a. A vessel or other device used for sprinkling water or other liquid.

1535 COVERDALE *Jer.* lii. 18 They toke awaye also the Cauldrons, shouels,..sprinklers, spones & all the brasen vessell. **1686** GOAD *Celest. Bodies* II. iii. 192 They are the Sprinklers, the Water-Pots of Heaven. **1874** H. H. COLE *Catal. Ind. Art S. Kens. Mus.* 137 Bottle, or Rose-water Sprinkler. **1875** KNIGHT *Dict. Mech.* 2292/1 A glass sprinkler found in Pompeii. **1882** *Rep. Prec. Metals U.S.*

152 Cold water..is forced through a fine sprinkler and falls upon them in a spray.

b. A machine or vehicle used for this purpose, esp. one for watering the roadway.

1879 COMSTOCK *Rep. Cotton Ins.* 252 Robinson's combined sprinkler and duster for destruction of the cotton worm. **1893** *Scribner's Mag.* June 708/1 In freezing weather the sprinkler is run [to make a frozen surface]. **1895** R. W. CHAMBERS *King in Yellow, Rue Barrée* ii, The watering carts and sprinklers spread freshness over the Boulevard.

c. An apparatus for extinguishing fires.

1887 *Pall Mall G.* 4 June 12/1. **1901** *Westm. Gaz.* 18 Oct. 7/1 When the Manchester cotton-spinners..first had sprinklers installed in their premises.

2. A brush for sprinkling holy water.

1577 tr. *Bullinger's Decades* (1592) 376 The holie cleansing water.., which they did sprinckle with a sprinckler made of hysope. **1656** W. DU GARD tr. *Comenius' Gate Lat. Unl.* 303 To sprinkle with Holy-water (taken out of a pot with a sprinkler). **1698** MOTTEUX *Quix.* (1733) I. 42 The House-keeper..return'd immediately with a Holy-water pot and a Sprinkler. **1816** [see HOLY WATER 2]. **1862** BORROW *Wild Wales* vi, Then drawing forth his sprinkler, he flung the holy water in the faces of the king and his people. **1896** tr. *Huysman's En Route* viii. 106 Dom Etienne took the sprinkler which a priest handed him.

3. a. A person who sprinkles.

1613 PURCHAS *Pilgrimage* (1614) 150 The Merissœans or Merists, which were (as the name importeth) sprinklers of their holy-water. **1818** in TODD. **1843** TIZARD *Brewing* Index 517 Sprinklers of malt, a majority. [*Ibid.* 68 Completely contradicting the assertion of the non-sprinklers.]

b. One who baptizes by sprinkling as opposed to immersion; an adherent of this practice.

1895 M. MATHER *Idylls* 321 (E.D.D.), Betty were a dipper an' I were a sprinkler. **1896** *Ch. Times* 1 May 505/1 Our reputation as 'the sprinklers' has been maintained..by the chaplains of the English congregations.

4. *attrib.* and *Comb.*, as (sense 1 c) ***sprinkler installation, system***; **sprinkler irrigation** = *spray irrigation* s.v. SPRAY *sb.*² 3 c.

1935 *Jrnl. R. Aeronaut. Soc.* XXXIX. 164 Sprinkler installation for air defence. **1967** *Guardian* 24 May 1/6 The store had no sprinkler installation. **1950** O. W. ISRAELSEN *Irrigation Princ. & Pract.* (ed. 2) vi. 142 Sprinkler irrigation systems may be divided into three groups according to the purpose for which they are used. **1955** MCCOLLY & MARTIN *Introd. Agric. Engin.* xxxvii. 531 Horizontal centrifugal pumps and turbine pumps are the common types used for sprinkler irrigation, as they give a steady flow of water. **1980** *Jrnl. R. Soc. Arts* Mar. 175/1 There are sophisticated forms of sprinkler irrigation..whereby the optimal nutrient content is fed to the crops at just the right moment. **1930** *Engineering* 28 Feb. 279/2 Sprinkler systems in various store rooms. **1973** *Scottish Sunday Express* 5 Aug. 1/2 Why was no sprinkler system installed in the Isle of Man Summerland entertainment centre in which 51 people died in one of Britain's worst-ever fires?

Hence **'sprinklered** *a.*, of or pertaining to a sprinkler system; *spec.* (chiefly *N. Amer.*), provided with or watered by a sprinkler system.

1930 F. E. WOLFE *Princ. Property Insurance* ix. 151 In Great Britain the principle is commonly applied to plural risks, to sprinklered and other fire-resisting risks. **1968** *Globe & Mail* (Toronto) 13 Feb. B11/6 (Advt.), 16,500 sq. ft. on second floor, vinyl tile floors, fully sprinklered, oil and steam heated,..air-conditioned offices. **1975** J. MONTAGUE *Slow Dance* 48 Our true Catholic world, a graveyard..water sprinklered grass, collapsing wreaths. **1978** *N.Y. Times* 29 Mar. D12/6 (Advt.), Over 50,000 sq. ft. now available in prime industrial location Complete burglar & fire alarm systems... Totally sprinklered.

'sprinklet. [f. SPRINKLE *sb.*¹] A slight sprinkle.

1882 *Garden* 11 Mar. 156/3 Deluge every position they [*sc.* crickets] occupy, not with mere sprinklets of water, but with sufficient to lie in pools.

'sprinkling, *vbl. sb.*¹ [f. SPRINKLE *v.*¹]

1. The action of the verb in various senses.

c **1440** *Alph. Tales* 83 With þe sprenclyng of his wengis, þe peper & þe sauce light vppon bathe thies gosseps. *c* **1440** *Promp. Parv.* 470/2 Sprenkelynge, or strenkelynge, *aspercio, conspercio.* **1535** COVERDALE *Heb.* xii. 24 The sprenklynge off bloude, that speaketh better then the bloude of Abel. **1608** BP. HALL *Epist.* 4 Your clericall shauings,..your crossings, creepings, censings, sprinklings, your cozening miracles. **1611** COTGR., *Espardement*, a scattering, sprinkling, dispersing, dissipation. **1726** AYLIFFE *Parergon* 103 Immersion is not strictly necessary unto Baptism; but it may be perform'd even by Effusion or Sprinkling. **1846** BAXTER *Libr. Pract. Agric.* II. 59 The frequent sprinkling of the gypsum upon stable floors. **1874** H. H. COLE *Catal. Ind. Art S. Kens. Mus.* App. 288 Rosewater Stand, surmounted by eight squirts for sprinkling.

2. A small quantity sprinkled or to be sprinkled.

1657 DAVENANT *Gondibert* II. i. 35 Bring Sprinklings, Lamp, and th' Altar's precious breath. *a* **1700** B. E. *Dict. Cant. Crew* s.v. *Dash*, A soft Shower, or a sprinkling of Rain. **1727** SWIFT *City Shower* Wks. 1755 III. II. 38 Such is that sprinkling, which some careless quean Flirts on you from her mop. **1760** R. BROWN *Compl. Farmer* II. 72 A little sprinkling of dung or mud upon rye-land will mightily advance a crop. **1835** W. IRVING *Tour Prairies* 125 As could be seen by sprinklings of blood here and there on the shrubs. **1842** LOUDON *Suburban Hort.* 667 A sprinkling of salt, or of wood ashes,..may be scattered on the surface of the beds. **1872** BLACK *Adv. Phaeton* iv. 36 A sprinkling of rain about his big brown beard.

3. *fig.* **a.** A small or slight quantity or amount.

1594 NASHE *Terrors of Night* Wks. (Grosart) III. 247 Men which haue had some little sprinkling of Grammer learning in their youth. **1600** HOLLAND *Livy* XLIV. xxvi. 1186 Himselfe brought with him..some litle sprinkling of gold to deale among a few of them. **1646** SIR T. BROWNE *Pseud. Epid.* 32 It containeth strange and singular relations, not without some spice or sprinckling of all learning. **1693** DRYDEN *Disc. Satire* Ess. (Ker) II. 108 Some sprinklings of this kind I had also formerly in my plays; but they were casual, and not designed. **1706** A. BEDFORD *Temple Mus.* iii. 62 The Noise may seem to pretend to a dash and sprinkling of Art. **1798** *Hull Advertiser* 23 June 4/4 Corn Exchange. We had a pretty sprinkling of wheat fresh in this morning. **1840** *Florist's Jrnl.* (1846) I. 152 We require a little sprinkling of philosophy. **1844** *Mem. Babylonian Princess* II. 190 Few of these people are without some sprinkling of knowledge.

b. A small number scattered or distributed here and there.

1621 BURTON *Anat. Mel.* I. ii. III. xv. 182 We haue a sprinkling of our Gentry, heere and there one, excellently well learned. **1706** E. GIBSON *Assize Serm. Popery* 3 A sprinkling of gray hairs foretels the approaches of old age. **1721** MORTIMER *Husb.* (ed. 2) II. 125 You may sow..a sprinkling of Carrots or Lettice between them the first Year. **1809** *European Mag.* LV. 20 There was a pretty good 'sprinkling' of genteel company..in the promenades. **1854** H. MILLER *Sch. & Schlm.* (1858) 51 My native town had possessed..its sprinkling of intelligent, book-consulting mechanics and tradesfolk. **1876** FREEMAN *Norm. Conq.* V. xxv. 545 Every man..to whom a sprinkling of foreign words seemed an ornament of speech.

4. *attrib.* and *Comb.*, as ***sprinkling-brush, -cart, glass, -machine, -pitcher, water***; **sprinkling irrigation** = *spray irrigation* s.v. SPRAY *sb.*² 3 c.

1596 NASHE *Saffron Walden* Wks. (Grosart) III. 142 Following him, with his sprinkling glasse,..from place to place. **1648** HEXHAM II, *Een Bespruyt-kruycke*, a Sprinkling, or a Spout-picher for gardens. *a* **1653** GOUGE *Comm. Heb.* ix. 9 There was also a sprinkling water to sprinkle on such as should be unclean. **1859** HOLMES *Aut. Breakf.-t.* ii. 24 A man driving a sprinkling-machine. **1876** L. STEPHEN *Eng. Th. 18th C.* I. IV. vi. 256 Even the same form of sprinkling-brush was retained. **1896** *Harper's Mag.* XCII. 812/2 He..got a job at driving a sprinkling-cart. **1927** *Bull. New Jersey Agric. Exper. Station* No. 453. 3 Three general methods of irrigation, known as surface, sub-, and sprinkling irrigation have been developed. *Ibid.*, Sprinkling irrigation, also known as overhead or Skinner irrigation, from the name of the inventor, is the method of watering crops by means of spray from small nozzles.

†**'sprinkling,** *vbl. sb.*² *Obs.* [f. SPRINKLE *v.*²] The fact of sparkling.

1548 ELYOT, *Scintillatio*,..a sprynclyng vp as newe wyne dooeth in the cuppe. **1582** BATMAN *Barth. De P.R.* VIII. xxxiii. 135 b/2 By chaunging of coulour, and sprinckelyng of beames.

'sprinkling, *ppl. a.* [f. SPRINKLE *v.*¹]

1. Scattering small drops or particles.

In quot. 1567 perh. 'sparkling', f. SPRINKLE *v.*²

1567 TURBERV. *Epit., Upon Death of R. Edwards* 78 b, Welles..Whose sprinklyng springs and golden streames ere this thou well didst knowe. **1621** W. SANDYS *Ovid's Met.* (1626) 110 Back to the shore she casts a heauy eye;..And from the sprinkling waues..shrinks her trembling feete. **1716** GAY *Trivia* II. 421 When..dex'trous damsels twirl the sprinkling mop. **1757** DYER *Fleece* I. 464 Lo! in the sprinkling clouds your bleating hills Rejoice with herbage. **1859** TENNYSON in Ld. H. Tennyson *Mem.* (1897) I. 456 A few sprinkling springlets by the wayside.

2. Falling in scattered drops.

1632 LITHGOW *Trav.* IV. 137 [Her] pittifull lookes, and sprinkling teares. **1666** BOGHURST *Loimographia* (1894) 29 There being no raine at all, but a little sprinkling Showre.

Hence **'sprinklingly** *adv.*

1615 H. CROOKE *Body of Man* 898 They offer also small shootes sprinklingly vnto the skin of the chest. **1657** J. SERGEANT *Schism Dispach't* 286 He speaks his non-sence, sleightly, sprinklingly.

sprint (sprınt), *sb.*¹ [f. SPRINT *v.*]

1. *dial.* (See quots.)

a **1790** PEGGE *Derbicisms* I. 66 A man layd hold of a hare upon her form, and she gave a sprint. *a* **1800** —— *Suppl. Grose, Sprunt*, or *Sprint*, a spring in leaping, and the leap itself. Derb.

2. A short spell of running, rowing, etc., at full speed.

1865- in Lanc. and Derb. glossaries. **1871** 'STONEHENGE' *Brit. Rur. Sports* (ed. 9) II. VII. i. 539/1 At the commencement of training for sprints. **1887** *Field* 19 Feb. 247/3 A strong wind..blowing down the straight, greatly interfered with the runners in the sprints. **1903** *Times* 14 Mar. 14/5 [They had] a few rowing sprints to vary their ordinary exercise work.

transf. **1895** *Westm. Gaz.* 23 Oct. 3/2 It may still seem..that there is too much of a 'sprint' in the last act.

3. *attrib.* and *Comb.*, as ***sprint course, race, -racing***, etc.; **sprint car** orig. *U.S.*, a type of racing car (see quot. 1969).

1864 *Saunders News Letter*, Sprint Race between Ford and Rogers. **1867** WAUGH *Owd Blanket* 82 Kempy..was a famous 'sprint-runner',..well known all over the country side. **1883** *Standard* 18 June 2/4 He..may..be dubbed the champion of the equine world over sprint courses. **1885** *Longman's Mag.* VI. 508 Summoning all my memories of the science of sprint-racing, I tore along. **1886** *Encycl. Brit.* XXI. 61/1 Sheffield..may be termed the home of sprint running. **1954** *Motorsport* June 19/2 Sprint cars were drawing big crowds at the half-mile speedways. **1955** *Sun* (Baltimore) 14 Apr. (B ed.) 18/7 Drivers for the latest entries are two Speedway veterans..and two rookies from the sprint-car circuit. **1961** [see DRAGSTER]. **1969** *Britannica Bk. of Year 1968* 801/1 *Sprint car*, a rugged racing automobile that is midway in size between midget racers and ordinary racers, has about the same horsepower as the larger racers, and is usually raced on a dirt track. **1981** *Telegraph* (Brisbane) 27 Nov. 18/3 The Queensland Bomber and National Sprintcar champion, Bob Kelly also will be having a crack at tonight's title.

sprint, *sb.*² *dial.* [var. of SPRENT *sb.*²]

1. A springe or snare.

1781 HUTTON *Tour to Caves* (ed. 2) Gloss., *Sprint*, a gin for catching birds with. **1892** *Fauna* 87 (E.D.D.), Used to set scores of sprints when a boy. **1897** MACPHERSON *Hist. Fowling* 246 The 'Sprint' employed in the north of England for catching Woodcock.

2. A spring. (Cf. SPRENT *sb.*² 2 b.)

1897 W. JAMIE in *Bards of Angus & Mearns* 235/1 Some queer auld knives wi' double sprint.

sprint (sprınt), *v.* [a. early Scand. **sprinta* (ON. and Icel. *spretta*, Sw. *spritta*): cf. SPRENT *v.*]

†**1.** *intr.* To dart or spring. *Obs.*⁻¹

1566 Is. W. *Copy of a Letter*, etc. xxix, Thy felowes chance that late such prety shift did make; That he from Fishers hooke did sprint before he could him take.

2. a. *dial.* (See quot.)

1862 C. C. ROBINSON *Dial. Leeds* 418 *Sprint*, to run on the toes. The sort of running practised in-doors.

b. To run, row, etc., at full speed, esp. for a short distance; to race in this manner.

1871- [implied in SPRINTING *vbl. sb.*]. **1889** H. O'REILLY *50 Yrs. on Trail* 177 By running and walking, or rather sprinting, the whole time. **1897** *Scotsman* 7 Oct. 7/1 He..sprinted at a good pace to where the observatory pathway commences.

transf. **1899** C. SCOTT *Drama of Yesterday* I. xvi. 555 If a journalist has trained himself to 'sprint', he is naturally employed..on other departments of the paper.

3. *Sc.* To sprout or grow. (Cf. SPRENT *v.* 1 d.)

a **1878** AINSLIE *Land of Burns* (1892) 303 Rare plants that beautify the Spring Aft sprint frae roughest spot.

4. *dial.* To spirt in small drops. Also *trans.*, to sprinkle.

1855- in dial. glossaries (Cumb., Yks., Notts., Linc.).

Hence **'sprinting** *vbl. sb.*

1871 'STONEHENGE' *Brit. Rur. Sports* (ed. 9) II. VII. i. 539/1 At Sheffield, the birthplace and nursery of professional sprinting. **1884** *Harper's Mag.* Jan. 302/2 They would do well to go in for..long-distance running rather than for sprinting.

sprinter ('sprıntə(r)). [f. SPRINT *v.*] One who sprints or engages in sprint-racing.

1871 'STONEHENGE' *Brit. Rur. Sports* (ed. 9) II. VII. i. 539/2 The best amateur sprinters of the present day. **1889** GUNTER *That Frenchman* vi. 65 He..runs wildly down the street, proving himself..a sprinter of first-rate speed. **1895** *Windsor Mag.* 120 [He] is probably the fastest sprinter ever seen on a safety.

transf. **1899** C. SCOTT *Drama of Yesterday* I. xvi. 555 The dramatic art has..suffered much at the hands of the 'sprinters' on the press.

†**sprintle.** *Obs.*⁻¹ A twig or shoot.

a **1225** *Ancr. R.* 276 Ofte druie sprintles bereð winberien?

sprisle, sprissel, obs. forms of SPRITSAIL.

sprit (sprıt), *sb.*¹ Forms: α. 1, 4 spreot, 4-5 sprete, 7-9 spreet. β. 4, 7 spret, 5-7 sprett(e. γ. 5-6 spryt, sprytt, spright, sprite (7 spright), 5, 7-8 spritt, 6- sprit. [OE. *spréot*, = MDu. (Du. and WFris.) *spriet*, MLG. *spryet, spriet*, (hence G. *spriet*) and *spreet*, NFris. *sprit, spret*, ultimately related to SPROTE¹ and SPROUT *v.*¹]

1. A pole, *esp.* one used for propelling a boat; a punting-pole; †a spear.

a c **725** *Corpus Gloss.* C 609 *Contis*, spreotum. *c* **1000** ÆLFRIC *Gloss.* in Wr.-Wülcker 143 *Trudes, uel amites*, spreotas. **1023** in Thorpe *Charters* 318 Anes mannes lenge þe healt anne spreot on his hand and strecþ hine swa feor swa he mæg aræcan into þere sæ. **13..** *St. Cristofer* 300 in Horstm. *Altengl. Leg.* (1881) 458 A lang sprete he bare in hande To strenghe him in þe water to stande. **13..** *K. Alis.* 858 (Linc. MS.), Þe þrid day þey gan aryue, þey swymmed wiþ spreot,..And bryngiþ schipes to þe lond. *c* **1400** *Laud Troy Bk.* 12653 Thei brende bothe mast & wynlase, Sterne & stere, ore & spretes. *c* **1440** *Promp. Parv.* 470/2 Sprete, or qvante,..*contus.*

β. *c* **1350** *Will. Palerne* 2754 Sone as þe schipmen seie him out lepen, hastili hent eche man a spret or an ore. *a* **1400** *Octouian* 601 A sprette ouyr the bord they caste. **1530** PALSGR. 274/2 Sprette for watermen, *picq.* **1609** HOLLAND *Amm. Marcell.* XVIII. v. 111 Antoninus..set his course against our State and Common-wealth, not (as they say) with spret nor oare, with shoouing, or haling,..but even with spred and full sayle. **1687** SHADWELL *Tenth Sat. Juvenal* 38 *Contus* signifies a Quant or Sprett, with which they shove Boats.

γ. *c* **1435** *Torr. Portugal* 181 Torrent undyr hys spryt [= spear] he sprent, And abowght the body he hyme hente. *a* **1450** *Octavian* 469 Some hente an oore,..some a sprytt, The lyenas for to meete. **1583** STOCKER *Civ. Warres Lowe C.* III. 126 b, This Arke..was rowed neither with sprites, nor ores,..but [driven] by wheeles wrought within her. **1606** HOLLAND *Sueton.* 116 A number of mariners, who with their sprits, poles and oares should beate..their carkasses. *a* **1825** FORBY *Voc. E. Anglia* 321 *Sprit*, a pole to push a boat forward. **1903** *Longman's Mag.* Jan. 216 You could not perceive when the flat bit of wood at the end of the sprit touched it [i.e. the bottom of a mere].

2. *Naut.* **a.** 'A small boom or pole which crosses the sail of a boat diagonally from the mast to the upper hindmost corner of the sail, which it is used to extend and elevate' (Falconer).

13.. *E.E. Allit. P.* C. 104 Wi3t at þe wyndas [they] we3en her ankres, Sprude spak to þe sprete þe spare bawe-lyne. **1399** *Rolls of Parlt.* III. 444/2 Par le rumper d'un cabel, rope, sprete, ou mast d'ascun Shoute. **1417** in *For. Acc. 8 Hen. V*, G/1, j dialle, j Soundynglyne, j Roffe Sprite in Balingera Regis. **1536** in Marsden *Sel. Pl. Crt. Adm.* (1894)

I. 54 Possessione virge, Anglice a yard or a spyryt [*sic*]. **1716** *Phil. Trans.* XXIX. 497 This Machine I suspended from the Mast of a Ship, by a Spritt which was sufficiently secured by Stays to the Mast-head. **1769** FALCONER *Dict. Marine* (1780) s.v., The lower end of the sprit rests in a sort of wreath or collar called the snotter. **1856** KANE *Arct. Expl.* I. xxiv. 316 A stouter mainsail of fourteen-feet lift with a spreet eighteen feet long. **1913** *Act 2 & 3 Geo. V*, c. 31 §39 A pilot flag.. to be placed at the mast head, or on a sprit or staff.

b. (See quot.)

1846 YOUNG *Naut. Dict.* 293 A *Sprit*, or *Spur*, in a sheer-hulk is a spar for keeping the sheers out to the required distance.

3. *attrib.*, as ***sprit pole, rig, staff, topmast, topsail, yard.***

1485 *Naval Acc. Hen. VII* (1896) 49 Spritt yerds, j; Spritte sailes, j. **1497** *Ibid.* 300 Fore yerdes, j; sprete yerdes, j. **1611** COTGR., *Miquelot*,.. a poore, pettie, vagabond Pedler, that with a spritstaffe crosses from place to place. **1627** CAPT. SMITH *Seaman's Gram.* vii. 31 Your Spret and Spret top-saile. **1769** FALCONER *Dict. Marine* (1780) s.v. *Yard*, Sprit-topsail yard equal to the fore top gallant-yard. **1894** *Outing* XXIV. 84/2 The sprit rig cannot be said to be pretty. **1903** *Longman's Mag.* Jan. 216 Under the influence of the silent sprit-pole it seemed to move by some voluntary self-contained power.

sprit (sprɪt), *sb.*[2] [f. SPRIT *v.*[1] Cf. SPIRT *sb.*[3] and SPURT *sb.*[2]] **a.** A young shoot of a plant or tree. **b.** A sprout of a seed or root.

1622 *Jrnl. Eng. Plantation Plymouth New England* 7 As we wandred we came to a tree, where a yong Spritt was bowed downe over a bow, and some Acornes strewed vnder neath. **1682** *Houghton's Lett. Husb. & Trade* I. 67 Sometimes.. I have known our Maltster stir his Barly-Couches.. till the Sprit begins to fork, five or six times a day. *Ibid.* 68 When the Sprits come forth at the Root end of the Corn, another Sprit, which we call the Acrospire, begins to stir at the same end. **1851** STERNBERG *Northampt. Dial.*, *Sprit*, a sprout; the awn of barley. **1886** HOLLAND *Cheshire Gloss.* 334 *Sprit*, a sprout from the eye of a potato, or the young radicle of corn when it first begins to grow.

sprit, *sb.*[3] *Sc.* = SPRET. Also *collect.*

1799 J. ROBERTSON *Agric. Perth* 268 It becomes instantly filled with sprits, rushes and other aquatics. **1807** *Ess. Highl. Soc.* III. 469 Bog ground is for the most part covered with sprit, of the smaller sort of which they make what they call bog hay. **1866** *Chambers's Encycl.* VIII. 373/2 Many marshy and boggy places abound in some of the species having leafy stems and the leaves jointed internally, popularly called Sprots or Sprits. **1883** G. M'MICHAEL *Notes Way thr. Ayrshire* 90 The Afton descends between rocky banks, mostly covered with bent and sprit.

sprit, *sb.*[4] *techn.* (See quot. 1880.)

1812 DUBOURDIEU *Antrim* 197 This substance, howsoever it may be acquired, and which by bleachers is called sprit, adheres so closely to the rind.. as to have eluded all the.. processes.. of the old mode of bleaching. **1880** *Spons' Encycl. Manuf.* I. 518 The object of the rubbing.. is to remove small specks of brownish matter called 'sprits', which may appear here and there throughout the piece.

sprit, *ppl. a.* [f. SPRIT *v.*[1]] (See quots.)

1688 HOLME *Armoury* III. 73/2 *Spritt*, or *Blasted*, when it [grass or grain] is beaten down by Rain, and through moisture begins to grow again. **1790** W. H. MARSHALL *Rur. Econ. Midl.* II. 443 *Sprit*, sprouted, as corn in the field. **1808** H. HOLLAND *Cheshire* 147 A potatoe is said to be well sprit, when it has a shoot from two to four inches long.

sprit (sprɪt), *v.*[1] Now *dial.* Forms: 1 spryttan, 3 sprutten, 7- sprit. [OE. *spryttan*:—**sprutjan*, f. the weak grade of the stem represented by SPROUT *v.*[1] Cf. SPIRT *v.*[2] and SPURT *v.*[2]] *intr.* To sprout or shoot; to germinate. Hence **'spritted** *ppl. a.*

*c*900 tr. *Baeda's Eccl. Hist.* I. xxi. (*heading*), Eft spryttendum [*v.r.* sprutendum] þam twigum ðæs Pelagianiscan woles. *c*1000 *Saxon Leechd.* II. 148 þonne treow & wyrta ærest up spryttað. *a*1225 *Ancr. R.* 86 Ase þe wiði þet sprutteð ut þe betere þet me hine ofte croppeð.

1669 WORLIDGE *Syst. Agric.* (1681) 60 Some affirm that Corn spritted a little,.. and then sowen, came up speedily. **1844** *Phytologist* I. 584 Do the seeds of pasture grasses ever germinate in the husk, like wheat, when it is said to 'sprit'? **1886–7** in Cheshire glossaries. **1911** D. H. LAWRENCE *White Peacock* II. viii. 335 We.. went along the wet furrows, sticking the spritted tubers in the cold ground.

sprit, *v.*[2] ? *Obs.* [Of obscure origin: cf. SPIRT *v.*[3]] *intr.* To spring, dart.

13.. *Gaw. & Gr. Knt.* 2316 He sprit forth spenne fote more þen a spere lenþe. **1836** HOOTON *Bilberry Thurland* I. vii. 142 The rabbits.. would.. sprit across to the field-sides in search of better herbage.

sprite (spraɪt), *sb.* Forms: α. 4, 5–7 *Sc.*, spreit (5 spreyt, spreyte), 5–6 sprete, 6 spreet(e; 5–6 spret, 6 sprette. β. 5, 7 spryt (6 sprijt), 5–7 spryte, 5–sprite. (See also SPRIGHT *sb.*[1]) γ. 5 spritte, 5–7 sprit, 8 sp'rit. [ad. OF. *esprit*, or similarly reduced from OF. *esperit(e*, AF. *spirit(e* SPIRIT *sb.* Cf. SPIRT *sb.*[1]]

1. † **a.** = SPIRIT *sb.* in various senses. *Obs.* exc. *arch.*

α. *a*1300 *Cursor M.* 15667 þof þe spreit ai redi be þe flesche be fus to plight. *c*1375 *Sc. Leg. Saints* xxxiii. (*George*) 796 As he hyr þis had talde, þe spret vn to god scho ȝald. *c*1400 *Destr. Troy* 5099 Eneas.. spake full dispitously with a sprete felle. *c*1450 HOLLAND *Howlat* 620 That terrible felloun my spreit affrayd. **1526** TINDALE *Acts* xvii. 16 His sprete was moved in hym. **1535** COVERDALE *Haggai* i. 14 So the Lorde waked vp the sprete of Zorobabel.. and the sprete of Iesua. **1584** HUDSON *Du Bartas' Judith* II. 467 Whose living spreet Reviving spreads, and through all things doth fleet. *c*1615 SIR W. MURE *Misc.* Wks. (S.T.S.) I. 30 Erect my puir dejected spreit, Prostrat befoir thy mercies feete.

β. *c*1375 *Sc. Leg. Saints* xxii. (*Lawrence*) 450 Fore contryt spryt euir ȝet was to my god thankful sacrifice. *c*1400 tr. *Secreta Secret., Gov. Lordsh.* 66 Rightwys philosophers.. lightend with godys spryt of wyt. **1502** ATKYNSON tr. *De Imitatione* I. v. (1893) 157 To rede the scripture with as great fervour of spryte as it was receyued firste. **1578** LYTE *Dodoens* 229 It is profitable for those that are.. troubled in sprite or minde. **1607** ROWLANDS *Earl of Warwick* (Hunterian Cl.) 7 This man compos'd of courage, full of sprite, Of hard adventures, and of great designs. **1669** STURMY *Mariner's Mag.* c4[1] Lord of Light, Without whose gracious Aid and constant Sprite No Labours prosper. **1730** SHENSTONE *Ode to Health* 43 Forth with jocund sprite, I run. **1761** GRAY *Odin* 29 Who thus afflicts my troubled sprite? [**1847** S. JUDD *Margaret* III. (1851) 417 So speaks my sprite.] **1928** R. CAMPBELL *Wayzgoose* ii. 53 As she bent above her chosen Knight A lovely fragrance ravished all his sprite.

γ. **14..** *Chaucer's L.G.W., Ariadne* 2069 (Camb. MS.), For whiche myn sprit goth to do me shame. **1442** *Cursor M.* 170 (Bedford MS.), Iesus after his fastyng long was temtid wiþ þe sprit [of] wrong. **1565** STAPLETON *Fort. Faith* 122 We see how farre the faith of the first vj. C. yeares, and the sprit of Protestants do agree. **1605** *1st Pt. Jeronimo* III. i. 73 This should not be mong men of vertuous sprit. Pay trybute thou, and receiue peace and writ. *a*1649 DRUMM. OF HAWTH. *Poems* Wks. (1711) 44/1 To his fair Spoils his Sprit again yet give.

† **b.** *pl.* = SPIRIT *sb.* 17. *Obs.*

α. *c*1470 HENRY *Wallace* XI. 176 He agayn in greiff him grippyt sayr, Quhill spretis failȝeid ner. **1533** BELLENDEN *Livy* Prol. (S.T.S.) I. 1 Quykin þe spretis of my dull Ingyne. **1566** DRANT *Horace, Sat.* IV. C, How say you, haue not comedies theyr vigors, and their spreets?

β. **1567** DRANT *Horace, Ep.* II. i. G vij, That poet.. That can stere vp my passions or quicke my sprytes at all. *c*1586 C'TESS PEMBROKE *Ps. David* CXIX. iii, I the pleasures of my sprites Will unto thy doctrine bind.

c. = SPIRIT *sb.* 9. *rare*[-1].

1844 DISRAELI *Coningsby* IV. xii. He generally contrived.. to steal down with some congenial sprites to the magical and illumined chamber [*sc.* the billiard-room].

2. = SPIRIT *sb.* 2 b and 3, SPRIGHT *sb.*[1] 2.

α. *a*1400–50 *Alexander* 4779 He was sodanly sesid & slane with a sprete. *c*1470 HENRY *Wallace* XI. 1262 Quhar art thow, spreyt? ansuer, sa God the sawe. **1526** TINDALE *Mark* vi. 49 They supposed yt had bene a sprete and cryed oute. **1575** *Gamm. Gurton* I. ii, As though they had been taken with fairies, or else with some ill spreet. **1611** SIR W. MURE *Misc.* Wks. (S.T.S.) I. 11 For he, now Cupid, now a spreit, did liue me.

β. **1340–70** *Alex. & Dind.* 623 God is spedful in speche & a spryt clene. *c*1375 *Sc. Leg. Saints* ix. (*Barthol.*) 88 Wikit spryt, trawale hym no mare! *c*1460 FORTESCUE *Absol. & Lim. Mon.* vi. (1885) 121 Wherfore the holy sprites and angels.. haue more poiar than we. *a*1513 FABYAN *Chron.* (1811) 325 Fyry dragons, and sprytys, were seen fleynge in the ayer. **1555** EDEN *Decades* (Arb.) 100 *marg. note*, A remedye ageynst walkyng sprites. **1610** HOLLAND *Camden's Brit.* 530, I wot not what sprites and fearefull apparitions. **1675** COTTON *Burlesque upon B.* 51 Where must I lye anights? For I am monstrous fraid of Sprites. **1728** YOUNG *Love of Fame* v. 509 In vain the cock has summon'd sprites away, She walks at noon. *a*1796 BURNS *'As on the Banks'* vi, 'Nae eastlin blast,' the sprite replied. *a*1845 BARHAM *Ingol. Leg.* Ser. III. *House-warming* 118 She verily thought that hobgoblins and sprites were there. **1877** MRS. FORRESTER *Mignon* I. 12 The most arch, mischievous, impertinent little sprite in the world.

Comb. **1609** SIR E. HOBY *Let. to Mr. T. H.* Pref. p. iii, They will not stick to set out our Ladies picture (as one of your sprite-speakers did) with one of your best faces.

γ. *c*1400 *Destr. Troy* 4297, I will tell.. How sprittis in hom spake to qwho þat spirre wold. **1565** STAPLETON *Fort. Faith* 85 The whole churche.. by no strength of wicked sprits.. can be ouerthrowen. **1728** RAMSAY *Monk & Miller's Wife* 245 Syne as the sp'rit gangs marching out, Be sure to lend him a sound rout.

† **3.** = SPIRIT *sb.* 6 and 6 b. *Obs.*

13.. *Coer de L.* 394 Upon his schelde a dove whyte, Sygnyfycacioun of the holy spryte. **1526** TINDALE *Eph.* iv. 30 Greve not the holy sprete off God. **1538** STARKEY *England* II. i. 143 By Hys Holy Spryte, from whom.. commyth al gudnes. *c*1600 FORMAN in *MS. Ashmole 802* fol. 143 b, Governe me with thy holy sprite.

† **sprite**, *v. Obs.* In 6 *Sc.* sprete. [f. prec.] *trans.* To inspire *with* courage.

1536 BELLENDEN *Cron. Scot.* (1821) II. 97 Aidane.. spretit thame with sic curage, that thay.. put the Saxonis.. to flicht. *Ibid.* 389 This victorie was sa plesand.. that every man wes spretit with new curage.

† **'sprited**, *a. Obs.* [f. SPRITE *sb.*]

1. = SPRIGHTED *a.*

1535 COVERDALE *Ps.* xxxvi. 11 The meke spreted shal possesse the earth. **1577** B. GOOGE *Heresbach's Husb.* III. (1586) 115 b, The whol body.. large, hie, liuely sprited, and well trussed. **1607** T. CAMPION *Maske* B 4 b, Mild sprited Zephyrus haile.

2. Having the form of a sprite.

*a*1586 SIDNEY *Astroph. & Stella* (1598) xcvi, In night, of sprites the gastly powers to stur; In thee, or sprites or sprited gastlinesse.

† **'spriteful**, *a. Obs.* [f. as prec.]

1. = SPRIGHTFUL *a.* 1.

*c*1650 HOWELL *Fam. Lett.* (1753) 458 The French nation is quick and spriteful. **1697** EVELYN *Numismata* ix. 308 Spriteful and Vigorous, striving to get the better of his little body.

b. = SPRIGHTFUL *a.* 1 b.

*c*1611 CHAPMAN *Iliad* XI. 246 His readie chariotere did scourge his spritefull horse.

2. = SPRIGHTFUL *a.* 2.

1606 SYLVESTER *Du Bartas* II. iv. II. *Magnificence* 1053 A thousand Flowrs spring in his spritefull pases. **1624** J. GEE *Foot out of Snare* 45 Considering, it hath been.. bedewed with their last spritefull breath. **1662** PLAYFORD *Skill Mus.* I. ii. (1674) 45 But much more spriteful will it appear.. by holding of a Note that falls not by one degree.

Hence † **'spritefully** *adv.*; † **'spritefulness.**

*c*1611 CHAPMAN *Iliad* XIII. 616 The Phthian and Epeian troopes did spritefully assaile The God-like Hector. **1651** JER. TAYLOR *Serm. for Year* II. ix. 113 Its memory was lost in the joyes and spritefulnesse of the morning.

'spritehood. [f. as prec.] The condition or state of being a sprite.

1882 NICHOL *Amer. Lit.* xi. 359 The same fascinating impishness, or spritehood, in both is allayed by a similar healing or converting process.

† **'spriteless**, *a. Obs.* [f. as prec.]

= SPRIGHTLESS *a.*

α. **1513** DOUGLAS *Æneid* IX. iii. 187 Quhilkis in thar weris previt sa spreytles men That Hector thaime delayit ȝeris ten. **1531** TINDALE *Expos. 1 John* (1537) 82 We.. beynge spretlesse.. serue God in the body. **1596** DALRYMPLE tr. *Leslie's Hist. Scot.* (S.T.S.) I. 314 Ane abiecte and spreitles harte.

β. *a*1547 SURREY *Æneid* IV. 896 Her sister Anne, spritelesse for dread to heare This fearefull sturre. *a*1618 J. DAVIES (Heref.) *Wit's Pilgr.* Wks. (Grosart) II. 36/2 It often proues such spritelesse heauy Stuffe. **1661** *Sir A. Haslerig's Last Will & Test.* Suppl. 6 So soon was his spriteless valour resolved into fear.

† **'spritelike**, *a. Obs.* [f. as prec.] Resembling a sprite or that of a sprite.

*c*1611 CHAPMAN *Iliad* XXI. 18 The Worthy,.. spritelike, did with his sword aduance Vp to the riuer. **1658** ROWLAND tr. *Moufet's Theat. Ins.* 924 Such spritelike courage hath Nature planted in them.

'spriteliness. Now *rare.* [f. SPRITELY *a.*]

= SPRIGHTLINESS.

1666 H. STUBBE *Mirac. Conformist* 2 A vivacitie and spriteliness that is nothing common. **1710** F. FULLER *Pharmacop.* 125 It.. puts new spriteliness into the clog'd Spirits. **1779** JOHNSON *L.P.*, *Pope* Wks. 1787 IV. 45 A Preface, written with great spriteliness and elegance. **1805** *Brathwait's Barnabees Jrnl.* Introd. (1818) 45 A very pleasing effusion of spriteliness. **1909** *Contemp. Rev.* Lit. Suppl. Nov. 6 Marred by the elephantine spriteliness of the style.

'spritely, *a.* and *adv.* Also 6 spritly, 7 -lye, sp'ritly. [f. SPRITE *sb.*]

A. *adj.* **1. a.** = SPRIGHTLY *a.* 1.

1606 SHAKS. *Tr. & Cr.* II. ii. 190 Yet nere the lesse, My spritely brethren, I propend to you In resolution to keepe Helen still. **1670** COTTON *Espernon* I. IV. 141 But the Commanders and Souldiers were such, that it was not possible to see any where a more complete, nor a more spritely Body. **1752** FIELDING *Amelia* Wks. 1755 X. 213, I fancy Mrs. Bennet hath been a very spritely woman: for.. she discovers by starts a great vivacity in her countenance.

b. = SPRIGHTLY *a.* 1 b.

1653 A. WILSON *Jas. I*, 246 Being a Spritlye Horse.. he saved both himself, and his Rider. **1680** *Spirit of Popery* 56 Not daring to Attack the Coachman, because his Whip did fright his spritely Horse. **1752** YOUNG *Nt. Th.* I. 437 The spritely lark's shrill mattin wakes the morn.

2. = SPRIGHTLY *a.* 2.

1654 WHITLOCK *Zootomia* 342 No doubt the Soule needs.. a well organiz'd Body, to exercise it[s] Functions with spritely Vigor. *a*1700 EVELYN *Diary* 10 Mar. 1685, An aire of spritely modestie not easily to be described. **1774** MITFORD *Ess. Harmony Lang.* 149 Where this is the case a monosyllabic line may be spritely in its motion. **1927** *Daily Tel.* 21 June 14/7 The programme was the usual compound of items serious and spritely—mostly spritely of course—and from time to time dancers and comedy cyclists flashed across the stage.

3. a. = SPRIGHTLY *a.* 3 a.

1602 ROWLANDS *Tis Merrie when Gossips meete* (Hunterian Cl.) 3 Not penny a quart, dull ale, nor drowsie Beere But spritely wine. **1669** DIGBY *Closet Opened* (1677) 7 It [the mead] will be very spritely, and quick and pleasant.

b. = SPRIGHTLY *a.* 3 b.

1598 MARSTON *Pygmal.*, *Sat.* iv, I see Th'art falne to wits extreamest pouerty, Sure in Consumption of the spritly part. **1638** BRATHWAIT *Barnabees Jrnl.* I. E, Furnish'd with their spritely weapons. **1821** LAMB *Elia* Ser. I. *Mrs. Battle's Opinions on Whist*, She could not conceive a *game* wanting the spritely infusion of chance. **1981** *N.Y. Times* 10 May XI. 23/1 The clams Casino.. covered with a spritely seasoned well-blended onion-garlic topping.

c. = SPRIGHTLY *a.* 3 c.

*c*1611 CHAPMAN *Iliad* XVIII. 449 Youthes, and maides,.. To whom the merrie Pipe and Harp the spritely sounds aduanc't. **1662** PLAYFORD *Skill Mus.* I. (1674) 60 Such effectual melody.. in such excellent Fug's and Spritely Ayres. **1789** BURNEY *Hist. Mus.* III. vii. 410 A Consort.. in 4 parts of a spritely kind such as were then called Fancies. **1977** *Monitor* (McAllen, Texas) 9 Jan. 5c/1 Instantly the room is filled with the spritely, bubbling sound of ragtime.

d. = SPRIGHTLY *a.* 3 d.

1662 PLAYFORD *Music* (1674) 109 The Treble-Violin is a cheerful and spritely Instrument. **1670** in *Term Catal.* (Arber) I. 49/2 Directions to learn to play upon that pleasant and spritely Instrument, the Flagollet.

B. *adv.* = SPRIGHTLY *adv.*

1606 SYLVESTER *Du Bartas* II. iv. II. *Magnificence* 924 There the Lord Zedec him more spritely bears, Milde, fair and pleasant. **1657** F. COCKIN *Div. Blossomes* 48 So lively glorious,.. So Spiritly vigorous and Soul-reviving. **1898** G. B. SHAW in *Sat. Rev.* 21 May 683/1 The younger generation is knocking at the door; and as I open it there steps spritely in the incomparable Max.

†**'spriten,** *v. Obs.*[−1] [f. as prec.] *trans.* To put spirit or life into; to enliven.

1614 C. BROOKE *Ghost Rich. III*, Poems (1872) 75 Griefe cast not downe, joy spritned not their eyes.

†**'spritiness.** *Obs.*[−1] [f. SPRITY *a.*] Sprightliness.

1607 MARKHAM *Cavel.* II. (1617) 260 You shal then..by the moouing of your bodie and legs forward with a liuelie spritines, thrust your horse into his galloppe.

'spriting, *vbl. sb. rare.* [f. SPRITE *sb.*] Acting as sprites; action appropriate to sprites.

?*c* **1570** *Buggbears* II. iv, Syng hegh hoe..a sprityng go we. **1610** SHAKS. *Temp.* I. ii. 298, I will be correspondent to command And doe my spryting, gently.

†**'spritish,** *a. Obs.* [f. as prec.] Impish, malicious, mischievous.

1569 in Ellis *Orig. Lett.* Ser. III. III. 367 To defend..you from the malitious practises of all your spritishe fooes. **1572** *Treat. Treas. agst. Q. Eliz.* 56 Euery man may..take al his whole tale for a wicked spritish lye. **1600** W. WATSON *Decacordon* (1602) 238 Thou daily dost minister new matter to increase our home persecutions, by thy spritish cruelty.

Hence †**'spritishly** *adv. Obs.*

1592 G. HARVEY *Four Lett.* 58 Ignis fatuus [was] never so spritishly busy.

spritsail, sprit-sail ('sprɪtseɪl, 'sprɪts(ə)l). *Naut.* Forms: (see SPRIT *sb.*[1] and SAIL *sb.*[1]); also 7 sprissel, sprisle. [f. SPRIT *sb.*[1] Cf. Du. *sprietzeil*, WFris. *-seil*, NFris. *spritseil*, *spretsaiel*, Da. *spritsejl*, Sw. *-segel*, G. *sprietsegel*.]

1. A sail extended by a sprit; formerly also a sail attached to a yard slung under the bowsprit of large vessels.

α. **1466** *Mann. & Househ. Exp.* 344 My mastyr paid to Willyam Elyse for to carye his sprete seyle of the kervelle to Yipswyche. **1497** *Naval Acc. Hen. VII* (1896) 303 Tyes for the Sprette Sayle. **1616** CAPT. SMITH *Descr. New Eng.* 49 Onely her spret saile remayned to spoon before the wind, till we had reaccommodated a Iury mast. **1627** —— *Seaman's Gram.* vii. 32 The Spret-saile is ⅜ parts the depth of the fore saile. **1694** MOTTEUX *Rabelais* IV. xviii. (1737) 76 He..made them..take in their Spreet-sail. **1750** BLANCKLEY *Naval Expos.* 150 Smacks are necessary Transporting Vessels, with one Mast and half Spreet-sail.

β. **1485** *Naval Acc. Hen. VII* (1896) 41 Spritt sailes feble, j. **1582** N. LICHEFIELD tr. *Castanheda's Conq. E. Ind.* I. xxix. 72 b, The Captaine generall commanded..to fardle up their sprits sailes. **1598** LODGE *Looking Gl. Lond. & Eng.* F ij b, Our topsailes vp, we trusse our spritsailes in. **1655** HEYWOOD & ROWLEY *Fortune by Land and Sea* IV, Our Spright-sayl, Top-sail, and Top-gallant..are hung with waving pendants. **1671** *Lond. Gaz.* No. 621/1 With great difficulty the Swallow,..having onely a Mainsayl and Sprit-sayl left,.. performed her Voyage. **1745** P. THOMAS *Jrnl. Anson's Voy.* 107 We unbent the Mizzen and Sprit-sail. **1794** *Rigging & Seamanship* 42 Barges, Pinnaces, and Yawls, with Sprit-sails. **1839** MARRYAT *Phant. Ship* viii. (Rtldg.) 66 She carried a square spritsail and sprit-topsail. **1891** *Spectator* 7 Feb. 211/1 The spritsail, the object of which is to get the advantage of a lofty peak and retain a short mast.

b. *ellipt.* A spritsail barge.

1881 *Standard* 22 June 3/7 The leading topsail barges at this part of the race overhauled the spritsails.

2. *attrib.* **a.** In the sense 'of or belonging to a spritsail', as ***spritsail brace, brails, clewline,*** etc.

1599 DALLAM in *Early Voy. Levant* (Hakluyt Soc.) 59 Myssen top, sprid saile top. **1626** CAPT. SMITH *Wks.* (Arb.) II. 793 The spret sayle top mast, the spret sayle top sayle yard. **1627** —— *Seaman's Gram.* 31 *marg.*, Spretsaile top-Saile. **1669** STURMY *Mariner's Mag.* 16 Let go the Sprit sail Breales, and hale aft the Sheets. *Ibid.* 17 Vere out..your Fore and Main-sheets, and Sprisle-sheets. **1676** WISEMAN *Surgery* VI. v. 425 Our men bravely quitted themselves of the Fire-ship by cutting the Sprit-sail-Tackle off with their short Hatchets. **1692** *Smith's Seaman's Gram.* I. xiv. 65 Spritsail Clewlines. **1698** in *MSS. Ho. Lords* New Ser. III. (1905) 34 The..rope was expended..for mizen top gallant mast and spritsail top gallant mast. **1711** W. SUTHERLAND *Shipbuild. Assist.* 112 Sprit-sail Lifts. **1750** BLANCKLEY *Naval Expos.* 12 Spritsail Sheat Blocks are turn'd. **1769** FALCONER *Dict. Marine* (1780) s.v., Formerly the spritsail-topsails were set on a mast, which was erected..on the end of the bowsprit. **1794** *Rigging & Seamanship* 135 Spritsail-Topgallant-sail is quadrilateral,..and is bent on the head, to the spritsail-topgallant-yard. *c* **1810** ADM. PATTON in *19th Cent.* (1899) 723 A seaman..let go the sprit-sail brace. **1860** *All Year Round* No. 66. 382 'Which knot?' asked Toby. 'Single or double wall,..spritsail-sheet, stopper, or shroud?' *c* **1860** H. STUART *Seaman's Catech.* 3 Spritsail gaff on bowsprit.

b. ***spritsail yard,*** a yard slung under the bowsprit to support a spritsail. Also *attrib.*

1627 CAPT. SMITH *Seaman's Gram.* iii. 16 The spret-saile Yard [must be] 16. yards long, and but 9. inches thicke. **1687** *Lond. Gaz.* No. 2246/4 A Sally Man of War,..with his Men on his Bowsprit and his Sprissel-yards along Ships. **1745** P. THOMAS *Jrnl. Anson's Voy.* 281 We..got our Spritsail yard fore and aft,..which is an infallible Sign of a Design to board the Enemy. **1797** S. JAMES *Narr. Voyage* 28 The boatswain, and others of the English seamen, were sitting at the spritsail yard. *c* **1810** ADM. PATTON in *19th Cent.* (1899) 723 Five of the enemy had got upon our starboard sprit-sail yard-arm. **1840** R. H. DANA *Bef. Mast* xxv. 83 The spritsail yard sprung in the slings.

c. In the sense 'carrying a spritsail', as ***spritsail barge, vessel.***

1798 *Ann. Reg., Chron.* 40/2 As a sprit-sail vessel..was coming up the river. **1885** *Daily Tel.* 27 Oct. (Encycl. Dict.), The well-known sprit-sail barge, a vessel with a mainsail that sets on a sprit.

Hence **spritsail-yard** *v. trans.*, to disable (a shark, dog-fish, etc.) by thrusting a spar or piece of wood through the snout or gills.

1835 MARRYAT *Pacha of Many Tales* ix. (Rtldg.) 111 The shark..had been caught and *spritsail-yarded*, as the seamen term it. **1867** SMYTH *Sailor's Word-bk.* 646 *Sprit-sail yarding*, a cruelty in which some fishermen wreak vengeance on sharks, dog-fish, etc., that encroach on their baits, and foul their nets.

†**'sprittle,** *sb. Obs.*[−1] In 4 spritell. [f. the stem of SPRIT *v.*[1] Cf. OE. *sprytele* chip, OHG. *spruzil* bar, MHG. *sprüzzel* stave, G. dial. *sprüssel* young shoot, stave (of a ladder).] A shoot or young twig.

a **1400** *Stockh. Med. MS.* i. 445 in *Anglia* XVIII. 306 Take to handfull of ȝonge elerne-spritell And schrape of þe ouerest bark with a qwetyll.

'sprittle, *v. Obs.* exc. *dial.* [Of obscure origin.] *trans.* To scrape or pick with some instrument; to dig *up* in this way.

1575 BANISTER *Chyrurg.* I. (1585) 254 Then with a brasse or yron pipe..thrust into the bottome of it, [they] do sprittle it up by the roots. **1904** in *Eng. Dial. Dict.* (Notts., Linc.).

sprittled: see SPRUTTLED *a.*

sprit-topsail: see SPRIT *sb.*[1]

spritty ('sprɪtɪ), *a. Sc.* [f. SPRIT *sb.*[3] + -Y.] Abounding in sprits or rushes.

1786 BURNS *To Auld Mare* xii, 'Till spritty knowes wad rair't an' risket, An' slypet owre. **1823** J. HOGG *Sheph. Cal.* (1829) I. 27 His dead master, who..was lying in a little spritty hollow. **1885** A. MUNRO *Siren Casket* 42 Large spritty clods from tearing hoofs In showers around them flew.

spritty ('sprɪtɪ), *sb. colloq.* Also sprittie. [f. SPRIT(SAIL + -Y[6].] A spritsail barge.

1948 H. BENHAM *Last Stronghold of Sail* ii. 27 The ketch barge skipper had no doubt of his superior status as compared with the sprittie sailorman... He admitted that in their own weather the spritties were faster. **1952** W. G. ARNOTT *Alde Estuary* vi. 46 The last spritties to visit Snape were the *Una* and *Beatrice Maud* about 1928. **1960** *Guardian* 1 July 7/5 The Cambria, the last 'spritty' to trade under sail as a coaster.

†**'spritual,** *a. Obs.* Forms: α. 5 **sprytwalle,** 6 **-ual;** 5–6 **spritual** (6 **-all**), 8 **sp'ritual.** β. 5–6 **spretuall.** [Reduced form of SPIRITUAL *a.*] Spiritual.

α. *c* **1420** *Chron. Vilod.* 1617 Two sprytwalle ladyus he ordeynede þo To ocupy þat worshipfulle state in hurre absens. **1526** TINDALE *1 Cor.* ii. 15 He that is spirituall discusseth all thynges. **1538** STARKEY *England* I. iv. 122 Wherfor..we may procede to the fautys in the sprytual parte. **1789** BURNS *Kirk's Alarm* xvii, Calvin's sons! Calvin's sons! Seize your sp'ritual guns.

β. **1498** *Reg. Privy Seal Scot.* (1908) I. 34/2 Ony uther courtis spretuall or temporall. **1526** TINDALE *1 Cor.* ii. 13 Makynge spretuall comparesons of spretuall thinges. **1554–9** H. SPONNER in *Songs & Ball., Phil. & Mary* (1860) 8 Musyck in spretuall rimes and psalms.

Hence †**spritu'ality;** †**'spritually** *adv. Obs.*

1526 TINDALE *1 Cor.* ii. 14 Nether can he preceave them because he is spretually examyned. **1567** *Reg. Privy Council Scot.* I. 537 Diverse of the Nobilitie, Sprituallitie, and Commissaris of burrowis.

'sprity, *a.* Now *dial.* Also 7 sprytie; *Sc.* 6 sprety, 8–9 spritty. [f. SPRITE *sb.*] **a.** Spirited. **b.** Spirituous.

1513 DOUGLAS *Æneid* XI. viii. 26 For eith it is for till assay, and se Quhat may our sprety fors in the melle. **1607** MARKHAM *Cavel.* II. (1617) 126 Till you see him euen with a sprytie furie and an actiue nimblenes, passe and repasse in his stalle. **1715** PENNECUIK *Misc. Sc. Poems* 10 Such spritty Liquor, cures us of all Sorrow. **1854** MISS BAKER *Northampt. Gloss., Sprity*, a term applied to wine or beer when the Mother or concreted matter is separated, and floats about in small particles.

spritz (sprɪts, ‖ʃprɪts), *v. U.S.* [f. G. *spritzen* to squirt.] *trans.* To sprinkle, squirt, or spray.

1917 *Dialect Notes* IV. 339 *Spritz*,..to sprinkle. 'Look out, I'll *spritz* you.' **1948** MENCKEN *Amer. Lang.* Suppl. II. 202 *Spritz*, to sprinkle or squirt. **1950** T. SHANE *Bar Guide* 156 Spritz seltzer over lemon juice, lime juice, grape juice, and sugar. **1976** N. THORNBURG *Cutter & Bone* i. 15 The dog, a male, was spritzing a dwarf palm tree. **1978** *Detroit Free Press* 16 Apr. D10/1 Pierre de France..maintains the stars tell which fragrances men and women should be spritzing on their bodies.

Hence **spritz** *sb.*; **'spritzing** *vbl. sb.*

1935 H. R. RUDD *Hocks & Moselles* x. 125 Light wine..often..possesses that natural sparkle or spritz that is so attractive in the Moselle wines. **1975** *High Times* Dec. 89/3 (Advt.), This spray will make any room smell like a candy store... A one-second spritz will mask any odour. **1976** *National Observer* (U.S.) 21 Aug. 12/3, I found myself inexplicably caught up by the nonsense..the inevitable spritzing of the seltzer bottle.

spritzer ('sprɪtsə(r), ‖ʃprɪtsər). Chiefly *N. Amer.* [a. G. *spritzer* a splash.] A mixture of wine and soda water; a drink of this mixture.

1961 in WEBSTER. **1964** *Vogue* Apr. 71/1 Drink *Spritzer* (dry white wine and soda). **1972** G. BAXT *Burning Sappho* iii. 50 Flo's [drink] was a white wine spritzer. **1979** *Toronto Star* 7 Apr. G1/6 Order a spritzer and never look at who you're talking to—something better could be walking in the door.

‖**spritzig** ('ʃprɪtsɪg), *a.* [Ger.] Of wines: sparkling, *pétillant*. Also as *sb.*

1949 T. A. LAYTON *Choose your Wine* (ed. 2) vii. 66 Sometimes the wines are shipped so that there is a delightful natural sparkle in them..called by the Germans *spritzig*. **1959** *Times* 21 Sept. 13/3 This is a wine that is *spritzig*, as the Germans say, or what the French call *pétillant*—that is, it has a slight prickle or sparkle. **1968** *Vogue* Dec. 141/1 A young moselle is a perfect aperitif, especially if it has that rare characteristic *spritzig*: an almost imperceptible touch of effervescence. **1972** *House & Garden* Feb. 100/4 KWV Late Vintage..is slightly *spritzig*, and has a very fresh taste. **1980** *Times* 9 Aug. 8/8 The wine is very big, with..a slight touch of spritzig on the palate.

sproat (sprəʊt). *Angling.* [f. the name of the inventor, W. H. *Sproat* of Ambleside.] ***sproatbend*** (***hook***), ***sproat hook,*** a light fish-hook with a wide and slightly flattened bend, short front, and point set well inwards.

[**1866** W. H. SPROAT in *Field* 1 Dec., I send..salmon hooks made by Messrs. Hutchinson and Son, of Kendal. They have affixed my name to them.] **1871** 'STONEHENGE' *Brit. Rur. Sports* (ed. 9) I. v. 276 The sproat-bend, which is intermediate between the round-bend and the Limerick, has also come a good deal into use of late for trout. **1883** *Cent. Mag.* July 378/1 He attached a sproat hook, No. 1½, with a gut snell eight inches long. **1888** GOODE *Amer. Fishes* 20 Thirty or forty yards of braided silk or linen line, and a Sproat-bend hook.

s-process: see S II. 9.

sprocket ('sprɒkɪt), *sb.* Also 6 **sprokett,** 6, 9 **sproket.** [Of obscure origin.]

1. *Carp.* and *Build.* A triangular piece of timber used in framing, esp. one fastened on the foot of a rafter in order to raise the level of the eaves.

1536 *MS. Acc. St. John's Hosp., Canterb.*, To Nycoles & Horton for makyng sprokettis & a grunsyll att Arnoldes, ij d. **1593** *MS. Churchw. Acc. St. Andrew's, Canterb.*, For setting vp a forme, nayles and sproketes, xiij d. **1703** [R. NEVE] *City & C. Purchaser* 121 A Coving-cornish..has a great Casement, or Hollow in it, which is commonly Lathed and Plaister'd upon Compass, Sprockets, or Brackets. **1880** LEANING *Quantity Survey.* 61 Sprockets.—State what size two are cut out of.

2. a. A projection (either forked or simple) from the rim of a wheel, engaging with the links of a chain.

1750 BLANCKLEY *Naval Expos.* 126 Sprockets are made not unlike a large Horse Shoe, drove into the Wheel, and the Chain works on them. **1875** KNIGHT *Dict. Mech.* 522/1 The sprockets on the wheel are adapted to receive the links of the chain successively. *Ibid.* 2292/2 The sprockets may be forked, and thus made to partially embrace the links of the chain. **1897** *C.T.C. Monthly Gaz.* Jan. 21 A roller-chain passing over ordinary sprockets.

b. *attrib.* and *Comb.*, as ***sprocket-wheel;*** **sprocket hole,** each of a line of holes along film or paper tape with which sprockets can engage to propel it or keep it correctly aligned.

1910 F. H. RICHARDSON *Motion Picture Handbk.* 101 Old, dry films jump because..the *sprocket holes are shrunken. **1931** B. BROWN *Talking Pictures* viii. 182 Bad tracking produces a loud hum due to either the picture or the sprocket holes running across the light beam. **1960** M. G. SAY et al. *Analogue & Digital Computers* ix. 263 A row of holes across the tape consists of one sprocket hole, 0·043 in. diameter.., and up to five information holes, 0·072 in. diameter. **1971** *Southerly* XXXI. 138, I could print those four or five with the sprocket holes still on the film. **1980** S. HOCKEY *Guide Computer Applic. Humanities* ii. 25 It is normally necessary to leave a foot or so of blank tape with only the sprocket holes punched at each end of a paper tape. **1769** FALCONER *Dict. Marine* (1780) s.v. *Pump*, The *sprocket-wheels, employed to wind it up from the ship's bottom. **1792** J. TOWNSEND *Journ. Spain* I. 170 It [the noria] consists of a band or girdle passing over a sprocket wheel. **1846** A. YOUNG *Naut. Dict.* 239 Above the upper extremities of these tubes there is fixed a sproket-wheel worked by crank-handles. *c* **1860** H. STUART *Seaman's Catech.* 54 It is rove round the sprocket-wheel of the capstan. **1896** *Westm. Gaz.* 21 Nov. 7/2 The chain, instead of acting direct on the driving wheel, passes from the sprocket wheel to another at the back of the saddle.

c. *ellipt.* A sprocket-wheel, esp. that of a cycle; and (*Cinemat.*), one that propels film by engaging with perforations along its edge.

1886 J. M. CAULFEILD *Seamanship Notes* 3 Parts of the Capstan. Drum head, barrel, sprocket. **1893** *Fortn. Rev.* No. 314. 241 The elliptical sprocket, or lower chain-wheel, has caused much discussion. **1910** F. H. RICHARDSON *Motion Picture Handbk.* 110 The intermittent sprocket..should be watched and promptly renewed when there are signs of serious wear. **1925** R. V. JOHNSON *Mod. Picture Theatre Electrical Equipment & Projection* 67 The intermittent sprocket pulls the film through the gate, and the bottom sprocket carries the film to the lower spool box. **1953** L. J. WHEELER *Princ. Cinemat.* vi. 181 It is reasonable to expect the sprocket dimensions to be different to those in the camera mechanism. **1977** D. MACKENZIE *Raven & Kamikaze* vi. 77 Slade unwound the film from the sprockets and put it back in the can.

attrib. **1897** *Outing* XXX. 277/2 A wheel, from handle-bar to sprocket-chain. *Ibid.* 370/2 A sprocket-lock, which was guaranteed to prevent any sprocket from revolving. *Ibid.* 371/1, I snapped in its place my sprocket-guard. **1910** F. H. RICHARDSON *Motion Picture Handbk.* 102 A machine with worn intermittent sprocket teeth. **1935** *Discovery* Nov. 325/2 Disturbances such as sprocket-tooth ripple.

3. *Naut.* One of the teeth of a pawl-rim.

1903 *Speaker* 7 Feb. 452/1 The Hermione capstans are of the dangerous old-fashioned type, fitted with the antiquated pawls and sprockets. **1906** *Temple Bar* Jan. 59 The little iron pawls..begin to click and clatter, as they pass over their sprockets.

Hence **'sprocketed** *a.*, furnished with sprockets or sprocket holes.

1895 *Queenslander* 7 Dec. 1071/1 The chain runs on and engages sprocketed wheels. **1967** P. Grosset *Compl. Bk. Amateur Film Making* viii. 143/2 You will need to use.. sprocketed tape (which cannot slip, shrink or stretch). **1978** [see next].

sprocketless ('sprɒkɪtlɪs), *a.* [f. SPROCKET *sb.* + -LESS.] Not employing or requiring sprockets.

1967 *Boston Sunday Herald* 26 Mar. VI. 2/8 The smooth, quick operation results from the projector's sprocketless film drive. **1978** *Broadcast* 23 Apr. 24/2 Synchronising sprocketed film..with sprocketless video tape.

sprod. *north. dial.* [Of obscure origin.] A salmon in its second year.

1617 *Shuttleworths' Acc.* (Chetham Soc.) 218 A salmon and sprodes and troutes. *a* **1672** Willughby *Hist. Pisc.* (1686) IV. iv. 189 Nostratibus in fluvio Ribble agri Eboracenis Salmones primo ætatis anno *Smelts* dicuntur; secundo *Sprods.* **1677** Johnson in Ray *Corresp.* (1848) 127, I am a little jealous that their Sprods are but Scurves. **1861** *Act 24 & 25 Vict.* c. 109 §4 All migratory fish of the genus salmon,..that is to say salmon,..tubs, yellow fin, sprod, herling [etc.]. **1884** *Westmorl. Gaz.* 1 Nov. 5/5 A good many morts and sprods have been landed from the lower reaches of the Kent.

sprog (sprɒg). [Cf. SPRAG *sb.*²]

1. *Services' slang.* A new recruit; a trainee; a novice. Also *occas.*, one of inferior or ordinary rank. Freq. *attrib.*

1941 *New Statesman* 30 Aug. 218/3 *Sprog* (R.A.F.), a tyro. **1942** *Word Study* Dec. 6/2 'Hey, *sprog*,' said the corporal, 'how about us gettin' another *cliner*?' **1943** J. Hillier in *Penguin New Writing* XVI. 23 Never mind, Wendy, you sprogs of 'B' flight will learn to fly yet—if you live long enough! **1946** J. Irving *Royal Navalese* 164 *Sprog*, a new entry. **1949** J. R. Cole *It was so Late* 62 Each time a new course of pilots arrived the sprog officers among them used to fall over themselves after her. **1970** C. Wood '*Terrible Hard' says Alice* ii. 31 Pasty-faced sprog subalterns. **1978** F. Branston *Sergeant Ritchie's Conscience* i. 12 Some sprog copper, so new he did not even recognize him.

2. *slang* (orig. *Naut.*). A youngster; a child, a baby.

1945 'Tackline' *Holiday Sailor* vii. 75, I can't deny him nothing. Always giving the sprog a tanner to nip off and buy himself some nutty. **1949** in Partridge *Dict. Slang* (ed. 3) Add. 1181/2 Nobby Clark's gone on leave, his wife's just had a sprog. **1968** 'O. Mills' *Sundry Fell Designs* x. 115 All those sprogs, and that ghastly earth-mother missus. **1973** M. Amis *Rachel Papers* 64 Here I attempted a few minutes' work, not easy because the fifty bawling sprogs had classes there in the afternoon. **1981** D. Clark *Longest Pleasure* ii. 14, I don't think he's been really with us since the sprog came along.

sproncy, var. SPRAUNCY *a.*

sprong. Now *dial.* Also 5 spronge. [Of obscure origin: cf. PRONG *sb.*²] = PRONG *sb.*² 1 and 2. Hence **sprongful**.

1492 Ryman *Poems* lxxxv. 5 in *Archiv Stud. neu. Spr.* LXXXIX. 255 When dredefull deth to the shal come And smyte the with his spronge. **1756** Toldervy *Hist. 2 Orphans* I. 146 She threw a fork at me that had three sprongs. **1870** Kennedy *Fireside Stories* 58 (E.D.D.), For every sprongfull he threw out, two came in. **1888** Elworthy *W. Somerset Word-bk.* 704 One o' the sprongs is a-brokt out o' the dung clow. *a* **1904** in *Eng. Dial. Dict.* (Kent and Somerset).

sprong, obs. f. pa. t. and pa. pple. SPRING *v.*

spronk¹. *Obs.* exc. *dial.* Also 1 spranca, 5 spronke. [OE. *spranca*; cf. WFlem. *spranke* branch of a vein or artery.]

†**1.** A shoot, sprout. *Obs. rare.*

c **1000** Ælfric *Voc.* in Wr.-Wülcker 139 *Stirps*, styb, *uel* spranca. *Ibid.* 149 *Plante*, treowes sprancan. *a* **1100** in Napier *O.E. Glosses.* 54/2 *Labruscas*, sprotu, sprancan. *c* **1440** *Pallad. on Husb.* XII. 116 After dayes vij vp hem [peaches] take; By thenne out wol a spronke of hem be lette Vppon the shelle.

2. *dial.* The stump of a tree or tooth.

1838 in Holloway. **1847-** in dial. glossaries (Kent, Sussex, Surrey).

†**spronk².** *Obs.*⁻¹ [Cf. SPRANK².] A spark.

c **1290** *S. Eng. Leg.* I. 205 Anon so he hadde þis word iseid, þat fuyr aqueinte ech spronke.

sprosser ('sprɒsə(r)). [Ger.] The thrush-nightingale, *Luscinia luscinia*, of the family Turdidæ, found in eastern Europe and Asia.

1871 Newton & Saunders *Yarrell's Hist. Brit. Birds* (ed. 4) I. 320 A second species of Nightingale occurs..long known to German bird-fanciers as the sprosser. **1912** Baxter & Rintoul *Rep. Scott. Ornithol. 1911* 3 Curiously enough, both the Common Nightingale..and the Northern Nightingale or Sprosser..were added in spring to the Scottish list. **1954** D. A. Bannerman *Birds Brit. Isles* III. 304 This [*sc.* the thrush-nightingale] is the 'sprosser' of Germany, inhabiting the same type of cover as its better known relative.

†**sprot¹.** *Obs.* Forms: α. 1–2, 4–7 sprot, 1, 4–6 sprott, 5–6 sprotte. β. 5–7 sprote. [OE. *sprot*, = Fris., MDu. and Du., MLG. *sprot* (hence G. *sprott*, †*sprotte*, obs. Da. *sprot, sprøt, spryt*).]

a. = SPRAT *sb.*¹ 1. **b.** A smelt.

α. *c* **1000** Ælfric *Lives Saints* xxxi. 1271 Hi ealle ne mihton, Ne fisceras ne he sylf, ȝefon ænne sprot. *c* **1055** *Byrhtferth's Handboc* in *Anglia* VIII. 310 Ða myclan hwælas and ða lytlan sprottas and eall fisc kynn. *c* **1110** in Napier *Contrib. O.E. Lexicog.* 14 *Silurus*, sprot, *glaucus*, hwitling. **1309–10** *Durh. Acc. Rolls* (Surtees) 8. **1328–9** *Exch. K.R. Mem.* m. 125, Piscem qui dicitur sprot. **14..** *Piers of Fulham* in Hartshorne *Anc. Metr. T.* 119 The cely fisshes can nat hem selff excuse; Tyll it be spitted like a sprotte. **1502** Arnolde *Chron.* (1811) 263 Rede sprottis: x cades maketh a last. **1535** *Act 27 Hen. VIII*, c. 3 Fisher men..vse commonly to conducte and conuey their hearing, sprottes, and other fyshe to..Kyngstone. **1601** Holland *Pliny* II. 434 Sprots salted haue a special propertie to heal the biting of the beetle or venomous fly Prester.

β. *c* **1475** *Cath. Angl.* 357/1 Sprote, *epimera, piscis est.* **1557** W. Turner *Ep.* in Gesner *Hist. Anim.* (1558) 1296 Apua quæ a Cantabrigensibus uocatur a Spirlyng, a Londinensibus, dum recens est, a Sprote; et infumata a rede Sprote, aut a dryed Sprote. **1583** *Shuttleworth's Acc.* (Chetham Soc.) 7 Rede heryngés and a hundrethe of sprotes, xij^d. **1609–10** *Ibid.* 186 A hundreth of sprotes, xj^d.

attrib. **1499** *Maldon Court Rolls* Bundle 58 No. 2 b, Pro le mesurage v. chaldre colys pro j sprotebote. **1500** *Ibid.* Bundle 59 No. 2, De custum, j sprotbote, iii. *d.*

sprot². *Sc.* (and *north.*). Also 9 sprote, sprott. [Cf. SPRAT *sb.*³] A coarse kind of rush or rush-like grass.

c **1600** *Lindesay's* (Pitscottie) *Chron.* (S.T.S.) I. 336 *note*, The fluir layd with greine scheirrittis, with sprottis, medwartis, and flouris. **1808** Jamieson s.v. *Sprat*, They are called sprotes [in] Ang[us]. **1825** *Ibid.* Suppl., *Fosset*,..a mat of rushes or *sprots*, laid on a horse. **1853** G. Johnston *Nat. Hist. E. Borders* 199 *Juncus acutiflorus.* Sprat or Sprot. **1883** G. M'Michael *Notes Way thr. Ayrshire* 78 All east of this is moorland, clad with bent, heath, and sprotts.

sprot³. *rare.* [Of obscure origin.] (See quot.)

1846 E. Jesse *Anecd. Dogs* 269 The otter swims and dives with great celerity, and in doing the latter, it throws up *sprots* or air bubbles.

sprot-barley, obs. variant of SPRAT-BARLEY.

sprote¹. *Obs.* exc. *dial.* Forms: 1 sprota, 4–5, 9 sprote, 5, 9 sprot, 9 spro(o)at. [Common Teut.: OE. *sprota*, = MDu. *sprote, sproot* (Du. *sport*), MLG. *sprote, sprate*, OHG. *sprozzo* (MHG. *sprozze*, G. *sprosse*), ON. *sproti*, related to SPROUT *v.* OE. had also *sprot* neut., which may be partly represented in the later form with short vowel.]

†**1.** A shoot, sprout, twig, rod. *Obs.*

c **1050** in Wr.-Wülcker 378 *Clauus*, næȝl oððe sprota. *a* **1100** in Napier *O.E. Glosses* 83 *Sarmentorum*, sprotena. *a* **1300** *Havelok* 1142, I ne haue hws, y ne haue cote, Ne I ne haue stikke, y ne haue sprote. *c* **1425** *Noah's Ark* in *Non-Cycle Mystery Plays* 22 For I have neither ruff nor ryff, Spyer, sprund, sprout, no sprot [*rime* boat]. *c* **1460** *Towneley Myst.* ii. 290, I wold that it were in thi throte, Fyr, & shefe, and ich a sprote.

b. *pl.* Small sticks or twigs; bits of branches blown from trees. Also ***sprote-wood***.

1825 in Jamieson *Suppl.* **1847** in Halliwell. **1854-** in dial. glossaries (Northampt., Yks., Sc.).

2. A chip, shiver, or splinter.

Freq. *c* 1400, in phr. ***in, into, on sprotes.***

c **1400** Maundev. (1839) xxii. 238 The Tronchouns flen in sprotes and peces alle aboute the Halle. *c* **1400** *Destr. Troy* 5783 Speiris into sprottes spronge ouer hede. *c* **1400** *Sege Jerus.* (E.E.T.S.) 554 Spakly her speres on sprotes þey ȝeden.

1825 Jamieson *Suppl.*, *Sprot*, a chip of wood, flying from the tool of a carpenter.

†**sprote².** *Obs.* [= MLG. (and LG.) *sprote, sprute*, MDu. *sproete* (Du. *sproet*), G. *sprosse*, †*sprusse*, perhaps related to prec.] A spot on the skin; a freckle. Hence †**sproted** *ppl. a.*, spotted. *Obs.*

a **1400–50** *Stockholm Med. MS.* 145 A good watir to purgyn a mannys face of sprotys. **1422** tr. *Secreta Secret.*, *Priv. Priv.* 233 Eyen that bene whit y-freklet, or i-sprotid, or blake.

sprottle ('sprɒt(ə)l), *v. dial.* [Cf. SPARTLE *v.*², SPRATTLE *v.*²] *intr.* To sprawl, to struggle helplessly. Hence **'sprottling** *ppl. a.*

1829 J. Hunter *Hallamshire Gloss.* 85 *Sprottle*, to struggle with inefficacious vehemence. **1839** A. Bywater *Sheffield Dial.* 15 An we sprottlin abaht to ger up. **1917** D. H. Lawrence *Look! We have come Through!* 97 Why do you spurt and sprottle like that, bunny? **1921** —— *Tortoises* 19 It goes right through him, the sprottling insect. **1937** A. Uttley *Ambush of Young Days* iv. 65 The lamb suddenly gave a tiny wailing 'Baa', and tried to struggle to its feet. 'It's sprottling. It'll be all right,' cried Josiah, our old manservant.

†**sproty**, *a.* *Obs.*⁻¹ [? f. SPROTE¹.] Small, thin, weak.

c **1425** *Eng. Conq. Irel.* 54 The Erl..was samroed, with grey eghen, wommanes vysage, & sproty smal spech [L. *voce exili*], short nek.

sprount (spraʊnt), *v. rare*⁻¹. [App. altered form of SPROUT *v.*¹; but cf. SPROUNTING *vbl. sb.*] *intr.* To sprout.

1939 Dylan Thomas *Map of Love* 64 The half-liquid plants sprounting from the bog.

†**sprounting**, *vbl. sb. Obs.*⁻¹ Spouting.

1691 Mrs. D'Anvers *Academia* 31 I've seen..Maudlin walks and Christ-Church Fountain, A thing that makes a mighty sprounting.

sprouse, var. SPROWSIE.

sprout (spraʊt), *sb.*¹ Also 4, 6 sproute, 7 sprowt(e, sproot(e. [Related to SPROUT *v.*¹ Cf. MDu. *sprute, spruyte* (Du. *spruit*, WFris. *sprút*), MLG. *sprute, spruut*, NFris. *spröt, spröd*.]

1. a. A shoot from a plant, root, or stump of a tree, shrub, or plant; a new growth developing from a bud into a branch, stalk, sucker, etc.

a **1300** *E.E. Psalter* lxxix. 12 He streked his pal[m]tres to þe se, And his sproutes to þe streme to be. **1602** Fulbecke *2nd Pt. Parall.* 53 If certaine sprowtes or braunches doe grow vpon the stocke, the cutting of these sprowtes or braunches or the destroying of them is wast. **1638** Wilkins *New World* xiv. (1707) 126 The Experiment of Trees cut down which will of themselves put forth Sprouts. **1693** Evelyn *De la Quint. Compl. Gard.* II. Refl. Agric. 63 The New Sprouts which shoot out at the Extremities of a Pruned Branch. *a* **1722** Lisle *Husb.* (1757) 376 Peach-trees are so difficult to be kept..if the gardener does not perfectly understand the way of cutting them, and taking their sprouts away. **1784** Cowper *Task* III. 528 He pinches from the second stalk A pimple, that portends a future sprout. **1849** Cupples *Green Hand* xvi. (1856) 159 The ferny sprouts of young cocoas. **1856** Olmstead *Slave States* 76 A large, square yard, growing full of Lombardy poplar sprouts, from the roots of eight or ten old trees.

fig. **1673** O. Walker *Educ.* viii. 68 No Nation civil or barbarous..that express not their joy and mirth by it [*sc.* dancing], which makes it seem a sprout of the Law of Nature. **1871** R. H. Hutton *Ess.* (1877) I. 64 All human minds are but sprouts from the same infinite source.

b. A rudimentary shoot of a seed; the acrospire of grain.

1610 Holland *Camden's Brit.* 485 The best barly, of which steeped in water and lying wet therein untill it spurt againe, then, after the said sprout is full come, dried and parched over a kill, they make store of mault. **1673–4** Grew *Anat. Pl., Anat. Trunks* II. i. (1682) 124 A Sprout from a Seed.

fig. **1640** Bp. Hall *Episc.* II. 167 So the rest of the Churches show, what sprouts they have of the Apostolike seed.

c. *pl.* Young or tender shoots or side-growths of various vegetables, esp. of the cabbage-kind.

1639 O. Wood *Alph. Bk. Secrets* 229 The juyce of young Sprowts of Nettles snuffed. **1698** M. Lister *Journ. Paris* (1699) 150, I never saw in all the Markets once Sprouts, that is, the tender Roots of Cabages. **1712** Addison *Spect.* No. 317 ⁋17 Dined on a Knuckle of Veal and Bacon. Mem. Sprouts wanting. **1721** Bailey, *Sprouts*, a Sort of young Coleworts. **1726** *Dict. Rust.*, *Sprouts*, small shoots of old Cabbage, in Winter, when they begin to Bloom and Head. **1842** Loudon *Suburban Hort.* 649 The roots, more especially those of the Swedish turnip,..will produce an abundance of delicate sprouts through February and March. **1858** Glenny *Gard. Everyday Bk.* 99/2 You may now clear away all the stems and remains of cabbages that have supplied you with sprouts. **1887** *Amer. Naturalist* XXI. 441 The tall [variety of Brussels sprouts] is quite distinct in habit and leaf from the dwarf, the former having less crowded 'sprouts'.

d. *ellipt.* for *Brussels sprouts* (see BRUSSELS).

1858 Glenny *Gard. Everyday Bk.* 271 Turnips, Sprouts, Spinach, Savoys.

e. *U.S.* A variety of potato.

1868 *Rep. U.S. Commissioner Agric.* (1869) 240 Michigan White Sprouts.

2. *transf.* **a.** Something resembling a sprout in appearance, formation, or growth.

1597 A. M. tr. *Guillemeau's Fr. Chirurg.* 22/2 An excrescence of fleshe, havinge divers small sproutes. **1822–7** Good *Study Med.* (1829) V. 611 The tegumental laminæ.. sometimes giving rise to sprouts or branches of a very grotesque appearance.

†**b.** A branch of a river. *Obs.* (Cf. SPROUT *v.*¹ 5.)

1794 Morse *Amer. Geog.* 378 To build a bridge over the sprouts of Mohawk river.

3. *fig.* **a.** Applied to persons: A scion.

1725 Ramsay *Gent. Sheph.* I. ii, When round the ingle-edge young sprouts are rife. **1779** J. Moore *View Soc. Fr.* II. l. 9 This kind of poison, being often poured upon the young sprouts of fortune and quality, gradually blasts the vigour of the plants. **1819** Scott *Ivanhoe* xxxii, The noble Athelstane, ..the last sprout of the sainted Confessor! *Ibid.* xlv, That resuscitated sprout of Saxon royalty. **1875** Tennyson *Q. Mary* I. v, Then the bastard sprout, My sister, is far fairer than myself.

b. *U.S. colloq.* and *slang.* A young person, a child.

1934 *Jrnl. Amer. Folk-Lore* Jan./Mar. 51 One time she was getting ready to go to a play-party. Some of the young sprouts were waiting for her. **1942** Berrey & Van den Bark *Amer. Thes. Slang* §383/2 Child..(little or young) sprout. **1950** R. Moore *Candlemas Bay* 24 I'm going to beat the living pickle out of this goddam sprout of mine. **1951** *Harper's Mag.* July 36/1 A girl out your way has married.. and is coming home with a sprout. **1983** *Verbatim* IX. III. 23/2 The young sprouts and broths of lads who feel their oats and are full of beans.

4. ***to put through a course of sprouts***, to beat, birch, or flog; to subject to a course of severe discipline or training. *U.S.*

1851 Mayne Reid *Scalp-Hunt.* ii. 15 See that he be put through a 'regular course of sprouts'. **1858** in Bartlett (1859) s.v., Any gentlemen who want to be put through the necessary course of preliminary sprouts. **1897** *Outing* XXIX. 484/1 He put the ladies [*sc.* dogs] through a course of sprouts which ultimately developed brilliant..working qualities.

5. The action of sprouting or of putting forth new growths. *rare.*

1586 T. B. *La Primaud. Fr. Acad.* I. 666 Every evill (as Cicero saith) in the first sprout thereof may be easily stopped. **1824** LAMB *Elia* II. *Blakesmoor in H——shire*, All Ovid on the walls, in colours vivider than his descriptions. Actæon in mid sprout, with the unappeasable prudery of Diana.

6. Special Combs.: †**sprout cauliflower**, sprouting broccoli (*obs.*); **sprout flow** *U.S.*, the first flow or flood of water sluiced into a rice-field, causing the seed to sprout; **sprout-hill** (see quot.); **sprout-land** *U.S.*, land covered with the sprouts of trees or shrubs.

1728 BRADLEY *Dict. Bot.* s.v. *Brocoli*, I call it in English, the Sprout Cauliflower, because the Brocoli..is the Flower stalk with the Flower bud at the End of it. **1766** *Museum Rust* VI. 317 In wet weather these insects [*sc.* ants] accumulate cavernous heaps of sandy particles amongst the grass, called by the labourers, sprout-hills. **1851** THOREAU *Jrnl.* 12 Feb. in *Writings* (1906) VIII. 156 It is refreshing to walk over sprout-lands, where oak and chestnut sprouts are mounting swiftly up again into the sky. **1856** OLMSTED *Slave States* 471 This is termed the 'sprout flow', and the water is left on the field until the seed [i.e. rice] sprouts. **1862** THOREAU *Excurs.* (1914) 219 About the second of October, these trees [i.e. maples]..are most brilliant, though many are still green. In 'sprout-lands' they seem to vie with one another. **1914** R. FROST *North of Boston* 87 A rock-strewn town where farming has fallen off, And sprout-lands flourish where the axe has gone.

†**sprout**, *sb.*² *Obs. rare.* Also sprut(t. [? Cf. Norw. *spruta* (Da. *blæksprutte*) cuttle-fish.] Some kind of fish.

c **1340** *Durh. Acc. Rolls* (Surtees) 36 In j sprutt et merling empt, xxjd. *Ibid.* 37, iiij kyling, j sprut, iijs. iijd. *Ibid.*, xxx keling, j leng, j sprout, et vij kodeling.

sprout (spraʊt), *v.*¹ Forms: α. 3 spruten, 4, 6 sprute, 6 spruit, spruyt. β. 5 sproutyn, 6–7 sproute, sprowt(e, 6– sprout. [OE. *sprūtan (cf. *āsproten* pa. pple.), = WFris. *sprute* (NFris. *spröt*), MDu. *spruten*, *spruyten* (Du. *spruiten*), MLG. *spruten*, MHG. *spriezen* (G. *spriessen*, †*spreussen*). Cf. OE. *sprȳtan* (rare) and *spryttan* SPRIT *v.*¹ The 16th cent. forms *spruit*, *spruyt*, are due to Du. *spruiten*.]

1. *intr.* To grow, issue, or proceed as a sprout or sprouts; to shoot forth or spring up by natural growth. Freq. in fig. context, and const. *of*, *out of*, *from*, etc.

c **1200** *Trin. Coll. Hom.* 217 An ȝerd sal spruten of iesse more. *c* **1230** *Hali Meid.* 11 Meidenhad is te blosme þat, beo ha eanes fulliche forcoruen, ne spruteð ha neauer eft. **1535** COVERDALE *Song Sol.* iv. 13 The frutes that sproute in the, are like a very paradyse of pomgranates with swete frutes. *c* **1572** GASCOIGNE *Fruites Warre* xvii, The bough, the braunch, the tree, From which do spring and sproute such fleshlie seedes. **1597** SHAKS. *2 Hen. IV*, II. iii. 60 To raine vpon Remembrance with mine Eyes, That it may grow, and sprowt, as high as Heauen. **1611** CORYAT *Crudities* 87 These vines I haue seene grow so high, that they haue sprowted cleane aboue the toppe of the tree. **1662** J. TATHAM *Aqua Triumph.* 1 A *Cornu-copia* out of which all sorts of Flowers seem to sprout. *a* **1708** BEVERIDGE *Priv. Th.* II. (1730) 65 If the Love of Money be the Root of so many Sins of Omission, how many Sins of Commission must needs sprout from it. **1762** FOOTE *Orator* I, The luscious fruit sprouting from the apex of each of my ramifications. **1879** B. TAYLOR *Germ. Lit.* 141 Verse sprouting from verse as simply as leaf from leaf. **1882** VINES tr. *Sachs' Bot.* 282 Since the filaments which produce the antheridia and oogonia sprout from it. **1904** HICHENS *Garden of Allah* Prel. iv, A straggling black moustache sprouted on his upper lip.

transf. **1832** G. DOWNES *Lett. Cont. Countries* I. 4 A light-blue striped pair of pantaloons, sprouting from an enormous pair of wooden boots.

b. Const. with adverbs, as *forth*, *out*, *up*.

1530 PALSGR. 730/2, I sprowte out, or spring out, as yonge floures, or buddes, or the grasse doth, *je poings*. **1604** E. G[RIMSTONE] *D'Acosta's Hist. Indies* IV. viii. 228 Like as out of the great armes of trees, there commonly sprout foorth lesse. **1626** BACON *Sylva* §407 That Leafe faded, but the young Buds did sprout on. **1665** HOOKE *Microgr.* 40 Neer the root of this Plant, were sprouted out several small Branches. **1774** GOLDSM. *Nat. Hist.* (1776) I. 293 Among their clifts..various substances sprout forward, which are either really vegetables, or the nests of insects. **1837** P. KEITH *Bot. Lex.* 92 The shoots or branches..are no sooner browsed or bitten off than an increased number of new ones begin to sprout up in their place. **1861** J. R. GREENE *Man. Anim. Kingd.*, *Cœlent.* 171 In most *Zoantharia* either five or six tentacles first sprout forth.

fig. **1596** DALRYMPLE tr. *Leslie's Hist. Scot.* I. 210 The ruites of the Pelagian hæresie, now spruitting vpe litle and litle. **1641** MILTON *Prel. Episc.* Wks. 1851 III. 84 The warme effusion of his last blood, that sprouted up into eternall Roses to crowne his Martyrdome. **1660** F. BROOKE tr. *Le Blanc's Trav.* 14 From this cursed Doctrine are sprouted forth many diverse Sects. **1677** YARRANTON *Eng. Improv.* 22 Out of such a Bank will sprout out many Lumber houses and smaller Banks, to quicken Trade. **1732** BERKELEY *Alciphr.* II. §23 You shall see natural and just ideas sprout forth of themselves.

transf. **1870** ROCK *Text. Fabr.* 63 Gold thread sprouting up like loops.

c. Of persons: To originate or spring.

1582 STANYHURST *Æneis* III. (Arb.) 75 From whence [*sc.* Hesperus] oure auncetrye sprouted. **1612** T. TAYLOR *Comm. Titus* Ded., Cham, of whome quickely sprowted that cursed race of the Cananites. *a* **1653** GOUGE *Comm. Heb.* ii. 17 The stock whence all men sprout was most impure and unholy.

2. Of a tree, plant, seed, etc.: To put forth, throw up or out, a sprout or sprouts; to develop new growths or shoots; to bud.

a **1300** *Cursor M.* 11216 He þat þe walud wand moght ger In a night leif and fruit ber,..And in a night sua did it sprute To flur and fruit. *c* **1440** *Promp. Parv.* 471/1 Sproutyn, or burionyn,..*pululo*. **1562** TURNER *Herbal* II. (1568) 156 Tribulus that hath the pricks in the leaues doth spruit or bud oute later. **1626** BACON *Sylva* §604 There be very few Creatures, that participate of the Nature of Plants, and Metalls both; Corall is one..: Another is Vitriol, for that is aptest to sprout with Moisture. **1632** SANDERSON *Serm.* 554 An egge may be hatched into a bird, and a kirnell sprowt and grow into a tree. **1765** *Museum Rust.* IV. 288 According to the time each sort of seed may require to sprout. *c* **1787** G. WHITE *Selborne* ii, The tree sprouted for a time, then withered and died. **1832** HT. MARTINEAU *Life in Wilds* ii. 27 Robertson lets the seed fall into the ground, and it sprouts. **1847** TENNYSON *Princ.* IV. 187 But his brows Had sprouted, and the branches thereupon spread out at top. **1862** GOULBURN *Pers. Relig.* ii. (1873) 11 If a branch does not sprout, and put forth leaf and blossom in the spring, we know that it is a dead branch.

fig. **1655** FULLER *Ch. Hist.* III. 25 Let him now get but the stump of a Crown, and with wise watering thereof, it would sprout afterwards. **1856** BOKER *Poems*, etc. (1857) II. 1 Should his money sprout and yield a thousand fold. **1878** T. L. CUYLER *Pointed Papers* 6 The evangelist let fall the only seed that can sprout into a true regeneration.

b. Const. with adverbs, as *forth*, *out*, *up*.

1589 R. ROBINSON *A Golden Mirrour* (Chetham Soc.) 20 Each spray was sprouted out with buds. **1610** HOLLAND *Camden's Brit.* 227 The Hawthorne, which upon Christmas-day sprouteth forth as well as in May. **1651** FRENCH *Distill.* v. 117 Untill the Wheat begin to germinate, or to sprout forth. **1711** ADDISON *Spect.* No. 98 ¶1 Like Trees new lopped and pruned, that will certainly sprout up and flourish with greater Heads than before. **1765** *Museum Rust.* IV. 256 The remaining part of the herb must be mowed close to the ground; after which it continueth to sprout out again. **1842** LOUDON *Suburban Hort.* 686 If they are cut off close to the collar of the plant, it will sprout out again. **1846** J. BAXTER *Libr. Pract. Agric.* (ed. 4) I. 259 The young plants..are thus encouraged to sprout out.

fig. **1657** *North's Plutarch, Add. Lives* (1676) 2 The Christians being settled in Peace again, the Church began to sprout out and flourish anew. **1743** J. DAVIDSON *Æneid* (1826) II. 135 Into so many shapes she turns herself,..with so many snakes the grim Fury sprouts up.

c. *spec.* To germinate, begin to grow, prematurely.

1685 *Rector's Bk. Clayworth* (1910) 70 The Harvest was wett, wch caused our wheat to sprout. **1763** MILLS *Pract. Husb.* II. 305 The error of sowing wheat that had sprouted. **1846** J. BAXTER *Libr. Pract. Agric.* (ed. 4) II. 213 Occasionally brushing off the eyes [of potatoes] if they have a tendency to sprout. **1860** *All Year Round* No. 74. 560 To lift some corn that was sprouting in the field in consequence of wet weather. **1886** *Pall Mall G.* 8 Nov. 2/2 Many a field of corn is sprouted which by a little more promptitude would have been saved with ease.

3. *transf.* Of earth, a surface, etc.: To bear, bring forth, or produce sprouts or sprout-like growths. Freq. const. *with* (a growth).

1591 SYLVESTER *Du Bartas* II. i. *Chaos* 555 The Night.. Moistens our Aire, and makes our Earth to sprout. **1822–7** GOOD *Study Med.* (1829) I. 479 Thus the strumous modification is sometimes found to have sprouted with fungous caruncles. **1854** ALLINGHAM *Day & Nt. Songs*, *Dirty Old Man* iii, The window-sills sprouted with mildewy grass. *a* **1884** T. WINTHROP *Love & Skates* (Cent.), After a shower a meadow sprouts with the yellow buds of the dandelion.

4. *trans.* To cause (branches, leaves, etc.) to grow or shoot; to bear or develop, to put or throw *forth* or *out*, as sprouts.

1601 DOLMAN *La Primaud. Fr. Acad.* (1618) III. 793 These mountaine Pines sprout their branches out of their roote close to the earth. **1626** BACON *Sylva* §585 [These trees] are more lasting than those which sprout their leaues early or shed them betimes. **1733** W. ELLIS *Chiltern & Vale Farm.* 198 That will cause it in a little time to sprout out a small Radicle. **1818** KEATS *Endym.* I. 14 Trees old, and young, sprouting a shady boon For simple sheep. **1827** HOOD *Mids. Fairies* ii, I..bade that bounteous season bloom again, And sprout fresh flowers in mine own domain.

b. *transf.* and *fig.*

1598 BARRET *Theor. Warres* IV. i. 120 Wealth bred their pride; their pride sprouted ambition. **1659** HAMMOND *On Ps.* ciii. 5 The new or young feathers, which the old Eagle yearly sprouts out. **1684** *Contempl. St. Man* I. v. (1699) 52 The Earth..sprouts out Miseries and Deaths even of whole Cities. **1711** W. SUTHERLAND *Shipbuild. Assist.* 2 How curiously their Fins are furl'd up, and again sprouted out at pleasure. **1819** LAMB *Elia* Ser. I. *On Acting of Munden*, When you think he has exhausted his battery of looks,.. suddenly he sprouts out an entirely new set of features, like Hydra. **1865** CARLYLE *Fredk. Gt.* XXI. iii. (1872) IX. 309 Several Lernean Hydras..getting their heads lopped off, and at the same time sprouting new ones.

†**5.** *refl.* To divide or ramify. *Obs.*$^{-1}$

1705 tr. *Bosman's Guinea* 426 This River sprouts it self into innumerable Branches.

6. a. To cause or induce (plants, seeds, etc.) to develop sprouts or shoots, esp. before planting or sowing them.

1770 *A. Hunter's Georg. Ess.* (1803) I. 62, I have sprouted all kinds of grain in a variety of steeps. **1840** J. BUEL *Farmer's Companion* 248 Another mode of preventing failure..in the growth of certain seeds—and that is, by *sprouting* them before they are planted. **1895** *Outing* XXVII. 18/2 The plants are sprouted within doors.

b. *dial.* and *U.S.* (See quot.)

1828 CARR *Craven Gloss.*, *Sprout*, to rub or break off the sprouts of potatoes. **1891** in *Cent. Dict.*

sprout, *v.*² *Obs.* exc. *dial.* [Cf. Norw. and Sw. *spruta*, Da. *sprude*, in sense 1, related to LG. *sprutten*, *sprütte* (hence Da. *sprutte*), MHG. and G. *sprützen*, and perh. identical in stem with prec.]

1. *trans.* To send forth in a spout or gush; to spout or pour *out*; to squirt.

1592 R. D. *Hypnerotomachia* 34 Her [the statue's] smal teates..did sprowt out smal streamings of pure..water. **1646** J. HALL *Poems* I. 65 What dost thou thinke I can retaine All this and sprout it out againe? As a surcharged Whale doth spew Old Rivers to receive in new. **1886–** in Lanc. and Yks. dialect use.

2. *intr.* To issue in a spout or gush. Also *transf.* of the sun: To pour down rays.

1611 COTGR., *Iallir*, to spurt out, sprowt vp,..as water forced out of a spout. **1614** GORGES *Lucan* VI. 242 The wether-beaten paunch she cast Out of the corpes, and then at last She lets the sunne thereon to sprout. **1624** WOTTON *Arch.* 112 By the turning of a cocke, they [i.e. pipes] did sprout ouer interchangeably from side to side. **1650** BULWER *Anthropomet.* 181 Who had such abundance of milk in hir breasts, as was not only sufficient to suckle a Child, but it moreover sprouted out exuberantly.

'sproutage. *rare.* [f. SPROUT *sb.*¹ + -AGE.] Sprouts collectively; new growth. In quot. *fig.*

1860 MASSON in *Macm. Mag.* II. 7 The rate of the [literary] growth, the amount of fresh sproutage that shall appear.

sprout-cale. (See quot.)

An erroneous rendering of older Flem. *sprock-kelle* (Du. *sprokkelmaand*, G. dial. *sporkel*, *spurkel*).

1778 G. WHITE *Selborne* lxxix, Our Saxon ancestors certainly had some sort of cabbage, because they call the month of February sprout-cale.

sprouted ('spraʊtɪd), *ppl. a.*¹ [f. SPROUT *v.*¹] That has developed a sprout or sprouts; *spec.* of corn that has germinated prematurely.

1483 *Cath. Angl.* 357/1 Sprowtyd benys, *fabefrese*. **1583** STUBBES *Anat. Abus.* II. (1882) 47 In the middest shall be neuer a good corne, but such as is mustie sprouted, and naught. **1763** MILLS *Pract. Husb.* II. 306 This was likewise sowed with sprouted corn. **1766** *Complete Farmer* s.v. *Madder*, I likewise sowed at the same time some of this sprouted seed. **1832** *Scoreby Farm Rep.* 8 in *Husb.* III. (L.U.K.), This..is not unfrequently the cause of a crop being sprouted and damp. **1842** LOUDON *Suburban Hort.* 641 Planting either sets, or sprouted sets,..will produce potatoes fit to gather about the end of May. **1883** *Knowledge* 20 July 43/2 It is..far better to plant sprouted [beet] seeds.

†**sprouted**, *ppl. a.*² *Obs.* [f. SPROUT *v.*²] Spouted, sprayed.

1644 DIGBY *Nat. Bodies* viii. §1. 53 And the like is of mistes; as also of the sprouted water to make a perfume.

'sprouter. [f. SPROUT *v.*¹] **1.** One who or that which causes plants, etc., to sprout. *rare.*

1585 JAS. I. *Ess. Poesie* (Arb.) 14 And first, ô Phœbus, when I do descriue The Springtyme sproutar of the herbes and flowris.

2. A container in which seeds (esp. of mung beans) are sprouted.

1971 *Health Food Age* June 33/2 (Advt.), Get more vitamins daily with a seed sprouter. *Ibid.*, Be one of the first to get a Miracle Seed Sprouter. **1977** C. MCFADDEN *Serial* (1978) xvii. 41/2 She was starting mung beans in her sprouter.

sprouting ('spraʊtɪŋ), *vbl. sb.*¹ [f. SPROUT *v.*¹]

1. The action of the verb, in various senses; an instance or occasion of this.

1547 BOORDE *Brev. Health* ccxc. 96 A sprowtyng or burstyng out in the secret places of manne and woman;.. some doth name it ych for the pacient must crache and clawe. **1580** HOLLYBAND *Treas. Fr. Tong*, *Germement*, a budding, a sprouting. **1635** SWAN *Spec. M.* vi. §1 (1643) 183 The third [matter] is pertinent to the sprouting and springing of the earth. **1677** GILPIN *Demonol.* (1867) 41 These sacrificings were used..at the sprouting of their corn. **1763** MILLS *Pract. Husb.* II. 336 The autumn was.. favourable to the sprouting of the corn. **1813** SIR H. DAVY *Agric. Chem.* (1814) 216 The process of malting should be carried on no farther than to produce the sprouting of the radicle. **1846** J. BAXTER *Libr. Pract. Agric.* (ed. 4) I. 87 A second sprouting [of cabbages] takes place at the end of March. **1906** *Brit. Med. Jrnl.* 13 Jan. 63 A periodical sprouting of irregular pale excrescences.

fig. **1640** BP. REYNOLDS *Passions* xv. 144 Though perhaps Feare may prevent the exercise and sproutings, nothing but Love can pluck up the root of sinne. **1673** O. WALKER *Educ.* ii. 19 Prevent the very first beginnings, and sprowtings of bad actions. **1768–74** TUCKER *Lt. Nat.* (1834) II. 630 Nor can you be too vigilant to watch the sprouting of evil weeds that may start up in them from time to time.

b. *attrib.*, as *sprouting condition*, *time*.

1601 HOLLAND *Pliny* I. 501 Winter raine principally is seasonable and good for all plants: and next to it the dewes and showers that fal immediatly before their sprouting time. **1733** W. ELLIS *Chiltern & Vale Farm.* 211 It is brought into a sprouting Condition.

2. A sprout, new growth, or shoot. Also *transf.*

1578 LYTE *Dodoens* 380 It hath small tender branches or spruytinges. *Ibid.* 383 The first springes or spruytinges are very good to be eaten. **1665** HOOKE *Microgr.* 194 Like the strings or sproutings of the herb Horse-tail. **1728** GARDINER *Rapin on Gardens* II. 70 The tender Sproutings only let them spare, For Shoots yet weak require protecting Care. **1762** R. GUY *Pract. Obs. Cancers* 123 In another Week the Sproutings of Flesh began to go away. **1822–7** GOOD *Study Med.* (1829) V. 612 The incrustation accompanied with horn-like, incurvated sproutings.

fig. **1649** BP. REYNOLDS *Hosea* vi. 87 The tender buds and sproutings of piety that are wrought within us. **1838** TUPPER *Proverb. Philos.* (1849) 245 Neither were the sproutings of his soul seared by the brand of superstition.

3. The spitting or sputtering of molten metal.

1891 in *Cent. Dict.*

ˈsprouting, *vbl. sb.*[2] *rare*−0. [f. SPROUT *v.*[2]] The action of sprouting.

1611 COTGR., *Iallissement*, a spurting, sprowting, spouting, or spinning vp (of water).

ˈsprouting, *ppl. a.* [f. SPROUT *v.*[1]] That sprouts, in senses of the verb.

1. Of buds, plants, etc.

1590 GREENE *Never too late* (1600) 20 His graue wisdom exceedes thy greene wit, and his ripened fruits thy sprouting blossomes. **1633** P. FLETCHER *Poet. Misc.*, *To Master W. C.*, Here thou and I, under the sprouting vine,.. Will sit. **1641** G. SANDYS *Paraphr. Song Solom.* II. iv, Green Figs on sprouting trees appear. **1721** RAMSAY *Content* 2 When genial beams..from the clod invite the sprouting corn. **1870** BRYANT *Iliad* VI. I. 189 The sprouting wood Puts forth another brood.

b. ***sprouting broccoli***, a kind of broccoli producing sprouts.

1852 G. W. JOHNSON *Cottage Gard. Dict.* 149 Purple or Green Brocoli:..4 Sprouting. *Syn.*, Italian Sprouting, Grange's Early Purple Sprouting [etc.]. **1895** *Daily News* 20 April 5/4 Sprouting broccoli and turnip tops are the cheapest green vegetables.

2. Of outgrowths from animal bodies.

1681 DRYDEN *Abs. & Achit.* 542 But a whole Hydra more Remains of sprouting heads too long to score. **1739** S. SHARP *Surg.* p. xix, Since Sloughs are flung off by the sprouting new Flesh underneath. **1771** *Encycl. Brit.* III. 644 Dry lint ..at the same time is an easy compress upon the sprouting fungus. **1822–7** GOOD *Study Med.* (1829) I. 394 The hemorrhoidal vessels..that form or supply the sprouting tumours. **1888** E. GERARD *Land beyond Forest* II. xlv. 236 He..had a small sallow face, a sprouting moustache, and dark eyes.

sproutling (ˈspraʊtlɪŋ). [f. SPROUT *sb.*[1] Cf. WFlem. *spruiteling*.] A little or young sprout. Also *attrib.* In quots. *fig.*

1838 *Blackw. Mag.* XLIII. 314 When Thiers the sproutling rebel began his career of rebellion at the soirées of M. Lafitte. **1876** T. S. EGAN tr. *Heine's Atta Troll*, etc. 30 My child, thou latest sproutling Of my loins.

Sprowese, variant of SPRUCE *sb.*

sprowl, obs. Sc. variant of SPRAWL *v.*

sprowsie (ˈspraʊzɪ). *slang.* Also **sprouse, sprowser.** [Prob. var. of SPRAZER.] Sixpence; a sixpenny piece.

1931 'G. ORWELL' in *Coll. Essays* (1968) I. 70 *Sprowsie, a*, a sixpence. **1933** —— *Down & Out in Paris & London* xxxii. 236 These..are some of the cant words now used in London... A hog—a shilling. A sprowsie—sixpence. **1960** A. PRIOR in *Pick of Today's Short Stories* XI. 180, I walked across to the record player and took some silver out of my pocket... 'Half-Nelson, do me a favour and put a sprouse in there for me... I've got no change.' **1966** F. SHAW et al. *Lern Yerself Scouse* 34/2 *Sprowser*, sixpenny piece.

Spruce (spruːs), *sb.* Also 4 **Sprws, Sprwys,** 5 **Sprewse,** 6 **Sprewce;** 5–7 **Sprusse,** 5–6 **Spruse,** 6 **Sprus,** 7 *Sc.* **Spruch.** [Alteration of PRUCE, Prussia: cf. SPRUCIA.]

I. †**1.** The country of Prussia. Also ***Spruce-land***.

See also PRUCE 2a, quot. 1377.

1378 *Durh. Acc. Rolls* (Surtees) 47 In xxiiij piscibus de sprws empt., ij *s.* **14..** *Chaucer's Dethe Blaunche* 1025 (MS. Bodl. 638), She wolde not..send men yn-to Walakye, To Sprewse & yn-to Tartarye. **1521** in Ellis *Orig. Lett.* Ser. II. I. 292 The expedition of the Gentlemen of Spruce. *c* **1550** BALE *K. Johan* (Camden) 9 In Sycell, in Naples, in Venys and Ytalye, In Pole, Spruse and Berne. **1639** FULLER *Holy War* v. iii. 233 They busied themselves in defending of Christendome,..as the Teutonick order defended Spruce-land against the Tartarian. **1656** G. ABBOT *Descr. World* 69 On the east and north corner of Germany lyeth a country called Prussia, in English Pruthen or Spruce.

†**b.** *attrib.* in the sense of 'brought or obtained from Prussia', as ***Spruce board, canvas, chest, coffer***, etc. *Obs.*

In some instances implying 'made of spruce fir'.

1497 *Naval Acc. Hen. VII* (1896) 321, vj *spruce bordes. **1545** *Rates of Customes* a v b, Canuas called *sprewce canuas the hundreth elles xx. s. **1640** in Entick *London* (1766) II. 167 Linnens: Gutting and spruce canvas. **1656** *Act Commw.* c. 20 Rates (1658) 470 Packing Canvas, Guttings, and Spruce Canvas. **1461** *Paston Lett.* II. 37 On of the canvas baggis in the gret cofir, or in the *spruse chest. **1540** *North Country Wills* (Surtees) 174 The spruse chest which is in my litle chamber. **1445** *Test. Ebor.* (Surtees) II. 195 j cistam vocatam *sprusse coffre. **1522** *Wills & Inv. N.C.* (Surtees, 1860) 106, I bequeathe to my said Wyffe..a spruse coffer. **1489** *Will of R. Parbrich* (P.C.C., 1 Dogett), My *spruce Compter and Euidences in the same. **1523** in *Visit. Southwell* (Camden) 121 A *spruce countre & a cup boorde. **1614** GENTLEMAN *Engl. Way to Wealth* 13 Tarre, mastes, and *Spruce-deales. **1626** CAPT. SMITH *Accid. Yng. Seamen* 10 Laying that Decke with spruce deale of 30 foot long. **1670** J. SMITH *Eng. Improv. Reviv'd* 190 Neer the Water are severall small Hutches made of boords for the *Spruce Ducks to lay their Eggs in. **1524** in *Rep. MSS. Ld. Middleton* (1911) 372 Item paid..for vj *spruce elles,..vj s. **1378** *Durh. Acc. Rolls* (Surtees) 47 In xl *sprwysfisc emp. vj s. viij *d.* **1493** *Bury Wills* (Camden) 82, I beqwethe to Anneys my doughter a litell *spruce forcer. **1550–1600** *Customs Duties* (B.M. Addit. MS. 25097), Iron. voc. Lewkes, or *spruse iron. **1649** *Eng. Farrier* xiii, Make your shooe of spruse or Spanish Iron. **1597** *N. Country Wills* (Surtees) II. 175 My best gowne and a *spruce jerkyn. **1464** *Mann. & Househ. Exp.* (Roxb.) 195 My mastyr lent hym a payr breganderys wyth *sprewse leder. **1530** PALSGR. 274/2 Spruse lether, *besane.* **1593** NASHE *Four Lett. Conf.* Wks. (Grosart) II. 221 A Broker, in a spruce leather ierkin with a great number of golde Rings on his fingers. **1656** G. ABBOT *Descr. World* 70 The English do..bring from thence a kinde of leather, which was wont to be used in Jerkins, and called by the name of Spruce-Leather-Jerkins. **1706** PHILLIPS (ed. Kersey), *Spruce-Leather*, a sort of Leather corruptly so call'd for Prussia Leather. **1553** in Daniel-Tyssen *Surrey Ch. Goods* (1869) 106 For vj dossen of *spruse oker. **1687** J. SMITH *Art Painting* (ed. 2) 22 Yellow-Oaker is of two sorts, one called Plain-Oaker, and the other Spruce-Oaker. **1875** BEDFORD *Sailor's Pocket Bk.* x. (ed. 2) 367 Stained with burnt umber, and spruce ochre ground in oil. **1570** in Raine *Richmondshire Wills* (Surtees) 228 For ij *sprowese skynes. **1656** *Act Commw.* c. 20 Rates (1658) 475 Spruce skins tawed. **1588** *Shipping Lists Dundee* (S.H.S.) 225 Ihone Jak hes of takill 14 *spruiss stains. **1597** SKENE *De Verb. Sign.* s.v. *Serplath*, Ilk Sprusse stane conteinis twentie aucht pound Trois weicht. **1497** *Naval Acc. Hen. VII* (1896) 241 A maste of a *spruce tree..bought for the foremast of the seid ship. *Ibid.*, An other Spruce tre mast. **1511** *Acc. Ld. High Treas. Scot.* IV. 284, lxiiij pulleis of coppir, weyand vj[c]lxxxxj pund of *Spruce wecht. **1656** *Act Commw.* c. 20 Rates (1658) 477 *Spruce or Muscovia-yarn. **1711** *Lond. Gaz.* No. 4898/2 Polonia-Wool, Hogs-Bristles, Spruce-Yarn. **1572** in Feuillerat *Revels Q. Eliz.* (1908) 178 Wylliam Lyzarde for syze,..*spruce yolow,..Gowlde [etc.].

2. *ellipt.* †**a.** A Spruce coffer or chest. †**b.** Spruce leather. **c.** Spruce beer. †**d.** Spruce ochre.

a. **1481–90** *Howard Househ. Bks.* (Roxb.) 273 Item a sprusse conteining ij. coffres of my Lordes. **1507** *Pilton Churchw. Acc.* (Som. Rec. Soc.) 54 Item one spruc.

b. **1570** LEVINS *Manip.* 182 Spruce, *corium pumicatum.* **1611** J. DAVIES (Heref.) *Sco. Folly* Wks. (Grosart) II. 63/1 What present haue we here? A booke... What stuffe contains it? Fustian, perfect spruce.

c. **1741** G. BERKELEY in *C'tess Suffolk's Lett.* (1824) II. 182, I may hope to drink a bottle of spruce with you on Saturday night. **1793** PEARCE *Hartford Bridge* II. i, *Waiter.* I'll be as brisk, your honour, as bottled spruce in warm weather. **1826** J. F. COOPER *Mohicans* vi, 'Come, friend,' said Hawk-eye,..'try a little spruce'. **1837** DICKENS *Pickw.* xx, Printed cards, bearing reference to Devonshire cyder and Dantzic spruce. **1891** *Daily News* 23 Sept. 3/5 Witness gave him some hot spruce and ginger brandy, which eased him.

d. **1761** J. WHITE *Art's Treasury* 75 Spanish brown, burnt spruce, and umber.

†**3.** *collect.* The Prussian people. *Obs.*

1640 SIR W. MURE *Counter-Buff* 101 Wks. (S.T.S.) II. 6 All vaste Teuton's states, the Spruch, the Dan, Dispatch.. some trustie man, Stercovius to pursue.

II. (Now with lower case initial.) **4.** *ellipt.* = SPRUCE FIR.

Freq. with specific epithets, as ***black, red, white, hemlock, Canadian, Norway, Sitka spruce.***

1670 EVELYN *Sylva* (ed. 2) xxii. 103 For masts, &c., those [firs] of Prussia, which we call Spruce, and Norway..are the best. **1717** *Petiveriana* III. 213 Spruce or Hemlock-tree. **1772** *Phil. Trans.* LXII. 390 In Winter they taste strongly of the pine spruce, upon which they feed. **1792** BELKNAP *Hist. New Hampsh.* III. 110 The black spruce is used only for beer... Of this spruce, is made the essence, which is as well known in Europe as in America. **1824** SCOTT in *Lockhart* (1839) VII. 258 One set of insects is eating the larch, another the Spruce. **1846** J. BAXTER *Libr. Pract. Agric.* (ed. 4) II. 331 The larch, spruce, and pine, require less space than the oak, chestnut, elm, &c. **1874** STEWART & BRANDIS *Flora N. West India* 526 On the south side of the Alps the Spruce forms large forests in Friaul.

b. A species, or a single tree, of spruce fir.

1832 *Planting* (L.U.K.) 124/2 The white, black, and red spruces are of inferior value to the Norway. **1857** A. GRAY *First Less. Bot.* (1866) 25 The main stem of Pines and Spruces..is carried on in a direct line throughout the whole growth of the tree. **1904** 'Q' (QUILLER COUCH) *Fort Amity* xxvii, The fragrance of the young spruces.

c. The wood of the spruce fir.

1853 SIR H. DOUGLAS *Milit. Bridges* (ed. 3) 39 The balks are of white pine, or spruce;..the chesses also are of spruce or white pine. **1894** *Outing* XXIV. 191/1 The white spruce is a tough, springy timber, similar to ash.

d. An oar made of this wood.

1892 *Sporting Life* 26 March 7/5 They were to use the new Ayling oars, and the 'spruces' went much better than on the preceding day.

5. *attrib.* (in sense 4), as ***spruce bark, -bough, -cone, forest, green***, etc.; **spruce budworm**, the brown larva of a tortricid moth, *Choristoneura fumiferana*, which damages the foliage of spruce trees in North America; **spruce grouse**, (*a*) the spotted Canada grouse; (*b*) Franklin's grouse, *Canachites canadensis*; **spruce hen**, a female spruce grouse; **spruce partridge** = *spruce grouse* (*a*); **spruce pine**, one of several North American conifers, formerly esp. the bog or black spruce, *Picea mariana*, but now usually *Pinus glabra*; **spruce tea**, an infusion of tender spruce shoots.

Also *U.S.* in names of insects which attack spruce trees, as ***spruce-borer, saw-fly.***

1784 M. CUTLER in *Life*, etc. (1888) I. 101 Our ax-men.. built us a very comfortable tent with *spruce bark. **1888** MEREDITH *Poems* (1898) II. 145 Seeing..Our household's twinkle of light Through *spruce-boughs. **1884** *Rep. Comm. Agric.* (U.S. Dept. Agric.) 378 The Reddish-Yellow *Spruce-Bud Worm..was found to be very injurious to the white spruce. **1925** [see BIOCŒNOSIS]. **1976** *Maclean's Mag.* 3 May 56/3 Except for its larva..the spruce budworm is an unexceptional creature. **1783** LATHAM *Gen. Synop. Birds* II. II. 736 In winter [they] feed on *spruce-cones and juniper-berries. **1874** STEWART & BRANDIS *Flora N. West India* 529 Silver Fir is found in some of the *Spruce forests of Saxony and Thuringia. **1939** *Sun* (Baltimore) 11 Feb. 20/2 Enrollees of the Civilian Conservation Corps will be attired in new uniforms..of 'forest' or '*spruce' green. **1844** J. E. DEKAY *Zool. N.Y.* II. 206 The *Spruce Grouse... The flesh is bitter, and has a peculiar taste as if boiled in turpentine. **1874** COUES *Birds N.W.* 394 *Tetrao Canadensis*,.. Franklin's Spruce Grouse. **1946** T. M. STANWELL-FLETCHER *Driftwood Valley* 13 Several times we've scared up coveys of spruce grouse along the trail. **1966** *Kingston* (Ontario) *Whig-Standard* 21 Jan. 11/1 The spruce grouse is so retiring ..that few people get to see one. **1868** *Rep. U.S. Commissioner Agric.* (1869) 176 Frames of canoes..covered with its bark, sewed with spruce or tamarack..roots, and the seams calked with *spruce gum. **1894** *Outing* XXIII. 391/2 The seams are payed with melted spruce-gum, which effectually prevents leakage. **1902** W. D. HULBERT *Forest Neighbors* 87 *Spruce hens and partridges. **1959** W. A. LEISING *Arctic Wings* 31, I had not seen the spruce hen until the shot bird came tumbling out of the tree. **1971** A. FRY *Long Journey* vii. 41 We came on half a dozen spruce hens. **1771** W. RICHARDSON *Jrnl.* in *Canad. Hist. Rev.* (1935) XVI. 57 There are more *spruce Partridges in the woods than I have seen anywhere in this country. **1774** *Phil. Trans.* LXIV. 377 The red-game, with a smaller sort which resemble them, called the spruce-partridge. **1783** LATHAM *Gen. Synop. Birds* II. II. 736 These [Spotted Grouse] are met with at Hudson's Bay, where they are called Wood or Spruce Partridges. **1872** COUES *N. Amer. Birds* 232 *Tetrao falcipennis* of Siberia, the representative of our spruce partridge. **1917** T. G. PEARSON *Birds Amer.* II. 15/1 There is no such bird as the Spruce Partridge. It is the Spruce Grouse. **1963** *Calgary Herald* 4 Oct. 27/7 Spruce partridge and Franklin's grouse season has been open since Aug. 31. **1765** J. BARTRAM *Jrnl.* 25 Sept. in *Trans. Amer. Philos. Soc.* (1942) XXXIII. 30/2 Y[e] 2 leaved or *spruice pine grows very large in swamps. **1842** M. CRAWFORD *Jrnl.* 10 Sept. (1897) 19, I noticed the White Pine and the Spruce Pine. **1886** *Outing* VIII. 60/2 One morning I entered a clump of bushes near a spruce-pine thicket. **1913** H. KEPHART *Our Southern Highlanders* xiii. 295 The hemlock tree is named spruce-pine. **1949** *Boston Globe Mag.* 4 Dec. 11/2 He went up to the white 'Honor Roll' board nailed to a big spruce pine. **1967** N. T. MIROV *Genus Pinus* iii. 183 *Pinus glabra* (spruce pine) is the least common pine of the southeastern United States. **1862** *Chambers's Encycl.* IV. 334/1 The true *Spruce Rosin flows spontaneously from the bark. **1783** in *New Brunswick Mag.* (1899) II. 320 Some chocolate is wanted for our Masting Camp for at present we use *Spruce Tea which causes sum murmuring. **1936** *Discovery* Jan. 31/1 That unpalatable beverage, spruce tea. **1956** *Beaver* Summer 18, I lashed out strong laxatives all round and ordered spruce tea to be brewed and administered constantly. **1782** RAYMOND *Statist. Mines & Mining* 152 A mountain thickly covered with pine and *spruce timber. **1870** MORRIS *Earthly Par.* II. III. 76 Midst rank grass a *spruce-tree stood. **1792** BELKNAP *Hist. New-Hampsh.* III. 265 In some of the new towns a liquor is made of *spruce twigs, boiled in maple sap. **1868** MORRIS *Earthly Par.* (1870) I. I. 171 Then with their melancholy sound The odorous *spruce woods met around.

spruce (spruːs), *a.* and *adv.* Also 6–7 **spruse,** 7 **sprewse,** 8–9 *Sc.* **sprush.** [perh. from SPRUCE *sb.* 1 b in the collocation *spruce* (*leather*) *jerkin*: cf. quot. 1609 in sense 2 b.]

†**1.** Brisk, smart, lively. *Obs.*

In early quots. probably implying sense 2.

1589 R. HARVEY *Pl. Perc.* 14 There steps me in a third tricksie, neat, nimble, spruse Artificer. **1598** E. GUILPIN *Skial.* (1878) 21 Fine spruce young Pansa's growne a malcontent. **1606** WARNER *Alb. Eng.* XVI. ci. (1612) 399 The sprewsest Citie-Lads for his would faine the Countrie-aire. **1691** WOOD *Ath. Oxon.* II. 496 He was a person..of a quick, warm, spruce and gay-fancy. **1705** HICKERINGILL *Priest-cr.* II. vii. 68 A Young Gentleman (of Spruce Natural Parts, and Ingenuous Disposition).

transf. **1634** MILTON *Comus* 985 Along the crisped shades and bowres Revels the spruce and jocond Spring. **1642** H. MORE *Song of Soul* IV. x, Here Aristophanes Doth maken sport with some spruce Comedy. **1749** CHESTERF. *Lett.* ccii. (1792) II. 265 A spruce, lively air, fashionable dress; and all the glitter that a young fellow should have.

2. Trim, neat, dapper; smart in appearance: **a.** Of persons, in respect of dress, etc. Also *transf.*

α. **1599** B. JONSON *Ev. Man out of Hum.* Charact. Persons, A Neat, spruce, affecting Courtier, one that weares clothes well, and in fashion. **1602** BRETON *Wonders Worth Hearing* Wks. (Grosart) II. 12/2 These youths of the parish, that are so spruse in their apparell, haue little money in their purses. *a* **1680** BUTLER *Rem.* (1759) II. 111 He fancies himself a dainty spruce Shepherd, with a Flock and a fine silken Shepherdess, that follows his Pipe. **1718** *Freethinker* No. 29. 206 Notwithstanding the Gilt Chariot,..the spruce Figure within is but an Idol. **1796** MME. D'ARBLAY *Camilla* IV. 163 He'll make himself so spruce, he says, we sha'n't know him again. **1818** CREEVEY in *C. Papers* (1904) I. 279 He was singularly smug and spruce in his attire,..in new cloaths from top to bottom. **1876** T. HARDY *Ethelberta* I. 209 Making themselves as spruce as bridegrooms of a mild kind, according to the rules of their newly-acquired town experience.

β. **1719** W. HAMILTON *Ep.* II. xii. in *Ramsay's Poems*, And then thou'd be sae far frae shabby, Thou'd look right sprush. *a* **1774** FERGUSSON *On Seeing a Butterfly* Poems (1845) 18 Kind Nature lent, but for a day, Her wings to mak ye sprush and gay. **1840** A. LAING *Wayside Flowers* (1878) 144 Mak' the bridegroom sprush and gay.

b. Of apparel, appearance, etc.

1609 DEKKER *Gull's Horn-bk.* Wks. (Grosart) II. 202 Euen he that iets vpon the neatest and sprucest leather..will be glad to fit themselues in Will Sommer his wardrob. **1653** W. RAMESEY *Astrol. Rest.* 242 [They] shall endeavour to live neatly and in a comely spruce manner. **1709** STEELE *Tatler* No. 49 ⁋8 The spruce Nightcap of his Valet. **1755** YOUNG *Centaur* ii. Wks. 1757 IV. 148 Your spruce appearance is a perfect forgery. **1828** SCOTT *F.M. Perth* viii, Altogether exhibiting an aspect..unlike the spruce and dapper importance of his ordinary appearance. **1853** C. BRONTË *Villette* v, Her spruce attire flaunted an easy scorn to my plain garb.

Comb. **1602** *2nd Pt. Return fr. Parnass.* II. v. 765 Wold it not gal a man to see a spruse gartered youth..be a broker for a liuing.

c. Of places, buildings, etc.

1639 FULLER *Holy War* v. xxii. 267 Norway in that age the sprucest of the three kingdomes of Scandia, and best tricked up with shipping. 1642 —— *Holy & Prof. St.* II. xxiii. 147 Commonly some new spruce town, not farre off, is grown out of the ashes thereof. 1682 WHELER *Journ. Greece* VI. 439 The Houses are more spruce here than ordinary. 1781 HAYLEY *Triumphs Temper* (1807) 30 Where spruce in motley pride, his villa stands. 1792 A. YOUNG *Trav. France* 249 What would a Watson.. or a Priestley say, upon a proposal to have their laboratories brushed out clean and spruce? 1856 EMERSON *Eng. Traits, Stonehenge* Wks. (Bohn) II. 127 The Cathedral [of Salisbury], which was finished 600 years ago, has even a spruce and modern air. 1865 DICKENS *Mut. Fr.* I. vi, Many a sprucer public-house.

d. In miscellaneous uses.

1648 J. BEAUMONT *Psyche* VI. xciii, Of younger Serpents an intangled fry Thick in the sprucer Networks twisted were. 1657 G. THORNLEY *Daphnis & Chloe* 171 These were encompassed with a spruce, thin hedge. 1706 J. PHILIPS *Imit. Milton* 121 Small need of art To form spruce architrave or cornice quaint. 1840 DICKENS *Old C. Shop* xl, Kit rubbed down the pony and made him as spruce as a race-horse. 1863 KINGLAKE *Crimea* (1877) III. i. 248 The spruce beauty of the slender red line.

e. Of immaterial things.

1602 MARSTON *Ant. & Mel.* Induct., He speakes with a spruce attick accent of adulterate Spanish. 1658 SIR T. BROWNE *Hydriot.* Ded., He that will illustrate the excellency of this order, may easily fall upon so spruce a Subject. 1687 MIÉGE *Gt. Fr. Dict.* II. s.v., A spruce Phrase, for a fine Phrase, *une belle Phrase*. 1822 HAZLITT *Table T.* xxvi, My sensations are all glossy, spruce, voluptuous, and fine.

Comb. 1721 RAMSAY *Answer to Burchet* 22 When the pride of sprush-new words are laid.

3. *adv.* = SPRUCELY *adv.*

*a*1618 J. DAVIES (Heref.) *Wit's Pilgr.* xci, Ile speake more spruce, yet call a Spade, a Spade. *a*1796 BURNS *Tither Morn* ii, His bonnet he, a thought ajee, Cock'd sprush when first he clasp'd me. 1824 SCOTT *Redgauntlet* ch. ix, Cock up your beaver, and cock it fu' sprush.

spruce (spruːs), *v.*[1] Also 7 spruse. [f. prec.]

1. *trans.* To make spruce, trim, or neat.

1594 NASHE *Terrors of Night* To Rdr., You shal haue them ..spend a whole twelue month in spunging & sprucing them. 1642 H. MORE *Song of Soul* I. II. 39 Then gan the learn'd and ag'd Don Psittaco..To spruse his plumes, and wisdome sage to show. 1671 tr. *Palafox's Conq. China* iv. 90 To cut off their hair which the Chinese love..and take great care to spruce and perfume it. 1756 *Gentl. Mag.* XXVI. 444 Paid Lavender's man for sprucing my garden. 1772 NUGENT *Hist. Fr. Gerund* I. 362 Our Friar Gerund was so.. smugged, and spruced, that it was a delight to behold his face.

refl. 1637 HEYWOOD *Pleas. Dial.* No. 4 Wks. 1874 VI. 191 Himselfe he spruceth, studieth to be fine. 1683 tr. *Erasm. Moriae Encomium* 44 Another shall spruce himself in a light periwig. 1703 *Rules Civility* 57 An old Man or Woman trimm'd up like young People of Eighteen, would make us believe they had spruc'd themselves so for no other end. 1903 J. CONRAD & HUEFFER *Romance* v. 40 He had spruced himself, but I seemed to see the rags still flutter about him.

b. With *up*.

1676 ETHEREDGE *Man of Mode* III. iii, I took particular notice of one that is alwaies spruc'd up with a deal of dirty sky-colur'd Ribband. *a*1704 T. BROWN *Lett. Ser. & Com.* Wks. 1709 III. 126 Madam D——, whom you are so angry with for..sprucing up her decay'd Person. 1748 LADY LUXBOROUGH *Lett. Shenstone* 27 June, My slovenly garden, which cannot be weeded, nor in the least spruced up, till my hay is all in. 1853 FELTON *Fam. Lett.* xlv. (1865) 336, I do not think you would have known my coat, hardly me, so spruced up were both of us. 1894 H. NISBET *Bush Girl's Rom.* 135 When washed and spruced up they looked and talked not unlike gentlemen.

fig. 1672 EACHARD *Lett.* 21 Out comes the Vindicationer, and spruces up this objection.

refl. 1621 BURTON *Anat. Mel.* III. ii. IV. i, Salmacis would not be seen of Hermaphroditus, till she had spruced up her self first. 1674 tr. *Scheffer's Lapland* 111 Woollen Cloth-Garments (such as they use to spruce themselves up withal, at their public Festivals, or more solemn affairs). 1749 MRS. DELANY *Life & Corr.* (1861) II. 532 Mrs. Foley's, where I was to spruce myself up a little before dinner. 1862 SALA *Seven Sons* II. v. 138 [She] spruced herself up to the extent of putting on..a black silk jacket. 1895 SNAITH *Mistress Dorothy Marvin* xli, Go spruce yourself up a bit.

†**2.** *intr.* With *it*: To be spruce or trim. *Obs. rare.*

1611 COTGR., *Faire la fringue*, to iet, brag, spruce it, wantonnize it. *Ibid.* s.v. *Garber*.

3. With *up* (or †*out*): To make oneself spruce.

1709 MRS. MANLEY *Secret Mem.* I. 176 His Father and grandfather are..profess'd Sparks, and spruce up in Cherry and other gaudy colour'd silk Stockings. 1746 MRS. DELANY *Life & Corr.* (1861) II. 443 We return home at two and spruce out, dinner at half an hour after two. 1833 [SEBA SMITH] *Lett. J. Downing* ii. (1835) 35 To-night we're goin to a quiltin at Uncle Josh's. Miss Willoby..is sprucin up for it. 1869 MRS. STOWE *Old Town* xvii, All of a sudden, Dench.. seemed to kind o' spruce up and have a deal o' money to spend.

spruce, *v.*[2] *slang* (orig. *Mil.*). [Of unknown origin.] **a.** *intr.* To lie, practise deception; to evade a duty, malinger. Also with quasi-obj. **b.** *trans.* To deceive.

1917 W. MUIR *Observ. Orderly* xiv. 230 To spruce is to dodge duty or to deceive. A man who contrived to slip out of the ranks of a squad when they were performing some distasteful task would be said to 'spruce off'. 1919 *Athenæum* 8 Aug. 728/1 *Spruce*, deceive. 1925 FRASER & GIBBONS *Soldier & Sailor Words* 267 *Spruce*.., to lie. To deceive. 1951 A. BARON *Rosie Hogarth* 222 Write your own cheque. It's yours for the asking..Go on! I ain't sprucing. 1967 G. M. WILSON *Cake for Caroline* vi. 71 Dr. Meunier's no fool, he'd have known if she was sprucing..Malingering. Faking tummy trouble. 1969 H. CARVIC *Miss Seeton draws Line* ix. 172 Them two old tarts at the Nut House, they spruced you proper. 1970 A. HUNTER *Gently with Innocents* xiii. 166 The coin is damning. He can't spruce his way round that. 1978 *Daily Tel.* 26 May 16 A kipper..by inference, should cost more than the untreated fish. Who is sprucing whom?

Hence **'sprucer**, one who tells tall stories, a trickster.

1917 W. MUIR *Observ. Orderly* xiv. 230 He would be denounced as a 'sprucer' if he managed to arrive late for his meal and yet, by a trick, to secure a front place in the waiting queue at the canteen. 1919 *Athenæum* 15 Aug. 759/1 'A sprucer' is a man who tells tall stories. A man who is 'ticked off' for wrong doing by his officer may escape further punishment by 'sprucing him up a yarn'. 1930 P. MACDONALD *Link* ix. 194 This is where the G.D. begins to show up for the sprucer that he is. 1968 *Listener* 25 Jan. 111/2, I suspect Peter Eckersley was pulling Cutforth's leg. He was a good 'sprucer', as they used to say in Swadlincote.

spruce beer. Also spruce-beer. [SPRUCE *sb.* The modern use is app. not due to, but rather the source of, the synonymous G. *sprossenbier*, f. *sprosse* shoot, sprout.] †**a.** Beer from Prussia. *Obs.* **b.** A fermented beverage made with an extract from the leaves and branches of the spruce fir.

*c*1500 *Colyn Blowbols Test.* 331 in Hazl. *E.P.P.* I. 106 Spruce beer, and the beer of Hambur, Whyche makyth oft tymes men to stambur. 1591 NASHE *Prognostication* 11 Many shall haue more Spruce Beere in their bellies, then wit in their heads. 1690 CHILD *Disc. Trade* (1698) 77 Foreign liquors made of corn, commonly called Mum, Spruce-Beer, and Rosteker-Beer. 1706 PHILLIPS (ed. Kersey), *Spruce-Beer*, a kind of Physical Drink, good for inward Bruises, &c. 1744 BERKELEY *Sec. Let. Tar-water* §4 Spruce-beer made of molasses, and the black spruce-fir. 1766 W. STORK *Acc. East-Florida* 44 The spruce fir here is quite a different tree from that to the northward, but answers the same end for making the spruce beer. 1834 T. J. GRAHAM *Dom. Med.* (ed. 6) 180 Spruce beer is a powerful diuretic and antiscorbutic, and is a wholesome beverage for the summer. 1893 LELAND *Mem.* I. 13 Selling doughnuts, spruce-beer, and gingerbread.

spruce fir. Also spruce-fir. [SPRUCE *sb.*]

1. A distinct species of fir (*Pinus* or *Abies*) comprising several clearly-marked varieties (cf. SPRUCE *sb.* 4); one or other of these varieties.

1731 MILLER *Gard. Dict.* s.v. *Abies*, The Common Firr, or Pitch Tree; sometimes called, The Norway or Spruce Firr. 1799 [A. YOUNG] *Agric. Lincoln.* 214 The spruce fir also grows well and large. 1812 J. SMYTH *Pract. of Customs* (1821) 85 This essence is extracted from the small twigs or sprouts of the black and white Spruce Fir. 1861 BENTLEY *Man. Bot.* 109 The whole will be shaped like a cone or pyramid, as in the Spruce Fir.

2. A tree belonging to this species.

1768 PENNANT *Brit. Zool.* II. 262 The last spring we discovered the nest of this bird in a spruce fir. 1774 GRAY *Corr.* (1843) 173 There you may see larches, Weymouth pines, and spruce firs that have risen by magic. 1842 LOUDON *Suburban Hort.* 317 Those remarkable rows of spruce-firs which line some of the avenues at Meudon. 1896 *Lloyd's Nat. Hist.* 58 The ordinary Crossbill devours the seeds of the larch and spruce-firs.

sprucely ('spruːslɪ), *adv.* [f. SPRUCE *a.* + -LY[2].] In a spruce manner; smartly, trimly, neatly.

1598 MARSTON *Pygmal.*, *Sat.* iii, Under that fayre Ruffe so sprucely set Appeares a fall, a falling-band forsooth. 1626 T. H[AWKINS] *Caussin's Holy Crt.* 186 We see men..who wast all their tyme..in striuing to haue their stockings sprucely put on. 1673 E. BROWN *Trav. Germ.* (1677) 179 Every Bastion is sprucely kept and covered within with green Turf. 1806 J. BERESFORD *Miseries Hum. Life* IV. xxxiii, As you walk forth freshly and sprucely dressed. 1854 EMERSON *Lett. & Soc. Aims, Poet. & Imag.* Wks. (Bohn) III. 160 A small, well-worn, sprucely brushed vocabulary serves him.

spruceness ('spruːsnɪs). [f. SPRUCE *a.*] The character or quality of being spruce; neatness.

1611 MIDDLETON & DEKKER *Roaring Girl* To Rdr., Now in the time of sprucenes, our plaies followe the nicenes of our Garments. 1653 W. RAMESAY *Astrol. Rest.* 60 An exceeding well-shaped body throughout, loving neatness, spruceness, trimming and the like. 1748 CHESTERF. *Lett.* clvi. (1792) II. 57 A spruceness of dress is also very proper and becoming at your age. 1833 HT. MARTINEAU *Briery Creek* v. 108 Not all his spruceness could hide it, if he was as spruce as ever. 1884 *Sat. Rev.* 7 June 745/2 There is an offensive spruceness about the whole picture.

'sprucery. *rare*⁻¹. [f. as prec. + -ERY.] = prec.

1844 *Fraser's Mag.* XXX. 351/2 There was a sprucery about almost every thing he did.

‖**'Sprucia.** *Obs.* Also 8 Sprutia. [Alteration of *Prucia* PRUCE: cf. SPRUCE *sb.*] The country of Prussia; also *attrib.* in *Sprucia deals*.

In Latin context the form occurs as early as 1419 in *North Country Wills* (Surtees) 23.

1614 GENTLEMAN *Engl. Way to Wealth* 6 For the Hollanders..are compelled to fetch..their hoopes and Barrell-boords out of Norway and Sprucia. 1705 *Lond. Gaz.* No. 4101/3 Friday the 16th, for Plank and Sprutia Deals.

†**'Sprucier.** *Obs.*⁻¹ [f. med.L. *Sprucia* (see prec.) or SPRUCE *sb.*] A Prussian.

1443 *Acts Privy Counc.* (1835) V. 233 My Lord Tres. hath declared..hou þat þe Spruciers & Hansze beth freer here in Ingland þan þe Kynges subgittes.

†**'sprucify,** *v. Obs.* [f. SPRUCE *a.*] *trans.* To make spruce. Also with *it* in refl. sense.

1611 COTGR., *Pimper*, to sprucifie, or finifie it; curiously to pranke, trimme, or tricke vp himselfe. 1661 K. W. *Conf. Charac., Cambr. Minion* (1860) 78 An emblematicall ass sprucefyed with the gorgeous trappings of a lofty beusephalus. 1676 *Poor Robin's Intell.* 15–22 Aug. 1/2 Sprucifying himself like a Country Bridegroom he came up to her brush'd and powder'd.

†**'sprucy,** *a. Obs.*⁻¹ = SPRUCE *a.* 2a.

1774 LANGHORNE *Country Justice* 121 Long had that anxious daughter sigh'd to know What Vellum's sprucy clerk, the valley's beau, Meant by those glances.

†**sprude,** *v. Obs.*⁻¹ [Of obscure origin.] *trans.* ? To attach, secure.

13.. *E.E. Allit. P.* C. 104 Cables þay fasten, Wiȝt at þe wyndas weȝen her ankres, Sprude spak to þe sprete þe spare bawe-lyne.

sprue (spruː), *sb.*[1] *Path.* Also sprew, *Sc.* sproo. [ad. Du. *spruw*, *sprouw* (older Flem. *sprouwe*, WFlem. *sproe*, = MLG. and LG. *sprüwe*), perh. related to Flem. *spruwen*, *sproeien* to sprinkle (cf. SPREW[1]).]

1. = THRUSH[2] 1. ? *Obs.*

Erroneously defined by Webster (1828–32) as 'a matter formed in the mouth in certain diseases'.

1825 JAMIESON *Suppl.*, *Sproo*, a disease affecting the mouths of very young children. 1847 WEBSTER, *Sprew*, a disease of the mucous membrane, consisting in a specific inflammation of the muciparous glands. *Ibid.*, *Sprue*,..this is sometimes a vicious orthography of *Sprew*, the name of the disease otherwise called *thrush*. 1899 *Syd. Soc. Lex.* s.v. *Thrush*, *Parasitic stomatitis*. Also called aphthæ, sprew, sprue.

2. A disease characterized by sore throat, raw tongue, and digestive disturbance, occurring esp. in tropical countries; psilosis.

1888 THIN (*title*), Psilosis or 'Sprue': its nature and treatment. 1897 *Allbutt's Syst. Med.* III. 777 Amongst the remoter causes of sprue prolonged residence in hot climates must be reckoned as the first.

attrib. 1897 *Allbutt's Syst. Med.* III. 778 One who has resided in a sprue country. *Ibid.* 790 In the debilitated condition of sprue patients. *Ibid.* 793 Nostrums used in Java by a class of charlatans who profess to be 'sprue doctors'.

sprue (spruː), *sb.*[2] *Founding.* [Of obscure origin.] **1. a.** A channel through which molten metal or plastic flows into a mould cavity or the runner supplying it. Also *attrib.*

Webster's definition is probably erroneous.

1828–32 WEBSTER, *Sprue*, in Scotland, that which is thrown off in casting metals; scoria. 1884 KNIGHT *Dict. Mech.* Suppl., *Sprue Hole*, a gate, ingate, or pouring-hole in a mold. 1884 W. H. GREENWOOD *Steel & Iron* 201 The smaller passages, often two or three in number, leading from the skimming gate to the mould are called sprues or sprue gates. 1939 J. OSBORNE *Dental Mechanics* xvi. 173 Sprues are necessary to convey the gold to the denture base. In order that this may be accomplished as quickly as possible it is usual to use three, four or even five sprues. 1943 SIMONDS & ELLIS *Handbk. Plastics* xv. 593 In a single-cavity mold, the sprue usually leads directly to the cavity, and there is no runner. 1979 L. J. BOUCHER *Comprehensive Rev. Dentistry* xxiii. 640/2 The sprues should be large enough that the molten metal in them will not solidify until after the metal in the casting has solidified.

b. A piece of metal or plastic attached to a casting, having solidified in the mould channel; *spec.* a stem joining a number of toys or other small items of moulded plastic.

1875 KNIGHT *Dict. Mech.* 1084/2 *Head*,..the sprue, sullage-piece, or riser on a casting, which is knocked off. 1911 G. H. WILSON *Dental Prosthetics* ix. 353 The investment is broken and brushed away from the casting... The sprues are snipped away and the edges filed. 1940 M. G. SWENSON *Complete Dentures* xxxiii. 576 The sprues..are removed by cutting with a carborundum disc or a jeweler's saw. 1966 *Airfix Mag.* June 308/1 Stretched sprue comes in very useful for numerous jobs. It is exceptionally rigid as compared with wire. 1971 W. R. MATTHEWS *Plastic Scale Model Aircraft* 72 Some practice is needed to master the technique and initially the failure rate is high—the plastic sprue just pulls in two. 1977 *Vole* I. 16/1 The sprue is the little plastic tree to which the functional bits of plastic are attached as in an aeroplane modelling kit.

c. An object used to form such a channel, e.g. by being withdrawn or by melting.

*a*1877 KNIGHT *Dict. Mech.* III. 2292/2 *Sprue*, a piece of metal or wood used by a molder in making the ingate through the sand. 1908 G. V. BLACK *Operative Dentistry* II. 353 The hole left connecting the mold with the little crucible by the removal of the sprue is too small for even the very highly heated gold to run through by its own weight. 1979 L. J. BOUCHER *Comprehensive Rev. Dentistry* xiv. 388/2 The wax sprue melts at the same time as the wax in the pattern.

2. *Comb.* **sprue former** *Dentistry*, (*a*) a wax channel for guiding moulding material into a mould; (*b*) = sense 1c above; (*c*) a tube or syringe for producing a wax channel.

1911 G. H. WILSON *Dental Prosthetics* x. 344 The completed wax model is prepared for flasking by attaching gate or sprue formers. 1920 *Ibid.* (ed. 4) x. 406 To operate the sprue former remove the screw plunger and fill the barrel with the desired wax. 1930 S. S. JAFFE in I. G. Nichols *Prosthetic Dentistry* xxx. 537 Make five sprue formers about the size of matchsticks. 1936 E. W. SKINNER *Sci. Dental Materials* xxix. 252 After obtaining the wax pattern, it is used for preparing a casting mold. A small length of wire, called the sprue former, is attached. 1961 J. N. ANDERSON *Applied Dental Materials* (ed. 2) xv. 141 The pattern may be removed by attaching a metal sprue former and then withdrawing the wax in a straight line away from the cavity. 1975 BREWER & MORROW *Overdentures* xiv. 197/1 The stainless steel sprue former is placed in the impression in the hydrocolloid formed by the cone attached to the master cast.

sprue (spruː), *sb.*[3] [Of obscure origin.] A poor or inferior quality of asparagus. Also *sprue grass*.

1846 Soyer *Cookery* 41 Throw in the sprue and let it boil very fast until tender. *Ibid.*, Get some fresh sprue grass. **1884** *Girl's Own Paper* Feb. 219/3 Long, thin straggling asparagus, commonly known as sprue. **1895** *Times* 3 April 3/4 Sprue, 9d. to 1s.; asparagus, 1s. 6d. to 3s. per bundle.

sprue, *v. Dentistry.* [f. sprue *sb.*[2]] *trans.* To furnish with a sprue or sprues.

1943 F. A. Peyton *Restorative Dental Materials* vii. 246/2 (*heading*) Spruing the pattern. **1949** *Brit. Dental Jrnl.* LXXXVI. 114/1 The wax pattern is thoroughly cleansed... It is sprued, the reservoir added and mounted on a rubber crucible former. **1963** J. Osborne *Dental Mechanics* (ed. 5) xiv. 319 If the pattern has been sprued from above then the mixed investment is coated over the pattern and sprues. **1975** Brewer & Morrow *Over-dentures* xiv. 201/1 After completion of the wax-up, the case is sprued.

So **'sprueing** *vbl. sb.*, provision of sprues.

1930 S. S. Jaffe in I. G. Nichols *Prosthetic Dentistry* xxx. 537 This method of 'sprueing' is only suitable for a centrifugal casting machine. **1979** L. J. Boucher *Comprehensive Rev. Dentistry* xxiii. 640/2, 8 to 12 gauge round wax forms are usually used for multiple sprueing of removable partial denture castings.

sprued (spruːd), *a. Dentistry.* [f. sprue *sb.*[2] + -ed[2].] Furnished with a sprue or sprues.

1930 S. S. Jaffe in I. G. Nichols *Prosthetic Dentistry* xxx. 538 Place the waxed and sprued model on the mix..and allow it to set. **1963** C. R. Cowell et al. *Inlays, Crowns, & Bridges* v. 46 The sprued pattern must be invested immediately because delay increases the chances of distortion due to the release of strains in the wax. **1979** L. J. Boucher *Comprehensive Rev. Dentistry* xxii. 579/1 The sprued pattern should be placed one-quarter inch from the end of the casting ring.

sprug, *sb. Sc.* and *north. dial.* Also sproug, sprog. [Of obscure origin: the form *spug* (with variant *spyug*) is also common in Sc. and Eng. dial.] A sparrow.

1815 Scott *Guy M.* xi, John Wilson was a blustering kind of chield, without the heart of a sprug. **1886-** in *Eng. Dial. Dict.*

sprug, *v. dial.* [? f. Sussex dial. *sprug* adj., smart, spruce: cf. sprig *a.*] *trans.* To deck or dress *up* smartly; to make smart or trim.

1622 T. Stoughton *Chr. Sacrif.* xv. 214 Some daintie Dames, euen sprugd vp of nothing, that are so long in dressing and attiring themselues in the morning. **1847** Halliw., *Sprug up*, to dress neatly. *Sussex.* **1875** Parish *Sussex Dial.* 112 *Sprug*, to smarten.

spruik (spruːk), *v. Austral.* and *N.Z. slang.* [Of unknown origin.] *intr.* Esp. of a showman: to deliver a speech, hold forth, speak in public.

1916 C. J. Dennis *Songs of Sentimental Bloke* 42 'E'll sigh and spruik, an' 'owl a love-sick vow. **1934** V. Palmer *Swayne Family* 250 Wonder you didn't get a job spruiking for the pictures down there in town. **1941** K. Tennant *Battlers* xiii. 143 The ampster's is an easy job. He stands in the front row of the listening crowd registering intense interest and enthusiasm while the showman 'spruiks'. **1955** D. Niland *Shiralee* 106 Kelly was chanting the count, banging the big drum, lining the fighters up on the board again, spruiking to the crowd. **1963** *Truth* (Wellington, N.Z.) 15 Oct., Announcers who spruik just for the sake of hearing themselves need to be mighty sure of their facts. **1975** H. Porter *Extra* 244 Hollow-chested men..who sell agitated toys on street corners or spruik outside strip-tease joints.

Hence **'spruiker,** a speaker employed to attract custom to a sideshow, a barker; a public speaker.

1924 *Truth* (Sydney) 27 Apr. 6 *Spruiker*, a speaker. **1933** *Bulletin* (Sydney) 2 Aug. 10/4 General Blamey's somewhat ill-advised efforts to prevent political spruikers addressing the Friday-night crowds. **1952** J. Cleary *Sundowners* 154 Rupe sounds like a spruiker from the Domain. **1959** J. Wright *Generations of Men* xvi. 203 Spruikers dressed in red flannel shirts..shouted and gestured in hoarse invitation. **1977** C. McCullough *Thorn Birds* v. 93 'Come on chaps, who'll take a glove?' the spruiker was braying. 'Who wants to have a go?'

‖**spruit** (sprœyt). *S. African.* [Du. *spruit* sprout *sb.*[1]] A small stream or water-course, usually almost or altogether dry except in the wet season.

1832 *Graham's Town Jrnl.* 13 Apr. 62 They were joined by Lieut. Warden and his party.., who had been ordered to come over the back of the mountains and rendezvous at the *Spruits* of the Keiskamma. **1850** N. J. Merriman *Jrnl.* in *Kafir, Hottentot & Frontier Farmer* (1854) 85 In two days more we found ourselves, just after sundown, at Carl Spruit, (a small stream,) about ten miles this side of Bloemfontein. **1863** W. C. Baldwin *Afr. Hunting* 207, I scraped my finger-nails off in making large holes in the dry spruits, but not one drop came. **1876** Lady Barker *Year's Housekeeping S. Africa* viii. 150 A real river, not..a capricious spruit, sometimes a ditch, and sometimes a lake. **1889** F. Oates *Matabele-Land* 66 Where we outspanned the boys made a fire in the hollow bed of a spruit.

sprule, north. or Sc. variant of sprawl *v.*

sprun. *north. dial.* [app. a metathetic var. of spurn *sb.*[2] 1 b.] (See quot. 1828.) Also *attrib.* in *sprun-vein*.

1737 Bracken *Farriery Impr.* (1756) I. 338 Bleeding in the Sprun-Vein. **1828** Carr *Craven Gloss.*, *Sprun*, 1. The fore part of a horse's hoof. 2. A sharp piece of iron fixed to the fore point of a horse's shoe to prevent him slipping on ice.

†**sprund.** *Obs.*$^{-1}$ [Cf. MSw. *sprund*, app. in a similar sense.] A spar or pole.

c **1425** *Noah's Ark* in *Non-Cycle Mystery Plays* 22 For I have neither ryff nor ruff, Spyer, sprund, sprout, no sprot.

sprung (sprʌŋ), *ppl. a.*[1] [pa. pple. of spring *v.*[1]]

1. That has sprung up or arisen. In combs. as *first-*, *high-*, *new-sprung*. Also with *up*.

1575 Gascoigne *Flowers, Dan Bartholmew* Wks. 1907 I. 101 God he knoweth..who pluckt hir first sprong rose. **1632** Lithgow *Trav.* ix. 415 The high sprung Woods, threatning the clouds. **1661** J. Davies *Civil Warres* 373 This utterly dissipated the power of the new sprung Committee of Safety. **1842** J. Aiton *Domest. Econ.* (1857) 150 The progress of his crops, from the scarce sprung-braird to the whitening harvest. **1895** *Daily News* 25 March 8/6 The newly sprung-up competition from the United States makers of this..tool.

2. Cracked, split.

1597 J. Payne *Royal Exch.* 33 Besyde myne acquayntans with your sprung masts, torne sales from the yarde. **1666** Dryden *Ann. Mirab.* cxliii, Tall Norway Fir, their masts in Battel spent, And English Oak sprung Leaks and Planks restore. **1781** *Naval Chron.* XI. 289 The main mast is a sprung mast. **1852** H. Newland *Tractarianism* 133 Some mixing mortar,..some strengthening the sprung beams. **1899** Eden Phillpotts *Human Boy* 12 Browne..made that noise in his throat like a sprung bat.

3. Made to fly up.

1598 Sylvester *Du Bartas* ii. ii. iii. *Colonies* 431 Out amaz'd first Grand-sires faintly fled, And, like sprung Partridge, every-where did spred.

4. *techn.* (See quot.)

1825 J. Nicholson *Operat. Mechanic* 601 The bevel..is termed the *spring of the plank*, and the edge thus bevelled is called the *sprung edge*.

5. a. *sprung rhythm*, a term coined by Gerard Manley Hopkins (1844–89) for a poetic metre used by him which approximates to the rhythm of speech and in which each foot consists of one stressed syllable either alone or followed by a varying number of unstressed syllables; hence applied to verse, etc., using this metre.

1877 G. M. Hopkins *Lett. to R. Bridges* (1955) 43 The *Deutschland*, though in sprung rhythm, is marked with accents. *Ibid.* 45, I do not of course claim to have invented *sprung rhythms* but only *sprung rhythm*; I mean that single lines and instances of it are not uncommon in English. *Ibid.*, The choruses in *Samson Agonistes* are intermediate between counterpointed and sprung rhythm. In reality they are sprung. *Ibid.* 46 Why do I employ sprung rhythm at all? Because it is the nearest to the rhythm of prose,..the least forced, the most rhetorical and emphatic of all possible rhythms. **1879** —— *Let.* 27 Feb./10 Mar. in Hopkins & Dixon *Corr.* (1935) 23, I shd. add that the word Sprung which I use for this rhythm means something like *abrupt* and applies by rights only where one stress follows another running, without syllable between. *c* **1883** —— *Poems* 3 Sprung Rhythm, as used in this book, is measured by feet of from one to four syllables, regularly, and for particular effects any number of weak or slack syllables may be used. *Ibid.* 6 Sprung rhythm..has..ceased to be used since the Elizabethan age, Greene being the last writer who can be said to have recognized it. **1935** W. B. Yeats *Let.* 16 Dec. (1954) 844, I think of writing for the first time in sprung verse (four stresses) with a certain amount of rhyme. **1940** H. S. Walpole *Roman Fountain* xi. 169 'But the metre——' 'This is sprung verse and you can run as many syllables into a line as you please.' **1961** *Listener* 23 Nov. 863/1 The myth is created in strikingly personal terms—a kind of sprung verse, for example, developed [by Isaac Rosenberg] quite independently of Hopkins. **1977** J. Milroy *Lang. of G. M. Hopkins* v. 116 Many 'sprung' lines can be quoted in which some of the metric feet have only one strongly stressed syllable.

b. *transf.* in *Mus.*

1944 M. Tippett *String Quartet No. 2 in F sharp* (verso front cover), The 4th *movement* needs a decisively sprung rhythm on which virtually the whole movement is based. **1959** *Listener* 8 Jan. 80/1 *The Heart's Assurance* was the first work in which Tippett's long-breathed melody and sprung rhythm flowered into what one might call creative ornamentation. **1975** *Gramophone* Jan. 1313/3 Even an early work like the Double Concerto..whose characteristic 'sprung-rhythm' style, derived from the Elizabethan and Jacobean madrigal,..demands from the string orchestra a litheness and an emancipation from the bar-line that were not common in those days.

6. Produced unexpectedly in order to disconcert (in quots., of an alibi which has been 'sprung' upon the prosecution in a court of law). Cf. spring *v.*[1] 21 d.

1966 *Listener* 1 Sept. 301/1 The sprung alibi in which the defence suddenly at the last minute..produces an alibi which has not been heard of before. **1973** Smith & Keenan *Eng. Law* (ed. 4) ii. 22 The abuse of 'sprung' or late alibis had been so widespread in criminal trials that Sect. 11 of the Criminal Justice Act, 1967, provides that, in general, notice of alibi must be given in advance of a trial on indictment. This is not required in summary trials because of the ease with which the prosecution can ask for an adjournment where the defendant 'springs' an alibi on the prosecution at the last moment.

sprung, *ppl. a.*[2] [Irreg. f. spring *v.*[2] by analogy with spring *v.*[1], sprung *ppl. a.*[1] The expected regular form, *springed*, is rare.]

1. Provided with a spring or springs. Also *Comb.*, as *sprung-edge(d)* adj.

1884 F. J. Britten *Watch & Clockm.* 246 Sprung above [or] Sprung over [is] a watch in which the balance spring is attached to the staff above the balance. **1909** *Westm. Gaz.* 11 Nov. 5/1 An entirely new form of suspension is to be introduced which is claimed not only to render the best sprung car extremely coarse in comparison, but which does away with springs altogether. **1916** 'Boyd Cable' *Action Front* 146 The longer but smoother journey in the sweetly-sprung motor ambulance. **1932** *Daily Tel.* 8 Oct. 19/6 (Advt.), 50 luxuriously sprung easy chairs in various coverings. **1948**, etc. [see *interior-sprung mattress* s.v. interior *a.* 4]. **1976** *Star* (Sheffield) 29 Oct. 3/3 (Advt.), 3 piece 10 cushioned traditional suite in high quality Dralon, incorporating sprung-edged seating. **1976** *Evening Standard* 29 Dec. 6 (Advt.), Pocketed spring mattress. Sprung-edge base.

2. Of a floor, esp. a dance floor: constructed so as to be resilient. Cf. *spring floor* s.v. spring *sb.*[1] 25 a.

1939 [implied in unsprung *ppl. a.*[2]]. **1966** J. B. Priestley *Salt is Leaving* xv. 202 Lights all colours. Sprung floor. Five-piece band. **1972** G. Hale *Floors* ix. 91 *Spring floors*, floors intended for dancing should have a degree of resilience and for this reason ballroom floors..are often fully sprung. **1978** *Daily Tel.* 31 Oct. 19/5 The hotel's sprung dance floor still exists.

†**sprunk.** *Obs.*$^{-1}$ [app. f. Du. *pronk*, or G. *prunk*: cf. next.] A display of wealth or grandeur.

c **1753** *The King's Disguise* xii. in Child *Ballads* III. 221/1 With fryars and monks, with their fine sprunks, I make my chiefest prey.

†**sprunking,** *vbl. sb. Obs.* [f. Du. *pronken* or G. *prunken*: cf. prec.] Personal adornment or beautifying. Also *attrib.* in *sprunking glass*.

1690 Evelyn *Mundus Muliebris* 6 The Pocket Sprunking Looking-Glass. *Ibid.* 19 The Table, Toilet, or Pocket Sprunking-Glass. **1694** N. H. *Ladies Dict.* 12 *A Sprunking Glass*, this sprunking is a Dutch word, the first as we hear of that Language, that ever came in fashion with Ladies.

'sprunny. Now *dial.* [Of obscure origin: some dialects have *sprunny* adj., spruce, smart.] A sweetheart.

1762 *Collins's Misc.* 111 Where if good Satan lays her on like thee, Whipp'd to some Purpose will thy Sprunny be. *a* **1800** Pegge *Suppl. Grose*, *Sprunny*, a sweetheart of either sex. **1814-** in midland and eastern dialects.

sprunt, *sb.*[1] Now *dial.* [f. sprunt *v.*] A convulsive movement; a start; a spring or bound.

1693 *Phil. Trans.* XVII. 876 Then (having just only opened her Eyes and made Two Sprunts, without speaking one word) [she] dyed immediately. *a* **1800** Pegge *Suppl. Grose*, *Sprunt*, or *Sprint*, a spring in leaping, and the leap itself. *Derb.* **1847-79** in dial. glossaries (Derby, Northampt., Shropsh., Warw.).

†**sprunt,** *sb.*[2] *Obs.*$^{-0}$ [cf. next.] 'Anything that is short and will not easily bend' (Johnson, 1755).

In the quot. applied to an obstinately curly lock of hair. *c* **1710** Congreve *Poems Sev. Occas.*, *Impossible Thing*, This Sprunt its Pertness sure will lose When laid (said he) to soak in Ooze.

sprunt, *a.* ? *Obs.* [prob. related to next.] Brisk, active, smart, spruce.

1616 [implied in sprUNTLY *adv.*]. *a* **1652** Brome *Mad Couple* v. ii, *La.* Pray Mr. Thrivewell entertaine the Lady. *Car.* Another sprunt youth. **1653** H. More *Antid. Ath.* i. xi. §8 That little sprunt Piece of the Brain which they call the Conarion. **1668** G. C. in H. More *Div. Dial.* Pref. 1. p. xii, This little sprunt Champion, called the Conarion,..within which the Soul is entirely cooped up. [**1687** Miége *Gt. Fr. Dict.* ii, Sprunt, wonderful active. **1706** Phillips (ed. Kersey), *Sprunt*, wonderful active, lively, or brisk. (Hence in Bailey.)] **1719** D'Urfey *Pills* I. 146 Nell dress'd as sprunt as a Daizy. *a* **1828** T. Bewick *The Upgetting* (1850) 13 Thou can get on thee sister's shoun..and mheyk thee sell leuk varra sprunt wouth them.

sprunt (sprʌnt), *v.* Now *dial.* [app. related to sprent *v.* and sprint *v.*] *intr.* To spring or start; to move in a quick or convulsive manner; to dart or run.

1601 Holland *Pliny* xxiii. vi, No sooner tast they of them, but the childe doth stir and sprunt in their wombe. **1603** —— *Plutarch's Mor.* 1277 The armie of Alexander, after it had lost and forgone him, did no more but sprunt, pant, struggle and strive for life. **1656** Trapp *Matt.* iv. 2 Beasts that have their death's wound, bite cruelly, sprunt exceedingly. **1690** C. Nesse *Hist. & Myst. O.N. Test.* i. 216 Those twins spurned and sprunted in her womb. **1740** Somerville *Hobbinol.* iii. 393 See! this sweet-simp'ring Babe, Dear Image of thyself; see! how it sprunts With Joy at thy Approach! **1789** Mrs. Piozzi *Journ. France* II. 193 Wonderfully indeed did the players struggle, and bounce, and sprunt. **1823** in *Spirit Public Jrnls.* 528 He sprunted about among their legs lustily. **1854-** in dialect glossaries (Yks., Derby, Northampt., Warw.). **1897** Ld. E. Hamilton *Outlaws of Marches* xvii. 187 I'll just sprunt up the water and cross abune the forkings.

Hence **'sprunting** *vbl. sb.*

1643 Trapp *Gen.* xxxii. 28 Their faint oppositions, and spruntings before death. **1647** —— *Rev.* xii. 8 Their late utmost endeavours..were but as the last spruntings, or bitter-bites of dying beasts.

'spruntly, *adv.* [f. sprunt *a.*] Smartly, sprucely, trimly.

1616 B. Jonson *Devil an Ass* iv. ii, How do I look to-day? Am I not drest Spruntly? **1651** H. More *Enthus. Tri.* (1656) 205 Provided thou wilt not prick up thy eares too, and look too spruntly upon the businesse. **1704** D'Urfey *Hell beyond Hell* 75 The pug appear'd, tall, spruntly dress'd, Powder'd all o'er, head, back, and breast.

†**sprusado.** *Obs.*⁻¹ [app. f. *spruse* SPRUCE *a.* + -ADO I.] A smartly-dressed person.
1665 BRATHWAIT *Comment Two Tales* (1901) 13 They put me in mind of the pregnant and present Answer of that Sprusado to a Judge in this Kingdom,..who seeing a neat Finical Divine come before him in a Cloak lined through with Plush [etc.].

spruse, sprush: see SPRUCE *sb.* and *a.*

sprut, *v.* Now *dial.* [var. of SPRIT *v.* Cf. SPURT *v.*²] **a.** *intr.* To sprout, germinate. †**b.** *trans.* To put forth by sprouting.
1523 FITZHERB. *Husb.* §13 Whan rayne cometh, than sprutteth that [corn] that lyeth aboue. **1559** *Mirr. Mag., Owen Glendour* xix, For like as drops engender mighty flouds, litle seedes sprut furth great leaues and buds. **1886–** in dialect glossaries, etc. (Lanc., Yks., Notts.).

sprut(t, variant of SPROUT *sb.*²

†**'spruttle,** *sb. Sc. Obs.* In 6 sprutill. [a. MLG. *sprut(e)le, sprotele, sprottel,* older Flem. *sproetel,* freckle.] A small spot; a speckle.
1513 DOUGLAS *Æneid* v. ii. 90 (1553), Of flekkit sprutillis [*v.r.* freklit spraiklis] all hir bak schone.

'spruttled, *a. Sc.* Also 8–9 sprit(t)led. [f. prec. See also SPURTLED *a.*] Speckled.
1513 DOUGLAS *Æneid* II. iv. 32 (1553), Bot thay..twys faldit thare sprutillit [*v.r.* spurtlit] skynnis, but dout, About his hals. *Ibid.* VII. iv. 91 (Small), Circes..in ane byrd him turnit, fut and hand, Wyth sprutlit wyngis. **1721** RAMSAY *Poems* Gloss., *Spruttl'd,* speckled, spotted. *a***1779** D. GRAHAM *Writ.* (1883) II. 35 Did I not send you my guid sprittled hen? **1807–10** TANNAHILL *Poems* (1846) 136 Mild blue spritled crowflower, nor wild woodland lily.

spry, *sb. Kentish dial.* [Special use of *spry* SPRAY *sb.*¹] A flat broom made of birch twigs.
1796 BOYS *Agric. Surv. Kent* 84 Wheat..is universally in Kent, cleaned with a casting-shovel, and flat broom, called a spry.

spry (spraɪ), *a.* and *adv.* Also *dial.* 8 sprey, 9 sprae, *Sc.* spree. [Of obscure origin. Current in English dialects, but more familiar as an Americanism.]
1. Active, nimble, smart, brisk; full of health and spirits.
Eng. and Sc. dial. instances are given under (*a*) and (*c*).
(*a*) **1746** *Exmoor Courtship* (E.D.S.) 579 A comely sprey vitty Vella vor enny keendest Theng. *Ibid.* 581 Thare's net a spreyer Vella in Challacomb. **1825** JENNINGS *Observ. Dial. W. Eng.* 72 *Spry,* nimble, active. **1844** W. BARNES *Poems* 48 Jump'd to zee who wer the spryest. **1866** *Gilbert Rugge* I. ii. 31 She's one o' them sort who's down one day and up and spry the next. **1870** VERNEY *Lettice Lisle* xx, He's so lusty and so spry he may give 'em all the slip.
(*b*) **1789** *Maryland Jrnl.* 10 Mar. (Thornton), [The snakes] were not so spry as in summer season, so none escaped being killed. **1815** *Massachusetts Spy* 28 June (Thornton), Pray be spry, sir, said I, for there's no knowing what my wife may do. **1833** [SEBA SMITH] *Lett. J. Downing* ii. (1835) 30 'And now,' says I, 'all on you be spry, and don't stop stirrin till the pudden's done'. **1869** SPURGEON *John Ploughman's Talk* 14 If some of the members..were a little more spry with their arms and legs when they are at labour. **1888** R. BUCHANAN *Heir of Linne* xiii, I'll have to be pretty spry, or they'll begin to discuss me.
(*c*) **1837** R. NICOLL *Poems* (1843) 164, I once was loved, —I loved again The spreest lad in a' our glen. **1892** J. LUMSDEN *Sheeph. & Trotters* 76 The wagtail, sae spree, In the golden evenings here shall linger.
b. Alert, clever.
1849 CUPPLES *Green Hand* xi. (1856) 106 And says Job Price,..'You're too cust spry for playin' jokes on, I calc'late, squire,' he says.
2. *dial.* Spruce, neat, smartly dressed.
1806 A. DOUGLAS *Poems* 144 Syne hame they gang..To busk themsels fu' trig and spree; For raggit they're an' dirty. **1854–** in dialect glossaries.
3. As *adv.* Nimbly, actively.
1855 HALIBURTON *Nature & Hum. Nat.* I. 227 They call us shakers, from shaking our feet so spry.
Hence **'spryly** *adv.*; **'spryness.**
1865 *Reader* No. 145. 393/2 A spryness of legs quite remarkable. **1905** MARY E. WILKINS *Debtor* 417 Then she hopped off as spryly as a sparrow.

spry (spraɪ), *v. rare.* [f. prec.]
1. *trans.* To smarten *up.*
1878 S. SMILES *Jerdan Ess. & Lyrics* 199 Robbie Bell, spried up and clean Wi' weel-spun hose and buckled shoon.
2. *intr.* To bustle or stir.
1885 *Harper's Mag.* April 707/2 She'll get over it, and be spryin' around to marry again.

spry(e, obs. forms of SPRAY *sb.*²

†**spualine.** *Obs.*⁻⁰ (See quot.)
1688 HOLME *Armoury* III. xvi. (Roxb.) 73/1 The principall games at cards:..Spualine an Irish game.

spuchour, obs. form of SPOUCHER.

spud (spʌd), *sb.* Also 5–6 spudde, 7 spudd. [Of obscure origin.]
†**1.** A short and poor knife or dagger. *Obs.*
*c***1440** *Promp. Parv.* 471/1 Spudde, *cultellus vilis.* *c***1450** *Cast. Persev.* 1402 With my spud of sorwe swote, I reche to þyne herte rote. **1530** PALSGR. 274/2 Spudde. **1589** FLEMING *Virg. Georg.* II. 24 The Volces also bearing darts (or spuds in shape like spits). **1609** HOLLAND *Amm. Marcell.* XXIX. i. 352 The one..with a spud or dagger was wounded almost to death. **1706** PHILLIPS (ed. Kersey), *Spud,* a short scurvy knife. **1823–4** in Poole *Wexford Gloss.* (1867) 69 *Spud,* a knife.
†**2.** An iron head or blade socketed on or fixed to a plough-staff. *Obs.*⁻¹
1613 MARKHAM *Eng. Husbandman* C, The Husbandman which liueth in durty and stiffe clayes, can neuer goe to plough without..the Aker-staffe,..a pretty bigge cudgell, of about a yarde in length, with an Iron spud at the end.
3. a. A digging or weeding implement of the spade-type, having a narrow chisel-shaped blade.
1667 PEPYS *Diary* 10 Oct., We..begun with a spudd to lift up the ground. **1728** SWIFT *Past. Dial.* Wks. 1755 III. II. 203 My spud these nettles from the stones can part; No knife so keen to weed thee from my heart. **1773** MRS. DELANY *Life & Corr.* (1861) I. 570, I sally'd out in a rage, arm'd with a spud. **1805** R. W. DICKSON *Pract. Agric.* II. 748 In making the pits or holes, the earth is taken out by a spade or spud. **1856** A. ANDREWS *Eighteenth Cent.* 24 It was of the length and size of the 'spud', an agricultural weapon which old farmers persist in carrying about with them in their war upon weeds. **1877** BLACKMORE *Cripps* xxxi, The Squire still looking very pale and feeble, but with the help of his favourite spud, managing to get along.
fig. *a***1876** M. COLLINS *Pen Sketches* (1879) II. 51 They reappear inevitably, though the heavy harrow of argument, and the light spud of wit have both been used upon them.
Comb. **1891** MISS DOWIE *Girl in Karp.* 226 She shook a bannock carefully from the spud-shaped spade to bake.
b. A digging fork with three broad prongs.
1805 R. W. DICKSON *Pract. Agric.* II. 757 The labourer makes use of a three-pronged fork, which in some places is termed a spud...each prong being about an inch and a half in breadth. **1848** *Jrnl. R. Agric. Soc.* IX. 551 Digging is done with a strong three-forked tool called a hop-spud. **1883** J. Y. STRATTON *Hops & Hop-pickers* 22 Kentish labourers dig with a spud or fork with three blade-like prongs.
attrib. **1848** *Jrnl. R. Agric. Soc.* IX. II. 560 Letting the earth fall loosely between the spud-spens.
c. *techn.* (See quot.)
1864 HOLTZAPFFEL *Turning* II. 813 As the veneer is sawn off, the attendant leads the veneer on to the guide, by means of a spud, or a thin blunt chisel.
d. A small instrument with enlarged end used in ocular and other surgery. Also *attrib.*
1869 G. LAWSON *Dis. Eye* 57 The foreign body..may be easily removed by a spud..or by a broad needle. **1895** *Arnold & Sons' Catal. Surg. Instrum.* 144 Spud and Gouge (combined), in screw ivory case. *Ibid.*, Spud Knife.
e. *U.S.* (See quots.)
1871 *Trans. Amer. Inst. Min. Engin.* I. 378 If the [surveying] station was intended to be a permanent one, a spud, as it is called, that is, a nail resembling a horseshoe nail with a hole in the head, is driven into the timbers over the station. **1875** KNIGHT *Dict. Mech.* 2292/2 *Spud,*..a spade-shaped implement, used in fishing for broken tools in a well.
f. *Forestry.* A chisel-like implement used to remove the bark from timber.
1914 MOON & BROWN *Elem. Forestry* 383 *Spud,* a tool for removing bark. **1919** N. C. BROWN *Forest Products* iii. 68 The spudder..proceeds to peel off the bark by inserting the spud between the bark and the wood, and gradually pries it off. **1966** A. E. WACKERMAN et al. *Harvesting Timber Crops* (ed. 2) viii. 198 Some [Redwood bark] is still removed by hand with spuds, but hydraulic methods are also in use. Mechanical power spuds are also used, as are tractors with spud attachments similar to dozer blades.
g. = *spade lug* s.v. SPADE *sb.*¹ 5.
1917 *Proc. Inst. Automobile Engineers* XII. 80 A machine with a 30 cwt. axle loading and short spuds pulls partly by adhesion and partly by grip. **1933** WATSON & MORE *Agriculture* (ed. 3) I. v. 157 A disadvantage of wheeled tractors is that the spuds or bars that are needed on the wheels for soft land are damaging to roads. **1950** C. DAVIES *Mechanized Agric.* vi. 39 There are many designs of this [skeleton wheel]—as, in fact, there are of wheel lugs, spuds and cleats.
h. *Thatching.* (See quots.)
1939 H. J. MASSINGHAM *Country Relics* i. 13 The equipment is the same when a roof is rethatched, except for the addition of a thatching spud still used by the older thatchers... It is a light, squarish slab of wood..with one end chamfered on both sides to an edge and an oblong slit cut out at the other end through which the fingers pass when the tool is grasped. It is thrust up into the old thatch at the eaves in order to make an opening for the new yealm to be made fast at its thin end. **1968** J. ARNOLD *Shell Book of Country Crafts* 185, I watched one man..driving home his pegs with a flat oblong board: this had a spade-like handle and was called a 'spud'. **1972** [see LEGGET].
4. A short or stumpy person or thing.
1687 MIÉGE *Gt. Fr. Dict.* II, A Spud, or little Fellow. **1706** PHILLIPS (ed. Kersey), *Spud,*..a Short-arse, or little despicable Fellow. *a***1825–** in dialect glossaries (E. Angl., Essex, Devon, Cornw.). **1847** HALLIW., *Spud,* a baby's hand. *Somerset.* **1900** *Daily News* 26 Apr. 3/1 That baby..everlastingly holds out its spuds of arms.
5. a. A potato. *slang* and *dial.*
Cf. *spuddy* as a nickname for 'a seller of bad potatoes' in Mayhew *Lond. Lab.* (1851) I. 24/2.
1845 E. J. WAKEFIELD *Adventure in N.Z.* I. xi. 319 Pigs and potatoes were respectively represented by '*grunters*' and '*spuds*'. **1860** *Slang Dict.* 225 In Scotland, a spud is a raw potato; and roasted spuds are those cooked in the cinders with their jackets on. **1868** *Good Wds.* Xmas No. 6/1 My..neighbour stretched out his hand to help himself to 'spuds'. **1898** *Westm. Gaz.* 6 Oct. 7/2 Three-quarters of a pound of meat and a pound of bread are the rations, spuds and pudding being thrown in.
b. = POTATO *sb.* 5 d. *slang.*
1960 I. MACCORMICK *Small Victory* 86 Are you any good at darning socks, Sister? I got a *spud* in my spare pair. **1978** M. DE LARRABEITI *Rose beyond Thames* 34 There were huge spuds in the heels of their socks.
6. Each of a number of poles that can be put out from a dredger and stuck into the bed or bank of the river so as to keep the vessel stationary.
1891 F. WYATT *Phosphates of America* iv. 51 The boats are held in position at the four corners by 'spuds' or strong square poles with iron points, which are dropped into the water before dredging is begun. **1912** C. PRELINI *Dredges & Dredging* xx. 166 The bow spuds are of great size, 43 in. square and 52 ft. long. **1925** G. W. PICKELS *Drainage & Flood-Control Engin.* xiv. 397 Spuds are devices for holding the hull still while the dredge is working. There are three of them, one at the center of the stern and one at each side near the front end. The rear spud is always vertical and consists of a heavy timber with a pointed iron shoe at its lower end which moves in a box or guide frame attached to the hull. When lowered, the pointed end is forced into the bottom of the ditch or river and prevents the rear end of the hull from moving. The spud is raised by a cable operated by the spud engine. The side spuds may be either vertical or inclined. *Ibid.* 398 Inclined spuds are fastened to the A-frame and their lower ends rest on the banks, hence they are called bank spuds. **1969** R. HAMMOND *Mod. Dredging Pract.* iv. 136 The spuds are provided with sliding collars in order to allow for the wide range of dredging depths.
7. *Plumbing.* A short length of pipe used as a connecting piece between two components or taking the form of a projection from a fitting to which a pipe may be screwed.
1905 *Internat. Libr. of Technol.* LXXI. §15. 68 The end..of the spud is threaded iron-pipe size for screwing into the tapping of an ordinary iron kitchen boiler. **1907** R. M. STARBUCK *Mod. Plumbing Illustr.* 123 Ventilation..consists in connecting a pipe from the local vent spud on the water-closet bowl to a heated flue. **1908** A. G. KING *Practical Steam & Hot Water Heating & Ventilation* xi. 105 The branches should be one size larger than the vertical pipe or 'spud' supplying the radiator valve, or one size larger than the riser which they feed. **1939** [see *spud wrench* in sense 8 below]. **1972** J. HASTINGS *Plumber's Compan.* 184 The 'spud connection' is a brass fitting comprising a socket on one end for receiving the nozzle and on the other end a male thread for connecting a pipe.
8. *attrib.* and *Comb.*, as **spud barber** *slang,* one who peels potatoes; **spud-bashing** *slang* (orig. *Mil.*), the peeling of potatoes; **spud can** *Oil Industry,* a structure that can be sunk into a soft sea-bottom by temporary ballasting and then used as the base of a tower platform extending above the surface of the water; **Spud Islander** *Canad. slang,* a native or inhabitant of Prince Edward Island, which is noted for its fine potatoes; **spud line**: in slang phr. *in the spud line,* pregnant; **spud wrench** (see quots. 1939, 1960¹).
1935 A. J. POLLOCK *Underworld Speaks* 112/2 *Spud barber,* a potato peeler (prison). **1961** G. FOULSER *Seaman's Voice* 48 The galley-boy [was] just a spudbarber after all. **1940,** etc. Spud-bashing [see BASHING *vbl. sb.* 3]. **1980** *Times* 13 Nov. 10/1 Between dashing home from the office..and having a bath, there is not much time for spud bashing. **1975** *Offshore* Sept. 49-04/3 Spud cans are designed for soft seabeds, giving minimum penetration. **1976** *Offshore Platforms & Pipelining* 53/3 The tower base consists of a truss-reinforced stiffened shell called a spud can... After the tower is uprighted, the spud can is artificially forced into the ocean bottom until the desired load-carrying capability is reached. **1957** *Globe Mag.* (Toronto) 29 June 4/2 (*caption*) Spud Islanders are known throughout Canada for the quality of their potatoes. **1962** G. MACEWAN *Blazing Old Cattle Trail* xxxiii. 222 In 1900, the twenty-four-year-old 'Spud Islander' journeyed to the far Northwest. **1937** J. CURTIS *There ain't no Justice* xxiv. 245 You mean she's in the spud line? **1967** H. W. SUTHERLAND *Magnie* vi. 80 It couldn't have been himself that put Kathleen Ertall in the spud line. **1939** W. T. WALTERS *Steam & Hot Water Fitting* x. 145 Spud Wrenches. This type of wrench is another handy tool. It is made to fit the spuds of the different sizes of the union radiator valves and traps. **1960** S. P. OPPENHEIMER *Erecting Structural Steel* vii. 93 The open-end spud wrench..is the most common... It is so called because the handle is formed into a long, heavy pin (or spud) that is thrust through and used by the erection men for matching up holes in connections to be fastened together. **1960** D. A. HALPERIN *Building with Steel* xii. 163/1 It is permissible to tighten the bolts with a long handled socket or spud wrench.

spud (spʌd), *v.* [f. prec. 3.]
1. *trans.* To dig *up* or *out,* to remove, by means of a spud.
1652 BLITHE *Eng. Improver Impr.* 121, I have found out a more certaine way which will destroy them at once, spudding up... I caused them to be spudded up by the root. **1839** E. FITZGERALD *Lett.* (1889) I. 50 Then a ride over hill and dale: then spudding up some weeds from the grass. **1842** *Penny Cycl.* XXIV. 21 He waits till the dog indicates the presence of the mole, and then spears or spuds the animal out as it moves in its run. **1884** *American* IX. 183 If he had spent a whole day in 'spudding' the thistles out of a small field.
2. To dig with a spud. Also *intr.*
1828–32 WEBSTER, *Spud,* v.t., to dig or loosen the earth with a spud. **1889** C. EDWARDES *Sardinia & the Sardes* 127 They spudded among the vines.
3. To begin to drill (a hole for an oil well) by imparting an up-and-down motion to the drilling bit. Now usu. more widely, to drill (a well) through the upper part of the overburden; also *absol.* Freq. const. *in* and occas. written *spud-in.* Also with *out.*
1886 *Sci. American* 21 Aug. 116 A 12 inch hole is usually drilled or spudded down to the rock. **1913** V. B. LEWES *Oil Fuel* 64 If the hole is not deep enough, it has to be 'spudded out' to the necessary depth. **1924** *Bull. Amer. Assoc. Petroleum Geologists* VIII. 643 The driller, with his hand on the brake and familiar with the action of his machinery and

pump since the well was 'spudded' in, is by far the best judge of the formation in which he is drilling. **1928** *Publ. Texas Folk-Lore Soc.* VII. 59 He had a 100,000 barrel gusher and was spudding in on another location. **1948** *Sun* (Baltimore) 16 Apr. 12/1 Drillers spudded in the first well of the big Leduc field in November, 1946. **1966** *Southern Reporter* CLXXX. 746/2 Substantial surface preparations to drill are sufficient to be considered 'commencement' of drilling operations for lease-clause purposes,.. provided that such preliminary operations are continued.. until well is actually spudded in. **1967** *Economist* 18 Nov. 788/2 The company has a world-wide business instrumentation for well-drilling.., whenever 'wildcats are spudded'. **1975** *BP Shield Internat.* May 1/2 BP's drilling contractors.. will spud and drill to completion the first Forties well. **1977** *Irish Times* 8 June 10/3 The Deminex consortium yesterday disclosed that it spudded-in its exploratory well in block 34/15, off the west coast, on Friday last.

'spudder[1]. *rare.* Now *dial.* Also 7 sputher. [Alteration of *pudder*, *puther* POTHER *sb.*] Fuss, disturbance, bother.

1650 A. B. *Mutat. Polemo* 38 These are to advance and keep some spudder in the North, to draw down a considerable party thitherward. **1661** BROME *Songs & Poems* 171 When we know all the Pretty sputher, Betwixt the one house and the other. **1880–2** in Cornwall glossaries.

spudder[2] ('spʌdə(r)). [f. SPUD *v.* + -ER[1].] A small drilling rig used for spudding.

1922 L. C. SANDS in D. T. Day *Handbk. Petroleum Industry* I. 250 These lighter outfits generally manipulate the drilling tools by the spudding principle and are often called 'spudders'. **1935** *Discovery* Apr. 119/1 The see-saw motion of the [rocking] 'beam'.. transmits to the tool a motion very similar to that of the spudder. **1960** *Pacific Reporter* CCCLIV. 444/2 Plaintiff.. purchased four small standard drilling rigs (commonly referred to as 'spudders') at an aggregate cost of $15,750. **1977** R. D. LANGENKAMP *Handbk. Oil Industry Terms & Phrases* (ed. 2) 160 Spudders are used in shallow-well workovers, for spudding in, or bringing in a rotary-drilled well.

'spudding, *vbl. sb.* [f. SPUD *v.* + -ING[1].]

1. The action of digging or removing with a spud. *spec.* the preliminary drilling of a well-hole through the upper part of the overburden (see SPUD *v.* 3 a); freq. as ***spudding in***, ***spudding-in***.

1885 *Engineering* 26 June 708/2 The bore is usually started by what is termed spudding—*i.e.*, working the tools direct from the Bull wheel, lifting and dropping by slacking or surging the rope on the wheel. **1891** *Daily News* 12 Sept. 3/6 This is followed by regular day work.. made up of thistle spudding,.. hop-branching, hay-making, harvesting, &c. **1901** *Munsey's Mag.* XXV. 746/2 The start is made by 'spudding', which is done by attaching the drill proper to the rope, and then skilfully tightening and loosening the coils on the drum by hand, thus raising the drill and letting it fall within the tube. **1922** A. BLUM *Petroleum* III. i. 162 The hole is started with a bit, eight to twenty inches across the cutting edge, the size depending upon the proposed depth of the hole... This is called 'spudding in'. **1929** BABBITT & DOLAND *Water Supply Engin.* vii. 160 The well hole is usually started by 'spudding', which consists in drilling without the walking beam because of the shorter length of tools and the lack of 'stretch' in the rope. **1967** *Sun* 22 Sept. 8/5 Exploratory drilling starts this weekend with the 'spudding-in' of a well 15 miles off the Lincolnshire coast. **1974** *Bull. Amer. Assoc. Petroleum Geologists* LVIII. 1124/2 The present drilling program began in 1971 with the spudding of the Eider well.

2. Special Comb.: **spudding bit**, a drilling bit used in spudding.

1907 *Internat. Libr. Technol.: Rock Boring* 16 The spudding bit in Fig. 16 is for drilling earth down to solid rock. **1924** L. C. UREN *Textbk. Petroleum Production Engin.* v. 125 A special spudding bit is used which is shorter than the usual pattern. **1939** D. HAGER *Fund. Petroleum Industry* ix. 225 With the Lucy spudding bit a cement plug is set at the bottom of the hole, and the bit, by being raised or lowered, digs a hole several feet deep into the side of the hole.

'spuddle, *v.* Now *dial.* [Alteration of PUDDLE *v.*; in later use partly f. SPUD *sb.* 3.]

1. *intr.* To puddle, in various senses; to work feebly or ineffectively.

1630 J. TAYLOR (Water P.) *Water Cormorant* Wks. III. 1/3 Hee grubs and spuddles for his prey in muddy holes and obscure cauernes. **1704** J. PITTS *Acc. Moham.* vii. 103 In the very place where the Child spuddled with his Feet, the Water flowed out. **1830** COBBETT *Rur. Rides* (1885) II. 314 The labourers who spuddle about the ground in the little *dips* between those sand-hills. **1883–** in dialect glossaries (Hants., Wilts., Som., Dev.).

2. *trans.* To turn over, dig up, stir or work at, lightly or superficially.

1805 R. W. DICKSON *Pract. Agric.* II. 600 This purpose is well accomplished.. by spuddling the land with a kind of plough. **1856** MORTON *Cycl. Agric.* II. 726 *Spuddling* (Kent); see *Broad-sharing* ['ploughing shallow and wide with a broad share, without turning it over']. **1875–** in dialect glossaries (Warw., Suss., Som., Dev.).

'spuddy, *a.* [f. SPUD *sb.* Cf. PUDDY *a.*] Short and stumpy or plump; thick-set.

a **1825** in FORBY *Voc. E. Anglia.* **1854** in MISS BAKER *Northampt. Gloss.* **1862** BORROW *Wales* II. xiii. 142 The other was a short spuddy fellow, with a broad ugly face. *Ibid.* 143 He was father of the spuddy military puppy. **1863** W. W. STORY *Roba di R.* II. ii. §29 [Jewesses] who fill.. the wide chair on which they sit, while they rest their spuddy hands on their knees.

spue, variant of SPEW *v.*

'spuffle, *v. E. Angl. dial.* [Imitative.]

1. *intr.* To fuss or bustle; to be in a flurry or in breathless haste.

a **1825** FORBY *Voc. E. Anglia* 321 I saw Mr. A. spuffling along. **1862** BORROW *Wales* xix, He spuffled and sputtered in a most extraordinary manner. **1869** *Spectator* 25 Dec. 1518 When a Suffolk man means to tell his friend that he is making.. too much fuss about anything,.. he says quietly, 'Now don't spuffle'.

2. *trans.* To utter thickly or indistinctly.

1861 *Temple Bar* III. 292 He finds her with her mouth crammed full of food, and incapable of spuffling out a word.

Hence **'spuffling** *vbl. sb.* and *ppl. a.*

1893 COZENS-HARDY *Brd. Norf.* 30, I am not sure whether spuffling is a practice peculiar to East Anglia. **1897** W. RYE *Norfolk Songs* 56 His spuffling overbearing ways did him harm.

spug (sparrow): see SPRUG.

spugslang, var. SPUUGSLANG.

spuilyie, -zie, variants of SPULYIE.

spule. *Sc.* [Of obscure origin: not a normal variant of SPAULD.]

1. A shoulder, esp. of an animal.

1803 SCOTT *Christie's Will* vi. in *Minstrelsy*, The spule o' the deer on the board he has set. The fattest that ran on the Hutton Lee.

2. *attrib.* in ***spule-blade***, ***-bone***.

1802 [see SPEAL-BONE]. **1818** SCOTT *Br. Lamm.* xviii, Then for dinner.. there's no muckle left on the spule-bane. **1824** —— *Redgauntlet* let. xi, His left hand [was] always on his right spule-blade, to hide the wound that the silver bullet had made.

spullar, -er, obs. forms of SPOOLER.

†**spult.** *north.* and *Sc. Obs. rare.* [Cf. WFlem. *spulten* to spout.] A spout.

1470–71 *Durh. Acc. Rolls* (Surtees) 643 Pro factura iiij[or] spultes eneis pro aqueducta hoc anno, xvj d. **1487–8** *Ibid.* 651 iiij[or] spultes cum j lavatory stone ad vj d. **15..** *Aberdeen Reg.* (Jam.), Ane spult of leyd. **1595** in *Scott. Hist. Rev.* Apr. (1913) 303 Item cheis shelf. Item ane brewing spult.

†**spulyiation.** *Sc. Obs. rare.* In 7 spuilzi-. [f. SPULYIE *v.*] Spoliation.

a **1688** G. DALLAS *Stiles* (1697) 266 Summonds of Spuilziation of Teinds. *Ibid.* 267 The said Pursuer having sufficient Right and Interest to prosecute.. the Action of Spuilziation after-specified.

spulyie ('spøljɪ, 'spølɪ), *sb.* *Sc.* Now *arch.* Forms: α. 5 spolȝe, 6 -ȝie, spoylȝe, -ȝie, spoillȝe, -ȝie, spoilȝe, -ȝie (7, 9 -zie), -ȝy; 6 spoylie, -llie, spoilie, spollie, 8 spoolie. β. 6 spulȝe (spuleȝe, -iȝe, spullȝe), 7– spulzie (8 -zy), 9 spulyie; 6 spuilȝe (spwilȝe), -ȝie, 7– spuilzie; 8 spulie, spuilie, 9 spuilly. [ad. OF. *espoille*, *espuille* SPOIL *sb.*]

1. The action of despoiling; spoliation; an instance of this.

1464–5 *Sc. Acts Parlt.* (1875) XII. 31/2 Þe lordis.. sall knaw apone.. all spolȝeis mayde sene the tyme of þe cessing of þe last sessionis. **1507** *Reg. Privy Seal Scot.* I. 205/1 Actioun.. for the spulȝe of the teynd schevez of the personage of Petcokkis. **1588** A. KING tr. *Canisius' Catech.* 39 All vnlauchfull.. vsurping of vthir mens geir be thift, spollie,.. iniust winning. **1678** SIR G. MACKENZIE *Crim. Laws Scot.* I. xxxi. §iii. (1690) 156 Like as by the constant Custom, many Actions of Spulzie were founded upon this Act. **1715** RAMSAY *Christ's Kirk Gr.* II. i, There had been mair blood and skaith, Sair harship and great spulie. **1765–8** ERSKINE *Inst. Law Scot.* III. vii. §16 When a spuilzie is committed, action lies against the delinquent [etc.]. **1814** SCOTT *Wav.* lxv, Doubtless officers cannot always keep the soldier's hand from depredation and spulzie. **1877** MISS YONGE *Cameos* III. i. 7 Graham further collected three hundred caterans in the Highlands, men always ready for bloodshed and spulzie. **1898** PATON *Castlebraes* 44 The yin o' us'll mak' a spuilly, or ma name's no Heather Jock.

†**b.** *Law.* An action for spoliation. *Obs.*

1678 SIR G. MACKENZIE *Crim. Laws Scot.* I. xxvi. §iv. (1699) 132 If the Executor did any wrong, he was lyable to a spuilzie, and his sentence was reduceable. **1686** in J. J. Vernon *Parish of Hawick* (1900) 197 Thomas Briggs.. was onlawed and amerciatt.. in ane Spuylyea for abstracting and resetting of lyme from the church style building. **1765–8** ERSKINE *Inst. Law Scot.* IV. i. §15 Spuilzie is not only competent against the *spoliator*,.. but against all abettors.

2. Spoil, booty, plunder.

1507 *Acc. Ld. High Treas.* III. 393 To Marchemond herald and his fallowis for the spulȝe of the feild, xx Franch crounis. **1513** DOUGLAS *Æneid* I. v. 106 Quham,.. Chergit with the spuilȝe of the orient, Amang the numer of goddis reskue thou sall. **1596** DALRYMPLE tr. *Leslie's Hist. Scot.* II. 280 Thay.. tak thair schipis to Ingland ladne with spoylȝie. **1719** HAMILTON *Ep. to Ramsay* III. viii, We'll bring aff but little spulzie In sic a barter. **1720** RAMSAY *Rise & Fall of Stocks* 120 There was odd scrambling for the spulzy. **1789** DAVIDSON *Seasons* 122 He got the spuilie to himsel' As they fled hame to toon. **1819** W. TENNANT *Papistry Storm'd* (1827) 192 Ha! Satan's toy-shop now is taen! Look up and see your spulzie! **1882** J. F. S. GORDON *Hist. Moray* II. 319 The *spulzie* taken or destroyed.. gives a good idea of the plenishing of a wealthy baron's residence in those days.

'spulyie, *v.* Chiefly *Sc.* Now *arch.* Forms: α. 4 spoly, 5 spolyon, 6 spolȝe (spoll-, spoulȝe), 7 spolze; 5 spoilȝe, 6 spoillȝe, -ȝie, spoylȝe, -ȝie, 6–7 spoylie, 7 spoilyie. β. 5–6 spulȝe (5 spwl-, 6 spvl-), 6 spuleȝe, -iȝe, spullȝe, 7 spulze; 6 spulȝie (spull-), 7– spulzie, 9 spulyie, -ye; 6 spuilȝe (spwil-), spuilȝie (spuill-), 8 spuilzie. [ad. OF. *espoillier* SPOIL *v.*]

1. *trans.* To despoil or plunder (persons, etc.).

1375 BARBOUR *Bruce* XIII. 459 Quhen thai nakit spulȝeit war That war slayne in the battale thar. *c* **1375** *Cursor M.* 2503 (Fairf.), Siþen þai spred to spoly þe lande. *c* **1440** *Promp. Parv.* 470/1 Spoylyn, or spolyon,.. *spolio, dispolio.* *c* **1470** HENRY *Wallace* III. 211 The Scottis.. Spoilȝeid the feld, gat gold and othir ger. **1533** BELLENDEN *Livy* III. ii. (S.T.S.) I. 247 At last he ischit at þe grete porte of his tentis, and spuleȝete his inemyis liand but ordoure. **1567** *Gude & Godlie B.* (S.T.S.) 59 He.. spolȝeit Sathan, hell and sin, And heuinlie gloir to vs hes win. **1588** A. KING tr. *Canisius' Catech.* 151 That widoues might becum thair pray, and that thay might spulȝie the fatherles. *a* **1670** SPALDING *Troub. Chas. I* (1850) I. 4 Thay.. first began to rob and spoilyie the Erllis tennentis. **1791** J. LEARMONT *Poems* 46 He spulzied fock and did them hang.

b. To despoil or deprive *of* something.

1508 DUNBAR *Tua Mariit Wemen* 397, I spittit quhen I saw That super spendit euill spreit, spvlȝeit of all vertu. **1513** DOUGLAS *Æneid* v. iv. 119 Syne Gyas schip.. gaif hym place alswa, For scho wes spulȝeit of hir sterisman. **1562** WINȜET *Wks.* (S.T.S.) I. 72 Qvhy spulȝe and denude ȝe ws of this part of our Catholik beleif? **1609** SKENE *Reg. Maj.* 55 He qvha is spolzeid of his possession, sould be first restored. **1834** H. MILLER *Scenes & Leg.* xxii. (1857) 316 Spulyieing women of their yarn.

2. To take as spoil or plunder.

c **1470** HENRY *Wallace* IV. 95 Syne spoilȝied thai the harnais or thai wend. **1508** KENNEDIE *Flyting w. Dunbar* 277 Than spulȝeit thay the haly stane of Scone. **1587** in *Scott. Hist. Rev.* July (1905) 358 He reft, spulzied, and took certaine wairs, guids, and geir out of a bark. **1609** SKENE *Reg. Maj.* ii. 16 The moueable gudes (spulzeit) or the land. **1754** ERSKINE *Princ. Sc. Law* (1809) 451 It is a relevant defence, that the defender.. made voluntary restitution.. of the goods spuilzied.

3. *intr.* To commit spoliation.

1834 H. MILLER *Scenes & Leg.* xxii. (1857) 317 They ate and drank, and then rose to spulzie. **1894** LATTO *Tam. Bodkin* i, The haill lot o' them reivin' an' thievin' an' spulyiein'.

Hence **'spulyied** *ppl. a.*

1838 W. BELL *Dict. Law Scot.* 934 The spuilzied property may be evicted from *bona fide* purchasers. **1875** *Sc. Acts Parlt.* Index 1137/2 The lords of session to have power to order the restoration of spulzied goods.

'spulyieing, *vbl. sb.* [f. SPULYIE *v.*] Spoiling, despoiling; spoliation.

1375 BARBOUR *Bruce* XIII. 457 Thai dispendit haly that day In spoulȝeing and riches taking. *c* **1440** *Promp. Parv.* 470 Spoylynge, or spolyynge, *spoliacio, depredacio.* **1647** *Extr. Burgh Recs. Stirling* 193 The actis and ordinances.. anent slotting and spuilyeing of flesche. **1691** *Jedburgh Council Records* 19 March (MS.), For his wrongous spulzieing and awaytakeing of certaine stones out of the Minister's yeard dyke.

'spulyier. *rare.* Also 5 spoliar, 6 spulyear. [f. as prec.] A spoiler.

c **1400** *Apol. Loll.* 7 Feiþful curats owen to sorowe as wel of þe spoling of þer sogetis, as also of þe synne of þe spoliars. **1562–3** *Reg. Privy Council Scot.* I. 231 The ressait.. makis the said Thomas expres spulyear and approvar of the spulye libellit. **1819** W. TENNANT *Papistry Storm'd* (1827) 62 They forc'd and flappit to the yird That spulyier and fae.

spumante (spuːˈmæntiː). Also erron. **spumanti**. [It., = 'sparkling'.] A sparkling (usu. sweet) white wine from Asti in Piedmont; in full, ***Asti Spumante***.

1908 C. E. HAWKER *Chats about Wine* 89 The Frenchman with his Sillery.. The Italian with his Asti Spumante, all favour sweetness. **1938** C. ISHERWOOD *Lions & Shadows* i. 37 To celebrate the achievement, Mr. Holmes has ordered Asti Spumanti. What a marvellous drink!.. So cool and fizzy and sweet. **1945** *Comment from Italy* (Three Arts Club) 22 It was beer issue night, and most of the groups had reinforced it with bottles of vino, vermouth, and spumanti as well. **1958** L. DURRELL *Balthazar* III. x. 206 Pursewarden was inveighing somewhat incoherently against the Cervonis for serving Spumante instead of champagne. **1971** *Country Life* 25 Nov. 1466/2 A dry spumante wine. **1982** *Sunday Tel.* (Colour Suppl.) 7 Mar. 38/3 The Spumanti was flowing in the officers' mess, everyone cheering.

spume (spjuːm), *sb.* Also 5 spome. [ad. OF. *spume*, *espume* (It. *spuma*, Sp. and Pg. *espuma*), or L. *spūma*.]

1. a. Foam, froth, frothy matter.

1390 GOWER *Conf.* II. 265 Sche sette a caldron on the fyr, ..And let it buile in such a plit, Til that sche sawh the spume whyt. *c* **1440** *Alph. Tales* 153 Þou seis I hafe no burnyng een, nor no spome at my mouthe. **1547** BOORDE *Brev. Health* xxxiii. 18 b, Take of the white of ii egges, beat it to a waterishe spume. **1576** G. BAKER *Gesner's Jewel of Health* 181 As soon as.. purple spumes or fomes swell or rise up to the brymme, increase the fyre. **1612** WOODALL *Surg. Mate* Wks. (1653) 37 English honey.. yeelding little spume in decocting. **1669** BOYLE *Cont. New Exp.* II. (1682) 96, I thrust a snail into it, who put forth much spume or froth. [*c* **1706** J. PHILIPS *Poems Style of Milton* (1762) 109 Sulphur, and nitrous spume, enkindling fierce.] **1710** T. FULLER *Pharm. Extemp.* 280 Both [litharges] are but a Spume blown off in the refining of Silver from Lead. **1727–46** THOMSON *Summer* 1108 Thence nitre, sulphur, and the fiery spume Of fat bitumen. **1826** KIRBY & SP. *Entomol.* xl. IV. 120 The abundant spume with which the larva.. envelopes itself. **1871** T. R. JONES *Anim. Kingd.* (ed. 4) 253 Two of these animals.. joined to each other by a quantity of frothy spume.

b. *spec.* Foam of the sea, etc.

Common from about 1850.

c **1440** *Gesta Rom.* xciv. 425 (Add. MS.), For all thing that are in the worlde are not but as a spume in the see. **1599** NASHE *Lenten Stuff* Wks. (Grosart) V. 209 They would no more liue vnder the yoke of the Sea, or haue their heads washt with his bubbly spume. **1615** G. Sandys *Trav.* 93 He [Nile] laves The stars with spume, all tremble with his waves. *a* **1687** Cotton *Night Quatrains* ii, His Steeds their flaming Nostrils cool in Spume of the Cerulean Pool. **1760** *Phil. Trans.* LII. 136 This bird therefore dipping so frequently into the spume of the sea, is probably for the food swimming amongst it, rather than to feed upon the spume itself. **1805** *Naval Chron.* XIII. 394 My forehead was wet with the spume of the spray. **1871** Longf. *Wayside Inn* II. *Musician's T.* IV. vii, A great rush of rain, Making the ocean white with spume. **1885** *Manch. Exam.* 2 May 6/2 Breezy seaside effects that breathe of the salt spume.

c. In fig. uses.

1608 Middleton *Trick to catch Old One* II. ii, A midnight surfeiter The spume of a brothel-house. **1651** Baxter *Inf. Bapt.* 124, I answer to this Objection, that it being but the spume of humane reason, I needed not to have given any other answer. **1836** Ruskin *Essay on Lit.* Wks. 1903 I. 374 These foul snails.., leaving their spume and filth on the fairest flowers of literature. **1861** Ld. Lytton & Fane *Tannhäuser* 14 That so august a Spirit.. Should.. Decline, to quench so bright a brilliancy In Hell's sick spume.

†**2.** = litharge 1, 1 b. *Obs.*

c **1400** Maundev. (Roxb.) xviii. 84 Þai take alde peper.. and strewez apon it spume of siluer or of leed. **1570** Levins *Manip.* 188 Ye spume of lead, *molybditis. Ibid.* Ye spume of syluer, *argyritis.* **1589** Fleming *Virg. Georg.* III. 51 They doo mingle therewith all The spume of argent, sulphur quicke, (or brimstone naturall). **1661** Lovell *Hist. Anim. & Min.* 118 With ceruse, or the spume of silver, it helps the colours of cicatrices.

3. *attrib.* and *Comb.*, as *spume-bow*; *spume-flake*, *-flecked* adj.; **spume-stone**, ? pumice-stone.

1831 Hodgson in Raine *Mem.* (1858) II. 217 There is much spume-stone like cinders and scoria in the middle. **1845** Browning *How they brought the Good News* v, The thick heavy spume-flakes which aye and anon His fierce lips shook upwards in galloping on. **1877** L. Morris *Epic Hades* I. 36 The spume-flecked waters.. Left dry the yellow shore. **1921** W. de la Mare *Veil* 15 With myriad spume-bows roaring ocean swills The cold profuse abundance of the rain.

spume (spju:m), *v.* [ad. L. *spūmāre* (hence It. *spumare*, Sp. and Pg. *espumar*, OF. *espumer*), f. *spūma* spume *sb.*]

1. *intr.* To foam or froth. Also with *out.*

13.. [see spuming *ppl. a.*]. **1582** Stanyhurst *Æneis* I. (Arb.) 41 At a blow hee lustelye swapping, Thee wyne fresh spuming with a draught swild vp to the bottom. **1610** Healey *St. Aug. Citie of God* (1620) 382 The fetching downe of the Moone, till (saith Lucan) she spume upon such hearbes as they desire. **1721** Bailey, *To Spume*, to froth or Foam. **1822** W. Irving *Braceb. Hall* (1845) 132 A small door, through the chinks of which came a glow of light, and smoke was spuming out. **1860** Mayne Reid *Wild Huntress* xxxv, A rushing torrent, that spumed against the banks. *fig.* **1904** *Blackw. Mag.* Apr. 588/1 Moore preferred that his should spume in his diary rather than his life.

2. *trans.* To send or cast *forth* like foam.

1859 Sala *Tw. round Clock* (1861) 173 Bedfordbury,.. whose tumble-down tenements and reeking courts spume forth plumps of animated rags. **1865** *Daily Tel.* 4 Dec. 5/4 Thus do these little people.. spume forth their venom day after day. **1883** R. Bridges *Prometheus* 599 The mountains .. from their swelling flanks spumed froth of fire.

Hence **'spuming** *ppl. a.*

13.. *E.E. Allit. P.* B. 1038 Þe spumande aspaltoun þat spyserez sellen. **1881** J. F. Keane *Six Months in Meccah* v. 105 While being laden it [the camel] gives vent to spuming, spluttering, bellows and whines. **1894** Sala *London up to Date* ii. 33 The spuming chalices.. having made the hearts of the guests glad within them. **1894** Max Pemberton *Sea Wolves* x, To plunge into the cavern of spuming water which lay between the crags.

spumed (spju:md), *ppl. a.* [f. spume *sb.* + -ed².] Flecked as with spume.

1923 D. H. Lawrence *Birds, Beasts & Flowers* 60 Cyclamen leaves.. Frost-filigreed Spumed with mud.

†**'spumeous**, *a. Obs.* [f. L. *spūme-us* (hence It. *spumeo*, Pg. *espumeo*), f. *spūma* spume *sb.*] Foamy, frothy; spumous, spumy.

1635 Person *Varieties* II. 55 These spumeous exhalations are such as are combustible and capable to bee kindled. **1664** Power *Exp. Philos.* I. 28 That spumeous froth or dew which here in the North we call Cuckow-Spittle. *a* **1670** Hacket *Cent. Serm.* (1675) 512 Far be it from us to think that it was not water,.. but a spumeous phlegmatic humour.

spumescence (spju:'mɛsəns). [See next and -ence.] Frothiness; the state of being foamy. Also *fig.*

1796 Kirwan *Elem. Min.* (ed. 2) I. 208 Before the blow-pipe it melts with a moderate spumescence into a white semitransparent enamel. **1903** *Speaker* 7 Feb. 489/2 His prose style always tends to spumescence.

spu'mescent, *a.* [See spume *v.* and -escent.] 'Having the appearance of foam or froth.'

1856 Henslow *Bot. Terms* 181.

†**'spumid**, *a. Obs.*$^{-0}$ [ad. L. *spūmid-us.*] 'Frothy or foamy' (Blount *Glossogr.*, 1656).

Hence **spumidness** in Bailey, 1727 (vol. II).

†**spu'miferous**, *a. Obs.*$^{-0}$ [f. L. *spūmifer.*] 'That bears foam, froth, or scum' (Blount).

spumification. *rare*$^{-1}$. [See spume *sb.* and -fication.] Production of froth.

1615 Crooke *Body of Man* 307 The least time of this processe of Nature is thirty dayes, sixe for Spumification, two for Delineation [etc.].

'spumiform, *a. rare*$^{-1}$. [See spume *sb.* and -form.] Froth-like, frothy.

1805 Weaver tr. *Werner* 201 The external form of friable fossils is.. spumiforn, as Red and Brown Scaly-Iron-Ores.

'spuminess. *rare*$^{-0}$. [f. spumy *a.*] 'Frothiness' (Bailey, vol. II, 1727).

spumoni (spu:'məʊnɪ). *U.S.* [ad. It. *spumone* (used in the same sense). f. *spuma* foam, spume.] A kind of ice-cream dessert (see quot. 1950).

1929 M. Lief *Hangover* v. 83 Mogador picked up a spoon and helped himself to some of the star's spumoni ice-cream. **1936** J. dos Passos *Big Money* 126 After they'd had their spumoni Mr. Barrow ordered himself brandy. **1950** Fransden & Nelson *Ice Cream & Other Frozen Desserts* xvii. 177 A special spumoni cup should be used. Press one-fourth of a spumoni cupful of vanilla ice cream around the sides and bottom to line the cup. Add chocolate ice cream. .. Finish filling with a mixture of fruit and whipped cream. **1968** P. Durst *Badge of Infamy* iv. 37 In addition to the minestrone and pizza there was a green salad.. spumoni and coffee. **1977** J. Wambaugh *Black Marble* (1978) xi. 246 Had her little two-year-old spumoni sucker *in the car* when I picked her up.

spumose (spju:'məʊs), *a. rare.* [ad. L. *spūmōs-us* (hence It. *spumoso*, Sp. and Pg. *espumoso*), f. *spūma* spume *sb.*] = spumous *a.*

1576 G. Baker *Gesner's Jewel of Health* 222 b, At any tyme .. may this water be drawne, and converted after into a spumose substaunce. **1683** Ray *Corr.* (1848) 132 A little spike of bright purple or red flowers, which afterwards turned to spumose vesicles. **1856–8** W. Clark *Van der Hoeven's Zool.* I. 798 A vesicular or spumose organ adhering to foot.

spumoso-, comb. form of L. *spūmōs-us* (see prec.), as in *spumoso-cellular* adj.

1846 Dana *Zooph.* (1848) 361 Texture of the sides and usually of the whole corallum spumoso-cellular.

spumous ('spju:məs), *a.* [ad. L. *spūmōs-us*: see spumose *a.* and cf. OF. *spumeux.*]

1. Of the nature of, having the appearance of, froth or foam.

c **1400** *Lanfranc's Cirurg.* 164 Þe blood þat goiþ out of þe wounde wole be spumous & cleer. *Ibid.* 201 Þere is engendrid þere a maner spumous substaunce. **1612** Woodall *Surg. Mate* Wks. (1653) 86 If.. the excrement which is voided from the mouth be spumous, pale, and crude. **1646** Sir T. Browne *Pseud. Ep.* 237 That spumous, frothy dew or exudation, or both, found upon Plants. **1710** T. Fuller *Pharm. Extemp.* 376 The Mass of Blood.. render'd spumous and sparkling. **1808** *Med. Jrnl.* XIX. 296 Had the blood proceeded from the lungs, he judged it would have been spumous, or mixed with air bubbles. **1846** Dana *Zooph.* (1848) 400 Corallum with very short calicles, truncate, rising from a spumous base.

2. Marked by foam; foaming.

1854 Dickens *Hard T.* II. i, Down upon the river.. rowed a crazy boat, which made a spumous track upon the water. **1876** R. F. Burton *Gorilla L.* II. 62 The fierce rollers of the spumous sea broke and recoiled.

spumy ('spju:mɪ), *a.* Also 6 spumye, 7 spumie. [f. spume *sb.*]

1. Covered with, throwing up, of the nature of, sea-foam.

1582 Stanyhurst *Æneis* III. (Arb.) 87 Thee rocks sternelye facing with salt fluds spumye be drumming. **1697** Dryden *Virg. Georg.* III. 368 The spumy Waves proclaim the watry War. **1741** H. Brooke *Constantia*, The Tiber now their spumy keels divide. **1797** T. Park *Sonn.* 7 High o'er the beech froths up the spumy spray. **1819** H. Busk *Banquet* II. 164 The spumy Rhone, or easy-winding Loire. **1894** *Outing* XXIV. 264/2 Great rollers, with their crest torn into spumy wreaths, rose higher and higher.

2. Of a frothy character or consistency; characterized by the presence of froth.

a **1618** Sylvester *Maiden's Blush* 1122 Swelling Clusters .., Whose spumy Juice in Pharao's cup I crush. **1621** G. Sandys *Ovid's Met.* VII. (1626) 137 Cerberus.. on the grasse his spumy poyson sheds. **1641** Wilkins *Mercury* Pref. (1707) 4 Though what the Author write prove spumy Froth. **1740** Somerville *Hobbinolia* III. 89 Matrons sage.. Grasp the capacious Bowl; nor cease to draw The spumy Nectar. **1788** Burns *Ep. R. Graham* iii, Some spumy, fiery, *ignis fatuus* matter. **1819** Keats *Song of Four Faeries* 16 Let me see the myriad shapes.. wrought by spumy bitumen.

spun (spʌn), *ppl. a.* [Pa. pple. of spin *v.*]

1. That has undergone the process of spinning; formed, fabricated, or prepared by spinning: **a.** Of wool, silk, or other material; also *spec.* of normally rigid materials, as glass. *Comb.*, esp. as *spun-dyed* adj., of materials coloured during spinning.

Also in earlier use as the second element in combs., as *evil-*, *ill-spun* (see those words).

1486 *Bk. St. Albans, Her.* fiij b, For as mych as weueris vse sich fusillys made of sponnyn woll. **1570** Levins *Manip.* 188 Spunne, *filatus.* **1608** Willet *Hexapla Exod.* 575 Women did spinne with their hands and brought the spunne worke. **1759** *Phil. Trans.* LI. 390 The stockings.. were wove of carded and spun silk. **1779** *Ibid.* LXX. 51 Long filaments of a vitrified matter like spun-glass. **1842** *Penny Cycl.* XXIV. 401/1 Two or more yarns, or simple spun threads, firmly united together by twisting. **1868** *Rep. U.S. Commissioner Agric.* (1869) 291 The Murray mill.. will be employed in weaving broad goods of net warps and 'spun' fillings. **1875** Knight *Dict. Mech.* 2292/2 *Spun-silk*, a cheap article produced from short-fibered and waste silk, in contradistinction to the long fibers wound from the cocoon and *thrown.* **1899** *Jrnl. Soc. Arts* XLVIII. 62/1 Spun glass is probably the earliest production which resembles natural silk. **1936** H. Miller *Black Spring* 192 Suddenly like spun-glass under a blue flame, the street quickens into tongues of fire. **1940** *Engineering* 1 Nov. 343/3 The advantages of such spun-concrete products as pipes and poles are well known. **1947** J. C. Rich *Materials & Methods of Sculpture* iv. 64 Spun-copper bowls are highly recommended for use in mixing plaster of Paris. **1980** *Nature* 14 Feb. p. xiii/2 The body is a spun steel bowl and lid on die cast iron base.

Comb. **1862** *Catal. Internat. Exhib., Brit.* II. No. 3900, Velvet and plush, made from spun silk waste. **1887** *Encycl. Brit.* XXII. 66/1 The spun-silk industry has chiefly developed in the Yorkshire and Lancashire textile centres. **1955** Cockett & Hilton *Basic Chem. Textile Colouring & Finishing* i. 34 Spun-coloured or pigmented fibres. These are sometimes known as spun-dyed fibres, although the method of colouration is not a dyeing process in the usual sense. **1975** R. H. Peters *Textile Chem.* III. i. 4 Other ways of colouring with insoluble compounds are to introduce them in fibre manufacture, i.e. in the polymer solution prior to extrusion giving 'spun-dyed' filaments.

b. *spun gold*, *silver*, a silk thread wound with gold, silver-gilt, or silver wire. Hence *spun-golden* adj.

1728 Chambers *Cycl.*, *Gold Thread*, or Spun Gold, is the flatted Gold wrapp'd, or laid over a Thread of Silk, by twisting it with a Wheel, and Iron Bobins. **1875** Knight *Dict. Mech.* 2292/2. **1966** T. Pynchon *Crying of Lot 49* i. 21 Frail girls with heart-shaped faces, huge eyes, spun-gold hair. **1978** S. Sheldon *Bloodline* ii. 40 She had spun-golden hair and skin as delicate as porcelain.

c. Of butter or sugar: Drawn out or worked up into a thread-like form, esp. for ornamenting confectionery or other dishes.

1834 Ht. Martineau *Farrers* ii. 20 A yellow lamb of spun butter. **1846** Soyer *Cookery* 549 You have previously formed some ropes of spun sugar. **1861** Geo. Eliot *Silas M.* iii, Spun butter in all its freshness. **1872** O. W. Holmes *Poet Breakf.-t.* iv, If you don't leave your spun-sugar confectionery business.

d. Applied to vegetable protein, esp. soya, that has been spun into fibres so as to resemble meat and to the meat substitutes made from it.

1973 *Guardian* 21 Apr. 12/3 'Spun steak.' Looks like steak .. only it is made of spun soya. **1976** T. Heald *Let Sleeping Dogs Die* v. 81 Canine comestibles... Doggy buckwheat.. spun protein tripe.

e. *ellipt.* Spun silk or yarn.

1868 *Rep. U.S. Commissioner Agric.* (1869) 290, 60,000 pounds of thrown silk, 60,000 pounds of 'patent spun', 100,000 pieces of belt ribbons [etc.]. **1892** *Daily News* 24 Sept. 2/6 Yarns, no improvement yet noted in position of dry spuns, wet spuns are in pretty good demand.

2. With *out.* Unduly prolonged or protracted.

1869 K. H. Digby *Little Low Bushes* 244 Carheil is like a long and spun-out speech. **1879** *Grove's Dict. Mus.* I. 645/2 We can pardon a few awkward or tedious phrases, a few spun-out passages.

spundge, obs. f. sponge *sb.*¹ and *v.*

spune, Sc. variant of spoon *sb.*

spung (spʌŋ), *sb. Sc.* [? Alteration of the earlier pung *sb.*¹] A purse; a fob.

1728 Ramsay *Last Sp. Miser* xiv, They bid us draw Our siller spungs, For this and that, to mak' them braw. **1728** —— *General Mistake* 167 [He] rarely has a shilling in his spung. **1836** M. Macintosh *Cottager's Daughter* 195, I to death hae some withstood To mak my spung and coffers guid. **1892** J. Lumsden *Sheephead & Trotters* 14 [He] took an enormous gold watch from his 'spung' and handed it toward me.

spung, *v. Sc.* [? f. prec.] *trans.* To rob.

1719 Ramsay *Ep. to Hamilton* II. xii, If that the gypsies dinna spung us. **1788** R. Galloway *Poems* 94 If you be not very sly, They'll spung you of your money.

spunge, -eous, -er, -iness, etc., obs. forms of sponge, -eous, sponger, sponginess, etc.

spunk (spʌŋk), *sb.* Forms: α. 6 sponke, 6–8 sponk, 7 sponck. β. 6 spounk, 6–7 spunck, 7 spunke, 6– spunk. [Of obscure history; prob. related to funk *sb.*¹ Cf. also punk *sb.*³]

1. *Sc.* and *dial.* A spark, in various senses.

Chiefly in fig. use: cf. spark *sb.*¹ 1 d and 2.

a. With *of* (some quality, fire, light, etc.).

α. **1536** Bellenden *Cron. Scot.* (1821) I. 211 For ane sponk of small occasioun of unkindness. *a* **1572** Knox *Hist. Ref.* Wks. 1846 I. 10 How mercyfullie God hath looked upoun this Realme, reteanyng within it some sponk of his light, evin in the tyme of grettast darkness. **1590** Davidson *Reply Bancroft* in *Wodrow Misc.* (1844) 508 If there had beene a sponke thereof [*sc.* charity] within him. *c* **1614** Sir W. Mure *Dido & Æneas* III. 446 Seazing on her death-seal'd lipps to knowe If any sponk of breath as ȝit remain'd.

β. **1599** A. Hume *His Recantation* 10, I feel no spunk of faith in me. **1629** Sir W. Mure *True Crucifix* 681 Loe, while ev'n his life's last spunke is spent, The Temple's vaile is to the bottome rent. **1647** Trapp *Com. Rev.* vi. 3 A Sea-coal fire, if not stirred up, will die of it self, so will our spark and spunk of light. **1653** Binning *Serm.* (1845) 622 He hath no more religion than a Spunk of desire. **1724** Ramsay *Vision* ii, Ilk creature.. That had a spunk of sense. **1785** Burns *1st Ep. J. L[aprai]k* xiv, O for a spunk o' Allan's glee. **1808** Stagg *Misc. Poems* 77 At length a wee bit spunk o' light Transfix'd his wand'ring eyes. **1886** Stevenson *Kidnapped* xviii, He has some spunks of decency.

b. Without const.

c **1585** Montgomerie *Misc. Poems* xiii. 40 Fy on that freik that can not love! He hes not worth a sponk of spreit. **1596** Dalrymple tr. *Leslie's Hist. Scot.* II. 57 He slokned out all occasioun of ciuil weir, and nychtbour fead, spunk and spark. **1669** R. Fleming *Fulfilling Script.* (1801) I. 172 That little spunk now under ashes must assuredly revive and blow up to a flame. **1818** Scott *Br. Lamm.* xxvi, Not a gleed of fire, then, except..maybe a spunk in Mysie's cutty-pipe. 1823- in dial. glossaries. 1827 J. Wilson Noct. Ambr. Wks. 1855 II. 31 As an Editor, he is, compared wi' Christopher North—but as a spunk to the Sun!

c. A small fire. Also in phr. ***a spunk of fire***.
1802 Sibbald Chron. S.P. Gloss. s.v., Spunk of fire, a very small fire. 1806 J. Nicol Poems I. 18 (Jam.), I see thee shiverin, wrinklet, auld, Cour owre a spunk that dies wi' cauld. 1815 Scott Guy M. xi, Ye may light a spunk o' fire in the red room. 1870 Verney Lettice Lisle xx, What, ain't there a spunk of fire?

d. *Sc.* and *north.* Applied to persons (see quots.).
1808 Jamieson s.v., A mere spunk, a lively creature; especially applied to one who has more spirit than bodily strength, or appearance of it. 1894 Heslop Northumbld. Gloss. s.v., He's a wee spunk o' a thing.

2. Touchwood; tinder, match, or amadou prepared from this.
1582 Stanyhurst Æneis I. (Arb.) 23 In spunck or tinder thee quick fyre he kindly receaued. 1646 Sir T. Browne Pseud. Ep. II. v. 89 To make white powder:..The best I know is by the powder of rotten willowes; spunck, or touchwood prepared, might perhaps make it russet. 1651 in Hartlib's Legacy (1655) 97 His Lordship told me the way of making of Spunk, or Touchwood. a 1691 Boyle Hist. Air (1692) 208 The burning of Match, Touchwood, Sponck, &c. 1723 Pres. St. Russia II. 13 They cure their wounds with Spunk or Tinder. 1754 Phil. Trans. XLVIII. 811 Of which [sc. fungus] touchwood or spunk, and the amadoue ordinaire of the French, is usually prepared. 1796 Hist. Ned Evans II. 141 By rubbing them with pounded gun-powder a little damped, he formed a kind of spunk, which kindled like a squib. 1841 Catlin N. Amer. Ind. xx. (1844) I. 147 It contained also his flint and steel, and spunk for lighting. Ibid. xxiii. I. 189 A spark of fire is seen and caught in a piece of spunk. 1858 Simmonds Dict. Trade s.v. Amadou, Amadou..dipped in a solution of saltpetre, forms the spunk or German tinder of commerce.

3. One or other of various fungi or fungoid growths on trees, esp. those of the species *Polyporus*, freq. used in the preparation of tinder. Cf. touchwood b.
1665 Hooke Microgr. 139 A kind of Jews-ear, or Mushroom, growing..on several sorts of Trees, such as Elders, Maples, Willows, etc.,..commonly called by the name of spunk. 1674 Josselyn Two Voy. 70 There is an excrescence growing out of the body of the Tree called spunck, or dead mens Caps. 1822-7 Good Study Med. (1829) I. 63 The best ordinary styptic is pressure with an elastic substance, as..touchwood, spunk, or some other spongy boletus. 1845-50 Mrs. Lincoln Lect. Bot. 199 The genus Boletus contains the touchwood, or spunk, which is sometimes used as tinder. 1866 Treas. Bot. 1089/1 Spunk, Polyporus igniarius.

4. *Sc.* (and *north.*). A slender slip of wood tipped with brimstone and used for conveying or producing fire; a match, a lucifer.
1755 Johnson, Sponk, a word in Edinburgh which denotes a match, or any thing dipt in sulphur that takes fire: as, any sponks will ye buy? 1788 G. Wilson Coll. Masonic Songs 52 The spunks tipt with brimstone he gropt for, In order to light him a candle. 1821 Scott Pirate vii, There is a gathering peat on the kitchen fire, and a spunk beside it —ye can light your ain candle. 1842 J. Aiton Domest. Econ. (1857) 263 The prowling thief enters the byre with a bag and brimstoned spunk. 1893 G. Travers Mona Maclean II. 127 Come and put a spunk to this fire.

5. a. Spirit, mettle; courage, pluck.
1773 Goldsm. Stoops to Conq. I, The squire has got spunk in him. 1775 S. J. Pratt Liberal Opin. cxvii. (1783) IV. 94 Those grave persons, who want taste, or (as these young gentlemen more elegantly term it) spunk, for such exercises. 1781 R. King Mod. Lond. Spy 24 They allowed that I had blood, but wanted spunk and spirit. 1802 Bentham Panopt. Wks. 1843 XI. 131 If Lord Henry had stuff and spunk enough in him for such business. 1857 Holland Bay Path xxiv. 285, I like your spunk, but it don't count in a fight with crazy folks and fools. 1890 Clark Russell My Shipmate Louise I. x. 213 Neither of them wanting spunk, at it they went!
transf. 1822 Galt Provost xxxi, The bailie, like a bantam cock in a passion, stotted out of his chair with the spunk of a birslet pea.

b. In phr. ***fellow, man***, etc., ***of*** (..) ***spunk***.
1774 Westm. Mag. II. 10 He is a fellow of Spanish spunk, and will run any man through the body, who dares to censure his portraits. 1785 Burns Jolly Beggars xliv, With an air That showed a man of spunk. 1812 Sporting Mag. XXXIX. 245 'Twas a shame That a lad of my spunk should be coop'd up so tame. 1833 [S. Smith] Lett. J. Downing xxii. (1835) 127 You are a man of spunk, Major, and I like you for it.

c. *coarse slang*. Seminal fluid.
For the sense development, compare the obs. slang *mettle*, which had the same meaning.
c 1888-94 My Secret Life I. 87 It seemed to me scarcely possible, that the sweet, well dressed, smooth-spoken ladies ..could let men put the spunk up their cunts. 1896 A. Beardsley Let. 21 Dec. (1970) 236 She played dirty tricks. .. Till the spunk trickled right down her femur. 1923 J. Manchon Le Slang 289 Spunk,..2° courage, vivacité, feu; on dit de préférence mettle, parce que 3° O[bscène] (= come, s.). 1971 B. W. Aldiss Soldier Erect 196 By sprawling right back on the seat and ignoring the stink of the shit-pit below me, I managed in no time to lob some spurts of spunk over my stomach, with some relief. 1978 J. Irving World according to Garp ii. 32 The boys were beating off, in turn, and rushing with their hot spunk in their hands to the microscopes in the infirmary lab—to see if they were sterile.

6. *attrib.*, chiefly in sense 4, as ***spunk-maker***, ***-seller***, ***-wood***; **spunk-box**, a tinder-box or matchbox; **spunk-fencer** *slang*, a match-seller; **spunk-flask**, a tinder-flask; **spunk-water** *U.S.*, rain-water that collects in hollow tree-stumps, popularly thought to be a cure for warts.
1721 Ramsay Lucky Spence v, Gin he likes to light his match At your spunk-box. 1828 Moir Mansie Wauch xx, Hiring beds at twopence a-night to..spunk-makers, and such like pick-pockets. 1835 Monteath Dunblane (1887) 122 His Spunk-flask at his hurdies hung. 1839 Slang Dict. 34 Spunk-fencers, match sellers. 1876 [see blame v. 7 d]. 1888 Barrie Auld Licht Idylls xii, An itinerant matchseller known..as the literary spunk-seller. 1888 Wardrop Poems & Sk. 213 I'll ding the business into spunkwood. 1949 Time 29 Aug. 7/2 Spunk-water, spunk-water, wash away my warts!

†spunk, *a. Obs.* = spunky *a.*
1788 J. Palmer in Parl. P. (1812-3) IV. 69, I hope the old woman may be spunk, and refuse to apologize. 1810 Spirit Publ. Jrnls. XIII. 177 Every thing spunk and giggish.

spunk (spʌŋk), *v.* [f. spunk *sb.*]
1. *intr.* To leak *out*, to become known. *Sc.*
1808 in Jamieson. 1820 Hogg Sheph. Cal. (1829) I. 28 It at last spunkit out that Rob Dodds had got hame safe enough. 1822 Galt Sir A. Wylie xxxviii, It might be detrimental if ony thing were to spunk out. 1857 Stewart Scot. Charact. 43 (E.D.D.), It spunkit oot I'd gat a letter frae Dr. Quibbles.

2. With *up*. a. *U.S.* To show spunk or spirit; to stand up, assert oneself spiritedly or courageously.
c 1850 'Dow jr.' in Jerdan Yankee Hum. (1853) 109 Just spunk up to the old codger—let him know you are not afraid of him. 1866 Harvard Mem. Biogr. II. 7 Sometimes I feel as if I must lie down;..but I 'spunk up' and have thus far held out. 1898 Westcott David Harum xxii, Then he spunked up some an' says [etc.].

b. *Sc.* To blaze or fire up in anger or passion.
1898 N. Munro J. Splendid viii. 86 He spunked up like tinder. 'Do you call me a liar?' he said.

spunkie (ˈspʌŋkɪ). *Sc.* Also 8 spunkey, 9 spunky. [f. spunk *sb.*]
1. A will o' the wisp.
1727 P. Walker Life R. Cameron in Biogr. Presbyt. (1827) I. 243 Some Willies with the Wisps, or Spunkies of Wild-fire. 1785 Burns Addr. to Deil xiii, An' aft your moss-traversing Spunkies Decoy the wight that late an' drunk is. 1816 Scott Bl. Dwarf ii, The scene of it had been avoided ..by all human beings, as being the ordinary resort of kelpies, spunkies, and other demons. 1855 Smedley Occult Sciences 75 The wily spunkie manœuvred so dexterously that the unhappy wanderer was speedily decoyed into the nearest morass. 1884 W. Sime To and Fro 170 The spunkie which showed the signal for freedom has disappeared.
Comb. 1898 Spence Poems 139 The spunkie-haunted bog, Where sank the shepherd and his dog.

2. Whisky or other spirituous drink. *rare.*
1786 Burns Epist. J. Kennedy iii, Gie me just a true good fallow,..And spunkie ance to make us mellow, And then we'll shine.

3. a. A spirited, mettlesome, or courageous person; a smart or lively fellow.
1806 J. Nicol Poems I. 148 (Jam.), An' frae his bow, the shafts, fu' snack, Pierc'd monie a spunkie's liver. 1901 G. Douglas House w. Gr. Shutters 182 Logan..thought him a hardy young spunkie.

b. A fiery, hot-tempered, or irritable person.
1821 Galt Ann. Parish xxvi, He was himself..a perfect spunkie of passion.

ˈspunkily, *adv.* [f. spunky *a.*] In a spunky manner; angrily, irritably. Also spiritedly, courageously (*U.S.*).
1890 Clark Russell Ocean Trag. II. xxiii. 228 The old chap very spunkily bestowed several emphatic nods upon her. 1949 J. Flanner in New Yorker 9 Apr. 58/2 A hundred artists, from all over Italy,..are spunkily giving their first show this month. 1976 Publishers Weekly 21 June 88/2 Judith hurries out to be with her sister and spunkily unravels the mystery.

ˈspunkless, *a.* [f. spunk *sb.*] Destitute of spunk; spiritless.
1882 J. Walker Jaunt to Auld Reekie, etc. 183 He disdained the spunkless martyrs. 1896 Snowden Web of Weaver vi, They all looked white in the face, and round-shouldered, and spunkless.

spunky (ˈspʌŋkɪ), *a.* Also 8 **spunkey**, 8-9 **spunkie**. [f. spunk *sb.* + -y.]
1. Full of spunk or spirit; courageous, mettlesome, spirited.
(*a*) 1786 Burns Earnest Cry & Prayer xiv, Erskine, a spunkie norland billie. 1793 in W. Roberts Looker-on (1794) II. 312 A strapping lassie, So spunky, brazen, bold, and saucy. 1805 Lamb Lett. (1888) I. 221 Vittoria Corombona, a spunky Italian lady, a Leonardo one, nicknamed the White Devil. 1829 Landor Imag. Conv. Wks. 1853 I. 520/1 They are grown again as young and spunky as undergraduates. 1884 Cent. Mag. 428 Spunk will sometimes carry a man through, and you can't say he ain't spunky.
(*b*) 1804 Charlotte Smith Conversations, etc. I. 26, I always get him upon a spunky horse, and the fun is to see his contrivances to stick fast, while I dash on, on purpose. 1856 Aird Poet. Wks. 130 All the year she sings.., The spunky little bird. 1873 C. Gibbon Lack of Gold x, He's a spunky wee beggar, that bantam.

b. Characterized by animation or spirit.
1831 Wilson in Blackw. Mag. XXX. 408 He..has repartee at his command, and occasionally rises into spunky declamation.

2. *Sc.* and *north.* Sparkling; burning or shining brightly.
1791 Nairne Poems 131 For rotton wood will give i' th' dark The spunkey semblance of a spark. 1802 R. Anderson Cumbld. Ball. 32 How neyce the spunky fire it burns. 1825 Brockett N.C. Gloss., Spunky, sparkling.

3. *dial.* and *U.S.* Angry, irritable, irascible.
1809 Debates in Congress (1853) 31 Jan. 1259 It may be a spunky spiteful child, but will have no strength. 1822 Galt Provost xxvi, The spunky nature of Mr. Hirple was certainly very disagreeable often to most of the council. 1873 W. Carleton Farm Ball. 7 We was both of us cross and spunky, and both too proud to speak.

spun-yarn, spunyarn. Also 4 *north.* **sponegarn.** [f. spun *ppl. a.*]
1. Yarn fabricated by the process of spinning.
1376 Durh. Acc. Rolls (Surtees) 584 In ij lib. de Sponegarn empt. per plumbar. pro aqua ductu ligand. iij s. 1541-2 Invent. in Lanc. & Chesh. Wills (Chetham Soc.) 81, xxx pond of sponnen fyne wollen yorne,..xx[ii] pound of spennen yorne. 1844 G. Dodd Textile Manuf. i. 21 The business of working up the spun-yarn into woven fabrics. 1856 Lever Martins of Cro' M. 78 A staid country-woman exchanging her spunyarn..for various commodities.

2. *Naut.* a. Line composed of two or more rope-yarns not laid but simply twisted together by a winch or by hand. Also *Comb.*, as ***spun-yarn major***, ***trick*** (slang): see quots. 1929, 1925; ***spun-yarn winch*** (see quot. 1846).
1627 Capt. Smith Seaman's Gram. v. 25 Spunyarne is nothing but rope yarne made small at the ends, and so spun one to another so long as you will with a winch. 1711 W. Sutherland Shipbuild. Assist. 155 Spun Yarn, for every Inch the Main Stay is in Di[ameter], allow 5 Hundred Weight. 1748 Anson's Voy. II. ii. 133 We had not a sufficient quantity of junk to make spun-yarn. 1769 Falconer Dict. Marine (1780) s.v. Pudening, It is..served with spun-yarn throughout its whole length. 1840 R. H. Dana Bef. Mast iii, He has to furnish them with spunyarn, marline, and all other stuffs that they need in their work. 1853 Kane Grinnell Exp. xxvii. (1856) 226 Although the chains of captivity, made of spun-yarn and leather, set hardly upon him.
Comb. 1772-84 Cook's Voy. (1790) IV. 1381 The bolt belonging to the spun-yarn winch. 1840 R. H. Dana Bef. Mast iii, Every vessel is furnished with a 'spun-yarn winch'. 1846 A. Young Naut. Dict. 368 A small winch with a fly wheel is used in making rope or spunyarn: it gets the name of a spunyarn-winch. 1916 In Northern Mists xvi. 63 The practice has been known of getting everything ready the night before and the proper fastenings replaced with pieces of spunyarn which can be cut with a sailor knife as soon as the signal is made. Of course, it is not playing the game: that's a 'spunyarn trick'. 1925 Fraser & Gibbons Soldier & Sailor Words 267 Spun yarn tricks, underhand dealing. 1929 F. Bowen Sea Slang 132 Spun-yarn major, a lieutenant-commander in the Navy. 1942 'Sea Wrack' Six Bells 163 Above her head sounded the drumming foot-steps of Tommy and his crew of spunyarn majors as they clattered round the decks securing stays.

b. A line or cord of this kind.
1685 Boteler Dial. Sea Service 163 As for the Spun-yarns, they are a kind of Rope-yarn [etc.]. 1805 Naval Chron. XIII 80 She did not strain a spun-yarn.

spur (spɜː(r)), *sb.*[1] Forms: α. 1-2 **spora**, 2-6 (9 *dial.*) **spore**, 4 **spor**, 5-6 **sporre**. β. 1 **spura**, 2-5, *north*, and *Sc.* 6-7 **spure** (5 *north.* **spvyre**), 6 **spoore**. γ. 6-7 **spurre** (7 **spirre**), 5- **spur** (6-7 **spurr**). [Common Teutonic: OE. *spora*, *spura*, = OFris. **spora* (WFris. *spoar*, NFris. *spöör*), OS. *spora* (MDu. *spore*, *spoor*; Du. *spoor*, WFlem. *spoore*, *sporre*), MLG. *spore*, *spare*, OHG. *sporo* (MHG. *spore*, *spor*, G. *sporen*, now *sporn*), ON. and Icel. *spori* (Norw. and Da. *spore*, Sw. *sporre*). The stem is possibly the same as that of spoor *sb.*[1]]

I. 1. a. A device for pricking the side of a horse in order to urge it forward, consisting of a small spike or spiked wheel attached to the rider's heel.
α. c 725 Corpus Gloss. (Hessels) C 93 Calcar, spora. a 1175 Cott. Hom. 243 Þu ahst to habben..swrd and spere, Stede and twei sporen. 1297 R. Glouc. (Rolls) 11280 He smot stede wiþ þe spore. 13.. K. Alis. 818 (Laud MS.), At þe yssue of þe doren Tholomeus dude on his sporen. 1390 Gower Conf. I. 40 Whan the scharpnesse of the spore The horse side smit so sore, It grieveth ofte. 1422 tr. Secreta Secret., Priv. Priv. 165 He smote the mule wyth the sporis. 1484 Caxton Chivalry 62 The spores ben gyuen to a knyght to sygnefye dylygence and swyftnesse. 1526 Skelton Magnyf. 575 Alasse, where is my botes and my spores? a 1533 Ld. Berners Huon lxxxxi. 292 He strake the good horse with the sporres.
β. c 1000 Ælfric On O. & N. Test. (Grein) 18 Iohannes þa heow þæt hors mid þam spuran. c 1205 Lay. 23772 He.. dude on his uoten spuren swiðe gode,..[and] leop on his stede. c 1300 Havelok 1676 þe stede, þat he onne sat, Smot Ubbe with spures faste, And forth awey. 1375 Barbour Bruce VIII. 79 With spurys he strak the steid of pris. 14.. Nom. in Wr.-Wülcker 703 Hec calcar, a spure. c 1475 Cath. Angl. 357/1 Spvyre,..calcar. 1547 Acc. Ld. High Treas. Scot. IX. 68 Brydill, spures, gyrthis, stirrep irnis. 1588 Lanc. & Cheshire Wills (Chetham Soc.) 149 One pair of spures. c 1657 Sir W. Mure Ho. of Rowallane Wks. (S.T.S.) II. 243 For yearlie payment of..ane paire of spures.
γ. c 1400 Destr. Troy 10942 Two spurres full spedely [they] spent on his heils. c 1470 Gol. & Gaw. 25 With spurris spedely thai speid Our fellis. 1523 Ld. Berners Froiss. I. cxxxiv. 161 He toke his horse with the spurres, and came on the skirmysshe warde. 1560 Daus tr. Sleidane's Comm. 235 He hearde the spurres strike on the stayres wham the murtherer ranne hastely downe. 1604 E. G[rimstone] D'Acosta's Hist. Indies III. ix. 147 Beasts..stay there, so as there is no spurre can make them goe forward. 1661 J. Childrey Brit. Baconica 44 They found nothing, but an old Spur. 1726 Dict. Rust. s.v., Obedience to the spurs is a necessary Quality of a good Horse. 1781 Cowper Anti-Thelyphth. 191 He spoke indignant, and his spurs applied.. to his good palfrey's side. 1815 Wellington in Gurw. Desp. (1838) XII. 552 A pair of Spurs taken from Buonaparte.

1863 Geo. Eliot *Romola* xvi, The horse wanted no spur under such a rider.

Prov. **1618** *Hist. Perkin Warbeck* in *Select. Harl. Misc.* (1793) 62 Little needed a spur, saith our proverb, to a forward horse.

b. Used in sing. in generalized sense.

1297 R. Glouc. (Rolls) 8169 Hor hors..nolde after wille Siwe noþer spore no bridel. *c* **1300** *Havelok* 2569 For he him dredde swiþe sore, So runci spore, and mikle more. **1390** Gower *Conf.* I. 321 This knihte..With spore made his hors to gon. **1580** Blundevil *Horsemanship* T v, If he be more slowe..in his trotting, or gallopping, harder of spurre than he was woont to be. **1596** Mascall *Govt. Cattle* 189 If spurre and wande will not profit. **1611** Shaks. *Wint. T.* I. ii. 96 You may ride's With one soft Kisse a thousand Furlongs, ere With Spur we heat an Acre. *a* **1802** *Kinmont Willie* xvii. in Scott *Minstrelsy*, He has called him forty Marchmen bauld With spur on heel, and splent on spauld. **1831** Youatt *Horse* 49 The [race-] horse,..without whip or spur, will generally exert his energies to the utmost to beat his opponent. **1859** Tennyson *Elaine* 455 They..Set lance in rest, strike spur, suddenly move.

Prov. c **1380** Wyclif *Sel. Wks.* III. 436 It is to hard to kyke aȝen þe spore. [Cf. prick *sb.* 13.] **1579** Tomson *Calvin's Serm. Tim.* 636/1 They..will get nothing by it, for they kicke against the spurre.

c. *gilt* (or †*gilded*) *spurs*, as the distinctive mark of a knight. Now *Hist.*

13.. *Coer de L.* 5346 Syxty thousand ther wer telde, Off gylte spores in the felde. **1377** Langl. *P. Pl.* B. xviii. 14 Þe kynde of a knyȝte þat cometh to be dubbed, To geten hem gylte spores. **1480** Caxton *Polychronicon* viii. xxvi, He toke sire Umfrayes salade and this brygantyns.., and also his gylt spores. *a* **1548** Hall *Chron., Edw. IV*, 191 He was disgraded of the high ordre of knighthode..by cuttyng of his gylt sporres. **1604** Marston & Dekker *Malcontent* i. iii, As your knight courts your city widow with jingling of his gilt spurs. **1641–54** Mennis & Smith *Mus. Deliciæ* (1817) II. 32 Gilded spurres do jingle at his heeles. **1728** Chambers *Cycl.* s.v., Anciently the Difference between the Knight and Esquire was, that the Knight wore gilt Spurs,..and the 'Squire silver'd ones. **1828** Scott *F.M. Perth* xxxii, Here, strike me this man's gilt spurs from his heels with thy cleaver. **1879** *Encycl. Brit.* IX. 544 The 'Day of the Spurs' was a fitting name for a carnage after which four thousand gilt spurs were hung as trophies in Courtrai cathedral.

attrib. **1641–54** Mennis & Smith *Mus. Deliciæ* (1817) II. 176 Battas believed..That yonder guilt-spur spruce and velvet youth Was some great personage.

d. With distinguishing terms, denoting various makes or kinds.

a **1400** *Octouian* 1447 A peyre sporys of Speyne. **1625–** [see Rippon]. **1688** Holme *Armoury* iii. 304/1 A Scotch Spur... This is an old way of making Spurs;..their Spurs were only armed with a sharp point like a Cocks Spur. *Ibid.* 325/1 Some term it a Gag Spur, others a Prick Spur. **1785** Grose in *Archaeol.* (1787) VIII. 111 The rouelle, or wheel spur (so called from the revolution of the spicula about its axis). **1824** Meyrick *Antient Armour* I. Introd. p. lxv, The [Anglo-Saxon] spur was formed..with a much longer neck, and was called the spear-spur. **1824, 1839** [see prick *sb.* 21]. *a* **1866** Fairholt *Costume* (1885) II. 377 The rowelled spur first appears..on the brass of Sir John de Creke, 1325.

†**e.** Used in some game or sport. *Obs.*$^{-1}$

c **1440** *Jacob's Well* 134 Þe v. inche is harlotrie, makyng iapys a-forn folk, in pleying at þe spore, at þe bene, at þe cat, in ledyng berys & apys.

f. *battle* (also *day* or †*journey*) *of* (*the*) *spurs*: (see quots. 1831 and 1837).

(*a*) *a* **1548** Hall *Chron., Hen. VIII*, 33 b, The Frenchemen call this battaylle the iourney of Spurres because they ranne awaye so faste on horssebacke. **1643** Baker *Chron., Hen. VIII*, 8 It was called the Battell of Spurres, for that they used more their Spurres in running away, then their Launces in fighting. **1831** Mackintosh *Hist. Eng.* II. iv. 118 [Hen. VIII] defeated the French army in an engagement [near Guinegate] on the 4th of August, 1513, afterwards called the Battle of the Spurs.

(*b*) **1837** *Penny Cycl.* VIII. 113/1 The Flemyngs, in 1302, ..encountered a French army near to Courtray, and found on the field, after the battle, about 4000 gilt spurs, which caused it to be called the battle of spurs. **1842** Longf. *Belfry of Bruges* xv, I beheld the Flemish Weavers..Marching homeward from the bloody battle of the Spurs of Gold. **1879** [see 1 c].

g. *Her.* The representation of a spur.

1688 Holme *Armoury* iii. 304/1 He beareth Gules, a Scotch Spur, Or. *Ibid.*, He beareth Vert, a Spur, Or; Leathered, Argent. *a* **1773** [see spurred *a.* 1 c]. **1882** Cussans *Her.* 122 *Spur*: This Charge may either be represented in its modern form, with a revolving rowel, or with a single point.

h. *transf.* One who wears spurs.

1821 Scott *Kenilw.* iii, I can..fling my gold as freely about as any of the jingling spurs and white feathers that are around me.

2. a. In various prepositional or elliptical phrases denoting speed, haste, eagerness, etc.

c **1374** Chaucer *Troylus* ii. 1427 Tristith wele that I Wole be her champioun with spore and yerd. **1592** Shaks. *Rom. & Jul.* ii. iv. 73 Swits and spurs, Swits and spurs, or Ile crie a match. **1601** —— *All's Well* ii. v. 40 You haue made shift to run into't, bootes and spurres and all. **1604** Dekker *Honest Wh.* Wks. 1873 II. 96 Wee shall ride switch and spurre. **1679** V. Alsop *Melius Inq.* Pref., As if they rod Post, all upon the switch and spur for a presentation to a warm Parsonage. **1708** Sewel ii, *Spoorslaags ryden*,..to ride switch and spur, to gallop with full speed. **1742** Pope *Dunciad* iv. 197 Each fierce Logician..Came whip and spur, and dash'd thro' thin and thick. **1782** Cowper *Mutual Forbearance* 22 What if he did ride whip and spur, 'Twas but a mile. **1900** *Daily Mail* 1 Feb. 4/3 The Government would have turned tail but for the fact that Lord Rosebery, in his famous Epsom speech, rode it 'with spurs'.

†**b.** *at the spur, at spurs*, = next. *Obs. rare.*

c **1450** *Merlin* xviii. 282 Than will we go down this ryver at the spore. **1535** *State P., Hen. VIII* (1834) II. 232 Wher Thomas Fitz Gerolde..was dreuen to flye at sporres, and lost dyvers of his men.

c. *on* or *upon the* (†*spurs* or) *spur* (also † *upon spur*), at full speed, in or with the utmost haste, in lit. or fig. use.

(*a*) **1525** Ld. Berners *Froiss.* II. viii. 18 Whan we be in the feldes, lette vs ryde on the spurres to Gaunte. **1577–87** Holinshed *Chron.* II. 537 He was rescued by certeine horssemen, which..came on the spurs..to the succour of their fellowes.

(*b*) **1560** Daus tr. *Sleidane's Comm.* 428 Ryding upon the spurre, [he] setteth upon them quickely. **1623** Bingham *Xenophon* 23 Lucius..returned and told him, that the enemie fled vpon the Spur. **1655** *Clarke Papers* (Camden) III. 30 The French Ambassadour seemes not to be all together uppon the spur to be gone. **1693** *Humours Town* 3 By this time our Horses must be ready, and we lose time till we are on the Spur. **1710** Shaftesb. *Charac.* (1737) III. 26 He is not presently upon the Spur, or in his full Career. **1775** S. J. Pratt *Liberal Opin.* xlviii. (1783) II. 31 The servant rode away on the spur, to alarm the family at the mansion-house. **1825** Scott *Betrothed* Concl., News are come on the spur from the Garde Doloureuse. **1847** Tennyson *Princ.* i. 150 And there, All wild to found an University For maidens, on the spur she fled.

(*c*) **1606** G. W[oodcocke] *Hist. Ivstine* xi. 49 Alexander.., following vpon spurre, had intelligence that [etc.]. **1643** Cromwell in Carlyle *Lett. & Sp.* (1861) IV. 252 Haste, —ride on spur. *Ibid.* 253 Haste, haste, on spur.

d. *on* (or *upon*) *the spur of the moment* (or *occasion*, etc.), without premeditation or deliberation; on a momentary impulse; impromptu, suddenly, instantly. Hence *spur-of-the-moment* attrib. phr.

(*a*) **1801** *Ann. Reg. 1799* ii. 27/1 Volunteers, with a party of the Surrey cavalry, attended and prevented the populace in general from taking that step, which, perhaps, the best feelings of human nature had, upon the spur of the moment dictated. **1806** A. Duncan *Nelson's Funeral* 43 The contrivance of Mr. Wyatt, on the spur of the moment. **1831** Blakey *Free Will* 152 A speaker who gives us a ready reply upon the spur of the moment. **1891** 'J. S. Winter' *Lumley* x, There's nothing like acting on the spur of the moment.

(*b*) **1809** Malkin *Gil Blas* ii. iii. ¶2 He carried me home on the spur of the occasion. [**1836** Sir H. Taylor *Statesman* xxxi. 237 Though compliments should arise naturally out of the occasion, they should not appear to be prompted by the spur of it. **1882** Hinsdale *Garfield & Educ.* ii. 312 Do not trust to what lazy men call the spur of the occasion.]

(*c*) **1834** Ht. Martineau *Moral* ii. 58 The utmost extent that ingenuity can devise on the spur of a great occasion. **1837** Carlyle *Fr. Rev.* ii. iii. vii, The Church..has been consecrated, by supreme decree, on the spur of this time, into a Pantheon.

(*d*) **1948** C. Day Lewis *Otterbury Incident* viii. 94 Toppy is tops at spur-of-the-moment tactics. **1958** C. Williams *Man in Motion* (1959) vii. 77 There's no such thing as a spur-of-the-moment suicide. **1978** M. Puzo *Fools Die* xv. 161 Junkies, alcoholics, amateur pimps, small-scale thieves and spur-of-the-moment rapists.

3. In phrases with verbs: **a.** *to win* (*one's* or †*the*) *spurs*, to gain knighthood by some act of valour; hence, to attain distinction, to achieve one's first honours. Chiefly *fig.* Also const. *against*, *from*, *of*.

c **1425** Lydg. *Assembly of Gods* 980 These xiiii knyghtes made Vyce that day; To wynne theyr spores they seyde they wold asay. **1539** Abp. Parker *Corr.* (1853) 13 The one to labour to win sporis of the other, and to allure the people's minds. **1551** T. Wilson *Logike* (1580) 74 b, Sennacherib that wicked kyng, thought..to winne his spurres against Jerusalem. **1595** *Enq. Tripe-wife* in Grosart *Eliz. Eng.* (1881) 171 It sufficeth that yee haue wonne the spurres from them all. **1600** Holland *Livy* xxx. xxxii. 762 Resolute that day either to winne the spurres or loose the saddle. **1837** *Penny Cycl.* IX. 291/2 His father nevertheless took him [the Black Prince] along with him to win his spurs..in July, 1346. **1862** Thornbury *Turner* I. 390 The painter.. executed his task with a patience..worthy of one who had to win his spurs.

b. *to put* or *set* (†*the*) *spurs to*, to impel or urge on by spurring; = spur *v.*[1] 1. Also *fig.*

(*a*) **1553** Brende *Q. Curtius* B b iij, He put spurres to his horse. **1561** Eden *Arte Nauig.* Pref. ¶iv b, I may..seme to put the spurres to a runnyng horse, as saith the Prouerbe. **1603** Knolles *Hist. Turks* (1621) 313 He..put spurres to his horse, and fiercely charged the front of Scanderbegs armie. **1770** Langhorne *Plutarch* (1851) II. 739/2 At the same time they put spurs to their horses. **1818** Scott *Br. Lamm.* xxi, I must have spurs put to Lady Ashton's motions. **1857** Holland *Bay Path* xix. 221 A motive force, by which the spurs were put to resolution. **1889** 'V. Fane' *Helen Davenant* I. 16 He put spurs to his horse as soon as he got outside upon the high road.

(*b*) **1565** Cooper *Thesaurus* s.v. *Incito*, Settyng spurres to his horse to gallop amonge his enemies. **1588** Kyd *Househ. Phil.* Wks. (1901) 239 Seeing the ayre wexe blacke,..I began to set spurs to my Horse. **1600** J. Pory tr. *Leo's Africa* ii. 70 Setting spurs to his horse-side, he cast himselfe..downe headlong. **1623** Lisle *Ælfric on O. & N. T.* 36 Iohn set spurs to his horse, and made after him. **1818** Scott *Br. Lamm.* xxii, The Captain proceeded..to set spurs to her resolution. **1889** Conan Doyle *M. Clarke* xxx. 313 He set spurs to his horse.

ellipt. **1598** Shaks. *Merry W.* iv. v. 70 They..set spurres, and away; like three Germane-diuels. **1652** J. Wright tr. *Camus Nat. Paradox* vii. 139 Hee set Spurs and hasted after his Companions. *a* **1700** Evelyn *Diary* (Chandos) 187 We set spurrs and endeavour'd to ride away. **1811** W. R. Spencer *Poems* 19 My spurs are set; Away, away. **1849** James *Woodman* xviii, Quick, spurs to your horse, and away for Sir William.

†**c.** *slang.* (See quot.) *Obs.*

1770 *Gentl. Mag.* XL. 560 To express the Condition of an Honest Fellow and no Flincher, under the Effects of good Fellowship, he is said to [have]..Got a spur in his head; this is said by brother jockies of each other.

4. a. A stimulus, incentive, or incitement. Also const. *of* (the particular influence, etc.) and *to* (a person or persons).

[**1526** *Pilgr. Perf.* (W. de W. 1531) 240 b, It is as a prycke or a spurre to set the slouthfull body forwarde in the seruyce of god.] **1551** Wilson *Logike* Ep. A iij, I professe it to be but a spurre, or a whetstone, to sharpe the pens of some other. *a* **1586** Sidney *Arcadia* iii. viii. (1912) 393 With the spurre of Courage, and the bitte of Respect. **1676** W. Mountagu in *Buccleuch MSS.* (Hist. MSS. Comm.) I. 323 It will not be proper..to make him any acknowledgments.., lest it be looked at for a spur, which I assure you his Lordship needs not. **1726** Shelvocke *Voy. round World* 28, I had no spur that they would be sensible of, but double allowance of brandy. **1771** *Junius Lett.* lix. (1788) 319 The spur of the press is wanted to give operation to the bounty. **1821** Lamb *Elia* i. *Grace before meat*, Our appetites, of one or another kind, are excellent spurs to our reason. **1842** S. Lover *Handy Andy* iii, How Andy runs! Fear's a fine spur. **1871** Blackie *Morals* i. 129 Human beings,..acting in masses, under the spur of great political or religious excitement.

b. Const. *to* or †*towards* (some quality, course of action, etc.). Also with inf.

1548 Udall *Erasm. Par.* Pref. 12 An encouragyng and spurre towardes ferther industrie. *a* **1593** H. Smith *Serm.* (1637) 585 Praise and honour are spurres to virtue. **1611** Shaks. *Wint. T.* iv. ii. 10 Which is another spurre to my departure. **1663** Patrick *Parab. Pilgrim* x. (1687) 54 The thoughts of this misery would be a sufficient spur to you to quicken the execution of it. **1716** Bentley *Serm.* xi. 382 Implanted in our Nature as a spur to mutual Beneficence. **1779** J. Moore *View of France* (1789) I. xxxi. 273 Emulation, the chief spur to diligence. **1800** Wellington in Gurw. *Desp.* (1837) I. 181 This will give a spur to the negotiation at Hydrabad. **1855** Bain *Senses & Int.* ii. iv. §31 The remembrance..is one source of the spur to preserve the stability of one's footing. **1888** Bryce *Amer. Commw.* II. xlvi. 195 This advantage..is a constant spur to the efforts of national politicians.

c. Similarly with *of* (= to).

Cf. 'þe spore of loue' as the title of a poem in the Vernon MS. (*Minor P.* I. 269).

1591 Spenser *Tears of Muses* 454 Due praise, that is the spur of dooing well. **1639** Fuller *Holy War* v. xiii. 252 Had the emulation betwixt those equall Princes onely been such as is the spurre of vertue. **1752** Hume *Ess. & Treat.* (1777) I. 96 Avarice, the spur of industry. **1824** Lamb *Elia* ii. *Capt. Jackson*, With many more such hospitable sayings, the spurs of appetite.

II. 5. a. *Zool.* A sharp, hard process or projection on the tarsus of the domestic cock and certain other fowls and birds; a back-claw.

1548 Elyot, *Calcaria*, the spurres of a cocke or an henne. **1577** B. Googe *Heresbach's Husb.* iv. (1586) 158 Their legges strong, wel armed with sharp and deadly spurres. **1601** Holland *Pliny* I. 276 As if they knew, that naturally they had spurs, as weapons, giuen them about their heeles, to try the quarrell. **1624** Capt. Smith *Virginia* ii. 31 Arrowes..headed with..the spurres of a Turkey, or the bill of some bird. **1661** Lovell *Hist. Anim. & Min.*, *Isagoge* b 3 b, Amongst Birds,..some have spurs, but not the crooked clawed. **1725** *Fam. Dict.* s.v. *Hen*, Those Hens that have Spurs break their Eggs, and generally will not hatch them. **1834** M'Murtrie tr. *Cuvier* 143 Their wings are short... Their thumb, reduced to a spur, cannot reach the ground. **1899** W. T. Greene *Cage-Birds* 38 The Woodlark ..differs from it in having a shorter tail and 'spur'—that is, the nail of the hind toe.

fig. **1571** R. Edwards *Damon & Pithias* (1906) 54 Though we are cockerels now, we shall have spurs one day. **1770** Langhorne *Plutarch* (1851) II. 858/1 If you design doing anything..you must do it quickly, before the spurs of this cockerel be grown.

b. *Zool.*, *Anat.*, and *Path.* A sharp-pointed or spur-like process, formation, or growth on some part of the body.

1681 Grew *Musæum* i. v. iii. 116 On each side his nether [jaw], two great Spikes or Spurs, hard and very sharp. **1722–7** Boyer *Dict. Royal* i, *Les ergots..d'un Chien*, a.. Dog's Spurs. **1760** [see *spur-fish* in 14 b]. **1785** Latham *Gen. Synop. Birds* III. i. 247 On the bend of the wing [are] two or three spurs half an inch in length. **1828** Stark *Elem. Nat. Hist.* II. 362 *Hesperides*. Posterior legs with two pairs of spurs. **1850** R. G. Cumming *Hunter's Life S. Afr.* (1902) I. 262 One of his [a buffalo's] hind legs being shot off above the spurs. **1899** *Allbutt's Syst. Med.* VIII. 686 Those [cicatrices] occurring after syphilis are said to be softer, less liable to encroach on the neighbouring skin or to produce spurs.

6. a. A sharp-pointed projection from the prow of a war-vessel.

1604 E. Grimstone *Siege Ostend* 171 One of them tooke him right vpon the sterne with his spurre or pointe. **1877** W. H. White *Man. Nav. Archit.* (1882) 320 Gaining such a depth below water as will enable the spur to pierce an enemy below the armour. **1889** Welch *Text Bk. Naval Archit.* vii. 98 Below water the stem is formed into a spur or ram, with a view to..piercing the thin bottom plating of an enemy's ship.

b. A metal needle or gaff for fastening to the leg of a gamecock for fighting purposes.

1688 R. Holme *Armoury* ii. 252/2 Gablocks are Spurs made of Iron, or Brass, or Silver, and are fixed on the Legs of such Cocks as want their natural Spurs; some call them Gaffs. **1706** Phillips (ed. Kersey), *Gaff*, an artificial Spur for a Cock. **1801** Strutt *Sports & Past.* iii. vii. 250 We frequently meet with paintings, representing cocks fighting; but I do not recollect to have seen in any of them the least indication of artificial spurs. **1841** Marryat *Poacher* iii, Having put on the animal his steel spurs, he..would.. throw down his gallant bird.

c. *Whaling.* One of a number of metal spikes in a boot-sole to prevent slipping.

1820 Scoresby *Acc. Arctic Regions* II. 298 The harpooners, having their feet armed with 'spurs',..to prevent them from slipping, descend upon the fish.

d. Any sharp or short projection, point, or spike suggestive of a spur. Freq. specific in technical use.

1872 J. RICKARDS *Wood-working* 193 The power is needed mainly to cross-cut the fibre with the spores. *Ibid.*, The spores [**1873** spurs] require frequent sharping. **1875** KNIGHT *Dict. Mech.* 2293/1 *Spur*, a prong on the arm of some forms of anchor, to assist in turning the lower arm from the shank. **1881** YOUNG *Ev. Man his own Mechanic* §399. 175 The two spurs, one on each section of the plane. **1888** JACOBI *Printers' Vocab.* 130 *Spur*, the short pin at the end of the point which pricks the hole in the sheet for registering purposes. **1889** WELCH *Text. Bk. Naval Archit.* xiii. 138 The lower pintle..being received into a spur projecting from the lower part of the sternpost. **1912** E. M. THOMPSON *Introd. Greek & Latin Palaeography* xix. 521 Long strokes [of letters]..are occasionally provided with an ornamental spur near the top of the vertical stems. **1976** *Visible Language* X. 44 *Spur*, a small projection, usually pointed, from a stroke or terminal.

7. a. A short or stunted branch or shoot, esp. one likely to produce fruit.

c **1700** *Compl. Gardiner* in *Dict. Rust.* (1726) s.v. *Pruning*, Tho' the Spurs are common and proper to be preserved, yet the Branches growing from them, will never be good for any thing. **1764** *Museum Rust.* IV. 15 Those little spurs which are only an inch or two long. **1796** C. MARSHALL *Gardening* xii. (1813) 162 The mode of bearing in pear trees is on short spurs, which..form themselves all along the branches. **1842** LOUDON *Suburban Hort.* 339 The great object in producing spurs is to obtain blossom-buds. **1858** GLENNY *Everyday-Bk. Gardening* 23/1 If they were to cut every inch of new wood back to a short spur, there would be fruit.

transf. **1912** F. BOND *Cathedrals* 287 The western bases have a 'spur' of leafage, a sign of late date.

b. *Bot.* A tubular expansion, resembling a cock's spur in form, of some more or less foliaceous part of a flower; a calcar.

1731 MILLER *Gard. Dict.* s.v. *Delphinium*, Many dissimilar Petals.., the uppermost of which is contracted, and ends in a Tail or Spur. **1796** WITHERING *Brit. Pl.* (ed. 3) II. 8 Bloss[om] gaping, ending in a spur. **1830** LINDLEY *Nat. Syst. Bot.* 141 Sepals..unequal; the lowermost elongated into a spur. **1855** MISS PRATT *Flower. Pl.* IV. 214 Spur conical, shorter than the limb of the corolla. **1874** LUBBOCK *Wild Fl.* iii. 53 The honey is in some cases.. situated at the end of a long spur.

c. A disease in rye and certain other cereals, in which the blighted ear resembles a cock's spur in form; = ERGOT 1.

1763 MILLS *Pract. Husb.* II. 405 The grains which have the spur are thicker and longer than the sound ones. **1828** A. NEALE (*title*), Researches respecting the Natural History.. of the Spur, or Ergot of Rye. **1837** P. KEITH *Bot. Lex.* 153 The most mysterious of all the maladies attacking the cereal grasses is that of the Ergot or Spur.

III. 8. a. A short strut or stay set diagonally to support an upright timber; a shore, prop, or sustaining pillar; a sloping buttress.

1529 *Sel. Cases Star Chamber* (Selden) II. 41 [They] cut vpp the yates, postes, and spores of the yates. **1594** PLAT *Jewell-ho.* III. 26 Two strong pillers..well propped with spurres. **1652** J. ENDECOTT in *Manip. Progr. Gosp. among Indians N. Eng.* 34 They have also built a foot bridge..with Groundsells and Spurres to vphold it. **1687** A. LOVELL tr. *Thevenot's Trav.* II. 124 A thick Wall, almost two Fathom broad, supported by two spurs of the same thickness. **1712** J. JAMES tr. *Le Blond's Gardening* 211 The..Wall should be supported..with Buttresses, or Spurs of Masonry. **1834** SOUTHEY *Doctor* (1862) 376 Murlooz is the name which they give to such spurs or stay-pillars. **1844** *Civil Eng. & Arch. Jrnl.* VII. 19/2 The spur [= prop] is then disengaged, and the wagon resumes its level position ready to be removed. **1851** TURNER *Dom. Archit.* II. iii. 91 The term spur is now applied to the carved timber work of the doorways of ancient houses supporting projecting upper stories. **1893** COZENS-HARDY *Broad Norf.* 25 He..supports his wall with a spore not a shore.

b. *Naut.* (See quots.)

1769 FALCONER *Dict. Marine* (1780) s.v. *Deck*, The spurs of the beams; being curved pieces of timber serving as half-beams to support the decks, where a whole beam cannot be placed on account of the hatch-ways. **1841** R. H. DANA *Seaman's Man.* 125 *Spurs*, pieces of timber fixed on the bilge-ways, their upper ends being bolted to the vessel's sides above the water. **1867** SMYTH *Sailor's Word-bk.* 647 *Spurs of the Bitts*, the same as standards.

c. *techn.* (See quots.)

1833 LOUDON *Encycl. Archit.* §1075 The spurs (lower stones of the raking part of the gable, called in England the summer stones). **1860** WHITE *Wrekin* p. xxvii, Stilts and spurs—bits of fireclay by means of which earthenware articles are kept separate during firing. **1875** KNIGHT *Dict. Mech.* s.v. *Pottery*, The *stilts* or *spurs* are generally of triangular form, and have sharp projecting points.

9. One of the principal roots of a tree. Cf. SPURN *sb.*[2] 2.

1610 SHAKS. *Temp.* v. i. 47 The strong bass'd promontorie Haue I made shake, and by the spurs pluckt vp The Pyne, and Cedar. **1677** PLOT *Oxfordshire* 159 The Tree without being 25 foot round above the spurs. **1740** SOMERVILLE *Hobbinolia* II. 89 If chance The cruel Woodman spy the friendly Spur, His only Hold. **1791** COWPER *Yardley Oak* 117 Yet is thy root sincere,.. A quarry of stout spurs, and knotted fangs, Which..clasp The stubborn soil. **1800–** in dial. glossaries (North Cy., Nhp., Chesh., Warw.).

fig. **1611** SHAKS. *Cymb.* IV. ii. 58, I do note, That greefe and patience rooted in them both, Mingle their spurres together.

10. †**a.** *Fortif.* An angular outwork or projection from the general face of a curtain or wall, to assist in the defence of this. *Obs.*

1575 CHURCHYARD *Chippes* (1817) 153 They did lose the Spurre, a place ful strong Which sore anoid the towne. **1598** BARRET *Theor. Warres* 125 The parts of a Bulwarke are..the front or Curtine; the Counter front or Spurres. **1604** E. G[RIMSTONE] *D'Acosta's Hist Indies* v. xiii. 364 Fortefied with great and large spurres or platformes. **1669** STAYNRED *Fortification* 12 In the middle of the Curtain you may make a Spur, or Point of a Bastion. **1687** J. RICHARDS *Jrnl. Siege of Buda* 12 We observ'd the Enemy at work on the East-Port, to which place they had advanc'd a Spurr. **1702** *Milit. Dict.* (1704), *Spurs*, are Walls that cross a part of the Rampart, and joyn to the Town Wall.

†**b.** An angular end of the pier of a bridge. *Obs.*

1736 HAWKSMOOR *London Bridge* 26 That the Becks or Spurs ought to be made in right Angles. **1742** LEONI *Palladio's Archit.* I. 92 The angle of the spurs, that cut the water, is a right angle.

c. An artificial projection from a river-bank serving to deflect the current.

1818 GARSTIN tr. *Frisi's Treat. Rivers* III. iii. 130, I have examined different sorts of spurs, and have found but few of them that were not shaken and damaged by the current. **1873** MEDLEY *Autumn Tour U.S. & Canada* ix. 149, I saw a large Spur which had been built to divert the stream under the bridge.

11. a. A range, ridge, mountain, hill, or part of this, projecting for some distance from the main system or mass; an offshoot or offset.

Freq. since 1850.

1652 HEYLYN *Cosmogr.* I. 37 The Alpes, and the Apennine, of which the residue in a manner are but spurs and branches. **1791** W. BARTRAM *Observ. Trav. Pennsylv.*, etc. 338 The upper end of this spacious green plain is divided by a promontory or spur of the ridges before me, which projects into it. **1796** MORSE *Amer. Geog.* I. 183 From these several ridges proceed innumerable nameless branches or spurs. **1837** W. IRVING *Capt. Bonneville* I. 96 A low and very rocky ridge, one of the most southern spurs of the Wind river mountains. **1863** KINGLAKE *Crimea* (1877) III. i. 198 A spur or rising ground at the base of the hills. **1874** H. R. REYNOLDS *John Bapt.* I. v. 48 The glittering palaces and flourishing cities in the Spurs of Lebanon.

b. An outshoot or projecting piece *of* ground, land, etc.

1851 MAYNE REID *Scalp Hunters* xxxii. 244 A spur of willows running out from the timber indicated the presence of water. **1852** GROTE *Greece* II. lxx. (1862) VI. 264 A spur of high and precipitous ground.

c. A branch of a lode, railway, etc.

1833 DARWIN *Jrnl.* 29 Jan. in *Voy. Beagle*, One side of the creek was formed by a spur of mica-slate. **1878** F. S. WILLIAMS *Midl. Railw.* 588 As we leave Newark we see the spur of line that runs down to the Great Northern Railway. **1881** RAYMOND *Mining Gloss.*, *Spur*, a branch leaving a vein, but not returning to it.

IV. 12. *attrib.* **a.** In sense 1, as ***spur-buckle***, ***-haste***, ***-mark***, etc.

1688 HOLME *Armoury* III. 304/2 The Second is termed a *Spur Buckle. **1911** E. POUND *Canzoni* 43 The silken trains go rustling, The *spur-clinks sound between. *a* **1649** DRUMM. OF HAWTH. *Hist. Jas. II*, Wks. (1711) 23 These with *spur-haste advanced the celebration of it. **1875** WHYTE MELVILLE *Riding Recoll.* iv, You may look in vain for a *spur-mark on their horses sides. **1688** C. TRENCHFIELD *Cap Grey Hairs* 52 'Tis no wise part of a man, *succumbere difficultatibus*,..but..like true *Spur-Nags,..strain hardest against the Hill. **1688** HOLME *Armoury* III. 304/2 A Buckle, with a *Spur Neck and Rowel fixed thereunto. **1842** 'NIMROD' *Horse & Hound* 331 The back-ribs..should also be deep, as in a strong-bodied horse, of which we say, when so formed, that he has a good '*spur place'. **1688** HOLME *Armoury* III. 325/1 A *Spur shank, with a Nail or sharp point. **1862** *Catal. Internat. Exhib., Brit.* II. No. 6151, Spurs and *spur sockets. **1814** SCOTT *Lord of Isles* VI. xxxiii, The *spur stroke fail'd to rouse the horse.

b. In senses 6 d, 8–11, as ***spur-brace***, ***-buttress***, ***-cog***, ***-dike***, ***-fork***, ***-piece***, etc.

1776 G. SEMPLE *Building in Water* 50 On those set-offs stretch your Plates, and on them rest your *Spur-braces. **1859** TURNER *Dom. Archit.* III. II. vii. 373 They are furnished with a variety, adapted to the shape, of the *spur-buttress. **1815** J. SMITH *Panorama Sci. & Art* II. 230 A horizontal wheel..with *spur-cogs. **1892** *Trans. Amer. Soc. Civ. Eng.* XXVI. 697 Where the velocity of the current is dangerous, we have sometimes used *spur-dikes. **1747** HOOSON *Miner's Dict.*, **Spur-fork*, a small sort of Fork, of Use only to keep some other Timber in its Place,..and sometimes used to hold Doorsteds in Drifts or at Sump-heads asunder. **1833** LOUDON *Encycl. Archit.* §889 Into grooves chiseled out of the *spur pieces..spiked to the sill and posts. **1825** J. NICHOLSON *Operative Mechanic* 73 The rollers..may..be formed into *spur pinions to fit the teeth. *Ibid.* 159 A *spur-rail, for strengthening the frame-work of the mill. **1871** KINGSLEY *At Last* xi, Around its great *spur-roots lay what had been its trunk and head. **1846** A. YOUNG *Naut. Dict.* 281 **Spur-shores*,..a name for shores placed in a horizontal position, or set up diagonally. **1889** *Daily News* 9 Oct. 6 The cost of the main thoroughfare..; the cost of the *spur street. **1871** *Routledge's Ev. Boy's Ann.* Sept. 535 Spaces between the links, into which the *spur-teeth fit. **1884** *Boston* (Mass.) *Jrnl.* 13 Sept., A *spur track from the Eastern Railroad freight yard. **1692** *Lond. Gaz.* No. 2774/3 They attack'd a kind of *Spur-work with Pallisadoes.

13. *Comb.*, with ppl. adjs. and vbl. sbs., as ***spur-finned***, ***-heeled***, ***-shaped***, ***-tailed***; ***spur-clad***, ***-driven***; ***spur-bearing***, ***-jingling***, ***-making***, etc.

1842 LOUDON *Suburban Hort.* 614 Shortening such wood on *spur-bearing trees. **1871** DARWIN *Desc. Man* II. xv. (1890) 450 The female progenitors of the existing spur-bearing species. **1847** WEBSTER, **Spur-clad*, wearing spurs. **1837** CARLYLE *Fr. Rev.* II. v. iii, The tired nag, *spur-driven, does take the River Sorgue. **1804** SHAW *Gen. Zool.* V. I. 110 *Spur-finned Pike, *Esox Chirocentrus*... Native of the Indian seas. **1803** *Ibid.* IV. II. 563 *Spur-gilled Holocentrus, *Holocentrus Calcarifer*... Native of Japan. **1829** H. HAWTHORN *Visit Babylon* 111 A tall,..*spur-heeled 'dead-weight' man. **1894** DU MAURIER *Trilby* iii. 42 The brutal sword-clanking, *spur-jingling aristocrats. *a* **1613** OVERBURY *A Wife*, etc. (1638) 173 The trade of *spurre-making had decay'd long since. **1837** P. KEITH *Bot. Lex.* 271 A *spur-shaped process issuing immediately from the corolla. **1894–5** LYDEKKER *Roy. Nat. Hist.* III. 245 *Spur-tailed Wallabies..having the extreme tip of the tail furnished with a horny spur or nail. **1896** *Ibid.* V. 286 The *spur-toed frogs (*Xenopus*).

14. a. Special Combs.: **spur blight**, a fungus disease of raspberries and loganberries causing discoloured patches on the stems and the death of buds at the nodes, and weakening the laterals; **spur-bow**, the solid spur-like prolongation of the lower part of the bow in certain warships; **spur box**, a special form of horseman's boot-heel, to which the rims of the spur are affixed; **spur centre**, a lathe-centre provided with spurs; †**spur-fire** *Pyrotech.* (see quots.); **spur gear**, **gearing** *Mech.*, gearing consisting of spur-wheels; **spur line**, a railway branch-line; **spur mark**, one of the marks left on the base of a glazed pot by the spurs (sense 8 c) on which it has rested during firing (see also quot. 1933); †**spur money**, a fine imposed by the choristers of certain privileged chapels on anyone entering with spurs on; = *spur silver*; **spur-nut** *Mech.*, a small spur-wheel; **spur pruning**, = SPURRING *vbl. sb.*[1] 2; **spur road**, (see quots. 1883, 1891); now applied to a connecting road that branches off from a motorway or main highway; **spur-shell**, (see quots.); †**spur silver** *Sc.*, = *spur money*; **spur-stone**, a stone fixed in the ground to support a post or to keep vehicles away from the footway, etc.; †**spur trochus**, a species of shell (cf. *spur-shell*); †**spur-vein**, a blood-vein in a horse's side where the spur usually strikes; **spur-way** *dial.* (see quot.); **spur-whang** *Sc.* and *dial.*, = SPUR-LEATHER 1.

1915 *Bull. Colorado Agric. Exper. Station* No. 206 (*title*) *Spur blight of the red raspberry caused by Sphaerella rubina. **1941** *Sun* (Baltimore) 18 Feb. 6/4 Anthracnose, spur blight on red raspberries and cane blight can be controlled by promptly removing and burning all old fruiting canes after harvest and spraying the new canes one to four times in the growing season. **1979** SCOPES & LEDIEU *Pest & Disease Control Handbk.* vi. 55 Some of the fungicides for spur blight will also control cane spot. **1877** W. H. WHITE *Man. Nav. Archit.* 232 Under-water projections, like the *spur-bows of ironclad rams, may also produce some limitation of pitching and 'scending. **1862** *Catal. Internat. Exhib., Brit.* II. No. 5007, The old *Spur Box, in which the boot heels are unsightly and the spur inconveniently near the ground. **1881** YOUNG *Ev. Man his own Mechanic* §592. 274 The following pieces are supplied with the lathe:..two plain centres, one *spur-centre for wood. **1765** R. JONES *Fireworks* ii. 27 When any of these *spur-fires are fired singly, they are called artificial flower pots. *Ibid.* 29 Called the spur-fire,..because the sparks it yields have a great resemblance to the rowel of a spur. **1823** BUCHANAN *Millwork* 28 By *spur geers is understood wheels acting together, and in the same plane, with their axes parallel. **1867–72** BURGH *Mod. Marine Engin.* 294 Spur gear motion for working slide valves. **1844** H. STEPHENS *Bk. Farm* III. 794 The motion of the main rollers..is communicated to the seed-distributor by means of *spur-geering. **1924** KIPLING *Debits & Credits* (1926) 166 'E 'ad us all screened in over in a cuttin' on a little *spur-line. **1977** H. FAST *Immigrants* 8 This great railroad..has begun the construction of a spur line to connect its main line with the City of San Francisco. **1895** R. MILLS *Catal. Blue & White Orient. Porc.* 52 '*Spur marks' are little projections of the paste, apparently to prevent the bottom of the vessel touching the oven. They are peculiar to Japanese porcelain. **1933** *Burlington Mag.* Oct. 160/2 On the bottom of the interior of the bowl will be found five spur marks where the pontil was broken off. **1972** *Trans. Oriental Ceramics Soc.* XXXVIII. 23 A ring of spur marks usually is to be seen on the base of proto-Yüeh pieces. **1566** in *N. & Q.* 1st Ser. I. 494/1 Every quorister sholde bringe with him to Churche a Testament..rather than spend their tyme in talk and hunting after *spur money. **1864** C. KNIGHT *Passages Work. Life* I. 77 Thus have I seen a stranger civilian stalk into the choir of St. George's Chapel. The spur was instantly detected; and when the bewildered man was surrounded by a bevy of white surplices..there was no help for him but to pay the spur-money. **1803** *Imison's Sci. & Art* I. 94 In common *spur-nuts, divide the pitch-line..into twice as many equal parts as you intend teeth. **1825** J. NICHOLSON *Operative Mechanic* 131 The four spur-nuts..at the end of the spindle..roll round the spur-wheel. **1842** LOUDON *Suburban Hort.* 541 *Spur Pruning, sixth year. **1883** GRESLEY *Gloss. Coal-m.* 233 **Spur road*, a branch way leading from a main level. **1891** *Hartland Gloss* 73 *Spur road*, a bridle path. Now obsolete in this sense, although the word remains in the name of a bye-road. **1958** *Times* 19 Mar. 10/3 The spur road to London Airport will be served by a flyover junction. **1963** *Listener* 31 Jan. 198/2 Heavy trucks rumble along the spur roads from the Alaska Highway to mining camps deep in the frozen interior. **1977** *Jrnl. R. Soc. Arts* CXXV. 359/1 These needs could be met by a six-lane spur road connecting with adjacent motorways. **1713** PETIVER *Aquat. Anim. Amboinæ* Tab. xi, *Calcar minor*,.. Small *Spur-shell. *Cassis verrucosa*, ..Great Spur-shell. **1752** HILL *Hist. Anim.* 129 The Spur-shell, with short spines. The gold-yellow Spur-shell, with a silvery white umbo. **1883** *Cassell's Nat. Hist.* V. 214 Genus *Imperator*. The shell is like a *Trochus*;..seen from above, it resembles the rowel of a spur, hence the name Spur-shell. **1500** *Acc. Ld. High Treas. Scot.* II. 97 Item, to the barnis in the Queir of Strivelin, of *spur silver, be the Kingis command, vs. **1545** *Ibid.* VIII. 411 Item, to the barnis of the quere in spur sylver, vs. **1848** *Gentl. Mag.* I. 248 An obelisk, ..part of it..having been above ground as a *spur-stone. **1880** *Daily News* 27 July 3/3 Accidents to the vehicles.. owing to the 'spur stones' that are fixed to..the refuges..at dangerous crossings. **1882** JEFFERIES *Bevis* I. x. 172 A small sarsen or boulder..put there as a spur-stone to force the careless carters to drive straight. **1753** *Chambers' Cycl.* Suppl. s.v. *Cochlea*, 11. The *spur trochus, with spines disposed in a regular circle. 12. The less aculeated spur trochus. **1607** Topsell *Four-f. Beasts* 351 Let him blood in his *spur vains, and his breast vaines. **1735** Burdon *Pocket Farrier* 38 Take.. Blood from the Spur Vein on each Side. **1691** Ray *S. & E. Co. Words* (ed. 2) 114 A **Spurre-way*, a Horse-way through a Man's Ground, which one may ride in by right of Custom. **1787–** in dial. glossaries (Norfolk, Essex, E. Anglia). **1684** in *Cloud of Witnesses* (1871) 393, I had not the worth of a *spur whang of any man's. **1820** Scott *Monast.* xxxvi, There are strapping lads enough would have rid us of him for the lucre of his spur-whang.

b. In the specific names of birds, fishes, or flowers, as **spur-dog**, a small spiny shark, *Squalus acanthias*, found in the Atlantic and the Mediterranean (see also quot. 1862); **spur-fish**, **-fowl**, etc. (see quots.).

1862 Couch *Brit. Fishes* I. 49 *Spur Dog. Bone Dog... Pre-eminently this fish is called The Dogfish. **1921** [see *nurse-hound* s.v. nurse *sb.*^{2} b]. **1959** A. C. Hardy *Open Sea* II. ix. 179 The spur-dog can easily be distinguished by the prominent spine immediately in front of each of its dorsal fins. **1976** *Evening Post* (Nottingham) 13 Dec. 7/2 Other trophies for the best specimen fish went to.. Eric Rawson for an 8¼ lb. spur dog, [etc.]. **1760** Edwards *Glean. Nat. Hist.* II. 153 The larger Fish I call the *Spur-fish, from the two odd pectinated sharp-pointed spurs on its upper and under sides. **1804** Shaw *Gen. Zool.* V. I. 194 Rondeletian Carp, *Cyprinus Rondeletii*... Spur-Fish. **1845** *Penny Cycl.* Suppl. I. 35/1 Guinea-fowls, *spur-fowls, quails, and bustards are very numerous [in Adal]. **1865** *Intellect. Obs.* No. 39. 224 Galloperdix Lunulosa,.. generally called the Spur-fowl. **1895** Lydekker *Roy. Nat. Hist.* IV. 416 The Indian spur-fowl are more pheasant-like. **1866** *Treas. Bot.* 550/1 Sea *spur grass, *Glyceria distans*. **1803** Shaw *Gen. Zool.* IV. II. 595 *Spur Mackrel. *Scomber Calcar*... Native of the African seas. **1866** *Treas. Bot.* 219 The shrubby Capsicum, or *Spur Pepper (*Capsicum frutescens*), is a native of the East Indies. **1910** *Encycl. Brit.* (ed. 11) XII. 203/2 Birds [of the Gold Coast].. include.. swallows, vultures and the *spur plover (the last-named rare). **1864** Grisebach *Flora Brit. W. Ind.* 787/2 *Spur-tree, *Petitia domingensis*. **1855** Miss Pratt *Flowering Pl.* III. 161 *Spur Valerian. Corolla 5-cleft, spurred at the base. **1863** Hogg & Johnson *Wild Fl. Gt. Brit.* II. Pl. 140 *Centranthus Ruber*, Red Spur-Valerian. Syn. Red Valerian. **1749** W. Ellis *Shepherd's Guide* 144 At Sidbury, Devonshire, 'they have a weed called *Spurwood or Spearwort, that they say runs up like a pike'. **1640** Franking *spurwort [see spurrey 1 b]. **1688** Holme *Armoury* II. 98/2 Francking Spurry, or Spurwort, [has].. small narrow leaves. **1796** Withering *Brit. Pl.* (ed. 3) II. 185 *Sherardia arvensis*... Little Field Madder. Little Spurwort.

†**spur**, *sb.*^{2} *Obs.* [f. spur *v.*^{1} 5.] A sharper's method of marking playing-cards.

1674 Cotton *Compl. Gamester* (1680) 95 In dealing these Rooks have a trick they call the *Spurr*, and that is, as good Cards come into their hand.. they give them a gentle touch with their nail. **1711** Puckle *Club* 23 The bent, the slick, the breef, the spur. [*Note*] Marking Putt-cards on the edge with the nail as they come to hand.

†**spur**, *sb.*^{3} *dial. Obs.* Also 7 spurre. [Of obscure origin.] The common tern, *Sterna hirundo* (or *fluviatilis*).

a **1672** Willughby *Ornith.* (1676) 269 In insula Caldey meridionali Cambriæ littori adjacente Spurres eas vocant, communi cum Argentinensibus nomine; et insulam ubi simul nidificant Spurre-Island. [Hence in Ray and later writers.]

spur, *sb.*^{4} *techn.* [Of obscure origin.] A set of folded sheets of paper.

1885 *Encycl. Brit.* XVIII. 225/1 After this the [hand-made] paper is hung in a drying loft on cow-hair ropes in spurs of three to five sheets thick until dry.

spur (spɜː(r)), *v.*^{1} Forms: α. 3 spurie, 4–5 spure(n), 6–7 spurre, 6– spur (9 spurr), 8 spir. β. 4–6 spore, 5–6 sporre. [ME. *spure*, *spore*, f. spur *sb.*^{1} Cf. MDu. and Du. *sporen*, MHG. *sporn*, *sporen* (obs. G. *sporen*, *spören*, G. *spornen*), NFris. *spöre*, Sw. *sporra*.]

I. *trans.* **1. a.** To prick (a horse, etc.) with the spur, in order to urge to a faster pace; to urge on by the use of spurs.

α. *c* **1205** Lay. 26480 Þe eorles gunnen riden & spureden heore steden. *c* **1250** *Gen. & Ex.* 3970 Balaam it spureð and smit ðor-on; And god vndede ðis asses muð. *c* **1470** Henry *Wallace* x. 417 For to fle he tuke no taryage; Spuryt the hors, quhilk ran in a gud randoun Till his awn folk. **1500–20** Dunbar *Poems* xxvii. 67 Thay spurrit thair hors on adir syd. **1530** Palsgr. 731/1, I dare not spurre my hors, he is so wylde. **1612** *Two Noble K.* III. i, When I spur My horse, I chide him not. **1679** Dryden *Troil. & Cress.* II. iii, Heaven made them horses, And thou.. rid'st and spurr'st them. **1740** Somerville *Hobbinolia* II. 218 He spur'd his sober Steed, grizled with Age. **1770** Langhorne *Plutarch* (1851) I. 408/1 He could scarcely make his horse go, though he spurred him continually. **1850** 'H. Hieover' *Pract. Horsemanship* 193 The horse being whipped, spurred, and rated at while galloping, of course supposes he is doing something wrong.

absol. **1607** Markham *Cavel.* II. (1617) 133 To bring your horse to a quicknesse vpon the spurre, is to spurre seldom, but when you spurre, to spurre most surely. **1823** Scott *Quentin D.* x, I am sure I spurred till his sides were furrowed.

β. *c* **1330** R. Brunne *Chron. Wace* (Rolls) 12719 He sporede his hors, forþ faste gan schake. *c* **1440** *Generydes* 217 He sporyd his hors and theder toke the way. *c* **1475** *Partenay* 4214 Gaffray that tyme.. his coursere spored. *a* **1532** Ld. Berners *Huon* lviii. 198 He spored blanchardyn & cam agynst Gerames. *Ibid.* lxxxxi. 292 He spored his horse that anone he ouer toke Huon.

b. With advs., as *away*, *forth*, *on*, *up*; or preps., as *against*, *at*, *into*, *through*, etc.

c **1450** *Merlin* xviii. 282 And whan thei saugh the cristin come thei sporred theire horse ouer the brigge at a brunt. *c* **1530** Ld. Berners *Arth. Lyt. Bryt.* (1814) 82 He sporred forth hys horse, and ranne into the thyckest of the prease. **1588** Shaks. *L.L.L.* IV. i. 1 Was that the King that spurd his horse so hard, Against the steepe vprising of the hill? **1664** H. More *Myst. Iniq.* 474 They gore and spurre up the Ass to goe that way. **1687** A. Lovell tr. *Thevenot's Trav.* III. 45 When the Rider spurs on his Horse to a full speed. **1770** Langhorne *Plutarch* (1851) I. 117/1 They spurred their horses to the encounter. **1788** Gibbon *Decl. & F.* lii. V. 357 He spurred his horse into the waves. **1812** Byron *Ch. Har.* II. lvii, Some high-capp'd Tartar spurr'd his steed away. **1848** Lytton *Harold* I. iii, Edward spurred his steed up to the boor. **1894** Baring-Gould *Des. S. France* II. 253 He spurred his horse to the side of the river.

c. *fig.* or in fig. context.

1500–20 Dunbar *Poems* xxi. 13 Quhen trewth gois on his fute abowt, And lak of spending dois him spur. **1575** Gascoigne *Glasse of Govt.* Wks. 1910 II. 26 Let shame of sinne, thy Childrens bridle be, And spurre them foorth, with bounty wisely used. **1602** Marston *Antonio's Rev.* I. v, Does thy hart With punching anguish spur thy galled ribs? **1846** Prescott *Ferd. & Isab.* II. vi. II. 371 This same impulse.. spurs guilty ambition along his bloody track. **1864** Tennyson *Aylmer's F.* 290 Him, glaring, by his own stale devil spurr'd, And, like a beast hard-ridden, breathing hard.

d. To make (one's way) by spurring.

1842 Lover *Handy Andy* xxxvii, The rider.. still spurred and plashed his headlong way through the heavy road.

2. *fig.* **a.** To drive on or hasten; to incite, impel, or stimulate; to urge or prompt. Freq. const. *to* (do something, or some course of action). Also occas., with an action or activity as object.

a **1225** *Juliana* 59 Heo as þe deouel spurede ham to donne, duden hit unsparliche. *c* **1230** *Hali Meid.* 13 Þe ilke sari wrecches.. beoð þe deuelles eaueres, þat rit ham & spureð ham to don al þat he wile. *a* **1548** Hall *Chron., Hen. VI*, 99 b, The Duke,.. somwhat spurred and quyckened with these noueltyes, retired backe. **1587** Golding *De Mornay* xx. (1592) 319 A desire of honor whereby we be spurred to do well. **1588** Shaks. *L.L.L.* II. i. 119 *Ber.* You must not be so quicke. *Rosa.* 'Tis long of you y^{t} spur me with such questions. **1633** G. Herbert *Temple, Storm* ii, A throbbing conscience spurred by remorse Hath a strange force. **1663** Patrick *Parab. Pilgrim* xxvii. (1687) 304 If these Joys do not spur you to Obedience,.. they are not of such value as you imagine. **1733** Cheyne *Eng. Malady* II. ix. (1734) 209 Any thing that will stimulate, rouze, and spur the dead and languishing Solids. **1769** E. Bancroft *Guiana* 371 They are spurred to industry by the whip of correction. **1803** Visct. Strangford *Poems of Camoens, Lusiad* VI. xl. (1810) 111 Some tale of joy, To spur the time that now so stilly stands. **1850** Dobell *Roman* iv, I spur my soul all day With thought of tyrants, woes and chains. **1874** Green *Short Hist.* i. §5. 48 The mention of Nero spurs him to an outbreak on the abuses of power. **1951** *Newsweek* 27 Sept. 74/3 Much of this expansion has been spurred by the government. **1976** *National Observer* (U.S.) 17 Apr. 7/2 Mae Craig,.. Liz Carpenter, and I spurred a move for the survivors of the Spruce Goose week end to entertain our millionaire host with an appreciation party.

absol. **1576** Gascoigne *Philomene* cciii, The flesh may spurre to euerlasting fire. **1611** B. Jonson *Catiline* III. iii, When need spurres, despaire will be call'd wisdome. **1738** Warburton *Div. Legat.* I. iv. I. 60 Self-interest.. spurring to Action, by Hopes and Fears.

b. With *on*.

1582 Stanyhurst *Æneis* II. (Arb.) 53 Too shock in coombats.. Mee my wyl on spurreth. **1624** Capt. Smith *Virginia* III. x. 83 With shame to spurre on the rest to amendment. **1663** Patrick *Parab. Pilgrim* xxiv. (1687) 259 And yet they spur on their hours, and would have them flye away faster than they do. **1672** Marvell *Reh. Transp.* I. 67 Two Friends who.. spurr'd him on perpetually with commendation. **1711** Swift *Jrnl. to Stella* 16 Nov., To spur on the French to be easy and sincere. *a* **1720** Sewel *Hist. Quakers* Pref., I was the more spurr'd on thereby to set down in due Order.. what I knew of the Matter. **1812** Cary *Dante, Parad.* IV. 14 Ire, that spurr'd him on to deeds unjust. **1854** *Poultry Chron.* 139/1 Spurred on with the certainty of a prize. **1874** Symonds *Sk. Italy & Greece* (1898) I. xii. 231 He is.. spurred on by yearnings after an unsearchable delight.

c. With *up*.

1645 Quarles *Sol. Recant.* XII. xi, The wise mans words are like to Goads, that doe Stir up the drowzy, and spur up the slow. **1656** Earl Monm. tr. *Boccalini's Advts. fr. Parnass.* II. vi. (1674) 145 Riches made proud, and spurr'd him up to commit faults. **1710** Swift *Jrnl. Stella* 9 Dec., Why did not you.. first spur up his recommendation to the height. **1732** Law *Serious C.* (ed. 2) xviii. 331 A youth that has been spurr'd up to all his industry by ambition. **1852** Mrs. Stowe *Uncle Tom's C.* ix, Spurring up the Legislature ..to pass more stringent resolutions against escaping fugitives. **1871** Burr *Ad Fidem* xv. 305 A strong faith, spurred up by approaching death.

3. To provide with a spur or spurs; to furnish with gaffs.

13.. *K. Alis.* 6650 (Laud MS.), His spere takeþ Perdicas; His helys sporeþ Emudus. **1694** Motteux *Rabelais* v. xxvii. (1737) 119 They.. began to boot and spur one another. **17..** *Young Hunting* in Child *Ball.* II. 144/2 She has booted an spird Young Hunting As he had been gan to ride. **1832** Marryat *N. Forster* xlv. (Rtldg.) 246 The proper way in which they [cocks] should be spurred... Two pairs of spurs were.. made.

4. Of a bird: To strike or wound with the spur. Also *transf.*

1631 T. Drue *Dutches of Suffolk* iv, Why the Cocke ale has spurd thee already. **1805** [see lark-spurred *a.*] **1863** Cowden Clarke *Shaks. Char.* vi. 145 That man's wife.. would so peck and spur him, that he was a totally different man when in her company.

†**5.** *Card-sharping.* (See quot.) *Obs.*$^{-1}$

1674 Cotton *Compl. Gamester* (1680) 95 They always fix half a score Packs of Cards.. by slicking them or spurring them, that is, giving them such marks that they shall certainly know every Card in the Pack.

II. *intr.* **6. a.** To ride quickly by urging on one's horse with the spur. Also with *it*.

1593 Shaks. *Rich. II*, II. i. 36 He tyres betimes, that spurs too fast betimes. **1596** Dalrymple tr. *Leslie's Hist. Scot.* II. 137 [He] than spurit with speid to Scotland, with lettres of commendatioun. **1697** Dryden *Virg. Georg.* III. 49 The Parthians.. spurring from the Fight, confess their Fear. —— *Æneid* XI. 923 Spurring at speed, to their own walls they drew. **1816** Byron *Siege Corinth* xxii, Mount ye, spur ye, skirr the plain. **1849** Macaulay *Hist. Eng.* ix. II. 436 Not a day passed on which he was not seen spurring from his villa to the Hague. **1891** *Cornhill Mag.* Oct. 416 His troop would spur it over the drawbridge with clatter of hoofs.

b. With advs., as *after*, *away*, *forward(s*, *on*, *up*.

1590 Spenser *F.Q.* III. i. 18 But all spurd after fast, as they mote fly. **1642** Fuller *Holy & Prof. State* IV. i. 241 He doth not alwayes spurre up close to the Kings side. **1697** Dryden *Æneid* v. 872 Ascanius took th' alarm,.. And, spurring on, his equals soon o'erpass'd. **1795** Southey *Joan of Arc* III. 81 Saying thus, he spurr'd away. **1829** Scott *Anne of G.* xxxv, Two or three Stradiots then spurred on to examine this defile. **1883** Pennell-Elmhirst *Cream of Leicestersh.* 135 [He] spurred forward to check the solitary hounds.

fig. *a* **1659** Bp. Browning *Serm.* (1674) I. xxx. 386 Obstinacy spurs on in spight of all perswasions. **1673** Marvell *Reh. Transp.* II. 82 The Gentleman thought it necessary to spur up again the next year with another new book.

c. *transf.* To hasten; to proceed hurriedly.

1513 Douglas *Æneid* II. xi. 31 A fair brycht sterne.. Markand the way quhidder at we suld spur. *Ibid.* VII. iv. 19 He.. fast gan spur.. To mark the fundment of his new citie. **1666** *Extr. St. Papers rel. Friends* Ser. III. (1912) 256, I shall be able to do more, goeing my owne way then by spurring to Fast. **1677** W. Mountagu in *Buccleuch MSS.* (Hist. MSS. Comm.) I. 324 The reason I had to spur on was, that.. I found Sir John Robinson there.

7. a. To strike out with the foot; to kick.

1590 Nashe *Martin Marprelate* Wks. (Grosart) I. 232 What is this,.. but to fall groueling to the earth.., and beeing downe,.. to kicke and spurre. *a* **1835** Hogg *Tales* (1866) 150/2 After gluthering and spurring a wee while, they cam to again. **1870** Emerson *Soc. & Sol., Domestic Life*, All day, between his three or four sleeps, he [an infant] sputters and spurs.

b. Of cocks, etc.: To fight with the spur; to strike *at*. Also *transf.*

a **1722** Lisle *Husb.* (1757) 346 If a sheep should come so near to a lark's nest as to tread on it, the lark will fly out, and spur at the sheep. **1838** T. Mitchell *Clouds of Aristophanes* 172 Two fighting-cocks.. spurring at each other. **1887** McNeill *Blawearie* 179 Examining the.. paws of the dog to see if he might be expected to spurr well.

c. *Sc.* (See quot.)

1825 Jamieson *Suppl.*, *To Spur*, v.n., to scrape, as a hen or cock on a dunghill.

III. *trans.* **8.** To support or prop up (a post, etc.) by means of a strut or spur; to strengthen with spurs.

1733 Tull *Horse-Hoeing Husb.* xxiii. 361 (Dubl.), These Standards ought to be braced (or spurr'd) before and behind. **1750** W. Ellis *Mod. Husb.* VI. I. 126 By spurring up a gate or stile-post before they are quite damaged, he may save a landlord a considerable charge. **1828–** in dial. glossaries (Yks., Chesh., Sussex, Hamps.).

9. To prune in (a side-shoot, etc.) so as to form a spur close to the stem. Chiefly with *in* or *back*.

1840 *Florist's Jrnl.* (1846) I. 104 Instead of being spurred-in closely,.. the shoots of the selected trees should be left somewhat longer. **1846** Baxter *Libr. Pract. Agric.* I. 184 Good lateral shoots may be spurred as before directed. **1849** *Beck's Florist* 54 Spur them back in a way best calculated to form a bushy head.

10. To affect with the disease spur or ergot.

1896 Lina Echenstein *Woman under Monasticism* 286 Bread containing rye spurred or diseased with ergot. **1897** *Allbutt's Syst. Med.* II. 796 Wagner reported one-fifth of a bulk of rye to be spurred.

spur, *v.*^{2} *north. dial.* Also 5 spirr, spyrr. [Special senses of *spir*, *spur* speer *v.*^{1} Cf. ask *v.* 20.]

1. *trans.* †**a.** To publish (the banns of marriage) in church. *Obs.*$^{-1}$

c **1400** *York Manual* (Surtees) p. xvi, Yet I spyrr y^{e} beynis off y^{e} forsayde N. and N.

b. In pa. pple. Of persons: To be proclaimed in church as having a purpose of marriage.

c **1400** *York Manual* (Surtees) p. xvi, N. and N... hase bene spirred thre solemne dayes in y^{e} kirke. **1705** Thoresby *Diary* (1830) I. 460 There were also two-and-twenty couples spurred (to use the local word) in order to marry this day. **1828–** in dial. glossaries, etc. (Yks., Lan., Der., Lincs.). **1852** *N. & Q.* 1st Ser. VI. 329/2 'To be spurred up' is to have had the banns published for three Sundays.

2. (See quot.) *Obs.*$^{-0}$

1674 Ray *N. Co. Words* 44 *To sparre*.. or *spurre*, to.. cry at the Market.

spur, obs. variant of speer *v.*^{1}

†**spurblind**, *a. Obs.* Forms: α. 6 spurr-, 6–7 spur(re)-. β. 6 spore, spoore. [App. an alteration of *purblind*.] = purblind *a.*

α. **1508** Stanbridge *Vulgaria* (W. de W.) B j b, *Luscus*, spurblynde. **1552** Latimer *Serm. Lord's Prayer* i. 4 They be spurre-blynd and sande blynd, they can not see so farre. **1584** Lyly *Sappho* II. ii, Madame, I craue pardon, I am spur-blind, I could scarce see. **1603** Florio *Montaigne* III. vii. 552 And such as flattered Dionysius in his owne presence did run and iustle one another,.. to inferre that they were as short-sighted or spur-blinde as he was.

fig. **1611** CHAPMAN *May Day* Wks. 1873 II. 370 O spur-blind affection. **1612** *Pasquil's Night-Cap* (1877) 16 Now if these spurre-blind Peasants could but see How much themselues they blemish and disgrace.

β. **1547** BOORDE *Brev. Health* ccliv. 86 There may be many impedimentes in the eye, as a blered eye,.. spore blynde, gogyll eyes. **1557** NORTH *Gueuara's Dial. of Pr.* I. xlvi. (1568) 79 b, He was deformed in his face, spoore blynde of his eyes, and exceading couetous of riches.

† **spurch.** *Obs. rare.* Also 9 *dial.* **spursher.** [Of obscure origin.] (See quot. 1823.)

1295 *Acc. Exch. K.R.* 5/8 memb. 8 Empcio meremii... Et xij. d. in .vij. spurches emptis de Roberto le piper. **1336–7** *Ibid.* 19/31 memb. 5 Et in xxviij. spurch' emptis, vij. s. Et in lvj. boltis ferri videlicet pro quolibet spurch' ij., iiij. s viij. d. **1823** E. MOOR *Suffolk Words, Spurshers*, straight young fir-trees, the same, I believe, as firbauks and gofers.

† **spur'cidical,** *a. Obs.*$^{-0}$ [f. L. *spurcidic-us*, f. *spurcus* foul, and *dicĕre* to speak.] (See quot.)

1656 BLOUNT *Glossogr.*, *Spurcidical*.., that speaks dishonestly or uncleanly, bawdy in talk.

† **spur'citious,** *a. Obs. rare.* [See next and -OUS.] Filthy, foul, obscene.

1628 FELTHAM *Resolves* II. i. Wks. (1677) 157 Loose and unrins'd expressions are the purulent and spurcitious exhalations of a corrupted mind. **1658** J. JONES *Ovid's Ibis* To Rdr., This Ibis was a spurcitious unclean bird of Egypt.

† **'spurcity.** *Obs.*$^{-1}$ [ad. L. *spurcitia*, f. *spurcus* dirty, foul, impure.] Impurity, obscenity.

1608 H. CLAPHAM *Err. Left Hand* 34 Rome is a Gehinnon for bloud-shed, a Sodome for all spurcicity [*sic*], an Hell for damnation.

spure, obs. variant of SPEER *v.*[1]

† **spur-gall,** *sb. Obs.* [f. next.] A gall caused or produced by the spur. Also *fig.*

1655 T. WHITE *Obed. Gov.* 117, I do not understand those spurgalls of honour, which disquiet their fiery humours. **1656** HEYLIN *Surv. France* 160 The very spur-gals had made such casements through their skin.

spur-gall, *v. Obs.* exc. *arch.* Also 6–7 **spurgal,** 7 **spurrgal,** *Sc.* **spurgaw.** [f. SPUR *sb.*[1] + GALL *v.*[1]]

1. *trans.* To gall (a horse, etc.) with the spur in riding; to injure or disable in this way.

Common from *c* 1590 to *c* 1600, freq. in fig. context.

1565 COOPER *Thesaurus* s.v. *Calx*, *Cruentare equum ferrata calce*, to spurgall. **1580** BLUNDEVIL *Horsemanship* T iiij b, When a Horse is shouldered by meanes of some outward cause,.. or his sides spurgalled. **1603** DEKKER *Wonderfull Yeare* Wks. (Grosart) I. 80 These are those ranck-riders of Art, that haue so spur-gald your lustie wingd Pegasus, that now he begins to be out of flesh. **1650** B. *Discolliminium* 17 Over-will'd Men, who, if they once Plot a Designe studiously, and conclusively, will spurgall all possibilities to the Bones. **1689** D. GRANVILLE *Lett.* (Surtees) 42 Our present Low Country cavaliers, who have mounted us (and shewn themselves allready soe ill riders as to have spur-galled us). **1705** HICKERINGILL *Priest-cr.* (1721) I. 55 Lest the Jade be spur-gall'd and tired, and throw us down. **1820** SCOTT *Monast.* xxiv, The lazy monks that have ridden us so long, and spur-galled us so hard.

absol. **1685** A. PEDEN in Walker *Biog. Presbyt.* (1827) I. 59 If I were uppermost again, I shall ride hard and Spurgaw well.

2. *fig.* To gall severely, in various senses.

a **1555** RIDLEY *Wks.* (Parker Soc.) 148 If I were as well learned as was St. Paul, I would not bestow much against them, further than to gall them, and spurgall too. **1596** NASHE *Saffron Walden* Wks. (Grosart) III. 187 Againe with the Atheist he spurgals mee, in that I iested at heauen. **1601** SIR W. CORNWALLIS *Ess.* II. xxviii. (1631) 22 Wee misuse all our actions, wee spur-gall and tyre them. **1630** J. TAYLOR (Water P.) *Wks.* III. 16/2 Like to a Post I'le runne through thicke and thin To scourge Iniquity and spurgall sinne. **1719** BAYNARD *Health* (1740) 46 For one half that dies Are spur-gall'd by his flies, And flay'd out of their lives.

Hence **spur-galling** *vbl. sb.*

1580 BLUNDEVIL *Horsemanship* E e iiij, The Farcin.. is.. ingendred in the bodie, or else of some outward hurt, as of spurgalling. **1602** *2nd Pt. Ret. fr. Parnassus* II. vi. 973 He is one.. that cannot ride a horse without spur-galling. **1639** T. DE GRAY *Compl. Farrier* 41 How commeth the farcin to the creature?.. sometimes by enter-firing, and hewing, and lastly by spur-galling. **1641** MILTON *Animadv.* Wks. 1851 III. 240 Spare your selfe, lest you bejade.. your owne opiniaster wit, and make the very conceit it selfe blush with spurgalling.

spur-galled, *ppl. a. Obs.* exc. *arch.* [f. prec.] Galled by spurs; having or suffering from a gall or galls caused by the spur.

1608 MACHIN *Dumbe Knt.* III, I am at my wits' end, and am made Duller than any spurgal'd, tyred Jade. **1641** J. DAY *Parl. Bees* v. (1881) 35 Tho' this, and such gald jades, Were [? *read* Mere] spurre-gald-hackneyes, kick at their betters. **1688** *Lond. Gaz.* No. 2382/4 A black Gelding, about 14 hands,.. spur gall'd on both sides. **1691** *Ibid.* 2709/4 A Spur gall'd, old poor Mare. **1821** LAMB *Elia* I. *My Relations*, A broken-winded or spur-galled horse is sure to find an advocate in him.

b. Freq. in fig. use.

c **1590** MONTGOMERIE *Misc. Poems* iii. 31 Then spurgald sporters they began to speill. *a* **1618** RALEIGH *Prerog. Parl.* (1628) 42 Your Lordship doth remember the spurgald proverbe, that necessitie hath no law. **1635** LAUD *Wks.* (1860) VII. 117, I am sorry the Bishopric of Fernes is so spurgalled. **1705** HICKERINGILL *Priest-cr.* IV. (1721) 225 When nothing will serve them but to get up and Ride the Spur-gall'd Laiety.

spurge (spɜːdʒ), *sb.*[1] Forms: α. 3– **spurge.** β. 5 **spowrge,** 5–6 **spourge.** γ. 5–6 **sporge.** [ad. OF. *espurge* (F. *épurge*), f. *espurgier* SPURGE *v.*[1]]

1. One or other of several species of plants belonging to the extensive genus *Euphorbia*, many of which are characterized by an acrid milky juice possessing purgative or medicinal properties.

α. **1387** *Sinon. Barthol.* (Anecd. Oxon.) 11 *Anabulla*, spurge. *c* **1410** *Master of Game* (MS. Digby 182) v, þei wroteth so depe in þe grounde, tille þei fynde þe rootes of þe ferne and of þe spurge and of oþer rootes. *c* **1450** *M.E. Med. Bk.* (Heinrich) 219 Tak betoyne, sawge, heihoue, vyolet, spurge, egrimoyne & hony. **1562** TURNER *Herbal* II. (1568) 31 Spurge purgeth thynne fleme vehemently. **1585** H. LLOYD *Treas. Health* K iij, Adde thereto Scamony, the herbe called spurge, and an ox gall. **1625** HART *Anat. Ur.* II. xi. 125 It was nothing else but a certaine kind of Spurge. **1651** BIGGS *New Disp.* ¶ 79 Celandin weepeth a golden juice, and spurge a milky one. **1762** B. STILLINGFLEET *Misc. Tracts* 98 The spurge, that is noxious to man, is a most wholesome nourishment to the caterpillar. **1794** GISBORNE *Walks Forest* (1796) 6 Changeful spurge, On redden'd stem with poisonous milk imbued. **1813** SIR H. DAVY *Agr. Chem.* (1814) 245 When a stalk of spurge.. is separated by two incisions from its leaves and roots, the milky fluid flows through both sections. **1872** TENNYSON *Last Tourn.* 356 That he can make Figs out of thistles,.. milk From burning spurge.

β. *c* **1425** *Voc.* in Wr.-Wülcker 645 *Hic tintimalius*,.. spowrge. *c* **1440** *Gesta Rom.* xlviii. 368 (Addit. MS.), Then the Crow toke Onyonus and Spourge, and made þerof a playster. **1483** *Cath. Angl.* 356/1 Spowrge, *herba est.* **1539** ELYOT *Cast. Helthe* (1541) 84 b, Spourge of the garden one handful. **1578** LYTE *Dodoens* 358 All the kindes of Tithymal or Spourge are most commonly in flower in June and July.

γ. **14..** *Nom.* in Wr.-Wülcker 713 *Hec spurgia*, a sporge. **1486** *Bk. St. Albans, Hawking* cv, Also take smale flambe rotis and polipodi and the cornes of sporge. **1530** PALSGR. 274/2 Sporge an herbe, *espovrge.*

b. With various distinguishing epithets.

For *caper, Cypress, myrtle, Portland, sea, sun, wood spurge*, etc., see these words.

1578 LYTE *Dodoens* 363 Peplos.. is called in English of some Wartwurt,.. also Pety Spurge. **1597** GERARDE *Herbal* cxxxii. 407 The sixt [kind of spurge is called] Pine Spurge; the seuenth shrub Spurge, the eight tree Mirtle Spurge..; the eleventh tree Spurge; the twelfe Broad leafed Spurge; the thirteenth and fowerteenth Quacksaluers Spurge. **1607** TOPSELL *Four-f. Beasts* (1658) 202 If a woman be.. troubled with a fever, let her take half a chœnix of pettispurge, and.. nettle-seed. **1611** COTGR., *Espurge*, Garden Spurge. **1671** SKINNER *Etymol.* I iii 2/2 Land-leapers-Spurge, *Esula major.* *a* **1705** RAY *Synop. Stirp.* (1724) 312 *Tithymalus segetum longifolius*,.. Long-leaved Corn Spurge. *c* **1711** PETIVER *Gazophyl.* VIII. §80 Luzone Dwarf Spurge. **1760** J. LEE *Introd. Bot.* App. 328 Spurge, Bastard, *Euphorbia.* **1777** JACOB *Catal. Plants* 113 *Euphorbia Exigua*, Dwarf Spurge, Small annual Spurge. *Ibid.* 114 *Euphorbia platyphyllos*, Broad leaved Spurge. **1796** WITHERING *Brit. Pl.* (ed. 3) II. 447 *Euphorbia peplis*, Purple Spurge. *Ibid.* 450 *E. hyberna*, Knotty-rooted Spurge. *Ibid.* 451 *E. characias*, Red Spurge. **1865** THOREAU *Cape Cod* vi. 101 The plants which I noticed here and there on the pure sandy shelf,.. were Sea Rocket,.. Saltwort,.. Seaside Spurge (*Euphorbia polygonifolia*).

2. A particular species or plant of this. Chiefly in pl.

1715 *Phil. Trans.* XXIX. 281 Dr. Tournefort says the Root of this Spurge is a proper Cathartick in Hydropick and Cachectic Bodies. **1741** *Compl. Family-Piece* II. iii. 374 Double Lady's-smock, Spurges of several kinds. **1785** MARTYN *Lett. Bot.* xx. (1794) 283 Spurges having little beauty, they are seldom cultivated in gardens. **1846** LINDLEY *Veget. Kingd.* 275 If.. we consider the separation of sexes a great physiological character, the Order of Spurges will join that of Nettles. **1886** *Pall Mall G.* 27 Aug. 4/1 If the stem or leaf of one of these spurges be broken, a fluid as white as milk will immediately run from it.

3. Applied, with distinguishing epithet, to a few plants related to or resembling spurge.

1854 GRISEBACH *Flora Brit. W. Ind.* 788/1 Spurge, branched, *Ernodea litoralis.* **1891** *Cent. Dict.* s.v. *Pachysandra*, The plant [*P. procumbens*] has also been called Alleghany-mountain spurge. *Ibid.*, *Slipper-spurge*, the slipper-plant.

4. As a moth-name (cf. *spurge-moth* in 5).

1832 J. RENNIE *Consp. Butterfl. & Moths* 80 The Spurge (*Acronycta Euphorbiæ*).. feeds on the Euphorbia esula, and E. cyparissias.

5. *attrib.*, as *spurge family, genus, oil, order*, etc.; † **spurge comfit**, a purgative comfit or sweet; **spurge Daphne**, the spurge laurel; **spurge flax, hawk, -moth, -nettle** (see quots.); **spurge-olive**, the shrub *Daphne mezereum*; † **spurge thyme**, petty spurge, *Euphorbia peplis.*

1619 DALTON *Countr. Just.* xciii. (1630) 241 So if one giveth to another *Spurge Comfits or other such thing in sport and not in malice. **1872** OLIVER *Elem. Bot.* II. 226 The berries of.. *Spurge Daphne are also said to be poisonous to all animals excepting birds. **1849** BALFOUR *Man. Bot.* §1016 *Euphorbiaceæ*, the *Spurge Family. **1678** PHILLIPS (ed. 4), **Spurge-flax* (Thymelæa), a sort of shrub, whereon grows that rich berry called *Coccum Gnidium.* **1796** WITHERING *Brit. Pl.* (ed. 3) II. 377 Mezereon. Spurge Olive. Spurge Flax. **1887** BENTLEY *Man. Bot.* 660 The bark of *Daphne Gnidium*, Spurge Flax, is likewise official in the Paris Codex. **1866** *Treas. Bot.* 476 *Euphorbia*, the *spurge genus, which gives its name to the order *Euphorbiaceæ*, comprises a very large number of species. **1832** J. RENNIE *Butterfl. & Moths* 25 The *Spurge Hawk (*Deilephila Euphorbiæ*).. feeds on various kinds of spurge. **1849** KINGSLEY *Misc.* (1859) II. 269 The great white *spurge-moths.. whirred like humming-birds over our heads. **1868** J. G. WOOD *Homes without H.* xiv. 293 These are moths, belonging to the genus Acronycta, and popularly called Spurge Moths on account of the plant on which they reside. **1847** DARLINGTON *Amer. Weeds* (1860) 289 *Cnidoscolus stimulosa*.., Stinging Cnidoscolus. *Spurge-nettle. Tread-softly. **1836** J. M. GULLY *Magendie's Formul.* (ed. 2) 162 Physical Properties of *Spurge Oil. It very much resembles castor oil, and has even the same colour. **1668** WILKINS *Real Charact.* 109 Bacciferous sempervirent shrubs:.. *Spurge Olive (*Thymælæa*). *a* **1689** MRS. BEHN tr. *Cowley's Plants* C.'s Wks. 1711 III. 339 Two lofty Plants or flowery Giants stand, Spurge-Olive one [etc.]. **1760** J. LEE *Introd. Bot.* App. 328 Spurge Olive, *Daphne.* **1796** [see *spurge flax* above]. **1802–3** tr. *Pallas's Trav.* (1812) I. 36 The most remarkable, perhaps, are.. the *Daphne mezereum*, or spurge-olive; and the mistletoe. **1887** BENTLEY *Man. Bot.* 672 *Euphorbiaceæ*, the *Spurge Order. **1548** TURNER *Names Herbes* (E.D.S.) 60, I neuer sawe peplum but once in Bonony; it had litle smal leaues lyke tyme, and in other facion lyke spourge, wherfore it may be called *spourge tyme in englishe, tyl we can fynde a better name.

† **spurge,** *sb.*[2] *Obs.*$^{-1}$ [f. SPURGE *v.*[2]] A shoot or sprout.

1630 BRATHWAIT *Eng. Gentlem.* 138 Cabbages of such huge proportion, as the very leaves thereof (so largely extended were the spurges) might.. give shadow to five hundred men.

spurge, *v.*[1] *Obs.* exc. *dial.* Forms: 4–6 **spourge,** 5 **spowrge,** 6 **sporge;** 5 **spurgyn,** 5–7, 9 *dial.* **spurge.** [ad. OF. *espurgier*:—L. *expurgāre*: cf. PURGE *v.*[1]]

† **1.** *trans.* To cleanse, purify (a person, the body, etc.); to free from or rid *of* impurity. Also *fig.*, to clear of guilt (= PURGE *v.*[1] 5). *Obs.*

1303 R. BRUNNE *Handl. Synne* 10917 Of flyes men mow hem weyl spourge. *a* **1320** *Sir Tristr.* 2226 At londen on a day Mark wald spourge þe quen. **1483** in *Lett. Rich. III & Hen. VII* (Rolls) I. 3 When that a king annoynted ys deceassed,.. his body [is] spurged. **1530** PALSGR. 729/1, I sporge, I clense, *jespurge. Ibid.*, I shall do the best I can to sporge it. **1546** in Strype *Ann. Ref.* (1824) VI. 267 Commandment was given to the apothecaries.. and others, to do their duties in spurging, cleansing, bowelling [etc.],.. the said corps.

† **2.** With *away* or *out.* To remove by some cleansing or purifying process. *Obs. rare.*

a **1395** HYLTON *Scala Perf.* II. xxix. (1494), Vntyll the wyne hath boylled & spourged oute all vnclennesse. **1483** CAXTON *G. de la Tour* i ij, Another ensample I shalle telle yow of Mary Magdalene whyche dyd wasshe and spurge awey her synnes and mysdedes by the water of her eyen.

3. *intr.* Of ale, wine, or other fermenting liquor: To emit or throw off impure matter by fermentation; to cleanse or purify itself in this way; to ferment or 'work'. Cf. PURGE *v.*[1] 7.

c **1440** *Promp. Parv.* 32/2 Bermyn, or spurgyn as ale, or other lyke, *spumo.* *c* **1440** *Gesta Rom.* xlv. 364 (Addit. MS.), A mouse on a tyme felle into a barell of newe ale, that spourgid, and myght not come oute. **1530** PALSGR. 731/1 This ale spurgeth a great deale better for the cariage. **1577** GOOGE *Heresbach's Husb.* (1586) 184 The hony,.. after the straining,.. worketh like newe wine, and spurgeth. **1658** tr. *Porta's Nat. Magick* IV. xi. 135 When these liquors are incorporated together, they wax hot, and begin to spurge. **1854** MISS BAKER *Northampt. Gloss.*, *Spurge*,.. to emit yeast from beer, when it is first tunned.

fig. **1626** B. JONSON *Staple of N.* Induct. (1905) 7 Yonder he is within,.. rowling himselfe vp and downe like a tun, i' the midst of 'hem, and spurges, neuer did vessel of wort or wine worke so!

b. *refl.* Of a vessel.

14.. *Medical MS.* in *Anglia* XIX. 85 Take of eytherys water and put it in-to sondre vessel; sythen put to eyþer barlyche and horssys dong, and whether wessel sporgyth hym, is noȝt bareyn.

† **c.** To come or rise *up* in fermentation or 'working'. *Obs.*$^{-1}$

1634 LEVETT *Ordering of Bees* 50 And if any rosse worketh or spurgeth up.

4. To empty or relieve the bowels by evacuation. Cf. PURGE *v.*[1] 4 b.

1530 PALSGR. 729/1, I sporge, I have a great laxe, *jay la foyre. Ibid.*, 730/2, I spurge, as a man dothe at the foundement after he is deed. *a* **1643** CARTWRIGHT *Siege* v. vi, The body's something noysome; 'tis a stale one; Good troth it spurgeth very monstrously.

† **spurge,** *v.*[2] *Obs.* Also **spourge.** [Ultimately ad. L. *exporgĕre, -porrigĕre* (cf. It. *sporgere*): see PURGE *v.*[2]]

1. *intr.* Of a tree: To shoot or sprout. *rare*$^{-1}$.

1422 tr. *Secreta Secret., Priv. Priv.* 243 In that tyme [spring] al thynnges begynnyth to renoue;.. the tren clothyn ham wyth lewis, botonyth and spourgyth.

2. To spout or gush *out* in a stream. **b.** *trans.* To cast *forth* copiously.

c **1470** HENRY *Wallace* VI. 167 Than fra the stowmpe the blud out spurgyt fast. **1582** STANYHURST *Æneis* II. (Arb.) 59 Not so great a ruffling the riuer strong flasshye reteyneth Through the breach owt spurging. *Ibid.* III. 77 They gripte in tallants the meat and furth spourged a stincking Foule carrayne sauoure.

† **spurgel.** *Obs. rare.* [? Related to prec.] A water cistern or tank.

c **1450** in *Archaeologia* (1902) LVIII. 306 Þis spurgell stondiþ in þe diche of þis same medue.

spurge laurel. Also **spurge-laurel.** [SPURGE *sb.*[1]] One or other of the shrubs belonging to the genus *Daphne*, esp. *D. laureola*, the dried bark of which is used in medicine.

1597 GERARDE *Herbal* 1218 Spurge Laurell is a shrub of a cubit high, oftentimes also of two. *Ibid.* 1219 *Laureola florens*, Laurell, or Spurge Laurell flowring. **1611** COTGR., *Laureole*, Lowrie, Lauriell, spurge Laurell, little Laurell. **1668** WILKINS *Real Char.* 109 Bacciferous sempervirent shrubs..: Spurge Laurel. **1725** *Fam. Dict.* s.v. *Laurel*, The Female Spurge Laurel, has Boughs which grow four Foot high. **1760** J. LEE *Introd. Bot.* App. 328 Spurge Laurel, *Daphne.* **1845** LINDLEY *Sch. Bot.* 113 *Daphne pontica* (Long-flowered Spurge Laurel). **1882** *Garden* 18 Feb. 112/1 The Spurge Laurel and Mezereon have highly fragrant flowers.

† **'spurger.** *Obs.*$^{-1}$ [f. SPURGE *v.*[1]] A purger or purgative.

1681 T. FLATMAN *Heraclitus Ridens* No. 3 (1713) I. 15 These are swinging Spurgers indeed, a weak stomach'd Conscience is not able to bear them.

spurget, variant of SPIRGET *Obs.*

spurge-wort. [f. SPURGE *sb.*[1] or *v.*[1]]

†**1.** The plant *Iris fœtidissima. Obs.*

1562 TURNER *Herbal* II. (1568) 171 This herbe is called in the yle of Purbek Spourgewurt, because the iuyce of it purgeth. **1578** LYTE *Dodoens* 195 This herbe is called..in English Stinking Gladyn, Spourgeworte, and wilde Ireos. **1588** L. M. tr. *Bk. Dyeing* 63 Take the yelow flag, some doe call it spurgewort.

2. *Bot.* Any plant belonging to the order *Euphorbiaceæ*. Also *attrib.*

1647 HEXHAM I. (Herbs), Spurge wort, *Duyvels Melck-kruydt.* **1845** LINDLEY *Sch. Bot.* 114 *Euphorbiaceæ.* Spurge-worts. **1846** —— *Veg. Kingd.* 275 In general the structure of Spurgeworts is very uniform. **1859** CAPERN *Ballads & Songs* 129 Where spurgewort and dog-mercury And cuckoo-flowers were found. **1866** *Treas. Bot.* 379/2 *Dactylostemon*, a genus of the spurge-wort family.

† **'spurging,** *vbl. sb. Obs.* [f. SPURGE *v.*[1]]

1. The action on the part of ale, wine, etc., of throwing off impurities by fermenting; fermentation. *Obs.*

c **1440** *Promp. Parv.* 470/1 Sporgynge, of ale or wyne *spumacio.* **1502** ARNOLDE *Chron.* (1811) 85 By cause such ale and biere hathe taken wynde in spurgyng. **1577** B. GOOGE *Heresbach's Husb.* I. (1586) 28b, That whiche commeth of the spurging, is kept both for brewing and baking. **1601** HOLLAND *Pliny* II. 153 The liquor of wine gets all the force and strength that it hath by working, spurging, and seething ..in the lees while it is Must. **1720** STRYPE *Stow's Surv.* v. xi. (1754) II 289/1 Such [vessels] as were carried in drays.. would be reason of spurging and working in the Carriage want near a gallon in every barrel.

2. Purgation, purging; matter purged out or exuded. *rare.*

a **1548** HALL *Chron., Hen. VIII*, 50b, Without any dreuelyng or spurgyng in any place of his body. **1609** B. JONSON *Masque of Queens* Wks. (1640) 166 The spurgings of a dead-mans eyes.

† **'spurging,** *ppl. a. Obs. rare.* [f. SPURGE *v.*[1]]

1. Fermenting, spuming.

1566 ADLINGTON *Apuleius* 44 The Goddesse whom..the froth of the spurging waves had nourished. **1570** GOOGE *Popish Kingd.* III. 38b, Saint Vrban makes the pleasant wine, and doth preserue it still, And spourging vessels all with Must continually doth fill.

2. Purging; purgative.

1632 BROME *Crt. Beggar* IV. ii, The Devill fright him next for a spurging skitterbrooke. *a* **1652** —— *Queenes Exch.* v. i, You do not remember How I behav'd my self upon the eating of Spurging Comfects.

spuria ('spjʊərɪə), *sb. pl.* [L., neut. pl. of *spurius* spurious: cf. TRIVIA *sb. pl.*] Spurious works, words, etc.

1918 E. MARSH *Rupert Brooke* 110, I hope this note will not start a vain hunt for *spuria* among the published poems. **1935** *Mind* XLIV. 105 There is a record of posthumously published remains and an interesting section on spuria. **1977** *Times Lit. Suppl.* 22 Apr. 496/4 The Platonic corpus (including spuria and doubtful works).

spuri'osity. *rare.* [f. next: see -OSITY.] The state or condition of being spurious; a spurious thing or production. Also *Comb.*

1863 KINGSLEY *Water-Babies* 168 A heavy tax on words over four syllables, as heterodoxy,..spuriosity, &c. **1894** *Athenæum* 6 Oct. 457/3 The horn-book..is at last receiving attention from the 'spuriosity' maker. *Ibid.*, How this spuriosity came into existence forms an amusing story.

spurious ('spjʊərɪəs), *a.* [f. L. *spuri-us* illegitimate, false. Cf. It. *spurio*, Sp. *espurio.*]

1. Of persons: Begot or born out of wedlock; illegitimate, bastard, adulterous.

1598 BP. HALL *Sat.* VI. i, But can it be aught but a spurious seed That grows so rife in such unlikely speed? **1604** T. WRIGHT *Passions* 166 Commonly such spurious ympes [bastards] follow the steppes of their bad parents. **1635** QUARLES *Embl.* I. v, Froth-born Venus and her brat, With all that spurious brood young Iove begat. **1651** W. G. tr. *Cowel's Inst.* 26 A spurious Issue may by silence and patience be rendred legitimate. **1734** tr. *Rollin's Rom. Hist.* (1827) III. 66 All children that were spurious and illegitimate were exempted from the same duty. **1768** WALPOLE *Hist. Doubts* 77 Henry came of the spurious stock of John of Gaunt. **1815** SOUTHEY *Roderick* VI. 89 The spurious race Whom in unhappy hour Favila's wife Brought forth for Spain. **1885** *Law Rep. 14 Q.B. Div.* 792 Adultery by the wife followed by the birth of a spurious child.

absol. **1628–30** BP. HACKET in Plume *Life* (1865) 30 The Lutherans..baptized none at home but the sick and the spurious.

b. *fig.* or in fig. context.

1598 MARSTON *Sco. Villanie* I. ii. 175 Pert Gallus slily slips along to wage Tilting encounters with some spurious seed Of marrow pies, and yawning Oysters breede. **1608** D. T. *Ess. Pol. & Mor.* 89 That love is but the spurious, and adulterate issue of a conscious and guilty feare. **1665** GLANVILL *Def. Van. Dogm.* 73 'Tis doubtful whither they are not the spurious issue of some more modern Author. **1764** REID *Inquiry* i. §2. 99 In those regions the offspring of fancy is legitimate, but in philosophy it is all spurious.

c. Characterized by bastardy or illegitimacy.

1770 LANGHORNE *Plutarch* (1851) II. 707/2 Aridæus..was of spurious birth. **1838** LYTTON *Calderon* i. 64 He knew not for what end Calderon had forced upon him the honours of spurious parentship. **1868** MILMAN *St. Paul's* viii. 203 Edmond Bonner was of obscure, according to his enemies .., of spurious birth, the son of a priest.

d. Supposititious. *rare.*

1833 MARRYAT *P. Simple* (1863) 214, I cannot help surmising, that my brother..has resolved to produce to the world a spurious child as his own.

2. Having an illegitimate or irregular origin; not properly qualified or constituted.

1601 B. JONSON *Poetaster* v. iii, Teach thy *incubus* to poetize; And throw abroad thy spurious snotteries, vpon that puft-vp lumpe of barmy froth. **1633** MASSINGER *Guardian* II. ii, I apprehend what thou wouldst say: I want all As means to quench the spurious fire that burns here. **1660** R. COKE *Power & Subj.* 2 That Providence should so direct those spurious and imperfect animals, and but of yesterdays being,..to fear and avoid those who are enemies and prey upon them. **1699** POMFRET *On a Marriage* 21 Achates' choice..from no spurious passion came, But was the product of a noble flame. **1781** GIBBON *Decl. & F.* xvii. (1787) II. 18 That a spurious race of strangers and plebeians was left to possess the solitude of the ancient capital.

Comb. **1668** H. MORE *Div. Dial.* IV. xxxiii. (1713) 384 An Adulterous Generation seeketh after a Sign, and a spurious-hearted Christian after a Prophecy.

3. Superficially resembling or simulating, but lacking the genuine character or qualities of, something; not true or genuine; false, sham, counterfeit: **a.** Of material things.

Freq. in more or less specific use in *Anat.*, *Bot.*, etc.

1615 H. CROOKE *Body of Man* 394 They are diuided into true or legitimate, & bastard or spurious ribs. **1665** *Phil. Trans.* I. 107 Making them a kind of Spurious Planets. **1668** CULPEPPER & COLE *Barthol. Anat.* IV. xvii. 353 The.. bastard Ribs..do stick one to the other,..the last excepted, which is the least, and sticks to none, and therefore 'tis truly spurious. **1782** COWPER *Self-diffidence* 37 Spurious gems our hopes entice, While we scorn the pearl of price. **1796** KIRWAN *Elem. Min.* (ed. 2) II. 57 Carbon bituminated, impregnated with a notable proportion of stony matter. Spurious Coal. **1807** J. E. SMITH *Phys. Bot.* 284 There are several spurious kinds of berries, whose pulp is not properly a part of the fruit, but originates from some other organ. **1827** ROBERTS *Voy. Centr. Amer.* 47 Traders..are often cheated, by having a kind of spurious, or bastard wood without dye, imposed upon them. **1857** HENFREY *Bot.* 123 False or spurious dissepiments occur occasionally both in compound and simple ovaries. **1892** GREENER *Breech-Loader* 52 The spurious gun may be either a gun represented as being of a quality it is not, or as a production of a maker other than the real one.

b. Of qualities, conditions, etc.

1646 MAXWELL *Burden of Issachar* 28 This scourge, which is gilded with the specious, but spurious compellation of a glorious, thorow, second Reformation. **1658** T. WALL *Charac. Enemies Ch.* 6 When this comes into competition that spurious concord which is knit by secular respects..is suddenly overthrown. **1713** SWIFT *Cadenus & Vanessa* Wks. 1751 III. II. 8 That spurious virtue in a maid, A virtue but at second-hand. **1728** MORGAN *Algiers* II. i. 211 The City known to us under the spurious name of Algiers. **1791** BURKE *Lett. Member Nat. Assembly* Wks. I. 483 States-men ..exist by every thing which is spurious, fictitious, and false. **1820** IRVING *Sketch Bk.* I. 205 It is only spurious pride that is morbid and sensitive. **1863** WHYTE MELVILLE *Gladiators* III. 152 He could lash himself into a spurious anger. **1875** JOWETT *Plato* (ed. 2) III 483 There appear to be three pleasures, one genuine and two spurious.

c. In the specific names of animals, birds, etc.

1781 PENNANT *Hist. Quad.* II. 37 In the southern and western provinces of Russia is a mixed breed of hares, between this and the common species. [*marg.*] Spurious [Hare]. **1787** LATHAM *Gen. Synop. Birds* Suppl. I. 214 The Wood Grous, as well as the Spurious Grous, were extant in Scotland. **1801** SHAW *Gen. Zool.* II II. 476 Spurious Narwhal (*Monodon Spurius*), a species most allied to the Narwhal, but not perhaps, strictly speaking, of the same genus. **1889** MAIDEN *Usef. Pl.* 579 *Notelæa ligustrina*, ..'Spurious Olive'.

d. In medical or pathological use.

1693 tr. *Blancard's Phys. Dict.* (ed. 2), *Spurii Morbi*, as Spurious fevers, a Pleurisie, a Bastard Quinsie, and the like. **1790** *Med. Comm.* II. 455 A woman in labour is to be treated as if suffering spurious pains, so long as the os uteri.. remains..close. **1803** *Med. Jrnl.* IX. 69 That sort of cow-pock, which had all the characteristics of the spurious kind. **1860** TANNER *Pregnancy* 126 Spurious pregnancy is by no means an unfrequent disorder. **1877** ROBERTS *Handbk. Med.* I. 29 It is necessary to mention certain morbid conditions which are known as spurious dropsies.

4. Of a writing, etc.: Not really proceeding from its reputed origin, source, or author; not genuine or authentic; forged.

1624 GATAKER *Transubst.* 43 Authors and writings, either justly suspected, or evidently spurious and counterfeit. **1682** BURNET *Rights Princes* ii. 72, I insist not on the spurious Treatises that are ascribed to him. *a* **1719** ADDISON *Evid. Chr. Relig.* I. vii, As for the spurious *Acts of Pilate*, now extant. **1790** PALEY *Horæ Paul.* i. 2 A situation in which it is more difficult to distinguish spurious from genuine writings. **1847** EMERSON *Repres. Men, Plato*, The vexed question concerning his reputed works—what are genuine, what spurious. **1868** FREEMAN *Norm. Conq.* (1877) II. App. 579 The writ is clearly spurious, but it is one of those cases in which a spurious document proves something.

b. Similarly of words or passages.

1651 BAXTER *Inf. Bapt.* 155 Though the place be most express for Infant Baptism,..yet it is either spurious or interpolate. **1699** BURNET *39 Articles* vi. (1700) 79 That he should be able to distinguish what is Genuine in them from what is Spurious. **1759** DILWORTH *Pope* 91 The lines, or even the words supposed to be spurious. **1861** PALEY *Æschylus, Choeph.* (ed. 2) 519 *note*, The words καὶ τὸν νύχιον had been marked as spurious in a former edition of this play.

5. Characterized by spuriousness or falseness.

c **1840** DE QUINCEY *Bentley* Wks. 1859 VII. 41 When instances of spurious pretensions came in his way. **1860** W. G. WARD *Nat. & Grace* I. 36 We may distinguish these true primary premisses from spurious counterfeits. **1892** *Photogr. Ann.* II. p. ci, Messrs... caution buyers against Spurious Imitations of their well-known Apparatus.

spuriously ('spjʊərɪəslɪ), *adv.* [f. prec.] In a bastard or spurious manner; with pretence or simulation; falsely.

1755 JOHNSON, *Bastardly*, in the manner of a bastard; spuriously. *a* **1818** in Todd s.v., The deposition.. confessing that the child had been spuriously passed upon Virginius for his own. **1845** BAILEY *Festus* (ed. 2) 83 How faith and fancy, in the mind of man, Have spuriously mingled. **1879** TROLLOPE in *19th Cent.* Jan. 39 She who is made interesting by exhibition of bold passion [will] teach others to be spuriously passionate.

b. *spec.* in *Bot.*

1830 LINDLEY *Nat. Syst. Bot.* 83 In Amelanchier the simple ovaria are spuriously 2-celled. **1861** BENTLEY *Man. Bot.* 547 Ovary inferior.., 1-celled, or spuriously 3-celled. **1872** OLIVER *Elem. Bot.* II. 133 The floral receptacle, which develops around, and adnate to the carpels, so that they become united into a spuriously syncarpous pistil.

spuriousness ('spjʊərɪəsnɪs). [f. as prec.]

1. Bastardy, illegitimacy. *rare.*

1668 WILKINS *Real Char.* 28. **1730** BAILEY (fol.), *Illegitimateness*, unlawfulness, baseness of Birth, spuriousness. **1828–32** in WEBSTER.

†**2.** ? Irregular or abnormal condition. *Obs.*$^{-1}$

1674 R. GODFREY *Inj. & Ab. Physic* 67 By enabling my stomach to master the food, whilst it destroy'd all inclinations to Spuriousness.

3. The state or quality of being spurious, false, or counterfeit: **a.** Of documents, writings, etc.

1678 CUDWORTH *Intell. Syst.* I. iv. 321 Several other Books..being unquestionably distinct from the Pæmander, and no signs of Spuriousness or Bastardy discovered in them. **1699** BENTLEY *Phal.* Introd. 20 The Spuriousness of Phalaris's Epistles. **1723** WATERLAND *Sec. Vind.* 124 Some considerable Testimonies in Ruinart's select Acts of Martyrs, which tho' not so certainly genuine..have yet no certain Mark of Spuriousness. **1790** PALEY *Horæ Paul.* i. 15 The internal marks of spuriousness and imposture which these compositions betray. **1830** D'ISRAELI *Chas. I*, III. vi. 91 [He] has been particluarly anxious to assert the spuriousness of some writings assigned to the King. **1884** *Manch. Exam.* 4 Nov. 5/1 The wretched article from the Paris paper, which carries the brand of spuriousness on its face.

b. In other contexts.

1818 BENTHAM *Parl. Ref. Catech.* 65 The necessity of secrecy, for securing freedom, and preventing spuriousness of suffrage. **1822–7** GOOD *Study Med.* (1829) I. 325 The pierres de Goa..were, at least generally, factitious bezoars of this kind; and their spuriousness was capable of proof. **1878** DOWDEN *Stud. Lit.* 40 In his romantic poems there is ..a note of spuriousness.

spurk, *v. E. Anglian.* [Of obscure origin. Cf. SPIRK.] *intr.* To shoot or spring *up.* Also of persons: To brighten or cheer *up.*

1691 RAY *S. & E. Co. Words* 115 To *Spurk* up, to Spring, shoot or brisk up. **1823** E. MOOR *Suffolk Words* s.v., Come spurk up, here's your sweet-hart a coming. **1847** HALLIW., *Spurk*, to rise up quickly. *East.*

† **spurket.** *Obs.* Also -ett, -it. (See quots.)

From one or other of these 17th cent. quots. the word and explanation are copied into subsequent dictionaries, the form being latterly altered to *spirket*, prob. by association with SPIRKETTING.

a **1625** *Nomenclator Navalis* (Harl. MS. 2301), Spurketts are the holes or spaces betwixt the Rungs by the Ships sides fore and aft above and below. **1627** CAPT. SMITH *Seaman's Gram.* ii. 3 The Spurkits are the spaces betwixt the timbers alongst the ship side in all parts, but them in Howle below the Sleepers are broad boords, which they take vp to cleare the Spurkits, if any thing get betwixt the timbers. *c* **1635** CAPT. BOTELER *Dial. Sea Services* (1685) 99 The Spaces betwixt the Futtocks, or betwixt the rungs by the Ships side, fore and aft, above and below, are named the Spurkets.

spurl, *v. Sc.* [Of obscure origin.] *intr.* To sprawl; to scramble.

1821 LIDDLE *Poems* 100 It kick'd and spurl'd sae Wi' its feet i' the air. **1825** in JAMIESON *Suppl.* **1891** *Blackw. Mag.* CL. 85 We mount up a steep crag.., slipping and spurling right over the ruined line of the Wall.

spur-leather. [f. SPUR *sb.*[1] + LEATHER *sb.* Cf. OE. *spurleþer*, OHG. *sporleder* (G. *spornleder*), MDu. *spore-*, *spoorleder*, Da. *sporelæder*, Sw. *sporrläder.*]

1. A leather strap for securing a spur to the foot.

1598 B. JONSON *Ev. Man in Hum.* II. i, I could eate my very spur-lethers for anger! **1620** J. WILKINSON *Courts Leet* 124 No man except he..is worth 200*l.* in goods ought to weare..girdle, scabberd, or spurleathers. **1673** [R. LEIGH] *Transp. Reh.* 122 When the rats gnaw'd his spur-leathers. **1890** 'R. BOLDREWOOD' *Col. Reformer* (1891) 279 From the well-brushed hat to lower spur-leather..he justified their appreciation.

2. *under spur-leather*, a subordinate, an attendant, a menial. Now *arch.*

1685 in Ellis *Orig. Lett.* Ser. II. IV. 83 The whole discourse both in the City, and amongst the under-spurr-leathers of the Court, is that Hambden is to die on Friday. **1707** J. STEVENS tr. *Quevedo's Com. Wks.* II. x, In came a parcel of strapping Scoundrels to wait at Table, whom the topping Bullies call Under-spurleathers. **1717** DENNIS *Rem. on Pope's Homer* P.'s Wks. 1751 V. 112 A notorious idiot, .. who from an under-spur-leather to the law is become an under-strapper to the playhouse. **1816** SCOTT *Bl. Dwarf* xii, I have opened house, not only for the gentry, but for the under spur-leathers whom we must necessarily employ. **1886** *Athenæum* 4 Sept. 300/1 It was an imitation of Swift's .. manner by one of his 'under spur-leathers'.

spurless (ˈspɜːlɪs), *a.* Also 4 sporeles, 5 sporles. [f. SPUR *sb.*[1] + -LESS. Cf. G. *spornlos.*]

1. Lacking a spur; having no spurs. Also in fig. context.

a **1300** *Pol. Songs* (Camden) 71 Thou shalt ride sporeles o thy lyard. *c* **1400** *Pilg. Sowle* (Caxton, 1483) v. x. 101 There come pryke forthe sporles Humylyte and ranne ageyne pryde.

1864 LOWELL *Fireside Trav.* 266 Digging at the sides of his mule with his spurless heels. **1880** in Mrs. Power O'Donoghue *Ladies on Horseback* (1881) 251 A spurless boot.

2. Of birds or their legs: Devoid of spurs.

1819 STEPHENS in Shaw's *Gen. Zool.* XI. I. 243 Argus: .. the tarsi spurless: the tail ascending. **1849** D. J. BROWNE *Amer. Poultry Yd.* (1855) 141 Bill and spurless legs less stout. **1859** DARWIN *Orig. Spec.* iv. (1860) 88 A hornless stag or spurless cock.

3. *Bot.* Having no spur or calcar.

1839 LINDLEY *Sch. Bot.* iv. 36 Petals 4; .. two convex and spurless. **1849** CRAIG, *Spurless-violet*, the plant Erpeton reniformis. **1855** MISS PRATT *Flower. Pl.* V. 196 Spurless Coral root.

4. Of branches: Destitute of fruiting-spurs.

1868 *Rep. U.S. Commissioner Agric.* (1869) 122 These long, spurless branches can be thinned out by removing them entirely.

spurlet. *rare*[-1]. [f. SPUR *sb.*[1] + -LET.] A small spur of a mountain or mountain-range.

1894 R. S. FERGUSON *Hist. Westmorland* 5 The waters from these two spurs and their subordinate spurlets (to coin a word) drain northwards.

spur-like, *a.* [f. SPUR *sb.*[1] + -LIKE.] Like or resembling a spur.

1829 T. CASTLE *Introd. Bot.* 83 Calcarate or spur-like [figure]—as in the larkspur, columbine, and snap-dragon. **1876** PAGE *Adv. Text-bk. Geol.* ii. 43 Stretching southward in long spur-like projections. **1896** LYDEKKER *Roy. Nat. Hist.* V. 286 Each of the three inner-toes is furnished with a sharp, spur-like nail.

spurling[1]. ? *Obs.* [var. of SPIRLING.] The smelt or spirling, *Osmerus eperlanus.* Also *attrib.*

a **1471** in N. F. Hele *Aldeburgh* (1870) vi. 65 Every boat .. going to fishing for sperling in spurling tyme. **1566** GASCOIGNE *Supposes* II. iv, A penieworth of cheese, and halfe a score spurlings. **1573** TUSSER *Husb.* (1878) 28 All Saints doe laie .. for sprats and spurlings for their house. **1601** CHESTER *Love's Mart.* (1878) 100 Here swimmes the Shad, the Spitfish, and the Spurling. **1655** MOUFET & BENNET *Health's Improv.* 169 Spurlings are but broad Sprats, taken chiefly upon our Northern coast. **1844** *Peter Parley's Ann.* V. 123 The little smelts or spurlings run up the softened rivers to spawn.

spurling[2] (ˈspɜːlɪŋ). *Naut.* [Origin unknown.] Only in Combs., as **spurling gate** (see quot. 1927); **spurling pipe** (see quot. 1962). Cf. SPURLING-LINE.

1927 G. BRADFORD *Gloss. Sea Terms* 169/2 *Spurling gate*, the iron casting set in the deck through which the anchor chain passes. **1938** F. A. WORSLEY *First Voyage* 217 The spurlingate pipes were now uncovered and the ends of the chain cables roused up. **1962** A. G. COURSE *Dict. Nautical Terms* 186 *Spurling pipe*, the pipe that encloses the anchor cable from windlass to cable locker.

spurling-line. *Naut.* (See quots.)

(*a*) **1823** CRABB *Technol. Dict.* II, *Spurling Line* (Mar.), the line which forms the communication between the wheel and the telltale. **1867** SMYTH *Sailor's Word-bk.* 646 [The] Spurling-line .. went round a small barrel, abaft the barrel of the wheel, and made the pointer show the position of the tiller.

(*b*) **1863** A. YOUNG *Naut. Dict.* (ed. 2) 365 *Spurling-line*, a line extended athwartships between the two foremast shrouds of a vessel, with thimbles spliced into it to serve as fairleaders for the running-rigging.

‖**spurlos versenkt** (ˈʃpuːrloːs fərˈzɛŋkt), *adj. phr.* [Ger., = sunk without trace.] Sunk without trace; usu. *fig.*, done for, lost from sight. Hence occas. (with partial translation) ***sunk spurlos.*** Cf. *to sink without trace* s.v. SINK *v.* 1 a.

The phrase became widely known as a result of the publication in September 1917 of a secret telegram sent in May of that year by Count Luxburg, the German minister in Buenos Aires, to Berlin, advising that Argentine shipping should be either turned back or sunk without trace.

1918 W. H. ALLEN in *Stories of Americans in World War* 24 He was merely seeking an excuse for the inhuman conduct he planned. The order 'spurlos versenkt'—to be sunk without leaving a trace—was to be obeyed. **1922** A. HUXLEY *Mortal Coils* 92 You're done for .. sunk—spurlos. **1928** H. CRANE *Let.* 23 Oct. (1965) 329, I haven't had a creative thought for so long that I feel quite lost and *spurlos versenkt.* **1930** W. F. SANDS *Undiplomatic Mem.* xv. 225 My plan for neutralization of Korea .. was sunk without trace, completely *spurlos.* **1946** W. S. CHURCHILL in *Compl. Speeches* (1974) VII. 7337 He has departed '*spurlos versengkt*' [*sic*] as the German expression says—sunk without leaving a trace behind. **1963** *Oxf. Med. School Gaz.* XV. 23 Many distinguished research workers have ceased production when they have become professors and like submarines in dangerous waters have been *spurlos versenkt.*

spur-maker. [f. SPUR *sb.*[1] + MAKER. Cf. MDu. *spor-*, MDu. and Du. *spoormaker, sporenmaker*, G. *spor(e)nmacher*, Da. *sporemager*, Sw. *sporrmaker.*] One who makes spurs; a spurrier.

1586 T. B. *La Primaud. Fr. Acad.* I. 698 So consequently armorers, .. spur-makers, smithes, and such like, are necessarie. **1598** FLORIO, *Speronaro*, a spurrier or spurmaker. **1676** *Dunfermline Kirk Session Rec.* (1865) 68 A complaint against W[m] bell spurrmaker. **1686** PLOT *Staffordsh.* 376 The Head or Spurr maker that makes the body of the Spurr .. with swan-necks. **1708** J. CHAMBERLAYNE *Pres. St. Gt. Brit.* (1710) 23 Rippon [is noted] for Clothiers and Spur-makers. **1797** *Encycl. Brit.* (ed. 3) XV. 37/1 [Silver-] Plating .. is said to have been invented by a spur-maker. **1881** *Instr. Census Clerks* (1885) 57 Harness: .. Spring Bar Maker, Spur Maker.

spurn (spɜːn), *sb.*[1] Also 4–7 spurne, 4–5 sporn. [f. SPURN *v.*[1]]

†**1.** A trip or stumble. *Obs.*

a **1300** *Cursor M.* 4324 Qua folus lang, wit-outen turn, Oft his fote sal find a spurn. *Ibid.* 4329. *a* **1375** *Joseph Arim.* 581 He hedde no space spedly him-seluen forto do him no dispit; þe sporn was his owne. ? *a* **1500** *Chester Pl.* I. 136 Beware yow of this Chayre, lest that yow have a fowle spurne. **1535** STEWART *Cron. Scot.* II. 150 Nocht wittand weill quhome to that tyid to turne, For lidder speid cumis of airlie spurne.

†**2. a.** *to hold (a) spurn*, to make successful resistance. *Obs.*[-1]

a **1300** *Cursor M.* 19414 Wit spec[h]e þai gaue him mani turn, Bot nan gain him moght hald spurn [*Gött*, a spurn].

†**b.** A pace or course (on horseback). *Obs.*[-1]

c **1330** R. BRUNNE *Chron. Wace* (Rolls) 12759 Wawayn .. byheld þat he cam so gret a spurne, He had no leyser his hors to turne.

†**c.** An encounter, fray. *Obs. rare.*

a **1500** *Chevy Chase* 136 in Child *Ballads* III. 310 At Otterburn begane this spurne, vppone a Monnynday.

3. A stroke with the foot; a kick.

a **1300** *Cursor M.* 23780 Qua herd a caitiuer crachun, þat will noght bide to giue a spurn? *c* **1440** *Gesta Rom.* lxx. 323 (Harl. MS.), He lifte vp his foote, and gafe him a spurne aȝen þe brest. **1542** UDALL *Erasm. Apoph.* b iij b, When a certain feloe had .. geuen him a spurne on the shynne, as he was gooyng on his waye in the strete. **1579** LYLY *Euphues* (Arb.) 145 A young man beeing peruerse in nature, .. gaue Socrates a spurne. **1622** MABBE tr. *Aleman's Guzman d'Alf.* II. 30 Hee should haue .. many a spurne and kicke with the foot. **1679** C. NESS *Antichrist* 46 Is not this like one of the spurns or kicks of the beast? **1708** SWIFT *Rem. upon Book* Wks. 1841 II. 182 Like the sick old lion in the fable, who .. took nothing so much to heart as to find himself at last insulted by the spurn of an ass. **1851** HELPS *Comp. Solit.* iv. 46 Alnaschar, .. who with an imaginary spurn .. disposed at once of all his splendid fortunes.

fig. *c* **1430** in *Reliq. Antiq.* I. 1 He gafe my mayden-hed a spurne. **1577** *F. de L'isle's Legendarie* F iij b, By this meanes they gaue so shrewd a spurne at the estate of this realme that it feleth it yet. **1612** WITHER *Juvenilia, Prince Hen. Obsequies* (1633) 297 'Tis true, I know, Death with an equall spurn The lofty Turret and low Cottage beats.

b. The act of kicking or spurning.

1641 MILTON *Reform.* II. Wks. 1851 III. 71 Where under .. the trample and spurne of all the other Damned .. they shall remaine in that plight for ever. **1650** BAXTER *Saints' R.* IV. iii, The spurn of a man's foot destroys all their labour. **1842** *Fraser's Mag.* XXVI. 479 The sweep of the arms and the spurn of the legs must always be made under the water. **1893** F. THOMPSON *Poems* 49 With flying lightnings round the spurn o' their feet.

Comb. **1676** *Doctrine of Devils* 196 The Magical Seals, &c., whereby men might be preserved Shot-free, and consequently Stick-free, Cane-free, Spurn-free, Kick-free.

4. The act of treating with disdain or contemptuous rejection; an instance of this.

1602 SHAKS. *Ham.* III. i. 73 The insolence of Office, and the Spurnes That patient merit of the vnworthy takes. **1646** JENKYN *Remora* 9 Do the rowlings of a fathers bowels deserve our spurn? *a* **1680** CHARNOCK *Attrib. God* (1834) II. 200 It is a spurn at God's sovereignty, and a slight of his goodness. **1875** LOWELL in *N. Amer. Rev.* CXX. 370 There is an exulting spurn of earth in it, as of a soul just loosed from its cage.

spurn (spɜːn), *sb.*[2] Also 6–7 spurne, 9 spern. [var. of SPUR *sb.*[1], prob. after prec. or SPURN *v.*[1]]

1. †**a.** The beak of a war-galley. *Obs.*[-1]

1553 BRENDE *Q. Curtius* G ij, They came agaynste her wyth two galeies crosse upon her side: wherof the one strake ful with her Spurne.

b. A sharp projection or edge on a horse-shoe. Now *dial.* or *Obs.* (Cf. SPRUN.)

1717 SIR W. HOPE *Solleysell's Compl. Horseman* I. xxxi. 301 He makes him a pair of hinder Shoes with long Spurns or Plates before the Toes. **1834** KNOWLSON *Cattle Doctor* (1843) 154 Some horses cut with the spurn of the foot, and some with the heel. **1849** *Teesdale Gloss.* 123 *Spurn.* The toe of a horse's shoe, when sharpened in time of frost, is so called.

2. An outward-growing root or rootlet; one of the main roots *of* a tree. *Obs.* exc. *dial.*

1601 HOLLAND *Pliny* I. 368 These Trees loue .. to haue the superfluous spurnes rid away from the root. **1613** MARKHAM *Eng. Husbandman* II. II. iv. (1635) 60 From the spurnes of the roote will arise new Spiers. **1793** *Trans. Soc. Arts* XI. 195 The butt or stem of an ash-tree, having the spurns left to it in felling. **1796–** in dialect glossaries, etc. (Midl., Chesh., Shropsh., Warw.).

fig. **1620** SANDERSON *Serm.* I. 160 If there be any sprigs or spurns of that root here. **1648** *Ibid.* II. 241 The flesh .. is ever and anon putting forth spurns of avarice, ambition, envy.

3. A slanting prop or stay; a spur or spur-stone.

1620–1 in *North Riding Soc.* (1885) III. 110 That a Wickham man be committed to the House of Corr[ectio]n for cutting downe a windemille spurne. **1847** in HALLIWELL (Linc.). **1866** PEACOCK *Eng. Ch. Furniture* 180 *note*, The fastenings or wooden supports—spurns, as a Lincolnshire man would say, of the 'shafte' or May-pole.

b. *Mining.* (See quots.)

1837 HEBERT *Engin. & Mech. Encycl.* I. 375 The spern, a small piece of coal left as a support to many tons above, which fall when this is taken away. **1860** *Eng. & For. Mining Gloss.* (ed. 2) 79 *Spurns*, small ties or connections, left between the coals hanging and the ribs and pillars. **1883** GRESLEY *Gloss. Coal-m.* 233 *Spurns*, narrow pillars or webs of coal between each holing, not cut away until the last thing before withdrawing the sprags.

†**spurn,** *sb.*[3] Variant of SPOORN. *Obs.*

1614 SELDEN *Titles Honor* 164 The spurne Lilith .. mentioned in holy Writ, which the Iews say is a Spirit very Dangerous to yong Children or Women in Childbirth. **1790** GROSE *Prov. Gloss.* (ed. 2), *Spurne*, an evil spirit. Dorsetsh[ire].

spurn (spɜːn), *v.*[1] Forms: 1 spurnan, spornan, 3–6 sporn(e, 3–7 spurne (5–6 spourne, 6 *Sc.* spwrne), 4– spurn (4 spourn, 5 *Sc.* spwrn, 6 spvrn). [OE. *spurnan, spornan* str. v. (pa. t. *spearn*, pa. pple. *-spornen*), = OS. *spurnan*, ON. **sporna* (pa. t. *sparn*), related to the weak vbs. OHG. *spornôn*, ON. *sporna*, OHG. *spurnan, -en*, ON. *spyrna*, and OHG. (*fir*)*spirnen*, ON. *sperna*, MSw. and Sw. *spjärna*. The stem is prob. that of SPUR *sb.*[1] In OE. the simple verb is less frequent than the compound *ætspurnan.*]

I. *intr.* †**1.** To strike against something with the foot; to trip or stumble. Also *fig.* *Obs.*

c **1000** *Ags. Psalter* (Thorpe) xc. 12 Þe læs þu fræcne on stan fote spurne. *a* **1225** *Ancr. R.* 186 A child, ȝif hit spurneð o summe þing, oðer hurteð him, me bet þet þing þet hit hurteð on. **1297** R. GLOUC. (Rolls) 7710 As he rod an honteþ & þar auntre is hors spurnde. *a* **1300** *Cursor M.* 3575 Quen þat [a man] sua bicums ald, .. þan es eth þe fote to spurn. **1388** WYCLIF *Jer.* xxxi. 9 Y schal brynge them .. in a riȝtful, weie, thei shulen not spurne therynne. *c* **1400** *Beryn* 2862, I shall make hem spurn, & have a sore falle. *c* **1449** PECOCK *Repr.* v. viii. 525 Lest if .. the hors where left to his fredom .. he schulde be in perel forto the oftir spurne. **1549–62** STERNHOLD & H. *Ps.* xci. 12 So that thy foote shall never chaunce to spurne at any stone. **1603** *Proph. of T. Rymour* (Bann. Cl.) 12 Where the water runnes bright and sheene Thair shal many steides spurne. **1639** FULLER *Holy War* IV. xxi. (1840) 218 And their legs so stand in men's way that few can go by them without spurning at them. **1714** GAY *Trivia* II. 211 How can ye Laugh, to see the Damsel spurn, Sink in your Frauds and her green Stocking mourn? **1734** ARBUTHNOT, etc. *Mart. Scriblerus* viii. (1756) 39 The maid .. ran up stairs, but spurning at the dead body, fell upon it in a swoon.

†**b.** In proverbial contrast with *speed.* Chiefly *Sc.*

1423 JAS. I *Kingis Q.* clxxxi, Quhen thai wald faynest speid, that thai may spurn. *c* **1440** *York Myst.* xxxix. 15, I sporne þer I was wonte to spede. *a* **1500** *Ratis Raving* II. 362 That garris thaim spwrn quhen thai suld speid. **1535** STEWART *Cron. Scot.* III. 226 Quha spurnis airlie cumis lidder speid.

†**2.** To strike or thrust with the foot; to kick (*at* something). *Obs.*

?*c* **1400** LYDG. *Æsop's Fab.* i. 52 [The cock] On a smal dunghill .. Gan to scrape and sporn. **15..** *Smith & his Dame* 301 in Hazl. *E.P.P.* III. 212 Than she spvrned at hym so, That hys shynnes bothe two In sonder she there brake. **1592** NASHE *P. Penilesse* (ed. 2) 3 b, Who spurneth not at a dead dogge? **1598** *Mucedorus* Induct. 32 Where I may see them wallow in there blood, To spurne at armes and legges quite shiuered off [etc.]. **1690** [see SPRUNT *v.*]. **1740** SOMERVILLE *Hobbinolia* II. 295 His Iron Fist descending crush'd his Skull, And left him spurning on the bloody Floor.

fig. *a* **1548** HALL *Chron., Hen. V*, 81 This prince was a capitaine against whome fortune never frowned nor mischance once spurned.

†**b.** In allusive phrases. *Obs.* (Cf. KICK *v.*[1] 1 c.)

c **1390** CHAUCER *Truth* 11 Bywar þerfore to spurne aȝeyns an al. *c* **1480** HENRYSON *Test. Cres.* 475 Quhy spurnis thow aganis the Wall? **1483** *Vulgaria* 26 It is a foly to sporn ageyns the pryk. **1513** MORE *Rich. III*, Wks. 70/2, I purpose not to spurne againste a prick. **1562** HEYWOOD *Prov. & Epigr.* (1867) 116 Folly to spurne or kycke against the harde wall. **1573** TUSSER *Husb.* (1878) 205 What profit then .. Against the prick to seeme to spurne? **1605** CAMDEN *Rem.* (1623) 268 Folly it is to spurne against a pricke. [**1816** SCOTT *Old Mort.* Introd., Waste not your strength by spurning against a castle wall.]

†**c.** To strike *at* with a weapon. *Obs.*[-1]

c **1400** *Destr. Troy* 4744 The grekes .. With speris full dispitiously spurnit at the yates.

†**d.** To dash; to drive quickly. *Obs.*

a **1400–50** *Alexander* 786 Now aithire stoure on þar stedis strikis to-gedire, Spurnes out spakly with speris in hand. *c* **1400** *St. Cuthbert* (Surtees) 4706 Thre grete wawes in spurned. *Ibid.* 6796 Þe shipp agayn to land spurned.

3. *fig.* To kick *against* or *at* something disliked or despised; to manifest opposition or antipathy, esp. in a scornful or disdainful manner.

(*a*) **1526** *Pilgr. Perf.* (W. de W. 1531) 17 b, Than they wyll sporne agaynst god, .. and vtterly refuse and forsake the batayle of vertue. **1559** *Mirr. Mag., Owen Glendour* xiii, Was none so bold durst once agaynst me spurne. **1605** STOW *Ann.* (ed. 2) 683 Wel knowing that the Queene would spurne against the conclusions. **1633** BP. HALL *Hard T., N.T.* 145 It is no boot for thee to struggle and spurne against my almighty power.

(*b*) **1549** LATIMER *3rd Serm. bef. Edw. VI*, G vi, They that be good wyl beare, and not spourne at the preachers; they that be faultye .. must amende, and neyther spourne, nor wynse, nor whyne. **1594** SHAKS. *Rich. III*, I. iv. 203 Will you then Spurne at his Edict, and fulfill a Mans? **1603** KNOLLES *Hist. Turks* (1621) 1321 Spurning at their bread and rice which was given them for their daily entertainement. **1660** *Extr. State Papers rel. Friends* Ser. II. (1911) 120 Anabaptists..will make advantage of the first opportunity to fly out, and spurne att his Maiesties Gouerment. **1753** H. WALPOLE in *World* No. 10, One must be an infidel indeed to spurn at such authority. *a* **1781** R. WATSON *Philip III* (1839) 119 They spurned at danger, and made several vigorous sallies on the enemy. **1839** T. MITCHELL *Frogs of Aristoph.* Introd. p. cxi, That parent required sacrifices of him, at which his genius evidently spurned.

II. *trans.* †**4.** To strike (the foot) against something. *Obs.*

a **1300** *E.E. Ps.* xc. 12 Þat thurgh hap þou ne spurn þi fote til stane. *c* **1430** *Hymns Virgin* (1867) 43 Lest þou spurne þi foot at a stoon.

5. To strike or tread (something) with the foot; to trample or kick.

In later use freq. with implication of contempt.

1390 GOWER *Conf.* II. 72 The ground he sporneth and he tranceth. *a* **1500** *Lyttel Geste of Robyn Hode* III. clxi, He sporned the dore with his fote. **1560** DAUS tr. *Sleidane's Comm.* 295 The people came running to it, jobbed it in with their daggers, and spurned it with their fete. **1609** HOLLAND *Amm. Marcell.* XIV. vii. 15 The foresaid governour..they layed at and spurned with their heeles. **1634** SIR T. HERBERT *Trav.* 20 With their Feet they spurne the yeelding sands. **1735** SOMERVILLE *Chase* III. 335 Wounded, he rears aloft,.. then bleeding spurns the Ground. **1743** FRANCIS tr. *Hor., Odes* III. v. 36 When..the hind shall turn Fierce on her hunters, he the prostrate foe may spurn In second fight. **1810** SCOTT *Lady of Lake* I. v, With flying foot the heath he spurned. **1848** MRS. JAMESON *Sacr. & Leg. Art* 219 Mary is spurning with her feet a casket of jewels. **1875** LONGF. *Masque of Pandora* IV, With one touch of my..feet, I spurn the solid Earth.

b. With advs. or advb. phrases, as *away, down, off, up*, etc. Also *fig.*

c **1386** CHAUCER *Sqr.'s T.* 608 He with his feet wol spurne adoun his cuppe. *c* **1450** *Merlin* xiii. 199 Galashin with his fote spurned his body to grounde. **1526** *Pilgr. Perf.* (W. de W. 1531) 264 Auaunce thy spirituall courage, and sporne away all dulnesse & slouth. **1590** SHAKS. *Com. Err.* II. i. 83 You spurne me hence, and he will spurne me hither. **1609** ROWLANDS *Knaue of Clubbes* (Hunterian Cl.) 6 Then with her feete she spurn'd them out of bed. **1642** D. ROGERS *Naaman* 30 The Pope treading on his necke, and spurning off his Crowne with his foot. **1700** DRYDEN *Cock & Fox* 85 If, spurning up the Ground, he sprung a Corn. **1727** SWIFT *Country Post* Wks. 1751 III. I. 178 The grave-stones of John Fry, Peter How, and Mary d'Urfey were spurned down. **1793** T. BEDDOES *Demonstr. Evid.* 110 It is said, that the statesman..is apt to spurn away the ladder by which he has mounted to power. **1836** H. ROGERS *J. Howe* ii. 30 There is no barrier to such inter-communion,..which the genuine spirit of charity will not spurn down. **1855** MACAULAY *Hist. Eng.* xiii. III. 360 The few who were so luxurious as to wear rude socks of untanned hide spurned them away. **1878** BROWNING *Poets Croisic* lii, To learn..how fate could puff Heaven-high.., then spurn To suds so big a bubble in some huff.

6. To reject with contempt or disdain; to treat contemptuously; to scorn or despise.

c **1000** ÆLFRIC *Saints' Lives* vii. 64 Æfter þæs mædenes spræce þe hine spearn mid wordum. *a* **1400-50** *Alexander* 3533 We sall neuer spise ȝow ne sporne in speche ne in dede. **1435** MISYN *Fire of Love* 44 Þat, vanite spisyd & spurnyd, to trewth vnpartyngly we draw. **1501** *Plumpton Corr.* (Camden) 155 He..wyll abyde by yt for his dede,..& so will shew to all men that spurns him any wher. *a* **1548** HALL *Chron., Hen. VI*, 98 b, Well knowyng, that the Quene would spurne and impugne the conclusions. **1591** SHAKS. *Two Gentl.* IV. ii. 14 The more she spurnes my loue, The more it growes. **1635** QUARLES *Embl.* V. 13 O how my soul would spurn this ball of clay, And loathe the dainties of earth's painful pleasure. **1697** DRYDEN *Virg. Georg.* IV. 339 The pleasing Pleiades appear, And springing upward spurn the briny Seas. **1791** BOSWELL *Johnson* II. 117 When he suspected that he was invited to be exhibited, he constantly spurned the invitation. **1848** DICKENS *Dombey* liii, I came back, weary and lame, to spurn your gift. **1868** FREEMAN *Norm. Conq.* (1877) II. 144 Every offer tending to conciliation had been spurned.

Hence **spurned** *ppl. a.*

1805 WORDSW. *Prelude* V. 278 He..draws..sweet honey out of spurned or dreaded weeds.

†**spurn,** *v.*[2] *Obs.* [Alteration of SPUR *v.*[1], after prec.] *trans.* To spur; to urge or incite.

1583 GOLDING *Calvin on Deut.* cxvii. 1114 Here Moses meant to spurne forward the slothfulnesse of the Jewes. **1590** SPENSER *F.Q.* III. i. 5 The Faery quickly raught His poinant speare, and sharpely gan to spurne His fomy steed. **1612** CAPT. SMITH *Proc. Virginia* 80 To encourage the good, and with shame to spurne on the rest to amendment.

†**spurn,** *v.*[3] *Obs.* [Of obscure origin. Modern south-western dialects have *spurl* and *spur* in the same sense.] *trans.* To spread or scatter.

a **1722** LISLE *Husb.* (1757) 21 Farmer Bond..flung no dung, in the spurning or spreading it, into the furrows. *Ibid.* 30 Spurning is throwing it [*sc.* lime] abroad on the earth just before sowed.

spurn, *v.*[4] Also 9 spern. [f. SPURN *sb.*[2] 3.]

1. *intr.* To serve as a prop or stay.

1783 J. OGDEN *Manchester* 16 Sawing strong deal balks through the middle, and letting in oak spars to spurn at obtuse angles upward.

2. *trans.* To prop or support with spurns.

1865 *Even. Standard* 7 Feb., Several of the men as well as deceased neglected to sprag or spern their work.

spurn-cow. *rare*$^{-1}$. [f. SPURN *v.*[1]] A cow-herd, 'cow-puncher'.

1614 RALEIGH *Hist. World* IV. (1634) 158 The Title and Charge of a Captaine hath been bestowed on euery Prique Bœuf or Spurn-Cow.

spurner ('spɜːnə(r)). [f. SPURN *v.*[1] Cf. OE. *spornere* 'fullo' (Ælfric).]

†**1.** One who strikes with the foot. *Obs.*

1562 J. HEYWOOD *Prov. & Epigr.* (1867) 166 Ageynst soft walles spurners spurne and kyck all. **1611** COTGR., *Regimber*, a winser, kicker, spurner.

2. One who rejects or despises; a scorner.

1863 KINGLAKE *Crimea* (1880) VI. xi. 420 Far from being a spurner of rules, she had so deep a sense of their worth. **1880** TENNYSON *Battle of Brunanburh* xi, Traitor and trickster And spurner of treaties. **1899** COULSON *Jester's Jingles* 50 Now bold grows the learner, Of fear quite a spurner.

spurning ('spɜːnɪŋ), *vbl. sb.*[1] [f. SPURN *v.*[1] Cf. OE. *sporning* 'offendiculum'.] The action of the verb, in various senses.

1382 WYCLIF *Rom.* ix. 33 Sothli thei offendiden in to the stoon of offencioun, or spurnynge. ?*c* **1400** LYDG. *Æsop's Fab.* i. 85 With scrapyng and spornyng al the long day The Cok was busy hym..to feede. *c* **1440** *Promp. Parv.* 470/1 Spornynge, or spurnynge, *calcitracio.* **1591** PERCIVALL *Sp. Dict., Puntillazo*, spurning with the feete. **1611** COTGR., *Regimbement*, a kicking, winsing, spurning. **1648** GAGE *West Ind.* 15 All our ships galleries would have been torn from us with the spurnings and blowes of that outragious Golfe. *Ibid.* 140 Some with blowes, some with spurnings, some with boxes on the ear. **1837** CARLYLE *Fr. Rev.* II. III. v, Accelerated by ignominious shovings,..by smitings, twitchings,—spurnings *à posteriori.* **1853** ROBERTSON *Serm.* Ser. IV. xviii. (1876) 204 There is love instead of spurning for him.

†'**spurning,** *vbl. sb.*[2] *Obs.*$^{-1}$ [f. SPURN *v.*[2]] Spurring.

1672 *Chaucer's Ghoast* 114 Then was there hot spurning and plucking up of Horses, and right so they came to the Fire.

'**spurning,** *ppl. a.* [f. SPURN *v.*[1] Cf. OE. *spornende* stumbling.] That spurns.

1697 DRYDEN *Virg. Past.* III. 135 A Bull he bred With spurning Heels, and with a butting Head. **1788** BURNS *Ep. R. Graham* v, Mark how their lofty independent spirit Soars on the spurning wing of injur'd merit!

†**spurn-point.** *Obs.* [f. SPURN *v.*[1]] An old game, perh. of the nature of hop-scotch.

1532 MORE *Confut. Tindale* Wks. 576/2 Albeit the old kindenesse of the father cannot lette the good chyld vttrely dyspayre, for all that he hath played at spurne poynte by the waye in goynge at scholewarde. **1627** W. HAWKINS *Apollo Shroving* III. iv. 49 If he were here, he would intreat Apollo to play at Quoits with me, or checkestone, or spurne-point. *a* **1643** LD. FALKLAND, etc. *Infallibility* (1646) 9 The Reader might almost think they had beene fallen out at Spurn-point or Ketle-pins.

spurn-water. *Naut.* [f. SPURN *v.*[1]] (See latest quot.)

1347-9 *Acc. Exch. K.R.* 25/32 Spornewaters. **1407** *Ibid.* 44/11 m. 6 In iij peciis maeremii..pro spurnewaters inde faciendis. **1828-32** in WEBSTER. *c* **1850** *Rudim. Navig.* (Weale) 151 *Spurn-water*, a channel left above the ends of a deck to prevent water from coming any farther.

spur-of-the-moment *attrib. phr.*: see SPUR *sb.*[1] 2 d.

spurre, obs. var. SPEER *v.*[1]; obs. f. SPUR.

spurred (spɜːd), *a.* [f. SPUR *sb.*[1]]

1. Wearing or provided with a spur or spurs:

a. In pred. use, chiefly in the phr. *booted* (or †*hosed*) *and spurred.*

c **1400** *Brut* cc. 227 In maner of an Erl, worthely arraied, ..and hosede and spored. *c* **1450** *Contin. Brut* 561 Þe Duyk of Burgeyn..was..slayne,..and after, put in-to a pitte, botit and spurret. **1632** MASSINGER *City Madam* II. ii, May the Great Fiend, booted & spurr'd,..Ride headlong down her throat. **1668** H. MORE *Div. Dial.* I. xxii. (1713) 47, I, and that booted and spurred too. **1678-1833** [see BOOTED *ppl. a.* 1 b]. **1864** *Chambers's Encycl.* VI. 296/2 Three legs of man in armour,..garnished and spurred. **1869** FREEMAN *Norm. Conq.* (1875) III. 138 Others came forth on foot, booted and spurred.

b. In attrib. use.

1688 J. GRUBB *Brit. Heroes* vii, Castor the flame of fiery steed With well spur'd boots took down. **1842** LYTTON *Zanoni* VII. xv, With his spurred heels on the table. **1900** *Times* 29 Jan. 10/3 In their..riding knickers, with brown.. riding leggings, spurred boots [etc.].

c. *spurred groat*: (see quot.).

a **1773** SNELLING *View Silver Coin Scot.* (1774) 6 From the mullet or spur in the quarters of the cross of this [David Bruce, 1329] and the two following kings, they were afterwards called Spurred Groats.

2. Furnished with sharp and hard spikes, claws, or the like.

1611 COTGR., *Ergoté*, spurred, or hauing spurres. **1648** HEXHAM II, *Als een Haen gespoort*, Spurred as a Cock. **1803** SHAW *Gen. Zool.* IV. II. 563 Subargenteous Holocentrus, with brownish back, large scales, and spurred gill-covers. **1884** *St. James's Gaz.* 27 Nov. 5/2 Spurred hens are often excellent hens.

b. In specific names, as *spurred centropyx, chameleon, lapwing, towhee bunting, tree frog.*

1831 GRIFFITH tr. *Cuvier* IX. Syn. 31 Spurred Centropyx, *Teius Calcaratus.* *c* **1882** *Cassell's Nat. Hist.* IV. 365 The Spurred Tree Frog has a flat, depressed triangular head. **1884** COUES *N. Amer. Birds* 397 *Pipilo maculatus megalonyx*, Spurred Towhee Bunting. **1887** *Cassell's Encycl. Dict.* s.v., Spurred-chameleon, *Chameleon calcarifer*, from the country round Aden. **1891** *Cent. Dict.* s.v. *Spur-winged*, Represented in South Africa by the black-backed spurred lapwing, *Hoplopterus speciosus.*

3. Of rye, etc.: Affected with ergot or spur.

1763 MILLS *Pract. Husb.* II. 405 When a spurred grain is broken. **1822-7** GOOD *Study Med.* (1829) V. 54 Spurred rye, or rye vitiated by being infested with the clavis or ergot, a parasitic plant. **1832** *Encycl. Metrop.* (1845) VI. 51/1 On breaking a spurred seed you find within it a matter of a dull white colour, adhering to the violet skin which surrounds it. **1876** BRISTOWE *Th. & Pract. Med.* (1878) 120 Amongst endemic affections may be included ergotism from the use of spurred rye as food.

4. *Bot.* Of the nature of, provided with, a spur or calcar; calcarate.

1824 R. K. GREVILLE *Flora Edin.* p. xlviii, A prominent or spurred nectary at the base. **1849** CRAIG, *Spurred valerian*, a plant belonging to the genus Centranthus. **1861** BENTLEY *Man. Bot.* 512 Sepals more or less valvate in æstivation, upper one spurred.

5. Of ships: Provided with a beak or ram.

1805 DUCKWORTH in Nicolas *Disp. Nelson* (1846) VII. 44 The Admiralty..giving me a spurred and doubled ship, the Formidable, yesterday out of dock.

spurred (spɜːd), *ppl. a.* [f. SPUR *v.*[1]] Pricked or urged on with a spur or spurs. Also *fig.*

1868 HEAVYSEGE *Jezebel* I. 258 Thine utmost speed will lag behind The spurred impatience whereon rides my soul. **1898** M. HEWLETT *Forest Lovers* xxviii, Prosper was abroad on a spurred horse.

'**spurrer.** [f. SPUR *sb.*[1] and *v.*[1] Cf. (in sense 1) MHG. *sporære* (G. *sporer*, †*spörer*).]

†**1.** A spurrier. *Obs.*$^{-0}$

1499 *Promp. Parv.* (Pynson), Sporer, *calcarius.*

2. One who spurs or urges. Also with *-on.*

1632 SHERWOOD, A spurrer, *piqueur.* **1728** SWIFT *Let. to Pope* 16 July, I doubt you want a spurrer-on to exercise and to amusements. **1848** BUCKLEY *Iliad* 83 Rush on, ye Trojans, spurrers of steeds!

spurrey, spurry ('spʌrɪ). Forms: 6 sperie, 6-7 spury, 6- spurry, 7- spurrey. [a. Du. *spurrie* (MDu. *sporie*; older Flem. *speurie, spurie*; WFris. *sparje, sparre*), prob. related in some way to med.L. *spergula* (whence G. *spergel, spörgel*, etc.).]

1. One or other of various species of herbaceous plants or weeds belonging to the genus *Spergula*, characterized by slender stems and very narrow leaves; esp. the common species corn spurrey (*S. arvensis*), occas. used as fodder for sheep and cattle; also, the genus to which these species belong.

α. **1577** B. GOOGE *Heresbach's Husb.* I. 38 b, The common people call it Spury, or Sperie. *Ibid.* 39 Such thinges as neede not muche moysture, are best sowed in lyght ground, as the great Clauer, Sperie, Chich. **1651** R. CHILD in *Hartlib's Legacy* (1655) 71 So we are ignorant what their Far or fine Bread Corn was, what their Lupine, Spury, and an hundred of this kind.

β. **1578** LYTE *Dodoens* 56 Spurry hath round stalkes, with three or foure knots or ioyntes. **1611** COTGR., *Spurrie*, Spurrie, or Franke; a Dutch hearbe, and an excellent fodder for cattell. **1706** PHILLIPS (ed. Kersey), *Spergula*,..an Herb call'd Spurry, or Frank; Wood-rose, a kind of Liver-wort. **1799** W. TOOKE *View Russian Emp.* III. 192 The pastures are richly furnished with spurry and golden clover. **1837** *Flemish Husb.* 37 in *Husb.* III. (L.U.K.), Spurry..is a plant which grows very rapidly in light sandy soils. **1879** *Cassell's Techn. Educ.* III. 28/1 Spurry..is used on the Continent as a winter food for sheep.

γ. **1671** PHILLIPS (ed. 3), *Spurrey*, a sort of herb called in Latin *Spergula.* **1683** *Lond. Gaz.* No. 1806/4 An excellent new sort of Grass-Seeds, called Spurrey. **1764** *Museum Rust.* IV. 45 Spurrey, by them [*sc.* Flemings] called Marian-grasse. **1766** *Compl. Farmer*, *Spurrey*, the name of a weed common in many parts of England. **1837** *Flemish Husb.* 14 in *Husb.* III. (L.U.K.), Those [seeds] which grow rapidly between the reaping of one crop and the sowing of another, such as spurrey or turnips. **1880** JEFFERIES *Hodge & Masters* I. 27 The spurrey that filled the spaces between the stalks below.

b. With distinguishing terms (see quots. and 2).

1640 PARKINSON *Theat. Bot.* 562 Both the Dutch and we in England call it Spurry or Franck Spurry, for the causes aforesaid, but I do a little more explaine the names, in calling it Francking Spurrewort. **1688** HOLME *Armorie* II. 98 Francking Spurry, or Spurwort. **1756** HILL *Hist. Plants* 185 Among the other useful plants cultivated in the neighbouring countries is the common spurrey. **1771** *Encycl. Brit.* III. 621/1 *Spergula arvensis*, or corn-spurrey. *Ibid.*, *Spergula pentandria*, or small spurrey.

c. *attrib.*, as *spurrey-sandwort, -seed.*

1644 G. PLATTES in *Hartlib's Legacy* (1655) 257 The Spurry-seed which you have gotten out of the Low-Countries. **1669** WORLIDGE *Syst. Agric.* (1681) 31 In the Low-Countries they usually sowe Spurrey-seed twice in a Summer. **1736** BAILEY *Househ. Dict.* s.v. *Poultry*, When fowls are near their laying-time, spurry seed, and buck wheat is an excellent strengthening for them. **1856** A. GRAY *Man. Bot.* (1860) 61 *Spergularia*, Spurrey-Sandwort... Low herbs, growing on or near the sea-coast. **1894** *Jrnl. R. Agric. Soc.* June 329 Adulterated..with spurry and other weed seeds.

d. *pl.* Plants of this genus.

1882 GRANT ALLEN *Colours of Flowers* ii. 39 Stitchworts.. and cornspurries.., which have open flowers of a very primitive character.

2. Applied, with distinguishing terms, to various species of plants allied to or resembling (and some formerly classed with) the genus *Spergula* (see quots.).

1828 SIR J. E. SMITH *Engl. Flora* II. 339 *Spergula saginoides.* Smooth *Awl-shaped Spurrey. **1842** *Penny Cycl.*

XXII. 333/2 *Spergula saginoides*, pearl-wort spurrey, and *S. subulata*, awl-shaped spurrey, are also natives of Great Britain. **1858** A. Irvine *Handbk. Brit. Plants* 768 *Sagina saxatilis*.. Smooth Awl-shaped Spurrey. **1887** *Field Spurrey [see *sandwort spurrey*]. **1753** *Chambers' Cycl.* Suppl. s.v. *Alsine*, The chickweed called the *greater spurry. **1771** *Encycl. Brit.* III. 621/1 *Spergula nodosa*, or *knotted spurrey. **1891** *Cent. Dict.* s.v., Knotted spurry, more properly called knotted pearlwort, is *Sagina nodosa*. The *lawn-spurry (or properly lawn-pearlwort) is *Sagina glabra*. **1797** *Encycl. Brit.* (ed. 3) XVII. 688/1 *Spergula saginoides*, *pearl-wort spurrey, has smooth, linear, opposite leaves. **1777** Jacob *Cat. Plants* 111 *Arenaria rubra*, *Purple Spurrey. **1796** Withering *Brit. Pl.* (ed. 3) II. 422 *Arenaria rubra*,.. Purple Spurrey, or Sandwort, [grows in] sandy meadows and corn-fields. **1866** *Treas. Bot.* 1089/1 *Sand Spurry. *Spergularia*. **1887** *Cassell's Encycl. Dict.* s.v. *Spergularia*, Two [species] are British: *Spergularia rubra*, Field, and *S. marina*, Sea-side *Sandwort Spurrey. Both have red flowers. **1756** Hill *Hist. Plants* 185/2 There is another species, the common *sea spurrey. **1777** Jacob *Cat. Plants* 110 *Arenaria marina*, Small flowered Sea-spurrey.

spur rial. Now *Hist.* Forms: 6 **spurr reyall, spurr(e) ryall,** 7 (9) **spur ryal,** 8– **spur rial** (9 **riall**); 6 **spur-rial,** 7 **-ryal(l;** 6 **spurriall** (8 **-al**), 7 **spurryal(l.** [f. SPUR *sb.*^{1} + RIAL *sb.*^{1}]

1. = SPUR-ROYAL.

1588 in *Aston's Manch. Guide* (1804) 26 A spurr reyall and an oulde piece of money, 00 16 00. **1593** Nashe *Christ's T.* 82 They must haue.. a few Spur-Rials to remedy deafnes. **1609** Dekker *Gull's Horn-bk.* Wks. (Grosart) II. 263 Two such Elizabeth twenty-shilling peeces, or foure such spur-ryals.. rid away amongst the rest. **1617** Moryson *Itin.* I. 283 Pieces of fifteene shillings called Spur Ryals. **1745** Fleetwood *Chron. Prec.* 18. **1853** Humphreys *Coin Coll. Man.* II. 465 Spur rials at 15 shillings each. *Ibid.*, The motto on the reverse of the rose rial and spur rial. **1899** Grueber *Coins Gt. Brit. & Irel. in B.M.* 102 The spur ryal.. received its name from the pointed form of the rays of the sun on the reverse, which looks like a spur.

¶**2.** *Her.* = SPUR-ROWEL 2.

1680 Mackenzie *Sci. Her.* 97 Though Bailzie of Lamingtons Arms are by some blazoned Mollets (Spurryals) yet.. they are Starrs.

spurrier ('spʌrɪə(r), 'spɜːrɪə(r)). Forms: α. 4–6 **sporyer,** 5 **-ier, sporyȝere,** 5 **sporyare,** 6 **-ar.** β. 5 **sporior, -iour, -your.** γ. 6 **spurriour, spouryor.** δ. 6 **spurryar,** 6– **spurrier.** [f. SPUR *sb.*^{1} + -IER. Cf. SPURRER 1.] A spur-maker.

α. **1389** in *Eng. Gilds* (1870) 42 Þese ordenaunce of fraternyte of Sadeleres and Sporyeres. *c* **1440** *Promp. Parv.* 470 Sporyare (*H.* sporyȝere), *calcarius.* *c* **1449** Pecock *Repr.* I. x. 50 As sporiers in Londoun gilden her sporis whiche thei maken. *c* **1500** *Cocke Lorell's B.* 8 Mercers, fletchers, and sporyers. **1575** *Gamm. Gurton* II. iv. 10 My goodly tossing sporyars neele chaue lost.

β. *c* **1400** *Destr. Troy* 1595 Sporiors, Spicers, Spynners of clothe. **1483** *Act 1 Rich. III*, c. xii. ¶1 The Artificers in greate nombre of this Royalme of Englond,.. that is to say, .. Blacksmythes, Sporiours [etc.].

γ. **1500** *Nottingham Rec.* III. 82 Georgius Othehay, spurriour. **1546** *Yorks. Chantry Surv.* (Surtees) 69 A chaumber.. in the tenure of Rychard Tomson, spouryor.

δ. **1530** Palsgr. 274/2 Spurryar, *esperonnier*. **1570** *Wills & Invent. N.C.* (Surtees, 1835) 332 Will'm Dagg of the towne of Gatisshed spurrier. **1609** *Shuttleworths' Acc.* (Chetham Soc.) 184 To the spurrier of Padiham, for a paire of spurres to my M^r, ij^s. **1688** R. Holme *Armoury* III. 304/1 From the Smith and Farrier, we proceed to the Spurrier and Loriner or Bit-maker. **1718** Bp. Hutchinson *Witchcraft* 260 A Black Dog.. that belong'd to one Clark, a Spurrier. **1764** R. Burn *Hist. Poor Laws* 10 Horse smiths, spurriers, tanners.. and other workmen, artificers and labourers. **1849** Macaulay *Hist. Eng.* I. iii. 380 It was vehemently argued.. that saddlers and spurriers would be ruined by hundreds. **1881** *Instr. Census Clerks* (1885) 57 Harness:.. Spurrier, Stirrup Maker.

†**spurriery.** *Obs.*$^{-1}$ In 5 **sporiorie.** [f. prec. + -Y.] The art or craft of a spurrier.

c **1449** Pecock *Repr.* I. x. 50 As thouȝ therfore sporiorie and cutellerie.. enterfereden with goldsmyth craft.

'spurring, *sb.* [f. SPUR *sb.*^{1} 11 c.] A railway side-track.

1842 *Civil Eng. & Arch. Jrnl.* V. 85/2 The sub-contractor .. had to.. lay down the temporary road, including turn-outs, shunts, crossings, boxes, spurrings, &c.

spurring ('spɜːrɪŋ), *vbl. sb.*^{1} [f. SPUR *v.*^{1}]

1. The action of pricking with a spur or spurs. Also *transf.*

a **1591** H. Smith *Wks.* (1867) II. 211 This gall will not hold spurring. **1593** Shaks. *Rich. II*, II. iii. 58 Here come the Lords of Rosse and Willoughby, Bloody with spurring, fierie red with haste. **1607** Markham *Cavel.* II. (1617) 74 These flancke spurrings,.. are the most preposterous motions that can be seen in a horseman. **1708** Sewel II, *Prikkeling*, a Pricking, a spurring on. **1837** Carlyle *Fr. Rev.* II. v. iii, The tired nag.. sticks in the middle of it;.. and will proceed no further for spurring! **1893** F. C. Selous *Trav. S.E. Africa* 172, I gave my sulky horse a good spurring.

attrib. **1677** *Lond. Gaz.* No. 1170/4 A black Mare 15 hands high,.. and on the off-side no hair in the spurring place.

b. The action of stimulating, inciting, or urging.

1611 Cotgr., *Stimulation*, a pricking, or spurring forward; a prouoking, egging, instigating, vrging. **1617** Hieron *Wks.* II. 276 When a man is so clay-like,.. and must haue a continuall spurring and prouoking,.. it is a wofull thing.

2. *spurring-in*, a mode of pruning fruit-trees in which side-shoots are shortened to a spur likely to produce fruit. Also *attrib.*

1829 Lindley *Encycl. Plants* 793 Hence the spurring-in method of pruning is the most successful in the production of fruit. **1846** Baxter *Libr. Pract. Agric.* (ed. 4) II. 381 A mode of pruning by spurring-in,.. as recommended by Mr. Griffin. **1852** G. W. Johnson *Cottage Gard. Dict.* 60 A regular series of these [side branches] should be left up the stem,.. practising what is termed 'spurring-in' by our nurserymen.

b. Similarly without *in*.

1844 *Florist's Jrnl.* (1846) V. 92 These evils are entirely obviated by short spurring, in doing which it is the practice .. to cut them in to the one nearest the stem. **1852** G. W. Johnson *Cottage Gard. Dict.* 842/2 *Spurring* is cutting the lateral or side-shoots, so as to leave only a few buds in length of them projecting from the main branches.

'spurring, *vbl. sb.*^{2} *dial.* Also 9 **sporring.** [f. SPUR *v.*^{2}]

1. *pl.* The banns of marriage published in church.

1787 Grose *Prov. Gloss.*, *Spurrings*, bans of marriage. **1829**– in dial. glossaries, etc. (Yks., Lanc., Derby, Linc., Rutland, Nottingham, Cornwall). **1862** *Life amongst Colliers* 172 Our maids were comely and apt, the young colliers gallant, so many spurrins went from our house.

2. (See quot.)

1888 T. North *Bells & Bell Lore* 94 At Barnoldby-le-Beck, Lea, and other places this ringing is called giving the [newly-wedded] couple their 'spurrings', or 'sporrings'.

spurring ('spɜːrɪŋ), *ppl. a.* [f. SPUR *v.*^{1}]

1. That spurs or pricks with a spur. Also *fig.* and *transf.*

1599 Middleton *Micro-cynicon* Wks. (Bullen) VIII. 135 A resolute ass! O for a spurring rider! **1649** G. Daniel *Trinarch.* To Rdr. 92 Hee without Cloake Is a Witt in Hutts, a pretty spurringe Cocke. **1819** Keats *Otho* I. iii. That unknown Mussulman After whose spurring heels he sent me forth. **1869** Ld. Lytton *Orval* 240 The spurring hour Posts to the bourne. **1881** J. F. Keane *Journ. Medinah* i. 15 The halters of such camels.. are fitted with an ingenious spurring-curb.

2. That impels, incites, or urges.

1648 J. Beaumont *Psyche* XXI. vii, Since by The spurring fervor of its natural Bent Above the third [stage] it aims. **1852** Disraeli *Ld. G. Bentinck* v. (1872) 61 So keen was the feeling of the Protectionists, and so spurring the point of honour.

spurrite ('spɜːraɪt). *Min.* [f. the name of Josiah E. *Spurr* (1870–1950), U.S. geologist + -ITE^1.] A monoclinic carbonate and silicate of calcium, $(Ca_2SiO_4)_2.CaCO_3$, which is a product of the contact metamorphism of limestone and usu. occurs as pale grey crystalline masses.

1908 F. E. Wright in *Amer. Jrnl. Sci.* CLXXVI. 551 Spurrite occurs in the hand specimens either in pure, unaltered state, except for minute inclusions of magnetite, or together with yellow garnet, calcite and gehlenite. **1938** *Mineral. Mag.* XXV. 38 Spurrite is.. a constituent not only of the silicated zone of the contact but also occurs isolated in calcite in the marbles derived from the chalk. **1968** I. Kostov *Mineralogy* 304 The minerals of the group are contact-metamorphic products in limestones, spurrite being a characteristic high-temperature mineral.

spur-rowel. Also 7 **-rowl,** 8 *Sc.* **-roll.** [f. SPUR *sb.*^{1} + ROWEL *sb.*]

1. The rowel or revolving pricking wheel of a spur. Also *Comb.*, and in fig. context.

1611 Cotgr., *Tartriere*, the Spurre-rowell-like instrument wherewith Pastissiers make indented iags. **1649** Davenant *Love & Hon.* I. i. 45 These bald chinnes are as familiar With their good starrs as with spur-rowells. *a* **1724** in Ramsay *Tea-table Misc.* (1876) II. 161 Curse on the spur-roll, Confounded be the upper-leather. **1816** Scott *Antiq.* xxi, Driving the spur-rowels o' the law up to the head into Sir Arthur's sides to gar him pay it. **1830** Skelton *Meyrick's Antient Arms & Armour* II. Pl. lxxxi, Spur-rowels were never of six points before the reign of Henry VI, nor of five till that of Charles I. **1866** *Even. Standard* 13 July 6 The more experienced Hungarian Hussars, jingling their monstrous spur-rowels.

2. *Her.* = MULLET^2 1.

1820 Scott *Monast.* Introd. Ep., The arms on the dexter side are those of Glendinning,.. and on the sinister three spur-rowels for those of Avenel.

spur-royal. Now *Hist.* or *arch.* Forms: 7 **spur(re) roial,** 7– **spur royal;** 6–7 **spur-roiall,** 7– **spur-royal** (7 **-all, spurroyal**). [f. SPUR *sb.*^{1} + ROYAL *sb.* Cf. SPUR-RIAL.] A gold coin of the value of fifteen shillings, chiefly coined in the reign of James I; so called from having on its reverse the form of the sun with rays, resembling a spur-rowel.

1600 Holland *Livy* 1424 *Aurei Romani*, Peeces of gold coine.. in round reckoning equivalent to our spur-roiall of 15 sh. **1639** Mayne *City Match* II. iii, Spur-royals, Harry-groats, or such odd coin Of husbandry, as in the King's reign now Would never pass. **1657** W. Rand tr. *Gassendi's Life Peiresc* I. 132 The *Solidus aureus*.. came at last.. to the Value of our usuall Shilling or Spur-roiall. **1704** *Lond. Gaz.* No. 4072/6 A red Sattin Purse, in which was a 5 Guinea Piece with a Spur Royal. **1711** Hearne *Collect.* (O.H.S.) III. 134 A small Gold Spur-royal shew'd me.. of Hen. VI. **1834** Mrs. Bray *Warleigh* xl. (1884) 298 A hundred spur royals must be your ransom: for I know your wealth. **1853** Humphreys *Coin Coll. Man.* II. 465 The old noble.. which was now termed a *spur* royal, from the resemblance of the rays to the rowels of a spur.

fig. *a* **1618** Sylvester *Little Bartas* 616 Wks. (Grosart) II. 90 Then was the Heav'n's Azure Pavilion spred, And with Spur-Royals spangled over-head.

spurry ('spɜːrɪ), *a.* [f. SPUR *sb.*^{1} + -Y.]

†**a.** Radiating like the points of a spur-rowel. *Obs.* **b.** Of the nature of a spur or prop. **c.** Having spur-like projections.

c **1611** Chapman *Iliad* XIX. 368 His crested helmet.. like a star.. cast a spurry ray. **1863** W. Lancaster *Præterita* 91 When the sick racking trees.. Tear up their spurry fastenings. **1875** Blackmore *Alice Lorraine* III. ix. 146 He quietly descended from the window, with the help of.. a spurry pear-tree.

spurt (spɜːt), *sb.*^{1} [var. of SPIRT *sb.*^{2}]

1. †**a.** A short spell *of* (something). *Obs.*

a **1566** R. Edwards *Damon & P.* F ij, It is very.. trimme, Tis Musselden ich weene; of fellowship let me haue an other spurt, Ich can drinke as easily now as if I sate in my shurte. **1613** Day *Dyall* (1614) 241 O how great injustice is it.. to.. deliver up that Soule to thy adversary the Divell, and all for a spurt of pleasure. *a* **1699** Bonnell in W. Hamilton *Life* (1703) II. 91 Those Qualities of Vanity and Worldliness, which I have contracted in this spurt of Health.

b. A short space of time; a brief period. Esp. in phr. ***for a spurt***.

Freq. in the 17th c.; now *dial.* Not always clearly separable from next.

a **1591** H. Smith *2nd Serm. Lord's Supper* (1611) 90 To amend thy euill life, not when age commeth, or for a spurt, but to begin now, and last till death. *a* **1618** Raleigh *Rem.* (1644) 121 To dispatch the whole manage of all eternity.. in so short a spurt. **1694** W. Salmon *Bate's Dispens.* (1713) 282/2 And such kind of Medicines are not to be given only for a little while, for a Spurt and away, but assiduously for several Weeks together. **1706** T. Baker *Tunbridge Walks* I. i, But this course of life, sister, is but for a spurt: we must now think of settling our condition. **1798** Mme. D'Arblay *Lett.* 10 Dec., Herschel has been in town for short spurts, and back again, two or three times. **1894** *Trans. Amer. Folk-lore Soc.* (E.D.D.), Excuse me for a spurt.

2. A brief and unsustained effort; a sudden outbreak or spell of activity or exertion.

a **1591** H. Smith *Serm.* (1592) 874 Some come to God as if they did fetch fire, a spurt and away, like a messenger which is gone before he haue his answeare. **1643** Tuckney *Balm of Gilead* 30 A short spurt doth not try me, but the length and hardnesse of the way will at last tell me what leg I halt on. **1654** Fuller *Comm. Ruth* (1868) 154 After a spurt in their calling for some few hours, they relapse again to laziness. **1774** Goldsm. *Nat. Hist.* II. 115 Although the savages held out,.. yet, for a spurt, the Englishmen were more nimble and speedy. **1883** *Pall Mall G.* 20 Dec. 2/1 Not with a fitful spurt, but year in, year out, do these thousands of.. lay helpers toil. **1885** Huxley in *Life* (1900) II. vi. 90 Quinine.. has given me a spurt for the last two days.

b. Const. *of.*

1791 R. Mylne *2nd Rep. Thames* 11 The Millers having a spurt of Business to do, were using all the Water as fast as possible. **1792** Mary Wollstonecr. *Rights Wom.* vii. 293, I do not forget the spurts of activity which sensibility produces. **1867** Trollope *Chron. Barset* II. lx. 172 One of those men who seem born to surprise the world by a spurt of prosperity. **1868** *Daily News* 8 July, Weak governments are like weak people; they put on spurts of energy and independence now and then.

c. A short spell of rapid movement; a marked or sudden increase of speed attained by special exertion.

1787 'G. Gambado' *Acad. Horsem.* (1809) 46 The Doctor went off at a spurt. **1858** O. W. Holmes *Aut. Breakf.-t.* xi, An easy gait—two, forty-five—Suits me;.. Perhaps, for just a single spurt, Some seconds less would do no hurt. **1861** Hughes *Tom Brown at Oxf.* xiv. (1889) 134 Their boat.. dipped a little when they put on anything like a severe spurt. **1898** *Allbutt's Syst. Med.* V. 844 It is hard to say what happens during [bicycling] spurts or at the outset of an excursion.

d. *transf.* A marked increase or improvement in business; a sudden advance or rise of prices, etc.; also, the period during which this lasts.

1814 *Stock Exchange Laid Open* 25 When the Jobbers find the spurt, as they call it, is over. **1880** *Sat. Rev.* 1 May 565 Men of business instinctively felt what was coming, and, buying up large stocks at the lowest quotations, realized fortunes when the spurt came. **1898** *Westm. Gaz.* 17 Nov. 10/1 It is clear that the recent spurt in the price of the shares was unwarranted.

e. A spell of gaiety; a frolic.

1885 'Mrs. Alexander' *At Bay* ix, After that spurt I went back to Melbourne. **1890** 'R. Boldrewood' *Colonial Reformer* (1891) 286 Puts me in mind of one of our Hurry-ghur dances. We used to have such jolly spurts at the old station.

3. *by spurts*: **a.** In or with brief unsustained or spasmodic efforts; fitfully, spasmodically. †Also *by fits and spurts*, by fits and starts.

1605 Chapman *All Fooles* II. i, [He] hath stolne, By his meere industry, and that by spurts, Such qualities as no wit else can match With plodding at perfection every houre. **1653** in *Verney Mem.* (1907) I. 523, I am like to bee 3 or 4 months in a yeare at Claydon & that only by fits & spurts. **1660** R. Coke *Just. Vind.* 21 Forsooth it is by spurts, and not long enough to be accounted a settled Magistrate. **1882** *Atlantic Monthly* L. 753 He [a negro] can work hard for a while by spurts.

b. In intermittent jets. (Cf. SPURT *sb.*^{3} 1.)

1644 Digby *Nat. Bodies* xxvi. (1658) 293 When a wound is made in the heart, blood will gush out by spurts at every shooting of the heart. **1789** W. Buchan *Dom. Med.* (1790) 507 A sudden constriction takes place, and the urine is voided by spurts, and sometimes by drops only.

4. *Naut.* A short spell *of* wind; = SPIRT *sb.*^{2} 2.

1699 Dampier *Voy.* II. III. iv. 37 When we come abreast of the Head-Lands, we.. see the Breez curling on the Water on both sides of us, and sometimes get a spurt of it to help us forward. **1745** P. Thomas *Jrnl. Anson's Voy.* 148 We made the best of every little Spurt of Wind.

5. *slang* or *dial.* A small amount or quantity.

1859 in *Slang Dict.* 100. **1889** in *Surrey Gloss.* (1893) 39, I had a little spurt of drink, that was all.

6. *U.S.* A quick and sudden dash on the part of wild-fowl; a flight of this nature.

1874 J. W. Long *Amer. Wild-fowl* i. 37 It is often desirable, where ducks are flying in spurts,.. to load as fast as possible.

spurt, *sb.*[2] Now *dial.* and *rare.* [Cf. SPIRT *sb.*[3]] A shoot or sprout.

1601 Holland *Pliny* II. 27 The Garden Sperages.. send out at first certaine greene spurts or buds peeping forth of the ground. *Ibid.* 196 The same yong springs eaten.. in a salad, in manner of the tender crops and spurts of the Colewort,.. do fasten the teeth.

spurt (spɜːt), *sb.*[3] [f. SPURT *v.*[1] (cf. SPIRT *sb.*[4]), and perhaps partly from SPURT *sb.*[1] 3 b.]

1. A stream or shower of water, etc., ejected or thrown up with some force and suddenness.

1775 Ash, *Spurt*, a sudden stream. **1828–32** Webster, *Spurt*, a sudden or violent ejection or gushing of a liquid substance from a tube, orifice, or other confined place. **1868** Morris *Earthly Paradise* (1870) I. I. 111 Then from light feet a spurt of dust there sprang. **1871** Rossetti *Poems, Dante at Verona* xxviii, The conduits round the gardens sing.. Where wearied damsels rest and hold Their hands in the wet spurt of gold. **1877** Black *Green Past.* xxxviii, As the Esquimaux began to receive shooting spurts of spray from the rocks overhead.

fig. **1864** Carlyle *Fredk. Gt.* XVI. xii. IV. 443 Thrice-private *Œuvre de Poésies*, in which are satirical spurts affecting more than one crowned head.

transf. **1881** Ruskin *Bible of Amiens* ii. §25 The rocks all the way from Rhine, thus far, are jets and spurts of basalt through irony sandstone. **1890** *Times* 17 May 13/3 An adaptation of the dots and dashes of the Morse alphabet to flashes of light and spurts of sound.

b. A spatter or splash made by a pen.

1871 G. Stephens in *Archaeologia* XLIII. 101 The spurts have been taken away in my woodcut.

2. A sudden outbreak or outburst *of* feeling, action, etc.

In this sense freq. suggestive of SPURT *sb.*[1] 2.

1859 Tennyson *Merlin & V.* 374 A sudden spurt of woman's jealousy. **1879** Froude *Cæsar* ix. 104 A spurt of insurrectionary fire had broken out in Italy. **1880** Miss Braddon *Just as I am* xix, Little spurts of angry feeling flashed out of her now and then in her talk.

spurt, *sb.*[4] *Coal-mining.* (See quot.)

1883 Gresley *Gloss. Coal-m.* 233 *Spurt*, a peculiar kind of stone, much disintegrated and mixed with colouring matter.

spurt (spɜːt), *v.*[1] [var. of SPIRT *v.*[1]]

1. *intr.* = SPIRT *v.*[1] I. Freq. with *out* and *up*.

1570 Foxe *A. & M.* 2287/1 He was.. so manacled that y[e] bloud spurt out of his fingers endes. **1578** Lyte *Dodoens* 76 Round huskes, the which do open of themselves, and the seede being ripe, it spurteth and skippeth away. **1611** Cotgr., *Surgeonner*, to shoot out, spring, spurt vp. **1684** tr. *Bonet's Merc. Compit.* XIV. 502 Hardly any [blood] would spurt out of the opened Vein. **1699** Dampier *Voy.* II. II. 89, I perceived two White Specks in the middle of the Boil; and squeezing it, two small white Worms spurted out. **1722–7** Boyer *Dict. Royal* I. s.v. *Rejaillir*, He made the Dirt spurt up, or fly into his Face. **1800** Coleridge *Piccolomini* I. iv, My blood shall spurt out for this Wallenstein. **1833** Ht. Martineau *Brooke Farm* vii. 89 The milk went on spurting and fizzing into the pail. **1887** Bowen *Æneid* v. 469 A crimsoning flood Spurts from his lips in a torrent.

fig. **1837** Carlyle *Fr. Rev.* II. I. i, Some sharpness of temper, spurting at times from a stagnating character. **1858** —— *Fredk. Gt.* IX. v. II. 453 Rumours are rife and eager, occasionally spurting-out into the Newspapers.

b. To sputter. *rare*[−1].

1854 Emerson *Lett. & Soc. Aims* iv. 119 Christmas hemlock spurting in the fire.

2. *trans.* = SPIRT *v.*[1] 2. Also const. *out, up.*

1601 Holland *Pliny* I. 441 The remedie to keepe Wespes from them, is to spurt or squirt oile out of a mans mouth vpon them. **1653** H. Cogan tr. *Pinto's Trav.* li. 201 The Chaubainhaa then took water in his mouth and spurted it on his wife. **1687** A. Lovell tr. *Thevenot's Trav.* II. 82 At every two fathoms distance there are Pipes which spurt up Water very high. **1725** *Fam. Dict.* s.v. *Headach*, In the next Place spurt Wine.. into his Nostrils. **1774** Goldsm. *Nat. Hist.* (1862) II. 166 They often fill their trunks with water.. to divert themselves by spurting it out like a fountain. **1886** Sheldon tr. *Flaubert's Salammbô* i. 7 A Lusitanian.. stalked about the tables, the while spurting fire from his nostrils.

fig. **1699** Bentley *Phal.* 122 His boyish Witticisms and doggeril Rhimes, which he has spurted here. **1827** Carlyle *Misc.* (1840) I. 34 His stream of meaning.. will not flow quietly along its channel; but is ever and anon spurting itself up into epigrams and antithetic jets.

Hence **'spurted** *ppl. a.*; **'spurter**.

1693 Evelyn *De la Quint. Compl. Gard.* II. 102 That Gum is nothing but a spurted Sap. **1890** *Blackw. Mag.* CXLVII. 420/2 It is only sentimentalists and spurters of rose-water that object to it.

spurt, *v.*[2] Now *dial.* and *rare.* [var. SPIRT *v.*[2] Cf. SPURT *sb.*[2]] *intr.* To sprout or shoot.

1601 Holland *Pliny* II. 22 By this means indeed last they [*sc.* onions] will longer without spurting. **1606** Marston *Fawne* II. i, *Nym.* But is not Faunus prefer'd with a right hand? *Her.* Did you euer see a fellow so spurted vp in a moment? **1610** [see SPROUT *sb.*[1] 1 b].

spurt (spɜːt), *v.*[3] [f. SPURT *sb.*[1] 2. Cf. SPIRT *v.*[3]]

1. *intr.* **a.** To make a spurt; to put on increased speed, to make greater exertions, for a short time.

1664 H. More *Myst. Iniq.* 549 To spurt out and run on in a career without attending the direction of their Superiours. [**1793** Burns *Let. to Ainslie* 26 Apr., I have written many a letter;.. but then—they were original matter—spurt-away! zig, here; zag, there.] **1861** Hughes *Tom Brown at Oxf.* xxvii, The crowd on both sides cheered, as the.. boat spurted from the Cherwell, and took the place of honour. **1897** *Allbutt's Syst. Med.* II. 841 It [i.e. alcohol] may enable a man 'to spurt' but not 'to stay'.

b. Of stocks and shares: to rise suddenly in price or value. Cf. SPURT *sb.*[1] 2 d.

1931 *Economist* 27 June 1385/2 Dunlops and Imperial Chemicals spurted on bear closing. **1977** *Belfast Tel.* 19 Jan. 4/1 Beecham 406p spurted 10p to 15p among top industrials. **1982** *Times* 27 Apr. 15/2 Building contractor J. Jarvis spurted 41p to 341p in response to a dawn raid.

2. *trans.* To cause to spurt; to overtake by means of a spurt. *rare.*

1888 P. Furnivall *Phys. Training* 7 If.. he decides to wait on the goer all through, and try to spurt him at the end, he should practise short, sharp bursts of speed,.. always finishing up with a sharp spurt.

'spurting, *vbl. sb.* [f. SPURT *v.*[1]] The action of the vb., in various senses.

1611 Cotgr., *Iallissement*, a spurting, sprowting, spouting, or spinning vp (of water). *Ibid.*, *Seringuement*, a squirting; an iniecting, or spurting of liquor by a Siringe. **1676** Wiseman *Surg. Treat.* (J.), If from a puncture.., the manner of the spurting out of the blood will shew it. **1677** Miège *Fr. Dict.* I, *Rejaillissement*, a spurting up. **1708** Sewell II, *Uytspatting*, a Spurting out, lanching out. **1822** Shelley *Scenes fr. Faust* ii. 213 What glimmering spurting, stinking, burning, As Heaven and Earth were over-turning. **1844** Emerson *Ess.* II. *Nature*, The crackling and spurting of hemlock in the flames. **1869** Day *Puddling* 5 in Rankine *Mach. & Hand-tools*, The spurting about of the metal.

'spurting, *ppl. a.* [f. SPURT *v.*[1]] That spurts; spirting.

1821 Clare *Vill. Minstr.* II. 187 The.. spurting dash Of muttering fountain. **1861** Paley *Æschylus, Choeph.* 260 *note*, Burning in the spurting pitch of the pyre of pine-wood. **1871** Stephens in *Archaeologia* XLIII. 101 What with the loose paper and the running ink, and the spurting pen.

b. ***spurting cucumber***: see SPIRTING *ppl. a.* 1 b.

1786 Abercrombie *Arr.* in *Gard. Assist.* 18 Hardy Annuals... Cucumber, spurting.

spurtle ('spɜːt(ə)l), *sb.*[1] *Sc.* and *north.* Also 6 spurtill, 9 -il, -el, spirtle, spurkle, etc. [Of doubtful origin: cf. SPARTLE *sb.*]

1. †**a.** A flat implement used for turning oatcakes, etc. *Obs.* **b.** A wooden stick for stirring porridge, etc.; a potstick or 'thivel'.

15.. in *Bannatyne MS.* (Hunter. Club) 388 Ane spurtill braid, and ane elwand. *a* **1572** Knox *Hist. Ref.* Wks. 1846 I. 38 The preast (said he).. standis up on Sounday, and cryes, 'Ane hes tynt a spurtill'. **1677** Nicolson in *Trans. R. Lit. Soc.* (1870) IX. 320 *Spurtle*, a piece of wood for turning oaten cakes. **1725** in Herd *Sc. Songs* (1776) II. 143 A spurtle and a sowen mug. **1776** '*Our Goodman*' Ibid. 173 Muckle hae I seen; But siller-handed spurtles Saw I never nane. *Ibid.* Gloss. 266 *Spurtle*, a flat iron for turning cakes. **1808** Jamieson s.v., A wooden or iron spattle, for turning bread, is called a *spirtle*, Ang[us]. **1839** Wilson *Tales* V. 370/1 The lid of the pot in one hand, and the 'spurtle' in the other. **1894** Crockett *Raiders* xxi. 190 [She was] standing with the porridge spurtle in her hand.

2. *transf.* A sword. Also *attrib.*

1670 J. Fraser *Polichron.* (S.H.S.) 486 Then the King will say,.. If't please your Grace put up your spurtle, Peter! **1789** Burns *On Capt. Grose* v, But now he's quat the spurtle-blade, And dog-skin wallet. **1822** Galt *Sir A. Wylie* lxxvi, 'The spurtle,' as he peevishly called the sword.

spurtle ('spɜːt(ə)l), *sb.*[2] [f. next. Cf. SPIRTLE *sb.*] The action or an act of spurtling.

1894 'Fiona Macleod' *Pharais* i, The spurtle of the sea-wrack,.. the cries of the gulls.

spurtle ('spɜːt(ə)l), *v.* [f. SPURT *v.*[1] + -LE. Cf. SPIRTLE *v.*]

1. *trans.* **a.** To besprinkle or bespatter. *rare.*

1633 J. Fisher *True Trojans* III. vii, The conduits of his vitall spring being ript, Spurtled my robes, solliciting Reuenge. **1868** R. W. Huntley *Cotswold* (Glouc.) *Dial.*, *Spurtle*, to sprinkle with any fluid.

b. To cause to spurt or spatter. *rare.*

1858 Caswall *Poems* 111 Around thee swarm Spirits of darkness fresh from yawning hell, Spurtling their fiery insatiate wrath on thy defenceless head.

2. *intr.* **a.** To burst or fly out in a small quantity or stream with some force or suddenness; to spirt or spurt.

1651 Ogilby *Æsop* (1665) 37 Whilst warm Blood spurtles in his face and eyes. **1656** W. Coles *Art of Simpling* 39 The seed will spurtle forth suddenly. **1899** J. G. Frazer in *Fortn. Rev.* April 660 Some young men,.. opening veins in their arms, allow the blood to spurtle over the edge of the rock.

b. To sputter.

1671 Grew *Anat. Pl.* I. (1682) 17 So Fenil-Seeds, held in the flame of a Candle, will spit and spurtle, like the Serum of Blood.

†**'spurtled**, *a. Sc. Obs.* [Metathetic form of SPRUTTLED *a.*] Speckled, spotted, variegated.

1513 Douglas *Æneid* II. iv. 32 (Small), Thai.. twyse faldis thair spurtlit skynnis, but dowt, About his hals. *Ibid.* VII. iv. 91 (1710), Ane byrd.. Wyth spourtlit wyngis, clepit ane Specht wyth vs.

spurtlet ('spɜːtlɪt). *rare*[−1]. [f. SPURT *sb.*[1] or *sb.*[3] + -LET.] A little spurt.

1921 E. M. Forster *Let.* 28 Sept. in *Hill of Devi* (1953) 132, I annoyed him.., and he had a spurtlet of temper and said I was not his friend.

'spurty, *a. rare.* [f. SPURT *sb.*[1] + -Y.] Characterized by spurts; intermittent, spasmodic.

1894 *Forum* May 305 In the relations of exercise to regimen and exposure, in the dangers of a spurty and erethic diathesis.

spur-wheel. Also spur wheel. [SPUR *sb.*[1]] A gear-wheel which has cogs or teeth on the periphery, projecting radially from the centre; a cog-wheel.

1731 *Phil. Trans.* XXXVII. 10 The Spur Wheel. **1764** J. Ferguson *Lect.* 78 A cog or spur-wheel may be placed upon each side of the water-wheel. **1805** Dickson *Pract. Agric.* I. Pl. xiv, On the axle of this water-wheel is fixed a large spur-wheel.. of 160 cogs. **1861** Smiles *Engineers* III. 97 The power of the two cylinders was combined by means of spurwheels. **1884** W. H. Greenwood *Steel & Iron* xi. 215 A spur-wheel, gearing into a pinion which is connected with a train of gearing driven by a small steam-engine.

fig. **1870** Mrs. Riddell *Austin Friars* iv, Love sets in motion the spur-wheel which turns all the other wheels of existence.

spur-wing, spurwing. *Ornith.* [Cf. next.] A spur-winged water-hen, goose, etc.

1842 *Penny Cycl.* XXII. 389/2 *Spur-wing*, the English name for species of the Genus *Parra.* **1855** Ogilvie *Suppl.*, *Spur-wing*; geese of the genus Plectropterus are also so called. They are natives of Africa, and have two strong spurs on the shoulder of the wing. **1900** Grogan & Sharp *Cape to Cairo* xxiii. 294 At my first shot I killed two large spurwings, and a few more rounds provided geese for all the camp.

attrib. **1897** Hinde *Congo Arabs* 270 The spur-wing geese seemed to be flocking preparatory to migrating.

spur-winged, *a. Ornith.* [f. SPUR *sb.*[1]] Having one or more stiff claws or spurs projecting from the pinion-bone of the wing. In specific names (see quots.).

a. **1668** Charleton *Onomast.* 116 *Anser Chilensis*,.. the Spur-wing'd Goose of America. **1785** Latham *Gen. Synop. Birds* III. II. 452 Spur-winged Goose, *Anas Gambensis.* **1865** Livingstone *Zambesi* xxi. 431 Occasionally we saw.. spurwinged geese. **1879** E. P. Wright *Anim. Life* 333 The Spur-winged Goose (*Plectropterus gambensis*) is a native of West Africa.

b. **1755** G. Edwards *Glean. Nat. Hist.* II. Pl. 280 The black-brested spur-winged Plover. **1785** Latham *Gen. Synop. Birds* III. I. 213 Spur-winged Plover, *Charadrius spinosus.* **1825** Waterton *Wand. S. Amer.* I. (1903) 32 The spur-winged plover, and a species of the curlew,.. frequently rise before you. **1899** F. V. Kirby *Sport E.C. Africa* i. 4 The spur-winged plovers not only warn the crocodiles,.. but act as tooth-picks for the saurians.

c. **1716** *Petiveriana* I. 284 The Spur-wing'd Lapwing. **1743** G. Edwards *Nat. Hist. Birds* I. Pl. 48 The spur-winged Water Hen. **1824** *Encycl. Metrop.* (1845) XVI. 537/1 The Jacana, or spur-winged water-hen (*Parra Chilensis*), is a beautiful bird with very long feet. **1829** Griffith tr. *Cuvier* VIII. 600 Spur-winged Swan, *Anas Gambensis.* **1897** *Daily News* 16 Nov. 6/2 The Spur-winged Lapwing of La Plata.

spus(e, obs. ff. SPOUSE *sb.* and *v.*

spusbreche, -bruche, varr. SPOUSE-BREACH[1] *Obs.*

†**sput**, *v. Obs. rare.* [Of obscure origin.] *trans.* To urge, incite.

c **1175** *Lamb. Hom.* 123 He hit forgulte.. þa þe he tuhte and spuhte [*sic*] þet folc to cristes cwale. *a* **1225** *Juliana* 58 (Royal MS.), Heo as þe feond sputte [*v.r.* spurede] ham te don hit, duden hit unsparlich. *a* **1225** *Ancr. R.* 196 þet flesch put [*v.r.* sput] propremen touward swetnesse & touward eise.

sput, pa. t. and pa. ppl. (now *dial.*) of SPIT *v.*[2]

‖**sputa**, pl. of SPUTUM.

†**spu'taminous**, *a. Obs. rare.* [f. L. *spūtāmin-*, *spūtāmen*, f. *spūtāre* to spit.] Of the nature of spittle; characterized by the presence or flow of saliva.

1597 A. M. tr. *Guillemeau's Fr. Chirurg.* 25 b/2 They retayne in them a certayne sputaminous humiditye which descendeth out of the header. *Ibid.* 51/1 Those which haue passede through the driveling or sputaminouse climate [= climacter].

†**sputania.** *Obs.* Also -anta. (See quots.)

1588–1617 Greene *Alcida* C, He became halfe lunaticke, as if hee had eaten of the seed of sputanta, that troubleth the braine with giddinesse. *Ibid.* G iv, Shee seemed to haue eaten of the herbe Sputania, which shutteth vp the stomake for a long season.

†**spu'tation.** *Obs.* [a. F. *sputation*, ad. L. **spūtātio*, f. *spūtāre*, frequentative of *spuĕre* to spit.] The action of spitting; expectoration.

1657 Tomlinson *Renou's Disp.* 166* Which may be easily excluded by frequent sputation. **1666** G. Harvey *Morb. Angl.* (1672) 89 This simple bloody sputation of the Lungs is difference from that, which concomitates a Pleurisie.

†**'sputative**, *a. Obs. rare.* [f. L. *spūt-āre*: see -ATIVE.] Of, characterized by, given to (excessive) spitting or salivation.

a **1639** Wotton in *Reliq.* (1672) 370 To see whether.. I could pick out any counsel to allay that Sputative Symptome which yet remaineth upon me from my obstruction of the spleen. **1656** Blount *Glossogr.*, *Sputative*, that spits often or much.

sputcheon (ˈspʌtʃən). [Of obscure origin.] (See quots.)

1842 Burn *Naval & Mil. Techn. Dict.* I, *Batte de la cuvette*, sputcheon of the mouth-piece of a sword-scabbard, or that part which retains the wooden scabbard. **1878** *Times* 19 Nov. 10/2 The metal 'sputcheon' or 'cup-lining' of the scabbard's mouth must come in contact with the blade-edge when the sword is drawn.

spute, obs. form of spout *sb.*

spute, *v.*[1] *Obs.* or *dial.* Also 4 spoute, 6 speut. [Aphetic form of dispute *v.*] *intr.* To dispute; to contend in disputation. Usu. const. *with.*

Modern instances from south-western dial. and U.S. are possibly of recent formation.

a **1225** *Leg. Kath.* 1308 Ne funde we nowhwer nan swa deope ilearet þat durste sputin wið us. *a* **1300** *Cursor M.* 19407 Vp þar ras to spute him with Men þat war o sundri kyth. **13..** *E.E. Allit P.* B. 845 Whatt! þay sputen & speken of so spitous fylþe. *a* **1400** *Hymns Virgin* (1867) 46 And ȝit oonis y siȝ him spute in þe scoole halle. *c* **1450** *Mirk's Festial* 109 Oure lady sputyd wyth þe angell of þe maner, and how scho schuld conceyue. **1556** J. Heywood *Spider & Fly* xxxix. 4, I forbad here all spouting in souostrie [= sophistry]. Now thei speut, in speuting who may speut most hie.

So †ˈ**sputing**, disputing, disputation. *Obs. rare.*

c **1250** *Owl & Night.* 1574 Þu ne schalt.. Onswere non þar-to fynde; Al þis sputing schal aswinde. **1556** [see above].

†**spute**, *v.*[2] *Obs.*[−1] [ad. L. *spūt-āre* to spit.] *trans.* To spit on (a person, etc.).

1382 Wyclif *Job* xxx. 10 To spute [L. *conspuere*] my face they shame not.

sputher, variant of spudder[1].

†ˈ**sputisoun.** *Obs.*[−1] [Aphetic form of disputisoun.] Disputation.

a **1375** *Joseph Arim.* 343 He sprong in his sputison, and speek harde wordes.

sputnik (ˈspʊtnɪk, ˈspʌt-). Also **Sputnik**. [a. Russ. *spútnik*, lit. 'travelling companion', f. *s* with + *put'* way, journey + *-nik*, agent suffix (cf. -nik).] An unmanned artificial earth satellite, esp. a Russian one; *spec.* (usu. with capital initial) the proper name of a series of such satellites launched by the Soviet Union between 1957 and 1961.

The first Sputnik, launched on 4 October 1957, was the first artificial satellite.

1957 *Times* 9 Oct. 10/6 Pride in the launching of the *sputnik* ('fellow-traveller'), as the satellite is called, as well as the guided missile, were reflected in a speech by Mr. Krushchev.. last night. *Ibid.* 30 Oct. 10/2 Mr. Khrushchev replied: 'To peace and to the *sputnik* as a symbol of peace!' *Ibid.* 4 Nov. 11/2 The régime which sends a second Sputnik girdling the earth has just emerged from another of its secretly contrived shifts of political power. **1958** A. Huxley *Let.* 15 Feb. (1969) 846 The technical advances in these psychological, physiological and bio-chemical fields are probably far more important.. than the physical and engineering advances which have put sputniks into the heavens. **1964** M. McLuhan *Understanding Media* iii. 44 When Sputnik had first gone into orbit a schoolteacher asked her second-graders to write some verse on the subject. **1971** *New Scientist* 10 June 638/1 China's remarkable progress in the field is underscored by the weight of its first sputnik (unmatched.. by any satellite launched by France or Japan). **1983** *N.Y. Times* 7 Jan. A1/4 It is not a dangerous situation.. and we have no worries about the fate of this sputnik.

b. *transf.* and *fig.*

1958 *Newsweek* 10 Feb. 25/1 We may find ourselves confronted with a sputnik in the chemical, biological, and radiological field, as we did in missiles. **1959** *Daily Tel.* 10 Dec. 16/7 Internal 'sputniks', pills containing miniature radio transmitters, which can travel around the intestines. **1963** *Punch* 17 Apr. 549/1 Such Hollywood *sputniks* as Frank Sinatra and Sammy Davis Jnr. **1968** [see loop *v.*[1] 6].

2. *attrib.* and *Comb.*, as ***sputnik diplomacy, race, town***; **Sputnik double** *Bridge*, a take-out double of a suit overcall of one's partner's opening bid; also *absol.* as ***Sputnik***.

1957 *N.Y. Times* 20 Oct. iv. 4/1 Since the Soviet space satellite has been in its orbit, Moscow has been showing what many are now calling sputnik diplomacy. **1959** *Listener* 15 Jan. 96/2 The rocket would set the stage for a diplomatic offensive [in Russia] similar to the sputnik diplomacy a year ago. **1958** *Bridge World* July 33/2 We noticed that the negative double ('Sputnik') would fit. **1976** *Country Life* 1 Apr. 846/2 A Sputnik double, if played, will lead to the same final contract. **1957** *Times Lit. Suppl.* 27 Dec. 782/4 America's defeat in the sputnik race. **1959** *Daily Tel.* 27 Apr. 10/2 The political sensationalism of the sputnik race. **1958** *Daily Mail* 7 June 5/5 Russian planners will deal with overspill population from big cities... They are planning 'sputnik' towns. **1966** *Listener* 19 May 729/3 In preparation for the creation of Moscow's own ring of 'Sputnik towns'—though this development may not happen until after 1980.

Hence ˈ**sputnik(e)ry**, **sputniˈkitis** (*nonce-wds.*).

1957 *Observer* 20 Oct. 14/2 We rang up Hamley's to see how Sputnikitis was hitting them... 'No, I'd not say our space toys were on the up... It's always in competition with cowboys and Red Indians, you see.' **1957** *Economist* 30 Nov. 762/1 The United States and the Soviet Union are pouring in money and scientists in an Antarctic form of sputnikitis. **1960** *Spectator* 10 June 826 The abnormal concentration of effort in such fields as 'sputnikery'. **1961** *New Scientist* 6 July 38/1 The narrower field of sputnikry.

†ˈ**sputous**, *a. Obs.*[−1] In 4 sputus, -wys-. [var. of spitous *a.*, perh. under the influence of spute *v.*[1]] = despitous *a.* Hence †ˈ**sputously** *adv. Obs.*[−1]

c **1420** *Chron. Vilod.* 4495 For Williham was a full sputus mon, y-wys, & nomely bokke-hunters in his tyme nad no rest. *c* **1450** *Mirk's Festial* 145 He.. grynd his teþe, and rebuked sputwyslyche þys oþyr Iew.

sputter (ˈspʌtə(r)), *sb.* [f. sputter *v.*]

1. a. Noisy or violent and confused speech or discourse; angry, excited, or fussy argument or protest; fuss, clamour; = splutter *sb.* 1 b.

1673 Wycherley *Gentl. Dancing Master* v. i, All the sputter I made was but to make this young man.. believe.. that it was not with my connivance or consent. **1676** Marvell *Mr. Smirke* 40 But he must make some sputter rather then be held to the terms of the Question. **1706** Baynard *Cold Baths* ii. 275 Z[oun]ds it will kill you (quoth he in Sputter and Passion). **1721** Steele *Conscious Lovers* iv. iii, What a deal of pother and sputter here is between my mistress and Mr. Myrtle from mere punctilio. **1760–72** H. Brooke *Fool of Qual.* (1809) III. 35 Weak or vapid tempers .. boil over in.. factious sputter and turbulence. **1812** D'Israeli *Calam. Auth.* (1867) 91 He has.. chronicled his suppressed feelings.. with all the flame and sputter of his strong prejudices. **1884** *Chr. Commonw.* 23 Oct. 20/3 What is there left when the chaff of sputter and jangle of platitude and puerility has been sifted away?

b. An instance or occasion of this. *rare.*

1692 Wagstaffe *Vind. Carolinæ* vi. 64 [He] makes such a Sputter about the old Law. **1721** Wodrow *Ch. Hist.* (1828) I. 340/1 [They] made a terrible sputter against private meetings and societies for prayer.

c. A state of bustling confusion or excitement.

1823 in *Spirit Publ. Jrnls.* 150 He will live in a sputter, And die in a gutter. *a* **1898** in *Eng. Dial. Dict.* s.v., *In a sputter*, in a fuss.

2. Matter ejected in or by sputtering. *rare.*

1748 Richardson *Clarissa* (1768) V. xxxi. 290 She pouted out her blubber-lips, as if to bellows up wind and sputter into her horse-nostrils. **1818** Todd, *Sputter*, moisture thrown out in small drops.

3. a. The action or an act of sputtering; the emission of small particles with some amount of explosive sound; the sound characteristic of or accompanying this. Freq. *fig.* or in fig. context.

1837 Carlyle *Fr. Rev.* I. iii. v, It is a quite new kind of contest this with the Parlement: no transitory sputter, as from collision of hard bodies. **1845** Alb. Smith *Fort. Scattergood Fam.* xxx. (1887) 97 Nothing breaking the silence but the occasional sputter of the rushlight. **1894** *Rev. of Reviews* Apr. 403/1 The peaceful partition of Africa.. is evidently going to be carried out amid a constant sputter of little wars.

b. A spattering or sprinkling.

1887 Ruskin *Præterita* II. 150 But, outside the ramparts, no more poor. A sputter, perhaps,.. along the Savoy road.

4. Special Comb.: **sputter ion pump** *Physics* [perh. f. the vb.], a pump in which the gas is absorbed by a getter that is deposited by sputtering it from a cathode.

1962 *Sci. Amer* Mar. 82/1 (*caption*) Sputter ion pump works by ionizing gas molecules and removing them from the chamber.. to be evacuated. **1980** J. F. O'Hanlon *User's Guide Vacuum Technol.* ix. 221 The sputter ion pump has the advantage of freedom from hydrocarbon contamination and ease of fault protecting but does suffer from the reemission of previously pumped gases.

sputter (ˈspʌtə(r)), *v.* [= Du. *sputteren*, WFris. *sputterje*, NFris. *sputteri*, *spūtere*, of imitative origin.]

1. a. *trans.* To spit out in small particles and with a characteristic explosive sound or a series of such sounds. Also in fig. context.

1598, 1602 [see sputtering *ppl. a.* 1]. **1697** Dryden *Æneid* ii. 279 Two serpents.. lick'd their hissing jaws, that sputter'd flame. **1720** Pope *Iliad* xxiii. 921 Thus sourly wail'd he, sputt'ring dirt and gore. **1791** Cowper *Iliad* xxiii. 972 He grasp'd his horn, and sputt'ring as he stood The ordure forth, the Argives thus bespake. **1835** T. Mitchell *Aristoph. Acharn.* 1041 *note*, A habit which he had of sputtering his saliva on bystanders.

b. *transf.* To scatter, throw up or about, in small particles.

1845 S. Judd *Margaret* i. xvii, One [sled] went giddying round and round, fraying and sputtering the snow, and dashed against a tree.

2. a. To utter hastily and with the emission of small particles of saliva; to ejaculate in a confused, indistinct, or uncontrolled manner, esp. from anger or excitement. Cf. splutter *v.* 1.

a **1677** Barrow *Serm.* Wks. 1716 I. 170 Nor out of.. inadvertency should we sputter our reproachful speech. **1681** H. Nevile *Plato Rediv.* 260, I have known some men so full of their own Notions, that they went up and down sputtering them in every Mans Face. **1753** Foote *Englishm. in Paris* i, Our pretty gentlemen.. sputter nothing but bad French in the side-boxes at home. **1817** Byron *Beppo* xliv, Like our harsh northern whistling, grunting guttural, Which we're obliged to hiss, and spit, and sputter all. **1841** Browning *Pippa Passes* Poems (1905) 169 So Luca.. lives to sputter His fulsome dotage on you. **1891** S. C. Scrivener *Our Fields & Cities* 172 Don't be a fool when you are talking to the managing clerk.., and go sputtering any of this rot to him.

b. With *out.*

1730 Swift *Vindic. Ld. Carteret* Wks. 1841 II. 113/2 Without the least pretended incitement [to] sputter out the basest and falsest accusations. **1783** Miss Burney *Early Diary* (1889) II. 310 This speech he sputtered out just as if his mouth had been full of beef and pudding. **1877** *Smith & Wace's Dict. Chr. Biog.* I. 469 Another desperate attempt to sputter out the guttural, Phthasuarsas, is found in Theophanes.

3. *intr.* Of persons: To eject from the mouth, to spit out, food or saliva in small particles with some force and in a noisy explosive manner.

1681 H. More *Expos. Dan.* 285 The Welch-man.. bit the Rine of the Orange into his mouth together with the Pulp, which made him sputter and make hard faces. **1683** Tryon *Way to Health* 305 They feed them till they sputter out of their Mouthes, and also cast it up. **1719** De Foe *Crusoe* i. (Globe) 216 Putting a little [salt] into his own Mouth, he seem'd to nauseate it, and would spit and sputter at it. **1792** Mme. D'Arblay *Diary* V. vii. 319 Putting her face close to mine, and sputtering at every word from excessive eagerness. **1845** Whitehead *R. Savage* 350 As a child sputters and wawls when physic is forced upon it. **1878** P. Bayne *Pur. Rev.* ii. 28 His tongue was too large for his mouth; he stuttered and sputtered.

4. To speak or talk hastily and confusedly or disjointedly.

Freq. with implication of prec. sense.

1681 T. Flatman *Heraclitus Ridens* No. 48 (1713) II. 53 He storms and sputters like—like any think. **1696** W. Mountagu *Holland* 4 The Servants.. sputter'd in Dutch, which they understood not. **1730** Swift *Traulus* i. 9 Why must he sputter, spawl, and slaver it In vain against the People's Fav'rite? *Ibid.* 63 Though he sputter through a session, It never makes the least impression. **1831** Trelawny *Adv. Younger Son* II. 160 Sputtering about the ignorance of womankind. **1852** H. Rogers *Eclipse of Faith* 167 They began to sputter at one another, on the supposition that each was mocking his neighbour. **1871** Tennyson *Last Tourn.* 65 Then, sputtering thro' the hedge of splinter'd teeth,.. said the maim'd churl.

transf. **1828** Scott *F.M. Perth* vii, The sea-gull, which flutters, screams, and sputters most at the commencement of a gale of wind.

5. a. To make or give out a sputtering sound or sounds, esp. under the influence of heat; with adv., to move *away*, come *in*, etc., with a sputtering sound; also *fig.*

1692 Dryden *Cleomenes* i. i, Like the Green Wood That sputtring in the Flame works outward into Tears. **1706** E. Ward *Wooden World Diss.* (1708) 79 Vex him then, and he shall swell and sputter like a roasted apple. **1866** Whittier *Snow-bound* 172 The mug of cider simmered slow, The apples sputtered in a row. **1936** L. C. Douglas *White Banners* ix. 200 The taxi sputtered away. **1977** N. Sahgal *Situation in New Delhi* xii. 123 Thank God no one was around as they sputtered in.

fig. **1879** McCarthy *Own Times* xviii. II. 16 Chartism bubbled and sputtered a little yet in some of the provincial towns. **1977** *Time* 11 Apr. 36/3 Terrorism sputters on, but Argentines have learned to cope with it, even ignore it.

b. Of a candle, fire, etc. Also with *out*, to sputter and die out (in quots., *fig.*). (Cf. the *ppl. a.* 2.)

1845 Alb. Smith *Fort. Scattergood Fam.* xxxii. (1887) 109 The candle.. was sputtering with the rain-drops. **1850** Dickens *Dav. Copp.* xx, The newly-kindled fire crackled and sputtered. **1889** D. C. Murray *Dangerous Catspaw* 20 A gas jet, which shrieked and sputtered as he applied the match. **1964** D. MacArthur *Reminiscences* vi. 162, I was certain that.. his advance would sputter out as it ran ahead of its supply line. **1974** H. L. Foster *Ribbin'* v. 228 In most cases, if teachers would not interfere, these incidents would sputter out.

6. *Physics.* **a.** To remove atoms of (a metal) *from* a cathode by bombarding it with fast positive ions; to deposit (metal removed in this way) *on* another surface.

1910 *Phil. Mag.* XX. 337 A relatively thick film was sputtered on a 1 mm. quartz plate. **1924** *Science* 31 Oct. 392/2 The cathode drop sputters tungsten from the cathode in an amount.. between 10^{-6} and 10^{-7} grams. **1949** S. Frankel in J. F. Blackburn *Components Handbk.* v. 182 A gold plating is sputtered on and is baked for at least one hour at 500°C. **1961** *Proc. IRE* XLIX. 1148/2 The gas is found in the metal which has been sputtered from the cathode. **1965** *Wireless World* Aug. 409/1 The positive plasma ions.. impinge with sufficient energy to sputter atoms onto an adjacent substrate. **1974** *Sci. Amer.* Apr. 35/1 The film can be sputtered onto the substrate in a vacuum chamber.

b. To cover (a surface) with metal by sputtering.

1910 *Phil. Mag.* XX. 331 Two plates were sputtered simultaneously so as to insure the same thickness for both films. **1962** *Sci. Amer.* Mar. 86/3 The steady hail of ions 'sputters' the surface. **1971** *Physics Bull.* Sept. 554/2 Pure silica glass surfaces have been sputtered by 20 keV argon ions at 0° incidence to the general plane.

sputtered (ˈspʌtəd), *ppl. a.* [f. prec. + -ed[1].] Formed by or resulting from sputtering (see sputtering *vbl. sb.* 2).

1910 *Phil. Mag.* XX. 337 A second blank quartz plate.. was now rigidly fastened to the blank side of the sputtered plate. **1921** *Physical Rev.* XVIII. 215 Sputtered films are crystalline. **1971** *Physics Bull.* Sept. 554/2 Redeposition of low energy sputtered particles on to adjacent surfaces.

ˈ**sputterer.** *rare.* [f. sputter *v.*] One who or that which sputters.

1687 Miège *Gt. Fr. Dict.* ii, Sputterer,.. *une personne qui crachote à force de parler vite.* **1755** in Johnson. **1881** *Punch* 15 Oct. 174/1 Whilst facts *be* facts, whilst truth its cold *douche* showers, Hydrants & squirts can ne'er be equal powers; One sturdy spout will spoil the sputterers all. **1935** A. J. Pollock *Underworld Speaks* 112/2 *Sputterer*, a person who has just begun opium smoking and smokes a small quantity daily, getting much satisfaction from the drug with the belief that he will never become addicted.

'sputtering, *vbl. sb.* [f. as prec.]

1. a. The action of the verb in various senses; an instance of this.

1719 BOYER *Dict. Royal* I, *Crachotement*,.. Sputtering, Spitting often. **1837** CARLYLE *Fr. Rev.* II. III. iv, A continual crackling and sputtering of riots from the whole face of France. **1844** DICKENS *Mart. Chuz.* iii, Such a smoking and sputtering of wood newly lighted in a damp chimney. **1884** *Fortn. Rev.* Mar. 326 Feeble little sputterings of mutual admiration or inane twaddle.

b. *pl.* Small particles sputtered out or emitted with some force and noise.

1894 HALL CAINE *Manxman* IV. xiv, Then Nancy began to fly about the kitchen like sputterings out of the frying-pan.

2. The removal of atoms from a substance subject to bombardment, esp. from a metallic cathode bombarded by positive ions, and usu. with subsequent deposition on an adjacent surface.

1902 *Phil. Mag.* IV. 653 The metallic films..were obtained by sputtering from a cathode *in vacuo* on glass strips. **1930** *Rev. Mod. Physics* II. 186 'Sputtering', or disintegration of an electrode subjected to positive ion bombardment is a well known and often troublesome phenomenon. **1948** L. D. SMULLIN in Smullin & Montgomery *Microwave Duplexers* v. 210 Sputtering is a process in which the cathode is heated by positive-ion bombardment to the point where particles are boiled out of the cathode and finally condense on the anode or on the tube walls. **1952** [see *ion bombardment* s.v. ION 2]. **1976** *Sci. Amer.* May 115/3 By the process known as sputtering, the impact of electrons and protons on the surface could chip away atoms and release them into the atmosphere, from which they would quickly escape.

'sputtering, *ppl. a.* [f. as prec.]

1. Emitting or ejecting saliva or spittle. Also in comb. ***venom-sputtering***.

1598 MARSTON *Sco. Villanie* III. xi. 229 Avaunt lewd curre, presume not speake Or with thy venome-sputtering chaps to barke Gainst well-pend poems. **1602** DEKKER *Satiro-m.* Wks. 1873 I. 244 Thy sputtering chappes yelpe, that Arrogance, and Impudence,.. are the essentiall parts of a Courtier.

2. Characterized by, burning with, making or giving out, a succession of explosive sounds accompanied by the emission of small particles, sparks, or bursts of flame.

1649 G. DANIEL *Trinarch., Hen. V*, cxx, The Despaireing flame Resigns its Sputtering light, ere the Time came. **1697** DRYDEN *Æneid* XII. 762 The laurels crackle in the sputt'ring fire. **1743** DAVIDSON *Æneid* VIII. 251 Others dip the sputtering Metals in the Trough. **1794** SCHMEISSER *Syst. Min.* I. 219 The so called sprudel stone or sputtering stone, from Carlsbad. **1837** CARLYLE *Fr. Rev.* III. v. vi, The wheels of Langres scream, amid their sputtering fire-halo. **1848** THACKERAY *Van. Fair* lxi, A sputtering tallow candle. **1880** GRANT *Hist. India* vi. 33/2 A sputtering fire of musketry was kept up for two hours.

b. Of sound, etc.

1825 JAMIESON *Suppl.*, *Sotter*,..the bubbling, crackling, or sputtering noise made by any thing in boiling or cooking. **1860** TYNDALL *Glac.* I. xxv. 189 My lamp..carried on a sputtering combustion. **1874** L. STEPHEN *Hours Libr.* (1892) I. iii. 94 His writings resemble those fireworks which.. suddenly break out again into sputtering explosions.

3. Of speech, etc., or of persons with reference to this: (see SPUTTER *v.* 4).

1691 *New Disc. Old Intreague* xxxiii. 33 Sir W——m W——ms first the Cause espous'd, And all his sputtering Eloquence he rous'd. **1756** MRS. DELANY *Life & Corr.* (1861) III. 411 To make out sputtering Hampden's observation. **1812** COMBE *Tour Picturesque* XXIII, Then..his shrill and sputt'ring speeches. *c* **1825** LD. COCKBURN *Mem.* iii. (1874) 135 His voice..got sputtering and screechy when he became excited. **1835** T. MITCHELL *Aristoph. Acharn.* 1041 *note*, It would have afforded the angry chorus a very appropriate quotation against their parsimonious and sputtering provider.

Hence **'sputteringly** *adv.*, in a sputtering manner; with a sputter or sputters.

1833 LAMB *Elia* II. *Barbara S——*, When she crammed a portion of it into her mouth, she was obliged sputteringly to reject it. **1861** *Temple Bar* III. 359 'But—but'—I exclaimed sputteringly.

sputtery ('spʌtərɪ), *a. rare.* [f. SPUTTER *v.* + -Y.] Inclined to sputter or burst out explosively; of a sputtering nature.

1858 CARLYLE *Fredk. Gt.* III. v. I. 232 This youth, very full of fire,..had been rather sputtery upon his Uncle. **1864** *Ibid.* XVI. ix. IV. 384 D'Argens..Has abundance of light sputtery wit, and Provençal fire and ingenuity. **1867** —— *Remin.* (1881) II. 59 His mood had really been splenetic, sputtery, and improper.

‖**sputum** ('spju:təm). *Med.* Pl. **sputa** ('spju:tə). [L. *spūtum* spit, spittle, neut. pa. pple. of *spuĕre* to spit.] Saliva or spittle mixed with mucus or purulent matter, and expectorated in certain diseased states of the lungs, chest, or throat; a mass or quantity of this. *spec.* (see quot. 1973[2]).

sing. **1693** tr. *Blancard's Phys. Dict.* (ed. 2), *Sputum*, a Liquor thicker than ordinary Spittle. **1784** *Med. Comm.* I. 397 The qualities of the sputum. **1803** *Med. Jrnl.* IX. 378 Although the cough continues, the expectoration is more free, the sputum being of a thicker consistence and milder quality. **1881** *Tablet* 28 Feb. 358 Some of the sputum left on the edge of the cup. **1973** *Lancet* 24 Feb. 420/1 Bacteriologists and exfoliative cytologists often report on a specimen sent as sputum: 'No sputum present, saliva only.' *Ibid.*, Sputum is material brought up from the trachea by the actions of coughing or hawking, or the same material spat out with (usually) an admixture of saliva. (Material hawked up into the pharynx and swallowed is generally referred to as swallowed sputum, so the first half of this definition is necessary—sputum is sputum even if it is not spat out.)

pl. **1829** COOPER *Good's Study Med.* II. 470 Frequently the characteristic sputa are observed only at the very beginning of the disease. **1876** BRISTOWE *Th. & Pract. Med.* (1878) 438 With the advance of the disease..the sputa usually become increased in quantity.

‖**spuugslang** ('spy:xslaŋ). *S. Afr.* Also **spoew-, spoog-, spug-, spuw-**, etc. [Afrikaans *spuugslang, spoegslang*, f. *spu(ug), spoe(g)* to spit + *slang* snake.] = RINGHALS.

1789 W. PATERSON *Narr. Four Journeys Country of Hottentots* 165 The Spoog Slang, or Spitting Snake. **1812** A. PLUMPTRE tr. *Lichtenstein's Trav. S. Afr.* I. I. vii. 95 A very rare sort of serpent, called here the *spugslang* (the spurting snake)..is from three to four feet long, of a black colour, and ..when attacked it will spurt out its venom. **1911** *Encycl. Brit.* XXV. 299/1 It shares with the cobra a third Dutch name, that of 'spuw slang' (spitting snake). **1923** KIPLING *Land & Sea Tales* 34 He gave us half-a-crown for a spuugh-slange—a kind of snake. **1931** R. L. DITMARS *Snakes of World* xiii. 172 Another name [for the ringhals] is Spoew-slang, applied from the reptile's 'spitting' its poison.

spuwe, obs. form of SPEW *v.*

spuying, obs. form of SPEWING *vbl. sb.*

spuyl(e, obs. forms of SPOIL *sb.* and *v.*[1]

spy (spaɪ), *sb.* Also 4–7 **spie, spye.** [ad. OF. *espie* (= Sp. and Pg. *espia*, It. *spia*) ESPY *sb.*; hence also MDu. *spie*. In sense 4 partly f. SPY *v.*]

1. a. One who spies upon or watches a person or persons secretly; a secret agent whose business it is to keep a person, place, etc., under close observation; esp. one employed by a government in order to obtain information relating to the military or naval affairs of other countries, or to collect intelligence of any kind. In joc. phr. ***one's spies***: one's private or unofficial sources of information.

c **1250** *Gen. & Ex.* 2169 It semet wel ðat ȝe spies ben, And in-to ðis lond cumen to sen, And..for to spien ur lord ðe king. *Ibid.* 2174 Spies were we neuer non. *c* **1380** WYCLIF *Wks.* (1880) 272 God haþ ȝouen a prest to be a spie to aspie þe sotil disceitis of þe fend & warne þe peple of hem. *c* **1384** CHAUCER *H. Fame* II. 196 Though that Fame had al the pies In al a Realme, and al the spies. *c* **1400** MAUNDEV. (1839) xi. 131 Whan the Spyes seen ony Cristene men comen upon hem, thei rennen to the Townes. *c* **1440** *Promp. Parv.* 469/1 Spy, or watare.., *explorator.* **1508** DUNBAR *Tua Mariit Wemen* 161 To speik, quoth scho, I sall nought spar; ther is no spy neir. **1592** SHAKS. *Ven. & Ad.* 655 This sour informer, this hate-breeding spy. **1617** MORYSON *Itin.* III. 13 Theeves have their spies commonly in all Innes, to inquire after the condition of passengers. **1667** MILTON *P.L.* II. 970, I come no Spie With purpose to explore or to disturb The secrets of your Realm. **1706–7** FARQUHAR *Beaux' Strat.* III. i, Why some think he's a Spy, some guess he's a Mountebank. **1797** MRS. RADCLIFFE *Italian* xiii, They are certainly spies from the Monastery. **1855** PRESCOTT *Philip II*, II. iii. I. 172 His spies were everywhere, mingling with the suspected and insinuating themselves into their confidence. **1882** J. H. BLUNT *Ref. Ch. Eng.* II. 122 John Hooper..and..William Latimer..informed against him to the Privy Council, having no doubt been sent as official spies. **1955** E. H. CLEMENTS *Discord in Air* iii. 32 He designed the engine... I got that from my spies. There's no secret about it, anyway. **1965** M. FRAYN *Tin Men* v. 31 The Queen's going to pay an official visit... So I'm told by my spies, anyway.

transf. and *fig.* **1590** SPENSER *F.Q.* I. ii. 17 Each others equall puissaunce enuies, And through their iron sides with cruell spies Does seeke to perce. *Ibid.* III. i. 36 And whilest he bath'd, with her two crafty spyes, She secretly would search each daintie lim. **1654** WHITLOCK *Zootomia* 560 Testimonies of dying Saints:..we may call them Intelligence from the Spies of Eternity, seeing..the Grapes of that Canaan. **1663** PATRICK *Parab. Pilgr.* xxi, If there be any thing of greater force than other to bring you acquainted with the joy and peace of Jerusalem,..this must be that happy Spy.

b. Const. *on, upon* (rarely *of*). Also *transf.*

1375 BARBOUR *Bruce* VII. 386 He to Carleill than vald ga, And a quhill thar-in soiorn ma, And haf his spyis on the kyng. **1623** WOTTON in Pearsall Smith *Life & Lett.* (1907) II. 237, I conceive it a duty to tell your Lordship first how we stand here at this date. For ambassadors (in our old Kentish language) are but spies of the time. **1680** N. TATE *Loyal General* Addr. E. Tayler A v, He was a most diligent Spie upon Nature. **1725** DE FOE *Voy. round World* (1840) 35 They had presently three Dutchmen, set by the Dutch captain, unperceived by them, to be spies upon them, and to mark exactly what they did. **1797** MRS. RADCLIFFE *Italian* ii, He suspected that this man was at once the spy of his steps and the defamer of his love. **1833** HT. MARTINEAU *Loom & Lugger* I. iii. 38 But these men are spies only upon those who break the laws. **1849** MACAULAY *Hist. Eng.* v. I. 533 There is strong reason to believe that he provided for his own safety by pretending at Whitehall to be a spy on the Whigs.

c. As the title of various periodicals, etc.

1644 The Spie, communicating Intelligence from Oxford. **1706** E. WARD, The London Spy. **1712** SWIFT *Let. Eng. Tongue* Wks. 1751 II. I. 189 Those monstrous productions, which under the name of trips, spies, amusements, and other conceited appellations, have over-run us for some years past. **1739** The Universal Spy, or London Weekly Magazine. **1810–1** [HOGG], The Spy. A periodical paper of literary amusement and instruction. **1854** *Poultry Chron.* II. 174 The 'Worcester Spy' says that the corn crop in Central Massachusetts, will be nearly or quite an average one.

†**d.** *black spy*, the Devil.

a **1700** in B. E. *Dict. Cant. Crew.*

2. *Mil.* A person employed in time of war to obtain secret information regarding the enemy; in early use esp. one venturing in disguise into the enemy's camp or territory.

13.. *K. Alis.* 3530 (Linc.), þe spies on boþe sydes goþ, An telliþ tales for soþ, Of Alisaundre, and eke Darie. **1338** R. BRUNNE *Chron.* (1810) 241 Had þei had a spie among þe Walssh oste,..þei had bien men lyuand, þat þer to dede went. *c* **1375** *Sc. Leg. Saints* xl. (*Ninian*) 905 þe Inglis.. vend þar spy betraisit had þame to þe knycht. *c* **1420** LYDG. *Assembly of Gods* 1022 Er he came at the felde he sent yet pryuyly Sensualyte before, in maner of a spy. *c* **1450** *Merlin* xviii. 290 On the morowe erly Gawein sente a spie for to se what the saisnes diden. **1533** TINDALE *Lord's Supper* Wks. (1573) 472/1 As if a souldier of our aduersaries part shoulde come in among vs with our Lordes badge,..we would..take him for a spye. *a* **1548** HALL *Chron., Hen. VIII*, 25 b, At a certayn foord shewed to them by a spy which serued ye yoman of ye tentes of vitailes. **1665** MANLEY *Grotius' Low-C. Wars* 267 Then they considered their danger, especially upon the Return of some that had been sent as Spies. **1699** TEMPLE *Hist. Eng.* 113 Upon approach of his Enemies he sent Spies into the Norman Camp, who were taken. **1777** in Sparks *Corr. Amer. Rev.* (1883) I. 428 My scouts and spies inform me, that the enemy's head-quarters and main body are at Saratoga. **1846** WRIGHT *Ess. Mid. Ages* II. xiii. 87 In the early romances, no disguise is so frequently used by a spy as that of a minstrel. **1899** *The Hague Conference* Art. 29, An individual can only be considered a spy if, acting clandestinely, or on false pretences, he obtains or seeks to obtain information in the zone of operations of a belligerent, with the intention of communicating it to the hostile party.

†**3.** An ambush, ambuscade, snare. *Obs. rare.* Cf. ESPY *sb.* 1 b.

c **1380** *Antecrist* in Todd *Three Treat. Wyclif* (1851) 116 He sitteþ in spies wiþ riche men þat he slee an innocent man in privee. **1382** WYCLIF *1 Kings* xvi. 20 The remnaunt..of the wordis of Zamry, and of the spies [1388 tresouns] of him, and of the tyraundise.

4. The action of spying; secret observation or watching; an instance or occasion of this. Chiefly in phrases.

c **1450** *Knt. de la Tour* (1868) 7 Hit happed that the lorde made spie how the gentill-woman was gone to hide her. **1605** SHAKS. *Macb.* III. i. 130, I will aduise you where to plant your selues, Acquaint you with the perfect Spy o' th' time, The moment on 't. **1751** *Female Foundling* I. 143 This young Baggage was on the Spy, and cannot hold her Tongue when she has done. **1857** A. MAYHEW *Paved with Gold* II. viii, But he's always at the window looking over your way, and if you keep a spy on her, there'll be some fun.

5. *attrib.* and *Comb.*, as ***spy-catcher, -catching, fever, -fiction, film, -government, -hunting, -knave, -like*** adj., ***-mania, movie, -net, network, novel, play, scandal, scare, school, series, story, -system, thriller, trial, work***, etc.; † **spy-boat**, a vessel used for purposes of observation; **spy in the cab** *colloq.* = TACHOGRAPH; **spy in the sky**, a satellite or aircraft used to gather intelligence; freq. *attrib.* (with hyphens); **spymaster**, the head of an organization of spies; **spy-money**, payment for the services of a spy; **spy plane**, an aircraft used to gather intelligence; **spy ring** = RING *sb.*[1] 11 c; **spy satellite**, a space satellite used to gather intelligence, usu. military; **spy-ship**, = *spy-boat*; **Spy Wednesday**, in Irish use, the Wednesday before Easter (in allusion, it is said, to Judas).

1637 HEYWOOD *Royall Ship* 10 A kind of *Spie-boates which waited upon a fleete at sea. **1693** LUTTRELL *Brief Rel.* (1857) III. 52 The German spy boat came upon the coast of France with a fleet of 16 French merchant men. **1704** *Lond. Gaz.* No. 4019/2 Her Majesty's Spy Boat the Chatham Prize. **1952** O. PINTO *Spy-Catcher* i. 7 There is indeed excitement at times in the life of a real *spy-catcher. **1976** *Eastern Evening News* (Norwich) 13 Dec. 1/1 Spycatcher ..'Jock' Wilson, head of London's C.I.D. **1978** CADOGAN & CRAIG *Women & Children First* x. 223 The most irresistible wartime subjects were evacuation and *spy-catching. *Ibid.* 225 The spy-catching tales of Dorita Fairlie Bruce. **1973** 'D. HALLIDAY' *Dolly & Starry Bird* xvi. 234 The *spy fever had spread like foot-and-mouth disease. **1963** *Times Lit. Suppl.* 8 Feb. 92/2 The famous heroes of British *spy-fiction..have seldom been professionals. **1942** *N.Y. Times* 13 June 11/2 A tautly intriguing and sometimes hair-raising *spy film. **1972** 'E. FERRARS' *Breath of Suspicion* iii. 46 It struck Richard, that this must be a spy film. **1929** D. H. LAWRENCE *Pansies* 127 The big, flamboyant Russia Might have been saved if a pair Of rebels like Anna and Vronsky Had blasted the sickly air Of Dostoevsky and Tchekov, And *spy-government everywhere. **1871** N. SHEPPARD *Shut up in Paris* 58 Crowd dissolves to wreak its wrath in *spy-hunting. **1968** J. KELSON in *Headlight* Sept. 15/3 The tachograph is a gadget that has been hotly argued over..but..against all.. obstacles to productivity and efficiency, the *Spy in the Cab is the crowning irrelevancy of the age. **1980** *Daily Tel.* 30 Dec. 1/1 The new rules on drivers' hours and the use of tachographs, the so-called 'Spy in the cab', will come into force on Thursday. **1960** *N.Y. Times* 12 June IV. 6/2 The U-2 reconnaissance 'over-flights' provided, by aerial photography and tape recording of Soviet radio and radar emissions, the most important intelligence gathered by the C.I.A. The '*spy in the sky' more than compensated for the very few spies on the ground that the United States has been able to infiltrate into Russia. **1961** *Time* 7 July 16 The spy-in-the-sky warning system. **1969** *Daily Tel.* 18 Apr. 24/8 The NSA..is responsible for ship, aircraft and 'spy-in-the-sky' satellite espionage. **1976** *Daily News* (N.Y.) 11 June (CB & Sound Suppl.) 2/1 *Spy in the Sky*, police aircraft. **1977** *Time* 23 May 33/2 A lot of the information is picked up by those spy-in-the-sky satellites. **1622** FLETCHER *Beggar's Bush* III. iii, You are sent here, Sirra, To discover certain Gentlemen, a *spy-knave. **1599** B. JONSON *Cynthia's Rev.* Prologue, *Spie-like suggestions, privie whisperings, And thousand such promooting sleights as these. **1668** *Extr. State Papers rel. Friends* Ser. III. (1912) 276 He may be imployed about busines from Holland, and soe spy like carry intelligence there. **1892** *Englishman in Paris* II. xii. 275 The *spy mania..became positively contagious. **1894** *Daily News* 21 Nov. 5/4 The recrudescence of the spy-mania in France. **1943** *Time* 18 Jan. 38/2 The Nazi *spymaster and Naval Attaché, Captain Dietrich Niebuhr. **1978** A. Neave *Nuremberg* xiii. 148 The older generation remembered him for his incompetence as a spy-master in the United States during the First World War. **1713** Addison *Guard.* No. 97 ¶4 *Spy-money to John Trott her footman, and Mrs. Sarah Wheedle, her companion. **1969** G. Lyall *Venus with Pistol* iii. 20 It's all a bit like some-thing out of a bad *spy movie. **1955** W. Tucker *Wild Talent* xvi. 215 A master *spy-net, efficiently directed. **1977** G. Markstein *Chance Awakening* xxv. 76 Hentoff is..a key figure in a British-based *spy network. **1919** C. Mackenzie *Sylvia & Michael* vi. 222 Our *spy-novels and spy-plays must have been of priceless assistance to the Germans. **1979** *Guardian* 1 Mar. 7/2 Literaturnaya Gazeta..cast doubt on the value of spy novels. **1960** *Aeroplane* XCVIII. 627/1 That the U-2 '*Spy-plane' operation is nothing new is evident from what I heard in America about three years ago. **1962** *Spectator* 14 Sept. 351 The Chinese..brought down an American spyplane. **1976** J. Poyer *Day of Reckoning* iv. 21 Wasn't there something about a spy plane—yes..the U-2 incident. **1919** *Spy-play [see *spy novel* above]. **1943** *Spy ring [see ring *sb.*[1] 11 c]. **1960** *Guardian* 22 July 1/2 The spy-ring members began checking on the habits of people working in radar.. establishments. **1980** *Times* 22 Jan. 15/1 General Miyanaga, the leader of the spy ring, had been a Russian-speaking specialist working in intelligence for many years. **1960** *Washington Post* 29 Mar. A16 Much of the money..will go for additional Atlas intercontinental ballistic missiles in hardened sites and for acceleration of the Midas, or '*spy' satellite development. **1976** W. H. Canaway *Willow-Pattern War* xx. 204 There's a camouflaged installation... You couldn't see it from a spy satellite. **1977** *Arab Times* 14 Dec. 1/1 Georg Leber, defending his role in a burgeoning *spy scandal. **1923** R. Macaulay *Told by Idiot* III. xxi. 257 The German *spy scare, the British spy scare, these fevers were worked up in the jingo press. **1976** J. Lee *Ninth Man* 74, I like an informed citizenry. Spy scares keep them alert. **1968** *Observer* 22 Dec. 11/2 New recruits..are sent for training to Group Four's headquarters... A large country house..it conjures up all the *spy-school images. **1975** *Listener* 28 Aug. 281/4 Drama..is supplied by *The Eiger Sanction*..but only so far as the most standard of television *spy series. **1858** tr. *Life of Xavier* 188 The *spy-ships which he had sent..to ascertain the fate of the contest between the Acheens and Portuguese. **1962** *Daily Tel.* 13 June 1/4 (*heading*) Fourth Soviet spyship watching U.S. tests. **1977** C. Forbes *Avalanche Express* xxiii. 242 The 17,000-ton Soviet freighter..the new pride of Soviet..spy ships. **1923** *Spy story [see daffy *a.*]. **1978** F. Maclean *Take Nine Spies* 333 The well-known story of the Watchmaker of Orkney..as neat a spy story as one could wish. **1823** T. Bewick *Memoir* (1975) xi. 103 This happy society was however, at length broken up, at the time when the War on behalf [of] despotism was raging & the *Spy system was set afloat. **1880** McCarthy *Own Times* liii. IV. 137 The spy system was soon flourishing in full force. **1952** I. Asimov *Stars, like Dust* iv. 48 All young fools who get their notions of interstellar intrigue from the video *spy thrillers are easily handled. **1977** *Amer. N. & Q.* XV. 76/2 Somehow, the categorization 'spy thriller'..seems to diminish the 'classic' quality. **1972** K. Benton *Spy in Chancery* xxi. 249, I don't hanker after another *spy trial, thank you. **1842** Lover *Handy Andy* xxiii, She spakes like a French spy,..and she was missin', I remember, all last *Spy-Wednesday. **1804** J. Larwood *No Gun Boats* 23 Her Emissaries are at the secret *spywork of observation and information. **1818** Cobbett *Pol. Reg.* XXXIII. 50 It appears..that the Duke of Montrose..highly approved of his spy-work. **1915** J. Buchan *Thirty-Nine Steps* vii. 184 It is ordinary spy work.

spy (spaɪ), *v.* Forms: 3–4 **spien**, 4–7 **spie** (4, 6 **spi**); 4–6 **spye** (4 **speiȝe**, 5 **spyȝe**, **spyyn**), 4– **spy**. Also 5 *pa. pple.* **spyne**. [ad. OF. *espier* espy *v.* Cf. MDu. *spêen* (Du. *spieden*), MLG. *spêen*, MSw. *speia*, *speya* (Sw. *speja*), ON. *speja*, *spæja*.]

I. *trans.* **1. a.** To watch (a person, etc.) in a secret or stealthy manner; to keep under observation with hostile intent; to act as a spy upon (one).

c **1250** *Gen. & Ex.* 2172 Cume ȝe for non oðer ðing, but for to spien ur lord ðe king. **1338** R. Brunne *Chron.* (1810) 40 Eilred ȝede þorgh his lond, priuely to spie Euerilkon þe Danes. *c* **1375** *Sc. Leg. Saints* ii. (*Paul*) 22 In Ierusalem he wes bofte, spyit, waitit, and bundyn ofte. *a* **1400** *Sqr. Lowe Degre* 641 The steward was ordeyned to spy And for to take them utterly. **1456** Sir G. Haye *Law Arms* (S.T.S.) 164 Men may..barate thair inymyes.., or ȝit ger spy thame, and se quhen thay ar in disaray. *a* **1533** Ld. Berners *Huon* clix. 612 The same tyme there was on the mountayne .vi. theues who laye to spye the marchauntes. **1617** Moryson *Itin.* II. 111 Sir Francis Staffords Lieutenant of his horse, sent by Sir Henri Daners to spy the rebels proceedings.

1870 *Pall Mall G.* 22 Oct. 12 Since the commencement of the Empire one half of France spied the other half. **1884** tr. *Gaboriau's Little Old Man* i, Indignantly declaring that he was not in the habit of 'spying' the tenants of the house.

b. To make stealthy observations in (a country or place) from hostile motives. Also with *out*, esp. in phr. ***to spy out the land***; freq. *fig.*

a **1300** *Cursor M.* 4824 Þan said ioseph,..'Bot er yee comen þe land to spi?' **13..** *Coer de L.* 7018 With velanye Ye be come my londe to spye, And sum treson me for to don! **1457** Harding *Chron.* in *Eng. Hist. Rev.* Oct. (1912) 751 [He] gafe me in commaundement Scotlonde to spye..How that it myght bene hostayed and distroyed. *c* **1470** Henry *Wallace* v. 490 The toune he spyit, and that forthocht we sone. **1535** Coverdale *Numb.* xiii. 16 The men, whom Moses sent forth to spye out the lande. *Ibid.* 21 They went vp, & spyed the lande. **1626** Gouge *Serm. Dignity Chivalry* §3 Those choice men which were..sent to spie the Land of Canaan. **1653** H. Cogan tr. *Pinto's Trav.* xxii. 77 He sente two small Barques..to spy the Port, and sound the depth of the river. **1913** Galsworthy *Dark Flower* III. v. 230 What had Dromore come for? To spy out the land, discover why Lennan and his wife thought nothing of the world 'outside'. **1936** A. Christie *ABC Murders* xv. 112 This man must have been spying out the land beforehand and discovered your brother's habit of taking an evening stroll. **1958** P. H. Newby *Ten Miles from Anywhere* 124 Maybe you think I'm up to no good? A poultry thief spying out the land. **1979** A. Boyle *Climate of Treason* i. 32 An unofficial representative of the new Soviet régime arrived in London to spy out the land not long after the 1918 Armistice.

c. To (seek to) discover or ascertain by stealthy observation. Usu. with dependent clause.

1338 R. Brunne *Chron.* (1810) 83 Roberd about did spie, if Malcolme wild haf wrouht. **1375** Barbour *Bruce* xv. 114 Thai gert spy That mony of schir Eduardis men War scalit in the cuntre then. *c* **1386** Chaucer *Frankl. T.* 778 For wel he spyed whan sche wolde go Out of hir hous to eny maner place. *a* **1400** *Pistill of Susan* 122 Spyes now specialy if þe ȝatis be sperid. *c* **1460** *Towneley Myst.* ix. 110 Luke that thou spy, both far and nere,..If thou here any saghes sere..Of that lad. *c* **1470** Henry *Wallace* vi. 467 Spyand full fast, quhar his awaill suld be. **1611** Bible *2 Kings* vi. 13 Goe and spie where he is, that I may send and fetch him.

1828 Lytton *Pelham* III. xix, Thornton..said he would go alone, to spy whether we might return. **1864** Tennyson *Aylmer's F.* 569 Some low fever ranging round to spy The weakness of a people or a house.

2. To look out for, to seek an opportunity for, in a close or stealthy manner. Now *rare.*

13.. *K. Alis.* 6998 (Laud MS.), Queed & harme he wil me spye. **13..** *E.E. Allit. P.* B. 1774 Þe prowde prynce of perce ..with ledes of armes, Þat now has spyed a space to spoyle Caldeez. **1382** Wyclif *Ecclus.* xii. 15 In his herte he spieth, that he turne thee vp so doun in to the dich. *c* **1400** *Destr. Troy* 5085 In speche may men spie the speker to know, And wete, by his wordes, the wit þat he beires. *a* **1425** *Cursor M.* 19715 Niȝte or day whenne þei myȝt spie Bi murþerment to do him diȝe.

1859 Meredith *Juggling Jerry* i, One that outjuggles all 's been spying Long to have me, and he has me now.

3. To look at, examine, or observe closely or carefully; to see or behold; in mod. use *spec.*, to investigate with a spy-glass or telescope.

c **1325** *Metr. Hom.* 13 His sawel gern spied he [*sc.* Satan], Yef he moht se or find thar inne Any filth or spotte of sinne. **1377** Langl. *P. Pl.* B. II. 225 Spiceres spoke with hym, to spien here ware. *c* **1440** *Ipomydon* 1730, I haue the spyed, sythe þou oute ȝede: Thou arte my lemman, as I haue thoght. **1508** Dunbar *Tua Mariit Wemen* 70, I suld at fairis be found, new faceis to spy. **1549** *Compl. Scot.* Prol. 11 Quhen he hed contemplit & spyit the proportions & propreteis of nature. **1590** Spenser *F.Q.* I. iv. 5 And all the hinder partes, that few could spie, Were ruinous and old, but painted cunningly. **1812** H. & J. Smith *Rej. Addr.* 35 Thy rival staggers; come and spy her Deep in the mud as thou art in the mire. **1871** B. Taylor *Faust* (1875) II. 52 Great Pan in cheerful mood stands by, Rejoiced the wondrous things to spy. **1893** Earl Dunmore *Pamirs* II. 78, I spied the whole ground, and never saw a beast.

4. a. To catch sight of; to descry or discover; to notice or observe. Cf. espy *v.* 2.

13.. *K. Alis.* 2183 (Laud MS.), A jolyf kyng ycleped barrys Spyeþ Alisaundres prys. **1375** Barbour *Bruce* xix. 528 The lord Dowglas has spyit a vay, How that he mycht about thame ryd. *c* **1380** *Sir Ferumb.* 1295 It miȝte hermye ȝow alle in cas if my fader miȝt it spie. **1404–8** *26 Pol. Poems* 29 [Let] No fende spot vppon þe spyȝe. *a* **1450** *Knt. de la Tour* (1868) 60 The theef..gothe and comithe till he be spied, and thanne is take. **1480** *Robt. Devyll* 823 in Hazl. *E.P.P.* I. 251 Themperoure..bade hys seruaunte throwe hym a bone. So he dyd, and whan Robert yt had spyne [etc.]. **1575** *Gamm. Gurton* II. iv, Good lord! shall never be my luck my nee'le again to spy? **1590** Spenser *F.Q.* I. i. 7 A shadie grove not farr away they spide. **1626** in Ellis *Orig. Lett.* Ser. I. III. 216 In my passage, spying a doore guarded by one,..I went, and..found an easie entrance. **1687** A. Lovell tr. *Thevenot's Trav.* I. 166 When they spie that Fish, they strike him on the back with Harping-Irons. **1719** De Foe *Crusoe* I. 80 Looking out to Sea in hopes of seeing a Ship, then fancy at a vast Distance I spy'd a Sail. **1774** Goldsm. *Nat. Hist.* (1776) V. 138 By dilating the pupil, the animal..is enabled to spy its prey..in the dark. **1849** *Sk. Nat. Hist., Mammalia* III. 13 There is great danger if the hippopotamus spies the huntsman before he can throw his spear. **1885–94** R. Bridges *Eros & Psyche* May xxv, It must end our love If they should hear or spy thee from above.

transf. *a* **1704** T. Brown *Dk. Ormond's Recovery* Wks. 1730 I. 51 His mind enlarg'd, and boundless as the sky, Shall unknown worlds and heaven's recesses spy.

b. With immaterial object.

c **1315** Shoreham I. 1851 Ȝyf þet one weddeþ þe þral,.. And ȝyf a spyet þat soþe prof [etc.]. *c* **1400** *Ywain & Gaw.* 3013 Our kyng..Passed thurgh many cuntre, Aventures to spir and spy. **1508** Dunbar *Tua Mariit Wemen* 271 Thought I dispytit thaim agane, thai spyit it na thing. **1549** E. Allen *Paraphr. Rev.* 4 Whan they spye any thing amysse in them selves. **1598** Drayton *Heroical Ep.* (1619) xxii, Feare seeing all, feares it of all is spy'd. **1667** Milton *P.L.* IV. 1005 The latter..kickt the beam; which Gabriel spying, thus bespake the Fiend. **1734** Watts *Reliq. Juv.* (1789) 95 Does nature find so much convenience, or spy so much decency in it? **1780** Cowper *Let.* 8 June, If you spy any fault in my Latin, tell me, for I am sometimes in doubt. **1810** Scott *Lady of L.* I. xix, Her kindness and her worth to spy, You need but gaze on Ellen's eye. **1813** —— *Trierm.* Introd. v, Too oft my anxious eye has spied That secret grief thou fain wouldst hide.

c. With clause as object.

c **1325** *Song of Yesterday* in *E.E.P.* (1862) 137 Whon þat he wol þe assayle, þat wost þou not, ne neuer may spye. *c* **1350** *Will. Palerne* 3399 Ac spacly þe spaynoles speiȝed he was slayne. *c* **1400** *Gamelyn* 490 Now I haue spied þat frendes haue I none. **1509** Hawes *Past. Pleas.* xxxv. 181 Besyde a ryver and a craggy roche This gyaunt was whyche spyed me approche. **1573** Tusser *Husb.* (1878) 60 Let Christmas spie yard cleane to lie. **1590** Lodge *Euphues Gold. Leg.* I 2 b, Aliena..spied where the hare was by the hounds, and could see day at a little hole. **1628** Milton *Vac. Exerc.* 61 Thy drowsie Nurse hath sworn she did them spie Come tripping to the Room. **1859** Tennyson *Guinevere* 31 For Sir Launcelot passing by Spied where he couch'd.

d. In the names of children's games: (*a*) ***hy-spy, I spy***: see hy-spy; (*b*) ***I spy (with my little eye)***, a game in which one player selects an object (visible to all) for the others to guess, giving them its colour or its initial letter with the words 'I spy with my little eye something (blue, etc.) *or* beginning with —'.

1946 R. Lehmann *Gipsy's Baby* 80 We remained below and played *I Spy*—with colours, not the alphabet, so that my brother could join in. **1969** I. & P. Opie *Children's Games* x. 275 Their participation in intellectual guessing games, even of the humble order of..'I Spy With My Little Eye', is apt to be limited to occasions when they are restricted and unable to play anything else. **1975** *Language for Life* (Dept. Educ. & Sci.) vi. 85 Stories, and such verbal games as 'I-spy' and 'Knock-knock', encourage children to explore speech sounds and help them develop a better intuitive understanding of these sounds.

5. To find *out*, to search or seek *out*, by observation or scrutiny.

1530 Tindale *Prol. Romans* ¶2 No man could spy out the intent, and meanyng of it. *a* **1533** Ld. Berners *Huon* lv. 188 As Huon foughte he spyed out the paynym that had gyuen him his swerde. **1584** Powel *Lloyd's Cambria* 151 The Normans began to spie out the Commodities of Wales. **1617** Moryson *Itin.* III. I The senses..are (as it were) our Sentinels and Watch-men, to spie out all dangers. **1650** Hubbert *Pill Formality* 69 They might spie out the Saints liberty. **1706** E. Ward *Wooden World Diss.* (1708) 72 He can spy out the Faults in the Structure of a Boat, sooner than those of himself. **1782** Mme. D'Arblay *Diary* 28 Oct., Lady Shelley, who spied us out, sent us an invitation to her party. **1848** Thackeray *Lett.* 28 July, I felt ashamed of myself for spying out their follies. **1893** Mrs. F. Elliot *Diary Constantinople* vi, One little black-eyed child..spied me out as I left the carriage.

II. *intr.* **6. a.** To make observations (now *spec.* with a spy-glass); to keep watch; to be on the look out.

a **1300** *Cursor M.* 27372 Þe preist bi-gin þan his franyng, Sua o ferrum for to spi Til he find quar þe roting ly. **13..** *E.E. Allit. P.* B. 780 Þere in longyng al nyȝt he lengez in wones, Whyl þe souerayn to Sodamas sende to spye. *c* **1375** *Sc. Leg. Saints* xiii. (*Mark*) 137 And sa eftyre spyit þai, þat þai fand hyme one pasck-day. *c* **1430** *Syr Gener.* (Roxb.) 2563 So long he spied day and night Til he hapened to haue a sight. **1508** Dunbar *Tua Mariit Wemen* 427 That I may spy, vnaspyit, a space me beside. **1530** Palsgr. 728/2, I spye for one, I lye awayte for hym, *je aguette.* *a* **1631** Donne *Songs & Sonnets, Break of day* ii, If it [*sc.* light] could speake as well as spie, This were the worst that it could say.

1883 *Longm. Mag.* Nov. 73 After a very cursory glance round with my own glass, I shut it up and began talking as Charlie spied.

b. Const. *at* (a thing).

1806 Beresford *Miseries Hum. Life* v. ix, While there was nothing in the house worth spying at. **1826** Hood *Mermaid of Margate* ii, On Margate beach,..Where urchins wander to pick up shells, And the Cit to spy at the ships.

7. a. To make stealthy or covert observations; to play the spy; to pry.

1456 Sir G. Haye *Law Arms* (S.T.S.) 238 [They may] travaill in were and pes..sa that thare be na coverit malice under, as to spy. **1593** Shaks. *Lucr.* 1086 Revealing day through every cranny spies. **1604** —— *Oth.* III. iii. 147 As I confess it is my Natures plague To spy into Abuses. **1611** Cotgr., *Mouscher*, to spy, pry, sneake into corners, thrust his nose into euery thing. *a* **1637** B. Jonson *Sad Sheph.* I. ii, But spy your worst, good spy, I will dispose of this where least you like!

b. Const. *on* or *upon* (a person, etc.).

1626 Donne *Lett.* (1651) 314 But this evening I will spie upon the B[ishop]. *a* **1774** Goldsm. *Hist. Greece* II. 102, I am come to spy upon your vanity and ambition. **1883** G. J. Cayley *Las Alforjas* II. 141 What do you mean, sir, by spying upon my movements? **1891** Farrar *Darkn. & Dawn* xiv, It is no such pleasure to be Emperor with you to spy on me.

†**spy**, variant of spi *int. Obs.*

c **1315** Shoreham I. 2035 Spy, felþe! Þer hy myȝte hyt do kendelyche, On-kende hys hare onselthe.

spy-, the stem of the vb. used in combs., in the sense of 'that spies' as ***spy-all***, ***-fault***, ***-maiden***, or 'from or through which one may spy, used for spying' as ***spy-camera***, ***-hole***, ***-house***, ***-microphone***, ***-mike***, ***-tower***, ***-window***. Also spy-glass.

(*a*) **1555** Watreman *Fardle Facions* II. xi. 256 Thei haue also certaine spiefaultes ordinarilie appoincted..that spie in euery shiere suche as be necligent. **1593** *Passionate Morrice* 80 This Honestie is such a pestilent spie-fault. **1631** Done *Polydoron* 117 A Criminal shall have faultie Spy-faults Enough going to Prison. **1706** E. Ward *Wooden World Diss.* (1708) 11 The first Thing he peeps at, thro' this trusty Spy-all, is, the Chase's Port-Holes. **1791** Cowper *Iliad* XI. 469 Archer shrew-tongued! spie-maiden! man of curls!

(*b*) **1717** Berkeley *Jrnl. Tour Italy* Wks. 1871 IV. 542 Towers..along the coast, being spy-towers against the Turks. **1755** S. Richardson *Let.* 15 Aug. in *Sel. Lett.* (1964) 321 My spy-window—Ay, that is the window of my vexation —workmen are—workmen... Only, that workmen I wish they were. **1867** P. Kennedy *Banks of Boro* xxxvii. 288, I got a..tumbler of punch sitting in my corner inside the spy-hole. **1888** Stevenson *Black Arrow* 125 Here and there, were spyholes, concealed, on the other side, by the carving of the cornice. **1896** *Allbutt's Syst. Med.* I. 312 *L* is a glass spy-hole through which the inmates can be watched. **1896** R. G. Moulton *Bk. Job* Introd. 38 The eagle in her spy-house of inaccessible crags. **1903** W. Ward *Probl. & Persons* 308 Another room at Moorfields, with a spy window. **1955**

POHL & KORNBLUTH *Space Merchants* i. 4 Nothing but the usual State Department and House of Representatives spy-mikes. **1960** *Sunday Express* 17 July 1 (*heading*) Spy-mikes sensation. Arms firms checked for 'listening walls'. **1960** *Sunday Express* 17 July 1 Tiny hidden spy-microphones planted by foreign agents. **1968** *Punch* 2 Oct. 495/1 Television spy-cameras, hooked to machines which will translate a visual image into patterns and templates, hooked to high-speed rotary presses, will start stamping out copies in all sizes. **1972** *Times* 14 Dec. 2/8 A Henry Moore bronze ..disappeared from the Lefevre Gallery..although a television 'spy' camera was operating. **1977** J. HEDGECOE *Photographer's Handbk.* 21 Made in Czechoslovakia the Mikroma 'spy camera'..has a seven speed shutter and a f3.5 lens.

spyal, spyar, obs. forms of SPIAL, SPIER.

spycarie, obs. form of SPICERY.

†**spyccard.** *Obs.*$^{-1}$ (Origin and meaning obscure. Cf. SPITTARD.)
1486 *Bk. St. Albans* f iv b, Ther be beestys of the chace of the swete fewte. And tho be the Bucke, the Doo, the Beere, the Reyndere, the Elke, the Spyccard, the Otre, and the Martron.

spyce, obs. form of SPICE.

'**spydom.** [f. SPY *sb.*] Spying; espionage; the world of spies.
1859 *Times* 27 Dec. 6/5 Should the practice of spydom become universal, farewell to all domestic confidence and happiness. **1862** *Morning Star* 18 June, The notion of spydom is so abhorrent to the English feeling. **1899** *Daily Tel.* 2 Sept. 10/5 The happy family of spydom assembled in Panizzardi's dining-room.

spyer, variant of SPIER.

spyere, obs. form of SPHERE *sb.*

spyghtful(l, obs. ff. SPITEFUL *a.*

spy-glass. Also spyglass. [f. SPY *v.* + GLASS *sb.*^{1} 10. Cf. SPYING-GLASS.]
1. A telescope; a field-glass.
1706 E. WARD *Wooden World Diss.* (1708) 11 He's never without a swinging large Spy-glass. **1753** *Phil. Trans.* XLVIII. 227 Turning the little end of a spy-glass, it appeared something like the ruins of Palmyra. **1814** SCOTT *Diary* 31 Aug. in *Lockhart* (1837) III. viii. 252 The whole, as seen with a spyglass, seems ruinous. **1840** MARRYAT *Poor Jack* xxi, A telescope, or spy-glass, as sailors generally call them. **1875** W. MCILWRAITH *Guide Wigtownshire* 50 Here with a spy-glass one may discern the entrance to Dirk Hatterick's cave.
2. *dial.* An eye-glass.
1883 R. CLELAND *Inchbracken* xi. 86, I have lost my gold spy-glass, something has caught the chain and broken it.

'**spying,** *vbl. sb.* [f. SPY *v.*] **a.** The action of the verb, in various senses.
1338 R. BRUNNE *Chron.* (1810) 338 Sir Jon de Waleis taken was in a pleyn, þorgh spiyng of Norreis. **1398** TREVISA *Barth. De P.R.* VIII. xxviii. (Bodl. MS.), Li3t..destroieth fals waitinges and spyinges. *c* **1430** *Syr Gener.* (Roxb.) 9138 But thei be armed in al maners..For auenture of ony spiyng. **1495** *Trevisa's Barth. De P.R.* XIV. xiii. 473 Mount Fasga is the hyll of spienge, of syghte, and of byholdynge. **1523** LD. BERNERS *Froiss.* I. liii. 75 None coulde yssue out without spyeng. *a* **1568** ASCHAM *Scholem.* II. (Arb.) 148 The spying of this fault now is not the curiositie of English eyes. **1611** COTGR., *Speculation*,..a viewing, watching, or spying out from a high place. **1883** *Longm. Mag.* Nov. 72 The Hill of Badeney..on ordinary days gave us our first vantage-ground for spying. **1907** *Athenæum* 6 July 6/2 His suspicions and spyings and petty meddlings certainly had required extraordinary patience.
b. *attrib.*, as ***spying-hole, -mission, -place, -point.***
1791 BENTHAM *Panopt.* I. Postscr. 97 A thin partition.. with blinded spying-holes running in the line level with the Inspector's eye. **1848** W. H. KELLY tr. *L. Blanc's Hist. Ten Y.* II. 448 Confident..that there was no truth in the spying mission attributed to Conseil. **1894** WEYMAN *Man in Black* 79 The closet was a spying-place, and these were Judas-holes. **1922** JOYCE *Ulysses* 254 What is it?..—Find out, Miss Douce retorted, leaving her spyingpoint.

spying-glass. [f. prec.]
1. = SPY-GLASS 1. Now *rare.*
1682 tr. *Glanius' Voy. Bengala* 28 Thus did they appear to us through our Spying-Glass, and every one..believed they saw very distinctly with it. **1739** *Wks. of Learned* I. 85 From whence Servius might conclude that he knew the Use of Spying-Glasses. **1770** BARETTI *Journ. Lond. to Genoa* I. x. 59, I saw through my spying-glass a ship that seemed to make towards us. **1803** *Naval Chron.* IX. 477 By the help of my spying-glass I had made a drawing. **1885** R. BUCHANAN *Annan Water* ix, I was up on the tower wi' my spying-glass.
†**2.** An opera-glass; an eye-glass. *Obs.*
1767 WARBURTON in W. & Hurd *Lett.* (1809) 405, I was accosted by a little, round, well-fed gentleman, with..a spying-glass dangling in a black ribbon at his button. **1780** *Ann. Reg.* II. 4 As they are masked, they do not scruple to reconnoitre the company with their spying-glasses. **1795** WOLCOT (P. Pindar) *Convention Bill* Wks. 1812 III. 380 And will it not be deem'd a daring thing To ogle through a spying-glass the King.

'**spyism.** [f. SPY *sb.*] Espionage.
1847 in WEBSTER. **1902** A. W. MARCHMONT *Sarita the Carlist* vi. 59 The episode was a part of that spyism she had declared so prevalent.

'**spyler.** *rare*$^{-1}$. [? f. SPILE *v.*^{2}] (See quot.)
1844 H. STEPHENS *Book of Farm* III. 921 This process is easiest done by inserting rolls of moulded cheese, extracted by the scoop or *spyler*, into holes previously made in the new cheese by the same scoop, an instrument usually employed by cheesemongers to taste cheese.

spylt, obs. form of SPELT *sb.*^{1}

†**spynist,** *ppl. a. Sc. Obs.*$^{-1}$ [For *spanist*: see SPANISH *v.*^{1}] Expanded, opened.
1508 DUNBAR *Tua Mariit Wemen* 29 New vpspred vpon spray, as new spynist rose.

spyr(e, spyrr, obs. forms of SPEER *v.*^{1}

spyse(r, obs. forms of SPICE, SPICER.

'**spyship.** [f. SPY *sb.*] The office or occupation of a spy.
1779 WARNER in Jesse *Selwyn & Contemp.* (1814) IV. 43 So, sir, there is an end of my affair and my spyship, for I do not think I can have anything else to say to you about it. **1825** LD. COCKBURN *Mem.* 327 The inconvenient fact of his having received considerable sums..from Government—not for his spyship. **1865** *Athenæum* No. 1956. 554/2 Personal spyship on the part of Jonson.

spysorye, obs. f. SPICERY.

spyte, obs. f. SPIT *sb.*^{1} and *v.*^{1}

spyttarde, var. SPITTARD *Obs.*

spytuously, -wysly, varr. SPITOUSLY *adv. Obs.*

†**sqawde**, var. of SCAWED *a. Obs.*
1578 WHETSTONE *2nd Pt. Promos & Cass.* IV. ii, What seekes thou good fellow? *Iohn.* My sqawde Mare.

sqn, abbrev. of SQUADRON *sb.*
1914 W. S. CHURCHILL *Let.* 26 Aug. in M. Gilbert *Winston S. Churchill* (1972) III. *Compan.* I. 55, I am trying to get the 3rd Sqn (yours I hope) for the Infantry division I am forming from Marines and Naval reservists. **1942** PARTRIDGE *Dict. Abbrev.* 91/2 *Sqn.*, squadron, whether naval or aerial. *Sqn Ldr.*, Squadron Leader. **1977** *R.A.F. News* 22 June–5 July 5/1 Sqn Ldr Sean Maffett..has been a commentator for nearly ten years.

squab (skwɒb), *sb.* Also 7, 9 *dial.*, squob, 8 squobb, squabb. [Of uncertain origin: cf. QUAB *sb.*^{1} and Sw. dial. *sqvabb* loose fat flesh, *sqvabba* a fat woman, *sqvabbig* flabby, Norw. dial. *skvabb* a soft wet mass.]
†**1.** A raw, inexperienced person. *Obs.*$^{-1}$
1640 BROME *Sparagus Gard.* II. ii, I warrant you, is he a trim youth? We must make him one Iacke, 'tis such a squab as thou never sawest; such a lumpe, we may make what we will of him.
2. a. A newly-hatched, unfledged, or very young bird. Also *fig.* of a person.
1682 SHADWELL *Medal John Bayes* 69 Should all thy borrow'd plumes we from thee tear, How truly Poet Squab would'st thou appear! *a* **1700** B. E. *Dict. Cant. Crew, Squab*, ..a new Hatcht Chick. **1736** W. ELLIS *New Exper.* 95 The earliest young ones [*i.e.* goslings] are commonly sent to London in March,..called squabs. **1838** HOLLOWAY *Prov. Dict., Squab*, an unfledged bird. **1853** KANE *Grinnell Exp.* xix. (1856) 146 Some of the men succeeded in reaching the squabs [= young auks] by introducing their arms. **1865** KINGSLEY *Herew.* v, At the bottom of each [pie] a squab or young cormorant.
b. *spec.* A young pigeon.
1694 MOTTEUX *Rabelais* IV. lix. 234 Pigeons, Squobbs, and Squeakers. **1765** *Treat. Dom. Pigeons* 50 This article, and the young squabs, will nearly, if not quite, maintain your Pigeons in food. **1854** *Poultry Chron.* I. 573/2 It is generally considered that a cock [pigeon] homes quickest when driving to nest, and a hen when she is feeding squabs. **1867** AUGUSTA WILSON *Vashti* xxvi, The gale blew down my pigeon-house and mashed all my squabs. **1902** R. W. CHAMBERS *Maids of Paradise* i, Among which generations of pigeons had built nests and raised countless broods of squealing squabs.
c. A young rabbit. *rare*$^{-0}$.
1838 HOLLOWAY *Prov. Dict., Squab*,..a young rabbit, before it is covered with hair.
3. A short fat person.
a **1700** B. E. *Dict. Cant. Crew, Squab*, a very fat, truss Person. **1710** POPE *Lett.* (1735) I. 152 We shall then see that the Prudes of this World..are naturally as arrant Squabs as those that went more loose. **1791** O'KEEFFE *Wild Oats* IV. i, Your figure is the most happy comedy squab I ever saw. **1809** MALKIN *Gil Blas* v. i. ¶29 A fat laughing squab of a woman. **1823** LADY GRANVILLE *Lett.* (1894) I. 240 He is a fat, sallow squab of a man. **1897** BARTRAM *People of Clopton* vii. 201 A great fat squab loike Lucy.
4. A sofa, ottoman, or couch.
1664 *Verney Mem.* (1907) II. 211 For a drawing-rome i should have 2 squobs, & 6 turned woden chars of the haith of the longe seates. **1689** *Lond Gaz.* No. 2495/4 The Covering of a large Squab, the upper side of Cloth of silver, the Ground white and toward a Filamot. *a* **1710** POPE *Imit., Artemisia* 10 On her large squab you find her spread, Like a fat corpse upon a bed. **1719** DE FOE *Crusoe* I. 178 Under this I had made me a Squab or Couch, with the Skins of the Creatures I had kill'd, and with other soft Things. **1788** W. H. MARSHALL *Yorksh.* II. 355 *Squab*, a couch, common in most farm 'houses'. **1867** *Morn. Star* 1 Jan. 2 In consequence of the fullness of the house the deceased was compelled to sleep on a sofa or squab in the bar. **1892** M. C. F. MORRIS *Yorksh. Folk Talk* 377 The squab is a roughly-made couch or long-settle with cushions, differing from the ordinary long-settle in that it has one arm instead of two.
5. a. A thick or soft cushion, *esp.* one serving to cover the seat of a chair or sofa.
1687 MIÉGE *Gt. Fr. Dict.*, A Squab, or very soft Cushion, *coussin fort moû*. **1706** PHILLIPS (ed. Kersey), *A Squab*, a soft stuffed Cushion or Stool. **1730** *Inv. R. Woolley's Goods* (1732) 8, 3 Pair of Window Curtains and 3 Squabs of the same. **1748** RICHARDSON *Clarissa* VI. 158 An old broken-bottomed cane couch, without a squab, or coverlid, sunk at one corner [etc.]. **1819** H. BUSK *Vestriad* IV. 1051 Bolstering his head with squabs, his mind with hope. **1839** DICKENS *Nickleby* x, Chairs, with turned legs and green chintz squabs to match the curtains. **1881** G. MACDONALD *Mary Marston* xxxvii, She was poking the little fists into the squab of the sofa.
transf. **1860** MAYHEW *Upper Rhine* v. 272 The apparatus appears to be more like a large squab of a watch-pocket.
b. A cushion forming part of the inside fittings of a carriage. Hence, in mod. use, the padded back or side of a car-seat.
1794 W. FELTON *Carriages* (1801) I. 145 A squab, or sleeping cushion;..occasionally added to the insides of those carriages, for the head or shoulders to incline against. **1844** HEWLETT *Parsons & Widows* vii, He looked into the carriage, turned up the squabs. **1888** FARR & THRUPP *Coach Trimming* vi. 75 Back Squabs are not usually fastened at the sides, and it is the custom to make the sides curving out from the straight line, that the squab may not when fixed appear narrower across the middle. **1904** *Car* 15 June 114/2 Two extra seats..fold up underneath the back squab. **1924** *Motor* 28 Oct. 700/1 Several different methods have been invented to enable the angle of the squab to be varied. **1966** 'A. HALL' *9th Directive* vii. 62, I slid back and rested my head on the rear squab... It was a big car, comfortable. **1972** *Drive* Spring 147/3 The height, legroom and squab level of the driver's seat can be adjusted.
6. *attrib.* **a.** In sense 2, as ***squab-condition, -gull, -pigeon, -virtuoso.***
1686 F. SPENCE tr. *Varillas' Ho. Medicis* 227 He nurs'd up these Squab-virtuoso's in Literature almost from the very Cradle. **1741** *Compl. Fam.-Piece* I. iii. 219 To pickle Sparrows or Squab-Pigeons. **1856** KANE *Arct. Expl.* I. xxiv. 320 The squab-gull of Hans Island has a well-earned reputation..for its delicious juices. **1877** NEWTON in *Encycl. Brit.* VI. 407 The young [of the cormorant]..remain for some time in the squab-condition.
b. In senses 4 and 5, as ***squab chair, cushion, -seat, sofa.***
1837 MARRYAT *Dog Fiend* xxiv, Seated on the squab sofa. **1849** ALB. SMITH *Pottleton Legacy* (1854) 263 There were squab seats all round the room. **1860** *All Year Round* No. 63. 306 An old mahogany Empire arm-chair, with squab cushion. **1864** *N. & Q.* 3rd Ser. VI. 136/2 Upholsterers make sofa and couch seats of three kinds, called respectively squab-seats, spring seats, and stuffed tight seats. **1867** O. W. HOLMES *Guardian Angel* ii, Nurse Byloe let herself drop into a flaccid squab chair.

squab (skwɒb), *a.* Also 7 squob, 8 squabb. [Cf. prec.]
1. Of persons: Short and stout; squat and plump.
1675 WYCHERLEY *Country Wife* IV. iii, I am now no more interruption to 'em..than a little squab French page who speaks no English. **1682** FLATMAN *Heracl. Ridens* (1713) II. 234 Do you know that same Squab Blade with the light Peruke? **1703** FARQUHAR *Inconstant* I. ii, A Dutch woman is squab. **1760** GOLDSM. *Cit. W.* lxviii, As Rock is remarkably squab, his great rival, Franks, is remarkably tall. **1827** T. HAMILTON *Cyril Thornton* (1845) 47 His lordship was a little squab man. **1865** *Reader* No. 122. 489/2 The squab yellow Hottentots. **1884** BESANT *Dorothy Forster* i, His eyes were large, his figure short and squab.
b. Having a thick clumsy form.
1723 CHAMBERS tr. *Le Clerc's Archit.* I. 46 The Capital.. wou'd be too flat and squab. **1818** SCOTT *Hrt. Midl.* xliv, Turning his squab nose up in the air. **1885** CLARK RUSSELL *Strange Voy.* v, A large three-masted ironclad, with low squab funnel. **1894** *Idler* Sept. 134 That ancient ship..with her..artillery running the fat squab length of her.
c. *Comb.*, as ***squab-faced, -looking, -shaped*** adjs.
1781 MME. D'ARBLAY *Diary* May, The Attorney-General, a most squat and squab-looking man. **1795** SOUTHEY *Lett. from Spain* (1799) 9 Its fountain ornamented with a squab-faced figure of Fame. **1865** ALEX. SMITH *Summer in Skye* ii, Comical squab-faced deities in silver and bronze. **1889** C. EDWARDES *Sardinia & the Sardes* 103 Mostly its buildings are low, squab-shaped, and of sun-dried brick.
2. Young and undeveloped; *esp.* of young birds, unfledged or not fully fledged, newly or lately hatched.
1706 PHILLIPS (ed. Kersey), A *Squab Rabbet* or *Chick*, one so young that 'tis scarce fit to be eaten. **1709** *Brit. Apollo* No. 46. 3/1 A Glazier..Came like a Squab-Rook flutt'ring down. **1774** G. WHITE *Selborne* lxi, I..found in each nest only two squab, naked *pulli*. **1789** *Ibid.*, The squab young we brought down and placed on the grass-plot. **1807–8** W. IRVING *Salmag.* (1824) 269 A nest-full of little squab Cupids.
†**3.** Reserved, quiet. *Obs.*$^{-1}$
1689 N. LEE *Princ. Cleve* III. i, Your demure Ladies that are so Squob in company, are Divels in a corner.
†**4.** Abrupt, blunt, curt. *Obs.*
1737 HERVEY *Mem.* II. 340 Most people blamed the Duke of Argyll for so squab an attack. *a* **1743** SAVAGE *An Author to be let* ¶8 Thus have I caused his Enemies..to libel him for my squab compliment. **1756** H. WALPOLE *Lett. Mann* (1833) III. 125 We have returned a *squab* answer, retorting the infraction of treaties. **1759** *Ibid.* 338 Lord Ligonier in words was more squab. 'If he wanted a court-martial, he might go seek it in Germany.'

squab (skwɒb), *v.* Also 9 *dial.* squob. [Cf. SQUAB *sb.* and *a.*]
1. *trans.* To knock or beat severely; to squash, squeeze flat. Now *dial.*
1668 WILKINS *Real Char.* Dict., *To Squab*, break, sp. by down casting. **1687** MIÉGE *Gt. Fr. Dict.* II, To Squab, or squelch one, to beat him to mash, *applatir quêcun de coups.* **1847–** in midl. and southern dial. use.
2. *refl.* To squat (oneself).

In mod. Leic. and Warw. dial., 'to squeeze (oneself) into a small space'.

1680 R. L'ESTRANGE *Erasm. Colloq.* (1711) 9 The Sea-Priest..squabs himself down directly upon our Shoulders.

3. *trans.* With *off*: To reject bluntly.

1812 *Sporting Mag.* XL. 41 Maslen..having most friends on the hill, he squabbed off these evasions.

4. To stuff or stuff up.

1819 H. BUSK *Dessert* 37 Ye whose divans, recesses, and whose piers, Are squabb'd with ottomans and chiffoniers. **1891** *Cent. Dict.*, *Squab*, v.t., to stuff thickly and catch through with thread at regular intervals, as a cushion.

5. *intr.* To fall or hang in a full or heavy manner.

1755 JOHNSON, *To Squab*, v.n., to fall down plump or flat. **1845** S. JUDD *Margaret* II. xi, Ladies in..short cloaks with hoods squabbing behind, known as cardinals.

squab, *int.* and *adv.* Also 9 *dial.* squob. [Imitative.] **a.** *int.* (See quot.)

a **1625** FLETCHER *Women Pleas'd* I. i, I should be loath to see ye Come fluttering down like a young Rook, cry squab, And take ye up with your brains beaten into your buttocks.

b. *adv.* With a heavy fall or squash.

1692 R. L'ESTRANGE *Fables, Eagle & Tort.* 192 The Eagle took him up a matter of Steeple-high into the Air, and..dropt him down, Squab upon a Rock. **1847** HALLIW. s.v. *Squob*, He throwed him down squob. *Sussex*. **1890** *Glouc. Gloss.* 149 Er came down squob.

squa'bash, *sb.* [A fanciful combination of *squash* and *bash*, prob. due to Prof. Wilson.] A crushing blow; a squashing.

1818 *Blackw. Mag.* III. 250 The Author of 'The Dentist' is most rash; If printed, 'twould secure him a squabash. **1832** WILSON *Ibid.* XXXI. 281 Here are some verses that give all such shallow and senseless critics the squabash!

squabash (skwɒˈbæʃ), *v.* [f. prec.] *trans.* To crush, squash, demolish.

1822 *Blackw. Mag.* XI. 88 When their darling was squabash'd At glorious Waterloo. **1827** SCOTT *Jrnl.* 17 Jan., His satire of the Baviad and Maeviad squabashed at one blow a set of coxcombs. **1843** BARHAM *Ingoldsby Leg.* (ed. 2) Pref., In order utterly to squabash and demolish every gainsayer. **1886** *Pall Mall G.* 23 Feb. 4/1 Mr. Ruskin is right in saying that J. S. Mill has been squabashed.

Hence **squa'basher**.

1827 *Blackw. Mag.* XXI. 650 That was a squabasher to the Elchee, who tried to back out of the argument. **1841** *Ibid.* L. 66 Sidney Smith,..squabasher of the cowardly..invention of the ballot-box.

squabbed, *a.* Also 7 squobb'd. [f. SQUAB *a.* or *v.*] Squat, dumpy.

1694 MOTTEUX *Rabelais* IV. ix. 38 A strapping, fusty squobb'd Dowdy. **1822** *Blackw. Mag.* XII. 70 What, that squabb'd thing? that's none of mine. **1893** *Westm. Gaz.* 7 Mar. 9/2 A 'squabbed' shape dome and an ordinary 'Ramsbottom' safety valve.

'squabbing. [f. SQUAB *sb.* 5 b.] Cushioning used in carriages.

1888 FARR & THRUPP *Coach Trimming* i. 6 Brown buckram, which is well adapted for marking purposes and the linings of squabbings. *Ibid.* vi. 73 Recesses..causing the sinking of the squabbing.

'squabbish, *a. rare.* [f. SQUAB *a.*] Somewhat squab or squat.

1666 G. HARVEY *Morb. Angl.* xii. 135 The dyets of two Nations..rendring those of a squabbish lardy habit of body; us of a thinner..appearance. **1784** J. BARRY *Lect. Art* ii. (1848) 94 Excesses and deficiencies in the human form,..squabbish and short.

squabble (ˈskwɒb(ə)l), *sb.* Also 7 squable, squabel, scwable. [prob. imitative: cf. next and Sw. dial. *sqvabbel*.] A wrangle, dispute, brawl; a petty quarrel.

1602 *How Chuse Good Wife* A iv b, Hoping Mistresse you will passe ouer all these Iarres and squabels in good health. *a* **1652** BROME *Mad Couple* II. i, I..have undersold a parcell of the best Commodities my husband had. And should hee know't wee should have such a scwable. **1690** C. NESSE *Hist. O. & N. Test.* I. 367 Whom possibly in some rude squabble ye have kill'd. **1748** H. WALPOLE *Corr.* (1846) II. 208 Except elections, and such tiresome squabbles,..it is all harmony. **1788** JEFFERSON *Writ.* (1859) II. 440 The squabbles, in which the pride, the dissipations, and the tyranny of kings, keep this hemisphere constantly embroiled. **1832** HT. MARTINEAU *Ireland* i. 8 The disputes..became so virulent that the agent could get no rest from squabbles and complaints. **1874** GREEN *Short Hist.* vii. 353 Politics were dying down into the squabbles of a knot of nobles.

squabble (ˈskwɒb(ə)l), *v.* Also 7 squob(b)le, 7–8 squable. [See prec.]

1. *intr.* To wrangle or brawl; to engage in a petty quarrel or dispute; to argue disagreeably or with heat. Freq. const. *about*, *for*, *over*, etc.

1604 SHAKS. *Oth.* II. iii. 281 Drunke? And speake Parrat? And squabble? Swagger? *a* **1677** BARROW *Serm.* Wks. 1716 I. 171 It agreeth to children..to squabble; to women of meanest rank to scold. **1693** *Humours Town* 46 They are launching out into the Sea of Politicks,..squabling to be Burgesses. **1730** *Lett. to Sir W. Strickland rel. to Coal Trade* 28 To deliver all the Coals out of the Ship first, and then squabble about the price. **1789** WOLCOT (P. Pindar) *Ep. to falling Minister* Wks. 1812 II. 118 Good places For which so oft the people squabble. **1839** THACKERAY *Fatal Boots* Dec., Her temper was dreadful, and we used to be squabbling from morning till night! **1873** MRS. WHITNEY *Other Girls* xxi, They've been squabbling over it these five minutes.

b. Const. *with* (another or others).

1655 CAPEL *Tentations* IV. iii. 27 As brethren out of envy will squabble one with another about a party coloured coat. **1660** H. MORE *Myst. Godl.* To Rdr. 15 My forbearing..to squable with every petty Sect. **1677** W. HUGHES *Man of Sin* II. ix. 148 The Devil comes again, and squabbles with him. **1740** CIBBER *Apol.* (1756) I. 290 They had forgot their former fatal mistake of squabling with their actors. **1831** TRELAWNY *Adv. Younger Son* I. 156 A yâk, or little cow, which was squabbling with the children about some fruit. **1889** *Cornh. Mag.* Feb. 118, I feel too miserable and too dejected to squabble with Frances.

c. *transf.* Of a stream. (Cf BRAWL *v.*[1] 3.)

1868 G. MACDONALD *R. Falconer* I. 241 On the grassy bank of the gently-flowing river, at the other edge of whose level the little canal squabbled along.

2. *trans.* In *Typog.*, to throw (type) out of line; to disarrange or disorder; to twist or skew so as to mix the lines.

1674 BLOUNT *Glossogr.* (ed. 4), *Squobble*, is a term among Printers, when the Compositor has set a Form, before it is Imposed, some lines happen to fall out of their order, they say it is squobled. **1683** MOXON *Mech. Exerc.*, *Printing* xxii. ¶3 He spreads and Squabbles the Shanks of the Letters between his Fingers askew. *Ibid.* 391 A Page or Form is Squabbled when the Letter of one or more Lines are got into any of the adjacent Lines; or that the Letter or Letters are twisted about out of their square Position. **1784** B. FRANKLIN in *Ann. Reg.*, *Chron.* (1817) 385 Every page of it being squabbled, and the whole ready to fall into pye. **1888** JACOBI *Printers' Vocab.* 130 *Squabble*, to break or upset type and thus make 'pie' of it.

b. *intr.* Of type: To get into disorder.

1683 MOXON *Mech. Exerc.*, *Printing* xxii. ¶2 Letter is less subject to Squabble between Line and Line..than it is between side and side.

Hence **'squabbled** *ppl. a.*

1886 *Science* VIII. 254 The letters do not range well, giving an irregular or 'squabbled' appearance to the line. **1888** JACOBI *Printers' Vocab.* 130 *Squashed*, another term for 'squabbled' type.

'squabblement. [f. SQUABBLE *v.*] Squabbling; petty quarrelling.

1731 *Gentl. Mag.* I. 125 Any..Rablement, Brabblement, or Squabblement. **1884** *Blackw. Mag.* Feb. 235 Cheating, swindling, peculation, Squabblement of Church and State.

squabbler (ˈskwɒblə(r)). [f. as prec.] One who squabbles or quarrels.

In quot. 1631 perh. a misprint for *squabbe* SQUAB *sb.* I.

1631 T. POWELL *Tom All Trades* 38 If he attaine..the knowledge of languages, and dispositions of foreigne Nations where he travailes and trades, he may rise from a Squabler to a Master. **1687** MIÉGE *Gt. Fr. Dict.* II, Squabbler, *quereleur*. **1702** *Burl. L'Estrange's Vis. Quev.* 65 Who in their Writings are such Squabblers, That they torment me Day and Night. **1876** L. STEPHEN *Eng. Th. 18th C.* II. x. §9. 234 It was possible..that the great families should become mere squabblers for place.

squabbling (ˈskwɒblɪŋ), *vbl. sb.* [f. as prec.] The action of the verb, in various senses.

1611 COTGR., *Noisette*,..a squabling, or small debate. **1664** H. MORE *Myst. Iniq.* 554 Their childish squabling about Nut-shells, Counters and Cherry-stones. **1683** MOXON *Mech. Exerc.*, *Printing* xxii. ¶7 The Breaking, Squabbling, or Hanging, &c. of the Page. **1740** RICHARDSON *Pamela* I. 239 Nothing offers these Days but Squabblings between Mrs. Jewkes and me. **1817** J. SCOTT *Paris Revisit.* (ed. 4) 181 The squabbling in Athens whether Demosthenes had passed his accounts properly. **1868** *Daily Tel.* 25 July, The usual squabbling ended with the usual postponement at a late hour.

'squabbling, *ppl. a.* [f. as prec.]

1. Engaging in, given to, petty quarrelling or wrangling.

1632 SHERWOOD, Squabbling, *noiseux*, *rioteux*. **1665** GLANVILL *Def. Van. Dogm.* p. vi, In a squabbling and contentious Age. **1771** BEATTIE *Minstr.* I. xvii, Nor cared [he] to mingle in the clamorous fray Of squabbling imps. **1841** DICKENS *Barn. Rudge* xliii, A dozen squabbling urchins made a very Babel in the air. **1894** ROOSEVELT in *Forum* Apr. 198 A squabbling multitude of revolution-ridden States.

2. Of the nature of, characterized by, dispute or wrangling.

1664 POWER *Exp. Philos.* III. 184 Ignorance..varnish'd over with a little squabling Sophistry. **1833** T. HOOK *Parson's Dau.* III. xii, There had arisen some squabbling differences amongst his noble passengers. **1879** FARRAR *St. Paul* (1883) 51 The partisans..thrust their squabbling Judaism even into the intercourse between a Paul and a Peter.

squabbly (ˈskwɒblɪ), *a.* [f. SQUABBLE *v.*] Given to squabbling; of a squabbling character.

1887 BARING-GOULD *Golden Feather* v, I do not like her to be at home with all those dirty, squabbley..savages. **1895** *Pall Mall G.* 11 Oct. 11/2 A family meeting where both parties..have a squabbly bargain.

squabby (ˈskwɒbɪ), *a.* [f. SQUAB *sb.* or *a.*] Low and stout; squat, thick-set.

1754 *Connoisseur* No. 5. 28 A short squabby gentleman of a gross and corpulent make. **1780** *Mirror* No. 88, Mrs. Deborah is..in her person thick and squabby. **1841** J. T. J. HEWLETT *Parish Clerk* I. 64 Judy was a good-looking girl, though of the species called squabby. **1845** *Tait's Mag.* XII. 39 The squabby cob maintained his even pace. **1875** G. MACDONALD *Malcolm* III. xv. 202 Over the kitchen-fire, like an evil spirit of the squabby order, crouched Mrs. Catanach.

Comb. **1848** GEO. ELIOT in Cross *Life* (1885) I. 171 You chubby-faced, squabby-nosed Europeans owe your commerce, your arts, your religion, to the Hebrews.

'squably, *adv. rare*[−1]. [f. SQUAB *a.*] Bluntly, abruptly.

1737 HERVEY *Mem.* II. 447 It was better to insinuate what those words meant than to express it so squabbly [*sic*].

squab-pie. Also squob-pie. [Cf. SQUAB *sb.* Chiefly current in western and south-western counties of England.] A pie chiefly composed of mutton, pork, apples, and onions, with a thick crust.

1708 W. KING *Cookery* 164 Cornwall squab-pye, and Devon white-pot brings. **1778** MORES *Diss. Typogr. Founders* 69 *note*, Probably he was a Gloucestershire man and remembered squab-pie, an *olla podrida* of horrible ingredients. **1800** SOUTHEY in Cottle *Rem. Coleridge & S.* (1847) 22 Neither Pilchards, White-ale or Squab-pie were to be obtained. **1865** KINGSLEY *Herew.* v, Most savoury of all the smell of fifty huge squab pies. **1880** *Adam & Eve* 281 Laden with the remnants of a squab-pie..and a couple of apple pasties.

fig. **1897** JANE *Lordship* xix. 209 The great matter being that I had made squob-pie of Robert.

'squacco. *Ornith.* Also 7–9 sguacco. [Local Italian *sguacco*.] A small crested species of heron, *Ardea ralloides* or *comata*.

α. [*a* **1672** WILLUGHBY *Ornith.* (1676) 206 Ardea quam Sguacco vocant in Vallibus dictis Malalbergi. Hence in Ray's translation (1678) 281.] **1785** LATHAM *Gen. Synop. Birds* III. I. 76 Castaneous Heron... It seems a mere variety of the Sguacco, if not differing in sex.

β. **1752** J. HILL *Hist. Anim.* 465 The yellowish Ardea, with the head and neck variegated with black, white, and yellow. [*Marg.*] The Squacco. **1785** LATHAM *Gen. Synop. Birds* III. I. 74 Squacco Heron... Size of the blue Heron. **1834** MUDIE *Feathered Tribes* II. 148 The Squacco Heron..has been more frequently met with in England than any of the former [species]. **1879** E. P. WRIGHT *Anim. Life* 327 The Squacco Heron (*A. comata*) is found in Asia, North Africa, South Europe, and a rare straggler now and then visits England.

squach, variant of SQUATCH *v. Obs.*

squad (skwɒd), *sb.*[1] [ad. F. *escouade*, earlier *esquade* (*esquouade*), var. of *esquadre* SQUADER.]

1. *Mil.* **a.** A small number of men, a subdivision or section of a company, formed for drill or told off for some special purpose.

1649 G. DANIEL *Trinarch.*, *Hen. V*, clxxxv, The Ragged Squad, whose Pay, ill-husbanded, Gives him nor Shooes nor Shirt. **1673** *Reg. Privy Counc. Scotl.* IV. 98 The commander of that squad of his Majesties troup of guardes, quartered at Bathgate. **1757** WASHINGTON *Writ.* (1889) I. 468 Divide your men into as many squads as there are Sergeants. **1811** *Regul. & Orders Army* 244 The Commanding Officer will cause them, by Squads of 20 or more, to move round the Vessel in double quick time, each Squad for ten or twelve minutes. **1844** *Ibid.* 133 The Subaltern Officers, to whom the Squads are entrusted, are responsible for the same to the Captain. **1877** *Field Exerc. Infantry* 4 Recruits formed into a Squad should be directed to observe the relative places they hold with each other.

b. ***awkward squad***: (see quot. 1802).

1796 BURNS in Cunningham *Wks. & Life B.* (1834) I. 344 John, don't let the awkward squad fire over me. **1802** JAMES *Milit. Dict.* s.v., The aukward squad consists not only of recruits at drill, but of formed soldiers that are ordered to exercise with them, in consequence of some irregularity under arms. **1842** MACAULAY *Ess.*, *Fredk. Gt.* (1877) 659 The household regiments of Versailles and St. James's would have appeared an awkward squad. **1878** BESANT & RICE *Celia's Arb.* v, The march and movement of troops,..the drill of the awkward squad, delighted his soul.

transf. **1797** S. JAMES *Narrative Voy.* 205 The butchers here are a truly aukward squad. **1816** [see AWKWARD *a.* 4 b]. **1856** P. THOMPSON *Hist. Boston* Provincialisms, They're a dirty squad, an awkward squad.

c. Without article.

1833 *Regul. & Instr. Cavalry* I. 9 Each Recruit must be trained..in squad.

†**2.** = SQUADRON *sb.* 3. *Obs. rare.*

1673 in *10th Rep. Hist. MSS. Comm.* App. I. 80 On Monday the fleets ingadged;..a whole squad surroundit Sir Edward Sprag, who was in the Royal Prince. **1676** Row *Contin. Blair's Autobiog.* xii. (1848) 509 All that the King was able to do was to set out some squads of small ships.

3. a. A small number, group, or party of persons.

1809 MALKIN *Gil Blas* IV. ix. ¶2 In my mistress's female squad there was a nymph named Portia. **1830** SCOTT *Demonol.* ix. 284 The witches of Auldearn were so numerous that they were told off into squads, or covines. **1841** CATLIN *N. Amer. Ind.* xxiv. (1844) I. 201 The same intelligence was soon communicated by little squads to every family. **1856** KANE *Arct. Expl.* I. xx. 243, I cannot realize that some may not yet be alive; that some small squad or squads..may not have found a hunting-ground.

b. Const. *of.* Also *transf.* and *fig.*

1818 KEATS *Lett.* Wks. 1889 III. 115, I am in a high way of being introduced to a squad of people, Peter Pindar, Mrs. Opie, Mrs. Scott. **1825** COBBETT *Rur. Rides* 83 We saw..squads of labourers..migrating from tract to tract. **1857** BORROW *Romany Rye* xlii, He had a very shabby squad of animals, without soul or spirit. **1896** E. A. KING *Ital. Highways* 91 A large squad of liveried servants. **1914** JOYCE *Dubliners* 244 Three squads of bottles of stout and ale and minerals, drawn up according to the colours of their uniforms. **1940** T. S. ELIOT *East Coker* v. 14 The general mess of imprecision of feeling Undisciplined squads of emotion. **1979** *N. & Q.* Feb. 83/2 The only unforgiveable fault is the abbreviation of titles to unpronounceable squads of initials.

c. In the phr. *in squads*.

a **1848** O. W. HOLMES *Stethoscope Song* 64 They every day her ribs did pound In squads of twenty. **1852** MOTLEY *Corr.* (1889) I. v. 132 People..making excursions into the country in small squads. **1869** Th. Rogers *Hist. Gleanings* I. 84 In the Georgian era men and women were hanged in squads.

4. a. A particular set or circle of people.

1786 Burns *To J. S.* xxviii, The hairum-scairum, ramstam boys, The rambling [1787 rattling] squad. **1809** Malkin *Gil Blas* iii. xi. ¶8 To study the feelings of authors ..would only be the way to spoil them. I know that contemptible squad. **1818** *Blackw. Mag.* III. 533 Tho' used by Hunt, and Keats, and all that squad.

b. *Sport* (orig. *U.S.*). A group of players forming a team or from which a team is chosen.

1902 *Harvard Bull.* 19 Mar. 2/2 The rest of the squad will leave the cage as soon as the ground is dry enough. **1920** W. Camp *Football without Coach* i. 17 A player should take the ball in his hands,..release it and pass it to the next player. This next man repeats the performance, and so it goes through the squad. **1950** *Daily Ardmoreite* (Ardmore, Okla.) 15 Jan. 14/3 It was the second loss of the season for the Tiger 'A' squad as the unbeaten Cougars took them 47 to 40. **1975** *Cricketer* May 4/1 Intikhab Alam..has been omitted from the squad of 19 from which the 14 will finally be chosen. **1981** G. Boycott *In Fast Lane* i. 7 Like everyone who has ever played or watched a cricket match I have my own views about the tour party—and I wouldn't have picked quite this squad.

c. A unit within a police force, organized to investigate or prevent a particular type of crime; freq. in ellipt. use for *flying squad* s.v. flying *ppl. a.* 4e (*b*). See also *fraud, murder, riot, vice squad* at first element.

1905 *N.Y. Times* 22 June 8/6 Commissioner McAdoo selected yesterday the men for the special squad which will arrest women in the streets. **1928** E. Wallace *Flying Squad* xv. 132 You do your best, eh? You did your best to put Bradley away, and draw the attention of the Squad to you and me! **1938** [see guy *v.*[4]]. **1939** 'N. West' *Day of Locust* xxvii. 221 A big squad of policemen was trying to keep a lane open between the front rank of the crowd and the façade of the theatre. **1962** *Daily Tel.* 15 June 22/5 Three detectives, two of them drug squad officers, flew to Gibralter from London yesterday to investigate the haul of illegal drugs found in the cruiser Belfast. **1980** *Times* 24 Jan. 5/3 Serious crime squads throughout Britain are searching for the inventor and manufacturer of a black box which contains a device that can reverse electricity meter readings.

5. *attrib.*, as ***squad car, -dance, drill, instructor, leader, room***, etc.; **squad bag** (see quot. 1876).

1869 E. A. Parkes *Pract. Hygiene* (ed. 3) 403 Squad bags are issued to infantry, four to each company. **1876** Voyle & Stevenson *Milit. Dict.* 398/1 *Squad Bags*, canvas bags provided for troops (one for every 25 men), for the purpose of relieving a soldier from carrying a complete kit on the line of march or in the field. **1864** *Daily Tel.* 14 March, A suttler ..is dispensing beer from squad barrels to a knot of thirsty labourers. **1938** F. D. Sharpe *Sharpe of Flying Squad* x. 120 A Squad car went down at once. **1956** D. G. Browne *Rise of Scotl. Yard* iii. xxv. 339 Squad cars, area cars, and 'Q' cars..kept in touch by wireless with the Information Room at Scotland Yard. **1970** G. F. Newman *Sir, You Bastard* iii. 109 Sneed parked behind the squad car, which had been directed via the information room. **1865** E. Burritt *Walk to Land's End* 171 Inaugurating a new term of service with.. squad-dances in the public street. **1891** *Macm. Mag.* Oct. 466/1 The best thing for them to do would be to go back to squad drill. **1899** Baldock *Cromwell as a Soldier* 24 The drill consisted of what we should now call 'squad drill'. **1859** *Musketry Instr.* 46 The squad instructor opposite the 50 yards point. **1953** *Amer. Speech* XXVIII. 23 A special group is formed by these military words and phrases...squad, squad leader, and training. **1967** tr. *Quotations from Chairman Mao Tsetung* (ed. 2) 106 The secretary of a Party committee must be good at being a 'squad leader'. **1844** *Regul. & Ord. Army* 121 In other Corps a Troop, Company, or Squad Police has been introduced. **1946** *Sun* (Baltimore) 3 July 15/4 John Moynahan, lockup keeper at the town hall police station, was puzzled as he watched Midnight, the seven-year-old station cat, leap madly around the squadroom. **1981** W. Marshall *Perfect End* 5 [He] went through the lobby and into the squadroom.

†squad, *sb.*[2] *Mining. Obs. rare.* Also 8 **squod.** = shoad.

1674 Ray *Coll. Words* 120 The tinners [in Cornwall] find the Mine by the Shoad (or as they call it *Squad*) which is loose stones of tin mixed with Earth. **1728** Chambers *Cycl.* s.v. *Shoaled*, Sometimes it [shoad] is called Squad, and Squod. *c* **1830** Mar. Edgeworth *Lame Jervas* ii, 'Loose ore of tin mixed with the earth, which in those days we used to call shoad or squad.'.. 'We call it squad to this day, master,' interrupted one of the miners.

squad, *sb.*[3] *dial.* Soft slimy mud.

1847 in Halliwell. **1866-** in dial. glossaries, etc. (Lincs., Leics.). **1880** Tennyson *Northern Cobbler* iv, I coom'd neck-an-crop..down i' the squad an' the muck.

†squad, *a. Obs. rare.* [Cf. squab *a.* and squat *a.*] = squaddy *a.*

1675 Covel in *Early Voy. Levant* (Hakluyt Soc.) 216 First there was a *bastanjé*, a middle-sized squad fellow, who shew a vast strength in tossing about weights. **1729** T. Cooke *Tales* 96 A short squad Figure, with a wadling Pace.

squad (skwɒd), *v.* [f. squad *sb.*[1]]

1. *trans.* To divide or form into squads; to draw up in a squad.

1802 James *Milit. Dict.*, *To Squad*, to divide a troop or company into certain parts, in order to drill the men separately, or in small bodies. **1841** Lever *C. O'Malley* lxxxvi. 416, I say, lads, squad your men and form on the road. **1884** *Pall Mall G.* 16 July 8/2 A few Lancashire and metropolitan corps are squadded first this morning.

2. To assign or allocate to a squad.

1802 James *Milit. Dict.* s.v., Recruits should always be quartered and squadded with old soldiers who are known to be steady and well behaved. *Ibid.*, The stables must likewise be squadded entire; that is, no one stable must be allotted to two separate squads.

Hence **'squadded** *ppl. a.*

1896 *Daily News* 18 July 6/4 Three Squadded Competitions have been finished this evening.

squaddie ('skwɒdɪ). *Services' slang.* Also **squaddy.** [f. squad *sb.*[1] + -ie, perh. influenced by swaddy *sb.*] A member of a squad; a private soldier; a recruit. Also *transf.*

1933 G. Ingram *Stir* xvi. 254 You get the screws and squaddies to shoot at us! Why, you're—well mad, you are. **1943** Hunt & Pringle *Service Slang* 61 *Squaddie*, recruit —new to the squad. **1959** I. Jefferies *Thirteen Days* viii. 105, I had a motley but effective army of luckless squaddies who had been selected by orderly sergeants. **1970** *Daily Tel.* (Colour Suppl.) 30 Oct. 25/4 Most of the Beatles have been seen several times, as have Danny Cohn-Bendit, Jean-Jacques Lebel, the CIA, of course, and drug squaddies with joss sticks and beards. **1978** J. B. Hilton *Some run Crooked* xi. 114 'It needn't have been a squaddy who'd lost the knife.' 'It was a soldier's knife.'

'squadding, *vbl. sb.* [f. squad *sb.*[1] or *v.*] The action of forming into or drawing up in squads. Also *attrib.*

1802 James *Milit. Dict.* s.v., The same rules for squadding hold good on a march, and in all situations whatever. **1868** *Daily News* 15 July, The squadding lists for the morning.. are scanned. **1882** *Pall Mall G.* 12 July 9/1 The squadding is arranged..so as to give every competitor a change of time ..when he fires at the different ranges.

'squaddy, *a.* Now *dial.* and *U.S.* [Cf. squad *a.*] Short and thick-set: squat, squab.

1593 Rich *Greenes Newes* G 3 b, He was a fatte squaddy Monke, that had beene well fedde in some Cloyster. **1840** Spurdens *Suppl. Voc. E. Anglia*, *Squaddy*, squoddy; short of stature, and sturdy. *a* **1848** 'Maj. J. Downing' *May-day* (Bartlett), I had hardly got seated, when in come a great, stout, fat, squaddy woman.

†'squader. *Obs.* [ad. older F. *esquadre* (*escoadre, escoydre*; also *squadre, scouadre*), mod.F. *escadre*, ad. It. *squadra* (Pg. *esquadra*, Sp. *escuadra*) square, company, squadron.] A squadron, company, squad.

1590 *Ordonances & Instructions for Musters* 31 Euery companie or squader of any companie. **1606** Birnie *Kirk-Buriall* (1833) xix, The next squader that commes in, are captanes of cheef. **1632** Lithgow *Trav.* x. 449 The Fleete was diuided in three Squaders. *Ibid.* 481 There being a Squader of his Maiesties Ships lying in the Road.

‖squadra ('skwadra). *Hist.* Pl. **squadre.** [It.; cf. squadron *sb.*] In Italy: a paramilitary squad organized to support and promulgate Fascism; a Fascist cadre.

1922 *English Rev.* XXXV. 558 When the Fascista army is mobilised..full authority is given to a secret military command. Their smallest unit is the 'manipolo'; then come the 'squadra', 'centuria', 'coörte', and 'legione'. **1924** K. L. Roberts *Black Magic* ii. 55 The smallest military unit of the Fascisti was the squadra of eight or ten or fifteen men—any small number. Three squadre made a manipolo. **1967** C. Seton-Watson *Italy from Liberalism to Fascism* xiii. 571 As the *squadre* grew in strength and boldness, they held up socialist local councils at the pistol point [*sic*] and forced them to resign. **1974** J. White tr. *Poulantzas's Fascism & Dictatorship* iii. iii. 126 Para-military *squadre* were also formed outside the *fasci*, even if most fascists took part in them.

†'squadrant, *sb.* and *a. Obs.* [ad. It. *squadrante*, pres. pple. of *squadrare* to square.]

A. *sb.* **1.** A square piece of something; a side of a square. Cf. quadrant *sb.*[2] 2 and 2 b.

1595 *Locrine* ii. v. 5 How brauely this yoong Brittain.., Mouing the massie squadrants of the ground, Heapes hills on hills. **1599** A. M. tr. *Gabelhouer's Bk. Physicke* 128/2 Put all this together in a little bagge, a qu. of an Elle in his squadrant.

2. A squadron of soldiers or ships.

1614 Sir R. Dudley in *Fortescue Papers* (Camden) 11 His Majesty maye make as manye of these as he please for his safetye and strenthe, but lesse then 6 were no fitt squadrant.

B. *adj.* Of a square form.

1599 A. M. tr. *Gabelhouer's Bk. Physicke* 310/2 Applye.. theron a squadrante boulster moystened in wine. **1642** Bird *Mag. Hon.* 136 A List shall be made in an even and plain ground, then Squadrant, that is to say, every Square 60 foot East, West, North, and South.

†'squadrate, *a. Obs. rare.* Also 7 *Sc.* **squadrat.** [ad. It. *squadrato, -ata*, pa. pple. of *squadrare* to square. Cf. quadrate *a.* 1.] Square-shaped, rectangular.

1632 Lithgow *Trav.* (1906) 386 At every spacious squadrat corner, there is a high Turret erected. *Ibid.* 387 A rotundo, with a wide leaden top, and on each side thereof a squadrat Steeple. **1784** J. Barry *Lect. Art* iii. (1848) 133 The hands..are a little mannered and squadrate.

†'squadrature. *Obs.*[−1] [ad. It. *squadratura*. Cf. quadrature 1.] A square figure or shape.

1592 R. D. *Hypnerotomachia* 42 b, Statues of fine mettal.. Which were fastened in a Marble, cut into a squadrature.

†squadrilla (skwɒ'drɪlə). *temporary.* [Blend of squadron *sb.* and flotilla. Cf. F. *escadrille.*] = squadron *sb.* 3 b.

1914 *Daily Mail* 28 Dec. 5/1 A squadrilla of five German aeroplanes caused a hundred casualties in the suburbs of Warsaw. **1916** *Glasgow Herald* 18 Aug. 8 Squadrillas of aeroplanes were sent forward to bring down or drive back the enemy aviators. **1917** *Daily Chron.* 11 Dec. 2/3 The strength of the German aviation services..rather more than 200 squadrillas.

squadrism ('skwɒdrɪz(ə)m). [ad. It. *squadrismo* (also used), f. squadra.] The organization and activities of the *squadre*.

1926 B. B. Carter tr. *L. Sturzo's Italy & Fascismo* ii. 46 The phenomenon of *arditismo* and *squadrismo*, or the use of armed irregular bands. **1932** H. R. Spencer *Govt. & Politics of Italy* xii. 115 After the March on Rome the existence of the *squadra* and the guerilla habit known as *squadrismo* constituted a serious difficulty for a régime that was seeking to regularize itself. **1940** *Ann. Reg. 1939* 195 All the new office-holders are old Fascists from the period of 'squadrism' (the earliest Fascist formation). **1954** B. & R. North tr. *Duverger's Pol. Parties* i. i. 39 Hitler reacted violently against the tendencies of Roehm, Mussolini against the excesses of squadrism. **1967** C. Seton-Watson *Italy from Liberalism to Fascism* xiii. 571 At the end of 1920 *squadrismo* spread from its training ground in Venezia Giulia to Emilia.

squadrist ('skwɒdrɪst). Pl. **‖squadristi** (skwa'dristi); **squadrists.** [ad. It. *squadrista*, f. as prec.] A member of a *squadra*. Also *attrib.*

1938 E. Ambler *Cause for Alarm* iv. 62 His father had been killed by the Squadristi in nineteen-twenty-three. **1957** *Encycl. Brit.* XII. 802/1 In the early years the *squadristi* had freely used rubber truncheons and castor oil. **1967** C. Seton-Watson *Italy from Liberalism to Fascism* xiii. 571 In July 1920..youths of the Trieste Fascio..burnt down the headquarters of the Slovene organisations... This was the first appearance of *squadristi*. **1973** *Times Lit. Suppl.* 2 Mar. 226/1 The *ras* of Cremona could claim the support of the 'squadrists'. *Ibid.*, The ultimate limit to Farinacci's squadrist ethic was its dependence upon Fascism's capacity to retain power. **1977** M. Walker *National Front* i. 19 They [*sc.* Mosley's army] had neither the numbers nor the organization of Hitler's *Sturmabteilung* or Mussolini's *Squadristi*.

squadrol ('skwɒdrəʊl). *U.S. slang.* [f. squad *sb.* + pat)rol *sb.*] A small police van.

1961 in Webster. **1965** J. McCormick *Bravo* ii. 44, I sat between them in the front seat of the squadrol, stone faced, my arms crossed, as we drove off under the thin pealing of noontime bells from Loyalty Chapel. **1972** B. Garfield *Line of Succession* (1974) i. 38 The Plymouth..was a block ahead when the squadrol, its red and blue lights flashing, came in sight on a collision course. **1976** *Tel.* (Brisbane) 21 Dec. 36/5 No one got excited when the small van, called a 'squadrol', pulled up in front of the Starr Hotel at 617 West Madison.

squadron ('skwɒdrən), *sb.* Also 6 **squadrone, -onne,** 7 *Sc.* **squadroun.** [ad. It. *squadrone* (f. *squadra* square), whence also Sp. *escuadron*, Pg. *esquadrão*, older F. *squadron* (*scadron*) and *esquadron* (mod.F. *escadron*).]

I. †1. *Mil.* A body of soldiers drawn up or arranged in square formation. *Obs.*

1562 J. Shute tr. *Cambini's Turk. War* Ep. Ded. *iiij b, There shalbe a squadrone ordered and in the myddest of the same shalbe a voyde space throughoute the squadrone. **1581** Styward *Mart. Discipl.* ii. 156 The poore Swizers,..not beeing able to furnishe themselues with horse, were the first deuisers of the pike and the Squadronnes. **1616** Bullokar *Eng. Expos.*, *Squadron*, a square forme in a battell. **1656** Blount *Glossogr.*, *Squadron*,..a certain number of Soldiers ranged into a square Body or Battalion. This word is most commonly appropriated to Horsmen.

2. *Mil.* **a.** A relatively small body or detachment of men.

1579 Digges *Stratiot.* 91 That euery Squadron or bodie of the watche haue theyr Armour..in readinesse. **1579** Fenton *Guicciard.* i. (1599) 27 His army contained little lesse then a hundreth squadrons of men at armes, accounting xx. men to a squadron. **1590** Sir J. Smyth *Disc. Weapons* 3 b, A squadron of armed men in the field being readie to encounter with another squadron. **1617** Moryson *Itin.* ii. 66 Leaving his foot in two squadrons of 250 each, himselfe with the horse passed to Dundalke. **1672** Villiers (Dk. Buckhm.) *Rehearsal* v. (Arb.) 121 To have a long relation of Squadrons here, and Squadrons there: what is that but a dull prolixity? **1720** Pope *Iliad* xx. 414 Through yon wide host this arm shall scatter fear, And thin the squadrons with my single spear. **1776** Mickle tr. *Camoen's Lusiad* iii. 111 The mountain echoes with the wild affright Of flying squadrons. **1810** Scott *Lady of L.* i. xxxi, Trump nor pibroch summon here Mustering clans, or squadrons tramping. **1878** B. Taylor *Deukalion* ii. iii. 68 In one squadron set To fight the world's long battle.

fig. **1656** Cowley *Pindar. Odes, Plagues Egypt* xi, All the full-charg'd clouds in ranged Squadrons move, And fill the spacious Plains above.

b. *spec.* A body of cavalry, usually composed of between one and two hundred men.

1702 *Milit. Dict.* (1704), *Squadron*, a Body of Horse, the number not fixt, but from an hundred to two hundred Men. **1768** Pennant *Brit. Zool.* I. 3 The enemy was broken through by the impetuous charge of our squadrons. **1832** *Regul. & Instr. Cavalry* iii. 45 Two or more Squadrons compose a Regiment. Squadrons are called 1st, 2d, 3d, &c., counting from the right of the Regiment. *Ibid.* 57 March past by Squadrons. **1893** *Times* 11 July 11/4 The march past followed, first in column of squadrons at a walk,..next at a canter by squadrons.

3. a. A division of a fleet forming one body under the command of a flag-officer; a detachment of warships told off for some particular duty. ***flying squadron***: see flying *ppl. a.* 4 d.

1588 Archdeacon tr. *True Discourse Army K. Spain* 17 Squadron of the Galeons of Portugall. *Ibid.* 19 There is in this Squadron 12 Vesselles. **1607** Dekker *Whore Babylon* Wks. 1873 II. 257 In the first Squadron twelue great

Galeons Floate like twelue moouing Castles. **1670** LASSELS *Voy. Italy* II. 271 [The kingdom of Naples'] ordinary squadron of gallyes are but 20. **1703** *Lond. Gaz.* No. 3937/3 He ordered the Captain of the Nonsuch to stretch a-head of the Squadron. **1743** BULKELEY & CUMMINS *Voy. S. Seas* 6 We judged this to be Admiral Pizarro's Squadron, sent out in Pursuit of Commodore Anson. **1800** WELLINGTON in Gurw. *Desp.* (1834) I. 135 The troops destined to sail with the squadron under Admiral Rainier. **1849–50** ALISON *Hist. Europe* V. xxxiii. §17. 494 A squadron of nine sail of the line, four bombs, and five frigates, was despatched to the Sound. **1865** H. PHILLIPS *Amer. Paper Curr.* II. 91 It was known that a French squadron was coming to America.

transf. **1807** J. BARLOW *Columb.* IV. 90 From Tago's bank, from Albion's rocky round, Commercing squadrons o'er the billows bound. ? **1878** B. HARTE *Man on Beach* 13 Low down the horizon still lingered a few white flecks—the flying squadrons of the storm.

b. *Air Force.* A small operational unit in an air force, consisting of aircraft and the personnel necessary to fly them.

1912 *Times* 9 May 14/5 A party of officers and non-commissioned officers..are to leave the Aviation School at Farnborough on May 15... These will form the nucleus of two flying squadrons of the new Royal Flying Corps. **1919** *Daily Mail Year Bk.* 46/2 The range of such raiding squadrons..tends to grow constantly from day to day. **1939** [see GROUP *sb.* 3 e]. **1942** T. RATTIGAN *Flare Path* I. 26 He was on a week's leave, and we were married before he went back to his Squadron. **1959** [see FLIGHT *sb.*[1] 1 h]. **1978** R. V. JONES *Most Secret War* xliv. 420 The main point, though, was the esprit de corps, and this was what Hartley had meant with his 'last *squadron* in the Air Force'.

†**4.** A squad (of a ship's company). *Obs.*

1626 CAPT. SMITH *Accid. Yng. Seamen* 7 Then diuide them into squadrons according to your numbers and burthen of your ship. **1627** —— *Seaman's Gram.* ix. 38 These are to..doe all duties each halfe, or each squadron for eight Glasses or foure houres which is a watch.

5. a. A comparatively large group or number of people, etc.; an organized body of persons. Also const. *of*.

1617 MORYSON *Itin.* I. 116 They say that Christ with the squadrons of the Fathers, passed this way when hee ascended from Hell. **1640** SIR W. MURE *Counterbuff* 96 That Esterne clyme..Where Squadrons of our Nation did abound. **1684** *Contempl. St. Man* II. ii. (1699) 173 The Hallelujahs which..the Squadrons of those blessed Spirits sing. **1713** J. WARDER *True Amazons* 25 They [*sc.* bees] send forth a Squadron to fetch in Honey. **1792** JEFFERSON *Writ.* (1830) IV. 470 These measures had established corruption in the legislature, where there was a squadron devoted to the nod of the Treasury. **1824** SOUTHEY *Sir T. More* (1831) I. 284 To join one or other of the numerous squadrons of dissent. **1897** MARY KINGSLEY *W. Africa* 484 The whole district will come, not in a squadron, but just when it suits them.

b. *transf.* A multitude *of* some thing or things.

1668 CULPEPPER & COLE *Barthol. Anat.* II. vi. 99 Yet that is false which Fallopius tells us, that a great Squadron of Nerves is spread up and down the Basis of the heart. **1680** ALSOP *Mischief Imposit.* xii. 96 He has..First, a Squadron of Considerations, and secondly, a Pacquet of Advices. **1930** T. S. ELIOT tr. *St.-J. Perse's Anabasis* 39 Squadrons of stars pass the edge of the world. **1978** J. A. MICHENER *Chesapeake* 759 What Steed did next, in the late 1950s, was to pension off his field hands and purchase a squadron of gigantic automatic corn harvesters.

†**6.** *U.S.* A division or ward of a town, community, or district. *Obs.*

1636 in *Cent. Dict.* s.v. **1671** *Town Records, Groton, Mass.* (Cent.), Agreed upon by the selectmen for the..calling out of their men to work, that is within their several squadrons. **1749** *Town Records, Marlborough, Mass.* (Ibid.), A committee of seven men to apportion the school in six societies or squadrons,..taking the northwesterly corner for one squadron.

7. A body of cardinals hovering between the main factions in a conclave. (Cf. SQUADRONIST.)

1670 G. H. *Hist. Cardinals* II. II. 161 He manag'd him-self so with his flying Squadron, that it gave no little disgust to the Crowns. **1906** *Edin. Rev.* Oct. 346 Cardinal de Retz and Cardinal Azzolino were of the squadron.

8. *attrib.*, as *squadron ball*, *form*, etc. *squadron commander*, *leader*, *officer*.

1862 *London Rev.* 16 Aug. 139 The squadron which is to go down Channel on the day after the squadron ball. **1907** R. HERMON-HODGE *Let.* 12 Jan. in R. S. Churchill *Winston S. Churchill* (1969) II. Compan. I. 640 In reporting on the Regiment in 1905 the GOC remarks 'I thought the Squadron Commanders exceptionally well qualified for their positions'. **1976** *Southern Even. Echo* (Southampton) 15 Nov. 9/2 If the junior NCO's are not doing their job properly it does not matter how good the squadron commander is. **1632** LITHGOW *Trav.* II. 49 When they enter the gates, they must deliuer their weapons to the Corporall of the Squadron company. **1894** *Outing* Sept. 477/2 These three gentlemen thoroughly understand the handling of a regatta and a squadron cruise. **1592** KYD *Sp. Trag.* I. ii. 32 Our battels both were pitcht in squadron forme. **1832** *Regul. & Instr. Cavalry* II. 20 The Squadron-Leader advances two horses' lengths. **1919** W. S. CHURCHILL *Let.* 8 Feb. in M. Gilbert *Winston S. Churchill* (1977) IV. Compan. I. 517 The ranks in contemplation are as follows:—Air Marshal: Air Commodore: Wing Commander: Squadron Leader: Flight Leader: Flying Officer or Observer. *a* **1944** K. DOUGLAS *Alamein to Zem Zem* (1946) II. 13 He now found himself second in command of a squadron whose squadron leader had been a subaltern under him before. **1972** A. PRICE *Col. Butler's Wolf* i. 9 Squadron Leader Roskill is a colleague of mine at the Ministry of Defence. **1796** *Instr. & Reg. Cavalry* (1813) 230 Some of the squadron flank officers who are otherwise disposed of. **1943** J. R. WILLIAMS *Aircraftwoman Grey* xiii. 146, I have asked Squadron Officer Hedley, the Group Officer, to call and see you. **1971** K. B. BEAUMAN *Partners in Blue* iv. 72 The Squadron Officer was one of six of this rank appointed on September 27th... She had joined the Directorate in August.

II. †**9.** A right-angled area, figure, etc.; a side of a square. *Obs.* Cf. SQUADRANT *sb.* 1.

1599 HAKLUYT *Voy.* II. 221 They sell the earth within the wall, for so much a squadron. **1599** A. M. tr. *Gabelhouer's Bk. Physicke* 153/2 About a quar. of a yarde in the squadrone therof.

†**10.** A square parenthesis-mark. *Obs.*$^{-1}$

1618 *Worthington's Anker Christian Doctr.* Printer to Rdr. 18 Because the holie Scriptures are very much cited in this Booke, I haue thought it better..to include them within two squadrons [ ].

'squadron, *v. rare.* [f. the sb.] *trans.* To form into, or as into, a squadron or squadrons.

1862 D. GRAY *Luggie*, etc. 19 By a furious wind Squadron'd, the hurrying clouds range the roused sky.

'squadronal, *a.* [f. SQUADRON *sb.* + -AL[1].] Of or pertaining to a squadron or squadrons.

1898 J. S. CORBETT *Drake & Tudor Navy* II. v. 177 Here we have the first trace of any squadronal organization. **1902** *Westm. Gaz.* 23 July 3/1 A diagram showing the squadronal flags of the English ships in colour.

‖**Squadrone** (skwa'drone). Now *Hist.* Also 8 *Sc.* -ronie, -rony. [a. It. *squadrone* (*volante*): cf. SQUADRON *sb.* 7.] A Scottish political party in the early years of the 18th century.

1707–14 *Lockhart Papers* (1817) I. 294 In the main the united Tories and Squadrone did not succeed so weel as they expected. **1708** *Caldwell Pap.* (Maitland) 215 If ye court be generous they'll at least procure for him ye fines for a wrongous imprisonment that is due by the squadrony. **1800** A. CARLYLE *Autob.* 40 By good-luck for the clergy, there was another party distinction among them,..viz., that of Argathelian and Squadrone.

†**b.** As *adj.* Hovering between two parties.

c **1720** WARDEN in *Wodrow's Corr.* (1843) II. 538, I am squadronie in that matter, being sometime on one side and sometime on another.

'squadroned, *ppl. a.* [f. SQUADRON *sb.*] Formed into squadrons; drawn up in a squadron. Also *transf.*

1667 MILTON *P.L.* XII. 367 They gladly thither haste, and by a Quire Of squadrond Angels hear his Carol sung. **1726** POPE *Odyss.* XXIV. 289 Thy squadron'd vineyards well thy art declare. **1792** J. BARLOW *Conspir. Kings* 85 See the long pomp in gorgeous glare display'd, The tinsel'd guards, the squadron'd horse parade. **1841** TUPPER *Twins* xxiv, As if the squadroned cavalry of heaven had charged across the seas. **1864** NEALE *Seatonian Poems* 65 Squadron'd forests, marshall'd as for fight, March o'er the land.

†**'squadronist.** *Obs.* [ad. F. *squadroniste* or It. *squadronista*, f. *squadrone* (*volante*): see SQUADRON *sb.* 7.] One of the cardinals belonging to the unattached party in a conclave.

1670 G. H. *Hist. Cardinals* III. III. 319 The Squadronists are all unanimously for Rospigliosi. **1670** *Lond. Gaz.* No. 4038/2 These Cardinals from France, who..have already gained to their party divers of the Squadronists.

†**squage,** *v. Obs.*$^{-1}$ [Of obscure origin.] *trans.* To dirty (? with handling).

a **1500** *Receipt* in *Rel. Ant.* I. 163 For to make clene thy boke yf yt be defowlyd or squaged.

squail (skweɪl), *sb.* [Of doubtful origin: cf. SQUAIL *v.*[2] and SKAYLES.]

1. *pl.* The game of ninepins; skittles. *s.w. dial.*

1847 in HALLIWELL (*Somerset*). **1883, 1888** in Hampshire and Somerset glossaries.

2. *pl.* A table-game in which counters or disks are propelled towards some mark by snapping.

App. introduced in 1857 by Mr. John Jaques, London.

1862 POLLOCK *Pers. Remembr.* (1887) II. 105 Drank tea with Faradays at Royal Institution, and played at squails. **1865** *Pall Mall G.* 12 June 11 Squails, or some such frivolous game, often serves to banish *ennui*.

b. A disk or counter used in this game.

1862 CALVERLEY *Verses & Transl.* 16 Or anon..Urge towards the table's centre, With unerring hand, the squail. **1900** UPWARD *Eben. Lobb* 153 An overcoat..with a driver's cape, and eighteen buttons, the size of squails, down the front.

3. = SQUAILER. (See also SQUOYLE.)

1883– in dial. glossaries (Hamps., Berks., Wilts.). **1899** *Outlook* 7 Jan. 714/1.

†**squail,** *v.*[1] *Obs.*$^{-1}$ [Imitative: cf. SQUEAL *v.*] *intr.* To make a shrill noise.

1526 *Pilgr. Perf.* (W. de W. 1531) 158 b, Not syngynge in ye nose as pygges, nor in the tethe as many women do, ne squaylynge, as maremaydes.

squail, *v.*[2] Chiefly *dial.* Also 7 squayle, 8– squale, 9 squoil, etc. [Of obscure origin.]

1. *intr.* To throw a (loaded) stick or similar missile (*at* some object).

c **1626** *Dick of Devon* II. iii. in Bullen *Old Pl.* (1883) II, Not soe much as the leg of a Spanyard left to squayle at their owne appletrees. **1787** GROSE *Prov. Gloss.*, *Squale*, to throw a stick as at a cock. **1795** in Mrs. Sandford *T. Poole & Friends* (1888) I. 112 They happened to meet some men carrying a hen up the street with the intention of squalling [*sic*] at her. **1821** SOUTHEY *Life & Corr.* (1849) I. 54 The boys were employed also to squail at the bannets. **1823–** in s.w. dial. glossaries (Somerset, Wilts., Dorset, Hamps., Isle of Wight). **1882** JEFFERIES *Bevis* II. v. 67 In the orchard Bevis and Mark squailed at the pears with short sticks. **1896** *Westm. Gaz.* 2 Dec. 2/1 The Marquis's gamekeepers did not love us, but we squailed in spite of them.

2. *trans.* To strike or hit by throwing a stick or squailer.

1844 W. BARNES *Poems Dorset Dial.* 143, I squâil'd her, though; an' miade her run. **1884** *Contemp. Rev.* Mar. 343 They 'squailed' fowls—that is to say, they tied them to stakes and hurled cudgels at them..on Shrove Tuesday, for a treat.

3. To cast or throw. Also *fig.*

1876 T. HARDY *Ethelberta* II. 240 These easterly rains..come wi' might enough to squail a man into his grave.

'squailer. Orig. *s.w. dial.* [f. prec.] A loaded stick, esp. used for throwing at small game or apples.

1847 in HALLIWELL. **1879** JEFFERIES *Amateur Poacher* iii, For making a 'squailer' a tea-cup was the best mould. **1896** *Westm. Gaz.* 2 Dec. 2/1 We used to use squailers at Marlborough... You held your squailer by the small end.

'squailing, *vbl. sb.* Also 8 **scailing.** [f. as prec.] The action of throwing a loaded stick (*at* a cock or other object).

1756 B. MARTIN *Misc. Corr.* Jan. 229 Cock-scailing, Cock-fighting, Bull-baiting, &c. are of a criminal Nature. **1795** *Sporting Mag.* VI. 157 The custom of squailing at cocks is very prevalent in the part of the country in which I reside [Ipswich]. **1825** JENNINGS *Observ. Dial. W. Eng.* 31 *Cock-squailing*, a barbarous game, consisting in tying a cock to a stake, and throwing a stick at him from a given distance, so as to destroy the bird. **1847** HALLIWELL s.v., Squailing therefore is often very awkwardly performed, because the thing thrown cannot be well directed. **1888** *Longman's Mag.* XIII. 516 Birds'-nesting, egg-stringing, squailing at birds, ..these of course were common.

squaimish(e, -ous, obs. ff. SQUEAMISH, -OUS.

squake, obs. variant of SQUEAK *v.*

†**'squalder.** *Obs. rare.* [Of obscure origin.] Some species of jelly-fish.

1659 DR. R. ROBINSON in Sir T. Browne *Wks.* (1835) I. 423 About us they [jelly-fish] are generally called squalders, but are indeed evidently fishes, although not described in any Ichthyology I have yet mett with. *a* **1682** SIR T. BROWNE *Norf. Fishes* Ibid. IV. 333 Sea stars in great plenty. ..Whether they be bred out of the urticus, squalders, or sea jellies, as many report, we cannot confirm.

squalene ('skweɪliːn). *Chem.* [f. SQUAL(US + -ENE.] A colourless, oily, liquid, triterpenoid hydrocarbon, $C_{30}H_{50}$, which in animals is an intermediate in the biosynthesis of cholesterol and occurs esp. in the liver oils of sharks and other elasmobranch fishes.

1916 M. TSUJIMOTO in *Jrnl. Industr. & Engin. Chem.* VIII. 896/2 From..the fact that the author has discovered the hydrocarbon first in the liver oils of the squaloid sharks, he proposes the name '*Squalene*' for the hydro-carbon. **1938** [see ŒSTRIN]. **1964** *New Scientist* 22 Oct. 221/1 These rearrangements occur as part of a marvellously complicated, concerted enzymic process by which the long molecule of squalene is folded and formed into rings. **1978** *Sci. Amer.* Sept. 94/1 Sterols, such as cholesterol and the steroid hormones, are flat, platelike molecules derived from the compound squalene.

†**squaleote,** *v. Obs.*$^{-1}$ (Meaning obscure.)

1562 LEIGH *Armorie* Pref. ¶iv b, His cote..was of cloth with a burgunian garde of bare velute, well bawdefied on the halfe placard, and squaleoted in the fore quarters.

squalid ('skwɒlɪd), *a.* Also 6–8 **squallid,** 7 **-ed.** [ad. L. *squālid-us*, f. *squālēre* to be dry, rough, dirty, etc. So It. *squallido*, OF. *squalide*, *scalide*, Pg. *esqualido*.]

I. 1. Naturally foul and repulsive by the presence of slime, mud, etc., and the absence of all cultivation or care.

1591 SPENSER *Virg. Gnat* 543 The squalid lakes of Tartarie, And griesly Feends of hell him terrifie. **1664** H. MORE *Myst. Iniq.* 565 Those that seek for Inspirations and Revelations in By-holes amongst the squallid Sepulchers of the dead. **1697** DRYDEN *Virg. Georg.* IV. 686 All these Cocytus bounds with squalid Reeds, With muddy Ditches, and with deadly Weeds. **1743** FRANCIS tr. *Horace, Odes* II. ix. I. 221 Nor everlasting Rain deforms The squalid Fields. **1887** RUSKIN *Præterita* II. 150 No squalid fields of mud and thistles.

b. In general use: Repulsive or loathsome to look at.

1620 DEKKER *Dreame* (1860) 31 Then clapping their obstreperous squallid wings, Each of them on the frozen ruffian dings Such bitter blasts. **1822–7** GOOD *Study Med.* (1829) III. 211 The skin will..be covered over with ecthyma, impetigo, or some other squalid eruption.

2. Foul through neglect or want of cleanliness; repulsively mean and filthy: **a.** Of clothing.

1596 SPENSER *F.Q.* v. i. 13 They saw a Squire in squallid weed, Lamenting sore his sorrowfull sad tyne. **1616** CHAPMAN *Homer's Hymn Pan* 131 Although a God he were Clad in a squallid sheepskinn. **1623** MASSINGER *Dk. Milan* III. i, Nor come I as a slave, Pinioned and fettered, in a squalid weed. **1726** POPE *Odyss.* XVII. 412 A figure despicable, old, and poor, In squalid vests, with many a gaping rent.

b. Of dwellings or similar places.

1628 T. MAY in Le Grys *Barclay's Argenis* 107 Those valiant Chiefes..In a darke squallid Dungeon must not dye. *a* **1700** EVELYN *Diary* 3 Aug. 1654, 'Tis a squalid den made in the rock. **1829** LYTTON *Disowned* 53 Some squalid and obscure quarter of the city. **1845** DISRAELI *Sybil* (1863) 198 The general appearance of the room, however, though dingy, was not squalid. **1891** FARRAR *Darkn. & Dawn* xii, The squalid taverns and lodging-houses of the poorest of that vast and mongrel populace.

c. Of persons, their appearance, etc.

1642 H. MORE *Song of Soul* III. App. lxii, Why gaze you thus on my sad squalid face. **1662** HIBBERT *Body Divinity* II. 17 When God beholds us as we are in our selves we appear vile and squallid. **1729** SHELVOCKE *Artillery* v. 338 Together with the Inferior Prisoners all Dirty, Dejected, Squallid, and as it were half starved. **1780** *Mirror* No. 70, The squalid and death-like appearance of the good old man. **1834** PRINGLE *Afr. Sk.* 302 The prisoners..exhibited a strange array of wild and swarthy visages, squalid with neglect and misery. **1847** EMERSON *Poems, Monadnoc* Wks. (Bohn) I. 433 Is yonder squalid peasant all That this proud nursery could breed? **1875** FARRAR *Silence & Voices* Ser. I. 5 The poorest and most squalid savage.

absol. **1840** HOOD *Kilmansegg, Marriage* xiii, Bravely she shone..As she sailed through the crowd of squalid and poor.

Comb. **1837** CARLYLE *Fr. Rev.* III. I. iv, Phantasms, squalid-horrid, shaking their dirk and muff.

3. Of qualities, conditions, etc.: Marked or characterized by filth, dirt, or squalor.

1621 BURTON *Anat. Mel.* I. ii. II. v, Winter is like vnto it, vgly, foule, squalid. **1638** SIR T. HERBERT *Trav.* (ed. 2) 242 Out of squallid wantonnesse they would overcharge their wide mouthes with pelo or other meat. **1784** COWPER *Task* I. 579 Strange! that a creature rational..should..prefer Such squalid sloth to honourable toil! **1822** SHELLEY *Chas. I*, I. 163 Here is health Followed by grim disease,..wealth by squalid want. **1849** MISS MULOCK *Ogilvies* xvii, While squalid poverty grovels in between. **1875** HELPS *Soc. Press.* iii. 51 Without which in great towns the life of man will always be barbarous, squalid, and most unsatisfactory.

4. *fig.* Wretched, miserable, morally repulsive or degraded.

a **1660** *Contemp. Hist. Irel.* (Ir. Archæol. Soc.) I. 277 To giue a luster unto the author and his squalled inuentions. **1797** BURKE *Regic. Peace* iii. Wks. 1808 VIII. 313 The rest of the squalid tribe of the representatives of degraded kings. **1856** EMERSON *Eng. Traits, Literature*, Squalid contentment with conventions..betray[s] the ebb of life and spirit. **1890** *Spectator* 16 Aug., What a morally squalid Session we have had!

II. †**5.** Dry, parched; marked by drought. *Obs.*

1615 CROOKE *Body of Man* 541 In a marrish and weeping ground no grasse is brought forth neither yet in a squallid and hot soile. **1621** BURTON *Anat. Mel.* I. i. I. i, If the earth be barren then for want of raine, if dry and squalid, it yeeld no fruit. **1661** LOVELL *Hist. Anim. & Min.* 194 They are great in autumne, and are best in a squalid yeare.

†**6.** Rough; shaggy; unkempt. *Obs.*

1628 BURTON *Anat. Mel.* (ed. 3) I. iii. II. iv. 193 The skin is many times rough, squalid, especially..about the armes. **1631** P. FLETCHER *Piscatory Eclog.* vi, [Diana] with a mighty spear Flings down a bristled bore, or els a squalid bear. **1664** EVELYN *Sylva* 3 Divers of those [young trees] which are found in Woods..being overdripp'd become squalid and mossie. **1722** WOLLASTON *Relig. Nat.* i. 17, I do not by this deny them to be poor, any more than I should deny a man to have a squalid beard by not shaving him.

7. Having a pinched and miserable appearance. Of complexion: Having a dull unhealthy look.

1661 LOVELL *Hist. Anim. & Min.* 225 Sprats. They are squalid, leane, and not of copious aliment. **1753** *Scots Mag.* Oct. 516/1 Such as were of a squallid, or pale swarthy complexion. *a* **1776** R. JAMES *Fevers* (1778) 123 [It causes] an uneasy sensation on the left side,..attended with a squalid countenance. **1823** J. BADCOCK *Dom. Amusem.* 31 Loaves made of adulterated flour are always low and squalid; *i.e.* they appear small for their weight. **1828** LYTTON *Pelham* li, His complexion sallow and squalid.

Hence ˈ**squalidly** *adv.*

a **1704** T. BROWN *Walk round Lond., Upon Compters* Wks. 1709 III. III. 53 Their Dress [was] squallidly neglected. **1847** WEBSTER, *Squalidly*, in a squalid, filthy manner.

squalidity (skwɒˈlɪdɪtɪ). [ad. L. *squāliditās*, or f. SQUALID *a.* + -ITY.] The quality or character of being foul or squalid; filthiness, squalidness.

1668 H. MORE *Div. Dial.* III. xxiii. (1713) 227 That horrid Squalidity in the Usages of the barbarous Nations presseth hard toward that Conclusion. **1721** BAILEY, *Squalidity*, filthiness, nastiness, ill-favouredness. **1773** *Observ. State Poor* 34 Rags and vermin, squalidity and disease. **1823** *Blackw. Mag.* XIV. 252 He has no keeping about him, excepting a sort of medium tint of squalidity. **1857** KINGSLEY *Misc.* (1859) II. 340 Ill-built rows of undrained cottages,..left to run into squalidity and disrepair. **1875** HELPS *Soc. Press.* iii. 53 The hideous difficulty and squalidity which beset those who are placed low down in the world.

ˈ**squalidize**, *v. rare*⁻¹. [f. SQUALID *a.* + -IZE.] *trans.* To render squalid or filthy.

1837 *New Monthly Mag.* L. 430 Rather than..squalidise himself into the Lazarus that had so long sat at his gate.

ˈ**squalidness.** [f. SQUALID *a.* + -NESS.] = SQUALIDITY.

1727 BAILEY (vol. II), *Squalidness*, Foulness, Nastiness, Slovenliness. **1751** F. COVENTRY *Hist. Pompey* II. x. 219 The cunning little Animal..made his Escape from this Scene of Misery, Squallidness, and Poetry. **1812** SHELLEY in Hogg *Life* (1858) II. 101 A spectacle of squalidness and misery. **1851** HELPS *Comp. Solit.* xii. (1853) 226 The poor should have some place free from..the squalidness of home. **1877** PLUMPTRE *Trag. Sophocles* 106 And this his garb, whose time-worn squalidness Matches the time-worn face.

†**squalino**, *v. slang. Obs.*⁻¹ [f. SQUALL *v.*¹] *intr.* To squeal or squall.

1810 *Sporting Mag.* XXXV. 147 While Blowzy squalino'd like entrapped rat.

†**squall**, *sb.*¹ *Obs.* [Of obscure origin.]

1. A small or insignificant person. Usu. as a term of abuse.

1570 *Marr. Wit & Sci.* v. iii, This it is that makes me loke so leane, That lettes my groth, and makes me seeme a squall. **1589** E. A. *Triumphs Love & Fortune* E, But, sirra, you must know this same squall is the Dukes sonne. **1591** HARRINGTON *Orl. Fur.* XLIII. iv, Some miser, base deformed squall That save his riches hath no worthy parts. **1607** MIDDLETON *Michaelmas Term* III. i, Who would think now this fine sophisticated squall came out of the bosom of a barn, and the loins of a hay-tosser? *c* **1630** EDW. FORD *Ballad Norfolk Farmer's Journ. London* xi, A woman that is mighty tall, And yet her spouse a little squall.

transf. **1614** GORGES *Lucan* IX. 405 As his owne breed those [young ones that can look at the sun] he [the Eagle] affects: But euery wincking squall reiects.

2. Applied to a girl: (see quots.).

1607 MIDDLETON *Michaelmas Term* I. ii, Wouldst thou, a pretty, beautiful, juicy squall, live in a poor thrummed house i' th' country? **1611** COTGR., *Obeseau*,..a young minx, or little proud squall. **1630** J. TAYLOR (Water P.) *Wks.* II. 112 The rich Gull Gallant calls her Deare and Loue, Ducke, Lambe, Squall, Sweetheart, Cony, and his Doue.

squall (skwɔːl), *sb.*² Also 8 **squawl**. [f. SQUALL *v.*¹]

1. A discordant or violent scream; a loud, harsh cry.

1709 W. KING *Misc.* 518 Betty distorts her Face with hideous Squawl, And Mouth of a Foot wide begins to bawl. **1768–74** TUCKER *Lt. Nat.* (1834) II. 443 Very bad music, badly executed, being rather roars or squalls than songs. **1782** WOLCOT (P. Pindar) *Odes to R.A.'s* xiii. Wks. 1812 I. 42 My lovely strangers, one and all, Gave, all at once, a diabolic squawl. **1821** CLARE *Vill. Minstr.* I. 94 The crowing pheasant..Betrays his lair with awkward squalls. **1833** HT. MARTINEAU *Manch. Strike* vi. 69 The passing squalls of the baby, who, however, allowed himself to be quickly hushed. **1883** *Century Mag.* XXVIII. 189 Away up the cañon, a wild-cat welcomed us with three discordant squalls.

b. The action or habit of squalling or talking in a shrill voice.

1755 *Connoisseur* No. 51 ¶3 He was determined, that the babe..should be put out to nurse,—he hated the squall of children. **1825** CREEVEY in *C. Papers* (1904) II. 87 Altho' these young ladies..have all more or less of the quality squall, yet their manners are particularly correct.

†**2.** *Cant.* (See quot.) *Obs.*

1725 *New Cant. Dict.*, *Squawl*, a Voice; as, *The Cove as a bien Squawl*, the Fellow has a good Voice.

squall (skwɔːl), *sb.*³ [Of obscure origin: perhaps connected with prec.]

1. a. A sudden and violent gust, a blast or short sharp storm, of wind. orig. *Naut.*

1719 *Boyer's Dict. Royal* I, *Rafale, Rafal*,..squall. **1725** DE FOE *Voy. round World* (1840) 128 It blew..not only by squalls and sudden flaws but a settled terrible tempest. **1745** P. THOMAS *Jrnl. Anson's Voy.* 346 A very violent and sudden Squall took us quite a-head. **1820** SCORESBY *Acc. Arctic Reg.* I. 402 The squalls continued from five minutes to half an hour at a time. **1841** ELPHINSTONE *Hist. Ind.* II. 7 He was drowned, with all his family, in a sudden squall on the Indus. **1886** *Pall Mall G.* 4 Oct. 8/2 A fishing boat..was upset by a squall on the same day, and its three occupants perished.

Comb. **1898** *Daily News* 19 April 3/2 The squall-beaten shores of the Basque Provinces.

b. Const. *of* (wind, rain, snow, etc.).

1748 *Anson's Voy.* I. viii. 78 We had frequent squalls of rain and snow. **1777** ROBERTSON *Hist. Amer.* (1783) I. 55 A sudden squall of wind..landed them on an unknown island. **1844** H. H. WILSON *Brit. India* I. 347 Captain Cole landed ..in a heavy squall of wind and rain, which effectually concealed his movements. **1879** BEERBOHM *Patagonia* v. 68 We encountered squalls of hailstones of unusual size.

transf. and *fig.* ?**1878** B. HARTE *Man on Beach* i. 7 A sudden flurry and gray squall of sand pipers. **1887** STEVENSON *J. Nicholson* vi, Squalls of anger and lulls of sick collapse.

c. With distinguishing terms (see quots.).

1801 *Naval Chron.* VI. 91 A white squall passed over. **1823** CRABB *Technol. Dict.* s.v., A *black squall* is attended with a dark cloud, in distinction from a *white squall*, where there are no clouds, and a *thick squall*, accompanied with hail, sleet, &c. **1846** A. YOUNG *Naut. Dict.* 293 The Arched Squall..is usually distinguished by the arched form of the clouds near the horizon. *Ibid.*, The Descending Squall issues from clouds which are formed in the lower parts of the atmosphere near the observer. **1889** STEVENSON *Lett.* (1899) II. 136 We had a black squall astern on the port side and a white squall ahead to starboard.

2. *fig.* A disturbance or commotion; a quarrel; a storm: **a.** In general use. (Chiefly *Sc.*)

1813 BRUCE *Poems* II. 19 (E.D.D.), Keep out o' ilka squall aye. **1826** D. ANDERSON *Poems* 69 (E.D.D.), In raisin' or in reddin' squals [they] Met wi' their death. **1900** 'ALLEN RAINE' *Garthowen* i, There was a squall when that was found out.

b. In the phr. ***look out for squalls***. orig. *Naut.*

1837 MARRYAT *Dog Fiend* xxiv, Look out for squalls, that's all. **1850** SMEDLEY *Frank Fairlegh* xxxi, Mind your eye, and look out for squalls, for that's a rasper and no mistake. **1902** ELIZ. BANKS *Newspaper Girl* 299 Ah! Now, I suppose, we must look out for squalls. I suppose in this book you..are going to pay off old scores.

c. *U.S.* A bad temper.

1807–8 W. IRVING *Salmag.* (1824) 96 The old gentleman came home in quite a squall.

3. Special Comb.: **squall line**, a line along which high winds and storms are occurring (see also quot. 1950).

1906 *Q. Jrnl. Meteorol. Soc.* XXXII. 264 From the Kew curves we might be led to suppose that the velocity in the squall was approximately of the same magnitude as the velocity of the squall line. **1923** N. SHAW *Air & its Ways* 75 The surface boundary of the polar front in this region is called the 'squall line'. **1950** *Jrnl. Meteorol.* VII. 21/1 The term *squall line* is among the oldest in meteorology and is perhaps the least clearly defined. Prior to the general adoption..of the frontal theory of cyclones, it was customary to designate as a squall line any line of storms projecting in a general southerly and easterly direction from a depression... With the advent of the frontal theory, some of these lines of storms were redesignated more descriptively as *cold fronts*... There remained the lines of storms which appear in general in the warm sector of cyclones, roughly parallel to the cold front, and along which there is intense convective activity. **1979** L. J. BATTAN *Fund. Meteorol.* ix. 187 Most often the storms regarded as being in the organized class are those that form in lines or bands of thunderstorms, sometimes called squall lines... They commonly are initiated along a cold front, or ahead of, and nearly parallel to it.

squall, *sb.*⁴ *local.* [Of obscure origin.] A boggy or springy piece of ground.

1784 *Young's Annals Agric.* II. 43 In many of their fields they are troubled with springs; they call the wet spots *squalls*. **1794** [see SPEW *sb.* 3]. **1794** GRIGGS *Agric. Essex* 21 Where there are squails [*sic*], with sand or drift gravel, the passages are apt to choak in a short time.

squall (skwɔːl), *v.*¹ Also 7–9 **squawl** (8 **squawll**). [Imitative: cf. SQUEAL *v.* It is doubtful whether there is any direct connexion with some Scand. forms having the stem *skval-* and denoting noise of various kinds.]

1. *intr.* To scream loudly or discordantly: **a.** Of birds or animals.

a **1631** DRAYTON *Noah's Flood* Wks. (1748) 467/1 The raven croaks, the carrion crow doth squall, The pye doth chatter, and the partridge call. *a* **1721** PRIOR *Turtle & Sp.* 422 Begone..And hear thy dirty Off-spring Squawl From Bottles on a Suburb-Wall. [**1759** *Ann. Reg.* 65 They said, that as he squalled like a cat, they would dispatch him likewise.] **1842** TENNYSON *Day-Dream* 144 The parrot scream'd, the peacock squall'd. **1859** MISS CARY *Country Life* (1876) 263 A flock of geese swimming in a shallow pond and squalling when he comes near. **1883** STEVENSON *Treas. Isl.* III. xiii, They..gave a cheer that..sent the birds once more flying and squalling round the anchorage.

b. Of persons, esp. children.

The common usage. Freq. with a touch of contempt.

1687 MIÈGE *Gt. Fr. Dict.* II. s.v., The least Thing that ails him makes him squawl. *a* **1700** B. E. *Dict. Cant. Crew*, *Squawl*,..to cry aloud. **1724** SWIFT *Corinna* Wks. 1751 III. II. 154 She seem'd to laugh and squawl in rhymes. **1760** GOLDSM. *Cit. W.* lxxxv, If they be for war,..I should advise them to have a public congress, and there fairly squall at each other. **1835** *Politeness & Gd.-breeding* 76 If any thing unpleasant happens at table,..do not squall out. **1848** THACKERAY *Van. Fair* xxxix, Seated at the piano with the utmost gravity, and squalling to the best of her power. **1883** STEVENSON *Treas. Isl.* I. v, Don't stand here squalling.

2. *trans.* To utter or sing in a loud discordant tone. Also with *out*.

1703 T. BAKER *Tunbridge-Walks* I, To hear a parcel of Italian Eunuchs, like so many Cats, squawll out somewhat you don't understand. **1762** *Phil. Trans.* LII. 475 The woman squalled out, all of a sudden, that an adder..had stung her by the finger. **1779** *Mirror* No. 34, She sung, or rather squalled, a song of Sacchini's. **1835** *Court Mag.* VI. 25/1 One of the common-place psalm tunes, squalled by charity children.

†**squall**, *v.*² *Obs. rare.* Also 8 **squawl**. [Of obscure origin.]

1. *intr.* To turn the feet outwards in walking.

a **1661** FULLER *Worthies, Monmouth.* IV. (1662) 54 He was not onely what the Latines call *compernis*, knocking his knees together, and going out squalling with his feet, but also haulted a little.

2. *trans.* (See quot.)

a **1700** B. E. *Dict. Cant. Crew*, *Squawl*, to throw a wry.

squaller (ˈskwɔːlə(r)). [f. SQUALL *v.*¹ + -ER¹.] One who squalls or screams; one addicted to squalling; *esp.* a screaming child.

1687 MIÈGE *Gt. Fr. Dict.* II, Squawler, *Celui. qui crie.* **1760** *Ann. Reg.* 220 Italian squallers oft disgrace the stage. **1796** HUNTER tr. *St.-Pierre's Stud. Nat.* (1799) II. 538, I don't mind nosegays, nor these little squallers [nightingales]. **1816** MRS. SHELLEY in Dowden *Life Shelley* (1887) II. 62 Tell me, shall you be happy to have another little squaller? **1841** HEWLETT *Parish Clerk* I. 24 Mothers always sent for him to calm refractory squallers. **1872** 'A. MERION' *Odd Echoes Oxf.* 42 Fifty babies too, Warranted loud squallers.

ˈ**squallery.** *rare*⁻¹. [f. SQUALL *sb.*² + -ERY.] Loud and shrill singing.

1895 MEREDITH *Amazing Marriage* xxxix, The goodly number of honest fellows in the house of music who detested 'squallery'.

squalling (ˈskwɔːlɪŋ), *vbl. sb.* [f. SQUALL *v.*¹] The action of the verb; loud discordant screaming.

1677 MIÈGE *Fr. Dict.* II, Squeaking, or squalling. **1712** STEELE *Spect.* No. 509 ¶2 With the Din of Squalings, Oaths and Cries of Beggars. **1740** RICHARDSON *Pamela* xxvi. (1824) I. 40, I intended no harm to her..if you'd have left your squallings. **1788** WESLEY *Wks.* (1872) VII. 93 That disagreeable noise, the squalling of young children. **1911** *Blackw. Mag.* Feb. 271/1 The squalling of a thousand cats.

ˈ**squalling**, *ppl. a.* [f. SQUALL *v.*¹] That squalls or screams.

Chiefly said of children, with contemptuous force.

1712 STEELE *Spect.* No. 479 ¶2 The Noise of those damned Nurses and squawling Brats. **1822–7** GOOD *Study Med.* (1829) I. 563 Squeaking voice. The voice shrill and squalling. **1828** SCOTT *F.M. Perth* xxii, I am glad I saved the squalling child's life. **1852** THACKERAY *Esmond* III. v. 140 Send that squalling little brat about his business.

† **'squally**, *a.*[1] *Obs.* [Of obscure origin.]

1. Of cloth: Defective (in some specific manner).

1552 *Act 5–6 Edw. VI*, c. 6 §19 Any Clothe whiche shalbe cockley, pursey, bandy, squally, rewy,.. evill burled [etc.]. **1601** *Act 43 Eliz.* c. 10 §1 The same Clothes being put in Water, are found to shrink, be rewey, pursey, squally, cockling, bandy, light, and notably faulty.

2. (See quot.)

1787 W. H. MARSHALL *Norfolk* Gloss. s.v. *Squally*, A crop of turneps, or of corn, which is broken by vacant unproductive patches, is said to be squally.

squally ('skwɔːlɪ), *a.*[2] Also 8 **squalley**. [f. SQUALL *sb.*[3]]

1. Characterized by the prevalence of squalls.

a. Of places, seasons, etc.

1719 *Boyer's Dict. Royal* I. s.v. *Rafale, Cote sujette aux rafales*, a squally Coast. **1830** HODGSON in Raine *Mem.* (1858) II. 175 The hills..in a squally evening look very black and dismal. **1848** CLOUGH *Amours de Voy.* III. 48 In the squally seas as we lay by Capraja and Elba. **1876** BLACK *Madcap Violet* xlv. 388 The day was squally enough, and might turn to showers.

b. Of weather.

1727 BAILEY, *Squalley*, inclinable to sudden Storms of Wind and Rain. **1745** P. THOMAS *Jrnl. Anson's Voy.* 25 Squally Weather, with Hail and Snow. **1782** NELSON 22 July in Nicolas *Disp.* (1846) VII. p. iv, I imagine we are just getting into the Gulf stream by its being so very squally. **1866** R. M. BALLANTYNE *Shifting Winds* xiv, The weather became thick and squally, and continued so for several days. **1890** *Science-Gossip* XXVI. 283 It was very squally at the time, with occasional showers of hail.

2. Of the wind: Blowing in sudden and violent gusts or blasts.

1748 *Anson's Voy.* III. i. 303 The wind proved squally, and blew so strong off shore [etc.]. **1797** NELSON 12 Apr. in Nicolas *Disp.* (1845) II. 379 The wind is either in from the sea, or squally with calms from the mountains. **1810** SHELLEY *Zastrozzi* xii, The towering pine-trees waved in the squally wind. **1883** STEVENSON *Silverado Sq.* 168 The wind veered..and began to blow squally from the mountain summit.

3. *fig.* Stormy, troublous, threatening. Chiefly *U.S.*, esp. in the phr. ***to look squally***.

1814 W. IRVING in *Life & Lett.* (1864) I. 315 Affairs, I am afraid, are about to look squally on our Canada frontier. **1833** 'MAJ. J. DOWNING' (Seba Smith) *Lett.* (1835) xiv. 87 The times are now gittin pretty squally, and if we don't look out sharp, things will go all to smash. **1853** KANE *Grinnell Exp.* xlv. (1856) 418 But for some hours things looked squally enough. **1876** MRS. H. WOOD *Parkwater* (1879) 284 In the midst of her squally bargaining with the fish-vendor.

squally ('skwɔːlɪ), *a.*[3] [f. SQUALL *sb.*[2] + -Y[1].] Of a child, etc.: that screams discordantly or shrilly; squalling, noisy.

1861 [see *mother's blessing* s.v. MOTHER *sb.*[1] 16 a]. **1947** D. RIESMAN in *University Observer* Winter 24/2, I prefer sensitive and cultivated people to squally brats on trains. **1958** *Listener* 25 Dec. 1093/3 Maria Callas seemed right out of the picture, squally and weak at climaxes.

† **squalm**. *Obs.*[−1] (Meaning obscure.)

c **1530** *Calisto & Melebea* 422, I haue..sene her trynkettys For payntyng, thyngys inumerable, Squalmys & balmys.

squalmish ('skwɑːmɪʃ, 'skwɔːmɪʃ), *a.* *U.S. colloq.* Also **squamish**, **squawmish**. [Var. QUALMISH *a.*, perh. influenced by SQUEAMISH *a.*] Nauseous, qualmish, queasy.

1867 'MARK TWAIN' *Notebk.* (1935) vi. 59, I am..very tired of being seasick... All I take an interest in is being squalmish and getting to shore again. **1902** S. CLAPIN *New Dict. Americanisms* 381 *Squawmish*, in parts of New England, said for queasy. **1944** H. WENTWORTH *Amer. Dial. Dict.* 590/1 *Squalmish, squamish*.., squeamish, qualmish. **1948** *Daily Progress* (Charlottesville, Va.) 24 Jan. 4/4, I am not only not interested in food but maybe a little squalmish at the very thought of it.

Squalodon ('skweɪlədɒn). *Palæont.* [mod.L. *Squalodon*, f. L. *squalus* SQUALUS + Gr. ὀδοντ-, ὀδούς tooth.] A genus of fossil cetaceans found in Miocene and early Pliocene formations; a cetacean belonging to this genus.

1872 DARWIN *Orig. Spec.* (ed. 6) xi. 302 The tertiary Zeuglodon and Squalodon..are considered by Professor Huxley to be undoubtedly cetaceans. *c* **1880** *Cassell's Nat. Hist.* II. 247 The Squalodons are known chiefly from the skull.

So **'squalodont**. Also *attrib.*

1889 NICHOLSON & LYDEKKER *Palæontology* (ed. 3) II. 1306 The extinct Squalodonts were formerly classed with the Zeuglodontidæ. **1899** *Proc. Zool. Soc.* 919 There is one detached tooth remaining, which is of the same Squalodont type.

squaloid ('skweɪlɔɪd), *a.* and *sb.* [f. L. *squalus* SQUALUS: see -OID.]

A. *adj.* Shark-like; comprising the sharks.

1836 BUCKLAND *Geol. & Min.* xiv. §13 (1837) I. 289 *note*, In the third, or Squaloid division of fossils of the family. **1852** ANSTED *Phys. Geog.* xii. in *Man. Geog. Sci.* I. 380 With the exception of the Squaloid, or Shark family.

B. *sb.* A fish of the shark family.

1836 BUCKLAND *Geol. & Min.* xiv. §13 (1837) I. 287 The third family of *Squaloids*, or true Sharks, commences with the Cretaceous formation. **1863** DANA *Man. Geol.* 278 The squaloids have an elongated body.

squalor ('skwɒlə(r), formerly also 'skweɪlə(r)). Also 7 **squalour**, 7–8 **squallor**. [a. L. *squālor*, f. *squālēre* to be dry, rough, dirty, etc. So It. *squallore*, OF. *squalleur*.]

1. a. The state or condition of being physically squalid; a combination of misery and dirt.

1621 BURTON *Anat. Mel.* 207 What can poverty giue els, but beggery, fulsome nastinesse, squalor,..drudgery, labor, vglinesse? **1635** SWAN *Spec. M.* vii. §3 (1643) 320 Without light..each parcel of the worlds fabrick [would] lie buried in ..dismall squalour. **1650** BULWER *Anthropomet.* 172 The Vice of this denominated Vertue is Squalor. **1714** MANDEVILLE *Fable Bees* (1733) I. 361 The dirt and squallor, ..his pastimes and recreations would be all abominable. **1858** HAWTHORNE *Fr. & It. Note-bks.* II. 198 Hovel piled upon hovel,—squalor immortalized in undecaying stone. **1877** BLACK *Green Past.* vii, These wretched people living in squalor and ignorance and misery.

b. *fig.* The quality of being morally squalid; the quality or state of being mentally squalid, or of lacking intellectual sensitivity and order.

1860 EMERSON *Cond. Life* vi. *Worship*, In creeds never was such levity; witness the..squalor of Mesmerism, the deliration of rappings. **1933** E. A. ROBERTSON *Ordinary Families* v. 88 The whole family is much the same. Lives Dangerously in mental squalor. **1941** A. HUXLEY *Grey Eminence* vi. 139 This strength and magnificence, so very different from our own weakness and mental squalor.

† **2.** Aridity or roughness. *Obs.*[−1]

a **1637** B. JONSON *Discov.* Wks. (1641) 116 Let them..no lesse take heed, that their new flowers and sweetnesse doe not as much corrupt, as the others drinesse, and squallor.

squalo'rology. [f. SQUALOR + -OLOGY.] The study of squalor, esp. as a supposed science. So **squaloro'logical** *a.*; **squalo'rologist**, a student of or a person particularly interested in squalor.

1956 *Observer* 7 Oct. 17/4 Toughish thriller about gigolo-adventurer smuggling between Venice and Yugoslavia. Distinguished by some sociological and squalorological realism. **1957** *Britannica Bk. of Year* 814/1 *Squalorologist*, a writer stressing unpleasant matters. (1955). **1958** *Observer* 27 Apr. 14/7 To congratulate Dan Farson on two vivid squalorogical [*sic*] scoops; one of methylated-spirit drinkers on a bomb-site.., the other of Soho's afternoon nudist shows. **1961** *John o' London's* 6 July 57/4 This [*sc.* a film] is a piece of glamourised squalorology. **1973** *Observer* 29 July 31/7 Himself an Ohio policeman and expert squalorologist.

† **squalper**, *v.* *Obs. rare*[−1]. [Cf. MSw. and Sw. *sqvalpa*, MDa. *sqvalpe*, to shake, agitate (a liquid).] *trans.* To agitate, disorder.

c **1530** *Judic. Urines* II. xii. 40 b, The humours..which afore were so squalpred & so distrublyd in yͤ body.

‖ **squalus** ('skweɪləs). Pl. **squali**. [L. *squalus*, some sea-fish.] A shark.

1753 *Chambers' Cycl.* Suppl. s.v., The *squalus* with a long-pointed and bony snout. *Ibid.*, The smooth *squalus* with granulous teeth. **1784** *Ann. Reg.* 241 The squalus or true tyger shark, uncommon on our coasts. **1816** TUCKEY *Narr. Exped. R. Zaire* ii. (1818) 40 We also took a small squalus, of a species new to us. **1854** BADHAM *Halieut.* 416 The ancients have left us many lively representations of the sanguinary proceedings of these ill-omened Squali.

† **squam**. *Obs. rare.* Also 7 **squamm**. [ad. L. *squāma*: see next and cf. SQUAME.] A scale.

1661 LOVELL *Hist. Anim. & Min.* 12 Therefore burnt, together with the floures, rust, and squamms it's kept by apothecaries to dry and bind. **1729** *Evelyn's Sylva* II. iii. 118 The Kernels and Nuts, which may be gotten out of their.. Cones, clogs, and squams by exposing them to the sun.

‖ **squama** ('skweɪmə). Pl. **squamæ**. Also 8 **squamma**. [L. *squāma* scale (in various senses): cf. SQUAME. So It. *squama, squamma*.]

1. *Zool.* A scale as part of the integument of a fish, reptile, or insect.

1706 PHILLIPS (ed. Kersey), *Squama*, the Scale of a Fish, Serpent, &c. **1728** [see 2]. **1817** KIRBY & SP. *Entomol.* II. xvii. 77 This species..borrowing the abdominal squama from the former [genus], and the sting from the latter. **1819** SAMOUELLE *Entomol. Compend.* 250 Very squamous, the squamæ porrected in bundles. **1856** W. CLARK *Van der Hoeven's Zool.* I. 321 Poisers covered with large squamæ.

b. *Path.* A small portion of epidermis morbidly developed in the form of a scale.

1876 BRISTOWE *Th. & Pract. Med.* (1878) 311 The squamæ also vary in colour, consistence, thickness and form.

2. *Anat.* A thin scaly portion of a bone, esp. of the temporal bone.

1728 CHAMBERS *Cycl.*, *Squammous*, in Anatomy, an Epithet given to the Spurious or false Sutures of the Skull; because composed of *Squammæ* or Scales like those of Fishes. **1866** HUXLEY *Prehist. Rem. Caithn.* 96 The upper part of the occipital squama is produced into a protuberance. **1877** BURNETT *Ear* 41 The canal is represented at that point by the curved lower edge of the squama.

3. *Bot.* = SCALE *sb.*[2] 3 d.

1738 *Gentl. Mag.* VIII. 140/2 As the Virtues of the Hop reside in the Squammæ, or subtile transparent Leaves. **1775** J. JENKINSON tr. *Linnæus' Brit. Pl.* 240 The cup..is a *squama*, growing out of the leaf. **1830** LINDLEY *Nat. Syst. Bot.* 277 The one-flowered species of Schœnus, in which a single naked flower is surrounded by several imbricated squamæ. **1842** *Penny Cycl.* XXII. 393/2 Examples of the squama are seen in those parts of the amentum or catkin which contain the organs of reproduction. **1861** BENTLEY *Man. Bot.* 190 The bracts of that kind of inflorescence called an Amentum or Catkin..are termed *squamæ* or *scales*.

Hence **squa'maceous** *a.*, furnished with scales.

1857 A. GRAY *First Less. Bot.* (1860) 231.

squamash, erron. variant of QUAMASH.

1849 BALFOUR *Man. Bot.* §1078 In the Oregon and Missouri districts of North America, the bulbs of *Gamassia esculenta*, Gamass or Squamash, are also employed in a similar manner.

squamate ('skweɪmət), *a.* [ad. L. *squāmātus*, f. *squāma* SQUAMA.] Provided or covered with squamæ or scales.

a. *Zool.* and *Ent.* **1826** KIRBY & SP. *Entomol.* IV. 338 *Squamate*,..wings covered with minute scales. Ex. *Lepidoptera*. **1841** *Penny Cycl.* XX. 460/2 Other very remarkable extinct terrestrial species of gigantic squamate Saurians. **1870** ROLLESTON *Anim. Life* Introd. 58 In the Squamate Reptiles..in which the heart has not four.. separate cavities.

b. *Bot.* **1848** LINDLEY *Introd. Bot.* (ed. 4) I. 314 The undisputed affinity with bulbs, whether tunicate or squamate. **1866** *Treas. Bot.* 1089/2 *Squamate*, covered with small scale-like leaves.

So **squamated** *a.* (In 8 squamm-.) *rare*[−1].

1752 J. HILL *Hist. Anim.* 58 The body is formed of eight squammated joints, or has so many separate folds.

squa'mation. *Zool.* [f. SQUAMA. See -ATION.] The condition or character of being covered with scales; a special mode or form of this.

1881 *Nature* No. 627. 2/1 A Palæoniscoid fish showing a condition of squamation almost identical with that of *Polyodon*. **1889** NICHOLSON & LYDEKKER *Palæontology* (ed. 3) II. 987 A fish from the Muschelkalk..has been made the type of the genus Prohalecites on account of peculiar features in its squamation. **1900** *Nature* 20 Sept. 507/1 *Eurynotus*..still retains the palæoniscid squamation.

squamato-, combining form, after L. types, of SQUAMATE *a.*, in the sense 'scaly and ——', as **squamato-granulous**, **-tuberculate**.

1852 DANA *Crust.* I. 423 The hand is minutely squamato-granulous. *Ibid.* I. 517 Surface of body without spines, squamato-tuberculate.

squame ('skweɪm). Also 5 **swame**, 7 **squamme**. [ad. OF. *esquame* (*escame*, also *scame*, *squamme*, mod.F. *squame*) or L. *squāma* SQUAMA.]

† **1.** A scale (of iron, or on the skin or eyes).

c **1386** CHAUCER *Can. Yeom. Prol. & T.* 206 What schulde I..besy me to telle yow the names, As orpiment, brent bones, yren squames, That into poudre grounden ben ful smal? *c* **1400** *Lanfranc's Cirurg.* 189 Furfurea ben a maner of squamis, i. schellis þat comeþ of brennyng þat is in þe skyn. *a* **1470** HARDING *Chron.* lxiii, In whose bloodde bathed he should haue been, His leprous swames [*v.r.* squamys] to haue washed of clene. *c* **1485** *Digby Myst.* (1882) II. 298 The swame ys fallyn from my eyes twayne. **1661** LOVELL *Hist. Anim. & Min.* 12 The flouers bind, represse excrescencies, and cleare the eyes of the Squamme.

fig. **1483** CAXTON *Gold. Leg.* 127/2 Take thynfirmytees of humanyte and caste away the squames of pryde.

† **2.** App. some species of fish or shell-fish. *Obs.*

1393 *Earl Derby's Exp.* (Camden) 215 Item pro pikerell et creuez, j duc. lxviij s; item pro squames, xl s; item pro kokkel, xxij s. *Ibid.* 216 Item pro squamez, xl s.

3. *Zool.* = SQUAMA I.

1877 HUXLEY *Anat. Inv. Anim.* vi. 339 In these genera the scaphocerite, or squame, usually attached to the base of the antenna, is absent. **1888** ROLLESTON & JACKSON *Anim. Life* 169 The second joint..bears an exopodite in the shape of a scale or 'squame'.

4. *Med.* **a.** A small flake of dead tissue shed from the surface of the skin in some disorders.

1911 M. MORRIS *Dis. Skin* (ed. 5) i. 16 The scale, or squame, is a dry and usually laminated exfoliation of the epidermis. **1953** S. BECKETT *Watt* 170 A..constipated man, covered with squames. **1975** *Sci. Amer.* Nov. 70/3 Finally they fuse into the flakes called squames, which are eventually shed from the surface.

b. A squamous cell (see SQUAMOUS *a.* 8).

1949 in *New Gould Med. Dict.* **1954** *Jrnl. Obstetr. & Gynecol.* LXI. 156/2 Smears of patients with erratic or inactive curves consist mainly of intermediate squames and have a high proportion of basal cells. **1973** *Gray's Anat.* (ed. 35) 27/2 Squamous (pavement) epithelium. This is composed of flattened, interlocking, polygonal cells (squames).

squa'mellate, *a.* *Bot.* [f. mod.L. *squāmella*, dim. of *squāma* SQUAMA.] 'Furnished with little scales.'

1857 A. GRAY *First Less. Bot.* 231.

'squameous, *a.* Now *rare* or *Obs.* Also 7, 9 **squamm-**. [ad. L. *squāmeus*, f. L. *squāma* SQUAMA.] Furnished or covered with scales; scaly.

1676 GREW *Anat. Pl.*, *Anat. Fl.* (1682) 175 Leaves are Membraneous, as the greater part; Squameous, as *Abies*, or Filamentous. **1677** PLOT *Oxfordsh.* 114 Such are the bones of Whales, Sea-horses, and the bones of all the squammeous kind. **1721** BAILEY, *Squameous*, scaly or like Scales. **1829** GRIFFITH tr. *Cuvier* VIII. 85 Squammeous Pigeon, *Columba Squamosa*.

squa'miferous, *a.* *Zool.* and *Bot.* [f. L. *squāmifer*: see SQUAMA and -FEROUS.] Bearing or provided with scales; squamigerous.

1748 MARTIN *Inst. Lang.*, *Squamiferous*, bearing scales. **1856** W. CLARK *Van der Hoeven's Zool.* I. 246 Feet destitute of squama..alternate with squamiferous feet. **1866** J. SMITH *Ferns Brit. & For.* (1879) 78 Fronds..rarely simple, smooth, villose, or squamiferous.

'squamiform, *a.* *Zool.* and *Bot.* [ad. mod.L. *squāmiformis*: see SQUAMA and -FORM. So F.

squamiforme.] Having the shape of a scale or scales.

1828–32 WEBSTER, *Squamiform*, having the form or shape of scales. **1828** STARK *Elem. Nat. Hist.* II. 165 The peduncle with squamiform teeth. **1852** DANA *Crust.* I. 518 The gastric [spine] has three or four squamiform tubercles, posterior to it.

'squamify, *v.* In 9 squamm-. [f. SQUAM-A + -(I)FY.] To make scales; to cover with scales.

1850 D. KING *Geol. & Relig.* 175 Until he became covered with scales from the squammifying power of the sea.

squa'migerous, *a.* [f. L. *squāmiger*: see SQUAMA and -GEROUS.] Scale-bearing; squamiferous.

1656 BLOUNT *Glossogr.*, *Squamigerous*, that hath or beareth scales; scaly. **1826** KIRBY & SP. *Entomol.* III. xxxvi. 711 The pedicle is..squamigerous in *Formica*. **1835** KIRBY *Hab. & Inst. Anim.* II. xvii. 151 The various piligerous, plumigerous, pennigerous, and squamigerous animals.

Squamish ('skwɔːmɪʃ), *sb.* and *a.* Also †**Skwamish**; **Squawmish**. [a Comox cognate of Squamish *sqxʷúʔmiš*.] **A.** *sb.* **a.** A (member of a) North American Indian people of the Coast Salish group of southwestern British Columbia. **b.** The language of this people. **B.** *adj.* Of, pertaining to, or characteristic of this people or their language.

1846 R. B. SAGE *Scenes in Rocky Mountains* 221 The Indians principally consist of the following tribes: the Snakes,..Squamishes, [etc.]. **1884** *Ann. Rep. Canad. Dept. Indian Affairs 1883* 189 (*table*) Fraser River Agency.. Squamish..Hon Sound..367. **1907** T. CROSBY *Among An-ko-me-nums* i. 10 The An-ko-me-nums..inhabit the valley of the Fraser River..and include the..Songees, Skwamish, Sumats. **1928** J. MOONEY *Aboriginal Population Amer. North of Mexico* 29 Squawmish tribes. **1934** WEBSTER, Squawmish. **1955** H. G. BARNETT *Coast Salish of British Columbia* 3 Aboriginally the Squamish made their homes on the river named after them at the head of Howe Sound. **1957** *Encycl. Brit.* XIX. 888/1 The principal [Salishan] groups or tribes are:..2, Coast Salish,..Nanaimo, Squawmish, Lummi, [etc.]. **1967** A. H. KUIPERS (*title*) The Squamish language. **1969** P. SEDLAK in *Working Papers on Language Universals* I. 24 *Squamish*..must be analyzed differently since the phonetic specification is not that indicated for the cases just discussed *Ibid.* 26 *Mandarin Chinese* involves two more features than those necessary to describe *Squamish*. **1977** H. LANDAR in T. A. Sebeok *Native Langs. of Americas* II. III. 356 Squamish. South Georgia Salish; 100 to 200 in British Columbia (1962).

squamish, var. SQUALMISH *a.*

squamo- ('skweɪməʊ), used as comb. form of SQUAMA, chiefly in terms of *Anat.* relating to the squamous bones, as ***squamo-occipital***, ***-parietal***, ***-sphenoidal***, ***-temporal***; also in the sense of 'scaly', as ***squamo-epithelial***. Cf. SQUAMOSO-.

1846 OWEN *Vertebrate Animals* I. 112 The squamo-temporal bone and the malar bone of higher animals. **1855** HOLDEN *Human Osteology* 93 The squamous part of the temporal is connected..to the great wing of the sphenoid by the 'squamo-sphenoidal' suture. **1878** T. BRYANT *Pract. Surg.* I. 135 Squamo-epithelial cancer extends to the glands, but not generally to the viscera. **1904** DUCKWORTH *Morphol. & Anthropol.* x. 229 The..point of confluence of the lambdoid, squamo-parietal and squamo-occipital sutures.

squamosal (skwə'məʊsəl), *a.* and *sb.* *Anat.* [f. next + -AL[1].]

A. *adj.* **1.** ***squamosal bone***, the squamous bone.

1849–52 *Todd's Cycl. Anat.* IV. 940/1 In all the mammalia it articulates..with the squamous element of the temporal —the squamosal bone. **1875** HUXLEY in *Encycl. Brit.* I. 754/1 The T-shaped squamosal bone..sends a broad, flat process inwards.

2. Of or pertaining to the squamous bone.

1863 HUXLEY *Evid. Man's Place Nat.* III. 142 Notwithstanding the great length of the skull..the squamosal suture is very straight. **1870** ROLLESTON *Anim. Life* Introd. 43 The lower jaw articulates directly with the squamosal element of the cranial walls.

B. *sb.* The squamosal bone or squamous portion of the temporal bone.

1848 OWEN *Homol. Vertebr. Skel.* 146 The chief bulk of this segment of the brain is protected..by the intercalated squamosals. **1866** HUXLEY *Prehist. Rem. Caithn.* 86 The upper contour of the squamosal is nearly straight. **1884** COUES *N. Amer. Birds* 157 The Squamosal..bounds the brain-box laterally.

squamose (skwə'məʊs), *a.* Also 7–9 squammose. [ad. L. *squāmōs-us*, f. *squāma* scale.]

1. Covered or furnished with scales; scaly.

1661 LOVELL *Hist. Anim. & Min.* Isagoge a 3, Fishes, which are..Marine and Fluviatile both, and are squammose, or scaled. **1695** WOODWARD *Nat. Hist. Earth* I. 32 The Teeth and Bones of the cartilaginous and squammose Fishes. **1752** J. HILL *Hist. Anim.* 221 There always stands a large fleshy and squammose apophysis at the top of each of these [fins]. **1826** KIRBY & SP. *Entomol.* IV. 274 *Squamose*, covered with minute scales. **1854** BADHAM *Halieut.* 259 No fish of the same inches is more broadly squamose than the Carp. **1856** W. CLARK *Van der Hoeven's Zool.* I. 298 Body depressed, squamose, not saltatory, terminated by 3 subequal setæ.

2. *Anat.* = SQUAMOUS *a.* 1 a, 1 b.

[**1699** *Phil. Trans.* XXI. 142 The Squammosa part of the Temporal Bones was wanting.] **1708** *Phil. Trans.* XXVI. 173 It was in the interior part of the Squamose Bone. **1758** J. S. *Le Dran's Observ. Surg.* (1771) Expl. Fig. 1, The Squamose Suture of the Temporal Bones. **1847** H. MILLER *Test. Rocks* vi. (1857) 214 It overrode by a squamose suture the lower plates with which it came in contact.

3. *Bot.* = SQUAMOUS *a.* 3.

1731 P. MILLER *Gard. Dict.* s.v. *Abies*, Soaking them all Night in Water..will cause their squamose Cells to open. **1760** J. LEE *Introd. Bot.* II. xxxi. (1765) 152 *Fritillaria*, with a squamose Bulb. **1857** HENFREY *Bot.* §47 Bulbs are named, according to the character of their leaf-scales, scaly or squamose, when these only partially overlap. **1857** M. J. BERKELEY *Cryptog. Bot.* 337 The outer coat assumes various forms, being floccose, furfuraceous, or squamose. **1879** A. GRAY *Struct. Bot.* (ed. 6) 40 The squamose (scale-like) character of this covering.

4. *Path.* = SQUAMOUS *a.* 6.

1822–7 GOOD *Study Med.* (1829) V. 547 Hence a great variety of superficial eruptions, papulous, pustulous, and ichorous, squammose, or furfuraceous. *Ibid.* 613 Various other species of squamose or leprous affections of the skin.

Hence **squa'mosely** *adv.*; **squa'moseness**.

1727 BAILEY, *Squamoseness*, Scaliness. **1822** J. PARKINSON *Outl. Oryctol.* 217 Backs squamosely serrated. *Ibid.* 223 Sides squamosely scabrous.

squa'mosity. *rare.* [f. SQUAMOSE *a.* + -ITY.] The state or character of being covered with scales.

1775 in ASH. **1904** *Ann. & Mag. Nat. Hist.* Aug. 107 Their series of punctures more regular and distinct, squamosity more infuscate.

squamoso- (skwə'məʊsəʊ), used as combining form of SQUAMOSE *a.*, in the sense 'squamous and ——', as ***squamoso-dentated***, ***-imbricated***, ***-radiate***; or in terms of *Anat.* relating to the squamous bones, as ***squamoso-maxillary***, ***-parietal***, ***-temporal***, ***-zygomatic***.

1822 J. PARKINSON *Outl. Oryctol.* 217 Ribs carinated, squamoso-dentated, rather rough. *Ibid.* 223 With twenty squamoso-imbricated rays. **1843** *Penny Cycl.* XXV. 269/2 The whorls turgidly convex, squamoso-radiate at the margin. **1875** *Encycl. Brit.* I. 874/1 The squamoso-temporal region of the skull.

squamous ('skweɪməs), *a.* Also 6 scamous, squamus, 8 squammous. [ad. L. *squāmōsus*, f. *squāma* SQUAMA. So It. *squamoso*, Sp. *escamoso*, OFr. *scamoux*, *scammeux*, F. *squam(m)eux*.]

1. *Anat.* **a.** ***squamous bone***, ***part***, ***portion***, the thin and scaly part of the temporal bone, situated in the temple.

1541 R. COPLAND *Guydon's Quest. Chirurg.* D iv b, Yᵉ bones that are called Petrous... Also they be called Scamous .., for they be conioynte in maner of the scales of a fysshe with the sayde parietalles.

1778 *Encycl. Brit.* (ed. 2) I. 345/2 One [part of the bone] ..is called the squamous, or scaly part. **1808** *Med. Jrnl.* XIX. 395 The Squamous portion of the Temporal Bone. **1842** *Penny Cycl.* XXII. 79/1 The squamous bone or portion has a roundish form. **1876** *Trans. Clinical Soc.* IX. 16 The skull narrows, leaving..prominent ridges which mark the junction between the squamous and parietal bones.

b. Of a suture: Formed by thin overlapping parts resembling scales.

1709 *Phil. Trans.* XXVII. 104 From thence it [the *Os Maxilla*] runs obliquely backward, and is articulated with the *Os Palati* by a broad squamous Suture. **1741** A. MONRO *Anat.* (ed. 3) 73 The Squamous Agglutinations or False Sutures are one of each Side, a little above the Ear. **1836** BUCKLAND *Geol. & Min.* II. 55 The overlapping, or squamous suture by which the Collar is fitted to..the calcareous Sheath of the Siphon. **1866** HUXLEY *Prehist. Rem. Caithn.* 151 The contained cerebral substance could only expand at the sides in the situation of the squamous sutures.

c. (See quot.)

1854 OWEN in *Orr's Circ. Sci.*, *Org. Nat.* I. 173 In the cod ..most of the bones..have what, in anatomy, is called the 'squamous' character and mode of union, being flattened, thinned off at the edge, and overlapping one another.

2. Containing scale-like particles. *rare*⁻¹.

1547 BOORDE *Brev. Health* lxxiii. 23 b, In this matter take good hede that thou do marke a furfurous uryne from a squamus water, and a squamus water from a skaly water.

3. *Bot.* Furnished or covered with, composed of, squamæ or scales.

1658 SIR T. BROWNE *Gard. Cyrus* iii, In the squamous heads of Scabious Knapweed,..and in the Scaly composure of the Oak-Rose. **1668** WILKINS *Real Char.* 73 Many squamous shining hollow heads hanging upon slender stalks. **1731** P. MILLER *Gard. Dict.* s.v. *Virga*, The Calyx (or Flower-cup) is squamous. **1785** MARTYN *Lett. Bot.* (1794) I. 24 [The root] of the lily is squamous, or composed of scales. **1861** HULME tr. *Moquin-Tandon* II. III. v. 152 The Squamous Gall, which Reaumur called Artichoke Gall, is.. found on the English Oak. **1870** BENTLEY *Man. Bot.* (ed. 2) 182 The bracts are described as *squamous* or *scaly*.

4. = SQUAMOSE *a.* 1.

1668 WILKINS *Real Char.* 142 Squamous River Fish. **1747** *Gentl. Mag.* XVII. 461 Others [*sc.* squares of skin] irregular and rough, and even squamous, like tubercles. **1796** MORSE *Amer. Geog.* I. 218 Blue bellied, squamous lizards, several varieties. **1819** H. BUSK *Vestriad* II. 84 The brawny Tritons, with their weedy hair, Their squamous tails, and slimy shoulders bare. **1854** S. P. WOODWARD *Mollusca* II. 281 The lower valves of some Spondyli are squamous or spiny,—the upper, plain.

5. Of substances: Composed of scales.

a **1728** WOODWARD *Fossils* I. 57 The squamous or foliaceous Talc and Mica. **1835–6** *Todd's Cycl. Anat.* I. 208/2 He considers each little band as being composed of two substances, one fleshy, which contracts upon drying, the other squamous.

6. *Path.* Of skin-diseases: Characterized by the development of scales or laminæ of skin.

1829 *Glasgow Med. Jrnl.* II. 327 These eruptions may be exanthematic, vesicular..or squamous. **1843** R. J. GRAVES *Syst. Clin. Med.* xx. 247 *note*, A copious eruption often combining the lichenous and the squamous forms. **1875** B. MEADOWS *Clin. Observ.* 60 A squamous eruption, not confined to any particular part, but especially affecting the chest. **1876** DUHRING *Dis. Skin* 164 Squamous eczema may be..merely an ephemeral stage of the disease.

7. Of armour: Scaly, scaled; laminated.

1845 C. H. SMITH in Kitto *Cycl. Bibl. Lit.* s.v. *Arms*, The term..'scales', in the case of Goliath's armour, denotes the squamous kind. **1858** KITTO *Daily Bible Illustr.* III. 225 The squamous arrangement of the pieces of metal.

8. *Med.* Designating epithelium that contains (or consists of) a layer of very thin, flattened cells, and the cells themselves. Also ***squamous-celled*** adj.

1860 TANNER *Pregnancy* ii. 79 The epithelium of the mucous coat..is of the tessellated or squamous variety. **1872** HUXLEY *Physiol.* xii. 275 Squamous epithelium generally consists of many layers of cells, one over the other. **1891** MOULLIN *Surg.* 139 The fatty change is common..in squamous-celled epitheliomata. **1908** *Practitioner* Sept. 355 Wherever the disease occurs, seeing that it is commonly a squamous-celled epitheliomatous ulcer, it is reasonable to suppose that it starts as the result of some previous lesion causing a denudation of the epithelium at one of these spots. **1937** E. E. HEWER *Text-bk. Histol.* ii. 9 Three types can be distinguished:—(1) Simple squamous epithelium... (2) Simple columnar and cubical epithelium... (3) Stratified epithelium. **1947** *Radiology* XLIX. 281/1 A variety of other tumors, such as..squamous-cell carcinomas of the vagina and fore-stomach..were observed. **1968** PASSMORE & ROBSON *Compan. Med. Stud.* I. xvii. 2/1 There are two varieties of stratified squamous epithelium, comified (keratinized) and non-comified (non-keratinized). **1978** *Jrnl. R. Soc. Med.* LXXI. 726 Metaplasis into stratified squamous-cell epithelium is very common in the middle ear.

Hence **'squamously** *adv.*; **'squamousness**.

1775 ASH, *Squamousness*, the state of being squamous. **1822** PARKINSON *Outl. Oryctol.* 223 *Pecten scabrellus*: sub-orbicular,..squamously denticulated.

‖**squamula** ('skweɪmjʊlə). *Zool.*, *Ent.*, and *Bot.* [L., dim. of *squāma* scale.] A small scale; a squamule.

1754 *Dict. Arts & Sci.* s.v. *Lepidoptera*, Four wings, which are covered with imbricated squamulæ. **1822** J. PARKINSON *Outl. Oryctol.* 15 The central part assumes the figure of a squamula. **1830** LINDLEY *Nat. Syst. Bot.* 294 In certain other genera, as Bambusa, and Stipa, a third squamula exists.

squamu'lation. [f. prec. or next.] An arrangement of small scales.

1886 P. L. SCLATER *Catal. Birds Brit. Mus.* XI. 122 Neck- and breast-feathers black edged with green or blue, forming squamulations.

squamule ('skweɪmjʊl). *Zool.* and *Bot.* [Anglicized f. SQUAMULA.] = SQUAMULA.

1858 W. CLARK *Van der Hoeven's Zool.* II. 71 Skin naked in the interstices, rough with small dispersed squamules. **1887** W. PHILLIPS *Brit. Discomycetes* 23 Stem..granular with minute squamules.

'squamuliform, *a.* [ad. mod.L. *squāmuliformis*: see SQUAMULA and -FORM.] Having the shape or character of a squamula.

1882 *Encycl. Brit.* XXII. 561/1 Thallus..squamuliform or granulose with the gonimia subsolitary.

squamu'lose, *a.* *Bot.* Also squamm-. [ad. mod.L. *squāmulōs-us*: see SQUAMULA and -OSE.] Furnished or covered with small scales.

1846 *Proc. Berw. Nat. Club* II. 174 Veil..thickly covered with the same powder as the pileus, but more distinctly squammulose. **1857** M. J. BERKELEY *Cryptog. Bot.* 418 Many other forms are assumed by the crusts of Lichens;.. the squamulose form an analogous hypertrophy. **1887** W. PHILLIPS *Brit. Discomycetes* 3 Stem..soft, white, squamulose on the surface.

† **'squamy**, *a.* *Obs. rare.* [f. L. *squāma* SQUAMA.] Covered with scales; scaly.

1592 R. D. *Hypnerotomachia* 28 b, A Dragon,..her squamy..hide trailing upon the flowerd pavement. **1599** NASHE *Lenten Stuffe* 27 This captaine of the squamy cattell [*sc.* the herring]. **1612** SHELTON *Quix.* II. vi. I. 97 The dreadful Howls Of ravening Wolf, and Hissing terrible Of squamy Serpent.

squander ('skwɒndə(r)), *sb.* [f. next.] The act of squandering; extravagant expenditure; an instance of this. Also *fig.*

1709 MRS. MANLEY *Secret Mem.* (1736) I. 27 Will he one Day set it all at Stake upon a Royal Cast, an Imperial Squander? Or descend to his Grave, choak'd with greediness of Gain? *Ibid.* IV. 136 He..did not care to make an ostentatious Squander of his own Person and Valour, and therefore would be manag'd. **1806** *Inq. St. Nation* 92 (Todd), The waste of our resources, and the squander of our opportunities. **1859** CORNWALLIS *New World* I. 27 He is a prodigal paymaster, and in the school of squander, completely takes the shine out of the 'Britishers'. **1893** F. F. MOORE *Gray Eye or So* II. 118 There's not much of a squander in the deal when I get value for it.

squander ('skwɒndə(r)), *v.* [Of obscure origin.]

1. *trans.* In pa. pple. **a.** Of things: To be scattered over a comparatively wide surface or area.

1596 SHAKS. *Merch. V.* I. iii. 22 He hath a third [ship] at Mexico, a fourth for England, and other ventures hee hath, squandred abroad. *c* **1645** Howell *Lett.* (1650) I. 267 The present condition of the Jews,..now grown contemptible, and strangely squandered up and down the world. *Ibid.* II. 20 In many thousand Islands that lye squandred in the vast Ocean. **1847** Halliwell s.v., 'His family are all grown up, and squandered about the country,' i.e. settled in different places. **1882** C. Elton *Orig. Eng. Hist.* ix. 223 The fallen timber obstructed the streams, the rivers were squandered in the reedy morasses.

b. Brought to disintegration or dissolution.

1610 *Gaultier's Rodomontados* D j b, She shall no sooner be falne downe there, but she shall be squandered into dust & pow[d]er. **1653** H. More *Antid. Ath.* II. vii. §4 And so they would rot upon the Ground before they be spent, or be squander'd away in a moment of Time.

2. To drive off in various directions; to cause to scatter or disperse.

1657 Sanderson *Serm.* (1674) 37 To tend his Forces.. against the strongest Troops of the enemy; and to squander and break through the thickest ranks. **1666** Dryden *Ann. Mirab.* lxvii, They charge, recharge, and all along the sea They drive and squander the huge Belgian fleet. **1697** —— *Æneid* II. 571 The troops we squander'd first, again appear From sev'ral quarters, and inclose the rear. **1818** Wilbraham *Chesh. Gloss.* s.v., To squander a covey of partridges. **1891** Atkinson *Last of Giant-killers* 96 The stones that had been laid in course, had been squandered about anyhow.

b. *Mining.* (See quot.)

1883 Gresley *Gloss. Coal-m.* 233 *Squander*, to beat or kill (extinguish) an underground fire.

3. To spend (money, goods, etc.) recklessly, prodigally, or lavishly; to expend extravagantly, profusely, or wastefully. Also const. *on*.

The most common usage. Freq. since 1810.

1593 Nashe *Christ's T.* 45 Fooles shall squander in an houre, all the auarice of their ambitious wise Auncesters. **1623** Cockeram I, *Squander*, lauishly to consume ones estate. **1727–46** Thomson *Summer* 1638 The cruel wretch, Who..has squandered vile, Upon his scoundrel train, what might have cheered A drooping family of modest worth. **1783** Burke *Rep. Aff. India* Wks. 1842 II. 33 The cultivators ..would squander part of the money, and not be able to complete their engagements to the full. **1849** Macaulay *Hist. Eng.* iii. I. 323 Of the great sums..part had been embezzled by cunning politicians, and part squandered on buffoons and foreign courtesans. **1881** W. G. Marshall *Through Amer.* i. 10 Millions of dollars..have been squandered over the work.

absol. **1710** Swift *Change in Queen Anne's Ministry* Wks. 1841 I. 283 He was grown needy by squandering upon his vices. **1863** Geo. Eliot *Romola* ix, To squander with one hand till they have been fain to beg with the other.

b. With *away*.

1611 Cotgr., *Fricasser*,..to spend, or squander all away. **1661** *Verney Mem.* (1907) II. 170, I have noe great mind to squander away £100. **1687** A. Lovell tr. *Thevenot's Trav.* I. 264 Don Philippo..soon squandered away two or three Thousand Crowns, that were lent him. *a* **1763** W. King *Polit. & Lit. Anecd.* (1819) 17 The public money is squandered away in pensions. **1789** J. Williams *Min. Kingd.* I. 204 Our schemes..will..squander away the public money upon unnecessary projects. **1855** Macaulay *Hist. Eng.* xx. IV. 489 Neale,..after squandering away two fortunes, had been glad to become groom porter at the palace. **1885** Miss Braddon *Wyllard's Weird* I. i. 19 He squandered every shilling of his small patrimony away.

4. To spend or employ (time) wastefully; to waste. Also with *away*.

1693 Stillingfl. *Serm.* (1698) III. x. 409 How much time is squandred away in Vanity and Folly? *a* **1721** Prior *Vicar of Bray & Sir T. Moor* 232 Alas how we squander away our Days without doing our Duty. **1757** Chesterf. *Lett.* cccxxiii. (1792) IV. 99 Have I employed my time, or have I squandered it? **1842** Borrow *Bible in Spain* i, They considered the time occupied in learning as so much squandered away. **1871** B. Taylor *Faust* (1875) I. 110 Such time I've squandered o'er the history.

5. To spend profusely, without securing adequate return; to use in a wasteful manner.

1716–7 Bentley *Serm.* xi. 389 If he squander his Talents in Luxury. **1758** Johnson *Idler* No. 1 ⁋11 No words are to be squandered in declaration of esteem, or confessions of inability. **1795** Burke *Regic. Peace* (1892) 89 If they were to send us far from the aid of our King,..to squander us away in the most pestilential climates. **1842** Lover *Handy Andy* xlvii, The extraordinary capers Tom cut on the occasion, and the unheard-of lies he squandered. **1857** Buckle *Civiliz.* I. xi. 625 The resources of the country were squandered to an unprecedented extent. **1900** G. T. Stokes *Worthies Irish Church* xii. 232 Much valuable enthusiasm was squandered.

6. *intr.* To roam about; to wander.

1630 J. Taylor (Water P.) *Wks.* I. 131/2 But at last (I squandring vp and downe)..I happened into a Caue. **1850** *Bentley's Misc.* Jan. 37 The way they squander about in pairs and single ones is edifying.

7. To disperse in various directions; to scatter.

1823 Jefferson *Writ.* (1830) IV. 367 Each shifted for him-self, and left his brethren to squander and do the same as they could. **1827** Scott in *Croker Papers* (1884) I. xi. 319 The disposition seems as if some Yankee general had given the command, 'Split and Squander'. **1861** Metcalfe *Oxonian in Iceland* 156 His reverence continues his mad career among the horses, who squander right and left in alarm.

squander-bug. *colloq.* Also squander bug, squanderbug. [f. squander *v.* + bug *sb.*[2] 3 a, after *jitterbug*, etc.] A symbol of reckless extravagance and waste, first used in government publicity campaigns to promote economy during the war of 1939–45 and represented as a devilish insect; a likeness of this. Also, one who is profligate with money or resources. Hence **'squanderbugging**.

Introduced in 1943 by the National Savings Committee.

1943 *Times* 8 Jan. 8/1 (Advt.), Beware the treacherous Squander Bug! He's the prince of fifth-columnists—doesn't believe in a nest-egg for the future—doesn't believe in making money fight for Britain... Join a Savings Group to defeat the Squander Bug! **1943** O. Lancaster *More Pocket Cartoons* 55 (*caption*) Oh, just look at this sweet little squander-bug in platinum and rubies that darling Boysy's just sent me. **1944** *Convoy* Feb. 26 A Government so dexterous, through its armies of Public Relations Depts., in persuading us to squash the squander bug or grow more onions or shave in tepid water. **1946** J. W. Day *Harvest Adventure* xvi. 268 That is the question to ask these rural squander-bugs. **1966** *Punch* 26 Jan. 108/2 The more favoured nations continue to outdo each other in squanderbugging. The new Russian satellite will have showers, electric razors, fresh linen and a load of other luxury items. What a blow to American prestige. **1976** *Listener* 23 Dec. 843/3 No initiative could be broached..for fear of earning the name of Squander-bugs.

'squandered, *ppl. a.* [f. squander *v.*]

1. Dispersed; scattered.

c **1645** Howell *Lett.* (1650) I. 329 This once select nation of God..is become now a scorned squandered people all the earth over. **1681** Dryden *Span. Friar* I. i, Upon the Skirts Of Arragon our squander'd Troops he rallies. **1692** Bentley *Boyle Lect.* vii. 231 'Tis necessary that these squander'd Atoms should convene and unite. **1820** Clare *Rural Life* (ed. 2) 118 Beckoning hints..That guide the squander'd covey home. **1883** Pennell-Elmhirst *Cream of Leicestersh.* 236 Six men were a quarter of a mile to the good of their squandered field.

2. Spent profusely or extravagantly.

1801 Southey *Thalaba* I. xxxii, What was to him the squander'd wealth? **1851** Helps *Comp. Solit.* x. 195 He sees what he might have done with the squandered resources.

transf. **1897** *Westm. Gaz.* 4 Sept. 2/3 Squandered love was never blessed.

squanderer ('skwɒndərə(r)). [f. as prec.] One who squanders or spends extravagantly.

1611 Cotgr., *Sacre*,..a spendall, vnthrift, squanderer. **1656** Earl Monm. tr. *Boccalini's Advts. fr. Parnass.* I. xix. (1674) 20 By giving past number or measure, they deserve rather to be esteemed foolish squanderers, than vertuously Liberal. **1741** Richardson *Pamela* IV. 369 This would.. instruct him..to avoid being a Squanderer or Waster. **1791** Cowper *Odyss.* xiv. 117 Witness how fast the squanderers use his wine. **1863** Cowden Clarke *Shaks. Char.* xvi. 406 Squanderers and gamblers have no sense of justice.

transf. *c* **1830** Landor *Prose Pieces* Wks. 1846 II. 465 Far differently ought we to estimate the squanderers of human blood, and the scorners of human tears.

'squandering, *vbl. sb.* [f. as prec.] The action of spending lavishly or prodigally. Also with *away*.

1632 Sherwood, A squandering, *bobance*, *bobans*. **1677** Miége *Fr. Dict.* II. s.v., A Squandering away. **1721** Bailey, *Profuseness*, a..lavishness or squandering of Money. **1753** *Scots Mag.* XV. 79/1 Our granting of a subsidy..would be worse than squandering. **1817–8** Cobbett *Resid. U.S.* (1822) 228 This squandering causes heavy taxes. **1859** Holland *Gold Foil* xxvi. 316 The squandering of precious means by organized bands of sane business men.

transf. and *fig.* **1763** D. Arnot in *Life M. Bruce* (1914) vii. 100 Nothing is more shameful than the squandering away of time. **1839–40** W. Irving *Chron. Wolfert's Roost* (1855) 65 He had experienced..its dissipation of the spirits, and squanderings of the heart.

'squandering, *ppl. a.* [f. as prec.]

1. a. Of persons: Given to squander; spending lavishly or extravagantly.

1589 Warner *Alb. Eng.* VI. xxx. 134 My wife..Shall not ywis be bused by the squandring Pollo so. **1668** Wilkins *Real Char.* II. i. §5. 42 Transcendental relations of Action... Squandring, lavish, profuse. **1708** King *Cookery* Wks. 1776 III. 78 Squandering of wealth, impatient of advice. **1845** Disraeli *Sybil* (1863) 53 All was certain;..the oaks [had not] to tremble at the axe of the squandering heir.

b. Of conduct, etc.: Characterized by extravagant expenditure.

1726 Bolingbroke *Study Hist.* viii. Wks. 1754 II. 472 The reign of false and squandering policy..will finally compleat our ruin. **1849** Craig, *Squanderingly*, in a squandering manner.

2. Straying, straggling; spreading abroad. Now *dial.*

1600 Shaks. *A.Y.L.* II. vii. 57 The Wise-mans folly is anathomiz'd Euen by the squandring glances of the foole. **1854–** in dial. glossaries (Nhp., Leics., Rutland). **1866** *N. & Q.* 3rd Ser. X. 27 It's a squandering farm; a field here and a field there; it don't lie together. **1886** *S.W. Linc. Gloss.* 140 It's a very squandering place.

Hence **'squanderingly** *adv.*

1847 in Webster.

'squanderlust. *U.S. slang.* [f. squander *v.*, after wanderlust.] A strong desire to spend money or to waste assets; also *loosely* = next.

1935 *Amer. Speech* X. 155/1 Louis Ludlow, member of Congress and former Washington correspondent..is the author of *America Go Bust*, which 'focuses attention on the bureaucratic *squanderlust*' of our times. **1960** *Wall St. Jrnl.* 5 May 8/2 Politicians.., moved..by an any-year philosophy of squanderlust, lead the country down the road to economic trouble. **1977** *Time* 18 July 72/3 No longer the ultimate expression of corporate and personal squanderlust, the private plane is now a ubiquitous..means of air travel to smaller cities.

squander'mania. *colloq.* [f. squander *v.* + -mania.] An insane desire or obsession to spend money recklessly or to waste assets. Hence **squander'maniac** *a.* and *sb.*

1920 *Public Opinion* 2 July 3/1 The public are deeply roused upon the Squandermania issue. **1921** *Glasgow Herald* 2 Apr. 7 The burden imposed upon him [*sc.* the tax-payer] by a 'Squandermaniac' Government. **1922** *Public Opinion* 10 Mar. 228/1 The real squandermaniac would be revealed in the man with an infinite capacity for standing at street corners. **1931** *Punch* 4 Nov. 481/1 The triumph of Reason over Squandermania. **1933** C. Mackenzie *Water on Brain* vii. 85 There cheek by jowl sat the squandermaniac and the suicidal junior clerk. **1956** *Sun* (Baltimore) 14 June (ed. B) 16/2 They think that people who support the provision of some military aid to our allies are 'soft' and afflicted with 'squandermania'. **1976** *Times* 16 Aug. 11/5 Sheer 'squander-mania'..has currently invaded our society.

† **squanging,** *ppl. a.* *Obs.*[−1] ? Sweeping.

1688 Holme *Armoury* III. 115/1 Swash Letters, are Italick Capitals, which have generally long dashing squanging stroaks in them, either at the head or foot.

† **squanter-squash.** *U.S. Obs. rare.* Also 7 isquouter, squonter-. [ad. Narragansett Indian *asqutasquash*: see squash *sb.*[2]] A squash.

1634 W. Wood *New Eng. Prosp.* 67 In Summer, when their [*sc.* the Indians'] corne is spent, Isquouter squashes is their best bread, a fruite like a young Pumpion. **1672** Josselyn *New Eng. Rarities* 57 Squashes, but more truly Squonter-squashes, a kind of Mellon, or rather Gourd. **1705** R. Beverley *Virginia* II. iv. (1722) 124 The Clypeatæ are sometimes call'd Cymnels.., from the Lenten Cake of that Name, which many of them very much resemble. Squash, or Squanter-Squash, is their Name among the Northern Indians, and so they are call'd in New-York and New-England.

squantum ('skwɒntəm). *U.S. local.* Also Squantum. [f. *Squantum*, the name of a seacoast village (now part of Quincy), in Norfolk Co., E. Mass: see also M. Mathews *Dict. Americanisms*.] In Massachusetts: a picnic, a 'clambake'; *spec.* an annual feast formerly held on the sea-shore at which sea-food was eaten.

1812 *Boston Gaz.* 24 Aug. 2/5 The Squantum Celebration Will be this day, (Monday) at the old celebrated spot... The Feast was postponed on Saturday on account of the weather. .. The antient Celebrators of the Squantum Feast, will be honored..with the presence of their illustrious friends. **1832** S. G. Goodrich *Syst. Universal Geogr.* 106 The feast of *Squantum* is held annually on the shore to the E. of Neponset Bridge, at a rocky point projecting into Boston Bay. **1855** H. A. Wise *Tales for Marines* i. 21, I wish to all hired smash I was..hazin' round with Charity Bunker and the rest o' the gals at a squantum. **1890** E. Bellamy *Six to One* vi. 60 The squantum was to be held at a point on the narrow peninsula..that divides the ocean from the broad lagoon.

squappe, obs. variant of swap *v.*

squarable ('skwɛərəb(ə)l), *a.* and *sb.* [f. square *v.*] **a.** *adj.* Capable of being squared. **b.** *sb.* A person who can be 'squared'.

1706 Phillips (ed. Kersey) s.v. *Contradictory Opposition*, The Circle is squarable, The Circle is not squarable. **1840** Riddle *Hutton's Recreat.* 169 This would be true, even if the figure A B C F A were not absolutely squarable. **1898** *Contemp. Rev.* Aug. 200 The receiver would be known by every promoting gang, as one of the 'squareables'.

square (skwɛə(r)), *sb.* Forms: α. 4 **sqwyr** (**swyer**), 4–6 **squyre**, 4–7 **squire** (4 **suire**), 5 **squir**, **sqvyȝer**, **sqvyyre**, **sqvyer**, 5–6 **squyer**, 6 **sqwier**, 6–7 **squier**; 6 **squere**. β. 5 **skwar**, **sqvar**, **sqware**, 6 **squair(e**, 5– **square**. [ad. OF. *esquire* (*esquierre*) and *esquare* (*es-*, *equarre*, also *escuerre*, *equerre*, mod.F. *équerre*):—pop. L. **exquadra* (see quadra), whence also It. *squadra*, Pg. *esquadra*, Sp. *escuadra*. Also (in sense 17) f. square *a.* The early form *squire* is chiefly employed in senses 1 and 3.]

I. 1. a. An implement or tool for determining, measuring, or setting out right angles, or for testing the exactness of artificers' work, usually consisting of two pieces or arms set at right angles to each other, but sometimes with the arms or sides hinged or pivoted so as to measure any angle; esp. one used by carpenters or joiners. Freq. without article in phr. *by square*.

bevel-, *mitre-*, *set-*, *T-* or *tee-*, *trial-* or *try-square*: see these words.

α. *a* **1300** *Cursor M.* 2231 Do we wel and make a toure Wit suire [*v. rr.* squire, squyre] and scantilon sa euen, þat may reche heghur þan heuen. *c* **1391** Chaucer *Astrol.* I. §12 Next the forseide cercle of the A. b. c...is Marked the skale, in Maner of 2 Squyres. **1426** Lydg. *De Guil. Pilgr.* 4906 Fyrst ye shal a squyre take, A Squyre off a carpenter; And ye shal vse thys maner. *c* **1449** Pecock *Repr.* II. i. 135 This werk is to be mad by cumpas, and thilk werk..bi squyer and suche othere. **1474** Caxton *Chesse* III. ii. (1883) 86 The carpenters ben signefyed by the dolabre or squyer. **1553** in *Archaeol.* (1796) XII. 341 John Keyme, smith, for 40 sockketts, 8 sqwiers, withe other necessaries. **1599** T. M[oufet] *Silkwormes* 35 Holding his file in right hand hansomly, In left his paire of compasses and squire. **1626** Bacon *Sylva* §373 Take a Turreted Lamp of Tinne, made in the forme of a Squire. **1656** W. Du Gard tr. *Comenius' Gate Lat. Unl.* 155 They search out..the straightness of a line, with a squire.

fig. **1582** Stanyhurst *Æneis* Ep. Ded. (Arb.) 5 Hauing no English writer beefore mee in this kind of poetrye with whose squire I should leauel my syllables. **1590** Spenser

F.Q. II. i. 58 But temperance..with golden squire Betwixt them both can measure out a meane. **1620** QUARLES *Feast of Wormes* (1638) 29 Fate..tels when dayes, and moneths, and termes expire, Meas'ring the lives of Mortals by her squire.

β. **1412** *York Fabric Rolls* (Surtees) 432/1 Pro levells, Squares, et reules, xx*d.* *a* **1562** in *Norf. Antiq. Misc.* II. 5 A square and a compass. **1579** GOSSON *Sch. Abuse* (Arb.) 57 This inforceth Magistrates..with vnskilful Carpenters, to vse the Square and the compasse,..not to builde, but to ouerthrow. **1618** *Barnevelt's Apol.* E 2 b, I beseech you, that the stone is to be fitted to the square, not the square to the stone. **1660** BARROW *Euclid* I. prop. 11 The practice of this and the following is easily performed by the help of a square. *a* **1763** SHENSTONE *Elegies* x. 35 The poor mechanic wanders home, Collects the square, the level, and the line. **1781** COWPER *Convers.* 789 A poet does not work by square or line, As smiths and joiners perfect a design. **1826** *Art Brewing* (ed. 2) 196 When you have made the face of the roller as true as the square and the chisel can render it. **1872–4** JEFFERIES *Toilers of Field* (1892) 173 A somewhat superior description is built in the shape of a carpenter's 'square'.

†**b.** *fig.* In phr. ***by the square***, with extreme accuracy or exactness; precisely, exactly. *Obs.*

1570 T. NORTON tr. *Nowel's Catech.* 51 b, He will not deale with vs after extremitie of lawe, nor call our doinges to exacte accompt, nor trie them as it were by the squire. **1588** SHAKS. *L.L.L.* v. ii. 475 Do not you know my Ladies foot by th' squier? **1633** B. JONSON *Tale Tub* IV. ii, Why you can tell us by the squire, neighbour, Whence he is call'd a constable.

†**c.** As a heraldic bearing. Also ***per square***, used to denote that a shield is divided by a line in the form of a carpenter's square. *Obs.*

1572 BOSSEWELL *Armorie* II. 117 He beareth Sable, a Squire direct from the chiefe, to the dexter parte of the shield de Argent. *Ibid.*, Note also, that there may be vsed particion per Squere, although it be rare seene. **1610** GUILLIM *Her.* 208 He beareth Argent, a Cheueron betweene three Carpenters Squires, Sable.

†**d.** A piece of ironwork, etc., having the form of a carpenter's square. *Obs.*

1530–1 *Rec. St. Mary at Hill* (1905) 354 Paid to the Smyth for a dogg of Iron for þe Roodloft... Paid for a Sqvyer for the same. **1551–2** in Feuillerat *Revels Edw. VI* (1914) 72, ij longe plates and two squiers for a geblot.

2. *fig.* A canon, criterion, or standard; a rule or guiding principle; a pattern or example. (Very common *c* 1550–1650.) **a.** Const. *of* (the thing serving as a standard, etc.). Now *rare* or *Obs.*

1549 E. ALLEN *Par. Leo Jude Rev.* 9 As the Christen religion shalbe restored and reformed after the rule and square of holy scripture. **1579** W. WILKINSON *Confut. Fam. Love* B ij, Judge all thinges according to the ballance of equitye, and trying squaire or measure line of righteousness. **1604** T. WRIGHT *Passions* I. iii. 13 To governe the body..by the square of prudence, and rule of reason. **1654** WHITLOCK *Zootomia* 24 Let thy Actions be justified by the Square of Religion and Justice. **1688** BUNYAN *Jerusalem Sinner Saved* (1886) 75 Upon the square, as I may call it, of the worthiness of the blood of Christ, grace acts. **1720** *Humourist* 64 My Countrymen must excuse me, if I say, upon the Square of right Reason we make as ill a Figure as they do in Italy or Asia. **1809** MALKIN *Gil Blas* x. viii. (Rtldg.) 357 They would not deal with Antonia upon the square of modern law and gospel.

†**b.** Const. *of* (the thing regulated or judged).

1567 JEWEL *Def. Apol.* v. 556 Syluester Prierias saith, that the Romishe Church is the Squier, and Rule of Truthe. **1594** WEST *2nd Pt. Symbol., Chancerie* §23 Lawes appointed to be rules and squares of mens actions. **1617** COLLINS *Def. Bp. Ely* II. viii. 322 The square of our faith is the Scripture, not the Fathers. **1642** FULLER *Holy & Prof. St.* III. xxv. 233 Is merit everywhere else made the exact square of preferment? *a* **1684** LEIGHTON *Serm.* Wks. (1868) 678 It is not the way to advance their Master's Kingdom, which end should be the Square of all their Contrivances.

†**c.** Without const. *Obs.*

c **1550** ROLLAND *Crt. Venus* III. 536 For in sic luif is nother reull nor squair..Bot blindid lufe. **1571** GOLDING *Calvin on Ps.* i. 6 Whose duetye it is to settle the state of the world according to the right squyre. **1603** DANIEL *Panegyric Congratulatory* xxviii. Wks. (Grosart) I. 152 And all will seeme compos'd by that same square By which they see the best and greatest are. **1616** BRETON *Good & Badde, Worthy Judge* Wks. (Grosart) II. 7/1 His study is a square for the keeping of proportion betwixt command and obedience. **1640** CAREW *Poems* Wks. (1824) 84 A life so straight, as it should shame the square Left in the rules of Katherine or Clare.

†**d.** Const. *of* (the person, etc., setting the standard). Also with possessives. *Obs.*

1602–3 DANIEL *Musophilus* 101 Wks. (Grosart) I. 228 Ignorance will liue By others square, as by example lost. **1607** J. DAVIES (Heref.) *Summa Totalis* Wks. (Grosart) I. 8/1 This Truth is not squar'd by Platoes squire. **1643** W. STAMPE *Serm. 18 Apr.* 18 The naturall square of the very Indians, is enough to condemne our want of obedience.

†**3.** *Geom.* **a.** A plane figure having the form of a carpenter's square. *Obs.*

1551 RECORDE *Pathw. Knowl.* I. No. 21 When any two quadrates be set forth, howe to make a squire about the one quadrate, whiche shall be equall to the other quadrate. *Ibid.* Defin., A syseangle..whose vse commeth often in Geometry, and is called a squire, is made of two long squares ioyned togither, as this example sheweth.

†**b.** ***in a square***, at right angles. *Obs.*

1571 DIGGES *Pantom.* I. xviii. F j, E is the fourth staffe running sydewise orthogonally or in a squire from the third.

II. †**4. a.** Rectangular or square shape or form. Chiefly without article in prep. phrases, as ***in*** or ***to square***. *Obs.*

1382 WYCLIF *Ezek.* xlviii. 20 Alle the premisses of fyue and twenti thousandis, by fyue and twenti thousandis in sqware [L. *in quadrum*], shuln be departid in to primisses of the sayntuarie. *a* **1513** FABYAN *Chron.* Prol. 3 The Prentyse that hewyth the rowgth stone, And bryngeth it to square, with harde strokes and many. **1591** SPENSER *Visions Bellay* iii, Then did a sharped spyre of Diamond bright, Ten feete each way in square, appeare to mee. **1615** TOMKIS *Albumazar* II. iii, I haue a parler Of a great square and height, as you desire it. **1663** GERBIER *Counsel* 77 The sawing, and bringing of the Timber to a square.

†**b.** *fig.* In phrases with preps or verbs.

In some cases not clearly distinct from sense 2.

1576 FLEMING *Panopl. Epist.* 91 Such be the present troubls and turmoyles, that nothing is left in iust square. **1597** BRETON *Wit's Trenchmour* Wks. (Grosart) II. 19/1 Her thoughts keepe the square of such discretion, that no idle humour dare enter the list of her conceit. **1606** SHAKS. *Ant. & Cl.* II. iii. 7, I haue not kept my square, but that to come Shall be done by th' Rule. **1610** HEALEY *St. Aug. Citie of God* II. 80 Budæus..was neuer drawne from his true square with any profit or study to augment his estate. *a* **1641** BP. MOUNTAGU *Acts & Mon.* (1642) 111 They have a Rule which will not hold square with his Position.

5. †**a.** A side of a square, rectangle, or polygon; a face of a cube. *Obs.*

c **1400** MAUNDEV. (Roxb.) vi. 21 It was made foure square, and ilka square contened sex myle or more. *c* **1440** *Jacob's Well* 91 þis wose of wrethe is foure-square: o sqware of wrethe is a ȝens god. *Ibid.*, An-oþer sqware of wrethe is aȝens þi-self. *Ibid.*, þe iij. sqware of wretthe is aȝens þi meyne. *c* **1593** *Rites Durham* (1903) 22 A foure squared stonn,..in euerye square a faire large Image. **1617** MORYSON *Itin.* I. 86 It is built foure square, each square containing forty foot. **1634** SIR T. HERBERT *Trav.* 112 The Sepulchre..is of foure Æquilaterall squares. **1656** HEYLIN *Surv. France* 196 The figure of it [a tower] is six square, every square of it being nine paces in length. **1753** HANWAY *Trav.* III. xxxiv. (1762) I. 157 This city is inclosed within a wall above a mile in each square.

b. The measurement of each side of a square object. *rare*$^{-1}$.

1771 LUCKOMBE *Hist. Printing* 294 Four inches..is the square of the Hind-post.

6. a. A square or quadrilateral space, esp. one of several marked out on a board, paper, or other surface for playing certain games or for purposes of measurement, etc.; a square surface or face.

magic, Nasik squares: see MAGIC *a.* 3, NASIK. ***square of Pegasus***: see PEGASUS 1 c.

c **1440** *Pallad. on Husb.* II. 110 An aker lond..therout of may be tolde Of squares x feet wide,..ccc square of x, and twyes twelue. **1483** *Cath. Angl.* 357/1 A Square,..*quadra.* **1551** SIR J. WILLIAMS *Accompte* (Abbotsf. Cl.) 101 For cutting and slyppinge of two greate saphures into many squares. **1611** COTGR., *Marelle*, a square in a chesseboord. **1667** MILTON *P.L.* v. 393 Rais'd of grassie terf Thir Table was,.. And on her ample Square from side to side All Autumn pil'd. **1694** MOTTEUX *Rabelais* v. xxiv. 108 So that the Golden King was on a White Square, the Silver'd King on a Yellow Square. **1735** BERTIN *Chess* 55 The queen gives a check in the black queen's second square. **1832** L. HUNT *Hero & Leander* ii. 104 The casement, at the dawn of light, Began to show a square of ghastly white. **1847** TENNYSON *Princ.* IV. ix, When unto dying eyes The casement slowly grows a glimmering square. **1898** *Eclectic Mag.* LXVII. 653 All white squares..belong to the government, and can be homesteaded.

fig. **1834** MAR. EDGEWORTH *Helen* iv, Whatever I may have been..on the great squares of politics, I believe I never have been accused..of being a manœuvrer on the small domestic scale.

†**b.** *fig.* Affairs, events, matters, proceedings. Only in the phr. ***how*** (***the***) ***squares go***. Now *Obs.*

Very common in the 17th c.

1607 MIDDLETON *Fam. Love* I. iii, How goes the squares. **1642** HOWELL *True Informer* 2, I pray be pleased to make me partaker of some forraigne news, and how the squares goe betwixt France and Spaine. **1678** J. PHILLIPS tr. *Tavernier's Trav.* v. ii. 203 Sha-Abbas,..to know how squares went in his kingdom,..oft'n disguis'd himself, and went about the City..to discover whether Merchants us'd false weights. **1692** R. L'ESTRANGE *Josephus, Antiq.* XVI. xvii. (1733) 451 He first gave him an account of what had passed at Berytus; and then ask'd him how Squares went at Rome. **1828** CARR *Craven Gloss.* II. 158 'How gang squares?' a familiar form of salutation, equivalent to 'how d' ye do'.

7. a. *Geom.* A plane rectilinear and rectangular figure with four equal sides; †a rectangle with unequal sides (cf. next).

1551 RECORDE *Pathw. Knowl.* II. No. 36 If a right line be parted into ij. partes..the square that is made of that whole line, is equall to bothe the squares that are made of the same line, and the twoo partes of it seuerally. **1571** DIGGES *Pantom.* I. B iij, If all the sides be equall, and al the angles right, than is that Paralelogramme called a square. **1660** BARROW *Euclid* I. Def. 29 Of Quadrilateral, or four-sided figures, a Square is that whose sides are equal, and angles right. **1728** CHAMBERS *Cycl.* s.v. *Geometry*, They observ'd, that God and Nature affect Perpendiculars, Parallels, Circles, Triangles, Squares, and harmonical Proportions. *a* **1777** FAWKES *Voy. to Planets* 32 An astrologer..decks the wall with triangles and squares. **1815** J. SMITH *Panorama Sci. & Art* II. 713 To obtain the perspective of a circle EFGH,..draw round it the square ABCD. Divide the square into small squares. **1854** *Poultry Chron.* II. 151 In shape the body divested of head, tail, and legs should give a square. **1881** ROUTLEDGE *Science* ii. 36 To find..the length of the side of a square which has precisely the same area as the circle.

fig. **1852** BAILEY *Festus* 493 Peace, piety, and innocence, and joy Made up the square of Being.

b. With qualifying term; esp. ***long*** or ***oblong square***, a rectangle. ? *Obs.*

1551 RECORDE *Pathw. Knowl.* II. No. 39 Nowe by the theoreme, that longe square F.G.M.O, with the iuste square L.M.O.P, muste bee equall to the greate square E.K.Q.L. **1611** COTGR., *Paralelogramme*, a Paralelogramme, or long Square. **1723** CHAMBERS tr. *Le Clerc's Archit.* I. 105 Windows..are usually long Squares; their height being sometimes double their width, or very neeral so. **1726** LEONI *Alberti's Archit.* II. 26/2 An equilateral and right-angled square. **1791** NEWTE *Tour Eng. & Scot.* 61 This castle formed an oblong square. **1842** LOUDON *Suburban Hort.* 159 They are made in frames in the following manner:—An oblong square..is formed of four laths [etc.].

†**c.** ***geometrical square***: see QUADRAT 1 b. *Obs.*

1571 DIGGES *Pantom.* I. xxix. I j b, The other plate wherein youre square Geometricall and Theodelitus was described. *Ibid.* I ij, The double scale is compound of two Geometricall squares. **1728** CHAMBERS *Cycl.*, *Quadrat*, call'd also Geometrical Square and Line of Shadows, is an additional Member on the Face of the common Gunter's and Sutton's Quadrants.

d. *Logic.* A square diagram used to illustrate the four kinds of logical opposition.

1864 BOWEN *Logic* vi. 168 That the various points in the doctrine of this sort of Immediate Inference might be more easily remembered, the old logicians contrived..the accompanying ingenious diagram, which may be called the Square of Opposition. **1891** *Pall Mall G.* 5 May 2/2 It is a logical square, and its squareness is supposed to carry some metaphysical virtue.

8. a. *Arith.*, *Alg.*, and *Geom.* The product of a number multiplied by itself; a second power.

1557 RECORDE *Whetst.* G iij b, Twoo multiplications doe make a Cubike nomber. Likewaies .3. multiplications doe giue a square of squares. **1571** DIGGES *Pantom.* I. xxx. K, Now square 2400 pase, so haue you 5760000, wherevnto yf you adioyne the square of HD the product will amount to 5763600. **1674** JEAKE *Arith.* (1696) 193 Then set down the Square of this Quotient figure. **1715** tr. *Gregory's Astron.* Pref. (1726) I. p. xii, He understood..that the Gravity of the Planets towards the Sun..were reciprocally as the Squares of their Distances from the Sun. **1764** J. FERGUSON *Lect.* ii. 21 The squares of the times of their going round are as the cubes of their distances from the centers of the circles they describe. **1838** DE MORGAN *Ess. Probab.* 62 Hence it follows, that when the number is large, the preceding fraction..is very nearly one half the square of that number. **1869** RANKINE *Machine & Hand-tools* App. 9 The square of the proof stress, divided by the modulus of elasticity, is called the Modulus of Resilience. **1885** WATSON & BURBURY *Electr. & Magn.* I. 258 The law of the inverse square in electric action.

b. ***method*** (or ***principle***) ***of least squares*** [tr. F. *méthode des moindres quarrés* (A.-M. Legendre *Nouvelles Méthodes pour la Détermination des Orbites des Comètes* (1806) 74)], the technique of estimating a quantity, fitting a graph to a set of experimental values, etc., so as to minimize the sum of the squares of the differences between the observed data and their estimated true values; so ***least square***(***s***) attrib., denoting estimates, regression lines, etc., obtained by this method, the method itself, and the processes which it involves.

[**1812** *Phil. Mag.* XXXIX. 242 M. Legendre had not in any way mentioned the method which he has denominated that of small squares, (*moindres carrées*,). *Ibid.* 243 The principle of the small squares.] **1825** *Ibid.* LXV. 10 The principle of least squares will hold good, whatever law of probability be adopted. **1830** POISSON in *Q. Jrnl. Sci., Lit. & Arts* VI. 96 This embarrassment..remained to the period when M. Legendre proposed a direct and uniform method of forming the final equations, which was generally adopted under the name of Method of least squares of the errors, which was assigned to it by its author. **1872** THOMSON & TAIT *Elem. Nat. Philos.* I. iii. 115 *A* and *B* are to be found by the method of least squares from values of *l* observed for different given values of *t*. **1916** L. D. WELD *Theory of Errors & Least Squares* v. 87 If more [observations] are made, least-square reduction may be applied to their adjustment. **1939** A. E. TRELOAR *Elem. Statistical Reasoning* iv. 59 'Least squares' solutions, or the minimizing of squared deviations to reach representative values, may be made with facility, whereas the minimizing of absolute deviations becomes so involved that the problems can rarely be solved that way. **1950** A. McF. MOOD *Introd. Theory Statistics* xiii. 311 The primary reason that the method of least squares is commonly used for curve fitting is merely that it leads to a simple linear system of equations for determining the coefficients. **1957** G. E. HUTCHINSON *Treat. Limnol.* I. vii. 469 *C* is determined from the distribution of temperatures by the method of least squares. **1970** *Jrnl. Gen. Psychol.* July 127 The principle of the method is to rotate one matrix (usually a principal-components matrix) as close as possible to a hypothesized factor matrix, in a least-square solution. **1974** *Encycl. Brit. Macropædia* VII. 967/1 Gauss developed a technique for calculating its orbital components with such accuracy that several astronomers late in 1801 and early in 1802 were able to locate Ceres again without difficulty. As part of his technique, Gauss used his method of least squares, developed about 1794.

9. *Mil.* **a.** A body of troops drawn up in a square formation, either with solid ranks or leaving an open space in the centre (see b).

1591 *Garrard's Art Warre* 1160 To defend and flanke the maine square. **1599** SHAKS. *Hen. V*, IV. ii. 28 Our superfluous Lacquies, and our Pesants, Who in vnnecessarie action swarme About our Squares of Battaile. **1602** MARSTON *Ant. & Mel.* III. Wks. 1856 I. 33 Huge troups of barbed steeds, Maine squares of pikes, millions of harguebush. **1606** SHAKS. *Ant. & Cl.* III. xi. 40 He alone Dealt on Lieutenantry, and no practise had In the braue squares of Warre. **1770** LANGHORNE *Plutarch* (1851) II. 599/2 He drew up the legions in a close square. **1791** COWPER *Iliad* xv. 751 In even square compact so firm they stood. **1815** WELLINGTON in Gurw. *Desp.* (1838) XII. 529, I had the infantry for some time in squares. **1847** TENNYSON *Princ.* v. 236 When we saw the embattled squares, And squadrons of the Prince, trampling the flowers With clamour. **1896** R. S. S. BADEN-POWELL *Matabele Campaign* vi, The square halted, and each man lay down to sleep just where he stood.

b. ***hollow, solid square*** (see quots. 1702, 1802).

1702 *Milit. Dict.* (1704) s.v., *Hollow Square*, a Body of Foot drawn up with an empty space in the middle for the Colours, Drums and Baggage, facing and cover'd by the Pikes every way, to oppose the Horse. **1711** *Lond. Gaz.* No. 4817/5 He..form'd the Foot..into hollow Squares. **1802** JAMES *Milit. Dict.* s.v., *Solid Square*, is a body of foot, where both ranks and files are equal. **1845** SYD. SMITH *Wks.* (1859) II. 334 It is..to be discussed in hollow squares, and refuted by battalions four deep. **1876** VOYLE & STEVENSON *Milit. Dict.* 398 The solid square, which faces outwards..to resist cavalry; and the hollow square, in which the men face inwards, for the purpose of hearing orders, &c. read.

c. Without article in phr. ***into square***.

1859 F. A. GRIFFITHS *Artill. Man.* (1862) 27 Men are formed into square to resist attacks of cavalry. *Ibid.*, A battalion may be formed into square two deep to protect baggage or treasure against infantry only.

10. †**a.** A square piece of material covering the bosom; the breast-piece of a dress. *Obs.*

1579 HAKE *Newes out of Powles* iv. (1872) D iv b, She must haue Partlet, Square & Lace, with Chaine about hir neck. **1600** FAIRFAX *Tasso* XII. lxiv, Betweene her brests the cruell weapon riues Her curious square, embost with swelling gold. **1611** SHAKS. *Wint. T.* IV. iv. 212. **1614** in *10th Rep. Hist. MSS. Comm.* App. I. 43 As for lace to be a band and cuffs, and square with long peaks, pleas yoor ladyship know that it is not the fashon to weare such now. *c* **1710** in J. Ashton *Reign Q. Anne* (1882) I. 173 A round Sable Tippet, ..with a piece of black Silk in the Square of the neck.

b. An object of a square (or approximately square) form or shape; a square or rectangular piece, block, etc.

1601 HOLLAND *Pliny* II. 447 Likewise morimals..and those sores which be filthy..are commonly healed with the old squares of the Tunie fish. **1662** J. DAVIES tr. *Mandelslo's Trav.* 4 The Sepulchre is in a little Chappel built of white marble, upon a high square of free-stonework. **1698** M. LISTER *Journ. Paris* (1699) 124, I saw a Picture here of about 6 inches over, finely painted in Mosaic, the very little squares were scarce visible to the naked Eyes. **1756** *Phil. Trans.* L. 111 Then they cut out the true peat,..in long pieces, vulgarly called long squares, about three inches and a half broad every way, and four feet long. **1794** MRS. RADCLIFFE *Myst. Udolpho* xliv, The floor inlaid with small squares of fine marble. **1815** SCOTT *Guy M.* xx, He..bolted his food down his capacious throat in squares of three inches. **1857** MILLER *Elem. Chem., Org.* vi. §1. 375 The distilled fat is..distributed in layers..upon squares of cocoa-nut matting. **1879** *Cassell's Techn. Educ.* IV. 338/1 The moulds themselves correspond in shape to the familiar tapering form of the 'squares' of salt, as they are called in shops.

†**c.** A surveying instrument made in the form of a square. *Obs. rare.*

1600 SURFLET *Countrie Farme* 655 In this figure you see the Squire and the Staffe each of them by themselues. **1712** J. JAMES tr. *Le Blond's Gardening* 82 The Square, or whole Circle,..an Instrument much made use of in..Surveying of Land.

d. A rectangular pane of glass.

1687 MIÉGE *Gt. Fr. Dict.* II, A Square of glass. **1714** S. SEWALL *Diary* 16 July (1882) III. 10 It..lifted up the Sash window, broke one of the squares. **1775** W. WILLIAMSON *Trials at York* 13/1 There were two squares of the window broke. **1842** LOUDON *Suburban Hort.* 219 Thus directing all the water..down the centre of the squares. **1877-** in Linc., Somerset, and Cornw. glossaries and texts.

e. A square piece of material used as a scarf or cravat.

1882 *Queen* 7 Oct. 334/2 Lace Bows... Lace Sets... Indian Muslin and Lace Squares, from 1s. 11d. to 12s. 6d. **1926** in C. W. Cunnington *Eng. Women's Clothing in Present Cent.* (1952) vi. 190 The latest scarf conceit is a square of chiffon caught round the neck. **1960** C. DALE *Spring of Love* iv. 94 Miss Burroughs [wearing]..a silk square over her shoulders against the draught. **1966** B. KIMENYE *Kalasanda Revisited* 60 Removing the georgette square which had been tightly binding her head. **1979** A. SCHOLEFIELD *Point of Honour* 142 Yellow knotted silk square at the throat.

11. a. A square or rectangular area or piece of ground; *spec.* a garden plot of this shape.

1615 W. LAWSON *Country Housew. Gard.* (1626) 10 If within one large square the Gardner shall make one round Labyrinth or Maze. **1623** MARKHAM *Country Housew. Gard.* III. i, This is the cause..that Gardners raise their squares. *a* **1700** EVELYN *Diary* 27 Feb. 1644, On one of these walkes, within a square of tall trees, is a basilisc of copper. **1706** LONDON & WISE *Retir'd Gard.* I. I. x, I now want to know how many Dwarfs I ought to have in the Squares of my Garden. **1746** FRANCIS tr. *Horace, Art Poetry* 47 One happier Artist of th' Æmilian Square. **1791** WASHINGTON *Lett.* Writ. 1892 XII. 90 It is of great importance..that the city should be laid out into squares and lots. **1800** WORDSW. *Hart-leap Well* 103 It chanced that I saw standing in a dell Three aspens at three corners of a square. **1850** TENNYSON *In Mem.* cxv, Now burgeons every maze of quick About the flowering squares. **1867** MORRIS *Jason* v. 38 But Jason and his fair folk..Came to a square shaded about by trees.

attrib. **1719** LONDON & WISE *Compl. Gard.* 288 Sow for the last time, your Square Peas in the middle of July.

b. *Cricket.* A closer-cut area at the centre of a ground, any strip of which may be prepared as a wicket.

1899 *Lawns* (Sutton & Sons, Reading) 32 The club purse must determine the extent of ground to be treated in the manner we recommend, but while the work is in progress it is worth while to strain the point to make the playing square sufficiently large, say, at the very least, forty yards in the line of the wickets, by thirty yards in width. **1924** H. DE SÉLINCOURT *Cricket Match* v. 110 As they reached the square, five Raveley men emerged, running, from the Pavilion, and called loudly for the ball. **1950** F. J. REED *Lawns & Playing Fields* xvii. 174 On established cricket squares mowing should commence as early as possible, setting the machine high and gradually lowering the cut as the season advances. **1976** J. SNOW *Cricket Rebel* 22 We were not to meet up as a side until we got on to the square.

c. *Mil. slang.* A parade ground.

1915 F. H. LAWRENCE in *Home Lett. T. E. Lawrence* (1954) 644 There were 10 officers on the square when I joined in September, and four of them are now dead, four wounded and one missing. **1925** FRASER & GIBBONS *Soldier & Sailor Words* 268 *Square*,..an army term for the drill or parade ground. In general, the Barrack Square. **1962** A. WESKER *Chips with Everything* I. iii. 17 This is the Square. We call it a square-bashing square. **1982** 'W. HAGGARD' *Mischief-Makers* ii. 21 He had failed to pass Sandhurst. He had failed to pass off the square and had been put back a term.

12. a. An open space or area (approximately quadrilateral and rectangular) in a town or city, enclosed by buildings or dwelling-houses, esp. of a superior or residential kind, freq. containing a garden or laid out with trees, etc.; more generally, any open space resembling this, esp. one formed at the meeting or intersection of streets; also, the group of houses surrounding an area of this kind.

1687 A. LOVELL tr. *Thevenot's Trav.* II. 79 There are many squares in Ispahan, but of all, that which is called the Meidan..is the greatest and finest place in the World. *a* **1700** EVELYN *Diary* 18 Apr. 1680, Going early from his house in the square of St. James. **1716** GAY *Trivia* I. 9, I.. the silent Court, and opening Square explore. **1782** MISS BURNEY *Cecilia* x. vii, She told the coachman, therefore, to drive to the corner of the square. **1816** SOUTHEY *Poet's Pilgr.* IV. liii, Methought that in a spacious Square Of some great town the goodly ornament, Three statues I beheld. **1849** MACAULAY *Hist. Eng.* iii. I. 358 We should greatly err if we were to suppose that any of the streets and squares then bore the same aspect as at present. **1886** C. E. PASCOE *Lond. of To-day* xxxiv. (ed. 3) 303 There is little to engage the wayfarer's interest westward of the Circus if we except some of the squares..lying on the north side.

attrib. **1883** BESANT *All in Garden Fair* II. iii, To end as his uncle was ending, with a square house and a one-horse carriage! **1893** *Daily News* 12 Jan. 3/1 Square-gardens innumerable will occur to every one—in Bloomsbury, in Mayfair, in Belgravia.

b. A rectangular building or block of buildings; *U.S.* a block of buildings bounded by streets.

a **1700** EVELYN *Diary* 23 May 1645, The house is a square of 4 pavilions. **1725** in Foley *Rec. Eng. Prov. S.J.* VII. Introd. p. xl, From thence it [the fire] communicated itself to the great square, or new building of the College on both sides. **1867** LATHAM *Black & White* 16 A square at Philadelphia means a solid block of houses, not an open space enclosed by buildings. **1891** *Cent. Dict.* s.v., The house is four or five squares further up-town.

13. An area of a hundred square feet, forming the measure or standard by which the price of flooring, roofing, tiling, or similar work is reckoned.

1663 GERBIER *Counsel* 63 Old Tiling at thirteen shillings foure pence a square. New Tiling at 1. pound 5 shillings a square. **1667** PRIMATT *City & C. Builder* 59 Carpenters do for the most part deal by the square, which is ten foot every way, and an hundred in all. **1703** R. NEVE *City & C. Purchaser* 23, 4s. per Square for Sawing the Boards..and.. 3s. 6d. per Square for Framing the Carcass. *c* **1738** in E. B. Jupp *Carpenters' Co.* (1887) 567 To do the new plain tyleing att £1. 6. 0 per square, and the Pan tyleing att 18s. per square. **1825** J. NICHOLSON *Operat. Mechanic* 550 A square of plain tiling will require a bundle of laths. **1883** *Law Times Rep.* XLIX. 139/1 The deceased had slated seven or eight houses,..and..had been paid..upon the terms that he was to have 4s. a square. **1894** *Times* 31 May 10/5 The flooring ..fetched 5s. 'a square'.

14. *Astrol.* and *Astr.* Quartile aspect; quadrature.

1667 MILTON *P.L.* x. 659 Thir planetarie motions and aspects In Sextile, Square, and Trine, and Opposite. **1686** GOAD *Celest. Bodies* I. xv. 97 Other causes may help to irritate that Passion, which the) in Square to the Sun inclineth to. **1690** LEYBOURN *Curs. Math.* 449 Mars..is observed by Kepler, when in Square with the Sun, to be Dichotomous,..at other times, between its Square and Opposition to the Sun to be Gibbous. **1819** J. WILSON *Compl. Dict. Astrol.* 379 *Square*, the quartile aspect, containing a quadrant or right angle. **1861** R. J. MORRISON *Hand-bk. Astrol.* I. I. iii. 8 When a sextile aspect or distance of *sixty* degrees falls in the latter, Ptolemy intimates that it has the effect of a square, or *ninety* degrees. And when a trine falls in signs of short ascension, he says that the effect is also that of a square aspect. **1929** V. E. ROBSON *Alan Leo's Dict. Astrol.* 188 The Square is the most critical and conflicting of aspects. *a* **1963** L. MACNEICE *Astrol.* (1964) viii. 258 Sextiles..are supposed to be 'good'..aspects, while the square (90°) is considered 'bad'. **1975** I. M. HICKEY *Astrol.* viii. 72 Squares represent the lessons we have failed to learn.

15. In various special or technical senses: †**a.** (See quots.) *Obs.*$^{-0}$ †**b.** *Arch.* A square moulding; an abacus. *Obs.* **c.** The squared part at the top of an anchor-shank. **d.** (Miscellaneous uses: see quots.) **e.** A thin piece of wood or metal, in the shape of a right-angled triangle, used as a bell-crank or connected with a tracker of an organ. **f.** *U.S.* A group of bracts surrounding the flower of the cotton-plant. Hence ***square-borer*** (an insect). **g.** *Bookbinding.* Usu. in *pl.* The portion of the cover of a bound book which projects beyond the leaves. **h.** A given space on the page of a newspaper, etc., considered as a unit of measurement for advertisements. *U.S.* (now *Hist.*).

a. 1688 HOLME *Armoury* III. xviii. (Roxb.) 134/2 The seuerall parts of the Barrell of a Muskett. The Barrell. The squares. The mullets. *Ibid.* 135/1 A screwed barrell, is when the bore is of six or eight squares, or thrids, all throughout.

b. 1703 T. N. *City & C. Purchaser* 5 Annulet... 'Tis the same Member as the Sieur Mauclerc, from Vitruvius, calls a Fillet,..and Brown from Scamozzi a..Square, and Rabit.

c. 1839 URE *Dict. Arts* 44 In fig. 7 A is the shank [of the anchor];..E, the square; F, the nut. **1852** BURN *Naval & Mil. Techn. Dict.* II. s.v., Square of an anchor, *carré de la verge*.

d. 1841 HARTSHORNE *Salop. Ant.* Gloss., *Squares*, broad hoops of iron which are used to hold coal in 'the Baskets', whilst being drawn up a pit. **1844** PARNELL *Appl. Chem.* II. 65 The furnaces for the melting-pots, and for the pots called the 'squares' or 'cuvettes',..are placed in a range along the middle of the room lengthways. **1875** KNIGHT *Dict. Mech.* 2294/2 *Square* (Horology), that portion of the arbor on which the winding-key is placed; a similar part on the arbor of the hands of a watch, whereby they are set. **1879** *Cassell's Techn. Educ.* IV. 398/1 The 'square' (the strong iron plate which connects the two parts of the carriage at the headstock).

e. 1881 C. A. EDWARDS *Organs* 74 Backfalls are dispensed with, and squares inserted in their stead. **1884** *Encycl. Brit.* XVII. 834/1 In square and trackerwork..the old squares were made of wood. They resemble in function the squares used for taking bell-wires round a corner.

f. 1895 in *Funk's Stand. Dict.* **1906** E. W. HILGARD *Soils* 503 The writer found a 'patch' of cotton with luxuriant stalks.., but almost devoid of 'squares' or blooms. **1906** *Westm. Gaz.* 19 Dec. 2/1 The devastation caused by..the cotton aphis, the web-worm, and the square-borer.

g. 1835 'J. A. ARNETT' *Bibliopegia* 207 Squares.—That portion of the boards of a volume which projects over the edges. **1876** *Encycl. Brit.* IV. 43/2 The same processes are followed with the sides and the 'squares' when any ornamentation is tooled upon them. **1901** D. COCKERELL *Bookbinding* ix. 131 If the book has been trimmed, or is to remain uncut, a little more must be allowed for the 'squares'. **1946** E. DIEHL *Bookbinding* II. xi. 148 If the squares are too large when the boards have been laced on, it is a simple matter to cut them down.

h. 1800 *Impartial Observer* (Natchez, Mississippi) 5 May 1/1 Advertisements..which exceed a square will be inserted at the same proportionate price. **1877** *Harper's Mag.* Dec. 111/1 These newspaper people set an extra-ordinary value on their squares, as they call them. **1943** C. CROW *Great Amer. Customer* 122 The standard space measurement [for advertising] was the 'square', which meant a space equal in depth to the width of a column—approximately two column inches.

16. Slang uses. **a.** One who is square (SQUARE *a.* 9 d); a person considered to hold conventional or old-fashioned views. orig. *U.S. Jazz.*

1944 *Sun* (Baltimore) 27 Jan. 10/5 *Square*, in musician's jargon, anyone who is not cognizant of the beauties of true jazz. **1944** D. BURLEY *Orig. Handbk. Harlem Jive* 70 Are you going to be a square all you days? **1947** [see HIP *v.*[2]]. **1952** 'E. Box' *Death in Fifth Position* (1954) i. 23 Though I might not be entirely a square I was.. hopelessly ignorant of all that.. mattered. **1959** H. HOBSON *Mission House Murder* ii. 15 The odd fifty million citizens who don't dig them are dead-beats —squares. **1965** G. HACKFORTH-JONES *Storm in Harbour* ix. 142 You and I are what the up and coming generation call squares. We live in the past and we don't like what we see of the present. **1968** T. WOLFE *Electric Kool-Aid Acid Test* xxvii. 386 We're in two different worlds. You're a hippie and I'm a square. **1974** *Howard Jrnl.* XIV. 101 The 'square' are women who are basically pro-authority, in favour of law and order, and share the values of 'respectable' society. **1977** J. D. DOUGLAS in Douglas & Johnson *Existential Sociol.* i. 42 Marihuana has been widely used for decades by artists and other groups, probably also as a way of expressing feelings against the squares.

b. A cigarette containing tobacco, rather than marijuana. *U.S.* (chiefly *Blacks'*).

1970 H. E. ROBERTS *Third Ear* 13/1 *Square*, a cigarette. **1971** *Black Scholar* Sept. 36/2 Why, why, he kept asking himself, as he lit a square.., why do I keep having that dream. **1974** *Black World* Nov. 57 Light me up a square, baby.

17. Elliptical uses of the adj.: A square meal (orig. and chiefly *U.S.*); a square piano; a square dance; a square drink, etc.

1882 O. MERDIAN *Let.* 20 Sept. in *Frontier* (1930) X. 252/1, I went in..and had some dinner..ate a square & talked awhile. **1883** *Daily News* 19 Sept. 1/7 A number of superior Secondhand Instruments,..including Grand Squares for India. **1893** *Family Herald* 131/1 'Which is the next [dance]?' 'A square, I think.' **1896** 'H. S. MERRIMAN' *Flotsam* xii. 136 The stoutest and most middle-aged civil servant, provided he was single, was accorded a 'square'. **1899** *N. & Q.* 7 Jan. 8/1 In several parts of Glamorgan 'a square of beer', measuring two-thirds of a pint, is also a favourite drink, so called, I have heard it said, because it is a 'square drink'. **1927** J. BARBICAN *Confess. Rum-Runner* xxiii. 260 We sure was hungry for the dough, for it was weeks since we had roped in our three squares a day. **1962** 'E. MCBAIN' *Like Love* ii. 21 But he had had a clean bed to sleep in, and three squares a day, as the saying goes. **1979** 'H. HOWARD' *Sealed Envelope* x. 135 Mine was a lousy job. There must be a better way of making three squares a day.

III. †**18.** A quarrel, dispute, wrangle; discord, dissension, quarrelling. *Obs.* (Cf. 19 and SQUARE *v.* 8.)

1545 *St. Papers Hen. VIII*, X. 721 We talked sumwhat vively, but without any square. **1579-80** NORTH *Plutarch* (1676) 66 Afterwards they fortuned to fall at jar one with the other,..yet this square bred no violent inconvenience between them. *a* **1603** T. CARTWRIGHT *Confut. Rhem. N.T.* (1618) 434 Thus through a perpetual square and iar, of the voice and of the hart, there can be no musique. **1627** MAGEOGHAGAN tr. *Ann. Clonmacnois* 39 They did agree without any Square at all.

IV. In various phrases.

to break a square, no square, etc.: see BREAK *v.* 46.

†**19.** ***at square***, in a state of disagreement, discord, or dissension; at variance; esp. ***to be*** or

to fall at (a) square, to quarrel, differ, or wrangle. *Obs.*

Freq. from *c* 1545 to *c* 1600.

(*a*) **1545** *St. Papers Hen. VIII*, X. 724 The Scottes, with whom they had amytie,..and never..but twyse wer at any square togithres. **1559** *Mirr. Mag., Malin* vi, My yongest brother,.. Whose hauty minde and mine were still at square. **1566** STAPLETON *Ret. Untr. Jewel* II. 47 M. Jewell is so at square with all Writers. *a* **1602** FORMAN *Diary* (Halliw.) 10 Oftentymes they too were also at square, insomuch that twise he had like to have killed hir.

(*b*) *a* **1548** HALL *Chron., Hen. VI*, 140 Yet their children and cosyns..fell so far at square, that the house of Burgoyne was spoyled of the fairest flower of his garland. **1568** GRAFTON *Chron.* II. 99 The Monkes of Cauntorbury now hauyng the whole election in their owne handes, fell also at a square among themselues. **1577–87** HOLINSHED *Chron.* I. 40/2 She falling at square with hir husband, married Uellocatus. **1602** CAREW *Cornwall* (1764) 103 She and hers fell at square, which discord..brake forth into a blow. [**1632** J. HAYWARD tr. *Biondi's Eromena* b 4, What? laid aside thy Compasse?..with the Circle art thou fallen at square?]

(*c*) **1549** COVERDALE, etc. *Erasm. Par. Rom.* 1 Leste either sectes or names of countreys put you now at square. **1577–87** HOLINSHED *Chron.* II. 54 Diuerse in Normandie desired nothing more than to set the two brethren at square.

20. *out of square*, out of the true, proper, or normal state or condition; out of (right) order or rule: **a.** In predicative use.

Very common from *c* 1540 to *c* 1630.

1542 UDALL *Erasm. Apoph.* 72 Neither shall the sense bee out of square, if ye take ye greke vocable λόγον..for reason. **1556** OLDE *Antichrist* 25 b, How great (and how out of square) this errour of yᵉ world is. **1612** *Two Noble K.* IV. iii. 109 This may..reduce what's now out of square in her, into their former law, and regiment. **1621** BP. MOUNTAGU *Diatribæ* 224 There are in Porphyrie two sorts of men irregular and out of square in the seruice of their gods. **1661** J. STEPHENS *Procurations* 129 That which..in him..seemeth *absonum*, untunable and out of square, and friendly compasse. **1850** CARLYLE *Latter-d. Pamph.* viii. (1872) 253 Something must be wrong in the inner man of the world, since its outer man is so terribly out of square!

b. With various verbs. In later use passing into the sense 'in or into disorder, irregularity, or confusion'.

1555 EDEN *Decades* 346 Wherin he speaketh not greatly owt of square. **1596** SPENSER *F.Q.* v. Introd. i, Me seemes the world is runne quite out of square. **1622** PEACHAM *Compl. Gent.* v. (1906) 39 The least disorder or ranknesse of any one flower, putteth a beautifull bed or well contrived knot out of square. **1650** HOWELL *Giraffi's Rev. Naples* I. 50 Had not a secret Treaty..against Masaniello, and his followers, bin discovered, which put all things again out of square. **1837** CARLYLE *Fr. Rev.* III. I. vii, This shrieking Confusion of a Soldiery, which we saw long since fallen all suicidally out of square, in suicidal collision. **1864** —— *Fredk. Gt.* IV. 74 All things..much fallen out of square.

c. In literal sense.

1576 FLEMING *Panopl. Epist.* 377 There was nothing in him that was out of square, but every joynte and limme, both in measure and in place,..passing hansome. **1603** FOWLDES *Homer's Battle Frogs & Mice* (1634) D 6 b, Exceeding were their [crabs'] shoulders out of square.

21. *square one*: the beginning, the starting-point. Freq. as ***back to*** (also ***in, on***) ***square one***.

Often said to derive from the notional division of an association football pitch into eight numbered sections for the purposes of early radio commentaries (see *Radio Times*, 1927, 28 Jan.). This suggestion cannot be upheld with any certainty, and the phrase may simply come from a board-game such as Snakes and Ladders.

1960 *Times* 21 May 9/2 As far as building up a basis for profitable negotiations is concerned the two sides are back in square one. **1965** *Listener* 24 June 930/2 Let us drop the logical knot that twin studies have tied us in and go back for a moment to square one. **1965** *Guardian* 13 Oct. 2/7 The city's medical officer..said they were still in 'square one', and would stay there till they got some real facts. **1966** J. I. M. STEWART *Aylwins* x. 126 That he had seized a chance to break off our interview at that point seemed to argue a refusal to abide by this judgement of the matter. We were back, so to speak, in Square One. **1970** G. F. NEWMAN *Sir, You Bastard* 279 A couple of wrong answers and Sneed knew he'd be right back on square one. **1973** G. TALBOT *Ten Seconds from Now* (1974) viii. 111 After each of those successful essays it was 'back to Square One'. **1977** 'M. INNES' *Honeybath's Haven* x. 98 Honeybath broke off in these bold proposals, suddenly aware that Edwin was weeping. It was like being back on square one. **1980** D. BOGARDE *Gentle Occupation* xii. 332 'Black is black, Moluccans.'..'Are coloured people. They are dark,' said Emmie with force. 'Well, don't let's *have* any blasted children'... 'But I do. I want.'..'Oh for God's sake. We're back to square one again.'

V. 22. *attrib.* and *Comb.*, as **square-bashing** *vbl. sb.* and *ppl. a. Mil. slang* [BASHING *vbl. sb.* 3], drilling; hence **square-basher**; **square-free** *a. Math.* [tr. G. *quadratfrei*], (of an integer) equal to the product of a set of different primes; not divisible by a perfect square; **square-pusher** *slang*, (*a*) a respectable girl; (*b*) a boyfriend; hence **square-pushing**, the act or practice of walking out with a girl (popularly associated with accompanying nursemaids, etc., about town squares); love-making; also as *pres. pple.*

1959 *Spectator* 21 Aug. 212/2 The transition away from the era of the square-basher and the char-and-wadder is painfully slow. **1943** Square-bashing [see BASHING *vbl. sb.* 3]. **1946** C. FRY *Phoenix too Frequent* 28 There, do you see her, you acorn-chewing infantryman? You've made her cry, you square-bashing barbarian. **1962** [see sense 11 c above]. **1975** 'G. BLACK' *Big Wind for Summer* ii. 20 Attached to a Malay regiment, supervising weapon training and square bashing. **1960** NIVEN & ZUCKERMAN *Introd. Theory Numbers* xi. 226 The set of square-free integers has natural density $6/\pi^2$. **1971** G. HIGMAN in Powell & Higman *Finite Simple Groups* vi. 209 All elements have square-free order. **1890** BARRÈRE & LELAND *Dict. Slang* II. 158/1 A square pusher is a girl of good reputation. **1922** JOYCE *Ulysses* 425, I seen you up Faithful place with your squarepusher, the greaser off the railway, in his cometobed hat. **1918** W. J. LOCKE *Rough Road* x. 116 'Go "square-pushing"?' said Doggie contemptuously, using the soldiers' slang for walking about with a young woman. **1922** JOYCE *Ulysses* 161 Squarepushing up against a backdoor. Maul her a bit. **1928** F. E. BAILY *Golden Vanity* xii. 178 Left me cold in a strange place to go square-pushing with some forward young woman. **1930** J. B. PRIESTLEY *Good Companions* I. iv. 134 'E wouldn't bother, though, too busy square-pushing, taking the girls out, see.

square (skwɛə(r)), *a.* Also 4–7 **squar**, 5 **sqware, squyer**, 6 **squear**, *Sc.* **squair, squayr**; 4–6 **sware** (4 **suare**, 6 **suar**). [ad. OF. *esquarré* (*escarré*), pa. pple. of *esquarrer* SQUARE *v.*, assimilated to this and to SQUARE *sb.*]

I. 1. a. Having a rectilinear and rectangular form of equal length and breadth; contained by four equal sides at right angles to each other; quadrate.

In early use freq. FOUR-SQUARE *a.* Cf. also THREE-, SIX-, EIGHT-SQUARE *sb.*

13.. *E.E. Allit. P.* A. 837 Lesande þe boke with leuezsware. *Ibid.* B. 1386 þe place..Was longe & ful large & euer ilych sware. *c* **1391** CHAUCER *Astrol.* I. §13 Thanne hastow a brod Rewle, þat hath on either ende a Square plate perced with a certein holes. *c* **1400** *Rom. Rose* 4158 Aboute it was founded square, An hundred fademe on every side; It was alle liche longe and wide. *c* **1440** *Palladius on Husb.* II. 107 A tabul square an aker lond to holde, Feet scoris nyne in lengthe, as fele in wide. **1509** HAWES *Past. Pleas.* XXXV. 179 On the thirde head, in a banner square, All of reade was wrytten Discomfort. **1557** in Feuillerat *Revels Q. Mary* (1914) 236 A square pece of waynscott. **1589** PUTTENHAM *Eng. Poesie* II. xi. (Arb.) 113 It will grow into the figure Trapezion, which is some portion longer then square. **1611** BIBLE *1 Kings* vii. 5 And all the doores and postes were square, with the windowes. **1667** MILTON *P.L.* II. 1048 To behold..th' Empyreal Heav'n, extended wide In circuit, undetermind square or round. **1715** tr. *Gregory's Astron.* (1726) I. 442 Because this given Rectangle..wants of a square Figure. **1784** COWPER *Task* I. 21 A massy slab, in fashion square or round. **1835** J. DUNCAN *Beetles* (Nat. Lib.) 128 The elytra..approach more to a square shape than is usual among the carabideous tribes. **1859** *Handbk. Turning* 127 Square patterns require great care in working them. **1892** *Photogr. Ann.* II. 489 An apparatus for trimming paper and prints..and enabling the user to be sure that they will be true and square.

transf. **1648** HEXHAM II, *Teerlingh-wijse*, after a Square manner. **1869** RANKINE *Machine & Hand-tools* Pl. P 8 The ordinary methods of hand or square centering now in general use. **1892** *Daily News* 28 July 6/7 The artillery moved up by square movements instead of in line.

b. *square inch, foot, yard*, etc., a rectangular space measuring an inch, foot, etc., either way. ***square mile***: also *spec.* a familiar term for the (heart of the) City of London.

In quot. 1667 'square Inches' are = 'cubic inches' (cf. 3 b), and in quot. 1715 the sense is 'of 36 square inches'.

1625 N. CARPENTER *Geogr. Del.* I. viii. (1635) 200 The product will shew the number of square miles in the face of the Terrestriall Globe. **1667** PRIMATT *City & C. Builder* 36 If you would let it by the square Foot,..it is worth twelve pence a Foot *per ann. Ibid.* 165 A Foot solid measure hath seventeen hundred twenty eight square Inches. **1691** T. H[ALE] *Acc. New Invent.* 59 To do the Work per Yard square. **1715** DESAGULIERS *Fires Impr.* 161 There are but few Cavities in this Construction, and those but 36 Inches square. **1774** GOLDSM. *Nat. Hist.* (1776) I. 302 A weight of fifteen pounds upon every square inch. **1837** J. T. SMITH tr. *Vicat's Mortars* 92 An absolute resistance of $5^k.43$ per centimetre square. **1846** BAXTER *Libr. Pract. Agric.* (ed. 4) II. 437 The result, in square chains and links, is converted into acres by a simple division by ten. **1868** G. DUFF *Pol. Surv.* 48 His territories in Asia cover 668,580 English square miles. **1966** L. SOUTHWORTH *Felon in Disguise* i. 13 Being a non-residential area, murders seldom occur in the square mile. **1971** *Guardian* 3 Mar. 18/4 Prince Charles was made a Freeman of the City of London yesterday... It was the kind of traditional occasion that the square mile does so well. **1975** *Times* 1 Mar. 12/2 The City Corporation hopes to have redeveloped 90 per cent of the square mile by 1980.

c. *square measure*, a unit of measurement consisting of a square space; a system of measures based on such units.

1728 CHAMBERS *Cycl.* s.v. *Measure*, English Square or Superficial Measures are raised from the Yard of 36 Inches, multiplied into itself. **1854** *Orr's Circle Sci., Math.* 19 Measures of Surface, or Square Measure.

2. a. *square number*, the product of a number multiplied by itself.

1557 RECORDE *Whetst.* C iij b, Square nombers are those, whiche maie be diuided by some one number, and haue the same number for the quotiente. **1570** BILLINGSLEY *Euclid* VII. def. 19. 187 It is called a square number, because..it representeth the figure of a square in Geometry. **1621** T. WILLIAMSON tr. *Goulart's Wise Vieillard* 41 Plato iudged the yeare eightie one, which is compounded of nine times nine, to be the Climactericall yeare,..which hee calleth the square number. **1646** SIR T. BROWNE *Pseud. Ep.* 215 Though it containeth both numbers..7. and 9. yet neither of them square or quadrate. **1674** JEAKE *Arith.* (1696) 193 Which Square Number set thereunder, and substract therefrom. **1751** JOHNSON *Rambler* No. 181 ¶5, I..considered even the square and cubick numbers through the lottery. **1846** DE MORGAN *Arith.* vii. §161 *note*, By square number I mean a number which has a square root. Thus 25 is a square number, but 26 is not.

b. *square root*, the number or quantity constituting such a base of a given number or quantity as to produce this when multiplied by itself.

1557 RECORDE *Whetst.* G iv, The roote of a square nombere, is called a Square roote. **1571** DIGGES *Pantom.* I. xxxiii. K ij b, The roote square of the remaynder ye must compare wyth the distaunce of the fyrste shyppe. **1633** MASSINGER *Guardian* I. i, They would have me..let him know No more than how to cipher well, or do His tricks by the square root. **1674** JEAKE *Arith.* (1696) 193 The Square Root of a Number is extracted commonly thus. **1715** tr. *Gregory's Astron.* (1726) I. 53 The Celerities of the Bodies are reciprocally as the Square Roots of the Radii. **1812–6** PLAYFAIR *Nat. Phil.* (1819) I. 195 The area of the orifice multiplied into the square-root of the depth. **1842** *Penny Cycl.* XXII. 394/1 The rule for the extraction of the square root is a tentative inverse process very much resembling division.

c. *square party*, a party of four persons.

In the first quot. after F. *partie carrée*, a party of two men and two women.

1851 WOLFF *Pict. Spanish Life* vi. 176 Remaining a 'square party',..we all four embarked in the little boat. **1893** G. ALLEN *Scallywag* I. vi. 79 The square party of pedestrians turned away along the sea front.

3. a. Having an equilateral rectangular section.

a **1300** *Cursor M.* 1664 A wessel..sal be wroght o suare tre. *c* **1386** CHAUCER *Knt.'s T.* 218 Many a barre Of iren greet and squar as eny sparre. *c* **1407** LYDG *Reson & Sens.* 5415 And arwes eke..With which, wher they be square or rounde, He kan hurte. **1459** *Paston Lett.* I. 490 Item, ij. grete square spittys. **1508** DUNBAR *Gold. Targe* 111 Wyth bow in hand..And dredefull arowis grundyn scharp and square. **1523** FITZHERB. *Husb.* §9 To plow a square forowe, the bredthe and the depenes all one. **1677** [see *square-bore* in 15]. **1728** CHAMBERS *Cycl.* s.v. *Stairs*, Square winding Stairs are such as wind round a square Newel, either Solid or open. **1796** WITHERING *Brit. Plants* (ed. 3) III. 531 Stems square, hairy. **1832** BREWSTER *Nat. Magic* viii. 188 One being a square rod, another a bent cylindrical one. **1846** HOLTZAPFFEL *Turning* II. 824 Square files, are used for small apertures, and those works to which the ordinary flat files are from their greater size less applicable. **1900** *Jrnl. Sch. Geog.* (U.S.) Jan. 11 A 'square tube' or long narrow box with an inside measurement of one inch square.

fig. **1862** MISS BRADDON *Lady Audley* xxv, The square men in the round holes are pushed into them by their wives. *c* **1870** TENNYSON in *Athenæum* 5 Nov. (1892) 631/1, I should but be..the square man in the round hole.

b. Having a form more or less approximating to a cube; rectangular and of three dimensions.

c **1420** *Liber Cocorum* (1862) 38 Cut [the mallard] in peses, as I þe kenne; Square as dises þou shalt hit make. **1600** *Sir John Oldcastle* IV. i, Giue vs square dice, weele keepe this courte of guard For al good fellowes. **1621** in Foster *Eng. Factories Ind.* (1906) I. 291 The square basketts are not made all of one biggnesse. **1650** BULWER *Anthropomet.* 11 These occidental Indian square-heads. **1726** LEONI *Alberti's Archit.* I. 38/1 Whether square Stone, or uneven Scantlings. **1760** R. BROWN *Compl. Farmer* II. 42 Steel-marle, which..is of it self apt to break into square cubical bits. **1832** BREWSTER *Nat. Magic* xi. 269 A large square chest or box, three feet and a half long, two feet deep, and two and a half high. **1884** KNIGHT *Dict. Mech.* Suppl., *Square Tank Coil*, a condensing coil of rectangular shape.

4. Of limbs, the body, etc.: Approximating to a square section or outline; stoutly and strongly built; solid, sturdy.

1375 BARBOUR *Bruce* III. 581 Newys that stalwart war & squar, That wont to spayn gret speris war. *c* **1400** *Destr. Troy* 3967 A hard brest hade þe buerne, & his back sware. *c* **1430** LYDG. *Min. Poems* (Percy Soc.) 200 Here greet shulderys, square and brood. **1513** DOUGLAS *Æneid* v. vii. 107 His lymmis squair, Baith big bonis and brawnis, [he] maid all bair. *a* **1548** HALL *Chron., Rich. III*, 3 b, To him he ioyned one John Dighton,..a bygge, broade, square, & strong knaue. **1596** DALRYMPLE tr. *Leslie's Hist. Scot.* II. 44 Quhen Æneas Syluius walde expreme the coniunctioun of his memberis, with the Maiestie of his persoune, he calis him squair. **1625** HART *Anat. Ur.* II. viii. 103 Yet was he of a reasonable square and corpulent body. **1709** *London Gaz.* No. 4536/4 He is a Square well-set Man. **1720** *Ibid.* No. 5898/9 A..well built, and square Mare. **1802** MAR. EDGEWORTH *Moral T.* (1816) I. x. 76 A square, thick, hard-working man. **1854** *Poultry Chron.* I. 239 What a glorious old hen she was! Large, wide, short-legged, square and compact.

5. Of (a stated) length on each of the four sides forming a square.

Regularly placed after the words giving the measurement. The usage in quot. 1448 is obsolete.

c **1400** MAUNDEV. (1839) v. 41 That Tour conteyned gret Contree in circuyt: For the Tour allone conteyned 10 Myle sqware. **1448** in Willis & Clark *Cambridge* (1886) II. 8 The Someres..shall be one side xij inch squar and on the other part xiiij inch squar; and all the Gistes shall be on the one part squar vi inches and on the other part viij inches. **1449** in *Cal. Proc. Chanc. Q. Eliz.* (1830) II. Pref. 55 þe gurdyng someres of þe same flore shull be xj inchis square. *a* **1550** *Droichis Part of Play* 44 in *Dunbar's Poems* (S.T.S.) 315 His teith wes ten myle squair. **1594** R. ASHLEY tr. *Loys le Roy* 41 b, In the midst there was an other place made of Carpenters worke,..and was large a hundred foote square, which is fower hundred foote round. **1619** in Foster *Eng. Factories Ind.* (1906) I. 163 Those peeces which content 30 ells square fall out but 20 covados square. **1659** LEAK *Waterwks.* 18 A straight Axeltree of wood, a foot square, and 60-foot high. **1728** CHAMBERS *Cycl.* s.v. *Diamond*, A Hole is made in a Wall, a foot-square. **1790** W. WRIGHTE *Grotesque Archit.* 4 An hermit's cell..eight feet square in the inside. **1842** LOUDON *Suburban Hort.* 427 This block, which may be six inches square, need not rise more than an inch above the surface. **1854** *Poultry Chron.* II. 142 The whole were reared in a back-yard not ten feet square. **1900** [see 3].

6. †**a.** Of an angle: Right. *Obs.*

1551 RECORDE *Pathw. Knowl.* I. Def., A blunt or brode corner, is greater then is a square angle, and his lines do parte more in sonder then in a right angle.

b. At right angles; rectangular in position or direction; perpendicular (*to* something).

1571 DIGGES *Pantom.* I. i. C, Thus drawe your plumbe or squire line FCG. *Ibid.* xxii. Giij, Drawe foure lines perpendiculare or squire the one to the other. **1656** H. PHILLIPS *Purch. Patt.* (1676) B viii b, In the square meeting of the Table. **1715** DESAGULIERS *Fires Impr.* 86 Whose sides are all square to one another. *Ibid.*, Draw HP square or perpendicular to GHA. **1769** FALCONER *Dict. Marine* (1780), *Square*, a term peculiarly appropriated to the yards and their sails, implying that they hang at right angles with the mast or keel. **1797** J. CURR *Coal Viewer* 11 In the main roads underground.. square turns are not necessary. **1833** M. SCOTT *Tom Cringle* xv. (1842) 379 A long low vessel,.. with immensely square yards. **1833** *Regul. & Instr. Cavalry* I. 49 Bodies to be quite square to the front. **1857** LIVINGSTONE *Trav.* ii. 40 The Bakwains have a curious inability to make or put things square. **1868** AIREY *Pop. Astron.* i. 15 *note*, When the expression perpendicular to the surface of the glass is used, it means what a workman would probably call square to the surface of the glass.

†**c.** *fig.* Diverging or deviating *from* something.

1549 L. COXE *Erasm. Par. Titus* 28 Teaching shamefull thinges and far square from the veritie of the gospell.

d. *Assoc. Football*, etc. Of a group of players: positioned in a line at right angles to the direction of play (*spec.* as a defensive weakness).

1972 G. GREEN *Great Moments in sport: Soccer* x. 97 Often, too, Mullen and Hancocks would find each other with long, cross-field passes which travelled from one touchline to the other during the course of an attack, with the result that opposing defences were often caught square offering vital openings to the forwards in the middle. **1977** *Times* 28 Feb. 8/3 They were goals Middlesbrough always looked like taking against Arsenal's soft, square defence.

7. a. Even, straight, level. Also const. *with.*

1814 D. H. O'BRIAN *Captivity & Escape* 7 On our arrival on board, the water was nearly square with the combings of the lower deck. **1884** F. J. BRITTEN *Watch & Clockm.* 201 Brass surfaces are.. rubbed square with blue stone.

b. *fig.* On equal terms; with all accounts settled. Freq. const. *with.*

1859 *Slang Dict.* 100 'To be square with a man,' to be revenged. **1867** TROLLOPE *Chron. Barset* I. xxxvii. 326 He's only going to give me my little bit of money.. and then he and I will be all square. **1883** *Contemp. Rev.* Sept. 358 Acred squires, who lay their heads.. on their pillows with self-approval that they are square with the world. **1892** 'R. BOLDREWOOD' *Nevermore* III. 68 I've got square with you so far, and.. I'll be more than even with you yet.

c. *Golfing.* Having equal scores. Also in other sports.

1887 in *Jamieson's Sc. Dict.* Suppl. 227/1. **1898** *Daily News* 22 Oct. 9/4 They were all square at the 18th, and no fewer than five extra holes had to be played before the Huddersfield man could claim a victory. **1955** *Times* 14 May 3/4 (*heading*) All square in Davis Cup.

8. *Mus.* Of rhythm: simple, straightforward.

1958 *Times* 27 Oct. 12/3 Attempts have been made.. in recent years to get away from the square style of playing that arose out of the hymns and other purely vocal music. **1967** A. L. LLOYD *Folk Song in England* iv. 170 The earlier melodies are more vigorous, squarer, franker in cast. **1976** *Early Music* July 270 The opening sinfonia for strings and trombones is remarkably like several opera overtures of the time, with square rhythms [etc.].

II. 9. Of actions: Just or equitable; fair, honest, honourable, straightforward: **a.** In the phrases ***square play*** or ***dealing, the square thing. square deal***: see DEAL *sb.*[2] 4 c.

(*a*) **1591** GREENE *Conny Catch.* (1859) 7 For feare of trouble I was fain to try my good hap at square play. **1604** TERILO *Fr. Bacon's Proph.* 214 in Hazl. *E.P.P.* IV. 276 And faire square plaie with yea and naie, Who lost the game would quickly paie. **1677** WYCHERLEY *Pl. Dealer* I. i, Why, don't you know.. that telling truth is a quality as prejudicial to a man that wou'd thrive in the World, as square Play to a Cheat? **1708** *Brit. Apollo* Supern. Paper No. 4. 1/2 Venturing my Money in any sort of Traffick, is much the same, as at Square Play.

(*b*) **1633** GERARD *Descr. Somerset* (1900) 115 Theis come as neere unto them as possibly with square dealing they can. **1692** BENTLEY *Boyle Lect.* i. 38 Would there then be kept that square-dealing in such a monstrous den of Thieves? **1884** *Harper's Mag.* June 56/2 Reputation for integrity and square dealing.

(*c*) *c* **1860** MRS. SPOFFORD in *Casquet of Literature* IV. 25/1 He had come to question.. whether it was just the square thing to.. shut her up all by herself. **1890** *Cent. Mag.* Feb. 527/1 You know I've tried to do the square thing by you.

b. In general use. (Cf. FAIR AND SQUARE *a.*)

1606 SHAKS. *Ant. & Cl.* II. ii. 190 She's a most triumphant Lady, if report be square to her. **1607** —— *Timon* V. iv. 36 For those that were, it is not square to take On those that are, Reuenge. **1679** HARBY *Key Script.* ii. 27 Much more must his Antitype.. be far from giving or receiving any right Counsel, and from all practice of Square Right. **1812** J. H. VAUX *Flash Dict.* s.v. **1885** *American* IX. 278 A desire to do something which, as they think, will be square all around. **1892** 'R. BOLDREWOOD' *Nevermore* xi, I may have doubted whether everything was quite square about him [a horse]; but I never thought for a moment that he was stolen.

10. Of persons: †**a.** Not readily moved or shaken in purpose, etc.; solid, steady, reliable. *Obs.*

1589 PUTTENHAM *Eng. Poesie* II. xi[i]. (Arb.) 113 [Aristotle] termeth a constant minded man.. a square man. **1612** T. TAYLOR *Comm. Titus* i. 7 This doctrine sheweth what a square and furnished man he had need be, who must stand vnder such a burden as this is. **1635** in Ellis *Orig. Lett.* Ser. II. III. 283 To make sure to keepe my self close and squaire in all to his Ma[ties] service. **1710** S. SEWALL *Diary* 3 Apr., I did not think him so square and stable a man.

†**b.** Solid or steady (at eating or drinking). *Obs.*

1611 COTGR., *Vn ferial beuveur*, a square drinker, a faithfull drunkard; one that will take his liquor soundly. *a* **1616** BEAUM. & FL. *Bonduca* II. iii, By —— square eaters, More meat I say:.. how terribly They charge upon their victuals.

c. Honest or straightforward in dealing with others; honourable, upright.

1646 QUARLES *Judgem. & Mercy* Wks. (Grosart) I. 93/2 Mistaking a lying or cousening knave for a square or honest man. **1667** TEMPLE *Let. Ld. Arlington* Wks. 1720 II. 49, I found him as plain, as direct, and square in the course of this Business, as any Man could be. *a* **1716** BLACKALL *Wks.* (1723) I. 165 When he sees that those Christians with whom he trades, are not.. so square and honest in their Dealings. **1811** *Lexicon-Balatronicum*, *Square*, honest, not roguish. **1852** MRS. STOWE *Uncle Tom's C.* i. 2 I've trusted him, since then, with everything I have—money, house, horses,—.. and I always found him true and square in everything. **1883** F. M. CRAWFORD *Dr. Claudius* ix, He amuses me, and he is very square on settling days.

d. Designating one who is out of touch with the ideas and conventions of a particular popular contemporary movement (orig. *Jazz*); conventional, old-fashioned. Formerly opp. HEP *a.* Also of things. *slang* (orig. *U.S.*).

1946 B. TREADWELL *Big Bk. Swing* 125/2 *Square*, not versed in Swing, puritanical. **1950** J. VEDEY *Band Leaders* 175 Consummate performer that Ellington is, he put these numbers over to the delight of all types of audience, young and old, sophisticated and 'square'. **1953** W. BURROUGHS *Junkie* (1972) x. 110 The other patients were a pretty square and sorry lot. **1959** N. MAILER *Advts. for Myself* (1961) 264 They wish this newspaper to be more conservative, more Square—I wish it to be more Hip. **1959** *Punch* 2 Sept. 103/1, I.. told her that the bang-opening was old-hat and a completely square method of writing these days. **1965** F. RAPHAEL *Darling* i. 7 You know books. Those things with pages very square people still occasionally read. **1971** B. MALAMUD *Tenants* 80, I didn't expect it to be that good, not from the square dude you are. **1977** P. G. WINSLOW *Witch Hill Murder* II. xvii. 219 He wants to be in with the law. Square at heart.

11. †**a.** Precise, prim, solemn. *Obs.*

c **1590** *Sir T. More* (Malone Soc.) 1425 Oh what formalitie, what square obseruance: liues in a little roome. **1599** B. JONSON *Cynthia's Rev.* II. iii, A serious, solemne, and supercilious face, full of formall and square gravitie. **1601** —— *Poetaster* IV. vi, And all their square pretext of grauitie [is] A meere vaine glorie.

†**b.** Solidly or firmly constituted; free from flaw or defect. *Obs.*

1628 STRAFFORD in Browning *Life* (1891) 293 We must apply a square courage to our proceedings, not fall away as water spilt upon the ground. **1672** OWEN *Disc. Evang. Love* v, Every undue presumption hath one or other lameness accompanying it: it is truth alone which is square and steady.

c. Precise, exact; †certain.

1632 LITHGOW *Trav.* v. 199 My conduct [= guide] still deceaued me, made it square Another Carauan, O! would come there. *Ibid.* IX. 415 Fit to gouerne others, and to direct him selfe with the square rules of wisdome and iudgement. *a* **1684** LEIGHTON *Wks.* (1868) 675 Framing them to an external and square carriage whereby the world.. is much advantaged. **1858** HAWTHORNE *Fr. & It. Note-bks.* (1871) II. 65 His ideas being square, solid and tangible, and therefore readily grasped and retained. **1884** J. PARKER *Apost. Life* II. 153 This is a square Gospel; it will have all things at right angles.

d. Straight, direct.

1804 M. CUTLER in *Life*, etc. (1888) II. 162 It was.. a square fight between the all-important head man of the party and another who ranks as his second. **1873** HALE *In His Name* vi. 57 [He] could not answer the square question put to him. **1896** *Daily News* 11 April 3/5 It may be.. foolish of the Transvaal to refuse the opportunity for a square talk, but it is strictly within its rights.

e. Right; in good order; on a proper footing. ***to call (it) square***, to regard as balanced or settled.

1825 H. WILSON *Mem.* (ed. 2) III. 360 As though I had been the Duchess's chosen daughter-in-law, for whom he was making all square. **1836** MARRYAT *Midsh. Easy* xviii, If she is unhappy for three months, she will be overjoyed for three more when she hears that I am alive, so it will be all square at the end of the six. **1853** DICKENS *Bleak Ho.* xx, I had confident expectations that things would come round and be all square. **1891** C. ROBERTS *Adrift Amer.* 163 Although he was willing to call it square, in reality he ought to make a claim.

f. Of meals: Full, solid, substantial. Of a drink: Copious; of full measure.

Orig. *U.S.*; common from about 1880.

1868 *All Year Round* 19 Sept. 354/2 Roadside hotel-keepers.. calling the miners' attention to their 'square meals': by which is meant full meals. **1876** *Daily News* 24 Oct. 1/3 This pot simmers from early morn till noon, when the one 'square meal' of the day is eaten. **1884** E. F. KNIGHT *Cruise Falcon* xi. 186 Mr. Wynn.. had prepared a good square supper for the travellers. **1899** [see SQUARE *sb.* 17].

III. *ellipt.* **12.** ***on*** or ***upon the square.*** **a.** With a square front; face to face; directly, openly. Now *rare.*

c **1611** CHAPMAN *Iliad* XIII. 138 But when he fell into the strengths the Grecians did maintain, And that they fought upon the square [Gr. ἀντίοι], he stood as fetter'd then. **1677** WYCHERLEY *Pl. Dealer* IV. i, Prithee bid 'em come up,.. captain, for now I can talk with her upon the square. **1691** DRYDEN *K. Arthur* v. i, How's this, a sally? Beyond my hopes, to meet them on the square. **1737** WHISTON *Josephus, Hist.* VI. vii. §2 Nor were [they] strong enough to fight with the Romans any longer upon the square. **1821** LAMB *Elia* I. *Old & New Schoolm.*, He is awkward, and out of place, in the society of his equals... He cannot meet you on the square.

b. In a fair, honest, or straightforward manner; without artifice, deceit, fraud, or trickery.

Very common from *c* 1670, freq. with reference to playing or gaming.

(*a*) **1667–8** DK. NEWCASTLE & DRYDEN *Sir Martin Marall* I. i, Scarce one woman in an hundred will play with you upon the square. **1680** COTTON *Compl. Gamester* (ed. 2) 4 These Rooks can do little harm in the day time at an Ordinary, being forc'd to play upon the Square. **1718** *Freethinker* No. 135, In an Age, wherein it is almost become the Glory of States to circumvent each other, who does not see the Necessity of playing upon the Square? **1748** SMOLLETT *R. Random* ix, He had played on the square with them. **1822** SCOTT *Nigel* xiii, While Lord Glenvarloch chose to play, men played with him regularly, or, according to the phrase, upon the square. **1844** THACKERAY *Barry Lyndon* xiii, No man could play with me through Europe, on the square.

(*b*) **1667** DRYDEN *Maid. Q.* IV. i, 'Gad, I love upon the square, I can endure no tricks to be used to me. **1689** T. R. *View Govt. Europe* 62 They no longer treated on the Square with their people. **1701** [DE FOE] *Villany of Stock-Jobbers* (ed. 2) 15 Then we shall Trade upon the square; Honesty and Industry will be the method of Thriving. **1736** LILLO *Fatal Curiosity* I. i, And he, who deals with mankind on the square,.. undoes himself. **1750** JOHNSON *Rambler* No. 75 ¶11 The greater part had indeed always professed to court, as it is termed, upon the square. **1809** MALKIN *Gil Blas* VIII. xii. ¶3, I shall act upon the square with you. **1851** MAYHEW *Lond. Lab.* I. 378 Some of the fraternity.. do not always deal 'upon the square'. **1866** G. MACDONALD *Ann. Q. Neighb.* xiii. (1878) 255, I could not help doubting if everything was done on the square, as they say.

†**c.** Upon terms of equality or friendship *with* another or others; also, even or 'quits' *with* another. *Obs.*

1692 WASHINGTON tr. *Milton's Def. People* x. M.'s Wks. 1851 VIII. 227 They chose rather to be lorded over once more by a Tyrant.. than endure their Brethren and Friends to be upon the square with them. **1693** DRYDEN *Juvenal* III. 179 We live not on the Square with such as these: Such are our Betters who can better please. **1707** *Reflex. upon Ridicule* 99 No body ventures to say in general, that he's upon the Square with Men of a great Merit. **1709** MRS. MANLEY *Secret Mem.* (1736) III. 30 They are now upon the Square with one another.

d. In predicative use without const.: Free from duplicity or unfairness; honest, straightforward, upright. Now *slang.*

1682 PENN in Dixon *Life* xxiii. (1872) 207 Keep upon the square, for God sees you. **1709** STEELE *Tatler* No. 39 ¶20 They us'd Seconds, who were to see that all was upon the Square. **1731** MEDLEY *Kolben's Cape G. Hope* 262 All of them trade.. in the most upright and friendly manner.. with the Europeans, whenever the latter are upon the square. **1839** in 'Ducange Anglicus' *Vulg. Tongue* (1857) 34 *On the square*, honest, square. **1867** TROLLOPE *Chron. Barset* I. xxxvii. 325 I'm not going to throw you over. I've always been on the square with you. **1892** E. REEVES *Homeward Bound* 53 An unfortunate stowaway, who.. was 'peached' on by a steerage passenger who he thought was 'on the square'.

e. ***to set on*** or ***upon the square***, to set or put right, or in proper order. *rare.*

1846 TRENCH *Mirac.* 255 Awaiting the great day when all things shall be set on the square. **1860** —— *Serm. Westm. Abbey* xxiii. 262 Leaving much.. to be redressed and adjusted and balanced, and finally set upon the square, on that great coming day.

f. In literal sense: At right angles; in a square or solid form.

1883 *Specif. Alnwick & Cornhill Rlwy.* 44 This Bridge is to be built under the Railway, on the square. **1904** *Daily Chron.* 1 Sept. 4/5 The Japanese soldier is never weedy. He is built on the square.

g. Having membership of the Freemasons; in accordance with the Masonic code.

1888 KIPLING *Man who would be King* in *Phantom 'Rickshaw* 73, I am hoping you will give him the message on the Square. **1927** —— *Limits & Renewals* (1932) 172, I told him I was something else besides a G.P... From then on he told the tale on the Square. **1974** *Times Educ. Suppl.* 21 June 2/4 How many local councils.. are riddled with freemasonry? At how many appointments are the best men .. passed over because they are not on the square?

IV. *attrib.* and *Comb.*

13. a. In parasynthetic combs., as ***square-barred, -based, -bladed, -bodied, -bracketed, -ended, -faced, -pupilled, -sectioned, -shaled,*** etc.; or with pa. pples., as ***square-built, -ground, -hewn, -hung, -made, -pied,*** etc.; also ***square footage; square-looking.***

1832 J. RENNIE *Consp. Butterfl. & M.* 164 *Square-barred Single Dot. **1857** MILLER *Elem. Chem., Org.* 605 It is deposited in *square-based anhydrous octohedra. **1611** COTGR., *Sang-de-dez*, little *square-bladed pocket daggers. **1643** R. BAKER *Chron.* (1653) 580 Sir Francis Drake,.. a short *square-bodied man. **1752** J. HILL *Hist. Anim.* 204 The square-bodied Syngnathus. **1970** *Guardian* 26 Nov. 13/4 Attention is focussed on the heavy-typed and *square-bracketed passages. **1843** JAMES *Forest Days* ii, A tall, powerful, and *square-browed man. **1687** MIÈGE *Gt. Fr. Dict.* II, *Square built, *bâti en carré.* **1825** J. NEAL *Bro. Jonathan* I. 191 He stood.. regarding his.. square-built brother opposite. **1891** *Tablet* 12 Sept. 437 Of contemporaneous design, like a square-built house. **1867** SMYTH *Sailor's Word-bk.*, **Square-Butted*, the yard-arms of small shipping so made that a sheave-hole can be cut through without weakening the yard. **1731** P. MILLER *Gard. Dict.* s.v. *Lotus*, Red *square-codded Birds-Foot Trefoil. **1849** CUPPLES *Green Hand* xix, As *square-countered and flat-breasted a ten-gun model as ever ran her nose under salt-water. **1805** R. W. DICKSON *Pract. Agric.* I. 540 The *square-eared wheat is a very productive kind. **1832** *Scoreby Farm Rep.* 9 in *Husb.* (L.U.K.) III, The square-eared, or some other of the coarse descriptions [of barley]. **1611** COTGR., *Escappe*, a small *square-edged circle, or fillet in a piller, &c. **1850** HOLTZAPFFEL *Turning* III. 1319 Applying the stone longitudinally upon a square-edged mill. **1792**

MARY WOLLSTONECR. *Rights Wom.* iv. 145 The *square-elbowed family drudge. **1923** *Trans. Scottish Ecclesiological Soc.* VII. 65 The Lady Chapel was..removed and a long *square-ended one substituted. **1936** W. FAULKNER *Absalom, Absalom!* 369 He saw then the square-ended saw chunk beside the wall. **1978** A. & G. RITCHIE *Anc. Monuments Orkney* 71 The church consisted of a rectangular nave with a porch at its W end and a square-ended chancel at the E end. **1872** GEO. ELIOT *Middlemarch* II. III. xxiv. 32 She was of the same curly-haired, *square-faced type as Mary. **1884** F. M. CRAWFORD *Rom. Singer* I. 108 This square-faced boy of mine was more than a match for her. **1607** TOPSELL *Four-f. Beasts* 460 The face of a Lyon is not round,..but rather it is *square figured. **1963** A. SMITH *Throw out Two Hands* i. 16 One man sitting down in a thing 3 feet 11 inches by 2 feet 11 inches tends to occupy the bulk of the available *square footage. **1879** MRS. A. E. JAMES *Ind. House-Managem.* 11, I actually once saw *square-fronted night-dresses! *c* **1330** R. BRUNNE *Chron. Wace* (Rolls) 15836 A wel longe pyk *Squar grounden, scharp, euenlyk. **1899** MARG. BENSON & GOURLAY *Temple of Mut* i. 2 The *square-hewn doorways of the tombs hollowed out in the face of the cliff. **1874** G. M. HOPKINS *Jrnls. & Papers* (1959) 255, I am not so sure of the tiles being *squarehung—they may have been lozenges. **1892** GUNTER *Miss Dividends* ix. 117 Two or three *square-jawed, full-lipped Mormon friends of his. **1833** LOUDON *Encycl. Archit.* §914 They are all to be *square-jointed at least 2 inches from the face. **1845** POE in *Godey's Lady's Bk.* Feb. 63/1 On the very tips of their heads were certain *square-looking boxes. **1853** LYNCH *Self-Improv.* 11 A rude square-looking country lad. **1820** SCOTT *Monast.* xxxv, Saunders was a short *square-made fellow. **1862** *Catal. Internat. Exhib., Brit.* II. No. 6963, *Square-mouthed travelling bags. **1894** LYDEKKER *Roy. Nat. Hist.* II. 479 The largest of the group is the square-mouthed, or Burchell's rhinoceros (*R. simus*). **1677** MOXON *Mech. Exerc.* i. 5 The *Square Nos'd Hand-Vice. **1868** G. M. HOPKINS *Jrnls. & Papers* (1959) 178 Like the skin of a white snake *square-pied with black. **1957** T. HUGHES *Hawk in Rain* 39 And looked down A *square-pupilled yellow-eyed look. **1964** W. L. GOODMAN *Hist. Woodworking Tools* 99 Another jack..with a similar casting screwed to a *square-sectioned wooden stock. **1592** GREENE *Upst. Courtier* (1871) 31 A *square set fellow, well fed and briskly appareled. **1888** EGGLESTON *Graysons* i. 6 Henry Miller was a square-set young fellow, without a spark of romance in him. **1816** SCOTT *Antiq.* xvii, That stretch of wall with *square-shafted windows. **1917** E. POUND *Lustra* 183 Breaking the riven waves On *square-shaled rocks. **1825** J. NEAL *Bro. Jonathan* II. 108 A dark, tall, *square-shouldered man. **1704** *Lond. Gaz.* No. 3984/4 A Neat's Leather Saddle, *square Skirted. **1860** HAWTHORNE *Fr. & It. Note-bks.* II. 303 Wig, square-skirted coat,..and all the queer costume of the period. **1822** *Hortus Anglicus* II. 71 *H. Nepetoides*, *Square-stalked Hyssop. Stem sharply quadrangular. **1872–4** JEFFERIES *Toilers of Field* (1892) 311 In the ditches the *square-stemmed figwort is conspicuous by its dark green. **1838** *Civil Eng. & Arch. Jrnl.* I. 279/2 The thread of a *square threaded screw. **1848** RICKMAN *Styles Archit.* 49 If it be *square-topt, it is called a tower. **1882** O'DONOVAN *Merv Oasis* I. 327 This village..consisting of little more than fifty square-topped huts. **1898** J. A. GIBBS *Cotswold Village* 3 A tiny village with its *square-towered Norman church.

b. ***square-maker*** (see quot.).

c **1850** *Rudim. Navig.* (Weale) 151 *A square-maker*, a shipwright who cuts the butts to receive the oakum, and prepares the work ready for the caulkers.

14. In collocations used attributively, as ***square-box house***, ***square-thread screw***, etc.

1819 SAMOUELLE *Entomol. Compend.* 421 *Noctua obeliscata.* The square-spot Dart. **1859** BOYD *Recreat. Country Parson* v. 188 The square-box house comes forward humbly. **1867** SMYTH *Sailor's Word-bk.*, *Square-Topsail Sloop*, sloops which carry standing yards. **1868** *Rep. U.S. Commissioner Agric.* (1869) 252 Specimens of square-top Osage thorn. **1869** RANKINE *Machine & Hand-tools* Pl. Q 16. 2 It is worked..by square-thread screws. **1893** *Times* 14 July 3/1 The same square-sett system of timbering.

15. a. In special collocations: **square battalion, battle, body** (see quots.); †**square book**, some variety of church song-book; †**square-bore** (see quot.), **bracket** (see BRACKET *sb.* 5); **square capital** *Palæogr.*, a form of rectilinear capital letter, *spec.* characterizing a script used in early Latin manuscripts (cf. RUSTIC *a.* 5 b); **square coupling**, (see quots.); **square cut**, (*a*) (see quot. 1850; cf. SQUARE-CUT *a.* 1); (*b*) *Cricket*, a cut hit square on the off-side; hence **square-cut** *v. trans.*, to cut (a ball) thus: **square cutter; square dance**, a dance in which four couples face inwards from four sides; also *loosely*, a country-dance; hence **square-dance** *v. intr.*; **square dancer, -dancing** *vbl. sb.*; **square dinkum**: see DINKUM *a.*; **square drive** *Cricket*, a drive hit square on the off-side; hence **square-drive** *v. trans.*, to drive (a ball or bowler) in this manner; **square engine**, an internal-combustion engine in which the length of the stroke is approximately equal to the bore of the cylinders; **square-eyed** *a. joc.*, affected by or given to excessive viewing of television; **square-face, frame, gin** (see quots.); **square-header**, a square-headed sail; **square Hebrew** *Palæogr.*, the standard Hebrew script which displaced the Aramaic form towards the end of the Biblical period, and has been adopted for use in printed texts; **square hit**, a hit at right angles to the wicket, esp. to square-leg; **square John** *N. Amer. slang*, an upright, respectable person; *spec.* one who is not a drug-addict; **square-joint, -knot** (see quots.); **square law** *Physics*, a law relating two variables one of which varies either directly or inversely as the square of the other (cf. *inverse square* (*law*) s.v. INVERSE *a.* 3 a); also used *attrib.* of a device whose action obeys the square law; **square-leg**, the position in the cricket-field to the left of the batsman and nearly in a line with the wicket; the fielder stationed at this point also *attrib.*; hence ***square-leg*** vb.; **square-lipped rhino(ceros** = *white rhino*(*ceros*) s.v. WHITE *a.* 11 a; **square main-sail, mark**, *Naut.* (see quots.); **square motor** = *square engine* above; **square-mouthed rhino(ceros** = *white rhino*(*ceros*) s.v. WHITE *a.* 11 a; †**square muscle**, one of the quadrate muscles of the loins; **square-net**, a fine net suspended so as to enclose a square, used in trapping hawks; †**square-pair** *Mining* (see quot. 1747); **square piano, pianoforte**, a piano of a rectangular form, now superseded by the upright or cottage piano; **square pin**: on an electrical plug, a pin with a rectangular rather than a circular cross-section; **square ribbon**, *Naut.* (see quots.); **square-rig**, (*a*) *Naut.* (see quot. 1875); (*b*) *Naut. slang*, the uniform of a naval rating (see also quot. 1942); **square-rigger**, a square-rigged vessel; a sailor on such a vessel; **square-roof** (see quot.); †**square rule**, = SQUARE *sb.* 1; **square serif** *Typogr.*, a type-face distinguished by straight serifs as thick as the other parts of the letters; **square sets, shoot**, (see quots.); **square-shooter** *slang* (orig. and chiefly *U.S.*), an honest, dependable, sound person; hence **square-shooting** *a.*, honest, respectable; **square staff, -stern, -tailing**, (see quots.); **square thread** *Mech.*, a screw thread which in cross-section is castellated in form, with the width and height of the thread equal to the width of the valley between threads; **square timbers, tuck, twelves**, (see quots.); **square wave** *Electronics*, (a voltage represented by) a periodic wave that varies abruptly in amplitude between two fixed values, spending equal times at each; **square well** *Nucl. Physics*, a potential well of square section; **square wheels**, used *joc.* of a set of wheels which give a jolting ride, as if they were square; also *fig.* **square work** (see quots.); **square-wright** *Sc.*, a carpenter whose work requires much use of the square; also *attrib.*; **square yards**, *Naut.* (see quots.)

Some of these have arisen by ellipse, as *square Hebrew* (sc. *characters*); also ***square manuscripts*** (i.e. written with these characters).

1710 J. HARRIS *Lex. Techn.* II, **Square Battel* or *Battalion* of Men, is one that hath an equal number of Men in Rank and File. **1770** LANGHORNE *Plutarch* (Rtldg.) 259/1 Not.. accustomed to draw up in a spiral form, but in the square battalion. **1711** *Milit. & Sea Dict.*, A **Square* Body; Which has as many Men in File as in Rank, and is equal whatsoever Way it faces. *c* **1850** *Rudim. Navig.* (Weale) 151 *Square body*, the figure which comprehends all the timbers whose areas or planes are perpendicular to the keel, which is all that portion of a ship between the cant bodies. **1537–8** *Rec. St. Mary at Hill* (1905) 378 Paid..for carolles for cristmas and for v *square bookes. **1538** *Accs. Wells Cath. Chapter* (MS.) 13 May, Libros cantuum crisporum sive diversorum, vulgariter nuncupatos square books and pricke song books. **1677** MOXON *Mech. Exerc.* 48 The *Square-bore, is a square Steel Point or shank, well temper'd, fitted into a square Socket in an Iron wimble... Its use is to open a Hole [etc.]. **1891** *Daily News* 14 May 5/2 They place notes of interrogation..or notes of exclamation within *square brackets. **1699** M. LISTER *Journey to Paris* 108 The same MS...is written in *Square Capitals and very short Lines. **1883** [see RUSTIC *a.* 5 b]. **1906** E. JOHNSTON *Writing & Illumin. & Lettering* I. i. 37 Square Capitals were formed, pen-made Roman Capitals, of the monumental type. **1831–3** *Encycl. Metrop.* (1845) VIII. 110/1 Even in small machines, the *square coupling has been in many cases supplanted by the cylindrical box. **1855** OGILVIE *Suppl.*, *Square-coupling*, in mill-work, a kind of permanent coupling, of which the coupling-box is made in halves and square. **1850** HOLTZAPFFEL *Turning* III. 1323 The *square cut, or trap cut, is the most simple form of cutting facets. **1897** K. S. RANJITSINHJI *Jubilee Bk. Cricket* iv. 164 A *square-cut travels somewhere between point and third-man. It is the commonest form of cut. **1906** A. E. KNIGHT *Complete Cricketer* ii. 77 Cuts are generally termed forward cuts, late cuts, and square cuts. **1956** N. CARDUS *Close of Play* 150 Those who saw him will cherish memories of his vehement hooking..his square-cuts. **1976** DEXTER & MAKINS *Testkill* 167 Hunt let the first ball go by, then square-cut the second with great majesty. **1920** D. J. KNIGHT in P. F. Warner *Cricket* 32 Another beautiful *square cutter is J. T. Tyldesley. **1870** L. M. ALCOTT *Old-Fashioned Girl* vii. 132 I'm going to begin with a redowa, because..it's better fun than *square dances. **1902** *Encycl. Brit.* XXVII. 375/2 'Dull Sir John' and 'Faine I would' were square dances popular in England three hundred years ago. **1955** *Times* 28 June 11/4 The term 'square dance' is the American equivalent of the English 'country dance'. **1959** *Manch. Guardian* 7 Aug. 6/4 The entire population turns out to *square-dance in the main streets. **1976** *West Lancs. Evening Gaz.* 15 Dec. 1. 8/2 One woman *square dancer had fallen on the polished floor of the hall. **1977** *Times* 24 Jan. 4/7 The mass free admission square dance..bore witness that *square dancing is alive and well across the continent. **1900** W. J. FORD *Cricketer on Cricket* xii. 140 His strokes are limited to the off-side, chiefly cuts and *square drives. **1954** J. FINGLETON *Ashes crown Year* 271 May brilliantly *square-drove him for 4. **1977** *Guardian* 3 Jan. 11/7 Amiss began the afternoon by square driving Bedi's first ball for four. **1930** *Engineering* 7 Mar. 303/2 He then analyses the main differences between a *square engine and one with a stroke:bore ratio of 2. **1964** J. BRAINE *Jealous God* viii. 136 '*Square-eyed sods,' he said. **1976** *Listener* 8 July 2/2 He called the television set 'the Devil's Box', claimed..that it would turn the bronzed, outdoor-loving youngster into a round-backed, square-eyed weakling. **1879** FORBES in *Daily News* 13 June 5/5 That potent fluid..that goes by the endearing name of '*Squareface', and that in reality is the rankest of schiedam. **1846** A. YOUNG *Naut. Dict.* 294 **Square frames*, in ship-building, those frames which are square with the line of the keel, having no bevelling upon them. **1888** CHURCHWARD *Blackbirding* 102 What they called the wine of the country—*square gin. **1892** 'R. BOLDREWOOD' *Nevermore* II. xvi, A glass of spirits, be it sound cognac,..or..good square gin. **1882** *Standard* 11 Aug. 6/6 Lorna and Chittywee last, the latter with a large jackyardtopsail set, the others having working *squareheaders. **1915** *N.E.D.* s.v. *Square* a. 15 a, *Square Hebrew. **1948** D. DIRINGER *Alphabet* 261 The Aramaic script therefore became the parent of the 'square Hebrew'. **1974** *Encycl. Brit. Micropædia* IV. 983/1 Between the 6th and 2nd centuries BC, Classical, or Square, Hebrew gradually displaced the Aramaic alphabet. **1837** *New Sporting Mag.* XI. 196 By swinging the bat nearly in the direction in which the umpire stands, making a *square hit. **1882** *Daily Tel.* 24 June, A square hit for 2 by Grace followed, which made up the century. **1934** *Detective Fiction Weekly* 21 Apr. 113/1 The man who works for a living..is generally referred to in terms of contempt such as working stiff, Honest John, *Square John, sucker or scissor bill. **1935** A. J. POLLOCK *Underworld Speaks* 112/2 *Square John*, a dope peddler who is not addicted. **1962** 'K. ORVIS' *Damned & Destroyed* ix. 62, I played it even safer with those uptown Square Johns. **1968** *Daily Colonist* (Victoria, B.C.) 2 Nov. 8/1 He kept saying that McWhirter was a 'square John'. 'What does a 'square John' mean? Does it mean an ordinary law-abiding citizen?' Mr. Owen-Flood asked. 'As far as I know,' Porter replied. **1875** KNIGHT *Dict. Mech.* 2294/2 **Square-joint*, a mode of joining wooden stuff in which the edges are brought squarely together, without rabbeting, tongue, or feather. **1867** SMYTH *Sailor's Word-bk.*, **Square-Knot*, the same as *reef-knot*. **1921** *Physical Rev.* XVIII. 263 For the weaker [magnetic] fields there is a decided curvature in the lines which gradually smooth out into practically straight lines. It is in this lower region that the '*square law', proposed by Sir J. J. Thomson, holds. **1945** *Electronic Engin.* XVII. 734/2 The valve will work satisfactorily as a square law rectifier. **1958** W. T. O'DEA *Social Hist. Lighting* i. 8 A room forty feet by thirty could be lit quite cheerfully by the candles and would be dismal by the light of a single bulb. The reason is the 'square law' so well known to anyone who has studied physics. Ten feet away from a light source the illumination per unit area is only one-hundredth of what it is one foot away, and so on. **1976** *Nature* 29 Jan. 294/2 The vector voltmeters had a bandwidth of 1 kHz and employed a square-law detector following the narrow-band filter. **1851** LILLYWHITE *Guide Cricketers* 21 The Long Leg for a '*square leg hitter' should stand parallel to the wicket. **1873** *Routledge's Young Gentlm. Mag.* May. 378/1 [He] was very nearly had at square leg the first 'slow' he got. **1894** *Times* 28 May 7/3 He made one particularly fine square-leg hit to the boundary. **1882** *Daily Tel.* 8 Sept. (Encycl. Dict.), [He] continued..by *square-legging both bowlers for a couple each time. [**1931** C. R. S. PITMAN *Game Warden among his Charges* i. 3 There is the huge, square mouth—from which it derives its sobriquet of 'square-lipped'.] **1961** *New Scientist* 9 Nov. 340/2 A rare animal, the white or *square-lipped rhino, is threatened by extinction. **1970** *Nature* 28 Mar. 1180/1 (*caption*) By 1966..there were about 800 southern square-lipped rhinoceroses in the Hluhluwe and Umfolozi reserves in Natal. **1867** SMYTH *Sailor's Word-bk.* 462 *Main-sail.* This, in a square-rigged vessel, is distinguished by the so-termed **square main-sail*. *Ibid.*, **Square* or *Squaring Marks*, marks placed upon the lifts and braces [as guides in squaring the yards]. **1912** C. B. HAYWARD *Pract. Aeronaut.* 349 Design in this field [*sc.* aircraft engines] has..gone back to automobile standards of several years ago when it was customary to build what are known as *square motors, i.e. those in which the bore and stroke are the same. **1881** *Proc. Zool. Soc.* 726 The *square-mouthed rhinoceros is a huge ungainly-looking beast. **1915** ROOSEVELT & HELLER *Life-Histories Afr. Game Animals* II. xxi. 662 The square-mouthed rhinos..seemed to be of a perceptibly lighter gray. **1615** CROOKE *Body of Man* 802 The first payre are called *Quadrati* the *square muscles;.. they..lye as it were square vpon the rackes of the loynes. **1856** 'STONEHENGE' *Brit. Sports* I. IV. i. 222 Haggards may be trapped in this country with the *square-net, or the bow-net. **1747** HOOSON *Miner's Dict.* Q 3, *Raising-Pair.* These differ from a *Squarepair in this, that instead of a Collar made on the Forks, we make Tenners, so that the Forks are Tennered at both Ends, and the Sliders are Slotted at both Ends to receive the Forks. **1853** DICKENS *Bleak Ho.* xxxviii. 379 A little jingling *square piano. **1938** R. FIELD *All this & Heaven Too* (1939) I. xvi. 208 One of the girls went to a square piano and began trying the keys. **1980** *Early Music* July 377/2 Included in the sale was the Zumpe square piano of 1766 (£3,200) the earliest known piano to have been made in England. **1787** *Brit. Patent* specn. 1596 (*caption*) This figure represents the movement of a *square Piano Forte. **1799** YOUNG in *Phil. Trans.* XC. 135 A square piano forte. **1840** *Penny Cycl.* XVIII. 139/2 The square piano-forte.. was taken from the clavichord, but..retains only its shape. **1875** STAINER & BARRETT *Dict. Mus. Terms* s.v. *Pianoforte*, Upright pianos have been called giraffes from their tall appearance, and horizontal ones have been called couched harp, or square pianoforte. **1965** P. HONEY *Planning Electricity in House* iii. 75 The 13-amp. plug has *square pins (which are superior to round pins) and will not fit any other size of socket. **1867** SMYTH *Sailor's Word-bk.*, **Square Ribbons*, a synonym of horizontal lines, or horizontal ribbons. **1875** KNIGHT *Dict. Mech.*, **Square-rig*, that rig in which the lower sails are suspended from horizontal yards, as distinguished from *fore-and-aft* rig. **1942** BERREY & VAN DEN BARK *Amer. Thes. Slang* §791/10 *Square rig* or *rigger*, a double-breasted uniform. **1951** N. COWARD *Star Quality* 24 Attired as they were in the usual 'Square-Rig' of British Ordinary Seamen, they caused a mild sensation. **1962** W. GRANVILLE *Dict. Sailors' Slang* 112/1 *Square rig*, uniform worn by 'men dressed as seamen', the jumper, flannel, jean collar and bell-bottomed trousers.

1979 *Navy News* Feb. 4/1 It is a once-only increase to enable these ratings to complete the replacement of old-pattern suits of square rig, without being out of pocket. **1855** C. Nordhoff *Merchant Vessel* 285 Our mate..had never before been in a '*square-rigger'. **1886** *Daily Tel.* 23 Apr. 2/3 There are many old square-riggers..who will be curious to know what there is for Jack on board a steamer to put his hand to. **1875** Knight *Dict. Mech.*, *Square-roof, one in which the principal rafters meet at a right angle. **1726** Leoni *Alberti's Archit.* I. 38/2 In making these Angles we must use a *Square Rule. **1940** H. F. Lock *Basic Typogr.* iii. 30 The modern *square-serif letters are derived from the 'Antiques' and 'Egyptians' of a century ago. **1967** E. Chambers *Photolitho-Offset* ii. 13 Leading the contemporary field are the square serif and the sans serif. **1978** S. Rice *Bk. Design* 214 *Sans serif*, typeface design not having the small bracketing accents at the ends of the letter strokes... Square serif letters do not properly belong to this grouping. **1881** Raymond *Mining Gloss.*, *Square sets, a kind of timbering used in large spaces. **1842** Gwilt *Archit.* Gloss., *Square Shoot, a wooden trough for discharging water from a building. **1914** Jackson & Hellyer *Vocab. Criminal Slang* 79 *Square-shooter,..a dependable person; a reliable, compact-keeping person. **1928** S. Lewis *Man who knew Coolidge* i. 51 There's a man that it's a pleasure to do business with, a square-shooter if ever there was one. **1937** Wyndham Lewis *Blasting & Bombardiering* i. vi. 63 My friend..was somehow treacherous and not at all the good sport and 'square-shooter' I had supposed him to be. **1962** E. Lucia *Klondike Kate* ii. 24 Kitty was looked upon as a 'square shooter' in the rough give-and-take game of the Dawson gambling joints. **1922** *Square shooting [see animal A. 6]. **1932** J. Dos Passos *1919* 428 One of them made a speech in English and another one in Sicilian saying that this was a squareshooting concern that had always treated laborers square. **1842** Gwilt *Archit.* Gloss., *Square staff, a piece of wood placed at the external angle of a projection in a room to secure the angle. **1875** Knight *Dict. Mech.*, *Square-stern, a build in which the wing-transom is at right angles to the stern-post, in contradistinction to *round* stern. **1881** *Gentl. Mag.* Jan. 62 Every five or six years there was a general muster technically termed *square-tailing,..to ascertain the precise number of cattle upon the station. **1908** E. Oberg *Handbk. Small Tools* i. 29 The Acme thread..has of late become widely used, having in most instances taken the place of the *square thread on account of its better wearing qualities. **1939** S. E. Winston *Machine Design* iii. 72 The Square Thread..is probably the most typical transmission screw thread, as its mechanical efficiency is considerably higher than that of such threads as the V thread. **1975** Bram & Downs *Manuf. Technol.* iv. 120 In the square thread the sides are parallel and normal to the axis of the screw. *c* **1850** *Rudim. Navig.* (Weale) 151 *Square timbers, the timbers which stand square with, or perpendicular to, the keel. **1846** A. Young *Naut. Dict.* 355 When the after part of the ship terminates in a straight plane which is nearly vertical, instead of the plank running up to the counter, she is said to have a *square tuck. **1888** Jacobi *Printers' Vocab.* 130 *Square twelves, twelvemo laid down in imposition the 'short' or 'square' way, in contradistinction to 'long twelves'. **1944** *Jrnl. Scientific Instruments* XXI. 64 (*heading*) A simple variable '*square-wave' stimulator for biological work. **1965** *Wireless World* Sept. 460/1 One popular method of amplifier stability assessment is 'square-wave testing' in which a suitable square wave is applied to the input, and the output inspected on an oscilloscope screen. **1975** G. J. King *Audio Handbk.* v. 120 It is assumed that the input waveform is a true square wave of very small rise time. **1939** *Physical Rev.* LVI. 890/1 The *square well fitting proton-proton scattering is not as deep as that fitting proton-neutron scattering. **1954** *Ibid.* XCVI. 461/1 The smoothing of the edges of the square-well potential was of significance for the interpretation of the elastic proton scattering with heavy nuclei. **1975** W. F. Hornyak *Nuclear Structure* iv. 242 Another simple potential well used to represent the average potential of the single-particle model is the three-dimensional square well. **1924** *Radio Times* 19 Dec. 594/1 (Advt.), Thousands of Wireless enthusiasts..are running their broadcasting reception on *square wheels, enduring..distortion... Are *you* getting square wheel reception? **1977** 'O. Jacks' *Autumn Heroes* viii. 111 It was almost impossible to stand upright. The truck was operating on square wheels. **1883** Gresley *Gloss. Coal-m.* 233 *Square work, an old system of working the Thick coal by getting the upper beds first and then the lower ones. *Ibid.*, *Square work*, a system of working a seam of coal by cutting it up into square blocks or pillars. **1752** *Records of Elgin* (New Spald. Cl.) I. 464 All chests, chairs, stools, spades, staves and other *squarewright work. **1825** Jamieson *Suppl.*, *Squarewricht*, a joiner who works in the finer kinds of furniture. Lanarks. **1769** Falconer *Dict. Marine* (1780), *Square, a term peculiarly appropriated to the yards and their sails, implying..that they are of greater extent than usual. **1794** *Rigging & Seamanship* 257 *Square. This term is applied to yards that are very long.

b. In specific or distinguishing names of plants, animals, etc., as **square barley**, **dory**, **-ear**, **fish**, **mussel**, etc.; **square flipper** [app. a folk etymologizing of Newfoundland dial. *fipper*, *fripper*, etc. (also used), of uncertain origin], the bearded seal, *Erignathus barbatus*, native to Arctic regions; **square-tail**, (*a*) (see quots. 1843, 1896); (*b*) the char or brook trout, *Salvelinus fontinalis*, native to eastern North America.

a **1722** Lisle *Husb.* (1757) 152 *Square-barley, or winter-barley..is commonly sown in the mountainous parts of northern countries. **1731** P. Miller *Gard. Dict.* s.v. *Hordeum*, Winter or Square Barley, or Bear Barley; by some call'd Big. **1803** Shaw *Gen. Zool.* IV. ii. 291 *Square Dory. *Zeus quadratus.* **1805** R. W. Dickson *Pract. Agric.* I. 540 The new sorts of wheat in that county are..the *square-ear, and the hoary brown. **1681** Grew *Musæum* i. v. ii. 110 The *Square-Fish. *Piscis quadrangularis.* **1774** G. Cartwright *Jrnl.* 12 Dec. (1792) II. 38 A *squarephripper was caught in a net to-day. **1784** T. Pennant *Arctic Zool.* 161 The Seal-hunters in Newfoundland have a large kind, which they call the Square Phipper, and say weighs five hundred pounds. **1832** J. McGregor *Hist. & Descr. Sk. Brit. Amer.* I. 108 The harp seal..the hooded seal..the square flipper, the blue seal, and the jar seal. **1842** J. B. Jukes *Excursions in Newfoundland* I. 312 The 'square fipper'..is, however, very rare. **1861** L. de Boilieu *Recoll. Labrador Life* 91 These seals are not like the Square Frippers. **1883** *Fisheries Exhib. Catal.* (ed. 4) 173 Hooded or Bladder Nose... Square Flipper. **1884** Goode *Nat. Hist. Aquat. Anim.* 65 *note*, The Bay Seal,..the Hooded Seal,..and the 'Square Flipper' (probably *Halichærus grypus*). **1911** D. M. Lindsay *Voyage to Arctic* iii. 39 Square flippers..are also found on the coast [of Newfoundland]. **1957** *Beaver* Spring 49/1 They were immensely strong and could carry off a square-flipper seal single-handed. **1681** Grew *Musæum* i. vi. ii. 146 The *Square-Muscle. *Concha Rhomboidea.* **1548** Turner *Names Herbes* 22 Bunium..may be called in englishe *square perseley. *Ibid.* 17 Ascyron..maye be called in english *square saint Johans grasse. **1832** J. Rennie *Consp. Butterfl. & Moths* 56 Dahl's *Square Spot... Wings..with a dusky square spot between the stigmata. **1843** Lowe *Fishes Madeira* 129 *Tetragonurus Atlanticus*... The *Square-tail, or Sea-raven. **1896** Lydekker *Roy. Nat. Hist.* V. 398 The curious Mediterranean and Atlantic fish known as Cuvier's square-tail (*Tetragonurus cuvieri*). **1935** B. Perry *And gladly Teach* vii. 151 The lake was perfect for bathing and boating. There were big 'square-tails' in it then. **1972** *Trout & Salmon* Feb. 14/2 It brought to mind an experience I had in Labrador this past summer when I was up there fishing for squaretail trout. **1548** Turner *Names Herbes* 36 Euonymus..maye be called in englishe Spyndle tree or *square tree. **1681** Grew *Musæum* i. vi. i. 130 The *Square-Wilk. *Buccina Rhomboidea.*

square (skwɛə(r)), *adv.* [f. prec.]

†**1.** So as to be squared (by multiplication). *Obs.*

1557 Recorde *Whetst.* E ij, And so moche doth 15 make, being multiplied square.

†**2.** Steadily, copiously. *Obs.*

1570 B. Googe *Pop. Kingd.* iv. 47 b, Foure dayes long they tipple square, & feede and neuer reast. **1603** Florio *Montaigne* ii. ii. 198 Iosephus reporteth that by making an Ambassador to tipple square whom his enemies had sent unto him, he wrested all his secrets out of him. **1608** Armin *Nest Ninn.* G 3, Hee..got downe into the Seller, and fell to it tipple square, till he was lost, and quite drunck.

3. a. Fairly, honestly; in a straightforward or direct manner. In later use *slang* or *colloq.*

1577–82 Breton *Toyes of an Idle Head* Wks. (Grosart) I. 29/1 If that Coggers all were barde,..And euery Gamster would play square: Then some men would hope well to fare. **1661** Feltham *Resolves* ii. xlii. 266 Nature implants a Moral Justice, which, unperverted, will deal square. **1851** Mayhew *Lond. Lab.* I. 324, I never thought of selling anything but tins. How could I, if I wished to do the thing square and proper? **1883** *Harper's Mag.* Jan. 212/1 He'll wonder what sort of a beast I be, When I tell him square out how it seemed to me. **1891** H. Herman *His Angel* 140, 'I reckon the boy means square,' muttered the old man.

Comb. **1891** C. Roberts *Adrift Amer.* 8 The old fellows..were what I should call very decent square-dealing men.

b. *colloq.* Solidly, without reserve.

1867 F. W. Newman in Sieveking *Mem.* (1909) ix. 198 N. C. comes out 'square' for the Republican party.

c. *colloq.* Properly, in correct form.

1889 'R. Boldrewood' *Robbery under Arms* xxviii, Here they were married, all square and regular, by the Scotch clergyman.

d. *U.S. colloq.* Completely, exactly.

1862 E. S. Philbrick *Let.* 2 Nov. in E. W. Pearson *Lett. from Port Royal* (1906) 103 His heart failed him and he backed square out. **1880** 'Mark Twain' *Tramp Abr.* xvii. 152 He..shot the dragon square in the center of his cavernous mouth. **1903** A. D. McFaul *Ike Glidden* xxvi. 236 Hain't I bin a-runnin' my legs right square off this four days? **1921** R. D. Paine *Comr. Rolling Ocean* i. 8 It surely did hit me square between the eyes.

e. *Mus.* In a square fashion (square *a.* 8).

1960 L. Bernstein *Joy of Music* 105 Now that you've heard what syncopation is like, let's see what that same Blues we heard before would sound like without it... *Played 'square' by sax, no vibrato.*

4. a. So as to be square; in a rectangular form or position; directly in line or in front.

1631 Chapman *Cæsar & Pompey* iii. i, Free minds, like dice, fall square whate'er the cast. **1678** Moxon *Mech. Exerc.* 66 Two edges of two boards, when thus shot, ly so exactly flat and square upon one another, that light will not be discerned betwixt them. **1683** —— *Printing* x. ¶9 The upper-sides of the Holes in the Iron Plates being square Bored. **1768** Sterne *Sent. Journ.*, *The Dwarf*, The German stood square in the most unaccommodating posture that can be imagined. **1821** Lamb *Elia* i. *Old Benchers*, He walked burly and square. **1852** Hawthorne *Blithedale Rom* xxiv, Logs..piled up square. **1852** Mrs. Stowe *Uncle Tom's C.* xvi, 'Well, cousin, are you ready to go to meeting?' said Miss Ophelia, turning square about on St. Clare.

b. *square on*: (*a*) *Cricket*, of a bowler: having one's body square to the batsman; (*b*) *fig.*, directly, honestly. Also as *adj. phr.*, straight-forward.

1963 A. Ross *Australia 63* ii. 65 His actual delivery, a shade reminiscent of George Tribe's, is made more square-on than is classical. **1968** K. Weatherly *Roo Shooter* 145 Jim, we've got to look at this square on. We haven't given the game away. It's given us away. **1977** *Lancashire Life* Dec. 60/2 Some of his more ambitious attempts, however, don't quite 'come off', while others are 'square-on' to the point of suggesting a lack of imagination.

5. a. At right angles. Freq. const. *to*, *with*, etc.

1680 Moxon *Mech. Exerc.* 213 To cut straight down all the way; that is, to cut it square down at right Angles with the outside of the Work. **1728** Chambers *Cycl.* s.v. *Roof*, Sometimes the roof,..instead of terminating in a Ridge or Angle,..is cut square off at a certain Heighth. **1792** Jefferson *Writ.* (1859) III. 337 In a position square with the streets. **1802** James *Milit. Dict.* s.v. *Gun*, The carriage..must be cast loose, and trained athwart-ship, square with the ship's sides. **1847** *Infantry Man.* (1854) 74 Pivot men..face square into the new direction. **1856** Olmsted *Slave States* 61 You'll find a path going square off to the right. **1878** Huxley *Physiogr.* xix. 332 The shadows of objects are distorted when the light does not fall square upon their surfaces.

b. *Cricket.* At right angles to the line of the delivery.

1851 J. Pycroft *Cricket Field* vii. 154 Practise diligently with leg-balls, till balls..a little wide of leg-stump go nearly square. **1891** [see fine *a.* 7 f]. **1909** W. Caffyn *Seventy-One not Out* viii. 90 He was a fine leg-hitter, generally hitting square. **1963** T. E. Bailey *Improve your Cricket* i. 38 (*caption*) The ball has been played behind square, but it can be played in front.

square (skwɛə(r)), *v.* Also 5 squaryn, sqvare, sqware, 6 squyer. [ad. OF. *esquarrer* (*escarrer*, *equarrer*), = Pg. *esquadrar*, Sp. *escuadrar*, It. *squadrare*:—pop.L. **exquadrāre*, f. L. *ex* out + *quadra* square. OF. had also *esquarrir* (*escarrir*, etc., mod.F. *équarrir*).]

I. *trans.* **1. a.** To make (a thing) square; to reduce to a square or rectangular form, by cutting or some similar process; to shape by reduction to straight lines and right angles.

Freq. implying the production of a form approaching to a cube.

1382 Wyclif *1 Kings* v. 17 The kyng comaundide, that thei shulden take the greet stoonus..and thei shulden square hem. **1398** Trevisa *Barth. De P.R.* xvi. lxxiv. (Bodl. MS.), Stones..itake oute of quarers and þanne þei beþ ihewe, planed and sqwared. *c* **1407** Lydg. *Reson & Sens.* 6100 The poyntes [were] squared eke so pleyn That the Ioynyng was nat sene. *c* **1460** J. Russell *Bk. Nurture* 52 The iij. [knife] sharpe & kene to smothe þe trenchurs and square. **1526** *Pilgr. Perf.* (W. de W. 1531) 142 b, The people of Israell..buylded a solemn temple..of stones precyous & quadrat or squared. **1555** Eden *Decades* (Arb.) 263 The Rubies..are scoured and made cleane... Yet can they not square and polyshe them. **1592** Greene *Def. Conny Catching* Wks. (Grosart) XI. 72 His beard squared with such Art. **1653** *Apol. for Goodwin* 4 But this Stone is so ill squar'd, that one way it will be found to narrow, and the other to broad. **1691** *Lond. Gaz.* No. 2668/4 Crown Window Glass..; which may be squared into all Sizes of Sashes for Windows and other Uses. **1754** *Dict. Arts & Sci.* s.v. *Book-binding*, After which the paste-boards are squared. **1801** Southey *Lett.* (1856) I. 169 A square hedge of thickset, squared most trimly by the shears of the garden-barber. **1849** Macaulay *Hist. Eng.* iii. I. 415 Those who..squared the Portland stone for Saint Paul's.

fig. **1647** N. Bacon *Disc. Govt. Eng.* i. xliii. (1739) 70 It was a regular frame in every part, squared and made even by Laws.

b. To make (timber, etc.) square or rectangular in cross-section.

1412–20 Lydg. *Chron. Troy* iv. 2432 With a spere, squared for to byte,..þe myȝty duke..Rood lyne riȝt..To Anthenor. **1503** *Acc. Ld. H. Treas. Scot.* II. 275 To the wrichtis that squarit the tymir in the Hieland. **1530** Palsgr. 731/1, I wyll square thyse ookes to make tymber of. **1560** Pilkington *Expos. Aggeus* (1562) 59 A carpenter which is not cunning to make the house, yet may he square trees. **1663** Gerbier *Counsel* 78 The Timber being squared before it be brought to London. **1725** Pope *Odyss.* v. 316 He smooth'd, and squar'd 'em [*sc.* trees], by the rule and line. **1791** W. Bartram *Carolina* 312, I have some men at work squaring Pine and Cypress timber for the West-Indian market. **1810** Scott *Lady L.* i. xxvi, [He] Lopp'd off their boughs, their hoar trunks bared, And by the hatchet rudely squared. **1869** Rankine *Machine & Hand-tools* Pl. H 8 The other end [of the tube] being squared to receive the handle.

c. To mark out as a square or in rectangular form; to convert into, draw up in, a square; to mark *off* or *out* in squares.

c **1440** *Pallad. on Husb.* ii. 109 A tabul square,..Feet scoris nyne in lengthe, as fele in wide; Let square hit so. **1530** Palsgr. 731/1, I squyer, I rule with a squyer, as a carpynter doyth his worke or he sawe it out, *je esquarre*. **1556** J. Heywood *Spider & Fly* xvii. 27 Whiche sqwyre shall square me, a scantlin well bent, For a right rewle, to show me innocent. **1667** Milton *P.L.* viii. 232 Squar'd in full Legion (such command we had) To see that none thence issu'd forth a spie. **1797** *Encycl. Brit.* (ed. 3) XVII. 392/1 Take also the round aft,..and square it down to the pencil line last drawn. **1800** *Phil. Trans.* XC. 541 The Master General has been pleased to issue his directions for the survey of Devonshire, and as much of Somersetshire and Cornwall as will square the work. **1864** Lowell *Fireside Trav.* 288 What frame..ever enclosed such a picture as is squared within the groundsel, side-posts, and lintel of a barn-door. **1877** Miss A. B. Edwards *Up Nile* vii. 176 The soil, squared off as usual like a gigantic chess-board.

d. With *out* (or *up*), in above senses. Also *fig.*

1565 Cooper *Thesaurus* s.v. *Exascio*, It is rough hewed or squared out, or it is begunne. **1632** Lithgow *Trav.* x. 443 This Pallace standeth alone, and founded vpon the skirt of a..hill.., squared out from a deualling steepnesse. **1642** H. More *Song of Soul* i. ii. lviii, A large green turf squar'd out, all fresh and fine. **1837** W. B. Adams *Carriages* 96 Two holes are then bored in each mortice in succession, after which they are squared out with proper chisels. **1869** Rankine *Machine & Hand-tools* Pl. Q 16. 2 Mortises are chased, and the ends squared-out. **1875** *Carpentry & Join.* 58 Take care to square up accurately the boards to form the front, back, and sides. **1930** T. S. Eliot tr. *St.-J. Perse's Anabasis* 53 The boundless unreckoned year, squared out with dawns and fires.

e. To form by making square; to cut in square or rectangular form. Also with *out*.

1584 B. R. tr. *Herodotus* ii. 94 Of the body of this thorne they sawe and square out certaine boardes two cubits longe. **1601** R. Johnson *Kingd. & Commw.* 133 Of the timber of these trees are squared all necessaries, as well for buildings as all other vses. **1606** *Choice, Chance*, etc. (1881) 38 For his proportion he was squared out of a timber logge, which was crooked at both ends. **1833** Loudon *Encycl. Archit.* §742 It is not intended that this wood shall be cut out of large trees, but that it shall be squared from young trees or branches.

2. a. To multiply (a number) by itself.

1571 DIGGES *Pantom.* I. xxx, Now square 2400 pase, so haue you 576000. *Ibid.* II. xii, The number proceeding of the perches squared. **1614** W. BEDWELL *Nat. Geom. Numbers* iv. 65, I square the quotient 2, that is, I multiply it by it selfe. **1674** JEAKE *Arith.* (1696) 193 Then do I square 6, and it is 36. **1766** *Compl. Farmer* s.v. *Surveying,* To square the diameter, and to multiply that square by 7854. **1804** HUTTON *Course Math.* (ed. 4) I. 8, 7^2 denotes that the number 7 is to be squared. **1894** *Act 57 & 58 Vict.* c. 60 Sch. 2 (2), To half the girth thus taken add half the main breadth; square the sum.

b. To convert (a circle) into an equivalent square; to measure exactly in terms of a square. Also *fig.*

1624 DONNE *Serm.* 14 Goe not Thou about to Square eyther circle [*sc.* God or thyself]. **1674** BOYLE *Excell. Theol.* I. iii. 104 Mr. Hobbs, after all the ways he has taken, and those he has proposed, to square the circle [etc.]. *a* **1704** T. BROWN *Amusem. Ser. & Com., Voy.* Wks. 1709 III. I. 12 You may as soon square the Circle, as reduce the several Branches.. under one single Head. **1717** PRIOR *Alma* III. 366 Circles to square, and Cubes to double, Would give a Man excessive Trouble. **1798** HUTTON *Course Math.* II. 311 To square the circle, or find its area. **1871** C. DAVIES *Metric Syst.* III. 68 The legislator.. cannot square the circle.

c. To reduce (measurements) to an equivalent square; to calculate in square measure.

1811 P. KELLY *Univ. Cambist* I. 260 In squaring the dimensions of artificers work, the Inch is divided into 12 parts. **1828** MOORE *Pract. Navig.* 26 In like manner may any dimensions be squared, and the content be found.

3. a. *Naut.* To lay (the yards) at right angles to the line of the keel by trimming with the braces; to set at right angles to, or parallel with, some other part.

a **1625** *Nomenclator Navalis* (MS. Harl. 2301) s.v. *Yard,* Wee square the Yards, that is make them hang either a Crosse and one Yard-arme not traversed more then th' other. **1669** STURMY *Mariner's Mag.* I. ii. 17 Hawl home the Top-sail Clue-lines, square the Yeard. **1769** FALCONER *Dict. Marine* (1780) s.v. *Lifts,* The yards are said to be squared by the lifts, when they hang at right angles with the mast. **1806** T. MOORE *Steersman's Song* iii, But see.., All hands are up the yards to square. **1832** MARRYAT *N. Forster* xii, The Estelle had squared her mainyard as a signal of submission. **1867** SMYTH *Sailor's Word-bk., Squaring the Dead-Eyes,* bringing them to a line parallel to the sheer of the ship. *Ibid., Squaring the Ratlines,* seeing that all are horizontal and shipshape. **1894** *Times* 10 July 11/1 Booms were squared off and spinnaker booms rigged.

b. To adjust so as to make rectilinear or rectangular or to set at right angles to something else. Also with *up.*

1690 in *Inchaffray Reg.* (Bann. Cl.) 140 To divide and appropriat the same.. as shall be necessary to square marches amongst the saids adjacent Heritors. **1796** *Instr. & Reg. Cavalry* (1813) 120 He.. gives his words,.. Halt! Dress! and corrects and squares his division. **1814** SCOTT *Lord of Isles* VI. xiii, The Monarch rode along the van,.. His line to marshal and to range, And ranks to square, and fronts to change. **1837** J. MORIER *Abel Allnutt* lvii, The clergyman drew forth his book and squared the table with two candles upon it. **1851** MAYNE REID *Scalp Hunt.* xxiii. 171 Having squared her [*sc.* the mare's] hips to the camp, he whispered something at her head. **1890** *Anthony's Photogr. Bull.* III. 206 To 'square' a print upon a mount turn it face down.

fig. **1814** CARY *Dante, Parad.* XVII. 25, I feel me on all sides Well squar'd to fortune's blows.

(*b*) **1794** *Rigging & Seamanship* 19 The butts of the coaks are then squared up. **1883** *Specif. Alnwick & Cornhill Rlwy.* 8 The stones to be roughly squared up in the beds and joints. **1892** *Photogr. Ann.* II. 369 This should be a useful appliance for squaring up hand cameras.

c. *Astrol.* To stand in quartile aspect in relation to (another sign).

1697 CREECH *Manilius* II. 70 The Icy Goat, the Crab which square the Scales. **1852** 'ZADKIEL' *Grammar Astrol.* 394 [On] June 4th, 1738, Mars was on the cusp of the meridian, squaring the ascendant.

d. To set or place (some part of the body) squarely.

1819 SCOTT *Ivanhoe* v, The Saxon domestics squared their shoulders. **1824** —— *St. Ronan's* xxxi, She does so stoop and lollop,.. so cross her legs and square her arms. **1829** LYTTON *Disowned* 149 Square your body a little more to your left. **1881** T. A. M'CARTHY *Calisth. & Drilling* 19 Square the heels and stand perfectly steady.

e. *refl.* To put oneself into a posture of defence. Also *fig.* Cf. sense 11. orig. *U.S.*

1823 J. F. COOPER *Pioneers* II. xv. 223 Square yourself, you lubber,.. and we'll soon know who's the better man. **1864** 'MARK TWAIN' *Celebrated Jumping Frog* (1867) 107 Caesar.. squared himself to receive his assailants. **1893** *Harper's Mag.* Mar. 643/1 With a look of determination on his face, [he] squared himself to write. **1977** J. I. M. STEWART *Madonna of Astrolabe* i. 28, I was squaring myself to the necessity of telling him that I was no good for the purpose he had in mind when our walk came suddenly to an end.

f. *Assoc. Football*, etc. To pass (the ball) across the pitch, esp. towards the centre.

1972 G. GREEN *Great Moments in Sport: Soccer* viii. 85 Bloomfield made it 2–3 from a squared header by Groves. **1976** E. DUNPHY *Only a Game?* iv. 113 Having to go round the back of the goal and square it back before you could score. **1978** *Times* 12 Jan. 10/3 Tait.. squared the ball into the stride of Rafferty who hit in a first-time shot.

II. 4. *fig.* **a.** To regulate, frame, arrange, or direct, *by*, *according to*, or *on* some standard or principle of action.

(*a*) **1531** TINDALE *Exp. 1 John* (1537) 2 To consente unto ye law that it is ryghteous, and good;.. and to rule and square all thy dedes therby. **1589** NASHE *Anat. Absurdity* Wks. (Grosart) I. 16 To eschew womens counsaile, and not to square our actions by their direction. **1620** E. BLOUNT *Horæ Subs.* 506 The very rules, by which all the actions of our life be squared and disposed. **1673** PENN *Christ. Quaker* vi. 540 A Light within, to know their Duty and Square their Lives by. **1712** BERKELEY *Pass. Obed.* §13 He who squares his actions by this rule can never do amiss. **1756** C. LUCAS *Ess. Waters* I. Ded., He squared all his political conduct by their counsil. **1823** SCOTT *Quentin D.* xiii, The path of royal policy cannot be always squared.. by the abstract maxims of religion and of morality. **1864** HAWTHORNE *S. Felton* (1883) 418 The habits of Sibyl Dacy were so wayward, and little squared by general rules, that nobody.. tried to account for them.

(*b*) **1603** SHAKS. *Meas. for M.* v. i. 487 Thou art said to haue a stubborne soule That apprehends no further then this world, And squar'st thy life according. **1682** NORRIS *Hierocles* 83 Having his mind always intent upon the Law of God, squares his life accordingly. **1705** tr. *Bosman's Guinea* 170 According to this Rule, I squared my Conduct in my Judges Office. **1752** FIELDING *Amelia* XII. v, The bailiff had squared his conscience exactly according to law. **1809** MALKIN *Gil Blas* x. vi. ¶13 They.. have squared their conduct for a length of time according to the maxims of their order. **1850** W. IRVING *Goldsmith* xxiii. 239 Peter was poor but punctilious, squaring his expenses according to his means.

(*c*) **1818** SCOTT *Hrt. Midl.* viii, An accommodating conscience of a military stamp, and which squared itself chiefly upon those of the Colonel and paymaster. **1850** W. IRVING *Mahomet* II. 104 He had shrewd maxims on which he squared his conduct.

b. To adjust or adapt, to cause to correspond *to*, or harmonize *with*, something.

(*a*) **1583** MELBANCKE *Philotimus* C iv, If thou canst.. square thy life to her direction, she will allowe thee two seruants. **1634** MILTON *Comus* 329 Eie me, blest Providence, and square my triall To my proportion'd strength. **1682** NORRIS *Hierocles* Pref. 29 Those Heathens who squared their actions to the law of natural reason. **1747** RICHARDSON *Clarissa* II. 166, I should not know how to square it to my own principles. **1819** KEATS *Otho* II. i, I cannot square my conduct to time, place, Or circumstance. *a* **1855** J. J. BLUNT *On Early Fathers* (1857) vi. 406, I am led to doubt if the testimony of the Fathers can be squared to it.

refl. **1715** M. DAVIES *Athen. Brit.* I. 169 The same Resolves, most of the Protestant Reformers Abroad, as well as our Protestant Dissenters at Home, thought themselves oblig'd to square themselves to.

(*b*) **1856** *N. Brit. Rev.* XXVI. 36 Not staying.. to square his belief with the stern realities of criticism. **1884** *Manch. Exam.* 19 Dec. 8/4 The promoters do not seek.. to square their mission with sociological theory. **1904** H. PAUL *Hist. Mod. Eng.* II. iv. 61 Evidence was produced which could not be squared with this plea.

c. To arrange, adjust, render appropriate or exact, etc.

1596 NASHE *Saffron Walden* Wks. (Grosart) III. 195 Your booke being readie for the Presse, Ile square & set it out in Pages. **1669** *Phil. Trans.* IV. 1134, I had no thought of squaring the comparison to agree in all circumstances. **1861** MAX MÜLLER *Sci. Lang.* Ser. I. (1864) 340 Any attempt at squaring the classification of races and tongues must necessarily fail. **1888** BRYCE *Amer. Commw.* I. xi. I. 144 When the majority belongs to the same party as the President, appointments are usually arranged, or to use a familiar expression, 'squared,' between them.

d. With *out* in above senses.

1578 *Chr. Prayers in Priv. Prayers* (1851) 514 That we.. may square out all our doings, words and thoughts, by thee. **1592** *Conspir. Pretended Ref.* 86 Doe not they.. exact and seeke to square out.. all ciuill policies.. vnto the Iudicials of Moyses. **1603** H. CROSSE *Vertues Commw.* C 2 b, No man is wise, happy, or any thing worth, if Temperance square not out the course of his life. **1628** PRYNNE *Love-lockes* 21 The rules for naturall, must regulate and square out the length of artificiall Haire. *a* **1661** FULLER *Worthies* (1662) I. xv. 45, I hope.. both being put together, may square out the most eminent of the Antient Gentry, in some tolerable proportion.

e. *colloq.* With *away*: to put in proper order, to tidy up, to 'sort out'.

1909 R. A. WASON *Happy Hawkins* (1912) xvi. 203 She had a head on her, Barbie had, an' when she got squared away, she made 'em all get down an' scratch. **1947** *Seafarers' Log* 19 Dec. 10/1 Motion carried that Ship's Delegate contact all tripcard men who have not acted in a way becoming to a Union man and get them squared away. **1956** H. KURNITZ *Invasion of Privacy* xiv. 87 Let's get you squared away, Mr. Jarrold. You knew damn well what you were doing.. didn't you? **1966** T. PYNCHON *Crying of Lot 49* i. 20 He outlined what she was in for.. decide what to liquidate and what to hold on to, pay off claims, square away taxes, distribute legacies. **1980** 'R. B. DOMINIC' *Attending Physician* ii. 12 We've got Mrs Bertilucci squared away... Sorry about her yelling at you.

5. To bring to an equality on both sides; to make even so as to leave no difference; to balance.

a. With *accounts* as object. Freq. *fig.*

1815 *Ann. Reg., Gen. Hist.* 22 For the purpose of squaring the civil list accounts. **1860** THACKERAY *Lovel* iv, She would accept benefits,.. but then she insulted her benefactors, and so squared accounts. **1888** SYMONDS *Life of B. Cellini* I. Introd. p. xlvii, He left the land of his adoption before he had properly squared accounts with King Francis.

b. With other objects.

1825 SCOTT *Jrnl.* 7 Dec., Square the odds, and good-night Sir Walter about sixty. **1828** *Ibid.* 23 Feb., On squaring his books and making allowance for bad debts [etc.]. **1853** R. S. SURTEES *Sponge's Sp. Tour* xviii. 87 If he couldn't square matters at short notice, he would have no better chance with an extension of time. **1868** CHESNEY in *Wellesley's Desp.* 813 The Directors.. still clung to trade as the only means of squaring their balance-sheet.

c. *colloq.* To put (a matter) straight; to settle satisfactorily, to compound.

1853 DICKENS *Bleak Ho.* xxii, 'I have squared it with the lad,' says Mr. Bucket, returning, 'and it's all right'. **1872** *Routledge's Ev. Boy's Ann.* 615 We always square it with the usher.

d. With *up*: To settle (a debt, etc.) by means of payment.

1821 J. A. QUITMAN *Let.* 4 Dec. in J. F. H. Claiborne *Life & Corr. J. A. Quitman* (1860) I. 69, I paid my $25, squared my bill, and departed. **1855** 'Q. K. P. DOESTICKS' *Doesticks, what he Says* xvii. 141 Damphool squared up his broad bill, and paid his washerwoman, which left him dead broke. **1862** MRS. H. WOOD *Mrs. Hallib. Troub.* III. xiv, I can square up some of my liabilities here. **1868** DICKENS *Lett.* (1880) II. 393 Square up everything whatsoever that it has been necessary to buy.

absol. **1904** *N. & Q.* 10th Ser. I. 62 It was high time for the young gentleman in the parlour to square up or to seek accommodation elsewhere.

e. *Sport.* To make the scores of (a match, etc.) equal. Also *absol.*

1923 *Daily Mail* 8 May 12 The American captain missed his chance to square at the 17th, where he had a putt of 4 feet to win the hole. **1926** WODEHOUSE *Heart of Goof* ii. 66 Bradbury, driving another long ball, won the fifteenth, squaring the match. **1955** *Times* 26 July 3/1 England, in fact, if they are to win.. must make 366 in six hours to-day, while South Africa, to square the rubber, have eight wickets yet to take. **1976** J. SNOW *Cricket Rebel* 54 The last few tense and dramatic overs later on in the final Test in Georgetown when the West Indies were pressing for victory to square the series.

6. *slang* or *colloq.* **a.** To conciliate, satisfy, or gain over (a person), *esp.* by some form of bribery or compensation; to get rid of (one) in this way.

1859 *Slang Dict.* 100 *Squaring his nibs,* giving a policeman money. **1861** HUGHES *Tom Brown at Oxf.* xlix, I told him the truth of the.. story, and I think he is squared. **1885** *Manch. Exam.* 7 Jan. 5/4 Rich offenders.. 'square the reporters' by giving them bribes on condition that their names shall not be printed in the newspapers.

b. To dispose of by murder.

1888 CHURCHWARD *Blackbirding* vii. 128 His 'getting square', meant cutting throats; and if he didn't lie, it would have taken a big ship to carry all the people he'd 'squared' up to date.

c. *Austral.* With *off*: to placate or conciliate (a person). Also *intr.*

1945 BAKER *Austral. Lang.* vi. 134 *Square off, to,* to apologize, to produce a glib explanation for some lapse or misdeameanour. **1969** *Courier-Mail* (Brisbane) 15 Jan. 7/3 Moloney said.. that he had been drinking at hotels... As they were driving home, he.. decided.. to buy beer to 'square off' with his wife. **1976** *Nature* 19 Feb. 519/2 Squaring off the proprietors of the three national chains of newspapers, whose unquestioning support he [*sc.* Mr. Fraser] enjoyed throughout the campaign.

III. *intr.* **†7. a.** To deviate or diverge, to vary (*from* something). *Obs.*

c **1450** in Aungier *Syon* (1840) 294 Sober, demewre, and chereful to speke to,.. who[se] sadnes is not wonte to suffer them notably to square in their demenynge. **1483** CAXTON *Gold. Leg.* 93/1 The blessyd Lucye hath.. Rightful goyng and deuocion to god with out squaryng out of the way. **1521** FISHER *Serm. agst. Luther* IV. Wks. (1876) 337 The prophetes somtyme left vnto themselfe dyd square from the trouthe. **1549** COVERDALE, etc. *Erasm. Par. Rom.* 19 Whiche froward minde,.. synce it squareth from Gods pleasure, cannot be but against him. **1582** STANYHURST *Æneis* To Rdr. (Arb.) 15, I made a prosodia too my selfe squaring soomwhat from thee Latin. **1609** HOLLAND *Amm. Marcell.* 204 Yet there is not a definitive sentence of his touching any controversie known, squaring from the truth.

†b. To digress from one's subject. *Obs.*

1567 MAPLET *Gr. Forest* 29 That thereby they might understand.. that I had not greatly squared, if I had pursued many moe diuisions. **1570** GOOGE *Pop. Kingd.* II. 18 The Preacher.. oft leauing it [*sc.* the Word], doth square And spend the tyme about complaints [etc.].

†c. To fall *out of* order. *Obs.*$^{-1}$

1583 STOCKER *Civ. Warres Lowe C.* IV. 66 b, The enemie [was].. so handled, as that his Souldiers squared somewhat out of order.

†8. a. To fall out, to be at variance or discord, to disagree or quarrel, *with* a person, etc.

1530 PALSGR. 731/1 Of all the men lyvyng I love not to square with hym. **1548** UDALL, etc. *Erasm. Par. Acts* 24 Sence your prohibicions doe vtterly square with his commaundementes, and that we cannot satisfie both the one and eke the other. **1561** T. HOBY tr. *Castiglione's Courtyer* III. (1577) R viij, See Madam, our enimies begin to breake and to square one wyth another.

†b. Without const. *Obs.*

1542 UDALL *Erasm. Apoph.* 255 Touchyng the stuffe wherof every of the saied garlandes was made, Gellius & Suetonius dooe square & disagree. **1580** SIR H. GIFFORD *Poems* (Grosart) 103 When men doe square for euery fly, To make them friends the women runne. **1593** NASHE *Christ's Tears* Wks. (Grosart) IV. 201 Lyke the Geometritians, they square about poynts and lynes, and the vtter shew of things. **1607** MIDDLETON *Fam. Love* IV. iii, Answer me roundly to the point, or else I'll square.

†c. To dissent or differ *from* a person. *Obs.*$^{-1}$

1600 HOLLAND *Livy* XXXIX. lii. 1056 But I accord neither with them nor with Valerius. From them I square, because I find [etc.].

9. a. To accord, concur, or correspond, to agree or fit, *with* something.

1592 WYRLEY *Armorie* 3 Wherein I may peraduenture not square in opinion with some others. **1608** D. T. *Ess. Pol. & Mor.* 118 b, True Vertue is alwaies like herselfe, she squares with euery accident. **1695** WOODWARD *Nat. Hist. Earth* I. (1723) 42 The present Circumstances of these Marine Bodies do not square with those Opinions. **1745** P. THOMAS *Jrnl. Anson's Voy.* 139 When any other Person's Account happens not to square exactly with what himself has observed. **1781** COWPER *Charity* 559 All disguises shall be rent away That square not truly with the scripture plan. **1843** LE FEVRE *Life Trav. Phys.* II. II. ii. 185 The apartment which he occupied squared well with its tenant. **1885** CLODD *Myths & Dr.* I. iii. 45 The theory may be pushed to extremes in compelling every fact to square with it.

†**b.** Const. *to* or *unto*. *Obs.*

1593 ABP. BANCROFT *Daungerous Pos.* IV. xv. 185 Thinges had not squared to their likings. **1642** SIR T. BROWNE *Relig. Med.* 8 There is no Church, whose every part so squares unto my Conscience. *a* **1691** BOYLE *Hist. Air* (1692) 71 These two notions..square to all other the instruments and phenomena in nature. **1724** A. COLLINS *Gr. Chr. Relig.* 251 Yet cannot this prophesy be made to square to the event.

c. Without const.

1600 W. WATSON *Decacordon* (1602) 29 In matters of life.., seeing they both square and differ herein from the Protestants [etc.]. **1687** DRYDEN *Hind & P.* II. 178, I set 'em by the rule, and as they square Or deviate from undoubted doctrine there, This Oral fiction, that old Faith declare. **1800** COLERIDGE *Piccolom.* v. ii, A joy it is To exercise the single apprehension Where the sums square in proof. **1849** CUPPLES *Green Hand* xiii. (1856) 133 Of all things in the world, that is the very thing where your views and mine happen to square.

10. To strut or swagger. *Obs.* exc. *dial.* †Also with *it* and *out*.

(*a*) **1590** GREENE *Neuer too Late* Wks. (Grosart) VIII. 165 Squaring in the streetes when thou shouldest bee meditating in thy chamber. **1591** SAVILE *Tacitus, Hist.* II. lxxx. 105 The Tribunes also and other captaines in terrible sort, with multitudes of armed men, went squaring and ietting the streetes. **1601** HOLLAND *Pliny* II. 115 Whereby..those gallants againe, squaring and ruffling thus in their colours, might court faire ladies. **1847-** in dial. glossaries (Devon, Lincs., Yorks.).

(*b*) **1592** GREENE *Upst. Courtier* B 3 b, As quayntlye as if some curious Florentine had trickte them vp to square it vp and downe the streetes before his Mistresse. **1626** BRETON *Fantastickes* Wks. (Grosart) II. 11/1 Now plummes and spice, Sugar and Honey, square it among pies and broth.

(*c*) *a* **1600** DELONEY *Gentle Craft* II. v, O the passion of my heart, how the villaine squares it out? **1605** CAMDEN *Rem.* (1623) 204 At another time, malapert boldnesse will square it out.

11. a. To put oneself into a posture of defence; to assume a boxing attitude.

1820 HOGG *Bridal Polmood* vi, He spit upon his hand and squared. **1823** MRS. SHERWOOD *Henry Milner* (ed. 2) III. xvi, Then beginning to square (to use an expression of Mr. Claydon's) the enemy took to his heels. **1861** HUGHES *Tom Brown at Oxf.* xi, Selecting the one most of his own size, he squared and advanced on him.

b. Const. *at* or *up to* (a person). Also *fig.*

1827 DE QUINCEY *Murder* Wks. 1854 IV. 24 Berkeley, feeling himself nettled by the waspishness of the old Frenchman, squared at him. **1848** in Bartlett *Dict. Amer.* 327 There were Polk and Cass fidgetting and squaring up to Queen Victoria. **1893** SELOUS *Trav. S.E. Africa* 3 He squared up to his adversary and..struck him a heavy blow.

c. To draw oneself *up* into a more compact attitude.

1897 *Westm. Gaz.* 26 Feb. 7/1 Mr. Rhodes..pulled himself together and squared up.

d. With *off*: to assume a fighting attitude. Also *fig.* orig. *U.S.*

1838 J. C. NEAL *Charcoal Sketches* 41 If he 'squares off' at a big fellow, he is obliged..to hit his antagonist on the knee. **1856** 'Q. K. P. DOESTICKS' *Plu-ri-bus-tah* xi. 126 Then, at once, squared off at Cuffee, Instantly 'sailed into' Cuffee. **1873** J. H. BEADLE *Undevel. West* xxxvi. 773 The bow appeared to be rearing up to square off at the midday sun. **1942** E. PAUL *Narrow St.* xxix. 267 The rest of the world were squaring off for a life-and-death struggle. **1960** T. MCLEAN *Kings of Rugby* 170 Wellington was still ahead, 6 to 3, as the two teams squared off for the second half. **1974** 'E. LATHEN' *Sweet & Low* iv. 49 The yelling started... It sounded to me like they were going to square off.

12. a. To measure (so much) on each of four sides forming a square; to yield a square of (the dimensions specified).

1789 *Trans. Soc. Arts* VII. 10 Spanish Chestnut Trees of a large size (one of them squared upward of two feet). **1792** *Ann. Reg., Nat. Hist.* 386 If it be cut when it squares only six inches, it will be as durable as an oak of six times its size and age. **1807** VANCOUVER *Agric. Devon* (1813) 255 The alder..frequently squaring a foot for twenty feet in height. **1840** SCHOMBURGK *Brit. Guiana* 93 Some of the blocks would square ten to twelve feet.

b. To increase in amount by squaring; to become square in form.

1854 *Chambers's Jrnl.* II. 280 The extravagant accounts..seem not only to square, but to cube spontaneously. **1902** RICKART *Cypress Swamp* 46 His face had squared and hardened in its lines.

c. *Naut.* To sail *away* with the yards squared. Also *fig.*, to get moving; to put oneself into shape; to make ready.

1849 N. KINGSLEY *Diary* 3 Sept. (1914) 57 The wind died away and soon sprung out from the South and [we] squared away before it. **1868** H. WOODRUFF *Trotting Horse Amer.* ix. 101 They must be wakened up from time to time, so as to make them get out of their sluggish habit and square away. **1887** in *Cassell's Encycl. Dict.* **1889** 'MARK TWAIN' *Connecticut Yankee* xxxvii. 479, I didn't waste any time..but squared away for business. **1894** *Outing* XXIV. 422/2 There, he rounds the buoy and squares away. **1899** F. T. BULLEN *Log Sea-Waif* 313 We squared away to a spanking breeze. **1961** 'E. LATHEN' *Banking on Death* (1962) xiii. 103 Miss Todd wasted no more time on idle chatter but squared away to her typewriter.

13. *colloq.* With *it*: To live or act honestly.

1873 in Taylor *Life David* vii. 91 Give a poor fellow a chance to square it for three months.

14. In Comb., as **square-up** *colloq.*, a quarrel.

? **1949** DYLAN THOMAS *Sel. Lett.* (1966) 339 Bert and I had a regular square-up, but he came over to my way of thinking.

square cap. Also square-cap. [SQUARE *a.*]

1. An academic cap with a square top; a mortar-board, trencher.

1584 LYLY *Sappho* I. iii, A square die in a pages pocket, is as decent as a square cap on a Graduates head. **1695** *Lond. Gaz.* No. 3049/4 Lost.., a Surplice, with a Doctors Hood and Square Cap, in a Past-board-Box. **1720** in *Leyborne-Popham MSS.* (Hist. MSS. Comm.) 261, I had [in 1677] a square cap given me for speaking, and was the first commoner, I think, that ever wore one in Oxford. **1728** CHAMBERS *Cycl.* s.v. *Cap*, Churchmen, and the Members of Universities, Students in Law, Physick, &c., as well as Graduates, wear square Caps. **1778** in *Lett. Radcliffe & James* (O.H.S.) 44 See me strutting in my new robes, with my square cap and tossel. **1796** [see TRENCHER-CAP].

†**2.** *transf.* A University man. *Obs.*

1642 [H. PEACHAM] (*title*), Square-Caps turned into Round-Heads: or the Bishops Vindication and the Brownists Conviction. **1651** CLEVELAND *Poems, Square Cap* i, Her suiters are many But shee'l have a Square-cap if ere she have any.

square-cut, *a.* [SQUARE *a.* or *adv.*]

1. Cut to or into a square form. Also *fig.*

1622 DRAYTON *Poly-olb.* xxiii. 192 Mosses, fleets, and fells,..Whose turf, and square-cut peat, is fuel good enough. **1820** KEATS *Cap & Bells* xvii, There's the square-cut chancellor, His son shall never touch that bishopric. **1848** CLOUGH *Bothie* I. 22 The grave man, nicknamed Adam,..with square cut antique waistcoat. **1879** MRS. A. E. JAMES *Ind. Househ. Managem.* 14 One good black silk, made with high, low, and square-cut bodices, you will certainly require.

2. *absol.* A coat with square skirts.

1893 *Westm. Gaz.* 21 Dec. 2/1 That one which you are looking at is a George I:..it is a true square-cut.

squared (skwɛəd), *ppl. a.* [f. SQUARE *v.*]

1. a. Made or fashioned square; reduced to a square form. Also with *off*.

1382 WYCLIF *1 Kings* vi. 35 And alle he couerde with goldyn platis, with squaryd werk at rewle. *c* **1410** *Master of Game* (MS. Digby 182) xiv, A grehounde shulde haue..þe thies gret and swared [*Bodl. MS.* squared] as an hare. **1416** *York Memo. Bk.* (Surtees) I. 213 Pur overer et faire.. flat salere, cowped salere, sqward salere. **1520** in *Archaeol.* (1892) LIII. 18 A pyxe of Every..havyng a squared steple yn the topp. **1577** B. GOOGE *Heresbach's Husb.* II. (1586) 106 b, The squared, and the round, or the whole timber. **1656** *Rites of Durh.* (1903) 84 A fair Ivory squared table covered with a green cloth. **1685** TEMPLE *Ess. Her. Virtue* Wks. 1720 I. 211 Another very long and large [highway], paved all with cut or squared Stone. **1707** SIBBALD *Scotland* (1739) I. 28 A Wall of squared and cut Stones. **1778** *Encycl. Brit.* (ed. 2) II. 1389/2 It is all of squared free stone, strong and lofty. **1809** CAMPBELL *Gert. Wyom.* III. xviii, Deep roars the innavigable gulf below Its squared rock. **1869** RANKINE *Machine & Hand-tools* Pl. H6, The screw, Z, which is likewise formed with a squared end to receive a winch handle or key. **1875** *Carpentry & Join.* 126 There can be 18 in. of the squared support above the pedestal. **1965** J. A. MICHENER *Source* (1966) 580 No square corners would be allowed, no neatly squared-off towers. **1973** D. MAY *Laughter in Djakarta* v. 83 Tapping some magazines into a squared-off pile.

fig. **1586** FERNE *Blaz. Gentrie* 83 Men seeming of such a squared conscience that they pretend all to run either to maintenance of superstition or vaine glory. **1594** *Selimus* Greene's Wks. (Grosart) XIV. 286 Your squared words And broad-mouth'd tearmes, can neuer conquer vs.

b. Drawn up in a square or squares.

1667 MILTON *P.L.* I. 758 Thir summons call'd From every Band and squared Regiment By place or choice the worthiest. **1798** in *Unit. Services Mag.* XIX. 464 They rushed on against our squared battalions. **1807** J. BARLOW *Columb.* III. 581 The troops in squared array Wait the wild hordes loose huddling to the fray. **1812** CARY *Dante, Purg.* XXIV. 64 Like as the birds, that winter near the Nile, In squared regiment direct their course.

c. Marked with squares.

1887 *Science* 11 Mar. 240/1 The graphic representation of the results will be readily understood. It is only necessary to take a sheet of 'squared' paper, or paper ruled in two directions at right angles to each other. **1902** *Westm. Gaz.* 21 June 3/1 Take on the squared paper two perpendicular lines.

2. Multiplied by itself. Also *fig.*

1557 RECORDE *Whetst.* G iv, That roote is called a Squared square roote, which maketh a square of squares in nomber. **1571** DIGGES *Pantom.* IV. xi. Y ij b, For the superficies ye shall augmente the squared square of the side by 3. **1613** TAPP *Pathw. Knowl.* 293 A squared square number is the product of any number multiplyed 3 times into it selfe. **1664** E. BUSHNELL *Compl. Shipwright* 31, 5 times 5 is a squared number. **1787** *Phil. Trans.* LXXVII. 228 The 4th power, or squared squares of the sines of the latitudes. **1964** J. W. LINNETT *Electronic Struct. Molecules* vi. 92 There will be five squared-terms..and twenty cross-terms..in the square of the total function. **1979** *Tucson* (Arizona) *Citizen* 20 Sept. 11A/1, I don't know if tarantulas are considered insects or just some form of spider..squared.

3. Adapted, suited. *rare.*

1698 FRYER *Acc. E. India & P.* 112 Such a subtile Generation is this, and so fitly squared a Place is Surat to exercise their Genius in. *Ibid.* 224.

Hence † **'squaredly** *adv. Obs. rare.*

1613 TAPP *Pathw. Knowl.* 322 Sq. of squ. squaredly square. **1674** JEAKE *Arith.* (1696) 272 A..Square of Squares Squaredly Squared. *Ibid.* 645 The Quotient shall be squaredly Quadratical.

'squarehead. *slang.* Also square-head. [SQUARE *a.* 9 c.] **1.** An honest person: one who is not a criminal (see quots.).

1890 BARRÈRE & LELAND *Dict. Slang* II. 293/1 'Honesty among thieves' is undoubtedly the production of a square-head or sham thief; a good thief will rob anybody. **1950** *Austral. Police Jrnl.* Apr. 119 *Square-head* (or *squarey*), one who has no convictions. **1977** *Courier-Mail* (Brisbane) 16 Feb. 5/1 Half an hour or so later a squarehead (criminal slang for someone who is going straight), who was minding the money in a bag for Blair, handed it over to one of the Toecutters.

2. A foreigner of Germanic extraction, esp. a German (spec. *Army slang* in the war of 1914–18) or Scandinavian.

1903 FARMER & HENLEY *Slang* VI. 333/1 *Squarehead*,..a German or Scandinavian. **1906** *Soldier Slang* in C. McGovern *Sarjint Larry an' Frinds*, *Square-head*, a soldier of German birth and addicted to the use of German idioms. **1918** H. C. WITWER in *Collier's* 16 Mar. 21/2 The English call 'em 'Uns..we call 'em squareheads. **1932** J. DOS PASSOS *1919* 61 She started firing across the North Star's bows with a small gun that the squareheads manned. **1942** C. BARRETT *On Wallaby* v. 95 A bunch of Germans with this mob behaved very differently: the square-heads were sullen and surly. **1953** *Times Lit. Suppl.* 23 Oct. 678/2 Those of Swedish extraction in America, known as squareheads, suffer the reputation of being dull, heavy, stupid, simple. **1973** D. JONES *Let.* 15 Apr. in R. Hague *Dai Greatcoat* (1980) iv. 244 In the ranks we often used 'Squarehead' of old Jerry—'That poor old 'squarehead' they brought in from last night's raid looked pretty far gone to me.'

3. In misc. *transf.* and *fig.* uses.

1919 *Dialect Notes* V. 62 *Square-head*, a dull, stupid person. **1949** *Sun* (Baltimore) 26 Oct. 10/3 A real 'square-head' seaman, who knows what it is like to drift for days without food. **1958** 'CASTLE' & 'HAILEY' *Flight into Danger* i. 13 This plane is crammed with squareheads who are going to Vancouver..to root like hell for their boys.

square-headed, *a.* [SQUARE *a.* 13.] Having the head or top fashioned or cut in a square form:

a. *Arch.* Of doors, windows, etc.

1815 J. SMITH *Panorama Sci. & Art* I. 169 An example of the square-headed door of the Perpendicular style. **1837** *Civil Eng. & Arch. Jrnl.* I. 19/1 Even the arch of the porch is not enclosed by a square-headed label. **1861** JAS. CAMPBELL *Balmerino & its Abbey* II. xii. 154 This apartment was originally lighted by two square-headed windows.

b. Of bolts or nails.

1825 SCOTT *Betrothed* iv, A volley of..square-headed bolts of great size and thickness. **1862** MISS BRADDON *Lady Audley* i, Old oak, studded with great square-headed iron nails.

c. In other applications.

1857 HUGHES *Tom Brown* i, They are a square-headed and snake-necked generation. **1883** *Harper's Mag.* Aug. 450/1 A large square-headed topsail. **1903** C. F. A. WILLIAMS *Notation* 93 The virga had become the square-headed note ꞁ, and the punctum either a square ■ or a lozenge ◆.

d. Level-headed, sensible.

1896 H. G. WELLS *Let.* 24 Jan. in *Exper. Autobiogr.* (1934) I. vi. 402 He's a first rate, square headed, thoroughly honest man. **1922** JOYCE *Ulysses* 82 Squareheaded chaps those must be in Rome: they work the whole show.

e. Stolid, dull.

1936 C. S. LEWIS *Allegory of Love* iv. 172 To believe thus is to attribute to Chaucer a square-headed vulgarity of thought and feeling.

f. Describing one of a Germanic race.

1942 E. PAUL *Narrow St.* xxix. 268 The square-headed, owl-like Nazis. **1979** O. SELA *Petrograd Consignment* 35 A big, square-headed man.

Hence **square-'headedness**.

1930 *Times Lit. Suppl.* 10 Apr. 321/1 An underlying sanity and square-headedness about Huneker's critical judgments.

square-leg: see SQUARE *a.* 15.

squarelike, *a. rare.* Also 7 squire-. [f. SQUARE *sb.*] Resembling a square; rectangular.

1557 RECORDE *Whetst.* G j b, Some menne delite more to call them squarelike figures. **1570** BILLINGSLEY *Euclid* I. def. 31. 5 A figure on the one syde longer, or squarelike, or as some call it, a long square. **1611** COTGR., *Buveau*, a kind of Squire, or Squire-like Instrument;..some call it a Beuell.

squarely ('skwɛəlɪ), *adv.* [f. SQUARE *a.*]

1. So as to be squared (by multiplication).

1557 RECORDE *Whetst.* D iij, The other sides beyng multiplied squarely (that is, by them selfes). **1594** BLUNDEVIL *Exerc.* I. (1636) 96 Which Root if you Multiply into it selfe squarely, the Product will be like unto the Number given. **1613** TAPP *Pathw. Knowl.* 303 Multiply the roote nearest found squarely. **1674** JEAKE *Arith.* (1696) 297 Then must 10 be multiplyed Squarely and 8 Cubically.

2. Honestly, fairly, in a straightforward manner.

1564 in Tytler *Hist. Scotl.* (1864) III. 138 To speak squarely our opinion, we think you could in fewer lines have comprehended matter more to our contentation. **1624** SANDERSON *Serm.* I. 247 Let us therefore deal squarely, as wise and honest merchants should do. **1640** HARSNET *Repent.* 166 True it is that many doe carry themselves very squarely and plausibly to the Eye of the World. *a* **1704** T. BROWN *Decl. Adv.* Wks. 1730 I. 41 If they dealt squarely with me..they'd scarce at all wonder. **1767** *Spirit Public Jrnls.* (1806) IX. 247 Act fairly and squarely,..For honesty sure is by far the best policy. **1876** STEDMAN *Victorian Poets* 59 The pleasure which comes from being in harness, and from duty squarely performed. **1884** *Chicago Times* 13 Jan., Lord Falmouth, one of the few sportsmen who never bet and who ran his horses squarely.

†**3.** Freely, copiously. *Obs.*[−1]

1611 COTGR. s.v. *Donné, Il s'en est bien donné*, he hath tipled squarely.

†4. Precisely, exactly. *Obs.*

1626 T. H[AWKINS] *Caussin's Holy Crt.* 6 The works are likewise the more feeble, not squarely answering to the modell of knowledge. **1637** GILLESPIE *Eng. Pop. Cerem.* Prol. C2b, Blindly to followe every opinion which is broached, and squarely to conforme unto every custome. **1684** OTWAY *Atheist* I. i, My Orders are to meet her fairly and squarely this Evening at Seven.

5. In a position directly square with, or opposite to, some line or object; in a straight or direct manner.

1802 JAMES *Milit. Dict.* s.v. *March*, The front-directing serjeant, after having placed himself perfectly and squarely in the rank, must [etc.]. **1883** B. HARTE *Carquinez Woods* viii. 186 She looked him squarely in the eyes without a word. **1894** MRS. F. ELLIOT *Roman Gossip* iv. 113 He sits squarely on his war-horse.

fig. **1867** AUGUSTA WILSON *Vashti* xv, She set this conjecture squarely before her, and forced herself to contemplate it. **1873** HALE *In His Name* ii. 8 They refuted it squarely.

b. At right angles to the length or height.

1873 SPON *Workshop Rec.* Ser. I. 7/1 The brush requires to be squarely and evenly cut. **1883** *Harper's Mag.* Jan. 200/2 We..saw that a bole fully six feet in diameter had broken squarely across.

c. *fig.* Plainly, unequivocally, firmly, solidly. Chiefly *U.S.*

1860 in Thornton *Amer. Gloss.* (1912) II. 845 [This] means simply and squarely, that you intend..to rule or ruin this Government. **1885** *Cent. Mag.* XXIX. 511 He stands squarely upon observation, experience, induction. **1900** LAPSLEY *Durham* 44 He..based his demand squarely on his royal power.

6. In a square form; so as to be square.

1828 W. FIELD *Mem. Dr. Parr* II. 355 He was about the middle height, squarely built, of strong athletic frame, not much inclined to corpulency. **1861** *Engl. Wom. Dom. Mag.* III. 219 Holding a squarely-folded note at arm's length before my eyes. **1864** MISS YONGE *Trial* II. 310 The squarely made,..handsome Averil Ward. **1882** *Jrnl. Linn. Soc.* XVI. 232 Aperture-papillae large and squarely oval.

'squareman. *Sc.* [SQUARE *sb.* I.] A carpenter, stone-cutter, or other workman who regularly uses a square for adjusting or testing his work.

c **1790** *Encycl. Brit.* (ed. 3) VI. 171/2 The incorporated trades [of Dumfries],..viz. square-men, smiths [etc.]. **1808** MAYNE *Siller Gun* I. xxvi, The squaremen follow'd i' the raw, And syne the weavers. **1837** CARLYLE *Fr. Rev.* III. v. i, How many hammermen and squaremen, bakers and brewers..must ply their old daily work. **1879** *Encycl. Brit.* IX. 750/1 There was probably a pass-word, such as the squareman word used in the 'brithering' of the wrights and slaters.

squareness ('skwɛənɪs). [f. SQUARE *a.*]

1. The quality of being square in form.

c **1400** MAUNDEV. (1839) xiv. 159 The Dyamand, be vertu of God, takethe squarenesse. **1474** CAXTON *Chesse* IV. i. (1883) 158 The seconde is wherfore the bordeur aboute is hyher than the squarenes of the poyntes. **1530** PALSGR. 201/1 Brede or squarenesse, *croisure*. **1590** STOCKWOOD *Rules Constr.* 48 The depth, length, thicknes, squarenes, roundnes of a thing. **1613** PURCHAS *Pilgrimage* (1614) 433 They made a thing being foure square, and in height and squarenesse of a chaire. **1690** LOCKE *Hum. Und.* II. xxi. §14 Liberty being as little applicable to the will, as swiftness of motion is to sleep, or squareness to vertue. **1768–74** TUCKER *Lt. Nat.* (1834) I. 278 When the wax is new moulded, the squareness it had is totally lost. **1818** *Art Bookbinding* 14 The beauty and squareness of the book greatly depend on having it well backed. **1855** *Poultry Chron.* II. 410 We should like to see amateurs..address great attention to compact squareness of form and shortness of leg. **1897** *Chr. Herald* (N. York) 15 Dec. 970/2 The shoulders had the awful squareness of a skeleton.

transf. **1873** H. C. BANISTER *Music* 175 Such devices serve to avert squareness, or tameness, especially in the development of musical ideas. **1885** *Mag. Art* Sept. 467 The determined character and consistent squareness of the touch.

2. Conformity to good principles.

1642 QUARLES *Observ. Princes & St.* lxiv, Let Princes be very carefull in the Choyce of their Counsellors, choosing.. by the Squarenesse of their actions. **1780** BURKE *Corr.* (1844) II. 356, I hope you will..bring the squareness, the manliness, and the decision of a judicial place into the house of parliament. **1817** KEATS *Lett.* Wks. 1889 III. 69, I am sure you are confident of my responsibility, and in the sense of squareness that is always in me.

3. a. Rectangular position in relation to some line or object.

1796 *Instr. & Reg. Cavalry* (1813) 11 On this squareness of man and horse both dressing and movement must essentially depend. **1802** JAMES *Milit. Dict.* s.v. *March*, Regularity of step, squareness of body, and precision of movement. **1847** *Infantry Man.* (1854) 3 The equal squareness of the shoulders and body to the front is the first ..principle of the position of a soldier. **1875** *Carpentry & Join.* 44 Plane this level, and then test its squareness to the first.

b. *Assoc. Football*, etc. Of a defence: the condition of being square. (SQUARE *a.* 6 d) and lacking in depth.

1978 *Guardian Weekly* 19 Nov. 23/5 Taking full advantage of Manchester United's inadequacy in the air and punishing the squareness of their defence on the ground.

4. Conventionality, dullness. Cf. SQUARE *a.* 9 d.

1961 *John o' London's* 16 Nov. 548/2 Where Squareness is the ultimate low, anything can get by if it proclaims itself Hip loudly enough. **1972** M. J. BOSSE *Incident at Naha* ii. 119, I was beginning to care about our Bostonian, even though he was capable of, like, ultimate squareness. **1977** P. USTINOV *Dear Me* xiii. 173 It is out of fear of what is known as squareness that we rarely say what we really think or feel.

squarer ('skwɛərə(r)). [f. SQUARE *v.*]

1. a. One who reduces wood, stone, etc., to a square form.

1422–3 *Foreign Acc. 1 Hen. VI*, i, Carpentarii vocati fellers & squarers. **1440** *Found. St. Bartholomew's* (E.E.T.S.) 29 Hewerrys of wode with axe and squarerys of tymbyr with chippynge axe. **1565** COOPER *Thesaurus, Quadratarius*, a squarer of marble. *c* **1601** KEYMOR *Observ. Dutch Fishing* (1664) 7 She imployeth..at Land..also Squarers of Timber,.. Carpenters, Shipwrights, Smiths. **1611** COTGR., *Esquarrisseur*, a squarer of stones, or timber.

b. With *out* (see quot.).

1611 FLORIO, *Squadra mondi*, a squarer out of worlds, an Astrologer.

c. One who aims at squaring the circle.

1852 DE MORGAN in Graves *Life Sir W. R. Hamilton* (1889) III. 350 A squarer of the circle said to me..about some lines [etc.]. **1865** —— in *Athenæum* Oct. 504 The new squarer who advertises..that, having read that the circular ratio was undetermined [etc.]. **1879** *Fortn. Rev.* Aug. 293 Mathematicians do not stop to argue with squarers of the circle or with reasoners that the earth is flat.

†2. A contentious or quarrelsome person. *Obs.*⁻¹

1599 SHAKS. *Much Ado* I. i. 82 Is there no young squarer now, that will make a voyage with him to the diuell?

3. *Sc.* 'One who squares his elbows for fighting; a sparrer' (Ogilvie, 1850).

4. *Electronics.* A device that converts a sinusoidal or other periodic wave into a square wave of the same period.

1965 *Wireless World* Aug. 402/1 If the square wave output is integrated and used to bias the first transistor, and if the squarer is d.c. coupled throughout and has an odd number of stages, then the feedback maintains the mark-to-space ratio constant. **1971** *Physics Bull.* July 427/1 The basic module was an inverter and was demonstrated as a squarer, then two or more were joined together to produce various logic gates and multivibrators.

square-rigged, *a.* [SQUARE *a.* 13.]

1. *Naut.* Having the yards and sails placed across the masts in contrast to fore and aft; †having exceptionally long yards (Falconer).

1769 FALCONER *Dict. Marine* (1780) s.v. *Xebec*, The crew of every xebec has..the labour of three square-rigged ships. **1802** *Hull Dock Act* 1503 Capable of containing seventy sail of ships or square-rigged vessels. **1840** R. H. DANA *Bef. Mast* xxiii, [He] was making his first voyage in a square-rigged vessel. **1895** *Oracle Encycl.* I. 503/2 *Brig*, the general term for a vessel with two masts, having a boom-mainsail, and otherwise square-rigged.

2. *transf.* (See quot.)

1851 MAYHEW *Lond. Lab.* I. 251/1 George and his two fellow-labourers were 'square-rigged'—that is, well dressed.

square sail. [SQUARE *a.*] a. A four-sided sail supported by a yard slung across the vessel. b. A flying sail set on the fore-mast of a schooner or the mast of a sloop or cutter.

1600 E. BLOUNT tr. *Conestaggio* 309 For which cause they shortned their yardes, prouiding square sailes. **1743** BULKELEY & CUMMINS *Voy. S. Seas* 117 As the Cutter was coming up to us, her square Sail splitted. **1769** FALCONER *Dict. Marine* (1780) s.v. *Scudding*, A ship..scuds with a sail extended on her fore-mast... In sloops and schooners, and other small vessels, the sail employed for this purpose is called the square-sail. **1794** *Rigging & Seamanship* 127 The cross-jack, or square-sail. **1846** MᶜCULLOCH *Acc. Brit. Empire* (1854) I. 37 The barges which navigate the Severn.. carry a square-sail, and have a mainmast and topmast. **1886** *Encycl. Brit.* XXI. 604/2 *Square sails*, those set upon such yards as have lifts and braces, regardless of their proportions.

attrib. **1794** *Rigging & Seamanship* 162 The Square-sail-boom is lashed across the deck of vessels with one mast, to spread the foot of the square-sail. **1823** CRABB *Technol. Dict.* II. s.v., A sloop's or cutter's sail, which hauls out to the lower yard, called the square-sail-yard. **1863** A. YOUNG *Naut. Dict.* 109 *Cross-jack-yard*..in a sloop or schooner also gets the name of the square sail yard. *Ibid.* 366 *Square sail boom*, a boom hooked on to an eye-bolt in the fore part of the foremast in any fore-and-aft-rigged vessel, for the purpose of booming out the square-sail, and setting the lower studding-sail.

†**square-square,** *a.* and *v. Obs.* [SQUARE *a.* and *v.*] a. *adj.* Biquadrate. b. *v. trans.* To biquadrate by multiplication.

1662 HOBBES *Seven Prob.* Wks. 1845 VII. 67 There be some numbers called plane, others solids, others plano-solid, others square, others cubic, others square-square. **1669** NEWTON in Rigaud *Corr. Sci. Men* (1841) II. 284 To which 6¼ square-squared, or multiplied three times into itself, is about equal.

square-sterned, *a.* [SQUARE *a.* 13.] Of vessels: Having a square stern (see quot. *c* 1850).

1676 *Lond. Gaz.* No. 1130/4 St Teresa of Dunkirk, Burthen 20 Tuns,..a square stern'd Sloop with a Deck. **1690** *Ibid.* No. 2562/4 The Ship Delight, English Built, Square-sterned, 130 Tuns. **1769** FALCONER *Dict. Marine* (1780), *Bastardes*, or *Batardelles*, square-sterned row-gallies. **1791** W. HUTCHINSON *Pract. Seamanship* 27 As square sterned ships..are found to answer all trades and purposes better than round or pink sterned ships. *c* **1850** *Rudim. Navig.* (Weale) 151 *Square-sterned*, a term applied to ships whose wing transom is at right angles, or nearly at right angles, with the stern-post... All British ships are now built upon this principle. **1867** SMYTH *Sailor's Word-bk.* 648 *Square-Sterned and British Built*, a phrase to express the peculiar excellence of our first-class merchantmen.

Squaresville ('skwɛəzvɪl). orig. *U.S.* Also **Squareville.** [f. SQUARE *sb.* or *a.*: see -VILLE.] An imaginary town characterized by dullness and conventionality. Also *attrib.* or as *adj.*

1956 'E. MCBAIN' *Cop Hater* (1958) viii. 75 This guy is from Squaresville, fellas, I'm telling you. He wouldn't know a ·45 from a cement mixer. **1961** *Times* 27 Apr. 17/2 To look round a crowded room and murmur 'Squareville' or 'Hicksville' may be elliptical, but is certainly more effective than the full form. **1967** P. WELLES *Babyhip* (1968) ii. 31 It's such squaresville talk. **1968** *Listener* 11 July 51/1 And they went away, more than ever convinced that the war between the generations was for real. And through the window there floated a querulous, puzzled voice. 'A queer fish, real squaresville.'

square-tailed, *a.* [SQUARE *a.* 13.] Having a square tail: a. Of animals, birds, etc.

1781 PENNANT *Hist. Quadrup.* II. 482 Square-tailed Shrew of a dusky cinereous color. **1819** *Pantologia* s.v. *Sorex*, The white footed, square tailed, carinated, and unicolor shrews. **1827** GRIFFITH tr. *Cuvier* V. 102 *Sorex Tetragonurus* (Square-tailed Shrew). **1891** *Science-Gossip* XXVII. 80/1 The Square-tailed Worm... Among our native worms there is one with a square tail (*Allurus tetraedrus*, Eisen). **1895** LYDEKKER *Roy. Nat. Hist.* IV. 54 The square-tailed bee-eaters (*Melittophagus*) are all of small size.

b. Of a coat.

1837 CARLYLE *Fr. Rev.* III. VII. ii, Young Valour in square-tailed coat eyes Beauty in Greek sandals.

square-toe. *attrib.* = SQUARE-TOED *a.* 1.

1706 *Lond. Gaz.* No. 4257/4 A pair of Square Toe Shoes.

square-toed, *a.* [SQUARE *a.* 13.]

1. a. Of shoes: Having broad square toes.

1785 GROSE *Dict. Vulgar T.* s.v. *Square toes*, Square-toed shoes were anciently worn in common, and long retained by old men. **1803** *Censor* 1 Apr. 47 In a superfine coat with waistcoat, and..hessian boots, or square-toed shoes. **1897** 'H. S. MERRIMAN' *In Kedar's Tents* xi, The priest had walked thither, as the dust on his square-toed shoes and black stockings would testify.

b. *transf.* in *U.S. Naut.* use. Now only *Hist.*

1851 H. MELVILLE *Moby Dick* I. xvi. 110 You may have seen many a quaint craft in your day, for aught I know: square-toed luggers, mountainous Japanese junks. **1886** *Forest & Stream* 13 May 316/3 Even the regular 'square-toed' schooner, supposed to be original to San Francisco, flourishes up the James. **1948** R. DE KERCHOVE *Internat. Maritime Dict.* (1958) 771/1 *Square-toed frigate*,..local name given in Quincy, Mass., to the scow sloops engaged in the granite trade. (Obsolete.)

2. *fig.* Old-fashioned, formal, precise.

1795 BURKE *Regic. Peace* iv. (C.P.S.) 294 We old people must retain some square-toed predilection for the fashions of our youth. **1803** PEGGE *Anecd. Eng. Lang.* 131 Square-toed and old fashioned as it may be, it certainly weeds the sense at once of all equivocation. **1846** MRS. GORE *Eng. Char.* (1852) 127 There are two leading classes of London Bankers—the square-toed and the pointed. **1880** MORLEY in *Daily News* 26 Mar. 2/6 A system of square-toed humdrum.

Hence **square-toedness.**

1846 MRS. GORE *Eng. Char.* (1852) 127 As regards this important distinction, however, neither square-toedness nor pointed-toedness is to be relied on.

square-toes. [SQUARE *a.*]

1. A precise, formal, old-fashioned person; one having strict or narrow ideas of conduct. Usu. qualified by *old*, and with initial capital.

1771 SMOLLETT *Humph. Cl.* (1815) 164, I could hardly keep my gravity on this ludicrous occasion; but old Squaretoes was differently affected. **1785** G. A. BELLAMY *Apology* (ed. 3) I. 195 He was sorry that old Square-toes was obliged..to go out of town immediately. **1819** 'RABELAIS THE YOUNGER' *Abeillard & H.* 219 Finding old Square-toes in the study Stern, gloomy, sulky, dark, and muddy. **1857** HUGHES *Tom Brown* Pref. p. xvi, Giving the idea that Arnold turned out a set of young square-toes. **1889** STEVENSON *Master of Ballantrae* 99 Even Square-Toes has a certain vivacity when his stake is imperilled.

2. Square-toed shoes.

1852 THACKERAY *Esmond* I. viii, The Doctor made a low bow..and walked off on his creaking square-toes after his patron.

squarewise, *adv.* Also square-wise; 6 squyre-, 6–7 squirewise. [f. SQUARE *a.*]

†1. After the fashion of a carpenter's square; at right angles, rectangularly. *Obs.*

1546 *State Papers Hen. VIII*, XI. 231, 2 boordes [= tables] being set squyrewise. **1571** DIGGES *Pantom.* I. xviii. Fb, Then go from it Orthogonally or Squirewise..200 foote. **1593** T. FALE *Art of Dialling* 13 Let the line of Contingence be drawn squarewise by the point F. **1598** R. HAYDOCKE tr. *Lomazzo* I. 111 From which point..vnto the great gate at the west ende, it woulde be extended square wise so much more. **1669** STURMY *Mariner's Mag.* VII. xxvii. 40 Draw the Line FBA squire wise to the Substiler Line. **1692** *Capt. Smith's Seaman's Gram.* II. 156 Two Sticks.. joyned together, Square-wise. **1725** *Fam. Dict.* s.v. *Cutting*, You must upon some Occasions cut Square-wise, and that is to be done to bushy dwarf Trees.

2. In the form of a square; squarely.

1611 SPEED *Theat. Gt. Brit.* (1614) 125/1 It lieth somewhat square-wise, not much different in length and breadth. **1725** *Fam. Dict.* s.v. *Watering*, You shall..knock four or five strong Stakes into the bottom of the Water, setting them Squarewise. **1853** G. J. CAYLEY *Las Alforjas* II. 254 By folding a silk handkerchief square-wise into a broad belt. **1891** CAYLEY *Math. Papers* (1897) XIII. 179 A circle is squarewise contractible into a point.

†**'squarier.** *Obs. rare.* [f. SQUARE *a.* or *v.*]

1. A square; a rule or standard.

1581 J. BELL *Haddon's Answ. Osor.* A vj b, The right squaryer of Christian fayth. *Ibid.* 411 b, If Luthers rule be agreably apporcioned accordyng to the infallible squarier of that holy standard.

2. A sort of false dice.

1591 GREENE *Conny Catch.* I. (1859) 4 Therefore had I cheates for the very sise, of the squariers, langrets, gourds, stoppe-dice, high-men, low-men, and dice barde for all advauntages.

ˈsquaring, *vbl. sb.* [f. SQUARE *v.*]

1. The action of making square or of reducing to a square form.

c **1440** *Promp. Parv.* 471 Squarynge, *quadracio, conquadracio.* **1476–7** *Sarum Ch.-w. Accs.* (Swayne, 1896) 363 The fellyng of ij Elms and swaryng, iiijd. **1529** MORE *Dyalogue* I. Wks. 155/1 Now consider, that ye make him by & by fall to yᵉ squaryng of his stones. **1552–3** in Willis & Clark *Cambridge* (1886) II. 52 Thomas Watson carpender for yᵉ squarynge, framynge, and settinge up..a wall of..timbre. **1634** SIR T. HERBERT *Trav.* 198 Ordnance of brasse ..very well proportioned in bore and squaring. **1683** MOXON *Mech. Exerc., Printing* xii. ¶6 The Squaring the Face and Stems of the Punch. **1725** W. HALFPENNY *Sound Building* 32 Enough for squaring of this Rail. **1841** R. H. DANA *Seaman's Man.* 125 Squaring by the lifts makes them [*sc.* yards] horizontal.

attrib. **1867** SMYTH *Sailor's Word-bk., Squaring Marks*, marks placed upon the lifts and braces [as guides in squaring the yards]. **1870** SAUZAY *Marvels Glass-making* 92 This.. fragile glass..[is] placed on wheels and rails, which will convey it still unpolished to the squaring room, where it will be examined, classified [and] cut. **1884** KNIGHT *Dict. Mech.* Suppl. 849/2 *Squaring Plow.* For squaring paper in book-work. *Ibid., Squaring Shears*,..a machine for squaring up tinned plate.

b. With *off*, *out*, or *up*. Also *attrib.*

(*a*) **1611** COTGR., *Equarrissement*, a measuring, or squaring out, by a Squire.

(*b*) **1846** A. YOUNG *Naut. Dict.* 294 *Squaring-off*, in ship-building, signifies plugging off and otherwise tightening the treenails [etc.]. **1884** KNIGHT *Dict. Mech.* Suppl., *Squaring-off Saw*, a circular saw,.. to square the ends of work.

(*c*) **1846** HOLTZAPFFEL *Turning* II. 501 When the works are planed with rebates, grooves, or mouldings, the squaring up of the four sides is always the preliminary step. **1869** RANKINE *Machine & Hand-tools* Pl. Q 16. 1 It is capable of performing..grooving, tongueing, and squaring-up. **1875** KNIGHT *Dict. Mech.* 2813/2 The squaring-up and facing tables are on the other side.

c. The manner in which a thing is squared or set square.

1832 MARRYAT *N. Forster* xxxvi, Look at..the squaring of her topsails.

†**2.** Dissension, wrangling, contention. *Obs.*

1580 NORTH *Plutarch* (1595) 197 Hanniball hearing of their iarre and squaring together [etc.]. **1598** FLORIO, *Rissa*, ..a quarrell,..a strife, a squaring. **1600** HOLLAND *Livy* XXIV. ix. 515 All the centuries besides without any squaring and variance elected the very same. **1621** J. REYNOLDS *God's Revenge* I. 153 Hee desired and sought some pretext..to bolster out and apologize his iarring and squaring with his wife.

3. Multiplication of a number by itself.

1579 DIGGES *Stratiot.* 52 Multiplication of moytie in itselfe whiche I name Squaring. **1694** [see BIQUADRATE *v.*].

4. The process of finding a square equivalent to another magnitude.

1704 J. HARRIS *Lex. Techn.* I. s.v., The Quadrature or Squaring of the Circle, is the finding a Square equal to the Area of a Circle. **1798** HUTTON *Course Math.* II. 95 It seems intended to make an allowance for the squaring of the tree. **1855** BREWSTER *Newton* I. ii. 22 Several articles on angular sections, and the squaring of curves. **1881** ROUTLEDGE *Science* ii. 36 This is the celebrated problem of the Squaring of the Circle.

5. Adaptation, adjustment.

1702 *English Theophrastus* 362 The squaring of a man's thoughts, wishes, and desires to the lot that providence has set out for us, is both a blessing and a duty. **1838** LYTTON *Alice* III. ii, I do not understand this new-fangled policy—this squaring of measures to please the Opposition.

6. Assumption of a boxing attitude.

1850 THACKERAY *Pendennis* xxxviii, He..started..into what is called an attitude of self-defence, and..began the operation which is entitled 'squaring'.

ˈsquaring, *ppl. a.* [f. SQUARE *v.*]

†**1.** Given to contention or wrangling. *Obs.*

1515 BARCLAY *Egloges* iii. (1570) C ij b/1 If thou be busy or squaring of language Thou mayst peradventure walke in the same passage. **1583** MELBANCKE *Philotimus* S j b, Nay holla squaring Dick, I am no but for euerie boult. **1598** FLORIO, *Dissentioso*,..contentious, squaring, quarrelsome.

2. ***squaring band, piece*** (see quots.).

c **1860** H. STUART *Seaman's Catech.* 74 The topmasts have squaring pieces at the heel, to fit the mast hole. **1879** *Cassell's Techn. Educ.* IV. 399/1 Upon the under side of the carriage there are wheels placed in a horizontal position, round which the 'squaring bands' are passed.

3. That multiplies a quantity by itself.

1961 *Technology* Feb. 44/2 An automatic neon overload indicator..detects signal peaks exceeding the range of the squaring unit. **1979** *Proc. London Math. Soc.* XXXVIII. 514 The squaring map $a \rightarrow a^2$, determined by this Jordan product, is the same as that determined by functional calculus.

ˈsquarish, *a.* Occas. square-ish. [f. SQUARE *a.*] Somewhat, more or less, or approximately, square.

1742 *De Foe's Tour Gt. Brit.* (ed. 3) I. 313 Rugemont-castle..is of a squarish Figure, not very large. **1763** *Phil. Trans.* LIII. 170 The mouth is a foot in width, and of a squarish form. **1784** J. BARRY *Lect. Art* iii. (1848) 141 The dry, lean, and (if such a term be allowable) squarish character and outline. **1815** KIRBY & SP. *Entomol.* (1816) I. 464 The habitation of a third larva..is composed of squarish pieces of the leaves of grass. **1843** *Florist's Jrnl.* (1846) IV. 200 The leaves narrow, ovate, with a squarish base, and serrated at the margin. **1872** COUES *N. Amer. Birds* 2 The rhachis is squarish, and tapers to a point. **1921** S. COLVIN *Memories & Notes* viii. 130 In spite of her squareish build she was supple and elastic in all her movements. **1950** M. PEAKE *Gormenghast* lxxvii. 417 A largish, square-ish room. **1981** *Times* 21 Apr. 14/5 Later, the mausoleum was superseded by a small squarish chapel.

squark (skwɑːk), *sb.* [Imitative.] A harsh croak; a squawk.

1860 SIMEON *Fishing* 244 If..a jay happens to catch sight of you, at his first warning squark every pheasant will..be off instanter. **1894** *Horse & Hound* II. 226 Perhaps the squarks of those young herns frightened that fox.

squark (skwɑːk), *v.* [Imitative: cf. prec. and QUARK *v.*]

1. *intr.* Of birds: To croak harshly; to squawk.

1871 W. MORRIS in Mackail *Life* (1899) I. 235, I heard a heron 'squark' just now. **1897** MARY KINGSLEY *W. Africa* 236 By no means all the birds here only screech and squark. Several of them have very lovely notes.

2. *trans.* To utter in croaks.

1891 *Chambers's Jrnl.* 31 Oct. 703 The crows will come and sit round, squarking sarcastic remarks.

Hence **ˈsquarking** *vbl. sb.*

1897 MARY KINGSLEY *W. Africa* 92 Save for this squarking of the parrots the swamps are silent all the day.

†**ˈsquarken**, *v. Obs. rare.* [Of obscure origin.] *trans.* To burn or scorch.

1530 PALSGR. 731/1, I squarkyn, I burne the utter part of a thyng agaynst the fyer, or roste mete unkyndly, *je ars. Ibid.*, This mete is nat rostyd, it is squarkynned.

squarrose (skwæˈrəʊs, skwɒˈrəʊs), *a.* [ad. L. *squarrōs-us* (rare), scurfy, scabby.]

1. *Bot.* **a.** Composed of, covered with, scales or other processes standing out at right angles or more widely.

1760 J. LEE *Introd. Bot.* I. xi. (1765) 23 *Squarrose*, that is, composed of Scales divaricated on all Sides. **1785** MARTYN *Lett. Bot.* xxvi. (1794) 398 An imbricate calyx, rather squarrose, or having a ragged appearance from the spreading of the tips of the scales. **1806** GALPINE *Brit. Bot.* 390 Spike oblong, somewhat decompound, squarrose. **1856** A. GRAY *Man. Bot.* (1860) 196 Scales of the hemispherical squarrose many-ranked involucre. **1870** HOOKER *Stud. Flora* 408 Spikelets few green squarrose.

b. Of scales: Standing out at right angles or to a greater degree.

1829 LOUDON *Encycl. Plants* (1836) 662 Invol[ucre] imbricated, the exterior scales somewhat squarrose. **1866** M. J. BERKELEY in *Intellectual Obs.* No. 50. 96 Covered with rough squarrose scales.

2. *Ent.* (See first quot.)

1826 KIRBY & SP. *Entomol.* IV. xlvi. 296 *Squarrose*, cut into laciniæ that are elevated above the plane of the surface. **1846** DANA *Zooph.* (1848) 452 Margin of the corallum squarrose.

Hence **squaˈrrosely** *adv.*

1849 CRAIG s.v., *Squarrosely-imbricated*, laid on in a squarrose manner. **1856** HENSLOW *Bot. Terms* 182 The incisions of laciniate and of pinnatifid leaves are squarrosely disposed.

squaˈrroso-, combining form of prec., as in ***squarroso-dentate*** (Worcester, 1860), ***-laciniate, -pinnatipartite, -pinnatisect*** (*Treas. Bot.* 1866) adjs.

ˈsquarrous, *a. Bot. rare.* = SQUARROSE *a.* 1.

1806 GALPINE *Brit. Bot.* 355 Cal[yx] squarrous; spines subulate. **1828–32** WEBSTER, A *squarrous* calyx consists of scales very widely divaricating; a *squarrous* leaf is divided into shreds or jags, raised above the plane of the leaf.

squarruˈlose, *a. Bot. rare.* [Dim. of SQUARROSE *a.*] Slightly squarrose.

1857 A. GRAY *First Less. Bot.* (1866) 231.

squarson (ˈskwɑːsən). [A jocular combination of SQUIRE *sb.* and PARSON.] A clergyman who also holds the position of squire in his parish.

The word is commonly attributed to Bishop Wilberforce (1805–73), but has also been credited to Sydney Smith and others. Cf. L. A. Tollemache *Old & Odd Mem.* (1908) 174. *Squishop*, similarly formed from *squire* and *bishop*, has also had some currency.

1876 FREEMAN in W. R. W. Stephens *Life & Lett.* (1895) II. 141 James Davies,..squebendary (cf. squarson and squishop) of Hereford. **1877** *Sat. Rev.* 10 March, A learned Bishop..instead of saying that they were squires and parsons combined was in the habit of joining the two words in one and defining them as squarsons. **1879** ESCOTT *England* I. 14 That combination of minister of the Church of England and territorial potentate which Sidney Smith has called Squarson. **1890** BARING-GOULD *Old Country Life* 136 A certain Bramston Staynes, who was a squarson in Essex.

attrib. **1895** *Q. Rev.* April 554 The average clergyman of the Squarson era.

Hence **ˈsquarsonage, squarsoˈnocracy**.

1886 A. LANG *Mark of Cain* ix. 109 She left the gray old squarsonage and went to town. **1893** *Westm. Gaz.* 22 March 1/2 The disestablishment of the Squarsonocracy.

squary (ˈskwɛərɪ), *a.* [f. SQUARE *sb.* + -Y.] Square-shaped; squarish.

1602 CAREW *Cornwall* 35 Some gutted and kept in pickle, as the lesser Whitings, Pollocks, Eeles, and Squarie Scads. *Ibid.* 320 Of flat [fish there are] Brets, Turbets, Dories,.. Squary Scad, Seale, Tunny, and many others. **1822** [G. WILKINS] *Body & Soul* (1824) I. 216 One whose broad and squary form had once ranked him among the strong. **1898** *Leeds Merc.* Suppl. 19 March, A squary piece of wood.

squasche, obs. form of SWASH (drum).

squash (skwɒʃ), *sb.*[1] [Related to, or directly from, SQUASH *v.*[1]]

I. 1. a. The unripe pod of a pea. Also applied contemptuously to persons. *Obs.* exc. *arch.*

1590 SHAKS. *Mids. N.* III. i. 191, I pray you commend mee to mistresse Squash, your mother, and to master Peascod your father. **1601** —— *Twel. N.* I. v. 166 As a squash is before tis a pescod. **1611** —— *Wint. T.* I. ii. 160 This Kernell, This squash, this Gentleman. [**1887** RUSKIN *Præterita* II. 34 The whole time..my mind was simply in the state of a squash before 'tis a peascod.]

b. *dial.* (See quot.)

1895 RYE *E. Angl. Gloss.* 210 *Squash*,..pea-pods which look full but are really empty.

†**2.** ***squash pear***, a variety of pear. ***squash perry***, a beverage made from this. *Obs.*

1678 WORLIDGE *Cyder* 219 Pears that are esteemed for their vinous juice in Worcestershire, and those adjacent parts, are the Red and Green Squash-pears. **1699** EVELYN *Kal. Hort.* (ed. 9) 170 Pears:..Red Squash, Bosbery, Watford, for Perry. **1766** *Compl. Farmer* s.v. *Perry*, Of these the Bosbury pear, the Bareland pear, and the horse pear, are the most esteemed for perry in Worcestershire, and the squash pear, as it is called, in Gloucestershire. **1826** *Art Brewing* (ed. 2) 167 Squash perry, in ordinary seasons, [sells] from £4 to £8 the hhd.

3. a. A soft india-rubber ball used in a form of the game of rackets (orig. at Harrow). Also *attrib.*, as ***squash-ball, -court, -racket*** (= the bat used in the game), ***-rackets*** (= the game); **squash tennis** *U.S.*, a game similar to squash rackets, played with a lawn-tennis ball.

1886 *Pall Mall G.* 17 May 14/1 The game in question, termed 'squash' rackets at Harrow if my memory serves me. .. There are the 'squashes'—that is, soft indiarubber balls —to be purchased. **1899** MILES *Lawn Tennis* 87 Turn that wall into a squash-racket court. **1899** *Westm. Gaz.* 10 Aug. 8/2 Mr. John Jacob Astor has built a private 'squash' court. **1901** E. MILES *Game of Squash* i. 16 Americans generally use a Lawn-Tennis ball, and a Squash-Tennis racket, which is like a miniature Lawn-Tennis racket. **1905** H. A. VACHELL *Hill* ii. 26 He bought..a 'squash' racquet, 'squash' balls, and a yard ball. **1917** *National Squash Tennis Assoc. Rules* 18 Description and specifications of a Squash Tennis Court, as adopted by the National Squash Tennis Association... The dimensions of a Standard Court shall be..Length 32 feet 6 inches Width 17 feet. **1928** *N.Y. Times* 12 Dec. 32/6 The success of the American players in the English squash racquets tournament... At the [American] colleges.. squash racquets became more popular. **1930** A. DANZIG *Racquet Game* III. i. 157 The two varieties of squash—squash tennis and squash racquets—have so much in common that they may be called first cousins. **1973** *Times* 28 Sept. 5/6 There is a wide disparity between the international and American versions of squash rackets. **1975** *Oxf. Compan. Sports & Games* 985/1 The squash racket is not as strong as the rackets racket. *Ibid.* 992/2 Squash tennis was born in a school in Concord, New Hampshire,..but..was refined by Feron, of New York, who first wrapped netting round the ball.

b. *ellipt.* for *squash rackets* or occas. (*U.S.*), *squash tennis.*

1899 *N.Y. World* 8 Aug. 14/4 'Squash'..is a variation of the time-honored court tennis. **1902** E. MILES (*title*) Racquets, tennis and squash. **1930** [see *squash tennis*, sense 3 a above]. **1952** J. B. PICK *Phoenix Dict. Games* 183 Squash is played with a rubber ball on a four-walled court. *Ibid.* 185 Service in squash is not the deadly weapon it is in rackets. **1975** *Oxf. Compan. Sports & Games* 986/1 Squash is derived from, and has much in common with, the much older game of rackets, and originated at Harrow School.

II. 4. a. The act of squashing; the fact or sound of some soft substance being crushed or dispersed.

1611 COTGR., *Escachure*,..a squash, crush, knock, or squeeze (wherby a thing is flatted, or beaten close together). **1739** R. BULL tr. *Dedekindus' Grobianus* 249 Anon, our Hero's Boots, well-soak'd with Wash, At ev'ry Step return'd a dreadful Squash.

b. The shock or impact occasioned by a soft heavy body falling upon a surface; the sound produced by this. Also in ***with a squash.***

1654 GAYTON *Pleas. Notes* III. ii. 74 The place, the fall, the squash, the hugge,..did so confound our Votary, that he could not containe. **1712** ARBUTHNOT *John Bull* II. xvi, I shall throw down the burden with a squash among them, take it up who dares. **1726** SWIFT *Gulliver* II. viii, My fall was stopped by a terrible squash that sounded louder to my ears than the cataract of Niagara. **1811** *Ora & Juliet* III. 131 This uncommon mass of mortality rolled on to a seat next to Zaire, on which she sunk with a mighty squash. **1812** H. & J. SMITH *Rej. Addr.*, *The Stranger*, Hearing a squash, he cried, Damn it, what's that?

c. ***to go to squash***, to become squashed or ruined.

1889 FROUDE *Table-t. Shirley* 205 It has all gone to squash.

5. a. *College Football slang.* = SCRIMMAGE *sb.* 4.

1857 SYMONDS *Let.* in H. F. Brown *Life* iii. (1903) 58 A squash is a large collection of boys, about twenty, with the football in the midst of them. **1867** *Routledge's Handbk. Football* 51 A disputed 'touch-down', in consequence of the ball having been carried in by a squash or otherwise.

b. A crush or crowd of persons, etc.; a large number.

1884 *Pall Mall G.* 27 May 4 Young Lord Horsewhipborough is just passing as slowly as the modern squash compels one to progress. **1884** W. C. SMITH *Kildrostan* I. ii. 178 Your father made a will, Only there was not anything to will Except a squash of sermons.

c. A social gathering; an informal religious or literary meeting.

1904 H. JAMES *Golden Bowl* I. III. xiv. 252 The intrinsic oddity of the London 'squash', a thing of vague, slow, senseless eddies. **1916** L. EINSTEIN *Let.* 31 July in *Holmes-Einstein Letters* (1964) II. 134 The season, however, which I loathe, was rendered nicer by the war.. no more fat squashes but agreeable dinners and luncheons. **1938** M. WHITLOW *J. Taylor Smith* xi. 114 The Intervarsity Christian Fellowship have a 'date' with him for a series of 'Squashes' at Oxford and Cambridge. **1977** L. GORDON *Eliot's Early Years* iii. 47 In 1912, Conrad Aiken took 'Prufrock' to a 'poetry squash' in London and showed it to Harold Monro. **1979** *PN Review 13* 19/1 Lord, you know that next week is the Freshers' Squash.

6. a. Something which is squashed or crushed.

1888 *Harper's Mag.* Dec. 80/2 It seemed churlish to pass him by without a sign, especially as he took off his squash of a hat to me.

b. *Biol.* A preparation of softened tissue that has been made thin for microscopic examination by pressing or tapping.

1942 DARLINGTON & LA COUR *Handling of Chromosomes* v. 40 Sections have now been largely replaced by smears and squashes for all but the smallest masses of material. **1971** *Nature* 18 June 452/2 Fifty cells of three females and thirty-two cells of four males were examined. A testis squash was also made to give meiotic figures. **1981** *Japanese Jrnl. Genetics* LVI. 529 This method enables the observation of both C-banding patterns and the karyotypes by aceto-orcein squash technique in the same chromosome complement.

7. Short for *lemon-squash* LEMON *sb.*[1] 7. Also, a drink made from the juice of crushed fruit other than lemons; = CRUSH *sb.* 4e. Freq. as second element of combinations: see *lime-squash* s.v. LIME *sb.*[2] 2, *orange squash* s.v. ORANGE *sb.*[1] 7 a.

1894 MRS. DYAN *Man's Keeping* (1899) 203 A smaller table held ices, squashes, and such. **1904** SLADEN *Lovers Japan* II. iv, She.. kept her mouth intently on the straw in her squash. **1914** C. MACKENZIE *Sinister Street* II. III. vii. 644 Will you have a squash and a biscuit? **1936** *Discovery* June 192/1 Fruit Squashes, containing the pulp of the fruit, were analogous to the well-known orange and lemon squashes. The blackcurrant squash was remarkable for its delicate flavour. **1939** A. P. HERBERT *Water Gipsies* (rev. ed.) x. 99 Jane suggested that they should.. have a lemon-squash... Ernest did not want a squash. **1967** *Coast to Coast 1965–6* 185 'Come on in and I'll make you a squash.'.. Meg squeezed a lemon for his drink. **1980** *Brit. Med. Jrnl.* 29 Mar. 913 Most fruit squashes are unsuitable for babies.

8. *attrib.* as **squash bite** *Dentistry*, an impression of the teeth made by biting the jaws together on a piece of plastic material.

1914 N. G. BENNETT *Sci. & Pract. Dental Surg.* xxxvii. 607/1 A 'squash bite' impression, or even one taken in the ordinary way in a tray, is very easily distorted in removing from the mouth. **1940** J. OSBORNE *Dental Mechanics* v. 47 It is usual if this type of block is used to have taken a 'squash bite' at the impression stage. **1963** C. R. COWELL et al. *Inlays, Crowns, & Bridges* ii. 10 The relationship of the prepared tooth to adjacent and opposing teeth must be recorded in the indirect technique with a wax or an alginate squash bite.

squash (skwɒʃ), *sb.*[2] Also 8 **squosh.** [Abbreviation of Narragansett Indian *asquutasquash*, f. *asq* raw, uncooked: cf. SQUANTER-SQUASH. (The *-ash* is a plural ending, as in *succotash*.)]

1. a. A gourd produced by one or other of various species of trailing herbaceous annual plants belonging to the genus *Cucurbita* or N. O. *Cucurbitaceæ*, esp. a fruit of the bush gourd, *C. Melopepo*.

1643 R. WILLIAMS *Key Ind. Lang.* 103 Askutasquash, their Vine aples, which the English from them call Squashes, about the bignesse of Apples, of severall colours, sweet, light, wholesome, refreshing. **1669** W. SIMPSON *Hydrol. Chym.* 259 In a weighed quantity of digged earth.. he set the seed of a squash. **1721** MORTIMER *Husb.* (ed. 4) II. 174 Squashes are a small sort of Pumpkin lately brought into request. **1764** T. HUTCHINSON *Hist. Mass.* I. (1765) 35 A dearth.. caused them to fall upon their pompions, squoshes, &c. before they were ripe. **1857** A. GRAY *First Less. Bot.* (1866) 10 It we strip off the coats from the large and flat seed of a Squash or Pumpkin, we find nothing but the embryo within. **1877** W. MATTHEWS *Ethn. & Phil. Hidatsa Ind.* 26 Squashes are cut in thin slices and dried; the dried squash is usually cooked by boiling.

b. Used in sing. with *the*, or without article.

1764 HARMER *Observ.* iv. §xxxii. 205 Dr. Russell tells us that the squash comes in towards the end of September, and continues all the year. **1878** BLACK *Green Past.* xl, Not at all desirous of eating at one and the same time boiled beans,.. green corn, squash and sweet potatoes. **1902** *Fortn. Rev.* June 1007 The divine 'sweet corn', and 'squash', and 'sweet potatoes'.

2. One or other species of *Cucurbita* producing the above fruit; the genus as a whole.

1661 BOYLE *Scept. Chem.* II. 107 A selected seed of.. Squash, which is an Indian kind of Pompion, that Growes a pace. **1731** P. MILLER *Gard. Dict.*, *Melopepo*, The Squash. **1766** J. BARTRAM *Jrnl.* 6 Jan. 26 Here is a native gourd or squash, which runs 20 foot up the trees. **1866** *Treas. Bot.* 358/1 *Cucurbita melopepo*, the Squash, forms a bush about 3 ft. high. **1884** *De Candolle's Orig. Cultivated Pl.* 252 The *Cucurbitaceæ* called squash by the Anglo-Americans.

3. With distinguishing terms: (see quots.).

1731 P. MILLER *Gard. Dict.* s.v. *Melopepo*, The common or flat Squash... The large white Squash... The Citron-shap'd Squash... The warted Squash. **1791** W. BARTRAM *Carolina* 137 It is exceedingly curious to behold the Wild Squash climbing over the lofty limbs of the trees. **1845–50** MRS. LINCOLN *Lect. Bot.* App. 95/2 *Cucurbita ovifera*, egg-squash. *Ibid.* 96/1 *C. verrucosa*, club squash. **1846–50** A. WOOD *Class-bk. Bot.* 272 *Cucurbita Melopepo*. Flat Squash. *Ibid.*, *C. verrucosa*. Warted Squash. Club Squash. Crook-neck Squash. **1847** DARLINGTON *Amer. Weeds*, etc. (1860) 142 *Cucurbita Melopepo*... Round Squash. **1866** *Treas. Bot.* 359/1 The Custard Marrow Squash, and the improved Custard Marrow or Bush Squash. **1874** *Ibid.* Suppl. 1344/1 Summer Squash, *Cucurbita Pepo*. Winter Squash, *Cucurbita maxima*.

4. *attrib.*, as ***squash bed, pie, seed, vine***, etc.; **squash-berry**, the red berry of *Viburnum pauciflorum*, a deciduous North American shrub; = *moose-berry* s.v. MOOSE[1] b; **squash blossom**, the flower of the plant on which squashes grow, applied *attrib.* to jewellery made by the Navajo which is characterized by designs (of Spanish, and ult. Moorish, derivation, representing pomegranates) resembling this flower; **squash-bug**, one or other of various insects infesting or injurious to squashes; **squash gourd, (-melon) pumpkin**, the common bush gourd or squash, *Cucurbita Melopepo*.

Also, in recent Amer. Dicts., ***squash-beetle, (-vine) borer, flea-beetle, ladybird***, and ***ladybug***, as names of insects infesting squashes.

1937 LADY ROCKLEY *Some Canadian Wild Flowers* 77 Its [sc. *Viburnum pauciflorum*'s] berries known as the '*Squash-berry' are gathered and make an excellent preserve. **1966** A. R. SCAMMELL *My Newfoundland* 32 He even shook his head at bakeapple jam, squashberry jelly and 'meshberries'. **1974** J. E. UNDERHILL *Wild Berries Pacific Northwest* 23 Huckleberries, Blueberries, Squash-berries, and many others, may be made into delicious jams. **1923** D. H. LAWRENCE *Birds, Beasts & Flowers* 19 The fig, the horseshoe, the *squash-blossom. Symbols. **1930** D. & M. R. COOLIDGE *Navajo Indians* xvi. 115 The beautiful squash-blossom pendants which the Hopis like so much. **1944** J. ADAIR *Navajo & Pueblo Silversmiths* v. 83, I watched Charie make other pieces. One of them was a squash-blossom bead. **1950** S. H. BABINGTON *Navajos, Gods & Tom-Toms* xv. 170 The pronged pieces in the beautiful so-called squash blossom necklace are the buttons which were sewed along the outside seams.. of Spanish army officers' pants. **1977** C. MCFADDEN *Serial* (1978) ii. 10/2 Carol.. had embellished it with her trademark jewelry: an authentic squash-blossom necklace. **1847** WEBSTER, **Squash-bug*, the common name of a bug injurious to squashes. **1866** MRS. STOWE *Little Foxes* 124 In the actual garden there are.. squash-bugs for all the melons. **1872** O. W. HOLMES *Poet Breakf.-t.* ix, Dor-bugs and squash-bugs and such undesirable objects of affection to all but naturalists. **1823** CRABB *Technol. Dict.* s.v., *Squash-gourd, the *Cucurbita melopepo* of Linnæus. **1842** LOUDON *Suburban Hort.* 605 The *Squash-melon pumpkin, or bush gourd. **1883** *Harper's Mag.* Jan. 213/1 Cranberry sauce, and thick *squash pies. **1823** SOUTHEY *Lett.* (1856) III. 391 With regard to these said quasheys (which, I believe, is their name,—first cousins to the *squash pumpkin). **1708** S. SEWALL *Diary* 15 Jan., This day Mr. Belchar brings me *Squash-Seeds from Dedham. **1725** S. WILLARD in *Early Rec. Lanc., Mass.* (1884) 238 They found 2 wigwarms;.. they also found a paddle and some *squash shells in one of them. **1751** J. BARTRAM *Observ. Trav. Pennsylv.*, etc. 62 We dined on Indian corn and *squash soop, and boiled bread. **1857** A. GRAY *First Less. Bot.* (1866) 39 The Cucumber and *Squash tribe. **1750** G. HUGHES *Barbados* 137 The *Squash-vine is long and trailing. **1855** *Poultry Chron.* III. 297 They will nearly get their living on insects without injuring the vegetables. Among squash vines they are indispensable.

†**squash**, *sb.*[3] *Obs.* [Aphetic f. MUSQUASH.] The musk-rat or musquash, *Fiber zibethicus*.

1678 PHILLIPS (ed. 4), *Squash*, a little Creature in some parts of America, somewhat resembling an Ichnumon or Indian Rat. **1699** DAMPIER *Voy.* II. II. 59 The Squash is a four-footed Beast, bigger than a Cat. **1774** GOLDSM. *Nat. Hist.* III. 380 But the smell of our weasels, and ermines, and polecats, is fragrance itself when compared to that of the squash and the skink. **1796** MORSE *Amer. Geog.* I. 201 Another stinkard, called the Squash, is said by Buffon to be found in some of the southern states. **1824** [see SKINK *sb.*[2]].

squash (skwɒʃ), *v.*[1] [ad. OF. *esquasser (escasser), esquacer (escacier)*, = It. *squassare*:—pop. L. **exquassāre*: see QUASH *v.* In some senses, however, perhaps partly or mainly of imitative origin.]

1. *trans.* To squeeze, press, or crush into a flat mass or pulp; to beat to, or dash in, pieces, etc. Also with preps., as *in, to*.

1565 STAPLETON tr. *Bede's Hist. Ch. Eng.* 61 Ye must, I saye, teare them, rent them, and squashe them to peeces. **1579–80** NORTH *Plutarch* (1895) III. 350 But the top of the gallery fell downe apon the boyes that were left, and squashed them all to death. **1601** HOLLAND *Pliny* I. 289 The hennes.. hide themselues from their males the cocks; for.. they would squash their egs. **1622** MABBE tr. *Aleman's Guzman d'Alf.* II. 277 Squashing and beating them vpon some stone,.. shee made our cloathes reasonable white. **1670** EVELYN *Sylva* (ed. 2) ix. 58 Note, that in sowing the Berry 'tis good to squash and bruise them with fine siefted Mould. **1726** SWIFT *Gulliver* II. i, One of the reapers.. made me apprehend that.. I should be squashed to death under his foot. **1806** J. BERESFORD *Miseries Hum. Life* III. xxvi, In shuffling the cards,.. squashing them together, breaking their edges [etc.]. **1827** HARE *Guesses* (1859) 144 There have indeed been.. men who have piled such a load of books on their heads, their brains have seemed to be squasht by them. **1897** MARY KINGSLEY *W. Africa* 327 There were eight elephants killed that day, but three burst through everything,.. squashing two men and a baby.

fig. **1613** tr. *Mexio's Treas. Anc. & Mod. Times* 24/1 More cleerly wil we yet reueale their grosse absurditie, and.. squash in pieces their unexcusable error. **1863** KINGSLEY *Water-bab.* 60 Between crinolines and theories, some of us would get squashed.

b. With advs., as *down, up*.

1611 COTGR., *Escraser*, to squash downe, beat flat. **1698** T. FROGER *Voy.* 105 A sort of wrought lime, which being squashed down upon the bridge.. has a most terrible effect. **1893** EARL DUNMORE *Pamirs* II. 320, I was not able to accompany my host, but had to be squashed up in the crowd.

c. To quash; to suppress or put down; to undo or destroy in a complete or summary manner.

Also, in recent colloq. use, to silence, discomfit, or repress (a person) in a very decisive or crushing way.

1762 FOOTE *Orator* II, I therefore humbly move to squash this indictment. **1850** KINGSLEY *A. Locke* xviii, I, to squash my convictions, to stultify my book for the sake of popularity, money, patronage! **1852** BRISTED *Five Yrs. Eng. Univ.* (ed. 2) 258 The report spread that I had broken down completely, or, as a Johnian elegantly expressed it, was squashed. **1895** *Law Times* XCVIII. 280/2 The Pharmaceutical Society made a strenuous attempt to squash the Stores as vendors of drugs.

†**2. a.** To press or squeeze *out*. *Obs. rare.*

1599 T. M[OUFET] *Silkwormes* 59 Now squashing out their bellies soft and round. **1600** HOLLAND *Livy* 372 The battalions troden under foot and their guts squashed out.

†**b.** To splash or dash (water) *upon* a person; to wet by splashing. *Obs. rare.*

a **1602–3** Q. ELIZ. in I. H. Jeayes *Cat. Charters Berkeley Castle* (1892) 323, I somewhat still doute that ther hath bene to greate abundance of the same [*sc.* water] squashed upon you. *a* **1825** FORBY *Voc. E. Anglia* 321 *Squash*, v., to splash; to moisten by plentiful affusion.

3. *intr.* To emit or make a splashing sound; to move, walk, etc., in this way; to splash.

1671 SALMON *Syn. Med.* I. lv. 142 *Ascites* is when much Water is heaped up between the Peritoneum and the Bowels, so that when it is struck it doth squash as it were. **1839** HOOD *Ode to St. Swithin* vii, Why upon snow-white table-cloths and sheets.. Come squashing? **1859** DICKENS *T. Two Cities* I. ii, Once more, the Dover mail struggled on, with the Jack-boots of its passengers squashing along by its side. **1893** *Outing* XXII. 139/1 Our feet 'squashing' as we step, for our boots are full of rain-water.

4. To be pressed into a flat mass on impact; to flatten *out* under pressure.

Cf. Florio's use of *squashing* ppl. a. (quot. 1611 below).

1858 GREENER *Gunnery* 121 Some other mixtures.. sufficiently strong to resist all tendency to squash; as the softer metals would inevitably do. **1893** *Scribner's Mag.* June 710/1 There must be the most skilful handling, lest the load 'squash out'.

Hence **'squasher**; **'squashing** *vbl. sb.* and *ppl. a.*

1598 FLORIO, *Squaccio*, a squashing, a hauocke. **1611** *Ibid.*, *Squala*,.. a kind of soft squashing Hazle-nut. **1611** COTGR., *Quasseur*, a squasher, breaker. *Ibid.*, *Escrasement*, a crushing flat, a squashing downe. **1865** S. FERGUSON *Forging of Anchor* ii, A hailing fount of fire is struck at every squashing blow.

squash, *v.*[2] *rare*[−1]. [f. SQUASH *sb.*[1] 5 b.] *intr.* To frequent crowded assemblies.

1867 MOTLEY *Corr.* (1887) II. 269 How anything can be done in London but breakfast, lunch, dine, and squash, if one really goes in for 'promiscuous Ned', I can't comprehend.

squash, *adv.* [f. SQUASH *v.*[1]] With or as with a squash. Freq. in *to go squash* (also *transf.*).

1766 [ANSTEY] *Bath Guide* iv. 55 His Wig had the Luck a Cathartic to meet, And Squash went the Gallipot under his Feet. **1859** F. E. PAGET *Curate Cumberworth* 246 He came down, in less than no time, squash on his nose, and broke it. **1886** G. ALLEN *Kalee's Shrine* ii, Some cottages may really go squash before long.

squash-, The verbal stem used in combs., in the sense 'having the appearance of being squashed', as **squash hat** (cf. SQUASHED *ppl. a.*), **nose**.

1861 MEREDITH *Evan Harrington* vi, I don't get took in again by a squash hat in a hurry. **1882** STEVENSON *New Arab. Nts.* (1884) 247 Admiring imbecility breathed from his squash nose and slobbering lips. **1900** *Daily News* 30 June 4/6 The million are going in for the broad-brimmed squash hat.

squashable ('skwɒʃəb(ə)l), *a.* [f. SQUASH *v.*[1]] Capable of being squashed. Hence **squasha'bility**, capability of being crushed together.

1875 GREEN *Lett.* (1901) IV. 416 The wonderful squashability of Roman buildings. **1902** *Contemp. Rev.* Oct. 502 It might be something squashable in the berry or jelly-fish line.

squashed, *ppl. a.* [f. SQUASH *v.*[1] + -ED[1].] **1.** In senses of the verb.

1857 DICKENS *Dorrit* ix, Such squashed hats and bonnets.. never were seen in Rag Fair.

2. Special collocations: **squashed fly (biscuit)** *colloq.* = GARIBALDI 3; **squashed tomato** *slang*, a name given in different localities to various children's games (see quots.).

1900 J. S. FARMER *Public School Word-bk.* 85 *Squashed flies*,.. biscuits with currants. **1909**, etc. [see GARIBALDI 3]. **1931** C. LITHGOW *Simple Sailor* v. 49 In 'the break', they grappled for their milk and bun, or 'squashed-fly' biscuit. **1977** K. M. E. MURRAY *Caught in Web of Words* xvii. 321 Gwyneth remembered her anguish as a little girl at finding nothing in her parcel but a Garibaldi ('squashed fly') biscuit. **1959** I. & P. OPIE *Lore & Lang. Schoolch.* xviii. 381 There are more than sixty established names for the pursuit of illegally knocking at doors... *Squashed tomato.* Wolverhampton. **1963** S. MARSHALL *Exper. in Educ.* ii. 56 The new look given to the age-old playground game which for some unknown reason has become 'Squashed Tomato' in the language of today... A voice was giving orders to the players. 'John, three scissors south towards Cambridge. Carol, two pigeon steps towards Newmarket [on a map painted on a school playground].' **1969** I. & P. OPIE

'Sardines', but also..'Squashed Sardines', and 'Squashed Tomatoes'. *Ibid.* vi. 189 *Squashed Tomato.* Both caller and called run towards each other, with arms crossed in front of them. The one advancing remains at the spot where they squash into each other. The caller returns to his place in front.

squashily (ˈskwɒʃɪlɪ), *adv.* [f. SQUASHY *a.* + -LY^2.] In a squashy or squelchy manner.
1922 *Blackw. Mag.* Oct. 485/2 A small damp object.. struck the ground squashily near where I was standing. **1924** 'L. MALET' *Dogs of Want* viii. 262 Upon the seat.. Mr. Noakes heavily, not to say squashily, subsided.

'squashiness. [f. SQUASHY *a.*] The condition or character of being squashy.
1846 LANDOR *Imag. Conv.* Wks. I. 79/2 Give a trifle of strength and austerity to the squashiness of our friend's poetry.

squash pear: see SQUASH *sb.*^{1} 2.

†**'squashy**, *sb. Obs.*$^{-1}$ [Cf. SQUASH *sb.*^{1} 1.] (See quot.)
1828 *Life Planter Jamaica* 211 A very small pea denominated by the negroes, okra, a kind of what is called squashies.

squashy (ˈskwɒʃɪ), *a.* [f. SQUASH *v.*^{1} or *sb.*^{1}]
1. Of fruit, etc.: Having a soft or pulpy consistency; lacking in firmness.
1698 FRYER *Acc. E. India & P.* 130 Having gone near Fifty Miles without eating more than a few squashy Figs. *Ibid.* 182 The Fruit.. squashy, of a better Relish than Smell. **1712** J. MORTON *Nat. Hist. Northamptonsh.* 478 The Ear [of wheat] was seemingly full and good; but it prov'd to be squashy, and had no Kernel. **1837** HOOK *Jack Brag* xx, A squashy French pie, made by a Cowes confectioner. **1847** HALLIW., *Squashy*, soft, pulpy, watery. *Warw[ick].* **1883** MISS WORBOISE *Sissie* xix, Squashy roly-poly pudding, with all the jam boiled out, and the water boiled in.
fig. **1859** GEO. ELIOT *A. Bede* xv, Them young gells are like th' unripe grain; they'll make good meal by-and-by, but they're squashy as yet.
2. Of ground, etc.: Soft with, full of, water; soaking, marshy.
1751 *England's Gazetteer* s.v. *Daventry*, The banks in it resemble those of ponds and canals, with a watry squashy ground between them. **1818** KEATS *Lett.* Wks. 1889 III. 163, I was damped by slipping one leg into a squashy hole. **1822** *Blackw. Mag.* XII. 335 A squashy knowe in an undrained quagmire. **1889** *Longman's Mag.* Aug. 379 Away we go again, floundering heavily through the squashy ground.
transf. **1877** W. S. GILBERT *Foggerty's Fairy* (1892) 302 We had a squashy walk over a pathless and furzy common.
3. Of the nature of a squash or squashing.
1865 E. BURRITT *Walk to Land's End* 284 That child.. comes down..in a squashy concussion with its forehead against the floor. **1873** *Spectator* 23 Aug. 1069 Alongside of you comes up an oozy, squashy sound of the advancing tide.
4. Having a squashed or flattened look.
1895 ZANGWILL *Master* II. iv, Matt pointed out that the eyes were wrong, that pupils should be round, not squashy.

†**squass.** *Obs.*$^{-1}$ In 6 sqwasse. [Related to SQUASH *v.*^{1} Cf. It. *squasso* a severe shake.] Pressure, squeezing.
1528 BP. CLERK *Let. to Wolsey* (MS. Cott. Cal. D. x. 227), He cannott ryed, his feett being n[ot able to] abyde the sqwasse of the sterope.

†**squa'ssation.** *Obs.*$^{-1}$ [f. It. *squassare* to shake severely: see SQUASH *v.*^{1}] A severe shaking.
1731 CHANDLER tr. *Limborch's Hist. Inquis.* II. 219 As to Squassation, 'tis thus performed:..on a sudden he is let down with a Jirk,..by which terrible Shake, his Arms and Legs are all disjointed.

squat (skwɒt), *sb.*^{1} Also 4 squate, 5, 7 squatte, 7 squatt, sqat, squot, 9 *dial.* swat. [f. SQUAT *v.* Cf. QUAT *sb.*^{2}]
1. a. A heavy fall or bump; a severe or violent jar or jolt. Now *north. dial.*
c **1350** *Ipomedon* (Kölbing) 4352 Yche myghte se, where he laye. I trowe, here leman had a squate [*rime* that]. **1513** DOUGLAS *Æneid* x. vii. 108 [He] tumlyt from hys hie cart chargit quhar he sat, And on the grund reboundis wyth a squat. **1545** RAYNALD *Byrth Mankynde* H h iij, Thone by a fal from her horse, the other by a violent thrust and squat on the buttocks vpon the hard stones. *Ibid.*, By the force of the fall and squat, the matrice vaynes brake. *a* **1633** G. HERBERT *Wks.* (1859) II. 298 Bruises and squats and falls which often kill others can bring little grief or hurt to those that are temperate. **1675** J. S[MITH] *Horolog. Dial.* 24 It might be some accidental injury in the conveiance from one place to another, as sometimes happens by jogs or Squats which loosen either pins, wedges or screws. **1812** *Sporting Mag.* XXXIX. 46 But ambling round an ugly post, A squat poor Bobby made. **1847-** in N. Cy. and Cumbld. glossaries (in form *swat*).
b. A bruise, contusion, or wound, esp. one caused by a fall; a dent or indentation. Now *dial.*
1578 LYTE *Dodoens* 238 The same herbe..is good to be layde on with wool upon squats or bruses. *a* **1691** AUBREY *Wilts.* (Royal Soc. MS. p. 127) (Halliw.), In our Western language squat is a bruise. **1697** R. PEIRCE *Bath Mem.* I. ix. 186 His Illness first came after a Sqat upon his Hand; to which fell a Humour, and made it a Running Sore. **1775** ASH, *Squat*,..a bruise, a hurt by falling; but this is a local sense. **1868-** in dial. glossaries (Glouc., Som., Wilts., Berks.).
†**c.** A heavy shower. *Obs.*$^{-1}$
c **1630** RISDON *Surv. Devon* (1810) 121 Haldon-Hill.., whereof the borderers..had this adage: When Haldon hath a hat, Let Kentowne beware a squat.
†**2.** A company *of* daubers. *Obs.*$^{-0}$
Only in lists of 'proper terms'.
c **1450** *Porkington MS. 10* in *Philol. Trans.* (1909) 54 A squat of davberis. **1486** *Bk. St. Albans* f vj b.
†**3.** *at* (*the* or *a*) *squat*, in a squatting or crouching attitude, esp. that assumed by a hare when sitting. *Obs.*
1580 LYLY *Euphues* (Arb.) 421 One runneth so fast you will neuer catch hir, the other is so at the squat, you can neuer finde hir. **1622** BRETON *Strange Newes* Wks. (Grosart) II 6/1 Hunting they vse little, but to finde a Hare at squat. **1670** J. SMITH *Eng. Improv. Reviv'd* 191 You may chance to see..on the ground a brace or two of Hares at squot. **1693** DRYDEN, etc. *Juvenal* x. (1697) 261 An old Grandam Ape, when, with a Grace, She sits at squat, and scrubs her leathern Face.
fig. **1623** WOTTON *Lett.* (1907) II. 280 The Rhetian business and the League depending thereon, which made so full a cry is, methinks, at a squat. **1732** POPE *Ep. Cobham* 56 And ev'ry child hates Shylock, tho' his soul Still sits at squat, and peeps not from its hole.
4. The act of squatting, crouching, or sitting down close to the ground, *spec.* on the part of a hare.
1584 in Cl. Robinson *Handful Pleas. Delights* (Arb.) 29 To see..Her [i.e. the hare's] trips and skips,..With squats and flats, which hath no pere. **1601** DEACON & WALKER *Spirits & D.* 208 You are like to the hunted Hare which scuddeth hither and thether, and standeth in feare at euerie squat. **1615** MARKHAM *Country Contentm.* I. i, The Huntsman cunning to undoe intricate doubles, Skips, Squats and windings. **1806** BLOOMFIELD *Wild Flowers* 43 Grace by the tumbril made a squat. **1838** HOLLOWAY *Prov. Dict.* s.v., A hare is said to Squat or go to Squat when she lies up in the chase. **1872** C. KING *Sierra Nevada* x. 214, I noticed one mule after another give a little squat.
†**5. a.** *to take squat*, to seek safety by squatting or hiding. *Obs.*
1580-3 GREENE *Mamillia* Wks. (Grosart) II. 63 The Foxe seeing his narrow almost kild with the dogges, is a foole, if he take not squat. **1592** —— *Philomela* Wks. (Grosart) XI. 138 Though the Hare take squat she is not lost at the first defaute.
†**b.** The place where an animal squats or crouches down in order to escape observation; *spec.* the form or lair of a hare. Also *fig. Obs.*
1590 COKAINE *Treat. Hunt.* B iv b, The Huntsman should blowe a call, that all that be in the field may repayre to him, and beate for the squat of the Hare. **1601** DEACON & WALKER *Answ. Darel* 163 You are to too afraid to tarrie ouer long in a squatte: the following crie of the Hounds is so hotte in your eares. **1624** QUARLES *Job Militant* xiii, Their deepe-mouth'd Art..ne'r could start..That Game, from squat, they terme, Felicity. **1673** HICKERINGILL *Greg. F. Greyb.* 8 Thou hadst better have sat For ever on thy squatt.
6. a. A squatting attitude or posture. *spec.* in Gymnastics and Weight-lifting (earlier called *crouch*).
1886 *Bicycling News* 24 Sept. 767/2 The cross-legged 'squat' is as natural an attitude to the sovereign as to the meanest beggar. **1954** M. FALLON *Muscle Building for Beginners* x. 56 Keep the head up and the back flat, and resist any temptation to lean forward, particularly at the lowest point of the squat. **1959** LOKEN & WILLOUGHBY *Compl. Bk. Gymnastics* iv. 35 *Squat Head Balance.* Start this stunt from a squat position with the hands on the mat and the inside of the knees resting on the elbows. **1964** G. C. KUNZLE *Parallel Bars* ii. 42 Simple squats on one bar. *Ibid.* 44 Complete the squat off by pushing away strongly with the arms and drawing the shoulders forwards. **1977** J. F. FIXX *Compl. Bk. Running* vii. 91 Some runners and coaches think weightlifting is essential to good performances. Emil Zatopek..used to do squats while holding his wife, Dana, on his shoulders.
b. *hot squat*: see HOT *a.* 1 e.
7. The fact of settling down in the water.
1905 *Sci. Amer.* 7 Jan. 7/1 To the loaded draft there should be added about four feet for 'squat', when running at full speed.
8. a. The illegal occupation of an uninhabited building (esp. by a group of homeless people organized for this purpose); the period of such an occupation.
1946 *Daily Mail* 20 Sept. 2/3 The Great Squat is over... Today at 1200 hours the rearguards of Squat-Force will retire. **1963** S. COOPER in Sissons & French *Age of Austerity* 44 Early in September 1946 Londoners were startled by what was christened the Great Sunday Squat. **1969** *Guardian* 27 Sept. 9/2 The Diggers have decided not to take part in any more hippie squats. **1970** N. SAUNDERS *Alternative London* xvii. 122 They then organised the squatters in East London, which has developed into the longest squat ever, lasting over ten months, in Arbour Square. **1975** *Times* 8 Jan. 3/6 This is the biggest squat ever, a serious attempt to house homeless people. **1981** *Daily Tel.* 3 Mar. 2/1 This squat cost the ratepayer £46,700—money we need not have spent had the squat not taken place.
b. A house, flat, or building occupied by squatters; a squatter's place of residence.
1975 *Guardian* 26 Sept. 5/8 He's at 14 Algernon Road. It's a squat. **1977** M. DRABBLE *Ice Age* II. 211 They'd been hosed out of their last squat. **1980** *Daily Tel.* 28 Oct. 17/3 A whipround among punks from a squat near the police station raised £12.50.

squat, *sb.*^{2} *Cornw.* [Perh. the same word as prec.] (See quots.)
1671 *Phil. Trans.* VI. 2098 Squatts are certain distinct places in the earth, not running in veins, differing from Bonnys..in this only that Squatts are flat, Bonnys are roundish. **1778** PRYCE *Min. Cornub.* 81 This kind of Fissure ..is wrongly called by the Tinners, a Floor or a Squat, which properly speaking is a hole or chasm impregnated with Metal, that makes no continued line of direction, or regular walls. **1860** *Eng. & For. Mining Gloss.* (ed. 2) 6 *Bunch*, or *Squat of ore*, a quantity of ore of small extent; more than a stone, and not so much as a course.

squat, *sb.*^{3} *U.S.* [Of doubtful origin.] The angel-fish, *Squatina angelus.*
1884 GOODE *Nat. Hist. Aquat. Anim.* 675.

squat (skwɒt), *sb.*^{4} *U.S. slang.* [Prob. f. slang *to squat* to void excrement.] Nothing at all; (following a negative construction) anything. Orig. as second element of phr. *doodly-squat* [prob. f. U.S. slang *doodle* excrement].
1934 Z. N. HURSTON *Jonah's Gourd Vine* xviii. 217 She ain't never had nothin'—not eben doodly-squat, and when she gits uh chance tuh git holt uh sumpin de ole buzzard is gone on uh rampage. **1946** MEZZROW & WOLFE *Really Blues* viii. 107 These cats weren't from doodlely-squat. *Ibid.* 373 *Doodlely-squat*, nothing, no more than the product of a child who squats to do his duty. **1967** WENTWORTH & FLEXNER *Dict. Amer. Slang* Suppl. 705/2 *Squat*,.. = zot. *Ibid.* 712/2 *Zot*,..a grade or a score of zero. **1975** G. V. HIGGINS *City on Hill* i. 18 A lot of people that didn't care squat about the war went with us on that point. **1977** *Rolling Stone* 30 June 82/1 Under no circumstances would I ask those..judges down in Oswego to give him back his shingle on the condition it doesn't mean doodly-squat. **1979** P. BENCHLEY *Island* ii. 26 It'll be another forecast-of-Armageddon cover that won't amount to squat.

squat (skwɒt), *pa. pple.* and (*ppl.*) *a.* Also 5 sqwat(e, 7, 9 *dial.*, squot, 9 *dial.* swat. [Pa. pple. of SQUAT *v.* Cf. QUAT *a.*]
I. 1. In predicative use: Seated in a squatting or crouching posture; sitting close to the ground.
a. Of a hare or other animal.
c **1410** *Master of Game* (MS. Digby 182) xxxiv, If it happe ..þat ony hunter fynde her sqwat,..he shall blowe a moot and rechate and stirt her. *Ibid.*, If it happe þat she be sqwate to fore hem. **1526** SKELTON *Magnyf.* 1315 So how,..the hare is squat! **1556** J. HEYWOOD *Spider & Fly* xxiv. 26 Neuer was there yet any larke or wat, Before hawke or dog, flatter darde or squat Then by this answere. **1602** ROWLANDS *Greenes Ghost* 43 The tumbler, who lies squat in the brakes till the Conie be come forth out of her burrow. **1695** BLACKMORE *Pr. Arth.* VI. 647 A Toad, squat on a Border, spies The Gardner passing by. **1795** WOLCOT (P. Pindar) *Royal Tour* Wks. 1816 III. 49 Squat on his speckled haunches gapes the Toad, And frogs affrighted hop along the road. **1897** *Christian Herald* (N.Y.) 4 Aug. 592/1 Does not the panther, squat in the grass, know a calf when he sees it?
b. Of persons.
In some contexts approaching to an advb. use.
1582 STANYHURST *Æneis* III. (Arb.) 73 Then to vs squat groueling in this wise the oracle auswerd. **1667** MILTON *P.L.* IV. 800 Him there they found Squat like a Toad, close at the eare of Eve. **1675** HOBBES *Odyssey* (1677) 268 Ulysses, to be sure that none remain Alive, and under seats or tables squat, Searcht well the hall. **1730** FIELDING *Tom Thumb* II. x, While the two stools her sitting-part confound, Between 'em both [to] fall squat upon the ground. **1748** SMOLLETT *R. Random* xxxix, Where I found her sitting squat on her hams on the floor. **1851** MAYNE REID *Scalp Hunt.* xxxi. 235 The earless trapper was sitting upon the prairie, squat on his hams. **1878** P. BAYNE *Purit. Rev.* v. 168 Satan, squat at his ear in the form of a sycophant priest, had told him [etc.].
Comb. **1897** GUNTER *Susan Turnbull* ii. 18 The..Eastern potentate, who sits squat-legged indulging in his nargileh.
c. Of things. *rare.*
1757 *Mrs. Montagu's Lett.* IV. 160 She has made them lie squat with some ivory thimbles. **1853** G. JOHNSTON *Nat. Hist. E. Bord.* I. 76 The shrub lies squat to the ground.
2. *dial.* Hidden from observation; quiet, still.
1841- in various dial. glossaries and texts (N. Cy., Yks., Lancs., Notts., E. Anglia, etc.). **1956** G. E. EVANS *Ask Fellows who cut Hay* xxv. 228 Another feature of the dialect is the expressive vigour of many of the words and phrases: ..*squat* (pronounced with a very broad *a*) hidden or quiet. **1962** M. PROCTER *Devil in Moonlight* xv. 155 We'll keep it squat and take a chance on having trouble later.
II. †**3.** Contused, crushed. *Obs.*$^{-1}$
1600 SURFLET *Countrie Farme* II. xliii. 280 This ointment ..is singular good in the curing of..brused or squat nailes, wounds old and new [etc.].
4. Short and thick; disproportionately broad or wide; podgy; thick-set: **a.** Of persons, animals, or their limbs, etc. ***squat lobster***, a crab-like marine animal belonging to the family Galatheidæ.
1630 *R. Johnson's Kingd. & Commw.* 12 The Tartar is a stubbed squat fellow, hard bred, and such are their horses. **1678** *Lond. Gaz.* No. 1308/4 A broad squot white beagle Bitch. **1717** PRIOR *Alma* I. 16 The Mind,..Throughout the Body squat or tall Is, *bonâ fide*, All in All. **1740** RICHARDSON *Pamela* (1824) I. 61 She is a broad, squat, pursy, fat thing, quite ugly. **1779** *Mirror* No. 2, A short squat man, with a carbuncled face. **1826** SCOTT *Woodst.* i, A squat broad Little John sort of figure. **1849** H. MILLER *Footpr. Creat* iii. (1874) 34 Squat, robust, strongly-built fishes. **1879** D. M. WALLACE *Australasia* v. 86 The nose..becomes broader and somewhat squat further down. **1902** *Encycl. Brit.* (ed. 10) XXXII. 111/1 Amongst other crustacea, the squat lobster (*Themis orientalis*) is..obtained by trawling in the southern waters. **1928** RUSSELL & YONGE *Seas* iii. 67 There are also squat-lobsters, which have long claws and broad, flattened bodies. **1978** *Sci. Amer.* Dec. 99/2 The galatheids (the squat-lobsters, a group intermediate between the macrurans and the true crabs) have reflecting superposition eyes with square facets.
b. In general use.
1684 *Lond. Gaz.* No. 1933/4 She is square before, with a square squat Stem. **1714** MANDEVILLE *Fab. Bees* (1733) I. 333 Little squat bibles clasp'd in brass. **1760** J. LEE *Introd. Bot.* Explan. Terms 389 *Sessiles*, squat, having no Foot-stalk. **1861** *Sat. Rev.* 21 Sept. 305 The [printing] type..is

somewhat squat and angular. **1865** Dickens *Mut. Fr.* III. vi, One of those squat, high-shouldered, short-necked glass bottles. **1885** Runciman *Skippers & Sh.* 103 Wilfrid joined a squat brig that crossed the Bay. **1891** E. Gosse *Gossip in Library* i. 10 A squat volume published two centuries ago.

c. Of buildings or parts of these.

1687 Miége *Gt. Fr. Dict.* II, A squat (or well compacted) House. *a* **1771** Gray *Wks.* (1843) V. 329 The capitals.. are all in general too squat and too gross for the pillars which they are meant to adorn. **1828** Duppa *Trav. Italy*, etc. 122 The arches are circular, and the columns squat. **1861** Beresf. Hope *Eng. Cathedr. 19th C.* vi. 224 The nave.. looks absolutely squat, owing to the lowness of the arcade. **1889** *John Bull* 2 Mar. 147/2 It must either be very low and squat in proportion, or it must be of such a scale in elevation as to rival the Abbey.

5. Characterized by squatness of form or structure.

1774 Goldsm. *Nat. Hist.* IV. 39 From its [*sc.* the marmot's] squat muscular make, it has great strength joined to great agility. **1789** Mrs. Piozzi *Journ. France* II. 82 [The palace] presents ideas rather of squat solidity, than of princely magnificence. **1858** Hawthorne *Fr. & It. Note-bks.* I. 133 The roof.. gives a very squat aspect to the temple. **1879** Green *Readings fr. Eng. Hist.* xxi. 108 Their buildings ..retained their primitive squat, low and meagre proportions.

6. *Comb.*, as ***squat-bodied, -built, -hatted.***

1705 *Lond. Gaz.* No. 4137/4 A dapple brown bay squat Bodied Mare. **1873** Greenwood *In Strange Company* 202 A sinister-looking, squat-built old gentleman. **1902** 'Linesman' *Words Eyewitness* 220 A string of cattle.. driven by dark, squat-hatted figures on horseback.

squat (skwɒt), *v.* Forms: 4–5 **sqwat**, 5 **sqwate**, 5–6 **squatte**, 6 **sqwatte**, 7 **squatt**, 9 **squot**, 5– **squat**. [ad. OF. *esquatir*, *esquater*, f. *es-* EX- + *quatir* QUAT *v.*[1] Cf. the early combs. *out-squat* OUT- 15 and TO-SQUAT *v.*]

I. 1. *trans.* To crush, flatten, or beat out of shape; to smash or squash; to bruise severely. Now *dial.*

a **1300** *E.E. Psalter* cix. 6 Sqwat sal he heuedes, blode and bane, In þe land of mani-ane. *c* **1380** Wyclif *Serm.* Sel. Wks. II. 68 Þis stoon shal falle on siche men, and squatte hem al to poudir. **1382** —— *2 Sam.* xxii. 8 The foundementis of hillis ben togidir smyten and squat. **1570** Redford *Marriage Wit & Sci.* 216 In twenty gobbetes I showld have squatted them. **1578** Lyte *Dodoens* 86 The same.. is good for such as are squatte and brused with falling from above. **1674** Ray *Coll. Words* 77 *To Squat*, to bruise or make flat by letting fall... *Suss.* *a* **1722** Lisle *Husb.* (1757) 189 Iron-clayted shoes do not well to thresh wheat in, especially if it be new corn; for such shoes squat and bruise it much. *Ibid.* 282 It often happens, that such a cow's knees fall against the side or flank of the cow with calf, and so squat the calf. **1825–** in many dial. glossaries and texts.

b. To dash down heavily or with some force; also, †to knock (gently). Now *dial.*

a **1400** *Leg. Rood* (1871) 142 But whon þe Roode ros and doun was squat, þe nayles renten him hondes and feete. **1519** Horman *Vulg.* 178 b, If it be gluishe.. and squatted on the grounde scatereth nat: it is a token of a fatte grounde. **1538** Elyot, *Allido*, to squatte or throw any thing agaynst the grounde or walles. **1599** T. M[oufet] *Silkwormes* 59 Now squatting them vppon the floore or ground, Now squashing out their bellies soft and round. **1609** Butler *Fem. Mon.* x. K vj, The Bees being dead, squat the hiue softly against the ground. **1828–** in Yks. glossaries.

†**c.** To knock *out* by smashing. *Obs.*[−1]

1553 *Respublica* (Brandl) v. vii. 28 Woulde ye have om sqwatte owt ous braine?

†**d.** To drive, force, or thrust violently or abruptly. *Obs.*

1655 Gurnall *Chr. in Arm.* II. 554 He saw the King like to recover, and he squatted his disease.. to his heart by the wet cloth. **1686** F. Spence tr. *Varilla's Ho. Medici* 110 The Cardinal-Nephew's continual Riots had squatted him in his Coffin at twenty-eight years old.

†**2.** *fig.* To suppress; to repress. *Obs. rare.*

1577 Stanyhurst *Descr. Ireland* iii. 11 b/1 in *Holinshed*, Saying that although lawes were squatted in warre, yet notwithstanding they ought to be reuiued in peace. **1582** —— *Æneis* I. (Arb.) 24 His grief deepe squatting, hoap he yeelds with phisnomye cheereful.

†**3.** *intr.* To fall or dash with some force or violence. *Obs. rare.*

1587 Daye *Daphnis & Chloe* (1890) 141 The yoong youth ..shooke the raskall off, and that so rudelie, as his pampered drunken carcas squatted against the ground. *c* **1590** in Hazl. *E.P.P.* IV. 218 Thou shalte be handled for the nonce, That all thy braynes on the ground shall squat.

II. 4. *refl.* To seat (oneself) upon the hams or haunches; to take one's seat in a crouching attitude or posture.

c **1410** *Master of Game* (MS. Digby 182) xxxiv, And if it happe.. þat she sqwat not her a forne þe houndes. **1737** Gray *Lett.* in Poems (1775) 24 At the foot of one of these squats me I. **1775** Mme. D'Arblay *Early Diary* 6 Dec., The Prince at last squatted himself on the corner of a form. **1836** W. Irving *Astoria* II. 29 An old man.. squatted himself near the door. **1842** Lover *Handy Andy* xxiii, He followed the cat, and off she went and squatted herself under the hedge.

fig. **1603** Florio *Montaigne* I. xxiii. (1632) 59 And seeking to squat himselfe [Fr. *se desrober*], hee the more enflamed and called them upon him.

b. Similarly with *down.* (Cf. 6 b.)

a **1535** More *Wks.* 1359/2 When thou hadest ietted thy fil, squat the down fair & wel in a chaire. **1583** Golding *Calvin on Deut.* 1050 Yet will they squatte them downe in their filthinesse. **1641** Smectymnuus *Answ. Humb. Rem.* (1653) Post. 88 The Archbishop of York, striving to sit above Canterbury, squatts him down on his lap. **1771** Smollett *Humph. Cl.* (1815) 172 Curtseying so low, that I thought she intended to squat herself down on the floor. **1772–84** *Cook's Voy.* (1790) IV. 1389 At the conclusion of each combat, the victor squatted himself down before the chief. **1806** J. Beresford *Miseries Hum. Life* IV. viii, Two friends, perfect strangers to you, squatting themselves down at your right and left hand. **1852** Mrs. Stowe *Uncle Tom's C.* xviii, She set down her basket, [and] squatted herself down.

c. With quasi-reflexive object. Also, to let (the tail) droop or fall.

1727 A. Hamilton *New Acc. E. Ind.* I. xxii. 262 As soon as he saw me, he squatted his Belly to the Ground,.. and crawled slowly towards me. **1739** R. Bull tr. *Dedekindus' Grobianus* 102 When Eloquence your Wrath has overcome, Then offer in a Chair to squat your Bum. **1801** Surr *Splendid Misery* I. 172 Foul imps of ignominy will squat their loathsome forms on my unbruised bones. **1825** *Mirror* V. 30/1 A mad dog.. generally goes.. in a straight line.. and never squats his tail.

5. *intr.* Of hares: To sit close to the ground in a crouching attitude; to crouch or cower down, esp. in order to avoid observation or capture.

c **1410** *Master of Game* (MS. Digby 182) i, And somtyme [the hare runs] a litell while and thenn abydith and squattith, and that done they ofte. **1576** Turberv. *Venerie* lix. 163 If she come to the side of any yong spring or groue, she will.. squat vnder the side thereof. *Ibid.* lxi. 172 Yet they will squatte vpon the outsides of the wayes or very neare to them. **1605** *Tryall Chev.* III. ii. in Bullen *Old Pl.* (1884) III, If they were hares as they are men, I should think them squatted. **1660** W. Secker *Nonsuch Prof.* 56 The fearful Hare squats at every noyse. **1711** Budgell *Spect.* No. 116 ¶7 The Hare now, after having squatted two or three Times, and been put up again as often [etc.]. **1731** Fielding *Grub St. Op.* I. iv, Poor puss's cunning, and shifting, and shunning!.. First this way, then that; First a stretch, and then squat. **1821** Clare *Vill. Minstr.* II. 196 The coy hare squats nestling in the corn. **1838** [see SQUAT *sb.*[1] 4].

fig. **1653** A. Wilson *Jas. I*, 248 Two great Favourites though of different Kingdoms could not well squat in one form. **1676** Hobbes *Iliad* 333 So coursed Hector was, Nor suffer'd was to double or to squat.

b. Of other animals, birds, etc.

c **1410** *Master of Game* (MS. Digby 182) ii, Þen he [the hart] maketh a ruse.. and þere he stalleth or squatteth. **1599** T. M[oufet] *Silkwormes* 36 Did euer thing do Cupid so much ill As once a Bee which on his hand did squat? **1601** Holland *Pliny* I. 262 He [*sc.* the ram-fish] squatteth close under the shade of bigge ships. **1611** Cotgr., *Blotir*, to squat, skowke, or ly close to the ground, like a daring Larke. **1665** Hooke *Microgr.* 184 It [*sc.* a fly] presently squats down, as it were, that it may be the more ready for its rise. **1826** Hood *Irish Schoolm.* vi, Also he schools some tame familiar fowls, Whereof, above his head, some two or three Sit darkly squatting. **1865** Livingstone *Zambesi* xv. 306 Then the Crocodiles squat on them till they are drowned. **1895** J. G. Millais *Breath fr. Veldt* (1899) 92 If then suddenly approached with a pointer, they become confused and squat well.

6. Of persons: To sit down with the legs closely drawn up beneath the hams or in front of the body; *esp.* to sit on the ground in this way or in a crouching attitude. Also jocularly, to sit (down).

Freq. const. with preps., esp. *on* or *upon* (the ground, hams, etc.).

1573 Tusser *Husb.* (1878) 43 Then squatteth the master, or trudgeth away, and after dog runneth as fast as he may. **1784** Russell *Hist. Mod. Europe* (1818) V. 186 Canadians and Indians.. squatted below bushes, or skulked behind trees. **1796** Morse *Amer. Geog.* II. 37 Men and women squat round this mat, which is covered with dishes. **1806** J. Beresford *Miseries Hum. Life* x. vi, Squatting plump on an unsuspected cat in your chair. **1865** Livingstone *Zambesi* viii. 174 The operator squatting, places his great toes on each end to keep all steady. **1878** Bosw. Smith *Carthage* 437 With groups of camels.. tended all night long by some swarthy Arab squatting on his haunches. **1883** Stevenson *Treas. Isl.* III. xiv, I crawled under cover of the nearest live-oak, and squatted there.

transf. **1895** Zangwill *Master* I. viii. 93 The rock that squatted on guard at the mouth of the harbour. **1906** Sir F. Treves *Highways Dorset* viii. 115 A commonplace town squatting soberly in the meadows.

b. With *down.* (Cf. 4 b.)

1609 Dekker *Gull's Horn Bk.* Wks. (Grosart) II. 207 Teach them both how to squat downe to their meat, and how to munch.. like Loobies. **1687** A. Lovell tr. *Thevenot's Trav.* I. 33 They squat down upon their heels, like Taylors, about the *Soffta.* **1768–74** Tucker *Lt. Nat.* (1834) I. 128 She squats down upon a chair. **1812** Combe *Syntax, Picturesque* III, Down on the grass the Doctor squatted. **1840** R. H. Dana *Bef. Mast* xiv, The lazy Indians.. squatting down upon their hams. **1901** D. B. Hall & Ld. A. Osborne *Sunshine & Surf* vi. 60 We would all squat down cross-legged, which is the correct way to sit at a native meal.

fig. **1760** Foote *Minor* II, Your gettings should be added to his estate, and my cousin Margery and I squat down together in the comfortable state of matrimony.

c. In pa. pple. used predicatively.

1577 Grange *Golden Aphroditis* L iij b, Thus squatted vpon this pleasaunt mount from mornyng to euenyng they spende their tyme. **1798** O'Keeffe *Wild Oats* v. iv, Leaving me, a chubby little fellow, squatted on a carpet. **1816** Tuckey *Narr. Exped. R. Zaire* iv. (1818) 137 The assembly was composed of about fifty persons squatted in the sand. **1867** Lady Herbert *Cradle L.* i. 15 The guests being seated, or rather squatted, on the divan. **1886** C. Scott *Sheep-farming* 82 Catch the ewe gently with the crook; lay her on her left side, yourself being squatted at her back.

†**d.** To crouch or lie down (*upon* the belly).

1650 T. B[ayley] *Worcester's Apoph.* 88 As soon as ever he came in sight of the enemy, he squatted upon his belly.

7. *trans.* To cause to squat; to put into, place in, a squatting attitude or posture. *rare.*

1600 Breton *Pasquil's Fooles-cap* lxxvi, Hee that squats a Hare within a furrowe, And sees how shee within her Muce doth Nuzzle. **1744** Gray in Gosse *Gray* (1882) 74 He came to meet me.., [and] squatted me into a fauteuil. **1850** *Bentley's Misc.* Nov. 507 They next squatted Sam upon the ground, and began to divest him of the hair of his head.

8. *intr.* †**a.** *fig.* To sink *into* (something lower or less important). *Obs.*[−1]

1641 Milton *Ch. Govt.* I. vi, The lofty minds.. thought it a poor indignity, that the high-rear'd Government of the Church should so on a sudden.. squat into a Presbytery.

†**b.** With *in*: To remain hid; to retire from view. *Obs.*

1655 Gurnall *Chr. in Arm.* xi. (1669) 43/2 Peter, whose grace that squatted in for a while, came forth with such a force [etc.]. *Ibid.* xv. 165/2 It makes all the joy which flusht out before, squat in on a sudden.

c. To sink in or down, in various uses.

1687 A. Lovell tr. *Thevenot's Trav.* II. 54 These Borrachios must be wet every half quarter of an hour, for fear they should squat for want of Wine. *a* **1722** Lisle *Husb.* (1757) 80 The inner parts of these lands bind and squat together below the harrow tinings. **1846** *Jrnl. R. Agric. Soc.* VII. II. 591 The peas soon shake hands across the furrow, and to attempt to hoe after they have done so, or have squatted, will [etc.].

9. To settle upon new, uncultivated, or unoccupied land without any legal title and without the payment of rent. Orig. *U.S.*

Freq. const. *on* or *upon* (land).

1800 *Mississippi Territorial Archives* (1906) 212, I wish also to be instructed for my Conduct towards those people Squatting or establishing themselves upon the Public Lands. **1829** Marryat *F. Mildmay* xxi, He was a Kentucky man, of the Ohio, where he had 'squatted', as we say. **1854** Thoreau *Walden* (1863) 70 As for a habitat, if I were not permitted still to squat, I might purchase one acre. **1884** *St. James's Gaz.* 20 June 6/1 The ancestors of many of the present freeholders began to squat upon the uncultivated slopes of the hills.

b. *Austr.* To rent or take up government or crown land for pasturage as a squatter.

1828 P. Cunningham *N.S. Wales* (ed. 3) II. 154 They have therefore.. much to gain by new settlers 'squatting' near their locations. **1852** Earp *Gold Col.* 98 The remaining mode of occupying land in New South Wales is to 'squat', i.e. to lease a large tract from the Government for purposes purely pastoral. **1870** *Daily News* 15 Feb., A tract of 160 acres of Government land, on which he 'squatted', with the right to buy it at five English shillings an acre.

c. To occupy an uninhabited building illegally (esp. said of a group of homeless people organized for this purpose); to live as a squatter (SQUATTER *sb.*[1] 1 d).

1880 Dixon *Windsor* IV. xxix. 269 Paupers had squatted in many of the towers. **1937** 'G. Orwell' *Road to Wigan Pier* v. 81 In one town I remember a whole colony of them who were squatting, more or less illicitly, in a derelict house which was practically falling down. **1946** *Daily Worker* 9 Sept. 4/3 We.. decided to assist homeless people to squat in certain of these buildings. **1969** *Listener* 15 May 665/1 No one expects to see 40,000 people squatting this year as there were 23 years ago. **1969** *Peace News* 13 June 5/1 One startling realisation.. is how few is the number of families that have had the courage to squat. **1980** *Oxf. Compan. Law* 1171/2 Persons may squat in buildings by reason of inability to find other accommodation and may do so deliberately as a protest against shortage of housing in the area.

d. *trans.* (*a*) To install (someone) as a squatter. (*b*) To occupy (a building) as a squatter.

1973 *Guardian* 23 Mar. 9/5 Shelter, the campaign for the homeless, has squatted a homeless family of six people in an Ealing council house.. reserved by the council for a homeless widow with four children. **1975** *Daily Tel.* 22 July 12 Much has been made of cases in which occupied privately-owned property has been squatted in the temporary absence of the owner. **1976** *Milton Keynes Express* 28 May 11/7 He added that he squats dozens of homeless people in corporations or council houses. **1977** *It* June 5/1 By January '76 the place was squatted by Enrique Ahriman, self-styled Demon of Confusion.

squat (skwɒt), *adv. rare*[−1]. [f. the (*ppl.*) *a.*] In a direct and straightforward manner, 'flat'.

1909 Kipling *Songs from Books* (1913) 24 Tell old Winter, if he doubt, Tell him squat and square-a!

squatarole ('skwætərəʊl). *Ornith.* Also **-olle.** [ad. mod.L. *Squatarola*, a. local It. *squatarola.*] The grey or Swiss plover, *Squatarola helvetica.*

1819 Stephens in Shaw *Gen. Zool.* XI. 505 Squatarolle with the body grey. **1870** Gilmore tr. *Figuier's Reptiles & Birds* 348 There are in Europe two species of this genus, the Lapwing and the Swiss Lapwing or Squatarole.

'squat board, squatboard. *Naut.* [f. SQUAT *v.* + BOARD *sb.*] (See quots.)

1905 *Rudder* Feb. 62/2 There is one institution on the St. Lawrence which, it is believed, is peculiar to it and but little known of elsewhere; the 'squat board'. This is an appendage in the form of a horizontal plane attached to the stern. **1953** M. V. Brewington *Chesapeake Bay: Pictorial Maritime Hist.* vi. 167 The stern settled so badly when underway 'squatboards' were necessary. **1955** J.-O. Traung *Fishing Boats of World* I. 8/2 To overcome the resulting 'squatting' or settling aft, 'squatboards' have been added. These are flat wooden fins or planes placed at and nearly parallel to the waterline under and abaft the stern, to hold the stern up when the boat is driven hard.

†**squatch,** *v. Obs.* Also 4 **squach, swatche.** [ad. OF. *esquachier* (*escachier*), to crush, break.] *trans.* To squash or smash; to quash or annul.

a **1325** *MS. Rawl. B.* 520 lf. 55 Lo nou is for te segge of þe ansueres ant of excepciouns þat squachez þe writ of Mort de auncestre. *c* **1380** in Horstm. *Altengl. Leg.* (1875) 224 Heo haþ sumwhat squached his tour þat we mihte not meue wiþ no stour. *a* **1400** *E.E. Psalter* cix. 7 Sqwat [*v. rr.* squatche, swatche] sal he heuedes, blode and bane.

'squatly, *adv.* [f. SQUAT *a.*] In a squat manner.

1894 CROCKETT *Lilac Sunbonnet* 257 [It] plunged down squatly among the dock-leaves.

'squatment. *rare.* [f. SQUAT *v.* 9.] The act of squatting; land occupied by squatting.

1860 *Chambers's Jrnl.* XIV. 39 The ghost of a squatter might prove a less unpleasant neighbour than the squatter himself, dispossessed of his squatment. **1887** F. W. MAITLAND in H. L. Fisher *Biogr. Sk.* (1910) 41 If ever I saw an untitled squatment it is now.

†**squatmore.** *Obs.* [f. SQUAT *sb.*[1] 1 b + MORE *sb.*[1]] The yellow horned poppy, *Glaucium luteum.*

In 19th c. southern dial. recorded as *squat(s.*

1691 AUBREY in *Ray's Corr.* (1848) 238 By the salt pits at Lymington..grows a plant called Squatmore, of wonderful effect for bruises. **1698** *Phil. Trans.* XX. 263 *Papaver Corniculatum Luteum*, or Horned Poppy, with a Yellow Flower, vulgarly called in Hampshire and Dorsetshire, Squatmore, or Bruseroot.

'squatness. [f. SQUAT *a.*] The quality of being squat.

1824 MISS MITFORD *Village* Ser. I. (1863) 119 Each of which artificial elevations..served equally to add to the squatness of the real machine. **1897** A. BALFOUR *Stroke of Sword* xv, This same squatness has served you well.

squat tag. *U.S.* [f. SQUAT *v.* + TAG *sb.*[2]] A version of the game of tag in which a player may gain temporary immunity by squatting on the ground.

1883 W. W. NEWELL *Games & Songs Amer. Children* xi. 159 In *squat-tag*, the fugitive is safe while in that position. **1960** V. WILLIAMS *Walk Egypt* 95 Half a dozen children played Squat Tag around a wagon.

squattage ('skwɒtɪdʒ). [f. SQUAT *v.* 9.]

1. A holding occupied by a squatter.

1862 G. DUFFY *Land Law Victoria* 10 Those..will necessarily desire to prevent any unfair absorption of the land, which must be speedily replaced out of their own squattages. **1864** W. WESTGARTH *Colony of Victoria* 272 The great Riverine district, which is one vast series of squattages. **1891** *Daily News* 11 Sept. 2/4 Their holdings being originally squattages or small enclosures made on commons and waste lands.

2. The occupation of ground, etc., by squatting.

1901 *Pall Mall G.* 1 July 3/1 The Piccadilly newsvendor, whose rights of squattage..that Office had not been prepared to acknowledge.

squatted ('skwɒtɪd), *ppl. a.* [f. SQUAT *v.*]

1. Pressed down, crushed.

a **1678** MARVELL *Wks.* (1786) III. 215 The nightingale.. adorns With music high the squatted thorns.

†**2.** *Bot.* = SESSILE *a.* 1 a. *Obs.*

1760 J. LEE *Introd. Bot.* I. xix. (1776) 53 A compound Flower is an aggregate one, comprehending many Florets that are sessile, squatted, or without Peduncles.

3. Settled down in a squatting posture.

1818 KEATS *Endym.* I. 264 To surprise The squatted hare while in half-sleeping fit. **1895** J. G. MILLAIS *Breath fr. Veldt* (1899) 49 A squatted covey, taken by surprise, will often rise singly or in pairs.

4. Occupied by squatters. Also with *in.*

1963 S. COOPER in Sissons & French *Age of Austerity* 46 The squatted-in camps were..a useful temporary stopgap for the housing problem. **1973** *Guardian* 5 Mar. 6/4 Everyone dropped in on another squatted house. **1975** *Time Out* 25 July 5/4 Islington Council is currently threatening to have electricity and gas supplies cut off to dozens of squatted houses in Finsbury Park. **1981** *Times* 14 July 2/4 According to Mrs Jean Styles..only two flats are empty and two 'squatted'.

squatter ('skwɒtə(r)), *sb.*[1] [f. SQUAT *v.*]

1. a. *U.S.* and early *Austral.* A settler having no formal or legal title to the land occupied by him, *esp.* one thus occupying land in a district not yet surveyed or apportioned by the government.

1788 J. MADISON in Sparks *Corr. Amer. Rev.* (1853) IV. 207 Many of them and their constituents are only squatters upon other people's land, and they are afraid of being brought to account. **1809** KENDALL *Trav.* III. lxxiv. 160 Upon visiting his lands, he finds..possession taken by a race of men, (the settlers and lumberers,) who in this view are called squatters. **1830** J. BETTS in *Occas. Papers Univ. Sydney Austral. Lang. Res. Cent.* (1965) No. 4. 13 A clan of people called 'Squatters'. These were generally emancipated convicts, or ticket-of-leave men, who, having obtained a small grant, under the old system, or without any grant at all, sat themselves down in remote situations, and maintained large flocks, obtained generally, in very nefarious ways, by having the run of all the surrounding country. **1833** W. H. BRETON *Excursions in N.S.W.* 442 There are likewise in the colony certain persons called 'squatters' (the term is American) who are commonly..of the lowest grade. **1834** PRINGLE *Afr. Sk.* iii. 162 Engelbrecht is what in America would be called a Squatter. He has no land of his own. **1835** *Sydney Gaz.* 28 Apr. 2 In every part of the country squatters without any reasonable means of maintaining themselves by honesty, have formed stations, and evidently pursued a predatory warfare against the flocks and herds in the vicinity. **1856** WHITTIER *Panorama* 478 The hunted bison tires, And dies o'ertaken by the squatter's fires.

b. An unauthorized occupant of land.

1849 MACAULAY *Hist. Eng.* iii. I. 359 At another time an impudent squatter settled himself there, and built a shed for rubbish. **1860** G. H. K. *Vac. Tour* 156 Hundreds of squatters from the neighbouring parts of Sutherland and Ross. **1874** JEFFERIES *Toilers of Field* (1892) 68 Commonly the squatters pitched on a piece of land..running parallel to the highway or lane.

c. In fig. uses.

1821 COLERIDGE in *Blackw. Mag.* X. 250 An intrusive supernumerary or squatter in the same tenement and workshop. **1897** BAILEY *Princ. Fruit-growing* 342 It will..be necessary to begin hunting for borers, and other squatters and campers.

d. One who occupies an uninhabited building illegally (esp. as a member of an organized group).

1880 W. H. DIXON *Royal Windsor* IV. xxix. 269 The King's house was a wreck; the fanatic, the pilferer, and the squatter, having been at work. **1946** *Times* 12 Aug. 2/3 Doncaster Rural District Council has turned on the water supply for a colony of its 'squatters' in military huts at Sprotborough. **1952** M. LASKI *Village* xiii. 185 The London squatters had moved into their flats and their hotels, and triumphantly held the police and all the authorities at bay. **1968** *Guardian* 2 Dec. 1/3 The London Squatters Campaign —formed three weeks ago. **1973** LD. DENNING in *All England Law Reports* III. 395 [McPhail v. Persons unknown]. What is a squatter? He is one who, without any colour of right, enters on an unoccupied house or land, intending to stay there as long as he can. **1980** *Oxf. Compan. Law* 1171/2 A squatter is a trespasser and liable to criminal penalties if he forces entry against the opposition of the lawful occupier or if, having been warned, he fails to leave.

2. *Austr.* and *N.Z.* One occupying a tract of pastoral land as a tenant of the crown; a grazier or sheep-farmer, esp. on a large scale.

In early Australian use (*c* 1835-) the term was employed as in sense 1.

1840 G. ARDEN *Austr. Felix* 109 Under this license the squatter is protected. **1847** LEICHHARDT *Jrnl.* Introd. p. xiv, We were received with the greatest kindness by my friends the 'Squatters', a class principally composed of young men of good education, gentlemanly habits, and high principles. **1872** M. A. BARKER *Christmas Cake in Four Quarters* IV. ii. 260 Amongst our most constant guests were the Scotch shepherds of a neighbouring 'squatter'. **1889** MRS. C. PRAED *Rom. Station* 12, I am glad to have married a squatter instead of a townsman. **1891, 1911, 1933** [see COCKY *sb.*[2] 2]. **1959** P. R. STEPHENS in A. McLintock *Descr. Atlas N.Z.* 38 The squatters soon became the dominant political force in the new country.

3. a. A squatting person or animal.

1824 CHALMERS in *Mem.* (1851) III. ii. 17 Dr. Haldane was not one of the squatters, but somehow his dusty back got into the view of the audience. **1872** SPURGEON *Treas. Dav.* Ps. lxviii. 13 Their enemies may have called them squatters among the pots. **1894** *Athenæum* 3 Feb. 144/1 The portrait of a toad 'from life' is creditable alike to the artist and the sitter—or rather *squatter*.

b. *Austr.* A bronze-wing pigeon of the genus *Phaps*, either *P. elegans* or *P. chalcoptera.*

1872 C. H. EDEN *In Queensland* 122 On the plains you find different kinds of pigeons, the squatters being most common,..crouching down to the ground quite motionless as you pass.

c. *Cricket.* A ball which remains low on pitching; a shooter.

1955 I. PEEBLES *On Ashes* 109 In Statham's first over to Miller there were three 'squatters'. **1959** *Times* 7 Aug. 4/4 Phelan failed by only a whisker to bowl Pataudi with a squatter.

4. *attrib.*, as ***squatter magistrate***; **squatter(s') camp** *S. Afr.*, an area in or around a town, occupied (usu. without permission) by the very poor for whom no housing provision has been made; **squatter pigeon** *Austr.*, = sense 3 b; **squatter's** (or **squatters'**; occas. †**squatter**) **right(s)** orig. *U.S.*, the right of a squatter to the land on which he has settled; also in extended and *fig.* use; **squatter sovereignty** *U.S.*, the right claimed by the inhabitants of newly-formed territories to settle for themselves the question of slavery or other institutions; **squatter state** (see quot.).

1956 T. HUDDLESTON *Naught for your Comfort* iii. 48 It is about ten or twelve miles from the centre of the city—a *squatters' camp..a conglomeration of lean-to, corrugated-iron and mud-brick dwellings. *Ibid.* vi. 106, I decided to fight it [*sc.* an eviction order]..even though it meant that the squatter camp, with all the inevitable hardships it must entail, would remain and would grow. **1970** *Stand. Encycl. S. Afr.* II. 141/1 That objective [*sc.* residential segregation] was realised in part by providing more and better housing for the Bantu and by demolishing squatters' camps and slums. **1986** *Daily Tel.* 7 Oct. 20/3 The Archbishop.. parading around the squatter camp of Crossroads in South Africa, apparently under the impression that it was typical of the way black South Africans have to live. **1894** H. NISBET *Bush Girl's Rom.* 214 To congratulate the *squatter magistrate on his good fortune. **1881** *Gentl. Mag.* Jan. 69 For the first time I saw the *squatter pigeon, a pretty little brown dove, that derives its name from its habit of squatting on the ground. **1854** H. D. THOREAU *Walden* i. 54 These are all the materials excepting the timber, stones and sand, which I claimed by *squatter's right. **1857** T. H. GLADSTONE *Englishman in Kansas* 168 The 'squatter-right' to a lot of ground is bought and sold on the strength of the law..which asserts its power by rifle and tomahawk. **1883** *Brandon* (Manitoba) *Daily Mail* 24 Feb. 4/2 The infernal row you are all making up there about grievances, monopolies, squatters' rights, etc. **1944** N. STREATFEILD *Curtain Up* xvi. 222 A talent once accepted acquired squatter's rights, as it were. **1958** B. HAMILTON *Too Much of Water* x. 209 They had, by constant use.., almost acquired squatters' rights over a small table in the aft corner. **1968** E. S. RUSSENHOLT *Heart of Continent* II. v. 76 Families already living along the Assiniboine, exercise 'squatter's rights', and lay claim to the newly-surveyed River Lots. **1973** 'TREVANIAN' *Loo Sanction* (1974) 207 The lone painter.. had come to assume over the years that the space, the stove, and the tea were his by squatter's right. **1854** in *Rep. 200, Ho. Representatives* 34th Congr., 1st Sess. 954 We are in favor of bona fide *squatter sovereignty. **1860** LOWELL *Election in Nov.* Prose Wks. 1890 V. 25 The Pro-Slavery party..here..represents Squatter-Sovereignty, and there the power of Congress over the Territories. **1894** J. FISKE *Hist. Amer.* 342 The doctrine of 'squatter sovereignty'; not Congress, but the 'squatters' were to be the supreme authority on the great question. It was the principle of 'local option' applied to slavery. **1872** DE VERE *Americanisms* 659 It [Kansas] appears occasionally as *Squatter State, from the pertinacity with which the squatter-sovereignty was discussed there.

'squatter, *sb.*[2] *Sc.* [f. SQUATTER *v.*] Sputtering, spatter; a loud fluttering noise.

1792 A. WILSON *Poems & Lit. Prose* (1876) II. 38 Frae his devilish mouth the froth Flew aff wi' squatter. **1834** M. SCOTT *Cruise Midge* (1859) 415 Such a squatter as a flock of a thousand teal..rose into the air with a loud rushing noise.

squatter ('skwɒtə(r)), *v.* [Prob. imitative.]

†**1.** *intr.* ? To be fussily busy. *Obs.*$^{-1}$

1593 G. HARVEY *New Letter* Wks. (Grosart) I. 282, I haue not bene squattering at my papers for nothing, and..I can dawbe with my incke like none of the Muses.

†**2.** = SQUITTER *v.* 2. *Obs.*$^{-0}$

1598 FLORIO, *Squaccarare*, to squatter, to squirt or lash it out behind after a purgation. **1611** COTGR., *Aller long*, to haue a squirt, to squatter out behind.

†**3.** *trans.* To scatter, disperse, spill. *Obs.*

1611 COTGR., *Escarter*, to sheed, squatter, throw about, or abroad. *Ibid.*, *Espancher*, to squatter, spill, sheed, or poure out disorderedly, or in hast. **1653** URQUHART *Rabelais* I. xxvii, To some others he..squattered into pieces the boughts or pestles of their thighs.

4. *intr.* To fly or run, to struggle along, to make one's way, among water or wet with much splashing or flapping. Const. *away*, *out of*, *through*, etc.

1785 BURNS *Address to Deil* viii, Awa ye squatter'd, like a drake, On whistling wings. **1790** A. WILSON *Poems & Lit. Prose* (1876) II. 103 Three years thro' muirs an' bogs I've squattert. **1825** SCOTT *Let.* in *Lockhart* (1839) VII. 354, I climbed Bennarty like a wild goat,..and squattered through your drains like a wild duck. **1853** C. BRONTE *Villette* xxv, A little callow gosling squattering out of bounds without leave. **1863** KINGSLEY *Water-Bab.* ii, Where the wild ducks squatter up from among the white water lilies. **1886** RUSKIN *Præterita* I. v. 143 He pitched the boy..into the canal,..but I believe the lad squattered to the bank without help.

b. To flutter, flap, or struggle among water or soft mud.

1808 JAMIESON, *To Squatter*, to flutter in water, as a wild duck, &c. **1833** M. SCOTT *Tom Cringle* i, A six-pound shot drove our boat into staves, and all hands were the next moment squattering in the water. **1897** MARY KINGSLEY *W. Africa* 259 We..were all soon squattering about on our own account in the elephant bath.

'squatterarchy. *Austr.* [f. SQUATTER *sb.*[1] 2.] = SQUATTOCRACY.

1881 MRS. C. PRAED *Policy & P.* I. 51 The squatterarchy of the Koorong rose up in a body. **1893** —— *Outlaw & Lawmaker* I. 246, I am not altogether at one with the squatterarchy, as you know.

'squatterdom. *Austr.* [f. SQUATTER *sb.*[1] 2.] The collective body of squatters.

c **1866** *Political Parody* (Morris), The ranks of squatterdom. **1873** *Contemp. Rev.* XXII. 701 The enormous domains of the old squatterdom. **1890** *Spectator* 22 Nov. 741/2 The scene is laid in Victoria, and from the picture of squatterdom given by the book [etc.].

'squattering, *vbl. sb.* [f. SQUATTER *v.*] The action of the verb, in various senses.

1598 FLORIO, *Squacquarata*,..a squattring, a squirting. **1611** COTGR., *Espanchement*, a disordered, or hastie squattering, spilling, sheeding, or pouring out. **1694** MOTTEUX *Rabelais* v. xvi. 68 The Devil of any thing we do, but fizzling, farting, funking, squattering, dozing. **1894** CROCKETT *Raiders* xiii. 121 We could hear..multitudinous squatterings in the water as of a thousand wounded wild ducks.

'squattering, *ppl. a.* [f. as prec.] That squatters, in senses of the verb.

1598 FLORIO, *Squacchera*, a squattring soft turd. **1603** —— *Montaigne* II. xvii. (1632) 361 It is a language.. squattering, dragling, and filthie. **1694** MOTTEUX *Rabelais* IV. lxvii. 270 From Eighteen squattering Bonasi. **1865** ALEX. SMITH *Summer in Skye* I. 108 As we approached, a duck burst from its face on 'squattering' wings.

‖**squattez-vous** ('skwɒteɪ,vuː), *imp. phr. slang.* [Joc. f. SQUAT *v.*, after Fr. *asseyez-vous* sit down.] Sit down.

1899 KIPLING *Stalky & Co.* 177 *Squattez-vous* on the floor, then!... I swear you aren't going to sit on *my* bed! **1959** R. POSTGATE *Every Man is God* xxiii. 216 'Squattez-vous' was an invitation to sit down—Captain Roddman offered it to tenants who called on him in his office.

'squattily, *adv.* [f. SQUATTY *a.*] In a squattish manner; somewhat squatly.

1859 MISS CARY *Country Life* (1876) 151 Two clumsy chimneys of stone showed squattily above the steep red gables.

'squatting, *vbl. sb.* [f. SQUAT *v.*]

1. The action of crushing or flattening. *rare.*

a **1400** *E.E. Psalter* cv. 29 Finees stode and quemed wele, And þe scathinge [*H.* swacching, *E.* sqwattinge; *L. quassatio*] lefte ilkadele. **1703** R. NEVE *City & C. Purchaser* 161 When 'tis laid on Sand, a very little Squating, *viz.* by jumping upon it with the Heals of ones Shooes will dent it.

2. The action of crouching or sitting close to the ground.

c **1410** *Master of Game* (MS. Digby 182) xxxiv, So þat.. at þe laste she be abyte with houndes notwithstondynge her rusyng, swattynge, and reiectynge. **1611** COTGR., *Tapissement*,.. a lurking, squatting, lying close. **1774** GOLDSM. *Nat. Hist.* (1776) IV. 17 The hare seems to have more various arts.. to escape its pursuers by doubling, squatting, and winding. **1782** J. WARTON *Ess. Pope* II. x. 166 The squatting down among the dead bodies till Dolon had passed. **1897** *Allbutt's Syst. Med.* III. 116 The child in squatting or crawling, begins to lean its weight on its hands.
attrib. c **1645** HOWELL *Lett.* I. xxxii, I do not like those squatting unseemly bold postures upon ones tail.

3. a. The action or fact of occupying land as a squatter. Also in sense 9 c of SQUAT *v.*

1832 *New England Mag.* III. 199 Tenants.. who occupied the land.. under that prescriptive tenure which we quaintly term squatting. **1839** MARRYAT *Diary Amer.* Ser. I. II. 75 Squatting, that is taking possession of land belonging to government and cultivating it. **1880** *Silver's Handbk. Australia* 146 But Victorian squatting is no occupation for the man of small capital. **1887** JESSOPP *Arcady* Introd. p. xiii, Days when squatting was not unusual. **1946** *Times* 17 Aug. 2/5 A new form of 'squatting' is reported from Gravesend, Kent. **1969** *Guardian* 27 Sept. 9/2 The Diggers will continue to support squatting by genuinely homeless families. **1976** *Times* 21 May 2/3 We publicly would not yield to the left.. on other issues, such as squatting.

b. *attrib.*, as ***squatting district, life***, etc.

1845 DISRAELI *Sybil* II. ii. (1863) 131 At the beginning of the revolutionary war, Wodgate was a sort of squatting district. **1847** J. D. LANG *Cooksland* 268 The large extent of land occupied by each Squatting Station. **1859** CORNWALLIS *New World* I. 155 Stations now were very different to what they had been in the early stage of squatting life. **1880** *Gentl. Mag.* CCXLVI. 64 He.. is now largely engaged in squatting pursuits in Queensland.

ˈsquatting, *ppl. a.* [f. SQUAT *v.*]

1. a. Occupying land as a squatter or squatters.

1839 W. IRVING *Chron. Wolfert's Roost* (1855) 4 The losel Yankees of Connecticut, those swapping, bargaining, squatting enemies of the Manhattoes. **1887** *Times* (weekly ed.) 25 Feb. 9/3 The numerous sub-tenants or squatting crofters.

b. Occupying an empty building as a squatter.

1963 S. COOPER in Sissons & French *Age of Austerity* 44 One of the squatting families. **1970** *Guardian* 12 Sept. 5/7 Last October the first four squatting families moved into flats which.. had been empty for up to two years.

2. Sitting closely to the ground; crouching.

1871 *Daily News* 5 Jan., Come nearer and look inside that ring of squatting men. **1883** *Congregationalist* Oct. 848 Further digging uncovered two parts of the statue of a squatting man.

ˈsquattingly, *adv. rare*$^{-0}$. [Cf. prec.] In a squatting posture.

1659 TORRIANO, *Catellone*, squattingly, closely, as a bitch upon her whelp. *Ibid.*, *Coccolone*, squattingly on the ground, as women do on their heeles.

ˈsquattish, *a.* [f. SQUAT *a.*] Somewhat or slightly squat.

1809 J. A. ANDERSEN *Dane's Excurs.* I. 10 He bent his squattish body into a most graceful curve. **1865** CARLYLE *Fredk. Gt.* XXI. iv. VI. 449 It is grace in a squattish form.

ˈsquattle, *v. rare.* [f. SQUAT *v.* + -LE.]

a. *intr.* To squat closely; to nestle. **b.** *trans.* To settle down squatly.

1786 BURNS *To a Louse* iii, Swith, in some beggar's haffet squattle. **1897** BLACKMORE *Dariel* xlvii, As a young cuckoo.. squattles his empty body down, and distends himself into one enormous gape.

squaˈttocracy. [f. SQUAT *v.* Cf. SQUATTERARCHY.] The class of squatters as a body possessed of social and political importance.

1846 C. P. HODGSON *Reminisc. Austr.* 118 Throughout the colony generally, English are the most numerous, then the Scotch, then the Irish, amongst the squattocracy. **1864** *Sat. Rev.* 19 Nov. 616 The aristocratic element of a large landed proprietary, which is already designated by the ingenious colonial title of a squattocracy. **1886** MRS. C. PRAED *Miss Jacobsen* I. i. 7 Female members of the squattocracy.

So **ˈsquattocratic** *a.*, of or pertaining to the squattocracy.

1854 *Melbourne Morning Herald* 18 Feb. 4/5 (Morris), Squattocratic Impudence.

squatty (ˈskwɒtɪ), *a.* [f. SQUAT *v.*] Somewhat squat; squattish.

1881 BURROUGHS *Pepacton* iii. (1884) 100 A few yards away stood another short, squatty hemlock. **1884** J. G. BOURKE *Snake Dance of Moquis* xxiii. 259 A low squatty plant, with thick, broad, dark-green leaves. **1890** W. R. NICOLL *J. MacDonell* i. 7 Every room in the low squatty Gordon Arms.
Comb. **1888** FENN *Dick o' the Fens* 110 A number of flat-looking squatty-shaped pochards.

ˈsquatwise, *adv.* [f. SQUAT *a.*] (See quot.)

1778 PRYCE *Min. Cornub.* 42 Pyritæ are to be met with.. Squat-wise, or in a horizontal position.

squauȝte, pa. t. of SQUETCH *v. Obs.*

squaw (skwɔː), *sb.* (and *a.*). Also 7–9 **squa**, 8 **squaa**. [a. Narragansett Indian *squaws*, Massachusetts *squa*, woman, with related forms in many other Algonquin dialects.]

1. a. A North American Indian woman or wife.

1634 W. WOOD *New England's Prosp.* II. xix, If her husband come to seeke for his Squaw. **1652** J. WILSON in *Progr. Gosp. among Indians* 18 The *Saneps* or men by themselves, and the *Squaes* or women by themselves. **1672** JOSSELYN *New Eng. Rarities* 99 The Indian Squa, or Female Indian. **1701** WOLLEY *Jrnl. New York* (1860) 36 Their Squaws or Wives and Female Sex manage their Harvest. **1756** WASHINGTON *Jrnl.* Writ. 1889 I. 401 Captn. Pear is came to town the other day with six Cherokees and two squaws. **1836** *Backwoods Canada* 160 The Indians are very expert in.. fishing; the squaws paddling the canoes with admirable skill. **1877** G. GIBBS *Tribes W. Washington* 193 The prairies are dotted over with squaws, each armed with a sharp stake and a basket.

b. Applied by Indians to white women.

1642 LECHFORD *Plain Dealing* 49 And when they [*sc.* Indians] see any of our English women sewing with their needles, or working quoifes, or such things, they will crie out, Lazie *squaes*! **1837** W. IRVING *Capt. Bonneville* III. 147 They.. were especially eloquent about the white squaws.

c. In general use: A wife or spouse. *rare.*

1823 BYRON *Juan* XIII. lxxix, Mrs. Rabbi, the rich banker's squaw.

†**2.** Used as *adj.* Female. *Obs.*$^{-1}$

1634 W. WOOD *New England's Prosp.* II. xv, They posted to the English to tell them how the case stood or hung with their squaw horse.

3. *transf.* An effeminate or weak person.

1807 PIKE *Sources Mississ.* (1810) 20, I directed my interpreter to ask how many scalps they had taken, they replied 'none'; he added they were all squaws, for which I reprimanded him. c **1890** A. WELCKER *Tales West* 24 By way of expressing their utter contempt for him they called him a 'squaw'.

4. ***old squaw***, the long-tailed duck.

1884 E. P. ROE *Nat. Ser. Story* vi, There is the old squaw, or long-tailed duck. **1894** [see OLD WIFE 2].

5. *attrib.* **a.** as ***squaw-axe, dance, hitch, mistress***; **squaw boot** (see quot. 1975); **squaw-man**, a White (or Negro) who marries a North American Indian woman; † **squaw-sachem**, a squaw chief in certain American Indian peoples; **squaw winter**, a short spell of winter-like weather which freq. precedes the Indian summer of Canada and the northern United States; **squaw wood** (see quot. 1944).

1896 *Harper's Mag.* XCII. 707/1 Such a settler.., watching his chance, fell on his captors.. and slew them 'with a *squaw-axe'. **1952** J. K. HOWARD *Strange Empire* 336 All the women had beaded ornaments and lavishly embroidered '*squaw boots'. **1975** C. CALASIBETTA *Fairchild's Dict. Fashion* 50/2 *Squaw boot*, below-the-knee boot made of buckskin with fringed turned down cuff at top, soft sole, no heel, worn by American Indian women and popular with young people in the 1960's. **1864** in *Beaver* (Winnipeg) (1963) Autumn 52/2 Oregon Jack gave a *squaw dance at which everybody got very drunk, I believe. **1894** *Outing* XXIV. 83/1 The short, choppy stepping of most squaw dances elsewhere. **1887** LEES & CLUTTERBUCK *British Columbia* 232 Other hitches there are of less fame than this, notably the '*Squaw Hitch', a comparatively simple affair. a **1901** A. ADAMS *Log Cowboy* iii, He showed me what he called a squaw hitch, with which you can lash a pack single-handed. **1866** *Rep. Indian Affairs* (U.S.) 91 White men, who have located in the vicinity of the reservation, and are known as *squaw men. **1877** R. I. DODGE *Hunting Grounds Gt. West* xliii. 427 Squaw men. This is the name given by Indians to those men, not of their tribe, who, by purchase of squaws (marriage), have been adopted by or are tolerated in it. **1884** *Pall Mall G.* 26 Aug. (Encycl. D.), The squaw-man—the miserable wretch of European blood who marries a Crow or a Blackfoot in order to take up land in the Indian Reservation. **1894** *Outing* XXIV. 87/2 A negro squaw-man (that is, one having an Indian wife) who went by the name of 'Smoky'. **1707** in Sewall *Diary* (1879) II. 60* She sent then unto a French Priest, that he would speak unto her *Squa Mistress. **1622** *Relat. Plantation Plymouth, New Eng.* 57 Also the *Squa Sachim, or Massachusets Queene was an enemy to him. **1716** B. CHURCH *Hist. Philip's War* (1865) I. 6 Amongst the rest he sent Six Men to Awashonks Squaw-Sachem of the Sogkonate Indians, to engage her in his Interests. **1861** *Amer. Agriculturist* XX. 321/2 The best authorities put them immediately after *Squaw Winter, which is the first cold snap that destroys tender vegetation. **1871** *Lakeside Monthly* V. 4/2 Those single-minded, grand old fellows.. kicked the light snow of 'squaw winter' from their Spanish-leather boots. **1901** in *Cent. Dict.* Suppl. (1909) s.v. *Winter*, Squaw winter is giving us a good long visit. **1914** *Outing* June 191/2 The cooking fire is only the beginning of the possibilities of '*squaw wood'. **1944** R. F. ADAMS *Western Words* 153/1 *Squaw wood*, a slang name for dried cow chips; also used in speaking of small, dry, easily broken sticks when used for fuel. **1968** C. HELMERICKS *Down Wild River North* I. vi. 100 Anything is squaw wood that you don't have to chop.

b. In names of plants, as **squaw-berry**, the edible berry of one of several shrubs, esp. the bear-berry, *Arctostaphylos uva-ursi*, an evergreen prostrate creeper; **squaw corn**, a variety of maize having soft grains of various colours; **squaw huckleberry, -root, -weed, whortleberry** (see quots.).

Also *squaw-bush, -carpet, -flower, -grass, -mint, -vine*, in recent Amer. Dicts.

1852 *Anglo-Amer. Mag.* I. 418/2 The partridge leads her young brood forth to feed upon the soft luscious fruits of the huckleberry and *squaw-berry. **1884** M. G. C. HALL *Lady's Life on Farm in Manitoba* 162 We have had jelly made of squawberries. **1956** V. FISHER *Pemmican* (1957) 161 Dried elderberry, or squawberry or wild currant he did not care for. **1824** J. DODDRIDGE *Notes Settlement Virginia* 90 How widely different is the large *squaw corn, in its size, and the period of its growth. **1914** E. STEWART *Lett. Woman Homesteader* 151 They had a small patch of land.. on which was raised the squaw corn that hung in bunches from the rafters. **1975** *Daily Colonist* (Victoria, B.C.) 5 Oct. 22/5 Nowadays, squaw corn is grown purely for its highly ornamental, variegated ears with kernels in purple, mauve, red, yellow, cream and black, very nice for Thanksgiving.. displays. **1856** A. GRAY *Man. Bot.* (1860) 248 *Vaccineum stamineum*, Deerberry. *Squaw Huckleberry. **1848** BARTLETT *Dict. Amer.* 328 **Squaw-root*,.. a medicinal plant put up by the Shakers. **1856** A. GRAY *Man. Bot.* (1860) 280 *Conopholis*. Squaw-root. Cancer-root. **1847** DARLINGTON *Amer. Weeds*, etc. (1860) 193 *Senecio aureus*... Golden Senecio. Golden Ragwort. *Squaw-weed. *Ibid.*, The var. *obovatus* (called 'Squaw-weed') has been denounced.. as being poisonous to sheep. **1872** DE VERE *Americanisms* 62 Squaw Root.. and Squaw Weed.. hold their place among the medicinal plants of the country, but owe their names to modern, not to Indian, usage. **1845–50** MRS. LINCOLN *Lect. Bot.* II. 181/1 *Vaccinium stamineum*, *squaw whortleberry.

c. **squaw-fish**, a fresh-water cyprinoid fish (*Ptychocheilus Oregonensis*) of the Western U.S.

1888 LEES & CLUTTERBUCK *B.C. 1887* (1892) xv. 147 We.. fished with fair success for the white-fish and squaw-fish which abound in it.

Hence **squawed** *pa. pple.*, married to a squaw.

1904 E. ROBINS *Magnetic North* 324 The old miners had nearly all got 'squawed'.

squawk (skwɔːk), *sb.* Also **skwawk**. [f. next.]

1. a. A loud grating call or cry; a hoarse squall.

1850 R. S. HAWKER in C. E. Byles *Life & Lett.* (1905) xiii. 212 There is.. the Squawk of the demon on every platform. **1863** READE *Hard Cash* II. 337 At sight of this lowering figure Hannah uttered a squawk, and fled with cheeks red as fire. **1889** CLARK RUSSELL *Marooned* (1890) 283 The harsh squawk of the macaw or some such fowl came like the edge of a saw out of the.. forest.

b. *fig.* A complaint, a protest, esp. in phr. ***to set*** (or ***put***) ***up a squawk***. *slang* (orig. and chiefly *U.S.*).

1909 C. B. CHRYSLER *White Slavery* ix. 70 'Snatchin' simps' is good enough for Little Willie, there is no 'fall', no squawk, all you have to do is to stall. **1914** JACKSON & HELLYER *Vocab. Criminal Slang* 79 *Squawk*,.. a protest; a vociferous demonstration, as an indignant repudiation of an injustice... 'If you don't put up a squawk they'll trim you.' **1948** M. LASKI *Tory Heaven* ix. 126 They was just told to shut down and shut down they did.. there wasn't a squawk out of none of them. **1973** 'B. MATHER' *Snowline* ii. 25 Our starry-eyed bleeding-hearts and permissives at home set up a squawk. **1976** 'R. B. DOMINIC' *Murder out of Commission* xvi. 147 How in God's name can we set up a squawk? We don't know what's going on.

2. *U.S.* (See quot.)

1872 COUES *N. Amer. Birds* 269 *Nyctiardea*, Night Heron. Qua-bird. Squawk.

squawk (skwɔːk), *v.* Also **squauk**. [Imitative. Cf. SQUARK *v.*]

1. a. *intr.* To call or cry with a loud harsh note; to squall or screech hoarsely.

1821 [implied in SQUAWKING *ppl. a.*]. **1847** HALLIWELL, *Squawk*, to squeak. **1879** MISS YONGE *Magnum Bonum* I. 120 A stately black Spaniard [fowl].. squauking and curtseying. **1881** RAE *White Sea Peninsula* v. 56 Clouds of gulls were hovering about,.. all hungry, some squawking hoarsely.

b. Of things: To give out a discordant sound; to creak or squeak harshly.

1859 MRS. STOWE *Min. Wooing* xxix. 275 That bedroom door squawks like a cat. **1869** 'MARK TWAIN' *Innoc. Abr.* iv. 29 A disreputable accordion, that had a leak somewhere and breathed louder than it squawked.

c. *U.S. slang.* To turn informer, to 'squeal'.

1872 G. P. BURNHAM *Memoirs U.S. Secret Service* p. vii, *Play baby*, to whine; 'squawk'; or assume innocence. **1929** W. R. BURNETT *Little Caesar* VI. v. 251 You know.. Joe squawked. **1935** *Amer. Speech* X. 12/2 *Belch*, to confess or carry information to the police. Modern to *squawk*. **1937** *Times Lit. Suppl.* 25 Dec. 974/4 The thief who 'squawks' is expelled as professionally infamous; his occupation's gone.

d. *U.S. slang.* To complain, protest.

1875 J. G. HOLLAND *Sevenoaks* xvii. 239 He mustn't squawk an' try to git another feller to help 'im out of 'is bargain. **1926** J. BLACK *You can't Win* iv. 41 Usually the sucker is a married man and can't squawk. But when he does squawk.. the only thing to do is to blow back his money. **1939** *Time* 23 Jan. 30/2 Since most Hummert ghosts are glad to add caviar to bread-&-butter from other jobs, they have seldom squawked. **1948** *Sun* (Baltimore) 7 Jan. 13/1 When you pass a law and hire somebody to enforce it, you can't squawk if your kids get pinched for violating it. **1951** E. PAUL *Springtime in Paris* vi. 121 The contractor had been getting away with plenty.. and would not dare squawk, no matter how high a bill was presented. **1976** M. MACHLIN *Pipeline* xxvii. 319 If the EPA ever finds out and squawks, they'll just fight it out in the courts.

2. *trans.* With *out*: To utter with or as with a squawk.

? **1856** MRS. WITCHER *Widow Bedott Papers* 208 (Bartlett), The way she squawked it out was a caution to old gates on a windy day.

ˈsquawk box. *U.S. slang.* Also with hyphen or as one word. [f. SQUAWK *sb.* or *v.* + BOX *sb.*[2]]

a. A loud-speaker or public-address system.

1945 *New Yorker* 17 Mar. 28/3 The squawk box became alive for that second before any message comes over. **1950** 'D. DIVINE' *King of Fassarai* xxv. 219 There was a radio blaring.. its music was punctuated with the hoarse stridencies of the squawk-box. **1973** *New Scientist* 20 Sept. 684/2 The squawk box emits two marginally different frequencies, almost out of audible range, through separate speakers. **1978** W. F. BUCKLEY *Stained Glass* xi. 104 The whistle stopped blowing, the passengers were all in their seats, the coordinators stopped speaking into their squawk boxes.

b. A speaker or receiving device which forms part of an intercommunication system, esp. in an office.

1954 *Sun* (Baltimore) 16 Apr. 27/2 Office buildings were deserted or skeleton staffed as interoffice 'squawk-boxes' carried in the doings on Thirty-third street by radio. **1962** L. DEIGHTON *Ipcress File* i. 15 Even over the squawk-box I could hear the lift in Alice's voice. **1964** P. GALLICO *Hand of Mary Constable* 48 To the right of the desk, on a small table, there was a squawk box with some dozen switches for inter-office communications. **1970** N. ARMSTRONG et al. *First on Moon* p. xiii, *Squawk box*, a small speaker, connected by telephone line to Mission Control, for home or office reception of live conversation between the spacecraft and earth. **1976** P. HARCOURT *Dance for Diplomats* ix. 96 The buzzer on my intercom made frantic noises... 'Coming,' I said into the squawk box.

squawk-duck. [f. SQUAWK *v.*] (See quot.)

1831 RENNIE *Montagu's Ornith. Dict.* 493 *Squauk Duck*, a name for the Bimaculated Duck.

'squawker. [f. SQUAWK *v.* + -ER.]

1. A toy wind-instrument for producing squawks.

1874 J. W. LONG *Amer. Wild-fowl* ix. 157, I like 'calling by mouth' much better than with a 'squawker', especially if the ducks are passing reasonably close. **1886** *Sci. Amer.* 25 Sept. 199 The small inflatable balloons applied to the toy squawkers.

2. One who squawks.

1891 in *Cent. Dict.* **1896** G. B. SHAW *Let.* 8 Dec. (1965) I. 712 Yes, Lena is a fascinating squawker. **1923** H. C. WITWER in *Collier's* 29 July 26/3 To show you what a cheap squawker this Rags is, Spence tells me he has just welshed on a bet with him.

3. A loudspeaker designed to reproduce accurately sounds in the middle of the audible range.

1959 N. H. CROWHURST *Basic Audio* I. 67 Many installations use two or more speakers of different sizes..: large speakers (woofers) for the low frequencies, medium-sized speakers (squawkers) for the mid-range, and small speakers (tweeters) for the high frequencies. **1975** G. J. KING *Audio Handbk.* vi. 150 The output..drives the middle-frequency unit (squawker) and the high-frequency unit (tweeter) via a 4 kHz frequency divider.

'squawking, *ppl. a.* [f. SQUAWK *v.*] That squawks, or utters hoarse squeaks; characterized by squawks or squawking.

1821 CLARE *Vill. Minst.* I. 90 Cow-boy's whoops, and squawking brawls, To urge the straggling heifers back. **1847** HALLIW., *Squawking-thrush*, the missel-thrush. *I. Wight.* **1899** F. T. BULLEN *Log Sea-waif* 208 The watch, up to their waists in water, splashed about collecting the squawking chickens.

'squawky, *a.* [f. SQUAWK *sb.* or *v.* + -Y.] Of the voice: Loud and harsh; hoarsely squeaky.

1898 *Westm. Gaz.* 12 May 1/3 She is to be married..to..a squawky-voiced curate.

squawl(er, obs. forms of SQUALL, SQUALLER.

squawmish, var. SQUALMISH.

squaymose, obs. f. SQUEAMOUS *a.*

squayne, obs. var. SWAIN.

squdde, obs. f. SCUD *v.*

squdge (skwʌdʒ), *v.* [Perh. blend of SQUEEZE *v.* or SQUASH *v.*[1] and PUDGE[1]; cf. next and SQUSH *v.*] *trans.* To squash or squeeze; to hug tightly. Also as *sb.*

1870 R. H. D. BARHAM *Life & Lett. R. H. Barham* II. vii. 27 At last he got so terrible bad surely nothing would ease him, so that we was forced to *squdge* him under the blankets. **1909** KIPLING *Rewards & Fairies* (1910) 5 They've put us into boots..and my toes are squdged together awfully. **1928** J. M. BARRIE *Peter Pan* v. ii. 159 Oh, Peter, how I wish I could take you up and squdge you! **1975** *New Society* 13 Nov. 388/1 Why does a large tube of toothpaste have a large hole? It is by length we judge the squdge of our brush, not by girth.

squdgy ('skwʌdʒɪ), *a.* [Perh. f. prec. + -Y[1], or blend of SQUASHY *a.* and PUDGY *a.*[1]] Soft and moist or yielding, squashy.

1892 KIPLING *Barrack-Room Ballads* 51 Elephints apilin' teak In the sludgy, squdgy creek. **1919** W. DEEPING *Second Youth* xvii. 145 He made haste to shake Joseph Bluett's squdgy hand and escape. **1959** M. STEEN *Woman in Back Seat* I. v. 97 'Don't you like babies?' Lavinia shook her head. .. 'They're so squdgy, and they haven't got any shape!'

squeak (skwiːk), *sb.* Also 8 **squeek.** [f. the vb.]

1. The act of squeaking. † ***to put to the squeak***, to cause to squeak.

1664 ETHEREDGE *Comical Revenge* IV. iii, (The women shriek within.) Hark! he puts them to the squeak. *a* **1700** *Songs Lond. Prentices* (Mackay) 92 They took my py-ball'd mare And put the carrion wench to th' squeak.

2. a. A short or slight sound, of a thin high-pitched character, made by animals or persons. Also *fig.* in neg. contexts (*colloq.*): cf. PEEP *sb.*[1] 2d.

1700 DRYDEN *Fables, Cock & Fox* 732 With many a deadly Grunt and doleful Squeak, Poor Swine, as if their pretty Hearts would break. **1710** STEELE *Tatler* No. 157 ¶7 With a great many skittish notes, affected squeaks, and studied inconsistencies. **1775** MME. D'ARBLAY *Early Diary* 14 Dec., We asked if he had been to the Opera? He immediately began a squeak, by way of imitation. **1827** SCOTT *Jrnl.* 17 April, Our party was enlivened by the squeaks of the wenches. **1866** R. M. BALLANTYNE *Shifting Winds* xxx. (1881) 342 The squeak of the pig caused the rest of the family to turn and fly from the fatal spot.

fig. **1847** L. HUNT *Men, Women, & B.* II. x. 252 There is something in the..frivolous and fragile celibacy of his life, which..gives a peculiarly revolting character to the perpetual squeak of his censoriousness. **1977** *Spare Rib* July 10/1 We've hardly heard a squeak out of them since. **1982** S. BRETT *Murder Unprompted* iv. 41 'I'm surprised you haven't heard anything about it... You sure you haven't heard anything?' 'Not a squeak.'

b. A thin, sharp sound produced by a musical instrument, etc.

1805 H. K. WHITE *Lett.* (1837) 276 The vile squeak of the Italian fiddle. **1832** BREWSTER *Nat. Magic* ix. 229 Vibrations of such frequency afford only a shrill squeak or chirp. **1883** J. GILMOUR *Mongols* xxvi. 309 Shrill above the boom of the temple drums..would come the squeak of the *thlimba.*

3. a. A slight, narrow, or bare chance *for* something.

1716 M. DAVIES *Athen. Brit.* II. 303 If we have success, you shall.., perchance, have a squeek for the renewing a great part, at least, of your old Hereditary Lease. **1737** BRACKEN *Farriery Impr.* (1757) II. 104 To caution my Readers, that they do not too hastily condemn what I advance, but to give me a Squeak for my Life (as the Saying is). **1806** J. BERESFORD *Miseries Hum. Life* XVI. Introd., I will give you—though I'm a fool for my pains—however I will give you one squeak more for your inheritance. **1868** *Chambers's Jrnl.* Oct. 675/2 See all ready with the boat,..it may give us a squeak for our lives, if a little one.

b. A narrow escape, a close shave. Usually with qualifying adjs. *narrow, near, tight.* Also const. *for* (one's life, etc.).

1822 SCOTT *Fam. Lett.* (1894) II. xviii. 149, I became extremely feverish myself, and had the disorder not terminated in a general rash..I should have had a squeak for it. **1833** M. SCOTT *Tom Cringle* xii, I have had more than one narrow squeak for it. *a* **1860** ALB. SMITH *Med. Student* (1861) 98, I had a tight squeak for it. **1867** TROLLOPE *Chron. Barset* II. 339 'It was a very narrow squeak,' Mr. Crawley said when he friend congratulated him on his escape. **1880** MRS. H. WOOD in *Argosy* XXIX. 191 At the last moment, when the ship was getting away, and I had given the captain up, he came on board... 'I've had a squeak for it, Johnny,' he laughed, as he shook my hand. **1889** STEVENSON *Lett.* (1899) II. 136 We had a near squeak, the wind suddenly coming calm. **1939** A. RANSOME *Secret Water* x. 121 You oughtn't to have waited. It's going to be a squeak getting home across the Wade.

4. † **a.** *Cant.* (See quot.) *Obs.*

1795 POTTER *Dict. Cant* (ed. 2), *Squeak*, a thief, who when taken up confesses and impeaches the rest of his companions.

b. A piece of incriminating information offered to the police; ***to put in the*** (or ***a***) ***squeak***: to turn informer, to inform *against.*

1922 [see FLATTY[2] 3]. **1936** J. CURTIS *Gilt Kid* ii. 22 You'll ..turn grass and put in the bleeding squeak against me. **1955** D. WEBB *Deadline for Crime* i. 14 Then the squeak goes in. A bent buyer grasses to the law. **1973** A. HUNTER *Gently French* iv. 33, I can see another villain putting a squeak in but knocking off Freddy would be just stupid.

5. *attrib.* as *adj.* Squeaky.

1818 MOORE *Mem.* (1853) II. 167 The Duke said, in his high, squeak tone of voice [etc.].

squeak (skwiːk), *v.* Also 4–6 squeke, 6–7 squeake, 7 sqweake, 7–8 squeek; 6–7 squake. [Imitative. Cf. Sw. *sqväka* to croak.]

1. *intr.* To emit a short or slight sound of a thin high-pitched character: **a.** Of persons.

1387 TREVISA *Higden* (Rolls) VII. 117 It byfel..þat a duke ..passynge þerby herde þe childe squeke. **1604** SHAKS. *Ham.* I. i. 116 (Q.[2]), The sheeted dead Did squeake and gibber in the Roman streets. **1634–5** BRERETON *Trav.* (Chetham Soc.) 6 Others..sung, screaming, and squeaking, and straining their voices. **1675** HOBBES *Odyssey* (1677) 219 Ulysses Irus struck just under th' ear:..He fell, squeakt, shed his teeth. **1733** POPE *Donne's 4th Sat.* 99 He lifts his hands and eyes, Squeaks like a high-stretch'd lutestring, and replies. **1831** TRELAWNY *Adv. Younger Son* I. 240 He never squeaked, or made a wry face. **1899** *Westm. Gaz.* 28 Aug. 3/1 There are also English girls who croak and squeak and chirp.

b. Of animals or birds.

1547 J. HARRISON *Exhort. Scottes* e viij, His aucthor is bewraied, as a Ratte is by squekyng. **1576** GASCOIGNE *Steele Gl.* Wks. 1910 II. 147 Since every janglyng byrd, Which squeaketh louder, shall never triumph so. **1634** SIR T. HERBERT *Trav.* 213 Bats..sqweake and call one the other. **1663** BUTLER *Hud.* I. i. 52 Beside, 'tis known he could speak Greek, As naturally as Pigs squeek. **1693** DRYDEN *Persius* I. Prol., Pies, Crows, and Daws, Poetick Presents bring: You say they squeak; but they will swear they Sing. **1774** G. WHITE *Selborne* lxi, Several [swifts]..squeaking as they go in a very clamorous manner. **1823** SCOTT *Quentin D.* iv, They loved better to hear the lark sing than the mouse squeak. **1848** DICKENS *Dombey* xxiii, Rats began to squeak and scuffle in the night time.

c. Of things.

1602 MARSTON *Ant. & Mel.* v. Wks. 1856 I. 59 My voice squeakes like a dry cork shoe. *c* **1628** DONNE *Serm.* 576 As a Cart that hath a plentifull load Squeaks and Whines the more for that Abundance. **1740** SOMERVILLE *Hobbinolia* I. 323 Shrill Fiddles squeak, Hoarse Bag-pipes roar. **1798** FERRIAR *Eng. Historians* 228 Till each attendant bagpipe squeak'd for fear. **1847** HALLIW., *Squeak*, to creak, as a door, &c. **1876** 'L. CARROLL' *Hunting the Snark* v. vii, The sound so exactly recalled to his mind A pencil that squeaks on a slate! **1892** GREENER *Breech Loader* 49 In cocking the locks, one will 'squeak', the other will make no sound.

2. *slang.* To confess; to turn informer; to 'split' or 'peach'. (Cf. SQUEAL *v.* 3.)

1690 DRYDEN *Don Sebastian* IV. i, If he be obstinate, put a civil Question to him upon the Rack, and he squeaks I warrant him. *a* **1734** NORTH *Examen* I. iii. (1740) 218 In continual Expectation that..some pusillanimous Wretch.. would squeak, as they called it, and own the Guilt. **1757** FOOTE *Author* I, Don't be afraid; I'll keep council;..when I was in the treasonable way, I never squeak'd. **1805** *European Mag.* XLVII. 122 Unless he had been allowed to squeak, i.e. turn evidence, it had been impossible to take his deposition. **1816** *Sporting Mag.* XLVIII. 30 Greenaway..confessed to him..that if any one squeaked he should be hanged. **1834** AINSWORTH *Rookwood* III. v, Never blow the gab, or squeak. **1874** *Slang Dict.* 307 *Squeak on a person*, to inform against, to peach.

3. a. *trans.* To utter, sing, or play in a squeaking manner or with a squeaky voice. Usu. derisively. Freq. with *out.*

1577 tr. *Bullinger's Decades* (1592) 241 For laughter is blame-worthy, if it be..childishly squeaked. **1592** NASHE *P. Penilesse* Wks. (Grosart) II. 108 The light vnconstaunt Multitude, that will..prefer a blinde harper that can squeake out a new horne-pipe. **1601** SHAKS. *Twel. N.* II. iii. 97 Ye squeak out your Coziers Catches without any mitigation or remorse of voice. **1687** MIÈGE *Gt. Fr. Dict.* II, To squeak out a sermon. **1700** CONGREVE *Way of World* V. v, Prophane Musick-meetings where the lewd Trebles squeek nothing but Bawdy, and the Bases roar Blasphemy. **1778** MISS BURNEY *Evelina* xxi, One of these outlandish gentry may..come on, and squeak out a song or two, and then pocket your money without further ceremony. **1840** DICKENS *Old C. Shop* xix, Fiddles..were squeaking out the tune to staggering feet.

b. With clause as object. Also with *out.*

1594 SHAKS. *Rich. III*, I. iv. 54 (Q.), He squakd out alowd, Clarence is come. **1828** SCOTT *F.M. Perth* vii, 'The Provost being himself a nobleman—' squeaked the Pottingar. **1848** THACKERAY *Van. Fair* lxvi, 'I will not hear it, I say,' squeaked out Jos at the top of his voice.

† **c.** ***to squeak beef***: (see quot.). *Obs.*

a **1700** B. E. *Dict. Cant. Crew, They Squeek beef upon us*, cry out Highway-men or Thieves after us.

4. a. To make (way) with squeaking.

1878 MRS. STOWE *Poganuc People* ix, The roads, through which the ox-sleds of the farmers crunched and squeaked their way.

b. To cause (something) to squeak.

1913 C. MACKENZIE *Sinister St.* I. II. xv. 401 Michael solemnly regarded the fair-haired boy of two who was squeaking an indiarubber horse. **1977** 'J. GASH' *Judas Pair* xv. 177 Could he see the curtain? I'd moved it without squeaking its noisy runners.

5. *intr.* **a.** ***to squeak through***: to get through by a narrow shave, to scrape through.

1938 H. NICOLSON *Diary* 1 Sept. (1966) 358 We may just squeak through. On the other hand, we may get into the same mess as in 1914. **1943** *Sun* (Baltimore) 22 Nov. 14/2 The Irish squeaked through to a 14-to-13 verdict over Iowa Pre-Flight. **1971** L. BISHOP *Days of Martin Luther King, Jr.* iv. 329 The President..said he was not optimistic about the passage of the civil rights bill. It would require strong bipartisan support to squeak through. **1977** *Time* 7 Mar. 24/2 Rabin only squeaked through by sweeping the votes allotted to Israel's conservative kibbutzim.

b. With preps.: to make one's way by a narrow shave, to scrape *by, into,* etc. Chiefly *U.S.*

a **1961** H. H. MARTIN in *Webster* s.v., By six months of hard cramming..he squeaked by the finals. **1966** *Economist* 27 Aug. 810/3 His Progressive Conservatives squeaked back into power with only 39 per cent of the votes. **1968** *Ibid.* 20 Apr. 20/3 The Bill squeaked out of the Rules Committee on a single vote. **1974** *Union* (S. Carolina) *Daily Times* 24 Apr. 1/4 Texaco..squeaked by Mobil last year to become the country's second biggest oil firm. **1977** *Monitor* (McAllen, Texas) 26 June 1B/5 Jimmy Connors squeaked past a valiant Stan Smith in five sets.

squeaker ('skwiːkə(r)). [f. the vb.]

1. a. One who plays on a squeaking instrument.

1641 COWLEY *Guardian* v. xi, Stay at the door, ye sempiternal squeakers. **1663** —— *Cutter Coleman St.* v. vi, Go home?..no, we'l Dance home; afore us Squeakers, that way.

b. One who squeaks.

1671 EACHARD *Obs. Answ. Cont. Clergy* 132 Mimical squeakers and bellowers, and the vain-glorious admirers only of themselves. **1702** MOTTEUX *Prol. to Farquhar's Inconstant*, Your rarity for the fair guest to gape on, Is your nice squeaker, or Italian capon. *c* **1753** FOX in *Trevelyan* (1880) ii. 45, I..found Harry in his nurse's arms... I called him Squeaker. **1823** BYRON *Juan* XI. lxxxv, I have seen the country gentlemen turn squeakers.

c. *slang.* (See quot.)

1676 COLES *Dict.*, *Squeeker*, a Barboy; also a Bastard, or any other child.

d. *Criminals' slang.* An informer. Cf. SQUEALER 2b.

1903 FARMER & HENLEY *Slang* VI. 335/1 *Squeaker*, (1) a blab.., and (2) an informer. **1924** E. WALLACE *Room 13* vii. 171, I want to talk with you, you dirty squeaker! You're the fellow that told the deputy I was getting tobacco in through a screw. **1930** *Observer* 19 Oct. 17 The recent attempt to murder him..was not due to..the impulse to remove rivals or 'squeakers'. **1950** [see GRASSER[2]]. **1973** A. HUNTER *Gently French* ii. 14 Dutt had been brooding over the tip-off mystery... The squeaker must have been Rampant.

2. A bird or animal which squeaks: **a.** A young pigeon, partridge, etc.

1654 GAYTON *Pleas. Notes* IV. ii. 179 Thou shalt lie upon thy pallat, and call to thy cook-maid, and say, dresse me that Squeeker for my breakfast. **1694** MOTTEUX *Rabelais* IV. lix. 234 Pigeons, Squobbs, and Squeakers. **1829** COL. HAWKER *Diary* (1893) II. 2, I actually brought home 24 partridges, 20 of which were old ones..and two squeakers. **1854** *Poultry Chron.* I. 263 Squeakers will often return home from long distances though they may have been kept in a considerable time. **1881** GREENER *Gun* 535 Mr. Campbell..succeeded in bagging 220 grouse by evening; every 'squeaker' was, however, counted.

b. *Ornith.* One or other of various birds characterized by their squeaking call.

1817 T. FORSTER *Nat. Hist. Swallow-tribe* (ed. 6) 9 *Hirundo Apus*,.. Black Swallow, Squeaker, Screamer, Deviling, or Shriek Owl. **1848** J. GOULD *Birds Australia* II. pl. 45 *Strepera Anaphonensis*, Grey Cow-Shrike; .. Squeaker of the Colonists. Its note is a piercing shriek. **1896** A. J. NORTH *List Insectiv. Birds N.S.W.* I. 1 For instance, *Corcorax melanorhampus*, *Xerophila leucopsis*, and *Myzantha garrula* are all locally known in different parts of the Colony by the name of 'Squeaker'.

c. *slang.* A foxhound.

1828 *Sporting Mag.* XXII. 23 He was often alone with the squeakers, and sometimes racing with the leaders.

d. *colloq.* A (young) pig.

1861 DICKENS *Gt. Expect.* iv, If you'd been born a Squeaker. **1889** BADEN-POWELL *Pigsticking* 28 At this period of his existence he is called a 'squeaker' and is not ridden.

e. *Zool.* (*a*) (See quots.) Also *attrib.* (*b*) = CICADA.

1887 GOODE *Fisheries U.S.* 651 The lady crab, sand crab, or squeaker crab (*Platyonichus ocellatus*), .. occurs on most sandy shores from Cape Cod to Mexico. **1897** 'NATALIAN' *S. Afr. Boy* viii. 76 The youthful genius who brought two squeakers—tree cicadæ—before school hours, and released one in each room. **1899** D. SHARP *Insects* 209 The adult *Pelobius tardus* is remarkable for its loud stridulation... The Insects are called squeakers in the Covent Garden market. **1959** S. J. BAKER *Drum* 147 Squeaker: A type of cicada.

3. a. *slang.* (See quot.)

1796 *Grose's Dict. Vulgar T.* (ed. 3) s.v., Organ pipes are likewise called squeakers.

b. A device or toy instrument for producing a squeaking sound; esp. as a party toy (see quot. 1980). Cf. SQUAWKER 1.

1878 *Grove's Dict. Music* I. 124 The 'squeaker' which children in the fields fashion out of joints in tall grass. **1894** *Westm. Gaz.* 8 March 6/3 A small wooden squeaker.. attached to an indiarubber balloon. **1930** [see *paper streamer* s.v. PAPER *sb.* 12]. **1939** N. COWARD *To step Aside* 49 She was seated on the knee of an Argentine with a paper fireman's hat on her head, blowing a squeaker. **1980** J. W. HILL *Intermediate Physics* v. 45 The party 'squeaker', a paper tube containing a weak coiled spring which uncoils when it is blown, works on the same principle.

4. *colloq.* **a.** A heavy blow. *rare*$^{-1}$.

1877 in *Casquet of Literature* I. 245/2 We must give him a squeaker quickly or all will go wrong, I tell you.

b. *N. Amer.* A game won by a very narrow margin.

1961 in WEBSTER. **1969** *Eugene* (Oregon) *Register-Guard* 3 Dec. 1D/1 Remember that 26–24 squeaker over Stanford, when the Indians kicked a field goal with 63 seconds left to 'win' the game. **1970** *Globe & Mail* (Toronto) 28 Sept. 18/8 Ottawa Rough Riders.. lost a squeaker to Montreal.

'squeakery. [f. SQUEAK *v.* + -ERY.] Squeaking character or quality.

1826 MISS MITFORD *Village* Ser. II. (1863) 377 It was the genuine man of puppets, the true squeakery, the 'real Simon Pure'. **1834** BECKFORD *Italy* II. 222 All these virtuosi.. were either contraltos of the softest note, or sopranos of the highest squeakery.

'squeaking, *vbl. sb.* [f. SQUEAK *v.*] The action of emitting or producing a squeak or squeaks.

1596 SHAKS. *Merch. V.* II. v. 30 (Q.[1]), When you heare the drumme, And the vile squealing of the wry-neckt Fife. **1653** H. MORE *Antid. Ath.* III. xiv. (1712) 130 The squeaking and roaring of tortured Beasts. *c* **1680** in *Verney Mem.* (1907) II. 321 There was fine squeeking and squeeling for a minute or two. **1770** LANGHORNE *Plutarch* (1851) I. 336/2 The squeaking of a rat.. [was] heard. **1786** MME. D'ARBLAY *Diary* 25 Dec., Now for the fiddlers!.. I.. hear over and over again all that fine squeaking, and then fall fast asleep. **1820** HAZLITT *Table-T.* xxviii, There is a mighty bustle at the door, a gibbering and squeaking in the lobbies. **1855** *Poultry Chron.* III. 536 It will save an incredible amount of.. squeaking, harsh grating, dismal creaking.

'squeaking, *ppl. a.* Also 6 **sweaking.** [f. SQUEAK *v.*]

1. a. Of the nature of a squeak or squeaks; characterized by squeaking.

1576 FLEMING *Panopl. Epist.* 277 Among these people,.. one.. made a harsh squeaking noyse. **1592** CHETTLE *Kindharts Dr.* (1841) 15 The one in a sweaking treble, the other in an ale-blowen base. *a* **1704** T. BROWN *Praise Drunkenness* Wks. 1730 I. 37 The drunkard's voice is hoarse and manly, not like the squeaking trils of an Eunuch. **1854** EMERSON *Lett. & Soc. Aims, Social Aims* Wks. (Bohn) III. 176 It seems to require several generations of education to train a squeaking.. habit out of a man.

b. Of the voice: Thin and shrill.

1803 *Med. Jrnl.* IX. 563 At an early period the voice was altered, and grew squeaking. **1828** SCOTT *F.M. Perth* viii, Said Dwining, with his squeaking voice. **1878** W. A. WRIGHT *Shaks. Jul. Cæsar* Notes 141 That ghosts had thin and squeaking voices was a belief in the time of Homer.

2. a. That squeaks; uttering squeaks.

1606 SHAKS. *Ant. & Cl.* v. ii. 220 And I shall see Some squeaking Cleopatra Boy my greatnesse. **1652** BENLOWES *Theoph.* v. viii. (1905) 368 Can squeaking reeds sound forth the organ's full delight. **1682** DRYDEN *Medal* 35 The loudest bagpipe of the squeaking train. *c* **1760** SMOLLETT *Burlesque Ode* 26 The squeaking pigs her bounty own'd. **1763** CHURCHILL *Poems, Apol.* Wks. 1767 I. 57 Italian fathers thus, with barb'rous rage, Fit helpless infants for the squeaking stage. **1802** MAR. EDGEWORTH *Moral T.* (1816) I. xiii. 106 The sound of a squeaking fiddle. **1837** CARLYLE *Fr. Rev.* II. IV. vii, A fanfaronading hollow Spectrum and squeaking and gibbering Shadow!

b. ***squeaking sand,*** sand that gives out a short, high-pitched sound when disturbed.

1966 *Sedimentology* VI. 136 A 'squeaking' sand was found by the writer in Gower, S. Wales and this has been used for comparison with the 'booming' sand of the desert. **1976** *Nature* 5 Feb. 368/2 The most common of the musical sediments is probably squeaking (otherwise known as singing, barking or whistling) sand which produces a high frequency note in the range 500–2,500 Hz.

Hence **'squeakingly** *adv.*

1611 COTGR., *Greslement*,.. shrilly, or sq[u]eakingly. *a* **1700** B. E. *Dict. Cant. Crew, To Whine*, to cry squeekingly, as at Conventicles.

'squeaklet. [-LET.] A little squeak.

1832 CARLYLE in *Fraser's Mag.* V. 379 Grating harsh thunder, or vehement shrew-mouse squeaklets.

squeaky ('skwi:kɪ), *a.* [f. SQUEAK *sb.* or *v.*]

a. Characterized by squeaking sounds; tending to squeak. Proverbial phr. ***the squeaky wheel gets the grease*** (and varr.): the person who makes the most fuss or trouble gets the attention.

1862 MISS YONGE *C'tess Kate* xii. (1880) 133 The loud squeaky key of the voice.. showed that she had worked herself up into a state of excitement. **1869** TOZER *Highl. Turkey* I. 219 They sang in nasal and squeaky tones. **1885** *Harper's Mag.* Dec. 78/1 What a scene of squeaky gossip in the moonlight! **1899** DOYLE *Duet* 238 An excellent piano.., but it is getting so squeaky in the upper notes.

[**1937** in J. Bartlett *Familiar Quotations* 518/2 The wheel that squeaks the loudest is the one that gets the grease. **1948** in B. Stevenson *Home Bk. Prov.* 2883/2, I hate to be a kicker, I always long for peace, But the wheel that does the squeaking is the one that gets the grease.] **1969** J. LA MARSH *Mem. Bird in Gilded Cage* x. 291 Mrs. Kinnear did.. put on a most relentless campaign over the years.. in line with the best of political principles—'the squeaky wheel got the grease'. **1974** *Hansard* (Canada) 17 Oct. 502/1 It is the old story: the squeaky wheel gets the grease.

b. Of the voice: = SQUEAKING *ppl. a.* 1 b.

1863 KINGSLEY *Water-Bab.* iii. 102 The tiniest, shrillest, squeakiest little voice you ever heard. **1881** MRS. MOLESWORTH *Adv. Herr Baby* 36 My little voice must have sounded very faint and squeaky from out of the trunk.

c. *Comb.* **squeaky clean** (also with hyphen), (of hair, etc.) washed and rinsed so clean that it squeaks; completely clean; freq. *fig.*, above criticism, beyond reproach.

1975 *Country Life* 8 May 1176/2 *No one*.. is in a position to criticise... No one is, in the current idiom, that squeaky-clean. **1976** N. THORNBURG *Cutter & Bone* i. 24 Still towelling his hair, Bone returned to the living room... 'Behold, the squeaky clean Richard Bone.' **1978** *Guardian Weekly* 13 Aug. 16/2 The [Ford Motor] company has denied making any illegal payments, claiming that it is 'squeaky clean' in this area. **1980** [see SET-ASIDE *sb. phr.*]. **1981** L. DEIGHTON *XPD* xvii. 155 His.. long dark hair was wavy and squeaky clean.

Hence **'squeakyish** *a.*

1832 WILSON in *Blackw. Mag.* XXXII. 865 Performers with.. punyish figures that must strut, and squeakyish voices that must crack.

squeal (skwi:l), *sb.* Also 8–9 **squeel**; *north. dial.* 8–9 **sweel**, 9 **sweeal**. [f. the vb.]

1. a. A more or less prolonged sharp cry; a shrill scream. Also *fig.*

1747 RELPH *Misc. Poems* 2 The shearers aw brast out In sweels of laughter. **1776** PENNANT *Brit. Zool.* (ed. 4) I. 85 It is observable that the male otters never make any noise when taken: but the pregnant females emit a most shrill squeal. **1786** BURNS *Holy Fair* xiii, His lengthen'd chin, his turn'd up snout, His eldritch squeel an' gestures. **1835** MARRYAT *J. Faithful* xix, All of a sudden we heard a rustling in the furze, and then a loud squeal. **1853** R. S. SURTEES *Sponge's Sp. Tour* ix. 42 Some of the more lively of the horses.. evinced their approbation of the move, by sundry squeals and capers. **1894** BIRRELL *Ess.* viii. 82 There is nothing.. [they] like better than to hear the squeal of some self-torturing atom of humanity.

b. A sharp shrill sound.

1867 MACGREGOR *Voy. Alone* (1868) 16 The shrill squeal of a pulley thrills my ear with pleasure. **1897** MARY KINGSLEY *W. Africa* 583 The shrill squeal of the wind, the roar of the thunder, and the rush of the rain.

2. *Sc.* A quarrel or broil.

1788 PICKEN *Poems* 65 Ye needna gang sae far afiel' To tell how Tea has bred a squeel.

3. *U.S.* **a.** *slang.* An act of informing against another.

1872 G. P. BURNHAM *Memoirs of U.S. Secret Service* 152 This 'squeal' among the 'queersmen' brings this foul business straight home to *you*. **1903** *N.Y. Sun* 5 Nov. 3 Ever since his so-called 'squeal' at the Lexow investigation he has been a marked man. **1907** 'O. HENRY' *Trimmed Lamp* 185, I always thought that Kike's squeal on his boss was about the lowest-down play that ever happened.

b. *Police slang.* A call for police assistance or investigation; a report of a case investigated by the police.

1949 S. KINGSLEY *Detective Story* I. 14 'This is Jim's squeal, ain't it?'.. 'Yeah, I'll take it... This is my partner's case.' *Ibid.* II. 86 Get me the old files on that Cottsworth squeal! **1960** 'E. MCBAIN' *See them Die* vii. 79 Parker's on the prowl, Hernandez is answering a squeal. **1972** B. GARFIELD *Line of Succession* (1974) I. 3 The first cop said, 'Do it. Send in a squeal—we'll want the wagon.' **1973** 'E. MCBAIN' *Hail to Chief* i. 6 The appearance of Homicide cops at the scene of a murder was mandatory, even though the subsequent investigation was handled by the precinct detectives catching the squeal.

squeal (skwi:l), *v.* Forms: 4–5, 7 **squele** (*north.* 4 **suele**, 5 **swele**), 6 *Sc.* **squeil(l**, 7–9 **squeel**, 7 **squeale**, 7– **squeal.** [Imitative.]

1. *intr.* To utter (or give *out*) a more or less prolonged loud sharp cry, esp. by reason of pain or sudden alarm; to scream shrilly:

a. Of persons.

a **1300** *Cursor M.* 1344 A new born barn lay in þe croppe, .. þar him þoght it lay suelland [*Gött.* squeland]. *c* **1375** *Sc. Leg. Saints* xxvii. (*Machor*) 145 He.. squelyt gret & raryt ȝarne, as kynd gaf to sic a barne. **1508** KENNEDIE *Flyting w. Dunbar* 39 Baith Iohne the Ross and thow sall squeill and skirle. **1535** STEWART *Cron. Scot.* II. 525 He ran.. Fra place to place,.. With mony schout ay squeilland like a kid. **1601** SHAKS. *Jul. C.* II. ii. 24 Ghosts did shrieke and squeale about the streets. **1671** SKINNER, To Squall or Squeal out. **1676** HOBBES *Iliad* 339 Enrag'd she.. threw it from her, tore her hair, and squeal'd. **1740** RICHARDSON *Pamela* I. 235 She.. took hold of my Arm, so roughly, and gave me such a Pull, as made me squeal out. **1778** MISS BURNEY *Evelina* xlii, They hide themselves, and run away, and squeel and squall, like any thing mad. **1846** LANDOR *Imag. Conv.* Wks. II. 92 He pinched my ear so bitterly, I was fain to squeel. **1851** D. JERROLD *St. Giles* xxxv, But for appearances,.. she'd have squealed no more than a rose-bud pulled from a bush.

b. Of animals or birds.

a **1400–50** [see SQUEALING *vbl. sb.*]. **1513** DOUGLAS *Æneid* VIII. vi. 112 The catell eik.. Baith squeill and low in thai ilk plenteus gatis. **1535** [see prec.]. **1684** *Lond. Gaz.* No. 1903/4 A Blood bay Stone Horse, between 14 and 15 hands high, being much given to bite and strike and squeel. **1688** R. HOLME *Armoury* II. 134/2 When he sendeth forth his Cry,.. a Rat Squeleth, or Squaketh. **1798** EDGEWORTH *Pract. Educ.* (1811) II. 450 He bit off the ear of a pig because it squealed when he was ringing it. **1856** KANE *Arct. Expl.* I. xxiii. 290 Tern were very numerous, hundreds of them squealing and screeching in flocks. **1879** BLACK *Macleod of D.* I. 167 You hear the rabbit squealing with fright long before the weasel is at him.

2. Of things: To emit or produce a shrill or strident sound.

1596 [see SQUEALING *vbl. sb.*]. **1658** tr. *Porta's Nat. Magic* XIX. 386 The voice is changed in divers tunes, one note is sweet and pleasant, two, squele and jar. **1727** SOMERVILLE *Fables* XIV. i, Here tortur'd cats-gut squeals amain, Guittars in softer notes complain. **1824** HEBER *Jrnl.* (1828) I. ix. 239 Different musical instruments were strumming, thumping, squeeling and rattling. **1859** JEPHSON *Brittany* vii. 99 Then the biniou or bagpipe squeals and grunts.

3. *slang.* To turn informer; to inform or 'peach' *on* a person. (Cf. SQUEAK *v.* 2.)

1846 *National Police Gaz.* (U.S.) 413/2 Some dozen of the infamous rogues, well known to them, who infest that city, will be 'pulled' until they find one that will 'squeal'. **1865** *Slang Dict.* 244 *Squeal*, to inform, peach. A north country variation of squeak. **1892** *Montreal Gaz.* 5 Nov. 8/2 This revelation led Gideon to 'squeal' and he to-day fortified his statement.. by much documentary evidence. **1896** *Boston* (Mass.) *Jrnl.* 29 Dec. 2/1 His pal,.. who is now serving time for counterfeiting, and who squealed on him.

4. *trans.* To utter or produce with a shrill, grating, or squeaking sound. Also with *out*.

1675 COVEL in *Early Voy. Levant* (Hakluyt Soc.) 211 There are trumpets, which come in onely now and then to squeel out a loud note or two. **1833** M. SCOTT *Tom Cringle* xii, 'Here, sir,' squealed Timothy. **1871** L. STEPHEN *Playgr. Eur.* xii. (1894) 294 Pigs.. squeal emphatic disapproval of their enforced journey. **1883** LD. R. GOWER *My Remin.* I. vii. 130 The fiddle squealed the old dance music of the old-fashioned quadrille.

5. Quasi-*adv.* With a squeal.

1849 MRS. CARLYLE *Lett.* II. 56 Squeal went the engine; we were off.

squeal, *a.* *s.w. dial.* ? *Obs.* [? Related to QUEAL *v.*] Feeble, frail.

1794 WOLCOT (P. Pindar) *J. Ploughshare's Royal Visit Exeter* Wks. 1816 III. 367 That he was weak, and ould, and squeal, And zeldom made a hearty meal. **1795** —— *Pindariana* Ibid. 336 Why should [he] be afraid of horns, Who married a poor squeal, starv'd cat, for money?

squealer ('skwi:lə(r)). [f. SQUEAL *v.*]

1. In bird-names: (see quots.).

1854 J. WARTER *Last of O. Squires* vii. 66 In the summer nothing broke the silence that reigned around, save the voice of the squealers—the country-name for swifts. **1879** MISS JACKSON *Shropsh. Word-bk.* 223 The Swift... This bird's loud piercing cry has obtained for it the name of *squealer*. **1888** G. TRUMBULL *Names Birds* 91 Harlequin Duck,.. known also as Squealer at Machias Port, Me. *Ibid.* 196 Golden Plover... Mr. Browne records Squealer in his list of gunners' names at Plymouth Bay.

2. One who or that which squeals. Also *transf.*

1865 *Slang Dict.* 244 *Squealer*,.. an illegitimate baby. **1897** *Daily News* 25 May 2/4 In one village a venerable squealer [a pig] was driven past a whole line of soldiers by a dog.

b. *slang.* An informer.

1865 in *Slang Dict.* 244. **1901** *Daily Chron.* 17 Sept. 7/2 It will not reap many 'squealers', because the men who might tell things to cause damage will not dare.

c. A complainer.

1889 *Columbus* (Ohio) *Dispatch*, In nine cases out of ten, the editor gives the squealer more privileges in the way of reply than he is entitled to by equity.

'squealing, *vbl. sb.* [f. SQUEAL *v.*] The action of the verb, in various senses.

c **1325** *Metr. Hom.* 167 For quen the childe es born, sal I Do it of daw sa priuely, That na wiht sal the squeling here. *a* **1400–50** *Alexander* 4112 For with þe sweling of þe swyne we sall þaim all voide. **1596** SHAKS. *Merch. V.* II. v. 30 The vile squealing of the wry-neckt Fife. *c* **1680** in *Verney Mem.* (1907) II. 321 There was fine squeeking and squeeling for a minute or two. **1791** HUDDESFORD *Salmagundi* 123 Upon a trestle Pig was laid And a sad squealing sure It made. 1837 CARLYLE *Fr. Rev.* I. II. ii, The cries, the squealings of children, of infirm persons, and other assistants. 1878 BLACK *Green Past.* xvi, They heard the squealing of a young cock outside.

'squealing, *ppl. a.* [f. as prec.]

1. That utters or emits squeals; screaming.

a 1300 *Cursor M.* 5626 þe kings doghter . . sagh þe vessel on þe flodd; . . A squeland child þer-in sco fand. *c* 1375 *Sc. Leg. Saints* xvi. (*Magdalene*) 484 To þis squeland barne ȝe [suld] spare. 1642 J. BALL *Answ. to Can* i. 143 Cathed. Churches . . where . . Singing men, . . Squealing Choristers, Organ-Players, . . &c. live in great idlenesse. 1689 R. COX *Hibernia Angl.* I. Apparatus 1 1 b, A Bagpipe, which is a squealing Engine, fit only for a Bear-Garden. 1709 STEELE *Tatler* No. 15 ¶2 She pinch'd me, and called me squealing Chit. 1879 GEO. ELIOT *Theo. Such* ii. 35 A small squealing black pig. 1897 MARY KINGSLEY *W. Africa* 586 A terrific rain-storm . . accompanied by a squealing, bitter cold wind.

b. ***squealing hawk***: (see quot.).

1884 *Harper's Mag.* March 622 The red-tailed hawk . . by some is called the squealing hawk.

2. Of the nature of a squeal.

1879 JEFFERIES *Wild Life* 338 Now and then a peculiar squealing sound may be heard proceeding from the grass. 1899 *Allbutt's Syst. Med.* VII. 506 Peculiar squealing cry.

squeam, *sb. rare.* [Back-formation from SQUEAMISH *a.*] A qualm or scruple (*of* conscience).

1798 *Geraldina* II. 240 Do not let any squeams of conscience prevent your attentions. 1888 *Interior* (Chicago) 5 Apr., Without squeam or apology, . . the mutual bearings of truths are to be . . unshrinkingly maintained.

†**squeam**, *v. Obs. rare.* [f. as prec., or from SQUEAMOUS *a.*] *intr.* To turn sick or squeamish.

1576 TURBERV. *Venerie* 363 And as for gaines men dive in every streame, All frawdes be fishe, their stomachs never squeame. 1765 C. SMART tr. *Phædrus* IV. vi, This threat is to the fools, that squeam At every thing of good esteem.

'squeamer. *rare*⁻¹. [Cf. prec.] One who turns squeamish or faint.

1887 W. S. GILBERT *Ruddigore* II, Coward, poltroon, shaker, squeamer.

squeamish ('skwiːmɪʃ), *a.*, *adv.*, and *sb.* Forms: α. 5 **squaymysch**, 6 **-ysh**, **-ish(e**, 6–7 **squaimish(e**; 6 **squeim-**, **squeymish**, **skeymishe**; 6–7 **squamish**, *north. dial.* 8–9 **swaimish**, 9 **swamish**. β. 6–7 **squemish(e**, 7 **squeemish** (9 *dial.* **skeemish**), 6– **squeamish**; *north. dial.* 7, 9 **sweamish**, 9 **sweemish**. [var. of *squaymes*, *squemes* SQUEAMOUS *a.*, by alteration of suffix.]

I. 1. Readily affected with nausea; easily turned sick or faint; physically unable to support or swallow anything disagreeable.

a. Of persons. †Also const. *of*.

c 1450 *Trevisa's Barth. De P.R.* v. xlv. (Bodl. MS.), And þerefor me schal not be squaymysch of vrine, for in many þinges it is profitable and leefe. 1584 GREENE *Arbasto* Wks. (Grosart) III. 192 Art thou so squemish that thou canst not see wine but thou must surfet? 1684 tr. *Bonet's Merc. Compit.* VI. 164 Purging Potions, taken by squeamish Persons, . . cause a Shivering. 1702 GAY *Achilles* III, She is so squeamish and so frequently out of order. 1744 BERKELEY *Siris* §3 Wks. 1871 II. 367 For children and squeamish persons it may be made weaker. 1777 COOK *Voy., Pacific* (1784) II. III. x. 186 We found that he was too squeamish to drink turtle's blood.

fig. 1614 RALEIGH *Hist. World* II. (1634) 486 Yet am I not so squeamish, that I can well enough digest a good Booke. 1740 CIBBER *Apol.* (1756) I. 11 As his patron knew the patient was squeamish, he was induced to sweeten the medicine to his taste.

transf. *a* 1677 BARROW *Serm.* Wks. 1686 III. 88 Thou hast a squeamish conscience, which cannot relish this, cannot digest that advantageous course of proceeding.

b. Of the stomach.

1620 VENNER *Via Recta* ii. 152 It is very good for such as haue squamish & waterie stomacks. *a* 1707 BP. PATRICK *Comm. 2 Sam.* xiii. 5 He would have him pretend that his stomach was so nice and squeamish, that he would like nothing that his servants dressed. 1851 THACKERAY *Eng. Hum.* v. (1876) 318 Their squeamish stomachs sickened at the rough fare.

fig. 1642 FULLER *Holy & Prof. State* v. ii. 363 The stomach of his Holinesse not being so squeamish, but that he would take a good almes from dirty hands. 1760 STERNE *Tr. Shandy* IV. xxxii, Nor do I value whose squeamish stomach takes offence at it. 1843 LOWELL *Glance behind the Curtain* 85 But now the uneasy stomach of the time Turns squeamish at them both.

2. Slightly affected with nausea; sickish, qualmish.

1660 PEPYS *Diary* 7 April, This day . . the wind grew high, and . . I began to be dizzy and squeamish. 1689 *Muses Farew. Popery* 81 When Satan was squeamish, and long'd for a Dainty, The Pope Fricasseed him this New Four-and-twenty. 1756 MRS. CALDERWOOD in *Coltness Collect.* (Maitland Club) 128 Then down I must go, and into bed as soon as possible, very very squeamish. I could not keep my feet in the cabin. 1817 J. EVANS *Excurs. Windsor*, etc. 485 Passed the North Foreland with a little swell, and most of the passengers were squeamish. 1887 *Poor Nellie* (1888) 411 You're feeling squeamish, I see, so take my advice and have a brandy-and-soda.

†**3.** Apt to produce qualms; = QUALMISH *a.* 3.

a 1571 JEWEL *Serm.* i. Wks. (1611) 974 When they had manna in their mouths, they thought it a loathsome and a squeamish meat.

4. Characterized by a sickish feeling. *rare.*

1670 COVEL in *Early Voy. Levant* (Hakluyt Soc.) 102 Our Freshmen passengers were all in a miserable, squeamish, and puking condition. 1748 THOMSON *Cast. Indol.* I. lxxvii, Fast by her side a listless maiden pin'd, With aching head, and squeamish heart-burnings.

II. †**5.** Averse, unwilling, or backward *to* do something. *Obs.*

1553 *Respublica* I. iii. 278, I shall tell Respublica ye can beste governe: bee not ye than skeymishe to take in hand the stern. 1589 PUTTENHAM *Eng. Poesie* I. viii. (Arb.) 38 Let none other meaner person . . be any whit squeimish to let it be publisht vnder their names, for reason serues it, and modestie doth not repugne.

6. Averse to freedom or familiarity of intercourse; distant, reserved, coy, cold.

Also, in mod. dial., modest, bashful, diffident, shy.

α. 1561 T. HOBY tr. *Castiglione's Courtyer* III. (1577) N vij, This woman ought not therefore . . [to] be so squeimish and make wise to abhorre both the company & the talke. 1565 COOPER *Thesaurus* s.v. *Delicium*, *Delicias facere*, to make strange and dally, because he would be intreated: to be squaymish. *a* 1586 SIDNEY *Arcadia* I. (1912) 118 Yet for countenance sake, he seemed very squeimish, in respect of the charge he had of the Princesse Pamela. 1788– in northern dial. glossaries (in form *swaimish* or *swamish*).

β. 1580 HOLLYBAND *Treas. Fr. Tong*, *Desdaigneux*, squemish, coye, disdainfull. 1584 LYLY *Sappho* I. iv. 7 Proud elfe! how squeamish he is become alreadie, vsing both disdaineful lookes, And imperious words. 1607 DEKKER & MARSTON *Northw. Hoe* IV. D.'s Wks. 1873 III. 59 A comely country mayd, not squeamish nor afraid, To let Gentlemen touch. *c* 1665 *Roxb. Ball.* (1886) VI. 256 Virgins, take my advice, be not disdainful; Neither be coy and nice, squemish nor scornful. 1710 PALMER *Proverbs* 115 A woman of virtue keeps a guard upon her eye, and yet don't affect to look soure, squeamish, and suspicious.

transf. 1583 MELBANCKE *Philotimus* C j b, As for Pallas, she is dainty, but not squemish, hard to be found, but easy to be intreated.

Comb. 1603 FLORIO *Montaigne* II. i. (1894) 166 Fair and soft, as squemish-honest as she seems, . . conclude not rashly an inviolable chastitie to be on your Mistresse.

†**b.** Const. *of*: Averse to being free or generous with (something). *Obs.*

1566 PAINTER *Pal. Pleas.* I. (1569) 195 The more she proved the King inflamed with her love, the more squeymish she was of her beautie. 1576 FLEMING *Panopl. Epist.* 37 You haue shewed your selfe . . not squemish or deintie of your singular beneuolence. *a* 1625 FLETCHER *Woman's Prize* v. i, *Petro.* I think 'twere well you would see her. *Row.* If you please, Sir; I am not squeamish of my visitation.

†**c.** Of actions, etc.: Characterized by coldness or coyness. *Obs.*

1577 STANYHURST *Descr. Irel.* Ep. Ded. in *Holinshed*, I was by them weied not to beare my selfe coy, by giuing my entier friends in so reasonable a request a squemish repulse. 1600 J. LANE *Tom Tel-troth* (1876) 119 Some gogle with the eyes, some squint-eyd looke, Some at their fellowes, squemish sheepes-eyes cast. 1603 FLORIO *Montaigne* I. xx. (1632) 42 Their wanton, squeamish, quarellous countenances, which setting us a fire, extinguish us.

7. Readily offended by anything approaching immodesty or indecency; easily shocked; prudish.

1567 HARMAN *Caveat* (1869) 55 Because the sight shoulde not abash her shamefast maydens, nether loth her squaymysh sight. 1677 W. HUGHES *Man of Sin* II. v. 94 If the good Man blush'd, . . he may be pardon'd for this once, being not so squeamish often. 1742 FIELDING *J. Andrews* I. xii, This the maid readily promised to perform, . . being . . not so squeamish as the lady. 1842 LOVER *Handy Andy* xvi, 'I'm not squeamish, sir,' said Miss Augusta; 'but it's dreadful to be shut up with a man who has no clothes on him'. 1858 HAWTHORNE *Fr. & It. Note-bks.* I. 217 As to the nudities, . . they might well have startled a not very squeamish eye. 1892 BARING-GOULD *Strange Survivals* x. 220 Riddles more or less good, some coarse, and some profane; but the age was not squeamish.

†**b.** Sensitive; shrinking from contact with anything rude or rough. *Obs.*

1707 *Curios. in Husb. & Gard.* 61 Sulphureous Matters that compose the Flowers . . are soon devour'd by the open Air, which destroys those frail and squeamish Beauties. 1782 COWPER *Poet, Oyster & Sensit. Pl.* 55 And, as for you, my Lady Squeamish, Who reckon ev'ry touch a blemish. 1785 BURKE *Sp. Nabob of Arcot's Debts* Wks. I. 345 The person so squeamish, so timid, so trembling lest the winds of heaven should visit too roughly.

8. Sensitively or excessively fastidious, scrupulous, particular, or punctilious, with regard to standards of action or belief.

1581 T. NEWTON *Seneca's Trag.* Ded., And whereas it is by some squeymish Areopagites surmyzed that the reading of these Tragedies . . cannot be digested without great danger [etc.]. 1602 MARSTON *Antonio's Rev.* II. i, High honour'd blood's too squemish to assent, And lend a hand to an ignoble act. 1676 W. ALLEN *Addr. Non-Conform.* 135 When they are nice, curious, and squeamish about undetermined circumstances in forms of administration. *c* 1690 LD. DELAMER *Disc. Incouragers of Popery* Wks. (1694) 93 Let then the high Church be more charitable, and the Dissenters less stiff and sweamish. 1724 WELTON *Chr. Faith & Pract.* 70 They were so squeamish upon the literal, and so loose and moderate in the moral sense. 1768–74 TUCKER *Lt. Nat.* (1834) I. 272 Another, who had not the same squeamish disposition, might have found enjoyments enow under general censure . . to make life desirable. 1829 A. CUNNINGHAM *Brit. Painters* i. 41 If Laud had not doated on trifles, and the Presbyterians had been squeamish about them. 1855 MACAULAY *Hist. Eng.* xiii. III. 274 Where enthusiasts are ready . . to be destroyed for trifles magnified into importance by a squeamish conscience. 1881 *Scribner's Mag.* XXII. 144 Some of the early American statesmen, doubtless, were not any too squeamish in their political maneuverings.

Comb. 1581 STUDLEY *Seneca's Agamemnon* A iij, Although as squemishe hearted men those priests in bedlem rage.

b. With preps., as *about*, *as to*, *at*, *of*.

1581 J. BELL *Haddon's Answ. Osorius* 417 But I will not be so squemish about these trifles. 1582 N. T. (Rhem.) p. xx, Why should we be squamish at newe wordes or phrases in the scripture which are necessarie. *a* 1660 *Contemp. Hist. Irel.* (Ir. Archæol. Soc.) I. 276 Neuer squemishe of any your proceedings. 1662 STILLINGFL. *Orig. Sacræ* III. i. §3 Those whose minds are so coy and squeamish as to any thing of Divine revelation. 1865 BRIGHT *Sp., Canada* 67 They are not so squeamish as to what they say about us. 1872 E. YATES *Castaway* II. vii, I don't pretend . . to be squeamish about such matters.

c. Marked or characterized by fastidiousness or scrupulousness.

1593 G. HARVEY *Pierce's Super.* Wks. (Grosart) II. 158 All resteth vpon a case of conscience, as nice and squeamish a scruple [etc.]. *a* 1658 CLEVELAND *Wks.* (1687) 99 Your pen is coy, and you ware the Holy Ground and Holy Coyn with a squeamish Pretention. 1776 COWPER *Let.* Wks. 1837 XV. 36 You perceive I have not made a squeamish use of your obliging offer. 1824 W. IRVING *T. Trav.* I. 10 In a bachelor's house . . there is no lady to stand upon squeamish points about lodging gentlemen in old holes and corners. 1884 BROWNING *Ferishtah* (1885) 73 So, with thy squeamish scruple.

9. Fastidious or dainty with respect to what one handles, uses, or comes in contact with.

1608 TOPSELL *Serpents* 789 If we would . . not be so squeamish as to refuse those wholesome medicines which are easie to be had. 1697 VANBRUGH *Prov. Wife* III. i, I'll warrant it's some squeamish minx as my wife, that's grown so dainty of late, she finds fault even with a dirty shirt. 1746 FRANCIS tr. *Hor., Sat.* II. vi. 176 If delicacies could invite My squeamish courtier's appetite, Who turn'd his nose at every dish. 1800 MISS EDGEWORTH *Belinda* xxii, I have heard . . that the passion of love, which can endure caprice, vice, [etc.] is notwithstanding so squeamish as to be instantaneously disgusted by the perception of folly in the object beloved. 1860 W. H. G. KINGSTON *Pirate Medit.* I. 12 He's the fellow to make your kid-glove wearing gentlemen dip their hands in the tar-bucket . . if he sees they are in any way squeamish about it. 1871 L. STEPHEN *Playgr. Eur.* (1894) ix. 206 Our nerves . . are unduly delicate, and our tastes too squeamish.

absol. 1828 (*title*), The Adventures of Doctor Comicus; . . a Comic Satirical Poem, for the Squeamish and the Queer.

†**10. a.** Having aversion or antipathy *at* or *towards* something. *Obs.*

1581 J. BELL *Haddon's Answer to Osorius* 249 b, Beyng squeymish at Luthers speache. 1654 WHITLOCK *Zootom.* 360 Squemish towards the present, and longing for Innovation.

†**b.** ***to make squeamish***, to hesitate or shrink; to show dislike. *Obs.*

1611 SPEED *Hist. Gt. Brit.* VII. xliii. §4. 355 This great Oracle made it not squemish to giue them this aduice. *a* 1617 BAYNE *Lect.* (1634) 197 If he [God] delight in us, what matter if the world make squemish of us?

'squeamishly, *adv.* [f. prec.]

†**1.** In a reserved or distant manner; coldly, disdainfully. *Obs.*

1571 GOLDING *Calvin on Ps.* lxxi. 15 Not to taste Gods goodnes lyghtly, and as it were squeymishly. 1580 HOLLYBAND *Treas. Fr. Tong*, *Par Mespris*, disdainefullye, squemishly. 1598 HAKLUYT *Voy.* I. I. 8 Squemishly, frowningly, or skornefully shunning the ragged and tattered sleeue of any suppliant. 1647 HEXHAM I, Squaimishly, *verachtelick ofte onwaerdighlick*.

2. Fastidiously, delicately, daintily.

1616 B. JONSON *Masques* Wks. 911 Howsoeuer some may squemishly crie out. *a* 1670 HACKET *Cent. Serm.* 219 But I marvel at those expositors who are squemishly conceited against that opinion. 1768–74 TUCKER *Lt. Nat.* (1834) II. 498 If the plea of conscience was admitted . . we should grow so squeamishly conscientious [etc.]. 1782 T. WARTON *Rowley Enq.* 70 The modern delicacy of the writer . . , who thus squeamishly introduces this tale of Saxon perfidy. 1838 DICKENS *Pickw.* xxxi, If she had been less proudly and squeamishly brought up. 1845 CAMPBELL *Lives Chancellors* (1857) V. cx. 148 Bolingbroke . . squeamishly says: 'The first regulation . . is decency'.

3. With a tendency to nausea or sickness.

1843 LE FEVRE *Life Trav. Phys.* III. i. III. 89, I sought my cot, . . rolled about for an hour rather squeamishly, and then fell asleep.

'squeamishness. [f. as prec. + -NESS.]

1. The state of being affected with nausea or qualms; sickishness.

a 1586 SIDNEY *Arcadia* II. (Sommer) 165 Mopsa . . at the first for squeamishnes going vp & downe, with her head like a boate in a storme. 1655 CULPEPPER, etc. tr. *Riverius* I. vii. 30 These are forerunners of our Epilepsy; disdain of meat, or immoderate Appetite, Squeamishness, heart-burning. 1692 E. WALKER tr. *Epictetus, Mor.* xxxv, You should consider . . Whether that Squeamishness you can forget, That makes you keep an Almanack for Meat. 1756 C. SMART tr. *Horace, Sat.* II. ii. (1826) II. 97 When exercise has worked off your squeamishness . . then let me see you despise mean viands. 1822–7 GOOD *Study Med.* (1829) I. 359 Pains in the stomach, nausea, squeamishness. 1878 J. MACGREGOR in F. Balfour *Life* (1912) xi. 331 We had a desperately rough passage, which in spite of one day's squeamishness I greatly enjoyed.

b. Const. *of* (the stomach). Also *fig.*

1648 GAGE *West Ind.* 102 The women of that City it seems pretend much weaknesse and squemishnesse of stomach. 1712 STEELE *Spect.* No. 286 ¶1 A good Constitution appears in the Soundness and Vigour of the Parts, not in the Squeamishness of the Stomach. 1715 tr. *Pancirollus' Memor. Things* I. Pref. 6 A voluminous Paraphrase not agreeing with the squeamishness of an Oxford Stomach.

†**2. a.** Disdainfulness; haughty reserve. *Obs.*

1580 HOLLYBAND *Treas. Fr. Tong*, *Desdaing*, disdaine, despite, squeamishnesse. 1611 COTGR. s.v. *Boutique*, A prouerbe taxing th' enuie, or squeamishnesse of cunning Artists, who . . conceale from the world their excellent gifts. 1647 HEXHAM I, Squaimishnesse, *verachtinge*.

†**b.** Modest reserve or coyness. *Obs.*⁻¹
1720 MRS. MANLEY *Power of Love* (1741) I. 41 If her Vertue and Squeamishness should reject the Offers of his Heart.

3. The quality or condition of being highly or excessively fastidious or dainty in some respect.
1654 WHITLOCK *Zootomia* 261 It being a Squeamishnesse to forbeare satisfying his Appetite.. because somewhat may be wanting in some Dishes Preparation. **1693** *Apol. Clergy Scotl.* 106 A Fanatick Squeamishness that will not allow the Title of Doctor to any Clergy Man. **1711** *Countrey-Man's Lett. Curat.* 58 They address'd His Majesty, and Roundly Condemn'd the Bishops for their Squeamishness. **1782** MISS BURNEY *Cecilia* VI. iv, Now pray speak the truth without squeamishness. **1839** DICKENS *Nickleby* xvi, I have undergone too much.. to feel pride or squeamishness now. **1885** *Law Times* LXXIX. 223/2 The squeamishness of certain judges has contributed not a little to the result.

'squeamous, *a.* Now *north. dial.* Forms: α. 4 scoymus, 5 -es, -os, -ous; 4–5 squoymous, 6 squymouse; 4–5 **skoymus**, 4–6 -ous, 4 -os, 5 -es, 6 -ys, -ose, 9 **skymous**. β. 4–6 **squeymous** (5 sqwey-), 4 squaymus, 5–6 -ous, 5 squaymes, -os(e, scaymes, skeymous, -ows(e; 5 sweymows, *north. dial.* 8 **swamas**, 8–9 **swamous**, 9 -us, swaim-, swaymous. γ. 5 squemes, 6 -ous. [a. AF. *escoymous*, *escomos*, of obscure origin. Cf. ESQUAYMOUS *a.*

Forms without initial *s* also occur, as *queymous* (see QUEIMISH *a.*) and *coymous* (see sense 3 β).]

1. = SQUEAMISH *a.* 1 a.
13.. *Coer de L.* 3485 Was non off hem that eete lyste; Kyng Richard.. sayde: Frendes, be nought squoymous. **1398** TREVISA *Barth. De P.R.* VII. lxvii. (Bodl. MS.), þey þat beþ y-bete with a wode hounde.. dredeþ watere most.. and beþ agrised þer of fulle sore and scoymos also. **1566** DRANT *Horace, Sat.* iv. G viij b, There must be brothe for squaymous folke, and spices all of pleasure. **1882** *Lanc. Gloss.* 243 *Skymous*, squeamish, fastidious in eating.

2. Distant, disdainful, fastidious.
c **1325** *Lai le Freine* 62 A proude dame and an envieous,.. Squeymous and eke scorning; To ich woman sche hadde envie. **13..** *E.E. Allit. P.* B. 21 Nif he nere scoymus & skyg & non scaþe louied, Hit were a meruayl. *c* **1440** *Promp. Parv.* 457/2 Skeymowse, or sweymows,.. *abhominativus*. **1847** HALLIWELL, *Squemous*, saucy. *Lanc.* **1886** *Rochdale Gloss.* 80 *Skymous*, squeamish; over-nice.

b. *north. dial.* Modest, shy.
1483 *Cath. Angl.* 357/1 Squaymose, *verecundus*. **1703** THORESBY *Let. to Ray*, *Swamous*, modest. **1790** MRS. WHEELER *Westmld. Dial.* (1821) 43 Ise nae way swamas. **1828** CARR *Craven Gloss.* II. 307 Poor Williams is a swamous, cowardly chap. **1847–** in dial. glossaries (Cumb., Yks.).

†**3.** Having or feeling abhorrence, repugnance, or detestation *of* something. *Obs.*
α. **13..** *E.E. Allit. P.* B. 598 He is so skoymos of þat skaþe, he scarrez bylyue. *Ibid.* 1148 So is he scoymus of scaþe þat scylful is euer. *a* **1400** *Prymer* (1891) 102 Wickednesse y hadde in hatrede and y was skoymes þer of. **1495** *Trevisa's De P.R.* VIII. xii. (W. de W.) 319 They that ben subgette to Saturnus.. ben not skoymous of foule and stynkyng clothynge.
β. *c* **1386** CHAUCER *Miller's T.* 151 He was somdel squaymous [*Camb.* coymous] Of fartyng, and of speche daungerous. **1398** TREVISA *Barth. De P.R.* VIII. xxiii. (Tollem. MS.), Not skeymous of foule and stynkynge cloþynge. **15..** *Piers of Fullham* 70 in Hazl. *E.P.P.* II. 4 Be alway squaymous of suche sklaunders.
γ. *c* **1410** LOVE *Bonavent. Mirr.* vi. (Gibbs' MS.), þei were not squemes of þe stable.. nor of heye nor of suche oþer abiecte sympolnes.

†**4.** = SQUEAMISH *a.* 5. *Obs.*
1387 TREVISA *Higden* (Rolls) VII. 461 Sche.. was nouȝt squaymus to wasche seke menis feet. *c* **1400** *Prymer* 7 Thou were not squoymous to take þe maidenes wombe to delyuere mankynde. *a* **1450** *Knt. de la Tour* 155 Atte sum tyme she wolde haue.. be right scoymous to haue do the seruice. **1535** in Loftie *Mem. Savoy* (1878) 10 Whether he be.. lovying to the poore, and not skoymys or lothesome to visite theym. *c* **1550** BALE *K. Johan* (E.E.D.S.) 184 Thou art not skoymose thy fantasy for to tell.

squeamy ('skwi:mɪ), *a.* orig. *U.S.* [f. SQUEAM(ISH *a.* + -Y¹.] = SQUEAMISH *a.*
1838 C. GILMAN *Recoll. Southern Matron* v. 44, I feel so squeamy-like at my stomach. **1863** 'E. KIRKE' *My Southern Friends* v. 76 Doan't be squeamy, gal; out with it. **1880** *Harper's Mag.* Sept. 582/1, I expect they'd eet so much sweet it kinder made 'em squeamy. **1908** H. G. WELLS *War in Air* v. 174 They're a bit squeamy now, but you wait till they've got their hands in.

†**squean,** *v. Obs. rare.* [Cf. SQUINNY *v.*¹ and dial. *squine* in the same sense.] *intr.* To look askance, to squint (*at* one).
1608 ARMIN *Nest Ninn.* (1880) 45 As the Philosopher squened at his curst wife in some feare, because of quiet. **1609** —— *Ital. Taylor* (1880) 175 As.. men amazde their sorrow flouts, By squeaning with the eye.

†**'squeasy,** *a. Obs.* Forms: 6 squeasye, 6–7 -ie (7 squeaysie), 8 squeasy; 7 squeazy, -ie. [Alteration of QUEASY *a.*]

1. Of times: Troublous; disturbed.
1583 MELBANCKE *Philotimus* D ij b, But now we are come to the last age, which as Ouid deuids it, is yᵉ 4, and the woorst, squeasye & dogged, & wrought of hard iron. *a* **1662** HEYLIN *Laud* (1668) 256 None of them in those squeasie and unsettled times being questioned for it.

2. Of the stomach: Readily nauseated, easily upset; = SQUEAMISH *a.* 1 b.
1596 LODGE *Wits Miserie* N iij, He driues him to be dainty of his meats, telling him his stomack is squeasie. **1640** HOWELL *Dodona's Gr.* 21, I use to have a squeazie stomacke on salt Water. **1655** FULLER *Ch. Hist.* VI. 299 My weak and squeazie stomack will hardly digest the wing of a small rabbet or chicken.
fig. **1620** MASON *Newfoundland* 5 Peraduenture some squeasie stomake will say, Fishing is a beastly trade and unseeming a Gentleman. **1656** EARL MONM. tr. *Boccalini's Advts. fr. Parnass.* I. ix. (1674) 11 It proves hard of digestion to the squeasie stomacks of modern weak-wits.
Comb. **1655** CULPEPPER, etc. tr. *Riverius* XIV. i. 372 These Patients are commonly squeazy stomached.

b. Readily unsettled or disturbed.
1611 *Coryat's Crudities, Panegyr. Verses*, The squeazie humour of his braine Before he parted from this maine Neare perished his skull.

3. Sparing *of* something.
1628 EARLE *Microcosm.* (Arb.) 56 Hee is as squeazy of his commendations as his courtesie.

Hence †'**squeasiness**, squeamishness. *Obs.*
a **1660** HAMMOND *Sermons* viii. Wks. 1684 IV. 614 A squeasiness and rising up of the heart against any mean.. condition of men. **1687** T. W. *Lett. to Dissenter* 6 After the squeaziness of starting at a Surplice, you must be forced to swallow Transubstantiation.

squebald, variant of SKEWBALD *a.*

squechon, obs. form of SCUTCHEON *sb.*¹

†**squeck.** *Obs.* [? Imitative.] A disease affecting fowls.
1577 B. GOOGE *Heresbach's Husb.* IV. (1586) 167 b, The greatest disease, that they are subiect vnto, as the Pippe and the Squecke, which must be holpen in like sorte as the Hennes.

squeege (skwi:dʒ), *v.* Also 8–9 squeedge. [Strengthened form of SQUEEZE *v.*]

1. *intr.* To press; to make one's way by pressure.
1782 MRS. H. COWLEY *Which is the Man?* v. ii, Such clattering, and squeedging down the gangway staircase. **1852** HOSKYNS *Talpa* xxi, Every time I see it [a plough], on stiff land, a-squeeging and pressing, and kneading its way along.

2. *trans.* To compress; to squeeze.
1787 in GROSE *Prov. Gloss.* **1848** DICKENS *Dombey* lii, Can't you be fond of a cove without squeedging and throttling of him! **1851** MAYHEW *Lond. Lab.* (1861) II. 530, I went, and I was nearly squeeged to death.

squeegee ('skwi:dʒi:, skwi:'dʒi:), *sb.* [? f. prec. Cf. SQUILGEE *sb.*]

1. a. A scraping implement, usually consisting of a straight-edged blade of india-rubber, gutta-percha, or the like, attached to the end of a long handle, for removing water, mud, etc.
1844 MRS. HOUSTON *Yacht Voy. Texas* I. 39 Holy-stoning the decks.. is the worst description of nervous torture of which I ever heard, excepting perhaps, the infliction of the squee gee. **1867** SMYTH *Sailor's Word-bk.* 648 *Squeegee*, an effective swabbing instrument, having a plate of gutta-percha fitted at the end of a broom handle. **1884** *Law Times Rep.* L. 635/2 They had swept mud in a state of batter to the side of a road by means of 'squeegees'.

b. A similar implement for cleaning windows, windscreens, etc., or for other purposes requiring smooth application of pressure.
1918 L. E. RUGGLES *Navy Explained* 130 Squeegee—.. used in civil life to clean windows. **1955** *Sci. News Let.* 2 Apr. 224/1 Resembling a window cleaner's squeegee, the sweeper is ribbed to fold gently back and forth when it is moved across the floor. **1955** *Sci. Amer.* Oct. 126/3 A small squeegee or an automobile windshield wiper will help in the cleaning job. **1962** *Which?* Oct. 314/1 The *Gnomist transfer* had to be stuck on with water and a squeegee, which the manufacturer provided. *a* **1977** *Harrison Mayer Ltd. Catal.* 15/1 The colour in paste form is forced by means of a squeegee through a fine mesh mounted on a frame.

2. *Photogr.* A strip of rubber mounted on a wooden frame which serves as a handle, for squeezing moisture from a print, pressing a film closer to its mount, etc.; a rubber roller serving this purpose; a squeezer.
1878 ABNEY *Photogr.* 170 The plate is then placed on a small low stool.. and the excess of water squeezed out by means of a squeegee. **1892** *Photogr. Ann.* II. 57 Use a Roller Squeegee.—After the print is applied to the mount,.. gently roll the squeegee over it.

3. *Comb.* **squeegee band** *Naut. colloq.*, an improvised band (see quots.). Cf. WASHBOARD 3 c.
1916 'TAFFRAIL' *Pincher Martin* x. 176 Before very long the 'squeegee band', composed of two drums, a dozen fifes, many mouth-organs, and an unholy number of mess kettles and other noisy utensils, was marching round the deck. **1979** A. C. HAMPSHIRE *Just Old Navy Custom* 225 *Squeegee band*, composed of instruments not usually found in a band, e.g. Jew's harp; mouth-organ; comb and paper, etc.

squeegee, *v.* [f. the sb.]

1. a. *trans.* To press, squeeze, or force, with a squeegee.
1885 C. G. W. LOCK *Workshop Rec.* Ser. IV. 346/2 When cold, squeegee the emulsion.. through muslin. *Ibid.* 411/2 A piece of American cloth to protect the print while squeegeeing. **1892** *Photogr. Ann.* II. 49 Take a print, put it face down on the glass and lightly squeegee it until it lies flat.

b. With advs. and preps., as *on, out, together*.
1883 *Hardwick's Photogr. Chem.* 347 It is then 'squeegeed' down on the glass and developed. **1889** *Anthony's Photogr. Bull.* II. 324 The two surfaces can be brought into contact and squeegeed together. **1890** *Ibid.* III. 259 It can be turned over and squeegeed out flat.

2. To scrape with a squeegee; = SQUILGEE *v.*
1886 *All Year Round* 4 Sept. 104 The decks were persistently holystoned, scrubbed, 'squeegéed', and swabbed.

3. *intr.* To use a squeegee.
1972 *Times* 20 Sept. 3/3 He washes, then squeegees. **1977** *Centuryan* (Office Cleaning Services) Christmas 17/2 Eva squeegeed off as first of the guest shiners.

Hence **squeegeed** *ppl. a.*, **squeegeeing** *vbl. sb.*
1892 *Photogr. Ann.* II. 435 The squeegeeing process.. is unsuitable for it. **1894** *Brit. Jrnl. Photogr.* XLI. 11 The squeegeeing is then gone on with. **1904** W. P. DRURY *Peradventures Priv. Pagett* 10 A sloppy road between two squeegeed banks of mud.

squeeza'bility. [f. next.] The condition or quality of being squeezable.
1882 in *Imperial Dict.* (citing *Spectator*). **1885** *Spectator* 25 July 961/1 There could be no worse policy than to show fresh squeezability in order to prevent being squeezed. **1893** *National Observer* 9 Sept. 418/2 Experiments on Ministerial squeezability as to Welsh Disestablishment.

squeezable ('skwi:zəb(ə)l), *a.* [f. SQUEEZE *v.*]

1. Capable of being compressed or squeezed. Also *transf.*
1813 SIR W. W. PEPYS in Roberts *Mem. Han. More* (1835) III. 398 One would like to keep it in squeezable order. **1844** H. STEPHENS *Bk. Farm* III. 1043 They must feel moist and clammy, and be squeezable in the hand.

b. Impressionable; susceptible.
1852 SAVAGE *R. Medlicott* I. I. v. 130 You are too versatile and too squeezable,.. you take impressions too readily.

2. Capable of being constrained or coerced to yield or grant something.
1837 *Ann. Reg., Hist.* 390/1 The ministers, at least, he regarded as squeezable commodities, out of which something good might, by compression, be extracted. **1852** W. JERDAN *Autobiog.* II. i. 7 As unlucky and squeezable by their more cunning competitors.. as the literary man. **1884** *Manch. Exam.* 23 Aug. 5/2 He hoped that China would be squeezable, and that the objects he had in view would be attained without war.

b. *esp.* From which money may be extracted.
1840 *Frazer's Mag.* XXI. 243 Not a farthing beyond what they could squeeze from any quarter squeezable. **1880** L. OLIPHANT *Land of Gilead* vi. 190 The result of their industry is only that they become more squeezable for taxes.

3. Capable of being extracted by pressure.
1843 *Tait's Mag.* X. 805 Their necessities compel them to exact the last penny squeezable out of the unfortunate tenantry.

Hence '**squeezableness**, = SQUEEZABILITY.
1844 *Blackw. Mag.* LV. 119 The issuing of that order would depend entirely on the strength or the necessity of the Minister: on his 'squeezableness'. **1871** *Standard* 12 Apr. 6 Mr. Gladstone's 'squeezableness'.

squeeze (skwi:z), *sb.* [f. SQUEEZE *v.*]

1. a. An act of squeezing; an application of strong or heavy pressure, or of force sufficient to compress.
1611 COTGR., *Escachure*,.. a squash, crush, knock, or squeeze, (wherby a thing is flatted, or beaten close together). **1708** J. PHILIPS *Cyder* II. 75 Let the tuneful Squeeze Of labouring Elbow rouze them [*sc.* 'imprison'd winds' of the bagpipes], out they fly Melodious. **1806** A. HUNTER *Culina* (ed. 3) 63 When sufficiently stewed, give it a gentle squeeze. **1835** SIR J. ROSS *Narr. 2nd Voy.* viii. 121 In attempting to pass between two large pieces of ice, they suddenly closed, so as to give us a considerable squeeze, but without any injury. **1843** HOLTZAPFFEL *Turning* I. 134 The final squeeze is given by the entire force of three men. **1869** RANKINE *Machine & Hand-tools* Pl. P 20, The punch;.. as it retires, after having given its squeeze, the point is lubricated.

b. In fig. use. Colloq. phr. (orig. *U.S.*) *to put the squeeze on* (someone): to exert influence on (someone) to act in a particular way, to 'pressurize' someone. Also without indirect obj.
1711 SWIFT *Lett.* (1767) III. 227 A rogue that writes a newspaper.. has reflected on me in one of his papers; but the secretary has taken him up, and he shall have a squeeze extraordinary. **1777** J. WEDGWOOD *Let.* 13 Apr. (1965) 204 Mrs. Du Burk's assurance in asking us to pay her debts is very great... It is another squeeze, and I would not pay a stiver. **1835** T. MITCHELL *Acharn. of Aristoph.* Introd. p. viii, A squeeze and a gripe too often advertised the towns beneath, that.. Athens had as much need of external as of native resources. **1850** LONGF. *Life* (1891) II. 182 It begins again, the old pressure and squeeze of books and old routine. **1887** *Spectator* 21 May 675/2 A gentle squeeze to the Sultan might effect some improvement. **1941** E. B. WHITE *Let.* 24 June (1967) 210, I am writing you direct to put the old personal squeeze on you. **1942** R. CHANDLER *High Window* (1943) xxxiii. 220 She hired me to.. put the squeeze on Linda for a divorce. **1949** *Ann. Reg. 1948* 6 The tension was not relaxed, for there now began the Russian 'squeeze' in Berlin. **1954** 'J. CHRISTOPHER' *22nd Century* 21 They're putting the squeeze on. But there's got to be an excuse before they can swallow us. **1969** A. G. FRANK *Latin Amer.* xxv. 394 The imperialist squeeze obliges them to react by squeezing their workers. **1978** S. BRILL *Teamsters* vi. 217 Spilotro's army of enforcers.. put the squeeze on hard-pressed loan-shark victims.

c. The pressure *of* a crowd of persons; a crush.
1802 BEDDOES *Hygëia* v. 55 Tea and coffee.. are frequently taken in the very stew and squeeze of a fashionable mob. **1805** BARONESS BUNSEN in Hare *Life* I. iii. 72, I never could have imagined what a real squeeze was until I found myself in the passage. **1854** *Poultry Chron.* I. 141, I shall never again believe what ladies say against a mob, after witnessing how many high-born, gentle, and feeble old ladies endured the squeeze at Birmingham.

d. *colloq.* A strong financial or commercial demand or pressure, esp. a restriction in the supply of money, credit, goods, etc.; *spec.* in

Stock Market usage, pressure applied to dealers in shorts to cause them to settle at a loss. Cf. *credit squeeze* s.v. CREDIT *sb.* 14.

1872 *Chicago Tribune* 23 Oct. 1/5 The Gold Room was treated to a slight sensation to-day in the shape of a 'squeeze' in cash gold, which was made as high as 3/8 per cent per diem for borrowing. **1890** *Daily News* 26 June 2/2 The middlemen who happened to have provided themselves with money in view of a 'squeeze'. **1894** *Times* 7 Mar. 5/4 The business of the New York Stock Market was marked to-day by a 'squeeze' in Sugar Trust certificates. **1924** G. G. Munn *Encycl. Banking & Finance* 523/1 A money squeeze refers to a temporary shortage in the supply of loanable funds accompanied by difficulty in borrowing and marking up of interest rates. **1927** W. H. Hubbard *Cotton & Cotton Market* (ed. 2) 396 While we have never had a corner since 1910, we have had in recent years a succession of annoying premiums on the near deliveries. The trade calls these minor corners a 'squeeze'. **1937** *Sun* (Baltimore) 25 Sept. 15/8 'Longs' are traders who in recent months have been accumulating contracts specifying delivery of corn to them in September. 'Shorts' are those who have sold these contracts, many of them reportedly without having possession of the corn to deliver. The attempt to make these 'shorts' pay a comparatively high price either to buy back their contracts or to buy the corn to deliver on them is known as a 'squeeze' in market parlance. **1943** [see ROLL BACK, ROLL-BACK, ROLLBACK 2]. **1958** J. K. Galbraith *Affluent Society* xvi. 184 A severe squeeze will ordinarily be placed on the capital requirements of smaller-scale firms. **1979** B. Hines *Price of Coal* I. 48 I'm talking about spending thousands of pounds of public money... I thought there was a squeeze on?

e. *Bridge.* A tactic used to force an opponent to discard or unguard a potentially winning card.

1926 *Work-Whitehead Auction Bridge Bull.* Jan. 117/1 The Squeeze is unquestionably the least understood of the several more or less rare plays arising from time to time in the proper play of Auction hands. **1933** *Sunday Times* 5 Feb. 5/1 The coup formerly only known as the 'Vienna Coup', but now, more appropriately, also termed the 'Squeeze'. **1959** *Listener* 5 Nov. 802/3 He played for a squeeze. **1976** *National Observer* (U.S.) 20 Nov. 21-A/2 Another 'cooked' story is behind this week's hand. It involved a refusal to finesse and ended with a very fancy squeeze.

2. a. A strong or firm pressure of the hand as a token of friendship or affection.

In quot. 1736 with allusion to the surreptitious passing of money in order to bribe.

1736 Fielding *Pasquin* I. i, I never had a civiller squeeze by the hand in my life... Ay, you have squeezed that out pretty well. **1760–72** H. Brooke *Fool of Qual.* (1809) III. 133 Harry seized him by the hand, and gave him..the squeeze and the look of love. **1819** Byron *Juan* I. cxi, Yet, there's no doubt she only meant to clasp His fingers with a pure Platonic squeeze. **1841** Thackeray *Gt. Hoggarty Diamond* iii, Lady Fanny..held me out her little hand, and gave mine such a squeeze. **1888** Burgon *Twelve Good Men* II. 265 Giving him an honest, hearty squeeze of the hand.

b. A close embrace; a hug.

1790 Wolcot (P. Pindar) *Epist. J. Bruce* Wks. 1812 II. 354 What bade the charming Lady Mary fly Marchesi's squeeze, for Pacchierotti's sigh? **1818** Keats *Endym.* III. 574 My tenderest squeeze is but a giant's clutch. **1848** Dickens *Dombey* xlvi, Drying the tears upon her shrivelled face, and giving him a tender squeeze. **1899** Doyle *Duet* 207 She threw her arms round his neck and gave him a hearty squeeze.

3. a. A (small) quantity or amount squeezed out; a few drops pressed out by squeezing.

1761 *Ann. Reg., Characters* 4/2 A little pimento, and the squeeze of an orange their only sauce. **1849** Macaulay in *Trevelyan* xii. (1913) II. 233 They are more than sufficiently eulogistic. In both there are squeezes of acid. **1864** *Reader* 12 Mar. 324/3 It is much relished with a squeeze of lemon-juice. **1907** *Westm. Gaz.* 12 Apr. 4/2 For the nearer colouring he would still serve himself out a liberal squeeze of burnt-sienna.

b. *techn.* in *Screw-cutting* (see quot.).

1846 Holtzapffel *Turning* II. 587 It appears..to be quite impolitic, entirely to expunge the surface-bearing, or squeeze, from the taps and dies, when these are applied to the ductile metals.

c. A forced exaction or impost made by Asiatic officials or servants; a percentage taken upon goods bought or sold; an illegal charge or levy.

1858 *Merc. Mar. Mag.* V. 42 The Transit Levies, or Mandarin 'Squeeze'. *Ibid.* 44 We should get our teas at a duty of..one thirty-fifth part of the present 'squeeze'. **1880** Miss Bird *Japan* I. 51 The practice common among native servants of getting a 'squeeze' out of every money transaction. *c* **1890** [A. Murdoch] *Yoshiwara Episode* 10 In his foolishness he was dreaming of 'squeezes', of looting temples, of marrying Japanese Princesses.

4. *colloq.* A crowded assembly or social gathering.

1779 Mrs. Barbauld *Wks.* (1825) II. 22 There is a squeeze, a fuss, a drum, a rout, and lastly a hurricane, when the whole house is full from top to bottom. **1793** [Earl Dundonald] *Descr. Estate of Culross* 53 Scots Coal and Wax Tapers forming two of the indispensably necessary attendants of Drums, Routs, and Squeezes. **1808** Lady S. Lyttelton *Corr.* (1912) i. 13 The weather is getting terribly hot for squeezes. **1818** Lady Morgan *Autob.* (1859) 191 Morgan swears I'll suffocate them all, as the French are wholly unused to a squeeze. **1893** F. F. Moore *I Forbid Banns* (1899) 149 He said he'd be hanged if he'd go to Madame Darius' squeeze—meaning this joyous entertainment.

5. *Coal-mining.* **a.** A gradual coming together of the floor and roof of a gallery or working; a place where this has occurred; a creep or nip.

1789 J. Williams *Min. Kingd.* I. 348 They are always sure that the vein will open again,..when they have cut through that squeeze or twitch. **1881** Raymond *Mining Gloss.*, *Squeeze*, the settling, without breaking, of the roof over a considerable area of workings. **1898** *Daily News* 5 July 2/5 Squeezes and falls are taking place in the levels and headings throughout the coalfield.

b. (See quot.)

1882 *Standard* 19 Aug. 3/5 There is no room for doubt that the explosion..was caused by the diffusion of a sudden 'squeeze' or outburst of gas.

6. *slang* or *Cant.* **a.** The neck.

1812 in J. H. Vaux *Flash Dict.* **1821** *Sporting Mag.* IX. 27 A prime yellow-man round his squeeze. **1828** Egan *Boxiana* IV. 158 Abbot appeared on the ground, with a blue bird's-eye round his squeeze. *c* **1866** in Farmer & Henley s.v. *Squeezer.*

b. Silk; an article made of this, a silk tie. Also *attrib.*

1839 'Ducange Anglicus' 34 *Squeeze*, silk. **1877** *Five Years' Penal Servitude* 240 He'd tog himself up in black, with a white 'squeeze', on a Sunday. **1877** in Farmer & Henley s.v., We got some squeeze dresses, and two sealskin jackets. **1888** *Times* 1 Dec. 4/4 He there saw Fife, who said, 'Did you hear about the load of "squeeze" (meaning silk) that was lost?'

c. A plan, work; see quot. 1865.

A few other slang uses are given by Farmer & Henley. *c* **1863** T. Taylor *Ticket-of-Leave Man* III. 59, I owe him one for spoiling my squeeze. **1865** *Slang Dict.* 241 'Precious rum squeeze at the spell,' *i.e.* a good evening's work at the theatre.

7. a. A moulding or cast of an object obtained by pressing some plastic substance round or over it; *spec.* in *Archæol.*, an impression or copy of an inscription, design, etc., taken by applying wet paper or other soft material in this way.

1857 Birch *Anc. Pottery* (1858) II. 277 Lamps were manufactured by means of moulds, which were modelled from a pattern lamp, in a harder and finer clay than the squeeze or pattern. **1870** Geo. Eliot in Cross *Life* III. 112, I saw squeezes of this [Moabite] stone for the first time. **1884** W. Wright *Hittites* iv. 45 Professor Sayce visited these sculptures. He made careful squeezes and copies of the inscription. **1890** W. J. Gordon *Foundry* 213 The wood..is used merely as a source of electrotypes. A squeeze in wax or some such substance is taken from it.

fig. **1894** *Times* 14 Mar. 7/3 Now we know that the policy of Lord Rosebery is the 'squeeze' of the policy of Mr. Gladstone.

b. *slang.* An impression of an object made for criminal purposes.

1882 *Sydney Slang Dict.* 8/2 *Squeeze*, an impression of a keyhole in wax. **1930** G. D. H. & M. Cole *Burglars in Bucks.* III. xxxiv. 135 Where did the dummy keys..come from?.. If they were forgeries it would be simpler, for Sir Hiram might remember if anyone had handled his keys long enough to take a squeeze. **1941** Baker *Dict. Austral. Slang* 71 *Squeeze*, an impression of a keyhole in wax.

8. Without article: The action of squeezing or the fact of being squeezed; pressure; constraint used to obtain a concession, gift, etc.

1862 Thackeray *Philip* xxvi, After four-and-twenty hours of squeeze in the diligence. **1898** *Westm. Rev.* May 479 It is on the knowledge of this fact that the policy of squeeze is based.

9. *colloq.* **a.** An escape, a 'squeak'.

1848 J. F. Cooper *Oak Openings* II. v. 78 In one instance, however, a young Indian had a still narrower 'squeeze' for his life. **1875** Wood & Lapham *Waiting for M.* 24 Jack had had..a still more narrow squeeze, for, had he been one minute sooner at the windlass, nothing could have saved him.

b. *at* or *upon a squeeze*, at a pinch.

1892 W. S. Gilbert *Mountebanks* I, I assist As soloist, Upon a squeeze. **1897** *Windsor Mag.* Jan. 277/2 The.. garden..contains only one..tennis-court, but at a squeeze could almost take in two.

c. A difficult situation.

1905 *Dialect Notes* III. 22 *Tight squeeze*,..a difficulty. **1972** *National Observer* (U.S.) 27 May 1/1 The safest drivers are those who know what their cars can do and how to make them do it in a squeeze.

10. *Baseball.* The use of squeeze play (SQUEEZE PLAY 1 a); a bunt made to try to bring home a runner from third base.

1908 *Spalding's Official Base Ball Guide* 279 Under Ned Hanlon the Cincinnati team worked the 'squeeze' nearly as well as the New York Americans. **1942** L. Fonseca *How to pitch Baseball* iii. i. 93 Another play for which the pitcher—and catcher, too—must always be on guard is the squeeze, one of baseball's most spectacular plays. **1976** *Billings* (Montana) *Gaz.* 30 June 2-E/6 In the eighth inning, the Royals tried to salvage the game with a squeeze with the bases loaded.

11. a. *attrib.* and *Comb.* in sense 7, as ***squeeze impression***, ***-taker***; in sense 3 c, as ***squeeze system***; **squeeze bunt** *Baseball*, the bunt (BUNT *sb.*[8] 2) made in squeeze play (SQUEEZE PLAY 1 a); also as *v. intr.*; **squeeze clout** *Cant* (see quot.); **squeeze-pidgin** *slang*, a bribe; **squeeze room**, a room in which 'squeezes' or assemblies are held.

1795 Potter *Dict. Cant* (ed. 2), *Squeeze clout*, a neck-cloth. **1850** Mrs. Trollope *Petticoat Gov.* 157 She ventured to whisper as they stood together in the squeeze room. **1871** *Q. Statem. Amer. Palest. Explor. Soc.*, We did not succeed in getting squeeze impressions. **1883** *Quiver* Dec. 89/1 Tourists' fingers, squeeze-takers, and the whole body of destroyers have done their work. **1898** *Morning Post* 9 Nov. 5/5 The official class, which religiously adheres to the time-honoured 'squeeze' system. **1946** J. Irving *Royal Navalese* 165 *Squeeze-pidgin*, a tip: a bribe. **1952** B. Feller *Pitching to Win* viii. 108 During the 1951 season, we had a number of squeeze bunts, those which score a runner from third base, beat us in several important ball games. **1955** P. Richards *Mod. Baseball Strategy* xi. 130 Many managers make a big mistake asking pitchers to squeeze-bunt. **1970** 'B. Mather' *Break in Line* i. 11 'What's a squeeze-pidgin?' ..'A bribe... Something you *squeeze* out of somebody.' **1974** *Cleveland* (Ohio) *Plain Dealer* 13 Oct. c. 1/2 The big run for the defending world champions came on a two-strike, suicide squeeze bunt by Bert Campaneris in the fifth inning.

b. *attrib.* uses in *Bridge* (sense 1 e above).

1936 E. H. Downes *Squeezes, Coups & End Plays* 10 The Squeeze trick must always be won in the hand opposite the final entry card. **1947** J. Brown *Winning Tricks* xxi. 233 A long suit is not necessarily for a squeeze, although long suits have come to be associated with squeeze positions. **1954** G. S. Coffin *Bridge Play from A to Z* 328 Many types of preparatory squeezes occur..such as the squeeze long-suit ..; the squeeze finesse, the squeeze strip, etc. **1964** Frey & Truscott *Official Encycl. Bridge* 526/1 The squeeze finesse is characterized by the presence of a symmetric menace which must be guarded with an equal number of cards by both opponents. **1974** *Times* 5 Jan. 8/7 The counter-attack by the declarer to keep one move ahead of the squeeze-breaking defence.

squeeze (skwi:z), *v.* Also 7 **squeez, squeaze, squease, squese,** 7–8 **squeese.** Also with *dial. preterite* and *pa. pple.* 9– **squoze**, *pa. pple.* 9 **squozen.** [perh. a strengthened form of QUEASE *v.*[1] Cf. also SQUIZE *v.*]

1. a. *trans.* To press or compress hard, esp. so as to flatten, crush, or force together.

a **1601** *Pasquil & Kath.* (1878) I. 117, I long not to be squeas'd with mine owne waight. **1634** Brereton *Trav.* (Chetham Soc.) 26 The devil..squeezed and bruised his body so as his death was thereby occasioned. **1697** Dryden *Virg. Georg.* IV. 208 He therefore first among the Swains was found, To..squeeze the Combs with Golden Liquor crown'd. **1727** *Philip Quarll* (1816) 81 He opened his windpipe by squeezing it the contrary way. *c* **1750** Coventry *Hist. Pompey* xv, A servant..heard him raving at the landlord because the bur was gone, and there was no lemon ready to squeeze over it. **1823** J. Badcock *Dom. Amusem.* 30 By your seizing a handful briskly, and squeezing it half a minute, it preserves the form of the cavity of the hand. **1892** *Photogr. Ann.* II. 397 Upon squeezing the ball the charge is blown very exactly through the flame. **1931** *Sun* (Baltimore) 1 Sept. 8/7 'Orange?' repeated Waitress No. 1. 'Do you want it squoze?' **1933** M. Lowry *Ultramarine* vi. 237 He just sort of *squoze* the rabbit.

fig. **1648** J. Beaumont *Psyche* XI. cxxviii, A Stone more ponderous he found Squeazing his Soul with full Damnation's Weight. **1681** Flavel *Method of Grace* v. 102 An unprincipled professor must be squeezed by some weight of affliction, ere he will yield one tear. **1823** W. Cobbett *Rural Rides* (1885) I. 320 The six hundred millions of Debt..are now squeezing the borough-mongers. **1845** Disraeli *Sybil* (1863) 312 You know something about somebody; I couldn't squeeze you then, but..I will have it out of you now.

†**b.** ***to squeeze wax***, to impress wax with a seal; to set one's seal to a document. *Obs.*

1658–9 in *Burton's Diary* (1828) III. 133 The people are not like a young heir that hath squeezed wax, by which being once bound, it is too late after for him to repent. **1677** Wycherley *Pl. Dealer* IV. i, *Wid.* When thou'rt of Age, thou wilt sign, seal and deliver too, wilt thou? *Jer.* Yes marry will I... *Wid.* O do not squeeze Wax, Son.

c. With complement: To reduce to, or bring into, a specified condition by pressure. ***to squeeze out*** (or †*forth*), to drain or exhaust in this way.

1660 H. More *Myst. Godl.* III. xiii. 85 The more Zealous of the people lye in the way to be squeezed to death by the wheels. **1683** Salmon *Doron Med.* I. 140 The fresh leaves of Asarabacca; bruise them,..squeez them forth strongly, and take it with care. **1697** Dampier *Voy.* I. 79 We caught several great Sharks;..and eat them all, boyling and squeezing them dry. **1825** Hazlitt *Spirit of Age* 142 He has ransacked old chronicles,..he has squeezed out musty records. **1848** Bailey *Festus* (ed. 3) 180 They have squeezed me black and blue. **1859** Dickens *T. Two Cities* I. v, Even with handkerchiefs..which were squeezed dry into infants' mouths. **1871** G. W. Curtis *Potiphar P.* i, To be squeezed flat against a wall.

fig. **1871** M. Collins *Marq. & Merch.* II. x. 293 When the [morning] paper was squeezed dry, the old lady usually settled down to take a nap. **1886** *World* 17 Nov. 14 The writer..says that Archer, by a fine bit of riding, squeezed Childeric home by a neck.

d. With advs., as *down*, *together*, *up*.

1716 Lady M. W. Montagu *Let. to C'tess Mar* 14 Sept., In order to that ceremony, I was squeezed up in a gown. **1833** Lardner *Manuf. Metal* II. 241 Placing them.. between polished pasteboards, and then squeezing them down very closely. **1852** Mrs. Stowe *Uncle Tom's C.* i. 5 She squeezed up her child in her arms. **1884** Bower & Scott *De Bary's Phaner.* 573 They press against the bast-plate, and squeeze it together, displacing and destroying its elements.

e. To press (the hand) in token of friendship or affection.

1687 Miége *Gt. Fr. Dict.* II. s.v., I squeezed her hand. **1751** Johnson *Rambler* No. 191 ¶6 Him that had once squeezed her hand. **1823** Scott *Quentin D.* xiv, The poor youth whose hand he squeezed affectionately. **1848** Thackeray *Van. Fair* xliv, Becky seized Pitt's hand... 'Thank you,' she said, squeezing it. **1878** *Roger Plowman's Excursion to London* ii. 21, I gently squoze hur 'and.

f. To fire *off* (a round, shot, etc.) from a gun. *colloq.*

1956 *Amer. Speech* XXXI. 192 A rifleman never fires a shot, he *squeezes off a round.* **1975** A. Price *Our Man in Camelot* vii. 136 He..got his gun clear just as Harry squeezed off his first shot.

g. To approach or 'push' (a certain age). *colloq.*

1976 *National Observer* (U.S.) 20 Nov. 24/1 But that takes a lot out of a man, particularly when he's squeezing 70. So sometimes he's pretty tired. **1978** *Guardian Weekly* 30 July 21/1 The original heroine, now squeezing forty.

2. a. To force by pressure. With advs. and preps., as *in*, *into*, *out* (*of*), *through*, etc.

1683 K. Digby *Chym. Secr.* 67 Mix these two Mercuries together and squeeze them through a leather. **1716** Lady M. W. Montagu *Let. to Lady X——* 1 Oct., A man, a little more slender than ordinary, might squeeze in his whole person. **1779** *Mirror* No. 12, Their bosoms..were squeezed up to their throats. **1829** *Chapters Phys. Sci.* 4 Squeezing the air into a small space in the upper part of the goblet. **1860** Tyndall *Glac.* I. ix. 62 The half-formed ice is squeezed through a precipitous gorge. **1866** J. T. Staton *Rays fro' Loominary* 107 Awd welly as lief they'd squozzen my guts eawt as speighlt my bonnet. **1892** Zangwill *Bow Myst.* 110 Crowl was squeezed into a corner behind a pillar.

refl. **1847** Tennyson *Princ.* Prol. 112 He had climb'd across the spikes, And he had squeezed himself betwixt the bars. **1860** Tyndall *Glac.* I. xix. 134 We had to squeeze ourselves through narrow fissures. **1883** *Cent. Mag.* Aug. 492 The frightened birds..crouch..so as to squeeze themselves into the smallest compass.

b. In more or less fig. use.

1658–9 in *Burton's Diary* (1828) IV. 225 Amidst that debate of Scotland was squeezed out a question about their withdrawing. **1694** in *Lett. Lit. Men* (Camden) 230 We shall be able to squeeze it into one [volume]. **1777** F. Burney *Early Diary* (1889) II. 210 She immediately complied, and I squeezed in my laughter with great decency. **1818** Cruise *Digest* (ed. 2) II. 239 This is not so strong as the case of tacking a third incumbrance to a first, in order to squeeze out a second. **1861** Gen. P. Thompson *Audi Alt. Part.* III. clxxvi. 211 It will very likely happen, that those who afterwards join, will squeeze him out of partnership. **1892** *Photogr. Ann.* II. 453 In last year's Annual I was just able to squeeze in a notice of this cheap and convenient erection. **1938** J. Agate *Diary* 17 Dec. in *Selective Ego* (1976) 115 Before going down to correct my proofs at the *S.T.* squeezed in a performance of the *Messiah*. Or, rather, Beecham squoze it in for me.

c. To force or push (one's way).

1864 Carlyle *Fredk. Gt.* xvi. xiii. (1872) VI. 298 His poor Wife had twice squeezed her way into the Royal Levee at Kensington. **1912** D. Crawford *Thinking Black* ii. 18 The terror o' mornings is to squeeze your way through this wet, matted tangle.

3. a. To press upon (a person, etc.) so as to exact or extort money; to fleece. Also const. *of*.

Cf. the fig. use illustrated s.v. sponge *sb.*[1] 9 c.

1639 Fuller *Holy War* iii. vi. (1840) 124 He made a new seal, wherewith he squeezed his subjects, and left a deep impression in their purses. **1674** Milton *Hist. Moscovia* i. Wks. 1851 VIII. 478 Being well enricht, he is sent at his own Charge to the Wars, and there squeez'd of his ill got wealth. **1700** J. Tyrrell *Hist. Eng.* II. 904 The Church had been so often squeezed by him. **1741** Middleton *Cicero* (1742) II. vii. 184 This King Ariobarzanes..had been miserably squeezed and drained by the Roman Generals and Governers. **1879** Froude *Cæsar* ix. 99 Squeezing the people ..of all the wealth that could be drained out of them. **1894** Baring-Gould *Deserts S. France* II. 193 The old corsair so squeezed these towns as to completely exhaust them.

†**b.** To subject to severe treatment. *Obs.*[−1]

1691 Sir R. Cox in *Sydney Papers* (1746) I. 168, I squeezd them hard, having killd and hangd not less than 3000 of them.

c. *slang.* To bring into trouble. ? *Obs.*

1804 *Revol. Plutarch* III. 232 The snuff-box for which I am now pinched, interrupted my career to the consulate for life, in the same manner as a gold bracelet squeezed me in 1796, and prevented me from being a Director.

d. To subject to strong constraint or pressure.

1888 *Christian Leader* 28 June 403/2 The sense of being squeezed makes even a pliant man stiffen his back and become obstinate. **1898** *Times* 15 Nov. 9/4 The notion that England can be 'squeezed' indefinitely and will submit to any humiliation.

e. To exert commercial or financial pressure on (someone); to restrict a supply of money, credit, goods, etc.; *spec.* in Stock Market usage, to force dealers in shorts to settle at a loss.

1885 *Harper's Mag.* Nov. 842/1 The bulls get a 'twist on the shorts' by artificially raising prices, and 'squeezing', or compelling the bears to settle at ruinous rates. **1900** S. A. Nelson *ABC Wall St.* 160 When shorts become frightened after having oversold and then are forced to violently bid up prices in competition with the owners of stocks they are said to have been squeezed. **1902** L. L. Bell *Hope Loring* xiv. 272 You squeezed me badly in '93. **1951** *Times* 3 Jan. 7/2 The domestic consumer of coal and coke is already being squeezed, but he often uses more gas and more electricity as a result. **1970** *Daily Tel.* 3 Sept. 3/2 The Government can scarcely ask banks to squeeze their customers when a State Corporation is advertising loans to attract business. **1978** *Jrnl. R. Soc. Arts* CXXVI. 390/2 Manufacturing industry's profits have been greatly squeezed.

4. a. With *out*: To press or force out; to cause to ooze or flow out by the application of pressure.

1599 B. Jonson *Ev. Man out of Hum.* Prol., To seize on vice, and..Squeeze out the humour of such spongie soules As lick up every idle vanity. **1602** Marston *Ant. & Mel.* iv. Wks. 1856 I. 49 Even this brinish marsh Shall squeeze out teares. **1696** Bp. Patrick *Comm. Exod.* xxvii. (1697) 526 Pure Oyl-olive,..not squeezed out by a Press or by a Mill, ..but..bruised with a Pestel. **1746** Francis tr. *Hor., Sat.* ii. v. 171 Squeeze out some teares. **1789** J. Williams *Min. Kingd.* I. 64 These troubles sometimes squeeze out one third, and at other times one half or more of the thickness of the coal. **1829** N. Arnott *Physics* (ed. 4) II. 12 It becomes instantly sensible on the condensation of any material mass, as if then squeezed out from the mass. **1854** Thackeray *Newcomes* xxviii, Lady Kew could..squeeze out a tear over a good novel too. **1892** *Garrett's Encycl. Cookery* II. 40 Squeeze out all the juice from the selected quantity of Seville Oranges.

b. In fig. use.

1641 Sir T. Roe in *Eng. Hist. Rev.* (1910) Apr. 273 My last remonstrance hath squeezed out an answere both from the emperor and the Spanish ambassador. **1704** Swift *Tale Tub* Author's Apol., From whence some have endeavoured to Squeeze out a dangerous meaning. **1821** V. Knox *Spirit of Despotism* (ed. 2) 36/1 *note*, Speeches in favour of the emperor, which the dread of impending evil squeezed out of many against their will and better judgment. **1835** *Gentl. Mag.* Nov. IV. 492 No old maids with their mouths, like purses, Squeezing out compliments like curses. **1837** Carlyle *Fr. Rev.* i. i. ii, Poverty invades even the Royal Exchequer, and Tax-farming can squeeze out no more.

5. a. To extort or exact, to obtain by force or pressure, *from* or *out of* a person, etc. Also rarely without const.

(*a*) **1602** Marston *Antonio's Rev.* ii. v. Wks. 1856 I. 103 Ile wring what may be squeas'd from out his use. **1693** *Humours Town* 24 The Jilt squeezes out of him a new Petticoat. **1700** Dr. Wallis *Collect.* (O.H.S.) I. 325 The rest serves..for a pretense to squeeze the more money from the gentleman. **1771** Nicholls in *Corr. w. Gray* (1843) 121 In four months I have only been able to squeeze two [letters] from you. **1802–12** Bentham *Ration. Judic. Evid.* (1827) IV. 65 *note*, The above..was the sum squeezed by the judge out of the clerk. **1848** Mill *Pol. Econ.* i. v. §9 (1876) 51 Food and necessaries, which they either go without, or squeeze by their competition from the shares of other labourers. **1865** Dickens *Mut. Fr.* iii. i, When it comes to squeezing a profit out of you.

(*b*) **1800** Wellington in Gurw. *Desp.* (1834) I. 273 The Nizam's horse are going about the country squeezing what they can get. **1898** *Daily News* 15 July 7/7 In cases where holders are pressed concessions can be squeezed.

b. To extract (juice, etc.) by pressure. (Cf. 4.)

1611 Cotgr., *Escrager*, to crush, or squeeze out of. **1700** Dryden *Flower & Leaf* 419 They squeez'd the juice, and cooling ointment made. **1710** Addison *Tatler* No. 131 ¶1 They can squeeze Bourdeaux out of the Sloe. **1758** Reid tr. *Macquer's Chym.* I. 136 To squeeze out of them all such parts of their substance as they will..part with. **1845** Budd *Dis. Liver* 359 From some of them a little pus, as well as bile, could be squeezed. **1891** Codrington *Melanesians* xvi. 316 The cream squeezed out from grated cocoa-nut.

c. To put or drop *in* (a fluid extracted by pressure).

1725 *Fam. Dict.* s.v. *Potage*, Squeezing in some Lemon Juice when served up. **1794** G. Adams *Nat. & Exper. Philos.* III. xxxii. 301 A viscous or slimy liquor that is squeesed in, as if from a sponge, between every joint.

d. To succeed in purchasing *out of* a sum.

1768 Sterne *Sent. Journ.*, *Le Dimanche*, He had squeez'd out of the money, moreover, a new bag and a solitaire.

e. *Bridge.* To force (an opponent) to discard a guarding or potentially winning card.

1926 *Work-Whitehead Auction Bridge Bull.* Jan. 118/2, I will give the three cards remaining in each of the four hands to show how South was squeezed by the lead of the Queen of Clubs. **1934** G. F. Hervey *Mod. Contract Bridge* xxi. 223 The Americans now call this coup [*sc.* the Vienna coup] Squeezing or Squeeze Play. The name is apt as the play of the declarer is such that he squeezes the opponents and forces them to discard and unguard a suit. **1949** H. G. Freehill *Squeeze at Bridge* i. 19 The essential features of the squeeze are three. First: there must be a squeeze-card. That is, a card to the lead of which the player who is squeezed has to discard. **1959** T. Reese *Bridge Player's Dict.* 209 Playing no trump, South lays down the ten of hearts and West is squeezed; he must either unguard spades of throw away the winning diamond. **1979** N. Squire *Squeeze Play Simplified* i. 4 The two menaces are on the left of the player to be squeezed, the squeeze card on his right.

6. *absol.* **a.** To press hard; to exert pressure, esp. with the hand.

1692 R. L'Estrange *Æsop* lv. 55 He [the fox] squeez'd hard to get out again; but the Hole was too Little for him. **1768** Gray *Comic* 3 For thee does Powell squeeze, and Marriot sputter. **1775** [Fitzpatrick] *Dorinda* (ed. 2) 6 And oh! what bliss, when each alike is pleas'd, The hand that squeezes, and the hand that's squeez'd! **1819** Scott *Leg. Montrose* xiii, If he offer to struggle or cry out, fail not..to squeeze doughtily. **1974** J. Gardner *Corner Men* xiii. 188 The man in the rear of the Merc fired once... Wright squeezed twice.

b. To take a squeeze or facsimile impression.

1890 *Athenæum* 4 Oct. 455/1 The overhang of the rock makes it extremely difficult to 'squeeze' satisfactorily.

7. *intr.* To yield to pressure; to admit of being squeezed. Also *fig.*

1683 Moxon *Mech. Exerc., Printing* xi. ¶1 Every Joynt between these are subject to squeeze by the force of a Pull. *Ibid.* xxiv. ¶5 Solid Blocks of Wood..will scarce Squeeze by the strength of a Pull. **1771** Luckombe *Hist. Print.* 327 Bran squeezes much more—But plaister of Paris not at all. **1844** Dickens *Mart. Chuz.* xliii, 'He's the sort of man,' added Mr. Tapley, musing, 'as would squeeze soft, I know'. **1892** *Labour Commission Gloss.* No. 3 s.v. *Creep*, The tendency of the roof, floor, and sides..in a mine to 'creep, crush, or squeeze together.

8. To force a way; to press or push; to succeed in passing by means of compression. With advs. and preps. as *in*, *into*, *out* (*of*), *through*, *up* (*to*), etc.

1704 Newton *Optics* ii. iii. prop. 8 (1721) 242 A concave Sphere of Gold filled with Water..has, upon pressing the Sphere with great force, let the Water squeeze through it. **1710** *Brit. Apollo* No. 83. 3/1 We squeez'd up the Stair-Case. **1738** *Gentl. Mag.* VIII. 34/1 There is always a confused Crowd about him... Now and then a Poet squeezes in. **1771** Smollett *Humph. Cl.* (1815) 117 The old duke..squeezing into the circle with a busy face of importance. **1810** Lady S. Lyttelton *Corr.* (1912) iv. 95, I saw Hartington as we were squeezing out of the theatre. **1831** Macaulay in *Trevelyan* iv. (1913) I. 235, I contrived to squeeze up to Lord Lansdowne. **1844** 'J. Slick' *High Life N.Y.* II. 195, I sot down on a bench runnin over with harnsome gals, that squoze close together and squinched themselves up to make room for me. **1848** L. Hunt *Jar of Honey* iv. 48 Don't stir an inch; and so We'll all squeeze in together. **1897** Mary Kingsley *W. Africa* 255 We squeeze through between the stakes so as not to let the trap off. **1928** A. A. Milne *House at Pooh Corner* viii. 143 He squeezed and he sqoze [*sic*], and then with one last squze he was out.

squeeze-, the verbal stem used (transitively) in combs., as **squeeze bottle**, a bottle made of flexible plastic, squeezed to expel the contents; **squeeze-box** *slang*, †(*a*) *Naut.*, a ship's harmonium (*obs.*); (*b*) an accordion or concertina; **squeeze cementing** *Oil Industry* (see quot. 1938); **squeeze-crab, -grape**, (see quots.); **squeeze lens** *Cinemat.* (orig. *U.S.*), an anamorphic lens attachment (cf. anamorphic *a.* 2); **squeeze toy**, a child's doll or similar toy which sounds when pressed; **squeeze tube** = tube *sb.* 2 d; a tube-shaped container which yields its contents when squeezed; **squeeze-wax** (see quot.).

1953 *Wall St. Jrnl.* 16 Sept. 23/4 The principal addition to the product line will be polyethyline, best known in its form of 'squeeze bottles' and transparent packaging material. **1964** V. E. Yarsley et al. *Cellulosic Plastics* i. 5 To-day 'squeeze-bottles' in polythene are used in increasing quantities all over the world. **1976** 'E. McBain' *Guns* (1977) vii. 177 The doctor..takes a squeeze-bottle..and then wets a piece of gauze. **1909** J. R. Ware *Passing Eng.* 232/1 *Squeeze-box*,..the ship harmonium—used in the hasty Sunday service. From the action of the feet. **1936** *Amer. Speech* XI. 280/1 *Squeeze-box*, an accordion. **1938** Auden & Isherwood *On Frontier* iii. i. 99 Get yer squeeze-box. [*First Soldier begins to play the accordion.*] **1942** E. Paul *Narrow St.* x. 77, I told my Marseilles accordion teacher that the experience had disabled me from practising the squeeze-box for a week. **1963** *Times* 26 Jan. 11/1 They imagine everyone spends their time dancing to squeezebox music and living on Knackwurst and Apfelstrudel. **1973** C. Bonington *Next Horizon* vii. 105 He was already ensconced in the bar at the Clachaig, his squeeze box out, a dram of whisky at his side and a cigarette in his mouth. **1938** *Oil Weekly* 28 Feb. 36/1 Squeeze cementing means that cement slurry is forced, or 'squeezed', by pressure into or against a permeable formation or through perforations in casing and liners for the purpose of shutting off water or for reducing gas/oil ratios. **1974** D. K. Smith in P. L. Moore et al. *Drilling Practices Man.* xvi. 400 Squeeze cementing is necessary for many reasons, but probably the most important use is to segregate hydrocarbon producing zones from those formations producing other fluids. **1785** Grose *Dict. Vulgar T.*, *Squeeze crab*, a sour looking shrivelled diminutive fellow. **1879** Miss Jackson *Shropsh. Word-bk.*, *Squeeze-crab*, a person of shrunk and withered appearance. **1622** Mabbe tr. *Aleman's Guzman d'Alf.* ii. 330 Hee was a notable squeeze-grape, a huge quaffer. **1957** *Amer. Cinematographer* Mar. 149/1 Focal distortion is practically eliminated by a technique that adds a squeeze (anamorphic) lens to the system that produces partial scene compression in the camera, with the remainder being effected in the printing process. **1977** J. Hedgecoe *Photographer's Handbk.* 31 *Squeeze lens.* This is an 'anamorphic' supplementary lens system continuing cylindrical lens elements. When mounted on a normal lens it squeezes the image by reducing either its vertical or its horizontal size without affecting the other dimension. **1954** *Toys & Novelties* Mar. 421 (Advt.), A complete new line of unique squeeze toys by Alan Jay. **1976** *National Observer* (U.S.) 25 Dec. 6/4 He would also like to see a uniform law covering sound levels of toys... 'I have been responsible for manufacturing more than 35 million squeeze toys in my career, and I have never run into anything like this,' Young says. **1872** S. Hale *Let.* 1 Oct. (1919) iv. 86 We went to Rowney's,—delicious!—and I bought two squeeze tubes..; there were watercolours there. **1962** J. Glenn in *Into Orbit* 201, I pulled a squeeze-tube of apple sauce out of its receptacle and parked it in the air in front of me. **1785** Grose *Dict. Vulgar T.*, *Squeeze wax*, a good-natured foolish fellow, ready to become security for another, under hand and seal.

squeezed (skwiːzd), *ppl. a.* [f. squeeze *v.*]

1. a. Subjected to pressure or compression.

1598 Florio, *Mizzi frutti*, rotten, withered, bruzed or squeazed fruites, mellowe. **1599** B. Jonson *Cynthia's Rev.* iv. i, His face is like a squeezed orange. **1648** J. Beaumont *Psyche* xv. lxii, That strange Pressure which the Rebel now Felt sealed sure upon his squeazed Brow. **1706** E. Ward *Wooden World Diss.* (1708) 99 More sapless than a squeez'd Lemon. **1784** Cowper *Task* vi. 672 The theatre too small, shall suffocate Its squeezed contents. **1800** Mrs. Hervey *Mourtray Fam.* I. 152 The gentleman was a little, thin, squeezed figure, with a pale peaked face. **1812** [see orange *sb.*[1] 1 b]. **1856** Kane *Arctic Explor.* II. xxiv. 246 There are ridges of squeezed ice between us and it.

transf. **1828** Walker *Pron. Dict.* 18/1 The squeezed sound of *ee* in *seen*.

fig. **1898** *Daily News* 21 Feb. 4/6 British Governments.. are squeezable, no doubt. But there comes a point at which even a squeezed Salisbury will turn.

b. With advs., as *in*, *out*, *up*.

1831 M. Edgeworth *Let.* 30 Apr. (1971) 533 A squeezed up poke bonnetted old mother. **1838** Dickens *O. Twist* iv, A short, thin, squeezed-up woman. **1880** in I. M. Tarbell *Hist. Standard Oil Co.* (1904) II. 325 This constitutes the only foundation for the oft-repeated expressions 'crushed out', 'squeezed out', and 'bulldozing'. **1889** Gunter *That Frenchman* xi. 132 One great, black mass of squeezed-in humanity. **1951** W. Faulkner *Requiem for Nun* 225 The long invincible arm of Progress..released him, not flung him away like a squeezed-out tube of paint, but rather.. merely opening its fingers.

2. Extracted or obtained by pressure. Also *fig.*, produced with difficulty, not spontaneous.

1601 B. Jonson *Poetaster* Prol., Take my snakes.., and eate, And while the squeez'd juice flowes in your blacke jawes, Helpe me to damne the Authour. **1683** Temple *Mem.* Wks. 1720 I. 471 Much more than any of those squeez'd or forced Strains of Wit that are in some Places so much in request. **1880** Browning *Dram. Idyls, Pan & Luna* 10 Fresh-squeezed yet fast-thickening poppy-juice.

ˈsqueezekin. [f. SQUEEZE *sb.* + -KIN.] A slight squeeze or pressure.

1862 Thackeray *Philip* xvii, A look or two, a squeezekin, perhaps, of a little handykin.

ˈsqueeze play. Also squeeze-play. [f. SQUEEZE *v.* + PLAY *sb.*] **1. a.** *Baseball.* A tactic whereby the batter bunts so that a runner at third base can attempt to reach home safely and score.

1905 *St. Louis Globe-Democrat* 2 July II. 8/5 Like the spit ball, the squeeze play is not strictly an invention of the present season. **1909** *Collier's* 15 May 29/2 The 'squeeze' play, of which we have heard so much in the past two or three years, is the method of scoring a man from third base on the hit-and-run system. **1949** *Chicago Tribune* 27 Sept. II. 1/8 The mighty sox..had to resort to the squeeze play to score their all-important victory. **1979** *Arizona Daily Star* 22 July c 4/4 Not many pitchers throw inside anymore. It's like the squeeze play. It's a lost art.

b. *transf.* and *fig.* An act of coercion or 'pressurizing'; the application of force or pressure to obtain an end. *colloq.* (chiefly *U.S.*).

1916 *Independent* (N.Y.) 5 June 410 (*heading*) The 'squeeze-play' at the capital. **1932** *Sun* (Baltimore) 14 Sept. 10/1 Most employers of relatively small numbers of workers, they appear to have been caught in an economic 'squeeze play' in which 'contract' shops..are played against each other in pursuit of the lowest bids. **1944** D. Wecter *When Johnny comes marching Home* IV. vii. 557 You perhaps mentioned the fact that Hitler was putting the squeeze play on Hindenburg a few years later. **1966** *Economist* 10 Sept. 1009/1 The real victims of the Franco government's squeeze-play—the Spaniards whose prospects of being allowed to go on crossing the border daily to work in Gibraltar are now in jeopardy. **1977** D. Anthony *Stud Game* xx. 122 She hinted that her partner had worked this squeeze-play once before, with..a pregnant girl..and a widow who paid off.

2. *Bridge.* The employment of a squeeze. Cf. SQUEEZE *sb.* 1 e.

1926 *Work-Whitehead Auction Bridge Bull.* May 50 The squeeze play is made when running a suit, by forcing an opponent to discard a number of times. **1934** G. F. Hervey *Contract Bridge Dict.* 139 Squeeze Play is the basis of practically all double-dummy problems. **1959** T. Reese *Bridge Player's Dict.* 209 The technique of squeeze play is complicated, and even in the simplest three-card ending.. certain basic elements have to be present, such as threat cards, entries, a squeeze card and correct timing. **1976** *Country Life* 19 Feb. 440/2 South did not understand squeeze play... When the Nine of Clubs falls from East, the squeeze against West is marked.

squeezer (ˈskwiːzə(r)). [f. SQUEEZE *v.*]

1. One who squeezes, in various senses.

1611 Cotgr., *Pressoireur*, a pressor, strainer, squeezer of iuyce, or liquor, out of things. **1679** T. Jordan *Lond. in Luster* 16 In that Scene below, I saw a fellow carried in a throng of Squeezers, upon Men's backs like a Pageant for the space of thirty Yards. **1694** Motteux *Rabelais* IV. xxxii. (1737) 136 Grinders and Squeezers of Livings. **1818** *Blackw. Mag.* III. 518 Item, 7 sitters, or rather squeezers, in the inside. **1824** Miss Mitford *Village* Ser. I. 178 'Aye,' rejoined the squeezer of lemons, 'poor Sidney!' **1825** J. Nicholson *Operat. Mechanic* 466 The moulds..are kept dry..so that the squeezer can often separate his work from them readily. **1894** *Daily News* 17 Feb. 5/4 Though the patrician 'squeezers' of the Coreans cannot apparently be 'mended' [etc.].

2. †**a.** A crowded assembly; a squeeze. *Obs.*$^{-1}$

1756 Mrs. F. Brooke *Old Maid* No. 16. 128 The day after my arrival, I went to the countess of ——s Squeezer, where I was sure of meeting her.

b. *slang.* The hangman's rope; the noose.

1836 Mahony *Rel. Father Prout* II. 115 For Larry was always the lad, When a friend was condemned to the squeezer.

c. A squeezing pressure.

1822 *Blackw. Mag.* XII. 101 Give the lemons a squeezer.

3. a. A mechanical device or apparatus, an implement, by which pressure can be applied. Also *attrib.*

1839 Ure *Dict. Arts* 133 The squeezing rollers or squeezers, for discharging the greater part of the water from the yarns and goods in the process of bleaching. *Ibid.* 233 The piece is drawn through by a pair of squeezer cylinders at the end of the trough. **1846** Holtzapffel *Turning* II. 919 This machine has also two squeezers for moulding pieces of iron when red-hot to the particular forms of the dies. **1879** *Cassell's Techn. Educ.* III. 327/1 A scraper or 'squeezer', made by securing a slip of india-rubber between two slips of wood.

b. *spec.* An apparatus by which a ball of puddled iron is reduced to a compact mass.

1843 Holtzapffel *Turning* I. 187 The shingling is sometimes performed by large squeezers, something like huge pliers. **1868** Joynson *Metals* 74 The loupes are then removed successively from the furnace, and placed either under the hammer or squeezer. **1890** W. J. Gordon *Foundry* 60 Drilling-machines, punchers, squeezers, shearers, all of mighty size.

4. Usu. *pl.* A playing-card which has its value indicated in one or two corners, so that a player may ascertain his hand while holding the cards closely arranged. (App. orig. used in poker, but now standard.)

1876 *Paper & Printing Trades Jrnl.* Sept. 8/1 The 'Squeezers' Playing Cards introduced by Messrs. Lawrence Brothers..are rapidly rising in popular estimation. **1888** *Amer. Humorist* 15 Sept. 3/1 The editor picked up his hand, slid the squeezers past his good eye, and began to softly whisper the 'Pirate King'. **1906** G. Frankau *X.Y.Z. of Bridge* 47 Horatius in a long frock-coat Rending two 'squeezer' packs. **1930** C. P. Hargrave *Hist. Playing Cards* xiii. 345 The New York Consolidated Card Company.. issued indexed cards..under the name of 'Squeezers'.

squeeziˈbility. *rare*$^{-1}$. = SQUEEZABILITY.

1848 *Westm. Rev.* Jan. 347 The Reform Act increased the squeezibility of the Legislature.

ˈsqueezing, *vbl. sb.* [f. SQUEEZE *v.*]

1. The action of pressing or compressing; the fact of being compressed. Also with *out.*

1611 Cotgr., *Pressement*, a pressing, squeezing, thrusting ..together. *Pressoirée*, a pressing, straining, squeezing out. **1648** Wilkins *Math. Mag.* I. ix. 57 It is chiefly applied to the squeezing or pressing of things downwards. **1683** Moxon *Mech. Exerc., Printing* xi. ¶1 The reason..for this coming down, is the squeezing of the several parts in the Press. **1730** Bailey (fol.), *Ecpiesmus*, a straining, wringing, or squeezing out. **1800** *Med. Jrnl.* IV. 330 The oppression and squeezing of the chest he felt during the greater part of the night. **1855** Bain *Senses & Intell.* II. ii. §5 That the squeezing or pinching of a nerve can produce sensibility is proved in many experiments. **1884** Q. Victoria *More Leaves* 317 There was a great crowding and squeezing, and some children screamed with fright.

fig. *a* **1700** *Dict. Cant. Crew*, *Squeezing of Wax*, being bound for any Body; also sealing of Writings.

b. That which is squeezed out.

a **1683** Oldham *Wks. & Rem.* (1686) 25 Heavens just pow'r thought fit To scourge this latter, and more sinful age With all the dregs, and squeesings of his rage. *a* **1719** Addison tr. *Virg. Georg.* iv. Wks. 1721 I. 23 His Bees first swarm'd, and made his vessels foam With the rich squeezing of the juicy comb.

2. The action of oppressing by exactions or extortion; the practice of extorting excessive or illicit gain.

1681 R. L'Estrange *Tully's Offices* 147 Publique Cheats, Oppressions, Squeezing of the people. **1693** *Humours Town* 32 Being better acquainted with the squeezing and harassing of their tenants. **1697** J. Collier *Ess. Mor. Subj.* II. (1709) 74 Let there nothing be said against..Spinning out of Causes, Squeesing of Clients. **1768** Foote *Devil* I. Wks. 1799 II. 252 He only suggested their cent. per cent. squeezings, and prompted the various modes of extortion and rapine. **1864** *Athenæum* No. 1923. 297/2 The squeezing, or black mail,..of the mandarins. **1892** *Daily News* 26 Oct. 5/7 From the highest official to the lowest all practise a system of unblushing robbery, called 'squeezing'.

3. *attrib.*, as ***squeezing action, noise, process***; **squeezing-box** (see quot. 1875); †**squeezing watch**, ? a repeating watch operated by pressing the mechanism.

1708 *Brit. Apollo* No. 30. 4/2 Lost..a Gold Squeezing-watch, with a Gold Chain to it. *Ibid.* No. 40. 4/2 Lost.., a Gold Sweezing Watch. **1853** Kane *Grinnell Exped.* xxxiii. (1856) 283 We could hear a squeezing noise among the ice-fields. **1868** *Rep. Munitions War* 285 Close the breech by a squeezing action. **1875** Knight *Dict. Mech.* 2295/2 *Squeezing-box*, a metallic cylinder having a hole in the bottom, through which clay is pressed for shaping the handles, etc., of earthenware. **1900** *Daily News* 24 Sept. 2/2 Now I hope the squeezing process has come to an end.

ˈsqueezing, *ppl. a.* [f. as prec.] That squeezes, in various senses; also, indicative of effort.

a **1687** Villiers (Dk. Buckhm.) *Poems* (1775) 144 His squeezing looks, his pangs of wit accuse, The very symptoms of a breeding muse. *a* **1726** in P. Walker *Life R. Cameron* in *Biogr. Presbyt.* (1827) I. 291 With squeezing Boots malignant Malice sported. **1727** Swift *Wonder of Wonders* Wks. 1751 II. II. 52 He hath the reputation to be a close, griping, squeezing fellow. **1839** [see SQUEEZER 3]. **1853** Kane *Grinnell Exped.* xxxix. (1856) 358 Followed by the peculiar swash of squeezing ice. **1897** *Westm. Gaz.* 15 Feb. 3 Would she..remain fixed to be crushed by the squeezing masses?

squeezy (ˈskwiːzɪ), *a.* [f. as prec.] Suggestive of, characterized by, squeezing; having a compressed or confined character. Also, capable of being squeezed, esp. as ***squeezy bottle***, squeeze bottle. Also *fig.*

1751 Gray *Lett.* (1900) I. 216 The Women are few here, squeezy & formal, and little skill'd in amusing themselves or other People. **1759** *Compl. Lett.-writer* (1768) 217 After her, ..by Way of Contrast, the squeezy Mrs Ellen Risborough, contracting her Minuteness to a Shadow, with Stays.. pinching her like [a] Pair of Nutcrackers. **1825** T. Lister *Granby* xvii. (1836) 110 And then another squeezy quadrille, and so on. **1843** Mrs. Romer *Rhone, Darro*, etc. II. 142 A squeezy little room just large enough to contain my bed. **1866** Miss Braddon *Lady's Mile* vii, The deliciously-squeezy little drawing-rooms and ante-chambers..in Mayfair. **1971** R. A. Percy *Charlesworth on Negligence* (ed. 5) xviii. 732 Using a squeezy bottle to squirt coolant liquid into the interior of a workpiece on a centre lathe. **1972** *Guardian* 5 Dec. 16/6 Strong colours ready mixed in squeezy bottles, a boon for..young children.

squegger (ˈskwɛgə(r)). *Electronics.* [Of uncertain origin: perh. a shortened respelling of *self-quench(ing* + -ER[1].] An oscillator whose oscillations build up to a certain amplitude and then cease for a time before beginning again; also, the production of such oscillations.

1921 *Radio Rev.* May 248 The production of notes by a high-frequency oscillating valve making use of a grid leak and condenser, and the factors governing the pitch of this note, were discussed. The application of this arrangement (termed by Major Prince a 'squegger') to a receiver..was also described. **1932** *Admiralty Handbk. Wireless Telegr. 1931* xvi. 727 Receivers in which..self-oscillations alternately build up and are damped out without the necessity of a separate circuit to vary the reaction. These are called self-quenching receivers or squeggers. **1932** Ladner & Stoner *Short Wave Wireless Communications* viii. 147 The presence of audible modulation..may also be brought about by a high resistance in the grid circuit... This effect ..was called originally a 'squegger'. **1932** *Wireless Engineer* IX. 186 In the super-regenerative class, two receivers were available, one of the self-quench (or squegger) type. **1946** C. A. Quarrington *Mod. Pract. Radio & Television* II. x. 156 Time bases employing the squegger principle are inclined to be affected unduly by working conditions.

Hence (as a back-formation) **squeg** *v. intr.*, (of an electrical circuit) to oscillate intermittently, to be self-quenching; †**ˈsqueggering** *vbl. sb.*; **ˈsquegging** *vbl. sb.* and *ppl. a.*

1933 *QST* Sept. 66/2 Coupling between this 'squegging' oscillator and the receiver is obtained. *Ibid.* Nov. 17/1 The receiver may be made..to operate as a super-regenerator, by increasing the screen voltage to the point where 'squegging' (low frequency oscillation) starts. **1938** *Television* XI. 540/3 The valve is allowed to oscillate continuously with pauses of quiescence ('squeggering'). **1939** *Radio Amateur's Handbk. 1940* (ed. 17) iv. 61/1 Too much feed-back will cause the oscillator to 'squeg', or operate at several frequencies simultaneously. **1942** *Electronic Engin.* XIV. 629/3 The great difficulty in ultra high frequency oscillators is to obtain sufficient oscillation amplitude without squeggering or dead-spots in the turning range. **1947** *Ibid.* XIX. 162 Increase of R_3 to successively greater values results in the oscillator squegging. **1959** K. Henney *Radio Engin. Handbk.* (ed. 5) xii. 22 The adjustment of the feedback to give oscillation without pulsing or squegging is very critical. **1973** *Simulation* XXI. 77/2 There are circumstances under which squegging is desirable, such as in a superregenerative receiver. *Ibid.* 79/2 A squegging oscillator is highly sensitive to the settings of certain parameters.

squelch (skwɛltʃ, skwɛlʃ), *sb.* Also 8 **squelsh.** [Imitative.]

1. a. A heavy crushing fall or blow acting on a soft body; the sound produced by this.

1620 Shelton *Quix.* III. iv. 25 The Stakes fail'd, and I got a good Squelch upon the Ground. **1656** Earl Monm. tr. *Boccalini's Advts. fr. Parnass.* I. xliii. 59 Giving their Adversaries such deadly squelches as they shall never rise again. **1719** Ozell tr. *Misson's Mem. Trav. Eng.* 25 A Turn of the [Bull's] Horn..puts him in Danger of a damnable Squelch when he comes down. **1760–72** H. Brooke *Fool of Qual.* (1809) II. 18 His shoulders and head came with a squelch to the earth. **1829** Marryat *F. Mildmay* xix, I heard a heavy squelch and a howl. **1854** H. Miller *Sch. & Schlm.* xxi. (1858) 467, I heard a peculiar sound,—a *squelch*, if I may employ such a word.

fig. **1685** F. Spence tr. *Varilla's Ho. Medicis* 301 The house of Medici now seem'd humbled by so terrible a squelch, that it cou'd not..get up again.

b. *fig.* A disconcerting surprise.

1815 Lamb *Corr.* 278 Just such a cold squelch as going down a plausible turning and suddenly reading 'No thoroughfare'.

c. A devastating argument or retort; a crushing blow. *slang* (orig. *U.S.*).

1942 Berrey & Van den Bark *Amer. Thes. Slang* §11/3 Something conclusive or decisive (as an argument, answer, blow, or the like),..squasher, squelch, squelcher. **1964** *Pix* (Australia) 4 Aug., *Pix* has added to its large collection of famous squelches with contributions from readers. **1977** *Amer. Speech 1975* L. 155 If I use *humdinger*, I have to face the derisive remark of my elder son, 'Nobody used that word since Theodore Roosevelt died'.., or the equally crushing squelch of the younger one, 'Papa, that is not even funny.'

2. A thing or mass that has the appearance of having been squelched or crushed. Also *fig.*

1837 Carlyle *Misc. Ess.* (1888) V. 195 A mangled squelch of gore, confusion and abomination. **1849** D. G. Rossetti *Let. to W. M. Rossetti* 24 Sept., Your surgeon..is a wretched sneak—quite a sniggering squelch of a fellow.

3. The sound made by a liquid when subjected to sudden or intermittent pressure.

1895 Snaith *Dorothy Marvin* xxviii, 'Twas sickening to feel the squelch of the blood at your sword point. **1897** *Allbutt's Syst. Med.* III. 476 To the expert physician the sounds are not closely alike; that of gastralgia is a squelch.

4. *Electronics.* A circuit that suppresses all input signals except ones of a predetermined character; *spec.* in *Radio*, a circuit that suppresses the noise output of a receiver when the signal strength falls below a predetermined level. Freq. *attrib.*

1937 [see QUIETING *vbl. sb.* 2 a]. **1945** *FM & Televison* Apr. 31/1 The feature of this squelch circuit is that sharp pulses of interference do not open the squelch... It has been found that a 1-microvolt signal can open the squelch, but noise pulses of considerable amplitude do not. **1950** J. K. Henney *Radio Engin. Handbk.* (ed. 4) xvii. 822 A signal of 140 db (0·1 μv) is sufficient to open the squelch of a police receiver. **1959** [see MUTING *vbl. sb.* b]. **1976** *CB Mag.* June 64/1 (Advt.), the transceiver is combined through a switchable standby circuit to interrupt the music when the adjustable squelch level is broken. **1981** *Daily Tel.* 5 Nov. 2 (Advt.), Ultra compact, yet has variable squelch to cut signal 'chopping'.

squelch (skwɛltʃ, skwɛlʃ), *v.* Also 7 **squelche,** 8–9 **squelsh.** [f. as prec. Cf. QUELCH *v.*]

1. a. *trans.* To fall, drop, or stamp upon (something soft) with crushing or squashing force; to crush in this way.

1624 Middleton *Game at Chess* v. iii, The Fat Bishop hath so overlaid me, So squelch'd and squeezed me, I've no verjuice left in me! *a* **1625** Fletcher *Nice Valour* v. i, Oh 'twas your luck and mine to be squelch'd, Mr. 'Has stamped my very puddings into Pancakes. **1719** Baynard *Health* (1740) 30 Besides your guts, if fat, it squelches, And causes fumes, and sour belches. **1825** Hone *Every-day Bk.* I. 1198 His left leg stood upon another dog squelched by his weight. **1850** Kingsley *Alton Locke* xxxvi. (1879) 377 My cousin, as he turned away, thrust the stone back with his foot, and squelched me flat. **1880** *Daily Tel.* 9 Dec., The smallest of the family of steam hammers will squelch it as thin as a six-pence at a single blow.

refl. **1859** *Blackw. Mag.* LXXXV. 302/1 Each man squelching himself..in the corner that best pleased him. *fig.* **1862** CARLYLE *Fredk. Gt.* XII. xi. (1872) IV. 250 Ambitious persons often..get squelched to pieces by bringing the Twelve Labours of Hercules on Unherculean backs.

b. *fig.* To squash or crush; to put down or suppress thoroughly or completely. Now chiefly *U.S.*

1864 *Temperance Spectator* 1 Dec. 184 We readily concede that the doctrine..has been utterly squelched by the Doctor's weighty arguments. **1872** H. W. BEECHER *Chr. World Pulpit* I. 207/3 The time is coming when you cannot squelch a barbarian horde in Pennsylvania without having it known throughout..the world. **1878** HUXLEY in *Life* (1900) I. xxxiii. 488 It would be so nice to squelch that pompous impostor. **1890** *Spectator* 8 Nov., The movement for 'reciprocity' in Canada..will be squelched at once. **1910** *Dialect Notes* III. 455 *Squelch, v. tr.*, to snub, to turn down. 'She *squelched* him.' **1936** L. C. DOUGLAS *White Banners* vi. 135 An inquisitive maid-of-all-work who might try to be chummy unless promptly squelched. **1960** *Wall St. Jrnl.* 15 Mar. 14 Recent attempts by other domestic unions to hurtle national boundaries have been squelched. **1978** H. WOUK *War & Remembrance* xxv. 252 That'll squelch him, I assure you, and he'll be as quiet as a mouse.

2. *intr.* †**a.** To make squelchy sounds. *Obs.*$^{-1}$

1709 *Brit. Apollo* No. 38. 3/2 Still Coughing or Squelching,..[She] is all that is ugly and old.

b. To fall with a squelch.

1755 JOHNSON, *To Squab*, v.n., to fall down plump or flat; to squelsh or squash. **1825** BRITTON *Beauties Wilts* III. 378 *Squelch*, to fall heavily. **1865-** in dial. glossaries, etc. (Derby, Warw., Wilts.).

c. To emit a squelch or squelches; to spout in squelches.

1834 J. WILSON *Noctes Ambr.* Wks. 1856 IV. 25 Their sodden corpses squelchin at every spang o' the flying dragons. **1892** STEVENSON & OSBOURNE *Wrecker* v. 68 My boots began to squelch and pipe along the restaurant floors. **1905** MCCARTHY *Dryad* 263 Water was squelching and oozing and bubbling over his horse's fetlocks.

d. To walk or tread heavily in water or wet ground, or with water in the shoes, so as to make a splashing sound.

1849 ALB. SMITH *Pottleton Legacy* xxiv. 254 You'd..pass all your time in squelching about soppy fields. **1851** HAWTHORNE *Amer. Note-Bks.* (1883) 404 He squelching along all the way, with his india-rubber shoes full of water. **1881** *Blackw. Mag.* July 110 In another moment [we] were squelching over the sloppy ground.

3. *trans. Electronics.* = QUIET *v.* 2 d.

1950 J. K. HENNEY *Radio Engin. Handbk.* (ed. 4) xvii. 822 This voltage drop biases the first audio amplifier beyond cutoff, thus squelching the set. **1976** *S9* (N.Y.) May/June 107/1 The light..then remains on (although the receiver may be squelched, it will then pick up all calls on the channel until it is reset by the firefighter).

Hence **squelched** *ppl. a.*

1837 CARLYLE *Misc.* (1840) V. 98, I behold thee..a squelched Putrefaction, here on London pavements. **1867** F. HARRISON *Autobiogr. Mem.* (1911) I. xviii. 343 Unmistakably..the squelched rats will squeal. **1914** 'HIGH JINKS, JR.' *Choice Slang* 18 *Squelched*, ignored, insulted, 'sat upon'. **1928** *Sat. Even. Post* 7 Jan. 20/2 Apparently squelched, she made no reply.

squelch, *adv.* [f. as prec.] With or as with a squelch or heavy squash.

1772 R. GRAVES *Spir. Quix.* (1783) III. 202 When he was got about seven or eight feet high, he made a sudden pause; and, squelch, he came down again. **1820** *Glenfergus* I. iv. 93 The maid lay squelch on the floor, rolled together, and blubbering and bawling hideously. **1823-** in dial. glossaries (Suffolk, Nhp., Leics., Hamps., Warw., Wilts.). **1851** BORROW *Lavengro* lxxxviii, He lost his wind, and falling squelch on the ground, do you see, he lost the battle.

'squelcher. *colloq.* [f. SQUELCH *v.*] One who, or that which, squelches; a squelching or crushing blow, leading article, etc.

1854 'C. BEDE' *Verdant Green* II. iv, There's a squelcher in the bread-basket, that'll stop your dancing! **1876** BESANT & RICE *Gold. Butterfly* xviii, I went back to the editor's room. He was going on again with his usual occupation of manufacturing squelchers. **1893** *Microcosm* (N.Y.) X. 192 He then asserts..that he has demolished our law by an overwhelming 'squelcher'.

'squelching, *vbl. sb.* [f. SQUELCH *v.*] The action of the verb, in various senses.

1709 *Brit. Apollo* No. 38. 3/2 Her Coughing and Squelching, Her F..ting and Belch[in]g, Ye Gods, what a Consort is here! **189.** KIPLING *Soldiers Three, Only a Subaltern*, There was an undecided squelching of heavy boots.

'squelching, *ppl. a.* [f. as prec.]

1. *dial.* Unusually big; burly.

1854 MISS BAKER *Northampt. Gloss.* s.v., A great squelching man. *a* **1904** in *Eng. Dial. Dict.* (Warw., Hants.).

2. That squelches under treading or pressure; emitting a squelchy sound.

1869 'BRADWOOD' [W. B. Woodgate] *The O.V.H.* I. xii. 210 The soil was rather holding and squelching. **1894** JANE BARLOW *Kerrigan* 110 He stepped up in his squelching brogues. **1895** K. GRAHAME *Golden Age* 14, I dug glad heels into the squelching soil.

3. Of sounds: Of the nature of a squelch; suggestive of squelching.

1881 *Cassell's Nat. Hist.* V. 177 When removed from the water they emit a peculiar 'squelching' noise. **1885** *Pall Mall G.* 5 May 4/2 Portions are dabbed on the plates with a slapping, squelching sound.

4. Crushing; squashing.

1885 *New Bk. Sports* 123 A straight downward blow, is delivered with a peculiarly 'squelching' effect.

squelchy ('skwɛltʃɪ, 'skwɛlʃɪ), *a.* [f. SQUELCH *sb.* or *v.*]

1. Liable to squelch or to emit a squelching sound. Cf. SQUELCHING *ppl. a.* 2.

1843 [JAMES] *Commissioner* 48 The peer was seen struggling to raise the squelchy rotundity of his abdomen over the wall. **1899** *Allbutt's Syst. Med.* VIII. 153 It is to be remembered that the squelchy stomachs, as I have called them,..of many neurasthenics may be taken for dilated organs. **1914** [see PAWPAW]. **1928** *Daily Express* 12 June 10/5 What Will Woman Do Next?.. Start an agitation, I shouldn't wonder, for the suppression of the word 'women'. Sober and dignified once.., the over-work of the last ten years has made a sickening, squelchy mess of it.

2. Of sounds: = SQUELCHING *ppl. a.* 3.

1897 *Allbutt's Syst. Med.* III. 475 Squelchy sounds on manipulation are not certain signs of ectasis. **1904** *Westm. Gaz.* 4 Feb. 1/3 At each stamp his shoes had made a squelchy squeak.

squelery, obs. form of SCULLERY.

†**squelter**, obs. variant of SWELTER *v.*

1595 *Locrine* II. vi, The slaughtered Troians, squeltring in their blood. *Ibid.* III. iv, The trecherous Scithians squeltring in their gore.

squench, *v.* Now *dial.* Also 6 **sqwenche**, 9 **squinch**. [f. QUENCH *v.* with prosthetic *s-*.]

1. *trans.* To extinguish, put out (a fire, etc.). Also *absol.*

1535 LAYTON in Ellis *Orig. Lett.* Ser. III. III. 165 The gret dynyng chambre..was sodenly fierede by sum fier-bronde... Asson as I hade sett men to sqwenche and to labor, I went into the Churche. **1541** PAYNELL *Catiline* vii. 11 Rather wyll a womanne squenche flame in a burnynge mouthe than kepe counsayle. **1600** *1st Pt. Contention* G 2 b, London bridge is a fire. Runne to Billingsgate, and fetch pitch and flaxe and squench [1619 quench] it. **1698** FRYER *Acc. E. India & P.* 152 One of the Factors..was blown up by a Cartrige of Pow[d]er, and squenched his Cloathes a-flame in the Ocean. **1823** E. MOOR *Suffolk Words, Squench*, to quench—fire or thirst. **1889** TENNYSON *Owd Roa* lix, I'll coom an' I'll squench the light.

2. To suppress, put an end to; to quell or stifle. *rare.*

1577 GRANGE *Golden Aphrod.* M iv b, Our sorrowes are squenched, with pleasaunt delight. **1606** WARNER *Alb. Eng.* XV. xcvi. 384 Babel is falne, Vr-Caldick squencht, Delphos in no request. *c* **1610** BEAUM. & FL. *Philaster* v. i, They'l flea him, and make Church Buckets on's skin to squench rebellion. **1865** *Punch* 20 May 200/2 Mr. Newdegate had a plan, whereof not much need be said, as it was squenched by 126 to 42. **1923** U. L. SILBERRAD *Let. Jean Armiter* iv. 100 You are not easily squenching Art, with a capital A, when it is once fairly talking.

3. To satisfy (the appetite, etc.); to slake (one's thirst).

1598 T. BASTARD *Chrestoleros* (1880) 53 Whome all the worlde which late they stood vpon Could not content nor squench their appetites. **1803** MARY CHARLTON *Wife & Mistress* IV. 50 Forbidding her a dish of tea to squinch her thirst. **1840** DICKENS *Old C. Shop* lviii, I wouldn't have taken much..—only enough to squench my hunger. **1876-** in various dial. glossaries.

4. To slake (lime).

1643 J. STEER tr. *Exp. Chyrurg.* vi. 24 Water, wherein Lime hath been squenched, is good for the same purpose.

5. *intr.* To become extinguished.

1643 J. STEER tr. *Exp. Chyrurg.* v. 14 Coals doe quickly squench if they are scattered about.

Hence **'squencher**, that which quenches.

1871 BLACK in W. Reid *Biogr.* (1902) iii. 95 If I had merely taken a squencher at Simpson's in Oxford Street. **1894** HESLOP *Northumberland Gloss.* 682 *Squinsher*, an extinguisher for a candle.

squene, variant of SQUEAN *v. Obs.*

†**squetch**, obs. variant of QUETCH *v.*

13.. *Sir Beues* 1753 þe medwe squauȝte of [*v.r.* quakyd with] her dentes, þe fur fleȝ out, so spark o flintes.

squeteague (skwɛ'ti:g). *U.S.* [Narragansett Indian.] The weak-fish or sea-salmon, *Cynoscion regalis* (†*Otolithus regalis*, †*Labrus Squeteague*), of the eastern United States. ***spotted squeteague*** (see quot. 1884).

1838 in D. H. Storer *Rep. Fishes Mass.* (1839) 33 The squeteague, or weak fish, have disappeared since the return of the blue fish, who are their avowed enemy. **1848** BARTLETT *Dict. Amer.* 328 *Squeteague*, or *Squetee*,..a very common fish in the waters of Long Island Sound and adjacent bays. **1871** in Good *Amer. Fishes* (1888) 113 Scup have disappeared from Narragansett Bay, but Squeteague have taken their place. **1884** GOODE *Nat. Hist. Aquatic Anim.* 365 The Spotted Squeteague, *Cynoscion maculatum*. This fish is..in every respect very unlike a trout, and the name 'Spotted Squeteague' has been proposed for it.

squetee: (see prec., quot. 1848).

squib (skwɪb), *sb.* Forms: 6 **squyb(e, sqwybe (skwybe, skuybe, scuibe, skybb)**, 7 **squybb**, 6–7 **squibb(e (7 sqib, squip)**, 6– **squib**. [Of obscure origin; perh. intended as imitative of an explosive sound.]

1. a. A common species of firework, in which the burning of the composition is usually terminated by a slight explosion.

'Squibs are straight cylindrical cases about 6 inches long, firmly closed at one end, tightly packed with a strong composition, and capped with touch-paper' (**1886** *Encycl. Brit.* XX. 136).

a **1530** HEYWOOD *Play of Love* 1293 (Stage-dir.), Here the vyse cometh in..with a hye copyn tank on his hed full of squybs fyred. **1551-2** in Feuillerat *Revels Edw. VI* (1914) 67 One hollowe clubb to burne squibbes in. **1582** N. LICHEFIELD tr. *Castanheda's Conq. E. Ind.* I. xii. 31 Our men made them a great feast, with much pastime also of Squibs, Gunne shot, and great and lowde cryes. **1623** in Ellis *Orig. Lett.* Ser. I. III. 160 Every College had a speech and one dish more at supper, and bonefires and squibbes in their Courts. **1673** BOYLE *Ess. Effluviums* II. 28 The irregular and wrigling motion of those fired Squibs that Boys are wont to make by ramming Gunpowder into Quills. **1721** AMHERST *Terræ Fil.* No. 22 (1726) I. 124 Several squibs were thrown in at the window, which burnt some of their cloaths. **1774** *Ann. Reg.* 151 Several people amused themselves with throwing squibs about the gates of the palace. **1808** *Beverley Lighting Act* 18 Crackers, squibs, serpents, rockets, or other fireworks. **1873** E. SPON *Workshop Receipts* Ser. I. 139/1 For squibs, before filling the case, ram in hard a thimbleful of coarse gun-powder.

b. In fig. context. (Cf. sense 3.)

1599 *Broughton's Lett.* 47 Your bookes [are] but squibs, compounds of gunpowder and pisse. **1623** HEXHAM *Tongue-combat* 50 [It] sets all Christendome in combustion, with a Romish squib of reseruation. **1644** QUARLES *Whipper Whipt* Wks. (Grosart) I. 164/1 If he cast no squibs in a Princes face, ..they say he hath no holy Fire in him. **1753** RICHARDSON *Grandison* (1781) II. 282, I could then throw my little squibs about me at pleasure; and not fear..the singeing of my own cloaths! *a* **1771** SMOLLETT *Humph. Cl.* (1815) 236 He..even threw such squibs at the immortality of the soul, as singed a little the whiskers of Mrs. Tabitha's faith. **1861** *Sat. Rev.* 30 Nov. 554 A talker of the highest order ought not to encourage the expectation of squibs and crackers as often as he opens his mouth. **1882** A. W. WARD *Dickens* iii. 68 In 1841 he had thrown a few squibs in the Examiner at Sir Robert Peel and the Tories.

†**c.** In fig. allusions to the display of such fireworks on a rope or line. *Obs.*

1647 CLEVELAND *Charac. Lond.-Diurn.* (1653) 81 But the Squib is run to the end of the Rope. **1649** G. DANIEL *Trinarch.* To Rdr. 39 Some Squibbs preparеing are, the Ropes are laid To entertaine the Gapers. **1679** DRYDEN *Limberham* v. i, Well, the squibs run to the end of the line, and now for the cracker.

d. *fig.* or in fig. contexts. ***damp squib***, something that fails ignominiously to satisfy the expectations aroused by it; an anti-climax, a disappointment.

1847 ALB. SMITH *Chr. Tadpole* i. (1879) 20 The literary gentleman having finished, like a damp squib with a good bang, resumed his seat. **1963** *Times* 6 Mar. 11/3 Possibly because too much was expected of it, the long-range study of Britain's transport needs by a Ministry of Transport group under Sir Robert Hall is something of a damp squib. **1976** *Yorkshire Even. Press* 9 Dec. 8/5, I came here thinking this Scarborough business would cause fireworks, but I have never known such a damp squib.

2. †**a.** An explosive device used as a missile or means of attack. *Obs.*

1589 R. HARVEY *Pl. Perc.* (1590) 7 Not to cast them like squibs & wild fire within your owne hatches. **1591** RALEIGH *Last Fight 'Revenge'* A 3 b, Their Nauy..consisting of 240 saile of ships..were..driuen with squibs from their anchors. **1598** FLORIO, *Petardo*, a squib or petard of gun powder vsed to burst vp gates or doores with. **1610** B. JONSON *Alch.* IV. iii, He speakes out of a fortification. 'Pray god, he ha' no squibs in those deepe sets. **1686** tr. *Chardin's Trav. Persia* 3 The Admiral coming to an Anchor, fir'd several Squibs from his Main-Top-Mast.

b. *slang.* A gun.

1839 G. W. M. REYNOLDS *Pickw. Abroad* xxvi. *Song*, A double-tongued [= double-barrelled] squib to keep in awe The chaps that flout at me.

c. *Mining.* (See quots.)

1881 RAYMOND *Mining Gloss.*, *Squib*, a slow-match or safety-fuse, used with a barrel. **1883** GRESLEY *Gloss. Coal-m.* 234 *Squib*, a straw, rush, paper, or quill tube filled with a priming of gunpowder,..and ignited by means of a smift.

3. A smart gird or hit; a sharp scoff or sarcasm; a short composition of a satirical and witty character; a lampoon.

c **1525** in Thoms *Anecd.* (Camden) 15 Purposing to put a grave slye squibbe upon him, 'Sir,' sayes he, 'this does not well'. **1593** NASHE *Four Lett. Conf.* Wks. (Grosart) II. 277 Thou must haue one squibbe more at the Deuils Orator,..or thy penne is not in cleane life. **1607** HIERON *Defence* I. 224 Observe..his squibb at M. B. for saying Austin not S. Austin. **1654** VILVAIN *Theorem. Theol.* iii. 87 'Tis a silly Sophisters squib to say, Bishops are called Elders, and contrarily. **1739** POPE *Let. to Warburton* 4 Jan., I see by certain squibs in the Miscellanies, that [etc.]. **1775** BINDLEY in *J. Granger's Lett.* (1805) 387 The little squib you sent me I thank you for; I think it lively enough. **1844** DISRAELI *Coningsby* I. ii, No one was more faithful to his early friends .., particularly if they could write a squib. **1882** SERGT. BALLANTINE *Exper.* xiii. 127 His tendency to uphold technical views gave rise to a very clever squib.

4. Applied to persons: **a.** A mean, insignificant, or paltry fellow; also, a short or thin person.

1586 ABP. LOFTUS in Froude *Eng.* (1870) XII. 201 *note*, They are all of them but a sort of beggars and squibbes, puppies, dogs, dunghill churles. **1591** SPENSER *M. Hubberd* 371 Its an hard case, when men of good deseruing Must.. be..asked for their pas by euerie squib, That list at will them to reuile or snib. **1599** NASHE *Lenten Stuff* Wks. (Grosart) V. 288 Out steps me an infant squib of the Innes of Court. *a* **1653** G. DANIEL *Idyll* i. 39 Away! Squibbs of Scurrilitie; 'twas Shame First taught vs cloths. **1898** *Leeds Mercury Suppl.* 26 Mar. (E.D.D.), Ah'll knock thee dahn, yo' little squib, if tha doesn't shut thi gob. **1979** *Courier-Mail* (Brisbane) 28 Apr. 17/2 We have numerous utility expressions for people such as..sparrow squib, nugget and streak, for men of varying sizes.

†**b.** A subordinate decoy in a gambling-house.
1731 *Gentl. Mag.* I. 25 A Squib is a Puff of a lower Rank, who serves at half salary.

c. A firer or thrower of squibs. *rare*⁻¹.
1759 H. WALPOLE *Lett.* (1846) III. 471 Every squib in town got drunk, and rioted about the streets till morning.

d. *Oxford slang.* erron. for SQUIL.
1866 *St. James's Mag.* Oct. 366 The simple seeming 'squib' was..a phrase used..by the privileged Christ Church man to designate any member of the university not a member of the..House. *Ibid.* 367 The supercilious *soubriquet* of 'squib' is practically extinct.

e. A horse lacking courage or endurance; hence, a coward. *Austral. slang.*
1908 [see MONTY]. **1924** *Truth* (Sydney) 27 Apr. 6 *Squib*, a coward. **1933** *Bulletin* (Sydney) 15 Nov. 8/4 In the result stayers reproducing the old-time qualities of the Australian thoroughbred became rare; but speedy squibs abounded. **1936** A. RUSSELL *Gone Nomad* 55 There's no place in this town for squibs. **1947** *Coast to Coast 1946* 217 'You're a bloody lot of squibs,' said Darky disgustedly. **1951** F. HARDY *Power without Glory* 160, I know these johnnys; they're all squibs. **1978** *Telegraph* (Brisbane) 8 Feb. 20/1 Don Ash is the sort of bloke who makes you feel a squib for crying off with some minor ache or pain from that daily canter around the block.

5. A squirt or syringe. Now *dial.*
1583 STUBBES *Anat. Abus.* II. (1882) 36 A squirt, or a squibbe, which little children vsed to squirt out water withall. **1854-** in dial. glossaries (Nhp., Leics., Worc., Kent, Glouc., Warw.).

†**6.** (See first quot.) *Obs.*
1611 COTGR., *Petereau*, a little fart, or Squib. **1653** URQUHART *Rabelais* I. xxv, Often-times thinking to let a squib, they did all-to-besquatter..themselves.

7. a. A small measure or quantity (*of* strong drink). Now *dial.*
1766 AMORY *Buncle* (1770) III. 208 He got me a good supper of trouts, fine ale, and a squib of punch. **1805** in *Spirit Public Jrnls.* IX. 312 We raised our spirits with a snack of the bacon, and a squib of gin each. **1844** W. H. MAXWELL *Wand. Highl.* iii. (1855) 52 You..rode your..match without a *squib*. **1869-** in dial. glossaries, etc. (Lancs., Yks., Westm.).

b. *slang.* A head of asparagus.
1851 MAYHEW *Lond. Lab.* I. 93/1, I buy all mine at Covent-garden, where it's sold in bundles,..containing from six to ten dozen squibs (heads).

c. *colloq.* A kind of sweet made up in a form resembling a squib.
1851 MAYHEW *Lond. Lab.* I. 203/2 'Hardbake', 'almond toffy', 'half-penny lollipops', 'black balls', the cheaper 'bulls eyes', and 'squibs' are all made of treacle.

d. *slang.* (See quot.)
1865 *Slang Dict.* 244 *Squibs*, paint-brushes.

8. *attrib.* and *Comb.*, as (in sense 1) ***squib-crack(er, -light, -maker, -powder***; (in sense 3) ***squib-teller, -writer***; †**squib-pear** (see quots. 1664–76).
c **1610** BEAUM. & FL. *Philaster* II, They talk of Jupiter, he's but a squib cracker to her. **1630** J. TAYLOR (Water P.) *Laugh and be Fat* Wks. I. 70 With squib-crack lightning, empty hogshead thundring, To maze the world with terror & with wondring. **1647** (*title*), A Fresh Whip for all scandalous Lyers; or, a true Description of the two eminent Pamphliteers, or Squib-tellers of this Kingdome. **1659** *England's Conf.* 16 Hab. Morley Squib-maker. **1664** EVELYN *Kal. Hort.* 80 Fruits in Prime, and yet lasting... The Squib-pear, Spindle-pear, Virgin. **1676** WORLIDGE *Cyder* (1691) 216 Dead mans pear, Bell-pear, the Squib-pear,..are all very good winter pears. **1837** W. B. ADAMS *Carriages* ii. 47 Their own poet Taylor..now and then assisted by a stray pamphleteer or squib-writer. **1893** *Westm. Gaz.* 7 Nov. 3/2 A sort of Lord Mayor's Show by torchlight and squib-light.

squib (skwɪb), *v.* Also 7 squibb(e. [f. the sb.]

I. *intr.* **1.** To use smart or sarcastic language; to utter, write, or publish a squib or squibs. Freq. const. *against*, *at*, *on*, *upon*.
1579–80 G. HARVEY *Lett.* Wks. (Grosart) I. 80 For squibbing and declayming against many fruitlesse Artes, and Craftes. **1607** HIERON *Defence* I. 224 Why is M, B, squibbed at, who observeth that course? **1682** BUNYAN *Greatness Soul* Wks. 1855 I. 138 It is a sport now to taunt and squib and deride at other men's virtues. **1718** *Entertainer* No. 40. 276 He has a deal of reason to be perpetually a squibbing upon the Romish Clergy. **1797** WOLCOT (P. Pindar) *Ode Sir J. Banks* Wks. 1812 III. 454 What a joke! ye certainly are squibbing. **1825** *New Monthly Mag.* XVI. 312 Now artists and actors the bardling engage To squib in the journals, and write for the stage. **1852** W. JERDAN *Autobiog.* II. iii. 26, I argued, and fought, and squibbed, and abused, with the hottest of my contemporaries.

2. a. To let off squibs; to go *on* doing this.
In the quot. a stage-direction for thunder.
1691 J. WILSON *Belphegor* I. i, I'd make him know, I fill my Orb my self...—Squib on—and say [etc.].

b. To fire a gun, etc.; to shoot. Also *fig.*
1831 *Lincoln Herald* 22 July 4/4 To go squibbing about with their guns, and putting in jeopardy the lives of his majesty's subjects. **1839** G. W. M. REYNOLDS *Pickw. Abroad* xxvi. *Song*, And if the swells resist our 'Stand!' We'll squib without a joke.

3. a. To move *about* like a squib.
1760–2 GOLDSM. *Cit. World* lxxxviii, A battered unmarried beau, who squibs about from place to place. **1886** *S.W. Linc. Gloss.* 140 Mary Ann does squib about; she nips about when she is playing.

b. With *on*: to betray or let down (someone). Also without const., to funk, to behave in a cowardly manner; to wriggle or squirm. *Austral. slang.*
1938 S. J. BAKER in *Observer* 13 Nov. 11/3 Rat on = to betray, let down. Squib on = ditto. **1941** —— *Dict. Austral. Slang* 71 *Squib, to*, to funk, to be afraid of something. **1945** *Coast to Coast 1944* 5 I'll let him through; it's better to squib than to wreck old Dutch and myself, too. **1947** K. TENNANT *Lost Haven* xvii. 292 You'll probably squib out of it at the last moment. **1962** *Coast to Coast 1961–62* 83 He could finish on a good wicket in anything. And never squib on a bloke.

4. To make a report like that of a squib.
1886 KIPLING *Departm. Ditties*, etc. (1899) 83 A Snider squibbed in the jungle.

II. *trans.* **5. a.** To cast or throw *forth*, *off*, *out* (a remark, quip, etc.) after the manner of a squib.
1596 NASHE *Saffron Walden* Wks. (Grosart) III. 184 Anie Frezeland, Dutch, or Almain scribe..that hath but squibd foorth a Latin *Puerilis* in Print. **1602** DEKKER *Satirom.* Wks. 1873 I. 235, I could make thine eares burne now that thou wouldst neuer squib out any new Salt-peter jestes against honest Tucca. **1649** G. DANIEL *Trinarch.*, *Rich. II*, cccxli, The Arch-Bishop still Flirting Divinitie against the Throne, ..Squibs the Worne moralls, Hope and Patience. **1853** W. JERDAN *Autobiog.* IV. xiii. 237 Hook squibbed off a few pleasantries.

b. To let off (a squib); to fire (a gun, etc.), esp. with the priming or powder only; †to shoot (an arrow).
1603 SIR C. HEYDON *Def. Jud. Astrol.* ii. 22 A child squibbes his arrows at random into the aire. **1811** *Spirit Public Jrnls.* XVI. 5 Squibbed our guns over the bridge. **1829** W. H. MAXWELL *Stories Waterloo, F. Kennedy* 223 The customary bows were formally interchanged between the respective belligerents,..pistols squibbed, loaded, and delivered to the principals. **1892** B. HINTON *Lord's Return* 194, I shall have all the squibs squibbed if I don't go.

†**c.** *fig.* To throw *in* as a squib. *Obs.*⁻¹
1655 FULLER *Hist. Camb.* 14 When Matthew Parker.. reports, how many deserting Oxford removed to Cambridge, he [Twine] squibs in this Parenthesis.

6. To assail or attack (a person) with squibs or witty sarcasm; to lampoon or satirize smartly.
1631 MAY tr. *Barclay's Mirr. Minds* II. 20 They..are squibbed with iests and taunts, which like little darts, are in daily discourse throwne against them. **1758** J. ADAMS *Diary* 29 Dec. Wks. 1850 II. 53 Lambert will laugh, no doubt, and will tell the story to every man he sees, and will squib me about it whenever he sees me. **1830** *Examiner* 2/1 He suffered himself to be squibbed to death. **1868** GREEN *Lett.* (1901) II. 202 The mendicant parson, whom I am so fond of squibbing. **1880** DISRAELI *Endym.* xxxiii, There is a cabinet minister;..I have been squibbing him for these two years.

7. To spatter with a squib or squirt.
1840 BARHAM *Ingol. Leg.* Ser. II. *Nurs. Rem.* vi, Billy Hawkins..with his pewter squirt Squibb'd my pantaloons and stockings Till they were all over dirt.

8. To avoid (a difficulty or responsibility); to funk, to shirk through fear or cowardice. *Austral. slang.*
1934 *Bulletin* (Sydney) 1 Aug. 46/4 He judges the dodger's done just what he'd do himself; squibbed it and dropped his load. **1936** F. CLUNE *Roaming round Darling* xv. 138 Oxley and Evans attempted to explore the Macquarie, but floundering about the marshes Oxley squibbed the job once more. **1940** N. MONKS *Squadrons Up* i. 26 The censor ..said that we should not let the enemy Command know their fighters were squibbing it [*sc.* avoiding combat]. **1955** D. NILAND *Shiralee* 50 The rough-and-tumble doesn't worry me. I'm not squibbing the issue.

†**squibals**, *sb. pl. Obs. rare.* [ad. med.L. *squibala*, ad. Gr. σκύβαλα (sing. σκύβαλον).] Hard excrement.
a **1425** tr. *Arderne's Treat. Fistula*, etc. 76 Water alon & salt boiled togidre and ȝette in by a clistrye bringeþ out squiballez. *Ibid.* 77 Þe egestions, wheþer it be blode or putride flemme &c, or wormes or squiballez indurate.

'squibarchy. [f. SQUIB *sb.* 4d.] The predominance of 'squibs'.
1866 *St. James's Mag.* Oct. 366 Professor-canons..who, in their persons, introduced Squibarchy into those sacred precincts.

'squibber. [f. SQUIB *v.*] One who writes or utters squibs.
1810 *Irish Mag.* Aug. 377/1 Nothing like a squibber writing of his own acquirements. **1824** *Blackw. Mag.* XVI. 347 Never disturb yourself about little squibs... If you want to annoy the squibber, pretend never to have heard of them. **1863** *Athenæum* 11 July 45/3 Of course we speak of Hook the novelist, not of the political squibber of the *John Bull.*

squibbery ('skwɪbərɪ). [f. SQUIB *sb.* + -ERY.]

1. The writing or production of squibs; satire in the form of squibs.
1820 MISS MITFORD in L'Estrange *Life* (1870) II. 115, I did not go to Reading; the squibbery there was too much to encounter. **1824** *Examiner* 739/1 Some allowable squibbery was delivered in the way of a candid admission of the absence of conveniences for a stud of horses. **1834** MOORE *Mem.* (1856) VII. 59 The verses having been declined in the usual quarter through which I discharged my squibbery.

2. Squibs (*sc.* fireworks) collectively.
1824 MISS MITFORD *Village* Ser. I. (1863) 57 The loyal conflagration of the arch traitor Guy Vaux,..accompanied with as much of squibbery and crackery as our boys can beg or borrow.

'squibbing, *vbl. sb.* [f. SQUIB *v.*]

1. The utterance or writing of squibs.
1607 S. COLLINS *Serm.* (1608) 70 Their squibbing at the Prelacie, yea and glancing sometimes at the soueraign authority. *a* **1849** POE *Thou art the Man* Wks. 1895 I. 148 Hereupon some little squibbing and bickering occurred among various members of the crowd. **1856** J. W. CROKER in *C. Papers* (1884) I. i. 5, I was an early dabbler in political squibbing.

2. The action of firing or letting off squibs, shooting with a gun, etc. Also with *off*.
1697 in *14th Rep. Hist. MSS. Comm.* App. II. 592 The Governors of the city have been very diligent to prevent the squibbing. **1729** SWIFT *To Delany* Wks. 1751 III. II. 228 When with squibbing, flashing, popping, He cannot see one creature dropping. **1814** *Sporting Mag.* XLIV. 108 Nothing is more absurd, if a gun has been washed, than dirtying it long before its time, by what is called 'squibbing'. **1830** *Poor Man's Guardian* 25 Dec. 5/1 The squibbing off a few pistols after the meeting. **1841** *Peter Parley's Annual* II. 63 He was thoughtless enough to go on the Green in the midst of the squibbing, with this large quantity of squibs and crackers about him.

b. In fig. context.
1825 T. HOOK *Sayings* Ser. II. *Doubts & F.* vii, Under the heavy fire of her self-gratulation, supported by the auxiliary squibbing of her dependant. **1840** MRS. GORE in *New Monthly Mag.* LX. 53 The solemn minute-guns of a quarterly review compared with the squibbings of a daily paper.

'squibbing, *ppl. a.* [f. SQUIB *v.*]

1. Uttering or composing squibs; of the nature of a squib or squibs; characterized by smart or satirical remarks.
c **1650** in Langbaine *Acc. Eng. Dram. Poets* (1691) 258 The squibbing Middleton, and Heywood Sage, Th' Apologetick Atlas of the Stage. *a* **1651** CLEVELAND *Poems* 41 But you're inchanted, Sir, you're doubly free From the great Guns and Squibbing Poetry. **1825** T. HOOK *Sayings* Ser. II. *Passion & Princ.* x, A squibbing conversation, which was carrying on between the mother and daughters at the top of the table.

2. Acting as squibs; explosive.
1710 J. DUNTON *Life & Err.* (1818) II. xv. 704 Our squibbing *Boutefeus*, that fill the Church with endless noise, and heat, and pother.

3. Moving in a jerky irregular manner.
1895 *Outing* XXVII. 195/2 When I tried to take him on with a squibbing pony for half a mile.

squibbish ('skwɪbɪʃ), *a.* [f. SQUIB *sb.*] Having something of the character of a squib.
1676 MACE *Musick's Mon.* 129 Toys, or Jiggs, are Light Squibbish Things. **1822** *Examiner* 697/2 The squibbish breadth of humour in the encounter is highly diverting. **1826** DISRAELI *V. Grey* III. viii, I had expected..something juvenile and squibbish, when lo! I was introduced to a corpulent individual.

†**'squibbler.** *Obs.*⁻¹ [Alteration of QUIBBLER, perh. after SQUIB.] A quibbling writer.
1671 EACHARD *Obs. Answ. Cont. Clergy* 4 He must be bound over to Westminster Squibblers, hard Thrusters and Reputation Wounders.

†**'squibbling**, *ppl. a. Obs.*⁻¹ [Cf. prec.] Of the nature of a quibble; equivocal.
1674 BUNYAN *Peaceable Princ.* Wks. 1853 II. 649 Your artificial squibbling suggestions to the world about myself.

'squiblet. *rare.* [f. SQUIB *sb.* + -LET.] A little squib; a jeu d'esprit.
1820 *Blackw. Mag.* VIII. 123, I enclose you a squiblet which was written when Sir J. E. Smith..made his grand charge on our Botanical Chair.

'squibling. *rare*⁻¹. [-LING.] = SQUIBLET.
1884 *Sat. Rev.* 8 Nov. 590/2 A burnt out and by no means clean squibling like Mr. Thorold Rogers's comparison of the House of Lords to the Cities of the Plain.

†**'squibster.** *Obs.*⁻¹ [f. SQUIB *sb.* + -STER.] One who fires or throws squibs.
1625 PURCHAS *Pilgrimes* II. 1823 After them came Squibsters, but how many in number I could not vnderstand.

squich, obs. f. SQUITCH *v.*; obs. var. SUCH *a.*

squid (skwɪd), *sb.* Also 7 **squide.** [Of obscure origin.]

1. One or other of various species of cephalopods belonging to the family *Loliginidæ*, *Teuthididæ*, or *Sepiidæ*, more esp. to the genus *Loligo*; a calamary, cuttle, or pen-fish: **a.** With *a* and pl.
1613 PURCHAS *Pilgrimage* (1614) 747 Smelts and Squids.. come on shore in great abundance, fleeing from the deuouring cod. **1620** MASON *Newfoundland* 5 What should I speake of..Squides a rare kind of fish at his mouth squirting mattere forth like Inke. **1791** *Phil. Trans.* LXXXI. 44, I send you..some of the bills of the fish called Squids (which are supposed to be the food of spermaceti whales). **1809** *Naval Chron.* XXI. 22 Squids, a squalid kind of fish. **1863** COUCH *Brit. Fishes* II. 46 From one example I took two Gobies and a Launce: from another a Squid, (*Loligo media*), five inches in length. **1888** GOODE *Amer. Fishes* 27 Hunting for crabs, shrimps, squids, and other invertebrate animals.

b. With *the*, in generic use.
1839 T. BEALE *Hist. Sperm Whale* 34 An animal of the cuttle-fish kind, called by sailors the 'squid', and by naturalists the 'sepia octopus'. **1859** HUXLEY in *Macm. Mag.* I. 145 'Loligo,' the squid of modern seas, appears in the lias, or at the bottom of the mesozoic series. **1880** in Morris *Austral Eng.* (1898) 435 The squid (*Sepioteuthis australis*) is highly appreciated.

c. Without article, esp. as a bait or food-stuff.
1865 THOREAU *Cape Cod* vi. 107 Their bait was a bullfrog or several small frogs in a bunch, for want of squid. **1880** MISS BIRD *Japan* II. 213 These lights are much used in fishing, specially for squid. **1883** *Cassell's Fam. Mag.* July

469/1 Neat little cuttle-fish..are dried whole, for inland carriage, and others are salted and sold as squid.

d. Also with capital initial. A ship-mounted anti-submarine mortar with three barrels, developed in the war of 1939–45.

1947 Crowther & Whiddington *Science at War* iv. 160 A three-barrelled mortar for throwing three projectiles each was developed, and named the Squid... The expenditure of ammunition required to sink a U-boat with the Squid was very much less than with depth charges. The production of the Squid was ordered direct from the drawing board in the urgency of the situation in 1943. **1962** W. Granville *Dict. Sailors' Slang* 112/2 *Squid box*, housing of a *squid*, a triple-barrelled mortar for firing depth charges. It is placed on the sterns of destroyers and frigates. **1973** J. Quick *Dict. Weapons* 418/3 *Squid*, a British shipborne surface-to-sub-surface medium-range antisubmarine mortar system. A triple-barreled mortar fires a pattern of three mortar bombs which are programmed to give a three dimensional explosive pattern ahead of the target.

2. With distinguishing terms, denoting various species.

1840 F. D. Bennett *Whaling Voy.* I. 269 The flying-squid rose from the sea in large flocks. **1851** S. P. Woodward *Mollusca* I. (1856) 73 The sailors call them 'sea-arrows' or 'flying squid' from their habit of leaping out of the water. **1861** *Chambers's Encycl.* II. 724/2 The Hook-squids of the South Seas.

3. a. A squid-bill (see quot.).

1822–7 Good *Study Med.* (1829) I. 334 The mass is usually loaded with hard bony fragments, by the seamen called squids, which are the beaks of the cuttle-fish, on which the whale is known to feed.

b. ***bone-squid***, an artificial bait made to imitate a squid.

1883 *Cent. Mag.* 383 Whether spoon-bait, bone-squid or other like lure.

4. A stable configuration of a parachute which is only partially extended.

1947 *Techn. Rep. Aeronaut. Res. Comm. 1946* II. 1465 If a parachute is released into an airstream and its speed relative to the air is greater than a certain critical speed, it will not open fully. Instead it will take up a dynamically-stable partly-open shape known as a 'squid'. **1949** *Jrnl. R. Aeronaut. Soc.* LIII. 1055/1 For a parachute in a steady squid state, the inflow to the canopy equals the outflow.

5. *attrib.* and *Comb.*, as ***squid-beak***, ***-bill***, ***-family***, ***line***, ***school***, ***-tentacle***; ***squid-catching***, ***-jigging***; **squid fish**, = sense 1; **squid-hound** (see quots.); also *attrib.*; **squid jig**, **-jigger**, **-thrower** (see quots.).

1884 Goode *Nat. Hist. Aquat. Anim.* 18 *Squid-beaks enough to fill two water-buckets were taken from the stomach. *Ibid.* 11 *note*, As *squid-bills are sometimes found in the lumps of ambergrease, it may be inferred, that ambergrease is some of the excrement from squid-food. **1881** *Cassell's Nat. Hist.* V. 170 In many stations more than a dozen boats are engaged in *Squid-catching. **1883** in Morris *Austral Eng.* (1898) 435 None of the *Squid family seems to be sought after, although certain kinds are somewhat abundant in our waters. **1725** *Phil. Trans.* XXXIII. 262 The Sperma Ceti Whale, besides other Fish, feeds much upon a small Fish that has a Bill; our Fishermen call them *Squid Fish. **1884** Goode *Nat. Hist. Aquat. Anim.* 11 *note*, Squid-fish, one of the Newfoundland baits for cod, are sometimes in Newfoundland cast ashore in quantities. **1794** A. Thomas *Newfoundland Jrnl.* (1968) 183 Whenever Squids are found is also found a Fish called Jumpers, or *Squid Hounds, from the avidity with which they pursue and eat squids. **1812** Southey *Omniana* I. 274 Accounts of the squid-hound from people who have been on the southern whale fishery. **1884** Goode *Nat. Hist. Aquat. Anim.* 425 The Striped Bass... Large sea-going individuals are sometimes known in New England by the names 'Green-head' and 'Squid-hound'. **1934** E. Reynard *Narrow Land* v. 250 Hut moved fast, almost as fast as the squidhound bass. **1883** *Fisheries Exhib. Catal.* 195 *Squid jigs used by Grand Bank Cod fishermen in the capture of squid for bait. **1875** Knight *Dict. Mech.* 2295/2 **Squid-jigger*, a trolling-hook for catching squids for bait. **1881** *Cassell's Nat. Hist.* V. 710 The fishermen go out in punts *Squid-jigging of an evening, to catch bait required for the next day's fishing. **1867** F. H. Ludlow *Little Brothers* 96 He can man his main-sheet with one hand, feel his *squid line with the other, and tend his tiller between his knees. **1884** Goode *Nat. Hist. Aquat. Anim.* 201 The '*Squid School' of Nantucket and other parts of the coast. **1897** Kipling *Capt. Cour.* 145 A little shiny piece of *squid-tentacle at the tip of a clam-baited hook. **1875** Knight *Dict. Mech.* 2295/2 **Squid-thrower*, a device..for throwing a fishing-line seaward, carrying the squid-bait.

SQUID (skwɪd), *sb.*[2] *Physics.* Also **Squid, squid.** [Acronym f. the initials of *s*uperconducting *qu*antum *i*nterference *d*evice.] A device consisting essentially of a superconducting ring containing one or more Josephson junctions, made the basis of a very sensitive magnetometer by utilizing the fact that a change in the magnetic flux linkage of the ring by one flux quantum produces a sharp change in the ring's impedance.

1967 W. S. Goree in *Proc. Symp. Physics of Superconducting Devices* (U.S. Naval Research Lab.) 9 One embodiment of this device is the SQUID originated by Mercerau and others, which is two Josephson junctions in a superconducting ring. **1972** *Cryogenics* XII. 28/1 SQUID magnetometers and related devices have been used to make quantitative measurements of thermal fluctuations at temperatures as low as 0·023 K. **1979** *Nature* 22 Feb. 643/1 The magnetisation was measured with a Squid magnetometer. **1979** *McGraw-Hill Yearbk. Sci. & Technol.* 379/2 The dc SQUID has recently been developed for fast switching applications, that is, as an electronic logic or memory element. **1982** *Economist* 3 Apr. 120/3 At the frontiers of R and D now being done into superfast computers..is a device that is known as a squid—which is short for superconducting quantum interference device.

squid, *v.* [f. squid *sb.*[1]]

1. *intr.* To fish with squid-bait. *U.S.*

a **1859** in Bartlett *Dict. Amer.* (1859) 442 The bluefish is taken by squidding in swift tideways.

2. Of a parachute: to achieve a stable configuration when only partially extended.

1943 *Rep. & Mem. Aeronaut. Res. Council* No. 2119. 4 A non-porous parachute will not squid. **1951** W. D. Brown *Parachutes* vii. 68 The mouth of the canopy will begin to collapse inward, and the parachute will squid. **1956** W. A. Heflin *U.S.A.F. Dict.* 148/1 *Critical closing speed*, in wind-tunnel tests, the airspeed at which an open parachute begins to squid, i.e. close or collapse into longitudinal shape.

Hence **'squidded** *ppl. a.*; **'squidding** *vbl. sb.*

1894 *Outing* XXIV. 54/1 The fly-fisher scoffs at squidding, trolling, bait-fishing, spearing and at.. everything save fly-fishing. **1943** *Rep. & Mem. Aeronaut. Res. Council* No. 2119. 1 Squidding obviously may be a source of trouble in applications of parachutes. *Ibid.* 5 If a parachute is taken in the squidded condition and the air-speed reduced, the effective permeability of the canopy falls. **1969** J. Gardner *Founder Member* viii. 132 A parachute training instructor went over all the elementary lessons.. recalling things like critical speeds, oscillation and squidding.

†**'squiddle,** *v. Obs.* = quiddle *v.* 1 a.

1824 Lady Granville *Lett.* (1894) I. 322, I sat squiddling with them for some time. **1834** *Ibid.* II. 157 Mrs. Damer and many others sit and squiddle in the first room.

squidge (skwɪdʒ), *sb.*[1] [Imitative. In dial. use also denoting 'a shove' and, as vb., 'to squeeze'.] The sound made by soft mud yielding to sudden pressure.

1897 Mary Kingsley *W. Africa* 111 My companion.. steers the boat up to it, and jumps out with a squidge into the black slime. **1905** D. Blackburn *R. Hartley* xvii, The moment he..heard the squidge of the mud, he realised his position and peril.

squidge, *sb.*[2] *U.S. slang. rare.* [Origin unknown.] One charged with performing troublesome duties for another (see quots.).

1907 Ade *Slim Princess* vii. 80 The squidge—that means the fellow who does all the worrying and gets nothing out of it. **1942** —— *Let.* 16 June (1973) 230 When Mr. and Mrs. Al Laflin and I traveled in distant countries, we always hired a 'squidge' the moment we arrived in a new town. His job was to stay with us and accept all the hardships and worries. **1953** [see patsy *sb.*]

squidge, *v.* [Cf. squidge *sb.*[1]; sense 2 may represent an independent imitative formation.)] *trans.* **1.** To squeeze; to squelch or to mix roughly; to press together, so as to make a sucking noise. Also *intr. dial.* and *colloq.*

1881 H. & C. R. Smith *Isle of Wight Words* 34 *Squidge*, to squeeze. **1939** J. Steinbeck *Grapes of Wrath* x. 136 The children squidged their toes in the red dust. **1947** —— *Wayward Bus* iii. 33 His shoes squidged sloppily on the floor. **1952** —— *East of Eden* xxxvi. 427 Now spit in your palm... Squidge the spit all together. **1969** *Guardian* 16 Aug. 3/8 Waiting for the day when lunch will be a blob of something squidged out of a tube. **1971** B. W. Aldiss *Soldier Erect* 242 The leeches were at me... I squidged them underfoot. **1977** *Basildon Yellow Advertiser* 19 May 5/2 To clean very dirty nails make a thick lather in a sponge and then 'squidge' your nails in the sponge—the suction will draw out the dirt.

2. *Tiddlywinks.* To play (a wink) by snapping it with a larger counter.

1955 *Sci. of Tiddlywinks* (Cambridge Univ. Tiddly-winks Club) 8 If the tiddlywink is squidged on the floor it will not rise more than an inch or two. **1962** *Time* 14 Sept. 56 A squopped wink cannot be squidged again until it is de-squopped. **1977** Sharp & Piggott *Bk. Games* 165 No player may squidge another's wink.

squidger ('skwɪdʒə(r)). *Tiddlywinks.* [f. prec. + -er[1].] **a.** The larger wink used to propel or flip a player's winks. **b.** One who propels winks with another wink of larger size. (*rare*).

1955 *Sci. of Tiddlywinks* (Cambridge Univ. Tiddly-winks Club) 6 The game is played with five variable factors..(3) The squidger (the instrument used to flick with; this is usually another round counter in normal games). **1958** *Sports Illustr.* 7 Apr. M5 Each tiddlywinker plays with two large and four medium-size winks and, to hoist them, uses a wink of suitable size. It is called a squidger. **1962** [see squopper]. **1975** *Sunday Mail Color Mag.* (Brisbane) 28 Sept. 21/2 The *squidger* is the tiddly-winker's most valuable tool—the large wink, with which he flips the smaller counters. **1977** [see squopped *ppl. a.*].

squidgy ('skwɪdʒɪ), *a.* [Cf. squidge *sb.*[1]]

1. Short and plump; podgy. Also *Comb.*

1891 Kipling *Life's Handicap* 30 There's a dale more in nature than your squidgy little legs have iver taken you to, Orth'ris, me son. **1892** —— *Barrack Room Ball.* 23 Yon squidgy-nosed old idol. **1893** —— *Many Invent.* 131 Come an' look at these squidgy ham-shanked beggars. **1942** G. Kersh *Nine Lives Bill Nelson* xi. 68 He..liked to get about with a few nice squidgy blondes. **1978** *Morecambe Guardian* 14 Mar. 6/2 (Advt.), Upholstery does not now rely on spectacular outlines to make its impact. Gone are the way-out 'squidgy' shapes that the Italians launched so successfully a few years ago, instead the line is neat and classical, with a strong accent on comfort.

2. Moist and pliant; squashy, soggy. Esp. of food. Cf. squdgy *a.*

1973 *Times* 17 May 18/6 We settled for sandwiches. This was not a good idea. They were made of squidgy and tasteless bread of the wrapped and sliced variety. **1976** U. Holden *String Horses* vi. 69 Her kiddies spread ketchup on their bread, liking squidgy food. **1977** *Times* 28 May 11/6 A nice squidgy fruit cake.

Hence **'squidgily** *adv.*

1933 E. A. Robertson *Ordinary Families* ix. 193 He turned out to be as squidgily repulsive as only an under-sized Italian can be.

squier(e, obs. ff. square *sb.*, squire *sb.*

squiery: see squiry.

†**squiff**[1]. *Obs.* [ad. F. *esquif.*] = skiff *sb.*[1] 1.

1594 R. Ashley tr. *Loys le Roy* 81 [Marius] hid himself in the marish about Minturnes, and went to sea in a squiffe without victuals. **1620** tr. *Boccacio* 52 b, What with the Tempests violence and ouerlading of the Squiffe, it sunke.

squiff[2]. *slang. rare.* [Of uncertain origin: perh. f. squiffy *a.*] **1.** A contemptible person.

1939 E. Pound *Let.* Feb. (1971) 322 Yes, do better than that squiff, that femme ouistiti and lowest degree of animal life (apart from Cambridge Eng. profs).

2. The head. In phr. ***off*** (one's) ***squiff*** = ***off*** (one's) ***head*** s.v. head *sb.*[1] 34.

1960 H. Pinter *Room* 115 Mr. Kidd: I don't know what I think. (He sits.) I think I'm going off my squiff.

squiffed, *a. slang.* [var. squiffy *a.*] Intoxicated, drunk.

a **1890** in Barrère & Leland *Dict. Slang* (1890) II. 295/1 He rolls home rather squiffed, just as the day is dawning. **1926** S. Howard *Lucky Sam McCarver* I. 36, I think I did meet you once before, though I was a bit squiffed at the time. **1961** [see chumble *v.*]. **1977** B. Garfield *Recoil* ii. 28 I'm already a little squiffed. Ought to go on the wagon.

squiffer ('skwɪfə(r)). *slang.* [Origin obscure.] A concertina; also, an organ-bellows or organ. Also *transf.* (see quot. 1934).

1914 G. B. Shaw *Fanny's First Play* I. 175 If you can get Holy Joe to sprint a hundred yards, I'll stand you that squiffer with the gold keys... What's a squiffer?..a concertina. **1934** 'I. Hay' *David & Destiny* v. 78 What exactly is a Squiffer... Strictly speaking, a concertina. By a process of excusable exaggeration, an organ-bellows, or even the organ itself. By a characteristic confusion of ideas, a person who blows an organ.

squiffy ('skwɪfɪ), *a. slang.* [Of fanciful formation.]

1. Intoxicated; drunk.

?**1855** Mrs. Gaskell *Lett.* (1966) 375 Curious enough there is a Lady Erskine, wife of Lord E, her husband's eldest brother living at Bollington, who tipples & 'gets squiffy' just like *this* Mrs E. **1874** *Slang Dict.* 307 *Squiffy*, slightly inebriated. **1884** Mrs. C. Praed *Zéro* viii, At night she is generally a little squiffy. **1894** G. W. Appleton *Co. Respondent* ii. 42 You're a bit squiffy, aren't you, Dick? No, I'm as sober as a water-spout.

2. Askew, skew-whiff.

1941 Baker *Dict. Austral. Slang* 71 *Squiffy*, askew. **1977** G. Melly *Rum, Bum & Concertina* vii. 85, I never associated it with an orgy, a term I felt to imply a Roman profusion of grapes, wine, buttocks, breasts, marble *chaises-longues*, and squiffy laurel crowns.

'squiggle, *sb.*[1] [Imitative.] A giggle or sniggle.

1898 B. Capes *Adv. Comte de la Muette* v. 92, I was betrayed into a squiggle of laughter.

squiggle ('skwɪg(ə)l), *sb.*[2] [f. next.]

1. A wriggly twist or curve; esp. a wavy or twisting line drawn on a surface.

1902 W. W. Jacobs *Lady of Barge* 10 'How does my hair look?' 'All wavy,..all little curls and squiggles.' **1928** *Daily Express* 9 July 10/3 No hieroglyphics in timetables to be looked up, no particular squiggle to be remembered lest one is unhooked from the express at Dijon or goes to Rome instead of Florence. **1934** R. Fry *Let.* 3 Aug. (1972) II. 692 The squiggles in the foreground represent runnels of water flowing everywhere. **1957** V. S. Naipaul *Mystic Masseur* v. 78 The handwriting became a hasty, tired squiggle, and the note-book was abandoned. **1979** *Listener* 3 May 603/3 From time to time, squiggles appeared on the screen which were interpreted by some as subliminal instructions to vote labour.

2. *Comb.*, as **squiggle-eyed** *adv.*: in phr. ***to look squiggle-eyed*** (***at*** someone), to view askance or unfavourably. Also as *adj.* (Only in P. G. Wodehouse.)

1927 Wodehouse *Meet Mr Mulliner* vi. 178 There is a certain stage in the progress of a man's love when he feels like curling up in a ball and making little bleating noises if the object of his affections so much as looks squiggle-eyed at him. **1941** —— *Berlin Broadcasts* in *Performing Flea* (1961) i. 265 The internee is always being told to show his passport, and if he has not got one, the authorities tend to look squiggle-eyed. **1960** —— *Jeeves in Offing* xii. 136 She's always been a bit squiggle-eyed about Phyllis, because in Switzerland she held the view that we were a shade too matey. **1972** —— *Pearls, Girls & Monty Bodkin* i. 9 He was very fond of her—in a brotherly way, of course, to which even Gertrude Butterwick, always inclined to look squiggle-eyed at his female friends, could not have taken exception.

'squiggle, *v.* Chiefly *dial.* and *U.S.* [Imitative: cf. sniggle *v.*[3] and wriggle *v.*]

1. *intr.* ? To work wavy or intricate embroidery. Hence **'squiggling** *vbl. sb.*

1804 in *Francis Lett.* (1901) II. 536 A pink velvet on her head—a good many necklaces—a vast deal of squiggling. *Ibid.* 549 Emily who had before thought her success depended very much on squiggling on a Worked Habit Shirt every afternoon.

2. To writhe about; to squirm or wriggle. Also *fig.*

1816 Pickering *Vocab. U.S.*, *To Squiggle*, to move about like an eel. **1895–9** in *Eng. Dial. Dict.* **1922** W. Stevens in *Dial* July 91 Our bawdiness..Is equally converted into palms, Squiggling like saxophones. **1978** *Detroit Free Press* 16 Apr. D11/1 Snitman..drew from the water a thin, blackish-brown worm that squiggled in his palm, trying to sink tiny teeth into his flesh.

3. *trans.* To shake about (a liquid); to write (something) in a squiggly manner, to scrawl; to squeeze or daub (paint) from a tube thus.

a **1825**– in dial. glossaries (E. Anglia, Essex, Nhp., Warw.). **1942** N. Balchin *Darkness falls from Air* vi. 108, I signed it. Lennox squiggled underneath, 'I foresee difficulties but the scheme is right in principle. J.L.' **1969** *Observer* 12 Jan. 8/5, I watched a little girl squiggle yellow and red paint on a piece of white paper. **1973** *Daily Tel.* 24 Oct. 17/2 It was the 15th tube [of paint], so I squiggled it on.

'squiggly, *a.* [f. prec.] Wavy, wriggly.

1902 Kipling *Just So Stories* 32 The squiggly things on the Parsee's hat are the rays of the sun.

† **squil** (skwɪl). *Oxford University Slang. Obs.* exc. *Hist.* Also **squill**. [Curtailed form of L. *Esquilīnus* of or pertaining to the Esquiline Hill, one of the seven hills of Rome (see quots.). The Esquiline was largely inhabited by low persons; it was used as a cemetery, ult. for paupers (cf. Hor. *Sat.* I. 8).] A name formerly used by Christ Church men to designate opprobriously any member of the university not a member of Christ Church (see also quot. 1970).

1721 [see hodman 3]. **1874** C. Wordsworth *Soc. Life Eng. Univ. 18th Cent.* 304 Ch. Ch. was unpopular:...the men gave themselves airs, with wonderful ignorance and conceit they claimed to belong to an House, not to a College; those of other Colleges were 'squils' and 'hodmen'. **1900** H. L. Thompson *Christ Church* vii. 151 The phrase 'Squils and Hodmen' needs some explanation. The first word is now happily forgotten, but was in use within the last twenty years, as a colloquial designation of members of other colleges. It was supposed to be a corruption of 'Ex-Collegees', or 'esquilini'. **1921** S. Paget *H. Scott Holland* iv. 82 He belonged to us, not to 'out-college men', whom some of us called Squills, *i.e.* dwellers on the Esquiline. **1970** Bill & Mason *Christ Church & Reform* p. ix, We are both non-gremial members of Christ Church, and in the abusive word of an earlier day are therefore 'squills'.

squilgee ('skwɪldʒiː, skwɪl'dʒiː), *sb. Naut.* Also **squillage, squiligee.** [Of obscure origin.] (See quots. 1867–75, and cf. squeegee *sb.* 1.)

1851 H. Melville *Moby Dick* III. viii. 66 Edgewise moved along the oily deck, it operates like a leathern squilgee. **1867** Smyth *Sailor's Word-bk.* 648 *Squilgee*, or *Squillage*, a small swab made of untwisted yarns. Figuratively, a lazy mean fellow. **1875** Knight *Dict. Mech.* 2295/2 *Squilgee*, an instrument like a hoe, covered with leather, to rub the decks after washing. **1890** W. C. Russell *Ocean Trag.* II. xvi. 68 Swabs and squiligees had been flung down.

Hence **squilgee** *v.*, to use a squilgee; to swab, clean, press, etc., with a squilgee; also *fig.* Also **squilgeeing** *vbl. sb.*

1840 R. H. Dana *Bef. Mast* xiv, The washing, swabbing, squilgeeing, etc., etc. lasts..until eight o'clock. **1905** J. C. Lincoln *Partners of Tide* vii. 147 That doctor squilgeein' my maintop with his physic stuff has made me feel A1 again.

squilk, variant of swilk *a. Obs.*

squill (skwɪl). Also 5 sqwylle, squylle, 6 squyll, 7 squille, 6–8 squil. [ad. L. *squilla*, var. *scilla*, a. Gr. σκίλλα. So F. *squille*, It. *squilla*, Pg. *esquilla*, Sp. *escila*]

1. a. A bulb or root of the sea-onion or other related plant (see 2). Chiefly in pl.

c **1400** *Lanfranc's Cirurg.* 195 Froting wiþ squillis is good þerfore. *Ibid.* 196 þou schalt frote wel þe place with squillis in a stewe. **1561** Hollybush *Hom. Apoth.* 20 Thrust a squill dipped in oyle into hys throte, to cause him perbreake. **1600** Surflet *Countrie Farme* 143 As for cornes and apostumes they must be killed with strong leauens, onions, lillies, or squils and vineger. **1626** Bacon *Sylva* §445 Put them into a Squill, (which is like a great Onion,) and they will come up much earlier than in the Earth it self. **1697** Dryden *Virg. Georg.* III. 689 Add to these..Hellebore, and Squills deep rooted in the Seas. **1725** *Fam. Dict.* s.v. *Venice-Treacle*, In the other part of the Wine infuse..green Squills for some time. **1738** Chambers *Cycl.* (1752) s.v. *Scilla*, There are two kinds of squills, the male and female,..also distinguished by the appellations of white squills..and red squills. **1807** Robinson *Archæol. Græca* III. iv. 211 By drawing round the person purified a squill, or sea-onion. **1838** Thomson *Chem. Org. Bodies* 716 Macerate dry squills in alcohol, decant, and distil. **1866** *Treas. Bot.* 1194/2 It has been supposed that the Red Squills are the produce of another species, *Urginea Pancration*, but this seems doubtful.

b. In the names of various preparations made from these bulbs.

1652 French *Yorkshire Spa* ix. 82 Let him..take some easie vomit, as of Oxymel, or wine of Squils. **1684** [see oxymel]. **1706** Phillips (ed. Kersey), *Scillites acetum*, Vinegar of Squills. **1712** tr. *Pomet's Hist. Drugs* I. 172 Galen ..gave it to a Dram in Oxymel or Honey of Squills. **1778** *Encycl. Brit.* (ed. 2) I. 311 A solution of gum ammoniac in vinegar of squills. **1810** Crabbe *Borough* vii. 248 A potent thing, 'twas said, to cure the ills Of ailing lungs—the oxymel of squills. **1879** *St. George's Hosp. Rep.* IX. 551 Oxymel of squills and compound tinct. of camphor.

c. *Pharm.* Without article, as a substance.

1725 *Fam. Dict.* s.v., Vinegar made of Squill or Scillitick Oximel. **1836** *Pharm. R. Coll. Phys.* 56 Squill contains a peculiar vegetable product to which the name of scillitin has been given. **1875** H. C. Wood *Therap.* (1879) 480 Clinical experience has established the fact that in small repeated doses squill is diuretic as well as expectorant. **1947** *Federation Proc.* VI. 333/1 The identity of the cardiac and the convulsant properties of red squill receives support from an experiment. **1963** *Times* 25 Jan. 13/7 The poisons are principally red squill, sodium fluoro-acetate, and rodenticides containing elemental phosphorus. **1974** M. C. Gerald *Pharmacol.* iii. 57 Strychnine and red squill have been used as rat poisons.

2. *Bot.* **a.** The bulbous-rooted sea-shore plant *Scilla* (or *Urginea*) *maritima*; the sea-onion; also, any other species of the genus *Scilla*.

c **1440** *Pallad. on Husb.* I. 856 Eek figtre askis oon on rukul throwith, Another hangith vp or sowith squylle. *Ibid.* IV. 340 To sowe ek squylle is kynde On euery side. *c* **1440** *Promp. Parv.* 471/1 Sqwylle, herbe, *cepa maris, bulbus.* **1516** *Grete Herball* ccccxiii. (1529) Y iv, A squyll or see onyon. **1562** Turner *Herbal* II. (1568) 62 It is meruelus that chanseth vnto the Squill or se vnyon & to Narcissus. **1629** Parkinson *Parad.* xi. 134 The Squill or Sea Onion is wholly vsed physically with us, because wee can receiue no pleasure from the sight of the flowers. **1725** *Fam. Dict.* s.v., Squill is of a sharp and corrosive Nature; they wrap up its Root in Paste or Fullers Earth, and bake it in an Oven. **1760** J. Lee *Introd. Bot.* App. 328 Squill, *scilla.* **1862** Ansted *Channel Isl.* II. viii. (ed. 2) 177 The picturesque little squill (*Scilla autumnalis*) will be found on the high ground. **1868** Gorrie *Summers & W. Orkneys* v. 222 The field-gentian, the bird's-eye primrose, and the squill.

b. With distinguishing terms.

1629 Parkinson *Parad.* (1656) 133 To taste of the red Squil. **1731** Miller *Gard. Dict.* s.v. *Scilla*, Common Red Squil. *Ibid.*, The White Squil. **1796** Withering *Brit. Plants* (ed. 3) II. 338 Autumnal Squill. *Ibid.*, Vernal Squill. **1811** A. T. Thomson *Lond. Disp.* (1818) 362 There are two varieties of the officinal squill, one with a white bulb and the other with a reddish bulb. **1842** *Penny Cycl.* XXII. 396/1 *Squilla maritima*, the maritime squill, has large roundish ovate bulbs. *Ibid.*, Roxburgh's Indian Squill (*Scilla Indica*). **1848** Johns *Week at Lizard* 279 *Scilla autumnalis*, Autumnal Squill, a plant very like the vernal species. **1901** *Speaker* 20 Apr. 86/2 The meagre turf was spangled with the vernal squill.

c. A plant of the sea-onion or related species. Chiefly *pl.* as a collective term.

1601 Holland *Pliny* II. 19 These Squilles or Sea-onions grow in exceeding great abundance..throughout all Spaine. **1698** Fryer *Acc. E. India & P.* 178 Near the Sea grow Squills, or Sea-Onions. **1718** Ozell tr. *Tournefort's Voy.* I. 152 The rest of the Mountain is spread with Cretan Thyme, ..Lentisques, Squills. **1767** Abercrombie *Ev. Man own Gardener* (1803) 727/2 Squills, sea onion, or lily hyacinth. **1846** Lindley *Veg. Kingd.* 202 With the *Scilleæ* or Squills, we reach a division of the Order [etc.]. **1882** *Garden* 4 Mar. 139/3 The early Squills, too, assert themselves boldly.

3. One or other of certain plants resembling the squill (see quots.).

1760 J. Lee *Introd. Bot.* App. 328 Squill, Lesser white, *Pancratium.* **1866** *Treas. Bot.* 1089/2 Chinese Squill, *Barnardia. Ibid.*, Roman Squill, *Bellevalia.*

4. *Zool.* The mantis-shrimp, *Squilla mantis.*

1710 Sibbald *Hist. Fife* 54 The Crustate Animals comprehend under them several Species, such as the Squills, the Crabs, the Lobsters, and the Sea-Vrchin. **1879** E. P. Wright *Anim. Life* 536 Here would be placed the curious Squill, so common in the Mediterranean (*Squilla mantis*).

5. *attrib.* and *Comb.*, as **squill bulb, pill, vinegar; squill-like; † squill-fish**, = sense 4; **† squill-head** (see quot.); **† squill-insect**, = squilla 3.

1650 Bulwer *Anthropomet.* 7 Sirnaming him Joult-head and Onions head, or as we should say Squil-head. **1681** Grew *Musæum* I. VII. iii. 176 The Squill-Insect... So called from some similitude to the Squill-Fish. *c* **1790** *Encycl. Brit.* (ed. 3) I. 622/2 Ammoniac..is an ingredient also in the squill pills. *Ibid.*, A plaster made of it and squill vinegar. **1811** A. T. Thomson *Lond. Disp.* (1818) 362 The squill bulb is inodorous. **1822** Good *Study Med.* IV. 402 When mixed, however, with the squill pill..it often succeeds. **1825** *Greenho. Comp.* I. 109 *Ixia scillaris*, squill-like flowers.

‖ **'squilla.** Pl. **squillæ.** [L. (see prec.).]

† 1. The squill or sea-onion. *Obs.*

1516 *Grete Herball* ccccxiii. Y iv, Squilla hath vertue to deuyde and sprede humours. **1539** Elyot *Cast. Helthe* (1541) 60 Digestiues of fleume,..Hony, Gynger, Squilla. **1563** Hyll *Art Garden.* (1593) 30 Certaine rather will, that you sow his hearbe in fashion to a big Onion, and named of the Apothecaries Squilla in the Garden. **1601** R. Chester *Love's Martyr* (1878) 87 And Squilla, that keepes men from foule despaire. **1611** Cotgr., *Scille*, the Squilla, or sea Onion.

† b. A plant or bulb of this. *Obs.*

1562 Turner *Herbal* II. (1568) 130 Take the squilla, and couer it round about wyth clay..., and put it into an ouen.

2. = prec. 4.

1658 Rowland tr. *Moufet's Theat. Insects* II. xxxvii. 1125 They leap quickly one upon the other as the Fishes Squillæ doe in coupling. **1752** J. Hill *Hist. Anim.* 28 The Squilla has ten legs, the foremost pair cheliform, or made for pinching and holding things. *Ibid.*, The long-tailed Squilla. **1818** Scoresby in *Life* (1861) vii. 140 The squillæ are very abundant in the Greenland Sea. **1839** T. Beale *Hist. Sperm Whale* 189 The common black whale's food, that consists of 'squillæ' and other small animals.

† 3. *Zool.* (See quot.) *Obs.*

1658 Rowland tr. *Moufet's Theat. Insects* II. xxxvii. 1124 The Squilla an Insect differs but little from the fish Squilla, but that it hath the sail-yards much shorter, and a more red colour, or rather a more earthly colour.

† **squillatic**, var. of squillitic *a. Obs.*

1516 *Grete Herball* ccccxiii. Y iv, Agaynst dropsy drynke oximel squillatyke.

† **squillecte.** *Obs.*[−1] [ad. OF. **escuillette*, = *cuillette, cueillette* culet[1] and quelet. Cf. OF. *escueillir* = *cueillir* to collect.] A collection (of money).

14.. *Forest Laws* in *MS. Douce 335*, fol. 72 b, If ther be ony forster or minister of the forest, that maketh ony congregacioun, skotfalles, squillectes, or extorcions.

† **'squiller.** *Obs.* Forms: 4 squyler, 5 sqwyllare, swyllere, 6 squyllare. [a. AF. *sciuler* (in the same sense), = OF. *esculier, escuillier, esquelier*, maker or seller of dishes, f. *escuele* (mod.F. *écuelle*):—L. *scutella* salver, dish-stand (whence med.L. *scutellarius*).] A servant having charge of the scullery.

1303 R. Brunne *Handl. Synne* 5911 Þe porter..Þys merueyle tolde hem alle, How þe squyler of þe kechyn [etc.]. *c* **1440** *Promp. Parv.* 471/1 Sqwyllare, dysche wescheare, *lixa.* **1469** in *Ord. R. Househ.* (1790) 93 The lardener, the squiller. *c* **1475** *Pict. Voc.* in Wr.-Wülcker 769 *Hic lixa*, a swyllere. **1522** *Rutland P.* (Camden) 100 To send thether a purveiour for cooles, and all suche other as shall long vnto the squyllare.

squillerie, obs. form of scullery.

'squillian. [f. squilla 3 + -ian.] A stomapod of the family *Squillidæ*; a squill.

1842 *Penny Cycl.* XXIII. 82/2 M. Milne Edwards divides this family into two small tribes, Erichthians and Squillians.

† **squi'llitic**, *a. Obs.* Forms: 6 squilytyke, squilityke, squilliticke, -ike, 7–8 -ick. [ad. med.L. *squilliticus*, var. of *scillīticus* scillitic *a.*] Made of squills; containing squill.

1544 Phaer *Regim. Life* (1553) F viij, The pacyente must drynke euerye mornynge the syrupe of oximell squilytyke. **1576** Baker *Gesner's Jewell Health* 88 Take of..squilliticke vinegar fower partes. **1601** Holland *Pliny* II. 376 A decoction of this kind of wormes sodden in squillitick vinegre. **1610** Barrough *Physick* III. xi. (1639) 116 Also squillitick vineger is good to soupe [in hiccup]. **1725** *Fam. Dict.* s.v. *Honey*, The Anacardine [Honey], made of Anacardins, and the Squillitick made of Squills.

'squilloid, *a.* and *sb. Zool.* [f. squilla 3 + -oid.] **a.** *adj.* Resembling the *Squilla* or mantis-shrimp. **b.** *sb.* A shrimp resembling the *Squilla*.

1852 Dana *Crust* I. 613 In the Squilloids, the ophthalmic and two antennary segments are distinctly marked. *Ibid.* 614 There is only a single type, the Squilloid, divisible.

† **squimble-squamble**, obs. var. skimble-skamble *adv.*

1611 Cotgr., *Griffe graffe*, by hooke or by crooke, squimble squamble, scamblingly, catch that catch may. [**1694** Motteux *Rabelais* v. xiv. 64 They all began to bestir their Claws, like a parcel of Fiddlers running a Division; and then fell to't, squimble squamble, catch that catch can.]

squin. Local var. of quin *sb.*[1] (scallop).

1864 P. H. Gosse in *Good Words* 95/1 She had never heard them called by any other name than 'Squins', though she understood they were called Scallops in some places.

† **squin.** *Obs.*[−1] In 5 skwyn. [Related to squint *a.*: cf. askoyne *adv.*] *of squin*, obliquely, slantingly.

c **1440** *York Myst.* viii. 74 Take high trees and hewe þame cleyne, All be sware and noght of skwyn.

squinacy. Now *dial.* Forms: 3 swinacie, 4 swynacy; 4–5 squynacy (4 -ase), 4 -acie, 5 -ye, sqwynacye, skwynecy; 5 squinaci, -acye, -aseye, 5, 7 squinacie, -asie, 7, 9 squinacy. [var. of squinancy, by early elision of the second *n*.] = squinsy.

c **1250** *Gen. & Exod.* 1188 His wif and oðere birðe beren, ða ðe swinacie gan him nunmor deren. *c* **1340** Hampole *Pr. Consc.* 2999 Som for glotoni sal haf þare, Als þe swynacy, þat greves ful sare. **1387** Trevisa *Higden* (Rolls) III. 335 Demoscenes come forþ wiþ wolle aboute his nekke, and seide þat he hadde the squynacy. *c* **1425** *St. Mary of Oignies* II. iii. in *Anglia* VIII. 157 A ful perlyous yuel, þat is aposteme of þe þroot, þat is callid þe squynacy. *c* **1450** *M.E. Med. Bk.* (Heinrich) 215 For þe squinaseye. **1483** *Cath. Angl.* 357/2 Þe Squynacy, *squinancia, guttura.* **1615** H. Crooke *Body of Man* 766 These inward muscles being inflamed the most acute and sharpe Squinasie is ingendred. **1629** Z. Boyd *Balm of Gilead* 70 There he will set down a squinacie, crowels, or boils. **1670** T. Brooks *Wks.* (1867) VI. 426 That one man dies..of an apoplexy in the head,.. one of a squinacy in the throat. **1880** *Antrim & Down Gloss.* 98 *Squinacy*, a quinsy. *a* **1904** in *Eng. Dial. Dict.*

† **squinance.** *Obs.* Also 5–6 squynance. [See next and -ance. So older F. (*e*)*squinance* (16th c.). Cf. squince.] = squinsy.

c **1450** *Trevisa's Barth. De P.R.* VII. xxviii. (Bodl. MS.), Þere beþ þre manere squynances. **1539** Elyot *Cast. Helthe* III. vii, It helpeth squynances, or quynces in the throte. **1578** Lyte *Dodoens* 272 It swageth the squinance. **1584** Cogan *Haven of Health* ccxi. 188 They shall be fettered with gowtes,..strangled with Squinances [**1596** Squinancies]. **1730** *Phil. Trans.* XXXVI. 451 The first..recorded History I can find of this Operation..is in the learned Anton. Musa Brasavolus,..who performed it in a desperate Squinance.

'squinancy. Now *rare.* Forms: α. 4 squyn-, 7 squinansy, 5–6 squynancy (5 sqyn-, sqwyn-), 5

-anci, 5–7 -ancie, 6– squinancy. *β.* 6 squinantie, -tye. [ad. med.L. *squinancia, -antia*, app. formed by confusion of Gr. συνάγχη and κυνάγχη CYNANCHE, both denoting diseases of the throat. Hence also F. *esquinancie, †squinancie, -tie* (MDu. *squinancie, -tie*), It. *squinanzia*, Sp. *esquinancia*, Pg. *esquinencia*.]

1. Quinsy; = SQUINSY 1.

a. **1398** TREVISA *Barth. De P.R.* v. xxiv. (Bodl. MS.), þis yuel mater.. bredith sqynancy þat sleep in on day. *a* **1400** in *Rel. Antiq.* I. 51 For hym that haves the squynansy. *c* **1530** *Judic. Urines* II. vii. 30 Humours that torneth in to apostume that is called *Squinancia* the squinancie. **1562** TURNER *Herbal* II. (1568) 164 It that is purple in the floure..is good for the squinancie or choukes. **1642** FULLER *Holy & Prof. State* v. XII. 408 A good cure for the squinancie, but no satisfaction for lying. **1676** *Phil. Trans.* XI. 672 The Squinancy,..frequent there among Children. **1748** tr. *Vegetius Renatus' Distempers of Horses* 70 From which arises a loathing of their Food, suffocation in the Chops, and the Squinansy. **1753** N. TORRIANO *Gangrene Sore Throat* 63 John Anthony Soglia..gave his Observations on the gangrenous Squinancy in 1563.

β. **1597** A. M. tr. *Guillemeau's Fr. Chirurg.* 6/1 A vehemente and great squinantie. *Ibid.* 29 b/2 Shee may be opened agaynst the Squinantye.

2. A form or attack of quinsy; = SQUINSY 2.

1596 [see SQUINANCE]. **1611** in Birch *Crt. & Times Jas. I* (1849) I. 134 The lord chamberlain was dangerously sick on the sudden of a squinancy, or quinsey. **1653** W. RAMESEY *Astrol. Restored* 170 If necessity inforceth, thou needest not stand to elect a time (as in Apoplexies and Squinancies). **1684** BOYLE *Porous. Anim. Bod.* iii. 29 The same Febril matter..causes in the first case a Pleurisie, in the 2^d^, a Squinancy.

3. Special Combs.: **squinancy berry**, the black currant, *Ribes nigrum*; **squinancy-wort** (also †**-woodruff**), the quinsy-wort or small woodruff, *Asperula cynanchica*.

1782 *Encycl. Brit.* (ed. 2) IX. 6712/1 The fruit [black currants] is often called *squinancy berries. **1863** PRIOR *Plant-n.*, *Squinancy berries*, black currants, from their use in the sore throat, *Ribes nigrum*. **1796** WITHERING *Brit. Pl.* (ed. 3) II. 186 *Asperula cynanchica*... *Squinancy Woodroof. *c* **1710** PETIVER *Cat. Ray's Eng. Herbal* §30, *Squinancy wort. **1763** *Museum Rusticum* I. 307 A wild madder that grows in Wales and England on barren grounds, called *Squinancy-wort*; formerly used by the apothecaries, for the cure of a sore throat. **1777** JACOB *Catal. Plants* 98 *Asperula Cynanchica*, Squinancy Wort. **1813** BREWER *Beauties Engl. & Wales* XII. II. 21 The botanist will find here a great quantity of the Squinancy wort, or *Synanchia Lugdunensis*. **1900** W. H. HUDSON *Nature in Downland* 54 Woodruff,.. curiously named squinancy-wort.

†**squinant.** *Bot. Obs.* Also 6 squynant, 6–7 squinanth. [ad. med.L. *squinantus, -anthus*, ad. late Gr. σχοίνανθος. So obs. F. *squinant*, It. *squinante, -anto*.] = SCHŒNANTH.

a. **1548** TURNER *Names Herbes* (E.D.S.) 45 Juncus odoratus sive rotundus, is called in greeke Schenos, in englishe squinant, in duche Kamelhewe. **1562** —— *Herbal* II. (1568) 24, I neuer sawe squynant growinge, sauinge only dryed. **1597** GERARDE *Herbal* I. xxix. 40 Camels haie is called ..in English Camels haie, and Squinant. **1656** BLOUNT *Glossogr.*, *Squinant*,..the sweet rush, which is very medicinable: Camels meat. *a* **1693** URQUHART *Rabelais* III. xxxii. 275 There is neither Squinant, Ginger nor Grains in it. **1706** PHILLIPS (ed. Kersey), *Squinanthus*, Squinant, a sweet-smelling Arabian Plant, otherwise call'd the sweet Rush and Camel's-Hay.

β. **1598** FLORIO, *Squinance*, squinanth, cammels meate, or sweet rush, which is very medicinable. **1601** HOLLAND *Pliny* II. 101 The medicinable vertues of the sweet Rush called Squinanth... Squinanth is round, of an hote and fiery taste. **1616** BULLOKAR *Eng. Exp.*, *Squinanth*, a kinde of round rush, which is sweet, and hath flowers very medicinable.

†**squinantic,** *a. Obs.*^−1^ In 6 squynantyke. [ad. med.L. **squinantic-us*, f. *squinantia* SQUINANCY.] That cures or allays the quinsy.

1516 *Grete Herball* ccviii, Herbe or grasse of vyne is otherwyse called herbe squynantyke.

†**squince.** *Obs.* Also 6 squynce. [Abbreviated form of SQUINANCE or of *squincie* SQUINSY. Cf. mod. dial. *squinches* and *squinges*.] = SQUINSY.

1538 ELYOT, *Cynanche*, a syckenes called the squynce, whiche is in the throte and iawes. **1563** HYLL *Arte Garden.* (1593) 64 The distilled water..aswageth the dangerous swelling of the throte, called the Squince. *a* **1610** G. BABINGTON *Wks.* (1622) II. 94 Demosthenes..pretended the disease in his throat called the Squince.

squinch (skwɪnʃ), *sb.*^1^ *Arch.* [var. SCUNCH *sb.*]

†**1.** A stone cut to serve as a scuncheon. *Obs.*

c **1500–18** *Acc. Building Louth Spire* in *Archaeol.* (1792) X. 80 Also paid to Nicholas Brancell for 100 foot achlere, and squinches of 18 inches high and 15 at the least.

2. A straight or arched support constructed across an angle in order to carry some superstructure.

It is not clear whether Parker had any authority for this use of the term.

1840 PARKER *Gloss. Arch.* (ed. 3) I. 203. **1850** *Ibid.* (ed. 5) I. 441 Because they have no tendency to expand the walls, which is always to be feared when the arched squinch is used. *Ibid.*, The straight squinch is often employed externally. **1886** *Archaeol. Cant.* XVI. p. lxvii, The squinch in the north-east corner of the tower, supporting the staircase.

attrib. **1850** PARKER *Gloss. Arch.* (ed. 5) II. 79 In the first example two of the squinch arches for carrying the octagonal faces of the spire are shewn. **1895** *Edin. Rev.* Apr. 466 The squinch-arch method is more elastic in this respect.

3. A small structure, with two triangular faces, sloping back from an angle of a tower against the superimposed side of a spire.

1848 RICKMAN *Architecture* p. xxxi, A good specimen of a plain tower, and broach-spire, with squinches and spire-lights. **1849** *Arch. Notes Ch. Archdeaconry Northampt.* 192 [The spire's] great height, the very small size of the squinches connecting it with the square Tower [etc.].

squinch, *sb.*^2^ [Of doubtful origin.]

1. A slit or narrow opening in a building. Cf. SQUINT *sb.* 5.

1602–3 in *Hartland Gloss.* (1891) 73 Item pd to Hughe the glasier for glasse for the litle Squinches of the Tower, xd. **1848** *Continental Ecclesiology* 95 Some open squinches looking into the synagogue, in three stages, are from the women's galleries. **1879** *Temple Bar* Aug. 470 Many of these little churches..are of very massive construction, with a squinch or hagioscope practised in the thickness of the wall.

2. *dial.* A crevice between floor-boards or the like; a crack.

1837– in Devonshire glossaries, etc.

squinch, *sb.*^3^ A strong grip, twist, or wrench.

1893 BARING-GOULD *Cheap Jack Zita* II. 18 That squinch of the wrist you gave me.

squinch, *v. U.S.* [Cf. prec. and SQUINT *v.*]

1. *trans.* To screw or distort (the face).

1840 HALIBURTON *Clockm.* Ser. III. (1862) 443 Lord! how she'll kick and squeel when I spread her out on the close-horse. How it will make her squinch her face, won't it? **1939** *Real Detective Mag.* Aug. 89 She squinched and twisted her too prominent nose in a way that was not at all becoming. **1956** R. ELLISON in W. King *Black Short Story Anthol.* (1972) 263 Buster stopped and looked at me, squinching up his eyes with his head cocked to one side. **1974** *Gen. Systems* XIX. 65/2 Within a few hours, the palsy paralyzes the seventh cranial nerve, squinching half the victim's face. The eye cannot close and it waters excessively. The lips displace, and the mouth corner sags.

2. *intr.* To squeeze up so as to occupy less place; to crouch. Also with advbs., as *down*, *over*, etc.

1843 'J. SLICK' *High Life in N.Y.* II. 195 Wal, she squinched a trifle and gin a leetle start. **1942** W. FAULKNER *Go down, Moses* ii. 158 The old woman was kind of squinched down in one corner. **1972** M. J. BOSSE *Incident at Naha* III. 144 Virgil..waited for me to move from the doorway, which I did not by rising but by squinching over.

squinch-owl. *U.S. local.* [SQUINCH *v.*] = SCREECH-OWL 1 b.

1880 J. C. HARRIS *Uncle Remus* xix. 89 Word went roun' dat de man Squinch Owl done kotch nudder watzizname. **1929** W. FAULKNER *Sound & Fury* 48, I heard a squinch owl that night. **1966** *Publ. Amer. Dial. Soc.* **1964** XLII. 23 *Screech* (or *scritch*, or *squeach*, or *squinch*, or *scrooch*) *owl*, *Otus asio*, each name of which suggests some characteristic of the little owl.

†'**squincing,** *ppl. a. Obs.* (Probably a purely fanciful formation without definite meaning.)

1641 COWLEY *Guardian* II. iii, Which of your spruce mincing squincing dames can make bonelace like her?

squink, obs. form of SWINK *v.*

squink-eyed, variant of SQUINT-EYED *a.*

Cf. '*Squink*, to squint or wink', in dialect use.

1632 LITHGOW *Trav.* (1906) 278 Whereat the squink-eyed Gunner perceiving his time drew the string;..off went the piece, and shot the Crocodile.

'**squinny,** *sb.*^1^ ? *Obs.* [Cf. SQUINNY *a.*^1^] (See quot. 1840.)

1716 *Coll. State Songs, Poems*, etc. 19 Soon a Pack was chose..Of Quacks and Squinnys, Rakes and Ninnys, Green and Grizled Beaus. **1840** SPURDENS *Suppl. Forby*, *Squinny*, a contemptible fellow.

'**squinny,** *sb.*^2^ [f. the vb.] A squint, glance.

1881– in dial. glossaries (Leic., Notts., Warw.). **1902** *Daily Chron.* 23 Sept. 3/4 Now and then heads were deliberately turned from us, and not a creature gave us more than a side-long squinny.

squinny ('skwɪnɪ), *a.*^1^ [Of obscure origin.] Very thin or slender; lean, meagre; narrow.

a. In the comb. *squinny-gut*(*s*. Also *Comb.*

1742 FIELDING *Andrews* II. iii, The coachman..was asked ..what passengers he had in his coach? A parcel of squinny-gut b——s (says he). **1791** CHARLOTTE SMITH *Celestina* (ed. 2) I. 134 Mayn't I talk to a handsome girl I wonder without your putting in your squinnygut opinion? **1823** E. MOOR *Suffolk Words*, *Squinny-guts*, a thin person. **1886** W. H. LONG *Isle of Wight Gloss.* 73 A regler squinny guts.

b. In general use.

1784 MME. D'ARBLAY *Early Diary*, *Lett.* 16 Jan., A German doctor..with a club [of hair] as thick as my two hands, and two squinney curls. **1838** [MISS MAITLAND] *Lett. fr. Madras* (1843) 175, I am very busy now, translating a story with my little squinny Moonshee. **1866** *Daily Tel.* 22 Feb. 5/4 The eleven thousand windows want height; they are mostly of 'squinny' proportions. **1871** KINGSLEY *At Last* iv, Those figures and faces, small, scrofulous, squinny, and haggard, which disgrace the so-called civilization of a British city.

'**squinny,** *a.*^2^ [Cf. next.] Squinting; looking askance; peering.

a **1825** FORBY *Voc. E. Anglia* 322 We talk also of having 'squinny eyes', and of being 'squinny-eyed'. **1850** *Poor Artist* v. 65 Don't sit all of a shrug up there, peering over with your squinny eyes. **1885** W. B. FORFAR *Poems* 20 We saw the queer Chineese. Their fa-aces are so white as milk, With little squinney eyes.

squinny ('skwɪnɪ), *v.*^1^ Also squiny. [Cf. SQUINNY *a.*^2^]

1. *intr.* To squint, look askance; to peer with partly closed eyes. Also const. *at* or *to*.

1605 SHAKS. *Lear* IV. vi. 140, I remember thine eyes well enough: dost thou squiny at me? **1608** ARMIN *Nest of Ninnies* (1842) 6 The World, queasie stomackt,..squinies at this, and lookes as one scorning. **1783** MME. D'ARBLAY *Diary* 4 Jan., Mr. P——, at last, spied me out, and came squinnying up to me. **1838** MISS MAITLAND *Lett. fr. Madras* (1843) 201 Squinnying cunningly at me the whole time, to see if I look as if I believe them. **1854** MISS BAKER *Northampt. Gloss.*, *Squiny*, to look askance.

2. *trans.* To direct (the eyes) obliquely; to close *up* partly in a short-sighted manner.

a **1825** FORBY *Voc. E. Anglia* 322 Child, do not squinny your eyes so. **1890** W. A. WALLACE *Only a Sister?* 35 So he 'squinnied' up his eyes, and pulled his huge moustaches.

squinny ('skwɪnɪ), *v.*^2^ [Of obscure origin.] *intr.* To weep or cry; to fret.

1847– in dial. glossaries (Hants, I. Wight). **1861** G. MEREDITH *Evan Harrington* xxi, You are crying!.. And you show the marks twice as long as any other, you fair women. Squinnying like this! **1885** RUNCIMAN *Skippers & Sh.* 245 Who'd have thought of seeing us two squinnying? Blowed if I didn't cry harder than you.

squinny-eyed, *a.* Chiefly *dial.* Also squin(n)ey-. [f. SQUINNY *a.*^2^] = SQUINT-EYED *a.*

a **1825–** in dial. glossaries (E. Anglia, Cornwall, Somerset, Devon). **1864** SALA in *Daily Tel.* 2 July, The bandy-legged columns,..the splay-footed pedestals,..the squinney-eyed windows of the Manhattan Hotel de Ville.

squinsy. Now *dial.* Forms: 5 sqwynsy, 6 squynsie, 6– squinsy, 6–9 -sey, 7 squinsie, 7–8 squinzie, 7 -zy; 6–8 squincy, 6–7 squincie. [Reduced form of SQUINACY.]

1. *Path.* Quinsy; suppurative tonsillitis.

silver squinsy (fig.): see SILVER *sb.* 21.

1499 *Promp. Parv.* (Pynson), Sqwynsy, sekenesse, *squinancia*. **1547** BOORDE *Brev. Health* xxi. 14 In englyshe it is named the Squincy. **1551** TURNER *Herbal* (1568) 2 Walnuttes..are good to be laide to the Squynsie wyth rue & oyle. **1606** HOLLAND *Sueton.* 201 Alleadging for an excuse the Squinsie whereof hee was sicke. **1694** WESTMACOTT *Script. Herb.* 223 Wormwood leaves discuss Tumors and Wind particularly in the Squinsie. **1725** *Fam. Dict.* s.v., Squincy, an Inflamation of the Throat. *Ibid.* s.v. *Violet*, A Sovereign Remedy against..the Squinsy. **1869–** in dial. glossaries (Lanc., Som., Devon).

2. A form or attack of this.

1591 PERCIVALL *Sp. Dict.*, *Esquinancia*,..a squincie. **1601** HOLLAND *Pliny* II. 301 Æschines, a Physitian of Athens, was wont to cure squinsies..with the ashes of a man or womans body burnt. **1688** ROKEBY *Mem.* (Surtees) 23 My sister Smithson is well recovered of a dangerous Squinsey which the doctor was afraid would have choked her. **1894** HALL CAINE *Manxman* 280 He'd break your face with laughing if it was bursting itself with a squinsey.

†**b.** *transf.* A halter; a rope. *Obs.*^−1^

1629 RANDOLPH *Jealous Lovers* III. xiv, Shall not we be suspected for the Murther, And choke with a hempen Squincy?

squint (skwɪnt), *sb.* [f. SQUINT *a.* or *v.*]

1. a. A permanent tendency in the eye to look obliquely or askant; defective coincidence of the optic axes; strabismus.

a **1652** BROME *Queenes Exch.* II. i, The dulnesse of the Eye, which here shews deadly But for a little squint it has. **1712–3** SWIFT *Jrnl. to Stella* 8 Feb., He has favoured her squint admirably; and you know I love a cast in the eye. **1764** REID *Inquiry* vi. §15 In the retinæ of those who have an involuntary squint. *Ibid.*, In those who have no squint. **1815** SCOTT *Guy M.* xxxiii, A stout bandy-legged fellow, with.. a most portentous squint of the left eye. **1839** THACKERAY *Fatal Boots* Jan., Nurse says that, when he is older, he will get rid of his squint. **1879** HARLAN *Eyesight* ii. 30 The operation for squint, or 'cross eye', consists in weakening the overacting muscle by cutting it.

fig. **1687** MIÉGE *Gt. Fr. Dict.* II, A disingenious Squint, that looks with an evil eye upon every Thing. **1875** *Galaxy* Apr. 560 Still, sometimes we manage to see things without a party squint, especially after election.

b. *Path.* With distinguishing terms.

1842 *Penny Cycl.* XXII. 396/2 Inward Squint, or *Strabismus convergens*. *Ibid.*, Outward Squint, or *Strabismus divergens*. **1867** *Chambers's Encycl.* IX. 69/1 The squint is said to be *convergent* when the eye or eyes are directed towards the nose, and *divergent* when they are directed towards the temple, and is termed *single* or *double* according as one eye or both are displaced. **1872** T. BRYANT *Man. Pract. Surg.* (1884) I. 409 Ordinary convergent or 'concomitant' squint has to be distinguished from ..'paralytic' squint. **1884** *Encycl. Brit.* XVII. 786/1 In periodic squint glasses to correct the hypermetropia ought to be given. **1887** *Brit. Med. Jrnl.* 23 Apr. 874/2 He had a well-marked external squint of the left eye. *Ibid.*, There was a slight internal squint.

c. *attrib.* in *squint-scissors* (used in operating for strabismus).

1879 *St. George's Hosp. Rep.* IX. 492 The mass was..so tough as to resist the insertion of the point of an ordinary pair of squint-scissors.

d. *Radar.* Lack of alignment between the axis of a transmitting aerial and the direction of maximum radiation, deliberately introduced in some systems. Freq. *attrib.*

1947 L. N. RIDENOUR *Radar Syst. Engin.* vi. 197 'Squint', which results from improper installation or trimming of antennas, has the same operational effect as crabbing of the aircraft in a cross-wind. **1969** BARTON & WARD *Handbk. Radar Measurement* ii. 31 The fall-off in energy ratio restricts the practical squint angles to about half the individual beamwidth. **1969** C. A. WILEY in Kayton & Fried *Avionics Navigation Syst.* viii. 370 (*caption*) Squint-mode window display.

2. A directing of the eyes obliquely; a sidelong look or glance; a hasty or casual look; a peep.

1673 [R. LEIGH] *Transp. Reh.* 14 Lacys best Grimaces were never so Artificial as the Squints of a Humiliation Saint. **1736** SWIFT *Propos. Regul. Quadrille* Wks. 1846 II. 131 To give damages for all opprobrious language, and especially for all hints, squints, innuendoes, leers, and shrugs. **1824** LADY GRANVILLE *Lett.* (1894) I. 245 He hopes to have another squint at me before I go. **1861** DICKENS *Gt. Expect.* xxxii, I have been down the road taking a squint at the scene of action. **1894** G. M. FENN *In Alpine Valley* I. 223 Better get back to him as soon as you've had your squint round.

3. An inclination or tendency towards some particular object; a drift or leaning; a covert aim.

1736 WEST *Let.* in *Gray's Poems* (1775) 15 The prophecy has certainly a squint that way. **1891** EGGLESTON *Faith Doctor* iv. 43 He lost interest even in the dinner parties, with a business squint, that he had been so fond of giving. **1895** *Funk's Stand. Dict.* s.v., A squint towards radicalism.

4. An oblique or perverse bent or tendency.

1774 ELIZ. CARTER *Lett.* 30 May (1809) IV. 112 Wit is a squint of the understanding which is mighty apt to set things in a wrong place. **1840** HARE *Vict. Faith* (1847) 45 This warping bent, this squint of our understandings.

5. a. *Arch.* = HAGIOSCOPE.

1839 [see HAGIOSCOPE]. **1850** PARKER *Gloss. Archit.* (ed. 5) I. 442 There seems to be no good or ancient authority for the name of squint applied to these openings, but it has been long in use. **1879** J. C. COX *Ch. of Derbysh.* IV. 21 At the east end of the south aisle is a genuine squint.

attrib. **1881** MACPHAIL *Relig. Ho. Pluscardyn* xix. 165 The squint window opening into the Lady's Chapel.

b. *transf.* (See quot.)

1891 *Science Gossip* XXVII. 39 We placed ourselves at squints, or peeping-holes, formed by thrusting short sticks through the reed fence.

squint (skwɪnt), *a.* [f. SQUINT *adv.*, or by inference from SQUINT-EYED *a.*]

1. Of eyes: Looking obliquely; having a cast or squint; affected with strabismus. Now *rare.*

In early quots. freq. implying envy or malice.

1579 SPENSER *Sheph. Cal.* Aug. 129 Heardgrome, I feare me, thou haue a squint eye. [*Gloss*, partiall iudgement.] **1590** GREENE *Mourn. Garm.* (1616) 68 Zoilus with his squint eyes will finde fault with the shape. **1601** HOLLAND *Pliny* I. 161 He was syrnamed already Strabo, for his squint eyes. **1602** *How to Choose a Good Wife* D 4, Gold can make limping Vulcan walke vpright, Make squint eyes looke strait. **1658** CRESHALD *Legacy* 15 The Survey and malevolent Aspect of some Squint and Blood-shot Eye. **1775** ADAIR *Amer. Ind.* 437 Hired speakers, who use their squint eyes and forked tongues like the chieftains of the snakes. **1903** LUMHOLTZ *Unknown Mexico* I. 245 Squint-eyes also afford them much amusement.

b. *fig.* (with *eye* = 'look, regard', and usually hyphened).

1623 FLETCHER *Rule a Wife* III, The pleasure I shall live in and the freedom Without the squint-eye of the law upon me. **1638** SIR T. HERBERT *Trav.* (ed. 2) 85 He beholds..his inferiors with a squint and supercilious eye of scorne and tyranny. **1715** J. CHAPPELOW *Rt. way Rich* (1717) 142 Now and then casting a squint-eye upon his money-bags. **1901** *Westm. Gaz.* 11 Dec. 9/2, I..hope to end my days without having used the squint-eye of prejudice in examining any fact whatever.

2. a. Of looks: Characterized by oblique vision.

1611 COTGR. s.v. *Gar*, *Vn regard à gar*, a squint looke. **1626** tr. *Boccalini's New-Found Politicke* 71 Her looke is squint, with which wishly beholding one, she fixedly looketh vpon another. **1714** R. SMITH *Poems of Controversy* (1853) 38 Thy squaint [*sic*] looks makes thee miss the mark. **1808** JAMIESON, *Gley*, a squint look.

b. *fig.* Of suspicion. *poet.*

In last quot. passing into next.

1634 MILTON *Comus* 413 My nature is That I encline to hope, rather then fear, And gladly banish squint suspicion. **1744** THOMSON *Tancred & Sigismunda* v. i, Henceforth, noble Osmond,..honour more my truth, Nor mark me with an eye of squint suspicion. **1784** COLMAN *Prose on Sev. Occas.* (1787) III. 250 While squint Suspicion holds her treacherous lamp.

c. Of persons: Squinting, squint-eyed.

1643 TRAPP *Comm. Gen.* xxix. 17 Leah was tender-eyed), Purblinde or squint, as one interprets it.

†**3.** Indirect. *Obs.*

1619 J. DYKE *Counterpoyson*, etc. (1620) 50 Out of a squint respect to your owne gaine. **1654** WHITLOCK *Zootomia* 370 To cleare ourselves of these Squint Aspects in our Services of Heaven, is a Perfection too Seraphicall for Earth. **1681** *Relig. Clerici* 56 Though 'tis not much to the purpose,..yet you may perceive it bears some squint relation to this discourse.

4. a. Characterized by obliquity of action.

c **1610** DONNE *Let. to C'tess of Bedford* Wks. 1912 I. 189 As although a squint left-handedness Be ungracious, yet we cannot want that hand.

b. Oblique; slanting.

1703 in E. Henderson *Ann. Dunfermline* (1879) 374 One squint cutt on one of the hinder legs. **1724** SIR W. HOPE *Vind. Art Self-defence* 131 The slop or squint motion of your arm near to the body. **1852** BURN *Naval & Mil. Techn. Dict.* II. s.v., Squint-quoin, *encognure oblique.* **1858** *Skyring's Builders' Prices* 66 Squint quoins, per foot run.

5. ***squint-minded***, having a perverse or depraved mind.

1653 URQUHART *Rabelais* II. xxxiv. 220 You and I both are farre more worthy of pardon, then a great rabble of squint-minded fellowes, dissembling and counterfeit Saints.

squint, *adv. rare.* [Aphetic for ASQUINT *adv.*] With a squint; obliquely, askant. Also in comb. ***squint-looker***.

1398 TREVISA *Barth. De P.R.* v. vi. (Tollem. MS.), Naþeles not euery squyntloker seþ so, þey his yen ben uneuen. **1621–31** LAUD *Serm.* (1847) 198 If 'justice and judgment' roll this eye aside,..they begin to look squint, and in part leave God.

squint (skwɪnt), *v.* [Aphetically f. ASQUINT *adv.* Cf. prec. and SQUINT *a.*]

1. a. *intr.* To have the axes of the eyes not coincident, so that one or both habitually look obliquely; to be affected with strabismus.

1611 COTGR., *Loucher*, to squint, sken, or looke askew. **1677** WYCHERLEY *Pl. Dealer* II. i, Can any one be call'd beautiful that squints? **1709** STEELE *Tatler* No. 5 ¶2 It is certainly a Mistake..to draw..Love, as a blind Boy; for his real Character is, a little Thief that squints. **1764** REID *Inquiry* vi. §15 Of those who squint, the far greater part have no distinct vision with one eye. **1808** *Med. Jrnl.* XIX. 314 The reason why those persons who squint, generally turn the weak eye towards the nose. **1852** THACKERAY *Esmond* I. vii, My lady's own waiting-woman squinted, and was marked with the smallpox. **1881** H. SMART *Race for Wife* ii, I heard one hideous old woman confide..that you squinted.

transf. **1829** *Chapters Phys. Sci.* 335 In this experiment the fingers may in a manner be said to squint.

b. Of the eyes.

1836 MARRYAT *Japhet* vi, One of his assistants had only one eye, the other squinted horribly. **1862** BORROW *Wild Wales* xxxiii, His eyes were grey and looked rather as if they squinted.

2. a. To look with the eyes differently directed; to glance obliquely or in other than the direct line of vision; also, to glance hastily or casually, to peep.

1610 G. FLETCHER *Christ's Vict.* II. xxvii, He..ever, as he crept, would squint aside, Lest him, perhaps, some Furie had espide. **1640** BROME *Asparagus Gard.* III. iv. 159 He gets a crick in his neck oft-times with squinting up at Windowes and Belconies. **1707** J. STEVENS tr. *Quevedo's Com. Wks.* (1709) 89 He drew near,..squinting upon the bundle. **1727** SWIFT *Further Acc. E. Curll* Wks. 1751 III. I. 157 Some turning away their heads..; others squinting with a leer that shewed at once fear and indignation. **1802** MRS. E. PARSONS *Myst. Visit* IV. 38 Squinting at Sir William with no little disdain. **1849** CUPPLES *Green Hand* xi. (1856) 107 Well, we squints up the hatchway, and see'd a young midshipman a-standing with his back to us. **1892** *Photogr. Ann* II. 41 Without having to squint at the ground glass with your nose nearly touching it.

fig. **1622** HAKEWILL *David's Vow* iii. 103 Hee could not at once intend two such distant objects; hee might glance, or squint upon both: but directly fix his eyes upon both hee could not. **1768–74** TUCKER *Lt. Nat.* (1834) I. 106 This we do by the power we have over our ideas to overlook, or, as it were, squint upon some, and hold others in a steadier view.

b. *fig.* To have a private eye to something. Const. *at* or *upon.*

1642 FULLER *Holy & Prof. St.* III. xxv. 233 Pity but his eyes were out that squints at his own ends in doing Gods work. **1692** SOUTHERNE *Fatal Marriage* I. i, That has a face of good nature, but it squints with both eyes upon your own interest. **1782** COWPER *To Rev. Wm. Bull* 12 Not meaning.. His pleasure, or his good alone, But squinting partly at my own.

c. *fig.* To glance *at*, *on*, or *upon* (a person or thing) with dislike or disapproval, or by means of some covert allusion, hint, or suggestion.

(*a*) **1652** BENLOWES *Theoph.* x. xlix. 185 He hates Superiors,..And on his Fellows squints, that are in joynt Command. **1654** WHITLOCK *Zootomia* 429 They will come to a bad Market too, in Times that squint on Ingenious Labours. **1706** *Drake's Secr. Mem. Earl of Leicester* Pref., [He] does not in the least squint upon the Earl as guilty of the fact.

(*b*) *a* **1732** GAY *Fables* II. iv, In prudence, too, you think my rhymes Should never squint at courtiers' crimes. **1742** FIELDING *J. Andrews* III. x, I hope you have a better opinion of my taste than to apprehend that I squinted at yourself. **1779** LOVELL in J. Adams *Wks.* (1854) IX. 481 R. H. Lee with H. Laurens are squinted at as two monsters..who pursue points in which the Southern States have no interest. **1894** BIRRELL *Ess.* ix. 99 The dramatists he squinted at were worse than they had any need to be.

3. *fig.* To have a side or covert reference, implication, bearing, or aim; to refer or bear indirectly; to incline or tend. Const. with *toward(s, that* (or *this*) *way*, or *at.*

1599 NASHE *Lenten Stuff* Wks. (Grosart) V. 243 There is a foule fault in the print escapt, that curstly squinteth and leereth that way. **1624** MOUNTAGU *New Gagg* 58 What neede I produce authority of Fathers?.. Name me but one that squinteth that way, 'nedum' that saith it positiuely. **1644** BULWER *Chiron.* 62 The Rubriques of the Romish Rites, which seeme a little to squint this way, prescribe three formes of Benediction. **1716** M. DAVIES *Athen. Brit.* III. 54 There be some short Passages in the holy Fathers, that seem to squint towards some of the Articles of Popery. **1768** *Woman of Honor* II. 54 Happened to drop something that squinted towards a reproach to his Lordship. **1895** *Funk's Stand. Dict.* s.v., The document squints toward treason. **1898** *Daily News* 26 Feb. 5/5 The President is prepared to veto any clap-trap measure which squints at war. **1902** J. F. RUSLING *European Days & Ways* 343 A goodly Wesleyan chapel,..not ambitious to be called a church yet, but squinting that way.

4. To move or branch off in an oblique direction.

1721 WODROW *Hist. Suff. Ch. Scot.* (1830) II. 30/2 Dalziel sends out a party of about fifty horse to squint along the edge of the hill, and attack their left wing. **1799** KIRWAN *Geol. Ess.* 288 That the vein in the inferior stratum of lime-stone ..squints 4 or five yards from the superior vein.

5. a. *trans.* To give a permanent or temporary cast to (the eye); to cause to look asquint or obliquely.

1605 SHAKS. *Lear* III. iv. 22 The foule Flibbertigibbet.. giues the Web and the Pin, squints the eye, and makes the Hare-lippe. **1637** HEYWOOD *Pleas. Dial.* xiii. Wks. 1874 VI. 226 Let him but use An unsway'd eye, not squinted with affections. **1852** R. S. SURTEES *Sponge's Sp. Tour* xxxiii, Our friend..was now squinting his eyes inside out with anger.

fig. **1622** BACON *Hen. VII* (1876) 166 Perkin..marched to Taunton; beginning already to squint one eye upon the crown, and another upon the sanctuary.

b. To cast or direct (a look, etc.) in a sidelong manner.

1631 CHAPMAN *Cæsar & Pompey* IV. v, What wild looks Are squinted at me from men's mere suspicions That I am wild myself. **1748** THOMSON *Cast. Indol.* I. xv, On others' ways they never squint a frown, Nor heed what haps in hamlet or in town.

6. a. To divert obliquely.

1789 J. PILKINGTON *Derbyshire* I. 58 In the language of the miners these veins are squinted 4 or 5 yards northwardly from their former direction, that is, they have departed so much from their perpendicular range.

b. To cross (a surface) obliquely.

1844 QUEEN VICTORIA *Jrnl.* 21 Sept. in D. Duff *Victoria in Highlands* (1968) I. 58 We then began our descent, 'squinting' the hill, the ponies going as safely..as possible. **1884** —— *More Leaves* 97 We first went along the road and then on the heather 'squinting' the hill.

†**squint-a-pipes.** *slang. Obs.*$^{-0}$ (See quot.)

1788 GROSE *Dict. Vulgar T.* (ed. 2), *Squint-a-pipes*, a squinting man or woman.

'**squinted**, *ppl. a.* [f. SQUINT *sb.* or *v.*]

1. Affected with strabismus or squint.

1591 FLORIO *2nd Fruites* 129 She is..halting of one foote, squinted of one eye, and the other goggled. **1596** SPENSER *F.Q.* IV. i. 27 Her face most fowle and filthy was to see, With squinted eyes contrarie wayes intended. **1637** G. DANIEL *Genius of this Isle* 601 Turne in your Squinted Eyes, and Seriouslie Learne how to prize the blessing you enioye.

2. *Radar.* Of an aerial: having squint (sense 1 d).

1966 R. W. BICKMORE in R. C. Hansen *Microwave Scanning Antennas* iv. 297 Resolution will suffer if a linear phase term is programmed into the processor to cause 'squinting' of the synthetic beam. This is due to the projected aperture effect and is true for all electrically squinted antennas. **1960** BARTON & WARD *Handbk. Radar Measurement* ii. 31 The feeds required for generation of slightly squinted beams must overlap in the focal plane.

squinter ('skwɪntə(r)). [f. SQUINT *v.*]

1. One who squints. Also *fig.*

1738 *Corr. betw. C'tess Hartford & C'tess Pomfret* (1805) I. 32 He bestows them on such a squinter as thou, and on such a halting cripple as myself. **1771** WARTON *Oxford Newsman* Poet. Wks. 1802 II. 217 Nor more..The triumphs of the patriot Squinter..Shall croud each column of our Journal. **1827** *Blackw. Mag.* XXI. 662, I was now a squinter...I squinted like an owl. **1861** J. G. SHEPPARD *Fall Rome* vi. 280 The son of Triar, or the 'Squinter', as he was sometimes called, one of the best captains of the age.

2. A squint eye.

1873 BLACKMORE *C. Nowell* xliii. (1883) 284 The cunning gleam from the black deep ambushed squinters.

squint-eye(s. [See SQUINT *a.* 1.] A person who has squinting eyes.

1653 R. SANDERS *Physiogn.* 173 Beware squint-eyes, for, of a hundred, there are not two faithfull. **1687** MIÉGE II, A squint-Eye, or one that is squint-eyed. **1839** THACKERAY *Fatal Boots* Apr., The men, though they affected to call me a poor little creature, squint-eyes, knock-knees, red-head, and so on, were evidently annoyed by my success.

squint-eyed ('skwɪntaɪd), *a.* [f. SQUINT *adv.*]

1. Of persons: Having squint eyes; affected with squint or strabismus.

1589 PUTTENHAM *Eng. Poesie* I. xiv. (Arb.) 48 He was squint eyed and had a very vnpleasant countenance. **1602** BRETON *Wonders Worth Hearing* Wks. (Grosart) II. 8/1 Though she were squinte eyed,..wry bodyed, and splay footed. **1656** EARL MONM. tr. *Boccalini's Advts. fr. Parnass.* II. viii. (1674) 147 Those glass-eyes which squint ey'd-people wore. **1726** LEONI *Alberti's Archit.* I. 6/2 People hump-back'd, squint-eyed, crooked and lame. **1753** TORRIANO *Gangr. Sore Throat* 37, I have since learned, that this Patient..became squint-ey'd and deformed. **1848** BUCKLEY *Iliad* 165 Daughters, halt, and wrinkled, and squint-eyed. **1872** BLACK *Adv. Phaeton* xix. 261 That squint-eyed publican who thrashes his wife.

b. In allusive or fig. use.

1563 A. NEVILL in Googe *Eglogs* (Arb.) 23 Defye them all. μισάνθρωποι and squynteyd Monsters ryght They are. **1591** HARINGTON *Orl. Fur.* Pref., Euerie blind corner hath a squint eyed Zoilus, that can looke a right vpon no mans doings. **1620–6** QUARLES *Feast for Wormes* 855 Wks. (Grosart) II. 17 Others, whom the squint-ey'd world counts holy. *Ibid.* 1482 (p. 22), Heart-gnawing Hatred, and Squint-ey'd Suspition. **1647** N. WARD *Simple Cobler* 21 All the squint-ey'd, wry-neck'd, and brazen-faced Errors that are.. of that litter. **1712** PARNELL *Spect.* No. 460 ¶3 Upon the broad Top of it resided squint-eyed Errour, and Popular Opinion with many Heads. **1755** BROWN *Barbarossa* I. i, In these walks..wakeful suspicion dwells, And squint-eyed jealousy.

2. Characterized by squint or oblique vision. Also *fig.*

1598 MARSTON *Pygmal.*, *Sat.* ii, Who would imagine that such squint-ey'd sight Could strike the worlds deformities so right. **1616** R. CARPENTER *Larum Love* 49 That squint-ey'd partialitie, so much condemned by the Apostle. 1656 Earl Monm. tr. *Boccalini's Pol. Touchstone* 401 A squint-ey'd look, wherewith while she seem to look fixedly upon one, she is very intent on observing another. 1661 Hickeringill *Jamaica* 71 To which squint-ey'd Mode in war Scanderbeg stands endebted for most of his Victories against the Ottomanes.

Hence **squint-eyedness**.

1591 Percivall *Sp. Dict.*, *Entortadura*,..squinteidnes, crookedness.

squint-hole. [f. squint *sb.* 5 or *v.*] (See quots.)

1889 W. Rye *Cromer* 111 A hagioscope or squint-hole. 1890 *Glouc. Gloss.* 149 *Squint-holes*, the long slits in the walls of barns to admit light and air.

†**squintifego.** *Obs. rare.* Also **-efuego.** [f. squint *a.* or *v.*] (See quot. *a* 1700.)

1693 Dryden *Persius* v. 271 The Timbrel, and the Squintifego Maid Of Isis, awe thee. *a* 1700 B. E. *Dict. Cant. Crew*, *Squinte-fuego*, one that Squints very much.

'squinting, *vbl. sb.* [f. squint *v.*]

1. The action of looking with a squint or side-glance. Also *fig.*

1611 Cotgr., *Louschement*, a squinting, or looking askew. 1654 Whitlock *Zootomia* 181 The Physitian halfe a Fee; the Mountebanke more than hee asketh, &c. with such like squintings on Desert. *a* 1721 Prior *Dial. Locke & Montaigne* ¶39 If again your Eyes were continually endeavoring [to] look one upon an other, you would only get a habit of Squinting. 1887 *Scottish Leader* 22 Nov. 6/1 A little political squinting might be allowable.

2. *spec.* The eye-disease strabismus; = squint *sb.* 1.

1626 Bacon *Sylva* ¶867 Both Eyes will moue Outwards; As affecting to see the Light, and so induce Squinting. 1763 Foote *Mayor of G.* i. Wks. 1799 I. 163 She has been cured of..squinting, by the Chevalier Taylor. 1799 Underwood *Dis. Childhood* (ed. 4) II. 248 Another, and a very common blemish is that called Squinting. 1822 Good *Study Med.* III. 237 It is obvious, therefore, that strabismus may have three varieties:..Habitual squinting... Atonic squinting... Organic squinting. 1851 Carpenter *Man. Phys.* 595 If..the conformity of the two eyes be restored (as by the operation for the cure of squinting). 1883 Millington *Are we to read backwards?* 23 Squinting..is usually produced by an abnormally flattened shape of the eyeball.

'squinting, *ppl. a.* [f. squint *v.*]

1. Of persons, the eyes, etc.: Looking obliquely or with a squint; affected with strabismus.

1611 Cotgr., *Biglesse*, a squinting wench. 1646 J. Hall *Satire* Poems (1906) 190 What rocks of diamonds presently arise In the soft quagmires of two squinting eyes. 1688 *Lond. Gaz.* No. 2371/4 Sam Cowling.., a squat bow-legged squinting Fellow. 1756 Mrs. Calderwood in *Coltness Collect.* (Maitland Club) 201 She was a little squinting beauty, very well painted. 1807 *Med. Jrnl.* XVII. 525 The focal points of direct vision do not ever correspond anatomically in squinting persons. 1848 Dickens *Dombey* xii, He..saw..squinting faces leering in the squares and diamonds of the floorcloth. 1879 *Cassell's Techn. Educ.* I. 160/1 The patient again suppresses the image of the squinting eye.

†**b.** Looking opposite ways. *Obs. rare.*

1598 Marston *Sco. Villanie* i. i. 173 Mylo doth hate Murder, Clodius Cuckolds, Marius the gate Of squinting Ianus shuts. 1651 Cleveland *Poems* 35 As in a picture, where the squinting paint Shews Fiend on this side, and on that side Saint.

2. Of looks, etc.: Characterized or accompanied by a squint or squints; oblique.

1600 Marlowe tr. *Lucan* i. 55 Whence thou shouldst view thy Roome with squinting beams. 1713 Berkeley *Guardian* No. 4, They all agreed in a squinting look, or cast of their eyes towards a certain person in a mask. 1822 Good *Study Med.* II. 332 The eye has a look peculiarly oblique or squinting. 1865 Dickens *Mut. Fr.* i. i, A man with a squinting leer.

3. That squints, in fig. senses of the verb.

1648 Fanshawe *Il Pastor Fido* (1676) 158 With a strait look, a squinting heart; and least Fidelity where greatest was profest. 1661 Boyle *Style of Script.* (1675) 136 Those dark and squinting oracles, that came..from the Prince of darkness and father of lies. 1693 *Humours Town* 74 You are lash'd in a Preface with a squinting Reflection that looks a hundred ways at once. 1826 Lamb *Conf. Drunkard* in *Elia* (1869) 393 To give pleasure and be paid with squinting malice.

So **'squintingly** *adv.*

1593 Nashe *Christ's Tears* Wks. (Grosart) IV. 183 O why should I but squintingly glance at these matters, when they are so admirably expatiated by auncient Writers? 1611 Cotgr., *Biglement*, squintingly, skenningly, askew. 1708 Sewel ii, *Loens*, asquint, squintingly. 1820 Hogg *Adv. Basil Lee* Tales (1866) 264 Her gray eyes softly and squintingly turned on me.

†**'squintly,** *adv. Obs.* [f. squint *adv.* + -ly².] In a squinting manner. Also *fig.*

1655 Emmot *Northern Blast* 12 The people who are not of the same opinion with us, we look squintly upon them. *a* 1677 Barrow *Treat.* (1680) 413 Looking squintly on others, or not well affected to them.

†**'squintness.** *Obs.* [f. as next.] Strabismus.

1656 Blount *Glossogr.*, *Strabism*, the squintness in the eyes. 1661 R. Lovell *Hist. Anim. & Min.* 417 The strabisme, or squintness, caused by evil conformation, custome, or disease.

'squinty, *a.* [f. squint *a.*]

†**1.** Oblique. *Obs.*⁻⁰

1598 Florio, *Bieco*, squintie, sidelin, crooked, twart, awrie.

2. a. Of persons: = squint-eyed *a.* 1 a, b.

[1819 Keats *Let.* 20 Sept. (1958) II. 204, I am like a squinti(n)g [squinty: 1931 ed.] gentleman who saying soft things to one Lady ogles another.] 1922 Joyce *Ulysses* 343 She knew right well..what made squinty Edy say that because of him cooling in his attentions. 1957 *Numbers* (N.Z.) Mar. 16, I was only a squinty little third-former.

b. Of the eyes: characterized by squint or oblique vision.

1925 T. Dreiser *Amer. Tragedy* II. i. ii. 174 The young girl with the yellow hair and squinty blue eyes. 1978 J. Irving *World according to Garp* ii. 37 The eyes..as red-lidded and squinty as a pig's.

squip, obs. f. squib *sb.*

squir, var. squirr *v.*

squirage ('skwaɪərɪdʒ). Also **squireage.** [f. squire *sb.* + -age.] The body of country squires; a book containing a list or account of these.

1837 J. Sinclair *Life Sir J. Sinclair* I. 187 Some one asked Mr. Bosville whether he intended purchasing 'the new Baronetage?'—'No,' replied the humourist, 'I am waiting till the *Squirage* comes out'. 1872 De Morgan *Budget of Paradoxes* 46 The old French aristocracy would have been as prosperous at this moment as the English peerage and squireage.

squiral ('skwaɪərəl), *a. rare.* [f. squire *sb.*] Of or belonging to, befitting, a squire; squirely.

1791 Anna Seward *Lett.* (1811) III. 99 The whole wide expanse is dotted over by white rough-cast cottages, and here and there a village-spire and squiral chateau. 1804 *Ibid.* VI. 198 The residence of squiral opulence.

squi'rality. *rare*⁻¹. = next (in sense b).

1759 Sterne *Tr. Shandy* i. xviii, I would effectually provide,..that such weight and influence be put thereby into the hands of the Squirality of my kingdom, as should counter-poise what..my Nobility are now taking from them.

squiralty ('skwaɪərəltɪ). Also **squirealty.** [f. squiral *a.* + -ty.]

a. The existence of squires as an institution. **b.** The body or class of squires. **c.** The position or status of a squire.

c 1856 *Denham Tracts* (Folk Lore Soc.) I. 332 It seems to have referred to the golden age of squirealty. 1886 Ruskin *Præterita* I. xi. 351 As a rule, the best of her [*i.e.* England's] squirealty passed necessarily through Christ Church. 1888 P. Cushing *Blacksmith of Voe* I. v. 144 It..went with the hall, and the crest,..and other notes of squiralty.

squire (skwaɪə(r)), *sb.* Forms: α. 3–7 **squier** (4 **-are**, 5 **-ere**), 3–6 **squyer** (4 **sqyer**, **squyȝer**, 5 **sqvyȝer**), 4–5 **squyere** (4 **-eer**), **squyar**; 4–5 **sqwyer** (5 **sqwier**), **sqwyar**, (5 *Sc.* **sqwhyare**), 5–6 **sqwyere**; 4 **scwyer**, **scwier**, **scoyer**, **skwier**, **skuyer** (4–5 **-ere**), 5 **skyer**; 4 **suier**, 4–6 **swyer**, 5 **swier(e**, **-ar**. β. 4 **squeyer**, 4–5 **squeer**; *Sc.* 5 **squear**, **sqwear**, **squere**, 6 **sqwere**. γ. 5 **swyr**, 6 **swyre**; 5 **squir**, 5–6 **squyre**, 6– **squire**. δ. 7– **'squire**. [ad. OF. *esquier*, *escuier*, etc., whence also the later form esquire *sb.*¹]

1. a. In the military organization of the later middle ages, a young man of good birth attendant upon a knight (= esquire 1 a); one ranking next to a knight under the feudal system of military service and tenure.

α. *c* 1290 *Beket* 2427 in *S. Eng. Leg.* 176 For-to honouri þis holi man þer cam folk i-novȝ;..Of Eorles and of barones and manie kniȝtes heom to; Of seriaunz and of squiers. 1297 R. Glouc. (Rolls) 7801 He let gadery is kniȝtes & is squiers al so. 13.. *K. Alis.* 6022 Theo kyngis ost..amounted fyve hundrod thousand Knyghtis.., withowte pages and skuyeris. 13.. *Gaw. & Gr. Knt.* 824 Knyȝtez & swyerez comen doun þenne. *c* 1380 Wyclif *Wks.* (1880) 362 Fro þe hiȝest knyȝte..to þe lowest sqwyer þat by wai of office of his state beriþ þe swerde. 1414 *Rolls of Parlt.* IV. 58/2 The freest Knight or Squyer of the Rewme..may be put in prison. *c* 1425 *Eng. Conq. Irel.* (1896) 8 He hade purueied hym of xxx^ti^ knyghtes and lx skyers. *c* 1530 Ld. Berners *Arthur Lyt. Bryt.* 134 He was served rychely with many goodly squyers, who dyd nothing elles but..served hym alwayes. 1568 Grafton *Chron.* II. 296 The Lord James Audeley with the ayde of his foure squiers, fought alwayes in the chiefe of the battayle.

β. *a* 1400 *R. Gloucester's Chron.* 3878 (Harl. MS. 201), Boþe kynges and dukes, and erles echon, Barons and knyȝtes, squeers monyon. *c* 1440 *Ipomydon* 320 And euery man sayd to other there, 'Will ye se þe proude squeer, Shall serue my lady of þe wyne?' 1474 *Acc. Ld. H. Treas. Scotl.* I. 69 For certane expensis maid..vpon the squere, the were man of the King of Denmarkis. 1490 *Exch. Rolls Scotl.* X. 663 Our traist and velebelovit cosingis and counsailouris, clerkis, and squearis.

γ. 1449 *Paston Lett.* I. 87 He harde sey of j. swyr of ij. c. marc be ȝere that [etc.]. *c* 1450 *Merlin* xiii. 191 Thei were wele armed, and hadde on hattes of stile as squyres vsed in tho dayes. 1515 *Scottish Field* (Chetham) 484 Many swyres full swiftelie were swapped to the deathe. *a* 1548 Hall *Chron.*, *Hen. IV*, 16 b, Owen Glendor a squire of Wales, perceiuyng the realme to be vnquieted,..entised and allured the wilde and vndiscrite Welshmen. 1595 Shaks. *K. John* i. i. 177 Goe, Faulconbridge.., A landlesse Knight makes thee a landed Squire. 1611 —— *Cymb.* ii. iii. 128 A Hilding for a Liuorie, a Squires Cloth, A Pantler. 1682 Burnet *Rights Princes* v. 147 Those of the better sort in the provinces, that were bound to come and serve as Auxiliary Troops, which was the Original of the Titles of Squires and Gentlemen. 1788 Gibbon *Decl. & F.* lviii. VI. 65 Each knight was attended to the field by four squires or archers on horseback. 1814 Scott *Lord of Isles* i. xxix, Where squire and yeoman, page and groom, Plied their loud revelry. 1859 Tennyson *Merlin & V.* 322, I once was looking for a magic weed, And found a fair young squire.

†**b.** Placed after the surname as a designation of rank. *Obs.*

Chiefly in formal documents.

1382 in Riley *Mem. Lond.* (1868) 456 [The said William Soys was attached to make answer to] Walter Begood, Squyer. *c* 1440 *Brut* ii. 370 To hym come Iohn Standisch, Squyer. *c* 1460 *Eng. Reg. Oseney* (1913) 138 Come John Wilcotys, squier, and all his tenauntes of þe Moore Barton. 1541 *Knaresborough Wills* (Surtees) I. 81 *note*, Thomas Middleton, squier, and John Pullayne, gentleman, supervisors. 1586 *Brasenose College Muniments* 22. 7 Richard Pultenham Squier, prisoner in the King his Bench.

c. A personal attendant or servant; a follower. Also *transf.*

c 1380 Wyclif *Wks.* (1880) 148 þei passen grete men in here gaye pellure..& tatrid squeyeres & oþere meyne. *c* 1386 Chaucer *Sompn. T.* 535 Now stood the lordes squier at the bord, That carf his mete. *c* 1410 *Master of Game* (MS. Digby 182) ii, Somtyme a gret hert hath an other felawe, þat is called his squyer. 1531 *Dial. on Laws Eng.* O iiij, The same is to be holden of a Captayne, that he shall be bounde for the offence of hys squyers. 1640 tr. *Verdere's Rom. of Rom.* i. 104 They boorded the Pagans ship all three together, leaving their Squires in guard of their bark. 1831 Macaulay *Biog.*, *Johnson* (1860) 122 Boswell importuned him to attempt the adventure and offered to be his squire. 1835 W. Irving *Tour Prairies* 35 He must have the young Osage as a companion and squire in his expedition into the wilderness. 1887 Ruskin *Præterita* II. 192 At Oxford, when it was thought becoming in a gentleman-commoner to have a squire to manage his scout.

†**d.** In contemptuous use. *Obs.*

Cf. *trencher-squire* s.v. trencher¹ 7.

1573 Tusser *Husb.* (1878) 62 Get trustie to tend them, not lubberlie squire, that all the day long hath his nose at the fire. 1596 Nashe *Saffron Walden* Wks. (Grosart) III. 71 O scabbed scald squire (Scythian Gabriell) as thou art. *a* 1618 Sylvester *Tobacco battered* 20 Wks. (Grosart) II. 267 Indian Tobacco, when due cause requires; Not the dry Dropsie, of Phantastick Squires.

†**e.** = apple-squire. *Obs.*

1610 B. Jonson *Alch.* Prol., No clime breeds better matter, for your whore, Bawd, squire, impostor,..Whose manners..feed the stage. 1617 Middleton & Rowley *Fair Quarrel.* iv. iv, When thou art dead, may twenty whores follow thee, that thou mayst go a squire to thy grave! 1622 Breton *Strange Newes* Wks. (Grosart) II. 6/2 Other kinde of close mates there are,..and they are called Squiers, but they are onely of the order of the Apple.

2. Applied to personages of ancient history or mythology regarded as holding a position or rank similar to that of the mediæval squire.

Freq., esp. in or after Biblical use, with the literal sense 'shield-bearer' or 'armour-bearer'.

a 1300 *Cursor M.* 6279 King ne knight, suier ne suain, O þam come neuer a fote again. *Ibid.* 7717 þe squier hight abysai, þat to þe tent com wit daui. 1382 Wyclif *1 Chron.* x. 4 And Saul seyde to his scquyer, Drawȝe out thi swerd. *c* 1400 *Destr. Troy* 6221 [They] were gouernet by a gome,.. A fyne squier & a fuerse,—Eufemius he hight. *c* 1450 *Mirour Saluacioun* (Roxb.) 132 Abymalech..saide thus til his sqwyere..out with thi swerde quod he and slee me hastily. 1483 Caxton *Gold. Leg.* 65 b/2 And his squyer wente to for hym & cryde ayenst them of Israhel. 1509 Fisher *7 Penit. Ps.* Wks. (1876) 281 A squyer also of kynge Saul whan he sawe his lorde & mayster deed..slewe hymselfe. 1582 Stanyhurst *Æneis* ii. (Arb.) 46 Then the squire emboldned dreadles thus coyned an aunswer. 1648 J. Beaumont *Psyche* xx. lxxxi, Bacchus's wrangling Squires, whose strange Contest Was, who should prove the best at being Beast. 1692 Dryden *St. Euremont's Ess.* 358 Except Ajax,..there was no considerable Warriour, that had not his God upon his Chariot, as well as his Squire: the God to conduct his Spear, the Squire for the management of his Horses. 1720 Pope *Iliad* xx. 565 The squire, who saw expiring on the ground His prostrate master.

3. †**a.** ***squire of*** (or ***for***) ***the body*** (or ***household***), an officer charged with personal attendance upon a sovereign, nobleman, or other high dignitary. *Obs.* Cf. esquire *sb.*¹ 1 c.

Used jestingly by Shaks. *1 Hen. IV.* i. ii. 27.

1450 *Rolls of Parlt.* V. 190/1 John Hampton Squier for oure body. 1477 *Exch. Rolls Scotl.* IX. 101 *note*, Our lovit familiare squear of houshald Johne of Ballone. 1536 *MS. Rawl. D.* 780 fol. 58 b, A new kay for the squyers of the bodys chambre. 1642 Milton *Apol. Smect.* Wks. 1851 III. 286 Some Squire of the body to his Prelat, one that serves not at the Altar only, but at the Court cupboard. 1706 Phillips (ed. Kersey), *Armiger*,..a Title of Dignity, properly an Armour-bearer to a Knight, an Esquire, a Squire of the Body. 1825 Scott *Betrothed* ii, Two squires of his body, who dedicated their whole attention to his service, stood at the Prince's back.

fig. and *transf.* 1649 Fuller *Just Man's Funeral* 17 A guiltie conscience, that Squire of the bodie, alwayes officious to attend a malefactour. 1665 R. Head *Eng. Rogue* (1874) I. ix. 71 From what Dunghil didst thou pick up this Shake-rag, this Squire of the body?

b. *transf.* In various humorous or jocular phrases.

† ***squire of the gimlet***, a tapster. † ***squire of the pad***: see pad *sb.*² 2. † ***squire of the placket***, a pimp. *Obs.*

1611 Cotgr., *Escuyer trenchant*, a caruer, or squire of the mouth. 1636 Davenant *Wits* ii, Squires of the placket, wee know you think us. 1679 T. Jordan *Lond. in Luster* 20 And a Drawer that Hath a good Pallat Shall be made Squire of the Gimlet. *a* 1721 M. Prior *Thief & Cordelier* ii, There the 'Squire of the Pad, and the Knight of the Post, Find their Pains no more balk'd, and their Hopes no more crost.

4. a. A man, esp. a young man, who attends upon, accompanies, or escorts a lady; a gallant or lover.

1590 Spenser *F.Q.* ii. i. 21 Archimago..eke himselfe had craftly deuisd To be her Squire, and do her seruice well aguisd. *a* **1625** BEAUM. & FL. *Wife for a Month* I. i, Has your young sanctity done railing, Madam, Against your innocent 'Squire? **1648** J. BEAUMONT *Psyche* XXII. xlvi, Is not brave Phylax forc'd to be her Squire, And dance attendance on that Brat's desire? **1664** COTTON *Scarron.* IV. (1715) 77 Turning strait his Eyes to Tyre, To look for Dido, and her Squire. **1676** WYCHERLEY *Pl. Dealer* II. E iv b, You are to pretend only to be her Squire, to arm her to her Lawyers Chambers.

b. ***squire of dames*** or ***ladies***, one who devotes himself to the service of ladies or pays marked attentions to them. †Also allusively, a pimp or pander.

1590 SPENSER *F.Q.* III. vii. 51 As for my name, it mistreth not to tell; Call me the Squyre of Dames, that me beseemeth well. **1619** FLETCHER *Mons. Thomas* I. i, *Val.* What, the old 'squire of Dames still! *Hyl.* Still the admirer of their goodness. **1624** MASSINGER *Parl. Love* IV. iii, And how, my honest squire o' dames? **1631** —— *Emp. East* I. ii, You are The squire of dames, devoted to the service Of gamesome ladies,.. their close bawd. **1886** *Illustr. Lond. News* 9 Jan. 31/2 Such attentions as would have been considered marked even in a 'Squire of ladies'. **1900** R. H. SAVAGE *Brought to Bay* vi. 105 It was no light-minded squire of dames who sat alone in the smoking-room.

5. a. Employed as a title and prefixed to the surname of a country gentleman, freq. forming part of his customary appellation. Now chiefly *colloq.*

Orig. applied to those having the rank of a squire in sense 1: (cf. 1 b).

1645 SYMONDS *Diary* (Camden) 169 The King lay at Bisbury,.. where Squire Gravenor (as they call him) lives. **1669** W. SIMPSON *Hydrol. Chym.* 363 That great naturalist, Squire Boyl. **1712** E. COOKE *Voy. S. Sea* 456 The principal Officers of the three Ships went ashore with 'Squire Hollidge. **1765** FOOTE *Commissary* I. Wks. 1799 II. 14 Our 'Squire Wou'd-be is violently bent upon matrimony. *c* **1795** ? BURNS *Poem on Pastoral Poetry* iv, Squire Pope but busks his skinklin patches O' heathen tatters! **1812** CRABBE *Tales* xii. 1 'Squire Thomas flatter'd long a wealthy aunt. **1857** HUGHES *Tom Brown* I, Here.. lived and stopped at home, Squire Brown, J.P. for the county of Berks. **1882** [see SQUIRESHIP 2].

b. A country gentleman or landed proprietor, *esp.* one who is the principal landowner in a village or district.

broom-squire: see BROOM *sb.* 6.

γ. **1676** WYCHERLEY *Plain Dealer* Dramatis Pers., Jerry-Blackacre, a true raw Squire under Age,.. bred to the Law. **1718** LADY M. W. MONTAGU *Lett.* 31 Oct. (1763) III. 129, I think the honest English squire more happy, who verily believes the Greek wines less delicious than March beer. **1771** SMOLLETT *Humph. Cl.* I. 17 And in the mean time I hobbled after the squire. **1818** SCOTT *Rob Roy* xiv, A bet or two.. placed me on an easy and familiar footing with all the young squires, except Thorncliff. **1855** *Poultry Chron.* II. 281/2 It was unanimously decided that 'the squire', who also was member for the borough, should be asked to act as patron. **1875** HAYWARD *Love agst. World* 2 The old squire held his head high among the aristocracy of the county.

δ. **1711** ADDISON *Spect.* No. 112 ¶7 The Parson is always preaching at the 'Squire, and the 'Squire.. never comes to Church. **1750** JOHNSON *Rambler* No. 30 ¶6, I was looked upon in every country parish as a kind of social bond between the 'squire, the parson, and the tenants. **1783** CRABBE *Village* II. 55 Here too the 'squire, or 'squire-like farmer, talk. **1826** in *Sheridaniana* 331 Sheridan was once on a visit to a great Norfolk 'Squire. **1841** E. MIALL *Nonconf.* I. 242 Little ignorant puffy 'squires propose to blow themselves out to these dimensions.

c. In various slang uses (see quots.).

[**1688** SHADWELL (*title*), The Squire of Alsatia.] *a* **1700** B. E. *Dict. Cant. Crew*, *Squire of Alsatia*, a Man of Fortune, drawn in.. and ruin'd by a pack of poor,.. spunging, bold Fellows that liv'd.. in White-Fryers. *Ibid.*, *The Squire*, a Sir Timothy Treat-all; also, a Sap-pate... *A fat Squire*, a rich Fool. **1785** GROSE *Dict. Vulgar T.*, *Squire of Alsatia*, a weak profligate spendthrift; *squire of the company*, one who pays the whole reckoning, or treats the company, called standing squire. **1834** H. AINSWORTH *Rookwood* IV. ii, I must insist upon standing Squire [*later edd.* Sam] upon the present occasion.

d. As a term of polite address to a gentleman not formally a squire. More recently, a jocular or familiar address to another man, not necessarily of different status.

1828 J. F. COOPER *Notions* I. 102 His usual address is 'friend', or sometimes he contemplates a stranger of a gentlemanly appearance, with the title of 'squire'. **1864** TROLLOPE *Can you forgive Her?* (1865) II. i. 6 'Well, Squire,' said Scruby, 'how is it to be?' **1959** [see LONG *a.*[1] 7 c]. **1962** C. WATSON *Hopjoy was Here* x. 111 You see, squire, it's reasonable. **1968** *Listener* 22 Feb. 255/3 At a garage in Paddington I overheard a very sleek young man.. ask the attendant to 'fill both tanks up'. 'Blimey, squire,' was the reply, 'you going all the way to Marble Arch?' **1977** N. J. CRISP *Odd Job Man* i. 6 'Good-night then, squire,' he said, to the barman. **1982** *Times* 15 May 14/6 (*caption*) Tell you what, squire—keep the pension and I'll take the cash!

6. *U.S.* A Justice of the Peace; also, a lawyer or judge. Also, applied more widely to any local dignitary.

1817 J. BRADBURY *Trav. Amer.* 320 He is not in the least danger of receiving a rude or uncivil answer, even if he should address himself to a *squire* (so justices are called). **1822** J. FLINT *Lett. fr. Amer.* 143 Squire, the appellation designating a Justice of the Peace, or Magistrate, is commonly retained for life, although out of office. **1848** *Knickerbocker* XVIII. 379 Every body is a squire in these days. **1859** BARTLETT *Dict. Amer.* (ed. 2) 442 *Squire*, the title of magistrates and lawyers. In New England it is given particularly to justices of the peace and judges. In Pennsylvania, to justices of the peace only. **1873** 'MARK TWAIN' & WARNER *Gilded Age* 17 'Squire' Hawkins got his title from being post-master of Obedstown. **1935** H. W. HORWILL *Dict. Mod. Amer. Usage* 301/1 In Am. the *squire* is primarily a justice of the peace, but the name is loosely given, most commonly as a title, to any prominent resident in a village. **1948** W. FAULKNER *Intruder in Dust* ii. 34 He had already telephoned Squire Fraser.

7. *Austr.* (See quot.)

1874 [see *count-fish* s.v. COUNT *sb.*[1] 9]. **1883** E. P. RAMSAY *Food Fishes N.S. Wales* 10 The carnivorous Sparidæ include the Schnapper, *Pagrus unicolor*, the immature young of which are known respectively as the 'squire' and red bream.

8. *attrib.* and *Comb.* **a.** Appositive, in early use chiefly in senses related to 3 a, as ***squire beadle*** (see BEADLE 3), ***carver***, ***fruiterer***, ***priest***, ***saddler***; in recent use in sense 5 b, as ***squire-farmer***, ***-parson***, ***-priest***.

(*a*) **1601** F. TATE *Househ. Ordin. Edw. II* (1876) 13 The squire fruiterer shal receve electuaries, confections, and other spiceries. **1615** *Caution-Book of Balliol Coll.* (MS.) fol. 11, I John Bell in the University of Oxon Squirebedle. **1618** *Stow's Surv.* 184 M. Thomas Cure, Sadler, and Squire Sadler to Queen Elizabeth. **1643** *Plain English* 14 They.. have.. made good Squire Priests prophesie. **1686** tr. *Chardin's Trav.* 227 From whence other Officers carry'd em [*sc.* dishes] before the Squire-carvers.

(*b*) **1850** THACKERAY *Pendennis* xxvi, The wine-merchants',.. solicitors', squire-farmers' daughters. **1863** A. BLOMFIELD *Mem. Bp. Blomfield* I. iv. 104 The treatment of the mere curate,.. and of the independent squire-parson of good family. **1888** DOWDEN *Transcripts* 189 The Chartist-peer, the lord-loving democrat, the squire-priest.

b. Misc., as **† squire-hart** (see quot. and sense 1 c, quot. *c* 1410); **squire-errant**, a squire who acts like a knight-errant; hence ***squire-errant*** vb., ***-errantry***; **squire-trap**, a soft spot or piece of ground into which one may sink while riding after hounds.

1607 TOPSELL *Four-f. Beasts* 135 Vntill he see.. the great Hart hauing.. his little squier-hart to attend him. **1733** FIELDING *Don Quix. in Eng.* II. i, The extreme difficulties.. of knight-errantry.. and of 'squire-errantry. *Ibid.* II. vi, I hate your squire-errants that carry arms about them. *Ibid.* III. ix, Ah, sir, I have been a squire-erranting to some purpose. **1859** G. A. LAWRENCE *Sword & Gown* ii. 14 Old Heathfield, who, when he is up to his girths in a squire-trap, never halloas 'ware bog', till five or six more are in it. **1861** WHYTE MELVILLE *Market Harb.* 88 Miss Dove was fast luring him into a country which.. was very cramped and blind, full of 'doubles', 'squire-traps', and other pit-falls for the unwary.

squire, obs. f. SQUARE *sb.*; var. SWIRE *Obs.*

squire (skwaɪə(r)), *v.* Forms: 4, 6 squier, 5 squyer (swyer), sqwier, 6 squyre, 6– squire, 8 'squire. [f. SQUIRE *sb.*]

1. *trans.* Of a man: To attend (a lady) as, or after the manner of, a squire; to accompany, conduct, or serve as escort to; to escort. (Freq. in the 17th and 18th c. Now more freq. in U.S. use.) **a.** With adverbs and preps.

c **1386** CHAUCER *Wife's Prol.* 305 And for he squiereth me bothe vp and doun, Yet hastow caught a fals suspecioun. **1588** E. D. *Xlth Idyl Theocritus* A 4, When I as Vsher, squirde you [*i.e.* Galatea] all the waie. **1606** DEKKER *Seven Deadly Sins* Wks. (Grosart) II. 45 Hee walkes vp and downe the streetes squiring old Midwiues to anie house. **1668** SHADWELL *Sullen Lovers* v, Will you please to squire me along? **1711** SWIFT *Jrnl. to Stella* 1 Oct., I squired his lady out of her chaise to-day, and must visit her in a day or two. **1751** ELIZA HEYWOOD *Betsy Thoughtless* I. 56 [She] suffered herself to be.. squir'd about to all public places, either by the rake, the man of honour, the wit, or the fool. **1821** SCOTT *Kenilw.* iv, Manhood enough to squire a proud dame-citizen to the lecture at Saint Antonlin's. **1857** DICKENS *Dorrit* II. vi. 373 Mr. Sparkler humbly offered his arm. Miss Fanny accepting it, was squired up the great staircase. **1866** R. CHAMBERS *Ess.* Ser. II. 93 He was.. fond of.. visits from ladies, whom.. he would squire about his garden. **1901** G. B. SHAW *Cæsar & Cleopatra* III, in *Three Plays for Puritans* 148 Ftatateeta comes to her. Apollonius offers to squire them into the palace. **1949** N. MITFORD *Love in Cold Climate* I. ix. 97 Squiring royal old ladies to the supper-room. **1967** *Boston Herald* 1 Apr. 20/5 You will squire Machree wherever she wants to go. **1977** I. SHAW *Beggarman, Thief* III. x. 334 The sight of his mother.. being squired.. off the plane by a man who seemed not much older than himself had disturbed him.

transf. **1686** GOAD *Celest. Bodies* III. iii. 456 That [star] of 1365.. was squired in by a Comet.

b. Without const.

1530 PALSGR. 731, I squier, I wayte upon, *je baille attendance. Ibid.*, Is he your servant, he can squyre you as well as ever you were in your lyfe. **1599** B. JONSON *Ev. Man out of Hum.* Dram. Pers., His chiefe exercises are taking the Whiffe, squiring a Cockatrice. **1639** MAYNE *City Match* II. vi, A Gentleman of valour who has been In Moore-fields often.. to squire his sisters. *a* **1692** SHADWELL *Volunteers* II. i. (1693) 20 Pray if you see my Daughter, do you Squire her. **1731** SWIFT *To Gay* Wks. 1751 IV. i. 168 To 'squire a royal girl of two years old. **1751** SMOLLETT *Per. Pickle* lxxx, Not a lady of fashion in the kingdom scrupled.. to be squired by him. **1800** A. CARLYLE *Autobiog.* 187 Lady Catherine Lyon, whom I squired that night, and with whom I danced. **1855** KINGSLEY *Westw. Ho!* xii, 'Escort me, sir.' 'It is but too great an honour to squire the Queen of Bideford,' said Cary, offering his hand. **1887** T. A. TROLLOPE *What I remember* I. xii. 254, I have since squired many fairer and younger dames. **1962** D. LESSING *Golden Notebk.* I. 120 That second night of dancing she was squired by Stanley while her husband drank in the bar until it closed. **1977** *Time* 31 Jan. 31/1 At least one of Carter's aides turned up: Pollster Pat Caddell, who squired Hugh Hefner's daughter Christie.

transf. **1838** MRS. BRAY *Trad. Devonsh.* I. 214 Some ladies who are not afraid of singularity, will occasionally squire one another when they are in want of a beau. **1896** *Westm. Gaz.* 28 Apr. 5/2 Sir Richard Webster, squired by Mr. Cuffe and Mr. Angus Lewis, made his appearance also in good time.

† c. *transf.* To act or serve as an escort or guard to; to convoy. *Obs.*

a **1578** LINDESAY (Pitscottie) *Chron. Scot.* (S.T.S.) I. 366 The king of France.. gart.. prepair schips and gallayis.. to squyre the king of Scottland his sone and his douchter throw the sie. **1599** NASHE *Lenten Stuff* Wks. (Grosart) V. 249 Robin hoode and little Iohn.. are industrious and carefull to squire and safe conduct him in. **1632** HOLLAND *Cyrupædia* 175 To imagine that we ought to entertaine others for the guard and safetie of our persons, and be not a guard to squire and defend ourselves.

2. *intr.* With *it*: To act as a squire; to play the squire; to rule or domineer *over* as a country squire.

1672 MARVELL *Reh. Transp.* I. 69 It were a wild thing for me to Squire it after this Knight. **1739** 'R. BULL' tr. *Dedekindus' Grobianus* 91 Survey the Great, in City, Town, or Court, Who 'squire or lord it o'er the meaner Sort.

3. *trans.* To entitle or call 'Squire' or 'Esquire'.

1832 TENNYSON in Ld. H. Tennyson *Mem.* (1897) I. 91 The title-page may be simply 'Poems By Alfred Tennyson' (don't let the printer squire me).

squirearch (ˈskwaɪərɑːk), *sb.* (and *a.*). [Back-formation from SQUIREARCHY[1], after *monarch*, etc.] A member of the squirearchy; a squire as a local magnate.

1831 LYTTON *E. Aram* II. ii, The wealthier but less honoured squirearchs of the county. **1848** —— *Caxtons* I. II. ix, The proudest of the neighbouring squirearchs always spoke of us as a very ancient family. **1893** MEREDITH *Lord Ormont* ii, Aldermen not at the feast, squirearchs not in the saddle.

b. *adj.* Squirearchal. *rare.*

1893 *Temple Bar Mag.* XCVII. 244 Portly and squirearch was her spouse.

squirearchal (skwaɪəˈrɑːkəl), *a.* Also **squirarchal.** [f. prec. + -AL[1].] Of or belonging to, characteristic of, the squirearchy or a squirearch.

Clark (1855) gives *squirarchial*, and Worcester (1860, citing Clark) *squirarcheal.*

α. **1833** J. S. MILL in *Jurist* IV. 15 Some stupid younger son of a squirearchal house. **1838** LYTTON *Alice* IV. x, We were all a squirearchal, farming, George the Third kind of people! **1864** *Reader* 8 Oct. 458/2 Deep, indeed, is the satire on the squirearchal administration of justice. **1867** FITZGERALD 75 *Brooke St.* II. 1 Sir John had been carried to his resting-place with all the pomp of squirearchal show.

β. **1830** CARLYLE *Misc.* (1857) II. 146 A certain fashionable, knowing, half-squirarchal air. **1889** MISS BETHAM-EDWARDS *A. Young* p. xxx, Nothing can be more squirarchal than the well-wooded park. **1897** H. S. COWPER *Register Bk. Hawkshead* p. lxxvi, Many representatives of the squirarchal families.

squire'archical, *a.* Also **squirarchical.** [f. as prec. + -ICAL.] = prec.

1845 *Tait's Mag.* XII. 67 The first move in the last campaign against squirearchical domination. **1855** *Househ. Wds.* XII. 172 The class I mean are respectably descended from old squirearchical families. **1893** G. ALLEN *Scallywag* iii, A large-built, well-dressed man of military bearing and most squirarchical proportions.

squirearchy[1] (ˈskwaɪərɑːkɪ). Also α. **'squire-archy, squire-archy.** β. **squirarchy, 'squir-archy.** [f. SQUIRE *sb.* after *hierarchy*, *monarchy*, etc. The spelling with *e* has been by far the more usual.]

1. a. The collective body of squires, landed proprietors, or country gentry; the class to which squires belong, regarded especially in respect of its political or social influence.

α. **1796** W. TONE *Autobiogr.* (1893) II. iii. 55 Such is the honesty of the Squirearchy of Ireland. **1804** *Spirit Public Jrnls.* VIII. 55 We look to the admiration and support of the Squirearchy of Old England. **1854** WARTER *Last of O. Squires* xvi. 167 He had lived amongst the old squirearchy of the midland counties. **1899** BARING-GOULD *Bk. of West* I. ii. 40 A very large number of old mansions, belonging to the squirearchy of Elizabethan days, remain.

β. **1819** SYD. SMITH in *Edin. Rev.* March 308 The new class of punishments which the Squirarchy have themselves enacted against depredations on game. **1861** FITZGERALD *Lett.* (1889) I. 277 We are split up into the pettiest possible Squirarchy, who want to make the utmost of their little territory.

b. Without article.

1858 BAILEY *Age* 5 Law, army, navy, physic, state and squirearchy. **1885** *Illustr. Lond. News* 14 Feb. 184/1 Keeping upon good terms with Squirearchy.

c. A class, body, or number of squires.

1830 *Examiner* 789/1 A gorgeous aristocracy, a pampered squirarchy, and a magnificent parson-archy. **1853** W. JERDAN *Autobiog.* IV. 146 The surrounding Cheshire gentry, about the.. best informed squirearchy in the kingdom. **1874** GREEN *Short Hist.* iv. §2. 167 To check this growth of a squirearchy.. the statute provided [etc.].

2. The position or dignity of a squire. *rare.*

1854 WARTER *Last of O. Squires* xii. 118 Always ready to explode when thwarted in his squirearchy, he not only could, but did, look inward continually.

3. Rule or government by a squire or squires.

1861 PYCROFT *Agony Point* (1862) 127 The form of polity in Brendon was a kind of Squirearchy.

'Squirearchy[2]. [f. the name of Sir John Collings *Squire* (1884–1958), Eng. poet and man of letters, punningly after prec.] The influential literary circle, composed principally of critics and poets, which surrounded Squire, esp.

during his editorship of the *London Mercury* (1919–34).

1930 J. ARROW *J. C. Squire v. D. H. Lawrence* 5 Mr. J. C. Squire has pronounced... The magnanimous verdict is that the work of which the 'Squirearchy' does not approve will be 'easily forgiven and even forgotten'. **1959** *Times Lit. Suppl.* 10 Apr. 210/1 When Dr. Leavis founded *Scrutiny* it was with the laudable intention of cleaning out the Augean Stables of the Squirearchy, and an academic Hercules indeed he proved to be. **1978** J. PEARSON *Façades* viii. 146 The next encounter [of] the Sitwells..was the battle with the group who called themselves..the 'Squirearchy'.

squiredom ('skwaɪədəm). [f. SQUIRE *sb.* + -DOM. Cf. ESQUIREDOM.]

1. The dignity, position, or status of a squire.

1650 B. *Discollim.* 34 The utmost title we must now expect, is a Gentleman; it may be if we straine hard, we may hap to vent a few Squiredomes. **1838** LYTTON *Alice* IV. x, I suppose you have been enjoying the sweet business of a squiredom. **1842** FITZGERALD *Lett.* (1889) I. 88, I always direct to you as 'Mr. Barton' because I know not if Quakers ought to endure Squiredom. **1897** LD. H. TENNYSON *Mem. Tennyson* I. v. 138 His son Charles Tennyson d'Eyncourt pressed to be installed in the squiredom.

2. The body of squires; squires collectively.

1842 *Blackw. Mag.* LI. 147 Groves, pheasantries, pineries, and the other fine things of modern squiredom. **1847** *Ibid.* LXI. 424 He never hunted..with the squiredom of the country. **1874** LISLE CARR *Judith Gwynne* I. i. 17 That tall..man..was an indubitable stranger, far removed from the ranks of ordinary squiredom.

squireen (skwaɪə'riːn). [f. SQUIRE *sb.* + *-een*, Ir. Gael. *-ín* diminutive suffix.] A petty squire; a small landowner or country gentleman.

The first group of quots. illustrates the orig. Irish usage.

(*a*) **1809–12** MAR. EDGEWORTH *Absentee* vii, Squireens are persons who, with good long leases or valuable farms, possess incomes from three to eight hundred a year, who keep a pack of hounds, take out a commission of the peace [etc.]. **1825** LOCKHART in *Scott's Fam. Lett.* (1894) II. 297 Warned by a Mr. Hutcheson (apparently a squireen) not to travel on the Drogheda road after 7 p.m. **1846** J. KEEGAN *Leg. & Poems* (1907) 421, I..said I would no longer be a slave to any squireen of them all. **1883** S. C. HALL *Retrospect* II. 314 The 'half-sirs' or 'squireens', a class peculiar to Ireland, are, I believe, unknown now.

attrib. **1841** LEVER *C. O'Malley* x, There were scores of squireen gentry.

(*b*) **1834** MEDWIN *Angler in Wales* II. 264 A young lout of a squireen took yesterday, with worms,..thirty pound of trout in one rapid. **1878** tr. *Dumas' Three Musketeers* ii, A reserve of courage, wit, and shrewdness, which often makes a Gascon squireen better off than the richest gentleman of other provinces. **1898** J. A. GIBBS *Cotswold Village* 67 Hunting, shooting, coursing, and sometimes fishing are enjoyed by most of these squireens.

Hence **squi'reeness**, a female squireen.

1872 *Contemp. Rev.* XX. 106 Can we not endeavour to dissociate the Irish nation from those Hibernian squireens and squireenesses?

squirehood ('skwaɪəhʊd). [f. SQUIRE *sb.*]

1. The position or status of a squire or esquire; squireship. Also used as a title.

a **1680** BUTLER *Rem.* (1759) II. 91 To which Purpose he brings his Squirehood and Groom to vouch. **1721** SWIFT *Lett. King at Arms* Wks. 1841 II. 70/2 If this should be the test of squirehood, it will go hard with a great number of my fraternity. **1801** *Spirit Pub. Jrnls.* V. 376 The rage of Squire-hood is now so universal, that one of my humble race, a simple Gent, is hardly to be met with in his Majesty's dominions! **1814** SCOTT *Chivalry* (1874) 34 The sumptuary laws of squirehood were not particularly attended to.

2. The body of squires; the squirearchy.

1792 BURKE *Corr.* (1844) III. 438 In the governing people, the old false principles were quite worn out. In the squire-hood, the pretence of them..still existed. **1831** GEN. P. THOMPSON *Exerc.* (1842) I. 331 Neither the squirehood nor the priesthood can persuade anybody to prop open his gates, that the pigs may run into his potato-field. **1850** SCARGILL *Eng. Sketch-Bk.* 6 Both these gentlemen had their intimacies among the squirehoods of their respective neighbourhoods.

squireless ('skwaɪəlɪs), *a.* [f. SQUIRE *sb.* + -LESS.] Unattended by a squire; having no squire or landed proprietor.

1828 S. ROGERS *Italy* II. 10 And thou, Sir Knight, hadst traversed hill and dale, Squire-less. **1887** *Macm. Mag.* Nov. 60 The vicar of a squireless parish denounces Dives with absolute impunity. **1897** *Westm. Gaz.* 9 Mar. 2/2 Some other school may get less [money] to enable the squireless school to go on.

squirelet ('skwaɪəlɪt). [f. as prec. + -LET.] A petty squire or small landowner; a squireling.

1832 CARLYLE *Misc.* (1857) III. 56 A Scottish squirelet, full of gulosity and gigmanity. **1862** —— *Fredk. Gt.* XII. xiii. (1872) IV. 288 A man born poor: son of some poor Squirelet in the Ruppin Country. **1891** G. PEACOCK *Narcissa Brendon* I. 82 The little squirelets of the county would be proud to know him.

squire-like, *a.* and *adv.* [SQUIRE *sb.*]

A. *adj.* Like a squire or that of a squire.

1749 FIELDING *Tom Jones* XII. ii, The two squires met, and in all squire-like greeting saluted each other. **1783** CRABBE *Village* II. 55 Here too the squire, or 'squire-like farmer, talk.

B. *adv.* In the manner of a squire or attendant; humbly, submissively. *rare*⁻¹.

1605 SHAKS. *Lear* II. iv. 217, I could as well be brought To knee his Throne, and Squire-like pension beg, To keepe base life a foote.

squireling ('skwaɪəlɪŋ). [f. SQUIRE *sb.*]

1. A petty squire; a squirelet.

1682 T. FLATMAN *Heraclitus Ridens* No. 80 (1713) II. 242 Great Care is desired in the Matter, because the Squirelings need the Commodity [*sc.* wit] extreamly. **1843** F. E. PAGET *Warden of Berkingholt* 31 The very thing to suit the idle tastes of a shooting, boozing squireling. **1855** TENNYSON *Maud* I. xx. ii, Our ponderous squire will give A grand political dinner To half the squirelings near. **1886** *Sat. Rev.* 11 Dec. 789 She succumbed to the blandishments of a pecunious squireling.

2. A young squire.

1834 *Tait's Mag.* I. 439 The country squire..despatches his squireling to a neighbouring grammar-school. **1834** *New Monthly Mag.* XLI. 327 The academic squireling would have been promenaded over half Europe.

squirely ('skwaɪəlɪ), *a.* [f. as prec. + -LY¹.] Of, belonging or relating to, a squire or the squirearchy; befitting a squire.

1612 SHELTON *Quix.* I. I. iv, One very fit for this purpose, and Squirely function, belonging to Knighthood. **1620** *Ibid.* II. II. xxviii. 188 Thou Preuaricator of the Squirely Laws of Knight-Errantry. **1834** *Fraser's Mag.* X. 126 He looked on the squirely family of Mr. Scott of Harden as the head of his house. **1850** *Tait's Mag.* XVII. 423/2 Some rural squirely squabble. **1892** *Review of Rev.* 15 July 36/2 Estates of squirely magnitude are sought.

'squirely, *adv. rare.* [f. as prec. + -LY².] In the manner of or befitting a squire.

c **1400** *Rom. Rose* 7415 His looking was..meke and ful peesible. About his necke he bar a Bible, And squierly forth gan he gon.

squireship ('skwaɪəʃɪp). [f. SQUIRE *sb.* + -SHIP. Cf. ESQUIRESHIP.]

1. The state, position, or dignity of a squire or esquire; squirehood.

1613 OVERBURY *Charact., Common Lawyer* Wks. (1856) 85 Then he begins to sticke his letters in his ground chamber-window; so that the superscription may make his squire-ship transparent. **1620** SHELTON *Quix.* II. IV. xxv, What profit hast thou reaped by this thy Squireship? **1698** FARQUHAR *Love & a Bottle* V. iii, I had only a mind to convince you of your squireship. **1730** SWIFT *Lett.* Wks. 1841 II. 633 By the terror of squireship frighting my agent to take what you graciously thought fit to give. **1799** *Spirit Pub. Jrnls.* III. 279 Is not this enough to sicken us of Squireship. **1868** LANIER *Poems, Jacquerie* ii. 137 Thou art first Squire to that most puissant knight, Lord Satan, who thy faithful squireship long Hath watched.

b. The estate of a squire.

1824 R. POLLOK in D. Pollok *Life* 236 He was more like an heir to a country squireship than a student in theology.

2. The personality of a squire. Chiefly with possessive pronouns.

1786 BURNS *On dining with Ld. Daer* ii, When mighty Squireships of the quorum, Their hydra-drouth did sloken! **1828** SCOTT *F.M. Perth* xxiv, And now, Buncle,..your valiant squireship knows your charge. **1882** *Pall Mall G.* 15 July 6/1 The waggonette of Squire Calthorpe..is driven up, bearing his squireship's butler, gardener, and groom.

squiress ('skwaɪərɛs, skwaɪə'rɛs), *sb.* [f. as prec. + -ESS¹. Cf. ESQUIRESS.] A female squire; the wife of a squire or country gentleman.

Freq. in 19th c., esp. coupled with *squire*.

1823 T. MOORE *Fables Holy Alliance* 176 The Squires and their Squiresses all, With young Squirinas just come out. **1834** RITCHIE *Wand. Seine* 68 An attorney's wife who suddenly finds herself..the squiress and lady of the manor. **1880** BURGON *Twelve Good Men* (1888) II. 35 The squiress who was also the Lady-Bountiful of the village.

So **squiress** *v. intr.* (with *it*), to play the squiress. *rare*⁻¹.

1786 ANNA SEWARD *Lett.* (1811) I. 109 Your old acquaintance,..who married a Warwickshire squire,.. squiresses it with much loquacious importance.

squiret ('skwaɪərɪt). [f. as prec. + -ET¹.] A squirelet, squireling.

1838 *Blackw. Mag.* XLIII. 372 He had in many a town in England assumed the character of a spruce, knowing squiret. **1841** J. T. HEWLETT *Parish Clerk* I. 82 Whom he.. considered perfect models of squirets.

squire-wise, obs. form of SQUAREWISE *adv.*

†**'squirgliting**, *a. Obs.* (Meaning obscure.)

1602 *Contention betw. Lib. & Prod.* Prol., As for the quirks of sage Philosophie, or points of squirgliting scurrilitie.

squi'riferous, *a.* [Irreg. f. SQUIRE *sb.*] Partaking of the character of squires.

1796 CHARLOTTE SMITH *Marchmont* I. 203 Squiriferous Parsons, young men in orders, who shoot, hunt, etc.

squirilitie, obs. variant of SCURRILITY.

squi'rina. *nonce-word.* [f. SQUIRE *sb.* + -INA¹.] The daughter of a squire.

1823 [see SQUIRESS].

'squiring, *vbl. sb.* [f. SQUIRE *v.*] The action of attending as a squire or escort.

1599 B. JONSON *Cynthia's Rev.* Palinode, From squiring to tilt-yards, play-houses, pageants, and all such publique places. **1639** MAYNE *City-Match* III. iv, I will cut your wizzel, And spoil your squiring in the dark. **1859** *Athenæum* 12 Mar. 349 Hand-kissings and effeminate squirings of ladies.

squirish ('skwaɪərɪʃ), *a.* [f. SQUIRE *sb.* + -ISH.]

†**1.** (See quot.) *Obs.*⁻⁰

a **1700** B. E. *Dict. Cant. Crew, Squirish*, foolish; also one that pretends to Pay all Reckonings, and is not strong enough in the Pocket.

2. Characteristic of or befitting a squire.

1755 SMOLLETT *Quix.* Pref. (1803) I. 8 Sancho Panza, in whom I think are united all the squirish graces. **1881** DUFFIELD *Don Quix.* I. cxxii, Plain attire and squirish speech.

3. Having the deportment, appearance, or character of a country squire.

1814 in *Parr's Wks.* (1828) VIII. 366 Nothing squirish, though so great a country gentleman. **1826** *Westm. Rev.* VI. 263 When lords were still more lordly, and squires still more squirish than they are at present. **1883** R. G. WHITE *W. Adams* 67 He's settled down into a mere squire, and has grown burly and squirish.

Comb. **1855** F. FRANCIS *Newton Dogvane* (1888) 260 Various yeoman-like and squirish-looking gentlemen.

squirism ('skwaɪərɪz(ə)m). [f. as prec. + -ISM.] Squiredom.

1819 W. S. ROSE *Lett.* I. 97 A trait of genuine squirism in the life of Obizzo. **1843** J. STERLING in Carlyle *Life* (1851) II. xiii. 327 Squirism had already, in that day, become the *caput mortuum* that it is now.

squirk. [Imitative.] **a.** A half-suppressed laugh. **b.** A sharp squeaking sound.

1882 'F. ANSTEY' *Vice Versa* iv. 64 Little gurgles and 'squirks' of laughter. **1902** P. FOUNTAIN *Mts. & Forests S. Amer.* ix. 260 [A thrush] occasionally uttering a squirk to attract my attention.

squirl (skwɜːl). *dial.* and *colloq.* [Perh. blend of SQUIGGLE *sb.*² and TWIRL *sb.* or WHIRL *sb.*] A flourish or twirl, esp. in handwriting.

1843 J. BALLANTINE *Gaberlunzie's Wallet* ix. 212 Look at the lang turns o' his L's, and the squirls o' his B's; he's been weel brought up. **1922** *Sunday at Home* Oct. 59/2 'What a squiggly handwriting,' she said... 'They would not let us write that way at school. But when I am grown up I shall make lots of squirls.' **1955** E. BOWEN *World of Love* iii. 58 They are simply signed with a squirl. **1971** H. R. LOYN *Wulfstan MS.* 22, S2 three times uses a distinctive squirl, rather like a reversed *c*, to show the end of a section before a blank half-line. **1979** *PN Rev.* 10 7/1 The anterior reinforcing board..has a similar but not identical configuration of interlaced and interlocking squirls.

†**squirle.** *Obs.*⁻¹ [A comb. of *lec* LEEK *sb.* (cf. ME. *garle* garlick), with obscure first element.] A plant of the leek-kind.

a **1400** *Stockh. Med. MS.* ii. 616 in *Anglia* XVIII. 322 Garlec þe ton, lec þe toþer, Squirle is þe grete broþer.

squirm (skwɜːm), *sb.* [f. the vb.]

a. A squirming or writhing movement; a wriggle. **b.** *Naut.* A twist in a rope. **c.** A twisting or curving form of decoration characteristic of *art nouveau*; hence *colloq.* (with *the*), the style itself.

1839 *Havana* (N.Y.) *Republican* 21 Aug. (Thornton), [The whale gave] a squirm, and roll'd over and over. **1867** SMYTH *Sailor's Word-bk.* 648 *Squirm*, a wriggling motion like that of an eel. Also, a twist in a rope. **1883** BARING-GOULD *J. Herring* II. xxiii. 39 The squirms and languishings of the redeyelashed heiress..were grotesque. **1909** [see *art nouveau* s.v. ART *sb.* VI. e]. **1972** F. MACCARTHY *All Things Bright & Beautiful* ii. 46 Art nouveau was called 'the squirm'. When 'the squirm' arrived in Britain..Lewis F. Day and Walter Crane were outraged.

squirm (skwɜːm), *v.* [app. imitative.]

1. *intr.* To wriggle or writhe: **a.** Of reptiles, etc. Chiefly *U.S.* and *dial.*

1691 RAY *S. & E.C. Words* 115 To *Squirm*, to move very nimbly about, after the manner of an Eel. It is spoken of an Eel. **1743** CATESBY *Nat. Hist.* II. 47 This harmless snake frequents the branches of Trees and very nimbly squirms among the leaves. **1828** WEBSTER s.v., *Squirm*..signifies to move as a *worm*. **1859** HAWTHORNE *Transform.* (1878) 156 He should press his foot hard down upon the old serpent,.. feeling him squirm mightily. **1885** H. C. MCCOOK *Tenants Old Farm* 389, I have seen specimens..hanging by a thread and squirming, bending and snapping their bodies in the oddest ways.

fig. **1885** *Pall Mall G.* 5 May 4/1 If you want definite ideas [about vermin] that will squirm in your brain for a lifetime.

b. Of persons.

1756 CLUBBE *Misc. Tracts, Physiognomy* (1770) I. 24 Let them squirm about as much as they will, and struggle to support their heads from sinking. **1860** HOLMES *Prof. Breakf.-t.* 177 They find out the red-handed.. undergraduate of bucolic antecedents as he squirms in his corner. **1879** G. MACDONALD *Sir Gibbie* I. x. 154 At length he could..bear his thirst no longer, and, squirming round on the floor, crept softly towards the other end of the loft. **1890** HUXLEY in *19th Cent.* XXVII. 9 These poor little mortals who have not even the capacity to do anything but squirm and squall.

c. Of things.

1872 *Routledge's Ev. Boy's Ann.* 25/1 If there are a few trees near, and the long leafless twigs of one of them twitters and squirms against the window panes. **1888** ABP. BENSON in *Life* (1899) II. 220 Leighton said he found it vain to try to remember the turns and angles at which these branches squirmed about. **1905** CATHERINE I. DODD *Vagrant Englishwoman* 78 The sausage squirmed, spluttered, and sang as the lively flames leapt around it.

2. a. To move, proceed, or go with a wriggling or writhing motion. Const. with advs. and preps., as *along*, *forward*, *in*, *out*, *round*, *to*, *up*.

1759 *Compl. Lett.-writer* (ed. 6) 224 Mrs. Langford.. puddled herself into a minuet, and squirmed round and round the room. **1882** *Cent. Mag.* July 348/1 If you insist upon going to the end.., you must squirm along on all fours.

1883 *Harper's Mag.* Jan. 186/2 The shark squirmed out, thrashing about and snapping its jaws. 1891 C. LL. MORGAN *Anim. Sketches* 235 Wriggling and squirming up a dark green vertical wall.

b. *trans.* To twist or contort (something) *into* a new form. *rare.*

1876 'MARK TWAIN' *Tom Sawyer* xxi. 171 A brain-racking effort was made to squirm it into some aspect or other that the moral and religious mind could contemplate with edification.

3. *fig.* To be painfully affected or sharply touched by something; to writhe under reproof, sarcasm, or the like.

1804 [see the *vbl. sb.*]. 1849 *Knickerb. Mag.* Jan. 64 The gambler 'squirmed' under the gospel truth; yet..he contrived to sit the sermon out. 1894 G. M. FENN *In Alpine Valley* I 36 I'll write my Lord..such a letter as shall make him squirm.

4. *trans.* With *out*: To utter with a squirm.

1889 GUNTER *That Frenchman* xxi. 286 Here Zamaroff squirms out: 'Do I look like a man who would kill anything?'

Hence **squirming** *vbl. sb.* and *ppl. a.*

1804 *Balance* 25 Dec. 410 (Thornton), Some of the late victorious party have discovered *squirmings of resentment. 1858 O. W. HOLMES *Aut. Breakf.-t.* (1883) 96 A terrible squirming and scattering of the..population. 1887 *Spectator* 15 Oct. 1378 The British will, after many delays and much squirming, ultimately pay the money. 1859 HAWTHORNE *Transform.* xv, What a spirit is conveyed into the ugliness of this strong, writhing, *squirming dragon under the Arch-angel's foot! 1865 *Cornh. Mag.* July 46 When a great nation..is stirred and shaken..we all know what squirming, slimy things run forth helter-skelter. 1885 *Harper's Mag.* Jan. 223/2 A squirming alligator some three feet long.

squirmer ('skwɜːmə(r)). [f. SQUIRM *v.* + -ER[1].] One who squirms or writhes, esp. with embarrassment; an evasive person.

1951 O. NASH *Family Reunion* 109 Ho, squirmers and writhers, how long will ye suffer The medical tyrant, the social rebuffer! 1977 P. DICKINSON *Walking Dead* iv. 59 He was anxious to pin the little squirmer down.

squirmy ('skwɜːmɪ), *a.* [f. SQUIRM *v.*]

1. Given to squirming or writhing; wriggly.

1836 HALIBURTON *Clockm.* Ser. I. xv, It makes them as squirmy as an eel. 1906 *Macm. Mag.* Sept. 810 You've got to put horrid squirmy things on to hooks.

2. Of the nature of a squirm.

1885 MRS. C. PRAED *Affinities* I. ii. 29 You can drive away the queer, squirmy sensation that has taken hold of me. 1922 E. RAYMOND *Tell England* I. ii. 46, I felt a pleasing, squirmy excitement to think that we were to walk on to the..field in the company of the great Middlesex amateur. 1943 D. POWELL *Time to be Born* viii. 182 It was a squirmy feeling and reminded Ken..that..the carapace should be a little thicker. 1982 BARR & YORK *Official Sloane Ranger Handbk.* 57/1 One would never talk about true feelings—excessive piety is rather squirmy.

squi'rocracy. *rare.* [f. SQUIRE *sb.* + -OCRACY.] = SQUIREARCHY[1].

1834 *Tait's Mag.* I. 276 How little of community of interest..exists between the people and the Squirocracy. 1890 C. MARTYN *W. Phillips* 159 Half a dozen prominent and elderly squires dominated it [Concord, Mass.]... The squirocracy naturally sympathized with the slavocracy.

squirr, *v.* Also squir. [var. of SKIRR *v.*] *trans.* To throw or cast with a rapid whirling or skimming motion. Also with *away.*

1710 ADDISON *Tatler* No. 249 ¶7 Having taken me [a shilling] in his Hand, and cursed me, he squirred me away from him as far as he could fling me. 1711 BUDGELL *Spect.* No. 77 ¶1, I saw him squirr away his Watch a considerable way into the Thames. 1803 COUPER *Tourifications* I. 102, I squirred the card into the fire. 1847 HALLIW. s.v., Boys *squir* pieces of tile or flat stones across ponds or brooks to make what are denominated *Ducks and drakes.* 1876 *Whitby Gloss.* 173 *Skew'd,* or *Squirr'd,* whirled away; squandered.

squirrel ('skwɪrəl), *sb.* Forms: α. 5 squirel, squyrel(l, -elle, -ylle, squvyrelle, 6 squirell, 8 *north. dial.* swirl; 5 squyrrel, 6 -ell, 6–7 squirrell (7 sqirrell), -ill, -ile, 7 -il, skuyrrell, 9 *north. dial.* swirrel; 5– squirrel. β. 5 squerel, 5–6 -ell(e, 5 sqwerylle, 9 *north. dial.* swerill; 7 squerrel, -ell, 9 *dial.* squerril. γ. 5 scorel, scurelle, *Sc.* skurel (6 skarale). [ad. AF. *esquirel,* OF. *esquireul, escureul, -ol,* etc. (mod.F. *écureuil*), = Prov. *escurols,* Sp. *esquirol,* med.L. (*e*)*scurellus, scurellius, scuriolus,* diminutives from pop.L. **scūrius,* for L. *sciūrus,* ad. Gr. σκίουρος, app. f. σκιά shade + οὐρά tail.

The pron. ('skwɪrəl) is not recognized by the earlier lexicographers of the 19th cent., who vary between ('skwerəl) and ('skwʌrəl).]

1. a. One or other of various species of slender, graceful, agile rodents (characterized by a long bushy tail, furry coat, and bright eyes), belonging to the genus *Sciurus,* or to the widely-distributed sub-family *Sciurina* including this; *esp.* the common species *Sciurus vulgaris,* native to Britain, Europe, and parts of Asia.

α. ?*a* 1366 CHAUCER *Rom. Rose* 1402 There myght menne does and roes y-se And of squyrels ful great plente, From bowe to bowe alwaye lepyng. *c* 1381 —— *Parl. Foules* 196 (Camb.), Squyrelis & bestes smale of gentil kynde. *c* 1400 MAUNDEV. (1839) xix. 206 Thei wolde lepen als lightly in to Trees..as it were Squyrelles. 1483 *Cath. Angl.* 357/2 A Squyrelle,..*sirogrillus.* 1530 PALSGR. 275/1 Squyrrell a beest, *escurevl, escuireau.* *c* 1592 BRETON *C'tess Pembroke's Passion* xcviii, The lambes and rabbots sweetlie rune at base, Whilst highest trees the litle squiriles clime. 1624 CAPT. SMITH *Virginia* II. 27 Their Squirrels some are neare as great as our smallest sort of wilde Rabbets, some blackish or blacke and white, but the most are gray. 1687 A. LOVELL tr. *Thevenot's Trav.* III. 12 Its Muzle is round and of a Flesh-colour, and hath a Tail like a Squirrel. 1726 SWIFT *Gulliver* IV. i, They climbed high Trees, as nimbly as a Squirrel. 1784 COWPER *Task* VI. 315 The squirrel, flippant, pert, and full of play. 1815 SHELLEY *Alastor* 100 The doves and squirrels would partake From his innocuous hand his bloodless food. 1855 *Orr's Circle Sci., Org. Nat.* III. 467 In the United States of America,..Squirrels abound to an extraordinary extent, and often cause great loss to the farmer. *c* 1880 *Cassell's Nat. Hist.* III. 87 Squirrels appear to be strictly monogamous, pairing for life, and constantly inhabiting the same dwelling.

β. 14.. *Chaucer's Parl. Foules* 196 (Harl.), Squerellis smale, and bestes of gentil kynde. 1423 JAS. I. *Kingis Q.* clv, The lytill squerell, full of besynesse. 1555 EDEN *Decades* (Arb.) 215 As it weare a grehounde shulde ouerturne a squerell. 1598 MANWOOD *Lawes Forest* v. (1615) 49 Any wild beast that is killed by hunting, as a squerrel. 1630 HIGGESON *New Engl. Plantation* B 3 b, Also here are great store of squerrels, some greater, and some smaller and lesser. 1860 GEO. ELIOT *Mill on Fl.* III. vi. 86 Bob Jakin.. as you went arter the squerrils with. 1876 *Whitby Gloss.* 191 *Swerill,*..the squirrel.

γ. *c* 1440 *Promp. Parv.* 450/1 Scorel, or squerel, beest, *esperiolus.* *c* 1475 *Pict. Voc.* in Wr.-Wülcker 759/29 *Hic scurellus,* a scurelle.

b. Without article, in collective sense; also = squirrel-skin, squirrel-fur.

1436 *Libel Eng. Policy* in *Pol. Poems* (Rolls) II. 186 Skynnes of otere, squerel,..Of shepe, lambe, and fox. 14.. in *Sc. Acts Parlt.* (1844) I. 667 Of þe tymmyr of skurel [*c* 1575 skarale], ij d. *Ibid.,* Of ane hundreth gray gryse and skurel dycht and letheryt, viij d.

c. Applied to other animals or to persons, usu. with contemptuous force.

c 1566 *Merie Tales of Skelton* in S.'s Wks. (1843) I. p. lxvi, Skelton dyd harnesse the doughtye squirell [a cobbler]. 1591 SHAKS. *Two Gent.* IV. iv. 59 The other Squirrill was stolne from me... And then I offer'd her mine owne, who is a dog As big as ten of yours. 1865 A. SMITH *Summer in Skye* I. 124 Lachlan Roy was a little, cheery, agile, red squirrel of a man.

2. a. With *the,* in generalized sense; also, the genus *Sciurus* or the sub-family *Sciurina* to which this belongs.

Many species or varieties are distinguished by specific epithets, as *Alpine, Barbary, Brazilian, Carolina,* etc., *black, grey, red, striped,* etc., *cat-, fox-, palm-squirrel.* See also FLYING SQUIRREL, GROUND SQUIRREL.

1591 SYLVESTER *Du Bartas* I. vi. 142 There skips the Squirrill, seeming Weather-wise. 1607 TOPSELL *Four-f. Beasts* 656 Of the Squirrell. 1668 CHARLETON *Onomast.* 21 *Sciurus,*..the Squirrel. 1768 PENNANT *Brit. Zool.* I. 93 Those vast leaps the squirrel takes from tree to tree. 1774 GOLDSM. *Nat. Hist.* (1824) II. 71 A few of the numerous varieties of the squirrel. 1801 SHAW *Gen. Zool.* II. I. 136 The Squirrel feeds on the buds and young shoots of trees, and is said to be particularly fond of those of the fir and pine. 1834 M'MURTRIE *Cuvier's Anim. Kingd.* 80 In the Squirrel, properly so called, the hairs of the tail are arranged on the sides, so as to resemble a feather.

b. *pl.* = prec.

1834 M'MURTRIE *Cuvier's Anim. Kingd.* 80 It is probable that we shall have to separate from the Squirrels certain species which have cheek pouches like the Hamsters. 1842 *Penny Cycl.* XXII. 397/2 The geographic range of the Squirrels is very wide both in the Old and New World. *c* 1880 *Cassell's Nat. Hist.* III. 91 The true Ground Squirrels (*Tamias*) are distinguished from the rest of the Squirrels (*Sciurinæ*), and approach the Marmots.

c. *ellipt.* A variety of squirrel skin. Also, squirrel-fur in fashionable use (in the 19th and 20th cent.). Also *ellipt.,* a coat of squirrel fur.

1827 *Manch. Guardian* 27 Oct. 1/2 (Advt.), A perfectly new, elegant..and fashionable assortment of Furs, consisting of Chinchilla, Russia Fitch,..Squirrel and Sable. 1895 *Army & Navy Co-op. Soc. Price List* 15 Sept. 1038 Cape, lined throughout with grey and white Squirrel. 1904 *Westm. Gaz.* 1 Dec. 8/2 This Russian squirrel..makes an excellent coat. 1930 P. HAMBLEDON *Straight Flame* iv. 169 A fur coat..fashioned of the softest silvery squirrel from Manchuria. 1978 *Country Life* 31 Aug. 598/3 There are.. squirrels and durable musquashes for the less well heeled.

†3. *U.S.* The prairie dog. *Obs. rare.*

1808 [see PRAIRIE-DOG]. 1814 BRACKENRIDGE *Views of Louisiana* 239, I happened on a village of barking squirrels, or prairie dogs, as they have been called.

4. *Ichth.* One or other of various species of fish belonging to the family *Holocentridæ,* esp. *Holocentrus erythræus* (*Holocentrum sogo*).

1734 *Phil. Trans.* XXXVIII. 315 *Perca marina rubra.* The Squirrel. It is a good eating Fish. 1876 GOODE *Fishes of Bermudas* 50 Their voracity is very great, and the tyro in angling usually finds his first prize to be a 'Squirrel'.

5. *techn.* (See quot.)

1839 URE *Dict. Arts* 348 Some cards [for carding cotton] consist entirely of cylinders, the central main cylinder being surrounded by a series of smaller ones called urchins or squirrels.

6. *attrib.* and *Comb.* **a.** Simple attrib., as ***squirrel bell, gun, hole, hunt,*** etc., or appositive, as ***squirrel family, tribe.***

1862 *Catal. Internat. Exhib., Brit.* II. No. 6364, Clang bells for cattle; ferret bells; *squirrel bells. 1894–5 LYDEKKER *Roy. Nat. Hist.* III. 70 The *Squirrel family.. includes the true flying squirrels, ordinary squirrels, marmots, and susliks. 1902 *Munsey's Mag.* XXVI. 513/1 Men armed with *squirrel guns..from the back counties of Georgia. 1851 *Zoologist* IX. 3298 There is a bird here which lives in the *squirrel-holes in the ground. 1817 J. BRADBURY *Trav. Amer.* 289 The squirrels..are prevented from an inordinate increase by the frequency of *squirrel hunts by the riflemen. 1860 MAYNE REID *Hunters' Feast* xix, To make a successful squirrel-hunt two persons at least are necessary. 1901 *Scribner's Mag.* XXIX. 389/1 Garnett himself fell with a bullet from a mountaineer's *squirrel rifle. 1844 EMERSON *Ess.* Ser. II. *Experience* (1901) 245 Western roads, which opened stately enough,..and ended in a *squirrel-track. 1860 MAYNE REID *Hunters' Feast* xix, The naturalist stated many facts in relation to the *squirrel tribe, that were new to most of us.

b. In the sense 'made of, obtained from, the squirrel', as ***squirrel fur, lock, pie, skin;*** also 'made of squirrel skin or fur', as ***squirrel coat, hat, lining.***

1936 E. M. DELAFIELD *Provincial Lady in Amer.* 235 Ella, elegant..in..grey *squirrel coat. 1969 L. HELLMAN *Unfinished Woman* xi. 153 A little girl in a fine squirrel coat and hat. 1882 CAULFEILD & SAWARD *Dict. Needlew.* 459/1 **Squirrel Fur*... There are seven varieties of this Fur. 1974 *Selfridge Xmas Catal.* 14 Leather coat with silvered racoon collar and *squirrel lining, £330.00. 1882 CAULFEILD & SAWARD *Dict. Needlew.* 459/2 **Squirrel Lock*..is that portion of the grey squirrels' fur that grows..on the belly. 1788 M. CUTLER in *Life,* etc. (1888) I. 419 Dined..on venison steak and *squirrel pie; very good dinner. 1883 *Sunday Mag.* Oct. 628/1 Squirrel-pie is a well-known luxury in some parts of England, and is far superior to rabbit-pie. 1689 *Lond. Gaz.* No. 2498/4 Stolen.., a red and white *Squirrel-skin Peticoat. 1710 *Tatler* No. 245 ¶2 A musk-coloured velvet mantle lined with squirrel skins. 1832 MᶜCULLOCH *Dict. Commerce* (1834) 203 *Calabar Skin,* ..the Siberian squirrel skin.

c. Comb. with vbl. sbs., (ppl.) adjs., and agent nouns, as ***squirrel-coloured, -limbed, -trimmed; squirrel-hunting, -shooting, -stoning; squirrel-hunter;*** also ***squirrel-like.***

1876 T. HARDY *Ethelberta* vi, The east gleamed upon Ethelberta's *squirrel-coloured hair. 1860 MAYNE REID *Hunters' Feast* xix, The height..is one of those marvels witnessed by every *squirrel-hunter. 1667 COTTON *Scarron.* IV. 78 Æneas and the Queen have made..A match to go.. Into the Woods a *Squirrel hunting. 1704 *Dict. Rust.* (1726), *Squirrel-hunting.* The proper time to hunt this little Animal, is at the fall of the Leaf. *c* 1790 *Encycl. Brit.* (ed. 3) VI. 666/1 Squirrel-hunting is a noted diversion in country places [in New England]. 1847 HALLIW., *Squirrel-hunting,* a curious Derbyshire custom [etc.]. 1849 *Sk. Nat. Hist., Mammalia* IV. 22 They lift their food to their mouths while sitting *squirrel-like. 1862 LYTTON *Str. Story* II. 271 The squirrel-like opossums frolicked on the feathery boughs. 1626 B. JONSON *Staple of N.* v. iii, H' has almost kill'd his maid,..But that she's Cat-liu'd, and *Squirrill-limb'd, with throwing bed-staues at her. 1860 MAYNE REID *Hunters' Feast* xix, *Squirrel-shooting is by no means poor sport.

7. a. Special combs.: **†squirrel's brains** (see quot. and cf. *squirrel-minded*); **squirrel-cage,** a cylindrical cage in which squirrels are confined, and which revolves as they move; also *transf.* a structure resembling this; spec. in *Electr.,* a form of rotor resembling a squirrel-cage, used in small electric motors (usu. *attrib.*); **squirrel card** (see quot. and sense 5); **squirrel-dog,** a dog used for hunting squirrels; **squirrel eyes,** sharp eyes like those of a squirrel; **squirrel-fish,** = sense 4 (*Cent. Dict.* 1891); **squirrel-headed, -minded,** shallow-brained *a.*; also **squirrel-headedness.**

1647 WARD *Simple Cobler* 26 Having nothing..but a few *Squirrils brains to help them frisk from one ill-favour'd fashion to another. 1821 SCOTT *Kenilw.* xxxviii, We shall never find them to-night amongst all these..*squirrel-cages and rabbit-holes. 1831 *Ann. Reg.* (1832) 323 He had a cage like a squirrel-cage, and two white mice in it. 1835 URE *Philos. Manuf.* 163 Over this casing..a fan is placed,.. which sucks out the dust through the wire or squirrel cage. 1887 W. CORY *Lett. & Jrnls.* (1897) 526 In a revolving squirrel-cage way. 1895 S. P. THOMPSON *Polyphase Electr. Currents* iv. 117 A solid cylinder of iron is improved [as a rotor] by surrounding it with a mantle of copper, or by a squirrel-cage of copper bars. 1920 *Whittaker's Electr. Engineer's Pocket-bk.* (ed. 4) 552 Motors with squirrel-cage rotors require special features in the rotor to obtain large starting torque without large losses at normal load. 1972 *Sci. Amer.* Oct. 114/2 The air is circulated and exhausted by a system of squirrel-cage blowers. 1851 *Art Jrnl. Illust. Catal.* p. iv**/2 The large card-drum is generally surrounded by urchin or *squirrel cards instead of tops. 1860 MAYNE REID *Hunters' Feast* xix, A good *squirrel-dog is a useful animal. 1600 ROWLANDS *Lett. Humours Blood* ii. 53 With narrow brow, and *Sqirrell eyes, he showes. 1637 J. WILLIAMS *Holy Table* 59 That *Squirrel-headed young man, that..would throw the Communion-table out of doores, and build him a close Altar, out of faction and singularity. 1953 *Sun* (Baltimore) 30 Jan. B4/1 Former President Harry S. Truman was quoted as saying..that action..to curb President Eisenhower's Government reorganisation powers 'was a squirrel-headed thing to do'. 1955 E. POUND *Section: Rock-Drill* lxxxv. 6 Not to pamper this *squirrel-headedness. 1837 SYD. SMITH *Lett. Singleton* Wks. 1859 II. 276/2 What a strange thing it is that such a man..should be so *squirrel-minded as to wish for a movement without object or end!

b. *Bot., Zool.,* and *Ichth.,* as **squirrel briar,** a name used in New England for either of two local species of *Smilax, S. glauca* or *S. rotundifolia,* deciduous prickly vines bearing blue-black berries; **squirrel-corn, -cup, -fish, flying phalanger, hake, hawk, monkey, mouse, opossum** (see quots.).

1910 C. B. GRAVES et al. *Catal. Flowering Plants & Ferns Connecticut* 125 Smilax glauca..Saw, Cat or *Squirrel Briar. Common. Dry or moist open woods and thickets. *Ibid.,* Smilax rotundifolia..Common Green Briar. Horse, Cat, Bull or Squirrel Briar. 1979 C. MACLEOD *Family Vault* viii. 53 Something grabbed her..but it was only a squirrel briar. 1856 A. Gray *Man. Bot.* (1860) 27 *Dicentra Canadensis*... *Squirrel-Corn. 1877 Bryant *Poems, Twenty-Seventh of March* 30 The *squirrel cups [= liverleaf], a graceful company, Hide in their bells, a soft aërial blue. 1803 Shaw *Gen. Zool.* IV. ii. 439 Squirrel Sparus... Size of a common Perch: native of the American seas, where it is known by the name of the Grunt, or *Squirrel-fish. 1867 Latham *Black & White* 122 Bastard snappers and squirrel-fish, the like of which I had never seen before. 1888 Goode *Amer. Fishes* 46 The Squirrel fish, *Serranus fascicularis*, is a beautifully colored species. *c* 1880 *Cassell's Nat. Hist.* III. 207 The *Squirrel Flying Phalanger,.. *Petaurus sciureus. Ibid.* 207 Probably it.. has been called the Squirrel Flying Phalanger by mistake. 1882 Jordan & Gilbert *Syn. Fishes N. Amer.* 799 *Phycis tenuis*, Codling; White hake; *Squirrel-hake. 1884 Coues *N. Amer. Birds* 551 *Archibuteo ferrugineus*,.. California *Squirrel Hawk. 1773 *Gentl. Mag.* XLIII. 219 Of these I noticed the following, viz. the *Squirrel Monkey [etc.]. 1827 Griffith tr. *Cuvier* I. 307 The Saïmiri, or Squirrel monkey, is a beautiful and elegant little animal found in Brazil, Cayenne, etc. 1879 E. P. Wright *Anim. Life* 49 The genus Saimaris (Chrysothrix) contains but three species. These Squirrel Monkeys are active little creatures. 1607 Topsell *Four-f. Beasts* 533 There is a flying Ponticke or Scythian Mouse, which we may call the broad *Squerrell-Mouse. 1800 Shaw *Gen. Zool.* I. ii. 498 *Squirrel Opossum. *Didelphis Sciurea.* 1827 Griffith tr. *Cuvier* V. 200 Norfolk Island Squirrel,.. Squirrel Opossum.

Hence **'squirrelish, 'squirrelline, squi'rrellian** *adjs.*

1834 Beckford *Italy* II. 363 Timoni, with his prying, squirrelish look, and malicious propensities. 1872 Ruskin *Fors Clav.* xviii, These three moist-throated men and the squirrelline boy. 1874 *Ibid.* xliv, This is.. their work in the world. When they rest from their squirrellian revolutions,.. these are what will follow them.

'squirrel, *v.* [f. the sb.]

†**1. a.** *intr.* To hunt squirrels. Also *fig.* **b.** *trans.* To hunt or chase like squirrels. Hence †**'squirreling** *ppl. a. Obs.*

1589 ? Lyly *Pappe w. Hatchet* B ij, Obscenitie? Naie, now I am too nice, squirrilitie were a better word: well, let me alone to squirrell them. *a* 1603 T. Cartwright *Confut. Rhem. N.T.* (1618) 540 Which we might worthely call a phrensie if it had not some support of grauer men, then are those squirriling Iesuits. 1667 Cotton *Scarron.* iv. 83 But young Ascanius, hops o' th' house, Car'd not for Squirreling a Louse.

c. *intr.* To go round in circles like a caged squirrel; to run or scurry (*round*) like a squirrel.

1921 *Sat. Westm. Gaz.* 29 Jan. 21/1 His deeply affectionate but explosive father inexhaustibly squirrelling round the cage of conventional ideas. 1953 A. Clarke *Coll. Plays* (1963) 374 My soul was waiting for me, so small, It wriggled and squirrelled to my shoulder. 1966 D. Francis *Flying Finish* xvii. 200 The useless thoughts squirrelled round and round, achieving nothing. 1983 'M. Yorke' *Find me Villain* v. 39 Nina's mind went on squirrelling round unhappily.

2. *trans.* To store *away* in the manner of a squirrel; to save, hoard; to cache. Rarely with *up* and without advb.

1939 J. Steinbeck *Grapes of Wrath* xxviii. 569, I been squirrelin' money away. 1949 M. Mead *Male & Female* vii. 145 Mouths first suck and later bite, and are capable of spitting, of squirrelling food in the cheek all night. 1953 J. Blish *Case of Conscience* in *If. Worlds of Sci. Fiction* I. iv. 40 I've got more plans to that effect squirrelled away. 1959 J. Braine *Vodi* vi. 95 Dick felt somehow provident, squirrelling up at least one good event to remember in the winter. 1965 G. Holden *Don't go it Alone* (1966) xvii. 141 He wasn't the type of person to squirrel away something and forget it. 1974 D. Smith *Look Back with Love* viii. 68, I started a bottom drawer, but it petered out after I had squirrelled one tea-cosy and a pen-wiper. 1981 N. Freeling *One Damn Thing after Another* viii. 58 Arlette.. was good at squirrelling away things in obscure places.

squirrelling, *vbl. sb.* [f. squirrel *v.*]

†**1.** Hunting squirrels. *Obs.*

1594 Lyly *Mother Bombie* ii. ii, I thinke Lucio be gone a squirelling, but Ile squirell him for it.

2. Hoarding, saving up; storing *away*.

1960 *Listener* 31 Mar. 564/2 Surplus hours.. used either to offset the effect of tight times, or as a safeguard against situations when.. work became short, and time had to be booked at the 'lower' time rate. I have heard this practice described as 'squirrelling' in other industries. 1965 *Wall St. Jrnl.* 17 Feb. 1 Presumably, the worsening could result from public hoarding of the new coins or the squirreling away of old ones as keepsakes. 1969 *Daily Tel.* 31 July 15/1 We resolved to resist all temptations to lay in 1969 supplies of anything which remained in bulk from 1968's feverish squirrelling. 1972 *Guardian* 25 Sept. 8/1 The specialist's squirrelling of facts.

squirrelly ('skwɪrəlɪ), *a.* Also squirrely. [f. squirrel *sb.* + -y^{1}.] **1.** Resembling or characteristic of a squirrel.

1925 D. H. Lawrence *Reflections on Death of Porcupine* 204 The chipmunks.. were little squirrely things with stripes down their backs. 1965 H. Gold *Man who was not with It* ii. 11, I saw that squirrelly look which says: 'Win it all back with the rent money.'

2. Inclined to rush this way and that, unpredictable. Of a person: demented, crazy; jumpy, nervy.

1928 O. Elton *Survey Eng. Lit.* (1730–80) I. iii. 70 Lady Sarah Lennox's letters are 'at first squirrelly and girlish'. 1934 M. H. Weseen *Dict. Amer. Slang* 198 *Squirrely*, abnormal; queer; crazy. 1960 *Spectator* 25 Mar. 438 Her description of contestants going 'squirrelly' (demented) with exhaustion.. makes an unpleasant sociological document. 1970 K. Platt *Pushbutton Butterfly* (1971) x. 117, I got all squirrelly after you left. I just couldn't sit around doing nothing. 1977 J. Wambaugh *Black Marble* (1978) viii. 108 Squirrelly dog, Pattie Mae... Squirrelly! Just like his goddamn owner. I never shoulda said I'd bring him today.

squirrel-tail. Also squirrel's tail.

1. The tail of a squirrel. In quot. *collect.*

c 1400 *Seuyn Sag.* (W.) 2777 He let him make a garnement,.. And heng theron squirel taile, A thousand and mo, withouten fail.

2. A species of lob-worm. ? *Obs.*

Walton's wording is repeated by later writers.

1653 Walton *Angler* 94 There be also of lob-worms, some called squirel-tails (a worm which has a red head, a streak down the back, and a broad tail). 1787 Best *Angling* (ed. 2) 16. 1839 T. C. Hofland *Brit. Angler's Man.* ii. (1841) 9.

3. ***squirrel-tail grass***, one or other of various species of grasses belonging to the genus *Hordeum*.

1777 W. Curtis *Flora Lond.* (1798) II. Pl. 23, We have been informed.. that in the Isle of Thanet this grass [*Hordeum murinum*] is well known to the inn-keepers, who call it *Squirrel-tail Grass*. 1796 Withering *Brit. Pl.* (ed. 3) II. 172 *Hordeum maritimum*. This is the true Squirrel-tail Grass of the Isle of Thanet, and not as Mr. Curtis says, the *Hord. murinum*. 1846–50 A. Wood *Class-bk. Bot.* 620 *Hordeum jubatum*. Squirrel-tail Grass. 1851 *Phytologist* IV. 10 *Hordeum pratense*... In the Monckton meadows [near Ryde].. the herbage consists mainly of the 'Squirrel-tail grass' [etc.].

b. *ellipt.* = *squirrel-tail grass*.

1796 Withering *Brit. Pl.* (ed. 3) II. 172 The stunted habit of the true Squirrel-tail. 1899 *Cumberland Gloss.* 310/2 *Squirrel's tail*, sea barley, *Hordeum maritimum*.

4. *Zool.* (See quot.)

1850 Miss Pratt *Comm. Things of Sea-side* iv. 250 Another [polyp] is called Squirrel's Tail, (*Sertularia argentea*), because it is so like the tail of our woodland animal.

squirrel-tailed, *a.* [f. squirrel *sb.* Cf. prec.] Having a tail resembling that of the squirrel in form or character.

1840 Hodgson *Hist. Northumb.* III. ii. 361/2 *Leucodon sciuroides*, Squirrel-tailed Leucodon. 1856 'Stonehenge' *Brit. Rur. Sports* 236/1 The tail [of the dew-worm] tapers somewhat, but in the squirrel-tailed variety it is flattened. 1894–5 Lydekker *Roy. Nat. Hist.* III. 107 Of the European species the largest is the squirrel-tailed dormouse (*Mus glis*).

squirrilitie, -ility, obs. varr. scurrility.

'squirry, *v. rare*$^{-1}$. = squirr *v.*

1825 *Examiner* 721/1 Mazurier.. followed with his impossible contortions; we fully expect some night to see him twitch off one of his legs, and squirry it up into the slips.

squirt (skwɜːt), *sb.* Forms: 5 **scqwyrt**, 6 **skurt, squyrt(e, squerte, squirte,** 6– **squirt** (9 *north. dial.* **swirt**). [f. squirt *v.*]

1. a. Diarrhœa; looseness or laxity of the bowels. Now *dial.* in *pl.*

c 1460 *Promp. Parv.* (Winch. MS.), Scqwyrt, *idem quod* flyx, *supra*. 1527 Andrew *Brunswyke's Distyll. Waters* K j b, The same is good for the squyrt, a cloute wet in the same and put behynde in the fondament. 1530 Palsgr. 317/1 Laxe as one that hath the flyxe or squyrte. *a* 1600 Deloney *Gentle Craft* ii. ix. Wks. (1912) 197 If euer I come to giue him Phisicke, if I make him not haue the squirt for fiue dayes, count me the veriest dunce. *a* 1651 Cleveland *Model of New Rel.* 40 A costive Dover gives the Saints the Squirt. 1719 D'Urfey *Pills* V. 311 The Cramp, the Stitch, the Squirt, the Itch. 1883 *Hampshire Gloss.* 88 To have the squirts. 1886 Elworthy *W. Somerset Word-bk.* 707 *Squirts*, diarrhœa... Called also *Wild-squirts*.

fig. 1639 Shirley *Ball* v. i, Your wit has got the squirt too. 1691 Wood *Ath. Oxon.* I. 356 He would preach and pray extempore.. insomuch that many were pleased to say he was troubled with the Divinity squirt.

†**b.** Thin excrement. *Obs.*

1580 Hollyband *Treas. Fr. Tong, Foire*, thin dung, skurt. 1611 Cotgr., *Foire*, squirt, thinne dung; a laske.

c. With *a*: An attack of diarrhœa.

1611 Cotgr., *Aller long*, to haue a squirt, to squatter out behind. 1641 (*title*), Taylor's Physicke has purged the Divel; or the Divell has got a Squirt. By Voluntas Ambulatoria. 1828 Carr *Craven Gloss.* II. 185 *Swirt*,.. a diarrhœa.

2. a. A small tubular instrument by which water may be squirted; a form of syringe.

1530 Palsgr. 275/1 Squyrt an instrument, *esguissovere*. 1552–3 in Feuillerat *Revels Edw. VI* (1914) 107, vj great woodden squertes by him turned and made for the combat of the lorde of misrule. 1632 tr. *Bruel's Praxis Med.* 90 If the patient bee vnwilling to take any medicines, wee must labour to put them into him with a squirt. 1697 J. Lewis *Mem. Dk. Glocester* (1789) 57 While we four men were to ply him well, in the Duke's sight, with syringes, and squirts of all sorts. 1712 J. James tr. *Le Blond's Gardening* 175 A little Pump or Squirt. 1828 Carr *Craven Gloss.* II. 185 *Swirt*, a syringe. 1840 Barham *Ingol. Leg.* Ser. ii. *Nurs. Rem.* vi, Billy Hawkins Came, and with his pewter squirt Squibb'd my pantaloons. 1871 L. Stephen *Playgr. Eur.* (1894) xiii. 316 To them.. foaming waterfalls are like streams from penny squirts.

fig. 1730 Young *Ep. Pope* i. 224 But when they have be-spatter'd all they may, The statesman throws his filthy squirts away! 1734 Pope *Let. to Swift* 6 Jan., There is a woman's war declared against me by a certain lord; his weapons are.. a pin to scratch, and a squirt to bespatter.

transf. 1855 Chamier *My Trav.* I. xviii. 321 The fountains were nothing but squirts. 1890 'R. Boldrewood' *Col. Reformer* (1891) 81 Casting the revolver away.. he.. said, 'Damn the—squirt!'

b. A larger instrument of the same type, used esp. as a fire-extinguisher.

In quot. *a* 1685 referring to the plunger-pump of Sir Samuel Morland.

1590 Lucar *Lucar Solace* 157 A squirt which hath been devised to cast much water upon a burning house. 1643 *Seasonable Adv. preventing Fire* in *Harl. Misc.* (Malh.) V. 348 Also it is necessary that every parish should have hooks, ladders, squirts, buckets, and scoops, in readiness, upon any occasion. 1667 in *Strype's Surv. Lond.* (1754) I. i. xxviii. 291/2 That every Alderman.. provide four and twenty buckets and one hand squirt of brass. *a* 1685 Duke *Ep. to Otway*, For once a squirt was rais'd by Windsor wall. 1866 C. F. T. Young *Fires, Fire Engines*, etc. vi. 69 Fire engines .. seem to have been altogether forgotten in the 'dark ages', and 'squirts' or portable syringes appear to have been the only contrivances in use.

†**c.** A kind of inflater or air-pump. *Obs.*$^{-0}$

1598 Florio, *Gonfiatoio*,.. a squirt of brasse that Balloniers vse to blowe their ballones full of winde.

d. A jet-propelled aeroplane, punningly after *jet. Air Force slang. temporary.*

1945 L. R. Gribble *Battle Stories of R.A.F.* xxiii. 59 To fly the squirts in combat meant the development of a new technique. 1948 *N.Y. World-Telegram* 30 Dec. 11/7 The plane itself is called a 'blow torch', a 'flame thrower', a 'squirt', [etc.].

3. a. A small quantity of liquid that is squirted; a small jet or spray; an act of squirting.

1626 Bacon *Sylva* §500 The Watring of those Lumps of Dung, with Squirts of an Infusion of the Medicine in Dunged water. 1760 Sterne *Tr. Shandy* iii. xxviii, How different from the rash jerks and hare-brained squirts thou art wont.. to transact it with in other humours,.. spurting thy ink about thy table and thy books. 1837 Carlyle *Fr. Rev.* ii. v. iii, And now in these new days such issues do come from a squirt of the pen by some foolish rhyming René. 1858 Hawthorne *Fr. & It. Note-bks.* I. 96 The water makes but the smallest part—a little squirt or two. 1878 Stevenson *Inland Voy.* 78 The rain kept coming in squirts and the wind in squalls.

b. *Math.* (See quot.)

1878 W. K. Clifford *Elem. Dynamic, Kinem.* 214 The point *s* is called a *source* of strength μ when the fluid streams out in all directions; when μ is negative, so that the fluid streams inwards, it is called a *sink*. The whole velocity-system here described may be called a *squirt*.

c. *transf. spec.* in *Air Force slang*, a burst of gun-fire.

1942 Brennan & Hesselyn *Spitfires over Malta* i. 28, I gave him a squirt with the scatter guns. 1948 *Welsh Rev.* Winter 287 There was another squirt of song and then silence. 1978 K. Amis *Jake's Thing* iv. 34 To be given the choice of two [buses].. was.. certainly welcome in the increasing rain and squirts of cold wind.

d. A compressed radio signal transmitted at high speed. Cf. sense 9 of the vb.

1968 M. Woodhouse *Rock Baby* vii. 64 It can't transmit continuously, though, surely... What does it do, transmit in squirts? 1974 'J. le Carré' *Tinker, Tailor, Soldier, Spy* vi. 50 Irina.. boiled down the microdots and played radio for him on a high-speed squirt to beat the listeners.

4. †**a.** The squirting or spirting cucumber. *Obs.*$^{-1}$

1753 *Chambers' Cycl.* Suppl. s.v. *Cucumis*, The wild cucumber, or squirt, called by authors, *cucumis asinus*, or the ass cucumber.

b. *slang.* (See quot.)

1859 *Slang Dict.* 100 *Squirt*, a doctor, or chemist.

c. *Zool.* An ascidian or sea-squirt.

1891 in *Cent. Dict.*

5. *colloq.* A paltry or contemptible person; a whipper-snapper; a fop. Also *spec.* a child or young person. orig. *U.S.*

a 1848 *Maj. Jones's Courtship* 160 (Bartlett), If they won't keep company with squirts and dandies. 1887 *S. Cheshire Gloss.* 370 What do I care for a little squirt like thee? 1914 G. Atherton *Perch of Devil* i. 39 She had 'sized him up' as a 'squirt'.., but he was 'a long sight better than nothing'. 1924 Kipling *Debits & Credits* (1926) 153 They both shook 'ands with the young squirt across the table. 1935 'N. Blake' *Question of Proof* i. 17 It's about time that squirt Wemyss was suppressed. 1955 M. Gilbert *Sky High* iii. 46 Most people who send letters like that are cowardly little squirts. 1958 B. Malamud *Magic Barrel* (1960) 138 George .. remembered him giving him nickels.. when he was a squirt. 1967 [see *half-portion* s.v. half- II. n]. 1977 J. Bingham *Marriage Bureau Murders* xi. 134 Sidney Shaw, the little squirt.. ought to be able to intercept a letter.

6. *U.S.* A display of rhetoric; a piece of fine writing verging on bombast.

1872 O. W. Holmes *Poet Breakf.-t.* ix, That sounds.. like what we college boys used to call a 'squirt'. *Ibid.*, I know what you are thinking—you're thinking this is a squirt.

squirt (skwɜːt), *v.* Also 5–6 squyrt, 6 squyrte, squirte, 9 *north. dial.* swirt. [Of obscure origin. Cf. LG. *swirtjen, swürtjen* (also EFriesl. *kwirtjen*) in senses 1 and 2.

For earlier evidence see squirting *vbl. sb.* In the 14th cent. *Nominale* (Skeat) 408 the F. *esclauotee* is rendered by 'be-squireid', prob. an error for 'be-squirtid'.]

I. *intr.* **1. a.** To eject or spirt out water in a jet or slight stream.

c 1460 J. Russell *Bk. Nurture* 293 in *Babees Bk.*, With youre mouthe ye vse nowþer to squyrt, nor spowt. 1530 Palsgr. 731/2, I holde the a grote that I squyrt over yonder wall with my squyrt. 1580 Hollyband *Treas. Fr. Tong, Caner*, to squirte. 1711 *New Map Trav. of High Church Apostle* 7 Two Cirenges hanging at his Saddle,.. to squirt in the Eyes of his Lowflyers. 1740 Cibber *Apol.* (1756) I. 35 It generally flew back into their faces as it happens to children when they squirt at their playfellows against the wind. 1837 Carlyle *Fr. Rev.* i. v. vi, The Firemen are here, squirting with their fire-pumps on the Invalides cannon, to wet the touchholes; they unfortunately cannot squirt so high. 1862 Miss Yonge *Countess Kate* iv, I squirted right through the window.

b. To void thin excrement; to have diarrhœa.
1530 PALSGR. 731/2, I squyrt, I have a lax, *jay le va va*. **1598** FLORIO, *Squaccarare*, to squatter, to squirt or lash it out behind after a purgation. **1611** COTGR., *Foirer*, to squirt, to shite thinne as in a laske. **1653** URQUHART *Rabelais* I. xxv. 115 For those that are costive..it will make them..squirt the length of a Hunters Staffe.

2. a. To move swiftly or quickly; to dart or frisk. Chiefly with advs., as *about, in, up and down*, or preps., as *among*.
1570 FOXE *A. & M.* 1243/1, I thought..to haue made easie iourneys,..and now come you squirtyng in post, and trouble all. **1607** MIDDLETON *Fam. Love* IV. i, Comes master doctor Glister, as his manner is, squirting in suddenly. *a* **1652** BROME *Covent Garden weeded* II. i, Let me see you squirting about without a weapon,..and I'le weapon you. **1692** L'ESTRANGE *Fables* (1694) 251 You are so..given to squirting up and down, and chattering, that the world would be apt to say I had chosen a Jackpudding for a Prime Minister. **1859–76** in dial. glossaries, etc. (Westm., Lancs., Yks.).

†**b.** ? To move jerkily up and down. *Obs.*
1611 COTGR. s.v. *Chevaucher, Chevaucher à la genette*, to sit squirting on horseback with legs drawn vp almost vnto the saddle.

3. To issue or be ejected in a jet-like stream; to spirt or spurt.
1858 HAWTHORNE *Fr. & It. Note-bks.* (1872) I. 57 The water squirts out of some fantastic piece of sculpture. **1863** READE *Hard Cash* I. i. 22 The oars seemed to lash the water savagely,..and the spray squirted at each vicious stroke. **1893** W. R. MACKINTOSH *Orkney Peat Fires* (1908) iii. 266 The blood was squirting from his finger-tips.

II. *trans.* **4. a.** To cause (liquid) to issue or stream (*out*) in a jet from a squirt or syringe.
1583 STUBBES *Anat. Abus.* II. (1882) 36 A squirt, or a squibbe, which little children vsed to squirt out water withall. **1590** LUCAR *Lucar Solace* IV. x. 157 This kinde of squirt may be..made to squirt out his water with great violence upon the fire. **1601** HOLLAND *Pliny* VIII. xxvii. I. 210 This bird having a crooked and hooked bill, useth it in steed of a syringe or pipe, to squirt water into that part. **1664** H. MORE *Myst. Iniq.* I. xvii. 64 This..will sooner quench all the fiery darts of the wicked, then whole pots of Holy-water squirted against him. **1688** WOOD *Life* (O.H.S.) III. 270 Mr. Philip Lewis appeared in the pulpit in the chappell and preached grining and laughing, and [they] had water squirted on them. **1712** ARBUTHNOT *John Bull* (1755) 32 She used to hire fellows to squirt kennel water upon him, as he passed along the streets. **1825** JAMIESON *Suppl.*, To *Skoot*,.. to squirt any liquid.

b. To eject or propel in a stream from a small orifice, etc. Chiefly with advs. or preps.
1601 HOLLAND *Pliny* I. 441 The remedie to keepe Wespes from them, is to spurt or squirt oile out of a mans mouth vpon them. **1607** TOPSELL *Four-f. Beasts* 207 They..would through their trunks squirt or cast a litle of their drink vpon their attendants. **1742** YOUNG *Nt. Th.* IX. 919 What childish toys, Thy watry columns squirted to the clouds! **1765** *Museum Rust.* IV. 332 Putting a bit of salt and butter up the cod instead of squirting up a little salt water. **1837** P. KEITH *Bot. Lex.* 376 It takes in a portion of water, which it has the power of squirting out again with considerable force. **1849** CUPPLES *Green Hand* i. (1856) 3 The emphatic way in which ..they squirted their tobacco-juice on the deck.

c. In fig. uses.
1606 J. DAY *Ile of Gulls* III. i, I had paraphrasticall admonitions of all sortes,—some against couetous Landlords, and that I would squirt amongst beggerlie Tennants. **1678** OTWAY *Friendship in Fashion* III. i, Comedy! no, I scorn to write comedy. I know several that can squirt comedy. **1702** BOYER *Dict. Royal* I, *Il chie de peur*, ..he squirts [his] wits, his heart is sunk into his breech. **1768–74** TUCKER *Lt. Nat.* (1834) II. 157 Versifiers squirting out careless rhapsodies of harmonious billingsgate. **1781** H. WALPOLE *Let. to H. S. Conway* 6 May, He lifted up his leg, and just squirted contempt on them. **1872** BLACKIE *Lays Highl.* 123 And you, poor shell fish, squirt your spiteful ban [etc.].

†**d.** Phr. *to squirt a mouldy*, to fire a torpedo. *Naut. slang. Obs.*
1916 [see MOULDY *sb.*].

5. To inject (a liquid) by means of a squirt or in a similar manner.
c **1550** H. LLOYD *Treas. Health* Cj, The joyce..put or squyrted into the eye doth put awaye the blemysshes of the same. **1577** B. GOOGE *Heresbach's Husb.* III. (1586) 122 Some woulde haue the licour of the lime Bitumen squirted in. **1610** [see SQUIRTFUL]. **1721** BAILEY, *To Syringe*, to squirt Liquors into the Ears, Sores, &c. **1841** HOOD *Tale of Trumpet* 144 The almond-oil she had tried,..Dabb'd, and dribbled, and squirted in. **1884** *Marshall's Tennis Cuts* 126 The bystanders took so lively an interest in his matches as to squirt tobacco-juice in his eyes.

6. To moisten or cover (a surface) with liquid by means of spirting or squirting; to bring into a certain state in this way.
1601 B. JONSON *Poetaster* To Rdr., They know, I dare To spurne, or baffull 'hem, or squirt their eyes With inke, or vrine: or I could doe worse. **1610** MARKHAM *Masterp.* II. xxii. 256 Either wash or squirt the soare place with it. **1909** *Daily Chron.* 1 April 4/4 Your first desire on beholding the outside of the building is to order up a few fire hoses and squirt it clean.

7. To cause to squirt or give out liquid.
1622 DRAYTON *Poly-olb.* xxiii. 262 Quoth warlike Warwickshire, 'I'll bind the sturdy Bear'. Quoth Worstershire again, 'And I will squirt the Pear'.

8. *techn.* To force or press (a viscous or ductile material) through a small orifice; to form or fashion in this manner.
1881 R. W. RAYMOND *Mining Gloss.*, *Squirting*, forcing lead by hydraulic pressure into the form of rods or pipes.

9. To transmit (information) in highly compressed or speeded-up form. Also *absol.*
1971 C. EGLETON *Last Post for Partisan* xii. 113, I should have been given the means to squirt... You prerecord the message and then push it through in a second, before they have a chance to find your frequency. **1977** P. VAN RJNDT *Blueprint* xiii. 231 The message is recorded on a separate tape which is then treated electronically in order to compress the message... The normal procedure is to 'squirt' it over radio transmission. **1979** C. MCCARRY *Better Angels* II. i. 106 Radio equipment..could squirt a million words from one continent to another via satellite in a droplet of electric energy that required less than a millisecond to send or receive.

squirt- (skwɜːt), the verbal stem in combination, chiefly in the sense 'that squirts, capable of squirting', as **squirt clam, -fish, -gun, -ring**; also †**squirt-fire**, a musket; **squirt-swimming**, swimming by propulsion produced by squirting of liquid; †**squirt-wit** (see quot. and SQUIRT *v.* 4 c).
Also *squirt-can, -oilcan*, in recent use.
1887 G. B. GOODE, etc. *Fisheries U.S.* II. 581 *Mya arenaria*... In Long Island Sound and at New York it is most spoken of as the 'long clam' and '*squirt clam'. **1678** BUTLER *Hud.* III. ii. 1169 One single Red-Coat Sentinel.. with his *Squirt-fire, could disperse Whole Troops. **1860** WRAXALL *Life in Sea* v. 110 The Javanese *Squirt-fish (*Chætodon rostratus*) catches its prey in a similar fashion. **1803** *Poet. Petit. agst. Tractorising Trumpery* 87 With glyster-pipe and *squirt-gun There will be dev'lish deal of hurt done. **1878** *Scribner's Mag.* Nov. 76/2 [He] made squirt-guns of the hollow metal pen-handles. **1877** W. JONES *Finger-ring* 494 In the Waterton Collection is a bronze *squirt-ring. **1861** P. P. CARPENTER in *Rep. Smithsonian Instit.* 1860 278 The *squirt-swimming of the Cuttles. **1632** HAUSTED *Rival Friends* Pref. A iij b, These *squirt-wits, who are able onely to bring forth a paper of verses in a yeere.

†**squirtel.** *Obs.*$^{-0}$ In 5 s(q)wyrtyl. [f. SQUIRT *v.*] A squirt or syringe.
c **1440** *Promp. Parv.* 471/1 Sqwyrtyl, or swyrtyl,..*sifon*.

squirter ('skwɜːtə(r)). [f. as prec.]
†**1.** One who shoots jerkily with the bow. *Obs.*$^{-1}$
1545 ASCHAM *Toxoph.* I. Wks. (1904) 59 If he giue it ouer, and not vse to shote,..he shal become of a fayre archer, a stark squyrter and dribber.

†**2.** One who has or suffers from diarrhœa. *Obs.*
1600 SURFLET *Countrie Farme* I. iv. 11 It oftentimes causeth bloudie fluxes,..if we beleeue Galen and them which for this cause call the inhabitants of Paris, squirters.

3. One who squirts or plies a squirt. Also *transf.*
1712 ARBUTHNOT *John Bull* III. vii, The Squirters were at it with their kennel water; for they were mad for the loss of their bubble. **1872** O. W. HOLMES *Poet Breakf.-t.* v, An over-dressed woman..at any rate..is better than the oil of vitriol squirter. **1878** *Scribner's Mag.* Nov. 76/2 [He] was a mysterious squirter of ink for four days before he was found out.

4. An apparatus for squirting.
1888 *Pall Mall G.* 21 Sept. 10/2 The patent oil squirter for calming the sea proved a failure. **1966** *Punch* 3 Aug. 193 The advertisements inviting operators to take up space at forthcoming fairs, feasts, wakes and well-dressings are full of cavillings like..'No squirters or confetti.' **1983** 'F. PARRISH' *Bait on Hook* ii. 29 You squirt it [*sc.* paint] out of a tin... You can't do a thin line easily with a squirter.

5. *slang.* A revolver.
1935 G. INGRAM *Cockney Cavalcade* xvi. 260 There've been reports..of some of you..doing that film stuff with squirters and handkerchiefs over your faces.

'**squirtful.** [f. SQUIRT *sb.*] The fill of a squirt.
1610 MARKHAM *Masterp.* I. lxxx. 165 With a large serring or squirt, squirt in three or foure squirtfull.

'**squirtical,** *a. nonce-word.* [f. as prec.] Concerned with a squirt or syringe.
1760 STERNE *Tr. Shandy* III. viii, Obadiah's was..a mixed case; for it was obstetrical,—scriptical, squirtical, papistical.

squirting ('skwɜːtɪŋ), *vbl. sb.* Also 4 **swirting.** [f. SQUIRT *v.*] The action of the verb; that which is squirted or spirted. Also *fig.*
c **1325** *Gloss. W. de Bibbesw.* in Wright *Voc.* 173 *Asset avera de esclautez*, of swirtingges. *Ibid.*, *Un garsoun esclaté*, bilagged wit swirting. **1598** FLORIO, *Squacquarata*, a dashing or blurring, a squattring, a squirting. **1607** TOPSELL *Four-f. Beasts* 361 Betwixt euery squirting, giue him liberty to hold downe his head. **1611** COTGR., *Injection*,..a squirting, or conueying of a liquid medicine, by Syringe, &c. into some part of the bodie. **1678** PHILLIPS (ed. 4), *Siringe*, ..an Instrument for the squirting of liquor into any wound. **1768–74** TUCKER *Lt. Nat.* (1834) II. 295 Party zeal..makes its last retreat in..occasional squirtings of the press.

squirting ('skwɜːtɪŋ), *ppl. a.* [f. as prec.]
1. Mean, contemptible, insignificant, trifling.
a. Of persons. Now *dial.*
1592 NASHE *P. Penilesse* Wks. (Grosart) II. 92 Our Players are not as the players beyond sea, a sort of squirting baudie Comedians. **1602** *2nd Pt. Return Parnass.* v. iv. 2174 Thou and thy squirting boy Endimion, Lies slauering still vpon a lawlesse couch. *a* **1658** CLEVELAND *Cl. Vind.* (1677) 107 Not such a squirting Scribe as this, that's troubled with the Rickets, and makes penny-worths of History. **1719** BOYER *Dict. Royal* II, A squirting (or pitiful) Fellow, *un pauvre homme, un petit genie*. **1803** T. CREEVEY in *C. Papers* (1904) I. 14 Such pitiful, squirting politicians as this accursed Apothecary. **1887** *S. Cheshire Gloss.* 370 A little squirtin' homnithom [= dwarf].

†**b.** Of things. *Obs. rare.*
1589 ? LYLY *Pappe w. Hatchet* E b, These fellowes can abide no pompe, and yet you see they cannot be without a little squirting plate. *a* **1625** FLETCHER *Love's Pilgr.* I. i, Did I or Mr. Dean of Civil..Ere reach our dignities in *cuerpo*, thinkst thou? In squirting hose and doublet? **1628** WITHER *Brit. Rememb.* 185 Their noblest mark is dieting a brace Of handsome Nags, to run a squirting race.

2. Issuing in a squirt or jet.
a **1694** *Urquhart's Rabelais* III. xxv. 211 On condition that he..should instantly with his squirting Spittle inluminate his Mustaches.

3. That ejects a jet-like stream of liquid.
1735 CLARE *Motion Fluids* 63 The common squirting Fire-Engine..is the Frame of a Lifting-pump, wrought by ..Leavers. **1744** DESAGULIERS *Exper. Philos.* II. 510 Which sort of Engines throwing the Water by Spirts are commonly, and not improperly, called Squirting Engines. **1821** SCOTT *Kenilw.* xxxviii, We shall never find them to-night amongst all these squirting funnels, squirrel-cages, and rabbit-holes. **1833** CHALMERS in Hanna *Mem.* (1851) III. xix. 375 Princess Victoria,..when asked on her visiting Chatsworth some months ago, which of all the things she had seen she liked best,..said it was the squirting tree.

4. *squirting cucumber*, the spirting cucumber, *Ecbalium agreste* (†*Momordica Elaterium*).
1802 PINKERTON *Mod. Geogr.* I. 278 The Momordica elaterium, squirting cucumber,..occurs in a truly wild state ..in Provence and Languedoc. **1849** BALFOUR *Man. Bot.* §872 The Wild or Squirting Cucumber is so called on account of the force with which its seeds are expelled when ripe. **1898** *Rev. Brit. Pharm.* 4 There are other articles in this category—*e.g.*, chalk, cevadilla, and squirting-cucumber.

'**squirtish,** *a. U.S.* [f. SQUIRT *sb.* 5.] Foppish, dandified.
1847 ROBB *Squatter Life* 73 These squirtish kind a fellars ..allers goes in fur aristocracy notions.

†'**squiry.** *Obs.* Forms: 4–6 squierie (4 -ye), 5 sqyrie, *Sc.* squyary, 6 squyry. [ad. OF. *escuierie, esquirie*, etc., f. *escuier* SQUIRE *sb.*] Squires collectively; a body or set of squires.
c **1327** *Pol. Poems* (Camden) 336 A new taille of squierie is nu in everi toun. *c* **1330** R. BRUNNE *Chron. Wace* (Rolls) 2405 My fader [Lear] in elde dotes To halde swylk a squierye. **1375** BARBOUR *Bruce* xx. 320 With ane nobill cumpany Of knychtis and of squyary. *c* **1475** *Rauf Coilȝear* 273 The King buskit him sone with scant of Squyary. Wachis and Wardroparis all war away. **1525** LD. BERNERS *Froiss.* II. clxxi. 505 It was nedefull for them within to make good defence, for against them was the floure of chyvalry and squyry.

squish (skwɪʃ), *sb.* [f. the vb.]
1. *Univ. slang.* Marmalade.
1874 *Slang Dict.* 307 *Squish*, common term among University men for marmalade. **1900** G. SWIFT *Somerley* 114 That *finale* of all college breakfasts and lunches, 'squish', otherwise known as marmalade.

2. A squishing sound.
1902 SNAITH *Wayfarers* xvi, The only sound from the great darkness that covered the land was the squish of the water under our feet.

3. *Engin.* In some internal-combustion engines, the forced radial flow of mixture from the cylinder into the combustion chamber as the piston approaches the cylinder head at the end of a stroke. Freq. *attrib.*
1934 *Proc. Inst. Mech. Engineers* CXXVIII. 155 Satisfactory mixing was brought about largely by the 'squish'. **1953** *Proc. Inst. Mech. Engineers: Automobile Division* 1951–2 103/2 Since squish occurs late in the compression stroke, it is not likely to affect maximum-power spark timing. **1957** *Encycl. Brit.* XII. 505/1 The squish turbulence..feeds most of the charge that would otherwise have been last to burn into the flame front. **1979** R. H. WARRING *Know Your Model Aero Engines* xii. 72 With a squish head, the outer section of the head is flat, with a smaller hemispherical combustion chamber in the middle.

squish (skwɪʃ), *v.* [Imitative: cf. SQUISH-SQUASH. In sense 1 perh. a modified form of SQUISS *v.* or SQUIZE *v.*]
1. *trans.* To squeeze, to squash. Now *dial.* and *colloq.*
1647 HEXHAM I, To Squise or squish, *wrijven*. **1888–** in dial. glossaries, etc. (Berks., Glouc., Hamps.). **1976** D. HEFFRON *Crusty Crossed* ix. 69 We squished our teeth into the berries in our mouths to stop giggling. **1977** G. DURRELL *Golden Bats & Pink Pigeons* v. 129 He [*sc.* an octopus] had wedged himself, or rather squished himself, into a small crevice.

2. a. *intr.* Of water, soft mud, etc.: To give out a peculiar gushing or splashing sound when walked in or on; to gush up, squirt out, with such a sound.
a **1825** FORBY *Voc. E. Anglia* s.v., The water squishes under our feet in the grass, if it be walked on too soon after rain. **1861** MISS YONGE *Young Stepmother* iii, She had made but few steps before the water squished under her feet. **1892** 'Q.' (QUILLER COUCH) *I saw three Ships* 35 The water in her shoes squishing at every step.

b. Of a person, etc.: to proceed or make *one's way* with a squishing sound. *colloq.*
1952 *Sun* (Baltimore) 9 July 30/4 (*caption*) Soaked to the point of not caring, this waterlogged pedestrian squishes his way across a downtown street. **1963** M. BEADLE *These Ruins are Inhabited* iii. 40 We squished down a rutted lane. **1965** F. KNEBEL *Night of Camp David* ii. 50 Tires squishing through the slush and spraying muddy water from little pools at the edge of the pavement. **1978** *Chicago* June 72/2 The highlight of Day is to squish around in the foam spread in a contained area by the Village Fire Department.

Hence '**squishing** *vbl. sb.*

1647 HEXHAM I, A squising or squishing together. *Ibid.*, A squising or squishing out.

squishop: see note to SQUARSON.

squish-squash, *adv.*, *sb.*, and *v.* [Imitative.]

A. *adv.* With the splashing or squashing sound made in walking through water or soft mud.

1789 CHARLOTTE SMITH *Ethelinde* I. 43, I thof of all things we should have been killed;..and then squish squash through such a deal of water! **1792** *Elvina* I. 150 Now we may go squish squash in the dark. **1881** in EVANS *Leics. Gloss.*

B. *sb.* The sound made in this way. Also *attrib.*

1821 CLARE *Vill. Minstr.* I. 23 He heard a squish-squash sound, As when one's shoes the drenching waters fill. **1838** HOLLOWAY *Prov. Dict.*, *Squish-squash* is a term used to express the noise made by the feet in walking over a loose, swampy, piece of ground. **1881** in EVANS *Leics. Gloss.*

C. *v.* = SQUISH *v.* 2.

1836 HALIBURTON *Clockm.* Ser. I. xxiii. (1839) 86 There he stands, all shiverin and shakin, and the water a squish-squashin in his shoes.

squishy ('skwɪʃɪ), *a.* [f. SQUISH *v.* + -Y.] Of a soft or wet nature; making, emitting, or characterized by a soft splashing sound or sounds. Also *fig.*

1847 HALLIW., *Squishy*, sloppy and dirty. *East.* **1879** JEFFERIES *Wild Life* vii. 147 The ploughing-engine be stuck fast up to the axle, the land be so soft and squishey. **1901** PRIOR *Forest Folk* xii. 128 The squishy tread of passing feet on the sodden grass. **1953** *Freckles* in *News & Observer* (Raleigh, N.C.) 9 Mar. 15/7 Everyone knows you're squishy about Miss Springtime! **1973** *Times Lit. Suppl.* 26 Oct. 1310/5 The very delicacy and respect for words in themselves which are radio's chief strengths do tend to make it rather a squishy medium. **1981** *Sunday Tel.* 8 Mar. 13/3 All the lovely squishy feeling flowed over us when we waved and the driver waved and tooted.

† **squiss**, *v. Obs. rare.* [Of obscure origin: cf. SQUISH *v.* I and SQUIZE *v.*] *trans.* To squeeze or crush. Hence † **squissed** *ppl. a.*

1558 WARDE tr. *Alexis' Secr.* (1568) 17 When ye have pressed and squissed them well,..cast them away. **1629** Z. BOYD *Last Battell* 701 My heart within me is so tossed to & fro, that it is come like a squissed egge, whose yolke is mingled with its white.

squit (skwɪt), *sb.*[1] *dial.* and *slang.* [Perh. related to SQUIT *v.* Cf. also SKIT *sb.*[2]]

1. A diminutive or insignificant person.

a **1825** FORBY *Voc. E. Anglia* 322 *Squit*, a word of supreme contempt for a very diminutive person. 'A paltry squit!' **1847** HALLIW. s.v., 'A little squit of a thing' is said disparagingly of a somewhat diminutive and not pleasing young woman. **1889** 'F. ANSTEY' *Pariah* III. viii, He's not half a bad little squit. **1909** G. B. SHAW *Let.* 4 Nov. in *Lett. to Granville Barker* (1956) 160 Some little squit of a nervous boy who can cry and scream like a burlesque of Eugene. **1928** A. HUXLEY *Point Counter Point* xxi. 389 Miserable scrofulous little squit! **1947** E. COXHEAD *Play Toward* iv. 102 It's impossible, darling. That—that little squit—and Peggy Jacques! **1976** J. SNOW *Cricket Rebel* 11, I was left in the hands of a second year prep boy, my 'nursemaid', to be introduced to the way of life of a new boy or 'squitt' as he was called.

2. Stupid or silly talk; nonsense.

1893 COZENS-HARDY *Brd. Norf.* 55 Some people may look upon this correspondence as a lot of squit and slaver. **1959** A. WESKER *Roots* I. 26 Love? I don't believe in any of that squit—we just got married. **1976** *Norwich Mercury* 19 Nov. 6/8 Dont talk squit.

squit (skwɪt), *sb.*[2] *U.S.* [? Shortened form of SQUETEAGUE or SQUETEE.] = SQUETEAGUE.

1884 GOODE *Nat. Hist. Aquat. Anim.* 362. **1902** D. S. JORDAN & B. W. EVERMANN *Amer. Food & Game Fishes* 260 It is done either from a sail-boat or row-boat, and a squit is a choice bait.

squit, *v.* Now *dial.* [? Imitative. Cf. SQUITTER *v.*] *trans.* To squirt.

1594 O. B. *Quest. Profit. Concern.* C iij, I doubt not but once in the yeare you squit out a commoditie to ingrate vpon the Gentlemans necessitie you meane. **1873-** in *Eng. Dial. Dict.*

squitch (skwɪtʃ), *sb.* [Altered form of QUITCH *sb.*[1] See also SCUTCH *sb.*[3]]

1. Couch-grass, *Triticum repens*; = COUCH *sb.* 2.

1785 *Young's Annals Agric.* IV. 415 A small close,..fuller I think of squitch than any field I had ever seen before. **1805** DICKSON *Pract. Agric.* I. 564 *Couch*, or what in many districts is better known by the name squitch, is a weed that is highly injurious to wheat crops. **1851-** in general dial. use (*E.D.D.*). **1885** *Pall Mall G.* 26 May 5/1 The time to burn rubbish is after the stubbles have been broken up, and the land cleaned of squitch and other weed.

attrib. **1846** LANDOR *Exam. Shaks.* Wks. II. 265 Two or three crops a year of that rank squitch-grass which it has become the fashion of late to call the people.

2. Applied to other plants of similar growth or habit, esp. to certain species of *Agrostis* (see quots.).

1792 *Young's Ann. Agric.* XVII. 38 Squitch, *Agrostis vulgaris.* **1796** WITHERING *Brit. Pl.* (ed. 3) II. 131 The 2d. 3d. and 4th [varieties of *Agrostis alba*], constitute the greater part of what is called squitch in light arable lands. In some places it is called white squitch, to distinguish it from the Agrostis nigra, and stolonifera, which are called black squitch, or couch. **1866** *Treas. Bot.* 1090/1 Squitch, ..*Agrostis stolonifera.*

squitch, *v.*[1] Now *dial.* Also 6 **squich.** [Variant of *quitch* QUETCH *v.*]

† **1.** *intr.* To move suddenly and quickly; to flinch or wince. *Obs.*

1570 *Marr. Wit & Sci.* v. iii, Mark how he from place to place will squich. **1592** *Soliman & Pers.* IV. ii. 24 They lopt a collop of my tendrest member. But thinke you Basilisco squicht for that?

2. *trans.* To twitch or jerk (*away*).

1680 *Honest Hodge & Ralph* 23 Do'st mind how he squitches the Church of England away too? calling it that Church that is rude to the Saints. **1880** *Cornwall Gloss.* 55 *Squitch*, to twitch; to jerk out of one's hand.

† **squitchin**, obs. form of SCUTCHEON.

1569 *Reg. Coll. Merton.* I June, A greate salte duble gylte with a cover square havinge a mane holdinge a squitchin with W. M.

'**squitchy**, *a. rare.* [Cf. dial. *squich*, var. of SQUISH *v.*] = SQUISHY *a.*

1851 MELVILLE *Whale* I. iii. 16 A boggy, soggy, squitchy picture truly, enough to drive a nervous man distracted.

'**squitter**, *sb.* [f. the vb. Cf. SKITTER *sb.*[1]] Now *dial.* and *colloq.*

1. Diarrhœa. Usually in pl. Cf. SKITTER *sb.*[1] I.

1664 COTTON *Scarron.* I. (1715) 7 It Bounces, Foams, and Froths and Flitters, As if 'twere troubled with the Squitters. **1691** MRS. D'ANVERS *Academia* 45 Then, as if troubled with the Squitters, Away they feque it to St. Peters. **1823** E. MOOR *Suffolk Words* 355 *Skutta, Skitta, Squitter*, these words are pretty nearly the same; and imply a lashness or diarrhœa, especially in a horse or cow. **1841-** in midland and southern dial. glossaries (in form *squitters*). **1958** P. SCOTT *Mark of Warrior* II. 131 'Aren't you sleeping?' 'I get the squitters pretty regularly.' **1976** A. PRICE *War Game* 13, I reckon squitters was queen [of the battlefield]. More of the poor bastards crapped themselves to death than killed each other. **1981** LD. HAREWOOD *Tongs & Bones* ii. 37 We went incessantly to those over-public latrines... My squitters were at their worst.

2. *Radar.* Random pulses produced by a transponder in the absence of interrogating signals.

1958 *Proc. Inst. Electr. Engineers* CV. B. Suppl. No. 8. 299/2 An average of 2700 pulses/sec are produced by the trigger circuit. These pulses are of constant amplitude and shape, but entirely random in time spacing and are known as 'squitter'. **1976** P. HONOLD *Secondary Radar* i. 67 If the dynamic characteristics of the receiver are too low, the message transmitted may be falsified.., should the signal level be very high. This..will also cause additional dead times—if these are triggered by interference pulses (squitter).

'**squitter**, *v.* Now *dial.* [Imitative (cf. SQUIT *v.*), or alteration of SKITTER *v.*[1]]

1. *trans.* and *intr.* To squirt; to spatter, splutter.

1596 NASHE *Saffron Walden* 102 Inck-squittring and printing against me. **1809** BATCHELOR *Anal. Eng. Lang.* 144 *Skwitter*, scatter, or sputter. **1828-** in dial. glossaries (Yks. and Som.). **1897** D'ESTERRE-KEELING *Return to Nature* viii, Then he said, looking at the squirt, 'This squittered'. 'You didn't make it squitter, did you?'

2. *intr.* To void thin excrement.

1611 FLORIO, *Squaccarare*, to squatter, to squirt or lash it out behind after a purgation; to squitter. **1071** SKINNER, To squitter, *forire.* **1719** D'URFEY *Pills* III. 313 And here the Mob make 'em squitter and tremble. **1719** BOYER *Dict. Royal* I, *Foirer*,..to squitter. **1886-** in dial. glossaries (Som., Devon, Derby).

Hence '**squitterer**, '**squittering** *vbl. sb.*

In quot. 1902 as imitative of a sound.

1611 FLORIO, *Squacchera*, a squattring soft turde, a squittring. **1737** OZELL *Rabelais* I. 255 *note*, The laxative Quality of the White Grape, called for that very Reason *Foirard* (Squitterer). **1902** SIR H. JOHNSTON *Uganda* I. i. 16 Hissings and squitterings and splashings..of those [birds] who are starting on flight.

† '**squitter-**, the verbal stem used in comb., as **squitter-book, -pulp, -wit**, a scribbler, a copious but worthless writer; **squitter-breech**, one who has or suffers from diarrhœa.

1594 NASHE *Unfort. Trav.* Wks. (Grosart) V. 70 The scolasticall *squitter bookes clout you vp cannopies & foot-clothes of verses. **1600** —— *Summers Last Will* Ibid. VI. 149 All this would not make me a squitter-booke. **1611** BEAUM. & FL. *King & No K.* II. ii, How now, goodman *squitter-breech, why do you lean on me? **1607** DAY *Parl. Bees* v. Wks. (1888) 235 Some lousy ballad! I cannot choose but laugh At these poor *squitter-pulps. **1615** J. H. *Worlds Folly* B iij, Those mercenary *squitter-wits, miscalled Poets.

'**squittling**, *vbl. sb.* [Variant of SCUTTLING *vbl. sb.*[1]] Scuttling; hurried or rapid movement.

1862 MISS MULOCK *Dom. Stories* 190 Hearing, as I passed the landing, much rustling of dresses and squittling away of little feet.

squiz (skwɪz), *sb. Austral.* and *N.Z. slang.* [f. QUIZ *sb.*[2], prob. blended with SQUINT *sb.*] A look or glance.

1916 C. J. DENNIS *Songs Sentimental Bloke* 130 *Squiz*, a brief glance. **1922** K. MANSFIELD *Garden Party* 72, I say Laura..you might just give a squiz at my coat before this afternoon. See if it wants pressing. **1948** V. PALMER *Golconda* xxx. 254 With one squiz at it [*sc.* the ore] he can tell how much it would crush to the ton. **1961** R. PARK *Hole in Hill* (1962) viii. 60 'All right, let's have a squiz.' They looked out very cautiously. **1972** J. MCCLURE *Caterpillar Cop* iv. 62 You won't find it there... I had a good squiz over the whole area.

squiz, *v. Austral.* and *N.Z. slang.* [f. prec.] *trans.* and *intr.* To look (at) or glance; to peer.

1941 BAKER *Dict. Austral. Slang* 71 *Squiz*, to look at, inspect. **1947** *Coast to Coast* 132 Kids, who used to slip up the lane behind our place and squiz through the cracks in the fence. **1948** D. W. BALLANTYNE *Cunninghams* (1963) xvi. 73 They walked down the passage and squizzed in the dining-room.

† **squize**, *v. Obs.* Forms: 6 **squyse**, 6–7 **squise**, 7 **squize.** [Of obscure origin: cf. SQUEEZE *v.*, SQUISS *v.*] *trans.* To squeeze, in various senses.

Common from *c* 1560 to *c* 1620.

α. **1548** ELYOT, *Presso*,..to presse or thruste together, to squise. **1574** HELLOWES *Gueuara's Fam. Ep.* (1577) 146, I began agaïne to squise out the matter. **1582** STANYHURST *Æneis* II. (Arb.) 50 Hee with his hands labored theyre knots too squise. **1614** GORGES *Lucan* IV. 159 He..with his teeth the throate doth squise, Not where the lurking poyson lies. **1647** HEXHAM I, To Squise out, *wt-wrijven.* **1648** *Ibid.* II, *Douwen*, to Presse, to Squise.

β. **1601** HOLLAND *Pliny* XVIII. xxxi. I. 606 Now when they purposed to squize out the grapes, they laid certain lids or planks thereupon. **1609** —— *Amm. Marcell.* 178 Some with stones that came tumbling downe upon them, were bruised and sore squized together. **1615** BRATHWAIT *Strappado* (1878) 216 To squize the poore that thou may better spend On wanton consorts. **1648** HEXHAM II, *Tsamen douwen*, to Presse, to Straine, Squize, or Wring together.

Hence † **squized** *ppl. a.*, † '**squizing** *vbl. sb.* and *ppl. a.*

1565 COOPER *Thesaurus*, *Collisus*, a squisinge, knockyng or thrustyng together. *Ibid.*, *Expressio*, a streignyng; a squising out. **1582** STANYHURST *Æneis* III. (Arb.) 89 Men say that Enceladus..here harbrouth, Dingd with this squising and massiue burthen of Ætna. **1621** BURTON *Anat. Mel.* III. ii. III, Every lover admires his mistress, though.. she looks like a squised cat. **1648** HEXHAM II, *Een douwinge*, a Pressing, a Squising.

squizzed (skwɪzd), *a. U.S. slang. rare.* [Orig. unknown.] Drunk, tipsy.

1845 *Knickerbocker* XXV. 75 He was rescued from the pyre..looking like a squizzed cat. **1941** *Sat. Rev. Lit.* 22 Mar. 5/1 A judge of good whiskey, who is, for the purpose of this narrative, slightly squizzed.

squizzle ('skwɪz(ə)l), *v. colloq.* and *dial.* Now *rare.* [Imitative.] *intr.* To squirt *out*, to squish. Hence '**squizzling** *ppl. a.*

1856 'J. PHŒNIX' *Phœnixiana* (ed. 11) xviii. 130 When the mouth is filled with the luscious fruit, and the..sweet though embarrassing juice is squizzling out all over the chin, and shirt-bosom. **1872** HARDY *Under Greenw. Tree* I. ii. 19 Such a squizzling and squirting job as 'tis in your hands. **1901** *Westm. Gaz.* 27 Feb. 1/3 Boots squeak and squizzle in the mud.

squunck, obs. form of SKUNK *sb.*

squob, obs. or dial. f. SQUAB *sb.*, *a.*, *v.*, etc.

squobble, obs. form of SQUABBLE *v.*

squodgy ('skwɒdʒɪ), *a. colloq.* Also **squodgey.** [Imitative: cf. SQUASHY *a.*] Soft and soggy; squelchy.

1970 *Daily Tel.* 15 June 11 Paper cups..tend to go squodgy and superimpose their own faint flavour to hot drinks. **1981** *Church of England Newspaper* 28 Aug. 10/3 One buries by pouring earth upon the deceased, rather than searching for squodgey ground in which to submerge the body.

squoggy ('skwɒgɪ), *a. colloq.* [Prob. blend of QUAGGY *a.* and SOGGY *a.*] Wet and miry.

1950 J. CANNAN *Murder Included* vi. 121 'These heelmarks.'.. 'The ground's too squoggy to tell whether they're male or female.'

squonyng, obs. form of SWOONING.

squop (skwɒp), *v. Tiddlywinks.* Also †**squallop** (pa. t. and pa. pple. †**squapt**). [Of unknown origin.]

1. *trans.* To cover and immobilize (another's wink) with one's own; also with another player as obj.

1956 *Minutes Cambr. Univ. Tiddlywinks Club* Mar. 12 in G. Consterdine *On Mat* (1967) 8 If both members of the team have all their winks either cupped or covered, then it shall be said that they are *squapt.* The verb shall be declined thus: *Present* I squallop..*Past* I squapt..*Past participle*—Squapt..*Noun*—squap. **1958** *Sunday Times* 2 Mar. 16/3 Mr. Harry Secombe squopted his own captain, who observed irritably that he was a Charlie. **1962** *Christian Sci. Monitor* 1 Oct. 13 In tournament play games are generally limited to 25 minutes, and a scoring system is instigated which takes account of how many winks a team has potted, squopped, etc. **1971** *Ottawa Citizen* 6 Feb. (Canadian Mag.) 24 You can't get something going for you if too many of your winks get squopped by an opponent's wink. **1978** *Boston Herald American* 25 Apr. 6 A gentle shot which either frees one of your winks or squops one of your opponent's winks is referred to as a 'piddle'.

2. *intr.* To cover an opponent's wink with one's own.

1963 *Observer* 22 Dec. 11/8 To squop is to cover an opponent's wink. **1971** *Philadelphia Evening Bull.* 13 Feb. 8 Squidgers in hand, the Hark Yon Tree Hath No Leaves But They Will Out Club is off to Toronto to squop and counter-squop for the North American Tiddlywinks Association Championship. **1977** *Cornell Alumni News* July 25 Sunshine tried to defuse the potential blitz by coming inside Drix's zone and threatening to squop.

Hence **squopped** *ppl. a.*, **'squopping** *vbl. sb.* and *ppl. a.*; **'squopper**, a player who squops.

1962 *N.Y. Times* 5 Aug. 23 It was in squopping that the British excelled. **1962** *Time* 14 Sept. 56 A squopped wink cannot be squidged again until it is de-squopped, either by the original squopper or by a squopped player's partner. **1962** *Life* 14 Dec. 122 Two-man units each with a powerful offensive squidger and a canny defensive squopper. **1971** *Ottawa Citizen* 22 Jan. 24/1 When it comes to squidging and squopping, Rosemary Wain and Andy Tomaszeuski are two of the best in the business. **1975** *Sunday Mail Color Mag.* (Brisbane) 28 Sept. 21/2 Squopping is the ability to flip one of your winks on top of your opponent's wink—and prevent him playing it. Then the squopped player tries to free his captive counter by squopping the counter on top. **1977** SHARP & PIGGOTT *Bk. of Games* 165 The owner of a squopped wink must wait until it is freed... The owner of a squopping wink..must ensure that his squidger first touched his own wink.

squop (skwɒp), *sb. Tiddlywinks.* [f. prec.] The act or achievement of covering an opponent's wink with one's own; a wink squopped in this way.

1962 *Time* 14 Sept. 56 The squop shot is entirely new to them. **1962** *N.Y. Times* 21 Oct. 83 The high point of the match was a septenary squop by Mr. Stein in which he immobilized seven winks with a single shot. **1979** *Harvard Mag.* May–June 40 The wink is shot into a key position, from which it can defend friendly squops, attack enemy squops, or set up a strategic zone.

squorge, squourge, obs. ff. SCOURGE *sb.* and *v.*

squoyle. Local var. of SQUAIL *sb.* 3.

1863 WISE *New Forest* xvi. 182 *Squoyle* in the New Forest ..properly signifies a short stick loaded at one end with lead, ..and is distinguished from a 'snog', which is only weighted with wood. **1865** TYLOR *Early Hist. Man.* vii. 186 The throwing cudgel, or, as a Hampshire man would call it, the squoyle of the Egyptian fowler. **1881** —— *Anthrop.* (1889) 193 Even in England the fowler's throwing-cudgel is not unknown in country parts, where it is called a squoyle.

squoze, squozen: see SQUEEZE *v.*

squrd, obs. form of SWORD.

sqush (skwʌʃ), *v. U.S. colloq.* and *dial. rare.* [Imitative: cf. SQUASH *v.*[1], SQUDGE *v.*, SQUISH *v.*]

1. *intr.* To collapse into a soft, pulpy mass.

1884 'MARK TWAIN' *Huck. Finn* xxix. 303 He'd a squshed down like a bluff bank that the river has cut under. **1955** E. POUND *Section: Rock-Drill* lxxxviii. 41 Belascio or Topaze, and not have it sqush, a 'throne', something God can sit on without having it sqush.

b. To squelch, squeeze messily.

1929 in H. Wentworth *Amer. Dial. Dict.* (1944) 592/1, I ..'squshed' through many a weary mile of mud. **1949** H. HORNSBY *Lonesome Valley* xix. 249 He could take off his shoes and walk around in the mud and let the mud ooze and sqush between his toes.

squuncke, obs. form of SKUNK *sb.*

squylery, squyllary, obs. ff. SCULLERY.

squylyon, obs. form of SCULLION.

squyngyl, obs. form of SWINGLE *v.*

squythe, obs. form of SWITHE.

squytherly: see SWIPPERLY.

sqw-, occas. ME. variant of SW-.

sqwyche, obs. form of SUCH *a.*

Sr., abbrev. of: ‖ **1.** SEÑOR 1 a, SIGNOR 1 a.

a **1912** W. T. ROGERS *Dict. Abbrev.* (1913) 182/1 *Sr.*,.. Señor. **1973** *Listener* 3 May 582/3 Sr Bassetti felt that the Italian Communist Party is not the ogre it used to be. **1977** 'D. CORY' *Bennett* ii. 43 My instructions with regard to the search for Sr Bennett are..unequivocal. **1982** *Listener* 14 Jan. 8/3 Sr Fraga won the recent elections in his native Galicia.

2. SENIOR *a.* 1 a. Chiefly *U.S.*

1936 *N.Y. Herald Tribune* 5 June 2/2 (*heading*) Extradition of Ellis Parker Sr. to await Republican Convention. **1973** D. AARON *Unwritten War* (1975) III. vii. 108 James Sr., for all his geniality and charm, was an opinionated and strong-minded man. **1977** D. DELMAN *Nice Murderers* iv. 53 Horowitz felt..a stab of sympathy for Kennicutt, Sr. Fathers and sons, he thought.

S[r]**,** obs. abbrev. of SIR *sb.*

sr-, occas. ME. or dial. variant of SHR-.

sraddha: see SHRADDHA.

Sranan ('srɑːnən). [Prob. Taki-Taki: in full *Sranan Tongo*, Surinam tongue (also used).] = TALKEE-TALKEE. Also *attrib.*

1953 L. L. E. RENS *Hist. & Social Background of Surinam's Negro-Eng.* x. 135 The term NE was used simply because none of the other appellations (takki-takki, Krioro, sranang tongo) was adequate. **1957** *Lingua* VI. 374 (*heading*) The verbal system of Sranan. **1964** *English Studies* XLV. 423 'Phonetic Interpretation', by which term he [*sc.* Echteld] means the substitution of Sranan phonemes for the original English ones. **1974** R. A. HALL *External Hist. Romance Languages* 45 The Portuguese element in Sranan. **1980** *English World-Wide* I. i. 6 This argument is valid even for such cases as Krio, Tok Pisin or Sranan.

Sri: see SHRI, SRI.

'sright: see 's 1 c.

Sri Lankan (ʃriː 'læŋkən, ʃrɪ'læŋkən, s-), *sb.* and *a.* [f. Skr. *Srī Laṅkā* name of the island known in English until 1972 as Ceylon (f. *śrī* SHRI, SRI, honorific prefix + *Laṅkā* name of (the chief town of) the island) + -AN.] **A.** *sb.* A native or inhabitant of Sri Lanka. **B.** *adj.* Of or pertaining to Sri Lanka or its people.

1973 *Advocate-News* (Barbados) 29 Dec. 7/2 (*heading*) Sri Lankan is world billiards champion. **1974** *Times* 9 Sept. 12/8 At the Edinburgh military tattoo, the Sri Lankan police reserve band have been giving a display. **1976** *Scotsman* 25 Nov. 3/5 BOC International are fighting the Sri Lankan plans to nationalise their Ceylon Oxygen offshoot. **1977** J. LAKER *One-Day Cricket* 66 The Sri Lankans rattled the score along. **1982** *Church Times* 29 Jan. 11/4 In all its life the Church there was both Anglican and totally Sri Lankan.

S-rope: see S 2 c.

‖**sruti** ('ʃrʊtɪ). *Mus.* [Skr. *śruti*, lit. hearing, listening.] A microtonal interval in Indian music.

1792 W. JONES in *Asiatick Researches* III. 69 They unanimously reckon twenty-two *śrutis*, or quarters and thirds of a tone, in their octave. **1891** [see GRAMA[2]]. **1954** *Grove's Dict. Mus.* (ed. 5) IV. 457/1 That disposes of the widely accepted view of the 'quartertone'—that it is half a semitone, and that Hindus have 22 of these *srutis* to make a melody with! What they have is five, six or seven notes to the octave, but 60 or more ways of disposing them. **1972** R. SHANKAR *Indian Music* iv. 135 The scale of twenty-two srutis is never sung chromatically, and the intervals are not important to one another but only as *groups* of intervals.

ss-, freq. ME. variant of SH-.

S-scroll(ed), -shaped, -sofa: see S 2 c.

st (st), *int.* Also 7 'st. [repr. a checked sibilation, instinctively felt as expressive; less exactly rendered by HIST, †IST *ints.* Cf. L. *st* (Plautus, Terence, etc.).]

1. An exclamation used to impose silence; = HUSH, WHIST.

1552 HULOET, *St*, a voyce of silence or taciturnitye or thus husht, or else it maye be sayde st, st, wherby dogges incited or prouoked to fight. **1598** FLORIO, *Zita*, an aduerbe to command or perswade silence, as we say isse, whosht or st. **1762** STERNE *Tr. Shandy* V. i. 14 St, st,—said a second,—hush, quoth a third. **1841** BROWNING *Pippa Passes* I, St—st!

†**b.** Used as *adj.* Hushed, silent. Cf. WHIST *a.*

1654 H. L'ESTRANGE *Chas. I* (1655) 69 For three dayes all was so 'st, so calm on both sides.

2. An exclamation used to drive away an animal, or to urge it to attack.

1552 [see 1]. **1841** S. WARREN *Ten Thou. a Year* III. ii. 36 Off! off!.. Go home! ah! ah!.. St! St!

st, 'st: see SHALL *v.* A 5 β.

1675 COTTON *Scoffer Scoft* 59 Hee st give me kisses half a score.

st. Abbreviation for various words: **a.** (with cap.) for SAINT prefixed to a name; **b.** (with cap. or small initial) for STREET preceded by a defining word, forming the name of a street; **c.** in references (*a*) for STANZA; (*b*) for STATUTE; **d.** for STONE (weight); **e.** for *stumped* (*by*) in *Cricket*. Cf. STUMP *v.*[1] 8.

staal, obs. var. STALE *sb.*; obs. pa. t. STEAL *v.*

staan, obs. variant of STONE *sb.* and *v.*

staar, obs. variant of STARE, a starling.

staare, obs. form of STARE *v.*

staat, staately, obs. ff. STATE *sb.*, STATELY.

stab (stæb), *sb.*[1] Also 5–7 stabbe, 6 stappe. [Related to STAB *v.* Cf. mod.Sc. *stab*, a large needle, a prickle.]

The form *stappe* in quot. 1583 may possibly be a distinct word, but has not been found elsewhere.

1. A wound produced by stabbing.

c **1440** *Promp. Parv.* 471/1 Stabbe, or wownde of smytynge, *stigma*. **1605** SHAKS. *Macb.* II. iii. 119 His gash'd stabs, look'd like a Breach in Nature, For Ruines wastfull entrance. **1826** S. COOPER *First Lines Surg.* (ed. 5) 134 An important punctured wound, such as the stab of a bayonet. **1841** DICKENS *Barn. Rudge* vi, You found me with this stab and an ugly bruise or two.

2. a. An act of stabbing; a thrust dealt with some sharp-pointed instrument producing a wound in the flesh.

1530 PALSGR. 275/1 Stabbe with a daggar, *coup destoc*. **1583** STOCKER *Civ. Warres Lowe C.* IV. 58b, After he was dead, the enemie gaue hym many a stappe with his dagger. **1610** SHAKS. *Temp.* III. iii. 63 The Elements..Of whom your swords are temper'd, may as well..with bemockt-at-Stabs Kill the still closing waters, as [etc.]. **1644** SIR E. DERING *Prop. Sacr.* b iiij b, A young fellow..did aim the stabbe of his knife into the Kings belly. **1722** DE FOE *Moll Flanders* (1840) 203 A stab that touched the vitals. **1746** HERVEY *Medit.* (1818) 27 A poisonous draught, or a deadly stab. **1830** TENNYSON *Oriana* 50 Oh! deathful stabs were dealt apace. **1867** F. FRANCIS *Angling* iii. (1880) 95 Master Perch..will resent rough..handling by a smart stab or two.

b. *fig.*

1594 SHAKS. *Rich. III*, III. ii. 89 This sudden stab of Rancour I misdoubt. **1746** WESLEY *Princ. Methodist* Pref., After many Stabs in the Dark, I was publickly attacked..by my own familiar Friend. **1796** BURKE *Let. to Mrs. Crewe* Corr. IV. 335 A stab was attempted on my reputation. **1894** WEYMAN *Man in Black* 201 This stab, that a little earlier would have pierced her very heart-strings, did but prick her. **1909** EDITH RICKERT *Beggar in Heart* 24 She remembered, with a stab of pain, the quiver in his voice.

c. *the stab*: death by stabbing. Also *fig.*

1610 HOLLAND *Camden's Brit* (1637) 124 With too silly arguments goe they about to give them the deadly stab. **1818** SCOTT *Br. Lamm.* xx, To kill one [raven] in their presence, is such bad luck that it deserves the stab. **1891** FARRAR *Darkn. & Dawn* xxxviii, Life—death—to-morrow; the *rudis* or the stab? Which shall it be?

d. *transf.* A vigorous thrust as if to stab some one.

1902 MABEL BARNES-GRUNDY *Thames Camp* 196 Sewing is rather restful; and you can give such vent to your feelings with each stab of the needle.

e. *fig.* A flash of bright colour against dark surroundings.

1894 *Superfl. Woman* (ed. 4) III. 4 The moving stabs of colour in passing trams and other vehicles. **1903** *Speaker* 17 Oct. 64/2 The blackbird in his jet-black dress, the stab of colour of his bill accentuating the hue.

f. In colloq. phr. *to make* (or *have*, etc.) *a stab at* (something), to try, attempt; to make a shot at. orig. *U.S.*

1895 W. C. GORE in *Inlander* Dec. 115 *Stab, to make a*, to make a blind attempt to answer a question. **1908** K. MCGAFFEY *Show Girl* 235, I..made a stab for the rail. **1915** WODEHOUSE *Something Fresh* xi. 315 'I *do* wish that this time you would endeavour..not to make a fool of yourself.'.. 'I'll have a jolly good stab at it, governor.' **1930** GALSWORTHY *Roof* vi. 96 D'you think you'll be able to travel the day after to-morrow?.. I'll have a good stab at it, as my more genial colleagues say. **1940** 'N. SHUTE' *Old Captivity* x. 294 We may have to come back again... But I think we'll have a stab at it. **1961** *Press Jrnl.* Apr. 10/3 Let's say you're going to take a stab at writing up the annual office picnic. **1973** 'S. WOODS' *Enter Corpse* 113 'Now that,' said Nelson, 'I can't believe.' 'You might have a stab at it,' Maitland suggested, 'It happens to be true.' **1980** W. MAXWELL *So Long, see You Tomorrow* (1981) ii. 7 She may have made a stab at being a mother to my older brother and me.

g. In fig. phr. *stab in the back*, a treacherous deed. Cf. sense 1 g of the vb.

1922 JOYCE *Ulysses* 621 That stab in the back touch was quite in keeping with those Italianos. **1934** R. H. LUTZ *Causes of German Collapse in 1918* v. 132 (*heading*) The 'stab-in-the-back' question. **1934** —— tr. von Kuhl in *Ibid.*, Some maintain that we lost the war owing to the stab in the back administered to the Army by those at home... On the other side the 'stab-in-the-back legend' is rejected as 'one of the most malignant and..stupidest legends'. **1953** J. W. WHEELER-BENNETT *Nemesis of Power* I. i. 67 For several days before his actual appearance..Hindenburg was closeted with..the extreme Nationalist leaders. In this brief period was crystallized the legend of the 'stab-in-the-back', in justification of which many innocent Germans were to suffer when the National Socialists came to power. *Ibid.*, The Marshal [*sc.* Hindenburg] testified..on November 18... He ..addressed himself to the German people. Their defeat, he told them, was not attributable to the Army but to the civilian demoralization and disunion. The irreproachable Army had received a 'stab-in-the-back' (*Dolchstoss*) from the Revolution. **1959** *Times* 21 Oct. 13/4 Professor Nordhoff, the managing director of Volkswagen, reacted as if he were the victim of another stab-in-the-back legend. **1971** A. BULLOCK *Twentieth Cent.* 25/1 Our knowledge of the recent past..will be based on hear-say, myths ('the Stab in the Back', for instance).

3. *Billiards.* A short, stiff stroke which causes the striker's ball to remain dead or to travel but slowly after striking the object ball; more fully *stab stroke*; hence *stab cannon*, *screw*, a cannon or screw made with this stroke.

1873 BENNETT & 'CAVENDISH' *Billiards* 192 There is another screw stroke called stab screw... If the striker desires to stop his own ball dead as soon as it strikes the object ball full,..the object is to be attained by means of stab. *Ibid.* 281 The best chance left is a stab cannon... The effect of the stab..is to carry the white slowly on to the spot-white. **1885** *Billiards Simplified* (1889) 157 The way to play the stroke is by means of what is known as a stab stroke.

4. *Oil Industry.* (See quot. 1975.)

1972 L. M. HARRIS *Introd. Deepwater Floating Drilling Operations* xii. 133 The integral marine-riser system has the choke and kill lines installed on the riser joints so that they are simultaneously stabbed and made up during the stab and make up of the marine-riser connector. **1975** L. CROOK *Oil Terms* 106 *Stab*, the operation of guiding one end of a pipe into the connection of another pipe to 'make up' a connection.

5. *Comb.* **stab-and-drag** *Archæol.*, a technique of ceramic decoration whereby a point is drawn along the surface of a pot and pushed in deeper at intervals (usu. *attrib.*); **stab-awl**, a shoemaker's tool used for piercing leather; **stab-cannon** (see sense 3); **stab-culture**, a CULTURE (3 c) in which the medium is inoculated by means of a needle thrust deeply into its substance; **stab-screw**, (see sense 3); **stab-stitch** *Needlework* (see quot. 1964); hence as *v. trans.* and **stab-stitching** *vbl. sb.*; **stab-stroke** (see sense 3); **stab-wort**, the wood-sorrel (*Oxalis acetosella*), believed to be so called with reference to its supposed healing properties (also STOBWORT, STUBWORT); **stab-wound**, a punctured wound produced by an act or the action of stabbing. Also *stab-like* adj.

1931 V. G. CHILDE in *Archæol. Jrnl.* LXXXVIII. 47 Handles and flat bases first make their appearance in Fort Harrouard II. In the same levels the fine incision of the early Chassey style gives place to deep incision, or *stab-and-drag. **1931** S. PIGGOTT in *Ibid.* 78 *Stab-and-drag* lines—made with a point that is drawn along the clay and pushed in deeper at intervals—occur only on certain Scottish pots, e.g., from Unstan. **1954** —— *Neolithic Cultures* vii. 204 Certain vessels with stab-and-drag motifs. **1978** *Proc. Prehist. Soc.* XLIV. 276 Decorated wall-sherd; fine vertical stab and drag lines. **1840** *Life Adam Clarke* iv. 94 He borrowed a *stab awl and a hammer from a shoe maker. **1889** *Science* 20 Dec. 418 The mere production of a direct *stab-culture from one organ, such as the spleen..affords very incomplete..information. **1887** CHRISTINA TYRRELL tr. *E. Werner's Her Son* I. 79 The contemptuous glance of those eyes penetrated with a *stab-like pain to his heart's core. **1917** E. R. HAMBRIDGE *Simple Dressmaking* I. 7/2 Back stitches should be frequent in stab tacking... *Cf.* Fig. 28 for *stab stitch, which is similarly worked. *Ibid.* I. 10/1 Running, run-stitching, and half back-stitching can also be stab-stitched, but strong thread or silk should be employed. *Ibid.*, Stab-stitching..is back-stitching, but worked with the needle placed vertically through the material..instead of horizontally. **1932** D. C. MINTER *Mod. Needlecraft* 159/2 Stab stitching..close to the fold of the felt..may be employed. *c* **1951** *Glovemaking* (Dryad Leaflet 31) 6 A hand-made glove..is almost always sewn on the right side, and various stitches can be used. The most popular of these is the 'prix' or stab-stitch. **1964** *McCall's Sewing* ii. 32/2 *Stab-stitch* a stitch in which the needle is brought in and out of the fabric at right angles. **1976** *Woman's Weekly* 6 Nov. 42/3 Stab-stitch the boots together in pairs. **1640** PARKINSON *Theat. Bot.* 747 We [call it] in English Wood Sorrell ..*Stabbewort. **1665** LOVELL *Herbal* (ed. 2) 419 Stubwort or Stabwort, see Wood sorrell. **1897** *Brit. Med. Jrnl.* 27 Mar. 774 A *stab wound in the right loin.

stab (stæb), *sb.*[2] *Sc.* and *dial.* [? Sc. variant of STOB *sb.*: cf. *tap* = top. But cf. also Da., Norw., Sw. dial. *stabbe*, mod.Icel. *stabbi* tree-stump, block, Da. dial. *stabb* peg.]

1. A stake, a wooden post.

stab and rice = *stake and rice*: see STAKE *sb.*[1] 2 a. *stab and stow*: completely, entirely.

1680 *Invent.* in *Scott. N. & Q.* IX. 95 Ane wall of stab and ryce..ane chimnay of stab and ryce. **1722** W. HAMILTON *Wallace* 259 (Jam.) Who set their lodgings all in a fair low About their ears and burnt them stab and stow. **1821** GALT *Ann. Parish* vi, The plantations supplied him with stabs to make stake and rice between his fields. **1842** J. AITON *Dom. Econ.* (1857) 160 The minister of a village..requested that a wall should be built round his glebe. 'Would stabs and railings not answer the purpose equally well?' asked one present. **1907** EPPIE FRAZER *Clodhopper* I. ii. 8 They've drawn the loosened paling stab.

2. A stump.

c **1800** HOWLETT in *Young's Agric. Essex* (1807) I. 180 As soon as the hedge is cut down, most of which [is] within an inch or two of the old stabb. *Ibid.*, With the young shoots of the parts cut off close to the stabbs.

3. A block (of wood, etc.) used as a seat.

1805 MCINDOE *Poems* 10 (E.D.D.) The seat, a stab, the heel pins rotten.

stab (stæb), *sb.*[3] *dial.* [Of obscure origin.] (See quot. 1838.)

1838 HOLLOWAY *Prov. Dict.*, *Stab*, a hole in the ground, in which the female rabbit secures her litter while they are very young. **1875** PARISH *Sussex Gloss.* s.v. *Stalled*, The old dog ..found a stab out in the field. **1888** *Sat. Rev.* 5 May 530/2 The rat..will draw the young rabbits out of the 'stabs'.

stab (stæb), *sb.*[4] *Printers' slang.* Also **'stab.** [Short for *establishment.*] = ESTABLISHMENT 10. Also *attrib.*

1865 *Hotten's Slang. Dict.* 244 On the stab. **1875** SOUTHWARD *Dict. Typogr.* s.v., A man who is 'on 'stab' receives establishment wages. **1888** JACOBI *Printers' Vocab.* 130 *Stab*, a term applied to establishment hands, i.e. workmen paid by the week and not by piece-work. **1890** *Scott. Leader* 10 June 5 Fleming was known as a stab man, as opposed to a man who was paid by the result of his labours. *Ibid.* 6 When he was dismissed he was a society-man, and was paid a stab wage of £2 3s a week.

stab (stæb), *sb.*[5] *Med.* [a. G. *stab* rod, after V. Schilling's use of G. *stabförmig* rod-shaped, *stabkern* rod-nucleus (*Zeitscher. f. exper. Path. u. Therapie* (1911) IX. 691, 692): cf. STAFF *sb.*[1]] Used *attrib.* and *absol.* to designate white blood cells characterized by a nucleus in the form of a single bent or twisted rod (orig. regarded as abnormal forms).

1929 R. B. H. GRADWOHL tr. *Schilling's Blood Picture* ii. 128 The neutrophilic degenerative stab or staff forms are not present in the normal blood picture. *Ibid.* 135 They [*sc.* degenerative forms] are practically insignificant, with the exception of the stabs..which deserve special mention as a degenerative phenomenon in the nuclear shift. **1938** W. MAGNER *Textbk. Hematol.* v. 79 Schilling divides the neutrophile leukocytes into the following classes. (1) Myelocytes. (2) Juvenile leukocytes or metamyelocytes. (3) Stab, staff or rod-nuclear cells. **1972** W. J. WILLIAMS et al. *Hematol.* iii. 27/2 (*heading*) Band form or stab cell. *Ibid.* lxvi. 562/2 The stab is the least mature cell of the granulocytic series found in the peripheral blood of normal persons.

stab (stæb), *v.* [Related to the synonymous STOB *v.*

The vb. has been found before 1530 only in Sc. writers; the related STAB *sb.*[1] occurs in *Promp. Parv.* (1440).]

1. a. *trans.* To wound (often to kill) with a thrust of a pointed weapon (chiefly, with a short weapon, as a dagger). Phrase, *to stab to* (†*at, into*) *the heart.*

1530 PALSGR. 731/2 He stabbyd hym with a daggar. **1585-7** KYD *Sp. Trag.* IV. i. 125 She..Did stab herselfe. **1588** SHAKS. *Tit. A.* V. ii. 47 Stab them, or teare them on thy Chariot wheeles. **1605** *Nottingham Rec.* IV. 276 A dagger to stabbe and kill Hugh Lenton. **1641** J. JACKSON *True Evang. T.* III. 201 Iohn Iames..did stab into the breast Peter Heywood Esquire. **1647** CLARENDON *Hist. Reb.* I. §9 Stabbed to the heart by the hand of an obscure villain. **1678** WANLEY *Wond. Lit. World* V. i. §100. 468/2 Henry the fourth King of France was stab'd by Ravilliac. **1713** ADDISON *Cato* III. ii, Think, thou seest thy dying brother Stabb'd at his heart. **1718** HEARNE *Collect.* (O.H.S.) VI. 247 A Stag.. meeting a Man as he was running along, he stabbed him with his Horns. **1764** *Museum Rust.* IV. 33 Some Remarks on stabbing Cattle hoved with Clover. **1771** BURROW *King's Bench Rep.* V. 2795 John Taylor instantly..stabbed the said James Smith. **1830** TENNYSON *Oriana* 55 They should have stabb'd me where I lay. **1891** FARRAR *Darkn. & Dawn* xlv, Scipio..stabbed himself.

†**b.** *to stab* (a person) *in* = sense 1. *Obs.*

1530 PALSGR. 731/2, I stabbe in with a dagger or any other scharpe wepyn, *je enferre.* **1561** NORTON & SACKV. *Gorboduc* IV. ii. 190 While slumbring on his carefull bed he restes His hart stabde in with knife is reft of life. **1565** COOPER *Thesaurus*, *Confossus*..wounded: stabbed in. **1587** HIGGINS *Mirr. Mag.*, *C. I. Cæsar* xlix, Hee stabde mee in, and so with daggers did the rest. **1587** GOLDING *De Mornay* xii. (1592) 173 This proud Peacocke [Cæsar]..is in one day stabbed in with infinite wounds.

c. *fig.*

1686 HORNECK *Crucif. Jesus* xxiv. 803 If he have often stabbed his neighbours by slanders. **1784** COWPER *Task* IV. 617 'Tis universal soldiership has stabb'd The heart of merit in the meaner class. **1813** SHELLEY *Q. Mab.* III. 200 He fabricates The sword which stabs his peace. *c* **1850** LOWELL *Leg. Brittany* II. xxiv, Her silence stabbed his conscience through and through.

d. *transf.* In various occasional uses.

a **1652** BROME *Queen & Concubine* III. viii. (1659) 64 Thou hear'st me say, I dare not speak her name, Yet thou dar'st stab mine Ears again, with it. *a* **1711** KEN *Psyche* Poet. Wks. IV. 234 As the Morning Cloud decays, When stab'd by the encroaching Rays. *a* **1800** *Dk. Athole's Nurse* xi. in Child *Ballads* IV. 152 O they stabbed the feather-bed all round and round. **1834** MAR. EDGEWORTH *Helen* II. ix, When they had stabbed the cushions, and torn the inside of my carriage all to pieces. **1895** *Outing* XXVI. 40/2 Fireflies stabbed the gloom with their darting flame.

†**e.** *slang.* (See quot.) *Obs.*

a **1661** FULLER *Worthies, Dorset* (1662) 278 Stab'd with a Byrdport Dagger. That is, hang'd... The best..Hemp.. growing about Byrdport.

†**f.** With obscene reference. *Obs.*

1597 SHAKS. *2 Hen. IV*, II. i. 15. **1601** —— *Jul. C.* I. ii. 277.

g. In fig. phr. *to stab* (a person, etc.) *in the back*, to harm or damage in a treacherous manner. Cf. BACK-STABBER.

1916 G. B. SHAW in *N. Y. Times Mag.* 9 Apr. 2/2 The cry that 'England's Difficulty Is Ireland's Opportunity' is raised in the old senseless, spiteful way as a recommendation to stab England in the back when she is fighting some one else. **1932** KIPLING *Limits & Renewals* 384 He makes my job ten times more difficult than it need be..stabs me in the back with his crazy schemes for betterment. **1956** N. NICOLSON *Diary* 4 Nov. in *Diaries & Lett. H. Nicolson* (1968) 315, I did not want to publish any letter until the crisis in Egypt had ended, as otherwise I might be accused of stabbing the troops in the back. **1979** F. OLBRICH *Sweet & Deadly* viii. 91 All these years with me he's been completely honest and now he stabs me in the back.

2. a. *absol.* and *intr.* To use a pointed weapon to wound or kill.

1375 BARBOUR *Bruce* XIX. 545 Than suld the laiff that forouth ar Stab doune with speres sturdely. *Ibid.* 565 Thai stabbit, stekit, and thai slew. **1597** SHAKS. *2 Hen. IV*, II. i. 13 It may chance cost some of vs our liues: he wil stab. **1607** *Lingua* II. i, If they heare my name abused, they stab for my sake. **1700** DRYDEN *Pal. & Arc.* III. 509 None shall dare With shortned Sword to stab in closer War. **1819** SHELLEY *Mask* lxxxiv, Let them ride among you there, Slash, and stab, and maim, and hew. **1847** TENNYSON *Princess* Concl. 61 The little boys begin to shoot and stab. **1887** GUNTER *Mr. Barnes* xxiii. 178 'My husband's body lies behind those curtains!' She stands with uplifted arm a moment, pointing to the draperies through which Tomasso has stabbed.

fig. **1597** SHAKS. *2 Hen. IV*, IV. v. 109 Thou hid'st a thousand Daggers in thy thoughts,..To stab at halfe an howre of my Life. **1599** —— *Much Ado* II. i. 255 Shee speakes poynyards, and euery word stabbes. **1762** LLOYD *Epist. to Churchill* 14 Critics of old..Boldly persu'd the free decisive task, Nor stabb'd, conceal'd beneath a ruffian's mask. **1769** *Junius Lett.* xxvi. 122 Suspicion is the foul weapon with which you..stab. **1871** MACDUFF *Mem. Patmos* xxi. 290 They stab at their neighbour's good name and reputation. **1883** *Harper's Mag.* Feb. 352/2 The baffled sun stabs wildly at the gale.

†**b.** *Sc.* To make thrusts with a staff or club.

1513 DOUGLAS *Æneis* III. x. 6 Poliphemus..A monstir.. Wanting his sycht, and com to stab and graip With his burdoun, that wes the greit fir tre [orig. *trunca manum pinus regit et vestigia firmat*].

c. To suffer a 'stab' of pain. ? *nonce-use.*

1865 ANNIE THOMAS *On Guard* xxxix, The reels of cotton danced aloud within it, making Stanley's head stab.

d. To make a hole *through* something. Also *fig.*, to pierce like a pointed weapon.

1897 KIPLING *Capt. Cour.* v. 112 The foregaff stabbed and ripped through the staysail. **1920** R. MACAULAY *Potterism* VI. v. 259 Gideon's fate pilloried on that placard had stabbed through him. **1946** D. C. PEATTIE *Road of Naturalist* ii. 33 Outside our mortal dusty sphere, Canopus must be a horrible, blinding searchlight stabbing through a black and icy void.

3. *trans.* To thrust (a weapon) into a person.

c **1610** ROWLANDS *Terrible Batt.* 10, I stab'd my dart, thus deepe into his side. **1639** S. DU VERGER tr. *Camus Admir. Events* 250 Liberat..gets upon him, stabs his poignard three or foure times in his belly. **1912** *19th Cent.* Dec. 1195 Women stab the daggers to their throats immediately.

4. To prick. Now *dial.* Cf. STOB *v.*

1570 LEVINS *Manip.* 1/26 To stab, pricke, *pungere, stimulare.* **1864** J. ROGERS *New Rush* II. 33 [He may] stab himself upon a Porcupine.

5. To hammer or pick (a hard surface) with a sharp tool, to roughen (a wall) with a pick before applying a coat of plaster.

1846 *Penny Cycl.* Suppl. II. 431/1 The surface of the brickwork must be stabbed or picked over to make it rough.

6. *Bookbinding.* To pierce (a collection of sheets) in order to make a hole for a binding thread or wire; to fasten the sheets of (a pamphlet, etc.) together in this way instead of by sewing.

1863 *Reader* 21 Nov. 600/1 Nor even stitched like a book, but 'stabbed' as an auction catalogue now is. **1888** JACOBI *Printer's Vocab.* 130 *Stabbed*, a form of stitching by piercing or stabbing, used mostly for cheap pamphlet work. **1901** *19th Cent.* Apr. 662 When enough sheets have been brought together they are stabbed at the open ends and form a volume.

7. *Oil Industry.* To guide (a length of pipe) so as to connect it properly to another member.

[**1922**: implied at STABBER 1 d.]. **1932** *Amer. Speech* VII. 271 *Stab*, to guide (pipe) in making connections so that the threads engage properly. **1948** *Petroleum Handbk.* (ed. 3) v. 85 As the empty elevator hook is hoisted the derrick man latches in a stand as it passes his level. The stand is picked up and 'stabbed' into the tool joint at the rotary table. **1976** *Offshore Platforms & Pipelining* 6/3 Only one pile add-on will have to be stabbed and welded to drive the sleeve piles.

†**sta'bado.** *Obs. rare*$^{-1}$. In pl. **stabadoes.** [f. STAB *v.* + -ADO.] A stab.

1607 WALKINGTON *Optic Glass* 47 This is a true wit.. hauing a priuy coate of pollicy and subtilty to shend it from all the intended stabadoes of any acute obiectionist.

‖**Stabat Mater** ('steɪbæt 'meɪtə(r), 'stɑːbat 'mɑːtə(r)). [From the opening words, L. *stabat mater dolorosa*, 'Stood the mother, full of grief'.] A sequence, composed by Jacobus de Benedictis in the 13th c., in commemoration of the sorrows of the Blessed Virgin Mary. Also a musical setting of this sequence.

There are other sequences beginning with the same words: 'Stabat mater regis nostri' (13–14th c.), 'Stabat mater anxiata' (1519), 'Stabat mater speciosa' (late 15th c.). None of these are in regular liturgical use, but some of them have well-known musical settings.

1867 LADY HERBERT *Cradle L.* iv. 120 While the low chant of the 'Stabat Mater' echoed through the deserted streets. **1883** ROCKSTRO in *Grove's Dict. Mus.* III. 684 The 'Stabat Mater' of Josquin des Prés, founded upon the Canto fermo just mentioned. *Ibid.*, Haydn's 'Stabat Mater' is a treasury of refined and graceful Melody.

stabbed (stæbd), *ppl. a.* [f. STAB *v.* + -ED[1].]

1. Wounded by stabbing.

1599 B. JONSON *Cynthia's Rev.* V. iv, S'foot, he makes a face like a stab'd Lucrece. **1884** 'V. LEE' *C'tess Albany* iii. 28 The Pretender's bride must often have met a knot of people conveying a stabbed man..to the nearest barber or apothecary.

Comb. **1612** CHAPMAN *Rev. Bussy d'Ambois* I. ii. 75 These tortur'd fingers and these stabb'd-through arms Keep that law in their wounds yet unobserv'd, And ever shall.

†**b.** Of a wound: Produced by stabbing. *Obs.*

1653 T. BRUGIS *Vade Mecum* (ed. 2) 57 It is good in wounds either incised, contused, or stabbed.

2. Perforated with punctured holes.

1862 *Catal. Internat. Exhib., Brit.* II. No. 6384, Stabbed iron for malt-kiln plates.

3. *Bookbinding.* (See STAB *v.* 6.)

stabber ('stæbə(r)). [f. STAB *v.* + -ER[1].]

1. a. One who stabs.

1589 *Pappe w. Hatchet* in *Lyly's Wks.* 1902 III. 399 One hath been an old stabber at passage. **1682** OTWAY *Venice Preserved* III. ii, Mix with hired Slaves, Bravoes, and Common stabbers? **1752** YOUNG *Brothers* III. i, Blood-thirsty stabbers. **1813** SCOTT *Rokeby* I. xxii, Despite his craft, he heard with awe This ruffian stabber fix the law. **1865** KINGSLEY *Herew.* i, Whoever called me stabber to you, lies.

b. *transf.*

1834 MAR. EDGEWORTH *Helen* II. ix. (1848) 240, I set at defiance all the searchers and stabbers and custom-house officers.

c. *fig.*

1603 DEKKER *Wonderf. Yr.* D 3 b, How sudden a stabber this ruffianly swaggerer, Death, is. **1737** *Gentl. Mag.* VII. 205/1, I leave the Reader to guess what such a Stabber of Reputations would stick to perpetrate. **1858** O. W. HOLMES *Two Armies* 23 The bloodless stabber [Death] calls by night. **1872** SPURGEON *Treas. David* Ps. lix. 12 Wretches who are persecutors in talk, burners and stabbers with the tongue. **1910** GOLDW. SMITH *Remin.* x. 181 The genius of the political stabber.

d. *Oil Industry.* One who stabs pipes (see STAB *v.* 7).

1922 F. M. TOWL in D. T. Day *Handbk. Petroleum Industry* I. 410 The joint is lifted into place, and a man, the 'stabber', standing by the end of the joint with a handspike, moves the joint until it is straight with the last joint laid. **1976** M. MACHLIN *Pipeline* iv. 50, I worked as a stabber—that's the man who sits on the end of the walking beam and holds the pipe straight.

2. a. Something which stabs, a knife, dagger, etc.

1581 DERRICKE *Image Irel.* II. F ij, Long stabbers plucke thei forthe, in steede of handsome kniues. **1585** HIGINS *Junius' Nomencl.* 275/1 *Sica*,..a priuye or close dagger: a stabber. **1913** *Engl. Rev.* Nov. 516 We've got his stabber and he can't do us any harm.

b. *spec.* (See quots.)

1794 *Rigging & Seamanship* I. 87 *Holes* in sails are made with an instrument, called a stabber or a pegging-awl. **1858** SIMMONDS *Dict. Trade*, *Stabber*, a marling-spike; a sailmaker's pricker. **1875** KNIGHT *Dict. Mech.*, *Stabber*, 1. (*Leather.*) A pegging-awl. A pricker. 2. (*Nautical.*) A marlinspike. 3. (*Domestic.*) A lady's awl for opening holes for eyelets.

3. (See quot.)

1854 MISS BAKER *Northampt. Gloss.*, *Stabber*, a person (generally a boy) who is employed to stitch the upper leathers of boots and shoes with an awl. **1881** *Leicestersh. Gloss.*

stabbing ('stæbɪŋ), *vbl. sb.* [-ING[1].]

1. a. The action or an act of STAB *v.* in various senses.

1375 BARBOUR *Bruce* XVII. 785 (Edinb. MS.) Off stabing, [*Camb. MS.* staffing], stoking, and striking Thar maid thai sturdy defending. *c* **1425** WYNTOUN *Cron.* VIII. 6534 For his hors rycht weill armyt was, That he þare stabyng dred weill les. **1604** SHAKS. *Oth.* III. iv. 6 He's a Soldier, and for me to say a Souldier lyes, 'tis stabbing. **1765** *Museum Rust.* IV. 90, I was obliged to perform the operation of stabbing in three several parts of the belly before the ox was relieved. **1769** BLACKSTONE *Comm.* IV. 193 This statute was made on account of the frequent quarrels and stabbings with short daggers.

b. *attrib.* **stabbing board** *Oil Industry* (see quot. 1932).

1837 W. B. ADAMS *Carriages* 152 An awl called a *stabbing awl. **1932** *Amer. Speech* VII. 271 **Stabbing-board*, a board in the derrick at the height of one joint, from which the derrick man stabs pipe. **1974** R. D. LANGENKAMP *Handbk. Oil Industry Terms & Phrases* 126 The derrick man stands on the stabbing board and assists in guiding the threaded end of the casing into the collar of the preceding joint that is hanging in the slips in the rotary table. **1894–5** KIPLING *2nd Jungle Bk.* 155 Kadlu..crossed the hut for his *stabbing-harpoon. **1875** KNIGHT *Dict. Mech.*, **Stabbing-machine*, a machine for perforating a pile of folded and gathered signatures for the insertion of the stitching-thread. **1858** SIMMONDS *Dict. Trade*, *Stabbing-press. **1875** KNIGHT *Dict. Mech.*, *Stabbing-press*, a bookbinder's press, in which pointed rods are driven through the folded sheets near the back, to stitch them together. **1892** RIDER HAGGARD *Nada* 33 Armed with the short *stabbing-spear.

†**2.** *Dicing.* (See quot.) *Obs.*

1680 COTTON *Compl. Gamester* (ed. 2) 12 Lastly, by *Stabbing*, that is, having a Smooth Box, and small in the bottom, you drop in both your Dice in such manner as you would have them sticking therein by reason of its narrowness [etc.].

stabbing ('stæbɪŋ), *ppl. a.* [-ING[2].]

1. Of a weapon: That stabs.

1611 SHAKS. *Wint. T.* IV. iv. 748 They often giue vs (Soldiers) the Lye, but wee pay them for it with stamped Coyne, not stabbing Steele. **1813** SCOTT *Rokeby* VI. xxxiii, But still his struggling force he rears, 'Gainst hacking brands and stabbing spears.

b. *fig.*

1599 B. JONSON *Ev. Man out of Hum.* IV. iv, Come, you'le never leave your stabbing similes. **1682** OWTRAM *Serm.* 403 That's a black and stabbing thought. *a* **1704** T. BROWN *Lett. to Gentl. & Ladies* Wks. 1709 III. II. 107, I dare trust my self no longer with such stabbing Ideas. **1745** ELIZA HAYWOOD *Female Spect.* No. 13 (1748) III. 15 Instead of reasoning with Zimene, and perswading her to moderation in so stabbing a circumstance.

2. Of pain: Sharp and sudden, characterized by twinges comparable to the effect of a stab.

1763 COLEBROOK in *Phil. Trans.* LIII. 347 She complained of most excruciating stabbing pains in both breasts. **1896** MARY BEAUMONT *Joan Seaton* 175 Unconscious of the stabbing pain in his foot.

Hence '**stabbingly** *adv.*

1673 S. PARKER *Reproof Reh. Transp.* 287 This intimation ..is as stabbingly suggested as the story of Sardanapalus.

stabble ('stæb(ə)l), *sb. dial.* [f. the verb.] Liquid mud caused by continuous traffic or treading with the feet; also dirty footmarks.

1825 COBBETT *Rur. Rides* 10 The street..has been kept in a sort of stabble by the flocks of sheep passing along. **1863** WISE *New Forest* Gloss., *Stabble*, marks, footprints, always used in the plural.

stabble ('stæb(ə)l), *v. dial.* [Perhaps a frequentative f. STAB *v.*: see -LE. (For the assumed sense-development cf. POACH *v.*[2] 4, 5; see also STABLE *v.*[3])] **a.** *trans.* To soil (a place) by treading dirt about. **b.** *intr.* To tread dirt *about*. **c.** *trans.* To reduce (ground) to mire or liquid mud by continual treading.

1838 HOLLOWAY *Provinc.*, To *stabble*, to dirty any place, by walking on it with wet and filthy shoes. *Hants.* **1856** MISS YONGE *Daisy Chain* xv. 148 The woman said she would not take half-a-crown a week to have a lot of children stabbling about, as she called it. **1858** HUGHES *Scour. White Horse* vii, 'T'aint a mossell o' use to bide stabbleing here [*Footnote.* 'Stabble'—to tread dirt about]. **1893** *Wiltshire Gloss.*, *Stabble*,..to poach up [ground] by continual treading, as near a field gateway.

stabilate ('steɪbɪleɪt). *Biol.* [f. L. *stabil-is* STABLE *a.* + *-ate*, after *filtrate*, *precipitate*, etc.] A sample of biological material from a homogeneous source which is preserved by freezing on a single occasion to serve as a standard, portions of it being restored as desired.

1965 LUMSDEN & HARDY in *Nature* 6 Mar. 1032/2 A separate term is now required to convey this implication of the stabilization of biological characters in preserved material and to distinguish preserved from 'strain' material. The word 'stabilate' is now proposed for this purpose. A 'stabilate' may be defined as a population of an organism preserved in viable condition on a unique occasion. **1970** *Ibid.* 19 Sept. 1255/1 A stabilate of infected blood was frozen to −70° at the start of each experiment to ensure that a strict homologous challenge of vaccinated animals was subsequently made. **1976** *Ibid.* 24 June 698/2 All eight surviving cattle were challenged with a similar injection of stabilate.

Hence as *v. trans.*, to make into a stabilate.

1978 *Tropenmedizin und Parasitologie* XXIX. 443/2 The isolate was needle-passaged once in a goat and then stabilated.

stabile ('steɪbɪl), *a.* [ad. L. *stabilis*: see STABLE *a.*

The examples of *stabile*, *stabil(l* occurring before English spelling became settled are to be referred to STABLE *a.*]

1. Firmly established, enduring, lasting. *rare.*

Used by a few writers to express more unequivocally the etymological sense of STABLE *a.*

1797 W. TAYLOR in *Monthly Rev.* XXIV. 524 That stabile conviction, which terminates the sweet toil of investigation. **1814** —— in *Monthly Mag.* XXXVII. 236/1 The poem is divided into short chapters,..it proves the stabile popularity of the first crusade. **1826** LANDOR *Imag. Conv.*, *Johnson & Tooke* Wks. 1846 I. 153 *Johnson.* You reformers will let nothing be great, nothing be stabile. **1864** SWINBURNE *Atalanta* 688 There is nothing stabile in the world But the gods break it. **1880** —— *Songs of Springtides*, *Thalassius* 71 This poor flash of sense in life,..More stabile than the world's own heart's root seems, By that strong faith.

2. Fixed in position; *spec.* in *Electro-therapeutics*, held firmly upon one point or over one part (as opposed to LABILE *a.* 4).

1896 *Allbutt's Syst. Med.* I. 364 An active electrode..is then moved over the affected region (labile application) or held firmly over one part (stabile method). **1899** *Ibid.* VII. 586 A stabile pupil on the same side as the abscess is an important sign.

stabile ('steɪbaɪl), *sb.* [f. L. *stabil-is* STABLE *a.*, after MOBILE *sb.*[3]] A rigid sculpture or similar construction of wire, sheet metal, etc., of a type first developed by Alexander Calder (1898–1976), Amer. sculptor and painter, opp. MOBILE *sb.*[3] 1 a. (The name was suggested by Jean Arp.)

1943 J. J. SWEENEY *Alexander Calder* 30 The sculpture which was exhibited at the Galerie Percier shows a full assimilation of his experiences... It was to this type of stationary abstract sculpture that Arp. a few months later, gave the name 'stabiles'. **1949** [see MOBILE *sb.*[3] 1 a]. **1957** [see KINETIC *a.* 6]. **1967** *Times* 28 Feb. (Canada Suppl.) 31 This 46-ton 'stabile' is conceived and created in nickel stainless steel. **1977** P. LEACH *Baby & Child* iii. 179 Her stabile will still be useful when she is in her cot.

stabilify (stə'bɪlɪfaɪ), *v. rare*[−1]. [f. L. *stabili-s* (see STABLE *a.*) + -FY.] *trans.* To make stable.

1871 BROWNING *Pr. Hohenstiel* 280 To..render solid and stabilify Mankind.

†**stabiliment.** *Obs.* In 4 **stablyment**. See also STABLEMENT. [ad. L. *stabilimentum*, f. *stabilī-re* to render stable, f. *stabili-s*: see STABLE *a.* and -MENT. Cf. OF. *establiment*, *establement.*] Something which gives stability or firmness; stay, support. *lit.* and *fig.*

1398 TREVISA *Barth. De P.R.* XVIII. xii. (1495) 768 The thyrde tyme they set more greter matere and thycke, and that is the stablyment and fastnynge of the hony combes. **1578** BANISTER *Hist. Man* I. 16 As a ground worke, or stabiliment to susteyne the whole worke. **1639** AINSWORTH *Annot. Ps. cv. 16.* 151 Staffe or stay, stabiliment: so bread is called. **1660** JER. TAYLOR *Duct. Dubit.* II. iii. rule 14 §37 Traditions..are no necessary or competent stabiliment of doctrine or manners, or if they were, themselves have no stabiliment. **1673** GREW *Anat. Plants* I. iii. (1682) 27 In the Trailing of the Trunk, they [the Claspers] serve for stabiliment, propagation and shade. **1684** PELLING *Serm.* 30 Jan. 30 The same laws which are the stabiliment of the church.

stabilimentum (stəbɪlɪ'mɛntəm). *Ent.* Pl. **-menta.** [See STABILIMENT.] A conspicuous broad band of silk running across the web of certain kinds of spider.

1912 J. H. COMSTOCK *Spider Bk.* iv. 203 Some of the orb-weavers strengthen their webs by spinning a zigzag ribbon across the centre or below the hub (Fig. 188). This ribbon has been termed the *stabilimentum.* **1952** T. H. SAVORY *Spider's Web* iv, In addition to radii and spirals there are certain accessory structures which most webs possess. Of these the most conspicuous, when present, is the stabilimentum. **1983** *New Scientist* 10 Feb. 366/1 It seems that stabilimenta are really early warning landmarks for birds.

stabilimeter (stæbɪ'lɪmɪtə(r)). [f. STABILI-TY = -METER.]

1. *Aeronautics.* A contrivance for ascertaining the stability of a model airship or aeroplane.

1907 G. H. BRYAN in *Cornhill Mag.* May 619 A stabilimeter..would enable any experimenter to test the stability of a complete model of his own flying machine. **1911** WEBSTER.

2. *Biol.* A device attached to or forming an animal's cage, the movement of which is recorded as a measure of the animal's activity.

1940 *Jrnl. Exper. Psychol.* XXVII. 91 A similar but smaller stabilimeter has been constructed for studies on spontaneous activity and conditioning in guinea pigs. **1954** *Jrnl. Compar. & Physiol. Psychol.* XLVII. 97 The basic apparatus unit was a stabilimeter-type activity recorder... It involves a circular living cage resting on a central pivot about which it can tilt slightly in any direction. **1972** A. K. BARTOSHUK in Kling & Riggs *Woodworth & Schlosberg's Exper. Psychol.* (ed. 3) xviii. 822/2 Stabilimeter activity increased markedly for the younger rats..but scarcely at all for 100-day rats.

stabilitate (stə'bɪlɪteɪt), *v. rare.* [L. *stabilitāt-* ppl. stem of *stabilitāre*, f. *stabilitās* STABILITY.] *trans.* To give stability to.

1642 H. MORE *Song of Soul* II. I. ii. 43 The soul about it self circumgyrates Her various forms, and what she most doth love She oft before herself stabilitates. **1657** BILLINGSLY *Brachy-Martyrol.* xxi. 73 Do you then..still think good For to stabilitate your throne with blood? **1804** W. TAYLOR in *Ann. Rev.* II. 335 These arguments all tend to stabilitate his institutions. **1835** *Blackw. Mag.* XXXVII. 280 Many sacred sympathies that will yet survive all this hubbub, and stabilitate the structure of social life. **1860** W. H. RUSSELL *Diary in India* xii. I. 180 The work reserved for him who shall come to stabilitate our empire in the East.

stability (stə'bɪlɪtɪ). Forms: α. 4 **stabylte, stabulte,** 4–5 **stablete,** 5 **stabiltee.** β. 5 **stabilite, stabilitee,** 5–6 **stabylyte,** 6–7 **stabilitie** (*Dict.* **stabylitie**), 7– **stability.** [ME. *stablete*, a. OF. (*e*)*stableté*, semi-popular ad. L. *stabilitās*, f. *stabili-s* STABLE *a.*: see -TY. The β forms (= F. *stabilité*, from 12th c.) are assimilated to the Latin form.] The quality or condition of being stable.

1. In physical senses. **a.** Power of remaining erect; freedom from liability to fall or be overthrown.

1426 LYDG. *De Guil. Pilgr.* 23472 Thyng that is maad by rule and lyne, In it self hath more beaute tendure, and mor stabilite. **1691** RAY *Creation* I. (1704) 119 The Roots [of a tree] for its stability and drawing Nourishment from the Earth. **1700** C. NESSE *Antid. Armin.* (1827) 22 The temple stood firmly upon those two pillars, Jachin and Boaz, i.e. stability and strength. **1712** BLACKMORE *Creation* I. 24 These subterranean Walls dispos'd with Art, Such Strength, and such Stability impart, That Storms..and Earthquakes..Break not the Pillars. **1746** HERVEY *Medit.* (1748) 231 The Strength of an Oak, or the Stability of a Pyramid. **1894** H. DRUMMOND *Ascent of Man* 414 The true function of the root is to give stability to the tree.

fig. **1585** C. FETHERSTONE tr. *Calvin on Acts* xv. 36. 381 There ought nothing..to bee more firme, than the spirituall building of faith, whose stabilitie is grounded in the very heauen. **1910** J. W. HARPER *Social Ideal* x. 117 Social jerry-building has no stability.

b. Fixity of position in space; freedom from liability to changes of place.

1625 N. CARPENTER *Geog. Del.* I. v. (1635) 115 The stability is an affection of the earth whereby the Terrestriall Spheare is firmely settled in his proper place. **1664** POWER *Exp. Philos.* III. 168 An Intrinsecal Tendency that it [the Magnet] has of its own, to bring all its parts to their right and determinate points, there to remain in a perfect Stability. **1681** COTTON *Wond. Peake* 45 He..began to try This, and that hanging stone's stability, To prove their firmness. **1831** BREWSTER *Newton* x. 136 *note*, The doctrine of the motion of the earth and the stability of the sun. **1853** SIR H. DOUGLAS *Milit. Bridges* 19 The gradual progress of rivers to their present state of comparative stability.

c. Ability to remain in the same relative place or position in spite of disturbing influences; capacity for resistance to displacement; the condition of being in stable equilibrium, tendency to recover the original position after displacement. Also, of a body in motion: Freedom from oscillation, steadiness.

a **1542** WYATT *Ps. xxxviii.* 13 Such is thi hand on me, yt in my fleshe for terrour of thy yre Is not on poynt of ferme stabilite. **1646** SIR T. BROWNE *Pseud. Ep.* II. ii. 57 Had they been acquainted with this principle, Anaxagoras, Socrates and Democritus had better made out the ground of this stability... Now whether the earth stand still, or moveth circularly, we may concede this Magneticall stability. **1794** G. ADAMS *Nat. & Exp. Philos.* III. xxviii. 162 Our motions ..serve..to preserve constant stability amidst a variety of causes which tend to destroy it. **1796** *Phil. Trans.* LXXXVI. 52 When a solid body floats..and external force is applied to incline it from its position, the resistance opposed to this inclination is termed the stability of floating. **1799** *Monthly Rev.* XXX. 501 A method..for ascertaining the degree of stability or stiffness of a ship. **1855** D. K. CLARK *Railway Mach.* 165/2 By steadiness or stability is meant the property of moving along the rail without any inclination from the centre-line of progression. **1877** W. H. WHITE *Man. Naval Archit.* iii. 63 The statical stability of a ship may be defined as the effort which she makes when inclined by external forces acting horizontally, and held steadily at that inclination, to return towards her natural position of equilibrium. *Ibid.* iv. 131 On this assumption..dynamical stability may be defined as the 'work' done in heeling the ship from her upright position to any angle of inclination. **1879** *Cassell's Techn. Educ.* II. 86/2 The spinning motion [of a top] gives a stability to the axis of rotation. **1883** *Encycl. Brit.* XV. 751/1 (art. *Mechanics*) Safety against displacement by turning is called stability of position; safety against displacement by sliding, stability of friction.

†**d.** 'Fixedness; not fluidity' (J.). *Obs. rare.*

1661 Boyle *Physiol. Ess.* (1669) 208 Since fluidness and stability being contrary qualities, are to be apprehended under contrary notions, we may conceive that the firmness or stability of a body consists principally in this, that the particles [etc.].

e. Of a system of bodies: Permanence of arrangement; power of resisting change of structure.

1855 Brewster *Newton* I. xiii. 358 This grand discovery ..securing the stability of the system, is doubtless one of the noblest in physical astronomy. 1869 Huxley in *Scientific Opinion* Apr. 464/2 Whereby all perturbations eventually reduced themselves to oscillations on each side of a mean position, and the stability of the solar system was secured.

f. Of a chemical compound or combination: Capacity to resist decomposition or disruption. Also of an atomic nucleus or sub-atomic particle.

1862 Miller *Elem. Chem., Org.* (ed. 2) 41 Such combinations are usually of small stability and are decomposed as rapidly as they are formed. 1877 J. Clerk Maxwell in *Encycl. Brit.* VI. 313 Now if such groups [of molecules] of greater stability are disseminated through the substance [etc.]. 1878 W. H. Wardell *Explosives* ibid. VIII. 808/1 The fulminates are among the most violent of all explosive compounds, their chemical stability being very small. 1955 J. A. Wheeler in W. Pauli *Niels Bohr* 163 (*heading*) Nuclear fission and nuclear stability.

g. Of a colour: Permanence.

1791 Hamilton *Berthollet's Dyeing* I. I. i. iii. 45 The stability of colour consists in its power of resisting the action of acids, alkalis, &c.

2. Of an immaterial thing: Immunity from destruction or essential change; enduring quality.

a. of government, institutions, customs, etc.

1470–85 Malory *Arthur* xx. xviii. 829, I wote wel in me was not alle the stabylyte of this realme. *c*1475 Henryson *Poems* III. 171/38 Now is stabilitee fundyn in na stage.. Peas is away, all in perplexitee. 1584 *Reg. Privy Council Scot.* III. 699 The cuntrie being brocht to a greittar stabilitie. 1624 Capt. Smith *Virginia* iv. 148 Where there was no honesty..in such a Countrey..there can bee no stabilitie. 1655 *Nicholas Papers* (Camden) II. 355 A progresse in the old way workes stability. 1767 A. Young *Farmer's Lett. to People* 15 The difference in stability of a commerce founded on the necessities or superfluities of life. 1800 Marq. Wellesley in Owen *Desp.* (1877) 732 The stability of our Government will bear a due proportion to its wisdom, liberality, and justice. 1858 Emerson *Lett. & Soc. Aims, Pers. Poetry* Wks. (Bohn) III. 237 Oriental life and society..stand in violent contrast with the..secular stability ..of the western nations. 1859 F. W. Newman *Let.* 5 May in Sieveking *Mem.* (1909) 172 He [Louis Napoleon] covets stability and the glory of liberating Italy. 1867 Smiles *Huguenots Eng.* xix. (1880) 354 That enterprising and industrious middle class which gives stability to every state. 1873 C. Robinson *N.S. Wales* 32 The stability and expansiveness of this industry is proved by its steady and uniformly progressive development. 1875 Jowett *Plato* (ed. 2) V. 123 He [Plato] is deeply struck with the stability of Egyptian institutions. 1882 Freeman *Lect. Amer. Audiences* II. v. 396 What I see in England, in America, in Switzerland, is stability, the power to make changes.. without pulling the whole political fabric down on the heads of the reformers.

b. of the Divine nature or attributes. ? *Obs.*

1594 Hooker *Eccl. Pol.* I. iii. §4 The naturall generation and processe of all things receyueth order of proceeding from the setled stabilitie of diuine vnderstanding. 1707 Norris *Treat. Humility* iii. 84 When he compares himself with the central stability and immoveable subsistence of that great and glorious Being.

c. of worldly estate, financial affairs.

*a*1628 Preston *New Covt.* (1629) 63 If you looke for stabilitie in your estate, and wonder why a change should come,..why didst thou expect stabilitie in that which is subject to vanitie? 1732 *Belle Assemblée* II. 295 Those devoted to Ambition; who seem, methinks, in a continual Whirl, are never in a state of Stability, or perfect Ease. 1814 Wordsw. *Excurs.* III. 386 [The hermit craving] a life of peace, Stability without regret or fear; That hath been, is, and shall be evermore! 1833 Ht. Martineau *Brooke Farm* v. 69 It is the resource on which the proprietor mainly relies for the stability of his fortune. 1865 Lever *Luttrell* xl, A great London banking firm was associated with the enterprise, which, of course, gave the air of stability to the operation. 1865 Miss Braddon *Only a Clod* xv, [He] suspends payment upon the first failure that affects his stability.

d. of a science, theory, covenant, etc.

1655–60 Stanley *Hist. Philos.* v. ii. (1687) 181/2 Science ..hath certitude, and Stability as being conversant in things certain and stable. *a*1687 H. More *Def. Cabbala* App. ii. (1713) 119 Which number [eight] being the first cube, is a fit hieroglyphick of the Stability of that Covenant made with the Jews in Circumcision. 1750 Johnson *Rambler* No. 158 ¶1 Criticism..has not yet attained the certainty and stability of science. 1751 Bp. Thomas in *10th Rep. Hist. MSS. Comm.* App. I. 306 The only Thing that could give Stability to their Proceedings. 1837 P. Keith *Bot. Lex.* 108 He will not admit that it shakes the stability of Mr. Knight's theory in the slightest degree. 1876 Mozley *Univ. Serm.* iv. 107 The Gospel language throws doubt upon the final stability of much that passes current here with respect to character. 1883 *Manch. Guard.* 22 Oct. 5/4 Some of his verses are purely occasional and have no claim to stability.

e. of natural laws or sequences of natural phenomena; also, of a physical property or the system possessing it.

1836 Emerson *Nature, Idealism* Wks. (Bohn) II. 160 The frivolous make themselves merry with the Ideal theory, as if it affected the stability of nature. 1860 Maury *Phys. Geog.* (Low) iv. 100 The two systems of trade-winds are very unequal both as to force and stability. 1880 A. R. Wallace *Isl. Life* 225 The result would be an epoch of exceptional stability of species. 1881 J. Hooker in *Nature* No. 619. 445 The belief in the stability of climatal conditions during the lifetime of the existing assemblages of animals and plants. 1925 W. Greenwood *Text-bk. Wireless Telegr. & Teleph.* vi. 121 Stability is essential [in a receiver]. By this is meant that the sensitivity must be capable of being controlled by the operator, and must not be liable to be upset by the reception of very strong signals. 1962 J. H. & P. J. Reyner *Radio Communication* iv. 153 Modern conditions call for high stability, the capacitance being required to remain constant with time. 1963 B. Fozard *Instrumentation & Control Nucl. Reactors* x. 122 For high quality equipments ..requiring a gain stability of 0·1% both H.T. and heater supplies must be stabilised. 1975 D. G. Fink *Electronics Engineers' Handbk.* XVII. 50 The stability of feedback systems is of great importance since an unstable system will not be effective in maintaining the controlled variable at approximately the desired value.

†**f.** Put for: Source or cause of stability. *Obs.*

1678 Cudworth *Intell. Syst.* 45 The Essential Goodness and Wisdom of the Deity is the only Stability of all things.

g. Something fixed or settled.

1833 Chalmers *Constit. Man* I. I. i. §1. 57 Just as much as the properties of a triangle are the enduring stabilities of mathematical science. 1847 Emerson *Repr. Men, Montaigne* Wks. (Bohn) I. 340 Adaptiveness is the peculiarity of human nature... We are golden averages, volitant stabilities, compensated or periodic errors.

3. a. Of a person, his character or dispositions: The condition of 'standing fast'; fixity of resolution or purpose; firmness, steadfastness. (The earliest recorded sense.)

13.. in *Hampole's Wks.* I. 75 Ihesu..Take my hert in till þi hand, sett me in stabylte. *a*1400 *Minor Poems fr. Vernon MS.* xxxii. 616 In al þe preyers he scholde in be Nis þer wiþ him [Lecherie] no stabulte. *c*1400 *Rom. Rose* 2940 And alle lovers that wole be Feithful, and ful of stabilite. *Ibid.* 5532 And for nought ellis wol he flee, If that he love in stabilitee. 1426 Lydg. *De Guil. Pilgr.* 1934 Look that ye In trouthe, & in stablete Yee loue to-gydre. 1535 Stewart *Cron. Scot.* II. 537 Tha war..So full of wisdome, gentres, and discretioun, With fredome, faith, and greit stabilitie. 1693 Owen *Holy Spirit* 71 It is hereon that our stability in Believing doth depend. 1784 Cowper *Task* I. 383 His firm stability to what he scorns. 1813 J. Jebb *Let.* 11 July in C. Forster *Corr. Jebb & Knox* (1834) II. 142 Whoever truly loves what is stable, will adhere to it with stability of affection. 1856 Emerson *Eng. Traits, Character* Wks. (Bohn) II. 63 The stability of England is the security of the modern world. If the English race were as mutable as the French, what reliance?

b. In the Benedictine order (tr. L. *stabilitas*): see quots.

1516 *Rule St. Benet* lviii. F6b, Whan she shall be reseyued she must..make a promisse of hir stabilite. 1657 Cressy *Father Baker's Sancta Sophia* III. iv. §18. 187 Let him that is to be receiued to a Religious Profession, promise ..1. A constant Stability in that state. 2. A conuersion of his Manners, and 3. Obedience... And as for Stability, it regards both these [2 and 3], adding to them a perseuerance and a continuall progresse in both to the end. 1883 R. F. Littledale in *Encycl. Brit.* XVI. 704/1 The method adopted [to extirpate irregular and vagrant monks] was the addition of a fourth vow, that of 'stability'... This fourth vow bound the monk to continuance in his profession, and even to residence for life at the monastery in which he was professed.

stabili'zation. [f. stabilize *v.*]

a. The action or process of stabilizing.

1887 *Mind* Oct. 602 With this 'fixation of force' goes the 'stabilisation of matter'. 1922 *World's Paper Trade Rev.* 10 Mar. 767/1 Stabilisation of wages is an urgent necessity in order that the industry might enjoy continued peace. 1945 *Electronic Industries* Sept. 226 *Stabilization*, a system for maintaining a radar beam in a desired direction in space despite the roll and pitch of the ship or aircraft. 1963 B. Fozard *Instrumentation & Control Nucl. Reactors* x. 122 Stabilisation of heater current is conveniently arranged by joining the valve heaters in series and supplying them with direct current from a regulated supply. 1975 *Petroleum Rev.* XXIX. 92/1 The stabilisation consists of the separation of light hydrocarbon components from the raw crude so that the 'stabilised' product is 'stable' in the sense that it can be stored and handled under atmospheric conditions.

b. *attrib.*

1940 *Times* 5 June 7/4 Inasmuch as the wage structure of the country has reached a stabilization point, the only justification for wage adjustments now will be in conditions common to all industry. 1958 *Spectator* 6 June 752/2 Sir Oliver Franks..called for a 'stabilisation' loan [from the U.S.] and the reinforcement of the IMF resources. 1969 *Advancement of Sci.* XXVI. 65/2 Management was thus seen as concerned primarily with stabilization policy and with the short-run, since stability is by definition a short-term affair. 1974 *Daily Tel.* 11 Mar. 18/5 The South African government may introduce a gold stabilisation fund.

stabilizator (steɪbɪlaɪ'zeɪtə(r)). *Aeronautics.* Also -isator. [ad. F. *stabilisateur*, f. *stabiliser*: see stabilize *v.* and -ator.] = stabilizer.

1902 Santos-Dumont in *Lond. Mag.* June 461 How much resistance will the guide-rope, which I shall use as a stabilizator, offer as it trails in the water? 1912 T. F. Farman in *Blackw. Mag.* Jan. 139/2 Securing its horizontal and lateral stability by working the stabilisator and the mechanism for warping the wings.

stabilize ('steɪbɪlaɪz), *v.* [ad. F. *stabiliser*, f. L. *stabili-s*: see stable *a.* and -ize.]

1. *trans.* To give stability to (a ship). Also with other objs. and *refl.*

1861 W. Froude *Rolling of Ships* (1862) 14 The ship, whether stabilised by breadth of beam or by deeply stowed ballast, would [etc.]. 1916 H. Barber *Aeroplane Speaks* 71 If an aeroplane was not stabilized in this way. 1938 G. H. Richter *Textbk. Org. Chem.* xxix. 595 The majority of the reactions of naphthalene are..the formation of unstable 1,4 addition products..which then stabilize themselves by the elimination of two atoms. 1958 *Times* 30 Aug. 6/1 The rocket during the whole of its flight was stabilized, to prevent rotation. 1975 *Petroleum Rev.* XXIX. 89/3 The raw crude oil will be stabilized and the natural gas liquids recovered.

2. To give a stable character or value to.

1875 Whitney *Life & Growth Lang.* ix. 158 Such forces ..fairly dominate the history of speech. The language is stabilized. 1907 *Daily Chron.* 7 Jan. 3/7 The Mexican dollar, which formerly varied in value from 35 cents to 50 cents, has been stabilised at 50 cents gold. 1909 [see stabilizing *vbl. sb.* below].

3. *intr.* To become stable; *esp.* to cease varying in value.

1961 in Webster. 1971 *Timber Trades Jrnl.* 21 Aug. 16/1 Lumber stabilises at approximately 15% moisture content under normal use conditions. 1974 *State* (Columbia, S. Carolina) 26 Apr. 19-A/2 The Nixon administration contends the economy will stabilize in the second quarter. 1981 *Times* 4 Feb. 16/7 He was obliged with his pilot to eject from a Javelin which had stabilized in an unrecoverable spin.

Hence **'stabilizing** *vbl. sb.*

1909 *Q. Rev.* Oct. 533 The pernicious effects of the fluctuations of exchange demand the stabilising of the gold value of currency.

'stabilized, *ppl. a.* **1.** Made stable. **a.** Prevented from oscillating or moving.

1887 *Mind* Oct. 602 Psychologically, what corresponds to 'fixed' force or 'stabilised' matter is [etc.]. 1958 *Times Rev. Industry* Sept. 96/1 The country's [*sc.* South Africa's] highways consist of gravelled or stabilized roads. 1968 R. W. Fairbridge *Encycl. Geomorphol.* 126/1 Sand-sized pellets from drying crusts of saline flats with 8% or more of clay..form stablized dunes. 1977 'D. Rutherford' *Return Load* ii. 40 The modern, stabilized vessel provided good accommodation for the drivers.

b. Prevented from fluctuating in value or quality.

1918 *Nation* (N.Y.) Feb. 129/2 To give every farmer just returns and stabilized prices.

2. Of cloth: treated in order to prevent stretching or shrinking.

1960 *Textile Terms & Definitions* (Textile Inst.) (ed. 4) 140 *Stabilized finish*, treatment applied to a textile material to increase its resistance to dimensional changes in laundering and use. 1977 *Austral. Sailing* Jan. 41/1 Cheret, Banks and Fogh spinnakers..are made from either ¾ oz or ½ oz stabilised or zephylite cloth.

3. Made stable in character or behaviour; *spec.* of a drug addict, able to live more or less normally on a repeated constant dose.

1961 *Drug Addiction* (Min. of Health) 11 Arising also..is the conception of a 'stabilised addict'... A careful scrutiny of the histories of more than a hundred persons classified as addicts reveals that many of them who have been taking small and regular doses for years show little evidence of tolerance and are often leading reasonably satisfactory lives. 1964 G. L. Cohen *What's Wrong with Hospitals?* vii. 152 They sit in one charabanc, and the stabilized male chronics in another. 1967 M. M. Glatt et al. *Drug Scene* vii. 81 The 'stabilized addict', i.e. a person who was able to maintain a fixed dose of the narcotic drug without the need for ever-increasing doses and who, at the same time, was able to follow his occupation. 1976 J. I. M. Stewart *Young Pattullo* viii. 188 Fish looked stabilized, at least until the following day, when I could take stock of his state again.

'stabilizer. [f. stabilize *v.* + -er[1].]

1. a. *Aeronautics.* A stabilizing apparatus or device.

1909 C. C. Turner *Aerial Navig. To-day* (1910) 315 *Stabilizer*, the tail of a flying-machine. 1910 *Times* 1 Nov. 4/5 The men removed the propellers, the 'stabilizer', and various parts of the fittings. 1911 G. C. Loening *Monoplanes & Biplanes* x. 136 A horizontal surface placed at the rear acts as a longitudinal stabilizer. 1918 J. M. Grider *War Birds* (1927) 221 He managed to land with his stabilizer wheel. 1920 *Discovery* Mar. 77/2 Captain Caquot solved the problem by fitting the peculiar large stabilisers, or tails, which give the balloon a conspicuous, almost an uncanny appearance. 1948 W. Ley *Rockets & Space Travel* vii. 180 Schaefer and I are inclined to believe that even a 1 *g* rocket might be able to do without a stabilizer. 1962 F. I. Ordway et al. *Basic Astronautics* ii. 17 The Dutch tried using small fins attached to the body of the rocket in order to do away with the unwieldy stabilizer stick. 1973 *Times* 21 Feb. 7/1 The stabilizer of the Soviet airliner..had jammed.

b. *Naut.* A device intended to reduce the rolling of a ship in heavy seas. Cf. *gyrostabilizer* s.v. gyro- b.

1913 *Engineering* 13 June 820/1 The perfect stabiliser must act against the forces which are acting on the ship in such a way as to always resist the effect of the sea in producing motion. 1946 *Nature* 24 Aug. 250/2 A chapter follows on the sperry gyro ship-stabilizer, in which each gyro rotor weighs 100 tons and spins at 800 revolutions a minute. 1958 *Engineering* 28 Mar. 386/3 The installation of anti-roll Denny-Brown stabilisers in the Cunard Liner Queen Mary has now been finished. 1968 W. J. Fox *Marine Auxiliary Machinery* (ed. 4) xvi. 461 It is in the provision of this form of [flume] control that the main differences lie between the flume stabilization system and the older types of passive tank stabilizer. 1983 *Listener* 14 July 12/1 We abruptly lurched... 'Technical proving of the stabiliser,' said the announcement.

c. Chiefly *N. Amer.* A stabilizing device on a motor vehicle or tractor; *spec.* = *sway bar* (*b*) s.v. sway-. Also ***stabilizer bar***.

1931 *Automobile Engineer* Nov. 481/3 The stabiliser bar on the Panhard-Levassow..is fitted transversely at the rear end of the chassis. 1939 *Audel's New Automotive Guide* xxxii. 827 Practically all modern cars are provided with stabilizers as standard equipment. 1949 Landon & Hafferkamp in Frazee & Bedell *Automotive Fundamentals* viii. 445 The stabilizer may be thought of as a third spring which connects the two individual suspensions. **1962** *Which? Car Suppl.* Oct. 138/1 Clamp bolts of stabiliser bar [were] slightly loose. **1966** SHIPPEN & TURNER *Basic Farm Machinery* I. viii. 94 *Stabilizers.* These are also used to prevent side to side movement of certain farm implements. They usually take the form of metal bars slightly cranked at each end and they fit between an anchorage point beneath the rear axle and the ends of the linkage bars. **1977** 'D. RUTHERFORD' *Return Load* ii. 32 She's got optional six-wheel drive with stabilizers operating on the front and rear axle.

d. *pl.* A pair of small supporting wheels fitted one at each side of the rear wheel of a child's bicycle, to keep it upright.

1960 A. L. PULLEN *Cycling Handbk.* (ed. 3) i. 10 (*caption*) Child's lightweight cycle with stabilizers. **1970** *Kay & Co.* (Worcester) *Catal.* 1970–71 Autumn/Winter 982/1 RSW 11 Cycle... It has a 12 inch frame, 11 inch pneumatic tyres, a spacious rear hold-all, and stabilizers. **1978** *Dumfries & Galloway Standard* 21 Oct. 21/7 (Advt.), Child's bicycle, with stabilisers, as new, to suit 3–6 years.

2. A substance added to an explosive to render it less liable to spontaneous decomposition (Webster, 1911). More widely, an additive which inhibits chemical or physical change in a substance, esp. one used to prevent the breaking of an emulsion.

1909 *Chem. Abstr.* III. 1342 Vaseline which was added originally to protect the gun has turned out to be a valuable stabilizer for the powder. **1932** *Discovery* Aug. 240/1 The coal was prevented from separating from the oil by the addition of a 'stabilizer'. **1940** *Thorpe's Dict. Appl. Chem.* (ed. 4) IV. 520/1 In the early days of smokeless powders a small amount of alkali was added as a stabiliser. **1948** J. OSBORNE *Dental Mech.* (ed. 2) xi. 183 Since the monomer will polymerize by the action of heat or light, it is necessary to prevent this occurring... An inhibitor, or stabilizer, is therefore added to all dental monomers. **1963** W. J. WOOLGAR *Plastics in Plumbing* v. 57 A small proportion of stabilizer is added, to prevent the P.V.C. from decomposing at processing temperatures. **1966** *Punch* 5 Jan. 9/1 Mrs. Joyce Butler..has introduced a Labelling of Food Bill which calls for a detailed specification..of anti-oxidants, emulsifiers and stabilisers in foods. **1977** *Lancet* 15 Oct. 780/2 Because it increases the viscosity of solutions guar gum is widely used in the food industry as a thickener and stabiliser of fat emulsions.

3. *Electronics.* **a.** A circuit or device for preventing unwanted feedback. **b.** A circuit that holds the output voltage of a power supply at a constant level despite changes in supply voltage or load, by comparison with a fixed reference voltage. Also *stabilizer circuit.*

1924 MOYER & WOSTREL *Practical Radio* viii. 119 A common stabilizer for all the radio-frequency stages is generally sufficient. **1936** *Physical Rev.* L. 1094/2 (*heading*) Electronic voltage stabilizers. **1958** D. G. A. THOMAS in O. R. Frisch *Nuclear Handbk.* xv. 24 The principle of.. stabilisers is to compare the output voltage (or fraction of it) with that of a voltage reference source, amplify the difference, and use it to control the output. **1974** HARVEY & BOHLMAN *Stereo F.M. Radio Handbk.* v. 82 An amplifier is not essential but its use improves the regulation of the stabilizer circuit.

4. *gen.* Something that reduces variation in the condition or behaviour of anything.

1955 *Times* 15 July 9/2 These stabilizers included increased social service payments, agricultural price supports..an easy credit policy..and a tax system which made tax liabilities fall faster than income during the recession. **1958** *Manch. Guardian* 21 Jan. 6/1 The 'built-in stabilisers' of the American economy are beginning to grip.

5. *Math.* A subgroup of a permutation group, being the group of elements that map some subset of the permuted elements on to itself.

1965 J. J. ROTMAN *Theory of Groups* iii. 49 If $x \in X$, then the set of all $t \in G$ that fix x forms a subgroup H_x of G (called the stabilizer of x). **1979** *Proc. London Math. Soc.* XXXVIII. 200 Hence the stabilizer of e, Stab $(e) = \{g \mid ge = e\}$ is finite.

stabilizing ('steɪbɪlaɪzɪŋ), *ppl. a.* [f. STABILIZE *v.* + -ING².] That stabilizes or gives stability; *spec.* in *Aeronautics*, that gives stability (to an aeroplane, etc.); that acts or may be used as a stabilizer.

1911 *Encycl. Sport* I. 16/2 In the Voisin machine there are vertical panels in the main planes, which..automatically check these oscillations, and a stabilising box at the rear. *Ibid.* 17/2 No really satisfactory stabilising device has yet been invented. **1911** *Daily Mail* 28 Oct. 5/7 A large stabilising vane fixed to the front of his aeroplane. **1935** H. A. L. FISHER *Hist. Europe* I. xii. 137 The Arabs were poets, dreamers, fighters, traders; they were not politicians. Nor had they found in religion a stabilizing or unifying power. **1954** P. MASON *Ess. Racial Tension* 141 Stabilizing devices are introduced to preserve the dominant position and genetic purity of the dominating race. **1960** C. DAY LEWIS *Buried Day* i. 18 For a rather rootless person like myself, there is something reassuring, if not stabilising, in the mere known existence of individual ancestors. **1981** *Sci. Amer.* Feb. 36/3 The ability to monitor Russian missile-carrying submarines could..be considered stabilizing in that it deters surprise attack.

Stabit ('stæbɪt). *Engin.* [Arbitrary, suggested by STABILITY.] A large mass of concrete so shaped that when large numbers are placed together they tend to interlock and form a strong barrier that will act as a break-water.

1962 *Dock & Harbour Authority* May 29/2 The Stabit is basically a hollow tetrahedron and, besides its use for breakwater construction, it is considered to be particularly suitable for beach and coast protection works. **1963** *Guardian* 30 Aug. 3/5 (*caption*) Six hundred concrete 'teeth' have been fixed in position to protect the root of Shoreham harbour's east breakwater from the pounding of heavy seas. The 'teeth'..are called Stabits, and are interlocking in a sloping, double layer. **1968** *Proc. 11th Conf. Coastal Engin.* II. 797 The number of 29 ton Stabits which have been used on the reconstructed moles at Benghazi is about 10,000.

stable ('steɪb(ə)l), *sb.*¹ Forms: 4–5 **stabille**, (5 **-ylle**), 4–5 **stabul**, 5 **stabull(e**, *Sc.* **stabill**, 5–6 **stabil**, 6 **stabell**, 7 **stabel**, 3– **stable**: *pl.* 4 **stablen**, 5 **stablis**, **stablez**, 6 **stabullys**, *Sc.* **stabulez**, 6– **stables**. [a. OF. *estable* masc. and fem., stable, also applied to a cowhouse, pigsty, etc. (mod.F. *étable* fem. cowhouse):—L. *stabulum* (also pop.L. *stabula* pl. used as fem. sing.) stable, stall, enclosure or fold for animals, lit. standing place, f. *sta-* root of *stāre* to stand. Cf. Sp. *establo*, Pg. *estabulo* stable, It. *stabbio* sheepfold, Rumanian *staul* (whence mod.Gr. σταῦλος).]

1. a. A building fitted with stalls, loose-boxes, rack and manger and harness appliances, in which horses are kept. Formerly used in a wider sense: †a building in which domestic animals, as cattle, goats, etc. are kept.

c **1250** *Owl & Night.* 629 Vor hors a stable, & oxe a stalle, boþ al þat hom wule þar falle. **1297** R. GLOUC. (Rolls) 5669 And þe hous of malmesbury..He made hit stable to his hors. **1340** *Ayenb.* 210 Huo..þet mest heþ hors mest him fayleþ gromes and stablen. *c* **1386** CHAUCER *Prol.* 168 Ful many a deyntee hors hadde he in stable. **1387** TREVISA *Higden* (Rolls) IV. 153 Also bestes þat were i-woned to lyve among men forsoke stable and lesewe. **1463** *Mann. & Househ. Exp.* (Roxb.) 152 My mastyre alowyd hys fermour ..ffor otys that he toke to my lordys stable..v.s. x.d. **1511** *Acc. Ld. High Treas. Scot.* IV. 262 Item, to ane grume of the stabulez of Falkland..xiij s. **1538** STARKEY *Dialogue* I. iii. (1871) 133 Wher hath byn many housys and churchys..you schal fynd no thyng but schypcotys and stabullys. **1588** *Exch. Rolls Scot.* XXI. 360 David Murray, ane of the kingis majesties maisteris of stabill. **1611** BIBLE *Ezek.* xxv. 5 And I will make Rabbah a stable for camels. **1660** F. BROOKE tr. *Le Blanc's Trav.* 139 'Twas thought the King distributed the best part of the horses in his stable. **1784** COWPER *Task* III. 463 The stable yields a stercoraceous heap. **1818** SCOTT *Br. Lamm.* xviii, I shall choose a better stable for my horse than the Kelpie's quick-sand. **1840** DICKENS *Old C. Shop* xvi, The whole house hurried away into an empty stable where the show stood. **1864** TENNYSON *Aylmer's F.* 126 When they ran To loose him [a dog] at the stables.

b. See AUGEAN *stable*.

1903 *Westm. Gaz.* 28 Jan. 9/1 Because the financiers.. have set themselves to clear up the stable, and put things upon a more honest and reputable footing. **1909** SIEVEKING *Mem. F. W. Newman* xiv. 301 Here is indeed the mind of a modern Hercules in its strong rational suggestions as to how this particular 'stable' must be swept out.

c. *to talk stable*: to talk of 'horsy' matters.

1855 SMEDLEY *H. Coverdale* viii, We shall have him on our hands, talking stable, and wishing we were dogs and horses, for a whole week!

d. *transf.* and *fig.* Also in phr. *straight from the stable* = *straight from the horse's mouth* s.v. HORSE *sb.* 26 c.

1907 LADY MONKSWELL *Jrnl.* 13 July in *Victorian Diarist* (1946) II. 188 The beautiful Surrey landscape looks down into this purgatory of motor stables & everything that motors require. **1922** JOYCE *Ulysses* 145 Tell him that straight from the stable. **1949** A. CHRISTIE *Crooked House* iii. 14 My information..came from the stable itself... She dined with me.

2. a. A collection (of horses) belonging to one stable.

1576 FLEMING *Panopl. Epist.* 373 If you take learning and knowledge from among men, what doe you else make of a publique bodye, but a stable of Asses. *a* **1700** EVELYN *Diary* Apr. an. 1646, He then shew'd us a stable of brave horses. **1776** in *Peterson Mag.* Jan. 60/1 The Congress seem to stumble at every step. I do not mean one or two of the cattle, but the whole stable.

b. *slang.* A group of prostitutes working for the same person or organization.

1937 [see KNOCK-DOWN *sb.* 5]. **1940** 'J. CRAD' *Traders in Women* i. 26 He..now runs a 'stable' of white women for coloured seamen in Cardiff. **1973** C. & R. MILNER *Black Players* ii. 35 Many players [*sc.* pimps] have several ladies, who constitute their stable. **1979** N. HYND *False Flags* xi. 91 The consulate maintained a stable of young women..whose only purposes were those of sexual entrapment.

c. *transf.* (In quots., of motor vehicles.)

1949 *Sun* (Baltimore) 29 July 12/3 The man who owned a stable of bulldozers laughed and said, 'We'll do it tomorrow morning.' **1974** *Spartanburg* (S. Carolina) *Herald* 18 Apr. C1/2 John Greenwood, a self-made millionaire, announced Wednesday that his stable of Corvettes would be running out of John Green Automotive garage on highway 221 at I-85.

3. a. An establishment where race-horses are trained; a racing-stable. Also, the horses belonging to a particular racing-stable; the proprietors and staff of such an establishment.

1810 *T. Holcroft's Mem.* xvi. (1856) 62 As the prize to be obtained was great, the whole stable was on the alert. **1865** LEVER *Luttrell* lvi, These were painful reflections, and made him think that very probably he had 'been backing the wrong stable'. **1868** *Field* 11 July 29/2 De Vere disappointed her stable very much by being the first beaten. **1884** H. SMART *Post to Finish* vi, William Greyson's is not a large stable; still he has a tolerable good string.

b. *transf.* An establishment where boxers are trained; a group of boxers under the same management.

1897 *Nat. Police Gaz.* (U.S.) 26 May 11/4 His boxing academy at..Dale End, Birmingham, is being largely supported, and some likely lads will shortly emerge from Anthony's stable. **1936** *Sun* (Baltimore) 16 Mar. 3/3 He insisted his occupation was manager of prizefighters, but the arresting detectives failed to recognize the pugilists he mentioned as his 'stable'. **1953** *Chicago Daily Sun-Times* 29 Dec. 40/5 Some years ago Rocky's hometown pal, Al Columbo, sent Marciano to New York as a candidate for membership in the Weill stable. **1976** *Scotsman* 24 Dec. 15/1 Maurice Hope..becomes the third member of the East London stable managed by Terry Lawless.

c. A team or organization which prepares motor cars for racing; a group of racing cars owned by the same enterprise.

1935 EYSTON & LYNDEN *Motor Racing & Record Breaking* ii. 20 The Italian term [*scuderia*] finds its equivalent in.. our own 'stable', and the formation of such terms among racing men is a development of very recent years. *Ibid.* vii. 65 Every important Continental racing stable was represented. **1957** S. MOSS *In Track of Speed* v. 61 He returned to Europe at the head of a racing stable of mechanics. **1966** *Publ. Amer. Dial. Soc.* 1964 XLII. 8 *Scuderia*.., a stable of cars, usually privately entered.

d. More widely, an establishment which trains or produces persons, etc., esp. of a characteristic quality or type. Also, a group *of* persons (*spec.* in publishing) under the same management or trained at the same place.

1942 *Tee Emm* (Air Ministry) II. 137 Robert..takes the lead in the latest offering from the Air Ministry Instructional Film stables. **1951** *Sun* (Baltimore) 19 June 7/2 Best known in the SRP's stable of führers is Remer. **1963** *Listener* 14 Mar. 458/1 The now-famous group centred on George Webb..which used to meet at the 'Red Barn', Bexleyheath, the stable out of which Humphrey Lyttelton came, played, typically, for a small audience of each other. **1970** C. L. CLINE *Lett. George Meredith* I. 37 Lucas recruited the best staff of artists in the business..mainly from the *Punch* stable. **1977** 'J. LE CARRÉ' *Hon. Schoolboy* i. 17 Luke..had been the star turn in his magazine's Saigon stable of war reporters.

e. In colloq. phr. *from the same stable*, from the same source.

1950 *Sun* (Baltimore) 6 Jan. 5 (*caption*) This jet plane is from the same stable as the Comet. **1959** *Listener* 2 July 36/1, I would be interested to hear a play from the same stable. **1962** H. E. BEECHENO *Introd. Business Stud.* v. 42 We find many competing products are coming from the same 'stables'. **1972** G. BELL *Villains Galore* xiv. 213 No one was quite sure who Boote actually was, except that he was from the same stable as Stallion.

4. *Mil.* Used in *pl.* for: Duty or work in the stables; also the bugle-call for this duty, stable-call.

1885 *Morning Post* 5 Feb. (Cass.), They seem always at stables, on parade, or out doing field-firing. **1908** *Animal Management* (Vet. Departm., War Office) 83 The usual hours for stables at Home are [etc.]. *Ibid.*, As soon as this is done 'Stables' should sound, when every man should be with his horse. *Ibid.* 84 At evening stables the horses are to be watered.

5. a. attrib. and Comb.: simple attrib., as *stable-bail* (BAIL *sb.*³ 4), *broom*, *brush*, *bucket*, †*chamber*, *-court*, *-dog*, *-door*, †*fee* (Sc.), *fittings*, *-fork*, *-gate*, *-girl*, *guard* (Mil.), *-jacket*, *jockey*, *lantern*, *-litter*, *loft*, *management*, *people*, *plank*, *post*, *slang*, *stuff*, *suit*, *-theatre*, *-wench*, *work*; *stable-like* adj.; locative, as *stable-born*, adj.

1737 HOPPUS *Salmon's Country Build. Estim.* (ed. 2) 103 Pins, Hooks, Chains, &c. to *Stable-Bails. **1648** J. BEAUMONT *Psyche* x. clx, A *stable-born and manger-cradeled Thing. **1819** SCOTT *Leg. Montrose* xviii, A bed as hard as a *stable broom. **1862** *Catal. Internat. Exhib.* Brit. II. No. 4535, *Stable brushes. **1842** LOVER *Handy Andy* i, But that's not nigh the full o' the *stable-bucket! **1582** *Durham Wills* (Surtees) II. 45 In the *stable chaumbre. In the chaumbre within the stable; one bedsteade [etc.]. **1816** *Gentl. Mag.* LXXXVI. I. 38 On the right, the chapel, *stable-court,..&c. **1850** THACKERAY *Pendennis* iv, Pen.. was presently heard riding out of the stable-court. **1865** *Our Young Folks* I. 461 It began to be remarked that this was a *stable-dog, educated for the coach-boy and stable. **1529** *Extracts Burgh Rec. Edin.* (1871) 6 At thai tak na *stabill fee fra the personis that lugis with thame. **1862** *Catal. Internat. Exhib.* Brit. II. No. 6106, *Stable fittings. **1837** CARLYLE *Fr. Rev.* II. IV. vi, The very Ostlers have *stable-forks and flails. **1602** *Narcissus* (1893) 264 It is too late, When steede is stolne to shutt the *stable gate [cf. STABLE DOOR.] **1967** N. FREELING *Strike out where not Applicable* 36 He blusters.. shouting at the *stable-girls. **1908** *Animal Management* (Vet. Departm., War Office) 84 A *stable guard should invariably be posted while the men are away from stables. **1852** C. M. YONGE *Two Guardians* i. 12 Edmund..seeing a boy in a *stable jacket, asked Marian if he should not let him lead the ponies round by the drive. **1884** H. SMART *Post to Finish* vi, A..lad, attired in a grey tweed stable-jacket, moleskin trousers,..and a tweed cap. **1971** D. FRANCIS *Bonecrack* xvi. 215 'You can stay on..if you like.'.. 'What as?' he said apprehensively... '*Stable jockey,' I said. **1892** ZANGWILL *Childr. Ghetto* i, The *stable-like doors of the kitchen. **1808** J. C. CURWEN *Econ. Feeding Stock* 242 Fresh *stable-litter being made use of. **1851** MAYHEW *Lond. Labour* I. 357/2 He allowed me..to sleep in the *stable-loft. **1856** 'STONEHENGE' *Brit. Rural Sports* II. I. ix. 349 Clothing, Dressing, and *Stable Management. **1800** MRS. HERVEY *Mourtray Fam.* IV. 195 He met one of the *stable people. **1595** SHAKS. *John* v. ii. 140 To crowch in litter of your *stable plankes. **1781** J. RIPLEY *Sel. Orig. Lett.* 101, I would have..tied both your hands together with a strong halter to one of the *stable-posts. **1894** *Stable slang [see LAD *sb.*¹ 2 c]. **1903** SOMERVILLE & 'ROSS' *All on Irish Shore* 269 His speech, what there is of it, is ungarnished with stable slang. **1551–2** in Aungier *Syon* (1840) 93 And the *stable stuffe and apparell for horsses to be delivered to thands of..our..

officers of our stable. **1849** *Bentley's Misc.* XXVI. 465 Stable-boys..at eight guineas a year, and a *stable-suit. **1928** T. S. Eliot *Dialogue on Poetic Drama* in *Dryden's Ess. Dram. Poesie* p. xxvi, We shall end with a..cosmopolitan little-theatre... What is..more likely is that nothing will be done at all. We are all too busy..to prance about in a *stable-theatre. **1847** Tennyson *Princess* ii. 223 A plump-arm'd Ostleress and a *stable wench Came running at the call. **1881** *Encycl. Brit.* XII. 193/1 *Stable work should commence early.

b. Special comb.: **stable block**, a building designed to house stables; **stable-boy**, a boy or man employed in or about a stable; **stable-call** *Mil.*, a bugle-call to stables (see 4); **stable-cleaner** (see quot.); **stable companion**, a horse from the same stable; also *transf.*; **stablecraft**, the knowledge and skill involved in the proper maintenance of stables and stable animals; **stable-dung**, dung from stables as distinguished from that collected in the foldyard or in the streets; **stable-fly** (see quots.); **stable groom** = GROOM *sb.*[1] 5; **stable-help, helper** = HELPER 2 *spec.*; **stable-horse** (see quot.); **stable hours**, the fixed times for work in the stable; **stable-keeper**, one who keeps a stable; one who provides stable-accommodation for horses; **stable-lad** = *stable-boy*; **stable-language**, the parlance of those who have the care and training of horses; **stableman**, one who is employed in a stable to groom, feed and otherwise look after the horses; **stable manure** = *stable-dung*; **stable-mate** = *stable companion*; **stable-meal** [MAIL *sb.*[2]] *Sc.*, 'the liquor consumed in an inn by farmers by way of remunerating the innkeeper for accommodating their horses during the day' (Jamieson, *Suppl.*); **stable room**, accommodation for horses or a horse in a stable; stabling; **stablewards** *adv.*, towards the stable or stables; **stable-yard**, the yard attached to a stable. Also STABLE DOOR.

1977 P. D. James *Death of Expert Witness* ii. i. 56 As she had come round the corner of the house from putting her bicycle in the old *stable block, Inspector Blakelock had been standing at the front door. **1729** Swift *Direct. Serv.* v. (1745) 66 Deliver your Horses to the *Stable-boy, and let him gallop them to the next Pond. **1898** J. Arch *Life* ii. 33 A wealthy banker..took me into his stables, made me a sort of stable-boy. **1889** *Century Mag.* Apr. 900 Will you go down to *stable-call and pick out a mount? **1875** Knight *Dict. Mech.*, **Stable-cleaner*, a manure-drag for removing used litter from stables. **1868** *Field* 11 July 29/3 Chatelherault winning..by a head from his *stable companion. **1892** *Strand Mag.* July 36/1 Its stable companion was the Challenge tricycle. **1920** Galsworthy *Tatterdemalion* xii. 179, I used to like very much his attitude to the young 'stable-companion' who had arrived with him. **1968** 'J. le Carré' *Small Town in Germany* xiii. 214 'Praschko was up there, was he? In Berlin? With the Russians and Aickman?' 'Stable companions.' **1931** *Times Lit. Suppl.* 25 June 502/3 His remarks on *stablecraft are also thoroughly sound. **1953** G. Brooke *(title)* Introduction to riding and stablecraft. **1763** *Museum Rust.* I. 257 Lime is a much sweeter manure than *stable-dung. **1842** Loudon *Suburban Hort.* 65 Street manure..has been used in forcing-gardens as a substitute for tanners bark and stable-dung. **1862** T. W. Harris *Insects Injur. Vegetation* (ed. 3) 16 The stinging *stable-flies (*Stomoxys*). **1884–5** *Riverside Nat. Hist.* (1888) II. 430 A very common and wide-spread species is the stable-fly, *Stomoxys calcitrans*... The larvæ live in fresh horse manure. **1910** *Encycl. Brit.* X. 584/1 The *Stomoxys calcitrans*, or stable-fly;..*Muscina stabulans*, another stable-fly. *c* **1485** *Digby Myst.* ii. 120 Now, *stabyll grom, shortly bryng forth away The best horse. **1638** Ford *Lady's Trial* ii. ii, And stable-grooms [have] reacht to some fair ones chambers. **1836** Haliburton *Clockm.* Ser. i. xxii. (1862) 105 Give up blood horses to them that can afford to keep *stable-helps to tend 'em. **1807** E. S. Barrett *Rising Sun* III. 30 Mrs. Secondhand..sent one of the *stable-helpers to fetch a chair. **1802** C. James *Milit. Dict.*, **Stable horse*, Ind. That part of Tippoo Sultaun's cavalry, which was best armed, accoutred, and most regularly disciplined. **1810** *T. Holcroft's Mem.* xii. (1856) 37 [The groom] was so attentive to *stable-hours, that..he was always to be found. **1844** *Regul. & Ord. Army* 352 The face, eyes, and nostrils of each horse are to be washed with a sponge and sea-water, at the regular stable-hours. *c* **1440** *Promp. Parv.* 471/2 *Stabul kepar, or hors kepar, *stabularius*. **1811** *Regul. & Ord. Army* 161 The Hay and Straw for Horses in Quarters..are furnished by the Stable-Keepers, &c. on whom they are billeted. **1856** 'Stonehenge' *Brit. Rural Sports* ii. i. ix. 352/2 Mischief..if not prevented will be indulged in by the *stable-lad towards his charge. **1856** Whyte Melville *Kate Coventry* xv, They were, what is termed in *stable language, very much above themselves. **1729** Swift *Direct. Serv.* i. (1745) 32 Get the Cook, the House-maid, the *Stable-men, etc...to stand in his Way to the Hall in a Line. **1629** J. Parkinson *Parad.* i. i. 2 Sandy loame..may soone be helped with old *stable manure of horses. **1864** Trollope *Small House at Allington* II. xxx. 306 There was..a vexed question between Hopkins and Joliffe the bailiff on the matter of—stable manure. **1973** 'I. Drummond' *Jaws of Watchdog* vii. 95 Give it plenty of muck... Stable manure is the best. **1941** Wyndham Lewis *Let.* May (1963) 288 The 'practical politicians' and..their *stable-mates the hardboiled business-men' have somehow or other to be tamed. **1958** *Daily Sketch* 2 June 15/3 Guersillus's stablemate, Paridel, will not now run in the Derby. **1979** J. Leasor *Love & Land Beyond* i. 13, I run a stable mate of the Cord, an Auburn 851 cabriolet. **1786** Burns *To Auld Mare* viii, When thou an' I were young an' skeigh An *stable-meals at fairs were dreigh. **1585** *Knaresb. Wills* (Surtees) I. 150 To my brother..sufficient hay for his horse..and *stable roome in my stable. **1753** *Chambers' Cycl.* Suppl., When there is stable-room enough partitions are to be made for several horses to stand in. **1838** Dickens *Nich. Nick.* v, [He] then lounged *stablewards. **1703** *Lond. Gaz.* No. 3899/4 Enquire at the *Stable Yard in St. Alban's street. **1837** Dickens *Pickw.* xxiii, In the vicinity of the stable-yard ..sat Mr. Weller senior.

stable ('steɪb(ə)l), *sb.*[2] *Coal Mining.* [Of uncertain origin: perh. the same word as prec.; cf. also STAPLE *sb.*[4]] An excavation in a face to accommodate a coal-cutting machine or loader working into it. Also ***stable hole***.

1906 *Trans. Inst. Mining Engin.* XXXI. 401 Coal-cutters, which have a disc or a chain-jib fixed to their longitudinal centre, cannot cut close to the ends of the face, and require a stable-hole or heading to be driven in advance at each end. **1914** G. L. Kerr *Practical Coal-Mining* (ed. 5) vi. 148 This avoids the necessity of making jib-holes or 'stables' at the start and finish of the cut. **1945** *Trans. Inst. Mining Engin.* CIV. 209 Stables to a depth of at least twice the depth of the cut are required at each end of the face. **1968** *Economist* 8 June 85/3 The great benefit of the machine is in avoiding the present concentration of men in the 'stable hole' the most dangerous part of the pit. **1973** L. J. Thomas *Introd. Mining* vii. 278 A longwall face stable was necessary so that the face cutting and loading machinery could stand in it..while the face conveyor was pushed over.

stable ('steɪb(ə)l), *a.* Also 3 **stabell**, 3, 5 **stabel**, 3–6 **stabul**, **stabil**, 4, 6 **stabile**, 4–6 **stabyll**, 5 **stabyl(le**, **stabull**, 5–6 **stabill**, (**sstabylle**), 5 (*Caxton*) **estable**. [a. OF. *stable*, *estable* (mod.F. *stable*):—L. *stabilem* f. *sta-* root of *stāre* to stand: see -BLE. Cf. Sp. *estable*, Pg. *estavel*, It. *stabile*.

The L. adj. has two primary etymological meanings: (1) with passive force of the suffix, that a person or thing can stand upon, firm as a support or foundation; (2) actively, able to stand, not liable to fall, secure; also (esp. of persons) standing one's ground, not to be driven back, steadfast. In figurative uses these senses are often blended. The Eng. word has most of the meanings of the Latin.]

1. a. Able to remain erect; secure against falling or being overthrown.

a **1300** *Cursor M.* 10121 Do me to passe þe dikes ouer, þar þe castel standes stable [*v.r.* stabil, stabul]. *a* **1591** H. Smith *Serm.* (1637) 268 He which is tottering himselfe, had neede leane unto a stable thing. **1872** Blackie *Lays Highl.* 76 The master-builder-bold Who reared this stable pile. **1909** C. C. Turner *Aerial Navig. of To-day* viii. (1910) 123 The bicycle is not stable. It depends upon motion and the manipulation of the handles.

fig. **1599** Davies *Nosce Teipsum* viii. xxxvii. (1714) 58 The perfect Angels were not stable, But had a Fall more desperate than we. **1869** McLaren *Serm.* Ser. ii. vii. 120 If we are to be stable amidst earthquakes and storms, we must be built on the Rock and build rock-like upon it.

Comb. **1725** Armstrong *Imit. Shaks.* 185 That rock the stable-planted towers.

b. Of a support or foundation: Firm, not likely to give way. *lit.* and *fig.*

1340–70 *Alex. & Dind.* 587 ȝe were alle..bred of þat modur þat is stable to stonde..And þe erþe is called. **1604** Earl Stirling *Aurora* Song iii. D 1, Hauing followed ore the stable ground. **1788** Priestley *Lect. Hist.* v. xlix. 364 The only stable foundation of most of the improvements in social life is Agriculture. **1801** Strutt *Sports & P.* iii. i. 126 The ground within hard, stable, and level. **1811** Pinkerton *Petral.* II. 338 Such pieces of scoriæ as..were capable of affording a stable support. **1820** Scoresby *Acc. Arctic Reg.* I. 256 It often affords a stable mooring to a ship. **1845** Darwin *Voy. Nat.* viii. (1879) 144 A government which as yet has never rested on any stable foundation. **1871** Blackie *Four Phases Morals* i. 24 A stable physical platform to stand on.

c. Firm in consistency, solid. Now *rare.*

1666 Boyle *Orig. Formes & Qual.* 76 The Texture, is.. vnlesse it be very stable and permanent,..very much alter'd. *Ibid.* 422 Alterations..mixtures can perform among Bodies, both of them fluid, as well as among those that were either both of them stable, or one of them stable and the other consistent. **1691** Ray *Creation* i. (1704) 70 Providence hath given to the solid and stable parts a two-fold Power. **1878** Stevenson *Inland Voy.* 103 The shadows lay as solid on the swift surface of the stream as on the stable meadows.

2. Stationary, keeping to one place.

†**a.** of persons or their dwellings. *Obs.*

a **1300** *Cursor M.* 15154 Iesus þam prechand ilk a dai Stable in temple stod. **13..** *E.E. Allit. P.* A. 597 He þat stod þe long day stable. **1422** Yonge tr. *Secreta Secret.* 215 Sum of the hoste shall stabill bene in oone Place. **1687** P. Ayres *Lyric Poems*, '*Spring*' (1906) 311 The stable mother [the sea] of those straggling sons [the rivers]. **1775** R. Chandler *Trav. Asia M.* (1825) I. 136 A people..not forming villages or towns with stable habitations, but flitting from place to place.

b. Of material things: Not shifting or fluctuating in position.

1853 Kane *Grinnell Exp.* xxxviii. (1856) 353 Some seventy miles from the nearest stable ice. **1861** Buckle *Civiliz.* II. vii. 368 The surface of our planet, even where it appears perfectly stable is constantly undergoing most extensive changes. **1862** Dana *Man. Geol.* 390 It, however, did not reach north to the Azoic of New York, which was still a portion of the stable part of the continent.

3. a. Of a material thing or its condition: Able to maintain its place or position; presenting resistance to displacement; not easily shaken or dislodged. ***stable equilibrium***: see EQUILIBRIUM 1.

1560 Bible (Geneva) *1 Chron.* xvi. 30 Surely the worlde shal be stable and not moue. **1829** *Nat. Philos., Mechanics* i. iv. 18 (U.K.S.) Of these two positions in which it is possible for the body to rest, the former is called instable, and the latter stable, equilibrium. **1871** B. Stewart *Heat* 45 That the particles may have time to assume their most stable position. **1889** Welch *Text Bk. Naval Archit.* ii. 19 If a ship when slightly inclined in any particular direction from her position of rest returns towards that position when the inclining forces are removed, it is said to be in stable equilibrium.

b. Of a system of bodies: Having a permanent structure or constitution; not liable to disintegration.

1839 Moseley *Astron.* lxxvii. (1854) 216 The system of Planets is stable, the System of Comets is unstable. **1845** Whewell *Indic. Creator* 52 The state of the solar system is stable.

c. Of a chemical compound or combination: Not at once decomposing.

stable dextrin: the fifth or remaining amylin group after the other four amylin groups in starch have been split off by the action of diastene.

1850 Daubeny *Atom. Theory* vii. (ed. 2) 190 These compounds are..much less stable, being decomposed by very slight causes. **1862** Spencer *First Princ.* ii. xiii. §101 (1875) 293 Stable compounds contain comparatively little molecular motion. **1900** *Jrnl. Soc. Dyers* XVI. 6 Causing the indigo white to separate out in a stable condition.

d. *Nucl. Physics.* Of an isotope: not subject to spontaneous radio-active decay, or decaying only very slowly.

1904 F. Soddy *Radio-Activity* viii. 126 The elements known to the chemist are stable *because* they exist and have survived. **1924** O. Lodge *Atoms & Rays* ii. 30 Even uranium is not quite stable... The element with 82 active pairs [of electrons] would be fairly or perhaps quite stable, and would be indistinguishable from lead. **1942** J. D. Stranathan '*Particles*' *of Mod. Physics* v. 167 Those elements with the greatest number of stable isotopes are Sn with 10 and Xe with 9. **1956** *Nature* 28 Jan. 159/2 Long-lived aluminium-26 may easily be confused with the stable aluminium-27 as product nucleus. **1977** J. L. Harper *Population Biol. of Plants* xi. 365 Small amounts of ^{15}N, a stable isotope, had been applied to the soil.

4. Not liable to fail or vary.

a. Of government, institutions, customs, etc.: Securely established; not liable to destruction or essential change. Often with fig. notion of 1.

c **1290** *St. Oswold* 5 in *S. Eng. Leg.* 45 For he was king are cristindom puyrliche stable were. **1390** Gower *Conf.* III. 233 Thei [pity and justice]..ben of vertu most vailable To make a kinges regne stable. *c* **1520** Nisbet *N.T., Epist. O. Test.* (S.T.S.) III. 277 And thar salbe na mark nor na terme of his kingdom, and he sal mak it stabile in the wed of beleue. **1574** *Mirr. Mag.*, *Albanact* lvi, But..as no state can stable stande for aye. *c* **1610** *Women Saints* 37 It was thought that this new kingdome would not be stable and firme for long continuance, vnlesse they had wiues of their owne nation. **1849–50** Alison *Hist. Europe* I. iv. §18. 446 Men..deemed present institutions stable, because they had never seen them shaken. **1856** Froude *Hist. Eng.* (1858) I. v. 412 His kingdom demanded the security of a stable succession. **1911** Seligmann *Veddas* i. 25 Vijaya found some sort of stable political organization on his arrival in the island [of Ceylon].

†**b.** Of a law, covenant, promise, etc.: Firm, not to be repealed or retracted. Phrases, ***to hold*** (something) ***stable***, ***to stand stable***. *Obs.*

1297 R. Glouc. (Rolls) 6430 Þis word was iholde stable & iloked uor dom. *c* **1386** Chaucer *Clerk's T.* 663 But now I woot youre lust and what ye wolde Al youre plesance ferme and stable I holde. *c* **1450** *Godstow Reg.* 31 Holdynge ferme & stable what euyr he wolde do ther-with, & neuyr to haue more clayme, ne eny of hys eyrys, for euyr-more. **1464** *Rolls of Parlt.* V. 529/2 That almaner Yeftes and Grauntes.. made, stand ferme and stable. **1474** Caxton *Chesse* ii. i. (1883) 21 Therfore hym ought to saye no thynge but yf hit were veritable and stable. **1533** *City Lond. Let. Bk.* O lf. 213 in *Vicary's Anat.* (1888) App. xiv. 264 This present graunte ..shall..be contynewed ferme and stable as concernyng the sayde Barbour-surgeons. **1543–4** *Act 35 Hen. VIII*, c. 9 The which order..shall stande firme and stable, and for a full determinate order. **1759** in *Nairne Peerage Evid.* (1874) 65 All which I oblige me to hold firm and stable without revocation.

†**c.** Of faith, resolve, love, friendship, etc.: Not changing, constant. *Obs.*

a **1300** *Cursor M.* 26158 We hope he sal haue for-giuenes, For þe trouth and stabil fai þat he was in in his last dai. *c* **1340** Hampole *Prose Treat.* 7 And for-thy I had na stabyll purpos in gude, na perfite contrycyone. **1402** Hoccleve *Let. Cupid* 447 In womman regneth stable constance. *c* **1450** *Mirk's Festial* 74 Full contricion wyth schryft, full charite wythout feynyng, and stabull fayth wythout flateryng. **1549–62** Sternhold & H. *Ps.* li. 10 (2nd vers.) Within my bowels Lord, renue a stable sprite. **1568** Grafton *Chron.* II. 484 There shal be from henceforward..stable friendship, betwene the same realmes. *c* **1610** *Women Saints* 51 An husband immortall, whose death may not grieue me, and whose loue shall be constant and stable.

†**d.** Of counsel, judgement, intellect: Trustworthy, sound. *Obs.*

1297 R. Glouc. (Rolls) 1245, & as he & is conseil stable conseil nome þe lettres he sende to Iuli þe emperour of rome. *Ibid.* 11489. *c* **1400** *Destr. Troy* 1423 Yche wegh þat is wise & of wit stable. **1477** Norton *Ordin. Alch.* i. in Ashm. (1652) 14 For his Trewth, Vertue, and for his stable Witt.

e. Of a doctrine, theory, conclusion: Securely established, not likely to be disproved or found wanting.

1480 Caxton *Myrr.* i. xiii. 42 Thus ben not the sciences muable but alleway ben estable and trewe. **1862** Ruskin *Unto this Last* Pref., It was..the first object of these papers to give an accurate and stable definition of wealth. **1891** *Hardwicke's Sci. Gossip* XXVII. 73/1 Even if with further research it led to no good and stable result.

†**f.** Permanent; of durable nature or quality.

a **1300** *Cursor M.* 26770 Bot þat þi stabil pes mai last To crist þou hald þi penance fast. *c* **1400** tr. *Secreta Secret.*, *Gov. Lordsh.* 57 Gete þe stabyl richesse, a lyf þat may noght be chaungyd, a kyngdome ay lastand dilatable. *Ibid.* 62 Brekand allyance stabyl ffor welfare and profyt of men. **1617** Moryson *Itin.* iii. 113 They bestow their money in stable things, to serve their posteritie. *c* **1645** HOWELL *Lett.* (1655) I. IV. vii. 172, I am not setled yet in any stable condition, but I lie Windbound at the Cape of Good Hope. **1660** STANLEY *Hist. Philos.* (1701) XIII. 615/1 Some pertain..to..the pleasure which consists in motion; others to felicity itself, (as that of indolence and tranquility or stable pleasure). **1683** SNAPE *Anat. Horse* (1686) App. I. i. 11 At the end of the fourth day, the Stalk tending upwards, (the outer or Sheath-leaf being loosened) puts forth the Stable-leaf [L. *folium stabile*] that is green and folded. **1742** YOUNG *Nt. Th.* I. 168 How I dreamt Of stable pleasures on the tossing wave?

†**g.** Of a language: Having fixed meanings. *Obs. rare.*

1679 DRYDEN *Troilus & Cr.* Ep. Ded., I am often put to a stand..And have no other way to clear my doubts, but by translating my English into Latine, and thereby trying what sence the words will bear in a more stable language.

†**h.** *Math.* = CONSTANT *a.* 5. *Obs.*

1727–41 CHAMBERS *Cycl.* s.v. *Calculus*, Stable Quantities being always express'd by the first Letters of the alphabet.

i. Of properties, movements, agencies, etc.: Persisting without essential or permanent change of character.

1742 HUME *Ess. & Treat.* (1777) I. 115 When the event is supposed to proceed from certain and stable causes. **1878** TAIT & STEWART *Unseen Univ.* vi. §179. 182 Two kinds, one of which makes use of the stable forces of nature and the other of the unstable. **1884** tr. *Lotze's Logic* 32 In..metal where there is no difficulty in regarding the marks of colour, brilliancy, and hardness as stable properties of that which they describe.

j. Of animal or vegetable species: Unvarying.

1889 A. R. WALLACE *Darwinism* (1890) 42 Wild animals and plants, it is said, are usually stable.

†**5.** Of look or countenance: Steady, unabashed.

c **1440** *Generydes* 1988 Beholdyng them with countenaunce right stabill. *c* **1475** *Babees Bk.* 65 And yf they speke withe yow at youre komynge, Withe stable Eye loke vpone theym Rihte. **1635** R. N. tr. *Camden's Hist. Eliz.* III. 329 The Queene of Scots..with a stable and stedfast countenance..gave thanks to God.

6. Of persons and their dispositions.

a. Steadfast in purpose or resolution; settled in character, not fickle, changeable, or frivolous. In early use also, †Trustworthy, sound in counsel or judgement. Phrase, † ***to stand stable***.

a **1275** *Prov. Alfred* 673 in *O.E. Misc.*, Ac nim þe to þe a stable mon, þat word and dede bi-sette con. *c* **1290** *Beket* 240 in *S. Eng. Leg.* 113 Of þe Ercedekne Thomas, Men tolden him sone i-nouȝ, hov he was stable Man and wis, and to alle guodnesse drouȝ. **1362** LANGL. *P. Pl.* A. x. 110 Hold þe stable and studefast And strengþe þi-seluen. **1398** TREVISA *Barth. De P.R.* VI. xii. (1495) 196 Men ben more wyse and wytty, more stedfaste and stable than wymmen. *c* **1400** *Rule St. Benet, Ord. Nuns* 142 To þam þat..standis stabill in-to þe purpose þat þa be-gane, it is [etc.]. *c* **1450** HOLLAND *Howlat* 174 Stable and steidfast, tender and trewe. **1500** *Ortus Vocab., Continens*, stable or chaste. **1500–20** DUNBAR *Poems* xx. 43 Hald God thy freind, evir stabill be him stand. **1526** *Pilgr. Perf.* (W. de W. 1531) 86 b, Let vs be stable and neuer loke backwarde agayne to the worlde. **1588** A. KING tr. *Canisius Catech.* 46 It is the Apostolicke doctrine, to stand firme, and stabill in ye traditions also quhilk ar nocht within.

†**b.** const. *of*, *in* (thoughts, purposes, words, etc.): cf. senses 4 c, 4 d. *Obs.*

c **1290** *St. Michael* 675 in *S. Eng. Leg.* 319 Ho so hath of þe eorþe mest he is slouȝ ase þe Asse,..Sone old and nouȝt willesfol stable and studefast of mod. *c* **1320** *Cast. Love* 384 þou art also so trewe a kyng, And stable of þouȝt in alle þyng. *a* **1375** *Joseph Arim.* 245 Bote beo ȝe stable in oure fei and foloweþ vre werkes. *c* **1400** MAUNDEV. (Roxb.) xxxi. 139 All gude Cristen men, þat er stable in þe faith, may ga in to þat valay. *c* **1400** *Destr. Troy* 10654 Ector..was stithist of stoure, stabill of hert. *c* **1477** CAXTON *Jason* 97 Considering the..promesse that he had made with Medea [Jason] abode ferme and stable in his firste purpoos. *c* **1500** *Lancelot* 1671 And of thi wordis beis trew and stable. **1552** *Bk. Com. Prayer, Ordering of Deacons*, Continuing euer stable and strong in thy sonne Christe. **1678** BUNYAN *Pilgr.* I. 34 Things to make me stable In what I have began to take in hand.

†**c.** Constant in affection. Const. *to*. *Obs.*

13.. *Cato* 214 in *Minor Poems fr. Vernon MS.* 570 Hose feyneþ him frend with word And not wiþ herte stable. *c* **1374** CHAUCER *Compl. Mars* 281 Ye, my ladyes, that ben true and stable. *c* **1386** —— *Clerk's T.* 931 And to hire housbonde euere meke and stable. **1390** GOWER *Conf.* II. 16 The god of love is favorable To hem that ben of love stable.

†**d.** In a bad sense: Persistent. *Obs.*

c **1440** *Promp. Parv.* 471/2 Stable, and a-bydyng yn malyce, *pervicax, pertinax*.

†**e.** Strong, capable of endurance. *Obs.*

a **1300** *Cursor M.* 13 His [*sc.* King Arthur's] knythes..Als wawan, cai, and other stabell. **13..** *Evang. Nicod.* 150 (MS. Harley) He bad þam tak men more myghty, Strang and stabyll of state. *c* **1430** LYDG. *Min. Poems* (Percy Soc.) 98 Holy Helyas..Made stronge in spirite fourty dayes went In his journay, the brede made hym so stable. *c* **1470** *Gol. & Gaw.* 741 Ane sterne knyght, stalwart and stabill.

†**f.** Of God or a deity: Unchangeable. *Obs.*

c **1385** CHAUCER *L.G.W.* 346 A god ne sholde nat be thus agreued But of hys deitee he shal be stable. *c* **1386** —— *Frankl. T.* 143 That semen rather a foul confusion Of werk than any fair creacion Of swich a parfit wys god and a stable. **1700** DRYDEN *Pal. & Arc.* III. 1046 He perfect, stable; but imperfect We, Subject to Change, and diff'rent in Degree.

†**stable**, *v.*[1] *Obs.* Also 3–4 stablen, 3–6 stabil, 3, 5–6 stabul, 4 stabil(l)e, 4–5 stabel, stabulle, 4–6 stabill, -yl, -yll(e, (stabelyn). [Variant of ESTABLE *v.*, a. OF. *establir*:—L. *stabilīre*, f. *stabili-s* STABLE *a.* Cf. ESTABLISH, STABLISH *vbs.*]

1. a. *trans.* To make stable, in various senses; to strengthen, render firm or fixed; to render steadfast; to bring into a secure or permanent condition; to confirm, ratify.

a **1300** *Birth of Jesus* 110 in Horstm. *Alteng. Leg.* (1875) 70 (Ashm. MS.) Vche ȝer also ioachim to þe temple wende þre siþe, to stable [*v.r.* stablen] his biheste, ȝif god him eny sende. *a* **1300** *Cursor M.* 19262 Cristen kirc, þan it bigan, Yeit was it noght stablid [*Fairf.* stabeled] þan. **1338** R. BRUNNE *Chron.* (1725) 244 Wardeyns gode he sette, to stabille þe lond. *c* **1380** WYCLIF *Sel. Wks.* II. 178 þis bileve shulde stable men to stonde stifly in Goddis cause. *c* **1386** CHAUCER *Merch. T.* 1161 (Harl. MS. 1758) Till that your sight stablid [*v.rr.* y-stabled, I-stabled, ysatled] be a while Ther may full many a sight you be-gile. *a* **1400–50** *Bk. Curtasye* 169 in *Babees Bk.*, When þou ministers at þe heghe autere, With bothe hondes þou serue þo prest in fere, þe ton to stabulle þe toþer Lest þou fayle, my dere broþer. *c* **1400** *Beryn* 1976 Sith I the fynde in suche plyte, our bargain for to stabill, Wee woll tofore þe Steward, þere we both shull have riȝte. *c* **1400** LOVE *Bonavent. Mirr.* (1907) 212 In feithe also he enformed hem and stabled hem more perfitely in byleue of his godhede. *c* **1440** *Promp. Parv.* 471/2 S(t)abelyn, or make stable and stede..*stabilio, solido*. *c* **1450** *Myrr. our Ladye* 297 Forsothe god hathe stabeled the erthe whiche shall not be meued. *c* **1485** *Digby Myst.* (1882) II. 569 Stabyll your syghtes, and look ye not stunt. **1501–2** *Acc. Ld. High Treas. Scot.* II. 140 To David Grame, to pas to Glasgo to stabill his procuratouris and to mak his expens on his pley, lvj s. **1538** STARKEY *England* I. ii. 42 Man, stablyd and confyrmyd wyth perfayt and sure hope. **1545** RAYNALD *Byrth Mankynde* 148 To stable & stedfast the teathe and to kepe the gumms in good case.

b. To base or ground (an argument, etc.) *upon*.

1521 FISHER *Serm. agst. Luther* i. Wks. (1876) 313, The fyrst .iij. instruccyons..shall vndermyne .iij. great groundes wher vpon Martyn doth stable in maner all his articles.

2. To put or set up in a certain position or place, or in a safe or firm place. *to stable up*: to collect and place; *pass.* to have taken one's stand.

a **1300** *Cursor M.* 24628 Fra me ne wald þai na wight tuin, Til i com til mi cosin in, þar stabild þai mi stall. *c* **1375** *Sc. Leg. Saints* xliv. (*Lucy*) 163 My patrimone haf I stablit in sa sekire place quhare foule corrupcion neuir ves. *a* **1400–50** *Wars Alex* 1091 May þou oȝt, lede, þe ȝonder lawe lyft on þi schulder, And stire it oute of þe stede & stable in a-nothire? *Ibid.* 1367 To stable vp a grete strenthe all on store schipis, Hugir be þe halfe dele & hiȝere þan þe toþire. *c* **1475** *Hunting Hare* 109 When that ye bin stabult up, I wylle ryde and putt her [the hare] vp.

3. To ordain permanently, establish, fix, institute; to appoint, settle.

a **1300** *Cursor M.* 25429 þou þat has þis werld all wroght, And stabuld it in skill. **1303** R. BRUNNE *Handl. Synne* 1604 þys [sixth] comaundment ys of prys, For hyt was stabled yn paradys. **1389** in *Eng. Gilds* (1870) 54 In septembre yis fraternite is funded & stabeled. **1423** *City Lond. Cal. Let. Bk. I* (1909) 294 It is ordeyned and stabled that payement be made anon upon such purveaunce made. **1516** in *Eng. Gilds* (1870) 328 Be hit [the ordinance] ordeynyd and stablyd, by þe M. and Wardens. **1538** STARKEY *England* I. i. 16 The same law..ys so stablyd and set, that [etc.]. **1538** ELYOT *Dict.*, *Statuo*, to ordayne, to determyne, to set faste, to stable a thinge.

4. a. To establish, install or secure in a possession, office, or dignity, etc.

1300–1400 R. GLOUC. (Rolls) App. xx. 400 þis king duc henri to sone þo nom & stablede him þer his eir of þis kingdom. *a* **1340** HAMPOLE *Ps.* ii. 6, I am stabild kynge [Vulg. *constitutus sum rex*]. **1473** *Rental Bk. Cupar-Angus* (1879) I. 190 Gif he thinks he ma do better to stabil hym in othir placis. **1513** DOUGLAS *Æneis* v. xii. 182 Ane hallowit schaw..as sanctuar, Plantit thai haif, and stabillit preistis thair.

b. To secure *to* (a person, or oneself).

1536 BELLENDEN *Cron. Scot.* III. vii. (1821) I. 87 This Guiderius, seing the realme stabillit to him, thocht hevy, that the Britonis suld leif under servitude of Romanis. *Ibid.* VI. xvii. 238 We mon othir be vincust..or ellis to be victouris, and stabill oure landis to us with glore, honoure, and permanent eis.

5. ? To hold fast.

c **1440** *York Myst.* xxiii. 187 Sir, oure strength myght not stabill tham stille. *a* **1593** MARLOWE *Ovid's Elegies* I. ix. 39 Mars in the deed the black-smithes net did stable.

6. *intr.* **a.** To come to a stand, cease from action; to refrain (from tears).

1377 LANGL. *P. Pl.* B. I. 120 Til god of his goodnesse gan stable [*v.r.* stablisse] and stynte. *c* **1400** *Destr. Troy* 3386 Who might stithly absteyne, or stable of teris, þat prestly were pricket with paynes so fele?

b. To become stable.

1399 LANGL. *Rich. Redeles* I. 10 Of alegeaunce now lerneth a lesson oþer tweyne Wher-by it standith and stablithe moste—By drede, or by dyntis or domes vntrewe [etc.]. *Ibid.* III. 249 Iche rewme vndir roff of þe reyne-bowe Sholde stable and stonde be þese þre degres.

stable ('steɪb(ə)l), *v.*[2] Also 5 stabel, 5–6 stabil, (6 stabble). [f. STABLE *sb.*[1] Cf. OF. *establer* (perh. the source); also L. *stabulāre*, *-ārī* intr.]

1. *trans.* To put (a horse) into a stable, or into a place which is used as a stable. Formerly also with *up* (rare). Also *transf.*

13.. *Coer de L.* 6770 At the gate he sette porters, And stablede up hys destrers. *c* **1380** *Sir Ferumb.* 3753 Wan þay had mad fast aboute & y-stablyd þe stede. **1475** *Bk. Noblesse* (Roxb.) 75 He on a tyme..stabled his hors in Salamon is Temple. **1513** DOUGLAS *Æneis* VI. iv. 102 The Centawris wer stabillit at this port. **1557** TUSSER 100 *Points Husb.* xxxviii, When pasture is gone,..then stable thy plough horse. **1598** SYLVESTER *Du Bartas* II. ii. IV. *Columnes* 461 Stabbling Thy smoaking Coursers under th' Earth, to bait. **1601** HOLLAND *Pliny* VIII. xliii. I. 223 Wheresoever they [asses] bee stabled, they love to lie at large and have roume ynough. **1688** CLAYTON in *Phil. Trans.* XVIII. 121 They never Shoe them, nor Stable them in general. *a* **1791** *Lochmaben Harper* iv. in Child *Ballads* IV. 18/2 Gae stable up the harper's mare. **1820** SCOTT *Monast.* xiv, Art thou there, old Truepenny? here, stable me these steeds, and see them well bedded. **1849** MACAULAY *Hist. Eng.* iii. I. 293 A third could never go into his parish church without being reminded..that Oliver's redcoats had once stabled their horses there. **1890** 'R. BOLDREWOOD' *Col. Reformer* (1891) 117 As soon as I have stabled the horses.

transf. *c* **1957–8** E. M. FORSTER *Life to Come* (1972) 175 British officers are never stabled with dagoes, never, it was too damn awkward for words. **1962** *Daily Tel.* 8 Jan. 15/7 The possibility of 'stabling' Underground trains in the tunnels instead of in the open at depots during periods of severe icy weather..unfortunately is unworkable.

b. Of a building: To afford stabling for.

1903 TALLENTYRE *Voltaire* xxxii. (1905) 338 An immense barn which stabled fifty cows and their calves.

2. *intr.* Of an animal: To live in a stable.

1508 *Extracts Burgh Rec. Edin.* (1869) I. 117 With.. sufficient lokkis..for thair duris, for the sure keping of the hors that stabillis with thame. **1601** HOLLAND *Pliny* IV. xi. I. 78 There, stood the towne Tinda, terrible for the horses of Diomedes that stabled there. **1878** BOSW. SMITH *Carthage* xxi. 423 The domestic animals of the Arabs are found stabling in the very buildings which may once, perhaps, have sheltered the Carthaginian Elephants.

b. *transf.* To live as in a stable.

1651 N. BACON *Disc. Govt. Eng.* II. xxx. 239 Forgetting their ancient yoke fellows the rural Presbyters, they stable with the King. **1667** MILTON *P.L.* XI. 748 In thir Palaces.. Sea-monsters whelp'd And stabl'd. **1774** J. BRYANT *Mythol.* I. 470 All the monsters of the sea stabled in the cavities at the foot the mountain. **1817** SHELLEY *Revolt Islam* II. iv, Tyrants dwelt side by side, And stabled in our homes. **1909** R. BRIDGES *Ibant obscuri* Poet. Wks. (1913) 449 [*Æneid* VI. 286] And many strange creatures of monstrous form and features Stable about th' entrance.

†**3.** To turn into a stable. *Obs. rare*[−1].

1649 J. TAYLOR (Water P.) *Wand. West* 19 Exeter..is a faire sweete City, a goodly Cathedrall Church (not yet quite spoyled or stabled).

†'**stable**, *v.*[3] *Obs.* [Perh. f. STABLE *a.* (in sense 2, stationary); but cf. the later STABBLE *v.*, which has some affinity of sense.] *passive* and *refl.* To stick fast in the mud. Also *fig.* *Obs.*

In quot. 1640 app. associated with STABLE *v.*[2]

1569 CAMPTON *Hist. Irel.* II. ix. (1633) 113 This is a doughty kinde of accusation, which they urge against mee, wherein they are stabled and myred at my first denyall. **1598** FLORIO *Dict.* Ep. Ded. 2, I many times in many words haue beene so stal'd and stabled. **1627** DRAYTON *Moon-calf*, *Batt. Agincourt*, etc. 184 They..In the stiffe mud are quickly stabled fast. **1629** GAULE *Holy Madn.* 196 Thoul't either jade, or stable thyselfe. **1640** E. DACRES tr. *Machiavelli's Prince* 268 The bottom proving rotten and miry, some of the Horse came over and over on their riders, and many stuck so fast in the mud that they were there stabled.

stable, obs. form of STAPLE.

stable, variant of STABLY *sb.* *Obs.*

†'**stabled**, *ppl. a.*[1] *Obs.* [f. STABLE *v.*[1] + -ED[1].] In senses of the verb.

c **1400** *Secreta Secret., Gov. Lordsh.* 66 Wete also þat stablyd planetys vnmooable ar a þousand twenty and nyne. *c* **1449** PECOCK *Repr.* II. iv. 156 For noon such fonnys opinioun..is eny long bifore stabilid gouernaunce to be left and to be leid aside. **1568** T. HOWELL *Arb. Amitie* (1879) 25 Then manhood makth a stabled minde, none youthly prancks we haue.

stabled ('steɪb(ə)ld), *ppl. a.*[2] [f. STABLE *sb.* or *v.*[2] + -ED.] Put into a stable, sheltered in a stable. Also *transf.*

1634 MILTON *Comus* 534 He and his monstrous rout are heard to howl Like stabl'd wolves. **1837** CARLYLE *Fr. Rev.* II. IV. iii, Motionless, as the brave stabled steed when conflagration rises. **1962** *Daily Tel.* 8 Jan. 15/8 No passenger service could start until the last stabled train had left.

stable door. The door of a stable. Prov. ***to shut*** (***lock***, etc.) ***the stable door when the horse is stolen***, to take preventive measures too late.

13.. *Sir Beues* 2152 At stable dore to him ȝhe sede [etc.]. **1848** THACKERAY *Van. Fair* xxxii, Isidor watched the stable-door constantly.

1390 GOWER *Conf.* II. 32 For whan the grete Stiede Is stole, thanne he [Negligence] taketh hiede, And makth the stable dore fast. *c* **1450** *Lat. & Eng. Prov.* (MS. Douce 52) lf. 16 When þe hors is stole steke þe stabull dore. **1509** WATSON *Ship of Fools* xii. (1517) D iv, The foole..shytteth the stable doore whan the horse is stolen. **1523** SKELTON *Garl. Laurel* 1435 When the stede is stolyn, sparr the stable dur. **1719** DE FOE *Crusoe* II. (Globe) 387 It was only shutting the Stable Door after the Stead was stoln. **1887** D. C. MURRAY *Old Blazer's Hero* iv, To lock the stable-door when the mare is stolen.

stableful ('steɪb(ə)lfʊl). *rare.* [f. STABLE *sb.* + -FULL.] As much or as many as fills a stable.

1858 TROLLOPE *Dr. Thorne* v. (1859) 63 The stableful of horses which had belonged to himself.

†**stablehead.** *Obs. rare*[−1]. [f. STABLE *a.* + -HEAD.] Stability.

c **1380** WYCLIF *Sel. Wks.* I. 69 þere is more stabilhede in wordis þat ben seid of Crist.

†'**stablement.** *Obs.* Also 5 **stabilement, establement.** [a. OF. *establement*, f. *establir*: see STABLE *v.* and -MENT. Cf. L. *stabilimentum.*]
a. An ordinance, regulation: = ESTABLISHMENT. **b.** Something that establishes or supports.

c **1400** tr. *Secreta Secret., Gov. Lordsh.* 55 First soueraynly it fallys to a kynge þat he attempre hym with trewe stablements & lawes. **1423** *City Lond. Cal. Let. Bk. I* (1909) 290 And if ony..wolde take onything ageyn this stabilement, no man be bounden to obeye to him. *Ibid.* 291 If any fele him greved ageyn this establement. **1481** *Tully of Old Age* (Caxton) i. 1 b (R.), The life to come is the stablement and the propre house of myne undedly soule. *a* **1603** T. CARTWRIGHT *Confut. Rhem. N.T.* (1618) 554 The Church of Rome is the pillar and stablement of truth.

stableness ('steɪb(ə)lnɪs). Now *rare.* Also 4–5 **stablynesse,** 6 **stablynes.** [f. STABLE *a.* + -NESS.] The quality or condition of being stable: = STABILITY.

a **1300** *Cursor M.* 23541 Bot in þat mikel stabilnes [*v.r.* stablenes, stabulnes], Sal nan yerne be bot þat he es. *c* **1374** CHAUCER *Boeth.* IV. vi. 30 Al that moeveth in any manere, taketh his causes..of the stablenesse of the divyne thoght. *c* **1400** *Rule St. Benet* (Prose) lxii. 40 þe reule of stabilnes. **1421** HOCCLEVE *Compl.* 9 Stablenes in this worlde is there none; there is no thinge but chaunge and variaunce. **1561** T. HOBY tr. *Castiglione's Courtyer* III. (1577) O iv, I impute it to the surenesse and stablenesse of the woman, and wauering of the man. **1605** SHAKS. *Macb.* IV. iii. 92. **1646** P. BULKELEY *Gospel Covt.* v. 360 He grounds the truth and certainty of the promise upon the stablenesse of God's counsell. **1702** EARL OF MARCHMONT in *Lond. Gaz.* No. 3819/3 Her Stableness in, and Fidelity to, the Protestant Religion. **1909** *19th Cent.* Oct. 677 Disconcerting to our sense of stableness and identity.

stabler ('steɪblə(r)). Now *Sc.* Forms: 5 **stabyler, (stabyller),** 6 **stabulare, stabillar,** 7 **staibler.** [a. OF. *establier*, f. *estable*: see STABLE *sb.* and -ER². Cf. L. *stabulārius.*] A stable-keeper.

14.. *Nom.* in Wr.-Wülcker 684/41 *Hic stabularius*, a stabyler. **1483** *Cath. Angl.* 357/2 A Stabyller, *stabularius.* **1508** *Extracts Burgh Rec. Edin.* (1869) I. 117 That all stabulares within this burgh haif thair stabilles weill and sufficientlie furnist with hek [and] manyger. **1529** *Ibid.* (1871) II. 6 All maner of stabillar within this burgh. **1611** *Extracts Rec. Convent. Burghs Scot.* (1870) II. 317 His maiesteis lieges wer gritlie abusit be the staiblers. **1676** ROW *Contin. Blair's Autobiog.* ix. (1848) 147 A pursuivant calling to a stabler, to provide against tomorrow morning two horses. **1722** DE FOE *Col. Jack* (1840) 109 The stabler, so they call the people at Edinburgh that take in horses to keep. **1821** *Blackw. Mag.* IX. 331 The humble dwelling of a stabler in the Grassmarket. *a* **1864** HAWTHORNE *Amer. Note-bks.* (1879) II. 173 They appear to be busy men, these stablers.

†**stable-stand.** [f. *stable* var. STABLY *sb.* + STAND *v.*] See quot.

The word was conjecturally substituted by Hanmer (1744) for *stables* in *Winter's Tale* II. i. 134; the passage with Hanmer's reading is quoted by Johnson as Shakspere's.

1598 MANWOOD *Laws of Forest* xviii. §9. 114 b, By the Assises of the Forrest of Lancaster [*margin* Assisa forestæ de Lancast. fol. 63], Taken with the maner, is when one is found in the kings Forrest in any one of these 4. degrees, viz. Stable stand Dogge drawe Back Beare and Bloudy hand. Stable stande is, when a man is found in any Forrest at his standing, with a Crosse bowe bent, ready to shoote at any Deere, or, with a Long bow, or els, standing close by a tree with Greyhounds in his lease, ready to let slip.

†'**stablet.** *Obs.*$^{-0}$ [a. OF. *establete*, dim. of *étable*: see STABLE *sb.*¹ and -ET¹.] A small stable, stall, pen.

1585 HIGINS *Junius' Nomencl.* 191/2 Stabulum..Estable, a stablet, a stal: a place for fodder.

†'**stabling,** *vbl. sb.*¹ *Obs.* [f. STABLE *v.*¹ + -ING¹.] The action of STABLE *v.*¹

c **1380** WYCLIF *Wks.* (1880) 229 þei techen opynly for worschipe of god & profit of þe reume and stablynge of þe kyngis pouer & distroynge of synne. *c* **1449** PECOCK *Repr.* I. xvi. 91 The firme stabiling of al the chirche. **1538** STARKEY *England* II. iii. 209 So the confyrmyng and stablyng of thys celestyal doctryne stondyth chefely in the offycerys therof.

stabling ('steɪblɪŋ), *vbl. sb.*² [f. STABLE *v.*² (? and *sb.*) + -ING¹.] The action of placing or accommodating (horses) in a stable; stable accommodation; stable-buildings collectively.

1481–90 *Howard Househ. Bks.* (Roxb.) 322 Item. for the stabilling of iiij. cartes iiij.d. **1494** in Aungier *Syon* (1840) 79 Fyndynge..to theym..mete, drynke, horsmete, loggynge, stablenge, and all other thyngs necessary. **1586** *Exch. Rolls Scot.* XXI. 617 The expensis requisit to his hienes hous and stabling. **1683** CHAS. II in *Buccleuch MSS.* (Hist. MSS. Comm.) I. 339 For whom our Harbingers are to provide lodging and stabling near our Court. **1735** THOMSON *Liberty* III. 370 A Stabling now for Wolves. **1782** R. CUMBERLAND *Anecd. Emin. Painters* II. 171 His Majesty is now adding wings and a corps of stabling, which are far advanced. **1813** *Sporting Mag.* XLII. 53 A very beautiful engraving of the Stabling at Errol House. **1841** DICKENS *Barn. Rudge* x, You can give my horse good stabling, can you. **1850** THACKERAY *Pendennis* lxxv, Excellent stabling and loose boxes for horses at the 'Clavering Arms'. **1886** *Pall Mall Gaz.* 10 Apr. 5/2 The chapel, guard-room, entrance tower, and stablings. **1890** 'R. BOLDREWOOD' *Col. Reformer* (1891) 276 The long range of stabling at no inconvenient distance.

attrib. **1899** *Daily News* 23 June 8/5 Comfortable stabling quarters.

stablish ('stæblɪʃ), *v.* Now *arch.* Forms: 3–5 **stablis,** 4 **stablys, stablisce,** 4–5 **stablisse,** 4, 6 **stablische,** 4–6 **stablisshe,** 5 **stablice, -esshe, -ych, -ysh,** 5–6 **stablysche, -ysshe,** 6 **stablyshe, -ishe, (stablyszshe),** 8–9 **'stablish,** 4– **stablish;** also *pa. t.* and *pa. pple.* 3–4 **stablist,** 4 **stablyste** (*Sc.* **stabelaste**), 4, 6 **stabliste.** [Variant of ESTABLISH *v.*] = ESTABLISH *v.* in various senses.

From the 16th c there seems to have been a tendency to confine the use of the form *stablish* to those uses in which the relation of meaning to *stable* adj. is apparent, i.e. where the notion is rather 'to strengthen or support (something existing)' than 'to found or set up'. The modern currency of the word is purely literary, and reminiscent of the Bible or Prayer Book.

1. *trans.* To place or set (a material thing) firmly in position; to station (a person) in a place. *Obs.* exc. in figurative context.

a **1300** *Cursor M.* 21288 Tuin axils [of an allegorical 'wain'] er tuin laghs, i-wiss,..þe carter self is iesus crist, His bodi es yock he has stablist. *a* **1325** *Prose Ps.* xxx[i]. 10 Ne þou ne shettest me nouȝt in þe hondes of þyn enemy; þou stabliced my fete in large stede. *c* **1450** *Merlin* iii. 59 Ye shall stablisshe the thirde table in the name of the trinite. *c* **1500** *Melusine* i. 17 There the lady Pressyne stablysshed a stronge geaunt to the sauegarde of the tresoure. **1650** *Sc. Psalms* xciii. 5 The world is also stablished, that it can not depart. **1845** BAILEY *Festus* (ed. 2) 198 Heaven's eternal base, Whereon God's throne is stablished.

2. To set (a person, etc.) permanently in an office, dignity, or condition.

c **1375** *Sc. Leg. Saints* xii. (Mathias) 318 Spedful thinge vare & gud, þat we stablyste ane in þe place, þe quhyle to supple of Iudas. **1439** *Charters, etc. Edin.* (1871) 64 We..be thir present lettres makis, stablissis, and ordanis..schir Robert Logane..oure baileye off fee. **1470–85** MALORY *Arthur* III. xv. 118 The kyng stablysshed all his knyghtes and gaf them that were of londes not ryche he gaf them londes. **1483** CAXTON *G. de la Tour* h j b, God chose and stablysshed [*c* **1450** lxxxvii. 111 ordeyned] hym [Moses] mayster and gouournour ouer alle his people. **1738** WESLEY *Ps.* CXXXII. iv, I will thy faithful seed increase, And 'stablish them on David's Throne. **1805–6** CARY *Dante, Inf.* II. 24 Both which..were ordain'd And 'stablish'd for the holy place, where sits Who to great Peter's sacred chair succeeds.

†**3.** To ordain permanently (a law, rule, etc.)

c **1386** CHAUCER *Knt.'s T.* 2137 That same prince..Hath stablissed in this wrecched world adoun Certeyne dayes and duracioun [etc.]. **1387–8** T. USK *Test. Love* I. v. (Skeat) 58 Wiste thou not wel that al the lawe of kynde is my lawe, and by god ordayned and stablisshed to dure by kynde resoun? *c* **1417** HOCCLEVE *De Reg. Princ.* 2232 By sotilte Brekynge bondes þat stablisshed were Mankynde to profite. *a* **1483** *Liber Niger* in *Househ. Ord.* (1790) 18 Hardeknoute was the furst that began iiii meales stablysshed in oon day. **1530** PALSGR. 731/2, I stablysshe, I make by acte, *je actifie.* **1561** T. NORTON *Calvin's Inst.* Pref. A v b, This bound they forgot, when they stablished..so many maisterly determinations without any woord of God. **1615** SYLVESTER *Job Triumphant* III. 329 For the raine hee stablisht a Decree.

†**4.** To set up or found securely (a government, a condition of things). *Obs.*

1591 SHAKS. *1 Hen. VI*, v. i. 10 And stablish quietnesse on euery side. **1612** T. TAYLOR *Comm. Titus* iii. 1 We haue stablished the regal power ouer all persons Ecclesiastical as well as others. **1855** SINGLETON *Virgil* II. 493 In suchlike words between them stablished they [*firmabant*] The leagues amid the nobles' view.

†**5.** To bring into settled order (a country, affairs, etc.). *Obs.*

1375 BARBOUR *Bruce* x. 303 He wex so wiss and avise, That his land first weill stablist he. **1470–85** MALORY *Arthur* I. vii. 44 Whanne..the kyng had stablisshed alle the countreyes aboute london. **1600** E. BLOUNT tr. *Conestaggio* 221 He now laboured to stablish the affaires.

6. To render indubitable, support by proof or testimony.

a **1325** *MS. Rawl. B.* 520 lf. 57 ȝif he stablisseth him to be lasse he ne sal noȝt ansuerien of ani tenement for acheson of possession or of prosprete are he be of plener age. **1530** PALSGR. 731/2 What so ever he saye, I wyll stablysche it. **1550** CRANMER *Def. Bath. Doctr.* title-p., A confutation of sundry errors concernyng the same, grounded and stablished upon Goddes holy woorde. **1561** T. NORTON *Calvin's Inst.* IV. 50 That whatsoeuer they shal determine on the one side or the other, maye be stablished and certayne to our mindes. **1885–94** R. BRIDGES *Eros & Psyche* July x, It is true That much hath hapt to stablish what ye teach.

7. To make secure, strengthen, reinforce.

1382 WYCLIF *Rom.* iii. 31 Therefore distrye we the lawe by the feith? Fer be it; but we stablischen [Vulg. *statuimus*] the lawe. *a* **1513** FABYAN *Chron.* I. (1811) 11 When Brute..sawe that he was stablysshed in his Realme quyetly, he..commaundyd [etc.]. **1586** MARLOWE *1st Pt. Tamburl.* IV. iv. (*ad fin.*), When holy Fates Shall stablish me in strong Egyptia. **1600** FAIRFAX *Tasso* x. liii, My weake estate to stablish come thou art. **1611** BIBLE *1 Chron.* xviii. 3 As hee went to stablish his dominion. **1667** MILTON *P.L.* XII. 347 Remembring..his Cov'nant sworn To David, stablisht as the dayes of Heav'n. **1696** TATE & BRADY *Ps.* xciii. 2 How surely stablisht is thy Throne! **1810** SOUTHEY *Kehama* XVIII. vi, Over Earth and Heaven my reign Is stablish'd. **1869** M. ARNOLD *Cult. & An.* ii. 92 It is stablishing the State on behalf of whatever great changes are needed.

8. To render stable in faith, virtue, etc.

1447 BOKENAM *Seyntys, Christina* 77 In þis [*sc.* faith] me stablych, lorde, I þe preye. **1535** COVERDALE *Ps.* li. 12 O geue me the comforte of thy helpe agayne, and stablish me with thy fre sprete. **1568** GRAFTON *Chron.* II. 662 For he himselfe, whether he were past all feare, or was not well stablished in his perfite minde,..boldely entred into Englande. **1611** BIBLE *1 Thess.* iii. 13 To the end hee may stablish your hearts vnblameable in holinesse. **1738** WESLEY *Ps.* LI. xiii, Stablish, and keep my faithful Heart. **1784** COWPER *Task* II. 343 He stablishes the strong, restores the weak. **1841** EMERSON *Ess.* Ser. I. viii. (1876) 208 Let him go home much, and stablish himself in those courses he approves. **1862** TRENCH *Poems, Justin Martyr* 15, I thought to arm my soul, And stablish it in self control.

Hence **stablished** *ppl. a.*, †**stablishing** *vbl. sb.*

a **1300** *Cursor M.* 27151 Wit stablising of hali kirck. *a* **1470** TIPTOFT *Cæsar* v. xiii. (1530) 16 þ^t nyghtys were shorter there than they be in the stablysshed lande [*in continente*]. **1570** T. NORTON tr. *Nowell's Catech.* 2 b, All these thinges serue..to the orderly stablishyng of the outward gouernance of the Chirch. **1655** G. FIRMIN (*title*) Stablishing against Shaking, or a Discovery of the Prince of Darknesse. **1709** COBB *Poems* (ed. 2) 5 Whose bold Presumption dares transgress Thy stablish'd Articles of Peace, Or disobey thy Law? **1885** R. BRIDGES *Nero* III. iv. 16/2 Thou..yet would'st dare..to thwart My stablished purpose?

†'**stablisher.** *Obs. rare.* [f. STABLISH *v.* + -ER¹.] One who stablishes.

1535 COVERDALE *Heb.* vii. 22 Thus is Iesus become a stabliszher of so moch a better Testamente. **1545** BRINKLOW *Compl.* 12 b, Thow art a stablissher of wicked lawes.

stablishment ('stæblɪʃmənt). *arch.* [var. of ESTABLISHMENT. Cf. STABLISH *v.* and -MENT.]

1. The action of stablishing or establishing; the condition of being established.

1444 *Rolls of Parlt.* V. 75/2 For the perpetuell stablesshement of the same College. **1526** *Pilgr. Perf.* (W. de W. 1531) 133 b, So the stablysshmentes in vertue, & the delectacyons in good workes..ben the fruytes of the holy goost. **1617** HIERON *Penance for Sin* Wks. 1620 II. 268 'Stablish mee with Thy free Spirit'. Here two things:..First, the particularity of the fauour which Dauid craues, stablishment, confirmation in good. **1677** GALE *Crt. Gentiles* IV. I. iv. 144 Not to be punished for sin is the stablissement of Sin. *a* **1711** KEN *Hymns Festiv.* Poet. Wks. 1721 I. 338 May we..Thy sacred Truth embrace, With strength of Faith, and Stablishment in Grace. **1898** S. EVANS *Holy Graal* 103 Prayer to God that He would recover back the walls in such stablishment as they were aforetime.

b. Confirmed possession.

1606 SHAKS. *Ant. & Cl.* III. vi. 9 Vnto her He gaue the stablishment of Egypt.

†**2.** Something established, a statute, ordinance.

1387–8 T. USK *Test. Love* III. i. (Skeat) 132 Under whiche lawe..bothe..arn..bounden..as by knotte of loves statutes and stablissshment in kynde. **1473** *Rolls of Parlt.* VI. 83/1 Any other Acte, Statute, Stablisshement or Ordenaunce, made or to be made in this present Parlement.

3. A means of establishing or strengthening.

1533 MORE *Confut. Tindale* VII. Wks. 665/1 To thentent that his catholike church may be to euery man that wil learne therof & giue credence therunto as himself commaundeth eueri man to do, a very sure stablishment and a stronge pyller of trouthe.

†'**stablishness.** *Obs. rare*$^{-0}$. [f. STABLISH *v.* + -NESS.] Stability.

1530 PALSGR. 275/1 Stablysshnesse, *establetė.*

†'**stably,** *sb. Obs.* Also 4–5 **stable.** [a. AF. *establie* (latinized *stabilia, stabilea, stablea*: see G. J. Turner, *Sel. Pleas of Forest*, Gloss.), f. *establir* to station, ESTABLISH. Cf. med.L. *stabilitiones venationum* (Domesday Book).]

1. *Hunting.* A besetting of a wood with men, hounds in leash, nets, etc. for the purpose of taking deer, etc.

13.. *Gaw. & Gr. Knt.* 1153 Bot heterly þay were Restayed with þe stablye, þat stoutly ascryed. *c* **1400** *Master of Game* (MS. Digby 182) xxxv, And if þe sette be wyde, þe forseyd forster..shulde warne þe Sherefe of þe Shyre..forto ordeyne stable suffisaunte and kartes eke forto brynge þe deer þat shulde be slayne. *c* **1425** WYNTOUN *Chron.* VI. xvi. 1609 As he past..In til huntynge hym to play,..On his gamyn al thouchty, þe stable [*MS. Wemyss* staill] and þe setis set.

2. A stand, halt (of armed men).

c **1450** *Merlin* xxii. 386 And ffrolle the Duke of Almayne come oute after and made his stablie vpon a litill river that is cleped Aroaise.

†'**stably,** *a.*¹ *Obs. rare*$^{-1}$. [a. OF. *establi*, pa. pple. of *establir*: see STABLE, STABLISH, ESTABLE, ESTABLISH *vbs.*] = STABLE *a.*

13.. in *Herrig's Archiv* LXXIX. 448/10 They stoode with stably steven in mayntenance of Moises law.

stably ('steɪblɪ), *a.*² *rare.* Also **stabley.** [f. STABLE *sb.* + -Y.] Characteristic of, having to do with, or pertaining to a stable or stables. Also *Comb.*, as *stably-smelling* adj.

1851 E. WARD *Jrnl.* 20 June (1951) III. 196 Slept at Wortley's on the floor—rather stably. **1864** *All Year Round* 30 Jan. 539 The boots..belonged to short-haired stably gentlemen in large white overcoats. **1884** YATES *Recoll.* I. vii. 251 Fresh air..which..seemed to me to have a somewhat stably twang. **1930** J. DOS PASSOS *42nd Parallel* I. 12 The musty stably smelling herdic cab. **1968** E. MCGIRR *Lead-Lined Coffin* iii. 100 The next [shed] had been a stable years ago: there was still a faint stably whiff attached to it.

stably ('steɪblɪ), *adv.* Forms: 3–4 **stabliche,** 3, 5 **stabili,** 3–5 **stabeliche,** 4 **stab(e)li,** 4–5 **stabely, stabilly, stabilli,** 5 **stabelike, stabely, stabyly, stabully,** 6 **stabilie,** 4– **stably.** [f. STABLE *a.* + -LY².] In a stable manner, firmly, †steadfastly, †constantly.

1297 R. GLOUC. (Rolls) 2611 þe king..bed hom..þat hii hom vnderstode & stabeliche helde to gadere to sauy þat lond. *c* **1300** *Beket* (Percy Soc.) 2172 Ac bihet him stabliche [*Laud MS.* studefastliche] to stonde al at here rede. **1338** R. BRUNNE *Chron.* (1725) 126 þat Steuen..suld bere coroun & his gyft certeyn be holden stabilly. *c* **1380** WYCLIF *Wks.* (1880) 75 A man þat meyntenep goddis lawe paciently & stably. *c* **1400** *Rule St. Benet* (Prose) xlvii. 32 Sho þat þabbes cumandis þis office [of reading], wid mekenes sal sho do it, And stabelike wid-vten pride. *c* **1400** *Master of Game* (MS. Digby 182) xxvi, And if he se an herte stondynge stabely, he muste looke wele what cuntre he shall goo to his leyr. *c* **1440** *York Myst.* xvii. 140 So shall ȝe stabely vndirstande þer mynde and þer menyng. *a* **1450** *Le Morte Arth.* 2663 By-twene you for to make pees Stabully euer for to stonde. **1488** CAXTON *Chastysing Goddes Chyld.* xi. 28 He only beholdeth hymselfe and stondeth stably upon his owne propre wyll. **1563** *Homilies* II. *Rogation Week* I. 236 Consider the huge substaunce of the earth... Howe coulde it so stande stably in the place as it doth, yf [etc.]? **1695** LD. PRESTON *Boeth.* IV. 193 Those are such things as are stably fixed near to the Divinity. **1895** JAS. ORR in *Advance* (Chicago) 25 Apr. 1066/1 Rome, stably seated on her seven hills. **1907** *Times* 5 Feb. 3/5 The Dean..contends that the teaching..ought to be stably standardized.

staboy, *int. U.S. nonce-wd.* Also ste(e)boy. [f. *sta boy* (also *stu boy, stub-boy*): see *Amer. Dial. Notes* 1900–4 II. 347–8; cf. *hist-a-boy*, HIST *int.* 2.] An exclamation addressed to hounds. Also as *v. trans.*, to urge on (hounds) with the cry 'sta boy'; occas. as *sb.*

1844 [W. T. THOMPSON] *Maj. Jones's Courtship* 55 (Bartlett) 'There it is..Steboy; catch him!' says he [to the dog]. **1848** LOWELL *Biglow P.* Ser. I. *Pious Editor's Creed*, As ..feeder of certain theologic dogmas, which, when occasion offers, he unkennels with a *staboy*. **1850** LOWELL *Unhappy Lot Mr. Knott* 60 Like dogs let loose upon a bear, Ten emulous styles *staboyed* with care, The whole among them seemed to tear. **1884** A. A. PUTNAM *Ten Yrs. Police Judge* xii. 86 They stand off and say stee-boy to the constables, who are only too ready to dog the dog-law breakers.

stabu'larian, *a. nonce-wd.* [f. L. *stabulāri-us* (f. *stabul-um*) + -AN.] Belonging to a stable.

1829 *Sport. Mag.* XXIII. 289, I must listen for half an hour to stabularian sibilations before I sit down to my own steak.

†**'stabulate**, *v. Obs.*[−0] [f. L. *stabulāt-*, *stabulāre, -ārī*, f. *stabulum*: see STABLE *sb.*] *intr.* (See quot.)

1656 BLOUNT *Glossogr.*, *Stabulate*, to stand or be as Cattell in a Stable or Stall, to be housed as Beasts are, to keep or stall up ones self.

stabu'lation. *rare.* [ad. L. *stabulātiōnem*, f. *stabulāre, -ārī*: see prec.] †'A harbouring of beasts' (Cockeram 1623). (*obs.*). Also, manner of housing in a stable.

1892 *Baily's Mag.* Apr. 225 The bad habits and vices of the horse..are more or less common and frequent. And many of them are due to, or consequent upon, stabulation.

'stabulist. *rare*[−1]. [f. L. *stabul-um* STABLE *sb.* + -IST.] ? One learned in stable management.

1826 *Sport. Mag.* XVII. 388 No stabulist taketh ought from it, since all it proves is the necessity of riding well-bred hunters.

stac, obs. var. STACK *sb.*; obs. pa. t. of STEEK, STICK *vbs.*

†**sta'ccado**. *Obs.* Also 7–8 stacado. [Incorrectly ad. Sp. *estacada* (whence F. *estacade*, ESTACADE), f. *estaca*, of Teut. origin: see STAKE *sb.*] A palisade or fencing of strong stakes, a STOCKADE.

1612 SHELTON *Quix.* II. v. (1620) 94 He entred into the Fortresse of Chiualrie..by leaping ouer the Staccado like a robber and a thiefe. **1688** HOLME *Armoury* III. xvi. (Roxb.) 97/1 Palizados: of which there are two sorts, those for a wall which stand with their sharp ends forwards... These for a gate which stand with the points vpright... Some terme these stacados or pickados erected. *a* **1774** GOLDSM. *Hist. Greece* I. 287 Gylippus,..not able to return into the staccado, landed. **1777** WATSON *Philip II*, XIX. (1812) III. 12 This part of the work, called the stacados or estacados.

transf. **1707** *Lond. Gaz.* No. 4349/3 To fortifie the Harbour, by..making in the midst of it a Staccado of Six Men of War of between 70 and 80 Guns.

‖**staccato** (stak'kato, stə'kɑːtəʊ), *a.* (*adv.*, *sb.*) *Mus.* [It., pa. pple. of *staccare*, shortened form of *distaccare*: see DETACH *v.*] Detached, disconnected, *i.e.* with breaks between successive notes. Used *adj.* or *advb.* as a direction to a performer to render a passage in this style; also as *sb.*, a succession of disconnected notes. Also *transf.* in all these uses.

1724 *Explic. For. Wds. in Mus. Bks.*, *Staccato*, or *Stoccato*. See the word *Spiccato*. **1787** BECKFORD *Italy*, etc. (1834) II. 40 The monotonous staccato of the guitar. **1806** J. ODELL *Ess.* 146 A certain staccato utterance of the emphatic syllables. **1844** HOOD *More Hullah-baloo* 54 A van with iron bars to play *staccato*. **1877** MORLEY *Crit. Misc.* Ser. II. 397 Turn to a page of Macaulay, and wince under..its unlovely staccato. **1883** BLACK *Shandon Bells* xxx, The staccato remarks about the probability of another..war,..developed into..abuse of the foreign policy.

b. Path. ***staccato speech***, ***utterance***: see SCANNING *ppl. a.* 2.

1898 *Syd. Soc. Lex.*, *Staccato utterance*. The same as *Scanning utterance*. **1899** *Allbutt's Syst. Med.* VII. 144 The staccato speech.

Hence **sta'ccato**, *v. trans.* To play (a piece of music) in a staccato manner; **sta'ccatoed**, *ppl. a.*

1814 J. T. COLERIDGE in Ld. Coleridge *Story Devon. Ho.* xvi. (1905) 231 It is always as if one should staccato a slow and pathetic air. **1818** BUSBY *Gram. Mus.* 445 By the intervention of *staccatoed* notes or short rests. **1882** MRS. A. EDWARDES *Ballroom Repent.* I. 147 The exclamation comes in staccatoed accents from Mrs. Dormer.

stachybotryotoxicosis (stækɪˌbɒtrɪəʊ tɒksɪ'kəʊsɪs). *Vet. Sci.* [f. mod.L. *Stachybotrys* (A. C. J. Corda *Icones Fungorum* (1837) I. 21/1), generic name (f. Gr. *στάχυς* ear of corn + *βότρυς* cluster) + TOXICOSIS.] Toxicosis caused by toxins of the graminivorous fungus *Stachybotrys alternans*, affecting esp. horses and characterized by hæmorrhage and necrosis.

1945 V. G. DROBOTKO in *Amer. Rev. Soviet Med.* II. 238 *Stachybotryotoxicosis* is the name we have given to a new disease of horses, of unknown etiology, which appeared in the Ukraine several years ago. **1970** JUBB & KENNEDY *Path. Domestic Animals* (ed. 2) I. iv. 352/2 Stachybotryotoxicosis is caused by preformed toxins of *Stachybotrys alter[n]ans* (*atra*) growing on substances rich in cellulose. **1978** *Bio Systems* X. 193/1 A group of toxins..produced by various species of *Fusarium*, *Trichoderma*,..and other genera [of fungi] are implicated in a number of mycotoxicoses. Among these are alimentary toxic aleukia and stachybotryotoxicosis.

stachyose ('stækɪəʊz). *Chem.* [a. G. *stachyose* (Von Planta & Schulze 1890, in *Ber. d. Deut. Chem. Ges.* XXIII. 1693): see STACHYS and -OSE[2].] A tetrasaccharide first isolated from the Chinese artichoke, *Stachys affinis*, and found in a number of plants of this genus and in the seeds of most leguminous plants.

1890 *Jrnl. Chem. Soc.* LVIII. II. 1089 The carbohydrate, for which the authors propose the name *stachyose*, has a slightly sweet taste, and forms a neutral solution. **1937** *Thorpe's Dict. Appl. Chem.* (ed. 4) I. 497/1 The characteristic carbohydrate is stachyose, $C_{24}H_{42}O_{21}$, $4H_2O$, yielding on hydrolysis one molecule of glucose, one molecule of fructose, and two molecules of galactose from one molecule of the carbohydrate. **1977** *Jrnl. Nutrition* CVII. 1861/1 A 1:1 mixture of soybean flour and sucrose would contain 2% stachyose.

‖**stachys** ('steɪkɪs). [L. *stachys* (Pliny), a. Gr. *στάχυς* (Dioscorides), a transferred use of *στάχυς* ear of corn.

The plant called *stachys* by Pliny is described as resembling a leek, with longer and more numerous leaves, a yellowish colour, and an agreeable smell; used as an emmenagogue. The reason for the modern application of the name is obscure.]

†**a.** In early use app. a name for clown's woundwort, *Stachys palustris*. *Obs.* **b.** *Bot.* A genus of plants of the N.O. *Labiatæ*, of which there are two British species, *S. palustris* (see a.) and *S. sylvatica*, popularly hedge nettle. Also a plant of this genus. Cf. RABBIT'S EAR I.

1562 TURNER *Herbal* II. 146 Stachis is a little bushe lyke vnto hore hounde. **1682** WHELER *Journ. Greece* I. 52 A kind of small Stachys, with silver leaves. **1789** W. AITON *Hortus Kewensis* II. 300 Wood Stachys, or Hedge-nettle.. Fl[owers] July and August. **1882** *Garden* 28 Oct. 385/3 The only species of Stachys that can really be termed a garden plant. **1876** *Pall Mall Gaz.* 18 Oct. 4/1 These places are where the corn stachys has overspread the ground.

stacioner, -cioun, obs. ff. STATIONER, STATION.

stack (stæk), *sb.* Forms: 3, 6 stac, 3–7 stak, (4 stagge), 5 sstakke, 5–6 stakk, stake, 5–7 stacke, 6 stayke, 4– stack. [a. ON. *stakk-r* haystack (MSw. *stakker*, Sw. *stack*, Da. *stak*, Norw. dial. *stakk*):—OTeut. type **stakko-z*, prob.:—pre-Teut. **stogno-s*: cf. Russian *stog* haystack.]

1. a. A pile, heap or group of things, esp. such a pile or heap with its constituents arranged in an orderly fashion.

a **1300** *Havelok* 814 He..cast a panier on his bac, With fish giueled als a stac. *c* **1440** *Promp. Parv.* 471/2 Stacke, or heep, *agger*. Stacke, *acervus*. **1570** LEVINS *Manip.* 5/20 A stacke, *strues*. **1581** LAMBARDE *Eiren.* I. vii. (1588) 37 Not Loades, but Stackes of Statutes. **1596** NASHE *Saffron Walden* 40 A stack of salt fish. **1698** FRYER *Acc. E. India & P.* 341 An huddled Stack of Buildings expatiated into a large Square in the middle of the Area. **1724** *Ramsay's Tea-T. Misc.* (ed. 9) I. 76, I ha' a good ha' house, a barn and a byer, A stack afore the door. **1856** KANE *Arctic Expl.* II. xiii. 132 Stacks of jointed meat are piled upon the ice-foot. **1888** JACOBI *Printers' Vocab.* 131 *Stacks*, paper or printed work arranged in 'stacks'.

b. *fig.* A quantity, a 'pile'. Also in *pl.* and as *advb. ellipt.*, a pile of money. *colloq.* (orig. *U.S.*).

1870 'MARK TWAIN' in *Galaxy* Sept. 425/2 Never saw 'such a stack of them on one establishment'. **1892** —— *Amer. Claim* xxiv. 236 Stacks of money had been placed in bank [*sic*] for him and Hawkins by the Yankee. **1894** A. ROBERTSON *Nuggets* 64 His uncle had left him a stack of money. **1896** MRS. CAFFYN *Quaker Grandmother* 126 You're a stack of conventions. **1904** W. N. HARBEN *Georgians* xxiii. 222 My boy, I had stacks an' stacks of fun on that trip. **1919** WODEHOUSE *My Man Jeeves* 15 I'm a bit foggy as to what jute is, but..Mr. Worple had made quite an indecently large stack out of it. **1952** E. F. DAVIES *Illyrian Venture* vii. 127 Chesshire had stacks of letters from a girl friend and decided to read one a day for a month. **1968** B. HINES *Kestrel for Knave* (1972) 81 I'm not that bad, I'm no worse than stacks o' kids, but they just seem to get away with it. *Ibid.* 83 It's stacks better than roamin' t'streets doin' nowt.

c. ***to swear on a stack of Bibles*** (see quot. 1909). *U.S. colloq.*

1866 M. REID *Headless Horseman* II. lvii. 287 I'll sware it on the crass—or a whole stack av Bibles if yez say so. **1909** *Dialect Notes* III. 378 *Swear on a stack of Bibles* (*a mile high*), ..an exaggerated or emphatic form of oath. **1926** M. J. ATKINSON in J. F. Dobie *Rainbow in Morning* (1965) 82, I would not believe him if he swore to it on a stack of Bibles as high as his head. **1956** B. HOLIDAY *Lady sings Blues* (1973) ii. 24 Mom..swore on a stack of Bibles I was eighteen.

d. A set of shelving on which books are arranged for storage, esp. in a library (also *book-stack* s.v. BOOK *sb.* 19); hence, a part of a library designed for the storage of books, and to which access by readers may be restricted. Freq. *attrib.* and in *pl.*

1879 C. A. CUTTER in *Library Jrnl.* IV. 235 The new wing ..consists of a perfectly uniform series of book stacks arranged like a gridiron. **1884** *Harper's Mag.* Nov. 828/1 The stack-rooms, in which the body of the collection..is packed. **1900** *Library Jrnl.* Nov. 679/2 Electric signals are also a part of the apparatus, and convenient elevators for passengers and freight are provided in the book-stacks. **1910** A. E. BOSTWICK *Amer. Public Library* 284 The relation of reading room to stack must be such as to make these [carriers] easily operable. **1933** *Times* 9 Nov. 9/2 Before leaving the building they paused to visit one of the new two-tier book-stacks on the ground floor. **1946** *Library Quarterly* Apr. 128/2 It is a modern brick building, five stories high, and contains, in addition to the stack space, a small reading room. **1956** 'C. BLACKSTOCK' *Dewey Death* i. 5 There were some seven thousand books... Barbara spent most of her spare time in the history section, wandering from stack to stack. **1966** C. POTOK *Chosen* (1967) II. viii. 152 Its stacks were filled mostly with bound volumes of scholarly journals and pamphlets. **1980** *Cosmopolitan* Dec. 221/1, I located a promising title for my Proust researches. 'Not on the open shelves.' I would have to order it to be fetched for me from the stacks of the library.

e. *Aeronaut.* A series of aeroplanes circling at different altitudes and awaiting landing instructions.

1947 *Britannica Bk. of Year* 841/2 As the bottom plane lands, each member of the stack drops 1,000 ft. and a new plane can then be brought in on top. **1952** *Jrnl. R. Aeronaut. Soc.* LVI. 615/2 Once an aircraft was in a stack it was difficult to bring it forward. **1965** *Observer* 31 Oct. 1/1 He came in for a third attempt after circling for a further 40 minutes in the Watford 'stack'. **1976** L. DEIGHTON *Twinkle, twinkle, Little Spy* x. 94 We joined the stack..and circled to await landing permission.

f. In a computer or calculator, a set of registers or storage locations which store data in such a way that the most recently stored item is the first to be retrieved; also, a list of items so stored, a push-down list.

1960 E. W. DIJKSTRA in *Numerische Math.* II. 312 The basic concept of the method is the so-called stack. One uses a stack for storing a sequence of information units that increases and decreases at one end only. **1963** *Ann. Rev. Automatic Programming* IV. 183 A stack is merely an area of storage with an associated administrative quantity, the 'stack pointer', which controls the addressing of the stack. **1973** C. W. GEAR *Introd. Computer Sci.* viii. 359 We can choose a section of memory at execution time to store this stack. **1976** *Sci. Amer.* June 88/1 (Advt.), HP's special logic system with four-register stack almost completely eliminates the need to re-enter data.

2. A pile of grain in the sheaf, of hay, straw, fodder, etc., gathered into a circular or rectangular form, and usually with a sloping thatched top to protect it from the weather.

a **1300** *Cursor M.* 6760 If fire be kyndeld and ouertak Thoru feld, or corn, or mou, or stak. *c* **1330** R. BRUNNE *Chron. Wace* (Rolls) 14690 In eueses þey crepte, & in þe þakkes, & in hey & in corn stakkes. *c* **1400** *Brut* cxcii. 212 þe Sccottes sette in fire iij stackes of hey. **1426** LYDG. *De Guil. Pilgr.* 17475, I resemble vn-to that hound Wych lyggeth in a stak off hay, Groynynge al the longe day. *c* **1440** *Promp. Parv.* 471/2 Stacke, *arconius*. **1513** DOUGLAS *Æneis* II. viii. 108 The corne graingis, and standand stakkis off hay. **1546–7** *Test. Ebor.* VI. 254 The þese stacke that I have bought. **1608** WILLETT *Hexapla Exod.* 495 The corne reaped and gathered into shockes or stackes. **1632** MILTON *L'Allegro* 51 While the Cock..to the stack, or the Barn dore, Stoutly struts his Dames before. **1795** COWPER *Needless Alarm* 23 But corn was hous'd, and beans were in the stack. **1816** J. SMITH *Panorama Sci. & Art* II. 624 The stacks should not be thatched till they have had about a week or a fortnight to settle. **1867** J. HATTON *Tallants* xv, The big yellow stacks peered out amongst the trees.

3. a. A pile of sticks, faggots, firewood, poles, etc.

1390 *Earl Derby's Exped.* (Camden) 66/9 Pro j stak focalis. *c* **1460** *Brut* ccli. 507 This same yere also, on New-yere day, at Baynard castell, fill down A stakk of wod sodenly at afternone. **1523–34** FITZHERB. *Husb.* §131 Whan thou shalt bryng them home to make a stacke of them [faggots], set the nethermoste course vpon the endes. **1625** BACON *Ess.*, *Custom & Educ.* (Arb.) 369 The Indians (I meane the Sect of their Wise Men) lay Themselves quietly upon a Stacke of Wood, and so Sacrifice themselves by Fire. *a* **1693** *Urquhart's Rabelais* III. lii. 427 A..Stack of Timber. **1711** *MS. Sessions Roll Durham* Oct. 1 Duas Strigas Ericarum anglice Stacks of Whinns. **1811** A. T. THOMSON *Lond. Disp.* (1818) 300 The stacks are generally built on the slope of a hill, so that the tar is easily collected, and put into barrels. **1838** JAMES *Robber* I. vi, On the edge of the moor was a low shed and a stack of fern. **1854** RONALDS & RICHARDSON *Chem. Techn.* (ed. 2) I. 11 An ordinary stack or pile of American wood. **1886** *Manch. Exam.* 8 Jan. 6/2 The stacks of timber, which are in close proximity, being saved from destruction.

†**b.** A pyre or burial pile. *Obs.*

a **1547** SURREY *Æneis* IV. 866 She rusheth in, and clam vp, as distraught, The buriall stack.

c. A measure of volume for wood and coal, usually 4 cubic yds. (108 cubic feet).

1651 *Publ. Gen. Acts* 1326 Such..of the said Coals as have been, or usually are sold by the Stack, Ruck, Fathom, or other uncertain Denomination. **1674** BLOUNT *Glossogr.* (ed. 4), *Stack of Wood*, in Essex, is fourteen foot in length, three foot in heighth, and three in breadth. **1706** PHILLIPS (ed. Kersey), *Stack of Wood*, (among Husband-men) a pile of Wood 3 Foot long, as many broad, and 12 Foot high. **1733** W. ELLIS *Chiltern & Vale Farm.* 92 Twenty one Stack of Fire-wood Billet, nine Stack of Roots. **1858** SIMMONDS *Dict. Trade* s.v., A stack of wood is 108 cubic feet.

4. *Brickmaking.* = CLAMP *sb.*[3] 1.

1816 J. SMITH *Panorama Sci. & Art* I. 186 The stacks or clamps are built of the bricks themselves.

5. a. A number of chimneys, flues, or pipes, standing together in one group.

1667 PEPYS *Diary* 29 Nov., She..heard a noise in the great stack of chimnies that goes from Sir J. Minnes's through our house. **1746** HERVEY *Medit.* (1818) 26 A stack of chimneys may tumble into the street, and crush the un-wary passenger. **1823** P. NICHOLSON *Pract. Builder* 434 When walls contain a great number of flues, they are called stacks of chimnies. **1842** LOUDON *Suburban Hort.* 197 It occupied a smaller space in the centre of the floor, with a stack of flues rising over it. **1882** *Worc. Exhib. Catal.* III. 5 One coil-end for stack of 2-in. pipes.

b. A chimney of a house, factory, etc.; the chimney or funnel of a locomotive or steamship; also, = *stack-furnace*. Cf. STALK *sb.*[1]

1825 J. NICHOLSON *Oper. Mech.* 357 In smelting by the reverberatory-furnace..the flame passes over the hearth, and enters into an oblique chimney, which terminates in a perpendicular one, called a stack, of considerable height. **1908** MISS ROBINS *Come & Find Me* 294 The big yellow stack belched out clouds of smoke.

c. In *fig.* phr. *to blow one's stack* = *to blow one's top* s.v. BLOW *v.*[1] 24 i. *slang* (orig. *U.S.*).

1947 BERREY & VAN DEN BARK *Amer. Thes. Slang* Suppl. §48/1 *Blow one's stack*, to become angry or excited. **1952** R. BISSELL *Monongahela* 189 When Andrew [Carnegie] received the minutes and read them he blew his stack a mile high. **1965** F. KNEBEL *Night of Camp David* xi. 173 O'Malley looked startled. 'Well, he..he was goddam mad. Frankly, he blew his stack.' **1979** W. H. CANAWAY *Solid Gold Buddha* xxiv. 156, I ain't whingeing, honest... I'm sorry I blew me stack.

†**6.** A set (of corn mills). *Obs.*

1772 *Jackson's Oxf. Jrnl.* 24 Oct., To be let—A compleat Stack of Corn Mills.

7. [Cf. Færoese *stakkur* 'high solitary rock in the sea'.] A columnar mass of rock, detached by the agency of water and weather from the main part of a cliff, and rising precipitously out of the sea. Cf. *sea-stack* s.v. SEA *sb.* 23 a. orig. *dial.*

[**1701** J. BRAND *Descr. Orkney* etc. viii. (1883) 164 At a little distance from Papa Stour, lyes a Rock encompassed with the Sea called *Frau-a-Stack*, which is a Danish word, and signifieth, *our Ladys Rock*.] **1769** PENNANT *Tour Scot.* (1771) 152 Great insulated columns, called here Stacks. **1822** HIBBERT *Descr. Shetl. Isl.* 568 After many unsuccessful attempts to bring the boat close in to the stack the unfortunate wight was left to his fate. **1851** STERNBERG *Northampt. Gloss.* s.v., In Pembrokeshire the insular rocks of the coast are locally termed 'stacks'. **1878** HUXLEY *Physiogr.* 168 [Rocks] completely isolated in the form of 'needles', 'stacks', and 'skerries'. **1889** *Hardwicke's Sci. Gossip* XXV. 205 On the coast [of Sutherland] the sea has deeply eroded and tunnelled into the land..leaving.. numerous stacks, islets, and spiry rocks. **1944** A. HOLMES *Princ. Physical Geol.* xiv. 287 Later the arch falls in, and the seaward portion of the headland then remains as an isolated stack. **1957** G. E. HUTCHINSON *Treat. Limnol.* I. ii. 173 Coastal islands formed by cutting behind promontories, so producing isolated stacks, occur along the margins of large lakes. **1975** [see SEVERE *a.* 9 b].

8. *attrib.* and *Comb.* **a.** Obvious combs.: simple attrib., as (sense 2) ***stack-cloth, -cover, -fire***, (sense 4 b) ***stack-pipe, -process***; objective, as ***stack-firer, -firing***; also ***stack-wise*** adv.; (sense 2) ***stack-shaped*** adj.

1832 *Boston Herald* 31 July 1 *Stack-Cloths of the same highly-approved-of description. **1799** *Hull Advertiser* 12 Oct. 2/1 Mill sails, waggon, cart, and *stack covers. **1898** *Westm. Gaz.* 16 Sept. 7/3 *Stack fires and the demolition of cottages owing to the thatch firing. **1831** *Lincoln Herald* 29 July 4/1 Serjeant Wilde has absolutely defended the magistracy against the bellowing of the *stack-firers. **1887** *Pall Mall Gaz.* 6 Sept. 6/2 A man..was charged yesterday at Arrington, Cambs, with *stack firing. **1833** LOUDON *Encycl. Archit.* §854 To put 3 inches lead rain-water *stack pipes, with cistern heads to bring the water to the ground in the angle of the north front. **1849** *Ecclesiologist* IX. 356 The stack-pipes will communicate with these main drains. **1884** *Chamb. Jrnl.* 8 Mar. 158/2 The old '*stack' process of white-lead manufacture. **1864** J. A. GRANT *Walk across Afr.* 62 Grain is housed under the eaves of *stack-shaped huts. **1921** *Glasgow Herald* 26 Mar. 7 About a dozen 18-pounder shell cases, some of which contained curious stack-shaped bombs. **1881** R. BUCHANAN *God & Man* III. 41 This [turf] I arranged *stack-wise.

b. Special comb.: **stack-bar**, a hurdle for fencing a stack (sense 2) standing in an open field; **stack-furnace**, a tall circular blast-furnace for smelting; **stack gas**, gas emitted by a chimney-stack; **stack-guard** (see quot. 1875); **stack-pole**, ? a pole round which sheaves are piled to form a stack; **stack-room** (see sense 1 d above); **stack-stand** (see quot. 1875); **stack-wood**, a faggot, usually *collect. sing.* a load of firewood; also *attrib.*; **stack-yard**, a rick-yard.

1657 *Knaresb. Wills* (Surtees) II. 223, 5 *stackbarrs. **1788** W. H. MARSHALL *Yorksh.* II. 355 *Stackbars*, large hurdles with which hay stacks in the field are generally fenced. **1877** RAYMOND *Statist. Mines & Mining* 289, 1 slag-furnace, and 2 *stack-furnaces. **1945** H. D. SMYTH *Gen. Acct. Devel. Atomic Energy Mil. Purposes* viii. 91 It became essential to know whether the *stack gases (at Clinton and at Hanford) would be likely to spread radioactive fission products in dangerous concentrations. **1973** H. GRUPPE *Truxton Cipher* xiii. 135 The smell of stack gas lay heavy upon the destroyer's upperworks. **1875** KNIGHT *Dict. Mech.*, **Stack-guard*, a temporary roof capable of elevation, and designed to protect a stack or rick of hay or grain in process of formation. **1816** *U.S. Coast Survey*, Deb. in Congress (1818) 2456, I began by erecting a signal..in form of a tripod, made of a ladder and two *stack-poles. **1893** OPIE READ *Emmett Bonlore* 343 He was almost as high as a stackpole, an' so slim. **1875** KNIGHT *Dict. Mech.*, **Stack-stand*, a device for supporting a stack of hay or grain at a sufficient distance above the ground to preserve it dry beneath and prevent the ravages of vermin. **1664** EVELYN *Sylva* 101 A round hole, which is to be formed in working up the *stack-wood, for a tunnel. **1785** J. PHILLIPS *Treat. Inland Navig.* 17 Stack-wood, for the London bakers. **1569** *Reg. Privy Council Scot.* II. 33 To teind, gadder, leid and place the saidis teind schaves in the *stak yaird. **1788** *Trans. Soc. Arts* VI. 82 Exposed to view in barns and stackyards. **1887** JESSOPP *Arcady* 11 All that this good man could make out of his stackyard in the best years.

stack (stæk), *v.*[1] Forms: see the sb. [f. STACK *sb.*]

1. a. *trans.* To pile (corn, fodder, etc.) into a stack; to make a stack of, to pile (something) up in the form of a stack.

c **1325** *Gloss. W. de Bibbesw.* in Wright *Voc.* 154 [*Dehors la graunge vos blez tassez* glossed,] stacke thi corn. *c* **1460** *Promp. Parv.* (Winch.) 464 Stakkyn, *arconiso.* **1483** *Cath. Angl.* 358/2 To Sstakke, *arconizare.* **1573** TUSSER *Husb.* (1878) 132 Stack pease vpon houell abrode in the yard. **1592** *Shuttleworths' Acc.* (Chetham Soc.) 74 Stackinge turffes towe dayes iij[d]. **1657** BILLINGSLY *Brachy-Martyrol.* II. viii. 211 Being in Harvest stacking of his corn. **1797** J. CURR *Coal Viewer* 11, I have adopted this mode of conveying coals above the ground also for stacking them. **1801** *Farmer's Mag.* Jan. 99, I do not think it proceeds from the crop yielding beyond what it had the appearance of when stacked. **1833** LOUDON *Encycl. Archit.* §1584 The boards to be prepared and stacked (horsed) by the 1st of September. **1859** GEO. ELIOT *Adam Bede* vi, At the far end, fleeces of wool stacked up. **1861** HUGHES *Tom Brown at Oxf.* x, The port which Tom employed the first hour after his return in stacking carefully away in his cellar. **1894** FENN *Real Gold* 314 Something serious was evidently going on by the spot where the packages had been stacked.

b. *Aeronaut.* To order (aircraft waiting to land) at different flight levels and in landing sequence above an airport; to place (an aeroplane) in a waiting stack (freq. with *up*). Also *intr.* (of aircraft), to form a stack.

1941 K. HENNEY *Radio Engin. Handbk.* (ed. 3) xvii. 616 The present practice of 'stacking' airplanes..limits the number of landings..to about 4 per hour. **1943** M. FEIGEN *Pocket Aviation Quiz Bk.* 55 Planes cruising above an airport at varying assigned altitudes in order not to collide while awaiting their turns to land are said to be: stacked up. **1949** *Sun* (Baltimore) 4 Nov. 2/6 Planes 'stack up' over the range station near Mount Vernon. **1965** P. WYLIE *They both were Naked* I. i. 4 We'd spent that interval..'stacked up' and waiting for planes..to be called down for landings. **1975** D. LODGE *Changing Places* vi. 218, I hope to hell we aren't stacked for hours over Kennedy.

2. a. *absol.* and *intr.* To put corn or hay into stacks; to make a stack or stacks.

a **1722** FOUNTAINHALL *Decis.* I. 548 The Lords found little matter of riot in the master's hindering his tenant to stack in that barn-yard. **1801** *Farmer's Mag.* Nov. 479 Some loss has occurred, from stacking too hastily. **1883** M. P. BALE *Saw-Mills* 237 If it [timber] is to be used for fencing posts and rails, &c., split at once and stack where there is a free circulation of air. **1894** HALL CAINE *Manxman* III. v. 137 It was her father stacking in the haggard.

b. To pile *up* one's chips at poker. Now usu. *fig.*, to present oneself, measure up; to arise, build up. *colloq.* (chiefly *U.S.*).

1896 ADE *Artie* ii. 10 He'd stack up, you know, an' feel in his pockets and then he'd say: 'I'm forty-seven cents loser.' **1911** R. D. SAUNDERS *Col. Todhunter* xiii. 198 Old Bill Strickland, of Nineveh, somehow don't seem to stack up the right way against the Honourable Stephen K. Vancey. **1921** R. D. PAINE *Comr. Rolling Ocean* iv. 71, I wish this trouble hadn't stacked up between us. **1938** *Sun* (Baltimore) 6 Apr. 11/5, I think every one will agree my record stacks up favourably enough with that of any other pro. past or present. **1951** M. MCLUHAN *Mech. Bride* (1967) 48/1 See how you stack up with your fellow men on the following issues. **1965** WODEHOUSE *Galahad at Blandings* x. 169 I've never been a brainy sort of guy, and what I want is a wife with about the same amount of grey matter I have, and that's how Vee stacks up. **1977** R. E. MEGILL *Introd. Risk Analysis* xv. 170 Dougherty and Nozaki ranked knowing your competitors as of equal value to knowing how well your own estimate stacks up.

3. *trans.* To make a pile of (weapons, etc.) by leaning one against another. (Cf. PILE *v.*[2] 1 b.)

1841 CATLIN *N. Amer. Ind.* xx. (1844) I. 144 The leader of the party with his arms stacked behind him. **1887** *Times* 9 Apr. 5/5 The men [military cyclists], having dismounted and stacked their machines.

4. *to stack up*: to pile materials on, to make up (a fire).

1892 RIDER HAGGARD *Nada* ix. 67 We stacked up the fire.

5. To fill with stacks of.

1652 BENLOWES *Theoph.* VI. xxvi, Whose Hands did stack The studded Orbs with Stars. **1913** *19th Cent.* Jan. 67 Calcutta was stacked with the rupees of 1907 still unissued.

6. a. To shuffle or arrange (playing-cards) dishonestly. In *fig.* phr. ***to stack the cards*** (etc.) ***against***: to reduce (a person or thing's) chance of success. Cf. PACK *v.*[2] 5, STOCK *v.*[1] 23 b. orig. *U.S.*

1825 in M. Bayard Smith *Forty Yrs. Washington Soc.* (1906) 186 John Randolph observed after counting the ballots, 'It was impossible to win the game, gentlemen, the cards were stacked.' **1896** J. F. LILLARD *Poker Stories* 54 The stranger got skinned right and left. The cards were stacked and marked on the back, so that he didn't have any chance at all to win. *c* **1926** 'MIXER' *Transport Workers' Song Bk.* 31 He'll know this when I stack the cards. **1941** B. SCHULBERG *What makes Sammy Run?* v. 81 You read the papers, you know how the cards are stacked against this nut. **1977** *New Yorker* 24 Oct. 37/1 He..confirmed our worst fear: the deck is stacked... He picked up a cardboard box containing several packs of cards. **1978** G. VAUGHAN *Belgrade Drop* x. 67 'Pin your ears back,' Yardly murmured. 'We've got a lot stacked against us.'

b. = PACK *v.*[2] 4. Also *fig.*

1948 *Durant* (Okla.) *Daily Democrat* 2 July 1/5 His young polltaker detected no signs of 'stacking' the poll for any candidate. **1963** *Wall St. Jrnl.* 25 Jan. 16/3 The government is now stacked from top to bottom with men who reflect their President's prejudices. **1970** *New Yorker* 28 Nov. 104/2 Legally, marriage is still stacked in favor of the man. **1975** *N.Y. Times* 10 Apr. 29/1 Gov. George C. Wallace of Alabama charged today that..efforts were being made..to stack delegate-selection procedures against him.

stack (stæk), *v.*[2] *Coal-mining.* [? f. LG. *stack* dam.] *trans.* See quot. 1883. (Chiefly with *out.*)

1832 HT. MARTINEAU *Hill & Valley* iv. 62 There is much labour in..stacking and loading the mine. **1883** GRESLEY *Gloss. Coal-mining* 234 *Stack out*, to dam off or shut up the entrance to a goaf by building a wall of stone or coal in front of it.

stack: see STICK *v.*, STAKE.

stackable ('stækəb(ə)l), *a.* [f. STACK *v.*[1] + -ABLE.] Able to be stacked or piled up: esp. of chairs and other furniture. Hence **stacka'bility**.

1958 *Archit. Rev.* CXXIII. 255 (*caption*) The chairs are stackable. **1960** *House & Garden* Oct. 80/2 Stackable Italian table..for use in large works canteens. **1969** *Jane's Freight Containers 1968–69* 490/3 Stackability... When the ends are folded down, five stacked together stand 8 ft high. **1973** J. ELSOM *Erotic Theatre* x. 209 Surrounded by a Brighton beach of stackable chairs. **1977** *Design Engin.* July 41/1 Stackable valves often introduce unacceptable pressure losses and fault finding often means dismantling the whole stack.

†**'stackage.** *Obs. rare.* [f. STACK *sb.* + -AGE.] A tax levied on stacks.

1587 HARRISON *England* II. v. (1877) 113 His Prædia in like manner were tributes, tolles,..stackage..& such like.

stacked (stækt), *ppl. a.* [f. STACK *v.* + -ED[1].]

1. Piled together.

1833 LOUDON *Encycl. Archit.* Gloss., *Stacked*, horsed. **1870** *Standard* 12 Dec., Those battalions that still remained and paced briskly to and fro by their stacked arms to warm themselves. **1905** TREVES *Other Side of Lantern* II. vii. (1906) 65 A place for stacked spears.

2. Piled into a 'stack' (senses 2, 3).

1901 *Westm. Gaz.* 17 Dec. 2/1 Clearings with stacked-up wood. **1908** MARY JOHNSTON *Lewis Rand* i. 10 Stretches of stacked corn appeared like tented plains.

3. Piled with goods.

1908 *Academy* 8 Feb. 441/1 A stacked trolley obsessed the tram-lines.

4. Of a female figure: well-rounded and attractively shaped. Also of a woman: having a prominent bosom. Similarly, ***stacked up, well-stacked***. *U.S. slang* (as a term of male approbation).

1942 BERREY & VAN DEN BARK *Amer. Thes. Slang* §37/14 *Shapely*,..stacked up nicely. **1952** *Esquire* June 131/2 The singer ain't a bad-looking broad, she's well-stacked and sort of young. **1954** *Amer. Speech* XXIX. 234 There is a present fashion of referring to an attractively proportioned woman as well stacked, or simply, stacked, period. **1965** *Liberator* (N.Y.) Aug. 22/3 Two stacked broads approached. Everyone attained a hip position. It consisted of pulling pants high, rolling the Hi-Lo collar, [etc.]. **1975** D. LODGE *Changing Places* v. 154 What about your wife?.. Is she well-stacked? **1981** 'D. SHANNON' *Murder Most Strange* vii. 147 A cute little blond chick..really stacked.

5. ***stacked head***, in a tape recorder: a head (HEAD *sb.*[1] 11 g) in which the gaps corresponding to the tracks in multi-channel recording are located one above another.

1954 C. A. TUTHILL *How to service Tape Recorders* iv. 45 Typical individual or stacked heads, currently being released by The Brush Development Company, are cast in synthetic resin. **1962** A. NISBETT *Technique Sound Studio* 267 For stereo, the first and third tracks are recorded at the same time, using a stacked head (one with both gaps in line). *a* **1975** *Tape Talk* (Sony Corporation) 3 *In-line heads*, arrangement of stereophonic heads on a tape recorder in which the head gaps are mounted one directly above the other. Also called 'stacked heads'.

6. ***stacked heel***, a heel built by stacking or appearing to stack thin layers of wood or other material. Also ***stacked-heeled*** adj.

[**1960** *Harper's Bazaar* Aug. 24 Stack-heeled moccasin in deep brown leather.] **1960** *Sunday Express* 11 Sept. 15/4 In Paris Dior..showed Cuban 'stacked' heels. **1964** in

Hamblett & Deverson *Generation X* 13 Mod girls have a short back-and-sides hair cut like men used to, wear shift-style dresses with round collars... Stacked heeled shoes, white stockings. **1966** T. PYNCHON *Crying of Lot 49* vi. 177 She turned, pivoting on one stacked heel. **1977** J. WAMBAUGH *Black Marble* (1978) v. 62 Comfortable loafers with low stacked heels in colors to match wool-knit pants and jackets.

7. ***stacked deck***, a pack of cards that has cheatingly been set in a prearranged order; also *fig.* Hence more widely (and without the implication of dishonesty), of odds. Cf. STACK *v.*[1] 6 a. Chiefly *U.S.*

1964 A. WYKES *Gambling* 329/1 *Stacked deck*, a pack of cards that a cheat has prearranged for his own benefit. **1971** P. O'DONNELL *Impossible Virgin* vii. 144 They worked alone, without hirelings, and so often went in against stacked odds. **1976** *Honolulu Star-Bull.* 21 Dec. H-3/1 The Minnesota Vikings, shooting to become the first National Football League team to make four Super Bowl appearances, will be playing with a stacked deck Sunday. **1978** E. TIDYMAN *Table Stakes* II. vii. 345 You played the game with a stacked deck. You had his daughter, his trust, and his face.

stacken-cloud. [App. arbitrarily f. STACK *sb.* + -EN.] A cloud which appears as though composed of piled up masses, a CUMULUS.

1823 T. FORSTER *Res. Atmospheric Phenomena* i. §3 (ed. 3) 9 Of the Cumulus or Stackencloud. **1844** H. STEPHENS *Bk. Farm* I. 246 Why the heap should be called the *stacken-cloud*,..is by no means obvious. **1867** SMYTH *Sailor's Word-bk.*, *Stacken Cloud*, the same as *cumulus*.

stacker ('stækə(r)), *sb.*[1] [f. STACK *v.*[1] + -ER[1].]

1. One who builds up a stack or pile.

1757 MRS. GRIFFITH *Lett. Henry & Frances* (1767) I. 249, I am, at present, sitting in the midst of a large field of barley, which I reaped the other day, and am taking care of the binders and stackers. **1834** *Brit. Husb.* I. 494 The common number of workpeople is five hay-makers to each mower, including tedders, loaders, pitchers, and stackers. **1880** *New Virginians* I. 180 None of the Virginians working for him were good stackers. **1883** GRESLEY *Gloss. Coal-mining* 234 *Stacker*, one who stacks coals, etc.

2. a. (See quot. 1875); more widely, any machine for raising individual items or bulk material and depositing them on a stack or pile; also, a stacker crane.

1875 KNIGHT *Dict. Mech.*, *Stacker*, a machine adapted for delivering straw from the threshing machine on to the stack, or hay from a wagon on to a stack or into a loft. **1887** *Sci. Amer.* 14 May 314/1 A hay stacker and loader. **1905** *Contemp. Rev.* July 98 There..the thresher and stacker has its home and works with long surges of droning sound which I love to hear. **1922** G. F. ZIMMER *Mech. Handling & Storing* (ed. 3) xxxviii. 654 A similar stacker is illustrated in Fig. 954; it is composed of a slat conveyor, and is for handling cases. **1950** W. STANIAR *Plant Engin. Handbk.* xx. 1417 A number of different types of portable elevators, stackers, or tiering machines are made with the lifting mechanism either motor or hand operated... Portable stackers are made for the handling of smaller units. **1979** *Belt Conveyors for Bulk Materials* (Conveyor Equipment Manufacturers Assoc., U.S.) (ed. 2) i. 7 Belt conveyors, with their stackers and reclaimers, have become the only practical means for large-scale stockpiling and reclaiming of such bulk materials as coal, ore, and taconite pellets.

b. A part of a data-processing machine in which punched cards are deposited in a stack after having passed through the machine.

1962 in *Gloss. Terms Automatic Data Processing* (*B.S.I.*) 90. **1969** P. B. JORDAIN *Condensed Computer Encycl.* 82 A card stacker ensures the correct sequencing of emerging cards. **1971** J. T. MURRAY *Introd. Computing* vii. 126 The input hopper provides the cards which are sorted into any of the six available stacker pockets.

3. Special Comb.: **stacker crane**, a hoist running on a fixed horizontal track for stacking and retrieving pallets or the like.

1959 W. STANIAR *Plant Engin. Handbk.* (ed. 2) XXVIII. 32 The makers of the stacker crane claim that it may be employed for safe stacking of materials to greater heights than with other forms of equipment. **1979** *Computers in Shell* (Shell Internat. Petroleum Co.) 6 A computer-controlled stacker crane takes the pallet and places it in one of the thousands of pallet spaces in the racks, the location being recorded by the computer.

stacker ('stækə(r)), *sb.*[2] *dial.* Also 7 *pl.* stakers, 9 stacher. [f. STACKER *v.*]

1. *pl.* = *staggers*: see STAGGER *sb.*[1] 2.

1610 *Shuttleworths' Acc.* (Chetham Soc.) 188 For letting the grissell mare blode for the stakers and giving her a drincke, xiiij[d]. **1828** [CARR] *Craven Gloss.*, *Stackers*, the staggers, a disease in horses, etc.

2. A reeling or tottering movement of the body, = STAGGER *sb.*

1870 J. K. HUNTER *Life Studies* xliv. 271 An attempt to ease the foot produced a stacher. **1877** 'SAXON' *Galloway Gossip* 358 He gied a great stacher and fell sprauchelling on the floor.

stacker ('stækə(r)), *v.* *Obs.* exc. *dial.* Forms: 3-6 staker, 4-6 stakker, 5 stakar, (stakeryn), stakyr, 5-6 stakir, 6 stakkir, 5-7, 9 (*dial.*) stacker (*Sc. dial.* 8-9 stacher, 9 staucher). [a. ON. *stakra* to stagger; freq. of *staka* to push, to stagger. The Sc. form *stacher* ('staxər) is difficult to account for. STAGGER *v.* is an altered form of *stacker*.]

1. *intr.* To totter, reel in one's gait, to stagger.

a **1300** *Cursor M.* 24032, I stakerd sua i moght not stand. *c* **1330** R. BRUNNE *Chron. Wace* (Rolls) 12377 Arthur was stoneyd, stakered, & stynt, But ȝut fel he nought for þat dynt. *c* **1385** CHAUCER *L.G.W.* 2687 She rist ȝit vp & stakerith her & ther. *c* **1400** *Song of Roland* 730 Then euery of them brest vpon other, that þer stedes stakered right euyn þer. *c* **1440** *York Myst.* xxx. 84 For scho may stakir in þe strete But scho stalworthely stande. **1535** COVERDALE *Ps.* cvi. 27 They stacker like a droncken man. *c* **1550** BALE *K. Johan* 1997 Of terryble deathe thu wylt stacker in the plashes. **1597** G. HARVEY *Trimming Nashe* Wks. (Grosart) III. 57 He eate the poyson, and presently (drunkard-like) stackered vp and downe, reeling backward and forward. **1597** MONTGOMERIE *Cherrie & Slae* 303, I stakkerit at the windilstrayis. **1785** BURNS *Death & Dr. Hornbook* iii, I stacher'd whyles but yet took tent ay To free the ditches. **1825** BROCKETT *N.C. Gloss.*, *Stacker*, to stagger.

b. *transf.*

1597 J. KING *On Jonas* (1618) 287 When hee had shipt himselfe, the vessell that bare him, stackered like a drunken man to and fro.

†2. To stammer, hesitate in speech. *Obs.*

1440 [see STACKERING *vbl. sb.*]. **1538** ELYOT *Dict.*, *Offensator*, He that stakereth in redinge, as if he were not perfyte in reding. *Ibid.*, *Titubo*, To stacker in speking or going, as a man being drunke or sycke.

†3. *fig.* a. To be insecure or in danger of ruin. b. To waver, to hesitate mentally in a state of indecision. *Obs.*

1402 *Pol. Poems* (Rolls) II. 40 Every state stakerth unstable in him silfe. **1526** TINDALE *Rom.* iv. 20 He stackered nott at the promes off God thorowe vnbelefe. **1533** MORE *Apol.* xxii. 134 b, Calanius perceuyng them begyn in the mater somwhat to staker and staye, persuaded them [etc.]. **1549** COVERDALE *Erasm. Par.*, *Jas.* 32 He..whiche stack-reth not to auenture in hys onely sonne whome he loued so syngularly.

stackering ('stækərɪŋ), *vbl. sb.* [f. STACKER *v.* + -ING[1].] The action of STACKER *v.*

c **1440** CAPGRAVE *Life St. Kath.* v. 1510 Make now noo stakeryng As in this mater. *c* **1440** *Promp. Parv.* 471/2 Stakerynge, in mevynge, *vacillacio*. *Ibid.*, Stakerynge, yn speche (or stamerynge), *titubacio*. **1555** WATREMAN *Fardle Facions* II. x. 229 Then must ye of necessitie be redy to do whatsoeuer I commaunde ye..without staieng or stackering.

stackering ('stækərɪŋ), *ppl. a.* [f. STACKER *v.* + -ING[2].] = STAGGERING *ppl. a.*

c **1550** ROLLAND *Crt. Venus* II. 363 Vp he rais into ane stakkerand stait. **1558** G. CAVENDISH *Poems* (1825) II. 170 My quaking hand my penne unnethe can hold, So dombe I ame of doctryn, lame of experience, Stakeryng in style, onsavery of sentence. **1566** DRANT *Horace, Sat.* II. vii. I iv b, Thy stackeringe stumpes thy corsey corps at lengthe will hardlie beare. **1584** HUDSON *Du Bartas' Judith* VI. 51 Then each of them, with stackring steps out went. **1597** MONTGOMERIE *Cherrie & Slae* 213 O quhat an stakkering stait! *c* **1600** *Burel's Pilgr.* in *Watson's Collect.* (1709) II. 34 Quhat stakren stait was this to me, To be in sick obscuritie? **1872** J. YOUNG *Lochlomond* 166 (E.D.D.) When staucherin' fou He fell an' brack his leg.

†'**stacket**, *sb.* *Sc.* *Obs.* [a. Du. *staket* (whence G. *stacket*); of Fr. origin, though the precise source is uncertain. Cf. OF. *estacade* (see STACCADO), also *estachete*, *estaquete* cord fencing in the lists, also post, stake.] A palisade.

1637 R. MONRO *Exped.* I. 51 We brake downe the Stacket, and the Towne not walled, we entred the broade side. **1819** SCOTT *Leg. Montrose* x, I would advise you to fortify the said sconce, not only by a foussie, or graffe, but also by certain stackets, or palisades.

Hence '**stacket**, *v.* *trans.*, to raise a palisade about.

1637 R. MONRO *Exped.* II. 8 We did worke all of us night and day, till we had Stacketed the Wall about, the height of a man above the Parapet.

stackfreed ('stækfriːd). *Hist.* [Of obscure origin; presumably corrupt Ger. or Du.

The word appears in the *Encyclopédie* (1756), s.v. *Fusée*, in the form *stochfred*. Berthoud *Hist. de la Mesure du Temps* (1802) I. 77 has *stackfreed*, and *staak-freed* occurs in a Fr. work of 1811 quoted in *Archæologia* XXXIII. 27 *note*.]

(See quot. 1884)

1819 REES *Cycl.* VIII. 3 S 1, s.v. *Clock*, This piece of mechanism.. was a German invention,..and was called *stack-freed*. **1884** F J. BRITTEN *Watch & Clockm.* 246 *Stack freed*, an eccentric wheel or cam attached to the barrels of watches before the invention of the fusee in order to equalize the force transmitted.

attrib. **1899** F J. BRITTEN *Old Clocks & Watches* 352 In 1764 Frederick Kehlhoff, of London, patented a centre seconds and going barrel watch with a stackfreed remontoire.

stackful ('stækfʊl). [f. STACK *sb.* + -FUL.] As much as is contained in a stack.

1868 SWINBURNE *Ess. & Stud.* (1875) 314 The huge mass of original designs..heaped and huddled in portfolios by the loose stackful.

stack-garth. *north.* Also 6-9 staggarth; 9 *dial.* stagarth, etc.: see *Eng. Dial. Dict.* [a. ON. *stakkgarð-r*: see STACK *sb.* and GARTH[1].] A stack-yard, rick-yard.

1293 *Durham Chapter MSS.*, Le Stakgarth in villa nostra de Hemingburg. **1402-3** *Durham Acc. Rolls.* (Surtees) 182 In alloc Rectori de Hemmyngburgh pro le Stakgarth, 2s. **1470-71** *Durham Chapter MSS.* 643 Circa inclusionem de lez Stakgarthez de Billyngham [etc.]. 20d. **1546** *Yorks. Chantry Surv.* (Surtees) 339 A stacke garthe, with a lee, iiij[s]. **1582** *Durham Wills* (Surtees) II. 45 In the staggarth, Sextene thraves of wheate. **1641** BEST *Farm. Bks.* (Surtees) 39 Of these [grasse cockes] the little Staggarth had seaven. *Ibid.* 60. **1842** GEN. P. THOMPSON *Exerc.* III. 42 *note*, He may know every part of it, as a farmer knows the corners in his own stack-garth. **1891** ATKINSON *Moorland Par.* (ed. 2) 357 Mighty loads of corn or hay as they are piled up in order to be taken..into the stack-garth.

stacking ('stækɪŋ), *vbl. sb.* Also 6 **staghynge**. [f. STACK *v.* + -ING[1].]

a. The action or an act of STACK *v.* in various senses.

1531-2 *Durham Househ. Bk.* (Surtees) 128 Pro le stakkynge [of corn] ibidem, per 2 dies 16d. **1532-3** *Ibid.* 165 Operantibus in collectione et staghynge decimarum de Harton. **1591** *Exch. Rolls Scot.* XXII. 145 For mawing, winning, leiding, stacking, and howsing of the hay of the new medowis of Falkland. **1707** MORTIMER *Husb.* (1721) II. 66 The Prices of which, and the stacking up of Wood, Roots, stumps of Timber Trees, &c. I shall give you an Account of hereafter. **1805** R. W. DICKSON *Pract. Agric.* I. 46 Where thrashing machines, and the practice of stacking, are properly held in estimation, large barns are quite unnecessary. **1880** [A. J. MUNBY] *Dorothy* 46 Reaping in harvest time; haymaking, stacking an' all. **1942** H. L. SMITH *Airways* 365 Since speed is the commodity sold by the air-line operator, he is interested in any system that can solve the problem of stacking. **1969** *Daily Tel.* 14 Nov. 1/7 Stacking over a 'holding area' while waiting a turn to land, is not uncommon. **1979** C. WOOD *James Bond & Moonraker* i. 13 If there were no stacking positions at Heathrow..he would be home in time to..eat supper with the family.

b. *attrib.* ***stacking chair***, ***-stage***, ***-swivel*** (see quots.); **stacking-elevator** = STACKER *sb.*[1] 2; **stacking fault** *Cryst.*, a break in the regular order of stacking of layers of atoms in a crystal.

1939 MARTIN & SPEIGHT *Flat Bk.* 101 *Stacking chair, by Alvar Aalto in natural birch or lacquered..20s od. **1951** *Catal. of Exhibits, South Bank Exhib., Festival of Britain* 87/2 Cantilevered all-purpose stacking chairs. **1982** E. DEWHURST *Whoever I Am* vii. 90 Motioning her niece to fetch up one of the stacking chairs. **1890** *Univ. Exhib. Guide* June 30/1 A *Stacking Elevator for straw, hay, sheaf corn, beans, &c., was shown. **1951** *Phil. Mag.* XLII. 815 The best-known examples of translation twinning are '*stacking faults' in the sphere-packing lattices, *i.e.* breaches of the stacking rules which lead to face-centred cubic or hexagonal close-packing. **1976** *Sci. Amer.* Nov. 105/2 In brass, bronze and certain stainless steels, for example, stacking faults extend over distances equivalent to many atomic diameters. **1805** R. W. DICKSON *Pract. Agric.* II. 799 It may likewise be useful, in building large corn ricks, to have a *stacking stage, so contrived as to be capable of standing close to their sides. **1875** KNIGHT *Dict. Mech.*, *Stacking-stage*, a scaffold used in building stacks. *Ibid.*, **Stacking-swivel*, a swivel attached to the upper band of a breech-loading rifle or carbine, to enable stacks to be formed without attaching the bayonet or using the wiper.

stackless ('stæklɪs), *a.* [f. STACK *sb.* + -LESS.] Without a 'stack' or chimney.

1883 *Harper's Mag.* Aug. 332/2 Eighteen locomotives [are] kept,..and several stackless ones for running into the ..mines.

†'**stacklet.** *Obs.* *rare*[−1]. [f. STACK *sb.* + -LET.] A small stack (of wheat, etc.).

1796 W. H. MARSHALL *West Eng.* II. 9 About Bodmin, the Wheat in general seems to be made into 'arrish mows', or field stacklets, of about a load each.

stack-up. [f. vbl. phr. *to stack up*: see STACK *v.*[1] 1 b.] The arrangement of objects in a stack or pile; a build-up. *spec.* in *Aeronaut.* = STACK *sb.* 1 e.

1945 F. WALTON *Airman's Almanac* 403 *Stack-up*, air-planes flying at different altitudes over an airport awaiting signal to land. **1948** *Jrnl. R. Aeronaut. Soc.* LII. 681/2 Once the diversion and 'stack up' problem is eliminated the plain jet..can become almost as cheap to operate as propeller-powered aircraft. **1950** *Daily Progress* (Charlottesville, Va.) 14 Dec. 1/8 The department has under study a plan for shifting first class surface mail to the air lines in order to avoid a stack-up of such mail. **1970** *Sci. Amer.* Mar. 86/1 Unsafe weather conditions at air-ports, forcing the stack-up and diversion of aircraft,..take an immense annual toll in inconvenience. **1976** *Lebende Sprachen* XXI. 153/2 The failure was caused by a build-up/stack-up of adverse manufacturing tolerances.

‖**stacte** ('stæktiː). Also 4-5 **stacten**, 7 **stact**, 8 **stackten**. [L. *stactē*, a. Gr. στακτή fem. of στακτός distilling in drops, f. σταγ-, στάζειν to drop. The form *stacten* represents the accus., treated in med.L. as indeclinable. (So G. *stacten*.)]

a. A fragrant spice referred to by ancient writers; properly, the finest kind of myrrh, the exudation of the living tree (Pliny *N.H.* XII. xxxv), but the name was also applied to a mixture of storax with fat. In the Bible used (after LXX and Vulgate) as the translation of Heb. *nāṭāph*, one of the ingredients of the incense prescribed for the Tabernacle worship, variously conjectured to be opobalsamum, myrrh, storax, or tragacanth. †b. *Pharmacy.* Formerly applied arbitrarily to LIQUIDAMBAR and perh. other preparations (the meaning in quot. 1715 is obscure).

1382 WYCLIF *Exod.* xxx. 34 Tak to thee swete smellynge thinges, stacten [**1535** COVERDALE stacte] and onycha, galbantum of good smel [etc.]. **1483** CAXTON *Golden Leg.*, *Joseph* 51 b, And gyue ye & presente to that man yeftes, a lytyl reysyns & hony, Scacten [*read* stacten], therebinthe & dates. **1600** B. JONSON *Cynthia's Rev.* v. iv, Stacte, opobalsamum, amomum, storax. **1631** WIDDOWES *Nat. Philos.* 33 The distilled liquor of fresh Myrrh was once called Stact, but now it is named Storax. **1715** LADY G. BAILLIE *Househ. Bk.* (1911) 98 For stacktens drops 2s. **1844** HOBLYN *Dict. Terms Med.* (ed. 2), *Stacte*,..Also, a more liquid kind of amber than is generally met with in the shops. **1887** BENTLEY *Man. Bot.* 506 The Stacte or Liquid Myrrh of the ancients.

stactometer (stæk'tɒmɪtə(r)). Also stakto-. [f. Gr. στακτό-ς (see prec.) + -METER.] (See quot.)
1842 *Encycl. Brit.* (ed. 7) XII. 25/1 (*Hydrodynamics*), Brewster's Staktometer. The Staktometer, or drop-measurer.. is a glass vessel four or five inches long, having a hollow bulb about half an inch in diameter. The instrument is filled by suction... The fluid is then allowed to discharge itself.. by drops, and the number of them is counted till the surface of the fluid descends to another fixed point.

stacyoner, obs. form of STATIONER.

‖**stad** (stat). *S. Africa.* Also stadt. [Du.] A town or village.
1896 *Daily News* 28 Dec. 5/3 The principal Stadt is in flames. **1900** *Ibid.* 23 May 5/6 Three hundred of the enemy entered and set fire to the native stad. **1906** *Blackw. Mag.* Sept. 390/2 The chief stad—as the native villages are curiously enough called in this country.

stad, obs. variant of STEAD *sb.*

stad(d, obs. pa. pple. of STEAD *v.*

stadda ('stædə). Also 7 **staddow**. [Of obscure origin.] (See quot. 1846.)
1688 HOLME *Armoury* III. 383/2 Two Tools belonging to a Comb-maker, *viz.*, the Turn-File, and the Staddow. **1846** HOLTZAPFFEL *Turning* II. 723 The comb-cutter's double saw.. is called a 'stadda', and has two blades so contrived as to give, with great facility and exactness, the intervals between the teeth of combs. **1875** KNIGHT *Dict. Mech.*

staddle ('stæd(ə)l), *sb.* Forms: 1 **staðol, -ul, steaðel, 1–3 staðel,** 6 **stathell(e, stadell,** 7 **staddel(l,** 6, 8–9 **stadle,** 8–9 **stathel,** 9 **stathle, steddle, stadel, staidel,** etc. (for other *dial.* forms see *Eng. Dial. Dict.*), 6– **staddle.** Also 8 **stavel** (whence STAFFOLD). [OE. *staðol* masc., foundation, base, support, trunk of a tree, also fixed position or state, corresponds formally to OFris. *-stathul* masc. foundation (WFris. *steal*, NFris. *stāl*), OS. *stadal* standing (MLG. *stadel*), OHG. *stadal* barn (MHG., mod.G. dial. *stadel* barn, storehouse, ON. *stǫðull* masc., milking-place (Norw. *støl*):—OTeut. **staþlo-z*:—pre-Teut. **statlo-s* f. *sta-* to STAND + *-tlo-* instrumental suffix.]

†**1.** A foundation. *lit.* and *fig. Obs.*
Very common in OE.: see examples in Bosworth-Toller. *a***900** tr. *Bæda's Eccl. Hist.* III. xxiii. (E.E.T.S.) 230 Se Drihtnes wer.. in þære stowe þa staðolas sette þæs mynstres. *a***1000** *Voc.* in Wr.-Wülcker 247/1 *Fundamentum uel fundamen, s. dictum quod fundus sit domui*, staþol. *c***1225** *Juliana* 72, & buldeð ower boldes uppon treowe staðele.

2. A young tree left standing when others are cut down. Also *dial.* the root or stump of a tree that has been felled.
1543 *Act 35 Hen. VIII*, c. 17 §1 (1544) The same stathilles or storers [*elsewhere in the section* standilles or storers]. **1559** *Boke Presidentes* 56 He.. shal leaue standyng in and vpon the foresaid landes.. competent and sufficient stathelles and storers. **1573** TUSSER *Husb.* (1878) 105 Leaue growing for stadles the likest and best. **1574** in Lipscomb *Hist. Bucks* (1847) III. 206 [Q. Elizabeth devised to Paul Wentworth] parcel of the monastery of Burnham except the great trees and staddells sufficient in every acre. **1577** HARRISON *England* II. xvi. 91 b, Those yong staddles which we leaue standing. **1612** BACON *Ess., Greatness Kingdoms* (Arb.) 476 Like as it is in copices, where if you leaue your staddels too thick, you shal neuer haue cleane vnderwood, but shrubbes and bushes. **1669** WORLIDGE *Syst. Agric.* 276 *Staddles*,.. Trees reserved at the Felling of Woods, for growth of Timber. **1733** *Lease* in *N.W. Linc. Gloss.* (1877) s.v. *Steddle*, Reserving all timber trees.. and also sufficient staddles in every acre of the said woodlands. *a***1763** in *Century Mag.* (1884) Jan. 448/1 To stubb all staddles. **1766** *Complete Farmer* s.v., *Stadle*,.. also signifies a tree suffered to grow for coarse and common uses, as posts or rails. **1845** JUDD *Margaret* II. v, At the edge of the woods, a rude structure had been thrown up, of staddles interlaced with boughs. **1863** *Trans. Essex Archæol. Soc.* II. 187 *Staddle*, the stump left by the wood cutters for the next crop of underwood to grow from.
appos. **1548** *Merton Coll. Rec.* No. 1071, All suche standers or stathell okes.

†**b.** ? A tree-trunk, ? a staff. *Obs. rare*$^{-1}$.
1590 SPENSER *F.Q.* I. vi. 14 His weake steps gouerning, And aged limbs on Cypresse stadle stout.

†**c.** *fig.*
1611 SPEED *Hist. Gt. Brit.* IX. xx. §66 Concerning his courses holden with his wiues kindred, (the laterall issues and staddles of the Plantagenets) it fell out thus.

3. a. The lower part of a stack of corn, hay, etc.
[Cf. STALL *sb.*[3]; also the following passage, where the word means the underside of a turf:—
*c***1000** *Sax. Leechd.* I. 398 Ðenim feower tyrf.. Nim ele.. and drype on ðone staðol ðara turfa.]
*c***1475** *Pict. Voc.* in Wr.-Wülcker 785/21 *Hic arcomus* [read *arconius*], a stathele. **1581** *Durham Wills* (Surtees) II. 28 A stadle of ottes.. covered with pease 24s. **1613** MARKHAM *Eng. Husbandman* II. II. vii. (1635) 73 The best [manure] is the rotten staddell of bottomes of Haystacks. **1623** —— *Eng. Housew.* v. [II. vii.] 216 Some being old Corne, some new Corne, some of the heart of the stacke, and some of the stadle. **1641** BEST *Farm. Bks.* (Surtees) 35 One goinge afore with a forke and makinge the staddle, and the other comming behinde with a rake. **1828** [CARR] *Craven Gloss., Staddle*, the bottom of a stack. **1894** *Northumbld. Gloss., Steadle, Steidel, Styeddle*, a portion of a stack begun and left unfinished on account of wet or other causes; or the part left standing after a portion has been carried into the barn.

b. A platform of timber, stone, etc. on which a stack or rick is placed. Also, in some districts, one of the stones with tapering tops and round flat under-surfaces, a number of which are placed on posts beneath ricks and granaries to raise them from the earth and keep rats out; also called *staddle-stones* or *rick-staddles*.
1729 P. WALKDEN *Diary* (1866) 30, I sodded the turf stack top, and dressed the mull from beside it, and from the staddle of our old one. **1735** SOMERVILLE *Chase* II. 56 His Barns are stor'd, And groaning Staddles bend beneath their Load. **1799** J. ROBERTSON *Agric. Perth* 52 The farmers have their stacks built upon stathels laid on pillars of stone or wood. **1805** R. W. DICKSON *Pract. Agric.* I. 67 It will be necessary to have proper stands or staddles provided for securing the corn. **1809** KENDALL *Trav.* II. 177 To protect the [hay] stacks, they are either built upon high ground, or, if in the marshes, upon stadles or piles. **1833** LOUDON *Encycl. Archit.* §1149 Two open lodges.. with stack staddles over their flat stone roofs. **1844** H. STEPHENS *Bk. Farm* I. 155 Stack-stools, or *stathels*, or *staddles*, as they are variously called, are sometimes made of cast-iron. **1848** LOWELL *Biglow P.* Ser. I. ix. 112 Lonesome ez steddles on a mash without no hay-ricks on. **1851** *Jrnl. R. Agric. Soc.* XII. II. 392 Few of the Lincolnshire ricks are built upon frames—a layer of straw being the usual 'steddle' or foundation. **1862** *Ibid.* XXIII. 215 Prepare your staddles (or stathels or brandreths, brandreys, or by whatever name the place for the stack is called) in the field. **1874** HARDY *Far fr. Mad. Crowd* vi, The corn stood on stone staddles.

c. *gen.* A supporting framework.
*a***1800** PEGGE *Suppl. Grose, Staddle*, anything that supports another is a staddle. **1823** E. MOOR *Suffolk Words, Staddle*, what any thing stands on.. the horse for casks, etc. **1883** GRESLEY *Gloss. Coal-mining* 234 *Staddle*, the foundation of a pack in iron-stone workings.

d. *Agric.* (see quots.) *dial.*
1749–50 W. ELLIS *Mod. Husbandm.* (E.D.D.), We put it [the grass] into staddles, load it and carry it away into a barn. **1798** J. MIDDLETON *View Agric. Middlesex* 239 The grass-cocks are to be well shaken out into staddles (or separate plats) of five or six yards diameter. **1881** *Leicestersh. Words* s.v., When hay-cocks are spread out and turned, the hay is said to be thrown into staddle.

†**4.** An upright timber, a post. *Obs.*
1633 T. JAMES *Voy.* 66 The Carpenter had set vp 17. ground timbers: and 34. Staddles.

†**5.** 'A building of timber standing on legs or *steddles*, to raise it out of the mud' (*Kent. Gloss.* 1887). *Obs.*
*c***1563** in *Archæol. Cant.* (1874) IX. 115 De viginti sex domibus que vulgariter vocantur the old staddeles or six and twentie houses.

6. *dial.* (See quots.)
1691 RAY *N.C. Words* 68 A *Staddle*; a mark or impression made on any thing by somewhat lying upon it. So scars or marks of the Small-Pox are called *Staddles.* **1825** BROCKETT *N.C. Gloss., Staddle*,.. a mark left in the grass by the long continuance of the hay in bad weather. **1828** [CARR] *Craven Gloss., Staddle*,.. the marks or scars left by the small-pox. **1847** HALLIWELL, *Staddle*, the stain left on metal after the rust is removed. *West.* **1856** P. THOMPSON *Hist. Boston* 725 The mark of anything remaining after the thing itself has been removed, is called its steddle.

†**7.** 'A place marked out on the surface of a field by a groove or course of sods' (*Eng. Dial. Dict.*). *Obs.*
1770–1803 A. HUNTER *Georg. Ess.* I. 385 Mark out a staddle, in proportion to the quantity of mud taken out.

8. *attrib.* and *Comb.*, as †**staddle barn, granary,** a barn supported on staddles; **staddle-burnt, -mark, -roof, -row, -stand** (see quots.); **staddle-stead,** †(*a*) the place where a stack or shock has stood; (*b*) *dial.* a mark, stain or blemish; **staddle-stones,** the stones on which a staddle or stack-frame is supported.
1794 T. DAVIS *Agric. Wilts* 96 A '*stavel barn' for wheat, built on stone pillars, to keep out rats and mice. **1889** *N.W. Linc. Gloss.*, **Steddle-burnt*, said of the seat of a hay-cock which has remained so long covered that the grass has dried or become bleached. **1816** *Ann. Reg., Chron.* 165/1 The lioness.. on hearing the voice of the keeper retired underneath a *staddle granary. **1876** *Mid-Yorksh. Gloss., Staddle*, an impression left on a surface by any object,.. the print being often called a *staddlemark. **1875** KNIGHT *Dict. Mech.*, **Staddle-roof*, a protection for a stack. **1847** HALLIWELL, **Staddle-row*, a large row of dried grass ready for quiling or carrying. *Derby.* **1875** KNIGHT *Dict. Mech.*, **Staddle-stand*, a stack stand. **1641** BEST *Farm. Bks.* (Surtees) 51 They.. gather togeather.. that which is lefte in the *staddle-stead wheare the stooke stoode. **1868** ATKINSON *Cleveland Gloss.*, Staddlestead. **1785** *Jackson's Oxf. Jrnl.* 5 Feb. 3/4 A Stump of Hay, Sets of *Staddle Stones.. and sundry other Articles. **1881** *Leicestersh. Words.*

staddle ('stæd(ə)l), *v. dial.* Also stadle, sted(d)le. [f. STADDLE *sb.* Cf. STATHEL *v.*, to found, establish (*Obs.* after early ME.).]

†**1.** *trans.* (See quots.) *Obs.*
1573 TUSSER *Husb.* (1878) 105 First see it well fenced er hewers begin, then see it well stadled, without and within. *Ibid. marg.*, Stadling of woods. **1787** GROSE *Prov. Gloss.*, *To stadle a wood*; i.e. in cutting a wood, to leave at certain distances a sufficient number of young plants to replenish it.

2. To stain, mark, leave an impression on.
1828 [CARR] *Craven Gloss.* s.v., A person's face is said to be staddled with measles. **1866** BROGDEN *Prov. Lincs.* 196 Don't stedle the cloth... How steddled my dress looks! **1892** M. C. F. MORRIS *Yorksh. Folk-Talk* 377 Inferior 'blue' is said to go *staddled* upon the linen.

staddling ('stædlɪŋ). Now *dial.* Forms: 5 **stadelyng, -ing,** 9– **staddling;** also 9 **staidlin, staddlen, stadelin, stadlin(g, steadlin, steddling,** etc. (see *Eng. Dial. Dict.*). [f. STADDLE *sb.* + -ING[1]. OE. had *staðolung, -ing*, vbl. sb. f. *staðolian* STATHEL *v.*]

†**1.** The starling or pier of a bridge. *Obs. rare.*
1461 in C. Welch *Tower Bridge* (1894) 89 For fishing next the stadelynges. **1481** *City Lond. Letter Bk. L* lf. 163 b, By casting of ankers in the Goleis and Stadelynges vnder þe brygge. **1482** in C. Welch *Tower Bridge* (1894) 89 Stadelinges and ground workys of the same brigge.

2. The materials used to form a foundation for a stack; the stand or foundation of a stack. Also (see quot. 1825).
?*a***1700** in Hodgson *Water Mellock* (1883) 33 (E.D.D.) None shall grave any turves for stadeling. **1825** BROCKETT *N.C. Words, Staidlin*, a part of a corn stack left standing. **1848** W. BARNES *Poems Rural Life* (ed. 2) 390 *Staddlen, Staddling*, stuff to make a staddle. **1866** BROGDEN *Prov. Lincs.* 194 *Staddling*, the bed or foundation upon which stacks of agricultural produce is placed.

staddow, obs. form of STADDA.

stade[1] (steɪd). [Anglicized form of STADIUM. Cf. F. *stade* and STADIE; also STAGE *sb.*]

1. a. An ancient measure of length; = STADIUM 1.
*c***1537** PAYNEL in De Benese *Measurynge Lande* Pref. + iiij, Famouse quantytes, as a fynger.. a pase, a perche, a stade and a myle. **1554** W. PRATTE *Aphrique* D viij b, Meroe .. is an Ilonde in forme of a tryangle.. and dothe extende almost thre thousand Stades. **1600** J. MELVILL *Autobiog. & Diary* (Wodrow Soc.) 420 A mightie erthquak.. reased the halff of the montean Eroge,.. and caried it four stades, that is, halff a myll. **1642** H. MORE *Song of Soul* II. App. 41 Distances.. such as were of yore, Measur'd by leagues, miles, stades. **1800** RENNELL *Geogr. Syst. Herodotus* ii. 13 In common acceptation we find a stade commensurate to a furlong. *Ibid.*, The Grecian itinerary stade. **1838** LEAKE in *Jrnl. R. Geog. Soc.* IX. 1 On the Stade, as a Linear Measure. **1869** TOZER *Highl. Turkey* II. 128 Strabo says that the ruins .. were situated above Demetrias, at seven stades distance from it. **1885–94** R. BRIDGES *Eros & Psyche* Jan. xxix, On the eastern coast, some forty stades, There stood a temple of her goddess foe.

b. A stadium or course for foot-racing. Also *attrib. rare.*
1875 BROWNING *Aristoph. Apol.* 16 When he had run life's proper race and worked Quite to the stade's end. *Ibid.* 18 He .. Turned stade-point but to face Activity.

†**2. a.** A stage in a journey. **b.** A stage in the progress of a disease: = STADIUM 3. *Obs.*
1616 J. LANE *Contn. Sqr.'s T.* VI. 91 Post horse he laid at everie fittinge stade. **1710** T. FULLER *Pharm. Extemp.* 274 Such a Consumption as is not yet gone beyond its first Stade.

3. *Geol.* (See quot. 1961); = STADIAL *sb.*, STADIUM 5.
1961 *Bull. Amer. Assoc. Petroleum Geologists* XLV. 660/2 A stade was a climatic episode within a glaciation during which a secondary advance of glaciers took place. **1964** *Prof. Papers U.S. Geol. Survey* No. 501-D. 104/2 Currently, the oldest group of moraines define the early stade of Bull Lake Glaciation, and the middle and youngest groups together define the late stade. **1974** *Nature* 26 Apr. 752/2 The 'cold' water fauna [belongs] to the period of the Loch Lomond readvance stade.

†**stade**[2]. *Obs.* [ad. Sp. *estado*:—L. *status* standing: see STATE *sb.*] A fathom.
1604 E. G[RIMSTONE] tr. *Acosta's Hist. Indies* III. xxi. 187 Of fifteene stades deepe, (which is the height of a man or more). *Ibid.* IV. vi. 223.

†**stade**[3]. *Obs. rare*$^{-1}$. [a. Du. *stad* (MDu. *stat*, inflected *stade.*] Chief town.
1481 CAXTON *Reynard* i. (Arb.) 5 The lyon.. wolde in the holy dayes of thys feeste holde on open Court at stade.

†**stade**[4]. *Obs.* [? *Stade*, name of a town in Hanover.] Some textile fabric.
1714 *French Bk. Rates* 82 Stuffs Stades per Piece of 18 Ells 08 00.

stadholder, stadtholder ('stædhəʊldə(r)). *Hist.* Forms: 6–8 **statholder,** 7 **state-holder,** (8 **stadhouder**), 7– **stadtholder,** 8– **stadholder.** [ad. Du. *stadhouder* (= G. *statthalter*) one who occupies another's place, a 'locum tenens', lieutenant, f. *stad* place (= G. *statt*; in Du. the word survives only in the sense 'city', = G. *stadt*, which is a mere graphic variant of *statt*) + *houder* HOLDER.]

†**1.** The governor of a fortress. *Obs. rare*$^{-1}$.
1591 HORSEY *Trav.* (Hakl. Soc.) 190 The centinell brought me to the statholder or liftenant of the castell.

2. *Netherlands Hist.* **a.** Originally, a viceroy or lieutenant governor of a province or provinces. **b.** The title borne by the chief magistrate of the Dutch republic.
In the latter use, the title was first conferred by the States-General on William of Orange in 1580, and implied a nominal recognition of the sovereignty of the king of Spain. When the independence of the republic was acknowledged, the title of the office (hereditary in the house of Orange) remained unchanged. The stadholdership was abolished in 1802.
1668 *Lond. Gaz.* No. 226/4 Zealand and Friezland are as yet for his admission as Stadtholder. **1673** H. STUBBE *Further Vind. Dutch War* To Rdr. 11 Twice we find the

State-holders to have acted Authoritatively. **1701** GREW *Cosmol. Sacra* III. i. 90 The United Provinces with their Statholder, and the Venetians, with their Doge. **1753** HANWAY *Trav.* II. I. ix. (1762) 49 William, sirnamed the great, was the first stadtholder, and may be properly called the founder of the republic. **1825** MACAULAY *Ess., Milton* (1850) I. 21 [Cromwell] demanded indeed the first place in the commonwealth; but with powers scarcely so great as those of a Dutch stadtholder or an American president. **1876** BANCROFT *Hist. U.S.* xxii. II. 36 The friends of the stadholder asserted sovereignty for the states-general.

3. Used to render the etymologically equivalent G. *statthalter*, Da. *statholder*, lieutenant-governor, viceroy.

1704 *Lond. Gaz.* No. 4015/2 The Emperor has Appointed the Count de Louvenstein,..to be Stadholder of the Upper Palatinate. **1886** T. MICHELL *Scot. Exped. Norway in 1612* I. vii. 52 The Norwegian Stadtholder.

Hence **stadholderess**, a female stadholder; the wife of a stadholder.

1737 [G. SMITH] *Cur. Relat.* I. 141 A free Pardon from Queen Mary, Sister to the Emperor Charles, then Stadtholderess.

stad'holderate. Also stadt-. [f. + -ATE[1].]

1. The office or dignity of stadholder.

1786 *Ann. Reg., St. Papers* 67/1 The Stadtholderate became extinct by the death of William III of England. **1825** JEFFERSON *Autobiog.* Wks. 1859 I. 75 He would take no part in the quarrel, unless an entire abolition of the Stadtholderate should be attempted. **1880** GREEN *Hist. Eng. People* IV. IX. iii. 300 The restoration of the Dutch Stadtholderate.

2. A state ruled by a stadholder, or by a chief with the status and powers of a stadholder.

1889 *Academy* 20 July 32/1 Making the revolted colonies into a stadtholderate under the Count of Broglie.

†**stadhol'derian,** *a.* and *sb. Obs.* [f. STADHOLDER + -IAN.] **a.** *adj.* Pertaining to a stadholder or to the office of stadholder; attached to the party of the stadholder. **b.** *sb.* A partisan of the stadholder.

1784–5 *Ann. Reg., Hist. Europe* 102/1 The hereditary enemies of the stadtholderian system of government. **1787** *Ibid., Chron.* 225/2 The houses of the Stadtholderians were not exempt from ravage. **1796** *Ibid., St. Papers* 194 The Netherlands were no longer under the stadtholderian yoke.

'stadholdership. [f. STADHOLDER + -SHIP.]

1. The office or dignity of a stadholder.

1668 *Lond. Gaz.* No. 238/3 The Deputies from the States General sent into Vriesland about the business of the Stateholdership. **1673** H. STUBBE *Further Vind. Dutch War* To Rdr. 7 The Election of Great Maurice to the said Stateholdership was purely a provincial act. *a* **1715** BURNET *Own Time* (1724) I. 273 To try what offices the King would do in order to his advancement to the Stadtholdership. **1723** *Lond. Gaz.* No. 6153/1 The Stadtholdership of that Province. **1837** *Foreign Q. Rev.* XIX. 173 The maintenance of the stadtholdership in the Netherlands. **1913** WILLCOCK *Sir H. Vane* xii. 203 During the time of his minority the Statthaltership was in abeyance.

†**2.** A district ruled by a stadholder. *Obs.*

1811 PINKERTON *Mod. Geog.* (ed. 3) 142 Of these twenty-three provinces [of Russia], forty-two stadtholderships were formed.

stadia ('steɪdɪə). [Of obscure history; prob. derived from STADIUM, and perhaps from the plural *stadia*. Cf. F. *stadia* (Littré *Suppl.*, with quot. of 1876).

It is doubtful in what country the word originated; the statement in the first quot. below lacks confirmation.]

An apparatus for measuring distance by optical means. **a.** *Mil.* An instrument consisting of a glass plate, or a brass plate with an opening of the form of an isosceles triangle, marked with figures showing the distance at which a foot- or horse-soldier will be when his image covers a certain height on the instrument held at arm's length. **b.** *Surveying.* An apparatus consisting of a rod or staff placed at one end of the distance to be measured and a pair of horizontal lines, hairs or wires on the diaphragm of a telescope placed at the other end. Also *attrib.* as in ***stadia hairs, lines, measurement, method, -rod, -surveying, telescope.***

By British surveyors *stadia* is commonly used as equivalent to 'stadia rod'; in the U.S. this use appears to be rare. The 'stadia method' has two varieties: in the one the staff is graduated and the telescope hairs fixed at a known distance apart; in the other the staff is of known length and the hairs are movable.

1865 MAYER in *Jrnl. Franklin Inst.* Jan. 4 The idea to measure the distances by a scale and the micrometer of a telescope was proposed by an Italian engineer about 45 years ago, and the name of Stadia (scale) was given by him to that kind of measure. *Ibid.* 5 Construction of a Stadia. *Ibid.*, To ..compute the error of the reading on the Stadia scale. **1865** S. W. ROBINSON *Ibid.* Feb. 74 The error of the stadia measurement has been found to be about one foot in 800 or 1000. *Ibid.* 75 A much more convenient arrangement than the rod and targets, is a flat surface of three or four inches width and the required length, painted in such a manner that the distance can be read to a foot by the observer himself. By the French this is called a *stadia*. **1871** *Trans. Amer. Inst. Min. Engin.* I. 377 An extra pair of hairs for stadia purposes. **1890** W. F. STANLEY *Surv. Instrum.* 321 For convenience the tangent is more generally taken upon a graduated stadia or staff which is erected for measurement perpendicularly to the horizon. **1899** W. G. BLIGH *Notes Instrum. Engin. Field-work* 122 The telescope fitted with stadia lines on a stop glass. *Ibid.* 124 Stadia hairs are horizontal lines, either hairs fixed to the diaphragm or else marked on a stop glass. **1900** H. M. WILSON *Topogr. Surveying* xii. 238 The stadia is a device for determining the distance of a point by means of a graduated rod, and the distance subtended on it by auxiliary wires in the telescope of a transit or alidade. *Ibid.*, The term *stadia surveying* is used to include not only the measurement of the horizontal distance, but also the determination of heights by means of vertical angles observed to a fixed point on the rod.

stadia: pl. of STADIUM.

'stadial, *a.* and *sb.* [ad. L. *stadiāl-is*, f. *stadi-um*: see STADIUM and -AL[1].]

A. *adj.* †**1.** Pertaining to a stadium in length. *Obs. rare*$^{-1}$.

1398 TREVISA *Barth. De P.R.* XIX. cxxix. (1495) 937 The Stadiall felde conteyneth syxe score pace and fyue.

2. a. *Geol.* Of or pertaining to a glacial stadium or stade; ***stadial moraine*** = ***recessional moraine*** s.v. RECESSIONAL *a.* 3.

1937 WOOLDRIDGE & MORGAN *Physical Basis of Geogr.* xxii. 378 Retreatal stages of the ice in the valleys are marked by 'stadial moraines'. **1970** R. J. SMALL *Study of Landforms* xi. 388 If the ice is affected by episodes of retreat, separated by stillstands, a number of smaller, sub-parallel ridges ('recessional' or 'stadial' moraines) will be formed. **1971** S. C. PORTER in K. K. Turekian *Late Cenozoic Glacial Ages* xi. 320 In the Puget Lowland only two stadial episodes have been determined for the Puget lobe. **1979** *Nature* 19 July 199/2 The landforms produced by the stadial glaciers in the Highlands are often clear and abundant.

b. *Archæol.* Pertaining to or expressed in terms of a series of successive stages into which a culture or period can be divided.

1959 *Science* 6 Feb. 305/2 Willey and Phillips' stadial conception of New World prehistory. **1968** L. R. BINFORD in S. R. & L. R. Binford *New Perspectives in Archeol.* I. i. 15 The application of such a scale to innumerable empirical cases..can never provide us with an understanding of the processes operative in the past which resulted in the stadial sequence. **1977** G. CLARK *World Prehistory* (ed. 3) ii. 41 The use of the term 'Neolithic' in this connection in itself poses a problem. If stadial terms are rarely used in contemporary archaeological discourse, it seems all the more important to be clear about their meaning.

B. *sb. Geol.* = STADE[1] 3.

1954 *Antiquity* XXVIII. 8 The tundra-like phase at the beginning of the third Würm stadial. **1964** K. W. BUTZER *Environment & Archeol.* xxvii. 395 It seems improbable that food-collectors at the Neanderthaler level would venture through thousands of kilometers of harsh environment at the height of any of the Würm stadials. **1979** SEYFERT & SIRKIN *Earth Hist. & Plate Tectonics* (ed. 2) xiv. 515/2 Glacial advances occurred during stadials.

stadic ('steɪdɪk), *a. rare.* [f. STAD-IA + -IC.] Pertaining to a stadia.

1901 A. P. DAVIS *Elevation and Stadic Tables* in *Nature* (1901) 28 Mar. 514/1 [Tables] for obtaining differences of altitude for all angles and distances, horizontal distances in stadic work, &c.

†**stadie.** *Obs. rare*$^{-1}$. [Anglicized form of STADIUM. Cf. STADE[1].] = STADIUM 2.

c **1374** CHAUCER *Boeth.* IV. pr. iii. (1868) 119 Yif a man renneþ in þe stadie or in þe forlonge for þe corone, þan lieþ þe mede in þe corone for whiche he renneþ.

stadiometer (steɪdɪ'ɒmɪtə(r)). [f. Gr. στάδιο-ν STADIUM + -METER. Cf. F. *stadiomètre*, according to Bouillet (1896) an improved stadia invented in 1861 by Dupuy de Podio.]

1. a. *Mil.* = STADIA a. **b.** (See quot. 1884.) **c.** *U.S. Surveying.* 'A modified theodolite in which the directions are not read off, but marked upon a small sheet, which is changed at each station' (*Cent. Dict.* 1891).

1862 *Catal. Internat. Exhib.* II. XI. 8 The stadiometer, for judging distance, has been adopted by Government. **1871** HEATHER *Math. Instrum.* III. 84 Edgeworth's Stadiometer or surveying instrument. **1884** KNIGHT *Dict. Mech.* Suppl. s.v., The geographic stadiometer..is designed to show at a single reading the measure of any line, right, curved, or broken, on maps or charts executed on any scale.

2. An apparatus for measuring a person's height.

1972 *Sunday Times* 22 Oct. 65/2 His product range does not end at anthropometers. There is a stadiometer for measuring height to a high degree of accuracy. **1980** *Brit. Med. Jrnl.* 29 Mar. 915 When the child is old enough to stand a special stadiometer can be used to measure height.

†**stadionicest.** *Obs. rare*$^{-1}$. [irreg. f. Gr. σταδιονίκης, f. στάδιο-ν STADIUM + νικᾶν to conquer.] A winner in the stadium or foot-race.

a **1656** USSHER *Ann.* (1658) 90 The Catalogue of the Stadionicests.

stadium ('steɪdɪəm). Pl. **stadia** ('steɪdɪə), **stadiums**; also 6 **stadias, stadios**, 8 **stadia's**, 7 **stadium's**, 7– **stadiums**. [L., ad. Gr. στάδιον.

A plural form *stadii* (after Gr. στάδιοι, L. accus. *stadios*) used by Byron *Sardanapalus* v. i, has been corrected in posthumous editions to *stadia*.]

1. An ancient Greek and Roman measure of length, varying according to time and place, but most commonly equal to 600 Greek or Roman feet, or one-eighth of a Roman mile. (In the English Bible rendered by *furlong*.)

1398 TREVISA *Barth. De P.R.* XIX. cxxix. (1495) 937 The Stadium is the eyghte parte of a myle. **1585** T. WASHINGTON tr. *Nicholay's Voy.* IV. xxix. 151 Amicle, distant twentie stadias from Lacedemon. **1600** PORY tr. *Leo's Africa* Introd. 11 Meroe..in length three thousand stadios or furlongs. **1601** HOLLAND *Pliny* II. xxiii. l. 14 A Stadium or Furlong maketh of our paces 125... Posidonius saith, That from the earth it is no lesse than fortie stadia to that height..wherein ..clouds doe engender. **1621** BURTON *Anat. Mel.* III. ii. I. i. (1624) 357 Two Palme trees..which were barren..till they came to see one another by growing vp higher, though many Stadiums asunder. **1657** G. THORNLEY *Daphnis & Chloe* 82 When he had born off to sea about ten stadium's. **1730** A. GORDON *Maffei's Amphith.* 325 The Circus..was three Stadia's in length.

2. A race-course for foot-racing, originally a stadium in length; hence *occas.* foot-racing as an exercise. In mod. use often in extended sense, a place for athletic exercises; *spec.* an enclosed area for sporting events equipped with tiers of seats for spectators. (The pl. *stadiums* is usual in this sense.)

1603 HOLLAND *Plutarch* Explan. Words, *Stadium*, a race or space of ground, conteining 625. foote. **1676** H. VERNON in *Phil. Trans.* XI. 579 There is the stadium yet to be seen. **1749** G. WEST *Pindar's Odes, Diss. Olympic Games* i. (1753) II. 10 Homer..introduces his greatest Heroes contending in the very same kind of Exercises, with those practised in the Stadium of Olympia. *Ibid.* vii. 61 The simple Foot-Race, named the Stadium, from the Length of the Course. **1833** SIR H. ELLIS *Elgin Marbles* I. 26 One of the greatest of the public works of Athens was the stadium of Herodes Atticus. **1834** BARON BERENGER (*title*) Particulars and Recommendations of the Stadium, or British National Arena for Manly and Defensive Exercises, Equestrian, Chivalric and Aquatic Games..at the Residence of the late Lord Cremorne. **1847** GROTE *Greece* II. xxviii. IV. 96 Kylon ..had gained the prize in the Olympic stadium. **1866** ALGER *Solit. Nat. & Man* II. 51 We always think of the oracles of the gods as dropping in grove and grotto, not in street and stadium. **1901** *Westm. Gaz.* 27 Feb. 8/2 The stadium for sports, covering ten acres, is one of the chief features of the [Pan-American] Exposition [at Buffalo]. **1928** *Times* 20 Apr. 6/6 It would be difficult to imagine a more impressive enclosure than the Stadium [*sc.* Wembley Stadium] for the holding of the greatest football festival of the year. **1938** L. MACNEICE *Earth Compels* 59 It's no go the picture palace, it's no go the stadium. **1972** G. GREEN *Great Moments in Sport: Soccer* iii. 44 As for Lenin Stadium itself, it was very much like Wembley before the cover went on, an elliptical concrete monster, liberally dotted with exits and entrances, and steeply tiered.

3. A stage of a process, disease, etc.

1669 W. SIMPSON *Hydrol. Chym.* 190 The several Stadiums of this Salt gives the various apparencies of growth, maturity, and old age of Plants. **1725** *Phil. Trans.* XXXIII. 391 Hence those Deliriums, Coma's, &c. so frequently threatening at this Stadium of the Disease. **1822–29** *Good's Study Med.* (ed. 3) IV. 77 Hence different stadia of life seem to exercise some control [over insanity]. **1860** GEO. ELIOT in Cross *Life* (1885) II. 282 We are still far off our last stadium of developement. **1876** BARTHOLOW *Mat. Med.* (1879) 176 Its good effects are limited, however, to that stadium of these maladies in which the morbid action is confined to the nasal passages. **1878** DOWDEN *Stud. Lit.* 36 A new stadium in the advance of the revolutionary idea commenced. **1888** J. MARTINEAU *Study Relig.* II. ii. II. 26 As the later stadia of her [Nature's] developments rise above the earlier. **1895** D. SHARP *Insects* I. 158 The intervals between the ecdyses are called stadia, the first stadium being the period between hatching and the first ecdysis.

4. *Surveying.* (See quots.) Cf. STADIA.

1861 in *Abridgm. Specif. Patents, Opt.* etc. *Instrum.* (1875) 363 An improved stadium or telemetre. **1871** HEATHER *Math. Instrum.* III. 79 The Stadium for measuring distances in rifle practice. **1884** KNIGHT *Dict. Mech.*, Suppl., *Stadium*, the leveling rod of a surveyor.

5. *Geol.* = STADE[1] 3. Now *Obs.* or *rare.*

1910 *Zeitschr. für Gletscherkunde* IV. 246 The later stages of glaciation in the scheme proposed by Geikie..may prove to correspond to the *stadia* of the Alpine region which are so clearly brought out by Penck and Brückner in their recent great work. **1914** W. B. WRIGHT *Quaternary Ice Age* vii. 156 An investigation of the stages of retreat in the Etsch district has shown that three main stadia can also be distinguished here. **1937** *Ibid.* (ed. 2) xi. 185 This stadium must..be dated back before the Swiss pile-dwellings, or in round numbers 7000 years ago.

stadt, variant of STAD.

‖**stadthaus** ('ʃtathaʊs). [G., f. *stadt* town + *haus* HOUSE *sb.*[1]] A German town-hall. Cf. STADTHOUSE.

1839 BARHAM *Ingold. Leg., St. Gengulphus*, They stuck up placards on the walls of the Stadthaus. **1848** THACKERAY *Van. Fair* lxiii, Georgy Osborne..came to the Stadthaus' ball in company of his uncle's courier.

stadtholder, variant of STADHOLDER.

stadthouse ('stæthaʊs). Also: 7 stat-, 8 stadhouse. [ad. G. *stadthaus* and Du. *stadhuis*, f. G. *stadt*, Du. *stad* town + G. *haus*, Du. *huis* HOUSE *sb.*] A town-hall, esp. one in a Dutch town (or Dutch colony).

1646 HOWELL *Lewis XIII*, ii. 42 A Stat-House in Delph in Holland, which had bin burnt in like maner and reedified. **1673** TEMPLE *Observ. United Prov.* ii. 86 The Magnificence of their Publique Buildings, as Stadthouse and Arsenals. **1704** *Lond. Gaz.* No. 4077/3 Having shewn his Grace their Famous Stadhouse. **1766** *Ann. Reg., Chron.* 94/1 A most terrible fire at Muskau in Upper Lusatia, which reduced to ashes, two churches, the stadthouse [etc.]. **1809** W. IRVING *Knickerb.* (1861) 131 A great banquet was served up in the stadthouse. **1849** MACAULAY *Hist. Eng.* v. I. 550 The Stadthouse of Amsterdam.

staeg, obs. form of STAG *sb.*[1]

†**'stafador.** *Obs. rare*[−1]. [ad. Sp. *estafador*, agent-n. f. *estafar* to swindle.] An impostor.
1638 W. M. *Garcia's Sonne Rogue* 246 For the first are the Robbers, next the Stafadours, then the Grumets, after these the Hobgoblins. *Ibid.* 249 A Robber, Staffador or Grumet.

stafesagre, obs. form of STAVESACRE.

staff (stɑːf, -æ-), *sb.*[1] Pl. **staves** (steɪvz), **staffs** (stɑːfs, -æ-). Forms: 1 stæb, (stab-, steb-), 1–2 stef, 1–4 stæf, 1–6 staf, 3 *oblique* stæve, steave, 3–4 *oblique* stave, 4–7 stafe, 4–8, (9 *arch.*) staffe, 5–6 *Sc.* staif, 6 stayffe, *Sc.* stalf, (stafte), 4–7 *genit. sing.* staves, 3– staff; *pl.* 1 stafas, 2 stafen, 2–5 stafes, 3 staven, *Ormin* stafess, 4 stafs, steves, (stavenes), 4–5 stafis, stawis, 4–6 stavis, -ys, 5–6 staffes, 6 stavez, *Sc.* staiffis, sta(l)ffis, 3–9 staves, 8– staffs. [Com. Teut.: OE. *stæf* masc. corresponds to OFris. *stef*, OS. *-staf* (MLG., MDu., Du. *staf*), OHG., MHG. *stap*, genit. *stabes* (mod.G. *stab*). ON. *staf-r* (Sw. *staf*, Da. *stav*):—OTeut. **stabo-z*; a variant type **stabi-* appears in Goth. **staf-s* (in dat. pl. *stabim*) rendering στοιχεῖον element; a third type, possibly ancient, is represented by early mod.Du. *stave*, now *staaf* fem., bar. Other probable derivatives from the Teut. **stab-* (? to be firm or fixed) are Da. *stabbe* (Icel. *stabbi*) STAB *sb.*[1]; ON. *stef* neut. (:—**stabjon-*) set or recurring time, refrain, *stefja* (:—**stabjon-*) to prevent, *stefna* fem. appointed time (:—**stabnjōn-*), STEVEN *sb.*; OHG. *stabên* (MHG. *staben*) to become stiff. The pre-Teut. type might be either **stapo-* (? f. **stā-* to stand, with suffix of causative import as in Sk. *sthāpāyati* makes to stand), or **stabho-*.
The plural form *staves* is now somewhat archaic, exc. in certain senses in which a sing. form STAVE has been developed from it; but it is still preferred in those senses that are confined to literary use.]

I. 1. a. A stick carried in the hand as an aid in walking or climbing. Now chiefly *literary* (e.g. in reference to 'pilgrims').
c **725** *Corpus Gloss.* 1441 *Olastrum*: stæb. *c* **888** ÆLFRED *Boeth.* xxxvi. §6 Ða cild ridað on hiora stafum. *c* **897** —— *Gregory's Past. C.* xvii. 126 Mid ʒierde mon bið beswungen, and mid stæfe he bið awreðed. *c* **1205** LAY. 30754 Þene staf he nom an honde and ferde ouer þan londe. *c* **1250** *Gen. & Ex.* 3149 Stondende, and staf on hond. **1377** LANGL. *P. Pl.* B. XVII. 36 Þe gome þat goth with o staf, he semeth in gretter hele þan he þat goth with two staues to syȝte of vs alle. *a* **1533** BERNERS *Huon* cxlvi. 545 Huon..aparelyd hymselfe lyke a pylgryme, with a stafe, and a bage abought his necke. *c* **1539** in Aungier *Syon* (1840) 131 They bare small staves in their honds to lepe over the watery playshes. **1590** SPENSER *F.Q.* I. viii. 30 An old old man..That on a staffe his feeble steps did frame. **1666** PEPYS *Diary* 20 July, He did present me with a varnished staffe, very fine and light to walk with. **1760–72** H. BROOKE *Fool of Qual.* (1809) IV. 139 With their staffs in their hands. **1803** JANE PORTER *Thaddeus* i, When we possessed no other property than the staffs which we hold in our hands. **1860** TYNDALL *Glac.* I. xiv. 95, I..dug my staff deeply into the snow. **1857** J. G. HOLLAND *Bay Path* vi. 78 Two or three pedestrians..swinging their sturdy staves. **1907** *Verney Mem.* I. 50 A curious pilgrim's staff.

b. *jocularly* as a type of thinness or leanness.
c **1386** CHAUCER *Prol.* 592 Ful longe were his legges and ful lene, Ylyk a staf, ther was no calf ysene. **1597** SHAKS. *2 Hen. IV*, v. i. 71 If I were saw'de into Quantities, I should make foure dozen of such bearded Hermites staues, as Master Shallow.

†**c.** Applied to a crutch. *Obs.*
1483 CAXTON *Gold. Leg.* 432/2 He coude not goo ne stande wythoute he had two crutches or staues under hys armes.

†**d.** A stick or rod, esp. one with a hooked end, used for tending sheep; a shepherd's crook. *Obs.*
For *shepherd's staff* used as a plant-name, after L. *virga pastoris*, see SHEPHERD *sb.* 8 d.
c **1475** *Pict. Voc.* in Wr.-Wülcker 814 *Hoc pedum*, a scheperdes stafe. **1530** PALSGR. 266/2 Schepherdes staffe, *hovlette.* **1538** ELYOT *Dict.*, *Agolum*, a staffe to dryue cattell with. **1577** GOOGE *Heresbach's Husb.* III. 141 They must be well ware in the driuing of them..that they guide them with theyr voyce, and shaking of theyr staffe.

e. A rod or wand used as an instrument of magic or divination.
1610 SHAKS. *Temp.* v. 54 I'le breake my staffe. **1656** S. HOLLAND *Don Zara* 67 Her Rod, Staff, and other implements of Sorcery stood by her on a Table of Abstersive Ebony. **1770** LANGHORNE *Plutarch, Camillus* (Rtldg.) 109/2 They discovered under a great heap of ashes the augural staff of Romulus. This staff is crooked at one end, and called *lituus.* **1836** THIRLWALL *Greece* xiv. II. 197 Diviners..who drew their knowledge of the future from the position of staves thrown on the ground.

f. *by staff and baton*: a formula of Scots Law, used when the vassal resigns his feu into the hands of his superior. (Cf. ROD *sb.*[1] 1 c.)
1499 *Reg. Privy Seal Scot.* I. 43/2 Resignit be his procuratouris in our soverane lordis handis..be staf and bastoun. **1596** in T. Morris *Provosts of Methven* (1875) 86 Thair in my name..be staff and bastoun, as vse is, to resigne ..in our said Souerane lordis handis..my mansioun. **1762** in *Nairne Peerage Evid.* (1874) 92 To resign surrender overgive and deliver duely and lawfully by staff and baton as use is all and haill the foresaids parts and portions of his baronies.

2. A stick, pole or club used as a weapon. (Cf. QUARTERSTAFF.)
The constable's staff (quot. 1583, etc.) is at once a weapon and a badge of office: see sense 7 and TIPSTAFF 1.
c **1000** ÆLFRIC *Gram.* ix. (Z.) 55 *Fustis* saʒol oððe stæf. *c* **1250** *Owl & Night.* 1167 Her-uore hit is þat me þe shuneþ, & þe to-toruep & to-buneþ Mid staue & stone & turf & clute. *c* **1290** *St. Lawrence* 114 in *S. Eng. Leg.* 343 He het heom with grete staues leggen on him to grounde. *a* **1300** *Cursor M.* 7528 His arms fra him did he suing, And tok bot a staf and a sling. **1340** *Ayenb.* 156 Þe sergons..nome steues and byete þane asse riȝt to þe uolle. **1382** WYCLIF *Mark* xiv. 48 As to a thef ȝe han gon out with swerdis and staues, for to take me. *c* **1386** CHAUCER *Knt.'s T.* 1652 Yemen on foote and communes many oon With shorte staues. **1421** *Cov. Leet Bk.* 28 That no bocher..ber no billys, ne gysarnez, ne no grett stauys within the Cite... Saue leefull be hit to euery bocher and othur man..comyng to market to dryve hur beestis with smale stavys and non othur. **1470–85** MALORY *Arthur* I. ix. 47 Thenne the comyns of Carlyon aroos with clubbis and stauys and slewe many knyghtes. **1583** *Nottingham Rec.* IV. 201, xxx. Cunstable stavez at xvd. a pece. **1663** KILLIGREW *Parson's Wedd.* IV. i, Constables staff, and Lanthorn. **1671** MILTON *Samson* 1123, I only with an Oak'n staff will meet thee. **1742** *Col. Rec. Pennsylv.* IV. 621 The Constables interposing with their Staves for some time kept off the Rioters. **1778** *Learning at a Loss* I. 103 In his Hand [was] a very inimical Oak staff of at least two Inches diameter. **1821** COMBE *Syntax, Wife* I. (1869) 267 But warrants, staves and mastiffs wait To guard the approaches to his gate. **1847** MRS. A. KERR tr. *Ranke's Hist. Servia* 32 We find them armed only with long staves.
fig. **1541** CROME in Strype *Eccl. Mem.* (1721) III. xi. 104 But, alack! this bold Beggar's Staf hath this Beggar of Rome left here behind him. Which Staf beateth both the Bodies and Souls of Men. **1577** *F. de Lisle's Legendarie* G vij, She looked to finde in him a new staffe wherewith to suppresse the Guisians.

3. a. The shaft of a spear or lance. *arch.* †**b.** A spear, lance, or similar armed weapon. ***to break a staff***, to tilt or contend *with* (an antagonist). *Obs.*
c **1205** LAY. 8155 Euelin..mid þan stæue to-draf, and smat Herigal a þon ribben þat þe stæf to-bræc amidden. *c* **1330** R. BRUNNE *Chron. Wace* (Rolls) 14806 Eyþer þorow pleyn bataille in feld, Or wyþ chaumpion staf & scheld. *c* **1400** *Brut* ccxxiii. 276 He fonde in a chambre aboue v C of grete stafes [CAXTON staues] of fyne oke, with longe pikes of yren and of stele. **1471** CAXTON *Recuyell* (Sommer) 157 Ther was..many an arowe shotte and many a staffe and guysarme broken. **1513** DOUGLAS *Æneis* VIII. xi. 45 Twa javilling speris, or than gyssarn stavis. *a* **1548** HALL *Chron.*, *Hen. VIII*, 6 There wer broken many staues and great praise geuen to the twoo straungers. **1597** SHAKS. *2 Hen. IV*, IV. i. 120 Their armed Staues in charge, their Beauers downe. **1599, 1624** [see TAINT *v.* A. 5 b]. **1600** HOLLAND *Livy* VIII. vii. 285 Wilt thou then..break a staffe with me in the meane time. **1605** SHAKS. *Macb.* v. iii. 48 Come, put mine Armour on: giue me my Staffe. **1611** BIBLE *1 Sam.* xvii. 7 The staffe of his speare was like a weauers beame. **1611** COTGR. s.v. *Manche, Le manche d'un espieu*, the staffe of a Bore-speare. **1868** MORRIS *Earthly Par.*, *Man born to be King* 1226 Who bore armed staves and coats of fence.

†**c.** with defining word, indicating some kind of spear or javelin, as ***horseman's***, ***hunter's***, ***hunting***, ***Jedburgh*** (***Jedworth***, ***Jedwood*** etc.) ***staff***. *Obs.*
1515–6 *Exchequer Rolls Scot.* XIV. 141 Halbertis, Leith axis, et Jedworth stauis [*printed* stanis]. **1538** ELYOT *Dict.*, *Venabulum*, a huntynge staffe. *a* **1547** SURREY *Æneid* IV. 167 The hunting staues with their brod heads of steele. **1560** WHITEHORN *Ord. Souldiours* xl. 45 Howe to make certayn fyreworke to tye at the poinctes of pykes or horsemenstaues. **1561** in *Maitland Club Misc.* III. 278 And for ye sam caws of set purpos ye person had Jedwod staiffis in ye qweyr. **1567** *Reg. Privy Council Scot.* I. 578 Stryking and schuting of culveringis and Jedburgh staffis. **1579–80** NORTH *Plutarch, Pelopidas* (1595) 309 Taking houndes with them, and hunters staues in their handes. **1611** COTGR., *Espieu*, a Boare-speare; a hunting staffe, or Iauelin. *a* **1625** FLETCHER *Hum. Lieut.* I. 1, And on Our Horsemans Staves, Death lookes as grimly as on your keene-edgd Swords. **1680** *Lyon Office Register of Arms* (MS.), A kynde of Launce (called the Jedburgh staff). **1708** MOTTEUX *Rabelais* v. ix. (1737) 35 Troutstaves,..and Hunting Staffs.

†**d.** ***Judas staff*** [cf. Mark xiv. 43] = JUDAS 2.
1488 in *Archæologia* XLV. 119 Ther bith vi Judas Staves for torches peynted.

4. a. *fig.* Something which serves as a support or stay.
1390 GOWER *Conf.* II. 145 Therof the Jelous takth non hiede, Bot as a man to love unkinde, He cast his staf, as doth the blinde, And fint defaulte where is non. *a* **1489** CAXTON *Blanchardyn* 213 And is she gon, the comfort of my youth, the staffe of my age. *a* **1591** H. SMITH *Serm.* (1637) 496 Take heed is a good staffe to stay upon. **1596** SHAKS. *Merch. V.* II. ii. 70 The boy was the verie staffe of my age, my verie prop. **1606** —— *Ant. & Cl.* III. xiii. 68 It much would please him, That of his Fortunes you should make a staffe To leane vpon. **1642** FULLER *Holy & Prof. St.* v. xiv. 415 Having lost his own legs, he relyes on the staff of his kinred. **1721** DE FOE *Mem. Cavalier* (1840) 256 They were the staff of the party. **1820** W. IRVING *Sketch Bk.* I. 223 They had one son, who had grown up to be the staff and pride of their age. **1830** SCOTT *Introd. Last Minstrel* ¶13, I determined that literature should be my staff, but not my crutch. **1876** HARDY *Ethelberta* xiii, Long before he adopted music as the staff of his pilgrimage.

b. In the Biblical phr. ***to break the staff of bread*** (literally from Heb. *mattēh 'leḥem*, Vulg. *baculum panis*), to diminish or cut off the supply of food.
1382, 1388 WYCLIF *Lev.* xxvi. 26. **1560** BIBLE (Geneva) *Lev.* xxvi. 26. *Ps.* cv. 16. *Ezek.* iv. 16. [And so **1611**.] *c* **1586** C'TESS PEMBROKE *Ps.* cv. iv, Scarse had he spoken, When famine came, the staff of bread was broken. **1596** BARLOW *Three Serm.* i. 121 God in his lawe threatneth that he will breake the staffe of bread, that is, bread shall not nourish them that eate it.

c. Hence ***the staff of life*** = bread (or similar staple food).
1638 PENKETHMAN *Artach.* A j b, Bread is worth all, being the Staffe of life. **1656** J. HAMMOND *Leah & Rachel* (1844) 9 Corn (the main staffe of life). **1698** FRYER *Acc. E. India & P.* 35 For Corn, they have Rice the Staff of the Land. **1860** *All Year Round* No. 45. 440 Barley bannocks and oat cake long remained the staff of life in villages in Scotland. **1901** D. SLADEN *In Sicily* I. 372 Broad beans form one of the staves of life in Sicily.

d. ***staff and staple***: the chief elements or ingredients.
1869 BUCKLE *Civiliz.* II. 171 Events of this sort though neglected by ordinary historians are among the staff and staple of history.

5. In proverbs and proverbial phrases.
†**a.** Various phrases of obvious meaning. *Obs.*
a **1300** *Cursor M.* 7322 Þat þai desire, þai sal it haue, To þair aun heued a staue. **1444** LYDG. in *Pol. Poems* (1859) II. 219 Whoo hath noon hors on a staff may ride. *a* **1450** *Knt. de la Tour* xv. 21 And sum saide it hadd be beter for her to holde her pees..and that she had bete her selff with her owne staffe. **1508** DUNBAR *Tua Mariit Wemen* 384 All thus enforsit he his fa And maid a stalwart staff to strik him selfe doune. **1546** J. HEYWOOD *Prov.* (1867) 21 The walkyng staffe hath caught warmth in your hand. **1579** FULKE *Heskins' Parl.* 519 These be all as good reasons as yt comon iest: The staffe standeth in the corner, therefore ye good man is not at home. **1593** SHAKS. *2 Hen. VI*, III. i. 171 A Staffe is quickly found to beat a Dogge. **1594** NASHE *Unfort. Trav.* Wks. (Grosart) V. 27, I warrant you are made while you liue, you neede not care which waie you staffe falles. **1659** N. R. *Prov., Eng. Fr.*, etc. 67 If you would know a knave give him a staff. *Ibid.* 74 Lean not to a broken staff. **1681** FOULIS *Rom. Treasons* 82 And though the Rule be but obscure, they are apt to take the staff by the wrong end, and apply it to their own pleasures.

†**b.** ***at*** (***the***) ***staves end*** or ***staff-end***: at a distance, away from close quarters or familiarity, on unfriendly terms. Chiefly in phr. ***to keep*** or ***hold*** (a person) ***at staves end***, ***to stand at staves end with*** (a person). (Cf. *at arm's end*, ARM *sb.*[1] 2 b.) *Obs.*
c **1374** CHAUCER *Anel. & Arc.* 184 (Fairf. MS.) His new lady holdeth him vp so narowe Vp by the bridil at the staves ende, That euery worde he dred hit as an arowe. **1546** J. HEYWOOD *Prov.* I. xi. (1867) 34 And now without them, I liue here at staues end. **1601** DENT *Pathw. Heauen* 175 So that wee both keepe Satan at the staues end, and also much sinne out of our soules. **1601** SHAKS. *Twel. N.* v. 292. **1640** HARSNET *God's Summons Repentance* 218 Hee keepes them a-while at the staves end, and speakes harshly unto them. **1650** I. AMBROSE *Ultima* (1654) 193 Whosoever they are that stand at the staffes end, he desires them to lay aside their weapons and come in. **1657** S. PURCHAS *Pol. Flying-Ins.* II. 322 Vaine and wicked thoughts..will presse..into the heart, but a good heart will not owne them,..but stands at staves end with them. **1680** BUNYAN *Mr. Badman* (1905) 66 Had I been his Father, I would have held him a little at staves-end, till I had had far better proof of his manners to be good. *a* **1780** SHIRREFS *Poems* (1790) 215 Fowks that ha'e power to mak' an' men', Sud keep sic lads at the staff-en'. **1816** SCOTT *Antiq.* xvi, I expect him here one of these days; but I will keep him at staff's end, I promise you.

†**c.** ***to have, get***, etc., ***the better*** (or ***worse***) ***end of the staff***: to come off best (or worst) in a contest, disputation, etc.; to have the advantage or the contrary. *Obs.* (Now STICK *sb.*)
1542 UDALL *Erasm. Apoph.* 306 As often as thei see theim selfes to haue the wurse ende of the staffe in their cause. **1546** J. HEYWOOD *Prov.* II. iii. (1867) 48 Who had the wurs ende of the staffe (quoth I) now? **1616** in *Cal. Colon. Papers, E. Ind.* 465 If others will be so foolish to cut their bellies for love (or rather lust) after whores, the worst end of the staff will be their own. **1626** JACKSON *Creed* VIII. viii. 71 He having gotten (as wee say) the better end of the staffe, did wrest our wills at his pleasure. *c* **1645** HOWELL *Lett.* (1650) II. II. 20 He was sure to keep the better end of the staff still to himself. **1688** BUNYAN *Christ as Advocate* 94, I am ashamed my self of mine own doings, and have given mine Enemy the best end of the Staff. **1753** RICHARDSON *Grandison* (1754) II. ii. 12 Miss Byron, I have had the better end of the staff, I believe?

†**d.** ***to set down*** (***the*** or ***one's***) ***staff***: to take up a fixed or settled position; to abide stedfastly by an opinion, decision, etc.; similarly ***to fix the staff*** (obs.). ***to set up*** (or †***in***) ***one's staff*** (***of rest***): to settle down in a place, take up one's abode.
1584 GREENE *Arbasto* Wks. (Grosart) III. 217 Setting downe the staff therefore on this secure periury thus it fell out. *a* **1610** HEALEY *Epictetus* (1636) 61 But sette downe thy staffe at this, whateuer the end bee, it noway concerneth thee. **1642** D. ROGERS *Naaman* 175 Yet till she rests there, and sets downe her stafe upon the promise, shee shall haue no rest. **1667** O. HEYWOOD *Heart-Treasure* xiv. 165 A sober solid wel-taught Christian hath fixt the Staffe, and you know where to finde him, and he knows where to finde his own Principles. **1828** [CARR] *Craven Gloss.* s.v., 'To put down one's staff in a place', to settle or take up his residence in it.
1590 SHAKS. *Com. Err.* III. i. 51 Haue at you with a prouerbe, Shall I set in my staffe. **1594** NASHE *Unfort. Trav.* Wks. (Grosart) V. 46 Here I was in good hope to set vp my staffe for some reasonable time. **1609** BODLEY *Life* (1647) 15, I concluded at the last to set up my Staffe at the Library doore in Oxford. **1760–72** H. BROOKE *Fool of Qual.* (1792) III. 71 This gentleman who has done us the honour to set up his staff of rest in our house. **1765** H. WALPOLE *Let. to Earl Strafford* 3 Sept., The Countesses of Carlisle and Berkeley ..will set up their staves there [in Paris] for some time. **1815** SCOTT *Guy M.* xix, Here, then, Mannering resolved, for some time at least, to set up the staff of his rest. **1840** DICKENS *Sk. Yng. Couples* 75 Old Mrs. Chopper, when her daughter married,..set up her staff of rest with Mr. and

Mrs. Merrywinkle. **1860** TROLLOPE *Framley P.* xlviii, They appeared in London and there set up their staff.

†**e.** *(one's) staff stands next the door*: it is (one's) turn next. *Obs.*

1548 HALL *Chron., 3 Hen. VII.* (1550) 13 The Prouerbe that sayth, when thy neighboures house is a fyer, thy staffe standeth nexte the dore. **1577–87** HARRISON *England* II. iii. 152/2 in *Holinshed*, For when the lands of colleges be gone, it shall be hard to saie, whose staffe shall stand next the doore.

†**f.** *to argue from the staff to the corner*: to shift a discussion to another issue. *Obs.*

1656 BRAMHALL *Replic.* ii. §9. 107 This is an argument from the Staffe to the Corner. I speak of a succession of holy Orders, and he of a succession of Opinions.

g. *to have the staff in (one's) own hand*: see quot. 1828.

1828 [CARR] *Craven Gloss.* s.v., 'To have the staff in one's own hand', to keep possession of his property, and, of consequence, to retain authority and obedience. 'To part with one's staff', the very reverse of the former phrase. **1852** MRS. STOWE *Uncle Tom's C.* xviii, And, of course, they know the staff is in their own hands. **1854** MISS BAKER *Northampt. Gloss.* s.v., To keep the staff in your own hand.

6. (Cf. sense 1 c.) Part of the insignia of the episcopal office, consisting of a rod or pole of wood, metal or ivory supporting a crook, or, in the case of metropolitans, a cross. See CROSE, CROSIER, CROSS-STAFF 1, and cf. PASTORAL *a.* 3.

The staff represents the possession of jurisdiction and was one of the insignia connected with INVESTITURE.

a **1122** *O.E. Chron.* (Laud MS.) an. 1047 Vif biscop com þær to, & for neah man sceolde tobrecan his stef. *Ibid.* an. 1102, Maniȝe Frencisce & Englisce þær heora stafas & rice for luron. *c* **1205** LAY. 22105 þene ærchebiscopes staf þer he Piram aȝaf. *c* **1400** *Apol. Loll.* 56 Prelats, wiþ þer stafis & oþer ornaments. **1535** STEWART *Cron. Scot.* II. 424 How the Bischopis Stalf tuke Neidfyre. **1535** BP. HILSEY in Ellis *Orig. Lett.* Ser. III. II. 352 Yff hytt may plese your Mastershypp to be soe good unto me as to geve my predecessours Myttre, Staff, and Seale. **1643** BAKER *Chron., Hen. I,* 55 That the King should receive homage of Bishops elect; but should not invest them by Staffe and Ring. **1851** MRS. BROWNING *Casa Guidi Wind.* I. 1006 With his pastoral ring and staff.

7. A rod or wand, of wood or ivory, borne as an ensign of office or authority; *spec.* as the badge of certain chief officers of the Crown.

Cf. *leading-staff* s.v. LEADING *vbl. sb.*[1] 6.

1535 COVERDALE *Ezek.* xix. 11 Hir stalkes were so stronge, that men might haue made staues therof for officers. **1593** SHAKS. *Rich. II,* II. ii. 59 The Earle of Worcester Hath broke his staffe, resign'd his Stewardship. **1605** *1st Pt. Jeronimo* I. i. 8 For honering me.. With this high staffe of office. *a* **1618** RALEIGH *Prerog. Parl.* 32 In his fifth yeare was the Treasurer againe changed, and the Staffe giuen to Segraue, and the Lord Chancellour was also changed, and the staffe giuen to the Lord Scroope. **1640** in *3rd Rep. Hist. MSS. Comm.* 80/2 Mr. Treasurer would not accept of the secretary's place until he was assured of holding his white staff also. **1642** G. MOUNTAGU in *Buccleuch MSS.* (Hist. MSS. Comm.) I. 299 These Lords, Holland and Essex,.. accordingly delivered their key and staff respectively to the Lord Falkland. **1711** SWIFT *Jrnl. to Stella* 31 May, I was bit about the two staves, for there is no new officer made to-day. **1716** HEARNE *Collect.* (O.H.S.) V. 283 By this Resignation of the.. place.. of Beadle.. I kept Possession of the Library, laying down the Staff before I went out. **1813** GEO. [IV] in Gurw. *Wellington Desp.* (1838) X. 552 You have sent me.. the Staff of a French Marshal, and I send you in return that of England. **1827** HALLAM *Const. Hist.* (1876) I. iv. 204 He kept the white staff of treasurer down to his death. **1843** PUGIN *Apol. Rev. Chr. Archit.* 52 A verge or cantor's staff. **1863** H. COX *Instit.* III. vii 694 Lord Godolphin, the Earl of Oxford, and the Duke of Shrewsbury successively received the Treasurer's staff.

8. a. A pole from which a flag is flown.

a **1613** [see FLAG-STAFF]. **1667** MILTON *P.L.* I. 535 Who forthwith from the glittering Staff unfurld Th' Imperial Ensign. **1702** [see JACK *sb.*[2]]. **1769** FALCONER *Dict. Marine* (1780) *Staff,* a light pole erected in different parts of a ship, whereon to hoist and display the colours. **1774** M. MACKENZIE *Maritime Surv.* 39 Setting perpendicular in a level Ground three Poles, or Staves, between four and five Feet high, with Flags flying at each, so as to form a Triangle. **1816** BYRON *Siege Cor.* xi, The banners droop'd along their staves. **1836** W. IRVING *Astoria* III. 228 They would willingly have nailed their colours to the staff, and defied the frigate. **1894** *pl.* staves [see JACK *sb.*[2]].

b. A rod or pole on which a processional cross was borne.

1431 *Rec. St. Mary at Hill* 27, ij staues [*printed* stanes] for þe principall crosses. *a* **1529** SKELTON *Ware the Hauke* 114 Cros, staffe, lectryne, and banner.

†**9. a.** A strong stick, pole, bar, rod or stake used for various purposes; e.g. for carrying burdens, to support a canopy, the stems of plants, etc. *Obs.*

c **1000** *Lamb Psalter* cvi. 16 *Vectes ferreos confregit,* stafas *vel* sahlas isenne tobræc. **1297** R. GLOUC. (Rolls) 2677 Ac some þat ofscapede.. mid staues of hegges defended hom aboute. **1382** WYCLIF *Exod.* xxv. 13 And thow shalt make berynge staues of the trees of Sychym. **1390** GOWER *Conf.* II. 294 Doun goth the corde into the pet, To which he hath at ende knet A staf, wherby, he seide, he wolde That Adrian him scholde holde. **1485** in *Rutland Papers* (Camden) 5 A seele of cloth of gold baudekyn with iiij staves gilte, to be borne alweis by iiij noble knights. **1523–34** FITZHERB. *Husb.* §21 Than muste ye haue a wedynge-hoke with a socket set vpon a lyttel staffe of a yarde longe. **1530** PALSGR. 275/1 Staffe to beare two peyles on, as they do in Fraunce, *une covrge.* **1538** ELYOT *Dict., Phalangæ,* staues, wherewith men doo carye packes, playne staues. **1552** in Daniel-Tyssen *Invent. Ch. Goods Surrey* (1869) 14 Item a canype with iiij staves. **1572** MASCALL *Plant. & Graff.* (1592) 13 How to set small staues by, to strengthen your Cions. **1643** BAKER *Chron., Rich. II,* 1 To beare the Kings Canopy, upon foure staves of silver, over the Kings head. **1688** HOLME *Armoury* III. 320/1 A Bearing Staff by which empty Barrels are carried by Servants from place to place. **1708** *Constit. Watermen's Co.* xxv, No Waterman.. shall stick up and lay his Boat at his Staff, so as to hinder.. due and orderly passing.. but shall.. stick up their said Staves clear of the said Stairs or Landing-places.

†**b.** A CHURN-STAFF; also = *pump-staff* (see PUMP *sb.*[1] 6). *Obs.*

1559 in *Richmond Wills* (Surtees) 134 A chirn with a staf. **1593** [see SHOE *sb.* 5 b]. **1609** *Balliol Coll. Acc.* (MS.), Item, staffe for mendinge the quadrangle pumpe.

†**c.** = PLOUGH-STAFF. *Obs.*

1538 ELYOT *Dict., Rulla,* the staffe, wherwith the ploughman clenseth his culter. **1565** COOPER *Thesaurus, Rallum,* the staffe wherewith plough men in tillyng put the earth from their share. **1577** GOOGE *Heresbach's Husb.* I. 21 With the Rodde or Staffe well poynted, the plowman maketh cleane his Coulter.

†**d.** = BOWSTAFF. *Obs.*

1545 ASCHAM *Toxoph.* II. (Arb.) 116 The boole of ye tree is.. best for a bow, yf the staues be euen clouen. **1583** *Rates Custom Ho.* A vj, Bowestaues the bundel containing xvi staues v s. **1688** HOLME *Armoury* III. 105/2 A Staff, the first cleeving out of the Timber, to make the Shaft. **1868** KIRK *Charles the Bold* III. IV. viii. 136 And 'bowiers' [were ordered] to make their staves into bows with all possible haste.

e. ? Each of two sticks fastened to the extremities of a fishing-net.

1823 J. F. COOPER *Pioneers* xxiii, Benjamin prided himself greatly on his skill in throwing the net... A loud splash in the water, as he threw away the 'staff', or 'stretcher'. *Ibid.,* 'I see the "staffs",' shouted Mr. Jones;—'gather in, boys, and away with it'... Elizabeth strained her eyes and saw the ends of the two sticks on the seine.

f. = *train staff (a)* s.v. TRAIN *sb.*[1] 22 b. Cf. TOKEN *sb.* 7 b.

1885 E. B. IVATTS *Railway Managem. at Stations* 559 *Staff (train),* a piece of wood or metal used on single lines, which.. confers the 'right of road' for an engine. **1902** *Encycl. Brit.* XXXII. 147/1 The staff.. is delivered to the engine-driver at station A, and constitutes his authority to occupy the main track between that station and station B. On reaching B he surrenders the staff, and receives another one which gives him the right to the road between B and C. **1931** D. L. SAYERS *Five Red Herrings* xxvii. 330 The station-master marched across, carrying the staff under his arm. **1974** J. S. HOLDEN *Watlington Branch* v. 87 One instance is recorded of the branch train being snowed up... A porter, despatched with the staff, had to make his way on foot.

10. a. *Surveying.* A rod for measuring distances and heights. Cf. JACOB'S STAFF 2 b; also *levelling staff* s.v. LEVELLING *vbl. sb.* 4.

[**1538** ELYOT *Dict., Pertica,* a staffe, a cogell, a perche or polle, wherwith grounde is mette.] **1556** DIGGES *Tecton.* (1592) title-p., An Instrument called the profitable Staffe. **1571** —— *Pantom.* I. xiv. D iv b, Heightes are ingeniously searched out by a staffe. **1590** BLAGRAVE (*title*) Baculum Familliare, Catholicon siue Generale. A Booke of the making and vse of a Staffe, newly invented by the Author, called the Familiar Staffe. As well for that it may be made vsually and familiarlie to walke with, as for that it performeth the Geometrical mensurations of all Altitudes, Longitudes, Latitudes, Distances and Profundities. **1610** A. HOPTON (*title*) Baculum Geodæticum, sive Viaticum. Or The Geodeticall Staffe. **1753** *Chambers' Cycl.* Suppl., *Staff.* This is used as an instrument for taking accessible, or inaccessible heights. *Ibid.* s.v., *Station-Staff,* in surveying. **1835** *Lond. Jrnl. Arts & Sci.* Conj. Ser. VI. 330 The graduated staffs or measuring rods being thus placed at the stations. **1880** L. D'A. JACKSON *Aids Surv.-Practice* 11 Telemetrical observation on graduated staves. A graduated staff is held vertically at the required distant point [etc.].

†**b.** (See quot. and cf. JACOB'S STAFF 2 c.)

For other uses see BACKSTAFF, CROSS-STAFF 2, FORE-STAFF, JACOB'S STAFF 2 a.

1728 CHAMBERS *Cycl., Staff,* in Surveying, a kind of Stand, whereon to mount a Theodolite, Circumferentor, plain Table, or the like, for use. It consists of Three Legs of Wood, joyned together at one End, whereon the Instrument is placed; and made pecked at the other, to enter the Ground.

†**c.** = *half-breadth staff* (see HALF- II. f).

1797 *Encycl. Brit.* (ed. 3) XVII. 407/1 The half breadth staff may be one inch square, and of any convenient length... Two sides of the staff are marked half breadths, and the other two sides heights of the sheer.

d. The gnomon of a sun-dial.

1669 STURMY *Mariner's Mag.* VI. iii. 123 The shadow being 83, the Gnomon or Staff 100. **1829** *Chapters Phys. Sci.* ix. 89 The sun dial, which marks the time by the shadow of a stile or staff.

11. *Her.* A representation of a stick, stake, bar, etc.; *spec.* = BATON *sb.* 3, FISSURE *sb.* 2 c. See also RAGGED STAFF 1.

1486 *Bk. St. Albans, Her.* e vij b, Ther be fyssuris or stauys playn ingradyt inueckyt and fusyllatit. **1874** PAPWORTH & MORANT *Dict. Coats of Arms* s.v. *Staff,* Arg. a hawk ppr... standing on a staff couped and raguled vert. *Ibid.,* Az. eight staves fretty and raguly or.

12. *Surg.* †**a.** The piston of a syringe. *Obs.*

1653 T. BRUGIS *Vade Mecum* (ed. 2) 148 In dangerous fluxes when we give comfortable Clysters, we oftentimes force them up as far as we can, I mean the Liquor by thrusting the staffe harder.

b. A grooved steel instrument used to guide the knife in lithotomy.

1698 LISTER *Journ. Paris* (1699) 233 He boldly thrusts in a broad Lancet.. till he joins the Catheter or Staff, or the Stone betwixt his Fingers. **1720** J. DOUGLAS *Lithotomia Douglas.* 14 That [operation] which Surgeons call Cutting on the Staffe, i.e. when a furrow'd Probe is pass'd into the Bladder, upon which they afterwards Cut. **1726** —— *Hist. Lateral Operation* 30 The Instruments he made Use of were first a Catheter or Staff. **1839** *Hooper's Lex. Med.* (ed. 7) 1216. **1895** *Arnold & Sons' Catal. Surg. Instrum.* 572 Stricture Staff (Syme's). *Ibid.* 625 Lithotomy Instruments.. Six Staffs, grooved.

13. *Arch.* **a.** = RUDENTURE.

1817 RICKMAN *Styles Archit.* 95 The square pedestal of the pinnacle being set with an angle to the front, is continued down, and on each side is set a small buttress of a smaller face than this pedestal, thus leaving a small staff between them.. this small staff at each set-off has the moulding to it.

b. (See quot. 1812.)

1812 P. NICHOLSON *Mech. Exerc.* 202 *Staff,* a piece of wood fixed to the external angle of the two upright sides of a wall for floating the plaster to, and for defending the angle against accidents. **1902** STURGIS *Dict. Archit* III. 593.

14. a. A rung of a ladder. ? *Obs.* Cf. STAVE.

c **1325** *Gloss. W. de Bibbesw.* in Wright *Voc.* 168 (Camb. MS.) [En les reideles vount les roilouns *glossed*] staves. *a* **1400–50** *Wars Alex.* 1438 On ilka staffe of a staire stike wald a cluster. *c* **1440** *Gesta Rom.* xlvi. 367 The goldyn laddere; of the which the fyrste staffe is contricion of herte. **1526** *Pilgr. Perf.* (W. de W. 1531) 68 b, Saynt Bernarde compareth them to a ladder of vii staues. **1563** *Homilies* II. *Repentance* II. 279 The first staffe or steppe of this ladder. *a* **1657** R. LOVEDAY *Lett.* (1663) 273 How many mount Fortunes ladder, and break the staves as they go up. **1657** J. WATTS *Scribe, Pharisee,* etc. III. 99 They fall off the Ladder at the lower staffe or step again. **1850** G. L. BANKS (*title*) Staves for the Human Ladder. **1858** SIMMONDS *Dict. Trade.* **1875** KNIGHT *Dict. Mech.*

b. A round cross-bar connecting the handles or stilts of a plough, or the legs of a chair; = ROUND *sb.*[1] 3 d. Also, each of the handles of a plough. *Obs.* or *dial.* Cf. STAVE.

1523–34 FITZHERB. *Husb.* §3 There be two roughe staues in euery ploughe in the hynder ende, set a-slope betwene the ploughe-tayle and the stilt, to holde out and kepe the plough abrode in the hynder ende, and the one lenger than the other. **1652** BLITH *Eng. Improver Improv.* II. xxviii. (1653) 190 But for the Plough-handles, some call them.. Hales, and some Staves. **1851** STERNBERG *Northampt. Gloss., Staff,* the spar or 'round' of a chair.

†**c.** A spoke of a wheel. *Obs.* exc. *Her.* (also applied to the 'rays' of a carbuncle).

1642 D. ROGERS *Naaman* 296 As then the spokes and staves cannot be wanting to a wheele. **1754** BOYER *Gt. Theat. Honour* (ed. 2) 116 Staves (is said of the Rays of the Carbuncle), *Rais, ou Bâtons d'Escarboucle.* **1847** *Gloss. Heraldry* 294 *Staff,* a word applied by some to the rays of an escarbuncle, and the spokes of a wheel.

†**d.** *Weaving.* = LAM *sb.*[2]

1338 in Dugdale *Monasticon* (1819) II. 585/2 Item pro weblomes emptis xx[s]. Et pro staves ad easdem vj[d]. **1797** *Encycl. Brit.* (ed. 3) XVIII. 835/1 The lams.. or, as they are called in some parts of Scotland, the hiddles, and in others the staves.

†**e.** A bar or rail used in the construction of a gridiron, gate, cart, cage, etc. *Obs.*

1459 *Paston Lett.* I. 468, j. roste iren with vij. staves. **1523–34** FITZHERB. *Husb.* §5 The bodye of the wayne of oke, the staues.. the keys and pikstaues. *Ibid.* §70 Make standynge cratches, to caste theyr fodder in, and the staues set nyghe ynough, togyther, for pullynge theyr fodder to hastely out. *Ibid.* §141 If any gate be broken down, or want any staues. **1596** MASCALL *Cattle, Horses* 120 When thou dost take any iourney, with thy horse and cart, thou must.. see the rath staues and struts be whole and sound & wel furnished, with staues of good strong holly, hasell, or oak. **1601** HOLLAND *Pliny* XXX. x. II. 388 The staves and windings, whereof the said cages are made.

†**f.** Each of the thin narrow pieces which compose a cask, barrel, tub, etc. *Obs.* (Now STAVE *sb.*)

The sing. has always been rare; for examples of pl. from 1398 onwards, see STAVE *sb.*

1531–2 *Act 23 Hen. VIII,* c. 4 §8 If any personne.. do mynysshe.. any maner of barrell.. by reason of.. takyng oute of any Staffe out or frome any suche vessell. **1599** DALLAM in *Early Voy. Levant* (Hakl. Soc.) 35 Ther weare marvalus greate peecis that weare made of hammered Iron, everie stafe at the leaste 3 inches square, and houped aboute lyke a barrell.

†**g.** The shank of an anchor. *Obs. rare*$^{-1}$.

1611 COTGR., *Stangue d' un' ancre,* the staffe of an Anchor.

h. *Mech.* Each of the cylindrical bars forming the teeth of a trundle or lantern; cf. STAVE *sb.*

1659, 1812–16 [see LANTERN *sb.* 7 d]. **1764, 1805** [see ROUND *sb.*[1] 3 d]. **1825** J. NICHOLSON *Oper. Mech.* 24 The semi-diameter of a staff of the trundle.

i. *Watchmaking.* An arbor or axle.

1860 E. B. DENISON *Clocks & Watches* (ed. 4) 285 The staff or arbor of the balance. **1885** LOCK *Workshop Rec.* Ser. IV. 339/1 Centre the point so that the body of the staff runs perfectly true. **1902** *Daily Chron.* 13 May 10/5 All Jobbers requiring pivots, staffs, cylinders, and complicated watch repairs.

†**15.** A pair (of cocks), a set of three (hawks).

1688 HOLME *Armoury* II. 252/2 Four staves of Cocks (or 16 Cocks). *Ibid.* 311/1 Three a staff of Hawks. **1691** RAY *S. & E.C. Words* 115 A Staffe of Cocks, a pair of Cocks. **1790** GROSE *Prov. Gloss.* (ed. 2), A *staffe* of cocks; a pair of cocks.

16. A bundle of 50 bunches of the heads of the teasel (*Dipsacus fullonum*) used for teasing cloth. (See also STAVE *sb.,* which occurs in Mortimer 1707.)

1794 GRIGGS *Agric. Essex* 19 These heads [of teasel] are.. bound up in small bunches, or gleans, of five and twenty heads each; the like number of which bunches, or gleans, constitute half a staff; which, after a few days sun, to harden and dry them, are tied together upon a stick or staff, of two feet and a half long, and in this form, carried to market. **1856** MORTON *Cycl. Agric.* II. 1126/2 *Staff,* of teazles (Essex), 50 bunches, or gleans of 25 each = 1250.

17. a. An enclosure or plot of pasture ground.
b. A measure of nine feet.

1786 *Jackson's Oxf. Jrnl.* 3 June 1/3 A Ham or Staff of rich Meadow Ground, in Kelmscott, containing ten Acres and a Half. **1796** W. H. Marshall *West Eng.* I. 330 *Staff*: a measure of nine feet; half a customary rod.

II. Letter, verse, musical staff.

These senses are here placed together because of their similarity of application, but it is doubtful whether they have any immediate connexion.

†**18. a.** A written character, a letter. *Obs.* Cf. BOCSTAFF, RUNE-STAVE.

c **888** Ælfred *Boeth.* xix, Hwæt is heora nu to lafe, butan .. se nama mid feaum stafum awriten? *c* **1000** Ælfric *Gram.* ii. (Z.) 4 Littera is stæf on englisc. *c* **1200** Ormin 16403–5 & off þatt name toc Drihhtin An staff Allfa ȝehatenn, To timmbrenn till þe firrste mann Hiss name off stafess fowwre.

†**b.** A mark made by, or as by writing. *Obs.*

c **1050** *Voc.* in Wr.-Wülcker 346/27 *Apicibus*, stafum. *c* **1205** Lay. 21154 þer wes innen igrauen mid rede golde stauen an on-licnes deore of drihtenes moder.

19. †**a.** A line of verse. *Obs.*

c **1450** in *Herrig's Archiv* CIV. 309 All be it the frenssh in foure staves be, The ynglissh sevyn kepith in degree. *c* **1475** *Partenay* 6555 As ny as metre can conclude sentence, Cereatly by rew in it haue I go. Nerehand stafe by staf. *Ibid.* 6581 Als the frensh staffes silabled be More breueloker and shorter also Then is the english lines. *c* **1540** *Pilgryms T.* 739 in Thynne *Animadv.* (1875) App. i. 98 Thes vi stauis .. whiche be chaucers own hand work.

†**b.** A stanza or set of lines. *Obs.* Cf. BASTON 2.

[There is no ground for the common statement that this is from ON. *stef* set or recurring time, refrain of a poem.]

a **1530** J. Heywood *Weather* (Brandl) 179* At thende of this staf the god hath a song played in his trone. *a* **1577** Gascoigne *Certayne Notes* ¶ 14 Wks. 1907 I. 471 Rythme royall is a verse of tenne sillables, and seven such verses make a staffe. *Ibid.*, The firste twelve do ryme in staves of foure lines by crosse meetre. **1582** T. Watson *Hekatompath.* lxxxviii. (Arb.) 124 The two first staffes (excepting onely the two first verses of all). **1586** W. Webbe *Eng. Poetrie* (Arb.) 59 Some of many rymes in one staffe (as they call it). *Ibid.* 62 The diuersities of the staues (which are the number of verses contained with the diuisions or partitions of a ditty). **1607** R. C[arew] tr. *Estienne's World of Wonders* 199 *marg.*, A staffe of eight verses. **1656** Cowley *Pindaric Odes, To Dr. Scarborough* Note ii, In the ninth staffe of the Nemeæan Ode. **1697** Dryden *Æneid* Ded. (f) 1 b, Mr. Cowley had found out that no kind of Staff is proper for a Heroick Poem; as being all too lirical.

c. A 'verse' or stanza of a song. Now STAVE.

1598 Yong *Diana* 257 These two last staeffs [sic] so liuely touched Parthenius that sung them. **1601** Holland *Pliny* x. xxix. I. 286 Yee shall have them listen attentively to the old birds when they sing, and to take out lessons as it were from them, whom they would seem to imitate staffe by staffe. **1601** B. Jonson *Poetaster* II. ii, I can sing but one staffe of the dittie neither. **1667** C. Simpson *Compend. Mus.* 21 The second Staff or Stanza is the same as the first; only it is broken into Crochets.

20. *Mus.* A set of horizontal lines (now five in number) on which, and in the spaces between, notes are placed so as to indicate pitch. Also STAVE.

In harmonic or concerted music two or more staffs are used together, connected by a brace.

1662 Playford *Skill Mus.* I. i. 4 But [for all] Lessons for the Organ, Virginals, or Harp, two staves of six lines together are required. **1688** Holme *Armoury* III. 157/1 [Follows Playford and adds:] They are called a Staff or Stansa. **1776** Burney *Hist. Mus.* (1789) II. 87 The regular staff of four lines. **1806** Calcott *Mus. Gram.* 1 The lines and spaces of the Staff are counted upwards. **1842** *Westm. Rev.* Jan. 34 *note*, There is a schism among musicians, whether this should be *staff* or *stave*, pronounced by some *staaf*. Authorities are mostly in favour of 'stave' but custom may be pleaded for 'staff' and 'staves' in the plural. **1873** H. C. Banister *Mus.* 2 Musical characters are written upon a series of parallel lines, termed a Stave or Staff.

attrib. **1881** Broadhouse *Mus. Acoustics* 365 The ordinary musical notation, or, as it is called, the 'staff notation'.

III. (Pl. always *staffs*.)

21. *Mil.* **a.** A body of officers appointed to assist a general, or other commanding officer, in the control of an army, brigade, regiment, etc., or in performing special duties (as the ***medical staff***). ***General Staff***, a body of officers controlling an army from headquarters under the commander-in-chief; hence ***Chief of the General Staff***. ***Chief of Staff***, the senior staff officer of a service or commander. [App. of continental Teut. origin. Cf. the like use of G. *stab* (also *generalstab*, *regimentsstab*, etc.), Du. *staf*; prob. developed from the sense 'baton' (= 7 above).]

[**1700** J. A. Astry tr. *Saavedra Faxardo* II. 249 The Germans call a Regiment, and all that belongs to it, the Colonel's Staff, (den Regiment oder Colonelstab,) for with that Soldiers are to be ruled.]

1781 Simes *Milit. Guide* (ed. 3) 7 Staff of the Army. *Ibid.*, The Staff properly exists only in the time of war. **1790** *Debates in Congress* 18 Jan. (1834) 2146 The legionary staff .. the brigade staff .. the regimental staff. *Ibid.* 2152 The United States to make an adequate provision .. for the following general staff. **1795** in *Ld. Auckland's Corr.* (1862) III. 328 My destiny is finally to act on the staff in the island of Corsica. **1801** *Med. Jrnl.* V. 185 The Medical Staff of the Armies acting in the West Indies. **1844** *Queen's Regul. Army* 5 Any Officer of the Regimental Staff. **1844** H. H. Wilson *Brit. India* II. 112 Several conferences ensued, not only with the Governor-General, but with members both of his civil and military staff. **1871** *Ann. Reg.* II. 95 The Duke of Cambridge, with his staff and the foreign officers attending the manœuvres, looked on from Bisley Common. **1875** *Encycl. Brit.* II. 577 Officers for the General Staff are selected exclusively from the regular army, and except in cases of proved abilities in the field, must have passed through the Staff College... Officers appointed to the Personal Staff are not required to pass through the Staff College. **1904** *Rep. War Office (Reconstruction) Committee* II. 22 in *Parl. Papers* (Cd. 1968) VIII. 121 In accordance with our recommendations, a Chief of the General Staff of the Army has been appointed. **1937** H. Nicolson *Diary* 21 Apr. (1966) 299 It is a man's dinner and consists mainly of the Cabinet and a few Chiefs-of-Staff. **1948** in M. McLuhan *Mech. Bride* (1951) 6/7 The artificial boundary line was decided upon by the joint chiefs of staffs during the war. *a* **1974** R. Crossman *Diaries* (1975) I. 595 Couldn't we have officials there as well, like the Chiefs of Staff?

b. *ellipt.* (chiefly with initial capital) = *staff sergeant*, sense 25.

1925 Fraser & Gibbons *Soldier & Sailor Words & Phrases* 269 *Staff*, staff-sergeant. **1943** *Yank* 8 Oct. 15 If all staffs are as shallow minded as this one, buck privates at the front are worth 10 staffs back home. **1958** P. Scott *Mark of Warrior* I. i. 23 A sergeant .. addressed them as 'Gentlemen' and told them to address him as 'Staff'. **1965** 'J. le Carré' *Looking-Glass War* xii. 136 'You call me "Staff",' the instructor said. **1978** J. Barnett *Head of Force* x. 88, I worked with Staff Gredek... The Staff was in charge of the depot.

22. a. *gen.* A body of persons employed, under the direction of a manager or chief, in the work of an establishment or the execution of some undertaking (e.g. a newspaper, hospital, government survey, school, etc.).

1837 Carlyle *Fr. Rev.* II. v. v, Subterranean Rivarol has Fifteen Hundred Men in King's pay ..; what he calls 'a staff of genius': Paragraph-writers, Placard Journalists; .. one of the strangest Staffs ever commanded by man. **1849** J. J. Blunt *Four Serm.* iii. (1850) 84 With what a staff would our colleges be furnished to carry on the same work! **1857** Trollope *Barchester T.* xliii, Those caterers for our morning repast, the staff of the Jupiter. **1875** Dawson *Dawn of Life* iii. 38 One of the explorers on the staff of the Survey. **1879** M. Arnold *Mixed Ess.* 152 The teaching staff have to furnish guarantees of their capacity to teach the matters of instruction confided to them. **1884** *Times* (weekly ed.) 26 Sept. 13/1 Besides their staff of clerks, book-keepers, &c., they employed about 300 ordinary hands. **1894** Conan Doyle *Mem. S. Holmes* 149 A coachman and two maids form the staff of servants.

b. Construed as *pl.*: members of a staff, employees. *Rarely*, an employee.

1931 E. M. Brent-Dyer *Chalet School & Jo* xvii. 220 You're almost a Staff, so that'll be all right. **1955** *Times* 10 May 17/4 A continuing supply of higher technical staff. **1970** *Daily Tel.* 4 May 2/4 A Yorkshire factory with 250 staff, nearly all women. **1979** P. Nihalani et al. *Indian & Brit. English* I. 166 The Director will introduce the new staff and ask him to say a few words.

c. *spec.* in a business organization: (*a*) the employees responsible for providing advisory and ancillary services to line managers and their subordinates; (*b*) salaried (as opp. to wage-earning) employees.

1915 C. E. Knoeppel *Installing Efficiency Methods* viii. 58 He [*sc.* the engineer] decides to create an organization to be known as the 'staff'—advisory in nature and without jurisdiction over any of the line officials. **1923** O. Sheldon *Philos. Managem.* iv. 114 A 'Staff and Line' organization .. is based upon a strict demarcation between thinking and doing; between the actual execution of production, which is the 'Line', and the business of analysing, testing, comparing, recording, making researches, co-ordinating information, and advising, which is the 'Staff'. **1960, 1964** [see LINE *sb.*[2] 19 d]. **1980** *Daily Tel.* 16 Feb. 25/3 Almost all the major companies pay more [in redundancy payments] than the statutory minimum and generally staff will enjoy more generous benefits than shopfloor workers.

23. ***Staff*** (***of Government***): in the Isle of Man, a court of justice presided over by the governor; since 1883 a Division of the High Court.

a **1700** *34th Customary Law* in Keble *Life Bp. Wilson* xvi. 511 No appeal shall be made from Church censures to the Staff, and none to be privileged from them. **1900** A. W. Moore *Hist. Isle of Man* 836 The courts existing prior to 1883, viz., the Staff of Government, Chancery, Exchequer .. [etc.] were united and formed into 'Divisions' of the 'High Court of Justice of the Isle of Man'... The 'Staff of Government Division' .. was deprived of all its original jurisdiction, and is now solely an appellate court.

IV. *attrib.* and *Comb.*

24. Objective, as ***staff-bearer***, ***-holder***, ***-maker***; instrumental, as ***staff-supported*** adj.

1553 in Kempe *Losely MSS.* (1836) 44 Touching the stafmaker .. I wyll see hym contented. **1611** Cotgr., *Bastonnier*, a staffe-bearer, or Vergier. **1814** Wordsw. *White Doe* I. 217 That bearded, staff-supported Sire. **1880** L. D'A. Jackson *Aids Surv. Pract.* 98 The staff-holders must .. be capable of holding the staff truly vertical.

25. a. In sense 'of or belonging to a military staff' (see 21), as ***staff appointment***, ***car***, ***duty***, ***job***, ***parade***, ***pay***, ***surgeon***, ***uniform***; **staff cap**, a flat-topped cap with a peak, such as forms part of various uniforms; **staff college**, a school in which officers are trained for staff appointments; **staff corps**, a body of officers and men organized to assist the commanding officer and his staff in various special departments; in India, a corps formed in each of the three presidencies to supply officers for service; **staff-ride** (see quot. 1902); hence ***staff-rider***; **staff sergeant** (see quot. 1876); **staff-wallah** *slang* [cf. WALLAH b], a disparaging term for a noncombatant army officer; **staff-work**, the supportive work of planning, organization, etc., done by staff officers for the commander; also in civilian contexts. Also STAFF OFFICER.

1802 J. Orrok *Let.* 22 July (1927) 23 I'm in hopes thro' his Interest to obtain a *Staff appointment there. **1825** T. Hook *Sayings* Ser. II. *Passion & Princ.* iii. II. 303 The Captain, habituated to India, 'held on', with staff appointments, as long as he could. **1875** *Encycl. Brit.* II. 577/2 Staff appointments are held for five years only. **1902** *Westm. Gaz.* 16 June 8/2 His Majesty, .. with hand raised to *staff-cap, in military salute. **1904** *Daily Chron.* 23 Aug. 8/1 The woman who depends upon a motor-car for recreation .. wears a staff-cap just as much as she who goes yachting. *a* **1944** K. Douglas *Alamein to Zem Zem* (1946) i. 11 A few staff and liaison officers in jeeps and *staff cars still passed. **1978** R. V. Jones *Most Secret War* xix. 155 Scott-Farnie himself would be going and would have a staff car. **1868** *Queen's Regul. Army* §220 No Officer will be appointed to the Staff, who shall not have passed the final examination of the *Staff College. **1911** W. S. Churchill in R. S. Churchill *Winston S. Churchill* (1969) II. Compan. II. xvi. 1283 You are authorized to apply to the War Office for the services of 25 Staff College Officers. **1974** A. Price *Other Paths to Glory* I. vi. 63 He had a lecture to give at the Staff College. **1811** *Regul. Army* 121 The Royal *Staff Corps. **1813** Wellington in Gurw. *Disp.* (1838) XI. 122, I have therefore had cut out the sheets .. containing the maps of the country immediately in my front, which I have had pasted upon linen by the Staff corps. **1853** Sir H. Douglas *Milit. Bridges* (ed. 3) 241 Two companies of the Staff Corps were accordingly sent, with a strong working party, to Baragona, to make a bridge across the Tietar. **1880** Gen. Adye in *19th Cent.* No. 38. 698 All officers now seeking what is called an Indian career in any capacity—regimental, staff, or civil—must enter one of the three Staff Corps. **1913** R. Meinertzhagen *Diary* 19 Dec. (1960) 57, I expected a better groundwork in *staff duties. **1916** F. M. Ford *Let.* Aug. (1965) 67 Bridges .. has written to Plumer to suggest that I ought to be given a *staff job. **1909** *Blackw. Mag.* Apr. 568/2 The adjutant inspected the *Staff parade. **1876** Voyle & Stevenson *Milit. Dict.* 401/1 **Staff Pay*, pay given to officers and soldiers in the government service, who perform duties either on the permanent staff of an army or in regimental or departmental employment. **1898** E. S. May *Field Artillery* 25 We have done the same sort of thing in this country in the form of '*staff-rides'. **1902** *Encycl. Brit.* (ed. 10) XXXIII. 7/1 'Staff-rides', as exercises on the ground without troops have come to be called, are just as effective a means of teaching strategy as field-days are of teaching tactics. **1910** *Contemp. Rev.* Jan. 46 No one had seen the alleged *staff riders. **1811** *Regul. Army* 147 *Staff Serjeants. **1851** *Ord. Royal Engin.* §26. 121 On no account is any Non-Commissioned Officer acting as a Staff-Serjeant to be employed as a Pay-Serjeant. **1876** Voyle & Stevenson *Milit. Dict.* 401/1 *Staff Sergeants*, non-commissioned officers employed on the staff of a regiment, district, or division. **1794** *Gentl. Mag.* Nov. 995/2 Whilst the regimental surgeons are thus engaged in the field of battle .. the new *staff-surgeons .. are to be found at the general hospital, perhaps .. 20 or 30 miles .. from the scene of action. **1803** Wellington in Gurw. *Disp.* (1844) I. 539 Mr. Gilmour, the Staff surgeon with this division of the army. **1809** Byron *Ch. Har.* II. lxii. *note*, I was dressed in a full suit of *staff uniform. **1951** R. Campbell *Light on Dark Horse* xi. 145 A family connection who was only a *staff-wallah, and jealous of my being a soldier. **1969** V. de S. Pinto *City that Shone* viii. 161 She's chock full of bleeding staff-wallahs. **1923** Kipling *Irish Guards in Gt. War* I. p. xi, Bad *staff-work or faulty generalship. **1933** W. S. Churchill *Marlborough* I. xxviii. 484 His private fortune was amassed upon the same principles as marked the staff-work of his campaigns. **1951** *Engineering* 2 Mar. 269/2 Consultations among .. executives, linked by 'staffwork'. **1980** *Sunday Tel.* 23 Mar. 17/8 [The new Archbishop of Canterbury] will need good staff work: some of his appointments in the past have been questioned, and he is by all accounts a bad delegator.

b. In the Navy used to designate a senior grade of officers, as ***staff captain***, ***commander***, ***surgeon***. Also in passenger ships.

1867 Smyth *Sailor's Word-bk.*, *Staff-Captain*, a designation conferred in 1863 upon masters of the fleet. *Ibid.*, *Staff-Commanders*, a designation conferred in 1863 on masters of fifteen years' seniority. **1875** Bedford *Sailor's Pocket Bk.* v. (ed. 2) 150 *note*, Staff-Commander Thomas A. Hull, R.N. **1913** *Times* 13 Aug. 4/1 The first paper .. was read by Staff-Surgeon Stewart, R.N. **1932** S. G. McNeil *In Great Waters* 136, I was to be the first holder of the newly created post of Staff-Captain. **1944** *New Yorker* 23 Dec. 26/1 One man who had this second feeling to a degree was Lemuel Watkins, staff captain and second in command to the *Marquette's* master. **1957** D. G. O. Baillie *Sea Affair* 111 In ships carrying anything over a thousand passengers, there is usually a Staff Captain who devotes his entire activities to their proper entertainment.

c. In sense 'belonging to the staff of a hospital, hotel, or other large establishment' (see 22). Similarly, ***staff member***. Also in sense 'of, provided or reserved for, arranged by, the staff of an establishment', as ***staff canteen***, ***dance***, etc.

1902 *Daily Chron.* 13 May 10/7 Woman (Strong, active) as staff maid... Apply Housekeeper, Hotel Windsor. **1940** R. S. Lambert *Ariel & all his Quality* i. 33 He fought shy of .. social gatherings, except for appearances at occasional staff dances. **1942** Wyndham Lewis *Let.* 27 Jan. (1963) 313 Your staff-member who has ended up a prisoner in Athens had an interesting journey. **1966** *Economist* 3 Sept. 888/1 The employers' habit of describing concessions of better pay and conditions to manual workers as creating 'staff conditions' for all has often meant that yet further concessions have been made to 'staff' employees, in order to preserve their differentials over the men on the shop floor. **1972** K. Benton *Spy in Chancery* xvii. 192 She probably had lunch there. There's a staff canteen. **1977** F. Branston *Up & Coming Man* xiv. 150 Freelancing .. binds you to a tighter routine than a staff job.

26. Special comb. (see also 25): **staff and ticket (system)** an elaboration of the staff system (below) allowing for the movement of several trains in one direction along a single line, whereby the last train carried the staff (sense 9 f above) and the preceding trains carried tickets pertaining to this (*Obs.* exc. *Hist.*); **staff-angle, -bead** = 13 b (cf. *angle-staff*, *angle-bead* s.v. ANGLE *sb.*[2] 8); hence **staff-beaded** *a.*; **staff-bismar**, a kind of steelyard; †**staff-drive** *v.* = *staff-herd*; **staff-head**, the upper end of a staff, carved, tipped with metal, etc.; the top of the tripod which supports a theodolite or other measuring-instrument; **staff-herd** *v. trans.*, to depasture sheep in charge of a shepherd upon common or forest land; **staffholster** *nonce-wd.*, a holster for a watchman's staff; **staff-hook**, 'a sharp hook fastened to a long handle to cut peas and beans and to trim hedges' (*I. of Wight Gloss.* 1881); **staff-land** *Isle of Man* [= med.L. *terra de baculo*], certain land in the parish of St. Maughold, also formerly in that of St. Patrick, the holder of which had the custody of the patron saint's pastoral staff; **staff-man** †(*a*) a man who wields a staff or cudgel; (*b*) a workman employed in silk-throwing (Simmonds *Dict. Trade* Suppl. 1883); (*c*) *Surveying* (see quot. 1940); (*d*) a member of a staff; **staff nurse**, a trained nurse in a hospital, ranking above a registered nurse and below a ward sister; **staff photographer**, a photographer on the staff of a newspaper or journal; **staff-room**, a common room for the use of the staff, as in a school; also *transf.*, the staff itself; †**staff-shide**, a billet of wood for fuel; †**staff-striker**, a sturdy beggar, tramp; **staff-student** *a.*, designating the relation between students and teaching staff; esp. in phr. ***staff-student ratio*** (cf. *pupil-teacher* adj. s.v. PUPIL *sb.*[1]); **staff system**, a block system on railways according to which an engine-driver may not proceed along a single line without carrying the staff (sense 9 f above) authorizing him to do so; **staff ticket**, a ticket used on railways to operate the staff and ticket system (see above); †**staff-torch**, a tall thick candle used for ceremonial purposes; **staff-tree**, the genus *Celastrus*; **staff-vine**, *Celastrus scandens* of U.S.; **staff writer**, a writer employed on the staff of a newspaper, radio or television station, or the like.

1887 C. E. STRETTON *Safe Railway Working* iii. 64 All other single lines should be worked under the train *staff and ticket system. **1889** W. M. ACWORTH *Railways of Eng.* x. 392 Single lines are commonly worked on what is known as the 'staff and ticket' system. **1927** E. T. MACDERMOT *Hist. Gt. Western Railway* I. II. xii. 611 The Wycombe Branch, on its extension to Thame in 1862, seems to have been the first on which the Train Staff and Ticket system was introduced. **1969** *Railway Mag.* Feb. 67 Up to 1892, all movement of trains was controlled by staff and ticket, which was replaced by the Webb-Thompson electric train staff. **1875** KNIGHT *Dict. Mech.*, **Staff-angle*. **1833** LOUDON *Encycl. Archit.* §239 The angles of the chimney breasts to have proper *staff beads. **1842** GWILT *Archit.* Gloss., Angle Bead, or Staff Bead. **1833** LOUDON *Encycl. Archit.* §1598 Fix 1-inch deal tongued and splayed and *staff-beaded linings to three windows. *a* **1733** *Shetland Acts* 31 in *Proc. Soc. Ant. Scot.* (1892) XXVI. 200 That none use *staff bismers, nor any other save such as are adjusted and marked to buy and sell on. **1566** in Hyslop *Ch. Stretton* (1904) II. 178 [John Nichols, who had taken cattle] cum baculis, videlicet, *Staff-dryve [over Whittington Heath to the injury of the township]. **1506** *Acc. Ld. High Treas. Scot.* III. 355, xij *staf hedis. **1766** *Complete Farmer* s.v. *Surveying* 7 I 1/2 Turn about the table upon the staff-head. **1862** *Catal. Internat. Exhib., Brit.* II. No. 2947 (Theodolite) The tripod and its staff-head. **1888** in *Archæologia* LI. 373 A staff-head of wood, coloured and gilded. **1563** in W. Nicolson *Leges Marchiarum* (1705) 138 If it shall happen the Cattel or Sheep of the one Realm to be *staff-herded, or to remain depasturing upon the ground of the opposite Realm. *Ibid., marg.* Staffherding of Cattel. **1595** in C. W. Hatfield *Hist. Notices Doncaster* (1866) I. 168 Doncaster time out of mind have made drives.. and staff hearded upon the moor. **1828** [CARR] *Craven Gloss.*, *Staff hird*, to have sheep under the care of a shepherd. **1922** JOYCE *Ulysses* 423 At a corner two night watch in shoulder capes, their hands upon their *staffholsters, loom tall. **1523** FITZHERB. *Husb.* §29 Pees and benes be.. reped or mowen some with sickles, some with hokes, and some with *staffe-hokes. **1890** A. W. MOORE *Surnames* etc. *Isle of Man* 122 *Staff lands. **1659** TORRIANO, *Bastoniére*.. also a cudgeler, a *staff-man. **1940** *Chambers's Techn. Dict.* 799/2 *Staffman* (Surv.), the surveyor's assistant whose duty it is to hold the levelling staff while the instrument is sighted upon it and readings are being taken. **1976** *Time* 27 Sept. 12/2 Says one Carter staffman: 'Jimmy has his good smiles and his bad smiles.' **1977** P. POLLACK *Pict. Hist. Photogr.* (rev. ed.) 138/1 The largest pool of talented recorders.. unsurprisingly, was to be found among the staffmen of *Life* magazine. **1888** HONNOR MORTEN *Sk. Hosp. Life* 6 An intelligent and capable woman can expect to rise by gradations from '*staff-nurse' to 'sister'. **1972** J. MCCLURE *Caterpillar Cop* xiii. 216 The staff nurse calls them from the other ward if she needs help. **1978** *Jrnl. R. Soc. Med.* LXXI. 401 This is presumably what the Briggs report implies when it recommends that staff nurses should be made head of ward teams whose teaching they themselves would undertake. **1941** *Times* (weekly ed.) 30 July 6/4 This special study was taken in the garden of 10, Downing Street by a *staff photographer. **1977** P. POLLACK *Pict. Hist. Photogr.* (rev. ed.) 134/2 In the Israeli-Arab War of June 1967, the first casualty was Paul Schutzer, staff photographer of *Life* magazine. **1925** W. DEEPING *Sorrell & Son* xxx. 297 There is a vacancy at the Northern Free, a junior surgeonship. Sir Ormsby told me about it to-day in the *staff-room. **1953** K. TENNANT *Joyful Condemned* xvi. 136 The staff-room was split over the sensational row between Miss Page and the Head. **1977** P. KEMP in *Winter's Tales* XXIII. 46 On the first day of the last term.. she hurried to the staff-room. **1411** *Rolls of Parlt.* III. 665/2 Tout le maresme & fuaile, autrement appelle *Staffes-hides [*sic*] & Kides. **1376** *Ibid.* II. 340/2 Et plusours de eux devenent *stafstrikers. **1468** *Maldon* (Essex) *Liber B.* lf. 12 b, Nyght-walkeres, stastrykeres [*sic*], and evesedropperes. **1969** H. PERKIN *Key Profession* iv. 130 After the immediate post-war crush an improved *staff-student ratio. *Ibid.* vi. 246 The A.U.T.'s policy on staff-student relations should stand firmly on the principle of a community of scholars. **1974** *Howard Jrnl.* XIV. 80 There is a good staff-student ratio as well as up-to-date teaching equipment. **1982** M. MILLAR *Mermaid* iv. 49 Staff-student romances.. can be a problem. **1887** C. E. STRETTON *Safe Railway Working* iii. 64 (*heading*) The train *staff system. **1902** *Encycl. Brit.* XXXII. 147/1 In the United Kingdom and in Australia the means for preventing collisions between trains running towards each other is the 'staff system'. **1966** K. MÖLLER *Amer. & Brit. Railway Eng.* 39 The.. staff system is still in use in Britain; every engine running over a certain section of a line must carry the corresponding token or staff. **1885** E. B. IVATT *Railway Managem. at Stations* 559 Two or three trains may be passed forward by '*staff ticket' in this way, but ultimately either a train, an engine, or a messenger must convey the staff to enable trains being sent in the opposite direction. **1532-3** *Rec. St. Mary at Hill* 361 Item, paid for iij *staf torches of wex, to hold at the levacion ijs vjd. **1556** *Chron. Grey Friars* (Camden) 54, ij C. powre men in blacke gownes holdynge staffe torches. **1580-1** *Act 23 Eliz.* c. 8 §3 Wares wrought with Waxe, as in Lightes, Staftorches. **1633** JOHNSON *Gerarde's Herbal* App. 1600 *Celastrus Theophrasti.* The *staffe tree. **1771** J. R. FORSTER *Flora Amer. Septentr.* 11 Celastrus bullatus. Staff tree, elegant. Virginia. **1884** W. MILLER *Plant-n.* 130 *Staff-vine, *Celastrus scandens.* **1914** *Staff writer [see CREDIT *sb.* 13 d]. **1941** W. ABBOT *Handbk. Broadcasting* (ed. 2) xxvi. 322 Staff writers prepare commercial continuity, talks, announcements, interviews, special-occasion scripts, original plays, adaptations, and often station publicity. **1967** E. E. WILLIS *Writing Television & Radio Programs* i. 11 Writers who are permanently attached to the staff of a broadcasting organization and are paid on a regular weekly or monthly basis instead of being paid per script are known as *staff writers.* **1977** D. GREENE in Bond & McLeod *Newslett. to Newspapers* II. 89 Cave's other early 'staff writers'.. were much more than Grub Street hacks.

staff (stɑːf, -æ-), *sb.*[2] [Of obscure origin.] A building material consisting of plaster mixed with fibre, used for temporary ornamental work.

1892 *Advance* (Chicago) May 19 When mixed the staff is rolled out into slabs to be nailed to the sides of buildings, or made up in blocks.. for statues, friezes or cornices. **1892** *Times* (weekly ed.) 21 Oct. 10/1 They [the Exhibition buildings at Chicago] are.. covered with the composition of plaster, cement, and hemp, or similar fibre, known as 'Staff'. *Ibid.*, The sculpture and decorations on the buildings are also chiefly of 'staff', being first modelled in clay. **1893** *Offic. Guide World's Columbian Expos.* 21 Staff was invented in France about 1876, and was first used in the buildings of the Paris Exposition in 1878.

staff (stɑːf, -æ-), *v.* [f. STAFF *sb.*[1]] *trans.* To provide with a staff of officers, teachers, servants, etc.

1859 *Times* 20 Aug. 7/6 We end by being efficiently and sensibly equipped, commanded and staffed. **1881** *19th Cent.* Apr. 656 Two or three such women, a care-taker, and a cook would adequately staff each home. **1888** MRS. H. WARD *R. Elsmere* V. xxxiii, A powerful church of the new type, staffed by friends and pupils of Pusey. **1895** *Naturalist* 132 It is a satisfaction to note how well the museum is staffed. **1904** *Catholic Times* 1 Jan. 8/3 To furnish and staff some three or four first class day schools for boys.

Hence **'staffing** *vbl. sb.*

1882 *19th Cent.* Nov. 788 The Board schools.. have.. many advantages, derived from.. their superior staffing, and more highly paid teachers. **1901** *Scotsman* 30 Oct. 12/4 The staffing of the offices at Castle Terrace.

‖**staffage** ('stafaːʒ). [Ger.: a pseudo-Fr. formation after G. *staffiren* to fit out, garnish, believed to be corruptly ad. OF. *estoffer*, f. *estoffe* STUFF *sb.*] The accessories of a picture. Also *transf.* and *fig.*

1872 B. TAYLOR in *Life & Lett.* (1884) II. 594 A forge where he [Schiller] studied the *staffage* for his ballad of 'Fridolin'. **1887** *Pall Mall Gaz.* 22 Nov. 3/1 The *staffage* to the little love-story is a fertile little oasis in the wide, bleak Cossack steppes. **1906** *Academy* 10 Nov. 480/1 But the seated figure is a needless piece of *staffage.* **1908** A. M. HIND *Short Hist. Engraving* 230 The *staffage* of some of Piranesi's dullest subjects.. discloses an irrepressible instinct for life.

staffage, Sc. variant of STAFFISH *a. Obs.*

staffed (stɑːft, -æ-), *ppl. a.* [f. STAFF *sb.*[1] + -ED[2].] In *Her.* (see quot. and STAFF *sb.*[1] 11).

1891 *Century Dict.* s.v., An amulet staffed, a ring from which staffs or scepters radiate.

staffelite ('stæfəlaɪt). *Min.* [ad. G. *staffelit* (C. A. Stein 1866, in *Jahrb. des Vereins für Naturkunde im Herzogthum Nassau* XIX-XX. 57), f. *Staffel*, name of a locality in Hesse, W. Germany: see -ITE[1].] A carbonate-containing variety of apatite found as colourless or yellow masses; carbonatefluorapatite; = FRANCOLITE.

1868 J. D. DANA *Syst. Mineral.* (ed. 5) 534 Staffelite of Stein.. occurs incrusting the phosphorite of Staffel, in botryoidal, reniform, or stalactitic masses. **1939** *Mineral. Mag.* XXV. 401 Francolite and staffelite are identical, and the name francolite has priority. **1977** V. GISSING tr. *Kouřimský's Illustr. Encycl. Minerals & Rocks* viii. 256 Staffelite.. is a stalactitic apatite and occurs in the Staffel deposits near Limburg, West Germany.

†**'staffer**[1]. *Obs. rare*[−1]. [? f. STAFF *sb.*[1] + -ER[1].] ? A kind of peashooter.

1688 HOLME *Armoury* III. xvi. (Roxb.) 82/2 Playes with Instruments... Shooting in a trunk staffer or spitter.

staffer[2] ('stɑːfə(r), -æ-). orig. and chiefly *U.S.* [f. STAFF *sb.*[1] + -ER[1].] A member of a staff.

a. Of a newspaper or journal: a staff writer.

1949 *Cavalier Daily* (Univ. of Virginia) 22 Oct. 4/2 Staffers of the Daily Pennsylvanian visited the Princetonian offices following the Penn-Princeton football game. **1952** G. REINHARDT *Crime without Punishment* 290 He knew.. what confidential memos had been passed between the managing editor and publisher of the *New York Times*—a fact doubtless not known to most *Times* staffers. **1973** E. B. WHITE *Let.* 24 May (1976) 648 The story of *The New Yorker* has yet to be *well* told. Many staffers were indignant about parts of the Thurber book.

b. More widely, of a business or other organization.

1950 in WEBSTER Add. **1962** *Housewife* (Ceylon) Apr. 34 (*caption*) Mr. Neale talks to staffers of a local advertising agency. **1966** *Economist* 3 Sept. 888/1 Clerks, foremen and other staffers. **1972** M. GLENNY tr. *Solzhenitsyn's August 1914* xi. 108 The younger General Staffers of recent vintage all knew each other and stuck together like members of a secret order. **1980** *Information Retrieval & Library Automation* XVI. 11/2 The issue of April 1980 for example contains a brief but informative report on 'interlending' in Czechoslovakia, prepared by a BLL staffer who spent two weeks surveying the Czech scene.

c. *spec.* of the President of the U.S.; a member of the President's White House staff.

1969 R. NEUSTADT in A. King *Brit. Prime Minister* 145 The functional equivalence between a British Cabinet and our set of influentials—whether Secretaries, Senators, White House staffers, Congressmen or others. **1976** *National Observer* (U.S.) 14 Feb. 16/6 The letter was written by a Carter staffer who misrepresented Carter's position. **1981** W. SAFIRE in *N.Y. Times Mag.* 29 Mar. 10/2 Some of the White House staffers at the time looked for a way round it.

staffette (stæ'fɛt). *Obs.* exc. *Hist.* Also 7 **staffett, staffeto.** [ad. It. *staffetta*, dim. of *staffa*, stirrup. Cf. ESTAFETTE.] A mounted courier.

1545 WOTTON in *St. Papers Hen. VIII*, X. 487, I have written thryse to you, twyse by the ordynarye staffette that goith weekelye to Andwerpe. **1633** *Cal. St. Papers, Dom.* 28 Jan. 521 [Orders.. to erect] staffette [or packet posts at fit stages]. *Ibid.* Apr. 39 [That letters should be sent by] staffeto. **1635** in *Rep. Secret Comm. Post-Office* App. (1844) 55 A Proposition for setling of Staffets or pacquet posts betwixt London and all parts of his Maiesties dominions. **1714** *Lond. Gaz.* No. 5263/2 We have Advices from Vienna which say, that a Staffette was arrived there with Letters from Constantinople. **1858** CARLYLE *Fredk. Gt.* IV. v. (1865) I. 307 Brief weekly report to his Majesty will be expected; staffettes, should cases of hot haste occur.

†**staff-full**, *a. Obs.* [? f. STAFF *sb.*[1] + FULL *a.* The original notion was perh. 'full to the brim but not heaped up', as when a staff has been passed across the brim. But cf. Norw. *stappfull* crammed full (Aasen), f. *stappa* to stamp, crush.]

Quite full.

13.. *Gaw. & Gr. Knt.* 494 Now ar þay stoken of sturne werk staf-ful her hond. *a* **1400-50** *Wars Alex.* 1543 A Mitre ..Stiȝt staffull of stanes þat straȝt out bemes. *c* **1420** *Liber Cocorum* 34 And do hit in a barel þenne; þe barel staf ful as I þe kenne.

'staffian, *a. nonce-wd.* [f. STAFF *sb.*[1] + -IAN.] Suited for making staffs.

1820 L. HUNT *Indicator* No. 35 (1822) I. 279 The ash.. hath been famous, time immemorial, for its staffian qualities.

†**staffier.** *Obs.* Forms: 6 **stafyre**, 7-8 **staffier.** [ad. It. *staffiero, -ere*, f. *staffa* stirrup, a. OHG. *stapho*: see STEP *v.* Cf. F. *estafier.*] 'A lacquey, that attends the stirrup' (Blount *Glossogr.*, 1674); a footman. Chiefly with reference to Italy.

1532 BONER in *St. Papers Hen. VIII*, VII. 396 The said old Abbot of Ferfa.. hath been of late at Rome with 3 score in companye, besides 20 stafyres. **1664** BUTLER *Hud.* II. ii. 650 Before the Dame, and round about, March'd Whifflers, and Staffiers on foot. *a* **1668** LASSELS *Voy. Italy* I. (1670) 12 The Italians.. value no bravery but that of Coach and Horses and Staffiers. **1673** RAY *Journ. Low C., Charac. Italians* 396 The Nobility.. chuse.. to spend their revenues in.. keeping coaches and horses and a great retinue of servants and staffiers. *a* **1734** NORTH *Exam.* III. vii. §89. 574 These figures were brought by the Mob in grand Procession, from the further End of London, with honourable Attendance of Staffiers and Link-Boys.

†**'staffish**, *a. Obs.* Also 6-9 *Sc.* **staffage.** [f. STAFF *sb.*[1] + -ISH.] **a.** Rigid, stiff, hard. **b.** *fig.* Stubborn, unmanageable.

1500-20 DUNBAR *Poems* lx. 17 Stuffettis, strekouris, and stafische strummellis. **1513** DOUGLAS *Æneis* XII. vi. 134 Thymetes, a man of full gret fors, Castyn from hys staffage, skeich and hedstrang hors. **1545** ASCHAM *Toxoph.* II. (Arb.) 118 An unfit and staffysh bow. *a* **1568** —— *Scholem.* I. (Arb.) 34 A witte in youth, that is not ouer dulle, heauie, knottie and lumpishe, but hard, rough, and though somwhat staffishe. *a* **1568** A. SCOTT *Poems* xxi. 17, I fand hir of ane staffage kynd, Bath staitly, strange, and he. **1802** J. SIBBALD *Chron. Scot. Poetry* IV. Gloss., *Staffage, Staffisch,* obstinate, obdurate, dry in the mouth, or not easily swallowed, like pease meal bannocks.

ˈstaffless, *a.*

1. Without a staff. *rare.*

a **1661** FULLER *Worthies, Kent* (1662) 67 Hereat the Queen in some passion snatching the staff out of his hand... The Lord waited Stafflesse almost a day..before the same was reconferred upon him.

2. Having no business or domestic staff; without employees. Also *transf.*

1957 'P. PORTOBELLO' *How to be Deb's Mum* 38 Her husband nursed the chef, a foreign refugee, back to health from influenza in an otherwise staffless but turreted castle. **1965** L. MEYNELL *Double Fault* II. iii. 126 In these almost staff-less days I can't tell you how comforting it is to lie awake in the morning and hear the gravel of the drive being raked. **1976** T. HEALD *Let Sleeping Dogs Die* ii. 46 You'll have to take pot luck... I'm staffless now..but I shall be able to rustle something up.

† **ˈstaffly**, *a. Obs.* [OE. *stæflic*: see STAFF *sb.*[1] and -LY[1]. Cf. ON. *stafligr*.] Literal. So † **ˈstaffly** *adv.* [see -LY[2]], literally.

c **1000** ÆLFRIC *Saints' Lives* xxv. 73 Hi..nellað understandan butan þæt steaflice [*v.r.* stæflice] andȝit. *c* **1200** ORMIN 11117 Forr to drinnkenn gastliȝ witt Ut off stafflike fetless. *Ibid.* 14419 Aȝȝ whil þatt menn þurrh flæshliȝ witt Stafflike itt unnderrstodenn. *Ibid.* 15055 Þa takesst tu gast-like witt Off staffliȝ witeȝhunnge.

staff officer.

† **1.** A high officer of the royal household, or minister of state, bearing a white staff. See STAFF *sb.*[1] 7. *Obs.*

1702 *Lond. Gaz.* No. 3862/1 The Duke of Ormond, being the Staff-Officer in waiting. **1728** CHAMBERS *Cycl.* s.v. *Officer, Staff Officers* are such as in the King's Presence bear a white Staff; and at other times, going abroad, have a white Staff borne before them by a Footman bare-headed. Such are the Lord Steward, Lord Chamberlain, Lord Treasurer, &c.

2. *Mil.* † **a.** A non-commissioned officer. *Obs.*

1702 *Milit. Dict.* (1704) s.v. *Officer, Warrant, and Staff-Officers*, those who have not the King's Commission, but are appointed by the Colonels and Captains, as Quarter-masters, Serjeants, Corporals. [*ed.* 4, 1711, *adds*: and in the same Number are included Chaplains and Surgeons]. **1706** FARQUHAR *Recruiting Officer* v. v, *Kite*. [A sergeant, addressing a constable] And then we are both staff-officers. **1709** *Lond. Gaz.* No. 4590/3 Forty-four Staff-Officers. **1727** H. BLAND *Milit. Discipl.* v. 61 The Staff-Officers, viz. Chaplain, Adjutant, Quarter-Master, Surgeon and Mate.

b. An officer doing duty with the general or departmental staff of an army, division, or brigade. Cf. G. *stabsoffizier*.

1777 SHERIDAN *Sch. Scand.* IV. i, Why then, he shall have him for ten pounds, and I'm sure that's not dear for a staff-officer. **1802** C. JAMES *Milit. Dict.* F ff 3/1 No officer must ride between the divisions on a march, except General and Staff officers. **1811** *Regul. & Orders Army* 29 Aides-de-Camp, Brigade-Majors, and other Staff Officers. **1864** [see SASHERY]. **1912** TREVELYAN *Geo. III & Fox* I. iii. 112 When he was a young staff officer on active service.

c. In the United States navy, an officer not exercising military command.

1891 in *Century Dict.*

staffold. *dial.* [Corrupt form (? after *scaffold*) of *stavel* STADDLE *sb.*] = STADDLE *sb.*

a **1722** LISLE *Husb.* (1757) 182 This method is not to be used where the wheat is designed for a staffold. **1764** *Museum Rust.* II. 221 Your said correspondent justly recommends the reek staval, or staffold, a frame of wood for the mow, placed on stones.

Stafford (ˈstæfəd). The name of a town in England (the county town of Staffordshire); also a surname derived from this. Used *attrib.* as in **Stafford blue**, some kind of blue cloth; **Stafford('s) knot** *Her.*, a knot used as a badge of the Stafford family; hence, a form of knot resembling this; † **Stafford law**, 'club law', with pun on *staff*; so † ***Stafford court***. Also used for STAFFORDSHIRE, as in **Stafford brick** (see quot. 1908).

c **1460** *Towneley Myst.* iii. 200 Thou were worthi be cled In *stafford blew; ffor thou art alway adred. **1908** *Animal Management* (Vet. Departm., War Office) 48 'Candy', 'blue *Stafford', 'Dutch', and 'adamantine clinkers' being the names of familiar varieties [of vitrified bricks]. **1611** COTGR. s.v. *Festin, Il a esté au festin de Martin baston*, He hath had a triall in *Stafford Court. **1552** *Invent. Ch. Goods York*, etc. (Surtees) 49, iij sewtes of vestmentes with *Stafforde knotes. **1828–40** BERRY *Encycl. Her.* I, *Stafford Knot*, a badge used by the family of *Stafford*. **1847** *Gloss. Heraldry* 197 *Stafford's Knot*. **1868** WALCOTT *Sacred Archæol.* 507 A true-love-knot..was the well-known Stafford knot. **1589** *Hay any Work* Aiij, I threatned him with blowes, and to deale by *stafford law. **1599** BRETON *Will of Wit*, etc. (Grosart) 29/1 And among souldiours Stafford law, martiall law, killing or hanging is soone learned. **1615** BEDWELL *Moham. Impost.* I. §26 The Alkoran of Mohammed established by Stafford law. **1647** M. CORBET *Sp.* 31 July 5 We have unlawfully erected Marshall Law, Club Law, Stafford Law, and such lawless Laws as make most for Treason.

Staffordshire (ˈstæfədʃə(r)). **a.** The name of a county of England, used *attrib.* as **Staffordshire bull terrier**, a small stocky terrier of the breed so called, first developed by crossing bulldogs and terriers, characterized by a fawn, blue, or brindle coat, often with white markings, and a short, broad head with dropped ears; **Staffordshire coke**, (see quots.); **Staffordshire cone**, a kind of pyrometric cone; **Staffordshire slack**, (see quot.); **Staffordshire ware**, earthenware and porcelain made in Staffordshire, hence ***Staffordshire warehouseman***. Also **Staffordshire knot** [? error for *Stafford knot*], (*a*) 'a knot used to ligature the pedicle in ovariotomy' (*Syd. Soc. Lex.* 1898); (*b*) also, a Stafford knot or half-hitch used as a craftsman's device or motif.

1765 J. WEDGWOOD *Let.* 17 June (1965) 34 An order from St. James's for a service of Staffordshire ware. **1784** H. WALPOLE *Descr. Strawberry H.* Wks. 1798 II. 414 Four green leaves of Staffordshire-ware. *Ibid.* 501 A Staffordshire Etruscan vase. **1813** *Examiner* 22 Feb. 119/1 J. Clarke, Tottenham-court-road, Staffordshire warehouse-man. **1827** FARADAY *Chem. Manip.* iv. (1842) 99 Of this kind is the Staffordshire coke, which may be obtained at some of the wharfs on the canals near London. **1857** J. MARRYAT *Pottery & Porcelain* (ed. 2) 149 The earliest specimens extant of the Staffordshire ware are the 'Butter-pots', and the Tygs or Tiggs. **1869** DAY *Puddling* 4 in Rankine *Machine & Hand-tools*, The thick coal called 'Staffordshire slack'. **1901** *Our Dogs* 13 July 47/2 (Advt.), Old Staffordshire red brindled Bull-Terrier Dog Pup, five weeks, makes 20lbs. **1904** *Ibid.* 2 Jan. 24/2 (Advt.), Grand Litter Staffordshire Bull-terrier Pups, gamest strain. **1908** B. W. WATSON *Old Silver Platers & their Marks* 9/2 (*table*) 1808 Feb. 4 Josh Gibbs... Staffordshire Knott. **1950** A. C. SMITH *Dogs since 1900* xi. 174 In 1935 the Staffordshire Bull Terrier Club was founded. **1967** M. CHANDLER *Ceramics in Mod. World* i. 38 Cones used in continental Europe are still known as Seger cones, the slightly modified cones used in America are called Orton cones, and those used in England—also slightly modified—are called Staffordshire cones. **1968** J. ARNOLD *Shell Bk. Country Crafts* 280 The figures represented by [Corn] Dollies cover a considerable variety... We may name a few... The Horn of Plenty,..the Staffordshire Knot, [etc.]. **1971** *Vogue* 15 Oct. p. LS ii, The strikingly unusual motif features Staffordshire knots. *a* **1977** *Harrison Mayer Ltd. Catal.* 70/1 Staffordshire Cones..are slender, Trihedral pyramids made of ceramic materials and are so constituted as to deform when subjected to elevated temperature for a period of time. *Ibid.*, 'Staffordshire Cones', have been manufactured in England for nearly fifty years. **1977** J. WAMBAUGH *Black Marble* (1978) viii. 126 Pattie Mae didn't do so well with the Staffordshire bull terrier.

b. *ellipt.* = *Staffordshire ware*. Also *sb. pl.* = *Staffordshire bricks*.

[**1770** H. WALPOLE *Let.* 6 May (1967) XXIII. 211 We have Etruscan vases, make of earthen ware in Staffordshire, from two to five guineas.] **1866** QUEEN VICTORIA *Let.* 16 May in R. Fulford *Your Dear Letter* (1971) 75, I send her a tea-set..which I hope she will often use. It is Staffordshire. **1898** *Daily News* 8 Feb. 3/5 Little stacks of various kinds of bricks—from London stocks to Staffordshires. **1908** *Daily Report* 25 Aug. 8/3 The 'Fitz-Gerald' sale of Staffordshire ware..came as a revelation, both as to the quality of old Staffordshire and the prices it now obtains.

c. *ellipt.* = *Staffordshire bull terrier*, sense a above. Also *attrib.*

1903 *Our Dogs* 27 June 944/1 (Advt.), Pure-bred Staffordshire Bitch, good guard, and very game. **1943** H. N. BEILBY *Staffordshire Bull Terrier* i. 3 The Staffordshire will, by his intelligence and general usefulness, make a very strong appeal. **1968** [see FILLED *ppl. a.* 2].

staff-sling. *Obs.* exc. *Hist.* [f. STAFF *sb.*[1] + SLING *sb.*[1] Cf. OHG. *stapaslinga* G. *stabschlinge*.] A sling (SLING *sb.*[1] 1) the cords or strings of which are attached to the end of a staff, used for hurling larger stones than the ordinary 'cord-sling'.

13.. *Coer de L.* 5226 (W.), With staffe-slynges that smyte wel. **1375** BARBOUR *Bruce* XVII. 344 Instrumentis..As scaffatis, ledderis..Pykis, howis, and ek staff-slyngis. *c* **1386** CHAUCER *Sir Thopas* 118 This geant at hym stones caste Out of a fel staf slynge. **1432–50** tr. *Higden* (Rolls) I. 297 Vsenge dartes and crosse bawes or staffe slynges. **1530** PALSGR. 275/1 Staffe slyng made of a clyftestycke, *ruant*. *c* **1550** ROLLAND *Crt. Venus* II. 226 Alswa he slew the Giant Golyas, In the foirheid with ane stane and stafsling. **1557–8** *Acc. Ld. High Treas. Scot.* X. 336 To big dikis and fowseis and to have stafe slungis in the reddines to the portis thairof. **1825** FOSBROKE *Encycl. Antiq.* 780 The Staff-sling, the Classical *Fustibalum*.

Hence † **staff-slinger**.

13.. *Coer de L.* 4454 (W.), Foremeste he sette hys arwe-blasteres, And aftyr that hys good archeres And aftyr hys staff-slyngeres And othir with scheeldes and with speeres.

† **staff-sword.** *Obs.* [Cf. OHG. *stapaswert*, MHG. *stab-*, *stapswert*, Du. *stafsweerd* (Kilian), etc.] A sword-stick.

c **1000** ÆLFRIC *Voc.* in Wr.-Wülcker 143/21 *Dolones*, stæf-sweord. *c* **1470** HENRY *Wallace* III. 178 With a staff suerd Boyd stekit him that tyde. *Ibid.* VI. 737 With a staff suerd off steill. *a* **1603** T. CARTWRIGHT *Confut. Rhem. N.T.* (1618) 543 Neither Aristotles..one shooe for both feet, nor Platoes staffe-sword.

stafisagre, obs. form of STAVESACRE.

stag (stæg), *sb.*[1] Forms: *α.* ? 2 *accus.* **staggon**, 4–7 **stagge, (4 staghe)**, 6–8 **stagg**, 4– **stag**. *β.* 5–7 **stage**; also (sense 2 only) 6 *north.* **staige**, 7 **staeg**, 5– *Sc.* **staig**. [Prob. repr. OE. **stacga* (*stagga*) wk. masc.; cf. various other names of animals, *docga* dog, *frocga* frog, **picga* pig, *wicga* beetle. The word seems to have meant properly a male animal in its prime; cf. the various senses below and the cognate ON. *steggi*, *stegg-r* (Norw. *stegg*) male bird, mod.Icel. *stegg-r* tom-cat, formerly also male fox: see STEG *sb.*

There is no ground for the current statement that *stag* is of Scandinavian origin, though some of the senses below may be due to confusion with STEG.]

1. a. The male of a deer, esp. of the red deer; spec. a hart or male deer of the fifth year. (In the 15th c. † ***stag of a hart***.)

α. ? *c* **1185** PSEUDO-CNUT *Constit. de Foresta* xxiv. in Liebermann *Gesetze der Ags.* (1903) I. 624 (Stowe MS., late 16th *c.*) Regalem feram, quam Angli a staggon [*Camb. MS. c.* 1570 Astaggon, *Harrison* 1577 staggon] appellant. *c* **1400** *Master of Game* (MS. Digby 182) ii, þe first yere þat thei [harts] be calfede, þei be ycalle a calfe þe secund yere a bulloke..þe thred yere a broket, þe iiii. yere a stagard, þe v. yere a stagge, þe vi. yere an herte of .x. **14..** *Chaucer's Sqr.'s T., heading of Part* 11, *MSS. Petworth & Corpus*, The Stag of an hert. **1473** *Rolls of Parlt.* VI. 98/2 Oure Graunte.., of a Tonne Wyne, and a Stagge of an Hert. **1576** TURBERV. *Venerie* xxii. (1908) 62 If you find together the footing of two stagges. *Ibid.* lxxix. 237 An Hart is called the firste yeare a Calfe..the fourth a Staggerd, the fifth a Stagge, and..the sixth..an Hart. **1584** POWELL *Lloyd's Cambria* 157 William Rufus was slaine by an Arrowe shot at a Stagge. **1596** SHAKS. *Tam. Shr.* Induct. ii. 50 Thy gray-hounds are as swift As breathed Stags I fleeter then the Roe. **1613** DRAYTON *Polyolb.* XII. 523 Those fallow Deere, and huge-hancht Stags that graz'd Vpon her shaggy Heaths. *c* **1643** LD. HERBERT *Autobiog.* (1824) 88 Forests and Chases which were well stored with wild Boar and Stag. **1667** MILTON *P.L.* VII. 469 The swift Stag from under ground Bore up his branching head. **1735** SOMERVILLE *Chase* I. 283 [The] stately Stag, that o'er the Woodland reigns. **1821** SHELLEY *Hellas* 537 The tiger leagues not with the stag at bay Against the hunter. **1863** LYELL *Antiq. Man* 23 Venison, or the flesh of the stag and roe, was more eaten. **1877** *Encycl. Brit.* VII. 23/2 The Red Deer or Stag..the largest of the British deer, is a native of the temperate regions of Europe and Northern Asia. **1908** *Blackw. Mag.* July 105/2 A herd of fourteen reindeer was seen... The horns of the entire band—for the hinds carry them as well as the stags—were still in velvet.

β. **1546** *Plumpton Corr.* (Camden) 250, I must..ride to Tankerslay..& se a showt at a stage, as my keper hath sent me wourd. *c* **1550** *Battle of Otterburn* iii. in Child *Ballads* III. 295/1 Vpon Grene Lynton they lyghted dowyn, Styrande many a stage [*rime* crage].

b. *fig.* Also in phrases † ***to go in stag***: To go naked. † ***to make*** (a husband) ***a stag, to make to wear the stag's crest*** = to cuckold. (*Obs.*)

1591 FLORIO *2nd Fruites* 143 What dooth she make him weare the staggs crest then? **1602** DEKKER *Satirom.* F 3, No, come my little Cub, doe not scorne mee because I goe in Stag, in Buffe, heer's veluet too. **1610** B. JONSON *Alch.* I. ii, *Dap.* Yes, but I'ld ha' you Vse Mr Doctor, with some more respect. *Fac.* Hang him proud Stagg, with his broad veluet head. **1659** T. PECKE *Parnassi Puerp.* 30 Paulina her first husband made a Stag. **1935** T. S. ELIOT *Murder in Cathedral* i. 29 Cabined in Canterbury, realmless ruler, Self-bound servant of a powerless Pope, The old stag, circled with hounds.

c. In the names of various species of the genus *Cervus*, as *Axis Stag*, an Indian deer (*C. axis*), *Carolina Stag*, the North American Wapiti (*C. canadensis*); see also quot. 1896.

1859 WOOD *Illustr. Nat. Hist.* I. 693 The Wapiti or Carolina Stag. **1895** *Outing* Apr. 4/2 An axis stag glanced across the nala. **1896** LYDEKKER *Brit. Mammals* 242 Of the allied species, we may mention by name the..Thian Shan Stag (*C. eustephanus*), the Kashmir Stag (*C. cashmirianus*)..and the Lhasa Stag (*C. thoroldi*).

d. The flesh of the stag; venison. *rare*$^{-1}$.

1787 A. C. BORRER *Diaries & Corr.* (1903) 71 He has given us twice Stag since I have been here.

e. The horn of the stag, as a material for handles of cutlery. Also *attrib.*

1876 CALLIS *Cutlery* (Brit. Manuf. Industr.) 173 Scales of wood and composition, pressed to imitate stag and buffalo, have been introduced for common goods.

† **f.** transf. ***flying stag***, the STAG-BEETLE. *Obs.*

1658 MOUFET *Theat. Ins.* I. xxi. 1005 The πλατύκερως, or Harts horn Beetle... Some call it the Bull, others the flying Stag... The French, *Cerf volant*; the English, Stag-fly, or Flying-fly.

2. *north.* and *Sc.* A young horse, esp. one unbroken.

α. **1318** *Durham Acc. Rolls* (Surtees) 373 In primis sunt..2 stagges masculi, 1 pullanus masculus. **1346–7** in *Finchale Priory Charters*, etc. (Surtees) p. xxvi, Item unus staggus masculi unius anni. **1363** *Ibid.* p. lxi, ij staghes ætatis duorum annorum. **1439–40** *Durham Acc. Rolls* (Surtees) 409 Item 1 equa cum 1 stag ijor annorum. *c* **1460** *Towneley Myst.* xxx. 227 Vnethes may I wag, man for wery in youre stabill Whiles I set my stag, man. **1483** *Cath. Angl.* 358/1 A sstagge, *pullus*. **1514** *Test. Ebor.* (Surtees) V. 60 To Thomas, my sone, a stagge to make hym an horrse off. **1522** *Wills & Inv. N.C.* (Surtees) I. 106 To John Cowndon..a colt stagge. **1565** *Ibid.* 245 Item I gyue to thomas peroson my graye fillie stagg. **1684** MERITON *Praise Ale* (1685) 105 A Stag is a young Colt. **1778** J. MILL *Diary* (S.H.S. 1889) 55 [The losses of horses and cattle] were soon supplied by the purchase of three cows and two pretty young staggs. **1788** W. H. MARSHALL *Yorksh.* II. 355 *Stag*; a young horse.

β. **1478** in *Acta Audit.* (1839) 82/1 For a meire & a staig xl s. **1540** *N.C. Wills* (Surtees) 170 To Mathew Hynde, xl s., a fely stage. **1558** in J. Croft *Excerpta Anat.* (1797) 28 Item, a Bay Stoned Staige. *a* **1585** MONTGOMERIE *Flyting w. Polwart* 395 Some [witches], on steid of a staig, ouer a starke monke straide. **1617** in *Extracts Rec. Convent. Burghs Scot.* (1878) III. 47 Ilk ox, kow, horse, stote, meir, staeg. **1654** *Ibid.* III. 388 Item, of ilk hors, meir or stage, going to the mercat, 1s. **1792** BURNS *Kellyburn Braes* iv, It's neither your stot nor your staig I shall crave..But gie me your wife, man. **1812** CHALMERS *Let.* in *Life* (1851) I. 309 The staigs were returned to the glebe.

Proverbs. **1857** J. MILLER *Alcohol* (1858) 123 Keep strong drink from the lad and the boy, 'Corn is not for staigs'. **1899**

J. SPENCE *Shetl. Folk-lore* 228 There's aye watter whaar the staig smores.

3. An animal castrated when full grown. **a.** A bull; more fully ***bull stag***. Now *dial.*, *Sc.* and *Australian.*

α. **1680, 1776** Bull stag [see BULL *sb.*[1] 11]. **1787** WINTER *Syst. Husb.* 284 A dairyman's six heavy bull stags..broke over a well secured fence into my field of wheat. **1884** 'R. BOLDREWOOD' *Melb. Mem.* xvii. 123, I just recollect that blue stag... Was he in the mob you saw? **1886** *W. Somerset Word-bk.*, *Stag*, a castrated bull. The term is applied to any animal emasculated after maturity. **1894** *Harper's Mag.* Feb. 354 They require work-steers to do their ploughing and Mr. Bell has brought up half a dozen old 'stags'.

β. **1818** SCOTT *Hrt. Midl.* xiv, He returned..muttering that he thought he heard the 'young staig loose in the byre'. **1822** —— *Pirate* xxx, The air and bearing of a bull-dog, whilk I have seen loosed at a fair upon a mad staig. **1856** MORTON *Cycl. Agric.* II. 726/1 In Scot., *Staig. Bull-staig* is a castrated bull.

b. A boar, hog, or ram. *dial.*

1784 [cf. *stag-hog* in 9 b]. **1811** T. DAVIS *Agric. Wilts* 260 Boar stag, a castrated boar. **1851** STERNBERG *Northampt. Gloss.*, *Stag*, an old boar. **1863** W. BARNES *Dorset Gloss.*, *Stag*, a castrated male animal; as, a ram-stag, a boar-stag, a bull-stag.

4. Applied to the male of various birds. (Cf. STEG.) **a.** A cock. *dial.* Also *spec.* in *Cockfighting*, a cock less than one year old.

1730 CHENY *Hist. List Horse-matches*, etc. 168 Each side shew'd some Cocks and some Staggs. **1758** [cf. *stag-match* in 9]. **1770** *Newcastle Chron.* Advt., To be fought for..on the 31st of December, Fifty pounds by cocks and stags, 3lbs. 14oz. **1815** *Sporting Mag.* XLVI. 59 The practice of running stags with cocks is unavoidable. **1823** 'JON BEE' *Dict. Turf.* s.v., A young game cock—is a stag. **1886** *Live Stock Jrnl.* 23 July 99/1 [Letter from *Devonshire*] Many people who keep hens for their eggs alone do not allow a stag with them. **1894** BARING-GOULD *Kitty Alone* I. 96 Bramber learned that day that a cock in Devonshire is entitled stag. **1902** *Lindsey & Lincolnsh. Star* 29 Nov. 5/2 Fowl stealing. .. In one case a fine buff Orpington stag has been taken.

b. A turkey-cock of two years and upwards.

1819 W. & H. RAINBIRD *Agric. Suff.* (1849) 300 (E.D.D.). *a* **1825** FORBY *Voc. E. Anglia*, *Stag*, a cock turkey, killed for the table in his second year. **1849** D. J. BROWNE *Amer. Poultry Yd.* (1855) 165 *note*, When a cock turkey arrives at the age of two years, he is called a 'stag'.

†**c.** A young swan. *Obs.* (Cf. STEG-*swan*.)

1544 *Will R. North* (Somerset Ho.), My Swanne marke w[t] all the Swannes Stagges & Signettes callid the Crow-fote.

5. *dial.* The wren.

a **1825** FORBY *Voc. E. Anglia*, *Stag*, a wren. **1885** SWAINSON *Prov. Names Birds* 35 Wren (*Troglodytes parvulus*), Stag, Tope (Norfolk; Cornwall). **1893** in Cozens-Hardy *Broad Norfolk* 51, Stag, Common Wren.

6. *dial.* and *colloq.* A big, romping girl; a bold woman.

1684 G. MERITON *Yorks. Dialogue* 55 Nea, nea, great stags, what a durdum thou macks! **1790** GROSE *Provinc. Gloss.* (ed. 2), *Stag*,..a romping girl. **1877** F. Ross et al. *Gloss. Words Holderness* 135/2 *Stag*,..a rude, romping girl. **1922** JOYCE *Ulysses* 425 The likes of her! Stag that one is. Stubborn as a mule! **1922** D. H. LAWRENCE *Aaron's Rod* iii. 33 She too was a tall stag of a thing.

7. *slang.* [Prob. from sense 1; but the reason for the use is obscure.] **a.** An informer; esp. in phrase ***to turn stag***. Also see quot. 1725.

1725 *New Canting Dict.*, *Stag*,..as, *I spy a Stag*, used by ..Shepherd, lately executed, when he first saw the Turnkey of Newgate, who pursu'd and took him. **1785** GROSE *Dict. Vulgar T.*, *Stag*, to turn stag, a rogue who impeaches his confederates. *a* **1826** J. HOLT *Mem.* (1838) II. 52 We had two disturbers of the harmony of the ship; I mean two stags or informers. **1834** AINSWORTH *Rookwood* I. viii. 217 As to clapping him in quod, he might prattle—might turn stag. **1846** J. KEEGAN *Leg. & Poems* (1907) 367 My father.. became a deserter, but he was not a coward, nor..a stag.

b. (See quots.)

1823 'JON BEE' *Dict. Turf*, s.v., Queer bail are 'stag': those men who being hired at a guinea or two per oath, to swear they are worth vast sums, stand about judges' chambers in term-time. **1848** BARTLETT *Dict. Amer.* 329 In the New York courts, a stag is the technical name for a man who is always ready to aid in proving an alibi, of course 'for a consideration'.

c. (See quot. 1857.)

1857 *Slang Dict.* 20 *Stag*, shilling. **1887** HENLEY *Villon's Straight Tip* 15 You cannot bank a single stag.

d. A spell of duty. (See also quot. 1881.)

1881 S. EVANS *A.B.E. Evans's Leicestershire Words* (new ed.) 255 A 'stag' is also one set to watch while his fellows are engaged in anything in which they wish not to be caught. **1931** BROPHY & PARTRIDGE *Songs & Slang Brit. Soldier: 1914–18* (ed. 3) 361 *Stag*, sentry-go. **1958** R. STOREY *Touch it Light* in J. C. Trewin *Plays of Year* XVIII. 341 There's seven stags in the hours o' darkness and only five of you to do 'em. Somebody has to do two. **1975** A. BEEVOR *Violent Brink* iv. 97 The films would be handed in for processing when they were relieved at the end of their two hour 'stag'.

e. *ellipt.* for *stag-dinner*, *-party*, etc. (sense 9 c.). *N. Amer.*

1904 *Brooklyn Eagle* 28 May 3 The Myrtle Fishing Club will have a stag at Hurman Hub's Park this evening. **1947** *Chicago Tribune* 19 Oct. (Comic Suppl.) 6 The marchin' and chowder club's throwin' a stag tonight. **1971** R. LEWIS *Fenokee Project* viii. 148 He's getting married tomorrow. Tonight he's holding his stag, and most of the men from the dam are going along.

f. *U.S.* A man who attends a social function without a female partner. Also quasi-*adv.* in phr. ***to go stag***.

1905 N. DAVIS *Northerner* 213 'No man not escorting a lady'—a stag, you know—could go upon the floor. **1905** *Dialect Notes* III. 21 Are you going to the dance stag? **1924** P. MARKS *Plastic Age* xix. 210 True, he was not 'dragging a woman', but several of the brothers were going 'stag'; so he felt completely at ease. **1928** *Daily Express* 14 Dec. 19 A needy or avaricious 'stag'—as male dancers are called in the United States. **1948** *This Week Mag.* 1 May 16/3 The sign read: 'No Stags Allowed'. **1979** R. JAFFE *Class Reunion* (1980) I. viii. 117 A lot of boys went to the parties stag. Social life was easy for them, not the way it was for girls, who had to wait..until someone called. **1980** R. L. DUNCAN *Brimstone* iii. 59 They're not going to let you in by yourself. They have a rule against stags.

8. *Comm. slang.* **a.** A person who applies for an allocation of shares in a joint-stock concern solely with a view to selling immediately at a profit.

1845 THACKERAY in *Punch* IX. 191 All the Stags in Capel Court. **1846** *Punch* X. 139 The bubble has in the mean time burst, the deposit is not paid, and the Stag..gives himself no more trouble about the scheme. **1857** SMILES *Stephenson* xxx. 408 Noble lords were pointed at as 'stags'..in the share markets. **1904** *Westm. Gaz.* 13 Apr. 9/1 Another point in the prospectus is the attempt to discriminate between the stag and the bona-fide investor.

b. (See quot.)

1854 H. AYRES *Fenn's Eng. & For. Funds* 109 A Stag is one who is not a Member of the Stock Exchange, but deals outside, and is sometimes called an 'Outsider'.

9. *attrib.* and *Comb.* **a.** similative, as ***stag-eyed***, ***-necked***, ***-sure*** adjs.

1826 HOOD *Stag-Eyed Lady* 42 Therefore he chose a lady for his love, Singling from out the herd one stag-eyed dear. **1793** HOLCROFT *Lavater's Physiogr.* xl. 213 The stag-necked horse. **1896** N. MUNRO *Lost Pibroch* 69 Girls..not with a flat slouching foot on the soil, but high in the instep, bounding and stag-sure.

b. quasi-*adj.* (*a*) = male, as ***stag-bird***, ***hartebeest***, ***-hog***, ***-moose***, ***-swan***, ***-turkey***. (*b*) in sense 2, as ***stag-bay***, ***-foal***, ***-horse***.

1606 *N. Riding Rec.* (1883) I. 55 Unum equum testiculatum, anglice a stoned *stagg bay. **1886** *W. Somerset Word-bk.* s.v. *Stag*, When applied to poultry *stag-bird is the usual term for a male kept for breeding purposes. **1883** R. M. FERGUSSON *Rambl. Sk. Far North* xv. 97 May a' your mares be well to foal, An' every ane be a *staig foal. **1850** R. G. CUMMING *Hunter's Life S. Afr.* (ed. 2) I. 188 He had observed an old *stag hartebeest standing in the shade of some tall green bushes. **1784** YOUNG *Ann. Agric.* I. 124 in Britten *Old Country Words* (1880) 110 **Stag-hog*, a boar. Suff. **1857** BORROW *Romany Rye* I. xi. 166, I..goes into a field, suppose by night, where there is a very fine *stag horse. **1721** DUDLEY *Moose-Deer* in *Phil. Trans.* XXXI. 166 Our Hunters have found a Buck, or *Stagg-Moose, of fourteen Spans in heighth from the Withers. **1892** TENNYSON *Church-Warden* vii. An' 'e torn'd as red as a *stag-turkey's wattles.

c. *slang* (orig. *U.S.*) = pertaining to or composed of males only, as ***stag-dance***, ***devilry***, ***-dinner***, ***-night***, ***-party***; freq. applied *spec.* to a celebration held on the eve of a man's marriage. Cf. *hen-party* s.v. HEN *sb.* 8.

1848 BARTLETT *Dict. Amer.* 330 **Stag-dance*, a dance performed by males only, in bar-rooms, &c. **1873** JOAQUIN MILLER *Life among Modocs* viii. 94 In one of the saloons.. men were wont to..have stag-dances. **1911** H. S. HARRISON *Queed* xv. 185 Buck Klinker, returning from some *stag devilry at the hour of two A.M. **1889** *Thompson St. Poker Club* 59 Mr. Tooter Williams had been to a *stag dinner in the early evening. **1965** *Listener* 9 Sept. 373/2 On '*stag nights' it [*sc.* the entertainment] is pretty blue. **1973** in E. Dunphy *Only a Game?* (1976) iv. 110 We went out this evening for his stag night. **1856** *Knickerbocker Mag.* Apr. 407 (Thornton *Amer. Gloss.*) A party of old bricks [*read* bucks], who, under pretence of looking at the picture, are keeping up a small *stag-party at the end of the room. **1923** 'BARTIMEUS' *Seaways* xii. 234 We don't want any women. We'll just have a stag party and talk Service shop and play pool afterwards. **1978** J. WAINWRIGHT *Thief of Time* 83, I know people... Class strippers. Stag-party hostesses. There's a real market.

10. a. Special comb.: **stag-book** *Comm. slang*, a book in which was entered the names of the stags or bogus shareholders (see 8); **stag-cart** = *deer-cart*, DEER 4 b; † **stag-chase** = *stag-hunting*; **stag-evil**, **-fever** (see quots.); **stag film** orig. *U.S.*, a pornographic film made for a male audience; † **stag-fly**, the stag-beetle; **stag-hafted**, **-handled** *adjs.*, furnished with a haft or handle of stag-horn; **stag-hog** = BABIROUSSA; **stag-hunt**, the chasing of a stag as a sport; **stag-hunter**, one who hunts the stag; also, a horse used in stag-hunting; **stag-hunting**, the sport of chasing the stag; an instance of this; **stag-like** *a.*, resembling a stag or that of a stag; **stag line** *U.S.*, the group of unattached young men at a social function; † **stag-match** *Cockfighting*, a match for young cocks (see 4 a); **stag movie** orig. *U.S.* = *stag film* above; † **stag-skin**, the prepared hide of a stag; † **stag-snake** = ELAPS; † **stag-worm** (see quot.).

1854 *Househ. Words* VIII. 470 You allotted to a great many stags, sir... Didn't you have any *stag-books when you allotted? **1894** *Daily News* 8 Feb. 2/6 A *stag-cart of the Mid-Kent staghounds. **1725** *Portland Papers* (Hist. MSS. Comm.) VI. 87 This [park] the Duke designed as the chief nursery for his *stag-chase. **1717** SOLLEYSELL *Compl. Horsem.*, *Stag's Evil. **1759** WALLIS *Farrier's Dict.*, s.v. *Convulsions*, Solleysell calls this malady the stag's evil, or palsy in the jaws. **1823** PURSGLOVE *Pract. Farriery* 81 In convulsions, or stag evil, the horse appears full of spirit. **1911** B. HOLLAND *Life Dk. Devonshire* II. xxiv. 237 He is said to have suffered at critical moments of the sport from the excitement known as *stag fever. **1968** *Wall St. Jrnl.* 11 Sept. 18/1 Pornography is not one of the nation's truly burning issues, and showing *stag films is not our idea of how to run the world's greatest deliberative body. **1977** *Gay News* 7–20 Apr. 23/2 She..made these very tame, anodyne stag films that she's always denying. **1634** MOUFET *Insect. Theatrum* I. xxi. 134 Anglis *Stag-flie. **1693** DALE *Pharmacol.* 538 Scarabæus cornutus, *Schrod*... The Stag-fly. **1797** *J. Robinson's Directory of Sheffield* 45 *Stag hafted penknife cutler. **1827** GRIFFITH tr. *Cuvier's Anim. Kingd.* III. 332 The Babiroussa, or *Stag Hog. **1842** LOVER *Handy Andy* lii, There was a *stag-hunt on the lake. **1855** MACAULAY *Hist. Eng.* xx. IV. 401 Without exposing himself to any risk greater than that of a staghunt at Fontainebleau. **1709** *Lond. Gaz.* No. 4540/8 Stoln or strayed.., a..Bay Gelding,..hath been a known and constant *Stag-Hunter in the Forest of Sherwood for 2 or 3 Years past. **1722** *Ibid.* No. 6112/1 There was a general *Stag hunting. **1845** YOUATT *Dog* iii. 86 Since the death of George III..stag-hunting has rapidly declined. **1627** MAY *Lucan* II. D 1 b, Along the hauens *stagge-like Hornes they runne Swiftly to shore. **1838** LYTTON *Leila* I. i, The small erect head and stag-like throat. **1934** J. O'HARA *Appointment in Samarra* i. 16 She would get twice around the dance floor with the same partner, then someone would step out of the *stag line and cut in. **1977** G. V. HIGGINS *Dreamland* v. 47 As a member of Porcellian I had been invited to the stag line at a gathering on Beacon Hill. **1758** *Lond. Chron.* 29 June 614/2 The *Stag Match between Sir Henry Grey, Bart., and Jennison Shafto, Esq. **1960** *Christian Herald* July 14/2 Teen-agers bought '*stag movies' for as much as $50 a reel. **1971** *Ink* 12 June 3/1 What he found was a hundred men having their mid-shift tea break and enjoying a stag movie. **1657** THORNLEY *Longus' Daphnis & Chloe* (1893) 60 She gave him a new Scrip of *Stag-skin. **1668** CHARLETON *Onomast.* 32 *Elaps*.. the *Stag-Snake. **1753** *Chambers' Cycl.* Suppl., **Stag-worms*,..a name given to a species of worms produced of the eggs of a fly, and lodged..behind, and under the palate of the stag.

b. In the names of plants: **stag bush** (see quot.); **stag fern** = staghorn fern (see STAGHORN 2 c); † **stag's garlic** (see GARLIC *sb.* 1 b).

1884 SARGENT *Rep. Forests N. Amer.* 94 *Viburnum prunifolium*..Black Haw. *Stag Bush. **1884** *Missionary Chron.* Apr. 102 Huge *stag ferns or fantastic shapes.

stag (stæg), *sb.*[2] ? variant of STACK *sb.* 6.

1775 *Ann. Reg.*, *Chron.* 185 The Abby,..having lately gone to pieces on the Stags near Kenrule, in Ireland, the captain, mate, and two common men..were cast upon the lower stags. **1867** SMYTH *Sailor's Word-bk.*, *Stag*, a name given to a rock..as off the Lizard, Castlehaven, &c.

stag (stæg), *sb.*[3] [? variant of STAKE *sb.*[1]]

1. A stake, pile. (Cf. STAG *v.*[2]) *dial.*

1881 *Leicestersh. Gloss.*, *Stag*, var. pron. of 'stake'. **1887** *Jamieson's Sc. Dict.* Suppl. 227/1 *Stag*, a stake, pile, fixed or for fixing in the ground. West of S.. Aberd[een].

†**2.** A tinman's tool = STAKE *sb.*[1] 5 a.

1688 HOLME *Armoury* III. xxii. (Roxb.) 269/2 He beareth Azure, a Small Stag, or a Round Stag, Argent. This..is for the raiseing of round filletts in Tyn for the Adornement of their Works. The second thing in this square is called a Creesing Stag.

†**stag**, *a.* *Obs.* Also stagg(e, stage. [Of obscure origin.] Of furs: Raw, unseasoned.

1545 *Rates Custom Ho.* a vij b, Callabre stagg. **1545** *Ibid.* b ij b, Foyne stagge. *Ibid.* d ij, Stagge the thousande. Stagge the hundreth. **1583** *Ibid.* A viij, Callaber stage. *a* **1618** *Rates of Merchandizes* G 2 b, Foynes wombes season'd... Foynes wombes stage. **1640** in Entick *London* II. 177 Coney skins grey, tawed, seasoned or stag.

stag, *v.*[1] Also 9 steg. [Prob. related to STAGGER *v.* Cf. ON. *staka* to push, stagger (whence *stakra* STAGGER *v.*). The identity of the word in the various senses below is uncertain.]

†**1.** *intr.* To stagger, waver. *Obs.*

1561 T. NORTON *Calvin's Inst.* III. ix. 156 b, For euen the Prophete confesseth that his fete stagged.

b. ? To flinch, yield, give way. *rare.*

1831 *Fraser's Mag.* III. 652 The House of Lords..are now making a loud clattering of their determination to stand against the bill—but it is no go. I lay you the long odds.. that their Lordships stag.

2. To walk with long strides. Hence ***stagged-up***, tired out with walking. *Sc.* and *dial.*

1823 MACTAGGART *Gallov. Encycl.* 311 His ghaist..was seen by many stegging about the estate. **1866** E. WAUGH *Ben an' th' Bantam* 66 Aw let on her [a traveller] o' tother side Yealey Ho'; quite stagged up. **1888** *Sheffield Gloss.*, *Stag*, to walk quickly. **1895** CROCKETT *Men of Moss-haggs* xxx, Auld Anton went stegging over the hills, till I was fair driven out of my breath.

†**stag**, *v.*[2] *Sc. Obs. rare*$^{-1}$. [? f. STAG *sb.*[3]; or var. of STAKE *v.*] *trans.* To support with piles.

1610 *Aberdeen Reg.* (1848) II. 300 The said brig to be staggit and branderit sufficiently in deipnes vnder the channall, to mak a sufficient ground to big vpoun.

stag (stæg), *v.*[3] [f. STAG *sb.*[1]]

1. *slang.* **a.** *trans.* To observe; to take particular notice of; to watch; also, to find out or discover by observation, to detect. Also *absol.* or *intr.*

1796 *Grose's Dict. Vulgar T.* (ed. 3), To *Stag*, to find, discover, observe. **1806** SURR *Winter in Lond.* (ed. 3) II. 120, I shall soon stag who they are. **1823** 'JON BEE' *Dict. Turf.* s.v., To 'stag' a thief, to look on, and spoil his sport: 'What's that cove a stagging there for? Down him, Billy'. **1854** MISS BAKER *Northampt. Gloss.* s.v., When workmen are taking beer clandestinely, one of them keeps on the look out, to watch or 'stag the master'. **1859** H. KINGSLEY *Geoffrey Hamlyn* v, So you've been stagging this gentleman and me, and listening, have you? **1897** G. BARTRAM *People of Clopton* v. 130 Who set ye on to watch me?.. And at last..he admitted that Master John had told him to keep an eye on me and Jenny—to 'stag' us if he saw us out together—and to get a witness to what went on between us.

b. (See quots.)

1811 *Sporting Mag.* XXXVII. 11 'I stagged him my Lord'.—'Stagged him, what do you mean by stagged him?' —'Why, my Lord, I mean I was down upon him'. **1870** *Daily News* 13 July, In the event of a man refusing or sloping, as it was termed, his line was what was called 'stagged', and when he went for an advance it was resolutely refused.

c. *intr.* To turn informer; to inform *against*.

1839 W. CARLETON *Fardorougha* xi. (1848) 161 But to stag against his companion and accomplice—this was looked upon as a crime. **1846** J. KEEGAN *Leg. & Poems* (1907) 380 She imagines that I played foul at New Ross,—that I stagged and betrayed as well as deserted.

d. (See quot.)

1860 *Hotten's Slang Dict.*, *Stag*, to demand money, to 'cadge'... Also, to dun, or demand payment.

2. *Comm. slang.* **a.** To deal in shares as a stag (see STAG *sb.*[1] 8).

1845 THACKERAY in *Punch* IX. 191 What! are ladies stagging it? **1845** —— [Implied in the *vbl. sb.* and *ppl. a.*].

b. *trans.* To deal in (shares) as a stag.

1935 *Times* 27 Nov. 19/2 The loan was heavily stagged, for the total applications exceeded £14,000,000. **1966** *New Statesman* 23 Sept. 456/3 The gilt-edged market has now improved to the point where the new issue of *ICI* loan stock seems likely to be stagged even more heavily than the last. **1981** *Daily Tel.* 20 July 15/2 The offer is likely to be subscribed although the opportunities for stagging the issue will be limited.

3. *dial.* (See quot. Cf. STAG-HEADED *a.*)

1854 MISS BAKER *Northampt. Gloss.*, *Stag*, to take off the top of a hedge without laying it down.

4. *intr.* To go to or attend a social occasion unaccompanied. Also const. *it*. *U.S. slang.*

1900 *Dialect Notes* II. 64 *To stag it*, to go to a party without escorting a lady. **1941** *Sat. Even. Post* 10 May 74/3 If you won't go with me to the picnic, I'll stag. **1973** *Lebende Sprachen* XVIII. 38/1 He had planned to stag at the class dance.

5. *trans.* To cut (trousers or other articles of clothing) off short. Also with *off*. *N. Amer.*

1902 [implied at *stagged* ppl. a. below]. **1905** *Terms Forestry & Logging* (U.S. Dept. Agric. Bureau Forestry) 49 *Stag*, to cut off trousers at the knee, or boots at the ankle. **1942** L. RICH *We took to Woods* vii. 188 One stags one's pants, one's shirt sleeves, anything that needs to be abbreviated quickly, even one's hair. **1953** R. MOON *This is Saskatchewan* 215 They [*sc.* the lumberjacks] wore pants stagged off or rolled half way to the knee so as not to be confused with mere city dwellers. **1972** *Islander* (Victoria, B.C.) 30 Apr. 16/1 He was always dressed in the same way ..heavy..underwear, tin pants stagged to the proper working length.

Hence **stagged** *ppl. a.*, (of trousers) cut off short; also with *off*; **'stagging** *vbl. sb.* and *ppl. a.* (*N. Amer.*)

1845 THACKERAY in *Punch* IX. 191 Her appearance created quite a sensation among the stagging gents. **1851** KINGSLEY *Yeast* ii, The Stock-Exchange and railway stagging,..and the frantic Mammon-hunting. **1902** S. E. WHITE *Blazed Trail* xxvii. 190 A gigantic young riverman in the conventional stagged (*i.e.* chopped off) trousers. **1905** A. J. SHAND *Days of Past* ix. 162 Everything went automatically to a premium, and systematic stagging was a profitable business. **1905** *Daily Chron.* 13 July 5/6 A peculiarity of the applications is the enormous number of them for £100. A great many of these are obviously of the 'stagging' order. **1933** E. HEMINGWAY *Winner take Nothing* 29 He wore stagged trousers and lumbermen's rubbers and a mackinaw shirt. **1956** H. S. M. KEMP *Northern Trader* 114 He had the mackinaw shirt and stagged-off pants, [etc.].

stag, stagard: see STEG, STAGGARD.

stagarth: see STACK-GARTH.

stag-beetle. [STAG *sb.*[1]] A beetle of the genus *Lucanus*, the males of which have large denticulated mandibles resembling the horns of a stag; esp. *L. cervus*, and, in U.S., *L. elaphus*.

1681 GREW *Musæum* I. §vii. ii. 163 The Stag-Beetle..hath his Name from his two Horns, which are branched like those of a Stag. **1816** KIRBY & SP. *Entomol.* xxi. (1818) II. 224 The terrific and protended jaws of the stag-beetle (*Lucanus Cervus*, L.) in Europe. **1859** DARWIN *Orig. Species* iv. 88 Male stag-beetles often bear wounds from the huge mandibles of other males. **1896** LYDEKKER *Roy. Nat. Hist.* VI. 141 The common stag-beetle (*Lucanus cervus*), one of the largest of European beetles.

stage (steɪdʒ), *sb.* Also 6 *north.* **stayge**, *Sc.* **staige**; pl. **stagies**. [ad. OF. *estage* masc. (mod.F. *étage*) = Pr. *estatge* (also *estatga* fem.), It. *staggio* station, dwelling (*obs.*), support for a net, side of a ladder, etc.:—popular L. **staticum*, f. L. *stāre* to stand (OF. *ester*, Prov. *estar*). From the etymological meaning standing, station, standing place, were developed in OF. many special senses, which passed into ME.; the only senses that have survived into mod.Fr. are 'story of a building' (= 1 a) and certain fig. applications of this. Mod.F. *stage*, the 'terms' to be kept before admission to certain professions, is ad. med.L. *stagium*, ad. OF. *estage*. In OF. *estage* was taken as the etymological equivalent of L. *stadium*, and used to render that word as denoting an ancient measure of distance (hence sense 7 below). Branch IV represents an English development of meaning, which seems to have begun about 1600, and for which it is not easy precisely to account. It may in some degree have been influenced by the notion of an etymological connexion of the word with L. *stadium*; at any rate this notion is distinctly traceable in the medical use 11 b.]

I. Standing-place; something to stand upon.

1. Each of the portions into which the height of a structure is divided; a horizontal partition.

a. A story or floor of a building.

a **1300** *Cursor M.* 1679 It [the ark] sal be made wit stages sere, Ilkon to serue o þair mistere. *Ibid.* 1691 In þe ouer-mast stage þi self sal be. *c* **1330** R. BRUNNE *Chron. Wace* (Rolls) 4579 He..dide hym make a merueyllous tour... Selcouþe stages ar þer-ynne. **1382** WYCLIF *Acts* xx. 9 He ledd by sleep fel down fro the thridde stage [Vulg. *de tertio cenaculo*]. *c* **1440** *York Myst.* viii. 127 Dyuerse stages must þer be [in the ark]. *c* **1477** CAXTON *Jason* 101 b, The ladyes and Damoyselles mounted & wente vpon the hyghe stages of the palays. **1513** DOUGLAS *Æneis* XII. Prol. 47 And ilke fair cite, Stude payntit, euery fyall, fane, and stage, Apon the plane grund, by thar awin vmbrage. **1828** DUPPA *Trav. Italy*, etc. 88 The Temple appears to have been divided into three stories or stages. **1870** F. R. WILSON *Ch. Lindisf.* 65 The lowest stage of a tower raised for the benefit of seafarers. **1884** W. ARMSTRONG tr. *G. Perrot & C. Chipiez' Hist. Art Chaldea & Assyria* I. iv. 386 Nothing but the first two stages..now remain at Nimroud of..the chief temple of Calah.

†**b.** *hall of stage*: an upper chamber. *Obs.*

1485 in *Descr. Cal. Anc. Deeds* (1890) I. 358 A mancion with a hall of stage. **1493** *Festivall* (W. de W. 1515) 44 [The apostles] wente in to the cyte of Jerusalem and there they were in an halle of stage.

c. *Arch.* (See quot. 1836.)

a **1400–50** *Wars Alex.* 4897 Þe windows on þe selfe wyse [of gold]..And þai ware coruen full clene & clustrid with gemmes, Stiȝt stafful of stanes stagis & othire. *c* **1450** *St. Cuthbert* 4146 Þe preste, graped felgyld vysage, As he saide, thurgh a wyndowe stage. *c* **1450** *Robin Hood & the Monk* xxxix. in Child *Ballads* III. 98/2 Litul John stode at a wyndow in þe mornyng, And lokid forþ at a stage. **1817** RICKMAN *Styles Archit.* 94 These [buttresses] differ very little from those of the last style, except that triangular heads to the stages are much less used. **1836** PARKER *Gloss. Archit.* (1850) I. 443 *Stage*,..the term is particularly applied to the spaces or divisions between the set-offs of buttresses in Gothic architecture, and to the horizontal divisions of windows which are intersected by transoms. **1891** FREEMAN *Sk. Fr. Travel* 268 A single corner buttress, finished with an oddly corbelled stage.

†**d.** A 'bank' or tier of rowers. *Obs. rare*$^{-1}$.

1382 WYCLIF *Isa.* xxxiii. 21 Ne the grete ship of thre stagis [L. *trieris*] shal not ouergon it.

†**e.** One of a series of levels rising stepwise one above the other; a step. *Obs.*

a **1500** *Assembly of Ladies* 477 And there I saw..A chayre set... And fyve stages it was set fro the ground. **1533** BELLENDEN *Livy* I. xv. (S.T.S.) I. 85 The ymage..was sett ..risand on certane stagis [L. *in gradibus ipsis*] towart þe left hand of þe counsel houss.

†**f.** A shelf or one of a series of shelves or horizontal divisions in a cupboard, etc.

1465, 1472 *Durham Acc. Rolls* (Surtees) 243, 245 Item j armoriolum cum sex stagys [**1465** *is doubtfully read stagerum*] duplicatis [= lined] pro cartis et munimentis conservandis. *a* **1505** in Kingsford *Chron. Lond.* (1905) 250 A cup-bourde of 6 stages height..garnysshed wt gilt plate. **1540** *Test Ebor.* (Surtees) VI. 94 One gret arke with a stayge in the middle thereof. *a* **1548** HALL *Chron., Hen. VIII* 96 A Cupperd of xii stages, all set with greate mightie plate al of golde. **1551** in *Rep. Comm. Publ. Rec. Irel.* (1815) 38 *note*, That [in the said Library] Presses or Stages..and all other necessaries shall be provided [for the Records and Muniments]. **1817** J. BRADBURY *Trav.* 139 The stages whereon they deposit the bodies of their dead.

g. A tier of shelves or platform for plants, esp. in a greenhouse; hence, a display of flowers on such a stage.

1802 MAR. EDGEWORTH *Dun* Wks. 1848 IV. 412 He sat down upon the corner of a stage of flowers [in Covent Garden]. **1824** LOUDON *Encycl. Gardening* §6166 In the interior of the green-house the principal object demanding attention is the stage, or platform for the plants. **1850** GLENNY *Handbk. Flower Garden* 8 A stage of these flowers is a beautiful sight. **1881** F. YOUNG *Ev. Man his own Mech.* §930 The simple stage [for flower-pots] of three, four, or more straight shelves rising one above another is easily made.

h. One of a series of layers or shelves of any material.

1837 P. KEITH *Bot. Lex.* 212 If you take a parcel of oranges, and place upon your table a first stage of six,..and over that a second stage, and over that a third stage. **1839** URE *Dict. Arts* 981 Another method of working coal of uncommon thickness, is by scaffoldings or stages of coals. **1869** FREEMAN *Norm. Conq.* (1876) III. xii. 151 Waterfalls bounding from one rocky stage to another.

i. *Geol.* (*a*) (Variously used: see quots. 1881, 1910.) In mod. use, a division of a stratigraphic series, composed of a number of zones and corresponding to an age in time; the rocks deposited during any particular age. [tr. F. *étage* (introduced in this sense by A. d'Orbigny 1841, in *Paléont. Française*: *Terrains Crétacés* I. 417).]

1859 DARWIN *Orig. Species* ix. 308 M. Barrande has lately added another and lower stage to the Silurian system, abounding with new and peculiar species. **1881** *Q. Jrnl. Geol. Soc.* XXXVIII. Proc. 3 The conclusions arrived at [by the International Commission for the Unification of Geological Nomenclature, 1880] were..that the term Group should be applied to the largest geological division of rocks,..Series to the third in order of magnitude, Stage to the fourth. **1898** [see GROUP *sb.* 4 b (iii)]. **1910** GEIKIE *Geol.* in *Encycl. Brit.* XI. 668/1 Two or more sets of beds or assises similarly related form a group or stage; a number of groups or stages make a series. **1915** C. SCHUCHERT *Text-bk. Geol.* II. xxx. 582 The epochs and series are further divided into ages (time) and stages (rocks), but these divisions have as yet no scientific precision. **1931** [see SERIES 11 a (ii)]. **1960** J. M. WELLER *Stratigr. Princ. & Pract.* 443 Biostratigraphic zones are combined to form larger units termed stages. **1966** D. T. DONOVAN *Stratigraphy* vii. 160 Thus we speak of Ordovician System or Ordovician Period, Albian Stage or Albian Age, according to whether we are referring to the rocks themselves or the time occupied by their accumulation. **1976** H. D. HEDBERG *Internat. Stratigraphic Guide* vii. 71 Currently recognized stages are variable in time span, but on the average they range from 3 to 10 million years as indicated by isotopic age determinations.

(*b*) A glacial or interglacial period.

1895 *Jrnl. Geol.* III. 247 These [flood-loams] cannot always be separated from the similar deposits of later glacial stages which must obviously have been deposited over the same tracts. **1939** A. K. LOBECK *Geomorphology* ix. 314 The following names have been given to the several stages of glaciation [in America]: Nebraskan, Kansan, Illinoian, Iowan, and Wisconsin... The world may now be in an interglacial period, to be followed by another glacial stage. **1969** R. V. RUHE *Quaternary Landscapes in Iowa* ii. 26 Four of the major units of the standard glacial and interglacial stages were established in Iowa.

j. *U.S.* A level (of water).

1814 BRACKENRIDGE *Views Louisiana* 43 There is a surprising difference in the navigation of this..river, in the ordinary stages of water and during..the floods. **1846** J. C. FREMONT *Narr. Explor. Exped. Rocky Mts.* 56 Even at its low stages, this river cannot be crossed at random. **1890** *Times* 14 Mar. 5/1 The Government officials report..that the stage of the Mississippi river from Cairo to Vicksburg.. will be one of the highest known.

†**2.** Station, position, seat, esp. with reference to relative height; each of a number of positions or stations one above the other. *Obs.*

1340 *Ayenb.* 122 And al alsuo ase ine heuene heþ þri stages of uolke ase zayt saynt denys huer-of þe on is heȝere þe oþer men þe þridde loȝest. *c* **1384** CHAUCER *H. Fame* 122 In whiche ther were moo ymages Of golde stondynge in sondry stages. **1390** GOWER *Conf.* III. 109 The Mones cercle so lowe is, Wherof the Sonne out of his stage Ne seth him noght with full visage. **1423** JAS. I *Kingis Quair* lxxix, Me thoght I sawe..martris and confessouris, Ech in his stage. *Ibid.* lxxxiii, A voce..said..ȝonder thou seis the hiest stage and gree Off agit folk. **1451** CAPGRAVE *Life St. Kath.* v. xx. 1151 Ye may haue wurship, ye may be sette in stage Ryght as a goddesse. **1509** BARCLAY *Ship of Fools* (1874) II. 262 Yet at the table another vse we se Whiche..ought nat vsed be That folys at the borde haue oft the hyest stage. **1513** DOUGLAS *Æneis* X. xii. 20 Bot he, lyke to a ferm rouk,..dois hym self defend,..Remanand onremovyt ferm in his stage. **1536** *Primer Engl. & Lat.* (Rouen) 80 The father..In this worlde gyues them wages, And a place in ye heuenly stages, In the kyngdome of excellence. **1625** BACON *Ess.*, *Viciss. Things* (Arb.) 573 The Changes and Vicissitude in Warres are many: But chiefly in three Things; In the Seats or Stages of the Warre [etc.].

†**3. a.** A degree or step in the 'ladder' of virtue, honour, etc.; a 'step' on Fortune's wheel. *Obs.*

a **1300** *Cursor M.* 25973 Thrifald aght þis soruing be, for it es sett in stages thre Bitter,..bitterer,..alþer-bitterest. *c* **1360** *Minor Poems fr. Vernon MS.* xxiii. 704 In to heuene vs up liftyng þorwh vertus, stage vp stage. **1500–20** DUNBAR *Poems* xxxv. 18 Vp-on my [Dame Fortune's] staigis or that thow ascend, Trest weill thy truble neir is at ane end. **1513** DOUGLAS *Æneis* X. v. 152 Bot Turnus hardy, stalwart, hie curage, For all this feyr demynist nevyr a stage. **1559** *Mirr. Mag.*, *Warwick* i, Among the heauy heape of happy knyghtes, Whom Fortune stalde vpon her stayles stage [etc.]. **1622–34** PEACHAM *Compl. Gentl.* x. (1906) 78 From the highest Stage of Honour, to the lowest staire of disgrace.

†**b.** A grade in rank. *Obs. rare*$^{-1}$.

1801 G. ROSE *Diaries* (1860) I. 348 He had thought it advisable to delay..to recommend any stage in the peerage to Lord Nelson.

4. A raised floor, platform, scaffold. **a.** A floor raised above the level of the ground for the exhibition of something to be viewed by spectators. Now *rare* or *Obs.* Cf. 5 a.

13.. *K. Alis.* 5569 (Laud MS.), And þer hij founden.. two grete ymages In þe Cee stonden on brasen stages. *c* **1400** MAUNDEV. (Roxb.) xi. 42 Ymiddez of þe temple es a stage of xxiiii. grecez hie. **1536–7** *Rec. St. Mary at Hill* 373 Item, paid to Wolston ffor makyng of ye stages ffor ye prophettes vj d. **1553** EDEN *Treat. New Ind.* (Arb.) 30 They founde certayne lowe cotages made of trees, lyke vnto stages. **1602** SHAKS. *Ham.* v. ii. 389 Giue order that these bodies High on a stage be placed to the view. **1610** HOLLAND *Camden's Brit.* (1637) 297 Athelstan, Edwin, and Etheldred were crowned kings upon an open stage in the market place. **1710** STEELE *Tatler* No. 240 ¶8, I have seen the whole front of a Mountebank's stage..faced with patents, certificates, medals, and Great Seals.

†**b.** A scaffold for execution or exposure in the pillory. *Obs.*

c **1400** *Brut* 240 He was draw and hongede on a stage made in mydes þe forsaide Sir Hughes galwes. **1586** *Verses of Praise of Joy, Kyd's Wks.* (1901) 341 For chaire of state, a stage of shame, and crows for crownes they haue. **1760** H. WALPOLE *Let. G. Montagu* 6 May (1857) III. 303 Lord Ferrers..was executed yesterday... There was a new contrivance for sinking the stage under him. **1781** COWPER *Hope* 556 Leuconomus..Stood pilloried on infamy's high stage.

†**c.** *fig.* ***to bring to, keep on the stage***: cf. STAGE *v.* 4. *Sc. Obs.*

1681 in J. H. Thomson *Cloud of Witnesses* (1871) 127, I.. being sentenced to die..thought fit to set down..the causes wherefore I suffer... I have never gotten the certainty of what hath brought me to the stage. **1725** in *Portland Papers* (Hist. MSS. Comm.) VI. 116 This staging process is made use of against any of the ministry..when..there is a *Fama Clamoza* against any person..and as the Kirk may be moved thereunto, he may be kept on the stage a year or more longer.

†**d.** Applied to a pulpit. *Obs. rare*$^{-1}$.

1483 *Wardr. Acc.* in Grose *Antiq. Repert.* (1807) I. 34 The stage otherwise called the pulpitt in Westminster.

e. A scaffold for workmen and their tools, materials, etc.; also (after sense 1) each of the levels of scaffolding.

c **1440** *Promp. Parv.* 471/2 Stage, or stondynge vp on (*v.r.* stage to stond on), *fala, machinalis, machinis.* **1535** in Willis & Clark *Cambridge* (1886) II. 453 Item to..carpenters..and laborers for syttyng vp the stage xxiij^{s} ij^{d}. **1719** De Foe *Crusoe* II. (Globe) 524 Our Men who were at Work on her Bottom, with Stages. **1739** Labelye *Short Acc. Piers Westm. Bridge* 18 Ballast was stow'd to make the Engine and its floating Stage as steady as possible. **1840** R. H. Dana *Bef. Mast* viii. 18 The outside is painted by lowering stages over the side by ropes. **1878** F. S. Williams *Midl. Railw.* 341 The gigantic travelling scaffold..made in 3 divisions, so that each part of either stage could be moved separately. **1906** *Westm. Gaz.* 4 Sept. 5/1 Two Blondin stages..have been erected to transport blocks of concrete.

f. An erection at a fishing station consisting of a platform and other apparatus for drying fish.

1535 in Weaver *Wells Wills* (1890) 132 Wm Yonge..ij stagis of fysshinge with iiij netts to them belongynge. **1634** W. Wood *New Eng. Prosp.* (1865) 35 Those which have had stages and make fishing voyages into those parts. **1698** *Act 10 Will. III*, c. 14 §1 [With] Liberty to goe on Shore on any part of Newfoundland..to cutt downe Wood and Trees there for building..Stages Shiprooms [etc.]. **1733** P. Lindsay *Interest Scot.* 218 The Cod and Ling..might be dried on our Beeches and Stages. **1820** Scoresby *Acc. Arctic Regions* II. 175 Two men..then carried it [blubber] piece by piece to a stage or platform erected by the side of the works, where a man, denominated a 'stage cutter'..sliced it into pieces. **1899** *19th Cent.* Aug. 236 Stages being used simply for the drying of cod-fish.

g. A platform used as a gangway, landing place, support or stand for materials, etc.

1773 *Cook's 1st Voy.* III. III. vii. 589 The bank so steep..that a ship may lie..so near the shore as to reach it with a stage. **1793** *Act 33 Geo III*, c. 96 §81 To be..unloaded without a Stage being laid upon the Gunwale of such..Vessel to the Bank of the said Canal. **1883** Gresley *Gloss. Coal-mining* 234 *Stage*, 1. A platform upon which trams stand. 2. The pit bank. **1888** Jacobi *Printers' Vocab.* 131 *Stage*, a wooden platform a few inches high used for building stacks of paper or printed work on. **1969** F. Mowat *Boat who wouldn't Float* iii. 24 We emerged at the base of a spindly and unbelievably rickety stage (as fishermen's wharves are called) made of peeled spruce poles.

h. A raised plate, ledge, or shelf to support an object, slide, etc. in a microscope or other instrument.

1797 *Encycl. Brit.* (ed. 3) XI. 711/2 The magnifier..may be easily made to traverse over any part of the object that lies on the stage or plate B. **1849** Noad *Electricity* 60 To the knob of a large jar A..screw a small metallic stage C, on which place a small jar B. **1875** Huxley & Martin *Pract. Biol.* (1879) 23 Place on the hot stage, and gradually warm up to 50° C. **1892** *Photogr. Ann.* II. 535 By means of a double changing stage, working vertically, any framed slides ..can be shown.

i. A boxing ring. Now *Hist.*

1829 P. Egan *Boxiana* 2nd Ser. II. 44 He was carried upon the shoulders of several men, from the stage to a private room in the Stand. **1954** F. C. Avis *Boxing Ref. Dict.* 106 *Stage*, the old name for the ring. **1982** S. B. Flexner *Listening to America* 105 *Broughton's rules* called for a 'stage' with a one-yard square chalked or scratched in the middle.

j. *Canad.* An erection on which meat is kept out of the reach of animals, or on which meat is dried.

1715 J. Knight *Let.* 30 June in *Lett. from Hudson Bay* (1965) 51 Wee were all forcd to leave the factory & to take our Selves to ye Woods & to gett on trees & Stages for Six Days. **1800** A. Henry *Jrnl.* 9 Sept. in E. Coues *New Light on Greater Northwest* (1897) I. iii. 91 We then arranged camp..and made a suitable stage near by, to hold fresh meat, etc. **1922** *Beaver* Mar. 39/2 Passing a considerable amount of jerked meat on a stage, I entered the wigwam. **1940** F. Niven *Mine Inheritance* 45 The erection of stages, platforms raised high on poles above the prairies on which food could be left beyond the reach of leaping wolves.

5. a. The platform in a theatre upon which spectacles, plays, etc. are exhibited; esp. a raised platform with its scenery and other apparatus upon which a theatrical performance takes place.

to take the stage (Theatr.): of an actor, to walk with dignity across the stage after concluding an impressive speech. ***to hold the stage***: see hold *v.* 6 g; ***to set the stage***: see set *v.* 74.

1551 R. Robynson tr. *More's Utopia* I. (1895) 98 Whyles a commodye of Plautus is playinge,..yf yowe shoulde sodenlye come vpon the stage in a philosophers apparrell. **1553** Eden *Treat. New Ind.* (Arb.) 16 The Romaynes..were wont to put them [Rhinoceros and Elephants] together vpon the theater or stage for a spectacle. **1567** R. Edwards *Damon & Pithias* (1906) 19 Pythagoras said, that this world was like a stage Whereon many play their parts. **1589** Puttenham *Eng. Poesie* I. xvii. (Arb.) 51 When Tragidies came vp they deuised to present them upon scaffoldes or stages of timber. **1593** Shaks. *Rich II*, v. ii. 24. **1623** B. Jonson in *Shaks. Wks.* A4, To heare thy Buskin tread, And shake a Stage. **1632** Milton *L'Allegro* 131 Then to the well-trod stage anon, If Jonsons learned Sock be on. **1774** Goldsm. *Retaliation* 101 On the stage, he was natural, simple, affecting; 'Twas only that when he was off, he was acting. **1858** [H. Aïdé] *Rita* I. x. 229 And having done what this virtuous woman considered to be her duty, she 'took the stage', as actors say, and swept to the further end of the room, with an air that said [etc.]. **1867** D. Cook *Nts. at the Play* (1883) I. 7 Miss Fanny Kemble used to rush from the back of the stage to the proscenium, as though driving the apparition before her. **1905** *Grand Mag.* Oct. 463 What we call 'taking the stage' on a heroic line is certain to induce a burst of applause;..but if one takes but one step too far down the stage..the applause will not be forthcoming.

b. In generalized use, e.g. ***to go on the stage***, i.e. to take up the profession of an actor. Hence (chiefly with *the*), the theatre, the acted drama, the dramatic profession.

1589 Puttenham *Eng. Poesie* I. xi. (Arb.) 41 There were also Poets that wrote onely for the stage, I meane playes and interludes. **1623** B. Jonson in *Shaks. Wks.* A4b, Shine forth, thou Starre of Poets, and with rage, Or influence, chide, or cheere the drooping Stage. **1693** Dryden *Juvenal* (1697) Ded. 3 Shakespear, who created the Stage among us. **1728** Pope *Dunc.* I. 109 Bays, form'd by nature Stage and Town to bless, And act, and be, a Coxcomb with success. *Ibid.* III. 142 And a new Cibber shall the stage adorn. **1781** Cowper *Retirem.* 685 Books..in which the stage gives vice a blow. **1822** Lamb *Elia* Ser. I. *On Artific. Comedy*, The artificial Comedy, or Comedy of manners, is quite extinct on our stage. **1849** Thackeray *Pendennis* iv, The stage had its traditional jewels as the Crown and all great families have. **1886** Adel. Sergeant *No Saint* I. xii. 229 If he had gone on the stage he would have made a good actor.

c. ***to bring*** (a person) ***on*** or ***to the stage***: to present (him) as a character in a play; to represent dramatically. ***to bring, put*** (an opera, a tragedy, etc.) ***on the stage***: to produce (it) in public.

1601 B. Jonson *Poetaster* III. iv, I heare, you'll bring mee o' the Stage there; you'll play mee, they say: I shall bee presented by a sorte of Copper-lac't Scoundrels of you. **1602** Dekker *Satirom.* C 2, They sweare they'll bring your life and death vpon'th stage like a Bricklayer in a play. *Ibid.* I 3b, What could I doe, out of a iust reuenge, But bring them to the Stage? **1721** *Lond. Gaz.* No. 6015/1 A new Opera..will be brought upon the publick Stage here. **1849** Macaulay *Hist. Eng.* vi. II. 74 A dramatist would scarcely venture to bring on the stage a grave prince, in the decline of life, ready to sacrifice his crown [etc.].

†d. The scene in which a play is set or the locality in which its events were supposed to have occurred. *Obs. rare.*

1639 Drumm. of Hawth. *Conv. betw. B. J. & W. D.* Wks. (1711) 224 [Ben Jonson] had also a design to write a Fisher or pastoral play, and make the stage of it in the Lomond lake.

e. *fig.*

1548 Udall, etc. *Erasm. Par. Matt.* v. 14–16 Ye haue a parte to playe in the stage of the whole world. **1581** Mulcaster *Positions* xxxix. (1887) 191, I do take publike [schools] to be simply the better: as being more vpon the stage, where faultes be more seene. **1600** Shaks. *A.Y.L.* II. vii. 139 All the world's a stage, And all the men and women, meerely Players. **1638** Sir T. Herbert *Trav.* (ed. 2) 72 We are now to present you upon the Asiatique stage, various scaenes compos'd of a miscelany of subjects. **1703** Maundrell *Journ. Jerus.* (1732) 38 A plain Field near the Sea, which is said to be the Stage on which St. George duell'd and kill'd the Dragon. **1780** Cowper *Progr. Error* 23 Plac'd for his trial on this bustling stage. **1823** Scott *Quentin D.* i, Actions for which his happier native country afforded no free stage. **1861** Bright *Sp., Amer.* 4 Dec. (1876) 88 There is no greater object of ambition on the political stage on which men are permitted to move. **1873** Burton *Hist. Scot.* VI. lxx. 186 The stage on which this scene was enacted was the Greyfriars' Churchyard.

f. ***stage left*** (or ***right***): (on) the left (or right) side of a stage (as considered from a position facing the audience). Similarly, ***stage centre***. Also *fig.*

1947 *Gloss. Techn. Theatr. Terms* (Strand Electr. & Engin. Co.) 28 *Stage left*, that half of the stage on the actor's left when facing the audience. **1961** Bowman & Ball *Theatre Lang.* 351 *Stage right*,..right stage, or right of stage. **1972** F. Warner *Lying Figures* III. 16 Epigyne..sits stage left in hanging basket chair. **1977** 'C. Aird' *Parting Breath* vi. 79 The Devil always enters stage left. **1979** *Internat. Jrnl. Sociol. of Law* Feb. 26 There are three things that are very evident already: one is that he brought to a 20th century anthropological stage-center classic legal problems that preoccupied Maine in the 19th century.

†II. 6. A period of time; a fixed or appointed date. *Obs.*

a **1300** *Cursor M.* 7339 Þat þai wit-in a tuel-moth stage, War put vte o þair heritage. *Ibid.* 21609. *a* **1325** in Horstm. *Altengl. Leg.* (1878) 143 Afterward a gret stage In his visage it was ysene. **1338** R. Brunne *Chron.* (1810) 164 Isaac wille not grante, to oblige him to þe, No to..ȝeld at terme & stage rent mykelle no lite. *Ibid.* 324. *a* **1400** *Minor Poems fr. Vernon MS.* xxxii. 641 Glotenye deseyueþ hym in luytel stage. *c* **1400** *Ywaine & Gaw.* 1068 Bot i have a wele rinand page, Wil stirt thider right in a stage. *Ibid.* 2501. *c* **1500** in Horstm. *Altengl. Leg.* (1881) 419 As they that gan approchen to the stage Off decrepitus.

†III. 7. = stadium 1. *Obs. rare.*

c **1375** *Sc. Leg. Saints* xvi. (Magdalene) 815 A cawe..þat twelfe stage was fra þe place,..& ilke stage,..Is of a myle þe auchtand parte. **1552** Lyndesay *Monarche* 2725 One hundreth and fyftye stagys That Citie wes of lenth. *Ibid.* 2731 The wallis..Four hundreth stageis and four score In circuit.

IV. Division of a journey or process.

8. a. A place in which rest is taken on a journey; a roadside inn for the accomodation of travellers riding post or by stage-coach; *esp.* a regular stopping place on a stage-coach route where horses are changed and travellers taken up and set down. More recently, as ***fare stage***, one of the principal stops on an omnibus or tram route, which marks the start of a new step in the fare structure: see fare *sb.*[1] 9.

1603 in *Rep. Secret Comm. Post-Office* App. (1844) 38 That the postemasters of every stage be aided..with fresh and able horses. *Ibid.* 39 Nor [to] ride them [*sc.* horses] further then the next immediate stage without changing, without the knowledge and consent of the Post of the stage. **1623** Massinger *Dk. Milan* IV. ii, He, that at euerie stage keeps liuerie Mistresses. **1635** in *Rep. Secret Comm. Post-Office* App. (1844) 56 The s^{d} Portmantle is to goe from Stage to Stage, night and day, till it shall come to Edenburgh. **1687** Lovell tr. *Thevenot's Trav.* I. 172 We..came to rest..at the place which we had made our first Stage, when we came from Suez. **1746** Francis tr. *Horace, Epist.* I. xv. 12 The Road we now must alter, and engage Th' unwilling Horse to pass his usual Stage. **1815** Scott *Guy M.* xlv, About three pounds of cold roast mutton which he had discussed at his mid-day stage. **1890** 'R. Boldrewood' *Col. Reformer* (1891) 273 He discovered that there was no other stage available without over-riding Osmund.

b. *transf.* and *fig.*

1770 Luckombe *Hist. Printing* 132 If any desire to know the motions and stages of the press, which printed these books; know, it was first set up at Moulsey,..thence conveyed to Fawsley, [etc.]. **1825** Scott *Betrothed* xxv, A small level plain, forming a sort of stage, or resting-place, between two very rough paths. **1851** T. T. Lynch *Lett. to Scattered* (1872) 143 Our Sundays are resting stages in the journey of life.

9. a. As much of a journey as is performed without stopping for rest, a change of horses, etc.; each of the several portions into which a road is divided for coaching or posting purposes; the distance travelled between two places of rest on a road.

1603 R. Johnson *Kingd. & Commw.* 162 They returne back againe towards the south (where they continue all the winter) by 10 miles a stage. **1622** Mabbe tr. *Aleman's Guzman d' Alf.* I. 48 Like your Post-horses when they haue runne their stage. **1703** Maundrell *Journ. Jerus.* (1732) 2 Our whole Stage this day was about five hours. **1792** Mme. D'Arblay *Diary* 5 Oct., Bradfield Hall..was but one stage of nineteen miles distant. **1828** Scott *Tapestr. Chamb.* (*init.*), In the conclusion of a morning stage, he found himself in the vicinity of a small country town. **1886** Ruskin *Præterita* I. vi. 183 Horses at each post-house..ready waiting, so that no time might be lost between stages. **1896** Baden-Powell *Matabele Campaign* xiii, Leaving Poore and the patrol..to follow on by slow stages. **1898** J. B. Crozier *My Inner Life* i. 6 We proceeded leisurely and by easy stages. **1907** *Verney Mem.* I. 465 He..had ridden a stage with Sir Henry on his journey back to Paris.

b. *transf.*

1660 Boyle *New Exp. Phys.-Mech.* xvii. 109 We were quickly hindred from accurately marking the Stages made by the Mercury in its descent, because it soon sunk below the top of the Receiver. **1664** Power *Exp. Philos.* I. 10 A Wood-Louse..has a swift motion and runs by starts or stages. **1687** Norris *Misc.* 71, I cannot like the Sun Each day the self same stage, and still unwearied, run. **1860** *Eng. & For. Mining Gloss., S. Staff. terms, Stage*, a particular distance that a horse travels along the gate-road and where candles are regularly placed.

c. Short for stage-coach. Also '*U.S.* an omnibus' (*Cent. Dict.*).

1671 in *Wood's Life* (O.H.S.) II. 221 The Stage begins Munday next. **1747** B. Hoadly *Suspicious Husb.* I. iii, It looks better than being drag'd to Town in the Stage. **1781** Cowper *Convers.* 305 'Tis like a parcel sent you by the stage. **1848** Thackeray *Van. Fair* xli, The London lamps flashed joyfully as the stage rolled into Piccadilly. **1853** 'Mark Twain' *Let.* 26 Oct. (1917) I. 28 The Phila. 'bus drivers cannot cheat. In the front of the stage is a thing like an office clock. **1883** Stevenson *Silverado Sq.* 179 The first of the two stages swooped upon the Toll House..in a cloud of dust. **1912** J. Milne *John Jonathan & Co.* 92 A fleet of motor-buses, which the New Yorkers call 'stages', short for stage-coaches, meanders up and down it [*sc.* Fifth Avenue]. **1939** *Nat. Geogr. Mag.* Feb. 133/2 Mammoth sleeper buses (which they still call 'stages'). **1973** R. Hayes *Hungarian Game* iii. 30 Nearly a dozen standbys had taken the stage back to Mammoth village.

10. a. A period of a journey through a subject, life, course of action, etc.

1608 Shaks. *Per.* IV. iv. 9 To teach you, The stages of our storie. **1621** T. Williamson tr. *Goulart's Wise Vieillard* 24 God hath appointed euery mans race of life how long it shall be, and the stages hee must passe before he come to the end of it, whereof old age is the last stage of all. **1648** W. Juxon in *Chas. I.'s Wks.* (1662) I. 456 There is but one Stage more, yet..it will carry you from Earth to Heaven. **1672** Cave *Prim. Chr.* III. v. 355 Having travelled through the several stages of the Subject. **1742** Young *Nt. Th.* ix. 674 In thy nocturnal rove, one moment halt, 'Twixt stage and stage, of riot and cabal. **1782** Cowper *Mut. Forbearance* 49 The love that cheers life's latest stage.

b. ***stage-by-stage*** adj. phr., that proceeds by stages; step-by-step.

1956 *Nature* 25 Feb. 391/1 Using the Townsend electron avalanche process in a gas in a stage-by-stage system. **1959** *Daily Tel.* 14 Apr. 22/3 (*heading*) Stage-by-stage atomic offer to Russia. **1962** E. Snow *Red China Today* (1963) xix. 139 An accurate stage-by-stage itinerary prepared for me by the First Army Corps showed a main trek of some 6,000 miles.

11. a. A period of development, a degree of progress, a step in a process.

1818 Hallam *Mid. Ages* (1872) I. 146 Such as travellers have found among nations in the same stage of manners throughout the world. **1852** Thackeray *Esmond* I. xii, 'Tis not to be imagined that Harry Esmond had all this experience at this early stage of his life. **1855** Macaulay *Hist. Eng.* xix. IV. 327 At every stage in the growth of that debt it has been seriously asserted by wise men that bankruptcy and ruin were at hand. **1862** Miller *Elem. Chem., Org.* (ed. 2) 155 It is difficult to prevent the oxidation from going a stage further. **1863** H. Cox *Instit.* I. vi. 43 It is necessary that at some stage of the Bill the consent of the Crown should be signified. **1875** Jowett *Plato* (ed. 2) IV. 13 The distinction..belongs to a stage of philosophy which has passed away. **1878** Browning *La Saisiaz* 49 As in one or other stage Of a torture writhe they. **1889** *Pall Mall Gaz.* 16 Oct. 1/2 Gradual development by stages, not complete transformation at a bound, is the law in the political, as in the natural, world. **1908** E. M. Forster *Room with View* x. 170 She was too great for all society, and had reached the stage where personal intercourse would alone satisfy her. **1940** J.

BUCHAN *Memory Hold-the-Door* ii. 39, I have used the word politics, but at this stage I was no politician, being interested only to a small degree in theories, and not at all in parties. **1956** W. S. CHURCHILL *Hist. Eng.-Speaking Peoples* II. xx. 247 It was at this stage that a group of lawyers and gentry decided to offer Cromwell the crown. **1966** *Oxf. Univ. Gaz.* 23 Dec. 429/1 This legislation will..come forward next term or in the following term, and it is at that stage that members of the House will be asked to take the responsibility of deciding [etc.]. **1977** J. THOMSON *Case Closed* i. 15 I'm not risking you making a balls-up of it at this stage in the game.

b. *Med.* A definite period in the development of a disease, marked by a specific group of symptoms. = STADIUM 3.

1747 tr. *Astruc's Fevers* 281 This stage holds from the fourth, and sometimes from the eighth day after the eruption, till the tenth or twelfth day. **1780** *Mirror* No. 70, I found him in the last stage of a dropsy. **1804** ABERNETHY *Surg. Observ.* 65 In the advanced stage of this disease. **1843** R. J. GRAVES *Syst. Med.* x. 113 During the stage of rigor. **1878** L. P. MEREDITH *Teeth* 154 The pulps of the teeth would..be exposed in the early stages of the disease.

c. *Biol.* Each of the several periods in the development and growth of animals and plants, frequently with qualifying word prefixed.

1882 G. ALLEN in *Nature* 17 Aug. 371 The flowers of gymnosperms (in their blossoming stage) are mostly composed of green scales or leaves. **1909** E. A. MILLS *Wild Life Rockies* 186 When this forest is in a sapling stage. **1925**, **1932** [see INSTAR *sb.*]. **1974** *Nature* 18 Jan. 154/2 The term 'stage' is here used as equivalent to the French term *étape* and is composed of several 'stadia' separated by a moult.

d. *slang.* A period of imprisonment during which privileges are allowed.

1932 'JOCK OF DARTMOOR' *Dartmoor from Within* ii. 56 In his fourth year he [*sc.* the convict] enters the highest stage. In this stage he is permitted a tobacco and cigarette ration. **1958** F. NORMAN *Bang to Rights* 30 My punishment was three days bread and water..and twenty eight days stage.

12. a. *Electronics.* A part of a circuit usu. comprising one transistor or valve, or two or more functioning as a single unit, and the associated resistors, capacitors, etc.

1920 *Jrnl. Inst. Electr. Engineers* LVIII. 65/1 This is the first attempt to deal comprehensively with the problems of the multiple-stage amplifier. **1930** *Proc. IRE* XVIII. 1715 It will be seen that there are two stages of push-pull high-frequency amplification. **1944** *Electronic Engin.* XVI. 392 A multivibrator functioning as a divider requires three valves per dividing stage. **1961** *Listener* 9 Nov. 776/2 The relatively poor amplifying stages..in even the most costly television sets [are] incapable of providing the full and almost distortion-free sound of a genuine 'high-fidelity' system. **1975** D. G. FINK *Electronics Engineers' Handbk.* XIII. 18 An amplifier may take the form of a single stage or a complex single stage or it may employ an interconnection of several stages... For a multistage amplifier, the individual stages may be essentially identical or radically different.

b. *Astronautics.* Each of two or more sections of a rocket that have their own engines and propellant and fall away in turn as their propellant becomes exhausted.

1935 C. S. PHILP *Stratosphere & Rocket Flight* xii. 62 The first method consists of a rocket built in two or more stages, the first stage being a relatively low-power engine for use in the lower parts of the earth's atmosphere, and the second stage, or subsequent multiple stages, of increased power for use in the higher and more rarefied regions. **1948** *Jrnl. Brit. Interplanetary Soc.* VII. 168 Into this section propellant from the 1st, 2nd and 3rd stage tanks is automatically transferred..so that as its own propellant is drawn off by the motor it is replaced and both the 4th and Final stages achieve 'release velocity' with tanks at capacity level. **1955** *Times* 4 Aug. 6/2 We shall be limited to one-stage rockets at first, but afterwards we may work on two-stage rockets which will reach greater heights. **1963** *Ann. Reg. 1962* 445 The satellite, weighing 170 lb., was placed in orbit by a three-stage Delta rocket. **1975** K. GATLAND *Missiles & Rockets* viii. 185 The first stage engines burnt for about 2½ minutes, boosting the Apollo astronauts to an altitude of 36 miles.

13. attrib. and Comb.: **a.** obvious combinations (senses 5, 5 b) 'pertaining to the stage', as ***stage-action, apparatus, -attire, boards, business, -carpenter, -carpentering, -clothes, crew, -curtain, design, designer, -hand, legend, lighting, machine, -novel, -performer, -performance, -picture, -piece, -poet, -poetry, -sentiment, show, -side, -tradition, -trap, trick, †-trotter, version, †-walker, -wardrobe, -writing***, etc.; that is seen on the stage or represented in drama as distinguished from what is seen in real life, as ***stage army, aside, death, -dialect, distraction, fighting, -gesture, hero, heroine, libertine, -lion, murderer, -villain, -whisper***, etc.; similarly ***stage Australian, Frenchman, Irishman***, etc.; ***stage Irish*** sb. and adj. Also rarely with adjs., as ***stage-mad***.

1697 DRYDEN *Æneid* Ded. (a) 2, There is no absolute necessity that the time of a *Stage-Action shou'd so strictly be confin'd to Twenty Four Hours. **1780** T. DAVIES *Garrick* (1781) I. xiv. 168 The second musick..put him [an actor] in mind, that it was time to think of the *stage-apparatus. **1922** C. S. CHURCHILL *Let.* 4 Jan. in M. Soames *Clementine Churchill* (1979) xiii. 203 All the sad events of last year culminating in Marigold passing and re-passing like a *stage Army through my sad heart. **1957** A. C. L. DAY *Outl. Monetary Economics* xiii. 177 There was, therefore, a stage army of cash moving from bank to bank through each week, helping improve appearances. **1813** M. EDGEWORTH *Let.* 16 May (1971) 53 Lady Derby he says is always *acting*—that there is continually a *stage *aside* which betrays her. **1945** *Essays & Studies 1944* XXX. 35 A dry unsympathetic comment delivered curtly like a stage-aside, 'Would he had blotted a thousand!' **1669** GALE *Crt. Gentiles* I. I. ii. 13 Poets have borrowed their best *stage-attire from the glorious Wardrobe of Israel. **1965** *Times Lit. Suppl.* 16 Sept. 812/1 Only the baggy trousers and the wide brimmed hat anchor him to the image of the '*stage' Australian, or the Boy from the Bush. **1831** LAMB *Elia* Ser. II. *Ellistoniana*, That harmonious fusion of the manners of the player into those of everyday life, which brought the *stage boards into streets and dining-parlours. **1825** *Ibid.*, *Stage Illusion*, In tragedy.. this undivided attention to his *stage business seems indispensable. **1826** O'KEEFFE *Recoll.* I. iv. 146 Years after, some such enthusiastic spirit possessed the *stage carpenters at Cork. **1856** DICKENS *Lett.* (1880) I. 459 Stage-carpenters. **1899** 'MARK TWAIN' in *Cosmopolitan* Oct. 593/2 He had to retire from his profession of stage-carpentering. **1630** *Stage-clothes [see STAGER 3]. **1959** *Guardian* 13 Nov. 9/3 The Banana Boat song was booming on the telly in the *stage-crew's room. **1975** *New Yorker* 21 Apr. 112/1 The theatre can devote all its resources—orchestra, singers, coaches, stage crews, lighting team—to the preparation and performance of the work. **1659** *Lady Alimony* I. ii, Be your *Stage-curtains artificially drawn. **1897** *Month* Apr. 363 If the death of Cæsar is but *stage-death, the murderer of Cæsar is but a stage-murderer. **1943** J. LEYDA tr. *S. Eisenstein's Film Sense* ii. 77 This is an important law which can be found in painting, in *stage design..of this period. **1977** J. AIKEN *Last Movement* vi. 116 Is that your profession—stage design? **1938** L. BEMELMANS *Life Class* II. iii. 141 An energetic hostess..will often arrive with a squadron of orchestra leaders, architects..and *stage designers. **1978** R. LUDLUM *Holcroft Covenant* xiii. 151 There was a man in London, a stage designer, who'd had a brief vogue as a decorator among the wealthy on both sides of the Atlantic. **1927** *New Republic* 12 Oct. 218/2 Mr. Wiley has a further advantage over his fellow craftsmen in being master of two *stage-dialects—pidgin English and Negro. **1966** G. N. LEECH *Eng. in Advertising* viii. 78 A music-hall comedian adopts a 'stage-dialect'. **1804** *European Mag.* XLV. 58/2 The youth..finding how he is abused, exhibits all the usual *stage distraction on the occasion. **1851** HELPS *Comp. Solit.* v. 73 Like the dialogues in a book, where, after much *stage-fighting, the author's opinion is always made to prevail. **1824** in A. Mathews *Mem. Charles Mathews* (1839) III. xx. 453 Talbot is the stock Morbleu, which he makes a monkey—a ballet-master—in short, a *stage Frenchman. *a* **1774** GOLDSM. in Hawkins *Life Johnson* (1787) 418 Sheridan the player, in order to improve himself in *stage-gestures, had looking-glasses,..hung about his room. **1885** F. LESLIE in *Entr'acte Ann.* 22/1 The *stage hands were non-expectorants, and the ladies were quite vexed at the clean condition of the stage. **1907** *Westm. Gaz.* 5 Feb. 7/2 As the accredited representatives of the artists, stage-hands, and musicians. **1751** WARBURTON *Note* Pope's Wks. (1751) IV. 165 (Jod.), Ranting, the common vice of *stage heroes. **1844** MARG. FULLER *Wom. 19th C.* (1862) 45 She had not the air and tone of a *stage-heroine. **1962** *Listener* 1 Mar. 387/3 These pages are littered with wild *stage-Irish cries of 'Jasez', 'begod', and the like. **1962** A. LURIE *Love & Friendship* xi. 208 'That's a gra-and idea,' Charley said, stage Irish. **1977** A. J. BLISS in D. O'Muirithe *Eng. Lang. in Ireland* 9 At this early date a conventional 'stage Irish' had been established. **1980** J. O'FAOLAIN *No Country for Young Men* v. 96 He must think he'd fallen into a stage-Irish household. **1860** *Players* I. 131 The dialect he assumed, though it may not have been so productive of laughter as that in which the '*stage Irishman' usually delivers himself. **1911** G. B. SHAW in *Evening Sun* (N.Y.) 9 Dec. 4/6 The stage Irishman of the nineteenth century, generous, drunken, thriftless, with a joke always on his lips and a sentimental tear always in his eye. **1973** J. ELSOM *Erotic Theatre* ii. 33 A stage actress—as recognizable a type as a stage Irishman and more frequently seen. **1849** THACKERAY *Pendennis* iv, He was attired in the tight pantaloons and Hessian boots which the *stage legend has given to that injured man. **1822** LAMB *Elia* Ser. I. *On Artific. Comedy*, We see a *stage libertine playing his loose pranks of two hours' duration. **1895** *New Budget* 4 Apr. 21/1 One would have practically to invent new methods of scene-painting and *stage-lighting. **1908** G. B. SHAW *Let.* 2 Aug. (1972) II. 804 There were some very clever tricks of stage lighting in the second act of Siegfried. **1983** 'J. LE CARRÉ' *Little Drummer Girl* iii. 51 The stage lighting was too good, she couldn't penetrate the haze. **1862** MEREDITH *Mod. Love* xv. Wks. (1912) 139 The Poet's black *stage-lion of wronged love. **1693** DRYDEN *Juvenal* IV. (1697) 86 So did [he] the Scenes and *Stage Machines admire. **1758** *Theatr. Rev.* 5 This *stage-mad age. **1897** *Stage-murderer [see *stage-death*]. *a* **1816** SHERIDAN *Rivals* Pref., Dram. Wks. 1902 I. 291, I.. might..have boasted that it [this comedy] had done more real service in its failure than the successful morality of a thousand *stage-novels will ever effect. **1714** FIDDES *Pract. Disc.* II. 379 Our *stage-performances, comedies especially, ..have tended..to corrupt..the bravest nation under heaven. **1801** STRUTT *Sports & Past.* III. v. 179, I may here mention a *stage-performer whose show is usually enlivened with mimicry, music, and tumbling; I mean the mountebank. **1920** W. B. YEATS *Poems* p. vii, When our *stage-pictures were made out of poor conventional scenery and hired costumes. **1949** F. FERGUSSON *Idea of Theatre* i. 28 The contemplation of the final stage-picture or epiphany. **1980** *Times* 29 Feb. 13/2 The WNO *Onegin* is..a procession of stage-pictures far beyond the everyday purview or opera production. **1912** F. HARRISON in *Engl. Rev.* Apr. 34 All this is enough to spoil any *stage-piece. **1658** SIR A. COKAIN *Poems* 186 Here Lies the *Stage-Poet Philip Massinger. **1693** DRYDEN *Juvenal* (1697) Ded. 10 [As the age] of Euripides..[was noted] for *Stage-Poetry amongst the Greeks. **1829** CARLYLE *Crit. & Misc. Ess.* (1840) II. 93 It is fair, well-ordered *stage-sentiment this of his. **1895** G. B. SHAW in *Sat. Rev.* 16 Feb. 217/1 *Stage shows with nothing to redeem their obvious silliness but a promise of as much lewdness as the audience will stand. **1982** N. FRYE *Great Code* v. 117 The Puritan and Jansenist prejudice against 'stage shows'. **1758** JOHNSON in Boswell *Life* (1909) I. 217 Doddy..went every night to the *stage-side, and cried at the distress of poor Cleone. **1823** SCOTT *Quentin D.* xxvi. *note*, This gesture..is also by *stage-tradition a distinction of Shakespeare's Richard III. **1852** MUNDY *Our Antipodes* (1857) 94 The 'poor ghosts' who..sink pale and silent through the *stage-trap of the cabin-stairs. **1776** *St. James's Chron.* 19 Oct., Allowing reasonably for *stage trick, this appears to us to be extravagantly over-done. **1895** G. B. SHAW *Let.* 28 Nov. (1965) I. 572 This is not one of my great plays..: it is only a display of my knowledge of stage tricks. **1614** R. TAILOR *Hog hath lost Pearl* I. i. B 3, *Pl[ayer]*. Nay, I pray sir be not angry; for as I am a true *stage-trotter, I meane honestly. **1856** A. C. RITCHIE *Mimic Life* 105 Desdemona, according to the *stage version (which omits her during the midnight brawl). **1955** *Radio Times* 22 Apr. 31/2 '*A Woman of No Importance*'..Adapted for radio from the stage version. **1885** A. EDWARDES *Girton Girl* II. xvii. 281 Dismissed as one occasionally sees the frustrated *stage villain, long before the final falling of the curtain! **1896** *Peterson Mag.* Jan. 103/2 With a stage-villain glance at the speaker. **1602** DEKKER *Satirom.* I 3 b, These part-takers ..(Players I meane) Theaterians pouch-mouth *Stage-walkers. **1837** CARLYLE *Fr. Rev.* I. I. ii, He has..his very Troop of Players, with their..*stage-wardrobes [etc.]. **1778** THEOBALD *Shaks. Wks.* VIII. 558 *note*, I never heard it so much as intimated, that he had turned his genius to *stage-writing before he associated with the players.

b. (sense 9, 9 c), as ***stage-boat, -carriage, -cart, -fly, -horn, -line, -office, post, -road, -route, -track, vehicle***; objective, as ***stage-driver, -robber***.

1753 HANWAY *Trav.* (1762) II. I. ix. 46 These *stage-boats are extremely commodious. **1839** W. PENNEFATHER *Let.* 7 Sept. in R. Braithwaite *Life* (1878) 79 The *stage car [Ireland] proceeded slowly. **1832** *Act 2 & 3 Will. IV* c. 120 §5 That every Carriage used..for..conveying Passengers for Hire,..and which shall travel at the Rate of Three Miles or more in the Hour, shall be deemed and taken to be a *Stage Carriage within the meaning of this Act. **1837–8** *Act 1 & 2 Vict.* c. 79 §1 And the Words 'Metropolitan Stage Carriage' shall include [etc.]. **1812–16** J. SMITH *Panorama Sci. & Art* I. 374 The London common *stage-carts have large wheels. **1825** J. NEAL *Bro. Jonathan* II. 36 Hourra! *stage-driver's blowin' away like fun. **1821** *Blackw. Mag.* X. 656 In going in the *stage-fly from my own parish to Kilmartin. **1825** J. NEAL *Bro. Jonathan* II. 112 A sound, like that of a *stage-horn, arose from the valley. **1830** *Williams's N.Y. Ann. Reg.* 115 Other principal *Stage lines from Albany. **1877** RAYMOND *Statist. Mines & Mining* 341 The route of the Butterfield stage-line..was through it. **1882** L. D'A. JACKSON *Mod. Metrol.* 43 The German *stage-miles do not follow this type. **1812** J. MCNAB *Jrnl.* 4 Mar. in *Beaver* (1973) Summer 9/2 We..inquired at the *stage office when the sleigh sets out for New York on Friday. **1872** 'MARK TWAIN' *Roughing It* 22 The first thing we did..was to hunt up the stage-office, and pay..for tickets per overland coach. **1690** *Lond. Gaz.* No. 2601/4 Late Servant at the Crane Inn at Edgworth.., and riding the *Stage Post between that Town and London. **1872** RAYMOND *Statist. Mines & Mining* 11 A distance of 42 miles by *stage-road. **1907** *Putnam's Monthly* July 486/1 Money..that was taken from Heinz by the *stage-robber. **1874** RAYMOND *6th Rep. Mines* 307 This valley is located on the *stage-route from Denver to Fair Play. **1890** L. C. D'OYLE *Notches* 61 Crossing the river at the old *stage-track. **1808** HAN. MORE *Cœlebs* I. xxiii. 338 An over stuffed *stage vehicle.

c. (sense 4 h), as ***stage condenser, forceps, micrometer, plate***.

1856 W. B. CARPENTER *Microscope* §66. 143 Every Microscope should be furnished with a pair of Stage-forceps for holding minute objects beneath the object-glass. *Ibid.* §67. 144 Glass Stage-Plate. **1857** BEALE *How to Work with Microscope* 22 Placing..the stage micrometer..under the object-glass. **1862** *Catal. Internat. Exhib., Brit.* II. No. 2947, Stage forceps,..stage condenser. **1864** *Chamb. Encycl.* VI. 443/1 Stage-plate, on which the object is placed [in a microscope].

14. Special comb.: **†stage-blanks**, dramatic blank verse (see BLANK *sb.* 8); **stage box**, each of the boxes over the proscenium of a theatre; **†stage cloth**, a carpet for the 'stage' or platform of an altar; **stage-craft**, that part of the art of dramatic composition which is concerned with the conditions of representation on the stage; **stage critic**, a critic of the drama; **†stage-cutter** (see quot. 1820 in sense 4 f); **stage direction**, (*a*) a direction inserted in a written or printed play where it is thought necessary to indicate the appropriate action, etc.; (*b*) stage-management (also *fig.*); **stage director** orig. *U.S.*, a stage-manager; also, more recently, a director (sense 1 g); **†stage-doctor**, a quack doctor who practised on a stage (see 4 a) in public; **stage-door**, (*a*) the entrance to that part of a theatre used by the players as distinguished from the public entrance; also, *attrib.*; †(*b*) a door at the side of the proscenium arch (*obs.*); **stage-door Johnny** *slang* (chiefly *U.S.*), a (young) gentleman who frequents stage-doors for the company of actresses; **stage-effect**, (*a*) effect on the spectators of what is shown on the stage; also *fig.*; (*b*) a spectacular effect exhibited on the stage; **stage-entrance** = *stage-door*; **stage-fever**, †(*a*) = *stage-fright* (*obs.*); (*b*) an intense desire to adopt the stage as a profession; **stage-fright**, nervousness experienced by an actor when appearing before an audience, esp. on his first appearance; **stage-gangway** (see quot.); **stage-head**, the head of a fishing stage (see 4 f); **stage-house**, †(*a*) a play-house, theatre (*obs.*); (*b*) *U.S.* a house of accommodation used as a regular stopping place for stage-coaches; **†stage-keeper**, (*a*) one who keeps or carries on a theatre; (*b*) ? a servant in a theatre employed to keep the stage in order; **stage-kiln** (see quot.);

stage-land, the 'world' of the stage and its occupants; **stage-like** *a.*, resembling that of drama or the stage; theatrical; **stageman**, †(*a*) an actor (*obs.*); (*b*) a workman engaged about the stage; **stagemanship** *nonce-wd.*, the profession of a stage-coachman; **stage name**, a professional name assumed by an actor; **stage-place**, the place where a play is acted (*obs.* or *arch.*); **stage presence**, the (forceful) impression made by a performer on an audience; **stage-property** = PROPERTY *sb.* 3, also *attrib.*; **stage pumping** (see quot.); **stage-right** (see quot.); **stage-room**, the locality or setting of a play; **stage-scene**, †(*a*) the scenery of a stage (*obs.*); (*b*) a scene in a play; **stage school**, an academy of drama; **stage-set** = SET *sb.*[1] 28; (also *transf.*); **stage-setter**, a practitioner of the art of stagesetting; **stage-setting**, the disposition of the persons of a play and the accessories on the stage; also *fig.*; †**stage-smitten** *a.* = *stage-struck*; **stage-stand** *U.S.*, a place on a stage-coach route where horses are changed; **stage-stricken** *a. rare* = next; **stage-struck** *a.*, smitten with love for the stage or drama or with the desire to become an actor; †**stage-wagon**, one of the wagons belonging to an organized system of conveyance for heavy goods and passengers by road; **stage-wait**, a delay or hitch in the course of a theatrical performance; **stage-whisper**, a conventional whisper used on the stage, purposely made audible to the spectators; hence as *v. trans.*, (*a*) to address (a person) in a stage-whisper; (*b*) with obj. as direct speech: to say (something) in a stage-whisper; **stage-whispered** *ppl. a.*, spoken in a stage-whisper; **stage-whispering** *ppl. a.*; **stage-work**, †(*a*) 'play-acting', histrionic ceremony (*obs.*); (*b*) the work of an actor or of a theatrical company; dramatic representation; also, a dramatic work; (*c*) the framework of a stage; (*d*) stage-coach work; **stage working** (see quot.); **stage-worthy** *a.*, worthy of representation on the stage; hence **stage-worthiness**; **stage-wright**, a dramatist, play-wright.

1635 MASSINGER *On death Chas. Ld. Herbert* 7, I..bit my star-crossed pen, Too busy in *stage-blanks and trifling rhyme. **1739** CIBBER *Apol.* (1889) II. xii. 85 The former lower Doors of Entrance for the Actors were brought down between the..Pilasters; in the Place of which Doors now the two *Stage-Boxes are fixt. **1857** H. MARTINEAU *Autobiogr.* I. IV. 388 [Mr. Macready] gave us the stage box, whenever we chose to ask for it. **1982** C. CASTLE *Folies Bergère* ii. 64 He was to be seen..accepting congratulations in a stage box. **1552** in *Archæologia* XLIII. 236, vj *stage clothes for the aulter, iij of blew, j of redd, vj of whight. **1882** *Society* 7 Oct. 12/1 Their ingenuity and knowledge of *stagecraft is wonderful. **1780** T. DAVIES *Garrick* (1781) I. i. 17 That gross illiberality which often disgraces the instructions of modern *stage criticks. **1790** MALONE *Pref. to Shaks.* I. p. lviii, The very few *stage directions which the old copies exhibit. **1833** R. DYER *Nine Years of Actor's Life* 78, I began a correspondence with the well-known Henry Lee, and finally agreed to take the stage direction of his theatres. **1858** THACKERAY *Virgin.* I. xvii. 130 But Lady Castlewood could not operate upon the said eyes then and there, like the barbarous monsters in the stage-direction in King Lear. **1962** V. NABOKOV *Pale Fire* 55 When morning finds us marching to the wall Under the stage direction of some goon Political, some uniformed baboon. **1782** T. HALL in G. O. Seilhamer *Hist. Amer. Theatre* (1889) II. v. 55 Before you see one of your *stage directors Or, if you please, one of those strange projectors. **1849** *Theatrical Mirror* 27 Aug. 101/1 Mr A. Harris, stage-director of the Royal Italian Opera, of Covent Garden, has been presented with a piece of plate. **1908** E. TERRY *Story of my Life* xiv. 326 It was not as an actor but as a stage director that he wanted to work. **1979** A. WILLIAMSON *Funeral March for Siegfried* ix. 42 'We'll have to chase up the stage staff,'..'I can give you the stage director's address.' **1774** ADAM SMITH *Let.* 20 Sept. in J. Thomson *Life W. Cullen* I. 476 *Stage-doctors do not much excite the indignation of the faculty; more reputable quacks do. **1761** A. MURPHY *Way to keep Him* (ed. 4) v. 101 Enter Lady Constant. *Lovemore* No way to escape?—[Attempts both *stage doors, and is prevented]. **1776** R. Y. WALSINGHAM *Let.* 6 Feb. in J. Boaden *Private Corresp. David Garrick* (1832) II. 134 That you will be so good as to pardon the stage-door keeper for admitting *me* last night. **1778** JOHNSON *L. P.*, *Fenton* (1781) III. 114 They determined all to see the Merry Wives of Windsor..; and Fenton, as a dramatick poet, took them to the stage door. **1829** H. FOOTE *Companion to Theatres* 33 At this time, the proscenium was altered; stage doors were introduced, there having been none in the original building. **1883** D. COOK *On Stage* I. ix. 187 Of such stage-doors as are here described there is no London theatre in possession. **1885** JEROME *On the Stage* 26 The mere announcement of my name had no visible effect upon the stage-door keeper. **1912** *Out West* Feb. 139/1 No theater can hope to do business without *stage door Johnnies. **1922** [see RICH *adv.* and *Comb.* 10 b]. **1952** GRANVILLE *Dict. Theatrical Terms* 169 *Stage-door Johnny*, the Victorian buck..who haunted the stage door of the Gaiety Theatre, London,..when some of the most beautiful women of the day were members of the chorus. **1976** BOTHAM & DONNELLY *Valentino* iv. 35 Two Ziegfield Follies girls who were doing the town with a pair of wealthy stage-door Johnnies. **1795** S. ROGERS *Words to be Spoken by Mrs. Siddons* 20 Every Woman studies *stage-effect. **1835** T. MITCHELL *Acharn. of Aristoph.* 164 *note*, The Σπονδαὶ are here evidently introduced on the stage, as mutes, characteristically habited. The same stage-effect occurs in the Equites, 1387–1395. **1830** J. BERNARD *Retrospections of Stage* II. ix. 273 He got the carpenter to fix a bucket on a swivel, over the *stage-entrance of the Theatre. **1956** B. HOLIDAY *Lady sings Blues* (1973) xii. 112 We were supposed to pick up all the cats at the Braddock Motel.., near the stage entrance of the Apollo. **1861** MAYHEW *Lond. Labour* III. 142/1 Some of the young chaps..get the *stage-fever and knocking in the knees. We've had to shove them on to the scene. **1882** ASHTON *Soc. Life Q. Anne* II. 21 He caught stage fever, ran away from school..and joined the theatre at Dublin. **1876** 'MARK TWAIN' *Tom Sawyer* xxi. 169 A ghastly *stage-fright seized him. **1878** MRS. COWDEN CLARKE *Recoll. Writers* 300 It proved to them that I was not liable to stage-fright. **1885** JEROME *On the Stage* viii. 72 Strange to say, I never experienced stage-fright at any time. **1867** SMYTH *Sailor's Word-bk.* s.v. *Brow*, A *stage-gangway for the accommodation of the shipwrights, in conveying.. articles on board. **1677** W. HUBBARD *Narrative* II. (1865) 46 Coming too near the *Stage head, they presently found themselves in danger of a surprizal. **1638** in Willis & Clark *Cambridge* (1886) II. 55 Tiles for ye new *Stagehouse. **1788** M. CUTLER in *Life*, etc. (1888) I. 431 Put up my horse at the stage-house in the street leading from Ordway's Market to Powles Hook Ferry. *a* **1586** SIDNEY *Apol. Poetrie* (Arb.) 44 Perchance it is the Comick, whom naughtie Play-makers and *Stage-keepers, have iustly made odious. **1637** SHIRLEY *Example* Prol., They..on whom, i' the Roman state, Some ill-looked stage-keepers, like lictors, wait, With pipes for fasces. **1910** *Encycl. Brit.* V. 655/1 (*Cement*) There are also *stage kilns..which consist of two vertical shafts, one above the other..connected by a horizontal channel. **1885** *Pall Mall Gaz.* 15 May 5/1 Mr. Jerome [in *On the stage—and off*] describes from a humorous point of view those lower levels of *stageland. **1893** *N. Amer. Rev.* Aug. 168 She had the convulsions which stageland arsenic brings on. **1561** T. NORTON *Calvin's Inst.* IV. 105 Leauing *stagelike pompes, which dasell the eyes of the simple. **1694** F. BRAGGE *Disc. Parables* xiv. 466 A strange kind of humiliation, that..does indeed look too Stage-like to be thought real by any discerning man. **1589** BRABINE in *Greene's Menaphon* In praise of Author, You witts that..striue to thunder from a *Stage-mans throate. **1887** *Pall Mall Gaz.* 9 Sept. 2/1 The class of stagemen employed in such places as these [theatres]. **1845** TALFOURD *Vacat. Rambles* I. 67 The departing race of English stage-coachmen, who shed a half-genteel grace on the last days of English *stagemanship. **1847** L. HUNT *Men, Women, & B.* (1876) 298 Lavinia Fenton sounds like a *stage-name. **1941** A. CHRISTIE *Evil under Sun* iv. 66 He doubted if Arlena Stuart, to give her her stage name, had ever wanted to be alone in her life. **1959** T. S. ELIOT *Elder Statesman* II. 51 You know I meant my stage name. The name by which you knew me. **1977** *Sounds* 9 July 28/1 *Stooges*..headed by James Osterburg—stage name Iggy Stooge. *a* **1564** BECON *Articles Chr. Relig.* xiv. Wks. II. 143 b, When thys Theatre or *stage place be once dissolued, then is there nomore deseruyng of Crownes. **1902** SIR E. ARNOLD *Nativity* xiv. in *Delineator* LX. 967 This Was scene and stage-place of the immortal story. **1929** *Melody Maker* Feb. 195/2 There was a wide gap between the *stage presence of the cornet soloist and the stage presence of the other artists. **1959** R. LONGRIGG *Wrong Number* iv. 49 Mrs. Proctor, in the soubrette part of the kitchen-maid, made up for her vocal uncertainty with a racy and convincing stage presence. **1977** *Zigzag* Aug. 16/1 Syl's got a lot of what directors call 'stage presence'. **1850** DYCE *Marlowe's Wks.* I. Introd. 17 *note*, Among the *stage-properties of the Lord Admiral's men we find 'j. dragon in fostes'. **1863** LE FANU *Ho. by Churchyard* I. x. 108 [He] viewed the wiglet with the eye of a stage-property man. **1883** GRESLEY *Gloss. Coal-mining* 234 **Stage Pumping*, draining a mine by means of two or more pumps placed at different levels. **1860** READE *8th Commandm.* 61 The copyrights only of French authors, not the *stage-rights, were to be protected. Copyright is the sole and exclusive right of printing. Stage-right the sole and exclusive right of representation on a public stage. **1642** MILTON *Apol. Smect.* 10 Whom no lesse then almost halfe the world could serve for *stage roome to play the Mime in. **1814** SCOTT *Let.* in *Lockhart* (1837) III. ix. 293 Reducing the knowledge I have acquired of the localities of the islands into scenery and stage-room for the 'Lord of the Isles'. **1664** POWER *Exp. Philos.* Pref. 18 Outside Fallacies; like our *Stage-scenes, or Perspectives, that shew things inwards, when they are but superficial paintings. **1822** SHELLEY *Chas. I*, i. 35 That stage-scene in which thou art Not a spectator but an actor. **1865** KINGSLEY *Herew.* xxvi, [A fire] breaking the bones of its prey with a horrible cracking uglier than all stage-scene glares. **1936** N. STREATFEILD *Ballet Shoes* iv. 55 She..ran an ordinary *stage school where the children learnt all kinds of dancing. **1977** S. BRETT *Star Trap* ii. 24 He came out of one of the stage schools... He may have been a child star in films. **1861** *Stage set [see SET *sb.*[1] 28]. **1947** J. C. RICH *Materials & Methods of Sculpture* i. 13 In designing for a garden..an excellent and highly recommended procedure is first to make a small three-dimensional scale model of the garden and its immediate environs, and to use this small 'stage-set' actively as an aid in determining the nature and placing of the garden ornament. **1958** S. SPENDER *Engaged in Writing* i. 13 A large, bare room with faded nineteenth-century murals, like the back of an operatic stage-set. **1977** *Proc. R. Soc. Med.* LXX. 427/2 A collaborative effort in which satirical comedy is fused with the sort of music, dance, lavish costumes and stage-sets used in court ballets. **1888** *Century Mag.* Feb. 544/2 M. Sardou is a born *stage-setter. **1881** C. C. HARRISON *Woman's Handiwork* III. 152 All the little invisible wires that control the scenery and '*stage setting' of a home-interior. **1905** C. F. KEARY in *Author* 1 Feb. 145 There is no harm in M. Antoine's realism of stage-setting. **1929** *Oxford Poetry* 10 For three-and-twenty years, he curled And drooped, on this stage-setting of the world. **1982** P. RABY '*Fair Ophelia*' iv. 48 Ciceri extended into the sphere of stage settings the reforms which Talma himself had introduced so far as historical accuracy of costume was concerned. **1682** MRS. BEHN *City Heiress* 8 Our *Stage-smitten Youth fall in love with a woman for Acting finely. **1856** MRS. STOWE *Dred* II. xii. 127 He pushed forward,..and, at the first *stage-stand, changed him [the horse] for a fresh one. **1838** DICKENS *Mem. Grimaldi* i, The *stage-stricken young gentlemen who..long to embrace the theatrical profession. **1813** SCOTT *Trierm.* II. ii, Or *stage-struck Juliet may presume To choose this bower for tiring-room. **1911** Stage struck [see RUMBLE *sb.* 6]. **1976** *Southern Even. Echo* (Southampton) 6 Nov., Despite warnings of financial trouble in the theatre,..she has remained stage-struck throughout her life after deciding at the age of four to become an actress. **1761** *Ann. Reg.*, *Chron.* 184 For robbing the Bath *stage waggon on the highway. **1849** MACAULAY *Hist. Eng.* iii. I. 376 Heavy articles were, in the time of Charles the Second, generally conveyed from place to place by stage waggons. **1865** MISS BRADDON *Only a Clod* II. i. 23 There were the usual number of dead pauses in the drama, technically known as '*stage-waits'. **1864** H. MORLEY *Jrnl.* 17 Dec. (1866) 355 His bedroom scene, spoken throughout in an oppressively ostentatious *stage whisper, is an intolerable blunder. **1865** *Hotten's Slang Dict.* 244 *Stage-whisper.* **1883** HOWELLS *Register* ii. in *Harper's Mag.*, Dec. 79/2 *Miss Reed*, in a stage-whisper. **1927** J. N. MCILWRAITH *Kinsmen at War* xx. 198 Mrs. Secord spoke in a stage whisper. **1960** J. RAE *Custard Boys* I. v. 52 'Who's your German friend?' he asked in a stage whisper. **1977** W. M. SPACKMAN *Armful of Warm Girl* 38 A huge handsome white-haired classmate flung himself jovially upon them.. to beg in a whooping and waggish stage-whisper. **1932** KIPLING *Limits & Renewals* 80 Private Gillock, who poses as a wit, was *stage-whispering me for leave to 'put a shot into his radiator'. **1941** B. SCHULBERG *What makes Sammy Run?* iii. 49 'What are you thinking about, honey?' Billie stage-whispered. **1979** R. LITTELL *Debriefing* iii. 33 'Do you have the pouch?' she stage-whispers. **1978** G. SIMS *Rex Mundi* iv. 26 The *stage-whispered duet started again... I made out only odd words. **1883** 'MARK TWAIN' *Life on Miss.* xxxi. 342 'The captain's voice, by G——!' said the *stage-whispering ruffian. **1649** MILTON *Eikon.* xix. 172 But the King and his Party..Canonize one another into Heav'n;.. but, as was sayd before, *Stage-work will not doe it. **1829** *Sporting Mag.* XXIII. 194 The antediluvian principle of 'any thing's good enough for stage-work'. **1898** *Daily News* 25 Oct. 8/5 Two large joists..had been placed in position in the stagework. **1906** *Macm. Mag.* June 595 The musical comedy..has wrought grave injury to all intelligent stage-work. **1913** *Illustr. Lond. News* 22 Feb. 230/2 That happiest and liveliest of all Oscar Wilde's stage-works. **1883** GRESLEY *Gloss. Coal-mining* 235 **Stage working*, a system of working minerals by open hole in which the various beds are removed in steps or stages. **1973** *Times Lit. Suppl.* 19 Oct. 1272/4 The recent Jonathan Miller production of *The Malcontent* has demonstrated that play's *stageworthiness. **1820** BYRON *Mar. Fal.* Pref., Were I capable of writing a play which could be deemed *stage-worthy. **1959** *Times* 4 Dec. 15/1 None of his [*sc.* Mussorgsky's] operatic undertakings is stageworthy. **1979** *Amer. N. & Q.* Nov. 40/1 In an effective and stageworthy central scene, the old miser's secrets..are discovered. **1630** *Stage-wright [see STAGER 3]. **1897** *Tablet* 18 Sept. 457 [Shakespere] our greatest stage-wright and philosopher.

stage (steɪdʒ), *v.* [f. STAGE *sb.*]

†**1.** *trans.* To erect, build. *Obs. rare*[−1].

c **1330** R. BRUNNE *Chron. Wace* (Rolls) 3090 Brugges ouer watres dide he stage.

2. To furnish with a stage or staging; in quots. with *about*. Now *rare* or *Obs.* †Also *absol.* or *intr.*, to set up a platform or scaffolding.

1506 *Justs of May & June* in Hazl. *E.P.P.* (1866) II. 114 A lady fayre..With seruauntes foure brought was into a place Staged about Whereon stode lordes and ladyes a grete route. **1526** *Dunmow Churchw. MS.* lf. 5 To purvay syce stufe as the workemen showlde nede, and to sett them a-worke, and helpe to stage. **1598** STOW *Surv.* 388 The great Hall..was richly hanged with Arras, and Staged about on both sides. **1879** J. D. LONG *Virgil's Æneid* IX. 690 A far-outlooking tower, staged high about, Stood in the way.

3. a. To put (a person) into a play; to satirize in drama; to represent (a character, an incident) on the stage. Sometimes in phr. *to stage to the crowd* or *show*.

1601 B. JONSON *Poetaster* III. iv, Death of Pluto, and you Stage mee, Stinkard; your Mansions shall sweate for't. **1606** SHAKS. *Ant. & Cl.* III. xiii. 30 Hye battel'd Cæsar will..be Stag'd to 'th 'shew Against a Sworder. *Ibid.* v. ii. 217 The quicke Comedians Extemporally will stage us. **1607** MIDDLETON *Five Gall.* IV. viii. H 3, *Gold.* What if we fiue presented our full shapes In a..maske? *Frip.* Some Poet must assist vs. *Go.* Poet? Youle take the direct line to haue vs sta'gde? **1621** J. TAYLOR (Water P.) *Superbiæ Flagellum* C 6 b, Cudgeld and bastinadoed at the Court, And Comically stag'de to make men sport. **1721** SOUTHERNE *Disappointment* III. i, O! may I be that hateful thing I scorn! The common, ridden cuckold of the Town, Stag'd to the crowd on publick theatres. **1879** SWINBURNE *Stud. Shaks.* (1880) 273 The next two scenes, in which the battle of Poitiers is so inadequately 'staged to the show'. **1898** G. WYNDHAM *Poems Shaks.* Introd. 61 Jonson staged Marston in Every Man out of His Humour (1599), as Carlo Buffone:—'a public, scurrilous and profane jester'.

b. *fig.*

1603 SHAKS. *Meas. for M.* I. i. 69 Ile priuily away: I loue the people, But doe not like to stage me to their eyes. **1784** BAGE *Barham Downs* II. 4 Too long I had staged me to their eyes in these my true habiliments.

c. To put (a play, etc.) upon the stage.

1879 *Theatre* Nov. 209 If an..author..permits a play of his to be mounted and staged without his permission. **1887** *Pall Mall Gaz.* 12 Sept. 5/2 As pretty a pastoral scene as has ever been staged, even at the Lyceum. **1894** *Times* 10 Sept. 10/3 The piece is staged in the most sumptuous manner imaginable.

d. *transf.* To mount or put on (a spectacle). Also, to effect (a recovery); *to stage a comeback*: see COME-BACK *sb.*[2] 2.

1924 F. J. HASKIN *Amer. Govt.* (rev. ed.) xxxvii. 437 In combating..bootlegging,..Federal agents..staged raids that revealed..the widespread extent of Volstead Law violations. **1951** *Sport* 27 Apr.–3 May 5/1 It is grand to think that the event can be staged at Wembley. **1956** A. H. COMPTON *Atomic Quest* 122 His Nazi-trained students staged a protest. **1973** *Daily Tel.* 15 Feb. 1/4 More than 500 students staged a sit-in at Cambridge University yesterday. **1981** *Times* 9 May 19/4 A gradual return of confidence saw equities and gilts stage a rally yesterday.

†**4.** *Sc.* To bring (a person) to trial for an offence (esp. before the ecclesiastical courts). Cf. STAGE *sb.* 4c. Const. *for*, *with* (an offence). Also *fig. Obs.*

1671 [R. MACWARD] *True Nonconf.* 223 All the regard to the powers, whereof..you..boast, doth not here in the least restrain you from staging these two Kings with us, as Monstruous imposers. **1681** in J. H. Thomson *Cloud of Witnesses* (1871) 119, I [Isobel Alison: see quot. 1722] told them, If they had staged me, they might remember my name. **1682** FOUNTAINHALL *Diary* Aug., in *Law's Memor.* (1818) 236 *note*, Kepperminshoo accused him of perjury. He was also staged with bribery. **1722** WODROW *Hist. Ch. Scot.* (1830) III. III. v. 275/2 Upon the 17th of January, I find Isabel Alison..and Marian Harvey..staged for their lives before the justiciary. **1729** in *Wodrow's Corr.* (1843) III. 429 He thought Mr Simson was staged for heretical opinions.

5. To put (plants) on a stage; to exhibit (plants or other objects) at a show. Also *absol.*

1850 *Beck's Florist* 249 There were several useful flowers staged, but few novelties. **1881** F. YOUNG *Ev. Man his own Mech.* §930 For staging auriculas the distance between the rows of shelves need not be so great as for pelargoniums. **1883** *Goole Weekly Times* 7 Sept. 8/2 With holyhocks, he has taken first and second prizes every time he has staged them. **1897** *C.T.C. Monthly Gaz.* Jan. 24 A few silver-plated models were staged.

6. a. *intr.* To travel by stage or stage-coach; to travel by stages; to journey *over* by stages; also *to stage it.*

1695 *Phil. Trans.* XIX. 144 This way..we assented to, as more eligible, than..to wander so far out of the Road, to have the same Ground to stage over again the next morning. **1698** FRYER *Acc. E. India & P.* 34 A Set of these Rascals [Coolies]..bait them generously shall stage it a Month together. **1713** [W. DARRELL] *Gentl. Instr.* III. vi. (ed. 5) 420 [A traveller]..learns the great Mystery of Foreign Governments;..he stages (if I may say so) into Politicks, and rides Post into Business. **1819** COLERIDGE *Lett., Convers.*, etc. I. 19 Riding, driving, or staging to London. **1840** MRS. TROLLOPE *Widow Married* xv, I wonder how the old lady came, whether she staged it, or posted? **1882** D. PIDGEON *Engineer's Holiday* I. 228, I staged three miles from its terminus to Leadville.

b. Of a pilot or aircraft: to make a brief landing in the course of a long journey.

1971 P. PURSER *Holy Father's Navy* I. iii. 17 The pilot [had]..staged in Iceland and was on his way to Norway. **1973** D. KYLE *Raft of Swords* (1974) I. iv. 32 The agent..was in time to join the Air Canada Hawaii to Montreal flight when it staged at Vancouver.

7. *trans. Astronautics.* To separate (a section or stage) from the upper or remaining part of a rocket. Also *intr.* of the stage.

1957 *Collier's Encycl. Year Bk. 1956* 264/1 After launching, when the propellants in the booster tanks are nearly exhausted, the three motors and the rear tanks will be staged, or shut down and separated from the missile. **1962** J. GLENN et al. *Into Orbit* 246 When one section of it [*sc.* a multi-stage booster] separates and is jettisoned.., the section is said to have staged. **1966** H. O. RUPPE *Introd. Astronaut.* I. iii. 91 It is possible to 'parallel-stage' tankage or engines only... E.g., a three-stage vehicle can have its first and second stages parallel staged, and the second and third stages tandem staged.

8. To cause (a person) to pass through stages; to bring about (something) in stages.

1957 A. C. CLARKE *Deep Range* ix. 83 We've got to haul him in around the hundred-and-fifty-foot level—no higher—and then start staging him in the air lock. **1962** E. SNOW *Red China Today* (1963) III. xxxviii. 279 We staged them through quick courses of training and retraining in the Ningtu technique. **1980** *Daily Tel.* 15 Mar. 1/7 The Government will 'stage' the payment of the increases to stay within its cash limits.

stage, variant of STAG *a. Obs.*

stageable ('steɪdʒəb(ə)l), *a. rare.* [f. STAGE *v.* + -ABLE.] That can be put upon the stage. Hence **stagea'bility**.

1907 *Mod. Lang. Notes* XXII. 225 (*title*) The stageability of Garnier's Tragedies. *Ibid.* 226 The play is stageable.

†'**stagean**, *a. nonce-wd.* [f. STAGE *sb.* + -AN.] Appropriate to the stage.

1600 W. WATSON *Decacordon* (1602) 15 A stagean countenance, as actors in the Pageant of a play.

stage-coach. [STAGE *sb.* 9.] **a.** A coach that runs daily or on specified days between two places for the conveyance of passengers, parcels, etc.

1658 *Mercurius Politicus* 1 Apr. 433 From the 26 day of April 1658, there will continue to go Stage Coaches from the George Inn. **1666** PEPYS *Diary* 26 Feb., Kate Joyce, in a stage-coach going towards London, called to me. **1781** COWPER *Retirem.* 492 And, if a shower approach, You find safe shelter in the next stage-coach. **1812** *Examiner* 28 Dec. 827/2 A stage-coach..usually carries six inside passengers, and is drawn by four horses. **1881** BESANT & RICE *Chapl. of Fl.* (1883) I. iii. 17 We came to the roadside inn where the stage-coach changed horses.

b. *U.S.* ? The name of a game in which the players scramble for new places.

1831 *Boston Transcript* 2 Aug. 2/3 The entertainment happened to be the 'Stage Coach', which was acted so wretchedly that it was impossible to make head or tail of it. **1872** 'S. COOLIDGE' *What Katy Did* (1873) v. 89 They all fell to playing 'Stage-coach'..in spite of close quarters and an occasional bump. **1892** *Nation* (N.Y.) 24 Nov. 397/3 What happened on the demise of the Grand Prince resembled a game of 'stage-coach', with swords thrown in.

c. *attrib.*

1791 O'KEEFFE *Wild Oats* II. iii, They've got your name down to the *stage-coach book. **1803** *Censor* 1 Mar. 27 A *stage-coach conveyance. **1840** DICKENS *Old C. Shop* xlvi, They allowed me..outside *stage-coach hire all the way. **1838** *Penny Cycl.* XII. 309/1 The horse of quick work, the *stage-coach horse and the poster. **1749** SMOLLETT *Gil Blas* II. iii. ¶2 The clerk of a *stage-coach office registers those who take places.

Hence **stage-coaching** *vbl. sb.*, the running or driving of stage-coaches (also *attrib.*); travelling by stage-coach. **stage-coachman**, the driver (also †the proprietor) of a stage-coach.

1756-7 tr. *Keysler's Trav.* (1760) I. 349 The *vetturini*, or stage-coachman, must..not go out of the country without a pass. **1757** LD. MANSFIELD in Burrow *Settlem. Cases* (1768) II. 424 This..is no more than the Case of the Oxford Stage-Coachman's Servant who gained a Settlement in Chipping-Wicomb. **1837** DICKENS *Pickw.* lv, They..wore as many clothes as possible, which is..a stage-coachman's idea of full dress. **1844** —— *Mart. Chuz.* xiii, A large stage-coaching establishment. **1856** OLMSTED *Slave States* ix. 547 Partly by rail and partly by rapid stage-coaching..I crossed the State. **1884** SALA *Journ. South* (1887) I. viii. 108 The virtual state of perfection to which English stage-coaching had attained.

staged (steɪdʒd), *ppl. a.* [f. STAGE *sb.* and *v.* + -ED.]

1. †**a.** That acts on or as on a stage. *Obs.*

1569 J. SANFORD tr. *Agrippa's Van. Artes* xxi. 32 b, [This Histrionical Rhetorike] is yet obserued of some staged Freers [*à scenicis aliquot fraterculis*]. **1586** J. HOOKER *Giraldus' Hist. Irel.* Pref., in *Holinshed*, But yet as a staged man can not alwaies dissemble and cloke himself, so this man, who [etc.].

b. Of a play: That is put upon the stage.

1904 N. HOWARD *Savonarola* Scenes, The Author has..permitted himself a fuller development, both of Theme and Character, than the staged Drama would require.

2. Of a building: Having a series of floors or stories one above another.

1884 W. ARMSTRONG tr. *G. Perrot & C. Chipiez' Hist. Art Chaldea & Assyria* I. iv. 369 Herodotus declares plainly that it [*i.e.* the temple of Bel] was a staged tower. **1885** *Athenæum* 21 Mar. 381/3 The lofty, staged towers of the Euphrates valley..must have been glorious to behold.

3. Of feathers: ? Arranged in order of length.

1828 STARK *Elem. Nat. Hist.* I. 208 Wings with the five first feathers staged; the sixth or seventh longest.

4. That proceeds by stages; = PHASED *ppl. a.* 2.

1960 *Economist* 15 Oct. 255/3 A group of commissioners who disagree with these proposals favour a traditional policy of staged development. **1969** *Daily Tel.* 16 May 1 A mutual and staged withdrawal of all foreign troops from South Vietnam. **1973** *Ibid.* 13 Dec. 2/8 New wage rates which would be introduced, with staged pay rises, over $2\frac{1}{2}$ years.

†'**stagely**, *a. Obs. rare.* [f. STAGE *sb.* + -LY[1].] Resembling (that of) the stage.

1656 *Artif. Handsom.* 168 Nor may this be called an histrionike parada, or stagely visard and hypocrisie.

'**stage-'manage**, *v.* [Back-formation f. STAGE-MANAGER.] *trans.* To arrange with a view to stage effect. Also *absol.*

1879 *Theatre* Nov. 209, I have never seen them stage-manage a play. **1906** *Daily Chron.* 8 May 5/1 The meeting was well stage-managed, care being taken to fill the front part of the hall with ticket-holders. **1910** WODEHOUSE *Psmith in City* i. 3 My pater wants to jump in and stage manage. **1924** J. BUCHAN *Three Hostages* viii. 118 'Now wake.' I was puzzled to know how to stage-manage that wakening. **1958** *Washington Post* 26 June 1/7 The United States..accused the Russian Government of stage-managing a demonstration against the U.S. Embassy in Moscow. **1964** 'E. MCBAIN' *Ax* ii. 36 We did it [*sc.* a play] in highschool... I stage-managed. **1980** D. LODGE *How Far can you Go?* vi. 218 The whole prank, she was now convinced, was being stage-managed..to get them all naked together.

Hence **stage-managed** *ppl. a.*

1930 *Times Lit. Suppl.* 1 May 359/3 In 1891 France and Russia had signalized their closer relations by the enthusiastic, though carefully stage-managed, reception given to the French fleet at Kronstadt. **1974** *Listener* 10 Oct. 461/3 These are not press conferences at all, but carefully stage-managed events, put on..for the audiences of BBC and ITV news.

'**stage-'management.** [f. prec. + -MENT.] The business of a stage-manager. Also *fig.*

1812 C. MATHEWS *Let.* 15 Jan. in A. Mathews *Mem. Charles Mathews* (1838) II. viii. 184 Mr Kemble is the proprietor. Whether he solely directs the stage management, or whether he does not at all interfere. **1879** *Theatre* Nov. 209, Stage-management. **1949** M. STEEN *Twilight on Floods* IV. i. 547 The sun, by one of the erratic tricks of Nature's stage-management, forced itself through the clouds. **1977** A. GIDDENS *Stud. in Social & Polit. Theory* ix. 329 Through the agency of Durkheim..the analysis of suicide became a critical issue in the struggle to establish sociology as a recognized academic discipline in France. This was, of course, largely due to Durkheim's own stage-management.

stage-manager. One whose office it is to superintend the production and performance of a play, and to regulate the arrangements of the stage. In mod. usage, restricted to mean: one who is in charge of the technical side of a production (see quot. 1961). Also *transf.* and *fig.*

1805 R. W. ELLISTON *Let.* 20 July in G. Raymond *Life & Enterprises of Robert William Elliston, Comedian* (1857) I. ii. 113 If to my office, as stage-manager, the term *officious* be applied. **1817** J. A. WILLIAMS *Mem. Kemble* 21 His appointment to the situation of stage manager..in 1788. **1837** CARLYLE *Fr. Rev.* I. III. vii, The World shall see one other Historical Scene; and so singular a man as Loménie de Brienne still the Stage-manager there. **1885** JEROME *On the Stage* 35, I don't know why stage managers are always surly, but they are. **1905** G. B. SHAW *Let.* in *Times* 3 July 8/2 My language was fairly moderate considering..the respectful ignorance of the dramatic points of the score exhibited by the conductor and the stage manager—if there is such a functionary at Covent Garden. **1906** E. DYSON *Fact'ry Ands* x. 121 Every woman in an astonishing frock is at heart a stage-manager. **1961** BOWMAN & BALL *Theatre Lang.* 349 *Stage manager*,..the head of the production staff, who assists the stage director, during rehearsals, in technical matters.., and who, once the production opens, takes complete charge of the stage, the actors.., and the crews. **1982** S. BRETT *Murder Unprompted* ii. 21 The Stage Manager's calming voice came over the loudspeaker, 'Beginners, Act One, please.'

Hence as *v. trans.*, to stage-manage (*rare*); **stage-manageress**, a female stage-manager; **stage-managership**, the post of stage-manager.

1817 COLERIDGE *Let. to J. Murray* Lett. (1895) 667 Mr. Dibdin..was likewise removed from the stage-managership. **1900** M. BEERBOHM *Let.* 11 Dec. (1964) 138 As stage-manageress she has been adsolutely intelligent and sweet and charming. **1902** G. B. SHAW *Let.* 9 Aug. (1972) II. 281 It is..very important to get the last scene well stage managered, with a big surging crowd. **1926** E. F. CROSSE *Let.* in *Times* 13 Apr. 15/5 There was no shyness and the stage manageress explained to me all details.

stage play. A dramatic performance; also, a dramatic composition adapted for representation on the stage. (Cf. PLAY *sb.* 15.)

1513 MORE *Rich. III* (1883) 79 And in a stage play all the people know right wel that he that playeth the sowdayne, is percase a sowter. **1605-6** *Act 3 Jas. I*, c. 21 For the preventing and avoyding of the greate Abuse of the Holy Name of God in Stageplayes..and such like. **1693** DRYDEN *Juvenal* (1697) Ded. 79 Stage-Plays, which are all of one Action, and one continu'd Series of Action. **1843** *Act 6 & 7 Vict.* c. 68 §23 The Word 'Stage-Play' shall be taken to include every Tragedy, Comedy, Farce, Opera, Burletta, Interlude, Melodrama, Pantomime, or other Entertainment of the Stage, or any Part thereof.

b. Dramatic acting, play-acting.

1872 MORLEY *Voltaire* (1886) 9 The contest was real, and not our present pantomimic stage-play.

c. *attrib.*

1819 KEATS *Otho* I. ii, I do not personate The stage-play emperor to entrap applause. **1908** *Stage Year Bk.* 26 Many provincial theatres also have..a stage play licence and a music and dancing licence.

stage-player. = PLAYER[1] 4.

1556 HOBY *Courtier* II. (1561) M b, A noble Stageplaier..that..would alwaies be the first to come furth to playe his parte. **1617** MORYSON *Itin.* III. 8 Rude Stage players, who..spend more time in putting on their apparrell, then in acting their Comedy. **1765** TUCKER *Lt. Nat.* (1834) II. 624 Tasks..which seem needful only to qualify them for stage players. *fig.* **1561** T. NORTON *Calvin's Inst.* IV. 150 In what point therfore wil these stageplaiers [*ces basteleurs*] say that they follow the Apostles.

stage-playing. Playing on the stage as an actor; play-acting.

1597 in *Engl. Studien* XLIII. 345 Wheras yor highnes said Subiectes..haue of longe tyme vsed and professed the Arte of Stageplayinge. **1643** BAKER *Chron., Jas. I*, 151 Edward Allin..having gotten his wealth by Stage-playing, converted it to this pious use. **1823** J. GILLIES tr. *Aristotle's Rhet.* III. i. 366 Stage-playing and rhetorical elocution are things highly natural.

stager ('steɪdʒə(r)). [f. STAGE *sb.* + -ER[1].

It is not wholly impossible that in the expression *old stager* (sense 1 below) the word may be ad. OF. *estagier* an inhabitant, resident (f. *estage* STAGE *sb.*), or med.L. *stagiārius* (see STAGIARY[1]) which is used in English monastic records (e.g. *Cust. St. Augustine's, Canterbury*, Henry Bradshaw Soc. Publ. XXIII) for an aged monk who was lodged permanently in the infirmary. Derivation from STAGE *sb.* is, however, more probable, but the precise notion seems difficult to determine. The usual explanation that the theatrical stage is alluded to ('one who has been long on the stage of life') finds no support in the 16th and 17th c. examples; the primary sense may be that indicated in the definition of sense 2, but this is supported only by a single quotation.]

1. a. *old stager*: one who has become graduated or qualified by long experience; one who has been long employed *in* an office, a profession, course of life, etc.; a veteran, an old hand. Also occas. of animals.

1570 FOXE *A. & M.* III. 1756/1 [They] betooke them to theyr legges..resembling in some part a spectacle not much vnlike to the old stagers of Oxford, worse feared then hurt, when as the Church there was noysed to be on fier. **1577** GOOGE *Heresbach's Husb.* IV. 181 They..doo..disdayne ye gouernment..of the old Bee..when the swarmes be great and lusty, and that the old stagers [orig. L. *veteres*] are disposed to send abroade their Colonies. **1648** HEYLIN *Relat. & Observ.* I. 10 It was worth observing to see how officiously some of the old Stagers took leave of the Publique Purse, before it came into Hucksters hands. **1665** M. NEDHAM *Med. Medicinæ* 284 The next Digestion..the old Stagers will needs have to be in the Veines of the Mesenterie. **1669** *Hist. Pope's Nephews* II. (1673) 135 'Tis a tedious thing to Princes Ministers, who are old Stagers in Councils and Affairs, to have to do with raw, unexperienced Persons. *a* **1734** NORTH *Life Ld. Keeper Guilford* (1742) 146 Some of the old Stagers of his Party told him plainly, he might take his Ease. **1737** BRACKEN *Farriery Impr.* (1756) I. 17 A young Horse, though he be more subject to Diseases than an old hardened Stager. **1748** CHESTERF. *Lett.* clxxii. (1792) II. 137 But here let me, as an old stager upon the theatre of the world, suggest one consideration to you. **1786-89** BENTHAM *Princ. Internat. Law* Wks. 1843 II. 549 True—but there are young beginners as well as old stagers. **1815** SCOTT *Guy M.* xxxv, You never come down to see your old acquaintance..you would find most of the old stagers still stationary there. **1833** MARRYAT *P. Simple* xxx, I'm an old stager in the West Indies, and I'll let you into a secret. **1841** PRESCOTT in *Life Longfellow* (1891) I. 411, I do not know that an old stager in authorship, like you, cares for anybody's opinion. **1895** SCULLY *Kafir Stories* 169 My horse was a steady old stager, not at all given to shying.

b. Hence *stager* simply, and with other adjs., as *cunning*, *sly*. Also (rarely) ***young stager***, one of small experience, a beginner.

1664 BUTLER *Hud.* II. i. 297 Quoth She, I've heard old cunning Stagers Say, Fools for Arguments use wagers. **1687** DRYDEN *Hind & P.* III. 497 'Tis true, some stagers of the wiser sort Made all these idle wonderments their sport. **1692** L'ESTRANGE *Fables* lxxxi. 79 At last, One Experienced Stager [a mouse] that had Baffled Twenty Traps and Tricks Before, Discover'd the Plot. **1709** SWIFT *Project Adv. Relig.* Misc. (1711) 190 The pert Pragmatical Demeanor of several young Stagers in Divinity. **1836** J. STRUTHERS *Dychmont* IV. Poet. Wks. (1850) II. 101 Where's the sly stager Gizzy Rags?

†**2.** One who has attained a definite stage or rank in his profession. *Obs. rare.*

1583 *Execution for Treason* 4 And them to send..under secret maskes,..with titles of Seminaries for some of the meaner sort, and of Iesuites for the stagers and ranker sort.

3. A stage-player. *Obs.* exc. *arch.*

1580 *2nd & 3rd Blast Plays & Theatres* 111 As for those stagers..are they not commonlie such kind of men in their conuersation, as they are in profession? **1601** B. JONSON *Poetaster* I. ii, What? shall I haue my son a Stager now? an Enghle for Players? a Gull? a Rooke? a Shot-clog? *Ibid.* III. iv, Suffer him not to droop, in prospect of a Player, a Rogue, a Stager. **1602** DEKKER *Satirom.* D 1 b, Thou borrowedst a gowne of Roscius the Stager,..and sentst it home lowsie. **1630** B. JONSON *New Inn* (1631) H 2 (*Just Indign. Author*), And safe in your stage-clothes, Dare quit, vpon your oathes, The stagers, and the stage-wrights too (your peeres) Of larding your large eares. **1873** BROWNING *Red Cott. Nt.-cap* 1264 Sganarelle,..That stager in the saint's correct costume.

†**4. a.** One who runs a stage or course. *Obs.*

1638 BRATHWAIT *Barnabee's Jrnl.* III. T 4, Thence to Towlerton, where those Stagers [*Stadiodromi*] Or Horse-coursers run for wagers. **1687** NORRIS *Misc.* 138 The Antient Stager of the Day Has run his minutes out, and number'd all his way.

b. A stage-coach or stage-coach horse.

1852 *Tait's Mag.* XIX. 656 The shock was so violent that the crazy stager, its conductor, its two horses and a single passenger rolled pell-mell in the..road. **1858** SIMMONDS *Dict. Trade*, *Stager*, a horse running in a stage carriage.

5. One who erects scaffolding in a shipyard. Cf. STAGE *sb.* 4 e.

1927 *Dict. Occupational Terms* §668 *Stager*,..erects staging on which workmen stand to work. **1974** *Socialist Worker* 26 Oct. 16/5 Management agreed that stagers in the Society of Boilermakers be made a skilled section with parity with packers and sheeters.

Hence †'**stageress** *Obs. rare*$^{-1}$, a play-actress.

1633 PRYNNE *Histrio-m.* 649 Hee who hath married a strumpet, or a woman-actor or stageresse, cannot be an Elder, a Bishop, or Deacon.

†**stagerite.** *jocular. nonce-wd.* [f. STAGER + -ITE; possibly with allusion to STAGIRITE.] An inhabitant of 'Stageland'.

1602 DEKKER *Satirom.* G 4, Thou hast forgot how thou..took'st mad Ieronimoes part, to get seruice among the Mimickes: and when the Stagerites banisht thee into the Ile of Dogs thou turn'dst Ban-dog.

stagery ('steɪdʒərɪ). [f. STAGE *sb.* + -ERY.] Exhibition on the stage; stage arrangements or contrivances.

1642 MILTON *Apol. Smect.* 9 [He] likening those grave controversies to a piece of Stagery, or Scene-worke where his owne Remonstrant whether in Buskin or Sock must of all right be counted the chiefe Player. **1886** HARDY *Mayor Casterbr.* I. i. 22 To watch it was like looking at some grand feat of stagery from a darkened auditorium.

stagese (steɪ'dʒi:z). [f. STAGE *sb.* + -ESE.] The 'dialect' peculiar to the stage.

1876 *Times* 6 Jan. 11/3 Such phrases as..'I would have speech with thee'..may..be described as accepted stagese. **1882** *Pall Mall Gaz.* 6 Dec. 4 The rest mopping and mowing in what was not to be called English but rather stagese.

stagey, stageyness: see STAGY, STAGINESS.

stagflation (stæg'fleɪʃən). *Econ.* [Blend of STAG(NATION and IN)FLATION: cf. SLUMPFLATION.] A state of the economy in which stagnant demand is accompanied by severe inflation.

1965 I. MACLEOD *Hansard Commons* 17 Nov. 1165/1 We now have the worst of both worlds—not just inflation on the one side or stagnation on the other, but both of them together. We have a sort of 'stagflation' situation. **1971** R. BOYSON *Down with Poor* 5 The result of all this extra state interference..has been..what might be called rampant stagflation, that is to say stagnation in production and raging inflation which..destroys belief in the future. **1974** W. REES-MOGG *Reigning Error* iv. 75 So-called stagflation and slumpflation are the inevitable reflection of the progressive divergence between a rising nominal and a falling real supply of money. **1976** F. ZWEIG *New Acquisitive Society* II. xi. 137 Even recession, stagnation, 'stag-flation' or steeply rising unemployment do not rule out wage explosions. **1979** *N.Y. Rev. Bks.* 25 Oct. 44/2 Stagflation ate away at prosperity. In 1975 industrial production fell.

staggard ('stægəd). *arch.* Also 5 **stagard**, 6–7 **staggerd**, 7 **staggarde**, 9 **staggart**. [f. STAG *sb.*¹ + -ARD.]

1. A stag in its fourth year.

c **1400** *Master of Game* (MS. Digby 182) ii, þe first yere þat thei be calfede, þei be ycalle a calfe.., þe iiii. yere a stagard. *Ibid.* xxii, An hynde commonlyche hathe hir traces more holowe þenne a staggard or a stagge. **1576** TURBERV. *Venerie* 235 An hart is called the firste yeare a Calfe, the seconde a Brocket, the thirde a spayde, the fourth a Staggerd the fifth a stagge. **1782** ELPHINSTON *Martial* I. II. xxxi. 26 The staggard [L. *cervi*] champs the golden bit. **1847** MARRYAT *Childr. N. Forest* iv, A stag is called a brocket until he is three years old; at four years he is a staggart. **1859** *Todd's Cycl. Anat.* V. 517/2 At this stage he [i.e. the deer] is styled a 'staggard'. **1891** CONAN DOYLE *White Company* iii, A lordly red staggard walked daintily out from among the tree-trunks.

†**2.** A swan (? above one year old). *Obs. rare*$^{-1}$.

1619 in Coates *Reading* (1802) 59 Swans..the signetts at 4*s.* 6*d.* a-piece, and the staggards at 6*s.* a-piece.

staggard, -arth, dial. var. ff. STACK-GARTH.

stagged (stægd), *a.* [f. STAG *sb.* + -ED².] = STAG-HEADED *a.* 2.

1891 *Pall Mall Gaz.* 30 Oct. 6/3 One or two 'old stagers' are no doubt decrepit, but, inasmuch as none are 'stagged' in the branches, their vitality cannot be seriously impaired.

staggeen (stæ'gi:n). *Anglo-Irish.* [f. STAG *sb.*¹ (sense 2) + Irish *-in* dim. suffix.] A colt.

1829 G. GRIFFIN *Collegians* I. vii. 135 A parcel of ould *staggeens*, sir, that's running for a saddle, that's all the races they'll have. **1899** SOMERVILLE & ROSS *Irish R.M.* 113 Is it that little staggeen from the mountains?

stagger ('stægə(r)), *sb.*¹ [f. STAGGER *v.*]

1. a. An act of staggering; a tottering or reeling motion of the body as if about to fall, as through feebleness, tripping, giddiness or intoxication.

1600 ROWLANDS *Lett. Humours Blood* ii. 8 Thus doth Sir Launcelot in his drunken stagger, Sweare, curse, & raile, threaten, protest, and swagger. **1615** T. ADAMS *Sacrif. Thankf.* 26 Their trepidations are more shaking then cold Ague-fittes; their staggers worse then a Drunkards. **1816** J. SCOTT *Vis. Paris* Pref. (ed. 5) 38 This throne has tumbled down like rotten wood under her stagger and fall. **1842** LOVER *Handy Andy* v, Making a sloping stagger towards the wall, [he] contrived by its support to scramble his way to the door. **1862** SALA *Ship-Chandler* iv. 72 The individual..advanced with a motion that alternated between a reel and a stagger, far more resembling that of a drunken man than of a labouring ship.

transf. **1599** B. JONSON *Cynthia's Rev.* v. iv, He hobbles too much.—'Tis call'd your court-staggers, sir.

b. *fig.* (Cf. STAGGER *v.* 2.)

1601 SHAKS. *All's Well* II. iii. 170, I will throw thee from my care for euer Into the staggers, and the carelesse lapse Of youth and ignorance. **1642** D. ROGERS *Naaman* 133 The ignorance of this causes the soule to bee in as deep a stagger after Christ is revealed, as it was before. **1782** PAINE *Let. Abbé Raynal* (1791) 55 Without shewing the least stagger in their fortitude. **1869** J. EADIE *Galat.* 70 The unbelief ascribed to Peter and Thomas was a momentary stagger.

2. a. *pl.* (const. as *sing.*) Used as a name for various diseases affecting domestic animals, of which a staggering gait is a symptom. Also with various defining words, indicating the characteristics or the supposed cause of the disease, e.g. ***blind, grass, mad, sleepy, stomach staggers***. Cf. STAVER *sb.*

The staggers in sheep is caused by the presence of a hydatid (*Cœnurus*, the larva of a tapeworm) in the brain.

1577 GOOGE *Heresbach's Husb.* III. 134 If he [a bullock] haue the staggers, he wyl looke very red about the eyes. **1596** MASCALL *Bk. Cattell, Hogges* 277 For the staggars in a hog. **1628** WITHER *Brit. Rememb.* VIII. 820 Some sheep..get the staggers; some the scab. **1667** PEPYS *Diary* 18 Aug., One of our coach-horses fell sick of the staggers, so as he was ready to fall down. *a* **1722** LISLE *Husb.* (1757) 413 The long-legged hogs, as it were double-jointed at the knee, are of a breed subject to the staggers. **1737** BRACKEN *Farriery Impr.* (1757) II. 279 A sort of Frenzy, resembling the Mad-staggers. **1753** BARTLET *Gentl. Farriery* ix. 77 Farriers generally include all distempers of the head under two general denominations, viz. Staggers, and Convulsions. **1831** YOUATT *Horse* vi. (1847) 113 The attack is usually sudden—the horse is dull, lethargic, and almost as comatose as in stomach-staggers. **1843** LEFEVRE *Life Trav. Phys.* II. I. xv. 72 Three of them [horses] were seized with the staggers, and..fell down dead. **1847** W. C. L. MARTIN *Ox* 130/2 Inflammation of the brain, phrensy, mad staggers or sough (phrenitis), and apoplexy. **1849** D. J. BROWNE *Amer. Poultry Yd.* (1855) 41 A correspondent in the London Agricultural Gazette..admits, that,..he had 'never brought up but two to be a'most hens', and that they took the megrims (staggers,) and died. **1858** J. HOGG *Microsc.* II. iii. (ed. 3) 441 If a lamb is the subject of a feeding experiment with *Tænia serrata*..within a fortnight symptoms of a disease known as 'staggers' are manifested. **1860** E. MAYHEW *Horse Doctor* 7 Sleepy staggers. **1868** *Rep. U.S. Commissioner Agric.* (1869) 41 Blind staggers has been somewhat fatal in the south and west. **1883** W. ROBERTSON *Equine Med.* 382 Grass staggers. **1897** *Allbutt's Syst. Med.* II. 1106 The allied organism Cœnurus, which produces the 'gid' or 'staggers'.

b. *allusively.* ***(to have) the staggers***: inability to walk steadily.

1599 PORTER *Angry Wom. Abington* (Percy Soc.) 44 He [the butler] hath got a horses desease, namely the staggers. **1603** DEKKER *Wonderf. Yr.* Wks. (Grosart) I. 136 This setter-vp of Malt-men, being troubled with the staggers, fell into the selfe-same graue. **1608** HEYWOOD *Lucrece* I. i, Heere's a giddie world, it Reeles, it hath got the staggers. **1611** SHAKS. *Cymb.* v. v. 233. **1620** *Hic Mulier* (title-p.) Being a Medicine to cure the Coltish Disease of the Staggers in the Masculine-Feminines of our Times. **1621** J. TAYLOR (Water P.) *Motto* A 4 b, Some with the staggers, cannot stand vpright. **1688** BUNYAN *Disc. Build. Ho. God* Wks. 1853 II. 582/1 Let them but feel your pulse, and they will tell You quickly whether you are sick or well. Have you the staggers? They can help you there. **1801** SIR T. MUNRO in Gleig *Life* ix. (1849) 165 It has given me the staggers, for I often reel when I get up as if I were drunk. **1837** TENNYSON in Ld. Tennyson *Mem.* (1897) I. 159 A nervous, morbidly-irritable man..stark-spoiled with the staggers of a mis-managed imagination.

3. *dial.* and *slang.* (See quots.)

1865 'MARK TWAIN' *Screamers* (1871) 149 He would make one more stagger at it anyway. **1880** *Antrim & Down Gloss.*, *Stagger*, an attempt. **1887** I. K. FUNK in *N.Y. Voice* (Extra) 1 Sept., It is a temperance party between drinks, and it makes a stagger at temperance reform. **1895** *Funk's Stand. Dict.*, *Stagger* (Telegrapher's Slang), a guess at an illegible word in a telegram. **1900** A. MᶜILROY *By Lone Craig-Linnie Burn* iii. 30 They gave their consent to the marriage, remarking to the neighbours that 'Oor Bessie's makin' a wunnerfu' stagger'.

4. A staggered arrangement or disposition; *spec.* in *Aeronaut.*, an arrangement of the wings of a biplane such that the leading edge of the upper wing is in front of or behind that of the lower wing.

1915 W. E. DOMMETT *Aeroplanes & Airships* 104 When the wings of a biplane are set with the upper one slightly ahead of, or abaft of the other, they are said to be staggered. The stagger is measured by the angle made by the line joining the leading edges with the normal to the fore and aft axis of the aeroplane. It is convenient to call the stagger positive if the upper wing is ahead of the lower. **1919** H. SHAW *Text-Bk. Aeronaut.* iii. 58 The effect of positive stagger on a biplane is to cause the lower plane to work in a slight downdraught from the upper plane, and so decreases its angle of incidence, giving the machine greater stability. **1937** *Times* 13 Nov. 13/5 All the footmarks lay on the same straight line with no 'stagger' right or left of it. **1950** R. G. BATSON *Roads* v. 83 A stagger interrupts the passage of traffic from one branch of the minor road to the other. **1957** L. L. BECKFORD *A.B.C. of Aeronaut.* 95/2 When the upper wing is placed behind the arrangement is known as Back Stagger. **1972** *Times* 14 Nov. 15/7 The method of arranging the 'stagger' was one of the matters on which Customs and Excise consulted a wide range of trade bodies. **1980** M. BOOTH *Bad Track* i. 17 At the head of the small approach road was a T-junction... At a stagger from the slip-road was another, going down the other side to join the motorway.

5. *attrib.* **a.** *gen.*, as **stagger-bush** *U.S.*, the shrub *Andromeda mariana*, supposed to give the staggers to sheep; **stagger-grass**, 'the atamasco-lily, *Zephyranthes Atamasco*: so called as supposed to cause staggers in horses' (*Cent. Dict.* 1891); **stagger-juice** *slang*, strong drink; **stagger tuning** *Electronics*, the tuning of different stages of an amplifier to slightly different frequencies so as to broaden the overall frequency response; so **stagger-tuned** *a.*; **stagger-weed** (see quot.); **staggerwort**, the ragwort, *Senecio Jacobæa*, supposed to cure staggers in horses.

1847 DARLINGTON *Amer. Weeds* (1860) 213 *A*[*ndromeda*] *Mariana*... *Stagger-bush... The farmers..allege that it is injurious to sheep, when the leaves are eaten by them,—producing a disease called the staggers. **1905** *Chambers's Jrnl.* Oct. 730/1 A liquor labelled Scotch whisky, but commonly known as '*stagger juice'. **1907** A. MACDONALD *In Land of Pearl & Gold* 22 Lor! Boss! if we didn't drink the stagger-juice no one would. **1947** F. E. TERMAN *Radio Engin.* (ed. 3) vii. 360 The behavior of such *stagger-tuned pairs under conditions corresponding to maximal flatness..is of particular interest. **1975** D. G. FINK *Electronics Engineers' Handbk.* XIII. 57 The simple shunt-compensated stage has found extensive use in stagger-tuned pulse-amplifier applications. **1953** FOWLER & LIPPERT *Television Fund.* vi. 121 Some of the later-model TV receivers make use of a single tuned inductance between tube sections of the i-f amplifier and obtain the necessary bandwidth by means of *stagger-tuning. **1979** G. M. MILLER *Handbk. Electronic Communication* ix. 285 The problem here is..how to get a wide-enough bandwidth but still have relatively sharp falloff at the pass-hand edges. Most TV IF amps solve this problem through the use of stagger tuning. **1855** DUNGLISON *Med. Lex.*, *Staggerweed, *Delphinium*. **1597** GERARDE *Herbal* II. xxvi. 219 The countrey people do call it [*Jacobæa*] *Stagger woort, and Stauerwoort, and also Ragwoorte. **1665** LOVELL *Herbal* (ed. 2) 415 Stagger wort or Stanner wort, see Rag wort.

b. That involves the implementation of a staggered arrangement, as ***stagger hours, schedule, plan***. Cf. sense 9 b of the vb. orig. *U.S.*

1918 *Dial* 2 Nov. 369/1 'Stagger' hours have been instituted—whereby one department goes to its work a half hour earlier than another, thus relieving the congestion of the street cars. **1933** *Sun* (Baltimore) 16 Aug. 4/2 The animals would be marketed..under a system of 'stagger' shipments to prevent swamping market and packing facilities. **1943** *Ibid.* 16 Nov. 11/3 State liquor stores went on a new 'stagger' schedule of hours..with doors opening at 9 a.m. and closing at 3 p.m. **1947** *News Chron.* 11 Apr. 4/6 (*heading*) Firms favour 'stagger' plan. **1960** *Wall St. Jrnl.* 7 Apr. 8 The stagger system is election of directors in classes for various terms of office.

†'**stagger**, *sb.*² *dial. Obs.* [? Connected with STAKE *sb.*¹; but cf. STAVER.] (See quot. 1879.)

1739 TULL *Horse-hoeing Husb.* i. (1762) 5 *note*, This Witch-Elm is a very old decay'd Stump, which is here called a Staggar. **1793** *Bailiff's Diary* 13 Dec. in Miss Jackson *Shropsh. Word-bk.* 408 Began to repair our fences, which is much wanted. Bought a load of staggers from Nuttree Bank to put in barren gapes. **1879** MISS JACKSON *Shropsh. Word-bk.*, *Staggers*, strong, well-grown thorn-bushes, hollybushes, &c.,—cropped for hedgerow purposes—taken up by the roots and replanted, sometimes to make a new fence, but more frequently to fill up gaps in an old one.

stagger, *sb.*³ [f. STAG *sb.*¹ + -ER¹.] One who hunts stags; *pl.* a pack of staghounds.

1865 *Dublin Univ. Mag.* II. 19 To wind up the season with a day or two after the 'staggers'. **1894** ASTLEY *50 Years Life* I. 113 The 'Surrey staggers' always met within easy reach.

'stagger, *sb.*⁴ *slang.* [f. STAG *v.*³ + -ER¹.]

1859 *Hotten's Slang Dict.*, *Stagger*, one who looks out, or watches.

stagger ('stægə(r)), *v.* Also 6 stagar, 6–7 stager, staggar, (8 staggir). [Altered form of STACKER *v.* Cf. early mod.Flem. *staggeren* (Kilian), Du. *staggelen* to stagger, G. *staggeln* to stammer.]

I. Intransitive uses.

1. a. Of a person or animal: To sway involuntarily from side to side when trying to stand or walk erect; to totter or reel as if about to fall; to walk with a swaying movement of the body and unsteady and devious steps, as from weakness, giddiness, intoxication, or the carrying of a heavy burden. Often with adv. or phrase indicating the direction of movement.

In mod. use always implying more or less movement from the spot; formerly this notion was sometimes absent: cf. sense 3.

1530 PALSGR. 732/1 Ar you nat a shamed to staggar thus as you go by the stretes. **1598** R. BERNARD tr. *Terence, Eunuch.* II. iii. 133 He comes running to me..very crooked, staggering and stammering for age. **1600** FAIRFAX *Tasso* XII. lxxx, Thither he staggred, reeling to and froe. **1611** BIBLE *Job* xii. 25 Hee maketh them to stagger like a drunken man. **1613** PURCHAS *Pilgrimage* (1614) 282 A wounded and halfe-dead Souldier..comming staggering as it were to begge his life. **1621** J. TAYLOR (Water P.) *Praise of Beggery* C 1 b, Drinke That neuer makes men stagger, reele and winke. *c* **1730** RAMSAY *Vision* xix, Staggirrand, and swaggirrand, They stoyter hame to sleip. **1810** CRABBE *Borough* i. 286 The tippling sailor, staggering home. **1860** TYNDALL *Glac.* I. xxv. 191 He..staggered like a drunken man, and fell upon the snow. **1886** G. R. SIMS *Ring o' Bells* Prol. 3 A young woman..staggered towards the landlady, and then fell down in a swoon.

b. said of the legs or feet.

1665 BOYLE *Occas. Refl.* IV. xviii. (1848) 277 My Head began to grow giddy, and my Leggs to stagger towards the River. **1828** LYTTON *Pelham* lxv, His feet staggered as he approached us.

c. In figurative context.

1579 J. FIELD tr. *Calvin's 4 Serm.* i. 10 b, For without this, man cannot come directly to God: but they stagger & reele, not knowing which way to turne themselues. **1598** FLORIO *Dict.* Ep. Ded. 3, I haue seene the best, yea naturall Italians, not onely stagger, but euen sticke fast in the myre. **1652** BP. HALL *Height Eloquence* p. xix, Great minds in their declination stagger into Fabling. **1837** CARLYLE *Fr. Rev.* II. v. v, The thing which the King's Government did do was to stagger distractedly from contradiction to contradiction. **1860** EMERSON *Cond. Life, Worship* Wks. (Bohn) II. 397 The churches stagger backward to the mummeries of the dark ages. **1887** L. J. JENNINGS *Gladstone* iii. 93 The 'greatest of orators' had once more staggered into a war which he was impotent to conduct.

d. As the result of a blow or encounter, or of carrying a heavy load. Const. *under*, *lit.* and *fig.*

1547 BOORDE *Brev. Health* II. (1557) 6 b, Gyue that knaue or drabbe a phylyp with a club that they do stagger at it. *a* **1548** HALL *Chron., Hen. VIII*, 49 b, The duke..with the but ende of the spere strake the Almayne that he staggared. **1682** BUNYAN *Holy War* 164 For the grace, the benefit..was sudden, glorious, and so big, that they were not able without staggering to stand up under it. **1707** ADDISON *Pres. State War* ¶ 14 The enemy staggers; if you follow your blow, he falls at your feet; but if you allow him respite, he will recover his strength. **1752** FIELDING *Amelia* 44 Without use and experience, the strongest minds and bodies both will stagger under a weight which habit might render easy and even contemptible. **1759** *Ann. Reg.* 48/1 This stroke, under which he was yet staggering. **1761** HUME *Hist. Eng.* lxxi. (1806) V. 299 The..King, who was already staggering with the violent shocks which he had received. **1823** SCOTT *Quentin D.* x, The first impulse of his surprise was to free his harquebuss by a violent exertion, which made the King stagger backward into the hall. **1850** R. G. CUMMING *Hunter's Life S. Afr.* (1902) 62/2 The eland staggered for a moment, and subsided in the dust. **1863** GEO. ELIOT *Romola* (1880) II. II. ii. 25 He had staggered under the weight of the thrust. **1874** L. STEPHEN *Hours in Library* (1892) I. x. 368 The bearers stagger under the heavy coffin and cry for help. **1896** BADEN-POWELL *Matabele Campaign* xii, Finding that their horses were but staggering on under them.

e. *transf.* Of a ship: To move unsteadily and with difficulty; esp. *under* a press of sail.

1840 R. H. DANA *Bef. Mast* xxv, With as much sail as she could stagger under. **1853** KANE *Grinnell Exp.* xxiii. (1856) 184 We are staggering along under all sail. **1867** SMYTH *Sailor's Word-bk.*, *Staggering under it*, a ship's labouring under as much canvas as she can bear. **1872** BLACKIE *Lays Highl.* 9 The wherry staggered through the fretted deep. **1890** CONAN DOYLE *White Company* xvii, The cog, battered and torn and well-nigh water-logged, staggered in for this haven of refuge.

f. Of the senses: To become unsteady. *rare.*

1826 HOOD *Fairy Tale* 117 The change was quite amazing; It made her senses stagger for a minute. **1846** LANDOR *Imag. Conv., Galileo, Milton & Dominican* (1891) IV. 384 My sight staggers; the walls shake; he must be—do angels ever come hither?

†**g.** To 'stumble' or blunder *into* (a place).

1803 J. BRISTED *Pedestrian Tour* II. 518 The lady soon gave us to understand, that we had staggered into a bagnio.

2. *fig.* **a.** To begin to doubt or waver in an argument, opinion, or purpose; to become less confident or determined; to hesitate or waver *at.* Now *rare.*

1533 MORE *Answ. Poysoned Bk.* IV. viii. Wks. 1112/1 Then the disciples and apostles..must nedes haue woondered, stonned, and staggered, and haue been more inquisitiue therin then they were. **1582** N. T. (Rheims) *Matt.* xxi. 21 If you shal haue faith, and stagger not. **1593** BILSON *Govt. Christ's Ch.* 96 They..caused the strong to stagger at the truth of Paules doctrine. **1628** PRYNNE *Cens. Cozens* 40 Wee need not doubt nor stager at this Conclusion. **1634** SIR T. HERBERT *Trav.* 158 Mahomet promised them his second glorious comming after a thousand yeares, which they seriously lately looking for, and seeing themselues guld by such credulity began to stagger. **1738** J. FISHER *Inestimable Value Div. Truth* (1803) 46 They who once begin to stagger are at the next Door to Apostasy. **1837** CARLYLE *Fr. Rev.* I. IV. i, They stagger at the Double Representation, at the Vote by Head. **1883** J. GILMOUR *Mongols* xvii. 202 A Buddhist..seems to stagger at the idea of a hell to the duration of which no period is assigned.

†**b.** const. *in, about.* Also with clause. *Obs.*

1555 BONNER *Homilies* 62 No appearaunce of reason to yᵉ contrary thereof, shoulde cause vs once to doute or stagger in any part of the same. **1570–6** LAMBARDE *Peramb. Kent* (1826) 486 Of latter yeers there hath beene some strong opposition, and seeing that now at this day some doe incline, and others doe stagger therein, I [etc.]. **1603** SHAKS. *Meas. for M.* I. ii. 169 Whether the Tirranny be in his place, Or in his Eminence that fills it vp I stagger in. **1606** WOTTON in *Life & Lett.* (1907) I. 353 A..letter..which I dare not adventure by the ordinary post; and I must confess I am at the present somewhat staggering whether I shall send it by an especial messenger. **1619** HIERON *Penance for Sin* xii. Wks. II. 194 To stagger about either of which, is no little sinne. **1642** D. ROGERS *Naaman* 6, I stagger much about this opinion. **1648** GAGE *West Ind.* 1 The people should not stagger in any lawfull doubts. **1686** tr. *Chardin's Coronat. Solyman* 100 They began to stagger in their Answers.

c. of purpose, opinion, faith, etc.

1617 MORYSON *Itin.* II. 64 Seeing no reason, why the Counsels of the warre should stagger upon his wel or ill doing. **1675** *Machiavelli's Prince* vi. (Rtldg.) 40 Their faith begins to stagger. **1800** MRS. HERVEY *Mourtray Fam.* IV. 204 Lady Bingfield's opinion staggered—she felt quite bewildered. **1813** SHELLEY *Q. Mab* i. 267 At whose immensity Even soaring fancy staggers.

3. Of an army, line of battle, etc.: To waver, become unsteady, give way.

1544 BETHAM *Precepts War* I. lxv. D iv b, To succour those companyes yᵗ begynne to stagger and faynte. *a* **1660** *Contemp. Hist. Irel.* (Ir. Archæol. Soc.) I. 155 Causinge the bould enemie to stager. **1719** DE FOE *Crusoe* II. (Globe) 568 The Chineses, our Guard on the Front,..who had talk'd so big the Day before, began to stagger. **1829** [implied in STAGGERED *ppl. a.*]

4. Of a material thing: To sway or rock from side to side; to shake, rock, or swing violently; to totter.

1530 PALSGR. 731/2 This house staggareth with every wynde. **1611** BIBLE *Ps.* xcix. 1 He sitteth betweene the Cherubims, let the earth be mooued [*marg.* Hebr. stagger]. **1633** P. FLETCHER *Purple Isl.* IV. vii, Her steddy race Staggers awhile, at length flies back apace. **1652** CRASHAW *Carmen Deo Nostro* Wks. (1904) 252 When starres themselves shall stagger. **1681** WITTIE *Surv. Heavens* 11 The Earth is so firmly establisht..in its proper place, that it cannot stagger. **1851** LONGF. *Golden Leg.* i, Beneath me I can feel The great earth stagger and reel.

†**5.** To stammer or falter in speaking. (Cf. STACKER *v.* 2.) *Obs.*

1565–98 [see STAGGERING *vbl. sb.*]

II. Transitive uses.

6. a. To cause (a person or animal) to reel or totter, esp. from a blow.

1593 SHAKS. *Rich. II*, V. v. 110 That hand shall burne in neuer-quenching fire, That staggers thus my person. *c* **1611** CHAPMAN *Iliad* v. 299 It staggerd him vpon his knees, and made th' Heroe stay His strooke-blind temples on his hand, his elbow on the earth. **1749** FIELDING *Tom Jones* XVI. x, Jones was a little staggered by the blow, which came somewhat unexpectedly. **1750** CARTE *Hist. Eng.* II. 474 Eustace de Ribaumont..staggered him twice with the force of his blows. **1836** MARRYAT *Japhet* xlv, I received a blow on the head from behind, which staggered me. **1863** W. C. BALDWIN *Afr. Hunting* viii. 331 My second barrel staggered him, and in fifty yards he fell. **1872** TENNYSON *Gareth & Lynette* 530, I have stagger'd thy strong Gawain in a tilt For pastime. **1879** STEVENSON *Trav. Cevennes* (1886) 114 It was a furious windy morning..and I wandered until dinner..sorely staggered and beaten up by the gale.

b. *transf.* and *fig.*

1602 MARSTON *Antonio's Rev.* IV. i, I could not thus run mad, As one confounded in a maze of mischiefe, Staggerd, starke feld with brusing stroke of chance. **1647** LILLY *Chr. Astrol.* To Rdr. 1 That yeer which afflicts me will stagger a Monarch and Kingdome. *a* **1711** KEN *Hymnotheo* Poet. Wks. 1721 III. 327 Both with like sensual Pleasure eat their Fill, Intoxicating Mind, and staggering Will. **1822** SHELLEY *Tri. Life* 197 Then like one who with the weight Of his own words is staggered, wearily He paused. **1872** SPURGEON *Treas. Dav.* Ps. lxxv. 6 That cup of spiced wine of vengeance, one draft of which shall stagger all his foes.

7. *fig.* **a.** To bewilder, perplex, nonplus; to render helpless by a shock of amazement (or *occas.* horror). In *passive*, to be perplexed or astonished *at.*

1556 J. HEYWOOD *Sp. & Flie* lxi. 81 Spiders harts it so perst, That it stagard and stonide all that hole bend. **1613** SHAKS. *Hen. VIII*, II. iv. 212 The question did at first so stagger me,..that [etc.]. **1653** RAMESEY *Astrol. Restored* 108 It hath staggered the learnedst Writers in Divinity. *a* **1700** EVELYN *Diary* 6 Dec. 1680, The consideration of this and some other circumstances began to stagger me. **1711** ADDISON *Spect.* No. 117 ¶ 8 Sir Roger was several times staggered with the Reports that had been brought him concerning this old Woman. **1737** FIELDING *Hist. Reg.* I. i, I am a little stagger'd at the name of your piece. **1760–72** H. BROOKE *Fool of Qual.* (1809) III. 38 This last argument staggered me. **1787** MME. D'ARBLAY *Diary* 16 Feb., He was staggered by this question. **1815** J. CORMACK *Abol. Fem. Infanticide Guzerat* viii. 121 The first aspect of the difficulties..was such as might be allowed to stagger the stoutest heart. **1865** DICKENS *Mut. Fr.* I. viii, 'Well!' said Mr. Boffin a little staggered. **1883** SIR T. MARTIN *Ld. Lyndhurst* xi. 298 The Ministry were for the moment staggered by the magnitude of their defeat. **1913** SIR T. BARLOW in *Times* 7 Aug. 8/2 We are staggered by the..calculated audacity of our brethren when sinuses of the skull are drained, cerebral abscesses evacuated, [etc.].

b. To shake the stability of (a country, a condition of things).

1613–18 DANIEL *Coll. Hist. Eng.* Wks. (Grosart) IV. 198 The report of Roberts returning from the Holy warres..might be noysed abroad to stagger the State. **1656** HEYLIN *Two Journ. France* 75 She will rather choose to leave her fine house uninhabited..then give the least opportunity to stagger her greatnesse. **1657** in *Burton's Diary* (1828) II. 41 Nor would I have any man's estate to be staggered or shaken by it. **1769** ROBERTSON *Chas. V*, III. VIII. 70 Such events..soon occurred, as staggered the credit which the Protestants had given to the Emperor's declarations. **1884** *N. Amer. Rev.* Dec. 515 Then strikes and lock-outs occur, which stagger the prosperity, not of the business merely, but of the state. **1889** STEVENSON *Edinburgh* 19 A dash that staggered Scotland to the heart.

c. Phrase. *to stagger belief*: to be incredible.

1756 BURKE *Vind. Nat. Soc.* Wks. I. 30 Which shocks our humanity, and almost staggers our belief. **1796** MORSE *Amer. Geog.* I. 758 A scene of barbarity..which shocks the human mind and almost staggers belief. **1802–12** BENTHAM *Ration. Judic. Evid.* (1827) V. 555 *note*, The technical system presents..enough to stagger belief. **1837** WHITTOCK *Bk. Trades* (1842) 409 (Soap Boiler) Such matters have been introduced to the Boilers as almost 'staggered' belief.

d. To shake, unsettle, cause to waver or falter (a person's faith, opinion, purpose, etc.).

1617 FLETCHER *Valentinian* III. i, *Æcius.* I have seen enough to stagger my obedience. **1659** RUSHW. *Hist. Collect.* I. 140 The notice of a sharp Petition against Popish Recusants..did a little stagger his Resolution. **1704** TRAPP *Abra-Mule* III. i. 1194 Your good Opinion of my Truth was stagger'd E'er you knew all. **1732** BERKELEY *Serm. S.P.G.* Wks. III. 246 The prevailing torrent of Infidelity, which staggers the faith of some. **1823** SCOTT *Quentin D.* xxi, His courage was not staggered, even for an instant. **1857** MAURICE *Epist. St. John* xiii. 204 Do not let this stagger your faith.

e. To cause (a person) to falter or waver (*in* his faith or purpose).

1627 in *Crt. & Times Chas. I* (1848) I. 268 My Lord of Holland..hath been a little staggered in the resolution of his journey. **1645** CHAS. I in Ellis *Orig. Lett.* Ser. I. III. 318 It nowais staggars me in that good opinion which I have ever had of you. **1667** PEPYS *Diary* 26 Mar., The Judge..did stagger us in our hopes, so as to make us despair of the success. **1709** ADDISON *Tatler* No. 108 ¶ 4 The son..began to establish a new religion in the family..; in which he succeeded so well, that he had..staggered his eldest sister. **1746** FRANCIS tr. *Horace, Sat.* II. v. 128 Whom all the Suitors amorously strove, In vain, to stagger in her plighted Love. **1791** 'GAMBADO' *Ann. Horsem.* ix. (1809) 105, I am a good deal stagger'd in my belief, and dare not, at present, make public my opinion. **1825** SCOTT *Talism.* xv, Richard..was once more staggered in his purpose by the dauntless determination of the criminal. **1848** GALLENGA *Italy* (1851) 271 The king and his advisers were not staggered in their warlike resolution. **1849** MACAULAY *Hist. Eng.* vi. II. 92 One of his parishioners who had been staggered by the arguments of Roman Catholic theologians.

†**f.** To cause to waver or fall *from* or *into.* *Obs.*

1658 WOMOCK *Exam. Tilenus* 14 And if they be not drunk with..strong drink, they think 'tis no matter though the spirit of pride and disobedience stagger them into any schisme or heresie. **1679** *Established Test* 7 Many were recalled whom the fear of Persecution had staggered from the Romish Religion.

†**g.** To throw doubt upon (a doctrine). *Obs.*

1646 SIR T. BROWNE *Pseud. Ep.* I. x. 42 He..staggereth the immortality of the soul. **1833** LAMB *Elia* Ser. II. *Barrenness Mod. Art*, The paintings..of a modern artist, have been urged as objections to the theory of our motto. They are of a character, we confess, to stagger it.

†**h.** To bring to nought, confound (plots, counsels). *Obs.*

1629 N. CARPENTER *Achitophel* II. (1640) 69 They would have heard the Lord often threatening..to stagger the counsell of the wicked. **1683** *Lond. Gaz.* 1856/5 Hereby the Machivilian contrivances of imbitter'd, envenom'd Mal-Contents..are Providentially detected, stagger'd, [etc.].

8. To cause to waver, throw into confusion (a line or body of troops).

1721 DE FOE *Mem. Cavalier* (1840) 178 He broke through the first line, and staggered the second. **1726** SHELVOCKE *Voy. round World* 262 This unexpected warm reception staggered a great many of my men. **1775** *Ann. Reg., Hist. Europe* 134* The king's forces seem to have been unusually staggered in this attack. **1778** COOK *3rd Voy.* IV. iii. (1784) II. 331 At this they were so much staggered, that they plainly discovered their ignorance of the effect of fire-arms.

9. a. To arrange in zig-zag order, or in positions alternately on the one side and the other of a median line. (See also quot. 1902.) Also, to position (things) at successively greater distances from the straight line they would otherwise form.

1856 *Patent Office Specif.* No. 1560 The other wheel on the shaft in question (staggered with the relation to the first wheel) closes a circuit through one of the two pairs of electro-magnets which work the indicator. **1875** KNIGHT *Dict. Mech.*, *Stagger*, to set spokes in a hub so that they are alternately on the respective sides of a median line, in order to give them a broader base, and a consequently greater stiffness to the wheel against lateral strain. **1902** STURGIS *Dict. Archit.* III. 593 *Stagger* (v.), to arrange in alternate order... By extension, to dispose floors so that each one is not continuous throughout the building, but so that they are arranged in two or more vertical series, each with its own independent system of heights. **1913** J. B. BISHOP *Panama Gateway* v. vi. 381 The lamps are staggered so as to illuminate both lock chambers. **1916** H. BARBER *Aeroplane Speaks* 63 By staggering the top surface forward..it is removed from the action of the lower surface and engages undisturbed air. **1937** *Memo. Lay-out & Constr. Roads* (Min. of Transport) No. 483. 13 Where a minor road crosses a major road constructed with a single carriageway the minor road should be staggered, preferably to the left. **1959** *Listener* 6 Aug. 208/2 Then the road engineers got to work and staggered the cross-roads.

b. To arrange (holidays, times, etc.) so that they do not coincide; to arrange (an event or action) so that its implementation is spread over a period of time, or so that it is performed by different persons at different times. orig. *U.S.*

1918 *Daily Chron.* 23 Apr. 4/2 In order to maintain efficient service for industrial traffic, it is urged by the Tramways..Committee that factories and other places of business should 'stagger' their times of opening and closing. **1929** *Sun* (Baltimore) 27 Sept. 12/3 The days of rest will be staggered, one-fifth of the workers presumably laying off each twenty-four hours. **1934** *Ibid.* 3 Nov. 2/2 Omitting their national shows and staggering the introduction of new models. **1946** in P. N. S. Mansergh *Const. Rel. between Brit. & India* (1979) VIII. 211 Though the departure of officers on proportionate pension could be 'staggered', the right to retire could not be taken away. **1951** *Engineering* 7 Sept. 302/2 A scheme for staggering working hours, to ease the..load at..peak hours. **1962** E. GODFREY *Retail Selling & Organ.* xvii. 172 Many firms have found it better to stagger stock-taking, so that all departments are not disrupted at the same time. **1978** L. DAVIDSON *Chelsea Murders* III. xxi. 122 Lunch was being staggered, the six of them dashing out individually for a sandwich.

staggerd, obs. form of STAGGARD.

'staggered, *ppl. a.* [f. STAGGER *v.*]

1. In senses of the verb.

1622 MALYNES *Anc. Law-Merch.* 434 Some cannot choose to become weake in faith, staggard or desperate, when there is no man to speake a word of comfort in due season. **1829** SCOTT *Anne of G.* xxxvi, A stately form, conspicuous in the front of the staggered column, raised up the fallen banner. **1911** *Blackw. Mag.* July 19/2 There was a staggered silence.

2. *spec.* **a.** Positioned alternately on one side and the other of a line, or obliquely at successively greater distances from it; also, composed of parts so placed.

1875 KNIGHT *Dict. Mech.*, *Staggered Wheel*, one whose spokes are set in and out alternately where they enter the hub. **1905** J. HORNER *Tools Engineers* 143 The tool is of the notched, or staggered type. **1909** V. LOUGHEED *Vehicles of Air* iv. 205 (*heading*) Staggered surfaces. **1930** *Engineering* 20 June 787/2 The removal of completely assembled portions of [railway] track would be awkward in the face of the general use of staggered joints. **1937** *Times* 13 Apr. (Motor Suppl.) p. x/1 Where this is not practicable staggered crossing or roundabouts are recommended. **1947** *Highway Engineers' Ref. Bk.* IV. 122/2 On straight roads side-mounted lanterns may be arranged either opposite to each other or in a staggered arrangement. **1960** C. H. GIBBS-SMITH *Aeroplane* I. xi. 69 The Goupy had staggered biplane wings with pivoting wing-tip ailerons. **1961** F. C. AVIS *Sportsman's Gloss.* 62/2 *Staggered start*, one in a race on an oval track..where the runner in the outside lane starts apparently in front of the runner in the inside lane, but only to compensate for the greater distance of the outside lane. **1968** BATSON & PROUDLOVE *Roads* (ed. 2) iv. 67 (*caption*) Layouts of T-junctions and staggered cross-roads on 2-way and divided roads. **1978** J. A. MICHENER *Chesapeake* xi. 654 From the woods came six doves, flying low in their wonderfully staggered fashion.

b. Arranged not to coincide in time; having starting and finishing times that overlap. Cf. STAGGER *sb.* 5 b.

1932 *Sun* (Baltimore) 8 Oct. 13/7 Severely curtailed appropriations, which necessitated recourse to a 'staggered' schedule of openings. **1940** *Ann. Reg. 1939* 358 A scheme of 'staggered' hours was evolved whereby some playhouses would be allowed to keep open till ten on condition that others still kept to the six o'clock rule. **1955** *Times* 12 Aug. 5/2 'Staggered' working hours for nearly 10,000 office workers in the West End of London may be introduced to ease the peak hour travelling problem. **1980** BABSON *Dangerous to Know* iii. 15 The rest of the staff arrived at staggered hours.

staggerer ('stægərə(r)). [f. STAGGER *v.* + -ER[1].]

1. One who staggers. *lit.* and *fig.*

1552 HULOET, Staggerer, *titubator.* **1597** J. PAYNE *Royal Exch.* 17 These staggerers..do call Gods providens and his regiment over all into question. *a* **1633** G. HERBERT *Jacula Prudentum* 517 The Lame goes as farre as your staggerer. **1642** D. ROGERS *Naaman* 92 Let me abhorre to play the timeserver,..staggerer, and revolter from Gods way.

2. Something that causes one to stagger; *fig.* a disconcerting incident, an argument admitting of no reply, etc.

1832 MARRYAT *N. Forster* xlvii, That broadside was a staggerer. **1872** C. KING *Sierra Nevada* v. 98 This was something of a staggerer to Susan and her father. **1874** HARDY *Far fr. Mad. Crowd* v, He knew to a hair's breadth the rate of trotting back from the ewes' tails that each call involved, if a staggerer with the sheep-crook was to be escaped. **1909** *Truth* Christmas No. 22/2 Still staggerer followed unceasing on staggerer.

staggering ('stægərɪŋ), *vbl. sb.* [-ING[1].]

1. In intransitive senses of STAGGER *v.*

a. Reeling, tottering, etc.

1530 PALSGR. 275/1 Stageryng or leanyng of an house, *bransle.* **1580** BLUNDEVIL *Horsemanship, Horses Dis.* xxi. 10 b, Dimnesse of sight the reeling and staggering of the Horse. **1598** SHAKS. *Merry W.* III. iii. 12 Without any pause or staggering take the basket on your shoulders. **1628** DUDLEY LD. CARLETON in Ellis *Orig. Lett.* Ser. I. III. 256 In his staggering he turn'd about, uttering onely this word 'Villaine'! **1732** ARBUTHNOT *Rules of Diet* iii. (1736) 370 The immediate Forerunners of an Apoplexy are commonly a Vertigo, Staggering, Loss of Memory [etc.]. **1867** RUSKIN *Sesame* ix. §47 The howlings and staggerings of men..in intoxication.

†**b.** Stammering, faltering in speech. *Obs. rare.*

1565 COOPER *Thesaurus*, *Volubilitas linguæ*, round or quicke speakyng, without impediment or staggerynge. **1575** R. B. *Apius & Virginia* C iv, And angerly to me (quoth he) wher hast thou ben walking. Without any staggeryng, I had ready my lye. **1598** GRENEWEY *Tacitus, Ann.* (1603) 99 Tiberius..cunningly premeditating his words, and with staggering and stammering delivering his minde.

c. *fig.* Wavering, vacillating; †a state of wavering or uncertainty.

c **1555** HARPSFIELD *Divorce Hen. VIII* (Camden) 235 Mr. Rowland.., being in a great dump and staggering, came to the King. **1565** JEWEL *Repl. Harding* (1611) 279, I thinke it best..they be abolished, and put away without scruple or staggering. **1607** TOPSELL *Four-f. Beasts* 96 If the mists of raine or sand, do neuer so much obscure the way from the rider, yet doeth shee remember the same without all staggering. **1681** FLAVEL *Meth. Grace* vii. 140, I have many staggerings and doubtings about the certainty and reality of these things. **1756** BURKE *Subl. & B.* Wks. I. 195 In this staggering and hurry of the mind. **1874** T. TAYLOR *Leic. Square* ii. 35 [He] complains of the staggering and irresolution of his nature.

2. In transitive senses.

a. Causing to totter or waver; unsettling.

a **1661** FULLER *Worthies* I. xvii. (1662) 51 The same Name hath been so often disguised unto the Staggering of many, who have mistook them for different. **1675** J. OWEN *Indwelling Sin* xvi. (1732) 223 The Power that the Holy Ghost puts forth by the Word, in the staggering and conviction of Sinners. **1686** F. SPENCER tr. *Varilla's Ho. Medicis* 26 The only persons from whom he need fear a second staggering of his fortune.

b. See STAGGER *v.* 9 a. Comb. *staggering-tool.*

1905 J. HORNER *Tools Engineers* 73 The staggering of teeth is variously done. **1905** *Athenæum* 26 Aug. 280/1 His [*sc.* J. Horner's] section on chisels..leads us..to the Fox-trimmer,..and other shearing and staggering tools.

c. See STAGGER *v.* 9 b.

1955 *Times* 19 May 7/3 Difficulties had arisen by all the pool mail being received in the same week and as a result 'staggering arrangements' were made to spread the traffic. **1959** *Ann. Reg. 1958* 507 He undertook to consider whether the staggering of hours should be made compulsory. **1971** *Timber Trades Jrnl.* 14 Aug. 53/1 The reduction in productivity..due to the staggering of holidays. **1979** *Daily Tel.* 15 Dec. 2/3 The inquest had been told that the staggering procedure under which the 32 [parachute] troops left opposite doors of their Hercules had gone out of synchronisation.

'staggering, *ppl. a.* [-ING[2].]

1. That staggers, in intransitive senses of the verb.

a. *lit.* Reeling, tottering, etc.

1575 GASCOIGNE *Posies, Flowers* (1907) 43 My stagring steppes eke tell the trueth, that nature fadeth fast. **1614** GORGES *Lucan* II. 73 Not trusting to his staggering troopes. **1684** BUNYAN *Pilgr.* II. Introd. 118 For Young, for Old, for Stagg'ring, and for Stable. **1797** DOWNING *Disord. Horned Cattle* 11 This giddiness and swimming in the head..gives a wavering and staggering motion of the body. **1818** SHELLEY *Homer's Hymn Castor & P.* 16 The staggering ship. **1839** THACKERAY *Fatal Boots* vi, We heard a heavy staggering step on the flags. **1895** SCULLY *Kafir Stories* 118 A disorganised mob of staggering men.

b. *transf.* and *fig.* In early use often, †Hesitating, undecided.

1576 GASCOIGNE *Kenelworth Castle* Wks. 1910 II. 115 To prop up so thy staging mind, Which in these sorrowes slides. **1597** J. PAYNE *Royal Exch.* 18 These new Saduces wth there staggeringe disciples. **1614** EARL STIRLING *Doomsday* I. lxxxv, A staggering courage, ruine still succeeds. **1627** E. F. *Hist. Edw. II* (1680) 14 Their staggering irresolution. **1654** in *Nicholas Papers* (Camden) II. 128 Our frends are very staggering till remedy in this point confirme them. **1678** CUDWORTH *Intell. Syst.* 745 St. Austine himself, is sometimes Staggering in this Point. **1742** RICHARDSON *Pamela* IV. 95 The staggering Doubts and Distress of Hermione, after she had ingaged Orestes in the Murder of Pyrrhus. **1838** LOCKHART *Scott* lxxix. VII. 235 Except the staggering penmanship,..there was scarcely any thing to indicate decayed vigour. **1867** SMILES *Huguenots Eng.* v. (1880) 84 The sack of Antwerp..gave the last blow to the staggering industry of that great city.

†**c.** Characterized by staggering. *Obs. rare*$^{-1}$.

1573 G. HARVEY *Letter-bk.* (Camden) 29 A kind of palsi.. or sum the like quivering and staggering diseases.

d. staggering bob *dial.* (see quots.).

1776 YOUNG *Tour Irel.* (1780) II. 274 Vast numbers of calves are killed at two or three days old for an execrable veal they call staggering bob, I suppose from the animal not being old enough to stand steady on its legs. **1818** WILBRAHAM *Chesh. Gloss.*, *Staggering Bob*, or Yellow Slippers, names given by butchers to very young calves. **1922** JOYCE *Ulysses* 413 Staggering bob in the vile parlance of our lower class licensed victuallers signifies the cookable and eatable flesh of a calf newly dropped from its mother. **1966** W. S. RAMSON *Austral. Eng.* iv. 70 *Staggering bob*, a widespread dialect phrase used either of a very young calf which has not yet found its legs or of the veal from such a calf.

2. In transitive senses: Causing to reel or totter; confounding, perplexing; hence in trivial use: amazing, astounding; enormous.

1565 J. PHILLIPS *Patient Grissell* (Malone Soc.) I. 63 The wandring Bucke by staggring strocke, of launch from blody boe..hath caught the ouer throe. **1769** BURKE *Corr.* (1844) I. 176 In this staggering situation, I imagine they [the ministers] would derive great comfort..by finding [etc.]. **1815** J. SMITH *Panorama Sci. & Art* II. 73 The remark..is rather staggering, and is calculated to throw the veil of doubt over all the rest. **1836** E. HOWARD *R. Reefer* xli, By noon we had a staggering breeze. **1840** DICKENS *Old C. Shop* xiii, He found himself complimented with two staggering blows. **1894** JEAFFRESON *Recoll.* II. 28 This rumour was a painful and staggering surprise. **1900** P. C. SIMPSON *Fact of Christ* iv. (1901) 115 The idea is utterly staggering and overwhelming. **1934** J. B. PRIESTLEY *Eng. Journey* vi. 202 He still controlled this staggering array of properties, extending from remote industrial villages in Yorkshire to Shaftesbury Avenue. **1939** [see BALLY *a.* and *adv.*]. **1951** *Sport* 30 Mar.–5 Apr. 9/1 Staggering offers have been made for Twentyman, a half-back of immense promise. **1958** P. H. GIBBS *Curtains of Yesterday* iv. 53 Summoning two of his men he had the lorry filled up with a staggering amount of food—cheese, bread, bully beef, hams, tinned food. **1978** *Lancashire Life* July 55/4 Rich man though he was..the High Sheriff must have faced a staggering bill.

'staggeringly, *adv.* [f. STAGGERING *ppl. a.* + -LY[2].] In a staggering manner; unsteadily, totteringly; also (*rarely*) so as to stagger or shock; hence in trivial use, amazingly; exceedingly.

1575 GASCOIGNE *Posies, Jocasta* III. i, To stay our state that staggringly doth stand. **1682** SIR T. BROWNE *Chr. Mor.* xxx. (1716) 36 While we are but staggeringly evil, we are not left without..merciful interventions, to recal us unto our selves. **1878** 'OUIDA' *Friendship* ii, Staggeringly and audaciously impossible. **1898** B. GREGORY *Side Lights* 489 We bore up staggeringly against wind and tide. **1976** J. COOPER *Harriet* xvi. 131 She felt staggeringly untogether... She had a blinding headache. **1979** *PN Rev.* 9 60/2 It is the mark of staggeringly few of the great pulpiteers. **1979** *Guardian* 3 Nov. 11/3 What he is going to say in his six lectures..is staggeringly banal.

'staggerment. *nonce-wd.* [f. STAGGER *v.* + -MENT.] Great amazement, astonishment.

1933 J. R. R. TOLKIEN *Let.* 16 Mar., (MS.) I have actually been presented by a well-wishing old gentleman with a complete N.E.D., to my staggerment, as I had quite given up hope of possessing one. **1937** —— *Hobbit* xii. 221 To say that Bilbo's breath was taken away is no description at all. There are no words left to express his staggerment. **1975** *Church Times* 31 Jan. 11/1 As I lifted my arms for the quick frisk, I was conscious of unjournalistic feelings of staggerment. I had been through this process often enough at airports across the world, but never before, ever in a cathedral for goodness' sake.

staggery ('stægərɪ), *a. colloq.* [f. STAGGER *sb.* and *v.* + -Y.] **a.** Of an animal: Affected with staggers. **b.** Liable to stagger; unsteady.

1778 [W. H. MARSHALL] *Minutes Agric.* 15 Oct. 1776, I found an exceedingly fine breed [of swine] upon the Farm.—But they were staggery. **1837** DICKENS *Pickw.* xvi, If I felt less like a walking brandy-bottle, I shouldn't be quite so staggery this mornin'. **1892** J. WILKINS *Autobiog. Gamekeeper* 225 Before he has got a hundred yards he [the dog] begins to feel very queer and staggery. **1907** C. D. STEWART *Partners of Providence* xxxiv. 436 A tired-out looking frame building that was as staggery as its shed.

staggon: see STAG *sb.*[1] and STAGON.

staggy ('stægɪ), *sb. Sc.* In 8–9 **stagie, staggie.** [dim. of STAG *sb.*[1] + -IE, -Y.] A colt.

1786 BURNS *To Auld Mare* i, Thou could hae gaen like ony staggie Out owre the lay. **1792** G. GALLOWAY *Poems* 42 Guide honest John ride frae Kilbagie, Upon a bonny dappl'd stagie. **1803** [SIR A. BOSWELL] *Songs* 13 When ilka bit laddie maun ha'e his bit stagie. **1910** *Blackw. Mag.* Feb. 263/1 One of them is only a wee bit staggie.

staggy ('stægɪ), *a.* [f. STAG *sb.*[1] + -Y[1].]

1. a. *N.Z.* and *N. Amer.* Of an animal or its meat: having the characteristics or appearance of a mature male (see quots.).

1933 *Press* (Christchurch, N.Z.) 9 Dec. 17/8 *Stag*, imperfectly, or late castrated male sheep or steer. Hence *staggy.* **1934** WEBSTER, *Staggy*, having the appearance of a mature male animal;—said of female domestic animals. **1950** *N.Z. Jrnl. Agric.* Sept. 201/3 Complaints about the proportion of 'staggy' New Zealand wether lamb carcasses have been received recently from the United Kingdom. **1974** *Globe & Mail* (Toronto) 12 Dec. 8/2 The quality of beef within a grade can vary, depending on whether an animal is staggy or whether it weighs less than 550 pounds or more than 700. A staggy steer exhibits bull-like characteristics and has tougher meat.

b. *Austral.* (See quot.)

1891 R. WALLACE *Rural Econ. Austral. & N.Z.* i. 30 Sometimes the [potato] sets remain fresh and do not decay in the soil after the haulms have developed; they remain 'staggy' or hard and woody.

2. a. Abounding in stags. *rare.*

1921 *Blackw. Mag.* July 34/2 Very staggy ground this. Indeed, a sambur grunted in covert which we watched.

b. *fig.* Of a tree, etc.: having bare branches. Cf. STAG-HEADED *a.* 2.

1933 R. CAMPBELL *Flowering Reeds* 21 Bare trees..Down the long avenue in staggy flight Are hunted by the hungers of the gale. **1961** P. WHITE *Riders in Chariot* i. 13 Slapped by a staggy elder-bush..Whipped by the little sarsaparilla vine. **1973** —— *Eye of Storm* vii. 322 Under the staggy orange trees, amongst the hummocks, in the green haze of Noamurra.

staghe, obs. form of STAG *sb.*[1]

stag head, stag's head. [STAG *sb.*[1]]

1. The head or skull and antlers of a stag.

1812 CRABBE *Tales* iv. 176 A stag's-head crest adorn'd the pictured case. **1908** HARPER *Rambles in Galloway* II. 28 Large stag heads..have been found in the bed of the loch.

2. ***stag-head*** or ***stag's head moss*** = *stag-horn moss* (see STAG-HORN 2 b).

1869 W. CORY *Lett. & Jrnls.* (1897) 266 Picking staghead moss and flowers. **1885** LADY BRASSEY *The Trades* 234 On the banks.. daisies and buttercups,.. stag's-head moss, and all kinds of familiar wild flowers flourished.

stag-headed, *a.*

1. Of an animal: Having a head shaped somewhat like that of a stag.

1683 *Lond. Gaz.* No. 1802/4 A Chesnut Nag, 14 hands high,.. Stag-headed. **18..** *Young's Annals Agric.* XXX. 333 in Britten *Old Country Words* (1880) 110 The horn is found neither drooping too low, nor rising too high, nor with points inverted, called here [Somerset] stag-headed.

2. Of a tree or forest of trees: Having the topmost branches bare and withered.

1769 *Phil. Trans.* LIX. 28 This grove of chesnuts.. begin to decay very much at the tops, being what the woodwards term stag-headed. **1790** W. H. MARSHALL *Midland Counties* II. 441 Stagheaded, as an old overgrown oak; having the stumps of boughs standing out of its top. **1843** *Jrnl. R. Agric. Soc.* IV. II. 396 Sometimes trees, which at first were good bearers, become stag-headed and unfruitful. **1882** *Garden* 14 Jan. 27/3 Some oaks are old and stag-headed at 100 years, while others are vigorous at 300 years.

stag-horn. Also stag's horn. [STAG *sb.*[1]]

1. a. In *pl.* The horns of a stag. **b.** In *sing.* The horn of a stag, as a material.

1663 BOYLE *Consid. Usef. Nat. Philos.* II. App. 356 In case Stags Horns cannot be procured for the preparation. **1815** J. SMITH *Panorama Sci. & Art* II. 499 Stag's horn and ivory are nearly the same as bone. **1843** HOLTZAPFFEL *Turning* I. 121 When short pieces of stag-horn are used entire, as for the handles of table-knives, the hollow cellular part is concealed. **1864** J. HUNT tr. *Vogt's Lect. Man* x. 263 When the articles became scarce they provided themselves with worked staghorns.

attrib. **1858** SIMMONDS *Dict. Trade, Stag-horn cutter*, a worker up of deer horn for knife handles, etc.

c. *transf.* in *pl.* The bare upper branches of a tree. *nonce-use.* Cf. STAG-HEADED *a.* 2.

1879 BROWNING *Ned Bratts* 172 That tree art thou!.. Thy stag-horns fright the sky, thy snake-roots sting the turf!

2. In the names of plants. **a.** The American or Virginian sumach, *Rhus typhina.* More fully ***stag('s horn tree, sumach.***

1753 *Chambers' Cycl.* Suppl. App., Stag's horn-tree, a name sometimes given to the rhus, or sumach. **1797** *Encycl. Brit.* (ed. 3) XVI. 228/1 The young branches [of the Virginian sumach] are covered with a soft velvet-like down, ..from whence the common people have given it the appellation of stag's horn. **1868** *Rep. U.S. Commissioner Agric.* (1869) 201 Stag-horn sumach (*Rhus typhina*). **1882** *Garden* 19 Aug. 163/3 The Stag's-horn Sumach.. has a very singular appearance just as the flower-spikes become prominent.

b. A kind of moss, esp. *Lycopodium clavatum.* More fully ***stag's horn*** (also ***staghorn***) ***moss.***

1741 DILLENIUS *Hist. Muscorum* 310 Hypnum cupressi, forme vulgare, foliis obtusis. The blunt Cypress-like Hypnum... Hisque notus est nomine Stags-Horn Moss. **1800** WORDSW. *Idle Shepherd-boys* 19 Or with that plant which in our dale We call stag-horn, or fox's tail, Their rusty hats they trim. **1844** E. NEWMAN *Brit. Ferns* etc. 353 The Common Club-moss, Wolf's-claw, or Stag's-horn, is the only species of Lycopodium that can be spoken of as abundant in Britain. **1855** M. ARNOLD *Tristram & Iseult* III. 24 Their little hands Are busy gathering..streams Of stagshorn for their hats. **1882** *Good Words* 165 Staghorn Moss.

c. A fern of the genus *Platycerium.* (In full ***staghorn fern.***)

1882 J. SMITH *Dict. Pop. Names Plants* 390 *Staghorn Fern* is represented by several species of Platycerium. **1893** MRS. C. PRAED *Outlaw & Lawmaker* II. 32 It was covered with a wonderful growth of ferns, birdsnests, and staghorns, with branching, antler-like fronds.

d. (See quot.)

1884 W. MILLER *Plant-n.* 122 Stag's-horn Saxifrage, *Saxifraga ceratophylla.*

3. a. In the names of insects, etc. (See quots.)

1816 KIRBY & SP. *Entomol.* xxi. (1818) II. 225 The stag-horn capricorn beetle (*Prionus cervicornis*, F.) in America. **1884** GOODE *Nat. Hist. Aquatic Anim.* 841 Among the true stony corals are the Stag-horn Corals (*Madrepora cervicornis, prolifera,* and *palmata*). **1896** LYDEKKER *Roy. Nat. Hist.* VI. 72 A curious representative from the Malay Archipelago, known as the staghorn-fly (*Elaphomyia*), takes its name from the development of the sides of the head into large branching horns.

b. stag('s) horn coral, a branching coral of the genus *Acropora.*

[**1785** in G. M. Millar *New Syst. Nat. Hist.* IV. ii. 286 The coral plants.. sometimes shoot out like trees without leaves in winter;.. sometimes they are found to resemble.. the antlers of a stag, with great exactness and regularity.] **1884** R. RATHBUN in G. B. Goode *Fisheries U.S.: Nat. Hist. Aquatic Animals* I. v. 841 Among the true stony corals are the Stag-horn Corals.. and many others. **1928** RUSSELL & YONGE *Seas* vii. pl. 59 (*caption*) Stag's Horn Coral. **1977** G. DURRELL *Golden Bats & Pink Pigeons* v. 123 The predominant coral was Stag's horn,.. like a great graveyard of all the finest Victorian deer trophies, decked out in white and electric blue.

4. *Naut.* (See quot. 1961.)

1923 *Man. Seamanship* (Admiralty) II. 87 The 15-in. cordite whips.. are either taken to the motor.. or to the special staghorn for lowering. **1961** F. H. BURGESS *Dict. Sailing* 196 *Staghorn*, a metal bollard with two horizontal arms.

5. *Path.* Used *attrib.* to designate a large calculus of the kidney having the branched form of the renal pelvis that it occupies.

1910 *Lippincott's New Med. Dict.* 924/1 Stag-horn calculus. **1926** YOUNG & DAVIS *Young's Pract. Urol.* I. vi. 377 In some extreme cases the kidney is only a thin sheet of dense scar tissue in which no trace of tubules or glomeruli can be found, overlying a large stag-horn calculus. **1961** R. D. BAKER *Essent. Path.* xvii. 441 (*caption*) The large staghorn calculus is a cast of the renal pelvis and of renal calyces. **1974** J. D. MAYNARD in R. M. Kirk et al. *Surgery* viii. 161 Renal calculi may be entirely symptomless, particularly the very large staghorn type filling most of the pelvicalyceal system.

Hence **stag-horned** *a.* (*a*) Epithet of a beetle (cf. prec. 3). (*b*) = STAG-HEADED *a.* 2.

1853 MRS. GORE *Dean's Daughter* III. i. 6 The oldest of the trees;—its branches, staghorned at the summit. **1867** R. S. HAWKER *Wks.* (1893) 127 A solemn grove of stag-horned trees. **1881** *Cassell's Nat. Hist.* V. Plate 59 The Stag-horned Longicorn (*Acanthophorus serraticornis*).

staghound ('stæghaʊnd). [f. STAG *sb.*[1] + HOUND *sb.*] = DEER-HOUND.

1707 *Lond. Gaz.* No. 4322/4 Lost.., a Couple of young Stag-hounds. **1810** SCOTT *Lady of Lake* II. vi, With.. his dark stag-hounds by his side. **1893** LYDEKKER *Roy. Nat. Hist.* I. 532 The true English staghound was a considerably larger animal than the foxhound.

stagiary ('steɪdʒɪərɪ), *sb.*[1] *Eccl. Hist.* [ad. med.L. *stagiārius*, f. *stagium* term of residence of a canon, ad. OF. *estage*: see STAGE *sb.*] A canon residentiary.

1868 MILMAN *St. Paul's* vii. 149 Still more important to the Revenues of the Dean and Stagiaries, so the Residentiaries were called. **1877** W. J. LOFTIE *London* vii. (1892) 154 The 'stagiaries' or resident canons conducted the services of the church. **1881** *8th Rep. Hist. MSS. Comm.* App. 634/1, 45 Edw. III. Compotus of dom. Amand Fithing, canon and stagiary of the church of St. Paul, London.. of moneys received from the box.

stagiary ('steɪdʒɪərɪ), *sb.*[2] and *a.* [ad. F. *stagiaire*, f. (after med.L. *stagiārius*: see prec.) *stage* period of probation, esp. terms to be kept by a student before admission to the bar, ad. med.L. *stagium*, ad. OF. *estage*: see STAGE *sb.*]

a. *sb.* A French law student (see quot. 1836). **b.** *adj.* In ***stagiary school***, a school in which, according to the French law of 1850, assistants could be employed who had no certificate of capacity, but only a certificate of three years' service (F. *stage*).

1836 *Blackw. Mag.* XL. 592 The Stagiaries form societies of their own body, under the title of conferences, in which they exercise themselves in pleading imaginary cases, and in discussing questions of law. **1861** M. ARNOLD *Pop. Educ. France* 143 Few departmental councils consented to authorise any stagiary schools at all.

stagily ('steɪdʒɪlɪ), *adv.* [f. STAGY *a.* + -LY[2].] In a stagy manner.

1867 *Athenæum* 26 Oct. 542/1 Weak, because stagily antipathetic, is the figure of the mother who places her child's body among the branches of a tree. **1900** *Pall Mall Gaz.* 13 Nov. 4/2 The rather perfunctory and stagily improbable rescue of Lance Carlyon from a watery grave.

staginess ('steɪdʒɪnɪs). Also stageyness. [f. STAGY *a.* + -NESS.]

1. Stagy character or style; the quality of being stagy; theatrical mannerism.

1864 *Reader* 7 May 598 There is not a trace of staginess to be detected. **1878** JEVONS *Methods Soc. Reform* 10 The crudeness and staginess of the play need to be subdued. **1882** A. W. WARD *Dickens* vii. 206 In his earlier writings.. there is much stageyness.

2. Of a seal or its skin (see STAGY *a.* 2).

1887 H. W. ELLIOTT in G. B. Goode *Fish. Industr. U.S.* v. II. 488 These [sea-otter] skins.. never show at any season those signs of shedding and staginess so marked in the seal. **1898** D. S. JORDAN *Fur Seals* I. 66 The trouble here arises from a misunderstanding of what is meant by 'staginess'. It does not designate any marked difference in quantity of the fur.

staging ('steɪdʒɪŋ), *vbl. sb.* Also 9 stageing. [f. STAGE *sb.* and *v.* + -ING[1].]

1. *concr.* **a.** A temporary platform or structure of posts and boards for support; scaffolding. Also, *spec.* shelving for plants in a greenhouse.

1323-4 *Ely Sacr. Rolls* (1907) II. 47 In xxiij arboribus de sapin empt. pro stagyngg *2l. 8s. od.* **1390-1** in W. Hudson *Leet Jurisd. Norwich* (Selden Soc.) 70 Rogerus Smyth depredavit c latthis de Herveo Skott et maremium et stagyngg murorum Civitatis. **1521** *Bury Wills* (Camden) 122 For a beme and stagyng in yᵉ chyrche, vij s. **1835-6** P. BARLOW in *Encycl. Metrop.* (1845) VIII. 87/1 A stageing is erected about seven feet above the deck. **1842** *Niles' Reg.* LXIII. 169/2 Governor Metcalfe appeared upon a staging erected upon the capitol steps, and returned his thanks. **1883** *Law Rep. 11 Q.B. Div.* 503 He supplied and put up the staging necessary to enable the outside of the vessel to be painted and repaired when in the dock. **1884** *Manch. Exam.* 7 Oct. 5/1 At the mass meetings.. two of the stagings gave way. **1886** *Bk. Garden Managem.* 437 The great desideratum in the arrangement of staging of any kind, as far as the plants themselves are concerned, is to bring them as close to the light as possible. **1929** *Radio Times* 8 Nov. 417/2 Chrysanthemums are now displaying.. bloom under glass. .. Be careful not to spill water on the floor and staging. **1974** *Country Life* 24 Jan. 150/2 *Tulipa humilis* and crocus.. have been moved to staging in an airy, unheated greenhouse.

attrib. **1535** in Willis & Clark *Cambridge* (1886) II. 453 Oon load of stagyng tymber. **1912** *Blackw. Mag.* Sept. 354/2 The slow waters of the river, purring around the stays and staging-piles.

b. *Arch.* The stages of a buttress collectively.

1865 *Athenæum* No. 1942. 57/3 Mediæval buttresses with their stagings.

2. †**a.** The action of mounting a stage. *Obs.*

1670 EACHARD *Cont. Clergy* 39 If getting into the pulpit were a kind of staging, where nothing was to be considered, but how much the sermon takes, and how much star'd at.

b. The action, process, or art of putting a play on the stage; stage-setting.

1884 *Sat. Rev.* 12 July 48 *Twelfth Night*.. was as brilliant and well ordered a piece of staging. **1884** *Times* (weekly ed.) 26 Sept. 6/1 The staging of a play is in itself a work of true art. **1901** SKRINE *Life Sir W. W. Hunter* xviii. 380 He did full justice to the staging [of 'Faust'], which was then unsurpassed in London.

3. The business of running or managing stage-coaches; the action of travelling by stage-coach or by stages. Also *attrib.* (Chiefly *Anglo-Indian* and *U.S.*) Now *rare.*

1840 *Southern Lit. Messenger* VI. 381/2 He does not follow the sea nor staging. **1850** OGILVIE. **1854** *Househ. Words* VIII. 367/2 A Dawk bungalow, or, as it is called officially, a staging bungalow. **1864** *Harper's Mag.* Oct. 563/1 In an ancient adobe building,.. Mr. Banning carried on his staging and teaming operations. **1894** *Outing* XXIV. 399/2 Stagin' in them days, stranger, was stagin'. **1896** SIR R. TEMPLE *Story My Life* I. 29 Halting in the hot hours of daylight, generally in the solitude of staging rest-houses. **1912** *Chamb. Jrnl.* Christmas No. 18/2, I jolted along in an old *dak ghari* (staging-carriage).

4. *Astronautics.* The arrangement of stages (STAGE *sb.* 12 b) in a rocket; the separation and falling away of a stage from the remainder of the rocket when its propellant is spent.

1959 H. S. SEIFERT *Space Technol.* xix. 19 In the staging operation the uncoupling of the two sections must take place smoothly so as not to put asymmetric loads on the continuing part of the structure. **1962** D. SLAYTON in J. Glenn et al. *Into Orbit* 26 About thirty seconds after staging ..the Atlas goes over into about a 14° pitch to get you headed into the precise angle for a good orbit. **1966** H. O. RUPPE *Introd. Astronaut.* I. iii. 88 In conventional 'tandem staging' or 'series staging' each complete stage burns and separates before the next stage ignites. In parallel staging, components (engines, tanks, or stages) operate simultaneously.

5. Used *attrib.* to designate a stopping-place or assembly-point at a place intermediate between a base and a destination, as ***staging-area, -point, -post.*** orig. and chiefly *Mil.*

1945 *Amer. Speech* XX. 259 Other terms are used metaphorically: some which are particularly adaptable are ..*ration allowance, staging area.* **1971** *Fremdsprachen* XV. 45 The states in the U.S. Coastal Zone contain most of the nation's population and industry, the gateway for maritime trade of about $40 billion, the staging area for the $500 million fish and crustacean industry. **1976** *New Yorker* 24 May 29/1 Almost all the American athletes will be 'processed' at a staging area on the premises of the State University College at Plattsburgh. **1955** *Times* 25 Aug. 9/2 Egypt is the vital staging point in air routes for the reinforcing of the Far East. **1969** H. HORWOOD *Newfoundland* i. 2 The point that I had reached had once been a meeting place for Indian bands, a summer staging-point. **1952** *Times* 21 Aug. 5/6 The American base in England is one of a number of strategic strongholds developed by the S.S.A.F. since the war. There are air bases, staging posts, and other installations in widely scattered places all over the world. **1959** *Listener* 1 Jan. 8/1 Explorers have met and drunk tea at the South Pole, as if it were just any other staging post. **1970** H. TREVELYAN *Middle East in Revolution* 154 All that was left at the revolution was an R.A.F. staging post and technicians helping to train the Iraqi Forces.

‖**stagione** (sta'dʒone). *Opera* and *Ballet.* [It., lit. 'season'.] (See quot. 1978.) Freq. *attrib.* Also in *Comb.*, as ‖**stagione lirica** [lit. 'lyrical season'], the opera season of an Italian theatre.

1946 E. BLOM *Everyman's Dict. Music, Stagione*,.. the term is used esp. for an opera season. **1963** *Times* 19 Feb. 15/3 Como's Teatro Sociale.. has opened its *stagione lirica* for 1963 with a work by Verdi. *Ibid.* 20 Feb. 16/7 The *stagione* and *abonnement* system (necessitating unvaried programmes on a subscription throughout the season), while working well for opera, is hard on the ballet. **1970** *Daily Tel.* 12 Oct. 11/5 He.. examined the problems of opera in English and the 'stagione' versus repertory systems. **1978** LD. DROGHEDA *Double Harness* xxi. 289 The repertory system meant running a large number of different operas on consecutive nights, whereas *stagione* (literally 'season' in Italian) meant grouping a series of performances of one opera fairly closely together, performed with basically identical casts and conductor.

†**Sta'girian**, *a.* and *sb. Obs. rare.* In 6 **Stagyrian.** [f. L. *Stagīra*: see next and -IAN.]

a. *adj.* Of or pertaining to Stagira or to Aristotle. **b.** *sb.* = STAGIRITE.

1591 SYLVESTER *Du Bartas* I. iii. 360 The Stagyrian Sage. *Ibid.* I. vii. 651 For house-hold Rules, read not the learned Writs Of the Stagyrian (glory of good Wits). *a* **1618** —— *Sonn.* Wks. (Grosart) II. 122/1 Little needs Hee the Stagyrian's store.

Stagirite ('stædʒɪraɪt). Also 8-9 *erron.* **Stagyrite.** [ad. L. *Stagīrītēs* (also *Stagērītes*), ad. Gr. Σταγειρίτης, f. Στάγειρος, also Στάγειρα (L. *Stagīra*) neut. pl.: see -ITE.] A native or inhabitant of Stagira, a city of Macedonia; *spec.* the philosopher Aristotle, who was born there.

c **1620** T. ROBINSON *Mary Magd.* 630 Yᵉ Stagirite by water came. **1656** COWLEY *Motto* 27 Welcome, great

Stagirite, and teach me now All I was born to know. *a* **1680** BUTLER *Rem.* (1759) I. 215 The Stagyrite, unable to expound The Euripus, leapt into it, and was drown'd. **1709** POPE *Ess. Crit.* 280. **1824** BYRON *Juan* XV. xxv, No lofty wing, Plumed by Longinus or the Stagyrite.

attrib. or *adj.* **1837** CARLYLE *Fr. Rev.* II. I. iii, The *Antre de Procope* has now other questions than the Three Stagyrite Unities to settle.

¶**b.** Used for: ? An authority on poetics (compared to Aristotle). *rare*$^{-1}$.

1834 CAMPBELL *Life Mrs. Siddons* II. ix. 219 The stagyrite, Augustus Wilhelm Schlegel, wrote this diatribe on Kotzebue.

Hence ˈ**Stagirism**, the philosophy of Aristotle; † **Stagiˈritic** *a.*, of or pertaining to Aristotle.

a **1711** KEN *Hymnotheo* Poet. Wks. 1721 III. 302 A sage.. Who stagiritick Errors had imbib'd, And to the World Eternity ascrib'd. **1875** *Encycl. Brit.* I. 466/2 But in those times of false Aristotelianism the *Spagirism* of Paracelsus was pitted against the *Stagyrism* of Aristotle.

‖ˈ**stagma.** *rare*$^{-0}$. [mod.L. a. Gr. στάγμα, f. σταγ-, στάζειν to drop, distil.] (See quots.)

1681 tr. *Willis' Rem. Med. Wks.* Vocab., *Stagmas*, the mixtures of metals, or other chymical things set together to ferment and operate one upon the other. **1693** tr. *Blancard's Phys. Dict.* (ed. 2), *Stagma*, Juices of Plants mixt together in order to Distillation. **1820** R. HOOPER *Lex.-Med.* (ed. 4) 838 *Stagma*, any distilled liquor. The vitriolic acid.

stagmoid (ˈstægmɔɪd), *a.* *rare*$^{-0}$. [f. Gr. στάγμα drop (STAGMA) + -OID.] (See quot.)

1859 MAYNE *Expos. Lex.*, *Stagmoides*,...resembling a drop; stagmoid.

stagnal (ˈstægnəl), *a.* *Nat. Hist.* [f. mod.L. *stagnālis*, f. L. *stagn-um* STAGNE, STAGNUM + -AL[1].] 'Living, growing, or delighting in a pond, marsh, or fen' (Mayne *Expos. Lex.* 1859).

ˈ**stagnance.** *rare.* [see -ANCE.] = next.

1850 S. DOBELL *Roman* vii. Poet. Wks. 1875 I. 122 The stagnance of the fosse.

stagnancy (ˈstægnənsɪ). [f. STAGNANT *a.*: see -ANCY.]

1. The condition of being stagnant or without motion, flow, or circulation.

1659 HAMMOND *On Ps.* cx. 7 The stagnancy or standing still of these waters. **1665** NEDHAM *Med. Medicinæ* 410 The bloud should be preserved from Stagnancy. **1853** RUSKIN *Stones Ven.* III. i §47. 31 We would not wantonly ..stay the mountain winds into pestilential stagnancy. **1873** MORLEY *Rousseau* I. vii. 263 Suddenly heated stagnancies of the blood. **1885** J. PAYN *Luck Darrells* II. xxiv. 161 The sleepy moat, preserved from stagnancy by a thread of running stream.

b. *transf.* and *fig.*

1837 CARLYLE *Fr. Rev.* I. v. v, When the long-enthralled soul, from amid its chains and squalid stagnancy, arises. **1849** ROBERTSON *Serm.* Ser. I. ii. (1866) 19 It stirs the stagnancy of our existence. **1903** F. W. H. MYERS *Human Personality* I. 6 That unseen world appeared..as a realm of law; a region not of mere emotional vagueness or stagnancy of adoration, but of definite progress.

2. Anything stagnant.

1681 COTTON *Wond. Peak* 55 For, though the Country People are so wise To call these Rivers, they'r but Stagnancies, Left by the flood. **1699** L. WAFER *Voy.* (1729) 310 The Stagnancies and Decliuities of the ground, and the very droppings of the trees, in the wet season, afford water enough. **1818** COLERIDGE *Let. to Mrs. Gillman* Lett. (1895) 692 The number of unnecessary fish ponds and other stagnancies immediately around the house.

b. *transf.* and *fig.*

1871 CARLYLE in Mrs. Carlyle *Lett.* I. 147 Those sad currents and sad stagnancies of thought. **1902** [see PECCANCY 1].

stagnant (ˈstægnənt), *a.* [ad. L. *stagnant-em* pres. pple. of *stagnāre*: see STAGNATE *v.* Cf. F. *stagnant* (1611 Cotgr.), It. *stagnante.*]

†**1.** Of a fluid: That is at rest in a vessel. *Obs.*

1666 BOYLE *Orig. Formes & Qual.* 32 A parcel of Stagnant Quicksilver. **1719** F. HAUKSBEE *Phys. Mech. Exper.* v. (ed. 2) 101 The Orifice of that shorter Leg of such a Tube, must always be at least as far below the Surface of the stagnant Fluid, as that Height amounts to. **1721** *Phil. Trans.* XXXI. 206 The Needle so touch'd, being laid gently on the Surface of a stagnant Water, floated.

2. a. Not flowing or running, of water, air, (the ice of) a glacier or ice sheet, etc.; without motion or current, as a pool. Often involving unwholesomeness.

1669 W. SIMPSON *Hydrol. Chym.* 326 Oaken vessels..if the water..were stagnant, could not move thereon half so well. **1699** DAMPIER *Voy.* II. II. iii. 82 Alligators..remain here till the Water drains off from the Land; and then confine themselves to the stagnant Ponds. **1773** *Cook's 1st Voy.* III. xii. in Hawkesw. *Voy.* III. 723 All but Tupia fell a sacrifice to the unwholesome, stagnant, putrid air of the country. **1862** MISS BRADDON *Lady Audley* i, The stagnant well. **1872** YEATS *Techn. Hist. Comm.* 308 Experience teaches that in a small level the air and powder-smoke lie stagnant. **1880** W. MACCORMAC *Antiseptic Surg.* 100 A stagnant and impure atmosphere and other such things were observed to influence their progress. **1902** *Geol. Survey New Jersey* V. iii. 86 Such isolated bodies of ice doubtless preserved their motion..for a time. But when they became small, or when the local topography was unfavorable to motion, they became stagnant, and all the drift they held was let down on the surface as the ice melted. **1949** *Amer. Jrnl. Sci.* CCXLVII. 291 The lower 9 miles of this glacier are stagnant, but the upper part and most of the tributary ice streams are active; some receding and some advancing. **1973** R. J. PRICE *Glacial & Fluvioglacial Landforms* viii. 206 Examples of downwasting, stagnant valley glaciers are known to have existed in the Scandinavian mountains.. during the last of the Pleistocene glaciations.

b. Applied to earth holding standing water.

1851 GLENNY *Handbk. Fl. Gard.* 10 These plants [Hepatica] require a well-drained border, and never succeed well in moist or stagnant earth.

3. *fig.* Void of activity, excitement, or interest.

1749 JOHNSON *Irene* III. viii, Immur'd, and buried in perpetual Sloth, That gloomy Slumber of the stagnant Soul. **1812** CRABBE *Tales* xxi. 274 To me refer the choice [of books], and you shall find The light break in upon your stagnant mind! **1827** POLLOK *Course of Time* VI. 204 The stagnant, dull, predestinated fool. **1837** CARLYLE *Fr. Rev.* I. IV. ii, Trade is stagnant. **1883** HARDY *Dorsetsh. Labourer* in *Longm. Mag.* July 263 It is too much to expect them to remain stagnant and old-fashioned.

4. *Comb.*

1843 DICKENS *Chr. Carol* iii. 82 The very gold and silver fish..though members of a dull and stagnant-blooded race. **1857** GRINDON *Life* xx. (ed. 2) 250 New doctrines always displease the small and stagnant-souled.

Hence ˈ**stagnantly** *adv.*

1837 CARLYLE *Fr. Rev.* I. I. ii, To pine stagnantly in thick obscuration, in squalid destitution and obstruction. **1847** WEBSTER, *Stagnantly*, in a still, motionless, inactive manner.

†ˈ**stagnate,** *a.* *Obs.* [ad. L. *stagnāt-us*: see STAGNATE *v.* and -ATE[2].] = STAGNANT *a.*

1706 DE FOE *Jure Div.* v. 13 The stagnate Vapours of the Flood. *Ibid.* 30 When..the Stagnate Brain Resolves on Death, our Application's vain. **1731** T. GORDON *Tacitus, Agricola* II. 360 This Sea [the Orkneys] they report to be slow and stagnate. **1761** *Ann. Reg.*, *Charac.* 41/1 The air becomes grosser and grosser until it becomes torpid and stagnate. **1794** MARY WOLLSTONECRAFT *View Fr. Rev.* I. 520 Lazy friars are driven out of their cells as stagnate bodies that corrupt society. **1813** J. C. HOBHOUSE *Journ.* (ed. 2) 683 The ancient port of Troas, a small circular basin, half choked up and stagnate. **1818** *Ann. Reg.*, *Chron.* 570 A large pool of stagnate water. *a* **1845** HOOD *Lamia* vii. 4 Such a calm As a shipmate curses on the stagnate sea Under the torrid zone.

stagnate (ˈstægneɪt, stægˈneɪt), *v.* [f. L. *stagnāt-* ppl. stem of *stagnāre* to stagnate, to be overflowed, f. *stagn-um* pool: see -ATE[3].]

1. *intr.* To be or become stagnant; to cease to flow, to stand without motion or current.

a. of water, air, (the ice of) a glacier or ice sheet, etc.

1669 W. SIMPSON *Hydrol. Chym.* 326 Motion keeps water from stagnating. **1681** J. SCOTT *Chr. Life* I. iii. §1 (1684) 55 Their unexercised Reason will..like standing water, stagnate and gather mire. **1682** WHELER *Journ. Greece* VI. 453 We past by a Fountain, that presently seems to stagnate into the Lake of Marathon. **1691** RAY *Creation* I. (1704) 88 The Air that stagnated in the Shaft. **1769** E. BANCROFT *Guiana* 20 The water..stagnates and corrupts during those months in which the rains intermit. **1789** W. BUCHAN *Dom. Med.* (1790) 77 Wherever air stagnates long, it becomes unwholesome. **1805–6** CARY *Dante, Inf.* IX. 111 Where Rhone stagnates on the plains of Arles. *a* **1845** BARHAM *Ingol. Leg.*, *House-warming*, The valley, where stagnates Fleet Ditch. **1924** *Bull. N.Y. State Mus.* No. 251. 159 If any general cause were to operate to deprive the whole glacier of a part of its pressure head, this part would be more likely to respond by stagnating. **1968** R. W. FAIRBRIDGE *Encycl. Geomorphol.* 1045/1 A variety of landforms have been interpreted as evidence that ice stagnated and melted over large areas during its retreat from various parts of Europe and North America.

transf. **1783** CRABBE *Village* I. 271 Or wipes the tear that stagnates in his eyes. **1866** *Cornh. Mag.* Aug. 137 The tea stagnating on a small table.

b. of the blood or other liquids of the body.

a **1687** COTTON *Anacreontick* Poems (1689) 88, I am fifty Winters old, Bloud then stagnates and grows cold. **1706** PHILLIPS (ed. Kersey), To *Stagnate*, to lie still after such a manner, to want a free Course, as the Blood does, when grown too thick. **1789** W. BUCHAN *Dom. Med.* (1790) 125 By stagnating in the bladder it [urine] becomes thicker. **1818** SCOTT *Hrt. Midl.* i, Nursing their revengeful passions just to keep their blood from stagnating. **1845** BUDD *Dis. Liver* 281 When it..causes the bile to stagnate in it, by narrowing the cystic or the common duct. **1878** BRISTOWE *Th. & Pract. Med.* 115 The blood tends to accumulate and to stagnate in the capillaries and veins.

2. a. *fig.* and in figurative context.

1709 STEELE & SWIFT *Tatler* No. 68 ¶1 Without this Impulse to Fame and Reputation, our Industry would stagnate. **1756** BURKE *Subl. & B.* I. xix, Nothing tends more to the corruption of science than to suffer it to stagnate. **1799** HT. LEE *Canterb. T.*, *Frenchm. T.* (ed. 2) I. 312 The stream of life now seemed to stagnate. **1818** BYRON *Juan* Ded. xv, Its very courage stagnates to a vice. **1850** TENNYSON *In Mem.* xxvii. 11, I envy not..The heart that never plighted troth But stagnates in the weeds of sloth. **1866** G. STEPHENS *Runic Mon.* I. 16 Dialects may stagnate for centuries, or may rapidly change, according to circumstances. **1874** H. R. REYNOLDS *John Bapt.* viii. 517 The faith of the Church would have stagnated.

b. Of a person or people: To subside into a stagnant mode of existence.

1774 NICHOLLS *Let.* in *Gray's Wks.* (1843) V. 175, I wish at my return very much to run down to you before I sit down to stagnate on the bank of my lake. **1838** PRESCOTT *Ferd. & Is.* Pref. (1846) I. 15 Better be hurried forward for a season on the wings of the tempest, than stagnate in a death-like calm. **1878** LIDDON in J. O. Johnston *Life* viii. (1904) 222 Mahommedanism condemns the races which it curses to stagnate in evil. **1911** MARETT *Anthropol.* iv. 120 The net result was that, despite a very fair environment..man [in Australia] on the whole stagnated.

c. *nonce-uses.* To be delayed in transit; to pass sluggishly *along*.

1787 JEFFERSON *Writ.* (1859) II. 255, I have sometimes suspected that my letters stagnate in the post-offices. **1837** CARLYLE *Fr. Rev.* I. VII. xi, [The procession] slow; stagnating along, like a shoreless Lake, yet with a noise like Niagara, Like Babel and Bedlam.

3. a. *trans.* To cause to be or become stagnant.

1693 J. EDWARDS *Author. O. & N. Test.* I. 134 Whence gushed out an Inundation of Water, that is here stagnated, and become a filthy Lake. **1708** *Brit. Apollo* No. 89. 2/2 The Blood is in a Manner stagnated. **1745** P. THOMAS *Jrnl. Anson's Voy.* 9 The Country being so very woody that the Air must needs be stagnated. **1750** G. HUGHES *Barbados* 3 We have neither bogs nor marshes to stagnate our waters. **1801** SOUTHEY *Let. to Lieut. Southey* 28 Mar. in C. C. Southey *Life* (1850) II. 130 The one river with its rush almost stagnates the other. **1806** *Med. Jrnl.* XV. 476 In which blood..remaining stagnated in its proper vessels, did not coagulate. **1818** KEATS *Endym.* II. 954 Cruel god, Desist! or my offended mistress' nod Will stagnate all thy fountains. **1842** LOUDON *Suburb. Hort.* 68 The power which these bodies have of stopping the transmission of heat depends on the air which is stagnated in their vacuities.

b. *transf.* and *fig.*

1745 *De Foe's Eng. Tradesman* vii. (1840) I. 47 His credit, the life and blood of his trade, is stagnated. **1756** WASHINGTON *Lett.* Writ. (1889) I. 331, I am so weak-handed here, that I could not, without stagnating the public works, spare a man to these people's assistance. **1906** *Daily Chron.* 18 Oct. 4/7 There is a tendency for age to stagnate a man's initiative, invention and energy.

4. To astonish, stagger. *dial.* and *U.S.*

1784 BELKNAP *Tour to White Mts.* (1876) 16 *note*, The most romantic imagination here finds itself surprized and stagnated. **1829** BROCKETT *N.C. Gloss.* (ed. 2), *Stagnate*, to astonish. 'I'll stagnate her wi' my story'. **1864** J. C. ATKINSON *Stanton Grange* 198 It was Bob's turn to be stagnated now.

stagnated (ˈstægneɪtɪd, stægˈneɪt-), *ppl. a.* [f. STAGNATE *v.* + -ED[1].] Rendered stagnant.

1703 R. NEVE *City & C. Purchaser* 58 A stagnated Pool. **1733** W. ELLIS *Chiltern & Vale Farm.* 235 They can emit a stagnated pestiferous Vapour. **1746** W. THOMPSON *R.N. Adv.* (1757) 41 So hanging them up to be ready for salting, with the stagnated..Blood for the Salt to purge out. **1748** *Anson's Voy.* II. v. 183 Tainted or stagnated air..is often produced by the continuance of great heats. **1805** LOUDON *Improv. Hot-Houses* 74 Heat passes..through wool or stagnated air more slowly than through any other body. **1846** J. BAXTER *Libr. Pract. Agric.* (ed. 4) II. 75 This method sets the stagnated bed in a fermentation, which makes the moisture run out of it. **1873** RALFE *Phys. Chem.* 103 Owing to the escape of the free carbonic acid..from the stagnated fluids of the part, the calcium salt is precipitated.

ˈ**stagnatile**, *a.* ? *Obs. rare.* [ad. late L. *stagnātilis* (Plinius Valerianus), f. L. *stagn-um* pool.] Of a bird: Stagnicolous.

1829 GRIFFITH tr. *Cuvier's Anim. Kingd.* VIII. 387 Stagnatile Snipe... *Totanus Stagnatilis.*

stagnating (ˈstægneɪtɪŋ, stægˈneɪtɪŋ), *ppl. a.* [f. STAGNATE *v.* + -ING[2].] Becoming or remaining stagnant.

1678–9 NEWTON *Let.* 28 Feb. in Birch *Life Boyle* (1744) 235 The cause of filtration, and of the rising of water in small glass pipes above the surface of the stagnating water they are dipped into. **1707** FLOYER *Physic. Pulse-Watch* 16 It gives that motion to the stagnating Blood which shakes the Artery and distends it. **1715** DESAGULIERS *Fires Impr.* 136 The.. unwholsomness of stagnating and vitiated Air. **1891** *Nature* 20 Aug. 370/2 A moory soil with stagnating and high-standing ground water. **1897** *Allbutt's Syst. Med.* IV. 35 In stagnating bile the bile salts were apt to undergo decomposition.

b. *fig.*

1837 CARLYLE *Fr. Rev.* II. I. i, Some sharpness of temper, spurting at times from a stagnating character. **1848** GALLENGA *Italy* I. pp. xxxii, The stagnating age that preceded the French revolution. **1905** A. I. SHAND *Days of Past* iii. 37 The dead-alive towns of stagnating Germany.

stagnation (stægˈneɪʃən). [f. STAGNATE *v.*: see -ATION.]

1. The condition of being stagnant; an instance of this. **a.** of water, ice or air.

1665 NEDHAM *Med. Medicinæ* 267 The Liquor is vindicated from Putrefaction, and Stagnation, that is to say, defect of motion. **1671** BOYLE *Three Tracts* III. 16 Sometimes at the Bottom of the Deep waters there seem'd to be a stagnation of the Sea for a great depth. *a* **1677** BARROW *Serm.* Wks. 1686 III. 205 If the water runneth, it holdeth clear, sweet, and fresh; but stagnation turneth it into a noisome puddle. **1702** SAVERY *Miner's Fr.* 74 Stagnation of air is the sole cause of this Inconvenience in Mines. **1783** JUSTAMOND tr. *Raynal's Hist. Indies* VIII. 82 A plain parcelled out and cut into channels by the stagnations of a small gulph, upon the slope of a low land. **1797** R. HERON *Scotland Descr.* 5 Some of them [i.e. the lakes] are formed by the stagnation of rivers in particular parts of their course. **1829** *Chapters Phys. Sci.* xiv. 147 Hydrostatics..denotes that science which treats of the mechanical properties of all fluids, considered more especially in a state of stagnation. **1844** H. STEPHENS *Bk. Farm* I. 518 The chief injury now sustained by the soil of Scotland arises from the stagnation of rain-water upon an impervious subsoil. **1929** *Geogr. Rev.* XIX. 256 (*heading*) The stagnation and dissipation of the last ice sheet. **1943** *Amer. Jrnl. Sci.* CCXLI. 97 When the ice finally disappeared, the gravel blanket..would be let down to form kames and hummocky gravel deposits such as have commonly been taken as indicators of general ice stagnation. **1973** R. J. PRICE *Glacial & Fluvioglacial Landforms* viii. 207 When stagnation of a valley glacier occurs, glacial erosion ceases.

transf. **1834** MARRYAT *P. Simple* xlvi, There appeared a total stagnation in the elements. **1913** *Times* 7 Aug. 8/4 The chances of the stagnation among the teeth of cereal food are enormous... Where coarse stagnation only was possible caries was far less frequent.

b. *Phys.* of blood, sap, etc. in a living body.
1707 FLOYER *Physic. Pulse-Watch* 65 They are subject to a Stagnation of Blood. **1816** T. A. KNIGHT in *Trans. Horticult. Soc.* II. 200 The stagnation in the branches and stock of a portion of that sap, which [etc.]. **1876** tr. *Wagner's Gen. Pathol.* 193 The causes of thrombosis consist either in stagnation of the blood, or in changes in the wall of the vessel.
attrib. **1899** *Allbutt's Syst. Med.* VI. 167 Thrombi attributed to slowing of the blood current..are called stagnation-thrombi.

2. *fig.* Unhealthy absence of activity, energy, etc. Also *spec.* in *Econ.*, an absence or low rate of growth.
1711 STEELE *Spect.* No. 260 ¶1 The Decay of my Faculties is a Stagnation of my Life. **1732** in *10th Rep. Hist. MSS. Comm.* App. I. 249 There will be a kind of Stagnation of all Business. **1798** SOPHIA LEE *Canterb. T., Yng. Lady's T.* II. 448 Such a collection of books as secured the mind from stagnation. **1869** TOZER *Highl. Turkey* I. 359 In an empire like Turkey..we see everywhere—neglect, stagnation, and decay. **1907** *Verney Mem.* I. 441 The dulness and stagnation of a French country town. **1938** A. H. HANSEN *Full Recovery or Stagnation* xx. 319 It ought to appear incongruous..to follow a chapter on secular stagnation with one on inflation. *Ibid.*, Paradoxical though it be, the more we sink into deep stagnation with vast unemployment of labor and resources, the more imminent is the danger of inflation. **1965** J. L. HANSON *Dict. Econ. & Commerce* 362/2 *Stagnation thesis*, the belief that in advanced economies saving might be so great as to make the maintenance of full employment difficult. **1972** *Oxf. Univ. Gaz.* CII. Suppl. No. 7 p. 4 Whereas the adoption of the I.M.F. prescriptions had apparently led to stagnation in Argentina. **1974** M. B. BROWN *Economics of Imperialism* ix. 224 Concentration..would be discouraged in periods of rapid economic growth and encouraged during stagnation or slump.

3. *Comb.* **stagnation point** *Aeronaut.*, a point on the leading edge of a moving aerofoil at which the air is at rest relative to the aerofoil.
1926 H. GLAUERT *Elements Aerofoil & Airscrew Theory* ii. 14 Consider first the pressure which occurs at a stagnation point, where the fluid is brought to rest at the nose of the body. **1955** *Sci. Amer.* Oct. 126/3 At what is called the 'stagnation' point, just in front of the model, the streamline splits in two, one half flowing around each side of the obstruction. **1979** BERTIN & SMITH *Aerodynamics for Engin.* vii. 269 We see that the temperature of the air at the stagnation point is sufficiently high that we could not use an aluminum structure.

stagnationist (stæg'neɪʃənɪst), *a.* and *sb.* Chiefly *Econ.* [f. STAGNATION + -IST.]
A. *adj.* Characterized by stagnation; promoting stagnation. **B.** *sb.* One who advocates or forecasts stagnation.
1951 A. KOESTLER *Age of Longing* v. 103 After some twenty million factory workers..had sent in resolutions calling for death to the 'stagnationist vermin', Edwards published another book. **1958** *Listener* 10 July 57/2 Mr. Nicholson..joins the ranks of the 'stagnationists'—those who would preserve forms when the functions have decayed. **1964** *Economist* 25 July 332/1 Consumption has moved into a stagnationist stage of the cycle. **1972** HUNT & SHERMAN *Economics* I. vi. 84 Marx..was not a 'stagnationist'—that is, he did not believe capitalism would suffer one long depression or that mass unemployment at high levels would last forever.

stagnator. *nonce-wd.* [f. STAGNATE *v.* + -OR.] One who denies the motion (of the earth).
1863 DE MORGAN in *Athenæum* 10 Oct. 467/3 Any squarer of the circle,..constructor of perpetual motion, subverter of gravitation, stagnator of the Earth, builder of the universe, &c.

stagnatory (stæg'neɪtərɪ), *a. Path.* [f. STAGNATE *v.*: see -ORY.] Produced by stagnation of the circulation.
1899 *Allbutt's Syst. Med.* VIII. 461 Hyperæmia is divided into two classes, congestive hyperæmia or erythema, and stagnatory hyperæmia or cyanosis. *Ibid.* 663 Unna.. classifies it [i.e. fœtal ichthyosis] among 'stagnatory tumours'.

stagnature. *nonce-wd.* [f. STAGNATE *v.* + -URE.] The state or condition of being stagnant.
1837 LOFFT *Self-formation* I. 122 You will find..his paper covered..with scratches, and blotches, and ink-puddles, signifying, by no obscure type, the coagulation and stagnature of his thoughts. *Ibid.* II. 106 Albeit the spirit may drag back and sink in stagnature.

†**stagne**, *sb. Obs.* [a refashioning of *stang*, STANK *sb.*, after L. *stagnum* pond. Cf. OF. *stagne* (one example in Godef.).] A pond, esp. a fish-pond; also, a weir or dam. = STANK *sb.*
c **1470** HARDING *Chron.* IV. iii, They gatte eche daye with nettes,..The fyshe in stagnes. **1471** CAXTON *Recuyell* (Sommer) 38 Menerue..shewid her self in this tyme by the stagne or riuer callid triton by the gretenes and subtilte of her engyne. **1483** —— *Golden Leg., St. Andrew* 83 b/2 After thys he called them the seconde tyme by the stagne of genezareth, whyche is named the see of galylee. **1512** *Helyas* in Thoms *Prose Rom.* (1828) III. 50 He arived nigh to a stagne or ponde where as he sawe vi. fayre swannes. **1562** *Act 5 Eliz.* c. 21 §1 Noblemen..have..made..Pooles, Stagnes, Stewis, Motes, Pittes or Pondes for thonelye encrease of Fishe. **1627** H. BURTON *Baiting of Pope's Bull* To Rdr. 4 Becomming as a stagne or pond, not stirring, for feare of discovering mine owne filth. **1636** *5th Rep. Hist. MSS. Comm.* 419/2 Bulkley..and Cheadle..have stayed and diuerted the said river by means of a stagne, placed across and athwart the stream. **1867** SMYTH *Sailor's Word-bk.*, *Stagnes*, a statute term for pools of standing water.

†**stagne**, *v. Obs. rare*⁻¹. [ad. L. *stagnāre* to STAGNATE.] *intr.* To form a pool.
a **1552** LELAND *Itin.* (1769) V. 90 Thes Pooles for the most part in Morisch Groundes..dreane the moist Places about them, and so having no Place to issue owt stagne there.

stagnicolous (stæg'nɪkələs), *a.* [f. mod.L. *stagnicol-us* (f. L. *stagn-um* pool + *col-ĕre* to inhabit) + -OUS.] Of a bird: Living in or inhabiting stagnant water.
1891 in *Century Dict.*; and in later Dicts.

†'**stagnize**, *v. Obs. rare*⁻¹. [f. L. *stagn-um* pool: see -IZE.] *trans.* To render stagnant: = STAGNATE *v.* 3.
1694 I. TURNER in *Phil. Trans.* XVIII. 16 The Blood in the Abdominal Vessels, had been stagniz'd for some time past.

‖'**stagnum.** *Obs. rare.* [mod.L. use of L. *stagnum* pool.] The mercury-cistern of a barometer.
1705 ADDISON *Italy, Antiq. near Naples* 232, I borrow'd a Weather-glass, and so fix'd it in the Grotto, that the *Stagnum* was wholly cover'd with the vapour. *a* **1734** NORTH *Life Ld. Keeper Guilford* (1742) 293 This must draw down the Tube into the Stagnum, till so much of the Glass Tube is immersed, as shall answer that Encrease of Weight.

†'**stagon, 'staggon.** *Obs. rare.* [a. late OE. *staggon* (12th c.) accusative of **stacga* STAG *sb.*[1] Treated as mod. Eng. by Harrison and later writers.] A stag or staggard.
[**1577** HARRISON *England* III. vii. 108 b/1 in *Holinshed*, The male of the red Deare was sometime called among the Saxons a staggon.] **1587** *Ibid.* III. iv. 226/1 In examining the condition of our red deere, I find that the yoong male is called in the first yeere a calfe..the fourth a stagon or stag.

'**stagship.** *nonce-wd.* [f. STAG *sb.*[1] + -SHIP.] The condition, dignity or state of being a stag.
1899 *Academy* 7 Oct. 375/2 From his [a red deer's] baby calfhood up to the later years of the proud stagship.

stagy, stagey ('steɪdʒɪ), *a.* [f. STAGE *sb.* + -Y.]
1. Of or pertaining to the stage; theatrical in appearance, manner, style, etc. (Chiefly in a depreciatory sense.) **a.** Resembling that used on the stage; dramatically artificial or exaggerated.
1860 *All Year Round* No. 71. 496 The foot-light air and stagey look which clings to the person of even the first tenor. **1862** F. W. ROBINSON *Owen* I. iii. 74 The woman..came hastily forth, and flung up both arms in rather a stagy manner. **1865** MEREDITH *Rhonda Fleming* xxii, He fooled and frowned like a stage hero in stagey heroics. **1882** J. C. MORISON *Macaulay* iv. 118 The stagey declamation which Macaulay has put into the mouth of Virginius.
b. Of a person: Given to the use or affectation of theatrical mannerisms in everyday affairs.
1864 F. W. ROBINSON *Mattie* III. 230 The Italian doctor was a man with a love of effect, one of those stagey beings whom we meet..more often on the Continent. **1870** LONGF. in *Life* (1891) III. 144 Lunched with Fields, to meet Fechter, the tragedian,—an agreeable man, and not at all stagey.
c. Of or pertaining to the stage. *rare.*
1895 MARIE CORELLI *Sorrows of Satan* xxx, Your place was the stage, Madam!.. You would have..had as many lovers, stagey and private as you pleased.
2. Of a seal or its skin: Out of condition from undergoing the change of coat.
1885 *Times* 22 May 3/3, 183 Japanese 'stagey' or immature seal skins. **1898** D. S. JORDAN *Fur Seals* I. 65 The stagy season. Between the middle of August and the middle of October the adult animals shed their hair and get a new coat. During this season the skins of seals are said to be stagy, and they are not taken on land... It has been held by those interested that no stagy seals were found at sea.

Stagyrite, erroneous form of STAGIRITE.

‖**Stahlhelm** ('ʃtaːlhɛlm). [Ger., lit. 'steel helmet'.] The Steel Helmet organization. Also *attrib.* Hence '**Stahlhelmer**, a member of this organization. See STEEL HELMET.
1927 *Daily Tel.* 16 Aug. 10/6 The Stahlhelm's boast that it mustered 80,000 members was grossly exaggerated. **1927** *Times* 29 Nov. 15/5 The Stahlhelm organization of ex-soldiers. **1928** *Times* 4 June 13/2 It is the Stahlhelmers' boast that they embody the traditions of the old Army. **1930** [see MINORITY 3 b]. **1934** *New Republic* 18 July 249/2 The *Stahlhelm*, the Steel Helmets, is a voluntary organization of khaki-uniformed veterans..tending..to be brought into semi-official relationship with the Nazi party. **1978** W. FEST *Dict. German Hist.* 150 *Stahlhelm*, association of ex-servicemen founded on 29 Dec. 1918... The Stahlhelm was anti-republican and from the late twenties it became militant in its demand for an authoritarian government... In 1934 it was converted into a 'National Socialist front-line fighters' union', but dissensions with the new Nazi members led to its dissolution in 1935.

Stahlian ('stɑːlɪən), *a.* and *sb.* [f. the name of G. E. *Stahl*, a German chemist 1660–1734 + -IAN.]
A. *adj.* Pertaining to Stahl or his doctrines.
a **1790** CULLEN *Wks.* (1827) I. 405 The Stahlian principle. *Ibid.* 406 The Stahlian system. **1822-9** *Good's Study Med.* (ed. 3) II. 71 Hoffman..omitted the metaphysical part of the Stahlian hypothesis. **1832** J. THOMSON *Life* etc. *Cullen* I. 179 The Stahlian practice.
B. *sb.* A follower of Stahl; an animist.
a **1790** CULLEN *Wks.* (1827) I. 22, I am equally remote from the materialists on the one hand, and the Stahlians on the other. **1839** *Hooper's Lex. Med.* (ed. 7) 1217 The Stahlians are also called Animists, and their school is called the Dynamic school. **1876** F. H. BUTLER in *Encycl. Brit.* V. 461/1 The Stahlians, however, met the difficulty by declaring that substance [phlogiston] to be the principle of levity or negative weight.

Stahlianism ('stɑːlɪənɪz(ə)m). *rare.* [f. prec. + -ISM.] The theory of vital action and of disease propounded by Stahl, animism.
1855 DUNGLISON *Med. Lex.*, *Stahlianism*, the doctrine of Stahl, which considered every vital action under the direction and presidency of the soul.

Stahlism ('stɑːlɪz(ə)m). *rare.* [f. *Stahl* (see STAHLIAN) + -ISM.] = prec.
1891 in *Century Dict.*

staid (steɪd), *a.* Forms: 6 sta(i)de, (steyed), 6-7 **staied, stayd,** 6-9 **staid, stayed.** [Adjectival use of *stayed*, pa. pple. of STAY *v.*]
1. Of beliefs, institutions, etc.: Fixed, permanent; settled, unchanging. Of a person's gaze: Fixed, set. Now *rare.*
1541 COPLAND *Guydon's Quest. Cyrurg.* Q iv, Than beholde..yf his [the lazar's] loke be steyed and horryble [orig. *aspectus fixus & horribilis*]. **1559** FECKNAM in Strype *Ann. Ref.* App. IX. (1709) I. 24 Your Honours must observe which of bothe these is the most stayed Religion, and allwayes forthe one, and agreeable with it self. **1584** POWEL *Lloyd's Cambria* 20 This was a troublesome time and as yet no staied government established in Wales. **1611** SPEED *Hist. Gt. Brit.* IX. iii. §2 The variable inclination of his owne mind carryed his actions past the limits of any stayed compasse. **1863** COWDEN CLARKE *Shaks. Char.* xvi. 393 His staid opinion. **1867** MACGREGOR *Voy. Alone* (1868) 38 That staid glazy eye which a hard-worked seaman generally has.
b. Of persons: Settled in faith, purpose, etc. ? *Obs.*
1631 WEEVER *Anc. Funeral Mon.* 104 So stayed in sacred resolutions as was Henry the fourth. **1812** CARY *Dante, Parad.* v. 73 Be ye more staid, O Christians! not like feather, by each wind Removeable.
2. Settled in character; of grave or sedate deportment; dignified and serious in demeanour or conduct; free from flightiness or caprice.
a. of a person, his actions, attributes, etc.
1557 NORTH *Gueuara's Diall Pr.* Ded. A j, By his stayed life God hath bene glorified. **1574** HELLOWES *Gueuara's Fam. Epist.* (1577) 285 A physician that is learned, wise, stayed, and of experience. **1579** SPENSER *Sheph. Cal.* June 38 But ryper age such pleasures doth reproue, My fancye eke from former follies moue To stayed steps. **1620** SHELTON *Don Quixote* II. xlii. 273 Hee..with a stayed voyce [orig. *con reposada voz*] said: I giue infinite thankes, friend Sancho, that [etc.]. **1638** BP. MOUNTAGUE *Art. Enq. Norwich* B 1 b, For his person and deportment, is he [your Minister] stayed, grave, humble, modest [etc.]? **1709** STEELE *Tatler* No. 61 ¶4 Not that she is against a more stay'd Conduct in others. **1756** WESLEY *Wks.* (1872) II. 360 The whole congregation appeared stayed and solid. **1807** CRABBE *Par. Reg.* I. 528 On widow fair and staid, He fixed his eye. *a* **1834** LAMB *Good Clerk* Misc. Wks. (1871) 386 His whole deportment is staid, modest, and civil. **1864** TENNYSON *En. Arden* 112 A grave and staid God-fearing man.
Comb. **1872** C. GIBBON *For King* iii, There spoke a lover, and not a staid-minded husband.
b. of things personified, their attributes, etc.
1622 DRAYTON *Poly-olb.* xxii. 18 Ouze hauing Ouleney past, From her first stayder course immediately doth gad. **1632** MILTON *Penseroso* 16 Ore laid with black staid Wisdoms hue. *a* **1839** PRAED *Poems* (1864) II. 335 Staid Order, gentle Peace, Twin-born of Justice, smiled.
c. of animals.
1618 BARET *Horsemanship* I. 13 There must be a time to reforme the will of the Horse, and after that to giue him a stayed body, and an euen carriage of the same. **1655** FULLER *Ch. Hist.* VI. 289 Thus husbandmen couple young colts with staid horses, that both together may draw the better. **1823** SCOTT *Quentin D.* ix, A staid and quiet palfrey.
d. Characterized by or indicating sedateness.
1567 DRANT *Horace, Art Poetry* A viij b, The stade Spondeus foote [*spondeos stabilis*]. **1820** L. HUNT *Indicator* No. 19 Prudence..Humanized into Pru. We suspect that these prodigiously staid names are apt to overshoot themselves, and disgust the possessor. **1865** LE FANU *Guy Deverell* xl. II. 169 Monsieur Varbarriere entered the staid mansion.
3. Of the intellect and intellectual operations: Sober, steady, well-regulated; free from extravagance or caprice.
1555 HOOPER in Coverdale *Lett. Martyrs* (1564) 160 Such as be of a right and stayed iudgement. *a* **1568** ASCHAM *Scholem.* II. (Arb.) 110 This exercise may bring moch profite to ripe heads, and stayd iudgementes. **1664** FLECKNOE *Discourse Engl. Stage* G 6, Wit being an exuberant thing.. but Judgement a stayed, and reposed thing. *a* **1676** HALE *Prim. Orig. Man.* I. ii. 57 Deliberation; a staid and attentive consideration of things to be known. **1870** J. BRUCE *Gideon* xiv. 246 A staid and considerate understanding.

staid, Sc. f. STADE; pa. t. and pple. of STAY *v.*

staidlin, variant of STADDLING *dial.*

staidly ('steɪdlɪ), *adv. rare.* [f. STAID *a.* + -LY[2].] In a staid manner; †constantly, fixedly (*obs.*); sedately, soberly.
1571 GOLDING *Calvin on Ps.* xxiii. 1. 85 Scarce the hundreth man keepeth himself stayedly in the feare of God. **1620** SHELTON *Don Quixote* II. xliii. 279 Walke softly, and speak stayedly. **1621** FLETCHER *Wild-Goose Chase* IV. ii, *Bel.* 'Tis well ye have manners: That Court'sie again, and hold your Countenance stai'dly; That look's too light. **1846** LANDOR *Exam. Shaks.* Wks. II. 263 His worship did look thereupon most staidly.

staidness ('steɪdnɪs). [f. STAID *a.* + -NESS.] The quality or fact of being staid (see the adj.)

1. Stability, permanence, constancy.

1553 GRIMALDE *Cicero's Offices* I. (1558) 57 b, Wherof comes a great presumption that they haue no staiednesse. **1581** PETTIE tr. *Guazzo's Civ. Conv.* II. (1586) 95 b, Her stayednesse in sticking to her friends. **1594** T. B. *La Primaud. Fr. Acad.* II. 155 This facultie of the fantasie is.. so farre from stayednes, that euen in the time of sleep it hardly taketh any rest. **1613** J. DAVIES (Heref.) *Muse's Tears* Wks. (Grosart) I. 13/2 Good Kings are least alone, when most alone; For stilnesse is the staidnesse of their Throne. **1631** LENTON *Charact.* G 12, He is a man of no staidnesse, for he leaues a Rocke to build vpon the Sand. **1661** GLANVILL *Van. Dogm.* 111 That serenity and fixed stayedness, which is necessary to so seuere an intentness. **1710** PRIDEAUX *Orig. Tithes* App. *Reasons for Bill* 8 Before they have.. stayedness of Mind to withstand Temptations.

2. Sobriety of character, manner, or conduct.

1561 HOBY tr. *Castiglione's Courtier* Yy 4 b, Staidenesse, noble courage [etc.]. **1571** GOLDING *Calvin on Ps.* xviii. 26. 62 His accustomed stayednesse. **1626** MIDDLETON *Anything for Quiet Life* I. i. 46 A matron's sober staidness in her eye. **1650** R. STAPYLTON *Strada's Low C. Wars* I. 19 His dexterity of wit, and staiedness of judgement, far riper then his years. **1685** CROWNE *Sir C. Nice* I. 5 Will you never learn staidness and gravity? *a* **1720** SEWEL *Hist. Quakers* (1795) I. 11 Endued with a gravity and staidness of mind, that is seldom seen in children. **1825** MRS. SHERWOOD *Old Times* I. 11 It compelled her to observe a stayedness of manner. **1842** BROWNING *In Gondola* 132 Where's a trace Of the staidness and reserve.. In the same child's playing-face? **1884** MAY CROMMELIN *Brown-Eyes* iv. 42 A sweet staidness noticeable in all the women of Marken.

staie, obs. form of STAY *sb.* and *v.*

staig, staige, Sc. and north. forms of STAG *sb.*[1]

staigh(e, obs. forms of STAY *sb.*

staik, Sc. form of STAKE *sb.* and *v.*

stail(e, variant forms of STALE *sb. dial.* handle.

stail(l, Sc. variant forms of STALE *sb.* and *v.*

staill, Sc. var. STALL *sb.*[4], obs. Sc. f. STELL *v.*

stain (steɪn), *sb.* Also 6–7 **staine, stayne,** 7 **steine, steigne.** [f. STAIN *v.*]

†**1.** The action of staining; pollution, disgrace.

1563 GOOGE *Cupido* Eglogs etc. (Arb.) 114 Vnhappy wretche that wolde Haue forced the Ladye of this forte with stayne of Royaltie To haue consented to his wyll in fylthye Lecherye. **1587** GREENE *Euphues* Wks. (Grosart) VI. 174 The staine of the one did ad a disgrace to the glorie of the other. **1607** SHAKS. *Timon* v. i. 176 Giuing our holy Virgins to the staine Of contumelious, beastly.. warre.

2. a. A discoloration produced by absorption of or contact with foreign matter; usually, one that penetrates below the surface and is not easily removable.

1583 L. M[ASCALL] *Prof. Bk.* 12 A good way to helpe all staynes in thinne silkes and woollen clothe. **1592** *Arden of Feversham* II. ii. 113 Seest thou this goare that cleaueth to my face? From hence nere will I wash this bloody staine, Til Ardens hart be panting in my hand. **1592** SHAKS. *Rom. & Jul.* II. iii. 75 Lo here vpon thy cheeke the staine doth sit, Of an old teare that is not washt off yet. *c* **1610** BEAUM. & FL. *Philaster* v. i. [iii], May their false lights.. discover presses, holes, stains, and oldness in their Stuffs. **1687** A. LOVELL *Thevenot's Trav.* I. 53 If by mischance Wine should be shed upon their cloaths, the greatest Drunkard that is, endeavours to get out the stain. **1798** FERRIAR *Illustr. Sterne* iii. 57 He should produce the portrait.. with all the stains and mouldiness of the last century. **1849** CUPPLES *Green Hand* xx. (1856) 193 Rusty stains at her hawse-holes. **1856** 'STONEHENGE' *Brit. Rural Sports* I. I. i. §4. 4/2 The coops ought to be moved daily, as the stain of the birds is injurious to them. **1877** 'RITA' *Vivienne* II. iii, I have not even waited to remove the stains and dust of my long journey before coming to see you.

b. A mark or discoloration on the skin; a blotch or sore.

1595 SHAKS. *John* III. i. 45 If thou.. wert grim Vgly.. Full of vnpleasing blots, and sightlesse staines,.. Patch'd with foule Moles.. I would not care. **1611** —— *Cymb.* II. iv. 139 You do remember This staine [a mole] vpon her? **1819** SHELLEY *Cenci* IV. i. 130 Let her food be Poison, until she be encrusted round With leprous stains! **1845** BUDD *Dis. Liver* 144 This [jaundice] had lessened a good deal, but there was still a light yellow stain of the skin. **1898** J. HUTCHINSON in *Arch. Surg.* IX. 334, I make him undress, and find him covered on limbs and trunk with blotches and papules and stains.

c. *Agric.* A spot (in an ear of corn) produced by mildew or damp.

1731 in *6th Rep. Dep. Kpr. Publ. Rec.* App. II. 119 A new Machine for cleaning Wheat.. contrived to take away the stains, smut bags, and other trumpery.

d. *transf.* A spot or patch of colour different from the ground. Common in *Nat. Hist.*

in fine stain: said of garden flowers with the characteristic markings finely shown.

1704 POPE *Windsor For.* 145 Swift trouts, diversified with crimson stains. **1712** ADDISON *Spect.* No. 412 ¶5 Those different Stains of Light that shew themselves in Clouds of a different Situation. **1784** COWPER *Task* VI. 241 Not a flow'r But shows some touch, in freckle, streak, or stain, Of his unrivall'd pencil. **1842** *Florist's Jrnl.* (1846) III. 130 In the bed were several Claudianas in very fine stain. **1860** RUSKIN *Mod. Paint.* VI. x. §25 V. 103 The gathering orange stain upon the edge of yonder western peak. **1890** R. BRIDGES *Shorter Poems* v. *Larks*, They In sunlight swim; above the furthest stain Of cloud attain.

†**e.** *fig.* A slight trace or tinge *of*. *Obs.*

1601 SHAKS. *All's Well* I. i. 123 You haue some staine of souldier in you. **1606** —— *Tr. & Cr.* I. ii. 27.

f. *Hunting.* = FOIL *sb.*[4] (Cf. STAIN *v.* 4 d.)

1832 *Q. Rev.* XLVII. 238 A short check from the stain of sheep makes everything comfortable; and the Squire having hit off his fox like a workman, thirteen men [etc.].

3. *fig.* (Often in phrases like *to wash, purge a stain.*) **a.** A morally defiling effect on the character or conscience; a grave blemish on a person's reputation; a mark of infamy or disgrace, a stigma.

1591 SHAKS. *1 Hen. VI*, IV. v. 42 Thy Fathers charge shal cleare thee from yt staine. **1593** —— *Lucr.* 1701 How may this forced staine be wip'd from me? **1598** R. BERNARD tr. *Terence, Phormio* v. ii, Studying to avoid the staine of niggardlines. **1610** HOLLAND *Camden's Brit* (1637) 525 A right ancient race of the Digbyes, which.. hath now caught a deepe steine by Sir Everard Digby drawne into that cursed crew. *c* **1610** *Women Saints* 55 Washing away the staynes of secular pleasures with flouds of teares. **1632** MILTON *Penseroso* 26 His daughter she (in Saturns raign, Such mixture was not held a stain). **1640** NABBES *Unfort. Mother* IV. G 1, A truth cleere as the innocence Of babes: after the holy ceremony Hath purg'd th' originall staine. **1781** COWPER *Expost.* 74 Till penitence had purg'd the public stain. **1800** MAR. EDGEWORTH *Moral T., Pruss. Vase* (1816) I. 224 No stain affixes to his honour from the accusation. **1838** JAMES *Robber* v, He would never speak so boldly and so tenderly of his mother, if there were any stain upon her name. **1871** FREEMAN *Norm. Conq.* (1876) IV. xviii. 143 The probable stain on their birth could hardly be thrown in their teeth in the days of William the bastard. **1882** J. H. BLUNT *Ref. Ch. Eng.* II. 484 But the stain of blood could not be washed out.

b. A person or thing that causes disgrace. Now *rare* or *Obs.*

1589 NASHE *Anat. Absurd.* Wks. (Grosart) I. 35 To send them to some other mechanicall Arte, that they might not thus be the staine of Arte. **1591** SHAKS. *1 Hen. VI*, IV. i. 45 Staine to thy countrymen, thou hear'st thy doom. **1598** BRANDON *Octavia* II. C 5, Stain of thy sexe, thy poisoned speech surcease. **1602** FULBECKE *Pandectes* vi. 31 b, Antiphon that vicious varlet, and steigne of Athens. **1649** DAVENANT *Love & Hon.* III. ii. 85 Hence from my sight, Thou birth ill gotten, and my marriage stain. **1725** POPE *Odyss.* XVIII. 4 A surly vagrant.., The stain of manhood.

†**c.** One who eclipses or casts into the shade.

a **1586** SIDNEY *Arcadia* I. xiv. (1912) 95 Hereby I will.. lead her that is the prayse, and yet the staine of all womankinde. **1592** SHAKS. *Ven. & Ad.* 9 Staine to all Nimphs, more louely then a man. **1605** EARL STIRLING *Alex. Trag.* III. ii, My sonne that was the glorie of his time, Staine of times past, and light of times to come.

†**4.** *Her.* (See quot.; and see STAINAND *a.*). *Obs.*

1586 FERNE *Blaz. Gentrie* I. 163 Notwithstanding I do with the french men, condemne the two last colours: that is to say, Tawney and sanguine, as no colours. But we will vouchsafe, to haue them called staines.

5. *Glass-painting.* (See quot. 1832.)

1832 G. R. PORTER *Porcelain & Gl.* xiv. 298 There are only three colours.. which can be floated on, and which are called stains to distinguish them from others which must be laid on by the strokes of a brush. These stains are orange, red, and lemon-yellow. *Ibid.*, Orange stain... In floating this stain upon the glass, a large camel-hair pencil.. must be used. **1838** *Civil Engin. & Arch. Jrnl.* I. 156/1 The stains are then put in, with the lights and shadows in enamel, and again passed through the fire.

6. A dye or colouring matter used in staining.

a. A liquid preparation used to colour wood, etc., differing from paint in being thinner, and in being absorbed into the pores of the material instead of forming a coating. (See also quot. 1880.)

1758 [DOSSIE] *Handmaid Arts* 435 A bright red stain for wood. **1875** E. A. DAVIDSON *House-painting*, etc. 364 The stain is to be applied with a sponge or large brush. **1880** *Cooley's Cycl. Pract. Receipts* (ed. 6) II. 1552 Stains, Confectioner's. *Ibid.* These stains are also used for cakes and pastry. **1895** ELEANOR ROWE *Chip Carving* 73 Should a very large quantity of the stain be required it would be cheaper to purchase the colours in powders. *Ibid.* 74 French polish must be used for oil-stains, but for water-stains.. wax and turpentine are simpler.

b. A dye or pigment used to render minute and transparent structures visible, or to differentiate tissue elements by colouring, for microscopic observations; or to produce specific micro-chemical reactions.

1880 GIBBES *Histol.* 23 Some tissues take in the stain very rapidly, others slowly. **1881** W. B. CARPENTER *Microscope* §202 (ed. 6) 248 A good blue stain.. is also given by the substance termed Indigo-Carmine. **1900–13** DORLAND *Med. Dict.* (ed. 7) 893/2 Anilin blue-black, an anilin dye used as a stain for the study of the central nervous system.

7. *attrib.* and *Comb.* as in *stain reaction, -spot*; *stain-bemoaned* adj.; †**stain-cloth** = STAINED *cloth*; **stain painting,** a style of painting in which diluted acrylic paints are applied to unsized canvas; a painting executed in this style; hence **stain painter,** an exponent of this style; **stain-resistance,** resistance to staining; hence **stain-resistant** *a.*

a **1711** KEN *Hymnarium* Poet. Wks. 1721 II. 79 Before the Judge enthron'd, Plead my Guilt, self-condemn'd, and *stain-bemoan'd. **1547** in *Archæol. Cant.* (1874) IX. 226 Item rec. of James Lake for a *stayne clothe that he bought, xvjd. Item rec. of John Sharpe for iij stayne clothes that he bought, xvjd. **1553–4** in Swayne *Sarum Churchw. Acc.* (1896) 98 Mr. Shorte ffor a stayne cloth iiijd. **1839** *Penny Cycl.* XV. 428/2 The effect of it [mosaic] may be obtained, and the beauty of its patterns produced, in stain-cloth flooring. **1965** *New Statesman* 30 Apr. 693/2 Some of the hard-edge and *stain painters are making matters worse by panicking themselves into the optical movement. **1965** *Stain painting [see *hard-edge* s.v. HARD *a.* (*sb.*) 22]. **1974** *Globe & Mail* (Toronto) 23 Oct. 14/8 Her big canvases.. are stain paintings (staining is a technique using acrylics mixed with water, on unsized canvas). **1898** *Allbutt's Syst. Med.* V. 413 *Stain reactions of the blood in diabetes. **1959** *Times* 12 Jan. 11/5 For use on wool, cotton, or synthetic fibres to improve oil, grease, and water *stain-resistance. **1960** *Farmer & Stockbreeder* Suppl. 12 Jan. 3/3 Casual coat by Salbry is in waterproof, *stain-resistant Norzon and has a fleecy wool lining. *a* **1670** HACKET *Life Abp. Williams* (1693) I. 159 But rip up all his Actions.. shew any *Stain-Spot in his Fidelity.

stain (steɪn), *v.* Forms: 4–6 **steyne,** 5–6 **steyn, stene,** 6 **steane,** 6–7 **stane,** 7 **stein;** 5 **stenyyn,** 6 *Sc.* **stenȝie, stainyie, steinȝie, steingyie, staingȝe, stinȝie;** 5–6 **stayne,** 6 **staine,** 6– **stain.** [aphetic a. OF. *desteign-, desteindre* (mod.F. *déteindre*), f. *des-* DIS- + *teindre* to dye: see DISTAIN *v.*, which appears in our quots. at the same time as the aphetic form. The vb. in Fr. and in the other Rom. langs. has only its etymological sense 'to remove the dye from', intr. 'to lose colour, fade, be washed out'. Some of the Eng. senses, both of *stain* and *distain*, are difficult to account for; it is possible that in AF. the prefix *des-* in *desteindre* may sometimes have been taken in the sense 'diversely, differently'; it is also possible that the verb of Fr. origin may have coalesced with an adoption of ON. *steina* to paint, f. *stein-n* paint, prob. identical with *steinn* stone.]

†**1.** *trans.* To deprive of colour. *Obs.*

[**1390** GOWER *Conf.* I. 65 Whan his visage is so desteigned.] *c* **1477** CAXTON *Jason* 42 b, I haue a seknes and maladye right secrete which shal first slee me er my face may be stayned or discouloured. **1530** PALSGR. 734/1, I stayne a thynge, I marre the colour, or glosse of it, *je destayns.* **1589** LODGE *Scillaes Metam.* E 2 b, Whereas vermillion hue Is stained in sight.

†**b.** Of the sun, etc.: To deprive (feebler luminaries) of their lustre. Also *fig.* of a person or thing: To throw into the shade by superior beauty or excellence; to eclipse. *Obs.* (Very common in the 16th c.)

1557 *Tottel's Misc.* (Arb.) 163 For here at hande approcheth one Whose face will staine you all. *a* **1586** SIDNEY *Arcadia* III. (1598) 344 O voice that doth the Thrush in shrilnesse staine. *c* **1586** C'TESS PEMBROKE *Ps.* LXXII. viii, The sunne.. all lights shall stayne. **1608** TOPSELL *Serpents* 94 In largenesse of body and greatnes of his hart.. he staineth all the rest. **1610** *Histrio-mastix* III. 137 This those excells as farre As glorious Tytan staines a silly Starre. **1613** HEYWOOD *Braz. Age* II. ii, How hath thy valour with thy fortune ioyn'd, To make thee staine the generall fortitude Of all the Princes we deriue from Greece. **1642** FULLER *Holy & Prof. St.* IV. ix. 282 He stains all other mens lives with the clearnesse of his own. *a* **1649** CRASHAW *Carmen Deo Nostro* Wks. (1904) 254 Thy Son Whose blush the moon beauteously marres And staines the timerous light of stares.

†**c.** To obscure the lustre of. *lit.* and *fig. Obs.*

1589 GREENE *Menaphon* (Arb.) 81 Sweete Natures pompe, if my deficient phraze Hath staind thy glories by too little skill, Yeeld pardon. **1594** J. DICKENSON *Arisbas* (1878) 41 A small clowde in a cleare day may somewhat stayne, not wholy stop the Sunnes light. **1596** DALRYMPLE *Leslie's Hist. Scot.* II. 45 O Detestable personnis, quha sa bricht a lycht blew out, stinȝeit sa honorable an ornament! **1634** PEACHAM *Compl. Gentl.* i. (1906) 10 Thirdly, whether Poverty impeacheth or staineth Nobility. **1657** AUSTEN *Fruit Trees* II. To Rdr., God.. is pleased to staine the pride of men.

†**2.** *intr.* To lose colour or lustre. *Obs.*

1387 TREVISA *Higden* (Rolls) II. 15 þe redenesse þerof is wonder fyn and stable, and steyneþ neuere wiþ colde ne with hete. *a* **1568** *Sat. Poems Reform.* xlviii. 15 My clayth will nocht stenȝie, Suppois ȝe weit it nycht and day. **1579** LYLY *Euphues* (Arb.) 82, I finde it nowe for a setled truth.. that the purple dye will neuer staine, that the pure Cyuet will neuer loose his sauour [etc.]. *a* **1609** SHAKS. *Sonn.* xxxiii, Suns of the world may staine when heauens sun staineth. **1614** T. GENTLEMAN *England's Way* 42 Wet and cold can not make them shrinke nor staine, that the North-seas.. haue dyed in graine, for such purposes.

3. Of something dyed or coloured: To impart its colour to (something in contact). Also in wider use (e.g. said of a chemical reagent), to alter the colour of (something to which it is applied).

[Cf. F. *déteindre sur quelque chose.*]

c **1440** *Promp. Parv.* 473/2 Steynyn, or stenyyn, as clothe þat lesythe hys coloure, *fuco, proprie in tertia persona tantum.* **1553** EDEN *Treat. New Ind.* (Arb.) 22 *Lacha, Lacca* or *Lacta*, which steyneth silke and cloth in high redde or crimison coloure. **1566** DRANT *Horace, Sat.* II. iv. Hj b, To rubbe thynges with thy purple cloth, I wis it woulde them steane. **1567** MAPLET *Gr. Forest* 37 Celedonie is an Herbe.. whose flower.. dyeth and stayneth the gatherers hande. **1576** FLEMING *Panopl. Epist.* 382 His lippes are alwayes staynd with the Juice of Bacchus his berries. **1583** L. M[ASCALL] *Prof Bk.* 14 Against clothes staynde with wine or vineger. **1750** *Leonardus' Mirr. Stones* 145 It stains the encircling air with its greenness. **1838** T. THOMSON *Chem. Org. Bodies* 790 Sap of the *musa paradisica*.. stains linen. **1844** G. BIRD *Urin. Deposits* (1857) 188 Several calculi.. with layers of urate of ammonia deeply stained with purpurine. **1901** TROWBRIDGE *Lett. her Mother to Eliz.* ii. 5 The rouge on her neck had stained her collar.

absol. **1805** WITHERING tr. *Werner's Ext. Char. Fossils* 191 Solid fossils that stain are not very common. **1887** 'MARK RUTHERFORD' *Revol. Tanner's Lane* ii. (ed. 8) 31 Tea doesn't stain; I hope it has not gone on your coat.

b. with complement denoting colour.

1750 *Apol. Life B. M. Carew* xi. (ed. 2) 132 They paint themselves with a Pecone-Root, which stains them of a reddish Colour. **1827** Faraday *Chem. Manip.* xii (1842) 280 Paper stained yellow by rhubarb. **1844** G. Bird *Urin. Deposits* (1857) 443 Urates, stained pink with purpurine. **1863** Lyell *Antiq. Man* xi. 203 There were many human bones, in old Indian graves in the same district, stained of as black a dye. **1900–13** Dorland *Med. Dict.* (ed. 7) s.v. *Stains*, Ehrlich's triacid stain..stains erythrocytes orange. **1912** W. G. Smith in *Man* XII. 197 It [the flint] is white in colour, but in parts very slightly stained ferruginous from adjacent red clay.

c. *transf.* Of the blood: To suffuse with colour. Also in *passive*, to be (naturally) spotted or streaked with colour.

1557 Surrey in *Tottel's Misc.* (Arb.) 6, I know how that the blood forsakes the face for dred: And how by shame it staines again the chekes with flaming red. **1567** Maplet *Gr. Forest* 76 He is bespotted and stayned dyuersely with diuers colours in a maner like ye Libard. **1768** Sterne *Sent. Journ.* (1778) II. 81 (Passport), That..which stains thy face with crimson, to copy in even thy study. **1831** James *Phil. Augustus* I. iv, His blue eyes would have been fine..had they not been..stained, as it were on the very iris, by some hazel spots in the midst of the blue.

d. *intr.* To absorb colouring matter, take a stain.

1877 Huxley & Martin *Elem. Biol.* 8 The protoplasm stains brown; the rest of the cell remains unstained. **1879** *St. George's Hosp. Rep.* IX. 691 They were of a very faintly granular appearance, staining feebly with log-wood. **1880** Gibbes *Histol.* 23 When the sections appear to have stained thoroughly remove them.

4. *trans.* To damage or blemish the appearance of (something) by colouring a part of its surface; to discolour by spots or streaks of blood, dirt, or other foreign matter not easily removed. In poetic use occasionally: To colour, defile (a river) with blood.

1382 Wyclif *Gen.* xxxvii. 31 Thei token the coote of hym, and in the blode of a kyde that thei hadden slayn steyneden [Vulg. *tinxerunt*]. *c* **1450** *Merlin* xxvii. 554 He and his horse were steyned with blode as he hadde fallen in a blody river. **1513** Douglas *Æneis* iii. i. 55 The blak droppis of bluide Distillit thairfra, that all the erd quhar it stuide Was spottit of the filth, and stenyt, alaik. **1535** Coverdale *Isa.* lxiii. 3 And their bloude sprange vpon my clothes, & so haue I stayned all my rayment [So later versions]. *Ibid.* lxiv. 6 All oure rightuousnesses are as the clothes stayned with the floures of a woman. **1538** Elyot *Dict.*, *Squaleo*, to be..soiled or stainid with som vnclene thing. **1596** Spenser *F.Q.* iii. iii. 22 Those same antique Peres..Which Greeke and Asian riuers stained with their blood. **1697** Dryden *Virg. Georg.* iii. 742 Scarcely the Knife was redden'd with his Gore, Or the black Poison stain'd the sandy Floor. **1718** Rowe tr. *Lucan* i. 550 See what Reward the grateful Senate yield, For the lost Blood which stains yon Northern Field. **1774** J. Bryant *Mythol.* II. 214 The birds were found to return with their feet stained with soil. **1791** Mrs. Radcliffe *Rom. Forest* viii, Upon a closer view it was spotted and stained with rust. **1839** Dickens *Nich. Nick.* viii, The walls were stained and discoloured. **1879** Farrar *St. Paul* (1883) 402 That bent and weary Jew..so stained with the dust of travel.

†**b.** To spoil (hay, grain) with damp. *Obs.*

1787 Winter *Syst. Husb.* 229 My barley, which was stained by the inclemency of the season in 1785, I had ground. *c* **1830** *Glouc. Farm Rep.* 15 in *Libr. Usef. Knowl., Husb.* III, The hay that has got stained.

†**c.** To spoil by intermixture. *Obs.*

1575 Gascoigne *Glasse Govt.* ii. Chor., Wks. 1910 II. 43 Such wicked means, malitious men can make The frutfull seede, with worthles weedes to stayne.

d. *Hunting.* = foil *v.*[1] 2.

1798 *Sporting Mag.* XI. 87 The ground so stained by running the foil that the scent lay with no certainty. **1897** *Encycl. Sport* I. 583/1 *Stained*, injured as regards scent by the previous passage of hounds, horses, or of cattle, &c.

5. *fig.* **a.** To defile or corrupt morally; to taint with guilt or vice.

1446 Lydg. *Nightingale P.* i. 287 Moch peple viciously Were in this age..thorgh theire vice destreied sore & steyned. **1570** Googe *Pop. Kingd.* i. 8b, Lest that he shoulde be periurde calde, and staynde with heresie. **1657** *Attest. Innocency Zach. Crofton* 14 A Master of a family this twelve year, or thereabouts, never stained with the least disorder or incivility. **1777** W. Cameron in *Sc. Paraphr.* xvii. vii, Though your guilty souls are stain'd with sins of crimson dye. **1847** Yeowell *Anc. Brit. Ch.* x. 104 The British kings were stained with every vice. **1841** Elphinstone *Hist. India* II. 649 Intrigues and combinations, which were stained with treachery and assassinations.

†**b.** To impair the beauty or excellence of. *Obs.*

1575–85 Abp. Sandys *Serm.* xiii. 219 Ought not we to doe the best we can to cast out all that steineth and marreth the perfect beautie of his Church? **1584** *Reg. Privy Council Scot.* III. 702 To blott and stainyie the gude word of God. **1633** P. Fletcher *Purple Isl.* ii. xv, Which my rude pencil will in limming stain.

c. To be or inflict a permanent reproach to or stigma upon; to blemish, soil (a person's reputation, honour, conscience, etc.); †to charge *with* something disgraceful. Also *intr.* of the conscience: †To suffer stain.

1513 More *Rich. III* (1883) 76 With which infami he wold not haue his honoure stayned for anye crowne. **1540–1** Elyot *Image Gov.* 32 If a knight..had used any unseemly thyng, appairing or steyninge the estimacion of the degree, whiche he represented. **1577** Kendall *Flowers of Epigr.* 102 Thei would not haue yᵉ Popedome staynde, with any more Pope Iones. *a* **1605** Montgomerie *Misc. Poems* ii. 5 Conscience stenȝies if he steill. **1610** Holland *Camden's Brit.* (1637) 545 Shee that by her light behaviour had not a little steined her good name. **1678** Dryden *All for L.* iii. i. 44, I have..stain'd the glory of my Royal House. **1682** Fountainhall *Hist. Observes* (Bannatyne Club) 80 It was also at this tyme..designed to stain him with briberie. *a* **1700** Evelyn *Diary* 17 Oct. 1644, This beautiful Citty [Genoa] is more stayn'd with such horrid acts of revenge..than any one place in Europ. *a* **1763** W. King *Polit. & Lit. Anecd.* (1819) 166 The bloody executions which he [Augustus] ordered..must stain his memory as long as his name shall be remembered. **1797** Mrs. Radcliffe *Italian* iii, One who did not scruple to stain the name of the innocent. **1869** Farrar *Fam. Speech* i. 28 One of the most infamous and arbitrary acts which stain the name of Napoleon. **1879** Froude *Cæsar* vii. 63 He won for himself a reputation which his later cruelties might stain, but could not efface.

d. Often used with double metaphor, esp. with reference to 'blood' = bloodguiltiness.

1577–87 Harrison *England* ii. xxi. (1877) I. 335, I held it unworthie that anie good man should staine his paper with such frivolous matters. *a* **1615** Mure *Wks.* I. 23 O spair In guiltles blood thy hands to stayne! **1700** Prior *Carmen Sec.* iii, Holding his Fasces stain'd with Filial Blood. **1865** Kingsley *Herew.* xxxiii, 'Heaven forbid,' he said, 'that the Church should stain her hands with the blood of the worst of sinners.' **1868** J. H. Blunt *Ref. Ch. Eng.* I. 365 After Wolsey's fall, every week of Henry's reign was stained with the blood of his subjects.

†**e.** *to stain* (a person's) *blood*: (*a*) to prove (him) of base descent; (*b*) to cause 'corruption of blood' (see corruption 2 b). *Obs.*

1568 Grafton *Chron.* II. 530 If he sayde contrarie, he..slaundered his mother, shamed himselfe, and steyned his blood. **1628** [see corrupt *v.* 1 b]. **1679** [see attaint *v.* 6]. **1766** Blackstone *Comm.* ii. xv. 252 The doctrine of escheat upon attainder,..is this: that the blood of the tenant, by the commission of any felony..is corrupted and stained.

†**f.** To vilify in words, abuse. *Obs.*

c **1450** *Cov. Myst.* (Shaks. Soc.) 385 Thorow here fayre speche oure lawys they steyn. **1642** H. More *Song of Soul* ii. i. ii. 41 The busie soul thus doth her reason strain To write or speak what envious tongue may never stain. **1691** *d'Emiliane's Frauds Rom. Monks* 63 The Officer very dexterously and freely stain'd the Priest with his Tongue.

†**g.** To 'obfuscate', make tipsy. *Obs.*

1614 B. Jonson *Barth. Fair* i. iii, Why? we were all a little stain'd last night, sprinckled with a cup or two.

†**6.** To ornament with coloured designs or patterns. *Obs.*

1426–7 *Rec. St. Mary at Hill* (1905) 64 Payd for betyng & steynynge of þe same penouns, vj s. *c* **1440** *Promp. Parv.* 473/2 Steynyn, as steynyowrys, *polo*. **1466** in *Archæologia* L. 42 Item j Rydyl steyned wᵗ a chalix and the figur of the sacrament on hyt and ij angell. **1482** *Cely Papers* (Camden) 118 The cortens be stayned bot on the ton syde. **1488** in *Archæologia* XLV. 117 Item, ij Clothes for the sepulchre, oon with the Passion and the other steyned full of whyte leves. **1506** in G. Oliver *Lives Bps. Exeter*, etc. (1861) 359, 1 front de lineo. stayned cum scriptura 'Honor Deo'. 1 front cum tuello annexo, stayned cum Crucifixo, Maria et Johanne, Petro et Paulo. **1555** in Feuillerat *Revels Q. Mary* (1914) 181, v longe garmentes the vpper Bodyes vpper baces of white cloth of syluer stayned with Collours. **1615** G. Sandys *Trav.* 133 The brests of divers [mummies] being stained with Hieroglyphicall characters.

absol. **1390** Gower *Conf.* I. 225, I wol me noght therof excuse, That I with such colour ne steyne.

†**b.** To depict in colour. *Obs.*

1519 *Registr. Aberdon.* (Maitland Club) II. 174 Ane grite arres bed..with þe kingis armes and bischoipe Willeam Elphinstone's stenȝeit be [blank]. *a* **1642** Kynaston *Leoline & Syd.* 1820 A carpet..On which the hyacinth and narcissus blue So naturally were stain'd, as if they grew.

fig. **1569** G. B. *Shippe Safegarde* D vij b, A follie therefore were it here for me, To touch that he with pencell once did staine.

7. To colour (esp. textile fabrics, paper, wood, stone) by the application of pigment that more or less penetrates the substance instead of forming a coating on the surface, or by means of chemical reagents. In microscopical and histological research: To colour (tissues, etc.) with some pigment so as to render the structure clearly visible.

1655 Terry *Voy. India* iii. 115 That pretty art of staining, or printing and fixing those variety of Colours in that white Cloth, the People of Asia have engrossed to themselves. **1660** F. Brooke tr. *Le Blanc's Trav.* 44 There are also made Calicoes, stained of divers colours. **1675** Covel in *Early Voy. Levant* (Hakl. Soc.) 236 Her nails were stein'd (as the custome is here) with *aleanna* of a golden red. **1712** *Lond. Gaz.* No. 5018/4 Any Person who..shall Print, Paint, or Stain, any Paper to serve for Hangings. **1712** *Ibid.* No. 5025/2 Any Person who shall Print, Paint, Stain or Dye any Callicoes, Silks or Stuffs. **1799** G. Smith *Laboratory* I. 338 An artificial marble formed by staining white marble with corrosive tincture. **1799** *Med. Jrnl.* I. 204 Experiments, made by Professor Beckmann, on staining wood. **1815** J. Smith *Panorama Sci. & Art* II. 398 Magistery of bismuth is sometimes mixed with pomatum for the purpose of staining the hair of a dark colour. **1873** J. Matthews *T. Davis's Prepar. Microsc. Obj.* (ed. 2) 8 The tissue may be subsequently stained with iodine. **1881** Young *Ev. Man own Mechanic* §1638. 731 Let us see what wallpaper is and how it is painted or technically speaking 'stained'. **1891** Farrar *Darkn. & Dawn* vii, There were rolls of vellum or papyrus, stained saffron-colour at the back. **1892** *Photogr. Ann.* II. 455 Finished in an altogether superior style..and the whole stained and varnished in imitation mahogany, 21/-.

b. To colour (glass) with transparent colours. Also *rarely* to depict in stained glass.

1797 *Encycl. Brit.* (ed. 3) VII. 779/1 The first thing to be done, in order to paint or stain glass..is to design..the whole subject on paper. **1815** J. Smith *Panorama Sci. & Art* II. 757 Of the Colours used in staining Glass. **1832** G. R. Porter *Porcelain & Gl.* xiv. 289 The invention of the art of painting on and staining glass..is..known to have existed for many centuries. **1893** Kath. L. Bates *Engl. Relig. Drama* 26 Some Christian hero, whose martyrdom was stained in window, carved in canopy.

stain, obs. form of stone.

stainable ('steɪnəb(ə)l), *a.* [f. stain *v.* + -able.] Capable of being stained. Hence **staina'bility**.

1884 *Proc. Boston Soc. Nat. Hist.* XXIII. 59 Two substances, one readily stainable, and one staining with difficulty. **1885** *Encycl. Brit.* XIX. 833/1 A very simple homogeneous corpuscle or vesicle of more readily stainable protoplasm. **1890** *Lond. Med. Recorder* 20 Apr. 144/2 Sometimes they appear in greater numbers within the nuclei, which thereby are puffed up and lose their stainability. **1898** P. Manson *Trop. Diseases* viii. 148 Those [plague bacilli] occurring in the blood..are stainable by Gram's method.

†**stainand**, *a.* *Her.* *Obs.* Also 6 **staynand**, 7 **staynant**, 7, 9 **stainant**. [app. a pres. pple. of stain *v.* (either northern ME. or repr. OF. *desteignant*).] An epithet of certain colours.

The precise sense and correct application are very doubtful, most of the successive writers having apparently copied from their predecessors with little understanding. The Book of St. Albans (quot. 1486 s.v. staining *ppl. a.*) seems to use 'steining colowre' for any tincture (whether 'colour' or 'metal') which presents a uniform tint in contradistinction to spots, etc.; according to this authority the 'steining' colours are the only ones that may appear on the shield of a gentleman. On the other hand, according to Legh (1562), 'staynande' colours are those which may *not* be used in armory; *tawny* or *tenné*, being the 'surest' of all the mixed colours, is the only one of them that is not 'staynande'; we may perhaps hence infer that Legh took the adj. to mean 'fugitive' (cf. stain *v.* 2), or rather 'indeterminate'. Guillim (1610) says that some heralds disallow the use of *tawny* and *murrey* (or *sanguine*) for fields, regarding them as 'staynande' (Ferne in 1586 speaks of these two as 'stains', not colours), but it is not clear how he interpreted the adj. The later notion that *staynand* means 'disgraceful', designating tinctures that are used for the purpose of 'abatement', appears to be entirely unfounded.

1562 Legh *Armory* 19 Tawney,..blazed by thys woorde, Tenne. It is a worshipfull colour... But very fewe Englishe men beare the same. Yet it is armorye, and so are all coloures, that are not staynandes. *Ibid.* 19 b, Tenne..is the surest colour..beeyng componed. For it is made of two bryghte coloures, whiche is Redde, and Yellowe. And ye shall not haue any colour so made emongest all yᵗ may be deuysed, and not to be staynande. **1610** Guillim *Heraldry* i. iii. 11 [Copies Legh and continues thus:—] The last of the seuen mixed colours, we doe commonly call Murrey, but in Blazon, Sanguine, and is (as most truly saith Leigh) a Princely Colour, being indeed one of the colors appertaining of ancient time to the Prince of Wales... Some Heralds of approued iudgement doe hardly admit these two last mentioned for Colours of Fields, in regard they are reckoned Staynand Colours. **1658** Phillips, *Stainand*-colours, in Heraldry are tawney and murrey. **1673** A. Walker *Leez Lachrym.* 25 Though a rough Herald would have found blots enough in Abner's Scutcheon, and a rude Pencil would have painted it with staynant Colours, or a Scotch Coal. **1689** Smithurst *Britain's Glory* 167 *Tenne*, Orange Colour; a Colour Stainant. **1845** Lower *Curios. Heraldry* 313 The stainant or disgraceful colours, tenné and sanguine.

stainch, obs. Sc. form of stanch *v.*

stainchell, obs. Sc. form of stanchel[1].

staincher, var. stancher[2].

staine, obs. form of stone.

stained (steɪnd), *ppl. a.* [f. stain *v.* + -ed[1].]

1. Discoloured with blood, dirt, etc.; having stains or blemishes. Also *fig.*, tainted with guilt, disgraced, etc. Often in comb. with a prefixed sb., as blood-stained, earth-stained, guilt-stained, travel-stained, etc.

1382 Wyclif *Isa.* lxiii. 1 Who is this that cam fro Edom, with steyned clothes from Bosra? **1538** Elyot *Dict.*, *Infectus*, infected, dyed, stayned, poysoned. **1592** *Arden of Feversham* iii. vi. 85 Then softly drawes she foorth her handkercher, And modestly she wypes her teare staind face. **1607** Lever *Crucifix* (Grosart) 49 O what is man whome Thou regardest so! A stayned cloth, a beauty withered. *a* **1628** F. Grevil *Monarchy* ccccclxxiv, Let Princes..Reform that common stained Discipline, Which is the Base of unprosperity. **1889** *Hardwicke's Sci. Gossip* XXV. 228/2 The chalk is full of iron-stained fissures. **1899** *Allbutt's Syst. Med.* VIII. 701 Patches of stained skin may be due to various local irritants.

†**2.** Ornamented with pictures or designs in colour: esp. in *stained cloth*. *Obs.*

1397 in *Finchale Priory Charters* etc. (Surtees) p. cxvii, Item j lectus stewynd cum tapete. **1413–14** *Durham Acc. Rolls* (Surtees) 224 Cum 2 steyned clothes emptis pro dicta capella. *c* **1449** Pecock *Repr.* ii. xviii. 258 In this steyned clooth ridith Hector of Troie; and here in this steyned clooth King Herri leieth a sege to Harflew. **1463** *Bury Wills* (Camden) 23 The steynyd clooth of the Coronacion of oure lady. *c* **1474** *Invent.* in *Paston Lett.* III. 407 Item, vj. steyned paperis, xij d. **15..** in *Northumbld. Househ. Bk.* (1770) 440, 1 Steyned Cloth of the Ymage of St. Nicholas. **1552** in Daniel-Tyssen *Invent. Ch. Goods Surrey* (1869) 15 Item one roode cloth of stayned canvas. **1627** Bp. Hall *Charac. Virtues & Vices* i. 181 He can make his cottage a Mannor;..his staind-cloth Arras. **1696** *MSS. Ho. Lords* (N.S.) II. 238 The wearing of wrought Silks, Bengals, and dyed, printed, or stained Calicoes, imported into the kingdom.

†**b.** *Comb.* (Cf. painter-stainer). *Obs.*

a **1618** J. Davies (Heref.) *Wit's Pilgr.* Wks. (Grosart) II. 26/2 Beauty..is the Signe where Grace doth vse to lie But if thrust out, the Inne is most amisse..And hath but meerely stained-painted Walls.

3. Coloured with liquid pigments that penetrate below the surface.

1562 J. Heywood *Prov. & Epigr.* (1867) 179 Walles, Som seeld,..som painted, som staind. **1712** *Lond. Gaz.* No. 5025/2 Such Printed, Painted, Stained or Dyed Silks. **1884** *Health Exhib. Catal.* 38 The stained leather is then taken to the drying-rooms [in glove-manufacture].

b. Prepared with a staining preparation, esp. for microscopic observation.

1889 *Hardwicke's Sci. Gossip* XXV. 31/1 A double stained-section of the plane wood. **1890** *Ibid.* XXVI. 101/2 Stained human muscle. **1899** tr. *Jaksch's Clin. Diagn.* viii. (ed. 4) 407 Such forms [of microbe] are to be discriminated by the behaviour of stained preparations in the presence of alcohol.

4. ***stained glass***: transparent coloured glass, formed into decorative mosaics, used in windows (esp. of churches). Also, less correctly, glass which has been decorated with vitrified pigments. So also ***stained window***.

1791 Mrs. Radcliffe *Rom. Forest* ii, Whose pointed arches still exhibited fragments of stained glass. **1834** L. Ritchie *Wand. by Seine* 159 The stained windows are very beautiful. **1859** Gullick & Timbs *Painting* 136 *Stained* glass must not be confounded with *painted* glass. In stained glass the colouring is not superficial, but pervades the substance of the glass. **1890** W. J. Gordon *Foundry* 142 The making of stained windows.

fig. **1909** J. Wells *Stewart of Lovedale* iii. 18 Though a zealous idealist, he did not look at present things through the stained glass of the imagination.

attrib. **1838** *Civil Engin. & Arch. Jrnl.* I. 155/2 The present want of encouragement to the stained glass artist. **1839** Ure *Dict. Arts* 1159 Stained-glass pigments. **1849** Rock *Ch. of Fathers* I. v. (1903) I. 280 Our stained-glass windows. **1881** W. S. Gilbert *Patience* II. (*Song, Bunthorne*), I am not fond of uttering platitudes In stained-glass attitudes.

stainer ('steɪnə(r)). Forms: 4-6 **steynour**, 5 **staynour, stener, stenyoure**, 6 **steyner**, 6-7 **stayner**, 6- **stainer**. [agent-n. f. stain *v.*: see -or 2 b, -er[1].]

1. One whose employment is staining; one who colours wood, etc. with pigments which penetrate below the surface; †a worker of 'stained cloths' (see stained *ppl. a.* 2). See also Painter-Stainer, paper-stainer.

1388 Wyclif *Exod.* xxxv. 35 That thei make the werkis of carpenter, of steynour [Vulg. *polymitarii*], and of broiderere. *c* **1430** Lydg. *Min. Poems* (Percy Soc.) 81 Peyntour, steynour, mason, nor carpentere. **1471** *Little Red Bk. Bristol* (1900) II. 131 John Sutton, Goldsmyth, and John Body, Staynour. **1489** *Acc.* in Sharp *Cov. Myst.* (1825) 196 Paid to the stener ffor workemanship ther-off [buckram for standards], x s. viij d. *a* **1513** Fabyan *Chron.* vii. 364 The tayllours helde yᵉ craft of stayners. **1538** Elyot *Dict.*, *Rhyparographus*, a paynter of tryfles, a Stayner. **1589** Lodge *Scillaes Metam.* Ep. Ded., From the shop of the Painter, shee is falne into the hands of the stainer. **1712** *Lond. Gaz.* No. 5018/4 All Printers, Painters and Stainers of Paper. *Ibid.* No. 5025/2 Silks, Callicoes, Linens and Stuffs which shall..be in the Possession of any private Painter, Stainer or Dyer to be printed.

2. One who or something which stains or calumniates.

1647 J. Norris (*title*) A Lash for a Lyar; Or, The Stayner Stayned, Being An Answer to a false and scandalous Pamphlet.

3. A tincture of colouring matter used in staining.

1891 in *Century Dict.*

Hence †**'staineress**, a female stainer.

c **1430** *Pilgr. Lyf. Manhode* III. xxvii. (1869) 150 þis hand is a steynowresse of corteynes and a makere. [A mistranslation; the orig. has *estendresse* stretcher.]

'stainful, *a. rare*⁻¹. [f. stain *sb.* or *v.* + -ful.] Polluting, disgraceful.

1765 J. Brown *Chr. Jrnl.* 55 Where the thoughtless fops keep their stainful plays.

stainierite ('steɪnɪəraɪt). *Min.* [ad. Du. *stainierit* (V. Cuvelier 1929, in *Natuurwetensch. Tijdschr.* XI. 177), f. the name of Xavier *Stainier* (b. 1865), Belgian geologist: see -ite[1].] A hydrous oxide of cobalt which is usu. found as black needles forming microcrystalline crusts on cobalt ores, and is now regarded as the same as heterogenite.

1930 *Mineral. Abstr.* IV. 248 This is regarded as the crystalline equivalent of the colloidal heterogenite, and is named stainierite. **1941** *Ibid.* VIII. 86 X-ray powder photographs of heterogenite, stainierite, mindigite, and trieuite from Katanga..show identical patterns, and these minerals are to be regarded as varieties of the heterogenite group, differing in the relative amounts of Co_2O_3 and CuO. **1962** [see heterogenite]. **1968** I. Kostov *Mineralogy* 228 The last mineral [*sc.* heterogenite] is also known as stainierite.

staining ('steɪnɪŋ), *vbl. sb.* [f. stain *v.* + -ing[1].] The action of the verb stain, in various senses; also *concr.* a result of this action.

1382 Wyclif *Job* xxviii. 19 Ne ther shal be maad euene to it topasie of Ethiope, ne to the most clene steynyng [Vulg. *tincturæ mundissimæ*] shal be comparisound. **1530** Rastell *Bk. Purgat.* III. viii. 2 The spottes and tokens of the steynynge whych remayne be than a great deformyte and eye sore. *c* **1586** C'tess Pembroke *Ps.* li. i, Clense still my spotts, still wash awaie my staynings. **1630** *R. Johnson's Kingd. & Commw.* 598 Their Painting is meere steyning or trowelling in respect of ours. **1652** Culverwel *Lt. Nature* xv. (1661) 128 Far be it from me to drop one word, that should tend to the staining, and eclipsing of that just glory. **1799** G. Smith *Laboratory* II. 79 This method of using water-colours is called painting; the other is called washing, or staining [*i.e.* tinting]. **1815** J. Smith *Panorama Sci. & Art* II. 753 The colouring of maps is in fact only a species of staining. **1842** Loudon *Suburban Hort.* 529 The wood..is well adapted..for staining. **1871** *Amer. Encycl. Printing* (ed. Ringwalt), *Staining*, in bookbinding, the coloring of the edges, fly-leaves, and backs of books, either in solid shades, or in the process styled marbling. **1881** W. B. Carpenter *Microscope* §202 (ed. 6) 247 For blue and green staining, the various Aniline dyes are principally used. **1907** J. A. Hodges *Elem. Photogr.* (ed. 6) 70 A more or less deep staining of the film results.

†**b.** A pigment used for staining. *Obs.*

1541 *Aberdeen Reg.* (1844) I. 175 Item, ane galkoit of stenyng, the price x s.

c. *attrib.*

1870 Power tr. *Stricker's Man. Histol.* I. Introd. p. xxxiii, The staining fluid. **1880** Gibbes *Histol.* 22 Of the staining agents, logwood is the most useful. **1884** *Health Exhib. Catal.* 38 Photograph No. 3 shows the men at work at the staining tables, and a portion of the staining room [glove-manufacture].

staining ('steɪnɪŋ), *ppl. a. rare.* [f. stain *v.* + -ing[2].] That stains, in senses of the verb.

For the use in quot. 1486 see stainand *ppl. a.*

1486 *Bk. St. Albans, Her.* b iij b, A gentilman mai not wear tokynys of armys bot of steining colowre, that is to say his cootarmure ynyat or ellis y geratt with preciouse stonys. **1601** Shaks. *All's Well* III. vii. 7, I..would not put my reputation now In any staining act. **1789** J. Williams *Min. Kingd.* I. 386 The better species of iron ores are generally accompanied with red staining soft soil, by which they are easily distinguished. **1880** Meredith *Tragic Com.* (1881) 281 She had no feminine horror of the staining epithet for that sex.

stainless ('steɪnlɪs), *a.* (and *sb.*) [f. stain *sb.* + -less.]

A. *adj.* **1.** Without stain, spot, or blemish.

a. *lit.*

a **1586** Sidney *Arcadia* II. xi. (1912) 221 The Phœnix wings are not so rare For faultlesse length, and stainelesse hewe. **1613-16** W. Browne *Brit. Past.* II. iii. 61 The Hare-bell for her stainlesse azur'd hue, Claimes to be worne of none but those are true. **1813** Shelley *Q. Mab* vi. 7 The stainless mirror of the lake Re-images the eastern gloom. **1867** Augusta Wilson *Vashti* xxxv, Robed in a soft stainless white muslin.

b. *fig.*

1592 Shaks. *Rom. & Jul.* III. ii. 13 Learne me how to loose a winning match, Plaid for a paire of stainlesse Maidenhoods. **1601** —— *Twel. N.* I. v. 278 Of fresh and stainlesse youth. **1743** Francis tr. *Hor., Odes* III. ii. 17 With stainless Lustre Virtue shines. **1814** Byron *Lara* II. viii, But that long absence from his native clime Had left him stainless of oppression's crime. **1819** Crabbe *Tales of Hall* VIII. 231 The very care he took to keep his name Stainless. **1889** Barrie *Window in Thrums* 176 Leeby, that stainless young woman. **1893** *Cath. News* 11 Nov. 2/3 The stainless Conception of the Blessed Virgin Mary.

2. Highly resistant to staining or corrosion. See also stainless steel.

1897 *Sears, Roebuck Catal.* 244/1 Ladies' Fast Black Cotton Hose... Fast color and stainless. **1921** *Engineer* 11 Nov. 504/2 Stainless iron may be easily forged by hand into such difficult objects as spurs. **1932** *Discovery* May 145/1 Low carbon stainless steel, frequently called stainless iron, contains less than 0·12 per cent of carbon and from 11 to 12 per cent of chromium. **1945** *ABC of Cookery* (Ministry of Food) i. 8 Any cutlery which is not stainless should be kept well polished. **1960** *Good Housek. Cookery Bk.* (rev. ed.) 574/1 A sharp-pointed, stainless vegetable knife. **1979** T. Motogoshi in M. Nurse *Stainless Steel* 19/1 The use of stainless tubes has been boosted by the increase in the erection of high rise buildings.

Hence '**stainlessly** *adv.*, '**stainlessness**.

1862 *Edin. Rev.* CXVI. 200 When the divorce was threatened, she again avowed her affection for Königsmark, and offered to take the sacrament on its stainlessness. **1882** Farrar *Early Chr.* I. 106 To represent the Christian Church as ideally pure, as stainlessly excellent and perfect, would be altogether a mistake. **1887** *Academy* 1 Jan. 16/3 Purity of heart, absolute stainlessness of soul.

B. *sb. ellipt.* for stainless steel; articles made of this.

1971 G. V. Higgins *Friends of Eddie Coyle* (1972) x. 64, I don't care whether it's the stainless or not... I got to have the stuff. **1975** *New Yorker* 26 May 111 (Advt.), Galax, a unique combination of solid brass and 18-8 stainless, is light-years ahead in function and design. **1977** C. McFadden *Serial* (1978) i. 8/2 They spent it rapidly on.. Dansk stainless and Rosenthal china.

stainless steel. [f. stainless *a.* + steel *sb.*[1]]

1. A chromium-steel alloy, usu. containing about 14 per cent of chromium when used for cutlery, etc., that does not rust or tarnish under oxidizing conditions because of the formation of a film of oxide on its surface. Freq. *attrib.*

1917 *Sci. Amer.* 31 Mar. 329/2 A steel that does not stain or tarnish is one of the latest new materials... It is called 'stainless steel'. **1920** *Glasgow Herald* 4 Aug. 9 Since the Armistice there has been an enormous sale of stainless steel for cutlery purposes. **1926** J. H. G. Monypenny *Stainless Iron & Steel* i. 6 Stainless steel was first introduced to the public in 1914 in the form of table cutlery. *Ibid.* 13 The discovery of the non-corrosive properties of stainless steel by Brearley, in 1913, was something entirely new in the history of chromium steels. **1932** *Discovery* May 145/1 There are three principal types of stainless steel. Low carbon stainless steel, frequently called stainless iron, contains less than 0·12 per cent of carbon and from 11 to 12 per cent of chromium... Cutlery steel, so called because it was first used for knives, contains 0·3 per cent of carbon and from 12 to 15 per cent of chromium... Austenitic stainless steel has the highest resistance of all to corrosion and is the most generally useful of the stainless steels. **1958** *Times Rev. Industry* Apr. 73/1 There were..many worthy examples of ..the application of newer materials, especially stainless steel and aluminium, to domestic requirements. **1979** V. S. Naipaul *Bend in River* v. 83 The stainless steel jug..had only a stale-looking trickle of powdered milk.

2. *fig.* or in fig. context: chiefly used *attrib.* with allusion to the qualities of brightness, hardness, coldness, etc., associated with stainless steel.

1963 *Times* 10 June 6/5 Miss Astrid Varney's Isolde has the hallmark of true greatness upon it, but sometimes the voice takes on a stainless steel quality that would be more suited to the role of Ortrud. **1964** G. Lyall *Most Dangerous Game* xxiii. 192, I was..searching for the stainless-steel glint of a river to fix my position. **1974** *Publishers Weekly* 25 Mar. 6/2 She is..married to Sir Alfred Ayer, the celebrated English philosopher, whom she describes affectionately as 'the man with the stainless steel mind'. **1978** R. Doliner *On the Edge* (1979) ix. 142 His ego was gleaming hard, made of stainless steel.

stainy ('steɪnɪ), *a. rare.* [f. stain *sb.* + -y.] Like a stain or something stained. Hence '**staininess**.

1864 Mrs. A. Gatty *Parab. Nature* Ser. IV. 23 The beets had an odd stainy look. **1905** Holman-Hunt *Pre-Raph.* I. 276 To correct the qualities of thinness and staininess which, over a dry ground, transparent colours would exhibit.

stainyell, Sc. var. staniel (bird).

stair (stɛə(r)), *sb.* Forms: 1 **stæᵹer**, 2-5 **steire**, 4-5 **steier** (5 **steiar**), 4 **steyᵹere**, 4-6 (9 *dial.*) **steyre**, 5-6 **steyr**, 4-6 **steyer**, 6 **steare, stare**, (7 **starre**), 6-7 **steer(e**, 4-8 **stayer** (6 **staigher, staygher**, 7 **stayor**), 4-7 **stayre**, 5-7 **stayr**, 6 **staier**, 5-7 **staire**, 6- **stair**. [OE. *stæᵹer* fem.:—OTeut. type **staiᵹrī*, f. **staiᵹ-*: **stiᵹ-* to climb: see sty *v.* Cf. (M)Du. *steiger* (WFlem. *steeger* staircase), LG. *steiger*, *steger* masc., scaffolding, landing-stage.]

1. a. An ascending series or 'flight' of steps leading from one level to another, esp. from one floor to another in a house; a staircase.

Still the ordinary use in Scotland, where 'up the stair', 'down the stair' are the usual equivalents for *upstairs*, *downstairs*, and '(to go up) six stairs' means what in England would be expressed by 'six flights of stairs'. (The whole series of steps between two successive floors counts, however, as a single 'stair', even when it consists of two or more 'flights' or portions separated by a landing.) In England the sing. in this sense is now very rare, exc. in phr. ***on the stair***, which is itself slightly archaic.

c **1000** Ælfric *Gloss.* in Wr.-Wülcker 126/9 *Ascensorium*, stæᵹer. *c* **1000** —— *Saints' Lives* (Skeat) v. 438 Sebastianus ..astah þa up to þære stæᵹre þe stod wiþ ðæs caseres botl. *Ibid.* xviii. 232 He feoll of anre stæᵹre, and forþy ᵹelæᵹ. *c* **1200** *Trin. Coll. Hom.* 165 þis holie maiden..þo hie was þreo ᵹier heold, [steᵹh] biforen þe temple on þe steire of fiftene stoples..wiðute mannes helpe. *c* **1374** Chaucer *Troylus* II. 813 Adoun þe steyre a-noon right þo she wente. **1387** Trevisa *Higden* (Rolls) III. 115 [Tarquinius] þrewe hym doun of a staire [L. *per gradus*]. **1427** *Rec. St. Mary at Hill* (1905) 66 For a mason & his man a day to make a stayer with iij stappes, xij d ob. **1449** in *Cal. Proc. Chanc. Q. Eliz.* (1830) II. Pref. 54 To the seid hous shullen be ij covenable steiers, þe on ledyng up from the ground in to þe furst flore, and that other [etc.]. *c* **1470** Henry *Wallace* vi. 248 The scherand suerd glaid til his coler bayne, Out our the stayr amang thaim is he gayne. *a* **1490** Botoner *Itin.* (1778) 176 A hygh grese called a steyr of xxxii steppys. *a* **1500** *Chaucer's Dreme* 1311, I..walkt..Til I a winding staire found. **1503** Hawes *Examp. Virt.* vii. cl, Than hardynes and fortune went downe the stayre. **1551** Ascham *Let.* 23 Feb., Wks. 1865 I. ii. 280 The houses be eight or nine stairs high, that a wonderful number of people may look out of windows. **1597** Drayton *Heroic. Epist., Q. Isab. to Mortimer* 39 Forth from my Pallace by a secret staire, I steale to Thames. **1632** in *10th Rep. Hist. MSS. Comm.* App. v. 480 The stayer of [the] little gate, and the stayer on the north syde of the greate gate. **1730** A. Gordon *Maffei's Amphith.* 290 A Stair of 20 Steps. **1755** Johnson s.v., *Stair* was anciently used for the whole order of steps; but *stair* now, if it be used at all, signifies, as in Milton, only one flight of steps. **1771** Smollett *Humph. Cl.* 1 July, There were two stairs in the house. **1781** J. Moore *View Soc. Italy* (1790) I. v. 53 The principal entrance is by a spacious stair called the Giant's stair. **1823** P. Nicholson *Pract. Build.* 441 A stair contained within a circular or elliptical wall is called a winding stair. **1831** Scott *Cast. Dang.* xvii, At length she became sensible that he descended by the regular steps of a stair. **1832** Macgillivray *Trav. Humboldt* xxiv. 372 A great stair of 57 steps conducts to the truncated summit. **1849** M. Arnold *Sick King Bokhara* 220 While I speak, O King, I hear the bearers on the stair. **1859** Tennyson *Marr. Geraint* 320 High above a piece of turret stair..wound. **1907** *Verney Mem.* I. 3 A concealed door leading to a small private stair.

†**b.** Vaguely used for: Something on which one ascends. *Obs.*

13.. *Disput. Mary & the Cross* 77 in *Min. Poems Vernon MS.* 614 Cros! he stikeþ nou on þi steir, Naked aᵹeyn þe wylde wynde.

†**c.** A ladder. *Obs.*

a **1400-50** *Wars Alex.* 1438 Sum stepis vp on sties to þe stone wallis, On ilka staffe of a staire stike wald a cluster. **1567-9** Jewel *Def. Apol.* IV. vii. §3 (1611) 376 *Cum Papa per Scalam ascendit*, &c. When the Pope taketh his staires to mount on Horsebacke.

d. *fig.* A means of ascending in rank, power, moral excellence, etc.

1570-6 Lambarde *Peramb. Kent* (1826) 422 Now hath he climbed the seconde steppe of this staire to the crowne. **1621**

J. TAYLOR (Water P.) *Superbiæ Flagellum* D 6 Humility is a most heauenly gift, The Stayre that doth (to Glory) men vp lift. **1627** E. F. *Hist. Edw. II* (1680) 9 Caring not what succeeds, so he may make it the Stair of his Preferment. **1677** GILPIN *Demonol.* (1867) 397 Pride was the stair by which he knew they must ascend to it. **1928** T. S. ELIOT *Song for Simon* 2 They shall praise Thee and suffer in every generation.. Light upon light, mounting the saints' stair. **1930** R. CAMPBELL *Poems* 4 All the gifts my faith has brought Along the secret stair of thought.

†**e.** An ascending series, scale. *Obs.*

1643 SIR T. BROWNE *Relig. Med.* I. §33. 73 There is in this Universe a Staire, or manifest Scale of creatures, rising not disorderly.. but with a comely method and proportion.

2. a. One of a succession of steps leading from one floor of a building to another.

Occurring earliest in figurative uses: see d.

1530 PALSGR. 275/1 Stayre or grece, *degré.* **1555** EDEN *Decades W. Ind.* III. XI. 150 To the fyrste porches of their houses.. they ascend by ten or twelue steares. **1617** MORYSON *Itin.* I. 145, I ascended the same by two hundred and forty staires of marble. **1624** WOTTON *Archit.* I. 57 That the breadth of euery single Step or Staire bee neuer lesse then one foote. **1846** DICKENS *Pict. Italy, Rome* 226 This man touched every stair with his forehead. **1854** tr. *Hettner's Athens* 8 The roof [of the Propylæa] is in ruins,.. the stairs are scattered about in isolated fragments.

†**b.** A step of a ladder. *Obs. rare.*

13.. *E.E. Allit. P.* C. 513 Wymmen vnwytte þat.. Bitwene þe stele and þe stayre disserne no3t cunen.

†**c.** Applied to a step cut in rock, to one of the successive levels in the ascent of a pyramid, etc.

1471 CAXTON *Recuyell* (Sommer) 330 They fonde a rooche entaillid and cutte in to steyers or grees.. hewyd out with chyselles. **1584** B. R. tr. *Herodotus* II. 104 They deuised certayne engines.. to heaue vp stones from the grounde to the fyrst stayre. **1600** PORY tr. *Leo's Africa* V. 240 They descend by certaine staires hewen out of the rocke.

†**d.** *fig.* A step or degree in a (metaphorical) ascent or in a scale of dignity. *Obs.*

a **1225** *Ancr. R.* 284 Þolemodnesse.. haueð þreo steiren —heie, & herre, & alre heixt, & nexst þe heie heouene. **1549** LATIMER *2nd Serm. bef. Edw. VI* (Arb.) 67 The thyrd stayer is thys. How shal they beleue in hym of whom they neuer heard? **1628** EARLE *Microcosm., Child*, The elder he growes, hee is a stayer lower from God. **1640** FULLER *Joseph's Coat* (1 Cor. xi. 21) 27 So *Summa hilaritas*, is *Ima ebrietas*, the highest staire of mirth, is the lowest step of drunkennesse.

†**e.** A high position. *Obs.*

1590 SPENSER *F.Q.* I. ii. 23 My dearest Lord fell from high honours staire Into the hands of his accursed fone. **1627** MAY *Lucan* V. 441 And.. yields at the peoples prayer To be dictator, honour's highest staire.

†**f.** A degree of a circle. *Obs.*

c **1374** CHAUCER *Compl. Mars* 129 He passeth but a steyre in dayes two.

3. *collective plural* (of sense 2). **a.** = sense 1. Also, in generalized sense, the steps of staircases. (In the latter use, the plural of sense 2 coincides in application with that of sense 1, and in many examples it is difficult to determine which of the two was intended by the writer.)

pair, flight of stairs: see PAIR *sb.*[1] 6 b, FLIGHT *sb.*[1] 7. *back stairs*: see BACKSTAIRS. *above, below stairs*: see the preps. *down, up stairs*: see DOWNSTAIRS, UPSTAIRS.

1398 TREVISA *Barth. De P.R.* XVII. clxv. (1495) 710 Thina ben certen trees.. and therof Salomon made steyers and grece [Vulg. *gradus* 2 Chron. ix. 11] and postys [Vulg. *fulcra* 3 Kings x. 11] in the house of our lorde. *c* **1489** CAXTON *Blanchardyn* xlvii. 180 [They] brought her doun the stayers of the paleys. **1556** in W. H. Turner *Select. Rec. Oxford* (1880) 247 The.. Coroners wer not thrust downe the stayers. **1565** COOPER *Thesaurus* s.v. *Conijcio, Sub scalas tabernæ librariæ se conijcere*, to hyde him selfe vnder the stayers. **1577–82** BRETON *Flourish upon Fancie* (Grosart) 21/1 Why didst thou throw him downe the Steares in such a sorte? **1631** GOUGE *God's Arrows* IV. §15. 395 The whole garret.. and top of staires were as full as could be. **1660** F. BROOKE tr. *Le Blanc's Trav.* 313 Not able to rest for ratlings and jinglings, both upon the stairs and in the Chamber. **1711** HEARNE *Collect.* (O.H.S.) III. 237 At the bottom of the Stayers. **1711** W. SUTHERLAND *Shipbuild. Assist.* 65 In lieu of such Stairs most Ships.. have only Ladders. **1712** J. JAMES tr. *Le Blond's Gardening* 126 The first Figure is the great Stairs in the Garden.. at S. Cloud. **1768** STERNE *Sent. Journ.* (1778) II. 44 (Address) The secretary look'd towards the stairs, as if he was about to leave me. **1825** T. HOOK *Sayings* Ser. II. *Passion & Princ.* ix. III. 154 At the foot of the stairs, the company was joined by Mr. Rodney. **1839** *Lamartine's Trav.* 116/1 Not far from the entrance of the temple, we found large openings and subterranean stairs which led us into lower constructions.

transf. **1667** MILTON *P.L.* III. 510 The Stairs were such as whereon Jacob saw Angels ascending and descending.

†**b.** construed as *sing.* A flight of steps, a staircase. *Obs.*

1536 *MS. Rawl. D. 780* lf. 62 Makyng of a new stayers for the Colehouse. **1565** COOPER *Thesaurus, Gradus*,.. a griese or steppe: a stayres. **1663** GERBIER *Counsel* 23 The composing of a fit and easy Staires being a Masterpiece. **1697** EVELYN *Architects & Archit.* Misc. Wks. (1825) 378 The perpendicular post of a winding staires. **1776** S. J. PRATT *Pupil of Pleas.* II. 242 It is a good way to any bed-chamber, and the stairs is steep. **1830** JAMES *Darnley* xxvi, He led the way up a little narrow stairs.

c. *fig.* and in fig. context; *esp.* applied to the means by which a person rises in rank or power. Now *rare* or *Obs.*

1576 GASCOIGNE *Steele Gl.* 16 Which.. make my backe, a ladder for their feete, By slaundrous steppes and stayres of tickle talke, To clyme the throne, wherin my selfe should sitte. **1600** HEYWOOD *If you know not me* (1605) A 3 b, The suffolke men my Lord, was to the Queene The very stayres, by which she did ascend. **1610** HOLLAND *Camden's Brit.* (1637) 397 Tyrants very often hew downe the staires and steps whereby they ascended. **1631** R. BOLTON *Comf. Affl. Consc.* xiv. (1635) 299 In a word to climbe up more merrily those staires of joy which are prest upon us by the holy Prophet. **1642** FULLER *Holy & Prof. St.* IV. iii. 249 By the stairs of a Parsonage or two he climbed up at last into the notice of Fox, Bishop of Winchester. **1648** J. BEAUMONT *Psyche* VIII. cxxxvii, By Virtue's daily Progress they shall build Up to the gate of Bliss their mystick stayers.

†**d.** *Dutch stairs*: app. a light winding staircase. *Obs.*

1649 in *Archæologia* X. 411 A roome within the turret of the west stayres, having a payre of round Dutch stayres, arising into the very midle of it. **1701** FARQUHAR *Sir H. Wildair* II. i, My bones ache this morning as if I had lain all night on a pair of Dutch stairs.

†**e.** Applied to the outside steps leading to the door of a building. *Obs.*

c **1481** CAXTON *Dialogues* 14/32 So goo to the halle Whiche is in the market; So goo vpon the steyres [Fr. *sy montes les degretz*]; There shall ye find the clothes. **1548** UDALL *Erasm. Par. Acts* xxi. 31–6 As Paule came to the stayghers of the castell. *Ibid.*, The multitude.. folowed, euen to the veray staighers of the castell.

4. *pl.* (rarely †*sing.*). **a.** A landing-stage, esp. on the Thames in and near London.

1517 in *Archæologia* XLVII. 312 For makyng of an upright steyer of assheler from the Themys as highe as the grounde afore the wacchehouse. **1555–6** in Feuillerat *Revels Q. Mary* (1914) 202 The blacke fryers stayre. **1598** DRAYTON *Heroic. Epist., El. Cobham to Duke Humph.* 54 When my Barge was launched from the stayre. **1643** BAKER *Chron., Hen. III*, 125 He commanded to be set ashore at the next Staires. **1687** LOVELL *Thevenot's Trav.* I. 20 This Town hath two and twenty Gates,.. five on the streight of the Propontis, having all their landing Places and Stairs. **1698–9** *Act 11 Will. III*, c. 21 §4 The said Rulers.. shall.. appoint the Watermen.. Stairs and Places of plying.. betweene Gravesend and Windsor. **1801** STRUTT *Sports & Past.* II. ii. 71 A vessel is moored at a distance from the stairs. **1904** A. GRIFFITHS *50 Yrs. Publ. Serv.* xiv. 205 Just opposite, on the riverside, were the Millbank stairs.

b. A flight of stone steps, or a steep lane or alley with steps at intervals, forming a passage from one street to another at a different level.

1585 T. WASHINGTON tr. *Nicholay's Voy.* IV. xv. 129 b, You doe discend by a faire stare, about 3. quarters of a myle. **1649** W. G. *Surv. Newcastle* 20 Neer this Street is two wayes which goes down into the Close, the long Staires and Tudhill Staires.

5. *attrib.* and *Comb.* **a.** simple attrib. as ***stair-arch***, ***-baluster***, ***-carpet***, ***-carpeting***, ***-door***, ***-newel***, ***-rail***, ***-top***, etc.; ***stair-like*** adj.; ***stair-wise*** adv.; ***stair-builder***, ***-building***, ***-climbing***. (Rarely ***stairs-***.)

1883 *Good Words* July 422/1 Marvellous 'bits' of broken *stair-arches. **1858** SIMMONDS *Dict. Trade*, **Stair-baluster manufacturer.* **1859** EASTERBROOK & MONCKTON (*title*) American *Stair Builder. **1892** *Nation* (N.Y.) 11 Aug. 99/2 Two stairbuilders from Boston. **1900** W. & A. MOWAT (*title*) A Treatise on *Stairbuilding and Handrailing. **1817** M. HOLYOKE in G. F. Dow *Holyoke Diaries* (1911) 167 Began to mend *Stair carpet. **1834** DICKENS *Sk. Boz, Boarding-ho.* ii, Mending a piece of stair-carpet off the first landing. **1862** *Catal. Internat. Exhib., Brit.* II. No. 4237 Twilled *stairs carpeting. **1874** H. H. COLE *Catal. Ind. Art S. Kens. Mus.* 249 Piece of stair-carpeting. **1898** *Allbutt's Syst. Med.* V. 893 All *stair-climbing being strictly forbidden. **1891** MEREDITH *One of our Conq.* xxv, A slam of the kitchen *stair-door restored her. **1896** A. MORRISON *Child Jago* i. 9 [He] climbed and reckoned his way up the first *stair-flight. **1848** RICKMAN *Archit.* 154 Windows in staircases, or *stair-lights, are also of a distinct character in all styles. **1863–65** J. THOMSON *Sunday at Hampstead* vii, Broad terrace-gardens *stairlike sank away. **1876** HARDY *Ethelberta* xx, She leant against the *stair-newel. **1848** THACKERAY *Van. Fair* lxvi, The narrow *stair passage. **1846** DICKENS *Cricket on Hearth* i, Deal doors, dressers, *stair-rails, bedposts. **1802** G. COLMAN *Br. Grins, Elder Bro.* (1819) 125 Being much nearer the *stair top. **1542** UDALL *Erasm. Apoph.* 50 b, The places, where open fightes wer exhibited, wer made circlewise round about with settles or benches of marble, *staier wise one aboue an other. **1871** W. KAY *Psalms* 403 The rhythmical structure of these Psalms [cxx. to cxxxiv] (in which one line is built up upon another stair-wise).

b. Special comb.: **stair-beak**, a Brazilian bird of the genus *Xenops*; **stair-cloth**, a fabric for covering stairs; **stair dancer** *slang*, a thief who steals from open buildings; cf. DANCER 6; **stairlift**, a device that can be built into a domestic staircase for the conveyance of disabled or infirm people up and down stairs; **stair-maid**, a maid-servant employed about the staircase in an hotel; **stair-pit** *Mining* (see quot. 1883); **stair-rod** (see quot. 1858); also (in *pl.*) a proverbial comparison for heavy rainfall; †**stairs-shell** ? = *staircase-shell*; †**stair-shide**, ? a side-piece for a stair-case; **stair-step** *sb.*, one of the steps in a flight of stairs; also *fig.* and as *adj.*, resembling a stair-step; also *attrib.* in ***stair-step curve***; **stair-step** *v.*, to furnish with a range of steps; also *intr.*, to resemble stair-steps; hence **stair-stepper**, **stairstepping** *ppl. a.*; **stair-tower**, a stair-turret; **stair-tread** = TREAD *sb.* 11; **stair-tree**, †(*a*) the sloping timber on or in which the ends of the steps of a wooden staircase are fixed; (*b*) (see quot. 1688); (*c*) a tree with steps in it to serve as a staircase; **stair-turret**, a turret with a staircase in it; **stairwell**, the shaft containing a flight of stairs, a well (WELL *sb.*[1] 8 a); **stair-wire**, a slender stair-rod of metal; **stair-work**, work made or done on or in connexion with stairs. See also STAIRCASE, STAIR-FOOT, STAIR-HEAD, STAIRWAY.

1869–73 T. R. JONES *Cassell's Bk. Birds* III. 19 The *Stair-beaks (*Xenops*) are a group of Brazilian birds. **1771** MRS. HAYWOOD *New Present* 254 If hair *stair-cloths are used. **1862** *Catal. Internat. Exhib., Brit.* II. No. 4247, Floor-cloths, table-covering, and stair-cloths. **1958** *Times* 10 Feb. 4/5 '*Stair dancer' is.. the name given by the police to the thief who walks in and out of City offices, looking for something to steal. **1977** 'E. CRISPIN' *Glimpses of Moon* xii. 235 Since he was a stair dancer, a walk-in thief, judges had been inclined to be lenient until the last occasion, when his offence had been said.. to have been aggravated by his having broken a window to 'effect an entrance'. **1977** *Hansard Commons* 24 Jan. 472 *Stairlift and personal passenger vertical lifts for the disabled. **1980** *BSI News* Aug. 13/1 Stairlifts and homelifts are now extensively used in domestic situations, where they can be an invaluable aid to the disabled or infirm person. **1895** *Daily News* 13 Feb. 10/7 Basementmaid or *Stairmaid.. in hotel or business house. **1883** GRESLEY *Gloss. Coal-mining*, **Stairpit*, a shallow shaft or staple in a mine fitted with a ladder or steps. **1887** MCNEILL *Blawearie* 95 We descended a stair-pit and breathed the peculiar air of the mines. **1843** DICKENS *Christmas Carol* iv. 130 The old man raked the fire together with an old *stair-rod. **1858** SIMMONDS *Dict. Trade*, *Stair-rods*, metal rods, usually of brass, fixed in eyes, to secure and keep a stair-carpet smooth in the bend of each step. **1879** *Cassell's Techn. Educ.* IV. 298/2 Stair rods are of solid iron, plated. **1963** *Times* 22 Apr. 4/6 During the morning the rain came down like stair-rods. During the match it turned to a swirling drizzle. **1977** D. MACKENZIE *Raven & Ratcatcher* i. 14 The rain was falling in stair rods. **1774** GOLDSM. *Nat. Hist.* VII. 10 The *Stairs shell. **1477–9** *Rec. St. Mary at Hill* (1905) 85 For ij pecis for *Steir shides, vj d. **1794** N. PARRY *Jrnl.* 26 June in *Kentucky Hist. Soc. Reg.* (1936) XXXIV. 386 Ky. hill on the south shore is exceeding bad, being long, steep, & broken with Limestone, somewhat resembling *stair-steps. **1833** LOUDON *Encycl. Archit.* §1089 Soles and lintels, stair-steps, crow-steps. **1904** *Brit. Med. Jrnl.* 10 Sept. 568/1 The neutralization, instead of the stair-step curve, as used by Ehrlich in his spectrum, could be represented by a very regular curve. **1925** C. R. COOPER *Lions 'n' Tigers* iv. 76 This was the district of 'stair-steps', of thin, narrow-shouldered women, trailed by processions of children, five and six in a line. **1944** S. PUTNAM tr. *E. da Cunha's Rebellion in Backlands* ix. 415 This position.. occupied a broad stairstep on the slope of the hill between Mount Mario.. and the Vasa-Barris. **1959** *Wall St. Jrnl.* (Eastern ed.) 12 Aug. 19/2 The 'stairstep' plan in use in Nashville calls for integration classes starting with the first grades and adding one grade each year. **1837** CARLYLE *Fr. Rev.* II. I. xi, Then our huge pyramidal Fatherland's-Altar, *Autel de la Patrie*, in the centre, also to be raised and *stair-stepped. **1961** WEBSTER, Stair-step *v. intr.* **1963** *Amer. Speech* XXXVIII. 203 Some of the English terms are literal equivalents of terms used by German-speaking skiers and might be called loan translations:.. *stair step*, Treppenschritt. **1976** *Billings* (Montana) *Gaz.* 11 July 1-c/3 Yellow clover which carpets the banks smells sweet, grassy rims stairstep against the distant horizon. **1925** C. R. COOPER *Lions 'n' Tigers* iv. 77 Don't need many ladders aroun' this country... All they have t'do is line up the kids and walk on their heads. Ever see so many *stair-steppers? **1972** *Nat. Geographic* Sept. 335 (*caption*) *Stairstepping head-waters of the.. river cascade out of a.. bog. **1886** STEVENSON *Kidnapped* iv. 32 The key of the *stair-tower at the far end of the house. **1919** *Brit. Manufacturer* Nov. 34/1 Sections.. such as are utilised for *stair-treads, cornices, etc. **1374** in Willis & Clark *Cambridge* (1886) I. 238 Ac etiam steires et *steyretres. **1688** HOLME *Armory* III. 340/2 The Stair Tree is the Post on which the Wheel [of the windmill] turns. **1848** tr. *Hoffmeister's Trav. Ceylon*, etc. xi. 437 The houses rest on basements of masonry, and the ascent to the low door-way is by means of a stair-tree. **1854** PETIT *Archit. Stud. France* 73 The western piers are carried up and form *stair-turrets. **1931** DOUGHERTY & KEARNEY *Fire* vii. 99 *Stair wells and other shafts extending from the first floor to the roof. **1958** 'W. HENRY' *Seven Men at Mimbres Springs* xiv. 164 Shortly, they heard his step on the stationhouse stairs, then saw his shadow rise out of the stairwell's greater blackness. **1977** B. BAINBRIDGE *Injury Time* xiii. 109 Lights burned on the stairwells of the flats and along the deserted balconies. **1834** DICKENS *Sk. Boz, Boarding-ho.* i, The very *stair-wires made your eyes wink, they were so glittering. **1611** SHAKS. *Wint. T.* III. iii. 75 This [child] has beene some *staire-worke, some Trunke-worke, some behinde-doore-worke. **1903** *Daily Mail* 11 Sept. 2/7 Many wives stay indoors more than they would through being tired by stair work.

†**stair**, *a. Obs.* exc. *dial.* In 4 stayre, 4–5 staire, 9 *dial.* stair, steer, etc.: (see *Eng. Dial. Dict.*) [OE. **stæᵹer* (in comb. *wiðer-stæᵹre* 'prerupti', *Voc. c* 1050 in Wr.-Wülcker 470):—OTeut. type **staiᵹrjo-*, f. **staiᵹ-*: see STAIR *sb.*] Steep.

a **1175** *Twelfth Cent. Hom.* (E.E.T.S.) 110 þe wæ3 is swiðe heah & swiðe stæ3er þe lædep us to heofene. **13..** *E.E. Allit. P.* A. 1022 Þise twelue de-gres wern brode & stayre. *a* **1400–50** *Wars Alex.* 4828 Till he was comen till a cliffe at to þe cloudis semed, þat was so staire & so stepe þe store me tellis. **16..** *As it befell one Saturday* 26 in *Percy Fol. MS.* (1867) I. 244 As I went vp Kelsall wood, & vp that banke that was soe staire, I looked ouer my left sholder where I was wont to see my deere.

†**stair**, *v.*[1] *Obs. rare.* [perh. f. STAIR *sb.*]

1. *trans.* To ascend.

a **1400–50** *Wars Alex.* 3923 Stayrand on þe staunke þe stour to asaill. *Ibid.* 4834 With þat stairis he forth þe stye þat stre3t to þe est.

2. *trans.* To make in the form of stairs.

? *a* **1412** LYDG. *Two Merchants* 635 Though to richesse ther be no grees i-steyred Tascenden vp.

†**stair**, *v.*[2] *Obs. rare. north.* and *Sc.* [? a. ON. **støyra* (mod.Norw. *støyra* to prick), f. *staur-r*

stake.] *trans.* To thrust (a person) *through*; to thrust (a weapon, etc.) into a person or thing.

a **1300** *Cursor M.* 7667 Dauid him gleud wit his harp, þe king þan hent a sper scarp To stair him thoru vnto þe wau. **1513** DOUGLAS *Æneis* III. iv. 56 All bair Full prevalie thair swerdis in thai stair. *Ibid.* XII. v. 197 On ane altar a birnand schyde hes hynt, And gan it rycht amyd his vissage stair, That blesit vp his lang berd of hair.

stair, obs. form of STAR *sb.*[2]

staircase ('stɛəkeɪs). [f. STAIR *sb.* + CASE *sb.*[2]]

1. a. Originally, 'The inclosure of a pair of Stairs, whether it be with Walls, or with Walls and Railes and Bannisters, &c.' (Moxon *Mech. Exerc.*, 1679, p. 172); now usually a flight (or sometimes a whole series of flights) of stairs with their supporting framework, balusters, etc. *spec.*, at Oxford and Cambridge, a college staircase and the rooms accessible from it; in *transf.* use, the people living in those rooms. ***moving staircase***: see MOVING *ppl. a.* 3.

1624 WOTTON *Archit.* I. 57 Of Staire-cases. **1634** BRERETON *Trav.* (Chetham Soc.) 32 Here is a dainty stair-case, there being two pair of stairs which come out of the hall. **1726** LEONI *Alberti's Archit.* I. 17b, Stair-cases therefore are of two sorts..that which has no Steps, but is mounted by a Sloping Ascent, and the other is that which is mounted by Steps. **1762** J. WESLEY *Jrnl.* 29 Mar., Who lived in the same staircase with me at Christchurch. **1777** ROBERTSON *Hist. Amer.* II. VII. 297 The ascent to it was by a stair-case of a hundred and fourteen steps. **1823** P. NICHOLSON *Pract. Build.* 184 The wall which supports the ends of the steps is called the stair-case. **1826** LAMB *Elia* Ser. II. *Pop. Fallacies* xi, The true Lady Marys and Lady Bettys ..are consigned to the staircase and the lumber-room. **1848** DICKENS *Dombey* xliii, Florence..crept down the staircase. **1861** T. HUGHES *Tom Brown at Oxford* I. i. 13 The rest is divided into staircases, on each of which are six or eight sets of rooms. **1878** BROWNING *La Saisiaz* 15 Till the landing on the staircase saw escape the latest spark. **1914** C. MACKENZIE *Sinister St.* II. III. x. 699 'Alan, who are these mysterious creatures that come down for cocoa at ten?'.. 'They'd bore you rather... They're people who live on this staircase. I don't see them any other time.' **1974** J. I. M. STEWART *Gaudy* ii. 26 The corridor is not an Oxford institution. One lives on a staircase: commonly one set of rooms on either hand, storey by storey, from ground floor to attics. A hospitable man will give a party for the whole staircase. **1977** K. BENTON *Red Hen Conspiracy* xvi. 130 He was one of my pupils... Leader of a very rowdy staircase.

b. *transf.*

a **1668** LASSELS *Voy. Italy* (1698) I. 46 When we came to Mount Sampion, one of the great stair-cases of Italy, we were forced..to go afoot. **1687** LOVELL *Thevenot's Trav.* I. 140 This Stair-case hath been made very easie to go down and up, for the convenience of the Oxen that go down to labour. **1781** GIBBON *Decl. & F.* xix. II. 156 A secret.. staircase, scooped out of the rock that hangs over the stream of the Tigris. **1860** TYNDALL *Glac.* II. xi. 290, I therefore took my axe,..and cut an oblique staircase up the wall of ice.

c. *fig.*

1641 BAKER *Apol.* 19 Doth not the whole staire case by which all Learning..is ascended up by, lye open before them? **1650** FULLER *Pisgah* IV. i. 17 Climax the mountain.., whose figure like that figure in Rhetorick ascends like a staire-case by degrees.

d. ***spirit*** (also ***bravery***) ***of the staircase***, phrases rendering Fr. *esprit de l'escalier* (see ESPRIT 2c). See also sense 4 below.

a **1906** J. MORLEY in H. W. & F. G. Fowler *King's English* (1906) i. 32, I thought afterwards, but it was *the spirit of the staircase*, what a pity it was that I did not stand at the door with a hat, saying, 'Give an obol to Belisarius.' **1906** [see ESPRIT 2c]. **1976** L. HELLMAN *Scoundrel Time* 110 Ah, the bravery you tell yourself was possible when it's all over, the bravery of the staircase.

e. *Electronics.* A voltage that alters in equal steps to a maximum or minimum value.

1956 *Electronics* Feb. 192/2 A..staircase generator which generates a negative-going staircase is shown in Fig. 1. **1959** *Ibid.* 23 Jan. 36/3 Each pulse in the train causes one step of the staircase. **1965** *Wireless World* Sept. 425/1 This signal.. consists of a 12·5 μs bar, a sine-squared pulse..and a five-step staircase.

†**2.** = *staircase-shell* (in 4). *Obs.*

1713 PETIVER *Aquat. Anim. Amboinæ* Tab. ii, *Buccinum scalare verum*..Royal Stair-Case. *Ibid.* Tab. xiii, *Buccinum scalare*..Small Stair-case. **1815** S. BROOKES *Conchol.* 157 Staircase. Trochus perspectivus.

3. *Phys.* A continuous series of responses to nerve stimuli, varying from a minimal to a maximal intensity. (*Syd. Soc. Lex.* citing Romanes.)

[**1871** BOWDITCH in *Ber. d. k. Sächs. Gesellsch. d. Wissensch., Math.-Phys.* XXIII. 669 Wir wollen eine so beschaffene Reihe von Zuckungen unter dem Namen einer Treppe zusammenfassen.] **1882** GASKELL in *Jrnl. Physiol.* IV. 106 In both the strip from the tortoise's auricle and the frog's ventricle..a series of single stimulations produces a 'staircase'. **1885** MCWILLIAM *Ibid.* VI. 209 This phenomenon has been termed a 'staircase of beats (aufsteigende Treppe)'.

4. *attrib.* and *Comb.*: ***staircase-gallery, -head; -like*** adj.; also with reference to sense 1 d, as ***staircase afterthought, thought, wit***; **staircase generator** *Electronics*, a signal generator whose output is a staircase (sense 1 e above); **staircase-shell**, a shell of the genus *Solarium*, any member of the family *Solariidæ*.

1964 *Guardian* 17 Jan. 11/6 The Senator, having written this last passage, decided not to deliver it, a *staircase afterthought that will cost him dear. **1848** DICKENS *Dombey* xlvii, She paced her own room, opened the door and paced the *staircase-gallery outside. **1956** *Staircase generator [see sense 1 e]. **1976** *Pract. Electronics* Oct. 812/2 The output from the staircase generator is then fed into one input of a comparator. **1802** G. COLMAN *Br. Grins, Elder Bro.* (1819) 123 Crow, in the dark, now, reached the *stair-case head. **1881** MRS. HOLMAN HUNT *Childr. Jerus.* 102 They made their way up and down such *staircase-like rocks as in England would seem impossible. **1830** SAY *Amer. Conchol.* Pl. 27 *Scalaria*..., a genus of very pretty shells, known by the name of *staircase shells by some collectors. **1896** LYDEKKER *Roy. Nat. Hist.* VI. 387 The so-called staircase-shells (*Solariidæ*). **1958** J. LODWICK *Bid Soldiers Shoot* II. vi. 210 'At what time did it start to snow that night, Lodwick?' He was referring..to the night of the parachutage... *Staircase thought makes me wish that I had suggested that they have a look at my companion's boots, to which the virginal blanket fallen from Heaven might still..be clinging. **1920** A. DOBSON in *National Rev.* July 654 *Staircase-wit. If you fail to understand a joke within twenty-four hours, your symptoms indicate sluggish apprehension... This is what the French call '*L'esprit de l'escalier*'.

Hence **'staircased** *a.*, furnished with a staircase; **'staircasing** *vbl. sb.*, supplying or providing with a staircase or staircases.

1729 in Willis & Clark *Cambridge* (1886) I. 563 At a Congregation..agreed to proceed in Covering flooring sashing staircasing of the new Building. **1909** *Engl. Rev.* Jan. 223 Each of the two balconied and staircased belfries.

staired (stɛəd), *a. rare.* [f. STAIR *sb.* + -ED[2].] Arranged like stairs, with one step above another; supplied with stairs or stairways.

1650 FULLER *Pisgah* II. v. 126 Our guesse is seconded by plenty of *Gradati montes*, Staired mountains, which goe up by degrees. **1804** COLERIDGE *Lett.* (1895) 482 Many of them [the streets of Malta] very steep—a few staired all across, and almost all..having the footway on each side so staired.

†**'stairer.** [f. STAIR *sb.* + -ER[1].] The keeper of the stairs (of a public building.)

1695 WOOD *Life* (O.H.S.) III. 496 Some rabble and townes-men that had got in by the connivance of the stairers.

stair-foot. Also *rarely* **stairs-, stair's-. a.** The foot of a staircase; the level space in front of the lowest step of a flight of stairs.

1470–85 MALORY *Arthur* XVIII. vii. 736 The other knyghte wente streyghte to the steyer foote where sat Kyng Arthur. **1513** MORE in *Grafton's Chron.* (1568) II. 804 He caused ye murtherers to bury them at the stayre foote. **1598** B. JONSON *Ev. Man in Hum.* III. iii, Or sit in the cold at the staire-foot for her. **1667** DRYDEN & DK. NEWCASTLE *Sir M. Mar-all* v. i, The gentle Guinea..which us'd as duly to steal into our hands at the Stair-foot, as into Mr. Doctor's at parting. **1722** DE FOE *Col. Jack* xv, I waited on her then to the stairfoot. **1848** DICKENS *Dombey* xliii, He had led her back to the stair-foot.

a **1562** G. CAVENDISH *Wolsey* (1893) 264 Whome they brought on his mewle to the stayers foote of his chamber, and ther lighted. **1757** *Hist. 2 Mod. Adventurers* II. 196 Waddling to the Stairs-foot; 'Moll, Moll', said she. **1868** 'HOLME LEE' *Basil Godfrey* v, She did not hear her mother call from the stair's-foot.

b. *attrib.*

1573–5 GASCOIGNE *Ferd. Jeronimi* Wks. 1907 I. 407 He having a large base court to passe over before he could recover his staire foote dore. **1607** TOURNEUR *Rev. Trag.* II. iii. 10 He and the Duchesse By night meete in their linnen, they haue beene seene By staire-foote pandars! **1665** WOOD *Life* (O.H.S.) II. 45 For a key to the starefoot door, 8*d.* **1914** D. H. LAWRENCE *Widowing of Mrs. Holroyd* I. ii. 22 At that instant the stairfoot door opens slowly, revealing the children.

stair-head, 'stairhead. Also formerly *rarely* **stairs-.** The level space at the top of a staircase or flight of stairs.

1534–5 *MS. Rawl. D.* 777 lf. 72 The Stayer hede goyng to the Quen's Juell hous. **1569** *Inv. Lanc. & Chesh. Wills* (Chetham Soc.) 36 In the chamber at the steare head. **1607** WOTTON in *Life & Lett.* (1907) I. 379 [The Doge of Venice] brought him afterwards down to the last stairhead of the place. **1634** BRERETON *Trav.* (Chetham Soc.) 32 Here is a dainty stair-case, there being two pair of stairs which come out of the hall, and land both at one stair-head, and lead into the best rooms. **1702** SAVERY *Miner's Friend* 43 This Pipe.. must be long enough to reach from the Landing-place or Stair-head. **1820** KEATS *Cap & Bells* lxx, He..scarce upright could reach The stair-head. **1849** CUPPLES *Green Hand* xv. (1856) 152 She stood with one little foot on the stair-head behind me. **1894** HALL CAINE *Manxman* v. iv. 294 He..crept out on to the stairhead, and listened.

1551–60 in H. Hall *Soc. Eliz. Age* (1886) 150 An olde cub-bord standing at the Stayers headd. **1588** PARKE tr. *Mendoza's Hist. China* 126 The first hall of the pallace which is at the staires heade. **1655** tr. *Sorel's Com. Hist. Francion* XII. 22 They took their ready way to the stairs head. **1748** RICHARDSON *Clarissa* VI. 258 She shot to the stairs-head to receive him.

attrib. **1851** MAYHEW *Lond. Labour* (1861) II. 378/2, I pay him 2*s.* 9*d.* a week for a little stair-head place with a bed in it. **1910** *Q. Rev.* Apr. 385 She was not a mere stairhead hostess.

stairless ('stɛəlɪs), *a. rare.* [f. STAIR *sb.* + -LESS.] Having no stairs.

1868 MACDONALD *R. Falconer* I. 283 Out at his eyes it would go, traverse the dim stairless space, and sport with the wind-blown monster. **1897** MARY KINGSLEY *W. Africa* 422 The population..has been..employed in hauling and hoisting the furniture on to the stairless verandah.

stairway ('stɛəweɪ). [f. STAIR *sb.* + WAY *sb.*]

a. A way up a flight of stairs, a staircase.

1767 T. HUTCHINSON *Hist. Mass.* (1795) II. iv. 387 Officers had planted themselves at the head of the stair-way with loaded carbines. **1847** PRESCOTT *Peru* IV. v. (1850) II. 339 Running down to the first landing on the stairway. **1872** M. COLLINS *P'cess Clarice* II. 92 He walked up the grim stairway of the hotel. **1892** BOYLE *County of Durham* 261 They were reached by a stairway from the triforium. **1906** MARJ. BOWEN *Viper of Milan* xx, It [the door] opened immediately on a black marble stairway.

b. *transf.* spec. in *Geomorphol.*, a series of abrupt changes of level in the floor of a glaciated valley.

c **1820** S. ROGERS *Italy, Jovasse* (1838) 23 His ancient carbine from his shoulder slung, His axe to hew a stair-way in the ice. **1894** *Westm. Gaz.* 1 Jan. 2/1 Here the old Duke of Bridgewater's canal makes junction with the Ship Canal by two long stairways of locks. **1904** *Jrnl. Geol.* XII. 570 The tread of the steps in the long stairway..greatly lengthened in down-canyon order. **1957** J. K. CHARLESWORTH *Quaternary Era* I. xiii. 297 Cirques in almost all glaciated regions frequently occur in tiers, the 'tandom cirque' or 'cirque stairway'.., each step often with its rock-basin and tarn. **1974** [see RISER 7b].

c. *fig.*

1879 E. ARNOLD *Lt. Asia* VIII. (1881) 229 Make golden stairways of your weakness. **1886** C. A. BRIGGS *Messianic Proph.* i. 26 The prophets as an order of..teachers constitute a grand stairway. **1909** *Edin. Rev.* July 40 Thus the soul ranges up and down the stairway of existence.

†**'stairy,** *a. Obs. rare.* [f. STAIR *sb.* + -Y.] Ascending or mounting like a flight of stairs.

1599 NASHE *Lenten Stuffe* 13 With wooden galleries in the Church that they haue, and stayry degrees of seates in them. **1602** [see CLIMACTERICAL *a.* 1].

stait(e, obs. forms of STATE *sb.*

staithe (steɪð), *sb.* Now *local.* Forms: 1 **stæþ** (*dat.* **staþe, stæþe**), 2 **steþ**, 3 **staþe**, 5–8 (9 *Dicts.*) **stathe**, 6 **stath**, 7 **stayth**, 8 **steath(e**, 6–9 **staith**, 6– **staithe**; also 9 *dial.* **steeth, stay,** etc.: see *Eng. Dial. Dict.* [In sense 1, repr. OE. *stæþ* neut. (?once masc.) = OS. *stad* bank, shore, OHG. *stad* masc., neut. (MHG. *stat*, inflected *stad-*, mod.G. dial. *staa*), Goth. *staþa* dat. (masc. or neut.):—OTeut. **staþo-* f. **sta-*: see STAND *v.* In senses 2 and 3, which are not evidenced in OE. and are current only in districts where Scandinavian influence is strong, the word prob. represents (or has coalesced with) the cognate ON. *stǫð* fem.(:—**staþwō*) landing-stage (Norw. *stød*). Cf. also OHG. *stado* wk. masc. (MHG. *stade*, mod.G. dial. *staden*) and MHG. *gistat* neut. (mod.G. *gestade*) landing-place.]

†**1.** The land bordering on water, a bank, shore.

c **893** ÆLFRED *Oros.* I. i. §22 Of ðæm mere ðe Truso standeð in staðe. *O.E. Chron.* (Parker MS.) an. 894, Æt Butting tune on Sæferne staþe. *a* **1000** *Riddles* iii. 6 (Gr.) Streamas staþu beatað. *Ibid.* xxiii. 19 Brohte hwæþre beornas ofer burnan & hyra bloncan mid from stæðe heaum. *c* **1050** *Suppl. Ælfric's Gloss.* in Wr.-Wülcker 177 *Ripa*, stæþ. [**11**.. *Ibid.* 546 steþ.] *c* **1205** LAY. 7 He wonede at Ernleȝe.. vppen Seuarne staþe.

2. A landing-stage, wharf; esp. a waterside depôt for coals brought from the collieries for shipment, furnished with staging and shoots for loading vessels.

1338 *Orig. Chartulary of Tinmouth Monastery* 172 in Brand *Hist. Newcastle* (1789) II. 255 Domus quam predictus prior et suus conventus..habent in predicta villa Novi Castri super le Stathes. *c* **1390** in Gross *Gild Merch.* II. 169 [Lynn Regis] *Unam communem placeam vocatam* le commen stathe *cum pertinenciis.* **1420** *Eng. Misc.* (Surtees) 17 We, serchours of the masons and wryghtes of the cite of York..awarde and deme yᵗ a lyne be drawn straight fra ye corner of ye stathe of ye chauntery..un to ye nexte corner of ye stathe of ye common place. *c* **1440** *Promp. Parv.* 473/1 Stathe, waterys syde, *stacio.* **1519** in *Archæologia* XXV. 418 For caryeng of yᵉ same ij cads [of Red Heryngs] to yᵉ Common Stathe, ij d. **1653** *Lilburn Tryed & Cast* 4 [He] sold a thousand pounds worth of Coales that were upon the Staithes. **1667** PRIMATT *City & C. Build.* 26 You may consider what Stayths or Wharffs there be upon the River. **1708** J. C. *Compl. Collier* (1845) 49 The Rivers are not Navigable for Ships, so high as they Keys or Coal-Steaths. **1833** HT. MARTINEAU *Tale of Tyne* i. 1 Train after train of coal-waggons slid by on the rail-road from the pit to the staithe. **1862** SMILES *Engineers* III. 11 Arrived at the staiths, the waggons are emptied at once into the ships waiting alongside for cargo. **1905** *Times* 4 Mar. 9/6 At midnight last night the River Tyne Commissioners' new staithes..were totally destroyed by fire.

3. An embankment.

1698 DE LA PRYME *Diary* (Surtees) 185 Their tyde..is fenced out with huge staithes, for if all the water might be suffered to come in that would, it would..dround..the whole Levels. **1839** STONEHOUSE *Axholme* 52 The fertility of the soil..would induce the inhabitants..by means of staiths and embankments, to reclaim the land thus formed. **1876** *Whitby Gloss.* s.v. *Steeath, Staithes*, masonry to prevent the ground as a foundation from being washed away.

staithe (steɪð), *v. dial.* [f. prec. sb.] *trans.* To furnish with a staithe; to embank.

1839 STONEHOUSE *Axholme* 20 Considerable attempts must have been made, even at this early period to staith and embank the Trent. **1876** *Whitby Gloss.* s.v. *Steeath*, It was well steeath'd; i.e. strengthened by masonry.

staithman ('steɪðmən). Also **staithsman.** [f. STAITH *sb.* + MAN *sb.*] (See quots.)

1667 PRIMATT *City & C. Build.* 27 By the Staithsmens accompts..you may find what quantity of Coles there hath been wrought. **1710** *Act 9 Anne* c. 28 §9 No Coal-Owner..

or his..Overman or Overmen, Staithman [etc.]. **1893–4** *Northumbld. Gloss.*, *Staithman, steethman*, the man who overlooks the shipping of coals.

staitly, obs. Sc. form of STATELY.

staive, staiver: see STAVE, STAVER *vbs.*

stak, obs. f. STACK *sb.*; obs. pa. t. of STICK *v.*

stake (steɪk), *sb.*[1] Forms: 1 **staca**, 5, 7 **stak**, 5–6 *Sc.* and *north.* **staik** (6 **steyk**), 6 **stack**, 6–7 **stacke**, 3– **stake**. [OE. *staca* wk. masc. corresponds to OFris., MDu. *stake* masc. and fem. (Du. *staak* masc.), (M)LG. *stake* (whence MHG., mod.G. *stake, staken*, and prob. MSw. *staki*, Sw., Norw. *stake*, Da. *stage*), f. **stak-* ablaut-var. of **stek-* to pierce, thrust in: see STEKE, STICK *vbs.* The Teut. word was adopted in Rom. as Pr., Sp., Pg. *estaca*, OF. *estaque, estache*, It. *stacca*: see STACKET, ESTACADE.]

1. a. A stout stick or post, usually of wood, with a pointed end for driving into the ground; used e.g. to mark a boundary or site, to support a plant, to secure an animal, to form one of the component parts of a fence, hedge, or the like.

c **893** ÆLFRED *Oros.* v. v, Ac þære ilcan niht þe mon on dæʒ hæfde þa burʒ mid stacum ʒemearcod, swa [etc.]. *c* **1000** *Sax. Leechd.* I. 395, & sleah ænne stacan on middan þam ymbhaʒan & leʒe þone stan on uppan þam stacan. *c* **1340** *Nominale* (Skeat) 338 On a stake of pere-tre. **1390** GOWER *Conf.* II. 83 A tente of cloth with corde and stake He sette up ferst. *c* **1420** *Avow. Arth.* xvii, The hed of that hardy, He sette on a stake. *a* **1440** *Sir Degrev.* 1120 Syxty stedus he wan, And brouȝth to stak. *c* **1440** [see STAKING *vbl. sb.* b]. **1523** *Act 14 & 15 Hen. VIII*, c. 13 Dyvers newe Weris, Gores, Stakes and Engyns have bene levyd and enhauncid; By reason wherof, the said Haven is greatly decayed ageyn. **1534** in J. Croft *Excerpta Ant.* (1797) 17 For a Steyk of vj Nyks for Stapys to a Grese, ij d. **1667** PRIMATT *City & C. Build.* 93 The Ground is not firm to build on, but doth require stakes to be driven. *a* **1674** CLARENDON *Hist. Reb.* xv. §144 The man was drawn by a horse to the gallows..and buried under it, with a stake driven through him, as is usual in the case of self-murderers. **1719** DE FOE *Crusoe* I. (Globe) 117, I set my Dog to guard it in the Night, tying him up to a Stake at the Gate. **1784** COWPER *Task* IV. 437 The farmer's hedge, Plash'd neatly, and secur'd with driven stakes Deep in the loamy bank. **1897** MARY KINGSLEY *W. Africa* 255 We find it completely fenced across with stout stakes.

fig. **1567** *Gude & Godlie Ball.* 186 O cankerit carionnis, and o ye rottin stakis. **1594** HOOKER *Eccl. Pol.* Pref. ii. §3 As the truth is, their ministers forrein estimation hitherto hath beene the best stake in their hedge. **1630** PRYNNE *Anti-Armin.* 123 Thus to plucke vp all the stakes, the bounds of Gods eternal Decrees.

Proverbial uses. a **1300** *Cursor M.* 7526 Bot þar he stod als still os stake. **1390** GOWER *Conf.* III. 8, I fro hire go Ne mai, bot as it were a stake, I stonde. **1546** J. HEYWOOD *Prov.* (1867) 29 For any great courtesie he doth make, It seemth the gentill man hath eaten a stake. *a* **1637** B. JONSON *Underwoods, Celebr. Charis* ix, Dressed, you still for man should take him! And not think h' had eat a stake.

b. A post upon which persons were bound for execution, esp. by burning. Hence ***the stake*** is used as a name for the punishment of death by burning.

c **1205** LAY. 16684 Samuel nom Agag þene king..& lette hine swiðe sterke to ane stake binde. *c* **1386** CHAUCER *Knt.'s T.* 1694 And he that is at meschief shal be take And noght slayn but be broght vn to the stake That shal ben ordeyned. *c* **1400** MAUNDEV. (Roxb.) ix. 35 Scho was..bun by a stake and fagotes of thornes..laide aboute hir. **1563–83** FOXE *A. & M.* II. 1623 When they came to the stake in Smithfielde to bee burned, M. Bradford lying prostrate on the one side of the stake, and..John Leafe on the other side. **1591** SHAKS. *1 Hen. VI*, v. iii. 44 Curse Miscreant, when thou comst to the stake. **1600** *Aberdeen Reg.* (1848) II. 209 The persoun convict thairof..sall be bund to ane staik within the floode merk during the space of thre houris, quhill the water flow round about him. **1642** FULLER *Holy & Prof. St.* II. xix. 125 When Religion is at the stake, there must be no lookers on. **1722** DE FOE *Moll Flanders* (1840) 277 To be burnt to death at a stake. **1829** HOOD *Eugene Aram* 204 And my red right hand grows raging hot, Like Cranmer's at the stake. **1852** THACKERAY *Esmond* I. v, 'I know I would go to the stake for you,' said Harry. **1872** MORLEY *Voltaire* (1886) 7 When..the fortunes of the fight do not hurry the combatant to dungeon or stake.

c. The post to which a bull or bear was fastened to be baited.

1546 J. HEYWOOD *Prov.* I. ix. (1867) 17 With as good will as a beare goth to the stake. **1601** SHAKS. *Jul. C.* IV. i. 48 *Octa.* Let vs do so: for we are at the stake, And bayed about with many Enemies. **1616** W. BROWNE *Brit. Past.* II. iv. 98 Saw you a lusty Mastiue at the stake Throwne from a cunning Bull.

d. A post pointed at both ends for use in military defensive work (see quot. 1876).

1297 R. GLOUC. *Chron.* (Rolls) 1171 Stakes of ire monion he piȝte in temese grounde Aboue ssarpe & kene inou bineþ grete & rounde. *c* **1450** *Brut* II. ccxliv. 378 He bade euery man to orden hym a stake of tre, and scharp both endis, þat þe stake myȝt be pyght yn the erthe a-slop, þat hir enymyez schulde not ouyr-ryde hem. **1634** MILTON *Comus* 491 Com not too neer, you fall on iron stakes else. **1876** VOYLE & STEVENSON *Milit. Dict.*, *Stakes*, small pieces of wood..used as an obstacle against the advance of an attacking force, being sharply pointed and driven into the ground until only 1 foot or 2 feet project.

e. *Phrases.* (U.S.) ***to pick up, pull up, move stakes***: to move one's habitation. Similarly ***to drive, set stakes, to stick one's stakes***: to pitch one's camp or tent, to settle. ***to tie*** (***someone***) ***to the stake***: see TIE *v.* 2.

1703 S. SEWALL *Diary* 15 Apr. (1879) II. 76 Went to my Bounds, asserted them,..then ordered Kibbe to pull up the Stakes. Told Mr. Lynde's Tenants what my Bounds were ..; forwarn'd them of coming there to set any Stakes. **1817** J. K. PAULDING *Lett. from South* I. 83 When they have exhausted one hunting-ground, [the Indians] pull up stakes, and incontinently march off to another. **1830** *Massachusetts Spy* 15 Dec. (Thornton *Amer. Gloss.* s.v. *Pull*), Our departed emigrants pulled up stakes, and returned post haste to the good old town of Springfield. **1869** BRET HARTE *Luck of Roaring Camp* 178 He built the shanty..lest titles should fall through, and we'd have to get up and move stakes farther down. **1872** DE VERE *Americanisms* 184 Where he settles, there he stakes or sticks his stakes. **1906** *Outing* (U.S.) Feb. 605/2 After drifting about several years I finally drove stakes on the Spokane River. **1924** 'R. DALY' *Outpost* xvii. 165 I've sometimes thought of pulling up stakes and pushing further into the mountains. **1949** *Boston Globe* 15 May (Fiction Mag.) 6/2 We'll set our stakes, an' I'll slip down to Dawson an' record the claim. **1974** M. ALLEN *Super Tour* (1975) i. 23 'I'm assuming you're in a position to pick up stakes in a hurry.' 'As long as it will take to pack two bags.' **1980** *Dallas Times Herald* 10 May (Week End Suppl.) 6/1 The economic incentive that Europeans once had to pull up stakes and move to America.

2. *collect. sing.* Stakes used as a framework or support in fencing and hedging; esp. as a basis for the intertwining, wattling, or plashing of brushwood or other materials.

a. ***stake*** (earlier †***stakes***) ***and rice*** (RICE *sb.* 2) *Sc.* and *north.*: a fence, hurdle, or partition made with these materials; also *attrib.*

1457 *Sc. Acts Jas. II*, §30 (1814) II. 51/2 þt na man mak gardes nor heggis of dry staikes na Rys or stykis. **1471–2** *Durh. Acc. Rolls* (Surtees) 644 Pro posicione del stakez et ryss. **1536** BELLENDEN *Cron. Scot.* (1821) I. 260 To big the wal betwix Abircorne and Dunbritane, with staik and rise. **1584** HUDSON *Du Bartas' Judith* iv, On stake and ryce hee knits the crooked vines, And snoddes their bowes. **1799** J. ROBERTSON *Agric. Perth* 278 Hurdles, (vulgarly called stake and rice) may be made round the links. **1821** [see STAB *sb.*[2] 1]. **1858** R. S. SURTEES *Ask Mamma* lxv. 295 Giving his horse a good dig with his spurs, he lifted him over a stiff stake-and-rice fence.

b. ***stake and band, bond, bound***: see quot. 1805.

1805 R. W. DICKSON *Pract. Agric.* I. Plate xxxiii, The form of dead hedge usually termed stake and band, and sometimes stake and rise. In it the dead materials are wattled in between strong stakes. *Ibid.* 141 A stake and band hedge. **1857** G. A. LAWRENCE *Guy Livingstone* iv, Instead of taking the stake-and-bound at the weakest place, he rode at the strongest. **1902** CORNISH *Naturalist on Thames* 161 This is the universal 'stake and bond' hedge of the shires, impenetrable to cattle.

c. ***stake and rider*** (see RIDER *sb.* 12 d), a fence made of stakes with a top bar; also *attrib.*; hence ***stake-and-ridered*** adj. Chiefly *N. Amer.*

1829 *Massachusetts Spy* 11 Feb. (Thornton *Amer. Gloss.*), [He met] a man in a lane with a stake-and-rider fence on each side. **1846** *Knickerbocker* XXVII. 208 Already the 'stake and ridered' fence was beginning to enclose the cleared land. **1859** BARTLETT *Dict. Amer.* (ed. 2) 443 Stake and rider, a species of fence higher and stronger than a 'worm fence'. **1884** G. W. CABLE *Dr. Sevier* II. liv. 175 Again they followed him along a line of stake-and-rider fence. **1895** *Century Mag.* Aug. 625/2 The stake-and-ridered fences everywhere. **1950** *Pennsylvania Dutchman* Jan. 3/3 He could do nothing better than to quickly place his gun behind him in a corner of a stake-and-rider fence.

†**3.** A rung (of a ladder). *Obs. rare.*

c **1440** *Jacob's Well* xxxiii. 215 He sytteth on þe netherest stake of þis laddere in helle. *Ibid.*, Iche of hem syttեth a-bouyn oþer on þis leddere on dyuers stakys.

†**4.** ? A stick (of a fan). *Obs. rare.*

1640–1 *Kirkcudbright War-Comm. Minute Bk.* (1855) 44 Delyverit..ane silver coupe, ane stak of ane fann, [etc.].

5. Technical uses.

a. A small anvil used by metal-workers, esp. one with a tang for fitting into a socket on a bench. Also, a tool used by watchmakers and jewellers (see quot. 1884).

1660 in *Archæologia* XI. 101 Armorers Tooles.. Tramping Stakes. Round stake. Welting stakes. **1677** MOXON *Mech. Exerc.* ii. 20 The Stake is a small Anvil.. which either stands upon a broad Iron foot..on the work-bench..or else it hath a strong Iron spike at bottom, which ..is let into..the work-bench. **1843** HOLTZAPFFEL *Turning* I. 386 The smaller anvils, which are called stakes,..are of progressively smaller sizes. **1884** F. J. BRITTON *Watch & Clockm.* 214 *Polishing Stake*, a square polished surface of steel on which red-stuff and other polishing material is mixed. It is usually enclosed in a box. *Ibid.* 228 *Riveting Stake*, a cube of steel..pierced with a series of different sized holes for the reception of arbors... A jointed stake.. hinged at one end..is handy in some cases. *Ibid.* 246 A stake with a beak to it.., a form much used by jewellers.

b. *Leather-manuf.* (See quot. 1897.)

1853 URE *Dict. Arts* (ed. 4) II. 63 The workman holding the extremities of the skin with both hands, pulls it in all directions..against the smoothing 'stake'. **1897** C. T. DAVIS *Manuf. Leather* xx. (ed. 2) 274 The hand stake..was an upright wooden stake, some two feet in length and eight inches in width into the tapering top of which was fixed a broad steel blade. The skin was drawn across this blade.

c. Each of the stanchions or posts which fit into sockets or staples on a trolley, wagon or boat to prevent the load from slipping off. Also *ellipt.* for *stake-body truck* (sense 7 below). *N. Amer. colloq.*

1875–84 KNIGHT *Dict. Mech.* **1968** *Globe & Mail* (Toronto) 17 Feb. 50/3 (Advt.), Immediate delivery on new pick-ups, panels, vans and stakes. *Ibid.*, Ford 2¼ ton stake with covered compartment for carrying personnel. **1978** *Detroit Free Press* 16 Apr. F13/7 (Advt.), 1978 Chevy truck sale. Pickups. Elcaminos. Stakes. Stepvans.

d. *Basket-making.* Each of the longest foundation-rods of a basket or the like. (Webster, 1911.)

1903, 1910 [see LEAGUE *sb.*[2] 4]. **1959** D. WRIGHT *Baskets & Basketry* vi. 136 *Stakes*, rods driven in with the bottom sticks to form the foundation of the sides of a basket. **1964** H. HODGES *Artifacts* x. 146 Most baskets were made by first weaving a base, although solid wooden bases drilled to take the uprights, or stakes, were occasionally used.

6. In the Mormon Church: A territorial division; the see or jurisdiction of a Mormon bishop. [? Suggested by Isa. liv. 2, 3.] Also ***Stake*** (***in*** or ***of***) ***Zion.***

[**1833** J. SMITH in Linn *Story of Mormons* (1902) 120 It is expedient in me that this Stake that I have set for the strength of Zion be made strong. **1839** *Ibid.*, I have other places which I will appoint unto them, and they shall be called Stakes for the curtains, or the strength of Zion.] **1843** H. CASWALL *Prophet of 19th Cent.* 90 Other 'churches' established by 'revelations' given to Smith, are called 'Stakes of Zion', or simply 'Stakes'. **1857** *Southern Illinoisian* (Shawneetown) 1 May 1/3 Throughout the States and Territories, at various and convenient locations, the Mormons have what are termed 'stakes in Zion', and each stake is governed by a Presidency. **1870** J. H. BEADLE *Life in Utah* 124 All the wealthy members were to follow him to western Pennsylvania, and establish a new 'stake' for the others to gather to! **1882–3** *Schaff's Encycl. Relig. Knowl.* II. 1578 Every city, or 'stake', including a chief town and surrounding towns. **1883** *Encycl. Brit.* XVI. 828 The [Mormon] church is made up of 23 stakes, each having a president. **1905** *Out West* Sept. 246 The Stakes of Zion, I will explain, are those gathering places of the Saints that are outside of Zion proper—Jackson county, Missouri, where the holy city it is believed will yet be built. **1961** *Guardian* 23 Jan. 2/3 The share of the Manchester 'stake' (stake is roughly the Mormon for diocese) is £2 million. **1976** *Times* 18 June (Spec. Rep. Mormons) p. iii/7 A stake is administered by four lay members.

7. *attrib.* and *Comb.*, as ***stake-beetle*** (BEETLE *sb.*[1] 1), ***-fence, -hedge, -hole, -pole, -rest***; (sense 6) ***stake centre, house, president***; **stake-boat**, a boat moored or otherwise fixed to serve as a starting-point or mark for racing boats; also, a fixed boat to which other boats may be moored; **stake-body** *U.S.*, a body for a lorry, etc., which has an open, flat platform fitted with removable stakes (sense 5 c) along the sides in order to retain the load; also *attrib.* in ***stake-body truck***, a lorry fitted with such a body; **stake-driver** *U.S.*, the bittern, *Botaurus mugitans*; **stake-fellow**, a fellow-sufferer at the stake; **stake-hang** *dial.*, **stake-head** (see quots.); **stake-iron**, (*a*) a nail-maker's stake (sense 5 a); (*b*) = sense 5 c; † **stake nail** (see quot.); **stake-net**, a fishing net usually set between tide-marks or in shallow water, secured in a vertical position by means of stakes; **stake-pocket**, a socket for a stake of a platform car (*Cent. Dict.* 1891); **stake-presidency**, the presidency of a Mormon stake (see sense 6); † **stake-stubber**, one who removes (boundary) stakes; † **stake-stuck** *a.*, that stands like a stake; **stake-truck** = *stake-body truck* above; † **stake willow**, a kind of willow used for the making of stakes.

1638–40 *Min. Archdeaconry of Essex* (MS.) 140b, He tooke two stakes and knockt them in with a *stake beetle. **1839** *Spirit of Times* 13 July 217/2 After a smart pull for it, she [*sc.* a boat] overhauled them one by one, passing the Washington about half way to the *stake-boat. **1884** *Pall Mall Gaz.* 4 Apr. 8 The Cambridge crew..paddled away.. to their stake-boat on the Middlesex side of the river. **1902** *Federal Reports* CXIII. 926 The tug left the tow in order to engage in other work, picking up light boats, and towing them down to a stake boat off Liberty Island. **1943** A. GIBBS *U-Boat Prisoner* 121 We went over to Jersey and took a motorboat to what he called a stake boat, where we found the barge. **1907** *Cycle & Auto. Trade Jrnl.* 1 Feb. 390 (*caption*) Studebaker 3½ ton paying load truck with *stake body. **1913** *Hub* July 123 (*caption*) Universal Chain Drive Stake Body Truck. **1976** *Washington Post* 19 Apr. D3/5 (Advt.), Discount center for stake bodies, step vans, medium duty trucks, [etc.]. **1978** J. GORES *Gone, no Forwarding* (1979) 4 He..opened the door of his stake-body truck. **1976** *Times* 18 June (Spec. Rep. Mormons) p. iii/7 Twenty stakes are now functioning, most of them headquartered in new *stake centre church buildings. **1872** COUES *N. Amer. Birds* 269 *Botaurus.* Bittern... *Stake-driver. **1889** H. SAUNDERS *Brit. Birds* 374 The note of the male..is..like the noise made by driving a stake in boggy soil, whence its common name of 'Stake-' or 'Post-driver'. **1577–87** HOLINSHED *Chron.* III. 1148/1 [He] bad his bedfellow and sworne *stakefellow.. maister Saunders farewell. **1882** W. D. HAY *Brighter Britain!* I. vii. 190 A *stake-fence ought to be proof against both pigs and cattle. **1913** J. MASEFIELD *Daffodil Fields* 46 Beside the stake-fence Lion stopped. **1825** J. JENNINGS *Observ. Dial. W. Eng.* 141 A knaw'd all about tha *stake-hangs Tha zalmon vor ta catch. *Ibid.* Gloss., *Stake-hang*,.. a kind of circular hedge made of stakes, forced into the sea-shore..for the purpose of catching salmon, and other fish. **1828–32** WEBSTER, **Stake-head*, in *rope-making*, a stake with wooden pins in the upper side to keep the strands apart. **1854** MISS BAKER *Northampt. Gloss.*, **Stake-hedge*, one made of thorns or wood,..wattled or ethered from three to four feet high. **1977** *Stake-hole [see POST-HOLE 1]. **1930** L. FOSTER *Larry* 131 Then we all paraded down to the *Stake House (Mormon Districts are called 'Stakes'), where there was a pioneer's meeting. **1832** BABBAGE *Econ. Manuf.* i. 14 He puts this [piece of red-hot iron] into a hole in a small *stake-iron immediately under a hammer connected with a treadle. 1875 Knight *Dict. Mech.*, *Stake-iron Bender*, a machine for bending stake-irons for the bolsters of wagons. 1688 Holme *Armoury* iii. 300/1 *Stake Nails, or Sadlers Tacks. 1836 Yarrell *Brit. Fishes* II. 23 It is not unusual to have *stake nets placed in the reverse position, with the courts open to the ebb-tide. 1936 *Sun* (Baltimore) 17 Feb. 7/1 A number of Rock Hall fishermen walked from their homes over the ice in the Chesapeake Bay to their stake nets near Tolchester Beach the past week, cut out their nets, and landed three hundred pounds of rock fish. 1973 W. Elmer *Terminol. Fishing* ii. 73 The stake net is a fixed net now only found on the south-west coast of Scotland. 1883 Moloney *W. Afr. Fisheries* (Fish. Exhib. Publ.) 24 These baskets are secured to *stake-poles or sticks, laid out in parallel lines. 1909 *Century Dict.* Suppl., **Stake-presidency*. 1947 G. S. Perry *Cities of Amer.* iii. 39 Each *stake president will parcel out the acreages he has agreed to accept among his bishops, and each bishop will divide his commitment among the Saints in his ward. 1891 *Century Dict.*, **Stake-rest*, on a railway platform car, a device for supporting a stake when turned down horizontally. 1562 J. Heywood *Prov.* (1867) 161 But if *stake stoobbers will not let stakis stand, Blame not the stake. 1741 in C. Whibley *In Cap & Gown* (1898) 37 Ev'n *stake-stuck Clarians strove to stoop. 1907 *Cycle & Auto. Trade Jrnl.* 1 Jan. 346a (*caption*) Five-ton Imperial *Stake Truck. 1975 C. Weston *Susannah Screaming* xxvi. 137 An old stake truck passed him, the back jammed with long-haired college-age kids. 1577 Googe *Heresbach's Husb.* ii. 103 b, The other kinde [of willow]..seruing for stayes to Vines..or stakes of Hedges, and is called *stake Wyllowe [L. *quæ perticalis dicitur*].

stake (steɪk), *sb.*[2] [Of uncertain etymology.

Perh. f. stake *v.*[3] On the alternative supposition that the sb. is the source of the vb., the former may be the same word as stake *sb.*[1] The peculiar use might have been developed from the phrase *on the stake*, which may originally have referred to a custom of placing on a 'stake' or post the object (an article of clothing or the like) hazarded on the event of a game or contest. There is, however, no evidence of the existence of such a custom; and in our quots. the first example of the phrase is dated 1592, while the use of the sb. to denote the money risked on a game of dice is more than half a century older.]

1. a. That which is placed at hazard; esp. a sum of money or other valuable commodity deposited or guaranteed, to be taken by the winner of a game, race, contest, etc.

1540 Palsgr. *Acolastus* iv. iii. Tj, All the stakes and settynges that be sette within the dyce borde, whiche lye on lyttell heapes. 1611 Shaks. *Wint. T.* i. ii. 248 A Foole, That seest a Game play'd home, the rich Stake drawne, And tak'st it all for ieast. 1630 *R. Johnson's Kingd. & Commw.* 41 He that winnes the game, gets not only the maine Stake, but all the Bets by follow the fortune of his hand. 1673 [R. Leigh] *Transp. Reh.* 88 Let who will be the gamesters, he is sure to sweep the stakes. 1808 Scott *Marmion* i. xxii, Full well at tables can he play And sweep at bowls the stake away. 1821 —— *Kenilw.* ii, Our landlord here shall hold stakes. 1878 H. Gibbs *Ombre* 9 Even at low stakes one may lose or gain enough to give interest to the game. 1884 Tennyson *Cup* i. iii. 79 [I] am no such gamester As, having won the stake, would dare the chance Of double or losing all.

b. *fig.* and in figurative context.

1581 J. Bell *Haddon's Answ. Osor.* 403 b, Upon what grew this inequabilitie and parcialitie of dispensation [of pardons], if there were no stakes layed doune for the game? 1601 Ld. Mountjoy in *Moryson's Itin.* (1617) ii. 145 For now *Jacta est alea* between England and Spaine and we that doe play the game have least interest in the stake. 1681 Dryden *Abs. & Achit.* i. 457 The Sword, Which for no less a Stake than Life you Draw. 1784 Cowper *Tiroc.* 863 Can'st thou..Lay such a stake upon the losing side, Merely to gratify so blind a guide? 1827 Hallam *Const. Hist.* (1876) II. x. 278 The royalists in England, who played so deep a stake on the king's account. 1878 Bosw. Smith *Carthage* 121 The prize was small..and the stake large, but they staked and lost it.

c. fig. *to have a stake in* (an event, a concern, etc.): to have something to gain or lose by the turn of events, to have an interest in; esp. in *to have a stake in the country* (said of those who hold landed property). Hence *spec.*, a shareholding (*in* a company).

1784 Sir A. Dick in *Boswell's Johnson* (1904) II. 526 With my most affectionate wishes for Dr. Johnson's recovery, in which his friends, his country, and all mankind have so deep a stake. 1807 Windham *Sp. Ho. Comm.* 22 July in *Hansard* IX. 897 Those entrusted with arms..should be persons of some substance and stake in the country. 1865 Livingstone *Zambesi* Introd. 8 And will probably always have the largest commercial stake in the African continent. 1911 H. Brown *Hist. Scot.* I. iv. viii. 281 Scotland came to have a stake in this struggle. 1955 *Times* 4 Aug. 12/1 Pilkington Brothers, famous the world over for plate and other kinds of glass, is proposing to increase its stake in another hardly less famous glass business. 1969 *Listener* 31 July 137/2 If the local paper has a stake in a local commercial station, this would tend to perpetuate the monopoly in local news and comment which has existed for too long in many provincial cities. 1981 *Times* 6 May 24/7 (*heading*) Trafalgar House buys 14.9 pc stake in French Kier.

d. Phrases. †*to part stakes*: see part *v.* 10 b. Similarly †*to share, divide stakes. to draw stakes*, to withdraw what is staked as a wager, etc.

1554 Philpot in Coverdale *Lett. Martyrs* (1564) 246 Communicate your necessities to me, and to others of his people, and God will make vs to deuide stakes. 1594 J. Dickenson *Arisbas* (1878) 56 But belike the god himselfe ment to share stakes. 1653 W. Ramesey *Astrol. Restored* 186 But after a tedious dispute they shall leave off and draw stakes. 1662 J. Davies tr. *Olearius' Voy. Ambass.* 300 The King of Persia farms out the Mint to private Persons, who gain most by it, and share stakes with the money-changers. 1708 [see draw *v.* 37]. 1758 Goldsm. *Mem. Protestant* (1895) I. 43 After two or three Conferences, he drew Stakes and declined the Dispute.

2. In certain phrases: The condition of being staked. *lit.* and *fig.*

In some of the early quots. the sb. in these phrases is taken (either by misapprehension or conscious word-play) as stake *sb.*[1] 1 b.

†**a.** ***to be, lie at*** or ***on the stake, to put, lay, lay down*** or ***set*** (a thing) ***at stake*** or ***at the stake***.

1592 Greene *Conny Catch.* 7 So they vie and reuie til some ten shillings be on the stake. 1601 Shaks. *All's Well* ii. iii. 156 *King.* My honor's at the stake. 1601 —— *Twel. N.* iii. i. 129 Haue you not set mine Honor at the stake, And baited it with all th' vnmuzled thoughts That tyrannous heart can think. 1604 —— *Oth.* iv. ii. 13 *Æmil.* I durst (my Lord) to wager, she is honest: Lay downe my Soule at stake. 1622 Bacon *Hen. VII* (1876) 34 He..saw plainly that his kingdom must again be put to the stake, and that he must fight for it. *a* 1660 *Contemp. Hist. Irel.* (Ir. Archæol. Soc.) III. 9 All that is deere unto us and our posteritie is now at the last fatall stacke. 1663 Butler *Hud.* i. i. 735 Are not our Liberties, our Lives, The Laws, Religion, and our Wives Enough at once to lye at stake? 1697 Dryden *Virg. Past.* iii. 40 My Brinded Heifer to the Stake I lay;..Now back your Singing with an equal Stake.

b. *fig.* (To be) ***at stake, to have at stake***.

1606 Shaks. *Tr. & Cr.* iii. iii. 227, I see my reputation is at stake My fame is shrowdly gored. 1722 Steele *Consc. Lovers* ii. i, I have more than Life at stake on your Fidelity. 1851 Dixon *W. Penn* x. (1872) 85 His private case was nothing, while so great a principle was at stake. 1875 Jowett *Plato* (ed. 2) IV. 227 He may be fairly appealed to, when the honour of his master is at stake.

3. a. *pl.* in *Horse-racing, Coursing*, etc., the sums of money staked or subscribed by the owners who enter horses or dogs for a contest, the whole to be received as the prize by the owner of the winner or divided among the owners of the animals 'placed', as declared in the conditions of the contest. Hence in *sing.* (cf. sweepstake) a race for money thus staked or subscribed. Also in *pl.* with defining words as the designation of particular races or classes of races in which the sum of money staked is the prize as distinguished from a Plate (see plate *sb.* 17), Cup, or the like.

produce stakes: (*a*) in *Horse-racing*, a race in which the runners must be the offspring of horses named and described at the time of entry; a produce race; (*b*) in *Coursing*, a race for puppies, i.e. for dogs of from one to two years of age; also called ***puppy stakes***. ***sapling stakes***: in *Coursing*, a race for saplings, i.e. dogs of less than one year old (see sapling 4 b). ***subscription stakes***: in *Horse-racing*, a race for which subscribers of a fixed amount annually have the right to enter one or more horses.

1696 *Lond. Gaz.* No. 3175/4 Strangers for the 30l. Plate are to put in 4l. and for the 20l. Plate, 2l. The Stakes are to go to the 2d Horse. 1730 J. Cheny *List Horse-Matches* 86 On..the following Day was a Purse of 20l. Sterling,..en. 2 Guineas, Stakes 10 Guineas. 1734 *Ibid.* 1 The following five Year Olds started for a Purse of 600 Guineas, call'd the Wallasey Stakes. 1778 in J. S. Fletcher *Hist. St. Leger Stakes* ii. 40 Tuesday, September 22.—The St. Leger Stakes of 25 gs. each, for three-year olds. 1833 Apperley *Turf* (1852) 124 The system lately adopted of produce-stakes for half-bred horses. *Ibid.* 129 There are upwards of a hundred horses besides himself named for the stake [*i.e.* the Derby]. 18.. *Turf Expositor* in Blaine *Encycl. Rural Sports* (1840) § 1268. 364 Cocktails are horses which appear as racers, but are understood not to be thorough-bred... They run for hunters' stakes, and also for what are called half-bred stakes. 1840 Blaine *Ibid.* § 1288. 369 By the winning of stakes alone, if honesty did but conduct the race, much money might be won, so as to remunerate..the vast sums which are expended in breeding, rearing, and training the best blood. 1856 'Stonehenge' *Brit. Rural Sports* i. iii. viii. 205/2 Puppy Stakes... In all produce stakes, the description of the puppy to contain its name, age, and pedigree [etc.]. 1895 *Westm. Gaz.* 30 Nov. 7/2 The cost [of horse-racing] is positively frightful in these days of heavy subscription stakes. 1898 *Encycl. Sport* I. 201/2 (Coursing), It was in the year 1836 that the proprietor of the Waterloo Hotel in Liverpool improvised an eight-dog stake, which he styled the Waterloo Cup.

b. *colloq.* Used *fig.* with defining words to denote a particular business or way of life in which success is attained through competition.

c 1885 A. W. Pinero *Magistrate* (1892) i. 24 You nominated yourself for the Matrimonial Stakes. Mr. Farringdon's The Widow, by Bereavement, out of Mourning, ten pounds extra. 1885 *Sat. Rev.* 7 Feb. 181/2 The hothouse kind of life..enabled this nervous, delicate, and curiously constituted competitor to win the Novel Stakes time after time. 1901 G. B. Shaw *Admirable Bashville* ii. i. 309 Yet so threadbare as to accept these consolation stakes. 1926 Galsworthy *Silver Spoon* ii. v. 145 He was not going to enter for the slander stakes. 1936 J. Curtis *Gilt Kid* iii. 34 Both the men looked as if they might be on the Jo Roncing [i.e. poncing] stakes. 1969 *Listener* 3 Apr. 470/1 No music is more recuperative than Mozart's and, in the therapy stakes, none runs it as close as Webern's. 1977 *Spare Rib* May 37/1 Energy and money were spent outdoing other girls in the beauty stakes.

4. *slang.* (See quot. 1812.) Also *N. Amer.*, a grub-stake; a sum of money earned or saved; a store of provisions or sum of money necessary for survival during a certain period.

1738 W. Byrd *Hist. Dividing Line* (1901) 178 [We] recommended to the men to manage this, their last stake, to best advantage. 1812 J. H. Vaux *Flash Dict.* s.v., A booty acquired by robbery, or a sum of money won at play, is called a stake, and if considerable, *a prime stake, a heavy stake*; a person alluding to any thing difficult to be procured ..would say, I consider it a stake to get it at all. 1853 'P. Paxton' *Yankee in Texas* 204 The horse is his last resource. .. When lost, the quondam owner is said to be flat broke or flat footed, and must beg, borrow, or steal, for a stake. 1873 J. H. Beadle *Undeveloped West* 510 It is a splendid country to travel through; a miserable poor one to stop in to make a 'stake'. 1891 C. Roberts *Adrift Amer.* 114 He had made a pretty good stake, and wanted to go east for the winter. 1899 'J. Flynt' *Tramping* i. i. 20 It is usually immaterial to him what happens to society as such so long as he [*sc.* a thief] can make a 'stake'. 1931 'D. Stiff' *Milk & Honey Route* xi. 117 A hobo may go to town with a stake and blow it in during two or three nights of slapping it up. 1946 E. O'Neill *Iceman Cometh* i. 53 I'll make my stake and get my new gamblin' house open before you boys leave. 1966 *Islander* (Victoria, B.C.) 21 Aug. 5/1 They [*sc.* loggers] seldom worked more than a few months in one place, just long enough to gather a stake, which they spent in a few days in town. 1978 J. Updike *Coup* (1979) vii. 279, I worked in that oil town in the Rift..and when I had a little stake I hitched back to Istiqlal.

5. *attrib.* and *Comb.*, as ***stake-money, -race***; **stakeholder**, (*a*) one who holds the stake or stakes of a wager, etc.; (*b*) one who has a stake (sense 1 c) in something, esp. a business; **stake-man** *U.S. slang*, a hobo, a tramp.

1708 *Brit. Apollo* No. 55. 2/1 Which will oblige Your Humble Servant **Stake Holder*. 1815 *Sporting Mag.* XLV. 231 A Bank of England note, which was lodged in the hands of a stake-holder as a deposit. 1858 Ld. St. Leonards *Handy-bk. Prop. Law* iv. 20 Where the deposit is directed to be paid to the auctioneer, he is entitled to retain it until the contract is completed,..because he is considered as a stakeholder or depositary. 1965 H. I. Ansoff *Corporate Strategy* iii. 34 The objectives of top management can and frequently do come in conflict with objectives of other stakeholders in the firm. 1975 *Economist* 11 Jan. 79/2 A good few of the smaller stake-holders in the North Sea are now trying to find buyers so that they can get out. 1976 R. E. Thomas *Government of Business* i. 22 Three approaches are considered here, the shareholder approach advocated by free enterprise theorists.., the stakeholder approach, as portrayed by Dahrendorf, and the Marxist approach. 1985 *Business Week* 3 June 94/2 The oil giant had arranged to buy out two other major stakeholders, gaining majority control. 1899 'J. Flynt' *Tramping* ii. v. 310 He learns to travel merely for travel's sake, and develops into a '*stake-man', who only works long enough to get a 'stake' and then go off on a trip again. 1901 Stake man [see bindle[2] a]. 1810 *Sporting Mag.* XXXVI. 123 He fought Dutch Sam for his own *stake money. 1896 H. M. Blossom *Checkers* ii. 20 Y' see, take a big *stake-race like this, where every horse is a 'cracker-jack',..and they've all got a chance. 1968 *Globe & Mail* (Toronto) 17 Feb. 1/5 Deep in the bush you can have just about all the comforts of home as the great uranium stake race enters its final two days.

stake (steɪk), *v.*[1] [f. stake *sb.*[1] MDu. (mod.Du. dial., WFlem.), G. *staken*.]

1. a. *trans.* To mark (land) with stakes. *N. Amer.*, to claim (land) by marking it with stakes; also *absol.*

c 1330 R. Brunne *Chron. Wace* (Rolls) 1852 Þey.. mesured lond, & dide hit stake þat ilkon dide his owen knowe. 1338 —— *Chron.* (1810) 309 [They] þat þorgh þe reame suld go, þe boundes forto stake. 1523 Fitzherb. *Surv.* 41 [Meadows] ought to be well staked bytwene euery mannes dole. 1715 *Maryland Laws* vi. (1723) 20 The Surveyor..shall have..Fees and Rewards of laying out and staking the Towns and Lots. 1716 in *Hist. Northfield, Mass.* (1875) 139 Each man's several quantities being set out and staked. 1908 M. A. Grainger *Woodsmen of West* 78 Now Billy Hewlitt was a 'timber-cruiser'—a man who sought for forest timber, to stake it. 1916 *Yukon Territory* (Canada Dept. Interior) 12 In a short time Bonanza was staked from end to end. 1945 *Clarke County Democrat* (Grove Hill, Alabama) 24 May 1/6 The California Oil Company..has staked a location for the drilling of a test well. 1959 M. Shand *Summit & Beyond* vii. 113 There was a report of a [gold] strike up White River. The men were talking of going to 'stake'. 1968 *Globe & Mail* (Toronto) 17 Feb. 1/7 It is land that was staked before in the madness of 1954, when it became known that one of the world's greatest concentrations of uranium ores had been uncovered.

b. with advs. *off, out*; esp. to mark *out* (land, a building site, etc.) with stakes or pegs. Also *fig.*

1445 in Willis & Clark *Cambridge* (1886) II. 404 The enlarging of garit hostell, as hit is now staked out. 1624 Capt. Smith *Hist. Virginia* vi. 232 We went to measure out the grounds: and so we cast lots where euery man should lie, which we staked out. 1710 in Picton *L'pool Munic. Rec.* (1886) II. 49 Thomas..has survey'd and stak'd out the same. 1885 *Manch. Exam.* 6 May 4/7 It will only remain to stake off the boundary through the intermediate districts.

c. Phr. ***to stake*** (***out***, †***off***) ***a claim***, to make or register a claim (to land) by marking it with stakes; freq. *fig.* orig. *U.S.*

1851 *State Jrnl.* (San Jose, Calif.) 15 Mar. 2/1 It was estimated that ten thousand people were on the ground staking off 'claims'. 1876 R. Bridges *Growth of Love* viii. Poet. Wks. (1912) 191 And against her shames Imagination stakes out heavenly claims. 1904 J. London *Daughter of Snows* xiii. 140 You staked that claim before he was dry behind the ears. 1928 H. Crane *Let.* 17 Apr. (1965) 324 Skepticism may stop there.., but I am not exactly satisfied by that... I still stake some claims on the pertinence of the intuitions. 1939 Wodehouse *Uncle Fred in Springtime* xiv. 199 Up till now, he had regarded Lord Emsworth as the most promising claim that any prospector for ore could hope to stake out. 1949 *Nat. Hist.* Apr. 189/3 Sometimes when the bee hunter finds a nest that has not yet reached its peak of honey production, he will 'stake his claim' by marking the tree so that other hunters will know of his prior discovery.

2. a. To protect, support, or obstruct with stakes.

a 1500 *Bale's Chron.* in Flenley *Six Town Chron.* (1911) 130 And they hadde merveilously staked all þe feeld aboute þeym that no power of horsmen shuld com and override theym. 1530 Palsgr. 732/1, I stake a hedge, *je mets des espieux en vne haye*. 1576 in W. H. Turner *Select. Rec. Oxford* 382 The water corse going to the howse of offyce.. shalbe staked and stopped uppe. 1591 Savile *Tacitus, Hist.*

II. xix. 63 Order was giuen that the camp should be entrenched and staked. **1602** LD. MOUNTJOY in *Moryson's Itin.* (1617) II. 213 Long traverses..staked on both sides with pallisades watled.

b. with advs. To close *up* or *in*, to keep *out*, to shut *off* with a barrier of stakes.

1597 BP. HALL *Sat.* v. iii. 73, I shall praise thee all the while So be, thou stake not vp the common stile; So be thou hedge in nought, but what's thine owne. **1627** DRAYTON *Agincourt* 19 The Duke of Glocester..Then caus'd his Ships the riuer vp to Stake, That none with Victuall should the Towne relieue. **1644** MILTON *Divorce* II. xvi. 62 No marvell any thing if letters must be turn'd into palisadoes to stake out all requisite sense from entring to their due enlargement. **1861** DICKENS *Gt. Expect.* iii, On the bank of loose stones above the mud and stakes that staked the tide out. **1883** H. DRUMMOND *Nat. Law in Spir. W.* (ed. 2) 71 This world of natural men is staked off from the Spiritual World by barriers which have never yet been crossed from within.

c. To put stakes or a stake to (a plant).

1664 EVELYN *Kal. Hort.* Mar. (1679) 13 Stake and bind up your weakest Plants and Flowers against the Winds. **1733** W. ELLIS *Chiltern & Vale Farm.* 90 They staked each Tree with four Poles, of about ten Foot long. **1812** SIR J. SINCLAIR *Syst. Husb. Scot.* I. 255 Beans answer excellently, to stake the tares intended for seed. **1846** J. BAXTER *Libr. Pract. Agric.* II. 200 All open standards should be staked as soon as planted.

3. To secure with or as with a stake. **a.** To bind or tie up (an animal) to a stake; to bind (a person) to the stake for execution. Also with *out*.

1544 in I. S. Leadam *Sel. Cases Crt. Requests* (1898) 79 His seruauntes dyd tedre and stayk thar horses vpon vj hawyns of Stokeleys. **1772** T. SIMPSON *Vermin-Killer* 22 The only method that can be taken is..by staking a chicken by the leg. **1845** DARWIN *Voy. Nat.* iv. 74 He ordered two soldiers to catch and stake me... This is a very severe punishment; four posts are driven into the ground, and the man is extended by his arms and legs horizontally, and there left to stretch for several hours. **1851** MAYNE REID *Scalp Hunt.* xlii. 328 Our horses were unsaddled and staked on the open plain. **1895** *Outing* (U.S.) XXVI. 403/1 We rode up as far toward the top of the ridge as we dared go and then staked out the ponies.

fig. **1846** LANDOR *Imag. Conv., Southey & Landor* Wks. 1853 II. 156/1 The poet is staked and faggoted by his surrounding brethren.

b. To fasten (a thing) *down*, *on* with a stake or with stakes.

1621 MARKHAM *Fowling* 114 These Nets being thus stakt downe with strong stakes. **1852** R. F. BURTON *Falconry Valley Indus* viii. 80 Strong fishing-nets, carefully staked down. **1825** J. NICHOLSON *Oper. Mech.* 44 In fixing the wheels and pullies upon a shaft, which is mostly done by driving wedges in the bush of the wheel or pulley, called staking them on.

†**c.** *fig.* To fasten securely as by a stake. Chiefly with *down*. *Obs.*

1592 SHAKS. *Rom. & Jul.* I. iv. 16, I haue a soale of Lead So stakes me to the ground, I cannot moue. **1596** NASHE *Saffron Walden* Wks. (Grosart) III. 195 Nere tell me of this or that he sayes I spake or did, except he particularize and stake downe the verie words. **1691** NORRIS *Pract. Disc.* 12 Men..that seem to be staked down and nailed fast to the Earth. **1702** C. MATHER *Magn. Chr.* II. vii. (1852) 147, I know not whether the terrors of my dreadful voyage hither might not be ordered by the Divine Providence to stake me in this land. *a* **1734** NORTH *Life Ld. Keeper Guilford* (1742) 14 His Mind was so airy and volatile, he could not have kept his Chamber, if he must needs be there staked down purely to the Drudgery of the Law.

4. a. To impale (a person) on a stake. Also with *up*. Also, to transfix and fasten down (a person) with a stake.

1577 HOLINSHED *Hist. Scot.* 203/2 *marg.*, The procurers of the murder were staked. *a* **1593** MARLOWE & NASHE *Dido* IV. i, That with the sharpnes of my edged sting, I might haue stakte them both vnto the earth. **1641** J. JACKSON *True Evang. T.* I. 24 Others [Nero] staked through, rosined and waxened over their bodies, and so set them lighted up, as torches. **1657** BILLINGSLY *Brachy-Martyrol.* vii. 26 Seven sons she had, all stak'd, rack'd and at last Thrust through, were into a deep pit cast. **1680** OTWAY *Caius Marius* I, Stake me, ye Gods, with thunder to the Earth. **1716** B. CHURCH *Hist. Philip's War* (1867) II. 129 His body being staked up, his head cut off, and a hogs head set in the room. **1786** WOLCOT (P. Pindar) *Odes to R.A.'s* i. Wks. 1812 I. 128 Stak'd through the body like a paltry Thief.

b. *pass.* Of a horse, etc.: To be injured by impalement on a hedge or fence stake. Also *refl.*; hence *trans.*, to cause a horse to stake himself.

1687 *Lond. Gaz.* No. 2281/4 A bright bay Gelding.., a..Scar on the far side near the Flank, (where he had been stak'd). **1741** *Compl. Fam.-Piece* II. i. 326 If any of these Dogs should happen to stake themselves, by brushing through Hedges. **1884** *Law Times* LXXVIII. 100/1 The animals..attempted to jump a fence. The foal was staked and had to be killed.

†**5.** To drive *in* (a pile, etc.) *Obs. rare*$^{-1}$.

1612 SIR D. CARLETON *Let.* 13 Apr. in *10th Rep. Hist. MSS. Comm.* App. I. 572 Hee hathe pulled up the piles, that yᵉ Ferraresi had staked in.

6. *Leather-manuf.* (See quot. 1853.)

1686 *Lond. Gaz.* No. 2124/4 Stolen.., about 350 of the best Kids, some ready pared, and some in the Crust not staked. **1853** URE *Dict. Arts* (ed. 4) II. 63 The tawed skins, when dry, are 'staked', that is stretched, scraped, and smoothed by friction against the blunt edge of a semi-circular knife.

7. 'To push with a stake or a pole, as a railroad car' (Webster, 1911). ? *U.S.*

8. *colloq.* (orig. *U.S.*). **a.** Usu. with adv. *out*. To maintain surveillance of (a place, etc.) in order to detect criminal activity or apprehend a suspect. Cf. STAKE-OUT.

1942 BERREY & VAN DEN BARK *Amer. Thes. Slang* §499/4 *Stake out*,..to surround a criminal retreat to spy upon or prevent escape. **1943** R. CHANDLER *Lady in Lake* (1944) xxix. 157 They had the house staked. **1962** L. DEIGHTON *Ipcress File* 221 When..the French police staked out the courier routes, they found..50,000 dollars of forged signed travellers' cheques. **1967** M. PROCTER *Exercise Hoodwink* xiii. 91 The house was 'staked out.'..A man called Whipper Slade emerged. 'Coo, he's a real deadleg,' said a detective who recognised him. **1974** *Black World* June 28/1 Places that are so staked out with doormen and electronic gadgets that only god can enter the lobby. **1981** *Daily Tel.* 6 July 2/2 Police were tipped off that trouble might occur with skinheads at nearby Greenford. They staked out a likely disco there.

b. *to be staked out*: to be set, or to set oneself, to maintain surveillance of a place.

1951 M. SPILLANE *Big Kill* vi. 122 He's been a cop a long time. He's been staked out often enough to spot it when he's being watched himself. **1974** J. A. MICHENER *Centennial* iv. 162 The Pawnee reacted as had been expected, with a countercharge of their own, and their leaders had covered only a short distance when they spotted Lame Beaver staked out, his rifle at the ready. **1979** H. KISSINGER *White House Years* xix. 756 David Bruce..came to the Embassy through the front door where the press was staked out.

†**stake**, *v.*² *Sc. Obs. rare*$^{-1}$. [? Cf. (M)Du. *staken* to fix, place, prob. related to OFris. *stak* stiff, firm.] *trans.* To place.

1513 DOUGLAS *Æneis* XII. iii. 72 And glaidy eik haue I nocht stakyt the Intill a party of the hevin alssua? [L. *scis ut te..cæli libens in parte locarim*].

stake (steɪk), *v.*³ [Of uncertain origin.

The verb appears in our quots. a little earlier than the related STAKE *sb.*², and may be its source. On this view it may be a. MDu. *staken* to fix, place (see prec.). On the other hand, it is possible that the vb. may be f. the sb.]

1. *intr.* To wager, hazard money, on the event of a game or contest. Now apprehended as absol. use of sense 3.

1530 PALSGR. 732/1, I stake in a play, *je boute*. I wyll nat play, except every mans take. **1591** [see 3]. **1631** HAUSTED *Rival Friends* II. ii, *Vrs.* What shall we play for? *Mer.* Two pinnes a game. *Vrs.* Stake then. **1708** *Yorkshire Racers* 10 And Tandem stakes both for himself and friend. **1896** *Spectator* 10 Oct. 480/1 As a rule a woman who plays cards for money feels like the cashier who is staking out of his master's till.

2. *trans. to stake down*: to deposit (a sum of money) as a wager or stake on the result of a game or contest. Also *absol.*

1565 COOPER *Thesaurus*, s.v. *Contendere, Pignore aliquo contendere*, to gage or stake downe somwhat and pay for it. **1596** SHAKS. *Merch. V.* III. ii. 218 *Gra.* Weele play..for a thousand ducats. *Ner.* What and stake downe? **1622** MALYNES *Anc. Law-Merch.* 198 So Wagers made by lookers on vpon other mens games are disallowed, which is the cause that Stipulations are made, putting the pawne or money downe, which is called, to stake downe. **1663** BUTLER *Hud.* II. i. 294 And if you doubt it to be true I'll stake myself down against you. **1821** SCOTT *Kenilw.* ii, Our landlord here shall hold stakes, and I will stake down gold till I send the linen.

3. To put at hazard (a sum of money, an article of value, etc.) upon the cast of dice, the result of a competition or game, the event of a contingency, etc.; to wager.

1591 FLORIO *2nd Fruites* 25 *T.* Let vs keepe the lawes of the court. *G.* That is, stake money vnder the line... *H.* Here is my monie, now stake you. **1611** SHAKS. *Cymb.* v. v. 188 He..No lesser of her Honour confident..stakes this Ring. **1754** JOHNSON *Connoisseur* No. 44 ¶1 Other Ladies of the family are staking their half-pence at Put or All-Fours in the kitchen. **1802** MAR. EDGEWORTH *Moral T., Forester, Bet*, Sir Philip staked his handsome horse Sawney against Archibald's sorry pony. **1847** TENNYSON *Princess* Prol. 168 I'll stake my ruby ring upon it you did. **1885** *Spectator* 25 July 977/2 The believer had the courage of his opinions and staked ten dollars on a magician whom he knew.

4. *fig.* To risk the loss of, to hazard.

1670 COTTON *Espernon* I. IV. 147 Men of Quality, who had generously stak'd their persons for the good of their fellow Citizens. **1766** GIBBON *Decl. & F.* v. (1782) I. 148 They had staked their lives against the chance of empire. **1868** STANLEY *Westm. Abbey* iv. 248 On it the sculptor Gibbs staked his immortality. **1874** GREEN *Short Hist.* vii. §4 (1882) 378 Mary had staked all on her union with Darnley.

5. *colloq.* (orig. *U.S.*) To furnish with money or supplies, etc.; to grub-stake. Also with compl. introduced by *with* or *to* indicating the commodity, etc., supplied.

1853 'P. PAXTON' *Stray Yankee in Texas* 219 The jofired mean whelp wouldn't stake me. **1894** 'MARK TWAIN' *Pudd'n-head Wilson* iv. 58 Tom staked him with marbles to play 'keeps' with. **1917** G. B. MCCUTCHEON *Green Fancy* 25 He staked her to a ticket to New York. **1934** R. GRAVES *I, Claudius* xxiii. 333 He gave me a purse of money and muttered in my ear: 'Tell nobody that I'm staking you, but put this on Scarlet.' **1942** Z. N. HURSTON in *Amer. Mercury* LV. 88 If Jelly really had had some money, he might have staked him..to a hot. Good Southern cornbread with a piano on a platter. **1969** *Coast to Coast 1967–68* 138 They would stake him, buy his grub, supply him with horses and packs, pay him a hundred pounds for her scalp. **1978** M. PUZO *Fools Die* ii. 38 He felt their happiness for him, and to repay it he said, 'Now let me stake you guys, you too, Diane. Twenty grand apiece.'

†**stake**, *v.*⁴ *Sc. Obs.* Also **staik**. [Of obscure origin; cf. STOCK *v.*, which has a similar sense, though etymological connexion is inadmissible.] *trans.* To supply the needs of; to stock or furnish sufficiently with something.

1547 *Reg. Privy Council Scot.* I. 80 And ordains the said Abbot and his convent religious men be honestlie stakit and furnist. **1565–6** *Ibid.* 426 That thai, on na wayis, sell ony part ..of the samyn wynis..unto the tyme thair Hienessis, the prelattis..and baronis be first stakit of thair necessaris thairof. **1573** *Satir. Poems Reform.* xlii. 162 Quhilk number [of preichers].. is sa small The Kirkis can not be stakit all. *a* **1578** LINDESAY (Pitscottie) *Chron. Scot.* (S.T.S.) II. 319 Collectouris maid in everie towne quhair salt vas maid to take vp sa mikill as to staik the cuntrie. **1583** *Leg. Bp. St. Androis* 170 in *Satir. Poems Reform.*, Perceaving weill St Androis vaikit and syne how sone the knave was staikit. **1641** D. FERGUSON *Sc. Prov.* (1785) 16 He's well staikit there-ben, that will neither borrow nor len.

b. Of a thing: To supply the wants of, to be sufficient for, to satisfy.

1550 *Rec. Elgin* (New Spalding Club 1903) I. 104 It salbe lesum to skynneris to pull samone voll skynnis as will staik tham to mak vark of within thair bothis. **1563** *Sc. Acts Mary* (1814) II. 539/1 That thay that ar appointit..haue the principall mans.., or samekill thairof as salbe fundin sufficient for staiking of thame. *a* **1568** A. SCOTT *Poems* xi. 32 Ȝe suld considdir or ȝe taik thame [*i.e.* lovers] That littill scheruice will noᵗ staik thame. **1589** R. BRUCE *Serm. Sacrament* ii. (1590) G 2, Be the naked and simple preaching of the worde ȝee get faith; sa the simple word may staike ȝou.

c. *intr.* To suffice.

1572 *Satir. Poems Reform.* xxx. 213 This Tragedie may staik, to tell the Lordis,..The thrid of marche was worthy Methwen slane. **1583** *Leg. Bp. St. Androis* 642 in *Sat. Poems Reform.*, To London Lowrie tuke the geat, With traine myᵗ staik for his esteat. **1585** JAS. I *Ess. Poesie* (Arb.) 31 Abusers, staikes it not to lurk in lust, Without [etc.].

Hence '**staking** *vbl. sb.*, (one's) fill.

1577–95 *Descr. Isles Scot.* in W. F. Skene *Celtic Scot.* (1880) III. App. 431 [They] saltis na fisches, but eittis thair staiking and castis the rest on the land.

stake, obs. form of STEAK.

stake, obs. pa. t. of STEEK, STICK *vbs.*

staked (steɪkt), *ppl. a.* [f. STAKE *v.*¹ + -ED¹.] In senses of the verb. ***staked-and-bound***: cf. STAKE *sb.*¹ 2 b. ***staked and ridered*** = *stake-and-ridered* adj. s.v. STAKE *sb.*¹ 2 c.

1531 *Rec. St. Mary at Hill* (1905) 37 Item, a stakyd fforme vjd. **1852** R. S. SURTEES *Sponge's Sp. Tour* (1893) 375 Now for the wall! It's five feet high.. in the staked-out part. **1852**, etc. [see RIDERED *a.* 2]. **1861** WHYTE MELVILLE *Mkt. Harb.* xxv, The last obstacle..consists of two ditches and a strong staked-and-bound fence on a bank. **1863** LYELL *Antiq. Man* 30 A staked inclosure had been raised round the cabin. **1865** A. SMITH *Summer in Skye* I. 155 Women in white caps..sat beside a staked cow or pony. **1901** W. N. HARBEN *Westerfelt* xx. 271 The scarecrow in the cornfield beyond the staked-and-ridered rail fence looked like the corpse of a human being flattened against the yellow sky.

stakement ('steɪkmənt). *Hist.* [f. STAKE *v.*¹ + -MENT.] The entitlement of tenants whose rents are in arrears to have their eviction delayed.

1904 M. BATESON *Borough Customs* I. II. 297 The 'stakement' appears to be the equivalent of the Germanic 'wiffatio'. **1927** J. S. FURLEY *Ancient Usages City of Winchester* 22 The *Usages* closes with an account of 'stakement'. When a tenant was in arrears with his rent the landlord could take no steps till after year and day. *Ibid.*, Stakement is symbolic... At Exeter the custom was to carry away a stone..but the stake was used at Reading, at Fordwich, and the other Cinque Ports. **1927** *Contemp. Rev.* Aug. 261 The procedure of 'Stakement', a court process that delayed adverse possession, is very early and full of interest. **1935** K. M. E. MURRAY *Constitutional Hist. Cinque Ports* ii. 16 Such is the practice of 'stakement' for rent arrears.

'**stake-out.** *colloq.* (orig. *U.S.*). Also as one word. [f. vbl. phr. *to stake out*: see STAKE *v.*¹ 8.] An act or period of surveillance of a place by police or investigative agents. Also *transf.* and *attrib.*

1942 BERREY & VAN DEN BARK *Amer. Thes. Slang* §499/2 *Stake-out*, a surrounding of a criminal retreat to spy upon or prevent the escape of criminals. **1943** R. CHANDLER *Lady in Lake* (1944) xl. 208 Somebody stood behind that green curtain..as silently as only a cop on a stake-out knows how to stand. **1955** *Sun* (Baltimore) (B ed.) 11 Jan. 26/8 Bergen was arrested..by..rookie policemen who were part of an extensive stakeout in the area which had been set up to trap the person or persons responsible for the large number of burglaries. **1960** *Washington Post* 15 Jan. A12 The success of the police in these instances has been largely due to the 'stake-out' system. **1966** J. GARDNER *Amber Nine* viii. 95 He had enjoyed that time as stake-out man at London Central: lurking, watching (and watching for) people. **1972** *New Yorker* 16 Jan. 27/1 A group of agents..who were conducting a stakeout of a house in suburban Wilmette. **1979** *Daily Tel.* 19 Sept 36/5 Father Frederick Linale..said police asked him last week if they could use the mission on a 'stake out'. **1983** *Times* 29 Jan. 6/8 President Reagan's impromptu visit to a Boston Irish pub for a quick beer broke up a stake-out by armed FBI agents.

staker¹ ('steɪkə(r)). [f. STAKE *v.*¹ + -ER¹.] **a.** One who drives in a stake; one who uses a stake.

1486 [see SENTRE]. **1897** C. T. DAVIS *Manuf. Leather* xx. (ed. 2) 274 Should this occur, the staker's balance would be lost, and he would be in danger of being impaled upon his stake.

†**b.** (See quot.) *Obs.*

1688 HOLME *Armoury* III. 261/1 Terms of Art used by Brick-Makers... Staker, is him that puts the Clay off the Ground, upon the Board.

c. *Canad.* One who stakes a (mining) claim.

1898 *Yukon Midnight Sun* (Dawson, Yukon Territory) 15 Aug. 1/3 He also said that until after September 1st no one but the original staker has any business upon these claims. **1921** *Daily Colonist* (Victoria, B.C.) 13 Oct. 2/4 The original stakers are reported to be taking out $35 a day in coarse gold, some very large nuggets being found. **1954** *North Star*

(Yellowknife, N.W. Territory) Aug. 2/1 Though a few stakers were 'made', it was generally the brokers and speculators who skimmed off the cream.

staker[2] ('steɪkə(r)). [f. STAKE *v.*[3] + -ER[1].] One who stakes or wagers money, etc.

1660 HEXHAM, *Een wedder*, A Wagerer, or a Staker. In mod. Dicts. **1975** J. SYMONS *Three Pipe Problem* vii. 45 Willie was a great staker of his reputation. **1976** *Sunday Times* (Lagos) 7 Nov. 21/3 (Advt.), Pools Magnet have won over ten million Naira for Stakers all over the world.

staker: see STACKER *sb.*[2] and *v.*

stakey ('steɪkɪ), *a. slang* (chiefly *Canad.*). Also **staky**. [f. STAKE *sb.*[2] + -Y[1].] Well provided with money; 'flush'.

1919 *Camp Worker* (Vancouver) 28 June 7/1 If they hold a job for a month they have done something out of the ordinary, and as a consequence, they are never very staky, and the question of funds comes first in most cases. **1927** *Amer. Speech* II. 392/1 When a *staky* worker comes to town, his giving money to his impecunious acquaintances is called the *pay-off*. **1960** *Weekend Mag.* (Montreal) 8 Oct. 28/1, I wasn't going to go in, because at the time I wasn't stakey. **1970** P. ST. PIERRE *Chilcotin Holiday* 31 On being assured that the prisoner was stakey, the mayor imposed a ten-dollar fine. **1973** B. BROADFOOT *Ten Lost Years* xv. 172 Why, we was making 15 cents a glass... Both of us were getting stakey as hell.

Stakhanovite (stə'kɑːnɒvaɪt), *sb.* and *a.* [f. the name of the Soviet coal-miner Alekséĭ Grigór'evich *Stakhánov* (1906–77) + -ITE[1]; cf. Russ. *stakhánovets* sb., *stakhánovskiĭ* adj.

The Soviet authorities publicized the prodigious output achieved by Stakhanov in 1935 as part of a campaign to increase industrial output.]

A. *sb.* In the U.S.S.R. during the 1930s and 1940s, a worker whose productivity exceeded the norms and who thus earned special privileges and rewards; *transf.*, one who is exceptionally hard-working and productive. **B.** *adj.* Designating, pertaining to, or characteristic of such a worker or such workers collectively.

1935 *Time* 16 Dec. 25/3 In the coal mine at Stalino two assistant foremen, a checkweighter and an electrician were arrested for the murder of a fast-working Stakhanovite. **1936** W. CITRINE *I search for Truth in Russia* 349 In the best building works the Stakhanovite builders have shown examples of high productivity of labour in bricklaying, beton work, plastering and excavating work. **1938** *Times Lit. Suppl.* 8 Jan. 18/4 The *udarnik* (or Stakhanovite, as he now is called) was 'curiously like the pep-it-up-team-work-factory-spirit fellows I knew at home, and equally detested by his clock-watching fellow-workers'. **1949** [see SHOCK *sb.*[3] 8 b]. **1952** [see NORM c]. **1959** *Times* 29 May 8/5 This conferring with East Anglian trade union leaders and stakhanovites of his party.. has probably been the most useful thing to come out of his [*sc.* Hugh Gaitskell's] tour. **1961** C. T. HSIA *Hist. Mod. Chinese Fiction* xviii. 495 The application of Stakhanovite methods to literary production could only mean further deterioration in quality. **1977** *Time* 1 Aug. 5/3 Though U.S. workers have been regularly chided at home for goofing off on the job, they are veritable Stakhanovites compared with some of their European counterparts.

Hence **Sta'khanovism**, a movement in the U.S.S.R. aimed at encouraging hard work and maximum output, following the example of Stakhanov; also *transf.*; **Sta'khanovist** *a.* and *sb.* = STAKHANOVITE *sb.* and *a.*

1936 V. M. MOLOTOV (*title*) What is Stakhanovism? **1937** *Nature* 27 Feb. 364/2 He outlined the development of the principles of scientific management from the pioneer work ..to such recent manifestations as 'Stakhanovism' in Russia. **1938** *Downside Rev.* LVI. 370 Before summing up the authors insert a valuable chapter on the Stakhanovist movement in Russia. **1940** *Manch. Guardian Weekly* 16 Feb. 130 News of what in the Soviet Union is called 'Socialist emulation' confirms again and again that certain 'Stakhanovists' accomplish 'norms' (their own normal production) of 260 to 400 per cent of normal. **1949** E. FITZGERALD tr. *Labin's Stalin's Russia* ii. 53 Stakhanovism (with all its serious industrial accidents) was introduced in Novosibirsk. **1954** *Encounter* Feb. 39/2 The tense, driving Stakhanovist atmosphere of Soviet Europe. **1957** *Times Lit. Suppl.* 25 Oct. 641/2 The romantic legend by which democracy lives, on the other hand, venerates Stakhanovism in high places. **1970** G. GREER *Female Eunuch* 123 Many others [*sc.* working wives] pride themselves on the way they manage to run a home and hold their own in a job at the same time, accepting the patronizing title of 'working wonders' in a kind of unofficial Stakhanovism. *Ibid.* 275 Women's literature is full of the trumpeting of female Stakhanovists.

staking ('steɪkɪŋ), *vbl. sb.* [f. STAKE *v.*[1] + -ING[1].]

a. The action of driving in a stake; the action of piercing with or impaling on a stake. Also *N. Amer.*, the action of STAKE *v.*[1] 1 a.

10.. *Poenit. Ecgberti* iv. 17 in Thorpe *Ags. Laws* (1840) II. 208 And ȝif se man for pære stacunge dead biþ þonne fæste he .vii. ȝear. **1420** in *For. Acc. 3 Hen. VI.* H, In diuersis peciis maeremii et ferri emptis .. et expenditis circa stakyng, Pyling et shoyng diuersorum pilorum in portu. **1630** LENNARD tr. *Charron's Wisd.* I. xlii. (1670) 156 Those tortures of the wheel, and staking of men alive, came from the North. **1664** EVELYN *Sylva* (1679) 12 To leave nothing omitted which may contribute to the stability of our Transplanted Trees, something is to be premis'd concerning their staking. **1707** MORTIMER *Husb.* (1721) II. 7 They will neither require staking nor watering. **1842** LOUDON *Suburban Hort.* 637 Very abundant crops of the scarlet runner are obtained without staking. **1897** *Outing* (U.S.) XXX. 137/2 If you coves'll lend me a hand at the 'staking', as he termed the fence building. **1952** *North Star* (Yellowknife, N.W. Territory) Nov. 3/2 There, the mineral claims map sheet is completely filled, so far as staking is concerned. **1968** *Globe & Mail* (Toronto) 17 Feb. 1/7 At noon on Monday, 100,000 acres of land beyond the geological formation that gave Elliot Lake 13 uranium mines in the 1950s, will be opened to staking. **1979** *Arizona Daily Star* 5 Aug. (Advt. Section) 4/3 You will be responsible for the acquisition of uranium mineral properties required through staking, bids, ..joint ventures and/or purchase.

†**b.** A stake. *Obs. rare*$^{-1}$.

c **1440** *Pallad. on Husb.* IV. 82 A sadder vyne a bigger stake olofte Mot holde; a lighter vyne is with a lesse Stakynge vpholde.

c. *Leather-manuf.* The action or process of drawing skins over the stake.

1852 MORFIT *Tanning & Currying* (1853) 411 The tanned skins.. are subjected to what is technically termed staking.

d. Comb.: **staking-iron**, a leather-dresser's stake (*Cent. Dict.* Suppl. 1909); **staking jaws**, the jaws of a staking-machine; **staking-machine**, a machine for softening leather by means of a blade drawn backwards and forwards over the skin; **staking rush** *Canad.*, a rush (RUSH *sb.*[2] 4) to stake (mining) claims.

1897 C. T. DAVIS *Manuf. Leather* xx. (ed. 2) 273 Staking machines... In addition they have two other sets of staking jaws, all different and giving different results. **1953** *North Star* (Yellowknife, N.W. Territory) July 1/1 There are possibilities of an additional poll in the Marion River area, where a staking rush is now under way. **1964** *North* (Ottawa) May–June 14 A miniature 'staking rush' to the Pine Point area took place during the following winter.

stakker, obs. form of STACKER *v.*

staktometer: see STACTOMETER.

staky, var. STAKEY *a.*

stal, obs. f. STALL; obs. pa. t. of STEAL *v.*

stalactic (stə'læktɪk), *a.* [ad. Gr. *σταλακτικός*, dropping, dripping, f. *σταλακ-*, *σταλάσσειν* to let drop, intr. to drop, drip.] Deposited by dripping water; pertaining to or consisting of stalactites. Cf. STALACTITIC *a.*

1756 P. BROWNE *Jamaica* (1789) 26 Most of the hills.. are chiefly composed of stalactic matter. **1828–32** WEBSTER. **1900** *Westm. Gaz.* 1 Sept. 4/2 Arrays of stalactic forms.

stalactical (stə'læktɪkəl), *a.* Now *rare*. [Formed as prec. + -AL[1].] Of the nature of a stalactite; resembling or pertaining to stalactites.

1714 DERHAM *Phys.-Theol.* II. i. (ed. 2) 64 A Cave, which ..was lined with those Stalactical Stones. *Ibid.*, This Sparry, Stalactical Substance. **1755** AMORY *Mem.* (1766) II. 212 The most elegant and beautiful stalactical figures the water has made. **1802** ACERBI *Trav.* I. 41 Stalactical ornaments of the same kind [*sc.* icicles].. were also attached to his nose and mouth. **1805** SAUNDERS *Min. Waters* 132 Natural caverns.. whose stalactical grottoes are great objects of curiosity to.. visitors. **1869** PHILLIPS *Vesuvius* v. 149 Salts of different kinds hang in stalactical shapes from the caverns.

stalactiform (stə'læktɪfɔːm), *a.* [f. STALACTITE + -(I)FORM.] Having the form of a stalactite.

1839 DE LA BECHE *Rep. Geol. Cornwall*, etc. ix. 262 The siliceous matter having infiltrated while in solution into cavities, and being there deposited in a stalactiform manner. **1853** TH. ROSS tr. *Humboldt's Trav.* III. xxix. 168 Stalactiform chalcedonies.

stalactital (stælæk'taɪtəl), *a.* Also 8 *erron.* **stall-**. [f. STALACTITE + -AL[1].] = STALACTITIC.

1789 J. WILLIAMS *Min. Kingd.* II. 378 Some of the stallactital productions. **1867** BAILEY *Univ. Hymn* 12 Huge halls Where stalactital mountains hang. **1874** *Hartwig's Aerial World* x. 154 The most magnificent stalactital grotto.

stalactite ('stælæktaɪt, stə'læktaɪt). Also 9 **stalactyte**. [Anglicized form of STALACTITES. Cf. F. *stalactit* (1752 in Hatz.-Darm.), G. *stalaktit*.

Here and in STALAGMITE some U.S. Dicts. recognize only the second of the two pronunciations given.]

1. a. An icicle-like formation of calcium carbonate, depending from the roof or sides of a cavern and produced by the dropping of waters which have percolated through, and partially dissolved, the overlying limestone.

1677 PLOT *Oxfordsh.* 96 Such are the stones made of nothing but such water, as it drops from the roofs and caverns of the Rocks, and therefore called Stalactites. **1789** MILLS in *Phil. Trans.* LXXX. 93 Some calcareous stalactites pendent from the roof. **1793** *Phil. Trans.* LXXXIV. 405 In one of them rises a stalactite of uncommon bigness. **1819** SHELLEY *Ode to Heaven* 31 Like weak insects in a cave, Lighted up by stalactites. **1847** DISRAELI *Tancred* v. v, With pendants of daring grace hanging like stalactites from some sparry cavern. **1877** W. BLACK *Green Past.* xxxvii. 295 They seem to be a stupendous semicircular wall of solid and motionless stalactites.

b. A similar formation of other material.

1801 J. BARROW *Trav. S. Africa* I. 164 From the under surfaces of the.. rotten sand-stone were suspended a great quantity of saline stalactites. **1802** ACERBI *Trav.* I. 44 All the rooms.. were embellished by long stalactites of multifarious shapes.. composed of the treacle and congealed water. **1860** TYNDALL *Glac.* I. xi. 77 A vertical precipice, from the coping of which vast stalactites of ice depended. **1890** E. S. DANA in *J. D. Dana's Charac. Volcanoes* 322 The delicate stalactites and stalagmites of lava which occur in the caverns. **1902** CORNISH *Naturalist on Thames* 101 Stalactites of finest meal-dust hung from every nail.. on the walls.

2. A general term for limestone found in this formation.

1796 KIRWAN *Elem. Min.* (ed. 2) I. 88 Stalactite, alabaster, sinter. **1823** BUCKLAND *Reliq. Diluv.* 10 The roof and sides were found to be partially studded and cased over with a coating of stalactite. **1839** DE LA BECHE *Rep. Geol. Cornwall*, etc. xiii. 413 More or less filled by loam, sand, or stalactite. **1908** *Blackw. Mag.* July 102/1 White crusts of stalactite.

3. *Arch.* (See quot. 1895.)

1851 W. IRVING *Alhambra* (rev. ed.) 76 The lofty ceiling was originally of the same favorite material, with the usual frostwork and pensile ornaments or stalactites. **1895** *Funk's Stand. Dict.*, *Stalactite*... A downward-projecting ornament of a vaulted surface. **1931** C. HILL *Moorish Towns in Spain* 147 We stand amid a small labyrinth of columns, under a roof of stalactites in stone. **1974** *Encycl. Brit. Micropædia* IX. 517/1 A peculiar type of faceted, crystal-shaped stalactite is found in Turkey; this form became the most common Turkish capital decoration.

4. *attrib.* and *Comb.*: **stalactite-work** *Arch.* (see quot. 1902).

1855 J. FERGUSSON *Illustr. Handbk. Archit.* I. IX. v. 463 Instead of the simple curves of the dome, the roofs are made up of honeycombed or stalactite patterns, which look more like natural rock-work than the forms of an art. **1864** J. HUNT tr. *Vogt's Lect. Man* ix. 247 A stalactite roof. **1881–2** CLARA BELL tr. *Ebers' Egypt* I. 227 The stalactite ornament, as it has been called—from a false idea that it was an imitation of those fantastical natural formations which [etc.]. *Ibid.* 228 Perso-Turkish Stalactite Capital [figured]. **1897** *Allbutt's Syst. Med.* IV. 798 Small stalactite-like projections. **1897** W. MILLAR *Plastering* 422 A stalactite-shaped cornice. *Ibid.* 425 Other mosques, palaces, and monuments with stalactite domes and cornices. **1902** STURGIS *Dict. Archit.* III. 612 *Stalactite work*, a system of corbelling of peculiar form or the imitation of such corbelling in wood and plaster.

stalactited ('stælæktaɪtɪd), *a.* [f. STALACTITE + -ED[2].] **a.** Covered or filled with stalactites. **b.** 'Formed in more or less semblance of stalactites' (*Cent. Dict.*).

1891 TALMAGE in *Voice* (N.Y.) Jan. 1, From cellar of stalactited cave, clear up to the silvery rafters of the star-lit dome. **1895** *Funk's Stand. Dict.*, *Stalactited*, 2. Ornamented in imitation of icicles: said of masonry.

‖**stalactites** (ˌstælæk'taɪtiːz). Now *rare*. Pl. **stalactitæ** (-tiː). [mod.L. (Olaus Wormius *a* 1654), f. Gr. *σταλακτ-ός* dropping, dripping (vbl. adj. f. *σταλακ-*, *σταλάσσειν* to let drip, intr. to drip), after names of stones in *-ītēs*: see -ITE[1].] = STALACTITE.

[*a* **1654** O. WORMIUS *Mus.* I. II. vi. (1655) 50 De Stalactite, Stalagmite, Osteocolla,..&c. Ad molliorum lapidum classem referimus Stalactitem, Norvegis Berg-drab]. **1681** GREW *Musæum* III. §i. v. 301 The Larger Hollow Stalactites, or Water-Pipe. **1695** WOODWARD *Nat. Hist. Earth* IV. 202 Sometimes Spar, and other crasser Minerals, are thus mounted up, and.. form Stalactitæ, or Sparry Iceycles hanging down from the Arches of the Grotto's. **1794** R. J. SULIVAN *View Nat.* I. 421 In caverns and fissures, stalactitæ, ..and other substances, crystallize in various forms.

stalactitic (ˌstælæk'tɪtɪk), *a.* [f. STALACTITE + -IC.]

1. Having the form or structure of a stalactite, resembling or pertaining to stalactites.

1778 *Ann. Reg.*, *Nat. Hist.* 103/1 A kind of sparry stalactitick shell. **1799** KIRWAN *Geol. Ess.* 127 Stalactitic concretions of modern formation. **1823** BUCKLAND *Reliq. Diluv.* 49 A hollow stalactitic tube. **1830** LYELL *Princ. Geol.* I. 384 It is of a hard stalactitic nature. **1877** *Erichsen's Surg.* (ed. 7) II. 228 Stalactitic masses of bone. **1886** G. P. MERRILL in *Ann. Rep. Smithsonian Inst.* II. (1889) 525 *Stalactitic marble*.. is a marble which is formed by the deposit of lime carbonates from waters percolating into cavities or caves.

2. Covered with, containing or consisting of stalactites.

1845 HIRST *Poems* 67 Stalactitic islands ever rise from out the waves of sound. *a* **1849** H. COLERIDGE *Ess.* (1851) I. 253 Stalactitic caves. **1849** DANA *Geol.* 272 The roof was very rough, though not stalactitic. **1872** W. S. SYMONDS *Rec. Rocks* ix. 351 A thin stalactitic floor, the results of the droppings of water.

stalactitical (stælæk'tɪtɪkəl), *a.* [f. STALACTITE + -IC + -AL[1].] = prec.

1770 LLOYD in *Phil. Trans.* LXI. 253 Some small stalactitical drops hanging from the roof. **1797** *Encycl. Brit.* (ed. 3) XII. 72/2 Stalactitical gypsum. *Gipsum sinter*. **1833–4** J. PHILLIPS *Geol.* in *Encycl. Metrop.* (1845) VI. 767/2 Calcedony.. sometimes appears in a stalactitical form hanging downwards. **1869** —— *Vesuvius* iii. 65 With a channelled surface and stalactitical shapes.

Hence **stalac'titically** *adv.*

1830 LYELL *Princ. Geol.* I. 384 From whence calcareous particles may be deposited stalactitically.

stalactitiform (stælæk'tɪtɪfɔːm), *a. rare*. [f. STALACTITE + -(I)FORM.] = STALACTIFORM.

1805 WITHERING tr. *Werner's Ext. Char. Fossils* 255 Stalactitiform (tropfsteinartig). **1823** W. PHILLIPS *Introd. Min.* (ed. 3) p. xcv, Stalactitiform minerals greatly resemble icicles in shape.

stalactitious (stælæk'tɪʃəs), *a. rare*$^{-1}$. [f. STALACTITE + -IOUS.] Containing stalactites.

1799 COLERIDGE in *New Monthly Mag.* (1835) XLV. 213 An enormous cavern.. dripping, stalactitious.

Stalag ('stɑːlæg, ‖'ʃtalak). [a. Ger., abbrev. of *stammlager* main camp.] In Nazi Germany: a prison-camp primarily for captured enemy private soldiers and non-commissioned officers. **Stalag Luft, Stalagluft** (-lʊft) [G. *luft* air], such a camp for Air Force personnel.

1940 *Times* 30 July 7/3 There are three types of camps for British prisoners known officially as Oflag, Stalag, and Dulag (contractions for Offizierslager, Stammlager, and Durchgangslager). **1941** [see ILAG]. **1944** V. G. GARVIN tr. *Gary's Forest of Anger* xxix. 141 The old man was sent to a Stalag in Poland. **1945** [see OFLAG]. **1947** *News Chron.* 24 Jan. 1/4 Scharpwinkel, who is believed to have ordered the murder of many of the 50 R.A.F., Commonwealth and Allied airmen after their escape from Stalagluft III in March 1944. **1959** W. FAULKNER *Mansion* xiii. 295 If it had been a..book instead of a war..they would have escaped. But he..never knew anyone who ever actually escaped from a genuine authentic stalag, so they had to wait for regular routine liberation. **1974** *Times* 18 Oct. 16/6 On at least first sight Long Kesh *looks* like one of the *Stalags*. **1978** R. V. JONES *Most Secret War* xxxi. 265 While in Stalag Luft 3 he not only concealed his knowledge of our new radar devices, but built a radio transmitter.

stalage, variant of STALLAGE.

‖**stalagma** (stəˈlægmə). [mod.L., a. Gr. στάλαγμα, drop, drip, f. σταλακ-, σταλάσσειν: see STALACTIC *a.*]

1. A distilled liquor. *rare*⁻⁰.

1693 tr. *Blancard's Phys. Dict.* (ed. 2), *Stalagma*, that which is Distilled from *Stagma*. **1706** PHILLIPS (ed. Kersey). **1855** DUNGLISON *Med. Lex.*, *Stalagma*, stagma.

2. = STALAGMITE 2.

1903 R. BRIDGES *Poems Class. Prosody* I. 358 Caves.. abandon'd Ages since to the drift and the drip, the cementing accretions Whence we now separate his bones buried in the stalagma.

stalagmite (ˈstælægmaɪt, stəˈlægmaɪt). Also 7 **stalagmites**. [a. mod.L. *stalagmītēs* (Olaus Wormius: see STALACTITES), f. Gr. στάλαγμα STALAGMA or σταλαγμός a dropping, f. σταλακ-, σταλάσσειν: see STALACTIC *a.* Cf. F. *stalagmite.*]

1. An incrustation or deposit, more or less like an inverted stalactite, on the floor of a cavern, formed by the dropping from the roof of some material in solution.

1681 GREW *Musæum* III. §i. v. 295 The Cluster'd Stalagmites. **1758** PLATT in *Phil. Trans.* L. 527 The stalactites and stalagmites, of which there is great variety. **1841** CATLIN *N. Amer. Ind.* (1844) II. lii. 148 The rich stalagmites that grew up from the bottom reflected a golden light through the water. **1878** HUXLEY *Physiogr.* viii. 122 As the stalagmite grows in height, it approaches the stalactite above which continues to grow downward.

2. Limestone deposited in this manner.

1815 AIKIN *Min.* (ed. 2) 159 Stalagmite occurs mammillated. **1823** BUCKLAND *Reliq. Diluv.* 12 The effect of the loam and stalagmite in preserving the bones from decomposition..has been very remarkable. **1882** GEIKIE *Text-bk. Geol.* II. II. vi. 113 The crust-like deposit known as stalagmite.

3. *attrib.* **stalagmite marble**, onyx marble.

1851 D. WILSON *Preh. Ann.* (1863) I. iv. 122 Extinct fauna buried beneath its stalagmite flooring. **1864** J. HUNT tr. *Vogt's Lect. Man* ix. 237 The stalagmite crust. **1895** *Funk's Stand. Dict.*, Stalagmite marble.

stalagmitic (stælægˈmɪtɪk), *a.* [f. STALAGMITE + -IC. Cf. F. *stalagmitique.*] Formed in the same way as a stalagmite, composed of stalagmites or having their form or character.

1772 BANKS in *Pennant's Tour Scot.* (1774) 302 A yellow stalagmitic matter has exuded. **1811** PINKERTON *Petral.* II. 501 More commonly this calcareous substance lines the cavities under the stalagmitic form. **1824** *Ann. Reg.* 238* A stalagmitic incrustation. **1862** D. WILSON *Preh. Man* iii. 46 A thick stalagmitic flooring. **1883** RUDLER in *Encycl. Brit.* XV. 529 Stalagmitic marbles.

stalagmitical (stælægˈmɪtɪkəl), *a.* [f. STALAGMITE + -IC + -AL¹.] = prec.

1809 J. KIDD *Min.* I. 15 Stalagmitical Marble. *Ibid.* 46 Stalagmitical depositions constituted the alabaster of the ancients. **1833–4** J. PHILLIPS *Geol.* in *Encycl. Metrop.* (1845) VI. 695/2 Stalagmitical carbonate of lime.

Hence **stalagˈmitically** *adv.*

1823 BUCKLAND *Reliq. Diluv.* 111 Ochreous concretions, formed stalagmitically.

ˌstalagˈmometer. [f. Gr. σταλαγμό-ς (see STALAGMITE) + -METER.] An apparatus for measuring drops. So **ˌstalagmoˈmetric** *a.*; **staˈlagmoscope**, [-SCOPE], an instrument for viewing drops.

1864 GUTHRIE in *Proc. Roy. Soc.* XIII. 477 In the cases of the still more proximate identity of isomeric bodies mentioned above..the stalagmometer may be used rather as a stalagmoscope, to render evident rather than to measure a difference of drop-size. **1910** *Chem. Abstr.* IV. 1765 (*heading*) The significance of the stalagmometric method. **1920** *Jrnl. Biol. Chem.* XLIV. 378 The amount of lipase in blood serum, determined by..the stalagmometric method. **1940** GLASSTONE *Text-bk. Physical Chem.* vii. 482 The weight of a definite number of drops is determined, or the number obtained from a given volume of liquid, as it flows between two marks on a stalagmometer, is counted. **1976** *Coll. Czech. Chem. Commun.* XLI. 1845 The dependence between the mass of the detached drop and the rate of its formation was determined by means of three stalagmometers with different sizes of the dripping area and with a different angle of the capillary edge.

stalan(d, stala(u)nt, obs. forms of STALLION.

stalboat, obs. form of STALL-BOAT.

†**stalch.** *Mining. Obs. rare.* [Of obscure origin.] A piece of ground left uncut though all around has been worked.

1747 HOOSON *Miner's Dict.* T 4, *Stalch*, a Piece of Wholes that is left uncut, yet we know it to be cut over the Top of it, and under, and at both Ends.

stald, var. *staled, stalled*: see STALE, STALL *vbs.*

stalder (ˈstɔːldə(r)). Also 7 **staulder**. [app. f. *stal-* root of OE. *stęllan* to place.]

†**1.** (See quot. 1611.) *Obs.*

1611 COTGR., *Buchier*, a stalder, wood-house, or woodpile. *Ibid.*, *Chantier de bois*, a staulder, woodstacke, pile of wood.

2. *dial.* A 'horse' or frame for casks to stand on.

1736 J. LEWIS *I. of Tenet* (ed. 2) 39 *Stalder*, a Stilling, or Frame to put Barrels on. **1853** W. D. COOPER *Sussex Gloss.* (ed. 2) 78. **1875** KNIGHT *Dict. Mech.*

stalding, erron. form of SCALDING *sb.*²

1577 HOLINSHED *Chron.* II. 835/2 Pollardes, Crocardes, Staldinges, Egles.

†**stale**, *sb.*¹ *Obs.* Forms: 1 **stalu**, *Northumb.* **stalo**, 2 **stala**, 2–4 **stale**. [OE. *stalu* str. fem. = OHG. *stala* fem. (mod.G. *-stahl* in *diebstahl* masc., theft), f. OTeut. **stal-*: **stel-*: see STEAL *v.*]

1. Theft, stealing.

c **950** *Lindisf. Gosp.* Matt. xix. 18 Ne doe ðu ðiofonto vel stalo. **971** *Blickling Hom.* 75 Þis þu cwist for þinre ȝitsunge & for þinre stale. *c* **1175** *Lamb. Hom.* 13 Stala and steorfa swiðe eow scal hene. *a* **1200** *Moral Ode* 253 Þa..þe luueden tening [*v.r.* reuing] and stale. **1340** *Ayenb.* 9 Ine þise heste is vorbode roberie, þiefþe, stale, and gavel.

2. *by stale* = by stealth.

a **1240** *Sawles Warde* in *Cott. Hom.* 249 Hire wune is to cumen bi stale..hwen me least cweneð.

stale (steɪl), *sb.*² Now *dial.* Forms: 1 **stalu**, 7 **staile, stayl**, 7, 9 **stail**, 3– **stale**. See also STEAL *sb.*¹ [OE. *stalu* str. fem., related by ablaut to the synonymous *stela* STEAL *sb.*¹ Cf. MFlem. *stael* (Kilian), WFlem. *staal* (De Bo), NFris. *stal*, *staal* masc., handle, WFris. *stâlle*.

The words *stale* and *steal* cannot be completely separated, as the spellings *stale, stail* may represent a dialectal pronunciation of *steal*, and on the other hand the sound which would be given in some dialects to *stale* would naturally be written *steal* by outsiders. For convenience, the examples with the spelling *stail(e stale* are placed here, and those with the spelling *steal, steele*, etc. under STEAL *sb.*¹]

†**1.** Each of the two upright sides of a ladder (*obs.*). Also (now *dial.*), a rung or step of a ladder. Also, the stave of a rack in a stable.

Cf. OE. *hearpanstala* 'ceminigi' (*a* **1000** in Wr.-Wülcker 203/36), perh. the side-pieces of a harp.

a **1225** *Ancr. R.* 354 Scheome and pine..beoð þe two leddre stalen þet beoð upriht to þe heouene, and bitweonen þeos stalen beoð þe tindes ivestned of alle gode þeawes, bi hwuche me climbeð to þe blisse of heouene. *c* **1315** SHOREHAM *Poems* I. 49 Þis ilke laddre is charite, þe stales gode þeawis. **1714** SAVAGE *Art Prudence* 172 The first Stale of this Ladder of Fortune. **1887** *Kent. Gloss.*, *Stales*, the staves, or risings of a ladder, or the staves of a rack in a stable. **1892** *Daily News* 13 Apr. 6/5 [Letter from a former labourer in Kent.] Give the labourer easy access to the land, and thereby put the stails very close together in the bottom of the social ladder.

†**b.** *fig.* Position in a series. *Obs. rare*⁻¹.

[This may perh. belong to STALL *sb.*¹]

13.. *E.E. Allit. P.* A. 1002 Iasper hyȝt ȝe fyrst gemme.. Saffer helde þe secounde stale.

2. A handle, esp. a long slender handle, as the handle of a rake, etc. Also, the stem of a pipe, etc.

a **1200** *Sidonius Glosses* in *Anecd. Oxon.* I. v. 59/22 *Ansae* et *ansulae* alicuius rei sunt illa eminentia in illa re per quam capi possit .i. 'stale'. *c* **1393** LANGL. *P. Pl.* C. XXII. 279 (Vesp. MS.) And lerede men a ladel bygge with a long stale [*v.r.* stele]. **1547** *MS. Harl.* 1419 If. 145 b, Twoo forkes of mettall guilte, the stales beinge of glasse. **1624** in Simpkinson *Washingtons* (1860) p. lvii, Pitch forke stailes. **1649–53** BLITHE *Eng. Improv. Impr.* (ed. 3) 71 Thy Stail need not be so long as a naturall Spade-stail. *a* **1652** BROME *Covent Gard.* I. i. stage-dir., A Table bottle, light, and Tobacco stales. **1675** WORLIDGE *Syst. Agric.* (ed. 2) 251 Which Net you hold strongly against the place, by the help of a Stail or handle that is fixed athwart the Bow. **1688** HOLME *Armoury* III. 343/1 The Mallet when it is large, and a long Stail or Handle, is termed a Maul by Wood Men. *Ibid.* III. xxi. (Roxb.) 253/2 He beareth Sable a Dung fork,..Argent, the shank or staile. **1742** *Lond. & Country Brew.* I. (ed. 4) 61 In Case your Cask is a Butt,..have ready boiling..Water, which put in, and, with a long Stale and a little Birch fastened to its End, scrub the Bottom. **1828** *Mech. Mag.* IX. 238 They are set like unto a hoe for a stroke with a straight stail (handle). **1890** *Manch. Guardian* 4 Feb. 12/3 You came to me with the axe head in one hand and the stale in the other.

3. A stalk or stem.

c **1440** *Pallad. on Husb.* XI. 194 And theryn do pistacis iij by tale, And of hem all vp wol ther ryse a stale [*germen*]. **1854** MISS BAKER *Northampt. Gloss.*, *Stail*, the stalk of a flower or fruit.

4. The stem of an arrow or spear.

1553 BRENDE *Q. Curtius* ix. 192 The Surgians cut of the stale of that shaft in suche wise, that they moued not the heade that was wythin the fleshe. **1585** HIGINS *Junius' Nomencl.* 276/1 *Hastile*,..a speare staffe or the shaft and stale of a iaueline. *c* **1611** CHAPMAN *Iliad* IV. 173 Seeing th'arrowes stale without.

stale (steɪl), *sb.*³ [Prob. a. AF. *estale, estal* (only in Bozon, 13th c.), applied to a pigeon used to entice a hawk into the net; that this word is not an adoption from English is rendered probable by the occurrence of the extended form *estalon* in continental Fr. with the same sense (Cotgrave 1611; Godefroy gives earlier instances spelt *estolon, etelon*). Of Teut. origin; cf. OE. *stælhrán* decoy reindeer, *stællo* (Northumbrian) catching (of fish), prob. from the root of *steall* place (STALL *sb.*¹) *stęllan* to place; for the sense cf. the rendering of *stale* by 'stacionaria' in the *Promptorium*, and G. *stellvogel* decoy-bird.

It has been usual to regard the *stæl-* in *stælhrán* as identical with the combining form of *stalu* theft (as in *stælȝiest* predatory guest, *stælhere* plundering army); but the difference of meaning renders this unlikely; and the current identification of ONorthumb. *stællo* with *stalu* seems inadmissible on grounds both of form and sense.]

1. A decoy-bird; a living bird used to entice other birds of its own species, or birds of prey, into a snare or net. Also, a stuffed bird or figure of a bird used for the same purpose. *Obs.* (? exc. *dial.*)

c **1440** *Promp. Parv.* 472/1 Stale, of fowlynge or byrdys takynge, *stacionaria*. *a* **1542** SURREY *Song*, 'Eche beast can chose' in *Tottel's Misc.* (Arb.) 220 As a faucon free..Which ..for no stale doth care. **1552** HULOET, Stale that fowlers vse, *incitabulum, mentita auis*. **1579–80** NORTH *Plutarch, Sylla* (1595) 515 Like vnto the fowlers, that by their stales draw other birdes into their nets. **1608** [TOFTE] *Ariosto's Sat.* IV. (1611) 52 A wife that's more then faire is like a stale, Or chanting whistle which brings birds to thrall. **1621** MARKHAM *Fowling* 31 You shal stake downe here and there a liue Stale, being either a Mallard, or a Widgon, or a Tayle. **1624** QUARLES *Job Militant* v. med. xxv, As the treacherous Fowler..doth first deuise To make a Bird his stale, at whose false Call, Others may chance into the selfe-same Thrall. **1675** WORLIDGE *Syst. Agric.* (ed. 2) 322 *Stale*, a living Fowl, put in any place to allure other Fowl, where they may be taken. **1681** FLAVEL *Meth. Grace* xxxv. 588 'Tis the living bird that makes the best stale to draw others into the net. **1768** PENNANT *Brit. Zool.* II. 365 The birds, enticed by a stale or stuffed bird, come under the nets. **1888** FENN *Dick o' the Fens* 53 If my live birds aren't all drownded and my stales spoiled.

attrib. **1725** *Bradley's Fam. Dict.* s.v. *Day-net*, When you have placed..your Gigs and Stales, go to the further End of your long Drawing-lines and Stale-lines, and [etc.].

b. in figurative context.

1579 STUBBES *Discov. Gaping Gulf* B 4 b, Her daughter Margerit was the stale to lure..them that otherwise flewe hyghe..and could not be gotten. **1584** STAFFORD in *Eng. Hist. Rev.* (1913) Jan. 44 *note*, I am more than half afraid that he [Sidney] is made but a stale to take a bird withal. **1614** JACKSON *Creed* III. ix. 97 Bellarmines distinctions..may hence be described to be but meere stales to catch guls. **1645** F. THORPE in *Hull Lett.* (1886) 120 But five yeares experience hath taught English men another lesson than to be Catcht twice with one Stale.

†**2.** *transf.* and *fig.* A deceptive means of allurement; a person or thing held out as a lure or bait to entrap a person. *Obs.*

a **1529** SKELTON *E. Rummyng* 324 It was a stale to take the devyl in a brake. **1530** TINDALE *Pract. Prelates* B ij, The chefest stale wherwith the cardinall caught the kynges grace. **1577** HOLINSHED *Hist. Eng.* I. 79/2 The Britaynes woulde oftentimes..lay their Cattell..in places conueniente, to bee as a stale to the Romaynes, and when the Romaynes should make to them to fetch the same away..they would fall vpon them. **1610** SHAKS. *Temp.* IV. i. 187 The trumpery in my house, goe bring it hither For stale to catch these theeues. **1615** G. SANDYS *Trav.* I. 66 Beautifull boyes, who serve as stales to procure them customers. **1670** EACHARD *Cont. Clergy* 88 Six-pence or a shilling to put into the Box, for a stale to decoy in the rest of the Parish. **1692** [J. WILSON] *Vindic. Carol.* xxvi. 132 Which yet they made use of but as a Stale to the Faction.

†**3.** A person who acts as a decoy; esp. the accomplice of a thief or sharper. *Obs.*

1526 *Pilgr. Perf.* (W. de W. 1531) 119 Theyr mynystres be false bretherne or false systerne, stales of yᵉ deuyll. **1579** GOSSON *Sch. Abuse* (Arb.) 36 Every Vawter in one blinde Tauerne or other, is Tenant at will,..and playes the stale to vtter their victualls. **1591** GREENE *Conny Catching* I. Wks. (Grosart) X. 38 He that faceth the man, the Stale. **1610** ROWLANDS *M. Mark-all* G 2, [He] was faine to liue among the wicked,..a stale for a foyst. **1622** J. TAYLOR (Water P.) *Water-Cormorant* D 2 b, He..Can play the Foist, the Nip, the Stale. **1633** MARMION *Fine Companion* III. iv, This is Captain Whibble, the Towne stale, For all cheating imployments.

†**4.** More fully *common stale*: a prostitute of the lowest class, employed as a decoy by thieves. Often (? associated with STALE *a.*) used *gen.* as a term of contempt for an unchaste woman. *Obs.*

1593 *Tell-Trothe's N. Y. Gift* (1876) 35 Can women want wit to frustrate a common stale. **1599** SHAKS. *Much Ado* II. ii. 26 Spare not to tell him, that hee hath wronged his Honor in marrying the renowned Claudio..to a contaminated stale. *Ibid.* IV. i. 66, I stand dishonour'd that haue gone about, To linke my deare friend to a common stale. **1605** DANIEL *Queen's Arcadia* II. i, But to be leaft for such a one as she, The stale of all, what will folke thinke of me? *a* **1641** BP. MOUNTAGU *Acts & Mon.* (1642) 265 Detesting as he said the insatiable impudency of a prostitute Stale.

fig. **1641** MILTON *Reform.* I. 10 The Bishops..suffer'd themselvs to be the common stales to countenance with their prostituted Gravities every Politick Fetch that was then on foot.

†**5.** A person or thing made use of as a means or tool for inducing some result, as a pretext for

some action, or as a cover for sinister designs. Cf. STALKING-HORSE. *Obs.*

1580 GRINDAL in Strype *Life* (1710) 252 That of the two nominated, one should be an unfit Man, and as it were a Stale, to bring the Office to the other. **1593** SHAKS. *3 Hen. VI*, III. iii. 260 Had he none else to make a stale but me? **1598–9** B. JONSON *Case Altered* v. iii, Was this your drift? to vse Fernezes name? Was he your fittest stale? **1606** HIERON *Truth's Purch.* ii. 45 Not to be (as it were) a stale, vnder the shadow whereof we may the more boldly giue our selues ouer to vngodlinesse. **1614** RALEIGH *Hist. World* IV. iii. §19. 239 Eurydice..meaning nothing lesse than to let her husband serue as a Stale, keeping the throne warme, till another were growne old enough to sit in it. **1620–6** QUARLES *Feast for Worms* 158 Lawyers arise, make not your righteous Lawes, A stale for Bribes. **1624** [SCOTT] *2nd Pt. Vox Populi* 14 Spaine hath..vsed their alliance and friendshippe but as a stale or stalking-horse ouer their backes to shoote at others. *c* **1640** SUCKLING *Brennoralt* II. i, Her health, is a stale, And helps us to make us drinke on. **1652** PEYTON *Catastr. Ho. Stuarts* (1731) 11 Giving it out for a Stale, that the Earl, with others, would have killed him. **1711** PUCKLE *Club* (1817) 20 A pretence of kindness is the universal stale to all base projects. **1774** *Ann. Reg., Hist. Europe* 20/1 Those people were only used as a stale for ambition and rapacity.

†**6.** A lover or mistress whose devotion is turned into ridicule for the amusement of a rival or rivals.

Some examples suggest allusion to some unknown sense relating to deer.

1579 LYLY *Euphues* (Arb.) 96, I perceiue Lucilla (said he) that I was made thy stale, and Philautus thy laughing stocke. **1588** T. HUGHES *Arthur* I. ii. 3 Was I then chose and wedded for his stale? **1590** SHAKS. *Com. Err.* II. i. 101 [A neglected wife says:] But, too vnruly Deere, he breakes the pale And feedes from home; poore I am but his stale. **1611** MIDDLETON & DEKKER *Roaring Girl* IV. ii. 154 Did I for this lose all my friends..to be made A stale to a common whore? *a* **1616** BEAUM. & FL. *Little Fr. Lawyer* III. i, This comes of rutting; Are we made stales to one another? **1635** RUTTER *Sheph. Holyday* v. ii. G 1 b, She would say, You have another mistresse, go to her, I wil not be her stale.

† **stale**, *sb.*[4] *Obs.* Also 4–6 staill, 6 stayll, stail(e, steill, (6–7 stall, 7 stal). [a. OF. *estal*, used in many specific applications of the senses (1) place, position, (2) something placed or fixed (mod.F. *étal* butcher's stall), a. OHG. *stal*: see STALL *sb.*[1]]

1. A fixed position or station. ***to hold*** or ***keep*** **(*one's*) *stale*** [= OF. *tenir* (*son*) *estal*]: to maintain one's position in battle.

1375 BARBOUR *Bruce* XVII. 97 [Thai] ordanit, that the mast party Of thair men suld gang sarraly With thar lordis, and hald a staill. *c* **1450** in Kingsford *Chron. London* (1905) 123 And at pavelen..þe Erle of Dorzet helde is stale, and þer he toke prisoners. **1470–85** MALORY *Arthur* v. xi. 179 And syr Florence with his C knyghtes alwey kepte the stale and foughte manly.

2. An ambush. ***in stale***: in ambush.

c **1425** WYNTOUN *Cron.* IX. viii. 811 And he in stale howyd al stil. **1513** DOUGLAS *Æneis* XI. x. 96 It is a stelling place and sovir harbry, Quhar ost in staill or embuschment may ly. *a* **1548** HALL *Chron., Hen. IV* (1809) 43 While he stode in a stale to lie in waite [**1568** GRAFTON *Chron.* II. 439 He lay in stale to waite] for the relefe that myght come from Caleis. **1557** EDGEWORTH *Serm.* 231 God badde him [Joshua] *Pone insidias vrbi post eam*, laye a stale behynde the citie. **1577** HOLINSHED *Hist. Eng.* II. 1479/2 The erle of Essex..with .ii. C. speares was layde in a stale, if the Frenchmen had come neerer. **1627** *Taking of Ship 'St. Esprit'* in *Harl. Misc.* (1810) V. 111 Which two noblemen..were drawn within danger by a stale made by twenty common soldiers.

3. A body of armed men posted in a particular place for ambush or otherwise, or detached for reconnoitring or other special service. Also (? chiefly *Sc.*) the main body of an army.

c **1350** in Nicolas *Hist. Royal Navy* (1847) II. 491 [Every time that it shall be ordered..that armed men..shall land on the enemy's coast to seek victuals.., then there shall be ordained a sufficient 'stale' of armed men and archers who shall wait together on the land until the 'forreiours' return to them]. *c* **1375** *Sc. Leg. Saints* xl. (Ninian) 1096 Brocht [þar pray] nere to þar stale þat þar abad nocht ful lang. ? *a* **1400** *Morte Arth.* 1355 [Gawayne] sterttes owtte to hys stede, and with his stale wendes. *c* **1400** *Laud Troy Bk.* 9647 Thei of Grece were gadered alle With-oute the diche be-fore the walle, In-myddis the feld ther standis her stale. **14..** in Nicolas *Hist. Royal Navy* (1847) II. 491 That no maner man goe for no forage, but it be with a stale, the whiche shall fowrth twise a weeke. *c* **1470** HENRY *Wallace* v. 32 Schyr Garrat Herroun in the staill can abide. **1513** LD. DACRE in Ellis *Orig. Lett.* Ser. I. I. 94 And I come with a stale to a place called the Dungyon. **1530** PALSGR. 275/1 Stale of horsmen in a felde, *guectevrs*. **1532** *St. Papers Hen. VIII*, IV. 626 Neveryeles I knaw asweill by Englisemen as Scottishmen that their stale was no les then thre thowsand men. **1543** *Ibid.* V. 315 Litle regardinge the service done by the foote men remayninge in the staile, but attributing all the prayse to theim selfes. *a* **1548** HALL *Chron., Hen. VIII*, 127 Sir Willyam FitzWillyam..in great haste sent for his stale of horsemen that he had left couered. **1565** GOLDING *Cæsar* v. 118 For they neuer fought in great companyes.., but scatteryinge.., and had stales lying in diuers places one to serue anothers turne. **1577** HOLINSHED *Hist. Scot.* 471/2 The lard of Drunlanrig lying al thys while in ambush.. forbare to breake out to gyue any charge vppon his enimies, doubting least the Earle of Lennox hadde kept a stale behynde. *a* **1578** LINDESAY (Pitscottie) *Chron. Scot.* (S.T.S.) I. 74 George Earl of Ormond was in the staill him self. **1579** CHURCHYARD *Gen. Rehearsal Wars* I j, He remained with the whole power of footemen nere the Blacke Neastes, as a stale to annoye the enemie.

b. ***in stale***: in battle array.

1513 DOUGLAS *Æneis* IV. viii. 123 King Pentheus, in his wod rage dotand, Thocht he beheld gret rowtis stand in staill Of the Ewmenydes.

c. ***flying stale***: a body of troops ordered to move rapidly to any part of the field in which help is required.

a **1500** *Harding's Chron.* ccxl. add. Harl. MS. (1812) 417 With fotemen in tho two erledomes with fleynge stales to releue theym. **1532** *St. Papers Hen. VIII*, IV. 628 And I did send for there strenght my cousyn Sir Arthur Darcy, being accompanied with 6 hundreth and above in a fleyng stale.

d. *transf.* A band of hunters.

c **1425** WYNTOUN *Cron.* VI. 1609 (Wemyss MS.) As he past apon a day In till his hunting him to play..The staill and þe settys set. **1536** BELLENDEN *Cron. Scot.* (1821) II. 298 The staill past throw the wod with sic noyis..that all the bestis wer rasit fra thair dennis.

stale (steɪl), *sb.*[5] Also 7 **stall.** [? f. STALE *v.* But cf. Du. *stalle*, MLG. *stal*, G. *stall.*]

1. Urine; now only of horses and cattle.

a **1400** *Stockh. Medical MS.* in *Anglia* XVIII. 299 In werd ben men & women..þat þer stale mown not holde. **1530** PALSGR. 275/1 Stale pysse, *escloy*. **1535** COVERDALE *Isa.* xxxvi. 12 That they be not compelled to eate their owne donge, and drinke their owne stale with you? **1548** RECORDE *Urin. Physick* xi. 89 The stale of Camels and Goats..is good for them that have the dropsie. **1583** MELBANCKE *Philotimus* O iij b, Or annoint thy selfe with the stale of a mule. **1606** SHAKS. *Ant. & Cl.* I. iv. 62 Thou did'st drinke The stale of Horses. **1662** GERBIER *Principles* 34 That his Stall doth not remain under him. **1698** FRYER *Acc. E. India & P.* 242 Mice and Weasels by their poysonous Stale infect the Trees so, that they produce Worms. **1733** W. ELLIS *Chiltern & Vale Farm.* 122 Sheep, whose Dung and Stale is of most Virtue in the Nourishment of all Trees. **1805** R. W. DICKSON *Pract. Agric.* I. 51 The stale of mares.

b. ***to have a rod in stale*** (? Anglo-Irish): = to have a rod in pickle: see PICKLE *sb.*[1] 1 b.

1837–8 KEEGAN *Leg. & Poems* (1907) 65, I have a rod in stale for him ever since the night he offinded me at the wake.

2. ***blood-stale, stale-foul*** a disease (see quot.).

1816 TOWNE *Farmer & Grazier's Guide* 21 The Blood-Stale in Horses, the Stale-foul, in Oxen, and the Red Water in Sheep, are Diseases..derived from very similar causes.

stale (steɪl), *sb.*[6] *Chess.* [a. AF. *estale*, perh. vbl. n. f. *estaler* STALE *v.*[3]] = STALEMATE.

1423 JAS. I *Kingis Q.* clxix, 'Off mate?' quod sche..'thou has fundin stale This mony day'. *c* **1470** *MS. Ashmole 344* lf. 18 b, þan draw thi fers in to e & þi other fers in to f as nye thy knyght as thow mayst savyng stale. **1591** FLORIO *2nd Fruites* 75 It is no check-mate, but a stale. **1625** BACON *Ess., Of Boldness* (Arb.) 519 They stand at a stay; Like a Stale at Chesse, where it is no Mate, but yet the Game cannot stirre. **1647** WARD *Simple Cobler* 57 When the Parliament shall give you a mate, though but a Stale. **1656** BEALE *Biochimo's Roy. Game Chess-play* 13 A stale is given when one King hath lost all his men and hath but one place left to fly into, if then the adversary bar him of that place without checking him, so that he being now out of check cannot remove but into check, it is then a stale, and he that giveth it to the distressed King loseth the Game.

stale (steɪl), *sb.*[7] *colloq.* [Absol. use of STALE *a.*[1]] A stale cake or loaf of bread, etc.

1874 HARDY *Madding Crowd* II. iii. 39, I went to Riggs's batty-cake shop, and asked 'em for a penneth of the cheapest and nicest stales, that were all but bluemouldy, but not quite. **1937** DEARMOND & GRAF *Route Sales Managem.* 4 The man who sells and delivers bread to the grocer must remove the stales each day. **1937** 'G. ORWELL' *Road to Wigan Pier* I. i. 15 Frayed-looking sweet-cakes..bought as 'stales' from the baker.

stale (steɪl), *a.*[1] [Of obscure history, but prob. ultimately f. the Teut. root **sta-* to STAND. Cf. Flem. *stel* in the same sense, said of beer and urine (Kilian; still used in WFlem., see De Bo).]

†**1.** Of malt liquor, mead, wine: That has stood long enough to clear; freed from dregs or lees; hence, old and strong. *Obs.*

c **1300** *K. Horn* 383 (Laud) Bi forn þe king abenche Red win to schenche And after mete stale Boþe win and ale. *c* **1386** CHAUCER *Sir Thopas* 52 Notemuge to putte in ale, Whether it be moyste or stale. **1398** TREVISA *Barth. De P.R.* XIX. lvii. (1495) 896 Yf meth is well sod and stale it is lykynge to the taste. *a* **1400** *Stockh. Medical MS.* in *Anglia* XVIII. 310 Good reed wyn þat be stale. **1421** *Cov. Leet Bk.* (1907) 25 When hit [ale] is good and stale. **1483** *Cath. Angl.* 358/1 Sstale As Ale, *defecatus*. *a* **1529** SKELTON *E. Rummyng* 367 And ye will gyve me a syppet Of your stale ale. *a* **1553** UDALL *Royster D.* I. iii. (Arb.) 19 Where good stale ale is will drinke no water I trust. **1586** COGAN *Haven Health* ccxviii. 221 Good ale..must be..made of good corne, well sodden, stale and well purged. **1709** ADDISON *Tatler* No. 162 ⁋ 1, I daily live in a very comfortable Affluence of Wine, Stale Beer, Hungary Water, Beef, Books, and Marrow-Bones. **1743** *Lond. & Country Brew.* IV. (ed. 2) 294 To turn Ale into stale Beer presently.

fig. **1709** O. DYKES *Eng. Prov. & Refl.* (ed. 2) Pref. 16 Proverbs scatter'd through all the Works of the Learned, like Salt, to give them a Relish, and to make them keep stale.

2. That has lost its freshness; altered by keeping.

a. of food or drink.

'Usually in disparaging sense; but when said of bread it is the ordinary opposite of *new*, without necessarily implying inferiority.' *N.E.D.*

1530 PALSGR. 325/2 Stale as breed or drinke is, *rassis*. Stale as meate is that begynneth to savoure, *viel*. *c* **1550** *Wyll of Deuill* (*c* 1825) C 2 b, New freshe blood to ouersprinkle their stale mete that it may seme..newly kylled. **1580** LYLY *Euphues* (Arb.) 386 Gestes and fish..are euer stale within three dayes. **1606** SHAKS. *Tr. & Cr.* v. iv. 11 That stole [*read* stale] old Mouse-eaten dry cheese, Nestor. **1726** SWIFT *Gulliver* II. v, To let out the Water when it began to grow stale. **1727** —— *Past. Dial. Richm. Hill* 53 To cry the Bread was stale, and mutter Complaints against the Royal Butter. **1759** R. BROWN *Compl. Farmer* 78 [A chicken will be] tender and green in the vent if stale. **1829** *Chapters Phys. Sci.* 251 The egg becomes stale or addled. **1845** JAMES *Arrah Neil* ii, I would as soon..eat stale cabbage. **1878** M. L. HOLBROOK *Hygiene Brain* 61 The bread should be stale. **1888** F. HUME *Mme. Midas* I. Prol., His companion collected the stale biscuits which had fallen out of the bag.

b. of urine, manure, straw, etc.

1577 GOOGE *Heresbach's Husb.* II. (1586) 83 Stale vrine. **1765** *Museum Rust.* IV. 255 Where dung is made use of, it must be very stale and rotten. **1865** DICKENS *Mut. Fr.* III. xi, An early public-house, haunted by unsavoury smells of musty hay and stale straw.

†**c.** of wounds. *Obs.*

1607 TOPSELL *Four-f. Beasts* 495 A very excellent remedy for the curing of wounds which are old and stale, and ful of putrifaction.

d. *Agric.*

a **1722** LISLE *Husb.* (1757) *Gloss.*, *Fallows-stale*, ground that has been ploughed some time, and lies in fallow. **1764** *Museum Rust.* II. 306 Lime would do very little or no good on stale ploughed lands. **1805** R. W. DICKSON *Pract. Agric.* II. 590 So that the crop may be put in upon a stale furrow.

3. a. *fig.* Of an immaterial thing: That has lost its freshness, novelty, or interest; hackneyed, worn out, out of date; effete. (Frequent in Shaks.)

1562 J. HEYWOOD *Prov. & Epigr.* (1867) 95 Better is..be it new or stale, A harmelesse lie, than a harmefull true tale. **1579** G. HARVEY *Letter-bk.* (Camden) 60 Doist thou smyle to reade this stale and beggarlye stuffe. **1596** SHAKS. *Merch. V.* II. v. 55 A prouerbe neuer stale in thriftie minde. **1602** —— *Ham.* I. ii. 133 How weary, stale, flat, and vnprofitable Seemes to me all the vses of this world? **1638** BAKER tr. *Balzac's Lett.* (vol. II) 16 A novelty that will quickly grow stale. **1716** ADDISON *Freeholder* No. 9 ⁋ 11 The Parliament of Great Britain, against whom you bring a stale accusation which has been used by every minority in the memory of man. **1780** MME. D'ARBLAY *Lett.* June, I hardly know what to tell you that won't be stale news. **1822** LAMB *Elia* I. *Distant Corresp.*, A two-days-old newspaper. You resent the stale thing as an affront. **1874** L. STEPHEN *Hours in Libr.* (1892) I. iii. 100 The commonplaces in which Pope takes such infinite delight have become very stale for us. **1880** *Macm. Mag.* No. 246. 518 She thought her chances of marriage at home were grown rather stale. **1908** *Outlook* 14 Nov. 651/1 When the memory of the last few weeks has grown stale.

b. *Law.* Of a claim or demand: That has been allowed to lie dormant for an unreasonable time.

1769 BLACKSTONE *Comm.* IV. xv. 211 The jury will rarely give credit to a stale complaint. **1884** *Law Rep.* 26 *Chanc. Div.* 119 The claims of the Plaintiffs had been barred..by the rules against stale claims. *Ibid.* 27 Chanc. Div. 530 Obligations..which he would never have incurred if he had had any reason to believe that this stale claim would be prosecuted.

c. *Comm.* That has remained inactive for a considerable time; (of a cheque) out-of-date.

1889 BARRÈRE & LELAND *Dict. Slang* II. 297/2 *Stale bear*, ..a man who has sold stock which he does not possess, and has not bought it back. A bear who has been short of stock for a considerable period... *Stale bull*, a man who has held stock for a long period without profit. **1901** C. DUGUID *How to read Money Article* viii. 37 The time comes when the 'bull campaign' turns into a 'stale bull account', that is, when the bulls are anxious to sell, even at a loss. **1901** *Business Terms & Phrases* (ed. 2) 199 *Stale cheque*,..a cheque which has remained unpaid for some considerable time. **1930** M. CLARK *Home Trade* 271 Stale bulls are those who come to the conclusion that they have waited long enough for a rise in price and who, therefore, sell out. **1939** F. LEE *City Page* iii. 61 Eventually every crossed cheque has to be paid into a banker's account, usually within a time limit of six months; otherwise the cheque is 'stale'. **1957** CLARK & GOTTFRIED *Dict. Business & Finance* (1967) 332/2 *Stale*,..in business, out of date, or outstanding for a long time. **1979** F. E. PERRY *Dict. Banking* 11/2 A banker receiving a cheque antedated by six months or more for payment would regard it as 'stale'.

†**4. a.** Of persons: Past the prime of life; having lost the vigour or attractiveness of youth. Of a bachelor or spinster: Past the fitting season for marriage. *Obs.*

c **1580** JEFFERIE *Bugbears* I. ii. 108 in *Archiv Stud. neu. Spr.* XCVIII. 309 Rosimunda..hathe an vncle a stale batcheler. **1585** HIGINS *Junius' Nomencl.* 19/1 *Virgo exoleta*,..an old stale maide past mariage. **1589** NASHE *Martin Marprelate* Wks. (Grosart) I. 108 Therein they are like to a stale Curtizan. **1598** HAKLUYT *Voy.* I. 99 Somtimes their maids are very stale before they be maried: for their parents alwaies keep them till they can sel them. **1609** ROWLANDS *Dr. Merrie-man* 10 An old stale Widdower, quite past the best. *a* **1643** CARTWRIGHT *Siedge* I. iv, I'm for your tender Maidenheads: I would not Venture my self with a stale Virgin, or A season'd Widow for a Kingdom. **1711** RAMSAY *On Maggy Johnstoun* xiv, She was..Right free of care, or toil, or strife, Till she was stale. **1742** SHORT *Dropsy* in *Phil. Trans.* XLII. 226 In barren Women, and stale Maids, Tapping should be very cautiously undertaken. **1748** SMOLLETT *Rod. Random* l. (1760) II. 136, I talked in raptures to the stale governante. **1858** HOGG *Life Shelley* I. 176, I found only two stale women; a stale middle-aged woman who acted as waiter and chambermaid, and an older and still staler woman, the landlady.

†**b.** of attributes. *Obs.*

1612 *Two Noble K.* v. i. 91 That may'st..induce Stale gravitie to daunce. **1771** SMOLLETT *Humph. Cl.* 5 May (1815) 63 The rancour of stale maidenhood.

5. a. *Sport.* Of an athlete, a racing animal, etc.: Out of condition through over-severe training or exertion too long continued. Phr. ***to go stale.***

1856 'STONEHENGE' *Brit. Rural Sports* II. I. vi. §7. 335 By this means the [horse's] legs are not made more stale than necessary. **1868** *Field* 4 July 15/1 In the third heat [rowing], Mair of Magdalen, easily beat Willan of Exeter, who seemed stale and gone off. **1885** *Truth* 28 May 853/2 Dame Agnes will probably be stale after her exertions in the Derby. **1889**

D. C. Murray *Dang. Catspaw* 38 William, though a little stale, turned out to be a past master in the art. *transf.* **1894** *Nation* (N.Y.) 22 Mar. 209/1 It sometimes happens that, in the strain of this part of the race [for Cambridge honours], the boy outgrows the brilliant precocity which put him ahead of his rivals, and emerges merely an ordinary young man with no further possibilities of use. This disaster is technically known as 'going stale'. **1903** W. T. Stead in *Rev. of Rev.* May 574 (Cent. Suppl.) In 1892, the Unionist administration having gone stale, it was turned out.

b. Of a bird: See quot.

1897 *Encycl. Sport* I. 301/1 (Decoys) *Stale birds*, fowl that have frequently visited the decoy, but have lost interest in the actions of the dog.

6. *Comb.*

1963 J. N. Harris *Weird World Wes Beattie* (1964) xv. 179 This check came along... It was *stale-dated, see? I mean it had been drawn the previous September, and this was about May. **1823** Egan *Grose's Dict. Vulgar T.* s.v., A person is said to be *stale drunk when they feel languid after a night's debauch. **1641** Milton *Animadv.* Wks. 1851 III. 234 O *stale-growne piety! O Gospell rated as cheap as thy Master, at thirtypence. **1819** Shelley *Cenci* iii. i. 159 Lay all bare So that my unpolluted fame should be With vilest gossips a *stale mouthed story. **1936** E. Wilson *Travels in Two Democracies* 286 They carried me into a *stale-smelling building. **1973** T. Pynchon *Gravity's Rainbow* i. 24 The city around them at once a big desolate ice-box, stale-smelling. **1593** Nashe *Christ's T.* Wks. (Grosart) IV. 92 Often reiterating hys *stale-worne note.

†**stale**, *a.*^{2} *Chess. Obs.* [f. stale *sb.*^{6}] Stalemated.

c **1470** *MS. Ashmole 344* lf. 21 b. Then drawith he & is stale.

stale (steɪl), *v.*^{1} *Obs.* exc. *arch.* and *dial.* Also 5 *Sc.* stal, 6 **staale**, *Sc.* **stail**; 7–9 *rare* **stall**. [Proximate source uncertain; perh. a. OF. *estaler* (once in Godef., with erroneous explanation) = It. *stallare*; either adopted from, or the source of, the Teut. word which appears as Du., LG., HG. *stallen* (MHG. in 14th c.), Sw. *stalla*, Da. *stalle*, to make water (said of horses).

Attempts have been made to identify the Teut. word with G. (Du., etc.) *stallen* to place in a stall, be lodged in a stall, also to come to a stand (see stall *sb.* and *v.*). For objections to these explanations see Grimm s.v. *stallen*.]

1. *intr.* To urinate, said esp. of horses or cattle.

14.. *Lawis Gild* x. in *Anc. Laws Scot.* (Burgh Rec. Soc.) 68 Gif ony stal in the yet of the gilde..he sall gif iiijd. to the mendis. *c* **1450** *Merlin* xxvii. 526 He turned be-side the wey to make his horse stale. **1530** Palsgr. 732/1 Tary a whyle, your hors wyll staale. **1596** Nashe *Saffron Walden* Wks. (Grosart) III. 206 Bringing in his great horse..into his Banquetting-house; to dung and stale amongst his guests. **1614** B. Jonson *Bart. Fair* i. iv, Why a pox o' your boxe, once again: let your little wife stale in it, and she will. *c* **1630** in *Law's Memor.* (1818) Introd. p. lv, He should pluck up a nettle by the root..and stale upon it three severall mornings. **1663** Killigrew *Parson's Wedd.* i. iii, I wonder he [the knight's son] doth not go on all four too, and hold up his Leg when he stales. **1735** Burdon *Pocket-Farrier* 22 Sometimes a Horse cannot stall, and will be in great Pain. **1795** T. Maurice *Hindostan* i. ix. (1820) I. 285 Observing the baboon to stale twelve times in the day. **1812** Skellett in H. Stephens *Bk. Farm* (1844) II. 477 She will be frequently dunging, stalling, and blaring. **1886** *W. Somerset Word-bk.*, *Stale*, to void urine—of horses only. **1891** Hardy *Tess* lii, While the horses stood to stale and breathe themselves. **1903** Kipling *5 Nations* (1903) 150 Cattle-dung where fuel failed; Water where the mules had staled; And sackcloth for their raiment.

†**2.** *trans.* To pass (blood) in the urine. *Obs.*

?*a* **1550** *Droichis Part of Play* 62 in *Dunbar's Poems* (S.T.S.) 316 Scho tuke the gravall and staild Craig Gorth. **1607** Topsell *Four-f. Beasts* 132 Anatolius approued beane meale sifted and sod with Harts marrow to be giuen to a horse which stalleth blood. **1647** J. C[leveland] *Char. Lond.-Diurn.* 2 For it casts the water of the State, ever since it staled bloud.

stale (steɪl), *v.*^{2} Also 6 *Sc.* **stail**, (7 **staule**). [f. stale *a.*^{1}]

1. *trans.* To render (beer or ale) 'stale'.

c **1440** *Promp. Parv.* 472/1 Stalyn, or make stale drynke, *defeco.* **1616** B. Jonson *Devil an Ass* i. i, You haue some plot, now, Vpon a tonning of Ale, to stale the yest. **1743** *Lond. & Country Brew.* iv. (ed. 2) 294 Like old October Beer staled through Time. **1826** *Art of Brewing* (ed. 2) 106 A stock of old porter should be kept, sufficient for staling the consumption of twelve months.

b. *intr.* Of beer: to become 'stale' or old.

1742 *Lond. & Country Brew.* i. (ed. 4) 64 The Drink from that Time flattens and stales. **1743** *Ibid.* iv. (ed. 2) 303 Secure a Butt of Beer from staling too soon.

2. *trans.* To render stale, out of date or uninteresting; to diminish interest in.

1599 B. Jonson *Cynthia's Rev.* Induct., Ile goe tell all the argument of his play aforehand, and so stale his inuention to the auditorie before it come forth. **1601** Shaks. *Jul. C.* iv. i. 38 Which out of vse, and stal'de by other men, Begin his fashion. **1606** —— *Ant. & Cl.* ii. ii. 240 Age cannot wither her, nor custome stale Her infinite variety. *a* **1616** Beaum. & Fl. *Q. Corinth* i. iii, Ile not stale them By giving up their characters, but leave you To make your own discoveries. **1768** *Woman of Honor* I. 10 Shame, that great engine of education, she employed with..attention not to stale its effect. **1822** Lamb *Elia* Ser. ii. *Detached Thoughts*, It may be, that the latter [names, Milton and Shakespeare] are more staled and rung upon in common discourse. **1863** W. W. Story *Roba di Roma* i. i. 7 Pictures and statues have been staled by copy and description. **1914** Marett in *Edin. Rev.* Apr. 397 Perhaps Dr. Frazer's theories have become for himself a little staled by dint of repetition.

†**b.** To lower (oneself, one's dignity) in estimation by excessive familiarity. *Obs.*

1598 B. Jonson *Ev. Man in Hum.* ii. i. 57 Not content To stale himselfe in all societies, He makes my house here common as a mart. **1606** Shaks. *Tr. & Cr.* ii. iii. 201 This ..right valiant Lord, Must not so staule his Palme. **1843** Lytton *Last Bar.* ii. ii, Henry the Fourth staled not his majesty to consultations with the mayor of his city.

c. *intr.* To grow stale; get out of fashion, become uninteresting.

1897 *Pall Mall Gaz.* 10 Nov. 2/3 The malicious tit-bit which he was treasuring with such eager anticipation would only stale by further delay. **1893** Q. (Quiller-Couch) *Delect. Duchy* 325 Philanthropy was beginning to stale.

†**3.** *Sc.* To affect with loathing or satiety. [Perh. another word: cf. stall *v.*]

1709 Wodrow *Corr.* (1842) I. 49 The abjuration oath.. will..stale a great many that we might otherwise have depended upon as friendly parties to us. **1717** E. Erskine *Serm.* Wks. (1791) 50/1 They have got so much of Christ as to be staled of his company.

stale, *v.*^{3} *Chess. rare.* Also 6 *Sc.* **stail**. [Perh. a. AF. *estaler*, ? of English origin: cf. stall *v.*]

a. *trans.* = stalemate *v.*

c **1470** *MS. Ashmole 344* lf. 7 He shall stale þe black kyng in the pointe þer the crosse standith. *Ibid.* lf. 17 Drau thou ther as thy pon stode, ande stale hym. **1903** H. J. R. Murray in *Brit. Chess. Mag.* 283 In China, however, a player who stales his opponent's King, wins the game.

b. *intr.* To undergo stalemate.

a **1585** Montgomerie *Cherrie & Slae* 216 For vnder cure I gat sik chek, Quhilk I micht nocht remuif nor nek, Bot eyther stail or mait.

†**stale**, *v.*^{4} *Obs. rare*$^{-1}$. [f. stale *sb.*^{2}] *trans.* To put rungs in (a ladder).

1492 in *Archæol. Cant.* XVI. 304 For stalyng of the ladders of the Churche xx d.

†**stale**, *v.*^{5} *Obs. rare.* [f. stale *sb.*^{3}] *trans.* To decoy, lure.

1557 *Tottel's Misc.* (Arb.) 198 The eye..Doth serue to stale her here and there where she doth come and go.

stale: see stall *sbs.*^{1}, ^{4}; obs. pa. t. of steal.

staled (steɪld), *ppl. a. rare.* [f. stale *v.*^{1} + -ed^1.] Rendered stale.

1862 Earl Lytton in Lady B. Balfour *L's. Lett.* (1906) I. 127 The staled and the spoiled experience. **1888** Stevenson *Across the Plains, Beggars* iii, The rant and cant of the staled beggar. **1897** F. Thompson *New Poems* 168 Once more A dull, new, staled amaze!

'stalely, *adv.* [f. stale *a.*^{1} + -ly^2.] In a stale, commonplace or hackneyed manner.

1598–9 B. Jonson *Case Altered* ii. iii, I will not sue stally to be your seruant, But a new tearme, will you be my refuge? **1611** —— *Catiline* ii. iii, Tut, all your promis'd Mountaines, And Seas, I am so stalely acquainted with. **1920** [see *class-jealousy* s.v. class *sb.* 9]. **1938** G. Greene *Brighton Rock* vii. i. 279 She smelt faintly, stalely, of Californian Poppy. **1957** 'M. M. Kaye' *Shadow of Moon* xxi. 326 The drawing-room smelt stalely of cigar smoke.

stalemate ('steɪlmeɪt), *sb. Chess.* [f. stale *sb.*^{6} + mate *sb.*^{1}

Strictly a misnomer, as the 'stale' (so called until 18th c.) is not really a mate.]

A position in which the player whose turn it is to move has no allowable move open to him, but has not his king in check.

According to modern rules, the game which ends in stalemate is drawn. In England from the 17th c. to the beginning of the 19th c. the player who received stalemate won the game. Various other rules have been in vogue at different times; sometimes the player giving stalemate won, either wholly or to the extent of half the stake; sometimes the last few moves had to be played over again until a mate resulted; sometimes the piece causing the obstruction was removed.

1765 Lambe *Hist. Chess* 91 When the King has no man whom he can play, and is not in check, yet is so blocked up, that he cannot move without going into check, this position is called a stale-mate, or Pat, in this case the King who is stale-mated wins the game. **1847** Staunton *Chess-Player's Handbk.* 33 He places the adverse King in the position..of stalemate.

b. *fig.*

1885 *Times* 15 Dec. 5 The Prince..will not..consent to the stalemate of mutual evacuation proposed by Servia. **1912** *Standard* 20 Sept. 6/4 So far as the public can see the match [between the two armies] ended in stalemate.

c. *attrib.*

1886 *Contemp. Rev.* Sept. 444 It would be disgraceful indeed if a great country like Russia should have run herself into such a stale-mate position. **1903** H. J. R. Murray in *Brit. Chess Mag.* 285 Several mediæval problems involve the condition that the one player forfeits his power of moving when his King is in a stalemate position.

stalemate ('steɪlmeɪt), *v. Chess.* [f. stalemate *sb.*] *trans.* To subject to a stalemate.

1765 Lambe *Hist. Chess* 91 In this case the King who is stalemated wins the game. **1813** Sarratt *Wks. Damiano* etc. 235 White cannot take the Rook without stalemating his adversary. **1879** Meredith *Egoist* xlvii, At the game of Chess it is the dishonour of our adversary when we are stale-mated.

fig. **1861** Hughes *Tom Brown at Oxf.* xli, You never saw a fellow look more puzzled, I had regularly stale-mated him. **1872** Geo. Eliot *Middlem.* i. xii, He spoke rather sulkily, feeling himself stalemated. **1910** *Edin. Rev.* Jan. 65 Pitt undertook to stalemate the French fleet.

Hence **stalemated** *ppl. a.* Also *fig.*

1903 H. J. R. Murray in *Brit. Chess Mag.* 282 Here [in Indian Rule] then we have the earliest convention: the stalemated King wins. **1952** D. MacArthur *Reminiscences* (1964) x. 409 The terrible blood tribute exacted by this type of stalemated attrition. **1965** *Economist* 9 Jan. 104/1 The United States accepted a stalemated substitute for victory in Korea. **1977** *Time* 31 Jan. 7/3 The Vice President also wants to know just what allied or U.S. initiatives Europeans would welcome to get the stalemated talks..going once again.

staleness ('steɪlnɪs). [f. stale *a.*^{1} + -ness.] The condition of being stale, in any sense of the adj.

1552 Huloet, Stalenes, *vetustas.* **1577–87** Holinshed *Hist. Eng.* I. 53/2 So that more than necessitie compelled him he could not eat, by reason that the stalenesse tooke awaie the pleasant tast thereof, and lesse prouoked his appetite. **1602** T. Phelippes in *St. Papers, Dom.* 1601–3 (1870) 227, I shall send you what [report] comes to hand, if staleness make it not like Rye fish, unfit for market. **1608** Shaks. *Per.* v. i. 58. **1620** Venner *Via Recta* ii. 39 If it [beer] be kept vntouched, till that it hath gotten a sufficient stalenesse. **1844** H. Stephens *Bk. Farm* II. 725 Failures in hatching arise from want of impregnation in the egg—from age, commonly called staleness. **1868** *Field* 4 July 14/2 Probably his continued rowing at Oxford nearly the whole year through may have tended to produce staleness. **1891** *Law Times* XCII. 127/2 The defence based on the staleness of the claim could not..prevail.

†**b.** *pl.* quasi-*concr.* Stale remarks or arguments.

1617 Collins *Def. Bp. Ely* ii. vi. 227 He is not ashamed to renew such motheaten stalenesses.

stalenge, var. stallenge *dial.*

stalewarde, staleword: see stalwart, stalworth.

Stalin ('stɑːlɪn). The name of Joseph *Stalin* (see Stalinism) used *attrib.* to designate things instituted by him or developed during his leadership of the Soviet Union, as ***Stalin Line, Prize, tank*** (see quots.); **Stalin organ** *Mil. slang*, a type of Soviet multi-barrelled mobile rocket launcher.

1942 *Foreign Affairs* XX. 317 The Stalin Line, with Kiev as a strong base behind it, runs along the Dniester and then through very easily defensible country in the direction of Zhitomir and Korosten. **1942** *Nature* 25 Apr. 475/1 The following awards of Stalin Prizes for outstanding scientific work in 1941 have been made. **1945** *Times* 1 Jan. 4/1 The Russians are using an entirely new type of tank... It is the super-heavy Stalin tank and has the biggest tank gun in the world. **1952** *Sun* (Baltimore) 16 May (B* ed.) 9/1 Eastern Germany, under Russian directions, is to help build a vast fortified 'Stalin line' defense belt across Eastern Europe including V-2 rocket bases and bomber fields. **1954** Koestler *Invisible Writing* ii. 29 Those who survived have ..become Stalin-prize court jesters. **1955** *Britannica Bk. of Year* 490/1 *Stalin organ*, a device for firing multiple rockets. **1977** *Time* 21 Feb. 21/1 Sakharov..won the Stalin Prize and was thrice awarded the country's highest civilian medal. **1982** *Daily Tel.* 5 Aug. 28/6 There was the characteristic, terrifying noise of 'Stalin organs' being fired—40 rockets going off within 10 seconds.

Stalinesque (stɑːlɪ'nɛsk), *a.* [f. as prec. + -esque.] Of, pertaining to, or characteristic of Joseph Stalin, his policies, activities, etc.; Stalinist.

1943 L. Adamic *My Native Land* 129 When I quoted to him a rumor that he was engaging in Stalinesque hold-ups to procure money for revolutionary purposes, he did not deny it. **1979** *Times* 14 Nov. 12/4 Stalin rebuilt the city [*sc.* Minsk] in Stalinesque style: a grandiose central avenue with a trade union palace.

†**'staling**, *sb. Obs. rare*$^{-1}$. [f. stale *sb.*^{3} + -ing^1.] = stale *sb.*^{3} 1.

1601 Deacon & Walker *Spirits & Divels* 230 [Like to] the craftie bird-catcher: who (while the silie poore birdes sit prying at, and playing with the whirligig, or staling before them) doth cunningly clap them..in his net.

staling ('steɪlɪŋ), *vbl. sb.* [f. stale *v.*^{1} + -ing^1.] The action of urinating; †*concr.* urine, esp. of horses or cattle.

c **1420** *Prose Life Alexander* (1913) 68 Sum ware at so grete meschefe þat þay dranke þaire awen stalynge. **1601** Holland *Pliny* viii. xlii. I. 222 Their [mares'] staling is no hinderance to their pace in running their carriere, as it doth the horse who must needs then stand still. **1613** Purchas *Pilgrimage* (1614) 311 A fountaine of water, which they say, sprang vp of the staling of Chederles horse. **1765** *Museum Rust.* IV. 185 That the staling of them [cattle] may not waste in its course. **1846** J. Baxter *Libr. Pract. Agric.* (ed. 4) I. 327 Mix a small quantity of salt with the food when feeding on furze, particularly for horses, as it..will sometimes affect their staling, which the salt will counteract.

attrib. **1759** *Brit. Chron.* 14 Sept. 261 The prisoner..has for many years been noted for begging at the staling-place for horses [*Ann. Reg.* (1759) 117/1 staling places].

staling ('steɪlɪŋ), *ppl. a. Bot.* [f. stale *v.*^{2} + -ing^2.] Of fungal products: diverting or inhibiting fungal growth.

1916 A. H. Graves in *Mem. N.Y. Bot. Gard.* VI. 326 The problem was now to obtain..this substance, which we may for convenience call the 'staling substance', free from mycelium. **1948** *Nature* Mar. 422/2 A similar effect is obtained when the metabolism of the latter [*sc.* a wound parasite of a plant] leads to the formation of substances ('staling substances') which by and by inhibit growth; hence the formation of lesions of limited size. **1979** *Experientia* XXXV. 200/2 This may possibly be due to reduction of growth of both interacting colonies caused by diffused staling products.

Stalinism (ˈstɑːlɪnɪz(ə)m). [f. Joseph *Stalin* (Russ. Íosif *Stálin*), the assumed name of Iosif Vissariónovich Dzhugashvíli (1879–1953), leader of the Soviet Communist Party and head of state of the Soviet Union + -ISM.] The policies pursued by Stalin, based on but later deviating from Leninism, esp. the formation of a centralized, totalitarian, objectivist government.

1927 *Daily Tel.* 22 Nov. 10/3 A violent denunciation of 'Stalinism' and its 'terrorising of the party'. **1941** KOESTLER *Scum of Earth* 23 We had realised that Stalinism had soiled and compromised the Socialist Utopia. **1947** C. MALAMUTH tr. *L. Trotski's Stalin* 422 On the theoretical plane every bit of 'Stalinism' has issued from the criticism of the theory of permanent revolution as it was formulated in 1905. **1955** *Times* 5 May 15/4 Indirectly the tenets of Stalinism and Trotskyism are being subjected in new tests at the conference tables of international diplomacy. **1958** *Times Lit. Suppl.* 7 Mar. 123/1 The Yugoslav system has relapsed into totalitarianism after a promising breakaway from Stalinism. **1968** *Russian Review* XXVII. 309 A formal definition of Stalinism would run something like this: a *one*-man dictatorship in which a single dictator ruling arbitrarily, uncontrolled by any party organs, is the sole interpreter of the Marxist-Leninist dogma, and is surrounded by the cult of his personality. A revised definition.. would be the same as above, but the single personality clause would be replaced by the CC Politburo collective leadership. **1971** I. DEUTSCHER *Marxism in our Time* (1972) 86 In the end the nonviolent meaning of Marxism was suppressed under the massive, crushing weight of Stalinism. **1977** *Time* 21 Mar. 12/2 In a bitter statement, Gui accused the Communists of practicing 'Stalinism', calling himself the victim of the chamber's 'will for my political execution'.

Stalinist (ˈstɑːlɪnɪst), *sb.* and *a.* [f. as prec. + -IST.] **A.** *sb.* A follower or supporter of Stalin or his policies. **B.** *adj.* Of, pertaining to, or characteristic of Stalin, his followers, or his policies.

1928 *Observer* 22 Jan. 14/5 Open calculations measured in advance by the Stalinists. **1930** *Times* 27 Mar. 13/3 The Stalinist group of Communist leaders. **1939** G. GREENE *Lawless Roads* iii. 107 The papers were full of a Stalinist plot. **1941** KOESTLER *Scum of Earth* 113 The sectarian hatred between Stalinists, Trotskists, and Reformists still existed. **1955** *Times* 2 Aug. 9/6 Khrushchev, the reputed Stalinist, goes on a mission to China. **1974** tr. *Wertheim's Evolution & Revolution* i. 70 In Stalinist Marxism.. there was no sign whatever that the Russian way was considered to be a deviation from the usual succession of phases. **1977** *Socialist Press* 2 Mar. 11/4 Their series of Conferences.. were 'bureaucratically controlled' as was that called by the Stalinist-led BLMC Combine Committee. **1978** I. B. SINGER *Shosha* xiii. 229 The designation.. as Fascist lackeys and agents of Hitler evoked protests even from sworn Stalinists.

Stalinite (ˈstɑːlɪnaɪt), *sb.* and *a.* *rare.* [f. as prec. + -ITE[1].] = STALINIST *sb.* and *a.*

1927 *Daily Tel.* 6 Dec. 11 The struggle between the Trotskists and the Stalinites. **1938** R. H. S. CROSSMAN in *New Statesman* 7 May 780/2 Unlike the Stalinites, he has learnt nothing from the experience of Fascism, and so can greet it as a positive advance towards the millennium. **1945** KOESTLER *Yogi & Commissar* III. i. 134 The *New Statesman and Nation's* interpretations of Stalinite policy display all the ingeniousness of the official Apologist. **1973** *Times* 19 Jan. 4/5 (*heading*) 'Almost Stalinite' to deny effective power to local parties.

Stalinize (ˈstɑːlɪnaɪz), *v.* [f. as prec. + -IZE.] *trans.* To transform, etc., in accordance with Stalin's policies and practices. Hence **Staliniˈzation**.

1949 I. DEUTSCHER *Stalin* 366 Even the spoken language became 'Stalinized' to a fantastic extent. **1954** KOESTLER *Invisible Writing* x. 110 The natives were drawn into the towns, educated, Russified and Stalinised. **1956** *Washington Post* 19 Nov. A21/1 Even today, after the unspeakable horror of the blood bath in Hungary, the betting is still somewhat against a 're-Stalinization'. **1959** *Manch. Guardian* 5 Aug. 10/3 Returning to Hungary.. in 1944 to take part in the 'Stalinisation' of his country. **1971** I. DEUTSCHER *Marxism in our Time* (1972) vi. 124 This was the first dangerous attack on the autonomy of the [Polish] Communist Party, the first act, as it turned out, of 'Stalinization'. **1979** *Dædalus* Winter 135 Mutual contamination or interpenetration between the Communist party (which had not been Stalinized in the first place..) and Italian society. **1981** *Guardian* 16 Feb. 4/5 Mr Gerald Kaufman.. said he did not regard 'the Stalinisation of the Labour Party as democracy'.

Stalinoid (ˈstɑːlɪnɔɪd), *a.* (and *sb.*). [f. as prec. + -OID.] Resembling or having some characteristics of Stalinism; loosely Stalinist. Also as *sb.*

1941 *Amer. Mercury* Apr. 498/2 Years of careful reading of the Stalinoid literature of hallucination. **1947** *Sun* (Baltimore) 4 Nov. 10/3 Food prices have come down—to the consternation of the Stalinoid cohorts. **1952** *Manch. Guardian Weekly* 16 Oct. 7/3 It is Marxist, hostile to 'Stalinoids and to modern Trotskyites'. **1952** P. SELZNICK *Organizational Weapon* vii. 297 The term 'stalinoid' is usually employed as a rough synonym for 'fellow traveler'. **1961** *Guardian* 26 May 6/5 The Stalinist intellectuals and the Stalinoid 'liberals'. **1977** *Daily Tel.* 12 Oct. 18 The Nobel Peace Prize has gone to some rum customers in its time, including Le Duc Tho, the villainous Stalinoid secretary of the North Vietnam Communist party.

stalk (stɔːk), *sb.*[1] Also 4–7 **stalke**, 7 **staulk**, 8 *Sc.* **stawk**. [ME. (14th c.) *stalke*, app. a dim. with *k* suffix f. *stal-* in STALE *sb.*[2] (? OE. *stalu*). The exact formal equivalent does not occur in the other Teut. langs., but a parallel formation from the ablaut-variant *stel-* (in OE. *stela* STEAL *sb.*, stem, handle, etc.) is found in NFris. *stelk*, MSw. *stiälke*, *stiälker* (mod.Sw. *stjelk*, *stjälk*), Norw. *stylk*, *stilk*, *stelk*, *stalk*, Da. *stilk*, mod.Icel. *stilk-ur*. Cf. Eng. dial. *stelch*, post, stake.]

1. a. The main stem of a herbaceous plant, bearing the flowers and leaves; also, a scape or flower-stem rising directly from the root.

a **1366** CHAUCER *Rom. Rose* 1701 The stalke [Fr. *la coe*] was as rysshe right And theron stode the knoppe vpright. **1382** WYCLIF *Hosea* viii. 7 A stondynge stalk [Vulg. *culmus stans*] is not in hem. **1398** TREVISA *Barth. De P.R.* XVII. clxvi. (1495) 711 The mydyll stalke of an herbe or of a tree highte Tirsus. **1412–20** LYDG. *Troy Bk.* I. 3106 Floures.. Vp-on her stalke gan splaie her levis wyde. **1483** *Cath. Angl.* 359/1 A Sstalke, *calamus*. **1538** ELYOT *Dict.*, *Frutex*, that which hath a great stalke and yet it is no tree, as fenelle. **1577** GOOGE *Heresbach's Husb.* I. 33 Beanes.. both the Coddes and the stalke, is a foode that cattel muche delightes in. **1591** SPENSER *Bellay's Ruines Rome* xxx, Like as the seeded field .. from greene grasse into a stalke doth spring, And from a stalke into an eare forth-growes. **1597** GERARDE *Herbal* II. li. 269 Dwale, or sleeping Night-shade hath round blackish stalks sixe foote high. **1624** CAPT. SMITH *Virginia* II. 28 Every stalke of their corne commonly beareth two eares. **1640** T. BRUGIS *Marrow Physicke* II. 147 To dry Lettice Stalkes, Artichocke Stalkes, or Cabbage Stalkes. **1667** MILTON *P.L.* V. 480 So from the root Springs lighter the green stalk, from thence the leaves More aerie. *c* **1680** BEVERIDGE *Serm.* (1729) I. 548 Having filled a sponge with vinegar.. they put it upon a stalk of hyssop. *c* **1730** RAMSAY *To D. Malloch* vii, Misty minds that plod And thresh for thought, but ne'er advance Their stawk aboon their clod. **1776** J. LEE *Introd. Bot.* Expl. Terms 378 Scapus, a Stalk, elevating the Fructification and not the Leaves. **1779** COWPER *Olney H.* I. lxxxv, We find a tall and sickly stalk But not the fruitful ear. **1833** HT. MARTINEAU *Briery Creek* iv. 92 The stalk of flax that waves in my field. **1839** FR. A. KEMBLE *Resid. Georgia* (1863) 87 It is a long green reed, like the stalk of the maize. **1910** *Blackw. Mag.* Feb. 263/2, I looked through the rough tangle of stalks and stems.

b. The woody core of hemp and flax.

1577 GOOGE *Heresbach's Husb.* I. 39 b, The Shales or Stalkes [of hemp] serue for the heating of Ouens. **1838** [see BOON *sb.*[2]].

†c. ? *nonce-use.* A bit of straw, a 'mote'.

c **1386** CHAUCER *Reeve's Prol.* 65 He kan wel in myn eye seen a stalke But in his owene he kan nat seen a balke.

2. a. The comparatively slender connecting part by which a vegetable organ is attached to the plant; the petiole of a leaf, the peduncle or pedicel of a flower, fruit, or inflorescence, the stipe of an ovary, or the like.

c **1325** *Gloss. W. de Bibbesw.* in Wright *Voc.* 150 Outez l'estiche et la parure [*gloss* the stalke and the paring], E lour donez la morsure [*gloss* the body of the appel]. *c* **1374** CHAUCER *Boeth.* I. met. vi. (1868) 26 þe stalkes of þe vine [L. *palmites*]. **1530** PALSGR. 275/1 Stalke of any frute, *queve*. **1538** ELYOT *Dict.*, *Pediculus*,.. the stalke of an apple or peare, or other frute. **1617** MORYSON *Itin.* III. 82 They gather a darke or blackish kind of cherry, and casting away the stalkes, put them into a great cauldron. **1632** MARMION *Holland's Leaguer* II. v, Have my love Shak'd off because 'tis ripe, but let me hang by The stalk of your mercy. **1808** SCOTT *Marm.* III. xvii, I on its stalk had left the rose. **1866** *Treas. Bot.* 1090/2 *Stalk*, the stem or support to an organ; as the petiole of a leaf, the peduncle or pedicel of a flower, &c. **1884** BOWER & SCOTT *De Bary's Phaner.* 105 The half-spindle-shaped ones [*sc.* cystoliths of Acanthaceæ] are attached by a very thin short stalk. **1909** G. K. CHESTERTON *Orthodoxy* iv. 89 The man of science says: Cut this stalk and the apple will fall.

b. A similar slender connecting part by which an animal organ or structure is attached or supported.

1826 KIRBY & SP. *Entomol.* III. xxxiii. 357 *Stipes* (the Stalk). The corneous base of the Maxilla, below the Palpus. **1866** TATE *Brit. Mollusks* iii. 47 The head bears two.. tentacles.. with the stalks bearing the eyes attached to them on the outside. **1899** D. SHARP *Insects* II. 317 When a portion of a nervure beyond the basal or primary portion serves as a common piece to two forked parts external to it, it is called a stalk. **1899** *Allbutt's Syst. Med.* VIII. 824 The 'stalk' of the tumour.

†3. The SHANK of a hawk. *Obs.*

c **1575** *Perf. Bk. Kepinge Sparhawkes* (1886) 5 Tokens of a good Hawke:.. stalke short and bygg: foot large, wyde, [etc.]. *Ibid.* 31 Good for any swellinge in fote or stalke.

4. Applied to various erect slender objects.

†a. The upright of a ladder: = STALE *sb.*[2] I.

c **1386** CHAUCER *Miller's T.* 439 His owene hand made laddres thre To clymben by the ronges and the stalkes In to the tubbes hangynge in the balkes.

b. The shaft of a chimney. Cf. STACK *sb.* 5 b.

1821 SCOTT *Kenilw.* iii, Twisted stalks of chimneys of heavy stone-work. **1838** *Civil Engin. & Arch. Jrnl.* I. 406/2 Vast improvements have been made.. in building stalks for steam boilers and chemical furnaces. **1839** URE *Dict. Arts* 280 To.. increase the solidity of an insulated stalk of this kind, it is built with three or more successive plinths, or recedures. **1885** R. L. & F. STEVENSON *Dynamiter* 134 A great stalk of chimneys.

c. A columnar rock; = STACK *sb.* 7. *local.*

1806 *Gazetteer Scot.* (ed. 2) 149 The Stalks of Dungisbay, as they are called, are two pyramidal pillars, of naked free-stone rock.

d. *coarse slang.* A penis, esp. one that is erect.

1597 SHAKES. *Lover's Compl.* (1609) l. 147 My wofull selfe .. Threw my affections in his charmed power, Reseru'd the stalke and gaue him al my flower. **1608** —— *Per.* IV. vi. 46 *Bawd.* Heere comes that which growes to the stalke, Neuer pluckt yet I can assure you. Is shee not a faire creature? [**1939** JOYCE *Finnegans Wake* (1964) ii. 236 Just so stylled with the nattes are their flowerheads now and each of all has a lovestalk onto herself.] **1961** PARTRIDGE *Dict. Slang* Suppl. 1293/2 *Stalk*,.. an erection. **1976** A. WHITE *Long Silence* iv. 37, I had a stalk on me long as my arm. A right handful, that one. **1978** J. UPDIKE *Coup* (1979) ii. 79 My stalk verged upon response, upon enlargement and erection. **1979** W. STYRON *Sophie's Choice* ii. 45 She.. prepared to take between those lips unkissed by my own the bone-rigid stalk of my passion.

5. a. The main part of anything long and slender, as distinguished from the extremities.

1530 PALSGR. 275/1 Stalke of a shafte, *fust*. **1607** TOPSELL *Four-f. Beasts* 221 The tops of the hair appeare blacke, the foot and stalke being white.

†b. The shaft of a quill; a quill. *Obs.*

c **1440** LYDG. *Hors, Shepe & G.* 183 Men plukke stalkes out of my weengis tweyn, Some to portraye, somme to noote & write. **1665** HOOKE *Microgr.* 172, I tried it by fixing the leggs of a Fly upon the top of the stalk of a feather. **1681** GREW *Musæum* I. §2. ii. 22 The Plume or Stalk of a Quill.

†c. The stem of a fork or spoon. *Obs.*

a **1423** in *Archæologia* LXI. 173, j fork of siluer w[t] a Dragouns hede holding up the stalk for grenynges. **1496** *Will of Dynham* (Somerset Ho.), A forke of siluer with a stalke of corall for grene ginger. **1522** *Will of P. Baynard* (ibid.), A doseyn sponys where p is in the stalk.

d. The tube or stem of a thermometer.

1833 N. ARNOTT *Physics* (ed. 5) II. 111 It is easy to proportion the bulb and the stalk to each other, so that [etc.].

e. *colloq.* A lever mounted on the floor or on the steering column of a motor vehicle, which controls the gears or such devices as horn, indicators, lights, windscreen wipers, etc.

1964 *Road & Track* Jan. 22/2 The gears are selected by an odd curved floor stalk which fouls the passenger seat but they go in all right. **1972** *Country Life* 15 June 1577/2 Steering-column stalks look after the windscreen washer and wiper. **1977** *Daily Tel.* 19 Jan. 12/6, I liked the cloth-trimmed seats and the control stalks on the steering column in place of the old rocker switches on the fascia.

6. A slender upright support; the stem of a wine-glass.

a **1864** HAWTHORNE *Amer. Note-Bks.* (1879) II. 88 Old drinking-glasses, with tall stalks. **1882** J. G. PHILLIP in *L. Shaw's Hist. Moray* I. 202 It is a chalice or cup [of the Bronze Period]... Its great peculiarity was that it had neither handle nor stalk. **1884** F. J. BRITTEN *Watch & Clockm.* 72 The teeth rise on stalks from the body of the escape wheel.

†7. *Sc.* Some appendage to a halter. *Obs.*

1497 *Acc. Ld. High Treas. Scot.* I. 328 Item, for ane doubil helter with tua stalkis. **1501** *Ibid.* II. 29, ij.. heltir stalkis.

8. *Ironfounding.* (See quot.)

1875 KNIGHT *Dict. Mech.*, *Stalk*, an iron rod armed with spikes, forming the nucleus of a core.

9. *Arch.* (See quot.)

1842 GWILT *Archit.* Gloss., *Stalk*, an ornament in the Corinthian capital, which is sometimes fluted, and resembles the stalk of a plant; from it spring the volutes and helices.

10. *attrib.* as ***stalk-like*** adj.; **stalk-borer** *U.S.*, the larva of a moth, *Gortyna nitela*, destructive to plants; **stalk-cutter** *U.S.*, an implement for cutting old maize stalks in the ground; **stalk-eyed** *a.*, having the eye at the end of a stalk, podophthalmate; **stalk-fruited** *a.* = PEDUNCULATE *a.*; **†stalk-legged** *a.*, long-legged, spindle-shanked; **stalk-puller**, an implement for pulling cotton and hemp stalks from the ground; **stalk switch**, a switch in the form of a stalk or lever mounted on the steering column of a motor vehicle (see sense 5 e above).

1885 *Riverside Nat. Hist.* (1888) II. 451 The *stalk-borer. **1875** KNIGHT *Dict. Mech.*, **Stalk-cutter*. **1853** T. BELL (*title*) A history of the British *stalk-eyed Crustacea. **1869** RANKINE *Machine & Hand-tools* App. 68 The old English Oak, or *Stalk-fruited Oak (*Quercus robur* or *Quercus pedunculata*), in which the acorns grow on stalks. **1659** TORRIANO, *Fuscello*, a spindle-shank, or *stalk-legged fellow. **1839–47** TODD *Cycl. Anat.* III. 678/1 The crura cerebri are seen.. to enter *stalk-like, into the inferior surface of the cerebral hemispheres. **1888** RUTLEY *Rock-forming Min.* 184 Stalk-like or reedy forms are likewise of frequent occurrence. **1875** KNIGHT *Dict. Mech.*, *Stalk-puller. **1976** *Evening Post* (Nottingham) 15 Dec. 10/8 *Stalk switches, within easy reach of fingers on the wheel, control the lights, wipers, wash and flasher, also horn and direction indicators.

stalk (stɔːk), *sb.*[2] Also 5–7 **stalke**, 7 **stauk**. [f. STALK *v.*]

1. An act of stalking game.

c **1450** in *Trans. Philol. Soc.* (1909) III. 53 A Stalke of ffostersse. **1470–85** MALORY *Arthur* XVIII. xxi. 764 They were shoters and coude wel kylle a dere bothe at the stalke & at the trest. **1621** MARKHAM *Fowling* viii. 53 Also you must obserue in the Stalke to turne that side [of the stalking-horse] euer vpon the Fowle which is plaine without splents. **1873** G. C. DAVIES *Mount. & Mere* x. 83 A careful stalk might have brought a shooter within shot. **1885** W. H. RUSSELL in *Harper's Mag.* Apr. 770/1 There may be a deer drive or a stalk at Glenmuick. **1907** J. H. PATTERSON *Man-Eaters of Tsavo* xx. 225 My stalk was crowned with success, the beautiful animal being bagged without much trouble.

b. *attrib.*, as **†*stalk-hound***.

1663 KILLIGREW *Pars. Wedd.* IV. i, A pox upon them for a couple of Stauk-hounds; have they killed at last?

2. A striding gait; a stately or pompous mode of walking.

1590 SPENSER *F.Q.* II. vii. 26 An vgly feend,.. The which with monstrous stalke behind him stept, And euer as he went, dew watch vpon him kept. **1599** B. JONSON *Cynthia's Rev.* v. iv, Leave him not so much as a looke, an eye, a stalke, or an imperfect oth, to expresse himselfe by. **1694** ADDISON *Greatest Brit. Poets* 56 Milton next, with high and haughty stalks, Unfetter'd in majestick numbers walks. **1751** JOHNSON *Rambler* No. 179 ⁋4 The sprightly trip, the stately stalk, and the lofty mien. **1787–89** WORDSW. *Even. Walk* 242 Then issuing often with unwieldy stalk, They [the swans] crush with broad black feet their flowery walk. **1869** LOWELL *Study Wind.*, *Gard. Acquaint.* (1871) 11 Their [the crow-blackbirds'] port is grave, and their stalk across the turf as martial as that of a second-rate ghost in Hamlet.

stalk (stɔːk), *v.*[1] Also 4–7 stalke, 6 stawk, 7 staulke, 7, 9 *dial.* stauk. [ME. *stalke*:—OE. **stealcian* (implied in *bistealcian* = sense 1 and *stealcung* STALKING *vbl. sb.*):—prehistoric **stalkōjan*, frequentative f. **stal-* (:**stel-*, see STEAL *v.*). Sense 4, which first appears in the 16th c., is perh. due to association with STALK *sb.*[1]; cf. Florio 1611, '*Fuscello*, a stub, a sprig, a stalk.. also spindle shankes or stalkeing legges'; also Norw. *stelk*, Icel. *stelkur*, a long-legged bird, the redshank.]

†**1.** *intr.* To walk softly, cautiously, or stealthily.

In quot. *a* 1300 either *refl.* or with dative of the subject.

[*c* **1000** ÆLFRIC *Saints' Lives* xxxii. 40 Hinguar færlice swa swa wulf on lande bestalcode and þa leode sloh. *c* **1000**: see STALKING *vbl. sb.*] *a* **1300** *Cursor M.* 3601 Esau.. Ga lok þi tacle be puruaid, And faand to stalk þe sa nere þat þou mai drep me sum dere. *c* **1300** *K. Horn* 1129 (Laud) He lokede in eche halke; Sey he nowere stalke Ayol hys trewe felawe. *a* **1320** *Sir Tristrem* 2578 Tristrem and þe quen Stalked to her play. *c* **1350** *Will. Palerne* 2728 þan hiȝed þei hem to þe hauen.. And stalkeden ful stilly þer stoden fele schippes. *c* **1374** CHAUCER *Troylus* II. 519 Tho gan I stalke softly hym by-hynde. *a* **1375** *How to hear Mass* 530 in *Minor Poems fr. Vernon MS.* 507 Whon he [*sc.* the priest] haþ waschen.. Priueliche and stille he stalkes To his Auter aȝeyn. *a* **1380** *Eufrosyne* 390 in Horstm. *Altengl. Leg.* (1878) 178, I stunte, I stonde, vnstabli I stalke. *c* **1400** *Beryn* 282 Madam! wol ye stalk pryuely into the garden to se the herbis grow. *c* **1440** *Promp. Parv.* 472/1 Stalkyn.. *serpo.* **1470–85** MALORY *Arthur* VII. xix. 243 He cam stylly stalkyng behynde the dwerf and plucked hym fast vnder his arme. *c* **1530** *Crt. of Love* 1030 And stalking soft with easy pase, I saw About the king ther stonden environ, Attendaunce, Diligence,.. and many oon. **1587** TURBERV. *Trag. Tales* (1837) 30 There stalkte he on, as softe as foote could tread.

†**b.** said of an animal. *Obs.*

1456 SIR G. HAYE *Law of Arms* (S.T.S.) 234 Quhen he herd ony wilde beste stalkand besyde him.

2. †To go stealthily *to*, *towards* (an animal) for the purpose of killing or capturing it (*obs.*). Hence, to pursue game by the method of stealthy approach, esp. by the use of a stalking-horse or of some device for concealing oneself from the view of the hunted animal.

a **1400** *King & Hermit* 321 Now, Crystes blyssing haue sych a frere, That þus canne ordeyn our soper, And stalke vnder þe wode bowe. *c* **1460** J. RUSSELL *Bk. Nurture* 21 His bowe he toke in hand toward þe deere to stalke. **1503–4** *Act 19 Hen. VII*, c. 11 That no person from hensforth stauke or cause eny other person to stalke with eny boussh or bestys to eny Deere. **1570** LEVINS *Manip.* 16/13 To stalke, *venari.* **1575** TURBERV. *Faulconrie* 193 Lette him.. carrye his hawke unhooded.. stawking towardes them untill he have gotten reasonably neare them. **1621** MARKHAM *Fowling* 55 To stalke with a Horse where no Horses liue or are bred.. is absurde and losse of labor. **1622** DRAYTON *Poly-olb.* xxv. 141 One vnderneath his Horse, to get a shoot doth stalke. **1624** CAPT. SMITH *Virginia* II. 32 Thus shrowding his body in the skinne [of a deer] by stalking, he approacheth the Deere. **1815** SCOTT *Ld. of Isles* III. xiii, Awhile their route they silent made, As men who stalk for mountain-deer. **1819** *Sporting Mag.* V. 118 A gamekeeper, who may be stalking, which is going behind a horse, whose head is kept down that he may appear to be grazing. **1863** W. C. BALDWIN *Afr. Hunting* iii. 77, I came up with the troop, stalked in upon them, and shot a fine young bull. **1907** J. H. PATTERSON *Man-Eaters of Tsavo* vi. 67 The roars completely ceased, and we knew that they [the lions] were stalking for their prey.

fig. **1599** SHAKS. *Much Ado* II. iii. 96 O I, stalke on, stalke on, the foule sits. I did neuer thinke that Lady would haue loued any man. **1603** B. JONSON *Sejanus* III. ii, His franke tongue Being lent the raines, will take away all thought Of malice, in your course against the rest. We must keepe him to stalke with. **1647** J. C[LEVELAND] *Char. Lond.-Diurn.* 5 He stalkes with Essex, and shoots under his belly. **1662** STILLINGFL. *Orig. Sacræ* III. i. §9 As well then may an Atheist say.. that religion is nothing but a design, because men may make it stalke to their private ends. **1692** R. L'ESTRANGE *Josephus*, *Antiq.* XVII. vii. (1733) 462 To get the Reputation of a tender and dutiful Son.. and so, to stalk under that Cloak, up to the King himself.

†**b.** *trans.* ? To involve by cunning devices, inveigle. *Obs. rare*⁻¹.

1626 in Rushw. *Hist. Coll.* (1659) I. 269 By the Artifices of the said Duke of Buckingham.. the said Earl hath been insensibly involved and stauked into the troubles he is now in.

3. *trans.* **a.** To pursue (game) by stealthy approach. *to stalk down*: to follow or track (an animal) stealthily until one comes within range.

1823 SCOTT *Peveril* xxv, And for shooting him from behind a wall, it is cruelly like to stalking a deer. **1845** *Zoologist* III. 971 He immediately proposed to a friend to get a horse and stalk them [wild swans]. **1847** MARRYAT *Childr. New Forest* iv, I intend to buy you a gun, that you may learn to stalk deer yourself. **1859** DARWIN *Orig. Spec.* vii. (1873) 178 No animal is more difficult to stalk than the giraffe. **1907** J. H. PATTERSON *Man-Eaters of Tsavo* ii. 25 Lions always stalk their prey in complete silence. *Ibid.* xxvii. 309 We dismounted and stalked them [the eland] carefully through the long grass.

transf. and *fig.* **1855** THACKERAY *Newcomes* II. 68 As he was pursuing the deer, she stalked his lordship. **1861** —— *Philip* ix, Mrs. Matcham's girl fished for Captain Woolcomb last year in Scotland,.. and stalked him to Paris. **1884** *Pall Mall Gaz.* 13 Nov. 5/2 Their [*sc.* torpedo boats'] special function is to stalk ironclads at night time. **1892** *Photogr. Ann.* II. 188 One would hardly care to make a study of animal photography with a larger-sized apparatus than 1/1-plate. To stalk a flock of sheep with a 15 × 12.. would .. be worse than futile. **1903** MORLEY *Gladstone* (1905) I. III. viii. 435 Whigs and Peelites.. were all ready at last to stalk down their crafty quarry.

b. To go through (a tract of country) stalking game.

1860 G. H. K. in Galton *Vac. Tour.* (1861) 122 The hills I am going to stalk are under sheep. **1890** 'R. BOLDREWOOD' *Col. Reformer* (1891) 211 The troopers, deciding to stalk the bush on foot,.. passed.. silently through the trees.

4. *intr.* To walk with stiff, high, measured steps, like a long-legged bird. Usually with disparaging notion, implying haughtiness, sullenness, indifference to one's surroundings, or the like. Also †*to stalk it.*

In dialect use, the predominant notion is often that of ungainliness.

1530 PALSGR. 732/1, I stalke, I go softly and make great strides, *je vas a grans pas.* He stalketh lyke a crane. *c* **1535** REDFORD *Play Wit & Sci.* (1848) 8 Yt is he playne That thus bold doth make hym Wythowt my lycence To stalke by my doore. **1576** GASCOIGNE *Steele Gl.* Epil. 21 The elder sorte, go stately stalking on. **1591** H. SMITH *Pride Nabuch.* 4 Then was hee stalking in his galleries, and thinking what sinne should be next. **1609** B. JONSON *Sil. Wom.* IV. i, Others that will stalke i' their gait like an Estrich. **1610** HOLLAND *Camden's Brit.* (1637) 491 Who stalking high upon stilts, apply their minds to grasing, fishing and fowling. **1612** *Benvenuto's Passenger* I. iv. 317 He replied that it was they, which there stalke it,.. with Ruffes, and blacke apparrell. **1667** MILTON *P.L.* IV. 402 About them round A Lion now he [Satan] stalkes with fierie glare. **1695** BLACKMORE *Pr. Arth.* VIII. 656 Like one of Anak's mighty Sons he stalk'd. *a* **1700** EVELYN *Diary* June 1645, The noblemen stalking with their ladys on *choppines.* **1748** *Anson's Voy.* III. x. 540 A soldier of unusual size.. stalkt about on the parapet. **1768** BEATTIE *Minstr.* I. xxxix, The whistling ploughman stalks afield. **1787** GROSE *Prov. Gloss.* L3b, Cambridgeshire camels... Some have supposed this term to have originated from the Fen-men, stalking through the marshes on their stilts. **1815** SCOTT *Guy M.* viii, The Dominie.. might be seen stalking about with a mathematical problem in his head, and his eye upon a child of five years old. **1855** MACAULAY *Hist. Eng.* xiii. III. 343 It was remembered but too well how the dragoons had stalked into the peasant's cottage, cursing and damning him, themselves, and each other at every second word. **1862** C. C. ROBINSON *Dial. Leeds* 421 *Stauk*, to walk in an awkward manner, unmindful of appearances. **1906** SIR F. TREVES *Highways Dorset* xi. 169 Its arched doorway, where pikemen stalked on guard.

fig. **1710** ADDISON *Whig-Exam.* No. 4 ⁋5 It stalks upon hard words and rattles through polysyllables. **1852** HAWTHORNE *Grandfather's Chair* II. iii. (1879) 85 One urchin shall hereafter.. stalk gravely through life. **1864** D. G. MITCHELL *Sev. Stor.* 264 Why should my fancy go stalking through that great Rubens Museum?

b. said of a bird or animal.

1600 *Maydes Metam.* I. in Bullen *O. Pl.* (1882) I. 113 Marke the Deare how they begin to stalke; When each.. Pricks vp his head and bears a Princely minde. **1601** HOLLAND *Pliny* x. xxiii. I. 281 These Cranes.. will.. run the round with their long shankes stualking full untowardly. **1697** DRYDEN *Virg. Georg.* III. 383 The Mother Lion.. Scours o'er the Plain;.. Demanding Rites of Love; she sternly stalks. **1820** W. IRVING *Sketch Bk.* II. 195 A vagrant deer stalking like a shadow across the opening. **1825** SCOTT *Betrothed* xxiii, No heron was seen stalking on the usual haunts of the bird. **1865** LIVINGSTONE *Zambesi* iv. 99 The stately stepping Marabout stalks slowly along the almost stagnant channels.

c. often said of ghosts, and *fig.* of quasi-personified maleficent agencies, as pestilence, famine, etc.

a **1593** MARLOWE tr. *1st Bk. Lucan* 570 Fowle Erinnis stalkt about the wals, Shaking her snakie haire and crooke pine With flaming Toppe. **1656** COWLEY *Misc.*, *On death W. Hervey* 22 As sullen Ghosts stalk speechless by Where their hid Treasures ly. **1719** YOUNG *Busiris* I. i, Illustrious shades! who nightly stalk around The tyrant's couch. *a* **1796** BURNS *Tam Glen* vii, The last Halloween I was waukin My droukit sark-sleeve, as ye ken; His likeness cam up the house staukin —The very grey breeks o' Tam Glen! **1826** DISRAELI *Viv. Grey* I. ix, That wild spirit of speculation which is now stalking abroad. **1846** MILL *Diss. & Disc.* (1859) II. 306 Ate .. is represented as a gigantic figure, who stalks forth furiously, diffusing ruin. **1850** HAWTHORNE *Scarlet L.* xiii, None so self-devoted as Hester, when pestilence stalked through the town. **1889** JESSOPP *Coming of Friars* v. 226 The plague was stalking grimly up and down the land.

d. *trans.* To march proudly through (a country, etc.). Also quasi-*trans.* with advb. accusative.

1610 G. FLETCHER *Christ's Tri.* I. xlvii, Two bloudy sunnes stalking the duskie sphear. **1612** J. TAYLOR (Water P.) *Sculler* D4b, With stately gate the peopled Burse he stalkes. **1742** COLLINS *Ode to Fear* 12 Danger.. Who stalks his round, an hideous form! **1841** W. H. AINSWORTH *Old St. Paul's* I. i, Like a hideous phantom stalking the streets at noon-day.

stalk (stɔːk), *v.*[2] [f. STALK *sb.*[1]]

1. *intr.* To put forth stalks. *rare*⁻¹.

1666 J. DAVIES *Hist. Caribbee Isles* 5 There is not strength enough left in the root to force it to staulk and knit in the ear.

2. *trans.* To remove the stalks from (fruit).

1902 *Daily Chron.* 5 July 8/4 Stalk three-quarters of a pound of fine fresh fruit, rub them through a hair sieve [etc.].

stalkable ('stɔːkəb(ə)l), *a.* [f. STALK *v.*[1] + -ABLE.] That may be stalked; admitting of stalking.

1893 EARL DUNMORE *Pamirs* II. 68, I observed two lots of Ovis Poli.. in a fairly stalkable place. **1899** *Blackw. Mag.* Aug. 186/2 They seemed in a kind of stalkable place. **1905** A. J. R. GLASFURD *Rifle in Ind. Jungle* 307 Our game may have shifted into some more stalkable position.

stalked (stɔːkt), *a.* [f. STALK *sb.*[1] + -ED[2].] Having a stalk or stalks; in *Nat. Hist.*, *Pathology*, etc. opposed to *sessile*. Also in parasynthetic combs., ***long-stalked***, ***red-stalked***, etc. (see the first element); in some of these some writers have ignorantly substituted an adv. for the first element, as ***firmly***, ***shortly stalked.***

1731 MILLER *Gard. Dict.* s.v. *Aloe*, The African stalk'd Aloe. **1806** J. GRAHAME *Birds Scot.* 19 A flower.. firmly stalked, of form Pyramidal. **1840** PEREIRA *Elem. Mat. Med.* II. 1266 *Sinapis nigra*... Lower leaves lyrate;.. stalked. **1847** STEELE *Field Bot.* 123 Flowers in stalked clusters. **1857** T. MOORE *Handbk. Brit. Ferns* (ed. 3) 68 Pinnæ opposite, the lower pair largest, obliquely triangular, shortly stalked. **1863** WOOD *Illustr. Nat. Hist.* III. 648 One species of Stalked Barnacle. **1874** LUBBOCK *Orig. Metam. Insects* iii. 59 The stalked Crinoids. **1883** *Encycl. Brit.* XVI. 669/2 The suckers are stalked and strengthened by a horny ring. **1897** *Allbutt's Syst. Med.* III. 955 Frequently they [i.e. islets of mucous membrane caused by ulceration] are more or less stalked because of the ulceration which undermines them.

b. *Her.* Of a plant: Having the stalk of a specified tincture.

1864 BOUTELL *Her. Hist. & Pop.* xix. (ed. 3) 304 A rose or, stalked ppr.

c. *Comb.*: **stalked-eyed** *a.* = *stalk-eyed* (see STALK *sb.*[1] 9).

1882 *Cassell's Nat. Hist.* VI. 206 Many species, both of the *Podophthalmia* (or stalked-eyed) and *Edriophthalmia* (or sessile-eyed) Crustacea.

stalker ('stɔːkə(r)). [f. STALK *v.*[1] + -ER[1].

The identity of the word in sense 1 is questionable.]

†**1.** A kind of net used by poachers. Also ***stalker net.*** *Obs.*

1389 *Act 13 Rich. II*, Stat. I. c. 19 §1 Qe null peschoʳ.. ne mette.. en les ewes de Thamise.. ascuns rees appelez stalkers.. par les quelles le frie.. des salmons.. purra.. pris ou destruit. **1584** [see TRINK *sb.*[1] d]. **1667** *Lond. Gaz.* No. 183/4 [They] did no more hurt then only by the taking up some few Stawkers or Nets laid for Lobsters.

†**2.** One who prowls about for purposes of theft.

1508 DUNBAR *Flyting* 156 And lyk twa stalkaris steilis in cokis and hennis, Thow plukkis the pultre, and scho pullis off the pennis.

3. One who stalks game. In early use only *Sc.*, one who stalks game illegally, a poacher (cf. sense 1). Also *fig.*

1424 *Sc. Acts 2 Jas. I*, §13 (1814) II. 7 It is ordanyt þat þe Justice clerk sall inquyre of stalkaris þat slais dere.. And als sone as ony stalkar may be conuict of slauchter of der he sal pay to þe king xl s. *c* **1575** in *Balfour's Practicks* (1754) 542 Stalkeris that slayis hart, hind, dae, rae. **1675** J. SMITH *Chr. Relig. App.* I. 21 Had it [the World] wanted the eye of Theology, a cunning Stalker might possibly have catcht it on its blind side. **1790** GROSE *Prov. Gloss.* (ed. 2) Suppl., *Stalker*, a fowler. **1872** *Daily News* 8 Oct. 3 The assembled stalkers and gillies. **1902** *Times* 13 Nov. 13/6 Self-denying stalkers.. have devoted several seasons to.. sparing the better class animals.

4. One who walks with long measured steps.

1585 HIGINS *Junius' Nomencl.* 522 *Grallator*.. a stalker: a goer vpon stilts or crutches. **1601** B. JONSON *Poetaster* III. iv, You, player, rogue, stalker, come backe here. **1604** *Meeting Gallants at Ordinarie* C1b, Away he went with himselfe as coragiously, as the best stalker in Europe. **1631** ANCHORAN *Comenius' Gate Tongues* 215 *Grallator*... A stalker makes great long strides with scatches or stilts and crowches. **1865** DICKENS *Mut. Fr.* IV. ix, The stately stalker stalked back.

b. †Used as the name of a bird found in N.W. Africa (*obs.*). Also in *Ornithology*, as the rendering of mod.L. *Gradatores*, an order of birds in certain now disused systems of classification.

Macgillivray (*Brit. Birds*, 1852) adopted the word as the rendering of *Aucupatores* (the name of an order in his own system), evidently associating it with sense 3.

1623 JOBSON *Golden Trade* 154 The greatest bird or fowle we see, is called a Stalker; who by reason of his long legs and necke, when he stands vpright, is in height taller then a man. **1872** COUES *N. Amer. Birds* 240 The birds stand in wait, or stalk stealthily along; hence they are sometimes called *Gradatores* (stalkers).

stalking ('stɔːkɪŋ), *vbl. sb.* [f. STALK *v.*[1] + -ING[1].] The action of STALK *v.*[1]; †stealthy movement (*obs.*); pursuit of game by the method of stealthy approach.

c **1000** ÆLFRIC *Hom.* (Th.) II. 138 On sumere nihte hlosnode sum oðer munuc his færeldes and mid sleaccre stalcunge his fotswaðum filiȝde. **1398** TREVISA *Barth. De P.R.* II. xix. (1495) 46 Yf the fende maye not dysceyue wyth stalkynge he puttyth to ferfull gastness and drede. *c* **1440** *Promp. Parv.* 472/1 Stalkynge, or soft and sly goynge, *serptura.* *c* **1460** *York Myst.* xxx. 157 With no stalkyng nor no striffe be ye stressed. **1503–4** *Act 19 Hen. VII*, c. 11 The grettest destruccion of Reed Deere and Falowe.. is with Nettis.. and stalking with beestis. **1533** in *Archæologia* XXV. 522 Item delyvered to my hosbond.. when he went a stalkynge for master tresurer. **1553** *Respublica* I. iii. 160 Theare was..such herkenynge, suche stalking, suche watching, such spyinge. **1853** KANE *Grinnell Exped.* xii. (1856) 86 The Esquimaux..by a patient process of stalking, succeed in getting within rifle shot.

b. *attrib.* as ***stalking engine, gelding, -ground, ox, -shoe, -system.*** Also STALKING-HORSE.

1531 *Privy Purse Exp. Hen. VIII* (1827) 112 Paied to a servant of my lorde lisles in Rewarde for bringing of the Stalking Oxe, x s. *Ibid.* 132 For the mete of the kingis white stalking guelding. **1621** MARKHAM *Fowling* x. 64 The last of these stalking Engines is the dead hedge of two or three yards long. **1850** R. G. CUMMING *Hunter's Life S. Afr.* (1902) 77/2, I resolved to try the stalking-system with these, and to hunt the troop of bulls with dogs and horses. **1860** G. H. K. in Galton *Vac. Tour.* (1861) 116 When we reach the stalking-ground. **1900** POLLOK & THOM *Sports Burma* 253 My stalking shoes.

stalking ('stɔːkɪŋ), *ppl. a.* [f. STALK *v.*^{1} + -ING^2.] That stalks.

†**1.** Stealthy. *Obs.*

a **1400** *Pol., Rel., & L. Poems* (1903) 254 [Death is] Stille and eke stalkinge.

2. Walking with great strides.

1560 PHAER *Æneid* IX. (1562) F fij b, With stalking doubtful steps. **1581** A. HALL *Iliad* III. 45 Paris with stalking pace aduauncde himself to the Greekes warde. **1590** SPENSER *F.Q.* I. vii. 10 His [the giant Orgoglio's] stalking steps are stayde Vpon a snaggy Oke. **1607** *Puritan* III. v. 84 Haue you neuer seene a stalking-stamping Player. **1700** DRYDEN *Ovid's Met.* XIII, *Acis, Pol. & Gal.* 44 Thus, warn'd in vain, with stalking pace he strode. **1757** SMOLLETT *Reprisal* I. vi. 18 That proud, stalking Highlander. **1909** CROCKETT *My Two Edinburghs*, A long-legged, stalking, wonder-stricken boy of fifteen.

b. said of long-legged birds.

1697 DRYDEN *Virg. Georg.* I. 413 That's the proper Time ..For stalking Cranes to set the guileful Snare. **1847** *Gloss. Heraldry* 294 *Stalking*, walking: a term applied to long-legged birds.

c. of ghosts. Also *fig.* of baleful agencies.

1697 DRYDEN *Virg. Past.* VIII. 142 To call from tombs the stalking Ghosts. **1792** MARY WOLLSTONECRAFT *Rights Wom.* vi. 266 Like some other stalking mischiefs. **1831** GEN. P. THOMPSON *Exerc.* (1842) I. 363 The grand stalking wrong, that was at the bottom of the well or ill directed resistance of the community.

†**d.** *fig.* Of style, etc.: Pompous, grandiloquent. *Obs.*

1601 B. JONSON *Poetaster* III. iv, Goe, he pens high, loftie, in a new stalking straine. **1806** W. TAYLOR in *Ann. Rev.* IV. 612 The stalking pomp of theatrical declamation.

Hence '**stalkingly** *adv.*

1891 MEREDITH *One of Conq.* II. v. 124 Contempt of any supposed affectation, which was not ostentatiously, stalkingly practised to subdue the sex.

'**stalking-horse.** [STALKING *vbl. sb.*]

1. A horse trained to allow a fowler to conceal himself behind it or under its coverings in order to get within easy range of the game without alarming it. Hence, a portable screen of canvas or other light material, made in the figure of a horse (or sometimes of other animals), similarly used for concealment in pursuing game.

1519 in *Archæologia* XXV. 420 Item p^d for Shoyng of Thomas Lawes Stawkyng horse..iij d. **1607** TOPSELL *Four-f. Beasts* 133 This is a beast standing amazed at euery strange sight, euen at the hunters bow and Arrowe, comming behind a stalking Horsse. **1611** COTGR., *Tonnelle*, a Tunnell, or staulking horse for Partridges. **1621** MARKHAM *Fowling* viii. 47, 49–50 The Stalking-Horse..is any old Iade trayned vp for that vse, which..will gently..walke vp and downe in the water..; and then..you shall shelter your selfe and your Peice behind his fore shoulder. Now forasmuch as these Stalking horses..are not euer in readinesse... In this case he may take any pieces of oulde Canuasse, and hauing made it in the shape or proportion of a Horse.., let it be painted as neere the colour of a Horse as you can deuise. **1621** BURTON *Anat. Mel.* II. ii. IV. (1624) 226 Fowling.., be it with guns, lime, nets, glades..stawking horses, setting-dogges, &c. *a* **1698** BLUNDELL *Cavalier's Note Bk.* (1880) 106 The use of stalking-horses is great... Horses are easily taught. Some do use to have a painted horse carried upon a frame. **1706** *Art Painting* (1744) 134 Giovanni d'Udine..is thought to have been the inventor of the stalking-horse, which poachers now use. **1780** PITT *Let.* in Stanhope *Life* (1863) I. i. 36 Your moor must be in the perfection of winter beauty; but I suppose with hardly any cattle upon it, except stalking horses. **1875** 'STONEHENGE' *Brit. Rural Sports* I. I. i. §5 He is enabled to drop his net over the place without the trouble of using the stalking-horse. **1902** CORNISH *Naturalist Thames* 7 The flats of the Upper Thames, where ..the wild duck are stalked with the stalking-horse, as of old.

2. *fig.* **a.** A person whose agency or participation in a proceeding is made use of to prevent its real design from being suspected.

1612 WEBSTER *White Devil* III. i. 41 You..were made his engine, and his stauking horse, To undo my sister. **1693** CONGREVE *Double Dealer* II. iv, Do you think her fit for nothing but to be a Stalking-Horse to stand before you, while you take aim at my Wife? *a* **1763** SHENSTONE *Progr. Taste* I. 78 Let me provide Some human form to grace my side: At hand,..An useful, pliant, stalking-horse! **1963** *Times* 12 Jan. 6/2 This meant that the Europeans would regard us as the stalking horse or paid hand of Uncle Sam and would not wish us to participate fully in European affairs. **1977** J. M. HARRISON in Bond & McLeod *Newslett. to Newspapers* III. 208 Zenger was actually a stalking horse for the group of wealthy politicians who owned the *New York Journal*. **1980** *Jewish Chron.* 15 Feb. 1/1 It raises the fear that the Irish may be acting as a stalking horse for the whole European Economic Community.

b. An underhand means or expedient for making an attack or attaining some sinister object; usually, a pretext put forward for this purpose.

1579 W. WILKINSON *Confut. Fam. Love* 70 b, Abusing the pretence of the Gospell as a stalking horse to leuell at others by. **1594** *Order for Prayer* To Rdr. A 4, Certaine who.. serue themselues of that idolatrous Romish religion, as of a Maske and stalking horse, therewith to couer the vnsatiable ambition..of vsurping the kingdoms of other Princes. **1600** SHAKS. *A.Y.L.* v. iv. 111 He uses his folly like a stalking-horse. **1624** GEE *New Shreds of Old Snare* 14 They made Religion a stalking horse to intend their own profit. **1792** LD. AUCKLAND in *Corr.* (1861) II. 423 The cause of Poland ..is..thought a good *mot de guerre*; and under that stalking-horse, the dissenters and levellers are preparing to attack us. **1827** SCOTT *Napoleon* Introd., Wks. 1870 VIII. 207 His.. popularity had..been the stalking-horse, through means of which, men..had taken aim at their own objects. **1835** SIR W. HAMILTON *Discuss.* (1852) 520 Their conscience is merely a stalking-horse, moved by their interest, and to conceal it. **1865** DICKENS *Lett.* (1880) II. 240 The cattle plague is the butcher's stalking-horse. **1880** L. STEPHEN *Pope* ii. 55 His [Pope's] indefensible use of Addison's fame as a stalking-horse in the attack upon Dennis.

stalkless ('stɔːklɪs), *a.* [f. STALK *sb.*^{1} + -LESS.] Having no stalk; chiefly of vegetable organs, sessile.

1698 PETIVER in *Phil. Trans.* XX. 400 They [*sc.* the leaves] are sharp at each end and stalkless. *c* **1711** —— *Gazophyl.* x. 95 Broad-leaved stalkless Dwarf-Moss. **1894** *Persian Pict.* 47 Stalkless jesamine blossoms.

stalklet ('stɔːklɪt). [f. STALK *sb.*^{1} + -LET.] A small stalk; in *Bot.* = PEDICEL.

1835 LINDLEY *Introd. Bot.* (1848) I. 272 Sometimes the leaflets themselves are subdivided. In this case..the small supports of the leaflets themselves [are called] stalklets. **1883** NASMYTH *Autobiog.* xviii. 343 To see all the delicate veins and stalklets thus brought to light again.

'**stalko.** *Anglo-Irish.* ? *Obs.* [? a. Irish *stócach* idler.] (See quot.)

1802 MAR. EDGEWORTH *Rosanna* iii. (1832) 332 Soft Simon had reduced himself to the lowest class of stalkoes or walking gentlemen, as they are termed; men who have nothing to do, and no fortune to support them, but who style themselves esquire. **1817** —— *Ormond* i. Wks. 1848 IX. 231.

stalky ('stɔːkɪ), *a.* [f. STALK *sb.*^{1} + -Y.] Consisting of or abounding in stalks; of the nature of a stalk or stalks; long and slender like a stalk.

1552 HULOET, Stalkye or stemmye herbes which be no trees and yet growe in height, as cawles, fenel, holiockes, humlockes and suche like. **1607** TOPSELL *Four-f. Beasts* 13 The *Bacchæ* or Satyres [are pictured] shaking togither their staulkie Iauelines and Paulmers. **1658** SIR T. BROWNE *Gard. Cyrus* iii. *Hydriot.* etc. 135 The folious and stalky emission distinguisheth herbs and trees. **1731** MILLER *Gard. Dict.* s.v. *Aloe*, The African stalky Aloe. **1825** E. HEWLETT *Cottage Comforts* viii. 104 Any pinks or carnations growing old and shabby, showing their brown stalky roots above the ground. **1887** *Daily News* 1 Dec. 3/8, Penang [*sc.* cloves]..; middling stalky at 11$\frac{1}{2}$d to 11$\frac{3}{4}$d. **1891** HARDY *Tess* v, Tess.. marching on upon long stalky legs.

stall (stɔːl), *sb.*^{1} Forms: 1 **steall, steal, stal,** 3–7 **stal, stalle,** 3 **steal,** 3–4 **stel,** 4–6 **stale,** (5 **stayle, stawll**), 6 **staull, stawle, stawyll,** 6–7 **staule,** 7 **staul,** 6–9 *Sc.* **staw,** 3– **stall.** [Com. Teut. (wanting in Gothic): OE. *steall* masc. standing, state, place, stall for cattle, corresponds to OFris. *stal* (WFris. *stâl*, NFris. *stal, staal*), MDu., mod.Du. *stal* masc., MLG. *stal* masc., neut. stall for cattle, OHG., MHG. *stal* masc., neut. place, dwelling, stall for cattle (mod.G. *stall* masc.), ON. *stall-r* masc. supporting block or slab, pedestal, stall for horse (MSw. *stalder*, Sw. *stall*, Da. *stald* stable):—OTeut. *stallo-*. The word passed into Romanic: It. *stallo* place, *stalla* stable, OF. *estal* place, position, stall for merchandise, etc. (mod.F. *étal* butcher's stall). Several of the English senses were probably adopted from Anglo-French, but this is not absolutely certain.

The OTeut. **stallo-*, according to the now prevailing view, represents an older **stadlo-*, f. root **sta-* to STAND. The pre-Teut. form of the suffix may have been either *-dhlo-* or *-tlo-*; on the former supposition the word would correspond formally to L. *stabulum* STABLE *sb.*; on the latter it would be a variant of **staplo-* STADDLE *sb.*]

†**1.** *gen.* Standing-place, place, position; place in a series, degree of rank; in OE. occas. state, condition. *Obs.*

in stead and stall (? corruptly ***in street and stall***), everywhere, continually (see STEAD *sb.*).

c **1000** ÆLFRIC *Gloss.* in Wr.-Wülcker 150 *Carceres*, horsa steal. **1042**, *c* **1220** [see STEAD *sb.*]. *c* **1200** ORMIN 2145 Þatt stannt wiþþ hire sune i stall þær heȝhesst iss inn heoffne. *Ibid.* 11854 To beon abufenn oþre menn I stalless & i sætess. *c* **1230** *Hali Meid.* 6 Of se swiðe heh stal, of se muche dignete, ..as hit is to beo godes spuse. *a* **1240** *Sawles Warde* in *Cott. Hom.* 263 Ha liuieð ..euer mare in a steal in al þat eauer god is. *a* **1300** *Cursor M.* 396 In þe ouermast element of all; þer þe fir he has his stall. *c* **1400** *Ywaine & Gaw.* 695 Als he was stoken in that stall, He herd byhind him, in a wall, A dor opend. *c* **1450** *Robin Hood & Monk* lxxxix. in Child *Ballads* III. 101/2 Robyn Hode is euer bond to hym, Bothe in strete and stalle. *c* **1460** *Towneley Myst.* ii. 375 In hell I wote mon be my stall. **1481** CAXTON *Godfrey* Prol. (1893) 3 The noble Godefroy of Boloyne whiche..was stalled in the thyrde stalle of the moost worthy of Cristen men. *a* **1618** SYLVESTER tr. *Panaretus* 1306 He found her out in a hot-humid Cell... The Angell..Made little stay in this unholesome Stall.

†**2.** Phrases. **a.** [Cf. OF. phrases with *estal*: see Godefr.] ***to bring to stall***: to bring to a stand, to fix, settle. ***to hold one's stall***: to stand firm, keep one's position. ***to make, take,*** etc., ***stall, to keep at stall***: to make a stand, take up a position, stop. ***to take*** (a tree) ***to stall***: to take up one's position (there). *Obs.*

c **1205** LAY. 1671 Þa Freinsce weoren isturmede & noðelas he stal makeden. *Ibid.* 21294 Whar Colgrim at-stod & æc stal wrohte. *c* **1330** R. BRUNNE *Chron. Wace* (Rolls) 5077 For eche man tok a tre to stal, As tristi as a castel wal. *Ibid.* 14144 Temese & Londone he passed al, At Wynchestre þer tok he stal. **1338** —— *Chron.* (1725) 146 Now has he brought to stalle, his lond stabled redy. *Ibid.* 156, I salle bring him to stalle, bot he mak me acquitance. *c* **1450** *Merlin* xviii. 286 Gaheries with his warde..kepte at stall a longe while, but in the fyn he mote yeve grounde a litill. **1523** BERNERS *Froiss.* I. lxxxi. 42 b/2 Y^e englysshmen drewe sagely to ye dykes, and ther made a stall tyll all their men wer in sauegard.

†**b.** [Perh. a distinct word (? OE. *stæl*): cf. OE. *on nánum stale béon* to be no help (to), Ælfred *Orosius* v. ix.] ***to stand*** (***much, great,*** etc.) ***stall, to stand much in stall***: to afford great help, be of use or service (const. *dative* of person). *Obs.*

c **1250** *Owl & Night.* 1632 Ah þu neuer mon to gode Lyues ne deþes stal ne stode. *a* **1272** *Luue Ron* 200 in *O.E. Misc.* 99 Hwo so cuþe hit to þan ende hit wolde him stonde muchel stel. **13..** *K. Alis.* 2748 (Laud MS.), It was no wonder gret stal he stood Amonge hem alle was non so good. *c* **1315** SHOREHAM *Poems* i. 746 Þe bone þat swych prest þer byȝt No stel ne schel hym stonde. **1399** *Pol. Poems* (Rolls) I. 365 The bag is ful of roton corne, So long ykep, hit is forlorne, hit wille stonde no stalle. *c* **1420** *Sir Amadace* (Camden) xxxix, A mon that hase alle way bynne kynde, Sum curtas mon ȝette may he fynde, That mekille may stonde in stalle. *c* **1440** *Ps. Penit.* (1894) 22 Envye and wrathe of herte..Schul stonde a man yn lytul stal, Whan he is clothed yn a clowt, To wone withynne a wormes wal.

3. a. [Cf. mod.F. *stalle.*] A standing-place for horses or cattle; a stable or cattle-shed; also each division for the accommodation of one animal in a stable, cattle-shed or cow-house; also, a manger.

c **725** *Corpus Gloss.* (Hessels) S 512 *Stabulum*, stal. *c* **1200** *Trin. Coll. Hom.* 113 On [stride he makede] of heuene into þe maidenes inneðe, Oðer þenne in to þe stalle. *c* **1250** *Owl & Night.* 629 Vor hors a stable & oxe a stalle. *c* **1300** *K. Alis.* 1885 For Alisaundre..Heom to sakyn heo gon calle, So bocher the hog in stalle. *c* **1390** CHAUCER *Truth* 18 Forþe, pylgryme, forþe, forþe beste out of þi stal. *c* **1420** *Anturs of Arth.* 447 His stede was sone stabillede, and lede to þe stalle. *c* **1440** *Ps. Penit.* (1894) 27 But seth thi flesch lord was perceyved, Ther hit was leid ful streit yn stalle Was ther no synful man deceyued That wolde to thy mercy calle. *c* **1440** *Promp. Parv.* 472/1 Stalle, of beestys stondynge, *boscar, presepe.* **1500–20** DUNBAR *Poems* lxi. 33 Great court horss puttis me fra the staw, To fang the fog be firthe and fald. **1596** SHAKS. *Tam. Shr.* II. i. 360, I haue..Sixe-score fat Oxen standing in my stalls. **1615** CHAPMAN *Odyss.* XIV. 156 Then fed he here, Eleuen faire stalles of Goats. **1697** DRYDEN *Virg. Georg.* III. 331 The youthful Bull must wander in the Wood; Or, in the Stall at home his Fodder find. **1782** *Phil. Trans.* LXXII. 370 At the west end is a stall for one horse. **1856** FROUDE *Hist. Eng.* I. i. 23 The art of fatting cattle in the stall was imperfectly understood. **1870** ROSSETTI *Poems, Stratton Water* ix, The Kine were in the byre that day, The nags were in the stall.

fig. **1601** B. JONSON *Poetaster* III. i. 114 This tyrannie Is strange, to take mine eares vp by commission, (Whether I will or no) and make them stalls To his lewd solœcismes, and worded trash.

b. *transf.* *U.S.* (See quot.)

1890 *T. M. Cooley's Railw. Amer.* 232 The earlier locomotives, like horses, were given proper names..; the compartments in the round-houses for sheltering locomotives are termed stalls.

c. A parking space for a motor vehicle, usu. marked out but not partitioned off. *U.S.*

1940 *College Topics* (Univ. of Virginia) 4 Nov., These stalls will be painted to facilitate parking and a time limit of one hour has been ordered for both sides of the street in this area between 8 a.m. and 6 p.m. **1955** J. H. SCHMITZ in Aldiss & Harrison *Decade the 1950s* (1976) 17 Cord hurriedly flew the skipboat round the station and rolled it back into its stall. **1976** C. WESTON *Rouse Demon* (1977) xxiii. 110 Her car was in its stall in the subterranean garage.

d. One of a series of urinals separated by divisions, in a men's lavatory; also, a compartment in a wash-room. Also ***urinal stall, toilet stall.***

1967 *Gloss. Sanitation Terms* (*B.S.I.*) 58 *Stall urinal*, a urinal having a back curved on plan to form a stall for the user... When stall urinals are fixed in ranges, divisions or cloaking pieces are provided between each stall. **1969** C. LOGUE *New Numbers* (1971) 62 Mechanical faucets drench a line of porcelain stalls. **1977** P. D. JAMES *Death of Expert Witness* II. vii. 90 The male washroom, apart from the urinal stalls, differed very little from the women's. **1978** R. LUDLUM *Holcroft Covenant* xxiii. 265 If they let the weapon through, he was to reassemble it immediately, in the toilet stall of a men's room.

†**4. a.** [So OF. *estal.*] A seat of office or dignity.

a **1300** *Cursor M.* 8582 Þar was he sett in king stall. **1399** GOWER *Praise of Peace* 383 Sette ek the righful Pope uppon his stalle. **14..** *Sir Beues* (C.) 1283 He broght hym yn to the halle And set hym at mete yn knyȝtes stalle. **1568** GRAFTON *Chron.* II. 663 He was set in the sure stall, stable throne, and vnmoveable Chayre of the crowne of his realme. **1638** W. LISLE *Heliodorus* x. 167 Persina [the Queen]..(rising from her stall) Entreats the King.

fig. *a* **1586** SIDNEY *Astroph. & Stella* lxxx, Sweet-swelling lip,..Nature's praise, Vertue's stall; Cupid's cold fire, Whence words, not words but heav'nly graces slide.

†**b.** Assigned quarters, privilege of residence (in an almshouse). *Obs.*

1595 in *Maitl. Club Misc.* (1833) I. 75 That gif evir heireafter David Moreson or Johnne Wilsoun sall injure be wordis Sir Bartilmo Simsone [the Master], thay salbe deposed fra thair stallis in the almoushous of Glasgw.

5. a. [Cf. med.L. *stallus, stallum, stalla*, OF. *estal(e*, mod.F. *stalle*.] A fixed seat enclosed, either wholly or partially, at the back and sides, esp. each of a row of seats in the choir of a church for the use of the clergy or religious, and, in a chapter-house, for the canons; also, each of the seats appropriated to knights of the higher orders of chivalry (e.g. the Knights of the Garter in St. George's Chapel, Windsor, the Knights of the Bath in Henry VII's Chapel, Westminster). Hence *occas.* the office, status, dignity or emolument connected with the occupancy of a (cathedral) stall; a canonry or the like.

a **1400–50** *Wars Alex.* 4543 Þe kirke of cupido is clenly a-rayed. Þe stallis & in all stedis strowid with Rose. *c* **1400** *Vesp. Ritual Ord. Nuns* in *Rule St. Benet* 145 Att þe bygynnyng of þe mese þe madyn þat salbe mayde nun sal sit in þe quere a-pon a stole be-for þe priores stayle. *c* **1450** in *Maitl. Club Misc.* III. 201 Item ane salter befor the Licentiatis stal strenyeit. **1522** [see STALLATION]. **1556** *Chron. Grey Friars* (Camden) 61 In the qwere in the byshoppes stalle that he was wonte to be stallyd in. **1571** GRINDAL *Injunct.* B ij b, Where the Churches are very small, it shall suffise that the Minister stande in his accustomed stall in the Queere. **1691** WOOD *Ath. Oxon.* I. 269 He was made Canon or Prebendary of the twelfth and last Stall in the collegiate Ch. at Westminster. **1756–7** tr. *Keysler's Trav.* (1760) IV. 84 The stalls of the monks in the choir are admirably carved. **1781** COWPER *Truth* 120 Though plac'd in golden Durham's second stall. **1788** *New Lond. Mag.* May 279/2 The eleven vacant stalls of the Most Honorable Order of the Bath. **1842** TENNYSON *Galahad* 31, I hear a voice, but none are there; The stalls are void, the doors are wide, The tapers burning fair. **1873** DIXON *Two Queens* XIX. ii. IV. 11 But Wolsey was not satisfied..with six prebendary stalls.

b. A long seat or doorless pew in a church; also a 'sitting'.

1580 *Churchw. Acc. Pittington*, etc. (Surtees) 119 Item of John Carter for a staule for himselfe, iiij d. **1584** *Ibid.* 15 Item for George Tayler, James Huntlye, John Wilkinson, and Jarrat Swalwell, the shorte stall on the north side of the quere doore. **1748** RICHARDSON *Clarissa* (1811) III. lxiii. 366, I have not been at church a great while; we shall sit in different stalls. **1788** W. H. MARSHALL *Yorksh.* II. 355 *Stall*; a doorless pew of a church. **1874** MICKLETHWAITE *Mod. Par. Churches* iii. 28 Of the pews. *Note.* I am quite aware that this word is dreadfully 'incorrect'... The 'correct' word is stalls, but unfortunately nave seats never are stalls.

c. [? After F. *stalle*, It. *stallo*.] Each of the chair-like seats arranged in rows in front of the pit in a theatre; also each of the corresponding seats in other places of entertainment.

1828 in *Sala's Jrnl.* (1892) 30 Apr. 22 An orchestra has been constructed [at the Lyceum]; that is, a separation of the best part of the pit to the extent of about one-third; each row divided into 'stalls' or single seats at half-a-guinea each. **1848** THACKERAY *Van. Fair* lxii, From our places in the stalls we could see our four friends..in the loge. **1892** KIPLING *Barrack-room Ballads, Tommy* 12 They sent me to the gallery, or round the music-'alls, But when it comes to fightin', Lord! they'll shove me in the stalls! **1901** TROWBRIDGE *Lett. her Mother to Eliz.* xviii. 89 The boxes were empty, and only a few of the orchestra stalls were taken.

d. *transf.* pl. Those who occupy the stalls in a theatre.

1901 G. B. SHAW *Three Plays for Puritans* Pref. p. viii, English influence on the theatre, as far as the stalls are concerned, does not exist. **1920** *Daily Mail* 17 Sept. 4/5 'I wonder whether we shall ever get our 'stalls' back,' a West End box-office manager remarked to me; the 'stalls' in the front-of-the-house vernacular signifying a particular class of playgoer. **1927** *Sunday Express* 10 Apr. 5/4 'Why should the stalls stand to oblige the pit?' asked a satellite near me.

6. a. [Cf. OF. *estal* (mod.F. *étal*), Flemish *stal*.] A bench, table, board or the like, esp. one in front of a shop, upon which goods are exposed for sale; a booth or covered stand for the sale of wares at a market, fair, or in the open street; a stand at a Fancy Fair.

1377 LANGL. *P. Pl.* B. XVI. 128 And knokked on hem with a corde and caste adown her stalles. *a* **1400** in *Engl. Gilds* (1870) 353 Also, no wollemongere, ne no man, ne may habbe no stal in þe heye-stret..bote he do war-fore. *c* **1400** *Destr. Troy* 1580 There were stallis by þe ſtrete stondyng for peopull, Werkmen into won, and þaire wares shewe. *c* **1450** *Godstow Reg.* 412 Iohn Curcy of Oxenford yaf..to hugh hore of Oxenford, mercer, a selde, with the stalle afore and a Celer vndir. **1581** FULKE in *Confer.* III. (1584) X iiij, I heard you at *Garbranges* staule in Oxenforde aske for *Irenæus* Epistles. **1590** SPENSER *F.Q.* I. v. 49 All these together in one heape were throwne, Like carkases of beasts in butchers stall. **1592** *Arden of Feversham* II. ii, *Prentise.* Tis very late; I were best shute vp my stall. **1644** DIGBY *Nat. Bodies* xix. (1658) 209, I have oftentimes seen in a Mercers shop, a great heap of massie gold lace lie upon their stall. **1714** GAY *Sheph. Week, Saturday* 73 How pedlar's stalls with glitt'ring toys are laid, The various fairings of the country maid. **1762–71** H. WALPOLE *Vertue's Anecd. Paint.* (1786) III. 124 The pocket-books were lost, but seven of them a friend of Vertue's met with on a stall, bought, and lent to him. **1822** SCOTT *Nigel* xiv, Though I was bred at a flesher's stall, I have not through my life had a constant intimacy with collops. **1848** THACKERAY *Van. Fair* lxvii, She is always having stalls at Fancy Fairs for the benefit of these hapless beings. **1894** HALL CAINE *Manxman* v. i, The market-place was covered with the carts and stalls of the country people.

? *Proverbial phrase.* **1697** *Verdicts conc. Virgil & Homer* i. 1 Sublime Notions,..which are not to be found in every Stall, are the Paterns to be imploy'd there [i.e. in an Heroic Poem].

†**b.** The booth or shed to shelter a cobbler at his work. *Obs.*

1692 R. L'ESTRANGE *Fables* II. cccci. 376 A Cobler turn'd Doctor,..What was it but the Brazen Face of the Quack.. that Advanc'd this Upstart from the Stall to the Stage? **1760–2** GOLDSM. *Cit. W.* lxv, A poor cobbler sat in his stall by the way-side.

†**7.** A stand for a cask. (Cf. STALLAGE 2 b, STELL *sb.*)

1538 in *Archæologia* XLIII. 226 The Buttery..j bread huche; j stalle to ley drynke on. **1630** *Maldon* (Essex) *Docum.* Bundle 217 No. 22, In the buttery, i beer stalle.

8. Applied to a sheath or receptacle of various kinds. **a.** Each of the several compartments or sheaths for the fingers in a glove.

1483– [cf. FINGER-STALL]. **1568** *Jacob & Esau* IV. viii, [*Rebecca to Jacob*] I haue brought sleues of kid... They be made glouelike, and for eche finger a stall.

†**b.** ***hammer stall***: see quots. *Obs.*

1802 C. JAMES *Milit. Dict.* s.v. *Stall, Hammer stall*, a piece of leather, which is made to cover the upper part of the lock belonging to a musquet. It is useful in wet weather. **1876** JAS. GRANT *Hist. India* I. lxv. 332/2 They had French firelocks, with a leather cover for the lock, known then, in our service, as a 'hammer-stall'.

c. Each of a set of cases for holding cartridges, attached to a tunic or waistcoat.

1906 *Advt.*, Automatic Stall Cartridge Holder... Each stall holds three cartridges, and the usual number of stalls on a coat or waistcoat is eight.

†**9.** Each of a series of 'screen' book-cases set at right angles to the walls of a library, each pair forming a bay or an alcove. *Obs.*

1709 HEARNE *Collect.* (O.H.S.) III. 318 All yᵉ Inner Part of yᵉ Library [of Exeter College] was quite destroy'd [by fire] & only one stall of Books or thereabouts secur'd. **1886** WILLIS & CLARK *Cambridge* II. 97 The Library..had seven 'stalls' or bookcases. We may assume that these were set at right angles to the walls,..with a window between each pair of cases.

10. *Metallurgy.* A 'walled area' or compartment between low walls in which ores are roasted.

1887 RÖHRIG *Technol. Wörterbuch* I. 586/1, *Röst-stadel* (Met.), stall, mound, walled-in area. **1891** *Century Dict.* **1911** WEBSTER.

11. [? A distinct word; cf. G. *stollen* (perh. the source).] *Coal-mining.* (See quot. 1883.)

pillar and stall: see PILLAR *sb.* 7. ***post and stall***: see POST *sb.*[1] 7 d. So also ***stall and room***.

1665 D. DUDLEY *Metallum Martis* (1851) 36 When they have wrought the Crutes or Staules, (as some Colliers call them) as broad and as far in under the ground, as they think fit. **1686** PLOT *Staffordsh.* iii. 148 In this Level He had five wallings or Stauls, out of which they dug the coal in great blocks. *Ibid.* Staules. **1883** GRESLEY *Gloss. Coalmining* 237 *Stall*, a working place in a mine, varying in length from a few feet to 80 yards or more, according to the thickness of the seam and system of working adopted. *Stall and Room work*, working the coal in compartments, or in isolated chambers or pillars.

12. [f. STALL *v.*[1] 14.] *Sc.* A surfeit, disrelish.

1782 SIR J. SINCLAIR *Observ. Sc. Dial.* 129 A staw. **1895** CROCKETT *Men Moss-Haggs* v, He had gotten a staw of the red soldiers.

13. [f. STALL *v.*[1] 9 d, e.] **a.** *Aeronaut.* The condition of an aircraft when the streamline flow over its wings breaks down, usu. owing to a low air speed or a high angle of attack; the sudden loss of lift (and height) associated with this.

1918 J. M. GRIDER *War Birds* (1927) 88 He went straight up three hundred feet and stalled and fell out of the stall right into the middle of the field. **1927** *Glasgow Herald* 31 Aug. 10 There is only one issue to the stall near the ground —a spin and a crash. **1928** [see LEVEL *v.*[1] 6]. **1966** M. WOODHOUSE *Tree Frog* xxv. 191 He couldn't slow down to my airspeed without..stalling and nobody..would risk a stall this close to the ground. **1976** W. GREATOREX *Crossover* 204 The big jet fell ten thousand feet..in a stall that would have turned into a spin..with a less-experienced captain.

b. The sudden stopping of an internal-combustion engine at low revolutions (see also quot. 1959).

1959 *Motor Manual* (ed. 36) iv. 83 The very simple torque converter..would work well only at one speed. It could, for instance, be designed to give quite high multiplication at 'stall' (the moment when the car is on the point of moving). **1973** R. ROSENBLUM *Mushroom Cave* (1974) 3 The [boat's] motor was finicky; tying off the cord had precipitated a coughing fit in the carburetor, followed by a stall.

14. *attrib.* and *Comb.* **a.** simple attrib., as ***stall-back, -collar, -drain, -elbow, -end, post, -produce, -ring, -woman***; ***stall-like*** adj.; (sense 13) ***stall warning*** (usu. *attrib.*).

1895 M. R. JAMES *Abbey S. Edmund* 131 The legends of saints are painted upon the wooden *stall-backs. **1844** H. STEPHENS *Bk. Farm* I. §31. 127 Each horse should be bound to his stall with a leather *stall-collar... Iron chains make the strongest stall-collar-shanks. **1805** R. W. DICKSON *Pract. Agric.* I. 51 The main drain, into which all the *stall-drains should empty themselves. **1882** *Archæol. Cant.* XIV. 115 Remnants of two *stall-elbows. **1512** *Test. Ebor.* (Surtees) V. 37 My body to be buried in the midd alye [of the church], at my *stale end. **1895** C. HOLLAND *My Japanese Wife* vii, The shops..have *stall-like extensions, encroaching upon the roadway. **1828** DARVILL *Race Horse* I. i. 31 Each *stall-post behind the horse's quarters should be placed at a distance from the north wall of the building..of ten feet, which will form the length of the stall. **1887** *Dict. Archit.* (Archit. Publ. Soc), *Stall post*, or hindpost of a stall. **1848** THACKERAY *Van. Fair* xxxviii, His grandpapa.. promised..not to give the child any cakes, lollipops, or *stall-produce whatever. **1844** H. STEPHENS *Bk. Farm* I. §31. 127 The best hempen cords..are..soon apt to wear out in running through the smoothest *stall-rings. **1958** *Chambers's Techn. Dict.* Add. 1016/1 **Stall-warning indicator*, a device fitted to aeroplanes which do not provide positive warning of the approach of a stall by buffeting. **1976** B. LELOMBER *Dead Weight* ii. 32 The stall-warning light blazed urgently as I tried to haul the shuddering nose up. *c* **1811** FUSELI *Lect. Art* iv. (1848) 441 The child had seen many *stall and market women.

b. Special comb.: **stall-board**, (*a*) the board in front of or behind a shop-window upon which goods are exposed for sale; (*b*) a hat-maker's ironing-board; (*c*) (see quot. 1875); (*d*) (see quot. 1887); **stall-edition**, a cheap edition of a work offered for sale on the bookstalls (cf. *stall-literature*); †**stall-epistle** (*nonce-use*), an 'open letter' or pamphlet sold on the stalls; **stall gate**, the road from a stall to the main road in a coal-mine; **stall-holder**, (*a*) the holder of an ecclesiastical stall; (*b*) one who is in charge of a stall at a bazaar, etc.; (*c*) one who occupies a seat in the stalls of a theatre, concert-hall, etc.; **stall-keeper**, †(*a*) one who provides stable accommodation for horses; †(*b*) (see quot. 1868); (*c*) one who keeps a stall for sale of goods; †**stall-learning**, learning acquired by the perusal of books on a bookstall; **stall-literature**, the cheap literature of the bookstalls (cf. *stall-edition*); **stall-man**, (*a*) a keeper of a book-stall; (*b*) a man who contracts for and works a stall in a coal-mine; also each of a company of men associated for that purpose; †**stall-master** [= G. *stallmeister*], a master of the horse; **stall plate** = *garter-plate* (see GARTER *sb.* 8 and cf. quot. 1522 in STALLATION); also, a similar plate bearing the arms of a knight of another Order; **stall-reader**, one who peruses the books on a bookstall; **stall seat**, a seat in the stalls of a theatre; **stall shower**, a shower-bath enclosed in a cubicle; **stall turn** *Aeronaut.*, a turn achieved by stalling one wing of an aircraft, causing increased drag on that wing and reduction of the radius of the turn; hence **stall-turn** *v. intr.*; **stall vicar**, ? a resident canon who also performed parochial duties, as distinguished from a parochial vicar; **stall-wages**, the payment due by a canon to the vicar who took charge of his parish during his term of residence; **stall-whimper** *slang* (see quot.); **stall-work** (*a*) the construction of choir stalls; (*b*) the working of coal in stalls.

1598 STOW *Surv.* 278 Before this Mountgodard streete, *stall boords were set vp by the Butchers, to shewe and to sell their flesh meate vpon. **1666** *Act 18 & 19 Chas. II*, c. 8 §12 It shall be lawfull for the Inhabitantes to suffer their Stall boards (when their Shop windowes are set open) to.. extend eleaven inches and noe more. **1745** *De Coetlogon's Hist. Arts & Sci.* II. 107/2 When steamed sufficiently and dried, we'll put it again off the Block, brush it, and iron it on our Stall-board. **1875** KNIGHT *Dict. Mech.*, *Stall-boards*, a series of floors on to which soil or ore is pitched successively in excavating. **1887** *Dict. Archit.* (Archit. Publ. Soc.), *Stall board*, the division between the housing places in a stable. **1898** FLETCHER *Carpentry & Joinery* xx. 222 [A ventilator] to prevent the condensation of the atmosphere against the glass, which would prevent the goods or articles on the stall-board being seen. **1854** H. MILLER *Sch. & Schm.* iii. (1857) 40 A common *stall-edition of Blind Harry's 'Wallace'. **1642** MILTON *Apol. Smect.* Wks. 1851 III. 297 So just is it in the language of *stall epistle non sense, that if [etc.]. **1883** GRESLEY *Gloss. Coal-mining* 237 *Stall gate. **1849** *Theatr. Programme* 34/2 The Committee have the honor to announce the following *Stall Holders:—The Duchess of Leeds, [etc.]. **1881** LADY M. E. HERBERT *Edith* vi, The stallholders [of the bazaar] were presented. **1895** *Dublin Rev.* July 217 The secular canons did not displace the ancient stall-holders before 1309. **1963** *Times* 10 Jan. 4/3 Last night's performance in the Albert Hall allowed stallholders, at least, to hear more of that detail than ever before. **1591** PERCIVALL *Sp. Dict.*, *Establerizo*, a horsekeeper, a *stall keeper, *Stabularius*. **1842** *Ainsworth's Mag.* II. 157 Went to keep a stall at the fancy fair. Threw all the other stall-keepers into the shade. **1865** J. B. HARWOOD *Lady Flavia* xvi, Tiresome men, they declared, expected stall-keepers [at a fancy-fair]..to smile incessantly at every coxcomb who might affect to cheapen a penwiper. **1868** WALCOTT *Sacred Archæol.* 560 At Lincoln they [the subsacrists] were called stall-keepers. **1914** *Daily News* 29 July 5 In several markets stall-keepers were assaulted. **1673** [R. LEIGH] *Transp. Reh.* 76 How well they have behav'd themselves..let..the Avenue-Readers, the Wall-Observers, and those that are acquainted with *Stall-Learning..testifie. **1831** CARLYLE *Sart. Res.* II. iii, My very copper pocket-money I laid out on *stall-literature. **1761** STERNE *Tr. Shandy* III. xxxv, There are not three *Bruscumbilles* in *Christendom*,—said the *stall-man. *a* **1608** DEE *Relat. Spir.* I. (1659) 230 Octavius Spinola, Chamberlain and *Stall-master. **1829** SCOTT *Anne of G.* xi, [They] scarce wondered at the fears of Caspar, the stall-master, when he found such a person in the stable. **1842** N. H. NICHOLAS *Hist. Order of Bath* 206 A copy of the

Inscriptions on some of the *Stall Plates of Knights of the Bath, will be found in the appendix. **1855** FRANKS in *Archæologia* XXXVI. 214 The Stall-plate of Sir William Parr. **1864** BOUTELL *Her. Hist. & Pop.* xiii. (ed. 3) 129 The Stall-Plates of the Garter are amongst the most interesting ..of Historical records. **1980** J. BROOKE-LITTLE *Royal Ceremonies of State* vii. 102/2 Henry VII's magnificent chapel at the East end of Westminster Abbey..makes a splendid setting for the installation of Knights Grand Cross who, like Garter Knights display banners and have stall plates. *c* **1645** MILTON *Sonn.* xi, A Book was writ of late call'd Tetrachordon;..Cries the *stall-reader, bless us! what a word on A title page is this! **1876** HARDY *Ethelberta* xli, Regarding her as a stall-reader regards the brilliant book he cannot afford to buy. **1920** *Daily Mail* 17 Sept. 4/5 Before the war approximately 90 per cent. of the occupants of *stall seats in a West End theatre of any repute were in evening dress. **1939** R. CHANDLER in *Dime Detective Mag.* Aug. 65/1 A glass *stall shower, monogrammed towels on a rack. **1978** S. SHELDON *Bloodline* xvii. 202 She walked through a tiled bathroom that included a marble bathtub and a stall shower. **1942** *R.A.F. Jrnl.* 3 Oct. 30 How insecure the safety belt seemed when called upon to do *stall turns in the back seat of a Hart. **1948** *Times* 9 Feb. 2/3 The aircraft..climbed steeply, stall-turned, and..burst into flames. **1952** A. Y. BRAMBLE *Air-Plane Flight* 205 The 'stall turn' is a useful manœuvre for changing to a reciprocal course (heading altered through 180°) in less time and space than by normal turning. **1898** A. F. LEACH *Beverley Acc. Bk.* (Surtees) I. Chapter Act Book 77 Though the parish was very large and many places in it very far off no regular vicarages had been instituted..; though *stall Vicars could not properly attend to them. **1868** WALCOTT *Sacred Archæol.* 330 At Hereford, where the Miserere was always sung after the investiture [of a canon]; and a bond to pay *stall-wages to his vicar was signed. **1676** COLES *Dict.*, *Stall-whimper*, a bastard. **1811** MILNER *Eccl. Archit. Eng.* Pref. 16 An..arcade of the most elegant *stall-work. **1883** GRESLEY *Gloss. Coal-mining* 237 Stall work. **1886** WILLIS & CLARK *Cambridge* I. 521 No attempt was made to complete the stall-work until the reign of Charles I.

stall (stɔːl), *sb.*^{2} Also 6 **staul(e**, 7 **stal**. [a. AF. *estal*, var. of *estale*: see STALE *sb.*^{3}]

†**1.** A decoy-bird. Chiefly *fig.* *Obs.*

? *a* **1500** *Chester Pl.* 102 (MSS. B.W.h) Send forth women of thie countrye, namely those that beautifull be, and to thie Enemyes lett them draw nye, as stalles to stand them before. **1577** KNEWSTUB *Confut.* (1579) 8 b, They seduce some goodly and zealous men.., placing them at the porch of their Synagogue,..to stand there as baites and stalles to deceiue others. **1584-7** GREENE *Carde of Fancie* Wks. (Grosart) IV. 91 Did I disdaine to looke at the lure, and shall I now stoope without stall? **1592** —— *Disput. He & She Cony-catchers* F 2, Sitting or standing at the doore [of a whore house] like a staule, to allure or draw in wanton passengers.

2. A pickpocket's helper who distracts the attention of the victim whose pocket is being rifled; also the action or an act of stalling (see STALL *v.*^{2} 1).

1591 GREENE *Conny Catching* II. Wks. (Grosart) X. 103 They see him drawe his purse, then spying in what place he puts it vppe, the stall or the shadowe beeing with the Foist or Nip, meets the man at some straight turne and iustles him. **1607** DEKKER & WILKINS *Jests* D.'s Wks. (Grosart) II. 328 The stall..gets before you, &..raggles himself too & fro, while the foyst dooing as much behind, they both disquiet you, & the one picks your pocket. **1812** J. H. VAUX *Flash Dict.*, *Stall*, a violent pressure in a crowd, made by pickpockets. **1881** *Daily Tel.* 30 Dec., I saw a woman..put her purse in her gown pocket, so I..said to my pal, 'Chuck me a stall, and I'll have that.' *Ibid.*, They go out with the clever ones, and do the 'stall' business for them.

3. *slang.* A pretext for something used as a pretext for thieving or imposition.

1851 MAYHEW *Lond. Labour* I. 254/1 He induced a woman to let him have a halfpenny for a 'stall', that is, as a pretext with which to enter a shop for the purpose of stealing. **1889** 'R. BOLDREWOOD' *Robbery under Arms* xli, Well, but how did they know it was true?.. It might have been only a stall.

4. a. ***stall off***: an act of stalling off (see STALL *v.*^{2} 2); an evasive story or trick. *slang.* More recently, without *off*.

1812 J. H. VAUX *Flash Dict.*, *Stall off*,.. generally it means a pretence, excuse, or prevarication—as a person..entering into some plausible story, to excuse himself, his friends or accusers would say, O yes, that's a good stall off. **1846** *Swell's Night Guide* 41 They are never at a loss for a stall. **1851** MAYHEW *Lond. Labour* I. 424/1 Women [fortune-tellers] who go about with a basket and a bit of driss (lace) in it, gammy lace, for a stall-off (a blind), in case they meet the master. **1931** W. FAULKNER *Sanctuary* xvii. 156 If it was a stall, dont common sense tell you I'd have invented a better one? **1939** E. S. GARDNER *D. A. draws Circle* (1940) vii. 98 'Sometimes when he'd be working, I'd take meals up to him. I think that was just a stall.' 'You mean the meals were for someone else?' 'Yes.'

b. An act of stalling (for time) or prevarication. Cf. STALL *v.*^{2} 3 a. *colloq.*

1945 *Sun* (Baltimore) 21 Nov. 1/1 The 200 delegates termed the company reply 'a stall pure and simple'. **1963** J. N. HARRIS *Weird World Wes Beattie* (1964) iv. 49 It was a very good stall, if you know Edgar... So he left the whole matter in abeyance. **1977** D. E. WESTLAKE *Nobody's Perfect* (1978) 141 It'll take me a while to get the cash together... This isn't a stall... I do have the money.

†**stall**, *sb.*^{3} *dial.* *Obs.* [Perh. a dialectal variant of *stavel*, STADDLE *sb.*

Cf. Sc. *stale*, *stail*, bottom of a stack (see *Eng. Dial. Dict.*), which is prob. a. ON. *stál* (Norw. *staal*) inside of a stack (? ultimately cogn. w. STADDLE *sb.*).]

(See quot.)

1688 HOLME *Armoury* III. 72/2 Terms used by the Mower and Haymaker... Raking the Bottom Stalls, is to Rake up all the scattered Hay about the Cocks, and cast it thereon.

stall (stɔːl), *sb.*^{4} Forms: α. *north.* and *Sc.* 6, 9 **stale**, 9 **staill**; β. 6-8 **stall**, 6-7 **stal**. [Prob. related to STADDLE *sb.*] A hive of bees; a 'stock' of bees in or for a hive; also, a bee-hive. (Cf. STALLER^3.)

α. **1505** *Acc. Ld. High Treas. Scot.* III. 159 Item, to the gardinar of Linlithgw to by viij stales of beis, viij Franch crounis. **1588** *Wills & Inv. N.C.* (Surtees) II. 312, iij wynter stales of bees, and the planck, 12s and empty hyves 4d. **1808** JAMIESON, s.v. *Stale, Staill*, or adj. *staill skep of bees*, S. denominated perhaps as being the principal skep, or mother-hive. **1824** MACTAGGART *Gallovid. Encycl.* 94 A beeman lang the chiel had been, Keep'd mony a winter stale.

β. **1531** ELYOT *Gov.* (1534) 7 b, For if..the bees may issue out of theyr stalles, with out peryl of raine..in the mornynge erely he callethe them. **1531** in Weaver *Wells Wills* 139 A stall of beyes. **1609** C. BUTLER *Fem. Mon.* iii. §23 Moue them not without urgent occasion: for often lifting vp the hiue.. doth discourage the stall. **1670** J. SMITH *Eng. Improv. Reviv'd* 180 On or at the North-west side of the Physick-garden..is built a Bee-house to contain 200 Stals, Stools, or Hives of Bees. **1743** WESLEY in *Wks.* (1872) XIII. 179 They destroyed five stalls of bees.

†**stall**, *a.* *Obs.* *rare.* [cogn. w. STALL *sb.*^{1}] Stubborn, resolute.

c **1205** LAY. 1841 Mid stocken & mid stanen stal [*c* 1275 strang] feht heo makeden. *Ibid.* 4143. *Ibid.* 10463 Heo nomen here uerden & comen to stal fehte. *c* **1400** *Destr. Troy* 9789 Noght stird hym þo stith in his stalle hert.

stall (stɔːl), *v.*^{1} Forms: 3-6 **stal**, (5 **stol**), 4-6 **stalle**, 6-7 **stawl(e**, **staule**, 3- **stall**. [Several distinct formations appear to have coalesced. The vb. partly represents a ME. adoption of OF. *estaller*, *estaler* (see STALE *v.*), ultimately f. Teut. **stallo-* STALL *sb.*^{1}, and partly an English formation on STALL *sb.*^{1} It is probable also that in some uses it was a back-formation from ME. *i-stald*, pa. pple. of *stellen* to place (see STELL *v.*), OE. *stęllan*, f. Teut. **stallo-* STALL *sb.*^{1}, and in others a shortening of INSTALL and FORESTALL. (OE. had *forþsteallian* intr., to take place, but the simple vb. is not recorded).]

I. To place.

1. *intr.* To have one's abode, dwell. *Obs.* exc. *dial.* in ***to stall with***, to tolerate the presence of (another), to get on with.

c **1315** SHOREHAM *Poems* III. 30 Þat hys þe blysse of heuene aboue, Þar holy soulen stalleþ. **1606** SHAKS. *Ant. & Cl.* v. i. 39 *Caesar* Oh Anthony..I must perforce Haue shewne to thee such a declining day, Or looke on thine: we could not stall together, In the whole world. **1897** J. GORDON *Village & Doctor* [iv.] 138 Varney wondered whether the pious farmer was after the mother or daughter. 'Depend on it,' he said to me one day, 'it is the young 'un; 'e never could stall with the old cat.'

2. *trans.* To assign a particular place to (a person or thing); to place.

1415 HOCCLEVE *Hen. V & Knts. Garter* 32 Dooth so and god in glorie shal yow stalle. **1423** JAS. I *Kingis Q.* 170 [Thow that] has all thing within thy hert[e] stallit, That may thy ȝouth oppressen or defade. **14..** LYDG. *Order of Fools* 116 in *Q. Eliz. Acad.* (1869) 83 Who..lowde lawghys whan he dothe morne, Amonge foles of riȝt he may be stallyd. *c* **1460** *Towneley Myst.* xxi. 202 Shall I neuer ete bred to that he be stald In the stokys. **1481** CAXTON *Godfrey* Prol. 2 But thystorye of the sayd Arthur is so gloryous and shynyng, that he is stalled in the fyrst place of the moost noble, beste and worthyest of the cristen men. **1513** DOUGLAS *Æneis* x. iv. 124 The mekle houk hym bayr was Tryton callit; For in hir foirstam was the monstre stallit. **1557** PHAER *Æneid* VI. (1558) Rj b, All her sisters out she calles, Infernall hideous haggs, and to their turmentes them she stalles. *Ibid.* VII. Tj, Now hie in heauen he sitts, and on the golden starrs is stalde. **1581** DERRICKE *Image Irel.* II. Fj b, In highest place of all: The Cheeftaine then this traitrous knaue, like honest man doeth stall. **1594** R. C[AREW] *Tasso* III. 134 To Dudon..A Sepulchre of Cipresse sweete they stall, Their Barricados neere.

†**3.** To fix, appoint beforehand. *Obs.*

14.. *Beryn* 2610 For hir lawis been so streyt, & peynous ordinaunce Is stallid [*but perh. read* stablid] for hir falshede. **1532** *Dice Play* (Percy Soc.) 5 As I roamed in the Church of Pauls..looking for certain my companions, that hither might have stalled a meeting. *a* **1555** GARDINER in Foxe *A. & M.* (1563) 739, I know your Grace cannot staye these matters so sodenly, and I esteme it a great matter that thinges be stauld hetherto thus.

†**4.** To agree to the payment of (a debt) by instalments; to fix (days) for payment by instalments. Cf. ESTALL *v.* *Obs.*

1491 in Studer *Oak Bk. S'hampton* (1910) I. 153 That.. no Meire, ne Auditours shall stall' no dayes with no persone, withoute graunte of comune Assemble. **1525** *St. Papers Hen. VIII*, VI. 462 *marg.*, They be also sufficiently instructed, howe they shal ordre themself for stalling of days for part of the money due by thEmperour. **1558-9** *Cat. Anc. Rec. Dublin* (1889) 484 The somme of sixe score eight pounds, eleven shillings, seven pence, stallid as a debt to this citte. **1585-6** EARL LEYCESTER *Corr.* (Camden) 45 Hir majesty refuseth ether to pardon hym..or to stall his dett. *c* **1640** J. SMYTH *Lives Berkeleys* (1883) I. 107 And the residue of his debts..were stalled to bee payd by this lord at fower-score pounds a yeare. *a* **1670** J. HACKET *Abp. Williams* II. (1693) 128 He petition'd, that His Majesty would stall his Fine, and take it up as his Estate would bear it, by a Thousand Pounds a year.

fig. **1591** SPENSER *M. Hubberd* 1245 And his false counsellor..[he chose] To damne to death, or dole perpetuall, From whence he neuer should be quit, nor stal'd. *a* **1631** DONNE *Serm.* Wks. 1839 IV. 154 Thou canst never promise thyself to sin..thriftly..and stall the fine; for thy soul, that is the price, is indivisible, and perishes entirely; and eternally at one payment.

†**5.** ***to stall forth***, ***out***: to display or expose to view. *Obs.* *rare.*

1547 *Bk. Merchauntes* c v b, They go fro town to town.. to make their mustres and stall theyr marchandise. **1580** HOLLYBAND *Treas. Fr. Tong*, *Estaler*, to stalle out, or shew wares. **1608** D. T[UVILL] *Ess. Pol. & Mor.* 101 Desirous (as it were) to stall foorth her treasures.

†**6.** To strengthen, stablish. *Obs.*

c **1400** *Destr. Troy* 5186 We mightily to Messam our men send, To fecche vs som fode..And abundantly broght with buernes betwene For to stall our astate and our strenght hold.

II. To place in a 'stall'.

†**7. a.** To induct formally into a seat of rule or dignity; to enthrone (a king, a bishop, etc.); *spec.* to induct (a canon, a knight of the Garter or Bath) into his 'stall'. Hence, to place in a high office or dignity. = INSTALL *v.* 1. *Obs.*

13.. *E.E. Allit. P.* B. 1334 Bot þenne þe bolde Baltazar, þat was his barn aldest, He was stalled in his stud, & stabled þe rengne. *c* **1384** CHAUCER *H. Fame* 1364 But al on hye, above a dees, Sitte in a see imperial,..Y saugh perpetually y-stalled A femynyne creature. **1387** TREVISA *Higden* (Rolls) VIII. 183 He was i-stalled at Lyncoln by þe arche-decon. *c* **1407** LYDG. *Reson & Sens.* 253 For this is she that is stallyd And the quene of kynde called. *c* **1440** *Brut* 466 Sir Robert Fitzhugh was stalled Bisshop of London in the see of Seint Paules. **1522** *Stat. Order Garter* xiii. in Ashmole *Inst.* etc. (1672) App. g 2/b And that all such straungers..shall sende ..a sufficient Deputie..to be stalled in his place. *a* **1562** G. CAVENDISH *Wolsey* (1893) 97 They had a specyall commyssion to creat and stalle the Kyng's Majestie in the Royall Order of Fraunce. **1565** JEWEL *Def. Apol.* (1611) 473 He..that being a wretched sinfull man, hath stalled himselfe in the place of God. *a* **1591** H. SMITH *Six Serm.* (1625) 91 When one stalleth vp another into Moses chaire, not hauing Moses Rod, nor Moses Spirit. **1594** SHAKS. *Rich. III*, I. iii. 206 Long may'st thou liue..And see another, as I see thee now, Deck'd in thy Rights, as thou art stall'd in mine. **1632** LITHGOW *Trav.* VI. 189 Where Kings were stall'd, disthron'd.., and crown'd. **1661** MORGAN *Sph. Gentry* IV. iii. 40 This favour is done and shewed to them which may not well come in their proper persons that they might be stalled by attourneys.

†**b.** *Cant.* esp. in ***to stall*** (a beggar) ***to the rogue***.

1567 HARMAN *Caveat* ii. (1869) 34 And if he mete any begger..he wyll demaund of him, whether euer he was stalled to the roge or no. If he saye he was, he wyll know.. his name that stalled hym. **1610** ROWLANDS *Martin Markall* F 4, He ordered, that euery one..taking vpon him the occupation of begging, shal be stauled to the order of rogues. **1622** FLETCHER *Beggars Bush* III. iii, *Higgen* [a beggar]. I.. stall thee by the Salmon into the clows, To mand on the pad.

8. a. To put (an animal) in a stall; to keep or confine in a stall, esp. for fattening; also ***to stall to*** (a particular kind of food), ***to stall up***.

1390 GOWER *Conf.* III. 124 A Monthe, which..The Plowed Oxe in wynter stalleth; And fyr into the halle he bringeth. **1500-20** DUNBAR *Poems* lxi. 28 (*Petit. Gray Horse*) I wald at ȝoull be housit and stald. **1530** PALSGR. 732/1, I stall an ox to fede him fatte, *je mets en estal.* **1588** KYD *Househ. Philos.* Wks. (1901) 246 The flesh of wild Beasts..is not so soone puft vp and fattened as those Beasts that commonly are stald and foddered. **1641** J. JACKSON *True Evang. T.* III. 205 So farre from..stalling the Oxe and Lyon together. **1764** *Museum Rust.* III. 7 As to oxen, we have them to the full as good, when stalled to turneps, carrots, etc. as if they were fed in the finest fatting grounds. **1837** *Flemish Husb.* 62 in *Libr. Usef. Kn.*, *Husb.* III, An ox kept stalled up for six or eight months and well fed, will double his original weight. **1850** *Jrnl. R. Agric. Soc.* XI. I. 89, I much prefer penning to stalling the sheep. **1894** K. GRAHAME *Pagan Papers* 79 On the other hand, can you stall the wild ass of the desert?

transf. and *fig.* **1553** EDEN *Treat. New Ind.* (Arb.) 30 *marg.*, Young men stalled to be made fatte. **1581** MULCASTER *Positions* vi. (1887) 41 Olde Asclepiades is by Galene confuted, and stawled for an asse. **1601** SHAKS. *All's Well* I. iii. 131 Praie you leaue mee, stall this in your bosome, and I thanke you for your honest care. **1839** BAILEY *Festus* (1848) 61, I saw the sun-god stall his flaming steeds In customary splendour.

b. *intr.* Of cattle: To be lodged in stalls.

1805-6 CARY *Dante, Inf.* xxv. 28 He [Cacus]..here must tread A different journey, for his fraudful theft Of the great herd that near him stall'd.

III. To come or bring to a stand.

9. *intr.* †**a.** Of a beast of the chase: To come to a stand. *Obs.* †**b.** Of an army: To take up a position for combat. *Obs.*

c **1400** *Master of Game* (MS. Digby 182) ii, And þen he maketh a ruse in some side and þere he stalleth or squatteth. *Ibid.* xxvi, Sometyme an herte wille stalle and looke aboute a gret while. *c* **1450** *Merlin* x. 161 And ther thei stalleden and foughten the ton vpon the tother. *a* **1562** G. CAVENDISH *Wolsey* (1893) 89 The boore issued owt of his denne, chaced with an hound in to the playn, and beyng there, stalled a whyle gasyng uppon the people.

c. Of a draught animal: To come to a halt because of mud or other impediment.

1807 C. W. JANSON *Stranger in Amer.* 172 The last time he passed, his horses *stalled*, that is, they were for some time unable to drag the wagon through the worst places. **1857** W. CHANDLESS *Visit to Salt Lake* II. vi. 233 His team were none too strong, and twice he 'stalled' hopelessly, and had to send to the nearest farm for a yoke of cattle.

d. Of an aircraft or its pilot: to enter a stall.

1910 R. LORAINE *Jrnl.* Apr. in W. Loraine *Robert Loraine* (1938) vi. 106 The machine leapt higher, so did my heart, higher still—then—puff!—I came to earth, having stalled and crashed. **1917** *Flying* 21 Feb. 136/1 An aeroplane can only reduce its flying speed to a certain minimum, after which it will stall. **1931** *Statesman* (Calcutta) 5 Dec., It is claimed that the autogiro cannot 'stall', or lose flying-speed. **1958** D. PIGGOTT *Gliding* vii. 34 The actual speed at which the glider stalls will be raised when the glider is being turned or manœuvred..or if a heavier load is being carried. **1975** L. J. CLANCY *Aerodynamics* v. 98 If a particular wing is such that it stalls too suddenly, it may be necessary to provide some artificial pre-stall warning device.

e. Of an engine or vehicle: to stop suddenly as if of its own accord. Also with the driver or the occupants of the vehicle as subj.

1914 R. & E. SHACKLETON *Four on Tour in Eng.* 204 A few miles beyond Chipping Norton we stalled near the foot of a hill—and found that it was because of an inexcusable forgetting of gasoline! **1932** *Birmingham Post* 17 Dec. 16/2 The men drove off in the van. A few minutes later the engine stalled. **1956** 'C. BLACKSTOCK' *Dewey Death* ix. 207, I share ..a car with a friend... She once stalled in the middle of Piccadilly Circus. **1973** R. ROSENBLUM *Mushroom Cave* (1974) 5 He let go of the throttle string, and the [boat's] motor stalled.

f. To loiter or linger *around* (also *along*); to 'hang about'. *U.S. colloq.*

1916 'B. M. BOWER' *Phantom Herd* i. 5 I've been stalling along and keeping the best of the bucks in the foreground. *Ibid.* xi. 194, I stalled around out there till my money gave out. **1976** P. G. WINSLOW *Witch Hill Murder* (1977) II. xv. 207, I hoped he might answer sort of friendly..and I've been kind of stalling around.

g. *transf.* and *fig.*

1923 R. D. PAINE *Comrades of Rolling Ocean* ii. 22 When things happened too fast, his mind stalled on a dead center. **1953** N. TINBERGEN *Herring Gull's World* i. 1 It stalls, makes a sharp turn and dives down. **1971** C. BONINGTON *Annapurna South Face* xvi. 199, I immediately noticed the lack of oxygen; once again my progress stalled into a crawl with rests at almost every step.

†**10.** *trans.* To bring (a hunted animal) to a stand. Also *transf.* (Cf. FORESTALL *v.* 1.) *Obs.*

13.. *E.E. Allit. P.* A. 188, I dred..Lest ho me eschaped þat I þer chos, Er I at steuen hir moȝt stalle. **1599** SHAKS., etc. *Pass. Pilgr.* xix, When as thine eye hath chose the dame, And stall'd the deer that thou shouldst strike.

†**11. a.** To bring to a standstill, render unable to proceed. *lit.* and *fig. Obs.*

c **1591** *Epit. Sidney* 2 in R.S. *Phœnix Nest* (1593) 10 Stald are my thoughts, which lou'd, and lost, the wonder of our age. **1598** FLORIO *Ital. Dict.* Ep. Ded. a4, If I, who many yeeres haue made profession of this toong,..in many wordes haue beene so stal'd, and stabled, as such sticking made me blushinglie confesse my ignorance [etc.]. **1603** B. JONSON *Sejanus* III. i. 393 [Silius stabs himself.] *Tib.* We are not pleased in this sad accident That thus hath stalled, and abus'd our mercy. **1650** MAY *Old Couple* III. (1658) 24 The time will be too short To get a pardon, specially as I Have lay'd some friends to stall it underhand. **1656** BAXTER *Reformed Pastor* viii. 465 See that you preach to such auditors as these, some higher points, that stall their understandings, and feel them not all with milk, but sometime with stronger meat. **1675** —— *Cath. Theol.* II. 98 And he that is stalled with the question, 'Can a Sinner leave his Sin, and love goodness?' would easily answer, [*sc.* if he understood the question to mean] 'Whether he be willing to do it? Yea.'

b. esp. in *pass.* To become stuck (in mud, mire, a snowdrift, etc.). Now only *U.S.* or *dial.* Also *fig.* (chiefly *U.S.*), of an assembly, plan, etc.: to be hindered or held up.

c **1460** *Towneley Myst.* III. 525 These floodis ar gone fader, behold... As still as a stone oure ship is stold. **1621** BURTON *Anat. Mel.* II. i. II. i. 291 Like him in Æsope, that when his cart was stalled, lay flat on his face and cryed aloud helpe Hercules. **1790** W. H. MARSHALL *Midlands* II. 443 To be stalled; to be set fast in a slough, or bad road. **1821** CLARE *Vill Minstr.* xliv, He knew no troubles waggoners have known, Of getting stall'd, and such disasters drear. **1864** LOWELL *McClellan's Rep.* Prose Wks. 1890 V. 100 He plunged into that Dismal Swamp of constitutional hermeneutics, in which the wheels of government were stalled at the outbreak of our rebellion. **1897** H. PORTER *Campaign. Grant* x. 164 A teamster whose waggon was stalled in a place where it was somewhat swampy. **1910** *Outlook* 2 July 473 Congress would have been stalled in its efforts to prepare certain legislation without their aid. **1953** *Times* 31 Oct. 3/6 General Thimayya said that 'explanations', which have been stalled for the past fortnight, were to be resumed to-morrow. **1970** G. F. NEWMAN *Sir, you Bastard* v. 143 Both their requests to make phone calls were stalled. **1978** *N.Y. Times* 29 Mar. A 8/3 The seventh session of the..conference was stalled at its beginning here today over the question of who would preside.

c. *Mech.* To cause (an aircraft, vehicle, engine, etc.) to stall.

1904 W. WRIGHT in M. McFarland *Papers Wilbur & Orville Wright* (1953) I. 442 He allowed the machine to turn up a little too much and it stalled it. **1914** HAMEL & TURNER *Flying* x. 198 He permitted the machine to lose speed until it had become what is known as 'stalled',—that momentary pause before the machine turns over on its side or nose and falls. **1918** BROKAW & STARR *Putnam's Automobile Handbk.* xxv. 167 Stalling the motor is the result of feeding too little gas with the accelerator. **1930** J. DOS PASSOS *42nd Parallel* iv. 266 He had to get out to crank the car as he had stalled the motor. **1947** F. S. HOLLIDGE *Driving Test Fully Explained* iii. 10 A timely change down will often prevent 'stalling' the engine. *c* **1965** A. CHRISTIE *Autobiogr.* (1977) VII. ii. 332, I stalled the engine once or twice..and I was rather chary about passing things. **1973** *Daily Tel.* 11 July 2/5 There was no structural failure in the Russian TU-144 supersonic airliner with until after the pilot had stalled it.

12. a. To take away (a person's) appetite; to satiate, surfeit *with*, *of*. Now *dial.* and *Sc.*

Prob. sometimes associated with sense 8; cf. the definition '*Stall*, to over-feed, to make fat, to stuff, etc.' (Dyche & Pardon, 1735).

1583 MELBANCKE *Philotimus* Mjb, Sith..you were stauled with yester dayes Disputation, I will prescribe you certaine Inductions to be performed at the Vniuersitie. **1690** W. WALKER *Idiomat. Anglo-Lat.* 139, I can never be stalled with that delight. **1787** BURNS *To Haggis* v, Is there that owre his french ragout, Or olio that wad staw a sow. **1816** SCOTT *Old Mort.* i, Which of them would sit six hours on a wet hill-side to hear a godly sermon? I trow an hour o't wad staw them. **1875** W. D. PARISH *Sussex Gloss.* s.v. *Stalled*, Aint you fairly stalled of waiting?

b. To cause aversion in, cause to turn away; also with *off*. Now *rare*.

1642 FULLER *Holy & Prof. St.* II. vii. 74 Mathematicks he moderately studieth to his great contentment. Using it as ballast for his soul, yet to fix it not to stall it. **1856** DICKENS *Lett.* (1880) I. 448 It conveyed..an idea of incompleteness ..and is likely to stall some readers off. **1874** *Slang Dict.* 308 *Stall*, to frighten or discourage.

c. To weary or tire; to fatigue. Usu. in *pass.* Chiefly *Sc.* and *north dial.*

1816, etc. in *Eng. Dial. Dict.* s.v. *Stall* v. 19. **1948** I. BROWN *No Idle Words* 108 Stalled, applied to depressed human beings, is a good old usage. 'You look stalled' is Yorkshire for 'You look dull'. **1967** J. WAINWRIGHT *Talent for Murder* 133 He was..cold, wet and fed-up—to use his own expression (as a Yorkshireman) he was 'stalled'.

†**13.** = FORESTALL *v.* 2 b. *Obs.*

1474 *Coventry Leet-bk.* 401 That no maner of man nor woman schall not stalle nor Regrate no markett.

IV. 14. To furnish (a choir, chancel) with stalls as seats.

1516 in Willis & Clark *Cambridge* (1886) II. 243 The Qwyer..shall be double staulled. **1857** *Yorksh. Archæol. Jrnl.* XV. 490 The chancel is stalled.

stall (stɔːl), *v.*[2] *slang.* [f. STALL *sb.*[2] Cf. STALE *v.*[5]]

1. a. *trans.* To screen (a pickpocket or his operations) from observation; also with *off*. Also, to close *up* or surround and hustle (a person who is to be robbed).

1592 GREENE *Disput. Conny-Catcher* Wks. (Grosart) X. 210, I either nip or foyst, or els staule an other while hee hath stroken, dispatcht, and gone. **1812** J. H. VAUX *Flash Dict.* s.v., *Stall off*, I wish you'd stall me off from that crib,.. meaning, walk in such a way as to cover or obscure me from notice. *Ibid.* s.v. *Stall up*, To stall a person up, (a term used by pickpockets) is to surround him..and by violence force his arms up, and keep them in that position while others of the gang rifle his pockets at pleasure.

b. *intr.* To screen a pickpocket's operation; to act as a look-out during a robbery or burglary.

1839 in 'Ducange Anglicus' *Vulgar T.* (1857) 34 To *stall*, to screen a robbery while it is being perpetrated. **1882** *Sydney Slang Dict.* 9/2, I pinched a swell of a fawney and fenced it for a double finnip and a cooter. My jomer stalled. **1926** J. BLACK *You can't Win* xxi. 338 Coppers located 'work' for burglars and stalled for them while they worked.

2. *to stall off.* **a.** To get rid of by evasive tactics, a trick, plausible tale or the like; also, in sporting parlance, to keep the upper hand of (a competitor).

1812 J. H. VAUX *Flash Dict.* s.v., To avoid or escape any impending evil or punishment by means of artifice, submission, bribe, or otherwise, is also called stalling it off. **1821** *Sporting Mag.* VIII. 151 The hardy mountaineer would not be stalled off. **1862** SALA *Seven Sons* III. viii. 157 [He] did his best..to..stall off the awful truth with discreet shrugs and simpers. **1883** *Daily News* 12 Sept. 6/1 To-day she ran very fast, but could not stall off the challenge by Florence, who won very easily at last. **1905** *Athenæum* 7 Oct. 464/2 His very preface should have stalled off denunciations of this kind.

b. To get off or extricate (a person) by artifice.

1812 J. H. VAUX *Flash Dict.* s.v., To extricate a person from any dilemma or save him from disgrace, is called stalling him off. **1828** LYTTON *Pelham* lxxxiii, Plant your stumps, Master Guinea Pig; you are going to stall off the Daw's baby in prime twig, eh?

3. a. *trans.* To put (someone) *off* for the time being. Now usu. without advb.

1829 P. EGAN *Boxiana* 2nd Ser. II. 345 He would not be '*stalled off*' by the most knowing of the knowing. **1930** *Sat. Even. Post* 26 July 26/1 We might be able to stall them for two or three days with the idea that Tony is in Washington tryin' to fix the rap against them. **1948** A. HYND *Pinkerton Case Bk.* 56 He kept stalling the woman off with one excuse or another. **1963** J. N. HARRIS *Weird World Wes Beattie* (1964) iii. 36 So I stalled him off. I said I couldn't remember meeting anyone at Mac's. **1977** J. CROSBY *Company of Friends* xx. 128 Elaine is in Paris. To bargain some more. It's the only way left to stall him. It's important to stall him.

b. *intr.* To prevaricate; to be evasive. Also, to play *for time* or temporize. Freq. in U.S. colloq. phr. ***quit stalling*** (usu. imp.). orig. *U.S.*

1903 A. H. LEWIS *Boss* 23 [If] Big Kennedy shows up to stall ag'inst you, why I should say [etc.]. **1932** W. FAULKNER *Light in August* ix. 202 'Quit stalling,' the stranger said. 'If you croaked the guy, say so.' **1934** D. RUNYON in *Collier's* 24 Nov. 52/2 All she can think of..is to stall for time. **1953** J. HILTON *Time & Time Again* III. 220 He was stalling for time. **1959** F. HOBSON *Death on Back-Bench* viii. 101 Just quit stalling..and come clean. **1969** *Listener* 9 Jan. 41/2 Suppose Mr Ransom suddenly seized Miss Gold and flung her down on the office table with a snarl of 'Quit stalling,' like one of her favourite film actors. **1980** S. NAIPAUL *Black & White* I. iii. 34 For more than a year the Guyanese courts had been stalling on the custody suit his parents had brought.

stall, obs. pa. t. of STEAL *v.*

stallage ('stɔːlɪdʒ). Also 4 stalage, 6 stalege. [ad. Anglo-L. *stallagium*, AF. *estalage* (mod.F. *étalage*), f. *estal* STALL *sb.*[1] In sense 3 formed on STALL *sb.*[1] + -AGE.]

1. A tax or toll levied for the liberty of erecting a stall in a fair or market; also attrib., as ***stallage rent***.

[*c* **1250** *Faringdon Acc.* (MS. Balow 49 [2] lf. 29), Reddit compotum..de vj s. viij d. de tolneto stallagiorum.] **1387** TREVISA *Higden* (Rolls) II. 97 Stalage, custom for stondynge in stretes in feyre tyme. *c* **1450** *Godstow Reg.* 665 And they shold be quyte þurgh all Ingelond by watir fro tol and passage and pountage and stallage and lastage and of all other customs. **1516** *Churchw. Acc. St. Marg., Westm.* (Nichols 1797) 8 Paid..for 24 ton of barnestone, with the pylage ankarage stallage custom and water carriage. **1705** HEARNE *Collect.* (O.H.S.) I. 28 Ye Toll and Stallage of Swyndon Market. **1763** in Picton *L'pool Munic. Rec.* (1886) II. 232 Rents, Dues and Stallage..And that all persons erecting stalls..do pay the customary stallage rents to the Corporation. **1774** *Ibid.* 227 The stallage Rents and other reversionary interest. **1833** *Boston* (Linc.) *Herald* 5 Feb. 4/2 The..right of the Lessee of the Corporation of this Borough, to his charge of one penny per foot for Stallage, upon all persons except freemen occupying ground with stalls in the Market-place..is at length decided.

2. [Cf. Du. *stellazje*, scaffold, stage.] †**a.** A stand, stage. *Obs. rare.* **b.** *dial.* A stand or support for a cask. (Cf. STALL *sb.*[1] 7, STILLAGE.)

c **1500** *Melusine* xvii. 54 And thenne the spouse & many other ladyes were sett vpon the scaffold or stalage. **1541** in W. H. Turner *Select. Rec. Oxford* (1880) 164 The howses, shoppys, stallys, stallagis, and standyngs now made..for the said fayre. **1838** HOLLOWAY *Prov. Dict.*, Stallage, a wooden trough, on which casks are placed, for the purpose of letting beer work. **1875** W. D. PARISH *Sussex Gloss. Stalder*, the stool on which casks are placed in a cellar. *Stallage.* (Same as Stalder.)

3. Accommodation for stalling (horses). *rare*$^{-1}$.

1861 WYNTER *Soc. Bees* 216 There are two of these [stables], containing stallage for 130 horses.

stalland, stallant, obs. forms of STALLION.

stallange: see STALLENGE.

'stallar, 'stallary.[1] *Scottish Eccl. Hist.* Also staller. [ad. med.L. *stallārius*, f. *stallum*, *stalla* STALL *sb.*[1]] (See quots.)

1561-2 in G. Chalmers *Caledonia* (1824) III. VI. viii. 664 [Out of this revenue, he had to pay a vicar pensioner, who did the parochial duty, and a] stallar [or vicar, who served for him in the choir of the cathedral]. **1861** C. INNES *Sk. Early Sc. Hist.* 82 The bishop and dignitaries were bound to provide priests as their cathedral vicars or stallers. **1875** A. SMITH *Hist. Aberdeensh.* I. 607 In 1437, the prebendary of Philorth was required to find a sub-deacon as his vicar, or 'stallar', to serve in the cathedral. **1885** R. NAISMITH *Stonehouse* 110 The 'stallers' or prebendaries of Bothwell. **1910** J. DOWDEN *Medieval Ch. Scot.* iv. 66 This deputy, was known as the canon's 'Vicar of the Choir', or 'Vicar Choral'. Another name frequently applied to this official is 'stallary' (*stallarius*), that is, vicar attached to the canon's stall in the cathedral, as distinguished from the vicar in charge of the canon's parish.

†**'stallary**[2]. *Sc. Obs.* [ad. med.L. *stallāria*, f. *stallārius*: see prec.] The office or position of a stall-vicar.

1612 *Sc. Acts Jas. VI* (1816) IV. 481/2 With..right of patronage of all benefices Chaiplanreis and Stallaries foundit and lyand within the boundis of Orknay and Zetland. **1624** *Reg. Mag. Sig. Scot.* 238/2 Cum..vicariis, capellaniis, prebendis, altaragiis et *lie stallaries*, decimis garbalibus, aliis decimis [etc.].

†**sta'llation.** *Obs.* Also -cion, -tioun. Aphetic form of INSTALLATION.

1447 *Shillingford Lett.* (Camden) 95 Byfore the stallacion of Leofrik in the said Cathedrall Church. **1522** *Stat. Order Garter* xxv. in Ashmole *Inst.* etc. (1672) App. hb/1 Every Knyght within the yere of his stallation shall cause to be made a Scouchon of his armes, and hachementis in a plate of metall.., and that it be surely sett upon the backe of his stall. **1537** *Acc. Ld. High Treas. Scot.* VI. 315 The tyme he was in Ingland for stallatioun of the Kingis grace in the ordour of the garter. **1661** MORGAN *Sph. Gentry* IV. iii. 44 In case that the said Soveraign be out in the country, to the which he cannot in propper person do that shall appertain to the Stallation, he may give power..to two of the fellows..to exercise it in his name. **1688** HOLME *Armoury* III. 54/1 The same Admission and Ceremonies shall be used at the Stallation of the said Noble Order to every Knight.

†**stall boat.** *Obs.* In 5 stallbote, 6 stalboat, 7 stale-boat, 8 (*Dict.*) stall-boat. [Prob. f. STALL *sb.*[1], in the sense of 'fixed station'.] A kind of fishing-boat, placed at anchor at the mouth of a river.

1328-9 *Exch. K. R. Memor.* m. 125 Quolibet piscante cum batello vocato stalbot. **1488** *Act 4 Hen. VII*, c. 22 §2 For a singuler covetyse and lucre in takyng of a fewe grete fysshes certeyne persones have used to set and ordeyne certeyne botes called Stallbotes festened with ankres. **1558** *Act 1 Eliz.* c. 17 §1 No person..withe any..Trimmenet, Trymebote, Stalbote, Weblyster..shall take..Spawne or Frye of Eeles, Salmon, Pyke or Pyckerel. **1584-5** *Act 27 Eliz.* c. 21 By the contynewall standinge of the saide Stalboates & usinge of the saide Nettes..the saide Haven and Gull..are become of muche lesse depthe. **1614** T. GENTLEMAN *England's Way* 19 These men..do set forth stale-boates, amongst the sands in the Theames mouth, for to take sprats, with great stale-nets. *Ibid.* 21 If that these men will needs vse their stale-boates and nets, let them go where the good Sprats be. **1706** PHILLIPS (ed. Kersey), *Stall-boat*, a kind of Fisher's Boat. **1720** STRYPE *Stow's Surv.* I. I. xv. 71/1 The Stal-boats, which are wont to belong to the Constable; and as yet do belong..[*margin* Ex Rotul. Claus. 9 R. II.].

stalle, obs. pa. t. of STEAL *v.*

stalled (stɔːld), *ppl. a.* [f. STALL *sb.*[1] and *v.*[1] + -ED.]

†**1.** Payable at fixed periods. Cf. STALL *v.*^{1} 4.

1553 *Act 7 Edw. VI* c. 1 §8 Collectoures of Customes, or certeyne and stalled Subsidies within any Porte [etc.].

2. Of a person: Endowed with or occupying a (church) stall. ? *Obs.*

1630 *R. Johnson's Kingd. & Commw.* 388 Certaine select & stalled persons. **1742** YOUNG *Nt. Th.* IV. 74 Was I as plump, as stall'd theology. **1829** I. TAYLOR *Enthus.* x. 262 Infidelity aggravated by stalled hypocrisy.

3. Of an animal: Confined to a stall; fattened in a stall for killing. *lit.* and *fig.*

1560 BIBLE (Geneva) *Prov.* xv. 17 Better is a dinner of grene herbes where loue is, then a stalled oxe and hatred therewith. **1638** PENKETHMAN *Artachthos* I 3 b, A fat stalled Cow 12s. **1734** tr. *Rollin's Anc. Hist.* XVII. ii. (1768) V. 511 To die a death worthy of Sparta, and not to wait as stalled victims, till it was thought proper to sacrifice them. **1886** STEVENSON *Prince Otto* I. iv. 56 About the stable all else was silent but the stamping of stalled horses. **1895** SIR H. MAXWELL *Dk. of Britain* xv, Stalled venison braised with prunes.

4. a. Divided into stalls or compartments for animals.

1825 HAZLITT *Spirit of Age* 6 He proposed at one time.. to make Milton's house.. a thoroughfare, like a three-stalled stable. **1839** BAILEY *Festus* (1852) 139 Through the foul-stalled stable of this world. **1898** J. K. FOWLER *Rec. Old Times* 108 The stables were stalled.

b. Archæol. ***stalled cairn***: on the Orkneys, a Neolithic cairn covering a burial-chamber which was divided into lateral cells by stone slabs projecting from the wall.

[**1934** J. G. CALLANDER in *Proc. Soc. Antiq. Scotl.* LXVIII. 320 (*heading*) A long stalled chambered cairn or mausoleum (Rousay type) near Midhowe, Rousay, Orkney.] **1937** C. S. T. CALDER in *Ibid.* LXXI. 117 (*caption*) Stalled cairn, Calf of Eday: plan and sections. **1954** S. PIGGOTT *Neolithic Cultures Brit. Isles* viii. 234 The *Camster* tombs.. are.. from the northern shores of the Moray Firth.. and thence up the coastal strip of Sutherland and Caithness. Their derivatives in Orkney, which include as the ultimate form the long 'Stalled Cairn' type.. are mostly concentrated in the islands of Rousay and Eday. **1963** *Field Archaeol.* (Ordnance Survey) (ed. 4) 31 Other peculiar features in Orkney are the 'stalled' cairns in which what is really a long and carefully-constructed cist is divided into as many as ten or more lateral cells. **1980** *Encounter* May 56/2 Renfrew and his team focused on the island of Rousay with its remarkable number of stalled cairns.

5. a. Of a vehicle, etc.: That has stuck fast.

1839 BAILEY *Festus* (1852) 335 It is they Who set their shoulders to the stalled world's wheel And give it a hitch forwards. **1851** MAYNE REID *Scalp-Hunt.* iii. 24 Now and then we were halted to help a 'stalled' wagon from its miry bed.

b. Of an aircraft or aerofoil: in an airflow that has ceased to be streamline. Also applied to flight in this condition.

1912 O. WRIGHT in M. McFarland *Papers Wilbur & Orville Wright* (1953) II. 1050 There is only one explanation that I can give and that is the one that you suggest, that the machine was 'stalled'. **1932** *Jrnl. R. Aeronaut. Soc.* XXXVI. 312 Two sensations are characteristic of stalled flying: first of all, a very noticeable increase in the rate of descent, and secondly the reversed effect of elevator control on the inclination of the gliding path. **1966** *McGraw-Hill Encycl. Sci. & Technol.* XIII. 228/2 For some wings, if the root section is placed at an angle near stall, the tip sections will probably be stalled. **1969** W. THOMSON *Thrust for Flight* 8 If the angle of attack is made too large.., flow becomes turbulent and the blade is said to be stalled.

c. Of a vehicle or engine: stopped through having stalled.

1966 B. H. DEAL *Fancy's Knell* (1967) x. 153 A man with a stalled pickup stood futilely beside it in the middle of the street. **1977** 'D. RUTHERFORD' *Return Load* i. 13 Sally restarted the stalled engine, engaged first gear and tentatively let in the clutch.

6. Glutted, satiated.

1740 DYCHE & PARDON *Dict.* (ed. 3), *Stalled*,.. also surfeited, or made to loath any particular food, by eating too much often of it. **1788** W. H. MARSHALL *Yorksh.* II. 355 *Stalled*; satiated with eating. **1798** ROSCOE tr. *Tansillo's Nurse* I. (1800) 33 Heedless what venom taints the stream she gives, So your stall'd offspring vegetates and lives.

†**'stallenge, 'stallange.** *Sc. Obs.* [Alteration of STALLAGE, after STALLENGER.] The fee, tax or toll paid by a STALLENGER = STALLAGE 1.

1509 *Reg. Mag. Sig. Scot.* (1882) 712/2 Et 3 merc[atas] ant[iquæ] ext[entæ] de Thanyfad.. cum *le Stallangis* edificiorum de dictis terris de Lokanis in via publica existen[tibus]. **1597** SKENE *De Verb. Sign.* (1641) s.v. *Stallangiatores*, And in the auld forme of customes, it is called, the stallenge of the mercat. **1605** *Reg. Mag. Sig. Scot.* (1890) 596/2 Unam croftam.. cum the stallange for brewing.

'stallenger. *Sc.* and *north. Obs.* exc. *Hist.* Forms: 4 **stallangear**, 5 **stallangar**, 7 **stallanger**; 5–7, 9 *Hist.* **stallenger**; 6 **stalinger**, 6, 9 *Hist.* **stallinger.** [Alteration of **stalager* (with inserted *n* as in *passenger*) a. OF. *estalagier*, f. *estalage* STALLAGE. (In Sc. Law-Latin *stallangiarius*, *stallangiator*.)] A stall-keeper, a petty trader who paid to the burgh a small sum for the privilege of setting up his stall in fair or market; also, a person not a freeman who paid a small sum to the corporation for the privilege of carrying on his business for one year. Also *attrib.*

a **1400** *Burgh Laws* xxxvii. (*Sc. Stat.* I), Of stallangearis and mersaris tol. Ilke stallangear sall mak fyne with þe borow greffis eftyr as þai may accord or ellis he sall geyf a halpeny ilke marcate day. **1433** *Seill of Caus*, Edin. 2d May, MS. (Jam.) Giue he beis sufficient of his craft, and not of power to mak his expenssis haistelie wpon his fredome, he sall bruik the priviledge of ane stallanger for ane yeir. **1523** *Morpeth Rec.* in *Archæol. Æliana* (1889) XIII. 214 And if it fortine anye stalinger to maike a fraye wthin the said boroughe, that then the officers aforesaid shall sett the same offenders in the Stox. **1597** SKENE *De Verb. Sign.* (1641) *Stallangiatores, à stallo*, Cremers, or Forraine merchandes, quha within Burgh, in the time of Faire or Mercat, payis certaine dewty for their stal or stand, in the quhilk place they sel their merchandice: For it is ordained, that ilk stallanger sal either agree with the Provest of the Burgh, in the best forme as he may; or else ilk mercat-day, sal pay to him ane halfe-pennie. **1857** *Gentl. Mag.* I. 351/1 [Sunderland.] It appears.. that one of the duties of the 'Grassmen', who were generally two or three of the defunct body of freemen and stallingers, was anciently to look after the hedges.

attrib. **1478–9** *Extracts Burgh Rec. Edin.* (1869) I. 36 Ilk stallenger puir body that occupeis the fredome of the towne.. and all stallangers that may be burges. **1481** *Ibid.* 40 Stallangars. **1598** *Aberd. Reg.* (Jam.) To pound all vnfremen for thair stallinger sylver.

staller^{1} ('stɔːlə(r)). *Hist.* [ad. late OE. *stallere*, **steallere* (in genit. contracted *stealres*, *steallres*), prob. f. *steall* STALL *sb.*^{1}, in imitation of L. *stabulārius*. Cf. ON. *stallari*, the title of a Norwegian court officer from the 10th c.] The title of a high officer in the reign of Edward the Confessor, equivalent to CONSTABLE 1.

a **1100** *O.E. Chron.* an 1047 (MS. D.) Her man utlagode Osgod stallere. **11..** *Charter* in Kemble *Cod. Dipl.* IV. 291 On Esgeres stealres, and on Raulfes steallres.. ȝewitnesse on Lincolne. *c* **1200** in Michel *Chron. Anglo-Norm.* II. 234 Esegarus regie procurator aule, qui et anglice dictus stallere, i.e. regni vexillifer. **1610** HOLLAND *Camden's Brit.* I. 439 Wee reade in the private historie of the place, The Kings Staller, that is, Standard Bearer.. first founded it. **1875** STUBBS *Const. Hist.* xi. (1897) I. 383 The constable.. succeeded to the duties of the Anglo-Saxon staller.

¶ Used vaguely for: Officer.

1638 H. SHIRLEY *Martyr'd Souldier* II. iii, Sit downe by me your Officiall: Or to come nearer to the efficacy of the word, Your undermost Iaylor, or staller; The word is Lordly and significant.

Hence **'stallership**, the office of a 'staller'.

1868 FREEMAN *Norm. Conq.* (1876) II. App. 684 A mere lad would hardly have been invested with a stallership.

staller^{2} ('stɔːlə(r)). *slang.* [f. STALL *v.*^{2} + -ER^{1}.]

1. ***staller (up)***: one who 'stalls up' or acts as confederate to a pickpocket (see STALL *v.*^{2} 1).

1812 J. H. VAUX *Flash Dict.*, s.v. *Stall*, The stallers up are gratified with such part of the gains acquired as the liberality of the knuckling gentlemen may prompt them to bestow. **1977** *New Society* 7 July 6/2 At first he was a staller. 'You get a woman trying to get on a train, someone goes in front of her, stalls her for ten to 15 seconds, and she's forgot about her bag.'

2. One who stalls or prevaricates; a person who gains time by obstructionism.

1937 PARTRIDGE *Dict. Slang* 823/1 *Staller*, a person constantly, or very good at, making excuses or playing for time. **1977** H. GREENE *FSO-1* ix. 76 You are.. one of the world's most transparent stallers... We are convened to talk about Larry. **1981** 'W. HAGGARD' *Money Men* vii. 74 He was an experienced staller. Postponing action was called good judgment.

†**'staller**^{3}. *Obs.* [f. STALL *sb.*^{4} + -ER^{1}.] = STALL *sb.*^{4}

1713 J. WARDER *True Amazons* iii. (1742) 44 In the Staller are left old sufficient Warriors to train up and discipline the young Amazons. *Ibid.* xiv. 135 You had better chuse a Staller of two Years old, than a light Swarm.

staller: see STALLAR.

'stall-fed, *a.* Also 6 **staulfed, stalfed,** (7 **stale feed**). [f. STALL *sb.*^{1} + FED *a.*] Of an animal to be fattened: Kept and fed in a stall.

1554 J. BRADFORD *Lett.* in Coverdale *Lett. Martyrs* (1564) 326 If you were for the Faire, you shoulde bee staulfed and wante no weale. **1557** TUSSER *100 Points Husb.* xxxiii, For Easter, at Martilmas hange vp a biefe: for pease fed and stall fed, play pickpurse the thiefe. **1615** CHAPMAN *Odyss.* XIV. 161 One beast, (the most fat, and best Of all the Stall-fed). **1688** HOLME *Armoury* II. 173/2 We call a fat Ox, a stale feed Ox. **1777** *Mass. Statute* 25 Jan., Stall-fed beef, well fatted, at fourpence a pound. **1890** *Farmer's Gaz.* 4 Jan. 1/1 Stall-fed cattle will now be on full keep.

b. *transf.* Of a person.

1589 GREENE *Masqverado* Wks. (Grosart) V. 243 Monkes, Friers,.. stall-fed with ease, and gluttony. **1626** B. JONSON *Staple of News* I. vi, You shall haue stall-fed Doctors, cram'd Diuines Make loue to her. **1635** BRERETON *Trav.* (1844) 51 We saw a man.. so stall-fed as that his legs were not able to support and carry his body. **1895** W. JAMES in *Will to believe*, etc. (1904) 43 Times.. when stall-fed officials of an established church could prove by the valves in the heart [etc.].

stall-feed, *v.* [f. STALL *sb.*^{1} + FEED *v.*]

1. *trans.* To feed (an animal) in a stall.

1763 MILLS *Pract. Husb.* III. 173 [The crop] will be sufficient to stall-feed four bullocks during the three winter months. **1861** WYNTER *Soc. Bees* 143 We stall-feed milch cows in upper stories in London houses.

2. Of an animal: To undergo feeding or fattening in a stall.

1766 *Complete Farmer* s.v. *Turnep* 7 Q 2/2, I have now two bullocks which are stall-feeding upon turnips.

Hence **stall-feeding** *vbl. sb.*

1805 R. W. DICKSON *Pract. Agric.* II. 1045 This.. is.. less advantageous in the point of fattening than that of wholly confining them to the stalls, or what is usually termed stall-feeding. **1865** TROLLOPE *Belton Est.* iv, The building of a shed for winter stall-feeding.

'stall-in. *U.S.* [f. STALL *v.*^{1} 11 c + -IN^{3}.] A form of protest in which participants block the roads with immobilized vehicles.

1964 [see *lie-in* s.v. LIE *sb.*^{2} 6]. **1977** *Time* 14 Nov. 21/3 They need hardly fear the kind of traffic stall-ins staged by New York City residents to protest the arrival of the Concorde.

stalling ('stɔːlɪŋ), *vbl. sb.*^{1} [f. STALL *v.*^{1} + -ING^{1}.]

†**1.** Induction into a stall; installation. *Obs.*

1387 TREVISA *Higden* (Rolls) VIII. 183 Whan he was i-stalled at Lyncoln by þe archedecon, me axede an hors oþer a kow for his stallynge. *c* **1440** *Alphabet of Tales* 60 This archedekyn was made bisshopp and made a grete feste at his stallyng. *c* **1535** in Gutch *Coll. Cur.* (1781) I. 207 Unto the first stalling of the Dean and Canons in the said College.

†**2.** The action of agreeing for the payment of a debt by instalments, or of fixing dates for payment; also, an instance of this. (See STALL *v.*^{1} 4.) *Obs.*

1525 *St. Papers Hen. VIII*, VI. 462 They be also sufficiently instructed, howe they shal ordre themself for stalling of days for part of the money due by the Emperour. **1563** *Repert. City Lond.* XV. f. 258 in *Eng. Hist. Rev.* (1900) July 451 My lord mayor &.. justices.. shall.. meete here for the stallynge & ratynge of the wages of artyficers & laborers according to the Acte. *a* **1631** DONNE *Serm.* Wks. 1839 V. 522 Yea it is not here only that they shall perish, in the future; that were a reprieve; it were a stalling of a debt. *c* **1640** J. SMYTH *Lives Berkeleys* (1883) I. 130 Of an other dett.. [he] could obtayne noe more, then the stallenge thereof to be payd by twenty marks a yeare.

3. The action or process of furnishing (a place) with stalls as seats; also concr., stall-work.

c **1515** in Willis & Clark *Cambridge* (1886) I. 482 The said werk is.. accomplished, except the pavyng, and stallyng and glasyng of the same. **1519** in *Fabric Rolls York Minster* (Surtees) 272 Our wher stallyng is defectiff in gronsoll. Our wher pavyng is fawty in stone.

4. Stall-accommodation (of or for an animal).

1535 COVERDALE *Isa.* lxv. 10 Saron shalbe a shepefolde, and the valley of Achor shal geue stallinge for the catell of my people, that feare me. **1600** SHAKS. *A.Y.L.* I. i. 11 Call you that keeping for a gentleman of my birth, that differs not from the stalling of an Oxe? **1859** TENNYSON *Geraint & Enid* 238 But hire us some fair chamber for the night, And stalling for the horses.

5. The event of coming to an unintended halt or stalling (STALL *v.*^{1} 9). In *Aeronaut.* freq. *attrib.*, as ***stalling point, speed.***

1808 M. L. WEEMS *Let.* 17 May in E. E. F. Skeel *M. L. Weems* (1929) II. 377 Stalling of Waggons, sweeping away of Stages, drowning of Horses &c. &c. are dreadful. **1888** J. KIRKLAND *McVeys* 220 The occurrence—the 'stalling' of a wagon and team, was common enough in those early days. **1912** O. WRIGHT in M. McFarland *Papers Wilbur & Orville Wright* (1953) II. 1052 The liability of the machine to dive in case of 'stalling' is present in every one. **1916** H. BARBER *Aeroplane Speaks* 89 If it [*sc.* the engine] is throttled down, then the course must be one of a steeper angle than B, or there will be danger of stalling. **1917** 'CONTACT' *Airman's Outings* iv. 100 At times he varied this method by lifting the machine almost to stalling point, letting her down again, and repeating the process. **1928** C. F. S. GAMBLE *North Sea Air Station* v. 84 An inherently stable machine was.. found to be of little value for aerial fighting, as the possession of a high degree of manœuvrability, combined with a low 'stalling' speed, are some of the essentials for this work. **1932** H. H. PRICE *Perception* vi. 149 A short-eared owl flying at just above stalling-point. **1952** L. NATHAN *Car Driving in Two Weeks* iii. 21 To prevent stalling of engine the following procedure is invaluable. **1966** D. FRANCIS *Flying Finish* 129 We touched down.. at a fraction above stalling speed. **1976** 'A. HALL' *Kobra Manifesto* i. 15 He reached the stalling-point and dropped tail first and bounced and tilted and.. then bucked forward.

6. *Surfing.* (See quots.)

1962 T. MASTERS *Surfing made Easy* 65 *Stalling a board*, stepping or leaning back on a board to slow it down. **1968** W. WARWICK *Surfriding in N.Z.* 10/2 Step back on your board and put it out of trim, this will slow your board down... This manoeuvre is called stalling.

stalling ('stɔːlɪŋ), *vbl. sb.*^{2} [f. STALL *v.*^{2} + -ING^{1}.]

1. The action of helping a pickpocket by distracting or jostling his victim. *Criminals' slang.*

1908 J. M. SULLIVAN *Criminal Slang* 24 *Stalling for a dip*, arranging [a pickpocket's] victims so that they can be successfully robbed. **1926** *Flynn's* 16 Jan. 638/1 The gay cat and spotters got 'em on location; then it was a case of palin', stick up, stallin' or rollin' in any way you please.

2. Prevaricating, temporizing; the action of being evasive or devious.

1927 *Vanity Fair* XXIX. 132/4 'The run-around' is stalling or failing to keep a promise. **1952** *Landfall* Sept. 227 Walk into a Saturday-afternoon bar and hear the noise; do you get the impression of *stalling*?

†**'stalling-ken.** *Thieves' cant. Obs.* Also 6 **stawlinge-, staulinge-,** 7 **stawling-, stuling-.** [f. *stalling*, vbl. sb. f. STALL *v.*^{2} + KEN *sb.*] (See quots.)

1567 HARMAN *Caveat* 32 Whych [pigs or poultry] they brynge to their stawlinge kens, which is their typplyng houses. *Ibid.* 83 A staulinge ken, a house that wyll receaue stolen ware. **1621** B. JONSON *Masque Gypsies* (1640) 48 Till.. he be able to beate it on the hoofe to the bene bouse, or the stauling Ken. **1624** BP. MOUNTAGU *Gagg* Pref. 17 They and their Trulls may meet at their stawling kenns with such clapper dogeons as your selfe. **1676** COLES *Dict.*, *Stalling-ken*, a brokers, or any house that receives stolen goods.

a 1700 B. E. *Dict. Cant. Crew, Stalling-ken. Ibid., Stuling-ken.* Also in later Dicts.

stallion ('stæljən). Forms: α. 4 **stalun**, 4–5 **staloun**, 4–6 **stalon**, (5 **stalan**, **stolon**, 6 *erron.* **stalume**), 6 **stallon(e**; β. 6 **stal(l)ant**, **stalland(e**, **staulande**, **stalaunt**; γ. (5 **stalyone**), 6–7 **stalion**, (7 **stallian**, **stallyon**), 6– **stallion**. [a. OF. *estalon* (mod.F. *étalon*), whence Anglo-L. *stalōnus*; corresp. to It. *stallone*:—popular L. **stallōnem*, f. Teut. **stallo-* stable, STALL *sb.*[1] The β forms appear to be due to confusion of the ending with the ppl. suffix -ANT (cf. *gallande, gallante* GALLON); the influence which produced the γ forms is obscure.]

1. a. A male horse not castrated, an entire horse, esp. one kept for the purpose of serving mares. Also *fig.*

α. 1388 WYCLIF *Eccl.* xxxiii. 6 An hors a staloun, so and a frend a scornere, neiȝeth vundur ech sittynge aboue. *Ibid.* Jer. v. 8 Thei be maad horsis, and stalouns, louyeris to wymmen. 1390 GOWER *Conf.* III. 280 Bot as a cock among the Hennes, Or as a Stalon in the Fennes, Which goth amonges al the Stod. *c* 1440 *Pallad. on Husb.* IV. 799 Fed stalons faat goth now to gentyl maris. *Ibid.* 802 Let euery stolon haue as he is abul. 14.. *Nom.* in Wr.-Wülcker 697/40 *Hic emissarius*, a stalan. 1530 PALSGR. 275/1 Stalume horse, *haras.* 1537 DARCY in *Lett. Suppress. Monasteries* (Camden) 158 For ssurly the breed of Gervayes ffor horses was the tryed breed in the northe, the stallones, and mares well ssoortyd.

β. 1519 HORMAN *Vulg.* 176, I wyll not sylle my stalant. 1530 PALSGR. 275/1 Stallant a horse, *haras.* 1541 *Act 33 Hen. VIII*, c. 5 Nobles..hauing parkes, should kepe mares, and finde staulandes for breed and encrease of horses. 1592 TIMME *Ten Eng. Lepers* I 3, In the desire of uncleane lust, they are become like unto stallandes.

γ. *c* 1440 *Promp. Parv.* 472/1 Stalyone, hors, *emissarius.* 1577 GOOGE *Heresbach's Husb.* III. (1586) 126 The stallion that you meane to haue for your race of moiles, must be as faire as you can get. 1607 TOPSELL *Four-f. Beasts* 297 The King of Babilon..had eight hundreth Stalions, which were admitted to couer sixe thousand Mares. 1697 DRYDEN *Virg. Georg.* III. 118 The Colt that for a Stallion is design'd, By sure Presages shows his generous Kind. 1774 GOLDSM. *Nat. Hist.* (1776) II. 352 March,..at which time the mares are given to the stallion. 1842 LONGF. *Slave's Dream* iv, At each leap he could feel his scabbard of steel Smiting his stallion's flank. 1861 *Times* 11 July, The first and highest legitimate vocation of a thorough-bred stallion is as a sire. 1924 R. CAMPBELL *Flaming Terrapin* ii. 27 He would hear the whinnying stallions of the wind career. 1940 L. MACNEICE *Last Ditch* 15 The stallions of the soul—Eager to take the fences That fence about my soul.

b. *transf.* Applied to a male dog or sheep with reference to its use for breeding.

1802 DANIEL *Rur. Sports* II. 490 Dash [a dog]..had the misfortune to break his leg, and was sent to Col. T. who.. considered him in that state a great acquisition as a stallion to breed from. 1842 [see *stallion-breeder* in 5].

c. As the name of a plant (see quot.).

1878 BRITTEN & HOLLAND *Plant-n.*, Stallions (Yks. W. Riding), or Stallions and Mares. Yks. (Wensleydale). *Arum maculatum*, L.

2. Applied to a person. †**a.** A begetter. *Obs.*

c 1305 *Land Cokaygne* 167 Þe monke þat wol be stalun gode..He schal hab wiþute danger .xii. wiues euche ȝere. 1621 BURTON *Anat. Mel.* I. ii. I. vi. 85 When no choice is had, but still the eldest must marry, as so many stallions of the Race.

b. A man of lascivious life; in 17th and 18th-c., a woman's hired paramour. Now only in former sense.

1553 tr. *Gardiner's De Vera Obed.* To Rdr. Bj, [They] thinke it more mete for wanton wagtaile weston to be turned out for a stalaunt,..than to vse ani kinde of communication among worthi ladies. 1623 MASSINGER *Dk. Milan* IV. ii, He ..that at euerie stage keeps liuerie Mistresses, The stallion of the State! 1676 SHADWELL *Virtuoso* IV, What are you, her Stallion, and her Bravo too? 1680 R. MANSELL *Narr. Popish Plot* 99 Her Mistress had got an ill Repute, by keeping Willoughby for her Stallion. 1714 T. LUCAS *Mem. Gamesters* (ed. 2) 193 A Marchioness in Naples..kept him as her Stallion. 1755 *Monitor* I. No. 15. 129 It was a complaint in our wars with Holland, that our losses were owing to the stallions and bastards of lewd women, who had interest at court. 1796 *Grose's Dict. Vulgar T.* (ed. 3), *Stallion*, a man kept by an old lady for secret services. 1933 D. PARKER *After Such Pleasures* 138 Go answer it, you damned—you damned *stallion*! 1978 L. MEYNELL *Papersnake* v. 70 Barton amused himself by keeping a tally of Lasting's women; 'that insatiable stallion' he called him.

†**3. a.** A courtesan. *Obs.*

[Perh. another word: cf. F. *estalon* (Cotgr.) a decoy; also STALE *sb.*[3] 4.]

1575 LANEHAM *Let.* (1871) 24 Then folloed the worshipfull Bride...But a stale stallion..God wot, and an il smelling, waz she. 1584 B. R. tr. *Herodotus* II. 102 b, Willing her..to abandon chastity for the time, making hirselfe a common stalant for all that would come. *Ibid.* 107. 1604 SHAKS. *Ham.* II. ii. 616 (2nd Qo.) That I..Must like a whore vnpacke my hart with words, And fall a cursing like a very drabbe; a stallyon, fie vppont, foh. [1603, 1st Qo. *reads* a scalion. *Ff. read* scullion.] 1635 *Life Long Meg of Westminster* iii. (1816) 6 Marry Master Vicar, quoth Meg, just fiue shillings and three pence. Fiue shillings and three pence, quoth he; why I tell thee foule Stallion, I owe but three shillings and a penny. *a* 1670 HACKET *Cent. Serm.* (1675) 600 Doth the Adulterer look for impunity that he walks to his stallion by twilight?

b. Among U.S. Blacks, a tall, good-looking girl or woman. *colloq.*

1970 C. MAJOR *Dict. Afro-Amer. Slang* 108 *Stallion*, a good-looking black woman. 1975 R. H. RIMMER *Premar Experiments* (1976) i. 148, I love you Samantha Brown. In black ghetto language, you're a lovely stallion.

4. ? A stand for showing goods.

[Possibly a distinct word, connected with STALL *sb.*[1] or OF. *estaler* to display. But cf. HORSE *sb.* 7.]

1752 *Gentl. Mag.* XXII. 348 Plate. The Porcelain Manufactory at Worcester. 10. (*b*). The eight windows in two large chambers, in which the ware is placed on stallions.

5. *attrib.* and *Comb.*, chiefly appositive, as ***stallion ass, horse, hound***, †***pen*** (fig.), ***steed***; objective, as ***stallion-breeder***; similative, as ***stallion-like*** adv.; †**stallion teeth**, the eye-teeth of a horse.

1607 TOPSELL *Four-f. Beasts* 558 It is most commodious and necessary to gett such a *Stalion Asse to the procreation of Mules. 1842 BISCHOFF *Woollen Manuf.* (1862) II. 385 There are a great many tup or *stallion-breeders too ready to omit this essential ceremony of inspection. 1889 T. T. STODDART *Angling Songs* 272 A merry fish on a *stallion hair 'Tis a pleasant thing to lead On May-days. 1607 TOPSELL *Four-f. Beasts* 297 Therefore it behooueth that a *Stalion Horsse be not vnder three yeares old when he coucreth a Mare. 1826 J. COOK *Fox-hunting* 10 A word now on the subject of *Stallion-hounds. 1904 J. A. THOMSON *Eighty Years Remin.* II. 134 A hound show took place at Haddington in July, 1876. In the class for..stallion hounds, Fife were first with 'Woodman'. 1605 SYLVESTER *Du Bartas* II. iii. I. *Vocation* 1155 Those..*Stallion-like, after their beauties neigh'd. 1737 M. GREEN *Spleen* 347 Nor, hir'd to praise with *stallion pen, Serve the ear-lechery of men. 1597 BP. HALL *Sat.* IV. i. 112 Some snout-fayre stripling..Whom staked vp like to some *stallion-steed They keepe with Egs and Oysters for the breed. 1607 TOPSELL *Four-f. Beasts* 285 It is a hard thing for a Horsse to haue a good mouth, except his *stallion teeth bee pulled out, for when he is chafed or heated, he cannot be helde backe by his rider.

† '**stallionize**, *v. Obs. rare.* [f. STALLION + -IZE.] *to stallionize it*, to act the stallion.

1694 MOTTEUX *Rabelais* v. viii. 38 Don't you [horses] Stallionize it sometimes here among your metal'd Fillies?

stallite ('stɔːlaɪt). [f. STALL *sb.*[1] + -ITE.] One who occupies a theatre-stall.

1887 *Sat. Rev.* 18 June 866/2 A rush from the dress-circle down these stairs would meet the rush of stallites.

†**stall net.** *Obs.* In 3 **stalnett**, 6 **stalnette**, 7 **stale-net**, **stall nett**. [Prob. f. STALL *sb.*[1]; cf. STALL-BOAT.] A stationary net laid across a river, esp. for sprat-fishing.

1246 *Charter Roll 31 Hen. III.* m. 13 in *Cal.* (1903) 310 [To fish in] hetun, dreynett, flodnett et stalnett. 1552 HULOET, Stalnette, *semiplagium.* 1614 T. GENTLEMAN *England's Way* 19 These men..do set forth stale-boates, amongst the sands in the Theames mouth, for to take sprats, with great stale-nets, with a great poake. *a* 1642 SIR W. MONSON *Naval Tracts* VI. (1704) 524/2 They are..entrapped by the Stale Nets, that use to take the Sprats. 1688 HOLME *Armoury* III. xxii. (Roxb.) 276/2 The Fourth..is termed a Stall Nett; these are netts of great length and breadth which are generally layd cross a River.

†**stallon.** *Obs. rare*[−1]. [? Misspelling of STOLON.] A slip, scion.

In the alleged earlier example from Palladius given in some Dicts. for *stalon* read *scalon* SCALLION.

1587 HARRISON *England* II. xix. [xx.] 210/2 in *Holinshed*, Such a one [*i.e.* rose] was to be seene in Antwarpe 1585..and I know who might have had a slip or stallon thereof, if he would haue ventured ten pounds.

stalloy (stə'lɔɪ). [App. arbitrarily f. ST(EEL) + ALLOY.] (See quots.)

1906 *Daily Chron.* 8 Dec. 3/5 The remarkable new steel alloy called 'stalloy'. 1911 J. A. FLEMING in *Encycl. Brit.* XXVII. 173/2 [The iron] must possess extremely small hysteresis loss, and various trade names, such as 'stalloy', 'lohys', are in use to describe certain brands.

stallworthe, var. form of STALWORTH *a.*

†**stalment.** *Obs.* Also **stallment.** [a. AF. *estallement* (Anglo-L. *stallamentum*), f. *estaller* STALL *v.*[1] (sense 4): see -MENT. Cf. ESTALLMENT.] The action of fixing terms of payment by instalments. Also, an instalment.

1484 in *Lett. Rich. III & Hen. VII* (Rolls) I. 81 No persone accomptable, ne other persone being in dette to the king, [shall] have any respet, stalment, or favor in the said court. 1491 in Studer *Oak Bk. S'hampton* (1910) I. 153 *marg.*, Townes monye in the Coffers and no stallmentt butt by comon Assentte. 1550 *Patent Roll 4 Edw. VI*, v. membr. 34 [Sir Philip Hobbye and Sir Thomas Speake stand bound in the sum of 200 mks. for surety of payment of 100l. part of 1100l. due] upon the stalment of the debts of the said Sir Phillip, to be paid [at Michaelmas]. 1657 HOWELL *Londinop.* 371 He (the Kings Remembrancer) taketh the stallment of Debts, and entreth them. 1721 STRYPE *Eccl. Mem.* II. I. xxxiii. 277 All which the King now forgave him..acquitting ..him, his heirs..and divers others standing bound with him for 1100l. due to the King for stalment of his debts.

b. *fig.* Apportionment.

1581 W. I. in *Rich's Farew. Milit. Profession* C ij b, Who seekes by Ladie fame to reape renoune, Must aske consent of worthie vertues grace: To her belonges the staulement of the croune.

stalon, obs. form of STALLION.

†**stalp.** *Sc. Obs.*[−1]. [Cf. WFris. *stap* trap, and STAMP *sb.*[5]] ? Some kind of trap.

1505 *Acc. Ld. High Treas. Scot.* III. 171 Item, for bigging of the deir fald in Faukland, xviij s. Item, for making of ane stalp and the irn graith to the samyn,..to sla foxes in the park of Faukland, vj s. vj d.

stalth(e, obs. forms of STEALTH.

† '**staltic**, *a. Obs. rare*[−1]. [ad. late L. *staltic-us* (Du Cange), a. Gr. σταλτικός capable of contracting, f. σταλ-, στέλλειν in sense to bring together, gather up, make to shrink.] Styptic.

1748 tr. *Vegetius' Distempers Horses* 166 The Wounds, may be thoroughly cured with Staltick Medicines.

stalume, obs. erron. form of STALLION.

stalwart ('stɔːlwət, 'stælwət), *a.* Now *literary.* Forms: 4 **stalouart**, **-wart**, (**stawlouart**), **stalawrt**, 4–5 **stallwart**, 5 **stal(l)uart**, **stalwert**, 4–6, 9 **stalwart**. [A 16th c. Sc. form of STALWORTH *a.*, brought into Eng. use by Scott.]

A. *adj.*

1. Of persons (†and animals): Strongly and stoutly built, sturdy, robust.

c 1450 HOLLAND *Howlat* 697 The Stork, stallwart and styth. *c* 1470 *Gol. & Gaw.* 555 On stedis stalwart and strang. 1825 BROCKETT *N.C. Gloss.*, *Stalwart*, stout, strong, hale. 1837 LOCKHART *Scott* IV. vi. 189 A tall and stalwart bag-piper. 1856 MISS MULOCK *J. Halifax* i. 1 What would I not have given to have been so stalwart and so tall.

2. Of inanimate things: Firmly made or established, strong. Now *rare.*

1375 BARBOUR *Bruce* III. 732 A rycht stalwart castell. *Ibid.* XIII. 14 With wapnys stalwart of steill Thai dang on thame with all thar mycht. *c* 1470 HENRY *Wallace* v. 1136 Tre wark thai brynt..Wallis brak doun that stalwart war off stanys. 1508 DUNBAR *Tua maritt wemen* 384 He..maid a stalwart staff to strik him selfe doune.

1858 HAWTHORNE *Fr. & It. Jrnls.* II. 80 Its old walls, however, are stalwart enough to outlast another set of frescos.

3. Of persons, their attributes, etc.: Resolute, unbending, determined. Chiefly *modern.*

c 1375 *Sc. Leg. Saints* l. (*Katherine*) 695 Bad hir be of stawlouart will.

1840 BARHAM *Ingol. Leg.*, *Black Mousquetaire*, The form whose stalwart pride But yester-morn was by his side. 1903 MORLEY *Gladstone* I. 69 The duke made his stalwart declaration in the House of Lords against all parliamentary reform. 1905 E. CLODD *Animism* §17. 99 The stalwart opponents of superstition refused his request.

†**b.** Of a fight: Stoutly contested, severe. *Obs.*

1375 BARBOUR *Bruce* I. 68 The Machabeys, That..Faucht into mony stallwart stour, For to delyvir thair countre. *c* 1420 WYNTOUN *Cron.* VIII. xxxiii. 5836 He fande þar hard [*v.r.* stalwart] barganynge. 1513 DOUGLAS *Æneis* X. v. 164 The tyme of batale reddy is at hand, Quhar strenth beis schawyn in stalwart stowr to stand.

4. Valiant in fight, brave, courageous.

c 1375 *Sc. Leg. Saints* xxix. (*Placidas*) 250 For-þi mon þu, as stalawrt knycht, to resist hym mak þe bown. *c* 1470 *Gol. & Gaw.* 353 Wondir staluart and strang, to striue in ane stour. ? *a* 1550 *Freiris Berwik* 507 in *Dunbar's Poems* II. 302 Sumthing effrayit, thocht stalwart was his hart.

1810 SCOTT *Lady of L.* I. xxviii, Whose stalwart arm might brook to wield A blade like this in battle-field. 1859 TENNYSON *Vivien* 332 But afterwards He made a stalwart knight.

†**5.** Of a storm, weather: Violent, tempestuous.

1528 LYNDESAY *Dreme* 80 With stalwart stormes hir sweitnes was suprisit. 1827 TENNANT *Papistry Storm'd* vi. 187 Siccan stalwart weather.

6. *Comb.*

1848 B. D. WALSH *Aristoph.*, *Knts.* IV. i, The stalwart-fathered goddess. 1871 PALGRAVE *Lyr. Poems* 51 Red-faced and stalwart-fashioned Point-blank they came on their foes.

B. *sb.*

1. A strong and valiant man.

Now only as nonce-use, after 2.

c 1470 *Gol. & Gaw.* 642 Thair wes na staluart vnstonait, so sterne wes the stound. *Ibid.* 767 Thair with the stalwartis in stour can stotin and stynt. 1891 *Academy* 3 Jan. 7/2 Emin's 'stalwarts'..proving to be for the most part brutal ruffians and abject cravens in the presence of danger.

2. A sturdy uncompromising partisan; esp. as a political designation.

In U.S. politics 1877 and subsequently, an extremist of the Republican party.

1881 *Nation* (N.Y.) XXXII. 415 The epithet 'Stalwart' as applied to a class of politicians was first used by Mr. Blaine in 1877 to designate those Republicans who were unwilling to give up hostility and distrust of the South as a political motive. 1890 *Times* 11 July 9/3 The 'stalwarts' of the Radical party, supported the resolution.

attrib. 1888 BRYCE *Amer. Commw.* II. xlvi. II. 203 The 'Stalwart' and 'Half-breed' sections of the Republican party. 1907 *National Church* 15 Oct. 262/1 The 'stalwart' section of militant Dissent.

b. One who is disposed to take an uncompromising position with regard to political, religious, and social questions in general; a 'doctrinaire'. *rare.*

1899 PATTEN *Developm. Engl. Thought* i. 27, I shall call them stalwarts from their love of doctrines, dogmas, and creeds, and from their inclination to subordinate policy to principle. *Ibid.* 28 Stalwarts are always impressed by ideals that are clear and simple, by principles that are bold and definite, by creeds that are rigid and exact, and by platforms that are plain and unmistakable.

stalwartism ('stɔːlwətɪz(ə)m). [f. STALWART + -ISM.] The principles or policy of the 'stalwarts'; the disposition characteristic of a 'stalwart' (see STALWART *sb.* 2, 2 b).

1879 *Nation* (N.Y.) 27 Nov. 355 (Cent.) Stalwartism. 1899 PATTEN *Developm. Engl. Thought* i. 29 In the eighteenth century, stalwartism became a political force through the democratic ideals which developed in harmony with frugal ideas.

stalwartize ('stɔːlwərtaɪz), *v. nonce-word.* [f. STALWART + -IZE.] *trans.* To turn (a political party) into 'stalwarts' (see STALWART *sb.* 2).

1882 *N.Y. Tribune* 12 Apr., An attempt is being made.. to stalwartize the Republican party,.. to convert its majority against its will from Garfield to Stalwart Republicanism.

'stalwartly, *adv.* Now *rare.* [f. STALWART *a.* + -LY².] In a stalwart manner, strongly, bravely.

1375 BARBOUR *Bruce* II. 66 [The king] swour In Ire, full stalwartly, That he suld drawyn and hangit be. *c* **1400** *Destr. Troy* 6873 þen gird in þe grekys with a grete wyll, Restoret þe stithe fight stalwertly þen. *c* **1475** *Rauf Coilȝear* 32 His steid aganis the storme staluartlie straid. **1887** in *Cassell's Encycl. Dict.*; and in later Dicts.

stalwartness ('stɔːlwətnɪs). *rare.* [f. STALWART *a.* + -NESS.] The quality or condition of being stalwart; robustness, strength.

1859 GEO. ELIOT *Adam Bede* I. i, In his tall stalwartness Adam Bede was a Saxon. **1888** *Athenæum* 14 Jan. 57/1 The glossy, well-filled skin of the cart-horse, his stalwartness and vigour.

'stalworth. *a.* and *sb. Obs.* exc. *arch.* Forms: *α.* 1 **stǽlwierðe, -wyrðe,** 2 **stele-,** 3 **stealewurðe;** 3 **stalwarþe,** 5– **warth;** 3 **stalewurðe;** 3–4 **stalwrthe;** 3–5 **stalworþe,** 4–6 **-worthe,** (5 **staloworth**), 6 **stalwoorth;** 4–5 **stallworthe, stalwurþe, -wurthe,** (5 **stalwort**), 4–7, 9 *arch.* **stalworth.** *β.* 3–5 **stalword(e.** *γ.* 3–5 **stalwarde,** 3 **stalewarde,** 4, 6, 8 *Sc.* **stalward.** (See also STALWART *a.*) *δ.* 3 **staðelwurðe.** [OE. *stǽlwierðe*, f. *stǽl* place + *wierðe* WORTH *a.*

The length of the vowel in the first syllable seems to be authenticated by some of the early ME. forms; the shortening of *ǽ* to *ă* in the first element of a compound is normal. The OE. *stǽl* (the quantity of which is certain from the three occurrences in poetry) appears not to be immediately connected with the synonymous *stæl* with short vowel (dat. *stale*); according to some scholars it represents a contraction of OTeut. **staþl-* or **stadl-*, the relation of OE. *stǽl* to *staðol* foundation (see STADDLE *sb.*) being considered parallel with that of *mǽl* speech to the synonymous *mæðel*. The 13th c. form *staðelwurðe*, occurring only once (see 3 δ) strongly confirms this view.

The early ME. forms with medial *e*, *stele-*, *steale-*, *stalewurðe* are difficult to account for.]

A. *adj.*

†**1.** (OE.) Of things: Serviceable. *Obs.*

O.E. Chron. an. 896, þa [scipu] þe þær stælwyrðe wæron binnan Lunden byriᵹ [hie] ᵹebrohton. *c* **897** ÆLFRED *Gregory's Past C.* xvii. (1871) 115 Se ðe ᵹeornlice conn onᵹietan ðæt he of him gadriᵹe ðat him stælwierðe sie [L. *quod adjuvat*]. *a* **1000** *Ælfred's Blooms* in Cockayne *Shrine* (1864) 192 He ᵹyfð.. gooda ᵹifa on þissa wurlda þeah hi eca ne sien hi beoð þeah stælwyrða þa hwile þe we on þisse wurlde beoð.

2. Of persons, and animals: Strongly and stoutly built, sturdy, robust.

α. c **1175** *Lamb. Hom.* 25 He.. þenchet ic em hal and fere and strong and stelewurðe ᵹet ic mei longe libben and alle mine sunne timliche ibeten. *c* **1350** *Will. Palerne* 1950 Alle on stalworth stedes stoutliche i-horsed. **13..** *Gaw. & Gr. Knt.* 846, On stal-worth schonkez. **1387** TREVISA *Higden* (Rolls) I. 263 þerfore þey haueþ staleworþe children and stronge. **1494** FABYAN *Chron.* v. lxxii. (1811) 50 Maximian ..was stalworth and mighty of his handes. **1565** GOLDING *Ovid's Met.* I. (1593) 25 A staleworth stripling strong and stout. **1600** *Fairfax Tasso* VII. xxvii, His stalworth steed the champion stout bestroad.

1847 LONGF. *Evang.* I. i. 43 Stalworth and stately in form was the man of seventy winters. **1864** LE FANU *Uncle Silas* I. xv. 168 The stalworth lady. **1890** D. C. MURRAY *John Vale* xxiv, We're a pretty stalworth set o' people.

β. **1375** BARBOUR *Bruce* XVIII. 310 Apon a stalward horss he raid.

3. Of persons, their actions, etc.: Brave, courageous, valiant, mighty.

α. a **1225** *Juliana* 44 þeo ilke þat beoð stalewurðe [*MS. Bodl.* stealewurðe]. *a* **1225** *Leg. Kath.* 702 A stalewurðe deð. *c* **1300** *Havelok* 25 He was þe stalworþeste man at nede, þat may riden on ani stede. **1303** R. BRUNNE *Handl. Synne* 9833 þat blessyng.. makeþ vs stalwurþe yn batayle whan þe fende wyl vs asayle. *c* **1400** *Rule St. Benet* (Verse) 276 For god makes þam so mekli of mayne And stalworth to stand him [þe deuel] a-gayne. *c* **1400** *Destr. Troy.* 365 Mony stalworth in stoure. **1577** HOLINSHED *Hist. Eng.* I. 286/1 Harolde aunswered, that they were not Priestes, but stalwoorth and hardie Souldiours. *a* **1650** *Turke & Gowin* 25 in *Percy Fol. MS.* (1867) I. 91 Giue thou be neuer soe stalworth of hand I shall bring thee to the ground.

1808 SCOTT *Marm.* I. v, He was a stalworth knight, and keen. **1853** ROCK *Ch. Fathers* I. ix. (1903) III. 251 England's most stalworth knights.

β. **1297** R. GLOUC. (Rolls) 3960 þe kniȝtes þe stalwordore & þe betere in hor dede. **1398** TREVISA *Barth. De P.R.* XV. lxxxvi. (1495) 522 The men..ben stalword men, stronge werryours and fyers. *a* **1400–50** *Wars Alex.* 3937 þa foule Backes, Als store & as stalword as þire sedill dowis.

γ. a **1225** *Ancren R.* 272 Hwon hit unstrencðeð, þet schulde beon monlich & stalewarde & kene ine treowe bileaue. **1297** R. GLOUC. (Rolls) 428 Vor godes loue stalwarde men armieþ ȝow vaste. **1375** BARBOUR *Bruce* XVI. 356 Till withstand Men that thame soucht vith stalvard hand. **1595** J. DAVIDSON in C. Rogers *Three Sc. Reform.* (1874) 104 John Knox that valyant Conqueror, That stood in many stalward stour. *c* **1750** D. GRAHAM *Hist. Rebell.* iii. Writ. 1883 I. 109 That stalward Duke.

δ. a **1225** *Ancr. R.* 272 (Cleop. MS.) Staðelwurðe [cf. *γ*].

†**4.** = STRONG in various applications. *Obs.*

α. a **1300** *Cursor M.* 17342 þai ledd ioseph.. To prisun in a stalworth hald. *a* **1340** HAMPOLE *Ps.* ii. 9 þis wand.. stalworth & lastand. **1340–70** *Alisaunder* 1230 þat stalworthe sted [Constantinople]. *c* **1400** tr. *Secreta Secret., Gov. Lordsh.* 68 Whanne a stomake ys hoot, stalworthe, and good.

γ. **1375** BARBOUR *Bruce* x. 491 Douglass the castell sesit all, At than wes closit vith stalward vall. *c* **1750** D. GRAHAM *Hist. Rebell.* ix. Writ. 1883 I. 158 Spey.. That rapid river and stalward stream.

†**B.** *sb.* A strong and valiant man. *Obs.*

13.. *Gaw. & Gr. Knt.* 1659 Wyth stille stollen countenance þat stalworth to plese. ? *a* **1500** *Chester Pl.* (Shaks. Soc.) II. 41 Suche a stalwarde before me never stood So stowte and stearne is he.

†**'stalworthhead.** *Obs.* In 3 **stalwardhede.** [f. STALWORTH *a.* + -HEAD.] Stalwartness, courage.

1297 R. GLOUC. (Rolls) 4337 þo hii to þe king come & ssewede hor stalwardhede. *Ibid.* 5548. *Ibid.* 5937.

†**'stalworthly,** *adv. Obs.* [+ -LY².]

1. Stoutly, strongly, etc.

c **1200** ORMIN 5520 The fihhtenn stallwurrliȝ Onnȝæn þe flæshess lusstess. *a* **1340** HAMPOLE *Ps.* xxvi. 12 With þe whilke i criyd till þe stalworthly. *a* **1400–50** *Wars Alex.* 1149 It was..sa strang & stalworthly wallid. *c* **1440** *York Myst.* xxx. 85 Scho may stakir in þe strete But scho stalworthely stande. **1508** DUNBAR *Tua maritt wemen* 485 Sum stalwardly steppis ben, with a stout curage.

¶**2.** ? Misused (through association with STALE *sb.*¹) for: Clandestinely, secretly.

The interpretation is not quite certain: the sense may be 'rigorously', 'resolutely' (in the second quot. designedly substituted for the 'secretly' of the older texts).

a **1300** *Cursor M.* 4310 Quen þou seis him busk to þe, þou do þe stallworthli to flei. *c* **1375** *Ibid.* 2517 (Fairf.) He dide to-gedder samyn his men.. and stalworþly [*v.rr.* Cott. dernlik; Gött. priuili] he made ham bide, til agayne þe euen-tide. *c* **1550** *Batt. Otterburn* vi. in Child *Ballads* III. 295/2, I rede we ryde to Newe Castell, So styll and stalworthlye.

'stalworthness. *Obs.* [f. STALWORTH *a.* + -NESS.] The quality of being 'stalworth'.

a **1340** HAMPOLE *Ps.* xvii. 40 Ay waxand in stalworthnes. **1382** WYCLIF *Jer.* xvi. 19 Lord, my strength and my stalwrthenesse. *c* **1425** *Eng. Conq. Irel.* (1896) 52 Geraud & Alexander.. throgh kynd stalwardnesse hertly smytten out to the formest, & many dydden to deth.

†**'stalworthy,** *a. Obs.* [Altered from STALWORTH *a.* after WORTHY *a.*] = STALWORTH *a.*

c **1250** *Gen. & Ex.* 864 Ðre hundred men.. Alle stalwurdi and witter of fiȝt. *c* **1300** *Havelok* 24 Haueloke, A stalworthi man in a flok. *c* **1400** *Secreta Secret., Gov. Lordsh.* 71 þanne ys þe stomak mad stalworthy to defye mete. *c* **1440** *Promp. Parv.* 472/1 *Sta[l] wurthy*, idem quod stronge, infra. **1522** *World & Child* 239, I am lorde bothe stalworthy and stoute. *c* **1522** SKELTON *Why not to Court?* 346 A stalworthy' stryplyng.

Hence †**'stalworthily** *adv.*, †**'stalworthiness.**

1387 TREVISA *Higden* (Rolls) III. 289 Riȝtwisnesse stalworþynesse and temperure. *Ibid.* V. 331 To fiȝte stalworthiliche in batayle.

†**stam,** *sb.*¹ *Obs.* Also 4 **stampne, stamyn(e.** [ME. **stamne*, a. ON. *stamn* stem, prow (also applied to the poop); for the ulterior etymology see STEM *sb.* Cf. FORESTAM.] The stem or prow of a ship. Also *attrib.* in ***stampneloker*** (? LOCKER *sb.*¹)

1336–7 *Acc. Exch. K.R.* 19/31 m. 5 Et in vno ligno empto pro. I. Stampneloker. *Ibid.*, In ij leopardis emptis.. cum puturacione eorundem positis super les stampnes. **13..** *E.E. Allit. P.* B. 486 On stamyn ho stod. ? *a* **1400** *Morte Arth.* 3659 [They] Standis styffe one the stamyne, steris one aftyre. *Ibid.* 3664 So stowttly þe forsterne one þe stam hyttis. **1513** DOUGLAS *Æneis* VIII. xii. 22 A crovne wyth stammys sik as schippis beris [L. *tempora navali fulgent rostrata corona*].

stam (stæm), *sb.*² *dial.* [Belongs to STAM *v.*; possibly cogn. w. OE. *stamm* adj., stammering: see STAMMER *v.*] A state of bewilderment.

1638 W. LISLE *Heliodorus* II. 32 O, then in what a stam Was theeuish, barb'rous, loue-sicke, angrie minde, That how to wreak his wrath could no way finde. **1674** N. FAIRFAX *Bulk & Selv.* 143 To break off from this so great a stamme to the mind. *a* **1825** FORBY *Voc. E. Anglia.*

stam (stæm), *sb.*³ *dial.* Also **stom, staum.** [Related to STEM *sb.*] A stem or stalk; a trunk or stump of a tree.

1839 SIR G. C. LEWIS *Heref. Gloss.*, *Stam*, or *Stom*, a stem. **1854** MISS BAKER *Northampt. Gloss.*, The bean staums run in my hand. **1892** 'SON OF THE MARSHES' *Within Hour of Lond.* xi. 209 No moss grows on their trunks, or 'stams', as they are generally called in woodland dialect.

b. *attrib.* **stam-wood,** the roots of trees removed from the earth.

1681 WORLIDGE *Syst. Agric.* (ed. 3) 332 *Stamwood*, the Roots of Trees grubbed up. **1851** STERNBERG *Dial. Northampt.* 104.

stam (stæm), *v. dial.* [See STAM *sb.*²] *trans.* To astonish; to overcome with amazement. Hence **'stamming** *ppl. a.*, fine, excellent; **'stammingly** *adv.*, extremely, excellently.

1578 *In Prayse rare beauty* in T. Proctor *Gorg. Gallery* H iiij, They with their Muses could not haue pronounst the fame, Of D. faire Dame, lo, a staming stock, the cheefe of natures frame. *a* **1800** PEGGE *Suppl. Grose*, *Stam'd*, amazed. Norf. and Suff. **1814** in Glyde *New Suffolk Garl.* (1866) 271 How stammin cow'd 'tis now-a-days. *Ibid.*, We're all stammenly set up about that there corn bill. *a* **1825** FORBY *Voc. E. Anglia* s.v. *Stam*, It is a stamming story indeed! **1893** in Cozens-Hardy *Broad Norf.* 7 Her wise husband would perhaps be stammed that she should be so careless.

stamber, obs. form of STAMMER.

‖**'stam-book.** *Obs. rare*⁻¹. [ad. G. *stammbuch*, orig. a family register, f. *stamm* STEM *sb.* + *buch* BOOK *sb.*] A memorandum book.

1662 GERBIER *Princ.* 10 The Germane Travellers.. did put in their Stam-books the Dimensions of.. the Amphitheaters.

Stambouline (stæmbuː'liːn), *a.* and *sb.* (Also **Stamboline, Stamboulina.**) [f. *Stamboul*, older form of Istanbul, Turkish name of Constantinople + -INE.]

a. *adj.* Of or pertaining to Stamboul. **b.** *sb.* (With lower-case initial.) A long frock-coat worn by Turkish officials.

1811 BYRON *Ch. Har.* II. App. D ii, *note*, Any of his Stamboline acquaintance. **1884** *Graphic* 4 Oct. 358/2 The ordinary Turkish or Stamboulina dress. **1886** *Pall Mall Gaz.* 22 Sept. 13/2 The gentry, dressed in coloured stamboulines or black caftans and fez, occupied the pit. **1900** *Harper's Mag.* Jan. 254 The stambouline.. is a queer single-breasted frock-coat, designed for all state occasions.

†**'stambuck.** *Obs. rare*⁻¹. [a. F. *stambouc* (*stanbouque*, Cotgr.), ad. G. *steinbock*, f. *stein* STONE *sb.* + *bock* BUCK *sb.*¹] A wild goat.

1591 FLORIO *2nd Fruits* 143 What matter is it for him then to bee a goate, or a stambuck [It. *stambecco*], a kid or a chamoise. **1694** MOTTEUX *Rabelais* IV. xxxii, He.. caught there.. Stamboucs [Fr. *Stamboucqs*].

stamele, -ell: see STAMMEL¹.

stamen ('steɪmən). Pl. **stamens;** also (now *rarely*) **stamina** ('steɪmɪnə). [a. L. *stāmen*, neut. (pl. *stāmina*) 'the warp in the upright loom of the ancients' (L. & Sh.), a thread of the warp, a thread or fibre in general, also (Pliny) applied to the stamens of the lily; corresponding formally to Gr. *στήμων* masc. warp, *στῆμα* neut., some part of a plant (Hesychius), Goth. *stōma* wk. masc., Skr. *sthāman* station, place, also strength :—Indo-germanic **st(h)āmon-*, *-en-*, f. **st(h)ā-* to STAND. Cf. It. *stame*, F. *étamine* (1690 in Hatz.-Darm.; repr. L. pl. *stamina*), Sp. *estambre*, Pg. *estame*.]

‖**1.** The warp of a textile fabric. Also *transf. Obs. rare.*

1650 FULLER *Pisgah* II. vi. i. 190 As in a web, the stamen, or Warp, is fast fixed, through which the woofe is cast, or woven. **1681** GREW *Musæum* I. § I. i. 6 Those whitest Fibers which.. make the stamen or warp of every Muscule.

†**2. a.** The thread spun by the Fates at a person's birth, on the length of which the duration of his life was suppose to depend. Hence, in popular physiology, the measure of vital impulse or capacity which it was supposed that each person possessed at birth, and on which the length of his life, unless cut short by violence or disease, was supposed to depend. **b.** The supposed germinal principle or impulse in which the future characteristics of any nascent existence are implicit. **c.** The fundamental or essential element of a thing. *Obs.* Cf. STAMINA.

a. 1701 C. WOLLEY *Jrnl. New York* (1860) 26 A person seemingly of a weakly Stamen and a valetudinary Constitution. **1709** *Tatler* No. 15 ¶ 1 All, who enter into human life, have a certain date or Stamen given to their being, which they only who die of age may be said to have arrived at. *a* **1745** J. RICHARDSON *Note on Milton's Lycidas* 75 Of the three fatal sisters the first prepar'd the flax upon the distaff, the stamen of human life. **1753** L. M. *Accompl. Woman* I. 246 Bad example hath not less influence upon education than a bad stamen upon the constitution.

b. 1718 CHAMBERLAYNE *Relig. Philos.* I. xvi. § 9. 306 All the Great Naturalists.. have been convinced.. that the Beginning of all Creatures consist in a *Stamen*. **1725** J. REYNOLDS *View Death* 16 *note*, Some suppose, that the soul takes away with it, the animal spirits, as the *stamen*, or ground of the vehicle, it is to assume.

c. 1758 BORLASE *Nat. Hist. Cornw.* 61 Earth is the general food and stamen of all bodies. **1794** R. J. SULIVAN *View Nat.* I. 305 Philosophers.. looked upon water as the elemental matter, or stamen of all things.

3. *Bot.* The male or fertilizing organ of a flowering plant, consisting of two parts, the *anther*, which is a double-celled sac containing the pollen, and the *filament*, a slender footstalk supporting the anther.

Although the L. *stamen* was applied by Pliny to the stamens of the lily, the technical use of the word in botany app. began with Spigelius (Adriaan van den Spieghel, died 1625), who defines *stamina* as 'partes oblongæ tenues veluti capillamenta.. quæ stylum (partem similiter oblongam sed paulo crassiorem).. ambiunt' (*Isagoge in Rem Herbariam*, ed. 1633, I. vi. p. 37).

α. sing.

1668 WILKINS *Real Char.* II. vi. 170 [Parts of the flower.] Stamen, tuft. **1764** BERKENHOUT *Clavis Angl. Bot.* s.v., Each *Stamen* consists of two distinct parts, viz. the *Filamentum*, and the *Anthera*. **1845** LINDLEY *Sch. Bot.* i. (1858) 15 The Stamen is one of the parts which stand next the corolla in the inside.

β. plural *stamina.*

1668 [see STAMINEOUS *a.*] **1683** RAY *Corr.* (1848) 131 A thrum of small flowers, which are vulgarly mistaken for stamina. **1760** J. LEE *Introd. Bot.* I. iv. (1765) 10 The Stamina are the Male Part of the Flower. **1858** BRIGHTWELL *Life Linnæus* 25 A close examination of the stamina and pistils. **1879** J. GRANT in *Cassell's Techn. Educ.* IV. 95/1 He showed that the *stamina*, or dust-threads, were the male.. parts of the plants.

γ. plural *stamens*.

1785 MARTYN tr. *Rousseau's Bot.* i. 25 Between the pistil and the corol [of a Lily] you find six other bodies..called the Stamens. **1807** J. E. SMITH *Phys. Bot.* 470 Class 21. *Monoecia.* Stamens and Pistils in separate flowers, but both growing on the same individual plant. **1875** BENNETT & DYER tr. *Sachs' Bot.* 791 The stamens of Berberis..lose their irritability *in vacuo*.

b. *Comb.*

1821 S. F. GRAY *Brit. Plants* I. 159 Gynophore... Stamen-bearing,..supporting the stamens also. **1829** T. CASTLE *Introd. Bot.* 170 The barren or stamen-bearing flowers. **1877** HUXLEY & MARTIN *Elem. Biol.* 84 The union of the filaments for three-fourths of their length to form the stamen-tube.

stamened ('steɪmənd), *a.* [f. STAMEN + -ED[2].] Having stamens. (In recent Dicts.)

[**1840** *Florist's Jrnl.* (1846) I. 124 All the florist's geraniums are pelargoniums having seven stamened flowers.]

stameniferous, variant of STAMINIFEROUS.

Stamford ('stæmfəd). The name of a town in Lincolnshire, used *attrib.*, as **Stamford ware** *Archæol.*, a kind of Saxo-Norman lead-glazed pottery made of estuarine clay from the vicinity of Stamford.

1956 G. C. DUNNING in D. B. Harden *Dark-Age Britain* III. 230 The term 'Stamford ware' may be proposed for the lead-glazed pottery of fine quality of the late Anglo-Saxon and Norman periods, provided it is clearly understood that this is a generic term for pottery made of..specific clays but at more than one centre within the area. **1956** *Proc. Cambridge Antiquarian Soc.* XLIX. 48 Saxo-Norman glaze only occurs on this Stamford ware. **1962** [see *lead-glazing* vbl. sb. s.v. LEAD *sb.*[1] 12]. **1974** M. INGATE *Sound of Weir* xx. 172 Stamford ware made from 900 to the 13th century from middle Jurassic esturine clay.

†**'stamin.** *Obs.* Forms: 3-7 **stamin**, 4-5 **stamyn**, 5-6 **stamyne**, 6 **-yng**, 6-7 **-en**, 7-8 **stamine**, 6-7 **stammyne**, 6-7 *Sc.* **stem(m)yng**, **-ing**, **stemnyn**, 7 *Sc.* **steimming**. See also ESTAMIN, ETAMINE, TAMIN. [Early ME. *stamin* (= Anglo-Latin *staminum*) a. OF. *estamin* (not in Godef. before 16th c.), parallel with *estamine* (12th c.; hence mod.F. *étamine*), app. a derivative (with suffix *-in*, *-ine*) of *estame*:—L. *stāmina* pl., warp threads (see STAMEN). The other Rom. langs. have in the same sense a cognate word of differing formation: Pr., Pg. *estamenha*, Sp. *estameña*, Cat. *estamenya*:—L. *staminea* fem. of *stāmineus* adj., f. *stāmin-* STAMEN. Med.L. had *stāminea*, *-eum*, *stāmen*, a rough woollen undergarment worn by monks.]

1. a. A coarse cloth of worsted; in earliest use usually an under garment made of this worn by ascetics. Cf. STAMMEL[1] 1.

a **1225** *Ancren R.* 418 Stamin habbe hwose wule. *c* **1290** *Beket* 2204 in *S. Eng. Leg.* I. 169 [Beket wore] Monekene Abite with Inne..boþe Covele and stamin. *c* **1385** CHAUCER *L.G.W.* 2360 She hadde I-wouyn In a stamyn large How she was brought from Athenys in a Barge. *c* **1386** —— *Pars. T.* 1052 In werynge of heyres or of stamyn, or of haubergeons on hire naked flessh. **1387** TREVISA *Higden* (Rolls) VII. 307 Þey wereþ nevere lynnen clooþ, noþer stamyn [L. *stamine*], but þe heer next þe flesche. *Ibid.* 401 Þei schal were no.. wollen þat is smal and softe as stamyn [L. *subtile quale est staminum*]. *c* **1425** *St. Mary of Oignies* I. xi. in *Anglia* VIII. 147 She vsed not next hir flesche a lynnen smok, but an harde sakke, þat is callid in open tunge stamyne. **1483** CAXTON *Golden Leg.* 432 b/2 He..ware for a shyrte a stamyn or streyner clothe.

b. In later use, a kind of woollen or worsted cloth, for outer garments, curtains, etc. for which Norfolk was formerly noted; = TAMIN, TAMMY.

c **1440** *Promp. Parv.* 472/1 Stamyn, clothe, *stamina.* **1493** *Will* in Cullum *Hawsted* (1784) 118 My payer of stamyns. **1495** *Act 11 Hen. VII*, c. 11 §2 Ther shuld no man take upon hym to shere Worstedes, called ten yerdes Stamyns ne any other Worstedes. **1496-7** *Act 12 Hen. VII*, c. 1 The due occupacion of makyng of Worstedys Sayes and Stamyns. **1533-4** *Act 25 Hen. VIII*, c. 5 §2 Any worstedes stamens or sayes. **1535** *Acc. Ld. High Treas. Scot.* VI. 246 Ane pair of hois, vj quarteris quhite steming. **1540** in *Archæologia* XLVI. 216 For stamyn & thred & gerdels vd. ob. **1579** *Extracts Burgh Rec. Edin.* (1872) IV. 117 Thre elnes of blak inglis stemyng to be thair hois. **1585** T. WASHINGTON tr. *Nicholay's Voy.* II. xxi. 58 b, Hee hath well soaped and rubbed your bodie..wyth a purse of Stammin, or Chamblet. **1594** BLUNDEVIL *Exerc.* v. iv. (1636) 539 The Merchandixes sent from England..are these, broad Clothes, Carsyes, Stamines. **1603** *Reg. Privy Council Scot.* 520 Fusteanis, stemingis, grogranis and other kynde of stuffe. **1621** *Sc. Acts Jas. VI* (1816) IV. 669/2 All Cloath stemming stuffes and Stokkingis maid in þ[r] said burgh. **1657** HOWELL *Londinop.* 60 Woollsteads, Jayes, Stamins. **1708** *Lond. Gaz.* No. 4482/4 For Sale..,..50 Pieces of Norwich Crapes..11 Pieces of Stamines. **1775** ASH, *Stamen, Stamin* (obsolete) [wrongly explained]. [**1818** in TODD; and in mod. Dicts.]

attrib. **1525** DK. NORFOLK in Ellis *Orig. Lett* Ser. III. I. 379 The living of theim of the Citie [of Norwich] was moste by worsted and stamen making. **1553** *Richmond Wills* (Surtees) 77 My blew stamyng jacket. **1570** *Satir. Poems Reform.* xxviii. 69 My Stemming Sark & Rokket was laid doun. **1574** *Reg. Privy Council Scot.* II. 374 Ane hors laid of Inglis steming clayth. **1580** *Aberdeen Reg.* (1848) II. 36 Thrie pair of steming breikis, ane blak, ane gray, ane browne. **1605** CHAPMAN etc. *Eastward Hoe* I. A 4, Your Stamen peticoate with two guardes. **1624** in *Archæologia* XLVIII. 144 A whole peece of 15 yardes and a halfe of stamin Carsey for a bed. **1664** in *Maitl. Club Miscell.* (1840) II. 509, 2 steming petticoatis.

2. Used to render F. *étamine*, a strainer.

1725 *Bradley's Fam. Dict.* s.v. *Blanc-manger*, You must pour it into a Stamine or thick Linnen-cloth.

stamina ('stæmɪnə). [a. L. *stāmina*, pl. of *stāmen*: see STAMEN 2. For *stamina* = stamens (*Bot.*) see STAMEN 3.

The senses explained below arise partly by direct metaphor from the original Latin sense 'warp of cloth', and partly from the frequent classical application of the word to the threads spun by the Fates (see STAMEN 2 a). In some examples the two notions appear to be blended.]

†**1.** (As *plural.*) The native or original (as distinguished from the adventitious) elements and constitution of anything; the nature, structure and qualities of an organism, as existing potentially in its nascent state; the rudiments or germs from which living beings or their organs are developed.

a **1676** HALE *Prim. Orig. Man.* 294 The greater and more comprehensive Rudiments and Stamina are laid..before the lesser and derivative parts are formed and compleated; as we shall have occasion to observe when we come to consider the *processus generationis* of Man and Brutes. **1684** T. BURNET *Th. Earth* I. 191 Others have thought that the long lives of those men of the old world proceeded from the strength of their stamina, or first principles of their bodies. **1692** BENTLEY *Boyle Lect.* v. 20 They must have had some rude kind of Organical Bodies, some *Stamina* of Life, though never so clumsy. **1718** CHAMBERLAYNE *Relig. Philos.* I. xvi. §10. 308 In almost all kinds of Plants and Living Creatures..the former have their Origin in a Seed, and the latter in *Stamina.* **1741** A. MONRO *Anat.* (ed. 3) 156 Different Stamina or Rudiments of Teeth are to be observed. **1768** STERNE *Sent. Journ.* (1775) I. 68 Every third man a pigmy!—from the first rudiments and *stamina* of their existence, never meant to grow higher. **1772** FLETCHER *Appeal* Wks. 1795 I. 14 Original sin..is as old as the first *stamina* of our frame. **1774** COOPER in *Phil. Trans.* LXV. 320 It..probably has its existence..originating,..in the first stamina of the embryo. **1801** *Med. Jrnl.* V. 568 The stamina of the teeth..are situated in the alveoli.

†**b.** *transf.* and *fig.* *Obs.*

1691 BAXTER *Nat. Ch.* Pref. A 2, They may yet become the Agents and *stamina* of a happy concordant Reformation. **1724** WATERLAND *Athan. Creed* xi. 158 Some few of the main *Stamina*, or chief Lines, were taken care of from the first, and made up the first Creeds: particularly the Doctrine of the Trinity briefly hinted. **1741** WARBURTON *Div. Legat.* II. 530 Job's whole dramatic life lies here in its *Stamina.* **1752** FIELDING *Amelia* IX. v, I am convinced there are good Stamina in the Nature of this very Man. **1779** JOHNSON in *Boswell* (1791) II. 300 Pope may have had from Bolingbroke the philosophick stamina of his Essay. **1795** BURKE *Reg. Peace* iv. (1892) 333 Enmity to us..is wrought into the very stamina of its constitution. **1798** *Monthly Mag.* June 430 One [charity]..whose growth, from its god-like stamina, has been gigantic... This is the orphan-house. **1816** *Sporting Mag.* XLVII. 295 In this group we do not see any thing very good, except certain hints, happy passages, and the *stamina* of possibly better pictures. **1816** J. GILCHRIST *Philos. Etym.* 238 He had the *stamina* of a good writer as well as sound thinker.

†**c.** *humorously.* *Obs.*

1824 LAMB *Elia* Ser. II. *Capt. Jackson*, A bare scrag.. carving could not lessen, nor helping diminish it—the stamina were left—the elemental bone still flourished.

†**2.** (As *plural*; rarely as *sing.*) The congenital vital capacities of a person or animal, on which (other things being equal) the duration of life was supposed to depend; natural constitution as affecting the duration of life or the power of resisting debilitating influences. *Obs.*

In 1665 Dr. R. Willis, 'being called to consult for one of his [the Duke of York's] sons, gave his opinion in these words, *mala stamina vitæ*, which gave such offence, that he was never called for afterwards' (Bp. Burnet, *Hist. Own Time*, ed. 1823 I. II. 228). Cf. the following:—

1542 LELAND *Naeniae* A v b, Atropos has illi laudes inuidit acerba, Infestaque manu vitalia stamina rupit.

1701 C. WOLLEY *Jrnl. New York* (1860) 60 Such as have the natural Stamina of a consumptive propagation in them. **1771** FOOTE *Maid of Bath* III. Wks. 1799 II. 230 Men have survived many years such disproportionate marriages as these... But then their stamina must be prodigiously strong. **1782** H. WALPOLE *Let. C'tess Ossory* 11 July, Though the relapse will be much more dangerous to Mr. Fox than to Mr. Fitzpatrick, whose stamina are of stouter texture. **1791** BOSWELL *Johnson* an. 1770, I. 344 He said..it was the bad stamina of the mind, which, like those of the body, were never rectified. **1806** *Med. Jrnl.* XV. 102 Persons with strong..constitutions..are much more slowly acted upon by medicine than those with weakly constitutions... This patient being of the former stamina, may [etc.]. **1823** GILLIES *Aristotle's Rhet.* I. v. 180 If the stamina are not sound, disease will soon ensue.

†**b.** *transf.* and *fig.* *Obs.*

1775 A. BURNABY *Trav.* 91 The northern colonies are of a stronger stamina. **1812** *Ann. Reg., Gen. Hist.* 107 Expressing his conviction that the stamina of the nation were still unimpaired. **1816** J. SCOTT *Vis. Paris* (ed. 5) p. xxv, Here thrive, beyond parallel, by means solely of the popular stamina, institutions for..improving the condition of mankind. **1862** MERIVALE *Rom. Emp.* lxviii. (1865) VIII. 359 The stamina of ancient life were healthier and stronger.

3. (Orig. as *plural*; now chiefly as *sing.*) Vigour of bodily constitution; power of sustaining fatigue or privation, of recovery from illness, and of resistance to debilitating influences; staying power.

1726 SWIFT *Let. Sheridan* 27 July Wks. 1841 II. 588/1, I indeed think her stamina could not last much longer when I saw she could take no nourishment. **1777** SHERIDAN *Sch. Scandal* I. i, Who avoid the least breath of air, and supply their want of stamina by care and circumspection. **1818** BYRON *Juan* I. cxxv, Some old lady or gentleman..Who've made 'us youth' wait..For an estate..Still breaking but with stamina so steady That all the Israelites are fit to mob its Next owner for their..post-obits. **1834** M. SCOTT *Cruise Midge* viii, Why, Sir Oliver, the man is exceedingly willing, ..but his stamina is gone entirely. **1853** ROBERTSON *Serm.* Ser. IV. xviii. (1876) 195 Those whose constitutions had less stamina than our own. **1865** DICKENS *Dr. Marigold* viii, Advising him to spend his legacy in getting up his stamina. **1880** COLBORNE *Hicks Pasha* 181 Had he been possessed of less stamina and less vitality he must have succumbed. **1880** W. DAY *Racehorse in Training* 225 Has he deteriorated in speed, size, or stamina? **1884** *Times* 28 Apr. 4/2 Lord Falmouth's horses seemed to possess more speed than stamina.

b. *transf.* and *fig.* In various applications: Intellectual or moral robustness and vigour; capacity for perseverance or endurance; also (of things, institutions, etc.) capacity for permanence.

1803 *Edin. Rev.* Jan. 452 Productions, which have scarcely *stamina* to subsist until their fruitful parent has furnished us with a new litter. **1828** ALFORD in *Life* (1873) 33, I have no stamina as yet of religious principle. **1844** H. STEPHENS *Bk. Farm* III. 1230 The stamina of the soil..is..its power of endurance under any system of cropping. **1860** W. COLLINS *Wom. White, V. Gilmore* iv. (1861) 121, I can't quarrel..I haven't stamina enough. **1861** T. A. TROLLOPE *La Beata* xix. II. 252 Not..calculated to encourage the growth of intellectual stamina. **1865** *Q. Rev.* CXVII. 549 The British Constitution has considerable stamina. **1869** GOULBURN *Purs. Holiness* vii. 63 It requires some stamina of character to feel this moral esteem for anyone. **1895** W. B. THOMSON *Remin. Med. Mission Work* xvii. 157 The stamina of the people was tested by a persecution that lasted for thirty years.

†**4.** (As *plur.* and *sing.*) Source of strength, main support, 'backbone'. *Obs.*

1779 A. HAMILTON *Wks.* (1886) VII. 577 The stamina of their military establishment are in this country. **1781** E. RUTLEDGE in Sparks *Corr. Amer. Rev.* (1853) III. 389 The Continentals, whom I consider as the stamina of the army. **1792** MARY WOLLSTONECRAFT *Vind. Rights Wom.* 110 The stamina of immortality, if I may be allowed the phrase, is the perfectibility of human reason. **1799** J. ROBERTSON *Agric. Perth* 450 The soil is the public stock, the great capital, the stamina of the nation.

staminal ('stæmɪnəl), *a.* [f. L. *stāmin-* STAMEN, STAMINA + -AL[1].]

1. †**a.** Forming part of the 'stamina' or original structure of the body. *Obs.*

1785 CULLEN *Instit. Med.* I. (ed. 3) 230 The gluten of the blood..is thus conveyed to every staminal fibre of the system.

b. Belonging to the stamina or natural constitution of a person or thing.

1798 J. BARRY *Let. Dilettanti Soc.* 32 The absurdity..of magnifying its accidental casual connexion with patronage, into something staminal and essential to its growth and perfection. **1805** SOUTHEY in *Robberds' Mem. W. Taylor* II. 77, I know myself to be free from these staminal defects. **1824-9** *Good's Study Med.* (ed. 3) V. 137 Where the intercourse has been so incessantly repeated as to break down the staminal strength. **1857** MILLER *Elem. Chem.* III. 738 The staminal principles or constituents of food may be further arranged as proposed by Liebig, according to the uses for which they are destined in the animal economy.

c. Constituting the 'stamina' or main outlines of a subject.

1845 J. MARTINEAU *Misc.* (1852) 92 An exposition of his staminal ideas on this subject.

¶**d.** As the trade designation of a class of prepared foods recommended as giving 'stamina' or bodily vigour.

1896 *Daily News* 3 Nov. 2/3 The supplies remaining over from the expedition, and consisting chiefly of large quantities of provisions, vegetables, staminal foods, and pemmicans, will be sold..on Monday.

†**2.** Pertaining to the fibrils of muscle. *Obs.*

1830 R. KNOX *Béclard's Anat.* 78 This last power also receives the names of fibrillar or staminal contractility, and tonicity.

3. *Bot.* Pertaining to or consisting of stamens.

1845 LINDLEY *Sch. Bot.* viii. (1858) 136 b, Staminal scales oblong-lanceolate acuminate. **1877** HUXLEY & MARTIN *Elem. Biol.* 70 Each of which [flowers] consists of a calyx, a corolla, a staminal tube and a central pistil. **1875** BENNETT & DYER tr. *Sachs' Bot.* 426 A leaf which bears pollen-sacs may be termed a Staminal Leaf or Stamen.

staminate ('stæmɪneɪt), *a.* *Bot.* [ad. L. *stāminātus* consisting of threads (mod.L. furnished with stamens), f. *stāmin-*, *stāmen*: see STAMEN and -ATE[2].] Furnished with or producing stamens. Of certain flowers: Having stamens but no pistils.

1845-50 MRS. LINCOLN *Lect. Bot.* Vocab., *Staminate*, having stamens without pistils. **1861** BENTLEY *Man. Bot.* 413 *Monœcia*, with staminate, pistillate, and hermaphrodite flowers on the same plant. **1870** LOWELL *Study Wind.* (1886) 141 There are staminate plants in literature, that make no fine show of fruit. **1883** *Science* I. 432/2 Staminate and pistillate flowers maturing at the same time.

†'**staminate.** *v. Obs. rare*$^{-1}$. [f. L. *stāmin-*, STAMEN + -ATE[3].] *trans.* To imbue with 'stamina' or vital force.

1720 S. PARKER *Biblioth. Biblica* I. 258 Persons..form'd and staminated, by the immediate hand of God, with peculiar Principles of Vitality.

stamineal (stə'mɪnɪəl), *a. Bot.* [f. L. *stāmine-us* (see next) + -AL[1].] (See quot.)

1856 HENSLOW *Bot. Terms, Stamineal*, having some marked reference to the stamens. As where the stamens are very prominent; or where perfect, and the corolla wanting. **1900** B. D. JACKSON *Gloss. Bot. Terms.*

stamineous (stə'mɪnɪəs), *a.* [f. L. *stāmine-us*, consisting of threads, f. *stāmin-*: see STAMEN and -EOUS.]

†**1.** (See quot.) *Obs.*

1661 BLOUNT *Glossogr.* (ed. 2), *Stamineous (stamineus)* pertaining to hemp or flax, or that hath shreds in it.

2. *Bot.* Consisting of, bearing, or pertaining to a stamen or stamens. Also of a flower: = STAMINEAL *a.*

1668 WILKINS *Real Char.* II. IV. §4 81 [Herbs] Stamineous; whose flower doth consist of threddy filaments or Stamina. **1704** J. HARRIS *Lex. Techn.* I, The Botanists call that a *Stamineous Flower*, which is so far imperfect, as to want..*Petala*, and consist only of the *Stylus* and *Stamina.* **1750** G. HUGHES *Barbados* 118 They discover innumerable small pale yellow stamineous flowers. **1760** J. LEE *Introd. Bot.* I. xii. (1765) 30 *Stamineous Nectaria*, such as attend the stamina. **1841** *Penny Cycl.* XXI. 174/1 Stamineous crown 5-leaved, with the leaflets compressed laterally.

‖**staminidium** (stæmɪ'nɪdɪəm). *Bot.* pl. **-ia.** [mod.L., f. L. *stāmin-*, STAMEN + Gr. -ίδιον dimin. ending.] The antheridium of cryptogamic plants, corresponding to a stamen.

1839 LINDLEY *Introd. Bot.* (ed. 3) 266 At the summit of some of the branches of many species are seated certain organs, which are called male flowers, but the true nature of which is not understood... By Hedwig they were called *spermatocystidia*; by others *staminidia* or *antheridia*. **1856** HENSLOW *Bot. Terms, Staminidium*, organs in some cryptogamous plants, which have been considered analogous to the anthers of Phanerogamic species.

staminiferous (stæmɪ'nɪfərəs), *a. Bot.* Also **stameniferous.** [f. L. *stāmin-* STAMEN: see -FEROUS.] Having or bearing stamens, applied to a flower having stamens but no pistils; also applied to a nectary having stamens growing on it.

1761 STILES in *Phil. Trans.* LV. 264 If the flowers of these plants be hermaphroditic, the staminiferous part doubtless falls off as soon as the impregnation is over. **1785** MARTYN *Rousseau's Bot.* ix. (1794) 95, I beg leave to coin two words, and to call those which have only the stamens staminiferous. **1796** WITHERING *Brit. Plants* (ed. 3) I. 371 The section of a stameniferous flower cut through perpendicularly. **1829** LOUDON *Encycl. Plants* 300 Nect[ary] 8-valved, staminiferous. **1889** *Hardwicke's Sci. Gossip* XXV. 130/2 The number of bees on stameniferous and pistiliferous plants.

staminigerous (stæmɪ'nɪdʒərəs), *a. Bot.* [Formed as prec.: see -GEROUS.] = prec.

1866 in *Treas. Bot.*

staminode ('stæmɪnəʊd). *Bot.* Anglicized form of next.

1857 HENFREY *Bot.* Index, Staminode, 113 [*text* staminodia]. **1866** *Treas. Bot.* Staminode. **1870** HOOKER *Stud. Flora* 350 Stratiotes, Water Soldier..Female. Staminodes many, a few antheriferous. **1896** G. HENSLOW *Wild Flowers* 36 It is represented without anthers or staminodes in some other members of the primrose family.

staminodium (stæmɪ'nəʊdɪəm). *Bot.* [mod.L., f. L. *stāmin-* STAMEN + mod.L. *-ōdium* (see -ODE[1]).]

a. A sterile or abortive stamen, or an organ resembling an abortive stamen, without its anther.

1821 S. F. GRAY *Brit. Plants* I. 158 *Staminodium*, appendages which appear to be abortive anthers. **1829** CLINTON tr. *A. Richard's Elem. Bot.* (ed. 4) 297 In general, these stamina are replaced by appendages which have received the name of staminodia. **1847** W. E. STEELE *Field Bot.* 142 Staminodium roundish, entire. **1859** MAYNE *Expos. Lex., Staminodium*, Term by L. C. Richard for appendages of the *gynostemium* of the *Orchideæ*, which appear to be the rudiments of aborted stamens.

b. The antheridium of a cryptogam.

1848 A. GRAY *Man. Bot.* p. xxxvi, (Jackson).

staminody ('stæmɪnəʊdɪ). *Bot.* [f. L. *stāmin-* STAMEN, after PHYLLODY.] The metamorphosis of other organs into stamens.

1869 M. T. MASTERS *Veget. Teratol.* 298 Staminody of the bracts... Staminody of the sepals and petals. **1880** A. GRAY *Struct. Bot.* 435 *Staminody*, name for the metamorphosis of other floral organs into stamens.

staminoid ('stæmɪnɔɪd), *a. Bot.* [f. L. *stāmin-*, STAMEN + -OID.] Of the nature of or resembling a stamen.

1869 M. T. MASTERS *Vegetable Teratology* 301 The scales that are met with in some plants, either as excrescences from the petals, or as imperfect representatives of stamens or other organs, are occasionally staminoid. **1930** *Jrnl. Genetics* XXIII. 107 A collection..in which the petals had become metamorphosed into stamens, showed every type of staminoid petal. **1974** *Flora* CLXIII. 405 (*heading*) Staminoid petals in *Geranium pratense* L. and their inheritance.

staminose ('stæmɪnəʊs), *a. Bot.* [ad. mod.L. *stāminōsus*, f. L. *stāmin-* STAMEN: see -OSE.] Applied to a flower 'when the stamens form a marked feature of the flower' (B. D. Jackson *Gloss. Bot. Terms* 1900). = STAMINEAL *a.*

†**staminous,** *a. Bot. Obs. rare*$^{-1}$. [ad. mod.L. *stāminōs-us*: see prec. and -OUS.] = prec.

1786 ABERCROMBIE *Gard. Assist., Arrangem.* 35 Staminous, or long stamened.

‖**Stammbaum** ('ʃtambaʊm). *Linguistics.* [Ger., family tree: the sense was introduced by A. Schleicher in *Darwinische Theorie u. die Sprachwissenschaft* (1863) 13.] A family tree of languages: see *family-tree* s.v. FAMILY *sb.* 11. Hence '**Stammbaumtheorie** (-ˌteori) (see quot. 1954).

1939 E. PROKOSCH *Compar. Gmc. Gram.* 21 August Schleicher conceived the Indo-European primitive language as the trunk of a linguistic 'Stammbaum'. **1954** M. A. PEI *Dict. Linguistics* 162 *Pedigree theory*, the theory (*Stammbaumtheorie*) formulated by August Schleicher in 1866, according to which a parent language split into two branches, each of which again bifurcated into two languages, etc. **1965** *Language* XLI. 106 Rodriguez stresses ..the ultimate reconcilability of the Stammbaumtheorie and the Wellentheorie. **1971** W. LABOV in W. O. Dingwall *Survey of Linguistic Science* 426 One of the classic unresolved dichotomies of historical linguistics is the opposition of the *Stammbaum* and *wave theories* of linguistic differentiation.

stammel[1] ('stæməl). Now only *arch.* or *Hist.* Also 6 **stamele, -ill,** ? *erron.* **stanel**(l, 6–7 **stamel**(l, **stammell.** [Corresponds to F. *estamel* (1611 in Godef.), mod. dial. *estamelle*, either f. *estame* + *-el, -elle*, or f. *estamine* STAMIN, by substitution of suffix; cf. the OF. synonyms *estamet, estamot*, formed with other dim. suffixes. The Eng. word may be a. F. *estamel(le* (though recorded earlier), but it may be an independent alteration of STAMIN.]

1. A coarse woollen cloth, or linsey-woolsey, usually dyed red; an under-garment of this material, worn by ascetics. Cf. STAMIN.

1530 PALSGR. 275/1 Stamell fyne worstede, *estamine.* **1534** in *Lett. Suppress. Monasteries* (Camden) 16 Another that had betyn hym zelfe so with roddes that his stamell was blody. **1542** BOORDE *Dyetary* viii. (1870) 249 In sommer use to were a skarlet petycote made of stamele or lynsye-wolsye. **1552** *Invent. Churches Surrey* 58 Item one cope of red stamill. **1606** CHAPMAN *Mons. D'Olive* II. i, Changeable creatures..now in Satten, To morrow next in Stammell. **1621** G. SANDYS *Ovid's Met.* XII. (1626) 239 Like a bull.. Whose dreadfull hornes the stammell, which prouokes His furie, tosse with still deluded strokes. **1623** COCKERAM *Dict.*, III, *Cutchoneale*,..wherewith Stammell is died. **1665** BRATHWAIT *Comm. Chaucer* 10 His Table with Stammel, or some other Carpet, [was] neatly covered.

fig. **1631** J. TAYLOR (Water P.) *Sudden Turn Fortune's Wheel* Advt. to Rdr., Knowinge the cause to be good, I adventured to piece a scarlet roabe with my coarse stammell; and though my lines are farr short of the other in elocution and ornate, still yet mine are more in number.

2. More fully ***stammel colour***: the shade of red in which the cloth was commonly dyed. Also *attrib.* or as adj. (Sometimes vaguely = 'red'.)

In the 17th c. often spoken of as cheaper than 'scarlet'.

1567 *Wills & Inv. N.C.* (Surtees) I. 273 Two peticotts thone of skerlet th' other of stamell xxx[s]. **1578** LYTE *Dodoens* II. iv. 151 The floures be..sometimes Carnation, Stamell, or Scarlet colour. *a* **1585** in *Eng. Hist. Rev.* (1914) XXIX. 518 Stanell Redes and lustie gallantes. *Ibid.* 519 You must have light skye collors.., fyne Redes and Stanells. **1591** SYLVESTER *Du Bartas* I. iii. 612 The Violet's purple, the sweet Rose's stammell. **1598** FLORIO, *Scarlatino*, the colour we call stammell red. **1633** B. JONSON *King's Entert. Welbeck* (1640) 276 Red-hood the first that doth appeare In Stamel. *Acc.* Scarlet is too deare. **1642** FULLER *Holy & Prof. St.* IV. xii. 296 As if the scarlet robes of their honour had a stain of the stamell die in them. **1657** LIGON *Barbadoes* 70 The body of a mixt red, partly Crimson, partly Stammell. **1658** W. SANDERSON *Graphice* 84 With breaks of Scarlet, or Stammell-colour. **1674** MILTON *Hist. Moscovia* iv. Wks. 1851 VIII. 493 They were spread under-foot with Cloth of Gold..the Bridges with Scarlet and Stammel-cloth. **1725** SLOANE *Jamaica* II. 54 Anoto-Berries dye a very fine Stammel colour. **1890** Æ. PRINCE *Palomide* 40 Comes a knight On lusty stammel steed. **1893** *Athenæum* 18 Nov. 706/1 Miss Gertrude Kingston, whose stammel tresses..are unbecoming and out of harmony with her face.

3. *attrib.* 'Of stammel', as ***stammel-weaver***; 'made of stammel', as ***stammel breeches, cloak, petticoat*** (but here often referring to the colour: see 2).

1591 HORSEY *Trav.* (Hakl. Soc.) 197 The ambassador.. with his 30 men livored in stamell cloakes. **1596** *Unton Invent.* (1841) 3 Five stamell cotes. **1601** MARSTON *Jack Drums Entert.* II. C 2, Mistresse Snuffe..hath newly put on her stamell petticoat. **1612** R. DABORNE *Christian turn'd Turke* 2143 That fellow in the stammell hose is one of them. **1615** G. SANDYS *Trav.* I. 48 The skirts of their coates..are gathered within long stammell broges. **1620** FLETCHER *Fr. Lawyer* I. i, But I'll not quarrell with this Gentleman For wearing stammell Breeches. **1634** EARL OF CORK *Diary* in *Lismore Papers* Ser. I. (1886) IV. 11 One whole peece..of very choice stammell cloath. **1820** SCOTT *Abbot* xix, She has a stammel waistcoat.

†'**stammel**[2]. *slang. Obs.* [In the first quot. perh. a use of prec. (with sense 'wearer of a stammel petticoat'); but cf. STRAMMEL.] (See quots.)

1597 DELONEY *Gentle Craft* II. Wks. (1912) 150 Out vpon her foule strammell (quoth she) he that takes her to his wife shall be sure of flesh enough. *a* **1700** B. E. *Dict. Cant. Crew, Stammel*, a brawny, lusty, strapping Wench. **1706** PHILLIPS (ed. Kersey), *Stammel* or *Stammel-Jade*, a great flouncing Mare; an over-grown bouncing Wench. **1735** DYCHE & PARDON *Dict., Stammel* or *Strammel*, a large flouncing Mare, or overgrown robust Wench.

stammer ('stæmə(r)), *sb.* [f. STAMMER *v.*] A stammering mode of utterance.

1773 GOLDSM. *Stoops to Conq.* II. i, This stammer in my address,..can never permit me to soar above the reach of a milliner's prentice. **1835** DICKENS *Sk. Boz, Parish* i, The beadle..states the case without a single stammer. **1842** *Penny Cycl.* XXII. 429/1 Stammer with this spasm distorts the utterance by an involuntary extension of some part of the syllable. *Ibid.*, In the looseness of language..all kinds of difficult and defective utterance are misnamed stammer... **1895** R. H. SHEPHERD in *N. & Q.* Ser. VIII. VII. 503 Lamb ..made the..witty retort, conveyed in his usual roll of stammers: 'I n-nev-never-h-heard-you-d-do-anything else'.

transf. **1898** KIPLING *Fleet in Being* iv. 45 The little demon [a Maxim gun] set up the 'irritating stammer' that the nine point two gun found so objectionable.

stammer ('stæmə(r)), *v.* Forms: *α.* 1 **stamerian, stomrian,** 2 **stamerie,** 4–5 **stamere,** 5 **stammery,** *Sc.* **stemer, stummer,** 4–7 **stamer,** 5– **stammer.** *β.* 6 **stamb(b)re, stambur,** 6–7 **stamber.** [OE. *stamerian, stǫmrian* = WFris. *stammerje*, NFris. *stamere*, (M)LG., (M)Du. *stameren*:—W.Ger. **stamrōjan*, f. **stamro-* (OE. *stamor* adj., NFris. *stamer* stammering) f. **stam-* (see STAM *a.*). A parallel formation with suffix *l* instead of *r* is found in (M)LG., (M)Du. *stamelen*, OHG. *stamalôn* (mod.G. *stammeln*) to stammer, f. WGer. **stamlo-* adj. (OHG. *stamal*), stammering. Other synonymous verbs from the same root are OHG. *stam(m)ên*, ON. *stama*, OE. *stǫmmettan.*]

1. *intr.* To falter or stumble in one's speech; *esp.* to make one or more involuntary repetitions of a consonant or vowel before being able to pass from it to the following sound. Cf. STUTTER *v.*

Stammering may be the result of indecision, or of sudden emotion (as fear, anger, delight, or grief), or may proceed from pathological conditions of the organs of speech or of the nervous system.

α. *c* **1000** *Prudentius Glosses* in *Germania* N.S. XI. 392/2 *Balbutit*, stamaraþ. *a* **1200** *Sidonius Glosses* in *Anecd. Oxon.* I. v. 43/15 *Balbutire* .i. stamerie. *c* **1330** *Arth. & Merl.* 2854 Ac he stamered a litel wiȝt. **1398** TREVISA *Barth. De P.R.* v. xxi. (1495) 128 Dronken men stamere whan they ben tomoche in moysture in the brayne. **1412–20** LYDG. *Chron. Troy* II. 4648 Neptolonius..in speche stamered whan he spak. **14..** *Lat.-Eng. Voc.* in Wr.-Wülcker 567/19 *Balbutio*, to stamery. **1522** *World & Child* 231, I shall myghtly make hym to stamer and stowpe. *a* **1529** SKELTON *E. Rummyng* 339 Her felow did stammer and stut. **1530** PALSGR. 732/1 It is a worlde to here hym stammer whan he is angryd. **1574** A. L. *Calvin's 4 Serm.* ii. D iiij, When he stammereth so in himself that he cannot draw foorth one only woord. **1638** JUNIUS *Paint. Ancients* 315 They..going about to tell a tale doe nothing but stutte and stammer. **1654** H. LESTRANGE *Chas. I*, 1 His vocall impediment..was..to wise men an index of his wisdome:..since there was never, or very rarely, known a fool that stammered. **1710** STEELE *Tatler* No. 244 ¶2 A Man that stammers, if he has Understanding, is to be attended with Patience. **1818** BYRON *Juan* I. clxiii, He stood in act to speak, or rather stammer. **1834** MACAULAY *Ess., Pitt* (1897) 311 He stammered, stopped, and sat down. **1848** DICKENS *Dombey* xli, Stammering and blushing, Mr. Toots affects amazement. **1879** FROUDE *Cæsar* xviii. 305 The eloquent tongue forgot its office. Cicero stammered, blundered, and sat down.

β. *c* **1500** *Col. Blowbol's Test.* 332 in Hazl. *E.E.P.* I. 106 Beer..Whiche makyth oft tymes men to stambur. **1526** TINDALE *Mark* vii. 32 They brought vnto him won that was deffe, and stambred [**1557**, *Geneva*, stambbred] in hys speche. **1570** LEVINS *Manip.* 79/6 To stamber, *titubare.*

b. *fig.* Also † ***to stammer it out.***

1616 R. JOHNSON *Kingd. & Comm.* 61 Neither doth he [*sc.* the Grand Seignor] stammer in his comparison of twenty Bashawes within his conquests [*i.e.* does not hesitate to assert each of them to be greater than our king]. **1653** LD. VAUX tr. *Godeau's St. Paul* 351 Although in his rapture he had seen the most profound mysteries of God, yet he accommodated himself to the weakness of his disciples, and stammered it out with them. **1818** KEATS *Endym.* I. 134 That I may dare, in wayfaring, To stammer where old Chaucer used to sing. **1822** BYRON *Vis. Judgem.* lvii, The grammar Of the last phrase, which makes the stanza stammer. **1837** EMERSON *Address Amer. Schol.* Wks. (Bohn) II. 183 Long he must stammer in his speech; often forego the living for the dead.

c. said of the tongue.

c **1050** *Malchus* in Assmann *Ags. Hom.* xviii. 380 Me þinceð, þæt me sio tunge stomriȝe. **14..** *Pol. Rel. & L. Poems* (1903) 253, & his Tonge shal stameren oþer famelen. **1628** WITHER *Brit. Rememb.* viii. 2545 The tongue, that stammers now, shall then speak plain. **1855** TENNYSON *Maud* I. VI. ix, The new strong wine of love, That made my tongue so stammer and trip.

d. *Path.* (See STAMMERING *vbl. sb.* 2.)

2. *trans.* To utter or say with a stammer.

α. **1810** SCOTT *Lady of L.* III. x, Childhood's babbling trill Of curses stammer'd slow. **1825** T. HOOK *Sayings* Ser. II. *Passion & Princ.* vii. III. 83 He stammered a few words which were as unintelligible as unmeaning, and resumed his chair. **1897** PEMBERTON *Queen of Jesters* iii. 118 The bailiff stammered an answer.

β. **1608** ARMIN *Nest Ninn.* (1880) 52 Playes on thoughts as girls with beads, When their masse they stamber.

b. with quoted words or clause as object.

1847 TENNYSON *Princess* iii. 190, I stammer'd that I knew him. **1859** —— *Elaine* 419 [It] Abash'd Lavaine.. But left him leave to stammer, 'is it indeed?' **1897** 'O. RHOSCOMYL' *White Rose Arno* 12 'Why—no,' stammered the young man. 'I—that is, sir——'.

c. with *forth*, *out*. Also *fig.*

1587 HIGGINS *Mirr. Mag.*, *Pinnar* Lenuoye ii, If hee vnstatelike stammer out the same, With staylesse staggering footed verse, by ame. **1782** MISS BURNEY *Cecilia* VIII. i, Cecilia.. stammered out, 'No, no——.' **1855** MACAULAY *Hist. Eng.* xvii. IV. 17 The judges.. had roared down the arguments feebly stammered forth by the prisoners. **1874** BURNAND *My time* viii. 68, I was about to stammer out an excuse. **1902** VIOLET JACOB *Sheep-Stealers* x, 'I was—I mean—I have been trying to get introduced to you for ever so long,' he stammered out at last.

transf. **1825** LAMB *Elia* Ser. II. *Superannuated Man*, I stammered out a bow, and.. went home.

3. *intr.* To stagger in walking; said especially of horses. Now *dial.*

c **1400** *Anturs Arth.* 109 Hit stemered, hit stonayde, hit stode as a stone. *c* **1440** [implied in STAMMERING *vbl. sb.* 1]. *c* **1470** *Gol. & Gaw.* 624 Thair stedis stakkerit in the stour, and stude stummerand. **1607** MARKHAM *Caval.* IV. (1617) 27 Giue him a good chocke in the mouth, that you may make him stammer and shuffle his legs confusedly together. **1707** J. STEVENS tr. *Quevedo's Com. Wks.* (1709) 380 My Legs naturally stammer. *a* **1774** R. FERGUSSON *Hallowfair* Poems (1845) 16 But if a birkie's oure weel sair'd [*i.e.* served (with drink)] It gars him often stammer To ploys that bring to the Guard And eke the Council Chammer. **1825** BROCKETT *N.C. Gloss.*, *Stammer*, to stagger. **1831** BLAKEY *Free Will* 62 The shot plied like hailstones round the old veteran... But he had the good fortune to escape unhurt, and when he was stammering back the Russians gave him three cheers.

†**4.** *trans.* To nonplus; = STAGGER *v.* 7. *Obs.*

1640 SANDERSON *Serm. Ad Aulam* xii. (1660) 232 If they should take away his life, that were indeed a sure course; but Nicodemus had stammered them all.. when he told them that they could not do it by law.

Hence ˈ**stammered** *ppl. a.*

a **1858** BRYANT *Burial of Love* vi, We shall.. miss.. The patter of his little feet, Sweet frowns and stammer'd phrases sweet. **1913** QUILLER-COUCH *Hetty Wesley* III. iii. 297 He would rise from the table on some stammered excuse.

stammerer[1] (ˈstæmərə(r)). [f. STAMMER *v.* + -ER[1].] One who stammers.

a. *a* **1513** *Fabyan's Chron.* VI. clxxiii. (1811) 170 Lodowycus Balbus, whiche is to meane Lewys yᵉ Stamerer. **1547** BOORDE *Brev. Health* xli. 21 If it [*i.e.* stuttering] do come with beyng in the company of a stutter or stamerer, a man must refrayne the company of a stutter. **1611** BIBLE *Isa.* xxxii. 4. *a* **1637** B. JONSON *Discoveries*, *De vita humana* (1640) 105 Like Children, that imitate the vices of Stammerers so long, till at last they become such. **1738** *Gentl. Mag.* VIII. 35/1 A Stammerer is generally of a Fiery Temper. **1899** *Allbutt's Syst. Med.* VII. 212 Cardiac defects are frequent in stammerers.

β. **1552** HULOET, Stambrer, *titubator.* Stambrer in readynge, *offensator.*

b. *fig.*

1580 G. HARVEY *Three Proper Lett.* iii. 45 A fewe suche stammerers as haue not the masterie of their owne Tongues. **1654** WHITLOCK *Zootomia* 150 What mighty lines hath Isaiah?.. read, and confesse Demosthenes and Cicero, but Stammerers at Eloquence. **1780** *Mirror* No. 97 She.. is a very stammerer in infidelity. **1868** GEO. ELIOT *Span. Gipsy* I. 135 Poor eager hope is but a stammerer.

† ˈ**stammerer**[2]. *Sc. Obs.* [Of obscure origin; cf. northern Sc. *stammerel* 'friable stone' (Jam.).] *pl.* Detached pieces of limestone.

1793 URE *Rutherglen* 259 Besides the regular strata, a great number of detached pieces, called Stammerers, are, in many places of the parish, found imbedded in clay. **1800** HEADRICK in *Commun. Board Agric.* II. 256 There are, however, water-worn limestones scattered here and there through land, called stammerers.

stammering (ˈstæmərɪŋ), *vbl. sb.* [-ING[1].]

1. The action of the verb STAMMER; hesitation and involuntary repetition in speech; also (now *dial.*) staggering and stumbling in gait. Also *fig.*

1357 *Lay Folks Catech.* (T.) 541 For idelnesse is enmy to cristen man saule Stepmodir and stameryng agayne gode thewes. *c* **1440** *Promp. Parv.* 472/1 Stameryynge, yn speche. *Ibid.*, Stamerynge, in goyng. **1584** LYLY *Campaspe* Epil. at Blacke Fryers, As Demosthenes with often breathing vp the hill amended his stammering. **1589** R. BRUCE *Serm. Sacr.* v. (1843) 148 He forgives thir doutings, he forgives thir stammerings. **1607** MARKHAM *Caval.* IV. (1617) 49 When you have brought him to the perfitnes of his pace, so that he will doe it.. without anie stammering or straining of his tramels. **1621** —— *Fowling* 270 That then presently he [the dog] doe the same, without any stamering, stay, or amazement. **1790** GOUV. MORRIS in Sparks *Life & Writ.* (1832) II. 15 There is also a confusion of language which resembles the stammering of one who endeavours to excuse a misdeed which he resolves to commit. **1856** SIR B. BRODIE *Psychol. Inq.* I. ii. 53 Cases of stammering, in which.. the organ of speech is more or less imperfect.

2. *transf.* in certain pathological uses.

1855 DUNGLISON *Med. Lex.*, Stammering of the Fingers. **1868** PAGET in *Brit. Med. Jrnl.* 24 Oct. 437/1 The stammering with the bladder occurs in just the same conditions as the stammering speech. *Ibid.* 437/2 The characters of stammering with the organs of deglutition may ..be recognised by their likeness to those of urinary stammering.

stammering (ˈstæmərɪŋ), *ppl. a.* [-ING[2].] That stammers. Often *transf.* and *fig.*

stammering micturition: see STAMMERING *vbl. sb.* 2.

1398 TREVISA *Barth. De P.R.* V. xxi. (1495) 128 Kyndly stameryynge men stamere for tomoche moisture of the brayne other of the tongue. *a* **1529** SKELTON *Sp. Parrot* 212 Parrot is no stameryng stare, that men call a starlyng. **1560** BIBLE (Geneva) *Isa.* xxviii. 11 A stammering tongue. **1579** G. HARVEY *Letter-bk.* (Camden) 74 Lett this stammringe letter suffize for a dutifull sollicitour. **1689** *Lond. Gaz.* No. 2453/4 He had a Scar in his left Cheek, and stammering Speech. **1704** STEELE *Tender Husb.* I. ii, I saw you.. prompt a stammering witness in Westminster Hall. **1818** COBBETT *Pol. Reg.* XXXIII. 273 Those maudling, stammering effusions which they call speeches. **1868** PAGET in *Brit. Med. Jrnl.* 24 Oct. 437/1 Stammering urinary organs. **1888** CHIENE in *Encycl. Brit.* XXIV. 191 The condition termed by Sir James Paget stammering micturition. **1899** *Allbutt's Syst. Med.* VII. 419 There may be a sort of stammering articulation for days.

Hence ˈ**stammeringly** *adv.*; also (*rare*) ˈ**stammeringness**.

1545 ELYOT *Dict.*, *Titubanter*, stameringly. **1637** LD. WARISTON *Diary* (1911) 276 Lord, thou knouest the stammeringnes, or rather the unskraiped overhaistings of my tongue. **1785** MME. D'ARBLAY *Diary* 16 Dec., I stammeringly answered—'I thought—sir—it would look very well in print!' **1868** BROWNING *Ring & Bk.* x. 53 Then one.. Spoke as he dared, set stammeringly forth... How nowise lacked there precedent for this.

† ˈ**stammet.** *Obs.* Forms: 6 *Sc.* **stemmet(t**, 7 **stam(m)ett.** [a. OF. *estamet*, f. *estame* + *-et* dim. suffix: see STAMMEL. Cf. Du. *stamet*, woollen yarn.] Some woollen fabric.

1531 *Acc. Ld. High Treas. Scot.* VI. 20 Ane pair of hois.. of.. broune stemmett. **1532** *Ibid.* 24, vij quartaris blak stemmet. **1618** in Foster *Eng. Factories Ind.* (1906) I. 43 Six pees of stametts. **1627** *Ibid.* III. 180 Most stammetts [reds].

‖**Stammtisch** (ˈʃtamtɪʃ). [Ger., f. *stamm* tree trunk, cadre + *tisch* table.] A table reserved for regular customers in a German restaurant, beer-hall, etc.

1938 L. BEMELMANS *Life Class* (1939) II. vii. 197 Political discourses at his *Stammtisch*, the table regularly reserved for him and his group of friends, at the Löwenbräu. **1940** G. FRANKAU *Self-Portrait* xi. 62 We lunched, with others of the same ilk, at his 'Stammtisch' (perpetually reserved table) in the Hamburg Rathskeller. **1964** I. FLEMING *You only live Twice* iv. 54 The quiet corner table that appeared to be his *Stammtisch.* **1970** L. DEIGHTON *Bomber* xxi. 312 The three best tables were marked with *Stammtisch* flags, so that only regulars would dare to sit there.

‖**stamnos** (ˈstæmnɒs). *Gr. Antiq.* [Gr. στάμνος, f. στα-, ἱστάναι to cause to stand.] A vessel resembling a hydria, but with a shorter neck.

1845 BIRCH in *Classical Museum* III. 418 On a stamnos of the more finished class, Medeia appears as before, holding up her hand. **1889** *Athenæum* 28 Sept. 424/2 A large double-handled vase, not unlike the shape of a *stamnos.*

stamock(e, obs. forms of STOMACH.

†**stamp**, *sb.*[1] *Obs. rare.* Also 4 **staumpe.** [ad. OF. *estampie*, corresp. to Pr., Sp., Pg. *estampida*, It. *stampita* song with accompaniment, also noise, f. Pr. *estampir* to resound, perh. cogn. w. Pr. *estampar* STAMP *v.*] Some kind of dance-music.

13.. *Sir Beues* 3908 Ʒhe hadde lerned of minstralcie, Vpon a fipele for to play Staumpes, notes, garibles gay. *c* **1407** LYDG. *Reson & Sens.* 5573 For ther wer.. Songes, stampes, and eke daunces, Dyuers plente of plesaunces.

†**stamp**, *sb.*[2] *Obs. rare*$^{-1}$. [Altered form of STANK *sb.*] A stank, pool (of water).

1338 R. BRUNNE *Chron.* (1725) 288 Sir James of Beauchamp.. In a water stampe he was dronkled fleand.

stamp (stæmp), *sb.*[3] [Partly f. STAMP *v.*, and partly ad. MF. *estampe* (mod.F. *estampe*, *étampe*), vbl. n. f. *estamper*: see STAMP *v.*]

I. An act of stamping.

1. a. A forcible downward blow with the foot.

1590 SHAKS. *Mids. N.* III. ii. 25 So at his sight, away his fellowes flye, And at our stampe, here ore and ore one fals. **1626** MIDDLETON *Women Beware Women* v. i, When thou hear'st me give a stamp, down with't. **1718** *Free-thinker* No. 17. 116 She rises with a Stamp and a loud Crack of her Fan. **1818** SCOTT *Br. Lamm.* xxxv, The repeated stamps of the heel of his heavy boot. **1827** HONE *Every day Bk.* II. 467 The 'tipsy toss' of that actor's head, his rollocking look, his stamps.. were worth the entirety of the drama. **1897** MARY KINGSLEY *W. Africa* 481 A dance.. which consists of a wriggle and a stamp.

b. *Fencing.*

1705 H. BLACKWELL *Engl. Fencing-Master* 16 For every Longe that is made, the Right Foot comes with a Stamp. **1809** ROLAND *Fencing* 100 Observe, that in making the appel or stamp, that it should be done upon a firm, steady position of the guard.

†**2.** A blow with the pestle in pounding. *Obs.*

1598 *Epulario* D j, Put it into a morter to beat, but giue it but two stampes.

3. *Dicing.* (See quot. 1777.)

1772 FOOTE *Nabob* II. (1778) 28 Seven, Sir is better nicked by a stamp... When you want to throw six and four.. you must take the long gallery, and whirl the dice to the end of the table. **1777** [T. SWIFT] *Gamblers* 22 *note*, The Stamp is, when the caster, with a certain elastic spring of the wrist, rappeth the cornet or box with vehemence on the table, the dice not as yet appearing from under the box.

4. A place where horses stand (cf. *stamping ground*: STAMPING *vbl. sb.*). *U.S. rare.*

1791 W. BARTRAM *Carolina* 355 A grand forest.. which we penetrated on foot a little distance to a horse-stamp.

II. An instrument for stamping.

5. a. An instrument for making impressions, marks, or imprints, on other bodies; a stamping-tool, an engraved block or die for impressing a mark, figure, design or the like, upon a softer material.

In quot. 1465 perh. = a branding-iron.

1465 *Finchale Priory Charters* etc. (Surtees) p. ccxcix, j hewyryn, j stampe, ij ponchonz [etc.]. **1548** *Acc. Ld. High Treas. Scot.* IX. 281 Item for ane stampe maid to my lorde governour. **1564** *Extracts Burgh Rec. Edin.* (1875) III. 187 That thair be maid ane stamp and the tounis armis thairapoun [for stamping cloth]. **1644** *Docq. Lett. Pat. at Oxf.* (1837) 123 To make and engraue Irons and Stampes with his Majestys Effigies.. and therewith to instampe and inprint all such Ingott Bullyon and plate of Gold. **1751** *Act 24 Geo. II*, c. 31. §21 Every Maker and Cutter of Stamps or Seals of any Kind for stamping of Cloth. **1827** SCOTT *Surg. Dau.* v, No, no—my old silver stamp, with the double G upon it, will serve my turn. **1837** R. HILL *Post Office Reform* 35 The marks being given by a tell-tale stamp, which would count the letters. *Ibid.* 58 It would be quite practicable to construct a stamp which at one blow should impress both the date and the required charge [etc.]. **1891** SLOANE *Rubber Hand Stamps* xiv. (1900) 113 Stamps made from a mixture of glue, glycerine, and molasses.. are adopted by the United States government for making dating stamps for use in the Post Office Department. **1904** BUDGE *3rd & 4th Egypt. Rooms Brit. Mus.* 109 A collection of wooden stamps used by plasterers and brickmakers.

b. *esp.* A die or the apparatus used in stamping a device upon a coin, token, medal or the like.

1572–3 in Swayne *Sarum Churchw. Acc.* (1896) 287 Altering of the stampe and striking of yᵉ tokins 6d. **1575** FENTON *Gold. Epist.* (1582) 280 In it was alwayes kept the stampe or minte of all the monie that serued the prouince. **1600** [see SEAL *sb.*[2] 3]. **1614** CAMDEN *Rem.* (ed. 2) 203 Mendlesham in Suffolke.. held in fee to make the coyning stampes seruing for all England. **1662** PEPYS *Diary* 24 Nov., Mr. Slingsby did show the King.. the stamps of the new money that is now to be made by Blondeau's fashion.

c. *transf.* and *fig.*

1607 SHAKS. *Cor.* II. ii. 111 His Sword, Deaths stampe, Where it did marke, it tooke from face to foot. **1645** WALLER *Loving at first sight* Poems 82 Some other Nymph with colours faint And pencil slow may Cupid paint..; She has a stamp and prints the Boy.

d. *Printers' slang.* (See quot.)

1875 SOUTHWARD *Dict. Typogr.*, *Stamp*, a colloquial synonym for types. *Stamps*, types. A common expression in the printing-office is 'picking up stamps', *i.e.* composing. **1888** in JACOBI *Printers' Vocab.*

†**6.** ? A printing press. *to put* (a book) *to stamp*: to print (it). *Obs.*

a **1548** HALL *Chron.*, *Hen. VIII*, 186 b, It will neuer be better as long as thei haue the letters and stampes, therefore it wer best for your lordshippe to bye the stampes to. *Ibid.* 221 b, A greate boke.. in a faire hand, redy to bee a copie to the printer, when the saied boke should be put to stampe. **1596** NASHE *Saffron Walden* L 4 b, The Doctor had some ierking Hexameters or other shortly after to passe the stampe. **1603** DANIEL *Def. Ryme* G 3, That mightie confluence of Learning.. which,.. heere meeting then with the new inuented stampe of Printing, spread it selfe [etc.].

7. A bookbinder's tool for embossing bindings. Also *transf.* an ornament produced by this.

1811 *Art Bookbinding* 40 A tool, or stamp, may be added between the bands, emblematic of the subject. **1818** *Ibid.* 2 Brass tools... Ornamental stamps and volume stamps. **1875** in KNIGHT *Dict. Mech.*

8. A machine for shaping articles made of sheet-metal; a drop-hammer, stamping-machine.

1839 URE *Dict. Arts* 999 Every one [of the shaped vessels of plated metal] of simple form is now made in dies struck with a drop-hammer or stamp. **1879** *Cassell's Techn. Educ.* IV. 263/1 It will be long before the 'old process of casting' is superseded by the stamp and die.

9. a. An iron-shod pestle of a mill for crushing ores, esp. each of the several pestles, usually five in number, forming the battery of a stamp-mill; chiefly in *pl.*, a battery of stamps, a stamp-mill.

1674 RAY *Collect. Words*, *Smelting Silver* 116 The slags or cinders of the first smelting they beat small with great stamps lifted up by a wheel moved with water, and falling by their own weight. **1875** J. H. COLLINS *Princ. Metal Mining* 107 The ore being broken down about the size of road stone, is now in a fit state for the action of the 'stamps'. **1901** *Munsey's Mag.* XXV. 662/2 A quartz mill.. with a varying number of stamps—beams of iron that are lifted and let fall in a sort of long mortar, in which are thrown the ore, water, and quicksilver.

b. Maize that has been crushed or pounded with a wooden pestle. *S. Afr.* Cf. *stamp mealies*, sense 20 below, and SAMP.

1923 *S. Afr. Pioneer* Dec. 143/2 All partook freely of the feast of meat and stamp. **1976** J. MCCLURE *Rogue Eagle* vi. 112 The price of mealie *stamp* in Maseru.

10. A machine for pounding hides to soften them. (Cf. STAMPER 3 d.)

1875 KNIGHT *Dict. Mech.*

11. *slang.* pl. (See quots.)

1567 HARMAN *Caveat* (1869) 82 Stampes, legges. **1609** DEKKER *Lanth. & Candle Lt.* C ij b, He sweares To put our stamps in the Harmans. **1785** GROSE *Dict. Vulgar T.*, *Stamps*, legs. **1812** J. H. VAUX *Flash Dict.*, *Stamps*, shoes.

III. The result of stamping.

12. The mark, impression, or imprint made with an engraved block or die.

a. An impressed mark used to certify or give validity to a document; an official mark certifying the quality or genuineness of goods.

1542 *Acts Privy Council* (1837) VII. 324 A lettre was sent under the stampe to the President and Cownsell in the northe for the giving to Sir Richarde Long his oth. **1545** in Rymer *Fœdera* XV. 81/2 Such Warrants as our said Counsail..shall undre our Stamp being sealed wyth our Signet, make [etc.]. **1578** *Extracts Rec. Convent. Burghs Scot.* (1870) I. 76 Thair wechtis..to be maid of bras, and markit with the tovnis stamp. **1621** in Foster *Eng. Factories India* (1906) I. 263, I having first told over all the bars of lead and carefully taken the contents of each bar according to the stampe marked on them. **1712** ARBUTHNOT *John Bull* I. iv, He sold goods, that were not marketable without the stamp. **1726** *Act 13 Geo. I*, c. 26. §19 It shall..be lawful to..the said Trustees [for the Linen Manufacture]..from Time to Time to direct such Stamp or Stamps to be made use of, as they shall think proper. **1771** *Junius Lett.* xlix. (1820) 254 The King had..affixed his stamp and given it currency among his subjects. **1800** tr. *Lagrange's Chem.* II. 126 The refiner has to deliver his opinion on a large mass of silver, and to attest its quality by a stamp. **1875** FORTNUM *Maiolica* i. 10 Remains of furnaces and fragments of Roman time and tiles with the stamp of Theodoric.

b. The design or combination of marks stamped by authority on a piece of metal in the process of minting or coining into money; the impressed design characteristic of a particular issue of coins of a certain value.

1555 EDEN *Decades* (Arb.) 211 The double ducades..are diminisshed of the goodnesse of their golde, with the stampe of youre maiestye chaunged. **1585** HIGINS *Junius' Nomencl.* 322/2 To coyne monie: to giue it the stampe. *Ibid.* 330/1 A crosse penie, so called of the stampe which it bare, being a crosse. **1628** in Foster *Eng. Factories Ind.* (1909) III. 241 All rup[ees] of Noor Jehann Beagams stampe are called in and not to bee uttered. **1660** F. BROOKE tr. *Le Blanc's Trav.* A 2, A Patron..whose Name in the Front, like a Princes stamp upon Lead, might give authority and make it currant coyne. **1665** GLANVILL *Scepsis Sci.* xxii. 139 The Stamp of Authority can make Leather as current as Gold. **1696** B. KENNETT *Romæ Antiq. Notitia* II. v. xiii. (1717) 372 Afterwards it had on one side the Beak of a Ship, on the other a Janus, and such were the Stamps of the As. **1712** J. MORTON *Nat. Hist. Northamptonsh.* 500 Eight or Nine [coins] of this very Prince of different Stamps. **1871** C. DAVIES *Metric Syst.* III. 150 The dollar, under its new stamp, has preserved its name and circulation. **1883** *Encycl. Brit.* XVI. 724/2 There are two distinct stages in the introduction of coining. In the first, only the quality or fineness of the metal is denoted by the stamp... In other words, the stamp acts as a kind of hall-mark... The second step was to certify the weight as well as the fineness of the metal.

in figurative context. **1596** SHAKS. *1 Hen. IV*, IV. i. 4 Such attribution should the Dowglas haue, As not a Souldiour of this seasons stampe, Should go so generall currant through the world. **1603** —— *Meas. for M.* II. iv. 46. **1690** LOCKE *Hum. Und.* III. xi. (1695) 293 For Words..being no Man's private possession, but the common measure of Commerce and Communication, 'tis not for any one, at pleasure, to change the Stamp they are current in. **1781** COWPER *Anti-Thelyph.* 156 Vice passing current by the stamp of law. **1795** BURNS *For a' that* i, The rank is but the guinea's stamp—The man's the gowd for a' that.

c. *gen.* Applied, e.g., to a postmark.

1661 H. BISHOPP in Hendy *Hist. Postmarks* (1905) Introd. 3 A stamp is invented, that is putt upon every letter shewing the day of the moneth that every letter comes to the office. **1867** AUGUSTA WILSON *Vashti* xxix, My letters always came back unopened, and bearing the London stamp.

13. In various figurative applications.

a. A certifying or distinguishing mark or imprint.

1611 SHAKS. *Cymb.* V. v. 366 *Cym.* Guiderius had Vpon his necke a Mole... *Bel.* This is he, Who hath vpon him still that naturall stampe. *a* **1646** BURROUGHES *Exp. Hosea* viii. (1652) 289 When God hath set his stamp upon any thing, we must take heed wee presume not to set our own stamp. **1781** COWPER *Expost.* 685 Blessings..giv'n Mark'd with the signature and stamp of heav'n, The word of prophesy. **1817** SHELLEY *Rev. Islam* 1060 Truth its radiant stamp Has fixed ..Upon her children's brow. **1874** SAYCE *Compar. Philol.* vi. 227 Conventional custom sets its stamp upon spoken speech.

b. The imprint or sign (*of* what is specified).

1596 SHAKS. *Merch. V.* II. ix. 39 For who shall goe about To cosen Fortune, and be honourable Without the stampe of merit. **1609** HEYWOOD *Troia Brit.* XII. l. 314 Great Hector.. fals vpon the next Greeke that he finds, And prints on him the bloudy stamp of death. *a* **1684** LEIGHTON *Comm. 1 Pet.* i. 10–12 (1693) 113 It carries the lively stamp of divine Inspiration. **1781** COWPER *Hope* 153 Hope sets the stamp of vanity on all That men have deem'd substantial since the fall. **1839** THIRLWALL *Greece* VI. lii. 271 In its leading outlines it bears the stamp of truth. **1891** F. HALL in *Nation* (N.Y.) LII. 297/2 Everything that had passed before me bore, to my apprehension, the stamp of intellectual obliquity.

c. 'Value derived from suffrage or attestation; authority, currency' (J.).

1632 LITHGOW *Trav.* Ded., Your auspicious Fauour, shall leaue a greater stampe to the Worke. **1686** W. HOPKINS tr. *Ratramnus* Dissert. iii. (1688) 53 Paschasius his Doctrine had not received as yet the stamp of publick Authority. **1738** SWIFT *Pol. Conversat.* Introd. 13 There is not one single witty Phrase,..which hath not received the Stamp and Approbation of at least one hundred Years. **1803** SYD. SMITH *Wks.* (1859) I. 19/1 The uproar even, and the confusion and the clamour of a popular election in England have their use: they give a stamp to the names, Liberty, Constitution, and People.

d. simply: Imprint, impression, mark.

a **1652** J. SMITH *Sel. Disc.* iv. 69 They are apt to acquire such deep stamps of material phantasms to themselves, that they cannot imagine their own being to be any other than material and divisible. **1673** DRYDEN *Marr. à la Mode* IV. i, You aggravate my griefs, and print them deeper In new and heavier stamps. **1817** SHELLEY *Rev. Islam* IV. viii. 2 The dead, who leave the stamp Of ever-burning thoughts on many a page. **1822** —— *Triumph Life* 409 The wolf..Leaves his stamp visibly upon the shore. **1838** CARLYLE *Misc.* (1857) IV. 206 Rahel Varnhagen von Ense..did not write. ..She left no stamp of herself on paper. **1858** HAWTHORNE *Fr. & It. Note-bks.* (1872) II. 29 The stamp of each new impression helps to obliterate a former one.

e. Character, kind; fashion, make; cast, type.

1573 G. HARVEY *Letter-bk.* (Camden) 9, I cannot tel how mani mo of this stamp frivolus and dogged iests. **1575** GASCOIGNE *Glass of Govt.* Wks. 1910 II. 37 Is shee of the right stampe? **1611** BIBLE *Transl. Pref.* ¶13 When the aboue named Radulphus happened to be at Rome, he found all the bookes to be new (of the new stampe). **1646** SIR T. BROWNE *Pseud. Ep.* II. iii. 67 But certainly false it is what is commonly affirmed [etc.]... Of the same stampe is that which is obtruded upon us by Authors..that an Adamant [etc.]. **1666** BOYLE *Orig. Forms & Qual.* 44, I would be understood to mean by it [Forme], not a real Substance distinct from Matter, but onely the Matter it selfe of a Natural Body, consider'd with its peculiar manner of Existence, which.. may..be call'd.., if you would have me expresse it in one word, its Stamp. **1709** HEARNE *Collect.* 1 Sept. (O.H.S.) II. 247 'Tis likely he is of the true Stamp for Principles. **1773** GOLDSM. *Stoops to Conq.* I. i, His acquaintance give him a very different character among creatures of another stamp. **1796** BURKE *Let. to Dudley North* Corr. IV. 551 He was exactly what we conceive of an English nobleman of the old stamp. **1831** D. E. WILLIAMS *Life & Corr. Sir T. Lawrence* II. 382 Men whose different stamps of genius and characters of intellect, were more singularly calculated to view their subjects through curious and diversified media. **1869** LECKY *Europ. Mor.* I. i. 161 Men of the stamp of a Washington or a Hampden. **1878** BOSW. SMITH *Carthage* 322 He struck a blow which showed that a general of a new stamp had appeared upon the scene.

f. Physical or outward form, cast.

a **1586** SIDNEY *Arcadia* III. (1598) 343 A yong maid, truly of the finest stamp of beautie. **1607** SHAKS. *Cor.* I. vi. 23 *Com.* Whose yonder. That doe's appeare as he were Flead? O Gods, He has the stampe of Martius. *a* **1704** T. BROWN *1st Sat. Persius* Wks. (1730) I. 53 A strange..birth: A glimpse of human stamp it has, the rest Is serpent fish and bird. **1877** MISS A. B. EDWARDS *Up Nile* xxi. 630 These early European settlers are seen with the Asiatic stamp of features.

14. a. An embossed or impressed mark placed by a government office on paper or parchment to certify that the duty chargeable in respect of what is thereon written or printed has been paid. Hence also, in recent times, an adhesive label (printed with a distinctive device) which is issued by the government for a fixed amount, and which when affixed to a document or other dutiable object serves the same purpose as an impressed stamp.

1694 *Act 5 & 6 Will. & Mary* c. 21. §5 [Stamp Act] And the said Commissioners shall..provide Six severall Markes or Stamps..for the severall and respective dutyes hereby granted with which severall Markes or Stamps all Velum Paper and Parchment upon which any of the severall and respective thinges herein before charged shall be ingrossed or written shall be stampt and impressed. **1712** ADDISON *Spect.* No. 445 ¶1, I am afraid that few of our weekly historians..will be able to subsist under the weight of a stamp. **1712** SWIFT *Jrnl. to Stella* 7 Aug., Have you seen the red stamp the papers are marked with? Methinks the stamping is worth a halfpenny. **1713** —— *Imit. Hor. Ep.* I. vii. 43 Of late indeed the Paper-Stamp Did very much his Genius cramp. **1802** *Med. Jrnl.* VIII. 136, I question whether an apothecary, who should make up parcels of ingredients..would not render himself liable to a confiscation..for selling them without stamps. **1817** W. SELWYN *Law Nisi Prius* (ed. 4) II. 886 It was holden that it [*sc.* a marine insurance policy] might be rectified by inserting the true name, without a fresh stamp. **1841** THACKERAY *Gt. Hoggarty Diamond* ii, Twenty-one pun five, Roundhand, and nothing for the stamp! There it is, sir, *re*-cipted. **1846** *Daily News* 21 Jan. 4/1 The stamp on newspapers is not like the stamp on Universal Medicine-Bottles, which licenses anything, however false and monstrous. **1881** BESANT & RICE *Chapl. Fleet* I. xiii, Your marriage is entered in my Register; I have the lines on a five-shilling stamp! **1911** *Act 1 & 2 Geo. V*, c. 55. §7 Subject to the provisions of this [National Insurance] Act, the Insurance Commissioners may make regulations providing for..payment of contributions whether by means of adhesive or other stamps affixed to or impressed upon books or cards, or otherwise.

b. *the Stamps* = the Stamp Office. ? *Obs.*

1820 BYRON *Blues* II. 59 *Sir Rich.* But this place ——... *Lady Bluem.* Excuse me—'tis one in the 'Stamps': He is made a collector. **1825** HONE *Every-day Bk.* I. 2 January 1. A close holiday at all public offices except the Excise, Customs, and Stamps.

c. *spec.* = POSTAGE STAMP.

1837 R. HILL in *Life* (1880) I. 271 Perhaps the difficulty [of the sender being unable to re-address the stamped cover purchased by him at the Post Office] might be obviated by using a bit of paper just large enough to bear the stamp, and covered at the back with a glutinous wash, which the bringer might..attach to the back of the letter. **1839** —— (*title*) On the Collection of Postage by means of Stamps. **1850** MRS. CARLYLE *Lett.* II. 105, I have little to tell you worth even a penny stamp. **1863** *Stamp-Collector's Mag.* I. 3/1 We cannot congratulate the designer of our penny and twopenny stamps on the display of any taste. **1896** *Punch* 7 Mar. 112/3, I have been writing letters broadcast. I prefer stamps to post-cards.

d. *pl.* (*U.S. slang.*) Money (properly, paper money).

1872 DE VERE *Americanisms* 296 Among the less generally known terms [for 'money'] are..*dyestuffs, charms,* and also the more modern designation of *stamps*. **1876** BESANT & RICE *Gold. Butterfly* x, 'But no Hand, dead or alive, shall ever get hold of my stamps.' 'Your stamps?' 'My stamps, sir; my greenbacks, my dollars.' **1885** R. L. & F. STEVENSON *Dynamiter* 195, I have neglected to supply myself with funds;..and without what is coarsely if vigorously called stamps,..it is impossible for me to pass the ocean.

e. = *insurance stamp* s.v. INSURANCE 5.

1912 [see *insurance stamp* s.v. INSURANCE 5]. **1946** *Act 9 & 10 Geo. VI* c. 67. 720 Contributions..are payable by means of adhesive stamps. **1974** *Times* 6 Feb. 14/2 The qualification test has been simplified for the emergency: a declaration that 26 stamps have been paid within the previous 12 months is enough to entitle people to the full rate for a year.

f. = *trading stamp* s.v. TRADING *vbl. sb.* b.

1933 in *Parl. Papers 1932–33, Rep. Cttee on Gift Coupons & Trading Stamps* 12 (Cmd. 4385) XII. 387 The stamps are given to the customer in proportion to the amount spent and are stuck by him into a collecting book... When the book is full..the stamps may be tendered in exchange for a gift. **1963** J. T. STORY *Something for Nothing* iii. 89 You get a grocer, you get a baker, you get a hairdresser and a chemist and a garage and a draper all giving stamps. **1976** A. GREY *Bulgarian Exclusive* I. i. 17 The two psychedelic gift mugs the garage..had given them in exchange for seven Heron stamps.

†**15.** Something marked with a device; a coin, medal. *Obs.*

1598 SHAKS. *Merry W.* III. iv. 16, I found thee of more valew Then stampes in Gold, or summes in sealed bagges. **1605** —— *Macb.* IV. iii. 153 People..The meere dispaire of Surgery, he cures, Hanging a golden stampe about their neckes. **1608–9** MIDDLETON *Widow* II. i, I will consume my self to the last stamp, Before thou gett'st me.

fig. **1588** SHAKS. *Tit. A.* IV. ii. 69 Here is the babe as loathsome as a toad,..The Empresse sends it thee, thy stampe, thy seale. **1594** —— *Rich. III*, I. iii. 256 *Queene Mother.* Peace Master Marquesse, you are malapert, Your fire-new stampe of Honor is scarce currant. **1633** G. HERBERT *Temple, Ch. Porch* lxiv, Man is Gods image; but a poore man is Christs stamp to boot; both images regard.

†**16.** A picture produced by printing from an engraved plate, an engraving, print. ***in stamp***: by means of engraving. [After It. *stampa*, F. *estampe*.] *Obs.*

1613 PURCHAS *Pilgrimage* V. ii. (1614) 463 He that will not onely reade, but in manner see,..may resort to Theodoricke and Israel de Bry, who haue in liuely stampes expressed these Nauigations. **1662** EVELYN *Sculptura* I. i. 9 The French call it [Etching] in particular *Taille douce*... The Italians *Intaglia*, or stamp, without Adjunct. *Ibid.* I. iv. 47 Ugo de Carpi did things in stamp, which appear'd as tender as any Drawings. **1705** ADDISON *Italy* 88 When I was at Venice they were putting out very curious Stamps of the several Edifices that are most famous for their Beauty. **1720** PRIOR in *Swift's Lett.* (1766) II. 11 Richardson..has made an excellent picture of me; from whence lord Harley (whose it is) has a stamp taken by Vertue. **1756** NUGENT *Gr. Tour, Italy* III. 26 At Rome, all sorts of fine stamps or prints, as of antiques, palaces..plans of towns, &c. **1780** J. ADAMS in *Fam. Lett.* (1876) 380 It is a description and a copper-plate of all the engravings upon precious stones... The stamps are extremely beautiful, and are representations of the gods and heroes of antiquity.

17. *Mining.* (See quots.)

1851 GREENWELL *Coal-trade Terms, Northumb. & Durh.* 50 *Stamp*, a hole made with a pick in the coal, in which to place a wedge. **1860** *Eng. & For. Mining Gloss.* (ed. 2) 80 (*S. Staffordsh. Terms*), *Stamp*, a mark cut in the roof or sides of the mine, as a point of reference, to show the amount of work done.

18. *Metallurgy.* (See quots.)

1880 *Encycl. Brit.* XIII. 319 (*Iron*) The first rough forged slabs are cut into pieces termed 'stamps', which are then reheated. **1881** RAYMOND *Mining Gloss.*, *Stamps*, S. Wales. The pieces into which the rough bars shingled from the finery ball are broken, to be piled for subsequent rolling into sheet-iron.

IV. *attrib.* and *Comb.*

19. Obvious combinations, as ***stamp-mark***, ***-seal***; objective and objective gen., as ***stamp-licker***, ***stamp-licking*** sb. and adj. (freq. with reference to menial office work), ***stamp-maker***, ***stamp-selling*** adj.

1928 F. LE GROS CLARK *Apparition* xiii. 176 You've never even held a commission. Bloody *stamp-licker in an office. **1978** J. UPDIKE *Coup* (1979) vii. 269 In the bureaucracy of Kush Amid so many posts for stamp-lickers and boot-lickers. **1913** *Punch* 14 May 382/3 There is something after all to be said for the *Stamp-licking Act. **1973** G. TALBOT *Ten Seconds from Now* (1974) ii. 22 At first the job was stamp-licking office boy on the commercial side. **1979** *Nature* 4 Jan. 7/1 A total paid staff of two people who do everything from typing, stamp-licking and driving to.. producing scholarly catalogues. **1858** SIMMONDS *Dict. Trade*, *Stamp-maker, a die sinker; a manufacturer of adhesive receipt or postage stamps. **1813** SHELLEY *Q. Mab* IV. 230 Red glows the tyrants *stamp-mark on its bloom. *Ibid.* v. 188 A public mart Of undisguising selfishness, that sets On each its price, the stamp-mark of her reign. **1758** J. BLAKE *Plan. regul. Marine Syst.* 3 Let her be provided with a screw *stamp-seal, having a device thereon. **1908** *Daily Chron.* 18 Apr. 4/6 An automatic *stamp-selling machine.

20. Special comb.: **Stamp Act**, each of the various Acts of Parliament for regulating the stamp duties; esp. that of 1765 (5 Geo. III, c. 12) for levying stamp duties in the American colonies; also, that of 1712 (10 Anne, c. 19, §101) imposing a stamp duty on newspapers; **stamp-album**, a book for the orderly arrangement and preservation of a collection of postage stamps; **stamp-battery**, a series of stamps in a stamp-mill; **stamp-bed**, the bed or bottom of a stamping machine upon which the lower die is placed; **Stamp-Bill**, a bill for imposing or regulating stamp duties; **stamp book** = *stamp-album*; **stamp-box**, (*a*) a receptacle for unused postage stamps; (*b*) the box in which the ore is pounded in a stamp-mill; **stamp-collecting**, (*a*) *sb.* = PHILATELY; (*b*) *adj.*, that practises philately; **stamp collection**, a philatelist's collection of postage stamps; also *fig.*; **stamp-collector**, (*a*) a collector or receiver of stamp duties; (*b*) a PHILATELIST; **stamp copper**, copper ore which is to be or has been crushed by stamping (*Funk's Stand. Dict.* 1895); **stamp-cutter** (see quot.); **stamp-dealer**, a dealer in postage stamps for collectors; **stamp-distributor**, an official who issues or sells government stamps; hence ***stamp distributorship***; **stamp duty**, any of the duties collected by means of stamps impressed on or affixed to the articles taxed; **stamp gold**, gold ore for stamping; **stamp-hammer**, the hammer of a stamping machine; **stamp-head**, (*a*) the head of a pestle of a stamp-mill; (*b*) the head of a cask upon which the brands are made (*Funk's Stand. Dict.*); †**stamp-house**, a house containing machinery for crushing ore; **stamp machine**, (*a*) *Paper-manuf.*, a machine for pulping rags (*Cent. Dict.* 1891); (*b*) a vending machine which supplies postage stamps; †**stamp-man** = *stamp-collector* (*a*); **stamps-man**, one who helps to work an ore-crushing stamp-mill; **stamp-master**, (*a*) an official appointed by the Trustees for the linen manufacture in Ireland (see quot. 1726); (*b*) an official appointed to adminster the Stamp Act; **stamp mealies** *S. Afr.* [ad. Afrikaans *stampmielies*] = sense 9 b above; cf. STAMPED *ppl. a.* 1 b; **stamp-mill**, (*a*) the apparatus used to crush ores by means of a pestle or series of pestles operated by machinery, also *attrib.*; (*b*) an oil-crushing mill of similar construction; **stamp note**, a permit from a Custom House official granting permission for the loading of goods on board ship; **stamp office**, an office where government stamps are issued and where stamp duties are received; **stamp officer**, one appointed to administer the Stamp Act; **stamp paper**, (*a*) paper having the government revenue stamp impressed on or affixed to it; (*b*) the marginal paper of a sheet of postage stamps (often used as sticking plaster, etc.); **stamp-press** (see quot.); **stamp rock**, ore suitable for treatment by stamping; **stamp-stem**, the stem of the pestle of a stamp-mill; **stamp-tax**, a tax imposed by a stamp act; **stamp war**, competition amongst retailers to attract custom by providing the best trading-stamp offer; an instance of this; **stamp-work** (see quot.).

1765 J. ADAMS *Diary* 18 Dec., Wks. 1850 II. 154 That enormous engine, fabricated by the British Parliament, for beating down all the rights and liberties of America, I mean the *Stamp Act. **1793** *Blackstone's Comm.* (ed. 12) I. 324 *note*, If each stamp-act declared the whole amount of the stamp at the time, it would prevent much confusion. **1862** *All Year Round* July 447/1 My *stamp album is worth twenty pounds. **1875** KNIGHT *Dict. Mech.*, **Stamp-battery*. **1877** RAYMOND *Statist. Mines & Mining* 451 The.. advantage in substituting a systematic crushing by steel rolls for stamp-batteries. **1879** *Cassell's Techn. Educ.* IV. 263/1 This block the stamper lays on the *stamp-bed, immediately under the descending hammer. **1765** J. INGERSOLL *Lett. Stamp-Act* (1766) 11 The *Stamp-Bill that has been preparing to lay before Parliament for taxing America. **1862** F. BOOTY *Stamp Coll. Guide* Introd., The *stamp book.. has also its utilitarian side. **1862** *Catal. Internat. Exhib., Brit.* II. No. 5825, Match-box, *stamp-box, and paper-knife, all *en suite*. **1872** W. W. SMYTH *Mining Statistics* 65 The amalgam obtained inside and outside the stamp boxes. **1862** F. BOOTY *Stamp Coll. Guide* Introd., It is curious to see how much public opinion has been modified lately, upon the subject of *stamp collecting. **1867** *Philatelist* I. 1/2 Not only in England, but in other stamp-collecting countries. [**1865** *Stamp-Collector's Mag.* 1 Jan. 2/1 When we first saw a postage-stamp collection, more than ten years past, it contained about a hundred and fifty specimens.] **1884** *Stamp Collectors' Jrnl.* 15 Jan. 19/1 The value of a *stamp collection does not depend entirely upon the amount of money expended for the album and the stamps. **1926** J. S. HUXLEY *Ess. Pop. Sci.* 164 This *corpus* of fact.. is only a vast stamp-collection, no more than a lumber-room, unless each generation in its turn will make it live. **1978** S. SHELDON *Bloodline* iv. 62 He was basically a retiring man, content to make a modest living, reside in a little apartment in Passy and tend to his small stamp collection. **1710** *Lond. Gaz.* No. 4673/3 All such Indentures.. to be sent.. either to the head Stamp-Office, or to some of the *Stamp Collectors. **1863** (*title*) The Stamp-Collector's Magazine. **1858** SIMMONDS *Dict. Trade*, **Stamp-cutter*, an engraver of dies on wood, stone, or metal. **1863** *Stamp-Collector's Mag.* I. 39/2 The *stamp dealers of Paris. **1765** *Universal Mag.* XXXVII. Suppl. 377/1 The *stamp distributor, or informer, may unrighteously get, from his Majesty's good American subjects, more than his Majesty, upon a balance, may get by the stamps. **1904** SPENCER *Autobiog.* II. 39 Of all posts likely to answer my purpose, that of stamp-distributor was the most promising. *Ibid.*, The *stamp-distributorship for Derby fell vacant, and I made an effort to obtain it. **1704** EVELYN *Diary* 16 Jan., The Lord Treasurer gave my grandson the office of Treasurer of the *Stamp duties. **1765** J. INGERSOLL *Lett. Stamp-Act* (1766) 28 'Tis said that it is intended to give the Business of collecting and paying the Stamp-Duty, to Americans. **1894** *Act 57–8 Vict.* c. 30. §6(1) Estate duty shall be a stamp duty collected and recovered as hereinafter mentioned. **1911** *Encycl. Brit.* XXV. 771/2 The death duties, the corporation duty, the duties on patent medicines and playing cards, and postage duties, are also technically 'stamp duties'; but in ordinary use the expression is limited to those imposed on the various classes of legal instruments, such as conveyances, leases,..&c., on bills of exchange,..bills of lading, and a few other documents. **1877** RAYMOND *Statist. Mines & Mining* 293 The Quartz Hill mines have furnished during the year about one-third of the *stamp-gold product of the county. **1837** HEBERT *Engin. & Mech. Encycl.* II. 190 By means of a blow from the *stamp hammer, the two needles between the dies are exactly impressed on both sides with the grooves. **1758** BORLASE *Nat. Hist. Cornw.* 178 The lifters.. are armed at the bottom with large masses of iron.. called *Stamp-heads. **1890** *Goldf. Victoria* 15 A battery of 26 stampheads. **1684** *Phil. Trans.* XVII. 745 Several persons were employed to bring the Refuse [copper ore] to the *Stamp-house, where it was stamped. **1944** J. D. CARR *Till Death do us Part* xviii. 191 There's no *stamp machine at the post office... Anyone who wants stamps must buy 'em.. over the counter. **1969** R. THOMAS *Singapore Wink* xxvi. 250 Trippet and I went in search of a stamp machine. We fed dimes and nickels and quarters into it until we had almost three dollars' worth. He helped me lick them. **1765** *Universal Mag.* XXXVII. 217/1 The *Stampman for that colony had appointed his Deputies. **1876** BANCROFT *Hist. U.S.* III. xx. 532 In Boston, the people dealt first with Andrew Oliver, who had received his commission as stamp-man. **1891** J. H. PEARCE *Esther Pentreath* I. i, The news of the accident spread like wildfire among..the *stamps'-men and spallers. **1712** in D. D. Black *Hist. Brechin* (1839) 125 [They were appointed by the council] to be *stamp-masters of this burgh for stamping all linen cloth. **1726** *Act 13 Geo. I*, c. 26. §20 All Dealers in Linen Cloth, before..they shall sell..any Linen Cloth.. shall carry the same..to the Place where such Lapper or Stamp-master..shall reside, there to be inspected, marked, lapped up and stamped by him. **1952** L. GREEN *Lords of Last Frontier* 79 We now live well and keep strong on *stamp mealies from Oorlog's place. **1749** *Phil. Trans.* XLVI. 226 After this Preparation it is brought to the *Stamp-mills. **1874** RAYMOND *6th Rep. Mines* 292 The stamp-mill ore is passed through the mill belonging to the mine. **1858** SIMMONDS *Dict. Trade*, *Stamp-note. **1710** *Lond. Gaz.* No. 4673/3 All such Indentures..to be sent..to the head *Stamp-Office. **1712** STEELE *Spect.* No. 555 ⁋5 The tax on each half-sheet has brought into the stamp-office one week with another above 20 l. **1765** *Universal Mag.* Oct. 218/2 His son, then in London, was appointed a *Stamp Officer for the said province. **1765** *Ibid.* XXXVII. Suppl. 378/2 A design ..to promote the taking of the *stamp-papers. **1814** SCOTT *Wav.* lxxi, It certainly related to stamp-paper and parchment. **1892** *Photogr. Ann.* II. 61 Get some gummed stamp paper, and punch through six or eight thicknesses at a time. **1875** KNIGHT *Dict. Mech.*, **Stamp-press*, one for attaching stamps to letters, envelopes, or other articles. **1872** RAYMOND *Statist. Mines & Mining* 314 The *stamp-rock, it is said, yields about one ounce of retorted amalgam per ton. **1882** *Rep. Precious Metals U.S.* 572 There is a momentum given to the stamp, *stamp-stem, and piston. **1825** J. NEAL *Bro. Jonathan* I. 160 We rose up as one man, against a paltry *stamp-tax. **1963** *Daily Tel.* 14 Oct. 1/4 (*heading*) *Stamp war challenge to Garfield Weston. **1972** *Guardian* 16 Oct. 9/5 In the early sixties the stamp war broke out. Different supermarket chains started offering different stamps, each one claiming to give better value and better gifts. **1881** RAYMOND *Mining Gloss.*, **Stamp-work*, Lake Superior. Rock containing disseminated native copper.

†**stamp**, *sb.*[4] *Obs. rare*$^{-1}$. [Of obscure origin; cf. ON. *stamp-r* large tub, LG. *stampe* drinking-glass with a thick stem, G. *stampf* mortar, also swill-tub.] Some kind of vessel for oil.

1552 *Invent. Ch. Goods* (Surtees) 65, ij pypes of everye, one with litle silver, the ole and creme in a stampe of latten, and the oyntment in a boke [? *read* boxe] covered with lether.

stamp (stæmp), *sb.*[5] *dial.* [Of obscure origin: cf. STALP.] A trap.

1788 PICKEN *Poems* 53 Mony a trap, an' stamp, an' snare, They hae their prey to catch in. **1827** *Sporting Mag.* XXI. 111 Some people catch foxes in stamps, and say it is done accidentally.

stamp (stæmp), *v.* Also 3–7 **stampe**, 4–5 **staumpe**, 6 **stampp**. [Early ME. *stampen* (? OE. **stampian*) = (M)LG., (M)D., WFris. *stampe*, NFris. *stampi* to stamp with the foot, to pound, OHG. *stamfôn* to pound (only once, gl. *comminuere*; MHG., mod.G. *stampfen* to stamp with the foot, to pound, bray in a mortar), ON. *stappa* (:—**stampa*) to stamp with the foot, to bray in a mortar, (M)Sw. *stampa*, (M)Da. *stampe*:—OTeut. **stampōjan*, f. **stampo-z* masc., pestle, mortar (MLG. *stamp*, OHG., MHG., mod.G. *stampf* masc.) A parallel formation from the same base is OE. *stęmpan* to bray in a mortar (occurring only once; cf. *á-stęmpan* to stamp with a die, *stęmping-isern* stamping-iron) = MLG. *stempen*, WFris. *stimpe*, NFris. *stemp*, MHG., mod.G. (? obs.) *stempfen*:—OTeut. type **stampjan*; cf. MLG., mod.G. *stempel*, MHG. *stempfel* stamp, die. The Teut. **stamp-* is the source of the Com. Rom. verb represented by It. *stampare* to tread, press, print, Pr., Sp., Pg. *estampar* to stamp, print, OF. *estamper* (mod.F. *estamper*, in some technical senses *étamper*) to stamp; whence the verbal noun It. *stampa* press, printing-press, Sp., Pg. *estampa*, F. *estampe* engraving, *estampe*, *étampe* stamp, die.

The view stated above seems on the whole more likely than the alternative supposition that the verb did not exist in OE., but is solely an adoption of OF. *estamper* (see above). At the same time there can be little doubt that the sense-development of the Eng. verb has been influenced by the uses of its Fr. cognate.

The Teut. root **stamp-* is prob. a nasalized form of **stap-* to tread; if so the primary sense of the verb would seem to be that of branch II below, from which the other senses might easily be derived. Some scholars regard the root (pre-Teut. **stomb-*) as cogn. w. Gr. *στέμβ-ειν* ? to shake, ? to maltreat (occurring only once); radical connexion with STUMP *sb.* has also been suggested.]

I. †**1.** *trans.* To bray in a mortar; to beat to a pulp or powder; to pound. Also *absol. Obs.*

[*c* **1000** *Sax. Leechd.* I. 378 Nim readstalede harhuna & ysopo, & stemp & do on ænne neowan pott.] *c* **1200** *Vices & Virtues* Hie [*sc.* rihte ȝeleaue] is ȝelich ðe seneueies corne... Æure ðe mann ðe hit more [*read* ðe more ðe hit mann] bat and stampeþ, ðe hit strengere and betre is. **13..** *K. Alis.* 332 Herbes he tok in an herber, And stamped heom in a morter. *c* **1386** CHAUCER *Pard. T.* 210 This Cookes, how they stampe and streyne and grynde, And turnen substaunce in to Accident. **1398** TREVISA *Barth. De P.R.* XVIII. lxxxix. (1495) 838 Coloquintida.. helpyth ayenst fleen yf it is stampyd and medlyd wyth water and spronge in the place there as many fleen ben. *c* **1400** *Lanfranc's Cirurg.* 56 Take malowe leues & leues of violet, & þe rote of holi-hocke; seþe hem weel in water, & staumpe hem. **1483** CAXTON *Gold. Leg.* 112 b, Yf all the espyces of the world had ben stamped to gydre it shold not haue smellyd so well. *c* **1489** —— *Sonnes of Aymon* vii. 169 Thenne toke Mawgis an herbe, & stamped it vpon a stone wyth the pomell of his swerde and tempered it wyth water. **1579** LANGHAM *Gard. Health* (1633) 602 Stamp good store of ripe Sloes. **1594** PLAT *Jewell-ho.* II. 46 Malaghie reasons.. either stampt or unstampt. **1607** TOPSELL *Four-f. Beasts* 386 Pelagonius would haue him to drink Parsly stampt with wine. **1613** PURCHAS *Pilgrimage* (1614) 650 They stamp their milia as we do spice. **1626** BACON *Sylva* §45, I conceiue that some Decoction of Bones, and Sinewes, stamped, and well strained, would bee a very Nourishing Broth. **1683** SALMON *Doron Med.* I. 113 Pultise is made of green Herbs stampt or of their juyces. *a* **1700** EVELYN *Diary* 24 Aug. 1678, They cull the raggs.. then they stamp them in troughs to a papp with pestles. **1719** DE FOE *Crusoe* I. (Globe) 123 A Stone Mortar to stamp or beat some Corn in. **1747** WESLEY *Prim. Physick* (1762) 116 A Plaister of Ground Ivy stampt. **1764** ELIZ. MOXON *Eng. Housew.* (ed. 9) 165 Stamp your berries and throw them into your water as you stamp them.

†**b.** To crush or press (fruit, esp. crabs) to extract the juice; to press (wine) out of grapes.

1387–8 T. USK *Test. Love* III. v. (Skeat) 114 But it the better be stamped, and the venomous jeuse out-wrongen, it is lykely to enpoysonen al tho that therof tasten. *c* **1450** *Mirour Saluacioun* (Roxb.) 134 Out of grapes stampyng the wyne. **1573** TUSSER *Husb.* (1878) 46 Stamp crabs that may, for rotting away. **1594** LYLY *Mother Bombie* III. iv, It was crabbs she stampt, and stole away one to make her a face. **1597** DELONEY *Gentle Craft* Wks. (1912) 151 Would you haue him to stampe the crab. **1618** W. LAWSON *New Orchard & Gard.* xvi. (1623) 52 Dresse euery Apple,.. stamp them, and straine them [etc.].

c. To thresh. *Obs.* exc. *dial.* 'to beat or break the awns from barley, etc., to thresh flax' (*Eng. Dial. Dict.*).

1388 WYCLIF *Isa.* xxv. 10 Moab schal be threischid vndur hym, as chaffis be stampid [Vulg. *teruntur*] in a wayn. **1856** MORTON *Cycl. Agric.* II. 103/2 Ordinarily the grain [barley] is spread on the floor of the barn, and stamped by either of the instruments [depicted].

d. To crush (ore); in mod. use, by means of the machine called a 'stamp'.

1568 in *Sel. Charters Trading Co.* (Selden Soc.) 18 The same ores.. to drain break stamp wash boil [etc.]. **1859** R. HUNT *Guide Mus. Pract. Geol.* (ed. 2) 261 The dressing floors, where the ores are stamped and prepared for the market.

e. To drive in (a blasting charge).

1899 *Allbutt's Syst. Med.* VII. 277 While engaged in stamping a blasting charge in a rock with a pointed iron bar .. the charge suddenly exploded.

II. To bring down the foot heavily. (Cf. STRAMP *v.*)

2. *intr.* **a.** To bring the sole of one's foot suddenly and forcibly down (*upon* the ground or floor, or some other object), with the object of crushing or beating down something.

1340 HAMPOLE *Pr. Consc.* 8590 Þe devels salle ay opon þam gang, And ay on þam stamp with þair feth omang. **1384** CHAUCER *H. Fame* 2154 Tho behynde.. troden fast on other heles And stampen as men doon aftir eles. **1719** YOUNG *Revenge* I. i, This usage is like stamping on the murder'd, When life is fled. **1818** SCOTT *Br. Lamm.* xxxiii, Stamping upon the coals with the heel of his boot.

b. To strike the ground or floor forcibly with the sole of one's foot, in order, e.g. to make a noise that will serve as a signal, to emphasize a command or an expression of firm resolve, to warm one's feet, etc. Phrase, ***to stamp with one's foot.***

1535 COVERDALE *Ezek.* vi. 11 Smyte thine hondes together, and stampe with thy fete. **1538** ELYOT *Dict.*, *Supplodo*, to stampe or make noise with the fete. **1548** HALL *Chron., Edw. IV* (1550) 43 b, The sayd Lewes conterfeited the fashion and gesture of the duke of Burgoyn, & began to stampe with his fote on the ground. **1662** GREENHALGH in Ellis *Orig. Lett.* Ser. II. IV. 15 When mention was made of the Edomites, Philistines, or any enemies of.. Israel's, they stamped strongly with their feet. **1705** H. BLACKWELL *Engl. Fencing-Master* 16 Must I stamp with my Foot when I make those Faints? **1756–7** tr. *Keysler's Trav.* (1760) III. 143 As far as can be conjectured from the sound caused by stamping with the foot against the bottom, there is another cavity under it. **1801** SOUTHEY *Thalaba* IX. xxviii, Thrice on the floor she stampt. **1815** SCOTT *Guy M.* liii, She paused an instant..and stamped upon the ground, which..shewed vestiges of having been recently moved. **1823** ROLAND *Fencing* 27 To ascertain whether you are firmly and correctly placed in this posture, it will be necessary to make an Appel. This is performed by stamping twice with the right foot. **1850** MERIVALE *Rom. Emp.* xiii. (1865) II. 114, I have only to stamp with my foot, he said,..to raise legions from the soil of Italy. **1860** TYNDALL *Glac.* I. xi. 78, I again resorted to stamping to secure a footing.

c. *esp.* as an instinctive expression of fury; formerly often †*to stamp and stare*. Hence (now only *U.S.*), to be very angry.

c **1375** *Sc. Leg. Saints* l. (Catherine) 1028 He..rathly ruschit to and fra,..& sturly stampit als, & steryt. **1530** PALSGR. 732/2, I stampe, I stare, as one doth that taketh on in his angyr, *je me demayne*. You never sawe man stampe as he dyd. *a* **1534** *Coventry Corpus Chr. Plays* I. 779, I stampe! I stare! I loke all abowt! **1560** DAUS tr. *Sleidane's Comm.* 185 Many men stamped [L. *fremebant enim plerique*] for the murther of Rincon and Fregose. **1577** KENDALL *Flowers of Epigr.*, *Trifles* 24 b, He stamps, he stares, he taketh on: he knowes not what to doe. **1657** BILLINGSLY *Brachy-Martyrol.* xii. 39 How he did stamp, did stare like one distracted. **1681** [DURFEY] *Progr. Honesty* viii. 9 And as a stubborn Child..Vext at some trifle, stamps, lies down and cries. **1712** STEELE *Spect.* No. 429 ¶17 The Petitioner swore, stamped, and threw down his Cards. **1842** LOVER *Handy Andy* xix, O'Grady stamped and swore with rage. **1866** 'L. CARROLL' *Alice in Wonderland* viii, The Queen..went stamping about, and shouting 'Off with his head!' **1872** DE VERE *Americanisms* 552 *Stamp*, to, commonly pronounced *stomp*, has, in the South especially, the meaning of being very angry. **1891** FARRAR *Darkn. & Dawn* liv, He stamped, and cursed the Christians by all his gods. **1891** E. ROPER *By Track & Trail* ii. 21 The Colonel stamped and groaned and swore.

d. said of a horse.

1509 HAWES *Past. Pleasure* xxviii. (Percy Soc.) 134 My stede Galantyse..began to stampe full marveylously. *c* **1611** CHAPMAN *Iliad* VIII. 72 The paine, so sore the courser stung, (Pierc't to the braine) he stampt and plung'd. **1810** SCOTT *Lady of L.* I. xxxi, Shouting clans or squadrons stamping. **1865** A. SMITH *Summer in Skye* II. 107 The horses stamped and pawed in their stables.

e. To walk with a heavy, 'pounding' tread; to walk noisily or laboriously, tramp.

c **1489** CAXTON *Sonnes of Aymon* iii. 93 Reynawde..asked who was there that maketh thys noyse?.. It is evyl doone for to go thus stampyng at this houre. **1523** BERNERS *Froiss.* I. ccccxv. 725 Yonder men of armes..haue all this laste day traueyled, and all this nyght stamped in the myre. **1581** PETTIE tr. *Guazzo's Civ. Conv.* II. (1586) 56 Men, who..come stamping in with their high clouted shooes, yet one of good understanding. **1753** MISS COLLIER *Art Torment.* I. ii. (1811) 63 Tell her you wonder how she can stamp about the floor in such a manner, as if she had wooden shoes on. **1833** M. SCOTT *Tom Cringle* iii, The capstan was manned, and the crew stamped round to a point of war. **1859** FITZGERALD *Omar* xvii, And Bahrám, that great Hunter—the Wild Ass Stamps o'er his Head, and he lies fast asleep.

f. Used *transf.* of a marine engine.

1892 KIPLING *Barrack-r. Ballads*, *L'Envoi* ix, And the engines stamp and ring, and the wet bows reel and swing. **1897** MARY KINGSLEY *W. Africa* 124 The *Mové*..stamps steadily along past the wooded shore.

3. *trans.* **a.** With complementary adv. or phrase: To affect in the specified way by stamping; *esp.* to trample violently *down*, *to the ground*.

c **1470** HENRY *Wallace* v. 270 Ane othir sone doune fra his hors he bar, Stampyt to grounde, and drownyt with outyn mar. **1552** HULOET, Stampe vnder fete, *pessundo*. **1659** D. PELL *Impr. Sea* 127 When..divisions are made in your ships, salve them up again, or else couragiously stamp them down. **1883** *Harper's Mag.* Dec. 51/2 Leonard was..heard stamping the snow from his boots. **1894** HALL CAINE *Manxman* III. xii, 'The Lord's blessing, Master Philip——' she began, but the horse's feet stamped out everything.

b. To bring down the sole or heel forcibly upon. Now somewhat *rare*. †Also with *off*.

1602 *Span. Trag.* Addit. III. xii. *a.* 19, I..Beat at the bushes, stampe our grandam earth Diue in the water, and stare vp to heauen, Yet cannot I behold my sonne Horatio. **1700** DRYDEN *Pal. & Arc.* I. 446 He frets, he fumes, he stares, he stamps the Ground. **1815** SCOTT *Guy M.* x, The short turf..was much trampled, as if stamped by the heels of men in a mortal struggle. **1892** *Daily News* 20 May 5/7 Hundreds of feet angrily stamped the ground. **1892** RIDER HAGGARD *Nada* 216 The Halakazi are no more a tribe, since Umslopogaas stamped them with his feet.

c. *to stamp one's foot* = sense 2.

1821 CLARE *Vill. Minstr.* I. 123 She furious stampt her shoeless foot aground. **1865** TROLLOPE *Belton Est* xx. 229 He would stamp his foot on the ground. **1875** B. TAYLOR *Faust* I. xiii. 146 Faust (stamping his foot). **1866** G. MACDONALD *Ann. Q. Neighb.* xxvii, She stamped her little foot.

d. *to stamp out*: to extinguish (a fire) by trampling on it. Hence, *transf.* to extirpate (a disease, a heresy, etc.), suppress (a rebellion) by resorting to vigorous measures; *occas.* to exterminate (a people).

1851 MRS. BROWNING *Casa Guidi Wind.* 107 Ye stamp no nation out, though day and night Ye tread them with that absolute heel which [etc.]. **1866** *Jrnl. R. Agric. Soc.* Ser. II. II. I. 271 Measures..by which, to use a now prevalent expression, the disease was 'stamped out'. **1868** SIR J. Y. SIMPSON in *Med. Times & Gaz.* 4 Jan. 5/2 The public mind has during the last two or three years become familiarised with the idea of 'stamping out' a disease, in the instance of the rinderpest. **1868** G. DUFF *Pol. Surv.* 78 The Taeping insurrection was stamped out utterly three years ago. *a* **1873** DEUTSCH *Lit. Rem.* 289 The very remembrance of it was stamped out. **1883** *Manch. Guardian* 17 Oct. 5/2 Earl Spencer..remarked that in Scotland they had, by a strict enforcement of the rules, stamped out the disease altogether. **1892** RIDER HAGGARD *Nada* 208 If these demands were granted, then he would spare them,..if not, he would stamp them out. **1899** J. MATHEW *Eaglehawk & Crow* ix. 117 Some fires had to be stamped out by the youths with their naked feet.

III. To strike an impression on something.

4. To impress with an embossed or intaglio device or lettering by means of a die and the impact of a hammer or machinery; to make (a coin, a medal) by this process.

1560 DAUS tr. *Sleidane's Comm.* 415 b, In his letters and coyne, that he stamped [*in..moneta quam cuderet*], used stil the name of elector. **1610** HOLLAND *Camden's Brit.* (1637) 75 He stamped certaine golden pieces of coine. **1617** MORYSON *Itin.* I. 284 Also they [the Irish] had silver groats, called crosse-keele groats, stamped with the Popes tripple Crowne. **1638** JUNIUS *Paint. Ancients* 177 Among many..sorts of coine anciently famous, the Cyziceni stateres were most of all renowned as being well stamped. **1670** PETTUS *Fodinæ Reg.* 41 Lastly, the Moniers, who are some to sheer the Monie,.. some to stamp or coin it. **1697** MAUNDRELL *Journ. Jerus.* (1707) 126 It's Gates are vastly large, and cover'd with Brass, stampt all over with Arab Characters. **1710** W. KING *Heathen Gods* vii. (1722) 15 Money of Brass was stamp'd, with a Ship on the one side..and the Figure of Janus with a double Face on the other. **1736** *Gentl. Mag.* VI. 683/2 There having been a great scarcity of Copper and Silver Coin in Ireland..Traders..hit on a Method of stamping Pieces of Silver bearing a promissory Note of three Pence each. **1818** STODDART *Gram.* in *Encycl. Metrop.* (1845) I. 156/1 A preposition is not like a piece of money stamped to pass for a certain value. **1862** STANLEY *Jew. Ch.* (1877) I. iii. 59 The pieces of money..are stamped with the earliest mark of coinage. **1865** STREET *Gothic Archit. Spain* 218 All the Moorish decorative work..was evidently cut and carved as if it had been stone, and seldom, if ever, I think, stamped or moulded, according to the mistaken practice of the present day.

transf. and *fig.* **1611** SHAKS. *Cymb.* II. v. 5 That most venerable man, which I Did call my Father, was, I know not where When I was stampt. Some Coyner with his Tooles Made me a counterfeit. **1614** J. TAYLOR (Water P.) *Nipping Abuses* B 3 b, My pulsiue braine no Art affoords, To mint, or stampe, or forge new coined words. **1799** CAMPBELL *Pleas. Hope* I. 498 Nature stamp'd us in a heavenly mould.

b. To impress (a device, lettering, etc.) by means of a die.

1613 PURCHAS *Pilgrimage* (1614) 598 The Cyrenæans to sooth this proud King..stamped his shape in their coynes. **1705** ADDISON *Italy*, *Rome* 351 But it is very well known that an Emperor often stamp'd on his Coins the Face or Ornaments of his Colledge. **1823** SCOTT *Quentin D.* viii, He now wore a hat, the band of which was garnished with..a dozen of little paltry figures of saints stamped in lead.

transf. and *fig.* **1589** GREENE *Menaphon* (Arb.) 43 So deepe were the characters stamped in my inwarde senses, that obliuion can neuer race out the forme of her excellence. *a* **1631** DONNE *Serm.* vii. (1640) 62 God stampeth his Image upon us, and so God is *Statuarius*, our Minter, our Statuary. **1692** R. L'ESTRANGE *Fables* ccxxvi. 198 She had the Flower-de-Luce Stamp'd, we must not say Branded upon her Shoulder. **1812** BYRON *Ch. Har.* II. xcviii, What is the worst of woes that wait on age? What stamps the wrinkle deeper on the brow?

c. *Bookbinding.* To impress a pattern on (leather) by means of dies.

1863 HOTTEN *Hand-bk. Topogr.* 103/2, 4to, old calf gilt, sides stamped.

d. To make by cutting out with a die.

1798 *Hull Advertiser* 18 Aug. 3/3 A man has invented an engine that will stamp or cut two hundred horse shoes in one hour. **1862** MORRALL *Needle Making* 17 In 1811, Abel and Michael Morrall..commenced stamping needles, and introduced the first eye into the needles by means of the stamp. What is meant by the first eye is an indenture half through the head of the needle.

e. *to stamp out*: to make (paste) into 'rounds', to fashion ('rounds' of paste) by pressure with a circular cutter.

1845 ELIZA ACTON *Mod. Cookery* (ed. 2) 457 Small rounds of bread stamped out with a plain..paste-cutter. **1877** *Cassell's Dict. Cookery* 17 Stamp out with a small cup-plate as many rounds as you wish to make pasties. *Ibid.* 19 Make a light sweet crust, stamp it out in small rounds.

5. To mark (paper or textile material) with a device either impressed in relief or intaglio, imparted to the surface by ink or pigment, or produced by both processes combined. Also, to impress (a device) on paper, etc. by means of a die or engraved plate. †Also with *off*.

1604 E. G[RIMSTONE] *D'Acosta's Hist. Indies* VI. v. 442 To make their impressions, they grave a boord or plank with the figures they will print, then do they stampe as many leaves of paper as they list. **1630** [see STAMPING *vbl. sb.* 1]. **1753** *Scots Mag.* Feb. 100/2 Each dozen of..hand-kerchiefs..are stamped twice. **1782** V. KNOX *Ess.* cxxxvii. ¶6 A few other books are extant, which are, on good reasons, judged to have been stamped, not printed *secundum artem*. **1828** LYTTON *Pelham* lxxxv, A letter was brought me, stamped with the foreign post mark. **1879** G. GLADSTONE *Calico Printing* in *Cassell's Techn. Educ.* I. 197/2 Block printing..consists in stamping the calico with a pattern raised in relief. **1885** 'MRS. ALEXANDER' *At Bay* xi, I know the paper and the crest stamped outside. **1885** 'H. CONWAY' *Family Affair* viii, This jacket..was stamped in various places with the government broad arrow. **1908** R. BAGOT *A. Cuthbert* xxi. 261 The address..was there in full, and she noticed that it was also stamped on the envelope.

†**b.** To print (a book, etc.). *Obs.* [Cf. It. *stampare*.]

1555 R. BRAHAM *Lydgate's Chron. Troy* To Rdr. 1/2 With ..great paynes causing the same to be perfected and stamped as it is nowe read. **1556** *Charter Stationers Co.* in Entick *London* (1766) IV. 225, Several seditious and heretical books,..are daily published, stamped and printed by divers..persons. **1609** W. BEDELL *Let. to Newton* 1 Jan. in *Two Biog. W.B.* (1902) 245 He told me further of a deliberation he had to remove himself..into Germany..to stamp that and sundry other things of the like nature. **1624** —— *Lett.* iv. 79 Wee had an Epistle stampt at Venice, pretended to bee written at Rome. *Ibid.* v. 85 These wordes Posseuine stamps in his former *Relation* in Capitall letters.

6. To impress with a device or lettering indicating genuineness, quality, or official inspection and approval; to impress (a device, etc.) on merchandise, weights or measures, or the like, for this purpose.

1564 *Extracts Burgh Rec. Edin.* (1875) III. 187 Quha..sall stamp samekill [cloth] as beis sufficient thairof with the said stamp in leid. **1631** *Letters patent Sir W. Russell* etc., That a stamp..to bee engraven with a Rose and Crown shall be stamped, sealed or marked on all the soapes..the better to distinguish the said soape from the counterfett soape. **1638** *Reg. Mag. Sig. Scot.* 315/1 To mark and stamp all firlottis, peckis, pund-wechtis, staine-wechtis, elnewandis [etc.]. **1795** FRANKLAND in *Phil. Trans.* LXXXV. 296 The Sheffield artists, who stamp much low-priced work with the title of cast steel. **1846** GREENER *Sci. Gunnery* 209 Such barrels are, of course, sent back unmarked. Those that are found satisfactory are duly stamped and taken home. **1885** KAY in *Law Times' Rep.* LIII. 490/2 The words..were never stamped on goods, or advertised as a trade mark. **1892** *Photogr. Ann.* II. Advt. p. cxxi, Messrs. —— warn customers before purchasing to see that every Lens is stamped with their Trade Mark.

7. To impress with an official stamp or mark indicating that a duty or tax has been paid. In later use also, to attach an adhesive 'stamp' to.

1765 BLACKSTONE *Comm.* I. viii. 313 A fifth branch of the perpetual revenue consists in the stamp duties... These imposts are very various, according to the nature of the thing stamped. **1837** R. HILL *Post Office Reform* 19 The duties of the Clerks in the London Office..are..to stamp the letters; to assort them for delivery [etc.]. **1854** *Poultry Chron.* II. 147 If you need a reply, send..an envelope directed and stamped. **1885** 'MRS. ALEXANDER' *At Bay* iii, He wrote a hasty line to the effect that [etc.]... When this had been sealed, stamped, and directed to Lambert, he rang and ordered his bill. **1892** HOLYOAKE *60 Yrs. Agitator's Life* I. liii. 287 Mr. Lloyd..was at once told he must stop or stamp. He stamped, raised his paper to twopence, and lost his circulation. I neither stopped nor stamped. **1907** G. JOHN *Voice from China* xi. 240 We..made another attempt to get the deed stamped.

8. In various uses, orig. figurative of senses 4–6.

†**a.** To fabricate (an inference) *out of* something. *Obs.*

1581 J. BELL *Haddon's Answ. Osor.* 82 b, Out of these two monstruous falsely forged propositions, he stampeth a conclusion..no lesse false then malicious. *Ibid.* 152, I awayte what this choppelogicke will stampe out hereof.

b. To declare or show to be of a certain quality or nature; sometimes in bad sense, to stigmatize.

1599 SHAKS. *Much Ado* I. ii. 7 *Leo*[*nato*] Are they [*sc.* the newes] good? *Old* [*Man*]. As the euents stamps them, but they haue a good couer. *a* **1720** SEWEL *Hist. Quakers* (1722) I. Pref. 3 Their Fear of doing or omitting anything which they judged would displease God, often hath been stampt with the odious Denomination of Stubbornness. **1853** MAURICE *Proph. & Kings* xix. 339 Their literal accomplishment..stamped them as sure decrees for Jerusalem and for euery other city of the earth in all generations to come. **1863** M. HOWITT tr. *Bremer's Greece* II. xii. 22 And this stamps them really as Greek islands. **1871** BLACKIE *Four Phases* i. 137 The death of Socrates must be stamped by the impartial historian as a great social crime. **1885** *Truth* 28 May 837/1 Not to like the picture is to stamp oneself as being no judge of painting.

c. To give a mark of authoritative approval to; †to convert by authorization *into*.

1681–6 J. SCOTT *Chr. Life* (1747) III. 450 By his own inherent Authority, as he was a King, he stamped those Doctrines into Laws which he taught and delivered as a Prophet. **1688** COMBER *Comp. Temple* (ed. 3) Pref. 2 Having ..undervalued these Devotions stampt by publick Authority. **1778** MME. D'ARBLAY *Diary* Sept., The sanction of his good opinion..would in a manner stamp the success of my book. **1809** PINKNEY *Trav. France* 268 Time has stampt his reputation. **1848** THACKERAY *Van. Fair* xlviii, No lady..can possess this desideratum, until she..has been presented to her Sovereign at Court. From that august interview they come out stamped as honest women. **1852** —— *Esmond* II. v, The famous Mr. Congreve had stamped with his high approval..this delightful person. *a* **1853** ROBERTSON *Serm.* Ser. III. xxi. 273 He has been stamped by his master's eulogy.

d. To impress with some permanent and conspicuous characteristic.

1780 BENTHAM *Princ. Legisl.* xiii. §4. 6 Falsehood stamps a character with a deep and degrading stain. **1836** J. MARTIN *Discourses* xv. 302 The Jewish priesthood must have seemed stamped by God with something of the mystery of His own nature. **1838** LYTTON *Leila* I. ii, Its beauty was singularly stamped with a grave and stately sadness. **1838** —— *Alice* II. i, The book that Evelyn could admire was sure to be stamped with the impress of the noble, the lovely, or the true!

e. To be a distinctive mark of; to characterize.

1833 TENNYSON *Lady Clara* 40 Her manners had not that repose which stamps the caste of Vere de Vere. **1837** CARLYLE *Fr. Rev.* I. iii. i, With that frankness of speech which stamps the independent man.

f. To impress or fix permanently (an idea, etc.) on the mind or memory.

1662 STILLINGFL. *Orig. Sacræ* III. i. §10 If God hath stamped an universal character of himself upon the minds of men. **1690** LOCKE *Hum. Und.* I. ii. §1 It is an established Opinion..That there are..some primary Notions,..

Characters; as it were stamped upon the Mind of Man. **1725** WATTS *Logic* IV. ii. (1726) 353 Give all Diligence..that your Words, as fast as you utter them, may stamp your own Ideas exactly on the Mind of the Hearer. **1818** BYRON *Ch. Har.* IV. xviii, And Otway, Radcliffe, Schiller, Shakspeare's art, Had stamp'd her image in me. **1872** MORLEY *Voltaire* (1886) 1 A new type of belief..was stamped by the impression of his character and work into the intelligence and feeling of his own and the following times. **1885** 'MRS. ALEXANDER' *At Bay* vi, The picture of the streets through which he was conducted..remained forever stamped upon his memory.

g. To impose permanently (an immaterial mark or sign); to impress the signs or traces of (some quality, event, etc.) *on* a person or thing; to place permanently *on* a record or the like.

1641 J. JACKSON *True Evang. T.* III. 211 The character of Antiquity, that is now stamped upon them. **1684** *Contempl. St. Man* II. vi. (1699) 191 This Infamy, by some Mark of Ugliness and Deformity, shall be stamped upon their Faces and Bodies. **1756** C. SMART tr. *Horace, Epist.* II. i. (1826) II. 275 If length of time makes poems better, as it does wine, I would fain know how many years will stamp a value upon writings. **1822** HAZLITT *Table-t.* I. xi. 249 Conquerors, statesmen, and kings live but by their names stamped on the page of history. **1826** DISRAELI *Vivian Grey* V. x, Despair was stamped on his distracted features. **1848** J. H. NEWMAN in W. Ward *Life* (1912) I. 240, I believe those long years of anxiety have stamped themselves on my face. **1850** MERIVALE *Rom. Emp.* (1865) I. i. 3 The native ferocity of the people is stamped upon its earliest traditions. **1867** J. H. PARKER *Introd. Gothic Archit.* (ed. 3) 256 The character of each century is stamped upon its architecture.

stampable ('stæmpəb(ə)l), *a.* [f. STAMP *v.* + -ABLE.] That may be stamped; (of goods) liable to stamp duty.

1803 *Med. Jrnl.* X. 168 Numbers of people..sold..stampable articles without stamps or licence.

stampage ('stæmpɪdʒ). [f. STAMP *v.* + -AGE. Cf. F. *estampage, étampage.*]

1. The crushing (of tin-ore).

1910 *Cal. Close Rolls* an. 1365, 113, 1,000 marks every year to be taken of the issue of the stampage of tin in Cornwall.

2. A copy or impression (of an inscription) made by stamping.

1880 *Encycl. Brit.* XIII. 118/2 No copy was obtained [of the rock inscription] until October 1838, when the traveller Masson..made a calico stampage and an eye copy.

3. The amount charged or paid for the stamp or stamps of a postal packet; postage.

1887 *Taken-in* 88, I must not forget the stampage expenses..two miles out of Christ Church, your letter will be 2*d.* **1888** *Athenæum* 16 June 762/1 It..costs..two or three times the amount of stampage for parcel post.

stamp and go. *Naut. phr.* [The vbs. in *imperative.*] **1.** An order given to sailors for the performance of certain duties (see quot. 1867); also, the action of performing such duties. Also, a shanty sung to accompany this action.

1830 MARRYAT *King's Own* xix, To stop my ears against the infernal stamp-and-go of the marines and after-guards, over my head. **1867** SMYTH *Sailor's Word-bk.*, *Stamp and Go!* the order to step out at the capstan, or with hawsers, topsail-haliards, &c., generally to the fife or fiddle. **1929** F. BOWEN *Sea Slang* 132 Stamp and Go. The shanty sung for a straight pull along the deck. 'What shall we do with the drunken sailor?' is probably the best known.

transf. **1899** KIPLING *Stalky* 38 The floor shook to the stamp-and-go of the ballet.

2. (Usu. with hyphens.) In the West Indies: a simple, quickly prepared codfish fritter (see also quot. 1893).

1893 C. SULLIVAN *Jamaica Cookery Bk.* 87 Stamp and go. These are rough cakes made with cornmeal and flour..salt fish and a little butter... The country people as they travel stop at the way-side shops and buy them... Hence the name. **1953** *Caribbean Q.* III. I. 11 *Stamp-and-go*,..a kind of codfish fritter that is quickly made. **1970** *New Yorker* 10 Jan. 54/3 (Advt.), A chief who can water your mouth with a ..native Stamp-and-Go.

'stampant *a.* [formed after *rampant.*] Stamping.

c **1730** RAMSAY *Vision* v, A stampant, and rampant, Ferss lyon in his hand.

stamped (stæmpt), *ppl. a.* [f. STAMP *v.* + -ED[1].]

1. a. Crushed by stamping; pounded with pestle and mortar; crushed or pounded in a stamp-mill; trodden hard with the feet.

1600 DEKKER *Shoomakers Holy-day* (1610) C j b, *Rose*... No doue was euer halfe so mild as he. *Sibil.* Mild? yea as a bushel of stampt crabs [*sc.* apples]. **1626** BACON *Sylva* §768 Putting it into great Jars of Stone, and Stirring it about with a few Stamped Almonds. **1778** PRYCE *Min. Cornub.* 238 Halvans stamped small, and then washed..is termed Stampt Ore. **1888** GERARD *Land beyond Forest* lv. 356 A heap of grey wood-ashes in the centre of the stamped earth floor.

b. *stamped mealies* = STAMP *sb.*[3] 9 b. *S. Afr.*

1911 A. B. LAMONT *Rural Reader for S. Afr.* 189 'Stamped mealies'—that is mealies from which the outer husk has been removed—are made by stamping the grain with a heavy wooden stick in a large bowl. **1937** C. R. PRANCE *Tante Rebella's Saga* 82 Oom Fanie and his family had just asked a blessing on their supper of pumpkin and stamped mealies.

2. Marked with a stamp or device. **a.** Of coin.

1581 *Cal. Laing Charters* (1899) 254 Stampit penneis and plakis being exceptit. **1611** SHAKS. *Wint. T.* IV. iv. 747 They often giue vs (Souldiers) the Lye, but wee pay them for it with stamped Coyne, not stabbing Steele. **1855** MACAULAY *Hist. Eng.* xxii. IV. 705 Nor did all the newly stamped silver pass into circulation.

b. Of paper: Furnished with a government revenue stamp; spec. in slang *stamped paper* = promissory notes. Of a National Health Insurance card: Having the required stamps affixed.

1710 SWIFT *Jrnl. Stella* 3 Oct., He is discovered to have counterfeited stampt paper, in which he was a commissioner. **1765** *Universal Mag.* XXXVII. Suppl. 375/2 A gallows was erected; on one end of which was suspended the effigy..; in his right hand he held a stamped bill of lading. **1809** R. LANGFORD *Introd. Trade* 5 Bills of Exchange ..must be written on stamped paper. **1848** THACKERAY *Van. Fair* xxx, But since I'm married..I've not touched a bit of stamped paper. **1855** *Literary Gaz.* 6 Jan. 1 *heading*, Price Fourpence. Stamped Edition, Fivepence. **1864** *Once a Week* 25 June 5/1 The money was paid, and the stamped warranty was given. **1913** *Times* 7 Aug. 3/3 They had become mere agents of the State for the receipt of stamped contribution cards.

c. Of an envelope or other postal wrapper: Having a postage stamp embossed or printed upon it or (in later use) attached to it. Also *stamped (and) addressed envelope*: a self-addressed envelope with a postage stamp affixed, enclosed with a letter so that the recipient may reply at the sender's expense. Freq. required by an organization of a private enquirer and often abbrev. *S.A.E., s.a.e.* (see S 4 a).

In the latter sense the word may now be considered f. STAMP *sb.*[3] + -ED[2].

1837 R. HILL in G. B. Hill *Life* (1880) I. 270 Let stamped covers and sheets of paper be supplied to the public from the Stamp Office or Post Office..and sold at such a price as to include the postage. **1839** —— *On the Collection of Postage by means of Stamps* ibid. 346 Small stamped detached labels —say about an inch square—which, if prepared with a glutinous wash on the back, may be attached without a wafer. **1852** *U.S. Stat.* X. 141 *margin*, Stamped letter envelopes to be printed. *Ibid.* X. 256 Stamped envelope,.. stamped or printed envelopes..stamped letter envelope. **1854** *Poultry Chron.* II. 242 All letters requiring a reply, must contain a stamped envelope. **1873** *Young Englishwoman* Apr. 208/1 We..will return your edging if you will send a stamped addressed envelope. **1949** N. MITFORD *Love in Cold Climate* I. xiii. 131 The fella says here to enclose a stamped and addressed envelope but I don't think I shall pander to him. *a* **1953** DYLAN THOMAS *Under Milk Wood* (1954) 39 Here's a letter for you with stamped and addressed envelope enclosed. **1977** *Graduate* 9 Dec. 14/2 (Advt.), Enquiries and applications, with stamped addressed envelope, to Mr P Austin, DoE Archaeological Services, Carlisle Castle, Carlisle, Cumbria. **1981** M. SPARK *Loitering with Intent* ii. 52 An unpublished poem..which.. had been rejected eight times, returning to roost in my own stamped addressed envelope.

d. Of notepaper: Having a device printed or embossed upon it.

1907 GALSWORTHY *Country Ho.* I. i. 1 A half-sheet of stamped and crested notepaper.

3. Ornamented with an embossed pattern or design.

stamped leather: an expensive kind of wall-hanging used in the 16th–17th c. consisting of leather covered with silver leaf, varnished with a yellow lacquer to represent gold, and embossed with figures, a pattern, etc., and painted.

1756 MRS. CALDERWOOD in *Coltness Collect.* (Maitl. Club) 264 The curtain..is made of a red stamped English stuff. **1818** SCOTT *Br. Lamm.* xxvi, The inferior landholders and clergy, who usually ornamented their state apartments with hangings of a sort of stamped leather, manufactured in the Netherlands, garnished with trees and animals executed in copper foil. **1865** WAY *Promp. Parv.* Pref. p. li, This MS. is in the original stamped binding with boards, probably of oak. **1874** H. H. COLE *Catal. Ind. Art S. Kens. Mus.* 150 Sword, iron hilted, with stamped leather scabbard. **1882** CAULFEILD & SAWARD *Dict. Needlework* 459/2 Stamped Velvet is employed for the making of dress bodices and trimmings. *Ibid.*, Stamped velvet work, a modern Embroidery that is both effective and easy.

4. Of a device, name, etc.: Impressed by means of a stamp.

1865 ANNIE THOMAS *On Guard* xxxv, Thinking the seal or stamped monogram would tell from whom it came. **1881–6** GROSART in *Greene's Wks.* V. Note to title of *Planetomachia*, Our text of 'Planetomachia' is from that in the Bodleian, which bears the well-known stamped name of 'George Steevens'.

5. Of metal-ware: Pressed into shape by means of a stamping machine.

1879 *Cassell's Techn. Educ.* IV. 263/1 The introduction of stamped brass-foundry created a new era in the trade.

stampede (ˌstæm'piːd), *sb.* Also †stampado, †stampedo, stampido. [Originally U.S.; ad. Mexican Sp. *estampida*, a peculiar use of Sp. *estampida*, also *estampido* crash, uproar: see STAMP *sb.*[1]] **1. a.** A sudden rush and flight of a body of panic-stricken cattle.

α. [**1826** T. FLINT *Francis Berrian* I. ii. 46 Instantly this prodigious multitude..took what the Spanish call the 'stompado'. With a trampling like the noise of thunder,.. they [*sc.* the horses] took to their heels.] **1828** in *Missouri Hist. Rev.* (1914) VIII. 187 A little before daylight, the mules made an abortive attempt to raise a stampido. **1834** *U.S. Exec. Docum.* 2nd Sess., 23rd Congr. I. 74 (Stanford) A stupid sentinel last night..alarmed the camp and sent off in a stampedo the rest of the horses. **1835** W. IRVING *Tour Prairies* xxvi. 230 About two hours before day there was a *stampedo*, or sudden rush of horses, along the purlieus of the camp. **1867** BURTON *Hist. Scot.* III. xxxi. 276 These visitations produced a serious practical result in a stampedo of horses.

β. **1844** G. W. KENDALL *Narr. Texan Santa Fé Exped.* I. 96 'A *stampede*!' shouted some of the old campaigners,.. running towards their frightened animals. *a* **1864** HAWTHORNE *Dr. Grimshawe* xviii. (1891) 227 Then, tossing their horns, they [the deer] set off on a stampede. **1884** *Times* 3 Mar. 5/1 The shells..fortunately doing no damage, only causing a stampede among the mules and horses.

b. In N. Amer., an exhibition of cowboy skills, a rodeo; *spec.* that held at Calgary, Alberta (usu. *Calgary Stampede*), for the first time in 1912 and annually since 1919.

1912 *Calgary* (Alta.) *Daily Herald* 31 Aug. 6/1 Calgary is on the eve of its Stampede festival. **1919** *Eye Opener* (Calgary, Alta.) 9 Aug. 4 Come to Calgary Stampede Week and have the time of your life. **1923** C. M. BARBEAU *Indian Days* 5 Picturesque stampedes take place every summer in the July celebrations at Banff. **1948** *Ada* (Okla.) *Even. News* 2 July 1/5 A capacity crowd was on hand for the opening performance of the Hereford Heaven Stampede. **1950** B. HUTCHISON *Fraser* xvii. 251 Here the ranchers and Indians gather once a year for the innocent fun of the stampede. **1974** *Sat. Rev. World* 2 Nov. 30/2 The Calgary Stampede during the first two weeks of each July..offer[s] competition in matches ranging from wild-cow milking to buffalo riding.

2. a. A sudden or unreasoning rush or flight of persons in a body or mass; in American politics, a sudden unconcerted rush of a political convention for a candidate who seems likely to win. Also *spec.* (N. Amer. Hist.), a concerted rush of prospectors to the goldfields.

α. **1862** T. A. TROLLOPE *Lenten Journ. Umbria* i. 4 The great lines, trodden smooth by the annual stampedo of northern travellers.

β. **1846** LONGF. *Life* (1891) II. 69 There is a great 'stampede' on Parnassus at the present moment. **1859** K. CORNWALLIS *Panorama New World* I. 352 A sort of stampede or unreasoning rush of about twelve thousand men, principally from Victoria, was the speedy consequence. **1872** R. W. RAYMOND *Statistics of Mines* III. iv. 202 Rocky Bar..has suffered somewhat from the stampede to the bars of the Snake River. **1883** LORD R. GOWER *Reminisc.* I. xiii. 236 We were stopped by a stampede of peasants, some on foot, others in carts and on horseback. **1888** BRYCE *Amer. Commw.* II. lxx. 568 [When the break comes, i.e. when the weaker factions, perceiving that the men of their first preference cannot succeed, transfer their votes to..one..likely to succeed]..battalion after battalion goes over to the victors... In the picturesquely technical language of politicians, it is a Stampede. **1893** *Nation* (N.Y.) 24 Aug. 140/3 Ward did not share the sanguine expectations of those converts who looked for an Anglican stampede into the Roman Church. **1916** *Yukon Territory* (Canada Dept. Interior) 11 In the autumn of 1886 coarse gold was discovered in the Fortymile River, and..the usual stampede occurred. **1937** C. L. ANDREWS *Pioneers & Nuggets of Verse they Panned* 17 The stampede to the gold fields of the Tanana Valley..caused an exodus from Dawson. **1965** *Canad. Geogr. Jrnl.* Apr. 119/1 Not only was it the last of the old-fashioned stampedes in which dog teams and men vied for space along the narrow trail, but it also ushered in the air age of prospecting.

b. (With initial capital.) An uproarious kind of dance. Also *Stampede Dance* (in quot., a dancing-party).

1856 *Spirit of Times* 13 Dec. 238/2 The following was the programme of dancing: Part the Fourth—Scotch Reel,.. French Four, General Stampede. **1870** J. C. DUVAL *Adventures Big-Foot Wallace* xlii. 263, I see you haven't yet introduced the Texas national dance—the Stampede. **1950** *Chicago Daily News* 10 May 10/1 The annual 'Stampede Dance' of the Order of the Builders, State of Illinois, will be held May 20.

stampede (ˌstæm'piːd), *v.* Also †stompede, †stampedo (*rare*). [f. STAMPEDE *sb.*]

1. a. *trans.* To cause a stampede amongst (cattle); to cause a stampede of (a person's) cattle.

α. **1848** *Blackw. Mag.* Nov. 593 The Chases [*i.e.* a family named Chase]..were stampedoed upon the waters of the Platte.

β. **1838** *Hesperian* Nov. 37/2 When we awoke, we found that the flies had *stompeded* our horses, to use the expression of the country, which means that they made them so restive that they broke loose from the hopples. **1844** J. GREGG *Commerce of Prairies* II. 35 A party of Mexicans..*stampeded* and carried away, not only their own horses, but those of the Texans. **1847** RUXTON *Adv. Mexico* xxii. 187 During the night our mulada, which was grazing at large in the prairie, was stampeded by the Indians. **1896** GEN. H. PORTER in *Century Mag.* Nov. 23 The mules, stampeded by the sound of battle raging about them, had broken loose..and run away. **1897** *Cavalry Tactics* 139 Against cavalry in bivouacs ..the party should be divided, some being told off to stampede the horses.

b. *transf.* and *fig.* To cause (a body of persons) to fly or rush away through fear or common impulse; in American politics, to induce (a political convention) to vote suddenly in a body (for a particular candidate). Cf. STAMPEDE *sb.* 2. Hence, to cause (an individual) to take precipitate action.

1868 VISCT. STRANGFORD *Select.* (1869) I. 204 The aforesaid people are as likely as not to go by default and be stampeded into rebellion. **1888** BRYCE *Amer. Commw.* II. lxx. 568 To stampede a convention is the steadily contemplated aim of every manager who knows he cannot win on the first ballot. **1889** *Boston* (Mass.) *Jrnl.* 7 Mar. 2/4 Efforts of the Bears to Stampede the New York Market. **1890** C. KING *Sunset Pass* 56 Don't get stampeded. Just keep cool; watch and listen. **1898** *Educat. Rev.* XV. 412 The crazes by which teachers are periodically stampeded. **1912** R. POCOCK *Man in Open* 104 The lady attracted attention by screaming, so the third shot stampeded poor Jones. **1924**

Machinists' Bull. (Winnipeg) Oct. 3/2 Efforts are being made by various agencies to use the present condition as a club to stampede the men and disgust them with their Organization. **1950** *Time* 3 Apr. 20/2 A solid, grey, calm man, never rushed to a conclusion, impossible to stampede.

2. a. *intr.* Of a herd of cattle: To become panic-stricken and take to flight.

1823 S. WILLIAMS in E. C. Barker *Austin Papers* (1924) I. 699 On the way..the Cavallada Stampeded and a part of the horses and mules were not recovered. **1859** MARCY *Prairie Trav.* xi. 69 My entire herd of about two hundred horses and mules all stampeded in the night. **1879** *Daily News* 1 Mar., If the Zulus attack they always try to make the cattle within the park stampede.

b. Of a company of persons: To rush with common impulse. Also *spec.* of a prospector: to rush to the goldfields.

1849 *N.Y. Tribune* 12 June (Bartlett *Dict. Amer.*), The Virginia Legislature, becoming frightened at the approach of the cholera, have finally stampeded toward the White Sulphur Springs. **1877** R. W. RAYMOND *Statistics of Mines* VIII. v. 263 Among the miners who had 'stampeded' to Cedar were many of the best prospectors in the Territory. **1884** A. FORBES *Chinese Gordon* xi. 108 The new regiment broke, stampeded into the other, and threw it into confusion. **1898** M. LANDREVILLE *Appeal of Yukon Miners* 23 Miners are prone to stampede to any district which has the appearance of greater richness than the one wherein they are at work. **1951** V. B. ANGIER *At Home in Woods* 41 The prospectors who stampeded through here around '98 on their way to the Yukon had a pretty good trick.

Hence **stam'peded** *ppl. a.*; **stam'peding** *vbl. sb.* and *ppl. a.*

1884 STANWOOD *Hist. Presid. Elections* xxiv. 315 Another rule [of the Republican convention of 1876] put an end to the practice of 'stampeding'. **1885** *Suakin* ix. 216 The enemy were still pursuing the stampeded camels. **1885** *Pall Mall Gaz.* 4 Nov. 4/2 He was nearly forced over a precipice by a stampeding herd of wild horses.

stampeder (stæm'piːdə(r)). *N. Amer.* [f. prec. + -ER[1].] **1.** One who takes part in a sudden or unreasoning rush of persons, esp. for gold.

1859 E. H. N. PATTERSON *Jrnl.* 22 May in L. Hafen *Overland Routes to Gold Fields* (1942) 143 In anything that I may have heretofore written that might be deemed disparaging of the 'stampeders', I do not wish to be understood as intentionally unjust or uncharitable. **1884** *Century Mag.* Oct. 844/2 In the days of the stampeders and the toboggan trains, this was the only house on the trail. **1891** *Daily News* 23 Sept. 5/1 In a short time we shall learn how many of Tuesday's stampeders found room in the new region. **1936** N. A. D. ARMSTRONG *Yukon Yesterdays* 13 No wonder that hundreds of the weaker stampeders returned to the base to take the first steamer back home! **1963** *Beaver* (Winnipeg) Summer 42/2 Before the turn of the century, hordes of rushing stampeders..had reason to curse the savage stretch of water.

2. One who causes a stampede amongst cattle or horses.

1862 *Harper's Mag.* Sept. 450/1 Horses..which, having been 'hobbled' beside the fires of their respective owners, had..escaped the notice of the stampeders.

†**stam'pee.** *Obs.* [? Corruptly a. F. *estampille* stamp, seal, a. Sp. *estampilla* dim. of *estampa* STAMP *sb.*[3]] A counterfeit coin formerly circulated in the West Indies.

1795 W. BULLOCK in *Naval Chron.* IX. 457 You was to have the stampees at 3*s.* per gross. **1797** *Ibid.* X. 128 Negro money called stampees, or black dogs.

stamper ('stæmpə(r)), *sb.* [f. STAMP *v.* + -ER[1].]

1. a. One who stamps with the feet; †one who treads (grapes). Also with *out* (cf. STAMP *v.* 3 d).

1388 WYCLIF *Amos* ix. 13 And the stampere [1382 treder] of grape schal take the man sowynge seed. **1913** E. C. BENTLEY *Trent's Last Case* 6 He stood in every eye as the unquestioned guardian of stability, the stamper-out of manipulated crises. **1914** J. H. SKRINE *Pastor Futurus* xxii. 180 Breaker of bruised reeds and stamper on smoking flax.

b. *Med.* (See quot.)

1901 DORLAND *Med. Dict.* (ed. 2) *Stamper*, a person affected with locomotor ataxia; so called because of the peculiar stamping gait of that disease.

c. *Ornith.* (See quot.)

1872 COUES *N. Amer. Birds* 240 Forced to rise by stamping with the feet on the ground; from this latter circumstance, the birds have been named *Calcatores* (stampers).

2. a. One who uses a stamp or works a stamping machine; one who marks an impression (on something) with a stamp. (In several trades the designation of a special class of workmen.) Also *fig.*

1556 *Charter Stationers' Co.* in Entick *London* (1766) IV. 227 Any stamper, printer, binder or seller of any manner of books. **1621** J. ARCHBOLD *Beauty of Holiness* 6 The Holy Ghost, as the immediate stamper of this impression of holinesse in the spirits of men. **1735** J. CHAMBERLAYNE *Pres. St. Gt. Brit.* II. III. (ed. 31) 90 [Officers for the Stamp Duties.] The Names of the Thirty-Nine Stampers. **1862** *Catal. Internat. Exhib. Brit.* II. No. 6449, The stampers [in needle manufacture] make a perforation partly through the wires. **1879** *Cassell's Techn. Educ.* IV. 263/1 The early stampers were timid, and used only shallow dies.

b. A postal employee who applies the postmark and obliterates the postage stamps on letters and postal packets.

1850 OGILVIE s.v., In the Glasgow post-office there are four stampers. **1901** *Scotsman* 26 Dec. 8/1 The swiftest stamper in the office..has obliterated [with the machine] the stamps of 268 faced letters in a minute.

3. An instrument used in stamping.

a. A pestle, rammer.

1483 CAXTON *G. de la Tour* f ij, He..took a stamper and brake the two legges of his wyf. **1600** SURFLET *Country Farm* III. lii. 551 Lay nutmegs on heapes, bray them with a wooden stamper. **1753** *Chambers' Cycl.* Suppl. s.v. *Beetle*, For the military use, beetles, called also stampers, are thick round pieces of wood... Their use is for beating or settling the earth of a parapet. **1869** A. R. WALLACE *Malay Archip.* vi. (1874) 92 [The Dyak woman] has an hour's work every evening to pound the rice with a heavy wooden stamper.

b. (Chiefly *pl.*) The pestle or each of several pestles in a crushing or pounding machine, esp. in a stamping mill = STAMP *sb.*[3] 9.

1602 CAREW *Cornwall* 12 Of late times they mostly vse wet stampers, and so haue no need of the crazing mils for their best stuffe. **1674** PETTY *Dupl. Proportion* 64 Water gushing out upon the floats of Under-shot Mills; as may be seen in the Stampers of Paper-Mills. **1791** SMEATON *Edystone L.* (1793) §201 It is beat by iron-headed Stampers upon an iron bed. **1872** W. W. SMYTH *Mining Statist.* 51 The crushing machine has 48 stampers, in twelve batteries of four stampers each. Each stamper weighs 6 cwt.

c. A hat-maker's tool: See quots.

1688 HOLME *Armoury* III. 386/1 The Felt-makers, (or more generally termed Hat-makers) Instrument called a Stamper. **1745** *De Coetlogon's Hist. Arts & Sci.* II. 106/2 A Stamper..is a Piece of Iron or Copper, bent. *Ibid.* 107/1 We'll proceed to give it the proper Form, by laying the conical Cap on a wooden Block of the intended Size of the Crown of the Hat; and thus tie it round with the Commander, which we'll beat and gradually drive down all round with the Stamper. **1837** WHITTOCK *Bk. Trades* (1842) 295 (*Hatter*), These inequalities are reduced..in which the assistance of a copper instrument called a 'stamper' is found available.

d. An instrument for beating leather. (Cf. STAMP *sb.*[3] 10.)

1852 MORFIT *Tanning & Currying* (1853) 227 The stamper leaves the surface of the leather [etc.].

e. A matrix or copy of an original disc recording used to press other copies of a gramophone record.

1918 [see MATRIX 4 c]. **1935** [see MASTER *sb.*[1] 10 a]. **1952** [see MOTHER *sb.*[1] 11]. **1975** G. J. KING *Audio Handbk.* vii. 154 Most gramophone records start as very high quality tape recordings, the edited material then being recorded in disc form on to a lacquer blank, from which the stamper is ultimately derived.

4. *slang.* pl. Shoes; feet. ? *Obs.*

1567 HARMAN *Caveat* (1869) 83 Stampers, shooes. **1652** BROME *Joviall Crew* I. Wks. III. 366 Strike up Piper a merry merry dance That we on our stampers may foot it and prance. **1673** R. HEAD *Canting Acad.* 20 From thy stampers then remove Thy Drawers [*i.e.* stockings]. **1676** COLES *Dict.*, *Stampers*, shoes or carriers. *a* **1700** B. E. *Dict. Cant. Crew*, *Deuseavile-Stampers*, County-Carriers. **1819** *Sporting Mag.* V. 123 Coster-mongers, in all their gradations, down to the Stampers. **1828** EGAN *Boxiana* IV. 164 The leaky stampers gave symptoms of ague touches to their miserable owners, who had not better soles for the trying occasion.

5. *Conch.* In book-names of certain shells. ? *Obs.*

c **1711** PETIVER *Gazophyl.* x. 98 Marbled Luzone Stamper, with a flesh-coloured and black Mouth. **1713** —— *Aquat. Anim. Amboinæ* Tab. ii, *Cylindrus*..Prince Stamper. *Voluta Musicalis*..Horn-Book Stamper.

6. *attrib.*, as ***stamper battery, box, press.***

1890 *Pall Mall Gaz.* 21 May 2/1 In a *stamper battery the stone is thrown into an oblong iron box, in which five bars of iron..are made to rise and fall alternately. **1872** W. W. SMYTH *Mining Statist.* 51 The *stamper boxes are fitted with false bottoms. **1875** KNIGHT *Dict. Mech.*, **Stamper-press*, a press for stamping sheet metal. **1911** *Encycl. Brit.* XX. 47/1 The Dutch or stamper press, invented in Holland in the 17th century, was up to the early years of the 19th century almost exclusively employed in Europe for pressing oil-seeds.

†**'stamper,** *v. Obs. rare*[−1]. [? var. of STAMMER *v.*] *intr.* To waver.

c **1425** *St. Eliz. of Spalbeck* in *Anglia* VIII. 114/28 ðit stumbiþ sche neuere ne stamperþe ne waggiþ.

Stampian ('stæmpɪən), *a. Geol.* [f. med.L. *Stamp-æ* Étampes (France).] = RUPELIAN *a.*

1893 GEIKIE *Text-bk. Geol.* (ed. 3) 989 Above it comes the Stampian [group]. **1910** *Encycl. Brit.* XI. 670 Oligocene... In continental Europe the following subdivisions have been established in descending order: (1) Aquitanian, (2) Stampian (Rupelian), 3 Tongrian (Sannoisian).

†**stampine.** An alleged name of a bird.

1579 HAKE *Newes out of Powles* iv. (1872) Dij b, Stent, Stockard, Stampine, Tantereuale, and Wigeon of the best.

stamping ('stæmpɪŋ), *vbl. sb.* [-ING[1].]

1. The action of STAMP *v.*, in various senses.

1375 BARBOUR *Bruce* VII. 269 Bot he had schort quhil at the met Sittyn, quhen he herd gret stampyng About the hous. *a* **1400–50** *Wars Alex.* 781 Quat of stamping of stedis & stering of bernes, All dymed þe dale & þe dust ryses. **1550** EDW. VI *Jrnl.* in Burnet *Hist. Ref.* II. II. II. (1681) 35 The Lords at London having tryed all kinds of Stamping,..proved that without any loss, but sufferable, the Coin might be brought to eleven ounces fine. **1630** *R. Johnson's Kingd. & Commw.* 598 (China) Their Printing is but stamping, like our great Letters or Gaies cut in wood; for they cut many words in one peece, and then stampe it off in paper. **1720** SWIFT *Poems, Irish Feast*, A mercy the ground Did not burst with their stamping. **1882** CAULFEILD & SAWARD *Dict. Needlework*, *Stamping*..is a method adopted for producing a pattern on cotton, silk, or woollen stuffs, having a stiff raised pile on the face. **1897** FLANDRAU *Harvard Episodes* 184 Such a cruel stamping out of youth and strength and happiness at the very beginning.

¶ The imposition of a stamp tax (on a country).

1766 FRANKLIN *Exam.* Wks. 1887 III. 450 While the stamping of America was under consideration, and before the bill was brought in.

2. *concr.* **a.** *pl.* The materials pounded or crushed.

1594 PLAT *Jewell-ho.* 71 Take the stampings of Crabs after the verjuice is expressed. **1678** *Evelyn's Pomona* (ed. 5) 403 For Water-cider, take your stampings when you press them from the first liquor, and put them into tubs. **1839** URE *Dict. Arts* 707 The balls [of iron] are first worked under the forge-hammer; and these stampings being afterwards heated..are passed through the roughing rollers.

b. An article fashioned by stamping.

1862 *Catal. Internat. Exhib., Brit.* II. No. 6189, Stampings and pressings of iron and steel for a variety of purposes. **1893** *Daily News* 10 Apr. 6/4 There is a brisk business..in large stampings in the shape of bowls, lard tins, &c.

c. Ornamentation produced by stamping; stamped work.

1889 *Amer. Publ. Weekly* 30 Mar. 489 The Work is..elegantly bound in imported cloth, gilt edge, with rich stamping in gold and silver. **1892** *Photogr. Ann.* II. 281 The fancy stamping all over the brasswork adding also considerably to a handsome appearance.

3. *attrib.* and *Comb.*, as ***stamping-die, -engine, hammer,*** †***-house, -iron*** (= pestle), ***-machine, -mill, -press, -rod;*** **stamping ground** orig. *U.S.*, an animal's habitual place of resort; also *transf.*; **stamping shop**, the 'shop' in a needle-factory containing machinery for punching the eyes of needles.

With *stamping-iron* cf. OE. *stęmpingisern* 'celon' (Wr.-Wülcker 203).

1845 *Penny Cycl.* Suppl. I. 221/2 Above is a press, to the lower end of which is attached the *stamping-die or device, face downwards. **1840** *Mechanics' Mag.* XXXIII. 504/1 On the *Stamping Engines in Cornwall. **1821** D. DUNKLIN *Let.* 25 Dec. in E. C. Barker *Austin Papers* (1924) I. 456 It is unnecessary to undertake to give you any details of affairs in your old *Stamping-ground. **1839** [H. R. HOWARD] *Hist. Virgil A. Stewart* 70 (R. H. Thornton *Amer. Gloss.*) I made my way from Milledgeville to Williamson County, the old stamping-ground. **1862** *Harper's Mag.* June 34/1, I found myself near one of these 'stamping grounds', and a simultaneous roar from five hundred infuriated animals gave notice of my danger. **1883** W. M. BAKER *New Timothy* 176 (Cent.) It's with them fellows as it is with wild animals. You can just keep clear of them if you want, stay far out of their stamping-ground. **1915** E. R. BURROUGHS *Return of Tarzan* xxiii. 326 The woman he loved was within a short journey of the stamping-ground of his tribe. **1955** *Times* 19 Aug. 2/5 Henry Wood used the Proms as a stamping ground for new music because there was little opportunity otherwise for making it known. **1977** J. I. M. STEWART *Madonna of Astrolabe* iv. 74 Tell Charles Atlas I'd have a go if asked—I suppose as Tutor for Admissions it's his stamping-ground. **1834–6** BARLOW in *Encycl. Metrop.* VIII. 676/2 All but the very largest [utensils] are raised or sunk by the *stamping hammer. **1706** J. STEVENS *Span.-Eng. Dict.* s.v. *Plata*, [The silver] is cast into Bars, and carry'd to the King's *Stamping-house, where it is try'd, and the Mark set upon it according to its Fineness. **1552** in P. H. Hore *Wexford* (1901) [II.] 243, 4 *Stamping Irons [for the stamping mill]. **1778** PRYCE *Min. Cornub.* 284 The Tin is..cool enough to sustain the stamping iron. **1839** URE *Dict. Arts* 1162 A *stamping-machine with dies. **1884** KNIGHT *Dict. Mech.* Suppl. *Stamping Machine*, for stamping the soles of boots and shoes with monogram or trade-mark. **1552** in P. H. Hore *Wexford* (1901) [II.] 243, 2 gret pecs of Iron for the *stampying myll. **1855** J. R. LEIFCHILD *Cornwall* 27 A stamping mill, worked by steam, was erected at the very bottom of the excavation. **1858** SIMMONDS *Dict. Trade*, **Stamping-press*, a press for imprinting, by a sunken die, bills of lading, notes, envelopes, drafts, etc.; [also] a crushing mill for ores. **1879** *Cassell's Techn. Educ.* III. 55 The rags, after macerating for many days.., were beaten by means of *stamping-rods shod with iron..; these worked in strong oak or stone mortars. **1862** *Catal. Internat. Exhib., Brit.* II. No. 6449, The wires are taken to the '*stamping shop', where the first germ of an eye is given to each half of every wire.

stamping ('stæmpɪŋ), *ppl. a.* [-ING[2].] That stamps with the feet; characterized by stamping with the feet. Hence **'stampingly** *adv.*

1594 NASHE *Unfort. Trav.* E 2, One as if he had ben playning a clay floore stampingly trode the stage so harde with his feete, that [etc.]. **1596** —— *Saffron Walden* O 2, Hee cald all the World asses..with the stampingest cursing and tearing he could vtter it. **1599** BRETON *Wil of Wit* (Grosart) 18/2 The gallant shewe of stamping steeds. **1709** STEELE *Tatler* No. 166 ¶8 The Stamping Dances of the West-Indians or Hottentots. **1899** *Allbutt's Syst. Med.* VII. 876 A stamping movement of the foot. **1903** KIPLING *Five Nations, White Horses* vi, By day with stamping squadrons, ..Creep up the wise White Horses.

ˌstampo'mania. The mania for collecting postage stamps. Hence **ˌstampo'maniac.**

1865 *Morning Star* 28 Aug., A few years ago, grey-haired people, as well as little children, were seized with the stampomania. **1886** *Daily News* 9 Dec. 5/2 In the other branches..the collector may be eager..for good things, but he can never know the passion of the stampomaniac.

stam-wood: see STAM *sb.*[3] b.

stan, obs. and dial. form of STAND *sb.* and *v.*; obs. var. STONE *sb.* and *v.* and STEND *sb.* (*dial.*).

Stancarian (stæŋ'kɛərɪən). *Hist.* [f. *Stancar-us* (see below) + -IAN.] One of those Protestants in the 16th c. who adopted the opinion of Stancarus (Francesco Stancari of Mantua, 1501–74) that the Atonement of Christ was wrought by His human nature only. Also *attrib.* or *adj.* (Cf. OSIANDRIAN.)

1565 HARDING *Confut. Apol.* III. iv. 141 b, The Osiandrines teach that Christ iustifieth a man by his diuine nature only. The Stancarians.. by his humaine nature only. 1655 J. OWEN *Vind. Evang.* Pref. 11, I do plainly Detest every Heretical blasphemy.. whether it be Arian, Servetian, Eunomian or Starcarian [*sic*].

So **Stan'carist.**

1882–3 SCHAFF *Encycl. Rel. Knowl.* III. 2235 [Stancaro] gathered some pupils, called 'Stancarists'.

†**stance,** *sb.*[1] *Obs.* Also 5 **stawnce,** 6–7 **staunce.** [Aphetic form of DISTANCE *sb.*] Dissension, dispute: = DISTANCE *sb.* 1. *withouten stance*: without dispute, undoubtedly.

14.. *Merita Missæ* 151 in *Lay Folks Mass Bk.* 152 Charlys wane All frawnce, And cristende spayne with-owtyn stawnce. 1566 GASCOIGNE *Supposes* II. iv, I will set such a staunce [It. *tanta discordia*] betweene him and Pasiphilo that all this towne shall not make them friendes. 1566 J. HEYWOOD *Spider & F.* xxxix. 11 Beginning of their comnicashin arose, Wherin they argde and fell at arging stance.

stance (stɑːns, -æ-), *sb.*[2] Also 6 **stanse** (sense 4), 7 **staunce,** 9 **stanch** (sense 1 c). [a. F. *stance* (now only in the sense 'stanza': see 4), ad. It. *stanza* station, stopping place, room, etc.: see STANZA.]

1. a. A standing-place, station, position.

1532 BONER in *St. Papers Hen. VIII*, VII. 396 Beyng at a stance, where oon way turneth to the Popes lodging, and the other to the Emperours, the Pope departed from the Emperour. *a* 1618 SYLVESTER *Panaretus* 473 If in Earth shee yet have any Stance, 'Tis with the Cynois, Turks, or Scythians. 1640 R. BAILLIE *Canterb. Self-convict.* 108 Yet now in our book it must change the place, and be brought to its owne old stance. 1816 SCOTT *Antiq.* iv, From this stance it is probable..that Julius Agricola beheld what our Beaumont has so admirably described! 1822 GALT *Provost* xxxiii, Getting out the fire-engine from its stance under the stair. 1862 BEVERIDGE *Hist. India* IV. iv. II. 143 One chapter is devoted to..stances for deities. 1891 ATKINSON *Moorland Par.* 319 One of my lads..shot fifteen of these depredators from one stance. 1895 CROCKETT *Sweetheart Trav.* 259 An empty stone-breaker's stance cut deep into the edge of the wood.

†**b.** *at a stance*: at a standstill. So *to put to a stance*. *Obs.*

c 1678 in *Kirkton's Hist. Ch. Scot.* (1817) 388 *note*, It seems your French trade, sir, is at a stance. 1697 W. CLELAND *Poems* 11 (Jam.) But here my fancie's at a stance. 1722 W. HAMILTON *Wallace* 167 (Jam.) Their sad misfortunes, and unlucky chance,.. Had put their measures to a stance.

c. A platform for a workman to stand on. Also *spec.* in *Mountaineering*, a ledge or foothold on which a climber can secure a belay.

1811 *Naval Chron.* XXV. 219 With a stanch six feet wide on the top, for the workmen to stand upon. 1886 BARROWMAN *Sc. Mining Terms* 63 *Stance*, a platform on which the men stand when working the lever in mineral boring. 1920 G. W. YOUNG *Mountain Craft* v. 218 It is.. vital for a leader to know what character of stance he requires in order to bring up his following safely. 1933 G. D. ABRAHAM *Mod. Mountaineering* viii. 154 The second man looped the rope behind him around the projection from a stance a few feet along the ledge. 1956 [see INTILTED *ppl. a.*]. 1971 C. BONINGTON *Annapurna South Face* xi. 127, I had to wait another hour while he safeguarded his stance with carefully placed pitons.

d. In *Golf* and other games: The position of the player's feet in playing a stroke. Also *transf.*, the position of the player's body in readiness or in playing a stroke. Similarly *gen.*, a standing attitude or way of positioning.

1897 *Outing* XXX. 426/1 The stance, the grip, the swing, that together make up, what they call a good style. 1897 *Encycl. Sport* I. 473/2 (Golf). 1913 *Blackw. Mag.* Dec. 832/2 When Jessop does not come off in batting, the peculiarities of his style and stance are calculated to accentuate the failure. 1929 M. LIEF *Hangover* 234 At dinner Mogador's young bride was plainly worried about her fork-stance. 1936 M. ALLINGHAM *Flowers for Judge* v. 84 No one who saw him could have dreamed for a moment that he regarded himself as anything else but the Head of the Firm. His poise and stance proclaimed it. 1965 'W. TREVOR' *Boarding-House* ii. 19 Gallelty and Mrs Slape stood close together..humble in their stance. 1970 J. G. FARRELL *Troubles* II. 220 Driscoll instantly dropped into a boxing stance, right fist guarding his chin, left fist pumping exaggeratedly back and forth.

e. *fig.* An attitude adopted in relation to a particular object of contemplation; a policy, 'posture'.

1960 *Amer. Speech* XXXV. 215 An 'unlinguistic' stance is evidenced in the view that some variants embody language 'corruption'. 1964 *Ann. Reg.* *1963* 216 In general those Parties in economically more advanced countries adopted a pro-Soviet stance, although several had dissident pro-Chinese minorities. 1972 [see RHETORICIZE *v.*]. 1977 J. I. M. STEWART *Madonna of Astrolabe* xx. 277 Moderate regret and underlying unconcern established itself as our public stance.

†**2.** A room, cell, cabinet. Also, a compartment in a shield. *Obs.* (Cf. STANZA 2.)

1632 LITHGOW *Trav.* x. 462 The Corregidor came out of his adioyning stance. *Ibid.* 476 The young English Priest entered my melancholly staunce. *Ibid.* 502 The third ioynd Staunce denotes to me a Galley.

3. a. A site; esp. an area for building upon. Also *building-stance.*

1631 *Reg. Mag. Sig. Scot.* 633/1 Molendinum..lie.. wattir-gang et stance ejusdem. 1649 *Presbyt. Rec.* in Campbell *Ch. & Par. Kirkcaldy* (1904) 161 The stance of the Kirk intendit to be built. 1793 *Statist. Acc. Scot.* VIII. 253 Every man had a dry gravellish stance whereon to found his house. 1823 SCOTT *Peveril* xi, The higher part of the level ground afforded a stance for an old house. 1844 H. STEPHENS *Bk. Farm* III. 972 A large oblong hay-stack should be built in this way:..The stance should be raised 1 foot above the ground. 1884 *North Brit. Daily Mail* 5 Aug. 6/5 Paisley Race Meeting... A few stances of Ground for Tents are still to let.

b. *Sc.* The pitch of a showman or street-trader; a location for a fair or market. Cf. STAND *sb.*[1] 15.

1814 *Farmer's Mag.* Nov. 466 If they are not in the market the night before, it is not often that a stance can be got after day-light in the morning. 1924 *Kelso Chron.* 25 July 4 This old-established Border fair was held on the usual stance on St Boswells Green on Friday. 1933 *Cases Court of Session* (Scotland) 65 A street trader shall not carry on business on any stance..unless he holds a permit from the chief constable for such stance. 1964 M. BANTON *Policeman in Community* ii. 31 He..can attend to less pressing matters such as an application for a news-vendor's stance.

c. *Sc.* A standing-place for (a row of) public vehicles; a bus-stop or taxi-rank. Cf. STAND *sb.*[1] 17.

1926 *Edinburgh Corp.* (*General Powers*) *Order Confirmation* 25 in *Bills Public* I. 461 'Stance' means a place where omnibuses may stop a longer time than is necessary for the taking up and setting down of passengers. 1931 A. A. MACGREGOR *Last Voyage* 24 The erection of stance poles [for tram-cars] along Princes St. 1978 *Dumfries Courier* 13 Oct. 6/2 Travellers will find that early buses and taxis are temporarily sitting in different stances than is usual.

†**4.** = STANZA 1. *Obs. rare.*

1596 HARINGTON *Apol. Ajax* Cc 6 b, They had quoted a stanse in Hary Osto beginning thus [etc.]. 1598 FLORIO, *Stanze*,..a stance or staffe of verses or songs. 1613 CHAPMAN *Mask Inns of Court* D 3, The Phœbades sing the first Stance of the second song.

stance (stans), *v. Sc.* [f. STANCE *sb.*[2]] *trans.* To place or station; to pen (cattle) for sale.

17.. *Sheriff-Muir* in *Ritson's Sc. Songs* (1794) II. 66 He ne'er advanc'd From the place he was stanc'd. 1887 *Scott. Leader* 19 Oct. 4 Three thousand head of cattle of all breeds were stanced at Dalkeith yesterday. *a* 1883 in R. Ford *Harp Perthsh.* 371 The fiddler loon..Was cannily stanced in his seat on a hill.

stanch, staunch (stɑːnʃ, -æ-, stɔːnʃ), *sb.*[1] Also 8 *Sc.* **stench.** [f. STANCH *v.*, or ad. the equivalent F. *estanche* (Cotgr. 1611; now *étanche*), which prob. existed in OF.]

†**1.** That which stops or allays, also a stopping.

a 1400–50 *Stockh. Med. MS.* 28 Staunch of lecherye. 1557 GRIMALDE in *Tottel's Misc.* (Arb.) 110 O frendship,..O sacred bond of blisfull peace, the stalworth staunch of strife. 1567 *Diurn. Occurr.* (Bannatyne Club) 110 It was rather done for the stanche of the mouthes of the peopill. 1613 JACKSON *Creed* I. x. §3 As it were, an ebbe or staunch in the affaires of the Kingdome of Israel. 1790 D. MORISON *Poems* 18 (E.D.D.) E'er their cravings got a stench, His pulse fu' sair was beatin'.

2. Something used for stanching blood, a styptic. †**a.** (Application uncertain). **b.** *dial.* Selenite or powdered gypsum. [Cf. F. *pierre d'estanche*, 'the bloud-stone' (Cotgr.).] **c.** *Anglo-Irish.* The leguminous plant *Anthyllis vulneraria.*

a. 1392 *Earl Derby's Exped.* (Camden) 164 Johanni leche pro camfor et staunche.

b. 1712 J. MORTON *Nat. Hist. Northamptonsh.* 178 Its Use in stopping excessive Bleeding has been try'd with very good Success at Kettering; on which Account it [*sc.* a variety of selenite] has there the Name of Stanch. 1748 HILL *Hist. Fossils* 129.

c. 1726 THRELKELD *Synopsis Stirp. Hibern.* A 6 b, *Anthyllis Leguminosa*..is sold in our Markets by the Name of Stanch, being astringent, as most of the Pulse Kind are.

†**3.** ? Drying effect (of fire). *Obs. rare*$^{-1}$.

1643 STEER tr. *Fabricius' Exper. Chirurg.* iii. 8 Sore by reason of the stretching of the skin, which is stretched and drawne together by the stanch of the fire.

4. A kind of after-damp in mines, etc.

1693 G. POOLEY in *Phil. Trans.* XVII. 674 In ancient Works,..Damps and Staunches sometimes arise. 1847 HALLIWELL, *Staunches*, damps or offensive vapours arising in underground works, mines, &c.

5. *Comb.*: **stanch-air** = sense 4; **stanch-grass** *Sc.* yarrow, *Achillea Millefolium.*

1768 ROSS *Helenore* 9 A' her washing cud na stench the bleed, In haste then Nory for the stench-girss yeed. 1874 R. BUCHANAN *Poet. Wks.* I. 196 No stanchgrass ever heal'd a wound so deep. 1883 GRESLEY *Gloss. Coal-mining* 237 Stanch-air.

stanch, staunch (stɑːnʃ, -æ-, stɔːnʃ), *sb.*[2] [a. OF. *estanche*, related to *estanc* STANK *sb.*] A lock or dam in a river.

1767 *Hull Navig. Act* 1054 Bridges, sluices, staunches, locks. 1866 BROGDEN *Prov. Lincs.*, *Stanch*, a lock or stop for water, much used in the fen districts. 1879 *Edin. Rev.* CL. 447 Rude temporary stanches, or flush-weirs. 1890 *Fishing Gaz.* 8 Nov. 242/3 This rather fast-running and weedy river—the staunches were up. *Ibid.* The swims at the first and second staunch.

Comb. 1794 RENNIE *Rep. Surv. Thames* 10 All the old stanch locks should be purchased, and proper gauge or pen wiers substituted in their place.

stanch, *a.*: see STAUNCH *a.* (the usual form).

stanch, staunch (stɑːnʃ, -æ-, stɔːnʃ), *v.* Forms: 4–6 **stanche, staunche,** 4–5 **stawnche, stonch,** 5 **staunge,** 6 **stainch, stayнche, stenche, stinch,** 6–7 **stench,** 4– **stanch, staunch.** [ad. OF. *estanchier* (mod.F. *étancher*) to stop the flow of (water), stanch (blood), stop up (a leak), make (a vessel) watertight, to quench (thirst), corresponding to Pr., Sp., Pg. *estancar* in similar senses (Pg. also to exhaust, weary), It. *stancare* to weary:—Com. Rom. **stancare*, according to some scholars a contraction of popular L. **stagnicāre*, f. *stagnum* pool, pond (whence STAGNATE *v.*, STAGNANT *a.*]

1. *trans.* To stop the flow of (water, etc.). Now only *poet.* (*rare*). Also, †to dam *up.*

1481 CAXTON *Myrr.* II. xxv. 118 Thus groweth the rayne And whan it is alle fallen to therthe & the grete moisture is staunched the clowde hath lost his broun colour. 1535 COVERDALE *Ezek.* xxxi. 15, I will staunch his floudes. 1576 FLEMING *Panopl. Epist.* 26 Those thinges, which could staunche the streames of my teares. 1642 BRIDGE *Wound. Consc. Cured* ii. 19 That Justice..may run down like water which hath been stanched up. 1876 SWINBURNE *Erectheus* 426 A living well of life nor stanched nor stained.

†**b.** *fig.* To dry up the springs of; to exhaust (one's credit). *Obs.*

1338 R. BRUNNE *Chron.* (1725) 197 For to stanch his foysoun homward haf I ment. 1380 *Lay Folks Catech.* (L) 1390 Ydylnesse is..stoppynge and staunchyng grace and good thewys. 1568 FULWEL *Like will to Like* E ij, My credit also is now quite staunched.

†**c.** *intr.* for *refl.* To cease flowing. *Obs.*

c 1400 tr. *Secreta Secret.*, *Gov. Lordsh.* 90 Water ys ouercomend in Planetys, and staunches noght but by dounshedyng. 1588 A. KING *Canisius' Catech.* in *Cath. Tract.* (S.T.S.) 187 The raine staincheit the 40 day efter Noa entereit in the ark.

2. *trans.* To stop the flow of (blood or other issue from the body); to stop the flow of blood from (a wound).

In the first two quots. possibly *intr.* for *refl.*: see c.

13.. *Seuyn Sag.* (W.) 1136 For al that heuer he mighte do, His menesoun might nowt staunche tho. ? *a* 1400 *Morte Arth.* 2577 For alle þe barbours of Bretayne salle noghte thy blode stawnche! 14.. *Sir Beues* (M.) 534 To the fresshe erth he laid hym flatt, For to staunche his woundus with that. *a* 1425 tr. *Arderne's Treat. Fistula*, etc. 47 Þe fluxe or þe rynnyng þer y-dried, or stopped, or staunched, þai dye sone after. 1599 BRETON *Will of Wit*, etc. (Grosart) 39/1 First the blood must bee stinched. 1610 G. FLETCHER *Christ's Vict. Earth* lix, *Ode*, Not all the skill his wounds can stench. 1684 tr. *Bonet's Merc. Compit.* II. 379 The flux could be stenched by no other Remedies. 1718 POPE *Iliad* IV. 229 Now seek some skilful Hand, whose pow'rful Art May stanch th' Effusion, and extract the Dart. *a* 1721 PRIOR *Dial. Locke & Montaigne* 657 A Cobweb is good..to..stanch cut thumbs. 1781 COWPER *Retirem.* 322 [To] staunch the bleedings of a broken heart. 1819 SCOTT *Ivanhoe* xxxvii, The bleeding was stanched, the wound was closed. 1859 TENNYSON *Elaine* 519 Then came the hermit out and..stanch'd his wound. 1872 DIXON *Switzers* xxxi. 315 They learn to staunch the flow of blood. 1890 R. BRIDGES *Shorter Poems* I. *Elegy* vii, The branches..bleed from unseen wounds that no sun stanches.

†**b.** To stop the bleeding or diarrhœa of (a person). *Obs.*

1470–85 MALORY *Arthur* XVII. xi. 706 Two felawes..lyfte her vp and staunched her but she had bled soo moche that she myght not lyue. 1530 PALSGR. 732/2 He fell a bledyng, but none coulde stanche hym tyll he was dede. 1561 HOLLYBUSH *Hom. Apoth.* 35 But if the siege be by reason a man hath eaten ought that is unwholsom, then ought he not to be staunched so sone.

c. *intr.* for *refl.*

c 1489 CAXTON *Sonnes of Aymon* i. 57 Whiche corps neuer staunched of bledynge by the space of viii myles. 1526 TINDALE *Luke* viii. 44 Immediatly her issue off bloud staunched. 1655 CULPEPER, etc. *Riverius* IV. vii. 118 Presently the blood stanched. 1599 A. M. tr. *Gabelhouer's Bk. Physicke* 317/1 Strewe of this pouldre theron, and keepe it alwayes on the wounde; if with the first time it will not stench, applye it theron the seconde time. 1850 ROBERTSON *Serm.* Ser. II. iii. (1864) 43 The heart will bleed, and stanch when it has bled enough.

†**3.** *trans.* To quench, allay, satisfy (thirst, hunger, desire, etc.); also, to repress, extinguish (appetite, hatred, anger, etc.). *Obs.*

c 1315 SHOREHAM *Poems* II. 96 Ine hys pyne hys stronge þerst Stanchede hy wyþ ȝalle. *c* 1374 CHAUCER *Boeth.* II. pr. ii. (1868) 34 Þe couetyse of men þat may not be staunched [L. *inexpleta cupiditas*]. *c* 1375 WYCLIF *Sel. Wks.* I. 183 If he staunche þis love and seie to þis þing þat he wole not love it so myche. *c* 1430 LYDG. *Min. Poems* (Percy Soc.) 14 The wyne of Mercy staunchithe be nature The gredy thristis of cruelle hastynes. *c* 1430 *Pilgr. Lyf Manhode* I. lxxxiii. (1869) 48 Fulfille it and saule it and staunche it [his desire] might not al the world. 1456 SIR G. HAYE *Law of Arms* (S.T.S.) 27 Ane unfillable gredy appetite..[that] never may be stanchit. 1513 DOUGLAS *Æneis* XII. vi. 9 O, stanch ȝour wraith for schame, or all is lorn! 1532 *Psalter of Jesus* ✠j, The desyre of my vnstable herte in tyme of prayer staunche I beseche the. 1581 N. BURNE *Disput.* 143 b, This maist honest refusal could nather stench his lust nor ambition. *c* 1610 *Women Saints* 80 Stanching hir hunger with herbes and barlie bredd, and her thirst with onelie water. 1679 DRYDEN *Œdipus* I. i, So will I seize and stanch The hunger of my love on this proud beauty. 1755 R. FORBES *Ajax' Sp.*, *Shop Bill* 39 Perhaps I may their greening stench, 'ere I hae done.

†**b.** To satisfy the appetite of. Also, to appease or cure (a person) *of* a desire or passion. *Obs.*

1340 *Alex. & Dind.* 938 Þanne wol he..wexe wilde of his wil & wikke to staunche. 1390 GOWER *Conf.* III. 11 For tastinge is defended me, And I can noght miselven staunche. 1440 SHIRLEY *Dethe K. James* (1818) 7 The..kynge..noght stanchid of his unsacionable and gredi avarice, ordeynd that tallage..upon his people, gretter..then ever..afore. *c* 1450 *Bk. Curtasye* 273 in *Babees Bk.*, Helpe to staunche hom of malice. 1486 *Bk. St. Albans*, *Hawking* c j b, Take hede the first day of to moch eetyng unto tyme that she be stawnchid.

4. To quench (a fire). *arch.*

*c*1450 Lovelich *Grail* liii. 279 God with hym schal senden his grace, and In this diche stawnchen this feer. *a*1513 *Fabyan's Chron.* vii. (1811) 512 Whiche fyre was scantly stenchyd in .viii. dayes after. 1860 M. Arnold *St. Brandan* 69, I stanch with ice my burning breast.

5. To arrest the progress of (a disease); to allay (pain); to relieve (a person) *of* pain.

*c*1375 *Sc. Leg. Saints* xliv. (Lucy) 20 Na scho mycht get na medycine, þat cuth hire stanche of þat pyne. 1398 Trevisa *Barth. De P.R.* xvii. clxxxii. (1495) 723 Grene grapes haue the vertue to binde and to staunche Coleryk perbrakynge. *a*1400 in *Rel. Ant.* (1841) I. 190 Fro basylica ..A branche veyn spryngeth..The cardiacle he wol stanche. 1551 Turner *Herbal* i. B vj, Aloe..stancheth the heade ake. 1809–10 Coleridge *Friend* (1865) 212 The patriot's sword may cut off the Hydra's head; but he possesses no brand to stanch the active corruption of the body. 1862 Goulburn *Pers. Relig.* iii. i. (1873) 155 Unless the moral malady be stanched in us by the Blood and Grace of Christ..salvation is for us out of the question. 1863 D. G. Mitchell *My Farm of Edgewood* 52, I haue sometimes availed myself of a curious bit of old narrative to staunch the pain of a sting.

†**6.** To put an end to (strife, enmity, rebellion, or any mischievous agency or condition). *Obs.*

1338 R. Brunne *Chron.* (1725) 253 If..holy kirke wild stanche sibred bituex þam tuo. *c*1375 *Sc. Leg. Saints* xxvi. (Nicholas) 329 Sic were to gere stanchit be, þe emperoure send princes thre. *c*1400 *26 Pol. Poems* iv. 17 Men may not staunche a comoun noys. 1409 *Exch. Rolls Scot.* IV. p. ccx, Gif thar happynnis ony discorde..[thai] sal lelily do thair power on aythir part to ger it be stanchit in lufely manere. *c*1430 *Life St. Kath.* (Roxb.) 5 He staunged soo by hys manly and vertuouse gouernaunce þat rebellioun. 1473–4 *Acc. Ld. High Treas. Scot.* I. 51 Lettres..to stanche thare gadering for the court of Forfare. 1533 Bellenden *Livy* II. 164 The Ire of goddis mon be first mesit to stanche þe said pest. 1573 G. Harvey *Letter-bk.* (Camden) 40 [He] cam downe himself..to stenche this strife. 1828 Scott *F.M. Perth* xiii, Their feud would be stanched by the death of one, or probably both, of the villains.

†**b.** To restrain *from* turbulence or violence; to put down, suppress (rebels, lawbreakers). *Sc.*

1513 Douglas *Æneis* i. ii. 21 The hie fadir Gaif thame [*sc.* the winds] ane kyng, quhilk as thar lord and juge, At certane tyme thame stanching and withhald. 1547 *Acc. Ld. High Treas. Scot.* IX. 75 With charges to the Maister of Maxwell ..to remane in Moffet ane moneth for stancheing of thevis. 1559 *Extracts Burgh Rec. Edin.* (1875) III. 50 All actis [etc.] ..set furth for stanching of sturdy beggeris. *a*1578 Lindesay (Pitscottie) *Chron. Scot.* (S.T.S.) I. 92 This wickit man that cuild na wayis be stenchit fra reffe and oppressioun. *Ibid.* 196 The king wschit out..to stenche thir twa lordis of thair combat and tuilzie. 1596 Dalrymple tr. *Leslie's Hist. Scot.* I. 10 Quha nathir in peace or weire can be stainchet from takeng the pray. *Ibid.* 172 He stanchet all seditious personnes.

†**c.** *intr.* for *refl.* Of storm, war, dissension: To come to an end, be allayed. Of persons: To cease from violence. *Obs.*

*c*1420 *Chron. Vilod.* 4549 And þe wynde stonchede & blew nomore. 1508 Kennedie *Flyting w. Dunbar* 543 Sterand the potis of hell, et newir stanchis. 1513 Douglas *Æneis* i. v. 110 The cruell tyme sone thereftir sall ceis, And weris stanch, all sal be rest and pece. *c*1560 Rolland *Seven Sages* 96 The first to spend he neuer stanches.

7. To stop up, to render water-tight or weatherproof. [After F. *étancher*.]

1776 G. Semple *Building in Water* 34 We got our Dam staunched as before mentioned. 1847 Emerson *Poems, Threnody* 84 The gathered sticks to staunch the wall Of the snow-tower, when snow should fall. *a*1862 O'Curry *Manners Anc. Irish* (1873) III. 32, I cannot say how they staunched the walls.., whether with clay, moss, or skins. 1892 P. H. Emerson *Son of Fens* xiv. 112 We'll go put the other board in now. I think we're stanched one.

8. *Comb.* †**stanch-blood,** (*a*) a blood-stone; (*b*) yarrow, *Achillea Millefolium.*

1567 Maplet *Gr. Forest* 7 b, Ematites..is called of some stench bloud. 1601 Holland *Pliny* xxvi. xii. II. 263 *marg.*, Stanch-bloud, a kind of Yarrow.

Hence **stanched** *ppl. a.* (in first quot. = ? cured of passion: see *vb.* 3 b), **'stanching** *ppl. a.*

1682 H. More *Annot. Glanvill's Lux O.* xiv. 147 It is unbeseeming either a sober and stanched man or a good Christian. 1852 Wiggins *Embanking* 19 Peat or bog is also a good material for a sea-bank, not only by reason of its staunching but also its adhesive qualities when packed. *Ibid.* 22 Such a material may also be..very hard and staunching when dry. 1865 A. Smith *Summer in Skye* I. 318 When the stanched rain-clouds were burning into a sullen red at sunset.

stanch, variant of stance *sb.*[2]

stanchel[1] ('stanʃəl). *Sc.* and *north.* ? *Obs.* Also 5 **stanchal,** 6 **sta(i)nchell,** 9 *dial.* **stanchil.** [An unexplained variant of staniel:—OE. *stánȝella*.] The staniel or kestrel, *Tinnunculus alaudarius.*

*c*1450 Holland *Howlat* 652 The hobby..Stanchalis, steropis. 1500–20 Dunbar *Poems* xxxiii. 82 The tarsall gaif him tug for tug, A stanchell hang in ilka lug. 1585 Jas. I *Ess. Poesie* (Arb.) 46 The Rauin, the Stainchell, and the Gled. ?*c*1730 in Maidment *N.C. Garland* (1824) 52 O Sir, ye're but a stanchel or else a ring-tail'd kite. 1818 Hogg *Brownie of Bodsbeck* I. xi. 208 That ever I sude hae lived to see..the stanchel and the merlin chatterin' frae the cushat's nest!

stanchel[2] ('stanʃəl). Now only *Sc.* Forms: 6 **stanchell, (stanshel,** 7 **stenchall,** 8 **-el,** 9 *dial.* **stanchil, staneshel),** 7, 9 **stanchel.** [? a. OF. *estanchele, estancele* (dim. of *estance* prop), recorded as the name of an object, variously of wood or iron, used in some game.] = stanchion *sb.*

1586 *Reg. Privy Council Scot.* IV. 95 [They] hes brokin doun and distroyit the haill corbellis, gestis and stanchellis of the rest of thair houssis. 1592 Greene *Def. Conny Catching* Wks. (Grosart) XI. 60 She nayled one eare fast to the windowe, and the other to the stanshel. 1658 in Campbell *Balmerino* (1899) 410 Ane new cupill,..half-doore,..ease-boards, and thereon stenchalls. 1687 G. Clerke *Spot-dial* 13 For the Length of the Frame and Glass that must be as the Jaume of the Window and *Stanchel* will give leave. 1727 P. Walker *Life Cameron* Biog. Presbyt. (1827) I. 300 Hanging some of them at the Stenchels of Windows. 1827 Tennant *Papistry Storm'd* 53 Some grippet..Great iron stanchels in their wraith. 1900 'R. Guthrie' *Kitty Fagan* 48 Meg was still at the door, half-leaning on the stanchel.

¶ ? Misused for: A large nail.

1832 G. Downes *Lett. Cont. Countries* I. 235 An old gate studded with stanchels.

stancher[1] ('stɑːnʃə(r), -æ-). [f. stanch *v.* + -er[1].] One who or that which stanches.

1453 in *14th Rep. Hist. MSS. Comm.* App. iii. 9 Reddaris and stanchearis of euill and debatis. 1611 Cotgr., *Estancheur*, a stancher. 1658 A. Fox tr. *Wurtz' Surg.* iv. iv. 320 This is the first and chiefest Bloud stencher. *a*1849 Mangan *Poems* (1859) 80 Friendship, stancher of our wounds and sorrows.

†**'stancher**[2]. *Sc. Obs.* Forms: 5 **stanssour,** 6 **stanch(e)o(u)r,** 7–8 **stencher,** 9 **staincher.** [? altered form of stanchion *sb.* Cf. stanchel[2].]

1. = stanchion *sb.* 1.

*c*1470 Henry *Wallace* iv. 507 Out off wyndowis stanssouris all thai drew. 1559 *Extracts Burgh Rec. Edin.* (1873) III. 78 To put in greit stancheouris of irne in all the wyndois. 1667 *Rec. Justiciary Crt. Edin.* (S.H.S.) I. 214 The stenchers of the windows. 1792 G. Galloway *Poems* 52 For standin' good for Willie Baird, He whistles through the stenchers, In Jail this day. 1823 Galt *Gilhaize* iii, A wicket was opened in the doors, ribbed with iron stainchers on the outside.

2. = stanchion *sb.* 2.

*a*1500 *Medulla Gram.*, *Calamarium*, an ynk horne or a stauncher.

†**'stanchgrain.** *Obs.* Forms: 5 **staunche greine,** 6 **-grayne, stounchegrey,** 7 **stainshgraine.** [f. stanch *sb.*[1] + grain *sb.*[1]] **a.** A composition used in preparing the smooth surface of parchment. **b.** ? *erron.* (see quot. 1530).

*c*1440 *Promp. Parv.* 472/2 Staunchegreyne, for wrytarys, *planula.* *a*1500 *Sloane MS.* 2584 lf. 10 (Promp. Parv. *note*) For to make staunchegreine. 1530 Palsgr. 275/2 Staunche grayne, an herbe. 1610 Folkingham *Art of Surv.* ii. vi. 58 It shal not be amisse to pounce the ground with a Stainsh-Graine of burnt Allome and a double quantity of pounded Rossin both finely searced.., thereby to preserue the Paper or Parchment from thorowe-piercing with the Colours.

†**'stanchier.** *Obs.* In 5 **staunchier.** [? Anglo-Fr., f. OF. *estanchier* stanch *v.*] ? An extinguisher.

1432 *Nottingham Rec.* II. 130 Torches, tortes, staunchiers, prikettes et pierchiers.

stanching ('stɑːnʃɪŋ, -æ-), *vbl. sb.* [-ing[1].] The action of the vb. stanch in various senses.

1387–8 T. Usk *Test. Love* iii. i. (Skeat) 50 It is nedeful and noble in staunching of bloode, there els to moche wolde out renne. *c*1400 *Brut* lxxv. (1906) I. 74 His breþ shal bene stanchyn of þerst to ham þat bene aþreste. 1456 Sir G. Haye *Law of Arms* (S.T.S.) 19 Thare is twa maner of fontaynis of the cristyn faith, ane is cummand fra God him self, that is but stanching. 1520 in *Charters*, etc. *Edin.* (1871) 204 For stancheing of trouibile hereftir. 1553 *Reg. Privy Council Scot.* I. 149 For..stancheing of malefactouris and ordorying of the Bordouris. 1621 N. Ward in *14th Rep. Hist. MSS. Comm.* App. ii. 14 The keeper..att the stenching of the blood, dyed. 1822 Scott *Nigel* ix, To..drink a blithe cup of kindness..to the stanching of feud, and perpetuation of amity. 1845–6 Trench *Huls. Lect.* Ser. ii. vi. 234 A binding up of hurts, a stanching of wounds.

Comb. 1658 A. Fox tr. *Wurtz' Surg.* iv. iv. 321 Then another broad and thin piece must be laid on the wound, or else Cotton wool, mingled with a little of stenching powder. [orig. Ger. *Pulver von Blutstellungen*.]

stanchion ('stɑːnʃən, -æ-), *sb.* Forms: 4–6 **stanchon** (5 **stanzon),** 6 **stancon;** 5–6 **staunchon** (5 **stauncyon, -son, stawncion),** 9 **stauncheon, -ion** (*Sc.* **-en);** 6 **stancion, -cyon,** 6 **stanchinge,** 7–9 **stantion,** 9 **stanchient, stantient,** 8–9 *dial.* **stansion;** 7 *Sc.* **stenchen,** 8, 9 **stancheon,** 7– **stanchion.** [a. OF. *estanchon, estançon* (mod.F. *étançon*), f. *estance* prop:—popular L. **stantia*: see stance *sb.*]

1. An upright bar, stay, prop or support.

a. *gen.*

[1343 in *Archæologia* LXIV. 148 In ij hominibus facientibus lacch' et stanchons ad idem.] 1433–4 in *Fabric Rolls York Minster* (Surtees) 53 Et iiij peciis pro stanzones. 1530 Palsgr. 275/2 Staunchon a proppe, *estancon.* 1532 in Bayley *Tower Lond.* i. App. p. xxij, A larder hous..w[t] planks rownde by the walls, and stancions w[t] pyns and hoks to hange the flesshe on. 1553 Brende *Q. Curtius* A iij, Least the earth washed upon with the raine might fall altogether, there were stanchinges of timbre putte betwixte to staie the whole worke. 1760–72 tr. *Juan & Ulloa's Voy.* (ed. 3) I. 181 The posts or stancheons by which the building is supported. 1791 Smeaton *Edystone L.* (1793) §97 The iron stanchions and particularities of each step. 1865 *Morn. Star* 3 Feb., Huge piles of balks were hurled with terrific violence from the stanchions which supported and held them in their places. 1875 Knight *Dict. Mech.*, *Stanchion.* 2. (Machinery) a principal post of a frame; especially one giving lateral support.

b. *spec.* of a window. Also see quot. 1836.

1472–3 *Durham Acc. Rolls* (Surtees) 247 Pro factura vij stawncions ferri pro nova fenestra ad scaccariam Elemos., vij d. 1530 in J. Croft *Excerpta Ant.* (1797) 16, vi Stancons for a bay Window. 1565 *Richmond Wills* (Surtees) 178, j stancyon of iron and a barre. 1609 Bible (Douay) *2 Kings* i. 2 Ochozias fel through the stanchions of his upper chamber. 1815 Scott *Guy M.* xxxiii, The stancheons on the window of the strong room..are wasted to pieces. 1836 Parker *Gloss. Archit.* (1850) I. 444 *Stanchion*, the upright iron bar between the mullions of a window, screen, &c... The name is also sometimes applied to mullions, and apparently to the quarters or studs of wooden partitions. 1840 Barham *Ingol. Leg.* Pref., An antiquated Manor house of Elizabethan architecture, with its gable ends, stone stanchions [etc.].

c. *Shipbuilding.*

1591 Horsey *Trav.* (Hakl. Soc.) 186 Everie shipe caries.. stancions for fights. 1627 Capt. Smith *Seaman's Gram.* vii. 32 The Roufe-trees..are..supported by Stantions that rest vpon the..Decke. 1703 Dampier *Voy.* III. i. 19 To keep the Boat thus with the Head to the Shore,..there are two strong Stantions set up in the Boat. 1769 Falconer *Dict. Marine* (1780), *Stanchion*, a sort of small pillar of wood or iron used for various purposes in a ship; as to support the decks, the quarter-rails, the nettings, the awnings, &c. 1805 *Shipwright's Vade-M.* 134 Stantions or Stantients. 1835 Marryat *Jacob Faithful* ix, At last the captain crawled up, and clung by the stanchions. *c*1850 *Rudim. Navig.* (Weale) 152 Stanchions or Stanchients.

d. *Mining.*

1855 Leifchild *Cornwall* 154 An upper joist..resting on two lateral upright posts, or stanchions. 1883 Gresley *Gloss. Coal-mining* 237.

e. (See quot.)

1875 Knight *Dict. Mech.*, *Stanchion.* 5. The vertical bars of a stall for cattle.

†**2.** A case for an inkhorn. *Obs.*

1404–5 *Durham Acc. Rolls* (Surtees) 400 Pro j stanchon' pro incausto pro scaccario, 18 d. *c*1440 *Promp. Parv.* 473/1 Staunchon, to set yn an ynke horne, *forulus.*

3. *attrib.* and *Comb.*: as ***stanchion-bar, -post, -rope, -waste*** (= *-rope waste*); **stanchion-gun,** a gun mounted in a boat for wild-fowl shooting.

1833 Loudon *Encycl. Archit.* §239 Window frames..with one-inch iron *stanchion bars. 1815 Col. Hawker *Diary* (1893) I. 140 Building a new canoe and *stanchion gun. 1889 A. Chapman *Bird-Life Borders* Pref., A long apprenticeship to rod, fowling-piece and stanchion-gun. 1875 Knight *Dict. Mech.*, *Stanchion.* 5. The vertical bars of a stall for cattle. In the example, the *stanchion-post is pivoted so as to swing horizontally. 1750 Blanckley *Naval Expos.* 136 *Stantion Ropes reeved through the Eyes of the Stantions. 1711 W. Sutherland *Shipbuild. Assist.* 131 Ropes..*Stancheon Waste, worn.

stanchion ('stɑːnʃən, -æ-), *v.* [f. stanchion *sb.*]

1. *trans.* To provide with stanchions, strengthen or support with stanchions.

1528 [see *vbl. sb.*]. 1802 *Trans. Soc. Arts* XX. 289 The thwarts are firmly stanchioned. 1853 Ruskin *Stones Ven.* II. vi. §70. 202 Cramped and stanchioned into such weight of grisly wall, as might..beat back the utmost storm of battle. 1871 Browning *Pr. Hohenst.* 1335 And see his system that's all true, except The one weak place that's stanchioned by a lie! 1907 H. Trench *New Poems* 4, I think some arm of the sea-gods Framed us her stormy frame, And ribbed and beamed and stanchioned her.

2. To fasten to, or by a stanchion.

1884 Allen *New Amer. Farm Bk.* 380 The cows tied, or stanchioned, as in their winter feeding.

Hence **'stanchioning** *vbl. sb.*

1528 *MS. Acc. St. John's Hosp., Canterb.*, Paid to a tyler for stanchonyng dobyng & vnderpynnyng of the store house.

stanchioned ('stɑːnʃənd, -æ-), *ppl. a.* [f. stanchion *sb.* or *v.* + -ed.] Provided with stanchions.

1839 W. Chambers *Tour Rhine* 59/1 Most of the best houses have strongly stauncheoned windows. 1852 Thackeray *Esmond* ii. i, Leaning against the great stanchioned door which the jailer had just closed upon them. 1914 *Blackw. Mag.* Mar. 368 The stanchioned under-story.

stanchless ('stɑːnʃlɪs, -æ-), *a.* Also 9 **staunch-.** [f. stanch *v.* + -less.] That may not be stanched.

1605 Shaks. *Macb.* iv. iii. 78 A stanchlesse Auarice. 1612 Drayton *Poly-olb.* i. 379 Where stanchlesse furie rap't The Grecians in so fast, that scarcely one escap't. 1820 Wiffen *Aonian Hours* (ed. 2) 82 We..cannot heal the stanchless wound. 1821 Shelley *Epipsych.* 320 Each word would be The key of staunchless tears.

stand (stænd), *sb.*[1] Also 4–5 **stonde,** 6 *arch.* **stond,** 7 **stande.** [f. stand *v.*

OE. had *stǫnd* masc., *stǫndo* (? fem.), delay (only once, see sense 1); equivalent formations, with the general sense 'standing, station, state', are LG., Du. *stand* masc. (in MLG. neut.), OHG. *-stand* in compounds (MHG., mod.G. *stand* masc.), Da., Norw., Icel. *stand*, Sw. *stånd* neut.).]

I. Action or condition of standing.

†**1.** A pause, delay. (OE. *rare*[−1].)

*c*950 *Lindisf. Gosp.* Mark vi. 35 Miððy..stando moniȝo wæs [L. *cum..mora* (bad reading for *hora*) *multa fieret*]. *c*975 *Rushw. Gosp.* ibid., Miððy..stondas moniȝe werun [L. *cum horæ multæ fierent*].

2. a. The action or an act of standing or coming to a position of rest; a pause, halt, esp. in the phrases ***to make a stand*** (rarely *to make stand*). †***fight of stand,*** a hand-to-hand encounter (*nonce-use*: cf. *stand-fight* in 31 b). Now *rare* or *Obs.* (cf. 4).

1592 SHAKS. *Rom. & Jul.* I. v. 52 The measure done, Ile watch her place of stand. **1596** —— *Merch. V.* II. vi. 2 This is the penthouse vnder which Lorenzo Desired vs to make a stand. **1602** MARSTON *Ant. & Mel.* I, Beeing entred, they make a stand in divided foyles. **1606** SHAKS. *Tr. & Cr.* III. iii. 252 Why he stalkes vp and downe like a Peacock, a stride and a stand. *c* **1611** CHAPMAN *Iliad* XIII. 290 Teucer..is great in fights of stand [Gr. ἐν σταδίῃ ὑσμίνῃ]. **1622** FLETCHER *Beggars Bush* IV. v, Why dost thou make These often stands? thou saidst thou knewst the way. **1622** F. MARKHAM *Bk. War* V. iii. §4. 171 To make stands (which some call Altoes or Hallts)..whereby the souldier may be refresht. **1633** P. FLETCHER *Purple Isl.* v. lvii, The idle Sunne stood still.., And pale-fac'd Cynthia at her word made stand. **1700** DRYDEN *Pal. & Arc.* 191 At ev'ry Turn she made a little Stand, And thrust among the Thorns her Lilly hand To draw the Rose. **1787** BURNS *Death & Dr. Hornbook* viii, It seem'd to mak a kind o' stan', But naething spak. **1807–8** WORDSW. *White Doe* vi. 29 He..made a sudden stand. **1827** D. JOHNSON *Ind. Field Sports* 208 He made a stand at one of them, and appeared to deposit something.

b. *fig.* A stop or pause (in speech, action, etc.).

1595 SHAKS. *John* IV. ii. 39 And we are all well pleas'd, Since all, and euery part of what we would Doth make a stand, at what your Highnesse will. *a* **1641** BP. MOUNTAGU *Acts & Mon.* (1642) 536 Had these narrators made a stand here,..they had found nor contradiction nor discommendation. **1709** STEELE *Tatler* No. 33 ¶7 But by Heaven, and all that's Sacred! If you could ——. Here he made a full Stand. **1726** BUTLER *Serm. Rolls Chapel* vii. 127 He run on headlong in Vice and Folly, without ever making a stand to ask himself what he was doing.

†**c.** ? A stage in a statement or argument. *Obs.*

1616 BP. ANDREWES *Serm. Holy Ghost* ix. Serm. (1629) 689, I proceed now to the second Combination, of breath, and the Holy Ghost... (I make two stands of it:) Breath and the Spirit: Christ's breath and the Holy Spirit. **1674** [see TEW *sb.*[2] 2].

†**d.** = EPODE 2. *Obs. rare*$^{-1}$.

a **1637** B. JONSON *Pindaric Ode Mem. Sir L. Cary*, The Turne... The Counter turne... The Stand.

e. *Theatr.* Each of the halts made on a tour to give performances; the place at which a halt is made; the performance itself; *transf.*, esp. in ***one-night stand***: see ONE *numeral a., pron.*, etc. 33.

1895 *N.Y. Dramatic News* 19 Oct. 11/1 Denver was the second stand of the week. **1896** *Peterson Mag.* N.S. VI. 273/2 Her managers, only depend on the one-night 'stands' to recoup their losses in the larger towns. One-night-stand audiences are not critical. **1900** *Free Lance* 6 Oct. 20, 1 (Farmer) This year I'm going with Grady—north and south—right through the big two week stands. **1910** *Stage Year Bk.* 49 In New Zealand, it may here be mentioned, the actor must be prepared for a number of one-night stands. **1931** *Amer. Speech* VI. 336 *Stand*, n., a town or city where a show stops to give performances. **1938** D. BAKER *Young Man with Horn* III. 149 He'd been making stands at moving-picture houses all over the country. **1959** *Times* 16 Dec. 3/2 A number of travelling road-shows do one or two-night stands at such unlikely places as the Constitution Hall. **1964** MRS. L. B. JOHNSON *White House Diary* 22 Apr. (1970) 115 Mrs. Eisenhower invited them in 1953, and had entertained around four thousand guests, about a four-hour stand. **1973** G. BEARE *Snake on Grave* ii. 12 When the Sands in Vegas offered her a stand she took Latch with her to play for her.

f. The mean sea-level at a given epoch in the past; also, the level of the sea at high or low tide.

1934 WEBSTER, *Stand*, the state of the tide at high or low water when there is no vertical movement. **1966** *Gloss. Oceanogr. Terms* (U.S. Naval Oceanographic Office) (ed. 2) 156/1 Where a double tide occurs, the stand may last for several hours even with a large range of tide. **1972** *Science* 13 Oct. 190/3 On Barbados, sedimentological considerations suggest that the high stand associated with the last interglacial (terrace III. 124,000 years ago) lasted no longer than about 5,000 years. **1978** *Nature* 18 May 185/3 At that time [*sc.* 22,000 years ago], sea-level was about 300 foot below its present stand because so much of the Earth's water was locked in glaciers.

†**3.** A standing in ambush or in cover. *Obs.*

1593 SHAKS. *3 Hen. VI*, III. i. 3 For through this Laund anon the Deere will come, And in this couert will we make our Stand. **1616** B. JONSON *Poetaster* Apol. Dial., Thefts, notable As Ocean pyracies, or high-way stands. **1621** MARKHAM *Fowling* 66 Now for these deade Engines [such as trees, bushes, hedges] which carry not the shape of any liuing creature, they are not altogether so necessary for the Stalke as the Stand. *Ibid.*, You must be carefull not to mooue them at all but to lye at the stand watching behinde them.

4. a. A holding one's ground against an opponent or enemy; a halt (of moving troops) to give battle or repel an attack; esp. in the phrase ***to make a*** (or ***one's***) ***stand***.

1590 SPENSER *F.Q.* II. xi. 15 On th'other side, th'assieged Castles ward Their steadfast stonds did mightily maintaine. **1607** SHAKS. *Cor.* I. vi. 2 Wel fought, we are come off, Like Romans, neither foolish in our stands, Nor Cowardly in retyre. **1609** HOLLAND *Amm. Marcell.* XVIII. xi. 118 We.. made a stand, and cast our selves into a round ring, as thinking it our safest way, neither to flye..nor to joyne battaile with them. **1736** *Milit. Hist. Pr. Eugene & Marlborough* I. 85 Instead of making any Stand they retreated continually. **1790** BEATSON *Nav. & Mil. Mem.* I. 269 He had raised a breast-work at a narrow pass, behind which he resolved to make his stand. **1817** JAS. MILL *Brit. India* II. v. vii. 613 After a slight stand at the outer intrenchment, the enemy fled through the fort. **1839** THIRLWALL *Greece* VI. xlvii. 115 The besieged made a short stand in the market-place. **1869** FREEMAN *Norm. Conq.* (1876) III. xii. 239 His last stand was made at Dinan.

b. *transf.* and *fig.*

1602 MARSTON *Ant. & Mel.* I, Take spirit;..make a firme stand. **1749** CHESTERF. *Let.* 12 Dec. (1870) 158 Mr. Hampden, to whose brave stand against the illegal demand of ship-money, we owe our present liberties. **1815** MME. D'ARBLAY *Diary* (1876) IV. lxiii. 286 He hoped a stand would be made against any obstinate revolt. **1833** HT. MARTINEAU *Brooke Farm* i. 13 We at once determined to make a stand against oppression. **1849** MACAULAY *Hist. Eng.* x. II. 668 Now, if ever, we ought to be able to appreciate the whole importance of the stand which was made by our forefathers against the House of Stuart. **1879** *Cassell's Techn. Educ.* IV. 13/1 Endeavouring..to make a public stand against it.

c. *Sporting.* A prolonged resistance. In *Cricket*, a prolonged stay at the wicket; now *spec.* a partnership between two batsmen at the crease.

1812 *Sporting Mag.* XXXIX. 187 [The pugilist] having made some good stands against first-raters. **1851** J. PYCROFT *Cricket Field* x. 189 Then comes the time when your great gun tumbles down his men: and that is the time that some sure, judgmatic batsman..comes calmly and composedly to the wicket and makes a stand. **1884** *Lillywhite's Cricket Ann.* 60 The longest stand ever made by two batsmen. **1912** P. F. WARNER *Eng. v. Austral.* iv. 29 Barnes and Strudwick made a capital last wicket stand. **1980** *Wisden Cricket Monthly* Mar. 6/3 Charlie Davis..was then joined by..Garfield Sobers, in a stand of 254 in 363 minutes.

5. a. A state of checked or arrested movement; a standstill; spec., the rigid attitude assumed by a dog on finding game. Chiefly in the phrases ***to be at a stand, to come to a stand, to bring*** or ***put to a stand***.

1618 W. LAWSON *New Orch. & Garden* (1623) 20 At the fal of the leafe..about that time is yᵉ greatest stand (but not descent) of sap. **1649** CROMWELL in Carlyle *Lett. & Sp.* (1850) II. 243 He could reach them with nothing but his horse, hoping to put them to a stand until his foot came up. **1698** FRYER *Acc. E. India & P.* 10 The Winds shrank upon us from off the Coast of Ginea..and had left us at a stand. *a* **1774** GOLDSM. *Hist. Greece* I. 139 Nor could he ever be persuaded to believe..that at the first pass he came to, his whole army would be put to a stand. **1837** CARLYLE *Fr. Rev.* II. IV. vii, For five-and-thirty minutes..the Berline is at a dead stand. **1856** STONEHENGE *Brit. Rural Sports* I. I. iii. 33 By increasing the encouragement in proportion to the increased length of stand, the dog becomes hourly improved. **1857** LIVINGSTONE *Trav.* xvii. 310 We were.. brought to a stand on this very plain by severe fever. **1883** *Century Mag.* Aug. 492 On our approach to the field, the dogs quartered it, but they did not come to a stand.

b. *Hunting phrase. U.S.*

1885 T. ROOSEVELT *Hunting Trips* 274 (Cent.) Occasionally these panic fits..make them [buffalo] run together and stand still in a stupid, frightened manner... When they are made to act thus it is called in hunters' parlance getting a stand on them.

c. (The performance of) a stallion or bull at stud. Also, a stud or stud-farm. *U.S.*

1797 E. CHAMBERS *Let.* 29 Nov. in J. Steele *Papers* (1924) I. 151 As a covering horse I am of Opinion he would make a very good Stand. **1836** *Russellville* (Kentucky) *Weekly Advertiser* 21 Jan. 3/3 (Advt.), Merlin is now at this stand in Elkton... Books are opened for those who may wish to enter their mares. **1959** W. FAULKNER *Mansion* i. 9 He had to lead the cow the three miles back..to claim a second stand from the bull.

d. = ERECTION 4. *slang.*

1867, etc. [see *cock-stand* s.v. COCK *sb.*[1] 23]. **1868** *Index Expurgatorius of Martial* 88 Maevius who while sleeping only gets A piss-proud stand that melts away on waking. **1903** FARMER & HENLEY *Slang* VI. 346/1 *Stand*,..(venery).—1. An *erectio penis*.

6. A state of being unable to proceed in thought, speech, or action; a state of perplexity or nonplus. Nearly always in the phrases ***to be at a stand, to put to a stand***, †***to set*** (***a person***) ***in a stand*** (*rare*$^{-1}$).

1599 SANDYS *Europæ Spec.* (1632) 71 Friers..being men of great marke..drew theyr Convents..with them; and thereby set the rest in such an amazement and stand, that the Pope grew in a generall great jealousie of them all. **1625** BACON *Ess., Truth* (Arb.) 499 One of the later Schoole of the Grecians, examineth the matter, and is at a stand, to thinke what should be in it, that men should loue Lies. **1652** G. HERBERT *Priest to Temple* xxii. (1671) 73 The Countrey Parson being to administer the Sacraments, is at a stand with himself, how or what behaviour to assume for so holy things. **1657** E. D'OYLEY in *Thurloe Papers* VI. 834 The prints telling me, that the heads of their people are..accounted conspirators..hath put me to some stand how to carry myself towards them. **1734** tr. *Rollin's Anc. Hist.* IV. IX. 321 There is one point however that puts me to a stand. **1790** BURKE *Fr. Rev.* Sel. Wks. 1898 II. 276 It remains only to consider the proofs of financial ability... Here I am a little at a stand; for credit, properly speaking, they have none. **1821** SCOTT *Kenilw.* xii, He is very ill at ease. The leeches are at a stand, and many of his household suspect foul practice. **1821** SHELLEY *Boat on Serchio* 85 With a bottle in one hand, As if his very soul were at a stand, Lionel stood.

7. A state of arrested progress (of affairs, institutions, natural processes or the like). Chiefly in the phrases ***to be at a stand, to come to a stand***; also †***to put*** (a hawk) ***unto a stand*** (*rare*$^{-1}$). Cf. STOND *sb.*

1614 LATHAM *Falconry* I. xi. 41 You shall find it wil suddenly put the soundest hawke that is vnto a stand, and by this onlie meanes, surfetted and spoiled manie a hawke. **1625** BACON *Ess., Of Usury* (Arb.) 543 The Greatest Part of Trade, is driuen by Young Merchants, vpon Borrowing at Interest: So as if the Vsurer, either call in, or keepe backe his Money, there will ensue presently a great Stand of Trade. *c* **1645** HOWELL *Lett.* (1650) I. 385 Nor did the pure Latin tongue continue long at a stand of perfection in Rome..but she received changes and corruption. **1664** FLECKNOE *Discourse Engl. Stage* G4b, We began before them [the French], and if since they seem to have out-stript us, 'tis because our Stage ha's stood at a stand this many years. *a* **1722** LISLE *Husb.* (1757) 141 My wheat, for want of rain, was at a stand in it's growth. **1789** *Ann. Reg., Hist.* 10 Public business was at a stand. **1796** MORSE *Amer. Geog.* I. 324 The effect [of attempting by law to regulate prices] was, a momentary apparent stand in the price of articles. **1814** SIR H. DAVY *Agric. Chem.* 255 In the northern winter, not only vegetable life, but likewise vegetable decay must be at a stand. **1833** NYREN *Yng. Cricketer's Tutor* (1902) 107 Then there was a dead stand for some time, and no runs were made. **1842** HAWTHORNE *Amer. Note-bks.* (1868) II. 143 Vegetation has quite come to a stand.

8. Manner of standing (of a thing). Now only *technical.*

a **1700** EVELYN *Diary* 23 July 1679, The stande [of the house], somewhat like Frascati as to its front. **1879** *Cassell's Techn. Educ.* IV. 190/1 To ensure the correct 'stand' of the timbers in relation to the keel.

9. A standing or upright posture (as distinguished from a crouching attitude). *rare.*

1893 *Outing* May 154/1 In the present season, scarcely a sprinter is to be found who runs from a stand. **1956** KUNZLE & THOMAS *Freestanding* i. 26 Also try jumps from stand, both from half knee bend and with very little knee bend. **1964** G. C. KUNZLE *Parallel Bars* ii. 50 Push away from the bars with the left hand to land in side stand.

10. *Leather-manuf.* (See quot.)

1883 R. HALDANE *Workshop Rec.* Ser. II. 372/1 The leather may have the quality known as Stand, that is to say, may be strongly stretched in either length or breadth without springing back.

II. Place of standing.

11. a. A place of standing, position, station; also in phr. ***to take one's stand***, poet. ***to take stand***.

a **1300** *Cursor M.* 1694 Siþen efter alþernest hand þe meke beistes sal haue þair stand. *c* **1450** *Mirk's Festial* 249 Come now wyth me, and stond on ȝondyr stonde befor þe and loke downeward. **1513** DOUGLAS *Æneis* v. 56 The stand thei [*sc.* competitors in a foot-race] leif, and flaw furth with a crak As windis blast. **1592** *Reg. Mag. Sig. Scot.* 697/1 Cum arca anguillarum et loco ejusdem (lie eill-ark and stand thairoff). **1599** DANIEL *Musophilus* 212 As if themselues had fortunately found Some stand from off the earth beyond our sight. **1601** SHAKS. *Jul. C.* II. iv. 25 *Por.* Is Cæsar yet gone to the Capitoll? *Sooth.* Madam, not yet, I go to take my stand, To see him passe. **1603** —— *Meas. for M.* IV. vi. 10 Come, I haue found you out a stand most fit, Where you may haue such vantage on the Duke He shall not passe you. **1667** MILTON *P.L.* IV. 395 Then from his loftie stand on that high Tree Down he alights. **1697** DRYDEN *Virg. Georg.* I. 498 Watchful Herons leave their watry Stand. **1704** POPE *Windsor Forest* 137 Beneath the quivering shade,..The patient fisher takes his silent stand. **1714** PARKYNS *Inn-Play* (ed. 2) 48 Shift your stand a little towards your Left. **1781** COWPER *Retirem.* 434 [He] Begins a long look-out for distant land, Nor quits, till ev'ning watch, his giddy stand. **1827** J. F. COOPER *Prairie* i, The low stands of the spectators exaggerated the distances. **1827** SCOTT *Surg. Dau.* iii, He saw from his lofty stand all the dumb show of gallantry. **1885–94** R. BRIDGES *Eros & Psyche* Mar. xxiii, She pass'd, and taking stand Upon its taper horn of furthest land, Lookt left and right.

b. *fig.*

1595 S. DANIEL *Civ. Wars* III. cxxv. 66 Nay father since your fortune did attaine So hye a stand: I meane not to descend, Replyes the Prince. **1648** G. DANIEL *Ode vpon Liricke Poesie of G. Herbert* 32 Wks. (Grosart) I. 214 This Stand, of Lirecks, Hee, the vtmost Fame Has gain'd. **1819** SIR J. MACKINTOSH *Sp. Ho. Comm.* 2 Mar., in Hansard *Parl. Deb.* 782 Accepting..the noble lord's concession,..here I might take my stand, and challenge him to drive me from this ground. **1850** *Tait's Mag.* XVII. 428/2 Their opponents take their stand on a quibble. **1874** GREEN *Short Hist.* vii. §4. 375 He [Philip] was preparing..to take a new political stand as the patron of Catholicism throughout the world.

†**c.** ***through lands and stands***: through many countries. *Obs.*

1380 WYCLIF *Sel. Wks.* III. 27 þei schulen go þoru liȝt of þin arrowis þat is, of þi þurlinge wordis, þoru londis and stondis.

d. The resting place of a salmon.

1886 *Q. Rev.* Oct. 359 *note*, A salmon is said to be swimming when he is moving up the river from pool to pool. At other times he is usually resting in his 'stand' or 'lie'.

†**e.** A degree of proficiency measured by achievement in school-work; a mark or grade awarded in assessment. *U.S. Educ. Obs.*

1900 *Dialect Notes* II. 64 *Stand*, degree of proficiency in college studies, as evidenced by marks and honors. **1904** *N.Y. Even. Post* 17 Mar. 7 The highest stand man of the non-elective scholastic period was Dean Wright of 1868, who attained a stand of 3·71 on a scale of 4·00. **1921** R. D. PAINE *Comrades of Rolling Ocean* i. 11, I had a rotten stand in your course.

12. a. The post or station of a soldier, sentinel, watchman, or the like.

1513 DOUGLAS *Æneis* IX. xi. 1 Endlang the wallis kyrnellis euery stand, The bruyt and clamour rais fra hand to hand. **1593** SHAKS. *3 Hen. VI*, IV. iii. 1, *1 Watch.* Come on my Masters, each man take his stand. **1624** CAPT. SMITH *Virginia* II. 37 At every halfe houre one from the *Corps du gard* doth hollow..; vnto whom every Sentinell doth answer round from his stand. **1760** JOHNSON *Idler* No. 95 ¶12 He.. comes home..with such thunders at the door as have more than once brought the watchmen from their stands.

b. The post or station of a sheep-shearer. *Austral.* and *N.Z.*

1893 S. NEWLAND *Paving Way* II. xviii. 339 As applicants for a 'stand' on the shearing-floor began to camp about, his audiences became more numerous. **1901** 'R. BOLDREWOOD' *In Bad Company* 21 It's hard on a chap, when he comes to a shed..to be told that all the stands is took up. **1922** C. G. TURNER *Happy Wanderer* 143 Four hundred men might answer the roll-call where only one hundred could 'get a stand'—i.e. a chance to shear. **1933** *Bulletin* (Sydney) 6 Sept. 20/2 They run a record long shearing, six stands being considered sufficient to cope with 60,000 sheep. **1949** D. WALKER *We went to Australia* 97 We watched them [*sc.* shearers] in the 'eight-stand' shed at Nareeb. **1956** G. BOWEN *Wool Away!* (ed. 2) x. 110, I have set out the plan of a three-stand shed.. which should meet the needs of a large cross-section of sheep farmers.

13. The standing-place from which a hunter or sportsman may shoot game; also in phr. *to take a* or *one's stand*.

c **1400** *Master of Game* (MS. Digby 182) xxxv, And þanne þe mayster forster or parker oweth to shewe hym þe kynges stonde. **1588** SHAKS. *L.L.L.* IV. i. 10 *For.* Hereby vpon the edge of yonder Coppice, A Stand where you may make the fairest shoote. **1611** —— *Cymb.* III. iv. 111 Why hast thou gone so farre To be vn-bent? when thou hast tane thy stand, Th' elected Deere before thee? **1639** FULLER *Holy War* III. xxii. (1640) 148 Using Gods cause as hunters do a stand, in it the more covertly to shoot at what game they please. **1679** BLOUNT *Anc. Tenures* 165 *Ad stabliamentum pro venatione capienda*. For driving Deer to a stand in order to shooting them. **1720** DE FOE *Capt. Singleton* xv. (1840) 257 Like an old decayed oak.., where the keepers in England take *a stand*, as they call it, to shoot a deer. **1791** W. GILPIN *Forest Scenery* II. 24 Here too, he had a banquetting-room built, like a stand, in a large tree. **1876** *Field* 9 Dec. in Greener *Breech-Loader* (1892) 270 My usual practice in grouse driving is to take two guns into the 'stands' (called by some butts). **1913** *Times* 12 Sept. 12/6 Equalization of sport by the drawing of numbers for each gun's stand.

†**14.** *Hawking.* An elevated resting place of a hawk; *spec.* as a 'fault', a position of rest from flight, esp. in the phrases ***to take stand, go to stand***, to settle. *Obs.*

1579 LYLY *Euphues* (Arb.) 80 Lucilla.. fearing he would take stand if the lure were not cast out, toke him by the hand, and.. began thus to comfort him. **1611** MARKHAM *Country Contentm.* I. viii. (1615) 93 If your long-winged hawke flying .. in champaine fields vse to take stand which is a foule fault you shal.. shunne flying neere trees or couert:.. when the hawke offers to goe to the stand, let him which is next her cast out his traine. *Ibid., margin*, Helps for faults in long winged hawkes, and first of the stand. **1678** RAY *Willughby's Ornithol.* 409.

15. a. A stall or booth.

1508 *Extracts Burgh Rec. Edin.* (1869) I. 114 [The fleshers] sall haif thair stall and standis weill tentit with fair canves. **1568** *Sat. Poems Reform.* xlviii. 88 To pay my buth maill and my stand. **1845** DISRAELI *Sybil* v. vi, The gas was beginning to glare in shops.. and the paper lanterns to adorn the stall and the stand. **1867** J. K. HUNTER *Retrospect Artist's Life* xxxi. (1912) 333 The shoe stands being erected in the Kirkyard.

b. A street vendor's habitual station or pitch.

1742 RICHARDSON *Pamela* III. 361 If I see them [beggars] often.. and so much in the same Place, as if they were as tenacious of their Stand, as others of their Freehold. **1929** [see MEET *sb.* 1 b.].

16. a. *U.S.* A position, site or building for a business.

1787 *Maryland Jrnl.* 25 Dec. (Thornton *Amer. Gloss.*), A Bargain will be given in that excellent stand now occupied by Mr. Mark Pringle. **1788** *Ibid.* 25 July (Ibid.), [Notice] to those who would wish for the best Stand for a Dry or Wet Store. **1856** EMERSON *Eng. Traits, Land* Wks. (Bohn) II. 17 The shopkeeping nation, to use a shop word, has a good stand. **1867** LOWELL *Study Wind., Gt. Publ. Char.* (1871) 64 Their historians.. have succeeded to the good-will as well as to the long-established stand, of the shop of glory.

b. *S. Afr.* A plot of land, a site (see quot. 1896).

1895 *Westm. Gaz.* 6 Sept. 6/1 It is announced by the British South Africa Company that the annual sale of stands in Rhodesia has now been completed. Township stands.. realised a total of £204,280. **1896** MÉLIOT *Eng.-Fr. Dict. Terms Finance*, etc. 222 In the Transvaal, a stand is a portion of any land measuring 150 × 150 feet, sold or let. **1914** *19th Cent.* Sept. 592 As far back as the year 1886 a township was surveyed and laid out in stands by the Government of that day.

17. A station for a row of vehicles plying for hire; also, the row of vehicles occupying a station.

1692 LUTTRELL *Brief Rel.* (1857) II. 411 A lieutenant of the marine regiment quarrelling with a coachman in the stand. **1768** *Act 8 Geo. III*, c. 21 §25 It shall.. be lawful.. for the said [Paving] Commissioners.. to direct.. how many Coaches shall be plied at each Stand. **1820** SHELLEY *Let. Maria Gisborne* 265 But what see you beside?—a shabby stand Of Hackney coaches. **1833** *Act 3 & 4 Will. IV*, c. 46 §113 Rules.. regulating the said hackney coaches.., and for fixing and altering their stands. **1841** DICKENS *Barn. Rudge* xvi, Long stands of hackney-chairs and groups of chairmen .. obstructed the way. **1865** RUSKIN *Arrows of Chase* (1880) II. 81 The just price of a cab at a stand involves an allowance to the cabman for having stood there.

18. A raised platform for spectators at open-air sports as race-meetings, football matches and the like, or for a company of musicians or performers. ***band stand***: see BAND *sb.*³ 7. ***grand stand***: see as main entry.

1615 in W. Sheardown *Doncaster Races, Hist. Notices* (1861) 4 It is agreed that the stand and the stoopes shall be pulled upp and imploied to some better purpose, and the race to be discontinued. *a* **1700** EVELYN *Diary* 20 July, 1654, Neere this is a pergola or stand, built to view the sports. **1842** *Niles' Reg.* 15 Oct. LXIII. 103/3 From a stand erected on Main Cross street, Mr. Clay.. reviewed a part of the procession. **1876** O. W. HOLMES *How old Horse won the Bet* 110 As.. The old horse nears the judges' stand. **1884** YATES *Recoll.* x. II. 47 Her Majesty then took up her station in the royal stand,.. and the entire mass of Volunteers marched past. **1885** *Daily Tel.* 11 Nov. 3/7 Many changes have taken place at Aintree, and, if the weather had permitted, the new stands would have been finished off. **1902** *Daily Mail* 7 Apr. 5/1 (*heading*) Stand collapses at a football match. **1977** *Evening Post* (Nottingham) 27 Jan. 20/4 There will be other rises with best seats in the stands going up to £1.40.

19. An elevated platform or standing place for a speaker; a rostrum, pulpit; *U.S.* the place where a witness stands to testify in court, more fully ***witness-stand***.

1840 *Niles' Reg.* 26 Sept. LIX. 56/2 Upon the stand, general Harrison was welcomed to Dayton, on behalf of the citizens.. by judge Crane. **1843** *Ibid.* 18 Nov. LXV. 184/2 Dr. Davis then again took the stand [at a barbecue in Indiana], and stated that [etc.]. **1865** LOWELL *Study Wind., Thoreau* (1871) 156 He had watched Nature like a detective who is to go upon the stand. **1885** W. WILSON *Congressional Govt.* ii. 128 Members [of the French Chamber] do not speak from their seats,.. but from the 'tribune'.. a box-like stand.

†**20.** The landing of a staircase. *Obs. rare*$^{-1}$.

1709 STEELE & ADDISON *Tatler* No. 86 ¶3 The simple Esquire made a sudden start to follow; but the Justice of the Quorum whipp'd between upon the Stand of the Stairs.

III. An appliance to stand something on.

21. a. A base, bracket, stool or the like upon which a utensil, ornament, or exhibit may be set; the base upon which an instrument is set up for use.

1664 in *Verney Mem.* (1907) II. 211 Be pleased to by a tabel and stands of the same coler. **1686** tr. *Chardin's Coronat. Solyman* 39 As we set our Candlesticks upon Tables or Stands. **1688** HOLME *Armoury* III. 316/1 An Oven .. having.. a stay or stand on the left side of it, to rest or set any thing out of the Oven thereon. *Ibid.* 346/1 He beareth Sable on a round foot or stand of two heights Argent, a pair of Broad Yarringle Blades. **1706** PHILLIPS (ed. Kersey), *Stand*,.. a Frame to set a Candle-stick on, or a Vessel in a Cellar, &c. **1727** DE FOE *Eng. Tradesm.* (1841) I. xxii. 207, 12 large high stands of rings, to place small dishes for tarts, jellies, at a feast. **1797** HT. LEE *Canterb. T., Frenchm. T.* (1799) I. 229 Stands for flowers were fixed on each side the dressing table. **1827** FARADAY *Chem. Manip.* xiii. (1842) 295 Stands of common earthenware are sold with crucibles; or the stand may be a small crucible about one inch and a half high, turned upside down. **1851** *Butler, Wine-dealer* etc. 9 In storing wine, the casks should be placed on stands. **1855** *Poultry Chron.* III. 206 Hives last several years; the same of covers and stands. **1878** ABNEY *Photogr.* xxx. 220 The essentials of a stand for landscape work consist of rigidity, lightness, and compactness when folded up. **1884** KNIGHT *Dict. Mech.* Suppl., *Stand*, 1. For holding materials for drawing or painting... 2. (*Microscopy.*) The framework of a microscope, usually implying all save the object glasses and the accessory apparatus.

b. *dial.* (See quot.)

1854 MISS BAKER *Northampt. Gloss.*, *Stand*, a small round pillar-and-claw table. **1862** C. C. ROBINSON *Dial. Leeds* 420.

22. A frame or piece of furniture upon which to stand or hang articles.

1692 DRYDEN *Cleomenes* Life 10 After Supper, a Stand was brought in with a brass Vessel full of Wine, two silver Pots,.. a few silver Cups. **1822** [M. A. KELTY] *Osmond* I. 256 Ornamented.. with stands of flowers and plants. **1823** J. BADCOCK *Dom. Amusem.* 100 A wooden stand, which has several ribs across to sustain the tobacco. **1839** DICKENS *Nich. Nick.* x, Some dresses, were arranged on stands. **1867** AUGUSTA WILSON *Vashti* xviii, She slowly descended the stairs, and took her hat from the stand in the hall. **1869** DICKENS *Mut. Fr.* III. iv, There were shelves and stands of books. **1875** SOUTHWARD *Dict. Typogr.*, *Stand*, otherwise frame. **1882** C. PEBODY *Eng. Journalism* xxii. 167 The *Times* .. and the *Daily Telegraph* are.. read at a stand in a club.

IV. Something which stands.

23. A complete set (of things).

a. *Sc.* (and *Anglo-Irish*). A set (of vestments, armour, or utensils); a suit (of clothes).

c **1450** *Reg. Vestments* etc. *St. Andrews* in *Maitland Club Misc.* III. 195 Of haill standis. Item in the fyrst of rede claith of gold, 1 stand. *Ibid.* 196 Of syngyll standis. *Ibid.* Item for lentryn iij singell standis of fustian. **1471** in *Acta Audit.* (1839) 12/2 The compleite stand of harnes quhilk he borrowit. **1516** in *3rd Rep. Hist. MSS. Comm.* 418/2 All the haill stand of the Mess except the Book. **1534** *Acc. Ld. High Treas. Scot.* VI. 185 To ane stand of bellis for the Kingis son, xx s. **1535** STEWART *Cron. Scot.* (Rolls) II. 425 And vestimentis of mony sindrie stand. *a* **1578** LINDESAY (Pitscottie) *Chron. Scot.* (S.T.S.) I. 367 He.. gart cheise our money standis of harneise that was dowbill ower-gilt. **1597** *Compt Buik D. Wedderburne* (S.H.S.) 164, 42 stand of gad iron. **1615** in *Reg. Privy Seal, Scot.* LXXXV. fol. 124 in *Proc. Soc. Ant. Scot.* (1896) XXX. 56 Ane honest stand of Cleithing ȝeirlie. **1642** in *10th Rep. Hist. MSS. Comm.* App. I. 51 And trewli for the present we hau not on stand of good curtteins. **1827** SCOTT *Chron. Canongate* vi, A full stand, as it is called in Scotland, of garments of a dark colour. **1880** *Antrim & Down Gloss.* s.v., Four knitting needles are a stand. **1896** CROCKETT *Grey Man* xvi. 122, I judged he wore a stand of chain mail underneath. **1898** J. PATON *Castlebraes* 302 They wummilt a staun' o' new Cairt rapes aneath his oxters, an' pooed him oot.

b. *Mil.* A set (of arms, colours).

Sometimes unchanged in plural (after numerals).

1721 DE FOE *Mem. Cavalier* (1840) 160 He had.. not a stand of arms. **1746** M. HUGHES *Jrnl. Late Rebell.* 14 They came riding into Edinburgh with the Stands of Cope's colours flying. **1794** LD. HOOD in Nicolas *Disp.* (1845) I. 401 *note*, By the first Ship.. I shall have the honour of sending the several stand of colours taken at Bastia. **1800** WELLINGTON in Gurw. *Desp.* (1837) I. 84, I will write to the Military Board, and recommend that I may be permitted to issue to Purneal 1000 stand of the repairable arms. **1837** CARLYLE *Fr. Rev.* III. I. i, Beaumarchais.. has commissioned sixty thousand stand of good arms out of Holland. **1876** VOYLE & STEVENSON *Milit. Dict.*, *Stand of Arms*, a single rifle or musket with bayonet complete. **1878** BOSW. SMITH *Carthage* 389 Long lines of waggons brought to the consuls.. two hundred thousand stands of arms.

c. *Metallurgy.* A set of rolls and their auxiliary fittings which during any one pass provide one gap for the metal being rolled.

1874 *Jrnl. Iron & Steel Inst.* I. 349 Space is left at the end of the train for two stands of merchant roughing and finishing rolls. **1958** A. D. MERRIMAN *Dict. Metallurgy* 338/2 A stand is usually.. described as 2-high, 3-high, [etc.] .. A rolling-mill may consist of a single stand or of several stands in series. **1973** G. F. BRYANT *Automation of Tandem Mills* ix. 160 In 1968, a fifth stand was added to the BSC Abbey Works tandem cold-rolling mill.

d. *Oil Industry.* A number of lengths of drill pipe (usually from one to four) joined together, esp. when being unscrewed from a string or racked in a derrick.

1913 B. REDWOOD *Petroleum* (ed. 3) I. v. 317 The casing with which it is desired to shut off the water must admit of being moved quite freely in the bore-hole, so that it may be raised or lowered the full length of a 'stand', that is, for a distance of, say, three lengths or joints. **1949** [see RACK *v.*² 4 a]. **1960** C. GATLIN *Petroleum Engin.* v. 52/2 Only two or three joints per stand will be pulled when using shorter derricks. **1973** J. W. JENNER in Hobson & Pohl *Mod. Petroleum Technol.* (ed. 4) iv. 120 The drawworks then hauls the blocks up the derrick until a stand of three joints of drill pipe is above the rotary table.

24. ***stand of pikes***: a compact group of pikemen. *Obs.* exc. *Hist.*

1598 BARRET *Theor. Warres* 69 Any troupe of shot, hauing no stand of pikes to succour them. **1647** CLARENDON *Hist. Reb.* VII. §89 Major general Chudleigh.. himself advanced, with a good stand of pikes, upon that party which was led by sir John Berkely. **1819** SCOTT *Leg. Montrose* xiv, And, comrade, you will be sure to keep your musketeers in advance of your stand of pikes.

transf. **1598** SYLVESTER *Du Bartas* I. iii. 843 The seed, to shut the wastefull Sparrows out, (In Harvest) hath a stand of Pikes about. *c* **1650** DENHAM *Of Old Age* III. 118 Drawn up in rancks, and files, the bearded spikes Guard it from birds as with a stand of pikes.

25. A drove or stud (of horses). ? *Obs.*

1711 P. H. *View 2 late Parlts.* 256 A milk-white virgin Palfrey was chosen out of the best Stands, to mount this Undefiled Prophet on.

26. *Sporting.* An assemblage or group (of certain game birds).

1851 W. KELLY *Excursion to California* I. v. 83 A stand of prairie plover most opportunely made their appearance as we pulled up. **1881** J. P. MAHAFFY in *Academy* 20 Aug. 133/3 But the bird is then always solitary.. and never in stands, as sports-men call them. **1882** BLACK *Shandon Bells* iii, Fitzgerald knew a great deal.. about the habits of a 'stand' of golden plover.

†**27.** *slang.* A thief's assistant who stands on watch. *Obs.*

1591 GREENE *Conny Catching* II. Wks. (Grosart) X. 128 The Black Arte is picking of Lockes, and to this busie trade two persons are required, the Charme and the Stand: the Charm is he that doth the feate, and the Stand is he that watcheth. *Ibid.* III. 157 A game, qd. he to his fellows, marke the stand. **1622** J. TAYLOR (Water P.) *Water-Cormorant* D 2 b, He.. Liues like a Gentleman, by sleight of hand; Can play the Foist, the Nip, the Stale, the Stand.

28. A young tree left standing for timber.

1787 W. H. MARSHALL *Norfolk* (1795) II. 389 *Stands.* Young Timber-trees under six inches timber girt, or twenty-four inches in circumference. **1823** E. MOOR *Suffolk Words*, *Stand* is also a young tree, unpolled.

29. orig. *U.S.* A standing growth or crop (of wheat, cotton, etc.); *spec.* one of trees. Also applied to natural assemblages of plants, esp. when only one species is present or considered.

1868 *Rep. U.S. Commissioner Agric.* (1869) 414 In the gullies and clayey places the stand [of wheat] was injured. **1887** *Century Mag.* Nov. 111/2 By the middle of April there should be a good 'stand' of the young sprouts [of sugar cane]. **1904** *Daily Record & Mail* 11 May 5 Reports of poor stands in the early planted cotton continue. **1905** *Terms Forestry & Logging* (U.S. Dept. Agric. Bureau Forestry) 22 *Stand*, all growing trees in a forest or in part of a forest. Syn.: growing stock. **1912** HAWLEY & HAWES *Forestry in New England* i. 8 The term 'stand' is the unit of description applied to any definite portion of a forest having a definite distinguishing characteristic. Thus in a certain type we may have a stand of young growth; a stand of diseased and damaged trees; a stand of exceptionally tall specimens, etc. These stands may be extensive, covering many acres or they may be confined each to a small part of an acre. **1947** K. TENNANT *Lost Haven* xvii. 284 Nice stand of trees, brushwood, coach-wood, white soapy box. **1967** M. J. COE *Ecol. Alpine Zone Mt. Kenya* 28 All the genera cited.. are.. obvious components of the alpine zone, with the megaphytic Senecios and Alchemilla scrub forming almost pure stands under suitable conditions. **1975** P. LIVELY *Going Back* i. 8 Old wooden chicken-houses half-submerged in grass and cow-parsley and stands of nettles. **1979** H. W. HOCKER *Introd. Forest Biol.* iv. 99 The stand is a basic unit of management and is important to planning silvicultural operations... In the terminology of plant ecology, a forest stand would be designated as a community, or an ecosystem. .. Foresters use the term stand to designate the tree portion of the ecosystem.

†**30.** A standing water. *Obs. rare*$^{-1}$.

[Possibly an error for, or etymologizing corruption of, *stang*, STANK *sb.*]

1612 *Benvenuto's Passenger* I. ii. 201 Not corrupted by the fogs, nor vapours of lakes, stands, marrishes [It. *laghi, stagni, e paludi*], caues, durt, nor dust.

31. *attrib.* and *Comb.*: **a.** simple attrib., as ***standholder, stand man, stairs, ticket***.

1887 *Daily News* 29 June 2/7 The London Grocery and Provision Exchange... There are already 140 *standholders. **1860** MAYNE REID *Hunters' Feast* xxiii, The '*stand men' remain quiet, with their guns in readiness. **1852** R. S. SURTEES *Sponge's Sp. Tour* (1893) 375 He swung down the *stand stairs, rushed to his horse, and.. struck across country. **1874** J. A. THOMSON *Remin.* (1904) II. iv. 105 As to the stand at Ascot..you can have the satisfaction of giving me a *stand-ticket.

b. Special comb., some of which may be combinations of the verb-stem: † **stand bed**, = *standing bed* (see STANDING *ppl. a.*); † **stand board** *Sc.*, a standing table, as opposed to a folding one (Jam.); **stand camera**, a camera for use on a tripod or other stand, as distinguished from a hand camera; **stand cask** *U.S.*, a cask for spirits to be set up and drawn from on the premises of a liquor dealer (*Funk's Stand. Dict.* 1895); **stand cock** = STAND-PIPE; **stand development** *Photogr.* (see quot.); † **stand-fight** (*nonce-wd.*), a hand-to-hand encounter (cf. *fight of stand* in sense 1 above); **stand-hand**, in the card-game of Napoleon, the player who 'stands' (see STAND *v.* 13) or declares how many tricks he will play for; **stand hawk** *dial.* (see quot.); **stand-heck** *Sc.* and *north.* = HECK *sb.*[1] 3; **stand-house**, the grand stand of a race-course with the buildings attached to it; † **stand ladder**, a step ladder; † **stand mail** *Sc.*, rent paid for a stand in a market; † **stand measure** *Sc.*, standard measure; **stand-rest** (see quot.); † **stand watch**, a guard of sentries. Also STAND-PIPE.

1489 *Acta Audit.* (1839) 132/1 For the wʳhaldin fra him of a hors & harnes, .a *stand bed, a pot [etc.]. **1658** *Knaresb. Wills* (Surtees) II. 243, 1 stand bed which I lye in. **1580** *Reg. Privy Council Scot.* III. 320 In the hall, thre *stand burdis sett on brandirs with thair furmes. **1892** *Photogr. Ann.* II. 280 Hand cameras..have appeared in battalions, although there is but little change to report in *stand cameras. **1844** *Civil Engin. & Arch. Jrnl.* VII. 86/1 The first experiment took place..by having lengths of..hose..attached to 6 *standcocks, placed into plugs. **1906** *Westm. Gaz.* 30 June 14/2 *Stand development, a method by which, say, a dozen plates may be developed together. Stand development is usually associated with the use of very dilute solutions, and subjecting the plates to these for an increased time. *c* **1611** CHAPMAN *Iliad* III. 258 Castor, the skilfull knight on horse, and Pollux, vncontrold For all *stand fights, and force of hand. **1884** *Encycl. Brit.* XVII. 229/1 If the *stand-hand succeeds in making at least the number of tricks he stood for he wins. **1885** SWAINSON *Provinc. Names Birds* 140 Kestrel (*Tinnunculus alaudarius*)... From its well-known habit of.. hovering and poising itself over a particular spot, are derived the names *Stand hawk (West Riding) [etc.]. **1570** *Richmond Wills* (Surtees) 229 One *stand hecke. **1576** *Ibid.* (Surtees) 260, ij stand hecks. **1620** [see HECK *sb.*[1] 3]. **1731** *Inventory of G. Bamforth, Sheffield*, Stand hecks. **1856** MORTON *Cycl. Agric.* II. 726/1 *Stand-heck* (Yorks.), a rack for straw in a farm-yard. **1859** LEVER *Dav. Dunn* lvi, You must be declared winner at the *stand-house before you have been seen on the ground. **1902** *Daily Chron.* 29 Apr. 7/1 Charles II..built a stand house, or what we should now call a grand stand [at Newmarket]. **1721** MORTIMER *Husb.* (ed. 2) I. 194 If they [hop-binds] forsake the Poles, a *Stand-Ladder is very useful in tying them up again. **1603** *Reg. Mag. Sig. Scot.* 515/1 With..*standmaillis baith of the land mercat, meill merket and clayth merket, with all uther custumes. **1654** *Extracts Rec. Convent. Burghs Scot.* (1878) III. 388 For ilk stand maill of ane daill length one thair weiklie mercat dayes, tuelue penyes. **1586** *Ibid.* (1882) IV. 475 As agreand to the awld and greitt *stand mesoure of this burgh. **1882** OGILVIE, **Stand-rest*, a kind of stool which supports a person behind while standing almost in an upright position at a desk, an easel, &c. **1579** DIGGES *Stratioticos* 100 It were requisite that a *stande watch be maintayned within and about the Ordinance.

stand (stænd), *sb.*[2] *Obs.* exc. *dial.* Also 3–5 stonde, 4–5 stoond(e, 6 stande (6 *pl.* stannes). [a. or cognate with (M)LG. *stande*, Flem. *stande* (16th c. in Kilian; mod.WFlem. in De Bo) = OHG. *stanta*, *standa* wk. fem. (MHG., mod.G. dial. *stande* fem.); f. the root of STAND *v.*]

1. An open tub; a barrel set on end.

c **1250** *Death* 110 in *O.E. Misc.* 174 Hwer is þi bred and þin ale, þi tunne and þine stonde. *a* **1390** WYCLIF *Jer.* lii. 19 Stoondis [1382 stenes, 1388 watir pottis, Vulg. *hydrias*]. *c* **1440** *Pallad. on Husb.* I. 1051 Or make an hyue of boordis lyk a stonde [L. *more cuparum*]. *c* **1440** *Promp. Parv.* 477/1 Stonde vessel (*v.rr.* ston vessel, stoonde vessel), *futula*, *cumula* [etc.]. *c* **1490** *5th Rep. Hist. MSS. Comm.* 445/2 Two stondys full of ale each of them conteyning 13 galons. **1559** in Nichols *Progr. Eliz.* (1823) I. 71 Item, for a stande of small ale 2s. od. **1582** *Inventory R. Best* in *Best's Farm. Bks.* (Surtees) 172 One gialfatte, 3 stannes 3s. **1588** *Marprel. Epist.* (Arb.) 38 At length sir Jefferie bethought him of a feat whereby he might both visit the alestond and also keepe his othe. **1594** LYLY *Mother Bombie* II. v, My wag-halter..shall learne the oddes betweene a stand and a hogs-head. **1603** DEKKER *Wonderf. Yeare* Wks. (Grosart) I. 124 The Tapster ..rapping out fiue or sixe plaine Country oathes, that hee would drowne himselfe in a most villanous Stand of Ale. **1673** SHADWELL *Epsom-Wells* I. 8, I have the rarest stand of Ale to drink out in the afternoon, with three or four honest Country fellows. **1679** *Lett. Gentl. Romish Rel. to his Brother* 28 That he may have leave to meet some few Neighbours to dust a stand of Ale. **1775** ADAIR *Amer. Ind.* 395 All his war store of provisions consisted in three stands of barbicued venison. *a* **1791** *Tom Line* xxxiv. in Child *Ballads* I. 344 First dip me in a stand o milk, And then a stand o water. **1854** MISS BAKER *Northampt. Gloss.*, *Stand*, a large barrel set on end under a spout for the purpose of receiving rain-water. **1899** DICKENSON & PREVOST *Cumbld. Gloss.*, *Stand*, the large washing tub in which the dolly is worked.

b. Comb.: † **standfat** = prec.

1593 *Wills & Inv. N.C.* (Surtees) II. 229 In the new house. One leade, ij standfattes, j troughe.

2. A certain weight (of pitch, coal).

1706 PHILLIPS (ed. Kersey), *Stand of Burgundy-Pitch*, (in Merchandize) a quantity from two and a half to three Hundred Weight. **1729** SWIFT *Lett. Irish Coal* 4 Aug., Wks. 1824 VII. 222 The common rate of the Kilkenny coal, at the pits, is sixteen pence the stand; the stand is five hundred, one quarter weight. **1858** SIMMONDS *Dict. Trade*, *Stond*,..a weight for pitch of $2\frac{1}{2}$ to 3 cwt.

stand (stænd), *v.* Forms: see below. [A Com. Teut. strong verb, in most of the Teut. langs. more or less defective, certain parts being supplied by a synonymous defective verb from the same ultimate root (see below). The OE. *standan* (*stǫndan*), pa. t. *stód*, *stódon*, pa. pple. *ȝestanden*, corresponds to OFris. *stônda*, pa. t. pl. *stôdon*, pa. pple. *stenden*; OS. *standan*, pa. t. *stôd* (*stuod*), *stôdun* (*stuodun*), pa. pple. *-standan*; MLG. imp. *stant*, pa. t. *stôt*, *stôden*, also nasalized *stunt*, *stunden* (mod.LG. pa. t. *stund*, *stunden*); MDu. *standen*, pa. t. *stond*, *stonden*, Flem. *stoet*, *stoeden*, pa. pple. †*gestanden* (mod.Du. pa. t. *stond*, *stonden*); OHG. *stantan*, pa. t. *stuont*, pl. *stuondum*, *-stuotun*, pa. pple. *-stantan* (MHG. inf. rare *standen*, pa. t. *stuont*, pa. pple. *gestanden*; mod.G. imp. †*stand*, pa. t. *stand*, pl. *standen*, earlier †*stund(e* etc., pl. †*stunden* etc., pa. pple. *gestanden*); ON. *standa*, pa. t. *stóþ*, pl. *stóþom*, pa. pple. *staþenn* (Norw. *standa*, pa. t. *stod*, pa. pple. *stadet*, *stande* etc.; MSw. *standa*, pa. t. *stóþ*, pl. *stóþo*, pa. pple. *standin*, also *staþin*; mod.Sw. pa. t. *stod*, pl. *stodo*, pa. pple. *stånden*; Da. †*stande*, *stonde*, pa. t. *stod*, pl. *stode*, pa. pple. †*standet*); Goth. *standan*, pa. t. *stōþ*, pl. *stōþum* (pa. pple. unrecorded).

In OTeut. the forms of the verb were probably as follows: pres.-stem *stand-*, perfect sing. *stōþ-*, plural *stōđ-*; formed, with suffix *-nd-* (:—pre-Teut. *-nt-*) in the present-stem, and *-þ-*, *đ* (:—pre-Teut. *-t-*) in the perfect stem, on the root **sta-*: *stō-*:—Indogermanic **st(h)ə-*: *st(h)ā-*, found in all branches of the family exc. Armenian and Albanian with the senses 'to stand', 'to cause to stand': cf. Skr. *sthā* (pres. ind. *tiṣṭhati*, inf. *sthātum*), Avestic *hištaiti*, Gr. *ἱστάναι*, L. *stāre*, *sistĕre*, Lith. *stojů-s* I set myself, OSl. *stojati*, *stati*, OIrish *táu*, *tó* I am (:—OCeltic **stāō*).

In Ger. and Du. the *n* of the present stem has within historical times passed into the pa. t. The pa. pple., which this vb. prob. did not possess in OTeut., has been variously supplied in the different langs.: the type **stađono-*, which conforms to the general rule of the *a*, *ō* conjugation, is represented in ON., Norw., MSw.; the other Teut. langs., so far as they do not take their pa. pple. from the shorter form of the verb (see below) have a formation based on the present stem, as in OE. (*ȝe*)*standen*. In English the regular form of the pa. pple., *standen* (with the variants *stande*, etc.) continued until the 16th c., when its place was taken by *stood* from the pa. t. A few examples of a weak form *standed* occur in writings of the 16th c.; in compounds (*understanded*, *withstanded*) this formation was less rare, and survived into the 17th c.

In all the Teut. langs. exc. English, Gothic, and Old Norse, the present stem has a shorter form, the OTeut. type of which varies between **stai-* and **stæ-* (WGer. **stā-*); in some of the langs. this is used exclusively, and in others along with the longer form **stand-*. In some of the languages the earlier form of pa. pple. has been wholly or partially superseded by a new formation from the shorter present stem. The dialectal range of the shorter type will appear from the following list of typical forms (minor variations being omitted): OS. inf. *stân* (rare; MLG. inf. *stân*, pa. pple. *gestân*; mod.LG. inf. *staan*, pa. pple. *staan*), OLow Frankish inf. *stân* (MDu. inf. *staen*, 3 pres. ind. *staet*, *steet*, pa. pple. *gestaen*; mod.Du. inf. *staan*, pa. pple. *gestaan*); OFris. inf. *stân*, *stên*, 3 pres. ind. *steet*, pa. pple. *stên* (WFris. inf., 1 pres. ind. *stean*); OHG. inf. *stân*, *stên* (MHG. inf. *stân*, *stên*, mod.G. *stehen*, *stehn*); MSw. inf. *stâ* (mod.Sw. *stå*, pa. pple. wk. *stådd*); Da. inf. *staa*, pa. pple. *staaet*; Norw. inf. *staa*, pres. *staar*, *stær*.

The remarkable parallel between the verbal stems **stæ-*, *stai-*, *stand-* and **gæ-*, *gai-*, *gang-* (see GO, GANG *vbs.*) strongly suggests that one of the two series has been assimilated to the other. The relation between the two, however, and the precise mode of formation of the shorter verbal stems from the roots, is very uncertain. For an outline of the different views, with references, see *Deutsches Wb.* ('Grimm') X. II. 1433.]

A. Illustration of Forms.

1. *Infinitive* (and Present stem). *α*. 1–2 **standan**, 3 *Orm.* **standenn**, 3–5 (7 *arch.*) **standen**, 4 **stan**, **standd**, 4–6 **stande**, (*mod. dial.* **stan**), 4– **stand**.

c **888** ÆLFRED *Boeth.* xxxvi. §3 Her ic wille nu standan fæste. *c* **1220** *Bestiary* 655 Hopeð he sal him don ut standen. *a* **1300** *Cursor M.* 10956 He..sagh an angel be him stand [*Gött.* standd]. *Ibid.* 23043 Þe formast rau sal stan him nere. **1642** H. MORE *Song of Soul* II. I. iii. 20 What things decay and cannot standen sure.

β. 1 **stondan**, 2–5 **stonden**, (4–5 **-yn**), 2–6 **stonde**, 4–5 **stonnd(e**, **stoond(en**, 5 **ston**, **stone**, 4–7 **stond**.

c **825** *Vesp. Psalter* xvii. 39 Ne hie maȝun stondan. *c* **1220** *Bestiary* 621 In water ȝe sal stonden. **1382** WYCLIF *Gen.* xxi. 29 The which thow hast maad stoond [**1388** stonde] asyde. *a* **1400–50** *Wars Alexander* 681 (Dubl.) As he by hym stonndes. *c* **1449** PECOCK *Repr.* III. xvii. 394 Alle the peple.. stoonden in caas of the firste trouthe. **1468** *Cal. Anc. Rec. Dublin* (1889) I. 329 The wiche [covenants] shall stone ferme and stable. **1469** *Yatton Church-w. Acc.* (Somerset Rec. Soc.) 105 Received of a chapman to ston in the porche, ob. **1543** *Star Chamber Cases* (Selden Soc.) II. 261 Others ..dyd refuse to stond to part of the covenauntes. **1642** H. MORE *Song of Soul* II. App. 54 A peck of peasen rudely poured out..To sight do in as seemly order stond.

2. *Pres. Indic.* (special forms). **a.** *2nd sing.* 3 **stonst**, **stondes**, 4 **standes**, 6 *Sc.* (*erron.*) **stant**.

a **1225** *Ancr. R.* 236 Iðet tentaciun þet tu stonst aȝean. *c* **1250** *Gen. & Ex.* 2782 Ðu stondes seli stede up-on. *a* **1300** *Cursor M.* 903 And þou, womman, þat standes her. **1500–20** DUNBAR *Poems* lxxxviii. 11 Imperiall as thou stant [*rime* Troynouaunt].

b. *3rd sing.* (contr.). 1–5 **stent**, 1, 3–5 **stond**, 2–4 **stand**, 2–5 **stont**, 3 **stænt**, **stend**, **steond**, **stunt**, 3–6 **stant**, (3 *Orm.* **stannt**), 4 **standt**, 4–5 **stante**, **stande**, **stonte**, **stonde**, 6 **standth**.

c **888** ÆLFRED *Boeth.* xxxix. §2 Sio unsælð stent on yfelra monna ȝeearnunga. *c* **1000** *Sax. Leechd.* III. 32 Stond heo wið attre. *c* **1200** *Trin. Coll. Hom.* 175 He..ne stont neure on one stede. *c* **1205** LAY. 4330 Nu stond [*c* **1275** steond] al þis muchele lond a Bailenes aȝere hond. *Ibid.* 15623 stunt. *Ibid.* 18850 stænt. *c* **1220** *Bestiary* 1 Ðe leun stant on hille. **1362** LANGL. *P. Pl.* A. x. 129 Þorw wedlac þe world stont. **1382** WYCLIF *Numb.* v. 18 Whanne the womman stondith [*v.rr.* stonte, stonde] in the siȝt of the Lord. **1390** GOWER *Conf.* II. 302 Or elles time com noght yit, Which standt upon thi destine. *c* **1420** *Chron. Vilod.* 3548 Ryȝt as hit stonte ȝet in-to þis same day. **1426** LYDG. *De Guil. Pilgr.* 4956 In the corner that stent lowe. **1471** CAXTON *Recuyell* (Sommer) 177 In the place where now stante the capytole of rome. *c* **1557** ABP. PARKER *Ps.* xlv. 132 As mete it stant. **1562** J. HEYWOOD *Prov. & Epigr.* (1867) 184 He standth well in his owne conceyte.

3. *Past Indic.* **a.** *sing.* 1 **stód**, 2–5 **stod**, 3 **stot**, 4 **stoed**, 4–6 **stode**, **stoode**, 5 **stodde**, 6 **stoade**, **stoud**, 3– **stood**; *north.* and *Sc.* 4–9 **stud(e**, 5–9 **stuid**, 6 **studd**, **stuide**.

Beowulf 1570 Leoht inne stod. *c* **1200** ORMIN 3340 Þatt enngell comm & stod hemm bi. *c* **1250** *Gen. & Ex.* 432 Wið dead him stood hinke and aȝe. *a* **1300** *Cursor M.* 1852 Þe streme it stud [*Gött.* stod, stode] ai still in-an. *c* **1386** CHAUCER *Prol.* 553 A werte, and ther on stood a toft of herys. *a* **1400** *St. Alexius* 439 (Laud 463) Out of his mouþ þer stoed a leom. *c* **1420** *Chron. Vilod.* 2160 Hurre modur stodde stylle. **1503** DUNBAR *Thistle & Rose* 97 On feild of gold he stude full mychtely. **1576** LAMBARDE *Peramb. Kent.* 92 While Priams state, and kingdome vpright stoade. **1595** in *Cath. Rec. Soc. Publ.* V. 289 [He] stoud to it manfully. **1611** SIR W. MURE *Misc. Poems* ii. 11, I stuid astonisch'd. **1789** BURNS *Laddies by Banks o' Nith* ii, The day he stude his country's friend.

b. *pl.* 1 **stódun**, **-on**, 1–2 **-an**, 2–5 **stoden**, 3 *Orm.* **stodenn**, 3–6 **stode**, 4–5 **stodyn**, **stooden**, **stod**, 4–6 **stoude**, 4–7 **stoode**, 7 **stowed** (sense B. 36), 4– **stood**; *north.* and *Sc.* as *sing.*

Beowulf 328 Garas stodon. *a* **1000** *Guthlac* 696 Ðearwe stodun hæftas hearsume. *a* **1225** *Leg. Kath.* 2033 As ha stoden & seten þer abuten. **1297** R. GLOUC. (Rolls) 3622 Þe saxons in her syde stode [*v.r.* stoden] euere aȝen vaste. **1375** BARBOUR *Bruce* XIV. 174 Thai stude with baneris all displayit. *c* **1386** CHAUCER *Clerk's T.* 1049 Of hem þat stooden [*v.rr.* stoden, stodyn] hire bisyde. **1557** in *Rep. Hist. MSS. Comm.* Var. Coll. IV. 223 The said writynges obligatorie wher in they stoude bounden. *a* **1578** LINDESAY (Pitscottie) *Chron. Scot.* (S.T.S.) I. 111 Thir men that stud about him. **1633** [see B. 36].

4. *Present Participle.* 1 **standende**, 1–4 **stondende**, 3 **stondinde**, 5 **-and(e**; *north.* and *Sc.* 4 **stan(n)and**, 4–5 **standande**, 4–6 **standand**, 5 **standdand**, 6 **standant**; 4–5 **stondeynge**, 5 **-eng**, 4–6 **standyng(e**, **stonding**, **stondyng(e**, 6 **standeng**, 4– **standing**.

c **900** *Bæda's Hist.* IV. iv. 571 Þa stondendan munecas þær. *c* **1000** *Ags. Gosp.* xx. 6 He..funde oþre standende. *a* **1225** Stondinde [see B 1]. *a* **1300** *Cursor M.* 4062 Hys breþer schaues he sagh lutand Til his allan þat was standand. *c* **1375** *Sc. Leg. Saints* ii. (Paul) 1034, & fand a multytud wele greit of Iowis, stanand at his yhat. **1382** WYCLIF *Ecclus.* l. 13 And he stondende biside the auter. *c* **1440** *Alphabet of Tales* 389 He contynued iij yere in his prayers, and all-way standdand. **1549** *Compl. Scot.* i. 20 At this tyme ther is nocht ane stane standant on ane vthir. *a* **1578** LINDESAY (Pitscottie) *Chron. Scot.* (S.T.S.) I. 188 Thair they fand the doore standand oppin.

5. *Past Participle.* 1–6 **standen**, 1–5 **stonden**, 2–5 **istonde**, 3 **istonden**, 3–5 **ystonde**, 4–5 **istounde**, **standyn(e**, 4–6 **stand(e**, **stond(e**, 5–6 **stondyn**; 6 **standed**, **stoode**, **stode** (*Sc.* and *north. dial.* **stooden**, **studden**), 6– **stood**.

a **1122** *O.E. Chron.* (Laud MS.) an. 1070 In þære cyrce ..þet ær hæfde standen fulle seofeniht for utan ælces cynnes riht. *c* **1175** *Lamb. Hom.* 47 Þa he hefede þer ane hwile istonde. *a* **1300** *Cursor M.* 9193 Þe tune o niniue..þat standen [*v.rr.* stondyn, stonden] had..Fourten hundret yeir. *c* **1386** CHAUCER *Merch. T.* 250, I haue stonden in ful greet degree. **1526** *Pilgr. Perf.* (W. de W. 1531) 178 Hath standed & stedfastly perseuered therin. *c* **1530** *Judic. Urines* I. ii. 3 Whan it hath well rested & stondyn. **1535** COVERDALE *Ps.* cv. 23 Had not Moses..stonde before him. **1577** GOOGE *Heresbach's Husb.* IV. (1586) 184 b, The waxe will be verie white after it hath stand in the sunne. **1579** Stode [see B. 72 d]. **1579** J. FIELD tr. *Calvin's 4 Serm.* I. 6 This article is much stoode vpon. **1596** DALRYMPLE tr. *Leslie's Hist. Scot.* I. VI. 310 Because stoutlie they had stande with him in his defence.

B. Signification and uses.

I. Of persons and animals, in lit. and fig. senses.

1. a. *intr.* To assume or maintain an erect attitude on one's feet (with distinction, expressed or understood, from *sit*, *lie*, *kneel*, etc.).

c **950** *Lindisf. Gosp.* John xx. 14 *Videt Iesum stantem* ȝesæh ðone hælend stondende. *c* **1205** LAY. 5863 Lihteð of eowre blanken and stondeð on eowre sconken. *a* **1225** *Ancr. R.* 34 Siggeð stondinde þesne psalm. *c* **1250** *Gen. & Ex.* 3149 Sod and girt, stondende, and staf on hond. *c* **1330** *Arth. & Merl.* 9276 Arthour, he seyd, þi kinde it nis To stond o fot. **1382** WYCLIF *2 Kings* xiii. 21 The man quyckened aȝeyn, and stode vpon his feet. *c* **1400** *Rule St. Benet* (Prose) 16 Standande alle for þe onur of the holy trinite. *Ibid.*, Þan sal alle stande for þe reuerence. **1529** RASTELL *Pastyme* (1811) 43 He ordeynid that men shuld stand while the gospell was reding. **1577** GOOGE *Heresbach's Husb.* 141 The shepheard ..must be well ware in the driuing of them,..that they neyther lye, nor sitte: for yf they goe not forwarde, they must stand. **1594** HOOKER *Eccl. Pol.* IV. xiii. §7 On all the Sundayes..their manner was to stand [*sc.* instead of kneeling] at prayer. **1610** SHAKS. *Temp.* III. ii. 47 Kneele, and repeate it, I will stand, and so shall Trinculo. **1629** WADSWORTH *Pilgr.* iii. 16 When they have ended the meale, the Rector..stands and sayes Grace. **1830** *Forrester* II. 111 Sit down, Ellen..see, you are keeping Lord Borrodale and Mr. Beamish standing. **1862** C. KNIGHT *Pop. Hist. Eng.* VIII. xvi. 299 He kept the two peers standing, contrary to usage, during their audience.

b. said of the feet.

c **825** *Vesp. Psalter* cxxi. 2 Stondende werun foet ure in ceafurtunum ðinum. *c* **1391** CHAUCER *Astrol.* II. §42 a. 57 Whan þou seest þe top of þe tour, sett a prikke þere-as þi foot stont. *c* **1430** *Prymer* (1895) 45 We schulen worschipe in þe place where hise feet stoden. **1535** COVERDALE *Ps.* cxxi. 2 Oure fete shal stonde in thy gates, O Jerusalem.

c. ***to stand to, up to, † in to the knees*** (or other specified part): to stand *in* water, mud, etc. which reaches to the knees (or other part).

c **1330** *Arth. & Merl.* 5195 In blod he stode..Of hors & man in to þe anclowe. *c* **1425** AUDELAY *Pains of Hell* 68 in *O.E. Misc.* 212 Sum stod vp to þe kne, And sum to þe armes a lytil laȝghere, And sum to þe lippis moche deppere. **1590** SIR J. SMYTHE *Disc. Weapons* Ded. 10 b, Where their souldiors in their watches and centinels stoode to the mid legges in dirt and myre.

d. With predicate: To be of a (specified) height when holding oneself upright. Said also of quadrupeds, etc.

1831 YOUATT *Horse* ii. 10 The Dongola horses stand full sixteen hands high. **1835** DICKENS *Sk. Boz*, *Mr. Watkins Tottle* i, He..stood four feet six inches and three-quarters in his socks. **1855** TENNYSON *Maud* I. XIII. i. Six foot two, as I think, he stands. **1884** *Graphic* 30 Aug. 219/2 He [the elephant] only stands five feet high. **1889** F. C. PHILIPS & WILLS *Fatal Phryne* I. 4 He only stood five feet ten in his stockings.

2. Used *fig.* in many phrases with literal wording; as ***to stand on one's own feet*** or ***legs***, ***upon a*** (specified) ***†foot*** or ***footing***, ***not to have a leg to stand on***, ***to stand in a person's*** or ***one's own light*** (see LIGHT *sb.* 1 g), ***in*** (another person's) ***shoes*** (see SHOE *sb.* 2 k), ***in the way*** (***of*** a person or thing: see WAY *sb.*).

c **1330** *Arth. & Merl.* 9271 Al þat in his way stode, He biheueded hem & lete hem blode. ? *c* **1450** LYDG. *Fl. Courtesy* 85 The whiche twayne ay stondeth in my wey Maliciously. *a* **1568** ASCHAM *Scholem.* I. (Arb.) 34 [They] stand by other mens feete, and not by their own. **1623** MASSINGER *Dk. Milan* II. i, The Duke stands now on his owne legs, and needs No nurse to leade him. **1666**, **1818** [see LEG *sb.* 2 c]. **1738** SWIFT *Pol. Conversat.* Introd. 66 Upon what Foot I stand with the present chief reigning Wits. **1767** [see SHOE *sb.* 2 k]. **1831** SCOTT *Nigel* Introd., The footing on which the bullies and thieves of the Sanctuary stood with their neighbours. **1872** H. KINGSLEY *Hornby Mills*, etc. I. 65 I cannot at present see that we have a leg to stand on. **1893** *Law Jrnl.* 4 Feb. 88/1 Courts of equity would not grant relief to under lessees unless they consented to stand in the shoes of the original lessees. **1893** *Nat. Observer* 7 Oct. 529/2 Cricket and football stand not upon the same footing.

3. a. Of a horse: To be kept in a stable or stall. Phr. ***to stand at livery*** (see LIVERY 1 c and *fig.*).

1465 *Paston Lett.* II. 254 As touching a stabil, Sir John Sparham and I have gote yow on ther your hors stode the last tyme ye were in this town. **1482** *Cely Papers* (Camden) 122 Lette hym [a horse] ron in a parke tyll Hallowtyd and then take hym wpe and ser hym and lette hym stand in the dede of whyntter. **1538** ELYOT *Dict.*, *Stabulo*, to stande as cattayle dothe in a stable. **1577** GOOGE *Heresbach's Husb.* 120 Laying fresh litter, so as they stand hard. **1607** TOPSELL *Four-f. Beasts* 374 Bring him into the stable, and ther let him stand on the bit..the space of two houres. **1676** *Lond. Gaz.* No. 1072/4 Gentlemens Accompts, for Horses standing in the Kings Head near Charing-cross. **1828** DARVILL *Race Horse* I. x. 240 The race-course, at Richmond..is the most convenient for horses which stand in the town to sweat over. **1892** *Field* 2 April 469/3 A horse standing at livery would always have the best of food.

b. Of a stallion: to be available as a stud-horse to serve mares (esp. *at* a certain place). Also, ***to stand at stud*** (cf. STUD *sb.*[2]). orig. *U.S.*

1766 *Virginia Gaz.* 4 Apr. 3/3 Merry Tom Stands at my house, and covers mares at a guinea the leap. **1788** W. LENOIR in N. E. Eliason *Tarheel Talk* (1956) 297 Whirligig will stand this season..& will cover Mares at Forty Shillings per season Twenty Shillings per cover. **1846** *Spirit of Times* 18 Apr. 94/1 Young Dread will stand this season at Watertown, Jefferson County, N.Y. **1891** J. L. KIPLING *Beast & Man in India* viii. 207 Importing English thoroughbreds, Arabs, and Norfolk trotters who stand as sires at the service of farmers. **1959** *Times* 31 Aug. 13/5 (*heading*) Shantung to stand in England. **1974** D. FRANCIS *Knock Down* xiv. 171 Nestegg is standing at stud in Ireland. **1974** *New Yorker* 29 Apr. 102/2 Go Man Go stands at stud at Buena Suerte Ranch. *Ibid.* 102/3 Tony B Deck's father, who stood in Perry, Oklahoma, was murdered in his stall. **1977** *N.Z. Herald* 5 Jan. 1–12/5 Aristoi is by Sir Gaylord from Attlea, by Mt Trouble from Athenia, by Pharamond II, and stands at the Preston Farm Stud.

4. a. To remain motionless on one's feet; to cease walking or moving on. More explicitly ***to stand fast, still***, etc.: see esp. STILL *adv.*

c **888** ÆLFRED *Boeth.* xxxv. §7 Wildu dior ðær woldon to irnan & stondan swilce hi tamu wæren. *Ibid.* xxxvi. §3 Her ic wille nu standan fæste; nelle ic nu næfre hionon. *a* **1300** *Cursor M.* 17131 Duell a quile and fond to stan, Bihald mi fote, bi-hald mi hand. *c* **1300** *K. Horn* 745 (Laud MS.) Ne stod he nowt to longe And ȝyede forþ ricte To reymyld þe bricte. **1362** LANGL. *P. Pl.* A. IV. 143 [They] stareden for studiing and stooden as Bestes. *c* **1475** *Rauf Coilȝear* 121 Quhen thay come to the dure, the King begouth to stand. **1611** BIBLE *Ezek.* i. 21, 24 When those went, these went, and when those stood, these stood. **1615** CHAPMAN *Odyss.* VI. 202 All but Nausicaa fled; but she fast stood. **1842** BROWNING *Pied Piper* xiii, The Mayor was dumb, and the Council stood As if they were changed into blocks of wood, Unable to move a step.

b. In imper., a command to come to a halt, e.g. as a sentry's challenge, a command to a horse, a highwayman's order to his victim (also ***stand and deliver!***).

1513 DOUGLAS *Æneis* VIII. iii. 38 To tham he callis: Stand, ȝing men, How! **1591** SHAKS. *Two Gent.* IV. i. 3 Stand sir, and throw vs that you haue about'ye. **1592** —— *Ven. & Ad.* 284 What recketh he his riders angrie sturre, His flattering holla, or his stand, I say? **1598** BARRET *Theor. Warres* IV. i. 103 Neither Captaine, Alferes, nor any other officer to passe the word, *stand*..vnlesse the necessitie be so vrgent [etc.]. **1635** *Long Meg of Westminster* ix. (1816) 17 One of the theeues with a good sword and buckler stept before, and said, Stand. **1714** A. SMITH *Lives Highwaymen* (ed. 2) I. 38 He order'd him to Stand and Deliver. **1727** H. BLAND *Milit. Discipl.* xii. 175 The Centinel..when he is answer'd by the Sergeant who attends the Round..is to say, *Stand Round*... No Round is to advance after the Centinel has Challeng'd and order'd them to stand. **1810** SCOTT *Lady of L.* V. xviii, 'Stand, Bayard, stand!'—the steed obeyed. **1821** —— *Kenilw.* xxiv, Are we commanded to stand and deliver on the King's highway? **1897** *Encycl. Sport* I. 610/1 (Lacrosse) The ball is dead when the referee calls 'stand'.

c. *Hunting.* Of a dog: To point. Const. *upon* (game).

1823 'JON BEE' *Dict. Turf* s.v., To *Stand* is also the position of pointers when they perceive their game. **1858** LEWIS in *Youatt's Dog* (N.Y.) ii. 53 He [the dog] might have been tutored..even sufficiently well to stand upon game.

5. a. With predicative extension: To remain erect on one's feet in a specified place, occupation, position, condition, etc.

For many phrases, e.g. *stand at attention, at ease, at gaze, on one's own bottom, (on) tiptoe, perdu, upright*, see the various words.

c **1000** *Ags. Gosp.* Matt. xx. 3 He ȝeseah oþre on stræte idele standan. *c* **1200** ORMIN 141 & al þe follc þær ute stod þatt while onn heore bene. **1297** R. GLOUC. 6816 A witesoneday as seint edward at is masse stod. **1390** GOWER *Conf.* III. 297 A Fisshere..sih a man ther naked stonde. **1530** PALSGR. 732/2, I Stande a strydlyng with my legges abrode. **1554** MACHYN *Diary* (Camden) 75 The xxiij day of November was a man and a woman stode on the pelery. **1678** J. S. *Unerrable Church* 327 When you stand with one foot in the grave. **1711** N. BLUNDELL *Diary* (1895) 93, I saw Peter Slinhead stand in yᵉ Pillery at Leverp[ool]. **1786** tr. *Beckford's Vathek* (1883) 118 The woodmen..stood aghast at the command of Carathis to set forward. **1878** BROWNING *La Saisiaz* 5 At last I stand upon the summit.

b. With inf. expressing the purposed or accompanying action.

c **1000** *Ags. Gosp.* Mark xi. 25 Þonne ȝe standað eow to ȝebiddenne. *c* **1200** ORMIN 3894 Enngless stanndenn aȝȝ occ aȝȝ To lofenn Godd & wurrþenn. **1591** NASHE *Prognost.* D 2, Diuerse spirites in white sheetes shall stand in Poules..to make their confessions. **1630** in Binnell *Descr. Thames* (1758) 72 No Trinck shall stand to fish above nine Tides in the Week. **1643** in *Fasti Aberd.* (1854) 422 [The college porter] shall suffer no children..to stand neir the yeat to mack urine. **1742** GRAY *Eton* 58 Ah, shew them where in ambush stand To seize their prey the murth'rous band! **1813** SCOTT *Trierm.* I. xiii, Upon the watch-towers airy round No warder stood his horn to sound. **1850** 'BAT' *Cricket Man.* 44 Long Leg..usually stands to save four runs. **1891** HARDY *Tess* lii, While the horses stood to stale and breathe themselves.

c. The accompanying action is often expressed by a verb in co-ordination, ***to stand and*** (do something).

So in many Bible passages, rendered literally from the Vulgate or the original.

c **1000** ÆLFRIC *Exod.* xiv. 13 Standað and ȝeseoð drihtnes mærða. *c* **1250** *Gen. & Ex.* 1019 Abraham stod and quamede hem wel. **1426** LYDG. *De Guil. Pilgr.* 4407 As a chaumberere, The syxte gate I stonde & kepe. **1601** SHAKS. *Jul. C.* IV. iii. 249 So please you, we will stand, And watch your pleasure. *c* **1655** MILTON *Sonn.* xvi, They also serve who only stand and waite. **1842** TENNYSON *St. Sim. Styl.* 34, I..sometimes saw An angel stand and watch me, as I sang. **1905** R. BAGOT *Passport* ii. 7 Don Agostino stood and gazed.

d. With pres. pple. as predicate.

a **1225** *Leg. Kath.* 743 Heo stod hercnende. **1470–85** MALORY *Arthur* IX. xxvii. 381 They stode thus talkynge at a bay wyndowe. **1566** *Pasquine in Traunce* 83 After I had stande a whyle diligently beholding such as entred in. **1697** DRYDEN *Virg. Past.* VIII. 4 The salvage Linxes listning stood. **1737** [S. BERINGTON] *G. de Lucca's Mem.* (1738) 32 It was a Shame to stand all Day firing at five Men. **1842** MACAULAY *Horatius* lx, Friends and foes in dumb surprise ..Stood gazing where he sank.

e. With sb. as predicate. e.g. ***to stand sentinel, sentry*** (see SENTINEL *sb.* 1, SENTRY *sb.*[1] 2), ***umpire***. ***to stand model***, to pose to artists. ***to stand pad***: see PAD *sb.*[2]

1866 *Routledge's Ev. Boy's Ann.* 322 [He] had consented to stand umpire. **1890** *Cornhill Mag.* Sept. 253 She has stood model to her mother's lodgers. **1890** *Universal Rev.* 15 Nov. 452 I've stood model in all the studios worth naming in London. **1898** J. A. GIBBS *Cotswold Village* xi. 229 His eldest son, Tom..generally stands umpire.

6. In various specific uses, contextual or arising from ellipsis:

a. To take up a position for fishing (*for*). In full, ***to stand to fish*** (cf. 5 b).

1630 in Binnell *Descr. Thames* (1758) 72 No Trincker shall stand for Smelts till the 21st Day of October... In Lent Time, they may stand every Day.

b. *Cricket* and other games: To act as umpire in the field. (Cf. 5 e.)

1846 W. DENISON *Sk. Players* Ded. 5 In almost every [cricket] match..where the Mary-le-bone, or equally.. impartial umpires do not stand. **1906** A. E. KNIGHT *Compl. Cricketer* vi. 195 No umpire who is the nominee of a particular county is eligible to stand in a game in which that county figures.

c. Of the penis: to become or remain erect.

? **1508** DUNBAR *Tua Mariit Wemen* sig. b ii, And a stif standand thing staiffis in mi neiff. *c* **1593** NASHE *Choise of Valentines* (1899) 12 'Unhappie me,' quoth shee, 'and wilt' not stand? Com, lett me rubb and chafe it with my hand!' **1762** T. BRIDGES *Homer Travestie* I. IV. 189 She guides his weapon where she list;..a touch of her soft hand, If fallen down, will make him stand. **1868** *Index Expurgatorius of Martial* 82 That's the way to make your Martial stand. **1903** FARMER & HENLEY *Slang* VI. 346/2 Also (proverbial) 'Stand always, as the girl said.'

7. With an adverb or advb. phr. implying change of place, distance, or the like, there often enters in the notion of movement as a preliminary to the static position; e.g. in ***to stand aside, back, down, forward, off, out of, up*** (see branch VII). Also ***to stand from under***: see UNDER *adv.* 4 c.

c **1520** SKELTON *Magnyf.* 763 Gyue this gentylman rome, syrs, stonde vtter! **1597** SHAKS. *2 Hen. IV*, IV. iv. 116 Stand from him, giue him ayre. **1691** *Humble Addr. Publicans New Eng.* in *Andros Tracts* (1869) II. 236 [At end of Proem] Stand clear, here comes the Address. **1731–8** SWIFT *Pol. Conversat.* 39 Come, pray, stand out of my spitting Place. *a* **1814** *Fam. Politics* v. iii. in *New Brit. Theatre* II. 247 Stand out of the way, Miss. **1852** BURN *Nav. & Milit. Dict.* II. s.v., Stand clear of the cable! **1867** SMYTH *Sailor's Word-bk.*, *Stand from under!* a notice given to those below to keep out of the way of anything being lowered down, or let fall from above.

8. ***to stand on one's head***: to take up an acrobatic position, with the crown of the head on the ground and heels in air; also *fig.* (to be ready) to do this as a sign of extreme delight. ***not to know whether one is standing on one's head or one's heels***: to be in a state of utter bewilderment.

1617 MORYSON *Itin.* I. 22 A Tumbler came in, and..stood upon his head. **1816** M. G. LEWIS *Jrnl. W. Ind.* (1834) 127 Cubina..having never heard a harsh word from me before, scarcely knew whether he stood upon his head or his heels. **1833** NYREN *Yng. Cricketer's Tutor* (1902) 58 The glory of this reward made me scarcely to know whether I stood on my head or my heels. **1886** MISS BROUGHTON *Dr. Cupid* II. iv. 103 Two years ago he would have stood on his head with joy at having the chance of going.

9. a. To remain firm or steady in an upright position, to support oneself erect on one's feet. Often in negative contexts. Also with adj. or adv., as *fast*, *firm*, *stiff*.

c **825** *Vesp. Psalter* xvii. 39 Ic swencu hio ne hie maȝun stondan. *a* **1300** *Cursor M.* 24618 On fote vnethes moght i stand, sua lam in lime and lith. **1362** LANGL. *P. Pl.* A. V. 196 He hedde no strengþe to stonde til he his staf hedde. *Ibid.* A. IX. 28 For stonde he neuere so stif he stumbleþ in þe waggyng [of the boat]. **1470–85** MALORY *Arthur* X. xxxvi. 472 This Malgryne..wounded hym wonderly sore that it was merueylle that euer he myghte stande. **1530** PALSGR. 733/1 Stande fast, for and you fall you ar but gone. **1592** in J. Morris *Troubles Cath. Forefathers* Ser. III. (1877) 17 The old man..by cold taken at that being in the hole, was never after able to go or stand. **1681** PRIDEAUX *Lett.* (Camden) 102 When they came unto him for their answer he could scarce speake or stand. **1897** A. E. HOUGHTON *Gilbert Murray* xiv. 230 His feet touched the floor before he knew, and to his amazement he found that he could stand.

b. *fig.* To remain stedfast, firm, secure, or the like. Also with adj. or adv.

c **1200** *Moral Ode* 316 in *Trin. Coll. Hom.* 229 For hit is strong te stonde longe and liht hit is to falle. *a* **1225** *Leg. Kath.* 1861 Beo stalewurðe & stond wel. **1362** LANGL. *P. Pl.* A. IX. 42 He strengþeþ þe to stonde, he stureþ þi soule. *c* **1380** WYCLIF *Sel. Wks.* III. 345 Þes monkes stoden awhile, and turneden souner to coveitise. *c* **1421** *26 Pol. Poems* xxi. 67 In goddis dome he stondis stable, Þat wrekiþ not all his owen wronges. **1552** HULOET, Stande stiffe or wilfull in opinion, *obstinare*. *c* **1588** in J. Morris *Troubles Cath. Forefathers* Ser. II. (1875) 318 Having heard much of the present..persecution of England and martyrdoms of such as have stood. **1605** BACON *Adv. Learn.* I. iii. §6 If they stand in seditions and violent alterations. **1657** BILLINGSLY *Brachy-Martyrol.* xi. 35 Though some thus fell away, others stood fast, Remaining glorious Martyrs to the last. **1667** MILTON *P.L.* III. 99, I made him just and right, Sufficient to have stood, though free to fall. **1697** DRYDEN *Ded. Æneid* (e) 4 They had great success at their first appearance; but, not being of God (as a Wit said formerly), they cou'd not stand. **1855** MACAULAY *Hist. Eng.* xvii. IV. 53 If it had seemed certain that William would stand, they would all have been for William. **1888** *Times* (weekly ed.) 29 June 8/1 They had stood true to the honour of Ireland. **1890** TOUT *Hist. Eng. fr. 1689*, 164 Eldon exhorted the king to stand firm.

c. ***to stand or fall***: often used *fig.* of a person or thing, to indicate that his or its fate is contingent on the fate of another person or thing, or must be governed by some event or rule. Const. *with* (a person or thing), *together*, also *by* (a rule, an uncertain event).

1683 D. A. *Art Converse* Pref., It shall stand or fall by your Verdict. **1743** BULKELEY & CUMMINS *Voy. S. Seas* 87 To be governed by the Rules of the Navy, and to stand or fall by them. **1771** *Junius Lett.* lix. 308, I know we must stand or fall together. **1818** CRUISE *Digest* Tit. xxxviii. vi. §37 The original and duplicate being but one will, they must stand or fall together. **1832** *Examiner* 82/1 We have Lord Grey's pledge to stand or fall with the bill. **1875** JOWETT *Plato* (ed. 2) I. 402 The pre-existence of the soul stands or falls with the doctrine of ideas. **1885** *Law Times Rep.* LIII. 481/2 In my opinion..the solicitors must stand or fall by the bills they have sent in.

10. To take up an offensive or defensive position against an enemy; to present a firm front; to await an onset and keep one's ground without budging. Of soldiers: To be drawn up in battle array.

Chiefly contextual or with predicative extension, as *to stand and fight*; *to stand fast, firm*, † *adversar*; *to stand at bay, at defiance, in the breach, in*, († *at*, † *on*) *defence*, *on* or *upon one's guard*, *on* or *upon the defensive* or *offensive*. See also *stand against* (67), *stand before* (69).

971 *Blickl. Hom.* 225 Ic mid þinum wæpnum ȝetrymed on þinum feþan fæste stande. *c* **1205** LAY. 1601 Nes þer nan swa stæðeli þat lengore mihte stonden. **13..** *Guy Warw.* 6751 Þer he [the boar] stod at a bay. *c* **1386** CHAUCER *Clerk's T.* 1139 Ye Archiwyues, stondeth at defense. *c* **1470** *Gol. & Gaw.* 575 Thoght thai war astonait, in that stour stithly thai stude. **1530** PALSGR. 732/2 Let them come, I shall stande at my defence. **1533** BELLENDEN *Livy* II. xx. (S.T.S.) I. 210 Incontinent þir twa fabis ruschit fordwart on þe first man þat stude aduersare to þame. **1577, 1610** [see GUARD *sb.* 5 a]. **1587** GOLDING *De Mornay* i. (1592) 11 Whosoeuer shoulde tell thee to the contrary, thou wouldest stand at defiance against him. **1611** [see BREACH *sb.* 7 c]. **1634** SIR T. HERBERT *Trav.* 32 [Queen Normall] immediately put into Battaglia, and stood in her owne defence. *a* **1700** EVELYN *Diary* 24 June 1690, It seemes the Irish in K. James's army would not stand, but the English-Irish and French made greate resistance. **1759** *Ann. Reg.* 52 M. Conflans had two choices, either to fly, or to stand and fight it out. **1793** R. HALL *Apol. Freedom Press* 43 They stood firm against a host of opponents. **1816** SCOTT *Old Mort.* xliii, Bidding foemen on the farther side stand at defiance. **1837** CARLYLE *Fr. Rev.* I. v. v, Hearing of which the Felons at the Châtelet..stand on the offensive. **1875** JOWETT *Plato* (ed. 2) I. 92 The Lacedaemonians..are said not to have been willing to stand and fight, and to have fled. **1890** TOUT *Hist. Eng. fr. 1689*, 8 The last Irish army stood at bay at Limerick.

11. a. ***to stand upon one's trial***, † ***to stand in doom*** or ***judgement***: to submit to judicial trial or sentence. See also *stand at* 68 a, *stand to* 76 a. ***to stand to the bar***: of an accused person, to stand up and come forward to hear the verdict of the court.

a **1300** *Cursor M.* 9492 Ne in na curt aght thral be herd, Ne stand in dom to be ansuerd. **1390** GOWER *Conf.* I. 91 How so thou be to wyte Of Branchus deth, men schal respite As now to take vengement, Be so thou stonde in juggement Upon certein condicioun. **14..** *Burgh Lawis* xxxi. in *Anc. Laws Scot.* (Burgh Rec. Soc.) 16 Ilke spousyt man may ansuer for his spousyt wyff and stande in iugement [*et stare in iudicio*] and do for hir all thyng at the court demys hym. *a* **1596** *Sir T. More* I. ii. 158 Lifter, stand to the barre: The jurie haue returnd thee guiltie. **1771** E. LONG in *Hone's Everyday Bk.* II. 202 The prisoner..stands upon his trial.

† **b.** ***to stand*** (***in judgement***), said of the judge or court: To hold session. *Obs.*

1560 DAUS tr. *Sleidane's Comm.* 7 b, That he [God] stand not in judgement agaynst us lest we be damned. *c* **1800** *Laird o Logie* xiv. in Child *Ballads* III. 453 The morn the Justice Court's to stand.

12. a. To appear as a candidate, to offer oneself as a candidate. Const. *for* (a post, office, †university degree); †*to be* (an office-holder); *against* (a rival candidate). †In early use ***to stand for the election*** (***of***), ***to stand in election*** (***for***), ***stand to be elected***; also ***to stand candidate***.

1551 ROBINSON tr. *More's Utopia* II. iii. (1895) 136 Owte of the .iiii. quarters of the citie there be .iiii. chosen..to stande for the election. **1562** in W. H. Turner *Select. Rec. Oxford* (1880) 291 The two fyrste persons..shall stonde..for the eleccyon of the Mayer. **1607** SHAKS. *Cor.* II. i. 248 Were he to stand for Consull. *Ibid.* II. ii. 2 How many stand for Consulships? **1631** WEEVER *Anc. Funeral Mon.* 540 Who stood in election for the Popedome. *a* **1635** NAUNTON *Fragm. Reg.* (Arb.) 54 None durst appear to stand for the place. **1674** WOOD *Life* (O.H.S.) II. 279 Thomas Thyn chose burgher for Oxon... Sir Ch. Wren stood against him. *Ibid.* Sir Georg Croke stood but he had very few votes. **1678** WALTON *Life Sanderson* b I b, In the year 1614. he stood to be elected one of the Proctors... They perswaded him, that if he would but stand for Proctor,..he would infallibly carry it against any Opposers. **1690** LOCKE *3rd Let. Toleration* i. (1692) 25 Had you stood to be Constable of your Parish. **1705** HEARNE *Collect.* 6 Oct. (O.H.S.) I. 52 Mr. Ellison stands Candidate for Fellow. *Ibid.* 17 Nov. 85 Dr. Hudson stood to be Library-Keeper. **1709** *Ibid.* 27 Oct. II. 293 [He] stood for ye Degree of Master of Arts. **1720** OZELL *Vertot's Rom. Rep.* II. XIII. 278 Those that stood Candidates brought their money openly to the Place of Election. **1803** *Gradus ad Cantabr.* 131 To stand for an honour. **1879** FROUDE *Cæsar* iv. 39 Marius began to be spoken of as a possible candidate. Marius consented to stand. **1890** *Blackw. Mag.* CXLVIII. 589/2 He did not stand for a fellowship.

b. ***to stand for a constituency*** or ***for Parliament***: to offer oneself for election as the representative of a constituency in the House of Commons; originally † ***to stand for burgess***, etc. (*obs.*). † ***to stand double***: of two candidates, to contest an election (*obs.*).

1676 LD. ROOS in *12th Rep. Hist. MSS. Comm.* App. v. 35 My uncle Mr. John Grey standing for Burgess for Leicester. **1690** LUTTRELL *Brief Rel.* (1857) II. 16 We hear from all parts the great contests that are about the election of parliament men, that there is hardly any county or town but they stand double. **1713** *Guardian* No. 58 ¶5, I design to stand for our Borough the next Election. **1714** LADY M. W. MONTAGU *Let. to W. Montagu* (1887) I. 89, I agree with you of the necessity of your standing this Parliament. **1844** DISRAELI *Coningsby* IV. xi, Tadpole wants me to stand for Birmingham. **1867** TROLLOPE *Last Chron. Barset* I. viii. 68 Dr. Thorne intended to stand for the county on the next vacancy. **1890** *Sat. Rev.* 3 May 526/2 Sir Charles..had never stood for Parliament.

13. *Card-playing.* To be willing, or announce one's willingness, to play with one's hand as dealt. Opposed to *pass*.

1824 MACTAGGART *Gallovid. Encycl.* 36 When one of the gamblers stands, that is to say, will play. **1879** H. JONES ('Cavendish') *Card Ess.* 58 [In the game of Prime,] Each then examined his hand and either stood or passed.

14. Chiefly *U.S.* **to stand pat**: (*a*) [Cf. prec. and *pat hand* s.v. PAT *adv.* and *a.* 3 b.] In *Poker*, to play, or declare one's intention of playing, one's hand just as it has been dealt, without drawing other cards. (*b*) *transf.* To adhere to an existing state of things or to an avowed policy (esp. a high tariff), refusing to consider proposals for change or reform. Hence **stand-pat** *sb.* and *a.*; **stand-patter, stand-pattism.**

1882 *Poker; how to play it* 12 The gentleman..failed to better his hand. The other stood pat. **1890** *Stock Grower & Farmer* 29 Mar. 7/1 When it came to them two accomplishments he stood pat. **1903** M. A. HANNA *Sp. at Akron, Ohio*, Now I say, Stand pat; you are not on the defensive. **1903** *Public Opin.* (U.S.) 8 Oct. 451/2 The Republican platform is principally noteworthy for the vehemence with which its framers 'stand pat' upon the tariff. The father of 'stand pattism' himself could not find fault with the declaration that no revision is needed now. **1904** *Evening Transcript* (Boston, Mass.) 16 Feb. 11/2 He..was an avowed stand-patter on the tariff. **1910** *Ibid.* 18 Aug. 10/5 The standpats in Iowa have been licked, and hereafter will either vote with the standpat Democrats or change their views. **1920** W. A. WHITE *Let.* 4 Feb. (1947) 204 He also has on [the Republican Platform Committee]..a lot of old high-binder standpatters who haven't had an idea since the fall of Babylon. **1922** *Nation* 18 Nov. 271/1 The Bonar Law Government..remains in power, but probably on a minority vote..This deprives it of the right to pursue the standpat Toryism on which it made the elections. **1952** W. D. JACOBS *William Barnes* v. 79 A sobering realization is that a certain antagonism to a new credo of language is plain stand-pattism. **1975** G. V. HIGGINS *City on Hill* vii. 202 The mood of the country may be such that a stand-patter is the only candidate who can be elected. **1977** *Daily Tel.* 17 Feb. 14/7 He is highly critical of stand-pat, counter-reformation Catholicism.

15. Uses in which the force of the verb is weakened and approaches that of a copula, the stress being on the complement or predicative extension. **a.** With sb. as complement: To take or hold the office, position, responsibility, etc. indicated by the sb.; to act as; e.g. ***to stand security, surety***; †formerly, ***to stand captain, king, officer***, etc. Also, to be ranked or regarded as, to have legal status as. Occas. with *as* before the sb.

1429 in *Cal. Pat. Rolls 8 Hen. VI*, 31 Non of the xxiiij aldermen xal..concentyn to be chosen er standen as an arbitrour..aghens any of the said xxiiij aldermen. **1442** in *Proc. King's Council Irel.* (Rolls) 275 For the tyme that they haue stonde your officers there. **1455** *Rolls of Parlt.* V. 308/2 All the tyme that the seid Duke stode Capitayn. *c* **1470** HARDING *Chron.* XXXI. vii, When he had stond so kyng by fourty yere. **1681** DRYDEN *Abs. & Achit.* 776 Then Kings are Slaves to those whom they command, And Tenants to their Peoples pleasure stand. *a* **1700** EVELYN *Diary* 1 May 1680, This yeare I would stand one of the collectors of their rents, to give example to others. **1713** STEELE *Englishman* No. 5. 31 The Pretender stands in our Law a Traytor to this Nation. **1776** *Trial of Nundocomar* 22/1 If I can get any one else to stand my security. **1857** J. W. DONALDSON *Chr. Orthod.* 116 Christianity stands surety for the divine origin of all that is spiritual in the creed of Moses. **1884** PIRKIS *Judith Wynne* III. xx. 238 Oscar, in the event of Wolf's decease, stood next heir. **1894** H. NISBET *Bush Girl's Rom.* 199 The future hope of standing an honest man.

b. ***to stand godfather, godmother, sponsor***; also ***to stand as*** or ***for godfather***, etc.; also simply ***to stand*** = to act as sponsor (*for* a child).

Sometimes †to be proxy *for* another person as sponsor.

1676 LADY CHAWORTH in *12th Rep. Hist. MSS. Comm.* App. v. 28 Mr. Hide is going..to Poland to stand for our King at the King's child's cristening. **1706** N. BLUNDELL *Diary* (1895) 44 My Doughter Frances was Christoned, Collo[nel] Butler stood Godfather for my Brother Lang. and Mrs. Mills stood for my Lady Gerard. **1709** *Lond. Gaz.* No. 4560/2 The King of Denmark and King Augustus stood as Godfathers to a Son of the Velt-Marshal. **1710–11** SWIFT *Jrnl. to Stella* 16 Jan., A girl..and died in a week..and was poor Stella forced to stand for godmother? **1742** RICHARDSON *Pamela* IV. 142 The Earl and Countess of C——, and Lord and Lady Davers, are here, to stand in Person at the Christening. **1766** GOLDSM. *Vic. W.* xx, To stand godfather to all the butler's children. **1809** MALKIN *Gil Blas* XI. i. (Rtldg.) 392 The governor's lady..stood for Scipio's daughter. **1846** D. JERROLD *Mrs. Caudle* xvi, Then she'd no right to stand for the child. **1856** MISS YONGE *Daisy Chain* I. viii, Richard hoped they would find sponsors by that time; and there Mrs. Taylor gave little hope;..there was no one she liked to ask to stand. **1877** —— *Cameos* Ser. III. xv. 132 Edward..stood as the godfather.

c. ***to stand one's friend***, to act the part of a friend to another. †Formerly in other similar phrases, as ***to stand good prince*** (***to***), ***to stand*** (one's) ***good lord***.

1461 *Mem. Hexham* (Surtees) I. Illustr. Docum. p. ci, Supposyng..that..Humfray hade stonde trew liegeman to Kyng Edward. **1483** in *Acts Parlt. Scotl.* (1875) XII. 32/1 That his hienez sal stand jn tyme tocum gude & graciouse prince to him. **1538** LONDON in *Lett. Suppress. Monasteries* (Camden) 217 Doctor Baskerfelde, to whom I do humblie besek your lordeschippe to stonde gudde lorde. **1571** in Feuillerat *Revels Q. Eliz.* (1908) 408 May it please your honour..to stand my good Lorde for the obtayning of the sayd office. **1598** R. BERNARD tr. *Terence, Phormio* v. iii, I pray thee stand my friend, and lend me a little mony once againe. **1605** SHAKS. *Lear* II. i. 42 Coniuring the Moone To stand auspicious Mistris. **1607** —— *Cor.* II. iii. 198 Standing your friendly Lord. **1662** HIBBERT *Body Divinity* II. 7 He stood our friend without flinching. **1677** DUGDALE in *Hatton Corr.* (Camden) 149 To intreate that you will please to stand my freind to his Ma[tie]. **1714** TYLDESLEY *Diary* (1873) 148 But honest Dick and Ben stud my ffreind. **1890** TOUT *Hist. Eng. fr. 1689*, 109 George II. and Queen Caroline stood his firm friends. **1890** *Murray's Mag.* Dec. 824 I'll stand your friend, and see you through it.

d. With pa. pple. as complement: To be or remain in the specified condition; e.g. ***to stand committed, indebted, pledged***. Also with adj. of state or condition, e.g. ***to stand free, to stand alone*** (in an opinion, a contest, course of action, etc.); ***to stand mute*** (see MUTE *a.* 1).

Usually with reference to a condition resulting from an engagement or a decision, or ascertained by survey of a situation. ***I stand corrected***: I accept or acknowledge the correction; so ***I stand reproved***.

c **1386** CHAUCER *Man of Law's T.* 557 An emperoures doughter stant allone. **1390** GOWER *Conf.* III. 317 Thus stant this lady justefied. *c* **1400** *Beryn* 2636 So stond I clene desperat, but ye con help ouȝt. **1442** *Rolls of Parlt.* V. 57/2 Tenementz that they stode enfeffed ynne. **1537** in *Archæologia* XXV. 506 A certen obligacyon wheryn my husband..stode bownde. **1590** *Knaresb. Wills* (Surtees) I. 168, 20 markes which he standethe indebted unto me. **1591** SHAKS. *Two Gent.* I. iii. 60 And how stand you affected to his wish? *a* **1593** MARLOWE *Edw. II*, IV. i, Stand gratious gloomie night to his deuice. **1643** H. LESLIE *Serm. St. Mary's, Oxford* 9 Feb. 26 Of all these crimes they stand indited by the Prophets. **1668** DRYDEN *Maiden Queen* v. i, I stand corrected, and myself reprove. **1717** in *Nairne Peerage Evid.* (1874) 29 He had been and stood attainted of high treason. **1720** WATERLAND *Eight Serm.* 109 To Him the very Angels owe..whatever Excellencies and perfections they stand possess'd of. **1829** *Examiner* 756/1 We stand almost alone in this expression of taste. **1849** GROTE *Greece* II. lv. (1862) V. 30 Alkibiades stood distinguished for personal bravery. **1868** FREEMAN *Norm. Conq.* (1876) II. vii. 147 Let the meeting stand adjourned. **1877** MISS YONGE *Cameos* Ser. III. iv. 37 Gloucester seems to have stood free from all suspicion. **1881** GARDINER & MULLINGER *Study Eng. Hist.* I. vi. 122 The Catholics stood alone in looking for direction to a head beyond the seas. **1891** *Murray's Mag.* Apr. 433 The delegates..stand pledged to a series of resolutions.

e. With adv. or advb. phrase: To be, to continue or remain in a specified state, position, etc.

e.g. ***to stand in doubt, danger***; ***to stand in a*** (certain) †***office, relation***; ***to stand well*** or ***high*** (= to be in high favour or esteem) ***with*** a person; ***to stand fair*** (= to be favourably situated, to have good chances) *for* something or *to do* something; ***how do you stand*** (financially)? For *to stand in awe* see 45.

c **1386** CHAUCER *Prol.* 88 In hope to stonden in his lady grace. **1390** GOWER *Conf.* I. 147 The more he caste his wit aboute, The more he stant therof in doute. *c* **1440** *Pallad. on Husb.* I. 23 If hit be cleer and hool, stond out of fere. **1453** *Cov. Leet Bk.* 275 Dureng the tyme that ye stonde in the seide offices. **1526** *Pilgr. Perf.* (W. de W. 1531) 20 b, Than the brother demaunded of hym in what case he stode. **1530** PALSGR. 733/1, I stande in dowt of a thyng, *je me doubte*. *a* **1578** LINDESAY (Pitscottie) *Chron. Scot.* (S.T.S.) I. 84 He stuide nocht lang in this credit. **1610** HOLLAND *Camden's Brit.* (1637) 329 Hee never stood in feare of them. **1662** J. DAVIES tr. *Mandelslo's Trav.* 112 They stood faire to become Master of the Island. **1697** COLLIER *Ess. Mor. Subj.* II. (1703) 117 Men naturally desire to stand fair in the opinion of others. **1723** *Lond. Gaz.* No. 6125/1 Baron Lagerberg..seems to stand fairest for that important Post. **1760–72** H. BROOKE *Fool of Qual.* (1809) II. 128, I stood at a high rent. **1823** BYRON *Juan* XIII. xxiv, Juan stood well, both with Ins and Outs. **1844** J. T. HEWLETT *Parsons & W.* xxi, I stand remarkably well for the Derby. **1848** THACKERAY *Van. Fair* xxi, Old Osborne stood in secret terror of his son. **1855** MACAULAY *Hist. Eng.* xi. III. 14 The relation in which the King stood to his Parliament and to his ministers. **1856** *Titan Mag.* Dec. 551/2, I stood very high with him; he was as fond of me as a son. **1890** CONAN DOYLE *Firm of Girdlestone* x. 78 How do you stand for money? **1893** *Ludgate Monthly* Jan. 244/2 Nobody quite knew how he stood financially; he might be rich or he might be poor.

16. Various figurative uses with *to* and infinitive.

† **a.** In a negative clause (or with *if*, etc.): To stay, stop, wait (in order to do something); to make a point of, insist upon (doing something).

1563 *Homilies* II. *Passion* II. 199 b, A thousande such examples are to be founde in Scripture, yf a man woulde stande to seeke them out. **1597** BEARD *Theatre God's Judgem.* (1612) 46 The truth of which storie, though I will not stand to auow, yet I doubt not but it might be true. **1605** BACON *Adv. Learn.* II. xxii. §8 The reason whereof we cannot nowe stande to discusse. **1652** J. WRIGHT tr. *Camus' Nat. Paradox* x. 261, I should swell this Volume too much, if I stood to relate the particulars. *a* **1676** HALE *Contempl.* I. 30, I do not stand to justifie this Opinion in all particulars. **1730** *Let. to*

Sir W. Strickland rel. to Coal Trade 28 How rare a thing was it to hear of any body who stood to talk about the Price before-hand at all? **1766** *Complete Farmer* s.v. *Surveying*, Which we cannot stand here to treat of. **1854** Miss Baker *Northampt. Gloss.* s.v., 'I never stand to do it': i.e. I do not take the trouble, I am not so particular.

†**b.** In a negative clause: To hesitate, scruple, refuse, be slow (to do something). *Obs.* (chiefly *Sc.*).

1563 J. Davidson in *Wodrow Soc. Misc.* (1844) 211, I wyll nocht stand to give Mr. Quintine the First part of this reasone grantit. **1698** *Season. Admon. Gen. Assembly* (1699) 11 Mr. John Hepburn standeth not to say, that some of them make a mock of serious Persons. **1712** *Caldwell Papers* (Maitl. Club) I. 229 He promised, that . . he would not stand to help him to purchase a place. **1728** Ramsay *Lure* 61 T' oblige ye, Friend, I winna stand. *a* **1800** *Dk. Athole's Nurse* xi. in Child *Ballads* IV. 152 And the curtains they neer stood to tear them.

†**c.** To have opportunity (to do something). Said of persons and things. *Obs.*

1589 Puttenham *Eng. Poesie* II. i. (Arb.) 78 That all things stand by proportion, and that without it nothing could stand to be good or beautiful. **1605** Daniel *Philotas* I. i, Seeing your owne designes not stand to square With your desires. **1612** Brinsley *Lud. Lit.* x. (1627) 158 Orations . . wherein Schollers stand to shew most art.

d. In betting, commercial speculation, etc.: To be in the position of being reasonably certain *to* (win or lose something or a specified amount); to have *to* (win or lose a certain amount in a specified contingency).

1861 *Temple Bar* II. 150 He stands to lose twenty thousand. **1871** *Punch* 19 Aug. 67/1 So hedging your bets . . that you stand to win sufficient gloves to last you the whole season. **1880** Mrs. Lynn Linton *Rebel of Family* i, She stood to lose all round. **1891** *Chamb. Jrnl.* 27 June 404/1 He stands to win either way. **1892** *Ibid.* 8 Oct. 648/1 If a man were reckless, . . he stood to dismast his ship and hopelessly ruin his chances of a smart passage.

II. Of things.

* To be set upright, to be in a definite position, etc.

17. a. To be in an upright position with the lower part resting on or fixed in the ground or other support; opposed to *lie*. Const. *on*, *upon* (the ground, a base, etc.). Cf. sense 1.

971 *Blickl. Hom.* 239 He þær ȝeseah swer standan. *c* **1200** Ormin 14412 Þa sexe waterrfetless þatt stodenn wiþþ þatt waterr þær. **1375** Barbour *Bruce* XVII. 135 Quhan thai the baner saw sympilly Swa standand. **1382** Wyclif *2 Kings* vi. 31 Thes thingis do to me God, and thes thingis adde, ȝif the heued of Helisee, the sone of Saphath, schulde stonden vpon hym to day. [Similarly **1611**, **1884**; lit. from Hebrew.] *c* **1386** Chaucer *Monk's T.* 419 But litel out of Pize stant a tour. **1470–85** Malory *Arthur* I. xvii. 62 One of the castels that stondyn in the forest of Sherewood. **1513** Douglas *Æneis* VI. x. 57 Thair speris stikking in the erd did stand. **1529** More *Dyaloge* II. ix. 59/1 How longe that ymage had stande in that olde tabernacle that coulde no man tell. **1585** Higins *Junius' Nomencl.* 183/2 *Textrina*, . . a weauers shop or workehouse where his loomes stand. **1594** Nashe *Unfort. Trav.* E 4 b, Wks. 1904 II. 256 Her house stood vppon vaultes. **1694** *Acc. Sev. Late Voy.* II. 22 When the Skies are not very clear, the Mountains stand, to about the middle, in the Clouds. **1710** Hearne *Collect.* (O.H.S.) III. 42 It [a volume] stands 4to T. 14. Art. **1735** Johnson *Lobo's Abyssinia* Descr. x. 103 Two rows of sharp Teeth, standing wide from each other. **1750** Gray *Long Story* 2 In Britain's Isle, no matter where, An ancient pile of buildings stands. **1823** Scott *Quentin D.* v, A flagon of champagne stood before them. **1886** Miss Sergeant *No Saint* I. i. 16 Behind the town-hall . . stood the parish church. **1889** *Century Mag.* June 177/2 One of its [the prison's] longer sides stands flush with the line of the street.

b. Of plants: To grow erect. Also with complement, ***to stand high, thick, thin***, etc. Said esp. of grass, corn, etc. when left uncut to ripen.

c **888** Ælfred *Boeth.* xxv. 57/21 Swa bið eac þam treowum þe him ȝecynde bið up heah to standanne. *c* **1205** Lay. 26058 And sturte him biaften ane treo þe þer stod [*c* **1275** stot] aneouste. *c* **1290** *S. Eng. Leg.* 18/598 A fair herbe, þat men cleopez letuse, heo i-saiȝ stonde bi þe weiȝe. **1382** Wyclif *Exod.* xxii. 6 If fyer . . cacche . . the corn stondynge in feeldis. **1573** Tusser *Husb.* (1878) 79 Such fewell as standing a late ye haue bought, now fell it. **1585** Higins *Junius' Nomencl.* 107/1 *Seges*, . . corne standing and vncut downe. **1618** W. Lawson *New Orch. & Gard.* viii. (1623) 22, I haue seene many trees stand so thicke, that one could not thriue for the throng of his neighbours. **1700** Dryden *Ovid's Met., Acis & Galatea* 110 Red Strawberries, in shades, expecting stand. **1765** *Museum Rust.* IV. 216 If the corn on this good land stood thin, we may safely conclude, that it was sown thin. **1837** Carlyle *Fr. Rev.* I. I. ii, The blossom of French Royalty . . was still standing with all its petals. **1842** Loudon *Suburban Hort.* 313 If the tree is to stand four or more years. **1847** *Jrnl. R. Agric. Soc.* VIII. I. 75 White wheats should stand somewhat longer. **1858** *Ibid.* XIX. I. 189 A piece of clover which was first mown and then allowed to stand for seed.

c. Hence, by hypallage, of land, ***to stand thick with*** or ***deep in***: To be covered with a rich standing crop. (Cf. 27 b.)

1535 Coverdale *Ps.* lxiv. (lxv.) 13 The valleys stonde so thicke with corne [Luther *stehen dick mit Korn*] yt they laugh and synge. **1641** J. Jackson *True Evang. T.* iii. 214 The lands stand thick with corn. **1899** Marg. Benson & Gourlay *Temple of Mut* i. 3 The fields . . stand deep in corn.

d. Of the hair: To grow stiff and erect like bristles. ***to stand on end, up, upright***: to rise up on the head as a result of fright or astonishment.

c **1386** Chaucer *Prol.* 555 Ther on stood a toft of herys Reed as the brustles of a sowes erys. **1530** Palsgr. 733/2 Whan I passed by the churche yarde my heares stode upright for feare. **1547** Boorde *Brev. Health* (1870) 75 The .183. Chapitre dothe shewe of standyng vp of mannes heare. **1592** Greene *Defence Conny-catching* Wks. (Grosart) XI. 72 His mustachies . . standing as stiffe as if he wore a Ruler in his mouth. *c* **1611** Chapman *Iliad* v. 593 This sight, when great Tydides saw, his haire stood vp on end. *a* **1691** Boyle *Hist. Air* (1692) 174 Their Horses Hair stood upright, like Bristles, with the vehement Cold. **1778** Miss Burney *Evelina* (1791) I. xl. 200 As for the particulars, I'm sure they'd make your hair stand on end to hear them. **1875** Jowett *Plato* (ed. 2) I. 249 When I speak of horrors, my hair stands on end.

e. To project in relief. (Cf. *stand out*, 99 i.)

1683 Moxon *Mech. Exerc., Printing* xiii. ¶4 [He] Sculps out the Steel between the . . Marks . . on the Face of the Punch, and leaves the Marks standing on the Face.

18. More loosely: To be set, placed or fixed; to rest, lie (with more or less notion of firmness and steadiness). Of a dish or its contents: To rest flat or on a flat base.

c **1200** Ormin 1030, & bi þatt allterr stodenn aȝȝ þatt follkess haliȝdomess, þatt wærenn inn an arrke þær Wel & wurrþlike ȝemmde. *c* **1420** ? Lydg. *Assembly of Gods* 357 A gymlot and a fauset theropon stood. **1459** *Paston Lett.* I. 490 Item, iij. pyllowes stondyng on the autre off rede felwet. **1551** Sir J. Williams *Accompte* (Abbotsf. Club) 24 Two collettes of golde, wherin standeth two course emeraldes. **1613** Purchas *Pilgrimage* (1614) 200 Milk must not stand on the table with flesh, nor touch it. **1681** Grew *Musæum* I. §5. i. 100 At the top of his Head, just under the Horn, stand his Eyes. **1818** Scott *Hrt. Midl.* xvii, Some food stood on the table. **1902** R. Bagot *Donna Diana* v. 42 On which [table] stood an inkstand. **1908** [Miss E. Fowler] *Betw. Trent & Ancholme* 24 A dial, of wood, stands upon an old hewn stone in the middle.

19. Of a place, country, piece of ground, dwelling, etc.: To be situated in a specified position or aspect. Now chiefly of a town or village (? as consisting of erect edifices).

c **893** Ælfred *Oros.* (1883) 19 He seȝlode on fif daȝan to þæm porte þe mon hæt æt Hæþum; se stent betuh Winedum & Seaxum & Angle. **971** *Blickl. Hom.* 77 Gaþ on þa wic þe beforan inc stondeð. *c* **1205** Lay. 125 Ful neh þan ilke stude þar Rome nou stondeð. **1297** R. Glouc. 3 Þe see geþ him al aboute, he [England] stond [*v.rr.* stont, stant] as in an yle. **13** . . *K. Alis.* 3269 Theo cite upon the see stod. **1340–70** *Alex. & Dind.* 114 Þanne he farus to a feld . . þat stod on an hie stede. *c* **1440** *Pallad. on Husb.* I. 28 Ek se thy londe Be fertile, and commodiously stonde. **1471** Caxton *Recuyell* (Sommer) 188 She and her susters soiourned in a cyte whiche stode on the ryuage. **1548** Hall *Chron., Edw. IV*, 233 b, The toune standeth lowe, and the Ryver passeth thorough. **1550** Crowley *Epigr.* 208 A Marchaunte Returned to his contrey, whiche in Europe standes. **1607** W. S. *Puritane* III. iv. 36 *Put.* O, it [a room] stands very pleasantly for a Scholler. **1612** Coverte *Voy.* 11 This place of our then ancoring standeth in the height of fiue Degrees and 20. minutes. *a* **1701** Maundrell *Journ. Jerus.* (1732) 7 The City stands Northerly. **1792** T. Twining *Recreat.* (1882) 160 The village stands pleasantly. **1849** Macaulay *Hist. Eng.* iii. I. 336 Large as Bristol might then appear, it occupied but a very small portion of the area on which it now stands. **1852** Thackeray *Esmond* I. iii, A large pleasant green flat, where the village of Castlewood stood, and stands.

20. a. With predicative extension or complement, indicating the manner or condition, the verb retaining more or less of its proper force (senses 17–19); e.g. ***to stand high, firm, open, ajar***.

c **897** Ælfred *Gregory's Past. C.* Pref. 5 Hu ða ciricean . . stodon maðma & boca ȝefyldæ. *c* **1205** Lay. 5352 Al þat liggende lond þat lið in to Rome . . þe nu stonded riche. *a* **1250** *Owl & Night.* 623 Myn hus stont briht & grene. **1375** Barbour *Bruce* VI. 77 He saw the brayis hye standand. *c* **1400**, *a* **1513**, **1786** [see ajar *adv.*[1]]. **1477–9** *Rec. St. Mary at Hill* (1905) 84 A tenement . . standyng void by the terme of Estir, Midsomer, and Mighelmasse. **1513** Douglas *Æneis* VI. ii. 104 The blak ȝettis of Pluto, and that dirk way Standis evir oppyne and patent nycht and day. **1675** J. S[mith] *Horolog. Dial.* 35 Fasten it [the clock] with another nail or two, that it may stand firm and not shake. **1697** Dryden *Virg. Georg.* III. 499 And open let thy Stacks all Winter stand. **1709** Steele *Tatler* No. 194 ¶5 The Gate stood open. **1735** Johnson *Lobo's Abyssinia* Descr. xi. 111 A large stone House . . which had stood uninhabited so long, that great Numbers of red Ants had taken Possession of it. **1857** Ruskin *Pol. Econ. Art* ii. §77, I have seen the hail fall in Italy till the forest branches stood stripped and bare. **1866** —— *Crown of Wild Olive* §57 My eye caught the title of a book standing open in a bookseller's window. **1894** *Amer. Dict. Printing, Stands high.* In printing, type or blocks which are higher than other types or than the normal height. **1910** Hogarth in *Encycl. Brit.* I. 248/2 The main chamber . . stands free, isolated from the rest of the plan by corridors. **1912** H. L. Cannon in *Eng. Hist. Rev.* Oct. 661 The 'cog' . . was lightly laden, and so stood high out of the water.

b. Of a house, etc., ***as it stands***: with all its furniture, decoration, etc.

1527 in *Test. Ebor.* (Surtees) VI. 14, I will a house to my wif in Scrayngham, and hir chamer as it standis. **1668** in *Rep. Hist. MSS. Comm.* Var. Coll. (1907) IV. 245 The bricke and materialls, or the house itselfe as it stands, to be solde.

†**c.** To be fixed or set or turned in a specified direction. *Obs.*

1471 Caxton *Recuyell* (Sommer) 409 His sayll that stode ouer ende by force of the wynde, was smyten full of hooles. *a* **1637** B. Jonson *Goodwife's Ale* in *Athenæum* (1904) 1 Oct. 447/2 My mouth did stand awry, just as it were Labouring to whisper somewhat in mine Eare. **1687** A. Lovell tr. *Thevenot's Trav.* II. 6 Its tail stands another way than the Tails of other fish which are forked upwards and downwards. **1694** *Acc. Sev. Late Voy.* II. 150 All the other Longboats row out before, and take notice which way the Line doth stand.

21. a. To be inscribed, drawn, painted, etc. (in a list, sheet, or the like). Hence of words or literary matter: To be set down, recorded, composed in a (specified) context or form.

871–889 *Charter* in *O.E. Texts* 452/43 Ðeos foresprec & þas ȝewriotu þe herbeufan awreotene stondað. *c* **1200** Ormin 315 All iss þwerrt ut soþ . . þatt stanndeþþ o þe Godd-spellboc. *Ibid.* 4986 þatt bocstaff . . þatt uppo Cristess name stannt Rihht allre nesst te firrste. **1362** Langl. *P. Pl.* A. I. 48 And he asked of hem, of whom spac þe lettre, And whom þe ymage was lyk þat þer-Inne stod. *a* **1400–50** *Wars Alex.* 279 In þe first compas . . Stude þe xij vndirstandings stoutly engrauen. *c* **1450** *Mirk's Festial* 45 Then, for þe ȝere ys rewlet and gouernet by þe kalender, and þis day stondeth yn þe begynnyng þerof, hit ys callet ȝeres-day. **1583** [see rubric *sb.* 3]. **1603** Shaks. *Meas. for M.* II. ii. 40 To fine the faults, whose fine stands in record. **1605** —— *Macb.* IV. i. 134 Let this pernitious houre Stand aye accursed in the Kalender. **1754** Sherlock *Disc.* (1759) I. ix. 251 These Words stand towards the Close of St. John's Gospel. **1801** Strutt *Sports & Past.* II. i. 44 The victories they obtained over their enemies . . stand upon record in the histories of this country. **1824** Scott *Redgauntlet* ch. x, I will not say but my name may stand on the list. **1832** *Examiner* 370/2 Mr. E. L. Bulwer's motion . . stands for Thursday next. **1890** *Harper's Mag.* June 44/2 Richard Garrard Fenwick—so his name stood on the club list. **1911** Jacques in *36th Prov. Mtg. Law Soc.* 269 Her husband of course has no vote as the house does not stand in his name.

b. esp. of numerical figures: To be set down or entered in a list, account, ledger, or the like. Hence of a sum, price, score; also of the game or player whose score is recorded. Const. *at* (a certain figure).

1537 *N. Country Wills* (Surtees) 153 That Roger Shawes sonne be forgiven the odde mony that standith in my boke more than lxvj s. viij d. **1579** Digges *Stratiot.* I. xvi. 26 Which all standeth thus 24/120. **1830** *Examiner* 538/2 At the close of the poll the numbers stood thus. **1878** R. H. Hutton *Scott* xv. 158 On the 17th of December, 1830, the liabilities stood at 54,000*l.* **1890** *Illustr. Lond. News* 26 Apr. 526/3 The prisoner had standing to his credit £57. **1890** *Field* 10 May 672/3 Streatfield . . played a very sound game, and stood at twenty-two when he lost his partner. *Ibid.* 673/1 The score standing at 123 for five wickets. **1892** *Chamb. Jrnl.* 1 Oct. 625/2 If a bank's shares stand at a good premium. **1913** *Oxf. Univ. Gaz.* 19 Feb. 493/2 The balance at the Bank stands . . at £50.

c. Of an account: To show a (specified) position of the parties with regard to debit and credit. Also, to continue on the books unsettled. Also *fig.*

1710–11 Swift *Jrnl. to Stella* 16 Jan., Let me know how accounts stand, that you may have your money betimes. **1776** *Pennsylv. Even. Post* 10 Aug. 398/1 Those whose accounts have stood beyond the customary time of payment, will please to take notice, that unless they are speedily discharged, I shall sue for the same. **1825** Scott *Betrothed* xxx, I will not accept favours from him in prosperity, who, in adversity, refused me his hand—our account stands yet open. *Mod.* At present, the account stands greatly in my favour.

d. Of a word, clause, etc.: To occupy a specified place in a verse or context, to be used in a specified inflexion or construction.

1693 Dryden *Persius* VI. note 8 But the word Empress wou'd not stand in that Verse: For which reason I Adjourn'd it to another. **1836** J. R. Major *Guide Grk. Trag.* 120 The rhythm is violated . . when the three last syllables of a word, which are capable of standing in the verse as an anapæst, are divided between a dactyl and the following foot. **1860** Goodwin *Grk. Moods & Tenses* 287 The Participles of impersonal Verbs stand in the Accusative Absolute, . . when other Participles would stand in the Genitive Absolute. **1861** Paley *Æschylus* (ed. 2) *Pers.* 618 *note*, In fact, χεροῖν could not possibly stand in this place.

22. Of water, etc.: To have the surface at a specified level. Of the mercury (or other liquid) in a thermometer, barometer, etc.: To reach to a certain height; hence said of the instrument itself.

c **1250** *Gen. & Ex.* 590 Fowerti dais and fowerti niȝt, So wex water wið maȝti miȝt . . And oðer fowerti ðore-to, Dais and niȝtes stodet so. **1686** Halley in *Phil. Trans.* XVI. 104 The Barometer standing at 30 Inches. *Ibid.* 110 In calm frosty weather the Mercury generally stands high. **1715** Desaguliers *Fires Impr.* 47 The Thermometer stands at the same height in deep Cellars at both Seasons. **1853** *Jrnl. R. Agric. Soc.* XIV. I. 165 The water in the sluice stands at 9 ft. **1890** Constance Smith *Riddle of Haviland* II. VI. iv. 241 The glass stood at set fair. **1891** *National Rev.* Jan. 656 The thermometer now stood at 20 Fah.

** With the notion of permanence, stability, etc.

23. a. Of an edifice, or the like: To remain erect and entire; to resist destruction or decay. Also with predicative adj. or adv., as *whole, sound, fast, stable*.

c **888** Ælfred *Boeth.* xii, Ne mæȝ hus naht lange standan on þam hean munte ȝif hit full unȝemetlic wind ȝestent. *a* **1122** *O.E. Chron.* (Laud MS.) an. 1009 & oft hi on þa burh Lund ne ȝefuhton. Ac si Gode lof þet heo ȝyt ȝesund stent. *c* **1205** Lay. 15532 Þenne mihte he [the wall] stonde to þere worlde longe. *c* **1290** *S. Eng. Leg.* 160/1889 Ich habbe a luytel Coffre þat stant hol and sount. *a* **1300** *Cursor M.* 10121 Þar þe castel standes stable. *c* **1400** *Brut* lx. 55 How Vortiger . . biganne þere a castel, þat wolde nouȝt stande wiþouten morter temprede wiþ mannes blode. **1542** Udall *Erasm. Apoph.* 281 b, The trenches and bulwerkes of his enemies campe was standing whole. **1562** Pilkington *Expos. Abdyas* Pref. 8 The winds blow boustously, yet stand faste the low busshes when the great ookes are overthrowen. **1567** *Gude & Godlie B.* (S.T.S.) 211 Had not ȝour self begun the weiris, ȝour stepillis had bene standand ȝit. **1610** Holland *Camden's Brit.* (1637) 636 Faire walles, which are partly yet standing. **1758** *Ann. Reg.* 100 Her masts [are] very much wounded: it is surprizing how they stood home. **1794–5** in B. Ward *Dawn Cath. Revival* (1909) II. 119 The rigging was damaged; but the vessel stood. **1798** in Nicolas *Disp. Nelson* (1846) VII. p. clvi, She had only a foremast standing at day-light. **1857** RUSKIN *Pol. Econ. Art* ii. §74 The marble would have stood its two thousand years as well in the polished statue as in the Parian cliff. **1879** M. J. GUEST *Lect. Eng. Hist.* x. 93 In that climate buildings stand much longer than they do in England. **1883** GRESLEY *Gloss. Coal-mining* 237 *Stand*, does not break down or require timbering. A rock or coal roof generally stands better than one composed of shale or clay.

fig. **1805** WORDSW. *Prelude* II. 280 The props of my affections were removed, And yet the building stood, as if sustained By its own spirit! **1834** J. WILSON *Noctes Ambr.* xxxvii. Wks. 1856 IV. 198 The Church doesna deserve to staun when sic atrocities are rife beneath its shelter.

b. Of the world: To exist; to remain stable, last.

Chiefly in phrase: cf. quot. 1526.

c **1205** LAY. 18850 Þe wile þe þis world stænt [*c* **1275** steond] ilæsten scal is worðmunt. *a* **1225** *Leg. Kath.* 1490 Of marbrestan a temple, þet schal aa stonden, hwil þet te world stont. **1340–70** *Alex. & Dind.* 587 ȝe were alle.. bred of þat modur þat is stable to stonde. **1526** TINDALE *1 Cor.* viii. 13 Whill the worlde stondeth [So **1611**; Gr. εἰς τὸν αἰῶνα]. **1598** R. BERNARD tr. *Terence, Adelphos* I. ii, Neuer was there since the world stood, any thing more vnreasonable.

c. Of any mechanism or contrivance: To hold together, resist wear or damage, keep its place.

1768 STERNE *Sent. Journ., The Wig*, But I fear, friend! said I, this buckle won't stand.

24. *Naut.* ***to let all stand***: to leave a ship fully rigged. ***all standing***, i.e. without dismantling or unrigging; *transf.* with one's clothes on, dressed; also *fig.* ***to pay off, bring up all standing***: see quot. 1867; ***to gybe all standing*** (see quot. 1976).

1669 STURMY *Mariner's Mag.* I. 17 Shall we get down our Top-masts? No, let all stand. **1791** SMEATON *Edystone L.* (1793) §259 We began to heave in our ground chain,.. and, it being nine P.M. concluded to let all stand till the next morning... Found all standing as we had left it. **1802** *Naval Chron.* VIII. 172 The Fisgard.. was paid off all standing, directly recommissioned. **1837** *Southern Lit. Messenger* III. 178 This reflection brought me up, as the sailors say, 'all standing'. **1840** R. H. DANA *Two Years before Mast* xxxi. 231 The mate.. turned in 'all standing', and was always on deck the moment he was called. **1867** SMYTH *Sailor's Word-bk.* s.v. *All, To be brought up all standing*, is to be suddenly checked or stopped, without any preparation. *Paid off all standing*, without unrigging or waiting to return stores; perhaps recommissioned the next day or hour. **1879** HARTIGAN & WALKER *Stray Leaves* 2nd Ser. 198 [They] gained their respective domiciles, and turned in 'regimental', or, as Jack has it, 'all standing', for their.. last night's rest in Old England. **1884** [see GYBE *sb.*[2]]. **1893** DUNMORE *Pamirs* II. 62, I dined, and after smoking a pipe, turned in all standing for the night. **1903** A. BENNETT *Let.* 27 Mar. (1966) 35 The close of the book, as it stands, will 'bring him up all standing'. **1924** A. J. SMALL *Frozen Gold* i. 13 A spring.. would take him from his chair, all-standing, sheer to the throat of the swaggering giant who held the gun. **1976** *Oxf. Compan. Ships & Sea* 365/2 To gybe without attending the runners, or to do so involuntarily, is known as to 'gybe all-standing', and is dangerous.

25. Of a pigment or dye: To keep its colour; also, not to blot or run.

1811 *Self Instructor* 531 All these three colours stand. **1815** J. SMITH *Panorama Sci. & Art* II. 731 Vermilion... Stands tolerably well if perfectly pure. **1883** R. HALDANE *Workshop Rec.* Ser. II. 336 Most of the black Indian ink.. blots when a damp brush is passed over it; or, as draughtsmen say, 'it does not stand'.

26. *Farriery.* Of the eye: To preserve its sight, to keep good sight.

1737 BRACKEN *Farriery Impr.* (1757) II. 13, I must return to a Description of the Eye that I think most likely to stand (as we term it).

*** To be still or stationary.

27. a. Of liquids: To cease flowing; *esp.* of water, to collect and remain motionless, be stagnant (cf. STANDING *ppl. a.*). (See also STILL *adv.*)

c **888** ÆLFRED *Boeth.* xxxv. §7 Se hearpere [*sc.* Orpheus].. hearpode ðæt.. þa ea stodon. **1382** WYCLIF *Luke* viii. 44 And a non the flix of hir blood stood [*v.r.* ceesed]. **1538** ELYOT *Dict., Stagno*, proprely of water is to stande and not to flowe. **1585** HIGINS *Junius' Nomencl.* 401/2 *Lacuna*,.. a ditch wherein water standeth. **1697** DRYDEN *Æneid* VII. 1093 Where Ufens glides along the lowly Lands, Or the black Water of Pomptina stands. **1852** *Jrnl. R. Agric. Soc.* XIII. I. 80 The stagnant water being permitted year after year to stand on the surface during the winter. **1882** *Unexpl. Baluchistan* 41 The water appeared to stand here some time, judging by the presence of many water weeds.

transf. **1899** MRS. E. COTES *Path of Star* xv. 160 The garden where heavy scents stood in the sun.

fig. **1842** TENNYSON *Sir Galahad* 10 When the tide of combat stands.

b. Of land, a ditch, etc.: ***to stand with***, to be full of (stagnant water). (Cf. 17 c.)

1601 HOLLAND *Pliny* VI. xxvii. I. 138 The countrey Elemais is so fennie, and standeth with water so wet, that there is no way through it to Persis. **1718** HEARNE *Collect.* (O.H.S.) VI. 229 The Ditch about the Camp stands with water, except in a dry time. **1848** *Jrnl. R. Agric. Soc.* IX. I. 242 It is not at all uncommon to see a clay pit stand with water.

28. a. Of tears: To remain collected (in the eyes) without falling. Of a humour, esp. perspiration: To remain in drops (*on* the skin, etc.).

1530 PALSGR. 733/1 He dyd nat wepe that I sawe, but the water stode in his eyes. **1581** A. HALL *Iliad* VI. 119 She smiles therewith, yet in hir eyes the water ful doth stand. **1627** MAY *Lucan* VI. L 3, She.. gathers poisonous filth, and slime that stands On the cold ioynts. **1675** HANNAH WOOLLEY *Gentlew. Comp.* 71 Do not venture to eat Spoon-meat so hot, that the tears stand in your eyes. **1719** DE FOE *Crusoe* I. (Globe) 230 This he spoke so earnestly, that I saw Tears stand in his Eyes. **1841** LONGF. *Excelsior* v, A tear stood in his bright blue eye. **1849** *Tait's Mag.* XVI. 226/1 Cold drops stood on my brow. **1891** *Strand Mag.* II. 509/2 The sweat stood in beads on his forehead.

†**b.** Of the eyes, ***to stand a-water***: to be filled with tears. *Obs.*

1605 CHAPMAN, etc. *Eastw. Hoe* II. C 3 b, *Gyr.* Gods my dignitie! as I am a Lady, if he did not make me blush so that mine eyes stood a water.

29. Of a liquid, etc.: To be kept in a vessel without shaking; of (a pot of) tea: to be left to draw.

c **1467** *Noble Bk. Cookry* (1882) 101 Sye it throughe a clothe and let yt stond and setelle. *c* **1550** LLOYD *Treas. Health* liii. R ij, Such thynges are neuer mynystred excepte they haue stonde [**1585** N iij b, stoode] setteled a good, whyle after commixtion. **1675** HANNAH WOOLLEY *Gentlew. Comp.* 136 Strain it [the Jelly], and so let it stand for your use. **1827** FARADAY *Chem. Manip.* xii. (1842) 275 The whole is to be closed up, and suffered to stand until cold. **1852** *Jrnl. R. Agric. Soc.* XIII. I. 37 The first milk is set.. to stand for cream. **1862** MILLER *Organ. Chem.* (ed. 2) 165 The liquid portion is removed by pressure, and after standing over chloride of calcium is rectified. **1933** E. A. ROBERTSON *Ordinary Families* vii. 162 Well, I'll get Olive to bring some fresh tea, then. This has been standing rather a long time. **1935** G. SANTAYANA *Last Puritan* III. v. 333 Don't keep this tea standing any longer... It will be poison. Make some fresh for the boys when they come down. **1976** L. HENDERSON *Major Enquiry* xii. 76 It will be ready soon. I like tea to stand properly, don't you?

†**30.** Of a mixture or confection: To be stiff, have a firm consistence. (Cf. STANDING *ppl. a.* 8 b.)

c **1450** *Two Cookery-bks.* 88 Loke that hit stonde well, with Gynger, Sugur. *Ibid.* 109.

31. Of a star: To appear fixed in the heavens. Of the sun or a planet: To be seen apparently motionless at any point of its course.

1382 WYCLIF *Josh.* x. 13 And the sunne and the mone stoden, to the tyme that [etc.]. **1398** TREVISA *Barth. De P.R.* VIII. xxi. (1495) 331 Stelle ben callyd sterres and haue that name of stando, stondyng, for though they moue alwaye, alwaye it semyth that they stonde. **1577** KENDALL *Flowers of Epigr.* 86 In heuen where starres do stand. **1629** MILTON *Nativity* 70 The Stars with deep amaze Stand fixt in stedfast gaze. **1833** TENNYSON *Lotos-Eaters* 7 Full-faced above the valley stood the moon.

32. a. Of a piece of machinery, an implement, a vehicle, etc.: To remain still or motionless; not to move or be operated; to cease moving, working, turning, etc. Of a timepiece: To cease 'going', to have stopped. Now somewhat *rare.* Cf. *to stand still*: see STILL *adv.*

1362 LANGL. *P. Pl.* A. VII. 105 At heiȝ prime perkyn lette þe plouȝ stonde. *c* **1386** CHAUCER *Friar's T.* 243 Deepe was the wey, for which the Carte stood. *c* **1400** *Anturs of Arth.* 266 Maye no mane stere hym of strenghe, whilles þe whele standis. **1549** LATIMER *Ploughers* (Arb.) 25 The ploughe standeth, there is no worke done. *a* **1696** P. HENRY in M. Henry *Life* x. (1825) 247 When the weight is off, the clock stands. **1772** FOOTE *Nabob* I. (1778) 22, I.. told him, the dog was mad, the parrot dead, and the clock stood. **1820** SCORESBY *Acc. Arctic Reg.* II. 476 During an hour.. the pumps were allowed to 'stand'. **1885** 'MRS. ALEXANDER' *At Bay* viii, Before his astonished companion could reply he was beside the vehicle, which was still standing.

b. Of a ship: To ride at anchor.

a **1300** *K. Horn* 1021 He let his schup stonde, & ȝede to londe. *Ibid.* 1437 His schup stod vnder ture. *c* **1350** *Will. Palerne* 2728 þan hiȝed þei hem to þe hauen.. þer stoden fele schippes.

c. Of a vehicle: To remain in a customary place waiting for a fare or for the time to start.

1665 in *Verney Mem.* (1907) II. 241 The Black Swan in Holborn where the Alisbury and other coaches stand. **1676** in J. Playford *Vade Mecum* (1679) 197 All Merchants.. may chuse what Carr they please, except such as stand for Wharf-work [etc.].. which are to be taken in turn.

d. Of a mine, factory, etc., also of the men employed: To stop working; to be at a standstill.

1733 *N. Riding Rec.* VIII. 202 The Treasurer to pay £22.15/ for the Milne standing tenn weeks. **1789** J. WILLIAMS *Min. Kingd.* I. 170 Several Cornish mines are now standing.. because they cannot be carried on with profit while coal is so dear. **1892** *Black & White* 12 Mar. 331/1 If they [the colliers] 'stand' for a fortnight. **1892** *Standard* 28 Apr. 7/5 Works which stood all last week for holidays being now restarted.

**** With some notion of motion or direction in a fixed or steady course.

†**33.** Of light (also rarely of vapour): To issue in a beam or shaft. *Obs.*

Beowulf 726 Him of eaȝum stod.. leoht unfæȝer. *c* **900** *Bæda's Hist.* v. xxiii. (1890) 476 Stod se leoma him of, swilce fyrenþecele. *c* **1000** ÆLFRIC *Hom.* (Th.) I. 86 Him stod stincende steam of ðam muðe. *a* **1300** *Cursor M.* 8160 A lem fra þe wandes stode. *c* **1300** *Havelok* 591 Of hise mouth it stod a stem, Als it were a sunnebem. *c* **1400** *St. Alexius* 439 (Laud 463) Out of his mouþ þer stoed a leom Brighter þan þe sonne beom.

†**34.** Of a weapon: To be fixed *at* or *on* the place to which it penetrates in wounding; to penetrate *through, unto.* Said also of the stroke or 'dint'. *Obs.*

Beowulf 1434 Sumne ðeata leod of flanboȝan feores ȝetwæfde,.. þæt him on aldre stod herestræl hearda. *a* **1300** *Cursor M.* 11371 þe suerd o soru thoru hir stode. *Ibid.* 24360 þe nails þat him fest on rode, thoru mi hend and fete þai stode. **13..** *King Alis.* 3709 He smot anothir,.. That he clef his basnet, At his chyn stod the dunt. *c* **1330** *Arth. & Merl.* 8134 King Malgar on þe heued he gert, þat þe dent stode at þe hert. **1390** GOWER *Conf.* III. 268 With his swerd droppende of blod, The which withinne his douhter stod.

35. Of the wind: To blow from a quarter indicated; also simply, to blow favourably, to continue to blow. Similarly of the weather. ? *Obs.* (Cf. SIT *v.* 13 d.)

c **1205** LAY. 1780 Wind stod on willen. *Ibid.* 25537 Weder stod on wille, wind wex an honde. *c* **1300** *Cursor M.* 24834 Forth þai floted on þat flod, For al to will þair bir þam stode. *c* **1300** *K. Horn* 784 (Laud MS.), þe whyȝt him gan stonde And drof tyl hirelonde. **1338** R. BRUNNE *Chron.* (1810) 145 þe next Marche folowand He suld take þat way, if wynde wild with him stand, At Marsile to aryue. **1412–20** LYDG. *Chron. Troy* I. 4392 Whan þei seye þat þe wedir stood, þe wynde also at her lust þei hadde, þei gan to saille. **1546** J. HEYWOOD *Prov.* (1867) 56 If the winde stande in that doore, it standth awry. **1635** BRERETON *Trav.* (Chetham Soc.) 77 The wind stood most easterly. **1669** STURMY *Mariner's Mag.* I. ii. 16 The Wind is fair, though but little; he comes well, as if he would stand. **1699** DAMPIER *Voy.* II. I. 155 If the gale stood. **1708** *Lond. Gaz.* No. 4417/2 [They] will sail for the River, as soon as the Wind stands fair.

36. a. *Naut.* Of a vessel (hence of the commander, sailors, etc.): To sail, steer, direct one's course (in a specified direction, to sea, into harbour, etc.).

See also *stand along, away*, etc. in branch VII; also *stand for* 71 k, *stand with* 79 d. (Note the pa. t. *stowed* in the 17th c., prob. due to misapprehension.)

1627 J. TAYLOR (Water P.) *Famous Fight* Wks. (1630) III. 39/1 We gaue him a whole broad-side.. tacking forthwith, and standing after him. **1633** T. JAMES *Voy.* 18 Wee stowed alongst it [floating ice], hoping to weather it. **1633** T. STAFFORD *Pac. Hib.* II. x. 189 The Spanish fleete.. standing to the Northward. *a* **1700** EVELYN *Diary* 16 Oct. 1644, The weather being still so fowle that for two houres at least we durst not stand into the haven. **1707** *Lond. Gaz.* No. 4312/2 They stood to Sea. **1745** P. THOMAS *Jrnl. Anson's Voy.* 280 We immediately.. stood towards her, and I believe if she had.. stood from us, we should have found it very difficult to have come up with her. **1748** *Anson's Voy.* III. ix. 386 This entrance he proposed to stand through next day. **1769** FALCONER *Dict. Marine* (1789) D 4 b, We discovered a fleet.. standing *athwart* us, i.e. steering across our way. **1823** W. SCORESBY *Jrnl.* 2 We took sail, and stood into the river. *a* **1860** in *Temple Bar* LVI. 353 We passed the bank, stood round the light, and sailed away to sea. **1867** SMYTH *Sailor's Word-bk., Stand in Shore*, to sail directly for the land. **1878** BOSW. SMITH *Carthage* 107 The Roman fleet.. stood right across the Mediterranean to the nearest point of Africa. **1892** *Black & White* 16 Jan. 78/1 The whole fleet put on good speed, and stood nearly due west.

With cognate object. **1705** tr. *Bosman's Guinea* 13 The Ship.. being bound to.. touch at Curacao before it stands its course homewards.

b. *transf.* Of a person: To go, proceed (in a specified direction).

a **1300** *K. Horn* 1179 Ifond horn child stonde To schupeward in londe. **1829** SHIPP *Mem.* II. 87 They bowed a hundred times..; then stood towards their village.

37. *Archery.* Of an arrow (see quot.).

1801 T. ROBERTS *Eng. Bowman* 294 An arrow is said to stand (or to stand in) a bow, when it flies from it steadily, and without shaking or flirting. *Ibid.*, To Stand in the wind, to stand across the wind.

***** Of immaterial things.

38. a. With adv., advb. phr., or adj. predicate: To be or remain in a specified condition, relation, situation, etc.

a **1122** *O.E. Chron.* an. 1093 þæt arcebrice on Cantwarbyrig, þe ær on his aȝenre hand stod. *c* **1315** SHOREHAM *Poems* I. 231 For ȝef þat water his kende lest, þat cristning stant te tealte. **14..** *26 Pol. Poems* 20/194 A cheuenteyn may fyȝte o day, þe victorye wiþ hym stande. *c* **1420** ? LYDG. *Assembly of Gods* 1887 Thy wytte stant a crooke. *c* **1470** *Gol. & Gaw.* 1056 Ane sair stonayand stour at thair hartis standis. **1548** HALL *Chron., Hen. IV*, 12 b, My life stoode in ieopardie. **1603** SHAKS. *Meas. for M.* V. i. 108 His Integritie Stands without blemish. **1688** *Lett. conc. Pres. State Italy* 170 The greatest part of the Revenue of this State stands engaged for the Interest that they pay. **1870** ROGERS *Hist. Glean.* Ser. II. 102 No reputation stood higher than that of Selden. **1875** JOWETT *Plato* (ed. 2) IV. 8 He cannot tell the relation in which abstract ideas stand to one another. **1891** *Standard* 16 June 3/2 Mr. Balfour's plan stands condemned in his eyes.

b. With a relative or demonstrative adv. as predicate; e.g. ***the case stands thus, as things*** or ***matters stand*** (= under present circumstances). Also impersonally, as ***it stands well***, † ***how stands?, how does it stand?*** (*with*, † *by*, † *of* a person or thing; † also with dat., ***him stands well***).

a **1000** *Boeth. Metr.* i. 28 Stod þraȝe on ðam. *c* **1300** *Havelok* 2983 Him stondes wel þat god child strenes. *c* **1380** WYCLIF *Sel. Wks.* III. 346 And þus it stondiþ in þe Chirche of þes newe servauntis þat ben brouȝt in. *c* **1386** CHAUCER *Shipman's T.* 114 It stant not so with me. *c* **1485** *Digby Myst.* (1882) IV. 1505 Sister! how standes with yow? *a* **1578** LINDESAY (Pitscottie) *Chron. Scot.* II. 25 The erle of glencairne returnit.. to the erle of lennox and schew him how all studd. **1591** SHAKS. *Two Gent.* II. v. 21 *Spee.* Why then, how stands the matter with them? *Lau.* Marry thus, when it stands well with him, it stands well with her. **1600** *Weakest goeth to Wall* H 3, My Lord of Bulloigne, thus then stands my case. **1612** *Benvenuto's Passenger* I. ii. 137 Sure sir, if it stood with you as he pleased, you should be in an euill case. **1672** PETTY *Pol. Anat.* (1691) 68 As things now stand. **1709** BERKELEY *Ess. Vision* §45 The truth of the matter, I find, stands thus. **1826** LAMB *Pop. Fallacies* xi, A hare, as the law now stands, makes many friends. **1837** CARLYLE *Fr. Rev.* III. VII. viii, Ill stands it with me if I have spoken falsely. **1862** *Temple Bar* VI. 401 How does it stand with your.. studies? **1898** 'MERRIMAN' *Roden's Corner* vii. 75 People did not know how matters stood between Joan Ferriby and Tony Cornish.

39. †**a.** With dative of person: To exist, be present (to one); e.g. ***me stondeþ raþe*** = I am in haste. Chiefly in (***me***, etc.) ***stands awe, need***: see 45, 46. *Obs.*

a **1300** *K. Horn* 554 For þi me stondeþ þe more rape. *a* **1300** *Cursor M.* 24220 Quen he þe sagh þis murning mak, sumthing to þe iwiss he spak if him stode ani steuen.

†**b.** *impers.* To be the case (*that*). ***it cannot stand but***, it cannot but be that... *Obs.*

1377 LANGL. *P. Pl.* B. XIV. 251 A strawe for þe stuwes! it stode nouȝt, I trowe, Had þei no þyng but of pore men, her houses were vntyled. **1561** *Reg. Privy Council Scot.* I. 173 It mycht stand that I had ressavit sum of the gudis libellit fra the thrid hand. **1644** MAXWELL *Prerog. Chr. Kings* ix. 99 It cannot stand but.. the like should hold.

c. *impers.* To behove (a person) *to do* (something). *rare.*

? A cutting down, or confused recollection, of *stand* (one) *in hand* (see 47) or *stand* (one) *upon* (see 78 q).

1857 TROLLOPE *Barchester T.* xlvi, He knew that it depended solely on his own wit whether or no he could throw the joke back upon the lady. He knew that it stood him to do so if he possibly could, but he had not a word. **1911** WEBSTER s.v., 19. To concern; to be of interest or advantage (to); as, it stood him to leave the country for a time.

40. Of a condition, process, or the like: To remain stationary or unchanged, neither progressing nor receding; to be at a standstill.

c **1386** CHAUCER *Merch. T.* 519 (Harl.), Now wolde God that it were woxe night, And that the night wold stonden [*v.r.* lasten] evermo. **1436** *Pol. Poems* (Rolls) II. 202 For whiche they muste dresse hem to pease in haste, Or ellis there thrifte to standen and to waste. *c* **1530** *Judic. Urines* II. xii. 40 But comynly in Homothena, the sekenes is stondyng tyll the seke man passe other to deth or to lyfe. **1658** SIR T. BROWNE *Hydriot.* v. 27 Every houre addes unto that current Arithmetique, which scarce stands one moment. **1723** SWIFT *Poems, Pethox* 52 And while his Fate is in thy Hands, The Bus'ness of the Nation stands.

41. To endure, last; to continue unimpaired; to flourish.

c **1000** *Ags. Gosp.* Matt. xii. 26 Hu mæȝ þonne hys rice standan. *c* **1200** ORMIN 18100 þatt ȝet ta stod stafflike witt Amang Judisskenn þede Off Moysæsess laȝheboc. *a* **1300** *Cursor M.* 9221 þair kingrik..þat had four hundret yeir stand. **1399** LANGL. *Rich. Redeles* III. 249 Iche rewme.. Sholde stable and stonde be þese þre degres. **1553** T. WILSON *Rhet.* (1580) 28 If in other thynges we should bee as negligente, this Realme could not long stande. **1865** M. ARNOLD *Ess. Crit.* ii. 60 Work done after men have reached this platform is classical; and that is the only work which, in the long run, can stand. *Ibid.* vii. 223 How little either of his poetry, or of his criticism, or of his philosophy, can we expect permanently to stand!

42. a. To be or remain valid or of force, hold good.

c **888** ÆLFRED *Boeth.* xxi, þa ȝesetennesse þa he læt standan þa hwile þe he wile. *a* **1122** *O.E. Chron.* (Laud MS.) an. 656 Ic bidde ealle þa ða æfter me cumen.. þæt ure ȝyfe mote standan. *c* **1275** LAY. 397 After þan heþene lawe þat stot in þan ilke dawe. *c* **1315** SHOREHAM *Poems* I. 238 For bote þat water his kende haue, þat cristnynge may nauȝt stonde. **1377** LANGL. *P. Pl.* B. XV. 573 Owre lorde wrote it [the Law] hym-selue, In stone, for it stydfast was and stonde sholde eure. *c* **1400** *Pilgr. Sowle* (Caxton) I. xxx. (1859) 34 Yf he byquethe al his good to his owne lord, standyth the testament? **1544** tr. *Littleton's Tenures* 39 The last deuyse and wyl made by him shal stande and abyde. **1568** GRAFTON *Chron.* II. 100 The yonger sort which had chosen Reignold their Subprior, would have that election to stande. *a* **1578** LINDESAY (Pitscottie) *Chron. Scot.* I. 343 Gif all promeisis had stand quhilk was maid be the king of scotland. **1719** DE FOE *Crusoe* II. (Globe) 432 A written Contract.. would stand. **1758** S. HAYWARD *Serm.* Introd. 19 The promise yet stands. **1855** MACAULAY *Hist. Eng.* xii. III. 211 No English Parliament.. would permit such laws as were now passing through the Irish Parliament to stand. **1879** *Nature* 20 Nov. 62/2 This result is so utterly opposed to fact that a theory which leads to it cannot stand for a moment. **1885** *Law Times Rep.* LII. 625/1, I think.. that the nonsuit ought not to stand. **1894** HALL CAINE *Manxman* III. xiii. 172 It was taken for granted that the old relations would stand.

b. With complement or predicative extension, as ***to stand good, in force,*** (†***for***) ***law***, etc.

a **1300** *Cursor M.* 6746 Qua stelis scep, or ox, or cu.. Oxen fiue for an he pai, For a scep four, it stand for lai. **1581** ALLEN *Apol.* 42 No statute then that stood in force. **1586** in J. Morris *Troubles Cath. Forefathers* Ser. III. (1877) 87 Which common presumption always standeth good by their own law until the contrary be plainly and evidently proved. **1633** BP. HALL *Hard Texts, Rom.* ix. 11 That the decree and purpose of God.. might stand in force. **1667** MILTON *P.L.* v. 602 Hear my Decree, which unrevok't shall stand. **1747** in *Nairne Peerage Evid.* (1874) 148 The said obligation was .. to stand in full force and virtue. **1890** *Chamb. Jrnl.* 27 Dec. 826/1 That charge of murder will not stand law. **1893** *Sat. Rev.* 11 Feb. 164/1 The chapter on planting.. stands good for all time.

43. Of a ceremony: To be performed, take place. *Sc.* ? *Obs.*

1649 LAMONT *Diary* (Maitl. Club) 5 The mariage feast stoode at the place of the Weyms in Fyfe. **1828** *Burd Isabel* ix. in Child *Ballads* IV. 420 Her kirking and her fair wedding Shall baith stand on ae day. *a* **1868** *Earl of Errol* i. ibid. V. 269 An they hae made a marrige o't, It stood at Earlstoon, O.

III. 44. To cost. (Cf. L. *stare, constare.*)

a. ***to stand*** (one) ***high***, to cost a high price. (Cf. G. *einem hoch zu stehen kommen.*) *rare.*

1362 LANGL. *P. Pl.* A. III. 49 We han a wyndow in worching wol stonden [*B. text* sitten] vs ful heiȝe. **1864** CARLYLE *Fredk. Gt.* XV. iii. IV. 41 His father and he have stood these Bavarian Countries very high. *Ibid.* XX. x. VI. 243 Carlos's War of ten months had stood him uncommonly high.

†**b.** ***to stand*** (one) ***on, upon, to*** (a price). *Obs.*

c **1440** *Jacob's Well* 38 þe seed stondyth þe on ij. s., þe rente stante þe on vj. d, þe gaderyng & þe repyng standyth þe on xij. d. **1471** *Paston Lett.* III. 31 The fense must stand yow over on xij. mark by the lest wey. **1641** BEST *Farm Bks.* (Surtees) 76 Sheepe that are fedde all the summer longe in our closes stande us to three shillings.. a peece. **1764** *Museum Rust.* III. 11 His stakes will not stand him, besides his labour, to more than half a farthing each.

c. ***to stand*** (one) ***in*** (a price, etc.). Formerly the ordinary construction; subsequently restricted in currency, being partly fashionable slang, partly dialectal.

Also *to stand* (a person) ***in at*** (an amount).

c **1460** FORTESCUE *Abs. & Lim. Mon.* vi. (1885) 122 Yet his highnes shall þan haue therfore a bouute his persone.. lordes, knyghtes, and sqviers.. to his charges peraduentur also gretly, as his houshold well ruled was wonned to stonde hym inne. **1488–9** *Act 4 Hen. VII*, c. 9 Where an hatte standeth not theym in xvj d. they woll sell it for iij s. or xl d. **1544** in *Lett. & Pap. Hen. VIII* (1903) XIX. I. 445 Here they shall stand the King not in one penny. **1551** ROBINSON tr. *More's Utopia* II. iv. (1895) 150 The same standeth them in muche lesse coste. **1625** in *Cosin's Corr.* (Surtees) I. 71 Boording and breakfest will stand him in 16li per annum. **1651** H. L'ESTRANGE *Answ. Mrq. Worcester* Ep. Ded., It will be in some sort an Answer to God for the time it stood me in. **1713** *Guardian* No. 84 ¶2 It has not stood me in above a Button. **1772** MME. D'ARBLAY *Early Diary* (1889) I. 160 Do you know, it stands me in a hundred a year for chaises? **1837** DICKENS *Pickw.* xli, It'll stand you in a pound a week. **1848** THACKERAY *Van. Fair* xiii, It stands me in eight shillings a bottle. **1875** MISS BRADDON *Hostages to Fortune* II. viii. 168 It only stands me in seven and six-pence. **1886** MRS. RANDOLPH *Mostly Fools* III. iv. 116 His town house.. stood him in at fifteen hundred a year.

d. With prep. as in b or c, but without indirect obj. of person. *rare.*

1457 *Paston Lett.* I. 414 That my maister shud be lerned whate hys housold standyth uppon yerlye. **1546** JOHNSON in Ellis *Orig. Lett.* Ser. II. II. 174 Thay stond in above 4li sterling a peise. **1583** STUBBES *Anat. Abus.* I. (1877) 61, I haue knowen the very nedle work of some one payre of these bootehose to stand, some in iiij pound, vj. pound, and some in x. pound a peece. **1737** BRACKEN *Farriery Impr.* (1756) I. 167 This Ball would stand in five or six Shillings a Day. **1845** *Jrnl. R. Agric. Soc.* VI. II. 526 This concern stands in 70l.

e. Without prep. before the word which denotes the price or cost. *rare.*

1542 in J. H. Glover *Kingsthorpiana* (1883) 82 An acre of lande sown in reye stondeth the tenant in sowing vii shillings at the lest. **1671** LAMONT *Diary* (Maitl. Club) 224 The new bake howse.. stood in workmanship, dales, iyronworke, and nayls, above 300 merks Scots. **1710** LUTTRELL *Brief Rel.* (1857) VI. 545 The company [were] ordered to bring in a modest computation of what their forts and castles have stood them. **1713** *Lond. Gaz.* No. 5137/10 The first.. will stand the Importer near 9s. and 6d. the Gallon. **1801** *Farmer's Mag.* Jan. 110 Good soup is delivered out at 1d. per quart, which stands the subscribers 2½d. **1808** JAMIESON, To *Stand* one, to cost; as, *It stood me a groat*, it cost fourpence. **1872** S. DE VERE *Americanisms* 552 This horse stands me two hundred dollars at least.

IV. Phrases and idiomatic uses.

45. to stand in awe.

†**a.** Orig. 'awe' was the nominative and the person affected in the dative: ***him (them, men,*** etc.) ***stands awe***; const. *of*, also *from, to, with* (the object of dread). Occas. with some other sb. of kindred meaning, as *doubt*. *Obs.*

c **1000** ÆLFRIC *Hom.* (Th.) I. 64 Swa micel eȝe stod deoflum fram eow. *c* **1200** *Trin. Coll. Hom.* 73 þer hem stod eie, þer hem ne sholde, þat is of idele þing. *c* **1205**, *c* **1250** [see AWE *sb.*1 4 a, β]. *a* **1300** *Cursor M.* 14805 Of him þam stod selcut gret agh. *c* **1320**, *c* **1380** [see AWE *sb.*1 4 a. β, α].

13.. *K. Alis.* 3426 (Laud MS.), At þat half stant hem no doute Of Alisaunder ne al his route. *c* **1330** *Arth. & Merl.* 4341 þat hem no stondeþ no doute Of þe payens no of her route.

†**b.** By inversion of const. the dative of the person became the subject and 'awe' the object of the verb: ***to stand awe*** (*of*, also *to do* something). Similarly ***to stand dread***. *Obs.*

c **1200** *Trin. Coll. Hom.* 39 He þat is recheles and non eiȝe ne stand of louerde. *Ibid.* 139 And te king stod eie of him for his holinesse. *a* **1300** *Cursor M.* 12091 þan suld þou sett him to sum scole, þar he moght lere o man stand agh. **1330**, *c* **1460** [see AWE *sb.*1 4 a, β]. *c* **1470** HENRY *Wallace* IX. 851 The Scottis defens so sykkyr was and keyn, Sotheroun stud aw to enter thaim amang. **1535** LYNDESAY *Satyre* 2520 Of na man we sould stand aw. **1597** MONTGOMERIE *Cherrie & Slae* 1053 Of vs ȝe stand na aw.

14.. *26 Pol. Poems* 19/140 Holy chirche stant of hem drede.

c. The modern const., ***to stand in awe***. Similarly ***to stand in dread, fear***, etc.

1413 [see AWE *sb.*1 4 a. β]. *a* **1425** *Cursor M.* 12091 (Trin.) þou most do sett him to þe scole For to lerne & stonde in awe. **1535** COVERDALE *Ps.* xcvi. 9 Let the whole earth stonde in awe of him. **1581** A. HALL *Iliad* IV. 70 Of whom stand you in awe? **1771** BURKE *Corr.* (1844) I. 325 He stood in some awe, though in no sort of fear of you. **1885** MRS. LYNN LINTON *Christ. Kirkland* I. x. 271, I stood in wholesome awe of him.

14.. *26 Pol. Poems* xiii. 6 Falsed stondis ay in drede. **1701** W. WOTTON *Hist. Rome* 302 The Brothers stood in fear of their Lives. **1885** J. PAYN *Luck of Darrells* I. xiv. 246 His aunt stands rather in fear of him.

46. to stand in need.

†**a.** Orig. in the form (***me, him,*** etc.) ***stands need*** = I (etc.) have need. Const. *till, to* (the thing required). (Corresponds to ***need is, is need***: see NEED *sb.* 4, 5.) *Obs.*

a **1300** *Cursor M.* 23983 Wede o welth wil i namar, Clething wil i me tak o care, þar-til [*Fairf.* þer-to] me standes nede. *a* **1400** *Sir Perc.* 184 A maydene scho tuke hir withalle, That scho myȝte appone calle, Whenne that hir nede stode.

b. In inverted const. (cf. 45 b), of a person, ***to stand need*** = to be in need (*of, to do* something). *Obs.* exc. *dial.*

1551 CROWLEY *Pleas. & Payne* Wks. 109 For aye, when I Stode nede of meate, ye gaue me fode. **1578** T. LUPTON *All for Money* 699 If you stoode neede of me you should finde me your friende. **1627** R. SIBTHORPE *Apostol. Obed.* 28 These, I say, and infinite others, neither will time permit, nor doth your experience stand need. **1657** J. SERGEANT *Schism Dispach't* 260 Though we have better grounds then to stand need to build upon it. **1664** MARVELL *Corr.* Wks. (Grosart) II. 180 If I stood need of witnesses, I would cite only Your own merits. **1877** *N.W. Linc. Gloss.*, *Stan' need*, stand in need of, ought [to do something]. **1886** *S.W. Linc. Gloss* s.v., One stans need to tak' care of one's lasses now-a-days.

c. Now (cf. 45 c), ***to stand in need***. Const. *of*, †*to do*.

1530 PALSGR. 733/2 If you stande in nede of me you shall fynde I am your frende. **1597** HOOKER *Eccl. Pol.* v. xlviii. §2 Petitionarie prayer belongeth only to such as.. stand in need of reliefe from others. **1600** J. PORY tr. *Leo's Africa* VI. 277 Their fields stand in neede of continuall watering. **1630** W. T. *Justif. Relig. now Professed* ix. 66 Who themselues stand in neede to bee saued. **1701** W. WOTTON *Hist. Rome* i. 15 His Mind truly stood in need of Instruction. **1849** MACAULAY *Hist. Eng.* x. II. 658 A realm of which these were the fundamental laws stood in no need of a new constitution. **1887** WESTALL *Capt. Trafalgar* xix. 245, I felt very tired and stood much in need of sleep.

47. to stand (one) in (†**on) hand.** Now *dial.*

Cf. the phrases *to lie* (one) *upon hand, in hand*: see HAND *sb.* 32 a, quot. 1548, 29 d quot. 1627.

a. Of the wind: To be favourable. *rare*$^{-1}$.

c **1205** LAY. 22313 Wind heom stod an honde.

b. To behove, concern; to be needful or necessary to; to be of importance or advantage to. Chiefly *impers.* with *it* and inf.

c **1400** *Beryn* 3173, I take no reward of othir mennys case, But oonlich of myne own, that stont me most an hond. **1470** *Paston Lett.* II. 400 Look that ye spare for no cost to do serche for itt, for it wyll stand yow on hand. **1523** BERNERS *Froiss.* I. ccxxii. 289 [They] fought valiantly, the whiche stode them well in hand to do, for ye naueroyse had caused them somwhat to recule. **1587** GOLDING *De Mornay* i. 9 To lay forth the proofes.. it would stand me in hand to ransacke the whole world. **1654** H. L'ESTRANGE *Chas. I* (1656) 89 The King.. conceived it stood him in hand to stand upon his guard. **1667** O. HEYWOOD *Heart-Treas.* vii. 54 It stands us all in hand to try our selves. *a* **1825** FORBY *Voc. E. Anglia* s.v., 'To stand in hand', to concern, behove, or interest. Ex. 'It stands you in hand to look to that'. **1848** BARTLETT *Dict. Amer.*, *To stand in hand*, to concern, to behoove.. This phrase is a colloquial one in New England. Ex. 'It stands you in hand to attend to your business'.

48. to stand in stead.

†**a.** To be of use or advantage, to be serviceable or profitable. Also with adj. qualifying *stead*, to be of (little, no, good) avail or service. *Obs.*

a **1300** *Cursor M.* 26512 It sal stand in sted sumquar. **13..** *Ibid.* 4114 (Gött.) Lat vs do him to dreri dede, Loke quat his drem sal stand in-sted. **1340** HAMPOLE *Pr. Consc.* 3648 His help thurgh hym-selfe standes in na stede, For he es als a lym þat es dede. **1399** *Pol. Poems* (Rolls) I. 365 The busch is bare and waxus sere, Hit may no lengur leves bere; now stont hit in no styde. *c* **1430** *Freemasonry* (Halliw. 1840) 679 They schul be told to stonde yn stede, When thou hast therto gret nede. **1544** BETHAM *Precepts War* I. cxci. 1iv b, But yf we must warre in playne and champyon countryes, then horsemen be moost necessarye. For fotemen wyll stande in lytle steade and vse. *c* **1645** HOWELL *Lett.* (1650) III. 12 If Love be fire, to light this Indian weed, The Donor's Love of fire may stand in steed. **1659** HAMMOND *On Ps.* lxii. 9 It standeth in no stead, and so disappoints those that depend on it. **1772** WHITEFIELD *Serm.* xxxii. Wks. VI. 11 Thy wealth and grandeur will stand in no stead.

b. More usually with indirect obj. (†rarely with *to*). ***to stand*** (one) ***in stead, in*** (***good,*** etc.) ***stead***: to be of service or benefit to; to help or avail. Now only with adj. (*good*, etc.), and that in literary rather than familiar use.

When without epithet, *in stead* was sometimes written or printed as one word.

1387 TREVISA *Higden* (Rolls) VII. 267 But for it stood hem but litel in stede [orig. *sed quia parum profecerunt*]. *c* **1440** *Sir Gowther* 658 He.. stode poure men in stede. **1513** MORE in *Grafton's Chron.* (1568) II. 785 Suche as they thought.. able to stande them in stead, eyther by power or by policie. **1577** KENDALL *Flowers of Epigr., Trifles* 5 The weake may stand the strong in sted. **1603–26** BRETON *Poste Mad Lett.* (Grosart) 39/1 Your kind promise vpon any urgent occasion to stand me instead. **1662** GERBIER *Principles* 1 Some Principles thereon, which may stand the lovers of it instead. **1730** *Lett. to Sir W. Strickland rel. to Coal Trade* 25 It will therefore stand them in stead to consider, whether they be likely to gain anything by the Exchange. **1802** MAR. EDGEWORTH *Moral T., Forester* (*The Bet*), That excuse sha'n't stand you in stead. **1826** DISRAELI *Viv. Grey* III. v, Your boasted knowledge of human nature shall not again stand you in stead.

1338 R. BRUNNE *Chron.* (1810) 202 Better is holy bede of man þat right lyues, & standes vs in more stede, þan alle þe gode he gyues. **13..** *Minor Poems fr. Vernon MS.* 674/90 Strengþe stont vs in no stide. *c* **1449** PECOCK *Repr.* v. vi. 514

If thilk gouernaunce..stondith to him in miche goostli stide. 1539 WRIOTHESLEY in *St. Papers Hen. VIII*, VIII. 160 Soo that his advise therein could stand them in small stede. 1577 HANMER *Anc. Eccl. Hist., Euseb.* III. ix. (1585) 44 Josephus him selfe, that hath stoode vs in so great stead, for the furnishing of this our present history. 1665 *Extr. St. Papers rel. Friends* Ser. III. (1912) 241 Our good intentions stand us in little stead. 1749 FIELDING *Tom Jones* v. viii, It is then he will find in what mighty stead that heathen goddess..will stand him. 1848 THACKERAY *Van. Fair* liv, A Johnson's Dictionary, which stood them in much stead. 1887 WESTALL *Capt. Trafalgar* i. 13 Continual practice stood me in better stead than whole volumes of theory. 1891 *Temple Bar* Oct. 177 His early training..stood him in good stead.

†**c.** Similarly *to stand* (one) *to* (good) *stead*. Also without prep., *to stand* (one) *stead*. *Obs. rare.*

1549 CHALONER *Erasm. Praise Folly* Bj, If ye aske me, what stede these stande me to? I aunsweare [etc.]. 1577 STANYHURST *Descr. Irel.* 1/2 in *Holinshed*, Thersites..being in outwarde feature so deformed, and in inwarde conditions so crooked, as he seemed to stande to no better steede, then to leade Apes in hell. 1581 A. HALL *Iliad* v. 95 What stead canst thou the Troyans stand?

†**d.** In various other phrases of like meaning, as *to stand* (a person) *in force*, *in profit*, *in vail*, *at* or *to avail*. *to stand stall*, *in stall*: see STALL *sb.*[1] 2 b. *Obs.*

c1400 *Pilgr. Sowle* (Caxton) I. xiii. (1859) 9 It maye hym stande nought in profite ne at none auaile. 1428 in *Engl. Misc.* (Surtees 1890) 7 For yt yair praiers suld stand John Lyllyng to availl. c1450 *Mirk's Festial* 76 What maner vertu þat a man haue, but yf he be yn charyte, hit stondys hym in no vayle. 1563 *Homilies* II. *Passion* II. 201 b, So the death of Christ shall stande vs in no force, vnlesse we applye it to our selues in suche sort, as God hath appoynted.

49. to stand in stead of, to take the place of, represent, do duty for; also ***instead of***, ***in the stead of***, ***in lieu of***. Also with indirect object.

a1500 *Gest of Robyn Hode* lxxxi. in Child *Ballads* III. 60 In a yeman's stede he may the stande, If thou greate nede haue. 1530 PALSGR. 733/2 Syns my lorde can nat be here him selfe to day, who shall stande in his stede. 1583 MELBANCKE *Philotimus* F iv b, Their banquet was ready..and Parmenio & Antigone stoode in steade of sewer and seruitours. 1612 *Benvenuto's Passenger* II. i. 395 Will stands instead of power, where wee cannot performe. 1847 C. BRONTË *J. Eyre* ii, To stand in the stead of a parent to a strange child she could not love. 1849 *Tait's Mag.* XVI. 58/1 Chemistry does not stand a man instead of dinner. 1870 DICKENS *E. Drood* xvii, I have undergone some mental distress..which has stood me in the stead of illness. 1882 STEVENSON *Fam. Stud.* 283 The rigidity of intricate metrical forms stood him in lieu of precise thought. 1893 *Temple Bar* XCIX. 68 A down-drawing of the corners of her mouth that stood her instead of a smile.

50. to let...stand. a. *lit.* To leave (a person or thing) undisturbed in an erect position. **b.** *fig.* To leave for the time without notice or discussion; to leave in abeyance, let alone.

For other literal examples, see 29, 32 a, 32 b.

c1205 LAY. 27159 An his riht honde he lette Lengres stonde. 1297 R. GLOUC. 1276 þe king þe wule londone bisegede uaste..Ac þo he hurde þat þe romeins icome were to þis londe, To hom he wende hasteliche & let londone stonde. a1300 *Cursor M.* 19601 Lat we nu þe prechurs stand, For to spek of a warraiand. a1300 *Harrow. Hell* 136 Ich lete hem [the gates of Hell] stonden and renne away. 1377 LANGL. *P. Pl.* B. xx. 101 Deth cam dryuende after and al to doust passhed..Lered ne lewed, he let no man stonde. c1400 *Beryn* 157 Pese, quod the hoost of Southwork, let stond þe wyndow glasid. 1535 COVERDALE *1 Sam.* xxiii. 13 Whan it was tolde Saul that Dauid was escaped from Cegila, he let his iourney stonde. a1810 TANNAHILL *Poems* (1846) 25 She has my vows, buy aye I let her stan', In hopes to win that bonnie lassie's han'. 1888 *Times* (weekly ed.) 22 June 13/3 To ask the Court to let the case stand. 1889 CONAN DOYLE *Micah Clarke* xi. 97 For my own claim, I let it stand for some time. 1898 H. NEWBOLT *He fell among Thieves* ii, Let the reckoning stand till day.

†**51.** The pres. pple. **standing**, placed before a sb. with which it agrees, or before a clause, has been used in certain 'absolute' constructions (cf. *during*, *pending*). **a.** = While (so-and-so) subsists, is retained, remains what it was. *Obs.*

c1380 WYCLIF *Sel. Wks.* III. 115 He [Christ] becom man, stondynge his godhed, þat he myȝt not leese. c1400 *Pilgr. Sowle* (Caxton) I. xiii. (1859) 9 Yet ouer this will I [Satan] preue by reson, that standing this filthe and dishoneste of synne with whiche he is entachyd, this lauure rather causeth hym to be juged to oure company. c1449 PECOCK *Repr.* v. xiii. 554 Not eny yuel, which mai not eesili be remedied, stonding al the good which bifore is rehercid to come bi the same bildingis. 1526 *Pilgr. Perf.* (W. de W. 1531) 205 b, For otherwyse (standynge the ordynate iustyce of god) he myght neuer haue..goten by meryt suche hye..dignitie. 1569 ABP. PARKER in *Corr.* (1853) 353, I think he should do this thing..better cheap than they may be bought from beyond the seas, standing the paper and goodness of his print.

b. = While (so-and-so) lasts; during. *Obs.*

c1500 MEDWALL *Nature* I. 323 (Brandl) Standyng the nonage of thys gentylman. 1512 in Willis & Clark *Cambridge* (1886) I. 609 Duryng the contynuaunce of the seid werkes and standyng the lyff and helth of the said John Wastell.

c. = When (so-and-so) is taken into account; considering, in view of. (The examples might be referred to a; but cf. d.) *Obs.*

c1528 WOLSEY in *Burnet's Hist. Ref.* (1679) I. Rec. II. 52 Which I suppose neither his Holiness nor any true Christian Man can do, standing the manifest occasions, presumptions, and apparent evidences to the contrary. 1532 MORE *Confut. Tindale* Wks. 720/1, I can not..perceyue what counsayle Tyndall can geue any manne towarde saluacion, standyng his frantike heresies agaynst free will.

d. As the first word of a clause (with or without *that*): The fact being that, considering *that*, since.

c1450 *Cov. Myst.* 190 Stondynge that ȝe be so wytty and wyse, Can ȝe owth tellyn how this werde was wrought? *Ibid.* 218 Stondynge ȝe wyl not graunt me grace, But for my synne that I xal dye, I pray ȝow kylle me here in this place. 1513 MORE *Rich. III* Wks. 59/1 And yt he could not well otherwise do, standing that ye Earle of warwik had so far moued already. 1526 *Pilgr. Perf.* (W. de W. 1531) 17 Thynkynge that it was impossyble for them to optayne and wynne the sayd lande, standynge that the people were so myghty and stronge.

V. Transitive senses.

* Originating from the conversion of an indirect into a direct object, from the omission of a prep., or from intrans. uses with cognate object.

52. To confront, face, oppose, encounter; to resist, withstand, bear the brunt of.

†**a.** an opponent. *Obs.*

c1325 *Chron. Eng.* 72 (Ritson) Yef the word of the spronge That eny mon the stode so longe,..Al thyn honour were leid adoun. c1435 *Torr. Portugal* 81 Full Euyll thow dourst hyme stond. c1450 HOLLAND *Howlat* 500 Was nane so stur in the steid micht stand him a start. 1470–85 MALORY *Arthur* x. lxxiv. 543 There myghte none stande hym a stroke. 1591 SHAKS. *1 Hen. VI*, I. i. 123 Hundreds he sent to Hell, and none durst stand him. c1611 CHAPMAN *Iliad* XXI. 508 This last heart, made him bold, To stand Achilles. 1615 —— *Odyss.* VI. 205 All but Nausicaa fled; but she fast stood...And still she stood him, as resolued to know What man he was. 1719 DE FOE *Crusoe* II. (Globe) 393 They resolved to stand them there. 1770 LANGHORNE *Plutarch, Crassus* (Rtldg.) 385/2 The young man cried out, 'They dare not stand us', and followed at full speed.

b. a blow or stroke, shot, attack, assault, siege, or the like; also laughter, raillery, indignation, etc.

c1330 *Arth. & Merl.* 9282 Non no miȝt stond his dent. 15.. *Adam Bel* 145 There myght no man stand hys stroke. 1605 SHAKS. *Lear* III. vii. 54, I am tyed to' th' Stake, And I must stand the Course. 1625 MASSINGER *New Way* IV. i, I, that haue liu'd a Souldier, And stood the enemies violent charge vndaunted. a1630 J. TAYLOR (Water P.) *Dog of War* B 2 b, He durst t'haue stood sterne Aiax frowne. 1670 DRYDEN *2nd Pt. Conq. Granada* III. i, The shock of such a curse I dare not stand. 1712 TICKELL *Spect.* No. 410 ¶4 My good Friend could not well stand the Raillery which was rising upon him. 1748 *Anson's Voy.* II. xiv. 286 Supposing that the troops..should..resolve to stand a general assault. 1803 *Pic Nic* No. 9 (1806) II. 87 Cecilia had stood a siege more than half as long as that of Troy. 1823 BYRON *Age of Bronze* xi, What is the simple standing of a shot, To listening long, and interrupting not? 1837 CARLYLE *Fr. Rev.* II. VI. i, He busy meanwhile training a few thousands to stand fire and be soldiers. 1890 *Illustr. Lond. News* 13 Sept. 331/1 These virgin walls have stood unmoved a hundred assaults. 1891 *Murray's Mag.* Sept. 382 She was ready to stand fire rather than retreat.

†**c.** To be exposed to (stress of weather, or the like). *Obs.*

1583 STUBBES *Anat. Abus.* II. 41 If the poore come to their houses, their gates be shut against them, where they standing frost and snow, haile, wind or raine whatsoeuer, are forced to tary two houres. 1607 SHAKS. *Cor.* v. iii. 74 Like a great Sea-marke standing euery flaw. 1726 LEONI *Alberti's Archit.* I. 45 *a*, Those parts..which stand all the changes of Weather..very soon decay.

53. a. To endure, undergo, be submitted to (a trial, test, ordeal, or the like). Usually (cf. sense 54), to come through or sustain successfully, (be able) to bear (a test, etc.). Said also of things.

1606 SHAKS. *Ant. & Cl.* I. iii. 74 And giue true euidence to his Loue, which stands An honourable Triall. 1610 —— *Temp.* IV. i. 7 All thy vexations Were but my trials of thy loue, and thou Hast strangely stood the test. 1712 ADDISON *Spect.* No. 409 ¶4 The celebrated Works of Antiquity, which have stood the Test of so many different Ages and Countries. 1742 BLAIR *Grave* 666 Pure as Silver from the Crucible, That twice has stood the Torture of the Fire And Inquisition of the Forge. 1814 MRS. J. WEST *Alicia de Lacy* IV. 217 'Of what shall we hereafter stand question', said the Earl of Hereford. 1822 LAMB *Elia* Ser. I. *Artif. Comedy* (init.), The business of their dramatic characters will not stand the moral test. 1825 *New Monthly Mag.* XV. 201 He has stood the ordeal of a London audience. 1890 *Blackw. Mag.* CXLVIII. 749/1 It would not be easy to get up a grievance which would stand a rigid examination.

b. spec. *to stand one's trial*: to be tried by a court for an offence. Also *slang*, in the same sense, *to stand the patter*. †*to stand suit*: to allow oneself to be sued.

1667 PEPYS *Diary* 27 Aug., Desiring that he may stand his trial in Parliament, if they will accuse him of any thing. 1685 P. HENRY *Diaries & Lett.* (1882) 344 Hee..sayes, hee wil stand suit, which if he doe, I know who wil get the better. 1726 SWIFT *Gulliver* I. vii, I sometimes thought of standing my trial. 1812 [see PATTER *sb.*[1] 1 b]. 1891 *Chamb. Jrnl.* 5 Sept. 571/1 He was obliged to stand his trial for forgery.

c. To submit to, offer to abide by (a judgement, decision, vote); to expose oneself to the chances of (a contested election: cf. 12).

a1700 EVELYN *Diary* 30 Nov. 1682, I was exceedingly indanger'd and importun'd to stand the election [for President of the R. S.]. 1713 ADDISON *Cato* II. ii, Bid him..Submit his actions to the publick censure, And stand the judgment of a Roman Senate. 1754 A. MURPHY *Gray's Inn Jrnl.* No. 86 ¶10 They would not be at a Loss for a proper Representative..whenever the Author of the *Polymetis* should be willing to stand the Poll. 1774 JOHNSON *Let. to G. Steevens* 21 Feb. in *Boswell*, I am desirous of nominating you, if you care to stand the ballot. 1789 MRS. PIOZZI *Journ. France* I. Pref. 5 [It] induces authors to venture forth, and stand a public decision. 1858 J. MARTINEAU *Stud. Chr.* 122 He who claims by the law, must stand the judgment of the law. 1889 GRETTON *Memory's Harkback* 244, I thought that the Prince Consort was lowering his position by standing a contest for the office. 1891 *Blackw. Mag.* CL. 147/1 All through his career he never stood a contested election.

d. *to stand one's chance*: to take one's chance, submit to what may befall one.

1796–7 JANE AUSTEN *Pride & Prej.* ii, Mrs. Long and her nieces must stand their chance.

†**e.** To abide by, obey, remain loyal to (an ordinance, etc.). *Obs. rare.*

c1450 *Merlin* vi. 99 The wise men and the high barouns..a-corded to stonde the ordenaunce of the archebisshop. 1573 *Reg. Privy Council Scot.* II. 265 Obleissis thame to stand and fulfill the injunctionis and articles quhilk wer aggreit be thame.

54. To face, encounter without flinching or retreating (an issue, hazard, etc.). Also in weaker sense, to be exposed or liable to (hazard, fortunes). (Cf. *stand to* 76 f.)

1594 SHAKS. *Rich. III* v. iv. 10 Slaue, I haue set my life vpon a cast, And I will stand the hazard of the Dye. 1607 —— *Timon* v. ii. 5 We stand much hazard, if they bring not Timon. a1619 FLETCHER *Knt. Malta* IV. ii, I am sorry ye are so poor, so weak a Gentleman, Able to stand no fortune. 1667 PEPYS *Diary* 2 Sept., He that serves a Prince must expect, and be contented to stand, all fortunes. 1705 COLLIER *Ess. Mor. Subj.* III. *Pain* 16 'Twas a noble Act of Faith to throw themselves upon Providence, to stand the Event, and face Death under the most frightful Form. 1792 CHARLOTTE SMITH *Desmond* I. 255 A gallant fellow, who had been in the former wars with the English, and stood the hazards of many a bloody day.

†**55.** To withstand, disobey, hold out against (a command). *Obs. rare.*

1605 SHAKS. *Lear* IV. i. 71 (Qo.) The superfluous and lust-dieted man That stands [*Fo.* slaues] your ordinance. c1800 *Bob Norice* vii. in Child *Ballads* II. 267 How daur you stand my bidding, Sir, When I bid you to flee?

56. ***to stand one's ground***: to maintain one's position against attack or opposition. Also *fig.*

1621 T. WILLIAMSON tr. *Goulart's Wise Vieillard* 99 Thou..wilt not from thy coullers flie, But stand thy ground couragiously. 1688 *Lett. conc. Pres. State Italy* 116 He could not have stood his ground in the Dispute. 1785 JEFFERSON *Corr.* Wks. 1859 I. 379, I have now no further fears of that Arret's standing its ground. 1804 NICHOLL in Owen *Wellesley Despatches* (1877) 530, I directed the picquets to stand their ground. 1849 MACAULAY *Hist. Eng.* vi. II. 115 He could not stand his ground against competitors who were willing to pay such a price for the favour of the court. 1891 *Strand Mag.* Jan. 77/1 The donkey..bravely stood his ground.

57. ***to stand a chance*** (also ***a good***, ***poor***, ***small***, etc. ***chance***; ***some***, ***little***, ***no chance***): to be likely to meet with some (specified or implied) piece of fortune, some danger, some good or ill luck. Const. *of* (something, doing something), *for*.

1725 *New Cant. Dict.* s.v. *Lay*, He stands a queer Lay; He stands an odd Chance, or is in great Danger. 1736 LEDIARD *Life of Marlborough* I. 319 The Duke stood a very ticklish Chance. 1803 *Pic Nic* No. 13 (1806) II. 211 They stood a fair chance of going to hell. 1845 M. PATTISON *Ess.* (1889) I. 18 Under such circumstances an obnoxious criminal stood..small chance of justice. 1848 *Jrnl. R. Agric. Soc.* IX. II. 281 He would have stood a fair chance for a prize. 1861 *Temple Bar* II. 539 Grey will stand no chance. 1889 F. C. PHILIPS *Ainslie's Courtship* I. vii. 100 He would stand no chance over the snow against your snow-shoes.

58. To endure (a physical trial, hardship, etc.) without hurt or damage, without succumbing or giving way: **a.** of persons and animals.

1839 T. MITCHELL *Frogs of Aristoph.* 73 *note*, A trumpet,..by which horses are proved, as to whether they will stand noises. 1853 LYTTON *My Novel* I. ix, 'But this climate—she could never stand it', said Riccabocca. 1887 *J. Coleman's Cattle* etc. *Gt. Brit.* 349 The Shropshire is a hardy sheep,..standing moisture better than severe cold. 1891 *Chamb. Jrnl.* 19 Sept. 608/1 Drivers have to stand all weathers. 1903 SIR M. G. GERARD *Leaves fr. Diaries* ii. 47 The great heat renders the tiger comparatively helpless—as he cannot stand the sun.

b. of things.

1756 C. LUCAS *Ess. Waters* I. 56 Common glass stands the utmost degree of fire without waste. 1777 [W. MARSHALL] *Minutes Agric.* 28 Apr., The green-cole and brown-cole stood the winter very well. 1864 *Jrnl. R. Agric. Soc.* XXV. II. 360 Turnips will stand almost any amount of frost. 1875 F. J. BIRD *Dyer's Hand-bk.* 45 Very fine shades of blue that will stand soaping. 1890 *Temple Bar* July 420 These dyes will not stand water.

fig. 1885 *Manch. Exam.* 13 July 5/3 These luxuriant growths of Liberal aspirations will stand pruning. 1885 *Law Times Rep.* LIII. 480/2 To avoid..the consequences of having sent in a bill which would not stand taxation.

59. a. To put up with, tolerate; (to be able or willing) to endure.

1626 G. SANDYS *Ovid's Met.* x. 198 A Stag..who..well pleas'd would stand The gentle strokings of a stranger's hand. 1710 STEELE *Tatler* No. 225 ¶2 It is often said, such an one cannot stand the Mention of such a Circumstance. 1750 CHESTERF. *Lett.* III. ccxxxvi. 76 Till I am satisfied in these particulars, you and I must by no means meet: I could not possibly stand it. 1816 SCOTT *Antiq.* xliv, Weel, I thought there was naething but what your honour could bae studden in the way o' agreeable conversation. 1821 [see NONSENSE 1 c]. 1831 PALMERSTON in Bulwer *Life* II. viii. 93 England never would stand the occupation of the Tagus by the French. 1858 CARLYLE *Fredk. Gt.* II. iv. (1872) I. 66 Baiern..could not stand to be balked after twenty-years possession. 1869 TROLLOPE *He Knew*, etc. lxv. (1878) 361 She..declared that she was not going to stand that kind of thing. 1891 *19th Cent.* Dec. 859 The Court cannot and will not stand..journalistic personalities about its members.

b. Familiarly in more trivial sense (with negative expressed or implied): To reconcile oneself to, be favourably disposed to, feel any liking for (a repugnant or distasteful object).

1879 Mrs. Oliphant *Within Precincts* xx. II. 60 She could not stand that Manager fellow. I could not stand him myself. **1919** Conrad *Arrow of Gold* iv. ii. 162 Captain Blunt jumped up. 'My mother can't stand tobacco smoke.' **1949** 'G. Orwell' *1984* ii. iii. 134 'I could have stood it if it hadn't been for one thing,' he said. **1964** I. Murdoch *Italian Girl* iii. 39 Do turn that music off, would you? I can't stand music in the background. **1981** E. A. Taylor *Cable Car Murder* (1983) xxiii. 170 Don't get me started on her; I can't stand her.

60. ***to stand watch, to stand a*** or ***one's watch***: to keep watch, perform the duty of a watch. Now chiefly *Naut.*, to take part in the duty of a 'watch' during a prescribed time.

1605 Shaks. *Macb.* v. v. 33 As I did stand my watch vpon the Hill. *c* **1730** Ramsay *Vision* iv, My wakryfe mynd..still stude watch. **1883** *Century Mag.* XXVI. 911/1 Fenton stood the first watch. **1890** *Chamb. Jrnl.* 21 June 389/1 He's the ship's carpenter, and stands watch as second officer.

61. a. colloq. ***to stand one's hand*** (***to***), ***to stand shot*** (***to***), rarely ***to stand the shot***: to meet the expenses, pay the bill (for all): see shot *sb.*[1] 23. Similarly ***to stand Sam, treat***: see Sam *sb.*[1] 1, treat *sb.*[1] 4 d.

1821 [see shot *sb.*[1] 23]. **1823–1887** [see Sam *sb.*[1] 1]. **1837–1885** [see treat *sb.*[1] 4 d]. **1883** J. Purves in *Contemp. Rev.* Sept. 356 At the one year's end and the beginning of the other, he must stand his hand like the rest. **1890** *Sat. Rev.* 3 May 61/2 Mr. Lowther..requested that his speech might be published..offering to take the consequences and stand the shot. **1892** H. Nisbet *Bushranger's Sweetheart* viii. 58, I used to see her..'standing her hand' liberally to all who happened to be in the bar.

b. To bear the expense of, make a present of, pay for (a treat); to put up or make a present of (a sum of money), esp. as part of a larger amount sought. Const. *to* or dative of the recipient. *colloq.*

1835 Dickens *Sk. Boz, Dancing Academy*, Mr. Augustus Cooper..'stood' considerable quantities of spirits-and-water. **1840** Thackeray *Shabby-genteel Story* ii, I'll stand glasses round to his jolly good health! **1844** Dickens *Let.* 22 July (1977) IV. 157 If you should decide to come, I will very gladly stand £10 of this Thirty. **1848** Thackeray *Van. Fair* xiii, I know my father will stand something handsome. **1890** *Lippincott's Mag.* May 633 I'll stand you a dinner. **1891** *Sat. Rev.* 18 Apr. 482/1 They..stood drinks promiscuously to all-comers. **1914** G. B. Shaw *Fanny's First Play* i. 177, I cant pay the fine and get him out; but if youll stand 3 pounds I'll stand one; and thatll do it. **1970** G. F. Newman *Sir, you Bastard* viii. 214 Friends able to stand five-thousand pounds surety for his bail.

c. With indirect obj. only = to stand drink for (a person or persons). *colloq.*

1894 Mrs. Dyan *All in Man's Keeping* (1899) 173 Sit down here, and I'll stand you both.

62. ***to stand the market***: to attend market in order to sell goods or to hire oneself out. *dial.*

Cf. *to overstand one's market* s.v. market *sb.* 6.

1866 W. Dobson *Diary of P. Walkden* 42 *note*, It was customary for carts with cannel to 'stand the market'. **1886** *Cheshire Gloss.* s.v., Farmers' wives call it *standing the market* when they sell their butter, eggs, &c., in the open market instead of taking them to shops or from house to house. **1886** *Ripon Chron.* 4 Sept. 3/5 The first harvest hirings were held at Malton on Saturday, when there was a good number of men 'standing the market'.

63. *Racing*, etc. **a.** To bet, wager (a sum of money) *on* or *about* a result. ? *Obs.*

1804 Chifney *Genius Genuine* 155 The fellow had asked him to stand fifty guineas with him on the match. **1825** *New Monthly Mag.* XVI. 375 Made up my mind..to stand something about the double event, if I could get any thing worth having.

b. To bet on the success of, 'back' (a horse).

1890 *Daily News* 10 Dec. 3/7 Backers were also well on the mark in standing Alfred for the Park selling Hurdle. **1891** *Standard* 9 Mar. 3/7, I shall stand Flower of the Forest for the..Hunters' Steeplechase. **1892** *Ibid.* 25 July 2/5, I shall stand him to carry his 12lb. penalty successfully.

64. *Hunting.* Of a dog: To set (game). Cf. 4 c.

1863 W. C. Baldwin *Afr. Hunting* viii. 333 Juno returns and stands them one after another. **1892** *Field* 7 May 671/3 He finds his birds, and stands them well.

** Causative.

65. a. To cause to stand; to place or leave standing; to set (a thing) upright; to place firmly or steadily in a specified position. Also with advs., as *up*. Only colloq. or in familiar writing.

1837 Dickens *Pickw.* xxvi, The pretty house-maid had stood the candle on the floor. **1848** —— *Dombey* ii, A plump and apple-faced boy, whom he stood down on the floor. **1848** *Jrnl. R. Agric. Soc.* IX. ii. 560 Sharpen the pole..and stand it in the ground. **1850** Dickens *David Copp.* xxxii A low iron [fender], with two flat bars at top to stand plates upon. **1873** M. Collins *Squire Silchester* I. i. 17 She would ..stand her in a corner if she gave herself airs. **1878** *Scribner's Monthly* XV. 763/1, I stood my rifle against a tree. **1889** 'Mrs. Alexander' *Crooked Path* I. v. 153 I've stood them [a chest of drawers] open all last night. **1892** *Illustr. Sporting & Dram. News* 17 Dec. 494/3 We recommend the driver to stand his horse in running water. **1894** *Jrnl. R. Agric. Soc.* June 230 Owners were compelled to resort to the fields near the borough to stand their horses. **1905** Wastell & Bayley *Hand Camera* 126 The negatives..may be stood up to dry... They must not be stood close together in a rack.

b. *refl. rare.*

1848 Dickens *Dombey* xxv, The Captain then stood himself up in a corner, against the wall.

VI. With prepositions. (The more literal and obvious meanings are left to be inferred from the simple senses above and those of the various prepositions.)

66. stand about ——.

a. *lit.* To surround; = L. *circumstare.*

c **1368** Chaucer *Compl. Pity* 36 Aboute hir herse there stoden lustely..Bounte parfyt [etc.]. **1535** Coverdale *Job* xxix. 4 When my housholde folkes stode aboute me. **1849** M. Arnold *Sick King Bokhara* 105 They who stood about the King.

†**b.** *fig.* To spend time upon, stay to consider, wait for (something to be done). *Obs.*

c **1555** Towrson in Hakluyt *Voy.* (1599) II. ii. 30 As for their arrowes, I haue not as yet seene any of them, for they had wrapped them up close, and because I was busie I could not stand about it, to haue them open them. **1579** Fulke *Refut. Rastell* 708, I will not stand about this trifling cauil.

67. stand against, † again(s ——.

a. To stand and face (an antagonist, etc.); to withstand, oppose, resist. Also, to resist successfully, hold one's ground against. Said also of things. (Cf. 10 and again-stand *v.*)

a **1122** *O.E. Chron.* (Laud MS.) an. 1048 þæh him lað wære þæt hi onȝean heora cyne-hlaford standan sceoldan. *c* **1200** Ormin 2785 He maȝȝ stanndenn wel onnȝæn þe deofell wiþþ swillc wæpenn. *a* **1300** *Cursor M.* 4096 þi bod i aght noght to stand agayn. *c* **1330** *Arth. & Merl.* 4842 Armes non, ywrouȝt wiþ hond, Oȝain his dent no miȝt stond. *a* **1400–50** *Wars Alex.* 1322 Was nane sa stiffe in þat stoure miȝt stand him agayn. *c* **1450** *Merlin* i Our strengthes..may nought..again him stonde in no diffence. **1593** Abp. Bancroft *Dang. Posit.* iv. xii. 173 That the people are inflamed with zeale, and that it is impossible to stand against it. **1687** Burnet *Contin. Reply to Varillas* 102 He finding that he was not able to stand against so strong a Party, submitted himself to them. **1820** Scott *Monast.* Introd. Ep., I hae fund something now that stands again' the spade, as if it were neither earth nor stane. **1833** Nyren *Yng. Cricketer's Tutor* 114 He [Aylward] had to stand against the finest bowling of the day—that of Lumpy. **1881** Mrs. Lynn Linton *My Love* II. viii. 156, I will not stand against your happiness. **1890** Conan Doyle *Firm of Girdlestone* xi. 85 No firm could stand against such a run of bad luck.

†**b.** To feel repugnance for. *Obs.*

1551 Robinson tr. *More's Utopia* i. (1895) 36 [Ought I to advance myself] to a welthyer condition..by that meanes that my mynde standethe cleane agaynst [*a qua abhorret animus*]?

68. stand at ——.

†**a.** To abide by, obey (a decree, etc.) (Cf. *stand to* 76 a.) *Obs.*

c **1290** *S. Eng. Leg.* 160/1874 þat heo don sikernesse for-to stonde at holi churche lawe And to þe lokinge of holi churche. *c* **1386** Chaucer *Prol.* 778 And if yow lyketh alle, by oon assent, ffor to stonden at my Iuggement. *c* **1480** Henryson *Fables, Fox, Wolf & Husbandman* 81 3e sall be sworne to stand at my decreit. **1581** *Exch. Rolls Scot.* XXI. 551 Bayth the saidis parties oblissis thame to stand and abyid thairat bot any reclaming.

†**b.** To assist or be present at. *Obs. rare*$^{-1}$.

1746 Hervey *Medit.* (1818) 79, I..must stand at the dissolution of all terrestrial things, and be an attendant on the burial of nature.

c. To stick, hesitate or scruple at; to allow oneself to be deterred, impeded or checked by.

1756–7 tr. *Keysler's Trav.* (1760) I. 2 Men of large fortunes stand at no price for Swiss cattle. **1808** *Sporting Mag.* XXXII. 122 We don't stand at a trifle. **1837** Carlyle *Fr. Rev.* III. v. v, To stand at no obstacles; to heed no considerations, human or divine. **1890** F. C. Philips & Wills *Sybil Ross* xx. 147 He is not a man who stands at trifles.

69. stand before ——.

a. To continue in the presence of, attend upon (a lord). Chiefly *Biblical*: see concordances.

c **1200** Ormin 206 Witt tu þatt icc amm Gabriæl þatt æfre & æfre stannde Biforenn Godd, to lutenn himm. *c* **1400** *Rule St. Benet* (Prose) 19 Loke ye do yure seruise als ye stode by-fore god almihti. *c* **1440** *Gesta Rom.* xlviii. 211 (Addit. MS.) [He] stode atte borde before the Erle, and served hym curtesly [*Harl.* gentilmanly stode afore him].

b. To come or be brought into the presence of, to confront (a person or assembly, a king, judge, tribunal, etc.).

a **1225** *Leg. Kath.* 632 Hwen ȝe stondeð biforen kinges & eorles, ne þenche ȝe neauer hwet ne hu ȝe schulen seggen. **1377** Langl. *P. Pl.* B. Prol. 183 A mous..Stroke forth sternly and stode biforn hem alle. *c* **1386** Chaucer *Man of Law's T.* 520 For as the lomb toward his deeth is brought So stant this Innocent bifore the kyng. *c* **1450** tr. *De Imitatione* i. xxiv. 32 In all þinges beholde þe ende, & how þou shalt stonde before þe rightwise Juge. **1526** Tindale *Rev.* xx. 12 And I sawe the deed, both grett and smale stonde before God. **1819** S. Rogers *Human Life* 586 Alone before his judges in array [He] Stands for his life.

c. To confront (an adversary). Usually with *can* etc. negatively or interrogatively: To maintain one's ground against. (Cf. 10.)

For Bible examples (lit. from Heb.), see concordances. *c* **1205** Lay. 21377 Her stondeð us biuoren vre ifan alle icoren. **1652** Needham tr. *Selden's Mare Cl.* 51 None was able to stand before him either by Sea or Land. **1721** De Foe *Mem. Cavalier* (1840) 87 Nothing could stand before them; the Spanish army..was every where defeated. **1879** M. J. Guest *Lect. Hist. Eng.* xlviii. 485 The Cavaliers could not stand before them.

†**d.** To protect, shield (a person) by placing oneself in front of him. *Obs. rare.*

c **1205** Lay. 25938 For ȝif he cumeð a-bolȝen mid his balu ræsen, nes he neuere iboren þe maȝen stonden þe biuoren.

e. *Hunting.* Of a fox: To hold out when pursued by (hounds). Cf. *stand up* 103 h.

1892 *Illustr. Sporting & Dram. News* 26 Nov. 400/3 A bag fox stood before hounds for two hours and a quarter till the pack were called off.

70. stand by ——.

a. *lit.* To station oneself or remain stationed beside (a person); usually as a helper, advocate, sympathizer, or the like (passing into sense c).

c **1250** *Gen. & Ex.* 3666 Ches ðe nu her seuenti Wise men to stonden ðe bi. *c* **1275** *Passion of our Lord* 163 in *O.E. Misc.* 42 þer com of heuene on engel and stod hym vaste by. **14..** *26 Pol. Poems* 53/77 And euere by trouþe stondes wreche, For wreche is goddis champioun. **1611** Bible *Zech.* iv. 14 These are the two annointed ones, that stand by the Lord of the whole earth. *a* **1700** Evelyn *Diary* 7 Dec. 1680, He had likewise the assistance of what Counsel he would, to direct him in his plea, who stood by him. **1849** Macaulay *Hist. Eng.* v. I. 666 His son and daughter stood by him at the bar.

b. *Naut.* To prepare to work (a gun, rope, etc.).

1669 Sturmy *Mariner's Mag.* v. xii. 46 When they be required to stand by a great Gun in time of Fight. **1867** Smyth *Sailor's Word-bk.*, To *stand by* a rope, is to take hold of it; *the anchor*, prepare to let go. **1897** Ansted *Dict. Sea Terms*, *Stand by.*—An order to be ready to do something; as 'Stand by the anchor', *i.e.* make ready to let go the anchor.

c. *fig.* (cf. a). To support, assist, protect, defend (a person, a cause, etc.); to uphold the interests of, take the side of, be faithful or loyal to.

1530 Palsgr. 733/1, I stande by, or I assyste a man in an acte, *je assiste*. Go to it, man, be nat a frayde, I wyll stande by the who so ever come. *a* **1586** Sidney *Ps.* x. vii, Lift up thy heav'nly hand, And by the silly stand. **1681** Nevile *Plato Rediv.* 263 That if they could make an honest Government, they should be stood by (as the Word then was) by the Army. **1687** Jas. II in *Magd. Coll.* (O.H.S.) 218, I will stand by them who stand by me. **1768** Boswell *Corsica* ii. 100 The house of Matra in Corsica, which stood by the republick. **1855** Macaulay *Hist. Eng.* xvii. IV. 54 To stand by the liberties of England and the Protestant religion, and, if necessary, to die for them. **1855** Trollope *Warden* iii, Surely he was bound to stand by his order. **1874** Stubbs *Const. Hist.* I. x. 316 The clergy stood by the king in his struggle with the feudatories.

†*Of a thing.* *a* **1770** Jortin *Serm.* (1787) IV. 35 This amiable quality will stand by him, will be a protector and benefactor to him in all stations.

d. To adhere to, maintain, abide by (a statement, agreement or the like).

c **1386** Chaucer *Wife's T.* 159 Thy lyf is sauf, for I wol stond therby, Vp-on my lyf, the queene wol seye as I. *c* **1400** *Brut* 329, & þese þingez þey profered hem self, if þe King wold, certey[n]ly to preue & stonde by. **1693** in Picton *L'pool. Munic. Rec.* (1883) I. 300 Whatever Ald[m] Clayton shall do..y[e] town will confirme and stand by. **1849** *Tait's Mag.* XVI. 158/1 We mean to stand by the assertion. **1891** *Review of Rev.* 15 Sept. 229/2 The Queen has..avowed her serious purpose to stand by her oath.

†**e.** To rest or depend upon; to be caused by, derived from, or owing to. *Obs.*

1471 *Paston Lett.* III. 31 And ther ayenst ye shold loose iij *li.* of the ferme of the maner yerly, whych standyth by undyr wood. **1477** *Rolls of Parlt.* VI. 188/1 The defense of this Lond stondeth moche by Archers. **1530** Palsgr. 733/1 This towne standeth by artificers: *ceste ville se mayntient par gens mecanicques*. **1547** Boorde *Introd. Knowl.* iv. (1870) 137 Muche of theyr lyuyng standeth by stelyng and robbyng. **1589** Puttenham *Eng. Poesie* ii. i. (Arb.) 78 It is said by such as professe the Mathematicall sciences, that all things stand by proportion.

†**f.** To approach in character or quality; to be nearly related to. *Obs. rare.*

c **1530** *Judic. Urines* ii. vii. 26 b, Vryne that is Ielowe and standet most by whyttenes. *Ibid.* ii. viii. 32 b, Color Citrine standith by color rubea & by fleume, but more by color rubea than by fleume.

71. stand for ——.

a. To uphold, defend (a cause, etc.); to support, take the part of (a person). Also, † ***to stand hard for***.

a **1300** *Cursor M.* 18933 To stand ai stitli for þe fai, And thrali preche al crist lai. *c* **1380** Wyclif *Wks.* (1880) 24 For to meyntene goddis lawe and stond for his worschipe. **1567** *Gude & Godlie B.* (S.T.S.) 142 For Christis word se ȝe stand for it. **1593** Abp. Bancroft *Dang. Posit.* iv. xiv. 179 Certaine ..men..would shortly take vpon them the defence of the cause, which he and his brethren in prison stood-for. **1642** *Prince Rupert his Declaration* 6 The Lord prosper the worke of their hands who stand for God and King Charles. **1711** Addison *Spect.* No. 34 ¶10 Every Man at first stood hard for his Friend. **1842** Browning *Cavalier Tunes* i. i, Kentish Sir Byng stood for his King. **1847** Tennyson *Princess* v. 169, I beheld her, when she rose..and storming in extremes, Stood for her cause.

†**b.** To insist on, urge (a view, proposal, etc.); to support, maintain (a theory, thesis); to strive for, try to obtain or bring about, insist on having. Also, ***to stand hard for. to stand for't***, ? to defend one's claim as against others. *Obs.*

1531 *Abstr. Protocols Town Clerks of Glasgow* (1897) IV. 39 Gaef sa beis that ther be ony mair Anwell tane nor fyf crownis..the sayd Robert or his airis sall pas to the toder part and stand for raleyf of the samyne. **1616** B. Jonson *Devil an Ass* i. vi. 36 All that pretend, to stand for't o' the Stage. **1618** Bolton *Florus* iii. xii. (1636) 212 What cause was there why the People of Rome should stand so hard for fields or food [*agros et cibaria flagitaret*]? **1643** Trapp *Comm. Gen.* xlviii. 19 The Jewish converts stood hard for a mixture of Christ and Moses. **1676** H. More *Remarks* Contents b v, That Experiment of Regius..can be no instance of such an Attraction and Rarefaction as this Author stands for. **1690** Norris *Beatitudes* (1694) I. 41 But that which I stand for is this, That we ought not [etc.]. **1726** Shelvocke *Voy. round World* 165 He stands more for his honour than any money.

†**c.** *I stand for it* (written also *foird*, *forde*), as parenthesis = I warrant, I'll go bail for it. *Sc.*

c **1480** HENRYSON *Mor. Fab.* III. (*Cock & Fox*) xxiv, Than will thay stint, I stand for it, and not steir. **1535** LYNDESAY *Satyre* 3982 Thou art an limmer, I stand foird. **1570** *Satir. Poems Reform.* xiv. 103, I stand forde.

†**d.** ***to stand in wax for***: to be legal security for (another). *Obs.*

1608 *Yorksh. Trag.* i, He has consumed al, pawnd his lands, and made his vniversitie brother stand in waxe for him—Thers a fine phrase for a scrivener.

†**e.** Of custom, sentiments: To be on the side of. *Obs.*

1581 MULCASTER *Positions* xxxviii. (1887) 168 Seeing my countrie giues me leaue, and her custome standes for me. **1788** *New London Mag.* 428 The King's affections standing for this disposition of the crown, he was gained at last to ouerlook his sisters and break through his father's will.

f. To be reckoned or alleged for; to be counted or considered as; to serve in lieu of. ***to stand for nothing***, to be worthless, of no avail; ***to stand for something***, to have some value or importance. Also with dative of person.

a **1300** *Cursor M.* 9972 It es vs sett als in þe marche, And standes vs for sceild and targe Agains all vre wiþerwyns. *Ibid.* 26601 And for þe scam man thinc scriuand, It sal for part o penance stand. *c* **1374** CHAUCER *Boeth.* IV. pr. ii. (1868) 112 Yif power faylеþ þe wille nis but in ydel and stant for nauȝt. **1563** BECON *Reliques of Rome* 211 b, For that daye yt he heareth a masse, .. if a man die: it shall stand hym for hys housell. **1579** GOSSON *Sch. Abuse* (Arb.) 51 Iupiter himself shall stand for example. **1659** N. R. *Prov., Eng. Fr.* etc. 54 He stands for a Cipher. **1686** tr. *Chardin's Trav. Persia* 23 The two Audiences which he had receiv'd should stand for nothing. **1863** MRS. OLIPHANT *Salem Chapel* ii. 28 He began to divine faintly, .. that external circumstances do stand for something.

†**g.** Of a money-payment: To be reckoned sufficient for, to free from obligation. *Obs.*

1389 in *Eng. Gilds* (1870) 10 And ȝif þe man wil haue his wyf a suster, þan schal þt paiement stonde for hem bothe.

h. To represent, be in the place of, take the place of, do duty for.

1567 SANDERS *Rocke of Churche* ii. 31 According to the Greeke phrase (where the comparatiue standeth for the superlatiue). **1595** W. W[ARNER] *Plautus' Menæcmi* I. ii. (1779) 119 *Cylindrus.* That's ten persons in all. *Erotium.* How many? *Cylindrus.* Ten, for I warrant you that Parasite may stand for eight at his vittels. **1596** SHAKS. *1 Hen. IV*, II. iv. 477 Doe thou stand for mee, and Ile play my Father. **1612** CHAPMAN *Rev. Bussy D'Ambois* III. iii. 5 You two onely Stand for our Armie. **1861** PALEY *Æschylus* (ed. 2) *Supplices* 968 *note*, Here therefore ταῦτα seems to stand for τάδε. **1889** CONAN DOYLE *Micah Clarke* xxxii. 359, I had now to attend to my appearance, for in truth I might have stood for one of those gory giants with whom [etc.].

i. To represent by way of symbol or sign; to be an expression or emblem of.

1612 BRINSLEY *Lud. Lit.* 25 As if you aske what [number] I. stands for, what V. what X. what L. &c. **1662** J. DAVIES tr. *Mandelslo's Trav.* 226 These Figures stand not for any word that hath any particular signification in their Language. **1729** BUTLER *Serm.* Wks. 1874 II. Pref. 7 It is impossible that words can always stand for the same ideas, even in the same author. **1823** *Mirror* I. 165/2 C stands for Cupid. **1911** PETRIE *Revolutions of Civilisation* v. 95 In architecture, Salisbury Cathedral stands for the perfect acquirement of freedom and grace without the least trace of over-elaboration.

j. To represent by way of specimen.

1593 SHAKS. *Lucr.* 1428 A hand, a foote, a face, a leg, a head, Stood for the whole to be imagined.

k. *Naut.* To sail or steer towards. (Cf. 36.)

1628 DIGBY *Voy. Mediterr.* (Camden) 13, I stood for the Barbarie shore. **1748** *Anson's Voy.* I. x. 105 We stood for the Island of Juan Fernandez. **1814** SCOTT *Diary* 11 Aug. in *Lockhart* (1837) III. 181 We are standing for some creek or harbour, called Ringholm-bay. **1861** SMILES *Engineers* II. 36 Wearing ship, they stood once more for the coast.

l. ***to stand*** (as candidate, as sponsor) ***for***: see senses 12, 15 b.

m. To endure, put up with, tolerate. Cf. sense 59. *colloq.* (orig. *U.S.*).

1896 ADE *Artie* xii. 107 They say they can't stand for that kind o' work. **1911** R. W. CHAMBERS *Common Law* x. 282 It's going to be hard for her. She can't stand for a mutt—and it's the only sort that will marry her. **1916** E. V. LUCAS *Vermilion Box* lxvi. 72 So crabbed and odd and disagreeable that the store let him go... Two weeks ago he lost his position in the country store. Even that place could not stand for him. **1927** *Punch* 20 Apr. 428/1 The English public, it appears, will only stand for American films. **1952** M. LASKI *Village* xix. 265 Me and Dad have stood for a lot of things .. but there's one thing we won't stand for and that's any hole-and-corner business. **1967** N. FREELING *Strike out where not Applicable* 77 Marguerite wouldn't have stood for being humiliated. **1973** E.-J. BAHR *Nice Neighbourhood* i. 6 He was a man who just purely couldn't stand for anyone .. to be asleep when he was awake.

72. stand in ——.

a. To be dressed in, to be actually wearing. ? *Obs.* (Cf. *stand up* 103 g.)

13.. *Coer de L.* 830 Sche rent the robe that sche in stod. *c* **1374** CHAUCER *Troylus* II. 534 So sore hath she me wounded That stod in blak wyth lokyng of here eyen. **1423** JAS. I *Kingis Q.* lxxxviii, Tho that thou seis stond in capis wyde. ? *a* **1500** *Merch. & Son* 206 in Hazl. *E.P.P.* I. 146 Gode had he no more, but ryght as he in stode. **1616** B. JONSON *Devil an Ass* I. vi. 64, I am, Sir, to inioy this cloake, I stand in, Freely, and as your gift.

†**b.** To persevere or persist in, remain obstinate or steadfast in (a state, course of action, purpose, opinion, assertion). *Obs.*

a **1300** *Cursor M.* 18697 Mistru noght þat es to tru, Bot stand in stedfast trouth fra nu. **1390** GOWER *Conf.* I. 141 The sinne Which thou hast longe stonden inne. *c* **1400** *Rule St. Benet*, etc. 143 Giffe sho standis in hir purpose eftir þe space of sex monethes. **1553** ASCHAM in *Lett. Lit. Men* (Camden) 14 And in this myne opinion I stand the more gladlie. **1586** H. BARROWE *Exam.* (1593) B iij, I said that sin, obstinatly stood in, did excommunicate. **1595** in *Cath. Rec. Soc. Publ.* V. 350 The martyr .. answered 'No', in which denialle he stoode before the Judges eaven to his last end. *a* **1632** T. TAYLOR *God's Judgements* I. I. x. (1642) 27 Trajan .. caused five holy Virgins to be burned for standing in the profession of the Truth.

†**c.** ***to stand in it***: to remain firm or obstinate, persist in one's purpose or attitude; esp. to persist in asserting, maintain stoutly (followed by clause with or without *that*). Similarly, ***to stand in this*** (***that*** ..). *Obs.*

1572 tr. *Buchanan's Detect. Mary Q. Scots* E iiij b, Quhen he had stoode in it a quhile and wald nat appeare .., at length constraynit with feare of exile and punitioun, he yelded. **1583** STOCKER *Civ. Warres Lowe C.* IV. 30 b, Except the Prior and three others of his Couent, who obstinately stood in it, and therefore were likewise .. tourned out of the Toune. **1610** HEALEY *St. Aug. Citie of God* XIII. xvii. (1620) 457 They stand in this also, that earthly bodies cannot be eternal. **1682** N. O. *Boileau's Lutrin* IV. Arg., This Counter-Scuffle, I dare stand in't, The Goddess Discord had a hand in't. **1682** BUNYAN *Holy War* (1905) 279 Both [= each] would stand in it that he told the truth. **1712** STEELE *Spect.* No. 534 ¶1 This cunning Hussey can lay Letters in my way .. and then stand in it she knows nothing of it.

†**d.** To dwell on, enlarge upon, discuss at large, insist on (a topic, a point in argument). Also ***to stand long in***. *Obs.*

a **1556** CHANCELOUR in Hakluyt *Voy.* (1598) I. 238, I will not stande in description of their buildinges. **1579** W. WILKINSON *Confut. Fam. Love* 16 b, Is ech circumstance to be sifted and stode in? **1606** G. WOODCOCKE *Hist. Ivstine* XII. 52 When Clytus .. defended the fame of Phillip, and stoode in the praise of his Noble and worthy acts. **1618** W. LAWSON *New Orch. & Garden* iii. (1623) 6, I haue stood somewhat long in this point.

†**e.** To insist upon having. *Obs. rare*$^{-1}$.

1588 SHAKS. *Tit. A.* IV. iv. 105 And if he stand in [*Fol. 4 and mod. edd.* on] Hostage for his safety, Bid him demaund what pledge will please him best.

†**f.** ***to stand in .. terms***: to be in a specified relation, on a certain footing *with* (a person). Also (without *with*), to be in a specified state or condition. *Obs.*

1543, 1653 [see TERM *sb.* 9 a]. **1600** HOLLAND *Livy* XXII. xxii. 445 Whiles Spaine stood in these tearms [*hoc statu rerum in Hispania*]. *Ibid.* XXXI. x. 779 He then addressed his letters unto the Senate, signifying in how bad termes the province stood [*quo in tumultu prouincia esset*]. **1633** BP. HALL *Hard Texts* Ps. li. 12 How can I, O Lord, be other then .. miserable, whiles I stand in these termes with thee?

†**g.** ***to stand in terms***: to dispute or contend *with* (a person). *Obs.*

a **1562** G. CAVENDISH *Wolsey* (1893) 178 Sir, I do not entend to stand in termes with yow in this matter. *a* **1568** ASCHAM *Scholem.* I. (Arb.) 58 To contrarie, or to stand in termes with an old man, was more heinous, than in som place, to rebuke and scolde with his owne father.

h. Of things: † To reside or inhere in; to be an attribute of (*obs.*); to rest or depend upon (something) as its ground of existence (*arch.*).

a **1300** *Cursor M.* 22251 O rome Imparre þe dignite Ne mai na wai al perist be, For in þaa kinges sal it stand Ai to-quils þai ar lastand. *c* **1380** WYCLIF *Wks.* (1880) 78 Whanne presthod stod in holy prestis of lif & studiouse & kunnynge. **1450–80** tr. *Secreta Secret.* xxvii. 20 It is well perilous when the lyf of a man stondith in the wille of oo persone. **1538** STARKEY *England* 79 In them [the yeomanry] stondyth the chefe defence of Englond. **1549** *Bk. Com. Prayer, Matins*, O God .. in knowledge of whome standeth oure eternall life. **1639** FULLER *Holy War* II. xl. (1640) 98 Victory standeth as little in the number of souldiers, as verity in the plurality of voyces. **1895** DENNEY *Stud. Theol.* ix. 223 A faith standing not in the wisdom of man but in the power of God.

†**i.** To consist of, have as its essence. *Obs.*

c **1386** CHAUCER *Merch. T.* 778 Somme clerkes holden that felicitee Stant in delit. *c* **1400** *Rom. Rose* 5581 Richesse stont in suffisaunce And no-thing in habundaunce. *c* **1460** FORTESCUE *Abs. & Lim. Mon.* vi. (1885) 120 The kynges yerely expenses stonden in charges ordinarie, and in charges extra ordinarie. **1526** *Pilgr. Perf.* (W. de W. 1531) 1 The selfe pilgrymage, which consysteth or standeth in vij dayes iourney. **1551** T. WILSON *Logic* (1580) 83 b, They fell to reasonyng with argumentes, that .. stoode in plaine buffettes. **1612** T. TAYLOR *Comm. Titus* i. 8. (1619) 177 The consecration stood likewise in fowre things.

†**73. stand of ——.**

a. To consist of. (Cf. 72 i.) *Obs.*

1390 GOWER *Conf.* II. 84 Of bodies sevene in special With foure spiritz joynt withal Stant the substance of this matiere. **1564–5** *Form Prayers Genev. & Scot.* (1584) M 8 b, Which Church we call vniuersall, because it consisteth and standeth of all tongues and Nations. **1600** HOLLAND *Livy* XXXII. xvi. 818 There were two Armadaes set out of Asia, the one .. consisting of foure and twentie saile of Quinqueremes: the other .. stood of twentie covert ships with decks and hatches. **1654** Z. COKE *Logick* 147 An induction standing of particular propositions.

b. By substitution of *of* for *on*: To dwell or insist on (a point); = *stand on* 74 j. *Obs.*

1599 THYNNE *Animadv.* (1875) 66 Whereof I wyll not stande at this tyme.

74. stand on ——.

†**a.** In fig. phrases with literal wording: see 78 a.

1579 LYLY *Euphues* (Arb.) 117 Stande thou on thy pantuffles, and shee will vayle bonnet. **1594** [see PANTOFLE b].

b. To base one's arguments or argumentative position on, 'take one's stand on'. Cf. 78 c.

1613 SHAKS. *Hen. VIII*, V. i. 123 The good I stand on, is my Truth and Honestie. **1693** CONGREVE *Old Bach.* Prol., So, standing only on his good Behaviour, He's very civil, and entreats your Favour. **1864** NEWMAN *Apol.* ii. (1904) 31/2 As to the Sacraments and Sacramental rites, I stood on the Prayer Book.

c. Of an immaterial thing: To be grounded or based on. †Also, to be contingent on; to consist in or arise from. *Obs.* Cf. 78 d.

c **888** ÆLFRED *Boeth.* xxxix. §2 Nu ic onȝite openlice ðæt sio soðe ȝesælð stent on godra monna ȝeearnunga. *c* **1386** CHAUCER *Pars. T.* 107 Penitence .. stant on [*Harl.* stondith in]. iij. thynges: Contricioun of herte, Confession of Mouth, and Satisfaccion. **1430–40** LYDG. *Bochas* IX. xiii. (1555) 25 All stant on chaunge. *c* **1449** PECOCK *Repr.* I. ii. 11 If this treuthe .. were knowe bi sum other thing than bi Holi Scripture .., thilk .. trouth were not groundid in Holi Scripture. Forwhi he stood not oonli ther on. *a* **1529** SKELTON *P. Sparowe* 366 Of fortune this the chaunce Standeth on varyaunce. **1662** STILLINGFL. *Orig. Sacræ* I. i. §15 The rational evidence which our faith doth stand on as to these things.

†**d.** Of a material thing: = 78 e. *Obs.*

1563 T. GALE *Antidot.* II. 7 b, Cataplasmes, be medicines standing on herbes, flowres, oiles [etc.].

†**e.** To give oneself to, practise (some kind of action or behaviour). *Obs.*

1590 SHAKS. *Com. Err.* I. ii. 80 Or I shall breake that merrie sconce of yours That stands on tricks, when I am vndispos'd. **1592** —— *Rom. & Jul.* II. iii. 93 O let us hence, I stand on sudden hast. **1600** ROWLANDS *Lett. Humours Blood* xxxvii. 44 Come nimbly foorth, Why stand you on delay? **1661** *Cal. St. Papers, Irel.* 406 Divers malefactors .. stood on their keeping, robbing and spoiling his Majesty's good subjects.

f. ***to stand on terms***, †***on condition***: see 78 f.

1561 NORTON & SACKV. *Gorboduc* V. i. 95 While we treate and stand on termes of grace. **1586** [see TERM *sb.* 8 b 6]. **1593** SHAKS. *Rich. II*, II. iii. 107 Let me know my Fault, On what Condition stands it, and wherein? **1599** —— *Hen. V*, III. vi. 78 What termes the Enemy stood on. **1611** COTGR., s.v. *Bout, Se tenir sur le haut bout*, to stand vpon his pantofles, or on high tearmes. **1639** FULLER *Holy War* III. x. 126 Whilest Guy stood on these ticklish terms, King Richard made a seasonable motion. **1824** SCOTT *St. Ronan's* xviii, We must stand, however, on more equal terms, my lord.

g. To be meticulously careful or scrupulous about, raise difficulties about (nice points, ceremony, etc.); = 78 g.

a **1593** MARLOWE *Edw. II* IV. vi. 1925 Stand not on titles, but obay th' arrest. **1593** SHAKS. *2 Hen. VI*, III. i. 261 And doe not stand on Quillets how to slay him. *c* **1611** CHAPMAN *Iliad* II. 355 Good Menelaus .. would not stand, on inuitation, But of himselfe came. **1682** N. O. *Boileau's Lutrin* II. 70 And if to gratifie thy Itch, (my Honey,) I stood not on th' nice points of Matrimony. **1753** MISS COLLIER *Art Torment., Gen. Rules* (1811) 189 People, who love civil freedom, and stand not on forms and ceremonies. **1837** CARLYLE *Fr. Rev.* II. I. ii, That is the precisest calculation, though one would not stand on a few hundreds. **1861** *Temple Bar* I. 500 Simple people, who never stood on ceremony with their friends. **1886** MRS. C. PRAED *Miss Jacobsen* II. xvii. 289, I'm not going to stand on nice points of law.

h. To assert, claim respect or credit for (one's rights, qualities, dignity, etc.); = 78 i.

1598 B. JONSON *Ev. Man in Hum.* I. i, Stand not so much on your gentility. **1616** [GAINSFORD] *Rich Cabinet* 54 Hee .. stands as tightly on his reputation, and hath his pedegree as perfect as any man. **1679** LUTTRELL *Brief Rel.* (1857) I. 17 Mr. Langhorn, who was lately executed on account of the plott, stood on his innocence to the last. **1820** SCOTT *Monast.* xiii, If they should stand on their pedigree and gentle race. **1823** A. CLARKE *Mem. Wesley Fam.* 521 Her uncle Matthew, who stood high on his honour. **1883** *Law Rep. 23 Chanc. Div.* 711 The facts are not such that we can say they have precluded themselves from standing on their strict rights. **1890** *Sat. Rev.* 19 July 76/1 Possibly he may stand on his dignity, being a self-respecting animal.

†**i.** To value, set store by (something external to oneself); = 78 j. *Obs.*

1601 SHAKS. *Jul. C.* II. ii. 13, I neuer stood on Ceremonies, Yet now they fright me.

†**j.** To dwell on, consider (a topic); to insist on (a point or argument); = 78 k. *Obs.*

1340 HAMPOLE *Pr. Consc.* 2684 On þis part I wille na langer stand, Bot passe to another neghest folowand. **1573** *New Custom* I. ii. B ij b, Standst thou with mee on schole poyntes, dost thou so in deede? *c* **1585** [R. BROWNE] *Answ. Cartwright* 34 How corrupt doctrine this is, I neede not heere stand on it. **1653** H. COGAN tr. *Pinto's Trav.* ix. 26 In a word, and not to stand long on that which past between them. **1658** *Whole Duty Man* xvi. 350 The great prevailing of this sin of uncharitablenesse has made me stand thus long on these considerations.

k. To insist on, as essential or necessary, urge, press for, demand; = 78 m. ? *Obs.*

1597 SHAKS. *2 Hen. IV* I. ii. 42 A Rascally-yea-forsooth-knaue, to beare a Gentleman in hand, and then stand vpon Security? **1616** B. JONSON *Devil an Ass* III. iii. 83 What is't? a hundred pound? *Eve.* No, th' Harpey, now, stands on a hundred pieces. **1816** SCOTT *Let.* in *Lockhart* (1837) IV. 19 He proposes I shall have twelve months' bills—I have always got six. However, I would not stand on that.

†**l.** *impers.* (It) behoves, is incumbent on; = 78 q.

1605 SHAKS. *Lear* V. i. 69 For my state, Stands on me to defend, not to debate. **1820** WILBRAHAM *Chesh. Gloss.*, *To Stand a person on*, is to be incumbent on him. It stands every one on to take care of himself.

m. In (chiefly imp.) phr. ***stand on me***, (you may) rely on me, believe me. Cf. *stand upon* sense 78 c. *slang.*

1933 *Cornh. Mag.* June 697 'E'll finish like a crab—stand on me fer that. **1935** WALLACE & CURTIS *Mouthpiece* i. 17 If any of your clients ever want to go abroad...in a hurry—never mind about passports, eh? Just stand on me. **1959** F. NORMAN (*title*) Stand on me, a true story of Soho. **1970** G. F. NEWMAN *Sir, you Bastard* i. 35 You'll be all right, stand on me.

75. stand over ——. To stand close by and watch or control (a person who is seated, lying down, or stationed on a lower level). Also *transf.* in extended use; *Austral. slang*, to intimidate or threaten; to extort money from (someone).

c **1330** *Amis & Amil.* 1972 The lazer lith vp in a wain... And ouer him stode a naked swain. **1737** *Gentl. Mag.* VII. 182/2 Sir Thomas is represented,..laid at Length on his Back, with the Figure of Time standing over him. **1851** RUSKIN *King of Golden River* iii. (1856) 32 Sobering them just enough to enable them to stand over Gluck, beating him very steadily for a quarter of an hour. **1932** V. WOOLF *Pargiters* (1978) 31 Miss Edwards, the small dressmaker,.. could cut out quite well, but one had to stand over her. **1939** K. TENNANT *Foveaux* 173, I just had Thompson in here and he stood over me for three quid. **1940** *Punch* 24 Apr. 449/2, I could *occasionally* leave her to wash up a few cups or something like that without actually standing over her the whole time. **1953** K. TENNANT *Joyful Condemned* iii. 21 There's many a man thought he was going to stand over some little lowie and now he's..looking through the bars. **1967** K. GILES *Death & Mr Prettyman* ii. 58 [Australian loq.] You could stand over—pardon, persecute me. **1978** D. FRANCIS *Trial Run* vii. 105, I should stand over them... Make yourself a bit of a nuisance, so they send it [*sc.* a Telex] to get rid of you.

76. stand to ——. (Also *unto*, †*till*, †*until*.)

†**a.** To submit oneself to, abide by (a trial, award); to obey, accede to, be bound by (another's judgement, decision, opinion, etc.). (Cf. *stand at* 68 a.) *Obs.*

c **1290** *S. Eng. Leg.* 160/1882 To holi churche heo wolden stonde and to is lokinge al-so. *a* **1300** *Cursor M.* 26249 To biscop dome þou agh to stand. **1338** R. BRUNNE *Chron.* (1725) 58 Þerfor Godwyn & his fro London went away, He stode vntille no more, defaute he mad þat day. *c* **1386** CHAUCER *Parson's T.* 483 To stonde gladly to the award of hise souereyns. **1457** HARDYNG *Chron.* in *Eng. Hist. Rev.* (1912) Oct. 747 Scottes..to Berwyke cam..And bonde thaym thar to stonde to his decre. **1584** LYLY *Campaspe* I. iii. 76 In kinges causes I will not stande to schollers arguments. **1616** CHAMPNEY *Voc. Bps.* 21 Such a Reformer is not bound to stand to the judgement of the Church. **1692** BENTLEY *Boyle Lect.* vi. 5 Will they not stand to the grand Verdict and Determination of the Universe? **1700** J. TYRRELL *Hist. Eng.* II. 889 The King summon'd [them] to appear.., and stand to the Law.

†**b.** To leave oneself dependent upon (another's mercy, courtesy, etc.). See COURTESY 2 b. *Obs.*

c **1449** PECOCK *Repr.* III. v. 305 Forto stonde to deuocioun of the peple in ȝeuing and offring. **1584** B. R. tr. *Herodotus* II. 103 That in case the party..woulde disclose himselfe, and stande to his mercy, he [the King] woulde..yeeld him free pardon. **1614** RICH *Honestie of Age* (1844) 13 He must stande to the mercy of twelue men; a jury shall passe vppon him. **1650** FULLER *Pisgah* II. ix. 187 He was contented to stand to the peoples courtesie, what they would bestow upon him. **1697** COLLIER *Ess.* II. (1703) 153 He that has the business of life at his own disposal..needs not stand to the curtesy of knavery and folly. **1722** [see COURTESY 2 b].

c. To apply oneself manfully to (a fight, contest, etc.). *Obs.* exc. in ***to stand to it***, to fight stoutly; also, to toil without flagging at painful or severe labour.

1338 R. BRUNNE *Chron.* (1725) 277 Þe Baliol was agast, for he stode tille no dede. *Ibid.*, Bot Sir Patrik Graham a while to bataile stode. **1544** BETHAM *Precepts War* I. cxxxv. G vj b, To comforte and encowrage hys men..fiercelye to fyght, and boldly to stande to it. **1579** FENTON *Guicciard.* I. (1599) 48 Some times he determined to stand to the defence of Rome. **1632** LITHGOW *Trav.* VII. 328 Saylers have the paine By drudging, pulling, hayling, standing to it In cold and raine. **1889** CONAN DOYLE *Micah Clarke* xvi. 144 The peasants stood to it like men.

d. Mil. ***to stand to one's arms***: to form up with arms presented. †***to stand to a guard***: to put oneself on guard. ***to stand to one's guns, one's colours***: to maintain one's position, not to retire before an attack; also *fig.* †***to stand to one's tackle*** or ***tackling***: see TACKLE *sb.* 4 b, TACKLING 3.

a **1548**, **1679** [see TACKLING 3]. **1581** J. BELL *Haddon's Answ. Osor.* 464 But yᵉ Carmelites standing hard to theyr tackle, recovered the victory at the last. **1583** STOCKER *Civ. Warres Lowe C.* IV. 55 The reste stoode stoutly to their tackle, so that..the trouble..was suppressed. **1644** PRYNNE & WALKER *Fiennes' Trial* App. 26 Gentlemen, under paine of death stand to your Armes. **1709** STEELE *Tatler* No. 6 ¶ 11 The Intendant had ordered some Companies of Marines,.. to stand to their Arms to protect him from Violence. **1815** SCOTT *Guy M.* xlvi, But Mr. Sampson stood to his guns. **1844** *Queen's Regul. Army* 364 In case of Alarm, the Guard is immediately to stand to their Arms. **1890** CONAN DOYLE *Firm of Girdlestone* xxxi. 244 Kate stood firmly to her colours. **1891** *Longman's Mag.* Oct. 598 They stood to their guns till their powder was all gone. **1893** *Law Times* XCIV. 599/1 Mr. Cayzer will have nothing more to do with the Bill. .. But the other nine supporters of the Bill stand to their guns.

e. To confront, present a bold front to (an enemy). (Cf. *stand forth* 93 a, *stand up* 103 p.) Now *rare.*

1562 MOUNTGOMERY in *Archæologia* XLVII. 240 The worthie souldior, that shall stande to the face of thenimye and abyde the threatninge of the canon. **1608** TOPSELL *Serpents* 220 The Salamander..is an audacious and bold creature, standing to his aduersary, and not flying the sight of a man. **1681** W. ROBERTSON *Phraseol. Gen.* 1166/1, I fear he will not be able to stand to him: *Metuo, ut substet.* **1844** THACKERAY *Barry Lyndon* ii, I never yet knew the man who stood to Captain Quin.

†**f.** To confront and take the consequences of (a chance, hazard, peril); to abide by (the issue or consequences of an event). Cf. sense 54. *Obs.* exc. *arch.*

a **1300** [see CHANCE *sb.* 11]. *c* **1330** R. BRUNNE *Chron. Wace* (Rolls) 6409 *note*, He seide he wolde assaye [*Petyt MS.* wild stande to] þe chaunce. *c* **1400** *Brut* 251 Þat þai shulde nouȝt feiȝt oppon þe Scottes..and if þai dede, þat þai shulde stande to [*v.r.* vnto] her owen peril. **14..** *26 Pol. Poems* 8/47, I gloser wil stonde to my chaunce. **1456** SIR G. HAYE *Law of Arms* (S.T.S.) 141 As men of were, thai mon stand to thair fortune. *Ibid.* 182 Lat him stand till his hap. **1579** [see CHANCE *sb.* 11, 12]. **1610** J. MORE in *Buccleuch MSS.* (Hist. MSS. Comm.) I. 87 Let all alone, and stand to all adventures. **1712** ADDISON *Spect.* No. 286 ¶ 6 It is very dangerous for a Nation to stand to its Chance, or to have its publick Happiness or Misery depend on the Virtues or Vices of a single Person. **1725** *Bradley's Fam. Dict.* s.v. *Horse-racing* ¶ 2 Without such Trials we must stand to the Hazard, and be at no Certainty to meet with good ones [*sc.* horses]. **1785** R. GRAVES *Eugenius* I. xvii. 117 The old lady..said she would make the governess produce her daughter, or stand to the consequences. **1935** T. S. ELIOT *Murder in Cathedral* i. 20 Do not ask us To stand to the doom on the house, the doom on the Archbishop.

†**g.** To endure, bear, put up with (harm, pain); to make good, bear the expense of (damage, loss); to defray, be answerable for (expenses); to accept liability for (a tribute or tax). *Obs.* (Cf. 57, 58.)

c **1386** CHAUCER *Miller's T.* 644 But stonde he moste vn to his owene harm. **1540** PALSGR. *Acolastus* II. iv. M iij b, He that putteth oone in truste, shall be fayne to stande to his owne harmes, if he be begyled. **1540** in *10th Rep. Hist. MSS. Comm.* App. v. 409 No person..shall not detayne nor keape any thinge of the comon rente for..debtes that the costome owith to any of them, but shall..stand to the costome of their own goodes. **1555** EDEN *Decades* (Arb.) 80 The inhabitantes..made humble supplication to the Admirall that they myght stande to theyr tribute. **1622** MABBE tr. *Aleman's Guzman d'Alf.* II. 150, I shall be content to stand to any losse that you shall suffer thereby. *a* **1633** G. HERBERT *Priest to Temple* xxvi. Rem. (1652) 111 Many think they are at more liberty then they are, as if they were Masters of their health, and so [= provided that] they will stand to the pain, all is well. But to eat to ones hurt, comprehends, besides the hurt, an act against reason. **1700** S. L. tr. *Fryke's Voy. E. Ind.* 150 He was obliged to defray all the charges my Patient had been at, and to stand to all damages. **1789** BENTHAM *Wks.* (1843) X. 108 The author's having three-fourths of the net profits..(he standing as before to the expense). **1809** E. S. BARRETT *Setting Sun* III. 50 If any of them decamp..the parish stands to the loss. **1809** MALKIN *Gil Blas* III. x. ¶ 5 Husband-like lovers, who expect to engross all the pleasures of a house, because they stand to the expenses.

h. To side with, help, back, support (a person); to maintain, uphold (a cause, interest, etc.); to remain faithful or loyal to.

1597 SHAKS. *2 Hen. IV* II. i. 70 Good my Lord be good to mee. I beseech you stand to me. **1607** —— *Cor.* III. i. 208 Or let vs stand to our Authoritie, Or let vs lose it. **1652** WADSWORTH tr. *Sandoval's Civ. Wars Spain* 258 They desired, that Valladolid would assist and stand to them, as they had promissed. **1725** DE FOE *Voy. round World* (1840) 72 The gunner was forced to fly with about twenty two men that stood to him. **1850** *Tait's Mag.* XVII. 489/1 We stood to our fellow student right loyally. **1887** MRS. C. PRAED *Bond of Wedlock* II. ix. 217 If he had the money he would always stand to a fellow.

i. To adhere to, abide by, carry out (a promise, vow, bargain, compact, etc.).

a **1547** SURREY *Æneid* II. 203 Kepe faith with me, and stand to thy behest. **1553** T. WILSON *Rhet.* 19 The one will make his felowe to stande to the bargain, though it be to his neighbors vndoyng. **1652** GAULE *Magastrom.* 252 She, having already obtained her desire, refused to stand to her promise. **1714** BUDGELL tr. *Theophrastus* vi. 23 He is always up to the Ears in Law,..some of his Suits he is forced to stand to, and works himself out of others by Perjury. **1765** BLACKSTONE *Comm.* I. 243 No wise prince will ever refuse to stand to a lawful contract. **1775** *Tender Father* I. 202, I am not one of those who make proposals which they never mean to stand to. **1860** READE *Cloister & H.* lvi. (1896) 169 When they have made a bad bargain drunk, they stand to it sober. **1892** *Sat. Rev.* 2 Jan. 8/2 He did not venture to stand to the promise he had given.

j. (*a*) To adhere to (a statement, etc.); to persist in affirming or asserting. †Rarely with *that* and clause. (*b*) ***to stand to it***: to insist upon or maintain a statement or assertion; often with *that* and clause (sometimes without *that*).

(*a*) **1562** *Child-Marriages* 119 Whether the said Margaret wold stand to the wordes she had spoken bie the said Katherine. **1597** J. PAYNE *Royal Exch.* 24 Let vs..to the deathe stand to, that Christ hathe the substans of God and the substans of man. *a* **1677** BARROW *Pope's Suprem.* (1687) 249 They..stood to the canonicalness of the former decision. **1688** *Lett. conc. Pres. State Italy* 184 He stood to his denial, and said, he knew nothing. **1737** [S. BERINGTON] *G. de Lucca's Mem.* (1738) To Rdr. 9 The Man stands to the Truth of it with a Steadfastness that is surprizing. **1893** *Strand Mag.* VI. 176/1 You will stand to the confession you have just made?

(*b*) **1581** A. HALL *Iliad* IV. 71, I dare auouch, and stand to't to your face. **1600** SHAKS. *A.Y.L.* I. ii. 69 Now Ile stand to it, the Pancakes were naught. **1612** FIELD *Woman a Weathercock* II. i, Lay the child to him—Stand stiffly to it. **1692** PATRICK *Answ. Touchstone* 175 This, I will stand to it, is an Interpretation they cannot confute. **1709** STEELE *Tatler* No. 171 ¶ 8 He would stand to it, that it was full Four Miles. **1887** JESSOPP *Arcady* ii. 36 They will stand to it that the present generation know nothing of the hard life their grandsires had experience of. **1889** ADEL. SERGEANT *Deveril's Diamond* III. viii. 170 He stood to it at first that he knew nothing.

†**k.** ***to stand to its duty***: to perform its work or function without giving way. *Obs.*

1726 LEONI *Alberti's Archit.* I. 53 *b* The..wedges also in ..the Arch, being justly counterpoised, will surely stand to their duty.

†**l.** Of desire, appetite, etc.: To be inclined to, hanker after. *Obs.*

c **1400** *Sir Cleges* 408 Wattsooeuer thou wolt haue, I will the graunte,..That thyne hart standyth to. **1551** R. ROBINSON tr. *More's Utopia* II. iv. (1895) 141 Yf a mans minde stonde to anny other [occupation]. **1561** HOLLYBUSH *Hom. Apoth.* 22 b, Then let hym eate that wherto his minde standeth best. **1601** HOLLAND *Pliny* XXIII. vi. II. 164 When their stomackes stand to coles, chalke, and such like stuffe. **1641** J. SHUTE *Sarah & Hagar* (1649) 150 Their hearts stood most to this. **1694** G. STANHOPE *Epictetus' Morals* Ep. Ded. A 2 b, Without these Qualifications..a Man's Palate can never stand to the following Reflections.

†**m.** To result or issue in, lead to, amount to. ***to stand to a person's pleasure***: to be allowed or approved by him. *Obs.*

1390 GOWER *Conf.* I. 86 Ful sore it stant to my grevance. *a* **1555** LATIMER in Foxe *A. & M.* (1563) 1309/2 Also I sayd yᵗ certayne Scriptures standeth some thyng to the same, vnlesse they bee yᵉ more warely vnderstanded and taken. **1558** Q. KENNEDY in *Wodrow Soc. Misc.* (1844) 135 As may stand to the weill of the Congregatioun. **1622** MASSINGER & DEKKER *Virg. Mart.* IV. ii, So it stand To great Cesaraes Gouernors high pleasure.

n. ***it stands to reason*** (formerly also † ***to good, great reason***; dial. ***to sense***): it is reasonable, it may reasonably be inferred or expected, it is natural, evident or certain (*that*). (Cf. 79 e.)

1620 ALURED in Gutch *Coll. Cur.* I. 173 Which stands to reason, and agrees with nature. **1632** [see REASON *sb.*[1] 12 b]. **1662** STILLINGFL. *Orig. Sacræ* II. i. § 1 It stands to the greatest reason that such a revelation should be so propounded. **1705** H. BLACKWELL *Engl. Fencing-Master* 34 *Schol.* What you say stands to a great deal of Reason, and I will observe your Directions. **1768–74** TUCKER *Lt. Nat.* (1834) II. 154 When we say a thing stands to reason, or is discordant from it. **1857** RUSKIN *Pol. Econ. Art* i. § 24 It stands to reason that a young man's work cannot be perfect. **1859** [see SENSE *sb.* 28]. **1865** TROLLOPE *Belton Est.* xxvii. 320 It stands to reason that in some things I must have had more experience than you. **1901** *Contemp. Rev.* Mar. 357 It 'stands to sense', as they say in the North of England, that [etc.].

o. To be related to.

1674 N. FAIRFAX *Bulk & Selv.* 54 Nor has bulk voideness or thickness but as it stands to body. **1856** *Titan Mag.* Dec. 551/2 He stood to me as a father. **1869** FREEMAN *Norm. Conq.* (1876) III. xii. 178 It would be hard to find any wife among the princely houses who did not stand to him within the forbidden degrees. **1890** *Longman's Mag.* Oct. 657 The Wantsum..stood to Rutupiæ as the Solent stands to Portsmouth.

†**p.** To face, be built opposite to. *Obs.*

1726 LEONI *Alberti's Archit.* I. 16 *a* We shou'd also observe what Suns our House stands to.

q. Of a mare: To admit or 'take' (the horse); to conceive after (horsing). ? *Obs.*

1759 BROWN *Compl. Farmer* 4 By which means they can see whether the mare will stand to the horse or not. *Ibid.*, When the stallion is dismounted, they commonly throw a pail of cold water on the mare, which they think makes her stand better to her horsing.

r. ***to stand to the hood*** (said of a hawk): to submit to being hooded.

1828 SIR J. S. SEBRIGHT *Hawking* 20 To accustom him to stand to the hood.

s. [tr. Ir. *seasamh do.*] To be to one's advantage, to sustain. *Anglo-Irish.*

1907 YEATS *Deirdre* 34 Women, if I die, If Naoise die this night, how will you praise? What words seek out? for that will stand to you; For being but dead we shall have many friends. **1914** JOYCE *Dubliners* 11 Why, when I was a nipper, every morning of my life I had a cold bath... That's what stands to me now. **1922** —— *Ulysses* 622 Through all those perils of the deep..there was one thing, he declared, stood to him..a pious medal he had that saved him.

77. stand under ——.

†**a.** To be ranged under (a lord, his banner).

c **1450** HOLLAND *Howlat* 133 The Pape commandit..to wryte in all landis..For all statis of kirk that wnder Crist standis To semble to his summondis. **1570** *Homilies* II. *Agst. Rebellion* VI. (1574) 609 Woulde they haue sworne fidelitie to the Dolphin of Fraunce,..and haue stande vnder the Dolphins banner?

b. To be exposed or subject or obnoxious to; to undergo, bear the burden or weight or incidence of; (to be able) to sustain (a charge, etc.).

1601 SHAKS. *Jul. C.* II. i. 52 Shall Rome stand vnder one mans awe? **1613** —— *Hen. VIII*, III. ii. 3 If you will now vnite in your Complaints, And force them with a Constancy the Cardinall Cannot stand vnder them. *Ibid.* V. i. 113 There's none stands vnder more calumnious tongues, Then I my selfe, poore man. **1667** MILTON *P.L.* VIII. 454 For now My earthly by his Heav'nly overpowerd, Which it had long stood under, streind to the highth In that celestial Colloquie sublime,..Dazl'd and spent, sunk down. **1891** in *Century Dict.* s.v., I stand under heavy obligations.

c. *Naut.* To make sail with (a specified display of canvas).

1707 *Lond. Gaz.* No. 4380/2 The Commadore made a Signal for the Line a-breast, standing under a pair of Topsails. **1834** M. SCOTT *Cruise Midge* i, I soon saw a large vessel, standing under easy sail, on the same tack.

d. Mil. ***to stand under arms***, to be ready for action (Voyle & Stevenson *Milit. Dict.* 1876).

☞ **stand until, unto** ——: see *stand to* 76.

78. stand upon ——. (Cf. *stand on* 74.)

a. In fig. phrases of which the wording is literal. †*to stand upon one's pantofles, slippers*: to give oneself airs. †*to stand upon stepping-stones*: to make gradual and cautious advances. *to stand upon thorns*: see THORN *sb.* 2.

1540 PALSGR. *Acolastus* I. iii. G j b, I see how thou standest vpon thornes. **1561** [see THORN *sb.* 2]. **1579** [cf. *stand on* 74 a]. **1591, 1685** [see PANTOFLE b]. *a* **1604** HANMER *Chron. Irel.* (1809) 334 They would talke and bragge of service,..stand upon the pantofles of their reputation. **1606** S. GARDINER *Bk. Angling* 36 The Donatists in Africa stood vpon their slippers. **1637** RUTHERFORD *Lett.* lxxxi. (1862) I. 205, I see that Christ will not prig with me nor stand upon stepping stones: but cometh in at the broadsides without ceremonies.

☛ *to stand upon the defensive, upon one's guard*, etc.: see sense 10.

†**b.** *to stand upon no ground*: of a horse, ? to rear, caper. *Obs.*

1590 PEELE *Polyhymnia* (Rtldg.) 572/1 The next came Nedham in on lusty horse, That, angry with delay, at trumpet's sound Would snort, and stamp, and stand upon no ground. **1594** LYLY *Mother Bombie* IV. ii, It was as lustie a nag as anie in Rochester, and one that would stand vpon no ground.

c. To rely upon, depend on, trust to. *Obs.* exc. in the sense: To take one's stand upon an argument, argumentative position or the like.

1390 GOWER *Conf.* I. 151 He..seith that he wol undertake Upon hire wordes forto stonde. **1565** ALLEN *Def. Purg.* I. vi. (1886) 79 Because we will not stand upon conjectures in so necessary a point. **1640** *Wits Recreat.* K 7, The Text which saith that man and wife are one, Was the chief argument they stood upon. **1726** SWIFT *Gulliver* I. v, The Emperor, standing upon the advantage he had got by the seizure of their fleet, obliged them to deliver their credentials. **1854** *Poultry Chron.* II. 206 'Faint heart ne'er won fair lady' is a good motto to stand upon.

d. Of an immaterial thing (also *impersonal*): To be grounded or based upon. †Also, to be dependent or contingent upon, hinge upon; to arise from, consist in.

1390 GOWER *Conf.* I. 11 The cherche keye in aventure Of armes and of brygantaille Stod nothing thanne upon bataille. *c* **1449** PECOCK *Repr.* I. ii. 11 No thing is ground and fundament of eny treuthe or conclusioun,..saue it upon which aloon al the gouernaunce, trouthe, or vertu stondith. *c* **1460** FORTESCUE *Abs. & Lim. Mon.* xii. (1885) 137 The reaume off Englond, wheroff the myght stondith most vppon archers. *c* **1500** *Lancelot* 1989 It stant apone thi will For to omend thi puple, or to spill. **1567** ALLEN *Def. Priesthood* Pref., The dishonoure and the derogation.. standeth vpon vnfaythfulnes, mistrust of Gods promise. **1577** HARRISON *England* III. iii. [II. ix.] 99 b, in *Holinshed*, The Common Lawe standeth vppon Sundrye Maximes or Princyples, and yeares or tearmes. *c* **1580** in *Eng. Hist. Rev.* (1914) July 520 Theyr trade standes upon woade and the same englishe comodities that sarveth for the one, sarveth for the other. **1596** SHAKS. *Merch. V.* III. ii. 203 Your fortune stood vpon the caskets there. **1602** —— *Ham.* I. i. 119 (1604 Qo.) The moist starre Vpon whose influence Neptunes Empier stands. **1608** T. MORTON *Preamble to Incounter* 40 Science standeth vpon demonstrable principles.

†**e.** Of a material thing: To consist of, be composed of; also, to contain as an ingredient.

1563 [cf. 74 d]. **1601** HOLLAND *Pliny* XXXI. vi. II. 412 Those waters which stand upon brimstone, bee good for the sinews. **1620** I. JONES *Stone-Heng* (1725) 4 The Druids chose..such Groves for their divine Service, as stood only upon Oaks.

f. *to stand upon terms*: (*a*) to be on a specified footing or in a specified situation or condition; (*b*) to insist upon conditions; also, *to stand upon conditions*; (*c*) to take a high line, to hold one's own, refuse to knuckle under.

1597 SHAKS. *2 Hen. IV*, IV. i. 165 Hath the Prince John a full Commission..To heare, and absolutely to determine Of what Conditions wee shall stand vpon? **1608** —— *Per.* IV. ii. 38 Besides the sore tearmes we stand vpon with the gods, wilbe strong with vs for giuing ore. **1611** [see TERM *sb.* 8 b 6]. **1661–2** PEPYS *Diary* 24 Jan., My uncle Thomas, who I hear by him do stand upon very high terms. **1673** DRYDEN *Marr. à-la-Mode* III. i. 32 Since we must live together, and both of us stand upon our terms. **1716** [see TERM *sb.* 8 b 6]. **1721** DE FOE *Mem. Cavalier* (1840) 36 They..hung back and stood upon terms.

g. To be careful or scrupulous in regard to (forms, ceremonies, nice points of behaviour); to be attentive to or observant of; to allow oneself to be unduly influenced or impeded by. Now *rare* exc. in negative contexts.

1549 CHALONER *Erasm. Praise Folly* F ij b, Standyng euer vppon narow poynctes of wysedome. **1605** SHAKS. *Macb.* III. iv. 119 Stand not vpon the order of your going, But go at once. **1607** TOPSELL *Four-f. Beasts* Ep. Ded. 2 Therefore I wil not stand vpon any mans obiections. *c* **1661** in *Verney Mem.* (1907) II. 219 These punctillios are not to be stood uppon by younger brothers. **1681** FLAVEL *Meth. Grace* viii. 177 You stand upon trifles with him, and yet call him your best and dearest friend. **1714** BUDGELL tr. *Theophrastus* xix. 57 He does not stand upon Decency in Conversation. **1751** JORTIN *Serm.* (1771) VII. xii. 250 There is no occasion to stand upon Complaisance and ceremony with writers who have done so much mischief. **1828** LYTTON *Pelham* lxxvi, Lady Glanville was a woman of the good old school, and stood somewhat upon forms and ceremonies. **1889** 'M. GRAY' *Reproach of Annesley* I. II. i. 145 You stand upon a fanciful punctilio. **1889** F. BARRETT *Under Strange Mask* II. x. 2 We were real friends, and only stood upon ceremony in our business relations.

†**h.** To hesitate at (expense), be sparing of (money). *Obs.*

1653 H. COGAN *Scarlet Gown* 162 When he was young, he delighted in taking all the pleasure that possibly he could, never standing upon mony. **1655** M. CASAUBON *Enthus.* iv. (1656) 242 There was a way of painting..very frequent among ancient Romans, who stood not upon any cost, either for pomp or pleasure.

i. To pride or value oneself upon; to urge, assert, make the most of, claim respect or consideration for, insist on the recognition of (one's qualities, rank, rights, possessions, dignity, etc.).

1588 SHAKS. *Tit. A.* II. iii. 124 This Minion stood vpon her chastity. **1608** WILLET *Hexapla Exod.* 321 The Pharisie that stood vpon his workes. *a* **1625** FLETCHER *Wit without Money* II. ii, This widow is the strangest thing, the stateliest, And stands so much upon her excellencies! **1683** KENNETT *Erasm. on Folly* 69 The Venetians stand upon their birth and Pedigree. **1840** THACKERAY *Shabby-genteel Story* i, She stood upon her rank. **1874** BLACKIE *Self-Cult.* 75 There are few things in social life more contemptible than a rich man who stands upon his riches. **1885** J. PAYN *Luck of Darrells* III. xxxi. 8 Langton would stand, and very properly, upon his legal rights. **1898** 'MERRIMAN' *Roden's Corner* vi. 60 Men who stand much upon their dignity have not, as a rule, much else to stand upon.

†**j.** To attach importance to, treat as important, give prominence or weight to; to value, set store by. *Obs.*

1598 R. BERNARD tr. *Terence, Andria* III. ii, The matter I stand most vpon, is the promise which my sonne himselfe made vnto me. **1607** SHAKS. *Cor.* IV. vi. 96 You, that stood so much Vpon the voyce of occupation, and The breath of Garlicke-eaters. **1629** BURTON *Babel no Bethel* 100 Shee stands not vpon inward holines, but is all for outward glory. **1651** *Life Father Sarpi* (1676) 15 The Dignities among Religious Men, being considered either by their profit, or their splendour, are not things to be stood upon. **1660** tr. *Amyraldus' Treat. conc. Relig.* III. viii. 471 We stand not greatly upon it, by which of these names they are termed. **1701** SWIFT *Poems, Mrs. Harris's Petit.* 42 'Tis not that I value the Money..But the thing I stand upon, is the Credit of the House. **1830** GEN. P. THOMPSON *Exerc.* (1842) I. 305 Free men do not stand upon family differences, when the object is to oppose a common despotism.

†**k.** To dwell with emphasis or at length upon (a topic, argument, etc.); to treat with insistence, urge; to discourse or dilate upon. *Obs.*

1565 ALLEN *Def. Purg.* Pref. (1886) 17 But I cannot now stand upon these points. **1605** BACON *Adv. Learn.* I. i. §3 As for the third point, it deserueth to be a little stood vpon, and not to be lightly passed ouer. **1608** DOD & CLEAVER *Expos. Prov.* xi–xii. 165 We purpose..to stand more largely upon it in the fifteenth chapter. **1638** JUNIUS *Paint. Ancients* 39 Seing then that this is a main point of Art, wee have also stood a little longer upon it. *a* **1715** BURNET *Own Time* III. (1724) I. 407 But he stood much upon this; that having once engaged with France in the war, he could not with honour turn against France, till it was at an end. **1732** BERKELEY *Minute Philos.* I. 66, I observe, said he, that you stand much upon the dignity of Human Nature.

†**l.** *to stand upon it*: to insist, maintain persistently (*that*). *Obs.*

1628 EARLE *Microcosm., Constable* (Arb.) 40 A Constable is a Vice-roy in the street and no man stands more vpon't that he is the Kings Officer. *a* **1715** BURNET *Own Time* (1897) I. 320 The presbyterians..stood upon it, that a law which excluded all that did not kneel from the sacrament was unlawful. *Ibid.* 362 Yet he always stood upon it, that he had the king's order by word of mouth for what he had done.

†**m.** To insist upon, treat or regard as necessary or indispensable, press for, demand. *to stand upon it to have*: to insist on having. *Obs.*

1634 SIR T. HERBERT *Trav.* 29 Had he stood vpon his Justification at the Court. **1653** AUSTEN *Fruit Trees* I. (1657) 67 Concerning Order in setting Trees, though it be not essentiall..yet if men stand upon it, they may measure out [etc.]. **1675** BROOKS *Gold. Key* Wks. 1867 V. 351 God the Father, in order to man's redemption and salvation, stands stiffly and peremptorily upon complete satisfaction. **1706** MRS. CENTLIVRE *Basset-Table* II. 18, I must say that of you Women of Quality, if there is but Money enough, you stand not upon Birth or Reputation, in either Sex. **1712** J. JAMES *Gardening* 17 Many stand upon it to have Palaces.

†**n.** Of the heart or inclination: To be bent or set on (some activity). (Cf. *stand to* 76 l.) *Obs.*

1390 GOWER *Conf.* I. 244 Tho Whos herte stod upon knyhthode.

†**o.** To be subjected to, submit to (amendment).

1390 GOWER *Conf.* I. 6 This bok, upon amendement To stonde at his commandement,..I sende unto myn oghne lord. *Ibid.* 179 If that it be thi wille To stonde upon amendement.

†**p.** *impers.* = It is a question of, it concerns, affects, involves. Similarly *the matter stands upon*.

1390 GOWER *Conf.* III. 220 Knihthode mot ben take on honde, Whan that it stant upon the nede. *a* **1553** UDALL *Royster D.* III. iii. 105 But now the matter standeth vpon your mariage, Ye must now take vnto you a lustie courage. **1590** SHAKS. *Com. Err.* IV. i. 68 Consider how it stands vpon my credit. **1616** B. JONSON *Devil an Ass* III. iii. 60 It stands vpon his being inuested In a new office. *a* **1625** FLETCHER *Noble Gent.* v. i, It stands upon my utter overthrow. **1630** J. ROGERS in *Winthrop's Hist. New Eng.* (1853) I. 56 In which I pray God move your heart to be very careful, for it stands upon their lives.

†**q.** *impers.* (It) concerns, behoves, is incumbent upon, is the duty of, is to the interest of, is urgent or necessary for (a person); occas. also with obj. a thing (one's credit, etc.) Const. *to* (do something). Usually in the form *it stands (one) upon* = one ought, one must needs. *Obs.* exc. *dial.*

1538 ELYOT *Dict.* Addit., *Abs te stat*, it standeth vppon the or it lyeth in the. **1602** WARNER *Alb. Eng.* XII. lxxiv. (1612) 306 For much it stood vpon Their Credits to be cautilous. **1611** *3rd Rep. Hist. MSS. Comm.* 58/2 It stands upon my reputation, being Governor of James-town, to keep a daily table for gentlemen of fashion about me. **1635** J. HAYWARD tr. *Biondi's Banish'd Virg.* 163, I know it stands upon us to wend us hence assone as we conveniently can. **1720–1** *Lett. Mist's Jrnl.* (1722) I. 260 It stands upon us to take off so heinous a Charge. **1749** BERKELEY *Word to Wise* Wks. III. 449 It stands upon you to act with vigour in this cause.

1549 CHALONER *Erasm. Praise Folly* R j b, My faire broode of doctours do enterprise to nippe of here and there foure or fiue woordes of the whole..(if it stande theim vpon). **1557** TUSSER *100 Points Husb.* xciii, Such season may hap, it shall stande the vpon: to till it againe, or the somer be gone. **1577** HOLINSHED *Chron.* II. 306/1 Now perceyuing that it stoode them vppon, either to vanquish or to fall into vtter ruine. **1603** KNOLLES *Hist. Turks* (1621) 1142 It now stood the great Turke upon to send another great armie to the aid of Mahomet. **1637** SANDERSON *Serm.* (1681) II. 91 He that would live a contented life..it standeth him upon to be frugal. **1690** LOCKE *Hum. Und.* IV. xix. §10 Does it not then stand them upon, to examine on what grounds they presume it to be a Revelation from God. **1887** *S. Cheshire Gloss.*, *Stond on, Stond upon*, to be incumbent on. 'It'll stond 'em upon to be moor careful another time.' The accusative of the person is always placed between the verb and the preposition.

79. stand with ——.

†**a.** To strive with, withstand (an adversary). Later, to contend with in argument, dispute with (also with *that* and clause); to haggle, make terms with (*for* something). *Obs.*

c **825** *Vesp. Psalter* xciii. 16 Hwelc stondeð mid mec wið wircendum unreht? *c* **1205** LAY. 23127 ȝif þe king me stont wiþ. *c* **1320** *Castle of Love* 701 Neuer schal fo him stonde wiþ. **1579** FULKE *Heskins' Parl.* 473, I might stande with him, that this is no interpretation. **1580** G. HARVEY in *Three Proper Lett.* 50 But I wil not stand greatly with you in your owne matters. **1616** *Marlowe's Faustus* (Brooke) 218 Well, I will not stand with thee, giue me the money. **1680** DRYDEN *Span. Fryar* I. i, However, I will not stand with you for a Sample. (*Lifts up her Veil.*) **1691** R. MEEKE *Diary* 3 Apr. (1874) 38, I do not usually stand with any for their wages. **1704** NORRIS *Ideal World* II. iii. 223 Whoever grants these two propositions..cannot stand with me about the consequence of our argument.

†**b.** To range oneself with (another), contend side by side with; to side with, make common cause with. *Obs.*

13.. *Cursor M.* 15499 (Gött.) Elleuen er we ȝeit to stand wid þe [*Cott.* to witstand wit þe], all redi bun. **14..** *26 Pol. Poems* xii. 8 Stonde wiþ þe kyng, mayntene þe croun. **1412–20** LYDG. *Troy Bk.* IV. 1691 To be willy, þoruȝ his chiualrie, With hem to stonde as he haþ do to-forn. **1596** DALRYMPLE tr. *Leslie's Hist. Scot.* I. 310 Because stoutlie thay had stande with him in his defence against his ennimies. **1601** SHAKS. *Jul. C.* II. i. 142, I think he will stand very strong with vs. **1605** —— *Macb.* III. iii. 4 But who did bid thee ioyne with vs?..Then stand with vs. **1654** BRAMHALL *Just Vind.* iv. 82 They..disavowed the Popes incroachments and offered the King to stand with him in these and all other cases touching his Crown.

†**c.** To stay with, be busied or converse with (a person). *Obs.*

1606 G. WOODCOCKE *Hist. Ivstine* XLII. 132 He would stand still as though he had stood with him [*cum illo loqui, cum illo consistere*]. **1631** DEKKER *Match mee* I. 3 A Barber stood with her on Saturday night very late..and as I thinke, came to trimme her.

d. *Naut.* To sail in the same direction as (another ship). (Cf. 36.) ? *Obs.*

c **1595** CAPT. WYATT *R. Dudley's Voy. W. Ind.* (Hakl. Soc.) 10 Wee might perceave a small saile to stande with us, and standinge in for the ilands as wee did. **1628** DIGBY *Voy. Mediterr.* (Camden) 21 Wee descryed a sayle standing with vs.

e. To be consistent or consonant with, agree or accord with. *Obs.* exc. *arch.*

to stand with (good) reason: cf. *stand to* (76 n) and REASON *sb.*[1] 12 b.

c **1380** WYCLIF *Wks.* (1880) 385 þe whiche stondiþ not wiþ þe plente of cristis perfection in prestis. *c* **1449** PECOCK *Repr.* III. iv. 304 It folewith that it stondith weel with the proces of Poul in this present processe, that bischopis haue endewing of vnmouable possessiouns. **1513** MORE *Rich. III*, Wks. 49/1 If it might stand with your pleasure to be in such place as might stande with their honour. **1515** *Star Chamber Cases* (Selden Soc.) II. 94 Whether their bying and selling.. doo stonde with the Comon Weale, or noo. **1603** KNOLLES *Hist. Turks* (1621) 337 [Mahomet II] kept no league, promise, or oath, longer than stood with his profit or pleasure. **1650** FULLER *Pisgah* I. iii. 8 Because it stands not with the State of a Prince to be his own purse-bearer. *a* **1656** HALES *Gold. Rem.* III. (1673) 59 It will seem a paradox that I shall speak unto you, yet will it stand with very good reason. **1710** O. SANSOM *Acc. Life* 39, I desired him, if it stood with his Freedom, to have a Meeting there that Evening. **1772** *Junius Lett.* lxviii, How an evasive, indirect reply will stand with your reputation..is worth your consideration. **1825** SCOTT *Talism.* xxvii, Would it stand with your pleasure that I prick forward?

†**f.** To co-exist with, go along with. *Obs.*

1396–7 in *Eng. Hist. Rev.* (1907) XXII. 296 He and his noble ȝiftis may not stonde with dedly synne in no manere persone. **1526** *Pilgr. Perf.* (W. de W. 1531) 30 b, All these may stande with deedly synne. **1572** J. JONES *Bathes* II. 11 Bycause great rarefaction standeth with great heate.

g. Of printing-type: To range with.

1770 LUCKOMBE *Hist. Printing* 223 The Letter of it would Stand with another Fount of the same Body.

VII. With adverbs.

☛ **stand aback**: see 88.

80. stand about.

a. Of a number of persons: To stand here and there, in casual positions or groups. Of an individual: To remain standing in a place without a fixed position or definite object.

1390 GOWER *Conf.* III. 337 And there in open Audience Of hem that stoden thanne aboute, He tolde hem [etc.]. 1847 C. BRONTË *Jane Eyre* xix, They stood about here and there in groups, their plates and glasses in their hands. 1872 *Punch* 30 Mar. 136 Wet trousers are unpleasant to stand about in. 1883 MRS. F. MANN *Parish of Hilby* xxv. 329 I've been standing about all day.

†**b.** To go about, endeavour *to* (do something). Cf. ABOUT A 10. *Obs.*

1549 LATIMER *4th Serm. bef. Edw. VI* (Arb.) 126 When we..acknowledge our faultes, and stand not about to defend them.

†**81. stand again.** To offer resistance or opposition. (Cf. 10.) *Obs.*

a 1122 *O.E. Chron.* (Laud MS.) an. 1010 þa stod Grantabrycgscir fæstlice ongean. *c* 1205 LAY. 26674 þa Bruttes auoten uaste aȝæin stoden. *c* 1250 *Gen. & Ex.* 3543 Aaron and vr stoden a-gen, And boden hem swilc ðhowtes leten. *a* 1250 *Owl & Night.* 1788, & if þe þinkþ þat ic mis-rempe, þu stond ayeyn and do me crempe. *a* 1300 *Cursor M.* 18090 Forces yow wit might and main Stalworthli to stand a-gain.

82. stand along. *Naut.* (See sense 36.) To sail in a given direction. Hence *gen.*, to proceed on a journey.

1653 *Fight Legorn-Road* 18 Supposing Captain Badily to have stood along to the relief of our Squadron. 1710 S. SEWALL *Diary* 27 Mar. (1879) II. 276 The Sun breaking out, I stood along about 10 m. 1714 *Ibid.* 12 Apr. 438 It began to Rain, [so] that I would have had the Horses set up again. But Mr. Thaxter and Mr. Denison were for standing along.

83. stand aloof. To stand away at, or withdraw to, some distance (*from*), keep away (*from*). Also *fig.*

1596 SHAKS. *Merch. V.* III. ii. 42 Nerryssa and the rest, stand all aloofe. 1602, 1611, etc. [see ALOOF *adv.* 5, 3]. 1605 SHAKS. *Lear* I. i. 242 Loue's not loue When it is mingled with regards, that stands Aloofe from th'intire point. 1704 SWIFT *T. Tub* i. 45 Our nearest Friends begin to stand aloof, as if they were half ashamed to own Us. 1881 GARDINER & MULLINGER *Study Eng. Hist.* I. v. 95 He himself stood aloof from such doctrines. 1893 LIDDON *Life Pusey* I. xi. 262 He stood somewhat aloof from the Movement in his later years.

84. stand apart. To stand separate or at a distance (*from* another or others). Also *fig.*

1538 ELYOT *Dict.*, *Distito*, to stande aparte, or be dystant one from an other. 1560 DAUS tr. *Sleidane's Comm.* 363 b, They were commaunded to stand apart. 1590 SHAKS. *Com. Err.* v. i. 364 Stay, stand apart, I know not which is which. 1840 *Penny Cycl.* XVII. 345/1 The plants [should be] thinned out by the hoe, so as to stand a foot or 15 inches apart. 1886 SHELDON tr. *Flaubert's Salammbô* 8 One of these slaves remained standing apart from the others. 1906 PETRIE *Relig. Anc. Egypt* viii. 58 Besides the classes of gods already described there are others who stand apart in their character, as embodying abstract ideas.

85. stand aside. To draw back or retire and stand apart from the general company or from what is going on. (See sense 7.)

c 1400, 1596 [see ASIDE *adv.* 9]. 1535 COVERDALE *Acts* iv. 15 Then commaunded they them to stonde asyde out of yᵉ Councell. 1703 CIBBER *She wou'd* etc. IV. 50 Stand aside, till I call for you. 1839 DICKENS *Nich. Nick.* liv, Stand aside, every one of you.

†**86. stand astrut.** See A-STRUT.

1540 PALSGR. *Acolastus* I. iv. G iij b, See howe my gyrdell swelleth .i. standeth a styrte. *Ibid.* IV. iv. T iv, Seest thou not my purses or bagges howe they be swollen or stande a stroute with moche golde?

87. stand away.

a. To withdraw to some distance. (See sense 7.)

1599 SHAKS. *Hen. V*, IV. viii. 14 Stand away Captaine Gower. 1601 —— *All's Well* v. ii. 17 Foh, prethee stand away.

b. *Naut.* To sail or steer away (from some coast, quarter, enemy, etc.) (See sense 36.)

1633 T. JAMES *Voy.* 18 The winde larged, and wee stowed away S.S.W. 1680 *Lond. Gaz.* No. 1551/4 They no sooner discovered the Guernsey to be a Man of War, but they Tacked and stood away with all the Sail they could make. 1725 DE FOE *Voy. round World* (1840) 9 We resolved to stand away from the Canaries to the coast of Brazil. 1845 J. COULTER *Adv. in Pacific* xi. 140 In two days more we left this anchorage, and stood away towards the north-east.

88. stand back. Also †*stand aback.* To withdraw and take up a position farther away from the front. (See sense 7.) Also *fig.*

a 1400 *Minor Poems fr. Vernon MS.* xxxiii. 195 He bad him stonde bac..þat he mihte sustene þat stynk. ? *a* 1500 *Robin Hood & Guy of Gisb.* liv, Stand abacke! stand abacke! sayd Robin: Why draw you mee soe neere? 1594 SHAKS. *Rich. III*, I. ii. 38 My Lord stand backe, and let the Coffin passe. 1637 [see ABACK *adv.* 2]. 1684 BUNYAN *Seasonable Counsel* 227 He saith..to all that are forward to revenge themselves; Give place, stand back, let me come. 1909 MAX BEERBOHM *Yet Again* 23 'Stand back, please'. The train was about to start, and I waved farewell to my friend.

89. stand behind. In literal senses (e.g. of one who waits at table). Used by Wyclif as an equivalent for 'apostatize'.

1380 WYCLIF *Sel. Wks.* III. 431 And ȝif apostasie is stondyng bihynde, hou myche stondiþ bihynde ilche siche þat shal be dampned? *Ibid.* 438 For þei stonden bihynde, and fyȝten not wiþ þe fend. 14.. *26 Pol. Poems* 78/171 When mede haþ leue to stande byhynde, þanne trewe loue his erande may spede. 1859 TENNYSON *Enid* 392 Enid..spread the board, And stood behind, and waited on the three.

90. stand beside. To stand by a person's side, as a looker-on, helper, etc.

14.. *26 Pol. Poems* xviii. 91 Suche towches..Wolde..ȝeue oþere cause, þat stonde bysyde, To wene it were a bargayn of synne. *c* 1520 SKELTON *Magnyf.* 1467, I can do nothynge but he stonde besyde.

91. stand by.

a. To stand near at hand; to be present. Now chiefly, to be present as an unconcerned spectator, without interfering or protesting.

c 1375 *Sc. Leg. Saints* xi. (Simon & Jude) 84 His fygur..In þat clath mycht be sene clerly, as he has standyne hymselfe by. *c* 1500 *Star Chamber Cases* (Selden Soc.) I. 105 Without that oone of the seid Erles seruantes shuld stand by and here what shuld be said. 1551 ROBINSON tr. *More's Utopia* I. (1895) 73 Ther chaunsed to stond by a certein iesting parasite. 1594 SHAKS. *Rich. III*, III. iii. 16 Now Margarets Curse is falne vpon our Heads,..For standing by, when Richard stab'd her Sonne. 1659 [H. NEVILE] *Game Pickquet* 6, I shall disturb you in the game if I stand by. 1678 BUNYAN *Pilgr.* I. (1900) 89 The Jury (who all this while stood by, to hear and observe). 1726 SWIFT *Gulliver* I. vi, A professor, who always standeth by on those occasions. 1831 SCOTT *Ct. Robt.* xviii, The most despicable of animals stands not by tamely and sees another assail his mate. 1861 *Temple Bar* II. 214 It did Philip good to stand by, and watch her animated face. 1876 MRS. OLIPHANT *Curate in Charge* xvi, Must we stand by and see all manner of wrong done and..think we..cannot help it?

b. = *stand aside* 85. Also *fig.*, to refrain from action.

1589 R. HARVEY *Pl. Perc.* 5 Stand by a trice, but looke you depart not the court. 1595 SHAKS. *John* IV. iii. 94 Stand by, or I shall gaul you Faulconbridge. 1647 WARD *Simple Cobler* (1843) 5 He..takes his Scepter out of his hand, and bids him stand by. 1764 FOOTE *Patron* III. Wks. 1799 I. 357 Rascals, stand by! I must, I will see him. 1836 MRS. SHERWOOD *Henry Milner* III. v, He was interrupted by the sound of horses' hoofs..followed by a shout of 'stand by, stand by there!' 1896 *Law Times* C. 357/1 To consider whether the beneficiary had stood by too long before he sought redress.

c. To be excluded (*from*). Now, of a juror: to withdraw from the jury, esp. at the challenge of the prosecution. Also *trans.* with juror as obj. Cf. CHALLENGE *sb.* 3 a.

1603 in *Buccleuch MSS.* (Hist. MSS. Comm.) I. 48 He had been before, and stood then by from being Jurate for his misbehaviour. 1828 *Act 9 Geo. IV* c. 54. 500 Nothing herein contained shall affect..the power of any court in Ireland to order any juror to stand by 1890 T. BRETT *Comm. Present Laws of Eng.* II. XIII. viii. 1162 The names of those ordered to 'stand by' are called again. 1925 W. J. BYRNE *Dict. Eng. Law* 167/1 The Crown, although it can challenge for cause, has no peremptory challenge, but it may order any person to 'stand by', and need not show cause. 1969 *Sunday Tel.* 12 Jan. 4/6 The defence..could have called 'Challenge!' 70 times without offering reasons. The prosecution called 'Stand by for the Crown!' nine times. (In a British court the phrase 'I object' does not arise in this context.)

trans. 1927 A. M. SULLIVAN *Old Ireland* ii. 41 If this infamous creature attempts to 'stand by' a single Nationalist juror, you will ram it down his throat! 1960 V. T. H. DELANY *Christopher Palles* xi. 101 The Crown 'stood by' 96 jurors, while the defence challenged 36. 1979 *Criminal Law Rev.* May 273 The Crown's right to 'stand-by' jurors is a term which refers to the Crown's power of challenge.

d. Of a thing: To be laid aside; *fig.* 'to be put aside with disregard' (J.).

1667 *Decay Chr. Piety* iv. 51 We make all our addresses to the promises, hug and caress them, and in the interim let the commands stand by neglected. 1683 MOXON *Mech. Exerc.*, *Printing* xxii. ¶7 The Wrought off Form is Stript..and stands by to Destribute. 1893 *Sketch* 15 Feb. 179/2 And now everything stands by for the discussion of Home Rule.

e. *Naut.* To hold oneself in readiness, be prepared (*for* something, *to* do something). Often in imperative = be ready! Also *gen.*

1669 STURMY *Mariner's Mag.* I. ii. 17 Come, stand by, take in our Top-sails. 1697 DAMPIER *Voy.* I. 17 He that stood by to clear it away, stopt the Line. 1759 *Ann. Reg.*, *Chron.* 62/1, I called to my people to stand by and do their duty. 1831 *Examiner* 178/2 Open the safety-valve, or stand by for the explosion. 1840 R. H. DANA *Bef. Mast* xxv, The starboard watch..left the ship to us for a couple of hours, yet with orders to stand by for a call. 1866 'MARK TWAIN' *Lett. from Hawaii* (1967) 117 Just as you take a sustaining breath and 'stand by' for the crash, his poor little rocket fizzes faintly in the zenith. 1890 *Chamb. Jrnl.* 7 June 356/2 Bring the boat close under, my lads,..and stand by to receive the lady. 1917 'CONTACT' *Airman's Outings* iv. 84 For thirty hours the flight had 'stood by' for a long reconnaissance... A slight but steady rain washed away all chance of an immediate job. 1943 *Ann. Reg. 1942* 28 The wastefulness of keeping so many men merely 'standing-by'. 1972 *Listener* 21 Dec. 852/1 Sequence of calls before a shot. Production Assistant: 'Quiet. Going for a take. Standing by.'

92. stand down.

a. Of a witness: To step down and leave the box after giving evidence. (Cf. sense 7.)

1681 *Trial S. Colledge* 74 Mr. Ser. *Jeff.* You say well, stand down. 1831 *Examiner* 732/2 Bench: Stand down.—Defendant: No, I shan't stand down, for you. 1837 DICKENS *Pickw.* xxxiii, I will not trouble the court by asking him any more questions. Stand down, Sir.

b. *Sport.* To withdraw from a game, match, or race; to give up one's place in a team, crew, or 'side'.

1890 *Field* 31 May 790/2 Charlton also stood down, and the vacant places were given to..Barrett and Trumble. *Ibid.* 15 Nov. 744/1 On the University side, Shiels stood down in favour of G. S. Thorn. 1912 *Throne* 7 Aug. 234/2 The first news was that Wootton had to stand down for the whole of August.

c. *Naut.* To sail with the wind or tide. (Cf. sense 36.)

1834 M. SCOTT *Cruise Midge* i, May I therefore request the favour of your standing down to her. 1885 *Times* (weekly ed.) 2 Oct. 14/4 Fishing boats..standing down with the ebb in midstream.

d. *Mil.* To come off duty; to relax after a state of alert (also *trans.*).

1916 I. GURNEY *Let.* 25 Oct. in *PN Review 29* (1982) 32/1 Our last orders were as follows.—From Stand to 5.30. Stand Down, clean rifles... Stand to 5–5.30. Stand Down. 1918 E. S. FARROW *Dict. Mil. Terms* s.v. *Stand to*, Stand down is the order countermanding 'stand-to'. 1919 W. H. DOWNING *Digger Dialects* 47 *Stand-down*, the order by which the period of intense armed vigilance is ended at daybreak, nightfall, or after the alarm of a threatened enemy attack has passed over. 1931 F. TILSLEY *Other Ranks* 108 They religiously stood-to and stood-down every dawn and dusk. 1973 *Daily Tel.* 29 Oct. 30/3 Pres. Nixon ordered..troops in Europe..to remain on the alert..but elsewhere round the world American forces were stood down. 1983 *Times* 12 Feb. 1/1 Acas officials were fighting to keep alive the proposal for a third-party intervention to settle the water workers' strike. But a lull in the peace process is expected over the weekend after the Acas conciliation team was stood down.

93. stand forth.

a. To step forward (in order to do something, make a speech, face a company, etc.); to come boldly or resolutely to the front or centre. (Cf. sense 7.) †*to stand forth to*, to confront.

a 1300 *Cursor M.* 10231 Joachim son forth can stand, And mad him bun wit his offrand. 1362 LANGL. *P. Pl.* A. II. 57 Now Simonye and Siuyle stondeð forþ boþe. *c* 1425 ? LYDG. *Assembly of Gods* 442 He stoode forthe boldly with grym countenaunce. 1526 TINDALE *Luke* vi. 8 Ryse vp and stonde forthe in the myddes. 1625 B. JONSON *Staple of N.* IV. iv, Now he treats of you, stand forth to him, faire. 1780 *Mirror* No. 68 In such a cause every man would stand forth. 1872 C. E. MAURICE *Stephen Langton* i. 28 The prophet who had stood forth to denounce the awful corruption. 1879 MORLEY *Burke* iv. 76 It needs valour and integrity to stand forth against a wrong to which our best friends are..committed.

†**b.** To persist *in* (a course of action). *Obs.*

c 1400 *Rom. Rose* 3547 To stonde forth in such duresse.

c. To make a conspicuous appearance, be prominent.

a 1764 LLOYD *Dial. Author & Friend* 17 Yes—it [his book] stands forth to public view. 1856 *N. Brit. Rev.* XXVI. 138 Sober, industrious, intellectual..he stands forth as one of the model workmen of Europe. 1862 *Temple Bar* VI. 356 No buildings are allowed to touch it, and thus it stands forth in its native gigantesque proportions.

94. stand forward. = *stand forth* 93 a.

1790 *Loiterer* 9 Jan. 7, I shall be happy to contribute my mite... I dare say his Lordship would stand forward [i.e. with a donation]. 1802 MAR. EDGEWORTH *Moral T.*, *Prussian Vase*, I applaud him, for standing forward in defence of his friend. 1820 MILNER *Suppl. Mem. Eng. Cath.* 313 Summoning all those who had signed the Protestation to stand forward in defence of its errors.

95. stand in.

†**a.** To strive, continue insistently *to* (do something). (Cf. L. *instare* and 98 a.) *Obs.*

c 1200 ORMIN 2149 I whillc an Crisstene mann..Birrþ standenn inn affterr hiss mihht To follȝhenn hire bisne. *Ibid.* 2617 þe deofell, þatt æfre & æfre standeþþ inn To screnkenn ure sawless.

†**b.** To impend, be imminent. (Rendering L. *instare*. Cf. 98 b.) *Obs.*

a 1390 *Wyclif's Bible*, *Jerem.* Prol. 343 Bifor that the tyme of destrucciouon shulde stonden in [*antequam depopulationis tempus instaret*].

†**c.** To join issue *with* (others in a dispute); to take part *in* (a controversy). *Obs.*

c 1540 R. MORICE in *Lett. Lit. Men* (Camden) 24 He never shranke from the facte but stowtlie stode in with them in disputation. 1555 RIDLEY *Treat. agst. Transubst.* E viij b, The controuersie..(wherin anye meane learned man either olde or newe doth stand in). [1865 *Hotten's Slang Dict.*, *Stand in*,..to take a side in a dispute.]

d. 'To make one of a party in a bet or other speculation' (*Slang Dict.* 1865). Usually const. *with*: To go shares with, join, be a partner with; in wider sense, to have a friendly or profitable understanding with, be in league with, be on good terms with. Also, to share chances with others *for* (a speculative event). Also *rarely*, to fall in *with* (a proposal).

1857 A. MAYHEW *Paved with Gold* III. xx, The policeman who 'stood in' for this robbery saw the rogues depart with their plunder. 1860 WHYTE MELVILLE *Mkt. Harb.* xv, The valet..who..made a point of 'standing in' with all the upper servants, treated the stud-groom with considerable deference. 1865 LEVER *Luttrell* xxxvi. 261 If I was quite sure that I 'stood in' for the double event..I almost think I'd do it. 1898 BESANT *Orange Girl* II. xii, The job was easy and should be done, but he should expect to stand in. 1898 *Edin. Rev.* Jan. 160 The policy of standing-in with both parties was the ruling idea of his political career. 1911 M. BEERBOHM *Zuleika Dobson* viii. 138 'Dorset,' he said huskily, 'I shall die too.'.. 'I stand in with that,' said Mr. Oover [an American]. 'So do I!' said Lord Sayes.

e. *Naut.* To direct one's course towards the shore. (See sense 36.)

c 1595 CAPT. WYATT *R. Dudley's Voy W. Ind.* (Hakl. Soc.) 10 Wee might perceave a small saile..standing in for the ilands as wee did. 1670–1 NARBOROUGH *Voy.* I. (1694) 181 We stood in for the Land. 1853 KANE *Grinnell Exp.* xix. (1856) 141 Wishing to fill up with water..we stood close in. 1892 *Chamb. Jrnl.* 27 Feb. 135/2 The captain,..noticing something strange, stood in to discover its meaning.

f. To fill the place of another (usu. temporarily); to deputize *for* (a person); *spec.* in *Cinemat.*, to act as a substitute *for* a principal actor. Cf. STAND-IN 2.

1904 in *Eng. Dial. Dict.* V. 725/2 *e. Ken.* Mrs. —— will stand in while Mrs. —— is ill. **1943** HUNT & PRINGLE *Service Slang* 62 *Stand-in*, a deputy; one who 'stands in' for you, or does your duty while you go out. **1955** *Times* 6 June 7/6 There is always a way, especially in Russia where queueing has had to be carried to a fine art. You can employ the willing services of an Armenian or Georgian or other agile-minded person who will stand in for you or will, in turn, get another to stand in for him. **1958** *Listener* 7 Aug. 210/2 The people who stand-in for the film stars when the rough stuff begins. **1978** 'B. GRAEME' *Double Trouble* ii. 20 She has to stand-in for the star while they are working out lighting, camera angles and so on... They try to have a stand-in as much like the star as possible.

96. stand off.

a. To remain at or retire to a distance; to draw back, go farther away. Chiefly in commands.

1631 B. JONSON *New Inn* IV. iii, *Fra.* She is some Giantess! Ile stand off, For feare she swallow me. **1717** POPE *Iliad* x. 93 Stand off, approach not, but thy Purpose tell. **1828** *Ann. Reg.* 26/2 Our party said, 'Stand off, or we will shoot you'. **1890** *Graphic* Summer No. 14/2 The rider.. told him with a curse to stand off.

†**b.** Of a thing: To remain apart or separate or at a distance (*from* some object). Also, *fig.*, to be separated in quality, differ. *Obs.*

1601 SHAKS. *All's Well* II. iii. 127 Strange is it that our bloods Of colour, waight, and heat, pour'd all together, Would quite confound distinction: yet stands off In differences so mightie. **1644** J. GOODWIN *Danger of fighting agst. God* 52 Your judgements stand off from the cause.. and you can see nothing of God in it. **1705** COLLIER *Ess. Mor. Subj.* III. *Pain* 16 The Flames being observ'd to stand off, and not touch his body.

c. *fig.* To hold aloof (from an offer or appeal, friendship, intercourse, sympathy, or the like); to be 'distant', uncomplying or unaccommodating.

1601 SHAKS. *All's Well* IV. ii. 34 Stand no more off, But giue thy selfe vnto my sicke desires. **1622** MABBE tr. *Aleman's Guzman d'Alf.* II. 265, I did not stand off, but gaue him all that he had giuen me. **1676** PHILLIPS *Purchasers Pattern* B 6 b, If any Tenant.. would have a longer lease.. I would not wish the Landlord to stand off. **1679** C. NESSE *Antichrist* 224 Aidanus, our own countreyman, who stood off not only from Romish primacy but from prelacy. **1705** tr. *Bosman's Guinea* 175 Though I desired nothing more, yet I stood off as though I was not to be perswaded to that. **1844** KINGLAKE *Eothen* xviii, I entreated him to stand off, telling him fairly how deeply I was 'compromised'. **1888** FLOR. WARDEN *Woman's Face* III. xxviii. 170 Stony eyes that bade sympathy stand off and be silent. **1889** *Univ. Rev.* Sept. 32 He has politicly stood off from her appeals.

d. Of a thing: To project, protrude, jut out (*from* a surface, etc.). Of a picture: To appear as if in relief. Also *fig.*, to be conspicuous or prominent. (Cf. *stand out* 99 i–k.)

1599 SHAKS. *Hen. V*, II. ii. 103 'Tis so strange, That though the truth of it stands off as grosse As blacke and white, my eye will scarsely see it. **1624** WOTTON *Archit.* II. 84 Picture is best when it standeth off, as if it were carued. **1737** BRACKEN *Farriery Impr.* (1757) II. 32 The farther the Back Sinew stands off from the Bone, the better it is. **1820** W. IRVING *Sketch Bk.* (1859) 157 A little, meagre, black-looking man, with a grizzled wig that was too wide, and stood off from each ear. **1843** *Jrnl. R. Agric. Soc.* IV. II. 471 The tines stand off from the beam so as to work to the depth of about 5 inches from the furrow-slice last turned.

e. *Naut.* To sail away from the shore. (Cf. *stand out* 99 h.)

1625 J. GLANVILLE *Voy. Cadiz* (Camden) 117 We tacked about againe and stood off to Sea. **1764** J. BYRON in Hawkesworth *Voy.* I. 13 Having stood off in the night, we now wore and stood in again. **1891** *Longman's Mag.* Oct. 591 Howard.. had to tack and stand off to sea.

f. *trans.* To keep off, keep at a distance; to repel, hold at bay; to put off, evade (a questioner, dun, etc.). *U.S. colloq.*

1878 J. H. BEADLE *Western Wilds* ii. 38 He offered him fifty thousand for it, and the feller stood him off for seventy-five thousand. **1883** J. HAY *Bread-Winners* xvii. 274 Come, come, Sam, don't stand me off that way. **1887** F. FRANCIS Jun. *Saddle & Mocassin* 181 Loop-holed! Well, the men who built this place expected occasionally to have to 'stand off' irate Mexicans. **1889** *Advance* (Chicago) 19 Dec., Standing off the hungry wolf from the door of the college. **1894** *Harper's Mag.* Feb. 391/1 Thankful to have stood her off, I asked how Reuben was looking.

g. To lay (an employee) off temporarily. Also *intr.* of an employee. Cf. LAY *v.*[1] 54 f.

1918 [implied at STAND-OFF *sb.* 5]. **1927** CARR-SAUNDERS & JONES *Soc. Struct. Eng. & Wales* 135 It is not uncommon for indentures to contain a clause enabling the employer to 'stand off' the apprentice without pay if there is no work for him. **1930** *Daily Express* 8 Sept. 11/4 Thirteen hundred Chislet miners.. went on strike.. as a protest against the standing-off of six men. **1940** H. G. WELLS *New World Order* § 5. 58 A state of five million people with half a million of useless hands, will be twice as unstable as forty million with two million standing off. **1952** M. LASKI *Village* i. 17 It wasn't very nice me having to go out to work when Mr. Wilson was stood off, and him staying at home to keep an eye on the children. **1960** G. E. EVANS *Horse in Furrow* i. 22 The day-men were liable to be *stood-off* on wet days. **1976** *Eastern Daily Press* (Norwich) 16 Dec., He was later stood off but went back there to work from 1962 to 1975.

97. stand off and on. *Naut.* (See quot. 1846.)

1666 [see OFF AND ON 2]. **1748** *Anson's Voy.* I. vi. 58 The weather made it dangerous to supply their ships by standing off and on. **1846** A. YOUNG *Naut. Dict.* 295 *Stand off and on*, alternately to recede from and approach the land while sailing by the wind.

transf. **1806–7** J. BERESFORD *Miseries Hum. Life* (1826) IV. xviii, Standing off and on in the street.. while the friend with whom you are walking talks to his friend.

98. stand on.

†**a.** To be urgent or insistent *to* (do something). (Cf. *stand in* 95 a.) *Obs.*

c **1440** *Pallad. on Husb.* I. 71 Coloured, stond not on to bisily To se thy lond, but rather fatte and swete.

†**b.** To impend, be imminent. (Cf. *stand in* 95 b.)

1382 WYCLIF *Isa.* xxi. 15 Fro the face of the swerd stondende on [*a facie gladii imminentis*]. *a* **1390** —— *Jerem.* Prol. 343 Now the caitifte stod on [*jam captivitas imminebat*].

c. *Naut.* (See sense 36.) To keep one's course, continue on the same tack. ***to stand on and off*** (*rare*) = 97.

1666 *Lond. Gaz.* No. 60/3 The whole Line tacked in the wake of him, and stood on till.. the Prince thought fit to keep the wind. *a* **1779** COOK *3rd Voy.* III. xi. (1784) II. 197 While the boats were occupied in examining the coast, we stood on and off with the ships, waiting for their return. **1790** BEATSON *Nav. & Mil. Mem.* I. 111 The Admiral continued, with a press of sail, standing on close to the wind. **1875** BEDFORD *Sailor's Pocket Bk.* iii. (ed. 2) 64 Is A to stand on; and if not, why not?

99. stand out.

a. To move away (from a company, shelter, etc.) and stand apart or in open view. (See sense 7.)

in first quot.? = *stand up.*

c **1220** *Bestiary* 655 Ðanne cumeð ðer on gangande, hopeð he sal him [a fallen elephant] don ut standen. **1753** RICHARDSON *Grandison* I. xiv. 86 To stand out to receive.. the first motions to an address of this awful nature. **1842** MACAULAY *Horatius* li, Yet one man for one moment Stood out before the crowd. **1849** JAMES *Woodman* iii, Stand out, and tell us who you are, creeping along there under the boughs. **1892** *Graphic* 17 Dec. 743/3 The master prefers.. to order the wrongdoer to 'stand out'.

b. Not to take part in (an undertaking, joint action, etc.); to refuse to come in or join others; to hold aloof (†*from* doing something); now *esp.* not to take part in a match, game or dance (cf. 92 b).

1599 B. JONSON *Cynthia's Rev.* I. iv, Though I affect not popularity, yet I would be lothe to stand out to any, whome you shall voutchsafe to call friend. **1601** SHAKS. *Twel. N.* III. iii. 35 It might haue since bene answer'd in repaying What we tooke from them, which for Traffiques sake Most of our City did. Only my selfe stood out. **1609** B. JONSON *Epicœne* I. i, Marry, the Chimney-sweepers will not be drawne in. *Cle.* No, nor the Broome-men: They stand out stiffely. **1640–1** *Kirkcudbr. War-Comm. Min. Bk.* (1855) 61 As for these that hes naither subscryvit nor will cum in, but stands owt, they are to be fyned. **1671** SHADWELL *Humourists* v, I am resolved to play at a small game, rather than stand out. **1687** BURNET *Contin. Reply Varillas* 19 Fisher being the only man that stood out a while, but even he at last concurred with the rest. **1690** LUTTRELL *Brief Rel.* II. 6 Dr. Timothy Hall, bishop of Oxon., has lately taken the oathes to their majesties, which he has stood out from doeing till the utmost time was come. **1890** *Field* 10 May 673/1 The captain and the secretary stood out on this occasion, but arranged twelve Seniors a-side. **1893** *Nat. Observer* 7 Oct. 535/2 The ladies proposed a dance.. The Captain himself stood out.

c. To resist, persist in opposition or resistance, refuse to yield or comply, hold out. Const. *against* (an opponent, proposal, etc.), *with* (an opponent).

1595 SHAKS. *John* v. ii. 71 His spirit is come in, That so stood out against the holy Church. **1601** BARLOW *Serm. Paules Crosse* 37 Nor will I mention his oft standing out with her if he were thwarted. **1698** FRYER *Acc. E. India & P.* vii, The Mountains in all Conquests the last that stand out. **1879** M. J. GUEST *Lect. Hist. Eng.* xxviii. 287 The Commons threw away their humility, and stood out boldly. **1887** SIMS *Mary Jane's Mem.* 296, I have had to stand out with my editor once or twice on that.. point. **1891** *Chamb. Jrnl.* 19 Sept. 594/2 It requires exceptional courage to stand out against a popular cry.

transf. **1806–7** J. BERESFORD *Miseries Hum. Life* (1826) x. lxi, The pullies resolutely standing out against all your efforts to turn them.

d. ***to stand it out*** = prec.

1607 TOPSELL *Four-f. Beasts* 571 When the fight is once begunne, there is none of both that may runne awaie, but standeth it out vntil one or both of them bee slaine to the ground. *a* **1694** TILLOTSON *Serm.* xxxv. (1742) III. 17 He is in good earnest, and will execute these threatnings upon them if they will obstinately stand it out with him. **1718** OCKLEY *Saracens* (1848) 219 Knowing very well how hard it would go with them if they should stand it out obstinately to the last, and be taken by storm. **1837** CARLYLE *Fr. Rev.* I. VII. xi, He, tough as tanned leather.. will stand it out for another year. **1866** RUSKIN *Crown of Wild Olive* iv. § 148, I.. stood it out to the end, and helped to carry four of my fellow students.. down stairs.

e. ***to stand out for***: to declare oneself for, contend on behalf of.

a **1600** *Raid of Reidswire* xviii. in Scott *Border Minstrelsy* (1869) 74 None stoutlier stood out for their laird, Nor did the lads of Liddisdail. **1633** BP. HALL *Hard Texts* Hos. v. 13 When Ahaz.. was in distresse, he sends to Tiglath Pileser, that should stand out for him. **1891** *Chamb. Jrnl.* 19 Sept. 593/2 He has not grit enough to stand out for justice and honesty.

f. To haggle, make difficulties about striking a bargain; to make an obstinate demand *for* (certain terms).

1766 GOLDSM. *Vic. W.* xii, He always stands out and higgles. **1816** SCOTT *Antiq.* xxiv, 'If the secret were mine,' said the mendicant, 'I wad stand out for a half.' **1889** RIDER HAGGARD *Col. Quaritch* xliii. 325, I am not going to stand out about the price. **1890** *Sat. Rev.* 20 Sept. 337/1 They stood out partly for more wages.

†**g.** Of a bill, debt, etc.: To remain unsettled or unpaid. (Cf. OUTSTANDING *ppl. a.* 4.) *Obs.*

1723 *Lond. Gaz.* No. 6183/2 Exchequer Bills (which are all that are now standing out and undischarged). **1736** *Gentl. Mag.* VI. 563/1 An Account of all the publick Debts.. due or standing out at Christmas, 1735.

h. *Naut.* (See sense 36.) To sail in a direction away from the shore. Usually ***to stand out to sea.*** Hence *gen.*, to start on a journey.

1718 ROWE *Lucan* iv. 717 *note*, Octavius stood out to sea. **1834** M. SCOTT *Cruise Midge* vi, The signal to weigh and stand out, sir. **1885** *Times* 18 Sept. 13/2 We stood out through the thickening rain. **1891** *Longman's Mag.* Oct. 596 They cut their cables.. and stood out into the Channel.

i. To jut out, project, protrude (*from* a surface); to be prominent.

1540 PALSGR. *Acolastus* II. i. H ij b, My chynne standynge out lyke as aged folkes lyppes do, that be totheles. **1558** PHAER *Æneid* VIII. (1562) Cc ij b, Agrippa loftie prince whose pendaunt streamers proud stand out. **1560** BIBLE (Geneva) *Ps.* lxxiii. 7 Their eyes stand out for fatnes. **1585** HIGINS *Junius' Nomencl.* 206/1 *Striæ*,.. those partes in furrowed pillers which stand out and swell as it were. *c* **1643** LD. HERBERT *Autobiog.* (1824) 100 The Pier of Dover, which stands out in the Sea. **1680** MOXON *Mech. Exerc.* xi. 202 The work.. is required to stand out free from the outer Flat of the Cheeks of the Coller. **1742** BLAIR *Grave* 274 Oh! how his Eyes stand out, and stare full ghastly! **1889** MRS. LYNN LINTON *Thro' Long Night* I. I. xiii. 207 Her ears stood out from her head like jug-handles. **1890** W. C. RUSSELL *Ocean Trag.* I. i. 6 The veins stood out like whipcord.

j. To be conspicuous; to be seen in contrast or relief *against* a dark object or background. Of figures in painting: To appear as if in relief.

1856 WHYTE MELVILLE *Kate Coventry* ix, Lucy's white face stood out in the lamplight. **1884** *Times* (weekly ed.) 29 Aug. 14/1 The white houses, sparkling in the sunshine, stood out against the dark background of woods. **1889** MRS. E. KENNARD *Landing a Prize* II. iv. 65 Red flannel shirts.. stood out in the distance as a brilliant spot of colour.

k. *fig.* To be prominent or conspicuous to the mental gaze.

1826 LAMB *Elia* Ser. II. *Genteel Style in Writing*, The man of rank is discernible in both writers; but in the one it is only insinuated gracefully, in the other it stands out offensively. **1874** GREEN *Short Hist.* viii. § 6. 518 John Pym.. stands out for all after time as the embodiment of law. **1891** *Chamb. Jrnl.* 7 Feb. 81/1 Two facts stand out in bold relief.

l. *trans.* To remain standing throughout (a performance). Also *Naut.* to 'stand watch' (see sense 60) during (a specified time).

1840 R. H. DANA *Bef. Mast* vii, We were then divided into three watches, and thus stood out the remainder of the night. **1890** CONSTANCE SMITH *Riddle Lawr. Haviland* II. III. iv. 90 He propped himself in an angle of the doorway, and prepared to stand out the performance.

m. To endure to the end, hold out under or against (a trial, ordeal, severe weather, etc.); to last out (a period of time).

1623 *Shaks. Wks.* To Rdrs., These Playes have had their triall alreadie, and stood out all Appeales. **1649** JER. TAYLOR *Gt. Exemp.* I. Ad. Sec. vi. 105 Jesus fled from the persecution; as he did not stand it out, so he did not stand out against it. **1676** PHILLIPS *Purchasers Pattern* 18 Houses.. many times cannot well stand out a long Lease. **1821** SCOTT *Kenilw.* vii, It is a sunburnt beauty,.. well qualified to stand out rain and wind. **1827** —— *Jrnl.* 28 Mar., I.. went out in as rough weather as I have seen, and stood out several snow blasts. **1855** FLOR. NIGHTINGALE in Sir E. Cook *Life* (1913) I. 283, I am ready to stand out the War with any man.

n. With object-clause: To maintain, insist, persist in asserting (*that*). Also ***to stand it out*** (*that*): cf. d.

1664 H. MORE *Myst. Iniq.* I. xiii. 42 They.. will stand it out as stoutly for their justification, as these professors of Christianity that they are no Idolaters. **1726** BERKELEY *Lett.* Wks. 1871 IV. 120 The latter still stands out.. that she never received.. any of Mrs. Mary's money. **1863** MRS. GASKELL *Sylvia's Lovers* xxxix, It were only yesterday at e'en she were standing out that he liked her better than you. **1898** BESANT *Orange Girl* II. xii, He.. stoutly stood it out that he was a gentleman of Cumberland.

o. *Sport.* To stick to (a bet) without hedging. (Cf. sense 63.)

1892 *Illustr. Sporting & Dram. News* 28 May 382/2 Personally I would not take 100 to 1, to stand it out. *Ibid.* 406/3 Still, mark my words, he will stand that bet out, if only for Julia's sake.

p. *dial.* To force or try to force (a person) by pertinacious assertion to believe or admit (the fact expressed by an object-clause).

1895 ALICIA A. LEITH *Plant of Lemon Verbena* v. 105 He tried t' stand me out 'twas a white caaf or a cow I'd zeen. **1895** JANE BARLOW *Strangers at Lisconnel* ii. 26, I question would any raisonable body stand me out I don't own her be rights.

100. stand over.

a. *Naut.* (See sense 36.) To leave one shore and sail towards another.

1699 DAMPIER *Voy.* II. I. 171 Yet we did not stand over towards Sumatra, but coasted along nearest the Malacca shore. **1855** MACAULAY *Hist. Eng.* xv. III. 604 He now stood over to the English shore.

b. To be left or reserved for treatment, consideration or settlement at a later date. (See OVER *adv.* 9.)

1822 M. EDGEWORTH *Let.* 30 May (1971) 404 A beef and pigeon pie that had stood over from the preceding week. **1824** *Examiner* 67/1 [He] directed the trial to stand over until the next morning. **1853** *Jrnl. R. Agric. Soc.* XIV. I. 30

Many acres..are left unsown, and must stand over for Lent corn. **1884** *Law Rep. 25 Chanc. Div.* 707 The motion was ordered to stand over for a fortnight. **1891** *Sat. Rev.* 22 Aug. 219/1 His accounts are balanced at the close of each season, and no bad debts are allowed to stand over.

101. stand to.

†**a.** To be present, 'assist'. *Obs.*

1540 PALSGR. *Acolastus* Peroration Bb iij b, You al.. whiche stand to here .i. all you, whiche stande here at this presente tyme.

†**b.** To set to work, fall to; *esp.* to begin eating. (See TO *adv.* 6.) *Obs.*

1605 SHAKS. *Macb.* II. iii. 38. **1610** —— *Temp.* III. iii. 49, 52, I will stand to, and feede..: my Lord, the Duke, Stand too, and doe as we.

c. *Mil. ellipt.* for *to stand to one's arms*, sense 76 d. Hence, to come or remain on duty. Cf. *stand-to*, sense 104 below.

1915 F. H. LAWRENCE *Let.* 7 Mar. in *Home Lett. T. E. Lawrence* (1954) 671, I thought the Germans were attacking us, so I passed the word along for all my men to stand to, as we call it. *a* **1918** W. OWEN *Poems* (1963) 60 Eh? What the 'ell! Stand to? Stand to! Jim, Give's a hand with pack on, lad. **1942** E. WAUGH *Put out More Flags* i. 22 She saw him as Siegfried Sassoon, an infantry subaltern in a mud-bogged trench, standing to at dawn,..waiting for zero hour. **1977** J. B. HILTON *Dead-Nettle* xv. 120 After days of pointless standing-to in dew-drenched hedge-bottoms, there was a cleaning-up of uniforms.

†**102. stand together.**

a. To agree, be consistent, harmonize. *Obs.*

1387–8 T. USK *Test. Love* III. ix. (Skeat) l. 26 As I was lerned how goddes before-weting and free choice of wil mowe stonden togider. *c* **1449** PECOCK *Repr.* II. xvi. 246 And so these ij. thingis whiche Scripture seith of ydolatrers stonden to gidere and ben trewe. **1565** HARDING *Answ. Jewel's Challenge* 137 Sith both these verities may well stande together. **1629** BURTON *Babel no Bethel* 96 The Arke and Dagon cannot stand together. **1711** FELTON *Diss. Classics* (1718) 9 Sprightly Youth and close Application will hardly stand together.

b. To consist *in, of.* (Rendering L. *constare* with ablative.) *Obs.*

c **1400** *Apol. Loll.* 47 We..striue to proue þe sacrifice of þe kirk to stond to gidre in two þingis, and to be maad in two þingis to gidre:..as þe persoun of Crist stondiþ to gidre of God and man.

103. stand up.

a. To assume an erect position; to rise, get up on one's feet.

a **1122** *O.E. Chron.* (Laud MS.) an. 656 Þa stod seo kyning up toforen ealle his ðæȝna & cwæd luddor stefne [etc.]. *c* **1200** ORMIN 16138 Þatt lufess fir..iss kinndledd i þatt herrte þatt..stanndeþþ upp biforenn follc,..To niþþrenn woh wiþþ all hiss mahht. *a* **1300** *Cursor M.* 16415 Pilate stode vp on his fete mid-ward þat gret gadring. **1535** COVERDALE *Song Sol.* v. 5, I stode vp to open vnto my beloued. **1667** *Answ. to Quest. out of North* 12 If any person coming to Church..do not Stand Up at the Creed. **1711** ADDISON *Spect.* No. 112 ⁋3 He..sometimes stands up when every Body else is upon their Knees. **1787** 'G. GAMBADO' *Acad. Horsem.* (1809) 34 The standing up in your stirrups, whilst trotting..has a most elegant and genteel effect. **1877** MISS YONGE *Cameos* Ser. III. xxxvi. 391 He stood up in the waggon and began to sing.

b. To remain erect and firm *under* (a crushing weight, or the like). (Cf. 77 b.)

1682 BUNYAN *Holy War* 164 For the grace, the benefit, the pardon, was sudden, glorious, and so big, that they were not able without staggering to stand up under it.

c. To take part in a dance; to dance *with* (a partner).

1766 GOLDSM. *Vic. W.* xxi, We were here interrupted by a servant who came to ask the Squire in to stand up at country-dances. **1796** JANE AUSTEN *Pride & Prej.* xviii, In vain did she entreat him to stand up with somebody else. **1804** —— *Watsons* (1879) 328, I thought you were to stand up with Mr. Tomlinson the two last dances.

d. To take up one's position to play an athletic game.

1884 *J. Marshall's Tennis Cuts* 169 He had a twist in his spine, which rendered him physically incapable of standing up to play more than one game a day. **1896** A. E. HOUSMAN *Shropsh. Lad* xxvii, Is football playing.., With lads to chase the leather, Now I stand up no more?

e. *dial.* (See quots.) Also, †to present oneself for marriage.

1842 *Amer. Pioneer* I. 314 They were married without any previous preparation..he standing up in a hunting dress, and she in a short gown and petticoat of homespun. **1886** *W. Somerset Word-bk.*, *Stand up for*, to undertake the office of God-parent at a baptism. **1891** *Century Dict.*, *To stand up with*, to act as groomsman or bridesmaid to: as, I stood up with him at his wedding. (Colloq.)

f. *colloq.* and *dial.* To take shelter from rain.

1836 DICKENS *Sk. Boz* (1st Ser.) I. 252 Nobody thought of 'standing up' under doorways or arches. **1887** 'MARK RUTHERFORD' *Revol. Tanner's Lane* xviii. (ed. 8) 271 Thomas, however,..proposed that they should stand up in a shed which had been used for faggot-making. The rain, which now came down heavily, enforced his arguments. **1893** in Cozens-Hardy *Broad Norf.* 13 Let us stand up out of the wet. **1908** G. K. CHESTERTON *Man who was Thursday* 126 Hoping..that the snow-shower might be slight, he stepped back..and stood up under the doorway of a..shop.

g. colloq. *to stand up in*, to be actually wearing; freq. in extended phr. (*only*) *the clothes one stands up in.* (Cf. *stand in* 72 a.)

1901 ALLDRIDGE *Sherbro* xxvii. 309 The boat returned.. bringing down Miss Mullen with only such things as she stood up in. **1937** 'G. ORWELL' *Road to Wigan Pier* ix. 182, I..planned..how one could..start out with no money and nothing but the clothes one stood up in. **1944** N. STREATFEILD *Curtain Up* vi. 71 Monsieur Manoff and most of his pupils..escaped to America... They had, of course, nothing but what they stood up in. **1981** E. LONGFORD *Queen Mother* v. 83 Queen Wilhelmina of the Netherlands ..brought only the clothes she stood up in plus a tin hat.

h. Of an animal: To hold out, endure (in a race or chase). †Also in *imper.* as a cry to urge on a horse.

1656 EARL MONM. tr. *Boccalini's Advts. fr. Parnass.* I. xxxi. (1674) 36 Coach-men..whipping their Horses, and.. crying, Stand up. **1891** *Field* 7 Nov. 695/3 A baker's dozen struggled on to the finish..but if our deer had stood up for another mile or two, the number would have been still further reduced. **1893** *Sat. Rev.* 7 Jan. 16/1 A dog who would lap after a course would have no chance of standing up in subsequent rounds.

i. Of things: To be set upright; to be or become erect. Of hair, spines, etc.: cf. sense 17 d.

a **1300** *Cursor M.* 3779 In slepe he sagh stand vp a sti, Fra his heued right to þe ski. *c* **1460** *Towneley Myst.* xxiii. 232 Vp with the tymbre fast on ende!.. A, it standys vp lyke a mast. **1549** *Compl. Scot.* xii. 102 And ane vthir speyr set & bundyn athort betuix the tua speyris that stude vp fra the eyrd lyik ane gallus. **1667** MILTON *P.L.* VII. 321 Up stood the cornie Reed Embattell'd in her field. **1815** J. SMITH *Panorama Sci. & Art* II. 182 Its apex rests upon the point of a steel pin standing up in the centre of the box. **1889** G. GISSING *Nether World* III. xii. 253 His hair stood up like stubble. **1896** tr. *Boas' Text-bk. Zool.* 391 The Sea Hedgehog (*Diodon*) is beset with bony spines, which stand up when the animal puffs itself out.

†**j.** Of flame, vapour: To rise up, issue upwards. (Cf. sense 33.) *Obs.* exc. *poet.*

c **1290** *S. Eng. Leg.* 233/501 Þe leiȝe stod op on heiȝ ase þei it a wal were. *c* **1330** R. BRUNNE *Chron. Wace* (Rolls) 1818 Þe stem stod vp, so þey blew. **1896** A. E. HOUSMAN *Shropshire Lad* vii. 11 When smoke stood up from Ludlow And mist blew off the Teme.

†**k.** Of a door: To remain open. *Obs.*

1550 CROWLEY *Epigr.* 118 In service tyme no dore standeth up, Where such men are wonte to fyll can and cuppe.

†**l.** *Naut.* Of a number of ships: To form up, assemble *together* in a given place or position. *Obs.*

1585 T. WASHINGTON tr. *Nicholay's Voy.* IV. xv. 130 The Cicilians..beeing acquainted with the seas,..Coursaries, and Skummers of the sea, stood vp in so great number, [etc.]. **1623** *Cal. St. Papers, Col.* 1622–4, 213 [The ships] Stood up altogether [in the road of Swally].

m. *Naut.* (See quot.)

1867 SMYTH *Sailor's Word-bk.*, *Standing up*, a ship in good trim, and well attended to, is said to stand well up to her canvas.

n. To hold oneself boldly erect to confront an opponent; to make a stand *against*. *lit.* and *fig.*

1601 SHAKS. *Jul. C.* II. i. 167 We all stand vp against the spirit of Cæsar. **1605** —— *Lear* III. vii. 80 Giue me thy Sword. A pezant stand vp thus? **1855** MACAULAY *Hist. Eng.* xv. III. 506 With the same spirit with which he had stood up against the Stuarts he had stood up against the Cromwells. **1890** TOUT *Hist. Eng. fr. 1689* 156 Lord Liverpool was not strong enough to stand up against Canning. **1897** A. E. HOUGHTON *Gilbert Murray* xvii. 273 The smaller boy, who, though still standing up pluckily, was getting decidedly the worst of it.

o. *to stand up for*: to defend, support, take the part of, champion (a person, a cause, etc.).

1605 SHAKS. *Lear* I. ii. 22 Now Gods, stand vp for Bastards. **1645** T. COLEMAN *Hopes Deferred* 30 His subjects stood up for their liberties. **1768–74** TUCKER *Lt. Nat.* (1834) II. 317 They..stand up for the honour of the nation. **1867** TROLLOPE *Chron. Barset* I. xvi. 136, I liked her for standing up for her husband. **1879** M. J. GUEST *Lect. Hist. Eng.* xxi. 208 All swore that they would stand up for their rights.

p. *to stand up to*: to confront or encounter boldly. Also *U.S.*, 'to meet fairly and fully (an obligation, one's word or promise)' (Webster, 1911). Also with impersonal subj.: to endure or withstand.

1624 FLETCHER *Rule a Wife* III. i, He stood up to me And mated my commands. **1823** 'JON BEE' *Dict. Turf* s.v., 'Stand up to him' (ring); do not flinch from the blows. **1827** SCOTT *Two Drovers* i, He found few antagonists able to stand up to him in the boxing ring. **1848** BARTLETT *Dict. Amer.* 331 *To stand up to the rack*, a metaphorical expression of the same meaning as the like choice phrases, 'to come to the scratch', 'to toe the mark'. **1889** 'M. GRAY' *Reproach of Annesley* I. I. vi. 136 How pluckily he stood up to the kicking horse! **1892** *Blackw. Mag.* CLI. 102/1 Few men..ventured to stand up boldly to such terrific bowling. **1894** *Speaker* 9 June 640/1 He knuckled under to any one who chose to stand up to him. **1921** G. B. SHAW *Back to Methuselah* p. lxxxv, I had seen Bible fetichism, after standing up to all the rationalistic batteries of Hume, Voltaire, and the rest, collapse before the onslaught of much less gifted Evolutionists. **1940** *Punch* 11 Dec. p. xiii, Nylon tufts will stand up to an incredible amount of hard use.

q. To fail to keep an appointment with (someone), esp. a social engagement or 'date' with a member of the opposite sex. *colloq.* (orig. *U.S.*).

1902 O. V. LIMERICK *Billy Burgundy's Opinions* 57, I am awfully sorry I had to stand you up last night. **1906** 'O. HENRY' *Four Million* 122 Rosy's stuck to the affirmative this time for two whole days. But it's five hours yet till the time, and I'm afraid she'll stand me up when it comes to the scratch. **1936** J. CURTIS *Gilt Kid* xxv. 244 It must be getting along. He didn't want Maisie to think that he was standing her up. **1940** R. CHANDLER *Farewell, my Lovely* xxxii. 246 You stood me up for an hour the other night. **1952** J. CANNAN *Body in Beck* ix. 186 Time and again..I stood up the chaps so as to climb with him. **1959** *New Statesman* 11 Apr. 519/2 It isn't long, however, before she discovers the canker in the bud, in the person of William, a young smoothie from Madison Avenue, who stands her up. **1978** L. THOMAS *Ormerod's Landing* iii. 43 'What about the other agent, the lady?'.. 'Stood you up, I shouldn't wonder,' laughed Charles.

r. In colloq. phr. *to stand up and* (also *to*) *be counted*, to show one's political colours; also more widely, to display one's conviction or sympathy, esp. when this requires courage. orig. *U.S.*

1904 *Hartford* (Connecticut) *Courant* 12 Aug. 10 Another democratic paper, the 'Sacramento Bee', follows the example of the 'Chicago Chronicle' and stands up to be counted for Roosevelt. **1945** *Somerset News* (Princess Anne, Maryland) 22 Mar. 1/3 Why then weren't Shore delegates men enough to stand up and be counted? **1968** *Listener* 1 Aug. 134/2, I suppose in the end it was having to stand up and be counted as part of 'The New Establishment'; being forced to own up that I earn my living and have my being in that world. **1969** *Ibid.* 13 Nov. 658/3, I was a great one for demos in my youth... I can remember a good deal of self-righteousness, in standing up to be counted with the saints. **1973** 'M. INNES' *Appleby's Answer* iv. 38 A mild-mannered man. But he felt he must stand up and be counted. **1977** D. JAMES *Spy at Evening* xxiv. 199 People like you haven't stood up to be counted.

s. To sustain close examination, to be tenable: esp. of a charge or theory.

1948 in M. McLuhan *Mech. Bride* (1967) 6/3 Authorities here voiced doubt..whether such a charge would 'stand up'. **1962** *Listener* 10 May 814/3 It will be interesting to see if this conclusion stands up when more results become available. **1976** N. FREELING *Lake Isle* xxxii. 232 It won't stand up in law, I tell you.

t. *will the real —— please stand up?*, a catch-phrase which requests that a person clarify his position or make himself known (often rhetorical). orig. *U.S.*

1971 *Black Scholar* June 32 (*heading*) Will the real black man please stand up? **1973** *Illustr. London News* July 76/3 Will the real Kate Brown please stand up and show herself? **1981** *Nature* 12 Mar. 89 (*heading*) Will the real Grenville Orogeny please stand up.

VIII. 104. Comb. in phrases used subst. or attrib., as **stand-alone** *a. Computers*, designating a part of a computer system that can be used independently; **stand-away** *a.*, (*a*) of a person: reserved, chilly, 'standoffish'; (*b*) of a collar, etc.: that lies or rises away from the neck of the wearer; also *absol.* as *sb.*; **stand-back** *rare*, (*a*) a source of reassurance or support; a dependable person; (*b*) one who holds back; **stand-down** *Mil.* (now esp. *Air Force*), the action or state of coming or remaining off duty or of relaxing from a period of vigilance; the end of a spell of duty; **stand-easy**, an assumption of the attitude directed by the command 'stand easy'; *fig.* a period of relaxation; also *attrib.*; †**stand far** (or **further**) **off**, a kind of cloth (see quots.); **stand-over**, (*a*) a plant that has been left standing beyond the normal time; (*b*) *Austral. slang*, used *attrib.* to designate the perpetrator of extortion by threat, a protection-racketeer, as *stand-over man*; or the process of such extortion; occas. *absol.* and *transf.*; **stand-to** *Mil.*, *ellipt.* for *stand-to-arms*; also, the time of coming on duty, as at dawn or dusk, or in preparation for an attack; also *attrib.*; **stand-to-arms**, the action of standing to arms; also, the period of standing to arms. Also STAND-BY, STANDFAST, STAND-OFF, STAND OUT, STAND-STILL, STAND-UP.

1966 C. J. SIPPL *Computer Dict. & Handbk.* 295/2 *Stand-alone capability*, a multiplexor designed to function independently of a host or master computer, either some of the time or all of the time. **1969** *Computers & Humanities* III. 137 A system for typing concordance output on an IBM Selectric typewriter is being developed for use with a stand-alone device which consists of a magnetic tape unit, keyboard, and heavy-duty selectric typewriter. **1977** *Sci. Amer.* Sept. 147/2 At the next level in the hierarchy of capability and function are the small computer systems that are prepackaged as stand-alone units... They have a self-contained power supply. **1938** J. CARY *Castle Corner* iii. 155 Rifty had Bridget for his partner but Bridget was even more standaway than usual. **1955** *Sun* (Baltimore) 3 Feb. (B ed.) 3/1 Most of Balenciaga's collars are simple turnover standaways. **1964** *McCall's Sewing* i. 12/1 Stand-away collars, collarless styles and V- or U-shaped necklines will make the neck seem longer. **1971** *Woman's Own* 27 Mar. 24/1 A stand-away collar is good for a thick neck. **1915** D. H. LAWRENCE *Rainbow* xii. 313 Gudrun was..a great comfort and shield to her... This was a great stand-back to Ursula, who suffered agonies when she thought a person disliked her. **1922** —— *Aaron's Rod* x. 122, I had a corporal called Wallace... He was my stand-back. **1946** J. W. DAY *Harvest Adventure* vi. 89 We've got a fine lot o' stand-backs to tell others to git forrad. **1919** W. H. DOWNING *Digger Dialects* 47 *Stand-down*, the hours at which the above orders [to go off duty] are regularly given each day. **1925** FRASER & GIBBONS *Soldier & Sailor Words* s.v. *Stand-to*, 'Stand-down' was the corresponding order at the end of the Danger Period, used in like manner as an expression for a definite point of time. **1945** C. H. WARD-JACKSON *It's Piece of Cake* (ed. 2) 57 *Stand-down*, time-off when flying is cancelled. **1949** W. S. CHURCHILL *Second World War* II. II. xvi. 297 On February 13, 1942, Admiral Raeder had his final interview on 'Sea Lion' and got Hitler to agree to a complete 'stand-down'. **1953** EARL WINTERTON *Orders of Day* xix. 270 Next morning at 'stand down', on a cold grey day, I went to have a look at where the place had been where I had spent so many years of my life [engaged in fire-watching]. **1978** H. WOUK *War & Remembrance* xxviii. 284 Then would come the bored wait, the stand-down, the recovery of aircraft, and the resumed plan of the day. **1898** *Daily News* 15 Feb. 8/3 The blue-jackets had by no means been idle in their 'stand easy' moments. **1899** F. M. HOLMES *Firemen* 97 Allowing for a 'stand easy' of fifteen minutes at eleven. **1906** *Daily Chron.* 14 July 6/2 They need holidays far more than civilians,..A 'stand-easy' is necessary to everyone. *a* **1661** FULLER *Worthies, Norwich* (1662) 274 In my child-hood there was one [stuff] called *Stand-far-of*,..which seemed pretty at competent distance, but discovered its coursness when nearer to the eye. **1613** J. TAYLOR (Water P.) *Eighth Wond.* Wks. (1630) II. 62 Certaine sonnets,..fashioned of diuers stuffs, as mockado, fustian, stand-further-off, and Motly. **1619** —— *Kicksey Winsey* B8b, I muse of what stuffe these men framed be, Most of them seeme Muckado vnto me: Some are Stand-further off, for they endeauer, Neuer to see me. **1847** *Simmonds's Colon. Mag.* Dec. 374 Old standover rattoons. *Ibid.* 375 The crop of sugar from these standovers is entirely lost for at least two years. **1939** K. TENNANT *Foveaux* 174 He didn't deserve to be a 'standover man' if he couldn't move quicker. **1941** BAKER *Dict. Austral. Slang* 71 *Standover* (*man*), a criminal who exacts toll from other lawbreakers or innocents. *Ibid.*, *Standover, work the*, to act as a 'stand-over man'. Also, a door-to-door hawker's term for bullying tactics adopted to intimidate housewives. **1954** L. H. EVERS *Pattern of Conquest* 198 Don't come the stand-over tactics you used with Charlie. **1977** *Daily News* (Perth, Austral.) 19 Jan. 16/5 Detectives believe the shooting is part of a war that has broken out amongst stand-over men in the massage parlour industry in Melbourne. **1915** in W. Wood *In Line of Battle* (1916) 217 At stand-to, 6 a.m. Much shelling. **1928** E. BLUNDEN *Undertones of War* ii. 21 Let me take you..back now..into the stand-to billets in Festubert village. **1942** *R.A.F. Jrnl.* 3 Oct. 31 There was that stand-to in the small hours one day. **1954** W. K. HANCOCK *Country & Calling* vii. 195 In the quiet middle years of the war we were allowed to lie down after our training until stand-to at 6 a.m. **1975** T. ALLBEURY *Special Collection* xi. 78 They made a permanent stand-to situation with just six of their anti-missile missiles. **1837** CARLYLE *Fr. Rev.* III. VII. iii, Whereupon also, on the Republican side, there will be rapid stand-to-arms. **1915** A. D. GILLESPIE *Let.* 11 Mar. in *Lett. from Flanders* (1916) 43 As I write, during the evening 'stand to arms', the birds are all singing in spite of the sniping.

☛ *Key to phrases, etc.*

Followed by an inf. 5 b, 12, 16; to let stand 50; to let all stand, all standing 24; as it stands 20 b; as things stand 38 b; how do you stand (financially)? 15 e; standing 51.

Stand aback 88; *s* about (*prep.*) 66, (*adv.*) 80; *s* again 81; *s* against 12, 67; *s* ajar 20; *s* alone 15 d; *s* along 82; *s* aloof 83; *s* and (do something) 5 c; *s* and deliver! 4 b; *s* and fight 10; *s* apart 84; *s* aside 85; *s* astrut 86; *s* at 68; *s* at (a figure or amount) 21 b; *s* at (a level or height) 22; *s* at attention 5; *s* at avail 48 d; *s* at bay, at defiance 10; *s* at ease, at gaze 5; *s* at livery 3 a; *s* at stud 3 b; *s* a-water 28 b; *s* away 87; *s* awe 45 b; *s* back 88; *s* before 69; *s* behind 89; *s* beside 90; *s* by (*prep.*) 70, (*adv.*) 91; *s* candidate 12; *s* captain 15 a; *s* a chance 57; *s* one's chance 53 d; *s* committed, corrected 15 d; *s* deep in 17 c; *s* double 12 b; *s* down 92; *s* dread 45 b; *s* fair (for, to do) 15 e; *s* fast 4, 9, 10, 23; *s* fire 52 b; *s* firm 9, 10, 20; *s* for 71; *s* (= fish) for 6 a; *s* for (an office, a constituency, etc.) 12, 12 b; *s* for law 42 b; *s* forth 93; *s* forward 94; *s* free 15 d; *s* (one's) friend 15 c; *s* godfather 15 b; *s* good 42 b; *s* (one's) good lord, prince 15 c; *s* one's ground 56; *s* one's hand 61; *s* a hazard 54; *s* high 17 b, 20; *s* (one) high 44 a; *s* high with 15 e; *s* in (*prep.*) 72, (*adv.*) 95; *s* (one) in (a price) 44 c, d; *s* in awe 45; *s* in the breach 10; *s* in danger 15 e; *s* in defence 10; *s* in doom 11 a; *s* in doubt 15 e; *s* in dread, in fear 45 c; *s* in force 42 b, 48 d; *s* (one) in hand 47; *s* in judgement 11 a, b; *s* in lieu of 49; *s* in one's light 2; *s* in need 46; *s* in profit 48 d; *s* in a (certain) relation 15 e, 38; *s* in (another's) shoes 2; *s* in stall 48 d; *s* in stead 48; *s* in stead of 49; *s* in vail 48 d; *s* in the way 2; *s* indebted 15 d; *s* instead of 49; *s* king 15 a; *s* law 42 b; *s* the market 62; *s* model 5 e; *s* mute 15 d; *s* (= consist) of 73; *s* off 96; *s* off and on 97; *s* officer 15 a; *s* on (*prep.*) 17, 74, (*adv.*) 98; *s* (one) on (a price) 44 b; *s* on one's own bottom 5; *s* on the defensive 10; *s* on end 17 d; *s* on one's own feet, on (upon) a foot, footing 2; *s* on one's guard 10; *s* (one) on hand 47; *s* on one's head 8; *s* on one's own legs 2; *s* on the offensive 10; *s* open 20; *s* or fall 9 c; *s* out 99; *s* over (*prep.*) 75, (*adv.*) 100; *s* pad 5 e; *s* pat 14; *s* the patter 53 b; *s* perdu 5; *s* pledged, reproved 15 d; *s* Sam 61; *s* security 15 a; *s* sentinel, sentry 5 e; *s* shot 52 b, 61; *s* sound 23; *s* sponsor 15 b; *s* stable 23; *s* stall 48 d; *s* stiff 9; *s* still 4, 27, 32; *s* suit 53 b; *s* surety 15 a; *s* thick 17 b, c; *s* till 76; *s* to (*prep.*) 76, (*adv.*) 101; *s* to (the knees, etc.) in 1 c; *s* (one) to (a price) 44 b; *s* to avail 48 d; *s* to the bar 11 a; *s* to lose, win 16 d; *s* together 102; *s* treat 61; *s* one's trial 53 b; *s* umpire 5 e; *s* under 77; *s* until, unto 76; *s* up 17 d, 103; *s* up to (the knees, etc.) in 1 c; *s* upon 17, 78; *s* (one) upon (a price) 44 b; *s* upon game 4 c; *s* upon one's trial 11 a; *s* upright 5, 17 d; *s* (a) watch 60; *s* well 15 e, 38 b; *s* whole 23; *s* with 79; *s* with water 27 b.

standage ('stændɪdʒ). In 6 stannage. [f. STAND *v.* + -AGE.]

1. Arrangements or accommodation for standing. Also, a charge for permission to stand.

1777 *Barmby Inclos. Act* 10 Settling the standage for the crops. **1848** *Jrnl. R. Agric. Soc.* IX. I. 120 The object is to give a firm standage for cattle drinking at the pond. **1896** *Times* 18 Dec. 13/5 The action was to recover..in respect of sidage or standage charged upon trucks..which remained more than four days upon..sidings. **1907** *Advt.* [Northumbld.], Standage for Motors and Cycles.

†**b.** A standing, stall. *Obs.*

1600 S. FORMAN *Autobiogr.* (1849) 8 They kept a stannage at our Ladie faier, and ther were many knavishe boies which were at play behinde the stannage, and often thruste downe their ware.

2. *Mining.* An underground reservoir for water.

1842 *1st Rep. Comm. Employmt. Childr. Mines* 59, 15 fathoms lower being sunk for 'standage', or for a reservoir of water. **1875** J. H. COLLINS *Princ. Metal Mining* 53 The space underneath serves as a water channel and standage or sump. **1883** GRESLEY *Gloss. Coal-mining* 237.

standage, obs. variant of STANDISH.

standard ('stændəd), *sb.* (*a.*) Also 4-6 **standarde**, 4-5 **stondard**, 4-6 **standerde**, 4-7 **standerd**, (6 **standred**), 4-7, 8 *rare* **standart**, 5-6 **standert** (5 **estandert**, 6 **standertt**), **stondart(e** (5 **stondert**), 6 **stander**, 7 *Sc.* **stender**. See also ESTANDARD. [aphetic a. OF. *estandard*, *-art*, *-estendard*, *-art* (mod.F. *étendard*) = med.L. *standardum*, *-us*, *standarium*, etc. Pr. *estandard*, *-art*, Sp., Pg. *estandarte*, It. *stendardo*; according to most scholars f. com. Rom. *estend-ere* (L. *extend-ĕre* to stretch out: see EXTEND *v.*) + -ARD; a parallel synonymous formation with different suffix is It. *stendale*, late OF. *estandale*, *-deille* (med.L. *standale*, *-ālis*). The Fr. word has passed into all the living Teut. langs.: MHG. *stanthart* (by popular etymology, as if 'stand hard'), later *standart*, *standert* (mod.G. *standarte*), MDu. *standaert* (mod.Du. *standaard*, *standerd*), Da. *standart*, Sw. *standar*.

The origin of sense 9 ('standard of measure or weight'), whence the other senses in branch II are derived, is somewhat obscure. It appears in AF. (*estaundart*) and Anglo-L. (*standardus*) in the 13th c., two centuries earlier than our earliest vernacular instance. It has not been found in continental OF.; the use of Du. *standaard* in this sense is believed to be imitated from English. It is noteworthy that in early instances the standard of measure is always either expressly or by implication called 'the king's standard', an expression which belongs to the older sense 1. It seems probable that sense 9 is a fig. use of sense 1; the king's standard being the point of reunion of the army, and the centre from which commands are issued.

The senses grouped as branch III are of doubtful, probably of various and in some instances of mixed origin. The notion of 'something conspicuously erected', involved in sense 1, would account for several of them; others may be referred to the idea of 'something permanent, fixed, or stationary', generalized from sense 9. Etymological association with STAND *v.* has, however, certainly affected the whole group, and it is possible that in some uses the word should be regarded as an alteration of STANDER. The senses of this branch are almost confined to English: OF. has *estandart* some kind of torch (*rare*$^{-1}$), and WFlem. has *standaart* mill-post (De Bo; *standaert*, Kilian); but the relation of these to the English uses is obscure.]

A. *sb.* **I.** A military or naval ensign.

1. a. A flag, sculptured figure, or other conspicuous object, raised on a pole to indicate the rallying-point of an army (or fleet), or of one of its component portions; the distinctive ensign of a king, great noble, or commander, or of a nation or city.

† *standard-general*: the principal standard of an army.

In Eng. the word appears first with reference to the 'Battle of the Standard' in 1138. A contemporary writer, Richard of Hexham, relating the story of the battle, describes the 'standard' there used as a mast of a ship, with flags at the top, mounted in the middle of a machine which was brought into the field. He quotes a Latin couplet written on the occasion, which says that the standard was so called from 'stand', because 'it was there that valour took its stand to conquer or die'.

1154 *O.E. Chron.* (Laud MS.) an. 1138, Him [*sc.* king David of Scotland] com to ȝænes Willelm eorl of Albamar.. mid fæu men &..flemden þe king æt te Standard. **1297** R. GLOUC. (Rolls) 6175 Edmond diȝte is stondard ware he ssolde him sulue abide. **13..** *K. Alis.* 2377 (Laud MS.), To ymagu hij turneden pas þer þe kynges standarde was. **1338** R. BRUNNE *Chron.* (1725) 115 Þise men lift ther standard, that stoute was & grim Ageyn Dauid wandelard, & disconfite him. *c* **1425** ? LYDG. *Assembly of Gods* 825 All these seuyn capteynes had standardes of pryce. **1483** *Cath. Angl.* 359/1 A Sstanderd or A bekyn, *statela*. *a* **1548** HALL *Chron., Hen. V*, 64 b, Banners, standers and penons of the kynges armes. **1588** PARKE tr. *Mendoza's Hist. China* 165 A watch towre..who had discouered our shippe, and knew the standard or flagge to bee the kings. **1594** SHAKS. *Rich. III*. v. iii. 263 Then in the name of God and all these rights, Aduance your Standards, draw your willing Swords. **1609** HOLLAND *Amm. Marcell.* xv. vii. 43 An high banke above which stood the maine standerds of Eagles and other ensignes. **1609** BIBLE (Douay) *Jer.* vi. 1 In Thecua sownd with the trumpet, and over Bethacarem lift up the standart. **1611** BIBLE *Num.* ii. 3. **1630** *R. Johnson's Kingd. & Commw.* 314 Every Citie hath his principall Standard, with their peculiar armes and devices therein, to distinguish one people from another. **1633** T. STAFFORD *Pac. Hib.* II. xxv. 252 The Burgesses..came to the Lord President, to beseech him to render unto them their Charter, Seale, Mace, and Standard. **1656** EARL MONM. tr. *Boccalini's Advts. fr. Parnass.* I. lxxxv. (1674) 112 Francisco Pico..was made Standard-bearer; and, in his Standard-General, bore the famous Ensign of an open Book. **1660** WATERHOUSE *Arms & Arm.* 45 *Vexilla* properly signifies the Standers of Kings and Chiefs. **1737** POPE *Hor. Ep.* II. ii. 41 He..Tore down a Standard, took the Fort and all. **1781** COWPER *Table T.* 454 The standards of all nations are unfurl'd. **1804** *Med. Jrnl.* XII. 46 The late dispute respecting the capture of the standard of the *Invincibles* before Alexandria. **1808** PIKE *Sources Mississ.* II. App. 23 They gave up the Spanish flag, and we had the pleasure to see the American Standard hoisted in its stead. **1831-3** E. BURTON *Eccl. Hist.* xxx. (1845) 643 From this time the imperial standards bore a device, which was composed of the two first letters of the name of Christ in Greek. **1864** PUSEY *Lect. Daniel* (1876) 114 The black eagle is the standard of Prussia. **1891** FARRAR *Darkn. & Dawn* iii, The tents and standards of the soldiers had been struck with fire from heaven.

transf. **1761** *Ann. Reg., Char.* 8/2 Every raja..appears.. mounted on an elephant, and is at once the general and ensign, or standard of that corps, who keep their eyes constantly on him.

b. In many phrases used with pregnant sense, the standard being taken as typifying the army or its leaders; e.g. ***to raise one's standard***, take up arms; ***under the standard of***, serving in the army of; so ***to join the standard of***; and the like.

c **1500** *Melusine* xxiv. 164 Your vassall & seruaunt shal I euer be vnder the standart of your gouernaunce. **1667** MILTON *P.L.* VII. 297 As Armies at the call Of Trumpet.. Troop to their Standard. **1697** DRYDEN *Virg. Georg.* IV. 102 With hoarse allarms the hollow Camp rebounds,..Then to their common Standard they repair. **1738** GLOVER *Leonidas* I. 155 They with dread Will shrink before your standards. **1838-43** ARNOLD *Hist. Rome* II. xxxvii. 481 All the nations of southern Italy were ready to join his standard. **1840** THIRLWALL *Greece* VII. lvii. 241 In a short time he..had a body of more than 2000 horse under his standard. **1842** W. C. TAYLOR *Anc. Hist.* xvii. §2 (ed. 3) 500 Wearied by the tyranny of Domitian, Lucius Antonius..raised the standard of revolt in his province. **1845** JAMES *Arrah Neil* vi, He would raise his standard at once, and march to London. **1852** SIR J. GRAHAM in C. S. Parker *Life & Lett.* (1907) II. 149 The rival camps under hostile standards will thus be pitched.

c. *fig.*

1532 MORE *Confut. Tindale* II. 105 Some that were heretyques in dede, and wolde..auaunce theyr owne heresyes forwarde vnder the name and standard of his [Origen's] famouse authoryte. **1613** PURCHAS *Pilgrimage* (1614) 87 No crueltie or sacriledge against God, or man, so irreligious..but Religion was pretended to be the cause, and bare the Standard to Destruction. **1688** JAS. II in Gutch *Coll. Cur.* I. 339, I tell you this is a Standard of Rebellion: I never saw such an address! **1856** *N. Brit. Rev.* XXVI. 250 [They] if they did not vote against him, at least deserted their standard, and did not vote at all. **1888** BRYCE *Amer. Commw.* II. lxx. 566 The gain of even twenty or thirty votes ..is so likely to bring fresh recruits to his standard.

2. a. In a more restricted sense, a military or naval flag of some particular kind.

Ordinarily, the *standard* is understood to be distinguished from a banner by being long and tapering instead of square, and from a pennon by its greater breadth. The British ***royal standard***, however, which is flown when the king or a member of the royal family is present, is now a square flag (thus technically a 'banner'), divided into four compartments bearing the emblems of England (twice), Scotland, and Ireland. In the British army, the regimental flags of the cavalry are called *standards*, those of the infantry being 'colours'. In the U.S. army the flag of a cavalry regiment is called its *standard*.

1375 BARBOUR *Bruce* XI. 465 Thai saw so fele browdyn baneris, Standartis, pennownys apon speris. **1471** CAXTON *Recuyell* (Sommer) 199 And than made dysplaye banyers, standardes & penons. **1523** BERNERS *Froiss.* I. xviii. 22 Euery man mounted, and the baners and standers folowed this new made knyght. *a* **1548** HALL *Chron., Hen. VII* 53 b, Barges garnished with standardes, stremers and penons. *a* **1577** SIR T. SMITH *Commw. Eng.* I. xviii. (1589) 33 Knights bannerets are made in the field, with the ceremonie of cutting off the poynt of his standert, and making it as it were a baner. **1644** [WALSINGHAM] *Effigies True Fortitude* 12 His Majesties Banner Royall, vulgarly called the Standard. **1700** TYRRELL *Hist. Eng.* II. 765 The Victors carried off his Standard Royal. **1811** *Regul. & Orders Army* 11 A Field Marshal is to be saluted with the Colours and Standards of all the Forces. **1814** WELLINGTON in Gurw. *Desp.* (1838) XII. 75 A request ..that the brigade of cavalry consisting of the 5th dragoon guards, and 3rd and 4th dragoons..should be permitted to bear the word 'Salamanca' on their Standards. *c* **1860** H. STUART *Seaman's Catech.* 12 Who attends the standard? **1868** *Queen's Regul. Army* §6 The Standards of Regiments of Dragoon Guards are to be of silk damask.

†**b.** In certain occasional uses. ***standard of trade***: a merchant ensign. ***standard of truce***: a flag of truce hoisted on a pole. *Obs.*

1449 *Paston Lett.* I. 85 Then they lonchyd a bote, and sette up a stondert of truesse. **1653** H. COGAN tr. *Pinto's Trav.* xvii. 59 A Standart of Trade hung out..to the end they might be taken for Merchants.

3. = STANDARD-BEARER.

13.. *K. Alis.* 1995 Sendith Ymagu, youre standard, And Archilaus in the furst ward! *c* **1400** *Sowdone Bab.* 2717 'Go forth' quod the stondart, 'thou getist noon here'. **1481** CAXTON *Godfrey* xcix. 150 Theyr estandart had ben longe seke by thoccasion of his hurte. **1610** SHAKS. *Temp.* III. ii. 19 Thou shalt bee my Lieutenant Monster, or my Standard. **1796** *Cavalry Instr.* (1813) 14 The standard must take care never to oblige the wheeling man to exceed a moderate gallop. **1832** *Prop. Reg. Instr. Cavalry* III. 101 The Standard and his Coverer resume their posts.

†**4.** A body of troops kept in reserve in the earlier part of an engagement. *Obs.*

1297 R. GLOUC. (Rolls) 8252 Þes tueye adde þe meste ost, þat as standard was þere Vor to helpe hor felawes, wanne hii weri were.

†**5.** A company of cavalry. *Obs.*

1580 HOLLYBAND *Treas. Fr. Tong, Vne Cornette de chevalliers*, a cornet or standard of horsemen. **1678** *Lond. Gaz.* No. 1313/3 The French have received a reinforcement of 15 Standards.

†**6.** Head-quarters. *Obs.*

1481 CAXTON *Myrr.* II. xviii. 106 There [in helle] deth holdeth his standard whiche sendeth out thurgh all the world for to fetche them that ben his.

7. *Bot.* The uppermost petal of a papilionaceous corolla: = VEXILLUM.

1776 J. LEE *Introd. Bot.* (ed. 3) 396 Papilionacea, butterfly-shaped... Vexillum, the Standard, or upper Petal ascending. **1785** MARTYN *Lett. Bot.* iii. (1794) 35 A large petal, covering the others, and occupying the upper part of the corolla [of a pea-blossom]; it is called the standard or banner. **1806** J. GALPINE *Brit. Bot.* 329 Legumes sessile..: standard villous. **1870** HOOKER *Stud. Flora* 103 Lathyrus hirsutus.. Flowers ½ in.; standard crimson.

8. *Ornith.* Each of the two lengthened wing-feathers characteristic of certain birds. Cf. STANDARD-WING.

1859 G. R. GRAY in *Proc. Zool. Soc.* XXVII. 130 It has, springing from the lesser coverts of each wing, two long shafts, both of which are webbed on each side at the apex. It is the possession of these peculiar winged standards that induces me to propose for it the subgeneric appellation of *Semioptera*. **1862** —— in *Ann. & Mag. Nat. Hist.* Ser. III. X. 445 The ninth feather (or, as it has been termed, 'standard feather') is the longest of all. **1864** P. L. SCLATER in *Ibis* VI. 115 The long 'standard feather'. **1903** W. L. SCLATER *Stark's Birds S. Africa* III. 42 The ninth [primary] is prolonged to about three times the length of the first and forms the so-called streamer or standard.

II. Exemplar of measure or weight.

9. a. The authorized exemplar of a unit of measure or weight; e.g. a measuring rod of unit length; a vessel of unit capacity, or a mass of metal of unit weight, preserved in the custody of public officers as a permanent evidence of the legally prescribed magnitude of the unit.

original standard: the standard of which the others are copies, and to which the ultimate appeal must be made.

1429 *Rolls of Parlt.* IV. 349/1 Weiȝtis.. acordant to ye standard of ye Chekier. *c* **1450** *Eng. Misc.* (Surtees) 61 The sayd Burgese schall haffe yᵉ standard, that is to say, the buschell, halff a buschell [etc.]... the qwhyche mesures schuld agre with the kynges standard. **1530** PALSGR. 276/2 Stondart to mesure bye, *maistresse mesure*. **1588** LAMBARD *Eiren.* IV. iv. 456 If they of the towne where the kings Standerd is appointed to remaine, haue not their common weights and measures signed. **1622** BACON *Hen. VII* 101 There was also a Statute, for the dispersing of the Standard of the Exchequor, throughout England; thereby to size Weights and Measures. **1624** MASSINGER *Renegado* III. iv, Let but any Indifferent gamester measure vs inch, by inch, Or waigh vs by the standard, I may passe I haue beene prou'd againe, true mettall. **1658** PHILLIPS, *Standard*.. also the standing measure of the King, or State, to which all other measures are framed. **1681** *Peace & Truth* 7 'Tis equally Treason to serve a Usurper, and to Usurp the Regalities of the Lawful Prince by forging new Standards of Commerce. **1694** J. SMITH *Horolog. Disquisit.* 45 A Royal Pendulum already Rectified, for a Standard to Adjust other Clocks by. **1728** CHAMBERS *Cycl.* s.v. *Measure*, The sealed Gallon at Guildhall, which is the Standard for Wines, Spirits, Oils, &c. **1774** BURN *Poor Laws* 244 The statute for ascertaining the measure of ale quarts and pints according to the standard, is seldom put in execution. **1856** W. H. MILLER in *Phil. Trans.* CXLVI. 753 History of the Standards of English Weight. **1870** *Pall Mall Gaz.* 2 Sept. 5 The annual report of the Warden of the Standards lately issued. **1871** C. DAVIES *Metric System* III. 101 These standards were kept in the royal exchequer.

fig. **1736** BUTLER *Anal.* II. viii. 399 An original standard of right and wrong in actions.

b. In abstract sense: The legal magnitude of a unit of measure or weight.

1540 *Act 32 Hen. VIII*, c. 13 §2 Euery handfull to contein .iiii. inches of the standerde. **1609** *Ev. Wom. in Hum.* I. C, *Citty wife*. I haue a Ruffe is a quarter deepe, measured by the yard. *Hostis*. Indeede by the yard! *Citty w.* By the standard.

c. A normal uniform size or amount; a prescribed minimum size or amount.

1625 BACON *Ess., Greatness Kingd.* (Arb.) 477 Making Farmes, and houses of Husbandry, of a Standard; That is, maintained with such a Proportion of Land vnto them, as may breed a Subiect, to liue in Conuenient Plenty. **1694** FALLE *Jersey* II. 68 Almost all our Trees are Pollards;.. The Husbandman being obliged to bring his Trees to a Standard, by Lopping of those.. Luxuriant branches which .. would cover his little Plots.

†d. A unit of measurement. *Obs. rare.*

1646 SIR T. BROWNE *Pseud. Ep.* VI. iii. 284 As for the divisions of the yeare, and the quartering out this remarkable standard of time, there have passed especially two distinctions. **1830** HERSCHEL *Study Nat. Phil.* 125 As a first preliminary towards effecting this, we fix on convenient standards of weight, dimension, time, &c.

¶ e. Sometimes misused for: Actual stature.

1833 NYREN *Yng. Cricketer's Tutor* (1902) 135 John was a stoutly-made man; his standard about five feet ten inches.

f. The substance or thing which is chosen to afford the unit measure of any physical quantity, such as specific gravity.

1805 R. JAMESON *Char. Min.* (1817) 266 Water is the standard with which all other bodies are compared. **1815** J. SMITH *Panorama Sci. & Art* II. 486 Water.. is employed as the standard of comparison in all tables of specific gravities. **1869** C. H. GILL *Chem. for Sch.* xxii. 274 Dalton.. adopted it [*sc.* hydrogen] as the unit or standard of atomic weight.

g. *Bowls.* A light reed or cane used to measure the distance of rival bowls from the jack.

1876 *Encycl. Brit.* IV. 180/2. **1897** *Encycl. Sport* I. 129/2.

10. a. (Originally *fig.* from 9.) An authoritative or recognized exemplar of correctness, perfection, or some definite degree of any quality.

1477 NORTON *Ord. Alch.* Proem., in Ashm. (1652) 9 This Boke; Named of Alkimy the Ordinall, The Crede mihi, the Standard perpetuall. **1665** BOYLE *Occas. Refl.* v. v. (1848) 316 Men will be asham'd to be unlike those, whose Customs and Deportments pass for the Standards, by which those of other Men are to be measur'd. **1676** HALE *Contempl.* I. 304 He was exhibited, as the common standard and pattern of a Christian's condition. **1691** T. H[ALE] *Acc. New Invent.* p. cvii, These Draughts of the Rivers serving as the Standards by which all future Enlargements or Diminutions.. may be guided. **1709** FELTON *Diss. Classics* (1718) 147 Among the Romans, Horace is the Standard of Lyric, and Virgil of Epic Poetry. **1710** *Caldwell Papers* (Maitl. Club) I. 219 They [at Hanover] believe themselves a standart that mankind should be guided by. **1742** WEST *Let.* in *Gray's Poems* (1775) 136 [Racine's] language is the language of the times, and that of the purest sort; so that his French is reckoned a standard. **1777** SIR W. JONES *Poems*, etc. Pref. 14 We always return to the writings of the ancients, as the standard of true taste. **1789** MRS. PIOZZI *Journ. France* II. 139 Let us learn better than to set up self, whether nation or individual, as a standard to which all others must be reduced. **1838–9** HALLAM *Hist. Lit.* IV. IV. vii. §11. 299 The Academy rendered this dictionary the most received standard of the French language.

b. A rule, principle, or means of judgement or estimation; a criterion, measure. Also *double standard*: see DOUBLE *a.* 6.

1563 WINZET *Bk. 83 Quest.* Wks. (S.T.S.) I. 53 At Pasche ..thai.. ministrate the sacraments til ws on the Catholik manere; and be Witsonday thai change thair standart in our plane contrare. **1673** DRYDEN *Amboyna* Ep. Ded. A 3 b, You have serv'd Him..: making His Greatness, and the true Interest of your Country, the standard and measure of your actions. **1681** —— *Abs. & Achit.* 785 Nor is the people's judgment always true:.. What standard is there in a fickle rout, Which, flowing to the mark, runs faster out? **1779** *Mirror* No. 30 ⁋8 Let them [the inexperienced] not believe that the scale of fortune is the standard of happiness. **1781** GIBBON *Decl. & F.* xx. (1787) II. 201 Personal interest is often the standard of our belief, as well as of our practice. **1790** BURKE *Fr. Rev.* 61 The degree of estimation in which any profession is held becomes the standard of the estimation in which the professors hold themselves. **1836** J. GILBERT *Chr. Atonem.* ii. (1852) 37 Without a prior standard somewhere presupposed, who shall ascertain the quality of what is willed? **1837** LOCKHART *Scott* II. iii. 86 Scott had by no means measured.. the character.. of great public functionaries, by the standard with which observation and experience subsequently furnished him. **1888** BRYCE *Amer. Commw.* I. x. 126 The English reader must be cautioned against applying his English standards to the examination of the American system.

c. *pl.* The books or documents accepted by a church as the authoritative statement of its creed. Hence *occas.* in *sing.*

1841 *Penny Cycl.* XXI. 175/1 All the divisions of the Seceders.. agree in adopting as their standards, in addition to the Westminster Confession of Faith [certain works of their founders]. **1848** G. STRUTHERS *Hist. Relief Ch.* 293 These considerations.. induced them simply to proclaim their adherence to the Westminster standards. **1881** J. MACPHERSON *Westm. Confess. of Faith* (1882) 1 A Confession of Faith.. is accepted by members of churches acknowledging it, simply as a subordinate standard.

11. a. Legal rate of intrinsic value for coins; also, the prescribed degree of fineness for gold or silver.

1463 *Ir. Acts, 3 Edw. IV*, c. 32 Forasmuche as the said moneis of silver may not continually be made according to his right estandert. **1551** SIR J. WILLIAMS *Accompte* (Abbotsf. Club) 91 Golde.. coyned into crownes of vs a pece, according to the standerde apperteyninge to the mynte. **1568** GRAFTON *Chron.* II. 121 At thys tyme was vsed to be coyned that standard and finenesse that was called sterling money. **1601** in *Stafford's Pac. Hib.* II. iv. (1633) 149 Being meerely dependant of our Prerogatiue to alter the Standerd of our Moneys at our pleasure. **1638** *Charter Goldsm. Co.* in A. Ryland *Assay Gold & Silver* (1852) 28 The standards for gold are 22 and 18 carats of pure metal in every ounce... The coinage is of the higher standard... The lower standard is used for all manufacturing purposes... The standards for silver are 11 oz. 10 dwt., and 11 oz. 2 dwt. of pure metal in every pound troy... The higher standard is never used. **1691** LOCKE *Consid. Raising Value Money* Wks. 1714 II. 68 That precise Weight and Fineness, by Law appropriated to the Pieces of each Denomination, is called the Standard. *a* **1700** EVELYN *Diary* 19 Sept. 1683, He said it must be finer than the standard, such as was old angel gold. **1702** *Lond. Gaz.* No. 3863/4 Lost.., a wrought Silver-Candlestick, old Standard. **1722** DE FOE *Col. Jack* (1840) 78 Good tower standard. **1757** HARRIS *Money & Coins* 36 Trade requires.. an indelible standard of money. **1772–3** *Act 13 Geo. III*, c. 52 §4 Plate, being of the standard of eleven ounces ten pennyweight of fine silver per pound troy [shall be marked with] the figure of.. Britannia.

fig. **1672** MARVELL *Reh. Transp.* I. 271 The wit of France and England.. hath at all times gone much after the same current Rate and Standard.

b. (Originally, *† standard of commerce*.) A commodity, the value of which is treated as invariable, in order that it may serve as a measure of value for all other commodities.

1683 *Brit. Spec.* 47 Some one or other Commodity was every where found out to be the Standard of Commerce and Traffick. **1757** HARRIS *Money & Coins* 84 In these parts of the world, silver is, and time immemorial hath been, the money standard. **1776** ADAM SMITH *W.N.* I. v. 43 Labour.. is.. the only standard by which we can compare the values of different commodities at all times and at all places. **1825** MᶜCULLOCH *Pol. Econ.* I. 25 Having been used.. as standards whereby to measure the relative value of different commodities.

12. a. A definite level of excellence, attainment, wealth, or the like, or a definite degree of any quality, viewed as a prescribed object of endeavour or as the measure of what is adequate for some purpose.

standard of living, life, comfort: the view prevailing in a community or class with regard to the minimum of material comfort with which it is reasonable to be content.

1711 SHAFTESBURY *Charact.* (1732) III. 138 'Twas thus they [the Greeks] brought their beautiful and comprehensive Language to a just Standard... The Standard was in the same proportion carry'd into other Arts. **1748** MELMOTH *Fitzosborne Lett.* lvii. (1749) II. 86 For may not publick happiness be estimated by the same standard as that of private? **1766** FORDYCE *Serm. Young Women* (1767) I. i. 11 Act up to the best standard of your sex. **1780** *Mirror* No. 79 ⁋18 We are told that those manners should be painted, not as they are found in nature, but according to an ideal standard of perfection in what is called the golden age. *c* **1800** PEGGE *Anecd. Eng. Lang.* (1803) 38 During his translation of Quintus Curtius.. it [*sc.* the French language] had varied so much that he was obliged to correct the former part of the work to bring it to the standard of the other. **1827** LYTTON *Falkland* I. 45 Neither in person nor in character was he much beneath or above the ordinary standard of men. **1879** A. & M. P. MARSHALL *Econ. Industry* II. vii. 102 The Standard of Comfort which young people are prudent enough to secure for themselves before they marry, varies from place to place and from time to time. **1898** B. BOSANQUET (*title*) Standard of life, and other studies. **1903** A. MCNEILL *Egregious English* xx. 186 The standard of living in England is an.. artificial standard. Practically every Englishman lives, or longs to live, beyond his means. **1907** G. B. SHAW *John Bull's Other Island* II. 41 He guesses Broadbent's standard of comfort a little more accurately than his sister does. **1936** J. M. KEYNES *Gen. Theory Employment, Interest & Money* xvi. 218 The position of equilibrium, under conditions of *laissez-faire*, will be one in which employment is low enough and the standard of life sufficiently miserable to bring savings to zero.

b. In British and Commonwealth elementary schools: Each of the recognized degrees of proficiency, as tested by examination, according to which school children may be classified. Also *transf.*, the form or class in which pupils are prepared for a particular standard.

The sixth used to be the highest standard which children were ordinarily required to pass, the seventh being intended mainly for those who were to become teachers.

1876 LUBBOCK *Elementary Educ.* in *Contemp. Rev.* June 79 The classes from which the children are examined in Standards II–VI. **1878** F. KILVERT *Jrnl.* 16 Jan. (1977) 300 Gave the upper standards at the school questions on paper on the Catechism. **1894** *Times* 22 Mar. 4/6 He.. was in the class of which defendant was teacher—viz., the seventh standard. **1899** *Allbutt's Syst. Med.* VIII. 204 In some schools there is a standard 0.. for dull or backward children. **1902** VIOLET JACOB *Sheep-Stealers* xv, When the village urchins are still wrestling with the fourth 'standard'. **1934** G. B. SHAW *On Rocks* Pref. 168 The likeliest outcome is an elaborate creed of useful illusions, to be discarded bit by bit as the child is promoted from standard to standard or from form to form. **1966** C. ACHEBE *Man of People* i. 2 Sixteen years or so he had been my teacher in standard three.

attrib. **1891** HARDY *Tess* xix, She was expressing in her own native phrases—assisted a little by her Sixth Standard training—feelings which [etc.]. **1903** A. MCNEILL *Egregious English* i. 9 Nature, like the seventh-standard boy in a board school, 'can get no higher'. **1915** D. H. LAWRENCE *Rainbow* xiii. 353 She made friends with the Standard Three teacher. **1973** *Express* (Trinidad & Tobago) 17 Mar. 7/1 He left Trinidad a Seventh standard pupil of the St. Helena C.M. School.

c. *Sporting.* (See quot.)

1897 *Encycl. Sport* I. 62/2 (Athletics) *Standard*, the time or distance assigned to each event at a championship meeting, by beating which a competitor becomes entitled to a medal.

13. † a. Some fixed numerical quantity. (? A quarter hundred, 25.) *Obs.*

1545 *Rates Custom Ho.* b vj, Knyues of collayne the groce xxx. s. Knyues of roue the standerde v. s.

b. A definite quantity of timber, differing in different countries. (Cf. *standard deal*, B. 1 c.)

1858 SIMMONDS *Dict. Trade*, *Standard*,.. a solid measure by which hewn timber is estimated, varying in different timber countries. **1864** *Daily Tel.* 17 Aug., A 'Petersburgh Standard'.. consists of 120 deals of 12 feet long by 11 inches wide and 1½ inch thick. [This = 165 cubic feet.] **1891** *Law Times* XCI. 192/2 The vessel contained about 1000 standards... A standard was 165 cubic feet of timber.

†14. A kind of arrow (distinguished from 'bearing arrow' and 'flight'). *Obs.*

Perh. short for 'standard arrow', which occurs in later citations of 16th c. documents. See quot. 1465.

[**1465** *Ir. Acts, 5 Edw. IV*, c. 4 (1786) I. 29 It is ordeyned ..That every Englishman.. shall have an English bow.. with twelve shafts of the length of three quarters of the standard.] **1557** *City of Lond. Jrnl.* 17 lf. 46 in *Vicary's Anat.* (1888) App. III. 177–8 Who will comme.. and take a longe bowe in his hande—having the standarde therin therefore prouyded,.. shall haue for the best game a Crown of golde. .. And for the best game of the bearing arrowe, he shall haue [etc.]... And for the best game of the flight, he shall haue [etc.]... And.. there shalbe a trumpett blowen at euerye shott, aswell of the standarde, as of the arrowe or flight. **1598** STOW *Surv. Lond.* 77 Of old time.. the Officers of the Citie ..were challengers of all men.. to shoote the Standarde, broade arrow, and flight, for games. [**1682** W. M. (W. Wood) *Remembr. Show & Shooting*, 1583, 51 Then came the Duke.. bearing a Standard Arrow in his hand.]

15. The market price per ton of copper in the ore.

1855 LEIFCHILD *Cornwall* 233 The term 'standard of copper'.. denotes the estimated value of the fine copper per ton, considered from the various assays to be in the ores sold; less a fixed sum per ton.. deducted for the cost of smelting. .. When I began this book the standard of copper was £125, 5*s*., but it has since varied considerably. **1913** *Times* 13 Sept. 18/5 London, Sept. 12.—Copper... Standard continued its advance on Monday.

16. Short for: **a.** *standard book* (see STANDARD *a.* 3 b);

1889 *Amer. Publ. Weekly* 30 Mar. 462 The old-fashioned book-store, with its supply of standards on the shelves tempting a customer to increase his library.

b. (*Dyeing*) *standard solution* (see STANDARD *a.* 1 b).

1882 CROOKES *Dyeing & Tissue-Printing* 379 A set of so-called 'standards'. These are mixtures of colouring matters and mordants not liable to undergo change or decomposition, and which merely require the addition of a thickener..to be ready for printing.

c. *standard lamp*, sense 30.

1910 H. G. WELLS *New Machiavelli* III. iii, in *English Rev.* Sept. 292 The light of the big electric standard in the corner. **1939** O. LANCASTER *Homes, Sweet Homes* 10 All over Europe the lights are going out..olde Tudor lanthorns, standards and wall-brackets. **1974** M. INGATE *Sound of Weir* ix. 74 Tall lamps, 'they're Standards,' said Iris, had large coloured shades.

d. A standard form of a language (see STANDARD *a.* 3 e). ***Modified*** (also ***Received***) ***Standard***: see the first element.

1913 *Mod. Lang. Teaching* Dec. 262/2 While within the London sphere of influence..Received Standard goes on quite gaily, the London type of Modified Standard has won the day in this area, among those sections of the community who might otherwise speak a Kentish..or Surrey type of Modified Standard. **1972** HARTMANN & STORK *Dict. Lang. & Linguistics* 218/1 Deviations from the respective established standards are called non-standard or sub-standard.

III. Senses associated with the verb *stand*.

†17. A lofty erection of timber or stone, containing a vertical conduit pipe with spouts and taps, for the supply of water to the public. *Obs.*

'The Standard in Cornhill' continued as the name of a point from which distances were measured, long after the 'standard' had disappeared.

1434 *Cov. Leet Bk.* 157 þat þe standard of þe cundyte in þe Smythford-strete..shall not be doon awaye. **1517** *Chron. Grey Friars* (Camden) 30 At the stondert in Cheppe. **1580** *Memoriall W. Lumbe* c ij, A standart with one cocke at Holborne bridge. **1598** STOW *Surv. Lond.* 316 A standard of timber with a cocke or cockes, deliuering fayre spring water to the inhabitants. **1616** B. JONSON *Devil an Ass* I. i, I will fetch thee a leape From the top of Pauls-steeple, to the Standard in Cheepe. **1665** SIR T. HERBERT *Trav.* (1677) 164 Towers, most of which are terrassed near the top like the Standard in Cheap-side. **1854** THACKERAY *Newcomes* ii, This paradise, five miles from the standard at Cornhill.

18. a. A tall candlestick. Now *spec.* a tall candlestick (or, in recent use, an upright gas candelabrum) rising directly from the floor of a church.

a **1420** *Aunters of Arthur* 451 (Thornton MS.) Sythene he ..clathes gune calle, Sanapes and salers..Preketes and broketes, and standertes [*Douce* stondardes, *Irel.* stondartis] by-twene. **1488** in *Archæologia* XLV. 116 A payre of Candelstyckks, greate standards for grete tapers, of tynne. **1538** *Ibid.* XLIII. 218, ij greate standers of laten; ij lampes. **1553** in Daniel-Tyssen *Surrey Ch. Goods* (1869) 97 Item ij stondardes of lattyn. **1605** TRESWELL *Journ. Earl Nottingham* 51 The roome was garnished with three hundred and twenty lights of wax, al set in standerds of siluer, of diuers fashions. **1851** PUGIN *Chancel Screens* 23 This screen is surmounted by standards for wax tapers. **1860** *Ecclesiologist* XXI. 72 The church is lighted with brass gas standards.

†b. (See quot.) Cf. OF. *estandart*, a kind of torch. *Obs.*

1611 FLORIO, *Doppione*, a great torch of waxe, which we call a standard or a quarrier.

19. a. An upright timber, bar, or rod; e.g. †a tall pole erected for display on an occasion of rejoicing or festivity (*obs.*); an upright scaffold pole; an upright bar for a window; an upright support or pedestal in various machines. In recent use often, a slender and lofty iron pillar carrying an electric or gas lamp, overhead electric wires, or the like.

c **1450** *Brut* 487 At the Ledenhall in Cornhill..a standard of tre was set in myddys of the pavement fast in the grounde, nayled with holme and Ive, for disport of Cristmasse to þe peple of the Cite. **1477–9** *Rec. St. Mary at Hill* (1905) 85 For xxv foote of Elmyn borde, for steppes and standardis for the same steyre, vj d. **1486** *Nottingham Rec.* III. 257 To ij. sawers for sawyng of þe standerdes of the chymney. **1502** *Privy Purse Exp. Eliz. York* (1830) 25 Item..to John Coneway smyth for four transoms and xij standardes. *c* **1580** in *Fabric Rolls York Minster* (Surtees) 118 For helping to carry into the wryghte housse standerdes, powles and boordes. **1587** MASCALL *Cattle* (1596) 72 Their standarts and posts to fasten them [oxen] by, would be round and smooth. **1609** HOLLAND *Amm. Marcell.* XXIII. iii. 222 Whereupon the standard [of a ballista: L. *stilus*] being now at libertie with that quicke stroke..hurleth out the stone. **1627** in *Maitl. Club Misc.* III. 369 *note*, For gilting the Cok and thanis and culloring of the same yallow with the glob and standart and stanes above the steiple heid. **1703** MOXON *Mech. Exerc.* 251 Fir Poles, of several lengths for Standards and Ledgers for Scaffolding. **1813** *Gentl. Mag.* LXXXIII. 227/2 The pyramidal iron lamp standards in the outer court. **1823** P. NICHOLSON *Pract. Build.* 593 Standards; the upright poles used in scaffolding. In joinery, the upright pieces of a plate-rack. **1839** URE *Dict. Arts* 268 An apparatus with cutters attached to a standard. **1840** F. WHISHAW *Railw. Gt. Brit. & Irel.* 128 The mile-standards are of wood,..and are placed at intervals of a quarter of a mile. *Ibid.* 391 The distances are marked from either end of the line on stone standards. **1856** HURLSTONE & GORDON *Exch. Rep.* XI. 183 The wires..for the..use of the railway company rest upon all the posts or standards in the respondent's township. **1869** RANKINE *Machine & Hand-tools* Pl. D 5, The same turning table also carries the standard, F, which supports the main gearing. **1883** *Law Times Rep.* XLIX. 139/1 The scaffolding in front was constructed of five standards or uprights and one ledger. **1885** *Act 48 & 49 Vict.* c. 50 §4 (iv), The purchase and erection of lamp standards. **1892** *Labour Commission Gloss.*, *Standards*, two standards, *i.e.*, two wooden legs with feet, which are often used instead of four legs to support the top frame of a table. **1907** H. WYNDHAM *Flare of Footlights* xxxiii, At intervals [along the Embankment] rose the tall standards of the electric lights.

b. *Naut.* An inverted knee-timber, having the vertical portion turned upwards.

1748 *Anson's Voy.* II. iv. 158 Two standards were broken. **1750** BLANCKLEY *Nav. Expositor*, Standards are a Sort of Knees fay'd from the Deck to the Sides of the Ship within-board, to strengthen her in the same Manner as Knees, but are bigger. **1769** FALCONER *Dict. Marine* (1780) s.v. *Architecture* D, The standard of the head which fastens it to the stem. **1874** THEARLE *Naval Archit.* III. xiii. 222 Standards are knees for connecting the stern posts to the deck beams of screw ships... Standards were fitted in sailing ships connecting the fore side of inner post with the after end of the keelson.

†c. *Coachmaking.* ? Each of the four corner posts of a coach. *Obs.*

1669 PEPYS *Diary* 26 Apr., I..do resolve upon having the standards of my coach gilt with this new sort of varnish. *Ibid.* 1 May, We went alone through the town with our new liveries..and the standards thus gilt with varnish.

d. In a plough: = SHEATH *sb.*[4]

1652 BLITHE *Eng. Improver Impr.* II. xxix. (1653) 205 By a Standard put into the end of it [*sc.* the plough-beam]. **1727** R. BRADLEY *Compl. Body Husb.* 43 in *Compl. Farmer* (1766) s.v. *Plough*, CC are the sheaths or standards.

e. *Figure-weaving.* (See quot.)

1831 G. R. PORTER *Silk Manuf.* 284 The leaves [of heddles in a gauze loom] numbered 1 and 2 which are called standards.

f. (See quot.)

1866 J. H. PARKER *Concise Gloss. Terms Archit.* 251 *Standard*..was also applied to the ends of the oak benches in churches, and that is the common use of the term now.

20. a. *Forestry.* A tree or shoot from a stump left standing when a coppice is cut down.

1473 SIR J. PASTON in *P. Lett.* III. 86 That the standardes off suche mesur as he and I comonyd off maye also be reservyd. I suppose it was xxx. inche, abowt a yerde from the grownde. **1577** B. GOOGE *Heresbach's Husb.* II. (1586) 95 b, I sette them on the outside of my Orchard, as standards to defend their fellowes from tempest and weather. **1669** WORLIDGE *Syst. Agric.* vi. 94 Felling of Coppices... Trimming up such as you spare for standards, as you go. **1677** PLOT *Oxfordsh.* 206 That ancient Standard in the high-Park, known of all by the name of the Kings Oak. **1799** J. ROBERTSON *Agric. Perth* 238 If the advantage of the copse alone is attended to, no standard should be left, except such seedlings as appear necessary to renew the stocks. **1832** *Planting* 91 in *Husbandry* (*Libr. Usef. Knowl.*) III, Standard.—The shoots of a coppice stool, selected from those cut down as underwood to remain for large poles or timber-trees.

transf. **1778** [W. MARSHALL] *Minutes Agric.* 31 July 1775, This pulled up the running weeds; the standards left, were readily drawn by hand.

b. *Gardening.* A tree or shrub growing on an erect stem of full height, not dwarfed or trained on a wall or espalier.

1625 BACON *Ess.*, *Gardens* (Arb.) 562 Part of which Heapes, to be with Standards, of little Bushes, prickt upon their Top... The Standards to be Roses; Iuniper; Holly [etc.]. **1685** TEMPLE *Gardening* Wks. 1770 III. 218 [Gardens] part laid out for flowers, others for fruits; some standards, some against walls or palisadoes. **1688** HOLME *Armoury* II. 86/2 Standards are trees standing of themselves, not on Wall sides. **1713** *Guardian* No. 173 (1756) II. 359 The trees, which were standards, and suffered to grow to their full height. **1846** BAXTER *Libr. Pract. Agric.* (ed. 4) I. 261 The fig-tree may be grown either as a standard, espalier, or against a wall. **1903** *Q. Rev.* Oct. 400 The only material difference between the experiments on dwarfs and standards respectively is that [etc.].

†21. A kind of collar of mail or plate armour. *Obs.* exc. *Hist.*

[**1371–3** *Acc. Exch. K.R.* 397/10 m. 3 Cxliiij standardis pro loricis.] **1465** *Will of T. Packet* in *Fairholt's Costume* (1885) II. 379 A standard of gesserant garnesshed with silver. **1465** MARG. PASTON in *P. Lett.* II. 190 Sertyn harnys... Inprimis;..a standard of mayle [etc.]. *c* **1490** in *5th Rep. Hist. MSS. Comm.* 445/1 Fower standardys with two gossetts of mayl. **1530** PALSGR. 275/2 Standart of mayle, *gorgerin*. **1885** *Fairholt's Costume* (ed. 3) I. 205 [On monuments 1391 and 1412] the camail is replaced by, or covered over with, a standard of plate.

†22. Some kind of service-book. *Obs.*

c **1400** in *Fabric Rolls York Minster* (Surtees) 244 Super librum vocatum standard. **1409** *Ibid.* 245 Standerdes, ac eciam libri processionales, [etc.]. **1503** *Visit. Southwell* (Camden) 71 Libri in choro vulgariter vocati le Standarths.

†23. A large packing-case or chest. *Obs.*

1371–3 *Acc. Exch. K.R.* 397/10 m. 3, j. standard magn[um] ferro ligatum, vj. Ciste magne ferro ligate. **1464** *Inv.* in *T. H. Turner's Dom. Archit.* (1859) III. 113 A square standarde, & covered with blaak letheir, & bowden with yrne, with 2 lokys... A grete red standerd, full of stuff... A gret standard of the chapell, bounde wth ierne, with 2 lokks. **1530** *Privy Purse Exp. Hen. VIII* (1827) 43 For ij standardes for to cary plate fro yorke place to hampton courte. *a* **1562** G. CAVENDISH *Wolsey* (1893) 183 The kyng caused to be sent hyme iii or iiii cartloods of stuffe, and most parte thereof was lokked in great standerds. **1663** *Cheque Bk. Chapel Royal* (Camden) 83 The Sergeant shall..deliver the Gentlemen their surplices out of the standard. *Ibid.* 93 Item, three standards, whereof one is for the song books of our sayd Chapell.

†24. *Coining.* ? = PILE *sb.*[4] 1. *Obs.*

1473 *Chancery Enrolments, Durham* 3/49 m. 6 (P.R.O.), We..haue..licencid..William Omorighe..to make graue and prynte ij dosene Trussellys and j dosene Standerdys for penys and .iiij. Standerdys and viiij. Trussellys for half penys. **1477** *Ibid.* 3/52 m. 4 (P.R.O.), To make..iij. dosen Trussels and .ij. dosen Standerdys for penys, and ij. dosen trussels and j. dosen Standerdys for halfpenys.

25. *s.w. dial.* 'A large standing tub used for washing purposes, for containing salted meat, etc.' (*Eng. Dial. Dict.*).

1535 in Weaver *Wells Wills* (1890) 116, ii. vates, a standerde, a barell and a kole.

26. †a. Something permanent; something that has lasted a long time. In *plural*, permanent or necessary furniture or apparatus (of a household, etc.). *Obs.*

1492 *Deed* A. 8331 in *Catal. Anc. Deeds P.R.O.* (1902) IV. 292 [She to have all the goods and chattels of the said Sir William] except the stondardys of howseholde [and all his growing corn, etc.]. **1506** *Will J. Cornwallis* in *Privy Purse Exp. Eliz. York* (1830) 224/2 All the brewyng vessells and standards in the brewhouse and bakehouse. **1639** FULLER *Holy War* I. xxiii. (1640) 35 The mountains..are standards too great..for either time or warre to remove. **1650** —— *Pisgah* v. 191 So there are certain standards in all visions, being the materiall and corporall ground-work, for a spirituall flourish..to improve itself thereupon. **1655** H. L'ESTRANGE *Reign K. Charles* 157 The Queen was loath to proscribe so long a standard as Episcopacy, to entertain such an upstart in-mate as Presbytery.

b. One who has been long in a position; an old resident, official, servant, etc. Now only ***old standard*** (rare exc. dial.).

a **1661** FULLER *Worthies, Gen.* xi. (1662) I. 38 The Ficklenesse and Fugitivenesse of such Servants, justly addeth a valuation to their Constancy, who are Standards in a Family. **1665** WOOD *Life* (O.H.S.) II. 45 This Dr. was an old standard..and at leisure times he would entertaine A. W. with old stories relating to the universitie. **1768** in *10th Rep. Hist. MSS. Comm.* App. I. 410, I believe [the new Cabinet will harmonize] well.., the old standards are usefull & I think makes every office better.

c. A tune or song of established popularity, esp. in *Jazz*.

1937 *Amer. Speech* XII. 184/1 *Standard*, a number whose popularity has withstood the test of time. **1938** 'JELLY ROLL' MORTON in *Downbeat* Aug. 31/1, I also transformed ..*After the Ball*, *Back Home in Indiana*, etc., and all standards that I saw fit. **1947** R. DE TOLEDANO *Frontiers of Jazz* p. xii, Half a dozen ancient Melrose stock arrangements of jazz standards 'as played by King Oliver'. **1959** 'F. NEWTON' *Jazz Scene* ii. 29 The repertoire [of jazz] consists of so-called 'standards'—themes which for one reason or another, lend themselves to profitable jazz playing. They may be drawn from any source, the traditional blues and the current popular song being the most important. **1971** C. FICK *Danziger Transcript* 95 There was a Cuban quartet in the garden playing light standards. **1980** M. BOOTH *Bad Track* v. 84 For an hour or so, the band jammed, ..before going into standards that they knew and admired.

†27. *Cookery.* (Of somewhat obscure meaning; usually explained as 'principal or standing dish'.)

1513 *Bk. Keruynge* in *Babees Bk.* 157 For standarde, venyson roste, kydde, fawne & cony [etc.]. *Ibid.* 166 The seconde course. Gelly whyte and rede..samon, dorrey, brytte, turbot, halybut; for standarde, base, troute [etc.]. **1526** in J. Croft *Excerpta Ant.* (1797) 79 Item, a Roe roasted for Standart. *Ibid.* 80 Item, for a Standart Cranes, two of a Dish.

†28. a. A suit (of clothes): = STAND *sb.*[1] 23 a. *Obs.*

1630 B. JONSON *New Inn*, Argt. II, The Lady had commanded a standard of her owne best apparrell to bee brought downe. *Ibid.* II. ii, We ha' brought a standard of apparrell, down, Because this Taylor fayld vs i' the maine.

b. ? A set (of plumes). *Obs.*

1578 *Invent. R. Wardr.* (1815) 238 Foure standeris of fedderis for the toppis of beddis.

IV. *attrib.* and *Comb.*

29. Simple attrib. **a.** in sense 1, as ***standard-car***, ***-flag***, ***-guard***, ***half-squadron***, ***-pole***, ***-shaft***, ***-sheet***, ***-spear***, ***-staff***.

1848 *W. Hemingburgh's Chronicon* I. 59 *note*, The carroccio, or great *standard-car, is said to have been invented..in the year 1035. **1821** *Sporting Mag.* VII. 196 When potent nature her *standard-flag rears. **1750** *Phil. Trans.* XLVII. 6 A soldier being confin'd to a tent call'd the *standard-guard. **1796** *Cavalry Instr.* (1813) 227 The commanding officer in the rear of the *standard half squadron. *a* **1700** EVELYN *Diary* 23 Nov. 1644, The ropes and cables which support the *standard-pole. **1497** *Naval Acc. Hen. VII* (1896) 89 *Standard shaftes. **1799** CAMPBELL *Pleas. Hope* II. 180 The stormy showers..Freeze every *standard-sheet. **1825** SCOTT *Talism.* xi, [He] laid his hand on the *standard-spear, as if to pluck it from the ground. **1560** PHAER *Æneid* IX. (1562) E e ij b, His fyriesmoking bronds on *standard-staff Mezentius shooke. **1802** C. JAMES *Milit. Dict.*, *Soc*, a machine..fixed near the stirrup, to receive the end of the standard staff. **1855** KINGSLEY *Westw. Ho!* xx, His left hand on the standard-staff, his sword pointed in his right.

b. in sense 9, as ***standard mark***.

1858 SIMMONDS *Dict. Trade*, *Standard-mark*, a legal assay mark for gold of 22 carats fine, and for silver of 11 oz. 2 dwts. **1884** F. J. BRITTEN *Watch & Clockm.* 116 The Standard Mark of the London Hall is a lion passant for sterling silver. **1889** GRETTON *Memory's Harkback* 73 In stature and in grasp of mind rather below standard-mark.

c. in sense 12 b.

1882 S. C. BUXTON in *19th Cent.* Nov. 792 The standard subjects are the three R's, while the class subjects include English grammar, geography..and needlework.

30. Special comb.: **standard-bred** *a.*, of horses, etc., bred up to the standard of excellence prescribed by some authority; also *N. Amer.* as *sb.*, a horse of this breed, developed esp. for harness racing (contrasted with *thoroughbred*); **standard-high** *a.*, of the height of a standard shrub (see B. 6); **standard lamp**, a lamp with a tall standard resting on the floor (either moveable, as a lamp for domestic use, or fixed, as in churches).

1888 G. W. CURTIS *Horses, Cattle, Sheep, & Swine* x. 56 When an animal meets the requirements of admission, and is duly registered, it should be accepted as a *standard bred trotting animal. **1901** *Westm. Gaz.* 28 Sept. 4/3 The standard-bred mare. **1948** *Sun* (Baltimore) 20 Aug. 18/1 The standardbreds..make running horses look like sissies. **1976** *National Observer* (U.S.) 2 Oct. 7/2, I grew up in..the western part of Illinois..and every farmer..had a standardbred, either trotter or pacer... They just tied sulky bikes to the backs of the nags and drove them around the track themselves. **1842** LOUDON *Suburban Hort.* 555 Standard cherry trees are generally budded *standard high, on free stocks of three years' growth from the seed. **1894** *Country Gentlemen's Catal.* 115/1 Wrought Iron *Standard Lamp, with copper Oil Container, 70/-. **1900** G. SWIFT *Somerley* 124 [He] came and stood with me under the light of the tall standard-lamp. **1932** R. LEHMANN *Invitation to Waltz* I. xi. 110 The light was very bright and white, coming from three brass standard lamps with white silk shades. **1980** A. N. WILSON *Healing Art* xvi. 195 By the fireplace.. gas blazed, and a standard lamp shone dimly.

B. *adj.* [Attributive use of the sb.]

I. 1. a. Serving as a standard of measurement, weight or value; conformed to the official standard of a unit of measure or weight. Also freq. in special scientific collocations, as ***standard atmosphere***, (*a*) a unit of atmospheric pressure, equal to 760 torr or 1013·25 millibars; (*b*) a hypothetical atmosphere with defined surface temperature and pressure and specified profile of temperature with altitude, used esp. in aviation and space research; ***standard cable***, a unit of attenuation formerly used in telephone engineering (see quot. 1963), now replaced by the BEL; ***standard candle***, a disused unit of luminous intensity, defined as the intensity of the flame of a spermaceti candle of specified properties (see quots.), now replaced by the CANDELA; also *transf.*; ***standard cell***, any of several forms of voltaic cell designed to produce a constant and reproducible electromotive force as long as the current drawn is not too large; ***standard deviation***: see DEVIATION 2d; ***standard error***, a measure of the statistical accuracy of an estimate, equal to the standard deviation which a large population of such estimates would have; ***standard wire gauge***, one of the series of standard thicknesses for wire and metal plates in the United Kingdom; any specific measure in this series; abbrev. *s.w.g.*, *S.W.G.* s.v. S 4a.

1622 MALYNES *Anc. Law-Merch.* 306 If it bee appointed of make a Standard peece of tenne ounces fine. **1669** BEALE in *Phil. Trans.* IV. 1113 A measure, taken exactly from the standard-foot of London. **1827** FARADAY *Chem. Manip.* iii. (1842) 67 The standard or imperial pint now to be used is larger than the wine pint. **1862** H. SPENCER *First Princ.* II. vi. §61 (1875) 192a, From the standard-measure preserved at Westminster, are derived the measures for trigonometrical surveys. **1870** JEVONS *Elem. Logic* xxxiii. 290 A yard or foot has no meaning unless there be a definite standard yard or foot which fixes the meaning. **1871** B. STEWART *Heat* (ed. 2) §25 The difference between mercurial and the standard air thermometer becomes very considerable at high temperatures. **1873** J. C. MAXWELL *Electr. & Magn.* (1881) II. 322 When it is intended to measure a current [electric] with the greatest accuracy in terms of standard units, it is called a Standard Galvanometer. **1878** JEVONS *Primer Pol. Econ.* 108 In the English system of money, gold is the standard money and the legal tender. **1884** KNIGHT *Dict. Mech.* Suppl., *Standard Battery* (Electricity). One to be used as a standard, having a perfectly constant electro-motive force.

1911 W. N. SHAW *Forecasting Weather* p. xi, The accepted normal pressure of the atmosphere, or 'standard atmosphere', is that of a column of mercury 76 centimetres high at the freezing-point of water under the conditions as to gravitation which are to be found in latitude 45°N. or S. **1924** *Official Bull. Internat. Comm. Air Navigation* VII. 34 The Commission decides: To adopt the Regulations set out hereunder concerning the definition of an international standard atmosphere. **1930** *Meteorol. Gloss.* (Met. Office) (ed. 2) 162 The International Standard Atmosphere which is used as the basis of graduation of altimeters assumes at mean sea level a temperature of 15°C., a pressure of 1,013·2 mb., and a lapse rate of 6·5°C. per kilometre from sea level up to 11 km., above which the temperature is assumed constant at − 56·5°C. **1963** JERRARD & MCNEILL *Dict. Sci. Units* 130 One standard atmosphere corresponds to a barometric pressure of 29·9213 inches or 760 mm of mercury of density 13·595 g cm^{-3}, where the acceleration due to gravity is 980·665 cm sec^{-2}... The ICAO [*sc.* International Civil Aviation Organisation] standard atmosphere was introduced about 1940. **1977** I. M. CAMPBELL *Energy & Atmosphere* iii. 47 The origin of the rising temperature from 11 to 50 km in the standard atmosphere is the degradation of a portion of the solar irradiance to thermal energy through the agency of primary absorption by ozone. **1906** J. POOLE *Pract. Telephone Handbk.* (ed. 3) xxvi. 413 Standard Cable and Equivalents. —In the agreement entered into in February 1905 between the British Post Office and the National Telephone Co. certain standards of telephonic transmission were stipulated, and these were to be measured by comparison with the transmission results obtained with standard telephone instruments through certain lengths of standard test cable. **1924** *Trans. Amer. Inst. Electr. Engineers* XLIII. 797/1 The 'mile of standard cable' has been used in telephone engineering in this country for over twenty years ..as the unit for expressing the transmission efficiency of telephone circuits and apparatus. **1963** JERRARD & MCNEILL *Dict. Sci. Units* 131 The unit compared the attenuation produced in the circuit under test with that in a standard cable which was defined as a theoretical cable one mile in length, resistance 88 ohms, capacitance 0·054 microfarad, inductance one millihenry and leakance 5 × 10^{-5} mho. The standard cable produced an attenuation of about 20% for a 800 c/s input. **1879** *Cassell's Techn. Educ.* II. 175 The *unit* of calculation adopted in practice is a sperm candle one-sixth of a pound in weight and burning 120 grains per hour; this is called a 'standard candle', and the 'standard burner' in use in London is Sugg's London Argand, Number 1. **1937** G. S. MONK *Light* v. 36 The standard candle was originally of sperm wax, weighing ⅙ lb., ⅞ in. diameter, and burning 120 grains per hr. **1959** *Listener* 2 July 14/2 By studying the period of a Cepheid, we can..find out its real luminosity; its apparent magnitude is easy to measure, and hence its distance may be determined, so that these convenient variables act as our standard candles in space. **1976** *New Scientist* 2 Dec. 530/1 The new finding opens the way to calibrate a new standard candle, namely, the absolute brightness of a galaxy by means of an easy measurement in radio astronomy. **1872** L. CLARK in *Proc. R. Soc.* XX. 447 We have therefore the mean value of the electromotive force of the standard-cells, as determined by the electrodynamometer, 18 observations..1·45735 Volt. **1920** *Whittaker's Electr. Engineer's Pocket-bk.* (ed. 4) 100 The original standard cell devised by Latimer Clark is a mercury-zinc cell using zinc and mercurous sulphates as electrolyte and depolarizer respectively. **1980** J. P. BROMBERG *Physical Chem.* xvii. 315 The voltage of the unknown cell..can be determined from the calibrated slide wire and the known voltage of the standard cell. **1897** G. U. YULE in *Jrnl. R. Statist. Soc.* LX. 821 We see that $\sigma_1\sqrt{(1-r^2)}$ is the standard error made in estimating *x*. **1956** J. H. BURN *Lect. Notes Pharmacol.* (ed. 4) 129 The standard error of the mean is proportional to the standard deviation and inversely proportional to the number of animals used. **1962** J. H. KINOSHITA et al. in A. Pirie *Lens Metabolism Rel. Cataract* 409 The results are given as the mean ± standard error of the mean of 12 determinations. **1858** J. WHITWORTH *Misc. Papers Mech. Subjects* 68 (*caption*) Standard wire-gauge. **1884** *Rep. Board of Trade on Proc. & Business Weights & Measures Act, 1878* 3 in *Parl. Papers* XXVIII. 851 The new standard wire-guage has been adopted by the War, Admiralty, and India Departments. **1941** *Trans Newcomen Soc.* XXI. 94 He [*sc.* Sir Joseph Whitworth] named it the 'Standard Wire Gauge'; it covered a range of 38 sizes of from 0·3 in. to 0·0018 in. diam. **1963** JERRARD & MCNEILL *Dict. Sci. Units* 151 The Standard Wire Gauge.. classifies wire diameters in geometrical progression. **1971** B. SCHARF *Engin. & its Lang.* ix. 75 In Great Britain the main gauges are the Standard Wire Gauge (S.W.G., s.w.g.), and the Birmingham Gauge (B.G.).

b. Having the prescribed or normal size, amount, power, degree of quality, etc. Also ***standard costs*** *Accountancy* (see quot. 1959); freq. *attrib.*, as ***standard cost card*** etc.; hence ***standard costing***; ***standard gauge*** *Railways*: see quot. 1884; also *attrib.* Also in parasynthetic adj., ***standard-rated***.

1807 T. THOMSON *Chem.* (ed. 2) 165 He calculated, that the increase of density, on mixing different quantities of standard acid and water, was [etc.]. **1813** J. THOMSON *Lect. Inflam.* 113 In hectic fever the temperature seldom rises two or three degrees above the natural or standard temperature. **1825** J. NICHOLSON *Oper. Mech.* 550 The standard thickness of a brick wall is 1½ brick laid lengthwise... A rod of standard brick-work..will require 4500 bricks. **1826** *Art of Brewing* (ed. 2) 17 To..evaporate the unnecessary quantity to a standard gravity. **1857** MILLER *Elem. Chem., Org.* 60 For the preparation of the standard copper solutions. **1878** STEWART & TAIT *Unseen Univ.* iii. §107. 120 That of boiling water under the standard pressure is 374°. **1881** *Chicago Times* 12 Mar., A standard-gauge railroad. **1884** KNIGHT *Dict. Mech.* Suppl. s.v., 'Standard gage' means 4' 8½" between centers of rails. **1889** *Hardwicke's Science-Gossip* XXV. 184/2 They are rectangular in shape, and are made of one standard size. **1900** P. N. HASLUCK *Model Engin. Handybk.* 43 All the small parts..would be made to some standard measurement. **1904** D. J. SHACKLETON *Sp. Ho. Comm.* 23 Mar. in *Hansard* 553 In using the words standard rate of wages in his Resolution, he desired the House to understand that he meant the trade union rate. *Ibid.* 557 That this House is of opinion that the wages paid to the unskilled workers in Government factories..should be not less than the standard rate of wages. **1917** W. N. POLAKOV in *Trans. Amer. Soc. Mech. Engineers* XXXVIII. 587 Carrying out the analysis of the economy limit to its logical conclusion, the standard cost of the product is arrived at. **1918** G. C. HARRISON in *Industrial Managem.* LVI. 393/2 In the 'Standard Cost Card' shown in Form I it will be seen that the estimated or standard cost of the bolts is $11·079 per thousand. **1921** (*title*) Standard costing principles & practices for the plywood industry. **1935** C. M. GILLESPIE *Accounting Procedure for Standard Costs* iv. 62 The structure of standard cost cards becomes complex. **1959** *Chambers's Encycl.* I. 39/2 Two major developments in cost accounting must be briefly mentioned. Firstly the introduction of standard costing. Standard costs are estimates made in detail for operations, processes of articles on the basis of predetermined standards. **1974** *Terminol. Managem. & Financial Accountancy* (Inst. Cost and Managem. Accountants) 15 *Standard cost rate*, a rate calculated by dividing the expected overhead cost attributable to a cost centre by the predetermined quantity of the base to which the rate is applied.

Comb. **1972** *V.A.T.: Gen. Guide* (H.M. Customs) 30 Where an amount payable covers both standard-rated and zero-rated goods or services, the amount must be split in fair proportion. **1977** *Jrnl. R. Soc. Arts* CXXV. 440/1 The most sensitive systems might have legislation applied at a luxury rate whilst others could be standard rated.

c. ***standard deal***: see quots.

1834 MCCULLOCH *Dict. Comm.* (ed. 2) 1150, 36½ Russian stand[ard] deals 12 ft. long, 1½ inch thick, 11 inch broad, make 1 load timber. **1867** SMYTH *Sailor's Word-bk.*, *Standard-Deals*, those planks of the pine or fir above 7 inches wide and 6 feet long.

d. Of bread (see quot.).

1851 MAYHEW *Lond. Labour* I. 178 Previously to 1815 bakers were restricted..to the baking of three kinds of bread —wheaten, standard wheaten, and household. The wheaten was made of the best flour, the standard wheaten of the different kinds of flour mixed together.

e. Bridge. ***Standard American***, the commonest system of bidding in the U.S.

1961 A. SHEINWOLD *Short Cut to winning Bridge* 13/1 Most of the hands in this book are bid according to the principles of 'Standard American'. **1963** H. SCHENKEN *Better Bidding* i. 16 The most popular system in this country is called Standard American... They all have one thing on common with Standard American: the opening bid of one in a suit is almost unlimited. **1968** ROTH & RUBENS *Mod. Bridge Bidding* p. xvi, Standard American is the most widely used although not..the best approach to bidding. **1976** *National Observer* (U.S.) 24 July 15/3 If you are playing under Precision's rules or by agreement in Standard American and you open light.., you can pass third hand with a subminimum count.

2. Of precious metals, coins: Conforming to the legal standard of fineness or intrinsic value. Also said of value or fineness.

1677 W. B. *Touchst. Gold & Silver* (title-p.), Discovering ..how to know Adulterated Wares from those made of the True Standard Alloy. **1691** LOCKE *Consid. Raising Value Money* Wks. 1714 II. 68 The Fineness of Standard Silver in England is eleven parts Silver, and one part Copper, near. **1706** PHILLIPS (ed. Kersey), *Jacobus*,..a Gold-coin..of two sorts, viz. the Broad Piece of Twenty Shillings Standard-value..and the 22s. Broad-Piece. **1790** KEIR in *Phil. Trans.* LXXX. 370, I added 144 grains of standard silver. **1809** R. LANGFORD *Introd. Trade* 38 Standard Gold contains 11 parts of pure Gold, and 1 part of alloy. Standard Silver contains 37 parts of pure Silver, and 3 parts of alloy. **1866** CRUMP *Banking* x. 230 The standard purity of the sovereign underwent many changes. **1879** *Cassell's Techn. Educ.* IV. 308/2 Standard gold which implies the quality used for coinage..is..what is called twenty-two carat.

3. a. Serving or fitted to serve as a standard of comparison or judgement.

1724 A. COLLINS *Gr. Chr. Relig.* 103 It seems incredible, that Origen..and other Christians of his time..should receive an Old Testament (and that with the greatest applause for its integrity, and as a standard Text) from enemies. **1776** BURNEY *Hist. Mus.* I. 276 *note*, We may suppose this sound to be the standard pitch, and fundamental note of the Mercurian lyre. **1845** DE MORGAN *Globes* 95 One hundred of these [*sc.* the fixed stars] are selected, among which are the *standard* stars, as they are called, being those which are best known and best adapted for the most accurate use.

b. Of a book, an author: That has a permanent rank as an authority, or as an exemplar of excellence.

1645 MILTON *Tetrach.* Wks. 1851 IV. 180 But Erasmus, who for having writ an excellent Treatise of Divorce, was wrote against by som burly standard Divine,..defends his former work. **1728** POPE *Dunc.* IV. 123 Let standard-authors, thus, like trophies born, Appear more glorious as more hack'd and torn. **1759** GOLDSM. *Bee* No. 8 *Acc. Augustan Age* ¶5 That he [L'Estrange] was a standard writer cannot be disowned, because a great many very eminent authors formed their style by his. **1783** H. BLAIR *Lect. Rhet.* xx. 408 The good sense, and good writing.. render it [Addison's Spectator] one of those standard books which have done the greatest honour to the English nation. **1821** HAZLITT in *London Mag.* Aug. 179/2 Pictures are scattered like stray gifts through the world... There are plenty of standard works still to be found in this country. **1849** C. BRONTË *Shirley* I. v. 94 One should not be apathetic in studying standard works. **1891** *Speaker* 2 May 534/1 A 'History of Chemistry', which..has rapidly won its way into recognition in scientific circles as a standard book on the subject. **1922** JOYCE *Ulysses* 628 You know the standard works on the subject. **1969** J. GROSS *Rise & Fall Man of Lett.* iv. 115 He goes on to supply a list of standard works, English and European,..which would certainly keep most ordinary readers tied up for as far ahead as they could plan.

c. Of a law: That has the chief authority with reference to a particular subject.

1752 C. LOUTHIAN *Form Process Scot.* 162 The Standard-law in England, concerning High Treason, is the Statute of the 25th of Edward III. cap. 2.

d. Of a maxim, etc.: Constantly repeated, standing, 'stock'.

1805 FOSTER *Ess.* III. i. 10 A standard expression of contemptuous dispatch. **1870** M. ARNOLD *St. Paul & Protest.* (1875) Pref. 36 Mr Miall's standard-maxim: The Dissidence of Dissent, and the Protestantism of the Protestant religion. **1885** *Spectator* 25 July 977/1 [He] has his oft-repeated little standard jokes.

e. Applied to that variety of a spoken or written language of a country or other linguistic area which is generally considered the most correct and acceptable form, as ***Standard English***, ***American***, etc.; Received Standard; also, ***standard pronunciation*** = *received pronunciation* s.v. RECEIVED *ppl. a.* 1b.

1836 *Q. Rev.* Feb. 356 It is, however, certain that there were in his [*sc.* Higden's] time, and probably long before, five distinctly marked forms, which may be classed as follows:—1. Southern or standard English, which in the fourteenth century was perhaps best spoken in Kent and Surrey by the body of the inhabitants. **1859** *Proposal Publ. New Eng. Dict.* 3 As soon as a standard language has been formed, which in England was the case after the Reformation, the lexicographer is bound to deal with that alone. **1878** J. A. H. MURRAY in *Encycl. Brit.* VIII. 396/2 Chaucer's language is well known to be more southern than standard English eventually became. **1908** H. SWEET *Sounds Eng.* 7 Standard English, like Standard French, is now a class-dialect more than a local dialect: it is the language of the educated all over Great Britain. **1909** D. JONES *Pronunc. Eng.* i. 1 Standard Pronunciation. **1919** G. P. KRAPP (*title*) The pronunciation of standard English in America. **1925**

—— *Eng. Lang. in Amer.* I. v. 296 The informal or local speech will often seem more penetrating, more genuine than the standard speech. **1947** PARTRIDGE *Usage & Abusage* 304/1 Standard English and Standard American are the speech of the educated classes in the British Empire and the United States. **1962** P. H. JOHNSON *Error of Judgment* ii. 5 Had spoken standard English varied by a few fancies such as 'crorss' for 'cross' and 'poyt' for 'poet'. **1975** *Times Lit. Suppl.* 7 Feb. 136/2 Local names pronounced in [Chinese] dialects widely different from 'Mandarin' or, as it must now be called, Standard Speech. **1978** *English Jrnl.* Dec. 7/1 There is also a kind of 'standard standard'. Some people call it 'broadcast' or 'publications' standard, because most newspapers and television news shows use it.

f. *standard time*: see TIME *sb.* 27.

4. *Math.* That does not involve infinitesimal quantities.

1961 A. ROBINSON in *Proc. K. Nederlandse Akad. v. Wetensch.* A. LXIV. 434 We consider in the first instance functions, relations, sets, etc. which are defined already in R_0 [*sc.* the set of all real numbers]... Such concepts will be called standard (functions, relations, sets, etc.). **1972** [see NON-STANDARD *a.* b].

II. 5. Upright, set up on end, or vertically.

standard-knee = STANDARD *sb.* 19 b.

1538 in *Lett. Suppress. Monasteries* (Camden) 276 Item, ij standert candelstyckes. **1627** CAPT. SMITH *Seaman's Gram.* ii. 14 All the beames to be bound with two knees at each end, and a standard knee at euery beames end vpon the Orlope. **1733** W. ELLIS *Chiltern & Vale Farm.* 318 Its Standard Iron Pin is twenty Inches long and one Inch Diameter. **1833** LOUDON *Encycl. Archit.* §981 Each fire-place to have.. standard grates (kitchen grates supporting themselves by feet in front). **1846** A. YOUNG *Naut. Dict.* 295 *Standard-knees.* **1865** *Morning Star* 27 Feb., The illumination is produced almost entirely by standard gas-burners. **1875** KNIGHT *Dict. Mech.*, *Standard-piles*, in a coffer-dam. Piles placed at regular intervals apart and connected by runners. **1901** *J. Black's Carp. & Builder, Scaffolding* 21 Each side of the inner square was divided into two by two upright poles, so that there were thirty-six standard poles on the outside, and sixteen on the inside.

6. Of a tree or shrub: Grown as a 'standard', not dwarfed or trained on a wall.

1685 TEMPLE *Ess. Gardens* Wks. 1731 I. 185 The Border is set with Standard Laurels. **1716** *Lond. Gaz.* No. 5488/8 Standard Trees of Cherries, Apples, &c. **1798** *Times* 28 June 4/2 Large walled Garden.. stocked with standard and wall fruit trees. **1842** *Florist's Jrnl.* (1846) III. 87 The habit.. does not make it answer so well as a standard rose. **1908** ELIZ. FOWLER *Betw. Trent & Ancholme* 17 A tall standard Rose.

Hence **'standardless** *a.* [-LESS], having no standard or standards; unprincipled; **'standardness** [-NESS].

1912 GALSWORTHY *Inn of Tranquillity* 217 How can we help it, seeing that we are undisciplined and standardless, seeing that we started without the backbone that schooling gives? **1944** AUDEN *Sea & Mirror* in *For Time Being* iii. 29 On the shuddering edge of the bohemian standardless abyss. **1972** J. L. DILLARD *Black English* vi. 238 A combination of age-grading, status-grading, and peer group influence causes a special feature to operate among young males at about the age of puberty. At that time, their graph of standardness will actually swing 'downward' a bit. **1973** *N.Y. Law Jrnl.* 2 Aug. 4/8 Such a subjective determination as is proposed here lacks the necessary standards to insure a nondiscriminatory result. The danger of discrimination which inheres in such a standardless approval is.. evidenced by the determination in question here.

standard ('stændərd), *v.* [f. prec. sb.] *trans.*

a. To ascertain the fineness of (precious metal). **b.** To establish or deposit as a standard of measure or weight.

1696 *Ord. Counc.* 24 Sept. in *Lond. Gaz.* No. 3222/1 The said Rate.. upon the Receiving, Melting and Standarding of the said Plate. **1817** HASSLER in J. Q. Adams *Rep. Weights & Meas.* (1821) 154 An iron metre standarded at Paris in 1799. **1820** G. G. CAREY *Guide to Funds* 98 Method of standarding coins and bullion.

standard-bearer.

1. An officer or soldier who bears the standard.

c **1450** *Brut* 538 In his retenewe.. v standart berers. **1538** in P. H. Hore *Hist. Wexford* (1900) I. 237 Watkyne and his followers did meth with Cahir McArtes Standarthe berrer. **1544** BETHAM *Precepts War* I. clxxv. H viij b, Plucke the standart from the standart bearer. **1611** BIBLE *Isa.* x. 18 They shall bee as when a standerd bearer fainteth. **1781** GIBBON *Decl. & F.* xxix. III. 129 As Mascezel advanced.. he encountered one of the foremost standard-bearers of the Africans. **1879** FROUDE *Cæsar* xvii. 278 The standard-bearer.. reached the fosse, flung the eagle over the rampart, [etc.].

b. As the title of an office of dignity. *Hist.*

1829 HEATH *Grocers' Comp.* (1869) 3 Lord Fitzwalter, hereditary chastellain banneret or standard-bearer of London. **1837** LOCKHART *Scott* I. ii. 71 A charter granted by Archibald Earl of Douglas.. to Henry de Haliburton, whom he designates as his standard-bearer.

c. One who carries a banner in a procession.

1495 *Acc.* in Sharp *Cov. Myst.* (1825) 196 Payd to the stondard-beyrres, & ffor poyntes xj d. **1844** tr. *M. T. Asmar's Mem. Babyl. P'cess* II. 72 Accompanied by standard-bearers, carrying banners of various colours. **1858** SIMMONDS *Dict. Trade, Standard-bearer*, an officer who carries a banner or colours in a procession.

2. *fig.* Chiefly, a conspicuous advocate of a cause; one who is in the forefront of a political or religious party.

1561 T. NORTON *Calvin's Inst.* IV. 7 They that are bolder than other, and as it were standerd bearers to make any departyng from the Churche. **1594** T. B. *La Primaud. Fr. Acad.* II. 543 Epicurus himselfe, the captaine and standard-bearer of all atheists and epicures. **1608** TOPSELL *Serpents* 65 Very seldome.. they [male bees, drones] stir out of doores, as those whom nature had pointed out to be the fittest to be stander-bearers, and to carry ancients in the camp of Venus. **1611** BIBLE *Cant.* v. 10 My beloved is.. the chiefest [*marg.*, a standard-bearer] among ten thousand. **1710** M. HENRY *Christianity no Sect* Wks. 1857 II. 449/1 Marvel not if the standard-bearers be most struck at. **1821** SCOTT *Kenilw.* vii, You, whom men call the standard-bearer of the true Protestant faith. **1900** G. C. BRODRICK *Mem.* 408 As though I had any claim to be treated as a standard-bearer of the party.

Hence **'standardbearership.**

1865 J. M. LUDLOW *Pop. Epics* II. 201 Aragon promises the standard-bearership of his kingdom to whosoever will take William.

'standardism. *rare.* [-ISM.] The system of educational 'standards' (see STANDARD *sb.* 12 b).

1878 T. SINCLAIR *Mount* 33 Ultra-centralising educationists with competition and standardism as whole code of youth's effort.

standardizable ('stændərdaɪzəb(ə)l), *a.* [f. STANDARDIZE *v.* + -ABLE.] That may be standardized.

1922 *19th Cent.* Feb. 185 The sale of the more standardisable profits. **1980** *U.S. News & World Rep.* 1 Dec. 45/1 Legal clinics offering adoptions, divorces, wills and other frequently cut-and-dried standardizable services at low cost are flourishing.

standardization (ˌstændədaɪˈzeɪʃən). [f. STANDARDIZE *v.* + -ATION.] The action of standardizing.

1896 *Allbutt's Syst. Med.* I. 226 The process of 'standardisation' which has been already adopted in two instances in the British Pharmacopœia. **1900** M. CRACKANTHORPE in *19th Cent.* Jan. 104 The 'standardisation' of punishment is not the same as its 'equalisation'. **1901** *Cyclists' Touring Club Gaz.* July 298/1 By all means, let us have standardisation of nuts and bolts. **1904** *Times* 20 Dec. 15/3 Standardization of waterpipes and fittings.

attrib. **1902** *Times* 31 Dec. 13/1, I know.. other standardization devices. **1908** *Brit. Pharmacop. Rep.* in *Chem. & Druggist* (1909) 20 Feb. 292/2 Standardisation experiments are in progress.

standardize ('stændədaɪz), *v.* [f. STANDARD *sb.* and *a.* + -IZE.]

1. *trans.* To bring to a standard or uniform size, strength, form of construction, proportion of ingredients, or the like.

1873 C. H. RALFE *Outl. Physiol. Chem.* 225 This solution must be standardized. **1889** *Daily News* 20 June 6/3 The supply of electrical energy under statutory powers could not be effectively carried out unless there was some method of standardising the meters and other instruments. **1904** *Brit. Med. Jrnl.* 10 Sept. 564 The emulsion was always made up to a uniform strength.. by standardizing it against an arbitrarily-chosen standard bacterial suspension. **1907** [see STABLY *adv.*].

b. *transf.*

1900 M. CRACKANTHORPE in *19th Cent.* Jan. 103 (*title*), Can sentences be standardised? **1906** *19th Cent.* June 990 Legislation is, to use an engineering expression, being standardised. **1911** F. HARRISON *Autobiog. Mem.* II. xxxvii. 314 Life and Society have been standardised.

2. To test by a standard.

1881 *Nature* 3 Nov. 17/2 This other mode of measurement should be standardised.. by comparison with Mr. Harcourt's air-gas flame, which should alone be taken as the official standard. **1898** *Longm. Mag.* Nov. 69 To standardise the poisonous principle contained in it [eel's blood].

3. (See quot. 1890.)

1889 *Tablet* 2 Nov. 688 For each instrument two plates will be standardised. **1890** *Anthony's Photogr. Bull.* III. 158 The Lick observatory plates were 'standardized.' That is, a portion of each plate was impressed with the light from a standard lamp shining for a known time through a small hole at a known distance.

Hence **'standardized** *ppl. a.*; **'standardizing** *vbl. sb.* (also *attrib.*).

1884 *Times* 14 Aug. 3 Standardized laudanum. **1889** *Daily News* 20 June 4/7 To advocate the establishment of an electrical standardizing laboratory. **1892** *Ibid.* 31 Mar. 6/8 The Electric Standardising, Testing, and Training Institution. **1913** *Contemp. Rev.* Dec. 776 Standardised voting cards are provided by the respective candidates.

'standardizer. [f. STANDARDIZE *v.* + -ER[1].]

a. One who standardizes. **b.** An apparatus for standardizing.

1889 *Lond., Edin. & Dublin Philos. Mag.* Feb. 86 The absolute values of the polarization.. should.. have been identical, but according to the standardizer they were always markedly different. [**1884** *Times* 14 Aug. 3 A serious error in analysis might lead to greater variations in strength than the pre-standardizers ever dreamt of.]

standardly ('stændədlɪ), *adv.* [f. STANDARD *a.* + -LY[2].] In a standard manner; according to common practice; normally, generally.

1957 *Proc. Aristotelian Soc.* LVII. 237 Knowledge of a particular event will standardly give one knowledge only of the location of its witnesses. **1978** A. RYAN in Hookway & Pettit *Action & Interpretation* 75 A game in which we are standardly beset by something like Prisoners' Dilemma problems.

standard-wing. [STANDARD *sb.* 8.]

1. A species of Bird of Paradise (*Semioptera wallacei*) discovered by Wallace in the island of Batchian.

1869 GOULD *Birds Austral.* Suppl. Pl. 52 *Semioptera wallacei*, G. R. Gray. Standard-wing. **1894–5** LYDEKKER *Roy. Nat. Hist.* III. 338 The standard-wing.. is characterised by.. the presence of two long projecting feathers from each wing. **1895** *Ibid.* IV. 43 Standard-winged Nightjar.

2. *attrib.* or *adj.* = STANDARD-WINGED.

1872 J. H. GURNEY *Andersson's Birds Damara Land* 45 *Cosmetornis vexillarius* (Gould). Standard-wing Goat-sucker. **1903** W. L. SCLATER *Stark's Birds S. Africa* III. 42 *Cosmetornis vexillarius.* Standard-wing Nightjar.

standard-winged, *a. Ornith.* [STANDARD *sb.* 8.] Of certain birds: Characterized by the possession of 'standards'.

1875–84 R. B. SHARPE *Layard's Birds S. Africa* 89 *Cosmetornis vexillarius.* Standard-winged Nightjar.

‖**Standartenführer** ('ʃtandaːrtənˌfyːrər). [Ger., lit. 'leader of the standard'.] Under the Third Reich, a commanding officer of a unit of the Schutzstaffel or Sturmabteilung.

1943 W. NECKER *German Army of To-day* IV. 168 *Staff Officers*:.. *SS-Standartenführer* = colonel. **1971** BENDER & TAYLOR *Uniforms, Organization & Hist. Waffen-SS* II. 72 SS-Standartenführer, promoted on Nov. 4, 1944 to SS Oberführer, Wilhelm Mohnke. **1973** 'D. JORDAN' *Nile Green* xliv. 225 He was on the staff of the SS Hauptamt. He ended the war as Standartenfuhrer. **1978** *Detroit Free Press* 16 Apr. (Record) 12/2 These strips had been collected by a German doctor who was writing a treatise on tatooes, and also by the 28-year-old wife of the Standartenfuehrer or commanding officer.

stand-by. [f. vbl. phr. *stand by*: see STAND *v.* 70, 91.]

I. 1. *Naut.* **a.** A vessel kept in attendance for emergencies.

1796 in Nicolas *Disp. Nelson* (1846) VII. p. xci, Meleager [a ship] is my only stand-by and every week I must send something to Genoa for news.

b. An order or signal for a boat to stand by (see STAND *v.* 91 e); *attrib.* in ***stand-by bell***, the ringing of a bell in the engine-room of a vessel as a signal to stop the engines.

1896 KIPLING *Seven Seas* 46 (M'Andrew's Hymn) Losh! Yon's the 'Stand-by' bell. Pilot so soon?

c. The state of being immediately available to come on duty if required; readiness for duty. Also *transf.* Usu. in phr. ***on stand-by***. orig. *Naut.*

1946 R. E. HIGGINBOTHAM *Wine for my Brothers* iv. 75 I'm on stand-by—take the wheel in fifteen minutes. **1959** WALLIS & BLAIR *Thunder Above* (ed. 2) ii. 13 With a full load we could use an extra stewardess. You're on stand-by, aren't you? **1960** *Times* 22 Mar. 12/1 Darkness brought peace to the riot areas, but an active citizen force was put on standby. **1971** W. KEENAN *Murder in Melancholy* v. 48 We'll use two of the vans every night, the other will be on standby. **1974** D. FRANCIS *Knock Down* iv. 45 I'm on stand-by from four this afternoon for twelve hours... Most stand-bys are just a bore.

d. *spec.* in civilian aviation, a stand-by passenger; ***on stand-by***, waiting for a stand-by seat; in possession of a stand-by ticket. See sense 9 below.

1961 'E. LATHEN' *Banking on Death* (1962) xix. 156 Four stand-bys who were convinced that by keeping in motion their chances of getting on a plane were improved. **1962** J. D. MACDONALD *Key to Suite* (1968) ii. 31 'You got in real early.' 'Earlier than I wanted to. But all they could do for me on anything later was to put me on standby.' **1970** *Guardian* 8 Sept. 11/4 All the flights are full. They're likely to be on standby half the night for seats on any plane. **1973** [see STAGE *sb.* 9 c].

2. One who stands by another to render assistance; esp. *fig.* one who upholds or seconds another; a staunch adherent or partisan.

1801 C. GADSDEN in *J. Adams' Wks.* (1854) IX. 578 But my duty to my country and to our old standbys.. compelled me in our late election to take up my feeble pen again. **1857** LADY CANNING in Hare *Two Noble Lives* (1893) II. 238 Neill is made a General, and joins General Havelock, and a capital stand-by he is. **1887** BARING-GOULD *Golden Feather* viii, His mother had always been his stand-by against the severity of his father. **1883** MRS. OLIPHANT *Sheridan* i. 34 The respectable brandy-merchant had been the family stand-by.

3. Something upon which one can rely; a main support; a chief resource.

1861 C. P. HODGSON *Resid. Nagasaki* iii. 70 We had that famous stand-bye [*sic*], a good ham, three fowls, sardines, bread and tea. **1882** STEVENSON *Lett.* 22 Feb., Art and marriage are two very good stand-by's. **1891** E. KINGLAKE *Australians at H.* 47 Old ladies are the great stand-by of the long established medicoes.

4. *ellipt.* for: **a.** *stand-by credit, loan*, etc.; **b.** a stand-by fare or ticket.

1959 *Daily Tel.* 18 Dec. 20/5 It was in December, 1956, after the Suez crisis, that Britain drew $561 million from the Fund and arranged for a 'stand-by' of $738 million.. to be drawn upon if necessary. **1975** *Offshore* Aug. 42/1 The Smit tug was lounging around, lapping up stand-by at a thousand dollars a day. **1980** *Daily Tel.* 29 Aug. 7/2 The £20 Scottish standby, the airline claims, is more than £5 cheaper than the second-class rail fare.

II. *attrib.* or as *adj.* **5. a.** Of a craft or vehicle held in reserve.

1882 *Pall Mall Gaz.* 21 June 5/1 To the 150 passengers was given the smaller 'stand-by' steamer. **1959** *Economist* 14 Mar. 992/2 In case of breakdown a 'standby' vehicle can be hired from the manufacturers when needed. **1974** *BP Shield Internat.* Oct. 20/1 I'm keeping in touch with our standby vessel, *Otterburn.* **1976** P. R. WHITE *Planning for Public Transport* viii. 183 It may be cheaper to move to direct sale coupled with retention of standby vehicles and crews to duplicate workings if required. **1982** *Times* 3 June 8/5 Several of the smaller frigates have been pulled out of standby fleets.

b. Of (a body of) persons: on stand-by; available to come on duty. More generally, ready to stand in for another if required. orig. *Naut.*

1891 CONSTANCE MACEWEN *Three Women in Boat* ix, She is a capital stand-by woman, holding her nerves as some people hold money—wisely and well. **1897** *Westm. Gaz.* 18 Dec. 5/3 Eight ordinary winches, each manœuvred by four men with 'stand by' labour at their elbow. **1933** J. H. MCCULLOCH *Million Miles* iii. 59 It was the standby man from the other watch, dragging us out again for another four-hour battle on the deck. **1937** *Amer. Speech* XII. 100 The public is..not so accustomed to *stand by organist* or *pianist*, an artist who remains on call for emergency work. **1946** R. E. HIGGINBOTHAM *Wine for my Brothers* 178 Dane was stand-by man, and he started over the catwalk for the bridge. **1958** *Economist* 16 Aug. 507/2 When he asked the assembly to create a United Nations 'standby' peace force, he was making a gesture of conciliation. **1974** *Sumter* (S. Carolina) *Daily Item* 18 Apr. 6B/1 The White House has secretly appointed wealthy campaign contributors to the standby corps, which would help run the country in case of war. **1981** G. CLARE *Last Waltz in Vienna* (1982) II. 144 My role was that of stand-by boy-friend very much playing second fiddle.

c. Of things: on which one can rely; esp. of machinery or equipment: kept in a position of reserve, *spec.* in case of failure of a primary device or supply.

1902 *Daily Chron.* 24 May 8/3 In Paris every summer foulard frocks re-appear with perennial freshness, and are made the stand-by gown of the woman of wisdom. **1908** *Sears, Roebuck Catal.* 205/2 The Stand-By Dry Batteries.. will produce more current and last longer. **1930** *Engineering* 28 Feb. 295/1 A standby machine of this type is also useful. **1942** *R.A.F. Jrnl.* 3 Oct. 25 From the..roof, electric lights and standy-by hurricane lamps are suspended. **1954** 'J. CHRISTOPHER' *Twenty-Second Cent.* 122, I knew they would have the standby generators on in a minute or two. **1969** *Gloss. Terms Magnetic Compasses & Binnacles* (*B.S.I.*) 4 *Stand-by steering compass*, a magnetic compass which provides a secondary heading reference for steering a ship. **1972** *Daily Tel.* 1 Mar. 2/6 Stand-by electric generators kept for emergencies have been packed ready for transport.

6. Of a charge for electricity: remaining constant, fixed; levied for the availability of an electrical supply in a given period, irrespective of the amount used; ***stand-by losses***: (see quot. 1940). Also *transf.*

1900 *Jrnl. Inst. Electr. Engineers* May 680 What are called the Standing or Stand-by Charges. Other items which might fairly be added to the stand-by charges are the rent, rates and taxes, and part of the management expenses. **1907** *Chambers's Jrnl.* 1 June 432/2 What are called the stand-by losses are also much reduced in the gas system. **1933** *Discovery* Feb. 65/1 The 'standby charges' of internal combustion cars are negligible, and therefore running costs are extremely low. **1940** *Chambers's Techn. Dict.* 800/2 *Stand-by losses*, that part of the power expended in a generating station in order to maintain plant in instant readiness to take a sudden load. **1973** *Gloss. Electrotechnical, Power Terms* (*B.S.I.*) II. vii. 7 *Standby charge*, a demand charge for the availability of a supply under the conditions of a standby tariff, to be paid by the consumer irrespective of whether or not he makes use of the standby supply.

7. Designating a state, condition, or position of readiness. Also ***stand-by duty***.

1922 *Wireless World* X. 355/1 The receiving telephones are hung on a special rest, this automatically putting the call-receiver in a stand-by position. **1944** *Daily Progress* (Charlottesville, Va.) 25 May 4/1 Ammunition plants which were closed or placed on a standby basis..have been ordered reopened. **1959** *Times* 11 Sept. 7/2 This new cell is specially designed for standby duties. **1977** *Cornish Times* 19 Aug. 15/3 The present Saltash ambulance station is manned from 7 a.m. to 11 p.m. each day with a stand-by-basis operating during the remaining eight hours.

8. Applied to an economic or financial measure prepared for implementation should certain conditions obtain; spec. ***stand-by credit***: an additional credit facility reserved at low interest which may be drawn upon at standard rates if needed; cf. *line of credit* s.v. LINE *sb.*[2] 30 c. Hence of loan arrangements, etc.

1947 *Sun* (Baltimore) 26 Nov. 14/3 The President's proposals for stand-by price-wage ceilings and rationing authority. **1957** *Encycl. Brit.* III. 56/2 It is a common practice for banks to grant their regular customers a 'line of credit' under which the bank agrees to extend loans up to a certain maximum... Borrowers sometimes pay a small interest charge, amounting to perhaps ½% of the unused part of the line of credit, under so-called 'stand-by' agreements. **1957** *Times* 17 Dec. 13/1 The decision to ask for an extension of the $739 standby credit with the International Monetary Fund..is a logical one. **1962** *Economist* 9 June 996/2 Ways to stimulate business..preferably by winning from Congress stand-by authority to cut taxes across the board. **1973** 'D. JORDAN' *Nile Green* xi. 50 We'd have to have some sort of standby agreement for the remaining $45m. **1977** *Time* 8 Aug. 18/2 Italy has repaid on schedule an International Monetary Fund stand-by loan.

9. In civilian aviation: designating a system of seat allocation whereby a passenger does not book in advance, but may board at a cheaper rate the next flight with spare unbooked capacity; also ***stand-by fare, passenger, ticket***, etc. Also as *adv.* Cf. sense 1 d above.

1963 *Guardian* 9 Feb. 12/2 BEA had proposed a one third cut in fares for stand-by passengers, namely, people prepared to chance obtaining a seat after booked passengers had boarded the plane. **1963** *Daily Tel.* 19 Feb. 1/8 Stand-by night tourist fares in April and May represent a rate of less than 2d a mile... The full cost of the stand-by ticket will be refunded to passengers who do not travel. **1968** 'A. YORK' *Predator* viii. 124, I had to come in as a standby tourist. But they've had a last-minute cancellation. **1970** D. HARPER *Hijacked* (1971) 6 We've been notified not to accept standby passengers for Flight 901. **1977** *Daily Tel.* 16 Sept. 1/3 The cost of travelling standby both ways is £149 as opposed to.. the normal return fare between London and New York of £392. **1978** *Times* 28 July 2/6 The argument over where to buy stand-by tickets was causing much confusion... Pan Am and TWA handled many..stand-by passengers at their London offices.

standee (stæn'diː). orig. and chiefly *U.S.* [f. STAND *v.* + -EE.]

1. (See quot. 1859.) Also *transf.* in *Theatr. U.S.*

1831 *American* (Harrodsbury, Kentucky) 25 Mar. 1/5 'I say Cap'en, what have I got?' 'A standee,' roared a dozen voices... 'Captain, I demand a berth.' **1849** G. G. FOSTER *N.Y. in Slices* xxiv. 90 Some police reporter..thus nobly earns the privilege of a seat in the dress circle..or a standee in the lobby on full nights. **1859** BARTLETT *Dict. Amer.* (ed. 2) 446 *Standee*, a standing bed-place in a steamer.

2. a. One who is compelled to stand; *spec.* a standing passenger in a public vehicle.

1856 *Knickerbocker* Mar. 278 Occasionally the car is brought to a full stop, and the 'standees' are thrown against each other like alley-pins by a 'ten-strike'. **1880** WEBSTER, *Standee*, one who is obliged to stand at a place of public amusement. (*Cant.*) (*U.S.*) **1901** POND *Eccentr. Genius* 313 Mr. Irving..having been one of the standees on that occasion. **1934** WODEHOUSE *Right Ho, Jeeves* xvii. 211, I wedged myself in among the standees at the back. **1942** *Sun* (Baltimore) 12 Aug. 9/2 Mr. Maxwell admitted that the bus left the terminal at Overlea with fourteen standees. **1954** E. E. CUMMINGS *Let.* 8 Dec. (1969) 238 A 9 o'clock, all 'standees' had to be given the seats of all ticketowners who ..hadn't appeared. **1964** N. MARSH *Dead Water* iii. 81 There were not enough chairs... Major Barrimore, Superintendent Coombe and Dr. Maine formed a rather ill-assorted group of standees. **1976** J. LEE *Ninth Man* 70 No seats were vacant, and standees stared angrily at the children for taking up so much space. **1982** S. B. FLEXNER *Listening to America* 109 The stands..seated 4,000 fans,..with over 20,000 added standees also watching.

b. *attrib.*, esp. of public transport vehicles, as ***standee bus***.

1937 *Sun* (Baltimore) 27 Oct. 5/2 Spectators began storming the playhouse long before curtain time, and by the time the show began, there was a standee audience. **1952** *Public Transport Assoc. Jrnl.* July 336 Large capacity single deck motor buses of special construction... The Minister had under review the whole question of standing passengers (including standing passengers on 'Standee' type vehicles). **1959** KITCHIN & WENLOCK *Road Transport Law* (ed. 12) 124 Laden weight of p.s.v. is total of vehicle with water, oil and fuel, plus 140 lb per seat (and, in the case of 'standee' vehicles registered after December 31, 1954, an additional 140 lb for each standing passenger in excess of eight). **1962** *Daily Tel.* 5 Nov. 10/2 The introduction of 'standee' buses, carrying 35 standing passengers and 35 seated. **1970** *Commercial Motor* 25 Sept. 122/2 The stanchions which one would expect in a standee bus are absent..to enable operators to suggest where handrails and stanchions would best be fitted. **1976** P. R. WHITE *Planning for Public Transport* iv. 80 The pattern of three or four sets of sliding doors per car..is related to an interior layout of limited seating capacity, often arranged longitudinally, and a high proportion of standee space. **1983** *Buses* Feb. 56/2 This [bus] was fitted with a dual exit and a standee area on the lower deck.

standel ('stændəl). Forms: 6 standill, 7 -dell, 8 -dal, -dall, 7–8 -dil, 7–8 standle, 7, 9 standel. [? f. STAND *v.* + -EL[1]. In sense 1 perh. an alteration of STADDLE influenced by STAND *v.* With sense 2 cf. MHG. *stendel*, early mod.G. *standel*.]

1. A young tree left standing for timber. (Cf. STANDER 8, STANDARD *sb.* 20 a.)

1543 *Act 35 Hen. VIII*, c. 17 §1 (1544) Dvj, There shalbe left standing..for euery acre of woode..xii. standilles or storers of oke..[or] of elme, ashe, or beche.., the same stathilles or storers to be of such standilles or storers, as haue been left there standyng at any the fellyng..in time past. **1602** CAREW *Cornwall* I. 21 The statute Standles commonly called Hawketrees. **1708** in Lyon *Chron. Finchampstead* (1895) 271 Provided always that sufficient Trees be left for standalls according to the Statutes in that case made. **1725** *Bradley's Fam. Dict.*, *Heyres*, young Timber-trees that are usually left for Standills in the felling of Coppices. **1762** in *Jrnls. Ho. Comm.* 13 Feb. 1792, 254/1 Leaving sufficient Standals or Stocks. **1793** W. H. MARSHALL *W. Eng.* (1796) II. 337 The purchaser to be allowed..a quarter of a perch, for each standle of the last cutting. **1884** *Lease* in *W. Somerset Word-bk.* s.v., All pollards and other trees, slips, saplings and standels.

fig. **1661** FULLER *Worthies, Northumbld.* (1662) 310 The Commissioners of this County..presenting no underwood, yea, no standels, but only tymber-oaks, men of great wealth.

†**2.** ? = STANDER 5.

1596 *Unton Inventories* 2 Two standells, and one joyned stoole.

†**standelwelks.** *Obs.* Also standweks. ? Blundered form of next.

a **1500** *MS. Bodl.* 536 lf. 36, Saturion..standweks. *a* **1500** *MS. Laud* 553 lf. 18 b, Saturion maior is an herbe þ[t] me clepuþ ȝekes or standelwelkes [*marg.* Standlewelkes]. **1597** GERARDE *Herbal* Suppl., Standelwelks is Satyrion.

†'**standelwort.** *Obs.* Also 7 standle, 9 (*Dicts.*) stander-. [a. MLG. *standel-*, *stendelwort* = MHG. *standel-*, *stendelwurz*, f. *standel*, *stendel* of the same meaning (f. root of STAND *v.*) + LG. *wort*, HG. *wurz* WORT *sb.*] = STANDERGRASS.

1578 LYTE *Dodoens* II. lvi. 217 Of Standelworte or Standergrasse..There are diuers sortes of Standergrasse called in Greeke Orchis. **1601** HOLLAND *Pliny* II. Table, Serapias, a kind of Orchis or Standelwort. **1866** *Treas. Bot.* 1090/2 Standerwort, *Orchis mascula*.

'**standenguss.** Now *dial.* (Som.) [? f. *standen* pa. pple. (? or *standend* pres. pple.) of STAND *v.* + **guss* a. F. *gousse* pod. Cf. Eng. dial. *gussets*, the *Orchis mascula*.] = STANDERGRASS. (In the 15th c. applied also erroneously to other plants.)

c **1450** *Alphita* (Anecd. Oxon.) 140, 158 Stondene-gousse (*v.r.* -gosse) [glosses *pes vituli, pes nisi, satirion*]. [**1881** *Hardwicke's Sci. Gossip* Nov. 258/1, I..showed them a flower. 'Oh', said they, 'we call them stannen-gusses.']

stander ('stændə(r)). [f. STAND *v.* + -ER[1].] One who or something which stands.

I. 1. a. One who stands, in the senses of the verb. Constr. with preps., as *before*, *on*.

In quot. 1423 used appositively, expressing the notion that the elephant was incapable of lying down.

1423 JAS. I *Kingis Q.* clvi, The standar oliphant. *c* **1550** *Fabric Rolls York Minster* (Surtees) 309 Four copes of crimson velvett..for standers. **1602** *Narcissus* (1893) 491 O, the hares a lusty stander, Follow apace. **1606** SHAKS. *Tr. & Cr.* III. iii. 84. **1635–56** COWLEY *Davideis* I. Note 28 One, τῶν ἑστηκότων, of the standers before God. **1657** J. WATTS *Scribe, Pharisee* etc. I. 13 Loyterers, and standers idle. **1788** MME. D'ARBLAY *Diary* 2 Feb., 'Tis indeed, to us standers, an amazing addition to fatigue to keep still. **1815** *Sporting Mag.* XLVI. 124 The crowd of sitters and standers gradually increases. **1850** *Tait's Mag.* XVII. 716/1 The most obstinate stander on old ways.

b. with advs.

1582 N. T. (Rhem.) *Mark* xiv. 47 And one certaine man of the standers about..smote the seruant of the cheefe priest. **1591** H. SMITH *Exam. Usurie* i. 13 The standers about said one to another, See how he loued him. *a* **1716** SOUTH *Serm.* (1727) VI. 114 Publick Spirits, Standers-up for their Country. **1885** LEFROY *Echoes fr. Theocritus* etc. II. xxix, And six tall lads break through the standers-round.

†**c.** *slang.* (See quots.) *Obs.*

1610 ROWLANDS *M. Mark-all* (1874) 41 A Stander, he that stands sentinel vpon the Pad or high-way to robbe. *Ibid.* 53 [He] was faine to liue..a stander for the padder.

d. One who 'stands' another a drink: see STAND *v.* 61 b. *nonce-use.*

1922 JOYCE *Ulysses* 419 Will immensely splendiferous stander permit one stooder..to terminate one expensive.. libation.

2. stander-by. a. One who stands by; one who looks on and abstains from interfering; one who stands aside from or has no concern in (a game, a quarrel, etc.); occas. a casual spectator or auditor, a bystander. Now *rare.*

1545 ASCHAM *Toxoph.* II. (Arb.) 120 Thys kynde of breakynge is mooste perilouse for the standers by. **1594** SHAKS. *Rich. III*, I. iii. 210 Riuers and Dorset, you were standers by..when my Sonne Was stab'd. **1606** —— *Tr. & Cr.* IV. v. 190 That I haue said vnto my standers by, Loe Iupiter is yonder, dealing life. **1612** NAUNTON in *Buccleuch MSS.* (Hist. MSS. Comm.) I. 113 Hereupon some standers by are apt to conceive that the King mea[neth] to keep these places in suspense. **1647** CLARENDON *Hist. Reb.* v. §155 It was thought strangely ridiculous by standers by that [etc.]. **1659** [H. NEVILE] *Game at Pickquet* 4, I shall be a kind of stander-by this time. **1709** STEELE *Tatler* No. 26 ¶8 If a Stander-by sees one at Play cheat, he has Right to come in for Shares. **1771** *Act 11 Geo. III*, c. 45 §29 In Default of a sufficient Number of Persons so impannelled, the said Sheriff shall return other honest and indifferent Men of the Standers-by. **1827** SCOTT *Surg. Dau.* iv, Will you, that are a stander-by, tell us, who are the unlucky players, what you think of this game of ours? **1870** MORRIS *Earthly Par.* II. III. 278 From off the poplar-block white chips would fly 'Neath some deft hand, watched of the standers-by.

Proverb. **1613** *Uncasing of Machiav.* 18 Standers by discerne more then gamsters can. **1768–74** TUCKER *Lt. Nat.* (1834) II. 303 It is commonly said that a stander-by sees more of the game than he that plays.

†**b.** *Naut.* A gunner's assistant. (Cf. *stand by*: STAND *v.* 70 b, 91 e.) *Obs.*

1669 STURMY *Mariner's Mag.* v. xii. 69 Standers by, or Matrosses. *Ibid.* 72 The standers by raise the Britch with Crows. *Ibid.* VII. xxx. 44 Let a stander by stop on the Glass a Thred.

¶**3.** Misused for CONSISTENT *sb.* 2. *rare.*

1885 *Encycl. Brit.* XVIII. 486 They are first defined in an epistle ascribed to Gregory Thaumaturgus about the year 258, and are as under: (1) Weepers..; (2) Hearers..; (3) Kneelers..; (4) Standers, who might remain throughout the entire rite, but were not suffered to communicate.

4. A person of long standing (in a profession, or place) as distinguished from a novice or newcomer; an old hand, an old resident. Only in ***old, ancient, long stander***. (Cf. STANDARD *sb.* 26 b; also STAGER 1.) ? *Obs.*

1589 R. HARVEY *Plain Perc.* 2 It moues me as much as the fatherly rebuke of an old stander moude that vniuersity post, which seemed to take the wall of a Senior. **1591** GREENE *Conny Catching* II. Wks. (Grosart) X. 174 Which did so much content him, as that he had beguiled so ancient a stander in that profession. **1681** R. KNOX *Hist. Relat. Ceylon* IV. xiii. 176 We begin with the Portugueze, who deserve the first place, being the oldest Standers there. **1699** DAMPIER *Voy.* II. I. iii. 49 [The Dutch] are the longest standers here by many years. **1732** BERKELEY *Alciphr.* II. §7 Our young proficients in the minute philosophy..do far outgo the old standers and professors of the sect. **1801** C. GADSDEN in *J. Adams' Wks.* (1854) IX. 579 Our old-standers and independent men of long well-tried patriotism, sound understanding, and good property. **1832** W. IRVING

Life & Lett. (1864) II. 486 It seems as if all the old standers of the city had called on me.

transf. **1646** W. HARINGTON in J. Hall *Poems*, A Genethliacon to the Infant Muse of his dearest Friend, A 6, Thus thy luxuriant Laurel-sprout As soon as it hath its head put out, Or'e tops old standers!

II. Something upright.

5. A pan or barrel set on end. *dial.* = STANDARD *sb.* 25. In quot. 1459 used appositively.

1459 *Paston Lett.* I. 490 Item, iij. grete standere pannes, j. bochers axe. **1882** FRANCISQUE-MICHEL *Crit. Inquir. Sc. Lang.* 427 *Staunder*, a barrel set on end for containing water or salted meat.

†**6. a.** An upright support; a supporting pillar, stem, and the like; also, a candlestick. (Cf. STANDARD *sb.* 17–19.)

1552 *Berksh. Ch. Goods* 39 A payre of grete Candylstyckes called Standers. **1605** in R. Welford *Hist. Newcastle* (1885) III. 170 [He] shall so work the mines as he leave standers for the upholding of the grounds thereof. **1648** GAGE *West Ind.* 149 [The idols] are placed upon standers gilded or painted, to be carried in procession upon mens shoulders. **1677** PLOT *Oxfordsh.* 257 To preserve their Ricks of Corn..they commonly place them in this Country, on standers and caps of stone; the standers being four Obeliscs about two foot high. **1711** W. SUTHERLAND *Shipbuild. Assist.* 164 Standers; Knees fitted upon any of the Decks; also Pieces placed to raise Stages or Scaffolds. **1860** *Song of Solomon in Lowland Scotch* v. 15 (E.D.D.) His shanks are as stanners o' merbel set on sockets o' fine gowd.

b. See quot. Cf. ORLOP^{2}. *Obs.*

1703 R. NEVE *City & C. Purch.* (1736) s.v. *Lead* §7 Of laying on Sheet-lead... They bend up the Edge of the Sheet, both for the Stander and Orlop... They bring them together, and proceed to make a Seam of them, by first turning the Orlop..over the Stander.

†**7.** Something which remains in a fixed position; a fixture. *Obs. rare.*

1642 FULLER *Holy & Prof. St.* II. iv. 62 Though he useth barbarous School-terms, which like standers are fixt to the controversie, yet in his moveable Latine..his style is pure. **1647** —— *Good Th. in Worse T.* 164 Mixt-Prayers.. Wherein the Standers,..remaine alwayes unaltered. Whilst the moveable petitions..are added..as Gods Spirit adviseth. **1666** J. SMITH *Solomon's Portr. Old Age* 76 There is necessary both these, viz. the firm stander, and the strong mover; the upper and the nether milstone.

8. †**a.** A tree left standing for timber (= STANDEL 1, STANDARD *sb.* 20a). *Obs.*

1548 [see STADDLE 1 *appos.*] *a* **1568** ASCHAM *Scholem.* II. (Arb.) 135 The fairest standers of all, were rooted vp, and cast into the fire. **1611** COTGR., *Balliveaux*, standers, or trees left standing after a wood sale. **1707** MORTIMER *Husb.* 427, I resolved to cut a Cart-way..to carry off both my Wood and Timber, which saved my Standers and Wood too very much. **1712** J. JAMES tr. *Le Blond's Gardening* 50 The old Standers left at the other Cuttings.

b. = STANDARD *sb.* 20b.

1685 PENN *Further Acc. Pennsylv.* 8 All sorts of English fruits..take mighty well for the time: The Peach Excellent, on standers.

†**III. 9.** Device on a coin, 'image and superscription'. *Obs. rare*$^{-1}$.

1579 FENTON *Guicciard.* VII. 375 He defaced out of their monies and coynes their auncient stampes, causing them for afterwards to beare his standers and stamp [It. has merely *il segno suo*] in signe of absolute superioritie.

stander: see STANDARD *sb.*

standergrass ('stændəgrɑːs, -æ-). Forms: 6 **standard-**, 7- **stander grass.** [f. *stander-* (alteration of *standel-* in STANDELWORT) + GRASS *sb.*] A name applied to *Orchis mascula* and allied plants.

1578 [see STANDELWORT]. **1579** LANGHAM *Gard. Health* 450 Orchis, or Standard grasse. **1597** GERARDE *Herbal* I. cii. 169 The first is called in Latine *Testiculus Odoratus*: in English..sweete Cullions and Standergrasse. **1610** FLETCHER *Faithful Sheph.* II. i, Therefore foule Standergrasse, from me and mine I banish thee, with lustful Turpentine. **1863** PRIOR *Plant-n.*, Standerwort, or Standergrass..*Orchis mascula.*

standfast ('stændfɑːst, -æ-), *a.* and *sb. rare.* [f. STAND *v.* (see 9b, 23) + FAST *adv.* Cf. HOLDFAST.]

A. *adj.* Stiff in opinion.

1716 M. DAVIES *Athen. Brit.* II. 369 Witness our own W. W. who sometimes seems very positive, and a standfast stickler for his Arianism even to Martyrdom.

B. *sb.* A fixed or stable position.

1846 HAWTHORNE *Mosses* II. ix. 162 It seems as if the whole world, both morally and physically, were detached from its old standfasts, and set in rapid motion.

†**stand-fra,** *a. Obs.* In 5 **standfray**, 7 **stanfra.** [f. STAND *v.* + *fra, fray*, FRO *adv.* Cf. STAND-OFF.] Inclined to stand aloof; refractory, rebellious; reserved, haughty.

c **1480** HENRYSON *Fables, Trial of Fox* 137 (Charteris) Angrie, austerne, and also vnamyabill To all that standfray ar to myne estait. **1683** *Yorke-sh. Dialogue* 9 Be neet Stanfra, but Loving and kind.

†'**standful.** *Obs.* [f. STAND *sb.*^{2}] A tubful.

1573 *Satir. Poems Reform.* xxxix. 88 Thay..keppit standfulis [of water] at the sklatis thair in. **1611** COTGR., *Tinée*, a Stand-full, or Soe-full.

'**standgale,** perverted form of STANIEL.

[**1834** MUDIE *Feathered Tribes* I. 93 'Stannel', or 'standgall', as it is sometimes pronounced, is 'stand-gale', and 'wind-hover' is 'hoverer in the wind', both of which express that wonderful power of poising..itself over a particular spot, despite the wind, which the kestrel possesses.] **1865** *Cornhill Mag.* July 41 With it may be compared another local name, 'stand-gale', and also 'crutch-tail', formerly applied to a kite.

'**stand-in.** [f. vbl. phr. *to stand in*: see STAND *v.* 95.] †**1.** A friendly or profitable understanding (*with* another), esp. a corrupt arrangement or 'put-up job'. *U.S. colloq. Obs.*

1870 *Food Jrnl.* 1 Nov. 523 The affair is settled amicably by a 'stand in', which means that the purchaser shall pay the other, or others, a certain sum not to bid against him. **1908** K. MCGAFFEY *Sorrows of Show Girl* 89 My heart went out to him the minute he said he had a stand in with three city editors. **1926** J. BLACK *You can't Win* iv. 41 The whole thing was a stand-in from the captain down. Everybody's satisfied. The sucker has his money, the girls are all out.

2. a. *Cinemat.* One who substitutes for a principal film actor while the cameras and lighting for a scene are set. Formerly, ***stand-in man.*** Chiefly *U.S.*

1928 *N.Y. Times* 11 Mar. VIII. 6/2 *Stand-in men*, substitute for the star used by the director while camera-men and electricians are testing the lights on a scene. **1935** *Evening Sun* (Baltimore) 21 May 16/2 Dorothy Granger, actress, and George Lollier, actor and 'stand-in' for Richard Dix, had a June wedding last year. **1937** *Daily Mirror* 16 Mar. 2/1 Frances is often described as Glenda's double, but 'I'm a good head taller,' she told me. 'Being a 'stand-in' does not necessarily mean that you must be exactly alike.' **1948** 'N. SHUTE' *No Highway* iv. 92 In Hollywood beauties were two a penny, and it was years before she got an inkling what it was that differentiated her from all the stand-ins and walkers-on. **1958** *People* 4 May 15/4 He won't use a stand-in for any of his roles. **1976** M. MAGUIRE *Scratchproof* ii. 22 The stand-ins were called for. The shot was lined up.

b. *gen.* One who fills the place of or substitutes for another. Also *transf.*

1937 D. RUNYON in *Collier's* 21 Aug. 32/1 Nobody cares much about this idea of a stand-in for Nicely-Nicely..and many citizens are in favor of pulling out of the contest altogether. **1940** *Punch* 7 Feb. 156/1 Easily bored by the polite functions that not even dictators can wholly avoid.. the German ruler has made..use of the 'stand-in' since he came to power. **1952** *Sun* (Baltimore) 19 Apr. (B ed.) 3/3 An absorbable gelatin sponge..may serve..as a stand-in for the liver when it becomes necessary to remove part of that organ. **1958** S. ELLIN *Eighth Circle* (1959) II. i. 32 His arrest was a fake; he was just a stand-in for the real culprit. **1968** T. STOPPARD *Real Inspector Hound* (1970) 11 An army of assistants and deputies, the seconds-in-command, the runners-up, the right-hand men..stand-ins of the world stand up! **1981** 'A. HALL' *Pekin Target* v. 45 A decoy, a scapegoat, a stand-in for us at the show trial.

c. *attrib.*

1938 *N.Y. Times* 28 Dec. 11/1 'Stand-in' ruse jails 3... Policy game collectors, with previous convictions on which they might receive long jail terms, were using 'stand-ins' to receive new sentences for them. **1958** *Engineering* 11 Apr. 457/3 Preliminary experiments were made on 'stand-in' compounds, which it was hoped would simulate the behaviour of plutonium compounds in reduction to the element. **1976** *Southern Even. Echo* (Southampton) 15 Nov. 15/4 Stand-in goalkeeper, Les Northrop, stood between Tonbridge and a hammering at the hands of unbeaten Salisbury.

standing ('stændɪŋ), *vbl. sb.* [f. STAND *v.* + -ING^{1}.]

1. a. The action of the vb. STAND, in various senses; an instance of this.

1382 WYCLIF *Ecclus.* xxvii. 15 The myche swering speche shal sette stonding [1388 schal make stondyng up] of heer, for fer, to the hed [Vulg. *horripilationem capiti statuet*]. **1398** TREVISA *Barth. de P.R.* XIII. ii. (1495) 440 Pytte water is thickest and worst to defye..for stondynge of the water. *c* **1440** *Promp. Parv.* 477/1 Stondynge, noþer syttynge ne walkynge, *status.* *c* **1450** [see SITTING *vbl. sb.* 1]. *c* **1530** *Judic. Urines* III. iii. 48 b, The standyng long tyme of ye burbels in ye vrinal sheweth that ye sekenes hath long tyme contynued. **1561** NORTON & SACKV. *Gorboduc* v. ii. 27 One sort that saw the dangerous successe Of stubborne standing in rebellious warre. **1678** WALTON *Life Sanderson* b 4, His former standing for a Proctors place, and being disappointed, must prove much displeasing. **1688** HOLME *Armoury* III. 382/1 A long piece of Copper..having the ends bent down..and then bent out again for its more steady standing. **1770** LANGHORNE *Plutarch, Marcus Crassus* (Rtldg.) 385/1 When they saw the depth of the Roman battalions..and the firmness of their standing, they drew back. **1840** BARHAM *Ingol. Leg. Jackd. Rheims*, He cursed him in sitting, in standing, in lying.

attrib. **1900** H. LAWSON *On Track* 38 Another timber, much inferior in grain and 'standing' quality, was plentiful.

b. With advs. (See STAND *v.* IV.) ***standing out***: †*concr.* a projection. (*Obs.*)

1608 TOPSELL *Serpents* 247 About the mouth there appeare and seeme to bud forth three eminenties or standings out. **1611** SHAKS. *Wint. T.* III. ii. 191 Poore Trespasses, More monstrous standing by. **1616** LANE *Contin. Sqr.'s Tale* x. 599 Other ancientes it [this towne] Rosalia call; others, the standinge vp of them which fall. **1622** FLETCHER *Beggars Bush* v. ii, And since the standing out of Bruges, where Hemskirk had hid her, till she was near lost. **1683** MOXON *Mech. Exerc., Printing* xvii. ¶ 3 They raise a Bur on the Face..to keep the Matrice off the Carriages and Bodies... But..the hollow standing off of the Face of the Matrice from the Carriages and Bodies, subjects the Mettal to run between them. **1884** *Law Rep. 26 Chanc. Div.* 790 In order to shew acquiescence he must shew a standing by with full knowledge of what was being done.

Winchester School. **1903** C. COLERIDGE *Life C. M. Yonge* iii. 98 It was the week before the 'Standing up' i.e. the repetition of an incredible number of lines of Latin or Greek Poetry.

c. The state of being without movement either progressive or retrogressive; the condition of being at a standstill. Also ***standing still.*** †***standing of the sun*** = SOLSTICE 1.

c **1440** *Pallad. on Husb.* VII. 71 Brasike is sowe at stondyng of the sonne. *c* **1530** *Judic. Urines* II. vi. 26 b, Yf the vryne come out in lesse quantyte..than it dede in the standyng or in the encresyng, or..in the begynnyng of the ague. **1552** HULOET s.v. *Heate, Solstitium*..is sometyme more aptlye taken for the staye or standynge of the sunne, whyche is twise in the yeare. **1648** HEXHAM II, *Den stil-standt der Zonne*, the Solstice, or the Standing still of the Sunne.

d. Erect position; condition of not falling or being overthrown. *lit.* and *fig.* Now *rare* or *Obs.*

1709 STANHOPE *Paraphr.* IV. 283 They..not only recover their Standing, but even profit themselves of their Fall. **1737** *Gentl. Mag.* VII. 556/2 He kick'd every one of them out of Office..except Buckingham, and he ow'd his Standing to the Prince. **1746–7** HERVEY *Medit. & Contempl.* (1818) 73 Afraid to plunge into the abyss of eternity, yet utterly unable to maintain their standing on the verge of life.

e. Phr. ***to be in good standing with*** = to stand well with, be in favour with: cf. STAND *v.* 15c.

1912 *Eng. Hist. Rev.* Oct. 652 For a number of years after this Eustace was in good standing with the English king.

†**2.** Manner of standing. **a.** Relative position (of a number of persons or things, or of one with reference to others.) **b.** Situation, site, aspect (of a building, etc.). **c.** Posture, attitude (of a person); position (of a thing) as erect, horizontal, etc. *Obs.*

a. *c* **1407** LYDG. *Reas. & Sens.* 6591 Y Haue declared.. The maner and the ordynaunce Of ther [i.e. the queen's pawns] stondyng. **1591** SAVILE *Tacitus, Hist.* III. xxii. 127 The order and standing of the Vitellian army I dare not for certaine auouch. **1600** SURFLET *Country Farm* III. xiv. 510 That you may fitly appoint the standings of trees. **1712** J. JAMES tr. *Le Blond's Gardening* 84 If the Eye be applied too near the Stick, a Defect in the standing of the others can't be so well perceived. **1733** W. ELLIS *Chiltern & Vale Farm.* 350 The double Rows were apt to heat each other by their close standing.

b. **1538** ELYOT *Dict.*, *Situs*,..also the settynge or standinge of a place, which is now called the syte. **1561** T. NORTON *Calvin's Inst.* I. xiv. (1634) 73 To set and fasten some of them [*sc.* stars] in their standings, and to other some, to grant a free course. **1647** CLARENDON *Hist. Reb.* IV. §8 They..resolved that the standing of the communion-table in all churches should be altered. **1665** SIR T. HERBERT *Trav.* (1677) 83 *Baroch* is visible by reason of her high standing a good way distant. **1682** 'R. BURTON' *Admir. Curios.* 67 Yet is the Structure better than the standing thereof, as being some-what low on the one side.

c. **1540** MORYSINE tr. *Vives' Introd. Wisd.* A viij b, A ryght gentyll man is he, whom nature hathe fashyoned and set, as it were in a standyng for the recepte of vertue. **1545** ASCHAM *Toxoph.* II. (Arb.) 147 The fyrste poynte is..to take suche footyng and standyng as shal be..cumlye to the eye. **1611** *Second Maiden's Trag.* 1041 (Malone Soc.), I like the standing of my head too well to haue it mended. **1683** MOXON *Mech. Exerc., Printing* xxiv. ¶ 2 [They] try whether the Stone lye truly Horizontal, which they know by the standing of the Water: For if the Water delate itself equally about the middle of the Stone, the Stone lies Horizontal. **1801** T. ROBERTS *Engl. Bowman* 294 The Standing, the posture in which an archer stands, when he shoots.

†**d.** The position of the indicator of a graduated instrument. *Obs.*

1669 STURMY *Mariner's Mag.* II. xiii. 82 Keeping in memory such standing of the Staff, I take off the one Cross, and set the Staff again. **1676** H. MORE *Remarks* Contents b 4 b, The various standing of the Mercury in the Tube, according to the change of weather. *a* **1734** NORTH *Life Ld. Keeper Guilford* (1742) 293 The standing of the Mercury, in the Tube, is always taken upon the Distance of the upper from the lower Superficies.

3. An act of standing erect on one's feet; a period during which one keeps a standing position.

1653 WALTON *Angler* ix. [xii.] 181 They may be at one standing, all catch'd one after another. **1850** LADY SARAH LYTTELTON *Corr.* xvi. (1912) 407, I never was more knocked up than last night, by..several long standings with Her Majesty. **1904** *Edin. Rev.* Jan. 112 The gentleman in Horace who could reel you off two hundred verses at a standing.

4. A standing-place, station; standing-room. **a.** The place in or upon which a person stands. Phrases *to take, keep one's standing.* ? *Obs.* Also, accommodation for one person to stand (at a show or the like); standing-room. Cf. STAND *sb.* 11.

1382 WYCLIF *Isa.* xxii. 19 And I shal putte thee out fro thi stonding, and fro thi seruyse I shal depose thee. **1542** BRINKLOW *Compl.* 34 b, Thei must take standings in Shoters Hill, in Newmarket Heath, and in Stangate Hole. **1571** DIGGES *Pantom.* I. xii. D iij, The Base being euen with your standing. *Ibid.*, The distance betweene the two standings is vndoubtedly the lengthe. **1586** MARLOWE *1st Pt. Tamburl.* I. ii, Keep all your standings and not stir a foot. *c* **1595** CAPT. WYATT *R. Dudley's Voy. W. Ind.* (Hakl. Soc.) 59 Himselfe toke his standinge on the open deck. **1598** R. BERNARD tr. *Terence* (1607) *Andria* II. ii, I got me vpon a high standing, and looked round about me. **1609** HOLLAND *Amm. Marcell.* XXIV. x. 255 The rest of the souldiors..gained the passing high and difficult bankes, and firmely kept their standing. *a* **1626** MIDDLETON *Women beware Women* I. iii, Now they come!.. You, sirrah, get a standing for your mistress. **1661** DRYDEN *To H.S. Majesty* 38 Your cavalcade the fair spectators view From their high standings, yet look up to you. **1719** DE FOE *Crusoe* II. (Globe) 392 In this [hollow] Tree they both took their Standing. **1795** COWPER *Needless Alarm* 120 We have at least commodious standing here. **1801** STRUTT *Sports & Past.* II. i. 61 His longest shot fell upwards of four hundred and eighty yards from his standing. **1809** MALKIN *Gil Blas* XII. i. (Rtldg.) 422 Along the streets where the procession was to pass were scaffolds, on one of which I purchased a standing.

b. *fig.*

1563–83 FOXE *A. & M.* 707/2 God..hath found a way by this facultie of Printing..to cast downe the foundation of his [the pope's] standing. **1656** CROMWELL *Sp.* 17 Sept., And so many as..do own your standings wherein the Providence of God hath set and called you to this work, will carry it on. **1669** O. SANSOM in *Acc. Life* (1710) 70 With earnest desires, that you would consider your own States and Standings, every one of you, whether you are not in the Broad way. **1676** W. ALLEN *Addr. Non-Conf.* 47 Some of them believed this; and so kept their standing in the Church. **1856** *N. Brit. Rev.* XXVI. 43 What should prevent our receding and taking a still lower standing?

†**c.** A hunter's station or stand from which to shoot game. *Obs.*

c **1400** *Master of Game* (MS. Digby 182) xxxv, þenne shulde þe maister of þe game..meete þe kynge and brynge hym to his stondynge and telle hym what game is withinne þe sette. **1551** SIR J. WILLIAMS *Accompte* (Abbotsf. Club) 87 For newe makinge a standinge in Combes parke. **1576** TURBERV. *Venerie* lxvi. 187 And thus you may trayne a foxe to a standing and kyll him in an evening with a Crossebowe. **1600** *Maids Metam.* III. i And yet my maister wayteth with his bowe, Within a standing, for to strike a Doe. **1616** *Manifest. Abp. of Spalato's Motives* App. III. 6 Imitating the Huntsman, who bending his bow to strike a faire Stagge, puts forth towards the Standing, for shew, other raskall Deere with him.

d. A place in which cattle and horses may stand under shelter; a stable; standing-accommodation for one animal; stable-accommodation for horses or a horse. Now *dial.*

c **1440** *Pallad. on Husb.* I. 523 Let make an hous for bestis. .. Of forkis, & of boord, & bouwes colde. A stondyng most be maad. **1510** STANBRIDGE *Vocabula* (W. de W.) C v, *Stabulum*, a stable or a stondynge. **1607** TOPSELL *Four-f. Beasts* 610 They also had a care to couer all the flower [of their sheep-stables] with strawe..to the end they might not be annoyed in their owne standings. **1714** T. ELLWOOD *Life* (1765) 66 Sir, don't you forget to pay for your Horse's standing? **1813** *Sporting Mag.* XLII. 54 Converting..all the loose stalls of a stable into loose standings. **1886** *W. Somerset Word-bk.* s.v., So John 've a-tookt the Dree Cups (Inn); I do year 'tis capical premises, an stannins for up thirty osses.
transf. **1798** *Times* 28 June 4/2 A Neat Cottage [with]..standing for chaise, stable and good garden.

†**e.** Stopping-place, goal. *Obs. rare.*

c **1510** *Gesta Rom.* (W. de W.) A ij, The whyle she was in takynge vp the thyrde balle, the knyght gate afore her, and was fyrst at the standynge.

†**f.** A place of settlement or encampment. *Obs.*

1598 GRENEWEY *Tacitus, Ann.* I. x. (1622) 19 The fift, and one and twentith legion, lodged in winter standings three-score miles of, at Vetera. **1611** SPEED *Theat. Gt. Brit.* (1614) 137/2 But then no longer able to hold out against them, they left their standings and departed the land.

g. A stand for carriages plying for hire.

1853 *Act 16 & 17 Vict.* c. 33 §6 The several standings for hackney carriages..within the Metropolitan district.

h. *Law* (orig. *U.S.*). A position from which one has the right to prosecute a claim or seek legal redress; the right itself; = *locus standi* s.v. LOCUS *sb.*[1] 4. (See also quot. 1962.)

1924 *Chicago Junction Case* in *U.S. Reports* CCLXIV. 271 Mr. Justice George Sutherland, dissenting... The complainants have no standing, to vindicate the rights of the public. **1962** *Stanford Law Rev.* May 433 Defined generally, if not very helpfully, in the context of this article 'standing' is the word of art for an interest which the federal courts hold worthy of legal protection from the effects of unconstitutional governmental action. **1967** H. W. R. WADE *Administrative Law* (ed. 2) iv. 126 These remedies are not restricted by the notion of *locus standi*. Every citizen has standing to invite the court to prevent some abuse of power. **1972** *N.Y. Law Jrnl.* 24 Oct. 3/3 It is sufficient for purposes of standing that plaintiff establish a causal connection between the violations alleged, be they fraud or breach of fiduciary duty, and plaintiff's loss. **1982** *Law Reports* (Appeal Cases) June 639 The rules as to 'standing' for the purpose of applying for prerogative orders..are not to be found in any statute.

5. A position for or occupied by a booth, stall, or the like; a booth or stall occupying such position. Now *dial.*

a **1547** in J. R. Boyle *Hedon* (1875) App. 80 Evrie man that hath a standing of vij. fote on Holyruddaie..shall paye ij.d. **1577** LEIGH *Surv.* (1596) D 3, Booths, Standings, shambles, and tolles,..of a weeklie market. **1626** in *10th Rep. Hist. MSS. Comm.* App. v. 338 If any..of the company of taylors ..shall departe his shopp or standing, to worke in any man's house. **1766** ENTICK *London* IV. 252 The clothiers..had their booths and standings within the church-yard. **1808** *Beverley Lighting Act* 16 Placing of stalls and standings on the market and fair days in the streets. **1858** SIMMONDS *Dict. Trade*, *Standing*, a stall placed in a market, or on the foot pavement in a street; a workman's loom in a lower flat or story. **1886** *W. Somerset Word-bk.* s.v., Butcher Morgan 've a-paid for a stan'in' in our market 'is number o' years.

†**6.** Something upon which a person or thing stands; a stage; a base, foundation. *Obs.*

1382 WYCLIF *2 Chron.* vi. 13 Salomon hadde maad the brasyn stondynge [1388 foundement, Vulg. *basis*], and hadde putte it in the mydil of the grete hous. **1556** *Chron. Grey Friars* (Camden) 71 Item the xxvj. of September [1551] was the stondynge at the tabulle in Powlles was removyd into the sowth. **1558** in Jupp *Carpenters' Co.* (1848) 51 Payd for the caryage of our standyng into fanchirche Strete at the commyng in of quene elizabeth vij d. **1585** HIGINS *Junius' Nomencl.* 190/2 *Fori*,..the galleries or standings for the beholders of plaies: the scaffoldes. *a* **1641** FINETT *For. Ambass.* (1656) 64 The French Ambassador in the first window..and the Spanish in a standing dressed up of purpose over the Porters lodge.

7. †**a.** Continuance in existence; duration. *Obs.*

1600 J. HAMILTON in *Cath. Tract.* (S.T.S.) 243 This heresie [adultery] baith repugnes to the trew law of God and is preiudiciable to the lawful standing of Noble houses. **1611** SHAKS. *Wint. T.* I. ii. 431 The Fabrick of his Folly, whose foundation Is pyl'd vpon his Faith, and will continue The standing of his Body. **1690** in *Nairne Peerage Evid.* (1874) 26 All..teynd duties payable furth of the estate during the standing of the marriage.

b. The state or fact of having existed for a longer or shorter period of time; degree of antiquity. (Now only of immaterial things.) Chiefly in phrases, *of old*, *ancient*, †*late standing*. Cf. LONG STANDING.

1656 EARL MONM. tr. *Boccalini's Advts. fr. Parnass.* I. l. (1674) 65 The Titolari were of much later standing than Doctors. **1674** N. FAIRFAX *Bulk & Selv.* 154 The next thing to be handled is, Of what standing the world may be. **1688** HOLME *Armoury* III. 318/2 Another fashion of Compasses.. not much differing from them though of an Elder standing. *c* **1710** CELIA FIENNES *Diary* (1888) 68 The Skull was whole and the teeth firme, tho' of so many yeares standing. **1780** *Mirror* No. 86 It expelled a gout, of thirty years standing. **1796** PEGGE *Anonym.* (1809) 49 This is reckoned a proverb of a late standing. **1801** STRUTT *Sports & Past.* I. i. 13 These privileges were of ancient standing. **1837** CARLYLE *Fr. Rev.* I. I. ii, There is a quarrel of twenty-five years' standing with the Parlement. **1888** BRYCE *Amer. Commw.* II. xl. 89 Other restrictions..such as the exclusion of clergy-men, which still exists in six States, and is of old standing. **1891** *Law Times* XC. 395/1 She was suffering from tuberculosis of long standing.

c. Age (of a tree).

1830 J. G. STRUTT *Sylva Brit.* 3 An oak of sixty years standing will in twenty-four years double its contents of timber. **1837** P. KEITH *Bot. Lex.* 245 If we estimate its [the oak's] standing upon the principle of the usual rule, we shall have to give it an antiquity of upwards of 2000 years.

8. a. Length of service, experience, or residence; position as determined by seniority in membership of a university, a profession, etc.

1580 G. HARVEY in Grosart *Spenser's Wks.* I. 436 What greater and more odious infamye for one of my standinge in the universitye and profession abroade then to be reckoned in the Beade-roule of Inglish Rimers. **1648** JENKYN *Blind Guide* i. 7 Sundry who exceed Master Goodwin in standing, and very much in understanding. **1651** LAMONT *Diary* (Maitl. Club) 26 They came in order to the king (from the youngest in standing to the eldest). **1711** STEELE *Spect.* No. 252 ¶3, I am a Practitioner in the Law of some standing, and have heard many eminent Pleaders in my time. **1713** *Guardian* (1756) I. No. 2. 14 He was sent for a little before he was of bachelor's standing. **1740** J. CLARKE *Educ. Youth* (ed. 3) 120 School-boys, of the oldest Standing. *a* **1790** T. WARTON in *Boswell's Johnson* an. 1754, One of the fellows, and of Johnson's standing. **1803** *Gradus ad Cantabr.* 131 *Standing*; academical age, or rank. 'Of what standing are you? I am a Senior Soph.' **1821** LAMB *Elia* Ser. I. *Old & New Schoolm.*, I know less geography than a school-boy of six weeks' standing. **1841** THACKERAY *Gt. Hoggarty Diam.* vi, The Company was only four years old, and the oldest clerk in it had not six months more standing in it than I. **1876** FIRTH *Munic. Lond.* 42 Such of the Liverymen of the various City Companies as are of one year's standing, free of the City. **1888** BURGON *12 Gd. Men* I. i. 69 He inquired after my standing in the University. **1892** *Law Times* XCIII. 550/1 To whose kind co-operation I, as a judge of long standing, feel that I ought to pay my tribute.

b. of a thing.

1885 R. L. & F. STEVENSON *Dynamiter* i, One of those gigantic Highlanders of wood which have almost risen to the standing of antiquities.

¶**c.** (A person's) age. *rare.*

1789 CHARLOTTE SMITH *Ethelinde* (1814) II. 113 You was considering how much younger you look than she does, though you are, I suppose, about the same standing.

9. a. Grade or rank in society, a profession, the world of commerce, religion, or the like; status.

1607 SHAKS. *Timon* I. i. 31 *Pain.* A Picture sir... *Poet.* Admirable: How this grace Speakes his owne standing: what a mentall power This eye shootes forth. **1727** DE FOE *Eng. Tradesm.* i. (1841) 7 The young Man should confine himself absolutely to such as are of like standing with himself. **1844** H. H. WILSON *Brit. India* III. ix. III. 529 Barristers of high standing. **1862** TROLLOPE *Orley Farm* xxxv, She also thought of Sir Peregrine's grey hairs, and of his proud standing in the county. **1866** CRUMP *Banking* i. 12 We must ..keep before us the commercial standing of the countries in which these banks were created. **1866** MRS. GASKELL *Wives & Dau.* xiii, She took standing with him as a young lady at once. **1867** SMILES *Huguenots* vii. (1880) 121 Satisfactory evidence was required of the character and religious standing of the new refugees. **1889** M. CREIGHTON *Hist. Ess.* vii. (1902) 232 Men of some standing in the neighbourhood were chosen. **1902** VIOLET JACOB *Sheep-Stealers* ix, Now that he had become a man of money and standing.

b. The position of a person or organization in a graduated table, esp. in *Sport* and *Educ.* Also, a score indicating this. Freq. *pl.* Chiefly *N. Amer.*

1881 *N.Y. Herald* 12 Sept. 11/5 The appended table will show the standing of the clubs up to date. **1904** *Spalding's Official Base Ball Guide* (ed. 28) 108 To find the Standing of the Clubs—Divide the number of games won by games played. Example: Pittsburgh, in 1903, played 140 games and won 91; 91 divided by 140 equals .650. **1917** R. EARLE *Life at U.S. Naval Academy* v. 113 Class standing is affected in some measure by conduct. **1938** K. BANNING *Annapolis Today* vii. 99 Their academic and conduct records..in combination with the aptitude marks..will become factors when their final class standings for the four-year course are computed. **1968** *Globe & Mail* (Toronto) 13 Feb. 8/1 The appointment leaves 10 vacancies in the 102-seat Senate. Standings now are: Liberal 60; Conservative 29; Independent 2; Independent Liberal 1. **1977** *Belfast Tel.* 24 Jan. 17/7 He now leads the world drivers' championship standings with 13 points.

†**10.** [Perh. from the *ppl. a.*] A tree left standing, a standard. Also, a supporting pole. *Obs.*

1580 in *Collect.* (O.H.S.) I. 237 He will always leave sufficient standards and standinges. **1800** *Hull Advertiser* 7 June 3/3 The country people went into the hop-gardens.. and some pulled down the standings.

11. *attrib.* and *Comb.*: †**standing-bar**, a bar which brings a person to a stand; **standing-bench**, a bench adapted for work to be done standing; **standing-ground**, ground upon which a contest is or may be fought or upon which a stand is or may be made, *lit.* and *fig.*; ground upon which a person or thing may (safely) stand, *lit.* and *fig.*; †**standing part**, the part or role of one who stands; **standing point** = STANDPOINT; **standing-post**, the spot where one stands; **standing room**, space in which to stand; accommodation for persons or a person standing; also in phr. *standing room only*, esp. in a theatre or similar place of resort (abbrev. *S.R.O.* s.v. S 4 a); †**standing stool**, a stool for the support of a child while learning to walk. Also STANDING PLACE.

1720 WATERLAND *Eight Serm.* viii. 319 Baptism; which was one of the Best Fences to the true Faith, and a *standing-Bar to most Heresies. **1866** *Chamb. Encycl.* VIII. 691/1 A simple..work-bench, at which shoes may be made standing. Of this *standing-bench, we offer a sketch. **1846** W. H. MILL *Five Serm.* (1848) 51 In opposing them we shall proceed..on that firm *standing-ground which all our truly great Divines have marked out, of adherence to the principles of the Ancient Church. **1864** HUXLEY *Compar. Anat.* vi. 87 Only those [systems of classification] published ..since our knowledge of the anatomy of these animals has approached completeness, have now any scientific standing-ground. **1865** KINGSLEY *Herew.* vii, How villainous for men on foot, not only to face knights but to bring them down to their own standing ground by basely cutting off their horses' heads! **1874** STUBBS *Const. Hist.* I. iv. 60 The concessions.. had given the invaders a standing-ground. **1895** *Educat. Rev.* Sept. 120 It offers us a sure standing-ground for our educational theory. **1611** B. JONSON *Catiline* v. ii, *Crassvs.* Let vs now take the *standing part. *Caesar.* We must... Yet I would faine helpe these wretched men. **1847** W. SMITH tr. *Fichte's Characteristics Present Age* xvii. 254 A view taken from the *standing-point of this Age itself. **1862** F. HALL *Hindu Philos. Syst.* 174 The Vedántins allege, that, from the standing-point of the true state of existence, Brahma alone is real. **1871** L. STEPHEN *Playgr. Eur.* (1894) iii. 81 A lovely and almost level ridge..connected it [the mountain top] with our standing-point. **1889** JESSOPP *Coming of Friars* vi. 294 We start from a standing-point..in advance of that of our forefathers. **1905** W. HOLMAN HUNT *Pre-Raphaelitism* I. xiv. 400 A track leading to it from our *standing-post. **1603** *Reg. Mag. Sig. Scot.* 514/2 To pay for *standand room, housmaill and uphalding of the saidis hallis and commowne merkett-place. **1807** *Cabinet* I. 344 To be rewarded at last.. by finding—'a little standing room'! **1812** H. & J. SMITH *Rej. Addr., Theatre*, No room for standing, mis-called standing-room. **1833** LOUDON *Encycl. Archit.* §757 The floor of the standing-room [in a cow-house] ought to be perfectly level. **1837** BARHAM *Ingol. Leg.*, *'Monstre' Balloon*, You'll scarcely get standing room, much less a seat. **1843** *Penny Cycl.* XXVII. 181/1 (*Weaving*.) Other persons are renters of what is termed a 'shop of frames', containing eight or ten frames, let, with standing-room, &c., to the workmen. **1856** 'STONEHENGE' *Brit. Sports* II. VIII. i. 462/2 The cabin is obliged to be left partially open, because there is not standing-room beneath the deck. **1889** G. B. SHAW *Fabian Ess. in Socialism* 11 The board is at the door, inscribed 'Only standing room left'. **1910** *National Police Gaz.* (U.S.) 5 Nov. 2/2 The Davenport Lady Minstrels opened their season in Asheville, N.C., recently, to standing room only. **1934** WODEHOUSE *Right Ho, Jeeves* ix. 101 The place being loaded down above the Plimsoll mark and standing room only as regarded tortured souls. **1964** MRS. L. B. JOHNSON *White House Diary* 5 June (1970) 154 A standing-room rally in the Senate caucus room. **1981** G. THOMPSON *Murder Mystery* xix. 146 That bar is mobbed. Standing room only. **1600** *Weakest goeth to Wall* F 3, Get him a *standing stoole, And then perhaps the child will learne to goe. **1656** R. FLETCHER *Martial's Epigr.* etc. 130 The elf dares peep abroad, the pretty foole Can wag without a truckling standing-stoole.

standing ('stændɪŋ), *ppl. a.* [f. STAND *v.* + -ING[2].]

I. That stands upright or on end.

1. a. Of a person, an animal, a statue: That keeps an upright stationary position on the feet. †Also *rarely* of the limb used. Also *fig.*

1576 FLEMING *Panopl. Epist.* 86 The standing image which he hath set in yᵉ Oratorie pulpit. **1611** BIBLE *Lev.* xxvi. 1 Ye shall make you no Idoles.., neither reare you vp a standing image. **1714** PARKYNS *Inn-Play* (ed. 2) 56 Throw your Lockt Leg against his standing Toe. *Ibid.* Your standing Leg. **1899** MARG. BENSON & GOURLAY *Temple of Mut* i. 8 Two colossal standing statues.
absol. *a* **1300** *Cursor M.* 27581 We may see bitide and ofsise þe standand fall, the falland rise.

b. *slang.* (See quots.)

a **1700** B. E. *Dict. Cant. Crew*, s.v. *Budge*, *Standing-Budge*, the Thieves Scout or Perdu. **1851** MAYHEW *Lond. Labour* I. 102 An elderly man..stood up to speak on behalf of the 'paper-workers' 'flying-stationers' and 'standing-patterers'. **1859** *Hotten's Slang Dict.* 101 *Standing patterers*, men who take a stand on the curb of a public thoroughfare, and deliver prepared speeches to effect a sale of any articles they have to vend.

c. said of posture.

1837 CARLYLE *Fr. Rev.* III. vi. v, And we..endeavoured to talk gallantly in a standing posture.

d. *transf.* Of an action: Performed in a standing posture.

1637 RUTHERFORD *Lett.* (1836) I. 324 Sometimes he [Jesus] sendeth me out a standing drink, and whispereth a word through the wall. **1667** MILTON *P.L.* VI. 243 That

Warr..sometimes on firm ground A standing fight, then soaring on main wing Tormented all the Air. **1856** Kane *Arct. Expl.* II. xxviii. 284 Now, with incessant labour and standing-hauls, she moved at a snail's pace. **1870** *Mil. Engineering* (1879) I. II. ix. §110 The mode of executing the sap..is done in two ways, called kneeling sap, and standing sap, from the attitude in which the leading sapper works.

e. *spec.* in *Sport* (esp. *Athletics*): performed from a standing position (cf. crouch *sb.*[2] b). Also ***standing start***, of a motor car, etc.: a start, esp. of a race or performance trial, from a stationary state.

1875 *Encycl. Brit.* III. 13/1 The running hop-step-and-jump, standing high-leaping, and standing wide-leaping. **1891** H. H. Griffin *Athletics* 85 The standing long and high jumps are rarely ever heard of. **1900** *Motor-Car World* Oct. 9/2 Jenatzy..covered..the first kilometre..with a standing start in 57 seconds. **1933** *Illustr. London News* 9 Dec. 962/1 (Advt.), Speed up Brooklands Test hill from a standing start, 16 m.p.h. **1951** D. W. Maurer in *Publ. Amer. Dial. Soc.* XVI. 60 *Standing start*, a type of start in which the horses line up exactly at the pole marking the distance they are to run and break at the starter's command... No starting gate is used. **1960** E. S. & W. J. Higham *High Speed Rugby* vii. 63 When a long pass is needed, the 'dive' pass, done properly, has advantages over the 'standing' pass. **1973** 'D. Rutherford' *Kick Start* vi. 138, I was making a standing start... The Norton Commando accelerates from 0 to 100 m.p.h. in 13 seconds.

f. ***standing ovation***: a rousing ovation conferred by an audience standing as a mark of enthusiastic approval, esp. after a speech.

1969 B. Russell *Autobiogr.* III. ii. 87, I was deeply touched by being given a standing ovation when I rose to speak. **1971** H. Wilson *Labour Govt.* xxvii. 564 At the end there was a spontaneous and wild standing ovation. **1981** S. Jackman *Game of Soldiers* II. iii. 175 The men gave him a standing ovation, whistling and stamping as he stood there grinning and bowing.

2. a. Of vegetation: That stands erect (in growth); growing (as distinguished from cut, felled or laid low by a storm or the like).

1382 Wyclif *Hos.* viii. 7 A stondynge stalk is not in hem. **1535** Coverdale *Judg.* xv. 5 And thus he brent ye stoukes and the stondinge corne. **1625** Massinger *New Way* II. i, I'le make my men breake ope his fences, Ride o're his standing corne. **1666** Dryden *Ann. Mirab.* cxii, When rolling Thunders roar, And sheets of Lightning blast the standing Field. **1707** Mortimer *Husb.* 427, I suppose I shall be asked how, in a standing Wood, I could carry the Path so streight. **1807** P. Gass *Jrnl.* 131 The hills come close in upon the banks of it, covered thick with standing timber and fallen trees. **1866** Rogers *Agric. & Prices* I. ii. 19 It was found advantageous to sell the standing grass.

b. (See quots.)

1884 W. Miller *Plant-n.* 208 *Ipomopsis elegans.* Standing Cypress. **1891** *Century Dict., Standing-cypress*, a common biennial garden-flower, *Gilia coronopifolia* (*Ipomopsis elegans*), native in the southern United States.

c. ***standing crop***, a growing crop; now used *spec.* in *Ecol.* to denote the total quantity of living things in an (esp. planktonic) ecosystem, or in some component of one.

1861 J. Brown *Forester* (ed. 3) vii. 477 There is great danger of having it [*sc.* the work] carelessly performed, and very often to the damage of a considerable portion of the standing crop. **1935** P. S. Welch *Limnol.* ix. 253 A quantitative measure of the production of a lake can be expressed in terms of (1) standing crop—the total amount of plankton present in the water on a selected date—and (2) annual crop. **1946** *Ecol. Monogr.* XVI. 324/2 The size of the standing crop at any time is the result of the summation of the excess of production over destruction from the beginning of the growth of the population to the moment of observation. **1957** G. E. Hutchinson *Treat. Limnol.* I. xii. 746 The addition of a large quantity of phosphorus in 1938 undoubtedly led to a considerable increase in the standing crop of plankton. **1979** R. Brewer *Princ. Ecol.* iv. 129 At any one time each trophic level contains some amount of energy stored as biomass, often referred to as the standing crop.

3. a. Of an inanimate thing: That stands up, upright, or on end; that is set in a vertical position. Also occas. ***standing-up***.

a **1539** *Cartul. Abb. de Rievalle* (Surtees) 339 Other iij wyndows w^{t} a standyng bar in euery wyndow and iii crosse barres. **1570** Billingsley *Euclid* XI. xxix. 341 Standing lines are called those fower right lines of euery parallelipipedon which ioyne together the angles of the vpper and nether bases of the same body. **1596** Shaks. *1 Hen. IV*, II. iv. 274 What is like thee? You Tailors yard,.. you vile standing tucke. **1611** Rowlands *Knave of Hearts* (1612) B3, Let vs haue standing Collers, in the fashion. **1846** Fairholt *Costume* (1885) II. 157 The fall..not being so readily put out of order as the large standing-lace ruff, inasmuch as it reposed on the shoulders. **1853** Surtees *Sponge's Sp. Tour* (1893) 9 His waistcoats..were..made with good honest standing-up stiff collars.

†**b.** ***standing strake***. Naut. (See quot. 1644.)

a **1618** Raleigh *Royal Navy* 12 We are forced to lye at trye with our maine Course and Missen, which with a deep keel and standing streake she will performe. **1644** Manwayring *Seamans Dict.* 102 Some ships are built, with a standing strake, or two, that is, when there is the whole bredth of a planck or two, rising from the keele, before they come to the floare timbers.

c. ***standing pillars***: the door posts of a carriage.

1837 W. B. Adams *Carriages* 88 In the central portion of the bottom sides are framed the door posts, called 'standing pillars'. **1912** H. J. Butler *Motor Bodies* 14 The toe of the front standing pillar.

d. Remaining erect; not fallen or overthrown. †Also, Already erected.

a **1700** Evelyn *Diary* 24 May 1695, We made a report of the state of Greenwich House, and how the standing part might be made serviceable at present for £6,000 and what ground would be requisite for the whole design. **1823** Scott *Quentin D.* v, [All] were killed in defending the castle; and there is not a burning hearth or a standing stone in all Glen-houlakin. **1892** P. Lindley *Tourist-Guide to Continent* (new ed.) 36 Broken flights of steps ascend..into yet standing fragments of the keep.

e. ***standing iron***, a metal spike on the collar of a sledge dog, to which a ribbon or similar decoration may be attached. *Canad.*

1934 P. H. Godsell *Arctic Trader* 39 Bells jangled as the dogs proudly tossed their massive heads and shook their beribboned standing-irons in the gusty breeze. **1939** *Beaver* Sept. 23 Fox tails and coloured ribbons decorated the leather collars and standing-irons. **1959** J. W. Godsell *I was no Lady* iv. 64 The fluttering rainbows of ribbons on the standing-irons of the harness.

4. a. Having a foot or feet, a base, or a stem and base upon which to stand, esp. in ***standing bowl, cup, nut*** (see nut *sb.*[1] 2), ***piece*** (of plate). *Obs.* exc. *Hist.*

1420 in *E.E. Wills* (1882) 46 A stondyng cuppe of seluer y-clepyd a chales cuppe. **1424** *Ibid.* 57 Also I wull þat Anneys my doughter haue þe standing pece þat was my faders, keuered. **1459** *Paston Lett.* I. 470 Item, ij. stondyng candilstikkes. *Ibid.* 486 Item, ij. staundyng aundyris. **1594** Greene & Lodge *Looking Gl.* (1598) D3b, Fetch me that sweet wine,..Powre it into a standing bowle of gold. **1601** Holland *Pliny* XXXIII. xii. II. 483 A broad goblet or standing peece there was of his making. **1608** Shaks. *Per.* II. iii. 65 Say wee drinke this standing boule of wine to him. **1820** Scott *Monast.* xxxiv, There was neither mazer-dish nor standing-cup upon the little table. **1843** Pugin *Apol. Rev. Chr. Arch.* 81b, On the step, two high standing candlesticks. *Ibid.* A standing altar cross. **1871** A. Nesbitt *Catal. Slade Coll. Glass* 70 Blue Standing Cup.

b. ***standing salt***: in medieval and later times, a large, often ornate, salt-cellar placed in the middle of a dining-table. Cf. salt *sb.*[1] 7a, b. *Hist.*

1878 W. J. Cripps *Old Eng. Plate* x. 255 A cylindrical standing salt, of the year 1554. **1931** E. Wenham *Domestic Silver* v. 42 The imposing standing-salts.., from the Middle Ages to the third quarter of the seventeenth century, were the symbols of social distinction. **1956** G. Taylor *Silver* ii. 42 The most important and often the most elaborate piece of table plate during the Middle Ages was the standing salt. **1972** *Times* 28 Nov. 24/1 (Advt.), An Elizabeth I silver-gilt standing-salt.

5. a. Of a piece of furniture: That rests upon its base when set up for use (as distinguished from 'hanging' or 'leaning'). ***standing ladder*** = step-ladder.

1485 *Rec. St. Mary at Hill* 29 A grete, new, standyng almerye with iij levys. **1503** *Maldon* (Essex) *Court Rolls* (Bundle 62, no. 7), 1 standyng cuppord. **1527** in *Archæologia* XXXVI. 223 Item too standyng deskes, too reide lessons off. **1726** Swift *Gulliver* II. vii, A kind of wooden machine,.. formed like a standing ladder. **1806–7** J. Beresford *Miseries Hum. Life* (1826) XX. ii, A standing screen which perpetually belies its name. **1834** Marryat *P. Simple* lii, I miss my regular watch very much..and I don't much fancy a standing bed-place... Nothing like a hammock, after all.

†**b.** ***standing bed*** (or ***bedstead***): a high bedstead, as distinguished from a truckle-bed. *Obs.*

1485 *Rec. St. Mary at Hill* 28 In the Cheffe Chaumbre a standyng bed, made with estrychborde. **1588** *Lanc. Wills* (1857) II. 75 The great standinge bedd wth the wheele bedd under yt in the greate chamber. **1598** Shaks. *Merry W.* IV. v. 7. **1624** in *Archæologia* XLVIII. 138 In the childrens chamber, a standing and a trundle bedsteed.

6. *naval Arch.* Of a bevel or bevelling: Forming an angle greater than a right angle; obtuse.

1754 M. Murray *Shipbuilding* in Falconer *Dict. Marine* (1780) s.v. *Bevelling*, But if the timber is not hewed square ..[and] if a square be applied to it, there will be wood wanting either at the upper or lower side... When the wood is deficient at the under-side, it is called under-bevelling; and when it is deficient in the upper side, it is called standing-bevelling. **1874** Thearle *Naval Arch.* I. iv. §44. 53 Their bevellings are always standing, or greater than a right angle.

II. That remains at rest or in a fixed position.

7. a. Of water, a piece of water: Still, not ebbing or flowing, stagnant; also *rarely* of air.

1398 Trevisa *Barth. De P.R.* XIV. liv. (1495) 487 In dyches is..bothe rennynge and stondynge water. *c* **1400** *Secreta Secret., Gov. Lordsh.* 79 þay ar vnhelfull, as þes stondyng waters. *c* **1440** *Promp. Parv.* 285/2 Lake, or stondynge watur, *lacus.* **1586** Marlowe *1st Pt. Tamburl.* V. ii, Noisome parbreak of the Stygian snakes, which fills the nooks of hell with standing air. **1596** Shaks. *Merch. V.* I. i. 89 There are a sort of men, whose visages Do creame and mantle like a standing pond. **1681** Dryden *Abs. & Achit.* I. 137 The standing Lake soon floats into a Floud. **1787** Best *Angling* (ed. 2) 5 But eels never breed in standing waters that are without springs. **1831** Brewster *Optics* iv. 33 If we suppose the surface BB' to be that of standing water, placed horizontally.

fig. **1601** Shaks. *Twel. N.* I. v. 168 Tis with him in standing water, betweene boy and man. **1874** L. Stephen *Hours in Library* (1892) II. iii. 71 Coleridge..threw a great stone into the standing pool of contemporary thought.

b. *Mining.* (See quots.)

1883 Gresley *Gloss. Coal-mining* 238 *Standing fire*, a fire in a mine continuing to smoulder for a long time. *Ibid., Standing gas*, a body of fire-damp known to exist in a mine, though fenced off.

†**8.** Stiff, rigid. **a.** Of a limb or member of the body. Also *rarely* of the eyes: Projecting. [? After L. *stantes oculi*, Ovid *Fasti* VI. 133.] *Obs.*

1340 *Ayenb.* 216 Ase byeþ þe fole wyfmen þet guoþ mid stondinde nhicke. *c* **1400** *Master of Game* (MS. Digby 182) xv, [Good wolf-hounds should have] stondyng eeres and sharpe aboue. **1649** Bp. Reynolds *Hosea* iv. 79 A hollow and standing eye.

b. *Cookery.* Of a stiff consistency (as distinguished from 'running'). *Obs.*

c **1420** *Liber Cocorum* (1862) 14 But loke þat hit be not to þyn, But stondand. *c* **1440** *Anc. Cookery* in *Househ. Ord.* (1790) 431 Thyck hit with floure of rys, that hit be welle stondynge.

9. a. Of a thing: At a standstill. Of a machine, tool, or the like: Not in operation.

1585 Higins *Junius' Nomenclator* 337 *Æquilibrium*,.. standing weight: euen weight. **1697** Dryden *Virg. Georg.* IV. 695 Ixion..leans attentive on his standing Wheel. **1883** Gresley *Gloss. Coal-mining* 237 *Standing*, not at work, not going forward, idle. *Ibid., Standing bobby*, an exploded shot which rips the coal but does not blow the stemming out.

†**b.** ***standing quoin***. (See quots.) *Obs.*

1626 [see canting *ppl. a.*[1] 2.] **1696** Phillips s.v. *Coin*, Standing Coins are Billets or Pipe-Stave to make the Cask fast that they cannot stir nor give way. **1711** *Milit. & Sea Dict.*, s.v. *Quoyn*, The standing Quoyns, made of Barrel-Boards, about four Fingers broad.

10. a. That is used in a fixed position.

1634 *Ir. Act 10 Chas. I*, c. 14 §1 Setting of stop-Nets, Still-Nets, or standing-Nets fixed upon posts. **1839** Ure *Dict. Arts* 749 The pieces of ore are sometimes merely stirred about with a shovel, in a trough filled with water. This is called a standing buddle. **1875** Knight *Dict. Mech.*, Standing-vise. **1895** G. J. Burns *Gloss. Archit.* etc., *Standing waste*, an overflow pipe fixed to the bottom of a cistern.

†**b.** ***standing prick***, a fixed archery target. *Obs.*

1468, **1541–2** [see rover[1] 1].

11. a. That remains in one spot; that is not moved or carried from place to place; stationary. *Obs.* exc. *Mil.* in ***standing camp***.

1469 in *Househ. Ord.* (1790) 98 The estate, rule & governaunce of the seid Prince in his ridinge, beinge departed from his standing housholde. *a* **1500** in Kingsford *Chron. London* (1905) 189 They were servid well..and as well seasoned mete as it had been dressed in a stondyng place. **1553–5** *Extracts Burgh Rec. Edin.* (1871) II. 289 The sowme..debursit be the farmorars of the commoun mylnis ..upon the standing grayth thairof. **1590** Sir J. Smythe *Disc. Weapons* 2b, The..standing watch (as we were wont to terme it) they now call after the French, or Wallons, *Corps du gard.* **1598** Stow *Surv.* 75 Besides the standing watches all in bright harnesse in euery warde..there was also a marching watch, that passed through the principall streetes thereof. **1603** R. Johnson *Kingd. & Commw.* 161 Townes they plant none, nor other standing buildings, but haue mooving houses. **1609** Holland *Amm. Marcell.* XXIV. xii. 258 We trusted upon our standing campe. **1642** *Docq. Lett. Pat. at Oxf.* (1837) 336 The Office of Keeper of his Majesties standinge Wardrobe within the Castle of Windsor. **1684** Wood *Life* July (O.H.S.) III. 102 Ralph Sheldon..spared not any mony to set up a standing library in his house at Weston. **1896** Baden-Powell *Matabele Campaign* ix, We got back to our standing camp outside the hills about mid-day.

†**b.** ***standing house, standing mansion-house***: a permanent or fixed dwelling-house; ***to keep, (take up one's) standing house***, to abstain from journeying. *Obs.*

1586 Harrison *England* II. vi. 167/2 The beere that is vsed at noble mens tables in their fixed and standing houses, is commonlie of a yeare old. **1589** *Mar-Martine* A2, Abbots were fat..The whoresons lov'de their ease, Yet standing house by them was kept. **1596** Norden *Progr. Piety* (1847) 161 Having thus far proceeded..we must be forced to take up our standing house, and for a time abide in the earthly mansions of our bodies. *c* **1645** Howell *Lett.* I. IV. xviii. (1890) 234 That your Grace would settle a standing Mansion-house and Family, that Suitors may know whither to repair constantly. **1671** E. Chamberlayne *Pres. St. Eng.* I. xiii. 203 The Yeomen of the Guard... Their Office is to wait upon the King in his standing Houses.

†**c.** Taken 'as it stands'. *Obs.*

1788 Jefferson *Writ.* (1853) II. 407 He rented a house with standing furniture, such as tables, chairs, presses, &c., and brought all other necessaries.

d. *Printing.* Applied to type not distributed after use (see quots.).

1770 Luckombe *Hist. Printing* 227 Irregular Bodied Letter of the smaller sizes sometimes serves the ends of proprietors of standing and selling Copies. **1875** J. Southward *Dict. Typogr.* (ed. 2) 129 *Standing matter*, composed matter remaining undistributed after it has been printed. **1888** Jacobi *Printers' Vocab.* 131 Formes not distributed after printing are said to be 'standing'. **1916** *Estimating for Printers* 24 If a job repeats and the printer has kept it standing without..rent, the job should be estimated as though it were reset, and the advantage of standing type kept by the printer. **1964** F. Bowers *Bibliogr. & Textual Crit.* I. v. 31 This homogeneity extended to the variants in the standing type..but not to their pages of reset type.

e. Physics. ***standing wave***, a wave in which the positions of maximum and minimum oscillation remain stationary; = *stationary wave* s.v. stationary *a.* 1e.

1896 *Knowledge* 1 June 136/1 Each wave crest maintains its position relative to the stone, and from this comes the term *standing wave.* **1905** *Trans. R. Soc. Edin.* XLI. 592 The remarkable analogy between the sound-vibrations of an elastic body and the light-vibrations of a radiating atom is at least suggestive. Is it not, for instance, conceivable that the latter are caused by 'standing waves' in the elastic system which constitutes the atom? **1947** A. E. Slater in A. C. Douglas *Gliding & Adv. Soaring* i. 29 Similar 'standing waves' have now been found, and soared in, elsewhere. For instance, in an experimental flight to leeward of the Alps a sailplane has reached 30,000 feet above sea level. **1962** A. Nisbett *Technique Sound Studio* ii. 46 If there are two parallel screens on opposite sides of the microphone a standing-wave pattern will be set up. **1977** A. HALLAM *Planet Earth* 55/2 Such features, called antidunes or standing waves, are often seen in streams running across beaches at low tide or in gutters during heavy rain.

12. a. That remains stationary while another part, or other parts, move.

1680 MOXON *Mech. Exerc.* (1703) 219 Then remove the standing point of the Compasses to either of the next Divisions..and in like manner describe another Circle. **1832** BREWSTER *Nat. Magic* ii. 27 The rotation should be effected round a standing axis by wheels and pinions. **1832** *Instr. & Reg. Cavalry* II. 11 Dressing is to the 'wheeling' flank, and distance of files is preserved from the 'standing' flank. **1881** GREENER *Gun* 266 Which process brings the breech ends of barrels nearer to the face of the standing-breech.

b. *Naut.* Chiefly in special collocations, as **standing rigging**, the fixed part of a vessel's rigging which serves as a support for the masts and is not hauled upon, as distinguished from the running rigging; **standing ropes** *pl.*, the ropes composing the standing rigging; so also in the names of various ropes and appliances, as ***standing backstay, block, bowsprit***, etc.; **standing part** (of a rope, sheet, etc.), that end of a thing which is made fast as distinguished from the end, hauled upon.

a **1625** *Nomenclator Navalis* (Harl. MS. 2301), Standing roapes. **1642** H. BOND *Boatswain's Art* 3, 2 Lanniards of the Spritsaile standing Lifts. **1644** MANWAYRING *Seamans Dict.* s.v., The standing parts are those parts of running roapes (or rather that end of a running roape) which is made fast to any part of the ship, to distinguish it from the other part, whereon we use to hale. *Ibid.*, *Standing roapes*, are counted all those roapes..which are not used to be removed, or to run in any blocks. **1745** *Observ. Conc. Navy* 64 Every Ship should have her standing Masts constantly in and rigg'd, with her Booms and Stores aboard, sufficient to compleat her other Rigging. **1748** *Anson's Voy.* I. v. 56 The other ships of the squadron fixed new standing rigging. **1791** SMEATON *Edystone L.* (1793) §143 We fixed the standing block to the stern timbers of our vessel,..bringing the chain along the deck to the moveable purchase block. **1846** A. YOUNG *Naut. Dict.* 25 Ropes extended from the..mast heads, to the after part of each channel for the support of these masts. They are distinguished by the name of Standing-Backstays. *Ibid.* 173 A large sail extended on the jib-stay to the extremity of..the jib-boom... It gets the name of the standing-jib, in contradistinction to the flying-jib. **1867** SMYTH *Sailor's Word-bk.*, *Standing Bowsprit*, one that is fixed permanently in its place, not the running-in bowsprit of a cutter. **1874** BEDFORD *Sailor's Pocket Bk.* vi. (1875) 214 Sling a dipping lug ⅓ from the foremost yard-arm; standing lug ¼.

III. That stands or continues.

13. a. Continuing without diminution or change; constant, permanent. Of colours: Permanent, unfading.

c **1375** *Sc. Leg. Saints* i. (*Peter*) 22 Peter of 'petra' may be tane..for men may a stane neuir bow;..and þis petir, abeove þe lafe, a stannand luf to criste can hafe. **1632** LITHGOW *Trav.* VI. 292 Pitching our Tents beside a source or standing Well. **1646** JENKYN *Remora* 16 A transient thought, becomes not a standing and a permanent mercy. **1716** ADDISON *Free-holder* No. 22 ¶2 The Landlord..worked up his complexion to a standing crimson by his zeal for the prosperity of the church. **1791** HAMILTON *Berthollet's Dyeing* I. I. II. iv. 200 This ground being a standing dye is not removed by the proof. **1831** CARLYLE *Sart. Res.* I. iii, His age, which was of that standing middle sort you could only guess at. **1900** R. GUTHRIE *Kitty Fagan* 183 Broon an' black, good stan'in' colours!

†**b.** *Math.* = CONSTANT *a.* 5. *Obs.*

1743 W. EMERSON *Fluxions* 4 The first Letters of the Alphabet, *a, b, c, &c.* are..put for standing Quantities; and the last, *x, y, z, &c.* for variable or flowing Quantities.

†**c.** Of a work of art or literature: Enduring, 'standard'. *Obs.*

1698 W. WOTTON in *Evelyn's Mem.* (1857) III. 372, I had almost forgotten to thank you for your honourable mention of my poor performances in so standing a work. **1710** SHAFTESB. *Charac.* (1737) I. IV. iii. 144 The standing Pieces of good Artists must be form'd after a more uniform way.

†**d.** ***standing measure***: a standard of measurement. *Obs.*

1668 DRYDEN *Ess. Dram. Poesie* 8 It was necessary, before they proceeded further, to take a standing measure of their Controversie. **1691** LOCKE *Lowering of Interest* Wks. 1714 II. 20 The value of any thing, compar'd with its self, or with a standing Measure. *Ibid.* 23 Supposing Wheat a standing Measure, that is, that there is constantly the same Quantity of it in Proportion to its vent.

14. a. Of employment, income, wages, prices, etc.: Fixed, settled, not casual, fluctuating, or occasional.

1473 *Rental Bk. Cupar-Angus* (1879) I. 190 He payand ..ȝerly to ws of standand male x[lb] of vsuale mone. *a* **1530** J. HEYWOOD *Play Weather* (1533) D ij b, I know not what god geueth in standynges fees [? *read* with *ed.* 1565 standyng fees] But the deuyls seruauntes haue casweltees A hundred tymes mo then goddes seruauntes haue. **1549** THOMAS *Hist. Italie* 5 Many of theim [*sc.* artificers] liue as well as they that haue standyng liuinges. **1622** *Pursuit Hist. Lazarillo* (1672) T 3, To hear her..threaten with such arrogancy, a man would have thought she had given me..thirty duckets a year standing wages. **1670** R. MONTAGU in *Buccleuch MSS.* (Hist. MSS. Comm.) I. 468 My standing allowance from Michaelmas last till Christmas. **1730** *Lett. to Sir W. Strickland rel. Coal Trade* 19 Keeping a Fleet in standing Pay. **1901** *Macm. Mag.* Apr. 455/1 There are some booksellers who have no standing-price for their wares, but rate them according to what they think each customer will give.

b. of attributes.

1640 BP. REYNOLDS *Passions* ii. Wks. (1658) 899 The Bias of Mens desires are often turned, by reason of some sudden or emergent Occurrences, contrary to the standing temper and complexion of the body. **1697** COLLIER *Ess. Mor. Subj.* II. (1709) 125 'Tis true, a Man cannot command the standing Features and Complexion; but the Diversities of Passion are under Disposal. **1835** STERLING in Carlyle *Life* II. ii. (1872) 98 Under this head, of language, may be mentioned..two standing characteristics of the Professor's style.

15. a. That continues in existence or operation that continues to be (what the noun specifies); that does not pass away. ***standing order***, (*a*) (Parliament), see quot. 1844; (*b*) (Mil.), see quot. 1802; (*c*) a written directive to a banker instructing that a regular payment be made from an account, usu. to another party; similarly, *transf.* in *Commerce*; ***standing rule*** (Mil.) = *standing order* (b).

1662 STILLINGFL. *Orig. Sacræ* II. v. §3 He layes this down as a standing rule among them. **1686** HORNECK *Crucif. Jesus* xiv. 326 The very Heathens..made it a standing maxim. That the Gods sold all their gifts for labour and industry. **1682** SHADWELL *Medal John Bayes* 3 Thou never mak'st, but art a standing Jest. **1710** PRIDEAUX *Orig. Tithes* ii. 42 The Decisions of Judges..are made the standing Rules. **1737** *Gentl. Mag.* VII. 583 The standing Order of the House, made Jan. 16, 1735, for restraining the Counsel at the Bar of that House..from offering Evidence. **1754** SHERLOCK *Disc.* (1759) I. x. 275 These are the standing Proofs of the Being and Goodness of God. **1780** BENTHAM *Princ. Legisl.* xix. §15 It is a standing topic of complaint. **1781** COWPER *Expost.* 110 Then God's own image on the soul impress'd Becomes a mock'ry, and a standing jest. **1802** C. JAMES *Milit. Dict.* s.v. *March* F ff 3/1 It is a standing rule in column, that every regiment should march with the same front, that the regiment does which precedes it. *Ibid.* s.v. *Order*, *Standing Orders*, certain general rules and instructions which are to be invariably followed, and are not subject to the temporary intervention of rank. **1844** MAY *Parlt.* II. vii. 131 Both houses have agreed, at various times, to standing orders, for the permanent guidance and order of their proceedings; which, if not vacated or rescinded, endure from one Parliament to another, and are of equal force in all. **1859** MILL *Liberty* ii. 40 The beliefs..have no safeguard to rest on, but a standing invitation to the whole world to prove them unfounded. **1864** C. KNIGHT *Passages Work. Life* I. i. 109 This is the standing joke nightly repeated. **1869** TYNDALL in *Fortn. Rev.* Feb. 237 The two great standing enigmas of meteorology—the colour of the sky, and the polarization of its light. **1874** L. STEPHEN *Hours in Library* (1892) II. ii. 39 Burke was..a standing refutation of the theory. **1879** *Cassell's Techn. Educ.* IV. 42/1 By referring to what is still the standing authority upon the question. **1913** BAGSHAW & HANNAFORD *Pract. Banking* ix. 144 Executing Standing Orders... A customer may instruct his banker to pay a certain sum at a stated time, and the main instances of this are in the payment of annual subscriptions to clubs. **1937** A. F. FERGUS *Pract. Branch Banking* xv. 207 All those regular periodical payments, such as rent, insurance premiums, club subscriptions..which are made by the Branch on the instructions of customers, come under the general description of 'Standing Orders'. **1962** D. FRANCIS *Dead Cert* xii. 134 I'll place a standing order with Interflora, for lilies. **1972** G. LYALL *Blame Dead* ix. 67 The standing orders were easy enough: they'd be payments to the life insurance companies and probably the rent on that flat.

†**b.** ***standing lottery***, one that remains open and undrawn for a specified long period. *Obs.*

1615 CAPT. SMITH *Virginia* IV. 117 We manifested our intents, to haue drawn out the great standing Lottery long before this. **1622** MALYNES *Anc. Law-Merch.* 207 There are two manner of Lotaries, namely, Standing Lotaries, and Running Lotaries; the first limitted for a continuance of time to bee drawne at the end thereof, without intermission by day and night; the latter to bee drawne daily.

†**c.** Of a building: Permanent, not temporary.

1624 *Issues Exchequer Jas. I.* (1836) 294 For making divers new ridings within his Majesty's park at Theobalds,..making of standing bridges, levelling of ground [etc.].

16. Habitually used; stock. ***standing dish***: see DISH *sb.* 2 b. †Of clothing or trappings: Ordinarily worn, 'everyday'.

1492 in *Bury Wills* (Camden) 75 My best stondyng gowne furred w[t] bever. **1533** *Acc. Ld. High Treas. Scot.* VI. 178 To be standing housouris to the grete hors, xviij elnis braid gray. **1541** *Ibid.* VIII. 28 Item,..To be standing howsis to the Kingis grace hors, lxxxiiij elnis thre quarteris braid gray. **1599** B. JONSON *Ev. Man out of Hum.* II. vi, He hath shift of names, sir: some call him Apple-John, some signior Whiffe; marry, his maine standing name is Cavalier Shift. **1667** O. HEYWOOD *Heart-Treas.* i. 7 A plain allusion to an housekeepers old store, which makes a daily standing dish. **1705** ADDISON *Italy*, *Venice* 101 There are Four Standing Characters that enter into every Piece that comes on the Stage, the Doctor, Harlequin, Pantalone and Coviello. **1758** JOHNSON *Idler* No. 12 ¶11 He had a standing elegy and epithalamium, of which only the first and last leaves were varied. **1776** R. TWISS *Tour Irel.* 37 Potatoes, which form a standing dish at every meal. **1861** T. A. TROLLOPE *La Beata* II. xv. 148 He was fain to plead the standing excuse of a bad headache. **1868** GLADSTONE *Juv. Mundi* ii. (1870) 31 The standing appellations of the army in the Iliad are these three, Danaoi, Argeioi, and Achaioi. **1868** FREEMAN *Norm. Conq.* (1876) II. App. 641 'Feri' seems to be a standing epithet for all Saxons.

17. a. Permanently and authoritatively fixed or set up; stated, established, organized, regular.

1549 COVERDALE, etc. *Erasm. Par. Gal.* v. 3-4 Whoso is content to receyue circumcision, muste lykewise therwith receyue sacrifices..standing fasting dayes, with suche other lyke. **1563** *Homilies* II. *Place & Time of Prayer* I. N nn j, The godly Christian people..began to chose them a standyng day in the weke, to come together in. **1578** in *Househ. Ord.* (1790) 250 Thirty standing posts appointed 18. 5. 0. **1609** in *Rep. Secret Comm. Post Office* App. (1844) 42 In..Kent, where the stages of our standing posts, are now established and appointed. **1649** MILTON *Eikon.* vi. 58 Which not onely the general Maxims of Policy gainsay, but eev'n our own standing Laws. *a* **1700** EVELYN *Diary* 23 Apr. 1661, [There followed, at the Coronation] Masters of standing offices being no Councellors. **1790** BURKE *Fr. Rev.* 269 This standing, unalterable, fundamental government would make..that territory truly and properly an whole. **1841** MYERS *Cath. Th.* IV. §29. 318 The Schools of the Prophets, and a standing Prophetic Order,..were formally established by Samuel. **1846** GROTE *Greece* (1862) II. xx. 493 A standing caravan commerce with Phenicia.

b. Of a legislative, administrative, or other body: Permanently constituted; esp. in ***standing committee***.

1625 BACON *Ess.*, *Counsel* (Arb.) 329, I commend also standing Commissions; As for Trade; for Treasure. *a* **1636** H. ELSYNGE *Expedicio Billarum Antiquitus* (1954) 23 Even this doth prove that there was one Standing Committee for all Bills in parlement. **1656** H. SCOBELL *Memorials* iii. 9 In Parliament there have usually been Five Standing Committees appointed in the beginning of the Parliament, and remaining during all the Session. *a* **1700** EVELYN *Diary* 10 Mar. 1671, To London about passing my patent as one of the standing Council for Plantations. **1735** BOLINGBROKE *Parties* 37 A standing Parliament, or the same Parliament long continued, changes the very Nature of the Constitution. **1739** BUTLER *Serm.* Wks. 1874 II. 217 A common form of Christian worship..with a standing ministry of instruction and discipline. **1810** BENTHAM *Packing* (1821) 155 In packing into a standing Board a set of dependent Commissioners. **1837** CARLYLE *Fr. Rev.* III. III. v, Five Judges; a standing Jury..: they are subject to no Appeal. **1868** ERSKINE MAY *Law of Parl.* (ed. 6) xiv. 379 There is further an exceptional class of committees, called standing committees. The only committee properly so termed is one whose appointment, being by standing order, is permanent, the nomination only being renewed from session to session. Such is the committee of public accounts, under a standing order of the 3rd April 1862. **1906** H. MONTGOMERY & CAMBRAY *Dict. Polit. Phr.* 72 Standing or Grand Committees [of the House of Commons]. Two in number were set up in 1883. One, the Standing Committee on Law,..The other, the Standing Committee on Trade. **1921** *Legislative Assembly Deb.* (Delhi) 1 Mar. 418 A Standing Finance Committee of this Assembly has been appointed. It is not proposed—at present at any rate—to appoint any other Standing Committee of the Legislature. **1967** J. D. LEES *Committee System U.S. Congr.* ii. 5 Standing committees..are permanent committees that continue from Congress to Congress... They are quite different from Standing Committees of the House of Commons which are not specialised and whose main purpose is to save time which would otherwise be spent by the House sitting as Committee of the Whole. **1978** *Nagel's Encycl.-Guide: China* 292 Out of session, the National People's Congress appoints a standing Committee. Theoretically at least, this committee (made up of a Chairman, 13 Vice-chairmen, 1 Secretary-general and 35 ordinary members) is all-powerful.

c. Of troops, etc.: Maintained on a permanent footing; esp. in ***standing army***: see ARMY 3 b; ***standing patrol***.

1603 KNOLLES *Hist. Turks* (1638) 235 He kept alwaies a standing army of forty thousand horse, and threescore thousand foot. **1655** *Clarke Papers* (Camden) III. 24 Commissions for raiseing of horse and foote, which are to bee in the nature of a standing Militia. **1673** TEMPLE *Observ. United Prov.* i. 22 The States first refused to raise any more moneys either for the Spaniards pay, or their own standing-Troops. *a* **1700** EVELYN *Diary* 9 Nov. 1685, The King in his speech required the continuance of a standing force instead of a militia. **1732** SWIFT *Beast's Confess.* (1738) 17 'Twas known..That, Standing Troops were his Aversion. **1734** POPE *Sat.* II. ii. 154 My Life's amusements have been just the same, Before, and after, Standing Armies came. **1838** THIRLWALL *Greece* xxxviii. V. 55 He kept a standing army of 6000 mercenaries in his pay. **1867** FREEMAN *Norm. Conq.* (1876) I. vi. 512 The standing navy of England consisted of sixteen ships. **1923** KIPLING *Irish Guards in Gt. War* I. 25 The Germans pushed a patrol through the wood and our standing-patrol went out and discovered one German under-officer..dead. **1941** P. RICHEY *Fighter Pilot* 35 Germans..maintained a standing patrol on their own side, only crossing over to our side occasionally, and always very high. **1959** P. FLEMING *Siege at Peking* xiii. 202 General Lineivitch..sent forward an advance-guard of one battalion and half a battery..to act as what used to be called a standing patrol.

d. Of an official: Holding permanent office.

1656 *Burton's Diary* (1828) I. 159 That there should be a standing treasurer. **1658** R. PARR *Judges Charge* 31 Sirs, you that are the standing Magistrates of the County, will it be for your honour (think you) to give license to [Tipling-houses]? **1659** WOOD *Life* 11 Feb. (O.H.S.) I. 268 Nath. Crew..brought..a petition, to present to the parliament against standing Visitors in the university. **1809** *Lond. Chron.* 15 July 50/3 An opinion which the Court of Directors had taken upon the subject from the Attorney and Solicitor General, and their standing Counsel, Mr. Adam. **1867** SMYTH *Sailor's Word-bk.*, *Standing Warrants*, those officers who remain with a ship in ordinary, or on the stocks, as the gunner, carpenter, boatswain, and cook, and till 1814 the purser. **1885** *Law Rep.* 15 *Q.B.D.* 374 A solicitor is not a standing agent for one who has been or may be his client, to receive [etc.].

†**e.** *U.S.* (See quot. 1911). *Obs.*

1861 *Contrib. Eccl. Hist. Connecticut* 253 There arose a class of churches..which though purely Congregational in their principles and practices were not in fellowship with the churches of 'the standing order'. **1911** WEBSTER, *Standing order*,..the denomination established by law;— a term formerly used in Connecticut of the Congregational Church, the State church until 1818.

†**IV. 18.** *predicatively.* Consistent *with*. *Obs.*

1511–2 *Act 3 Hen. VIII*, c. 23 §5 It is not convenient nor standing with good..ordre that [etc.]. **1542** UDALL *Erasm. Apoph.* 77 The oratours..wer buisie enough to speake thynges standyng with right & justice. *Ibid.* 288 b, Thy dooynges o Cato dooen more nere approche vnto the spirite of prophecie, but myne are muche better standyng with frendeship. **1553** T. WILSON *Rhet.* (1909) 34 But such stubburnesse.. is not standing with Iustice.

19. Naut. ***all standing***: see STAND *v.* 24.

Hence †'**standingly** *adv.*, as a regular thing.
a **1641** BP. MOUNTAGU *Acts & Mon.* (1642) 460 They used to pray, at the third, the sixth, the ninth houre,.. standingly, besides other times and houres occasionally.

'standing-place. [f. STANDING *vbl. sb.*]
1. A place prepared or assigned for a person or thing to stand in; a place to accommodate persons standing.
c **1440** *Promp. Parv.* 477/1 Stondynge place, where men stondyn, *stacio.* **1561** CLOUGH in *Burgon's Life Gresham* (1839) I. 378 In the makyng of pagents, and standyng plasys to stande uppon, to geve judgement, who shalle wyn the pryse. **1585** HIGINS *Junius' Nomencl.* 189/2 *Caueа*,.. the court or low standing place before the stage, where the people stoode or sat togither. *Ibid.* 287/1 *Statio*,.. the soldiours station or standing place, which they are appointed to keepe in the time of warre. **1869** 'MARK TWAIN' *Innoc. Abroad* xiii. (1881) 103 A speculator bridged a couple of barrels with a board and we hired standing-places on it.
fig. **1889** *Spectator* 21 Sept., If this portion of by no means the largest of the Republics of South America has so much spare room in it, there is no need to despair of people finding standing-places in the world.
2. A place where a person takes his stand.
1736 C. WESLEY *Let. Lady Oglethorpe* in J. Telford *Methodist Hymn-bk.* (1906) 429 The vastness of the watery waste, as compared with my standing-place, called to mind the briefness of human life and the immensity of its consequences. **1856** STANLEY *Sinai & Pal.* vii. (1858) 300 A high place dedicated to the heathen Nebo, as Balaam's standing-place had been consecrated to Peor.

standing stone. [STANDING *ppl. a.*] A large block of stone set upright; a menhir, monolith.
?*c* **1200** *Newminster Cartul.* (Surtees) 36 Et j acram versus le north de Standenstan. **13..** *Childh. Jesus* 842 in *Archiv Stud. neu. Spr.* LXXIV. 338 In a Mowntayne he gane it hele Reghte in a standande stane. *c* **1470** HENRY *Wallace* v. 298 He.. left him thus besyde the standand stanys. **1601** *Reg. Mag. Sig. Scot.* 391/2 Ane lang standand stane quhilk standis in direct line betuix the said Sadill-stane and the utter merche stane. **1814** SCOTT *Diary* 7 Aug. in *Lockhart* (1837) III. iv. 158 Ride down the loch to Scalloway.... Pass a huge standing stone, or pillar. Here, it is said, the son of an old Earl of the Orkneys met his fate. **1851** D. WILSON *Preh. Ann.* (1863) I. v. 130 The most primitive of these ancient memorials are the unhewn columns, or standing stones, as they are called.

standish ('stændɪʃ). *Obs.* exc. *Hist.* or *arch.* Forms: α. 5–6 **standisshe**, 6 **-ys(s)he**, **(-yche)**, 6–7 **standishe**, 8–9 **stand-dish**, 6– **standish**. β. (7 **standage**, **-ege**, 8 **standidge**.) [Commonly believed to be f. STAND *v.* + DISH *sb.*; but evidence is wanting for such a use of *dish* as would account for the assumed combination.] A stand containing ink, pens and other writing materials and accessories (see quots.); an inkstand; also, an inkpot.
α. **1474–5** in Swayne *Sarum Church-w. Acc.* (1896) 17 Et in j quartari paupiri & in j standisshe viij d. **1480** *Wardr. Acc. Edw. IV.* (1830) 131 Standisshes with weightes and scales iij. **1590** LODGE *Euphues Gold. Leg.* ⁋2, Reaching to her standish, she tooke penne and paper, and wrote a letter. **1607** BEAUMONT *Woman Hater* v. i, Secretary, fetch.. the standish I answer French Letters with. **1688** HOLME *Armoury* III. xiv. (Roxb.) 20/1 This fashion of Horne.. is now converted into Lead, and hath the denomination of a standish: or of tyn and soe haue both Inke place, sand box, candlestick and a long box to lay wax, pens and knife in: all fixt togather, yet all but a standish. **1747** RICHARDSON *Clarissa* (1811) II. 249 Away went the dear girl.. carrying down with her my standish, and all its furniture, and a little parcel of pens beside. **1789** MRS. PIOZZI *Journ. France* II. 361 His.. writing-table.. was contrived.. with a square hole for the standish to drop into and not spill the ink. **1841** DICKENS *Barn. Rudge* x, He wanted pen, ink, and paper. There was an old standish on the high mantel shelf containing a dusty apology for all three. **1852** THACKERAY *Esmond* II. x, Pouring out his flame and his passion.. pacing the room.. twisting and breaking into bits the wax out of the stand-dish. **1864** *Athenæum* 11 June 801 When the veteran, .. is about to lay his pen to rest in the standish.
β. **1605** *Tryall Chev.* v. i, in Bullen *Old Pl.* (1884) III. 340 The incke that's in the standage doth looke blacke. **1609** *Louth Rec.* (1891) 156 Item for a pewter standege for the Chamber iij s. iiij d. **1772** in *Cath. Rec. Soc. Publ.* I. 138 A Leathern Standidge.
¶**b.** (See quot.)
1727 A. HAMILTON *New Acc. E. Ind.* I. xi. 120 A Glass Pipe for his Tobacco, and an embroider'd Standish for it to stand in.

standle, obs. variant of STANDEL.

'stand-off. *attrib. phrase*, *a.* and *sb.* [f. vbl. phr. *stand off*: see STAND *v.* 96.]
A. *attrib. phrase* and *adj.*
1. That holds aloof from familiar intercourse; contemptuously distant in manner; reserved, unsocial.
1837 MOORE *Mem.* 12 Oct. (1856) VII. 203 Lady Lansdowne objected to the number of dirty houses that come up quite close to the Castle [of Windsor]. This Lord John said.. he preferred.. to the insulation of the great houses of the present day... [I] was all for the stand-off system of Lady Lansdowne; each rank in its own station. **1859** LEVER *Dav. Dunn* xxiv, I want to know what he is personally; is he stiff, haughty, grave, gay, stand-off, or affable? **1888** MRS. H. WARD *Robert Elsmere* i, People generally like the other two much better. Catherine is so stand-off. **1889** F. E. GRETTON *Memory's Harkback* 102 Your fellow-passengers are rarely discourteous: but there is almost always the 'stand-off' habit with them. **1889** MRS. LYNN LINTON *Thro' Long Night* II. II. xi. 161 She.. was as stiff and stand-off as a grenadier. **1894** SALA *Things Seen* I. i. 40 His occasional propensity to treat people in a distant stand-off manner.
2. *Rugby Football.* (See quot. 1910.)
1909 E. GWYN NICHOLLS *Mod. Rugby Game* iii. 40 He must be capable of adequately filling the position of stand-off and of scrum half. *Ibid.* 43 The scrum half's pass should go to his stand-off colleague. **1910** *Encycl. Brit.* X. 620/2 One [half-back] stands fairly close to the scrummage and is known as the 'scrum-half', the other takes a position between the latter and the three-quarters, and is termed the stand-off-half.
3. Of an object: that projects or is positioned a short distance away from a surface or another object; that serves to hold something in such a position.
1952 *Chambers's Jrnl.* Feb. 128/2 The well at the base of the shower-unit has a stand-off waste-pipe and the well can be used as a foot-bath. **1962** *Air-Cushion Vehicles* I. 58/2 On top of the trusses are secured box-section full-length longerons, known as 'stand-off booms', which are braced together and complete the primary structure. **1964** R. F. FICCHI *Electr. Interference* v. 52 Component manufacturers have developed the ceramic stand-off, or stud-type, capacitor in an effort to reduce the internal and lead-in inductance of the capacitor. **1977** *Gramophone* Oct. 743/1 The GC300.. is finished with a.. matt charcoal plastic base with four stand-off feet.
4. *Mil.* Of a guided missile: designed to be launched against its target from an aircraft at long range, esp. as ***stand-off bomb***. Also ***stand-off range***.
1957 *Times Survey British Aviation* Sept. 2/1 Improved marks of the V-class bombers will carry a powered guided bomb (the so-called stand-off bomb) and will form the foundation of our striking force for many years. **1960** A. BALL *Ballistic & Guided Missiles* iv. 62 Already there are short-range missiles.., often called 'stand-off bombs'. **1969** *Times* 30 Apr. 27/3 The Swingfire anti-tank weapon is now being delivered to the British Army, and we hope that the Division will shortly obtain a contract to develop Swingfire further by exploiting its ability to 'kill' armour from the air and at long stand-off range. **1971** E. LUTTWAK *Dict. Mod. War* 181/1 *Stand-off missile*, a missile, generally fitted with a nuclear warhead, which is launched by a bomber and substitutes for the latter in the final phase of the attack. **1978** R. V. JONES *Most Secret War* xlvi. 463 A long-range glider bomb, the BV 246.. was thus an early example of a 'stand-off' missile. **1982** *Navy News* Mar. 18/2 With its considerable 'stand-off' range, it is designed to destroy or disable enemy warships up to the largest-known size.
B. *sb.* Chiefly *U.S.*
1. Aversion to associate with others; aloofness.
1865 TROLLOPE *Can You forgive Her?* II. xxiv. 183 There's a stand-off about some women—what the men call a 'nollimy tangere'. **1885** D. D. PORTER *Incid. Civil War* xiv. 143 (Funk) There was a kind of 'stand-off' between the army and the navy when acting together, which prevented them from working in harmony.
2. a. Something which counterbalances.
1888 *Microcosm.* (N.Y.) Dec. 7 We are willing to allow this judicial estimate.. to count as a stand-off against all the subsidized commendations. **1890** *Atlantic Monthly* Nov. 672/1 When therefore the lawyer hears the curses.. of his impatient clients, the preferences of other clients.. make a complete stand-off; and he feels that the law's delay is both bad and good.
b. ***Mexican stand-off***, no chance to benefit (or *spec.* to defend oneself); hence, a general stalemate (cf. sense 3). *slang.*
1891 *N.Y. Sporting Times* 19 Sept. 4/3 'Monk' Cline, who got a Mexican stand-off from Dave Rowe has signed with Louisville. **1929** HOSTETTER & BEESLEY *It's a Racket!* 231 *Mexican stand-off*, to kill in cold blood. **1935** J. O'HARA *Appointment in Samarra* vii. 222 The men were the victims of the St. Valentine's Day massacre in Chicago, when seven men were given the Mexican stand-off against the inside wall of a gang garage. **1958** 'W. HENRY' *Seven Men at Mimbres Springs* xvi. 189, I rightly and firmly believe we've taken some of the flap out of Mangas's shirttails and can turn this thing into a Mexican stand-off, given any luck at all. **1979** D. MACKENZIE *Raven settles Score* 26 As things stood it was a Mexican standoff. He couldn't go to the law but.. nor could the Koreans.
c. In *gen.* use, any uneasy stalemate or deadlock; an impasse. Freq. in *Pol.* contexts.
1958 *Spectator* 31 Oct. 588/2 On the Fuchs-Hillary standoff whether to continue to Scott Base or not.. Sir Vivian tactfully writes: 'Unfortunately this exchange became known publicly.' **1971** T. W. ROBINSON *Cultural Revolution in China* i. 15 The standoff with Cambodia was precipitated by the propaganda activities of the Chinese embassy and the New China News Agency. **1974** *Spartanburg* (S. Carolina) *Herald* 19 Apr. A1/5 A 29-year-old Colombian.. died in a hail of police bullets after a four-hour standoff. **1981** 'E. V. CUNNINGHAM' *Case of Sliding Pool* (1982) xii. 145 We can't do anything, neither can he. It's a standoff.
3. 'A draw or tie, as in a game; a set-off; as, the contestants agreed to call it a stand-off' (*Funk's Stand. Dict.* 1895.)
1843 J. H. GREENE *Exposure Arts Gambling* 187 Thus, if a man bets on the ace and deuce, and the ace comes to his side, and the deuce to the dealer's side, it is a stand-off, and neither wins. **1893** 'MARK TWAIN' in *St. Nicholas* Nov. 21/2 It was about a stand-off; so both of them had to whoop up their dangerous adventures, and try to get ahead *that* way. **1938** *Sun* (Baltimore) 17 May 14/5 Supreme Court decisions were about a standoff. There was a ruling against the General Electric in a patent suit... The High Court agreed to consider the validity of the TVA on an appeal by eighteen Southeastern utilities. **1964** F. BOWERS *Bibliogr. & Textual Crit.* IV. iii. 115 But in *Old Fortunatus* the evidence is a stand-off... In the 11 extant copies, 5 contain the uncorrected state of A and 6 the uncorrected state of B. **1974** *Cleveland* (Ohio) *Plain Dealer* 26 Oct. 7-D/7 Cleveland Benedictine and Cambridge battled to a 0–0 standoff in a non-league football game here Friday night.
4. *slang.* 'Extension of time imposed on a creditor; postponement of payment; as, he gave me a stand-off' (*Funk's Stand. Dict.* 1895). Also *fig. U.S.* Now *rare.*
1883 B. HARTE *Carquinez Woods* 65, I reckon you'd better make it [*sc.* a bet] a stand-off for twenty-four hours, and I'll find out and let you know. **1891** M. E. RYAN *Told in Hills* IV. viii. 350, I got a stand-off on the hostilities—till your return. **1906** 'O. HENRY' in *Everybody's Mag.* Aug. 166/2 I've negotiated a stand-off at a delicatessen hut down-town.
5. A rest; a temporary cessation from work. Cf. STAND *v.* 96 g. *rare.*
1918 *Jrnl. R. Naval Med. Service* IV. 181 He should have four months 'stand off'. **1930** C. R. SANSOM *Fights & Flights* 100 He told me.. to give my cars a stand-off for the rest of the day.
6. Rugby Football. *ellipt.* for *stand-off half.* Cf. *fly-half* s.v. FLY *sb.*² 8.
1922 *Daily Mail* 15 Nov. 11 Cassels at stand-off seeming to be able to take any sort of pass. **1939** *Daily Tel.* 18 Dec. 11/3 Their backs, with the exception of P. Hodgson, at stand-off, were disappointing. **1969** *Listener* 15 May 700/3 Castleford.. are captained by their stand-off Alan Hardisty. **1980** *Sunday Times* 21 Sept. 29 Even now, 100 days later, it's still something of a whirl for the Lions stand-off.
7. Something serving to hold an object clear of a surface or another object.
1967 *Boston Sunday Herald* 26 Mar. I. 22/1 (Advt.), Two mast strap standoffs... Four $3\frac{1}{2}''$ wood screw stand-offs. **1974** *Physics Bull.* Dec. 592/2 Two quartz blocks are positioned adjacent to the device, and a preformed gold tape is bonded across the quartz standoffs and the back contact of the diode. **1977** *Engin. Materials & Design* Aug. 56/2 The brochure details a selection of fasteners, from a plain self-clinching nut or stud, to standoffs, self-locking, floating and miniature types, having thread sizes from M2 to M12.
Hence **stand-'offish** *a.* = sense A. 1; **stand-'offishness**, stand-off behaviour.
1860 *All Year Round* No. 66. 374 We are.. not aristocratic, perhaps, but decidedly rich, and on that account rather high and stand-off-ish. **1881** MISS BRADDON *Asphodel* II. 172 She has been very stand-offish to me ever since. **1886** P. ROBINSON *Teetotum Trees* 144 He even becomes a trifle haughty, and affects a stand-offishness which sits grotesquely upon him. **1888** D. C. MURRAY *Weaker Vessel* xxxii, I told him I did not like this pride and stand-offishness between man and man.

stand oil. Also 'standoil. [tr. G. *standöl*: see STAND *sb.*¹, OIL *sb.*¹ So called from its formerly being prepared by allowing linseed oil to stand.] Linseed oil or another drying oil that has been thickened by heating, used in paints, varnishes, and printing inks.
1908 LIVACHE & MCINTOSH *Manuf. Varnishes & Kindred Industries* (ed. 2) II. vii. 153 Reb's Stock Mixing Varnishes... The different ingredients are prepared as follows. (1) Linseed oil, 'stand oil'.—Raw oil is heated without driers until it deposits mucilage and clarifies, after which it is tanked for three to four weeks before use. **1934** H. HILER *Notes on Technique of Painting* iii. 234 A good varnish containing some standoil (and a hard resin). **1955** W. GADDIS *Recognitions* I. iii. 124 This Van Eyck,.. how sharp the lines are, look how smoothly they flow, it's perfect painting in stand oil, isn't it. **1981** *National Gallery Report 1980–81* 69 The problem of distinguishing, in the dried state, between raw and heat-treated oils (stand oils) remains obstinately unresolved.

stand out, *sb.* (and *adj.*) *phr.* Now usu. **standout** or with hyphen. [f. vbl. phr. *stand out*: see STAND *v.* 99.] **1.** [After *lock-out.*] A workmen's strike.
1898 *Westm. Gaz.* 12 Jan. 2/2 They are all protected by a strike clause, which says that a 'strike or stand out' by their workmen may be a sufficient excuse for non-completion of their contract. **1901** R. MURRAY *Hist. Hawick* I. 95 Hawick had hitherto been free from strikes, or 'stands oot', as they were called.
2. a. One who stands out from the crowd; an outstanding or conspicuous person or thing. *N. Amer. colloq.*
1928 *Collier's* 29 Dec. 26/2 When the show opened, this girl had improved in her dancing so amazingly that she was a distinct 'standout'. **1936** *Sun* (Baltimore) 13 July 4/1 The smash-ups are staged realistically, the standout being that in which an apparently new.. car hurtles over a parapet and arcs one hundred feet or so through the air. **1938** D. BAKER *Young Man with Horn* III. ii. 145 He was blessed above the run of band leaders. It isn't given to all organizers to have a stand-out in their organizations. **1944** *Sat. Rev. Lit.* (U.S.) 8 Jan. 14/3 John Hersey's novel about the AMG in Italy, 'A Bell for Adano', is likely to be one of the action stand-outs of the new season. **1958** *Times* 24 Nov. (Canad. Suppl.) p. xii/6, If they see a boy who is a standout,.. they can't go wrong by putting him down as a good prospect. **1979** *Time* 8 Jan. 46/2 Another campus standout, Phyllis Wallace, now in her 50s, has been burdened by prejudice against blacks as well as women.
b. *attrib. phr.* or as *adj.*
1932 *Sun* (Baltimore) 15 Aug. 9/1 California's rowing triumph and Japan's first swimming conquest were the stand-out performances. **1955** KEEPNEWS & GRAUER *Pictorial Hist. Jazz* xi. 117/2 Red Nichols and Miff Mole were the stand-out figures in this phase. **1978** J. IRVING *World according to Garp* viii. 162 Robert Muldoon, a standout tight end for the Philadelphia Eagles.

stand-pat, etc.: see STAND *v.* 14.

'stand-pipe, *sb.* [f. STAND *v.*]
1. A vertical pipe for the conveyance of water, gas, steam or the like to a higher level.

1850 OGILVIE. **1875** KNIGHT *Dict. Mech.* **1879** *Cassell's Techn. Educ.* I. 209 [In a low-pressure engine] water is.. commonly supplied by means of a vertical stand-pipe with a small cistern at the upper end. **1889** WELCH *Text Bk. Naval Archit.* xi. 127 To empty the double bottom spaces [of a ship], a suction known as a stand pipe is led from each compartment to a valve chest. *Ibid.* 129 The standpipe valve chest.

2. A pipe for attachment to a water-main furnished with a spout or nozzle to which a hose may be fixed or with a tap.

1850 OGILVIE. **1866** *Tomlinson's Cycl. Useful Arts* I. 3/1 A stand-pipe, with a flexible hose, is placed in one corner of the slaughter-house. **1883** *Pall Mall Gaz.* 5 July 7/2 The presence of several firemen with a standpipe in readiness was deemed desirable during the night.

Hence **'standpipe** *v. trans.*, to supply (a water-main) with stand-pipes.

1895 *Daily News* 22 Mar. 3/7 The Company caused the district to be stand-piped. *Ibid.*, The special operations of stand-piping and of providing for the increased draught.

standpoint ('stændpɔɪnt). [f. STAND *v.* + POINT *sb.*[1], after G. *standpunkt.*]

1. A fixed point of standing; the position at which a person stands to view an object, scene or the like; a point of view.

1829 MILL *Hum. Mind* (1869) II. xiv. §6. 150 As often as the movement [of the eyes] is repeated from the same stand-point, the optical series is repeated. **1868** LOCKYER *Guillemin's Heavens* (ed. 3) 475 We want to know the distance of this tower from our stand-point without actually measuring or stepping the distance. **1907** J. A. HODGES *Elem. Photogr.* (ed. 6) 142 A suitable stand-point having been selected.

2. A mental point of view; the position (with respect to degree of information, direction of sympathies or prejudices, assumed fundamental principles, or the like) which a person occupies in relation to any object of mental contemplation.

[**1836** G. C. LEWIS *Lett.* (1870) 53 The letters are.. those ..of a woman viewing the facts from the supposed standpunct of Mdlle. de Morell.] **1854** GEO. ELIOT tr. *Feuerbach's Essence Christianity* ix. 96 This abstraction.. is determined by the essential standpoint of man. **1858** H. SPENCER *Ess.* I. 169 His stand-point is far remote from the one usually regarded as scientific. **1874** L. STEPHEN *Hours in Library* (1892) I. iii. 100, I am content to look at it for the time from Pope's stand-point. **1884** H. JENNINGS *Phall.* xiv. 150 He deals with the subject simply from the orthodox and academic standpoint. **1894** DRUMMOND *Ascent Man* 12 The whole mistake of naturalism has been to interpret Nature from the standpoint of the atom.

3. A position in life or in the world. *rare*$^{-1}$.

1874 HELPS *Soc. Press.* iii. 54 They direct all, or the greatest part of, their efforts to insure a most favourable standpoint for their children.

'stand-still, 'standstill, *sb.* and *a.* [f. vbl. phrase *to stand still*: see STILL *a.*] **A.** *sb.*

1. A state of cessation of movement; a halt, pause. *lit.* and *fig.* Chiefly in ***to come, bring to a standstill, to be at a standstill.***

1702 C. MATHER *Magn. Chr.* VII. App. (1852) 597 We will here.. come to a little stand still, and with mournful hearts look upon the condition of the captives. **1786** MME. D'ARBLAY *Diary* 23 Dec., I had advanced straight forward ..; a matter contrary to all etiquette, which exacts a dead stand-still, and retiring to the side of the walls or houses, when any of the Royal Family appear. **1809** WELLINGTON in Gurw. *Desp.* (1837) IV. 346 If the army was not most successful this very circumstance would probably bring us to a stand-still. **1849** ROBERTSON *Serm.* Ser. I. iv. (1866) 66 The business would be at a standstill. **1852** C. W. HOSKYNS *Talpa* i. (1854) 3 The plough comes to a standstill. **1870** LOWELL *Study Wind.* (1886) 47 Those stand-stills of the air ..forebode a change of weather. **1878** M. FOSTER *Physiol.* III. v. §2. 479 Stimulation with a strong constant current causes a stand still in diastole. **1882** VINES tr. *Sachs' Bot.* 875 The growth of the motile zone is by no means at a standstill when the flowers are not performing any movements. **1890** A. W. DU BRAY *Upland Shooting* 433 When the shooter is at a standstill—be it in a blind, boat or on a pass.

2. The state of being unable to proceed, owing to exhaustion; in phrases ***to ride*** (a horse) ***to a standstill, to row*** (a competitor) ***to a standstill,*** and the like.

1811 *Sporting Mag.* XXXVII. 168 Osbaldeston rode his horse to a stand-still. **1912** *Throne* 7 Aug. 227/1 Barry.. rowed the New Zealander to a standstill a hundred yards from the winning post.

B. *adj.* **1.** That stands still; that is deficient in advancement or progress.

1856 MISS WARNER *Hills Shatemuc* xii, 'Taint a stand-still world, this; what's up to-day is down to-morrow. **1876** J. PARKER *Paracl.* II. Epil. 387 A standstill policy is in its very essence a blunder and a crime. **1876** GEO. ELIOT *Dan. Der.* xlii, They are a stand-still people.

2. a. Characterized by the absence or restriction of movement.

1829 P. EGAN *Boxiana* 2nd Ser. II. 233 Jem had now reduced the 'big one' to his own weight, and had also placed him upon the stand-still system. **1852** J. REYNOLDS *Hist. Illinois* 266 The cotillions, or stand still dances, were not then known. **1927** *Daily Express* 27 Dec. 1 A 'standstill' order prohibiting all movements of cattle, sheep, pigs, or goats in thirteen counties. **1975** J. G. EVANS *Environment Early Man Brit. Isles* ii. 46 Intervening organic horizons represent standstill phases when the climate ameliorated sufficiently for a continuous vegetation cover to form.

b. *Econ.* Of an agreement, etc.: that seeks to maintain the present state of affairs, esp. by deferring the necessity to repay an international debt. Also *transf.* and of the debt itself.

The original *standstill agreement* was concluded in 1931 between German and U.S. and other Allied banking and commercial concerns, and allowed for the postponement of German short-term credit repayments in the light of the country's severe economic plight.

1931 *Times* 17 Aug. 9/2 The agreements negotiated between the national 'standstill' committees and the German bankers will.. be mentioned in the report. *Ibid.* 20 Aug. 9/1 The 'standstill' agreement for the prolongation of short-term credits to Germany was signed.. today. **1932** *Sun* (Baltimore) 12 Sept. 7/4 The standstill agreement.. was designed to lift the pressure of world creditors on Germany until that nation could nurse its financial affairs back into something like normal vigor. **1938** H. V. HODSON *Slump & Recovery* ix. 331 The story of Germany's 'standstill' debt in this period. **1940** *Economist* 10 Aug. 191/2 The new standstill agreement was signed on behalf of the British, American and Swiss Banking Committees. **1955** *Ann. Reg. 1954* 425 Although further 'reactivation' of standstill debts was effected during the war, the amount of standstill debts declined substantially. **1970** *Internat. & Compar. Law Q.* 4th Ser. XIX. II. 270 Even an obligation of member States merely to abstain—a so-called standstill clause.. must be clear enough as to permit its direct application. **1980** *Wall St. Jrnl.* 6 June 1/2 Diamond International disclosed that it is discussing several courses of action that include a 'standstill agreement' with Cavenham Holdings.

Hence **stand-stillism.** (*nonce-wd.*)

1863 W. PHILLIPS *Speeches* xxiv. 560 The stupid stand-still-ism of the Cabinet.

stand-up, *a.* and *sb.* [f. vbl. phrase *stand up*: see STAND *v.* 103.] **A.** *adj.*

1. a. That stands erect; esp. of a collar, upright as distinguished from one folded over or turned down.

1812 *Sporting Mag.* XXXIX. 167 The stand-up Infantry Feather. **1813** in R. J. Macdonald *Hist. Dress R.A.* (1899) 48 A false stand-up collar of Belgian fashion. **1890** M. S. WILLIAMS *Leaves Life* II. xviii. 160 He wore a low stand-up collar and a dark cravat. **1897** *Westm. Gaz.* 24 Dec. 4/1 A whole series of fanciful 'stand-up' cards.

b. Of a person: Standing up boldly. Also *transf.* (jocular) of beer. *rare.*

1841 DICKENS *Barn. Rudge* xxxix, He was.. one of the finest, stand-up men, you ever see. **1844** —— *Martin Chuz.* xxv, An atmosphere of steak, and strong, stout, stand-up English beer.

c. Projecting; spec. in *Book-binding* (see quot.).

1818 *Art Bookbinding* 2 *Stand-up-bands*, the bands that the sheets are sewed too, projecting from the back.

d. ***stand-up comic*** (also ***comedian***), a comedian whose act consists of standing before an audience and telling a succession of jokes.

1966 *Listener* 11 Aug. 194/1 In television complex sentences need to be eschewed, especially by stand-up comics. **1969** *Ibid.* 24 Apr. 588/2 The audience, used to jazz singers, satire companies or stand-up comedians, could make nothing of his work. **1969** *New Yorker* 14 June 92/2 Bruce had just begun to surface as a standup comic. *a* **1975** WODEHOUSE *Sunset at Blandings* (1977) vi. 44 I've known Home Secretaries who were as cheerful as stand-up comics. **1980** D. MACKENZIE *Raven & Paperhangers* i. 9 Playing straight man to a stand-up comic in a Vegas night club.

2. a. Performed in a standing posture. Of a meal or other refreshment: Taken standing. Also, designating a cafeteria or other establishment at which patrons stand at a counter to eat or drink; and applied to the counter itself.

1862 *Macm. Mag.* May 28 Generally, the receptions end with stand-up suppers. **1899** *Daily News* 10 Jan. 2/7 The encouragement of hurried, stand-up drinking at a counter. **1900** *Ibid.* 1 Sept. 5/1 Double Canadian canoe race, stand-up canoe race. **1920** H. G. WELLS *Outl. Hist.* xviii. 130/2 A stand-up buffet for light refreshments. **1971** R. J. WHITE *Second-Hand Tomb* v. 59 Jasper.. took a peep into the stand-up bar. **1981** M. C. SMITH *Gorky Park* I. vii. 87 A stand-up cafeteria next to the children's store.

b. Of a vehicle: Having standing accommodation only.

1840 *Civil Engin. & Arch. Jrnl.* III. 39/1 The fare for travelling in the stand-up-carriages amounts only to one penny a mile.

3. *Pugilism.* Of a contest: In which the combatants stand up fairly to one another without wrestling, flinching or evasion; esp. in (***a fair, square,*** etc.) ***stand-up fight.***

1811 [see SPARRING *vbl. sb.*[2] 1]. **1860** LD. W. LENNOX *Pict. Sporting Life* II. 7 A regular slashing mill.. no manœuvering—no dodging..; a real stand-up affair—foot to foot—front to front. **1881** *Sportsman's Year-bk.* 310 Rules for Boxing. The match to be a fair stand-up boxing match, in a 24-ft. ring. **1898** W. H. BULLOCK-HALL *Romans on Riviera* v. 46 In a stand-up fight a Ligurian was considered a match for a Gaul twice his size.

fig. **1849** STOVEL *Canne's Necess.* 90 The conflict of the Puritans became a direct stand-up fight with legalized.. episcopal domination. **1872** O. W. HOLMES *Poet at Breakf.-t.* i, His face marked with strong manly furrows, records of hard thinking and square stand-up fights with life.

B. *sb.*

†**1.** *pl.* ? Long boots. (Cf. STARTUP.) *Obs.*

1590 GREENE *Never too late* (1600) O 1, His holy day roabes went on, his standvps new blackt, his cap faire brusht.

2. A dance. (Cf. STAND *v.* 103 c.) *vulgar.*

1861 MAYHEW *Lond. Labour* III. 202/1 It was a penny a dance for each of 'em as danced, and each stand-up took a quarter of an hour.

3. A stand-up fight.

1867 J. K. HUNTER *Retrosp. Artist's Life* xi. (1912) 112 A stand-up of one round was commenced, in which Tam got twa blue een.

4. A function or meal at which one stands. Also *rarely*, a counter at which stand-up refreshment can be obtained and consumed.

1884 HAWEIS *Musical Life* I. iii. 80 Whewell's evening parties—called by the freshmen Whewell's 'Stand-ups', because undergraduates were not supposed to 'sit' on these solemn occasions. **1897** 'MARK TWAIN' *Following Equator* xiii. 143 He halted in front of the best restaurant, then glanced at his clothes and passed on, and got his breakfast at a 'stand-up'. **1902** *Westm. Gaz.* 4 June 1/1 Luncheon is to be provided.. and there will also be a 'stand up' at the buffet.

5. Short for *stand-up collar.*

1905 'H. HALIBURTON' *Excurs.* 36 Starched stand-ups.

6. An act of failing to keep an engagement or 'date' with another; also, ***to give*** (someone) ***the stand-up.*** Cf. STAND *v.* 103 q. *slang* (orig. *U.S.*).

1921 A. G. EMPEY *Madonna of Hills* vii. 56, I wonder if that jane's double-crossed me and and given me the stand-up? **1940** R. CHANDLER *Farewell, my Lovely* xxxix. 297 'It's a little late, but I've had a lot to do.' 'Another stand-up?' Her voice got cool. **1961** J. MACLAREN-ROSS *Doomsday Bk.* II. vii. 172 Find out where he's ringing from if it's another stand-up. **1977** D. RAMSAY *You can't call it Murder* I. 15 We made a dinner date... He didn't show up... I'd write it off as an ordinary stand-up, except that he left that ten-gallon job [*sc.* hat] behind.

7. A police indentification parade. *U.S. slang.*

1935 A. J. POLLOCK *Underworld Speaks* 113/2 *Stand-up*, the police line-up; show-up. **1949** *Philadelphia Even. Bull.* 14 Apr. 2/4 Jackson was brought to City Hall last night to take a look at Norman in a police standup, but he could not positively identify the prisoner.

stane, obs. form of STONE *sb.* and *v.*

stanene, variant of STONEN *a. Obs.*

staneraw ('stenrɑ), *sb.* and *a. Sc.* Also 9 stani-, steinraw. [f. *stane* STONE *sb.* + *raw*:—OE. *raȝu* lichen. Cf. Sc. *aikraw* lichen (f. *aik* = oak).]

A. *sb.* The stone-lichen *Parmelia saxatilis*, used for dyeing (see quot. 1861).

1777 J. LIGHTFOOT *Flora Scot.* II. 816 *Lichen saxatilis*.. Staneraw. **1806** P. NEILL *Tour Orkneys* etc. 50 Lichen saxatilis.. throughout the north of Scotland called Steinraw. **1861** H. MACMILLAN *Footn. Page Nat.* 118 The common stone lichen.. is still collected abundantly by the Scottish peasantry, under the name of *staneraw*, to dye woollen stuff of a dirty purple or reddish-brown colour.

B. *adj.* Dyed reddish-brown with staneraw.

1820 HOGG *Winter Tales* I. 316 (Jam.) The staniraw stockings and red garters, in his hurry, he took in his teeth.

stanerie, obs. form of STANNERY *a. Sc.*

stanery, obs. form of STANNARY.

Stanford-Binet ('stænfəd 'bi:neɪ). *Psychol.* The names of *Stanford* University and Alfred *Binet* (1857–1911), used *attrib.* and *absol.* to designate the revision and extension of the Binet-Simon intelligence tests (see BINET-SIMON) undertaken by L. M. Terman and first published in 1916, which established the concept of an intelligence quotient.

1918 CUNEO & TERMAN in *Pedagogical Seminary* Dec. 414 The purposes of this study were.. to correlate the results of Stanford-Binet tests with school marks. *Ibid.* 428 The Stanford-Binet scale was given to 112 representative school children. **1937** TERMAN & MERRILL *Measuring Intelligence* iii. 51 The old Stanford-Binet.. yields mental ages slightly too high at the younger ages. **1939** *Brit. Jrnl. Psychol.* XXX. 8 The Stanford-Binet test gives a good estimate of general intelligence though it gives verbal ability undue weight. **1954** A. ANASTASI *Psychol. Testing* i. 11 In America, a number of revisions were prepared, the most famous of which is.. known as the Stanford-Binet. **1974** R. M. PIRSIG *Zen & Art of Motorcycle Maintenance* (1976) I. vii. 80 His Stanford-Binet IQ, which is essentially a record of skill at analytic manipulation, was recorded at 170.

stang (stæŋ), *sb.*[1] *dial.* Forms: 3 stong, (7 stonge), 4–7 stange, 6–7 stangue, 8 steng, 3– stang. [a. ON. *stǫng* fem., genit. *stangar* (Sw. *stång*, Da. *stang*), cogn. w. OE. *stæng, stęng* masc., pole (see STING *sb.*[1]), OS. *stanga* fem. (MLG. *stange*), MDu. *stanghe* fem. (mod.Du. *stang*; also *steng*, earlier *stenge* fem.), OHG. *stanga* fem. (MHG., mod.G. *stange*); the OTeut. types are **staŋgō*, **staŋgjō* fem., **staŋgi-z* masc., f. the root **steŋg-* to pierce: see STING *v.*

The It. *stanga* bar (whence Fr. *stangue* shaft of an anchor) is an adoption of the Teut. word.]

1. A pole or stake, a wooden bar or beam. Also in various specific uses (see quots.).

a **1300** *Cursor M.* 24029 Þai draf him forth wit staf and stong. **13..** *Ibid.* 21144 (Gött.) A wicked iuu.. Smate him wid a walker stang [*v.r.* (Fairf.) a saa stange]. **13..** *Gaw. & Gr. Knt.* 1614, & syþen on a stif stange stoutly hem henges. **1481–90** *Howard Househ. Bks.* (Roxb.) 102 To by stanges for my Lord xvj. d. **1599** FITCH in Hakluyt *Voy.* II. I. 258 A kind of Coches.. caried vpon a stang betweene 3. or 4. men. **1613** MARKHAM *Eng. Husb.* I. II. ix. (1635) 167 In those large baskets.. carry them [apples] upon cole-staves, or stangs, betwixt two men. **1709** in *D. Beveridge's Culross & Tulliallan* (1885) II. 52 Four pounds Scotts to be payed to Alexr. Birnay, wright, for erecting the stang for the scollers in August last. **1781** J. HUTTON *Tour to Caves* (ed. 2) Gloss. 96 *Stangs*, the shafts of a cart. **1816** SCOTT *Antiq.* xxvi, He has braw broad shouthers, and I just took the measure o' them wi' the stang. **1824** [CARR] *Craven Gloss.*, *Stang*, a pole applied as a lever to press on a cart wheel, to prevent too great a velocity in rapid descents. **1828** *Ibid.*, *Stang*, a strong piece of wood on which the carcases of beasts are suspended by the sinews of the hind legs. **1900** C. MURRAY *Hamewith* 73 This is the ferry, an' I'm the lord An' king o' the boat an' stang.

b. *to ride the stang*: to be mounted astride of a pole borne on the shoulders of two men, and carried through the streets for the derision of the spectators.

In some places in Scotland and the north of England, one who has in certain ways incurred the indignation of his or her fellow-villagers is compelled to 'ride the stang' (either personally, in effigy, or by proxy), accompanied by a jeering crowd and sometimes 'rough music'. There is also a New Year's day custom by which every one met by the mob has either to 'ride the stang' or pay a forfeit.

1718 RAMSAY *Christ's Kirk Gr.* III. xviii, Ane mounted wi' a bang, Betwisht twa's shoulders..and rade the stang On her that day. **1740** in Cramond *Ann. Banff* (1891) I. 152 Sundry riotous persons fin'd for carrying Ann Miln from her own house and causing her to ride the stang. **1782** CALLANDER *Two Anc. Scott. Poems* 154 When they cannot lay hold of the culprit himself, they put some young fellow on the stang or pole, who proclaims that it is not on his own account that he is thus treated, but on that of another person, whom he names. **1865** *Athenæum* 2 Sept. 313/3 An attempt was recently made, in Barnsley..to revive the old custom of 'riding the stang'. That is, hoisting an offending man on to a staff, or a woman into a basket, and carrying them till the victims ransom themselves by paying a fine, spent in 'drink'. **1893** *Westm. Gaz.* 17 Oct. 5/2 On Thursday night the villagers expressed their indignation by the ceremony known as 'riding the stang'. This consists of carrying an effigy of the person in question round the village. **1896** DITCHFIELD *Old Eng. Cust.* 181 All who were found at work on the day of the feast had to ride the stang or pay a forfeit.

†**2.** A measure of land. **a.** = ROOD *sb.* 8. **b.** In Wales, an acre. *Obs.*

[**1249** in *Cal. Charter Rolls* (1903) I. 343 Tres stangas.] **1326** *Black Bk. St. David's* (1902) 18 Philippus Curteys tenet j acram terre et stang et reddit per annum ij d. **1570** in *11th Rep. Dep. Kpr. Rec. Irel.* 233 A stang called No-man's land, and 1 acre called Bodyngs acre. **1603** OWEN *Pembrokeshire* (1892) 133, 8 poles in bredth and xx in length or 4 in bredth and 40 in length maketh a stange. **1652** in *Gentl. Mag.* (1861) Nov. 507, 32 acres and three stonge of beanes and pease. **1682** PIERS *Descr. W. Meath* (1770) 116 They divide usually one field into acres, half-acres, stangs, that is roods. **1726** SWIFT *Gulliver* I. ii, These fields were intermingled with woods of half a stang. **1777** *Tunstall Inclos. Act* 10 Five acres and three stengs of land in the said East Field.

3. (See quot.)

1734 in D. D. Black *Hist. Brechin* vii. (1839) 140 [The price of the] stang or standing stone for the top of the cross.

4. *Comb.*, as **stang-ball**, a variety of bar-shot.

1802 C. JAMES *Milit. Dict.* s.v. *Ball*, Stang Balls.

stang (stæŋ), *sb.*[2] *Obs.* exc. *Sc.* and *north.* Also 4-5 **stong(e**. [f. STANG *v.*[1]]

1. A sting.

a **1300** *Cursor M.* 18115 To ded i said, 'quar es þi stang?' *Ibid.* 20960 Þe nedder..wit hir stang. **1382** WYCLIF *Exod.* xxiii. 28 Stynggynge flies, that ben sprungun of deed bodies, hauynge the stonges enuenymd. **1500–20** DUNBAR *Poems* xxxviii. 10 The crewall serpent with the mortall stang. **1556** J. HEYWOOD *Spider & F.* lvi. 34 Should it not sting him like stang of an adder? **1567** *Gude & Godlie Ball.* 108 Thow sall stampe on the edderis stang. **1851** *Cumberld. Gloss.*

b. The punctured wound caused by a sting.

c **1800** *Ye hae lien a' wrang* in *Burns' Poems*, But in herrying o' a bee byke, I'm rad ye've got a stang.

c. A sharp pain such as is caused by a sting.

1513 DOUGLAS *Æneis* XI. ix. 18 The greif and ire dyd fast habound, Rasit wyth breithfull stangis full onsound. **1526** *Pilgr. Perf.* (W. de W. 1531) 260 b, Remember here also the sharpe stanges & panges that our lorde suffred for our synnes. **1530** LYNDESAY *Test. Papyngo* 1140 It war to lang to mak narratioun Off sychis sore, with mony stang and stound. **1789** BURNS *Addr. Toothache* 1 My curse upon thy venom'd stang, That shoots my tortur'd gums alang. **1822** GALT *Provost* xxxvii, Such a stang as I got on entering the house, when I heard his mother wailing that he was dead. **1891** R. FORD *Thistledown* xvi. 299 My conscience yet gies me sair stangs when I think about her.

2. A name for certain fishes: **a.** The pipe-fish, *Syngnathus acus*; **b.** the lesser weever, *Trachinus vipera*.

1803 *Sibbald's Fife & Kinross* 127 *note*, Syngnathus acus, Shorter Pipe-fish; our fishers call it the Stang or Sting. **1880** DAY *Fishes Gt. Brit.* I. 82 Little- or lesser-weever:.. Stangster or Stang, Moray Firth.

3. An eel-spear. Also Comb. *stong-gad*.

1847 HALLIWELL, *Stang*, an eel-spear. *North.* **1866** BROGDEN *Prov. Lincs.* **1888** FENN *Dick o' the Fens* xii. 189 Mester Hickathrift has got the stong gad to mend. One of the tines is off, and it wants a noo ash pole.

4. *Sc.* The awn or beard of grain.

1808 JAMIESON.

5. The tongue of a 'trump' or jews harp; also *fig.* (see quot. 1808).

1803 JAMIESON, *Stang of the trump*, a proverbial phrase, used to denote one who is preferred to others viewed collectively; as the best member of a family. **1909** C. MURRAY *Hamewith* (ed. 2) 21 Trumps wi' double stang.

6. *Comb.*, as *stang-fish* (cf. sense 2 and STING-FISH).

1838 JOHNSTON in *Proc. Berw. Nat. Club* I. No. vi. 170 Lesser Weaver, *Yarr.* Stang-fish, *Prov.*

stang (stæŋ), *v.*[1] Also 3-4 **stange**, (4 **stayng**), 9 *dial.* **steng**. [a. ON. *stanga* to prick, goad, to spear (fish), to butt with the horns, f. *stang-*, *stǫng* stake: see STANG *sb.*[1]]

1. †*trans.* To pierce (a person) with a weapon. *Obs.*

c **1340** HAMPOLE *Pr. Consc.* 5293 Þe spere..þat staynged [*v.r.* stanged] Crist until þe hert rote. *c* **1400** MAUNDEV. (Roxb.) ii. 7 Þe schaft of þe spere with whilk Criste was stanged to þe hert.

b. *dial.* To spear (eels).

1856 P. THOMPSON *Hist. Boston* 725 *Stang*, an instrument to catch eels with, by 'stanging'.

2. To sting. *lit.* and *fig.*

a **1300** *Cursor M.* 22014 Dane..neder in strete, waitand hors to stang in fete. *c* **1375** *Sc. Leg. Saints* xviii. (*Mary of Egypt*) 427 Ane edir þat wald hym stang. *c* **1460** *Towneley Myst.* xxiii. 426 If thou will my harte stang. **1724** RAMSAY *Royal Archers Shooting* i, Serpents that wad stang The hand that gies them food. **1862** C. C. ROBINSON *Dial. Leeds* 421 It'll steng thah if thah touches it.

b. *absol.*

c **1375** *Cursor M.* 24357 (Fairf.) Þai stokid him wiþ a spere wiþ wrange þat þorou mi hert I felde hit stange. *c* **1475** HENRYSON *Orpheus & Euryd.* 324 The serpent stangis that is dedely syn. **1785** BURNS *Jolly Beggars* lii, But for how lang the flie may stang, Let inclination law that. **1786** —— *Epist. to Major Logan* vi, As the clegs o' feeling stang.

3. *intr.* To shoot or throb with pain. *dial.*

1788 W. H. MARSHALL *Yorksh.* II. 355. **1825** BROCKETT *N.C. Gloss.* **1856** P. THOMPSON *Hist. Boston* 725.

Hence **stanged** *ppl. a.*; **'stanging** *vbl. sb.* and *ppl. a.*

a **1300** *Cursor M.* 21688 Quen þe stanged men moght se þe nedder on þe tre þat hang, þai war all warist of þair stang. *Ibid.* 24540 In sterin stanging was i stadd. *c* **1460** *Towneley Myst.* xxi. 11 We haue had for the mekill hart stangyng. **1508** DUNBAR *Two Mariit Wemen* 266 With a terrebill tail be stangand as edderis. **1513** DOUGLAS *Æneis* VII. xiii. 124 Thair wraith and vennom culd he dant and meys And heill thair stanging. **1602** *2nd Pt. Return fr. Parnassus* Prol. 33 Its a Christmas toy indeede, as good a conceit as stanging hotcockles, or blinde-man buffe. **1863** *Specim. Yorksh. Dial.*, I had such a stanging pain from the tooth-ache. **1881** J. MURRAY in *Mod. Sc. Poets* III. 154 The doctors pondered lang and sair To rid me o' the stangin' o't.

stang (stæŋ), *v.*[2] [f. STANG *sb.*[1]]

†**1.** *trans.* To fasten with a 'stang', to bar.

1598 FLORIO, *Stangare*, to barre, to sprang, to stang a dore.

†**2.** To cause to ride the stang. Cf. STANG *sb.*[1] 1 b.

1674 RAY *N.C. Words* 44 This Word is still used in some Colleges in..Cambridge; to stang Scholars in Christmas, being to cause them to ride on a colt-staff, or pole, for missing of Chappel. **1777** BRAND *Pop. Antiq.* App. 410.

3. To carry (produce) on stangs.

1829 GLOVER *Hist. Derby* I. 203 In very steep or small inclosures, hay continues here to be carried to the stack, by a method called stanging... Corn crops from similar situations are also stanged.

stang, pa. t. (obs.) of STING *v.*

stang(e, obs. ff. STANK *sb.*

stangster ('stæŋstə(r)). *dial.* [f. STANG *sb.*[2] + -STER.] = STANG *sb.*[2] 2 b.

1880 [see STANG *sb.*[2] 2].

Stanhope ('stænhəʊp, 'stænəp). [f. the proper name *Stanhope* (see below).]

1. a. A light open one-seated vehicle, formerly made with two wheels, but subsequently commonly with four. First made for the Hon. and Rev. Fitzroy Stanhope (1787–1864). Often written with small initial.

1825 C. M. WESTMACOTT *Engl. Spy* I. 86 Or in a stanhope come it strong. **1837** W. B. ADAMS *Carriages* 128 The two-wheeled carriage called a Stanhope is suspended on four of these springs. **1837** DICKENS *Pickw.* xl, The vehicle was not exactly a gig, neither was it a stanhope. **1891** 'J. S. WINTER' *Lumley* 13 They found the Stanhope drawn by a big grey awaiting them.

b. *Comb.*: **stanhope horse**, one suitable for a stanhope; **stanhope phaeton**, a variety of the stanhope.

1836 SIR G. STEPHEN *Search of Horse* ix. (1841) 137, I would suggest that the form of a stanhope horse be carefully considered. **1901** SKRINE *Life Sir W. Hunter* xiii. 245 He had purchased a Stanhope phaeton.

2. Stanhope lens, a lens of small diameter with two convex faces of different radii, inclosed in a metallic tube (Knight). Invented by Charles 3rd Earl Stanhope (1753–1816).

1850 W. KING *Permian Fossils* 143 In others..they [the punctures] cannot be detected so readily without a Stanhope lens. **1862** *J. Wylde's Circ. Sci.* I. 65/1 A Stanhope lens of the ordinary form.

3. Stanhope press, a hand printing-press invented by the 3rd Earl Stanhope (1753–1816).

c **1805** EARL STANHOPE in *Collect.* Ser. III. (O.H.S.) 400 The high price of the Stanhope press (compared with that of the common wooden ones) has, by many, been considered as likely to check the sale of them. **1841** *Penny Cycl.* XIX. 18/1 The accompanying diagram of the Stanhope press.

4. The name of the historian Philip Henry *Stanhope* (1805–75), 5th Earl Stanhope, used *attrib.* and *absol.* to designate the historical essay prize founded by him at Oxford University in 1855, or essays associated with this prize.

[**1856** *Oxford Univ. Calendar* 273 Earl Stanhope's Prize. In a Convocation holden on Friday, December 14, 1855, the following Regulations for a Prize founded by the Right Hon. Earl Stanhope, with a view to the full development and the continued growth and welfare of the School of Law and Modern History, and accepted by Convocation on the 20th day of June, 1855, were agreed upon.] **1861** J. A. SYMONDS *Let.* 17 Apr. (1967) I. 285 Conington..declares the Stanhope to be about as much too long. *Ibid.* 1 June 296, I confess to being a little anxious myself about the Stanhope, though one ought never to be disturbed on account of Prizes. **1863** *Oxford Univ. Calendar* 105 (*heading*) Stanhope historical essay. **1896** J. BUCHAN in W. Buchan *John Buchan* (1982) iv. 81 Get the Newdigate. Get the Stanhope. **1915** A. HUXLEY *Let.* 8 June (1969) 71, I may come up here in September to do some reading in Bodley for the Stanhope Prize. **1916** *Ibid.* 18 June 101, I trust I don't have to read the Stanhope at the Encaenia. **1934** *Oxford Univ. Gaz.* 21 Nov. 140/2 Stanhope Essay Prize, 1935. The subject for 1935 is '*Edward, the Black Prince.*' **1976** M. GREEN *Children of Sun* ii. 51 John Buchan..went to Oxford, where he won the Stanhope Essay Prize, the Newdigate Poetry Prize..and a first-class degree.

So **Stan'hopian** *a.*

1808 STOWER *Printer's Gram.* 54 Judging from former times, when ligatures..were used, and abolished because they encumbered the compositor,..we much fear the Stanhopian introduction of an, in, of, &c. will not be found to meet with a much more favourable reception. *Ibid.* 302, 506.

stanhopea (stæn'həʊpɪə). [mod.L. (J. Frost 1829, in *Curtis's Bot. Mag.* LVI. 2948), f. the name of Philip Henry *Stanhope* (1781–1855), 4th Earl Stanhope, President of the Medico-Botanical Society.] An epiphytic orchid of the genus of that name, native to tropical America and bearing large, often fragrant, flowers.

1829 *Curtis's Bot. Mag.* LVI. 2948 (*heading*) Splendid Stanhopea. **1890** W. WATSON *Orchids* lxi. 465 Some cultivators use nothing but sphagnum for Stanhopeas. **1917** L. H. BAILEY *Stand. Cycl. Hort.* VI. 3222/2 Stanhopeas enjoy a shady, moist location. **1962** *Amateur Gardening* 7 Apr. 6/1 The stanhopeas have large highly scented wax-like flowers.

Stanhoscope ('stænəskəʊp). [f. the name *Stanhope* (in *Stanhope lens*) + -SCOPE.] A magnifying lens like the Stanhope lens, but plane on the side farther from the eye.

1866 *Q. Jrnl. Microsc. Sci.* VI. 263 These Stanhoscopes.. are, of course, not in every instance so perfect optically as is desirable. **1868** W. B. CARPENTER *Microscope* (ed. 4) 22 A modified form of the 'Stanhope' lens..has been brought out in France under the name of 'Stanhoscope'.

staniel, stannel ('stænjəl, 'stænəl). Forms: α. 1 **stánezella, stánzella, -zilla, -zylla**, 5 **stanyel**, 7-8 **staniel**, 7 **stanniell**, 9 *dial.* **stanniel**, 7-9 *Sc.* **stainyell**; also *corruptly* 7 **stallion**. β. 7 **stannell**, 7-9 **stannel**. See also STANCHEL, STONEGALL. [OE. *stánezella*, *stánzella*, lit. 'stone-yeller' f. *stán* STONE *sb.* + **zella* agent-n. f. *zellan* to YELL (in OE. poetry used of the cry of the hawk).

The corrupt form *stallion* (quot. 1601 in 1 a) may have had dialectal currency; cf. the converse mispronunciation *staniel* for *stallion*, which is common in rustic speech. The spurious forms *standgale*, *-gall*, given in some recent dictionaries, are evolved from the etymologizing conjecture 'stand-in-gale' (Swainson, *Prov. Names of Birds*). The alleged Ger. synonym *steingall*, commonly cited by etymologists as cognate, is of doubtful genuineness. The 19th c. lexicographers seem to have obtained it, directly or indirectly, from the *Vocabula* of Peucer and Eber (1549). But although in this glossary the word is treated as German, its source appears to be William Turner's *Avium Historia* (Cologne 1544), where *steingall* is said to be the English word for *tinnunculus*. Turner's *steingall* prob. represents **steingall*; Gesner (1555) says that it is northern English. The English ornithologists of the 17th c., following Gesner, give *steingall* as an English name of the bird; Willughby's *stone-gall* is an etymologizing alteration of this.]

The kestrel, *Tinnunculus alaudarius*. Also applied contemptuously to a person, in allusion to the uselessness of the kestrel for the purposes of falconry. (Cf. KESTREL b.)

In OE. a mistranslation of L. *pellicanus* (pelecanus) pelican.

α. *c* **825** *Vesp. Psalter* ci. 7 Ðelic zeworden ic eam stanezellan [L. *pellicano*] in woestenne. *a* **1100** *Ags. Voc.* in Wr.-Wülcker 287/10 *Pellicanus*, stanzella and wanfota. *c* **1475** *Pict. Voc.* ibid. 758/32 *Hic odorincicus*, a stanyel. **1590** BUREL *Pilgr.* in *Watson's Collect.* (1709) II. 28 The Stainzell and the Schakerstane. **1601** SHAKS. *Twel. N.* II. v. 124 And with what wing the stallion checks at it? **1630** BRATHWAIT *Engl. Gentlem.* (1641) 178 Owles, cuckowes, staniels and Popinjayes. **1659** *Lady Alimony* I. iii. B 1, This Musæus is a Martiallist; and if I had not held him a feverish white-liver'd staniel..that Knight of the Sun, who imploy'd me should have done his errand himself. **1838** HOLLOWAY *Prov. Dict.*, *Stanniel*, a hawk.

β. **1601** HOLLAND *Pliny* x. xxxvii. I. 291 A Kestrill, or Stannell. **1678** RAY *Willughby's Ornithol.* 84 The Kestrel, Stannel, or Stonegall. **1688** CLAYTON *Virginia* iv. in *Phil. Trans.* XVII. 989 There are several sorts of the lesser kind of Stannels. **1863** H. G. ADAMS *Birds of Prey* 47 The Kestrel ..Stonegall, Steingall or Stannel.

Comb. **1797** BEWICK *Brit. Birds* I. 36 The Kestrel... Stannel Hawk.

Hence †**'stanielry**, staniel-like cowardice.

1659 *Lady Alimony* v. ii. I 4, All that Puny-pen feather'd Ayry of Buzardisme and Stanielry.

stanine ('stænaɪn). *Psychol.* [Blend of STANDARD *sb.* and NINE *sb.*] A nine-point scale on which test scores can be grouped in descending order of achievement, first developed by the

United States Air Force in 1942 (see quot. 1968); also, a score on such a scale. Freq. *attrib.*

1945 *Sun* (Baltimore) 1 Oct. 6/5 The result..was a 'stanine' rating (stanine being an invented word, from 'standard of nine'). **1957** E. R. HILGARD *Introd. Psychol.* (ed. 2) xvi. 400/2 A score of..650 on a Graduate Record Examination, or 8 on the Air Force stanine scale is above that achieved by 93 per cent of those on whom the test was calibrated. **1961** A. ANASTASI *Psychol. Testing* (ed. 2) iv. 93 Raw scores can readily be converted to stanines by arranging the original scores in order of size and then assigning stanines in accordance with the normal curve percentages. **1968** *Internat. Encycl. Social Sci.* I. 38/1 Single-digit standard scores, ranging from 1 to 9, with a mean of 5 and a standard deviation of 2 are called *stanines* (*standard nines*). **1976** *Word 1971* XXVII. 330 The performance of the Experimental children placed them at the second stanine with respect to French-speaking children in Montreal. **1976** *Woman's Day* (U.S.) Nov. 62/2 But few educators use such simple terms anymore. Instead, we may be unnecessarily confused by a *stanine* score.

Stanislavsky (stænɪˈslævskɪ). *Theatr.* Also Stanislavski. The name of the Russian actor and director Konstantin *Stanislavsky* (1863–1938), used *attrib.* to designate the style and technique of acting practised and taught by him: see METHOD *sb.* 2 e.

1924 J. J. ROBINS tr. *Stanislavsky's My Life in Art* xxxiii. 351 Chekhov gave that inner truth to the art of the stage which served as the foundation for what was later called the Stanislavsky System. **1958** *Spectator* 22 Aug. 248/3 The success of the Bolshoi Theatre Ballet rests on the application to dancing of the Stanislavsky technique. **1972** *Village Voice* (N.Y.) 1 June 55/4 The Stanislavski approach may meet one of its greatest challenges in a Stein play. **1974** T. P. WHITNEY tr. *Solzhenitsyn's Gulag Archipelago* I. I. x. 387 Krylenko abandoned the Stanislavsky method, didn't assign the roles, relied on improvisation.

Hence **Staniˈslavskian, -yan** *a.*

1958 *Spectator* 20 June 813/1 Stanislavskyan acting was being practised by Schepkin fifty years before the genesis of the System. **1965** *New Statesman* 8 Oct. 537/1 Gielgud..is the outstanding Stanislavskian actor in the West. **1979** A. WILLIAMSON *Funeral March for Siegfried* x. 50 He would have thought most [singers]..incapable of expressing so lucid a Stanislavskian principle.

‖**stanitza** (stæˈnɪtzə). Also 7 staniza. [Russian *stanitsa*, dim. of *stan* station, district.] A Cossack community or township.

1662 J. DAVIES tr. *Olearius' Voy. Ambass.* 420 There went away a Staniza or Caravan, of about 200. persons. **1799** [see SOTNIK]. **1837** *Penny Cycl.* VIII. 79/2 Each [Cossack] regiment is drawn from one or more stanitzas or districts. **1895** *Daily News* 13 June 5/4 It were well, too, that a large number of Cossack stanitzas should be intermingled with the new colonists.

stank (stæŋk), *sb.* Forms: α. 4 **stanc**, 4, 7 **stanck(e**, 4–5 **staunk(e**, (5 **stonke**), 5, 7 **stanke**, (7 *Sc.* **stunk**), 9 *dial.* **stenk**, 3– **stank**. β. 3–6 **stang**, 5–6 **stange**, (6 **staung**). [a. OF. *estanc* (mod.F. *étang*) = Pr. *estanc-s*, Sp. *estanque*, Pg. *estanque*, *estanco*:—Com. Rom. **stanco*, prob. vbl. noun to **stancare* to dam up (:—popular L. **stagnicāre* f. *stagnum* pond): see STANCH *v.*]

1. A pond or pool. Also a ditch or dyke of slowly-moving water, a moat. Now *Sc.* and *dial.*

α. *a* **1300** *Cursor M.* 5922 On stank and burn and well. **1338** R. BRUNNE *Chron.* (1725) 68 Þei lighted & abiden biside a water stank [*rime* lang]. **13..** *E.E. Allit. P.* B. 1018 A stynkande stanc. *c* **1400** MAUNDEV. (1839) xix. 209 Bestes, taughte of men to gon in to Watres..and in to depe Stankes, for to take Fysche. **1450** *Paston Lett.* I. 170 Sir John Bukk ..physshed my stankys at Dedham, and holp brake my damme. *c* **1450** *St. Cuthbert* (Surtees) 2982 In an Ile he duelt ..Whar þan was a grete staunk; Of derwent watir þare is þe hede. **1535** STEWART *Cron. Scot.* (Rolls) I. 208 Ane nobill toun..That wallit wes about with lyme and stone, With dowbill stank and fowsseis mony one. **1603** J. DAVIES (Heref.) *Microcosmos* Wks. (Grosart) I. 32/1 Stanckes, Moores, and Lakes that never ryn. *c* **1630** in *Macfarlane's Geogr. Collect.* (1907) II. 165 It is now one little Logh being but ane stunk before when the Illand was in the midst of it. *c* **1690** in *Roxb. Ball.* (1888) VI. 616 O'er ditch and stank, he staik amang them a' then. **1786** BURNS *Auld Mare* iii, Thou ance..could hae flown out owre a stank, Like onie bird. **1807** STAGG *Poems* 3 Wi' whup an' spur, thro' stenk an' stoore, [they] Set off, a jolly party. **1825** CARLYLE *Let.* in Froude *Life* (1882) I. 296 If he..is made to plash and sprawl ..through every stank to which their love of provant leads them. **1871** W. ALEXANDER *Johnny Gibb* (1873) 31, I b'lieve ye he'll no loup the stank so easy wi' Maister Saun'ers.

β. *a* **1300** *Cursor M.* 8936 Ilk dai..þar lighted dun of heuen ture Angels..For to stir þe stang bidene. *a* **1340** HAMPOLE *Ps.* cxiii. 8 That turnys the stanys in stangis of watirs. **1484** CAXTON *Fables of Æsop* V. x, A stange or pond where as was a fayr mylle. *c* **1530** BERNERS *Arth. Lyt. Bryt.* (1814) 7 The stang or ponde of the forest. **1588** PARKE tr. *Mendoza's Hist. China* 205 They haue their stanges for the most part full of fish. *c* **1595** NORDEN *Spec. Brit., Cornw.* (1728) 71 Ther standeth a Stange or Poole of water.

transf. **13..** *Cursor M.* 23191 (Gött.) Sathanas..sal casten be,..a stinckand stanck of fire. *c* **1386** CHAUCER *Pars. T.* 841 Seint Iohn seith that Auowtiers shullen been in helle, in a stank brennynge of fyr and of Brymston.

2. A dam to hold back water, a weir or floodgate. Now *dial.* and *techn.*

1604 *Jrnls. Ho. Comm.* 23 June, All Weres, Kiddells, Stanks, and other Obstructions in..navigable Rivers. **1610** VAUGHAN in *J. Davies' Wks.* (Grosart) II. 4/1 The Brookes runne murmuring by their parched Brincks..and chide against the Stancks. **1633** in *N. Riding Rec.* (1885) III. II. 347 Att the stancke or damm of the abovenamed mill. **1656** R. FLETCHER *Martial's Epigr.* etc. 167 An inundation that ore-bears the banks And bounds of all religion; If some stancks Shew their emergent heads? Like Seth's fam'd stone, Th'are monuments of thy devotion gone! **1763** in J. Lloyd *Old S. Wales Iron Works* (1906) 73 To make such.. channels..pondheads, stanks, and wears as they shall think fit. **1855** GAWTHROP *Fraser's Guide to L'pool* 235 Crossing the stank, or bar, between Seacombe and Woodside. **1865** *Jrnl. R. Agric. Soc.* Ser. II. I. II. 277 The cutting through one of these subterranean stanks or ridges will often lay a large tract immediately dry. **1883** GRESLEY *Gloss. Coal-mining* 238 *Stank*, a water-tight stopping; generally a well built brick wall.

3. *attrib.* and *Comb.* as ***stank-head***, ***-side***; **stank-brae**, the edge of a stank; **stank-hen**, the moorhen, *Gallinula chloropus*; **stank-meadow**, a meadow containing a pool.

1579 in *Reg. Mag. Sig. Scot.* 1581, 73/1 The *stank bra on the eist syde. *c* **1680** J. RUSSELL in *Kirkton's Hist. Ch. Scot.* (1817) 443 Presently Clavers advanced all in a body to the stank bree. **1412–13** *Durham Acc. Rolls* (Surtees) 610 Pro reparacione de le *Stankhede apud Ketton, 4s. **1766** REID *Let.* Wks. I. 47/2 A bird called a *stankhen. It is a water fowl, less than a duck [etc.]. **1831** *Montagu's Ornith. Dict.* 188 Gallinule. Provincial.—Moor-hen... Stank-hen. **1358** *Durham Acc. Rolls* (Surtees) 561 In diversis foveis et gutturis factis in le *Staunkmedowe de Pityngton, 12s. 1d. **14..** *Prose Life Alexander* 71 Þay..went to þe *stanke-syde & drewe fisches & elez oute of þe water, & ete þam. **1903** A. WHYTE *Apostle Paul* x. 111 It is then that I sit down at a stank-side with poor Lord Brodie.

†**stank**, *a. Obs. rare*[−1]. In 6 **stanck, stanke**. [ad. It. *stanco* = OF. *estanc*, related to It. *stancare*, OF. *estancher*: see STANCH *v.*] Weary, faint, exhausted.

1579 SPENSER *Sheph. Cal.* Sept. 47, I am so stiffe, and so stanck [*gloss.* wearie or fainte]. **1598** FLORIO, *Stanco*, wearie, tyred, faint, ouerlaboured, stanke.

stank (stæŋk), *v. dial.* and *techn.* [f. STANK *sb.*] trans. **a.** To dam or strengthen the banks of a stream. Also to ***stank back***, ***up*** (water). †**b.** To surround with a moat. *Obs.*

a. 1656 R. FLETCHER *Martial's Epigr.* etc. 154 I'le..stanck up the salt Conducts of mine eyes To watch thy shame, and weep mine obsequies. **1829** in Ashbee *Last Rec. Cotswold Community* (1904) 6 Jno. Steel stanking the water and mounding in meadow. 0. 1. 6. **1839** SIR G. C. LEWIS *Gloss. Heref.* s.v., A man shutting down a floodgate would stank back the water. **1881** CUSSANS *Hist. Hertfordsh., Cashio* 321 Water-courses are stanked where they take a sharp turn.

b. *a* **1670** SPALDING *Troub. Chas. I* (Bannatyne Club) II. 315 Sir William Forbes..plantis sum soldiouris thairin, being stankit about and of good defens.

Hence **ˈstanking** *vbl. sb.* = STANK *sb.* 2.

1883 GRESLEY *Gloss. Coal-mining* 238 Stanking.

Stanley (ˈstænlɪ). The name of Edward Smith *Stanley* (1775–1851), 13th Earl of Derby, zoologist, used *attrib.* to denote birds named in his honour, as **Stanley bustard**, a large black and brown bustard, *Neotis denhami* (formerly *Otis stanleyi*), native to south-eastern Africa; **Stanley crane** = *paradise crane* s.v. PARADISE *sb.* 8; (*Tetrapteryx paradisea*, formerly *Anthropoides stanleyanus*).

1831 J. E. GRAY *Zool. Misc.* 12 Stanley Bustard. *Otis Stanleyi.* Above vermiculated, black and white. **1884** R. B. SHARPE *Layard's Birds S. Afr.* (ed. 2) 634 Stanley Bustard.. is common in the northern portions of the colony. **1912** J. STEVENSON-HAMILTON *Anim. Life Afr.* xvii. 273 The Stanley Bustard..is partial to..the high country of East and South Africa. **1979** K. B. NEWMAN *Birdlife in S. Afr.* xii. 134/2 Both the Kori Bustard and the second largest, the Stanley Bustard, perform rather grand courtship displays. **1867** E. L. LAYARD *Birds S. Afr.* 303 The 'Stanley' or 'Blue' Crane is not abundant in any locality. **1937** *N. & Q.* 19 June 450/2 A Stanley Crane, elegant in dove-like grey. **1958** [see *paradise crane* s.v. PARADISE *sb.* 8]. **1966** E. PALMER *Plains of Camdeboo* xi. 187 Our blue crane is also known as the Stanley crane. It belongs only to South Africa.

†**stanmarch.** *Hist.* Forms: 1 **stánmerce**, 4–6 **stanmarche**, 5–6 ? *erron.* **stammarche**, 5 **stanmerche**, **-mers(c)h**, 5– **stanmarch**. [OE. *stánmerce*, f. *stán* STONE *sb.* + *merce* MARCH *sb.*[1]] The umbelliferous plant *Smyrnium Olusatrum*, also called alexanders and horse-parsley.

c **1000** ÆLFRIC *Gloss.* in Wr.-Wülcker 134/36 *Petrosilion*, stanmerce. *a* **1387** *Sinon. Barthol.* (Anecd. Oxon.) 10 *Alexandria*, i. stanmarche. *c* **1450** *M.E. Med. Bk.* (Heinrich) 196 Tak morel. stanmerche. smalache. & malewes. *c* **1450** *Alphita* (Anecd. Oxon.) 5 Alexander uel olixatrum..anglice stanmersh. **1516** *Gt. Herbal* viii. (1529) A iv b, De Apio. Smalache or stammarche. **1597** GERARDE *Herbal* Suppl., Stanmarch is Alisander. **1665** LOVELL *Herbal* (ed. 2) 415 Stan march. **1863** PRIOR *Plant-n.*

attrib. *c* **1500** *Arnolde's Chron.* (1811) 172 Stanmarch seede.

stannary (ˈstænərɪ). Forms: 5–7 **stannarie**, 6 **stanery, steinery, steynery**, 7 **stannery**, (**stanary**), 7– **stannary**. See also STANNIER. [ad. med.L. *stannāria* (1198 in G. R. Lewis *Stannaries* App. 233), f. L. *stann-um* tin: see -ARY. An AF. form *estei(g)nerie* (whence some of the forms above) occurs 1328 in *Rolls of Parlt.* II. 19.]

1. ***the Stannaries***: The districts comprising the tin mines and smelting works of Cornwall and Devon formerly under the jurisdiction of the Stannary courts; also, the customs and privileges attached to the mines.

1455 *Rolls of Parlt.* V. 293/2 Delyvered to the said Prynce ..the said Duchie of Cornewayll, and all..Cunage of Tynne, Stannaries, Marlsettes, [etc.]. **1485** *Ibid.* VI. 382/1 The Office of Wardeyn of the Stannaries in the said Countie of Devynshire. *c* **1630** RISDON *Surv. Devon* §91 (1810) 88 Steward of the Stanneries. **1670** PETTUS *Fodinæ Reg.* 12 The King for advancement of the Stannaries in Cornwall frees the Tinners from all pleas of the Natives touching the Court. **1776** ADAM SMITH *W.N.* I. I. xi. 180 Vice-Warden of the Stannaries. **1869** BLACKMORE *Lorna D.* xx, He came as captain of a gang from one of the Cornish stannaries. **1908** J. MARTINEAU *Life H. Pelham* x. 330 In February 1862, the office of Lord Warden of the Stannaries was conferred upon him.

b. *sing.* (*a*) *collect.* = pl.; (*b*) *rarely*, an individual district in the Stannaries.

1467–8 *Rolls of Parlt.* V. 610 Th' office of Baillif of oure Stannarie of Penwith and Kerye. **1514** FITZHERB. *Justice of Peace* (1538) 140 b, Yf any person be indyted..in hys tyn workes goodes or cattels by any minister of the court of Stanery. **1564** T. HARDING *Answ. Jewel's Challenge* xiii. 139 They may not vnfittely be likened to a Judge of the Stemerie [? *read* Steinerie] at Lidford in Deuonshire, who [etc.]. **1611** SPEED *Hist. Gt. Brit.* IX. xvi. §95 The title of Duke of Cornwall..is reputed vnto the Kings eldest sonne..he.. hauing his royalties in the Stannarie, Wrackes at Sea, Customes &c.

2. Tin; tin-ware; a locality in a mart or fair appropriated to the sale of tin-ware. *Obs.* exc. *Hist.*

1668 WILKINS *Real. Char.* II. iii. 65 Tinn, Stannery. **1864** *Times* 16 Sept. 8/4 The fair formed a kind of temporary city ..consisting of whole streets appropriate to the sale of particular commodities, and distinguished..as the drapery, the pottery, the spicery, the stannary, &c. *Ibid.*, In the reign of Henry VI. this celebrated mart appeared to be on the decline, the lands appropriated to those who brought articles of stannary from Cornwall not being fully occupied.

3. *attrib.*, as ***stannary artillery***, ***castle***, ***cause***, ***charter***, ***district***, ***law***, ***man***, ***parliament***, ***town***, ***troop***, ***weight***.

1812 *Examiner* 7 Sept. 570/1 Lieut. Moyle, of the Royal *Stannary Artillery. **1810** *Risdon's Surv. Devon* 405 The *Stannary Castle, containing the room where the courts were held,..is at Lydford. **1602** CAREW *Cornwall* I. 18 The Gayle for *stannery causes is kept at Lostwithiel. **1856** J. ALLEN *Hist. Liskeard* iii. 32 Many of the old *stannary charters were destroyed in the revolutionary war. **1758** BORLASE *Nat. Hist. Cornw.* 193 The four principal towns of the *stannary districts. **1899** BARING-GOULD *Bk. West* II. v. 59 The Danish freebooters..carried fire and sword through the stannary districts of Devon. **1633** T. ADAMS *Exp. 2 Pet.* ii. 3. 470 That old scandall of the *Stanneries Law; that hanged a man in the forenoone, and sate in judgement on him in the afternoone. **1796** MORSE *Amer. Geog.* II. 103 Those tin-works are under..the stannary laws. **1610** HOLLAND *Camden's Brit.* (1637) 196 The *Stannarie men of Cornwall and Denshire. **1877** *Encycl. Brit.* VI. 426 1 The last Cornish *stannary parliament was held at Truro in 1752. **1705** *Addr. Lostwithiel* in *Lond. Gaz.* No. 4087/1 We are Members of Your Majesty's Ancient and Chiefest *Stannary Town. **1690** *Lond. Gaz.* No. 2579/3 The Lord Lansdowne..came hither on the 25th with the *Stanary Troop. **1703** *Ibid.* No. 3951/1 Her Majesty is..pleased to offer..to take Sixteen hundred Tuns of Tinn at the Price of Three Pounds Ten Shillings per Cent. *Stannary Weight.

b. ***stannary courts***: The courts of law for the administration of justice in the Stannaries.

Stannaria curia occurs 1337 in a charter of Edward III: see Du Cange. By the Stannaries Courts Abolition Act of 1896 the jurisdiction of these courts was transferred to the County Court.

1602 CAREW *Cornwall* I. 18 They are termed Stannery Courts, of the latine word *Stannum*, in English Tynne. **1641** (*title*) An Act against diverse Incroachments and Oppressions in the Stannarie Courts. **1768** BLACKSTONE *Comm.* III. vi. 80 The stannary courts in Devonshire and Cornwall for the administration of justice among the tinners therein, are also courts of record. **1877** *Encycl. Brit.* VI. 426/1 By ancient charters, the tinners of Cornwall were exempt from all other jurisdiction than that of the stannary courts, except in cases affecting land, life, and limb.

stannate (ˈstæneɪt). *Chem.* [f. STANN-UM + -ATE[4].] A salt of stannic acid.

1839 URE *Dict. Arts* 608 By the second [agent], stannate of potash forms. **1841** BRANDE *Chem.* (ed. 5) 781 The compounds of peroxide of tin with bases have sometimes been called stannates.

stannator (stæˈneɪtə(r)). [ad. med.L. *stannātor* (*stagnātor* 1198 in G. R. Lewis *Stannaries* App. 233) irreg. f. late L. *stannum* (*stagnum*) tin.] A member of the Stannary convocation or parliament.

1686 in *Cal. Treas. Papers* (1868) I. 19 Precepts to the four Cornish Mayors, for meeting at Lostwithiel,..to choose their respective stannators. **1703** *Lond. Gaz.* No. 3951/1 Her Majesty having been pleased to grant Her Commission to the Rt. Hon. the Lord Granville, Lord Warden of the Stannaries, to hold a Convocation, or Parliament of Stannators, according to ancient Custom. **1877** *Encycl. Brit.* VI. 426/1 Twenty-four stannators were returned for the whole of Cornwall. Their meeting was termed a parliament, and when they assembled they chose a speaker.

stannel: see STANIEL.

stanners (ˈstænəz), *sb. pl. Sc.* Also 6 **stannirs**, 8 **staners**. [App. a derivative of OE. *stán* STONE *sb.*; cf. ONorthumb. *stǽner* (inflected *stǽnere*, *stǽnero*), rendering *petrosa* stony places, Matt. xiii. 5, 20 and Mark iv. 5, 16.] 'The small stones and gravel on the margin of a river or lake, or forming a sea-beach; applied also to those within the channel of a river, which are occasionally dry' (Jam.).

1508 DUNBAR *Gold. Targe* 36 The bruke vas full of bremys, The stanneris clere as stern in frosty nycht. **1513** DOUGLAS *Æneis* XII. Prol. 60 The new cullour alychtnyng all the landis, Forgane thir stannyris schane the beryall strandis. **1549** *Compl. Scot.* vi. (1873) 39 Than vndir ane hingand heuch, i herd mony hurlis of stannirs & stanes that tumlit doune vitht the land rusche. *a* **1670** SPALDING *Troub. Chas. I* (Spalding Club) I. 174 Dugar.. carryes over his men to the Staners whilk is in the midst of the watter of Spey. **1802** JAMIESON *Water-Kelpie* xx, Yestreen the water was in spate, The stanners aw war cur'd. **1805** *State, Leslie of Powis*, etc. 94 (Jam.) At low water the net comes ashore on the stanners, and at high water on the grass. **1867** G. W. DONALD *Poems* (1879) 3/1 Sae lang's the tide shall ebb or jaw Upo' the stanners.

stannery ('stænərɪ), *a.* Now *Sc.* Forms: (5 stanry), 6 *Sc.* stanerie, (stendirrie), 8- **stannery**. [f. *stanner*, STANNERS + -Y.] = STONY *a.*

c **1440** *Pallad. on Husb.* III. 708 A stanry pere [L. *lapidosi generis pyra*] is seyd to chaunge his mete In esy lond ygraffed yf he be. **1501** DOUGLAS *Pal. Hon.* II. xlii, The beriall stremis rinnand ouir stanerie greis Made sober noyis. **1579** *Reg. Privy Council Scot.* III. 129 The ground.. is sandy and stanerie. **1795** *Statist. Acc. Scot.* XV. 316 One meets with boggy, stannery, croft, and clay ground, almost in every farm. **1805** *State, Leslie of Powis* etc. 109 (Jam.) The said dike.. lies upon a stannery and sandy bed.

fig. **1563** WINZET *Wks.* II. 54 Ar thai ony found.. of sa stanerie stubburnes, quha suld not submit thame selfis to sa gret plentuousnes of thir heuinlie wordis. **1596** DALRYMPLE tr. *Leslie's Hist. Scot.* I. 261 Perceiueng in how dangerous ane state now the Realme was, how Scopulous, stendirrie, or stanie, was the stedd, quhairon thay than stude.

stannic ('stænɪk), *a. Chem.* [f. STANN-UM + -IC.] Of a compound: Containing tin as a quadrivalent element. Cf. STANNOUS.

1790 KERR tr. *Lavoisier's Elem. Chem.* xvii. 166 Stannic [acid]. **1849** D. CAMPBELL *Inorg. Chem.* 240 Binoxide of tin .. is known, also, as the stannic oxide, and generally as the peroxide. **1868**: see STANNO-, STANNOSO-. **1873** WATTS *Fownes' Chem.* (ed. 11) 593 Stannic Ethide.. is produced by the action of zinc ethide on stannic chloride.

stannicle, dial. var. STANSTICKLE.

† '**stannide.** *Chem. Obs.* [f. STANN-UM + -IDE.] A primary combination of an element with tin.

1862 MILLER *Elem. Chem., Org.* (ed. 2) 221 Stannide of sodium.

† '**stannier.** *Obs.* [ad. (? through some AF. form) of med.L. *stannāria* STANNARY.] = STANNARY; only in the title ***Warden of the Stanniers***.

1610 HOLLAND *Camden's Brit.* (1637) 185 A warden called L. Warden of the Stanniers [*margin*, L. Warden of the Stannary]. **1611** SPEED *Theat. Gt. Brit.* xi. (1614) 21/1 The Common-weale of Tinne-workes from one body was divided into foure, and a Lord Warden of the Stanniers appointed their Judge.

stanniferous (stæ'nɪfərəs), *a.* [f. late L. *stann-um* tin + -FEROUS.] Producing tin. ¶ Also incorrectly applied to designate enamels or glazes containing tin, and pottery treated with these.

1823 J. J. CONYBEARE *Geol. Devon & Cornw.* in *Ann. Philos.* N.S. V. 185, I venture to propose the following division of the principal rock masses.. 1. Granite... 2. Metalliferous, or, more strictly, cupriferous and stanniferous slate... 3. Slate [etc.]. **1855** J. R. LEIFCHILD *Cornwall* 25 The St. Austell mining district is principally stanniferous. **1859** GULLICK & TIMBS *Painting* 132 An opaque stanniferous enamel was known to the Arabs of Spain. **1875** FORTNUM *Maiolica* i. 4 Stanniferous or tin-glazed wares.

'**stannified,** *ppl. a. rare*$^{-1}$. [f. late L. *stannum* tin + -(I)FY + -ED[1].] Impregnated with tin.

1855 J. R. LEIFCHILD *Cornwall* 38 The term stannified granite was applied to it—which the plain reader may call tinnified granite.

stannine ('stænɪn). *Min.* [f. STANN-UM + -INE.] Native sulphide of tin.

1843 CHAPMAN *Pract. Min.* 146 Stannine. **1871** tr. *Hartwig's Subterr. World* xxvii. 335 There are only two ores of tin—the peroxide, or tinstone, and the pyrites, or stannine.

stannite ('stænaɪt). [f. STANN-UM + -ITE.]

1. *Chem.* A salt of stannous acid.

1851 WATTS tr. *Gmelin's Hist. Chem.* V. 95 Stannite of Potash. *Ibid.* 98 Stannite of Soda. **1853** URE *Dict. Arts* II. 711 Stannates and stannites of alkalis are valuable mordants in calico printing.

2. *Min.* Sulphide of tin, copper, iron and zinc, found in steel-grey masses. [ad. F. *stannine* (F. S. Beudant *Traité élémentaire de Minéralogie* (ed. 2, 1832) II. 416).]

1868 J. D. DANA *Syst. Mineral.* (ed. 5) 68 Stannite... Probably tetragonal, and hemihedral like chalcopyrite. **1896** CHESTER *Dict. Min.* **1900** L. FLETCHER in *Brit. Mus. Return* 156 Complex twinned crystals of the very rarely crystallised mineral Stannite.. have been investigated. **1976** [see STANNOIDITE].

stanno- (stænəʊ), before a vowel also **stann-**, used as combining form of late L. *stann-um* tin, in *Chem.*, as **stannamyl**, a compound produced by the action of amylic iodide on an alloy of sodium and tin; **stannethyl**, a compound of ethyl and tin; **stannofluoride** (see quot. 1868).

1857 WATTS tr. *Gmelin's Hist. Chem.* XI. 131 *Stannamyl. $C^{10}H^{11}Sn$. [**1852** E. FRANKLAND in *Phil. Trans.* CXLII. 422 *Stanethylium.] **1854** *Fowne's Chem.* (ed. 5) 446 Stannethyl. A series of substances have been lately described by Frankland and by Loewig, which contain the elements of ethyl, associated with the metal tin. **1880** CLEMINSHAW *Wurtz' Atom. Theory* 271 Stannethyl has just as much claim to be considered as a radical as stannous iodide. **1868** *Fownes' Chem.* (ed. 10) 446 Stannic flouride, Sn F_4.. unites with other metallic flourides, forming crystalline compounds called *stannofluorides or fluostannates.

stannoidite ('stænɔɪdaɪt). *Min.* [f. STANN(ITE + -OID + -ITE[1].] A sulphide of copper, tin, iron, and zinc, Cu_8 $(Fe,Zn)_3Sn_2S_{12}$, found as yellow-brown orthorhombic crystals having a metallic lustre, superficially resembling those of stannite.

1969 A. KATO in *Bull. Nat. Sci. Mus. Japan* XII. 165 (*heading*) Stannoidite,.. a new stannite-like mineral from the Konjo Mine, Okayama Prefecture, Japan. **1975** *Econ. Geol.* LXX. 834 Mawsonite and stannoidite characteristically occur with bornite and chalcopyrite in xeno-thermal ore deposits in Japan. **1976** *Nature* 10 June 482/2 The Japanese ores, however, contain tin minerals other than cassiterite (for instance, stannite, stannoidite, and mawsonite).

† **stannolite** ('stænəʊlaɪt). *Min. Obs.* [f. late L. *stann-um* tin + -LITE.] = CASSITERITE.

1843 CHAPMAN *Pract. Min.* 111 Cassiterite... Stannolite.

stannoso- (stæ'nəʊsəʊ), *Chem.*, used as combining form of mod.L. *stannōs-us* STANNOUS.

1868 *Fownes' Chem.* (ed. 10) 445 Tin.. forms two well-defined classes of compounds, namely, the stannous compounds, in which it is bivalent,.. and the stannic compounds, in which it is quadrivalent..; also a few compounds called stannoso-stannic compounds, of intermediate composition. **1873** WATTS *Fownes' Chem.* (ed. 11) 444 Stannous Chloride unites with the chlorides of the alkali-metals forming crystallisable double salts,.. called Stannosochlorides.

stannotype ('stænəʊtaɪp). [f. late L. *stann-um* tin + Gr. τύπος impression, print, TYPE.] A simplified form of the Woodbury process of photo-mechanical engraving in which a mould obtained from a positive instead of a negative is coated with tinfoil. Also *attrib.*

1883 *T. F. Hardwich's Photogr. Chem.* (ed. 9) 360 The Stannotype.. is the invention of Mr. Woodbury. **1891** WOODBURY *Encycl. Photogr.* 666 The object of the stannotype process was to do away with all this costly machinery [*i.e.* the hydraulic press of the Woodbury process].

stannous ('stænəs), *a. Chem.* [f. STANN-UM + -OUS.] Of a compound: Containing tin as a bivalent element. Cf. STANNIC *a.*

1849 D. CAMPBELL *Inorg. Chem.* 239 This oxide [hydrated protoxide of tin] is in many works distinguished as the stannous oxide. **1868** *Fownes' Chem.* (ed. 10) 445 The dichloride, or Stannous chloride, Sn Cl_2. **1868** Stannous compound: see STANNOSO-.

‖**stannum** ('stænəm). *Chem. rare* in Eng. context. [mod.L. use of late L. *stannum* tin, in earlier use an alloy of silver and lead; app. an altered form of the synonymous *stāgnum*, whence the Rom. forms, It. *stagno*, Sp. *estaño*, Pg. *estanho*, Pr. *estanh-s*, OF. *estain* (mod.F. *étain*), tin.] The chemical Latin name for tin. (Hence the symbol Sn.)

1783 WITHERING tr. *Bergman's Outl. Min.* 98 Stannum or Tin. **1812** SIR H. DAVY *Chem. Philos.* 379 Tin or Stannum.

stanol ('steɪnɒl). *Chem.* [f. ST(ER)OL about -AN(E, after *cholestanol*, *ergostanol*, etc. (the respective saturated derivatives of CHOLESTEROL, ERGOSTEROL, etc.).] Any fully saturated sterol.

1949 L. F. & M. FIESER *Nat. Products related to Phenanthrene* (ed. 3) iii. 93 Members of the sterol series that are fully saturated, like cholestanol, are conveniently described as stanols; those that contain one double bond are stenols. **1958** C. W. SHOPPEE *Chem. Steroids* ii. 78 The test is positive with stenols, negative with stanols. **1972** *Nature* 21 July 149/1 Although stanols have been shown to occur in *Sphagnum* moss and in a pollen mixture they are extremely rare in the rest of the contemporary plant kingdom. **1979** *Experientia* XXXV. 186/1 Saturated sterols (stanols) comprise 50–75% of the total sterols of this insect.

stanpic(c)he, obs. ff. STONE-*pitch*.

stansel, obs. form of STENCIL *v.*

stanssour, variant of STANCHER.[2] *Sc. Obs.*

stanstickle ('stænstɪk(ə)l). *dial.* Also stannicle. [Alteration of BANSTICKLE, due to alliterative association with STONE *sb.*] = STICKLEBACK.

a **1300** NECKAM *De Utensilibus* in Wright *Voc.* 98 *Gamarus, pinosche*, stanstikel. *c* **1620** *New Metamorphosis* (MS.) (Nares), To stansticles he did them all transforme, A fishe noe bigger then a prety worme. *a* **1825** FORBY *Voc. E. Anglia.* **1893** in Cozens-Hardy *Broad Norf.* 35 The stickleback is a stannicle.

stant, variant of STENT.

stantient, -ion, var. ff. STANCHION.

Stanton ('stæntən). [Name of Sir Thomas Edward *Stanton* (1865–1931), English engineer.] ***Stanton number***, a dimensionless measure of heat transfer used in forced convection studies, equivalent to the ratio of the Nusselt number to the product of the Reynolds and Prandtl numbers, viz. $h/c_p\rho u$, where h is the heat transfer coefficient of the fluid, c_p is its heat capacity at constant pressure, ρ is its density, and u is its velocity.

Defined as the reciprocal of the Prandtl number in some dictionaries, but no textual evidence for this has been found.

1942 W. H. MCADAMS *Heat Transmission* (ed. 2) iv. 95 Stanton number. **1966** W. M. KAYS *Convective Heat & Mass Transfer* xi. 248 The decrease in Stanton number noted here occurs in what still seems to be essentially a turbulent boundary layer. **1978** *Internat. Jrnl. Heat & Mass Transfer* XXI. 282/2 From the results for the Nusselt number, the dimensionless heat transfer, expressed as the Stanton number, can be determined: $St = Nu/Re\ Pr$.

† '**stanty.** *Obs.* Forms: 5 stantyf, 7 stant(e)y. [Late ME. *stantyf*, ad. med.L. *stantīvus* standing erect, f. *stant-em* pr. pple. of *stāre* to stand: see -IVE.] ***stanty hedge***: a stake-and-rice fence.

1446 *Crt. Roll Gt. Waltham Manor, Essex* 9 June, Thomas Gossyb appropriavit de regia via.. unam peciam.. super quam posuit unum stantyfhegge ad nocumentum. **1659** GAUDEN *Tears Ch.* IV. vii. 438 A setting up a stanty hedge, instead of a good quick-set or a brick-wall, for the fense of Christs vineyard. **1664** SPELMAN *Gloss.* s.v. *Assis*, Quoad sepem stantariam, nos.. *A stantey hedge*, vocamus, quod non e surculis vivis, sed e perticis & viminibus componitur, absque fossa.

stanza ('stænzə). Forms: α. 6–7 **stanze**, (6 **stands**); β. 6–7 **stanzo**; γ. 6- **stanza**. See also STANCE *sb.*[2] 4. [a. It. *stanza* standing, stopping place, room, stanza, corresp. to Sp. Pg. *estancia* dwelling, room, Pr. *estansa* position, OF. *estance* (mod.F. *étance*) stay, support:—popular L. **stantia*, f. L. *stant-em* pr. pple. of *stāre* to stand. The It. word was adapted in Fr. as *stance*, whence STANCE *sb.*[2]; also in Ger. as *stanze*.]

1. *Versification.* A group of lines of verse (usually not less than four), arranged according to a definite scheme which regulates the number of lines, the metre, and (in rhymed poetry) the sequence of rhymes; normally forming a division of a song or poem consisting of a series of such groups constructed according to the same scheme. Also, any of the particular types of structure according to which stanzas are framed.

α. **1588** SHAKS. *L.L.L.* IV. ii. 107 Let me heare a staffe, a stanze, a verse, *Lege domine.* **1596** LODGE *Margarite of Amer.* K 4, The first stands is the complaint, the second the counsel. **1605** CHAPMAN etc. *Eastward Hoe* v. H 3 b, This Stanze now following alludes to the storie of Mannington.

β. **1589** GREENE *Menaphon To Gentlm. Stud.* (Arb.) 15 Euerie stanzo they pen after dinner, is full poynted with a stabbe. **1600** SHAKS. *A.Y.L.* II. v. 18 Come, more, another stanzo: Cal you'em stanzo's? **1609** HEYWOOD *Brit. Troy* v. iii. 108 From Calliope hie Stanzoes flow. **1611** COTGR., *Sestine*, a Sestine, or stanzo of six verses. **1660** F. BROOKE tr. *Le Blanc's Trav.* 144 The musick changes to a very solemn base.. with certain stanzoes sung in praise of their deceased Ancestors.

γ. [**1589** PUTTENHAM *Eng. Poesie* II. ii. (Arb.) 79 Staffe in our vulgare Poesie I know not why it should be so called... The Italian called it *Stanza*, as if we should say a resting place.] **1595** E. C. *Emaricdulfe* Sonn. xxxix. in *Lamport Garl.* (Roxb.), Thy name, thy honour, and loues puritie, With Stanzas, Layes and Hymnes Ile stellifie. **1603** DRAYTON *Bar. Wars* To Rdr., Therefore.. I chose Ariostos stanza of all other the most complete and best proportioned, consisting of eight, sixe interwouen, and a couplet in base. **1612** *Benvenuto's Passenger* II. i. 417 In euery corner they recite the pleasant Stanzaes of the gentle *Furioso*. **1621** T. WILLIAMSON tr. *Goulart's Wise Vieillard* 89, I will heereunto add further this Stanza of verses of the same quill. **1674** PLAYFORD *Skill Mus.* I. ii. 35 The double Bars are set to divide the several Strains or Stanzaes of the Songs and Lessons. **1693** DRYDEN *Juvenal* (1697) Ded. p. lxxxii, The *Secchia Rapita* is an Italian Poem.. 'Tis written in the Stanza of Eight. **1706** CONGREVE *Pindarique Ode* Disc. A 1 b, The Poet having made choice of a certain Number of Verses to constitute his Strophé, or first Stanza, was oblig'd to observe the same in his Antistrophé, or second Stanza. **1741** POPE *Ess. Crit.* 423 And each exalted stanza teems with thought! **1817** SHELLEY *Rev. Islam* Pref., I have adopted the stanza of Spenser (a measure inexpressibly beautiful). **1842** TENNYSON *Talking Oak* 135 She came.. And sang to me the whole Of those three stanzas that you made About my 'giant bole'. **1856** EMERSON *Eng. Traits, Lit.* Wks. (Bohn) II. 115 A stanza of the song of nature the Oxonian has no ear for.

2. In Italy, an apartment, chamber, room; *spec.* in pl. ‖*stanze* ('stantse), applied to certain rooms in the Vatican.

1648 J. RAYMOND *Voy. Italy* 34 At the right hand of this gallerie are severall stanzas full of Curiosities. **1670** G. H. *Hist. Cardinals* I. III. 79 The Agents of Serene Princes.. have half a Stanza [in the Vatican]. **1823** LADY MORGAN *Salvator Rosa* (1824) I. iii. 90 A certain sympathy.. between the brothers-in-law frequently carried Salvator to the *stanza* or work-room of Francesco. *Ibid.* 95 Having.. studied or worked in the galleries, churches, or *stanze* of the eminent masters in Rome. **1878** MRS. JOS. BUTLER *Catharine of Siena*

vii. 200 It forms the subject of a fresco in one of the stanze of the Vatican.

†**3.** (See quot.) *Obs.*

1675 COVEL in *Early Voy. Levant* (Hakluyt Soc.) 219 Upon every stanza [*i.e.* 'branch' of an acrobat's pole] he would set a cup of water; then raysing it, he would dance with all these in like manner without spilling one drop.

4. *Sport.* A half or other session of a game.

1945 S. J. BAKER *Austral. Lang.* xvii. 299 In football news we find..*first* or *second stanza*, the first or second half of a game. **1974** *News & Reporter* (Chester, S. Carolina) 22 Apr. 10-A/5 Comfort Control warmed their bats up in the final three stanzas to gain the victory. **1981** *National Times* (Austral.) 25–31 Jan. 23/3 There is also a growing habit of describing the next half or quarter of a football match as a 'stanza'—perhaps because it is so poetic.

5. *Comb.*, as **stanza-form**, the form of a stanza (sense 1); arrangement in stanzas.

1927 E. V. GORDON *Introd. Old Norse* 293 There were variants of the normal stanza-forms. **1957** E. T. CONE in N. Frye *Sound & Poetry* 1. 6 Zelter, keeping close to the unusual stanza-form..produces a top-heavy musical period. **1976** *Classical Q.* XXVI. 16 The catalectic effect in English or German is a function of the particular stanza-form. **1978** *Early Music* Oct. 629/1 A large number of 'wasted pages'..are taken up with setting out the poetic texts in stanza form.

Hence **'stanzaed** *a.* (in parasynthetic derivatives), having (a specified number of) stanzas; **'stanza** *v.* (*nonce-wd.*) *trans.*, to write stanzas upon.

1755 J. SHEBBEARE *Lydia* (1769) II. 78 He..hit off an epigram or a three stanzaed song with some reputation. **1796** LAMB *Final Mem.* i. 199 (To Coleridge) Dyer stanza'd him in one of the papers t'other day. **1868** *Chronicle* No. 43. 67/1 The nine-stanzaed hymn.

stanzaic (stæn'zeɪɪk), *a.* [f. STANZA *sb.* + -IC.] Of, belonging to or of the nature of poetry composed in the form of stanzas.

1816 *Q. Rev.* XIV. 403 Thus the Lady of the Lake has stanzaic introductions. **1869** *Athenæum* 24 July 108/2 Even those odes which are manifestly stanzaic are not printed in stanzas. **1891** E. GOSSE *Gossip in Libr.* xx. 261 The stanzaic form in which the two pieces are written is identical.

So **stan'zaical** *a.* Hence **stan'zaically** *adv.*

1883 HALL CAINE in *Academy* 1 Sept. 138 The printer has been instructed to make a stanzaical division for the eye. **1883** *Athenæum* 17 Nov. 628/2 Work produced in any of the more stringent metres or stanzaical structures. **1908** *Q. Rev.* Apr. 363 The 'long measure' is not even treated stanzaically, but presents to the eye a series of dull-looking columns of verse.

stanzic, *a. rare.* = STANZAIC.

1869 E. WADHAM *Eng. Versif.* xii. 92 The Lay. In one stanzic measure the rhymes are allowed to assume every possible variation of arrangement.

stap (stæp), *sb. Sc.* and *north.* Forms: 6 **steppe**, 9 **staup, stawp, step, stap.** [Of obscure origin.] A stave of a tub or cask. Chiefly in fig. phrases: see quots.

1587 *Sc. Acts Jas. VI* (1814) III. 522/1 þat þe steppis of þe said firlot be of þe auld proportione, in thiknes of bayth the burdis, ane insche and ane half. **1808** JAMIESON, *Stap, Steppe*, a stave. *I'll tak a stap out of your coag*, S. Prov., I'll put you on shorter allowance. **1821** *Blackw. Mag.* VIII. 432 But stoups are needed, tubs, and pails, and knaps, For all the old are 'gisand' into staps. **1825** JAMIESON s.v., *To fa' a' staps*, to become extremely debilitated, *q*[*uasi*] to fall to pieces, like a vessel made of staves. **1825** BROCKETT *N.C. Gloss.*, *Stap*, the stave of a tub. **1829** HOGG *Sheph. Cal.* I. vi. 170 Else I should take a staup out o' their punch cogs the night. **1846** *Brockett's N.C. Gloss.* (ed. 3) s.v., 'To take a stap out of your bicker' means to humble you. **1891** H. JOHNSTON *Kilmallie* I. 96 It behoved me and the likes o' me to keep a calm sough, if we didna want a step taen oot o' our cog.

stap, affected pronunciation of STOP *v.*, in the phrase ***stap my vitals***, used as an exclamation of surprise, anger, etc., or as an asseveration.

Prob. the first quot. is the source of the phrase. Lord Foppington, the speaker, pronounces *a* for *o* throughout. Cf. GAD, EGAD, and the pronunciations 'Laard', 'plaat' (for Lord, plot) attributed to Titus Oates.

1696 VANBRUGH *Relapse* I. iii, Well, 'tis Ten Thousand Pawnd well given—stap my Vitals. **1716–20** *Lett. Mist's Jrnl.* (1722) I. 50 Thou art one of the most comical Dogs, stap my Vitals! that ever set Pen to Paper. **1730** FIELDING *Author's Farce* III. 34 My Life went out in a Hiss—Stap my Breath. *Ibid.* 46 And so all my Puns, and Quibbles, and Conundrums are quite forgotten, stap my Vitals. **1839** THACKERAY *Catherine* i, Stap my vitals, my dear, but there was a lady..who had a hoop as big as a tent. **1901** *Graphic* Christmas No. 24/2 'Tis a trick of theirs. Stap me, we shall have 'em yet.

stap, Sc. form of STOP *sb.* and *v.*

stape (steɪp). *s.w. dial.* [Altered form of STAPLE.] = STAPLE *sb.*[1]

1512 *Stratton* (Cornw.) *Churchw. Acc.* in *Archæologia* XLVI. 201 Paid to wylliam Jule for a stape to the stepyll dore iij d. **1629–30** *Hartland Church Acc.* in *Hartland* (Devon) *Gloss.* (1891) s.v., Pd Charles Bagilholl for 2 stapes of iron to make fast y^e^ leads ag^t^ the Tower iii d. **1891** *Hartland* (Devon) *Gloss.*, *Stape*, a staple. (Always.)

stapedectomy (stæpɪ'dɛktəmɪ). *Surg.* [f. mod.L. *staped-* STAPES + -ECTOMY.] Excision of the stapes.

1894 J. C. GORDON in *Amer. Annals of Deaf* Oct. 265 While stapedectomy may be rarely resorted to.

stapedial (stə'piːdɪəl), *a. Anat.* [f. mod.L. *stapedi-us* (see STAPEDIUS) + -AL[1].] Pertaining to the stapes.

1875 HUXLEY in *Encycl. Brit.* I. 757/1 The posterior.. branch of the seventh nerve passes back..above the stapedial ligament. **1884** COUES *N. Amer. Birds* 154 This stapedial cartilage. *Ibid.* 186 An extremely delicate rod, stepped into the fenestra ovalis by its foot..and bearing..its hammer-like..stapedial elements.

stapediform (stə'pɛdɪfɔːm), *a. Anat.* [f. *staped-* STAPES + -(I)FORM.] Stirrup-shaped.

1856 W. CLARK *Van der Hoeven's Zool.* I. 200 Two stapediform maxillæ, with teeth transversely incumbent.

‖**stapedius** (stə'piːdɪəs). *Anat.* [mod.L., elliptical use of *stapedius* adj. (sc. *musculus*), f. *staped-* STAPES.] (More fully ***stapedius muscle.***) The small muscle attached to the neck of the stapes.

1788 *Encycl. Brit.* (ed. 3) I. 764 Little muscle, the stapedeus [sic]. **1808** *Med. Jrnl.* XIX. 398 The muscle usually called Stapideus [sic]. **1844** HOBLYN *Dict. Terms Med.* (ed. 2), Stapedius. **1847** TODD & BOWMAN *Phys. Anat.* II. 106 The facial nerve gives off the following branches... 2. A twig to the stapedius muscle. **1899** *Allbutt's Syst. Med.* VIII. 41 Spasm of the stapedius.

stapelia (stə'piːlɪə). *Bot.* [mod.L. (Linnæus 1737) f. name of Jan Bode van *Stapel*, a Dutch botanist (died 1636): see -IA.] A South African genus of apocynaceous plants, remarkable for the fetid smell of the flowers, whence one species (*S. hirsuta*) is called Carrion-flower. Also, a plant of this genus.

1785 MARTYN *Rousseau's Bot.* xvi. (1794) 217 *Stapelia*.. has a very large wheel-shaped corolla. **1834** *Penny Cycl.* II. 440/2 The leafless succulent stapelias. **1860** *All Year Round* No. 63. 295 The carrion-scented flowers of stapelias.

Comb. **1842** *Florist's Jrnl.* (1846) III. 76 *Maxillaria stapeliflora*, stapelia-flowered.

Hence **sta'peliad**, a plant belonging to one of a group of closely related genera including *Stapelia* and others formerly considered part of it.

1933 WHITE & SLOANE *Stapelieae* 1 The corolla of Stapeliads is usually fleshy. **1966** E. PALMER *Plains of Camdeboo* xvi. 261 Among the great plant travellers are the Stapeliads of the family Asclepiadaceæ. **1977** W. P. U. JACKSON *Wild Flowers Table Mt.* 48/2 *Orbea variegata*..is the only Stapeliad in the Cape Peninsula.

‖**stapes** ('steɪpiːz). [mod.L. use of med.L. *stapēs* (*staped-*) stirrup. Cf. It. *stapede* (sense 1).

In the 16th c. *stapes* was regarded as the standard Latin word for stirrup (for which there was no word in classical Latin, as stirrups were not used by the ancients); it is in Estienne, Cooper, and two Latin-Ger. dictionaries cited by Diefenbach. Du Cange has one example of *stapes*, and one each of *stapedium* (1314), *stapeda*, and *strapes*. The word may perh. be an alteration of med.L. *stapha*, *staffa* (= It. *staffa* stirrup), after L. *stāre* to stand and *ped-em*, *pēs* foot.]

1. The innermost of the three ossicles in the tympanum of the ear in mammals; named from its stirrup-like shape.

The Sicilian anatomist J. Ph. Ingrassia (died 1580), in his posthumous notes to Galen *De Ossibus* (1603), claims the discovery of this bone, and says that he called it *stapha*, but others, more solicitous about Latinity, preferred *stapes* or *strapeda*. In 1564 Eustachius (*De Auditus Organis*, Opusc. Anat. 153) asserts that he made the discovery before Ingrassia did, and states that some call the ossicle *staffa* or *stapes*.

1670 *Phil. Trans.* V. 2060 The Stapes of the Ear. **1705** *Ibid.* XXV. 1983 The Sides or Branches of the Stapes are furrowed on the inside. **1877** BURNETT *Ear* 75 The smallest bone in the body..is the stapes or stirrup.

2. *Surg.* (See quot.)

1875 KNIGHT *Dict. Mech.*, *Stapes*, a bandage for the foot, making a figure-of-8 round the ankle.

staph (stæf). Colloq. abbrev. of mod.L. *Staphylococcus*, name of a genus of pathogenic bacteria.

1933 PARTRIDGE *Slang To-day & Yesterday* III. iii. 190 *Staph*, staphylococcus, one of the commonest types of bacteria. **1956** A. HUXLEY *Let.* 13 Aug. (1969) 804 The average mortality after surgery was twenty-nine per cent, with peaks, during epidemics of streps and staphs, of over fifty per cent. **1978** J. IRVING *World according to Garp* ii. 47 He later went through Harvard Business School, a staph infection, and a divorce.

staphisacre, -ager, -agria: see STAVESACRE.

staphisagriated (stæfɪ'seɪgrɪeɪtɪd), *ppl. a. Pharm.* [f. mod.L. *staphisagria* (see next) + -ATE[3] + -ED[1].] Impregnated with the juice of stavesacre seeds: said of lard used in an ointment for destroying animal parasites.

1898 *Rev. Brit. Pharm.* 39.

staphisagrine (stæfɪ'seɪgraɪn). *Chem.* Also -in. [f. mod.L. *staphisagria* STAVESACRE + -INE. (Substituted for the earlier STAPHISAÏNE, which is abnormally formed.)] One of the alkaloids found in the seeds of stavesacre (*Delphinium Staphisagria*).

1868 WATTS *Dict. Chem.* V. 406.

staphisaïne (stæ'fɪseɪaɪn). *Chem.* Also -aïn. [ad. F. *staphisain* (Couerbe 1833, *Ann. de Chimie et de Physique* LII. 363), f. *staphisaigre* STAVESACRE: see -INE.] = STAPHISAGRINE.

1842 *Penny Cycl.* XXII. 445/1 Staphisaïn. **1876** HARLEY *Mat. Med.* (ed. 6) 769 The seeds also contain a second alkaloid called staphisaïne.

‖**staphyle** ('stæfɪliː). *Anat.* [mod.L., a. Gr. σταφυλή bunch of grapes, also the uvula when swollen by disease.] A rare synonym for UVULA.

1808 BARCLAY *Muscular Motions* 506 When the mouth is opened, it is seen extending from right to left in the form of an arch, with the staphyle or uvula suspended in the middle. **1890** G. M. GOULD *New Med. Dict.*

staphyline ('stæfɪlaɪn), *a.* [ad. late Gr. σταφύλινος, pertaining to a bunch of grapes, f. σταφυλή: see prec.]

1. *Min.* Having the form of a bunch of grapes; = BOTRYOIDAL *a.*

1820 MOHS *Char. Min.* 46 Staphyline-Malachite. **1837** DANA *Syst. Min.* 238 Uncleavable Staphyline-Malachite.

2. *Anat.* 'Pertaining to the uvula or the whole palate'. (*Syd. Soc. Lex.*)

1859 MAYNE *Expos. Lex.* s.v. *Staphylinus.*

staphylinid (stæfɪ'lɪnɪd), *sb.* and *a. Ent.* [ad. mod.L. *Staphylīnidæ*, f. *Staphylīn-us* a. Gr. σταφυλῖνος a kind of insect (Aristotle), prob. f. σταφυλή bunch of grapes: see -ID.] **a.** *sb.* An insect belonging to the *Staphylinidæ* or rove-beetles, a coleopterous order of which the typical genus is *Staphylinus.* **b.** *adj.* Belonging to the *Staphylinidæ*. Also **staphyli'nideous** *a.*

1848 HARDY in *Proc. Berw. Nat. Club* II. No. 6. 336 A Staphylinideous insect. **1891** *Century Dict.*, *Staphylinid.* **1925** A. D. IMMS *Gen. Textbk. Entomol.* III. 481 Staphylinid larvæ are typically campodeiform. **1965** B. E. FREEMAN tr. *Vandel's Biospeleology* xiii. 208 The staphylinids found in caves belong to three ecological categories. **1978** *Nature* 16 Mar. 209/1 Among the many other examples are various species of staphylinid beetles that march with army ants.

‖**staphylococcus** (ˌstæfɪləʊ'kɒkəs). *Bacteriology.* Pl. -cocci (-'kɒksaɪ). [mod.L., f. Gr. σταφυλή bunch of grapes + κόκκος berry.] A form of pus-producing bacteria composed of cocci grouped in irregular masses.

1887 GARNSEY & BALFOUR *De Bary's Lect. Bacteria* 168 In the others the cells separate from the rows after division, and form aggregations which Ogston has compared with a bunch of grapes, and he has expressed the resemblance by the name Staphylococcus. **1895** *Pop. Sci. Monthly* Feb. 513 Organisms, such as..staphylococci. **1897** *Trans. Amer. Pediatric Soc.* IX. 191 A bacteriological examination.. showed the staphylococcus in pure culture.

attrib. **1897** *Allbutt's Syst. Med.* II. 575 It is usually distinguishable from staphylococcus pus. **1901** OSLER *Princ. & Pract. Med.* (ed. 4) 162 The common streptococcus and staphylococcus infection is as a rule first local.

Hence **staphylococcal** (-'kɒkəl), **-coccic** (-'kɒksɪk) *adjs.*, pertaining to or produced by staphylococcus.

1900 *Brit. Med. Jrnl.* 5 May 72 Injections of staphylococcal toxins. **1904** *Ibid.* 10 Sept. 582 The pus from staphylococcic or tuberculous abscesses.

staphylolysin (stæfɪ'lɒlɪsɪn). *Bacteriology.* [f. *staphylo-* (in STAPHYLOCOCCUS) + LYSIN.] The hæmolysin of staphylococcus toxin.

1904 *Brit. Med. Jrnl.* 10 Sept. 571 Walbum and I have examined the neutralization curves of several other bodies and their antibodies: the rennet.., the vibriolysin, the staphylolysin, and the streptolysin.

‖**staphyloma** (stæfɪ'ləʊmə). *Path.* In 6 anglicized **staphylome.** [mod.L., a. Gr. σταφύλωμα, 'a disease in the eye inside the cornea' (L. & Sc.), f. σταφυλή bunch of grapes.] Protrusion of the cornea or sclera, resulting from inflammation.

1597 A. M. tr. *Guillemeau's Fr. Chirurg.* C ij b/1 The portraycture of an Eye, wherin is presentede a Staphylome. **1676** J. COOKE *Marrow Chirurg.* 713 In its progress it receives several Names... If the protuberance be..great, 'tis called Staphyloma, because like a Grape-Stone. **1797** *Phil. Trans.* LXXXVII. 22 In the substance of the cornea, round the basis of the staphyloma, I have frequently seen vessels carrying red blood. **1878** T. BRYANT *Pract. Surg.* I. 320 Staphyloma may be met with in the ciliary region. **1879** P. SMITH *Glaucoma* 19 The very frequent association of glaucomatous tension with corneal staphyloma.

Hence **staphy'lomatous** *a.*, of the nature of or pertaining to staphyloma.

1753 *Chambers' Cycl.* Suppl., s.v. *Mylon*, Tumours of the staphylomatous kind. **1875** H. WALTON *Dis. Eye* 354 Staphylomatous enlargement of the sclerotica.

staphyloplasty (ˌstæfɪləʊ'plæstɪ). [f. Gr. σταφυλή (see STAPHYLE) + -PLASTY.] (See quot. 1890.) So **ˌstaphylo'plastic** *a.*

1846 [see STAPHYLORRHAPHY]. **1855** DUNGLISON *Med. Lex.*, *Staphyloplastic*, an epithet applied to the operation for replacing the soft palate, when it has been lost. **1890** G. M. GOULD *New Med. Dict.*, *Staphyloplasty*, a plastic operation for the closure of cleft palate.

staphylorrhaphy (stæfɪˈlɒrəfɪ). *Surg.* Also -o(r)raphy. [ad. assumed Gr. *σταφυλορραφία, f. σταφυλή (see STAPHYLE) + ῥαφή sewing, suture.] The surgical closure of a cleft palate.

1835 *Lancet* 31 Jan. 648/1 In the operation of staphyloraphy,.. if care be not taken to leave the ends of the sutures rather long..the knots will readily untie. **1846** BRITTAN tr. *Malgaigne's Man. Oper. Surg.* 363 When there is only a narrow fissure in the velum, we have staphyloraphy, properly so called; when this cleft, very much separated, simulates a loss of substance, staphyloplasty. **1855** DUNGLISON *Med. Lex., Staphylorraphy*..consists in paring the edges of the cleft; passing ligatures through them, and bringing them together. **1878** L. P. MEREDITH *Teeth* 242 The operation of staphyloraphy. **1898** ROSE & CARLESS *Man. Surg.* 722 In dealing with clefts of the soft palate alone, a modification of the above operation may be performed, called staphylorraphy.

attrib. **1895** *Arnold & Sons' Catal. Surg. Instrum.* 232 Suture Needles for Staphyloraphy operations.

Hence **staphyloˈrrhaphic** *a.*, pertaining to or used in staphylorrhaphy.

1875 KNIGHT *Dict. Mech.*, Staphyloraphic Instruments.

ˈstaphylotome. *rare*⁻⁰. [ad. Gr. σταφυλοτόμον knife for cutting the uvula, f. σταφυλή (see STAPHYLE) + -τόμο- that cuts.] See quot.

The explanation in Dunglison *Med. Lex.* 1876, 'A knife adapted to the operation for staphyloma', appears to be unfounded.

1875 KNIGHT *Dict. Mech.*, *Staphylotome*, a knife for operating upon the uvula or palate.

staphyˈlotomy. *Surg.* *rare*⁻⁰. [ad. mod.L. *staphylotomia*, as if a. Gr. *σταφυλοτομία f. σταφυλή STAPHYLE + -τομία cutting.]

1. Amputation of the uvula.

1855 DUNGLISON *Med. Lex.* **1890** G. M. GOULD *New Med. Dict.*

¶**2.** 'The removal of a staphyloma by cutting' (Dorland *Med. Dict.* 1913).

staphylotoxin (ˌstæfɪləʊˈtɒksɪn). *Bacteriology.* [f. *staphylo-* (in STAPHYLOCOCCUS) + TOXIN.] A toxin occurring in cultures of staphylococci.

1902 *Brit. Med. Jrnl.* 12 Apr. 920 M. Neisser, and Wechsberg [have studied] staphylotoxin.

staple (ˈsteɪp(ə)l), *sb.*¹ Forms: 1, 4 **stapol**, 1–5 **stapul, stapel,** 3 **stapil, stapple,** 5 **stapill, stapyl(l,** 6 **stapylle,** 5–6 **stapulle,** 6 **stappill,** 4, 7 **stable,** 7 *Sc.* **staiple,** 4– **staple.** [OE. *stapol* str. masc. (a wk. form *stapole* is doubtful) corresponds to OFris. *stapul, stapel* stem or visible part of a tooth, also block for executions (WFris. *steapel,* NFris. *stabel* heap), OS. *stapal, stapel,* candle, small tub (MLG. *stapel* pillar, post, candle, block for executions, platform, stocks for shipbuilding, heap; hence MHG. and mod.G. *stapel* stake, beam, stocks for shipbuilding, and prob. Sw. *stapel,* Da. *stabel* in the same senses), MDu. *stapel* foundation, support, stem of a plant, heap (mod.Du. *stapel* leg of a chair, stocks, heap), OHG. *staffal* (gl. 'basis'; the fem. *staffala,* mod.G. *staffel* step, rung of a ladder, is prob. a separate formation), ON. *stǫpull* steeple, tower, once pillar:—OTeut. **stapulo-z.*

The various applications of the word in the Teut. langs. seem traceable to a general sense of 'something supporting'; the root **stap-* is prob. identical with that of STEP *sb.*¹ and *v.*

In addition to the sense 1 below, OE. seems to have had those of foundation (gl. *batis,* perh. error for *basis*) and steps or raised platform in front of an outer door (see Beowulf 926 and the gloss 'stapel, *patronus*', prob. for *petronus*: cf. F. *perron*), but these did not survive into ME. Sense 2 is not found in continental Teut., and its evolution is not easy to explain; the identity of the word is not certain.]

1. †**a.** A post, pillar, column (of wood, stone, metal). *Obs.*

Beowulf 2718 þa stanboȝan stapulum fæste. *c* **950** *Lindisf. Gosp.* Matt. xxi. 12 Staplas [glosses *columbas* mistaken for *columnas*]. *a* **1000** *Andreas* 1062 Oð ðæt he ȝemette.. standan stræte neah stapul ærenne. *a* **1000** *Gloss.* in *Wr.-Wülcker* 205/5 *Cione,* stapole. *a* **1300** *Cursor M.* 8288 Vnder þis tre.. A stapul was o marbul grai. **13..** *Seuyn Sages* (W.) 201 Leues thai tok, sextene, Of iuy.. Under ech stapel of his bed..four thai hid. **1387** TREVISA *Higden* (Rolls) V. 273 But Edol, duke of Gloucestre, cauȝte a stable, [L. *arrepto palo*: v.rr. pale, stake] and defended hym manliche.

†**b.** Used for STEEPLE. *Obs. rare*⁻¹.

Perh. an error; but cf. ON. *stǫpull.*

1470–1 in *Oxf. Stud. Soc. & Legal Hist.* (1914) IV. 225 In Bylddyng of..the Chyrche Stapill in the Town of Latton.

c. *Mining.* A pillar of coal left as a temporary support for a superincumbent mass.

1839 URE *Dict. Arts* etc. 979 As a further precaution staples of coal, about 10 inches square, are left.

2. a. A short rod or bar of iron or other metal bent into the form of a U or of three sides of a rectangle, and pointed at the ends, to be driven into a post, plank, wall, or other surface, in order to serve as a hold for a hasp, hook, or bolt to secure a door or box, or as an attachment for a rope or the like. Also applied to other contrivances of similar shape or function, as the box or case into which the bolt of a lock is shot.

For *hasp and staple* (Law), see HASP *sb.* 1 d.

1295 *MS. Acc. Exch. K.R.* 5/8 m. 10 Et .ij. s. ix. d. in stipendiis Hugonis Fabri pro stapples et hespes fabricandis. *c* **1340** *Nominale* (Skeat) 467 *Et graps et appenduz* Stapul and haspe. *Ibid.* 471 *Sere veroil et cerrure* Barre slot and stapul. **1344–5** *MS. Acc. Exch. K.R.* 492/24 Facientis unum haspe et unum stapel pro hostio stabuli. *c* **1380** *Sir Ferumb.* 2181 þe henges boþe barste & þe stapel þar-with out sprong. *a* **1400–50** *Wars Alex.* 1081 Of ilka bild,..barred was þe ȝatis, Stoken stifly with-out with stapilis & cheynes. *c* **1440** *Promp. Parv.* 472/2 Stapylle of a schyttynge (*v.r.* stapul), *stapellum.* **1485** *Nottingham Rec.* III. 231 A newe staple of iren to þe same yeate. **1495** *Naval Acc. Hen. VII* (1896) 150 Staples & clampes of yron ffor a carte. **1541** *Act 33 Hen. VIII,* c. 12 §3 The Sergeant..shall bringe to the saide place of execucion a blocke withe a betill a staple and cordes to bynde the saide hande vpon the blocke. *a* **1552** LELAND *Itin.* VII. 56 Men alyve have sene Rynges and Staples yn the Walles as yt had bene Stayes or Holdes for Shyppes. **1560** *Ludlow Churchw. Acc.* (Camden) 96 A stapulle and a haspe for the..chest. **1606** SHAKS. *Tr. & Cr.* Prol. 17 With massie Staples And corresponsiue and fulfilling Bolts. **1626** CAPT. SMITH *Accid. Yng. Seamen* 12 Grummets, and staples for all yeards. **1643** LIGHTFOOT *Glean. Exod.* 41 Staples of Gold were fastned in every planke. **1660** BOYLE *New Exp. Phys.-Mech.* Proem 14 A small Iron nut,..which is fastened by two staples..to the under side of the board. **1677** MOXON *Mech. Exerc.* ii. 28 You must with square Staples, just fit to contain the Bolt with an easie play, fasten these staples, by rivetting them with the Bolt within them..to the Main-plate. **1688** HOLME *Armoury* III. 462/1 The Crown Stable, that to which the Clapper [of the Bell] is hung. *Ibid.* IV. v. (Roxb.) 309/2 A demy Ape..holding a stable by the tanges with both his hands, Sable. **1691** T. H[ALE] *Acc. New Invent.* 46 Her Rudder-Irons Stirrups, Staples, etc. **1725** POPE *Odyss.* XXI. 48 The bolt..Forsakes the staple as she pulls the ring. **1746** WATSON in *Phil. Trans.* XLIV. 714 Cork'd, with a Staple of small Wire running through each Cork into the Water. **1810** SHELLEY *Zastrozzi* i. Pr. Wks. (1888) I. 5 His limbs..were fixed by immense staples to the flinty floor. *c* **1850** *Rudim. Navig.* (Weale) 152 *Staples,* crooked fastenings made of copper, from 6 to 12 inches long, with a jagged hook at each end. **1863** GEO. ELIOT *Romola* I. xvi, Fastening the old bridle..to an iron staple in the wall. **1884** *Manch. Exam.* 6 Oct. 5/4 The deceased was drawing the staples by which the ladders were held. **1898** M. HEWLETT *Forest Lovers* xxx, A girdle made of bright steel in which was a staple.

fig. **1809–10** COLERIDGE *Friend* (ed. 3) III. 118 The uneducated..talker overlooks all mental relations... Hence the nearer the..incidents in time and place, the more distant, disjointed [etc.]..will they appear in his narrative.. and this from the want of a staple or starting-post in the narrator himself. **1827** HARE *Guesses* Ser. II. (1873) 324 A philosopher..must be a staple firmly and deeply fixt—in the adamantine walls of Truth.

†**b.** A clasp or fastening for armour. *Obs.* [Cf. STAPLED *ppl. a.* quot. 13..]

a **1420** *Aunturs of Arthur* 591 (Douce MS.) Stiþe stapeles [*v.r.* stapuls] of stele þey strike done seiȝte. **1535** STEWART *Cron. Scot.* (1858) I. 382 Thair freikis fell with mony forcie flap, Quhill ruvis raif and steill stapillis out lap.

c. A snout-ring.

1688 HOLME *Armoury* II. 181/2 Rings, or Staples to put into their [swine's] Noses to keep them from Rooting. **1875** [see *snout-ring,* SNOUT *sb.*¹ 7].

d. A piece of thin wire (characteristically shaped in the form of three sides of a rectangle), driven through papers, etc., and clinched to bind them.

1895 *Army & Navy Co-op. Soc. Price List* 540/2 Patent Staple Presses (For Fastening Papers &c.)..Wire Staples. Size ¼ inch, per 1000 0/6. **1898** G. B. SHAW *Let.* 4 Mar. (1972) II. 11 Come along & bring some long staples (⅝" will do) with you. **1907** *Yesterday's Shopping* (1969) 349/1 The Self-Feeding Automatic Staple Press. Holds 25 staples which travel automatically. Staples are in strips of 25, as shown in illustration. **1926–7** *Army & Navy Stores Catal.* 369/3 The 'Longdon' Combined Stapler..only one staple can pass at a time. **1940** *Brit. Stationer Ann.* 2 (Advt.), Ace Stapling Machines..Staples: ¼ in...7/2 per box of 5,000. **1967** *New Yorker* 15 July 26/3, I..dropped into a stationery store..looking for a mechanism of sorts with which to run a staple into my thumb. **1981** H. ENGEL *Ransom Game* (1982) iii. 21, I wondered how could I possibly discuss anything with a man who called staples Bostitch pins.

3. a. The upright body of a hand printing press.

1833 J. HOLLAND *Manuf. Metal* II. 208 A is the upright body of the press, called the staple.

b. *Mus.* A metal tube on to which the double reed of a wind instrument is tied.

1880 GROVE *Dict. Mus.* II. 486/2 It [*sc.* the oboe] is usually made in three pieces, a top, bottom, and bell joints, to which is added a short metal tube, the staple, on which the reed.. is attached by means of silk. **1908** *Ibid.* (ed. 2) IV. 42/2 The bassoon reed is placed directly upon the 'crook' of the instrument, but the oboe reed is built up upon a small tube or 'staple'. **1953** E. ROTHWELL *Oboe Technique* 49 The part of the cane from the tip downwards which has been scraped and thinned with the knife after tying the cane on the staple, is known as the 'scrape' (or sometimes as the 'lay'). **1976** D. MUNROW *Instr. Middle Ages & Renaissance* i. 8/4 The [shawm] player presses his lips against a metal disc at the base of the staple, taking the entire reed inside his mouth. *Ibid.* vi. 39/3 (*caption*) Set of modern rackett reeds mounted on their staples.

4. *attrib.* and *Comb.* (sense 2), as ***staple-driver, -fastener, -pin, -punch***; ***staple-headed, -shaped*** adjs.; ***staple-fashion, -wise*** advs.: also †**staple-bar,** ? a bar to which a staple is fixed; **staple gun,** a hand-held device for driving staples home; hence (hyphened) as *v. trans.*; **staple isinglass,** isinglass in staple-shaped pieces; **staple-knee** *Naut.* (see quot.); †**staple press** = STAPLER²; **staple-ring** = sense 2 c; **staple-vice,** a bench-vice.

1339–40 *Ely Sacrist Rolls* (1907) II. 96 Item solut. Johanni Amyot pro *stapolbarris fabricandis de iiijˣˣ peciis ferri Dni. pro pec. iijd. £1. os. 3d. **1399** *Ms. Acc. Exch. K.R.* 473/11 m. 3 Pro .viij. Soudletles .ij Stapulbarres pro fenestris eiusdem noue domus. **1884** KNIGHT *Dict. Mech.* Suppl., **Staple-driver,* an instrument for driving the staples in window-blinds. **1895** *Montgomery Ward Catal.* Spring & Summer 116/3 Staple Driver, for binding books, papers, pamphlets, etc...staple is placed in holder, driven to place. **1869** E. J. REED *Shipbuilding* ii. 42 The angle-irons on the upper edge are forged *staple fashion. **1884** KNIGHT *Dict. Mech.* Suppl., **Staple Fastener,* a spring punch for driving and clinching a staple against an anvil block beneath. **1960** G. LEWIS *Handbk. Crafts* 350 A *staple gun can be useful, but is not essential. **1975** *Harpers & Queen* May 128/3 Looks like some faggot decorator went nuts in here with a staple gun. **1977** J. FRASER *Hearts Ease* ix. 107 The heavy squad..had staple-gunned plastic sheets to cover the hole. **1819** FOSBROKE *Hist. Glouc.* 119 Massy round Columns, with *staple-headed arches. **1879** SIMMONDS *Commerc. Products Sea* 243 Isinglass..drawn out in a serpentine manner into the form of a heart, horseshoe, or lyre (long and short *staple) between three pegs. **1883** R. HALDANE *Workshop Rec.* Ser. II. 355/1 The isinglass comes into commerce under the names of..'staple', 'book', 'pipe',.. and other designations, according to its form. **1846** A. YOUNG *Naut. Dict.* 295 *Standard-knees*... These..are also called *Staple-knees, or Staple-lodging knees. **1835** URE *Philos. Manuf.* 145 It has a *staple pin at its inner end. **1895**, **1907** *Staple press [see sense 2 d above]. **1875** KNIGHT *Dict. Mech.* s.v., The *staple-punch has two points, and is used to prick blind-rods and slats for the reception of the staples which connect them. **1707** *Lond. Gaz.* No. 4377/4 A black Mare..,wring'd with a *staple Ring. **1874** THEARLE *Naval Archit.* §258. 275 An intercostal *staple-shaped angle-iron. **1881** YOUNG *Ev. Man his own Mech.* §280 The best black *staple vices are sold, according to weight, at 7d per lb. *Mod. Tool-maker's Price-list,* Vices. Staple Leg Vices. **1596** MASCALL *Bk. Cattle, Hogs* 275 Make it sharpe at both ends, and bow it *staple-wise with two corners nigh an inch wide.

staple (ˈsteɪp(ə)l), *sb.*² Also 5–6 **stapull, stapyll,** 6 **stapul,** 5–6 **stapill,** 8 **stapple.** Also 5 **estapell, estaple.** [a. OF. *estaple* fem. emporium, mart (mod.F. *étape* halting-place):—med.L. *stapula,* also *staplus,* ad. MLG. *stapol, stapel*: see STAPLE *sb.*¹

The (M)LG., (M)Du. *stapel,* and hence the G. and Sw. *stapel,* Da. *stabel,* have the sense 'emporium, mart', in addition to the senses mentioned under the preceding sb. It is, however, uncertain whether this sense was developed in MLG., or whether it originated in OF., and was thence adopted into MLG. The precise relation of this sense to the other senses of the Teut. word is also uncertain. It has been usually held to have been developed from the sense 'heap, pile'. This is not impossible; but, on the other hand, in the Frankish laws *regis stapulus* meant the place where the king or his representative administered judgement; the original notion may have been that of 'raised platform'. The transition would be easy from the Frankish sense of *regis stapulus* to that of the 'king's staple' for the collection of duties on merchandise.]

1. a. A town or place, appointed by royal authority, in which was a body of merchants having the exclusive right of purchase of certain classes of goods destined for export; also, the body of merchants so privileged. Now only *Hist.*

The English word has not been found earlier than 1423; the AF. *estaple* and the Anglo-L. *stapula,* however, occur in statutes and official documents from the reign of Edw. II onwards, and these contain evidence that the institution of the staple was of older date. Each staple had a mayor and constables, appointed by the king, and in early times distinct from the municipal authorities, though latterly the mayor of some boroughs was *ex officio* mayor of the staple. At various times the chief staple was oversea, usually at Bruges or Calais; from about 1390 to 1558 it was at Calais, which is often called 'The Staple'. There were also staples in many important towns of England, Wales, and Ireland, the list of which varied greatly at different periods. ***Statute of the Staple***: the ordinance 27 Edw. III (1353), which established staples in various English towns, and at Carmarthen, Dublin, Waterford, Cork, and Drogheda, and contained regulations for their form of government and the conduct of their business. (For *statute of the staple* in another application, see STATUTE STAPLE.)

1423 *Rolls of Parlt.* IV. 249/1 They may bey Wolle..atte the Stapull of Calais. **1429** *Ibid.* IV. 359/2 And yat ye Maire of ye Staple for the tyme beyng, have power..to make due serch. **1450** *Ibid.* V. 189/1 Nygh to oure Staple there [*sc.* the Palace at Westminster]. *c* **1450** *Brut* ccxxix. 305 In þe same ȝere þe Kyng reuoked..þe staple of wolles out of Flaundres into Engelond. **1473** *Paston Lett.* III. 97 To the Mayre, Lieutenant, and felaship of the staple. **1480** *Cely Papers* (Camden) 33 George Cely merchand of the estapell at Calleys. **1481** *Ibid.* 63 Merchant of the estaple. ?**1482** *Ibid.* 130 Bryn[g]yng my ij oblygacyons of the Stapyll to Cales. **1525** BERNERS *Froiss.* II. xx. 18 The kyng..gaue hym an hundred marke sterlynge, yerely to be payed out of the Staple of the wolles in London. **1538** STARKEY *England* II. i. 173 The caryage out of wolle to the stapul ys a grete hurte to the pepul of Englond. *a* **1548** HALL *Chron., Hen. VI* 131 Ther [in Ghent] was the staple of woolles, tynne, leade and other merchaundise. **1568** GRAFTON *Chron.* II. 169 In the xix yere of this king, the staple of woolles was kept at Sandwiche, which afterwarde was kept at Caleys as long as it was Englishe, but now it is holden at Bridges in Flaunders. **1577** HOLINSHED *Hist. Eng.* II. 519/2 He had borrowed a great summe of monie of the Marchants of the Staple. *Ibid.* 1771/1 Edmonde Hall one of the Conestables of the Staple. **1599** *N.C. Wills* (Surtees) II. 185 The worshipfull companie of marchauntes of the staple of Englande. **1610** HOLLAND *Camden's Brit.* (1637) 540 The Staple, as they tearme it, that is, the Mart, of Wooll, Leather, Lead, etc. **1615** BRATHWAIT *Strappado* (1878) 196 You ayme at no Monopoly, No priuate staples, but desire to sell,.. Your Ware in publique places. **1617** MORYSON *Itin.* I. 50 This City is the Staple of all Merchandise, excepting Rhenish wine, for which by old priviledge Dorte is the Staple. **1621** ELSING *Debates Ho. Lords* (Camden) 110 *Hodie 2 vice lecta Billa* for the merchantes of the Staple. **1650** Jer. Taylor *Serm. for Yr.* 165 By weight and measure of the staple. **1875** Stubbs *Const. Hist.* II. xvi. 411 The system of the staple was..a combination of the principle of the guild and of the royal privilege of establishing fairs and markets. **1890** Gross *Gild Merch.* I. 144 It is evident that the staple was primarily a fiscal organ of the crown, facilitating the collection of the royal customs. It also ensured the quality of the goods exported by providing a machinery for viewing and marking them.

b. †(*a*) A town or country which is the principal market or entrepôt for some particular class of merchandise (*obs.*). (*b*) A commercial centre, a chief place of business in a country or district. (Now somewhat *arch.*)

1436 *Libel Eng. Policy* in *Pol. Poems* (Rolls) II. 160 Saffron, quiksilver..Is into Flaundres shypped fulle craftylye, Unto Bruges, as to here staple fayre. *Ibid.* 162 The lytelle londe of Flaundres is But a staple to other londes.. And alle that groweth in Flaundres..May not a moneth ffynde hem mete of brede. *c* **1511** *1st Eng. Bk. Amer.* (Arb.) Introd. p. xxix/1 [Punctuation corrected.] There groeth much peper, and the properest stapell therof, that kingdom of Colen, is xxiiij myles from there. **1612** in *Eng. Hist. Rev.* (1914) Apr. 251 In time this Kingdom will become the staple of those easterne commodities, from whence they may be dispersed into France, Germaine, [etc.] **1630** *R. Johnson's Kingd. & Commw.* 224 They enjoy also Malaca, which..is..the staple of the Traffique..of the East Ocean. *c* **1645** Howell *Lett.* iv. i. (1655) I. 167 The Spaniards notwithstanding they are the Masters of the Staple of Jewels, stood astonish'd at the beuty of these. **1650** Fuller *Pisgah* iii. i. 315 God intended not Jerusalem for a staple of trade but for a Royal Exchange of Religion. **1723** *Pres. State Russia* I. 117 Novgorod..was comprehended in the League of the Hans-Towns, and was the Staple of the inferior Towns. **1737** G. Smith *Cur. Relat.* I. i. 81 The rest is sold to the People or Merchants at Ucienjen, this being the greatest Staple for Porcelain in all China. **1776** Gibbon *Decl. & F.* xiii. I. 380 That the city of Nisibis might be established for the place of mutual exchange, or, as we should formerly have termed it, for the staple of trade, between the two empires. **1836** Thirlwall *Greece* II. xii. 202 The position..was well adapted for a great staple of commerce between the Thracian tribes..and the Greek cities. **1850** W. Irving *Mahomet* iii. (1853) 10 Its seaports.. were the staples of an opulent and widely extended Commerce. **1865** Carlyle *Fredk. Gt.* vii. v. II. 293 Old Nürnberg..Trading Staple of the German world in old days.

c. *fig.*

1594 Lyly *Mother Bombie* ii. v, A tauerne is the Randeuous, the Exchange, the staple for good fellowes. **1621** Donne *Serm.* xv. (1640) 152 There is a Trade driven, a Staple established betweene Heaven and earth;..Thither have we sent our flesh, and hither hath he sent his Spirit. **1626** B. Jonson *Staple of N.* i. ii, *Tho.* O Sir, a staple of newes! Or the New Staple, which you please. *P. Iv.* What's that? *Fas.* An..Office set vp... *P. Iv.* For what? *Tho.* To enter all the Newes, Sir, o' the time. *c* **1645** Howell *Lett.* i. v. (1655) I. 9 This City of Amsterdam, though she be a great Staple of News, yet I can impart none unto you at this time. **1647** Ward *Simple Cobler* 9 That Country which hath been the Staple of Truth to all Christendome. **1699** T. C[ockman] tr. *Tully's Offices* (1706) 236 Since you are gone as 'twere to a Staple and Mart of good Literature. *a* **1718** Prior *Engl. Padlock* 62 A Staple of Romance and Lies. **1849** Macaulay *Hist. Eng.* iii. I. 366 Whitehall naturally became the chief staple of news.

†**d.** A 'factory' or authorized place of trade for merchants of a foreign country. *Obs.*

1617 Moryson *Itin.* i. 61 Meluin is a little and faire City, ..and at this time grew rich by the English Merchants having their staple in the same. **1634** W. Haig *Let.* in J. Russell *Haigs* (1881) 468 Mr. John Forbes, a minister..of the English that are about their staple in that place. **1668** Sir W. Temple *Lett.* i. (1699) 8 Attempts of removing the Scotch Staple from Teweet to Dort. **1698** Fryer *Acc. E. India & P.* 25 The English Factory..being under the Tutelage of the Natives, as also are the Portugals and Flemmings (who each have here their Staples). **1861** M. Pattison *Ess.* (1889) I. 41 This original factory and staple of the German merchants, vulgarly called 'The Steelyard' (*Stahlhof*) still stands on the banks of the Thames. **1892** Cochran-Patrick *Mediæval Scot.* vii. 133 The establishment of the Scottish staple at Middleburgh in 1347 was followed by more cordial relations between Scotland and England.

†**2. a.** A dêpot or storehouse for provisions, war material, etc. *Obs.*

1523 *St. Papers Hen. VIII*, VI. 171 The Kinges Grace hathe prepared the power of the north parties to a great nomber, whiche..may..either invade or defende, as they shal be commaunded, and vitailles ordred in staples for that purpose. **1552** Edw. VI *Jrnl.* Lit. Rem. (Roxb.) II. 421 Duke Maurice toke..50 peces of ordinaunce, which he conveyed to Auspurg, for that toune he fortefied and made it his staple of provision. **1688** Holme *Armoury* iii. xix. (Roxb.) 202/1 There must be choise made of some place, Citty or Towne, to make the Staple of Ammunition.

b. A stock, quantity of provisions or material stored up. *Obs.*

1549 Thomas *Hist. Italie* 75 Hauyng suche a staple of tymber (whiche in the water within Th'arsenale hath lien a seasonyng, some .20. yere, some .40. some an .100. and some I wote not how longe). **1586** Hooker *Holinshed's Chron. Irel.* 165/2 That a storehouse be prouided alwais in the towne for a staple of vittels to be kept there at all times. **1603** R. Johnson *Kingd. & Commw.* 118 In their Arsenal they continually maintaine two hundred gallies, and such a staple of timber, that for every day in the yeare, they are able to builde a newe galley.

3. [Short for *staple-ware*, etc. (see 4), and elliptical use of staple *a.*] A staple commodity.

†**a.** An article of merchandise the trade in which is subjected to the regulations of the Staple. *Obs.*

1690 Child *Disc. Trade* (1698) 161 Except such species only as his Majesty and the Parliament shall think fit to make Staples, as suppose Colchester Bayes, Perpetuanoes, Cheanyes,..to be allowed the honour of a publick Seal, by which to be bought and sold here, and beyond seas, as if it were upon the publick faith of England.

b. A principal industrial product of a country, town, or district; *occas.* the commodity principally dealt in by a person or class of persons. Also, the principal or basic food on which a community lives.

1616 Capt. Smith *Descr. New Eng.* 10 The maine Staple ..is fish. **1640** Howell *Dodona's Grove* 7 Corne, Wine, and Salt, her three rich staples doe so abound in her. **1733** P. Lindsay *Interest Scot.* 143 Linen is out Staple, &c. but it has been wofully neglected. **1789** *Ann. Reg., Brit. & For. Hist.* 167 Mr. Pitt introduced it [the subject] by observing that tobacco was now to be considered as the smuggler's staple. **1806** *Gazetteer Scot.* (ed. 2) 323 The manufacture of cotton ..has long been the staple of this county. **1834** Ht. Martineau *Demerara* iii. 42 Sugar is our staple and sugar we must grow. **1840** Hood *Up Rhine* 163 Villages..built by some speculating timber-merchant, who found his staple quite a drug in the market. **1843** Prescott *Mexico* vii. ii. (1864) 424 The sugar-cane..formed a more desirable staple for the colony than its precious metals. **1883** *Century Mag.* Oct. 818/1 Barley is always a staple, and averages twenty bushels to the acre. **1883** *Stubbs' Merc. Circular* 8 Nov. 982/2 Grey shirtings show a falling-off..and..it is to be feared that the trade in this once flourishing staple will continue to decrease. **1912** *Times* 19 Dec. 19/2 Good returns should also be obtained from the cultivation of maize (which was the staple of Rhodesia). **1970** C. Furtado in I. L. Horowitz *Masses in Lat. Amer.* ii. 33 In the case of exported staples, there occasionally appeared competitive productive areas which were better situated geographically or which had access to protected markets. **1971** *Sci. Amer.* Sept. 113/1 Except for the staples and tea, tobacco and candy, there is no strong desire for non-Eskimo foods. *Ibid.* Oct. 21/1 It is only recently that human populations have come to depend heavily on a single cultivated plant staple for food. **1977** *N.Y. Rev. Bks.* 23 June 16/1 Much of this inflation can be attributed to a rise in the world price of oil and food staples.

c. *transf.* and *fig.* The thing chiefly 'dealt in'; the principal object of employment, thought, or discourse. Sometimes (? with mixture of staple *sb.*[3], sense 2) used for: The chief component element, the 'substance', 'bulk'.

1826 Syd. Smith *Wks.* (1859) II. 74/1 An unconquerable aversion to..that train of meteorological questions and answers which forms the great staple of polite English conversation. **1844** Dickens *Mart. Chuz.* xvi, The poultry ..may perhaps be considered to have formed the staple of the entertainment. **1849** W. Irving *Goldsmith* xviii. 205 Conversation was the great staple there. **1857** Buckle *Civiliz.* I. x. 616 Events of this sort, though neglected by ordinary historians, are among the staff and staple of history. **1865** Tylor *Early Hist. Man.* iv. 63 It may be said that action,..forms the staple of that part of the gesture-language. **1907** C. Hill-Tout *Brit. N. Amer., Far West* v. 100 These staples were everywhere supplemented by the flesh of other animals which varied with the habitat.

4. *attrib.* (Cf. staple *a.*) 'of or pertaining to the Staple' (sense 1), as ***staple-court***, ***-register***, ***-roll***, ***seal***; 'that is a staple' (senses 1, 1 b), as ***staple place***, ***port***, ***town***; †**staple-good** = *staple-ware*; †**staple-hand** *Sc.* (sense obscure: ***mercats of stapillhand*** = 'markets of staple-ware'); **staple-house**, a warehouse where commodities chargeable with export duties were stored; †**staple-merchandise** = *staple-ware*; †**staple rate**, ? a price fixed by the Staple, a monopoly price; in quot. *fig.*; †**staple-traffic**, an organized branch of trade (*fig.*); †**staple-ware(s**, such goods as were the monopoly of the Staple (in England wool, woolfells, leather, lead, and tin).

1433 in *10th Rep. Hist. MSS. Comm* App. v. 296 In defraude of the courte..of Watirforde, or of the *staple courte of the Kynge. **1574** *Ibid.* 335 The Sergeants may arrest anny challendged in the Staple-court. **1455** in *Charters* etc. *Edin.* (1871) 80 Ony merchandice that is *staple gude. **1482** *Extracts Burgh Rec. Edin.* (1869) I. 46 That na maner of stapill gudis of strangearis remane.. langare in Leyth..than it may be caritt and brocht to the toun. **1593** *Reg. Mag. Sig. Scot.* 797/2 *Cum libertate*..de lie paking, peilling, loising or laidning be sey of stapill guddis or wairis. **1811** P. Kelly *Univ. Cambist* II. 310 *Staple goods*, such as are sold at a staple. The term is however mostly aplied to goods that are not of a perishable nature, as wool, lead, &c. **1364** in *Reg. Episc. Brechinensis* (Bannatyne Club) II. 380 Ane Inchibitioun for halding off mercats of *Stapillhand at Brechine and Fordoune. **1876** F. Martin *Hist. Lloyds* i. 2 In their large *staple-house on the Thames ..were stored the collections of raw produce..which England sent away to foreign countries. **1721** Strype *Eccl. Mem.* II. 259 Paying no more..than for so much Goods of *Staple Merchandize as they shall..transport unto the Staple of Calais. **1650** Fuller *Pisgah* iii. iii. 322 Indeed Tyre,..was the *staple place which furnished it with fish. **1838** *Murray's Handbk. N. Germ.* 247 Coblenz..forms the natural staple place of the Rhine and Mosel wines. **1727** A. Hamilton *New Acc. E. Ind.* I. vi. 53 It [Aden] continued many Years after the *Stapple Port for the Red Sea Commerce. **1730** A. Gordon *Maffei's Amphith.* 378 The Staple-Port for Merchandize of the East. *a* **1628** F. Grevil *Cælica* lxxviii, So States proue sicke, where toyes beare *Staple-rates. **1483–4** *Cely Papers* (Camden) 147 Thys entercourse ys entryd in the *stappull Regester of old tyme. **1890** Gross *Gild Merch.* I. 144 The *Staple Rolls in the Record Office. **1482** *Cely Papers* (Camden) 114 Ther shall be made vj oblijgaschons under the *stapell seal. **1617** *Nottingham Rec.* IV. 355 The matter of makinge this towne a *staple towne. **1756** Nugent tr. *Montesquieu's Spirit Laws* xxi. xi. (1758) II. 51 The barbarians obliged the Romans to establish staple-towns. **1908** *Athenæum* 14 Nov. 610/3 The Statute of the Staple, 1353,..established a number of Staple towns where the wools, &c., were to be weighed and sealed, the duty paid [etc.]. *a* **1618** Sylvester *All's not gold* xii. Wks. (Grosart) II. 254 That Ignatian-Latian Colledge, Where..They study State and Stratagems; Making a *Staple-Trafick of it..To murther Kings, and mangle Realms. **1432** *Rolls of Parlt.* IV. 417/2 Grete substaunce of marchaundises, nat *Staple ware, but other. **1587** *Reg. Privy Council Scot.* IV. 237 To transporte thair guidis and staple wairis to uthuris townis. **1720** Strype *Stow's Surv.* i. xxxi. I. 306/1 King James..incorporated himself into the Clothworkers: as men dealing in the Principal and Noblest Staple Wares of all these Islands, viz. Woollen Cloths.

staple (ˈsteɪp(ə)l), *sb.*[3] Also 7 **stapple**. [Of uncertain origin; perh. a back-formation from staple *v.*[2] or stapler[1], the sorting of wool according to quality being part of the business of the stapler.]

1. a. The fibre of any particular variety or sample of wool (in later use also of cotton, flax, or other material for textile processes) considered with regard to its length and fineness; a particular length and degree of fineness in the fibre of wool, cotton, etc.

1481 *Cely Papers* (Camden) 66 They causyd me to kep hyt [your new wool] iiij or v dayes and then the sayd the staple therof was to schoorte. *c* **1580** in *Eng. Hist. Rev.* (1914) July 523 Theyr woolles beinge of so course a staple that it will not ronne in threde unles they mingle our woolles withall. **1596** Mascall *Bk. Cattle, Sheep* (1627) 200 Ye must see that ye buy no Ram nor other Sheepe that hath a thin staple, or small store of wooll. **1601** Holland *Pliny* viii. xlviii. I. 227 The wooll of Apulia is of a short staple, and specially in request for cloakes and mantles, and nothing else. **1610** Folkingham *Feudigr.* 9 Lemster Ore merits the preheminence (though it be short) for a purely-fine, soft and crisped Staple. **1641** Best *Farm. Bks.* (Surtees) 9 To cutt of all the shaggie hairy woll..by which meanes they make them seeme more snodde and of a better stapple. **1675** Grew *Anat. Plants* (1682) 140 The Qualities..of the best Tow..are that the Staple be long, small, tough, and white. **1754** in *6th Rep. Dep. Kpr. Publ. Rec.* App. ii. 128 An Engine ..which will..lay the Harle or Staple of the Wool more straight and close than any Yarn yet produced. **1825** J. Nicholson *Oper. Mech.* 389 Some difficulty might be expected to occur in adapting the rollers to different staples. **1861** *Times* 27 Sept., That straight staple and open fleece which the Lincoln long-wool grazier avoids. **1879** *Cassell's Techn. Educ.* IV. 261/2 The staple of mohair is from five to six inches long. **1886** C. Scott *Sheep-Farming* 180 It is essential to the character of a good wool, that there should be an evenness of staple. **1897** Mary Kingsley *W. Africa* 323 The fibre from which these nets are made has a long staple.

b. A lock of wool.

1805 Luccock *Nat. Wool* 134 In such coats the..staples separate easily from each other, and the wool dies in the bowl. **1884** McLaren *Spinning* (ed. 2) 15 This can be done ..by pulling a staple out of the fleece. If it be a wether, the staple will come clean out without interfering to any extent with the surrounding staples; but if it be a hog, some of the fibres of the other staples will adhere to the bottom of the one being pulled. **1885** F. H. Bowman *Struct. Wool* Gloss., *Staple*, the lock of wool or hair which is formed by the aggregation of fibres in the fleece.

c. Unmanufactured wool.

1885 *Wool Trade Circular* Jan., The situation as regards cross-bred staple has proved somewhat exceptional. **1897** *Ibid.*, Jan., Though crossbreds were somewhat neglected, prices for merino staple rose 7½ per cent. *Ibid.*, All grades of staple fell 10 per cent. in value.

2. The fibre of which a thread or a textile fabric is composed. Hence *gen.* the material of which anything is made. Also *fig.*

1588 Shaks. *L.L.L.* v. i. 19 He draweth out the thred of his verbositie finer then the staple of his argument. **1682** Grew *Anat. Plants* Ep. Ded. 2 The Staple of the Stuff is so exquisitely fine, that no Silk-worm is able to draw any thing near so small a Thred. **1755** *Phil. Trans.* XLIX. 208 The substance [*sc.* a kind of paper]..appears to be of a coarser grain, a shorter staple, and of a much looser texture. **1824** Johnson *Typogr.* II. 644 Producing a good paper in appearance, from an inferior staple. **1831** G. R. Porter *Silk Manuf.* 206 Even when the injury occurring to the staple of the thread is less apparent. **1845–6** Trench *Hulsean Lect.* Ser. i. ii. 34 The staple out of which its whole web is woven. **1850** Merivale *Rom. Emp.* xxii. (1865) III. 40 Lucilius himself could not refrain from interweaving Greek words with the homely staple of his Latin style. **1882** Annie Edwardes *Ballroom Repent.* I. 227 The coaching that teaches you how to find staple for conversation out of the slightest materials.

3. The stratum of vegetable mould overlying the rock; a particular depth or quality of this.

a **1722** Lisle *Husb.* (1757) 70 A shallow grete or staple. *Ibid.* 263 The tops of such grass will be coarse and sour, as running to a length beyond what the staple of the ground can well carry. **1771** Burke *Corr.* (1844) I. 265 The general objection of farmers against ploughing up the dead earth, or going beyond what is called the staple; that is, that body of dark-coloured mould, which seems to be in part formed of rotten vegetables and animal substances. **1793** A. Young *Agric. Sussex* 10 Advancing down the hills, the soil becomes of a deeper staple. **1802** R. Brookes *Gazetteer* (ed. 12) s.v. *Rutlandshire*, The e and se parts are of a shallow staple upon limestone rock. **1813** Vancouver *Agric. Devon* 29 The country through Ashton..consists of a brown tender mould of a good staple on a Dunstone rubble. **1861** *Times* 11 July, In a clover-ley field, where plenty of stone showed itself at 6 inches or 7 inches depth, under a hard and tough staple.

4. *attrib.* and *Comb.*, as (sense 1) ***staple-end***, ***fibre***, ***yarn***; **staple-rope** (see quot. 1794); **staple-soil** = sense 3; **staple-threaded** *a.*, composed of thread of selected staple.

1884 McLaren *Spinning* (ed. 2) 15 By examining the *staple-ends to see whether they are pointed or thick. **1928**

E. Fyleman tr. *Hottenroth's Artificial Silk* i. 16 *Staple fibre ..consists of artificial silk, the thread of which is cut into sections of about the length of cotton or worsted staple. **1974** *Sci. Amer.* Apr. 57/3 The viscose-rayon process.. regenerates pure cellulose..as a continuous filament or a staple fiber. **1794** *Rigging & Seamanship* 57 *Staple-ropes, a term for ropes made of hemp not inferior to clean Petersburgh. **1847** *Jrnl. R. Agric. Soc.* VIII. ii. 317 This is chiefly a deep *staple soil. **1856** *Farmer's Mag.* Jan. 20 His practice never advanced further than to lay bare the subsoil in the intervals' by gathering the staple-soil into the wheat ridges. **1896** *Daily News* 9 Apr. 6/5 Woven with a double warp and a *staple-threaded weft of the strongest wools. **1955** *Times* 10 May 18/3 More inquiry continues to come forward for filament rayon and *staple yarns. **1968** J. Ironside *Fashion Alphabet* 209 The filaments are bunched together, cut into short lengths, combed, drawn and spun into spun or staple yarn, which is fuzzier and is made into fabrics.

staple ('stæpl), *sb.*[4] *north.* Also stapple. [Of obscure origin.] (See quots.) Also *staple-pit.*

1818 J. Adley *Coal Trade* 8 With sinking staples and driving drifts You're often put to all your shifts. **1849** Greenwell *Gloss. Terms Coal Trade* (1851) 51 *Staple*, a small pit, sunk upwards or downwards from one seam to another underground. **1862** *Times* 28 Jan., A 'staple', or narrow shaft communicating with the upper seam. **1883** Gresley *Gloss. Coal-mining* 238 *Staple* or *Staple pit*, a shallow shaft within a mine. **1883** *Chamb. Jrnl.* 733, I was near done when I got out, and then had to travel round and get out by a stapple. **1887** P. McNeill *Blawearie* 131 Bob Pringle has fa'en into a stapple fu' o' water in the great-seam waste. **1900** *Engineering Mag.* XIX. 714 Into all of these operations—cutting the coal by machinery,..hoisting trams up small 'staple' pits from one seam to another,..electricity now enters very largely.

staple (steɪp(ə)l), *a.* [From the attributive use of staple *sb.*[2], as in *staple-ware.*]

1. Originally, qualifying *commodity* or words of similar meaning: Having a foremost place among the products exported by a country or place. Hence, in wider sense: Having the chief place among the articles of production or consumption, the industries, employments, etc. of a place, a people, or an individual, or among the constituent elements of anything.

1615 G. Sandys *Trav.* 221 The staple commodities are cotton woolles..chamolets, salt and sope-ashes. **1633** Sir J. Boroughs *Sov. Brit. Seas* (1651) 150 Wee may as easily grow expert in the Art of Fishing, and in time make it a staple commodity of our owne. *a***1661** Fuller *Worthies, Glouc.* (1662) 351 The staple use of Sider is at Sea, where it quencheth thirst better than other liquor. **1699** Sir W. Temple *Ess. Pop. Discont.* Wks. 1731 I. 263 Woollen manufacture..ought to be ever the Staple Trade of England, as that of Linnen ought to be of Ireland. **1715** Bentley *Serm.* x. 371 Nothing but Mass-books and Rosaries..shall then be the staple commodities, even in an University. **1765** *Museum Rust.* IV. 201 Agriculture is..that art..from which the most staple commodities must proceed, to wit, corn and wool. **1841** L. Hunt *Seer* (1864) 25 We confined ourselues to tea, because it is the staple drink. **1845** Darwin *Voy. Nat.* xi. (1879) 236 The only country in the world where a cryptogamic plant affords a staple article of food. **1859** C. Barker *Assoc. Princ.* ii. 44 Woollen cloth, which the King sought to make the staple manufacture of his own dominions. **1875** Whitney *Life Lang.* vii. 112 Their staple subjects of thought. **1872** Jenkinson *Engl. Lake Distr.* (1879) 129 The staple trade of Keswick. **1900** Elworthy *Horns of Honour* ii. 89 The staple accusation made by these wretches against their victims [witches] was that of being in compact with the devil.

†**b.** Of a book, an author: Standard. *Obs.*

1642 Fuller *Holy & Prof. State* iii. xviii. 200 Proportion an houres meditation to an houres reading of a staple Authour. *a***1730** Fenton *Poems, To Knt. Sable Shield* 28 And while each little author struts In calves-skin gilt, adorn'd with cuts; I, vouching, pass 'em off as dear As any staple-classic ware. **1745** P. Thomas *Jrnl. Anson's Voy.* 223 The Chinese..say by heart all their Staple Books without Hesitation.

†**c.** Home-grown, native; characteristic of the country. *Obs.*

[**1648** *Art. Peace* xiv. in *Milton's Wks.* (1851) IV. 519 Certain Articles added to the same Act, all concerning staple or native Commodities of this Kingdom, shall be repealed.] **1771** *Junius Lett.* lvii. 295 Pernicious influence..banishes the staple virtues of the Country.

†**2.** (? Confused with stable *a.*) Permanent, stable. *Obs.*

1621 Bp. Mountagu *Diatribæ* 536 The Athenians gaue the Tenth, not onely of spoyles for once, and no more, but of land, to be a standing staple Tithe for euer. *a***1641** —— *Acts & Mon.* (1642) 11 For sacrifice, in shedding of bloud, was the principall staple, standing Service of God in Nature. [Often in Mountagu.] *a***1642** Sir W. Monson *Naval Tracts* v. (1704) 454/1 [He] will be sure to make his Foundation firm and staple. **1794** G. Adams *Nat. & Exper. Phil.* III. xxix. 196 Time cannot be applied to any being of staple and permanent duration.

†**3.** In statute staple the adj. replaces the phrase *of the Staple*, on the analogy of *statute merchant* (see statute *sb.*); hence also in ***recognisance staple***, a recognisance taken before the mayor of the staple. *Obs.*

1586 Hooker *Holinshed's Chron. Irel.* 139/2 They haue a maior and officers of the staple..who haue the liberties for taking of statutes and recognisances staple, not onelie within their owne towne..but also of sundrie townes in Leinster and Mounster, and the counties of Waterford, Kilkennie, Wexford, and Tipporarie.

staple ('steɪp(ə)l), *v.*[1] [f. staple *sb.*[1]] *trans.*

†**a.** To clasp, fasten (a helmet): cf. staple *sb.*[1] 1 c. *Obs.* **b.** To secure with or as with a staple.

13.. *Gaw & Gr. Knt.* 606 þenne hentes he þe helme..þat was stapled stifly, & stoffed wyth-inne. *c***1470** Henry *Wallace* i. 125 [He] Brocht it till Scwne, and stapill maid it thar, Quhar kingis was cround viij hundyr ȝer and mar, Befor the tyme at king Eduuard it fand. **1742** Woodroofe in *Hanway's Trav.* (1762) I. ii. xxiii. 98 They cover them with canvass well tarred, and lay battins over it every three or four inches, stapling them fast with a kind of crooked nail. **1748** Smollett *Rod. Random* I. xxix. 190, I was loaded with irons and stapled to the deck. **1760–72** H. Brooke *Fool of Qual.* (1809) IV. 2 An iron ring that was stapled into a post. **1896** *Strand Mag.* XII. 323/2 The standing ways are securely stapled to heavy cross-blocks of timber. **1964** R. Petrie *Murder by Precedent* vi. 87 At no time after stapling the copies did I move any sheets apart. **1975** D. Ramsay *Descent into Dark* iv. 130 You were stapling that article on abortion together.

staple ('steɪp(ə)l), *v.*[2] *Obs.* exc. *Hist.* [f. staple *sb.*[2]]

1. *trans.* To receive (export goods) at a staple; to cause to be weighed, inspected, and sealed in accordance with the regulations of the staple.

1472–3 *Rolls of Parlt.* VI. 59/2 That all the Wolles..be shipt and conveyed to the said Staple at Caleys and there to be stapled. **1601** J. Wheeler *Treat. Comm.* 14 The Company settled themselues in the Towne of Bridges, and stapled their commodities there.

2. *intr.* To establish a staple.

1580 Hakluyt *Voy.* (1599) I. 437 It were good that we did seeke out some small Island..where we might plant, fortifie, and staple safely, from whence..wee might feed those heathen nations with our commodities.

Hence '**stapling** *vbl. sb.* (in quot. *attrib.*)

1908 Atton & Holland *King's Customs* 26 To gain possession of the stapling privilege.

stapled ('steɪp(ə)ld), *a.*[1] [f. staple *sb.*[3] + -ed[2].] Having a staple (of a certain kind). Chiefly in parasynthetic formations, as in ***long-, short-stapled***; ***thin-stapled***; also ***well-stapled.***

a. Of wool, sheep; also of cotton, silk, etc.: see staple *sb.*[3] 1.

1594 Greene *Friar Bacon* 1514 My flockes, Yeelding forth fleeces stapled with such woole, As Lempster cannot yeelde more finer stuffe. **1805** Luccock *Nat. Wool* 346 Of the fifteen millions of short stapled ones [*sc.* fleeces], which the kingdom produces, there are not five hundred thousand which even border upon perfection. **1851** *Art Jrnl. Illustr. Catal.* p. iv**, Coarser and shorter stapled cottons. **1865** *Reader* 8 July 47/1 He had himself seen, in Pekin, warehouses stored with..fine tobacco, short-stapled silk, paper [etc.].

b. Of soil: see staple *sb.*[3] 3.

1773 *Gentl. Mag.* XLIII. 130 Taking away small stones and flints is detrimental to..thin stapled light lands, and to all lands of a binding nature. **1795** Vancouver *Agric. Essex* 27 A well stapled gravelly loam. **1844** *Jrnl. R. Agric. Soc.* V. i. 17 The thin-stapled lands of this district.

stapled ('steɪp(ə)ld), *a.*[2] [f. staple *sb.*[1] + -ed[2].] Furnished with a staple or staples (staple *sb.*[1] 2); *spec.* of papers, fastened together with a staple or staples.

1845 Browning *Confessional* xii, That horrible black scaffold dressed, That stapled block..God sink the rest! **1868** J. Greenwood in *Morn. Star* 3 Feb., It is two years and a week or so since I applied at that stapled knocker and traversed the chaste hall. **1956** S. Bellow *Seize Day* (1957) i. 32 Several pages of blue hectographed script, stapled together. **1958** *N. & Q.* Jan. 46/2 The cost of this book by English standards ($1.50 for a text in stapled paper cover) is prohibitive. **1974** 'P. B. Yuill' *Bornless Keeper* xii. 113 He picked up the wad of stapled foolscap sheets.

†**staple fish.** *Obs.* [? staple *sb.*[2]; but the precise reference is not clear.] Fish not thoroughly cured; = green-fish 1.

1477 *Pat. Roll 16 Edw. IV*, ii. 17 d, Nauis..le Jacob de Hamburghe..cum viginti et sex Milibus Stokfisshe duobus Milibus Staplefisshe et nouem doliis de Trane ad valenciam Sexcentarum librarum in partibus Islandie onusta. **1545** *Rates Custom Ho.* c vj, Staple fysshe. **1563** *Norwich Deposit.* (1905) 72 A firkin of eels, and 600 staplefish, shipped at Amsterdam. *a***1661** Fuller *Worthies, Gen.* viii. 23 As for Staple or Salt-Fish, there are those..who will maintain, that it will..set up the Fishery as high as ever it was, if every one in England able to dispend a Hundred Pounds per annum, were enjoyned to lay out Twenty Shillings a Year, in staple-fish. *c***1682** J. Collins *Making Salt Eng.* 90 Green-fish (*alias* Staple Fish as they call it,) cured with a good Salt, proves excellent.

stapler[1] ('steɪplə(r)). Also 6 stapeler, stapuller. [f. staple *sb.*[2] + -er[1]. Cf. med.L. *stapulārius.*]

1. (More fully ***merchant stapler.***) A merchant of the Staple. (See quot. 1908.)

*a***1513** Fabyan *Chron.* (1811) 465 In the whiche [parlyament]..was graunted, to the mayntenaunce of his warres, l. s. of a sak of woll, for the terme of .vi. yeres; but it contynued lenger, though the marchauntes staplers ther at grudgyd. *Ibid.* 652 Whan kyng Edwarde was thus stablysshed in this realme, great sute and labour was made to hym for the repayment of the foresayd. xviii. M. li. to hym and other dyleueryd by the stapelers. **1568** Grafton *Chron.* II. 659 The Lordes borowed of the Marchantes of the Staple .xviij. thousand pound, the which money the Staplers did nowe sue for vnto King Edwarde to be repayed vnto them. **1585–6** Leycester *Corr.* (Camden) 398 Our staplers of late complayned for the burden layd uppon ther wares at Midleborough. **1601** J. Wheeler *Treat. Comm.* 82 The Staplers Companie haue drawne the trade of English Wooll into their owne hands onely. **1607** Middleton *Fam. Love* i. iii. 84 Yon merchants were wont to be merchant staplers. *c***1645** Howell *Lett.* vi. iii. (1655) I. 242 They..so divided themselves (though they be now but one) to Staplers and Merchant-Adventurers. *Ibid.* lii. 298 The Staplers of Hamborough and Rotterdam. **1651** N. Bacon *Disc. Govt. Eng.* ii. vii. (1739) 44 Nor doth it appear to me that the Staplers in these times used such a course, or were other than mere Officers for the regulating of the Staple. **1890** Gross *Gild Merch.* I. 140 The staplers were merchants who had the monopoly of exporting the principal raw commodities of the realm. **1893** *Dict. Nat. Biogr.* XXXIV. 425 McBride, John..was admitted a free stapler of Belfast on 8 April 1644. **1908** H. O. Meredith *Econom. Hist. Eng.* 153 During the first half of the fifteenth century the Merchant Staplers were a powerful company, whose members lived either in English ports or in Calais, who directed the export trade of the country. **1912** *Eng. Hist. Rev.* Oct. 811 This strengthens the hypothesis that the staplers and the adventurers sprang from a common root.

†**b.** A dealer in 'staple-ware'. *Obs.*

1532–3 in E. Law *Hampton Crt. Pal.* (1885) 347 Payd to Thomas Ostley, stapuller, for 18 ffother, 12 cwt. 3 qrs. 21 lb. of leade to cover the Kynges New Hall. **1890** Gross *Gild Merch.* I. 148 The staplers, who dealt in certain raw materials.

2. A trader who buys wool from the grower to sell to the manufacturer: = woolstapler.

*a***1552** Leland *Itin.* (1769) IV. 113 Norton is a pretty uplandish Towne in Worcestershire, and there be fayre Houses in it of Staplers, that use to buy Wooll. **1600** Holland *Livy, Topogr. Rome* 1376 Æquimelium is betweene Velabrum and the Capitoll, neere to the staplers wooll shops. **1667** O. Heywood *Heart Treas.* ii. 9 Every Trades-man lays up that which is fit for his Calling; Cloathiers, Staplers, Tanners, Husbandmen, have all their peculiar provisions, suited to their vocations. **1707** *Lond. Gaz.* No. 4341/4 George Wagstaffe, of Glossop.., Stapler. **1805** Luccock *Nat. Wool* 133 If the opinion of the staplers be correct, the sheep in extreme old age appears to lose the faculty of producing a valuable wool. **1863** Fawcett *Pol. Econ.* iii. vi. (1876) 367 The Leeds manufacturer, who purchases wool from the stapler, pays for it by a cheque. **1881** *Daily News* 29 Aug. 3/6 Spinners buy with hesitation and caution... Staplers, however, maintain quotations with a tolerable degree of firmness. **1885** F. H. Bowman *Struct. Wool* Gloss., *Stapler*, a merchant who buys wool from the farmer and sorts it into its various qualities for the manufacturer.

stapler[2] ('steɪplə(r)). [f. staple *sb.*[1] 2 d + -er[1].] A device for fastening together papers, etc., with a staple or staples.

1951 *Catal. of Exhibits, South Bank Exhib., Festival of Britain* 64 Office equipment..'Velos' plier stapler. **1969** 'C. Keith' *Missing Book-Keeper* iv. 48 The shallow centre drawer..contained..some extra staples for the stapler on top of the desk. **1973** *Sci. Amer.* July 113/2 Edges of the foil can be fastened together with tape or with a stapler. **1978** *Detroit Free Press* 16 Apr. (Advt. Suppl.) 1/4 Full-size standard stapler with open-channel loading.

stapling ('steɪplɪŋ), *vbl. sb.* [f. staple *v.*[1] + -ing[1].] The action of the verb, esp. that of fastening papers together with staples; the fastening so made.

1898 G. B. Shaw *Let.* 4 Mar. (1972) II. 11 The plays.. require endless cutting & folding and stapling into brown paper covers. **1940** [see staple *sb.*[1] 2 d]. **1961** *Lebende Sprachen* VI. 104/1 Stapling machine, stapler. **1970** *Guardian* 5 May 4/5 He looked at his report again and noticed the stapling had been interfered with. **1973** D. Miller *Chinese Jade Affair* xix. 190 The secretary came in with..official seals, a stapling gadget, sealing-wax.

stappe, obs. f. step *sb.*[1] and *v.*

stapte, obs. pa. t. of step *v.*

star (stɑː(r)), *sb.*[1] Forms: 1 steorra, stiorra, *Northumb.* stearra, sterra, 2–3 steore, storre, 2–4 steorre, 2–6 sterre, 3 stor, sturre, 4–6 stere, 5–7 stare, 6 ster, 6–7 starr(e, 6– star. [Com. WGer.: OE. *steorra* wk. masc. corresponds to OFris. *stera* (NFris. *stear, stêar, stiar*), OS. *sterro* (MLG. *sterre*), MDu. *sterre, starre* (mod.Du. *ster, star* fem.), OHG. *sterro* (MHG. *sterre*):—OTeut. type **sterron-*, f. **ster-* cogn. w. L. *stella* (:—**ster-la*), Gr. ἀ-στερ-, ἀστήρ, ἄ-στρ-ον, Cornish, Bret. *steren*, Welsh *seren* (pl. *sêr*), Sk. *star*, Zend *stare.* A parallel OTeut. formation, **sternōn-* fem. (also *-non-* masc.), with suffix as in **sunnōn-* sun *sb.*[1], is represented in several Teut. langs., and was adopted from ON. into northern Eng. and Sc. dialects: see stern *sb.*[2]]

I. 1. a. Any one of the many celestial bodies appearing as luminous points in the night sky. Now usually restricted (in scientific and to some extent in popular language), to the *fixed stars* as distinguished from planets (exc. in evening-*star*, morning star), comets, and meteors (exc. in falling star, shooting star). See also seven stars.

*c***825** *Vesp. Ps.* cxlviii. 3 Herȝað hine alle steorran & leht. *O.E. Chron.* an. 892, þy ilcan ȝeare..æteowde se steorra þe mon on boclæden hæt cometa, same men cweþaþ on Englisc þæt hit sie feaxede steorra. *c***1200** *Moral Ode* 279 (Trin. Coll. MS.) Nafre sunne þar ne sineð ne mone ne storre. *c***1205** Lay. 17870 þe steorre is ihate a latin comete. *c***1340** *Ayenb.* 164 And þus him þingþ al þe wordle lite, ase a sterre hit þincþ to ous. *c***1386** Chaucer *Prol.* 268 His eyen twynkled in his heed aryght As doon the sterres in the frosty nyght. *c***1449** Pecock *Repr.* ii. xvi. 242 The vij. planetis.. and..the fix sterris. **1588** Kyd *Househ. Philos.* Wks. (1901)

262 Euen as the Moone and the Starres receiue light by participation with the sunne. **1784** COWPER *Task* III. 158 And tell us whence the stars; why some are fix'd, And planetary some. **1813** W. BAKEWELL *Introd. Geol.* (1815) 432 It is well known to astronomers, that new stars have suddenly appeared with a brilliancy exceeding that of Jupiter. **1842** *Penny Cycl.* XXII. 447/1 We distinguish the stars from the planets in much the same way as our ancestors did before us. **1892** TENNYSON *Death Œnone* 82 And the dream Wail'd in her, when she woke beneath the stars.

b. In proverbial phrases, similes, etc.

c **1000** *Sax. Leechd.* I. 164 Ðeos wyrt scineð on nihte swilce steorra on heofone. *c* **1200** *Trin. Coll. Hom.* 153 No man hit ne mihte tellen, nan more þene men muȝen tellen þe sterres on heuene. *a* **1225** *St. Marher.* 9 Ant his twa ehnen steappre þene steorren. *c* **1381** CHAUCER *Parl. Foules* 595 There been mo sterris god wot than a payre. *c* **1450** *Mirk's Festial* 17 And at yche 'Aue' scho set a rose yn þe garlond þat schon as bryght as a sterre. **1513** MORE *Rich. III* in *Grafton's Chron.* (1568) 807 They extolled and praysed him farre aboue the starres. **1581** A. HALL *Iliad* II. 18 Casting how he Achilles fame vnto the starres might raise. **1596** SPENSER *F.Q.* IV. xi. 53 More eath it were for mortall wight To tell the sands, or count the starres on hye. **1754** RICHARDSON *Grandison* VII. iii. 11 Since she has already one foot among the stars, and can look down with pity..on all those who [etc.]. **1782** MRS. H. COWLEY *Bold Stroke for Husband* II. ii, To take up all the fine apartments, and send poor little Livy to lodge next the stars. **1799** WORDSW. '*She dwelt*' 7 Fair as a star, when only one Is shining in the sky. **1802** —— *Sonn. to Liberty* I. xiv. 9 Thy soul was like a Star, and dwelt apart.

c. With reference to the pagan belief that the souls of illustrious persons after death appear as new stars in the heavens.

c **1384** CHAUCER *H. Fame* 599 For Ioues ys not ther aboute ..To make of the as yet a sterre. **1591** SHAKS. *1 Hen. VI*, I. i. 55 A farre more glorious Starre thy Soule will make, Then Iulius Cæsar. **1608** —— *Per.* v. iii. 79 Heauens make a Starre of him! **1598** T. ROGERS *Celest. Elegies* C 4 in *Lamport Garl.* (Roxb.), She to a starre is metamorphosed And with the golden Twinns in heauen enstald.

d. *poet.* = LODESTAR, POLE-STAR.

1599 SHAKS. *Much Ado* III. iv. 58 Well, and you be not turn'd Turke, there's no more sayling by the starre. *c* **1600** —— *Sonn.* cxvi. 7 Loue..is the star to euery wandring barke. **1663** COWLEY *Ess.* vii. Wks. (1906) 441 [Gold] The Ensign 'tis at Land, and 'tis the Seamans Star.

e. *transf.* (Chiefly in *colloq. phrase*: see quot. 1891.)

1609 HEYWOOD *Brit. Troy* VII. lxxv. 157 Those that but late incompast him about, And with their steele strooke Stars out of his Crest. **1839** *Spirit of Times* 16 Nov. 434/1 She fetched me a slap in the face that made me see stars. **1891** *Century Dict.* s.v. *Star*, *To see stars*, to have a sensation as of flashes of light, produced by a sudden jarring of the head, as by a direct blow. **1894** SIR J. ASTLEY *Fifty Yrs. Life* I. 142 Quicker than thought, in comes his right, and if you only see stars you are pretty lucky. **1924** GALSWORTHY *White Monkey* II. xi. 206 '*Per ardua ad astra*,' 'Through hard knocks we shall see stars.' **1966** D. VARADAY *Gara-Yaka's Domain* xiv. 160 Had it been daylight I would still have seen the stars caused by the searing pain I felt in my thumb! **1977** *Cleethorpes News* 27 May 32/3 Already three fighters have seen stars as they have been sent crashing to the canvas.

2. In extended sense, any one of the heavenly bodies, including the sun and moon; sometimes in pl. as a vague designation for the abode of departed spirits; so occas. ***this star***, the earth regarded along with other 'stars' as a place of habitation. Chiefly *poet.*; cf. L. *sīdus*.

diurnal star, star of day, of noon: the sun.

a **1225** *Leg. Kath.* 714, & mid tet ilke step up, & steah to þe steorren. *a* **1240** *Ureisun* in *Lamb. Hom.* 187 Ne wene na mon to stihen wið este to þe steorren. *c* **1375** *Sc. Leg. Saints* xxxi. (*Eugenia*) 252 þai..sad þat goddis had hir tane & ymang þe sterris with hir gane. **1602** DOLMAN *La Primaud. Fr. Acad.* (1618) III. 799 There are some [trees] which naturally follow the Sunne,..hauing a sympathy and secret inclination to this Starre. **1616** R. C. *Times' Whistle* (1871) 113 The blazing bright beamd starre, Sol. **1667** MILTON *P.L.* x. 1071 Ere this diurnal Starr Leave cold the Night. **1697** J. SERGEANT *Solid Philos.* 118 Providence has left us no Means to know what is done in the Moon, or other Stars. **1737** *Gentl. Mag.* VII. 63/1 He adds, that they see the Sun at Midnight,..And as that Star [etc.]. **1742** YOUNG *Nt. Th.* IX. 1683 Worlds conceal'd by day Behind the proud and envious star of noon! **1808** MACAULAY in Trevelyan *Life & Lett.* (1880) I. 32 The star of day had reached the West. **1841** DICKENS *Barn. Rudge* ix, Perhaps she wondered what star was destined for her habitation when she had run her little course below. **1870** R. S. HAWKER in C. E. Byles *Life* (1905) 588 No, my fate is fixed. Here on this Star nothing of any palm: it is reserved for another Sphere, a far-away world.

3. a. In Astrology, used of the planets and zodiacal constellations as supposed to influence human affairs. ***one's star*** or ***stars***: the planet or constellation which, by its position at the moment of a person's birth, sways his destinies, moulds his temperament, etc. Now often in metaphorical quasi-adoption of astrological beliefs.

c **1250** *Owl & Night.* 1321 Hwat constu, wrecche þing, of storre? **1375** BARBOUR *Bruce* IV. 675 As it wes vounderfull, perfay, How ony man throu steris may Knaw the thingis that ar to cum. **14..** *Life St. Bridget* in *Myrr. our Ladye* p. xlix, The sykenes of this childe is nat of the sterres. **1542** BOORDE *Dyetary* iii. (1870) 236 Many thynges doth infect.. the ayre, as the influence of sondry sterres. **1601** SHAKS. *All's Well* I. i. 205 You were borne vnder a charitable starre. **1601** —— *Jul. C.* I. ii. 140 The fault (deere Brutus) is not in our Starres, But in our Selues, that we are vnderlings. **1686** tr. *Chardin's Trav. Persia* 19 What unlucky Star brought him to Constantinople. **1698** [W. KING] *Sorbiere's Journ. Lond.* 25 There are people that can pick Pockets, and afterwards by Consulting the Stars, tell you who it was that did it. **1726** SWIFT *Gulliver* II. i, My good star would have it that he appeared pleased with my voice. **1728–46** THOMSON *Spring* 1113 But happy they..Whom gentler stars unite. **1831** LYTTON *Godolphin* xxvi, In a word, he was a reader of the stars. *Ibid.*, As the stars (which night had been spent in reading) began to wink and fade. **1845** SARAH AUSTIN *Ranke's Hist. Ref.* III. 477 Suleiman recognized the ascendancy of the star of his rival. **1886** RUSKIN *Præterita* I. x. 308 Another segment of my learning..might have had better consequence than ever came of it, had the stars so pleased. **1888** BRYCE *Amer. Commw.* lxxx. III. 51 It is natural for them to believe in their star.

b. In phrases and adjurations as ***to thank, bless, curse one's stars; my stars!*** usually a trivial expression of astonishment; ***to thank*** (or ***praise***) ***one's lucky stars***: see LUCKY *a.* 3; also †***good stars!*** and jocularly ***my stars and garters!*** (cf. 8).

a **1593** MARLOWE *Edw. II*, IV. vi, O my starres! Why do you lowre vnkindly on a king? **1599** B. JONSON *Ev. Man out of Hum.* I. iii, I thanke my Starres for it. **1609** DEKKER *Gull's Horn-bk.* v. 23 That you are (thankes to your starres) in mightie credit. **1686** W. DE BRITAINE *Hum. Prud.* xxii. 105, I am not (I bless my Stars) disturbed at any thing. **1706** E. WARD *Wooden World Diss.* (1708) 37 He has oft-times thank'd his good Stars for it. **1711** M. HENRY *Hope & Fear Balanced* 16 Then 'twill be Folly to curse your Stars (as some profanely speak). **1728** VANBR. & CIB. *Prov. Husb.* III. i. 51 My Stars! and you would really live in London half the Year, to be sober in it? **1760** H. WALPOLE *Let. to Mann* 24 May, It costs, the stars know what! **1782** MISS BURNEY *Cecilia* VII. ix, 'Your dog!' cried Morrice, looking aghast, 'good stars! I never thought of him!' **1807–8** W. IRVING *Salmag.* i. (1860) 19, I..blessed my stars that I was a bachelor. **1819** M. WILMOT *Let.* 24 Oct. (1935) 24 O ye stars and garters how often do I wish for Mary and a green Lawn!!! **1841** DICKENS *Barn. Rudge* xxii, My stars, Simmun!.. You frighten me to death! **1850** R. G. CUMMING *Hunter's Life S. Afr.* (ed. 2) I. 213 My stars and garters! what sort of man is this? **1865** J. HATTON *Bitter Sweets* xiv, You may thank your stars, my lad, that I followed Master Barns to-night. **1913** [see BOBBY-DAZZLER]. **1931** F. L. ALLEN *Only Yesterday* ix. 237 In any café in Paris one might find an American expatriate thanking his stars that he was free from standardization at last. **1976** M. MILLAR *Ask for me Tomorrow* (1977) ix. 77 My stars, you needn't shout.

c. *transf.* A person's fortune, rank, or destiny, disposition or temperament, viewed as determined by the stars.

1601 SHAKS. *Twel. N.* II. v. 156 In my stars I am aboue thee, but be not affraid of greatnesse. **1602** —— *Ham.* II. ii. 141 Lord Hamlet is a Prince out of thy Starre. **1643** SIR T. BROWNE *Relig. Med.* II. §13, I was not borne unto riches, neither is it I thinke my Starre to be wealthy. **1646** BUCK *Rich. III*, I. 4 Geoffry Plantagenet..had so amorous a Star, That Philippe le Grosse..suspected him for too familiar commerce with his bed.

4. In various figurative and similative contexts.

Star of the sea = *Stella maris*, a title given to the Virgin Mary; cf. SEA-STAR 1.

c **1230** *Hali Meid.* 11 Meidenhad is te steorre þat, beo ha eanes of þe east igan adun to þe west, neauer eft ne ariseð ha. *a* **1400** *Minor Poems fr. Vernon MS.* 735/1 Heil, sterre of þe See so briht! **1538** STARKEY *England* i. 12 Where fyrst we schal se the gudly cytes, castellys, and townys..pleasauntly set as they were sterrys apon erthe. **1631** T. ADAMS in *Lett. Lit. Men* (Camden) 148 Our learned and bright shining star Mr. Holsworth. **1653** *Apol. for Goodwin* 5 The light of Nature in his Astronomy, is a Star of the first magnitude. **1697** DRYDEN *Æneis* Ded. (b) 1 b, These are the single Stars which are sprinkled through the Æneis: But there are whole Constellations of them in the Fifth Book. **1769** GRAY *Installation Ode* 93 The Star of Brunswick smiles serene, And gilds the horrors of the deep. **1833** LAMB *Elia* Ser. II. *Imagin. Faculty*, Quixote—the errant Star of Knighthood, made more tender by eclipse. **1845** R. W. HAMILTON *Pop. Educ.* vii. (ed. 2) 174 Education is the star of their hope and their guidance. That star is fixed. **1889** GRETTON *Memory's Harkback* 129, I suppose he was not reckoned among the stars of greater magnitude, but he was very full of light.

5. *fig.* A person of brilliant reputation or talents.

a. An actor, singer, etc. of exceptional celebrity, or one whose name is prominently advertised as a special attraction to the public. ***film star***: see FILM *sb.* 7 c; ***movie star***: see MOVIE b. orig. *Theatr.*

[**1779** WARNER in Jesse *Selwyn & Contemp.* (1844) IV. 30 The little stars, who hid their diminished rays in his [Garrick's] presence, begin to abuse him.] **1824** *Compl. Hist. Murder Mr. Weare* 219 Carter..was at a loss for a star in the pugilistic hemisphere to produce him a crowded house. **1827** *Edin. Weekly Jrnl.* 28 Feb. in *Scott's Chron. Canongate* Introd. App., He had hitherto been speaking of what, in theatrical language, was called *stars*. **1833** MOTLEY *Corr.* (1889) I. ii. 31 The great tragedy star of Berlin and of Germany, Devrient, is dead. **1864** C. KNIGHT *Passages Work. Life* I. v. 218 Our theatre was..commodious; but the manager could not draw audiences without stars. **1883** *Athenæum* 8 Sept. 313/1 A ballad concert in which the 'stars' took part. **1919** G. B. SHAW *Annajanska* in *Heartbreak House* 265 You still want to be a circus star. **1941** *Picturegoer & Film Weekly* 6 Sept. 3/1 Barbara Mullen is no longer unknown. It would be an exaggeration to say *Jeannie* makes her a star. It needs more than one part to do that. **1946** *R.A.F. Jrnl.* May 175 The British Forces Network finds new stars of radio from the ranks of the R.A.F. **1976** *Oxf. Compan. Film* 468/2 Hayley..has been the more prominent in films, scoring a success as a teenage star, notably in *Tiger Bay*.

b. *gen.* (Chiefly *colloq.*) One who 'shines' in society, or is distinguished in some branch of art, industry, science, etc.

1829 G. GRIFFIN *Collegians* II. xx. 103 Anne Chute..was, beyond all competition, the star of the evening. **1850** S. G. OSBORNE *Glean.* 228, I have attended many such meetings in England, to meet English Agricultural stars. **1876** GLADSTONE *Glean.* (1879) 266 The historian, the poet, the great social star. **1880** MISS BROUGHTON *Second Thoughts* II. vii, A tiny foreign princekin who is the star and lion of the evening. **1881** C. E. PASCOE *Everyday Life in our Public Schools* 218 The Torpid game is reserved as a sphere for young 'stars' who come up to Harrow with a reputation. **1973** *Art Internat.* Mar. 55/1 George Washington Wilson's *The Brig and Cliffs, Filey, From the North Landing*..was for me the star of the group [of photographs]. **1975** *Nature* 16 Oct. 531/3 It was supported by a galaxy of scientific stars, including 14 Nobel Prizewinners.

c. *Sport.* An outstanding performer.

1916 [see *clay court* s.v. CLAY *sb.* 9]. **1928** E. O'NEILL *Strange Interlude* VI. 210 I'm going to start in training him ..so he'll be a crack athlete when he goes to college... I want him to..be a bigger star than Gordon ever was. **1930** *Sun* (Baltimore) 26 Dec. 11/7 No player is now on the field more than half of that, so even a star averages only about a half hour's real work throughout the year. **1964** G. C. KUNZLE *Parallel Bars* ix. 407 The content of five difficulties and one superior difficulty was more than most international stars had at that time. **1979** R. JAFFE *Class Reunion* (1980) III. iii. 318 Emma..was the star of her gymnastics class.

6. a. An image or figure of a star.

It is conventionally represented by a number of rays diverging from a central point or circle; or by a geometrical figure of five or more radiating points, such as is formed by producing the sides of a pentagon, hexagon, etc.

13.. *King Alis.* 134 Of gold he made a table, Al ful of steorren, saun fable. *c* **1400** *Wycliffite Bible* Lev. xi. 30 *marg.*, *Stellio*, that is, a worme peyntid as with sterris. **1431** *Rec. St. Mary at Hill* 26 A hole vestement of blu veluet with sterres & mones of golde. **1538** in *Archæologia* XLIII. 215, i cope of oulde redd velvett spotted wyth sters. **1599** SHAKS. *Hen. V*, III. vii. 74 The Armour that I saw in your Tent to night, are those Starres or Sunnes vpon it? **1705** ADDISON *Italy, Ferrara* 124 A Circle of Stars glew'd to the Canvas over the Head of the Figure [of the Virgin]. **1795** DENNE in *Archæologia* XII. 114 A star of eight points within a double circle, the device of John Tate, supposed to have been the first Paper-maker in England. **1818** *Art Bookbinding* 31 Stamped with a star or any device, to fancy. **1846** SOYER *Cookery* 424 When partly set form a rosette or star upon each, with fillets of hard-boiled white of eggs and truffles. **1890** MOUNTENEY-JEPHSON *Emin Pasha* 290 His own flag with the crescent and three stars,..was flying at the fore. **1899** MISS MASTERS *Bk. Stitches* 100 Small rings or stars, for sprinkling over a background,..may be very successfully made in buttonhole stitch.

b. ***stars and stripes***; the popular name for the United States flag. ***stars and bars***, the flag of the Confederate States.

The American flag, when first adopted by Congress (14th June 1777), contained 13 stripes and 13 stars, representing the 13 States of the Union. It now contains 13 stripes and 50 stars.

1782 E. WATSON *Men & Times Revol.* (1861) 203 He.. attached to the ship the stars and stripes. **1830** *Debates in Congress* 24 Feb. 193 This alone can account..for the exhortation against enlistments, against joining the stars and stripes of their country. **1840** R. H. DANA *Bef. Mast* xiv. 32 We..ran the stars and stripes up to the peak. **1859** THACKERAY *Virginians* lxix. II. 171 All accents are pretty from pretty lips, and who shall set the standard up? Shall it be a rose, or a thistle, or a shamrock, or a star and stripe? **1863** WHITTIER *Barbara Frietchie* 13 Forty flags with their silver stars, Forty flags with their crimson bars.

c. A badge of rank, authority, or military service.

1890 [see PACK *v.*[1] 9 a]. **1895** *Montgomery Ward Catal.* Spring & Summer 296/3 Policemen's regulation rubber coats..pocket for billy and shield for star. **1908** W. H. DAVIES *Autobiogr. Super-Tramp* 48 With that the marshal of the town stood before the open door, showing the star of his authority on his dark clothes. **1924** C. J. TOLLEY *Mod. Golfer* 6, I passed on from there in '16 with a second lieutenant's star in that regiment. **1942** [see SAM BROWNE]. **1946** W. S. CHURCHILL *Victory* 143 Two new stars for operations in the East will also mark the service of those who have gone out..to finish the war against the Japanese. **1977** R. LUDLUM *Chancellor Manuscript* xxix. 312 My permanent rank is brigadier-general. I will undoubtedly receive my second star in June.

d. A small star of coloured paper, awarded to a (usu. primary) schoolchild for a good piece of work. (The star is often stuck alongside the work in an exercise book, or displayed on a wall-chart.)

1977 *Cleethorpes News* 6 May 17/2 The books were all very neat and dotted with gold stars on nearly every page. The stars are worth house points which build up over the term. **1978** *Jrnl. R. Soc. Arts* CXXVI. 351/1 If they get 80 per cent or over, they get a blue star, 90 per cent or over a gold star. And ten lessons with stars will win them a prize.

7. *Pyrotechny.* A small piece of combustible composition, used in rockets, mines, etc., which as seen burning high in the air resembles a star.

1634 J. B[ATE] *Myst. Nat.* II. 57 [Of Fire-works.] Such as operate in the ayre, as Rockets,..Stars, [etc.]. **1669** STURMY *Mariner's Mag.* v. xiii. 89 When you have divers Rockets,.. let one be with a Report, another with Starrs, another with Golden Hair or Rain. **1797** *Encycl. Brit.* (ed. 3) XV. 688/1 (*Pyrotechny*) If the sparks, which are called *stars*, or *pinks*, come out in clusters..it is a sign of its being good. *Ibid.* 702/2 Strung stars..Tailed stars..Drove stars. **1842** *Penny Cycl.* XX. 54/1 (*Rocket*) A conical case containing the composition for producing the explosions or *stars* of light which constitute the signal. **1876** VOYLE & STEVENSON *Milit. Dict.* 139/2 The variety of stars and colours observed in fireworks is formed principally of metallic filings.

b. A kind of match for lighting cigars.

1863 ABEL in *Lond.* etc. *Phil. Mag.* Nov. 358 Cigar lights (known as Vesuvians, Etnas, Stars, &c.).

8. An ornament, usually of precious metal, representing a star, worn as part of the insignia of an order of knighthood, or as a military decoration. Also occas. applied to the holder or wearer of this decoration.

1712–14 POPE *Rape Lock* I. 85 While Peers, and Dukes, and all their sweeping train, And Garters, Stars, and Coronets appear. **1731** SWIFT *Poems, On his Death* 323 He ..Despised the fools with stars and garters, So often seen caressing Chartres. **1795** BURNS *For a' that* iii, For a' that, and a' that, His ribband, star, and a' that. **1844** DISRAELI *Coningsby* III. ii, A Field Marshal covered with stars? **1862** THACKERAY *Philip* i, Lord Ascot in his star and ribbon.. walked with his arm in the doctor's into chapel. **1901** *Essex Weekly News* 15 Mar. 2/4 Deceased..wore the Egyptian medal and the Khedive's star.

9. a. A natural object resembling or likened to a star; e.g. the open corolla (or corolla and disk) of a flower.

a **1635** RANDOLPH *Muse's Looking-Gl.* IV. i, Nature adornes The Peacocks taile with starres. **1777** CAVALLO *Electricity* 207 The Star and Pencil of electric Light. **1784** COWPER *Task* VI. 176 [Jasmine] The bright profusion of her scatter'd stars. **1796** WITHERING *Brit. Plants* (ed. 3) III. 364 Leaves upright..those at the end forming a star. **1815** SCOTT *Guy M.* xxvi, Now the light diminished to a distant star that seemed to twinkle on the waters. **1851** MEREDITH *Love in Valley* xiv, Jasmine winds the porch with stars two and three. **1859** TENNYSON *Enid* 313 His charger trampling many a prickly star Of sprouted thistle on the broken stones. **1890** BRIDGES *Shorter Poems* II. viii. ii, From hour to hour unfold A thousand buds and beads In stars and cups of gold.

b. A spot or patch of white hair on the forehead of a horse or ox.

c **1380** *Sir Ferumb.* 3925 Hys hors..bar a sterre on his forhed. **1390** GOWER *Conf.* II. 47 Thus was the hors in sori plit, Bot for al that a sterre whit Amiddes in the front he had. **1607** MARKHAM *Caval.* I. (1617) 22 The pure black, with white star, white foote, or white rach. **1676** *Lond. Gaz.* No. 1103/4 A large brown Bay Coach Gelding..with a made star in the forehead. **1697** DRYDEN *Virg. Georg.* III. 97 The Mother Cow..Her ample Forehead with a Star is crown'd. **1737** BRACKEN *Farriery Impr.* (1757) II. 118 In a Hunter or Road Horse, a Star and Snip makes them look more lightsome. **1842** BORROW *Bible in Spain* xviii, It was of a bright bay colour, with a star in its forehead. **1859** TENNYSON *Enid* 1605 She Kiss'd the white star upon his noble front.

attrib. **1692** *Lond. Gaz.* No. 2800/4 A bright bay Mare,.. some grey Hairs in the Star-place.

c. *Palmistry.*

1653 R. SANDERS *Physiogn.* 24 If upon the mount of Saturn there be any of these marks, as a star or demy-cross. *Ibid.* 43, 57.

d. A star-like crystalline pattern which appears on the surface of antimony in the process of refining.

1660 J. H. *Basil Valentine's Tri. Chariot of Antimony* 150 If thou hast proceeded aright,..thou shalt have a white star shining like to pure silver, and divided, as if the most accurate Painter had described it with its Radij or Beames. *Ibid.*, This Regulus or Star may be often distilled by the fire, [etc.]. **1661** BOYLE *Cert. Physiol. Ess.* (1669) 56 He..shew'd me his Regulus [of Antimony] adorned with a more conspicuous Star than I have seen in several Stellate Regulusses of both Antimony and Mars. **1868** CROOKES & RÖHRIG *Kerl's Metallurgy* I. 546 The appearance of a star upon the surface of the regulus [of antimony] indicates a certain degree of purity.

e. *Zool.* A star-shaped zoophyte or its cell. Also, a stellate sponge-spicule.

1755 J. ELLIS *Corallines* 83 When I applied my Glass to it [a Sea-fig], I found the whole Surface covered with small Stars of six Rays, like small Polypes of six claws. **1839** *Penny Cycl.* XIV. 266/2 *Caryophyllia.* Animals actiniform,.. provided with..tentacula, which project from the surface of stars of cylindriconical cells. **1858** BAIRD *Cycl. Nat. Hist.* s.v. *Anthozoa* 36/2 When the animals are simple and solitary, and only a single star is visible, they form the genus *Fungia*... In some, the whole surface of the coral is roughened with little stars, showing the numbers of animals living in society.

f. = STAR-FISH. ***brittle star*** = OPHIURAN *sb.*

1601 HOLLAND *Pliny* IX. lx. I. 269 Of the sea fishes called Starres... The Starre in the sea..is..a very little fish, made like a starre. **1843, 1863** [see BRITTLE *a.* 4]. **1864** Feather-star [see FEATHER *sb.* 19]. **1890** *Hardwicke's Science-Gossip* XXVI. 199 The brittle stars and star-fishes.

10. a. = ASTERISK 3. (Cf. F. *étoile.*)

1382 WYCLIF *Prol. Job* p. 670 And Origenes alle the volumes of the Olde Testament markide with signe of a ȝerde, and with signe of a sterre [*obelis asteriscisque*]. *Ibid.*, Tho thingus, that vnder sterre signe ben addid.

1557 N. T. (Genev.) To Rdr. **iij, If the bookes do alter in the sentence then it is noted with this starre *. **1571** DIGGES *Pantometria* I. xxxiv. Kiij b, Making thereon a Starre or suche like marke. **1659** C. SIMPSON *Division-Violist* I. 4 Those two Notes marked with little Stars over their Figures. **1662** *H. Broughton's Wks.* 733 Where the Figures are repeated, one Asterisk (or Star, *), is prefixed. **1724** WATTS *Logic* I. v. (1726) 75 What Remarks you find there worthy of your riper Observation, you may note them with a marginal Star. **1830** *Forrester* I. 135 The names must certainly have been supplied by stars, out of consideration to the feelings of families, I suppose. **1847** L. HUNT *Men, Women, & Bks.* II. xi. 267 There were no stars, or other typographical symbols, indicating the passages omitted. **1904** A. MORRISON *Green Diamond* II. ii, Here you are. Lot 87 star, one magnum real old Imperial Tokay... Lot 88 star, ditto.

b. In lists of stockholders, an asterisk prefixed or appended to a person's name when his holding exceeds a certain amount.

In East India stock each vote to which a stockholder was entitled was denoted by a star; one star meant a holding of over £1,000, two stars over £3,000, three stars over £6,000, and four stars over £10,000.

1845 DISRAELI *Sybil* IV. xi, 'The only stars I have got', said Mr. Ormsby, demurely, 'are four stars in India stock'. **1848** THACKERAY *Van. Fair* xx, She was reported to have..three stars to her name in the East India stockholders' list.

c. In guidebooks, one of a number of stars or asterisks against the name of a hotel, restaurant, resort, etc., indicating its rank in a grading system. Cf. *four-star*, *five-star*, etc., under the first elements.

[**1886** S. COOLIDGE *What Katy did Next* vi. 138 'Following a star', in their choice of a hotel..they had decided upon one of those thus distinguished in Baedeker's guide-book.] **1905** E. M. FORSTER *Where Angels fear to Tread* vi. 172 Giotto.. has painted two frescoes... That is why Baedeker gives the place a star. **1939** J. B. PRIESTLEY *Let People Sing* v. 99 A bad inn that is given two stars in the Automobile Association's handbook. **1963** R. CARRIER *Great Dishes of World* 128 If one gave stars to the regions of France—as well as to their better restaurants—for the excellence of their cooking, Burgundy would have an unchallenged 'three'. **1974** *Guardian* 20 Mar. 1/1 The Michelin Guide..said that no [British] restaurants had been awarded two to three stars.

d. Used in various other grading systems, as for cognac, refrigerators, petrol, etc.

1922 JOYCE *Ulysses* 498 It was in consequence of a portwine beverage on top of Hennessy's three stars. **1951** R. POSTGATE *Plain Man's Guide to Wine* ix. 125 'Three Stars' indicates the standard and satisfactory degree of distillation. .. Five Stars should indicate a good brandy. **1968** S. E. ELLACOTT *Everyday Things in England 1914–68* ii. 42 Frozen foods and refrigerators were graded with stars according to the length of time they could be kept fresh. One star denoted a week, two stars a month, and three stars three months. **1971** *Homes & Gardens* Aug. 86/1 Two stars indicate that the temperature is about 10 deg. F. (−12 deg. C.) and frozen food will last for up to four weeks. **1982** *Sunday Tel.* 1 Aug. 6/1 My correspondent objects to the use of star petrol ratings in place of octane numbers.

11. a. The mark of a fracture in a surface of glass or ice, consisting of a central hole or smash with lines of cracks radiating from it.

1842 LEVER *J. Hinton* iii, An ominous-looking star in the looking-glass bore witness to the bullet of a pistol. **1842** TENNYSON *Epic* 12 Where, three times slipping from the outer edge, I bump'd the ice into three several stars.

b. *Thieves' slang.* The act of 'starring the glaze': see STAR *v.* 5.

1812 J. H. VAUX *Flash Dict.* s.v., *The star* is a *game* chiefly practised by young boys,..although the offence is capital... A person convicted of this offence, is said to have been *done for a star*.

c. A blemish in paper.

c **1865** J. WYLDE in *Circ. Sci.* I. 153/2 We..find unaccountable spots, and what are called 'stars' on the surface.

d. *Physics.* A photographic image consisting of a number of lines emanating from a central point, which represent the paths of sub-atomic particles produced by the impact of a cosmic ray or other energetic particle.

1938 *Nature* 1 Oct. 613/1 After an exposure of five months the plates have now been developed and examined. They present singular tracks and stars like those reported in previous papers. **1948** *Science* 26 Nov. 588/2 Approximately 75% of the heavy negative mesons give rise to stars when they come to rest in the emulsion. **1957** G. E. HUTCHINSON *Treat. Limnol.* I. iii. 212 Reactions in which a number of particles are produced.., when they are recorded in a photographic emulsion, are recognized as cosmic ray 'stars'. **1974** *Encycl. Brit. Macropædia* V. 201/2 Interaction of the cosmic-ray particle with the constituents of the emulsion can often be observed as a 'star' in the emulsion; *i.e.*, a spot from which secondary particles are emitted.

12. Applied to various objects shaped or arranged in the conventional form of a star (see 6).

a. *Arch.* A Norman moulding.

1836 H. G. KNIGHT *Archit. Tour Normandy* 199 The most common mouldings are the billet,..hatchet, nebule, star, rope. **1851** E. SHARPE *Seven Periods Archit.* 13 Ornaments of different kinds,—such as the billet, the saw-tooth, the star, and the chevron.

b. *Lace-making.* A kind of stitch.

1882 CAULFEILD & SAWARD *Dict. Needlework* 235 Etoile Stitch. Also known as Star, and made to fill in nine or sixteen squares of a netted foundation, with combinations of Slip Stitch, Point de Toile [etc.]..arranged so to form stars.

c. = *star-fort* (see 20).

1672 LACY tr. *Tacquet's Milit. Archit.* 41 The Banck opposite to the Town..may be fortified with less Works; To wit, with a half sexangular Star, or with a plain Bulwork. *Ibid.* 46 Redoubts and Stars. **1704** J. HARRIS *Lex. Techn.* I.

d. A wheel or pulley in a silk-winding machine. Cf. *star-pulley*, *-wheel* in 20.

1777 in *Phil. Trans.* LXVII. 462 note *a*, The nucleus..is the smaller end of that part of a silk engine called a star. **1835** URE *Philos. Manuf.* 269 The long driving-shaft..on which are fixed a series of light wheels called stars, which bear the bobbin-pulleys, and turn them round by friction.

e. (See quot.)

1875 KNIGHT *Dict. Mech.*, *Star*, a series of radial spokes, forming handles, on the roller of a copperplate or lithographic printing-press.

f. An iron pin used to secure a bird-net.

1851 MAYHEW *Lond. Lab.* II. 66.

†**g.** A number of streets, avenues, or the like, made to converge in one centre. *Obs.*

a **1700** EVELYN *Diary* 1 Apr. 1644, A grove of tall elmes cutt into a starr, every ray being a walk, whose center is a large fountaine. *Ibid.* 5 Oct. 1694, I went also to see the building beginning neere St. Giles's, where 7 streetes make a star from a Doric pillar plac'd in the middle of a circular area. **1762** KAMES *Elem. Crit.* (1763) III. xxiv. 339 A common centre of walks, termed a star.

h. An assemblage of objects arranged so as to form a star.

1831 TRELAWNY *Adv. Younger Son* xxiv, In the spaces between them and the upper deck were two stars of pistols.

i. *Electr. Engin.* A star-connected set of windings; ***in star***, by means of a star connection.

1907 [see NEUTRAL *a.* 4 f]. **1924** A. L. COOK *Elem. Electr. Engin.* xviii. 509 When starting, the three groups of coils are connected in star (or Y). **1962** *Newnes Conc. Encycl. Electr. Engin.* 709/1 A 4-branch star converts to a 6-branch mesh. **1974** HOWATSON & LUND *Princ. Heavy Current Engin.* 109 It is possible to connect star to delta but..no fourth wire can be used and so the calculations become tedious if the system is not balanced. **1976** F. DE LA C. CHARD *Electricity Supply* v. 147 Transformers for 3-phase duty..may have both primary and secondary windings connected in delta or star.

13. *Billiards.* The act of 'starring' (see STAR *v.* 9).

1850 *Bohn's Handbk. Games* (1867) 609 (Rules of Pool), 15. The first person who loses his three lives is entitled to purchase, or, as it is called, to star (a star being the mark placed against his lives on the board, to denote that he has purchased), by paying into the pool the same sum as at the commencement... 17. Only one star is allowed in a Pool.

14. *colloq.* A person who wears a star as a badge (cf. 6); e.g. a police-officer (see quot. 1859); a prisoner of the 'star-class' (see 18).

1859 BARTLETT *Dict. Amer.* (ed. 2) 446 *Stars*, the officers of the new police in the city of New York are so called from their badge, a brass star. **1903** LD. W. NEVILLE *Penal Serv.* xi. 146, I as a 'star' had nothing to do with him directly. **1928** *Notes on Imprisonment* (Home Office) 11 Promotion to the Third Stage may be earned after 12 months, or by 'Stars' after six months. **1945** *Prisons & Borstals* (Home Office) ii. 18 An Ordinary Class prisoner comes into the Second Stage after 12 weeks, a Star after 4 weeks. **1962** 'J. BELL' *Crime in Our Time* VI. ii. 170 Nowadays, the 'stars' as a general rule are by no means first offenders. **1976** A. MILLER *Inside Outside* iv. 48 Several..said that if that was what one-time Stars became, they were cured of returning.

II. *attrib.* and *Comb.*

15. a. In obvious attrib. use.

1821 SHELLEY *Epipsych.* 505 With moonlight patches, or star atoms keen. **1837** CARLYLE *Fr. Rev.* II. III. i, From beyond the Star-galaxies. *a* **1849** E. A. POE *Ulalume* 31 And now, as the night was senescent, And star-dials hinted of morn. **1869** DUNKIN *Midnight Sky* 85 The bright star-group of Cassiopeia. **1870** T. W. HIGGINSON *Army Life in Black Regiment* ix. 209, I know moon-rise, I know star-rise, Lay dis body down. **1890** AGNES M. CLERKE *Syst. Stars* 238 Star-groupings of singularly definite forms are often met with. **1904** *Nature* 9 June 135/2 The error inherent in the star-images. *a* **1918** W. OWEN *Poems* (1963) 95 And tiring after beauty through star-crowds, Dared I go side by side with you. **1920** A. S. EDDINGTON *Space, Time & Gravitation* viii. 127 The measurement of the displacement of the star-image on the photographic plate. **1952** C. DAY LEWIS tr. *Virgil's Aeneid* IV. 82 Often as star-rise, the troubled ghost of my father, Anchises, Comes to me in my dreams. **1954** J. R. R. TOLKIEN *Fellowship of Ring* II. ix. 402 In the star-glimmer they must have offered their cunning foes some mark. **1961** WEBSTER, *Star field*, a region of the sky containing stars either as seen in a telescope or recorded on a photograph. *a* **1963** S. PLATH *Crossing Water* (1971) 63 The pale, star-distance faces. **1968** P. MOORE tr. *E. L. Schatzman's Struct. Universe* i. 11 In 1838 F. W. Bessel.. measured the first star-distance. **1976** *Houston* (Texas) *Chron.* 22 Sept. VII. 1/2 Sumner's first lecture covers the starfield, with the movements of the sun, moon, planets illustrated and explained.

b. objective, as ***star-watcher***; ***star-bearing***, ***-wearing*** adjs.

c **1611** CHAPMAN *Iliad* IV. 54 Heauens starre-bearing hill. **1649** OGILBY *Virg. Æneis* IV. (1684) 204 My Reputation and Star-climbing Fame. **1672** WILD *Poet. Licentia* 39 But hark-you Will, Star-poching is not fair. **1742** BLAIR *Grave* 287 The Star-surveying Sage. **1777** POTTER *Æschylus, Prometh. Chain'd* 44 Passing those star-aspiring heights. **1835** WILLIS *Pencillings* I. iv. 30 Half-a-dozen star-wearing dukes, counts, and marquises. **1869** DUNKIN *Midnight Sky* 5 The star-watcher at an Australian midnight. **1877** BLACKIE *Wise Men Greece* 351 The arts of field-measuring and star-measuring.

c. instrumental, as ***star-embroidered***, ***star-led*** adjs.; instrumental or locative in ***star-born*** adj. Also STAR-SPANGLED.

1597 DRAYTON *Heroic. Ep., John to Matilda* 124 Her star-bestuded crowne. **1599** R. LINCHE *Anc. Fict.* G iv, In a gorgeous and starre-bespotted chariot. **1601** WEEVER *Mirr. Mart.* (Roxb.) 179 Vpon the bosom of the star-deckt skie. **1616** DRUMMOND *Madrigals* l. 4 Night, to this flowrie Globe Ne're show for mee thy starre-embrodred Robe. **1629** MILTON *Ode Nativ.* iv, The Star-led Wisards. **1638** RANDOLPH *Poems* 54 [To Astrologers] But farewell now You hungry star-fed Tribe. **1667** MILTON *P.L.* IV. 976 In progress through the rode of Heav'n Star-pav'd. **1735** THOMSON *Liberty* IV. 424 With star-directed prow, To dare the middle deep. **1786** T. DWIGHT *Amer. Poems* (1793) I. 39 Let every sage and seer, Dreamer of dreams, and star-taught prophet hear! **1791** WOLCOT (P. Pindar) *Remonstrance* 12 The star-bedizen'd sycophants of state. **1798** COLERIDGE *Anc. Mar.* III. xv, The star-dogged Moon. **1799** CAMPBELL *Pleas. Hope* II. 272 On heavenly winds..Float the sweet tones of star-born melody. **1817** MOORE *Lalla Rookh, Veiled Proph.* I. 127 The flying throne of star-taught Soliman! **1821** SHELLEY *To Night* ii, Wrap thy form in a mantle gray Star-inwrought! **1835** TENNYSON *Day-Dream* 85 The silk star-broider'd coverlid. **1863** I. WILLIAMS *Baptistery* II. xxvii. (1874) 129 The sky, with its star-peopled space. **1868** J. R. LOWELL in *Atlantic Monthly* May 627 It is wider Than the star-sown vague of space. **1886** W. B. YEATS *Mosada* 2 For Azolar The star-taught Moor said thus it was decreed. **1895** M. H. KINGSLEY *Diary* 5 June in *Trav. W. Afr.* (1897) vii. 124 The hills silhouetted against the star-powdered purple sky. **1896** A. E. HOUSMAN *Shropshire Lad* 87 The star-filled seas are smooth to-night. **1897** *Atlantic Monthly* Jan. 35 When he [*sc.* Emerson] came to put together his star-born ideas, they fitted well..because they were all part of the same idea. **1901** H. G. WELLS *First Men in Moon* v. 62 That airless, star-dusted sky! **1915** G. FRANKAU *Tid'apa* v. 25 Blue-dark against star-strown turquoise, rose the ramparts of Lallong Ridge. **1920** J. GREGORY *Man to Man* xxiv. 284 The field of star-strewn sky. **1930** J. MASEFIELD *Wanderer of Liverpool* 87 Star-lighted, star-guided, the sea-gleaming beautiful thing. *a* **1936** A. E. HOUSMAN *More Poems* (1936) 166 No star is lost at all From all the star-sown sky. **1945** W. DE LA MARE *Burning-Glass* 11 Ev'n happier in watch of.. A star-strewn nightfall. **1958** *People* 4 May 19/5 Star-studded with ex-League players. **1962** *Daily Tel.* 28 Arp. 20 (*heading*) U.S. seeking 'star-guided' missile for NATO. **1977** *New Yorker* 29 Aug. 20/2 It's Mickey Mouse, imprisoned inside a star-dusted transparent balloon. **1978** *Listener* 16 Mar. 339/1 In an otherwise star-studded cast, the lead characters are not quite up to their role.

d. similative, as ***star-distant, -eyed, -leaved, -shaped, -sweet*** adjs.; ***star-wise*** adv.

1608 TOPSELL *Serpents* 247 That kind of Spyder.. is more knowne by his little spots made starre-wise. **1642** H. MORE *Song of Soul* II. App. xcix, Ruby-lip'd, pearl-teeth'd, stare-eyn'd. *c* **1711** PETIVER *Gazophyl.* VI. lvi, Star-leaved Persia Chickweed. *Ibid.* IX. lxxxii, Star-flowred Globe Cats-foot. **1799** UNDERWOOD *Dis. Childhood* (ed. 4) II. 133 Three or four strips of adhesive plaster, applied star-wise. **1799** CAMPBELL *Pleas. Hope* II. 325 Oh! star-eyed Science. **1812** *New Bot. Gard.* I. 24 Adorned with many star-shaped flowers. **1821** S. F. GRAY *Brit. Plants* I. 75 Leaves.. Star-ribbed, *stellinervia*. **1855** TENNYSON *Maud* I. III, Passionless, pale, cold face, star-sweet on a gloom profound. **1859** FITZGERALD *Omar* lxxv, Among the Guests Star-scatter'd on the grass. **1859** LD. LYTTON *Wanderer* (ed. 2) 285 At dawn star-distant thou wilt be. **1861** P. P. CARPENTER in *Rep. Smithsonian Instit.* 1860, 278 In *Botryllus*, the breathing-holes are star-shaped. **1878** G. M. HOPKINS *Poems* (1967) 77 Star-eyed straw-berry-breasted Throstle. **1883** *Encycl. Brit.* XVI. 681/2 Each chromatophore-cell has from six to ten muscular bands attached to its walls, radiating from it star-wise. **1884** SARGENT *Rep. Forests N. Amer.* 86 *Liquidambar Styraciflua*.. Star-leaved Gum. **1900** W. B. YEATS *Shadowy Waters* 9 More shining winds, more star-glimmering ponds? **1943** S. SPENDER *Spiritual Exercises* 6 Outside, the eternal star-tall mountains gleam.

16. a. With reference to the knowledge of astrology or astronomy, as ***star-craft, -lore,*** †***-read*** [REDE *sb.*[1]], ***-skill; star-read, -skilled, -wise*** adjs.; in designations (some jocular or contemptuous) of an astrologer or astronomer, as ***star-catcher, -clerk, -conner, -man, -master, -monger, -peeper,*** †***-tooter.***

a **1250** *Owl & Night.* 1318 Þe mon mot beo well storre [*Jesus MS.* sturre]-wis. **1573** R. LEVER *Arte Reason* 6 The arte of measuring, witcrafte, speachcraft, starre-craft, &c. **1575** GASCOIGNE *Fruites of Warre* xv. Wks. 1907 I. 144 If Mars moove warre, as Starcoonners can tel. **1583** STUBBES *Anat. Abus.* II. (1882) 57 As these foolish starre tooters promised. **1591** SYLVESTER *Du Bartas* I. iii. 494 If, at the least, Star-Clarks be credit worth. **1593** NASHE *Four Lett. Conf.* Wks. (Grosart) II. 252 Pierce Pennilesse is a better Star-munger than a Diuelmunger. **1596** SPENSER *F.Q.* v. Proem viii, Those Ægyptian wisards old, Which in Star-read were wont haue best insight. **1599** B. JONSON *Ev. Man out of Hum.* III. vii, These star-monger knaves, who would trust 'hem? **1602** WARNER *Alb. Eng.* XIII. lxxvii. 319 Obseruing which of Images, he hous'd himselfe them in, And, star-skil'd, opportunely there did Oracles begin. **1606** SYLVESTER *Du Bartas* II. iv. I. *Tropheis* 796 The Star-wise sometimes calculates (By an Eclipse) the death of Potentates. **1607** DEKKER *Knt.'s Conjur.* (1842) 9 The celestiall bodies for any thing star-catchers knew, were in very good health. **1610** HEALEY *St. Aug. Citie of God* XVIII. viii. Vives 667 That star-skil that Abraham taught the Phænicians. **1620** MELTON *Astrolog.* 24 Hearing a Starre-catcher make a long.. discourse about the Celestiall Signes. *c* **1640** H. BELL *Luther's Colloq. Mens.* (1652) 505 An astrologer or Star-peeper. **1654** GATAKER *Disc. Apol.* 4 So would I fain know of this great Star-master, how it comes to pass, that [etc.]. **1708** SWIFT *Poems, Grub St. Elegy* Epitaph, A cobbler, starmonger, and quack. **1821** BYRON *Sardanap.* II. i. 12 The star-read Chaldean. **1836** R. FURNESS *Astrologer* II. Wks. (1858) 149 Which brought the star-man to the realms below. **1871** B. TAYLOR *Faust* II. II. iii. 134 Hast thou in star-lore any power? **1871** TYLOR *Prim. Cult.* II. 402 Our astronomers may only find in the starcraft of the lower races an uninstructive combination of myth and common-place.

b. With reference to 'nebular' or other theories of the formation of the stars.

1839 BAILEY *Festus* (1852) 516 Then there came A voice, as of a star-cloud in the sky. **1870** PROCTOR *Other Worlds* xii. 287 The region where those nebulæ appear has been drained of star-material, so to speak, in order to form them. **1870** —— *Pleas. Ways Sci.* (1879) 145 Star-mist, under which head I include all orders of nebulæ. **1885** PATER *Marius* (1910) I. v. 61 Apuleius had gathered into it the floating star-matter of many a delightful story. **1899** C. F. D'ARCY *Idealism & Theol.* i. 50 From star-cloud to civilisation, all is the result of slow development. **1900** *Edin. Rev.* Apr. 462 The 'lucid matter' of space is neither more nor less than star-spawn. **1902** *Blackw. Mag.* July 66 What force could twist a great mass of star-stuff—we have no better name for it—into the form of a spiral. **1905** AGNES CLERKE *Mod. Cosmogonies* 54 If space contained only full-grown stars and no stars in the making—no star-spawn, no star-protoplasm.

17. With the sense 'shaped like a conventional star', 'arranged in the form of a star', 'ornamented with stars' (see 6).

1590 *Acc. Bk. W. Wray* in *Antiquary* XXXII. 374, ii dosse' great stare buttons. **1613** in *Heriot's Mem.* App. VII. (1822) 220 A starre pendant set with diamonds. **1681** GREW *Musæum* III. §i. iii. 281 A Piece of Fungites with Great Star-Work. **1812** *Sporting Mag.* XXXIX. 168 A cocked hat with a star-loop. **1851** RUSKIN *Stones Venice* I. App. 8. 364 The salt sea winds have eaten away the fair shafting of its star window into a skeleton of crumbling rays. **1882** CAULFEILD & SAWARD *Dict. Needlework* 30 Double Stitch.. is also known by the name of 'star stitch'. *Ibid.* 460 *Star Braid*, a kind of Braid.. made in blue and red, and having a white star. **1883** GRESLEY *Gloss. Coal-mining* 238 *Star reamer*, a tool for regulating the diameter of or straightening a borehole, made star-shaped at the base. **1895** ELEANOR ROWE *Chip Carving* 69 A small star punch was used instead of the single-pointed one.

18. With the sense 'marked or distinguished by a star or asterisk'. In *Prison slang*, with reference to the badge worn by 'first offenders'.

1814 *Hist. Univ. Oxford* II. 259 This is the dress of business; it is used.. in the morning at church, excepting star days. **1882** *Daily News* 6 Feb. 3/5 The new category to be distinguished by the title of 'Star-class Prisoners'. **1888** *Encycl. Brit.* XXIII. 783/2 The 'star-routes'.. gave rise to.. great scandals. **1890** C. L. NORTON *Polit. Americanisms* 108 *Star Routes*.. are post-office routes which are not self-supporting, and are designated by asterisks in the 'Postal Guide'. **1891** *Pall Mall Mag.* Nov. 454 'Star' prisoners are generally, but not always, first offenders. **1903** LD. W. NEVILLE *Penal Serv.* vi. 66 There were only five parties in which 'star' men were allowed to work.

19. In senses 5 a, b, c.

1839 F. MARRYAT *Diary in Amer.* II. II. xiii. 121 They look for importations of star actors from this country. **1849** *Athenæum* 30 June 677/2 Mr. Lumley, resolute in star-chasing, has absolutely succeeded in luring Madame Rossi back. **1864** *Reader* 19 Nov. 650/3 Mdlle. Nillson, the new star-soprano at this theatre. **1876** 'MARK TWAIN' *Tom Sawyer* iv. 50 He had been around among the star pupils inquiring. **1879** C. E. PASCOE *Dramatic Notes* 68 What is known as 'star-acting' usually forms the principal feature of the bills of this theatre. **1890** W. JAMES *Princ. Psychol.* I. xi. 453 The laws of stimulation and association.. *may* at times simply form the background for a 'star-performer', who is no more their 'inert accompaniment' or their 'incidental product' than Hamlet is Horatio's or Ophelia's. **1904** MRS. ALEC TWEEDIE *Behind Footlights* vi. 123 She.. has played many star parts in the provinces. **1905** VACHELL *Hill* viii, It's a star-performance, I tell you. **1905** *Sat. Rev.* 28 Oct. 545 He finds himself now spectator instead of star performer. **1909** *Times* 24 Aug. 15/6 The engaging of outside 'star' players to strengthen a county [cricket] side. **1917** T. E. LAWRENCE *Lett.* (1938) 219 The star film showed the Pyramids. **1927** *Melody Maker* Sept. 923/1 The all too few star performers in this country. **1933** J. CARY *Amer. Visitor* xiii. 169 Uli turned out one of the star pupils. **1943** N. COWARD *Middle East Diary* (1944) 23 He must possess.. what is described in the theatre as 'star quality'... Complete authority, a direct eye, and a compelling economy of gesture. **1950** *Sport* 22–28 Sept. 12/4 Have too many star players been allowed to drift away from the Swansea Town fold? **1961** *Ann. Reg. 1960* 446 Star acting was also the chief merit of *The Last Angry Man*. **1972** *Vogue* Feb. 89/3 Twiggy's got this rather mysterious presence. Star quality. **1977** *New Yorker* 19 Sept. 75/1 I'm sure Mme. Dorfmann is furious with the review, because he's her star pupil. **1978** J. GARDNER *Dancing Dodo* xxxii. 256 You're playing the star role—Hercule Poirot—and I've got to coach you. **1982** *London Review Bks.* IV. xxiv. 20/2 Star quality, however, was not at all what was looked for in those who played opposite a superstar like Kean.

20. Special comb.: **star-back** *slang*, an expensive, reserved seat at a circus; **star bill**, a poster advertising a theatrical star; **star billing** = *top billing* s.v. BILLING *vbl. sb.*[3] b; also *transf.* and *fig.*; †**star-blasting**, the pernicious influence of malign stars; **star boarder** *U.S.*, a boarder, usu. of long standing, having or regarded as having special privileges; also used euphemistically of more complicated relationships; **star-burst**, (*a*) an explosion of a star or stars, or an explosion producing an appearance of stars; (*b*) *Photogr.*, a lens attachment which causes a bright light source to appear in a photograph with added star-like rays; also, the effect so produced; usu. *attrib.*; **star-catalogue**, a list of stars, with their position, magnitude, etc.; **star-chart**, a chart which shows the stars in a certain portion of the sky; **star-clock**, a sidereal clock; **star cloud**, a region of the sky where stars appear to be especially numerous and close together; **star-cluster**, a number of stars closely grouped together; **star connection** *Electr. Engin.*, an arrangement in a polyphase system in motors and the like by which one end of each phase winding is connected to a common point; so **star-connected** *a.*; **star count**, a statistical survey of the stars in various directions in space to ascertain the numerical distribution across the sky of stars brighter than some given magnitude; †**star-cross** *a.* = *star-crossed adj.*; **star-crossed** *a.*, thwarted by a malign star; **star-cut** *a.*, of a diamond, cut with star-facets; *sb.*, this style of cutting; also in extended uses (see quots.); **star-delta** *Electr. Engin.*, used *attrib.* with reference to the use of star connection when an induction motor is started with a change to delta connection for continuous running; **star drag** *Angling* (see quot. 1960); **star-drift**, a proper motion common to a group of stars; **star-facet**, one of the eight small triangular facets which surround the table of a brilliant; †**star-fashion** *a.* (of a flower), star-shaped; †**star-flint**, ? cf. STAR-STONE; **star-fort**, a small fort having alternate salient and reentrant angles; **star fracture** *Med.*, a fracture with radiating fissures; **star-gauge**, (*a*) a determination by the average of a number of observations of the number of stars visible in a given portion of the heavens; (*b*) a gauge with radiating steel points for measuring the bore of a cannon at any part of its length; **star-gauging** = prec. (*a*); †**star-gem**, ? the cat's-eye; **star-glint** (see quot.); **star-god**, a star or planet worshipped as a deity (cf. *star-worship*); **star lot**, an item in a sale catalogue added after the numbering is completed, and therefore designated by a starred number; **star-map**, a projection of the whole or part of the heavens, showing the position of the stars; **star network**, a data or communication network in which all terminals are independently connected to one central unit; **Star of David** = MAGEN DAVID; **star-pagoda**, an Indian gold coin (cf. PAGODA 3); **star point** *Electr. Engin.*, the common junction of the windings in a star-connected system; **star-proof** *a.*, impervious to starlight; also *transf.*; **star-pulley** = *star-wheel* (b); **star quad** *Telecommunications*, a quad (QUAD *sb.*[6]) in which the four conductors are all twisted around a common axis, with members of each pair being diametrically opposite each other; usu. *attrib.*; **star-queen** *poet.*, the moon; †**star-real, -rial** = SPUR-RIAL; †**star-redoubt, -sconce** = *star-fort*; **star-shake**, a shake in timber consisting of radial fissures; **star-shell** *Mil.*, a shell which on bursting releases a shower of stars, to illuminate the enemy's position at night; **star-shooter, -shooting**, jocularly used with reference to taking the altitude of stars; **star-shower**, a shower of falling meteors; †**star-staring** *pres. pple.* and *ppl. a.* = STAR-GAZING; **star stream**, †(*a*) a narrow band of the sky that is rich in stars; (*b*) each of the two groups of stars in star streaming; **star streaming**, the phenomenon (explained by the rotation of the galaxy) in which stars show a broad tendency to have proper motions in one or other of two opposite directions, thus falling approximately into two intermingled groups ('streams'); **star-stroke** (see quot.); **star system**, (*a*) in the world of film and theatrical entertainment, the practice of promoting an eminent artiste in leading roles; (*b*) a large structured collection of stars, a galaxy; **star-tracker**, a self-regulating device which maintains its orientation relative to a star, used in the control systems of spacecraft; so **star-tracking** *vbl. sb.*; **star-trap** *Theatr.*, a trap in the stage-floor consisting of five or more wedge-shaped pieces which part when pressure is applied to the centre, used for the sudden appearance or disappearance of a gymnastic performer; **star turn**, the principal or most important item in an entertainment; also *fig.*; **star-vehicle**, a play or film designed especially to show off the talents of a particular actor or actress; **Star Wars** (also with lower-case initials), the title of a popular science-fiction film released in 1977, used (chiefly *attrib.*) as the informal name for a military defence strategy proposed by U.S. President Reagan in 1983, in which enemy weapons would be destroyed in space by lasers, antiballistic missiles, etc., launched or directed from orbiting military satellites; cf. *SDI* s.v. S 4 a; **star-wheel**, †(*a*) a firework combining the shapes of a wheel and a star; (*b*) a wheel with radial projections or teeth, used in winding-machines, clockwork, etc.; **star witness**, the principal or most important witness in a trial; **star-worship** = SABAISM; hence **star-worshipper**; †**star-ypointing** *ppl. a.* [erroneously formed], pointing to the stars.

1931 *Amer. Mercury* Nov. 354/1 *Starbacks, the reserved seat section. **1933** E. SEAGO *Circus Company* iii. 23 He sat with me in the 'star backs'. **1965** M. STEWART *Airs above Ground* vi. 72 Tim had no difficulty in getting what he called 'starback' seats... These, the best seats, were rather comfortable portable chairs.. right at the ring-side. **1901** A. CHEVALIER *Before I Forget* 157 Just ordered fresh stock of special printing, *star bills, &c. **1956** H. KURNITZ *Invasion of Privacy* iii. 27 One picture a year... *Star billing. **1959** *Listener* 5 Feb. 238/1 The Chinese still give credit to the Russians for their technical aid, but there has been a change in the star billing. Now they say these things were done by Chinese engineers with Soviet assistance. **1967** *Amer. N. & Q.* June 156/1 *Behind Spanish American Footlights* is the key reference tool in its field, and as such rates star billing. **1979** *Listener* 25 Oct. 547/3 The *Radio Times*.. gives Ted Heath (1970–74) star billing. **1605** SHAKS. *Lear* III. iv. 60 Blisse thee from Whirle-Windes, *Starre-blasting, and taking. **1877** in H. Asbury *Gem of Prairie* (1940) iv. 135 Jessie Curtis, *star boarder, is still at 519 State Street. **1897** *Boston Jrnl.* 16 Jan. 6/5 'I'm afraid you are about to be dethroned.' The Star Boarder—'Why?' **1908** J. M. SULLIVAN *Criminal Slang* 24 *Star boarder or lodger*, a boarder.. in good financial standing who has all the privileges of a husband. **1922** N. B. TARKINGTON *Gentle Julia* 113 The pill-boxes [for insects].. evidently contained star boarders, for they were pierced with 'breathing holes'. 1935 J. Hargan Gloss. Prison Lang. 8 Star-boarder, a lifer. 1935 A. J. Pollock Underworld Speaks 113/2 Star boarder, the inmate of a house of prostitution, who earns the most money. 1976 'O. Bleeck' No Questions Asked xii. 137 He lived here and we split expenses... He was sort of a star boarder. 1965 G. McInnes Road to Gundagai iii. 56 Rockets whooshed skyward ending in great parabolic *starbursts. 1977 G. Michanowsky Once & Future Star i. 3 At the dawn of human history,.. this starburst occurred and briefly became visible as a.. second sun in our sky. 1977 J. Hedgecoe Photographer's Handbk. 181 A clear sky can be filled with diverging lines if the sun is spread by means of a starburst filter. 1978 Amateur Photographer 2 Aug. 110/1 Sparkling highlights are emphasized with a cross screen (star-burst). 1979 Ibid. 30 May 92/3 A very special filter which not only gives a star-burst effect, but rays of the starburst are tinged with the colours of the spectrum. 1830 Carlyle Richter & De Stael Ess. 1840 II. 405 A lively people.. can at least use *star-catalogues, and some planisphere thereof. 1866 Proctor Handbk. Stars 44 Aided by well-constructed *star-charts. 1878 Huxley Physiogr. xx. 341, 23 hours, 56 minutes, and 4 seconds would be a day by the '*star-clock'. 1924 Proc. Amer. Acad. Arts & Sciences LIX. 217 Fainter stars of division A reveal through their distribution the relative nearness of the *star clouds in Cygnus. 1947 Astrophysical Jrnl. CV. 257 The regions of the star clouds in Sagittarius and Ophiuchus are rich in clearly marked globules. 1870 Proctor Other Worlds xii. 288 In fact, each of the Nubeculæ is at once a *star-cluster and a cluster of nebulæ. 1896 D. C. & J. P. Jackson Alternating Currents II. viii. 395 If the armature is *star connected, the pressure between rings is equal to the vector sum of the pressure developed in the two coils. 1976 F. de la C. Chard Electr. Supply v. 145 A star-connected winding has only $1/\sqrt{3}$ times the line voltage across each phase but carries the full line current. 1894 G. Kapp Electric Transmission of Energy (ed. 4) xii. 418 The armature is drum wound with *star connection. 1969 Power System Protection (Electr. Council) II. xi. 404 Busbar reactors. (b) Tie bar connected. Two methods are commonly adopted and may be classified as (i) the star connection.., and (ii) the ring connection. 1889 Nature 8 Aug. 345/1 For simple *star-counts, we have only to substitute star-counts by magnitudes over selected areas of the sky. 1933 Discovery Feb. 41/2 The modern method employed for thus studying the distribution of stars is the statistical one of 'star-counts'. 1947 Astrophysical Jrnl. CV. 257 Stoddard has made star counts according to photographic and photovisual magnitudes for four large globules. 1608 Middleton Fam. Love iv. ii. G 1, Since these proiects haue had so *star crosse euents. 1592 Shaks. Rom. & Jul. Prol. 6 A paire of *starre-crost louers, take their life. 1600 Dekker Fortunatus H 1, The star-crost sonne of Fortunatus. 1962 C. Oman Mary of Modena v. 172 Abbé Armand Jean de Bouthillier de Rancé of La Trappe had, according to rumour, well known star-crost love before he suddenly renounced the world at the age of thirty-six. 1973 Alberta Hist. Rev. Winter 12/1 But if Uncle Charlie's first motivation was star-crossed love, his second was certainly horses. 1977 W. M. Spackman Armful of Warm Girl 18 She wailed in star-crossed despair. 1704 Lond. Gaz. No. 4046/4 Another [Ring] with 3 Diamonds, *Star-cut. 1850 Holtzapffel Turning III. 1331 Generally the trap cut, or the star cut, is employed on the back, and the stone is then said to have a.. star-cut back. 1967 Wodehouse Company for Henry iii. 45 Clichy double overlay weight,.. the top flattened by a large window, star-cut base. 1972 J. Howard-Williams Sails (ed. 3) xii. 172 The genniker (or spanker, or star-cut spinnaker) is.. a cross between a genoa and a spinnaker... It is primarily a racing sail... It is cut rather like a storm spinnaker, with full width foot tapering to the rule minimum 75 per cent at mid-girth, with narrow shoulders from there up. 1976 Yachting World Oct. 72/1 Spinnakers are sewn in a special corner of Hood's loft with a five-step machine. This sews a unique five-stitch seam on star-cut spinnakers. 1908 W. B. Hird Elem. Dynamo Design ix. 260 If the *star-delta method of connection is used [in the starting of a squirrel-cage motor], the ratio must be 1 to 1·73, and no other choice can be made. 1962 Newnes Conc. Encycl. Electr. Engin. 517/1 Star-delta starting is one method of reducing starting current of 3-phase motors. 1976 F. de la C. Chard Electr. Supply v. 148 A star-delta connection for a step-down transformer is normally used. 1950 N.Y. Times 30 Dec. 18/8 While you could stand a heavier bait rod and a reel with *star drag, the regulation bait rod will suffice. 1960 C. Willock Angler's Encycl., Star-drag, adjustable tension device often built into big sea multiplying reels. Tension is varied by means of a star-shaped nut. 1979 Angling July 33/1 (Advt.), Rugged star drag design with white-oak leather washers for smooth line control. 1870 Proctor in Proc. Roy. Soc. XVIII. 169 When the proper motions are indicated in maps,.. the *star-drift (as the phenomenon may be termed) becomes very evident. 1751 *Star facets [see skill sb.[1] 9]. 1813 Mawe Diamonds (1823) 79 The triangles on the bizel, adjacent to the girdle, are called skill facets, and those which join the table, star facets. 1597 Gerarde Herbal ii. cxxv. 393 Stalks.. whereupon do grow faire yellow flowers, *star fashion. 1640 Parkinson Theat. Bot. 132 The flower is purple, starre fashion, and yellow in the middle. c1711 Petiver Gazophyl. vii. lxviii, Wiltshire *Star-flint... This Fossil is represented, as cut, polisht, and designed for a Snuff-box. 1704 J. Harris Lex. Techn. I, *Star-fort. 1783 Justamond tr. Raynal's Hist. Indies VI. 117 Fort Lewis.. is but a wretched star-fort, incapable of much resistance. 1834-47 J. S. Macaulay Field Fortif. (1851) 20 Star forts are usually constructed either on a triangle or on a square. 1892 Daily News 27 May 3/4 There was a mark on the right temple.. and from this point a fracture of the skull started. This ran round to the left side, where there was a *star fracture. 1784 Sir W. Herschel Sci. Papers (1912) I. 162, I call it Gaging the Heavens, or the *Star-Gage. It consists in repeatedly taking the number of stars in ten fields of view of my reflector very near each other, and by adding their sums, and cutting off one decimal on the right. 1847 Sir J. Herschel Astron. Observ. Cape 373 A system of star-gauges was set on foot. 1875 Knight Dict. Mech. 2310/2 Star-Gage (Ordnance). 1870 Proctor Other Worlds Pref. 8 The fact that Sir William Herschel adopted an erroneous hypothesis as the basis of his system of *star-gauging. 1693 Dale Pharmacol. 100 Asteria gemma, Offic. The Bastard-Opal or *Star-Gemm. 1867 Smyth Sailor's Word-bk., *Star-Glint, a meteorite. 1879 Proctor Flowers of Sky ii. 24 note, The worship of *star-gods. 1905 Budge Egypt. Heaven & Hell II. 263 Three bearded beings, the 'Star-gods'. 1854 Poultry Chron. I. 80/1 Two young Brahma Pootra fowls, not included in the catalogue (introduced as *star lots). 1866 Proctor Handbk. Stars 11 The projection and construction of *star-maps. 1900 W. B. Blaikie (title) Monthly Star Maps for the Year 1900. 1977 Financial Times 21 Feb. 13/1 Modern data networks have come a long way since the banks first started installing their enormous *star networks, consisting of one or two very big computer centres serving several thousand simple terminals installed in branch back offices. 1979 T. Housley Data Communications & Teleprocessing Systems ii. 52 There are four basic network configurations that can be used: the star network, the ring network, the mesh network, and the hierarchical network. The star network.. is probably the most common. 1941 M. Samuel tr. Bein's Theodore Herzl ii. vii. 229 At one side hung a flag: a white field with two blue stripes and the *Star of David. 1979 N.Y. Rev. Bks. 25 Oct. 3/2 Jan Friedländer's book plates displayed a score by Chopin set within a Star of David. 1799 Hull Advertiser 21 Dec. 4/1 The prize fund amounted.. to *star pagodas 25 lacks 34.804. 1858 Beveridge Hist. India II. vi. v. 711 One lac of star pagodas (£40,000). 1908 W. B. Hird Elem. Dynamo Design vii. 186 The *star point.. is usually connected to earth, both at the generator and at the load end. 1969 Power System Protection (Electr. Council) II. xi. 404 Each section of busbar is connected via a reactor to a common star point, and if the feeders and generators are suitably arranged little or no current need flow through the reactors. a1645 Milton Arcades 89 Under the shady roof Of branching Elm *Star-proof. 1871 Swinburne Songs bef. Sunrise Prelude 101 Star-proof trees. 1873 Lytton Ken. Chillingly i. xi, To all female fascinations he had been hitherto star-proof. 1839 Ure Dict. Arts 1109 The *star pulleys c, c. 1930 Gloss. Terms Telegraphs & Telephones (B.S.I.) 31 *Star quad cable, a cable containing a number of quads, each quad formed by twisting together four insulated conductors about a common axis. 1958 J. R. G. Smith Elem. Telecommunications Pract. v. 73 Other features of star-quad cables are that in some cables certain of the pairs are screened by being wrapped in metallized paper..; they are placed in the centre of the core and used for music. 1970 P. Norman in T. L. Squires Telecomm. Pocket Bk. v. 53 Some 4,000 miles of these [balanced pair] systems are installed in this country, consisting mainly of 24-pair, 40 lb per mile conductors in star-quad formation. 1818 Keats Endymion iv. 589 The *Star-Queen's crescent [cf. Horace Carm. Saec. 35 siderum regina bicornis]. 1580 Fermor Acc. in Archæol. Jrnl. (1851) VIII. 185 It. rec. of old gold, one *staw [sic] ryall, a duckett [etc.]. 1606 Holland Sueton. Annot. 34 Our olde Edward Star-Reals, or fifteene shilling peeces. 1702 Milit. Dict. (1704) *Star-Redoute, of four, of five, of six, or of more points, otherwise call'd an Estoile. 1632 Swed. Intelligencer i. 112 The great *Starre-Sconce or Toll-house by the old Elue. 1875 Laslett Timber 178 The chief defect in Mexican Mahogany is the prevalence of *star-shake. 1883 M. P. Bale Saw-Mills 336 Star shake, consists of clefts which radiate from the pith or centre of the tree towards the circumference or bark. 1876 Will & Dalton Artill. Handbk. Ref. 224 The *star shell... The interior is filled with 13 stars. The stars are paper cylinders filled with a composition which burns about 18 seconds and gives a brilliant light. 1899 Daily News 1 Dec. 3/4 There is also on board a large quantity of star shell. 1863 Athenæum 21 Nov. 63 When navigators first began to make observations with instruments on deck, the self-sufficient called them *star-shooters and when the star's altitude was taken would ask if they had hit it. 1898 Daily News 14 Apr. 2/3 After a good deal of *star-shooting and other scientific operations. 1818 Shelley Stanzas Written in Deject. ii, I see the waves upon the shore, Like light dissolved in *star-showers, thrown. 1869 Dunkin Midnight Sky 137 The memorable star-showers of November 1866, 1867, and 1868. 1621 Brathwait Nat. Embassie (1877) 20 *Star-staring earthling, puff'd with insolence. a1661 Fuller Worthies, Worc. (1662) 182 They saw You gone, but whether could not tell, Star-staring, though they ask'd both Heaven and Hell. 1894 Knowledge 1 June 133/1 The streams are in most cases accompanied by narrow black channels in the general nebulosity, which run parallel to and alongside of the *star streams. 1904 J. C. Kapteyn in H. J. Rogers Congress of Arts & Science (1906) IV. 418 Here we have a clear indication that we have to do with two star-streams. 1925 Ark. f. Mat., Astr. och Fysik XIXa. xxi. 1, I have tried to find a clue to a possible connection between the star-streaming discovered by Kapteyn, 'the two star-streams', and the asymmetrical drift of high stellar velocities. 1968 W. M. Smart Riddle of Universe vi. 106 Kapteyn's star-streams are consistent with the phenomenon of galactic rotation and are indeed explained by it. 1906 Rep. Brit. Assoc. Adv. Sci. 1905 257 (heading) *Star streaming. 1921 Discovery Feb. 36/1 In 1904 Professor Kapteyn.. read at the Astronomical Congress at St. Louis, U.S.A., a paper of far-reaching importance, in which he announced the discovery of star-streaming. 1979 Lang & Gingerich Source Bk. Astron. & Astrophysics lxxvii. 514 Karl Schwarzschild showed that it was unnecessary to think of two star streams and that the phenomenon of star streaming could be explained by assuming that the individual motions of the stars are distributed in an ellipsoid with the long axis in the direction of motion of Kapteyn's two star streams. 1855 Dunglison Med. Lex., Coup de Soleil,.. Stroke of the sun, Ægyptian *Starstroke or Sunstroke. 1832 Rep. Sel. Comm. on Dramatic Lit. in Parl. Papers 1831-32 VII. 30 The *star system that has been adopted by the two great theatres. 1870 R. A. Proctor Other Worlds than Ours 256 To return for a moment to fig. 2, it will be seen at once that an aperture extending laterally through a star system so shaped must have a particular direction and be perfectly straight in order to be visible to observers placed, as we are supposed to be, in the central opening. 1890 G. B. Shaw in Star 18 Apr. 2/3 The familiar star system trick of making the minor characters slur their work in order to leave plenty of time for the mock pregnant pauses.. of the leading actor. 1928 A. S. Eddington Nature Physical World viii. 167 The first partitions [of the gaseous nebulae] are the star-systems such as our galactic system. 1937 A. Calder-Marshall in C. Day Lewis Mind in Chains 71 This tendency.. has led to the star-system deplored by film critics almost without exception. 1967 P. Moore Amat. Astronomer's Gloss. 89 Nubeculæ (or Magellanic Clouds), the nearest of the external star-systems, and so the brightest as seen with the naked eye. 1971 Guardian 5 June 9/4 Hollywood was devising the 'star system', the big solo buildup, the personality cult of the silent screen. 1962 Aeroplane & Commercial Aviation News CIII. 32/1 The main outstanding problem in the provision of such a system is the development of a suitable daylight *star-tracker. 1978 Nature 5 Oct. 378/2 The star tracker in the scientific instrument can identify and guide on stars brighter than 14 mag. 1964 Discovery Oct. 7/3 A *star-tracking ability can readily be developed from the same system. 1873 Routledge's Young Gentl. Mag. 279/1 A *star trap is circular in form. 1898 A. M. Binstead Pink 'Un & Pelican ii. 44 The '*star turns' in the entertainment, which took place twice every day, were the then unknown Paul Cinquevalli, Batty, the natty horseman.. the 'Beautiful Geraldine', and two savage and sullen brown bears. 1906 E. Dyson Fact'ry 'Ands vii. 78 In fact the packer soon found that waiting was Eric's 'star turn'. 1909 Flight 3 July 398/1 M. Bleriot.. is the 'star turn' at the Brayelle aerodrome at Douai just now. 1915 H. G. Wells Boon 328 'Inevitably,' said the Bishop, 'this theatricalism, this star-turn business, with its extreme spiritual excitements,.. leads to such a breakdown as afflicts you.' 1951 J. G. Fennessy Sonnet if Bottle iv. iv. 116 You're our star turn, it's up to you. 1977 'E. Crispin' Glimpses of Moon xii. 232 His normal chief recreation.. is watching other people at work. And in this.. it is the two workmen who are the star turns. 1932 New Yorker 9 Jan. 43/1 As a spectacle it is a typical *star vehicle hitched up to a singer with.. a weak larynx. 1953 K. Reisz Technique Film Editing i. 60 Many of the films built round the personality of Greta Garbo.. are little more than ingeniously contrived star-vehicles, yet they cannot be dismissed as worthless. 1974 Listener 2 May 580/2 Few self-respecting dramatists want to construct star-vehicles nowadays, and so Robert Morley.. has written one for himself. [1977 Washington Post 4 Sept. A12/2 Four decks above the tow, the Bernard G.'s pilot house looks more like something from Star Wars than from Mark Twain. 1982 Space World Aug.-Sept. 10 (heading) The real star wars. Ibid. 10/1 The years from now to the end of the century will be critical in the real 'star war' to determine who will exercise control of earth through dominance of space.] 1983 Time 4 Apr. 19/2 The first question is one of commitment: whether Ronald Reagan understands what it takes to nudge a doubting, cash-short nation into serious consideration of his *star wars defense concept. 1984 Times 3 July 1/8 The Foreign Secretary.. urged the Soviet Union to discuss 'star wars' weapons with America. 1984 Daily Tel. 27 Oct. 6/3 'Star Wars' is the term that has been applied to various defensive systems designed to destroy enemy weapons outside the earth's atmosphere. 1985 Radio Times 1 July 36/4 President Reagan believes his 'Star Wars' defence initiative may end the threat from nuclear weapons. 1797 Encycl. Brit. (ed. 3) XV. 716/1 The *Star-wheel illuminated. 1848 Archæologia XXXIII. 32 The wheel B carries 6 pins, which act upon the star-wheel C of 12 rays, and cause it to revolve in 48 hours. 1876 Preece & Sivewright Telegraphy 117 They admit the teeth of a little star wheel. 1924 W. M. Raine Troubled Waters xvii. 183 Haight [sc. a district attorney] was very gentle and considerate of his *star witness. 1978 P. Moyes Who is Simon Warwick? xi. 137 The prosecutors were.. satisfied with the evidence. Susan Benedict was to be their star witness. 1860 Pusey Min. Proph. 243 That favourite study of the Chaldæans, astrology, 'the mysteries', *star-worship. Ibid. 447 The milder form of idolatry, the *star-worshippers. 1630 Milton Shaks. 4 Under a *Star-ypointing Pyramid.

21. In names of animals: **star-buzzard**, an American hawk of the genus *Asturina*; † **star-cake**, ? some flattish species of sea-urchin; **star-coral**, a coral of the family *Astræidæ*; **star-cowry** (see quot.); **star-finch**, the redstart; † **star-hawk**, a goshawk (*Astur*); † **star-lizard**, a lizard of the genus *Stellio*; **star-mouthed**, epithet of the family *Strongylidæ* of nematoid worms; **star-nose**, **-nosed**, epithet of certain moles, esp. *Condylura cristata*; † **star-spider**, the *asterion* of Pliny; **star-tail**, the tropic bird; **star-throat**, a humming-bird of the genus *Heliomaster*; also **star-throated** *a.* See also STAR-FISH.

1884 Coues N. Amer. Birds 551 Asturina, *Star Buzzards. 1713 Petiver Aquat. Anim. Amboinæ Tab. i, Echinus planus .. Wrinkled *Star-cake. 1856 Page Adv. Text-bk. Geol. xiv. (1876) 245 *Star-corals. 1884 Goode Nat. Hist. Aquatic Anim. 841 The Star Corals (Orbicella annularis and cavernosa). 1815 S. Brookes Conchol. 157 *Star Cowry. Cypræa Helvola. 1752 Hill Hist. Anim. 507 Authors call it the Ruticilla and Phœnicurus; we, the Fire-tail, the *Star-finch, and the Red-start. 1668 Charleton Onomast. 64 Accipiter Asterias, Astur.. the *Star-hawk, or Egret. 1601 Holland Pliny xxix. iv. II. 361 Our Stellions or *Star-lizards here in Italie. 1854 A. Adams etc. Man. Nat. Hist. 350 *Star-mouthed Worms (Strongylidæ). 1837 Penny Cycl. VII. 443/1 Condylura macroura (Harlan). Thick-tailed, *star-nose. 1859 Wood Illustr. Nat. Hist. I. 429 Radiated Mole, or *Star-nosed Mole, Astromyctes cristatus. 1608 Topsell Serpents 250 Of the wounding of the *Starre-Spyder feeblenes and weakenes followeth. 1862 Wood Illustr. Nat. Hist. II. 756 They also call it [sc. the Tropic Bird] by the name of *Startail, on account of the long projecting tail-feathers. 1862 Ibid. 243 The *Star-throats. Ibid. The *Star-throated Humming-birds.

22. a. In names of plants: **star-anemone**, *Anemone stellata* (or *hortensis*); **star-anise**, *Illicium anisatum* or its fruit (from the stellate arrangement of the carpels); also, *Illicium verum*, a small evergreen tree found in southern China; the fruit of this tree, or the oil or spice obtained from it; **star-bush** (see quot.); **star-cucumber**, *Sicyos angulatus* of N. America; **star-fruit**, *Damasonium stellatum*; **star-hyacinth**, *Scilla amœna*; **star-pepper**, *Xanthoxylon Daniellii* (*Treas. Bot.* 1866); **star-plum** (see quot.); **star-primula**, *Primula* *stellata*; **star tulip**, a glabrous perennial bulbous plant belonging to any of several species of the genus *Calochortus* (family Liliaceæ), native to temperate western N. America; (formerly distinguished from Mariposa lilies, but now sometimes used synonymously for the whole genus). See also STAR-APPLE, -FLOWER, -GRASS, -HEAD, -THISTLE, -WORT.

1812 *New Bot. Gard.* I. 28 The best *Star-Anemones are said to come from Brittany. **1882** *Garden* 14 Jan. 14/2 The Star Anemone in some of its more distinct colours should be freely grown. **1838** *Penny Cycl.* XII. 445/1 *Illicium anisatum* ..of which the fruit is exported from Canton, and well known in commerce by the name of *Star anise. **1883** Star anise [see *coffin-wood* s.v. COFFIN *sb.* 13]. **1972** K. LO *Chinese Food* I. 12 One or two pieces of star-anise and a sprinkling of cinnamon. **1884** W. MILLER *Plant-n.* 201 *Grewia occidentalis*, African *Star-bush. **1856** A. GRAY *Man. Bot.* 138 *Sicyos*, L. One-seeded *Star-Cucumber. **1857** MISS PRATT *Flowering Pl.* V. 307 *Actinocarpus* (*Star-fruit). **1758** BORLASE *Nat. Hist. Cornw.* 233 Lesser autumnal *star-hyacinth. **1859** BARTLETT *Dict. Amer.* (ed. 2) 446 *Star-plum (*Chrysophillum monopyrenum*). A kind of star-apple, also called a Barbadoes Damson plum. **1904** *Nature* 25 Aug. 408/1 The graceful *Star Primula. **1895** W. ROBINSON *English Flower Garden* (ed. 4) II. 347/2 One of the most experienced growers of the Calochorti, Dr. Wallace, of Colchester, writes of the family thus:..'Other dwarf forms among the *Star Tulips lasted well up to the end of June, when the beautiful Mariposa Lilies continued the display with their tall spikes.' **1921** M. HAMPDEN *Bulb Gardening* xvii. 185 Every garden should contain Calochorti... They consist of three groups, but I consider two only fit for the amateur gardener's patronage; these are known as Mariposa, or Butterfly Tulips, and Star Tulips. **1925** [see MARIPOSA LILY]. **1974** H. G. W. FOGG *Compl. Handbk. Bulbs* vii. 49/2 Of those described as star tulips, *C[alochortus] benthami*, clear yellow with dark central blotch, and *C. maweanus* 'Major'..are among the finest.

b. In names for nostoc (as supposed to be shed from the stars): ***star-jelly***, ***-slime***, ***-slough***, ***-slubber***, ***-slutch***: also ***star-fallen***, ***-falling***, and STAR-SHOT.

c **1440** *Promp. Parv.* 474/2 Sterre slyme, *assub.* **1552** *Elyot's Dict.*, *Aporrhocæ*, certayne impressions in the ayer, which we call starre fallyng, because it so appereth to our sightes. **1712** J. MORTON *Nat. Hist. Northamptonsh.* 353 That gelatinous Body call'd Star-Gelly, Star-shot, or Star-fall'n, so named because vulgarly believ'd to fall from a Star. **1756** W. WATSON *Leicestersh. Plants* in *Phil. Trans.* XLIX. 8 o Our country people call it Tar-slough [? read Star-slough] and some of them, as it is principally seen after rain, suppose..that it drops from the clouds. **1766** Star Gelly [see JELLY *sb.*[1] 2b]. **1779** *Gentl. Mag.* XLIX. 489 Dr. Lister conceived that star-slime is nothing but frogs dissolved and putrified in the air. **1781** J. HUTTON *Tour to Caves* (ed. 2) Gloss. 96 *Starslubber*, frog spawn. **1791** *Gentl. Mag.* LXI. I. 467 *Tremella Nostoch*..is in that county [Cheshire] called *star-slutch*. **1796** WITHERING *Brit. Plants* (ed. 3) IV. 80 *Star-slough*. **1878** *Cumbld. Gloss.*, Star-slime. **1882** J. SMITH *Dict. Pop. Names Plants* 391 Star Jelly, *Nostoc commune* and *N. edule*, gelatinous cryptogams.., springing up often on gravel walks after rain in round patches.

c. star of Bethlehem (also † ***Bethlem star***), the genus *Ornithogalum*, esp. *O. umbellatum* abundant in Palestine, with white stellate flowers; applied also to *Stellaria Holostea*, *Hypoxis decumbens*, and other plants; **star of the earth**, *Plantago Coronopus*; **star of Jerusalem**, *Tragopogon pratensis* or *T. porrifolius*; **star of night**, *Clusia rosea* (Grisebach *Flora W. Ind.* 1864, 788).

1573 TUSSER *Husb.* (1878) 96 Star of Bethelem. **1597** GERARDE *Herbal* I. lxxxiii. 131 There be sundrie sorts of wilde field-onions called Star of Bethlehem. **1678** SALMON *Pharm. Lond.* 84 Bethlem star, temperate: It is not much used in Physick, but the Root serves for meat or food being rosted in Embers, mixt with honey. **1755** *Gentl. Mag.* XXV. 407 The *Ornithogalums*, or *stars of Bethlehem*. *a* **1806** CHARLOTTE SMITH *Flora's Horologe* viii, Pale as a pensive cloistered nun, The Bethlem star her face unveils. **1845** S. JUDD *Margaret* I. xiv, She got bunch-berries, and star-of-Bethlehems. **1847** JERDON in *Proc. Berw. Nat. Club* II. v. 212, I beg to send you..two specimens of the Yellow Star of Bethlehem (*Ornithogalum luteum*, Lin.). **1864** GRISEBACH *Flora W. Ind. Islands* 788 Star-of-Bethlehem, *Hypoxis decumbens*.

1651 T. DE GREY *Compl. Horseman* (1656) 160 A third Cure [for the bite of a mad dog]... Take the Hearbe which groweth in dry and barren Hils, called *The Starre of the earth*. **1671–2** *Roy. Soc. Jrnl.-Bks.* in *Phil. Trans.* (1736) XXXIX. 360 Sir Robert Moray mentioned that a whole Kennel of Dogs, belonging to his Royal Highness, were bitten by a mad Dog, and had been lately cured by a certain Herb called *Stellaria*, or Star of the Earth. **1738** STEWARD in *Phil. Trans.* XL. 458 In Norfolk, my native County,..the *Coronopus* is called *the Star of the Earth*.

1573 TUSSER *Husb.* (1878) 96 Star of Jerusalem. **1665** LOVELL *Herbal* (ed. 2) 415 Starres of Jerusalem, see Josephs-flower.

23. *Min.* The names of precious stones which exhibit asterism, as ***star diamond***, ***quartz***, ***ruby***, ***sapphire***; STAR-STONE.

1805–17 R. JAMESON *Char. Min.* 256 Star-sapphire. **1829** CRAWFURD *Jrnl. Emb. Crt. of Ava* (1834) II. 201 The star ruby. **1887** *Cassell's Encycl. Dict.*, *Star-diamond*. **1896** CHESTER *Dict. Min.*, *Star-quartz*, a var. of quartz which exhibits asterism. **1976** *Sci. Amer.* Apr. 94/2 A type of opal new to us has recently been mined near Spencer, Idaho. It is a star opal that shows streaks of colour in symmetrically arranged angular patterns similar to the rays of a star sapphire.

star, *sb.*[2] Now *dial.* Forms: 4–5 **starre**, (? 5 **stair**), 5, 9 **stare**, 8–9 **starr**, 4– **star**. [a. ON. *stǫr-r* fem. (gen. *starar*; Norw. *storr*, Sw. *starr*, Da. *stær*).] A name given locally to various coarse seaside grasses and sedges, as *Psamma arenaria* and *Carex arenaria*. Also ***star-grass***.

c **1300** *Havelok* 939 He bar þe turues, he bar þe star. **1322** *Bolton Priory Compotus* 445 [455] Pro starre empt' et cariat' ad grangiam de Penisthorpe vs. **1419** *Mem. Ripon* (Surtees) III. 147 Et in iiij carect. de Star empt. cum car. ejusdem. *c* **1440** *Promp. Parv.* 64/2 Cegge, or stare [*Winch.* starre], *carix*. *a* **1550** in *Archæologia* I. 175 Item in Marisco potest Dominus habere *Stair*, pro coopertura domorum. **1712** N. BLUNDELL *Diary* (1895) 100 As I was going to my Setters of Star to hinder ye Sand from recking up my Grand Watercourse. **1722** *Ibid.* 186 For Cuting the Starr. **1742** *Act 15 Geo. II* c. 33 §6 A certain Rush or Shrub called Starr or Bent. **1792** LIGHTFOOT *Flora Scot.* II. 560 Turfy-pink-leav'd Carex. *Anglis.* Starr. *Scotis.* **1823** MOOR *Suffolk Words* s.v. *Bent*, Bent or Starr. **1881** GREGOR *Folk-Lore* ix. 51 A bunch of stars or bruckles to redd the tobacco pipes. **1895** 'M. E. FRANCIS' *Frieze & Fustian* 284 It is on the sand-hills that I generally find him, bundles of blue-green star-grass, ready to be planted, lying about him. *a* **1897** J. MACDONALD *Place Names W. Aberd.* (1899) 308 In this part of the country the name Starrs is applied to rushes.

† **star**, *sb.*[3] *Obs.* [Of obscure origin.]

a. ? A crack or fissure in the skin. **b.** ? A swelling or tumour in horses.

1607 TOPSELL *Four-f. Beasts* 28 If any be hurt by the starres, wash them in asses stale mingled with Spiknard. *Ibid.* 654 The dust of lambs bones is very much..vsed for Vlcers which haue no chops or stars in them. **1710** *Lond. Gaz.* No. 4768/4 A Star or Bunch, with no Hair on it, on the far Leg behind.

star (stɑː(r)), *v.* [f. STAR *sb.*[1]]

† **1.** *intr.* Of a planet: To be in the ascendant.

1592 WARNER *Alb. Eng.* VII. xxxvi. (1612) 172 Dull malcontented Saturne rulde the houre when I was borne. Had Iupiter then starr'd I had not liued now forlorne.

2. *trans.* (*poet. nonce-uses.*) To fix as a star in the heavens; to transform (a person) into a star. Also *fig.*

1610 G. FLETCHER *Christ's Tri.* II. xxvii, The seeling gay, Starred aloft the guilded knobs embrave. **1632** [see STARRED *ppl. a.* 5]. **1819** WIFFEN *Aonian Hours* (1820) 96 His love he told, A feeling pity in her eyes was starred.

3. To mark (a horse) with a star. (See STAR *sb.*[1] 9b.)

1592 GREENE *Conny Catch.* II. 4 They will straight spot him by sundry pollicies, and in a blacke horse, marke saddle spots, or star him in the forehead.

4. a. To adorn with an ornament likened to a star or a number of stars; to bespangle as with stars. Also with *over*, *round*.

The verb is perhaps implied at an earlier date in some of the instances of STARRED *ppl. a.*, q.v.

1718 POPE *Iliad* I. 326 His Sceptre starr'd with golden Studs around. **1742** YOUNG *Nt. Th.* IX. 562 Like a sable curtain starr'd with gold. **1777** POTTER *Æschylus, Supplicants* 88 An herdsman..starr'd round with eyes... The earth-born Argus. **1820** SHELLEY *Prom. Unb.* III. iii. 138 Blooms Which star the winds with points of coloured light. **1884** A. LANG in *Century Mag.* Jan. 340/2 The primroses starred the banks. **1885** B. HARTE *Maruja* iii, Pretty women, with roses starring their dark hair.

b. To decorate with the star of an order.

1845 DISRAELI *Sybil* IV. xi, And now he is a quasi ambassador, and ribboned, and starred to the chin.

5. a. To make a radiating crack or fracture in (a surface of glass, ice, etc.). Cf. STAR *sb.*[1] 11.

to star the glaze (Thieves' slang): see quot. 1788.

1788 GROSE *Dict. Vulgar T.* (ed. 2), *To Star the Glaze*, to break and rob a jeweller's show glass. *Cant.* **1813** MRS. PIOZZI in *Jrnls. & Corr. Whalley* (1863) II. 364 The ice is starred, as skaters call it, by the fall of the French in Spain. **1824** *Mechanic's Mag.* No. 19. 300 A pane of window-glass, perforated completely through..without the glass being, as it is technically called, starred. **1873** *Chamb. Jrnl.* 30 Aug. 547/2 The next [pebble]..not only hit the window, but starred one of the panes with a loud crash. **1884** *Manch. Exam.* 19 Dec. 5/2 As the granite around the hole is starred in all directions, it is Major Majendie's opinion that a large quantity of dynamite was used.

b. *intr.* To become fractured in this way.

1842 *Civ. Engin. & Arch. Jrnl.* V. 368/1 The iron of which vessels is composed has been found to become brittle in the course of years, so that..it will..star like glass when struck by a hard and sharp body. **1894** *Athenæum* 3 Mar. 282/1 Sir J. Evans suggested that the meaning of this was 'I will not star', or crack, like a glass bottle.

c. *trans.* (*Geol.*) To diversify (strata) by cracks or veins radiating from a centre.

1839 MURCHISON *Silur. Syst.* I. xx. 261 The highly inclined and dislocated strata of purple schist and sandstone ..are starred through in many directions by veins of white crystallized quartz. **1842** SEDGWICK in *Hudson's Guide Lakes* (1843) 227 In the progress of elevation, mountain masses were torn asunder and starred by diverging lines of 'fault'.

6. a. *trans.* To produce the 'stars' on (antimony) in the process of refining. Cf. STAR *sb.* 9d. **b.** *intr.* Of antimony: To form 'stars' when solidifying. (Webster 1911.)

1889 BERINGER *Text-bk. Assaying* 186 Briefly, the process consists of the three ordinary operations of—(*a*) Singling or removing most of the antimony from the ore; (*b*) Doubling: (*c*) Refining or 'starring'.

7. To distinguish (a written or printed word, name, etc.) by an affixed star or asterisk. Hence, to single out for special notice or recommendation.

1827 *Gardener's Mag.* II. 105, I wonder indeed that members of a (professedly) liberal society should quietly submit to be classed and regulated, and starred and scheduled, like the items in a paper of assessed taxes. **1897** *Daily News* 29 July 3/1 He maintained that..if the Government meant to proceed with these Bills they ought to have 'starred' them, meaning that an asterisk should be placed by them on the Order Paper, as is the case with Bills in charge of Ministers. **1897** *Ibid.* 4 Nov. 7/1 The defendant complained that his name was not starred on the play bills and programmes. **1898** *Q. Rev.* July 192 This recommendation amounts to 'starring' the several codices, just as individual charters have..been 'starred' by the editor of our first 'Codex'. **1913** J. M. JONES *Welsh Gram.* p. xxvii, The form need not have been starred.

8. a. *intr.* Of an actor, singer, etc.: To appear as a 'star', perform the leading part (see STAR *sb.*[1] 5a); to make a tour in the provinces as the 'star' of a dramatic company. Also *to star it*, and quasi-trans. ***to star the provinces***. Also in sport, to play a star role in a team.

1824 W. IRVING *T. Trav.* II. 36 The great actors, who came down starring..from London. **1825** *New Monthly Mag.* XV. 393 Mr. Fitzwilliam is 'starring' it among them. **1850** THACKERAY *Pendennis* xix, She..had starred the provinces with great éclat. **1891** R. FORD *Thistledown* xvi. 298 He attaches himself to a band of strolling players, and 'stars' it through part of the country of Fife. **1933** *Radio Times* 14 Apr. 73/1 There may have been two Zazels, one of whom..retired before 1890, when the other took over the name and 'starred' at the Westminster Aquarium. **1972** J. MOSEDALE *Football* viii. 116 Turner..starred from 1940 through 1952. **1976** *Oxf. Compan. Film* 633/2 She returned to Britain to star in *Say Hello to Yesterday*. **1978** *Dumfries Courier* 20 Oct. 5/3 Carson starred on the right wing, and was the mainspring of a lively Queens side.

b. said of any notable or distinguished personage when appearing in public. Also jocularly (see quot. 1852).

1852 MOTLEY *Corr.* (1889) I. v. 129, I don't know where he [the sun] is, probably engaged elsewhere, starring it in some more profitable region. **1887** HUXLEY in L. Huxley *Life* (1900) II. 151, I have been 'starring' at the Mansion House. **1893** *Bookman* June 86/1 This Russian baroness.. starring it in Russian embassies and Paris salons.

c. *trans.* To furnish with 'stars', provide a run of 'stars' for.

1831 *Lincoln Herald* 7 Oct. 4 We were extremely sorry to see so thin a house: sad encouragement for the manager in starring the season.

d. To advertise as a film or theatrical star; to give a star part to (an actor or actress); (with a film, etc., as subject) to present in a leading role.

1895 G. B. SHAW *Let.* 27 Mar. (1965) I. 508 It is good business to star Janet. **1922** *Encycl. Brit.* XXX. 699/2 He appeared in a minor rôle on the New York stage in 1901; later he was 'starred' in several comedies and musical pieces. **1929** A. C. & C. EDINGTON *Studio Murder Mystery* viii. 102 Already ve are going to star her! Already ve haff bought a story, just for her. **1936** [see FEATURE *v.* 4c]. **1951** 'N. SHUTE' *Lonely Road* (ed. 2) p. v, In 1936 a film was made..starring Clive Brook. **1962** E. ALBEE *Who's afraid of Virginia Woolf?* (1964) I. 5 *Chicago* was a 'thirties musical, starring little Miss Alice *Faye*. Don't you know *anything*? **1980** *Sunday Times* 21 Sept. 14 Since then he has earned an international reputation with plays..and The Faith Healer, which starred James Mason last year on Broadway.

9. *Billiards.* In the game of Pool, to buy an additional life or lives (see STAR *sb.*[1] 13). Similarly in *Dominoes*. Also quasi-*trans.*

1850 *Bohn's Handbk. Games* (1867) 609 (Rules of Pool) If the first person out refuse to star, the second person may do it,..and so on, until only two persons are left in the pool, in which case the privilege of starring ceases. **1870** HARDY & WARE *Mod. Hoyle, Dominoes* 100 He who 'stars' re-commences at the number which the player holds who is in the worst position. **1875** G. F. PARDON in *Encycl. Brit.* III. 677/1 The first player who loses all his three lives can 'star'; that is, by paying into the pool a sum equal to his original stake, he is entitled to as many lives as the lowest number on the marking board. Thus if the lowest number be two, he stars two; if one, he stars one.

staragen, obs. form of TARRAGON (sense 1).

1765 STERNE *Tr. Shandy* VIII. xii, 'Tis all pepper, garlick, staragen, [etc.].

star-apple (ˈstɑːrˌæp(ə)l). The fruit of any tree of the genus *Chrysophyllum*; the tree itself (also ***star-apple tree***).

The fruit is the size of a large apple, and when cut across shows ten cells forming a star-like figure.

1697 DAMPIER *Voy.* I. 204 The Star Apple Tree grows much like the Quince Tree, but much bigger. **1725** SLOANE *Jamaica* II. 170 Star Apple-Tree... If the Fruit be cut athwart the Places where the Seeds were lodg'd will represent a Star. **1823** SABINE *Edible Fruits Sierra Leone* in *Trans. Hort. Soc.* (1824) V. 458 Long-leaved Star-Apple. Chrysophyllum macrophyllum. *Ibid.* Obovate-leaved Star Apple. Chrysophyllum obovatum. **1887** *Standard* 16 Sept. 5/3 How many..Britons have eaten..of the star-apple?

ˈstar-beam. Chiefly *poet.* A ray of starlight.

a **1425** *Cursor M.* 11435 (Trin.) þei followed on þe sterre beme [*earlier texts* o þis stern þe leme] Til þei coom to Ierusalem. **1700** BLACKMORE *Job* 11 Shut every Starbeam out from mortals sight. **1794** COLERIDGE *Monody on Death of Chatterton* 120 Like star-beam on the slow sequester'd tide Lone-glittering. **1817** BYRON *Manfred* I. i. 57 On a star-beam I have ridden. **1874** REYNOLDS *John Bapt.* i. 11 The immeasurable difference between the star-beam and the noon-tide splendour. **1884** BROWNING *Ferishtah's Fancies* 87 How twinks thine eye, my Love, Blue as yon star-beam.

starboard (ˈstɑːbɔəd, -bəd), *sb.* (and *a.*) *Naut.* Forms: 1 **stéorbord**, 4 **stere-b(o)urde**, 5 **sterbord(e**, 6 **steereboord**, **-board**, **steirburd** (*Sc.*), **starbourd**, (7 **stereboard**), 6–7 **starboord**, **starrebord(e**, 7 **starr-boord**, **-board**, **starbord**, (stanbur), 7- starboard. [OE. *stéorbord*, f. *stéor* steering paddle, rudder, STEER *sb.* + *bord* BOARD *sb.* Equivalent compounds (some of which do not strictly correspond in form) are MDu. *stierbord*, *stuyrbord* (Du. *stuurboord*), MHG. *stiurbort* (mod.G. *steuerbord*), OIcel., mod.Icel. *stjórnborði* (now pronounced *stjórborði*), Sw., Da. *styrbord*. The Rom. langs. have adopted the word from one or other of the Teut. langs.: OF. *estribord* (mod.F. *tribord*), Sp. *estribor(d*, Pg. *estribordo*, usually *estibordo*, It. *stribordo*.

The etymological sense of the word refers to the mode of steering the early Teutonic ships, by means of a paddle worked over the right side of the vessel. The left or larboard side, to which the steersman turned his back, was in several Teut. langs. called 'back-board', whence F. *bâbord*: see BABURD.]

A. *sb.* **a.** The right-hand side of a ship, as distinguished from the LARBOARD or PORT side; the side upon which in early types of ships the steering apparatus was worked. (See LARBOARD *note.*) Also used with reference to aircraft. Often in the phrases †*a, on, upon, to starboard.*

c **893** ÆLFRED *Oros.* I. i. §14 Let him ealne weȝ þæt weste land on ðæt steorbord, & þa widsæ on ðæt bæcbord þrie daȝas. *Ibid.*, Ac him wæs ealne weȝ weste land on þæt steorbord..& him wæs a widsæ on ðæt bæcbord. ?*a* **1400** *Morte Arth.* 745 Frekes..Standez appone stere-bourde. *Ibid.* 3665 So stowttly the forsterne one the stam hyttis, That stokkes of the stere-burde strykkys in peces! **1495, 1591, 1598, 1698** [see LARBOARD]. **1568** *Satir. Poems Reform.* xlvi. 6 Se that hir hatchis be handlit richt, W[t] steirburd, baburd, luf and lie. **1622** R. HAWKINS *Voy. S. Sea* (1847) 83 He commaunded him at the helme, to put it close a starbourd. **1633** T. STAFFORD *Pac. Hib.* III. viii. 312 He..ordered it so, that with two takles hee might steere the Hoy either to Starboard, or to Port. **1687** A. LOVELL tr. *Thevenot's Trav.* I. 16 When we were got out to Sea, we bore away to the starboard. **1762** FALCONER *Shipwr.* II. 819 Brace fore and aft to starboard every yard. **1833** TENNYSON *Lotos-Eaters* viii. 7 We, Roll'd to starboard, roll'd to larboard, when the surge was seething free. **1874** BEDFORD *Sailor's Pocket Bk.* iii. 48 If to your starboard red appear, It is your duty to keep clear. **1891** FARRAR *Darkn. & Dawn* xxxv, Those who had not been warned..rushed to the starboard. **1909** F. T. JANE *All World's Air-Ships* 142 Motor-3-cylinder 10–12 h.p. Buchet, mounted directly on the lower plane, a little to starboard of centre line. **1977** J. CLEARY *High Road to China* ii. 65 The Bristol slid to starboard, kept sliding and I let it go, feeling I was getting it under control.

b. as *adv.* To or on the starboard side.

1634–5 BRERETON *Trav.* (Chetham Soc.) 169 Starboard, that is to the right hand. **1644** MANWAYRING *Seamans Dict.* 28 Then he who conds uses these termes to him at the helme, starr-boord, larboord, the helme a mid-ships. **1647, 1663** [see LARBOARD b]. **1669** STURMY *Mariner's Mag.* I. ii. 20 Give fire Starboard. **1883** BURTON & CAMERON *Gold Coast* I. i. 4 Starboard rose black Ithaca, fronting the black mountain of Cephalonia.

B. *attrib.* passing into adj. Of, belonging to or situated on the right side of a boat, vessel, or aircraft.

1495 *Naval Acc. Hen. VII* (1896) 192 Sterborde Bowers —j, Latheborde Bowers—j. **1538** *Admiralty Crt. Exam.* 28 May 2 The Thomas with the loreborde buttock touched the fore parte of the shippe..at a place callyd the starrebord luffe. **1540** *Sel. Pleas Crt. Admiralty* (Selden Soc.) I. 91 The said shippe..dydd hange..soo violentle upon starreborde sydd of the said shippe..that the cable..dydd breake. **1594** NASHE *Terrors Nt.* Wks. (Grosart) III. 270 Fellowes..that ..knew..what belongs to haling of bolings yare, and falling on the star-boord buttocke. **1626** P. NICHOLS *Drake Revived* (1628) 21 One [pinnace] on the starboord bough, the other on the starboord quarter..forthwith boarded her. **1627** CAPT. SMITH *Sea Gram.* ix. 42 Hale off your star-boord sheats. **1635** J. HAYWARD tr. *Biondi's Banish'd Virgin* 156 Causing him to be at the self-same time boarded on both the Starbur and Larbur-sides. **1644** MANWAYRING *Seamans Dict.* 114 The ships company is divided into two parts, the one called the Star-boord-watch, the other the Lar-boord-watch. **1669** STURMY *Mariner's Mag.* I. ii. 20 Give him our Starboard Broad-side. **1697** DAMPIER *Voy.* I. 452 The fury of the Wind..took the Ship on the Starboard bow with such violence, that it snapt off the Boltsprit. **1747** *Gentl. Mag.* VII. 247/1 We..began to form the line on the starboard tack. **1798** in Nicolas *Disp. Nelson* (1846) VII. p. cliv, We wore gradually round..till we brought the wind on the starboard beam. **1833** MARRYAT *P. Simple* iii, He flogged the whole starboard watch. *Ibid.* xii, 'Sail on the starboard-bow!' cried the look-out man. **1874** BEDFORD *Sailor's Pocket Bk.* i. 18 The Starboard Columns of a formation [of ships] are the alternate Columns, commencing from the right. **1877** BLACK *Green Past.* xxvii, Who gave us that piece of advice about choosing a starboard berth. **1917** [see PORT *sb.*[6] (*a.*) 2 a]. **1948** 'N. SHUTE' *No Highway* iii. 61 The second pilot..came down into the cabin... Then he said: 'Which is the boffin?'..'Sitting on the starboard side, near the front.' **1976** B. LECOMBER *Dead Weight* iii. 45 The tailwheel lock had broken... The starboard prop had run away.

starboard ('stɑːbɔəd, -bəd), *v. Naut.* [f. STARBOARD *sb.*] *trans.* To put over or turn (the helm) to the starboard side of the ship. Chiefly in the command ***Starboard (the helm)!***

1598 SYLVESTER *Du Bartas* II. i. III. *Furies* 43 He hails us threatfully, Star-boord our helm. **1627** CAPT. SMITH *Sea Gram.* ix. 37 Starboord the Helme, is to put the Helme a Starboord, then the ship will goe to the Larboord. **1759** *Ann. Reg., Chron.* 121/1 We then immediately star-boarded our helm, and ran right down upon her. **1888** *Times* 23 Aug. 8/6 A red light is always a signal not to starboard the helm.

ellipt. **1669** STURMY *Mariner's Mag.* I. ii. 19 Starboord, the Chase pays away more room, Starboard hard; ..Stereboard hard. **1673** HICKERINGILL *Gregory* 141 Look to your Ship then, hard at Helm, Starboard, or else we overwhelm. **1762** FALCONER *Shipwr.* III. 69 'Starboard again!' the watchful pilot cries. **1884** CAPT. POLLARD in *Western Morn. News* 2 Aug. 8/1 The course which the Valiant was steering before starboarding was south-west.

Hence '**starboarding** *vbl. sb.*

1902 *Daily Chron.* 18 June 10/1 The starboarding of the Cambridge in the circumstances of the case was wrong.

starbolins ('stɑːbəlɪnz), *sb. pl. Naut.* Also **starbowlines.** [? For **starboardlings*, f. STARBOARD *sb.* + -LING[1]. Cf. LARBOLINS.] (See quots.)

1769 FALCONER *Dict. Marine* II. (1776), *Tribordais*, starbowlines; a cant term for the starboard watch. **1840** R. H. DANA *Bef. Mast.* v. 10 The cry of 'All starbowlines ahoy!' summoned our watch on deck. **1867** SMYTH *Sailor's Word-bk.*, *Star-Bolins*, the old familiar term for the men of the starboard watch.

'**star-bright,** *a.* Also **star bright. a.** Bright as a star; bright with stars. Chiefly *poet.*

1560 PHAER *Æneid* x. (1562) F fiij, The father of gods.. him selfe doth councell call into the starbright seat. **1561** NUCE *Seneca's Octavia* II. ii. E j, So is Augustus prince and father cald, Of country first, in starbright throne ystald. **1606** SYLVESTER *Du Bartas* II. iv. II. *Magnificence* 840 Their star-bright eye seems vail'd. **1667** MILTON *P.L.* x. 450 At last as from a Cloud his fulgent head And shape Starr-bright appeer'd. **1817** SHELLEY *Rev. Islam* I. xviii, Loosening her star-bright robe and shadowy hair. **1828** COLERIDGE *Gard. Boccaccio* 77 Florence!..Thou brightest star of star-bright Italy!

b. Of wine and cider: perfectly clear and free from sediment (see quot. 1979).

1833 LOUDON *Encycl. Archit.* §1324 When it [cider] has remained a short time quiet,..if not perfectly star-bright, which it seldom is, it should be fined with isinglass. **1923** A. L. SIMON *Supply, Care & Sale of Wine* xvi. 109 Before bottling any wine, you must make sure:—..That the wine is star-bright. *Ibid.* 110 These..conditions are, to my mind, rules without exception, but there are bottlers who make an exception to the 'star-bright bottling' rule when they bottle Vintage Ports. **1945** *Wine & Spirit Trade Rec.* 18 June 650/1 A device that helps the examination of Wines is to paint sheets of tin..with black pigment..and to fix it in an angle of the cellar walls where a short gas jet can be lit behind the bottle so that the Wine can be seen..under the best conditions for discovering whether the Wine is 'star bright' or not. **1973** *Times* 20 Oct. 14/2 Modern vinification makes the majority of wines 'star bright' but the presence of a little deposit in many fine wines means quality. **1979** TURNER & ROYCROFT *Winemaker's Encycl.* 167 Wines which are brilliantly clear and reflect highlights when in the bottle are said to be 'star-bright'. All wines that are entered in competitions or are otherwise exhibited publicly should be star-bright.

starch (stɑːtʃ), *sb.* Forms: 5–6 sterch(e, 5–7 starche, 7 startch, 6– starch. [In 15th c. *sterche*, f. *sterche* STARCH *v.* to stiffen. Cf. MDu. *stercke*, MHG. *sterke* (once, 13th c.), mod.G. *stärke* starch (from 17th c.), also in the same sense MHG. (13th c.) *sterch-chlei* (= **sterk-klîe*), early mod.G. *starkmel* 'amidum' (Diefenbach).]

1. A substance obtained from flour by removing some of its constituents (now also from other vegetable sources containing 'starch' in sense 2), used, in the form of a gummy liquid or paste made with water, to stiffen linen or cotton fabrics in the process of laundry-work, to give a finish to the surface of textile materials, to size paper, and for various other purposes. Also, the gummy liquid or paste made from this substance to prepare it for use.

Starch in its solid form is a white or yellowish white powder (often aggregated in shapeless granules or lumps), odourless, tasteless, and soft to the touch.

c **1440** *Promp. Parv.* 472/2 Starche, for kyrcheys, *stibium, gersa.* **14..** *Lat.-Eng. Voc.* in Wr.-Wülcker 568/48 *Brella*, sterche. **1530** TINDALE *Answ. More's Dial.* Wks. (1573) 324/1 About which was no smale question in Oxforde.. whether it were bread or none: some affirming that the floure with long lying in water was turned to starch, and had lost his nature. **1530** PALSGR. 275/2 Starche for lawne, *folle flevr.* **1549** *Act 3 & 4 Edw. VI* c. 2 §6 Noe person..shall..put any Flockes, chalke, flower or sterche..upon any sett Clothe. **1583** STUBBES *Anat. Abus.* D viij, A certaine kinde of liquide matter which they call Starch, wherin the deuill hath willed them to wash and diue his ruffes wel. **1591** GREENE *Conny Catch.* (1592) 16 Rufs of the largest size, quarter and halfe deep, gloried richly with blew starch. **1605** TIMME *Quersit.* III. 188 Doe you not see how paste, a glutinous matter, and starch also, are made onely with flower and water? **1612** PEACHAM *Gentl. Exerc.* I. xxv. 94 With starch thinne laid on, and the skinne well stretched,..prepare your ground or tablet [for a picture]. **1614** B. JONSON *Barth. Fair* II. iv, A delicate ballad o' the Ferret and the Coney... Another of Goose-greene-starch, and the Deuill. *c* **1645** HOWELL *Lett.* (1655) I. I. ii. 4 Mistris Turner, the first inventresse of yellow-Starch. **1683** PEPYS *Diary at Tangier* in *Life* (1841) I. 422 Conge..which is like our water-starch. **1713** STEELE *Englishman* No. 17. 113 Queen Elizabeth was a mortal Enemy to the Use of blue Starch in making up Linnen. **1848** DICKENS *Dombey* viii, Mr. Dombey stiff with starch and arrogance. **1855** T. F. HARDWICH *Man. Photogr. Chem.* II. v. 277 The French [photographic papers] are sized with starch. **1882** L. CAMPBELL *Life Clerk Maxwell* v. 105 He had a rooted objection to the vanities of starch and gloves. **1893** *Laundry Management* ix. 61 Indian corn or maize is now much used for procuring laundry starches. **1903** *Westm. Gaz.* 6 Aug. 3/2 For things that need a very slight stiffening there is what is called ecru starch. **1913** E. THORPE *Dict. Applied Chem.* V. 174/1 The starch [from potatoes] dried in this manner [*i.e.* on shelves made of bars of wood] is known as 'hurdle starch'.

2. *Chem.* An organic compound found in plant-cells (a member of the amylose group of carbohydrates) being the chief constituent of 'starch' as described under sense 1.

1812–16 J. SMITH *Panorama Sci. & Art* II. 610 The lime tending to hasten the ripening of the seed, and to convert mucilage into starch. **1839** URE *Dict. Arts* 1163 Three kinds of starch have been distinguished by chemists; that of wheat, that called *inuline*, and lichen starch. **1849** BALFOUR *Man. Bot.* §17 Starch exists in the form of granules, which are minute cells..in which nutritious matter is stored up. **1870** YEATS *Nat. Hist. Comm.* 139 Starch is turned blue by iodine, an excellent test for detecting its presence in plants. **1882** VINES *Sachs' Bot.* 56 Starch always appears in an organised form as solid grains having a concentrically stratified structure, which arise at first as minute dots in the protoplasm, and continue to grow while lying in it.

3. *transf.* A glutinous mass or substance.

†**a.** (See quot.) *Obs.*

a **1625** FLETCHER *Nice Valour* III. i, I'm but froath;..or come more nearer sir, Y'ave seen a Cluster of Frog-spawns in April, E'ne such a starche am I.

b. *dial.* The jelly-fish. More fully ***starch-fish.***

1850 MISS PRATT *Comm. Things of Sea-side* v. 326 At Dover they [jelly-fishes] are very generally called Starch-fishes. **1887** *Kent Gloss.*, *Sea starch*, jelly-fish. Dover. **1889** *Hardwicke's Sci.-Gossip* XXV. 71 Wanted, British and foreign sponges... Also starches (genuine), large spines of echinodermata.

4. *fig.* Stiffness; esp. of manner or conduct; stiffening. Freq. in phr. ***to take the starch out of*** (a person or thing): to remove the stiffness, formality, or pompousness from (someone, etc.), esp. by ridicule; to deflate.

1705 J. DUNTON *Life & Err.* 461 His Language is always Neat and Fine, but unaffected, free from Starch, or Intricacy. **1712** ADDISON *Spect.* No. 305 ¶14 This Professor is to give the Society their Stiffening, and infuse into their Manners that beautiful Political Starch, which may qualifie them for Levees, Conferences, Visits. **1840** *Spirit of Times* 25 Apr. 90/1 There is something in training in these parts that will be very apt to 'take the starch out' of any 'conceit' they may have. **1846** *Punch* X. 139 The panic has begun to take the starch out of the provisional committee-man. **1876** GEO. ELIOT *Dan. Der.* I. iv, Her quick mind had taken readily that strong starch of unexplained rules and disconnected facts which saves ignorance from any painful sense of limpness. **1889** G. B. SHAW in *Hawk* 13 Aug. 172/1 This is the sort of thing that takes the starch out of the most bumptious critic. **1922** *Daily Mail* 20 Nov. 12 The home forwards were unquestioned masters, and on the day's play would have taken the starch out of any other pack in the country. **1936** V. W. BROOKS *Flowering of New England* vi. 113 The British reviews were cold and formal... The great Romantic critics had not appeared, to take the starch out of their pompous manners.

5. *attrib.* and *Comb.* **a.** simple attrib., as ***starch box, liquid, -mush*** (see MUSH *sb.*[1] 1), ***pan, paste, -powder, -works,*** †***-yard***; objective and obj. genitive, as ***starchmaker, starchmaking*** vbl. sb., ***starch-free, -producing*** adjs.; instrumental, as ***starch-sized*** adj.; similative, as ***starch-like*** adj.

1617 *Shuttleworths' Acc.* (Chetham Soc.) 213 For the *starche boxe vj[d]. **1939** A. THIRKELL *Before Lunch* iv. 88 Miss Starter is on a diet and has to have a special bread called Kornog, which is practically *starch-free. **1971** *Guardian* 29 June 13/2 Anyone on a starch-free diet should seek some other country [than Scotland]. **1899** CAGNEY tr. *Jaksch's Clin. Diagn.* iv. (ed. 4) 123 *Starch-like formations. **1893** *Laundry Management* ix. 66 If a large quantity of *starch liquid is used in a machine. **1586** *St. Papers Eliz., Dom.* 372 [Richard Young to Walsyngham..sends an account of proceedings against the *starch-makers.] **1663** *Canterb. Marriage Licences* (MS.), John Loft of All Saints, Canterbury, starch-maker. **1775** ASH, **Starchmaking*, the act or process of making starch. **1894** *Nation* (U.S.) 14 June LVIII. 451/3 To become proficient in the art of shooting fish, Indians have to live an entire month solely on *starch-mush. **1504** *Will of Goodyer* (Somerset Ho.), A *starche panne. **1857** MILLER *Elem. Chem., Org.* 74 The *starch paste ..does not, when evaporated, recover its former insolubility. **1886** [see MOUNTANT]. **1601** HOLLAND *Pliny* XXII. xxv. II. 140 As touching Amylum or *starch pouder, it dimmeth the eyesight. **1736** *Cal. Treas. Books & Papers* 160 Those..who make wigs only and use starch powder, must pray an abatement of duty on starch. **1846** SOYER *Cookery* 483 Have an equal quantity of starch-powder, and powdered sugar. **1871** KINGSLEY *At Last* xvi, The *starch-producing plants of the West Indies. **1851–3** *Tomlinson's Cycl. Usef. Arts* (1867) II. 298/1 The *starch-sized paper is generally thought to be preferable to the other kind. **1885** *Manch. Exam.* 11 June 4/6 A destructive fire occurred..in the *starchworks. **1706** *Lond. Gaz.* No. 4216/4 The White Lead-House at Rotherhith,..fit for a Deal-yard, *Starch-yard, or Brew-house, to be Let.

b. Special comb.: **starch bandage**, a bandage rubbed with starch paste, to serve as a splint; also *attrib.*; **starch bath**, a medicinal bath or lotion made with starch; **starch blocker**, a dietary preparation that supposedly affects the metabolism of starch so that it does not contribute to a gain in weight; **starch blue**, cellulose (see quots.); **starch-corn** = SPELT *sb.*[1] 1; **starch fish**, a jelly-fish (see 3 b); †**starch-flour**, starch in its solid form (see sense 1 *note*); **starch gel**, a gel made from starch and an aqueous buffer solution, used as the supporting medium in a method of zone electrophoresis; so ***starch-gel electrophoresis***; **starch glaze**, a preparation for producing a glossy surface on starched goods; **starch grain, granule**, each of the grains or granules of which starch consists; **starch-gum** = DEXTRIN; **starch hyacinth**, a small bulbous plant, *Muscari neglectum*, belonging to the family Liliaceæ, native to Europe and western Asia, and bearing spikes of dark blue, strongly scented flowers; **starch iodide**, a compound of iodine and starch; **starch jelly** = *starch mucilage*; †**starchman**, a starch manufacturer; **starch mucilage**, a paste made of wheat starch, used alone or as a vehicle in pharmacy; **starch-reduced** *a.*, processed so as to contain less than the normal proportion of starch; **starch root** (see quot., cf. *starchwort*); †**starch-ruffed** *a.*, that wears a starched ruff; **starch splint**, a splint made with a starch bandage (q.v.); **starch sugar** = DEXTROSE; **starch-water**, a solution of starch and water; †**starch wench**, a young woman employed as a starcher; †**starchwoman**, a woman who sells starch; **starchwort** (see quots.).

1846 *Lancet* 28 Feb. 240/1 The *appareil amidonné*, or *starch bandage. **1895** *Arnold & Sons' Catal. Surg. Instrum.* 684 Starch Bandage Shears.. Starch Bandage Cutter. **1899** *Allbutt's Syst. Med.* VIII. 605 In very acute cases [of lichen] ..Vidal recommends a litre of vinegar in a *starch bath. **1981** *Arizona Med.* XXXVIII. 848/1 A new product has appeared on the market... It is not a drug, but a processed food made from a certain type of bean. It is also called NBE (Northern Bean Extract) or The *Starch Blocker. **1983** *Daily Tel.* 14 Apr. 6/5 Slimmers who use starch blockers.. are wasting their money... Experts.. say they do not affect the quantity of starch digested and could have unpleasant effects if they did work. **1797** *Encycl. Brit.* (ed. 3) II. 707/2 Azure is employed to colour starch; hence it has also been called **starch-blue*. **1880** BESSEY *Bot.* §70 From two to six per cent of the whole [starch] grain..bears some resemblance to cellulose; it is distinguished as *starch-cellulose. **1597** GERARDE *Herbal* I. xliii. 63 Triticum Amyleum. *Starche corne. **1866** *Treas. Bot.* 1092/2 Starch-corn, *Triticum Spelta*. **1540** *MSS. Duke Rutland* (Hist. MSS. Comm.) IV. 301 Payd for *sterche flour, ij*d*. **1601** HOLLAND *Pliny* XVIII. vii. I. 562 Touching Starch-flower called Amylum, it may be made of all kinds of wheat. **1955** O. SMITHIES in *Biochem. Jrnl.* 630/1 A *starch gel containing the desired buffer is prepared in a suitable plastic tray. *Ibid.* 635/1 α_1-Globulin does not appear as a definite band between α_2-globulin and albumin in starch gel electrophoresis. **1961** *Lancet* 5 Aug. 291/1 On electrophoresis in starch gel, no macroglobulin moved out from the point of insertion. **1978** *Jrnl. R. Soc. Med.* LXXI. 192 Investigations into this isoenzyme composition of the circulating CK using starch-gel electrophoresis. **1893** *Laundry Management* ix. 64 Some *starch glazes are sold as powders, others as paste. **1849** BALFOUR *Man. Bot.* 8 Cell of Potato, containing striated *starch grains. **1857** HENFREY *Bot.* § 683 *Starch-granules..occur either singly or collected in masses of definite shape. **1854** tr. *Pereira's Polarized Light* (ed. 2) 278 The substance called dextrine is *starch-gum. **1790** *Curtis's Bot. Mag.* IV. 122 We have thought it better to call this species the *Starch Hyacinth, the smell of the flower in the general opinion resembling that substance. **1808** J. E. SMITH *Eng. Bot.* XXVII. 1931 Starch Hyacinth..is so abundantly wild in many places. **1900** G. BELL *Let.* 11 Jan. (1927) I. v. 61, I went there yesterday afternoon for starch hyacinths and cyclamen and had a tremendous scramble. **1927** F. B. YOUNG *Portrait of Claire* IV. iii. 372 In sheltered crevices gentian, starch-hyacinth and chionodoxa mocked with their living blue the surly Midland winter. **1878** ABNEY *Photogr.* xxi. 151 A dark blue colour due to *starch iodide. **1899** *Allbutt's Syst. Med.* VIII. 520 *Starch jelly is used for similar purposes. **1728** CHAMBERS *Cycl.* s.v. *Starch*, Such as require very fine Starch, don't content themselves, like the *Starch-men, with the Refuse of Wheat, but use the finest grain. **1898** *Allbutt's Syst. Med.* V. 241 A tea-spoonful of oil of turpentine suspended in two ounces of *starch mucilage. **1939** A. THIRKWELL *Before Lunch* iv. 89 Pepso is only *starch-reduced. **1972** 'G. NORTH' *Sgt. Cluff rings True* ix. 76 Sugar substitutes, starch-reduced biscuits and breads, low-calorie soups. **1853** T. B. GROVES in *Pharm. Jrnl.* XIII. 60 The *Arum maculatum* is commonly called arrow-root or *starch root [Isle of Portland]. **1783** COLMAN *Capricious Lady* Epil., in *Prose on Sev. Occas.* (1787) III. 237 The *Starch-Ruff'd Maidens of Queen Bess's reign. **1869** B. HILL *Essent. Bandaging* iii. 85 In six weeks the *starch splint may usually be discarded. **1844** *Starch sugar [see GLUCOSE 1]. **1839** URE *Dict. Arts* 1166 The starch thus obtained.. may be used..in the moist state..for the preparation of dextrine, and *starch syrup. **1825** J. NICHOLSON *Oper. Mech.* 347 This reel is sometimes placed..in a tub containing *starch-water. **1893** *Laundry Management* ix. 66 Muslins ought merely to be dipped in very weak starch water. *a* **1626** BRETON *Figure of Four* II. (Grosart) 6/2 A needle wench, and a *starch wench. **1604** MIDDLETON *Father Hubburd's T.* E 4, Trulls passing too and fro in the wash-shape of Laundresses, as your Bawdes about London in the manner of *Starch-women. **1597** GERARDE *Herbal* II. ccxc. 685 The common Cockow pint is called in Latin *Arum*: ..in English Cockow pint,..and of some *Starchwoort. **1866** *Treas. Bot.* 1092/2 Starchwort, *Arum maculatum*.

starch (stɑːtʃ), *a.* Somewhat *arch.* [f. STARCH *sb.*

A supposed 13th c. instance of this word, in the form *sterch* (*Long Life* in *OE. Misc.* 156) quoted in some Dicts., is illusory; the scribe makes mistakes like *drinche* for *drinke*, and the other texts read *starc*, *sterk*.]

Of a person, his bearing, etc.: Stiff, unbending; formal.

1717 J. KILLINGBECK 18 *Serm.* xi. 230 'Tis but misrepresenting Sobriety as a Starch and Formal, and Vertue as a Laborious and Slavish thing. *a* **1720** SHEFFIELD (Dk. Buckhm.) *Wks.* (1753) I. 146 Then Ph...ps came forth, as starch as a quaker, Whose simple profession's a pastoral-maker. **1721** RAMSAY *Tartana* 249 Lest, O fair nymphs, you should our patience tire, And starch reserve extinguish generous fire. **1762–71** H. WALPOLE *Vertue's Anecd. Paint.* (1786) IV. 1 Holbein and the Flemish masters, who..saw nothing but the starch and unpliant habits of the times. **1809** MALKIN *Gil Blas* VI. i. ¶12 A man who puts on all the starch formalities of an inveterate religionist. **1822** LAMB *Elia* Ser. I. *Some old Actors*, [Bensley as Malvolio] was starch, spruce, opinionated, but his superstructure of pride seemed bottomed upon a sense of worth. **1837** DISRAELI *Venetia* I. xi, His housekeeper,..as precise and starch as an old picture. **1904** H. PAUL *Hist. Mod. Eng.* II. x. 261 That stiff and starch publicist Vattel.

starch (stɑːtʃ), *v.* Forms: 5 **sterch(e, starche,** (7 **startche, stars),** 7– **starch.** [ME. *sterche*:—OE. **stercan* to make rigid (the pa. pple. is found in *stercedferhþ* adj., fixed or resolute of mind), f. *stearc* stiff, rigid: see STARK *a.* The mod.G. *stärken* to starch is known no earlier than the 17th c.; Sw. has *stärka* to starch (app. already in 14th c.), and the derivative *stärkelse* starch (= WFlem. *sterksel*, a kind of starch used by weavers).

The formally equivalent OHG. *sterchen* (MHG. *sterken*, mod.G. *stärken*), OS. *sterkian* (MLG. *sterken*), (M)Du. *sterken*, (M)Sw. (? from LG.) *stärka*, have the sense 'to strengthen'.]

†**1.** *trans.* To stiffen, make rigid; to compose (one's countenance) to a severe or formal expression. *Obs.*

1402 *Pol. Poems* (Rolls) II. 50 Who tytheth bot ȝe the anet and the mente, sterching ȝour faces [cf. Matt. vi. 16, *exterminant* (v.r. *demoliuntur*) *facies suas*], to be holden holi. ? *c* **1600** *Distr. Emperor* III. i. in Bullen *Old Pl.* (1884) III. 209 Dothe not fawne, Nor croutche, nor crynge, nor startche his countenance.

2. To stiffen (linen, etc.) with starch.

14.. *Lat.-Eng. Voc.* in Wr.-Wülcker 613/31 *Stibio*, to starche. *c* **1450** in Aungier *Syon* (1840) 367 Whan the sexteyn..hathe wasche the corporas ones, sche..schal wasche them, sterche them, drye them. **1601** B. JONSON *Poetaster* IV. i, And aske you, where you bought your lawne? And..who starches you? *c* **1625** in *Songs & Poems Costume* (Percy Soc.) 111 About his neck a flaunting ruff,..Starched with white and blew. **1698** [see CONJEE]. **1718** *Free-thinker* No. 28. 197 A Milliner in the Neighbourhood..Starches his Ruffs. **1881** BESANT & RICE *Chapl. of Fleet* I. iv, White bands, clean and freshly starched, and a very full wig.

absol. **1614** STOW *Ann.* 869/1 [They] made them cambrick Ruffes, and sent them to Mist. Dinghen, to starch... And then they began to send their Daughters..to learne how to starch. **1624** J. TAYLOR (Water P.) *Praise Cl. Linen* Wks. (1630) II. 169/1 She wrings, she folds, she pleits, she smoothes, she starches.

†**b.** with object the beard or moustache. *Obs.*

1589 NASHE *Pref. Greene's Menaphon* (Arb.) 10 Sufficeth them.., hauing starched their beardes most curiouslie, to make a peripateticall path into the inner parts of the Citie. **1642** HOWELL *For. Trav.* v. 68 If the one hath a Fancy to stars his mustachos. **1664** BUTLER *Hud.* II. i. 171 It [your beard] does your visage more adorn, Than if 'twere prun'd, and starcht, and lander'd, And cut square by the Russian Standard. **1731** MRS. ELIZ. THOMAS *Life Corinna* p. xxi, His Valet being some Hours every Morning, in Starching his Beard, and Curling his Whiskers.

†**c.** *fig.* To make rigid, formal, or precise; to frame (a discourse) in formal or pretentious terms. Also with *up*. *Obs.*

1615 A. NICCHOLES *Disc. Marriage & Wiving* vii. 21 But as to please woman hath much starched vp man from his slouenry, so to delight man..hath the woman thus increased in prides. **1644** MILTON *Areop.* (Arb.) 64 How to be wisht were such an obedient unanimity as this, what a fine conformity would it starch us all into? **1677** GILPIN *Demonol.* (1867) 161 A quaint discourse starched up in the dress of common rhetoric. **1680** C. NESSE *Ch. Hist.* 141 Hushai..did defeat his counsel..by starching an oration every way accommodated to Absaloms ambitious humour. **1763** *Brit. Mag.* IV. 495 Tho' with prudish airs she starch her, Still she longs. **1771** SMOLLETT *Humphry Cl.* 12 Sept., She starched up her behaviour with a double portion of reserve. **1814** JANE AUSTEN *Mansf. Park* I. ix. 180 Starched up into seeming piety, but with heads full of something very different.

absol. **1698** M. HENRY *Life P. Henry* viii. (1699) 117 He us'd to say, he could not Starch in his Preaching;..knowing where the Language..is stiff, and forced, and fine (as they call it) it doth not reach the greatest part of the Hearers.

3. †**a.** To fasten or stick with starch paste; also with *on*, *up*. *Obs.*

1602 DEKKER *Satiro-m.* E 3, I haue a set of letters readie starcht to my hands. **1673** HICKERINGILL *Gregory* 28 Some of the Common Herd of mankind..would quietly..pass by this Title-Page, (when starch'd up with the Play-house Bills). **1676** T. MILLER *Modellist* 4 In starching three or four sheets of paper together. **1717** S. SEWALL *Diary* 8 Jan. (1882) III. 116 A virulent Libel was starch'd on upon the Three Doors of the Meeting House. *a* **1721** PRIOR *Sat. Poets* 66 And find'st thy Picture starch'd 'gainst Suburb Wall.

b. To apply a starch paste mountant to (a photographic print).

1892 *Photogr. Ann.* II. 53 The print should be mounted dry, by starching the back and allowing it to dry and moistening the mount.

Star-chamber, †**starred chamber.** Also (nonce-form) **chamber of stars.** [f. STAR *sb.*[1], STARRED *a.*; rendering Anglo-L. *camera stellata* (14th c.), AF. *chambre d'estoiles, des esteilles, esteillee* (14th c.).

The conjecture of Sir T. Smith (*Commonw. Eng.* III. iv, *a* 1577) that the chamber was so called 'because at the first all the roofe thereof was decked with images of starres gilted', appears to have no confirmatory evidence, but is highly probable. The notion, made popular by Blackstone, that the chamber had been the depository of 'starrs' or Jewish bonds (see STARR) has no claim to consideration.]

1. The appellation of an apartment in the royal palace at Westminster, in which during the 14th and the 15th c. the chancellor, treasurer, justices, and other members of the king's council sat to exercise jurisdiction.

α. **1398** *Acc. Exch. K.R.* 470/17 m. 3 Circa reparationem tecture domus vocate Sterred chambre infra palacium predictum. **1426** *Rolls of Parlt.* V. 409/2 In the Sterred Chambre at Westmynstre, it was said and declared vnto my Lorde of Bedford [etc.]. **1433** *Ibid.* IV. 424/2 Lordes of ye Kyngs Counseil, beyng assembled in ye Sterrid Chambre. **1505** *Star Chamber Cases* (Selden Soc.) I. 225 The king our souerain Lordes moste honorable and most discrete Counsell in the starryd Chamber. **1533–4** *Act 25 Hen. VIII* c. 1 §2 To appere before the kynges Highnes, and the Lordis of hys most honorable Counsell in the Sterred Chambre at Westmynster.

β. **1422** *Close Roll 1 Hen. VI.* m. 21 b, In quadam camera vocata le Sterne-chamere infra palacium domini Regis Westm. **1427** *Rolls of Parlt.* IV. 334/2 En presence des plusours Seignours du Conseill nostre dit Sr. le Roi.. esteantz en le Sterre chambre de Westm[r]. **1450** *Ibid.* V. 179/1 Sittyng in your Counseill in the Sterre Chambre, in your Paleis. *a* **1548** HALL *Chron., Hen. VI*, 157 b, The same Duke sayde openly in the starre chamber before the lordes of the Counsail, that [etc.]. **1560** *Procl.* in Cardwell *Docum. Ann.* (1839) I. 260 To certify her majesty's privy council, or the council in the starchamber at Westminster. **1591** LAMBARDE *Archeion* (1635) 148 So the Councell-Chamber of that Palace..hath beene of long time called the Star-Chamber.

2. a. (More fully ***Court of Star-chamber.***) A court, chiefly of criminal jurisdiction, developed in the 15th c. from the judicial sittings of the King's Council in the Star Chamber at Westminster. The judges were the Lord Chancellor or Lord Keeper, the Lord Treasurer, the Lord Privy Seal, and any peers that chose to attend. The rules of procedure of the court rendered it a powerful instrument in the hands of a sovereign or a ministry desirous of using it for purposes of tyranny, and the abuse of it under James I and Charles I have made it a proverbial type of an arbitrary and oppressive tribunal. It was abolished by an Act of the Long Parliament in 1641.

1487 *Act 3 Hen. VII* c. 1 Pro Camera Stellata. An Acte geving the Court of Starchamber Authority to punnyshe Mydemeanors [*sic*]. **1522** SKELTON *Why not to Court* 185 In the Chambre of Starres All maters there he marres. **1534** *Star Chamber Cases* (Selden Soc.) II. 315 A bille ageynst the seid mulsho in the kynges most honorable Courte of Sterred Chamber. **1604** BACON *Apol.* 41, I was absent that day at the Starre-chamber. **1622** —— *Hen. VII*, 64 As the Chancerie had the Pretorian power for Equitie; So the Star-chamber had the Censorian power for Offences, vnder the degree of Capitall. **1637** (*title*) A Decree of Starre-Chamber, concerning Printing. **1655** FULLER *Ch. Hist.* IX. 187 The most sturdy and refractory Non-conformists (especially if they had any visible Estates) were brought into the Star-Chamber, the power whereof was above dispute. **1692** [J. WILSON] *Vindic. Carol.* 21 The taking away the several Courts of the Star-chamber. **1764** CHURCHILL *Gotham* II. 490 Curs'd Star-Chambers made, or rul'd the law.

b. *transf.* (allusively) and *fig.*

1596 *Edw. III*, II. ii. 165 When to the great Starre-chamber ore our heads The vniuersell Sessions cals to count This packing euill, we both shall tremble for it. *a* **1625** WEBSTER *Appius & Virg.* I. iii. (1654) 7 This three months did we never house our heads, but in yon great star-chamber. *a* **1633** AUSTIN *Medit.* (1635) 194 Sent, as Messengers from the Star-chamber of heaven. **1896** W. C. GORE in *Inlander* Jan. 150 *Star chamber*, an oral examination given to a student privately. **1934** [see GAY-PAY-OO]. **1958** M. KENNEDY *Outlaws on Parnassus* xiii. 208 A large group of [novelists]..will never allow that the novel can be subjected to legislation. If some Star Chamber has been set up, they ..will have none of it. **1973** *Times* 4 Dec. 17/6 The constitutional propriety of the present industrial star chamber is dubious. **1975** 'S. MARLOWE' *Cawthorn Jrnls.* (1976) xviii. 150 Mexican law's based on the Code Napoleon... You could say the courtroom's a Star Chamber instead of a field of forensic battle.

c. *attrib.*

1596 *Lett. Lit. Men* (Camd.) 95 The last starrchamber day of this terme. **1598** SHAKS. *Merry W.* I. i. 2 Sir Hugh, perswade me not: I will make a Star-Chamber matter of it. **1647** CLARENDON *Hist. Reb.* III. §211 The two bills for the taking away the Star Chamber court and the High Commission. **1659** RUSHW. *Hist. Coll.* I. 671 To acknowledge his offence at the Council-board, the Star-Chamber-Bar, and Exchange. **1800** *Asiatic Ann. Reg.* II. *St. Papers* etc. 82/2 They would steadily oppose the reviving of a nefarious star-chamber process. **1822** SCOTT *Nigel* xvi, Are you aware this is a Star Chamber business, young gentleman?

transf. **1888** *Daily News* 23 June 6/2 The defendants' solicitor was furnished..with the transcript of the shorthand writer's notes, taken at a 'Star Chamber' inquiry of four of the witnesses examined.

Hence (*nonce-wd.*) ˈ**Starchamber** *v. trans.* to bring before the Star-chamber.

1640 SHIRLEY *Constant Maid* v. I 3, You have conspired to rob, cheat, and undo me; I'll have you all Star-chamber'd.

starched (stɑːtʃt), *ppl. a.* [f. STARCH *v.* + -ED[1].]

1. Stiffened with or as with starch. **a.** of linen, etc. Also with *out*. Hence, of a person.

1617 B. RICH *Irish Hubbub* 9 Wee haue conuerted the coller of steele to a yellow-starched-band. **1707** J. STEVENS tr. *Quevedo's Com. Wks.* (1709) 223 My curious starch'd Band. **1818** SCOTT *Rob Roy* i, The ex-minister, as bolt upright as a starched ruff and laced cassock could make him. **1862** MRS. H. WOOD *Channings* xxxvi, Martha wore a crinoline.., and a starched-out muslin gown over it. **1891**

HARDY *Tess* xxv, A broad-brimmed hat and highly-starched cambric morning-gown.

†**b.** of the beard or hair. *Obs.*

1599 B. JONSON *Ev. Man out of Hum.* IV. iv, Who? this i' the starcht beard? **1633** P. FLETCHER *Purple Isl.* VII. 71 Some with black terrours his faint conscience baited, That wide he star'd, and starched hair did stand.

2. *fig.* Stiff, formal, precise. **a.** of a person, his countenance, behaviour, etc.

1599 B. JONSON *Ev. Man out of Hum.* I. ii, And when you come to Playes, be humorous, looke with a good starcht face and ruffle your brow like a new boot. **1607** *Puritan* I. iv. 54 Good Cocks-combe! what makes that pure, starch'd foole here? **1626** SHIRLEY *Brothers* v. i, One boisterous fellow, With a starched voice and a worse vizard.. quoited me Into the coach again. **1661** WOOD *Life* 3 May (O.H.S.) I. 395 John Haselwood, a proud, starch'd, formal and sycophantizing clisterpipe. **1662** E. HOPKINS *Serm. Funeral A. Grevil* (1663) 35 This taught him to outstrip in true wisdome, temperance and fortitude.. whatsoever those starch't and formall moralists did. **1708** SWIFT *Abol. Chr.* Misc. (1711) 172 Does the Gospel any where prescribe a starched squeezed Countenance, a Stiff formal Gate. **1749** SMOLLETT *Gil Blas* VIII. ix. (1782) III. 192 A parcel of insolent fellows, with their self-sufficient starched airs! **1771** —— *Humphry Cl.* 2 Apr., A maiden of forty-five, exceedingly starched, vain, and ridiculous. **1822** W. IRVING *Braceb. Hall* xxvi. 235 Mrs. Hannah moved about with starched dignity among the rustics. **1837** DICKENS *Pickw.* xxvii, His looks were starched, but his white neckerchief was not. **1862** SALA *Accepted Addr.* 5, I was seriously afraid that I should be married to some starched old maid.

b. of an oration, ceremony.

1659 WOOD *Life* Dec. (O.H.S.) I. 300 And 'scandalus' it was to have a formall starcht prayer before it. **1672** GALE *Crt. Gentiles* I. III. x. (ed. 2) 108 Aristotle tels us, that it [an oration] must be natural, not feigned, artificial or starched. **1693** *Humours Town* 31 Syllogising, that damn'd starch'd method of the Schools. *a* **1734** NORTH *Exam.* II. v. §133 (1740) 398 And they wrote it as he spoke it, which useth not to be in any starched Method. **1792** MARY WOLLSTONECRAFT *Rights Wom.* v. 217 A cultivated understanding and an affectionate heart will never want starched rules of decorum. **1883** R. RITCHIE *Bk. Sibyls* i. 28 A contrast to prim, starched scholastic life. **1884** *Christian World* 19 June 463/4 The stiff starched 'order of service', the rented pews, with the odious distinction of free seats.

Hence **'starchedly** *adv.*, **'starchedness.**

1671 L. ADDISON *West Barbary* 105 Don Diego de Palma ..chanceing to smile at the Moors Deportment, as not answering the starch'dness of his own Nation. **1702** C. MATHER *Magn. Chr.* VII. ii. (1852) 496 The fierceness of his talking in publick, and the starchtness of his living in private. **1705** J. DUNTON *Life* 145 'Twas the Vitals of Religion that she minded, and not Forms and Modes; and.. she did not think her self oblig'd to such a Starch'dness of Carriage as is usual amongst the Bostonians. **1873** BROWNING *Red Cott. Nt.-Cap* 379 See, the church With its white steeple,.. Starchedly warrants all beneath is matched By all above, one snowy innocence!

starcher ('stɑːtʃə(r)). [f. STARCH *v.* and *sb.* + -ER[1].]

1. One whose employment or trade is to starch linen.

c **1515** *Cocke Lorell's B.* (Percy Soc.) 10 Butlers, sterchers, and musterde makers. **1598** FLORIO, *Amitatrice*, a starcher. **1614** STOW *Ann.* 869/1 [In 1564] Mistris Dinghen.. came to London.. and there professed herselfe a starcher. **1669** E. CHAMBERLAYNE *Pres. State Eng.* I. xiv. 302 Of the Queen Consorts Court... A Laundress, a Semstress, a Starcher. **1725** *Bradley's Family Dict.* s.v. *Clear Starching*, Most Starchers boil their Muslins, which they should not by reason it wears them out. **1893** *Laundry Management* ix. 63 People of inventive turns of mind have stepped in the breach to help the starchers, offering them prepared glazes.

2. A starched neckcloth; also *attrib.*

1818 (*title*) Neckclothitania; or, Tietania: being an Essay on Starchers. *Ibid.* 38 If this be true.. a furious effort must be made unanimously by all starcher-wearers, to stop it in its birth. **1852** R. S. SURTEES *Sponge's Sp. Tour* i. 3 If [he wore] a striped waistcoat, then the starcher would be imbued with somewhat of the same colour and pattern.

3. A starching machine.

1893 *Laundry Management* ix. 65 In machine starching, the liquid starch is poured into a dash-wheel revolving washer or special starcher. **1909** *Daily Chron.* 3 Sept. 6/6 Contents of Laundry, 6 washing machines, two starchers.

starching ('stɑːtʃɪŋ), *vbl. sb.* [f. STARCH *v.* + -ING[1].]

1. The action of the verb STARCH.

1390-1 *Norwich Sacrist's Roll* (MS.), Vestiarium. Pro Coole pro starchyng, viij d. **1444** *Compota Domest.* (Abbotsf. Club) 23 Furfur.. Liberantur lotrici de camera pro sterchyng velaminum domine et generosarum suarum hoc anno.. j quarterium. **1529-30** *Rec. St. Mary at Hill* (1905) 350 Paid for wasshyng & Starchyng of þe pix clothe ij d. **1671** DRYDEN *Assign.* III. i, A Waiting-woman.. with mighty Golls, rough-Grain'd, and red with Starching. **1837** WHITTOCK *Bk. Trades* (1842) 32 (Bleacher) The next process is 'starching and bluing'. **1893** *Laundry Management* ix. 65 Starching may be done either by hand or by machine.

b. *attrib.*

1583 STUBBES *Anat. Abus.* II. 35 They haue their starching houses.. the better to trimme and dresse their ruffes. **1688** HOLME *Armoury* III. 348/1 The Weavers Starching Brush, is a long square Bristle Brush; with it he Starcheth the Yarn. **1839** URE *Dict. Arts* 1167 Starching and Steam-drying Apparatus. *Ibid.* **1168** C, is the cloth-beam, from which the starching roller draws forward the goods. **1875** J. PATON in *Encycl. Brit.* III. 817/2 [Bleaching.] The starching mangle and drying-machine are seen together in fig. 10. **1893** *Laundry Management* xviii. 152 Starching machines are virtually the same as the above [blueing machines].

†**2.** *concr.* Starch. *Obs.*

1612 WOODALL *Surg. Mate* Wks. (1653) 201 The excrements being of a yellowish colour in young men (like their starching now adayes). **1775** ASH, *Starching*,.. the starch put in cloaths to make them stiff.

starchly ('stɑːtʃlɪ), *adv.* [f. STARCH *a.* + -LY[2].] In a stiff, formal or precise manner.

1704 SWIFT *Let. Tisdall* 20 Apr., Wks. 1841 II. 439/2 In answer to all this, I might with good pretence enough talk starchly, and affect ignorance of what you would be at. **1755** JOHNSON, *Starchly*, stiffly, precisely.

starchness ('stɑːtʃnɪs). [f. STARCH *a.* + -NESS.] Stiffness of manner, formality, preciseness.

1683 J. H. tr. *10th Sat. Juv.* Ep. Ded. 1 Without any manner of Starchness or Ceremony, I may write what I please to you with the greatest freedom and liberty that can be. **1713** *Guardian* No. 29 ¶4 The Coquet in her turn laughs at the Starchness and awkward Affectation of the Prude. **1860** A. L. WINDSOR *Ethica* vii. 388 That academical starchness and that academical affectation which dons and tutors love to see in their undergraduates.

starchy ('stɑːtʃɪ), *a.* [f. STARCH *sb.* + -Y.]

1. Of or belonging to starch; resembling that of starch.

1802 COLERIDGE *Lett., To W. Sotheby* (1895) 384 This [cloud] is of a starchy grey. **1811** A. T. THOMSON *Lond. Disp.* (1818) 406 The pieces.. break with a short starchy fracture.

2. a. Of the nature of starch; composed of or containing starch-grains.

1838 T. THOMSON *Chem. Org. Bodies* 667 The solution of diastase.. separates amidin from all starchy substances containing it. **1861** BENTLEY *Bot.* 343 The albumen is described as mealy, starchy, or farinaceous, when its cells are filled with starch-grains. **1867** *Chamb. Encycl.* IX. 86/1 Limit the diet of the patient.. to a purely starchy diet, such as arrowroot. **1913** E. THORPE *Dict. Applied Chem.* V. 172/2 The starchy liquor as it comes from the sieves generally contains some sand.

b. Of food: containing much starch.

1948 *Good Housek. Cookery Bk.* I. 12 *Carbohydrates.* These comprise starchy foods and sugars. **1977** C. MCCULLOUGH *Thorn Birds* i. 13 No one carried a pound of superfluous flesh, in spite of the vast quantities of starchy food.

3. Of linen, etc.: Stiffened with starch.

1865 [implied in *starchiness*: see below].

4. *fig.* Of a person: Stiff, formal, precise. Also *transf.*

1828-32 WEBSTER, *Starchy*, stiff, precise. **1859** *Hotten's Slang Dict.* 101 *Starchy*, stuck-up, high-notioned, showily dressed, disdainful, cross. **1864** F. W. ROBINSON *Mattie* II. 286 He was the poor relation, he fancied, and some of these starchy beings scented his poverty by instinct. **1874** 'MARK TWAIN' *Lett. to Publishers* (1967) 81 It will thus be a mighty starchy book. **1880** 'OUIDA' *Moths* xiv, London had got so much nicer, she said, so much less starchy. **1897** W. C. HAZLITT *Four Generations* II. IV. vii. 149 My father.. got into trouble by asking some rather starchy people to meet them at dinner. **1977** E. W. HILDICK *Loop* xxiv. 164 Maybe that's putting it a bit too formal, Ralph, just a bit starchy.

Hence **'starchily** *adv.*, **'starchiness.**

1859 F. FRANCIS *Newton Dogvane* III. ii. 51 Ned rode after her, rather piqued at what he termed 'his sisters' starchiness'. **1865** *Daily Tel.* 6 May, The night-dress.. had all the freshness and starchiness of one which had only just been taken for use. **1876** GEO. ELIOT *Dan. Der.* I. iii, There were no distinctively clerical lines in the face,.. no tricks of starchiness or of affected ease. **1882** OGILVIE, *Starchily.* **1886** G. R. SIMS *Ring o' Bells* 98 Primness and starchiness are not always the signs of a bad heart.

starck, obs. form of STARK.

'stardom. [-DOM.] The world or status of 'star' actors; the status of a celebrity or star performer in other spheres of activity. Also *fig.*

1865 *Times* 6 Sept. 12 The theatres of New York differ from each other in their power of giving lustre to Stardom. **1901** C. MORRIS *Life on Stage* xxv. 203 At the curtain's fall her stardom was over. **1927** *Radio Times* 21 Oct. 143/2 From a clerkship in an insurance office to 'stardom' at a Royal Variety Performance is a long step. **1941** 'N. BLAKE' *Case of Abominable Snowman* xvi. 177 'I fancy lady Macbeth had put in a good deal of quiet work before the play opens, telling her husband what a worm he was.' 'Grooming him for evil stardom?' **1951** *Sport* 16-22 Mar. 13/3 Quietly plodding the hard road to stardom is Terry Webster, goalkeeper of Derby County. **1977** *New Yorker* 9 May 143/2 The media.. impel a Prime Minister to seek stardom at the expense of the Cabinet. **1979** *Tucson* (Arizona) *Citizen* 20 Sept. 1D/3 Giangardella has been tackling opponents since he was a fourth grader at Mt. Carmel Elementary School back in Niles. He went on to stardom at Niles McKinley High School.

star-dust. Also stardust.

1. *Astr.* Innumerable minute stars, likened, as seen in the telescope, to particles of dust.

1844 SMYTH *Cycle Celestial Obj.* I. 307 In some straggling clusters the components are nearly of the same magnitude, but in others they are extremely different, the brighter individuals being apparently on a ground, as it were, of star dust, really 'powdered with stars'. **1850** NICHOL *Archit. Heavens* 52 Masses still farther off may best be likened to a handful of golden sand, or, as it is aptly termed, *star-dust.* **1878** NEWCOMB *Pop. Astron.* IV. i. 443 Many of them [these clusters] are so distant that the most powerful telescopes.. show them only as a patch of star-dust.

2. Meteoric matter in fine particles supposed to fall upon the earth from space; 'cosmic dust'.

1879 A. GEIKIE *Geol. Sk.* xiii. (1882) 323 Mud gathers on the floor of these abysses [of the ocean].. so slowly that the very star-dust which falls from outer space forms an appreciable part of it.

3. *fig.* That which is illusory or insubstantial. Freq. in phr. ***to have stardust in one's eyes*** and varr.

1933 E. SITWELL *English Eccentrics* iv. 116 Here comes the star-dust, the noisy chattering crowd of tipsters and smaller racing men. **1934** V. WOOLF *Walter Sickert* 20 His [*sc.* Sickert's] paint has a tangible quality; it is made not of air and star-dust but of oil and earth. **1967** WODEHOUSE *Company for Henry* iii. 45 Clichy double overlay weight.. centred by a pink rose within a ring of white stardust canes. **1975** A. HUNTER *Gently with Love* xxii. 81 'You had a different opinion of her once.'.. 'I must have had some stardust in my eyes.' **1977** *New Yorker* 4 July 82/3 There is the silliness of the movie's plangency: hard to feel soupy about a talented couple giving up their love because of the stardust in their eyes.

stare (stɛə(r)), *sb.*[1] Now *arch.* and *dial.* Forms: 1 stær, (stear, star), 5 staar, 6 star, staare, 7 steare, 8 stear, 4- stare. [OE. *stær* masc. = MLG. *star* masc., OHG. *star* masc., *stara* fem. (mod.G. *star*, also written *staar*, *stahr*), OIcel. *stari* (Edda Gl.; Sw., Norw. *stare*, Da. *stær*):—OTeut. **staro-z*, *starŏn-*, cogn. w. L. *sturnus* of the same meaning.] A bird of the genus *Sturnus*: = STARLING.

c **725** *Corpus Gloss.*, *Sturnus*, staer. *c* **950** *Lindisf. Gosp.* Matt. x. 29 Tuoeȝe staras *vel* hronsparuas. *c* **1381** CHAUCER *Parl. Foules* 348 The stare that the counsell can bewrey. *c* **1400** *Pilgr. Sowle* (Caxton 1483) v. v. (1859) 76 Thenne I bethought me vppon the byrdes as thrusshes, and thrustels, and stares. **1486** *Bk. St. Albans* f vi b, A Murmuracion of stares. **1530** PALSGR. 275/2 Staare a byrde, *estourneau.* *c* **1532** DU WES *Introd. Fr.* ibid. 912 The star, *lesprohon.* **1542** BOORDE *Dyetary* xv. (1870) 271 Rasis and Isaac prayseth yonge staares. **1639** SIR R. GORDON *Gen. Hist. Earldom Sutherland* 3 Steares or stirlings,.. and all other kinds of wildfowl and birds. **1673** DRYDEN *Marr. à la Mode* III. i, He taught a prating Stare to speak my name. *a* **1721** PRIOR *Poems, Turtle & Sparrow* 356 An honest Rook Told it a Snipe, who told a Stear Who told it those, who told it her. **1768** PENNANT *Brit. Zool.* I. 231 The Stare breeds in hollow trees, eaves of houses &c. **1845** *New Stat. Acc. Scot.* XIV. 189 (Ross & Cromarty) The stare is also a rare bird. **1868** MORRIS *Earthly Par.* I. i. 167 And plovers cry about the meads, And the stares chatter. **1910** *Spectator* 26 Mar. 506/1 Whitethroat and willow-wren and whistling stare Singing together.

b. *Ornith.* With prefixed word, denoting some particular species of the genus *Sturnus*.

1678 RAY *Willughby's Ornith.* II. xix. 196 Bontius his Indian Stare. [Willughby *Sturnus Indicus Bontii.*] **1787** LATHAM *Suppl. Gen. Syn. Birds* I. 137 Common Stare, *Sturnus vulgaris.* Silk Stare. Length eight inches. **1829** GRIFFITH tr. *Cuvier* VII. 173 Cape Stare, *Sturnus Capensis.*

stare (stɛə(r)), *sb.*[2] Also 5-6 *Sc.* stair. [f. STARE *v.*]

†**1.** Power of seeing. *Obs. rare*$^{-1}$.

13.. *E.E. Allit. P.* B. 583 He þat stykked vche a stare in vche steppe yȝe.

†**2.** A condition of amazement, horror, admiration, etc., indicated by staring. *Obs.*

c **1480** HENRYSON *Mor. Fables* IV. (*Fox's Confess.*) xviii, Astonist all still into ane stair he stude. **1513** DOUGLAS *Æneis* IV. ii. 58 Sche.. in a stair behaldis hym for joy. **1610** SHAKS. *Temp.* III. iii. 94 Why stand you In this strange stare? **1904** M. HEWLETT *Queen's Quair* III. iv, She was in a stare. 'I am going to the King'.

3. An act or a habit of staring; a fixed gaze with the eyes wide open.

1700 DRYDEN *Pal. & Arc.* III. 43 He look'd a Lion with a gloomy Stare. **1778** MISS BURNEY *Evelina* (1791) II. 112 She cast her languishing eyes round the room with a vacant stare. **1796** *Plain Sense* III. 78 With a broad stare of incomprehension, she was answered. **1840** DICKENS *Old C. Shop* ii, After bestowing a stare and a frown on me. **1855** TENNYSON *Maud* I. xiii. 22 [He] gorgonised me from head to foot With a stony British stare. **1911** GALSWORTHY *Patrician* II. ii. 179 Unmoved by the stares of the audience, Barbara sat absorbed in moody thoughts.

b. generalized use. *rare.*

1785 COWPER *Task* II. 430 Avaunt all attitude, and stare, And start theatric, practised at the glass!

c. ***to make a stare***: to make people stare, excite astonishment. † ***to be on the stare***: to be staring.

1804 WOLCOT (P. Pindar) *Epist. to Ld. Mayor* Wks. 1812 V. 203 We have been upon the stare For your Address. **1808** —— *One More Peep at R. Acad.* ibid. 359 A vulgar World delights in glare Adores whatever makes a stare.

d. Used for: The object stared at.

1753 E. MOOR in *World* No. 43 ¶8 She never hears the word Infidel mentioned from the pulpit, without fancying herself the stare of the whole rabble of believers.

†**stare**, *sb.*[3] *Obs.* Also 7 starre. [ad. It. †*stara*, *staro* (also *staio*); the med.L. forms are *stara*, *starium*, *starius*; perh. shortened from L. *sextārius*: see SESTER, SEXTAR, SEXTARY.] An Italian measure of grain, etc., corresponding to the bushel, but varying according to locality or the kind of substance measured. Also as a weight (see quot. 1622).

1540 *St. Papers Hen. VIII*, VIII. 235 ThEmperour hath given this State licence to draw owt of the realme of Naples abowt 80000 staris of wete. **1622** MALYNES *Anc. Law-Merch.* 26 Italie. They doe also weigh.. by starre of 220 lb. weight. **1698** *Phil. Trans.* XX. 286 Ashes drawn from a Stare and a half of Bran, burnt.. in the Furnace with Sulphur. [**1811** P. KELLY *Univ. Cambist* I. 312 Modena... Corn is measured by the Staro or Staja, 4 of which are nearly equivalent to an English Quarter.]

stare (stɛə(r)), *v.* Pa. t. and pa. pple. **stared** (stɛəd). Also 6 **stayre**, **staar**. [OE. *starian*, corresp. to (M)LG., Du. *staren*, OHG. *starên* (MHG. *starn*), ON. *stara* (Norw. *stara*), f. OTeut. **staro-* (see STAREBLIND *a.*).

In mod.Ger. the vb. has disappeared, being merged in the cognate vb. *starren* (OHG. *starrên*) to be rigid; the sense 'to look fixedly, stare' being capable of being regarded as a particular application of the general meaning. A vb. of identical meaning, and prob. cognate, though the phonological relation is obscure, exists in several Teut. langs.: On. *stira* (Da. *stirre*, Sw. *stirra*), mod.G. *stieren*.]

1. a. *intr.* To gaze fixedly and with eyes wide open. Said also of the eyes. Const. in mod. use chiefly *at* (also in *indirect passive*), *in* (a person's face), and occas. *after*, *into*, *through*; formerly (now *arch.*) *on*, *upon*. Also with advs. *about*, *around*, or advb. phr. denoting direction.

In modern use the verb ordinarily implies rudeness, or is otherwise disparaging; hence many of the older examples would now be differently expressed.

Beowulf 1781 þæt ic on þone hafelan heorodreorigne.. eaȝum starige. *c* **1000** ÆLFRIC *Lives Saints* xv. 199 Forðan þe se earn..mæȝ swyðost starian on þære sunnan leoman. *a* **1300** *Cursor M.* 13557 Quen men him sagh þat kneu him are, Fast þai can on him to stare. *c* **1340** *Nominale* (Skeat) 176 *Homme doile guenyle*, M. with ee starith. **13..** *E.E. Allit. P.* A. 149 Abowte me con I stote & stare To fynde a forþe. **13..** *Ibid.* B. 389 Summe styȝe to a stud & stared to þe heuen. **1362** LANGL. *P. Pl.* A. XII. 61, I stode stille in a stodie and stared a-bowte. *c* **1374** CHAUCER *Troylus* II. 1142 This Pandarus gan on here for to stare. *a* **1400–50** *Wars Alex.* 263 He in his sege lened In stody still as a stane, & starid in hire face. *c* **1400** *Destr. Troy* 8627 He stode þus in stid, starit hym vpon. **1412** LYDG. *Troy Bk.* 1337 þei wern so rude to staren and to gase To gape & loke, as it wer on a mase. *c* **1430** *Hymns Virg.* (1867) 37 Summe staren broode & moun not se. *c* **1440** *Promp. Parv.* 472/2 Staryn, wythe brode eyne, *patentibus oculis respicere*. **1557** *Tottel's Misc.* (Arb.) 241 For had he come in golden garmentes bright, Or so as men mought haue starde on the sight. **1570** LEVINS *Manip.* 252/45 To stayre, *aspicere, contemplare*. *a* **1586** SIDNEY *Arcadia* I. xiii. §4 Standing upon his tip-toes, and staring as though he would have a mote pulled out of his eie. **1589** PUTTENHAM *Engl. Poesie* III. xxiv. (Arb.) 300 King Henry th'eight..could not abide to haue any man stare in his face. **1602** MARSTON *Antonio's Rev.* IV. iii, Her bright eyes gan ope, And starde upon him. **1697** DRYDEN *Virg. Past.* VI. 34 He stares around, with stupid Eyes. *Ibid., Georg.* IV. 370 With hagger'd Eyes they stare, Lean are their Looks, and shagged is their Hair. **1703** CIBBER *She wou'd* etc. v. 68 How shall I be star'd at when I give an Account of this to my Father, or your Friends in Sevil? **1806** H. SIDDONS *Maid, Wife, & Widow* I. 95, I sat for hours together staring on the fire. **1817** KEATS *Sonn.* xi, Like stout Cortez when with eagle eyes He star'd at the Pacific. **1818** SCOTT *Hrt. Midl.* ix, There was..scarce a maiden on whom he did not stare. **1820** W. IRVING *Sketch Bk.* I. 73 They..stared at him with fixed statue-like gaze. **1835** MARRYAT *Jacob Faithful* xii, She'd a roguish eye, and liked to be stared at, as most pretty women do, because it flatters their vanities. **1848** DICKENS *Dombey* iv, By having stared for three or four days successively through every optical instrument in his shop. **1859** TENNYSON *Geraint & Enid* 267 Two wild men supporters of a shield, Painted, who stare at open space. **1859** FITZGERALD *Omar* xxiv, Alike for those who for To-day prepare, And those that after a To-morrow stare. **1865** LIVINGSTONE *Zambesi* xvi. 326 They [the hippopotami] stare with peculiar stolid looks. **1878** MISS BRADDON *Eleanor's Vict.* i, A few hurried off to the Market-place, to stare at the Cathedral Church of Saint Jacques. **1880** 'OUIDA' *Moths* I. 21 And be kind enough not to stand here and stare; everybody is listening. **1907** J. A. HODGES *Elem. Photogr.* (ed. 6) 119 The sitter should never be allowed to stare into the lens.

b. *colloquial phrases.*

1694 MOTTEUX *Rabelais* v. ix. 41 Panurge star'd at him like a dead Pig. **1714** GAY *What d'ye call it?* I. i, His loving mother left him to my care Fine child, as like his dad as he could stare. **1796** JANE AUSTEN *Sense & Sens.* xiii, Oh! yes; and as like him as she can stare. **1809** MALKIN *Gil Blas* x. x. (Rtldg.) 373 He stared like a stuck pig at my equipment!

¶**c.** In poetry used (on account of rhyme or alliteration) for: To look. *Obs.* Cf. STARE *sb.*[2] 1.

1390 GOWER *Conf.* III. 7 Whanne I mai upon hire stare, ..Myn herte is full of such gladnesse. *c* **1400** *Destr. Troy* 5551 Wo so staris on þis story, or stodis þerin, Take hede on þe harmys & the hard lures.

d. *transf.* and *fig.* Of things: To be obtrusively conspicuous. Also in obvious transferred uses with comparison of lights or windows to eyes.

1657 BILLINGSLY *Brachy-Martyrol.* iii. 12 So said, thus rack'd, into a fire he's thrown, And now his wasting bowels stared on The Tyrants face. **1825** LAMB *Elia* Ser. II. *Barbara S——*, And then came staring upon her the figures of her little stockingless and shoeless sisters. **1863** COWDEN CLARKE *Shaks. Char.* iii. 84 Their subtleties of character stare out like the bones of a starved beast. **1895** P. HEMINGWAY *Out of Egypt* II. 175 One evening, as I stood watching a vessel in the harbour, that stared townwards with a hundred round unblinking eyes. **1909** BRIDGES *Paraphr. Æn.* VI. Poems (1913) 457 Right i' the front stareth the columnar gate adamantine.

2. quasi-*trans.* with complement.

a. With adv., adj., or phrase expressing the result of staring at a person or thing; *esp.* in *to stare* (a person) *out of countenance* (see COUNTENANCE *sb.* 6 b).

1672 VILLIERS (Dk. Buckhm.) *Rehearsal* IV. i. (Arb.) 103 Who e'er to gulp one drop of this dares think I'l stare away his very pow'r to drink. **1719** D'URFEY *Pills* III. 319 The.. Stone..stares Deucalions..Boys, into..Pebbles. **1833** LYTTON *Godolphin* xxiii, She did not stare young men out of countenance. **1844** MRS. BROWNING *Poems, Dead Pan* x, Thou art staring the stars pale. **1857** [see COUNTENANCE *sb.* 6 b].

b. *to stare* (a person) *in the face* [after the older phrase in LOOK *v.* 1 e]: to stare at (his) face; also *fig.* of a thing, to be glaringly obvious to, to force itself on the notice of; to be apparently obvious but nevertheless overlooked.

1690 LOCKE *Hum. Und.* I. iii. §13 Whether it be possible, for People..to offend against a Law..that stares them in the Face, whilst they are breaking it? **1692** R. L'ESTRANGE *Fables* cclxxx. 245 But to come now to the Ungrateful Point, the Bare Innuendo of it would stare so many People in the Face, that [etc.]. **1698** FRYER *Acc. E. India & P.* 9 They staring one in the Face, and in the mean time..steal a Handkerchief. **1727** BOLINGBROKE *Occas. Writer* ii. 44 This terrible Object stares our speculative Enquirer in the Face, and disturbs his Head. **1769** *Junius Lett.* xix. 82 The contradiction was unexpectedly urged and stared him in the face. **1790** BUCHAN *Dom. Med.* 569 Few people will submit to the extirpation till death stares them in the face. **1817** LD. ELLENBOROUGH in *Maule & Selwyn's Rep.* VI. 316 When he knew himself insolvent, and when ruin and bankruptcy were staring him in the face. **1846** GREENER *Sci. Gunnery* 98 The mock sales..that stare us in the face at every turning. **1855** ABP. THOMSON *Laws of Thought* §46 A man stares his friend in the face without recognising him. **1912** *Throne* 7 Aug. 205/1 To minimise the severity of the defeat which Ministers see staring them in the face. **1966** J. B. PRIESTLEY *Salt is Leaving* iii. 43 She found the Mahler album... 'It must have been staring you in the face,' she added. **1972** 'G. NORTH' *Sgt. Cluff rings True* xvi. 120 'It was staring me in the face,' the Sergeant said, and he should have seen it sooner. **1979** A. BOYLE *Climate of Treason* viii. 236 The over-caution of Cowgill in fumbling for conclusions that stared him in the face demanded some patience.

c. *to stare* (a person) *up and down*: to survey with a stare from head to foot.

1889 MAY CROMMELIN & J. M. BROWN *Violet Vyvian* III. i. 6 She always stares me up and down at the meets. **1891** H. S. MERRIMAN *Prisoners & Captives* II. 78 They are staring me up and down like a wild animal.

d. *to stare* (someone) *down, out*: to stare at someone without being first to blink or lower one's gaze, usu. as an expression of resistance or hostility; to outstare. Also *fig.*

1856 DICKENS *Little Dorrit* (1857) I. xxiv. 215 'She looked at the Princess, and the Princess looked at her.' 'Like trying to stare one another out,' said Maggy. **1946** T. H. WHITE *Mistress Masham's Repose* xiv. 115 Miss Brown searched out her pupil's eyes and fixed them with her own. She had a.. trick of staring Maria down. **1965** 'T. HINDE' *Games of Chance* I. iv. 110 That made me shout at Kenny a lot, and mimic him, and stare him out. **1972** R. THOMAS *Porkchoppers* (1974) xii. 107 He spent nearly a minute staring at Goff. Goff had stared back, thinking that he was damned if he'd let any pal of Cloke's stare him down. **1979** *Guardian* 12 Jan. 8/5 Some measure of fiscal 'mid-term adjustment'..is called for. So is a serious attempt to stare down the local government workers. **1979** G. SEYMOUR *Red Fox* iv. 56 The maid in the starched apron stared him out.

3. Used with implication of a mental state.

†**a.** To open the eyes wide in madness or fury; to glare. Often in alliterative phrases, e.g. *scowl and stare*, *stamp and stare* (see STAMP *v.* 2 c), *swear and stare*, denoting the indications of uncontrolled rage. *Obs.*

c **1250** *Death* 234 in *O.E. Misc.*, He [*sc.* the Devil] ȝeoneþ mid his muþe and stareþ mid his eȝe. *c* **1250** *Owl & Night.* 77 þu starest so þu wille abyten. *a* **1300** *Havelok* 508 Starinde als he were wod. **1340** HAMPOLE *Pr. Consc.* 2225 Als wode lyons thai [the devils] sal than fare, And raumpe on hym, and skoul and stare. *c* **1360** *Song of Yesterday* 53 in *E.E.P.* (1862) 134 Nis..non so styf to stunt ne stare... þat he naþ warnynges to be ware. **1390** GOWER *Conf.* II. 63 He gan to fare Into the field and loke and stare, As he which feigneth to be wod. **1399** LANGL. *Rich. Redeles* III. 189 This makyth men..to stroute and to stare and stryue aȝeyn vertu. *a* **1400** *Minor Poems fr. Vernon MS.* xxix. ii. 75 þe Ieuh bigon to stare and swere And seide þer com non such child þere. **1530** PALSGR. 733/2, I stare, as a mans eyes stare for anger. *a* **1548** HALL *Chron., Hen. VI*, 131 b, Lorde how the Flemines bragged..that Calice should be wonne.. swearyng and staryng, that thei would haue it, within thre daies at the moste. **1579** NORTHBROOKE *Dicing* (1843) 8 If he can sweare and stare they say hee hath a stout courage. **1590** SPENSER *F.Q.* I. iv. 33 His eies..stared sterne on all that him beheld. *Ibid.* III. vii. 39 Her firie eyes with furious sparkes did stare. **1615** J. TAYLOR (Water P.) *Taylor's Rev.* Wks. (1630) II. 145/2 Some laught, some swore, some star'd and stamp'd and curst. **1667** STURMY *Mariner's Mag.* Friendly Advt. (1669) c 3 b, They..will swear and stare, crack and boast, That they have done all things according to Art. **1837** A. TENNENT *Force of Imag.* 64 His eye-balls stared with vicious scowl.

b. To open the eyes wide in astonishment; hence, to be amazed.

1399 LANGL. *Rich. Redeles* II. 8 Some stode astonyed and stared for drede. *c* **1400** *Rowland & O.* 551 Drondale felle so sadde and sare þat þe Saraȝene bi-gane to stare. *a* **1400** *Pistill of Susan* 285 (MS. Phillipps) Tho criede þat ferly [*read* frely] fode: 'Why spillist þou innocent blode?' And all þei starid [*v.rr.* stoteyd, stynted, were a-stonyed] and stode. **1716** LADY M. W. MONTAGU *Lett.* I. iii. 12, I was yesterday at the French Church, and stared very much at their manner of service. **1782** COWPER *Gilpin* 194 Said John, It is my wedding day And all the world would stare If wife should dine at Edmonton And I should dine at Ware! **1789** PITT in *G. Rose's Diaries* (1860) I. 98 You will stare a good deal at the circumstance which makes me write this letter. **1815** SCOTT *Guy M.* lviii, Mac-Morlan will stare when he sees the bill. **1820** BYRON *Juan* III. lxxxi, Even good men like to make the public stare. **1849** MACAULAY *Hist. Eng.* vii. II. 194 Mordaunt wanted merely to enjoy the excitement of conflict, and to make men stare. **1850** MRS. JAMESON *Leg. Monast. Ord.* (1863) 429 To produce such illusions as make the vulgar stare. **1855** MACAULAY *Hist. Eng.* xv. III. 605 The other councillors stared, but remained silent. **1902** VIOLET JACOB *Sheep-Stealers* viii, Bumpett stared blankly. For once in his life he was quite taken aback.

†**4.** To shine. *Obs.*

13.. *E.E. Allit. P.* A. 116 As stremande sternez..Staren in welkyn in wynter nyȝt. *c* **1394** *P. Pl. Crede* 553 þei ben y-sewed wiþ whiȝt silk..Y-stongen wiþ stitches þat stareþ as siluer. *a* **1400–50** *Wars Alex.* 3796 As ai stremand sternes stared all þaire wedis. *c* **1400** *Destr. Troy* 7349 The sternes full stithly starond o lofte. *c* **1440** *Promp. Parv.* 472/2 Staryn, or schynyn, and glyderyn, *niteo, rutilo*.

5. Of hair, a horse's coat, feathers, fibres of any kind: To stand on end. [So mod.G. *starren*.] Now chiefly *technical*. Also, †to spread out.

1523–34 FITZHERB. *Husb.* §56 Loke well, that the heare stare not. **1560** PHAER *Æneid* IX. (1562) Dd iij, Thou sawest ..how his helmet crest did streaming stare? **1565** COOPER *Thesaurus* s.v. *Coma*, *Horror comas erexit*, feare made his heare to stare. **1590** COCKAINE *Treat. Hunting* D j, His coate also will stare and frise so vppon him, as you may easely knowe him thereby. **1603** OWEN *Pembrokeshire* (1892) 127 The here of the seale stareth at the South windes. **1614** *Life & Death Geninges* 55 His face glowed, and as he thought his hayre stared. **1621** BURTON *Anat. Mel.* I. ii. IV. iii. 195 There was such an hideous noyse..that their haire stared for feare. **1676** DURFEY *Madam Fickle* III. iii, See how his Perriwig stares with his wild passion. *a* **1722** LISLE *Husb.* (1757) 319 Their skins would turn scurfy and starky, and their wool stare and grow thin. **1748** RICHARDSON *Clarissa* VI. 157 Four old turkey-worked chairs, bursten-bottomed, the stuffing staring out. **1753** BARTLET *Gentl. Farriery* xxxvi. 278 So that the hair stares up, and is what some term pen-feathered. **1788** *New Lond. Mag.* 624 When the whole is dry, dress the feathers round the outline that may chance to stare a little. **1806–7** J. BERESFORD *Miseries Hum. Life* (1826) x. §69 Its few remaining hairs [said of an old toothbrush] staring off horizontally on all sides. **1808** SCOTT *Marmion* II. xxxii, The locks that wont her brow to shade, Star'd up erectly from her head. **1860** *All Year Round* No. 49. 531 One drink of hard water would put the favourite horse out of condition, make his coat 'stare'. **1888** *Lancet* 14 Jan. 96/1 The affected cows were restless and irritable; their coats 'stared.' **1891** *Labour Commission Gloss.* s.v. *Nap*, [Filaments of cotton yarn] are very sensitive to electrical conditions, hence the importance of means to make them lie as smooth as possible, otherwise they polarise in all directions, that is 'stare'.

6. *Comb.* † **stare-about**, one who stares about; **stare-cat** *U.S.* (see quot.); **stare-you-out**, the activity of staring someone out (see sense 2 d above), esp. as a chlldren's game; also *attrib.*

1614 B. JONSON *Barth. Fair* III. v, They stick not the Stare-abouts purses to take. **1859** BARTLETT *Dict. Amer.* (ed. 2) 448 *Stare-cat*, a woman or girl who amuses herself with gazing at her neighbors. **1962** E. O'BRIEN *Lonely Girl* ix. 107 In the village..people stopped to look..with savage stare-you-out eyes. **1972** J. QUARTERMAIN *Rock of Diamonds* xxvi. 140 She held her expression... I grinned and played 'Stare-you-out'. But I blinked first. **1977** D. MORRIS *Manwatching* 75 (*caption*) Such is the impact of the close-quarters gaze that the schoolboy game of stare-you-out is extremely difficult to maintain over a long period of time.

stare, obs. f. STAR *sb.*[1], var. STAR *sb.*[2]

†**stareblind**, *a.* *Obs.* [OE. *stær(e)blind* = OFris. *staru-*, *stare-*, *starblind*, MDu. *staerblint* (mod.Du. *staarblind*), OHG. *staraplint* (MHG. *starblint*, mod.G. *staar-*, *star-*, *starrblind*), ON. *starblind-r* (Sw. *starrblind*, Da. *stærblind*); f. OTeut. **staro-* found as MDu. *star* rigidity (of the eyes in death), mod.G. *staar*, *star*, Du. *staar*, Sw. *starr*, Da. *stær* cataract in the eyes; app. cogn. w. OHG. *starrên* (mod.G. *starren*) to be stiff or rigid, MHG. *stärre*, *sterre* (mod.G. *starr*) stiff, rigid.] ? Blind without perceptible lesion of the eyes.

c **725** *Corpus Gloss.* S 134 *Scotomaticus*, staerblind. *c* **1000** in Cockayne *Shrine* (1864) 187 ðyf he enyȝ wiht ȝeseon mæȝ, buton he stare blind si. *Ibid.*, Sume beoð stære blinde. *c* **1250** *Owl & Night.* 241 Bi daye þu art stare-blynd.

‖**stare decisis** ('stɛəriː dɪ'saɪzɪs, 'stɑːreɪ dɪ'siːsɪs). *Law.* [L., lit. to stand by things decided.] The legal principle of determining points in litigation according to precedent; properly as *vbl. phr.*, to be bound by precedents.

1782 F. BULLER in E. H. East *Rep. King's Bench* (1801) I. 495 The rule *stare decisis* is one of the most sacred in the law. **1811** *Q. Rev.* Dec. 434 The learned judge..professes his anxiety 'stare decisis', and to abide by authorities. **1845** H. BROOM *Legal Maxims* ii. 61 It is..an established rule to abide by former precedents, *stare decisis*, where the same points come again into litigation. **1936** J. C. GARDNER *Judicial Precedent Scots Law* iii. 41 It probably cannot be said that the *stare decisis* doctrine had no part in the operation of precedent on the inferior Courts in Scotland. **1970** *Internat. & Compar. Law Q.* XIX. I. 145 A rigid adherence to *stare decisis*..is of little assistance where the law hopes to offer an answer to the people it serves. **1982** *Sci. Amer.* June 20/2 The doctrine of *stare decisis* (namely that precedents should be followed) may be imposed at the players' option, or it may arise without explicit amendment, as successive judges feel impelled to treat 'similarly situated' persons 'similarly'.

staree (stɛə'riː). *nonce-wd.* [f. STARE *v.* + -EE.] The person stared at.

1800 MAR. EDGEWORTH *Belinda* iii, We were mutually agreeable to each other—I as starer, and she as staree.

starer ('stɛərə(r)). [f. STARE *v.* + -ER[1].]

1. A person who stares.

1663 BOYLE *Usef. Exp. Nat. Philos.* I. v. 116 The vulgar astonishment of an unlettered Starer. **1711** STEELE *Spect.* No. 20 ¶2 A kind of Men, whom I choose to call Starers, that without any Regard to Time, Place, or Modesty, disturb a large Company with their impertinent Eyes. **1767**

S. Paterson *Another Trav.* I. 338 Exhibiting their mummeries..to thousands of stupid starers. **1796** Mme. D'Arblay *Camilla* IV. 218 They regularly drew forth either the master or the man to make another starer at their singular proceedings. **1865** W. G. Palgrave *Arabia* I. 140 We passed down the street, lined with starers at the King and us. **1880** Browning *Dram. Idyls* Ser. II. *Clive* 154 I'll engage no glance was sent That way by a single starer.

2. *pl.* Eye-glasses with a long handle. *colloq.*

1904 Mrs. A. Sidgwick *Scenes Jewish Life* 135 His mother put up her 'starers', and addressed Eva in French. **1905** Miss Broughton *Waif's Progr.* xi. 128 She sat with the 'starers' she had taken off lying in her lap.

‖**starets, staretz** ('starjɛts). Pl. **startsy, startzy** ('startsɪ). [Russ., = (venerable) old man, elder.] In the Russian Orthodox Church, a spiritual leader or counsellor. Also *transf.*

1923 G. Buchanan *My Mission to Russia* I. xviii. 240 Rasputin..thus gradually acquired the reputation of a holy man, or elder (*staretz*), and was credited with the gifts of healing and prophecy. **1955** J. D. Salinger in *New Yorker* 29 Jan. 36/2 He meets this person called a starets—some sort of terribly advanced religious person—and the starets tells him about a book called the 'Philokalia'. **1966** A. Bloom *Living Prayer* v. 73 The Staretz Ambrose of Optina had the kind of vision which allowed him to see a person's real good. **1975** *Christian* III. 91 The Startsy became enormously influential in the last hundred years of Tsarism. **1976** *Ibid.* III. 150 She was meeting..a man who was himself the spiritual soul of one of the greatest *startzy* (spiritual fathers) of the nineteenth century West, the Abbé Huvelin. **1981** A. Edwards *Sonya* 492 Rasputin..'cured' Tsarevich Alexis's hemophilia in 1904. Thereafter, with each recurrence of her son's illness, the Tsarina grew more dependent upon this starets. **1983** *Church Times* 4 Feb. 7/1 They tell us of the hidden work of the *Startsy*, the 'elders' or spiritual fathers, whose counsel and prayer is an inspiration to many.

starey ('stɛərɪ), *a.* Also **stary**. [f. stare *v.* + -y[1].]

1. Inclined to stare; giving the appearance of staring.

1924 *Chambers's Jrnl.* Aug. 557 A bit flushed and starey about the eyes but still breathing. **1950** T. E. Lawrence *Mint* xiv. 50 Her eyes were starey, like a haddock's. **1960** P. Coleridge *Running Footsteps* 170 Did he go blind at the end? He was getting very stary, very vacant, like. **1975** *Listener* 9 Oct. 479/1 Vanessa Redgrave, very starey and earnest. **1980** S. King *Firestarter* I. 57 There was something starey in her eyes that made him think about those combat-fatigue stories you heard during wartime.

2. = staring *ppl. a.* 3.

1955 W. W. Denlinger *Complete Boston* I. 94 They [*sc.* internal parasites] reflect themselves in a dull starey coat.

starf, obs. pa. t. of starve *v.*

star-fish, starfish ('stɑːfɪʃ). Pl. **-fish, -fishes.** [Cf. sea-star 2.]

1. Any echinoderm of the genus *Asterias* or of the class *Asteroidea*, having a flattened body, normally consisting of lobes or rays (usually five), radiating from a central disc. These rays are sometimes very short or altogether absent, the body having the form of a pentagonal disc. The common star-fish is *Asterias* (*Asteracanthion*) *rubens*.

1538 Elyot *Dict.*, *Stella*, a sterre, also a sterrefyshe. **1611** Cotgr., *Arbre marin*.., the greatest of Starre-fishes. **1672** W. Hughes *Amer. Physit.* 9 Of the Sea-Star-Fish, or by some called the Sea-Star. **1672** Josselyn *New-Eng. Rarities* 95 The Star Fish, having five points like a Star, the whole Fish no bigger than the Palm of a Mans hand. **1774** Goldsm. *Nat. Hist.* VIII. 174. **1836–9** *Todd's Cycl. Anat.* II. 34/1 The star-fish has the power of slowly moving its rays. **1896** Lydekker *Roy. Nat. Hist.* VI. 305 Star-fish are sluggish animals.

attrib. **1868** M. W. Taylor in *Trans. Cumb. & Westm. Antiq. & Archæol. Soc.* I. 166 Imparting..a kind of star-fish appearance to the structure. **1885** —— *Ibid.* VIII. 331 The White Raise or Star-fish cairn.

2. *transf.* A name for certain species of Stapelia.

1840 Paxton *Bot. Dict.*, Star fish,..*Stapelia Asterias.* **1884** W. Miller *Plant-n.* 130 Star-fish-flower, *Stapelia Asterias* and other species.

3. Special Comb.: **starfish bed** *Geol.*, a stratum rich in starfish fossils; (usu. with capital initial(s) as a proper name).

1863 *Q. Jrnl. Geol. Soc.* XIX. 289 Capping these, in Down Cliffs, is the Starfish-bed, above which begin the Middle Lias Sands. **1935** J. Pringle *South of Scotland* ii. 34 Near the head of the Lady Burn the mudstones are underlain by a hard greenish-grey calcareous sandstone, the well-known Starfish Bed. **1970** R. M. Black *Elements Palaeont.* x. 141 While, in general, they are rare fossils, in some horizons (referred to as 'starfish' beds) they are relatively numerous, e.g. in the Upper Ordovician, Girvan and in the Lower Ludlow in Herefordshire. **1977** J. W. Perkins *Geol. explained in Dorset* xi. 138 The base of the Starfish Bed forms a strong spring-line, and hillsides below this level are often cut by deep wooded gullies as a result.

Hence '**star-fishy** *a.* (*nonce-wd.*).

1875 Ruskin *Fors. Clav.* lxi, A population mostly of.. bagmen..nothing else but bags;—sloppy, star-fishy, seven-suckered stomachs of indiscriminate covetousness.

'**star-flower.**

1. A name given to a number of plants with bright stellate flowers, as *Ornithogalum umbellatum* and other species, (in U.S.) *Trientalis americana*, etc. Also as a book-name for *Stellaria* and *Aster*.

1629 Parkinson *Paradisus* 134 The kindes of Starre-flowers, or Starres of Bethlehem, as they are called. **1664** Evelyn *Kal. Hort.* May (1679) 17 Stock-gilly-flowers, Spanish Nut, Star-flower [etc.]. **1707** Mortimer *Husb.* (1721) II. 236 Star-Flowers are of several sorts, as the Star-Flower of Arabia, the great white Star-Flower of Bethlehem [etc]. *c* **1711** Petiver *Gazophyl.* ix. lxxxv, Blush Cape Star-flower. **1771** J. R. Forster *Flora Amer. Septentr.* 15 Hypoxis erecta. Bastard star-flower, upright. Virginia. **1845–50** Mrs. Lincoln *Lect. Bot.* 185 The star-flower, (Aster). **1856** A. Gray *Man. Bot.* 272 *Trientalis Americana* ..Star-flower. **1890** *Sarum Dioc. Gaz.* Jan. 6/1 'Star-flower' prettily describes the golden spangles of the Tormentil.

†**2.** *Zool.*

a **1776** J. Ellis *Zoophytes* (1786) 3 *Actinia gemmacea.* Studded Sea Star-flower. *Ibid.* 6 *Actinia Aster.* Sea Star-flower with a smooth stem.

'**starful**, *a. poet. rare.* Full of stars.

1605 Sylvester *Du Bartas* II. iii. I. *Vocation* 889 Heav'n's starfull Canapey. *a* **1631** Donne *Progr. Soule, 2nd Anniv.* 80 The starfull Northern pole. **1850** Lynch *Theoph. Trinal* viii. 141 So Time the wave, Eternity the deep, Shines starful.

'**star-gaze**, *v.* [Back-formation from next or star-gazing.] *intr.* To gaze at or study the stars. Also *transf.* and *fig.*; esp. to gaze intently at something compared to a star.

1626 Shirley *Maid's Rev.* I. i. (1639) B4b, How now Antonio,..Strucke dead with Ladies eyes?—I could star-gaze For ever thus. **1640** —— *Arcadia* I. i. B4, Her eyes Are fixt upon't, and my poore soule could heere Star-gaze for ever. **1692** R. L'Estrange *Fables* clxxxix. 159 The Mischief is, that we are..star-gazing after Futurities; when in truth, our Bus'ness lies just under our Noses. *a* **1704** T. Brown *Wks.* (1711) IV. 210 Madam, while I was Star-gazing t'other Night at your Window. **1778** *Hist. Eliza Warwick* II. 101 He could not remove his eyes from my face. Lady Norfolk, observing it, asked him whether he intended to sup, or to stargaze all night? **1830** Miss Mitford *Village* Ser. IV. 179 The sky prospect from her apartment being rather limited, she used..to come star-gazing to mine. **1857** Hughes *Tom Brown* II. iii, 'Very odd birds, kestrels', said East, looking waggishly at his victim, who was still star-gazing.

†**b.** with indirect question depending on the vb.

1691 *d'Emiliane's Frauds Rom. Monks* 226 The Abbot himself went out after Supper, to Star-gaze what Weather they were like to have the next day.

c. quasi-*refl.* with complementary phrase.

1678 T. P[orter] *Fr. Conjurer* III. 15 He has talkt and stargazed himself into..favour with my Master. **1871** Ruskin *Fors Clav.* i, Their present eagerness for instruction in painting and astronomy proceeds from an impression in their minds that, somehow, they may paint or star-gaze themselves into clothes and victuals.

'**star-gazer.**

1. One who gazes at the stars. Often used as a familiar or contemptuous substitute for *astrologer* or *astronomer*.

1560 Bible (Geneva) *Isa.* xlvii. 13 Let now the astrologers, the starre gasers & pronosticatours stand vp. **1583** Stubbes *Anat. Abus.* II. 62 These star-gaisers, who teach that man is drawne to good or euill by the..influence of stars. **1611** Speed *Hist. Gt. Brit.* VI. viii. §5. 72 His Astrologers and Star-gazers forwarding him with their vaine predictions. *a* **1700** Evelyn *Diary* 29 Apr. 1652, Knavish and ignorant star-gazers. **1727** De Foe *Syst. Magic* I. iii. (1840) 73 As the eminent Dr. H—— may be called the king's astronomer, or as the more eminent Flamstead usually called himself, the king's star-gazer. **1842** Emerson *Transcendentalist* Wks. (Bohn) II. 280 The materialist.. mocks at..star-gazers and dreamers. **1876** Chambers *Astron.* p. v, The mere star-gazer who is an Astronomer simply in the respect that he is the owner of a telescope.

2. The fish *Uranoscopus scaber*, which has eyes set on the top of the head and directed vertically; also, any fish of this genus or of the family *Uranoscopidæ*.

1661 Lovell *Hist. Anim. & Min.* 225 Starre-gazer. *Vranoscopus.* **1740** R. Brookes *Art of Angling* II. lxviii. 189 The Star-Gazer..is often taken in the Mediterranean Sea. **1881** *Cassell's Nat. Hist.* V. 92 The best known genus, Uranoscopus, comprises about ten species, which are familiarly termed star-gazers. **1882** Jordan & Gilbert *Syn. Fishes N. Amer.* 627 *Uranoscopidæ* (The Star Gazers).

b. Applied to other fishes: see quots.

1863 Wood *Illustr. Nat. Hist.* III. 330 Stargazer, *Anableps tetrophthalmus. Ibid.* 331 The Stargazer is a native of Surinam. **1878** A. M. Ross *Catal. Mammals* etc. *Canada* 11/1 *Uranidea gracilis*, Little Star Gazer.

3. *slang.* (See quots.)

1785 Grose *Dict. Vulgar T.*, *Star gazer*, a horse who throws up his head. **1831** Youatt *Horse* ix. 156 The back of the head being thus pulled back,..the horse..will become what is technically called a star-gazer.

4. *Naut.* (See quots.)

1867 Smyth *Sailor's Word-bk.* 630 *Sky-scraper*, a triangular sail set above the skysail; if square it would be a moon-sail, and if set above that, a star-gazer, &c. **1883** Clark Russell *Sailors' Lang.* 137 *Star-gazer*, an imaginary sail, like sky-scraper.

'**star-gazing**, *vbl. sb.* The action of gazing at or studying the stars.

1576 Fleming *Panopl. Epist.* 205 At such time as he went out a stargazing. **1613** Purchas *Pilgrimage* (1614) 63 One beginning of Idolatrie did arise of this curious and superstitious Starre-gazing. *a* **1618** Sylvester *Little Bartas* 381 Wks. (Grosart) II. 88 Who, by Star-gazing, or ought else below, Dare arrogate the Future to foreknow. **1878** Lockyer (*title*) Stargazing, past and present. **1884** F. Harrison in *19th Cent.* Mar. 501 Religion is not a thing of star-gazing and staring.

'**star-gazing**, *ppl. a.* That gazes at the stars; given to study of the stars.

1593 Nashe *Christ's T.* 19b, All the starre-gazing Townes. **1596** Bp. W. Barlow *Three Serm.* i. 10 The like predictions of starre-gasing diuiners. **1669** Sturmy *Mariner's Mag.* II. 45 Perhaps you'l say, 'Tis a Star-gazing Age. **1708** Partridge *Bickerstaff detected* 4 A certain Star-gazing Squire. **1823** Scott *Quentin D.* xxviii, The quack-salving, word-mongering, star-gazing, lie-coining impostor.

star-gazy, stargazy, stargazey ('stɑːgeɪzɪ), *a.* Also **star-a-gaze, starry-gazey, starry-gazy.** [f. star-gaze *v.* + -y[1].] ***star-gazy pie***, a kind of fish pie traditionally made in Cornwall (see quots.).

1847 J. O. Halliwell *Dict. Archaic & Provinc. Words* II. 799/1 Starry-gazy-pie. A pie made of pilchards and leeks, the heads of the pilchards appearing through the crust as if they were studying the stars. *Cornw.* **1864** F. T. O'Donoghue *St. Knighton's Keive: a Cornish Tale* Gloss. 303 *Star-a-gaze pie*, a mackerel pie with the heads above the paste, gazing upwards, as it were. **1954** D. Hartley *Food in England* x. 246 *Stargazey pies.* These are properly made of pilchards... The cooks covered the body of the fish—but left the head sticking out. **1966** *Punch* 14 Sept. 385/1 To provide the dishes that one's forbears ate—roast saddle of hare,..or stargazy pie, or syllabub—would be to proclaim oneself madly affected. **1970** A. Pascoe *Cornish Recipes Old & New* 30 (*heading*) Star-gazy pie. **1980** *ABMR* Feb. 75/1, I now believe that heavy cake, like starry-gazey pie, was originally made from pilchards.

starge, obs. (*erron.*) Sc. var. of stark *a.*

'**star-grass.** [star *sb.*[1] Cf. *star-grass* in star *sb.*[2]] A name for various grass-like plants with stellate flowers or stellate arrangement of leaves; as *Aletris farinosa*, *Callitriche verna* and *C. aquatica*, *Hypoxis erecta*, *Rhynchospora Vahliana*, etc.

1687 Clayton *Virginia* in *Phil. Trans.* XLI. 158 There is another Root of the Species of Hyacinths, the Leaves whereof are grass-like..and spread like a Star upon the Ground... Some call it Ague-grass, others Ague-root, others Star-grass. **1796** Withering *Brit. Plants* (ed. 3) II. 5 *Callitriche verna.* Vernal Stargrass. Water Starwort. **1831** J. Davies *Manual Mat. Med.* 117 Mealy-star-wort. Star-grass. *Aletris farinosa.* **1845–50** Mrs. Lincoln *Lect. Bot.* 39 The water star-grass, *Callitriche aquatica. Ibid.* App. 113/2 *Hypoxis erecta*, (star-grass). **1864** Grisebach *Flora W. Ind. Islands* 788 Star-grass, *Rhynchospora Vahliana.* **1866** *Treas. Bot.* 35/2 *Aletris farinosa*, called Colic root and Star grass.

'**star-head.**

†**1.** *Zool.* A species of *Echinus*. *Obs.*

1713 Petiver *Aquat. Anim. Amboinæ* i, *Echinus sulcatus*... Sea Furrowed Star-head.

2. *Bot.* The genus *Asterocephalus*.

1852 G. W. Johnson *Cottage Gard. Dict.* **1866** *Treas. Bot.*

'**star-,headed**, *a.*

Headed with a star; having a head like a star; *spec.* as an epithet of certain stellate flowers.

c **1710** Petiver *Catal. Ray's Eng. Herbal* §42 Bur and Star-headed Plants. **1777** Jacob *Catal. Plants* 111 *Callitriche verna*,..Star-headed Chickweed. **1814** Roxburgh *Hort. Bengal* 58 *Trifolium stellatum.* Star-headed trefoil. **1855** Bailey *Mystic* 39 Aiming star-headed arrow winged with light.

staring ('stɛərɪŋ), *vbl. sb.* [-ing[1].] The action of the verb stare; gazing fixedly with eyes wide open, standing up (of hair), etc.

c **1440** *Promp. Parv.* 472/2 Starynge, brode lokynge, *patentacio oculorum.* *c* **1515** *Cocke Lorell's B.* 13 They songe and daunsed full merely, With swerynge, and starynge heuen hye. *a* **1548** Hall *Chron., Hen. VIII*, 50b, We found the body of the sayde Hun..w[t] his eyen & mouth fayre closed, withoute any staryng, gapyng or frownyng. **1549** Udall etc. *Erasm. Par. 1 Thess.* ii. 1–8 We came not vnto you, with bragging and staring. **1563** Sackville *Induct. Mirr. Mag.* xxxiv, His cap borne vp with staring of his heare. **1598** Shaks. *Merry W.* v. v. 168 [One that is given] to drinkings and swearings, and starings. **1682** Norris *Hierocles* Pref. 32 A resolution of all our faculties into sweetnesses, affections and starings upon the Divine beauty. **1766** *Complete Farmer* s.v. *Roup*, Roup, the name of a filthy disease in poultry..known by the staring, or turning back of the feathers. **1817** Byron *Beppo* lxxxi, Could staring win a woman, this had won her. **1897** *Allbutt's Syst. Med.* II. 689 In cattle these [symptoms] are slight dulness, shivering, ..'staring of the coat', and stiffness in movement.

staring ('stɛərɪŋ), *ppl. a.* [f. stare *v.* + -ing[2].] That stares, in senses of the verb.

1. That looks fixedly with wide open eyes.

a **1547** Surrey in *Tottel's Misc.* (Arb.) 17 He cast on me a staring loke, with colour pale and ded. **1588** Shaks. *L.L.L.* v. ii. 927 Then nightly sings the staring Owle, Tu-whit to-who. **1590** Spenser *F.Q.* II. vii. 37 Their staring eyes sparckling with feruent fire And vgly shapes did nigh the man dismay. **1592** Shaks. *Ven. & Ad.* 1149 The staring ruffian shall it keepe in quiet. **1682** N. O. *Boileau's Lutrin* ii. 17 With hollow Cheeks, and staring Eyes she view'd him. **1747** Richardson *Clarissa* (1811) I. xvi. 102 The man is a very confident, he is a very bold, staring man! **1809** *Med. Jrnl.* XXI. 221 The countenance is wild, the eyes red and staring. **1816** Scott *Old Mort.* xxxiv, 'How came the fellow here?—Speak, you staring fool', he added. **1845** Disraeli *Sybil* IV. i, I have sent his vulgar wife and great staring daughter a card for next Wednesday! **1859** Tennyson *Marr. Geraint* 356 Turn, turn thy wheel above the staring crowd. **1861** Dickens *Lett.* (1880) II. 152 They were an intent and staring audience. **1899** *Allbutt's Syst. Med.* VI. 120 Powell describes a slightly staring, suffused, and anxious expression of countenance as most common.

transf. **1646** CRASHAW *Sospetto d'Herode* vii, Such his fell glances as the fatall Light Of staring Comets, that looke Kingdomes dead.

†**b.** Frantic, wild. *Obs.*

c **1449** PECOCK *Repr.* III. xiv. 371 In wantowne and nyse disgisingis of araies (and so forth of many othere [staryng *added by a later hand*] gouernancis, semyng summe wijlde woode). **1607** WALKINGTON *Optic Glass* iii. 21 Who knowes not that..goggle eyes [denotate] a starke-staring foole? **1839** BAILEY *Festus* (ed. 3) 309 The staring madness when we wake and find That what we have loved..is not that We meant to love.

c. *Proverbs.* (App. often used with no definite meaning; perh. orig. ellipt. for the combs. in 5.)

1546 J. HEYWOOD *Prov.* (1867) 67 The difference betwene staryng and starke blynde The wise man at all tymes to folow can fynde. **1579** LYLY *Euphues* (Arb.) 154 Descende into your owne consciences, consider with your selues the great difference between staring and starke blynde, witte and wisedome, loue and lust. **1629** FORD *Lover's Mel.* II. ii, *Mel.* Am I starke mad? *Troll.* No, no, you are but a little staring —there's difference betweene staring and starke mad. **1738** SWIFT *Pol. Conversat.* 200 There's Difference between staring and stark mad. **1787** WOLCOT (P. Pindar) *Ode upon Ode* Wks. 1812 I. 440 There's odds 'twixt staring and stark mad.

†**2.** Shining; bright-coloured. *Obs.*

c **1400** *Destr. Troy* 3037 Shynyng full shene as þe shire sternys, Or any staring stone. *a* **1400–50** *Wars Alex.* 2880 He ..Strad vp him selfe on a stede, in starand wedis. *Ibid.* 3615 He stendis vp in his stereps in starand maylis. *Ibid.* 5396 He saȝe a dym cloude Full of starand sternes. **1425** *Ord. Whittington's Alms-house* in Entick *London* (1766) IV. 354 That the overcloathing..be dark and brown of colour, and not staring ne blaising. *c* **1440** *Promp. Parv.* 472/2 Starynge, or schynynge, as gaye thyngys, *rutilans, rutilus, nitidus*. *c* **1495** *Epitaffe* etc. in *Skelton's Wks.* (1843) II. 391 His starynge standarde..nowe set is on a wall. *c* **1500** MEDWALL *Nature* (Brandl) I. 749 A staryng colour of scarlet red.

3. Of hair, feathers, etc.: Standing up, bristling.

1562 J. HEYWOOD *Prov. & Epigr.* (1867) 182 Vncomde staryng heades. **1578** LYTE *Dodoens* v. xvi. 569 It layeth downe the staring heares of the eyebrowes. **1609** C. BUTLER *Fem. Mon.* iii. (1623) F 1, Take away all those staring strawes, twigs, and other offensive jagges that are fast in the Hiues. **1674** *Scheffer's Lapland* 136 Mountain Mice..which Wormius describes with short tails and staring hair. **1697** DRYDEN *Virg. Georg.* III. 813 The Water-Snake..With staring Scales lyes poyson'd in his Bed. **1730** BURDON *Pocket Farrier* (1735) 63 If your Horse is brought to you with a staring Coat and hollow Flank. **1860** E. MAYHEW *Horse Doctor* 7 The eye is closed; the skin cold, and the coat staring. **1869** E. A. PARKES *Pract. Hygiene* (ed. 3) 66 Grooms object to give hard water to their horses, on the ground that it makes the coat staring and rough.

4. That obtrudes itself on the view or attention; glaringly conspicuous.

a **1513** FABYAN *Chron.* VI. clix. (1811) 149 At those dayes in Fraunce was vsyd of prestes, and men of the Church, precious and shewynge vesture, and goldyn and ryche starynge gyrdellys, with rynges, and other ornamentis of golde. **1542** UDALL *Erasm. Apoph.* 252 She..perceiued his yies to bee offended with hir ouer wanton and staryng araie. **1709** BERKELEY *Ess. Vision* § 125 Made up of manifest staring contradictions. **1719** DE FOE *Crusoe* I. (Globe) 258 Friday.. not making quite so staring a Spectre-like Figure as I did. **1773** GOLDSM. *Stoops to Conquer* II, And at last to blurt out the broad staring question of, Madam, will you marry me? **1849** DICKENS *Barn. Rudge* iv, A modest building..with great staring windows. **1850** BLACKIE *Æschylus* II. 8 Not to mention the staring absurdity of the idea. **1859** JEPHSON *Brittany* ii. 15 The staring modern chapels. **1880** MRS. J. H. RIDDELL *Palace Gard.* ii. 20 A staring new terrace built on the ground which the old house covered. **1894** BRIDGES *Shorter Poems* v. xv. (1912) 316 That sickly, staring shore. **1902** O. WISTER *Virginian* xxxv, The rustlers..were a staring menace to Wyoming.

†**b.** Of a story: 'Sensational'. *Obs.*

1753 *Scots Mag.* Oct. 492/1, I..could..tell a staring story, and humbug with..skill. **1781** MME. D'ARBLAY *Diary* Aug., He told us a thousand strange staring stories. **1789** MRS. PIOZZI *France & Italy* II. 144 One must not judge from staring stories told one.

5. quasi-*adv.* as in ***staring blind, mad*** (cf. 1 c), ***plain, sober***. Usually ***stark staring***: see STARK *adv.* 2 b.

[**1546**, **1579**: see 1 c.] **1589** *Whip for Ape* A 4, I am a rimer of the Irish race, And haue alreadie rimde thee staring mad. *a* **1861** T. WOOLNER *My Beautiful Lady, Storm* iv, Familiar things, that staring plain had been, Fade into mists away. **1886** STEVENSON *Treas. Isl.* iii, At one look the rum went out of him, and left him staring sober.

staringly ('stɛərɪŋlɪ), *adv.* [f. prec. + -LY².]

1. With a stare or open-eyed fixed gaze.

1580 HOLLYBAND *Treas. Fr. Tong, Errailler les yeux*,..to open ones eyes wide, staringly. **1598** FLORIO, *Rabbuffare*, .. to looke staringlie as a mad man. **1602** MANNINGHAM *Diary* (Camden) 53 That long swaggerer..staringly demaunding what he ment..said the gent., 'I tooke you for a May pole'. **1615** CROOKE *Body of Man* 545 Like as when we would open the eye more staringly the muscles of the forehead doe much helpe vs. **1883** *Harper's Mag.* Oct. 805/1 [They] heard my questions staringly.

†**2.** Wildly, frantically. *Obs.*

1667 H. MORE *Div. Dial.* III. xvii. (1713) 218 So staringly mad that the eye of Reason seems to have quite started out of their head. **1670** EACHARD *Cont. Clergy* 43 Not by talking staringly, and casting a mist before the peoples eyes.

3. In a manner that 'stares one in the face'; glaringly.

1817–18 COBBETT *Resid. U.S.* 316 There is in this statement something..so ridiculously and staringly untrue, that [etc.]. **1824** *Blackw. Mag.* XVI. 293 The veil is now.. staringly, and strikingly transparent. **1833** COBBETT *Eng. Gram.* xviii. § 221 These are staringly absurd. **1879** STEVENSON *Lay Morals* (1911) 7 The universe..is plain, patent and staringly comprehensible.

†**stark**, *sb.*¹ *Sc. Obs.* [? Corrupt form of STAKE *sb.*¹ (sense 5 b; in our quots. not before 1853).] Some implement used in dressing leather.

1541 *Aberdeen Reg.* (1844) I. 176 Item, ane stark to vork the ledder vpoun, with thair feytt.

†**stark**, *sb.*² *Obs.*—⁰. [? Corruption of *start* in REDSTART.] The redstart.

1611 COTGR., *Rossignol de muraille*, a Starke, a Red-tayle.

Stark (stɑːk), *sb.*³ *Physics.* The name of Johannes *Stark* (1874–1957), German physicist, used *attrib.* with reference to an effect observed by him (*Sitzungsber. der k. Preuss. Akad. der Wissensch.* (1913) 20 Nov. 932) in which spectral lines of a gas are broadened, split, or shifted when the source is in an electrostatic field (either applied externally or due to charged particles within it). Cf. ZEEMAN.

1914 *Science* 2 Oct. 493/2 The Stark-electric effect differs from the Zeeman effect in that the various lines of the same series are not equally affected. **1939** *Nature* 20 May 834/1 The spectroscopy team is drawn from an even wider area,..dealing..with atomic spectra, hyper-fine structure, Stark effect and related phenomena. **1962** G. M. BARROW *Introd. Molecular Spectrosc.* v. 92 Some dipole-moment determinations that have been made using the Stark effect in rotational spectra. **1979** *Physical Rev.* A. XX. 504/2 Stark-broadening parameters for the brighter isolated tin lines are given in Table VI.

stark (stɑːk), *a.* and *adv.* Forms: 1–2 **stearc**, 1 **starc**, 2–3 **sterc**, 2–6 **sterke**, 3 **stærc**, **starc**, *Ormin* **starrc** (*pl.* **starrke**), 3–4 **starck**, 3–6 **sterk**, (3 **sterch**, 6 *Sc.* **starge**), 4–7 **starcke**, **starke**, 3– **stark**. [Com. Teut.: OE. *stearc* corresponds to OFris. *sterk* (WFris. *sterk*, NFris. *stark*), OS. *stark* (MLG. *stark*, *sterk*), OHG. *stark*, *starach* (MHG. *stark*, *starch*, mod.G. *stark*), ON. *sterk-r* (Da. *sterk*), OSw. *stark-er* (Sw. *stark*):—OTeut. **starku-*; the declension is attested by the fluctuation between umlaut and non-umlaut forms. The weak grade of the root (OTeut. **sturk-*) is found in Goth. *gastaurknan*, OHG. *kistorchanên* to grow rigid, Icel. *storkna* to coagulate, ON. *styrk-r* strength, *styrk-r* strong. Outside Teut., probable cognates are Lith. *stregti* to become frozen, mod.Pers. *suturg* strong.

Some of the cognates suggest that the sense 'stiff, rigid', which is rare exc. in English, may be more original than the sense 'strong', which prevails in the other Teut. langs.]

A. *adj.*

1. Hard, unyielding.

†**a.** Of a material substance: Hard, rigid. *Obs.*

c **1000** ÆLFRIC *Saints' Lives* I. 196 Stanas maȝon hnexian and þæt starce isen on leades ȝelicnysse. *c* **1200** ORMIN 999 & oþerr stund itt bakenn wass Full harrd & starrc inn ofne.

b. Of a person, his heart, etc.: Hard, obdurate. Also in good sense, firm, unyielding. *Obs.* exc. *arch.*

a **900** CYNEWULF *Elene* 565 (Gr.) Heo wæron stærce, stane heardran, noldon þæt ȝeryne rihte cyðan. *c* **1175** *Lamb. Hom.* 5 Ne beo þu þereuore prud ne wilde ne sterc ne wemod ne ouer modi. *c* **1200** ORMIN 1596, & ȝiff þin heorrte iss harrd & starrc, & stedefasst o Criste. *c* **1205** LAY. 23678 Strong mon wes Frolle and sterc mon on mode. *c* **1400** *Cato's Morals* in *Cursor M.* App. iv. 33. 1669 If richesse come þe rife..be noȝt starke to freindis, spende þou fulle hertli..þi gift wiþþe weindis. *c* **1440** *Ps. Penit.* (1894) 43 Crist ihesu..was nothur starke ne stef, But ever was louly in word and chere. **1589** R. BRUCE *Serm.* (1590) S 5, Swa then, wald thou knaw, quhither thy faith be strong or not, quhither thy perswasion of Gods mercie, be starke or not? **1836** GEN. P. THOMPSON *Exerc.* (1842) IV. 91 Against Tallow-plots, however, the Whig government was stark.

†**c.** Of a judgement: Stern, inflexible. *Obs.*

c **1200** ORMIN 8802 He ȝifeþþ himm..witt & mihht to drædenn Godd & hise starrke domess. *a* **1225** *Ancr. R.* 144 þe sterke dom of domesdei.

†**d.** *Sc.* Of a question, a science: Hard, difficult. *Obs.*

1456 SIR G. HAYE *Bk. Gov. Princes* (S.T.S.) 111 No traist nocht in ignorant mennis wordis that sais..that the science of thaim [*sc.* the stars] is sa stark that nane may knaw it. *Ibid.* 140 Here speris the doctour a stark questioun.

2. Violent, harsh, severe.

†**a.** Of natural agencies: Fierce or violent in operation; hard, harsh, rough, severe.

a **1000** *Colloq. Ælfric* in Wr.-Wülcker 90 Nys hyt swa stearc winter [*aspera hyems*] þæt ic durre lutian æt ham. *a* **1225** *St. Marher.* 9 Ant al warð þat stude of strong and starc stench. *a* **1225** *Juliana* 78 þer arisen stormes starcke & stronge & breken þe schipes bord. *a* **1240** *Lofsong* in *Cott. Hom.* 211 þeo sterke stremes and þet flod þet fleaw of þine wunden moncun uor to helen. *c* **1250** *Owl & Night.* 524 Ac hwenne nyhtes cumeþ longe, & bryngeþ forstes starke & stronge. *c* **1320** *Seuyn Sag.* (W.) 2123 The clerkes to the stage stale, And bet a fir strong and sterk. **1338** R. BRUNNE *Chron.* (1725) 174 þe hungre was so grete, & þe cold so stark. **1460** *Lybeaus Disc.* 1766 A fere stark and store Was lyght and brende bryght. **1597** MONTGOMERIE *Cherrie & Slae* 1529 The streim is thair sae stark,..It suld be idle wark. **1606** A. CRAIG *Amor. Songs* (1872) 133 And though the streams be stark, I through the waltring waues shall swim.

†**b.** Of persons: Stern, harsh, severe. (Cf. sense 1 b.) *Obs.* exc. *arch.* in echoes of quot. *a* 1122.

c **1000** ÆLFRIC *Hom.* I. 362 He [John Baptist] ða heardheortan Iudeiscre ðeode mid stearcre ðreale and stiðre myngunge to lifes weȝe ȝebiȝde. *a* **1122** *O.E. Chron.* (Laud MS.) an. 1086, He wæs..ofer eall ȝemett stearc þam mannum þe wiðcwædon his willan. *c* **1205** LAY. 9197 Ah he wes swiðe sturne & stærc wið þeon folke. **1869** FREEMAN *Norm. Conq.* (1876) III. xii. 183 William was already beginning to show himself..beyond measure stark to all who withstood his will. **1876** TENNYSON *Harold* II. ii, For he is only debonair to those That follow where he leads, but stark as death To those that cross him. **1891** *Q. Rev.* July 190 This great Emperor was stark to all the opponents of Christianity.

†**c.** Of living, treatment, circumstances, etc.: Attended with hardship, harsh, severe. Of a wound: Severe. *Obs.*

c **1000** ÆLFRIC *Hom.* I. 148 He nolde awendan his ȝewunelican biȝleofan..ac ða stiðnyssa his stearcan biȝleofan..on his life ȝeheold. *c* **1290** *St. Sebastian* 48 in *S. Eng. Leg.* 179 With quareles and with Arewene: heo maden him woundes starke. **1338** R. BRUNNE *Chron.* (1725) 21 Tille Elfride oure kyng com tiþinges starke. *Ibid.* 98 Bot Henry þink it stark, þat he is charged so.

†**d.** Of an instrument of torture or punishment: Inflicting severe pain, cruel. *Obs.*

c **1000** ÆLFRIC *Hom.* I. 428 Ða het he hine wædum bereafian, and mid stearcum stengum beatan. *c* **1200** *Trin. Coll. Hom.* 127 Weste was his wunienge and stark haire of oluente his wede. *a* **1225** *Leg. Kath.* 1925, & let þurhdriuen þrefter þe spaken & te felien mid irnene gadien; swa þat te pikes & te irnene preones se scharpe & se starke borien þurh. *c* **1380** *Sir Ferumb.* 2118 Furst sche tok out þe croune sterk; þat crist on is heued let. **1500–20** DUNBAR *Poems* xxxiv. 77 God, that evir I chaip, Nor ane stark widdy gar me gaip, Bot I in hell for geir wald be. **1508** KENNEDIE *Flyting w. Dunbar* 413 A stark gallowis, ane wedy, and a pyn, The hede poynt of thyne elderis armes ar. **1549** *Compl. Scot.* iii. 28 Than the father takkis ane batton or sum vthir sterk vappin to puneise his sonne.

†**e.** Of fighting or contention: Vehement, fierce. *Obs.*

c **1205** LAY. 4171 þat fæht wes swuðe strong & swuðe stær [*c* **1275** starc] & swuðe longe. *Ibid.* 4036 Sterce weren þe reæmes mid stronge raflake. *c* **1250** *Owl & Night.* 5 (Jesus MS.) þat playd wes stif & starc & strong. *Ibid.* 1176 þe vle ..yef answere stark & stronge. *c* **1380** *Sir Ferumb.* 3241 þan at þe furste þe Assaut by-gan sterk & strait to be. **1456** SIR G. HAYE *Law Arms* (S.T.S.) 121 He wist wele, and he had scapit, he wald nocht have cessit to mak him starkare were than before.

f. Of climate or weather: Harsh, inclement. (See quot. 1878.) Now *dial.*

1611 B. JONSON *Catiline* I. i, *Cet.* The North is not so starke, and cold. **1878** DICKINSON *Cumbld. Gloss.*, *Stark weather*, continued dry and cold north and east winds. **1913** *Daily Graphic* 24 Mar. 12/1 The season is early, the weather stark and unpromising.

†**g.** ***stark at the rent*** (see quot.). *dial. Obs.*

1683 G. M[ERITON] *Praise of Ale* 51 And yet you say your Farme is starke att'th Rent [ed. 1685 starke 'oth Rent; *but Gloss. has* Stark at the Rent, is very dear at the Rent.]

3. Strong, stout, powerful.

†**a.** Of a structure or material: Strong, substantial. *Obs.*

c **1205** LAY. 189 He makede enne stronge castel mid starke ston walle. *c* **1290** *St. Brendan* 124 in *S. Eng. Leg.* 223 þis hound ladde þis holi man to an halle..Gret & starc. *c* **1375** *Sc. Leg. Saints* xlv. (*Christina*) 10 He mad a toure of lyme & stane, a starkare mocht be fundine nan. **1460** *Lybeaus Disc.* 710 Thanne sawe they yn a park A castell stout and stark. **1529** *Registr. Aberdon.* (Maitland Club) I. 396 To big agan þe said brig..als stark and substantious as we resave þe samyn. **1535** STEWART *Cron. Scot.* II. 685 Anwik castell thet was starge and strang. *a* **1572** KNOX *Hist. Ref.* Wks. 1846 I. 177 [He] cryed, 'Fyre, fyre,' (for the door was verray stark). **1609** *Extracts Rec. Convent. Burghs Scot.* (1870) II. 284 All cowperis sall mak their hering barrellis ticht, stark, and sufficient treyis. **1755** R. FORBES *Ajax' Sp.*, *Shop Bill* vii, Fare may be had..The starkest hose that can be made. **1794** [W. ANDERSON] *Piper of Peebles* 6 (E.D.D.) The sarks were few, An' very stark, but no that saft.

b. Of a weapon: Strong, massive, stout. *arch.*

c **1205** LAY. 21227 Arður þe ræie Ron [*i.e.* his spear] nom an honde he stræhte scaft stærcne stiðimoden king. *a* **1300** *Havelock* 380 In his hand a spere stark. *c* **1375** *Sc. Leg. Saints* xix. (*Christopher*) 339 Quhen þat christofore þis prayere had mad..his staf, þat was sture & stark, was cled with lewis, & with bark. **1895** CROCKETT *Men of Moss-Hags* vi. 47 The crossbar and simple Italian guard of Wat Gordon's lighter weapon seemed as if it must instantly be beaten down by the starker weapon of the dragoon.

c. Physically strong or powerful; lusty, robust, sturdy, vigorous; occas. †strong (of sight). *arch.*

c **1250** *Long Life* 11 in *O.E. Misc.*, Nis non so strong ne sterch [*v.r.* sterk] ne kene þat mai ago deaþes wiþer-blench. *a* **1310** in Wright *Lyric P.* xxx. 87 Ne is no quene so stark ne stour,..that ded ne shal by-glyde. **13..** *K. Alis.* 5527 Ich wil thee yiue of golde a mark, And a stede strong and stark. *c* **1384** CHAUCER *H. Fame* 545 Me caryinge in his clawes starke. **1552** ABP. HAMILTON *Catech.* (1884) 24 Lat nocht the sterk man glore in his strenth. **1589** PUTTENHAM *Eng. Poesie* III. xix. (Arb.) 249 There be some fowles of sight so prowd and starke, As can behold the sunne, and neuer shrinke. **1641** BEST *Farm. Bks.* (Surtees) 19 Throwe..your lambes oute of the penne, for feare that your starke sheepe treade them under foote. **1721** RAMSAY *Prospect of Plenty* 183 A nation, healthfu' wise, and stark. **1787** BURNS *Old Farmer's Salut. Mare* iv, He gied me thee An' fifty mark; Tho' it was sma' 'twas weel-won gear, An' thou was stark. **1805** SCOTT *Last Minstr.* I. xxi, A stark moss-trooping Scott was he. **1836** W. IRVING *Astoria* (1849) 158 The loss of two stark hunters and prime riflemen was a serious affair to the party. **1895** CROCKETT *Men of Moss-Hags* xxv, The dragoons were stark fellows and had seen service.

†**d.** Strong in authority, dominion, rule, arms; powerful, mighty. *Obs.*

a **1300** *Havelok* 341 In þat time..Was in þe lon[d] of Denemark, A riche King, and swyþe stark. **1303** R. BRUNNE *Handl. Synne* 6840 He was bysshope and patryarke Of Constatynē, noble starke. **1338** —— *Chron.* (1725) 45 Now rises Eilred, & gadres oste stark. **1456** SIR G. HAYE *Law Arms* (S.T.S.) 13 The maa miraclis, the starkar was haly kirk. For ay the faith grewe starkar and starkare. *Ibid.* 28 For the office of knychthede suld have stark place in governaunce. **1543** *St. Papers Hen. VIII*, V. 588 All that be His Highnes servauntes and frendes must make theim starke, and to make the most frendes they can. **1596** DALRYMPLE tr. *Leslie's Hist. Scot.* (S.T.S.) I. 138 Frome yrland he sayles to Scotland, wt a strang and starke armie. **1807** J. BARLOW *Columb.* VII. 339 Now roll, with kindling haste, the long stark lines, From wing to wing the sounding battle joins.

†**e.** Of a cause of wonder, also (*Sc.*) of a reason: Strong. *Obs.*

c **1250** *Owl & Night.* 1473 Wunder me þinkþ stark & sor [*MS. Cott.* starc & stor] Hw enymon [etc.]. **1456** SIR G. HAYE *Law Arms* (S.T.S.) 120 And ȝit ane othir mare stark resoun is for the decreis sais that [etc.]. **1587–8** *Reg. Privy Council Scot.* IV. 242 Upoun bettir avisement and starkare ressonis. **1596** DALRYMPLE tr. *Leslie's Hist. Scot.* (S.T.S.) I. 50 Of quhilke a stark rasone they vse to collecte, that in.. riueris in Irland, quhilkes..ar bath maist cleir, and maist pure, Salmonte in gretter number thair ar takne.

†**f.** Of action: Vigorous. *Sc. Obs.*

a **1557** *Diurn. Occur.* (Bannatyne Club) 11 And in this mene tyme was stark watcheing in Edinh about kingis grace. *a* **1578** LINDESAY (Pitscottie) *Chron. Scot.* (S.T.S.) II. 195 That nycht the towne of Edinburgh keipit ane stark watch in the towne.

g. Of liquor, †poison: Strong, potent. *Obs.* exc. *Sc.*

1542 UDALL *Erasm. Apoph.* 103 b, Cantharis is a litle litle vermyn..but hauyng in it starke poyson. *a* **1578** LINDESAY (Pitscottie) *Chron. Scot.* (S.T.S.) I. 186 The Duik of Albanie send his..servand..for the wyne and prayit him to send of the best and starkest. **1622** FLETCHER *Beggars Bush* III. i, [*Second Boor*] Stark beer boy, stout and strong beer. **1633** *Orkney Witch Trial* in Dalyell *Darker Superst. Scot.* (1834) 153 Becaus the oyle was not stark enuch, he gat some aquavite to make it starker. **1870** J. K. HUNTER *Life Studies of Char.* vi. 40 The gudeman and his wife had several tastings till it came to the right thing, the wife remarking that it was a stark dram [of whisky]. **1898** CROCKETT *Standard Bearer* xiv, Doon at the clachans the stark Hollands flowed like water in a running spate.

†**h.** Of colour: Strong, dark. *Obs.*

1547 RECORDE *Urinal Physick* 67 Greene is a compownde colour of blew and yellow..and the right greene have I in this booke called a starke greene.

4. Rigid, stiff, incapable of movement.

a. Of the (muscles of the) body or limbs: Lacking suppleness and pliability (through weakness or over-exertion, fear, age, cold, or the like); †also, of the senses, the blood, the eyes (*obs.*).

c **1300–20** *Pol., Rel., & L. Poems* (1903) 243 Starke waren his armes Hi-spred opon þe rode. *c* **1325** *Gloss. W. de Bibbesw.* in Wright *Voc.* 148 De genuler serroynt trop redz [*gloss* stiffe *v.r., MS.* Camb. starke]. *a* **1340** HAMPOLE *Psalter, Canticles* (1884) 506 *Obriguerunt omnes habitatores chanaan*... All þe woners of chanaan wex starke... þai sall wax stark for drede & wa. *c* **1440** *York Myst.* xxxviii. 395 [*Soldier.*] I myght not stande, so was I starke [with fright]. *c* **1460** *Towneley Myst.* iii. 268 My bonys ar so stark, No wonder if thay wark, ffor I am full old. *c* **1520** SKELTON *Magnyf.* 481 A knokylbonyarde wyll counterfet a clarke; He wolde trotte gentylly, but he is to starke. **1542** BOORDE *Dyetary* viii. (1870) 247, I do aduertyse you not to..syt by the fyre..for fyre..doth make sterke the synewes & ioyntes of man. **1590** SPENSER *F.Q.* I. i. 44 And downe did lay His heauie head,..Whose sences all were straight benumbd and starke. **1607** TOPSELL *Four-f. Beasts* 402 [The Mallander] will make a horse go stark, and stumble much. **1647** H. MORE *Cupid's Conflict* lxxvii, The clearest truths may well seem dark When sloathfull men have eyes so dimme and stark. **1660** F. BROOKE tr. *Le Blanc's Trav.* 334 We had not strength to make another [bridge of planks] we were so num'd and stark [*printed* strark], with the cold. *a* **1800** PEGGE *Suppl. Grose, Stark*, stiff, from too much exercise, or from the rheumatism, &c. **1817** SHELLEY *Revolt Islam* III. xviii, I sought to close mine eyes, But like the balls, their lids were stiff and stark. **1838** BARHAM *Ingol. Leg.* Ser. I. *Nurse's Story*, But, ere he can vent one inquisitive sniff, That little pug-dog stands stark and stiff. **1886** *S.W. Linc. Gloss.* s.v., The rheumatis' has left my leg a bit stark.

b. Rigid, stiff (in death).

1592 SHAKS. *Rom. & Jul.* IV. i. 103 Each part depriu'd of supple gouernment, Shall stiffe and starke, and cold appeare like death. **1611** —— *Cymb.* IV. ii. 209 [*Enter Aruiragus, with Imogen dead.*] *Bel.* How found you him? *Arui.* Starke, as you see. **1609** HOLLAND *Amm. Marcell.* 136 The bodies of the Persians slaine, waxe drie and starke as stakes. **1839** LONGF. *Wreck Hesperus* xiii, A frozen corpse was he. Lashed to the helm all stiff and stark. **1865** KINGSLEY *Herew.* vi, They left nought behind them save stark corpses.

c. Of material things: Rigid, stiff; not supple or flexible.

a **1400** *Stockh. Medical MS.* i. 64 in *Anglia* XVIII. 296 Ley it on þe hed þat hath gret werk, And het yt ageyn, whann it is stark. *c* **1450** *St. Cuthbert* (Surtees) 926 How cuthbert child stode on his croune..; In his playng a wondir harke, his clathes aboute his leggys stode starke. *Ibid.* 950. **1591** G. FLETCHER *Russe Commw.* ii. 4 You shall sensibly feele your breath to waxe starke, and euen stifeling with the colde, as you draw it in and out. **1713** DERHAM *Phys.-Theol.* x. i. 453 So soon as this spring is become stark enough, it suddenly breaks the Case into two Halfs..and so flings the Seed. **1854** MISS BAKER *Northampt. Gloss., Stark* or *Starky*, stiff, dry. **1883** BRIDGES *Prometheus* 1271 O heavenly fire,..O spirit of rage and might, Who canst unchain the links of winter stark. **1889** *N.W. Linc. Gloss.* s.v., This smock's a deal oher stark, I can't wear it while [= until] its weshed.

d. *transf.* of immaterial things.

1847 EMERSON *Repr. Men* iv. *Montaigne* Wks. (Bohn) I. 340 The Spartan and Stoic schemes are too stark and stiff for our occasion. **1851** GLADSTONE *Glean.* VI. xlii. 29 We seem to require an elasticity of system..which is in entire contrast with our rather stark and rigid methods. **1876** F. HARRISON *Choice Books* (1886) 53 There is much in the method and genius of the French drama which falls chill and stark on ears accustomed to the abounding life of a Shakspearean play.

e. Of a rope, etc.: Taut, tight, not slack. *north.*

1641 BEST *Farm. Bks.* (Surtees) 61 For that the bandes will blowe aside with the winde, and the riggings blowe away, if you do not minde to pull the bandes downe starke. **1788** W. H. MARSHALL *Yorksh.* II. 356 *Stark*; tight;..as a stark rope.

f. Of land: Hard with drought. *dial.*

c **1740** A. ALLEN *MS. Gl.* (E.D.D.) When ye ground is parch't and chop't wth droughth, they say ye ground is stark. **1854** MISS BAKER *Northampt. Gloss.* s.v., The ground is so stark, the seeds will not come up.

g. Of landscape or an object in a landscape: Stiff in outine or formation; hence, bare, barren, desolate.

1833 HT. MARTINEAU *Charmed Sea* iv. 64 Snow was heaped on the eastern mountains, and tumbled in huge masses among the stark, black rocks at their base. **1847** EMERSON *Poems* (1857) 199 Not of adamant and gold Built he heaven stark and cold. **1872** C. KING *Sierra Nevada* xii. 258 Among rigid crater rims and stark fields of volcanic sand. **1898** CONAN DOYLE *Trag. Korosko* v, How cool and beautiful that green looked in the stark, abominable wilderness!

5. a. Sheer, absolute, unqualified.

c **1400** *Rom. Rose* 7292 But unto you dar I not lye: But mighte I felen..That ye perceyved it no-thyng, Ye shulden have a stark lesing Right in your hond. **1530** *Proper Dyaloge* 509 in *Rede Me* etc. (Arb.) 149 By seynt mary syr that is a starcke lye. *a* **1553** UDALL *Royster D.* I. iii, But it will be starke nyght before I shall haue done. **1594** CAREW *Huarte's Exam. Wits* xv. (1596) 309 The whole..is in my conceit a starcke leasing, and verie mockerie. **1611** B. JONSON *Catiline* I. i. 693 Consider first the starke securitie The common wealth is in now. *a* **1661** HOLYDAY *Juvenal* (1673) 182 To escape starke beggery. **1701** COLLIER *M. Anton.* (1726) 292 Let all this be done out of stark love and kindness. **1776** JOHNSON in Boswell *Life* an. 1728, *Boswell*: That, Sir, was great fortitude of mind. *Johnson*: No, Sir; stark insensibility. **1820** SHELLEY *Vis. Sea* 3 From the stark night of vapours the dim rain is driven. **1839** W. IRVING *Chron. Wolfert's Roost* (1855) 185 It was stark midnight before they landed at Communipaw. **1852** H. ROGERS *Eclipse of Faith* 373 [They were convinced] that the only orthodox belief in such a world was stark Atheism. **1898** F. T. BULLEN *Cruise 'Cachalot'* 333 When a stark calm left the surface of the bay as smooth as a river.

b. Qualifying an unfavourable appellation of a person: Arrant, thorough, unmitigated.

c **1375** *Sc. Leg. Saints* v. (*John*) 401 He lefit þe bischope, & vent þan to sterk thefis. **1529** MORE *Dyaloge* II. Wks. 181/2 He..neuer can be cast out being a stark heretique. **1530** RASTELL *Bk. Purgat.* III. xv. 5 He shall be proved a very stark fole that wyll beleve that there is no purgatorye. **1545** ASCHAM *Toxoph.* I. (Arb.) 94 Yet if he giue it ouer, and not vse to shote..he shal become of a fayre archer, a stark squyrter and dribber. **1641** BROME *Joviall Crew*, II, I mean stark, errant, downright Beggars, I, Without equivocation; Statute Beggars. *a* **1711** KEN *Serm.* Wks. (1838) 123 Beauty is often incident to stark fools. **1817** SHELLEY *Revolt Islam* XI. xii, 'Tis but a crowd of maniacs stark. **1877** TALMAGE *Serm.* 260 Before we make stark fools of ourselves, let us stop pressing this everlasting 'Why'.

6. = STARK NAKED.

1762 H. WALPOLE *Let. C'tess Ailesbury* 5 Mar., What dreadful discoveries will be made both on fat and lean! I recommend to you the idea of Mrs. Cavendish, when half-stark. **1817** SHELLEY *Revolt Islam* III. xiii, They bore me to a cavern..And one did strip me stark. **1885–94** BRIDGES *Eros & Psyche* March xxx, Behind came Tritons..Green-bearded, tail'd like fish, all sleek and stark. **1898** J. BUCHAN *John Burnet of Barns* III. vii. 255 Slowly..they began to disrobe themselves..till they stood before me..as stark as the day they were born.

fig. **1876** M. ARNOLD *Lit. & Dogma* 55 If all the law they were thinking of stood, stark and written, before their eyes already? **1891** HARDY *Tess* v, He felt the necessity of recommencing with a name..less commonplace than the two original bald stark words.

B. *adv.* (In 13th c. with advb. ending †*sterke*.)

1. In a 'stark' manner; †firmly, strongly (*obs.*); strenuously, vigorously, 'hard'; boldly, stoutly.

c **1205** LAY. 16683 Samuel nom Agag..& lædde hine a þan cheping & lette hine swiðe sterke to ane stake binde. **1794** *Har'st Rig* lxv, Now kempen fo'k, they dinae lo'e They work sae stark. **1900** C. LEE *Cynthia in West* v. 82 One young chap asked a maid the question, and she said 'no', and said it brave and stark.

2. To the fullest extent or degree; absolutely, utterly, quite. Cf. STARK *a.* 5.

a. qualifying an adj., esp. *mad* (occas. *wild, wood*), *drunk, dumb*; also Naut. in ***stark calm.*** Also STARK NAKED, STARK NAUGHT.

This use seems to have begun with STARK BLIND, and to have arisen through taking *stark* in STARK DEAD as an intensive adverb. The adv. is often hyphened with the following adj., esp. when used attributively.

1489 SKELTON *Death Earl Northumbld.* 50 I say, ye comoners, why wer ye so stark mad? **1561** DAUS tr. *Bullinger on Apoc.* (1573) 125 Our Religion is true, and yours starke false. **1573** G. HARVEY *Letter Bk.* (Camden) 133 If the marke I not hitt Saye he is starke wood. **1579–80** NORTH *Plutarch, Lycurgus* (1595) 63 They forced them sometimes to drinke wine..till they had made them starke drunke. **1590** SHAKS. *Com. Err.* II. i. 59. **1593** G. HARVEY *Pierce's Super.* Wks. (Grosart) II. 235 Iwis hee mought haue spied a difference..betwene raging, and starke-madd. **1593** NASHE *Four Lett. Conf.* Wks. (Grosart) II. 261 His conscience accuseth him, hee is stroke starke dumbe. *c* **1595** CAPT. WYATT *R. Dudley's Voy. W. Ind.* (Hakl. Soc.) 52 Havinge somtimes most soden gustes and againe in a moment beinge starke becalmed. **1596** SHAKS. *Tam. Shr.* I. i. 69. *Ibid.* III. ii. 55 His horse..starke spoyl'd with the Staggers. **1620** DEKKER *Dream* 26 Ten thousand Salamanders (whose chill thawing Puts Bonfires out), their starke-stiffe lunges were gnawing. **1624** CAPT. SMITH *Virginia* v. 182 In the evening it grew starke calme. **1661** PEPYS *Diary* 23 Apr., We drank the King's health..till one of the gentlemen fell down stark drunk, and there lay. **1683** P. LORRAIN tr. *Muret's Rites of Funeral* 191 In his days it seem'd to be yet stark new. **1719** DE FOE *Crusoe* I. (Globe) 19 Going a fishing in a stark calm Morning. *a* **1721** PRIOR *Poems, Cromwell & Porter* 281 You may study among the Law givers without being stark wild about Ordinances and Proclamations. **1818** SCOTT *Hrt. Midl.* vi, But every body was, for the moment, stark-mad on the subject of Porteous. **1823** W. SCORESBY *Jrnl.* 390 It fell stark calm. **1870** MORRIS *Earthly Par.* II. III. 45 And, stark awake, with beating heart He put the hawthorn twigs apart.

b. qualifying *staring, raving* ppl. adjs., sometimes used quasi-*advb.*, esp. in ***stark raving*** or ***staring mad.*** Also ***stark ravers*** (slang): see RAVERS *a.*

In later use the collocation *stark staring* is often felt as a mere strengthening of *stark* adv. or adj.

1532 *Dice Play* A viij, *R.* Euery Player..payeth a Crowne ..towards the house charges. *M.* Ye may fare well of that price at the stark-staring stews. **1548** UDALL etc. *Erasm. Par. Luke* vi. 6–11 Thei are turned into stercke staryng madnesse. **1562** J. HEYWOOD *Prov. & Epigr.* P, I thinke it as good, by ought I can deuise, To be starke staryng blinde, as thus to haue eies. **1575** GASCOIGNE *Posies, Fruites Warre* cvii, The tide skarce good, the winde starke staring naught. **1648** J. BEAUMONT *Psyche* XII. xxxii, Stark raving she and roaring prov'd. **1693** DRYDEN *Persius* v. 212 Art thou of Bethlem's Noble College free? Stark, staring mad. **1734** FIELDING *Intriguing Chambermaid* II. vi. I find I am distracted! I am stark raving mad! **1788** WESLEY *Wks.* (1872) VI. 322 It is such stark-staring nonsense, as every man of sense ought to be utterly ashamed of. **1839** HOOD *Lost Heir* 23 Oh Lord! oh dear, my heart will break, I shall go stick stark staring wild! **1849** CUPPLES *Green Hand* viii. (1856) 71 One morning when Westwood and I went on deck, it was a stark staring calm. **1870** MISS BRIDGMAN *R. Lynne* I. xi. 189 He must be stark staring mad. **1894** MRS. H. WARD *Marcella* II. 263 The whole thing is stark staring lunacy. **1958** E. DUNDY *Dud Avocado* III. vi. 270 My first thought was that I had gone stark raving mad..and that I was now hallucinating in a looney bin. **1968** [see COOL *v.* 5 b].

†**c.** qualifying *tire, weary* vbs. (Cf. STARK *a.* 4.)

1553 T. WILSON *Rhet.* 75 Antisthenes made suche a long oracion, that he starke weried all his hearers. *a* **1661** HOLYDAY *Juvenal* (1673) 146 Whiles he strives to perfect the boy, he starke tires himself.

d. qualifying an adv. or advb. phrase.

1668 SHADWELL *Sullen Lovers* II. i, O' my conscience thou art stark out of thy wits. **1863** KINGLAKE *Crimea* II. 307 No other light infantry men were thrown forward in their stead, and the whole body went stark on with bare front. **1899** 'ZACK' [Gwendoline Keats] *On Trail* xvii. 148 I've half a mind to turn him stark out o' the house.

stark (stɑːk), *v.* Also 6 starck, 6–7 sterk. [OE. *stearcian*, f. *stearc* STARK *a.* Cf. OHG. *starcên* to become strong.]

†**1.** *intr.* To become stiff or rigid; to coagulate, solidify. *Obs.*

c **1000** *Gloss. Prud.* in *Germania* (1878) XI. 402/56 *Riget*, stearcode. *a* **1300** *Cursor M.* 1845 Þe stormes starked wit þe wind. *c* **1325** *Gloss. W. de Bibbesw.* in Wright *Voc.* 149 Les nerfs de bewor engurdisst [*gloss*] starken. **14..** *Pol., Rel., & L. Poems* (1903) 250 Wonne..þin hew dunnet: and þi sennewess starket. *c* **1530** *Judic. Urines* II. vi. 27 It causeth rigor Anglice starkyng and racchyng for colde. *a* **1618** SYLVESTER *Hymn of Alms* 185 Wks. (Grosart) II. 210 To stark for Cold, to starve for Food.

2. *trans.* To make stiff. *arch.*

1862 SIR H. TAYLOR *St. Clement's Eve* v. v. Wks. 1864 III. 198 Arise, if horror have not stark'd your limbs.

†**3.** To strengthen, make stout or strong. *Obs.*

c **1470** HENRY *Wallace* XI. 892 And Iohn Wallang, was than schyreff off Fyff, Till Wallace past, starkyt him in that stryff. **1562** TURNER *Baths* 8 This bath..sterketh and streyngtheneth verye muche the broken place.

Hence †**starked** *ppl. a.*, hardened, stiffened.

c **1425** LYDG. *Horse, Goose & Sheep* 388 It..Causith men starkid bonys to recure; Dede synnewis restorith a-geyn to live.

stark blind, *a.* Also β. 4–5 start-, storte-. [f. STARK *adv.* 2 (advb. use of STARK *a.* 4); an alteration of STAREBLIND (after STARK DEAD). The β forms are due to association with START-NAKED.] Quite blind. *lit.* and *fig.*

1387 TREVISA *Higden* (Rolls) III. 97 He put out his eiȝen in Reblata, and lad hym (so) in Babilon streiȝt blynde. [MSS. α and γ start blynde. Caxton & β stark blynde.] *a* **1400** *Minor Poems fr. Vernon MS.* xxix. i. 70 Þei woxe start-blynde anon-riht. *c* **1400** *Sege Jerus.* 576 For þe doust & þe dyn..alle..storte-blynde wexen. **1534** MORE *Comf. agst. Trib.* I. Wks. 1145/1 Christe..threw hym to the ground, and strake hym starke blynde. **1666** J. DAVIES *Hist. Caribby Isl.* 251 In the Streets they have met with many one-eyed, and many stark blind people. **1704** EVELYN *Diary* May, He was 86 years of age, stark blind, deafe, and memory lost. **1781** COWPER *Charity* 404 She sees a world stark blind to what employs Her eager thought.

Hence **stark-blind** *v.*, to make stark blind.

a **1618** SYLVESTER *Tri. Faith* IV. ix, By Faith, Saint Paul stark-blinded Elymas.

stark dead, *a.* [prob. orig. STARK *a.* (sense 4); afterwards taken as STARK *adv.* 2.] Quite dead. *lit.* and *fig.*

a **1375** *Joseph Arim.* 567 [He] Baar him doun of his hors and..strok him stark ded þat he sturede neuere. **1390** GOWER *Conf.* II. 105 Stark ded, his armes sprad, sche syh Hire lord fleetende upon the wawe. **1470–85** MALORY *Arthur* XXI. iv. 847 Therwythall syr Mordred fyl starke deed to the erthe. *a* **1595** R. SOUTHWELL *Hundred Medit.* (1873) 221 The soul..waxeth cold, and proud, and stark dead..when it is deprived of this Thy holy love. **1615** CROOKE *Body of Man* 420 When I came, I found the man starke dead. **1728** CHAMBERS *Cycl.* s.v. *Damps*, The Maid going down to call her Master, found them all in their digging Postures: but stark dead.

†**b.** of night. *Obs.*

1602 MARSTON *Antonio's Rev.* III. i, Tis now starke deade night.

starken (ˈstɑːk(ə)n), *v.* [f. STARK *a.* + -EN[5].

The forms *sturken*, *storken* (Yorkshire dial.: see quot. 1862 in sense 1) represent a different though cognate word, a. ON. *storkna*, referred to under STARK *a.*]

1. *intr.* = STARK *v.* 1.

14.. *Pol., Rel., & L. Poems* (1903) 253/6 [Signs of Death.] His nese shal sharpen, & his skyn shal starken. **1563–83** FOXE *A. & M.* 1895/1 He..wyth the ryghte hande being somewhat starckned knocked vpon his brest softly. **1664** POWER *Exp. Philos.* I. 38 Which..was their nutrimental juice coagulated there, like the bloud starkn'd in the veins of dead Animals. **1862** C. C. ROBINSON *Dial. Leeds* 420 *Starken, Sturken, Storken*, to stiffen. Boiled treacle or rendered fat 'starkens' as it cools. **1876** T. S. EGAN tr. *Heine's Atta Troll* 146 They now lie mute and like unto the dead, Starkened and cold.

2. *trans.* To make stark or inflexible.

1842 SIR H. TAYLOR *Edwin the Fair* IV. iv. Wks. 1864 II. 103 If thy lust of kingly power Outbid thine other lusts, and starken thee In grasping of that shadow of a sceptre That still is left thee.

starkers (ˈstɑːkəz), *a. slang.* [f. STARK *adv.*: cf. -ER[6].] **1.** = STARK NAKED *a.*

1923 J. MANCHON *Le Slang* 292 *Starko*,.. = *stark naked* = *starkers*, tout nu. **1952** M. ALLINGHAM *Tiger in Smoke* vi. 105 We was all starkers and painted black. **1963** *Guardian* 20 Apr. 12/6 There was no stripping... The girls were starkers all the time. **1972** 'D. DEVINE' *Three Green Bottles* 12, I dare you to go in starkers. **1981** *Times Lit. Suppl.* 11 Sept. 1046/3 There is also Rosemary Martin as the Art School model in David Storey's *Life Class*, and Cathy Kessler, similarly starkers in *Lay-By*.

2. Stark raving mad. Cf. STARK *adv.* 2 b

1962 E. GRIERSON *Massingham Affair* v. i. 245 She's..a bit starkers, poor soul, and driving Matron..up the wall. **1972** L. P. DAVIES *What did I do Tomorrow?* iii. 38 You belted out of that room... They thought you were starkers.

†**ˈstarkle**, *v. Obs.* Forms: 6 starcle, starkel, 7 starckle, 6–7 starkle. [app. a variant of STARTLE *v.*] *intr.* To make a stir; to use threatening gestures; to show signs of fear, quake, be afraid.

1527 *Caxton's Trevisa* II. xii. 69 b, That bole hete Apis that was wonte to come out of yᵉ Riuer Nylus & warne by his pleyng and starclynge [L. *gesticulatione sua*; Trevisa and Caxton startelynge] what was to comynge. **1544** H. STALBRYDGES *Epistle* 25 Yowe sturdye strouggelers wyll somwhat starkle at thys my homelye wrytynge, yet shall not that make me leaue of. **1550** BALE *Eng. Votaries* II. 93 b, Than stirt up Becket, and starkeled lyke a lyon, sekynge..to brynge the kynge vndre. **1550** —— *Image Both Ch.* Pref. (1560) B b, The boystouse tyrauntes of Sodoma..wyll sturre about them... Oure worldlye wyse brethren also, which are neither hote nor colde, wyl starcle a course at the matter. **1571** GOLDING *Calvin on Ps.* lxxi. 7. 265 b/2 Although men starkled at him as at a monster [*quamvis instar prodigii execrati sint eum homines*]. **1600** HOLLAND *Livy* II. xli. 71 This act of his made diuerse of the senatours..to starkle for feare of hazarding their estate. **1609** —— *Amm. Marcell.* XIV. ii. 6 Intelligences thereof continually given one after another had made Gallus Cæsar to starckle. *a* **1624** M. SMITH *Serm.* (1632) 72 If those condemne you for altering of your course, I cannot blame you to starkle.

†**ˈstarkled**, *a. Obs. rare*[−1]. [f. **starkle* v. (f. STARK *a.* + -LE; cf. STARKEN *v.*) + -ED[1].] Of the blood: Congealed.

1628 *Robin Good-fellow* II. (Percy Soc.) 23 [Robin, as a night-raven to an old usurer.] I doe come to doe thee good; Recall thy wits and starkled blood.

†**ˈstarkly**, *a. Obs.* In 3 sterclich, starclich. [f. STARK *a.* + -LY[1].] Violent, fierce.

c **1205** LAY. 25330 And astured weoren Romweren alle mid sterclichere wræððe. *c* **1275** —— 7505 And hii him to wende mid star[c]liche [*c* **1205** ladliche] fihte. *Ibid.* 23956 Mid starcliche maine [*c* **1205** mid feondliche lechen].

starkly (ˈstɑːklɪ), *adv.* Forms: 2 stearclice, stercliche, 3 sterk-, stærc-, sterc-, starc-, starchliche, starliche, -lige, 5–6 starklie, (6 starkli, starckly, starkely), 4– starkly. [f. STARK *a.* + -LY[2].]

†**1.** Stoutly, boldly; strongly, powerfully; strenuously; harshly, sternly. *Obs.*

c **1100** *O.E. Chron.* (MS. D.) an. 1016, Þa ȝewende se here to Lundenne & þa buruh utan ymbesæton & hyre stearclice on feaht æȝðær ȝe be wætere ȝe be lande. *c* **1175** *Lamb. Hom.* 121 Summe þer weren þet his eȝan bundan and hine on þet neb mid heore hondan stercliche beoten. *c* **1205** LAY. 21178 Nu fusen we hom to, & stærcliche [*c* **1275** starlige] heom leggen on. *a* **1225** *Leg. Kath.* 717 Þeos meiden..stod, þurh þeos steuene starcliche istrenget. *c* **1375** *Sc. Leg. Saints* xxiii. (*Seven Sleepers*) 128, & þai cane ete, to ma þame stark, confort to get to þat end, and in entent þat starklyare to thole þe torment. *c* **1480** HENRYSON *Test. Cress.* 280, I say this by ȝone wretchit Cresseid, The quhilk..Me and my Mother starklie can reprufe. **1520** M. NISBET *N.T. Scots* Acts xix. 20 So starkli the word of God waxit, and was confermyt. *a* **1578** LINDESAY (Pitscottie) *Chron. Scot.* (S.T.S.) I. 281 Bot his freindis advertissit thairof watchit starklie that night. **1596** DALRYMPLE tr. *Leslie's Hist. Scot.* II. 305 The Castel of Dunbar starklie, and stoutlie suld be defendet with the ffrenche wappounes. *a* **1802** *Jamie Telfer* xxviii. in Scott *Minstrelsy* I. 86 The Scots they rade, the Scots they ran, Sae starkly and sae steadilie. **1816** SCOTT *Old Mort.* xix, Was ever wight so starky made But time and years would overthrow? **1900** C. MURRAY *Hamewith* 51 An' starky did he gie him 't back.

2. Stiffly, rigidly.

1523–34 FITZHERB. *Husb.* §65 There be beastes, that wyll haue the goute..in the hynder fete, and it wyll cause them to halt, and go starkely. **1557** PHAER *Æneid* VII. (1558) V ij, And euery feeld with swordes vpright, As stubble starckly stands. **1603** SHAKS. *Meas. for M.* IV. ii. 70 *Pro.* Where's Barnardine. *Cla.* As fast lock'd vp in sleepe, as guiltlesse labour, When it lies starkly in the Trauellers bones. **1828** CARR *Craven Gloss.*, *Starkly*, stiffly. **1870** B. HARTE *Luck of Roaring Camp* 5 The low bunk..on which the figure of the mother was starkly outlined below the blankets. **1871** R. ELLIS *Catullus* lxvii. 6 A corpse outstretch'd starkly.

b. Tightly, firmly.

1818 BYRON *Mazeppa* xvi, With feeble effort still I tried To rend the bonds so starkly tied. **1820** SHELLEY *Hymn Merc.* lxx, The withy bands, though starkly interknit, Fell at the feet of the immortal child.

3. Barely, nakedly.

1850 MERIVALE *Rom. Emp.* lv. (1865) VII. 49 Many noble trees were stripped of their branches under the Caesars as starkly as the Caesars themselves. **1913** *Blackw. Mag.* Sept. 309/2 The place was starkly furnished.

stark naked, *a.* (and *sb.*) [f. STARK *adv.* 2; altered from the earlier START-NAKED.]

1. Of a person: Absolutely without clothing.

1530 PALSGR. 842/1 Starke bely naked, *tout fin mere nud*... Starke naked, *tout fin nud.* **1560** DAUS tr. *Sleidane's Comm.* 356 They left them starcke naked. **1606** SHAKS. *Ant. & Cl.* v. ii. 59 Rather on Nylus mudde Lay me starke-nak'd. **1771** ROBERTSON *Hist. Amer.* (1778) I. 474 Both sexes go stark-naked. **1840** R. H. DANA *Bef. Mast* xvi. 44 The little children were running about among the huts, stark naked. **1913** SIR H. JOHNSTON *Pioneers Australia* vii. 227 These stark-naked savages.

b. *transf.* and *fig.*

1601 SHAKS. *Twel. N.* III. iv. 274 Therefore on, or strippe your sword starke naked. **1712** STEELE *Spect.* No. 268 ¶9, I came to my Mistress's Toilet this Morning, for I am admitted when her Face is stark naked. **1765** H. WALPOLE *Let. to Miss A. Pitt* 25 Dec., The rest of the room is stark naked. **1779** WARNER in Jesse *Selwyn & Contemp.* (1844) IV. 246 A great stark-naked new house on an eminence, without a morsel of anything green about it. **1881** *Athenæum* 27 Aug. 267/2 This is the essential difficulty, stated in its simplest and stark-naked form. **1895** *Dialect Notes* (Amer. Dial. Soc. 1896) I. VIII. 379 *Naked, starknaked*: of tea without milk or sugar,—pure, undiluted.

2. *sb.* Unadulterated spirit; esp. raw gin. *slang.*

1820 J. H. REYNOLDS *Fancy* (1906) 83 To take of Deady's bright stark naked A glass or so. **1830** LYTTON *Paul Clifford* iv, His 'bingo' was unexceptionable; and as for his stark-naked, it was voted the most brilliant thing in nature. **1860** *Hotten's Slang Dict.* 227 *Stark-naked*,..raw gin.

stark naught, *a.* Now *rare* or *arch.* [STARK *adv.* 2.] Utterly worthless or valueless; †utterly bad, vicious, hurtful, etc. (see NAUGHT *a.*).

a **1543** BECON *David's Harp* Wks. 1564 I. 150 b, He is none of those, that say all is well, when altogyther is starke nought. **1577** GOOGE *Heresbach's Husb.* I. (1586) 20 b, But long vse of it, in the ende bringes the grounde to be starke nought. **1607** *Lingua* II. i, Ah heres a youth starke naught at a trench, but old dog at a trencher. **1647** FULLER *Good Th. in Worse T.* 78 No man can be starke naught at once. Let us stop the progresse of sin in our Soule at the first Stage. **1658** A. FOX tr. *Wurtz' Surg.* III. xiii. 258 This abuse is partly committed, by stitching, which is stark nought to be used here. **1738** SWIFT *Pol. Conversat.* II. 163, I have heard 'em say, that too good is stark naught. **1741** RICHARDSON *Pamela* I. 213 But both [Letters] are stark naught, abominably bad. *Ibid.* II. 76 No, said he, I have been stark naught, and it is she, I hope, will be very forgiving. **1808** BENTHAM *Sc. Reform* 48 The self-same mode or procedure or..the self-same courts, are stark naught for a debt of 5*l.* 1*s.* **1840** THACKERAY *Paris Sk. Bk.* (1869) 43 All the good its students have done, as students, it is stark naught. **1882** *Times* 6 Feb., But these influences..are stark naught to those [etc.].

†**b.** as *sb.* Something utterly worthless. *Obs.*

1562 TURNER *Herbal* II. 105 But they [*sc.* plums] that ar litle ones and harde and harrish tarte ar sterk noughts.

starkness (ˈstɑːknɪs). [f. STARK *a.* + -NESS.]

1. Rigidity, stiffness (of the body or limbs).

c **1440** *Promp. Parv.* 472/2 Starkenese (or styfnesse) *rigor, rigiditas, artitudo.* **1544** PHAER *Regim. Life* (1560) R vj b, Of the stifnes or starckenes of limmes. **1627** [R. BERNARD] *Guide to Grand Jury Men* I. ii. 17 With a generall starknesse and stiffenesse. **1846** TRENCH *Mirac.* xxvii. (1862) 368 *note*, The stiffness and starkness, the unnatural rigescence of the limbs in the accesses of the disorder. *a* **1893** CHRISTINA ROSSETTI *Verses* 135 Night for the dead in their stiffness and starkness!

†**2.** ? 'Stark' or utter privation. *Obs.*

1544 BETHAM *Precepts War* I. lxxvii. E j b, His souldiours ..were wyllynge to fyght, fastyng and undyned: wherby the mooste parte of them clunged for colde, was rather by starknesse of meat, than by yᵉ violence of theyr enemies slayne. **1616** J. LANE *Contn. Sqr.'s T.* VI. 86 So tooke hee order how his campe and shipps shoold bee revictualld, ear them starcnes nipps.

3. Sternness, harshness. *arch.* (See STARK *a.* 2 b.)

1884 M. CREIGHTON *Hist. Ess.* viii. (1902) 248 He [William I] let men feel his starkness by his remorseless harrying of the north.

4. Absoluteness, utterness.

1641 MILTON *Animadv.* Wks. 1851 III. 220 How should wee have yeelded to his heavenly call, had we beene taken, as they were, in the starknes of our ignorance. **1849** H. ROGERS *Ess.* (1860) III. 252 Those legislative pedants..who would propose to give New Zealanders and Hottentots in the starkness of their savage ignorance, the complex forms of the British Constitution.

5. Bareness, nakedness.

a **1849** MANGAN *Poems* (1859) 415 The rocks with their steepness, And the earth with its starkness. **1896** MRS. CAFFYN *Quaker Grandmother* 101 It would go hard with her before that thought, with anything of the starkness of fact about it, could so much as enter into her mind.

starko (ˈstɑːkəʊ), *a. slang.* [f. STARK (NAKED + -O[2].] = STARK NAKED *a.*

1923 [see STARKERS *a.* 1]. **1935** L. LUARD *Conquering Seas* iii. 40 They'll be stripping us starko next. **1946** B. MARSHALL *George Brown's Schooldays* iv. 16 Doing a bundle means getting dressed from starko in five minutes. **1961** J. PUDNEY *Thin Air* xv. 197 Leave him in his birthday suit. Miss bloody Garth can walk back to Midsomer starko and explain to the folks that she's been a man all the time. **1979** C. BRAND *Rose in Darkness* iv. 25 She opened the door, practically starko, and couldn't think what the lady was so surprised about.

starky (ˈstɑːkɪ), *a. dial.* [f. STARK *a.* + -Y.] Stiff and hard; not pliable or workable.

1697 R. PIERCE *Bath Mem.* II. v. 312 His Hands would be as hard, dry and starky, as if he had wrought for his Living, at Cleaving of Wood. *a* **1722** LISLE *Husb.* (1757) 50 If the ground be dry and starky,..so much the better. *Ibid.* 426 Wool..when three years old..grows starkey and dry, and will not lie smooth in the spinning. **1787** GROSE *Prov. Gloss.*, *Starky*, dry, shrivelled up. **1863** WISE *New Forest* 287 Gloss., *Starky*, used particularly of land which is stiff or unworkable, especially after rain.

†**starle, starll.** *Obs.* [? Dim. of STARE *sb.*[1] Cf. G. dial. *starl*, *stärl*.] A starling.

1555 GESNER *Hist. Anim.* III. 715 Sturnus auis.. Anglicum a sterlyng, a starll, a stare. **1562** WITHALS *Dict.* 5/1 A stare or starle, *sturnus.*

starless (ˈstɑːlɪs), *a.* [-LESS.]

1. Destitute of stars or starlight; having no stars visible.

1390 GOWER *Conf.* III. 119 This Bole is ek with sterres set, Thurgh whiche he hath hise hornes knet Unto the tail of Aries, So is he noght ther sterreles. **1638** COWLEY *Love's Riddle* I, Though I were blacker then a starlesse night. **1667** MILTON *P.L.* III. 425. **1728** MALLET *Excursion* I. 288 Night by Night, beneath the starless Dusk. **1818** BYRON *Mazeppa* v, With starless skies my canopy. **1877** 'RITA' *Vivienne* III. ix, The sky was black and starless.

2. In nonce-uses. **a.** Having no star or badge of honour on the breast. **b.** Not made into a star, having no star named after oneself. **c.** Not born under a good or favourable star, luckless.

1814 BYRON *Frag. Ep. T. Moore*, The Czar..wore but a starless blue coat. **1853** D. JERROLD *Chron. Clovernook* Wks. 1864 IV. 403 Bacchus,..with all his great bounty, is starless and unhonoured. **1873** DIXON *Two Queens* I. Pref., Two crowned and starless women.

Hence **ˈstarlessly** *adv.*, **ˈstarlessness.**

1842 *Tait's Mag.* IX. 726 Night sternly and starlessly appears. **1888** MEREDITH *Poems, Hard Weather* 103 Nor in her starlessness of night Peruse her with the craven nerve.

starlet (ˈstɑːlɪt). [-LET.]

1. A small star. Also *transf.* of a flower.

1830 CARLYLE *Richter Again* Ess. 1840 II. 363 The evening star..hovers..above the rosy red, and, modest as a bride, deprives no single starlet of its light. **1863** H. SPENCER *Ess.* II. 8 Nebulæ may be comparatively near, though the starlets of which they are made up appear extremely minute. **1881** BLACKIE *Lay Serm.* vii. 224 The smallest yellow starlet that peeps out from a grassy carpet in the spring.

2. A star-fish of the genus *Asterina.*

1854 A. ADAMS etc. *Man. Nat. Hist.* 325 Full grown Starlets (Asterina). **1863** WOOD *Illustr. Nat. Hist.* III. 732 Gibbous Starlet, *Asterina gibbosa.*

3. A young promising performer (usu. an actress) in the world of entertainment; also used in sport, etc. Cf. STAR *sb.*[1] 5 a, c.

1920 J. FERGUSON in *Northern Numbers* 97 Some 'starlet' sings, Into the footlights' glare. **1938** *Life* 29 Aug. 37 When Hollywood uncovers a starlet with a unique personality, like Marie Wilson, they turn her over to the still-picture department for a publicity 'build-up'. **1951** M. MCLUHAN *Mech. Bride* (1967) 24/1 As much time goes into the search for a title of some indigestible cold lard as in launching a starlet. **1959** ANON. *Streetwalker* iii. 48 A paragraph about a film starlet catches my eye. **1976** *Star* (Sheffield) 29 Oct. 28/1 Sheffield United manager Jimmy Sirrel produced another starlet from his club's youth policy today when he named Gary Hamson in his side. **1978** J. WAINWRIGHT *Thief of Time* 105 Very few 'starlets' end up as stars. They stay there—chocolate-box perfection with nil personality.

ˈstar-light, ˈstarlight, *sb.* and *a.*

1. a. The light of the stars; *occas.* the time when the stars shine.

c **1374** CHAUCER *Boeth.* II. met. iii. (1868) 39 Þan þe sterre ydimmyd paleþ hir white cheres, by þe flamus of þe sonne þat ouer comeþ þe sterre lyȝt. **1390** GOWER *Conf.* II. 259 Upon a nyht, Whan ther was noght bot sterreliht. **1565** COOPER *Thesaurus*, s.v. *Tenebræ*, The sterre light did put away darkenesse. **1590** SHAKS. *Mids. N.* II. i. 29 By fountaine cleere, or spangled star-light sheene. **1634** MILTON *Comus* 308 In such a scant allowance of Star-light. *a* **1637** B. JONSON *Sad Sheph.* II. iii, A Gypsan Ladie..

Wrought it by Moone-shine for mee, and Star-light. **1670** EACHARD *Cont. Clergy* 90 An hardy and labouring clergy.. that can foot it five or six miles in the dirt, and preach till star-light for as many shillings. **1799** HT. LEE *Canterb. T., Old Woman's T.* (ed. 2) I. 387 They at length emerged to star-light and the open country. **1840** R. H. DANA *Bef. Mast* xxix. 99 At work, from the grey of the morning till starlight. **1914** *Blackw. Mag.* Aug. 176/2 He went all night to the southward by starlight only.

b. *transf.* and *fig.*

1530 TINDALE *Prol. Levit.*, And though also that all the ceremonies and sacrifices haue as it were a sterrelyght of Christ, yet some there be that haue as it were the lighte of the brode daye a litle before the sonne risinge. **1600** FAIRFAX *Tasso* IX. lxxxvi, He saw waxe dim the starre-light of his eies.

2. A cluster of artificial lights arranged in the form of a star.

1884 *Baptist Yr.-Bk.* 357 Star-lights and brackets supply good artificial lighting.

3. a. *attrib.* and *adj.* Of or pertaining to starlight; bright as the stars; appearing or accompanied by starlight; lighted by the stars. [? Partly f. LIGHT *a.*^{2}]

1585 HIGINS *Junius' Nomencl.* 375/2 A cleare and starre-light night. **1665** SIR T. HERBERT *Trav.* (1677) 174 It is due North from Spahawn, as we observed in our star-light travel. **1697** DRYDEN *Virg. Georg.* I. 548 A Star-light Evening, and a Morning fair. **1803** VISCT. STRANGFORD *Poems of Camoens, Madrigal* (1810) 41 Starlight eyes, and heaving snows. **1819** BYRON *Juan* II. clxxxviii, The silent ocean, and the starlight bay. **1852** MRS. STOWE *Uncle Tom's C.* xvii. 163 The night was clear starlight. **1869** DUNKIN *Midnight Sky* 22 These two stars being never absent from our view on starlight nights.

b. Special Comb.: **starlight scope** *Mil.*, a device incorporating an image intensifier for use as a gun sight or telescope when there is little light.

1969 I. KEMP *Brit. G.I. in Vietnam* vii. 146 The North Vietnamese found two very valuable, expensive, and secret items of equipment, known as 'Starlightscopes'. The Starlightscope is an infra-red telescope for observation at night, which can also be fixed to a rifle for shooting in the dark. **1973** T. O'BRIEN *If I die in Combat Zone* iv. 28 Look at this... It's a starlight scope... Supposed to let you see in the dark. **1977** *Time* 23 May 33/2 There's the 90-mm. recoilless rifle with a 'starlight' scope for enhanced visibility.

'star-lighted, *ppl. a.* [f. STAR *sb.* + LIGHTED *ppl. a.* after STAR-LIGHT *sb.*] Star-lit.

1825 J. NEAL *Bro. Jonathan* I. 30 They run about laughing and shouting in the star-lighted wood. **1855** DICKENS *Holly Tree* Christm. Stor. (1874) 22 The bleak, star-lighted sky. **1895** KIPLING *2nd Jungle Bk.* 213 His voice could be heard in all sorts of wet star-lighted blossoming places.

star-like, *a.* and *adv.* **A.** *adj.*

1. Resembling a star; shining like a star.

1591 HARINGTON *Orl. Fur.* xxxv. ii, Those two starrlike eyn. **1611** COTGR. s.v. *Estoille, Pierre d'estoilles*, a.. Carbuncle, wherein.. many golden, sparkling, and starre-like drops may be discerned. **1652** [see SKY-LIKE]. **1860** PIESSE *Lab. Chem. Wonders* 3 This touch-wood.. will shine with a star-like light. **1870** BRYANT *Iliad* XVI. 173 The breastplate of the swift Æacides With star-like points.

b. *transf.* and *fig.*

1607 SHAKS. *Timon* V. i. 66 What, to you, Whose Starre-like Noblenesse gaue life and influence To their whole being? **1833** TENNYSON *Dream Fair Wom.* xxiii, She turning on my face The star-like sorrows of immortal eyes. **1883** *Mrs. Carlyle's Lett.* II. 274 With a certain star-like radiance and grace. **1884** *Christian World* 21 Feb. 139/5 This star-like serenity in all the tumult of his stormy life.

c. Countless as the stars. *nonce-use.*

1630 [see *sand-like* s.v. SAND *sb.*^{2} 9 e].

2. Shaped like a conventional star; stellate, radiate.

1611 COTGR., *Estoillé*, the Lizard Stellio, whose necke is full of starre-like spots. **1633** JOHNSON *Gerarde's Herbal* II. xcvi. (1636) 418 At the top whereof stand many pretty starre-like skinny seed-vessels. **1753** *Chambers' Cycl.* Suppl. s.v. *Hair*, The quills of the hedge-hog and porcupine have somewhat of a pith in a starlike form. **1847** C. BRONTË *Jane Eyre* xxxiv, A soft turf,.. spangled with a star-like yellow blossom. **1906** HICKSON in *Hartog's Protozoa* etc. (Camb. Nat. Hist.) 332 The position of the zooids in the colony is indicated only by star-like holes.

B. *adv.* Like a star.

1613 SHAKS. *Hen. VIII*, V. v. 47 So shall she leaue her Blessednesse to One.. Who, from the sacred Ashes of her Honour Shall Star-like rise. *a* **1678** CHALKHILL *Thealma & Clearchus* 104 So Star-like bright they shone. **1725** *Bradley's Family Dict.* s.v. *Saffron* (*Bastard*), This Plant produces staring Heads.. with some Leaves, opening underneath Star-like. **1842** TENNYSON *Sir Galahad* 48 As down dark tides the glory slides, And star-like mingles with the stars.

starling^1 (ˈstɑːlɪŋ). Forms: 1 **stærlinc**, 4–5 **sterling(e**, **-yng(e**, 5–6 **starlinge**, 5–6, 7–8 *Sc.* **stirling**, 6 **starlyng**, *Sc.* **stirlene**, **styrlyng**, 7 **sterling**, 4– **starling**. Also *dial.* STARNEL. [OE. *stærlinc*, f. *stær* STARE *sb.*^{1}: see -LING^1.]

1. Any bird of the passerine genus *Sturnus*, esp. *S. vulgaris*. Now also applied in wider sense to any bird of the family *Sturnidæ*.

a **1050** *Gloss.* (MS. Harl. 107) in *Zeitschr. für deutsches Alterth.* XXXIII. 241 Stærlinc, *sturnus*. *a* **1300** *Cursor M.* 1789 Þe sparhauk flough be pe sterling [*Gött.* starling]. *c* **1325** *Gloss. W. de Bibbesw.* in Wright *Voc.* 151 Soundre de porks et d'estourneus [*glossed* sterlinges]. *c* **1450** HOLLAND *Howlat* 713 The Maviss and the Merle syngis, Osillis and Stirlingis. *c* **1450** *Merlin* ix. 135 Thei smote in a-monge hem as faucouns amonge starlinges. **1513** DOUGLAS *Æneis* XII. Prol. 238 The styrlyng changis diuers stevynnys nys. **1549** *Compl. Scot.* VI. (1873) 39 The garruling of the stirlene gart the sparrou cheip. **1596** SHAKS. *1 Hen. IV*, I. iii. 224 Ile haue a Starling shall be taught to speake Nothing but 'Mortimer'. **1667–8** PEPYS *Diary* 1 Mar., A starling which.. do whistle and talk the most and best that ever I heard anything in my life. **1670** EACHARD *Cont. Clergy* 86 Then, after all this, came the jackdaws and sterlings (idle birds that they are!). **1724** RAMSAY *Tea-t. Misc.* (1733) II. 137 Of all the birds.. I far prefer the stirling's notes. **1768** STERNE *Sent. Journ.* (1778) II. 25 (Hotel at Paris), 'I can't get out', said the starling. **1880** *Cassell's Nat. Hist.* IV. 103 The Starlings are found only in the Old World, where they form a very large and natural Group. **1880** W. CARNEGIE *Pract. Trapping* 40 It is not generally known what a delicious bird the starling is to eat. **1894–5** LYDEKKER *Roy. Nat. Hist.* III. 343 Starlings.. all agree in possessing a wing with five primary quills, and twelve tail-feathers.

b. With prefixed word designating a particular species, genus, or group belonging to the family *Sturnidæ*.

1734 ALBIN *Nat. Hist. Birds* II. 38 The yellow Starling from Bengall. **1743** G. EDWARDS *Nat. Hist. Birds* I. 19 The Chinese Starling or Black-Bird. **1821** BEWICK *Brit. Birds* Suppl. I. 14 The Rose Coloured Starling. **1829** GRIFFITH tr. *Cuvier* VII. 37 The.. collared stare, Persian starling, and Alpine warbler. **1869–73** T. R. JONES *Cassell's Bk. Birds* I. 227 The Sardinian Starling (*Sturnus unicolor*). *Ibid.* The Rose Starling or Shepherd-bird (*Pastor roseus*). *Ibid.* 232 The Glossy Starlings (*Lamprotornithes*). *Ibid.* 234 The True Glossy Starlings (*Lamprocolii*). **1898** MORRIS *Austral Eng.* 435 The Shining Starling, *Calornis metailica*.

c. Applied to birds of the American family *Icteridæ*.

1731 CATESBY *Nat. Hist. Carolina* (1754) I. 13 The red-wing'd Starling. **1839** AUDUBON *Ornith. Biog.* V. 487 Red-winged Starling, *Icterus phœniceus*. **1869–73** T. R. JONES *Cassell's Bk. Birds* I. 215 The Yellow or Golden Starlings.

2. A kind of pigeon. Also ***starling-pigeon***.

1867 TEGETMEIER *Pigeons* xxi. 174 The Starlings are dark-coloured birds, white barred, with a speckled, crescent-shaped band across the crop. **1881** LYELL *Pigeons* 97 The Starling pigeon is a Continental variety, and in Germany it goes by the name of Der Staarenhals, or the starling neck. *Ibid.* 98 With age the starling often loses its marking to a great extent.

3. (See quot.)

1884 GOODE *Nat. Hist. Aquat. Anim.* 267 Boregata (*Hexagrammus Stelleri*)... The name 'Starling' is applied to some fish, supposed by us to be this species, in the Straits of Fuca.

4. *slang.* (See quot.)

a **1700** B. E. *Dict. Cant. Crew*, *Brother-starling*, that Lies with the same Woman.

5. *Comb.* as ***starling-breasted***, ***-like***, adjs.

1855 *Poultry Chron.* III. 272 The starling-breasted pigeon. **1880** *Cassell's Nat. Hist.* IV. 101 The first family of the starling-like perching birds. The Weaver Birds (*Ploceidæ*).

starling^2 (ˈstɑːlɪŋ). Forms: 8 **steerling**, **stirling**, 8–9 **sterling**, 7– **starling**. [Possibly a corruption of STADDLING.] An outwork of piles, projecting in front of the lower part of the pier of a bridge, so as to form a protection for the pier against the force of the stream or to secure it from damage by the impact of vessels or floating objects.

c **1684** *Old Ballads Gt. Frost* (Percy Soc.) 29 And on the starlings [was] kept the brandy trade. **1714** MACKY *Journ. Eng.* I. xiii. 192 Arches.. fenced with large Sterlings for the keeping off the Force of the Tide. **1724** DE FOE *Tour Gt. Brit.* I. III. 124 The Islands of Scilly.. are plac'd like Outworks to resist the first Assaults of this Enemy [the ocean].. as the Piles or Starlings (as they are call'd) are plac'd before the solid Stone-work of London-bridge, to fence off the Force, either of the Water or Ice, or [etc.]. **1739** LABELYE *Short Acc. Piers Westm. Bridge* 42 There must be .. a necessity of building Steerlings to preserve the Piers. **1773** NOORTHOUCK *Hist. Lond.* 561 The passage under the arches [of old London Bridge] was contracted by enormous platforms, built round the decaying piers, called sterlings. **1776** G. SEMPLE *Building in Water* 49 We laid three Beams stretching the whole Length of the Pier from Sterling to Sterling. **1778** H. BOWMAN *Trav.* 337 The stream still more streightened by starlings filled with large stones placed round the bottoms of the peers. **1840** *Civil Engin. & Arch. Jrnl.* III. 106/2 Piers and.. ponts or chests.. made salient at each end like the starlings of a bridge. **1878** STEVENSON *Inland Voy.* 17 They perched upon sterlings and buttresses. **1879** *Cassell's Techn. Educ.* IV. 405 The starling is that portion of the pier which faces the direction of the stream, and acts like the cutwater of a ship.

starling^3 (ˈstɑːlɪŋ). *nonce-wd.* [f. STAR *sb.*^{1} + -LING.] An inhabitant of a star.

1839 BAILEY *Festus* xiv. (1848) 150 Thou shouldest have been a starling, friend, And not an earthling.

starling, obs. form of STERLING *sb.*^{1}

star-lit, starlit (ˈstɑːlɪt), *ppl. a.* [LIT *ppl. a.*] Lit up or lighted by the stars.

1827–35 N. P. WILLIS *Confessional* 66 The bewitch'd caique, That o'er the star-lit waters flew. **1852** M. ARNOLD *Poems, Future* 47 When he lay in the night by his flock On the starlit Arabian waste. **1870** PROCTOR *Other Worlds* xii. 273 The whole of the star-lit sky.

'star-litten, *ppl. a.* [LITTEN *ppl. a.*] = prec.

1895 KIPLING *2nd Jungle Bk.* 150 That dim, star-litten sky.

starn, var. STERN *sb.*^{2} *Obs.* and *dial.*, star.

starnel (ˈstɑːnəl). *dial.* [A metathetic form of STARLING^1. Not from OE. *stearn* some bird, perh. the starling (gl. *beacita*, *sturnus*).] A starling.

a **1800** PEGGE *Suppl. Grose*, *Starnel*, a starling. North. **1856** P. THOMPSON *Hist. Boston* 725. **1888** FENN *Dick o' the Fens* 158 Look at the starnels sattling down on the reeds.

'starnie. *Sc.* [f. *starn*, STERN *sb.*^{2} + -IE.] A little star.

a **1774** FERGUSSON *Hallowfair* Poems (1845) 13 At Hallowmas when nights grow lang And starnies shine fu' clear. **1790** BURNS '*O death! thou tyrant*' xiv, Ye twinkling starnies bright. **1815** G. BEATTIE *John o' Arnha'* (1826) 12 Or modern Dux, wi' noddin' crest, An' starnies glancin' on his breast. **1833** *Chamb. Jrnl.* No. 69. 136 In nights when the starnies were broonding wi' frost.

‖**starosta** (ˈstærɒstə). Pl. **starosti**. Also anglicized 6 **starust**, 8 **stahrost**, 7–9 **starost(e**. [Russian *starosta*, Polish *starosta*, lit. 'elder'.]

1. In Russia, the head man of a village community.

1591 G. FLETCHER *Russe Commw.* x. 33 Besides these.. there are Starusts or Aldermen for euerie seuerall companie. **1796** MORSE *Amer. Geog.* II. 84 One family, whose chief.. performs the functions of staroste, or magistrate of the village. **1799** W. TOOKE *View Russ. Emp.* I. 460 Their elders, whom they still.. style Starosts. **1810** E. D. CLARKE *Trav. Russia* (1839) 37/1 Any person arriving in a town or village, must produce his [passport] to the starosta. **1833** R. PINKERTON *Russia* 281 They.. are governed by their own elders or starosti. **1901** *Scotsman* 5 Apr. 7/2 At Nijni Novgorod.. the starosta, or chief of the village artel, comes to buy the supply of material.

2. In the former kingdom of Poland, a noble holding a castle and domain bestowed by the Crown.

1670 *Lond. Gaz.* No. 504/1 Major-General Bokumbs.. has been lately killed by a Peasant, who was hired to commit the murther by a Staroste. **1827** BOWRING *Specim. Polish Poets* 137 His father was the starost of Korytnik. **1896** *Cosmopolitan* XX. 445 She assures us that she and her sisters have the bearing 'becoming young ladies of high station, and daughters of a Staroste'.

‖**starosty** (ˈstærɒstɪ). Also 8 **starostie**, 9 **starostee**. [ad. G. *starostei* or F. *starostie*, f. *starost* STAROSTA. The Polish word is *starostwo*.] In the former kingdom of Poland, the domain of a starosta.

1710 *Lond. Gaz.* No. 4656/2 They write from Wilda.. that the Chancellor Dewitz had taken Possession of the Starostie of Orsla. **1768** *Ann. Reg.* 19 Whole starosties, districts, towns, villages were sackt and burnt. **1774** *Ibid.* 20 She bestows upon him, in hereditary possession four starosties (which are governments of castles with the districts belonging to them). **1775** WRAXALL *Tour N. Europe* 378, I saw an original charter of Sigismund Augustus, dated in 1507, which grants it as royal starosty to Andreas Gorsley. **1795** *Ann. Reg., Hist.* 6 The starosties, the name given to those lands and estates bestowed by the Crown upon individuals, for their public services or expenses. **1840** *Penny Cycl.* XVIII. 325/2 Starosts without jurisdiction, who were only holders of starostees, or crown estates.

‖**starover** (starəˈvjer). Pl. **starovers**, **starovery**. [Russ.] = OLD BELIEVER.

1861 A. P. STANLEY *Lectures on Hist. Eastern Church* xii. 471 The real force, the permanent interest, of the Rascolniks lies in the eight millions of souls who call themselves *Starovers*; that is, 'the Old Believers'. **1957** *Oxf. Dict. Chr. Ch.* 1287/1 *Starovery*, another name for the Russian sect of the Old Believers. **1963** N. V. RIASANOVSKY *Hist. Russia* xix. 220 The Old Believers or Old Ritualists—*starovery* or *staroobriadtsy*—rejected the new sign of the cross, the corrected spelling of the name of Jesus, the tripling instead of the doubling of the 'Hallelujah' and other similar emendations.

starquake (ˈstɑːkweɪk). *Astr.* [f. STAR *sb.*^{1} after EARTHQUAKE.] A sudden change of shape or structure undergone by a neutron star, pulsar, etc.

1969 *Nature* 9 Aug. 598/1 Neutron stars which satisfy the criterion, $\omega \geqq 10^3\ s^{-1}$, should have starquakes as they slow up. **1970** *New Scientist* 4 June 465/3 After the starquake, the pulsar readjusts its shape and speeds up. **1976** *Sci. Amer.* Oct. 78/3 In still other neutron-star models the source of the gamma rays is ascribed to 'starquakes', volcanic activity or other sudden changes in size or shape. **1978** PASACHOFF & KUTNER *University Astron.* xi. 314 As a result of this 'starquake', the matter would then be distributed slightly closer to the center of the star.

starr. *Hist.* Also 7 **starre**, **star**. [ad. med.L. *starrum*, ad. late Heb. *sh'ṭār* a writing.] A Jewish deed or bond, esp. one of release or acquittance of debt.

1614 SELDEN *Titles Honor* 328 Whence the word *Starrum* or *Starre* for Acquitances or writen testimonies of Contracts is vsd. **1617** PURCHAS *Pilgrimage* II. x. §7 (ed. 3) 172 Any such Starres or Deeds. **1656** PRYNNE *2nd Pt. Short Demurrer Jews* 11 All their Deeds, Obligations, and Releases were usually called *Stars*, and *Starra*, *Starrum*, *Starr*. **1875** J. T. FOWLER in *Yorks. Archæol. Jrnl.* III. 57 Starrs were written in Hebrew, Latin, or French. **1902** J. M. RIGG *Sel. Pleas*, etc. *Jews* Introd. p. xix, A starr of acquittance entitled the debtor to cancellation and delivery of the duplicate or 'foot' (pes) of the chirograph.

starr(e, variant forms of STAR *sbs.* and *v.*

starre, variant of STARE *sb.*^{3} *Obs.*

starred (stɑːd), *ppl. a.* Forms: 3 stirred, 4 stared, 4–5 sterred, 5 sterrid, -yd, 6 stered, *Sc.* sterrit, 6– starred. [f. STAR *sb.*^{1} and *v.* + -ED.]

1. Of the heavens, the sky, etc.: Studded with stars, starry.

a **1225** *St. Marher.* 22 þe gast anan riht steh up in to þe stirrede bur bliðe to heouene. **1390** GOWER *Conf.* III. 375 Enclosid in a sterred sky. *c* **1485** *Digby Myst.* I. 397 From the sterrid hevyn, lord, thu list come down. **1513** DOUGLAS *Æneis* I. v. 55 The sterrit sky. **1610** BOLTON *Elem. Armories* 150 Azure being the colour of the starred heauen. **1794–6** COLERIDGE *Relig. Musings* 19 Nor the starred azure, nor the sovran sun. **1820** KEATS *Hyperion* I. 118 Upon all space: space starr'd, and lorn of light. **1883** MEREDITH *Lucifer in Starlight* 1 On a starred night, Prince Lucifer uprose.

2. a. Marked with the representation or figure of a star; studded or adorned with star-like figures. Of a horse or cow: Having a star on the forehead (see STAR *sb.*^{1} 9 b).

13.. *E.E. Allit. P.* B. 1506 Nov is alle þis guere geten glotounes to serue; Stad in a ryche stal & stared ful bryȝtȝ. *c* **1380** *Sir Ferumb.* 3987 Hastelich aȝen on ys stede he wond, þe sterrede he takeþ on ys hond, & leteþ hem boþe renne. **1570** *Bury Wills* (Camden) 156 One blacke stered heckforde of the age of two yeres. **1681** GREW *Musæum* III. §i. v. 305 The Starred-Stone. *Astroites.* So called, for that being tabulated, or polish'd to a plain, it appears adorned with little Stars. **1688** HOLME *Armoury* II. 355/1 A Starred Ray, ..the fins and body is adorned with painted Stars. **1831** GRIFFITH tr. *Cuvier* IX. Syn. 4 Starred Tortoise, *Testudo Stellata.* **1854** A. ADAMS etc. *Man. Nat. Hist.* 356 Starred Corals (Caryophylliidæ).

†**b.** ***starred chamber***: see STAR-CHAMBER.

†**c.** Epithet of an order of monks or friars.

Cf. COTGR. *Estoillins*, an Order of Friers, that weare starres on the breasts of their gownes.

1537 *Orig. & Sprynge of Sectes* 33 The order of Starred monkes... They weare an honest blacke garment with a starre sewed theron, wherby they maye be knowen. *Ibid.* Starred freres. **1563–83** FOXE *A. & M.* 154/2 Some Flagellants..: some starred Monkes.

d. Decorated with the star of an order.

1826 DISRAELI *Viv. Grey* II. xii, Gartered peers, and starred ambassadors. **1856** LEVER *Martins of Cro' M.* xxiv. 263 Your starred and cordoned agitator of the Bourse. **1900** E. WALLACE *Writ in Barracks* 113 O the starred and gartered Levee!

e. Marked or distinguished with an asterisk. *spec.*, in order to indicate some special category or merit.

1893 *Daily News* 20 Dec. 5/7 Does the right hon. gentleman expect candidates to count 1,169 starred voters? **1914** *Hansard Lords* 24 Nov. 459 My original arrangement with Lord Kitchener was that a starred man should neither be solicited for recruitment nor accepted for the Army if he offered himself. **1927, 1937** [see NAP *sb.*^{5} 2 c]. **1940** *Hansard Lords* 6 Aug. 148 As far as I remember, the starred question was introduced at the instance of the late Lord Curzon about twenty years ago, and the object was to enable noble Lords to put down questions which they would wish to see mentioned in the House, rather than dealt with by a written reply, but upon which no debate should take place. **1964** F. WHITE *West of Rhone* xxii. 233, I stopped at a starred hotel. .. It deserved its star, for it was very good. **1970** R. LOWELL *Notebk.* 104 Four stone inkfish, thrice stepped on, lifting the spout—Not starred in any guidebook. **1971** *Guardian* 19 July 8/2 Margaret Drabble..whom he much admires for.. her starred first. **1974** R. QUIRK *Linguist & Eng. Lang.* xi. 158 American English items [in a dictionary] are prefixed by a warning asterisk (an unhappy emblem when we consider what a starred form means in linguistics). **1976** N. ROBERTS *Face of France* xix. 185 The starred items on the menu.

f. Of glass or ice: see quot. and STAR *v.* 5. Similarly of a radiating 'splash' of liquid, and *spec.* of a shattered vehicle windscreen of splinterproof glass.

1849 CRAIG, *Starred*,..cracked in the form of a star, as a starred bottle, or pane of glass. **1896** J. CONRAD *Outcast of the Islands* IV. iii, A single big drop of rain..struck loudly the dry ground between them in a starred splash. **1960** *B.S.I. News* Mar. 8/2 A windscreen of laminated glass may crack under impact but it will hold together, though 'starred', and remain in one place except in the most violent of collisions. **1979** R. PERRY *Bishop's Pawn* ix. 153, I continued driving blind, unable to see through the starred windscreen.

3. a. Star-shaped; arranged in the form of a star; stellate. Chiefly *Bot.*

1725 *Bradley's Family Dict.* s.v. *Narcissus*, The most common in France are..the crennell'd, the yellow, the starr'd wild [etc.]. **1821** S. F. GRAY *Brit. Plants* I. 88 Hairs ..Starred, *stellati.* **1870** MORRIS *Earthly Par.* III. IV. 368 The first starred yellow blossoms of the spring. **1874** LADY HERBERT tr. *Hübner's Ramble* II. iv. (1878) 324 Maples with their fine starred leaves.

†**b.** ***starred wheel*** = *star-wheel* (*b*), STAR *sb.*^{1} 20.

1696 MANDEY & MOXON *Mech. Powers* IX. i. (1699) 176 A Starred Wheel is that whose Circumference is furnished with three sided Prismes having each side equal.

4. Influenced by the stars; born under a (lucky or unlucky) star. Only with defining adv., or in parasynthetic comb. with adj. (as ILL-STARRED).

1611 SHAKS. *Wint. T.* III. ii. 100 My third comfort (Star'd most vnluckily). **1786** BURNS *To Mountain-Daisy* vii, Such is the fate of simple Bard, On Life's rough ocean luckless starr'd! **1824** HOOD *Ode on Clapham Academy* 67 Some brightly starr'd,—some evil born. **1855** SINGLETON *Virgil* II. 434 O nations, happy starred.

5. Of a person: Made into a star or constellation; elevated to the region of the stars. (Cf. STAR *v.* 2.)

1632 MILTON *Penseroso* 19 That Starr'd Ethiope Queen [Cassiopeia]. **1832** LYTTON *Eugene Aram* V. vi, The confession..of a starred soul that had wandered from how proud an orbit. **1898** MEREDITH *Odes Fr. Hist.* 79 In the ranks of the starred, she is one.

6. Placed in or allocated to a star. *nonce-use.*

1742 YOUNG *Nt. Th.* IX. 777 Ye Starr'd, and Planeted, Inhabitants!

starrer ('stɑːə(r)). [f. STAR *v.* + -ER^1.] **1.** One who marks a material with stars. *local*

1870 *Inquiry, Yorksh. Deaf & Dumb* 16 She is employed ..as a starrer, that is putting the roses in the corner of the blankets.

2. *slang.* A play or film which provides an impressive leading role for an actor or actress.

1951 GREEN & LAURIE *Show Biz* 571/2 *Starrer*, starring vehicle. **1978** M. PUZO *Fools Die* xxvii. 311 A Kellino starrer would get the studio's two million back.

†**'starrify**, *v. Obs. rare.* [f. STAR *sb.*^{1} + -(I)FY. Cf. STELLIFY *v.*] *trans.* **a.** To mark with a star, decorate with stars. **b.** To make (a person) into a star or constellation.

1598 SYLVESTER *Du. Bartas* II. i. IV. *Handicrafts* 413 [Description of a horse] his fore-head starrifi'd. **1675** T. JORDAN *Triumphs of London* 11 A skie-colour'd Mantle starrified with Gold. **1681** W. ROBERTSON *Phraseol. Gen.* 1160/1 Amalthæa..put it to Jupiter's mouth, for which he starrified his nurse.

starrigan ('stærɪgən). *Newfoundland.* Also starigan. [Perh. ad. Ir. *stairricín* stump, stick.] A young, stunted, or decayed evergreen tree (chiefly fir), esp. cut for firewood; a stick, branch, or stump of this.

1895 *Jrnl. Amer. Folk-Lore* VIII. 39 *Starrigan*, a young fir-tree, which is neither good for firewood nor large enough to be used for timber, hence applied with contempt to anything constructed of unsuitable materials. *c* **1900** in *Regional Lang. Stud. Newfoundland* (1978) VIII. 26 *Starrigan*, a green stick, especially a var of small dimensions. **1903** *Newfoundland Q.* Dec. 5 He could get nothin' there but a few green var starrigans..or dun boughs. **1920** GRENFELL & SPALDING *Le Petit Nord* 94 Light snow has fallen during the night, and every 'starigan', every patch of 'tuckamore' is 'decked in sparkling raiment white'. **1964** *Newfoundland Herald* 26 Jan., *Starrigans*, actually dry tree stumps which formed an important source of fuel in the depression days. **1977** *Decks Awash* Sept. 64 De bull would get de tacklin An off 'e'd go for starrigans Wid frosty snow acracklin. **1981** *Publ. Amer. Dial. Soc.* LXVIII. 43 *Starrigan*.., very sappy fir, this name usually applied only when cut for firewood.

starrily ('stɑːrɪlɪ), *adv. rare.* [-LY^2.] In a starry manner.

c **1825** BEDDOES *Bridal Serenade* Poems 180 Starrily clothed in a garment white. *a* **1849** MANGAN *Poems* (1859) 361 Garments so starrily shining.

'starriness. *rare.* [-NESS.] Starry quality.

1727 BAILEY vol. II, *Starriness*, Fulness of Stars. **1830** *Blackw. Mag.* XXVII. 848 Let the heaven of thy imagination be spanned in its starriness by that most celestial Evanescence. **1879** MEREDITH *Egoist* v, She had money and health and beauty, the triune of perfect starriness, which makes all men astronomers. **1910** BRIDGES *Later Poems* No. 8 As she drifteth free Between the starriness of the air And the starry lea.

starring ('stɑːrɪŋ), *vbl. sb.* [-ING^1.] The action of the verb STAR; *spec.* the acting or touring of a 'star' performer.

1841 *Punch* 17 July 12/1 We consider Mr. Phelps' opposition to this ruinous system of 'starring' as commendable and manly. **1849** *Theatrical Programme* 25 June 38 Queen's Theatre, Hull... Starring is the order of the day here. **1859** F. FOWLER *Southern Lights* 36, I heard that Mr. Brooke had netted upwards of 30,000*l.* during his 'starring' career in the colony. **1864** DASENT *Jest & Earnest* (1873) I. 180 In London, where the starring system prevails to a stifling extent, we have sometimes one good actor, supported, like a sweet pea, by sticks. **1868** MISS BRADDON *Dead Sea Fr.* xxvi. II. 287 He was the enchantress's *alter ego*,..arranging her starring engagements. **1882–3** SCHAFF *Encycl. Relig. Knowl.* II. 1358 He made a second starring-tour as rhetorician. **1940** *Illustr. London News* CXCVI. 188/2 This kind of 'starring' I regard as a foolish departure at a theatre which has built up a reputation as a repertory with a first-rate team.

†**'starrulet.** *Obs. rare*$^{-1}$. [irreg. f. STAR *sb.*^{1}, after *annulet*, *rivulet.*] A little star.

1610 BOLTON *Elem. Armories* 123 But why haue you noted some with Asterisks or Starrulets? **1656** BLOUNT *Glossogr.*, *Starrulet*, a little Star.

starry ('stɑːrɪ), *a.* Forms: 4–5 sterry, 5 sterri, 6 sterrie, starrye, 6–7 starrie, 6– starry. [f. STAR *sb.*^{1} + -Y.]

1. Of the sky, night, etc.: Full of stars, spangled or lit up with stars.

The phrases ***starry heaven, sphere***, etc. were formerly used spec. = the 'sphere' of the fixed stars.

c **1374** CHAUCER *Boeth.* II. met. ii. (Camb. MS.) (1886) 24 As many rychesses as ther shynyn bryhte sterres in heuene on the sterry nyhtes. *c* **1403** LYDG. *Temple of Glas* 1100 Nou blisful goddes, doun fro þi sterri sete, Vs to fortune, caste ȝour stremes shene. **1551** RECORDE *Cast. Knowl.* (1556) 7 The Firmament..hath in it an infinite numbre of starres, wherof it is called the Starrye skie. **1590** SHAKS. *Mids. N.* III. ii. 356 The starrie Welkin couer thou anon With drooping fogge. **1617** MORYSON *Itin.* I. 208 Many times we lay in the field under the starry canopy. **1667** MILTON *P.L.* IV. 992 The Starrie Cope Of Heav'n. **1684** *Contempl. St. Man* II. i. (1699) 137 The only thickness of the starry Sphere is said to contain as much as the whole space betwixt that and the Earth. **1709** ADDISON *Tatler* No. 119 ¶2 While you are admiring the Sky in a Starry Night. **1875** JOWETT *Plato* (ed. 2) III. 417 The starry heaven which we behold.

fig. **1657** J. WATTS *Scribe, Pharisee* etc. III. 51 Those starry times of the Apostles, and those Sunshining dayes of Christ Jesus. **1864** SWINBURNE *Atalanta* 1077 Shall they..like flowers Be shed and shine before the starriest hours..?

2. a. Of or relating to the stars; consisting of stars.

1594 BARNFIELD *Affect. Sheph.* II. ix, By the bright glimmering of the Starrie light. **1645** W. LILLY (*title*) The Starry Messenger. **1651** DAVENANT *Gondibert* III. vi. 31 Night had put all her Starry Jewels on. **1700** MOXON *Math. Dict.* (ed. 2) s.v. *Solar*, The Sidereal or Starry year, is the space wherein the Sun comes back to any particular fixed Star. **1805** HERSCHEL in *Phil. Trans.* XCV. 58, I saw the asteroid, which in its true starry form has left the place where I saw it Sept. 29th. **1826** DISRAELI *Viv. Grey* III. vi, The bright moon with her starry court. **1878** NEWCOMB *Pop. Astron.* IV. ii. 461 The starry system.

b. Relating to, or caused by, the 'influence' of the stars.

1831 LYTTON *Godolphin* xxvii, We must do our best to contradict the starry evils by our own internal philosophy.

c. applied to an astronomer. *nonce-use.*

1818 BYRON *Ch. Har.* IV. liv, The starry Galileo.

d. Of or pertaining to stars in the world of entertainment.

1907 G. B. SHAW *Let.* 24 May (1972) II. 690, I have.. utterly rejected the starry part of it [*sc.* a production of *Man & Superman*]. **1918** R. WAGNER *Film Folk* 8 The starry firmament of Los Angeles. **1929** H. G. WELLS *King who was King* i. 30 The film *entrepreneur*..has to secure the services of a starry lady. **1959** *Manch. Guardian* 30 Jan. 7/1 One of the most persistent critical complaints about Miss Dresdel has been her tendency to shine too brightly even in the starriest company. **1981** *Times* 24 Jan. 7/2 Gertrude Lawrence..needed something very big, something very starry.

3. Shining like a star or like stars, bright as a star, star-like.

1608 D. T[UVILL] *Ess. Pol. & Mor.* 101 Captivated by the powerfull attraction of their [*sc.* women's] starry looks. *c* **1630** MILTON *Passion* 18 His starry front low-rooft beneath the skies. **1636** SHIRLEY *Duke's Mistr.* IV. i. (1638) H 1 b, Bright in thy sorrowes, on whom every teare Sits like a wealthy Diamond, and inherits A Starry lustre from the eye that shed it. **1667** MILTON *P.L.* VII. 446 And th' other whose gay Traine Adorns him, colour'd with the Florid hue Of Rainbows and Starrie Eyes. **1757** GRAY *Bard* 112 Sublime their starry fronts they rear. **1866** LYTTON *Lost Tales of Miletus, Oread's Son* xvi. 96 The fountain stirred, And from it rose a mist of starry spray. **1867** AUGUSTA WILSON *Vashti* xxv, There was a dangerous, starry sparkle in her eyes.

fig. *c* **1610** *Women Saints* 103 This starrie gemme shall ere long be taken from vs into the Saints contrie. **1840** BROWNING *Sordello* I. 282 Rather, test qualities to heart's content; Summon them, thrice selected, near and far; Compress the starriest into one star. **1862** SWINBURNE *Sonn. to J. Nichol* 13 The starry spirit of Dobell.

4. Shaped like the conventional figure of a star with rays projecting from a centre; arranged in the form of a star; in *Bot.* = STELLATE.

1606 SYLVESTER *Du Bartas* II. iv. II. *Magnif.* 662 The starry-flowers. **1629** PARKINSON *Paradisus* 131 The early blew starry Iacinth. **1755** J. ELLIS *Corallines* Introd. 12 Till the Polypes had extended themselves out of their starry Cells. **1781** COWPER *Charity* 552 Guns, halberts, swords, and pistols, great and small, In starry forms dispos'd upon the wall. **1794** KIRWAN *Min.* (ed. 2) I. 88 The striæ.. diverging as from a common center, or starry. **1873** LIVINGSTONE in Blaikie *Life* xxii. (1881) 440 Grasses with white starry seed-vessels.

5. Sprinkled or studded with star-like forms. Chiefly *Nat. Hist.*

† ***starry coral, stone*** = STAR-STONE 2.

1611 COTGR., *Raye estelée*, the starrie Skate, the rugged Ray. **1653** R. SANDERS *Physiogn.* 56 If [this line of the Head] be starry towards the plain of Mars. **1661** BOYLE *Cert. Physiol. Ess.* (1669) 56 Eminent Chymists..have often failed in their endeavours to make the Starry Regulus of Mars and Antimony. **1677** PLOT *Oxfordsh.* 87 *Astroites* or starry-stones, such as in bulk are irregular, but adorned all over with many stars. **1681** GREW *Musæum* I. §ii. iii. 45 Stellio, or the Starry-Lizard. **1695** WOODWARD *Nat. Hist. Earth* IV. 177 The *Astroites*, or Starry-Stone, as well that sort with the Prominent, as that with the Concave Stars. **1712** J. MORTON *Nat. Hist. Northamptonsh.* 183 Some Sorts of Starry Coral. **1781** LATHAM *Gen. Synop. Birds* I. I. 79 Starry Falcon..marked with spots resembling stars. **1835** JENYNS *Man. Brit. Vertebr.* 517 *Raia radiata*, Don. (Starry Ray). **1861** *All Year Round* 1 June 237 Spring meadows starry with primroses. **1884** GOODE *Nat. Hist. Aquat. Anim.* 184 The Starry Flounder, *Pleuronectes stellatus.* **1884** COUES *N. Amer. Birds* 465 *Stellula*, Starry Hummers.

6. *Comb.*

1591 SYLVESTER *Du Bartas* I. iv. 201 His azure wings, and Starry-golden tail. **1633** JOHNSON *Gerarde's Herbal* II. xcvi. (1636) 417 Starry headed small Water Plantaine. **1652** GAULE *Magastrom.* 66 The night..not cloudy, but starry-bright. **1753** *Chambers' Cycl.* Suppl. s.v. *Thistle*, The Calcitrapa, or starry-headed Thistle. **1814** SIR W. HERSCHEL *Sci. Papers* (1912) II. 526 Starry-nebulous patches.

starry-eyed, *a.* [f. STARRY *a.* + EYED *ppl. a.*]

a. Of persons: idealistic, uplifted, romantic: ingenuous, naïve.

1936 M. MITCHELL *Gone with Wind* xxix. 489 She had never stood starry-eyed when the Stars and Bars ran up a pole. **1945** NELSON & WRIGHT *Tomorrow's House* xviii. 206/2 Starry-eyed prospective home builders. **1955** M. DICKENS *Winds of Heaven* v. 130 Holding hands and being starry-eyed over bottles of Chianti in romantic little cafés.

1958 *Spectator* 10 Jan. 37/3 He can hardly be so starry-eyed as to suppose that a similar enterprise on a national scale would be blessed by the whole hierarchy. **1964** S. Brittan *Treasury under Tories* II. vii. 208 He understood both businessmen and bureaucrats too well to be starry-eyed about either. **1979** *Dædalus* Summer 107 A starry-eyed bachelor woos the kitchen maid.

b. *transf.* and *fig.*

[**1928** 'Brent of Bin Bin' *Up Country* x. 163 She expressed starry-eyed sympathy with his loss, having a struggle to keep back the tears.] **1947** A. L. Rowse *End of Epoch* i. 14 The starry-eyed vacuity of the unteachable and the uneducable. **1958** *Listener* 25 Sept. 476/2 All too often United States policy-makers..tend to hover between a starry-eyed idealism and a dangerous brinkmanship. **1973** *Times Lit. Suppl.* 3 Aug. 891/4 Mr Grunberger's account is balanced, but..his conclusion is starry-eyed. **1978** *Jrnl. R. Soc. Arts* CXXVI. 345/2 It is just not possible to accomplish anything like so starry-eyed a concept.

starscape (ˈstɑːskeɪp). [f. star *sb.*[1], after landscape.] A view or prospect of a sky filled with stars. Also *fig.*

1926 S. Leslie *Cantab* (ed. 2) xiii. 163 He stared through the window at the Sussex star-scape. **1947** *Horizon* Aug. 100 He [*sc.* Paalen]..leads us into 'star-scapes', a happy nomenclature invented by him. **1958** L. Durrell *Balthazar* I. i. 13 Winter: freezing snow, cool sand..clear sky panels ...magnificent starscapes. **1965** *Spectator* 1 Jan. 16/1 One of those golden, glittering Covent Garden starscapes which ..are so fascinating to diagnose through opera glasses. **1968** A. C. Clarke *2001: Space Odyssey* xliv. 210 The scurrying flecks of light no longer moved across the redly-glowing starscape still thousands of miles below.

ˈstar-shine, ˈstarshine. = star-light.

1581 Dee *Diary* (Camden) 12 All the skye clere about, and fayre starshyne. **1830** Tennyson *Oriana* 24 By star-shine and by moonlight. **1855** Browning *Last Ride* iii, Cloud, sunset, moonrise, star-shine too. **1883** *Century Mag.* XXVII. 39 A faint, diffused starshine came into the room like mist.

attrib. **1591** Florio *2nd Fruites* 165 This wilbe a faire moone and starre-shine night.

star-ship. Also **star ship, starship.** [f. star *sb.*[1] + ship *sb.*[1]]

1. The Southern constellation Argo Navis.

1606 Sylvester *Du Bartas* II. iv. I. *Tropheis* 216 'Twixt Eridanus And th' Heav'nly Star-Ship. **1849** Cupples *Green Hand* xviii. (1856) 178 The great star-ship down in the south.

2. *Sci. Fiction.* A large manned spacecraft designed for interstellar travel.

1934 *Astounding Stories* Dec. 9 To start the year we offer you *Star Ship Invincible*, by Frank K. Kelly. **1956** F. Pohl *Alternating Currents* 77 A particle of meteoric matter slammed into *Starship Terra II* in hyperspace. **1967** J. Blish *Star Trek* 40 Capt. James Kirk of the star-ship *Enterprise*..had seen more planets than most men knew existed. **1972** H. C. Rae *Shooting Gallery* iv. 242 Now he was to be..flung, like one of those plastic star-ships, out into a galaxy of worlds which didn't really exist. **1978** *Listener* 30 Mar. 405/1 Smaller monitor screens were scattered about. It could have been the bridge of a star-ship. **1980** *Daily Tel.* 14 Jan. 8/1 Could star ships ever be propelled by the violent mutual annihilation of matter and anti-matter?

ˈstar-shot. In 7 -shoot, -shut. [shot *sb.*[1] With sense 1 cf. WFris. *stjerreskot*, MDu. *sterrenschot* (Kilian), Du. *sterreschot*, Sw. *stjärnskott*, Da. *stjerneskud*. Gawin Douglas (1513) has 'sterne schot' = shooting star: see stern *sb.*[2]]

1. A popular name for nostoc, which is supposed to fall from the stars, or to be the remains of a shooting star. ? *Obs.* (For other names see star *sb.*[1] 22 b.)

1653 *Goughe's Queen* I. B 3 b, Why, look, look ye, we are all made, or let me be stew'd in Star-shut. **1661** Boyle *Cert. Physiol. Ess.* (1669) 175 That jelly that is sometimes found on the ground, and by the Vulgar call'd a Star-shoot, as if it remain'd upon the extinction of a falling Star. **1701–2** Star Shot Gelly [see nostoc]. **1768** Pennant *Brit. Zool.* II. 424. **1804** Bewick *Brit. Birds* II. 211. **1866** Brogden *Prov. Lincs.*

†**2.** A kind of chain-shot. *Obs.*

1769 Falconer *Dict. Marine* (1789) Mm 2 [described].

star-spangled, *ppl. a.* **1.** Spangled with stars.

1591 Sylvester *Du Bartas* I. ii. 1172 Above the Heavn's Star-spangled Canopy. *a* **1593** Marlowe *Ovid's Elegies* III. ix. [x.] 21 He who rules the worlds starre-spangled towers. **1647** C. Harvey *Schola Cordis* xxxiii. 12 Thy piercing eye Whose light outvieth the star-spangled skie. **1777** Potter *Æschylus, Agamem.* 234 Heaven's star-spangled plain. **1814** F. S. Key (*title of song*) The Star-spangled Banner. **1896** Baden-Powell *Matabele Campaign* vi, And then you take a last look at the glorious star-spangled ceiling overhead.

2. ***star-spangled banner.*** **a.** The national flag of the United States of America. Also *fig.* Cf. *stars and stripes* s.v. star *sb.*[1] 6 b.

1814 F. S. Key in *Baltimore Patriot* 20 Sept. 2/1 The star-spangled banner in triumph shall wave. **1843** Dickens *Martin Chuzzlewit* (1844) xxi. 261, I thank you, sir, in the name of the star-spangled banner of the Great United States. **1869** 'Mark Twain' *Innoc. Abr.* xlix. 515 A robe.. that was a very star-spangled banner of curved and sinuous bars of black and white. **1887** —— *Let.* 18 Dec. (1917) II. 480 It had bought them of the star spangled banner Masterthief. **1949** *Chicago Daily News* 15 Dec. 3 Was the Star-Spangled Banner made in a brewery?

b. With capital initials: the name of the U.S. national anthem.

1814 [see sense 1]. **1843** *Quincy* (Illinois) *Herald* 3 Mar. 1/1 It is a most beautiful history of that national ballad, 'The Star Spangled Banner'. **1899** Kipling *From Sea to Sea* II. xxv. 15 When we had chanted 'The Star-Spangled Banner' not more than eight times, we adjourned. **1936** *Nation* 10 Oct. 419/2 As the band played the Star Spangled Banner at the end,..the President stood erect. **1977** G. Markstein *Chance Awakening* xliii. 128 He was on his feet..with 17,000 other people in the stadium as the Star Spangled Banner thundered out of the loudspeakers.

star-stone. [star *sb.*[1]]

1. A name for the pentagonal or star-shaped vertebral joints of pentacrinites.

1658 Ray *Itin.* Sel. Rem. (1760) 107 Hereabout [Shuckborough, Warw.] are found Star-Stones. **1666** Merrett *Pinax* 211 *Astroites*, the Star-stone. **1673** Ray *Journ. Low C.* 116 Those they call Star-Stones (because they run out into five Angles like so many Rays as they use to picture Stars with). **1748** J. Hill *Hist. Fossils* 653 Nearly allied to the Entrochi and Volvulæ, are the Asteriæ or Star-stones, well known in most of the Northern counties of England. **1836** Buckland *Geol. & Min.* (1837) I. 435 All the joints of the [vertebral] column [of Pentacrinites], when seen transversely, present various modifications of pentagonal star-like forms; hence their name of Asteriæ, or star-stones. **1908** [Miss E. Fowler] *Betw. Trent & Ancholme* 36 We used to gather 'star stones', pentracrinites.

†**2.** A fossil coral studded with star-like forms. (Cf. starry *a.* 5.)

1668 Charleton *Onomast* 262 *Astroites, Lapis Stellaris*, Germanis *Sternenstein*; the Star-stone (quia stellulis undiquaque insignitus nigricantibus). **1748** J. Hill *Hist. Fossils* 641 The *Astroites* or Star-Stone is ally'd also to these [corals]. **1755** J. Ellis *Corallines* 102 The Polypes inhabiting the Corallines, Corals, Star-Stones,..and the like.

3. A precious stone which exhibits asterism; a star-sapphire or star-ruby.

1798 *Phil. Trans.* LXXXVIII. 448 When the reflection is compounded of rays which intersect each other, and appear to diverge from a common centre, I call them star-stones, as red, blue, or greyish star-stones, or star-sapphires. **1802** *Ibid.* XCII. 273 That beautiful reflection of light, in the form of a star with six rays, which is frequently given, by cutting, to oriental rubies, sapphires, &c. and which causes those stones to be then called by the name of *star-stones.* **1879** *Cassell's Techn. Educ.* II. 123/2 Star-stones... These gems are essentially crystallised alumina, and are known as star or asterias rubies or sapphires, according to their colour.

start (stɑːt), *sb.*[1] Forms: 1 **steort**, (3 **steort-** in comb.), 3–7 **stert,** 4–6 **sterte,** 5 **storte,** 6 **starte,** 6– **start.** [Com. Teut.: OE. *steort* masc. corresponds to OFris. *stert, stirt* (WFris. *stirt*, NFris. *stört*), (M)LG. *stert*, MDu. *staert* (mod.Du. *staart*), OHG., mod.G. *sterz*, ON. *stert-r* (Sw. Da. *stjert*):—OTeut. **sterto-z.*]

†**1.** The tail of an animal. *Obs.*

The explanation 'tail' is given in many dictionaries from the 17th c. onwards, and in many modern dialect glossaries, but app. only as an assumed general or primary meaning accounting for the specific senses and the use in *redstart.* Evidence of any modern currency of sense 1 is wanting.

c **725** *Corpus Gloss.* C 196 *Cauda*, steort. *c* **888** Ælfred *Boeth.* xxxv. §7 Ceruerus..ongan onfægnian mid his steorte & pleȝian wiþ hine. *c* **1220** *Bestiary* 9 Ðe leun..Draȝeð dust wið his stert. *a* **1300** *Havelok* 2823 Demden him to binden faste Vp on an asse..His nose went unto þet stert.

2. A handle (of a vessel, handbell, broom, etc.).

c **1325** *Gloss. W. de Bibbesw.* in Wright *Voc.* 168 *Le manuel e le tenoun*, [*glossed*] the handele and the sterte. *c* **1440** *Promp. Parv.* 474/2 Stert, of a handylle of a vessel, *ansa.* **1512** in *Archæologia* XLI. 344 For..mending yᵉ start of yᵉ sanctus bell ix d. **1521** *Test. Ebor.* (Surtees) V. 129 To ychon of my broder sonys a sylver spoyne with cuttid starttis. **1562** in J. R. Boyle *Hedon* (1875) App. 206 An olde panne with a start and a candelsticke. **1566** *Engl. Ch. Furniture* (Peacock 1866) 33 Item one handbell broken the start of yt and sold to Johnne Chamberlaine and he haith made a morter thereof. **1657** Tomlinson *Renou's Disp.* 483 A Pottenger.. where-unto a long start..is suffixed. **1828** Carr *Craven Gloss.*, *Start*, a handle, as 'beesom start'. **1862** C. C. Robinson *Dial. Leeds* 420 *Start*, the handle of a vessel. 'Pot-start'.

†**b.** The tail of a plough: = plough-start.

c **1440** *Promp. Parv.* 474/2 Stert, of a plowe (or plowstert), *stiua* [printed *stina*]. **1530** Palsgr. 276/1 Stert of a plow, *queue de la chareue.*

†**3.** The footstalk of a fruit. *Obs.*

c **1440** *Promp. Parv.* 474/2 Stert, of an appull or oþer frute, *pediculus.* *c* **1440** *Pallad. on Husb.* IV. 387 Or make a diche in long, and take a rynde As long as hit; in that the storte [*v.r.* stortes] doo Of pomgarnat. **1530** Palsgr. 276/1 Stert of frute, *queue de frvit.* **1600** Surflet *Country Farm* III. 1. 543 Choose the fairest sowre cherries..cutting off their starts at the halfe, and afterward boile them. **1672** Hoole *Comenius' Vis. World* xiv. 30 The Cherry hangeth by a long start [*pediolo*].

†**b.** The stalk of a plant. *Obs. rare.*

1523–34 Fitzherb. *Husb.* §20 Dernolde groweth vp streyght lyke an hye grasse, and hath longe sedes on eyther syde the sterte.

†**c.** The stem (of a candlestick). *Obs.*

1696 Patrick *Comm. Exod.* xxv. (1697) 502 Here is nothing said of the foot of it [*sc.* the candlestick]... Nor doth he mention the length of the start or trunk.

†**4.** An outgrowth, a projecting point or spur; *esp.* a point of a stag's horn. *Obs.*

Perhaps this may belong to start *sb.*[2]

1575 Turberv. *Faulconrie* 283 The second..shall serue to cawterise yᵉ nares without danger or hurt to yᵉ little stert yᵗ groweth vp in the midle of the nares. **1578** Lyte *Dodoens* I. lxiv. 93 The first Crowfoote..bringeth forth vpon each side of the leafe three or foure shorte startes or branches. **1623** Cockeram, I. *s.v. Pollard*, Beame is that whereon the starts of the head growes. **1633** Gerard *Part. Descr. Somerset* (1900) 222 Ingotts of copper..rudely cast having on yᵉ back side some 5 sterts or points, some fewer. **1658** Phillips, *Torch-Royal*,..the next start in a Stag's head growing above the Royal. **1721** Bailey, *Brow-Antler*, the first Start that grows on the head of a Stag.

5. *Mech.* **a.** The innermost segment of the bucket of a water-wheel.

1547 *Rec. Elgin* (New Spalding Club 1903) I. 90 He cuttit thwa startis to ane mylln quhyll. **1611** Cotgr., *Les rayeres d'un moulin à eau*, the armes, or starts of the wheele of a water-mill. **1797** *Encycl. Brit.* (ed. 3) XVIII. 904/2 The bucket consists of a start AB, an arm BC, and a wrest CD, concentric with the rim. **1825** J. Nicholson *Oper. Mech.* 75 The partitions, which determine the form of the buckets, consist of three different planes or boards... We have heard them called the start or shoulder, the arm, and the wrest. **1829** *Nat. Philos.* I. *Mech.* (U.K.S.) I. v. 20 This bucket is formed of three planes; AB is in the direction of the radius of the wheel, and is called the start, or shoulder.

b. The shaft or lever of a horse-mill.

1771 *Gentl. Mag.* XLI. 57 The upper end or spindle of the shaft..with a square tenon fixes into a mortice in the start or leaver..very securely by a crank of iron which is screwed upon this start. **1812** Sir J. Sinclair *Syst. Husb. Scot.* I. 75 A piece of wood was fixed to the beam, or what is commonly called the start of the mill, and the oxen were yoked to it by chains. **1812** Hodgson in Raine *Mem.* (1857) I. 101 The starts or shafts of the gin. **1883** Gresley *Gloss. Coal-mining* 238 *Start*, a lever for working a gin to which the horse is attached.

6. Comb. †**start-pan**, a pan with a handle; **start-post**, the arm carrying the float of a scoop-wheel used in draining; †**start-rope** (meaning obscure).

1459 *Paston Lett.* I. 489 Item, j. lytyll *stert panne of sylver. **1888** W. H. Wheeler *Drainage Fens & Low Lands* v. 73 The rim is cast with sockets, in which are fixed with pins, oak arms, or '*start posts'. To the start posts are bolted boards. **1356** in *Pipe Roll 32 Edw. III* m. 34/1 Reddit compotum..de x. *stertropes, xlij vptieghes, xliij bowlynes [etc.]. *Ibid.* m. 34/2, j copula de baksteys, i sterterope.

start (stɑːt), *sb.*[2] Forms: ? 3, 4–6 **stert(e,** 5 **stertte, stirt,** 6 **styrt,** 5–6 **styrte, starte,** 6 **startte,** 6– **start.** [f. start *v.*]

1. a. A short space of time, a moment. Often used adverbially. *Obs.*

[*a* **1225**: see *start-while* in 12.] *a* **1300** *Cursor M.* 14298 Iesus beheild þan hir a stert, And had gret reuthnes in his hert. *c* **1375** *Sc. Troy-bk.* (Horstm.) I. 64 All wrath ande angry ine hys hert Stude studeande a litill stert. **14..** *Erthe upon Erthe* (1911) 24 Man, amende þe betyme, þi lyfe ys but a starte. *c* **1440** *Promp. Parv.* 476/1 Styrt, or lytyl whyle, *momentum.* *c* **1450** *St. Cuthbert* (Surtees) 894 In þat place duelt cuthbert With religiouse men a stert. *c* **1450** Holland *Howlat* 500 Was nane so stur in the steid micht stand him a start. *c* **1470** *Rauf Coilȝear* 892 This wickit warld is bot ane start. **1530** Palsgr. 854/1 A preaty start a go, *une petite espace de temps.* *a* **1552** Leland *Itin.* I. 119 An old manor place, wher in tymes paste sum of the Moulbrays lay for a starte. **1620** E. Blount *Ep. Ded.* in *Shelton's Quixote* II, His study being to sweeten those short starts of your retirement from publique affaires.

†**b.** A (short or long) distance. *Obs.*

a **1552** Leland *Itin.* III. 31 First I markid a litle start above the haven mouth on the west side of it, a creeke caullid Stoken Teigne Hed. *a* **1553** Udall *Royster D.* IV. v. (Arb.) 67 Indeede he dwelleth hence a good stert I confesse. **1580** Lyly *Euphues Eng.* To Gentl. Rdrs. (Arb.) 223 Secondly, being a great start from Athens to England, he thought to staye for the aduantage of a Leape yeare.

2. a. A sudden and transient effort of movement; in early use, †a leap, a rush. †***at a start***: with a bound, in an instant.

c **1386** Chaucer *Knt.'s T.* 847 This duc his courser with his spores smoot And at a stert he was bitwix hem two. *c* **1412** Hoccleve *De Reg. Princ.* 1109 And at a stirt, withouten tarying, Vn-to his cofre he dressith hym in hye. *c* **1440** *Generydes* 6699 Vnto hir chaunber sone he made a stert, And curtesly of hir his leve he toke. *c* **1440** *Promp. Parv.* 476/1 Styrte, or skyppe, *saltus. Ibid.* Styrte, of sodeyne mevynge, *assultus.* **1530** Palsgr. 276/2 Styrt a lepe, *course.* **1664** Power *Exp. Philos.* I. 10 A Wood-Louse..has a swift motion, and runs by starts or stages. **1845** Darwin *Voy. Nat.* i. (1852) 16 The animals move with the narrow apex forwards by the aid of their vibratory ciliae, and generally by rapid starts.

b. Sc. ***start and owerloup***: the leaping of cattle over a fence into an adjoining pasture.

1707 Fountainhall *Decis.* (1761) II. 408 If they [cattle], in their transient passage, do any skaith by start and o'erloup. **1827** Scott *Two Drovers* ii, The cattle..derived their subsistence..sometimes by the tempting opportunity of a start and owerloup, or invasion of the neighbouring pasture.

†**c.** A sudden journey; a sudden flight, invasion, etc. ***to take the start***: to decamp, run away. *Obs.*

'The Start', applied by historians to the flight from Perth of Charles II in 1650, is derived from quot. 1650, where however the use of the word is not in any way special.

1593 Shaks. *2 Hen. VI*, IV. viii. 45 Wer't not a shame, that ..The fearfull French..Should make a start ore-seas, and vanquish you? **1596** —— *Merch. V.* II. ii. 6 The fiend.. tempts me, saying to me, Iobbe,..vse your legs, take the start, run awaie. **1650** R. Baillie *Lett. & Jrnls.* (Bannatyne Club) III. 117 The King..did willinglie returne, exceedinglie confounded and dejected for that ill-advysed start. *a* **1674** Clarendon *Hist. Reb.* XIII. §48 It was indeed a very empty and unprepared design,..and might well have ruined the King, and was afterwards called the Start. **1804** M. Laing *Hist. Scot.* III. 437 This incident was termed the Start. **1894** Gardiner *Commw. & Protectorate* I. 376 Such was Charles's escapade, to which Scottish writers give the name of 'The Start'.

d. A sudden acceleration of progress or growth.

1817 Malthus *Popul.* I. 365 The population of Norway.. has made a start within the last ten or fifteen years. **1877** G.

F. Chambers *Astron.* (ed. 3) 37 Of late years the study of the sun has taken a remarkable start.

3. a. A sudden involuntary movement of the body, occasioned by surprise, terror, joy or grief, or the recollection of something forgotten. Phrase, ***to give a start.***

c **1374** Chaucer *Troylus* v. 254 And ther-with-al his body sholde sterte, and wiþ þe stert al sodeynlych a-wake. **1605** Shaks. *Macb.* iii. iv. 63 O, these flawes and starts.. would well become A womans story. **1700** Dryden *Pal. & Arc.* i. 555 The fright awaken'd Arcite with a start. **1750** Johnson *Rambler* No. 109 ⁋2, I imagine the start of attention awakened. **1809** Malkin *Gil Blas* x. vi. (Rtldg.) 351 He assumed the start of a man who all at once hits upon a circumstance which had hitherto escaped his recollection. **1825** Scott *Betrothed* Introd., In the general start and exclamation which followed this annunciation, Mr. Oldbuck dropped his snuff-box. **1863** Geo. Eliot *Romola* ii. xxiv, He gave a start of astonishment, and stood still. **1897** A. E. Houghton *Gilbert Murray* xix. 291 His eyes wandered to the ring. What a start he gave! **1902** R. Bagot *Donna Diana* xvi. 196 One or two old men were dozing upon their chairs, waking up every now and then with a start.

with adv. **1840** Browning *Sordello* iii. 638 Thus do I interpret the significance Of the bard's start aside and look askance.

b. ***to give*** (a person) ***a start***: to startle.

1816 Scott *Old Mort.* xxxix, What for did ye come creepin' to your ain house as if ye had been an unco body, to gie poor auld Ailie sic a start?

4. a. A starting into activity; a sudden and transient effort or display of energy.

1605 Shaks. *Lear* i. i. 304 Such vnconstant starts are we like to have from him, as this of Kents banishment. **1847** Tennyson *Princess* i. 53 A gentleman of broken means.. but given to starts and bursts Of revel. **1849** Macaulay *Hist. Eng.* ii. I. 205 He continued to the very last to show, by occasional starts and struggles, his impatience of the French yoke.

b. ***by starts***, † ***at starts***, later chiefly † ***by starts and fits***, now ***by fits and starts*** (see fit *sb.*[2] 4 c): intermittently, not continuously or with sustained effort.

The earliest examples may be referred to sense 1.

1421–2 Hoccleve *Dialog* 505 By stirtes when þat a fressh lust me takith, Wole I me bisye now and now a lyte. **1515** Barclay *Eglog* ii. (1570) B ij, To hir mayst thou come but onely nowe and then, By stealth and startes as priuily as thou can. **1530** Palsgr. 858/1 At startes, *par foys*. **1557** P. Hoby in *Burgon's Life Gresham* (1839) I. 225 But you come so by sterts, as to-night you are here, and tomorrowe you are gone. **1586** Hooker *Hist. Irel.* in *Holinshed* II. 83/1 They [*sc.* the Irish].. performed by starts (as their manner is) the dutie of good subiects. **1603** Holland *Plutarch's Mor.* 51 This little Treatise.. being gathered and compiled by starts, as my leysure would serve. **1621** T. Williamson tr. *Goulart's Wise Vieillard* A 2 b, I took vp my Pen againe, and at starts and tymes finished it. **1630** Rutherford *Lett.* (1862) I. 53 So we at starts do assent to the sweet and precious promises. **1640** Wilkins *New Planet* viii. (1707) 223 The Motion of the Earth is always equal and like it self; not by starts and fits. **1681** Dryden *Abs. & Achit.* i. 548 Was Every thing by starts, and Nothing long. **1728** Earl of Ailesbury *Mem.* (1890) 261 But I knew he had by starts great notions of generosity. **1747** Collins *Ode Passions* 28 'Twas sad by fits, by starts 'twas wild. **1799** Ht. Lee *Canterb. Tales, Frenchm. Tale* (ed. 2) I. 239 The letters he daily received.. induced him, by starts, to betray [etc.]. **1817** Coleridge *Biogr. Lit.* II. xxii. 131 Let it likewise be shown how far the influence has acted; whether diffusively, or only by starts. **1841** Dickens *Barn. Rudge* lxvi, He.. had watched with little intermission for some weeks past, sleeping only in the day by starts and snatches.

†**c.** ***on the start***: ? suddenly, without warning.

1601 Shaks. *All's Well* iii. ii. 52, I haue felt so many quirkes of ioy and greefe, That the first face of neither on the start can woman me vntoo't. *a* **1637** B. Jonson *Sad Shepherd* iii. iv, My men shall hunt you too upon the start, And course you soundly.

d. A sudden fit of passion, grief, joy, madness, etc.; an outburst, sally, or flight of wit, humour, or fancy. Now *rare* or *Obs.*

1596 Shaks. *1 Hen. IV*, iii. ii. 125 Thou, that art like enough, through.. the start of spleene, To fight against me. *a* **1652** Brome *Queen & Concubine* i. iii. (1659) 7 This is one of his un-to-be-examin'd hastie Humours, one of his starts. **1682** Dryden *Duke of Guise* ii. i, I've heard you say, You'd arm against the League; why do you not? The thoughts of such as you, are starts divine. **1692** L'Estrange *Fables* ccixiii. 230 There are several Starts of Fancy, that Off-hand look well enough; but [etc.]. **1713** *Guardian* No. 103 ⁋6 We were well enough pleased with this Start of Thought. **1772** Miss Burney *Early Diary* (1889) I. 143 In defiance of the gloom his misfortunes have cast over him, some starts of his former, his native vivacity break out. **1790** Cowper *In Mem. J. Thornton* 41 Such was thy Charity; no sudden start, After long sleep of passion in the heart, But steadfast principle. **1802** H. Martin *Helen of Glenross* II. 134 Did you then know your sister liable to occasional starts of the infirmity that afterwards became rooted and declared incurable? **1816** L. Hunt *Rimini* iv. 131 A passionate start Of tears and kindness. **1823** J. Simpson *Ricardo the Outlaw* II. 29 It was not a start of momentary passion, but an oath calmly, and deliberately taken.

e. A sudden broken utterance or burst of sound.

1601 Shaks. *Twel. N.* ii. ii. 22 Me thought her eyes had lost her tongue, For she did speake in starts distractedly. **1816** L. Hunt *Rimini* i. 103 Another start of trumpets, with reply. **1878** Gilder *Poet & Master* 57 Where he might listen to the starts and thrills Of birds that sang and rustled in the trees.

5. a. A beginning to move; a setting out on a journey or a race; the beginning of a career, of a course of action, a series of events, etc.

false start: in Racing, a wrong start, necessitating return to the starting-point; hence *gen.* an unsuccessful attempt to begin something (e.g. a speech, a song, a business).

1566 Gresham in Burgon *Life* (1839) II. 109 Beinge within xiiii mile of my howse of Rinxall, (whereas I make all my provision for my timber for the Burse,) I was so bolde [as] to make a starte to vewe the same. *c* **1586** C'tess Pembroke *Ps.* lxxxix. x, While circling time, still ending and beginning, Shall runne the race where stopp nor start appeares. **1693** Prideaux *Lett.* (Camden) 165 We have a young nobleman of our countey that now makes his first start in London. **1811** *Sporting Mag.* XXXVIII. 109 A great number of genteel folks attended the start. **1834** Marryat *P. Simple* xxi, The new moon's quartered in with foul weather; if it holds, prepare for a start. **1845** Ford *Handbk. Spain* i. 63 There is nothing in life like making a good start. **1850** Smedley *Frank Fairlegh* xxxi. 260 Pilkington.. was partly coaxed, partly coerced into attempting the only song he knew,.. in which performance, after making four false starts,.. he contrived.. to get as far as the words [etc.]. **1856** 'Stonehenge' *Brit. Rural Sports* 370 If any jockey is evidently and wilfully the cause of a false start, the starter reports the same to the stewards, who have power to fine him. **1876** Mozley *Univ. Serm.* iv. (1877) 87 In the eyes of others too, his goodness would appear to have taken a fresh start. **1879** B. Taylor *Ger. Lit.* 167 We found ourselves at the start in a rough land of mountains. **1911** G. P. Gooch *Hist. Our Time* x. 234 Women have voted in County Council elections from the start.

b. Phr. ***from start to finish.*** Also ***start-to-stop***, used (usu. *attrib.*) with reference to train journeys or their schedules.

1868 *Field* 4 July 14/3 A slashing race was rowed from start to finish between the two former [boats]. **1894** *Illustr. Lond. News* Christmas No. 22/3 The whole thing was unusual, from start to finish. **1896** *Spectator* 25 Apr. 580 The plot interest.. is sustained from start to finish. **1899** *Railway Mag.* IV. 375/1 They comprise one of the best start-to-stop runs I have ever had on a British line. **1931** *Times Educ. Suppl.* 19 Sept. (Home & Classroom Section) p. ii/2 (*caption*) The Great Western Railway Company regained this week the record for the fastest start-to-stop journey in the world. **1936** *Discovery* Nov. 356/1 Two or three runs booked, start-to-stop, at over 80 miles an hour. **1968** O. S. Nock *Railway Enthusiast's Encycl.* 279 The run of the 'Silver Jubilee' from King's Cross to Darlington is also tabulated; and finally that of the 'Coronation', introduced in 1937, with the fastest start-to-stop schedule ever tabled with steam in Great Britain.

†**c.** ***to strain*** or ***draw on the start***: of hounds, to strain on the leash. *Obs.*

1599 Shaks. *Hen. V*, iii. i. 32, I see you stand like Greyhounds in the slips, Straying [*Rowe* straining] vpon the Start. **1622** Drayton *Poly-olb.* xxiii. 338 And whilst the eager dogs vpon the Start doe draw, Shee riseth from her seat.

d. An act of setting in motion; an impulse to movement; a signal for starting in a race, etc.

1602 Shaks. *Ham.* iv. vii. 194 How much I had to doe to calme his rage? Now feare I this will giue it start againe. *c* **1612** in *Hore's Hist. Newmarket* (1885) I. 331 Lastlie, for giving of the starte, either Mr. Sheriffes for the time being, or whom Mr. Maior will appointe. **1891** N. Gould *Double Event* xvi. 123 The six starters were now at the post, and at the second attempt Mr. Watson let the flag go to one of his best starts. **1892** *Photogr. Ann.* II. 273 If plates are slightly larger than ordinary, they may be slow in moving, and it might be necessary to tap the camera to effect the start. **1897** *Encycl. Sport* I. 65/1 [In the Tug-of-War] The start shall be by word of mouth. **1904** E. H. Coleridge *Life Ld. Coleridge* II. 107 If.. Keble's sermon on 'National Apostacy'.. was the start or set-off of the Catholic Revival.

e. An opportunity or an assistance given for starting or entering on a career or course of action. Often ***a start in life.***

1849 Ht. Martineau *Hist. Peace* iv. x. (1877) III. 75 All were to have a fresh start—to be allowed the free use of their best powers. **1871** Freeman *Norm. Conq.* (1876) IV. xviii. 171 The Norman Conquest may very well have given the native element a fresh start. **1888** Bryce *Amer. Commw.* lviii. II. 405 Nobody can get an early and easy start on the strength of his name and connections. **1902** Eliz. Banks *Newsp. Girl* xxviii. 310 Then, as I was not to be turned back, he took me on and gave me my start—a better start.. than falls to the lot of many girls who begin the life journalistic. **1907** *Verney Mem.* I. 95 He was given a fresh start by his long-suffering father. **1908** *Times* 20 July 19/4 It does not affect the special funds.. for helping towards the education or start in life of clergy children.

f. The starting-point (of a journey).

1881 in *J. Hatton's New Ceylon* vi. 166 From the morning's start, the rapids, we only covered six miles.

g. *Sport.* By synedoche, a contest, race, or game. Chiefly *N. Amer.*

1944 *Sun* (Baltimore) 23 Feb. 12/3 Davis is a welter-weight... Davis isn't that good. At least he never has been in most of his previous starts. **1949** *Richmond* (Va.) *Times-Despatch* 10 Oct. 13/2 The Rebels, in gaining their third win in four league starts.. won it as convincingly as the score would indicate. **1966** *Telegraph* (Brisbane) 22 Jan. 5/2 He [*sc.* a horse] started racing in November, and in five starts has tallied a win, second, and a third. **1970** *Globe & Mail* (Toronto) 25 Sept. 32/3 Winless in 14 previous starts this season, Miss Ella Cinders had little trouble with Sandy Hawley up last Saturday as she galloped to a 12-length win. **1970** *Washington Post* 30 Sept. D1/7 The hapless, helpless Nats.. couldn't hold off the East Division champions, who have captured nine consecutive starts.

h. The act of beginning to build a house. Also ***housing start.***

1946 *Sun* (Baltimore) 20 Aug. 8/2 The Wyatt office claims about 406,000 'starts' of dwelling units in the first five months of the year. **1955** *Times* 30 May 11/1 New housing 'starts' rose in April but by less than they usually do over March. **1966** *New Statesman* 25 Nov. 769/2 What is worrying is that the starts are falling in the private sector and, as a house takes an average of about a year to build, the effects will be projected into next year's figures. **1976** *National Observer* (U.S.) 22 May 8/3 Around 28 to 29 per cent of all single-family housing starts.

i. Phr. ***for a start***: to begin with. *colloq.* Cf. starter 3.

1951 E. Paul *Springtime in Paris* iii. 56, I.. found Montherlant's *Les Célibataires*... 'That's a good one for a start.' **1971** *Radio Times* 21 Aug. 47/3 What makes Raven unusual? *For a start* he's 46, and.. he was a ballet dancer, a lieutenant of infantry, a classical actor and a television producer. **1978** L. Thomas *Ormerod's Landing* iii. 48 Everybody else knows... The submarine crew know for a start.

6. a. Advantage gained by starting first in a race or on a journey; in wider sense, position in advance of competitors whether obtained at the beginning or in the course of a race, etc. Hence *gen.* priority or position in advance of others in any competitive undertaking. Chiefly in ***to get, have,*** †***take the start*** (*of* a competitor); also with words indicating the amount in time or distance of the advantage, as in ***ten minutes start, ten yards start.***

1580 Lyly *Euphues* (Arb.) 418 Those, who hauing gotten the starte in a race, thinke none to be neere their heeles. **1598** Shaks. *Merry W.* v. v. 171 You have the start of me. **1601** —— *Jul. C.* i. ii. 130 It doth amaze me, A man of such a feeble temper should So get the start of the Maiesticke world. **1608** D. T[uvill] *Ess. Pol. & Mor.* 45 b, As they haue the start of all men in the one: so loue they not to bee out-stript by any in the other. **1609** Holland *Amm. Marcell.* xv. v. 39 But for all the running hast we made, a certaine wandering and flying fame had gotten the start of us. **1614** Raleigh *Hist. World* i. viii. §2. 131 Hauing withall the start of 130 yeares, to raise themselues without controlement. **1665** Bunyan *Holy Citie* (1669) 98 The Twelve will have the start of him; for they both had the Spirit as he, and more then he. **1682** Ken *Serm.* Wks. (1838) 127 We were all travelling the same way, as pilgrims towards our heavenly country, she has only got the start of us, is gone before, and is happy first. **1720** De Foe *Capt. Singleton* vi. (1840) 108 Having.. about three hundred yards the start of the lion. **1726** Swift *Gulliver* ii. i, Our men had the start of him half a league. **1732** Kames *Decis. Crt. Sess. 1730–52* (1799) 11 Several of these creditors, taking the start, laid arrestments in the hands of the accepters of these bills. **1733** W. Ellis *Chiltern & Vale Farm.* 278 Twitch-grass and other Weeds.. got the start of the St. Foyn and kill'd it. **1746** Francis tr. *Hor., Sat.* ii. vi. 50 Be nimble to perform your part, Lest any rival get the start. **1809** Malkin *Gil Blas* x. vi. (Rtldg.) 351, I remained motionless for some seconds, which gave him time to get the start of me. **1812** Southey *Lett.* (1856) II. 309, I have got start enough with Ballantyne to lay the Debates aside, and take a spell at Abella's documents. **1826** Lamb *Pop. Fallacies* xiv, It is flattering to get the start of a lazy world. **1841** Thackeray *Gt. Hoggarty Diamond* iv, I did not go to the office till half an hour after opening time... I was not sorry to let Hoskins have the start of me, and tell the chaps what had taken place. **1861** K. H. Digby *Chapel of St. John* (1863) 169 She never suffered her imagination to get the start of her judgment. **1885** 'Mrs. Alexander' *At Bay* v, The hopelessness of the search in the face of nearly twenty-four hours' start. **1897** Mary Kingsley *W. Africa* 258 Ngouta and the Ajumba used to sit down.. and I also, for a few minutes,.. and then I would go on alone, thus getting a good start.

¶**b.** In early use sometimes loosely: Superiority.

1611 B. Jonson *Catiline* iii. ii, Here is a Lady, that hath got the start In piety, of vs all. *c* **1645** Howell *Lett.* (1650) I. v. xxvii. 164, I have bin shewn for Irish and Bascuence Imperfect rules couchd in an Accidence: But I find none of these can take the start Of Davies. *Ibid.* I. vi. xxxv. 224 Dr. Jorden hath got the start of any that ever wrote of this subject.

†**7.** A starting aside; a deviation or digression.

1534 Whitinton *Tullyes Offices* i. B 2, For all the laude of vertue standeth in effectuall exercyse, fro the whiche not withstandynge a sterte or pause maye be made [*a qua tamen saepe fit intermissio*]. **1576** Fleming tr. *Caius' Engl. Dogges* v. (1880) 37 A starte to outlandishe Dogges in this conclusion, not impertinent to the Authors purpose.

8. *Mining.* = leap *sb.*[1] 6.

1778 W. Pryce *Min. Cornub.* 106 The most considerable disorder which Lodes are liable to.. is what is termed a Start, a Leap. **1789** J. Williams *Min. Kingd.* I. 354 The horizontal start or joint which cuts off the vein as they go down in it, does not cut if off in the true horizontal line, but leans or declines a little some way. **1797** *Encycl. Brit.* (ed. 3) XII. 40/2 Sometimes a vein will suddenly disappear without giving any warning by becoming narrower or of worse quality; which by the miners is called a *start* or *leap*.

†**9.** *U.S.* The name of some game. *Obs.*

1788 J. Q. Adams *Diary* (1903) 91 Afterwards play'd a number of very amusing sports, such as start.

10. *Whaling.* (See quots.)

Cf. sense 1 b; but direct connexion seems very unlikely.

1836 *Uncle Philip's Convers. Whale Fishery* 48 When the fish rises within two hundred yards of [the boat, it].. is then said to 'come up within a start'. **1846** A. Young *Naut. Dict.* 146 The boats meanwhile separate.. in order that one at least may be within 'a start'—that is, about two hundred yards from the point of its rising.

11. *slang.* **a.** A prison, esp. Newgate.

1756 J. Cox *Narr. Thief-taker* 66 The Prisoner replied, that he was going to the Start for nimming a Cull in his Eye. **1796** *Grose's Dict. Vulgar T.* (ed. 3), *Start*, or the *Old Start*, Newgate. **1823** 'Jon Bee' *Dict. Turf* s.v., *The Start.* Newgate is thus termed, *par excellence.* But every felon-prison would be equally *a start.*

b. ***the Start***: a vagrants' name for London.

1851 Mayhew *Lond. Labour* I. 312 All the 'regular bang-up fakes' are manufactured in the 'Start' (metropolis). **1860** *Hotten's Slang Dict.* 227 'The *start*', London,—the great starting point for beggars and tramps. **1862** *Cornhill Mag.* Nov. 648, I will send a few thickuns to bring you and your tamtart up to Start.

c. A proceeding or incident that causes surprise; = GO *sb.*[1] 3.

1837 DICKENS *Pickw.* xxii, What with your mother-in-law a worrying me to go, and what with my looking for'ard to seein' some queer starts if I did, I put my name down for a ticket. **1853** —— *Bleak Ho.* xi, Being asked what he thinks of the proceedings, [Little Swills] characterises them (his strength lying in a slangular direction) as 'a rummy start'. **1857** A. MAYHEW *Paved with Gold* III. xiv, Here's a start! a reg'lar twicer! **1880** PAYN *Confid. Agent* I. 138 That's the rummest start I ever knew. **1905** VACHELL *Hill* vi. 136 Of all the queer starts I——.

12. Comb.: **start button**, a switch that is pressed in order to set a machine or process in action; † **start-hole**, the hole in which an animal takes shelter; = STARTING-HOLE; **start-line** = *starting-line* s.v. STARTING *vbl. sb.* 2b; chiefly *transf.* and *fig.*, esp. in *Mil.* use (see quot. 1961); **start-point** *rare* = *starting-point*; † **start-while** = sense 1.

1964 *Start button [see *control register* s.v. CONTROL *sb.* 5]. **1968** *Brit. Med. Bull.* XXIV. 190/1 When the start-button of the machine is pressed, it simply causes the programmed procedure to operate on the data, giving rise to an action which will depend entirely on the data and the procedure. **1977** D. MACKENZIE *Raven & Kamikaze* iii. 40 He.. plugged the cable into a wall-socket and thumbed the start button. **1624** HEYWOOD *Captives* I. iii. in Bullen *Old Plays* IV. 125 France shall not conteine them But I will finde theire *start-holes. **1945** E. WAUGH *Brideshead Revisited* 224, I would.. think at such and such a time.. I shall cross the *start-line and open my attack for better or worse... With Julia there were no phases, no start-line, no tactics at all. **1946** G. MILLAR *Horned Pigeon* ii. 32 Rommel's Afrika Korps were on the start line of their long advance. **1961** W. VAUGHAN-THOMAS *Anzio* v. 69 The concept of a start line —an essential part of infantry tactics—is simply a matter of applied common sense... Just as in a race in athletics all competitors must line up at a starting-point.. so, in the infinitely more exacting race of an infantry attack, the unit —be it battalion, brigade or division—needs some feature on the ground along which the troops can be lined for the take off. **1982** J. WAINWRIGHT *Anatomy of Riot* 15 In Army parlance he was going to be the field commander when the war left the start-line. **1876** RUSKIN *Fors Clav.* lxii. 59, I find myself.. without any *start-point for attempt to understand them. *a* **1225** *Ancr. R.* 336 Þe þeof o þe rode.. in one *sterthwule hefde of him milce.

† **start**, *sb.*[3] *Obs. rare.* Also stert. [Perh. a. Du. *staart*, tail, in allusion to the old accusation that Englishmen had tails. But cf. WFlemish *drilsteert*, *plaagstaert*, a bore, *vraagsteert* a prying person.] A supposed Dutch term of contempt for an Englishman.

1673 DRYDEN *Amboyna* I. i. 3 Hang 'em base English sterts. *Ibid.* v. i. (end) Then in full Romers, and with joyful Hearts We'l drink confusion to all English Starts.

START (stɑːt), *sb.*[4] orig. and chiefly *U.S.* [Acronym.] Strategic Arms Reduction Talks (superseding SALT *sb.*[2] in 1981) held esp. between the U.S. and the U.S.S.R.; also, the Strategic Arms Reduction Treaty signed by the United States and the Soviet Union in December 1987.

1981 *Washington Post* 23 June A2/4 Rostow suggested that the well-known acronym SALT, which stands for Strategic Arms Limitation Talks, now become START, for Strategic Arms Reduction Talks. **1984** S. TALBOTT *Deadly Gambits* xii. 235 By the time the National Security Council finally buckled down to START in the spring of 1982, Perle was advocating one ceiling of 4,000 ballistic-missile warheads [etc.]. **1986** *Ann. Reg. 1985* 373 Three groups were set up to discuss intermediate nuclear forces (INF), strategic nuclear forces (START) and space weapons. **1987** *New Scientist* 19 Nov. 48/1 If the US and USSR sign.. a strategic arms reduction treaty (START) then the superpowers will have to take the unprecedented step of reducing their armouries of nuclear weaponry.

start (stɑːt), *v.* Pa. t. and pa. pple. **started**. Forms: (? 1 *north.* pr. pple. **sturtende**), 3–6 **sterte**, 3 **-storte**, (3 3rd sing. pres. **start, stard**), 4–6 **styrt**, 4–7 **stirt(e**, (5 3rd sing. pres. **stirt**), 4–7 **sturt(e**, **stert, starte**, 6 *Sc.* **stairt**, 4– **start**. Pa. t. 3–5 **sturte, stirt(e**, 3 **storte**, 3–6 **sterte**, 4–5 **sturt**, 4–6 **stert**, 4–7 **start(e, styrte**, 6 **stertt, styrtt, steart**; 5 **stirted**, 6 **sterted**, 6– **started**. Pa. pple. 4 **stirt, styrt**, 4–6 **stert(e**, 5 **stirte**, 6–7 **start**; 6– **started**. [App. two formations representing different ablaut-grades of the Teut. root **stert-* (: *start-*: *sturt-*). The OE. *styrtan* (only once, in pres. ppl. *styrtende*, miswritten *stvrtende*) corresponds formally to (M)LG. *störten*, (M)Du. *storten*, WFris. *stoarte*, NFris. *stört*, OHG. *sturzen* (MHG., mod.G. *stürzen*), MSw. *styrta*, *störta*, (mod.Sw. *störta*, Da. *styrte*):—OTeut. **sturtjan*. The verb in continental Teut. has the senses: To overthrow, precipitate, overturn; to empty by overturning, to pour out; also *intr.* to rush, to fall headlong, to gush out. (The mod.Fris. forms are certainly from Du. and LG.; the word may possibly be native in Scandinavian, but the senses in Sw. and Da. are largely adopted from Ger.)

The ME. *sterte* (whence mod.Eng. *start*) is, so far as it is a southern form, explicable as the Kentish representative of OE. *styrtan*, whence in other ME. dialects *sturte*, *stirte*, etc. But the occurrence of *sterte* in early northern English, and of its normal phonetic descendants in mod.Sc. and northern dialects, points to the existence of a form (? OE. **steortian*, ? **stiertan*) corresponding to MHG. *sterzen* (also *starzen*) trans. and intr. to set up (or stand) stiffly, to move briskly.

Other derivatives of the root are START *sb.*[1] (f. **stert-*), OE. *steartlian* (f. **start-*) to stumble: see STARTLE *v.* No cognates outside Teut. are known.]

I. Intransitive uses.

† **1.** To leap, jump, caper; also, to leap or spring *upon* a horse, *into* water, etc. *Obs.*

a **1000** *Rit. Dunelm.* 57/27 *Exiliens claudus stetit* stvrtende se halta ʒistod. *c* **1240** *Cuckoo Song*, Bulluc sterteþ.

c **1250** *Owl & Night.* 379 He [*sc.* the hare] huphþ & start [*Cott.* stard] swiþe cove & sécheþ paþes to þe groue. *a* **1366** CHAUCER *Rom. Rose* 344 Him luste not to play ne sterte Ne for to dauncen, ne to synge. **1375** BARBOUR *Bruce* VIII. 471 In gret hy thair hors hint thai, And stert apon thame sturdely. *c* **1385** CHAUCER *L.G.W.* 697 And with that word nakyd with ful good herte Among the serpentis in the pit sche styrte. **1387** TREVISA *Higden* (Rolls) VI. 35 Þanne þe camel.. gan to lepe and [to] sterte. *c* **1440** *Gesta Rom.* xxx. 110 (Harl. MS.) Abowte the sydes of þe diche wer iiij frogges sterting. *c* **1440** *Promp. Parv.* 476/1 Styrtyn, or skyppyn, *salto*. **1470–85** MALORY *Arthur* XVI. xv. 684 Therfore starte vpon thy hors. **1480** *Robt. Devyll* 813 in Hazl. *E.P.P.* I. 250 So daunced and leapt [he,] and aboute so starte. *c* **1500** *Lancelot* 994 He, to qwham the presone hath ben smart, With glaid desir apone his cursour start. **1567** *Gude & Godlie B.* 109 Quhat gart ȝow montanis lyke rammis stert & stend?

2. a. To move with a bound or sudden violent impulse from a position of rest; to come suddenly *from*, *out of* a place of concealment. Also with *out*.

c **1290** *S. Eng. Leg.* 86/91 He sturte out of þis deope Roche. *a* **1300** *Cursor M.* 12527 A nedder stert vte of þe sand. *a* **1300** *Floris & Bl.* 457 (Camb. MS.) Into þe cupe he sterte aȝen, And wiþ þe flures he hudde him. *c* **1375** *Sc. Leg. Saints* viii. (Philip) 17 A fel dragone, lyk to be wod, come startand owt al sudanly. *c* **1386** CHAUCER *Knt.'s T.* 1826 Out of the ground a furie Infernal sterte. *c* **1386** —— *Merch. T.* 909 This Damyan thanne hath opened the wyket And In he stirte. *c* **1412** HOCCLEVE *De Reg. Princ.* 131 He sterte unto me, and seide, 'Slepest thou, man'? *c* **1440** *Promp. Parv.* 476/1 Styrtyn, or sodenly mevyn, *impeto*. **1470–85** MALORY *Arthur* I. xx. 66 There with he sterte vnto the kynges hors and mounted in to the sadel. **1483** CAXTON *Gold. Leg.* 83/1 Thenne Vago.. wente into the tabernacle of Judith and fonde her not and sterte out to the peple. **1568** GRAFTON *Chron.* II. 338 With those wordes he had thought to haue lept agayne to his horse, but he fayled of the Styrop, and the horse sterted awaye. **1591** SHAKS. *1 Hen. VI*, IV. vii. 12 Dizzie-ey'd Furie.. Suddenly made him from my side to start Into the clustring Battaile of the French. **1623** J. MEADE in Ellis *Orig. Lett.* Ser. I. III. 119 The King awakened with this noise, start out of his bed, and cryed 'Treason, Treason'. **1671** MILTON *P.R.* IV. 449 Out of the wood he starts in wonted shape. **1697** DRYDEN *Virg. Georg.* IV. 496 Starting at once from their green Seats, they rise; Fear in their Heart, Amazement in their Eyes. *a* **1700** EVELYN *Diary* 11 May 1652, At a place call'd the Procession Oake, two cut-throates started out. **1815** SCOTT *Guy M.* x, She had seen Meg Merrilies.. start suddenly out of a thicket. **1829** *Chapters Phys. Sci.* 22 If a horse that was standing still suddenly starts forward. **1837** CARLYLE *Fr. Rev.* II. III. iii, For one moment.. he starts aloft.. to sink then for evermore! **1859** TENNYSON *Enid* 1331 Who saw the chargers.. Start from their fallen lords, and wildly fly.

b. To spring *on*, *upon one's feet*.

c **1400** *Destr. Troy* 10977 And ho stithly in the stoure start vppon fote. *c* **1420** ? LYDG. *Assembly of Gods* 566 Than Pheb[e] styrt vppon her fete And seyd [etc.]. *a* **1605** MONTGOMERIE *Misc. Poems* xxxiii. 21 Vpon my feet incontinent I start. **1847** TENNYSON *Princess* I. 59 He started on his feet.

† **c.** To make a sudden attack (*upon*). *Obs.*

c **1440** *Ps. Penit.* (1894) 16 Lat never the fend.. Sterte upon me with no stelthe. *c* **1440** *Promp. Parv.* 476/1 Styrtyn, or brunton, or sodenly comyn a-ȝen a enmy,.. *insilio, irruo*.

d. To awake suddenly *from*, *out of*, †*out* (sleep, reverie).

c **1386** CHAUCER *Clerk's T.* 1004 She ferde, as she had stert out of a sleepe. *a* **1450** *Knt. de la Tour* 68 And for the fere that the Ermite hadde, he sterte and waked oute of his auisyon. *c* **1566** *Merie Tales of Skelton* in *S.'s Wks.* (1843) I. p. lxix, The preest, hearyng the bell tolle, starte oute of his slepe. **1581** A. HALL *Iliad* x. 176 He starteth out his sleepe, and vp to them he thus began. **1591** GREENE *Maiden's Dream* in *Shaks. Soc. Papers* (1845) II. 145 The people shouted such a screame, That I awooke, and start out of my dreame. *c* **1611** CHAPMAN *Iliad* xxiv. 612 This said, the king (affraid) Start from his sleepe. **1737** [S. BERINGTON] *G. de Lucca's Mem.* (1738) 51, I started out of my Reveries as if I had awak'd from a real Dream. **1770** M. BRUCE in J. Mackenzie *Life & Wks.* (1914) 173 Strait all the chatt'ring tribe obey; Start from their trance and wing away. **1837** CARLYLE *Fr. Rev.* I. v. iv, Let Paris court a little fever-sleep; .. or from time to time start awake, and look out, palpitating, in its nightcap. **1885** 'MRS. ALEXANDER' *At Bay* vii, 'Yes', he exclaimed, starting from his thoughts, 'I have heard, but.. not taken in the sense of what you have been saying.' **1906** E. A. ABBOTT *Silanus* iv. 41, The cock was still crowing when I started out of my dream.

e. To move suddenly from one's place, as to avoid a danger; hence *fig.* to flinch or recoil *from* something in alarm or repugnance. Chiefly with adv., *back* (†*on back*, *aback*), *aside*.

a **1300** *Cursor M.* 8901 Þe tre sco stert al gloppend fra. *c* **1450** *Mirk's Festial* 226 And anon þe fend was aferd, and starte on bakke. *c* **1489** CAXTON *Sonnes of Aymon* xiv. 328 He toke a staff, & caste it after Estorfawde but Estorfawd sterte from his place. **1508** DUNBAR *Tua Mariit Wemen* 234 Scho suld not stert for his straik a stray breid of erd. **1530** PALSGR. 733/2, I starte asyde, as one dothe that shrinketh with his bodye when he seeth a daunger towardes. ? *a* **1550** *Freiris Berwik* 568 in *Dunbar's Poems* 304 With that Freir Robert stert abak and saw [etc.]. **1657** BILLINGSLY *Brachy-Martyrol.* II. vii. 177 By God's grace, I will nothing start aside. **1679** DRYDEN *Œdipus* I. i. 5 Nature her self start back when thou wert born. **1698** CHILCOT *Evil Thoughts* iv. 96 Like a Man that accidentally treads upon an Adder, starts back immediately, and strives to make no more approaches to it. **1701** NORRIS *Ideal World* I. ii. 17 Even the men that talk at this rate shall presently start from it as from a bugbear or apparition. **1831** SCOTT *Cast. Dang.* xiv, The horse, too, upon which the lady rode, started back. **1861** MRS. H. WOOD *Shadow of Ashlydyat* I. ii, There ensued a proposal to knight him. He started from it with aversion. **1867** TROLLOPE *Chron. Barset* I. xiii. 113 [He] started back, appalled at the energy of the words used to him.

f. In various figurative uses: To come suddenly *into* a condition; to go *out of* (one's wits); to burst *into* (anger); to emerge suddenly *into* (life, activity, etc.).

c **1385** CHAUCER *L.G.W.* 660 And for dispeyr out of his wit he sterte. *c* **1400** *Destr. Troy* 5871 He, stithely astonyt, stert into yre. *a* **1600** KYD *Sp. Trag.* III. xii. A. 1948 Starting in a rage. **1784** COWPER *Task* VI. 199 When all creation started into birth. *Ibid.* 550 His horse.. Snorting, and starting into sudden rage. **1794** MRS. RADCLIFFE *Myst. Udolpho* xlvii, I have sometimes known her argue.. with acuteness, and then in a moment start off into madness. **1802** *Noble Wanderers* I. 51 When kindred minds meet.. they instantly start into amity, and become incorporated in affection. **1816** BYRON *Ch. Har.* III. lxxxvii, At intervals, some bird from out the brakes Starts into voice a moment, then is still. **1863** COWDEN CLARKE *Shaks. Char.* ix. 217 The characters start into light, life, and identity.

3. a. Of an inanimate thing: To issue suddenly and violently; to fly, flow, or be projected by a sudden impulse. Of tears: To burst *out* suddenly; to rise suddenly *to* the eyes.

c **1385** CHAUCER *L.G.W.* 1301 Therwith hise false terys out they sterte. *Ibid.* 851 The blod out of the wounde as brode sterte As watyr whan the condit brokyn is. *c* **1400** *Pilgr. Sowle* (Caxton 1483) III. viii. 55 They maden them for to hurtlen ageyn a pyler, so that.. hit semed as theyr brayne sturt oute. *a* **1425** tr. *Arderne's Treat. Fistula* etc. 77 In ȝettyng in þe liquore with þe clistery þe liquor alsone stirt out vpon þe handez of þe leche. **1508** DUNBAR *Tua Mariit Wemen* 339 Than with a stew stert out the stoppell of my hals. **1648** J. BEAUMONT *Psyche* VII. clxxix, She Seemd in that breast he suck'd alone to live: For thither leap'd her soul, and scarce could stop It self from sturting out with every drop. **1678** R. L'ESTRANGE *Seneca's Mor.* II. ix. (1696) 198 The Clawing of an Itch till the Blood starts. **1739** LABELYE *Short Acc. Piers Westm. Bridge* 46 Some Springs unluckily starting in their Foundation, which they.. could neither stop nor master. **1757** W. WILKIE *Epigoniad* v. 154 A flood of sorrow started to his eyes. **1812** BYRON *Ch. Har.* I. vi, 'Tis said, at times the sullen tear would start, But Pride congeal'd the drop within his ee. **1831** JAMES *Phil. Augustus* I. iii, Over one edge thereof poured a small but beautiful cascade, starting from mass to mass of volcanic rock. **1832** BREWSTER *Nat. Magic* ii. 35 The chip of wax.. had started into my eye when breaking the seal of a letter.

b. Of the eyes: To burst out, escape *from* their sockets. Chiefly in hyperbolical use, expressing the effect of horror or fury.

1526 WHYTFORD *Martiloge* 76 Of some theyr tongues rotted, & of some the eyes stert out of theyr hedes. **1602** SHAKS. *Ham.* I. v. 17, I could a Tale vnfold, whose lightest word Would.. Make thy two eyes like Starres, start from their Spheres. **1605** —— *Macb.* IV. i. 116 Why do you shew me this?—A fourth? Start eyes! **1828** *Ann. Reg.* 375/1 The eyes [of the murdered woman] were not started, nor did the tongue hang out. **1863** MRS. H. WOOD *Verner's Pride* xlvi, His eyes were starting.. and his hair rose up on end. **1894** HALL CAINE *Manxman* v. vii. 304 Philip's blood-shot eyes seemed to be starting from his head.

c. *start out*: to project; to become visible or conspicuous, burst into view.

1825 R. CHAMBERS *Tradit. Edin.* I. 236 The pin.. was formed of a small rod of iron, twisted or notched, which was placed perpendicularly, starting out a little from the door, and bore a small ring of the same metal. **1831** JAMES *Phil. Augustus* I. ii, The road.. now showed, now concealed, the abrupt mountain-peaks starting out from their thick vesture of wood. **1863** J. HUGHES *Pract. Photogr.* (1866) 21 If it [the image] start out at once, directly the developer has flowed over the plate, the exposure has been too long.

d. Of a plant: To spring up suddenly. *rare.*

1720 RAMSAY *Prosp. Plenty* 225 A' the beauties o' the year Which start wi' ease frae the obedient soil. **1820** SHELLEY *Sensit. Pl.* III. 62 And agarics and fungi.. Started like mist from the wet ground old.

e. In figurative uses: cf. 2f. Also with *forth* (*arch.* and *poet.*): cf. sense 4b.

1303 R. BRUNNE *Handl. Synne* 425 Dremys.. been but as glasyng glemys þat yn þe þouȝt stertys & lepys. *c* **1480** HENRYSON *Test. Cresseid* 538 Quhen Cresseid vnderstude that it was he, Stiffer than steill thair stert ane bitter stound. **1683** DRYDEN *Dk. Guise* I. i. 5 My Blood stands still. My Spirits start an end for Guise's Fate. **1764** GOLDSM. *Trav.* 389 Fear, pity, justice, indignation start. **1817** KEATS *I stood tip-toe* 26, I was light-hearted, And many pleasures to my vision started. **1833** NEWMAN *Arians* v. ii. (1876) 374 Theological subtleties were for ever starting into existence among the Greek Christians. **1842** LOUDON *Suburban Hort.* 447 When they are wanted to start into fruit, expected to be matured by June 1, we begin by [etc.]. **1916** JOYCE *Portrait of Artist* ii. 86 All day the stream of gloomy tenderness within him had started forth and returned upon itself in dark courses and eddies. *Ibid.* iv. 171 He seemed.. to see the amount of his purchase start forth immediately in heaven.. as a frail column of incense. **1939** C. S. LEWIS in M. Black *Importance of Lang.* (1962) 37 A new metaphor simply starts forth, under the pressure of composition or argument.

† **f.** Of a commodity: To rise suddenly in price.

a **1661** FULLER *Worthies, Essex* (1662) 318 No commodity starteth so soon and sinketh so suddainly in the price. **1767** T. HUTCHINSON *Hist. Mass.* (1795) II. ii. 174 The extravagant price to which provisions had started.

†**4. a.** To go or come swiftly or hastily; to rush, hasten. In ME. verse occas. = to go. *Obs.*

a **1300** *Cursor M.* 8629 Vntil hir fere sco stert [*Gött.* stirt] in hij. *c* **1350** *Will. Palerne* 3600 He dede þen his stef stede stert a god spede. *c* **1374** CHAUCER *Troylus* II. 1094 This Pandarus tok þe lettre and þat by tyme A morwe and to his Neces paleys sterte. **1393** LANGL. *P. Pl.* C. xx. 297 Þre þynges þer beoþ þat doþ a man to sterte Out of his owene hous. *a* **1400** *Minor Poems fr. Vernon MS.* xlix. 39 Ofte to churche loke þow sterte. ? *a* **1400** *Festivals of Ch.* 124 in *Leg. Rood* App. 214 To poure in prisoun þou schalt sterte. *c* **1410** *Master of Game* (MS. Digby 182) xxxiv, And whan she hath be wele ychased.. so þat.. she be abyte with houndes.. who so is nexte shulde sterte to geete her hoole fro hem. *c* **1440** *Gesta Rom.* 8 He stirte to þe bord, and tooke a faire gilt cowpe. *c* **1475** *Babees Bk.* 61 Stert nat Rudely; komme Inne an esy pace. **15..** *Adam Bel* 321 in Hazl. *E.P.P.* II. 152 Wyllyam sterte to an offycer of yᵉ towne, Hys axe out of hys hande he wronge. **1575** *Gammer Gurton* IV. ii. 26 When ich saw this, ich was wrothe, see now, And start betwene them twaine, see now. **1637** RUTHERFORD *Lett.* (1664) 198 O how joyfull would my soul be to hear you start to the gate, and contend for the crown.

b. with advs., as *away, forth, in, to.* In ME. sometimes with dative of reflexive pronoun. *Obs.*

1297 R. GLOUC. (Rolls) 4311 Þe romeyns sturte [*v.r.* stertte] to anon hor prince vor to aere. *a* **1300** *Cursor M.* 15782 Þai stert þam forth ilkan. *c* **1300** *Havelok* 873 Hauelok ..stirte forth to þe kok. *c* **1320** *Sir Tristr.* 2977 As ganhardin stert oway, His heued he brac þo, As he fleiȝe. **1382** WYCLIF *1 Kings* ii. 46 The kyng comaundide to Banaye,.. the which stert to [Vulg. *egressus*], smoot hym, and he is deed. *a* **1400** *St. Alexius* 410 (Vernon MS.) Eufemian sturte him forþ as tit. **1481** CAXTON *Reynard* xxx. (Arb.) 75 The man sterte awaye and was a ferde. **1518** *Star Chamber Cases* (Selden Soc.) II. 140 And then styrtt forth John powur Water Baker [etc.]..the whyche seyd to me [etc.]. *a* **1529** SKELTON *E. Rummyng* 412 Than sterte in mad Kyt, That had lyttle wyt. **1538** ELYOT *Dict.*, *Fugitiuarius*, startyng away, flyttyng. **1596** SHAKS. *1 Hen. IV*, I. iii. 216 You start away, And lend no eare vnto my purposes.

c. ***to start abroad, astray***: to desert one's place. *Obs.*

13.. *Gaw. & Gr. Knt.* 1716 He blenched aȝayn bilyue, & stifly start onstray. *c* **1400** *Destr. Troy* 6258 If any stert vpon stray, strike hym to dethe. *c* **1470** *Gol. & Gaw.* 19 Mony sterne our the streit stertis on stray. **1488** CAXTON *Chast. Goddes Chyldern* 18 Somtyme sharply he smyteth to kepe in his chyldern that they shold not sterte abrode fro the scole.

d. ***to start to*** (a weapon): to seize it hastily.

1340–70 *Alex. & Dind.* 127 Þanne [buskede] a bold kniht & to a bow stirte. *c* **1400** *Melayne* 331 And Rowland styrte þan to a brande And hastily hent it owte of a sarazene hande. **1567** *Sat. Poems Reform.* iii. 163 For the Quhilk cause vnto ane brand sho start, And slew hir self.

e. Of immaterial things: To depart, pass away. *Obs.*

c **1386** CHAUCER *Man of Law's T.* 237 The lyf shal rather out of my body sterte Than Makometes lawe out of myn herte. **1546** J. HEYWOOD *Prov.* I. iv. (1867) 9 Who hopeth in Gods helpe, his helpe can not starte. **1558** BULLEIN *Gov. Health* A v b, Apoploxia and Vertigo, will neuer fro the starte, Vntill the vital blode, be killed in the harte. *c* **1560** PULLAIN *Ps.* cxlix. in Farr *S.P. Eliz.* (1845) II. 495 The Lord's pleasure is in them that are his, Not willing to start; But all meanes do seke to succour the meke. **1577** KENDALL *Flowers of Epigr.* 29 b, Leude is the loue that doeth not last, but startyng, taketh ende.

5. a. To undergo a sudden involuntary movement of the body, resulting from surprise, fright, sudden pain, etc. Hence *occas.* to feel startled.

a **1529** SKELTON *Bouge of Court* 502 Thenne I, astonyed of that sodeyne fraye, Sterte all at ones. **1530** PALSGR. 735/1, I sterte, I styrre, as one dothe for feare. **1590** *Tarlton's News Purgatory* To Rdrs., So fareth it with mee, for neuer before beeing in print I start at the sight of the Presse. *a* **1592** T. WATSON *Poems* (Arb.) 201 Which hauing seene as one agast shee start. **1598** SHAKS. *Merry W.* V. v. 90 If he be chaste, the flame will.. turne him to no paine: but if he start, It is the flesh of a corrupted hart. **1613** —— *Hen. VIII*, III. ii. 113 Some strange Commotion Is in his braine: He bites his lip, and starts. **1695** BLACKMORE *Pr. Arth.* II. 456 He starts at every Noise. **1735** JOHNSON *Lobo's Abyssinia* Voy. ii. 13, I started, and ask'd what he wanted? he told me to Bleed me. **1738** SWIFT *Pol. Conversat.* 20 Hold up your Head, Girl; (*Miss starts*). **1742** BLAIR *Grave* 693 Then why, like ill-condition'd Children, Start we at transient Hardships? **1818** SCOTT *Br. Lamm.* xix, You are no fool to start at shadows. **1829** —— *Anne of G.* xxix, It is by giving fair names to foul actions, that those who would start at real vice are led to practise its lessons. **1865** TROLLOPE *Belton Est.* xiv. 162 Will Belton started so violently, and assumed on a sudden so manifest a look of anger, [etc.]. **1906** CHARL. MANSFIELD *Girl & Gods* xi, Margaret started guiltily as though detected in an indecency. **1908** R. BAGOT *A. Cuthbert* vii. 68 Jim started. 'How did you know my name?' he asked.

b. said of a horse. Also, ***to start aside***, to swerve suddenly from its course.

1594 SHAKS. *Rich. III*, III. iv. 87 Three times to-day my Foot-Cloth-Horse did stumble, And started, when he look'd vpon the Tower. **1638** JUNIUS *Paint. Ancients* 136 In the heat of the fight they [*sc.* the horses] should start aside, affrighted. **1690** R. MEEKE *Diary* 17 Nov. (1874) 31 As I rode home my horse starting at a stoop in the way, gave me a fall. **1726** SWIFT *Gulliver* I. iii, The horses.. were no longer shy, but would come up to my very feet without starting. **1847** LEVER *Knt. Gwynne* xviii, He [a horse] starts, or shies, or something of that sort—don't he? **1870** BRYANT *Iliad* v. 360 His fiery steeds Started aside with fright.

†**6.** To escape. Cf. ASTART *v. Obs.*

a **1300** *Cursor M.* 7168 Vte o þair handes son he stert. *c* **1386** CHAUCER *Knt.'s T.* 1592 (Camb. MS.) Þow þat I no wepene haue in þis place But out of prisoun am styrt [*v.rr.* astert(e, I-stert] by grace. *c* **1403** LYDG. *Temple of Glas* 584 Fro þe dep, I trow, I mai not stert. *c* **1430** *Pol. Rel. & L. Poems* (1903) 209 On doomysday þou schalt not starte. *a* **1542** WYATT *Poems, Go burning Sighs* 7 Take with the payn ..And eke the flame from which I cannot stert. **1622** J. TAYLOR (Water P.) *Water-Cormorant* E 2, And thence [*sc.* from the jail] he gets not, there he shall not start, Till the last drop of blood's wrong from his heart.

†**7.** To desert or revolt *from* (a leader, a party; to swerve *from* (a course, purpose, principle); to withdraw *from* (a promise, a treaty). Also with *aside, back. Obs.*

1542 LD. LISLE *Let.* in Tytler *Hist. Scot.* (1864) III. 5 *note*, He durst not move the matter as yet to none of them; for if he shuld, he is sure they wolde starte from them. **1556** OLDE *Antichrist* 199 b, He commaundeth us.. not to starte fro them [the scriptures] one ynche. **1570** J. PHILLIP *Frendly Larum* in Farr *S.P. Eliz.* (1845) II. 531 That from thy truth and testament No daunger cause us start. **1576** FLEMING *Panopl. Epist.* 114 Neither wil I yeald so farre to the inuasions of feare, as to revolt and start back from my professed humanitie. **1581** A. HALL *Iliad* IV. 67 That we abate the Troyan glorious pride, By which, and by their arrogance from stricken pact they start. **1597** BEARD *Theatre God's Judgem.* (1612) 501 Francis Pizarre.. interrupted all their agreements by starting from his promises, and rekindled the halfe quenched fire of warre by his owne ambition. **1639** FULLER *Holy War* II. xxv. 76 But here Baronius, who hitherto had leaned on Tyrius his authority, now starteth from it. **1652** NEDHAM tr. *Selden's Mare Cl.* title-p., Go on (great State) and make it known Thou never wilt forsake thine own, nor from thy purpose start. **1663** PATRICK *Pilgr.* xviii. (1687) 175 The greedy humour of the world, who catch at all that presents it self, though they start out of their way to get it. **1781** COWPER *Conversat.* 452 No —nature unsophisticate by man, Starts not aside from her Creator's plan.

8. Of a material thing: To break away from its place; to be displaced by pressure or shrinkage; to get loose. Chiefly in technical uses.

1526 *Pilgr. Perf.* (W. de W. 1531) 274 b, The hopes kepeth fast the bordes of the vessell, yᵗ they disseuer not, & holdeth in yᵉ endes that they start not. **1570** LEVINS *Manip.* 33/35 To starte, *dissilire.* **1631** B. JONSON *New Inn* II. vi, The best bow may start, And th' hand may vary. **1683** MOXON *Mech. Exerc., Printing* xxiv ¶8 Drawing and straining the Skin tighter, he drives in.. Nails.. to keep the Skin from starting as it Dries. **1748** *Anson's Voy.* III. ii. 317 A but-end or a plank might start, and we might go down immediately. **1758** BORLASE *Nat. Hist. Cornw.* 64 This ruddle.. made a very good red,.. and.. would not start, nor alter its colour. *a* **1779** COOK *3rd Voy.* III. xi. (1784) II. 219 About seven o'clock.. the anchor of the Resolution started, and she drove off the bank. **1793** SMEATON *Edystone L.* §318 The mortar in the joints had started. **1818** *Art Bookbinding* 12 The book must not be put to the fire to dry, as that would cause the foldings to start. **1869** SIR E. J. REED *Shipbuild.* i. 11 Just as the ship floated several rivets started again. **1888** JACOBI *Printers' Vocab.* 131 *Start*, leaves of books are said to 'start' when the sewing is defective, and the leaves are loose. **1894** HALL CAINE *Manxman* III. xi. 168 I've summered and wintered the man, haven't I? He's timber that doesn't start. **1912** *Westm. Gaz.* 17 Apr. 10/1 The force of the shock was so tremendous that the 'Titanic' started in every joint.

9. Of a beast of the chase: To leave its lair; to be 'started'. (Cf. sense 17.)

c **1400** *Master of Game* (MS. Digby 182) xxxiii, To se if þe deer þat is herbowrede wolde sterte and steele away or þe lymer meved hym. **1576** TURBERV. *Venerie* lix. 164 As soone as euer she [the hare] hearde the horne, she starte. **1714** TYLDESLEY *Diary* (1873) 172 Mopey seated us a hare wʰ beet us ffor 3 howʳˢ, but a fresh on started and savᵈ her life.

10. 'To set out from the barrier at a race' (J.). Also in figurative context.

to start fair: to start on equal terms in a race, etc.

1645 WALLER *Poems, To a Friend* 3 Faire course of Passion, where two Lovers start And run together, heart still yoakt in heart! **1697** DRYDEN *Virg. Georg.* III. 165 When from the Goal they start, The Youthful Charioteers with beating Heart, Rush to the Race. **1704** CIBBER *Careless Husb.* III. i. 24 Nay, Madam, let's start Fair. **1727** BOYER *Eng.-Fr. Dict.*, To start (or begin to run) *Partir.* **1730** CHENY *List Horse-Matches* 5 The following four Year olds started for a Prize of 800 Guineas. **1870** *Pall Mall Gaz.* 23 Sept. 9/1 Hendre Claiming Stakes... Four started... County Members' Plate... Three started.

fig. **1780** *Mirror* No. 82 The King of Prussia [as the sign of an inn] began to give place a little to two popular favourites, who started at the same time, I mean Prince Ferdinand, and the Marquis of Granby.

11. a. To set out, to begin a journey; to begin to move, to leave the point of departure in any kind of progression. Said of a person or animal; also of a vehicle, ship, etc. Also with *off*, (orig. *U.S.*) *out*, rarely *away*. Cf. sense 12 d.

1821 SCOTT *Kenilw.* xxiv, 'To-morrow, madam', he said to his charge, 'we will, with your leave, again start early'. **1827** —— *Surg. Dau.* i, The good-daughter of Peg Thomson started off with an activity worthy of her mother-in-law. **1837** CARLYLE *Fr. Rev.* I. I. iv, These, with torches.. start from Versailles on the second evening, with their leaden bier. **1843** DICKENS *Chr. Carol* ii. 60 New top couple starting off again, as soon as they got there. **1855** MACAULAY *Hist. Eng.* xx. IV. 413 In February 1693, near four hundred ships were ready to start. **1858** MᶜCOMBIE *Hist. Victoria* xv. 234 Immigrants who had not means to start for the diggings. **1860** TYNDALL *Glac.* I. iii. 23 Next morning I started with this man up the valley. **1885** *Law Rep., Weekly Notes* 146/1 The ship loaded the coals.. and.. started on her voyage to Bombay. **1896** BADEN-POWELL *Matabele Campaign* x, Ridley's column started to-day for the Shangani. **1898** FLOR. MONTGOMERY *Tony* 13 Mother! *do* just get in with me for a few minutes till the train starts. **1901** ALLDRIDGE *Sherbro* xxiii. 242 A pilot was provided for me.. and the next morning at 6.30 I started away. **1925** E. O'NEILL *Desire under Elms* in *Compl. Wks.* II. 170 We're free, old man.. an' we're startin' out for the gold fields of Californi—a! **1933** —— *Ah, Wilderness!* II. 71 He dared me to race him... So I said all right and we started out. We swam and swam and were pretty evenly matched. **1978** W. F. BUCKLEY *Stained Glass* xii. 117 There are escort vessels, and it is quite a muddle if every boat decides for itself when to start out.

b. To begin one's journey *in* or *from* a certain place.

1879 R. K. DOUGLAS *Confucianism* iii. 90 A mountaineer .. in order to reach the top of the peak, has to start from the foot. **1912** J. L. MYRES *Dawn Hist.* ix. 191 The grassland heart of Asia Minor.. is in fact as open as Hungary.. to intruders who started in Turkestan.

c. Of a motor vehicle or its engine: to begin to operate. Also with *up*.

1902 A. C. HARMSWORTH *Motors & Motor-Driving* ix. 165 A petrol engine will generally start most easily with all the cold-air inlets closed. **1904** J. F. GILL *How to build Petrol Motor* 57 When a speed of about four miles per hour has been obtained, the current may be switched on, after which, the motor should start. **1932** D. L. SAYERS *Have his Carcase* xii. 145 The Morgan wouldn't start, not for toffee... On their.. putting in a new one [*sc.* lead], the engine had started up at once. **1971** *Daily Tel.* 27 Oct. 13/5 The engine would start instantly from cold without using the choke control. **1973** L. COOPER *Tea on Sunday* iii. 44, I left early.. because of the bad weather. I was afraid my car might not start.

12. a. To begin a career, course of action, process, etc. Also of a process: To begin.

1798 WORDSW. *Peter Bell* I. 200 Who Peter was, let that be told, And start from the beginning. **1801** *Farmer's Mag.* Jan. 85 Wheat started at 48s. and 50s. per boll, and has now got up to 63s. **1818** SCOTT *Rob Roy* viii, The high tone with which the tune started, died away in a quaver of consternation. **1868** *Field* 4 July 9/2 Each bowler started with a maiden. **1874** L. STEPHEN *Hours in Library* (1892) I. iii. 102 A modern essayist starts where Addison or Johnson left off.

b. With reference to reasoning. ***to start from*** or ***with***: to assume as one's point of departure.

1870 NEWMAN *Gram. Assent* II. x. 408 They and I start from the same principles, and what is proof to me is a proof to them. **1871** R. H. HUTTON *Ess.* (1877) I. 51 The Darwinian theory starts from the assumption of organic types competent to reproduce themselves.

c. Of a trader, a trading firm or company: To begin one's career. More fully ***to start in business***.

1872 R. B. SMYTH *Min. & Min. Statist.* 59 The Majestic Company was formed in February, 1861, from the previous company, known as Sim and Company, who started in 1857. **1875** H. J. BYRON *Our Boys* I, When I first started in business I'd the finest stock in Lambeth. **1879** *Cassell's Techn. Educ.* IV. 62/2 He started in business on his own account.

d. With adverbs. ***to start in*** colloq. (orig. *U.S.*): to begin; also ***to start in on***; ***to start out***: to set oneself, begin *to do* something; also const. *prep.*; ***to start over*** (U.S.): to begin again.

1872 'MARK TWAIN' *Innoc. at Home* ii. (1882) 270 So when some roughs jumped the Catholic bone-yard and started in to stake out town lots in it, he went for 'em. **1885** *Lisbon* (Dakota) *Star* 2 Jan. 7/1 The United States commissioner for Dakota.. started in to give the world a comprehensive idea of the resources.. of the territory. **1892** 'MARK TWAIN' *Amer. Claimant* 138 He had started out on a high emprise. **1897** *Sat. Rev.* 19 June 597/1 If Mr. Clive Holland started out to write this story without knowing [etc.]. **1902** WISTER *Virginian* xxix, I was starting in to die when she found me. **1912** WODEHOUSE *Prince & Betty* iv. 53 Then we start in. **1924** F. SCOTT FITZGERALD *Let.* 27 Oct. (1964) 168 I'm tired of being the author of *This Side of Paradise* and I want to start over. **1925** J. BUCHAN *John Macnab* vii. 144 In this country, once you start in on politics you're fixed in a class and members of a hierarchy. **1929** D. H. LAWRENCE *Pansies* 20 Then I am willing to fight, I will roll my sleeves up And start in. **1951** M. MCLUHAN *Mech. Bride* (1967) 68/2 She started out as a Tillie the Toiler. **1957** O. NASH *You can't get there from Here* 84 Once they start in on ideas and ideals they'll end up spouting ideologies and isms. **1965** M. BRADBURY *Stepping Westward* ii. 112 Now go back to the beginning and start over. **1976** *National Observer* (U.S.) 26 June 8/6 If it doesn't work, throw the whole mess out and start over, adding a teaspoon of active dry yeast and a few drops of vinegar at the beginning. **1978** T. ALLBEURY *Lantern Network* vii. 87 Chaland had started in straight-away. 'Bonnier your group is far too big.'

e. ***to start with*** (advb. phr.): = 'to begin with'; at the beginning.

1866 MRS. OLIPHANT *Agnes* I. xxii. 280 Her mind.. was of a much higher order than his to start with.

f. To begin to go *to* (school). *U.S.*

1836 W. SEWALL *Diary* 10 Aug. (1930) 172/1 Henry and Catherine started to school. **1898** C. A. BATES *Clothing Bk.* No. 1279 That boy.. will have to start to school soon. **1931** *Amer. Speech* VII. 20 *Start*, begin to go. Used mainly in the one expression, start to school. 'I started to school when I was five.' (Widespread.)

g. ***to start (in) on***: to attack; to nag or bully. Cf. sense 12 d above. *colloq.*

1907 G. B. SHAW *Major Barbara* II. 214 When trade is bad .. and the employers az to sack arf their men, they generally start on me. **1953** K. TENNANT *Joyful Condemned* iii. 23 I'll give you five minutes, and then I'll start in on you. So hand over the two quid. **1967** J. MORRISON in *Coast to Coast 1965–6* 140 The minute I mentioned it she started on me. **1968** BETHELL & BURG tr. *Solzhenitsyn's Cancer Ward* I. xxi. 332 The critics may start in on you.

h. Colloq. phr. ***don't you start***, expressing exasperation at hearing sentiments (of praise, criticism, advice, etc.) repeated by another speaker.

1934 N. MARSH *Man lay Dead* x. 167 'You're a—a wonder,' finished Nigel seriously. 'Don't you start!' said Mrs North. **1956** P. SCOTT *Male Child* II. v. 157 'She ought to get out more.' He grinned. 'Now don't you start.' **1974**

'S. Woods' *Done to Death* 129 'She's a spinster.'.. 'Don't you start!' said Hugh explosively.

13. start up. a. To rise suddenly; to spring to an erect position (in ME. occas. †with dative of refl. pron.); also *fig.* to arise suddenly from inaction, bestir oneself.

c **1205** Lay 23951 Þær Bruttes wolden ouer water buȝen ȝif Arður up ne sturte [*c* **1275** storte] strecliche sone. *c* **1250** *Gen. & Ex.* 2931 And pharaon stirte up a-non, And for-bed ðis folc to gon. **1297** R. Glouc. (Rolls) 6581 Þis grete louerd sturte him vp Þo he oþer ne sey. *a* **1330** *Roland & V.* 816 When rouland herd Þat steuen He stirt him vp ful euen & fauȝt wiþ hert fre. *c* **1386** Chaucer *Pard. T.* 377 And vp they stirte, and dronken in this rage. *c* **1440** *Alphabet of Tales* 83 Þis cokk starte vpp with his fedurs on, & clappid samen hys wengis & krew. **1526** Tindale *Acts* xiv. 10 And he stert vppe, and walked. **1530** Palsgr. 735/1, I sterte up sodaynly out of my bedde. **1592** Shaks. *Rom. & Jul.* iii. iii. 100 She ..now fals on her bed, and then starts vp. **1603** Knolles *Hist. Turks* (1621) 48 Andronicus..in great rage start up and said. **1653** Dorothy Osborne *Lett.* (1888) 176, I, that had not said a word all night, started up at that, and desired they would say a little more on't, for I had not marked the beginning. **1667** Milton *P.L.* iv. 813 Up he starts Discoverd and surpriz'd. **1816** Scott *Old Mort.* xxxviii, 'The de'il, woman!' exclaimed Cuddie, starting up, 'trow ye that I am blind?' **1840** Thackeray *Shabby-genteel Story* iii, 'This is too bad!' said Mrs. G. starting up. **1849–50** Alison *Hist. Europe* lvii. IX. 31 Prussia..would start up the moment that a serious reverse befell their [Austria's] eagles. **1875** Jowett *Plato* (ed. 2) I. 9 Chaerephon..started up and ran to me, seizing my hand.

b. Of the hair: To stand suddenly on end.

1602 Shaks. *Ham.* iii. iv. 122 Your bedded haire..Start vp, and stand an end. **1660** F. Brooke tr. *Le Blanc's Trav.* 249 The hair of my head so started up, that it threw my cap on the ground.

c. To rise suddenly to power or importance; to become suddenly conspicuous.

1556 Olde *Antichrist* 51 Anon Boniface of Rome the thrid of that name steart up. **1592** Timme *Ten Eng. Lepers* B 3 b, There hath start up false Christes. **1603** Knolles *Hist. Turks* (1621) 22 Up start the Turks, a vagrant, fierce, and cruell people.

d. Of things: To come suddenly into being or notice, to spring up. Also *loosely*, to begin.

1596 Dalrymple tr. *Leslie's Hist. Scot.* I. 77 Litle an litle thair forces beginning to florishe weirs of new startis vpe. **1596** Bacon *Use Com. Law* (1635) 47 Since..these notable Statutes..there is start up a device called Perpetuity. **1651** Hobbes *Leviath.* iv. xlvii. 386 So did the Papacy start up on a Sudden out of the Ruines. **1673** Cave *Prim. Chr.* i. ii. 18 You are wont to object to us..that our Religion is novel, start up not many days ago. **1775** Earl Carlisle in Jesse *Selwyn & Contemp.* (1844) III. 132, I am surrounded by difficulties, and as fast as I get the better of one another starts up. **1780** *Mirror* No. 102 Half a dozen societies have started up this winter, in which female speakers exercise their powers of elocution. **1836** [Mrs. Traill] *Backw. Canada* 257 A village has started up where formerly a thick pinewood covered the ground. **1979** *Southern Star* (Eire) 29 Sept. 3/4 Mr. McCarthy also told Mr. Coleman that £160,000 had been allocated for further work on the Cork-Brandon road and the Viaduct aided by the EEC Regional Development Fund and would start up in two weeks after the meeting. **1981** E. North *Dames* viii. 138 The music started up and played..a tango.

†**e.** Of children: To grow up rapidly. *Obs.*

1650 Fuller *Pisgah* iv. vi. 103 From a child he starts up a youth, and becomes a stripling. **1753** Richardson *Grandison* (1754) II. viii. 51 Girls will start up, and look up, and parents cannot help it.

f. Of a hill: To rise abruptly from the ground.

1820 Scott *Monast.* ii, A beautiful green knoll, which started up suddenly in the very throat of a..narrow glen.

II. Transitive uses.

†**14.** To escape. (Cf. sense 6.) *Obs. rare.*

1450 *Knt. de la Tour* (1868) 113 Atte the dredfulle day he wolle axe acomptes where as there shalle none sterte to yelde ansuere. *c* **1460** *Pol. Rel. & L. Poems* (1903) 292 Lord, Þi iugement we may not sterte.

15. †**a.** To cause to start or flinch; to startle. *Obs.*

c **1440** *Ps. Penit.* (1894) 31 Ther was no scorn, spotul, ne speche, Despit, ne stroke, that him sterte. **1456** Sir G. Haye *Law Arms* (S.T.S.) 256 Quhen a man or beste is sudaynly stert, thair naturale inclinacioun gevis thame of thair complexioun to a brethe. **1597** J. King *On Jonas* (1618) 91 Do you tarry to be started with the shrillest trumpet that euer blew? **1601** Shaks. *All's Well* v. iii. 233 You boggle shrewdly, euery feather starts you. **1604** —— *Oth.* i. i. 101 And now..dost thou come To start my quiet. **1625** B. Jonson *Staple of N.* iii. iv, Stage-dir., He is started with Broker's comming back. **1706** Estcourt *Fair Example* iv. i. 43 'Twill heighten my Revenge, when she thinks I come to make fresh Offers of my Love, to start her with Neglect and Scorn. **1756** Mrs. Calderwood in *Coltness Collect.* (Maitl. Club) 225 What started me most was the bare plaister wall. **1822** Scott *Peveril* xxv, If my news have not frightened away Lance Outram too, whom they used to say nothing could start. **1871** R. Ellis *Catullus* lxv. 22 Soon as a mother's step starts her.

b. To awaken out of sleep.

1753 Miss Collier *Art Torment.* i. i. (1811) 33 She made such a noise as to start you suddenly out of your sleep. **1799** Campbell *Pleas. Hope* ii. 349 How can thy words from balmy slumber start Reposing Virtue, pillow'd on the heart!

†**16.** To ride (a horse) at full speed. *Obs.*

c **1470** Henry *Wallace* v. 251 Till him he stert the courser wondyr wicht, Drew out a suerd, so maid [hym] for to lycht.

17. a. *Hunting.* To force (an animal, esp. a hare) to leave its lair, form, or resting-place. †Also with *out.*

c **1384** Chaucer *H. Fame* 681 But as a blende man stert an hare. *c* **1410** *Master of Game* (MS. Digby 182) xxxiv, And whenne she [the hare] is founde and stirt, he shall blowe a moot and rechate. **1473** *Paston Lett.* (1897) III. 83 Raff Blaundrehasset wer a name to styrte an hare. I warrant ther shall come no suche name in owr bokys, ner in owr house; it myght per case styrt xx^ti harys at onys. **1519** Horman *Vulg.* 283 b, I haue nede of a feret, to let into this beery to styrt out the conies: that they may be take aboue ground. **1576** Turberv. *Venerie* xxxvii. 100 An Hare started and a Fox vnkennelled. **1595** *Locrine* v. iv. 31 What, is the tigre started from his caue? **1659** N. R. *Prov., Eng. Fr.* etc. 73 Little dogs start the hare, the great one gets her. **1749** Fielding *Tom Jones* vii. iii, The squire, however, sent after his sister the same holla which attends the departure of a hare, when she is first started before the hounds. **1769** E. Bancroft *Guiana* 177 They..when started, fly with a loud noise. **1817** Selwyn *Law Nisi Prius* (ed. 4) II. 833 If A. start a hare in the ground of B., and hunt and kill it there. **1850** R. G. Cumming *Hunter's Life S. Afr.* (ed. 2) I. 224 Shortly before outspanning we started three leopards that were consuming a duiker. **1883** *Century Mag.* Oct. 923/2 For a week or two at a time, the meadows may be worked over without starting a bird.

b. *transf.*

1593 Marlowe *Edw. II*, 1848 They shalbe started thence I doubt it not. **1595** Shaks. *John* v. ii. 167 Do but start An eccho with the clamor of thy drumme. **1603** Holland *Plutarch's Mor.* 100 If we be not altogether ignorant of our selves, and wilfully blinde,..we can not choose but start and finde out a flatterer. **1716** B. Church *Philip's War* (1865) 43 They had not March'd above a quarter of a Mile before they started Three of the Enemy. **1852** Mrs. Stowe *Uncle Tom's C.* xix, The dogs bayed and howled, and we rode and scampered, and finally we started him [*sc.* a hunted negro].

†**c.** *fig.*

a **1763** Shenstone *Elegies* xi. 58 We start false joys, and urge the devious race. **1781** Cowper *Retirement* 693 Learn'd philologists, who chase A panting syllable through time and space, Start it at home, and hunt it in the dark.

†**d.** *to start up* (fig.): to track to its hiding-place. Also, to discover suddenly. *Obs.*

1566 Drant *Horace, Sat.* i. v. C 4, To sterte vp in astrologie the casuals of men. *a* **1652** J. Smith *Sel. Disc.* viii. i. (1821) 378 The minds of men..are ever and anon roving after religion; and as they casually and fortuitously start up any models and ideas of it, they are presently prone to believe themselves to have found out this only pearl of price. **1674** *Essex Papers* (Camden) I. 203 Now that this is almost consented to..a Patent of Sr Thomas Armstrong's is started up to obstruct it. [Quot. 1674 may belong to 13 d.]

18. To propound (a question, an objection); to introduce (a subject of discussion). Also const. *forth* (*rare*).

1643 Sir T. Browne *Relig. Med.* ii. iii, For then reason, like a bad hound, spends upon a false sent, and forsakes the question first started. **1656** H. Phillips *Purch. Pattern* (1676) 13, I start this question. **1673** Hickeringill *Greg. Father Greyb.* 230 Methinks I hear the proverb started. **1678** Cudworth *Intell. Syst.* 231 This Paradox, was both late started amongst the Greeks, and quickly cried down by the Succession of their Philosophers. **1710** Prideaux *Orig. Tithes* ii. 112 From what I last said another objection lies very obvious to be started. **1719** De Foe *Crusoe* (1840) II. vi. 155 Will you give me liberty to start one difficulty here? **1786** Mme. D'Arblay *Diary* Aug., Having..explained herself, she finished the subject, and has never started it since. *a* **1817** Jane Austen *Northanger Abbey* (1818) II. xiii. 245 She took the first opportunity..to start forth her obligation of going away very soon. **1828** Scott *F.M. Perth* xxviii, He prepared to apply himself..to his food, without starting another topic. *a* **1853** Robertson *Serm.* Ser. iii. xiii. 160 Many difficulties arose; such for instance as the one here started. **1877** Freeman *Norm. Conq.* I. App. 604 The charter of 934 starts a point of quite another kind.

†**19.** *to start out*: to put forth (a projection) abruptly. *Obs.*

1662 J. Davies tr. *Mandelslo's Trav.* 260 It is somewhat strange, that at so great a distance from the Continent, the Sea should start out an Island about 7. Leagues in compass.

20. a. To discharge the contents of, empty (a vessel); to pour or shoot (liquids, coal, etc.) from one vessel into another.

a **1700** B. E. *Dict. Cant. Crew, Start,* (Drink) Brewers emptying several Barrels into a great Tub; and thence conveying it through a Leather-pipe down the Cellar into the Butts. **1729** Capt. W. Wriglesworth *MS. Log-bk. of the 'Lyell'* 27 Oct., Took in 15 Puncheons of Water and started them into the Empty Butts in the Hold. **1743** Bulkeley & Cummins *Voy. S. Seas* 88 The Captain told him not to start the Powder..without his Orders. **1799** *Hull Advertiser* 16 Mar. 4/2 Every exertion was..made to lighten the ship, by starting the water. **1820** Scoresby *Acc. Arctic Reg.* II. 399 Which fenk-back is sometimes provided with a clough..for 'starting' the fenks into a barge or lighter placed below. **1823** J. Badcock *Dom. Amusem.* 24 Charcoal might be started at once from its charring place to close vessels. *Ibid.* 102 The wine was anciently started into lead cisterns. **1826** *Art of Brewing* (ed. 2) 65 A stock of old beer can thus be increased expeditiously: start half of one full vat, when it is getting a little age, into another, and fill up both with new beer. **1830** Marryat *King's Own* xvi, The cocoa was in the tub,..but they started it all in the lee-scuppers. *c* **1850** *Rudim. Navig.* (Weale) 118 A small place..wherein the powder is started.

fig. **1879** L. Stephen *Hours in Libr.* Ser. iii. 273 When the cares of life begin to press, they start their cargo of classical lumber and fill the void with law or politics.

b. *Naut.* (See quot. 1846.)

1744 J. Philips *Jrnl. Exped. Anson* 152 At Daylight observing our Ship had started her Anchors, we lowered our Yards. **1846** A. Young *Naut. Dict.* 296 *Start an Anchor*, to make it lose its hold of the ground... *Start a tack*, or a sheet, to slack it off a little.

21. a. To cause (a material thing) to 'start' or break away from its place; to displace by pressure or strain. Of a ship. To suffer the starting or giving way of (a plank, etc.).

1676 Wiseman *Chirurg. Treat.* vii. iv. 485 Another having by accident of a Fall in wrastling started the end of the Clavicle from the Sternon. **1711** W. Sutherland *Ship-build. Assist.* 46 Which may be of dangerous consequence.. in starting the But. **1748** *Anson's Voy.* i. iii. (ed. 4) 33 The ship in rolling..started the butt ends of her planking. **1753** *Phil. Trans.* XLVIII. 91 A plank of this door was started, and beat in. **1839** Marryat *Phant. Ship* xii, She had started one of her planks, and filled. **1840** *Civil Engin. & Arch. Jrnl.* III. 137/2 The damage she sustained was trifling,..not a rivet was started.

b. *Mining.* To displace (a vein) horizontally: said of another vein intersecting it.

1758 Borlase *Nat. Hist. Cornwall* 157 Guessing then from their experience in like cases that the lode is heaved, or more properly speaking started.

22. a. To cause (a person, an animal, a vehicle) to start or set out in a race, on a journey; to cause to begin moving in any kind of progression. Also with *off.*

1725 *Bradley's Fam. Dict.* s.v. *Horse-racing*, Start him off roundly, and run him to the very Top of what he can do. **1850** Scoresby *Cheever's Whalem. Adv.* i. (1858) 7 Her unprecedented success started numbers on her track. **1865** Carlyle *Fredk. Gt.* xxi. vi. VI. 597 Draught-horses.. whom..you would see spring at the ropes..thirty of them to a gun, when started and gee-ho'd to. **1885** *Law Rep. 10 Prob. Div.* 100 The vessel was started again on her voyage with the machinery unaltered. **1890** Mrs. Kingscote *Tales of Sun* x. 125 This she gave to the brothers to eat on their way, and started them off to the woods.

fig. **1781** Cowper *Charity* 565 So self starts nothing but what tends apace Home to the goal where it began the race.

b. To enter (a horse) for a race.

1885 *Truth* 28 May 853/2 The Payne Stakes, for which Lord Hastings very wisely started Melton.

23. To cause to begin to act or operate. **a.** To cause or enable (a person) to start or enter on some course of action; to set up or establish in business.

1735 Dyche & Pardon *Dict.*, *Start*..in the Brewers Trade, 'tis to supply a Customer with a Cellar of Beer, Ale, &c. in order to keep, settle, and refine some Months before it be drawn, &c. **1757** Foote *Author* i. Wks. 1799 I. 138, I intend giving him the run of Jonathan's for three months to understand trade and the funds; and then I'll start him. **1854** *Poultry Chron.* I. 69 The plan for starting the cottager in business..may appear tardy in its results.

b. To set on foot, initiate, be the first to move in (a business); to set (a rumour) in circulation; †to originate, be the first to practise (an art).

1666 Pepys *Diary* 24 June, He started a discourse of a talk he hears about the town. **1699** Bentley *Phalaris* 237 Allowing then, that this Epigenes..started Tragedy before Thespis; still [etc.]. **1723** Waterland *2nd Vind. Christ's Divin.* 95 Before the Arian Controversy was started. **1777** Burke *Let. to E. Perry* Wks. 1842 II. 405 The fair part, which the Whigs had acted in a business, which, though first started by them, was supposed equally acceptable to all sides. **1782** Priestley *Corrupt. Chr.* I. iv. 380 The Canons of Lyons started the opinion. **1902** R. Bagot *Donna Diana* xx. 242 No doubt it is honourable—according to the conception of honour existing among those who have started the story.

c. To set going, cause to begin to operate; to set (machinery) in motion. Also with complementary infinitive or gerund, and with *up* (occas. *absol.*).

1841 in *Loudon's Suburban Hort.* (1842) 511 Cucumbers will succeed beautifully, trained against a south wall, if planted in a little good soil to start them. **1846** Soyer *Cookery* 330 Start it to boil over the fire. **1850** *Mech. Mag.* 20 Apr. 315 At the slightest tap of one of these bells, these enormous engines are stopped, or started or reversed. **1865** *Intell. Observ.* No. 36. 419 By the time I had started my fire. **1885** *Law Times Rep.* LIII. 52/1 The small quantity of.. black smoke necessary to start the fires. **1901** *Daily Express* 28 Feb. 5/1 The private member..started the ball rolling by attacking the government [etc.]. **1910** *Marine Oil Engine Handbk.* 14 It is possible to start up from cold on petrol. *Ibid.* 57 There is little difficulty about starting up small engines. **1945** C. S. Lewis *That Hideous Strength* xiv. 383 He started his engine up and they drove away. **1979** D. Clark *Heberden's Seat* i. 8 A car with a set of jump leads to start me up would do it.

d. To set (a person) going in conversation, to induce to begin to talk on some subject.

1877 Mrs. Argles *Phyllis* xx, I would back mamma, once started, to hold her own against any of those Billingsgate ladies one hears of. **1885** 'Mrs. Alexander' *Valerie's Fate* ii, Miss Riddell,..by a judicious question or two, started the old gentleman on one of his favorite topics.

e. To set on foot (an institution), establish. Also, to set *up* a business (occas. *absol.*). Cf. sense 12 c.

1859 Lever *Dav. Dunn* lxxvi. 669 What a head it must have been that..started companies, opened banks, worked mines, [etc.]. **1864** *Sat. Rev.* 27 Aug. 257/1 The list of possible religions is closed in France, and no one is permitted to start a new one. **1874** R. Tyrwhitt *Sketch Club* 2 Nothing is easier than to start an art-club. **1884** E. Yates *Recoll.* II. 322 You don't mean to say..that you actually mean to start a paper of the kind set forth? **1974** McArthur & Atkins *Dict. Eng. Phrasal Verbs & their Idioms* 215 He has started up a new business. **1975** Cowie & Mackin *Oxf. Dict. Current Idiomatic Eng.* I. 305/2 He *started up* a successful car hire firm. *Ibid.*, They were thinking of *starting up in* the fruit and vegetable trade.

f. To begin to keep as part of one's establishment; to 'set up' (e.g. a horse, a carriage).

1851 D. Jerrold *St. Giles* viii. 78 His wife suggested he should forthwith start a horse and very genteel cart. **1866** Annie Thomas *Walter Goring* I. xvii. 251, I often thought it a pity that your uncle did not keep up the kennels..I wish you'd start them again! **1873** Black *Pr. Thule* xxv. 415 He is sure to start a yacht for one thing.

g. To conceive (a baby), to succeed in conceiving (a child). Also, *to start a family*.

1931 N. MITCHISON *Corn King & Spring Queen* III. vii. 306 She wanted to start another baby at once, but he was very anxious that she should be as strong and well as possible at Plowing Eve. **1934** H. G. WELLS *Exper. Autobiogr.* II. viii. 638 We were now justified in starting a family. **1938** E. BOWEN *Death of Heart* I. i. 24 Irene had started Portia. **1956** *Mademoiselle* Sept. 185/1 After the apple farm was started we were going to start a child. **1973** G. GREENE *Honorary Consul.* II. iii. 96 'He wanted to marry... And if there's a child—' 'Have you started one?' 'No.' **1975** M. BABSON *There must be some Mistake* xiv. 107 We would have married immediately, perhaps have started a family. **1977** *Listener* 25 Aug. 227/1 When a couple have become used to a two-wage standard of living, how do they give it up to start a family?

h. To begin to suffer from or succumb to an illness, esp. a cold.

1932 E. M. DELAFIELD *Thank Heaven Fasting* I. i. 14, I think Cecily's starting a cold. **1943** J. B. PRIESTLEY *Daylight on Saturday* xi. 68 The very sight of her streaming face.. had made him feel that at any minute he would start a cold too. **1958** P. KEMP *No Colours or Crest* vii. 147 He himself was recovering from the malaria he had started at Arborie, but was still very weak.

24. a. To begin (some action or operation). Often with obj. a gerund; also with infinitive. Also said of a thing.

1833 NEWMAN *Lett.* (1891) I. 434, I had before this written to Rose how we had best start agitating. **1873** BLACK *Pr. Thule* i. 10 The young fellow.. started another ballad. **1884** *Manch. Exam.* 20 May 5/2 He started business on a capital which he would now-a-days consider ridiculously small. **1891** C. ROBERTS *Adrift Amer.* 181 There would be no chance of crossing it [the river] for some days.., even if it started to go down at once. **1902** W. W. JACOBS *Lady of Barge* (1908) 10 Miss Harris.. waved the amorous Ted on deck, and started work on her disarranged hair. **1914** R. CURLE *Life a Dream* 256 It was most unfortunate that at that instant the outer door bell of his flat should start ringing.

b. Phr. *to start something*: to cause some trouble, agitation, etc. *colloq.* (orig. *U.S.*).

1917 U. B. SINCLAIR *King Coal* 78 Either the man was an agitator, seeking to 'start something', or else he was a detective sent in by the company. **1917** WODEHOUSE *Uneasy Money* xvi. 179 You certainly did the wrong thing. You started something! **1924** E. O'NEILL *Welded* I. 97 We're not 'starting something' now, are we—after our promise? **1943** F. J. BELL *Condition Red* 59 The Japs.. slunk by without starting anything.

†**25.** ? To provide, supply. *Obs.*

1826 H. N. COLERIDGE *Six Months W. Indies* 27 They start you an exquisite luncheon.. at each [country residence].

26. *slang.* (See quot.)

1825 *Gentl. Mag.* XCV. I. 397, 'I started him.' To start is to apply a smart word to an idle or forgetful person.

†**27.** *Naut.* To flog with a rope's end. *Obs.*

[**1801**: see STARTING *vbl. sb.* I.] **1813** SIR F. BURDETT in *Hansard's Parl. Deb.* XXV. 390 To.. make him sweep the ship, and if he did not, to get him well started (beaten with a rope's end). **1824** *Ann. Reg., Chron.* 33 The charge of severely starting marines and seamen, and flogging others on their breech. **1836** 'JACK NASTY-FACE' *Naut. Econ.* 119 Upwards of three hundred men had been flogged or started.

III. 28. The verb-stem in combination: **start-away**, †(*a*) a renegade, deserter (*obs.*); (*b*) a starting away, sudden deviation from a course; **start-back**, †(*a*) a deserter (*obs.*); (*b*) an act of starting back; **start-stop**, used *attrib.* with reference to an electric telegraph system in which each group of elements transmitted is respectively begun and ended with signals activating and deactivating the receiving mechanism.

1578 TIMME *Calvin on Gen.* xv. 318 Being degenerate and *start-awayes from the faith of their fathers. **1840** BROWNING *Sordello* III. 632 Some slight weariness, some looking-off Or start-away. **1600** HOLLAND *Livy* XXIII. xviii. 486 These *start-backs had no other place of haunt to lurke in, but Capua. **1626** BACON *Sylva* § 179 So we see in Strings; the more they are wound vp, and strained; (And thereby giue a more quicke Start-backe;) the more Treble is the Sound. **1922** *Electrician* 8 Sept. 265/2 The teletype.. is a '*start-stop' printer. **1937** *Sci. Abstr.* B. XL. 48 A machine for correcting start-stop 5-unit signals. **1974** R. N. RENTON *Internat. Telex Service* iii. 12/2 In the start-stop system, although the driving motors may be running, the sending and receiving devices are normally held at rest in a zero-phase position.

Hence **'started**, *ppl. a.*, in senses of the verb; also with adv. as *started-up*.

1646 CRASHAW *Steps to Temple* 43 Why blusht the day? Why ran the started aire trembling away? **1679** LONGUEVILLE in *Hatton Corr.* (Camden) I. 181 This new started question about their Speaker. **1764** H. WALPOLE *Otranto* iv. (1765) 166 Whoever weds Isabella, it shall not be Father Falconara's started up son. They start up, said the Friar, who are suddenly beheld in the seat of lawful Princes. **1902** S. SHELDON & H. MASON *Altern.-Current Machines* 23 Magnetic Energy of a Started Current.

startability (stɑːtəˈbɪlɪtɪ). [f. START *v.* + -ABILITY.] **a.** Of a fuel: the degree to which it facilitates the starting of an engine. **b.** Of an engine: the degree to which it can be readily started.

1933 *Petroleum Handbk.* (R. Dutch-Shell Group) viii. 131 The exact point in the distillation curve which controls 'startability' varies considerably with the atmospheric temperature and the particular engine in which the gasoline is used. **1935** *Jrnl. R. Aeronaut. Soc.* XXXIX. 907 Experimental evidence has shown that until very low temperatures are reached the startability of a gasoline is roughly dependent upon the percentage distilling to 100°C. **1971** *Good Motoring* Sept. 4/3 Checking startability on steep hills. **1976** *Drive* Sept.-Oct. 114/2 The Beetle has a deserved reputation for.. unfailing startability in all weathers.

†**'started,** *a. Obs.* [f. START *sb.*[1] + -ED[2].] Having a 'start', handle, or stalk. Also in parasynthetic formation *short-started*.

1468 *Will* in *Ripon Chapter Acts* (Surtees) 137 Unam ollam enniam sterttydd. **1600** SURFLET *Country Farm* I. xii. 56 To eate one or two short started apples.

starter (ˈstɑːtə(r)). Also 6 **sterter, startar.** [f. START *v.* + -ER[1].] One who or something which starts. **I.** In intransitive senses of the verb.

†**1.** One who 'starts' or goes away. Chiefly in phr. *to be no starter*. **a.** A deserter *from* a principle or cause; one who is given to 'starting' from or abandoning his purposes; a fickle or inconstant person. **b.** One given to wandering; one that cannot abide long in one spot. **c.** One who runs away, a flincher, coward, shirker. *Obs.*

a. 1536 STARKEY *Let.* in *Life & Lett.* (1871) p. xxxix, From thys truthe you schal fynd me my lord to be no sterter, wauerar nor hengar in the wynd. **1561** T. HOBY tr. *Castiglione's Courtyer* IV. (1577) Y iij b, I recken him a waueryng starter. **1609** HOLLAND *Amm. Marcell.* XXIX. v. 373 He advised the Generall, who of his owne disposition was no starter, but constant and resolute, That [etc.]. **1680** *Reflect. late Libel on Curse-ye-Meroz* 28 The Author had (in all probability) been Lecturer there at this day, (for he is no Starter, nor Shifter, nor Swapper of Livings.) *a* **1704** T. BROWN *Sat. Fr. King* Wks. 1730 I. 59 Were I thy confessor, .. Dost think that I'd allow thee any quarter? No—thou should'st find what 'tis to be a starter.

b. 1579 LYLY *Euphues* (Arb.) 57 Canst thou prefer a stranger before thy countryman? a starter before thy companion? **1600** HEYWOOD *If you know not me* (1605) C 4 b, Nay, nay, you need not bolt & locke so fast, Shee is no starter. *c* **1613** MIDDLETON *No Wit like Woman's* V. i. 226 My miseries are no starters; when they come, Stick longer by me. **1621** J. TAYLOR (Water P.) *Praise Beggery* C 3 b, A Lowse.. She's not a starter like the dust-bred-Flea. **1705** DUNTON *Life & Errors* (1818) I. vii. 244 He was no starter, having lived forty years in the same house.

c. *c* **1620** FLETCHER & MASS. *Double Marr.* II. i, We'll spare her our main top-sail, He shall not look us long, we are no starters. **1663** BUTLER *Hud.* I. iii. 606 I'll sooner Stand to it boldly, and take quarter, To let them see I am no starter. *a* **1700** B. E. *Dict. Cant. Crew* s.v., *I am no Starter*; I shan't flinch, or cry to go Home. **1731** C. D'ANVERS *Pacification* 26 Poems 6 St. Dunstan's Clock struck One, And all the sober Cuffs were gone; The rest.. Call'd for a Bottle and to pay; The Doctor and the Bard made two, Who are no Starters, you all know.

d. With adverb.

1538 ELYOT *Dict.*, *Errones*, startars asyde, vagabundes.

2. a. One who starts or sets out in a race, on a journey; *esp.* a person, animal, yacht, etc. that is to start or has started in a race. Also *transf.* and *fig.*; *spec.* an idea that deserves initial consideration (only in neg. contexts: cf. NON-STARTER).

1818 SCOTT *Rob Roy* xxxv, We are early starters in the dawn, even when we have the luck to have good beds to sleep in. **1825** —— *Fam. Lett.* 18 July (1894) II. 310, I speak for security, for ladies are rarely early starters. **1847** *Illustr. Lond. News* 10 July 23/1 Yachts that would take up their station as starters. **1860** HUGHES *Tom Brown Oxf.* xxiv, The private tutors [compared to Newmarket trainers] watch the examiners.. to see what line they take.. that they may handle the rest of their starters accordingly. **1881** *Daily News* 5 Aug. 6/4 In the Yawl Race the starters were Fleur de Lys, Curlew, Opal, Lizzie, Raven, and Arethusa. **1891** N. GOULD *Double Event* xvii. 122 These [horses] comprised the six starters. **1917** 'I. HAY' *Carrying On* iv. 93 That exasperating race of bad starters but great stayers, the British people. **1947** G. B. SHAW in *Musical Times* Jan. 10/1 They can all sing passably in tune and are selected.. because they are good readers and good starters. **1948** M. ALLINGHAM *More Work for Undertaker* xiii. 166 The tip about Brownies [*sc.* shares] was never even a likely starter. **1960** *Times* 7 July 13/2 'Bevanism' was never a starter as a political philosophy or programme. **1976** *Listener* 18 Nov. 641/2 The objections to it are so strong that it isn't a starter.

b. With qualifying adj.: a motor vehicle or engine which starts (well, slowly, etc.). Cf. sense 11 c of the vb.

1952 M. STEEN *Phoenix Rising* viii. 179 That's my car..; it's the easiest starter... Get in and start the engine. **1975** *Country Life* 27 Feb. 508/3, I found the Lancia a good starter with no need for choke.

3. a. Phr. *as* or *for a starter, for starters*: to begin with, for a start. *colloq.* (orig. *U.S.*).

1873 J. H. BEADLE *Undeveloped West* xxii. 450 He gave me twenty drops of laudanum as a starter. **1902** G. H. LORIMER *Lett. Self-Made Merchant* v. 64 All that he ever needed was a few hundred for a starter. **1947** *Chicago Tribune* 3 Sept. 6/3 As a starter, agents have begun a canvass of small independent food wholesalers. **1950** *Manch. Guardian Weekly* 9 Nov. 7 He wired how many frogs' legs did they think they could handle. They told him ten thousand as a starter. **1969** D. FRANCIS *Enquiry* xii. 168, I fell with a crash. 'That's for starters,' he said. **1970** *New Yorker* 5 Dec. 142/1 (Advt.), For starters, here's the line-up of Knicks and Rangers games for the rest of the month. **1973** *Listener* 6 Dec. 767/3 The vehicles for enlargement could be found in new stations or wave-lengths.. but what happens is likely to require as a starter some change in current assumptions. **1978** *Globe & Mail* (Toronto) 11 Jan. 8/1 For starters, do not call us scalpers. We are ticket hosts.

b. A dish eaten as the first course of a meal, before the main course (also in *pl.*). *colloq.*

1966 [see DESSERT 1 b]. **1966** *Sunday Express* 16 Oct. 18/3 You get a three-course dinner, with four 'starter' courses and seven main dishes to choose from, and a sweet. **1966** *Vogue* Nov. 154/3 Starters include fish soup, cock-a-leekie, duck-liver pâté. **1968** *New Society* 22 Aug. 266/1 The first course of a meal is sometimes called a 'starter', which is perhaps not so much non-U as jargon. **1969** P. HIGHSMITH *Tremor of Forgery* xvii. 155 'Try this Tunisian starter. Turns up on every menu.' He meant the antipasto of tuna, olives, and tomatoes. **1975** *Reveille* 20 June 2/2 They are equally good as a 'starter' or served with salad. **1979** V. CANNING *Satan Sampler* ii. 30 There was avocado pear for what some people disgustingly called 'starters'.

II. In transitive senses.

4. a. A person or animal that starts game.

1607 TOPSELL *Four-f. Beasts* 217 Strabo.. speaking of the Conies of Spaine, and of their hunters and starters out of their holes. **1829** [J. L. KNAPP] *Jrnl. Nat.* (ed. 2) 247 In the evening.. the wagtail resorts to the pastures, feeding under the very.. noses of the cattle, who now become the starters of his game.

b. A dog trained for starting game. Also *fig.*

1748 RICHARDSON *Clarissa* (1811) VIII. 267 In short, Belford, thou wert an excellent starter and setter. **1754** DELANY *Observ. Ld. Orrery's Rem. Swift* 107 If he [Sheridan] was not the stanchest hound in the pack, he was at least the best starter. **1768** PENNANT *Brit. Zool.* I. 54 There were two varieties of this kind [of dog], the first used in hawking, to spring the game, which are the same with our starters.

5. a. The person who starts or initiates something.

1699 BENTLEY *Phal.* Pref. 19 The Starters of this Calumny. **1729** SWIFT *Let. on McCulla's Project* Wks. 1905 VII. 184 Mr. McCulla, as being the first starter of the scheme, might be.. rewarded by such a society. **1893** H. T. FISHER in *King's Business* 385 An untold number of starters or converts of revivals.

b. *N. Amer. Sport.* The player in a team game who starts the game; in Baseball *spec.* the pitcher.

1967 *Boston Herald* 8 May 16/6 The victory gave Atlanta starter Pat Jarvis a 3-0 record. **1968** *Globe & Mail* (Toronto) 3 Feb. 35/2 Two of our starters are in Quebec City on an exchange visit, one player is away sick and Bill Edwards is still injured. **1974** *State* (Columbia, S. Carolina) 3 Mar. 3-D/4 Collins.. led the way with 20 points as again all starters hit in double figures. **1976** *Billings* (Montana) *Gaz.* 16 June 3-C/7 The Phillies jumped on starter Ed Halicki and reliever Dave Heaverlo for an eight-run lead after two innings.

6. a. One who gives the signal to start (in a race). Also, an official who gives the signal to start a train. Freq. in phr. *under starter's orders* (*Horseracing*): subject to the instruction of the starter, ready to begin a race. Also *transf.* and *fig.* Cf. ORDER *sb.* 23 a.

1622 in *Hore's Hist. Newmarket* (1885) I. 347 John Wagget onely the starter. **1852** *Bentley's Misc.* XXXI. 120 The starter.. drops his flag with the word 'Go!' **1859** H. KINGSLEY *G. Hamlyn* xv, 'Back, Velocipede; back, Lara!' says the starter; down goes the flag, they dart away, [etc.]. **1860** LD. W. LENNOX *Pict. Sporting Life* II. 23, 'I shall give the words, One, two, three, and away', said the starter, placing me ten yards in advance. **1885** *Manch. Exam.* 7 Apr. 5/1 On a well-managed line there are starters and station officials to give the word of command. **1965** M. SPARK *Mandelbaum Gate* vi. 197 Freddy has said to tell you we are under starter's orders; what is starter's orders? **1973** P. MALLOCH *Kirkback* i. 10 'Drink it up, chum. I forgot we were under starter's orders.' Gilchrist drank it. Five minutes later they were on their way. **1974** *Times* 27 Jan. 10/5 With the first day of the £44,000 Philadelphia indoor tennis tournament only half over, six of the 16 seeds were already out of the running. Nastase, Newcombe and Orantes were all injured and, like five other entrants, did not even come under starter's orders. **1976** *Milton Keynes Express* 11 June 3/2 Show jumping commentator Dorian Williams put the horses under starter's orders. **1979** REESE & FLINT *Trick 13* 82 They're under starter's orders... They're off!

b. *U.S.* (*a*) One who directs the operation of lifts in a large building; (*b*) an employee of a hotel, station, etc., who organizes transport for patrons (see also quot. 1917).

1909 *Pacific Monthly* Feb. 123/1 Thanks to the crowd in the lobby, the uniformed 'starter' had not seen the bum and come over from the elevators to order him away. **1917** *Street Railway Employment in U.S.* (U.S. Bureau of Labor Statistics) 14 *Starters.*—See that cars leave terminal points on scheduled time.. reroute cars to straighten schedules and perform duties of inspectors. **1922** S. LEWIS *Babbitt* 32 The little unknown people who inhabited the Reeves Building corridors—elevator-runners, starter..—were in no way city-dwellers. **1931** WODEHOUSE *Let.* 19 May in *Performing Flea* (1961) 66 A man standing in the crowd outside a movie theatre here after a big opening hears the carriage starter calling for 'Mr Warner's automobile'. **1932** *Making Bus Operations Pay* iv. 77 The station is kept open 24 hours a day by a force of eleven paid employees and three redcaps to handle baggage. Included in the paid force is a station manager, three ticket managers.. and a special officer who also acts as a taxi starter. **1978** R. LUDLUM *Holcroft Covenant* 541 She was given a number on the twelfth floor, the top floor, but as it was the lunch hour, the starter doubted anyone was there. **1981** *Washington Post Mag.* 22 Mar. 8/4 'A *starter*,' she said. 'You know, the man who gets a guest a taxi.'

7. a. An apparatus for starting a machine.

1875 KNIGHT *Dict. Mech.* 2310. **1909** *Stage Year Bk.* 56 The motor is controlled by a Siemens ironclad automatic starter. **1926** W. FAULKNER *Soldiers' Pay* ii. 86 She turned the switch and tried to reach the starter with her foot. **1934** *Discovery* Nov. 324/2 A hand starter is provided on the engine, or it may be started from a car battery. **1969** G. MACBETH *War Quartet* 30 When we kicked the starters, drove On across other countries.. I remembered all Who fought. **1970** K. BALL *Fiat 600, 600D Autobook* xi. 135/2

Dismantling of the starter is a simple task and is similar to that for the generator. **1977** [see SHOCK *sb.*[3] 7].

b. An automatic switch forming part of the auxiliary circuit of some fluorescent lamps, the purpose of which is to enable the electrodes to become hot enough for a discharge to occur after it becomes inactive. Also ***starter switch***.

1942 C. L. AMICK *Fluorescent Lighting Man.* ii. 22 Each lamp requires a separate starter and a separate ballast. *Ibid.* 23 The heat from the discharge itself keeps the cathodes hot during normal operation, hence the starter switch can remain open. **1962** *Newnes Conc. Encycl. Electr. Engin.* 433/2 In place of the starter switch..a cathode-heating transformer can be used, so avoiding the need for replacement parts. **1967** P. HONEY *Household Electricity* 44 Fluorescent lamps..generally need a special circuit with what is called a starter, a device which heats up the electrodes for a second or two after the current is switched on.

8. A culture containing bacteria, yeast, or the like, used to initiate souring or fermentation in the making of butter, cheese, dough, etc.

1896 *Vermont Agric. Rep. 1895* 67 This may be done..by using a 'starter' made from cream. **1908** J. P. SHELDON *Farm & Dairy* (ed. 4) 76 The modern..method is to ripen the cream artificially by means of a pure culture of the lactic acid bacillus, technically called a 'starter'. **1935** *Discovery* Nov. 340/2 In the manufacture of butter 'starters' are employed to sour the cream under controlled conditions. **1939** K. PINKERTON *Wilderness Wife* vii. 74 At least sour dough bread was sure... Robert had sponsored it by making the 'starter', a mixture of flour and water which grabbed its yeast germs from the air. **1950** *N.Z. Jrnl. Agric.* Jan. 27/2 Quick granulation is achieved by the addition of a 'starter' and the storing of the packed honey immediately in a consistent temperature of about 56 degrees F. **1973** W. H. T. TAYLEUR *Home Brewing & Wine-Making* vii. 55 The optimum amount of starter in wine-making is about 1 to 15.

9. *attrib.* and *Comb.*, as (sense 7) ***starter button, cord, motor, switch***; **starter home** orig. *U.S.*, a first home, usu. one bought by a young couple; also *ellipt.*; **starter set** orig. *U.S.*, a small set of china intended to be the basis of a larger collection; also *transf.*

1971 Starter button [see *starter motor* below]. **1977** D. BEATTY *Excellency* vi. 80 He primed the engines, pressed the starter button, heard the propeller creak round. **1971** *Scope* (S. Afr.) 19 Mar. 65/2 Damned engine doesn't have a starting handle, just a starter cord. **1976** *Billings* (Montana) *Gaz.* 27 June 5-D/7 (Advt.), Also a fenced back yard makes it a great starter home. **1979** *Arizona Daily Star* 5 Aug. (Advt. Section) 21/2 This 3 bedroom, 1 bath home will make a super starter for a young family. **1980** *Times* 6 Feb. 6/6 Local authorities and builders should provide more 'starter' homes to meet the demand for lower priced small homes for sale, Mr John Stanley, Minister for Housing and Construction, said yesterday. **1928** *Correct Lubrication* 39 Starter motor spins without turning engine. **1971** R. DENTRY *Encounter at Kharmel* vi. 100 Pepper..leaned hard on the starter button. The starter motor set up a pulsating, piercing shriek. **1946** *Time* 29 July 64/2 It was inexpensive —a 20-piece 'starter set' sold for about $6. **1970** *Guardian* 17 Dec. 9/5 A starter set consisting of four soup bowls, four 10½-inch plates, four eight-inch plates, [etc.]. **1977** *Montgomery Ward Catal.* Spring-Summer 510/3 Men's starter set [of golf clubs]. **1925** *Morris Owner's Man.* 9 The starter switch should immediately be released. **1965** PRIESTLEY & WISDOM *Good Driving* ii. 19 The starter switch usually takes the form of a knob or button which is either pressed or pulled out.

Hence '**startership**.

1889 *Star* 10 Jan. 3/5 When the vacancy for the startership to the Jockey Club occurred, Lord Marcus Beresford was appointed to succeed the late Mr. McGeorge.

startful ('stɑːtfʊl), *a.* [f. START *sb.* or *v.* + -FUL.]

a. Apt to start, easily startled, timorous. **b.** Proceeding by starts, fitful.

1790 WOLCOT (P. Pindar), *Rowland for Oliver* Wks. 1812 II. 310 Say, Virgin, where dost thou delight to dwell? With Maids of Honour, startful Virgin? Tell. **1796** COLERIDGE *Destiny of Nations* 255 The Maid Brooded with moving lips, mute, startful, dark! **1837** C. LOFFT *Self-formation* I. 226 The growth of each is capricious and startful, often making a sudden push from no apparent motive.

Hence '**startfulness**.

1803 BEDDOES *Hygeia* IX. 141 Palpitations, startfulness, disposition to be terrified, exist more or less strongly.

star-thistle. [STAR *sb.*[1]; cf. G. *sterndistel.*] A name for the weed *Centaurea Calcitrapa*, the flowers of which are surrounded by radiating spines; also for *C. solstitialis*, and as a book-name for the whole genus.

1578 LYTE *Dodoens* IV. lix. 521 This herbe is nowe called in Latine *Carduus stellatus*, and *Stellaria*, also *Calcitrapa*:.. they call it..in base Almaigne, Sterre distel: in English Starre Thistel or Caltrop. **1597** GERARDE *Herbal* II. ccccl xx. 1003 The Star Thistle, called *Carduus stellatus*, hath many soft frized leaues. **1753** *Chambers' Cycl.* Suppl. App., *Star-thistle*, the English name of a species of centaury, called by some *calcitrapa*. **1822** *Hortus Anglicus* II. 418 *C. Solstitialis*. St. Barnaby's Star Thistle. **1863** PRIOR *Plant-n.*, Star-Thistle, from its spiny involucre, resembling the weapon called a morning star, *Centaurea solstitialis*.

'**starting**, *vbl. sb.* [f. START *v.* + -ING[1].]

1. a. The action of the verb in various senses. Also with *off* and *up* in some senses. Freq. *attrib.*

† *starting of the navel*: umbilical rupture.

1398 TREVISA *Barth. de P.R.* XVIII. xxx. (1495) 793 A hart ..lepyth thwart ouer wayes..and stertyth wyth contrary lepynges and stertynges. *c* **1430** *Syr Gener.* (Roxb.) 7317 [Generides] stert a-side thoo; In the sterting the knife was nigh. **1602** *Archpriest Controv.* (Camden) II. 221 Which action, without waveringe or startinge, I did earnestly prosecute. **1626** BACON *Sylva* §713 Starting is both an Apprehension of the Thing feared;.. And likewise an Inquisition, in the beginning, what the Matter should be. *a* **1653** JER. TAYLOR *Serm.* I. i. 8 Thy falshod to God and startings from thy holy promises..shall be laid open before all the world. **1694** J. PECHEY *Compl. Herbal* 164 The Starting of the Navel has been cured in many Children, with a Cataplasm made with [etc.]. **1798** R. JACKSON *Hist. & Cure Fever* 239 Tremors, startings, and the various irregular motions, which often appear in fever, are undoubtedly dangerous. **1801** *Ann. Reg., Chron.* 44 [He] called to the boatswain to bring a point (a rope doubled with knots at the end), and give the plaintiff a 'starting'. **1821** M. EDGEWORTH *Let.* 29 Jan. (1971) 235, I hope this can be arranged as I found it a starting off point and I could not conclude the agreement without it. **1828** A. B. GRANVILLE *St. Petersburgh* II. 454 There is, moreover, another species of corporal punishment in the British navy... It is vulgarly called 'starting', or the 'rope's end'. **1850** NEWMAN *Difficulties Anglicans* I. ii. (1891) I. 59 They..relieve their feelings by gestures and cries, and startings to and fro. **1885** PATER *Marius* IV. xx. II. 100 Those noises in the house all supper-time..were they only startings in the old rafters? **1895** KIPLING in *Century Mag.* LI. 265/2 There was the same 'starting-off place'—a pile of brushwood. **1912** *Motor Man.* (ed. 14) iii. 108 Cars having compressed air starting-up devices are always equipped for rapid tyre inflation from the air pressure cylinder. **1927** [see ACTIVATION]. **1946** *Happy Landings* July 1/1 The engine was not turned by hand through one cycle before the starting-up operation. **1959** *Times* 12 June 17/5 Extraordinary starting-up costs at the Company's new borate refinery. **1967** E. SHORT *Embroidery & Fabric Collage* i. 28 There is a definite starting-off point, namely the subject, which then has to be translated into a suitable flat pattern.

b. Phrase, *at starting*: *lit.* at the beginning of a race or journey; *fig.* at the outset.

[**1656** EARL MONM. tr. *Boccalini's Advts. fr. Parnass.* I. xxxi. (1674) 35 Many Charrets appearing at the first starting with new Wheels well greased.] **1834** NEWMAN *Par. Serm.* I. ix. 134 It is given you in order that you may find it easy to obey at starting. **1861** READE *Cloister & H.* i, Let me remind him that even Christians loved one another at first starting. **1868** *Field* 18 July 49/1 The favourite, taking a clear lead at starting, made all the running, and won in a canter by a couple of lengths. **1880** SWINBURNE *Stud. Shaks.* 103 None of these had better luck in that line at starting than *King Henry IV.* **1883** ANNIE THOMAS *Mod. Housew.* 144 At starting let me say that [etc.].

2. *attrib.* and *Comb.* **a.** Simple attrib., of appliances for starting machinery, as ***starting-bar, cord, -gear, panel, platform, -valve, -wheel***; relating to the starting of horses in a race, as ***starting-list, -machine,*** †***-stoop***; relating to the starting of railway trains, as ***starting-signal***.

1875 KNIGHT *Dict. Mech.*, **Starting-bar*, a hand-lever for starting the valve-gear of a steam-engine. **1977** D. MACKENZIE *Raven & Ratcatcher* viii. 114 He whipped the *starting cord on the small outboard motor. It caught at the second attempt. **1867** BURGH *Mod. Marine Engin.* 295 *Starting Gear. **1898** *Encycl. Sport* II. 190/1 (Racing) The Starter's duties are at present threatened with supersession by the introduction of the '*starting machine', a colonial invention. **1913** J. B. BISHOP *Panama Gateway* V. v. 376 A *starting panel containing contractors by which current is applied to the motor. **1869** RANKINE *Machine & Hand-tools* Pl. F 5, The hammer can be regulated and easily worked by one man, at the lever, F, on the *starting platform. **1889** G. FINDLAY *Eng. Railway* 68 *Starting signals are usually placed at the end of the platform at a staion..and they indicate to the driver when he may start his train. **1708** *Lond. Gaz.* No. 4450/4 The Horses to be enter'd at the *Starting-Stoop 10 Days before the Race. **1865** BOURNE *Rec. Improv. Steam Eng.* 35 In 1852 I introduced *starting valves. **1867** BURGH *Mod. Marine Engin.* 55 The correct locality of the *starting wheel.

b. Special comb.: **starting-back** *Whaling* [BACK *sb.*[2]] (see quot.); †**starting-beer**, beer used for the purpose of starting or reviving stale beer; **starting block**, (usu. *pl.*) a shaped rigid block for bracing the feet of a runner at the start of a race; also *fig.*; **starting-bolt** *Naut.* (see quot.); **starting gate** *Sport*, (*a*) a barrier device used at the beginning of a race (esp. of horses) to ensure a simultaneous start for all competitors; (*b*) a point from which individual runs are timed, as in skiing etc.; also *transf.* and *fig.*; **starting grid** = GRID 6 c; **starting ground**, a basis from which an argument or a development starts; **starting handle**, a handle used to start a machine; *spec.* a detachable one that is turned to start the engine of a motor vehicle; **starting line**, a real or imaginary line used to mark the place from which a race starts; also *fig.*; **starting-note** *Sc.*, an extra note or anacrusis at the beginning of a melody, preceding an accented note; also *fig.*; **starting pistol**, a pistol used to give the signal at the start of a race; **starting-place**, the place occupied at starting by a competitor in a race; the place from which a person or thing starts; **starting-point**, the point from which a person or thing starts; a point of departure in a journey, argument, narration, development, etc.; **starting-post**, a post which marks the place from which the competitors in a race should start; also *fig.*; **starting powder** *Fireworks* (see quot.); **starting-price**, (*a*) the price at which the bidding at an auction is started; (*b*) *Racing*, the final odds on a horse at the time of starting; also *attrib.*; **starting salary**, the salary (on a pay-scale) earned at first by an employee taking up a new post. See also STARTING-HOLE.

1820 SCORESBY *Acc. Arctic Reg.* II. 398 An oblong wooden cistern, called the '*starting-back', is usually erected, for containing blubber. **1742** *Lond. & Country Brew* I. (ed. 4) 23 For brewing common brown Ale and *Starting-beer. **1937** BRESNAHAN & TUTTLE *Track & Field Athletics* iii. 54 There are two opinions on the matter of support for the feet at the start of the sprints. One is that holes in the track be used as a means of foot support, while the other is that *starting blocks on top of the track be used. *Ibid.* xvi. 455 Those who prefer to employ starting blocks rather than holes in the track claim that blocks have the advantage in that they protect the track and make adjustments..easier. **1961** F. C. AVIS *Sportsman's Gloss.* 63 *Starting blocks*, triangular pieces of wood fixed to the track and against which the sprinter's heels are pushed at the start of a race. **1977** J. WAINWRIGHT *Pool of Tears* 205 He crouched, like a sprinter on starting-blocks. **1983** *Listener* 29 Sept. 4/2 All the Opposition parties are poised nervously on the starting-blocks of the new political year. **1867** SMYTH *Sailor's Word-bk.*, **Starting-Bolt*, or *Drift-bolt*, a bolt used to drive out another; it is usually a trifle smaller. **1898** T. HAYDON *Sporting Reminisc.* 29 There is another Australian invention..the *Starting Gate. **1930** *Times* 24 Mar. 4/2 Numbered saddle cloths, the starting-gate, and the totalisator are among the reforms which came from them. **1940** C. DAY LEWIS tr. *Virgil's Georgics* I. 31 When racing chariots have rushed from the starting-gate. **1950** *Sun* (Baltimore) 18 Feb. 12/1 The competitors fear for life and limb when they are encased in the gate, which resembles the starting gate used for horses, and is designed to eliminate false starts. **1968** *Globe & Mail* (Toronto) 5 Feb. 19/3 The 18-year-old student was assessed a one-second penalty by the jury panel, which reviewed a claim by two officials that Debbie was too quick out of the starting gate. **1971** *Language* XLVII. 5 Acceptance of this very general position, how-ever, does little more than put one in the proper starting gate. **1976** *New Yorker* 8 Mar. 105/1 Mount Sterling stumbled coming out of the starting gate, unseating his rider, Maple. **1957** *Starting grid [see GRID 6 c]. **1978** 'D. RUTHERFORD' *Collision Course* 100 Positions on the starting grid are allocated on practice times. **1869** DK. OF ARGYLL *Primeval Man* IV. 145 Man..must always have had instincts which afford all that is required as a *starting-ground for advance in the mechanical arts. **1873** M. ARNOLD *Lit. & Dogma* (1876) 63 The more we meditate on this starting-ground of theirs, the more we shall find that there is solidity in it. **1876** PREECE & SIVEWRIGHT *Telegraphy* 131 The receiver has also a switch in connection with the *starting handle. **1886** D. CLERK *Gas Engine* ix. 242 The starting handle is then let go, and the motor piston runs over its ports. **1932** D. L. SAYERS *Have his Carcase* xii. 145 After.. exercise on the starting-handle, they had diagnosed trouble with the ignition. **1973** P. AUDEMARS *Delicate Dust of Death* x. 136 They left the bus... Perhaps they could not start it. .. I tried the starting handle myself. It was jammed. **1906** *Starting-line [see *repair station* s.v. REPAIR *sb.*[2]]. **1920** [see BATON *sb.* 2 b]. **1962** A. NISBETT *Technique Sound Studio* x. 173 Anything but sheer surrealism was doomed to remain stickily on the starting-line. **1974** *Howard Jrnl.* XIV. 84 In a meritocratic society those whose powers of oral and written expression are extremely limited are left at the starting line in the race for social status. **1982** J. JARVER *Athletics Fundamentals* 20/1 The aim of the sprint start is to get the athlete away from the starting line as fast as possible. **1793** BURNS *Let. to Thomson* Sept. (Globe) 536 The old way, and the way to give most effect, is to have no *starting-note, as the fiddlers call it, but to burst at once into the pathos. **1829** CUNNINGHAM *Brit. Painters* I. 275 Most of the songs of Burns..are constructed on the stray verse or vagrant line of some forgotten bard. But then the poet only employed those as the starting notes to his own inimitable strains. **1935** 'N. BLAKE' *Question of Proof* ii. 30 Get set! Go!! That was the *starting-pistol you heard. **1962** A. NISBETT *Technique Sound Studio* x. 178 A modified revolver is better than a starting pistol. **1656** EARL MONM. tr. *Boccalini's Advts. fr. Parnass.* I. xxxi. (1674) 36 Injustice was used in the inequality of the *starting-places. **1837** CARLYLE *Fr. Rev.* II. VI. iii, Paris and every City of them, starting-place, course, and goal of said sacrilegious forced march, shall [etc.]. **1874** MARQ. DUFFERIN in Sir A. Lyall *Life* (1906) I. 238 Our original starting-place was Quebec. **1875** JOWETT *Plato* (ed. 2) III. 510 Runners, who run well from the starting-place to the goal. **1840** MILL *Coleridge* Diss. 1859 I. 403 Every consistent scheme of philosophy requires as its *starting-point, a theory [etc.]. **1844** KINGLAKE *Eothen* xvii, Here we met in the wilderness at about half-way from our respective starting-points. **1848** R. I. WILBERFORCE *Doctr. Incarnation* i. (1852) 10 Rationalism makes the individual the starting-point for all improvement, whereas the Church's starting-point is Christ. **1858** LADY MORGAN *Autobiog.* (1859) Pref. 8 My original intention was to publish an autobiography from my starting-point on a certain Christmas Day. **1874** GREEN *Short Hist.* ii. §1. 60 The countries of Scandinavia which had so long been the mere starting-points of the pirate-bands. **1899** *Allbutt's Syst. Med.* VIII. 502 A neuro-paralytic hyperæmia..is sometimes the starting-point of eczema. **1758** JOHNSON *Idler* No. 6 ¶8 Let an equestrian statue of this heroine be erected near the *starting post on the heath of Newmarket. **1819** BYRON *Juan* III. xxi, All feelings which o'erleap the years long lost, And bring our hearts back to their starting-post. **1852** J. F. BATEMAN *Aquatic Notes* 41 The starting-posts were 140 feet apart. **1892** WESTCOTT *Gospel of Life* 46 It is as true in metaphysics as it is in physics that the goal of yesterday is the starting-post of to-day. **1910** *Encycl. Brit.* X. 422/1 Such are the *starting-powder, which first catches fire, the bursting powder which causes the final explosion, and the quick-match [of a firework]. **1854** *Poultry Chron.* II. 127 A great number of the lots were claimed at the *starting price, 5s. **1891** *Daily News* 17 Nov. 7/1 The plaintiff was a starting-price bookmaker. **1901** *Westm. Gaz.* 20 Nov. 7/3 Mr. Hawke promises to bring very telling testimony.. before the Select Committee..particularly with regard to starting-price betting. **1969** H. PERKIN *Key Profession* iv. 138 New assistant lecturers and junior lecturers..came in.. at *starting salaries much lower than those in schoolteaching. **1973** *Nature* 7 Dec. p. i, Starting salary would be in the vicinity of £3,000.

starting ('stɑːtɪŋ), *ppl. a.* [f. START *v.* + -ING².] That starts, in various senses of the verb: †leaping, bounding, hence full of energy; making sudden movements; suffering displacement or disintegration, etc.

c **1420** *Anturs of Arthur* 511 (Thornton MS.) One a stirtande stede he strykes one straye. **1545** JOYE *Exp. Dan.* vii. P vij b, The scole doctors of diuinite.. what new strange sterting termes they haue invented. **1545** ASCHAM *Toxoph.* ii. (Arb.) 125 Againe Hulder, black thorne, Serues tree [etc.] make holow, starting, studding, gaddynge shaftes. **1598** DALLINGTON *Meth. Trav.* G 4, [Henri IV] his nature stirting and full of life, like a true French man. **1606** SHAKS. *Tr. & Cr.* IV. v. 2 With starting courage, Giue with thy Trumpet a loud note to Troy. **1608** DEKKER *Dead Term* Wks. (Grosart) IV. 44 The eyes of euery Straunger, and of euery starting Passenger be cast vp vppon mee. **1628** FELTHAM *Resolves* I. x. 26 What feares and cares affright the starting sleepes of the couetous? **1648** HEXHAM II, *Een schouw-peerdt*, a starting Horse. **1712** STEELE *Spect.* No. 398 ¶6 Your starting Manner of Writing,..has in it something very unaccountable. **1718** ROWE tr. *Lucan* I. 364 Stiff rose his starting hair, he stood dismay'd. **1757** W. WILKIE *Epigoniad* III. 72 Behind his ear the starting weapon shone. **1787** POLWHELE *Engl. Orator* II. 209 When now the starting Tear Of filial Duty trembles. **1817** SHELLEY *Rev. Islam* XI. viii, But still there clung One hope, like a keen sword on starting threads uphung. **1878** BOSW. SMITH *Carthage* 89 The starting timbers of the unseasoned wood of which the ships were built.

Hence '**startingly** *adv.*, with a start; by starts; †impetuously, fitfully.

1604 SHAKS. *Oth.* III. iv. 79 Why do you speake so startingly and rash? **1636** FEATLY *Serm.* in *Strict. Lyndom.* (1638) II. 174 In a Fever..it [the pulse] beateth unevenly and startingly. *a* **1693** *Urquhart's Rabelais* III. xiv. 119 You startingly awaked. **1827** MOORE *Alciphron* III. 127 As startingly her eyes she rais'd. **1841** *Fraser's Mag.* XXIII. 315 Then startingly the pheasant springeth forth.

†**starting-hole.** *Obs.* [f. STARTING *vbl. sb.* (Cf. START *v.* 6).]

1. A hole in which a hunted animal takes refuge; *transf.* a place in which a criminal or a hunted enemy finds refuge.

1530 PALSGR. 276/1 Stertyng hole, *ung tapynet, lieu de refuge.* **1537** LAYTON in *Lett. Suppress. Monasteries* (Camden) 76 Lyke a cony clapper fulle of startyng hoilles. **1559** AYLMER *Harborowe* F j, Least the contrary side might haue their refuge and startinge hole there. **1565** STAPLETON tr. *Bede's Hist. Ch. Eng.* 99 To erect a monastery in the high and desert mountaines. Where before that time were rather starting holes for theues and dennes for wilde bestes, then mete mansion places for men. **1577–87** HOLINSHED *Chron.* III. 257/1 The Welshmen..brake vpon him out of their starting-holes and places of refuge through the marishes. *a* **1593** MARLOWE *Edw. II* 1436 Aduaunce your standard Edward in the field, And marche to fire them from their starting holes. **1609** HOLLAND *Amm. Marcell.* XVII. xvi. 103 The others to avoid the danger were driven to flye for refuge unto their starting holes among the blind marishes. **1613–16** W. BROWNE *Brit. Past.* I. v. 105 Th' insnared fish..with his franticke fits so scares the shole, That each one takes his hyde, or starting hole. **1617** MORYSON *Itin.* II. 272 He had razed Hen. Ovingtons Castle, and Mac Hughes Iland, which both had been neasts and starting holes for theeves. **1618** BOLTON *Florus* II. iii. (1636) 87 The Deceates..thus for a long time shifted for themselves by advantage of their woods, wayes, and starting holes.

2. *fig.* A means of evasion; a loophole.

Extraordinarily frequent in the 16th and 17th c.

1531 ELYOT *Governor* II. ix. (1880) II. 100 Perauenture some, which seke for sterting holes to mainteine their vices, will obiecte. *a* **1533** FRITH *Answ. Rastell* Wks. (1573) 32/1 If they would here fayne a glose (as their maner is) when they are in a straite euer to seeke a startyng hole. **1591** GREENE *Conny Catching* II. Wks. (Grosart) X. 78 There is no Act, Statute, nor Lawe so strickt conueyed, but there be straight found starting holes to auoide it. **1596** SHAKS. *1 Hen. IV*, II. iv. 290. **1610** HOLLAND *Camden's Brit.* (1637) 147 He thought that Harold thereby sought starting holes for to hide his perjurie. **1674** HICKMAN *Quinquart. Hist.* (ed. 2) 46 That the poor Jansenists might have no starting hole, by slipping into which to avoid the force of this condemnation. **1688** BUNYAN *Heavenly Footman* (1886) 170 Because they are not willing, how many shifts and starting-holes will they have. **1696** C. LESLIE *Snake in Grass* (1697) 260, I see the Starting-hole that they have left, (as in all their Writings) whereby to escape from what I have before Quoted. **1801** W. HUNTINGTON *God Guardian of Poor* Ded. 6 And dry forms of devotion..are no better than..a starting hole to shun the cross.

startish ('stɑːtɪʃ), *a. rare.* [f. START *v.* + -ISH.] Apt to start or jib.

1730 BAILEY (fol.) *Startish, Startly*, apt to start as some Horses, &c. **1768** TUCKER *Lt. Nat.* (1834) I. 203 Sometimes he [the horse] may prove startish or restive, turning out of the way, or running into a pond to drink. **1791** NAIRNE *Poems* 79 The startish beast took fright, and flop The mad-brain'd rider tumbled, neck and crop!

startle ('stɑːt(ə)l), *sb.* [f. STARTLE *v.*]

1. An experience of being startled; a start or shock of surprise or alarm. Also (predicatively), something that startles.

1714 *Spect.* No. 599 ¶4 After having recovered myself from my first Startle, I was very well pleas'd at the Accident which had befallen me. **1823** BYRON *Juan* X. i, Newton.. found In that slight startle from his contemplation..A mode of proving that [etc.]. **1836** R. H. FROUDE *Rem.* (1838) I. 426 Burton's death.. was quite a startle to me. **1844** H. STEPHENS *Bk. Farm* III. 1029 [The colt] bearing, without a startle, the fall of the pail-handle, [etc.]. **1894** CROCKETT *Raiders* (ed. 3) 166 This gave me a great startle.

b. *nonce-use.* A startling perception *of* something.

1854 LOWELL *Jrnl. Italy* Pr. Wks. 1890 I. 191 You receive hints and startles of it through the senses first.

2. A sudden rush (of water).

1912 MASEFIELD in *Engl. Rev.* Oct. 369 Startles of water made the swing ports gush.

†'**startle,** *a. Obs. rare.* In 5 styrtyl, -el. [f. START *v.* + -LE.] Actuated by sudden impulse.

c **1440** *Promp. Parv.* 447/1 Schytylle, styrtyl [*Winch.* styrtel], or hasty, *preceps. Ibid.* 476/1 Styrtyl, or hasty, *preceps.*

startle ('stɑːt(ə)l), *v.* Also 1 steartlian, 4 stertel, 4, 6, 9 *dial.* stertle, 5 stertylle, 6 startell, -yll, 6–7 startel, 9 *dial.* sturtle. [OE. *steartlian* :—**startlōjan*, f. **start-* (: **stert-*: **sturt-*) see START *v.* The ME. *stertle* (whence the mod. word) may however be a new formation on *stert-* START *v.*]

†**1.** *intr.* In OE.: To kick, struggle. *Obs.*

a **1100** *Aldhelm Gloss* in Napier *O.E. Glosses* i. 2438 *Ut non calcitres (.i. ut non pugnes)* þæt þu ne spear[n]last, steartlast. *Ibid.* ii. 82 (*Same lemma.*) þæt þu ne steartlige.

2. To rush, move swiftly; to caper. Now *dial.*

In mod. dialects chiefly said of cows rushing wildly about under a burning sun: see *Eng. Dial. Dict.*

a **1300** *Body & Soul* in *Map's Poems* (Camden) 335 Thouȝ art unsemly for to se,.. Thouȝ ne havest frend that ne wolde fle, come thouȝ stertlinde in the strete. *c* **1385** CHAUCER *L.G.W.* 1741 (Seld. MS.) Hir husbond Colatyn Or sche was of him war com stertlyng In. **1387** TREVISA *Higden* (Rolls) VIII. 55 þerynne [*sc.* on a carved casket] it semeþ þat geantes fiȝten, bestes stertelleþ [L. *gestus animalium.. conspiciuntur*], foules fleeþ. **1398** —— *Barth. De P.R.* XVIII. cix. (1495) 851 Whan a cowe is stonge wyth a grete flye thenne she..stertelyth as she were wood abowte feldes and playnes. **1483** *Cath. Angl.* 363/1 To Stertylle, *exilire, prosilire.* *c* **1520** SKELTON *Magnyf.* 751, I make them to startyll and sparkyll lyke a bronde. **1526** TINDALE *Mark* v. 13 And the heerd starteled [Gr. ὥρμησεν], and ran hedlyng into the see. **1549** *Compl. Scot.* vi. (1873) 37, I beheld the pretty fische vantounly stertland vitht there rede vermeil fynnis. **1555** WATREMAN *Fardle Facions* I. iv. 40 Emong their priestes, loke whome they sawe startle aboute as haulfe wood, him did they iudge of all other mooste holy. **1583** MELBANCKE *Philotimus* S iij, The Leopard pursues his pray leaping and startling. **1616** J. LANE *Contn. Sqr.'s T.* IV. 312 Then the horse gann startel, tripp, and goe. **1637** RUTHERFORD *Lett.* (1664) 66 We see oxen goe to the shambles leaping and startling. **1786** BURNS *Twa Dogs* 163 He..down Italian Vista startles [*rhyme* myrtles].

3. a. To start, to undergo a sudden involuntary movement of the body, caused by surprise, alarm, acute pain, etc. Of a horse: To shy. **b.** To feel sudden astonishment or alarm; to take fright, be shocked *at* something. Now *rare* (superseded by passive of sense 5).

1530 PALSGR. 734/1, I startell, as a man dothe that is amased sodaynly, or that hath some inwarde colde. **1540** —— *Acolastus* B iv, Thou begynnest to wynche or to startle on this facion. **1562** COOPER *Answ. Def. Truth* Pref., And in dede..a man maye thinke they had good cause to startle at the matter. **1591** SAVILE *Tacitus, Hist.* II. lxxiii. 95 Oftentimes as hee [Vespasian] was named, Vitellius would startle. **1600** SHAKS. *A.Y.L.* IV. iii. 13 Patience her selfe would startle at this letter, And play the swaggerer. **1603** HARSNET *Pop. Impost.* 136 To teach her..gnash her teeth, startle with her body, [etc.]. **1614** WITHER *Sat. to King* Juvenilia (1633) 326 Make them, when their Villanies are blazed, Shudder and startle as men halfe amazed. **1629** GAULE *Holy Madn.* 206 His Head startles, Haires bristle, Browes wrinkle. **1634** SIR T. HERBERT *Trav.* 30 His pampered horse startled at him. **1641** *Vind. Smectymnuus* 31 Our loyall hearts startle to think of a repetition of the words. **1660** T. M. *C. Walker's Hist. Independency* IV. 12 But the Dutch [denied]..to vaill to the English because they were the younger State..hereat the English (though yet but an Embrio) begin to startle. *a* **1704** T. BROWN *Char. Jacobite Clergy* Wks. 1711 IV. 269 You must either leave them, or else, after the squeamishness of startling at a Surplice, be forc'd to swallow Transubstantiation. **1719** YOUNG *Revenge* II. i, Yet to ask it Has something shocking to a generous mind; At least Alonzo's spirit startles at it. **1732** *Lond. Mag.* I. 240 Like Moon-blind horses are apt to startle at every object. **1785** MISS FIELDING *Ophelia* xxx, She..startled at me, as if I had been a monster. **1792** WORDSW. *Descr. Sk.* 60 The cloister startles at the gleam of arms. **1815** J. SMITH *Panorama Sci. & Art* I. 614 The horses..crowded close to us, startling with great surprise. **1826** LAMB *Let. to B. Barton* 20 Mar., A good lady, a friend's wife, whom I really love (don't startle, I mean in a licit way). **1835** TALFOURD *Ion* III. ii, Which the pirates' nest..would startle at! **1961** R. GRAVES *More Poems* 42 In the course of travel, you must have startled at Some coign of true felicity. **1972** R. ADAMS *Watership Down* v. 18 To rabbits, everything unknown is dangerous. The first reaction is to startle, the second to bolt. Again and again they startled, until they were close to exhaustion.

†const. *into.* **1649** LOVELACE *Lucasta* 72 The Robber and the Murderer in 'spite Of his red spots shal startle into White.

†**c.** *indirect passive. Obs.*

1665 NEDHAM *Med. Medicinæ* 215 Oure Dogmatical Methodists can now vouchsafe to use such Medicaments as were startled at before. **1673** *Lady's Calling* II. §1 ¶18 The liberties that are taken now, would then have been startled at.

†**d.** To awake with a start; to start *up* suddenly; to move as if surprised or frightened. *to startle back*: to recoil, move backwards in terror.

1576 GASCOIGNE *Philomene* Wks. 1910 II. 189 And startling from her traunce, I wil revenge (quoth she). **1608** H. CLAPHAM *Errour Left Hand* 56 Why startlest thou back? why lookes thou agast? **1613** HEYWOOD *Brazen Age* I 1, My father..startles vp to thunder-strike the lad, And lets me fall. **1631** GOUGE *God's Arrows* IV. §8. 385 Be not so affrighted..as upon the sight of painted fire to startle backe into true burning fire. **1798** COLERIDGE *Lewti* 58 The river-swans have heard my tread, And startle from their reedy bed. **1813** SCOTT *Trierm.* III. xxxix, Gyneth startles from her sleep. **1847** JAMES *Castle of Ehrenstein* xli. III. 198 The Count of Ehrenstein startled up and laid his hand upon his sword.

e. Of inanimate things: To move or change suddenly as if startled.

1812 CRABBE *Tales* vii. 107 And sordid pictures from the fancy pass, As the breath startles from the polish'd glass. **1815** SHELLEY *Alastor* 476 The grass that sprung Startled and glanced and trembled even to feel An unaccustomed presence. **1888** LOWELL *Poems, Broken Tryst* 5 If a dead leaf startle behind me, I think 'tis your garment's hem.

†**f.** Of the eyes: To 'start from their sockets'.

1632 LITHGOW *Trav.* x. 463 Now mine eyes begun to startle, my mouth to foame and froath, and my teeth to chatter.

†**4.** To swerve, deviate *from* a purpose: = START *v.* 7. *Obs.*

1649 MILTON *Tenure Kings* 4, I shall..exhort them not to startle from the just and pious resolution of adhering with all their assistance to the present Parlament and Army.

5. a. *trans.* To cause to start; to frighten; to surprise greatly; †to give offence to, to shock.

1595 SHAKS. *John* IV. ii. 25 It makes the course of thoughts to fetch about, Startles, and frights consideration. **1608** —— *Per.* V. i. 147 Thou little knowst howe thou doest startle me to call thy selfe Marina. **1598** CHAPMAN *Blind Begg. Alexandria* F 3 b, How now my Lords doth beauty startle you. *c* **1611** —— *Iliad* XVI. 437 His ruine startl'd th' other steeds. **1634** MILTON *Comus* 210 These thoughts may startle well, but not astound The vertuous mind. **1655** FULLER *Ch. Hist.* III. 108 Not long after, he was arraigned again at the Kings Bench, the news whereof so startled the Clergie, that [etc.]. **1710** *Tatler* No. 257 ¶2, I was startled with a Flourish of many Musical Instruments. **1817** KEATS *Sonn.*, '*O Solitude*', Where the deer's swift leap Startles the wild bee from the fox-glove bell. **1818** —— *Isabella* v, If looks speak love-laws, I will drink her tears, And at the least 'twill startle off her cares. **1823** SCOTT *Peveril* xiv, The shrill neigh with which she startled the female inmates of the parlour. **1828** LYTTON *Pelham* xlii, There was a..licentiousness in his opinions, which startled even me (used as I had been to rakes of all schools). **1829** W. IRVING *Granada* I. v. 35 The garrison, startled from sleep, found the enemy already masters of the towers. **1856** FROUDE *Hist. Eng.* (1858) I. ii. 93 On the return of a settled government, they were startled for a moment in their security. **1879** MᶜCARTHY *Own Times* xx. II. 76 Such an act as that done by the Pope might have startled them back to their old attitude. **1903** A. WHYTE *Apostle Paul* i. 21 It startles and staggers us to hear it.

fig. **1632** MILTON *L'Allegro* 42 To hear the Lark..singing startle the dull night. **1822** LAMB *Elia* Ser. I. *Praise Chimney-sw.*, Hundreds of grinning teeth startled the night with their brightness. **1849** WOOLNER *My Beautiful Lady* (1887) 36 Grateful, in her deep silence, one loud thrush Startled the air with song. **1862** B. TAYLOR *Poet's Jrnl.* (1866) 39 And the drowsy air is startled.

†**b.** *to startle out*: to cause sudden shedding of (blood). *Obs.* (? *nonce-use.*)

1605 *1st Pt. Jeronimo* I. i. 79 Ile wake the Court, or startle out some bloud.

†**6.** To cause to waver; to shake (a person, his resolution, faith, etc.). *Obs.*

1643 SIR T. BROWNE *Relig. Med.* I. §21 I have perused them all, and can discover nothing that may startle a discreet beliefe. **1647** CLARENDON *Hist. Reb.* IV. §293 His known affections to the King's service, from which it was not possible to remove or startle him. **1687** LOVELL tr. *Thevenot's Trav.* I. 2 He explained the..Old Testament with so much advantage to our Faith..that I dare be bold to say, he startled and shook most of them. *a* **1701** MAUNDRELL *Journ. Jerus.* (1732) 65 It almost startles their Faith. **1710** O. SANSOM *Acc. Life* 52 When he saw them [the Neighbours] flock in, he in his Rage (thinking to startle me) asked me before them, Whether [etc.]. **1784** P. WRIGHT *New Bk. Martyrs* 798/2 At Axminster one also was executed,..he had great resolution, and not at all startled with the fear of death.

†**7.** To rouse, excite. *Obs.*

1601 B. JONSON *Poetaster* IV. v, What, doe we nod, fellow Gods? sound musicke, and let us startle our spirits with a song.

8. *Comb.* †**startle-brain**, something that upsets the brain.

1653 BROME *Damoiselle* I. i, The care of children's such a Startle-braine.

Hence '**startlement**, the state or condition of being startled, alarm; hence, something that gives rise to this.

1927 *Chambers's Jrnl.* Feb. 92/2 No startlement was in her face by now. **1960** 'S. HARVESTER' *Chinese Hammer* i. 10 A strange expression of startlement came into her cool dark eyes. **1975** *Islander* (Victoria, B.C.) 4 May 3/3 Even so he [*sc.* a mouse] was dreadfully nervous and would leap like a miniature kangaroo at the least startlement.

startled ('stɑːt(ə)ld), *ppl. a.* [f. STARTLE *v.* + -ED¹.] In senses of the verb.

c **1611** CHAPMAN *Iliad* XVII. 269 The same hand giuing wing To martiall Phorcis startled soule. **1648** J. BEAUMONT *Psyche* IX. xlvii, All upright staring stand her startled Hairs Of one another's touch in jealous dread. **1764** *Oxf. Sausage* 59 Whether the plaintive Voice Of Laundress shrill awake my startled Ear; Or [etc.]. **1808** SCOTT *Marmion* II. Introd. 43 The startled quarry bounds amain. **1860** TYNDALL *Glac.* I. xi. 84 Uttering a startled shout as he went down the declivity. **1885** 'MRS. ALEXANDER' *At Bay* vi, He woke with a startled sense of wrong-doing.

startler (ˈstɑːtlə(r)). [f. STARTLE *v.* + -ER[1].] One who or something which startles.

†**1.** One who takes offence *at* something; one who awakes with a start. *Obs.*

1671 [R. MacWard] *True Non-Conf.* 268 None, but such phantastick Formalists as you will prove startlers at this sure and acceptable simplicity. **1810** Scott *Lady of L.* II. xxi, When, dazzled by the eastern glow, Such startler cast his glance below.

2. One who does startling things.

1873 Leland *Egypt. Sketch-Bk.* 309 Let us suppose that an artist—like many great modern startlers in paint—simply attempts to [etc.].

3. Something which startles; a startling thing.

1864 'Artemus Ward' *Among Mormons* v. Wks. (1871) 205 This careless manner of carting off solid silver is rather of a startler. **1889** Jerome *Idle Thoughts* 63 A subject the discussion of which will come upon the world in the nature of a startler. **1892** *Photogr. Ann.* II. 881 He heads the article in question appropriately, 'An Optical Startler'.

†**ˈstartless**, *a.* *Obs.*—[1]. [f. START *sb.*[2] + -LESS.] Without a start; giving no start.

1633 T. Adams *Exp. 2 Peter* ii. 12. 837 The Horse is valiant, startlesse at the drumme.

startling (ˈstɑːtlɪŋ), *vbl. sb.* [f. STARTLE *v.* + -ING[1].] The action of the verb STARTLE.

†**1.** A moving about; a rushing about. *Obs.*

1375 Barbour *Bruce* III. 704 A gret stertling he mycht haiff seyne Off schippys. **1387** Trevisa *Higden* (Rolls) II. 307 Þat bole heet Apis, þat was i-woned to..warne by his pleyenge and stertelynge what was to comynge. *a***1513** *Fabyan's Chron.* VII. ccxxxviii. (1811) 277 Stertlynge of beestys.

†**2.** The action of starting suddenly through surprise, alarm, etc.; an instance of this, a sudden start. *Obs.*

1624 Donne *Serm.* xix. (1640) 188 It is rather a startling in our sleep, then any awaking at all, to have a sudden remorse,..and no constant perseverance. **1652** Kirkman *Clerio & Lozia* 34 Her trembling body, her unaccustomed startlings and disquietness. **1677** Gilpin *Demonol.* (1867) 193 Custom doth by degrees take off the startling of conscience. **1825** Warman *Tremaine* III. xvii. 317 Why.. this shrinking of the soul back on herself, this startling at destruction?

3. The action of causing surprise or sudden fear.

1797 Coleridge *Remorse* I. ii. 329 If..our rude startling Drove you to this, your not ungentle, wildness. **1880** Meredith *Tragic Com.* (1881) 244 She has a turn for startling.

ˈstartling, *ppl. a.* [f. STARTLE *v.* + -ING[2].]

†**1.** Capering, prancing. *Obs.*

The phrase *startling steed* was apparently interpreted by Dryden in sense 3.

[*c***1385** Chaucer *L.G.W.* 1204 Vp on a courser stertelynge as the fyr..Sit Enyas.] *c***1450** *Merlin* xvi. 257 With vij hundred Knyghtes vpon startelinge stedes. **1513** Douglas *Æneis* IV. iv. 56 The child, amyde the planis, Joyus and blyth his stertling steid to assay. **1566** Gascoigne *Jocasta* v. ii. 104 Downe our duke dismountes From of his startling steede. [**1700** Dryden *Pal. & Arc.* III. 701 The startling Steed was seiz'd with sudden Fright.]

†**2.** Fickle, irresolute. Cf. STARTLE *v.* 4. *Obs.*

1645 Milton *Tetrach.* 25 Unless wee imagine Moses weaker then every negligent and startling Politician.

3. Starting with terror; easily terrified or shocked; timorous. Of sleep: Disturbed. Now *rare* or *Obs.*

1599 T. M[oufet] *Silkwormes* 2 That we resembled melancholique hares Or startling stagges, whom euerie shadow scares. *a***1718** Prior *Poems, Power* 824 In broken Rest, and startling Sleep to mourn. **1792** S. Rogers *Pleas. Mem.* I. 44 Oft, fancy-led, at midnight's fearful hour, With startling step we scaled the lonely tower. **1810** T. L. Peacock *Genius of Thames* p. vi, When in the startling grove The battle-blast was blown. **1813** Shelley *Q. Mab* IX. 175 'Tis but..The transient gulf-dream of a startling sleep. **1821** Clare *Vill. Minstr.* II. 121 The startling peewits.. Scream joyous whirring over-head.

†**4.** Of eyes: 'Starting from their sockets', protruding. *Obs.*

1648 Gage *West Ind.* 173 His look was grim with a wrinkled forehead, and broad startling eyes.

5. That causes a shock of surprise; that suddenly and forcibly compels attention.

1714 T. Lucas *Mem. Gamesters* (ed. 2) 275 He receiv'd the startling News, that his Lady was gone to London with the Lord M——n. **1826** Lamb *Pop. Fallacies* ix, If by worst be only meant the most far-fetched and startling, we agree to it. **1866** J. Martineau *Ess.* I. 30 The statement is as false as it is startling. **1884** *Punch* 27 Dec. 305/2 Read the startlingest of tracts! Get 'The Truth about the Navy'. **1911** H. Brown *Hist. Scot.* I. IV. vii. 244 Some of their tenets were certainly startling.

Hence **ˈstartlingly** *adv.*, **ˈstartlingness**.

1840 L. Blanchard in *New Monthly Mag.* LIX. 413 So strangely, so startlingly like. **1859** Meredith *R. Feverel* xxxviii, She could make you forget she was a woman, and then bring the fact startlingly home to you. **1871** Mozley *Univ. Serm.* v. (1876) 97 We have suddenly become alive to the strangeness and startlingness of the fact. **1886** *Harper's Mag.* Dec. 26, I rapped at the door somewhat startlingly.

startlish (ˈstɑːtlɪʃ), *a.* [f. STARTLE *v.* + -ISH.] Easily startled; apt to take fright; esp. said of a horse. Hence **ˈstartlishness**.

1740 Dyche & Pardon *Dict.* (ed. 3), *Startlish* [ed. 1735 *Startish*] or *Startly*. **1807** Southey *Espriella's Lett.* (1814) II. 273 Both were spirited beasts..;—both were startlish, and the mare vicious. *Ibid.* III. 339 All night I remained wakeful—not in that state of feverish startlishness which the expectation of an early call occasions, but [etc.]. **1836** *Blackw. Mag.* XL. 618 The cab-horse had exhibited symptoms of startlishness. **1863** Mrs. H. Wood *Verner's Pride* xlv, The sudden entrance startled her, albeit she was not of a startlish temperament.

startly (ˈstɑːtlɪ), *a.* [f. STARTLE *v.* + -Y.] = STARTLISH.

1727 Bailey vol. II, *Startly*, apt to start. **1735** Dyche & Pardon *Dict.*, *Startish* or *Startly*, fearful, timorous, apt to jump, leap, &c. upon every Noise, &c. **1840** Card. Manning *Let.* in Purcell *Life* (1895) I. 167 Don't be so startly, or you will frighten me. **1889** Gretton *Memory's Harkback* 148, I soon found that she [a mare] was scared and startly.

†**ˈstartmeal**, *a.* *Obs. rare*—[1]. In 5 **stirtemeel**. [f. START *sb.*[2] + -MEAL.] By starts.

*c***1425** Hoccleve *Learn to Die* 660 Stirtemeel gooth my pows.

start naked, *a.* *Obs.* exc. *dial.* Forms: 3 **steortnaket, steor(t)naked, stert naked,** (4 **star naked**), 4, 9 *dial.* **start naked.** [App. f. START *sb.*[1] + NAKED *a.*

The literal sense would seem to be 'naked even to the tail'. *Start* has not been found in Eng. with the sense 'buttocks' (= TAIL *sb.*[1] 5), but the MDu. and Ger. equivalents are so used.]

Entirely naked; = STARK-NAKED *a.*

*a***1225** *Juliana* 16 (Roy. MS.), & he het hatterliche strupen hire steortnaket [Bodl. MS. steort naket]. *a***1225** *Ancr. R.* 148 Heo haueð bipiled mine figer..despoiled hire stert [*printed* sterc] naked, & iworpen awei [etc.]. *Ibid.* 316 Bicleope þine sunne steornaked; þet is, ne hele þu nowiht of al þet lip þer abuten. **13..** *Pol. Songs* (Camden) 336 Sholde he for everi fals uth lese kirtel or kote,..He sholde stonde start [*printed* starc] naked twye o day or eve. *c***1320** *Cast. Love* 431 in *Minor Poems fr. Vernon MS.* xxxviii, And I-strupt him al start-naked. *a***1325** in Horstm. *Altengl. Leg.* (1878) 140 þai lay þerin all star naked. **1892** *Dialect Notes* (Amer. Dial. Soc. 1896) I. v. 234 *Start-naked*: stark naked. 'He is a start-naked villain.'.. Mr. A. W. Long, of North Carolina, reports that he never heard any other form than *start-naked* used in conversation in that state; and that two of his friends—one from Virginia, and the other from South Carolina—make the same statement for those two states. **1896** *Warwicksh. Gloss.*

startup (ˈstɑːtʌp), *sb.*[1] *Obs.* exc. *dial.* and *Hist.* Also 6 **startop(p)e, -uppe, stertup,** 6–7 **startop.** Also *pl.* 6 **stertops, stert-, startuppes, styrtoppes, stertyppes.** [f. vbl. phr. *start up* (see START *v.* 13); as if 'a shoe that starts up to the middle of the leg'.] Originally, a kind of 'high-low' or boot, worn by rustics; in later use, a kind of gaiter or legging. Chiefly in *plural.*

1517 *Test. Ebor.* (Surtees) V. 83, j par sotularium quæ dicuntur stertuppes. **1530** Palsgr. 251/1 Payre of startoppes, *hovssettes*. **1551–2** *Act 5 & 6 Edw. VI* c. 15 §5 Any Shoes, Boots, Buskyns, Styrtoppes or Slippers. **1558** in Feuillerat *Revels Q. Eliz.* (1908) 35 Imployed into edging of Stertyppes for the Patriarkes. **1572** *Ibid.* 159, viii payer of white startops of cloth of sylver. **1573** Baret *Alv.* S 328 A high shooe of rawe leather called a stertvp, *pero*. **1574** *Withals' Dict.* 54 b, In a maner all husbande men doe weare stertups. **1591** Greene *Farew. Follie* Wks. (Grosart) IX. 265 His pompes were a little too heauie, being trimmed start-vps made of a paire of boote legges. **1600** Pory *Leo's Africa* III. 156 The streetes are so mirie, that you cannot walk in them without startups. *c***1605** Drayton *Pastorals*, Ecl. ix. 9 (1619) 467 When not a Shepheard any thing that could, But greaz'd his start-ups black as Autumns Sloe. **1608** Sylvester *Du Bartas* II. iv. IV. *Decay* 114 Her neat, fit, Startups of green Velvet bee, Flourisht with silver. *a***1626** Moryson *Itin.* IV. (1903) 451 [Italian] Gentlewemen.. weare high Startups or Pantofills of wood, so as they cannot goe without helpe. **1667** Cotton *Scarron.* IV. 124 Yet she made shift to stuff each start-up, And tie 'um to the rest on's Wardope. **1688** Holme *Armory* IV. vii. (Roxb.) 325/2 Startops or hose foulded downe belowe the knees. **1777** *Horæ Subsec.* [MS., Devon dialect] 411 (E.D.D.) *Start-ups*, a kind of button'd buskins. Not high shoes as Littleton represents them. **1821** Scott *Kenilw.* xxiv, This was a stupid lout,.. with..his hose about his heels, and huge startups upon his feet. **1836** R. Furness *Astrologer* I. Wks. (1858) 137 Thor's knitted cap, suspended on a wire, And hoddin start-ups warm'd above the fire. **1854** Miss Baker *Northampt. Gloss.*, *Start-ups*, short gaiters: long ones being styled leggings.

start-up, *ppl. a.* and *sb.*[2] Also **startup.** [f. *start* pa. pple. of START *v.* + UP *adv.*: see START *v.* 13.]

†**A.** *ppl. a.* That has suddenly 'started up' into existence, notice, or importance; upstart, parvenu. *Obs.*

a. With adv., *new, newly, fresh, late, first.*

1557 Traheron *Expos. S. John* title-p., The wicked enterprises of new sterte vp Arians in Englande. **1573–80** G. Harvey *Lett.* Wks. (Grosart) I. 125 To sende..my lord Ritches players, or sum other freshe starteupp comedanties unto me. **1628** in *Cath. Tract.* (S.T.S.) 275 These first start-up apostats and runnagats redacted it [Abbirbroth] to such desolation & ruines, as may be seene. **1634** Sir T. Herbert *Trav.* 139 Shewing no more..beautie then neighbouring and late start-up-townes about her. **1687** [Shields] *Hind let loose* 176 A newly start up opinion. **1762** Warburton *Doctr. Grace* III. Wks. 1788 IV. 686 A new Start-up Sect.

b. *simply.*

1567 Drant *Horace, Ep.* II. i. G iiij, Eche man is burning hote To be a startevp wryter straighte. **1597** *Return fr. Parnass.* IV. i. 1340 Each start-upp clowne. **1601** Sir W. Cornwallis *Ess.* II. xlii. (1631) 197 Like start-up Gentlemen, Gentlemen without a pedegree. **1616** J. Lane *Contn. Sqr.'s T.* IX. p. 139 *note*, Wheare prowd Fregilea lies with all her start vp statelie palaces. **1704** Swift *Tale Tub* i. 43 Two Junior start-up Societies. **1801** Eliz. Helme *St. Marg. Cave* (1819) II. xii. 219 A start-up baron of yesterday.

B. *sb.*

†**1.** An upstart; a low-born person who has risen to wealth or power. *Obs.*

1599 Jas. I *Basil. Doron* II. (1603) 70 Delight to be serued with men of the noblest bloud..for besides that their seruice shall breede you great good-will and least enuie, contrary to that of start-ups; yee shall oft finde vertue follow noble race. **1599** Shaks. *Much Ado* I. iii. 69 That young start-vp hath all the glorie of my overthrow. *a***1652** Brome *Queen & Concubine* II. i. (1659) 24 His Marriage with that Start-up.

2. [A distinct word; subst. use of phrase *to start up*: see START *v.* 23c, e.] An instance of 'starting up'; *spec.* the action or process of starting up a series of operations, a piece of machinery, a business, etc. Also *attrib.*

1845 Disraeli *Sybil* IV. xiii, I am used to these start-ups. **1945** H. D. Smyth *Gen. Acct. Devel. Atomic Energy Mil. Purposes* ix. 94 In estimating time schedules this 'start-up' or 'equilibrium' time must be added to the time of construction of the plant. **1954** *Trans. IRE on Nuclear Sci.* I. 3/1 During startup the behavior of the reactor is similar to that of an amplifier with positive feedback. **1959** *Wall St. Jrnl.* (Eastern ed.) 18 Dec. 9/1 Start-up expenses connected with new store openings have been heavy. **1968** *Globe & Mail* (Toronto) 13 Jan. B 5/4 Production target is late 1969 with startup to have cost more than $90-million. **1975** P. R. F. Mathijsen *Guide to European Community Law* II. iv. 87 It is proposed that modern agricultural enterprises be set up with special aids such as start-up grants, investment aid and guaranteed credits. **1976** B. Jackson *Flameout* (1977) iv. 63 The flight data recorder..tape-recorded engine start-up, takeoff, climb-out, [etc.]. **1980** *Daily Tel.* 20 Mar. 28 (Advt.), They will assume responsibility for the start-up, management, organisation, and profitability of large work sites. **1983** *Sunday Times* 23 Jan. 56/1 The fund is designed to take advantage of the tax relief introduced in 1981 for investors putting up to £20,000 a year into start-ups. **1983** *Times* 19 Feb. 15 (*heading*) Business start-up funds worth the risk for top taxpayers.

starty (ˈstɑːtɪ), *a.* *dial.* [f. START *v.* + -Y.] Apt to start, easily frightened.

1861 Mrs. Stowe *Pearl of Orr's Island* I. ix. 70 The little feller was very starty and fretful in his sleep last night. **1864** *Realm* 2 Mar. 1 'Tis feared their political creed might be somewhat too skittish and starty.

starvation (stɑːˈveɪʃən). [f. STARVE *v.* + -ATION. Except *flirtation* (1718), this is the oldest of the many sbs. in *-ation* formed on native Eng. vbs.

App. first used with reference to the bill of 1775 'for restraining Trade and Commerce with the New England Colonies', which the Opposition denounced as intended to combat the rebellion by producing a famine in which the innocent would suffer equally with the guilty. The remark of Mr. Dundas (*Hansard's Deb.*, 6 Mar. 1775), that he was 'afraid' that the famine spoken of 'would not be produced by this Act', excited great indignation, and in 1781–2 Walpole and Mason call him by the nicknames 'Starvation Dundas' and 'Starvation'. The statement of Mitford (*Corr. Walpole & Mason*, 1851, II. 396) that Dundas himself used the word is in itself not improbable, but appears to lack confirmation. The verb *starve* occurs several times in the reports of speeches on the bill, but the sb. does not appear.]

1. The action of starving or subjecting to famine.

1778 Lady Craven in *Ann. Reg., Characters* etc. 204 Behold, our ministers..Who talk of peace, of taxes, and starvation. **1782** W. Mason in *Corr. Walpole & Mason* (1851) II. 310 If it be true that Jenkinson has been closeted ..and if..he comes into any ostensible office, I shall not wait for the advent of *Starvation* from Edinburgh to settle my judgment. **1791–3** in *Spirit Publ. Jrnls.* (1799) I. 260 *Starvation.* A curious experiment, which, after being tried in America and France, has succeeded tolerably well at home. **1854** Milman *Lat. Chr.* II. 395 Somewhat later he alludes to the starvation of Rome.

attrib. **1802** in *Spirit Publ. Jrnls.* VI. 371, I have a long catalogue to offer to your choice... 7. The Starvation War. 8. The Financial War [etc.].

2. a. The condition of being starved or having too little food to sustain life or health.

1802 *Sporting Mag.* XX. 292 Here are no symptoms of starvation, the hounds are well fed. **1813** Wellington in Gurw. *Desp.* (1838) X. 367 The French..live in countries in Spain, in which the Spaniards starve; and..the starvation of the Spanish armies is more burthensome to the country than the plentiful mode of living of the French. **1822** *Sporting Mag.* IX. 218 The parish horses must otherwise actually have perished by starvation. **1866** Mrs. Oliphant *Agnes* I. xvii. 213 But then was not a married curate the emblem of starvation all the world over? **1867** H. Latham *Black & White* 37 When Lee surrendered, we had come to simple starvation.

b. *attrib.*, as *starvation diet, line, point, rations*, etc.

1848 Mill *Pol. Econ.* I. II. xii. 433 Wages may fall below starvation point. **1867** J. Campbell *Balmerino* III. i. 166 The minister was placed on a starvation allowance. **1869** J. Greenwood *Seven Curses of London* iii. 46 The child is welcome to live on starvation diet just as long as it may. **1886** Besant *Childr. Gibeon* II. xxiii, In allowing an employer to pay starvation wages to girls. **1897** Mary Kingsley *W. Africa* 313 The two or three Kruboys on a starvation beach can fairly well fend for themselves. **1915** Mrs Belloc Lowndes *Diary* 3 Mar. (1971) 56 British prisoners..have one cup of coffee with no milk or sugar..a 2 lb. loaf of bread for two days..Practically starvation rations. **1925** Joyce *Let.* 25 Mar. (1966) III. 117, I have now been put on a starvation diet by way of adding to my present pleasures. **1937** 'G. Orwell' *Road to Wigan Pier* v. 80 A man and wife on twenty-three shillings a week are not far from the starvation line. **1957** P. Worsley *Trumpets shall Sound* 15 This does not mean that Melanesians always live near the starvation-line. **1977** D. Williams *Treasure by Degrees* i. 16 The production of pure food..unadulterated by mechanical or chemical intervention..would have put the nation on a starvation diet. **1977** D. Francis *Risk* v. 56

If he caught me..he'd..leave me in the dark on starvation rations.

c. quasi-*advb.* So as to cause starvation. *colloq.*

1892 KIPLING *Barrack-room Ballads, Tommy* 18 Yes, makin' mock o' uniforms that guard you while you sleep Is cheaper than them uniforms, an' they're starvation cheap.

d. *transf.* Deprivation or insufficient supply of something necessary to life.

1866 HUXLEY *Physiol.* iv. §31. 103 Two deadly influences ..are co-operating; one is the deprivation of oxygen, the other is the excessive accumulation of carbonic acid in the blood. Oxygen starvation and carbonic acid poisoning..are at work together. *Ibid.* vi. §7. 142 Whether an animal be herbivorous or carnivorous, it begins to starve from the moment its vital food-stuffs consist of pure amyloids or fats, or any mixture of them. It suffers from what may be called nitrogen starvation. **1891** G. S. WOODHEAD *Bacteria* 117 In one case the yeast-cells die of starvation, although large quantities of sugar are present.

3. starvation (cold), very cold. *dial.* and *colloq.*

1893 *Wiltsh. Gloss.* Add., *Starvation cold*, extremely cold. **1899** *N.W. Linc. Gloss.*, *Starvation*, suffering from cold. **1967** E. GRIERSON *Crime of One's Own* xi. 89 Queer day to leave it open. It's starvation. **1977** *Lancashire Life* Mar. 68/3 They mostly had open top decks and open staircases, and it was starvation in the winter.

†**starve**, *sb. Obs. rare.* In 3 steorve. [OE. *steorfa* wk. masc., related to *steorfan* STARVE *v.* Cf. OS. *man-sterbo* pestilence.] Pestilence, mortality; also a pestilent being (applied to the devil).

a **1023** WULFSTAN *Hom.* xiii. (1883) 86 Eac sceal aspringan wide and side..stric and steorfa and fela unȝelimpa. *c* **1175** *Lamb. Hom.* 13 Stala and steorfa swiðe eow scal hene. *a* **1225** *Juliana* 49, & stondinde o þe steorue nom hire ahne bondes & bigon to beaten þen belial of helle. *a* **1225** *St. Marher.* 12 Stute nu earme steorue ant swic nuðe lanhure swikele swarte deouel þat tu ne derue me na mare.

starve (stɑːv), *v. Pa. t.* and *pa. pple.* **starved.** Forms: 1 steorfan, 2 stærfan, 2, 4–5 sterven, 3 sterfen, 3–4 steorve, 3–4, 6 storve, 4–7 sterve, 5 *Sc.* sterwe, 6 sterf, (sterff), *Sc.* sterv, 6– starve. *Pa. t.* 1 stearf, 2 sturfe, sturve, 3–5 starf, 4–5 starfe, 3–5 sterf, (5 sterfe); 5 stervet, stervid (? *error* sterevid), 6 stervit, starvit, 7 sterved, 6– starved. *Pa. pple.* 1 storfen, 3–4 istorve, 4 ystorve, 3 isterve, 3–6 storven, 4, 6 storve, 5 storvyn, (storvun); 6–7 sterved, 6– starved. [A Com. WGer. str. verb, which has become weak in mod.Eng.: OE. *steorfan* (pa. t. *stearf*, pl. *sturfon*, pa. pple. *storfen*) corresponds to OFris. *sterva* (WFris. *stjerre*, NFris. *sterwe*), OS. *sterban*, (M)LG., (M)Du. *sterven*, OHG. *sterban* (MHG., mod.G. *sterben*), to die, f. Teut. root **sterb-* (:—*starb-* :—*sturb-*).

A root of identical form, and possibly of identical origin, occurs in ON. *stiarfe* wk. masc., ? epilepsy, *stiarf-r*, *stir-finn* obstinate, *starf* toil, effort, *starfa* to toil. It has been suggested that the primitive sense of the root may have been 'to be rigid', which might account both for the sense 'to die' of the WGer. verb and for the meanings of the ON. words. On the other hand, as the Teut. form may equally well represent pre-Teut. **sterp-* and **sterbh-*, it is possible that the WGer. and the ON. words may be unconnected.

The conjugation of the verb has remained strong in the continental Teut. langs. In English the strong forms of the pa. t. became obsolete in the 15th century, and those of the pa. pple. in the 16th c. The transitive (causative) use, which arose in English in the 16th c., is not paralleled in the other langs.]

I. Intransitive uses.

1. To die. Said of a person or animal. In late use app. to die a lingering death, as from hunger, cold, grief, or slow disease. Also, in spiritual sense, of the soul. *Obs.*

c **1000** ÆLFRIC *Hom.* I. 398 Annanias and Saphiran..mid færlicum deaðe ætforan ðam apostolum steorfende afeollon. *c* **1175** *Lamb. Hom.* 71 þole us to bi-wepen ure sunne þet we ne steruen noht þer inne. *a* **1225** *Ancr. R.* 222 He..pineð so hire licome þet to soule steorueð. *c* **1250** *Gen. & Ex.* 1893 Starf ysaac quan he was hold .ix. score ȝer and fiue told. *c* **1290** *St. Clement* 146 in *S. Eng. Leg.* 327 He wende þat huy a-dronke weren oþur i-storue bi þe weie. *c* **1374** CHAUCER *Troylus* v. 1844 [Christ] Vpon a cros oure soules for to beye First starf, and ros, and sit yn heuene a-boue. *c* **1450** *Mirk's Festial* 104 þys Perys sterfe yn hys bede. *a* **1542** WYATT in *Tottel's Misc.* (Arb.) 78 What so befall, tyll that I sterue By proofe full well it shall be knowne. **1578** *Narsetus* 90 in T. Proctor *Gorg. Gallery* B iiij, A thousand deathes I do desire, in wretched state to starue. **1590** SPENSER *F.Q.* II. vi. 34 These armes,..the which doe men in bale to sterue. *a* **1657** SIR W. MURE *Sonn. to Margaret* ii. Wks. (S.T.S.) I. 48 Margrait..Quho with thy eyes, (least my puir lyfe sould sterue), Wouchaiffes to look wt pitty on my paine.

2. With various constructions, specifying the cause of death. In later use with modified sense: To be brought gradually nearer to death, to be in process of being killed; to suffer extremely. Now only *dial.*

†**a.** const. *for*, *of*, *with* (grief, love, pestilence, and the like). *Obs.*

c **1330** *Arth. & Merl.* 692 Anon he starf for diol, ywis. *c* **1385** CHAUCER *L.G.W.* 1277 There as he was in paril for to sterue For hungyr & for myschif in the se. *c* **1386** —— *Knt.'s T.* 1156 A thousand slayn, and nat oon of qualm ystorue. **1513** DOUGLAS *Æneis* IV. Prol. 51 For luff thow stervist maist dowchtie Achill. **1584** POWEL *Lloyd's Cambria* 109 Meredyth..whome Blethyn pursued so straightlie, that he starued for cold and hunger vpon the mountaines.

†**b.** const. *of*, *with* (hunger), *for* (hunger, food, meat). *Obs.* (Cf. sense 4; also HUNGER-STARVE *v.*)

1124 *O.E. Chron.* (Laud MS.), Se man þe æni god heafde him me hit be ræfode..þe nan ne heafde stærf of hungor. **1154** *Ibid.* (Laud MS.) an. 1137. *c* **1175** *Cott. Hom.* 233 þa were cofe abruden into þesternesse þe hi sturfe hungre. **1528** ROY *Rede Me* (Arb.) 86 Playnly for honger they shulde sterve, Excepte they wolde to laboure fall. *a* **1618** SYLVESTER *Hymn of Alms* 185 To stark for Cold, to starve for Food, to perish In Penury. **1650** LAMONT *Diary* (Maitland Club) 24 A collectione..for supplying the prisoners in England.. that were sterueing for famine. **1707** PRIOR *Sat. Poets* 153 Starving for Meat, not surfeiting on Praise. **1735** ARBUTHNOT *Aliments* ii. §8. 48 An Animal that starves of Hunger, dies feverish and delirious.

c. const. †*for*, †*of*, *with* (cold).

c **1380** WYCLIF *Wks.* (1880) I. 14 Here children steruen for cold. **1526** *Pilgr. Perf.* (W. de W. 1531) 140 All bathed in rayne & frosen with yce, & nere storuen for colde. *a* **1604** HANMER *Chron. Irel.* (1809) 393 We starve for cold, wanting our winter garments. *a* **1619** FOTHERBY *Atheom.* I. xi. §4 (1622) 117 Friget Venus. Poore Venus staru's with cold, & soone will dye. **1737** POPE *Sat. Donne* ii. 72 His Office keeps your Parchment fates entire, He starves with cold to save them from the fire. **1756** MRS. CALDERWOOD in *Coltness Collect.* (Maitl. Club) 151 In summer she is like to starve of cold, and in winter like to die with heat. **1867** P. KENNEDY *Banks of Boro* xiv. 70 [He'll] be obleeged to bring the shakedown near the fire..to keep her from starving with the cold.

†**3.** Of plants or their parts: To die, wither. Of a material substance: To lose its characteristic quality, spoil, deteriorate. *Obs.*

1393 LANGL. *P. Pl.* C. XIII. 179 Bote yf þe sed þat sowen is in þe sloh sterue [L. *mortuum fuerit*], Shal neuere spir springen vp. *a* **1400–50** *Bk. Curtasye* 766 in *Babees Bk.* 203 þe potage fyrst with brede y-coruyn, [the sewer] Couerys hom agayn lest þey ben storuyn. **1466** in Willis & Clark *Cambridge* (1886) III. 93 This tymbir shalbe white oke, not doted, nor storvyn, nor sappy. **1578** LYTE *Dodoens* IV. lxii. 525 [Our Ladyes Thistell] floweth in June and July,..and when it hath brought foorth his seede, it decayeth and starueth. **1607** J. CARPENTER *Plaine Mans Plough* 220 The trees which grow not sterue, or are very neare to steruing. **1669** A. BROWNE *Ars Pictoria* 90 When your silver either with long keeping or moistness of the Air becomes starved and rusty; you must..before you lay the silver Cover over the place with a little Juice of Garlick, which will preserve it. **1695** WOODWARD *Nat. Hist. Earth* VI. (1723) 288 Had the seeds of the pepper-plant been borne from Java to these northern countries, they must all have starved for want of Sun. *a* **1722** LISLE *Husb.* (1757) 148 In our hill-country.. the straw breaks or starves three or four weeks before harvest.

4. a. [Orig. *ellipt.* = 2 b.] To die of hunger; to perish or be in process of perishing from lack or insufficiency of food; to suffer extreme poverty and want; more emphatically ***to starve to death***. Also hyperbolically in colloquial use: To be extremely hungry.

[**1124–1735** to starve for, of, with hunger: see 2 b.] **1578** WHETSTONE *2nd Pt. Promos & Cass.* I. vii, Better the purce then body starue of twayne. **1596** SHAKS. *1 Hen. IV*, I. iii. 89 No: on the barren Mountaine let him sterue. **1604** BRETON *Passionate Sheph.* (Grosart) 8/2 That thou wilt no foode reserue, But my flockes and I shall sterue. **1647** E. PORTER in *Nicholas Papers* (Camden) I. 70 Were it not for an Irish Barber that was once my servaunt I might have starved for want of bredd. **1655** I. S. *Brief Jrnl. W. Ind.* 24 Which in common reason may seem strange that (of all men) Souldiers should starve in a Cooks shop (as the saying is). **1734** POPE *Ess. Man* IV. 149 But sometimes Virtue starves, while Vice is fed. **1775** *Ann. Reg., Hist. Europe* *88/1 It was said, that they [the Americans] had no alternative but to starve or to rebel. **1784** COWPER *Tiroc.* 402 Let rev'rend churls his ignorance rebuke, Who starve upon a dog's-ear'd Pentateuch. **1820** W. IRVING *Sketch Bk.* I. 63 [He] would rather starve on a penny than work for a pound. **1842** TENNYSON *Godiva* 20 If they pay this tax, they starve. **1885** 'MRS. ALEXANDER' *At Bay* i, Pot luck, my dear fellow, but you shan't starve. **1910** ASHTON HILLIERS *Master Girl* i. 24 The man was starving to death. Water he did not want.

Proverb. *a* **1536** *Proverbs* in *Songs, Carols* etc. (1907) 128 While the grasse grwith, the hors sterwith.

b. *transf.* Of an animal or plant: To die or lose vitality for lack of proper nutriment.

a **1680** BUTLER *Rem.* (1759) II. 23 Thorns and Thistles flourish on barren Grounds, where nobler Plants would starve. **1866** HUXLEY *Physiol.* vi. §7. 142 An animal..begins to starve from the moment its vital food-stuffs consist of pure amyloids or fats.

c. *fig.*

1590 SHAKS. *Com. Err.* II. i. 88 His company must do his minions grace, Whil'st I at home starue for a merrie looke. **1616** R. C. *Times Whistle* i. 398 Though our soules doe sterve For want of Knowledge, we doe litle care. **1872** KINGSLEY *Lett.* (1878) II. 388 The scheme might starve without such more liberal assistance at first. **1884** BROWNING *Ferishtah* (1885) 7 Which lacks food the more, Body or soul in me? I starve in soul.

5. a. [Orig. *ellipt.* = 2 c.] To die of exposure to cold; chiefly used hyperbolically, to suffer extreme cold, to be benumbed or 'dead' with cold. Now only *north.*

[**1380–1604** to starve for cold, **1756** to starve of cold, **1619–1867** to starve with cold: see 2 c.] **1602** ROWLANDS *Greenes Ghost* (1872) 27 So out of doores go they with his clothes..and left Nicholas Nouice staruing and quaking in that doghole. **1710** SWIFT *Jrnl. to Stella* 30 Dec., The weather grows cold... I'll go rise, for my hands are starving while I write in bed. **1731** POPE *Ep. Boyle* 38 Imitating-Fools..Shall call the winds thro' long arcades to roar,.. And, if they starve, they starve by rules of art. **1772** J. W. FLETCHER *Appeal* III. Wks. 1826 I. 77 Whether they starve in the snows of Lapland, or burn in the sands of Guinea?

†**b.** quasi-trans. ***to starve out***: to endure in perishing cold. *Obs.*

1606 SHAKS. *Tr. & Cr.* V. x. 2 Stand hoe, yet are we maisters of the field, Neuer goe home; here starue we out the night.

II. Transitive uses.

†**6. a.** To cause to die, to kill, destroy. Const. *by*, *for*, *with*. *Obs.*

a **1529** SKELTON *Duke of Albany* 251 The fynde of hell mot sterue the! *c* **1550** R. BIESTON *Bayte Fortune* B ij b, Both Emperour and Kyng at last by death he sterueth. **1560** DAUS tr. *Sleidane's Comm.* 434 He..also sterued them for honger and cold, so that many died. **1629** MAXWELL tr. *Herodian* (1635) 398 That the Souldiers might perish for lacke of water, and be starved with thirst. **1690** C. NESSE *Hist. & Myst. O. & N.T.* I. 341 There to starve him with cold as well as with hunger. **1707** [E. WARD] *Hudibras Rediv.* VI. 27 Thus almost starv'd with Wind and Weather, I left 'em marching all together.

†**b.** To cause (a plant, bodily limb or organ) to wither or perish. *Obs.* Cf. 8.

1580 [see STARVED *ppl. a.* 1]. **1591** SHAKS. *Two Gent.* IV. iv. 159 But since she..threw her Sun-expelling Masque away, The ayre hath staru'd the roses in her cheekes. **1607** —— *Timon* I. i. 257 Aches contract, and sterue your supple ioynts.

7. a. To cause to perish of hunger; to deprive of or keep scantily supplied with food; †also with *up*; †more definitely ***to starve for hunger*** or ***meat***; more emphatically ***to starve to death***.

1530 PALSGR. 734/1, I starve one for honger, *je affame.* **1544** BETHAM *Precepts War* II. lxxxiv. M iij, For yf they be sterued for hungre, vnpossible it is that they shoulde do anye thynge vyliauntly. **1552** HULOET, Storue wyth hunger, *victum alicui subducere.* **1570** LEVINS *Manip.* 83/9 To sterue, actiue, *cibum subducere.* **1573** TUSSER *Husb.* (1878) 89 Who abuseth his cattle and starues them for meat. **1583** STOCKER *Civ. Warres Lowe C.* III. 130 b, The young children which were staruen to death, said,..Where is the bread, where is the wine. **1596** SHAKS. *Tam. Shr.* IV. iii. 9 But I..Am staru'd for meate, giddie for lacke of sleepe. **1635** R. JOHNSON *Hist. Tom a Lincolne* (1828) 106 Wherein was left but onely the Red Rose Knight, in his Palmer's weed (for all the rest were starved up for want of food). *a* **1641** BP. MOUNTAGU *Acts & Mon.* (1642) 462, I..had rather perish by, and with that Thracian sport you speak of then here in this Countrey to bee starved up with your religious fasts. **1684** BURNET tr. *More's Utopia* 140 Such as are wrought on by these Perswasions, do either starve themselves of their own accord [L. *inedia sponte vitam finiunt*], or they take Opium. **1718** PRIOR *Alma* III. 257 To starve a man, in law is murther. **1775** *Ann. Reg., Hist. Europe* *88/1 The object of consideration was not, whether the Americans were to be starved or not; but [etc.]. **1784** COWPER *Task* IV. 463 Oh for a law to noose the villain's neck Who starves his own. **1861** FLOR. NIGHTINGALE *Notes on Nursing* 46 Thousands of patients are annually starved in the midst of plenty.

b. To subdue by famine or low diet; also with *down*, *out*; to force *into* (a course of action) by starvation.

a **1625** FLETCHER *Womans Prize* I. iv, We will beleagure 'em, and either starve 'em out, or make 'em recreant. **1705** ARBUTHNOT *Coins* (1727) 278 There was one Attalus, who endeavoured to starve Italy by stopping their Convoy of Provisions from Africa. **1775** MARQ. ROCKINGHAM *Sp. Ho. Lords* 16 Mar., in *Hansard* 431 They..were to be starved into compliance. **1839** DICKENS *Nich. Nick.* viii, Every young and healthy feeling flogged and starved down.

c. To cure (a disease) by abstemious diet; also with *out*.

1617 MORYSON *Itin.* III. 159 They..give themselves to the keeping of Irish women, who starve the ague, giving the sick man no meate. **1700** DRYDEN *Fables, Theodore & Hon.* 37 As men by fasting starve the untamed disease. **1737** [see STARVING *vbl. sb.* 2]. **1784** COWPER *Tiroc.* 768 Disease.. Prevented much by diet neat and plain; Or, if it enter, soon starv'd out again. **1839** J. W. CROKER in *C. Papers* 21 Nov. (1884) I. xxi. 358 Last week he [Wellington] had been what he called starving a cold. **1885** *Brit. Med. Jrnl.* 26 Sept. 611/1 Feeding and Starving in the treatment of disease.

d. *transf.* and *fig.*

1581 G. PETTIE tr. *Guazzo's Civ. Conv.* (1586) I. 3 b, In steede of consuming and staruing your euil, you giue it nourishment. **1588** SHAKS. *L.L.L.* II. i. 11 When she did starue the generall world beside, And prodigally gaue them [*sc.* graces] all to you. **1590** —— *Mids. N.* I. i. 222 We must starue our sight, From louers foode, till morrow deepe midnight. **1599** DRAYTON *Sonet* xxxiv. Minor P. (1907) 38 Marvaile not Loue..That I am onely staru'd in my desire. **1603** —— *To his coy Love* i. Ibid. 78 These poore halfe Kisses kill me quite; Was euer man thus serued? Amidst an Ocean of Delight, For Pleasure to be starued. **1628** GAULE *Pract. Theories Panegyr.* (1629) 403 Neither should his absence starue them, nor his presence cloy them. **1675** BAXTER *Cath. Theol.* II. xiii. 292 And so you starve out and destroy true piety, by calling off the peoples minds to Controversie. **1704** M. HENRY *Communic. Comp.* Wks. 1855 I. 309 The soul that is starved is as certainly murdered as the soul that is stabbed. **1810** S. PERCEVAL in S. Walpole *Life & Corr.* (1874) II. iv. 133 If you thought they were starving the great cause [Peninsular War] by any mistaken economy. **1878** D. KEMP *Yacht & Boat Sailing* 371 *Starved of Wind* —when a vessel is sailed so near the wind that she does not have enough of it, or feel the weight of it.

e. Phr. ***starve the crows*** and varr. = *stone the crows* s.v. CROW *sb.*[1] 3 d. *Austral. slang.*

1918 H. MATTHEWS *Saints & Soldiers* 116 'Starve the crows,' howled Bluey in that agonised screech of his. **1936** A. RUSSELL *Gone Nomad* vi. 46 Starve the crows! I laugh ev'ry time I think of it. **1966** G. W. TURNER *Eng. Lang. Austral. & N.Z.* vi. 118 The well-known *stone the crows*.. occurs in such forms as *starve the wombats..starve the ninnies* and several more. **1966** 'J. HACKSTON' *Father clears Out* 156 Trooper Newbigun turned his horse's head and rode off with such dignity that Albert Horne said, just like an Australian, 'Gawd starve the crows!' **1968** *Courier-Mail* (Brisbane) 18 Nov. 10/7 Though the Dad and Dave expression 'Starve the lizards' is well enough known it has taken the spring of 1968 to bring about a similar but far from fanciful phrase for the flying foxes.

8. To produce atrophy in (a plant, an animal or vegetable organ, a morbid growth) by withholding nutriment. Also *fig.* with immaterial object. So *to starve out*, to destroy by absorbing all the available nutriment.

1633 Bp. Hall *Occas. Medit.* xi. 26, I do not love to see an Infancy over-hopeful; in these pregnant beginnings, one facultie starves another, and, at last, leaves the minde saplesse, and barren. *a* 1682 Sir T. Browne *Misc. Tracts* i. (1683) 76 This, in the Pathology of Plants, may be the Disease of..superfoliation..whereby the fructifying Juice is starved by the excess of Leaves. 1709 Shaftesb. *Moralists* ii. iv. 118 The Anatomy of the Creature shews it..to be, as it were, all Wing..: these Parts of theirs being made in such superiour proportion, as in a manner to starve their Companions. 1766 H. Walpole *Let. to Mann* 9 Sept., Our harvest..turns out ill, the preceding rains having starved it with weeds. 1781 Cowper *Retirem.* 44 Invet'rate habits.. Their fibres..draining its nutritious pow'rs to feed Their noxious growth, starve ev'ry better seed. 1855 Bain *Senses & Int.* iii. ii. §11. (1864) 474 The whole soul, passing into one sense, aggrandizes that sense and starves the rest. 1866 Livingstone *Jrnl.* (1873) I. i. 19 Where bamboos prevail they have starved out the woody trees. 1899 *Allbutt's Syst. Med.* VIII. 780 To endeavour to starve the growth by coagulating the blood-vessels at the base.

9. a. To cause to die of cold, to kill with cold; also hyperbolically, to benumb with cold; more emphatically *to starve to death*. Chiefly *pass.* *Obs.* exc. *dial.*

1600 Holland *Livy* xxi. lviii. 427 Many a man and beast, and seven Elephants..were starved and perished [owing to the intolerable cold]. 1636 Cowley *Sylva* 486 No flower or herbe is neere it found, But a perpetuall winter sterves the ground. *a* 1639 Carew *Poems, To Saxham* 11 The cold and frozen ayr had sterv'd Much poore, if not by thee preserv'd. 1662 J. Davies tr. *Olearius' Voy. Ambass.* 37 Their cloaths being all wet about them, most of them would have been starv'd to death in the snow. 1667 Milton *P.L.* ii. 600 Thither..the damn'd Are brought:..From Beds of raging Fire to starve in Ice Thir soft Ethereal warmth. *a* 1676 Hale *Prim. Orig. Man.* ii. ix. (1677) 208 The Winter cold, which starves very many, either for want of heat or food. 1697 *C'tess D'Aunoy's Trav.* (1706) 57 What occasion was there..to put me into such an open place to starve me? 1770 Lady Mary Coke *Jrnl.* 12 Jan. (1892) III. 203 There is not a window or door that shuts; I am starved to death at my fire side. 1891 *Leeds Mercury* 14 Dec. 5/6 A man starved to death at Farsley. 1893 J. K. Snowden *Tales Yorksh. Wolds* 158 Willie was rubbing his hands slowly before the roaring fire. 'I'm fearful starved', he said.

b. (See quot. 1886.)

1766 *Museum Rust.* VI. 84 Considerable parts of each land, towards each furrow, are starved by the coldness of the water dripping from the higher parts of the lands. 1886 *Chesh. Gloss.* s.v., Land is also said to be starved when it is cold for want of drainage.

10. *Comb.*: **starve-acre** *sb.* (see quot. 1886); *a.*, that produces poor crops; †**starve-crow**, †**starve-yoad** *dial.* [YAUD, horse] formerly used as field-names; †**starve-gutted** *a.*, famished.

1672 Eachard *Hobbes' St. Nat. Consid.* 112 Because Jonas Moore is not as yet come to divide, and set out the ground, and to call this piece starve-crow, and t'other long acre. 1726 *Diss. Dumpling* 22 The Enemies of good Eating, the Starve-gutted Authors of Grub-street. 1755 in *N. & Q.* 7th Ser. (1886) II. 408/1 Monkhouse has been at Newton, to have t'other view of Starve-yoad. 1886 Britten & Holland *Plant-n.*, Starveacre. *Ranunculus arvensis*, L. 1891 Hardy *Tess* xlii, 'Tis a starve-acre place. Corn and swedes are all they grow.

starved (stɑːvd), *ppl. a.* [f. STARVE *v.* + -ED[1].]

1. Of a plant-stem, branch of a tree: Dead, dry, withered. *Obs.* exc. *Her.*

1580 R. Parsons *Reas. Catholiques refuse Church* 50 b, As dead..as a starued stake in the hedge, from bearing of flowers. [1585: cf. STARVING *ppl. a.* 3.] 1610 Guillim *Her.* iii. vii. 106 He beareth Argent, three sterued branches, slipped Sable... This Example is of different nature..being mortified and vnuested of the verdour which sometimes it had. 1754 Boyer *Gt. Theat. Honour* (ed. 2) 116 *Starved*, Adj. (or dead, speaking of Branches of Trees without Leaves), *Mort, Sec.* 1828–40 Berry *Encycl. Her.* I, *Starved*, a term used by heralds to denote a branch of a tree when stripped of all its leaves.

2. a. That suffers want of food or the necessaries of life; famished; poverty-stricken. *starved out*: driven out by poverty.

1559 *Mirr. Mag., Owen Glendour* i, My body and fame she [*sc.* Fortune] hathe made leane and slender, For I, poore wretch am sterved Owen Glendour. 1596 Shaks. *Merch. V.* v. i. 295 Faire Ladies you drop Manna in the way Of starued people. 1673 R. Stapylton *Juvenal* Sat. xiv. 168 And thy sterv'd droves, thou send'st into his Corn. 1709 Pope *Ess. Crit.* 419 What woful stuff this madrigal would be, In some starv'd hackney sonneteer, or me? 1823 Scott *Quentin D.* ii, This youth will do as much honour to it as a starved mouse to a housewife's cheese. 1878 J. Davidson *Inverurie & Earld. Garioch* v. 155 Leslie..was occupied in 1600 by William Forbes, the starved-out minister of Kintore.

b. *transf.* and *fig.*

1590 Spenser *F.Q.* iii. iii. 34 And the greene grasse, that groweth, they shall bren, That euen the wild beast shall dy in starued den. 1826 Lamb *Elia, Pop. Fallacies* xii, For a starved grate, and a scanty firing..he finds [at the alehouse] in the depths of winter always a blazing hearth. 1856 Kane *Arct. Expl.* I. viii. 81 Scanty as this starved flora may seem to the botanists of more favored zones. 1912 J. S. Black & G. Chrystal *Life W. R. Smith* xii. 505 Here and there were a few meagre patches of starved wheat or barley.

c. Atrophied.

1832 Lindley *Introd. Bot.* 419 Starved (*depauperatus*); when some part is less perfectly developed than is usual with plants of the same family. Thus, when the lower scales of a head of a Cyperaceous plant produce no flowers, these scales are said to be starved. 1856 Henslow *Dict. Bot. Terms.* 1899 *Allbutt's Syst. Med.* VIII. 816 Essentially the same formation as a small starved wart upon the horny finger of a workman.

3. a. Emaciated with or as with want of food, lean, thin.

1597 Shaks. *2 Hen. IV*, iii. ii. 327 This same staru'd Iustice [Shallow]. *a* 1637 B. Jonson *Sad Shepherd* i. vii, A starv'd Muttons carkasse Would better fit their palates. 1638 Junius *Paint. Ancients* 35 They are puffed up, not stately; starved, not delicate. 1819 Keats *La belle Dame sans Merci* xi, I saw their starved lips in the gloam, With horrid warning gaped wide. 1885 *Riverside Nat. Hist.* (1888) V. 81 The American Pika, or 'Little Chief' Hare (*Lagomys princeps*)... The miners and hunters in the West know these oddities as 'conies' and 'starved rats'.

b. *transf.* and *fig.* Meagre, poor, jejune.

1747 Wesley *Char. Methodist* 6 May the Lord God of my Fathers preserve me, from such a poor, starved Religion as This! 1870 F. R. Wilson *Ch. Lindisf.* 34 A nave..with a small, stiff, starved tower. 1874 Micklethwaite *Mod. Par. Churches* 130 Logs [of wood] tortured into the forms of starved masonry. 1874 Mahaffy *Soc. Life Greece* v. 134 Mr. Müller Strübing shows..how wretchedly poor and starved are the allusions of Thucydides.

c. Of soil: Poor in fertilizing elements.

a 1591 H. Smith *2nd Serm. Jonah's Punishm.* (1675) 624 Say not, I have a stony, or a starved, or a thorny ground. 1763 *Museum Rust.* (ed. 2) I. 93 We are obliged to dig deep for a poorer or more starved kind [of gravel].

d. *Pottery.* Of a glaze: lacking the expected brilliance after firing.

1964 H. Hodges *Artifacts* ii. 52 Under-firing may result in starved glazes which have a dull appearance. 1968 H. Powell *Pottery Handbk. Clay, Glaze & Colour* ii. 56 A starved glaze is lacking in shine. *a* 1977 *Harrison Mayer Ltd. Catal.* 18/2 Starved glaze. The glaze surface is dull in areas which have been adjacent to porous refractories during firing. As the term implies glaze volatiles are sucked away from the surface of the glaze by the porous refractory.

4. Perished with cold. Now chiefly *dial.* and *poet.*

1581 Sidney *Apol. Poetrie* (Arb.) 68 So is that honny-flowing Matron Eloquence, apparelled..with figures and flowers, extreamelie winter-starued. 1588 Shaks. *Tit. A.* iii. i. 252 Alas poore hart that kisse is comfortlesse, As frozen water to a starued snake. 1593 —— *2 Hen. VI*, iii. i. 343, I feare me, you but warme the starued Snake. 1667 Milton *P.L.* iv. 769 [The] Serenate, which the starv'd Lover sings To his proud fair. 1847 C. Bronte *Jane Eyre* vii, Behind them the younger children crouched in groups, wrapping their starved arms in their pinafores. 1878 Browning *Poets Croisic* Prol. i Such a starved bank of moss Till that May-morn Blue ran the flash across: Violets were born! 1894 Bridges *Palm Willow* i, See, whirling snow sprinkles the starved fields. 1898 J. Hutchinson *Archives Surg.* IX. 302 When I get a cold I never shew it, but only feel chilly and starved.

5. *Comb.*, as *starved-looking* adj.; †**starved-gut** *a.*, famished.

a 1653 *Goughe's Queen* i. 131 (Bang) *Muret.* You are a stinking starv'd-gut star-gazer. 1888 E. Gerard *Land beyond Forest* II. xlvii. 255 Starved-looking daisies, and spiritless, emaciated camomiles, are all the flowers to be seen. 1895 W. C. Scully *Kafir Stories* 23 His dog, Sibi—a starved-looking mongrel greyhound.

Hence 'starvedly *adv.*

1606 Bp. Hall *Medit. & Vows* iii. §24. 54 Like some boasting housekeeper, which keepeth open doors for one day with much cheer, & liues staruedly al the yeer after. 1865 *Athenæum* 28 Jan. 122/2 But our lively lady..is 'driven wild' by the sight of hepaticas in myriads, which only grow at home starvedly.

starveling ('stɑːvlɪŋ), *sb.* and *a.* [f. STARVE *v.* + -LING.]

A. *sb.* A starved person or animal; one who habitually starves or is stinted of food; one who is emaciated for lack of nutriment.

1546 *Supplic. Poore Commons* (1871) 64 If none should be alowed meat in your Highnes house, but suche as were clothed in veluet... What steruelynges would your seruantes be aboue all other? 1557 Tusser *Husb.* (1878) 226 The fewe [swine] that she kepe, much the better shal bee: of all thing, one good is worth steruelinges three. 1596 Shaks. *1 Hen. IV*, ii. iv. 76 If I hang, Ile make a fat payre of Gallowes. For, if I hang, old sir Iohn hangs with mee, and thou know'st hee's no Staruelinge. 1674 Marvell *Reh. Transp.* ii. 49 But the more hungrey starvelings generally look'd upon it as an immediate Call to a Benefice. 1830 M. Donovan *Dom. Econ.* II. 119 Some [hogs] will fatten where others would remain starvelings. 1854 Mrs. Gaskell *North & S.* xxii, And now they've frightened these poor Irish starvelings so with their threats. 1871 B. Taylor *Faust* (1875) II. i. iii. 47 What will the lean fool do? Has he, so dry a starveling, humour?

b. *transf.* of a plant, etc.

1600 Surflet *Country Farm* iii. xvi. 453 You may graft.. two or three scutcheons, prouided that they be all of one side: for they would not be equally set together in height, because that so they might all become staruelings. 1664 Evelyn *Sylva* xxi. §3 (1679) 92 Some of the outward skirts [of the wood] were nothing save shrubs and miserable stervlings. 1709 Shaftesb. *Moralists* ii. iv. 118 What think you of the Brain in this Partition? Is it not like to prove a Starveling?

c. *fig.*

1579 Tomson *Calvin's Serm. Tim.* 610/2 Therfore as oft as we play the lingerers, & cold staruelinges..let vs take this Exhortation. *a* 1652 J. Smith *Sel. Disc.* v. 157 As if rather some blind fortune had bestowed her blessings carelessly till she had no more left, and thereby made so many starvlings. 1861 J. G. Holland *Lessons in Life* xxiii. 331 An irreligious man..is always a starveling.

B. *adj.*

1. That lacks a sufficiency of food; hence, lean and weak for want of nutriment; ill-fed, hungry.

1597 Bp. Hall *Sat.* ii. i, So lauish ope-tyde causeth fasting-lents, And staruling Famine comes of large expence. 1617 Moryson *Itin.* i. 239 Starveling flies sucke much more, then those that are fully gorged. *a* 1660 *Contemp. Hist. Irel.* (Ir. Archæol. Soc.) I. 152 The poore starulinge souldiers, after theire longe and tedious marche, fell eagerly to eate and drinke. 1693 Evelyn *De la Quint. Compl. Gard.* I. 175 If any Trees..have all their Leaves lesser, and more starveling than they should be. 1787 Beckford *Lett. Italy*, etc. II. 263 The stems of starveling pines. 1850 S. Dobell *Roman* vi, The very meanest starveling hound. 1883 Symonds *Ital. Byways* iii. 61 The palace has become a granary for country produce in a starveling land.

fig. 1642 Milton *Apol. Smect.* Wks. 1851 III. 325 Sending heards of souls starvling to Hell, while they feast and riot upon the labours of hireling Curats. 1675 J. Owen *Indwelling Sin* xv. (1732) 199 They..perform Duties with as much constancy as ever they did, but yet have poor lean starvling Souls.

2. Poverty-stricken. Of circumstances, etc.: Characterized by or exhibiting poverty.

1638 Featly *Transubst.* 9 To another a Cardinals hat was given, but with so thinne lining..that he was commonly called the starveling Cardinal. 1728 Pope *Dunciad* ii. 36 No meagre, muse-rid mope, adust and thin,..But such a bulk as no twelve bards could raise, Twelve starveling bards of these degen'rate days. 1822 W. Irving *Braceb. Hall* xxii. 188 [He] then cast a glance upon his own threadbare and starveling condition. 1850 —— *Goldsm.* vi. 89 The book-sellers, who gave him occasional, though starveling, employment. 1874 F. C. Burnand *My time* xxxi. 309 There was a starveling air about the place.

fig. 1841–9 J. C. Hare *Par. Serm.* II. 190 Our hearts are too poor and starveling..to find food and room for all these thoughts and feelings.

3. Perishing (with cold and exposure). *rare.*

1697 Dampier *Voy.* I. 498 In this wet starveling plight we spent the tedious night. 1805 Wordsw. *Waggoner* iv. 260 And babes in wet and starveling plight; Which once, be weather as it might, Had still a nest within a nest.

4. *fig.* Poor in quality or quantity, lean, thin, meagre, scanty.

a 1641 Bp. Mountagu *Acts & Mon.* (1642) 117 It is a starveling conceit of Innovating brain-pans. *a* 1665 J. Goodwin *Being filled with the Spirit* (1670) 79 The expressions of such a man, whether by words or actions, will be lean and starveling. 1768–78 Tucker *Lt. Nat.* (1834) II. 484 We talk..of a meagre and starveling style, of crudities in expressions. 1816 Coleridge *Statesman's Man.* 36 A hunger-bitten and idea-less philosophy naturally produces a starveling and comfortless religion. 1843 Gladstone in *For. & Col. Q. Rev.* II. 565 They are so much at variance with the fixed formularies of the Church, from the narrow and starveling form of their doctrine, that they [etc.]. 1859 R. F. Burton *Centr. Afr.* in *Jrnl. Geog. Soc.* XXIX. 195 Beyond Uyogo is Usange, a starveling settlement of Wanyamwezi. 1889 C. Edwardes *Sardinia* 297 A starveling little group of pines.

5. *Comb.*: †*starveling-brained* adj.

1638 Ford *Ladies Trial* i. ii, Leave such poore out-side helpes to puling lovers, Such as Fulgoso your weake rivall is, That starveling braind-companion.

starven ('stɑːv(ə)n), *ppl. a.* *Obs.* exc. *dial.* Also 6–7 sterven. [irregular str. pa. pple. of STARVE *v.* Cf. STORVEN *ppl. a.*]

1. = STARVED *ppl. a.* in various uses.

a 1533–98 [see *hunger-starven* s.v. HUNGER-STARVE *v.*]. 1563 Sackville *Induct. Mirr. Mag.* li, Shee [Famine] fayne would so sustayne Her staruen corps. 1592 *Arden of Feversham* ii. ii. 118 But, giue me..Such mercy as the staruen Lyones, When she is dry suckt of her eager young. 1642 D. Rogers *Naaman* 170 Those sterven Egyptians beholding Iosephs store of corne. 1653 Austen *Fruit Trees* ii. (1657) 60 Their starven love to the saints, and their.. serious pursuite of their owne interests, in things of the world..prove their Earthly mindednesse. 1686 Plot *Staffordsh.* 204 It advances all starven weak Cattle above any thing yet known. 1887 *S. Cheshire Gloss.*, *Starven*, sensitive to cold. 'It's a nesh, starven little thing.' 1893 *S.-E. Worcester Gloss.*

†2. Of cattle: That have died of disease. *Obs.*

1584 R. Scot *Discov. Witchcr.* vi. iv. 95 [He] bargained.. for all their hides which were of Sterven cattell.

starver ('stɑːvə(r)). [f. STARVE *v.* + -ER[1].]

1. One who or that which starves, in the senses of the verb. **a.** One who causes starvation. **b.** One who suffers starvation. **c.** Something that kills or numbs with cold.

a. 1709 Shaftesb. *Moralists* ii. iv. 118 The Brain certainly is a great Starver, where it abounds. *Ibid.* 119 What shall we say of our..Dancers, Tennis-players, and such like? 'Tis the Body surely is the Starver here: and if the Brain were such a terrible Devourer in the other way [etc.]. 1859 Mill *Liberty* iii. 100 An opinion that corn-dealers are starvers of the poor..may justly incur punishment when delivered orally to an excited mob. 1870 *Pall Mall Gaz.* 5 Dec. 2 Should the Germans be hemmed in and their communications cut, the starver may become the starved.

b. 1839 Hood *Fugitive Lines on Pawning Watch* vii, So long I have wander'd a starver, I'm getting as keen as a hawk. 1897 Blackmore *Dariel* xlvii, The unfortunate starver..tore the cake from Cator.

c. 1844 Hood *Forge* i. viii, Flapping his arms to keep him warm, For the breeze from the North is a regular starver.

2. *Austral. slang.* A saveloy.

1941 Baker *Dict. Austral. Slang* 71 *Starver*, a saveloy. 1959 D. Niland *Big Smoke* 211, I know what the things I eat cost me. Starvers, crumpets, stale cakes, speckled fruit, pies.

starving ('stɑːvɪŋ), *vbl. sb.* [f. STARVE *v.* + -ING[1].] The action of STARVE *v.*

†1. Dying, death. *Obs.*

a 1300 *E.E. Psalter* cvi. 20 He sent his worde, and heled þam, And fra þar steruinges he þam nam. 1340 *Ayenb.* 73 Voryet þi body ones a day, guo in-to helle ine þine libbinde: þet þou ne guo ine þine steruinge. *Ibid.* 165 Ase zaiþ þe sauter ydelnesse be steruinge. *c* **1440** *Promp. Parv.* 475/1 Stervynge, or deyynge, *mors, expiracio*.

2. The condition of suffering privation of food.

1549 CHEKE *Hurt Sedit.* (1641) 34 The pore..who in a common scarcitie, lyueth most scarcely, and feeleth quickliest the sharpenesse of staruing. **1737** POPE *Sat. Donne* ii. 10, I grant that Poetry's a crying sin..Catch'd like the Plague,..the Lord knows how, But that the cure is starving, all allow. **1820** SHELLEY *Œdipus* II. ii. 6 We call thee Famine! Goddess of fasts and feasts, starving and cramming. **1842** F. TROLLOPE *Vis. Italy* II. ix. 163 Our starvings, &c. did not begin..till after we had quitted the beaten track.

allusively. **1844** W. PENNEFATHER in *Life & Lett.* (1879) 171, I have been offered a pretty little living... Its value is £92 per annum..my father will call it a *starving*. **1861** PYCROFT *Ways & Words* 274 It is not a living a man can earn there; it is a starving.

b. *attrib.*

1843 S. C. HALL *Ireland* III. 354 Particular periods of the year which may be rightly termed 'starving seasons'. **1905** *Pearson's Mag.* July 104/2 Frail women and children, who have to work long hours at a starving wage.

3. The action of depriving of food.

1665 MANLEY *Grotius's Low-C. Wars* 233 [He] was sent with part of the Army to see if he could reduce it, either by force or starving. **1883** *Congregat. Yr. Bk.* 73 The starving of the body has a relation to the starving of the mind.

†**4.** The stripping of the branches (of trees). *Obs.*

1585 HIGINS *Junius' Nomencl.* 144/2 *Articulatio*,..the staruing of trees as when by the force of tempestes the young shootes of vines are beaten off, or hurt through vnskilfulnes, or naughtilye lopped.

'starving, *ppl. a.* [f. STARVE *v.* + -ING[2].]

†**1.** Of death: ? Lingering, languishing. *Obs.*

1387-8 T. USK *Test. Love* I. i. (Skeat) 5 Certes, her absence is to me an helle; my sterving deth thus in wo it myneth, that endeles care is throughout myne herte clenched.

†**2.** Causing death, killing. *Obs.*

a **1605** MONTGOMERIE *Misc. Poems* xlv. 11 Come, gentill Death,..Thy sterving straik with force thou let out flie, And light on me, to end my peirles pyne.

3. That is dying of hunger; that lacks the necessaries of life; also *absol.*

1719 DE FOE *Crusoe* II. (Globe) 339, I also forgot not the starving Crew..but order'd my own Boat..to carry them a Sack of Bread. **1732** POPE *Ess. Man* II. 269 The starving chemist in his golden views Supremely blest. **1817** SHELLEY *Rev. Islam* x. xv, All night, the lean hyaenas their sad case Like starving infants wailed. **1886** W. J. TUCKER *Eastern Europe* xxxi. 315 How beneficially all this luxuriance.. might be applied to the cravings of the needy and starving.

4. That causes or entails starvation or famine; also, that treats disease by stinting the patient of food.

1590 SIR J. SMYTHE *Disc. Weapons* 1 The tumultuarie, licentious, and staruing warres of the Low Countries. **1693** *Humours Town* 22 Modesty is a starving Quality, and only another Name for Folly. **1731** *Gentl. Mag.* I. 118 The whole income remaining to the Church is but 15, 20, or 30l. Yearly; which is but a starving Support. **1824** SCOTT *St. Ronan's* vii, Then he is a starving doctor, Mrs. Blower—reduces diseases as soldiers do towns—by famine. **1899** *Westm. Gaz.* 26 June 7/3 Starving trades—that was to say, trades that were starving those who had their capital invested in them—must ultimately also starve the workpeople.

b. That causes one to starve with cold. *rare.*

1684 OTWAY *Prol. to N. Lee's Constantine* 32 Under the starving sign of Capricorn. **1721** AMHERST *Terræ Fil.* No. 13 (1726) I. 72 [He] found him in his lodgings by a little starving fire, with a rush light candle before him. **1897** T. H. WARREN *By Severn Sea* 41 On sullen earth, clogged flood and starving air.

†**'starvy**, *a. Obs. rare.* [f. STARVE *v.* + -Y.] Poor in quality, starved. **a.** of land. **b.** of fruit.

1647 C. HARVEY *Schola Cordis* xxvii. 21 Apply Thy plow be-time; now now beginne To furrow up my stiffe and starvy heart. **1656** HARTLIB *Herefordsh. Orchards* (1724) 6 The rough starvy ground (which in this country we wrongfully call marle). *Ibid.*, Under this starvy ground it finds a more congenial and richer nourishment. **1680** ALLEN *Peace & Unity* 137 If you would yield the Lord the.. pleasant Fruit of all his cost, and not such as is starvy, harsh, and unsavoury.

starward ('stɑːwəd), *adv.* [-WARD.] Towards the stars. Also *attrib.* or *adj.*

1831 CARLYLE *Sartor Res.* II. vi, Its white steeple is then truly a starward-pointing finger. **1839** BAILEY *Festus* 232 As on they sped upon their starward course. **1845** HIRST *Poems* 53 When the mists were star-ward creeping. **1865** E. BURRITT *Walk to Land's End* 9 The sparks going up starward. **1872** BLACKIE *Lays Highl.* 92, I clomb thy starward peak not long ago.

starwort ('stɑːwɜːt). Also 5-6 ster-, sterre-, 6-7 (? *erron.*) stir(e-. [f. STAR *sb.*[1] + WORT *sb.*]

1. The genus *Stellaria*, with white starry flowers; esp. *S. Holostea*.

In the 15th c. quots. perhaps *Alchemilla vulgaris*.

a **1400-50** *Stockh. Med. MS.* p. 156 Sterrewort: *stellaria maior*. *a* **1500** *MS. Laud* 553 lf. 19 Stellaria maior is an herbe þ[t] me clepuþ sterwort... Stellaria minor is an herbe þ[t] me clepuþ lasse sterrewort. **1845-50** MRS. LINCOLN *Lect. Bot.* App. 173/2 *Stellaria longifolia* (long-leafed starwort). **1878** SUSAN PHILLIPS *On Seaboard* 89 The poppy, like a scarlet flame, By snowy starwort blazes. **1899** BRIDGES *New Poems, Idle Flowers*, And in the shady lanes..Starwort and Celandine.

2. A book-name for the genus *Aster*; esp. *A. Tripolium*, Sea Starwort; *A. Amellus*, Italian Starwort.

1578 LYTE *Dodoens* I. xxiv. 36 *Aster Atticus*..is called..in English Sharewurte or Sterrewurte. **1585** HIGINS *Junius' Nomencl.* 118/1 *Aster atticus*..stirwoort. **1597** GERARDE *Herbal* II. lxxxviii. 334 *Aster Marinus*, or *Amellus Marinus*: in English Sea Starwort,..of some Blew Daisies. *Ibid.* II. cxxv. 391 There be diuers sorts of the Asters or Starwoorts. *Ibid.*, Italian Starrewoort. **1647** HEXHAM I. (Herbs) Stirewort, *sterren kruydt*. **1693** DALE *Pharmacol.* 175 Aster Atticus..Golden Star-wort. **1728** BRADLEY *Dict. Bot.*, *Amellus*..appears plainly to be the Flower call'd Asteratticus Italorum, call'd in English, Purple Italian Star-wort, or Purple Marygold. **1785** MARTYN *Lett. Bot.* xxvi. (1794) 392 Large flowering or Catesby's Starwort (Aster grandiflorus *Lin.*), is one of the handsomest [of the American asters]. **1812** *New Bot. Gard.* I. 65 *Aster Chinensis*, China Aster, or Chinese Starwort. **1862** T. W. HARRIS *Insects Injur. Vegetation* (ed. 3) 620 Our native asters or star-worts. **1882** *Garden* 11 Feb. 90/1 The American Starworts.

3. **water starwort**, the genus *Callitriche*.

1597 GERARDE *Herbal* II. cclxxxviii. 681 There is likewise another herbe of small reckoning that floteth vpon the water called *Stellaria aquatica* or water Starwoort. **1796** WITHERING *Brit. Plants* (ed. 3) II. 5 *Callitriche verna*.. Water Starwort. **1861** S. THOMSON *Wild Flowers* (ed. 4) I. 65 The water star-wort..has its anthers but one-celled.

4. The name of a moth, *Cucullia Asteris*.

1819 SAMOUELLE *Entomol. Compend.* 419 *Noctua Asteris*. The Starwort. **1832** J. RENNIE *Consp. Butterfl. & Moths* 90 The Starwort (*Cucullia Asteris*). **1869** E. NEWMAN *Brit. Moths* 433.

stary ('stɛərɪ), *a.* [f. STARE *v.* (sense 5) + -Y. Cf. G. dial. *starrig*.] (See quot. 1886.)

1884 W. S. B. MCLAREN *Spinning* 171 The projecting fibres, which would make it stary and lack lustre, in passing beneath the cap get laid along the yarn and twisted into the body of it. **1886** *W. Somerset Word-bk.*, *Stary*... Thread-bare. A word used technically of cloth in which the separate threads are plainly to be seen.

stash (stæʃ), *v. slang.* Also **stach**. [Of obscure origin.] **1.** *trans.* To bring to an end, stop, desist from (a matter, a practice); to quit (a place). Often imp. ***stash it! stash that!*** †***to stash the glim***: to cease using the light. ***to stash up***: to bring to an abrupt end. Also *absol.*

1794 *Sessions Papers* 17 Sept. 1200/2 He says, Miller, it is, *stash*, I am satisfied. **1811** *Lex. Balatr.* s.v., The cove tipped the prosecutor fifty quid to stash the business. **1812** J. H. VAUX *Flash Dict.* s.v., Thus a thief determined to leave off his vicious courses will declare that he means to stash (or stow) prigging... To stash drinking, card-playing, or any other employment you may be engaged in for the time present. *Ibid.*, *Stash it*: see *Stow it*. **1823** 'JON BEE' *Dict. Turf* s.v., 'Stash the glim', to put out lights, or to place an extinguisher on the candle. **1889** 'R. BOLDREWOOD' *Robbery under Arms* (1890) 99 The rest of us..as they was sold, stashed the camp and cleared out different ways. **1903** W. CRAIG *Adv. Austral. Goldf.* 229 She is requested to 'stash' tragedy and give them comedy. **1909** H. G. WELLS *Tono-Bungay* III. iv, She brought her [piano] playing to an end by —as schoolboys say—'stashing it up'.

2. To conceal, to hide; to put aside for safe keeping; to stow or store. Freq. with *away*. Formerly *Criminals' slang*; orig. *U.S.* in revived mod. use.

1797 *Humphry Potter's Dict. Cant & Flash Lang.* (ed. 3) 55 *Stach*, to conceal a robbery. **1821** *Sessions Papers* 14 Dec. 66/1 He begged of me to *stash* it, which means say nothing about it. **1914** JACKSON & HELLYER *Vocab. Criminal Slang* 80 *Stash*,..to hide;..to cease talking; to 'plant'. **1927** *Dialect Notes* V. 477 Billy he done stashed the jug in th' brush, an' now the damned ol' fool caint find hit! **1937** C. R. COOPER *Here's to Crime* v. 102 A friend of mine had it stached in his cellar, in a fruit jar. **1937** D. RUNYON in *Collier's* 16 Jan. 9/4 She must have some scratch of her own stashed away somewhere. **1944** *Daily Progress* (Charlottesville, Va.) 25 May 6/6 A customer at least has a sporting chance to pick up a bottle of brandy, gin, or rum if the dealer doesn't have a bottle of old Kentucky corn julep stashed away under the counter for him. **1952** *Manch. Guardian Weekly* 20 Mar. 4/3 The big gift already stashed away in the farmers' bank accounts. **1962** J. HELLER *Catch-22* vi. 51 Just when I was all set to really start stashing it away they had to manufacture fascism and start a war. **1970** R. PRICE *Howling Arctic* i. 15 Travel proved too difficult after a while so they stashed the sledges and walked on. **1974** F. FORSYTH *Dogs of War* (1975) I. i. 39 With all fees paid, he netted a cool £500,000, which was still stashed in the Zwingli Bank. **1978** J. A. MICHENER *Chesapeake* 670 The watermen ferried dead birds to the ice shelf, stashed them and returned to fetch others.

stash (stæʃ), *sb. slang* (orig. and chiefly *U.S.*). Also **stach**. [f. the vb.]

1. a. Something, or a collection of things, stashed away; a hoard, stock; a cache.

1914 JACKSON & HELLYER *Vocab. Criminal Slang* 80 *Stash*, ..used as a noun in the sense of something cached. **1942** BERREY & VAN DEN BARK *Amer. Thes. Slang* §207/5 *Cache*.. stach, stash, stash-away. **1954** WEBSTER, *Stash*,..something stashed away or the place where it is stashed. **1969** *New Yorker* 31 May 90/1, I liked..the stash of Pucci shifts. **1970** G. JACKSON *Let.* 26 Mar. in *Soledad Brother* (1971) 199, I *want* my food and drink from the people's stash. **1975** B. GARFIELD *Hopscotch* xxv. 257 If he told Oakly the truth about going to ground then he'll want to clean out his stash ..he's..got to have money. **1979** *Daily Tel.* 10 Apr. 3/2 Chief Insp. Newark said he was satisfied Barnes had no stashes of money hidden away. **1980** *Encounter* May 37 Even crane-crews angle For a share of the stash, Their lines urging up A grey, enormous catch.

b. A cache of an (illegal) drug; a quantity (of a drug); the drug itself. (See also quot. 1942.)

1942 BERREY & VAN DEN BARK *Amer. Thes. Slang* §509/12 *Stash*, concealed equipment for taking narcotics. **1953** W. BURROUGHS *Junkie* iii. 36 Taking junk hidden by another junkie is known as 'making him for his stash'. It is difficult to guard against this form of theft because junkies know where to look for a stash. **1959** [see BUST *sb.*[3] f]. **1967** *Trans-Action* Apr. 11/1 Someone cruises by in a car and brings a nice 'stash' of 'weed'. **1968** T. WOLFE *Electric Kool-Aid Acid Test* xi. 133 The Hermit...was..keeper of the communal acid stash down there in the cave. **1975** *High Times* Dec. 11/1 Anyone who turns stash knows that most people will pay any price to get high. **1978** *N.Y. Times* 30 Mar. B1/2 A number of dubious substances, such as 'African Yohimbe Smokestuff'. This, the label said, should be added 'to your regular stash to turn your domestic green into African Red'. **1982** *Guardian* 14 Dec. 11/6 The hairy young man in Lee Cooper jeans..asking 'Anyone seen my stash?'

2. *slang* (orig. *Criminals'*). A hiding-place, a hide-out; a rendezvous; a dwelling, 'pad'.

1927 *Amer. Speech* II. 390/2 A *stash* is a hiding-place. **1930** R. CHADWICK in *Liberty* 23 Aug. 33/2 If we were on a bank job in a strange city the stash would be in a room we had rented several weeks in advance. In a small town, though, you don't have any stash, because an hour after you moved in everybody in the burg would be checking in. **1946** MEZZROW & WOLFE *Really Blues* viii. 132 No Hotel Ritz for us this time; our stash was over some kind of feed store. **1963** L. DEIGHTON *Horse under Water* xviii. 77 We set up 'Art for the Average Guy, Inc.', just a little stash on East 12th. **1965** *Listener* 7 Jan. 31/2 Susan Sontag went to see Philip Johnson, the New York architect, or rather she 'moseyed along to his stash on Park'.

†**'stasiarch**. *Obs. rare.* [ad. Gr. στασί-αρχος, f. στάσι-ς sedition + -αρχος ruler.] A ringleader in sedition.

1655 H. LESTRANGE *Reign K. Chas.* 57 With the conjunction of these seven English,..Lewes brake furiously in upon Subize the Stasiarch, the chief Rebel. **1666** SIR G. WHARTON *Calend. Carolinum* Nov., But know (Ingrateful Stasiarchs!) you must Stoop, and..lick Our English Dust.

†**stasi'metric**, *a. Surveying. Obs.* [f. Gr. στάσι-ς standing, station (see STASIS) + μέτρ-ον measure + -IC.] (See quots.)

1774 M. MACKENZIE *Treat. Surveying* (1819) Introd. 14 A Stasimetric Survey, is, when the mutual distances of three, or more, proper objects are carefully measured; and by means of these objects, the position and distance of all stations along the coast determined trigonometrically, each at its respective station alone, independent of one another. **1824** W. H. SMYTH *Mem. Sicily*, etc. iv. 145, I therefore deduce the height [of Ætna]..from stasimetric points previously ascertained on shore.

‖**stasimon** ('stæsɪmən). Pl. **stasima**, **stasimons**. [Gr. στάσιμον neut. (agreeing with μέλος song) of στάσιμος stationary, f. στα- to stand.

Some think that the 'stationary song' was so called because it began after the chorus had taken their places; others because it was continued without interruption.]

In ancient Greek tragedy, a song of the Chorus, occurring after the PARODE, continued without the interruption of dialogue or anapaestics.

1861 PALEY *Æschylus* (ed. 2) *Supplices 1 note*, 1-39. The parode, or anapaestic recitation of the chorus as they enter the orchestra, the stasimon commencing with v. 40. **1876** W. CORY *Lett. & Jrnls.* (1897) 413 [Swinburne's] chorus is altogether too sugary, luxuriant, and unbridled in the *stasima* or set pieces. **1904** M. HEWLETT *Queen's Quair* II. vii. 283 Recalling critically..the stasimons of the late tragic scene.

stasimorphy ('stæsɪmɔːfɪ). *Biol.* [f. Gr. στάσι-ς (see STASIS) + μορφ-ή form + -Y.] (See quot. 1869.) Hence **stasi'morphic** *a.*

1869 M. T. MASTERS *Veget. Teratol.* 216 Stasimorphy. Deviation from the ordinary form of organs arising from stasis or arrest of development are included under this heading. *Ibid.*, Stasimorphic changes affecting principally the relative size of organs. **1873** COOK *Man. Bot. Terms* (ed. 2).

stasiology (stæsɪ'ɒlədʒɪ). *rare.* [tr. F. *stasiologie* (see quot. 1954), f. Gr. στάσι-ς party, faction (see STASIS): see -OLOGY.] The science or study of political parties.

1954 B. & R. NORTH tr. *M. Duverger's Pol. Parties* 422 The development of the science of political parties (it could perhaps be called *stasiology*). **1966** K. WEST *Power in Liberal Party* p. vii, There is now a field of academic enterprise known as analytical stasiology whose practitioners believe that by constructing a series of conceptual frameworks one may arrive at a 'science' of political parties.

stasipatric (stæsɪ'pætrɪk), *a. Biol.* [f. Gr. στάσις STASIS + πάτρα fatherland (f. πατήρ father) + -IC.] Applied to a form of speciation in which new taxa are considered to arise within the geographical range of the parent species, each part of which comes to be occupied by one of the new taxa. Hence **stasi'patrically** *adv.*

1967 M. J. D. WHITE et al. in *Austral. Jrnl. Zool.* XV. 298 If a term, equivalent to allopatric and sympatric, is needed to describe the process of direct conversion of an essentially continuous population into a number of contiguous taxa (races, semispecies, or species) by the spread of chromosomal rearrangements around which isolating mechanisms develop, one might perhaps choose the adjective *stasipatric*, which is intended to indicate the essentially unchanging geographic range of the superspecies. **1968** *Science* 8 Mar. 1069/1 In the case of a chromosomal rearrangement which first establishes itself near the edge of a species distribution, one can imagine it spreading both inwards through the range of the species (stasipatrically) and outwards into previously unoccupied territory (allopatrically). **1973** L. S. DILLON *Evolution* x. 138/2 The stasipatric model is not designed to displace the established ones but to supplement them.

stasis ('stæsɪs, 'steɪsɪs). [mod.L., a. Gr. στάσις, standing, station, stoppage, f. στα- to stand.]

1. a. *Path.* A stagnation or stoppage of the circulation of any of the fluids of the body, esp. of the blood in some part of the blood-vessels.

1745 R. JAMES *Med. Dict.* III, *Stasis*, .. a Stagnation. **1753** *Chambers' Cycl.* Suppl., *Stasis*, a word used by physicians to express a stagnation of the humors. **1835–6** *Todd's Cycl. Anat.* I. 745/2 Previously to the establishment of osteitis [of the cranium] .. there is found that stasis of the blood which always precedes inflammation. **1899** *Allbutt's Syst. Med.* VIII. 380 In many cases there seems to be an over-fulness of the cerebral venous system and probably a lymphatic stasis. **1913** SIR T. BARLOW in *Times* 7 Aug. 8/2 A strong case has been made out for intestinal stasis as a cause of various forms of malnutrition.

b. *gen.* Inactivity; stagnation; a state of motionless or unchanging equilibrium.

1920 *Glasgow Herald* 30 Nov. 9 The prevailing mood of Labour is indefinite; a condition of stasis has been caused by the coal strike and the dread of unemployment. **1930** W. EMPSON *Seven Types of Ambiguity* vii. 245 He is drawn taut between the two similar impulses into the stasis of appreciation. **1933** T. S. ELIOT *Use of Poetry & Use of Criticism* vi. 103 Arnold represents a period of stasis; of relative and precarious stability, it is true, a brief halt in the endless march of humanity in some, or in any direction. **1940** E. MUIR *Story & Fable* v. 186 This could be done by so controlling the chemical processes of the body as to produce a self-subsistent balance, an everlasting, living stasis. **1943** *Sewanee Review* LI. II. 337 Art, according to Dedalus-Joyce, tends toward the achievement of *stasis*, which implies a state of contemplation, of detachment from the *kinesis* of life. **1972** *Times Lit. Suppl.* 1 Sept. 1020/3 We see him in the moment of stasis before action. **1978** J. UPDIKE *Coup* (1979) iii. 91 A religion whose antipodes are motion and stasis.

c. In the psychoanalytical theory of Wilhelm Reich (see REICHIAN *sb.* and *a.*), a hypothetical accumulation of unused or repressed sexual energy.

1942 T. P. WOLFE tr. *Reich's Function of Orgasm* iii. 58 The role of sexual stasis in increasing antisocial and perverse sexual impulses. *Ibid.* 361 *Stasis*, the damming-up of sexual energy in the organism, thus the source of energy for the neuroses. **1953** in *Wilhelm Reich: Sel. Writings* (1961) 12 *Stasis neurosis*, all somatic disturbances which are the immediate result of the stasis of sexual energy, with stasis anxiety at its core. **1973** D. BOADELLA *W. Reich* vii. 194 There are two fundamental biological responses to sexual stasis, or any other blockage to emotional functioning.

2. [Gr. στάσις in sense 'faction, discord'.] Party faction, civil strife.

1933 R. J. BONNER *Aspects of Athenian Democracy* v. 91 Solon tried to strengthen the government against sedition, or *stasis*, as the Greeks called it, by requiring every citizen to take one side or another in case of serious party strife. **1956** A. W. GOMME *Commentary on Thucydides* II. 374 From *stasis* in Kerkyra to *stasis* in the Greek world generally .. to universal conditions of *stasis* and war as its stimulus. **1963** M. I. FINLEY *Anc. Greeks* 51 The dividing-line between politics and sedition (*stasis* the Greeks called it) was a thin one in classical Greece, and often enough *stasis* grew into ruthless war. **1975** N. G. L. HAMMOND *Classical Age of Greece* 166 The weakening of traditional obligations and the revolution in the economy which arose from the war were among the factors which led to the outbreak of *stasis*, civil war, in 411 and 410 at Athens.

stassfurtite ('stæsfɜːtaɪt). *Min.* Also **stassfurthite**. [Named (Ger. *stassfurtit*) in 1856 after *Stassfurt* in Prussia, its locality: see -ITE.] A massive variety of boracite.

1858 J. NICOL *Elem. Mineral* 212 Stassfurthite. **1865** P. H. LAWRENCE *Lithol.* 95 Boracite (Stassfurtite).

stasyon, obs. form of STATION.

stat (stæt), *sb.*[1] Colloq. abbrev. of PHOTOSTAT b.

1960 'E. MCBAIN' *Give Boys Great Big Hand* v. 40 Here are the stats, kid. **1971** C. FICK *Danziger Transcript* (1973) 81 Make stats of all the graduation and group pictures. **1977** J. AIKEN *Last Movement* i. 33 Wonderful reviews... I'll send you stats of all the notices.

stat (stæt), *sb.*[2] Colloq. abbrev. of STATISTIC *sb.*, STATISTICS. Cf. MATH[3]. orig. and chiefly *U.S.*

1961 WEBSTER, *Stat*, .. statistics. **1973** *Amer. Speech* 1970 XLV. 86 *Stat*, Elementary Statistics. **1976** *Springfield* (Mass.) *Daily News* 22 Apr. 39/1 A key stat: Marcel Dionne had only two shots Tuesday night. He scored on one, had another in the second period. **1977** *Rolling Stone* 5 May 46/3 Certainly, his stats in spring training were not impressive; his earned run average was over 4.00.

stat. (stæt), *adv. Pharm.* [Abbrev. of L. *statim.*] On a prescription: immediately.

1875 W. H. GRIFFITHS *Lessons on Prescriptions* iv. 18 *Stat.*, immediately. **1971** *Lancet* 25 Sept. 700/2 *Stat.*, to be given at once.

stat- (stæt), *prefix.* [f. STAT(IC *a.* and *sb.*] Used in combination with the names of the practical electrical units to form the C.G.S. electrostatic system of units, as ***statampere***, ***statcoulomb***, ***statfarad***, ***statgauss***, ***statohm***, ***statvolt***.

[**1903** A. E. KENNELLY in *Trans. Amer. Inst. Electr. Engin.* XXII. 534 In a comprehensive system of electromagnetic terminology, the electric C.G.S. units should also be christened... They might be denoted by the prefix *abstat*. Thus the C.G.S. electric unit of e.m.f. would be the abstatvolt.] **1920** *Proc. Amer. Philos. Soc.* LIX. 365 B_e is the electric flux density in 'statgausses'. **1925** W. H. TIMBIE *Elements of Electricity* xvi. 584 A statcoulomb is a small unit of charge, one coulomb being equal to 3×10^9 statcoulombs. **1932** S. S. ATTWOOD *Electric & Magnetic Fields* i. 19 The unit of potential is an erg per statcoulomb and is called the statvolt in the electrostatic C.G.S. system. **1937** H. L. CURTIS *Electr. Measurements* ii. 11 The prefixes *ab* and *abstat* were proposed by Kennelly... The latter has generally been shortened to *stat*. No one of the proposed names has been adopted by any international organization. **1939** J. B. WHITEHEAD *Electricity & Magnetism* vi. 62 The name of the electrostatic unit of capacitance is the statfarad. One farad is equal to 9×10^{11} statfarads. **1958** CONDON & ODISHAW *Handbk. Physics* A-9/2 The cgs unit of charge is called the esu or the statcoulomb. It is the unit defined by using dynes of force and cm of distance and adopting $4\pi\epsilon_0 = 1$. The corresponding unit of current is called the statampere, defined as the flow of one statcoulomb per second. *Ibid.* A-11/1, 1 statohm $= c^2/10^9$ ohms .. with $c = 2{\cdot}997930 \times 10^{10}$ cm/sec. **1963** JERRARD & MCNEILL *Dict. Sci. Units* 12 In recent years the prefix stat has sometimes been used to denote electrostatic units, thus 1 stat volt = 300 practical volts, 1 stat ampere $= (1/3) \times 10^{-9}$ ampere. This prefix is an abbreviation for abstat which was proposed for electrostatic units at the same time as ab was suggested for electromagnetic units.

-stat, the terminal element in certain names of scientific instruments, *aerostat*, *heliostat*, *hydrostat*, *klinostat*, *thermostat*. The earliest example of this formation is *heliostat*, ad. mod.L. *hēliostata* ('s Gravesande *a* 1742), app. repr. an assumed Gr. type *ἡλιοστάτης (cf. ὑδροστάτης hydrostatic balance), intended to mean an instrument for causing the sun to appear stationary, f. ἥλιο-ς sun + -στατης agent-n. f. στα- root of ἱστάναι to cause to stand, set. This word is directly imitated in *siderostat* (hybrid, f. L. *sīder-* star). The F. *aérostat* (whence Eng. *aerostat*) may be a back-formation from *aérostatique* (formed after *hydrostatique*), but owes its form to the example of *héliostat*. The later words have been formed on the analogy of *heliostat*, app. with some reference to the Gr. στατός standing, stationary, which is given in Fr. and Eng. dicts. as the source of the ending.

statable ('steɪtəb(ə)l), *a.* Also **stateable**. [f. STATE *v.* + -ABLE.] Capable of being stated.

1802 CANNING in *Earl Malmesbury's Diaries & Corr.* (1844) IV. 117, I will .. send you .. one or two trifling alterations more, and will then state to you the *statable* reasons for this last change. **1859** DICKENS *Christmas Stor.*, *Haunted House* i, For all these reasons, and for others less easily and briefly statable, I find [etc.]. **1877** RUSKIN *Fors Clav.* lxxvi. 119 Those are the clearly stateable and memorable heads of expenditure. **1887** *Century Mag.* Mar. 921 The *rationale* of this is simple, and statable in brief form.

statal ('steɪtəl), *a.* [f. STATE *sb.* + -AL[1].]

1. Of or pertaining to a State (of the U.S. or other federation), as distinguished from *national*. *rare*.

1862 E. BATES in *Official Opinions Attorneys Gen.* X. 388 I have no knowledge of any other kind of political citizenship, higher or lower, statal or national. **1880** A. TOURGÉE *Fool's Errand & Invisible Empire* II. xi. 489 Public education flourished as a part of the statal economy. **1949** *Times* 7 Feb. 5/3 All the states outside this special category have already been merged with provinces or have joined one or another of the six great statal groups.

2. *Linguistics.* Of a passive verbal form: expressing a state or condition rather than an action (opp. ACTIONAL *a.*).

1935 [see ACTIONAL *a.*]. **1961** R. B. LONG *Sentence & its Parts* v. 119 Thus *have* has no passive when it is statal. **1968** *Language* XLIV. 236 The 'statal passives' are quite different in their internal representations from the true passives, and actually are not passives at all. **1975** *Ibid.* LI. 362 The ambiguity is between the 'statal' and 'dynamic passive' meaning.

statalon, var. STATOLON.

statant ('steɪtənt), *a. Her.* [app. irreg. f. L. *stat-* ppl. stem of *stāre* to stand + -ANT.] Of an animal, esp. a lion: Standing in profile with all four feet on the ground.

c **1500** *Sc. Poem on Her.* 127 in *Q. Eliz. Acad.* 98 First, a lionne statant. **1688** HOLME *Armoury* II. 144/1 The sundry ways that Beasts are besides born in Arms. Statant or standing, when all the feet are down. **1864** BOUTELL *Her. Hist. & Pop.* x. 59 A Lion Statant, having his Tail extended in a right line, is the Crest of the Duke of Northumberland.

†sta'tarian, *a. Obs. rare.* [f. L. *statāri-us* (see next) + -AN.] = next 2. Hence **sta'tarianly** *adv.*

1768–74 TUCKER *Lt. Nat.* (1834) I. 473 Your skirmishing parties .. shall never drive my statarianly disciplined battalion from its ground. *Ibid.* 474, I have made bold to bring a new adopted son of mine to beg a detachment of your statarian soldiers to escort him.

statary ('steɪtərɪ), *a.* Also 7 *erron.* **statory**. [ad. L. *statāri-us*, f. *stat-* ppl. stem of *stāre* to stand.]

†1. Standing fast or firm, established; stated, fixed; having a fixed position, stationary. *Obs.*

1581 MULCASTER *Positions* xxxix. 199 Both a gentleman, and a common man .. may be either rich or poore: landed or vnlanded, which is either the hauing or wanting of the most statarie substance. **1617** COLLINS *Def. Bp. Ely* I. i. 47 What is this to the Popedome? what to a Monarchie? what, I say not to their stately, but euen statarie and ordinarie supremacie in the Church? **1646** SIR T. BROWNE *Pseud. Ep.* v. xxi. 266 The set and statary times of payring of nailes, and cutting of haire. *Ibid.* VI. ii. 287 The observation of festivities and statary solemnities. **1650** FULLER *Pisgah* v. xxi. 184, I will not plead that a tent is also termed an house .. that statory, or long standing tents were quilted with timber.

†2. Of soldiers: Equipped for stationary combat as opposed to skirmishing. *Obs.*

1623 BINGHAM *Xenophon, Compar. Lipsius*, The Battalions haue their spaces and intervals, and the Velites in them or before them. So that the Statarie Souldier serueth the Velites for retreat.

3. *Ent.* Pertaining to or designating army ants during that phase of their life cycle when they return to a fixed colony each night.

1933 *Jrnl. Compar. & Physiol. Psychol.* XV. 297 When in the 'statary' condition, [ant] colonies do not appear as susceptible to the atmospheric changes that apparently furnish the stimuli for the bivouac-change movements of nomad colonies. **1940** *Jrnl. Compar. Psychol.* XXIX. 434 Swarm division is exceptional in a statary colony, but is a regular morning event in a nomadic colony. *Ibid.* 435 Smaller swarms .. characterize the statary period. **1972** *Sci. Amer.* Nov. 73/3 The actual regulator of the ants' nomadic and statary behavior, as Schneirla eventually demonstrated, was not some external influence but the breeding cycle within the colony.

state (steɪt), *sb.* Forms: 3–6 **stat**, (4 **stade**, *pl.* **stas** (?)), 4–5 **staat**, 4–5, 7 **statt**, 4–6 **statte**, 4, 5–7 *Sc.* **stait(e**, 5–6 *Sc.* **stayt(e**, 6 *Sc.* **staet**, **steat**, 7 *Sc.* **staitt**, 4– **state**. [Partly var. of ESTATE *sb.* a. OF. *estat* (mod.F. *état*) = Pr. *estat-z*, Sp., Pg. *estado*, It. *stato*, ad. L. *status* (*u* stem), manner of standing, condition, n. of action f. *sta-*, *stāre* to stand; partly direct adaptation from the Latin source. The word in the Rom. langs. has or has had most of the senses of the Eng. *state* and *estate*; in the mod. Teut. langs. it has been adopted in forms derived from Latin or It. (G., Du. *staat*, Sw., Da. *stat*) chiefly in the political senses, though other uses also exist; Sw. has the form *ståt* in the sense ceremonial grandeur, pomp (sense 17 below).]

I. Condition, manner of existing.

1. a. A combination of circumstances or attributes belonging for the time being to a person or thing; a particular manner or way of existing, as defined by the presence of certain circumstances or attributes; a condition. Sometimes qualified by an adj. or a following phrasal genitive.

state of nature: see NATURE *sb.* 14. ***state of siege***: the condition of undergoing investment by a hostile army; also *transf.*

a **1225** *Ancr. R.* 204 Þet is riht religiun, þet euerich, efter his stat, boruwe et tisse urakele worlde so lutel so heo euer mei. *c* **1400** MAUNDEV. (Roxb.) vi. 21 Þat he schuld bring it [the Euphrates] to swilke a state þat wymmen schuld mow wade ouer and noȝt wete þaire kneesse. *c* **1450** *Reg. Godstow Nunnery* (1911) 415 That the forsaid ser Thomas shold susteyne the forsaid halle .. in all so good a state or better than he resceived hit. *c* **1460** *Oseney Reg.* 161 That þe waye Bitwene þe londe of þe same Roger and my londe .. be in þe same state in þe which it whas i-purueyed .. In the tyme of theobalde of Bray. **1500–20** DUNBAR *Poems* lxxii. 130 To keip the house in sicker stait. *c* **1600** SHAKS. *Sonn.* xxix. 2, I all alone beweepe my out-cast state. **1735** H. WALPOLE *Let.* 5 Sept. in *10th Rep. Hist. MSS. Comm.* App. I. 259 Ye violent & desperate state of their affairs. **1750** JOHNSON *Rambler* No. 28 ¶13 Adversity has ever been considered as the state in which a man most easily becomes acquainted with himself. **1791** COWPER *Let. to Lady Hesketh* 26 June, Olney is also itself in a state of beautification. **1793** SMEATON *Edystone L.* §324 Concerning the State and Condition of the Edystone Lighthouse. **1809** *Lond. Chron.* 1 July 4/2 He .. saw the young lady opposite to him .. in a state of nature, quite naked. **1815** J. SMITH *Panorama Sci. & Art* II. 833 The changes which it exhibits according to the state of the weather. **1843** WORDSWORTH in Chr. Wordsw. *Mem.* (1851) I. 97 A successful play would in the then state of my finances have been a most welcome piece of good fortune. **1847** TENNYSON in Ld. Tennyson *Mem.* (1897) I. xi. 244 My pen is .. in a state of hopeless splittage and divarication. **1848**, **1873** [see SIEGE *sb.* 6 b]. **1880** *Encycl. Brit.* XIII. 190/2 International law regards the states of the world as being either in a state of war or in a state of peace. **1890** *Law Times Rep.* LXIII. 766/2 Owing to the crowded state of the port. **1891** *Law Times* XC. 411/2 Allowing a foundry and other property to fall into .. a state of disrepair.

b. in regard to welfare or prosperity (worldly, moral or spiritual). Now somewhat *rare*.

a **1300** *Cursor M.* 5059 'How fars', he said, 'our fadir state?' **13..** *Sir Beues* 1990 Þai kiste hem anon wiþ þat And aþer askede of oþeres stat. *c* **1325** *Poem temp. Edw. II* (Percy) vii, Erchebisshopes and byshopes, That schuld trewly enquere Of al men of holy cherche In what stat thei were. *c* **1386** CHAUCER *Prol.* 572 Algate he wayted so in his Achaat That he was ay biforn and in good staat. **1632** MASSINGER *Maid of Honour* II. iii, If we come off, It is not amisse, if not, my state is settl'd. **1849** MACAULAY *Hist. Eng.* iii. I. 415 The great criterion of the state of the common people is the amount of their wages.

†c. *for the state of* = for the welfare of (a person prayed for). *Obs.* Cf. 27.

1395 *E.E. Wills* 8 To preye for my lordes soule..and for the stat of my sone forseid. [**1399** Gower *Eng. Wks.* (Macaulay) II. 492 Et nunc sequitur epistola in qua idem Ioannes pro statu et salute dicti domini sui apud altissimum deuocius exorat.] *c* **1460** *Oseney Reg.* 70 For þe stabulnese of all þe reame and state and welth of our Kyng ande quene.

d. as regards health of mind and body.

† *state of mortality*: a fatal epidemic.

a **1300** *Cursor M.* 28496 Womman ner hir chiltyng state. *c* **1375** *Sc. Leg. Saints* xli. (*Agnes*) 71 His fadir send.. medicinaris, his stat to se. **1538** Starkey *England* 35 Yet yf hyt be deformyd..the body hath not hys perfayt state and vertue. **1591** Savile *Tacitus, Hist.* II. xciii. 108 The Germans and Frenchmen lying by the Tiber..vtterly ouerthrew the state of their body with too much swimming in the riuer and impatience of heate. *c* **1600** Shaks. *Sonn.* cxviii. 11 And brought to medicine a healthfull state. **1700** in *Jrnl. Friends' Hist. Soc.* (1914) Oct. 180 A letter..from my sister..who..advises of a state of mortality in ther Country attended with a sort of feauor. **1813** Jane Austen *Lett.* (1884) II. 202 It is but roughish weather for any one in a tender state. **1854** J. C. Bucknill *Unsoundness of Mind* 89 He was fully conscious of his state, and had great hopes of being cured in the asylum. **1899** *Allbutt's Syst. Med.* VIII. 492 Urticaria occurs as a premonitory..or concomitant phenomenon in a great number of morbid states. **1908** R. Bagot *A. Cuthbert* xxviii. 370 It was in vain that he attempted to deceive his patient as to her state.

†**e.** as regards means of livelihood, riches or possessions. *Obs.* Cf. sense 36 and estate *sb.* 2.

1389 in *Eng. Gilds* (1870) 20 If eny brother or sister falle in pouert,..his state shal bene holpen, of euery brother and sister of ye gilde, wt a ferthyng in ye woke. *a* **1425** tr. *Arderne's Treat. Fistula*, etc. (1910) 5 þan after þat þe state of þe pacient askeþ aske he boldly more or lesse. *c* **1430** *How Good Wife taught Dau.* 149 in Hazl. *E.P.P.* I. 190 Ilke a man after his state, and ȝeue the pouere atte nede. **1557** F. Seager *Sch. Vertue* 1088 in *Babees Bk.*, Ye that are poore, with your state be contente. *c* **1590** Greene *Fr. Bacon* 588 Ile giue Liuing and lands to strength thy colledge state. **1611** Tourneur *Ath. Trag.* II. i, Yow shall doe well if yow be sicke to set Your state in present order. **1763** Churchill *Conference* 109 My Credit at last gasp, my State undone.

f. *colloq.* Used for 'a dreadful state' (of dirt, untidiness, etc.). Cf. 2 c.

1879 F. W. Robinson *Coward Consc.* II. vii, Just look what a [dirty] state I am in!

2. a. A condition (of mind or feeling); the mental or emotional condition in which a person finds himself at a particular time.

1538 Starkey *England* 43 When prosperyte ys wel vsyd, hyt ys a mean to set mannys mynd in that state, wherby he schal attayne hyar felycyte. **1638** Junius *Paint. Ancients* 292 The motions of the countenance doe best expresse the state of the mind. **1728** Law *Serious Call* ix, Covetousness.. supposes a foolish and unreasonable state of mind. **1751** Johnson *Rambler* No. 155 ¶2 It seems generally believed, that, as the eye cannot see itself, the mind has no faculties by which it can contemplate its own state. **1820** Southey *Wesley* I. 329 England was but in too apt a state for receiving the poison. **1848** Thackeray *Van. Fair* lviii, He..brought Mr. Jos..to a very good state of feeling regarding his relatives in Europe. **1865** Ruskin *Sesame* i. §31 No reading is possible for a people with its mind in this state. **1882** Pebody *Eng. Journalism* xx. 149 The whole country was in a state of white heat about the Roman Catholic claims. **1890** tr. *Moll's Hypnotism* 48 From the above examples it appears that the various hypnotic states differ much from one another.

b. as a technical term of psychology; esp. in *state of mind*, *state of consciousness*.

1749 D. Hartley *Observ. Man* I. Introd. p. iii, The Will is that State of Mind, which is immediately previous to, and causes, those express Acts of Memory, Fancy, and bodily Motion, which are termed voluntary. *c* **1790** Reid *Lett. to Gregory* Wks. (1846) 85 The reason why madness, idiotism, &c., are called states of mind, while its acts and operations are not, is because mankind have always conceived the mind to be passive in the former and active in the later. *c* **1810** T. Brown *Lect. Philos. Hum. Mind* (1820) I. 245 To the whole series of states of the mind, then, whatever the individual momentary successive states may be, I give the name of our *consciousness*. **1836–7** Sir W. Hamilton *Lect. Metaphysics* (1859) I. 203 We are conscious of one mental state only as we contradistinguish it from another. *c* **1837** —— *Reid's Wks.* (1846) 85 *note*, The term *State* has, more especially of late years, and principally by Necessitarian philosophers, been applied to all modifications of mind indifferently. **1862** Spencer *First Princ.* I. iii. §19. (1875) 61 It is..beyond question that our states of consciousness occur in succession. **1866** [see consciousness 4].

c. Used *colloq.* for: An agitated or excited state of mind or feeling. Cf. 1 f.

1837 Marryat *Perc. Keene* xxii, Lord, what a state I shall be in till I know what has taken place. **1890–91** *Boston* (Mass.) *Jrnl.*, There is no concealing the fact that English printers and publishers are in a state of mind over the International Copyright bill. **1902** Violet Jacob *Sheep-Stealers* xiv, Don't you remember when she went away, what a state you were in and how you raged?

†**d.** Condition of mind or feeling as displayed in one's manner or behaviour. *Obs.*

13.. *Bonaventura's Medit.* 391 þan cryst answered, with mylde state. **1375** Barbour *Bruce* VII. 128 Thai changit contenanss and late, And held nocht in the first stat..For thai var fayis to the kyng.

3. The mode of existence of a spiritual being; a particular mode or phase of (spiritual) existence.

future state: see future *a.* 1 b.

c **1300** *S. Eng. Leg.* 439/275 (Harl. MS.) Of þe pure stat of crist & of his mageste. *Ibid.* 281 þe gretteste clerkes..Ne poȝte þat eni vrþlich man so furforþ miȝte go Ne wite so moche of godes stat bote hit angel were. *c* **1380** Wyclif *Sel. Wks.* I. 132 þis aungel..telliþ hem how now Crist is sittynge in hevene, for his staat here in erþe is fulli performed. *a* **1400** *Minor Poems fr. Vernon MS.* xxiii. 958 Beo we translated in to blis Of wel better state. **1533** More *Confut. Tindale* VII. Wks. 720/1 The state of this present life. **1565** Allen *Def. Purg.* xvi. 280 All that passe hense in the happy state of grace. *a* **1667** [see nature *sb.* 14]. **1675** R. Burthogge *Causa Dei* 61 Is not the State of Hell in Scripture called the Second Death? **1684** Norris *Poems*, etc. 70 Are we affraid of making too nigh advances to the State of Angels? **1719** De Foe *Crusoe* II. (Globe) 443 It is a clear Evidence of God, and of a future State. *a* **1805** Paley *Serm. Sev. Subj.* v. 635/1 Our new bodies will be infinitely superior to those which we carry about with us in our present state. **1850** Tennyson *In Mem.* lxxxii. 6 From state to state the spirit walks. *Ibid.* lxxxv. 22 The great Intelligences fair That range above our mortal state. **1883** [see future *a.* 1 b]. **1907** F. Weston *The One Christ* 53 First, the Incarnation involved a state of being that is quite inferior to the divine state.

4. a. Physical condition as regards internal make or constitution, molecular form or structure, and the like. Also, one of several forms or conditions in which an object—animal, vegetable, or mineral—is found to exist; a phase or stage of existence. Also in generalized or abstract sense: each of the possible modes of existence of a system; the condition of a device that determines what output it produces for a given input.

c **1290** *S. Eng. Leg.* 239/701 þe eyr was euere in o stat, naþur to hot ne to cold. *a* **1300** *Leg. Rood* II. 100 þo hi were iwoxe to þe lengþe of an elne ich wene In þulke stat hi stode longe and euermore grene. **1340** *Ayenb.* 28 þanne by þe godspelle þet corn heþ þri stas, uor hit is uerst ase ine gerse, efterward ine yere, efterward is uol of frut. **1545** Elyot *Dict.*, *Amphicyrtos*, is the state of the moone, as wel whan he is somwhat increased..as also whan he is in the wane. **1721** Bradley *Philos. Acc. Wks. Nat.* 156, I have found it a little difficult to bring Water and Pepper into a right State of yielding these Insects. *a* **1805** Paley *Serm. Sev. Subj.* v. 634/1 When an animal changes its state, it changes its body. **1815** J. Smith *Panorama Sci. & Art* II. 243 Water, in the state of vapour. **1823** Scoresby *Jrnl.* 411, I do not consider it different from a dwarf state of V. uliginosum. **1849** J. F. Wood *Midland Florist* iii. 122 Bulbs in a breeder state throw up stronger and bolder flowers than when in colour. **1859** Ruskin *Two Paths* iv. §143 The most perfect and useful state of it [iron] is that of ochreous stain. **1876** Tait *Rec. Adv. Phys. Sci.* ix. 219 Some black body..which may be either in a solid or in a liquid state,—possibly even in the state of extremely compressed gas. **1937** A. M. Turing in *Proc. London Math. Soc.* XLII. 250 We know the state of the system if we know the sequence of symbols on the tape, which of these are observed by the computer.., and the state of mind of the computer. **1942**, etc. [see Markov]. **1954** *Jrnl. Franklin Inst.* CCLVII. 170 Once a stable state has been reached for all secondary relays, then further circuit changes can occur only if modification is made in the input state. **1961** F. M. Reza *Introd. Information Theory* ii. 54 Let an experiment have a finite number of *n* possible outcomes, $a_1, a_2, \ldots,$ and a_n, called states. We assume the process to be of the finite Markov type and initially in the state *k*. **1962** A. Gill *Introd. Theory of Finite-State Machines* i. 6 Roughly, the state of a finite-state machine at any given sampling time is that variable which, together with the input symbol, enables one to predict the output symbol. *Ibid.* iv. 130 Let *M* be an *n*-state machine with the input alphabet $X = \{\xi_1, \xi_2, \ldots, \xi_p\}$. **1964** F. L. Westwater *Electronic Computers* ii. 21 The reliable and stable electronic devices are so far two-state devices... If we had a three-state device we could..develop a ternary system of arithmetic. **1979** J. R. Gibson *Electronic Logic Circuits* i. 5 Logic elements may be combined to form multiple-state systems and the states of such systems may be used to represent numbers in systems other than the binary one.

b. *spec.* in *Physics*, a condition of an atom or other quantized system described by a particular set of quantum numbers; *esp.* one characterized by the quantum numbers *n*, *L*, *S*, *J*, and *m*. Cf. level *sb.* 3 e.

1913 N. Bohr in *Phil. Mag.* XXVI. 5 If in these expressions we give τ, different values, we get a series of values for W, ω, and *a* corresponding to a series of configurations of the system. According to the above considerations, we are led to assume that these configurations will correspond to states of the system in which there is no radiation of energy; states which consequently will be stationary as long as the system is not disturbed from outside. **1925** *Astrophysical Jrnl.* LXI. 39 Every spectral line is now believed to be emitted (or absorbed) in connection with the transition of an atom (or molecule) between two definite (quantized) states, of different energy-content—the frequency of the radiation being exactly proportional to the change of energy. **1929** N. V. Sidgwick *Electronic Theory of Valency* ii. 18 These states are distinguished by the fact that in them the electron possesses an integral number..of quanta of energy. **1935** P. A. M. Dirac *Princ. Quantum Mech.* (ed. 2) i. 11 A state of a system may be defined as an undisturbed motion that is restricted by as many conditions or data as are theoretically possible without mutual interference or contradiction. **1935** Condon & Shortley *Theory Atomic Spectra* iv. 122 The terms are designated as ^2S (doublet *S*), ^2P, ^{2}D,...according to the *P* value of the configuration from which they arise. The separate levels are designated by adding the value of *j* as a superscript, thus $^2S_{\frac{1}{2}}$...To specify an individual state the value of *m* is given as a superscript. **1955** E. B. Wilson et al. *Molecular Vibrations* x. 246 The selection rules for overtone frequencies will next be considered. These are transitions between the ground vibrational state and an excited state in which one quantum number is greater than one and all other quantum numbers are zero. **1970** [see level *sb.* 3 e]. **1972** De Puy & Chapman *Molec. Reactions & Photochem.* iii. 43 Formaldehyde, which is planar in its ground state, distorts slightly toward a pyramidal structure in the S_1 state. **1978** P. W. Atkins *Physical Chem.* xix. 631 The isotope ^{57}Co decays slowly..and forms an excited nuclear state of ^{57}Fe.

5. a. *the* (or *a*) *state of things* or *affairs*: the way in which events or circumstances stand disposed (at a particular time or within a particular sphere). *spec.* in the philosophy of L. Wittgenstein (1889–1951): see quots. 1922, 1962.

Cf. L. *status rerum*, in reference to public or political affairs; and quot. 1387 in b.

1555 Eden *Decades* (Arb.) 114 Thalteracion of the state of thynges in Vraba. **1580** Campion in Allen *Martyrdom* (1908) 21, I thought it good to give you intelligence..of the present stat of things here. **1607** Chapman *Bussy d'Ambois* I. i. 1 Fortune, not Reason, rules the state of things. **1776** *St. James's Chron.* 23–25 May 4/1 Administration had, to the Scandal of all good Government, suppressed every Thing relative to the true State of Affairs in America. **1794** Burke *Corr.* (1844) IV. 253 This is an unfortunate state of things; but it is your state, and you must conform to it. **1856** Froude *Hist. Eng.* (1858) I. i. 87 We have seen a state of things in which the principles of political economy were.. contradicted. **1871** Freeman *Norm. Conq.* IV. xvii. (1876) 64 In Herefordshire and on the Welsh border the state of things was very unsettled. **1909** G. B. Shaw *Press Cuttings* 31 We [women] should lose our influence completely under such a state of affairs. **1911** E. L. Thorndike *Animal Intelligence* vi. 245 By a satisfying state of affairs is meant one which the animal does nothing to avoid. **1922** tr. *Wittgenstein's Tractatus* 31 It would..appear as an accident, when to a thing that could exist alone on its own account, subsequently a state of affairs could be made to fit. *Ibid.* 35 Objects contain the possibility of all states of affairs. *Ibid.* 43 The picture contains the possibility of the state of affairs which it represents. **1958** R. L. Green *Land of Lord High Tiger* ii. 33 Sad affairs of State! Sad state of affairs! Affairs in a sad state! **1962** M. Cranston tr. *Hartnack's Wittgenstein & Mod. Philos.* ii. 13 A 'state of affairs' is a fact that in itself does not consist of facts... A state of affairs is a combination of possible facts. *Ibid.* 14 If an elementary sentence, or, better, an elementary proposition is true, then the state of affairs which is spoken of exists. **1973** A. Kenny *Wittgenstein* v. 73 States of affairs, we are told, are independent of one another.

†**b.** A dispensation or system of divine government during a particular era. Also, *state of things*.

1387 Trevisa *Higden* I. 31 Descrypcions of places, states of thynges, distinccion of tymes. *Ibid.* Touchynge þe secounde take hede of tweie states, oon from þe bygynnynge of þe world to Criste, and is i-cleped þe staat of mysgoynge; the secounde staat from Criste to þe worldes end, and is i-cleped þe state of grace and of mercy.

†**c.** *state of time* or *times*: a juncture or posture of affairs. *Obs.*

1594 Shaks. *Rich. III*, IV. iv. 416 Vrge the Necessity and state of times. **1596** —— *1 Hen. IV.* IV. i. 25, I would the state of time had first beene whole, Ere he by sicknesse had beene visited. **1662** Stillingfl. *Orig. Sacræ* II. i. §5 How can we conceive the Nation of the Jews would have ever embraced such a Law, had it not been of Moses his enacting among them in that state of time when he did?

d. *the state of the case*: the facts and circumstances of a particular affair, question, etc.

1729 Butler *Serm.* Wks. 1850 II. Pref. p. xvii, The taking in this consideration totally changes the whole state of the case. **1848** Thackeray *Van. Fair* xiii, And the real state of the case would never have been known at all in the regiment but for Captain Dobbin's indiscretion. *a* **1873** Deutsch *Lit. Rem.* (1874) 365 This is the simple state of the case.

e. *state of the art*: the current stage of development of a practical or technological subject; freq. (esp. in *attrib.* use) implying the use of the latest techniques in a product or activity.

[**1889**: see status 4.] **1910** H. H. Suplee *Gas Turbine* 6 It has therefore been thought desirable to gather under one cover the most important papers... In the present state of the art this is all that can be done. **1955** *Jrnl. R. Aeronaut. Soc.* LIX. 471/1 Flight instruments and flight techniques of human pilots had to be brought up to a state where automatic flying could be fitted into a consistent state-of-the-art picture. **1957** R. A. Heinlein *Door into Summer* (1960) v. 69 Engineering is the art of the practical and depends more on the total state of the art than it does on the individual engineer. **1967** *Technology Week* 23 Jan. 18/1 (Advt.), Poseidon's requirements range from weapon effects on electronics to the design and use of state-of-the-art test checkout equipment. **1970** J. Earl *Tuners & Amplifiers* iv. 79 An average magnetic cartridge at the current state of the art produces an output of 1 mV per channel for each velocity unit of 1 cm/S. **1970** *Daily Tel.* (Colour Suppl.) 9 Oct. 7 Our highly sophisticated, technological defence establishment is advancing the state-of-the-art weaponry into new and therefore secret areas. **1975** *Language* LI. 1009 What emerges about the state of the art in linguistics is incidental to the presentation of L[abov]'s analysis of language use in various speech communities. **1976** *National Observer* (U.S.) 27 Mar. 15/2 State-of-the-art solar research is well advanced in New Mexico. **1976** *Offshore Platforms & Pipelining* 16/3 Except for an innovation or two, the platform is state-of-the-art and no more than an extension of existing capabilities. **1978** *Sci. Amer.* Apr. 64/3 In the 1950's C. Miller Fisher..proposed that anastomosis, or joining, of cerebral arteries beyond the point of occlusion might be appropriate in some stroke cases, but such manipulations were then still beyond the state of the art. **1978** *SLR Camera* Aug. 54/1 It is still not so easy to produce decent pictures at such a venue, even when one is replete with 'state of the art' cameras, long lenses and fast film.

f. *State of the Union message*: a yearly address delivered by the President of the U.S. to Congress, giving the Administration's view of the state of the nation and its plans for legislation.

[**1787** *Constitution as formed for U.S.* II. iii. 10 He shall from time to time give to the Congress information of the state of the union.] **1945** *Newsweek* 15 Jan. 30 (*caption*) Three days before the President's State of the Union message, the 79th Congress takes its oath of office. **1959**

Ann. Reg. 1958 182 The President appeared in person before both Houses of Congress on 9 January to deliver his State of the Union Message. **1968** W. Safire *New Lang. Politics* 427 State of the Union *messages* (preferred over speeches, addresses, or reports..) have inclined to be lengthy statements of legislative intent. **1974** *Guardian* 31 Jan. 2/7 President Nixon's sixth—and very possibly his last—State of the Union message.

g. ***the state of play***: the position in which a matter or business stands at a particular time.

1966 *Rep. Comm. Inquiry Univ. Oxf.* II. 56 Receiving applications..and keeping colleges informed on the 'state of play' on each candidate. **1971** A. Garve *Late Bill Smith* i. 38 You know the state of play, you can handle everything. **1979** R. Mutch *Gemstone* v. 56 Write me a short report... I want the state of play. I want it accurate and I want it now.

†**6.** With contextual implication: **a.** Original, proper or normal condition; a sound, healthy, flourishing, prosperous condition. (Cf. estate *sb.* 1 d.) Chiefly in phrases, as ***to be*** (or ***stand***) ***in state***: to be firmly established or flourishing; to be intact; also, to remain 'in statu quo'. ***to bring in, to*** (***one's***) ***state***: to reinstate, restore. ***to put of, out of state***, to deprive of one's position or status, disinherit, degrade. *Obs.*

1297 R. Glouc. (Rolls) 254 Atte laste þo he in stat was & him þo3te þat is per in þe world nas. *a* **1300** *Cursor M.* 9219 Þe Iuues now er put o state, And þair kingrik translate. *Ibid.* 20958 To halt o ganging gaf he stat. *c* **1320** *Cast. Loue* 1206 Þorw whom þe fend was al mat, And þe world for-bou3t and brou3t in stat. **1340–70** *Alex. & Dind.* 686 A soþ god..þat haþ þe stomak in stat stifly to kepe. **1375** Barbour *Bruce* I. 297 Bot wondirly hard thing is fell Till him, or he till state wes brocht. **1387** Trevisa *Higden* III. 165 Þat Tarquinius schulde be brou3t to his state and in to þe citee a3en. *c* **1470** Henry *Wallace* v. 340 He bad thaim se giff that place stud in stait; Tharoff to her he had full gret desyr, Be caus he thocht that it was all in fyr. **1531** in *Archæologia* XLVII. 62 Sharing some dishe from thyn own bord and likewise from thy chanons till tyme thou bring thy said house in state agayne. **1605** Bacon *Adv. Learn.* I. iv. § 1 To scandalize and depraue that which retaineth the state and vertue, by taking aduantage vpon that which is corrupt and degenerate. *Ibid.* II. xxi. § 2 To preserue in state is the lesse, to preserue with aduancement is the greater. **1638** Earl Manch. in *Buccleuch MSS.* (Hist. MSS. Comm.) I. 278 Things here rest as yet in state as they were.

†**b.** Fixed or stable condition. *Obs.*

1597 Bacon *Coulers Good & Evill* ix. ¶ 1 In the fauours of others or the good windes of fortune we haue no state or certainty, in our endeuours or abilities we haue. **1605** —— *Adv. Learn.* II. xxi. § 1 If wee mought haue a perpetuity and Certainty in our pleasures, the State of them would aduance their price.

†**7.** The height or chief stage of a process; the condition of full vigour. Chiefly *Path.*, the crisis or 'acme' of disease. *Obs.* Cf. status 1.

1607 Topsell *Four-f. Beasts* 342 To euery disease or malady, belongeth foure seuerall times, that is to say, the beginning, the increasing, the state, and declination. **1656** Blount *Glossogr.*, *Catastasis*, the third part of a Comedy, and signifies the state and full vigour of it. **1656** Ridgley *Pract. Physick* 257 In the augmentation and the state, Cordials and such things as expel. **1665** G. Harvey *Adv. agst. Plague* 11 At present it is in the Augment, and likely to attain to a state about the latter end of August. **1717** J. Keill *Anim. Oecon.* (1738) 189 When all the peccant matter is thrown out, the disease generally proceeds to its state without any ill accident. **1913** Dorland *Med. Dict.*, *State*.. the crisis or turning-point of an attack of disease.

†**8. a.** Existence. ***to hold state***, to continue or persist in being; ***to hold in state***, to maintain in existence. ***to have state***, to consist *in* (something).

a **1300** *Cursor M.* 314 His sun his wisdom es, þat wat All þinges, þat haldes stat [*Gött.* For all þe werld he haldis in state]. *c* **1440** *Pallad. on Husb.* xii. 599, xiij is thridde, and firthe in x hath state. **1447** Bokenham *Seynts, Magd.* 756 If ..god also my state so longe, Tyl yt be doon, vouchesaf to prolong. **1615** Chapman *Odyss.* ii. 333 If dead I heare him, nor of more state [εἰ δέ κε τεθνηῶτος ἀκούσω μηδ' ἔτ' ἐόντος].

†**b.** ? A possibility, possible means. *Obs.*

a **1300** *Cursor M.* 14149 Quen þai sagh þat þar was nanoþer Stat o couering o þair broþer.

†**9. a.** Stature, bodily form or contour. *Obs. rare.* (So L. *status*, OF. *estat* in Godefroy.)

1387 Trevisa *Higden* (Rolls) III. 223 Þere is no fairenesse of body wheþer it be in state [*v.r.* staat] of body as in schap of lengþe and brede [*sive in statu corporis consistat, sicut est figura*], oþer in meouynge as in song, but suche as þe inwitte of man deemeþ. **1538** Elyot *Dict.*, *Habitus*, the fourme or state of the body. **1623** Fletcher & Rowley *Maid in Mill* v. ii, If't please ye (Madam) let me see the state of your body; I'll fit you instantly.

†**b.** A person's proper form, shape or nature. *Obs. rare.*

c **1330** *Arthur & Merl.* 2584 Þe king wiþ water þer he wesche, His owhen stat he hadde, ywis. ? *a* **1550** *Freiris Berwik* 475 in *Dunbar's Poems* (1893) 301 Him to translait or ellis dissagyiss Fra his awin kynd in-to ane vder stait.

†**10. a.** A kind, sort or species. *Obs. rare*⁻¹.

a **1400–50** *Wars Alex.* 5646 Þan with stanes of ilka state wall [? *read* was] þe stoure clustrid.

b. *Bot.* 'A form or phase of a particular plant' (*Cent. Dict.*).

1872 Tuckerman *Genera Lichenum* 35 (Cent.) Sticta linita ..was recognized as occurring in the United States by Delise,..and Dr. Nylander (Syn. p. 353) speaks of a state from Arctic America. **1900** B. D. Jackson *Gloss. Bot. Terms*, *State*, the most trivial variation from the type.

11. Phrases. †**a.** ***to hold no state of***: to disregard, have no respect for. (Cf. F. *faire état de*, to set store by.) *Obs.*

a **1300** *Cursor M.* 13584 O godd him semes ha na perti þat haldes of hali-dai na stat.

†**b.** ***to make state*** (*to* do something): to expect (to do), count (on doing). [A mere Gallicism.]

1691 *d' Emiliane's Frauds Rom. Monks* 56 Telling him, That he was an Abbot accurs'd of God; that Damnation would be his portion, and that all those who lived under his Conduct, might make State to go to Hell with him.

†**c.** ***in state***, later ***in a state*** (now ***in a fit state***) followed by infinitive: fit, likely, ready *to do* or *be* something. Cf. F. *en état* (*de*).

a **1562** Ld. Vaux *Instab. Youth* iv, Thou that didst saue the theefe in state to sterue. **1585** T. Washington tr. *Nicholay's Voy.* i. xv. 16 Hee had two faire daughters then beyng in state to be marryed. **1592** *Arden of Feversham* iii. vi. 93 Your pretty tale beguiles the weary way; I would you were in state to tell it out. **1776** *Trial of Nundocomar* 23/1 He has not for a long time been in a state able to go out of the house. **1789** Charlotte Smith *Ethelinde* IV. 192 She had a good deal of fever, and was not in a state to be removed. **1835** I. Taylor *Spir. Despot.* vi. 244 To assume..that the political rulers of the body were still in a state to be spoiled. **1857** Trollope *Barchester T.* xxxiv, He..went on thinking of her till he was almost in a state to drown himself in the little brook.

†**12.** *Rhet.* (after L. *status*). The point in question or debate between contending parties, as it emerges from their pleadings; the issue or main question. In full ***state of the cause***, ***of the plea***. *Obs.*

c **1450** Holland *Howlat* 266 The circumstance and the stait all couth thai argewe. *c* **1530** Cox *Rhet.* (1899) 71 In these [judicial] oracions the fyrste is to fynde out the state of the cause, whiche is a short proposicion conteynynge the hole effect of all the controuersies. *Ibid.* 72 The state of the plee. **1549** Latimer *5th Serm. bef. Edw. VI* (Arb.) 134 *margin*, The scope or state of the boke, tendes to dysuade the kinge from hys supremycye. **1553** T. Wilson *Rhet.* 47 b, Of the foundacion, or rather principall poincte in euery debated matter, called of the Rhetoricians the State, or constitucion of the Cause. *Ibid.* 48 b, A State therfore in matters of iudgement is that thyng whiche doeth arise vpon the first demaunde and denial made betwixt men... I cannot better terme it in Englishe than by the name of an issue. **1609** R. Barnerd *Faithf. Sheph.* 20 The scope or principall intendment of the Holy Ghost in that place; from which scope ariseth the principall proposition, called of Rhetoricians the State, of Lawyers the Issue. **1611** Cotgr., *Estat*..the state, head, issue, knot, principall point of a matter in controuersie. **1776** B. Martin *Bibl. Technol.* (ed. 4) 129 *margin*, The several states of the cause.

13. *Gram.* **a.** [= mod.L. *status*.] In the grammar of the Semitic langs., a noun is said to be in the ***construct state*** (or ***state of construction***) when it governs a following genitive, and in the ***absolute state*** when it does not; the two 'states' being usually distinguished flexionally. In Aramaic grammar, a noun is in the *emphatic* (or, in some recent books, the *definite*) state when it has the suffix which originally served the purpose of a definite article, but in Syriac became unmeaning.

1752 P. Petit *Hebr. Guide, View Chaldaic* 4 Nouns in an absolute state are sometimes found in the construct form, and *vice versa*, as in Hebrew. **1837** G. Phillips *Syriac Gram.* 24 To the absolute and constructive state of nouns, which the Hebrews have, the Syrians add a third, the Definite. **1853** P. H. Mason & Bernard *Hebr. Gram.* I. 100 A Noun in the State of Construction. **1874** A. B. Davidson *Introd. Hebr. Gram.* 35.

†**b.** By some English grammarians of the 18th c., ***foregoing*** or ***leading state*** and ***following state*** were used for the nominative and objective cases respectively, the term *case* being regarded as inapplicable to English. *Obs.*

1711 J. Greenwood *Ess. Pract. Eng. Gram.* 104 The Pronouns have a twofold State... The first State we shall call the Foregoing State, as I, We; the second State we shall call the Following State, as Me, Us. **1809** *Lindley Murray Examined* 5 What has, for ages, been called the *nominative case*, is by one Grammarian called the *leading state*.

c. ***positive state*** is used by Lindley Murray for 'positive degree'.

1800 L. Murray *Engl. Gram.* (ed. 6) 48.

14. a. *Engraving.* An impression taken from a plate at a particular stage of its progress and recognizable by special marks.

1874 Ruskin *Stones Venice* I. Pref. p. ix, The present edition..containing the best states of the old plates now procurable. **1899** E. F. Benson *Mammon & Co.* vii. 97 Mrs. Siddons was a first state with the coveted blotted edge.

b. *Bibliography.* (See quots. 1931.)

1931 P. H. Muir *Points* 12 A word is still needed to describe changes made before any publication takes place. These changes may be made while the entire edition is still in the publisher's hands, they may take place at the printer's, at the binder's, or even at a stage intermediate between the issue of some of the review copies and the actual date of publication. Any differences that may arise before that time will be referred to as 'states'. *Ibid.* 13 It is probable that copies of the book in all three states will be issued on the same day. They will all be 'first issues'; but some will be first, some second, and others again third 'states' of the first edition. **1931** G. Worthington *Bibliogr. Waverley Novels* p. viii, I have..decided to use the word 'State' whenever between two copies of a first edition there are differences of sufficient importance to be noticed; and my 'First State' is the variety which I believe to be preferable..to any other. *Ibid.* 37 Guy Mannering... There are four States of the first edition. **1949**, etc. [see issue *sb.* 15 b (ii)]. **1972** *Scholarly Publishing* III. 123 The text was published almost simultaneously in English, French, and German, all with the same title. To distinguish between the various states and issues is nearly hopeless.

II. Status; high rank; pomp.

†**15. a.** A person's condition or position in life; a person's natural, social or legal status, profession or calling, rank or degree. *Obs.*

c **1290** *S. Eng. Leg.* 98/212 Þench op-on þi noble stat, of alle Maidenes þov art flour. **1303** R. Brunne *Handl. Synne* 1679 3yf..þou art yn state of prest. *c* **1330** —— *Chron. Wace* (Rolls) 11202 Wyþ hym, of Rome cam þe legat; And oþer bischopes of mener stat. **1399** Langl. *R. Redeles* iii. 174 3it blame I no burne to be, as him ou3te, In comliche cloþinge as his statt axith. **1450** *Rolls of Parlt.* V. 211/2 Any persone, beyng under state of Lorde. *c* **1470** Henry *Wallace* vi. 588 Quha best did than, he had the heast stait. **1538** Starkey *England* 55 What so euer state, offyce, or degree, any man be of. **1549** *Bk. Comm. Prayer, Catechism*, To doe my duetie in that state of life: vnto which it shal please God to cal me. **1601** Barlow *Serm. Paules Crosse* 35 Could he..haue beene contented with his great state. *a* **1616** Beaumont *To B. Jonson*, 'Tis that which keeps our minds fit for our states. **1630** Pagitt *Christianogr.* i. ii. (1636) 85 He..freed these Indians from slaverie and gave them the state of free men. **1741** Kames *Decis. Crt. Sess.* 1730–52 (1799) 37 Having died in the state of apparency.

†**b.** A person's condition or status as determined by his years. ***man's state*** = manhood; cf. estate *sb.* 1 b and L. phr. *ad statum suum pervenire*.

c **1315** Shoreham *Poems* i. 15 And hondred winter 3ef a leueþe, þat his lyf mid þe lengeste. Onneþe creft eny þat stat. **1460–70** *Bk. Quintessence* 15 Wiþinne a fewe dayes he schal so hool þat he schal fele him silf of þe statt and þe strenkþe of xl 3eer; and he schal haue greet ioie þat he is come to þe statt of 3ongþe. *c* **1475** Henryson *Poems* III. 108 The state of youth I repute for na gude, For in that state sik perilis now I see. **1553** T. Wilson *Rhet.* 118 When they come to mans state. **1579–80** North *Plutarch, Theseus* (1595) 3 The yong men after their..growth to mans state.

c. Condition or status as married or single.

c **1380** Wyclif *Sel. Wks.* III. 184 And to þes þree ben þre oþere, comyn and leeful bi Goddis lawe—state of virgyns, and state of wedloke, and þe state of widewis. **1712** Steele *Tatler* No. 278 ¶ 2 When I enter into a married State. **1812**, **1836** [see single *a.* 8 b].

†**16.** *contextually.* A high rank or exalted position; an office of power or importance. *Obs.*

c **1290** *S. Eng. Leg.* 133/920 He..wole..bi-nime þe þi stat and perantur bringue þe out of londe. **1297** R. Glouc. (Rolls) 1261 Þer vore ich bidde þat ich mowe mi stat holde þoru þe. **1338** R. Brunne *Chron.* (1725) 73 Þe archbisshop Stigand, of Inglond primate, þat tyme was suspended, þe pape reft him þe state. **1390** Gower *Conf.* I. 260 And thus the man and noght the stat The Frensche schopen be her miht To grieve. **1544** Betham *Precepts War* ii. xvi. K iij, That fault is augmented by the state and honour of the capitayne. *a* **1586** Sidney *Arcadia* iv. (1598) 401 The Queene, to whom besides the obedient duetie they ow'de to her state, they had alwayes caried a singular loue. **1605** Bacon *Adv. Learn* i. To the King § 1 The businesse of your Crowne and State. **1622** J. Taylor (Water P.) *Thief* Wks. (1630) ii. 117/2 And many a mitred Pope and Cardinall This way haue got their state Pontificall. **1642** D. Rogers *Naaman* 29 Forgetting his state, and being at the curtesie of the Prophet for his cure.

†**b.** In generalized sense: High rank, greatness, power. *Obs.*

c **1400** *Destr. Troy* 9099 Prinses, That most were of might & of mayn state. *c* **1470** Henry *Wallace* x. 274 We will nocht stryff for stayt. *c* **1590** Greene *Fr. Bacon* v. iii. 2027 Great Potentates, earths miracles for state. *c* **1590** Marlowe *Faustus* Chorus 4 In courts of Kings where state is ouer-turnd. **1608** Chapman *Byron's Consp.* iv. i. 114 You make all state before Utterly obsolete. **1630** Wadsworth *Pres. Estate Spain* 33 Don Alphonso..did Conquer Toledo,..and was the first King that established this Arch-Bishopricke, in this great state and estate. *c* **1640** Shirley *Cont. Ajax & Ulysses* (1659) 127 The glories of our blood and state.

†**c.** ***to bear*** (***great***) ***state***, to hold (high) office; *fig.* (of a thing), to be of importance, involve great consequences. *Obs.*

a **1300** *Cursor M.* 6949 Bot quen aaron was ded, þe priste, His sun eliazar was neist, And bar state of his fader-hade. **1340** Hampole *Pr. Consc.* i. 883 Emperour, kyng, duke, ne caysere, Ne other þat bers grete state here. **1613** Shaks. *Hen. VIII*, ii. iv. 213 The question did at first so stagger me, Bearing a State of mighty moment in't, And consequence of dread.

†**d.** ***man of state***: one of high rank or dignity. Cf. estate *sb.* 3. *Obs.*

13.. *Guy Warw.* (1891) 420 A man y was of state sum stounde, & holden a lord of gret mounde. **1338** R. Brunne *Chron.* (1725) 258 Sir Hugh was man of state, he said as I salle rede. **1582** Stanyhurst *Æneis* etc. (Arb.) 129 Thee Prophet layeth downe an exhortation too theese men of state.

17. a. Costly and imposing display, such as befits persons of rank and wealth; splendour, magnificence (in manner of life, clothing, furniture, buildings, retinue, etc.); 'solemn pomp, appearance of greatness' (J.).

c **1330** *Amis. & Amil.* 1906 That riche douke..As a prince serued he was, With riche coupes of gold: And that brought him to that state Stode bischet, withouten the gate, Wel sore of-hungred and cold. *c* **1400** Maundev. (Roxb.) vi. 22 Of his state and magestee I think to speke afterwardes. **1596** Shaks. *Merch. V.* v. i. 95 A substitute shines brightly as a King Vntill a King be by, and then his state Empties it selfe, as doth an inland brooke Into the maine of waters. **1616–17** in *Crt. & Times Jas. I* (1848) I. 466 Our new lord keeper goes with great state, having a world of followers put upon him. **1625** Bacon *Ess.*, *Masques* (Arb.) 540 Double Masques, one of Men, another of Ladies, addeth State, and Variety. **1639** Fuller *Holy War* iv. viii. (1640) 182 Richard fortified Askelon.., not onely to strength but state, with marble pillars and statues. *a* **1661** —— *Worthies, Gen.* ix. 24

The Brasen-Andirons stand only for state, to entertain the Eyes. *a* **1700** EVELYN *Diary* 22 July 1670, It does onely well in very small and trifling roomes, but takes from the state of greater. **1725** POPE *Odyss.* VI. 46 In pomp ride forth; for pomp becomes the great, And Majesty derives a grace from State. **1728** LAW *Serious Call* ii. (1732) 20 Or remove him from a shop, to a life of state and pleasure. **1756–7** tr. *Keysler's Trav.* (1760) IV. 468 The former duke..had fifty gentlemen of the bed-chamber; however that state could not have been kept up, had the salaries been on the same extravagant footing as in other courts. **1842** TENNYSON *Ld. of Burleigh* 32 Ancient homes of lord and lady, Built for pleasure and for state. **1848** DICKENS *Dombey* iii, It was a house of dismal state. **1849** MACAULAY *Hist. Eng.* iii. I. 354 The gilded coach, indeed, which is now annually admired by the crowd, was not yet a part of his state. **1915** *Eng. Hist. Rev.* Jan. 168 The royal vault where he [Charles I] had been laid with so little state after his execution.

b. Phr. ***of state***; as in ***bed*** or ***chair of state***. Otherwise expressed by the attributive use (see 39); thus ***bed, rooms of state*** are = state-bed, state-rooms.

1503 *Acc. Ld. High Treas. Scot.* II. 213 The Quenis gret bed of stait. **1593** SHAKS. *3 Hen. VI*, I. i. 51 My Lords, looke where the sturdie Rebell sits, Euen in the Chayre of State. **1667** MILTON *P.L.* II. 1 High on a Throne of Royal State. *a* **1700** EVELYN *Diary* 16 Oct. 1671, The chambers and roomes of state. **1786** ABIGAIL ADAMS *Lett* (1848) 296 Here, upon a superb bed of state, lay the remains of his Grace. **1865** KINGSLEY *Herew.* xiv, The queen-countess sat in her chair of state in the midst. **1903** A. SMELLIE *Men of Covenant* xix. 222 He rode in his carriage of state drawn by six horses. *transf.* **1579** SPENSER *Sheph. Cal.* Feb. 146 And his trees of state in compasse rownd.

c. ***in state***: with great pomp and solemnity; with a great train; with splendid or honorific trappings and insignia.

to lie in state: of a dead body, to be ceremoniously exposed to view before interment.

1592 SHAKS. *Rom. & Jul.* I. iv. 70 And in this state she gallops night by night. **1687** A. LOVELL tr. *Thevenot's Trav.* I. 86 The Grand Signior..resolved to go through the City in State. **1700** T. BROWN *Amusem. Ser. & Com.* 93 See a Consult of them marching in State to a Patient. **1705** *Lond. Gaz.* No. 4096/2 Her Majesty is to lie in State at Hanover. **1847** C. BRONTE *Jane Eyre* ii, It was in this chamber he breathed his last; here he lay in state. **1849** MACAULAY *Hist. Eng.* i. I. 76 Abroad the ambassadors of Elizabeth and James went in state to the very worship which Elizabeth and James persecuted at home. **1883** J. GILMOUR *Mongols* xxiv. 295 Lamas in state coming to the temple.

18. a. Dignity of demeanour or presence; dignified appearance, stateliness of bearing. Now *rare*.

a **1586** SIDNEY *Astroph. & Stella* Song I. ii, Who hath the eyes which marrie state with pleasure! **1609** B. JONSON *Epicœne* II. i, This is not, onely, fit modestie in a Seruant, but good state, and discretion in a Master. **1642** FULLER *Holy & Prof. St.* III. vi. 164 True, there is a state sometimes in decent plainnesse. **1754** GRAY *Progr. Poesy* 39 In gliding state she wins her easy way. **1763** CHURCHILL *Poems, Night* 141 How many from appearance borrow state. **1808** SCOTT *Marmion* v. xxxi, The Abbess, seeing strife was vain, Assumed her wonted state again—For much of state she had. **1822** LAMB *Elia* Ser. I. *Dream-Children*, A great sulky pike hanging mid-way down the water in silent state. **1875** SWINBURNE *Ess. & Stud.* 356 A sketch of Lucrezia seated with legs bare, perfect in shapeliness and state.

†**b.** Dignified observance of form or ceremony.

1604 E. G[RIMSTONE] *D'Acosta's Hist. Indies* VI. xii. 455 They observed one custome very great & full of state. **1642** FULLER *Holy & Prof. St.* I. vii. 17 The lion out of state will not run whilst any one looks upon him. **1654** —— *Two Serm.* 52 He [God] reciteth downe mens Actions, not out of any necessitie to helpe himselfe to remember them; but partly out of State (as Ioseph made use of an Interpreter though understanding his Brothers language). **1671** tr. *Frejus' Voy. Mauritania* 82 Although the King very well understood the interpretation of my Discourse given by Jacob Pariente, nevertheless, as a piece of State, Cheq Amar..repeated unto him the words.

19. Phrases. **a.** ***to keep state, one's state***: to observe the pomp and ceremony befitting a high position; to keep one's dignity, behave in a dignified manner. Now *rare*.

1599 B. JONSON *Cynthia's Rev.* II. iii, The woorst in her is want of keeping state, and to much descending into inferior and base offices. **1601** SHAKS. *Jul. C.* I. ii. 160 There was a Brutus once, that would haue brook'd Th' eternall Diuell to keepe his State in Rome, As easily as a King. **1625** B. JONSON *Staple of N.* III. i, Keep your state, stoupe only to the Infanta. **1652** NEDHAM tr. *Selden's Mare Cl.* 82 Andronicus Palæologus, one that kept the State of an Emperor. **1818** SCOTT *Br. Lamm.* xviii, But keep your ain state wi' them..they will think the mair o' ye. **1847** TENNYSON *Princess* III. 213 O Vashti, noble Vashti! Summon'd out She kept her state.

†**b.** ***to take state upon one***: to assume an appearance of grandeur or dignity; to affect superiority, give oneself airs; to be reserved and haughty. *Obs.*

1608 DOD & CLEAVER *Expos. Prov.* ix–x. 37 And yet she goeth not as an ordinarie strumpet,..but taketh state upon her like a courtizan. **1611** COTGR. s.v. *Haultain, Faire le haultain*, to be high in th' instup,..take state vpon him. *a* **1635** SIBBES *Breathing after God* (1639) 28 It is the nature of excellent things, except we desire them in the chiefe place, they take state upon them. **1660** F. BROOKE tr. *Le Blanc's Trav.* 29 A Portuguais, who took state upon him, his man still carrying after him a guilt sword. **1767** *Woman of Fashion* II. 43 Now the pretty Fool takes State upon her, forsooth.

c. ***to hold one's state***, to appear in pomp and splendour. *arch.* or *Obs.*

1613 SHAKS. *Hen. VIII*, v. ii. 24 The high promotion of his Grace of Canterbury, Who holds his State at dore 'mongst Purseuants, Pages, and Foot-boyes. *a* **1806** H. K. WHITE *To Morning* v, The mists which on old Night await, Far to the west they hold their state. **1862** 'F. G. TRAFFORD' *City & Sub.* iv, The Earls of Oxford had once held state [there].

†**20. a.** A raised chair with a canopy, etc.; a throne; = *chair of state* in 17 b. (Cf. ESTATE *sb.* 4 d.) *Obs.*

1421 *Order of Guests* in *Q. Eliz. Acad.* 89 The kyng off Scottes yn A State. *c* **1435** *Torr. Portugal* 1729 In to a state they hym brought. **1596** SHAKS. *1 Hen. IV*, II. iv. 416 This Chayre shall bee my State. *a* **1700** EVELYN *Diary* 4 May 1645, The Pope, sitting on an elevated state or throne. **1712** ARBUTHNOT *John Bull* III. i. 7 As she affected not the Grandeur of a State with a Canopy, she thought there was no Offence in an Elbow-Chair.

†**b.** A canopy. *Obs.*

a **1626** BACON *New Atl.* 19 Over the Chair is a state made round or oval. **1648** HERRICK *Hesper., Parl. Roses*, Over the which a State was drawne Of Tiffanie, or Cob-web Lawne. **1656** HARRINGTON *Oceana* (1700) 121 At the upper end hangs a rich State overshadowing the greater part of a large Throne. **1667** MILTON *P.L.* x. 445. **1828** SCOTT *F.M. Perth* ix, The King had moved..to the cushioned chair, which, under a state or canopy, stood prepared for his accommodation.

III. A class, rank; a person of rank.

†**21.** A class, rank, order, sort or body *of* persons; a 'condition', profession, or occupation; the members of a class or profession collectively. Cf. ESTATE *sb.* 5 and F. *état*. *Obs.*

1340 *Ayenb.* 122 Alsuo ase ine heuene heþ þri stages of uolke... In þo manere..heþ he þri states of godes zone ine erþe. *c* **1380** WYCLIF *Wks.* (1880) 25 Generaly ypocrisie regneþ among alle statis of cristen men. *c* **1425** *Cast. Persev.* 3616 Lytyl & mekyl, þe more & þe les, all þe statis of þe werld is at myn renoun. *a* **1568** A. SCOTT *Poems* i. 170 Caus everye stait to þair vocatioun go. **1589** *Whip for Ape* A 2, This iesting Jacke..With his Asse heeles presumes all States to strike. **1596** *Shirburn Ballads* lx. 3 They comforted our ould men; they spared our feeble women; noe state they did abuse. **1625** BACON *Ess., Greatness Kingd.* (Arb.) 477 Neither is that State [*illa pars populi*]..to be passed ouer; I meane the State of Free Seruants and Attendants vpon Noblemen and Gentlemen.

†**22.** An order or class of persons regarded as part of the body politic and as participating in the government; an ESTATE of the realm. *Obs.*

c **1380** WYCLIF *Sel. Wks.* III. 184 Þer ben in þe Chirche þre statis þat God haþe ordeyned; state of prestis, and state of knyȝtis, and þe þridd is staat of comunys. **1390** GOWER *Conf.* III. 379 Ther ys no staat in his degree That noughte to desire pes. **1399** *Rolls of Parlt.* III. 451 Salvation and seurete of other States of the Reaume. *c* **1450** HOLLAND *Howlat* 283 So that the Spirituale staite, And the secular consait, Mycht all gang in a gait. **1553** Q. JANE in Strype *Eccl. Mem.* (1721) III. App. ii. 4 This our most lawful Possession of the Crown, with the free Consent of the Nobility of our Realm and other the States of the same. **1562** WINȜET *Wks.* I. 5 The maist part of vs of the Eclesiasticall Stait. **1625** BACON *Ess., Empire* (Arb.) 305 For their Prelates;..The danger is not from that State, but where it hath a dependance of forraine Authority. **1641** W. HAKEWILL *Libertie Subj.* 25 In full assembly of the three States. **1667–84** E. CHAMBERLAYNE *Pres. St. Eng.* I. 241 All the subjects of England are divided into Clergy and Laity, the Laity subdivided into Nobility and Commonalty. These are called *Ordines Regni*, or the Three States. **1689** *Acts Parlt. Scot.* (1875) XII. 71/1 The vote þen stated whither ane or more of every state should be sent with the offer of the Crown and carried for one of every state. **1700** SIR D. HUME *Diary Parl. Scot.* (Bannatyne Club) 3 Proceeded to chuse 9 of every State for the Committee of Security.

23. a. *pl.* (= F. *états*, Du. *staaten*, etc.) The 'estates of the realm' met to form a constitutional assembly; the princes, dukes, nobles, etc., together with the delegates or representatives of the several ranks, orders, chief cities, etc. of a country, assembled in a parliament or diet; e.g. in the United Netherlands (and the several provinces), France before the Revolution, Scotland before the Union, the Holy Roman Empire (and its several members), Hungary, Poland. Now only *Hist.*, exc. as the title of the legislatures of Jersey and Guernsey. See also ESTATE *sb.* 6 b and STATES GENERAL.

In 16–17th c. 'the States' often means: the men at the head of affairs in the United Netherlands; the Dutch government as a European power.

1399 *Rolls of Parlt.* III. 451/2 Byfore the Kyng and all the States in this present Parlement. **1560** DAUS tr. *Sleidane's Comm.* 109 Letters wrytten to the states of the Empyre. *Ibid.* 183 b, The .XXI. day of July the Princes and states [*principes ac ordines*] all go to themperoure. **1560** GRESHAM in Burgon *Life* (1839) I. 298 They say playne here, that the States of the lande [the Low Countries] will never consent to have war with Ingland. **1578** *Cecil Papers* (Hist. MSS. Comm.) II. 180 To remembre unto the States [*sc.* of the Netherlands] what aydes the Queen's Majesty hath alredy gyven them. **1587** *Acts Privy Counc.* (N.S.) XIV. 306 An agreement made between the Erle of Leycester and the Deputies of the States of the United Provinces. **1618** in *Falle's Jersey* (1694) 194 There shall be no Assembly of the States without the consent of the Governor. **1670** R. COKE *Disc. Trade* 2 Who are the Dutch States? They who govern Trade in the United Netherlands. *a* **1674** CLARENDON *Hist. Reb.* XII. §23 The States, especially those of Holland, let fall somewhat every day in their councils and consultations, that the King's residing in the Hague would be very inconvenient to them. **1682** WARBURTON *Hist. Guernsey* (1822) 77 The assembly of the States is composed of the bailiff and jurats, the ministers of each parish, and the constables, who represent the rest of the inhabitants of their parish. **1768** STERNE *Sent. Journ.* (1778) II. 55 (*The Sword*) When the states were assembled at Rennes. **1792** A. YOUNG *Trav. France* 105 To..appeal to the King to dissolve the states. **1804** M. LAING *Hist. Scot.* III. 437 *note*, Had the committee of states [in Scotland, 1650] known the extent of the conspiracy,..it is not probable that they would have so easily forgiven the Start. **1828** TYTLER *Hist. Scot.* I. 68 The States of Scotland undertook, before receiving their queen, to find security to the King of England, that the said lady should not marry without his counsel and consent. **1844** LD. BROUGHAM *Brit. Const.* iii. (1862) 54 The French States at no time attained the regularity of the English Parliament. **1845** SARAH AUSTIN *Ranke's Hist. Ref.* I. 133 The States of the empire gradually assembled in Lindau. **1862** ANSTED *Channel Isl.* IV. xxiii. 526 In Jersey, besides the Royal Court, there is only one Assembly. It is called the States... In Guernsey,..the States consist of two bodies, one called the Elective and the other the Deliberative States. **1915** F. M. HUEFFER *When Blood is Argt.* I. ii. 25 The Elector Frederick William III in 1701, in an assembly of the States, was accorded the title of King in Prussia.

†**b.** Delegates or members of the Dutch government as individuals. (Cf. 24, 25.) *Obs.*

1590 SIR R. WILLIAMS *Disc. Warre* 55 Although our masters the States be for the most part honest and vertuous personages. **1607** J. CHAMBERLAIN in *Crt. & Times Jas. I* (1848) I. 68 The States took their leave yesterday, and shall be presented with chains of five or six hundred crowns a-piece. **1618** SIR D. CARLETON *Lett.* (1775) 259 For his adjuncts..he will have four of the states, whereof two shall be of Holland,..one of Zealand, and one of Friesland. **1653** in *Nicholas Papers* (Camden) II. 8, I have spoken with several of the States here touching their expediting an Ambassador into Germany. **1705** DUNTON *Life & Errors* (1818) I. 149 When there is any Synod called, two of the States are always present, to watch them that they may not meddle with the Government; and if the Clergy do but drop a word that has any reference that way, the States immediately cry, 'Ho, la, Miin Heeren Predicanten!' **1708** SEWEL *Du.-Eng. Dict.*, *Staat*.., One of the States, a Representative of the Country. **1767** S. PATERSON *Another Trav.* I. 103 [Public canal-barge from Ostend to Bruges]. The cabin in the stern is always reserved for the states of the province and is therefore called the States-cabin.

†**24.** A person of standing, importance or high rank; a great man, personage, dignitary; a noble, lord, prince. (Cf. ESTATE *sb.* 3 c.) *Obs.*

c **1400** *Beryn* 404 The statis þat wer a-bove had of þe feyrest endreyte. *c* **1400** *Song of Roland* 22 With-in xvj days thedur he wille hym hye, and all the hethyn statis in his company. *a* **1450** *Cov. Myst.* 384 Owre worthy prynsis,..That are statis of this lond, hye men of degre. *c* **1490** CAXTON *Rule St. Benet* 126 Yf we shulde make ony suggestion to a state temporall, we wolde not presume to doo it but with mekenes & reuerence. **1509** BARCLAY *Shyp of Folys* (1570) 19 Some thinkes him selfe a gentleman or state Though he a knaue, caitiff, and bonde churle be. **1535** STEWART *Cron. Scot.* I. 69 The grittest stait that wes in all that stound, In his bodie buir mony deidlie wound. **1549** LATIMER *4th Serm. bef. Edw. VI* (Arb.) 126 Thys fayth is a great state, a Ladye, a Dutches. **1562** J. HEYWOOD *Prov. & Epigr.* (1867) 192 In sommer when states sit from fire in the coole. *c* **1620** MASSINGER *Unnat. Combat* III. i, Our great Admirall With other States, being invited ghests. **1667** MILTON *P.L.* II. 387 The bold design Pleas'd highly those infernal States.

†**25.** *pl.* The magnates, dignitaries or authorities of a town or district. *Obs.*

1421 *Coventry Leet Bk.* 35 To the reuerent and wurschipfull states that her byn, and to all wurthy men of this grett Lete. *c* **1440** *Gesta Rom.* i. 3 When þe Meyre and þe statys sawe þis doyng. *c* **1450** *Reg. Godstow Nunnery* 659 To all statis and to the baillifs of Gloucestre. **1517** in *10th Rep. Hist. MSS. Comm.* App. v. 397 After the election of the Maior a Michalmas daye..all the stattes and worship[f]ull shall ffolowe the Mayor to his doore. **1609** HOLLAND *Amm. Marcell.* XXVII. vi. 315 He had given commandement that the States [*marg.* or principall Burgesses *Ordines*, or Senators] of three townes should be massacred.

†**26.** *collect. sing.* **a.** The rulers, nobles, or great men of a realm; the government, ruling body, grand council, or court. *Obs.*

1581 A. HALL *Iliad* IV. 64, I know ere long Troy shal to wracke, & Priam with his state Shal passe the sword. **1597** SHAKS. *2 Hen. IV*, v. ii. 142 Our Coronation done, we will accite..all our State. **1604** —— *Oth.* I. ii. 96 The Duke himselfe, Or any of my Brothers of the State. **1606** —— *Tr. & Cr.* IV. ii. 69 *Troy.* Is it concluded so? *Æne.* By Priam, and the generall state of Troy. They are at hand, and ready to effect it. **1612** BACON *Ess., Judicature* (Arb.) 458 It is an happy thing in a State, when Kings and States doe often consult with Iudges; and againe, when Iudges doe often consult with the King and State. **1617** MORYSON *Itin.* II. 8 That Kingdome was..peaceable and quiet, (so as any the greatest Lord called by letter or messenger, readily came to the State there..). *Ibid.* 12 Sir Henrie Bagnoll, Marshall of Ireland, had formerly exhibited to the State diuers articles of treason practised by the Earle of Tyrone, who now would not come to the State without a protection.

†**b.** The governing body of a town; the city magnates collectively. (Cf. sense 25.) *Obs.*

1516 in *10th Rep. Hist. MSS. Comm.* App. v. 396 Every of the statte of this town, when they are warnid to come to the courte-housse, shall sit every man acording his degre and callinge. **1575** in W. H. Turner *Select. Rec. Oxford* (1880) 377 Dysobedyens wch they have commytted agaynst Mr. Mayor and the state of thys Cytie. **1582** *Burgh Rec.* in Campbell *Kirk & Par. Kirkcaldy* (1904) 63 Yat ye kirk dykes be putt up and sic as ye syt of ye steat and ye assemblie. *c* **1648–50** BRATHWAIT *Barnabees Jrnl.* III. (1818) 143 Thence to Kendall, pure her state is, Prudent too her magistrate is.

IV. 'Common weal'; commonwealth, polity.

†**27.** The condition of the Church, a country, realm, etc. in regard to its welfare and polity. Sometimes, a condition of prosperity, of order

and settled government. *Obs.* with any specific force.

So L. *status rei publicæ, status civitatis, status ecclesiæ.*
c **1290** *S. Eng. Leg.* 280/92, 93 He þou3te þat þe stat of holi churche swuyþe i-febled were And þat cristine-dom in Manie studes in ri3t guod stat it nere. **1297** R. GLOUC. (Rolls) 10080 þo þe king adde normandie in god stat ibrou3t al. *c* **1375** *Lay Folks Mass Bk.* 361 Lord, þenk on þo state of holy kirk. **1387** TREVISA *Higden* (Rolls) V. 199 þis Gracianus, whan he sigh þat þe staat of þe empere was almost afalle [L. *statum rei publicae paene collapsum*]. **1389** in *Eng. Gilds* (1870) 71 Yei shul haue ye preyurs for ye pees and ye state of holy chirche. *c* **1450** *Mirk's Festial* 11 And also 3e schull pray for þe state of all holy chyrch. *c* **1450** *Reg. Godstow Nunnery* 535 For the helth of the sowles of her lord Geffrey..and her, and for the state of the kyngdome of Englond. *c* **1460** *Oseney Reg.* 25 For þe state and welefare of all þe realme. **1549** *Bk. Com. Prayer, Commun.*, 127 b, Let us praie for the whole state of Christes churche. **1573** *Reg. Privy Council Scot.* II. 271 And sall do nor attempt na thing ..aganis the stait of the Christiane religioun publictlie precheit and establishit within this realme. **1587** R. CROMPTON *Short Decl. End Traytors* E ij, Yᵉ great benefits & profittes which growe by yᵉ same [*sc.* law and justice] to the Common wealth & state of euerie kingdome. **1593** SHAKS. *Rich. II*, IV. i. 225 These grieuous Crymes, Committed by your Person, and your followers, Against the State, and Profit of this Land. **1594** KYD *Cornelia* Argt., Caesar (after he had ordred the affayres of Egipt and the state of Rome). *a* **1600** HOOKER *Eccl. Pol.* VIII. vi. §8 As now the state of the Church doth stand. **1651** HOBBES *Leviathan* IV. xlv. 365 He [Romulus] would be propitious to the State of their new City.

†**28. a.** A particular form of polity or government. ***the state***, the form of government and constitution established in a country; e.g. ***the popular state***, democracy (cf. F. *état populaire*). ***state royal***: a monarchy. *Obs.*

1538 STARKEY *England* 56 Ther ys the veray and true commyn wele; ther ys the most prosperouse and perfayt state, that in any cuntrey, cyte, or towne, by pollycy and wysdom, may be stablyschyd and set. *Ibid.* 67 They..dow not only saue other wych be vnder the same gouernaunce and state, but also themselfe. **1551** ROBINSON tr. *More's Utopia* (1895) 13 (*title*) A fruteful and pleasaunt worke of the beste state of a publyque weale. **1555** RIDLEY *Err. Transubst.* (1556) 55 Yt beganne to subuerte Christes gospell, and to turne the state that Christ and his Apostles sett in the church, vpside down. **1630** LENNARD tr. *Charron's Wisd.* I. xviii. (1670) 66 We may compare man to a Commonweal, and the state of the soul to a state-royal. *a* **1680** BUTLER *Char., Republican* (1908) 24 And therefore 'tis probable, the State of Venice would be no more the same in any other Country, if introduced, than their Trade of Glassmaking. **1701** SWIFT *Contests Nobles & Commons* ii. Misc. (1711) 19 Theseus is the first who is Recorded..to have establish'd the Popular State in Athens.

†**b.** A republic, non-monarchical commonwealth. *Obs.*

1656 WALLER *To Evelyn* 2 Lucretius, with a stork-like fate, Born and translated in a State, Comes to proclaim in English verse No Monarch rules the universe. **1651** HOBBES *Leviathan* IV. xlv. 365 When Augustus Cæsar changed the State into a Monarchy. **1673** DRYDEN *Amboyna* Prol. 22 Well, Monarchys may own Religions name, But States are Atheists in their very frame.

†**c.** *transf.* Applied to a University. *Obs.*

c **1590** GREENE *Fr. Bacon* I. ii. 177 Now Maisters of our Academicke State, That rule in Oxford Vizroies in your place.

29. a. ***the state***: the body politic as organized for supreme civil rule and government; the political organization which is the basis of civil government (either generally and abstractly, or in a particular country); hence, the supreme civil power and government vested in a country or nation.

1538 STARKEY *England* 48 The kyng, prynce, and rular of the state... The gouernance of the commynalty and polytyke state... He or they wych haue authoryte apon the hole state. *Ibid.* 53 Whether the state of the commynalty be gouernyd by a prynce, by certayn wyse men, or by the hole multytude. **1590** in *Cath. Rec. Soc. Publ.* V. 179 For the better understanding of the trewthe of matters agenst her Maiestie and the Stayte. **1594** [see PILLAR *sb.* 3 b]. **1617** MORYSON *Itin.* II. 17 Which may concerne the good of the State. *a* **1618** RALEIGH *Rem.* (1644) 2 State is the frame or set order of a Common-wealth, or of the Governours that rule the same, especially of the chief and Sovereign Governour that commandeth the rest. The State or Soveraignty consisteth in five points. 1. Making or annulling of Laws. **1622** BACON *Hen. VII* 8 As one that hauing beene somtimes an Enimie to the whole State, and a Proscribed person. **1681** DRYDEN *Abs. & Achit.* I. 174 Resolv'd to Ruine or to Rule the State. **1697** —— *Virg. Georg.* IV. 229 All is the State's, the State provides for all. **1834** ARNOLD in Stanley *Life* (1844) I. vii. 376 The State, being the only power sovereign over human life, has for its legitimate object the happiness of its people. **1879** M. ARNOLD *Democracy* Mixed Ess. 42 The State is properly..the nation in its collective and corporate capacity. **1884** SPENCER (*title*) The Man *versus* the State. **1891** C. LOWE in *19th Cent.* Dec. 858 The railways..in Prussia are now all in the hands of the State.

fig. **1598** SHAKS. *Merry W.* V. v. 245 In Loue, the heauens themselues do guide the state.

b. distinguished from 'the church' or ecclesiastical organization and authority. In the phr. ***church and state*** the article is dropped.

1589 *Whip for Ape* A 3 b, That is, destroy both Church, and State, and all. **1650** in *Sir J. Balfour's Ann.* (1825) IV. 146 At last, quhen nather kirke nor staite did giue ther concurrence therin, he deserted the counsailles of the kingdome. *a* **1674** CLARENDON *Hist. Reb.* XII. §27 To preserve and maintain the government of Church and State in that kingdom as it is established by the laws thereof. **1761** GRAY *Sketch* 6 He..left Church and State to Charles Townshend and Squire. **1844** LINGARD *Anglo-Sax. Ch.* (1858) I. ii. 91 In addition to the rank and rights which the bishop held in the church, he also derived..important privileges from the state. **1864** TENNYSON *North. Farmer, Old Style* iv, I hallus voäted wi' Squoire an' choorch an' staäte.

30. a. A body of people occupying a defined territory and organized under a sovereign government. Hence *occas.* the territory occupied by such a body.

1568 GRAFTON *Chron.* II. 760 Such a pestilent Serpent is ambition,..which among states where he once entereth, creepeth so farre forth, till with diuision and variaunce he turneth all to mischiefe. **1587** R. CROMPTON *Short Decl. End Traytors* E ij, For there is no Common wealth, state, or societie of man kind, that can continue, where there is not superiority or preheminence in gouernment. **1625** BACON *Ess., Greatness Kingd.* (Arb.) 481 Never any State was..so open to receive Strangers, into their Body, as were the Romans. **1673** TEMPLE *Observ. United Prov.* ii. 75 Each of these Provinces is likewise composed of many little States or Cities, which have several marks of Soveraign Power within themselves, and are not subject to the Soveraignty of their Province. **1705** ADDISON *Italy* Pref., Lassels may be useful in giving us the Names of such Writers as haue treated of the seueral States through which he pass'd. **1769** ROBERTSON *Chas. V*, v. iii. Wks. 1851 III. 523 The Italian states were no less desirous of peace than the pope. **1781** SIR W. JONES *Ode in Imit. Alcæus* 1 What constitutes a State? **1841** W. SPALDING *Italy* III. 351 The state of Parma, formed of the three duchies of Parma, Piacenza, and Guastalla, is divided into five provinces. **1844** H. H. WILSON *Brit. India* II. 458 Those compacts which had been formed by the English,..with the independent native States. **1880** *Encycl. Brit.* XIII. 190/2 The theory of international law contemplates the world as divided into independent states... States are sovereign within their own territories, independent of other states, and equal as between themselves.

¶**b.** Used (from similarity of sound) to render G. *stadt*, city.

1800 COLERIDGE *Death Wallenstein* III. vii. 69 Say, shall we have the State illuminated In honour of the Swede?

31. a. The territory, or one of the territories, ruled by a particular sovereign. ***hereditary states***: spec. (= G. *Erbstaaten*) the kingdoms or principalities held hereditarily by any head of the Holy Roman Empire.

1602 CHETTLE *Hoffman* IV. (1631) H 4, Since neyther Ferdinand, nor Saxony, Haue any heires, to sway their seuerall states; Ile work what lies in me to make thee Duke. **1845** SARAH AUSTIN *Ranke's Hist. Ref.* I. 89 The emperor was driven out of his hereditary states, and wandered about the other parts of the empire as a fugitive.

b. *pl.* (*Hist.*) Applied (? after It. *stati*) to the cities and territories included in an Italian principality or republic, esp. the grand-duchy of Tuscany and the republic of Venice. Also in ***States of the Church, Papal States*** (also *sing.*), titles of the former temporal dominions in Italy of the Holy See.

1797 *Encycl. Brit.* (ed. 3) XV. 381/1 *Pope's Dominions*, or *Ecclesiastical States*, a country of Italy, bounded on the north by the gulph of Venice [etc.]. **1828** [H. BEST] *Italy as it is* 357 Less persecution has taken place in the States of the Church than in any other state. **1831** J. CONDER *Italy* I. 19 *note*, The states of Parma consist of the dutchy of that name and the territories of Placentia and Guastalla. **1840** *Penny Cycl.* XVII. 195 *Papal State, Stato Pontificio*, called also *stato della Chiesa*. **1851** MRS. BROWNING *Casa Guidi Wind.* I. 1062 Which..our Florence in her prime Turned boldly on all comers to her states. **1857** J. BRIGHT in G. M. Trevelyan *Life* (1913) 257, I would rather spend three months in the United States of America than in the States of the Church.

c. One of a number of polities, each more or less sovereign and independent in regard to internal affairs, which together make up a supreme federal government; as in the United States of America or the Commonwealth of Australia.

1634 *Mass. Bay Rec.* (1853) I. 117 When I shalbe called to give my voice touching any such matter of this state, wherein ffreemen are to deale, [etc.]. **1774** JEFFERSON *Writ.* (1892) I. 420 A proper device (instead of arms) for the American states united would be the Father presenting the bundle of rods to his son. **1776** ABIGAIL ADAMS in *Fam. Lett.* (1876) 204 Thus ends royal authority in this State [Massachusetts]. **1777** A. HAMILTON *Wks.* (1886) VII. 487 A treaty..between the Court of France and the States of America. **1816** WHEATON *Cases Supreme Crt. U.S.* I. 91 A citizen of a territory cannot sue a citizen of a state, in the courts of the United States. **1851** DIXON *W. Penn.* xxi. (1872) 183 This colony was the beginning of a state. **1901** *Empire Rev.* I. 443 The governors of Australian colonies, or states as they are now called.

d. *the States*: the United States of America.

1777 J. ADAMS in *Fam. Lett.* (1876) 301 The enemy are in possession of the Head of Elk,..in which they found a quantity of corn and oats belonging to the States. **1856** MRS. BROWNING *Aur. Leigh* v, Delia Dobbs, the lecturer from 'the States' Upon the 'Woman's Question'. **1890** A. LANG *Sir Stafford Northcote* II. 25 He thus found himself a prophet in the States, if not in his own country.

32. (Without article.) All that concerns the government or ruling power of a country; the sphere of supreme political power and administration. The adjectival phr. *of state* (= F. *d'état*, It. *di stato*) is otherwise expressed by the attributive use (see 38). †***in state***, in the sphere of government or politics.

reason of state: see REASON *sb.*¹ 5 b. ***Secretary of State*** (Gt. Britain and U.S.): see SECRETARY *sb.*¹ 3. ***Department of State*** (U.S.): see DEPARTMENT 3 b; formerly † ***Office of State***.

1582 ALLEN *Martyrdom Campion* (1908) 9 To alter the question from controversie in religion to the cause of the Prince and matter of state. **1591** HARINGTON *Orlando* Apol. Poetrie ¶ vj, How much good matter, yea and matter of state, is there in that Comedie cald the play of the Cards? **1600** E. BLOUNT tr. *Conestaggio* 6 According vnto reason of State. **1601** SHAKS. *Twel. N.* II. v. 164 Let thy tongue tang arguments of state. **1612** BACON *Ess., Reg. Health* (Arb.) 59 It is a secret both in nature and state, that it is safer to change many things then one. **1625** N. CARPENTER *Geogr. Delin.* II. xiv. (1635) 243, I speake here onely of matters of state and policy. **1651** HOBBES *Leviathan* IV. xlv. 365 The Supreme Power both in State, and Religion. **1673** TEMPLE *Observ. United Prov.* ii. 101 The Council of State is composed of Deputies from the several Provinces. **1694** (*title*) Letters of State, written by Mr. John Milton to most of the Sovereign Princes and Republicks of Europe. **1708** SWIFT *Sentim. Ch. Eng. Man* Wks. 1755 II. I. 72, I believe it may pass for a maxim in state, that the administration cannot be placed in too few hands, nor the legislature in too many. **1795** BURKE *Regic. Peace* iv. Sel. Wks. III. 344 The Ministers of State and the Judges of the Bench. *Ibid.* 345 They were made an affair of state. **1796** WASHINGTON *Lett. Writ.* (1892) XIII. 213 From the office of State you will receive every thing that relates to business. **1845** DISRAELI *Sybil* v. viii, She was on her way to Bow Street to be examined as a prisoner of state. **1878** BEACONSFIELD in *Times* 11 Nov. 10/4 My Lord Mayor, I have observed that the month of October is often rife with high secrets of State.

33. a. Short for *state-letter* (see 41). ? *Obs.*

a **1879** SIR R. HILL *Life* (1880) II. 107 Sorting out the letters for Government and foreign ambassadors resident in London, letters technically called 'States'.

b. Short for *State Department* (sense 41 a below). *U.S.*

1955 W. TUCKER *Wild Talent* xi. 151 Somebody down at State had to soothe his ruffled feelings. **1971** R. LUDLUM *Scarlatti Inheritance* I. ii. 18 It took an executive order from the President to get it out of State. **1979** H. KISSINGER *White House Years* ii. 29 The new President wanted to change the negotiating instructions on Vietnam drafted at State that reflected the approach of the previous Administration.

c. Preceded by the name of a State: short for *state university* (sense 38 e below).

1928 *Time* 29 Oct. 28/3 Penn mauled Penn State, 14-0. **1975** J. WYLLIE *Butterfly Flood* (1977) xxiv. 177, I can outswim you any time at all. I used to swim for Penn State. **1980** 'R. B. DOMINIC' *Attending Physician* ii. 11 Two students in Ohio State sweatshirts.

V. Interest in property; possessions.

†**34.** *Law.* **a.** The interest which any one has in a property; right or title to property; = ESTATE 11.

1439 *E.E. Wills* (1882) 115, I..bequeth..to þe saide Iohn my wyfe, the termys and state comyng of & in all the tenement. *c* **1450** *Reg. Godstow Nunnery* 613 Aliz wynnynge ..surrendred to þe Abbas & couent of Godestowe all þe state, þat she had of the same Abbas & couent. **1502** *Will of J. Hutton* (Somerset Ho.) Lond..in the which I haue a state. **1523** FITZHERB. *Surv.* 15 b, Where they haue no state of inherytaunce. **1596** SPENSER *F.Q.* v. xi. 3 He..bad Deliuer him his owne,..To which they had no right, nor any wrongfull state. **1621** BURTON *Anat. Mel.* III. ii. v. v. (1624) 455 State of liues in coppy holds. **1660** R. COKE *Power & Subj.* 25 *Do* or *Dedi*, to A. and the heires of his body lawfully begotten,..creates a state taile.

fig. **1616** B. JONSON *Epigr.* lxx, He makes a state In life, that can employ it.

†**b. *to make a state* (*of* property) *to*** (a person): to give a legal right or title to. Also (without *of*): to make a (specified or understood) gift, grant or settlement. (Cf. ESTATE *sb.* 11 b.)

1445 *Test. Ebor.* (Surtees) II. 155, I require my seid feffes ..that they make a state of the Maner of Kirklyngton vnto Elizabeth Chaworth. *c* **1445** in *Oxf. Stud. Soc. & Legal Hist.* (1914) IV. 194 Without any state maide to the saide personez so named Feffes of the saide landez and tenementz. **1455** *Rolls of Parlt.* V. 306/1 Eny Advousons or Patronages in which eny persone or persones..have enfeoffed us, or yerof made eny Graunte or state unto us. **1521** *Test. Ebor.* (Surtees) VI. 5 That my said feoffes make a state to the saide William Vescy of all my landes in Cateby. **1541** *Ibid.* 135, I will that my heres make alway a newe state at the ende of xxj yeres agayne to ane honeste preste to singe [etc.]. **1559** *Boke Presidentes* 53 b, There is no maner of states made of free lande by pol deede, or dede indented, but ther may be made the same of copy landes by copy. **1606** CHAPMAN *Gentl. Usher* III. ii. 40 What state hath your lord made you for your service?

†**35.** *Law.* **a.** Possession (of property); as ***to give, deliver, receive state and seisin.*** Chiefly *Sc. Obs.*

1338 R. BRUNNE *Chron.* (1725) 83 Kyng Steuen..þat withouten reson Of þis land had þe state, & conquered þe coroun. **1461** *Paston Lett.* II. 37 That whan I com homwar I mygh..mak seson and stat to be take whil I wer ther. **1501** *Reg. Privy Seal Scot.* I. 107/2 Quhill the lauchful are or aeris ..recover lachfull state, sessing and possessioun. **1520** *Perth Hammermen Bk.* (1889) 13 Item till Constantine Arthur for the staits giffin of the annuels and for his travell to Sanct Androis at the command of the Craft. **1524** Q. MARGARET in *St. Papers Hen. VIII*, IV. 112 To schawe His Grace how and in quhat maner We haf downe in this Parliament, and yat ye Kyng my sone is put to his stayt and governans be all his Lordis and Barrowns wyth his Prelattis and Commouns. **1606** *Reg. Mag. Sig. Scot.* 662/2, I will and chairgis yow.. ye delyver staitt and seasing [etc.]. **1710** in *Nairne Peerage Evid.* (1874) 45 And there give and deliver heritable state and sasine actuall reall and corporall possession of the foresaid. **1765–8** ERSKINE *Inst. Law Scot.* II. iii. §35 Lastly, The vassal..takes instruments in the hand of the notary, before witnesses, that he hath received state and seisin of the lands in due form.

†**b. *to put in state***: to put (a person) in possession (of). ***to be in state***, to be seised (of).

1474 *Acc. Ld. High Treas. Scot.* I. 4 To put his sone and ayre in state of his landis. **1531** *Abstr. Protocols Town Clerks*

Glasgow (1897) IV. 28 George Elquhistoune, beand in stait of the said land.

†**c.** ***in state***: held in (a person's) ownership or possession. *Obs.*

1592 *Arden of Feversham* I. 467 The lands are his in state. *Ibid.* 484 So as he shall wishe the Abby lands Had rested still within their former state.

†**36.** Property, possessions; one's private means; = ESTATE *sb.* 12. *Obs.*

13.. *Sir Beues* 3483 Now haþ Beues al is stat. *c* **1430** LYDG. *Min. Poems* 212 Ne were the plough no staat myght endure, The large feeldys shulde be bareyn. **1500–20** DUNBAR *Poems* lxvi. 37 The temporall stait to gryp and gather, The sone disheris wald the father. **1598** SHAKS. *Merry W.* III. iv. 5 My state being gall'd with my expence. **1612** BACON *Ess.*, *Riches* (Arb.) 240 A great state left to an heire, is as a lure to al the birds of prey round about, to seise on him. **1634** W. WOOD *New Eng. Prosp.* (1865) 61 There are some noble spirits that devote their states, and their persons, to the common good of their king and country. **1694** WOOD *Life* (O.H.S.) III. 448 He kept his coach and horses, and had no visible state. **1790** MRS. WHEELER *Westmld. Dial.* 75 Yee kna heeas a Staat, an nae daut will be for a girt Portion. **1899** *Cumberld. Gloss.*, '*State*, the land or property of a *statesman*.

VI. A statement. (? Partly from STATE *v.*)

†**37. a.** A statement, account, description, report (*of* a transaction, events, a legal case, etc.). *Obs.* in general use (partly superseded by STATEMENT).

c **1611** CHAPMAN *Iliad* XV. 33 This frighted the offending Queene, who, with this state, excusde Her kind vnkindnesse. *c* **1643** in *13th Rep. Hist. MSS. Comm.* App. IV. 281 [Notes on the] State of the Tynfarmers' Case. **1647** CLARENDON *Hist. Reb.* II. §123 The next error to this was, that at the meeting of the Great Council at York.. there was not a state made, and information given, of the whole proceedings in Scotland. **1657** in *Burton's Diary* (1828) II. 62 You have had a fair state of the case by this honourable person. **1751** H. WALPOLE *Mem. Geo. II* (1822) I. 55 Sir Henry Erskine then presented his charge against General Anstruther, which he called only a state of his own case. **1772** *Ann. Reg.* *76 He wrote a long state of the whole transaction.. to the court of Petersburg. **1791** BOSWELL *Johnson* (1816) III. 425 His state of the evidence as to the ghost did not satisfy me. **1802** MARIA EDGEWORTH *Moral T.*, *Forester* xii, Convinced of the woman's innocence, he had drawn up a state of her case. **1805** (*title*) *State, Leslie of Powis*, &c. **1814** SCOTT *Wav.* li, Waverley therefore wrote a short state of what had happened, to his uncle and father.

†**b.** A detailed enumeration or report of particulars or items; esp. a statement of items of cost or outlay, of actual or estimated expenses. (Cf. STATE *v.* 7 d.) *Obs.*

1671 R. MONTAGU in *Buccleuch MSS.* (Hist. MSS. Comm.) I. 505 The King command[ed] Mr. de Louvoy to make a state of the expense of the war. **1673** TEMPLE *Observ. United Prov.* ii. 102 Towards the end of every year, this Council forms a state of the Expence they conceive will be necessary for the year ensuing. **1691** T. H[ALE] *Acc. New Invent.* 28 A more strict and Annual State to be had of all their respective Hulls, Masts, and Yards. **1701** EVELYN *Diary* 27 Jan., I laid before the Speaker the state of what had ben receiv'd and paid towards the building of Greenwich Hospital. **1727** [W. PULTENEY] (*title*) A state of the national debt as it stood Dec. 24, 1716. **1785** BURKE *Sp. Nabob of Arcot's Debts* Wks. 1842 I. 342 Possibly at the time of the chairman's state they might have been as high. **1786** JEFFERSON *Writ.* (1859) II. 61 They.. have asked me to procure a state of the advantages of that place. **1788** GIBBON *Decl. & F.* lx. VI. 173 *note*, We are indebted to him [Ramusio] for a correct state of the [Venetian] fleet. **1805** FORSYTH *Beauties Scot.* III. 281 That the commerce has.. been gradually increasing here [Glasgow], will appear from the following states. **1818** SCOTT *Rob Roy* xxiv, He.. sate down to examine Mr. Owen's states, which the other thought it most prudent to communicate to him without reserve.

c. *Mil.* A report of the numbers of a corps, regiment, etc. in the field, with details of casualties.

1802 C. JAMES *Milit. Dict.* s.v., A weekly state of a regiment,.. The difference between the state of a corps or detachment, and a mere return of the same, consists in this, that the former comprehends the specific casualties, &c. that have occurred. **1813** WELLINGTON in Gurwood *Desp.* (1838) X. 569 If your Lordship will do me the favor.. to look over the morning states which I send every week to the Secretary of State. **1854** BENNETT in *Kinglake's Crimea* (1877) VI. App. 499 The.. officer whose duty it was to make out the duty 'States'. **1863** KINGLAKE *Crimea* II. 237 *note*, The 'morning state'.. gives as present under arms (without including the cavalry, of which there was no 'state') a total of 26,004 officers and men. **1889** *Infantry Drill* 451 The commander-in-chief.. will himself deliver a state of the troops to that Royal Personage. **1915** *Times* 5 Apr. 4/2 The parade state showed that 61 officers and 975 rank and file took part in the march.

†**d.** ***state of a vote***: the framing or putting a question in the form in which it is to be voted upon. (Cf. STATE *v.* 7 e.) *Sc. Obs.*

1701 SIR D. HUME *Diary Parl. Scot.* (Bannatyne Club) 44 After a long debate about these two states, moved it might be put to the vote, Which of these two should be the vote. **1703** *Ibid.* 101 Then Salton proposed the state of a vote, Whether to give the Act for the Cess a first reading, or to proceed to make Acts for the Security of our Religion, Liberties, and some added, Trade. **1758** SMOLLETT *Hist. Eng.* (1759) IX. 315.

VII. *attrib.* and *Comb.*

38. Attributive uses of senses 29–32. **a.** in sense: Of or belonging to the State, body politic, or civil government; made by, issuing from the State; employed by, in the service of, the State; recognized, supported or enforced by the State. Often equivalent to 'of state' (sense 32).

1491 *Cartular. S. Nich. Aberdon.* (New Spalding Club) I. 255 Gife yai be.. occupiet in Stet erandis. **1605** SHAKS. *Oth.* I. iii. 190 Pleese it your Grace, on to the State Affaires. **1612** SELDEN *Illustr. Drayton's Poly-olb.* xvi. 253 Such as were receiued into State-fauour and friendship by the Roman. **1634** FORD *Perk. Warbeck* II. ii, A State-Informers Character. **1667** MILTON *P.L.* I. 775 They.. expatiate and confer Thir State affairs. **1690** SIR W. TEMPLE *Misc.* II. *Ess. Poetry* 58 So many Pretenders to Business and State-Imployments. **1700** EVELYN *Diary* 24 Apr., This weeke there was a greate change of State Officers. **1755** JOHNSON, s.v. *Pension*, In England it is generally understood to mean pay given to a state hireling for treason to his country. **1775** *Lond. Chron.* 23–25 May 495/1 In the last State Lottery there were only 81 prizes above 100l. **1828** [H. BEST] *Italy as it is* 427 The supporters of state religions are shrewdly suspected, too, of holding that one religion is as good as another. **1836** THIRLWALL *Greece* xxv. III. 390 On his return to Catana he found there the state-galley, the Salaminia. **1859** MILL *Liberty* 190 The objections which are urged with reason against State education. **1860** PUSEY *Min. Proph.* 34 Jeroboam made a state-worship at Bethel. **1881** E. W. HAMILTON *Diary* 5 June (1972) I. 144 It is certainly a great misfortune that the three foremost men on the front Opposition bench should be dependent on State aid. **1885** State school [see REAL *a.*[2] 10]. **1886** *Encycl. Brit.* XX. 241/1 The State Railways of India. **1892** *Bk. Comm. Prayer* 1662, Publ. Pref. 8 The titles of.. the three State Services [*sc.* those for 5 Nov., 30 Jan., 29 May]. **1905** *Act 5 Edw. VII*, c. 19 (*title*) The construction.. of Railways in India, by State Agency, or through the Agency of Companies. **1917** A. S. NEILL *Dominie Dismissed* ii. 27 Our rulers.. send the rest of the sons of the community to State schools where they are trained to be disciplined and content with their lot. **1937** *Discovery* Oct. 305/2 State aid.. might ultimately be the only hope of British agriculture. **1943** KOESTLER *Arrival & Departure* IV. 165 State-bureaucracies and managers establish themselves in vital hedgehog positions. **1944** WYNDHAM LEWIS *Let.* 20 Aug. (1963) 378 But Stalin has a working state-system, with the air purged of humbug. **1948** J. TOWSTER *Political Theory in U.S.S.R.* iii. 42 The Party.. was not yet equipped to substitute collective-farm and state-farm production for kulak production. **1972** *Listener* 23 Nov. 690/2 With the inevitable rise in food prices.. the Government.. [should] introduce state subsidies to stabilise prices. *a* **1974** R. CROSSMAN *Diaries* (1975) I. 351 If he stays in the state system—in the village school and then in Banbury. **1977** B. FREEMANTLE *Charlie Muffin* iv. 43 Had she been born in a council house.. and attended a state school.. Janet would have been a slag.

b. In a wider or generalized sense: Relating to politics or the art of government; concerned with or depending on political considerations.

Very common in the 17th c.; sometimes with unfavourable implication, e.g. of crafty or tortuous or time-serving policy.

c **1610** BEAUM. & FL. *Philaster* I. i, My ignorance in state policy. **1623** DONNE *Serm.* xviii. (1640) 177 State Divinity, that obeyes affections of persons. **1637–50** ROW *Hist. Kirk* (Wodrow Soc.) 399 It seemeth to be als well aganis State-wisdome as it is evidentlie aganis religion. **1649** MILTON *Eikon.* xv. 141 Had he as well known how to distinguish between.. the wholsome heat of well Governing, and the feverous rage of Tyrannizing, his judgment in State-physic, had bin of more autoritie. **1655** FULLER *Ch. Hist.* IX. 181 The State Historian. **1661** R. DAVENPORT *City Nightcap* III. 29 My Lord would have made an excellent state-sophister. **1678** CUDWORTH *Intell. Syst.* I. v. 692 That Religion is nothing but a meer State-juggle and political imposture. **1680** BUTLER *Rem.* (1759) II. 59 A State-Quack, that.. vapours what Cures he could do on the Body politic. *c* **1681** DUKE *Review* 83 That new state-maxim he invented first. *a* **1700** EVELYN *Diary* 2 Oct. 1685, Upon some politic and state reasons. **1709** STEELE *Tatler* No. 11 ¶3 Mr. D...y generally writes State-Plays. **1711** ADDISON *Spect.* No. 105 ¶6 The State-Pedant is wrapt up in News, and lost in Politicks. **1742** YOUNG *Nt. Th.* VIII. 344 How curious to contemplate two state-rooks, Studious their nests to feather in a trice. **1755** *Dict. Arts & Sci.* s.v. *Sibyls*, it is the opinion of Prideaux, that the story of the three books of the sibyls, sold to Tarquin, was a state-trick or fetch of politics. **1757** *Monitor* No. 79. II. 265 The languid commonwealth.. which has been almost brought to its last gasp, under the cruel hands of our late state-quacks. **1809–10** COLERIDGE *Friend* (1865) 131 The venerable state-moralist. **1827** HARE *Guesses* Ser. I. (1873) 198 Our statequacks of late years haue thought fit to style themselues Radical Reformers. **1832** J. A. HERAUD *Voy. & Mem. Midshipman* iii. (1837) 52 No doubt a state-necessity, or a state-expediency, might be made out, for the purpose of producing an apparent uniformity in religious worship. **1909** *Hibbert Jrnl.* Jan. 434 The statecraft and state-morality of China and Japan.

†**c.** with reference to affected solemnity of countenance, as of one ostensibly burdened by secrets of state. *Obs.*

1611 B. JONSON *Challenge at Tilt* Wks. (1616) 998 There shall not the greatest pretender, to a state-face, liuing, put on a more supercilious looke then I will doe vpon you. **1639** GLAPTHORNE *Wallenstein* II. ii, You must not then accost her .. in the Spanish garbe, with a state face. **1728** SWIFT *Dial. Mad Mullinix & Timothy* 50 Thy screw'd-up front, thy state-grimace.

d. with reference to offences against the State and their punishment; as ***state-crime***, ***-criminal***, ***-offence***, ***-offender***, ***-prisoner***, ***-trial***.

1642 FULLER *Holy & Prof. St.* v. ix. 391 This State-sinne Jehu must commit to maintain his kingdome. **1682** DRYDEN *Duke of Guise* v. i, Where no ambition, nor state-crime, the happier spirits prove. **1692** SIR B. SHOWER *Reasons New Bill Rights* 6 What Harm can accrue to the Publick.. that in Case of State Treason Councel should be allowed to the Accused. **1726** SWIFT *Gulliver* I. vii, Having in my life perused many state-trials, which I ever observed to terminate as the judges thought fit to direct. **1766** SMOLLETT *Trav.* II. 227 The isles Marguerites, where state-prisoners are confined. **1798** HELEN M. WILLIAMS *Tour Switz.* I. 122 A castle, which is the northern bastile of the canton of Berne for state-offenders. **1837** CARLYLE *Fr. Rev.* III. I. vi, As for the Orléans Prisoners, they are State Criminals. **1839** LYTTON *Richelieu* II. i. 70 Who ever Heard of its being a state-offence to kiss The hand of one's own wife. **1886** C. E. PASCOE *Lond. To-day* xxvii. (ed. 3) 255 The little Chapel.. was long used by the state prisoners in the Tower. **1893** BADDELEY *Joanna I of Naples* 4 His just indignation at this state-crime.

e. *U.S.* Of or belonging to a State of the Union.

For numerous other *attrib.* uses see *D.A.E.* and *D.A.*

1780 ABIGAIL ADAMS in *Fam. Lett.* (1876) 388 Our State affairs are thus. **1784** *Acts & Laws Connecticut* 219 The Law relating to the gathering and collecting the State Rates. **1790** M. CUTLER in *Life, Jrnls. & Corr.* (1888) I. 460 Congress are still on the question, whether the State debts shall be assumed. **1831** J. M. PECK *Guide for Emigrants* 256 One sixth part is to be.. bestowed on a state college or university. *a* **1857** *Michigan Gen. Statutes* (1882) I. 171 The board of state auditors are hereby authorized.. to procure plans, drawings and estimates for a state capitol. **1885** State park [see *land-jobbing* s.v. LAND *sb.*[1] 12]. **1888** BRYCE *Amer. Commw.* II. xliv. 153 As the frame of a State government generally resembles the National government, so a State legislature resembles Congress. **1925** L. S. DUNAWAY *What Preacher Saw* 81 Jeff Davis declared that the ground on which the new state capitol was constructed was 'too poor for two Irishmen to raise a row on!' **1941** *N.Y. Times Mag.* 26 Jan. 19/3 Police work forms only part of the State trooper's duties. **1952** *Mind* LXI. 471 Suppose we then see him in earnest conversation with a scout from the state university. **1964** M. BANTON *Policeman in Community* iv. 94 Many of the State police forces again are very different. The men wear big hats like the Canadian mounties and concentrate upon highway patrol. **1969** C. BURKE *God is Beautiful, Man* (1970) 30 They took a trip to a place that looked like a state park. **1976** *National Observer* (U.S.) 1 May B5/4 The bulk of the newly admitted enjoyed a style of training, in junior and state colleges, little superior to that of the high school. **1976** A. PRICE *War Game* I. ix. 173 He's a New Englander... He left his state university nine years ago.

39. (Attributive use of sense 17.) Belonging to, employed on, reserved for, occasions of state or ceremony; accompanied with pomp and ceremony; richly or splendidly decorated, furnished, etc. (Equivalent to 'of state': see 17 b). Also STATE-ROOM.

1549 LATIMER *4th Serm. bef. Edw. VI* (Arb.) 126 As Chryste when he counterfayted a state goyng to Hierusalem. **1591** SYLVESTER *Du Bartas* I. vi. 472 Under starry State-Clothes. **1609** MARKHAM *Famous Wh.* (1868) 22 State-chambers richly deckt and furnished. **1615** CHAPMAN *Odyss.* IV. 171 She tooke her State-chaire. **1664–5** PEPYS *Diary* 21 Mar., A couple of state cups, very large, coming, I suppose, each to about £6 a piece. **1704** *Acc. Innov. Abp. Dublin* 17 The Governments Chaplains always Preach'd upon State-days. **1761** *Brit. Mag.* II. 602 Their Majesties last, in the old state-coach. **1812** H. & J. SMITH *Rej. Addr.*, *Macbeth Trav.* (1852) 173 King Duncan, in grand majesty, Has got my state-bed for a snooze. **1835** DICKENS *Sk. Boz*, *Mr. Watkins Tottle* ii, Referring to the gold watch, which was wound up on state occasions, whether it required it or not. **1843** FAIRHOLT *Ld. Mayors' Pageants* 152 These courts were held in the state barge. **1846** DICKENS *Pict. Italy* 74 A public promenade, where.. the Genoese nobility ride round, and round, and round, in state-clothes and coaches. **1846** MRS. GORE *Engl. Char.* (1852) 111 A state-coachman is one of the most prominent embodyings of national character in the metropolis. **1855** TIMBS *Curios. Lond.* 686 The State Carriage now used by the sovereign. **1858** SIMMONDS *Dict. Trade*, *State-bed*, an elaborately carved or decorated bed. **1883** MRS. ARMYTAGE *Old Court Customs* 178 Court or state balls are given during the season. **1915** *Times* 26 Mar. 11/4 Lord Wimborne has fixed April 14 for his State entry into Dublin.

40. Objective and instrumental uses of sense 29.

a. objective.

1598 T. ROGERS *Celest. Elegies* D 2 in *Lamport Garl.* (Roxb.), To royall princes and State-ruling peeres. **1600** W. WATSON *Decacordon* (1602) 152 Knowing themselues most innocent of all state-medlings. **1601** *2nd Pt. Return fr. Parnass.* III. i, Such busie state-prying fellowes. **1627** MAY *Lucan* I. B 1, State-changing comets dire. **1629** H. BURTON *Babel no Bethel* Ded. 5 Imposters, state-treachers, troublers, and betrayers. **1657** FLATMAN *Cordial* 11, I care not what your state confounders do. **1735** THOMSON *Liberty* III. 468 All the state wielding magick of his tongue. **1768–74** TUCKER *Lt. Nat.* (1834) I. 391 The state-mending citizen. **1792** LD. WESTMORLAND in *Lecky's Hist. Eng. 18th C.* (1887) VI. 531 The present Statemaking mania of the world. **1913** *Engl. Rev.* Jan. 284 The Mongols are not state-builders.

b. instrumental, chiefly with pa. pples.

1616 J. LANE *Contn. Sqr.'s T.* IX. 288 Th' prize of state-caused strife. **1650** B. *Discolliminium* 8 They have gotten some yeers on their back, and are able to make a profession of some State-establishment. **1833** J. S. MILL in *Jurist* IV. 14 Let the State endowments be once withdrawn from the church of England. **1842** MIALL in *Nonconf.* II. 193 An authorised, a state-provisioned clergy. **1842** J. S. MILL in *Morning Chron.* 13 Jan. 3/6 If an established church is not to be independent of state control, no established church ought to exist. **1848** in A. Prentice *Tour in U.S.* viii. 76 A real, state-paid bishop, whilome a minister of the Scotch Relief Kirk. **1856** GEO. ELIOT in *Westm. Rev.* X. 64 Its patent machinery of state-appointed functionaries. **1872** YEATS *Growth Comm.* 58 The poor citizens.. became state-fed paupers. **1876** *Fortn. Rev.* 1 Apr. 630 Proof that, as the *Katheder-Socialisten* maintain in Germany, the part of state-intervention will go on steadily increasing. **1882** M. ARNOLD *Irish Ess.* 97 State-aided elementary schools. **1887** G. B. SHAW *Let.* 8 June (1965) I. 173 The sweeping away of our.. wicked workhouse prisons in favour of State-owned farms and factories. **1891** H. SPENCER *Justice* 270 Under the existing system of ownership, those who manage the land, experience a direct connexion between effort and benefit; while, were it under State-ownership, those who managed it would experience no such direct connexion. **1897** *Westm. Gaz.* 3 Sept. 8/1 The very atmosphere of State-ridden

Germany is fast becoming unbreathable to English lungs. **1899** W. S. CHURCHILL in *Morning Post* 6 Dec. 5/7 There will be those who will dream another dream of a brave system of State-aided—almost State-compelled—emigration. **1901** *Edin. Rev.* Apr. 453 In Germany we have seen a State-paid clergy help to create and keep on foot the great parliamentary party of the Centre. **1912** W. B. SELBIE *Nonconformity* xii. 226 The principle of the State establishment of religion. **1926** H. SHEEHY-SKEFFINGTON *Let.* 15 Feb. in *Lett. of Sean O'Casey* (1975) I. 168 In no country save in Ireland could a State-subsidized theatre presume on popular patience. **1927** CARR-SAUNDERS & JONES *Social Structure Eng. & Wales* 148 To complete the tale of State-provided benefits that school children may receive. **1927** A. HUXLEY *Proper Studies* 220 In most modern countries the only state-supported orthodoxy is a sexual orthodoxy. **1942** *Contemp. Jewish Rec.* V. 274 The state-controlled *Kolkhoz* or *Sovkhos* systems in Soviet Russia. **1946** J. W. DAY *Harvest Adventure* xviii. 301 No National Park or State-planned 'lung' could offer lovelier scenery so near a manufacturing area. **1946** State-run [see PRIVATE *a.* 4d]. **1952** C. P. BLACKER *Eugenics: Galton & After* 185 France has a Minister for Population and a state-sponsored National Institute of Demographic Studies. **1958** A. QUINTON in *Victorian Stud.* I. 254 [T. H.] Green's defence of state intervention is now generally recognised as an important intellectual preparation for the British Labour Party. **1973** *Listener* 17 May 635/1 That section of the Left which wants greater equality without a massive increase in state ownership. **1977** *N.Y. Rev. Bks.* 31 Mar. 22/3 On state control of industry, the pivotal socialist issue, he had no consistent views. **1978** S. SHELDON *Bloodline* iv. 69 He borrowed money on the real jewelry from the Crédit Municipal, the state-owned pawnshop. **1979** *Jrnl. R. Soc. Arts* CXXVII. 125/2 There was now state-aided scientific research.

41. a. Special comb.: **state-cabin** = STATE-ROOM 2, 3 (cf. *states-cabin*, quot. 1767, 23b); **state capitalism**, a system of socialism whereby the State exerts exclusive control over a substantial proportion of the means of production, and over the deployment of capital created by this; hence **state-capitalist, -capitalistic** *adjs.*; **state-centred** *a.*, that centres on the State; **state-church**, a church established by the state; hence **state-churchism, -churchman**; **State Council**, the highest administrative and executive body of the People's Republic of China; **State Department** *U.S.*, the federal department for foreign affairs, presided over by the Secretary of State, = *Department of State* s.v. DEPARTMENT *sb.* 3b; **State Enrolled Nurse**, a nurse enrolled on a State register and having a qualification lower than that of a State Registered Nurse; †**state-fallen** *a.*, fallen from high estate; **state-letter**, a letter written officially by a secretary of state; †**state-like** *a.*, stately, magnificent; **state line** *U.S.*, the boundary line of a State; †**state-making**, conveyance of an estate (see 34b); **state-oriented** *a.*, directed towards the State; **state-paper**, an official document in which some matter concerning the government or the nation is published or expounded; also *attrib.* in *State Paper Office*; **state-prayers**, the prayers for the king and royal family in the order for morning and evening prayer; **state-prison**, (*a*) a prison for political offenders (cf. 38d); (*b*) *U.S.* and *Austral.*, a prison maintained by a State for the penal confinement of criminals; in *U.S.* also *state's prison*; **state-quake** *jocular*, a convulsion of the state; **State Registered Nurse**, a nurse enrolled on a State register, and better qualified than a State Enrolled Nurse; **State rights**, the rights and powers vested in the separate States under the Federal constitution of the U.S.A. and other federal nations; also *attrib.*; **State Scholarship**, a scholarship awarded by the State for study at a university; **state secret**, a matter kept secret by the government; *jocularly*, an important secret; **state socialism**, socialism achieved by State ownership of public utilities and industry; hence **state socialist** *a.* and *sb.*; **state-socialistic** *a.*; **state-statue** *nonce-wd.*, a mere image of a statesman; **state vector** *Physics*, a vector in a space whose dimensions correspond to all the independent wave-functions of a system, the instantaneous value of the vector conveying all possible information about the state of the system at that instant; **state visit**, a visit by a head of state to a foreign country for ceremonial rather than official purposes; also *fig.*; †**state-ward**, one's post as 'watchman for the state'; **state-wide** *a.*, of, pertaining to, or extending over a whole state (usu. in sense 31c; occas. sense 30); also as *adv.*; †**statewise** *adv.*, in regard to the State.

1760–72 H. BROOKE *Fool of Qual.* (1809) III. 85 Going down to the *state-cabin. **1838** *Civil Engin. & Arch. Jrnl.* I. 167/2 Each side [of the saloon is] occupied with State cabins. **1903** D. MODELL tr. *P. Kropotkin's Mod. Science & Anarchism* x. 94 Anarchism cannot see in the next coming revolution a mere exchange of monetary symbols for labor-checks, or an exchange of present Capitalism for *State-capitalism. **1928** E. & C. PAUL tr. *Stalin's Leninism* 436 The left-wing communists were of opinion that State capitalism is incompatible with the system of the proletarian dictatorship. **1978** LD. HAILSHAM *Dilemma of Democracy* xvii. 110 Modern capitalism is the state capitalism of the Coal Board, British Rail or the Post Office. **1965** B. PEARCE tr. *Preobrazhensky's New Economics* 153 In the Entente countries the economic system of the war period was *state-capitalist to a considerably smaller extent. **1945** KOESTLER *Yogi & Commissar* III. iii. 201 Soviet Russia is a *State-Capitalistic totalitarian autocracy. **1957** K. A. WITTFOGEL *Oriental Despotism* 33 The *state-centered system of land grants as it prevailed in early China. **1977** *Dædalus* Summer 53 Is the state-centered concept of international politics.. still relevant to the age of interdependence? **1726** TRAPP *Popery* I. 63 They call our church and Religion, a *State-Church, and Religion. **1888** SCHAFF *Hist. Chr. Ch., Mod. Chr.* I. 83 Christianity flourishes best without a state-church. **1862** R. VAUGHAN *Nonconformity* 391 *State-churchism in any form was not in logical accordance with the leading principle of their polity. **1845** MIALL in *Nonconf.* V. 397 Government officials, who, of course, will be *state-churchmen to a man. **1969** PLANO & OLTON *Internat. Relations Dict.* 179 **State Council*, the highest executive decision-making body of the state apparatus, comparable to the Council of Ministers in the Soviet Union. **1978** tr. *Documents 1st Sess. 5th National Congr. People's Republic of China* 153 The State Council is the Central People's Government and the executive organ of the highest organ of state power. **1790** *Deb. Congress U.S.* 1 Apr. (1834) 1505 The resolution laid on the table yesterday, respecting the *State Department. **1836** in *Ann. Rep. Amer. Hist. Assoc. 1907* (1908) II. 117 This morning..I went to the State Department, to have a conference with the present Acting Secretary of State. **1930** *Times* (Weekly ed.) 9 Jan. 35/1 On the eve of its meeting the State Department published the New Year greetings exchanged between King George and President Hoover. **1970** E. SNOW *Red China Today* (new ed.) 26 Under pressure he had himself made a State Department-accredited 'correspondent'. **1978** R. LUDLUM *Holcroft Covenant* iii. 41 'It's the State Department. For you.' 'State? This is Lieutenant Miles, NYPA police.' **1961** *Nursing Mirror & Midwives' Jrnl.* 23 June 1143/2 The lettering on badges and certificates of existing State Enrolled Assistant Nurses will not be altered when the title is changed to *State Enrolled Nurse as from June 28 this year. **1974** *Encycl. Brit. Macropædia* XIII. 399/1 Legislation in 1960 changed the title of a less qualified grade from state-enrolled assistant nurse to state-enrolled nurse. **1845** E. WARBURTON *Crescent & Cross* II. 287 Every thing about this *state-fallen prince wore an appearance of poverty and sadness. **1692** *Post Office patent to T. Neale* 17 Feb. (MS.) All letters commonly called *State letters which are usually carried Postage ffree here in England shall pass free thorow all our Plantations and Iselands. **1738** BIRCH *Life Milton* Wks. 1738 I. 59 Besides the Works already mentioned, he was prevail'd upon..to get his State-Letters transcrib'd. **1659** W. CHAMBERLAYNE *Pharronida* I. 38 A magestick Vest Of *state-like red. **1783** *Virginia Gaz.* 20 Dec. 2/3 George R. Clark, Surveyor *State Line. **1868** *Harper's Mag.* June 123/2 He pronounced 'good-by' to the Prairie State, at the State line. **1973** R. L. SIMON *Big Fix* (1974) xviii. 132, I was..driving into a desert dawn. I had already crossed the state line. **1487** *Rolls of Parlt.* VI. 394/1 By means of any Feoffeement, *State makyng or Relees. **1961** *Encounter* Sept. 24/1 The political self-consciousness of the individual citizen is *State-oriented. **1740** S. HAYNES (*title*) A Collection of *State Papers. **1849** MACAULAY *Hist. Eng.* ii. I. 172 No man wrote abler state papers. **1915** H. JENKINSON *Palaeogr.* 4 Almost at the same time [*temp.* Hen. VII] appears a new class of Administration..the Department, the Office of the Secretary of State; whose Records are State Papers, with, very soon, a special home of their own in the State Paper Office. **1831** W. L. BOWLES *Life Bp. Ken* II. 246 Even at Long-Leat, the *state-prayers, as they were called, disturbed his mind, so as to prevent his attending the chapel. **1723** BLACKMORE *Alfred* x. 365 Judg'd Guilty and condemn'd they were convey'd To the *State Prisons. **1828–32** WEBSTER s.v. *Prison*, We have state-prisons, for the confinement of criminals by way of punishment. **1832** G. DOWNES *Lett. Cont. Countries* I. 158 Out in the lake is a state-prison called the Wellenberg. **1867** C. H. PEARSON in Brodrick *Ess. Reform* 193 They..are filling the State prisons in Victoria and New South Wales. **1645** *State-quake [see CHURCH-QUAKE]. **1655** FULLER *Ch. Hist.* IX. 130 Untill it hath vented itself with a State-quake of those countries. **1766** H. WALPOLE *Let. to G. Montagu* 12 Dec., We have had..many grumbles of a state-quake. **1920** *Nursing Mirror & Midwives' Jrnl.* 17 July 270/1 A Bill for the State Registration of Nurses was drafted by the College in which it was provided that..all the nurses on the College Register would automatically become *State-registered nurses without further fee. **1965** D. EDWARDS-REES *Story of Nursing* vi. 66 From 1925 onwards the only way for a new-comer to become a state-registered nurse was to take a three-year course and to pass the state examination at the end of it. **1977** P. HILL *Liars* ix. 117 On the mantelshelf were pictures ..one..of Rose in the full uniform of a State Registered Nurse. **1798** *Debates in Congress* 21 June (1851) 2022 The powers of our general Government are checked by *State rights. **1846** S. M. MAURY *Statesmen Amer.* 370 The struggle which ended in the triumph of the State rights party. **1890** C. L. NORTON *Polit. Americanisms* 109 *State Rights.* The political creed which favours the retention of independent powers by individual States as opposed to 'Centralization'. **1907** W. S. CHURCHILL in R. S. Churchill *Winston S. Churchill* (1969) II. Compan. I. 627 A more practical explanation of any inconsistency in the attitude of the States is to be found in the growing cleavage upon the question of State rights *versus* Federal authority. **1930** W. K. HANCOCK *Australia* vi. 121 In truth, Australian public opinion (even that section of it which is disposed to favour 'State rights') has only a fitful, ineffective interest in maintaining the Federal balance. **1944** *Ann. Reg. 1943* 63 *State Scholarships to universities should be of such a value as to enable the holder to take full part in the life of the university. **1966** *Rep. Comm. Inquiry Univ. Oxf.* II. 27 Source of financial assistance... A college scholarship or exhibition and a State Scholarship or LEA award. **1822** GALT *Provost* xlvi, I told it to Mrs. Pawkie as a *state secret. **1831** SCOTT *Ct. Robt.* xxix, It was considered as a state secret of the greatest importance. **1879** G. J. HOLYOAKE in *19th Cent.* June 1114 *State socialism is one of the diseases of despotism. *Ibid.*, State Socialism, so far as any taste for it exists in England, is a growth of Toryism. **1930** W. K. HANCOCK *Australia* vii. 137 Mr. Eggleston says that the Victorians are destroying their State socialism by political sabotage. **1968** H. W. LAIDLER *Hist. Socialism* xliii. 739 The social legislation of Bismarck has often been referred to as state socialism. **1879** G. J. HOLYOAKE in *19th Cent.* 1116 True co-operators are no *State Socialists. **1912** State socialist [see RADICAL *sb.* 5a]. **1968** H. W. LAIDLER *Hist. Socialism* xliii. 742 Mr. Hillquit's distinction between government ownership and collective ownership..was.. the distinction made between the state socialist and the democratic socialist approach. **1879** G. J. HOLYOAKE in *19th Cent.* 1115 The only persons in this country likely to be suspected of the *State Socialistic craze are the working class co-operators. **1613** SHAKS. *Hen. VIII*, I. ii. 88 If we shall stand still, In feare our motion will be mock'd, or carp'd at, We should take roote here, where we sit, or sit *State-Statues onely. **1929** CONDON & MORSE *Quantum Mechanics* vi. 205 The components of the *state vector along the different principal axes multiplied by their complex conjugates give the probabilities of each value for the state in question. **1951** *Physical Rev.* LXXXII. 914/1 Quantum mechanics involves two distinct sets of hypotheses—the general mathematical scheme of linear operators and state vectors with its associated probability interpretation and the commutation relations and equations of motion for specific dynamical systems. **1970** D. T. GILLESPIE *Quantum Mechanics Primer* iv. 41 The state of the system is completely described by the state vector in the sense that anything which is in principle knowable about the system at time *t* can be learned from the function $\Psi t(x)$. **1794** H. WILSON *Let.* 12 Apr. in *Fingall Papers* (Nat. Libr. Ireland MS. 8023(5)), I think your resolution as to a certain complimentory *State Visit is perfectly correct, both as to yourself and your Lady. **1857** C. M. YONGE *Dynevor Terrace* I. xiv. 218 On Monday we go to Leffingham... After that, more state visits, unless I can escape to Oxford. **1914** W. OWEN *Let.* 1 Jan. (1967) 225, I had to buy a waistcoat today, to complete the black suit: for the State Visit to Mr. Aumont which French Politeness imposes. **1966** *Listener* 23 June 900/2 President de Gaulle arrives in Moscow for twelve-day state visit. **1979** G. ST. AUBYN *Edward VII* vii. 320 He [*sc.* the King]..decided that he wished to pay a State Visit abroad. *a* **1625** FLETCHER *Bloody Bro.* IV. i, I, ist so? at your *stateward, sir? [*Cf. infra*, A watchman for the State]. **1911** C. E. PERSONS et al. *Labor Laws* 62 A *state-wide organization was sufficient to bring the necessary pressure to bear. **1927** [see RODEO 3b]. **1948** J. TOWSTER *Political Power in U.S.S.R.* iv. 86 Maximum unification of all economic activity by one state-wide plan. **1954** W. FAULKNER *Fable* 189 A horde of Federal agents and sheriffs and special officers like the converging packs of a state- or nation-wide foxhunt. **1974** *Hartsville* (S. Carolina) *Messenger* 2 Apr. 2-A/5 The American Patriot Reading Club will offer youngsters statewide the opportunity to become better acquainted with the men, women, places and events, which have been prominent in the history of our state and the nation. **1980** *News & Observer* (Raleigh, N. Carolina) 28 Oct. 22/3 That immunization of cats against rabies be required statewide, and that the N.C. Wildlife Resources Commission be permitted to hunt and trap foxes for rabies control. **1642** BRIDGE *Wound. Consc. Cured* §2. 17 It is lawfull for the Subjects considered *statewise to rayse an army to defend themselves.

b. Combinations of the genitive or pl.: **State's attorney** *U.S.*, a lawyer commissioned to represent the State in the courts, esp. in criminal actions; **state's evidence**: see EVIDENCE *sb.* 7c; **states-folk**, †(*a*) persons of (great) estate or position; (*b*) *dial.* yeomen-farmers, owners of small estates (cf. STATESMAN[1] 2); **states-people** *dial.* = prec. (*b*); **States rights** = *State rights* in sense a; hence **States-righter**, an advocate of States rights in the *U.S.* or other federal nations; **states-system** (tr. G. *staaten-system*), the federation of a number of states with the object of preserving the actual balance of power.

1809 KENDALL *Trav.* III. 251 There is in Vermont..an attorney-general, or, as it is called, a *states attorney, for each particular county. **1906** W. WALKER *Calvin* xii. 335 The prosecution now fell into the charge of the states-attorney of the city, Claude Rigot, a friend of Calvin. ? **1727** SWIFT *Gulliver, Let. Capt. Gulliver*, I see myself accused of reflecting upon great *States-Folk. **1902** *Pall Mall Mag.* Sept. 53 The statesfolk too, and the townsfolk—true, a worshipful company! **1887** CAINE *Deemster* iii, The robustious *states-people from twenty miles around. **1858** HAMILTON *Sp.* 27 Oct. (Bartlett), Having been all my life.. an ardent '*States-rights' man. **1948** *States' Rights* (Birmingham, Alabama) 26 July 1/1 *States' Righters is all right, but the term, 'Dixiecrats', leaves the wrong impression. **1959** *Times Lit. Suppl.* 28 Aug. 491/3 It undoubtedly rallied every states-righter and virtually every Southerner, however progressive, behind Governor Faubus. **1972** *Accountant* 30 Mar. 405/2 Mr Macaw is regarded as a devout 'States-righter', who is firmly opposed to the creation of any Federal body to control the securities industry [in Australia]. **1834** tr. *Heeren's Man. Hist. Polit. Syst. Europe* I. Pref. p. vii, The history of any particular *states-system (by which we mean the union of several contiguous states, resembling each other in their manners, religion, and degree of social improvement, and cemented together by a reciprocity of interests). **1864** BRYCE *Holy Rom. Emp.* xix. (1876) 340 The Peace of Westphalia is the first..of those attempts to reconstruct by diplomacy the European states-system which have played so large a part in modern history.

†**state**, *a.*[1] *Obs.* *rare*$^{-1}$. [ad. L. *status*, pa. pple. of *sistĕre* to place, set.] = STATED *ppl. a.*

1581 J. BELL *Haddon's Answ. Osor.* 313 Neither doe we enforce any person to state tymes of the yeare [orig. *nec statis temporum præscriptis quenquam astringimus*]. *Ibid.* 323 The long processe therfore that you made of state feasts, and other gaddyng holydayes in y^e yeare [*Quæ igitur de* *consecratis anni temporibus, & festorum distributione hactenus commemorasti*].

†**state**, *a.*[2] or quasi-*adv. Obs. rare*$^{-1}$. [? After STATE *sb. attrib.*] (See quot.)

1579 SPENSER *Sheph. Cal.* Sept. 45 They..bearen the cragge so stiffe and so state [*gloss.* stoutely].

state (steɪt), *v.* Also 7 *Sc.* **steat.** [f. STATE *sb.*]

1. *trans.* To place, station. *rare.*

c **1590** MARLOWE *Jew of Malta* II, The Christian Ile of Rhodes, from whence you came, Was lately lost, and you were stated here To be at deadly enmity with Turkes. *a* **1734** NORTH *Exam.* III. vii. §8 (1740) 510 The capital Practice in the Court of King's Bench, wherein he was stated before he had any Preferment. **1742** *De Foe's Tour Gt. Brit.* (ed. 3) II. 129 As the Court is now stated, all the Offices and Places for Business are scatter'd about, here and there. **1845** BAILEY *Festus* i. (ed. 2) 5 Some vast temptation calmly comes And states itself before it, like the sun Low looming in the west.

†**b.** In *passive*, of a quality: To reside, inhere *in* a subject. *Obs.*

1678 BARCLAY *Apol.* VII. vii. 216 The Adjective [Just].. signifies a Man..in whom this Quality of Justice is stated.

†**2.** To give a certain rank or position to, to rank; also in *pass.*, to have a position, to be ranked. *Obs.*

1592 *Arden of Feversham* III. v. 84, I haue neglected matters of import That would have stated me aboue thy state. **1631** R. H. *Arraignm. Whole Creature* Ep. Ded., Some of you are in a high manner, and all of You in some sort seated and stated. **1632** HEYWOOD *2nd Pt. Iron Age* IV. i, Shall hee inioy my birth-right, or inherite Where I am heire apparant?..where I am stated, sit? **1669** PENN *No Cross no Crown* I. ix. §31 (1857) 122 The aspiring fallen angels, that affected to be greater and better than they were made and stated by the great Lord of all. *a* **1715** BURNET *Own Time* III. xiii. (1900) II. 314 The two religions, popish and protestant, were so equally stated in his mind, that a few grains of loyalty..turned the balance with him.

†**b.** ? To assign a value to, have an opinion upon. *Obs.*

1671 MILTON *Samson* 424 Thou didst plead Divine impulsion prompting how thou might'st Find some occasion to infest our Foes. I state not that; this I am sure, our Foes Found soon occasion [etc.].

†**c.** With complement: To constitute, to give (a person) the status of. *Sc. Obs.*

1689 in *Sc. Acts* (1875) XII. 58/2 That..The clerks should not be allowed to call the Earle of Selkirk before him least þat myght steat him ane petitorie.

†**3.** To place in a specified condition; in early use chiefly to settle, place in safety or quiet. *Obs.*

1605 B. JONSON *Volpone* III. ix, On which [violence done to his parent] the Law should take sufficient hold, And you be stated in a double hope. **1628** FELTHAM *Resolves* II. lii. 152 Then, the soule stated in a deepe repose, bewrayed her true affections. **1640** SHIRLEY *Constant Maid* II. ii, My next work Shall be..To state her body in that modest temper She was possessed of. **1642** FULLER *Holy & Prof. St.* II. x. 90 An excellent Chirurgeon he was at joynting of a broken soul, and at stating of a doubtfull conscience. **1654** H. L'ESTRANGE *Chas. I* (1655) 53 This answer of the Duke to his impeachment..seemed to state him in impunity. *c* **1681** T. HUNT *Def. Charter Lond.* 37 Which put many thousand Persons well stated to starving. **1685** COTTON tr. *Montaigne* I. 495, I see nowhere..a house more nobly and constantly maintain'd than his, happy in this to have stated his affairs to so just a proportion, that his estate is sufficient to do it without his care or trouble. **1722** DE FOE *Plague* (1756) 142, I mean especially, as you and I are stated, without a Dwelling-House of our own. **1786** A. GIB *Sacred Contempl.* I. iv. 147 His will was stated in a wicked contradiction to the authority and will of God.

†**b.** To bring about (a state of things). *Obs.*

1654 J. OWEN *Saints Persev.* viii. §16. 197 Take a Cyon.. bind it on as close as possible, yet 'tis not united to the Tree, untill the Sappe..be communicated to it, which communication states the union.

4. To place, install *in* a dignity, office, right, etc.

1617 MIDDLETON & ROWLEY *Fair Quarrel* I. i, Heere you boaste to mee Of a great reuenew, a large substance Wherein you would endow & state my daughter. **1625** GILL *Sacred Philos.* iv. 35 In which right, If He had not fully stated mankind, then had the benefit of His purchase beene utterly lost. **1648** J. BEAUMONT *Psyche* IX. xcix, No Proxy He, nor stated in his Might Barely by Patent, but by Native Right. **1651** BAXTER *Inf. Bapt.* 24 Either members must be baptized at their admission, or else after they are stated in the Church. **1654** in *Burton's Diary* (1828) I. 81 To state him in the right of disposing of the forces.

†**b.** To confer or settle (a possession, right, etc.) *upon*, vest *in* a person, etc. *Obs.*

1633 BP. HALL *Hard Texts* Eph. i. 14 Untill that purchased possession of eternall life may be fully accomplished and stated upon us. **1638** BRATHWAIT *Barnabees Jrnl.* III. (1818) 101 These [*i.e.* the Little Gidding community] hold and walke together wholly, And state their lands on uses holy. *a* **1641** BP. MOUNTAGU *Acts & Mon.* (1642) 107 The Scepter..was not stated upon them of the Tribe of Iudah. **1678** SANDERSON *9 Cases* 104, I acknowledge the Soveraign Power of this Nation..to be rightly stated in the House of Commons.

†**5.** To set in state, to treat with ceremony of state. *Obs.*

1613 HEYWOOD *Braz. Age* II. ii, Oh you Gods! or make her mine, Stated with vs the Calidonian Queene. **1622** BACON *Hen. VII*, 80 For shee was not onely publikely contracted, but stated as a Bride, and solemnly Bedded. *a* **1625** FLETCHER *Noble Gent.* III. i, 'Twill be rarely strange To see him stated thus, as though he went A shroving through the City.

†**b.** *to state it*: to affect the attributes of rank; to go or live in state. *Obs.*

1631 J. TAYLOR (Water P.) *Sudden Turn Fortunes Wheel* (1848) 23 Nassau,..you did gather The fearfull rebells into warlike bands, Who now do state it in the Netherlands. **1655** FULLER *Ch. Hist.* v. xvi. 178 Wolsey began to state it at York as high as ever before. **1663** KILLIGREW *Pars. Wedding* III. v, These Gentlemen are quickly satisfi'd; what an ugly Whore they have got! how she states it!

†**6.** To settle, or regulate, by authority. *Obs.*

1647 WARD *Simp. Cobler* 28, I seriously feare, if the pious Parliament doe not finde a time to state fashions,..God will hardly finde a time to state Religion or Peace. **1699** *Plea agst. Price of Corn* 16 Suppose, for instance in the Southern parts of England,..Corn were stated at 5s. per Bushel for Wheat. **1714** in *Hist. Northfield* (Mass.) (1875) 133 The said Committee are further impowered to state the place of the town upon small lots so as it may be made defensible.

†**b.** ? To fix, make dependent *upon*. *Obs.*

1671 J. LIVINGSTONE *Let.* 7 Oct. in *Sel. Biogr.* (Wodrow Soc. 1845) I. 242 Persecution [is] bended against all who go not alongs in that apostacie and perjury; and is not, then, suffering stated on as important a quarrel as ever was since the foundation of the world? **1692** SOUTH *Serm.* (1697) I. 14 One of the grand duties of which [*sc.* Religion] is stated upon Repentance.

7. To set out (a question, problem, etc.) in proper form; spec. in *Logic*.

a **1641** BP. MOUNTAGU *Acts & Mon.* (1642) 110 First the question is not rightly stated in the Conclusion. **1662** JER. TAYLOR *Via Intell.* 8 We find by a sad experience, that few Questions are well stated. **1680** DRYDEN *Ovid's Ep.* Pref., To state it fairly; imitation of an author is the most advantageous way for a translator to show himself, [etc.]. **1795** *Gentl. Mag.* LXV. II. 543/2 Permit me to state a few queries to your Correspondents in general. **1826** WHATELY *Logic* I. i. §2 (1827) 24 An argument thus stated regularly and at full length, is called a Syllogism. **1869** J. MARTINEAU *Ess.* II. 6 A problem must be stated in order to be solved. **1883** *Manch. Guard.* 22 Oct. 5/3 The question is surely one which, stated in this way, needs no answer.

b. *Arithmetic.* (See quot. 1740.)

1740 DYCHE & PARDON *Dict.* (ed. 3), *State v.*..in Arithmetick, it is the arranging numbers in such order, that the question may be truly answered. **1797** *Encycl. Brit.* (ed. 3) II. 302 (*Compound Proportion*), The above question may therefore be stated and wrought as follows: Men 18:24::6 bolls [etc.]... In general, state the several particulars on which the question depends, as so many simple proportions, [etc.].

c. *to state a case*: to set out the facts of a matter or pleading for consideration by a court. Said of a pleader or advocate; also of a court when allowing an appeal from its own judgement; also *gen.*

1692 *Cal. Treas. Papers* 265 Mr. Lowndes to state his case to be laid before the King. **1710** ADDISON *Whig-Exam.* No. 5 ¶3, I must observe, that the Advocates for this doctrine have stated the case in the softest and most palatable terms that it will bear. **1857** *Act 20 & 21 Vict.* c. 43 §4 If the.. justices be of opinion that the application is merely frivolous ..they may refuse to state a case. **1879** *Act 42 & 43 Vict.* c. 49 § 33 Any person aggrieved who desires to question a conviction..of a court of summary jurisdiction..may apply to such court to state a special case.

d. *to state an account* or *accounts*: to set down formally the debits and credits arising in a course of business transactions. Also *fig.*

1648 HEYLIN *Relat. & Observ.* I. 83 About the beginning of March, was given to Col. Sydenham and Col. Bingham 1000 l. apiece, as part of their Arrears; their Accounts not yet stated. *c* **1685** *Cal. Treas. Papers* 16 To be referred to Mr. Surveyor to state y[e] accompt and examine y[e] bills and report it to y[e] Lords Commissioners. **1690** *Jrnls. Ho. Lords* XIV. 606/1 An Act for appointing and enabling Commissioners to examine, take, and state, the Public Accompts of the Kingdom. **1712** ARBUTHNOT *John Bull* I. xi, John spent several Weeks in looking over his Bills, and by comparing and stating his Accompts he discovered, that..he had been egregiously Cheated. **1718** *Freethinker* No. 33 ¶9 After this, when he finds himself most in Temper, let him coolly state the Accompts of his Love, by computing..the Profits and the Losses, arising from it.

†**e.** *to state a vote, a question*: to frame a question in the form in which it is intended to vote upon it. *Sc.*

1700 SIR D. HUME *Diary Parl. Scot.* (Bannatyne Club) 9 And then the vote came to be stated, Whether the Parliament should proceed to the Sheriff's procedure, or the Lords' their coming in, under these words Lords or Sheriff. Carried by one vote Sheriffs. *Ibid.* 33 Then the question was offered to be stated To allow the exportation..or Not. *a* **1712** FOUNTAINHALL *Decis.* (1759) II. 420 Then the vote was stated, If Sir Andrew Kennedy's taking Conservator dues..was relevant to infer deprivation.

8. To declare in words; to represent (a matter) in all the circumstances of modification; to set out fully or in a definite form.

1647 CLARENDON *Hist. Reb.* I. §34 Whereupon it was thought fit that the whole affair..should be stated and enlarged upon in a conference between the two Houses. **1667** BOYLE *Orig. Formes & Qual.* (ed. 2) 332 Themes, where the names that are of very common and necessary use have (yet) their significations very little stated or agreed upon. **1764** GOLDSM. *Trav.* 361 Yet think not, thus when Freedom's ills I state, I mean to flatter kings, or court the great. **1781** COWPER *Convers.* 816 It has indeed been told me (with what weight, How credible, 'tis hard for me to state) That [etc.]. **1802** MARIA EDGEWORTH *Mor. Tales, Forester* xii. (1848) 57 The facts were so plainly and forcibly stated, that his hopes even from law began to falter. **1810** SCOTT *Let.* in *Lockhart* (1837) II. viii. 284 The only purpose which I suppose Lord Lauderdale had in view was to state charges which could neither be understood nor refuted. **1860** TYNDALL *Glac.* II. i. 224 It will not be a useless labour..to state..our present views of light and heat. **1862** KALISCH *Hebr. Gram.* I. 19 Exercise vii. State the reasons why metheg is employed in the following words. **1891** *Law Times* XC. 463/1 The contents of the deed were falsely stated.

b. Const. (*a*) with a clause (introduced by *that*) as object; (*b*) with object followed by the inf., chiefly *pass.*

(*a*) **1801** *Farmer's Mag.* Apr. 137 It has already been stated, that 3,000,000 of acres are required to be in wheat. **1850** GLADSTONE *Glean.* (1879) II. 123 We may state that his father was known..to be a man of extreme opinions. **1866** THIRLWALL *Lett.* (1881) II. 77 Diego then stated that he was going to the university of Salamanca.

(*b*) **1838** LINDLEY *Flora Med.* 57 Conium is stated by Aretæus to be anti-aphrodisiac. **1839** FR. A. KEMBLE *Resid. in Georgia* (1863) 13 Upon an English lady's stating it to be her intention to visit these persons. **1846** *Penny Cycl.* Suppl. II. 502/2 The inhabitants, whose number is stated not to exceed a thousand. **1857** GLADSTONE *Glean.* (1879) VI. 89 It is sometimes stated to have been owing to accident.

c. To specify (a number, price, etc.).

1789 *New Lond. Mag.* July 370/2 Fifteen thousand men effective are stated. **1823** SOUTHEY *Penins. War* I. 373 The numbers of the Spanish army have been variously stated from 14,000 to 40,000. **1842** BISCHOFF *Woollen Manuf.* (1862) II. 169 To enable the manufacturers to afford the cloths at the prices I have stated. **1854** *Poultry Chron.* II. 147 State your profession, especially if a clergyman. **1859** RANKINE *Steam Engine* etc. 428 The vacuum in the condenser being often measured by a mercurial gauge, is sometimes stated in *inches of mercury*.

stateable: see STATABLE.

statecraft (ˈsteɪtkrɑːft, -æ-). [f. STATE *sb.* + CRAFT.] The art of conducting state affairs; statesmanship. Sometimes with sinister implication: Crafty or overreaching statesmanship.

1642 FULLER *Holy & Prof. St.* IV. v. 263 Some plead that dissembling is Lawfull in the State-craft, upon the presupposition that men must meet with others which dissemble. **1719** OLDISWORTH *Callipædia* IV. 582 Well verst in State-Craft, the mysterious Trade, They know to gild and paint a pious Fraud. **1745** FIELDING *True Patriot* No. 9 ¶16 Nor can I help observing..another piece of state craft..; for while we sent for this troop of singers into England, we left several troops of our soldiers abroad. **1798** W. TAYLOR in *Monthly Mag.* V. 352 To avoid a civil, wage a foreign war, is an old adage of profligate state-craft. **1855** MACAULAY *Hist. Eng.* xviii. IV. 163 A double treason, such as would have been thought a masterpiece of statecraft by the great Italian politicians of the fifteenth century. **1861** TULLOCH *Engl. Purit.* I. 2 The English Reformation..was also the creature of statecraft, and royal policy. **1873** SYMONDS *Grk. Poets* i. 16 The men who rose to the greatest eminence in statecraft are to be reckoned among the primitive philosophers of Greece. **1886** *Manch. Exam.* 18 Jan. 5/5 It savours more of statecraft than of statesmanship. **1887** LOWELL *Democracy* etc. 34 Statecraft is no longer looked upon as a mystery, but as a business.

So **state-craftsman**, an expert in statecraft.

1809–10 COLERIDGE *Friend* II. 185 Whatever study or doctrine bears upon..a certain Phantom of a State *in toto*, which is every where and no where, this shall be deemed most useful and wise; and all else is the state-craftsman's scorn. **1914** WELLS in *Engl. Rev.* Jan. 202 State-craftsmen sat with their historical candles burning.

stated (ˈsteɪtɪd), *ppl. a.* [f. STATE *v.* + -ED[1]. In early use perh. rather f. L. *stat-us* appointed, fixed, regular (see STATE *a.*) + -ED[1].]

†**1.** Fixed, regular in operation or occurrence; not occasional or fluctuating. *Obs.*

a **1641** BP. MOUNTAGU *Acts & Mon.* (1642) 124 Extraordinary singular courses, sometimes intervenient in naturall processes, alter not the generall, stated, habituall course of nature. **1719** DE FOE *Crusoe* I. (Globe) 162 That altho' there were no stated Inhabitants who liv'd on the Spot; yet that there might sometimes come Boats off from the Shore. **1752** JOHNSON *Rambler* No. 188 ¶2 The pleasure which men are able to give in conversation, holds no stated proportion to their knowledge or their virtue. *a* **1774** GOLDSM. *Surv. Exper. Philos.* II. 134 Thus every four-and-twenty hours they have two regular and stated winds.

2. a. Of times, amounts, etc.: Fixed or settled by authority, agreement, custom, promise, or prearrangement.

1667 O. HEYWOOD *Heart-Treas.* xi. 129 'Tis good for a Christian to keep up set and stated times of prayer. **1690** CHILD *Disc. Trade* i. 30 If a low stated Interest by Law be the cause of Riches, no Country would be poor,..all having it in their power to state their Interest as low as they please by Law. **1771** GOLDSM. *Hist. Eng.* IV. 341 None but men already possessed of a stated fortune, were allowed a privilege of carrying a gun. **1784** COWPER *Tiroc.* 606 'Tis not enough that Greek and Roman page, At stated hours, his freakish thoughts engage. **1804** J. GRAHAME *Sabbath* (1823) 30 [He] Opens the book, and reverentially The stated portion reads. **1821** BAYLEY *Tower Lond.* I. 194 A keeper, appointed by the king's letters patent, with a stated salary. **1823** SOUTHEY *Penins. War* I. 387 All the French troops in Andalusia were to proceed by stated journies. **1884** E. YATES *Recoll.* II. 202, I should get rid of the long familiar life of the Office, with its stated hours of attendance.

b. Of an action, ceremony, observance, etc.: Having its fixed time and manner; 'set', not casual.

stated meeting, one of the regular periodical meetings (of a society, an Oxford College) as distinguished from meetings occasionally called.

1697 (*title*), Stated Christian Conference asserted to be a Christian duty; or A plea for stated Conference. **1698** M. HENRY *Life P. Henry* x. (1699) 165 It is of use in stated Prayer, ordinarily to observe a Method, according to the several Parts of Prayer. **1734** WATTS *Reliq. Juv.* (1789) 49 When a whole family sits down together, to make a regular and stated meal. **1856** *N. Brit. Rev.* XXVI. 61 This..is the proper course to be taken by ordinary Christian teachers, in their stated expositions of Scripture. **1866** *Harper's Mag.* Apr. 676/2 At one of their stated weekly meetings recently there was a large attendance. **1867** RUSKIN *Time & Tide* iii. §12 Invite trustworthy persons of other classes to join your council; appoint time and place for its stated sittings. **1907** *Colonial Soc. Massachusetts* Apr. 280 A Stated Meeting of the Society was held..on Thursday. *Ibid.*, The Records of the last Stated Meeting were read and approved. **1915** (16 June) in *Oxf. Univ. Gaz.*, At a Stated General Meeting held to-day the College [Brasenose] made a grant of £100 to the General Fund of the University.

c. Of a functionary, an employment: Recognized, regular, official.

1752 WESLEY *Wks.* (1872) II. 251 W. Harding who..was a stated Preacher. **1808** W. WILSON *Dissenting Churches* II. 28 The relish of his labour excited a desire after a stated ministry. **1861** *Contrib. Eccl. Hist. Connecticut* 221 There is a disposition to supersede this ministry of pastors, by a ministry of stated supplies;—men employed to perform the duties of a pastor, but not inducted, in any appropriate way into the pastoral office. **1911** WEBSTER s.v., *Stated clerk*, in the Presbyterian churches of the United States, the secretary of a court.

†**d.** Definitely recognizable, decided; declared, avowed. *Obs.*

1651 BAXTER *Inf. Bapt.* 82 If Holiness of state here be a stated separation of the person from the world, to God. **1680** *Spirit of Popery* 51 He..saith, That the King Erects a Papacy in himself more absurdly than the Pope did; and saith, That he is a stated Antichrist. **1687** [SHIELDS] *Hind let loose* 411 Nay, we are by this obliged, if ever we be in case, to bring these stated Enemies to God and the Country to condign punishment. **1719** DE FOE *Crusoe* I. (Globe) 225 To carry me directly on to..Repentance..and..to a stated Reformation.

3. (In senses 7, 8 of the vb.) **a.** Of a law, rule, penalty: Formulated, explicitly set forth.

1681–6 J. SCOTT *Chr. Life* (1747) III. 461 Now the Law obliges us under a certain stated Penalty to do and forbear what it commands and forbids. **1694** COLLIER *Ess. Mor. Subj.* I. (1709) 133 Particular Satisfaction for every Affront in Conversation cannot be Awarded by Stated Laws. **1765** BLACKSTONE *Comm.* I. 92 What equity is, and how impossible in it's very essence to be reduced to stated rules, hath been shewn. *Ibid.* 238 [Oppressions springing from sovereign power] must necessarily be out of the reach of any stated rule, or express legal provision. **1768** *Ibid.* III. xxvii. 435 A penalty in the nature of stated damages; as a rent of 5*l.* an acre for ploughing up antient meadow.

b. Narrated, alleged as fact.

1787 POLWHELE *Engl. Orator* II. 339 Adhere To stated Facts. **1909** *Spectator* 25 Dec. 1093/1 In poetry, history, biography, and even in Holy Writ, we continually find the page..drawing its light and meaning from the stated words of quite unknown speakers.

c. ***stated account***: a statement of account that has been agreed to by the parties to a suit.

1765 J. T. ATKYNS *Chanc. Rep.* (1781) II. 1 When the defendant sets forth a stated account he shall not be obliged to go on upon a general one, because very often a stated account would unravel a perplexed affair. **1787** J. MITFORD *Plead. Suits Chanc.* (ed. 2) 208 A plea of a stated account is a good bar to a bill for an account. **1862** WATERSTON *Man. Commerce* 303 *Stated Account*, in the English law of accounts, is an account settled whether it be signed or not.

d. Law. ***stated case, case stated***: A summary of the points in dispute, drawn up by agreement of the parties to an action, to be presented to a court or an arbitrator in order to facilitate a speedy decision.

1899 *Daily News* 15 May 11/2 We [a firm of solicitors] take the liberty of sending you a print of a stated case herein, and of the decision of the Court of Session thereon.

statedly (ˈsteɪtɪdlɪ), *adv.* [f. STATED *ppl. a.* + -LY².]

1. With regularity, as a regular practice, constantly, not occasionally or spasmodically.

1670 BAXTER *Cure Ch.-divisions* 52 The Profession it self, or open covenanting with God is the thing statedly necessary to the being of visible Christianity. **1743** J. MORRIS *Serm.* viii. 216 That profession of faith in Jesus Christ, which is made at baptism, is statedly renewed at the Lord's supper. **1799** UNDERWOOD *Treat. Dis. Childhood* (ed. 4) I. 55 *note*, Numerous children..from their infancy have been for several days without a motion; nor would any gentle means procure it statedly. **1828** W. FIELD *Mem. Dr. Parr* I. 120 It will long be remembered by those who were statedly or occasionally his hearers. **1855** BROWNING *Bp. Blougram's Apol.* 945 You, Gigadibs, who, thirty years of age, Write statedly for Blackwood's Magazine. **1894** CROCKETT *Raiders* (ed. 3) 25 Men..who met statedly for their diets of worship.

2. According to what is stated or alleged.

1867 RUSKIN *Time & Tide* §37. viii. (1904) 46 A passage from the statedly authoritative portions of the Bible.

stateful (ˈsteɪtfʊl), *a.* Now *rare* or *Obs.* [f. STATE *sb.* + -FUL.] Full of state or dignity, stately.

1591 SYLVESTER *Du Bartas* I. vi. 342 To humble suiters neither stern nor statefull. **1624** T. GOKIN *Medit. Lord's Prayer* in Farr *Sel. Poetry Jas. I* (1848) 324 Thou lookest down from heaven, thy stateful throne.

Hence ˈ**statefully** *adv.*, ˈ**statefulness**.

1655 FULLER *Hist. Camb.* 79 It is not worthy to carry the books after Oxford Library for the statefulness of the Edifice. **1891** SARA J. DUNCAN *American Girl in Lond.* 68, I was rolling up Regent Street statefully in the carriage of Mrs. Torquilin.

statehood (ˈsteɪthʊd). [f. STATE *sb.* + -HOOD.] The condition or status of a political state (see STATE *sb.* 30, 31). Orig. with reference to the U.S.

1868 *New York Times* 8 June, Why indeed should the Federal Senate be organized on the basis of an extinct statehood? **1881** J. DAVIS *Rise & Fall Confed. Govt.* I. 291 The comparative claims of Statehood and Union. **1906** *Outlook* 29 Dec. 819/1 That indiscriminate turmoil through which Russia has yet to fight her way to coherent statehood. **1911** *Times* 19 Apr. 8/4 Utah was admitted to Statehood in 1896. **1952** *Times* 9 Dec. 9 (*heading*) Solid achievements [by Israel] after four years of Statehood. **1971** I. DEUTSCHER *Marxism in Our Time* (1972) v. 99 In a vast part of the continent a struggle was indeed going on for the achievement of independent statehood and nationhood. **1976** *Time* 27 Dec. 14/3 What the Palestinians want most of all is the sense of national identity that would arise from statehood.

State-house. Also with lower-case initial. [f. STATE *sb.* + HOUSE *sb.* Prob. suggested by Du. *stathuis* (now *stadhuis*) STADTHOUSE.]

†**1. a.** A house of state; a building appropriated to state-ceremonies. **b.** = SENATE HOUSE 1. *Obs.*

1593 NASHE *Christ's T.* 65 b, Humaine writers haue theyr vse of reprouing vices, as well as the Scriptures. It is an easie matter to prayse God, in that wherein hee hath placed the especiall state-house of his praises. **1614** RALEIGH *Hist. World* II. xxiii. §4. 574 Pacuuius in Capua..lockt the Senators vp within the State-house, and offered their liues to the Peoples mercie.

†**2.** A town hall; = STADTHOUSE. *Obs.*

1627 BP. HALL *Apol. agst. Brownists* §9 Wks. (1628) 578 Is it no Citie, if there be mud-walles halfe-broken, low Cottages vnequally built, no State-house? **1634** BRERETON *Trav.* (Chetham Soc.) 19 Delph hath..the finest state-house said to be in all the seventeen provinces. **1686** *Col. Laws N. York* I. 182 The Citty Hall or State House with the Ground thereunto belonging. **1756** MRS. CALDERWOOD *Lett. & Jrnls.* (1884) 111 The State-house [at Amsterdam] you have seen a print of.

3. a. In some of the North American colonies before 1776, the building in which the public affairs of the colony or province were transacted. Also applied to the building used by an Indian people for its deliberative assemblies. *Obs.* exc. *Hist.*

1639 in *Virginia Mag.* III. 30 A Levye..is raised for the building of a State howse at James Cittie. **1654** E. JOHNSON *Wonder-working Provid.* 109 The Indian King..gathered together his chiefe Counsellors, and..afterward gave them Audience, in a State-house, round, about fifty foot wide, made of long poles stuck in the ground. **1662** *Archives of Maryland* I. 434 The Vpper howse took into Consideracion the place for the Seateing of the State howse. **1709** J. LAWSON *New Voy. Carolina* 37 In these [Indian] State-Houses is transacted all Publick and Private Business, relating to the Affairs of the Government. **1725** *New Hampsh. St. Papers* XVIII. 1 The s^d Dishonour and Inconv[en]ience may both be remedyed by building a State house for holding the s^d General Assem^y and Courts. **1770** J. ADAMS *Diary* 13 July, Wks. 1850 II. 247 This Tilton's is just behind the State House.

b. *U.S.* The building in which the legislature of a State of the Union has its sessions; a State capitol.

1786 E. WATSON *Men & T. Revolution* (1861) 282 The State House, the Capitol of Maryland. **1821** T. DWIGHT *Trav.* I. 495 The State-house [at Boston, Mass.]..has a most noble and commanding position. **1908** W. CHURCHILL *Mr. Crewe's Career* ix. 134 I'll call in on you at the State-house day after to-morrow.

c. *attrib.*

1671 *Rec. N. Amsterdam* VI. 308 The Stone Well in the State-House-Yard. **1830** O. W. HOLMES *Dorchester Giant* 10 Then he brought them a pudding..As big as the State-House dome. **1908** W. CHURCHILL *Mr. Crewe's Career* xi. 167 Austen took his way slowly across the State-house park.

4. *N.Z.* (As two words.) A house owned and let by the government.

1941 W. B. SUTCH *Poverty & Progress in N.Z.* vii. 153 In the building of State houses of high quality a suggestion as to necessary standards has been made. **1964** B. CRUMP in *N.Z. Listener* 11 Dec. 5/3 It was a state house with shrubs and flowers in a street full of state houses with flowers and shrubs. **1978** B. MASON in *Islands* Aug. 15 After years of waiting, they got a State house last summer.

stateless (ˈsteɪtlɪs), *a.* [f. STATE *sb.* + -LESS.]

a. Without a state or political community. **b.** Destitute of state or ceremonial display.

† *stateless state*: a state not worthy of the name.

1609 F. GREVIL *Mustapha* v. iij, What soule then..Would hold a life of such a statelesse State. **1611** SPEED *Hist. Gt. Brit.* VII. xl. §5. 346 The Northumbrians expulsing their stateless Hericus..so pacified the King, that [etc.]. **1638** DRUMM. OF HAWTH. *Irene* Wks. (1711) 169 Cast not your selves into a voluntary Servitude; turn not your selves into a stateless State. **1843** D. JERROLD *Punch's Lett.* Ded., Wks. 1864 III. 450 Ye who have..with kindly conjurations given state to stateless Kings. **1902** B. KIDD *Princ. Western Civiliz.* x. 343 In the section of which England is the centre we catch sight..of a conception round which a practical system of world-politics..is actually slowly beginning to centre; namely, the ideal of a stateless competition of all the individuals of every land.

c. Not being a citizen of any state; having no nationality.

1930 E. F. W. GEY VAN PITTIUS *Nationality within Brit. Commonw.* xiii. 133 A person of dual nationality can at least enter more than one country and seek protection from both while abroad. Not so the stateless person. **1957** C. DAY LEWIS *Pegasus* 36 He travels on, not only blind But a stateless person. **1968** J. LOCK *Lady Policeman* xv. 132 The alien—a forty-seven year old Jugoslav-born stateless person —looked at her blankly. **1981** G. MARKSTEIN *Ultimate Issue* 153 In the absence of valid documents, we must grade a suspect stateless.

Hence ˈ**statelessness**, the condition of having no nationality.

1930 E. F. W. GEY VAN PITTIUS *Nationality within Brit. Commonw.* xiii. 132 In case of statelessness, which is the reverse of dual nationality or multiple nationality, an unfortunate individual is placed in the unenviable position of being without any country at all. **1959** *Times* 24 Mar. 9/5 The fundamental theory that statelessness should be overcome or reduced by the application of the principle of *jus soli* (the law of the soil) under which the nationality of a State is acquired by birth on its territory. **1963** H. ARENDT *Eichmann in Jerusalem* x. 155 This was one of the few cases in which statelessness turned out to be an asset.

statelet (ˈsteɪtlɪt). [f. STATE *sb.* + -LET.] A small state.

1865 *Morn. Star* 14 Nov., The innumerable currencies [in Germany twenty-five years ago], each Statelet having a little system of its own. **1900** CROCKETT *Joan of Sword Hand* i. 7 That cluster of hill statelets which is called collectively Masurenland.

‖ˈ**statelich**, *adv. Obs. rare*⁻¹. [G. *statlich* (now *stattlich*: see STATELY). The folio (1616) has the word in black letter as foreign.] In a stately manner.

1610 B. JONSON *Alch.* II. iv, *Svb.* Dol, my Lord Whachums Sister, you must now Beare your selfe statelich. *Dol.* O, let me alone... I'll keep my distance, laugh, and talke aloud; Haue all the tricks of a proud sciruy Lady.

ˈ**statelihood.** [See -HOOD.] Stateliness.

1845 *Tait's Mag.* XII. 208 With solemn statelihood, the camel's head o'erlooks the press. **1906** S. W. MITCHELL *Pearl* 27 In statelihood of mighty place She stood.

†ˈ**statelike**, *adv. Obs. rare.* [f. STATE *sb.* + -LIKE.] In a stately manner.

1456 SIR G. HAYE *Law Arms* (S.T.S.) 302 Quhen he wrytis, his writtis suld be wele and statelyke devisit and dytit. **1639** DU VERGER tr. *Camus' Admir. Events* 62 He caused them to carry him..into a chamber most state-like furnished.

statelily (ˈsteɪtlɪlɪ), *adv.* Now *rare.* [f. STATELY *a.* + -LY².] In a stately manner.

1611 COTGR., *Sublimement*, loftily, highly, haughtily, statelily. **1672** EACHARD *Hobbes' State Nat.* 18 It sounds, I must confess, somewhat statelily. **1796** *Mod. Gulliver* 16 Walking in statelily himself, he beckoned me to follow. **1859** TENNYSON *Marr. Geraint* 175 She, Sweetly and statelily, and with all grace Of womanhood and queenhood, answer'd him. **1903** KIPLING in *Windsor Mag.* Sept. 370/1 The Head Chief bowed solemnly and statelily before Taffy.

stateliness (ˈsteɪtlɪnɪs). [f. STATELY *a.* + -NESS.]

†**1.** Haughtiness, arrogance. *Obs.*

1509 BARCLAY *Shyp of Folys* 90 Suche as foloweth shamefull wantonnes, Ungoodly luste, and statelynes of mynde. **1513** BRADSHAW *St. Werburge* I. 1860 Pryde, statelenes, and sensualyte Were not in her founde. **1530** PALSGR. 275/2 Statelynesse, *arrogance, bourgoisie.* **1582** BENTLEY *Mon. Matrones* 96 Thou hast meekened me,..to put from me all manner of presumption, and statelinesse of hart. **1644** MILTON *Areop.* (Arb.) 33 Did they but know how much better I find ye esteem it to imitate the old and elegant humanity of Greece, then the barbarick pride of a Hunnish and Norwegian stateliness.

2. Lofty dignity of manner or behaviour. Sometimes with unfavourable notion: Repellent dignity, stiffness or formality of manners.

a **1586** SIDNEY *Arcadia* II. ii. (Sommer) 103 b, It pleased the Princesse (in whom indeede statelines shines through courtesie) to let fall some gratious looke vpon me. **1654** COKAINE *Dianea* I. 19 Her entreaties were delivered with such an inbred statelinesse, that they seemed rather commands then prayers. *a* **1700** EVELYN *Diary* 14 Jan. 1682, He told him likewise of his stateliness and difficulty of accesse. **1740** RICHARDSON *Pamela* II. 310 They rallied him on the Stateliness of his Temper. **1828** D'ISRAELI *Chas. I*, III. ii. 17 There was a cold reserve in his speech, and a stateliness in his habits. **1879** MORLEY *Burke* i. 9 A certain inborn stateliness of nature, which made him unwilling to waste thoughts on the less dignified parts of life.

†**3.** Loftiness of position or rank. Also, as a title of dignity. *Obs.*

1576 FLEMING *Panopl. Epist.* 332 For some haue beene aduaunced to degrees of statelynesse, through the noblenesse of their byrth. **1638** W. LISLE *Heliodorus* VII. 112 And when he came her Statelinesse [the Princess] before, They will'd him, yet he would not her adore.

4. Nobleness of proportion or design; grandeur, magnificence.

1577–87 HOLINSHED *Chron.* III. 431/1 The said dukes house of the Sauoie, to the which in beautie and statelinesse of building..there was not any other in the realme comparable. **1615** G. SANDYS *Trav.* I. 31 Mosaike painting ..composed of little square pieces of marble; gilded and coloured..: which set together, as if imbossed, present an vnexpressible statelinesse. **1748** *Anson's Voy.* III. ii. 313 The stateliness, freshness, and fragrance of its woods. **1869** FREEMAN *Norm. Conq.* (1876) III. xii. 236 Its walls indeed crown..a height great enough to give the minster yet further stateliness in the view from the lower ground. **1914** *Blackw. Mag.* Feb. 243/2 A monument of amazing stateliness.

5. Imposing dignity of personal aspect or carriage.

a **1667** COWLEY *Ess.*, *Of Greatness* (1906) 429 Like a Daughter of great Jupiter for the stateliness and largeness of her person. **1784** COWPER *Task* v. 76 The cock foregoes His wonted strut; and..seems to resent His alter'd gait and stateliness retrench'd. **1833** TENNYSON *Eleänore* iv, How many measured words adore The full-flowing harmony Of thy swan-like stateliness Eleänore? **1885** *Manch. Exam.* 20 Mar. 8/6 His bearing had always a kind of stateliness, utterly free from pomp or pretence.

6. Loftiness of diction, dignity of style in speech or writing.

1591 HARINGTON *Orl. Fur.* Pref. ¶iij b, Heroicall Poesie, that with her sweet statelinesse doth erect the mind. **1649** F. ROBERTS *Clavis Bibl.* 404 The Princely statelinesse of his stile hath inclined some to believe that he [Isaiah] was of the blood-Royal. **1789** BELSHAM *Ess.* I. xii. 231 The Spenserian stanza must be allowed to exhibit a certain air of stateliness. **1884** R. W. CHURCH *Bacon* ix. 222 The stateliness and dignity of the Latin corresponded to the proud claims which he made for his conception of the knowledge which was to be.

stately ('steɪtlɪ), *a.* and *adv.* Forms: 4–8 **statly**, 5–7 **statelie**, 5–6 **-lye**, 5–7 *Sc.* **staitly**, 5– **stately**. [f. STATE *sb.* + -LY. Cf. the equivalent ESTATELY *a.* and *adv.* in 14–15th c.

The G. *staatlich* of identical formation has now in the literary language only the sense 'pertaining to a (political) state or to the State'. In dialects, however, and in early mod. German, it has the meanings of the Eng. word, which in standard German have been transferred to *stattlich*, f. *statt* = STEAD *sb.* Cf. Du. *statelijk*, Sw. *ståtlig*, stately, magnificent.]

A. *adj.*

1. a. Of personal appearance or demeanour, and of persons with reference to these. In early use, Befitting or indicating high estate, princely, noble, majestic. In later use, Imposingly dignified. (Occasionally said of animals: cf. 4 b.)

c **1385** CHAUCER *L.G.W.* 1372 Thou rote of false lovers, duk Iasoun!.. Thow madist thyn recleymyng & thyn luris To ladyis of thyn statly aparaunce. *c* **1430** LYDG. *Min. Poems* (Percy Soc.) 11 Sapience, To-fore whos face, most statly and rialle, Were the vij. science callyd libereallе. *Ibid.* 213 This stately fowle most imperial,.. Callid in Scripture the fowle celestial. **1724** RAMSAY *Vision* xi, He, with.. staitly air, did me rebuke. **1877** MISS YONGE *Cameos* Ser. III. xi. 94 She was a good, sensible, and learned woman, but the stateliest of dames.

absol. **1868** TENNYSON *Lucretius* 172 That council-hall Where sit the best and stateliest of the land.

b. Of movement, a person or animal in movement: Dignified, deliberate.

1593 SHAKS. *Rich. II*, v. ii. 10 Bullingbrooke, Mounted vpon a hot and fierie Steed,.. With slow, but stately pace, kept on his course. **1826** DISRAELI *Viv. Grey* VI. ii, A whole flock of stately geese issued in solemn pomp from another gate.

2. Of persons, their dispositions or actions.

†**a.** Haughty, domineering, arrogant. *Obs.*

c **1440** *Alphabet of Tales* lxxx. 62 And sho was a passand fayr mayden emang all oþer, & with þat sho was passand statelie & prowde, & thoght skorn be evur ilk common man. *Ibid.* dcxlii. 428 He was neuer prowde nor statelye. *c* **1450** in Aungier *Syon* (1840) 361 For often tymes statly and unreligious porte causeth murmur and grudgynge to other. **1544** BETHAM *Precepts War* I. clxx. H vij b, The multitude neuer iustly ne egally can beare rule and offyce thorough theyr arrogaunte, stubburne, and stately conditions. **1577** HANMER *Anc. Eccl. Hist.* (1619) 180 He presumed to waxe stately against his fellow Emperours. **1599** HAYWARD *1st Pt. Life & Reign Hen. IV* 4 Neither did the continuance of his Raigne bring him to a proude port and stately esteeming of himselfe, but in his latter yeares he remained so gentle and faire in cariage, that [etc.]. **1607** TOPSELL *Four-f. Beasts* 658 Such is the stately mind of this little Beast, that while her limbes and strength lasteth, she tarrieth & saueth her self in the tops of tal trees.

b. In milder sense: Showing a sense of superiority; repellently dignified; not affable or approachable. In recent use a euphemistic application of sense 1.

a **1625** FLETCHER *Wit without M.* II. ii, This widow is the strangest thing, the stateliest, and stands so much upon her excellencies. **1688** PENTON *Guardian's Instr.* 22 When I say I would have my eldest son a little stately: I do not mean any degree of that gross imperious Pride which God and Man hates. **1712** SWIFT *Let. to D'hess of Ormond* 20 Dec., [Your grace's picture] will set me labouring upon majestic, sublime ideas..; and will make those who come to visit me think I am grown on the sudden wonderful stately and reserved. **1841** JAMES *Brigand* vii, When we did meet, he was distant and stately in his manner. **1848** THACKERAY *Van. Fair* xlix, Their ladyships made three stately curtsies.

absol. **1707** *Refl. Ridicule* 88 There are Women who think to act the Stately by affronting every body.

3. a. Of things: Appertaining to or befitting a person of high estate; magnificent, splendid.

c **1430** LYDG. *Min. Poems* (Percy Soc.) 3 In statly wise whan thei were mett, Eche oone welle horsed, made no delay, But with her mayer rood forthe in her way. **1433** —— *S. Edmund* I. 134 The statly royal date Whan I first gan on this translacioun. **1447** BOKENAM *Saints, Magd.* 870 Thou lyist here in a statly paleys, Bewrappyd in clothys of sylk & gold. **1555** *Act 2 & 3 Phil. & Mar.* c. 20 § 1 The Duchie of Lancastree, being one of the most famous Princeliest & Stateliest peeces of our said Soveraigne Ladie the Quenes auncyent Enheritance. **1583** STUBBES *Anat. Abus.* (1585) 65 Golde silke or silver lace of stately price. **1639** FULLER *Holy War* IV. xii. 188 [Lewis the ninth] arrived in Cyprus; where Alexius Lusignan King of the Island entertained him according to the stateliest hospitality. **1756** NUGENT *Gr. Tour, Germany* II. 256 In winter they have races in stately sledges, besides masquerading and splendid balls. **1842** TENNYSON *Ld. of Burleigh* 43 A gateway she discerns With armorial bearings stately.

b. of ceremonies, etc.

1593 SHAKS. *3 Hen. VI*, v. vii. 43 That we spend the time With stately Triumphes, mirthfull Comicke shewes. **1648** GAGE *West Ind.* 16 The Dominicans.. invited all the Jesuites.. to a stately dinner both of Fish and Flesh. **1891** E. PEACOCK *N. Brendon* I. 53 The most stately ritual that can be devised. **1899** A. C. BENSON *Life E. W. Benson* I. xvii. 635 The circumstances of his life placed him in stately spheres of activity. **1911** W. W. FOWLER *Relig. Exp. Rom. People* ix. 218 Meaningless as they were, the stately processions remained.

4. Imposing or majestic in size and proportions.

a. of inanimate things, a building, town, tree, mountain, etc. Also of a ship, now usually with some reference to its motion: see 1 b. *stately home*: originally in allusion to quot. 1827; now a fixed phrase designating a great country-house; also *attrib.* and *Comb.*

c **1450** in Kingsford *Chron. London* (1905) 142 And many moo good tovnys and stately villagis. **1586** A. DAY *Eng. Secretary* I. (1625) 23 Woods high and decked with Stately trees. **1591** SHAKS. *1 Hen. VI*, I. vi. 21 A statelyer Pyramis to her Ile reare, Then Rhodophes or Memphis euer was. **1613–16** W. BROWNE *Brit. Past.* I. i. 10 Or the Nymph of Kent, That statelyest Ships to sea hath euer sent. **1632** LITHGOW *Trav.* I. 25 This Prouince is mainely watered through the middle with stately Po. **1667** MILTON *P.L.* IV. 142 And as the ranks ascend Shade above shade, a woodie Theatre Of stateliest view. **1700** R. CROMWELL in *Eng. Hist. Rev.* (1898) XIII. 116 A statly chine, accompaned with a fatt Turkey. **1784** JOHNSON in *Boswell* (1904) II. 569 When somebody talked of being imposed on in the purchase of tea and sugar, and such articles: 'That will not be the case', said he, 'if you go to a stately shop, as I always do.' **1827** F. HEMANS in *Blackw. Mag.* Apr. 392 The stately Homes of England, How beautiful they stand! **1831** J. BROWN *Let.* 26 Oct. (1912) 26 There is certainly something unapproachable in the 'stately homes of England'. **1842** TENNYSON *Locksley Hall* 37 Many an evening by the waters did we watch the stately ships. **1848** A. BRONTË *Tenant of Wildfell Hall* III. xv. 311, I.. looked back, for one last view of her stately home. **1874** JEWITT & HALL (*title*) The stately homes of England.. illustrated with 210 engravings on wood. **1914** *Blackw. Mag.* Sept. 301/1 From the walls of stately cathedrals and monuments, they being dead may yet speak. **1920** D. H. LAWRENCE *Touch & Go* III. i. 68 This is what happens to the stately homes of England—they buzz with inky clerks, or their equivalent. **1934** WODEHOUSE *Right Ho, Jeeves* xiv. 167 Some stately-home owners of the name of Stretchley-Budd, hanging out in a joint called Kingham Manor. **1938** N. COWARD *Operette* I. vii. 54 The Stately Homes of England How beautiful they stand, To prove the upper classes Have still the upper hand. **1945** B. GOOLDEN *Ichabod* ix. 50 A group of persons restricted to the Services, the stately homes of England, and a line running roughly from Stanhope Gate to Eaton Square. **1959** DUKE OF BEDFORD *Silver-Plated Spoon* xi. 215 We had jumped straight into the front rank of the stately homes business. **1977** B. PYM *Quartet in Autumn* v. 45 There would be visits to a safari park and to the stately homes that offered the best attractions.

b. of a person or animal. (Cf. 1 b.)

1653 WALTON *Angler* I. ix, The Carp is the Queen of Rivers: a stately, a good, and a very subtle Fish. **1687** A. LOVELL tr. *Thevenot's Trav.* I. 148 After them, came.. at length the Basha himself, mounted on a stately Horse. **1815** BYRON *Hebr. Mel., Wild Gazelle* ii, The Cedars wave on Lebanon, But Judah's statelier maids are gone! **1825** SCOTT *Betrothed* xiii, Fourscore years had not quenched the brightness of her eyes, or bent an inch of her stately height. **1849** W. E. AYTOUN *Lays Scott. Cavaliers* 113 When they scent the stately deer. **1851** TENNYSON *Sonn. Macready*, Garrick and statelier Kemble, and the rest Who made a nation purer through their art. **1863** GEO. ELIOT *Romola* I. xix, She looked up with one of her happy, loving smiles at the stately old man. **1907** *Verney Mem.* II. 488 A tall, dignified woman.. and the mode in which her black hair towered above her forehead made her statelier still.

c. Of sound: Impressive, majestic.

1655 STANLEY *Hist. Philos.* III. (1687) 102/2 Good Heavens, what voice is this, how strange and stately? *a* **1661** FULLER *Worthies, Cornw.* (1662) 196 The hall (rising above the rest) yieldeth a stately sound as one entereth it. **1850** KINGSLEY *Misc.* (1860) I. 228 The stately calmness of the wood-dove's note.

5. a. Of speech or writing or its style; hence of a speaker or writer: Elevated in thought or expression, dignified, majestic.

1579 LODGE *Def. Poetry* 23 Yf you had wanted your Mysteries of nature, & your stately storyes, your booke would haue scarce bene fedde wyth matter. **1583** MELBANCKE *Philotimus* E iij, He might tricke his speech with a few superficiall colours, but all his statly style were not woorth a strawe. **1685** DRYDEN *Sylvæ* Pref. A 6, Virgil.. maintains Majesty in the midst of plainess;.. and is stately without ambition, which is the vice of Lucan. **1802** WORDSW. *Resolution & Indep.* 96 Choice word and measured phrase, above the reach Of ordinary men; a stately speech. **1849** MACAULAY *Hist. Eng.* iii. I. 404 That deficiency he did his best to conceal.. by stately declamation.

absol. **1809** MALKIN *Gil Blas* XI. v. (Rtldg.) 404 He preferred the stately, or rather the grotesque in writing.

b. of a subject.

1602 WARNER *Alb. Eng.* x. lx. 266 Of which [Fleets and their commerce] shall be digested here the Progresse,.. Though stately be the Subiect, and to slender be our Arte. **1644** MILTON *Educ.* 5 Then will the choise Histories,.. and Attic tragedies of statliest, and most regal argument.. offer themselves.

†**6.** Powerful, effectual. *Obs.*

With quot. 1662 cf. G. *stattlich*, in early mod.G. said of medicines (Grimm s.v., II. 1. *c*).

1587 TURBERV. *Trag. Tales* 142 b, So statelie is the stroke of Cupids bow. **1662** R. MATHEW *Unl. Alch.* 78 Make a Lixivium or stronge lye of *Chalkes vive*, or White-lime for this is most stately, and operates very potently. *Ibid.* 177 One of the most potent, stateliest Medicines that I think is attainable in the World.

†**7.** Pertaining to the state or body politic. (*nonce-use.*) *Obs.*

1641 MILTON *Reform.* 73 What a perversenesse would it be in us of all others to retain forcibly a kind of imperious, and stately Election in our Church?

8. *Comb.*

a **1618** SYLVESTER *Woodman's Bear* xli, Shee was Strait proportion'd, stately-pased. **1777** T. WARTON *Poems* 79 Whate'er adorns the stately-storied hall.

B. *adv.* In a stately manner. Now *rare.*

†**1.** With splendid ceremonial or surroundings; in state. *Obs.*

c **1407** LYDG. *Reson & Sens.* 2662 Where that love, as I ha tolde, Stately holdeth his housholde With his meyne in gladnesse. **1568** GRAFTON *Chron.* II. 378 The King sitting in a Pauilion stately apparelled. **1648** GAGE *West Ind.* 84 Spaniards who thought nothing too good for us, and would entertain us stately.

†**2.** In a domineering or arrogant manner. *Obs.*

1449 *Paston Lett.* (1900) Suppl. 24 And ther to Mariot seyd stately, that myght not be performed. **1538** ELYOT *Dict.*, *Imperiose*, stately, rigorously. **1539** BP. TONSTALL *Serm. Palme Sundaye* (1823) 33 Whyles a noble manne.. dyd prostrate hym selfe.. and kyssed his shoo, whyche he stately suffered to be doone, as of duetie.

†**3.** In a noble or dignified form or style; so as to have a stately appearance. *Obs.*

1582 STANYHURST *Æneis* I. (Arb.) 17 Martyred in battayls, ere towne could statelye be buylded, Or Gods theare setled. **1625** BACON *Ess., Gardens* (Arb.) 555 When Ages grow to Ciuility and Elegancie, Men come to build Stately, sooner then to Garden Finely. **1633** BP. HALL *Hard Texts, Ps.* cxxii. 3 Ierusalem is stately built. **1640** tr. *Verdere's Rom. of Rom.* III. 50 He met with a house very stately built.

4. With stately or dignified bearing, movement, or expression.

1584 LYLY *Campaspe* III. iv, How stately she passeth bye, yet how soberly! **1602** SHAKS. *Ham.* I. ii. 202 A figure.. Appeares before them, and with sollemne march Goes slow and stately. **1794** MRS. RADCLIFFE *Myst. Udolpho* xxv, A tall signor.. who walks so stately. **1821** SCOTT *Kenilw.* xvi, Both Earls moved slowly and stately towards the entrance. **1858** G. MACDONALD *Phantastes* iii, Tiny, gaily decorated forms, .. moving stately on.

†**5.** In a fitting manner, properly. *Obs.*

c **1440** *York Myst.* xxvi. 82 We! þare sir, he skelpte oute of score [of money-changers in the Temple] þat stately stode selland þer store. **1513** *Bk. Keruynge* in *Babees Bk.* (1868) 269 And yf ye wyll wrappe your soueraynes brede stately, ye muste square and proporcyon your brede.

6. *Comb.*

1591 SYLVESTER *Du Bartas* I. v. 891 The fair Peacock.. Proud, portly-strouting, stalking, stately-grave. **1592** KYD *Sp. Trag.* IV. i. 158 But to present a Kingly troupe withall, Giue me a stately written Tragedie. **1648** J. BEAUMONT *Psyche* VI. lxxxix, The Glass.. weep'd to see its stately-beautious face Dissolv'd by one short Touch. **1728** THOMPSON *Spring* 777 The stately-sailing swan.

statement ('steɪtmənt). [f. STATE *v.* + -MENT]

1. a. The action or an act of stating, alleging, or enunciating; the manner in which something is stated.

1789 *Polit. Geog.; Introd. Statist. Tables Europe* 7 Not from an imaginary picture,.. but exhibited in the sober garb of exact statement, backed with the irresistible force of arithmetical demonstration. **1841** MACAULAY *Ess., Ld. Holland* (1897) 600 In statement, the late Lord Holland was not successful; his chief excellence lay in reply. **1885** PEARSON in *Law Rep. 29 Chanc. Div.* 558, I think Mr. Farwell's statement of the law is correct. *Mod.* The book is a model of cautious and accurate statement.

b. *Mus.* A presentation of a subject or theme in a composition.

1883 *Grove's Dict. Mus.* III. 568/2 Occasionally the middle repeats [of the theme] are variations, and the first and last statements simple and identical. **1887** *Daily News* 22 Nov. 3/2 The Overture.. is very brief, and bears few signs of maturity, although in the first statement of the second subject.. occur some charming examples of [etc.].

2. a. Something that is stated; an allegation, declaration. Also *transf.* and *fig.*

1775 ASH *Suppl.*, *Statement*, the thing stated. **1787** MALONE *Diss. Three Pts. K. Hen. VI*, 37 This statement was taken from the old quarto play; and, from carelessness, was adopted by Shakspeare without any material alteration. **1796** JANE AUSTEN *Pride & Prej.* xxxvi. (1906) 176 She put down the letter, weighed every circumstance..—deliberated on the probability of each statement—but with little success. **1833** CRUSE *Eusebius* I. vii. 32 Neither of the gospels has made a false statement. **1838** *Civ. Engin. & Arch. Jrnl.* I. 239/1 There is much useful matter.. to be culled from the statements of both parties. **1875** JOWETT *Plato* (ed. 2) IV. 258 The moderns have certainly no reason to acquiesce in the statement, that truth is appearance only. **1905** J. B. BURY *Life St. Patrick* App. 279 The statement that he was ordained in his twenty-fifth year seems to stand alone. **1953** W. M. IVINS *Prints & Visual Communication* i. 3 Since the invention of writing there has been no more important invention than that of the exactly repeatable pictorial statement. **1958** *Listener* 18 Sept. 437/3 Apart from some inherent nastiness in the story there is a fundamental weakness in its theatrical statement. **1970** *New Yorker* 26 Sept. 29/3 We had in mind thirty or forty people making a quiet statement by riding together. **1977** C. MCFADDEN *Serial* (1978) xl. 86/2, I wish you'd stop shaving your goddamn legs. You might not know it, but you're making a *statement.*

b. *Computers.* An expression in a program language that specifies some operation or task, corresponding to one or more instructions according to the context and the level of the language.

1957 *Proc. Western Joint Computer Conf.* 188/2 He.. programmed the job in four hours, using 47 FORTRAN statements. **1957** D. D. MCCRACKEN *Digital Computer Programming* xviii. 215 The automatic coding systems directed toward scientific calculations accept problem statements in a form similar to ordinary mathematical language. **1959** M. H. WRUBEL *Primer of Programming for Digital Computers* vi. 126 There are statements for performing arithmetic; statements for branching and looping; and input and output statements. **1967** W. F. SHARPE *Introd. Computer Programming using BASIC Lang.* i. 6 Every statement must begin with a legal command (after the line number, if any). **1973** J. K. HUGHES *PL/I Programming* i. 8 The statement to input the data..should be specified. This could be accomplished with the statement GET LIST (A, B, C, D, E); Notice how all PL/I statements are ended with a semicolon. **1981** MONDS & MCLAUGHLIN *Introd. Mini & Micro Computers* vii. 99/1 An assembler translates a machine oriented language, ie, a language where, in general, one statement gives rise to one machine instruction... A compiler translates a problem-oriented language..into machine code. Each statement in the language usually gives rise to more than one, and sometimes many, machine instructions.

3. a. A written or oral communication setting forth facts, arguments, demands, or the like.

1787 MALONE *Diss. Three Pts. K. Hen. VI*, 15 A correct statement of the issue of King Edward the Third..is given in *The first part of K. Henry VI*. **1863** H. COX *Instit.* III. vii. 696 His annual statement to the House of Commons of the financial condition of the Kingdom. **1891** S. C. SCRIVENER *Our Fields & Cities* 43 Some of the farmers avoid paying taxes; they make a 'statement' instead. **1898** W. J. GREENWOOD *Commerc. Corresp.* (ed. 2) 155, I have decided to call a meeting of my creditors..when I shall submit to them a statement of my affairs. **1912** *Times* 19 Dec. 2/5 The plaintiff alleged by his statement of claim that [etc.].

b. *Comm.* (More fully ***statement of account***): a document setting out the items of debit and credit between two parties.

1885 W. WHITMAN *Daybks. & Notebks.* (1978) II. 375 Half-annual 'Statement' from D Mckay $20.71 'ts for 6 mo's preceding Dec 1, '85. **1897** F. HOOPER & J. GRAHAM *Mod. Business Methods* 38 The next step is to send in what is called a Statement. This, as its name implies, is a short statement of account between the parties. **1910** FIELDHOUSE *Business Methods* 115 It is customary for the Creditor..to send to the Debtor..a statement, which is an account, rendered at certain periods..giving dates and amounts only (no details) of each delivery of goods since the last Statement or balancing.

c. statement of affairs *Accounting*, a list of assets and liabilities not expressed as a formal balance sheet.

1895 *Reports Tax Cases* (1907) III. 456 Every man and every company having foreign or colonial investments, of course, knows of the interest arising from them, takes note of it and enters it in any statement of affairs which may require to be made up. **1928** R. G. WILLIAMS *Elem. Bk.-Keeping* xiv. 240 The preparation of the statement of affairs may possibly depend upon information which is not supplied by the books of account, and often undue reliance must be placed upon the trader's memory. **1978** J. KELLOCK *Elem. Accounting* xi. 184 The term 'statement of affairs' is one commonly used in the subject of incomplete records and may be defined as a list of assets and liabilities. **1981** *Daily Tel.* 19 Dec. 17/6 In the statement of affairs presented at the creditors' meeting £31,000 of client account balances appeared as part of the net assets of the company. **1983** *Ibid.* 12 Mar. 19/1 Not only was there a complete absence of a statement of affairs—the receiver said that he had been unable to lay his hands on any of the company's books—but it was apparent from the scant information he was able to provide that the liabilities are far in excess of known assets.

4. *Comm.* In certain branches of industry, a document periodically issued, setting forth the prices to be paid to workmen for various kinds of piece-work. Also *attrib.* as ***statement price***, ***wages***.

1889 D. F. SCHLOSS in *Charity Org. Rev.* Jan. 7 These workmen receive a rate of wages fixed by the Union and embodied in a 'statement'. **1897** *Daily News* 12 Apr. 2/5 In several cases manufacturers have offered..an increase of ten per cent. above statement wages. **1900** C. RUSSELL & H. S. LEWIS *Jew in Lond.* 79 [In the boot and shoe trade] the better class of work is still done by Englishmen under 'statement' prices.

5. Special Comb. (in sense 2): **statement-form** *Logic* = *propositional function* s.v. PROPOSITIONAL *a.* b.

1942 J. FINDLAY in *Mind* LI. 261 A statement-form is an expression containing variables such as X, Y, etc., which gives rise to statements when expressions with a constant meaning are substituted for those variables. Thus 'x is long' is a statement-form. **1950** M. G. WHITE in M. Farber *Philosophic Thought in France & U.S.* 711 How shall we define or make clear the meaning of the statement-form '*x* is a history of *y*'? **1961** E. NAGEL *Structure of Sci.* v. 95 Instead of being statement-forms the postulates of the theory appear to be statements.

statemental (steɪt'mɛntəl), *a.* [f. STATEMENT + -AL.] That makes, consists of, or is characterized by a statement or statements.

1939 C. W. MORRIS in *Kenyon Rev.* I. 413 Scientific discourse is, in summary, statemental or predictive in character. **1955** J. L. AUSTIN *How to do Things with Words* (1962) vi. 72 The primary or primitive use of sentences must be..statemental or constative. **1976** [see SENTENTIAL *a.* 2 b].

state-monger, states-monger. Now *rare* or *arch.* [See MONGER *sb.*[1]] A contemptuous designation for: A projector of political constitutions; a pretender to political science.

1616 J. LANE *Contn. Sqr.'s T.* IV. 375 Some mockd at somme, for state-mongers absurd, till scarce one of them all had one wise word. **1622** LD. KEEPER WILLIAMS *Let.* 17 Sept., in *Cabala* (1654) 111, I would therefore see the most subtile State-monger in the world chalk out a way for his Majestie to mediate for Grace, and favour for the Protestants. **1678** BUTLER *Hud.* III. ii. 999 This said; the impatient States-monger Could now contain himself no longer. **1682** D'URFEY *Butler's Ghost* 125 He finding that the warpt Statemonger Would preach his Canting Treason longer, Resolv'd [etc.]. **1816** SOUTHEY *Ess.* (1832) I. 347 The old balsam of memory should be prescribed for such state-mongers. [**1844** DISRAELI *Coningsby* II. i, The Arch-Mediocrity..though not a statesman, might be classed among those whom the Lord Keeper Williams used to call 'statemongers'.] **1891** F. W. BAIN *Antichrist* I. 53 The Revolutionary statesmongers were far too much in a hurry. **1965** C. CAMPOS *View of France* x. 241 Perhaps..France is the source of light, as a certain tall statemonger would have it. Or perhaps Arnold was right after all and the English are a more earnest nation.

‖**stater**[1] ('steɪtə(r)). *Antiq.* [a. L. *stater*, a. Gr. στατήρ, f. στα-, ἱστάναι (see STAND *v.*) in the sense 'to weigh'.]

1. An ancient weight.

According to Isidore *Etym.* XVI. xxv. it was half an ounce. In antiquity it was variously 2, 3, and 4 drachmæ.

1382 WYCLIF *Ezek.* iv. 10 Thi meet..shal be in weiȝt twenti stateris [1611 shekels (lit. from Heb.), LXX. σίκλους, Vulg. *stateres*] that is ten ouncis. **1631** ANCHORAN *Comenius' Gate Tongues* 170 A statere [L. *statera*] is a weauers or clothiers pound to be carried.

2. A name of various ancient coins.

The gold coins so called were the Persian stater or DARIC, the Athenian stater, the Cyzicene stater. The name was also applied to various silver coins; in Roman times chiefly to the TETRADRACHM, as in Matt. xvii. 27.

1382 WYCLIF *Matt.* xvii. 27 His [*sc.* the fish's] mouth openyd, thou shalt fynde stater, that is, a certeyn of moneye. **1483** CAXTON *Golden Leg.* 202/4 He fond the Statere or piece of money in the fisshes mouth. **1646** SIR T. BROWNE *Pseud. Ep.* I. viii. 32 Antoninus, whose apprehensions so honoured his Poems, that..for every verse, hee assigned him a Stater of gold. **1771** M. RAPER *Anc. Money* in *Phil. Trans.* LXI. 480 The silver Stater, or Tetradrachm, is the most common Attic coin now remaining. **1854** J. D. BURNS *Vis. Prophecy* 49 A fish to Peter's hook the Stater brings. **1881** JOWETT *Thucyd.* I. 216 The penalty was fixed at a stater. *Note.* If the gold stater, about 16*s.*; if the silver Athenian stater, about 3*s.* 3*d.*; if the silver Corinthian stater (ten Aeginetan obols), about 2*s.* 2*d.*

stater[2] ('steɪtə(r)). [f. STATE *v.* + -ER[1].] One who states. ***average stater*** = average-adjuster: see AVERAGE *sb.*[2] 4 b.

1702 *3rd Let. to Gentl. in Country* 21 The Stater of the Case..makes me to affirm the Former. **1702** R. CROSFEILD *Affection of People* 6 Those Gentlemen that were then the Publick Staters of Accounts. **1820** LADY GRANVILLE *Let.* 6 Sept., Lett. (1894) I. 179 It is of no use what is stated when people are resolved not to believe the staters. **1884** *Times* 5 Apr. 5 Mr. Smith..for many years carried on business at Glasgow as an average stater.

Stater[3] ('steɪtə(r)). *Irish Hist.* [f. STATE *sb.* + -ER[1].] A member of the Irish Free State army.

1925 S. O'CASEY *Juno & Paycock* III. 111 Ah, why didn't I remember that then he wasn't a Die-hard or a Stater, but only a poor dead son! **1936** 'N. BLAKE' *Thou Shell of Death* xiii. 239 During the Civil War..the Staters and the Republicans had a battle in the garden. **1965** L. FLEMING *Head or Harp* x. 83 The streets themselves were full of 'Staters'.

‖**sta'tera.** *Obs.* Pl. -æ. [L. *statēra*, prob. a. Gr. στατῆρα, accus. of στατήρ STATER[1], in the unrecorded (but etymologically probable) sense of 'balance'. Cf. It. *stadera.*] A steelyard.

1669 BOYLE *Contn. New Exp.* I. 23 The Weight..being taken off, and weighed in a Statera amounted to abovt 28 Pounds. **1793** *Statist. Acc. Scot.* VII. 563 The instruments they have for the purpose of weighing, are a kind of staterae or steelyards. **1822** IMISON *Sci. & Art* I. 35 The Statera, or Roman steel-yard, is a lever of the first kind.

state-room.

1. A state apartment; a room in a palace, great house, hotel, etc., splendidly decorated and furnished, and used only on ceremonial occasions.

1703 *Lond. Gaz.* No. 3943/4 Several Tables were plentifully covered in the State-Room, and in the Guildhall. **1742** YOUNG *Love of Fame* I. 170 When lo! my Lord to some small corner runs, And leaves state-rooms to strangers and to duns. **1853** FELTON *Fam. Lett.* vi. (1865) 40, I have seen but few places yet; but have passed through the state-rooms of the Tuileries. **1886** RUSKIN *Præterita* I. x. 308 A grand military dinner in the state room of the Sussex, at Tunbridge Wells. **1912** *Blackw. Mag.* Oct. 501/2 Prince Arthur..stayed twice in the College, probably in the Founder's state-rooms.

fig. **1817** COLERIDGE *Biog. Lit.* II. 79 *note*, The mechanical system of philosophy..leaves the idea of omnipresence a mere abstract notion in the state room of our reason.

2. A captain's or superior officer's room on board ship. (Cf. *state-cabin*, STATE *sb.* 41.)

1660 PEPYS *Diary* 24 Apr., Very pleasant we were on board the *London* which hath a state-room much bigger than the *Nazeby*, but not so rich. **1694** *Lond. Gaz.* No. 2982/3 The Yacht having lost in this Rencounter but 3 men, who were killed by one great Shot in the State-Room. **1748** SMOLLETT *Rod. Random* xxxv, A cabbin was made for him contiguous to the state-room, where Whiffle slept. **1834** M. SCOTT *Cruise Midge* xvii, The cabin had two state-rooms, as they are called in merchantmen, opening off it. **1836** MARRYAT *Midsh. Easy* xiv, In the captain's state-room they had found fourteen thousand dollars in bags.

3. *U.S.* **a.** A sleeping apartment with one or two berths on a passenger steamer.

1774 J. SCHAW *Jrnl. Lady of Quality* (1921) i. 22 Our Bed chamber which is dignified with the title of State Room, is about five foot wide and six long. **1832** F. TROLLOPE *Domestic Manners of Americans* (ed. 2) I. xvii. 259 They occupied a state-room which Captain Hall had secured for his party. **1837** HT. MARTINEAU *Soc. Amer.* III. 152 On board steam-boats which have not separate state-rooms, there are no means of preserving sufficient cleanliness and health. **1842** DICKENS *Amer. Notes* (1850) 1/1 This state-room had been specially engaged for 'Charles Dickens, Esquire, and Lady'. **1852** MRS. STOWE *Uncle Tom's C.* xv, There she is, sitting now in her state room, surrounded by ..little and big carpet-bags, boxes, baskets. **1873** MEDLEY *Autumn Tour U.S. & Canada* v. 77 On the middle deck [of the steamer] is a splendid saloon,..with most comfortable sleeping cabins on both sides, which, by the way, are always called 'State-rooms'.

b. A private compartment in a railway train.

1853 *Southern Standard* (Charleston, S. Carolina) 31 Aug. 2/5 Messrs. Eaton & Gilbert..have built a beautiful car for the Hudson River Railroad which is divided into state rooms of eight feet square. **1867** W. H. DIXON *New Amer.* II. 291 On the Pennsylvania central line, a lady entered into my state-room. **1872** DE VERE *Americanisms* 359 In the new Palace Cars they pay more, if they engage a state-room. **1884** E. YATES *Recoll.* II. 264, I used to engage a 'state-room', *i.e.* a private compartment, on the train.

4. *Boating.* (See quot.)

1857 P. COLQUHOUN *Comp. Oarsman's Guide* 29 Seats termed 'thwarts', forward, midship, after, and backward thwart; the state-room being the space between the back-board or after, and the midship thwart.

†**'statery.** *Obs. rare*[−1]. In 7 statrie. [See -RY.] Affairs of state.

1606 WARNER *Alb. Eng.* XIV. lxxxii. 345 The Stories Nationall of Picts and Scots, once Kingdomes twaine Within the same... Of Picts, Scots, Welsh be now abridg'd, such Turnes as times did see, Howbeit little Statrie.

States General. *Hist.* Also 6 **general states.** [= F. *états généraux*, Du. *staaten generaal.*] A legislative assembly representing the three estates, viz. clergy, nobles, and commons or burghers of a whole realm, principality, or commonwealth (distinguished from *states provincial*): **a.** in France before the Revolution; **b.** in the Netherlands from the 15th c. to 1796.

1585 J. NORRIS in *Eng. Hist. Rev.* (1903) Apr. 317 The Councell established in this towne for the generall states. *Ibid.* 318, I haue deferred to send..myndinge to morrowe.. to repaire to the states generall in Hollande. **1646** HOWELL *Lewis XIII*, ii. 40 The Assembly of the States General. **1673** TEMPLE *Observ. United Prov.* ii. 75 As the States-General cannot make War or Peace..without the consent of every Province; so cannot the States-Provincial conclude any of those points without the consent of each of the Cities. **1677** DRYDEN *State Innoc.* I. i, Most high and mighty Lords, who better fell From Heav'n, to rise States-General of Hell. **1680** BUTLER *Rem.* (1759) II. 345 A Rabble is a Congregation, or Assembly of the States-General sent from their several and respective Shops, Stalls, and Garrets. **1792** A. YOUNG *Trav. France* 108 They..assert that his letting the king go to the states-general, before their powers were verified,..was madness. **1875** STUBBS *Const. Hist.* II. xv. 265 The States General answer to the parliament of the three estates. **1876** BANCROFT *Hist. U.S.* I. viii. 240 Under the command of the stadholder and the states general.

stateship ('steɪtʃɪp). *Irish Hist.* [f. STATE *sb.* + -SHIP.] = TUATH.

1917 D. FIGGIS *Gaelic State Past & Future* 11 To make more easy the general administration of the country, he [*sc.* Cormac] regrouped the administrative units of the country. Until then the nation had consisted of a number of separate stateships. **1918** —— in *Studies* VII. 259 For the unit of the Irish polity—sometimes spoken of as the Gaelic State—was the Tuath. It was at once a political and an economic unit; a stateship of a state. **1918** A. DE BLACAM *Towards Republic* iii. 24 Along the western counties, where the Irish language still predominates, traces of the life of the stateships linger to this day.

'Stateside, stateside, *a.* and *adv. colloq.* (orig. and chiefly *U.S.*). Also **states side** and hyphened. [f. *State-s* (STATE *sb.* 31 d) + SIDE *sb.*[1] 15 b.] **A.** *adj.* Of, in, or pertaining to the continental United States of America.

1944 KARIG & KELLEY *Battle Report* I. vii. 151 Hearing that several United States news correspondents were in Soerabaja it occurred to him that Stateside newspapers might carry stories of the air attack. **1952** *Chambers's Jrnl.* Aug. 486/1 After the biennial yacht-race to Honolulu is over ..the problem of how to return the yachts to their stateside ports can no longer be postponed. **1960** *Encounter* Feb. 31/2 The kids keep up with the latest Stateside fad. **1967** A. DIMENT *Dolly Dolly Spy* vi. 80 She was tall and slim, as most of those Stateside career women are. **1975** tr. *Melchoir's Sleeper Agent* II. 148 Larry numbly examined his mangled, disfigured hands. 'I..guess I bought myself a Stateside ticket.' **1979** *Sci. Amer.* Feb. 27/2 Agent Orange and its stateside analogues, much used defoliants for weeds and forest cover.

B. *adv.* Towards or in the continental United States of America.

1945 *Sun* (Baltimore) 12 Mar. 9-0/6 'Stateside' is a mighty popular word out here [*sc.* in Guam] because a service man going 'stateside' is going home. **1950** 'D. DIVINE' *King of Fassarai* xvi. 137 You're just fresh from States-side. You'll see what I mean when you've been on the island for a week. **1963** L. DEIGHTON *Horse under Water* xliv. 176 Fernie fixed the consignment to a ship heading stateside. I notified my contacts in New York. **1966** E. MCGIRR *Funeral was in Spain* 74 I'm going back states side in a few days. **1969** *Oz* Apr. 27/2 This guy knew some of the Angels State-side, or at least he thinks he knows. **1976** M. MACHLIN *Pipeline* xxxix. 426 I'm willing to cash in my chips, drag up stateside, and get going on something else.

statesman[1] ('steɪtsmən). [f. *state's* genitive of STATE *sb.* + MAN *sb.*, after F. *homme d'état.* Cf. G. *staatsmann*, Du. *staatsman*, Sw. *statsman*, Da. *statsmand.* In sense 2, a separate formation on STATE *sb.* 34.]

1. a. One who takes a leading part in the affairs of a state or body politic; esp. one who is skilled in the management of public affairs. ***elder statesman***: see ELDER *a.* 1 c.

1592 *No-body & Someb.* A 3 b, Your words are dangerous, good honest subiect, Old reuerent states-man, faithful seruitor. **1599** B. JONSON *Ev. Man out of Hum.* II. vi, For that were to affirme, that a man writing of Nero, should meane all Emperours: or speaking of Machiauel, comprehend all States-men. **1600** W. WATSON *Decacordon* (1602) 222 A gentlewoman.. saide to a secular priest.. if you once become statesmen, and haue dealings with the Lords of the Counsell.. then I haue done with you. **1638** *Diary of Ld. Warriston* (S.H.S.) 295 Thou prayed earnestly for the Lords direction.. about.. the hol busines to be trusted to the staits-men. *a* **1661** FULLER *Worthies, Gen.* vi. (1662) 16 The word Statesmen is of great Latitude, sometimes signifying such who are able to manage Offices of State, though never actually called thereunto. **1681** DRYDEN *Abs. & Achit.* I. 550 He.. in the course of one revolving Moon, Was Chymist, Fidler, States-man, and Buffoon. *c* **1730** RAMSAY *Some of the Contents* iv, Lethington the statisman courts the Nine. **1774** GOLDSM. *Retal* 38 Too nice for a statesman, too proud for a wit. **1839** LYTTON *Richelieu* I. ii. 213 Where the lion's skin fell short, he eked it Out with the fox's! A great states-man, Joseph, That same Lysander. **1891** *Times* 9 Dec. 5 [Lord Dufferin's] wide and varied training had made him not a politician but a statesman able to take Imperial views. **1912** J. H. ROSE in *Eng. Hist. Rev.* Oct. 702 The optimism which was the glory of Pitt as a man, but not seldom his weakness as a statesman.

attrib. **1728** SWIFT *Dial. Mad Mullinix & Timothy* 17 An able statesman-bishop. **1852** TENNYSON *Ode Wellington* 25 The statesman-warrior, moderate, resolute. **1906** E. G. SANDFORD *Mem. Abp. Temple* I. 260 He is also the greatest of the statesmen-bishops of Exeter.

b. *humorously.*

1718 *Freethinker* No. 8 (1733) I. 31 Numbers, who were present at his Tryal and Execution (not excepting our News-Writers and Garret-Statesmen) have not been able to agree about him. **1770** GOLDSM. *Des. Vill.* 223 Where village statesmen talked with looks profound, And news much older than their ale went round.

2. *dial.* (See quots.) Cf. ESTATESMAN.

A doubtful instance of this sense, much earlier than our quots., is found in a letter dated Oxford 16 July 1695 from James Fleming to his brother Robert Fleming ('att Rydall'), which begins 'Quondam Staits Man', and concludes 'I am Your affectionate Statets Man'.

1787 W. H. MARSHALL *Norfolk* II. 389 *Statesmen.* Yeomen; small owners. **1794** A. PRINGLE *Agric. Westmorland* 30 The great number of small land-holders, or statesmen above-mentioned.. doing the work upon their own estates, with their own hands and those of their families. **1794** T. BROWN *Agric. Derby* 14 The smaller landowners, provincially statesmen. **1813** MARY LEADBEATER *Ann. Ballitore* (1862) 339 A statesman, which means in Cumberland phrase one who owns the fee-simple of his land, but works on it himself. *a* **1825** FORBY *Voc. E. Anglia, Statesman*, the proprietor of an estate. **1827** *Sporting Mag.* XXI. 27 What in this part of the world [Durham] is called a Statesman—Anglicè, a Yeoman. **1866** BROGDEN *Prov. Lincs.* **1890** *Leeds Mercury* 21 Feb., At Westmoreland Assizes.. yesterday.. John Metcalfe, the son of a farmer and 'statesman' residing at Longmarton, was charged with [etc.].

† **'statesman**[2]. *Obs.* [f. *States* (see STATE *sb.* 23) + -MAN.] A subject of the States of Holland.

1665 MANLEY *Grotius's Low C. Warres* 679 The Enemies Horse.. violently falling into the Flank of the Statesmen, made a great slaughter.

'statesmancraft. *rare*⁻¹. [See CRAFT *sb.*] The art of statesmanship.

a **1894** SIR A. H. LAYARD *Autobiogr.* (1903) II. iv. 93 He had qualities fitting him for practical statesmancraft.

'statesmanlike, *a.* [f. STATESMAN[1] + -LIKE.] Having the qualities characteristic of a statesman; befitting or worthy of a statesman.

1801 W. TAYLOR in *Monthly Mag.* XII. 588 The admirable statesmanlike pamphlet of the Earl of Liverpool. **1838** DICKENS *Nich. Nick.* xvi, A statesmanlike habit of keeping his feelings under control. **1855** MACAULAY *Hist. Eng.* xi. III. 31 The orator who took the most statesmanlike view of the subject was old Maynard. **1885** *Public Opin.* 9 Jan. 34/2 Mr. Chamberlain.. spoke with statesmanlike prudence and emphasis.

'statesmanly, *a.* [f. STATESMAN[1] + -LY[1].] Pertaining to or characteristic of a statesman; befitting a statesman.

1845 R. W. HAMILTON *Pop. Educ.* v. (ed. 2) 95 There are patriots, statesmanly and philosophic, who would not for a moment touch that right. **1848** HARE *Guesses* Ser. II. 215 This is one of the main elements of the historical genius, as it is of the statesmanly. **1898** B. GREGORY *Side Lights* 497 A sagacious and statesmanly stroke.

'statesmanship. [-SHIP.] The activity or skill of a statesman; skilful management of public affairs.

1764 CHURCHILL *Candidate* 286 We saw Thee nimbly vault.. Into the seat of pow'r, at one bold leap, A perfect Connoisseur in Statemanship. **1849** MACAULAY *Hist. Eng.* ix. II. 417 The whole history of ancient and of modern times records no other such triumph of statesmanship. **1905** LD. E. FITZMAURICE *Life Ld. Granville* I. xiv. 402 British Statesmanship had lost all reliance on the good intentions of the French Emperor. **1906** F. S. OLIVER *Alex. Hamilton* III. vi. 240 His idea of good statesmanship was good stewardship.

stateswoman ('steɪtswʊmən). Pl. **-women** (-wimen). [f. *state's* genitive of STATE *sb.* + WOMAN, after STATESMAN[1].] A woman who takes part in the conduct of public affairs; a woman with statesmanlike ability.

1609 B. JONSON *Epicœne* II. ii, So she may.. be a Stateswoman, know all the Newes, [etc.]. **1715** ADDISON *Freeholder* No. 45 ¶9 Of this kind are the Passions of our Stateswomen, and the Reasonings of our Fox-hunters. **1845** DISRAELI *Sybil* II. xi, Lady Firebrace, a great stateswoman among the tories. **1885** *Society in Lond.* vii. 164 The Queen is a theologian as well as a stateswoman. **1912** E. RUSSELL *Maitland of Lethington* i. 14 The politic Regent.. was stateswoman enough to appreciate these qualities.

transf. **1826** MISS MITFORD *Village* II. 88 She was.. a perfect stateswoman; wound the whole school round her finger; and wanted nothing of art but the art to conceal it.

Hence **'stateswomanship; 'stateswomanlike, -ly** *adjs.*

1850 THACKERAY *Pendennis* II. vi. 62 She.. discharges I don't know what more duties of British stateswomanship. **1959** C. PANKHURST *Unshackled* xii. 205 The signatories of this stateswomanly letter included Viscountess Acheson, the Hon. Mrs. Guy Baring. **1966** *Punch* 30 Mar. 442/1 Mrs. Indira Gandhi.. will 'meet and talk with the Prime Minister', either at the airport or a nearby hotel. With stateswomanlike caution, of course, she'll be rehearsing her formal greeting with a blank after the Mister.

stath(e: see STAITHE.

† **stathe,** *v. Obs. rare*⁻¹. [a. ON. **staðwa* (Icel. *stǫðva*, MSw. *staþva*, Norw. *stødva*, *stada*), f. OTeut. **stad-*: see STAND *v.*] *trans.* To put an end to, stop, still.

c **1200** *Trin. Coll. Hom.* 147 Hem was staðed wop, and turnden here wop to blisse.

† **'stathel,** *v. Obs.* Forms: 1 (ȝe-)staðolian, (ȝe)staðelian, 2 (i-)staðel(e. [OE. (*ȝe*)*staðolian*, f. *staðol* foundation: see STADDLE *sb.*] *trans.* To place on a foundation (*lit.* and *fig.*); to establish.

971 *Blickl. Hom.* 111, þone rihtan ȝeleafan fæste staðelian on urum heortum. *c* **1175** *Lamb. Hom.* 115 Ðes kingges rihtwisnesse arereð his kine setle and his sodfestnesse istaþeleð þes folkes stere. *c* **1200** *Trin. Coll. Hom.* 127 He makede his wuniende in þe wilderne and staðelede his liflode on fode and on shrude swo þat he was bicumelich to his wuninge. *c* **1205** LAY. 6777 þis lond wes istaðeled, & stod i þon ilke fulle ten ȝere. *a* **1300** *E.E. Psalter* viii. 4 (Egerton MS.), The mone and sternes.. þat þou staþeled for to be [*Harl.* þat þou staþheled swa; *Vesp.* þat þou grounded to be swa]. *Ibid.* xx. 12 þai þought redes þat staþel þai ne might.

stathel(e, obs. and dial. forms of STADDLE *sb.*

† **'stathelfast,** *a. Obs.* Forms: 1 staðolfæst, 3 staðelvæst, -fest. [OE. *staðolfæst*, f. *staðol* foundation (see STADDLE *sb.*) + *fæst* FAST *a.*] Firm, steadfast.

c **888** ÆLFRED *Boeth.* xxxv. §3 He is ana staðolfæst wealdend & stiora. *c* **950** *Lindisf. Gosp.* Matt., Pref. (1887) 5/15 Cirica.. ofer staðolfæst stan.. ȝeseted is. *c* **1205** LAY. 9819 þu hauest mucle treow-scipe treowðe staðelæste. *a* **1225** *Leg. Kath.* 71 In þis ilke burh wes wuniende a meiden .. steðelfest wiðinnen, of treowe bileaue.

† **'stathelness.** *Obs.* [f. STATHEL *v.* + -NESS.] Solidity, firmness.

a **1300** *E.E. Psalter* lxviii. 3, I am festened in slime depe esse, And es þare na staþelnesse. *Ibid.* cxxxviii. 15 And þe staþelnes ofe me In netherest ofe erthe to be.

† **'stathely,** *a. Obs.* [OE. **staðolig*, f. *staðol* foundation: see STADDLE *sb.* and -Y.] Steadfast, firm.

c **1205** LAY. 1600 Nes þer nan swa stæðeli þat lengore mihte stonden.

stathmograph ('stæθməgrɑːf, -æ-). *rare*⁻⁰. [f. Gr. σταθμός in the sense 'day's journey, stage' + -GRAPH.] (See quot.)

1884 KNIGHT *Dict. Mech.* Suppl., *Stathmograph*, an instrument invented by Dato, of Cassel, for recording the velocity of railway trains.

stathmokinesis (ˌstæθməʊkɪ'niːsɪs). *Biol.* and *Med.* [ad. F. *stathmocinèse* (A.-P. Dustin 1938, in *Compt. Rend. de l'Assoc. des Anatomistes* XXXIII. 209), f. Gr. σταθμό-ς station, stage + κίνησις motion.] The type of cell division produced by substances such as colchicine, characterized by a halt or long delay at metaphase. Hence **ˌstathmoki'netic** *a.*, (of a drug) that produces stathmokinesis; applied also to the method of measuring rates of cell division by means of such a drug.

1945 *Bot. Rev.* XI. 148 While some cells showed complete pycnosis, normal telophase stages and cytoses occurred. Some cells assumed normal telophase stages and formed giant or polyploid nuclei. Dustin proposed the name of 'stathmocinesis' for this type of indirect division and applied the name of 'stathmocinetic poison' to colchicine. He contended that the arrest of the nuclear division in the metaphase was preceded by a phase of excitation which distinguished this poison from those which merely inhibited division. **1971** *Brit. Jrnl. Cancer* XXV. 692 Since the stathmokinetic method we used cannot provide information about the proportion of cells actually in the proliferative cycle, the proportion or index of arrested metaphases.. can only be used to find the potential doubling time.. of the tumour cell population. **1977** W. A. AHERNE et al. *Introd. Cell Population Kinetics* iii. 18 (*heading*) Metaphase arrest (stathmokinesis). *Ibid.*, The stathmokinetic agents in use today are colchicine, its derivative Colcemid, and the increasingly popular vinca alkaloids vinblastine and vincristine.

static ('stætɪk), *a.* and *sb.* Also 7–8 **statick**, 7 **statique.** [ad. mod.L. *staticus*, a. Gr. στατικός causing to stand, also pertaining to or skilled in weighing, f. στα-, ἱστάναι to cause to stand, to weigh. The *sb.* (= F. *statique*, It. *statica*) is ad. mod.L. *statica*, ad. Gr. στατική (*sc.* τέχνη) the art of weighing, ellipt. use of the adj.]

A. *adj.*

† **1.** Of or pertaining to weighing or the use of the balance: = STATICAL *a.* 1. *Obs.*

static barometer = *statical baroscope*: see STATICAL 1. ***static chair***: the Sanctorian weighing chair (see SANCTORIAN *a.*) for determining the amount of insensible perspiration by weighing the body; ***static medicine***, the branch of medical science concerned with the study of the variations of insensible perspiration as thus determined.

1646 SIR T. BROWNE *Pseud. Ep.* IV. vii. 196 In the middle of summer,.. a man weigheth some pounds lesse then in the heighth of winter, according to.. the statick aphorismes of Sanctorius. **1676** J. DAVIES tr. *Sanctorius' Med. Statica*, Acc. Weighing Chair A 6, That perspiration which is commodiously weigh'd by the Chair, any one may easily understand by our Book of Statick Medicine. **1733** TULL *Horse-Hoeing Husb.* ii. 16 Sanctorious by his Statick-Chair, found Five Eights of the Nourishment.. pass off by insensible Perspiration. *a* **1734** NORTH *Life Ld. Keeper Guilford* (1742) 293 About this Time [*c* **1675**].. Sir Samuel Moreland publish'd a Piece, containing a Device... This he call'd a statick Barometer.

† **2. a.** Pertaining to the effect of weight or the conditions of the equilibrium of weight: often said of experiments for determining specific gravity. Of a power or principle: Operative in the production of equilibrium; also *fig. Obs.*

1638 WILKINS *New World* I. (1684) 170 And that upon this Statick Principle; any Brass or Iron Vessel whose Substance is much Heavier than that of the Water, yet being Filled with the Lighter Air, it will.. not Sink. **1659** H. MORE *Immort. Soul.* III. iii. §10. 361 If we consider the nature of the Windes, the nature of these Vehicles, & the Statick power of the Soule. **1664** POWER *Exp. Philos.* II. 105 After a few vibrations up and down (as is Observable in all Statick Experiments) they arrive at a Counterpoise. **1668** HOWE *Bless. Righteous* i. 3 He.. subjoyns some account of himself, in this his closure of the Psalm: *As for me*, Here he is at his statique point. *Ibid.* viii. 145 And if Philosophy and.. Christianity, Reason and Faith have that statique power, can so compose the soul.. in the midst of storms and tempests: how [etc.]. **1681–6** J. SCOTT *Chr. Life* II. vii. §9 Wks. 1718 I. 444 Our City-Companies.. still retain the same Laws and Charters, which are the statique Principles or Forms that individuate them, and keep them still the same. **1775** SIR E. BARRY *Observ. Wines* 391 It is very evident from Statick experiments, that [etc.].

† **b.** Of a mental condition: Balanced, stable. *Obs. rare.*

1652 EVELYN *St. France* Pref. Let. B, It is.. a thing extreamly difficult to be at all times, and in all places thus reserved, and as it were obliged to Temper so Statick and exact among all conversations.

3. a. Pertaining to forces in equilibrium, or to bodies at rest: opposed to *dynamic*.

1850 GROVE *Corr. Phys. Forces* (ed. 2) 74, I have used.. the terms dynamic and static to represent the different states of magnetism. **1857** *Edin. Rev.* July 36 The Voltaic battery reproduces the tension, and the earth repeats the neutralisation, and so the force which was static in the wire is rendered dynamic. *a* **1878** SIR G. SCOTT *Lect. Archit.* (1879) II. 303 Thus, purely trabeated architecture sleeps in safety, while arcuated architecture never ceases to exert force. The one is static, the other a dynamic style—only becoming static when its abutments are of undoubted sufficiency. **1881** O. J. LODGE in *Nature* XXIII. 303 Electrical energy may exist in.. the static form, when [etc.].

b. Applied *spec.* to designate frictional as opposed to voltaic electricity. Cf. STATICAL *a.* 4 b.

1839 FARADAY *Exp. Res. Electr.* I. 534 *heading*, Theory of static induction. **1876** F. GUTHRIE *Magnetism & Electr.* (title of Book 1), Frictional or Static Electricity. **1898** *Westm. Gaz.* 6 Jan. 2/1 A static current, such as produced by the Holtz machine, will be sent over the wires. **1890** G. M. GOULD *New Med. Dict.* s.v., *Static Breeze*, a method of administration of static electricity.

c. ***static friction*** (see quot. 1878).

1878 *Phil. Trans. R. Soc.* CLXVII. 509 Coulomb pointed out the necessity of distinguishing between the friction which resists the relative movement of surfaces already in motion, or what is now called kinetic friction, and the friction which tends to prevent surfaces at rest from being set in motion, or what is now called static friction. **1922** GLAZEBROOK *Dict. Appl. Physics* I. 389/2 The subject of static friction is of considerable importance in the theory of the stability of engineering structures. **1980** J. W. HILL *Intermediate Physics* iv. 29 The block should, in absolutely frictionless conditions, begin to move however small the applied force but in practice static friction opposes the movement.

d. *Econ.* Of or pertaining to an economic system in a state of equilibrium. Cf. STATICS 1 d.

1899 J. B. CLARK *Distrib. of Wealth* iii. 31 What a static theory openly and intentionally puts out of sight—namely, changes that alter the mode of production. *Ibid.* v. 60 The study of the unreal static state is a heroic.. use of the isolating method of study. **1904** J. N. KEYNES *Scope & Method Pol. Econ.* (ed. 3) iv. 147 An economic theory is termed *static* if it is based on the assumption of.. a state in which there occurs no essential modification of the general conditions under which production and consumption, distribution and exchange, are carried on. **1947** P. A. SAMUELSON *Foundations Econ. Analysis* xi. 312 Gustav Cassel.. considers Economic Dynamics to be a third stage of analysis, following a pure Static Economy and a 'quasi-static'. Uniformly Progressive Economy. **1974** A. S. CAMPAGNA *Macroeconomics* iii. 50 Static analysis is concerned with states of equilibrium, and static models inquire into the forces leading to, maintaining, and reestablishing, if necessary, the equilibrium condition.

4. a. *transf.* and *fig.* = STATICAL *a.* 5.

1856 DOVE *Logic Chr. Faith* III. §1. 129 Causation may be viewed either as static or dynamic. **1889** J. M. ROBERTSON *Ess. Critical Method* 5 It was very natural that the fresh mediaeval intelligence, to which the recovered past came as a splendid treasure-trove, should.. set up the old standards of static criticism, to last till the influx of new knowledge.. wrought [etc.]. **1897** A. B. WALKLEY *Maeterlinck's Treas. Humble* Introd. 13 M. Maeterlinck boldly asks whether a 'static' theatre is impossible, a theatre of mood not of movement. **1904** *Edin. Rev.* Oct. 307 By a 'static' character we mean one that is a fixed quantity in the play; essentially the same force in magnitude and direction from the rise to the fall of the curtain. **1907** J. B. CLARK *Essent. Economic Theory* viii. 128 The Sign of a Static State.—The sign of the existence of a static condition is, therefore, that labor and capital, though they are perfectly free to move from one employment to another,.. still do not move. *Ibid.* 131 Influences that disturb the Static Equilibrium. **1909** W. R. INGE *Faith* vii. 122 Revelation, like inspiration, is a process, not a static condition.

b. *Gram.* Expressive of a state as distinguished from an action or process.

1871 B. H. KENNEDY *Publ. Sch. Lat. Gram.* §127 Many Static Verbs take the cause or motive of the state as an Object, and so become Transitive.

c. *Phonetics.* Of consonants, = CONTINUANT *a.* 2; of tones, not changing pitch during utterance.

1931 [see KINETIC *a.* 5]. **1939** L. H. GRAY *Foundations Lang.* 53 All consonants can be uttered by themselves whether they are *static* (or *continuant*), i.e., can be held continuously without changing quality (notably nasal, lateral, rolled, fricative, and sibilant sounds..); or are *kinetic*, i.e., cannot be so held. **1958** R. KINGDON *Groundwork Eng. Intonation* p. xxii, *Static tone*, a tone in which the voice remains steady on a given pitch throughout its duration. *Ibid.* 4 The Static Tones are the level tones, accompanied by stress, which are used on the words to which it is desired to give prominence in the sentence, but to which no particular feeling is attached. **1961** [see KINETIC *a.* 5]. **1968** B. M. H. STRANG *Mod. Eng. Structure* (ed. 2) vi. 92 Kingdon divides the notes and tunes of English speech into two kinds, the level or Static Tones, and the moving or Kinetic Tones. **1969** D. CRYSTAL *Prosodic Systems & Intonation in English* iv. 158 *Stress.* Perceivable increase in loudness accompanied by unmarked pitch movement (the norm in the pitch-range system, static tone).

5. *Path.* and *Phys.* in various applications.

a. (See quot.) *rare*$^{-0}$.

1855 DUNGLISON *Med. Lex.*, *Static*, an epithet applied to the physical phenomena presented by organized bodies in contradistinction to the organic or vital.

b. Structural or organic as opposed to *functional*.

1855 J. R. REYNOLDS *Diagn. Dis. Brain* II. ix. 126 Although post mortem examination can reveal no static (anatomical) change, the simple fact of convulsion is proof of dynamic (functional) disease. **1897** *Allbutt's Syst. Med.* III. 639 We must avoid any confusion between the static results of past peritonitis and the slowly progressive changes of the chronic disease. **1899** *Ibid.* VII. 238 One of those anomalous fatal instances in which the medulla has been found apparently free from static disease.

c. Of a disease, etc.: Characterized by STASIS.

1878 T. BRYANT *Pract. Surg.* (1884) I. 92 Static or venous gangrene includes those [cases] in which stagnation of blood is caused by the mechanical arrest of the circulation through the veins.

d. Of or pertaining to a standing posture.

1898 *Syd. Soc. Lex.*, *Static ataxia*, the failure of muscular coördination in standing still, or in any fixed position of the limbs. **1899** *Allbutt's Syst. Med.* VII. 900 Saltatory spasm. Syn.—Saltatoric spasm; Static reflex spasm.

e. (See quot.)

1899 *Allbutt's Syst. Med.* VI. 829 There is no mental stimulus to the combination of the retinal images, and the eyes remain in their static or resting position.

f. Tending to maintain equilibrium.

1899 *Allbutt's Syst. Med.* VII. 372 The cerebellum normally exerts on the apparatus of movement, a sthenic, tonic and static influence.

6. *Machinery.* **a.** (See quot.)

1911 *Encycl. Brit.* XXII. 237/1 [Power transmission (Electr.)] Such disturbances [as minor surges] when trivial are commonly referred to as 'static'.

b. Of an electric transformer or generator: Having all its parts stationary, non-rotary.

1903 *Nature* 15 Jan. 248/1 The Hewitt Mercury Lamp and Static Converter. **1911** *Encycl. Brit.* XXVII. 173/1 [In a continuous current transformer] some part of the machine must revolve, whereas in the alternating current transformer all parts are stationary; hence the former is generally called a rotary transformer, and the latter a static transformer.

c. *Computers.* Applied to a store in which the data are held at fixed positions in the device, and any location can be accessed at any moment.

1947 A. W. BURKS et al. in *Coll. Wks. J. von Neumann* V. 44 We distinguish two broad types of such devices: static, and dynamic or pulse-type accumulators. **1970** O. DOPPING *Computers & Data Processing* x. 134 A ferrite core memory .. is an example of a static memory, while a drum memory .. is a dynamic memory in which a particular memory can be read or written only when the continuously rotating drum is at a certain angular position. **1977** J. C. BOYCE *Digital Computer Fund.* viii. 212 The basic building block of the static memory discussed in this section is a 16-pin integrated circuit.

7. Special collocations (mostly in sense 3): ***static characteristic*** (***curve***) (Electronics), a graph showing the relationship between two parameters of a valve, transistor, etc., measured under steady conditions (strictly at zero frequency and with no load impedance); ***static line***, a line connecting a parachute to the body of an aircraft and serving to open and release it automatically when tensioned by the movement of the parachutist away from the aircraft; ***static pressure***, the pressure of a fluid on a body when the latter is at rest relative to it; ***static-pressure tube*** = *static tube* below; ***static test***, a test of a device or object in a stationary position, or under conditions that are constant or change only gradually; so ***static-test*** vb. trans.; ***static testing*** vbl. sb.; ***static thrust***, thrust generated by a stationary aero-engine or rocket engine; ***static tube*** (Aeronaut.), the part of the pitot-static head that registers static pressure, consisting of a tube aligned parallel to the airflow, closed at the forward end, and having holes along its length; ***static water***: during the war of 1939–45, a store of water with no pressure of its own intended for use as an emergency supply, esp. in fighting fires.; freq. *attrib.*, as ***static-water tank***.

1919 *Wireless World* May 77/2 From the *static characteristic of a valve.. it is clear that if the grid voltage varies between sufficiently small limits, the law of variation will be exactly reproduced in the anode circuit. **1939** H. J. REICH *Theory & Applications Electron Tubes* iii. 43 Strictly a static characteristic is one obtained with steady voltages, whereas a dynamic characteristic is one obtained with alternating voltages. **1975** D. G. FINK *Electronics Engineers' Handbk.* VII. 39 The performance of a transistor over wide ranges of current and voltage is determined from static characteristic curves. **1930** C. DIXON *Parachutes for Airmen* ii. 20 The 'Guardian Angel' was a typical example of the 'automatic' design. It was fitted into a tube fixed at the side of the aeroplane, with a *static line attached to the harness on the airman. **1966** M. R. D. FOOT *SOE in France* iv. 78 All a parachutist has to do is to jump through the hole; his parachute is opened automatically by a thin wire called a 'static line' which his own weight breaks. **1977** *R.A.F. News* 30 Mar.–12 Apr. 3/3 If new members decide they want to move on to free-fall parachuting, they must first make six static line jumps. **1915** W. E. DOMMETT *Aeroplanes & Airships* 103 *Pressure head*, a combination of pitot tube and *static pressure or suction tube. **1923** GLAZEBROOK *Dict. Appl. Physics* V. 66/2 The air thus blows tangentially past these holes, and the pressure within the tube is equal to the static pressure of the surrounding air. **1948** C. E. CHAPEL *Aircraft Basic Sci.* i. 21/1 The center of pressure can be located for each angle of attack by installing parallel rows of static pressure tubes at right angles to the leading edge of a wing flush with the upper and lower surfaces. **1978** J. D. ANDERSON *Introd. Flight* iv. 95 Static pressure is a consequence of just the purely random motion of the molecules. **1905** *Jrnl. Iron & Steel Inst.* LXVII. 486 Overheating.. will produce brittleness under shock or vibratory stress, although *static tests may have given fairly satisfactory results. **1918** COWLEY & LEVY *Aeronautics* ix. 176 Fig. 97 gives thrust and torque required to drive the propeller for a 'static test', i.e. when the forward speed is zero. **1961** *Time* (Atlantic ed.) 24 Feb. 12/2 The Saturn has been static-tested, but will not be operational until 1965. **1962** *B.S.I. News* July 9/1 The 'static' test used.. in approving well over a million Kite-marked safety belts is extremely effective in finding out any weakness. **1966** *McGraw-Hill Encycl. Sci. & Technol.* XI. 610a/2 The static test facilities must be capable of handling and disposing of the hot gases.. that are expelled from the rocket. **1968** A. E. ROY tr. *T. de Galiana's Conc. Encycl. Astronautics* 259/1 The complete rocket, held in a test-stand, is then static tested. **1950** G. G. SMITH *Gas Turbines & Jet Propulsion* (ed. 5) xii. 205 (*heading*) *Static testing. **1958** F. A. WARREN *Rocket Propellants* x. 173 Because of the dangers involved in static testing, special precautions must be taken to protect personnel. **1962** F. I. ORDWAY et al. *Basic Astronautics* vii. 319 Static testing may be divided into two categories: powerplant static testing and vehicle capture firing. **1916** M. A. S. RIACH *Air-Screws* vii. 89 The '*Static' thrust of an air-screw on an aeroplane is usually measured by attaching a spring balance to the rear portion of the machine and attaching a rope from the spring balance to some fixed support. **1952** A. Y. BRAMBLE *Air-Plane Flight* x. 153 The problem of providing the essential static thrust for take-off found its solution in the variable-pitch propeller. **1962** F. I. ORDWAY et al. *Basic Astronautics* vii. 319 Some of the common measurements made.. are given below. (1) Thrust (static thrust developed by the engine) [etc.]. **1923** GLAZEBROOK *Dict. Appl. Physics* V. 66/1 A 'head', consisting of two parts—the 'pressure' or 'Pitot' tube and the '*static' tube—is fixed on some exposed part of the aircraft. **1940** A. C. KERMODE *Mechanics of Flight* (ed. 4) ii. 29 In modern types the Pitot tube is connected to the inside of a capsule.. while the Static tube is connected to the casing of the instrument. **1965** V. H. BRIX tr. *Martynov's Pract. Aerodynamics* vi. 141 The most widely used instrument for measuring static pressure is the static tube or sonde. **1944** *Ourselves in Wartime* 108/2 Thousands of *static water tanks were established in parks, squares and in the basements of bombed buildings, so that never again would there be a shortage of water through the destruction of the mains by the enemy. **1958** L. W. TANCOCK in *Aspects of Translation* 31 You may remember those tanks of water stored in our towns against fires caused by enemy action. We had none in North Wales, but.. near where we lived a torrent came tumbling down the valley and a large notice stood by indicating that this was *static water*. **1976** 'J. CHARLTON' *Remington Set* xxiii. 119 This place used to be an airfield in the war... Under here there's a big static water tank.

B. *sb.*

1. = STATICS. Now *rare.*

1570 DEE *Math. Pref.* biiij, Statike, is an Arte Mathematicall, which demonstrateth the causes of heauynes, and lightnes of all thynges: and of motions and properties, to heauynes and lightnes, belonging. **1578** W. BOURNE *Treas. Trav.* IV. 2 The which Art or Science, called Staticke, dooth shewe the heauinesse or lightnesse of any thing. *a* **1583** in Halliwell *Rara Mathem.* (1841) 33 Youre Honoure had some speeche with mee, as touching measuring the moulde of a shipp. Whiche gave mee occasyon to wryte a litle Boke of Statick. **1873** [see DYNAMIC *sb.*].

2. The metrology of weights. *Obs. rare.*

1699 BENTLEY *Phalaris* 456 Talent originally is a word of Static [*printed* Statics, *but see Errata*], and means lx pound weight of any thing.

†**3.** (See quot.) *Obs.*$^{-0}$

1728 CHAMBERS *Cycl.*, *Staticks, Statici*, in Medicine, a kind of Epilepticks, or Persons seiz'd with Epilepsies. The Staticks differ from the Catalepticks, in that, these last [etc.].

4. a. Atmospherics; radio noise.

1913 *Wireless World* Nov. 508/2 Communication will also be had with New Orleans, which the static formerly prevented. **1938** D. CANFIELD *Fables for Parents* II. 124 That woman who talks about cooking is coming on splendidly. Not a speck of static. Wouldn't you like to bring your sewing over and listen? **1950** 'N. SHUTE' *Town like Alice* v. 156 He wanted to see a live broadcast of 'Much-Binding-in-the-Marsh' which he listened to on short wave from Brisbane when the static permitted. **1960** *Practical Wireless* XXXVI. 413/1 The background noise caused by external static can be troublesome. **1978** R. LUDLUM *Holcroft Covenant* xvii. 196 There was a sudden burst of static from a radio speaker beneath the dashboard.

b. In *fig.* use, 'aggravation' or interference; confusion, fuss, trouble, criticism. *slang* (orig. *U.S.*).

1926 MAINES & GRANT *Wise-Crack Dict.* 8/1 *Full of static*, not worth listening to. **1953** W. BURROUGHS *Junkie* (1972) viii. 77 An Sol said, 'Hell, I love junk... But if I can't use it without I get static all the time from the law, I'll get off junk and stay off.' **1969** C. YOUNG *Todd Dossier* 154 If I notified Security it would just mean a lot of fuss,.. where was the requisition, all that static. **1974** L. DEIGHTON *Spy Story* xvii. 186 Spare me the static... Why didn't you lay it on for me, about working for the goddam Brits? **1979** D. ANTHONY *Long Hard Cure* v. 42 The words are full of static, a reaction to that attack.

5. Static electricity. Freq. *attrib.*

1916 'B. M. BOWER' *Phantom Herd* xiv. 233 All that negative I took to-day is chock full of 'static'. **1951** KOESTLER *Age of Longing* 195 The umbrellas.. had a tendency to charge the people who carried them with static, which sometimes discharged itself in crackling sparks at a handshake, kiss or other bodily contact. **1956** *Planning* XXII. 128 Static elimination is the removal of the harmful electric charges which accumulate on fibres and thin sheets during manufacturing processes. **1978** *Hi-Fi News* Sept. 130/1 (Advt.), Not unlike a common magnet attracting iron particles, static scavenges and draws dust particles onto the record surface. **1979** *Globe & Mail* (Toronto) 5 May 8/1 The winter smell of the settlement has become that of laundry aids—fluffers and static eradicators—whose smells are wafted into the icy air.

-static, formative element (f. Gr. στατικός causing to stand, stopping: see STATIC *a.* and *sb.*) used in the senses (*a*) 'inhibiting flow', as in HÆMOSTATIC *a.* and *sb.*; (*b*) 'inhibiting growth', as in BACTERIOSTATIC *a.*, FUNGISTATIC *a.*

statical ('stætɪkəl), *a.* Also 6 **-all.** [formed as STATIC *a.* and *sb.* + -AL[1].]

†**1.** Pertaining to the action or process of weighing: = STATIC *a.* 1. *Obs.*

statical baroscope: a baroscope in which the varying weight of the air was rendered observable by the movements of a balance; so ***statical hygroscope***. ***statical chair*** = *static chair*: see STATIC *a.* 1.

1570 DEE *Math. Pref.* cjb *marg.*, The practise Staticall, to know the proportion, betwene the Cube, and the Sphære. **1578** W. BOURNE *Treas. Trav.* IV. 6, I wyll shewe vnto you a more pleasaunter.. waye (by the Arte Staticall).. for to know the true wayghte of any Shyp. **1666** BOYLE in *Phil. Trans.* I. 233 So that I had oftentimes the satisfaction by looking first upon the Statical Baroscope (as for distinctions sake it may be call'd) to foretell, whether in the Mercurial Baroscope the Liquor were high or low. **1669** *Phil. Trans.* IV. 897 The Ingenious Sanctorius hath not exhausted all the results of Statical Indications. **1673** BOYLE (*title*) A Statical Hygroscope Proposed to be further tryed. **1732** ARBUTHNOT *Rules of Diet* in *Aliments*, etc. I. 401 If such a one by a statical Engine could regulate his insensible Perspiration.. he might often.. shorten his fit. **1753** *Chambers' Cycl.* Suppl., *Statical* is sometimes applied in a peculiar sense to the experiments made as to the quantity of perspiration and other excretions of the human body. **1779** J. ADAMS *Wks.* (1854) IX. 508 Suppose you should make a statical chair, and try whether perspiration is most copious in a warm bed, or stark naked in the open air. **1780** *Mirror* No. 79 To devise.. some.. statical balance which should shew the difference of weight and solidity of such objects as have a similar appearance.

2. Of or pertaining to STATICS.

1660 BOYLE *New Exp. Phys. Mech.* xxxvi. 299 The Atmosphere may.. for ought can be determin'd by our Statical and Mechanical Experiments, rise to the height of Five and twenty German Leagues. **1685** —— *Free Enq.* 253 This Ascension is made.. by the Pressure of the Atmosphere, acting upon the Water, according to Statical Rules. **1820** SHELLEY *Let. Maria Gisborne* 83 Then comes a range of mathematical Instruments, for plans nautical and statical. *a* **1878** SIR G. SCOTT *Lect. Archit.* (1879) I. 61 A careful study of the monuments in which it [the pointed arch] is first systematically used clearly shows that its introduction was from statical, and neither geometrical nor merely æsthetical motives. **1880** *Nature* XXI. 369 Any true theory of the constitution of the ether would be something totally different from statical theories of this kind.

†**b.** ? *transf.* (Sense obscure.) *Obs. rare.*

a **1656** HALES *Gold. Rem.* (1673) 271 There are in Story two things especially considerable. First, the Order of the Story it self: and secondly, Moral, or Statical observations, for common life and practise.

†**3.** Pertaining to weight or the equilibrium of weight. *Obs.*

1714 Parkyns *Inn-Play* (ed. 2) 23 For all other Statical Motions of humane Bodies, such as are curious may find them abridg'd, from Alphonsus Borellus [Quotation follows].

†**b.** Of analysis, etc.: Gravimetrical. *Obs.*

1727 S. Hales *Statical Ess.* Introd. (1731) 2 The most considerable and rational accounts of it [the animal œconomy] have been chiefly owing to the statical examination of its fluids. **1784** J. Richardson (*title*) Statical Estimates of the materials of Brewing. **1813** Sir H. Davy *Agric. Chem.* i. (1814) 14 The true statical analysis of the atmosphere is comparatively a recent labour.

c. Pertaining to the metrology of weight. Cf. static *sb.* 2.

1846 Grote *Greece* II. iv. II. 425 The..information contained in M. Boeckh's recent publication on Metrology has thrown new light upon these monetary and statical scales.

4. Of or pertaining to forces in equilibrium or the condition of rest in bodies. Of forces: Operating to produce or maintain equilibrium.

1802 Playfair *Illustr. Huttonian Theory* 43 Whenever, therefore, we meet with rocks, disposed in layers quite parallel to one another, we may rest assured, that..no cause has interrupted the statical tendency above explained. **1830** Lyell *Princ. Geol.* II. xviii. (1835) II. 352 Let us, however, concede that the statical figure [of the earth] may be a modification of some other pre-existing form. **1837** Whewell *Hist. Induct. Sci.* (1857) II. 13 This includes the principle of the Composition of Statical Forces. **1839** G. Roberts *Dict. Geol.*, *Statical Figure*.., the figure which results from the equilibrium of forces. **1867** Thomson & Tait *Treat. Nat. Philos.* I. §451. 340 This, which is called Statical Friction, is thus capable of opposing a tangential resistance to motion which may be of any requisite amount up to μR. **1868** H. Spencer *Princ. Psychol.* (1872) II. vi. xi. 141 The statical attributes shape, size and position. **1869** J. Martineau *Ess.* II. 167 All forces..are dynamical..till.. they become statical. **1871** B. Stewart *Heat* §195 The equilibrium suggested by Prevost is not therefore a statical or tensional equilibrium..but it is essentially an equilibrium of action. **1889** Welch *Test Bk. Naval Archit.* ii. 22 This effort of the ship to right herself when inclined at any angle, is called her statical stability at that angle.

b. Applied to frictional electricity: = static *a.* 3 b.

1837 Faraday in *Phil. Trans.* CXXVIII. 20 Inductive effects produced by electricity, not in currents, but in its statical state. **1845** *Proc. Amer. Phil. Soc.* IV. 208 Statical induction takes place at great distances. **1849** Noad *Electricity* (ed. 3) 187 The intensity of voltaic Electricity, as compared with statical, is exceedingly low. **1870** R. M. Ferguson *Electricity* 107 Galvanic electricity..can be made to manifest the attractions and repulsions of statical electricity.

c. ***statical chemistry***: see quot.

1866 Odling *Anim. Chem.* i. 1 (*heading*) Statical chemistry concerned only with the composition of parts... Dynamical chemistry concerned with the changes of composition undergone by various parts from time to time.

5. *transf.* and *fig.* Of or pertaining to a fixed or stable condition, as distinguished from a state of progress or change.

1855 G. Brimley *Ess.* (1858) 196 Of all science viewed in its statical aspect, apart from the experience of change and the idea of cause, this classification, naming, and definition are the ultimate processes. **1874** Fiske *Cosmic Philos.* II. 371 The crude philosophies current..take what we may call a statical view of things. Hence they suppose that God created the world a few thousand years ago in nearly the same condition in which we now behold it. **1886** Maine *Pop. Govt.* 47 The fund by which the life of the human race..is sustained, is never in a statical condition.

6. *Math.* Concerned with magnitude alone, without regard to direction. *rare.*

1859 A. J. Ellis in *Proc. R. Soc.* X. 87 The object of the statical algebra of fractions is to reduce all combinations of numerical fractions to numerical fractions... This algebra applied to geometry allows of the investigation of all statical relations.

7. *Med.* Structural, organic.

1896 *Allbutt's Syst. Med.* I. 236 In most cases, however, our power to remove a cause by drugs ceases as soon as it consists of definite statical tissue change. **1898** *Ibid.* V. 481 We have in this chapter to deal with anæmia in its dynamical rather than in its statical aspects.

statically (ˈstætɪkəlɪ), *adv.* [f. statical *a.* + -ly².] With reference to static conditions; by means of static electricity.

1854 Faraday *Exp. Res. Electr.* (1855) III. 511 The copper wire becomes charged statically with that electricity which the pole of the battery connected with it can supply. **1859** A. J. Ellis in *Proc. R. Soc.* X. 86 The problem of mathematics is, first, to discover the laws of these successions as respects results (that is, statically), by means of considerations drawn from contemplating operations (that is dynamical). **1862** Maxwell *Sci. Papers* (1890) I. 498 Now let η_1 and η_2 be the same quantities of electricity measured statically. **1867** *Contemp. Rev.* VI. 410 Both [Catholicism and Feudalism] worked for good equally by their organization and by their action, or, to use more convenient technical words, statically and dynamically. **1870** R. M. Ferguson *Electricity* 244 A telegraphic line may be charged statically. **1873** Maxwell *Electr. & Magn.* II. xi. §641. 254 The force arising from a system of stress of which these are the components will be statically equivalent, in its effects on each element of the body, with the forces arising from the magnetization and electric currents.

Comb. **1881** *Nature* XXIV. 616/1 According to this theory the earth-current consists in the return currents produced by the statically-induced change on the surface of the earth.

‖**Statice** (ˈstætɪsiː). [L. *staticē*, a. Gr. στατική, orig. fem. of στατικός causing to stand still (see static *a.*) in the specific sense 'stopping flow of blood'.] A genus of herbaceous perennial plants, typical of the tribe *Staticeæ*, N.O. *Plumbaginaceæ*; a plant of this genus, esp. Sea Lavender.

1731 Miller *Gard. Dict.*, *Statice*; Thrift or Sea Pink. **1745** R. James *Med. Dict.* III. s.v., Dodonæus pretends that the *Statice* is of no Use in Medicine, but that the Flowers are beautiful enough in Garlands. **1837** P. Keith *Bot. Lex.* 166 In some plants a single flower produces only a single seed, as in Statice or Thrift. **1873** Tristram *Moab* xviii. 353 Now pale lilac from a statice, now as softly red from the sorrel in flower. **1881** *Encycl. Brit.* XII. 262/1 [Greenhouse Plants.] Statices include some very highly ornamental plants. **1882** *Garden* 22 July 64/3 The Statice is a cloud of bluish grey.

staticisor (ˈstætɪsaɪzə(r)). *Computers.* [f. static *a.* + -ise¹ + -or.] A device which converts a succession of bits into an array of simultaneous states, thereby storing them.

1949 Williams & Kilburn in *Proc. Inst. Electr. Engineers* XCVI. iii. 82 Information may be represented 'dynamically' by pulses, which only exist transiently, or 'statically' by d.c. coupled flip-flop circuits, which retain the information until purposely reset to a standard condition... The set of flip-flop circuits is called a 'staticisor'. **1956** *Electronic Engin.* XXVIII. 154/2 The diodes in one horizontal row store the binary digits of the same significance in each of the words, and all have access to the trigger V_2 in the input-output staticizor. **1960** Haley & Scott *Analogue & Digital Computers* vii. 191 The digits are transient and must therefore be stored or converted into a static form by setting a row of five staticisors.

So **ˈstaticize** *v. trans.*, to store by means of a staticisor.

1952 *Electronic Engin.* XXIV. 30/1 In almost every design, a modest number of electronic triggers is retained since they allow words to be set up ('staticized') or discharged ('dynamicized') at different rates. **1960** Haley & Scott *Analogue & Digital Computers* vii. 193 Once the function digits have been 'staticised' there comes the problem of decoding.

statics (ˈstætɪks). [Alteration of static *sb.*, after names of sciences in -ics.] **1. a.** Originally, the science relating to weight and its mechanical effects, and to the conditions of equilibrium as resulting from the distribution of weight. In modern use, the branch of physical science concerned with the action of forces in producing equilibrium or relative rest, in contradistinction to *Dynamics* in its older sense as the science of the action of forces in producing motion. In recent terminology, Statics and Kinetics (= the older Dynamics) are the two branches of Dynamics.

1656 Blount *Glossogr.*, *Staticks* (Gr.) the science of weights and measures; a species of Mechanicks. **1664** Butler *Hud.* II. iii. 206 He had been long t'wards Mathematicks, Opticks, Philosophy, and Staticks. **1681** Colvil *Whigs Supplic.* (1751) 83 Like some attempting tricks in Statics, Not vers'd in Euclid's mathematics. **1691** Norris *Pract. Disc.* 24 There is more Force and Vertue in one Single *Now*, than in many *Hereafters*. 'Tis not in the Moral as in Physical Statics;..here the nearer the Weight, the stronger is its Power. **1692** Bentley *Confut. Atheism* II. 11 Now this is a Catholick Rule of Statics; That if any Body be bulk for bulk heavier than a Fluid, it will sink to the bottom of that Fluid. **1700** Moxon *Math. Dict.*, *Staticks*, the Science of Weights and Measures, a Species of the Mechanicks, shewing the Properties and Motion of Ponderosity, or Heaviness and Lightness of Bodies, &c. **1837** Whewell *Hist. Induct. Sci.* (1857) I. 73 The mechanical doctrine of Equilibrium, is Statics. **1867** Thomson & Tait *Treat. Nat. Philos.* I. §454. 342 We naturally divide Statics into two parts—the equilibrium of a particle, and that of a rigid or elastic body or system of particles. **1882** G. M. Minchin *Unipl. Kinemat.* 201 There are methods in Statics for calculating the resultant attraction of matter, or its components, without finding the potential.

b. with qualifying word.

chemical statics, the statics of chemical bodies or systems of bodies. ***graphic(al statics***, the investigation of statical problems by means of drawings made to scale. †***vegetable statics***, the study of the laws of the circulation of the fluids in plants.

1727 S. Hales (*title*) Statical Essays: containing Vegetable Staticks; Or, An Account of some Statical Experiments on the Sap in Vegetables. **1780** M. Cutler in *Life, Jrnls. & Corr.* (1888) I. 80 The Doctor's discoveries in his vegetable statics..must be very useful in the culture and improvement of vegetables and fruit trees. **1876** Maxwell *Sci. Papers* (1890) II. 492 On Bow's method of drawing diagrams in graphical statics. **1910** *Encycl. Brit.* VIII. 147/2 The most useful of these applications, collectively termed Graphic Statics, relates to the equilibrium of plane framed structures.

c. *transf.*; esp. in ***social statics*** (see quots. 1843, 1851).

1843 Mill *Logic* vi. x. §5 [With Comte] Social Dynamics is the theory of Society considered in a state of progressive movement; while Social Statics is the theory of the *consensus* already spoken of as existing among the different parts of the social organism. **1845** Graves *Roman Law* in *Encycl. Metrop.* II. 768/1 Gaius..treats rather of the dynamics than of the statics of law—rather of those events or forces by which classes of rights begin, are modified or terminate, than of those rights and duties which accompany a given stationary legal relation. **1851** Spencer *Soc. Stat.* xxx. §1 Social philosophy may be aptly divided..into statics and dynamics; the first treating of the equilibrium of a perfect society, the second of the forces by which society is advanced towards perfection.

d. *Econ.* That part of economic theory which examines the forces and conditions obtaining at a state of equilibrium in an economic system, without consideration of changes through time; esp. as ***comparative statics*** (see quot. 1974).

1871 W. S. Jevons *Theory Pol. Econ.* p. viii, The nature of Wealth and Value is explained by the consideration of indefinitely small amounts of pleasure and pain, just as the theory of Statics is made to rest upon the equality of indefinitely small amounts of energy. **1891** J. N. Keynes *Scope & Method in Pol. Econ.* iv. 141 In so-called economic statics we are frequently engaged in examining the effects of particular changes. **1920** A. Marshall *Princ. Econ.* (ed. 8) v. v. 366 The problem of normal value belongs to economic Dynamics: partly because Statics is really but a branch of Dynamics. **1947** P. A. Samuelson *Foundations Econ. Analysis* ii. 8 This method of comparative statics is but one special application of the more general practice of scientific deduction in which the behavior of a system (possibly through time) is defined in terms of a given set of functional equations and initial conditions. **1954** W. Jaffé tr. *Walras's Elem. Pure Economics* viii. 117 Had I supposed utility to be a *variable* functionally related to time, then time would have had to figure explicitly in the problem. And we should then have passed from economic *statics* to economic *dynamics*. **1963** R. E. Kuenne *Theory of Gen. Econ. Equilibrium* i. 15 Comparative statics is a *method* of employing static models analytically by imposing changes upon the data of the model. **1974** A. S. Campagna *Macroeconomics* iii. 50 With a model in equilibrium any change in the variables will cause the model to react until a new equilibrium is reached. The comparison of these two equilibrium states is called comparative statics.

†**2.** = static *sb.* 4 a. *Obs.*

1918 in Webster Add. **1921** *Sci. Abstr.* B. XXIV. 156 On the North Atlantic coast the statics come in large proportion from the S.W. **1926** *Glasgow Herald* 15 May 4 A wall of 'statics' may be responsible for the fact that no wireless messages have been received from the airship for some time.

stating (ˈsteɪtɪŋ), *vbl. sb.* [f. state *v.* + -ing¹.] The action of the verb state.

1652 in *Verney Mem.* (1904) I. 519 W. R. had done nothing in order to yᵉ stating of the accounts. **1652** Nedham tr. *Selden's Mare Cl.* 167 The Ancient Orators,..whilst they allege Examples about the stating of Questions in pleading, do mingle [etc.]. **1654** Hammond *Of Fundamentals* ix. §9. 9 Many other inconveniences there are consequent to this stating of the question. **1662** Jer. Taylor *Via Intell.* 8 Many of our Controversies and peevish wranglings are kept up by the ill stating of the Question. **1780** Burke *Corr.* (1844) II. 333 When any new propositions are made without their explanations, their qualifications, and a full stating of their grounds. **1798** Hutton *Course Math.* I. 49 Compound Proportion teaches how to resolve such questions as require two or more statings by Simple Proportion.

stating (ˈsteɪtɪŋ), *ppl. a.* [f. state *v.* + -ing².] That states; *spec.* in *Law* (see quots.).

1787 J. Mitford *Plead. Suits Chanc.* (ed. 2) 42 The third part contains the case of the plaintiffs, and is commonly called the stating part of the bill. **1796** C. Barton *Suit Equity* 27 The Premises, or, as more usually stiled, the Stating Part of the Bill. **1838** J. Story *Comm. Equity Plead.* §27. 20.

station (ˈsteɪʃən), *sb.* Forms: 4–6 stacio(u)n, 5 stacon, stacyoun, stasyon, 5–6 stacyon, 6 statyon, 6– station. [a. F. *station* (12th c.) ad. L. *station-em*, noun of action f. *sta-*, *stāre* to stand. Cf. Sp. *estacion*, Pg. *estação*, It. *stazione*, and the popular form It. *stagione* season.]

I. Action or condition of standing.

1. The action or posture of standing on the feet; manner of standing. Now only in scientific and technical uses: see quots. 1891 and 1913.

bipedal, quadrupedal station (Zool.) [= F. *station bipède, quadrupède*]: the having two or four feet respectively.

1526 *Pilgr. Perf.* (W. de W. 1531) 65 These cerimonyes that this doctour calleth but small thynges, I suppose they be as stacyons, inclynacyons, gestures..& suche other. **1599** B. Jonson *Cynthia's Rev.* II. v, If [she be] reguardant, then maintaine your station,..shew the supple motion of your pliant bodie. **1602** Shaks. *Ham.* III. iv. 58 A Station, like the Herald Mercurie New lighted on a heauen kissing hill. **1650** Bulwer *Anthropomet.* xxi. 234 Nature..allowes us two feet for the firmer station. **1861** Hulme tr. *Moquin-Tandon* I. iii. 20 The quadrupedal station. **1891** *Century Dict.*, *Station*,.. the manner of standing or the attitude of live stock, particularly of exhibition game fowls: as, a duck-wing game-cock of standard high station. **1913** Dorland *Med. Dict.* (ed. 7) 901 *Station*, the manner of standing; in ataxic conditions it is sometimes pathognomonic.

2. The condition or fact of standing still; assumption of or continuance in a stationary condition: opposed to *motion*. Now *rare*.

1606 Shaks. *Ant. & Cl.* III. iii. 22 Her motion, and her station are as one. She shewes a body, rather then a life. *a* **1619** Fotherby *Atheom.* II. xi. §1 (1622) 310 The vacuity of both Heauinesse and Lightnesse..is rather the principle of station, then of Motion. **1643** Sir T. Browne *Relig. Med.* 32 The natural motion of the Sun made them more admire him, than its supernatural station did the Children of Israel. **1658** Owen *Temptation* iii. 53 If it [peace] be lost for a season, it may be obtained againe; I will not solicite its station any more;..and a thousand such pleas there are. **1660** Stanley *Hist. Philos.* XIII. iv. (1687) 910/1 That Pleasure, wherein Felicity consists, is of the first kind, the stable, or that which is in station. **1841** Emerson *Ess.*, *Compensation* 122 His life is a progress, and not a station.

3. A halt; a stand. Now *rare* or *Obs.*

1604 E. G[rimstone] *D'Acosta's Hist. Indies* v. xxiv. 394 Presently they went from thence with like diligence, to go to a place..where they made their second station. **1609** J. Davies *Holy Roode* F 3 b, But now, my Soule, here let vs make a Station, To view perspicuously this sad aspect. **1657** Heylin *Eccl. Vind.* II. ii. 117 A portable Temple..which might be carried and removed, according to the stations and removes of Israel. **1845** J. Coulter *Adv. in Pacific* viii. 100

After having enjoyed my first station here, I prepared my morning meal of terrapin, . . and . . I again commenced my march.

†**4. a.** An act of a pageant or a mystery play. *Obs.*

1474 *Cov. Leet. Bk.* 391 And at Babulake yate there ordeyned a stacion, therin beyng kyng Richard with xiij other arrayed lyke as Dukes, Markises, Erles [etc.]. *c* **1485** *Digby Myst.* (1882) II. 155 Fynally of this stacon thus we mak a conclusyon.

†**b.** In Ireland: Some municipal ceremony. *Obs.*

[**1560**: see *station-day* in 29.]

5. *Astr.* The apparent standing still of a planet at its apogee and perigee.

1412–20 LYDG. *Troy-bk.* IV. 3366 Whan þe shene sonne In þe Crabbe had his cours I-ronne To þe hiȝest of his ascencioun, Whiche called is þe somer staciuon. **1551** RECORDE *Cast. Knowl.* (1556) 279 The progression, retrogradation, and station of the Planetes. **1647** CUDWORTH *Serm. 1 John* ii. 3–4. 56 Those upper Planets in the Heaven . . have their Stations and Retrogradations, as well as their Direct Motions. **1667** MILTON *P.L.* VII. 563 The Planets in thir stations list'ning stood. **1704** J. HARRIS *Lex. Techn.* I, *Points of Station*, in Astronomy, are those Degrees of the Zodiack, in which a Planet seems to stand quite still, and not to move at all. **1812** WOODHOUSE *Astron.* xxiii. 249 In speaking of the stations and retrogradations of the planets. **1819** J. WILSON *Dict. Astrol.* 379 *Stations*, those parts in the orbit of a planet where it becomes either retrograde or direct, because it remains for a while there stationary before it changes its course.

†**6.** *Path.* The stationary point, crisis, a height (of a disease). Cf. STATE *sb.* 7, STATUS I. *Obs.*

1661 LOVELL *Hist. Anim. & Min.* 437 Of the times of diseases, of the beginning, lesse considerable injury of action. . . In the augmentation worse. . . In the station worst. . . In the declination better.

II. Standing-place, position.

* In literal applications.

7. a. A place to stand in; *esp.* a position assigned to a man on duty, or in games.

1556 N. SMYTH *Herodian* I. 10 b, Yea, and the footemen whyche had stations within the cyte, came to rescue the people againste the horsemen. **1601** MOUNTJOY in *Moryson's Itin.* (1617) II. 157 The weather is so extreme, that many times we bring our Sentinels dead from the stations. **1607** SHAKS. *Cor.* II. i. 231 Seld-showne Flamins Doe presse among the popular Throngs and puffe To winne a vulgar station. **1651** HOBBES *Leviath.* II. xxv. 136 Able Seconds at Tennis play, placed in their proper stations. **1665** MANLEY *Grotius' Low C. Wars* 251 Armed men stood round about in the Station, at the top of the Mast. **1679** M. RUSDEN *Further Discov. Bees* 93 Every particular Bee taketh notice of his Station. *a* **1700** EVELYN *Diary* 29 Jan. 1689, I got a station . . at the doore of the lobby to the House, and heard much of the debate. **1760–2** GOLDSM. *Cit. W.* lix, I placed my self on my former station in hopes of a repeated visit. **1784** COWPER *Task* II. 624 A man o' th' town dines late, but soon enough . . T'ensure a side-box station at half price. **1833** NYREN *Yng. Cricketer's Tutor* (1902) 11 The . . description of their different stations in the field, and of the importance of each in his station, will convince the young practitioner that [etc.]. **1867** SMYTH *Sailor's Word-bk* s.v., In most merchantmen the cry of 'Every man to his station, and the cook to the fore-sheet', is calling the hands and the idlers. *Ibid.*, *Stations for Stays!* repair to your posts to tack ship.

In fig. context. **1609** DANIEL *Civ. Wars* VIII. civ, It were a Cowards part, to fly Now from my Holde, . . It be'ing the Station of my life, where I Am set to serue, and stand as Sentinell. *a* **1669** DENHAM *Cato Major, Of Old Age* IV. 79 Pythagoras bids us in our station stand, Till God, our general, shall us disband.

b. Phrases, ***to take* (*up*), *keep* (*one's*) *station, on station.***

1667 MILTON *P.L.* XII. Argt., The Cherubim taking their Stations to guard the Place. **1719** DE FOE *Crusoe* (1840) II. iv. 91 They kept their station for a while. **1797** MRS. RADCLIFFE *Italian* i, They took their station under a balcony that overhung the lattice. **1840** DICKENS *Old C. Shop* xlvi, Even when she . . sat pensively waiting for their friend, she took her station where she could still look upon them. **1849** HELPS *Friends in C.* II. i. (1854) I. 258 A gorgeous peacock that took his station on the low wall bounding the lawn. **1882** E. O'DONOVAN *Merv Oasis* xliv. II. 249 One of our companions took his station as sentinel upon the tomb of the little mosque. **1923** *Man. Seamanship* (Admiralty) (ed. 2) II. x. 176 The leading ship should therefore at once reduce speed, even though the other is keeping station on her. **1939** *War Illustr.* 2 Dec. 372/3 The absolute necessity of maintaining the order in which their ships are placed in the convoy, i.e. to keep station, and not to alter course except at the order of the commodore of the convoy. **1972** *Lebende Sprachen* XVII. 149/1 *On station*, the status of an ocean station vessel when within the limits of the assigned ocean station. **1979** *Courier-Mail* (Brisbane) 1 Jan. 15/4 Quentin Fogarty managed to get film on the return flight of a large glowing orange object keeping station with the aircraft about 8 km away. **1982** *Times* 31 Mar. 4/4 HMS Endurance will remain on station as long as is necessary.

c. A point at which one stands or may stand to obtain a view.

1822 'BARRY CORNWALL' *Poems, Flood of Thessaly* I. 138 From that high station Jove doth watch the world Its happiness and woe. **1858** HAWTHORNE *Fr. & It. Note-bks.* (1872) I. 50 Seven different views of the city, from as many stations. **1872** JENKINSON *Engl. Lake Distr.* (1879) 13 The three best stations are, at the foot of the lake, on its eastern side, and from near Tarn Hows. **1878** BROWNING *La Saisiaz* 11 Can there be a lovelier station than this spot where now we stand?

d. In wider sense: Position occupied (in other postures than standing). *rare.*

1667 KATH. PHILIPS *Lucasia & Rosania* Poems 127 I'd dwell within thine arms Could I my station chuse. **1770** W. SHIRLEY *Hymn, 'Sweet the Moments'*, Truly blessed is this station, Low before his cross to lie. **1822** SCOTT *Nigel* xii, The two friends, being seated in the most honourable station at the board.

e. *Boat-racing.* The position (at one side or the other of the river) occupied by a competing crew at starting.

1864 *Field* 2 July 2/1 The Oxford boat had the better station, and twice led by a length. **1868** *Ibid.* 4 July 14/3 University had the best or Berkshire station. *Ibid.*, A change of station might have altered the result.

f. The correct position of a vessel in a squadron. (Cf. *station-keeping* in 29.)

1911 WEBSTER.

8. *Surveying*, etc. Each of the selected points at which observations are taken. Formerly also †*place, point of station.*

1571 DIGGES *Pantometria* I. xvii. E iv, And thus proceede from station to station. *Ibid.* I. xxv. Hj, A the toppe of the hill, B the foote, C my station or the place of mine eie. **1590** BLAGRAVE *Baculum Fam.* xviii. 27 Marke that station on the ground. . . Then measure exactly the distance betweene those two stations. **1610** HOPTON *Baculum Geodæt.* III. vii. 68 Appoint thy first station, and there place thy staffe, and take the angle of altitude, [etc.]. **1712** J. JAMES tr. *Le Blond's Gardening* 118 Station, is the Place where the Level is set for performing the Work of Leveling, so that one Cast of the Level is contained between two Stations. **1774** M. MACKENZIE *Marit. Surv.* 19 Draw out the Line C D, and it will cut the Circle in S, the Point of Station required. *c* **1791** *Encycl. Brit.* (ed. 3) VII. 674/2 Drawn from two points A and B, to the place of station C. **1875** *Encycl. Brit.* III. 387 s.v. *Barometer*, The heights read off from the pressures should be corrected for observations of temperature carefully taken at the upper and lower stations. **1880** L. D'A. JACKSON *Aids Surv.-Pract.* 112 A base line is measured, . . and a network of triangles conveniently arranged by choosing suitable positions for stations.

9. a. The place in which a thing stands or is appointed to stand. Now *rare* or *Obs.*

c **1440** *Pallad. on Husb.* XIII. 18 Vlpike and oynouns in their stacioun To growe. **1626** CAPT. SMITH *Accid. Yng. Seamen* 11 The gunwayle, stations for the nettings, a chaine through the stations, or brest-ropes. **1669** J. ROSE *Eng. Vineyard Vind.* (1675) 25 This will likewise maintain them cold and fresh in summer, till they have struck and taken hold of their stations. **1687** DRYDEN *Song St. Cecilia's Day* 9 Then cold, and hot, and moist, and dry, In order to their Stations leap, And Musick's pow'r obey. **1693** EVELYN *De La Quint. Compl. Gard., Cult. Orange Trees* 19 As soon therefore as you bring forth your Trees, and have Rang'd them in the Stations where they are to continue, bestow upon them as plentiful a Watering as [etc.]. *a* **1701** MAUNDRELL *Journ. Jerus.* (1732) 78 Whether they were cut out of the Rock, . . or whether they were brought, and fix'd in their station like other doors. **1711** ADDISON *Spectator* No. 98 ¶5 The Head has the most beautiful Appearance, as well as the highest Station, in a human Figure. **1792** *Baron Munchausen* xii. 39 With this balloon . . I played many tricks, such as taking one house from its station, and placing another in its stead. **1831** SCOTT *Cast. Dang.* ii, Groups of alder-trees . . which had maintained their stations in the recesses of the valley.

†**b.** The height at which the barometer stands.

1666 BOYLE in *Phil. Trans.* I. 237 When the Mercury . . is either very high, or very low, or at a middle station between its greatest and least height. **1753** *Scots Mag.* XV. 16/2 [Barometer] Common station 30 1/10.

†**c.** *Arith.* = PLACE *sb.* 10. *Obs.*

1709–29 V. MANDEY *Syst. Math., Arith.* 17 The Divisor being removed one station, repeat this Process, until all the figures of the Dividend be wasted.

d. *Biol.* The kind of place in which an animal or a plant is fitted to live, the nature or essential characteristics of its habitat.

1721 BRADLEY *Philos. Acc. Wks. Nat.* 49 Which is the same case with that which I have mention'd to be natural to Plants, which are each of them confin'd to their several Stations. **1832** LYELL *Princ. Geol.* II. 69 Station indicates the peculiar nature of the locality where each species is accustomed to grow, and has reference to climate, soil, humidity, light, elevation above the sea, and other analogous circumstances; whereas by habitation is meant a general indication of the country where a plant grows wild. **1854** STARK *Brit. Mosses* 59 Giving such explanation of the terms as will . . enable the tyro Muscologist, . . to assign their proper station and name to the mosses he may pick up. **1871** DARWIN *Desc. Man* I. xi. 403 Males and females of the same species of butterfly are known in several cases to inhabit different stations.

e. *Shipbuilding.* (See quot. 1913.)

1869 E. J. REED *Shipbuild.* ii. 29 An elevation of this Keel is given in Fig. 27. . . The stations are drawn in dotted lines. **1913** *Board of Trade Instr. Tonnage Measurement*, Rule 13. Points of division of length, or stations of the transverse areas.

10. *Naut.* **a.** More fully ***naval station.*** In early use, a port, harbour, or roadstead for ships. In modern use, a place at which ships of the Navy are regularly stationed.

1382 WYCLIF *Gen.* xlix. 13 Zabulon in the brynke of the see shal dwelle, and in the stacioun of shippes. **1615** G. SANDYS *Trav.* 22 The ruines [of Troy] . . are . . too neare the navall station to affoord a field for such dispersed encounters. *Ibid.* 38 At the West end thereof the Grand Signiors Gallies have a dry station. **1656** BLOUNT *Glossogr.*, *Station*, a standing place, a Bay or Rode for ships to rest in. **1697** DRYDEN *Virg. Georg.* IV. 608 A large Recess, . . A Station safe for Ships, when Tempests roar. *a* **1700** EVELYN *Diary* 10 Sept. 1677, Then we saw the Haven. . . The tide runs out every day, but the bedding being soft mudd it is safe for shipping and a station. **1708** J. CHAMBERLAYNE *St. Gt. Brit.* I. I. iii. (1743) 15 At Chatham is a Station for the Navy Royal. **1885** *Encycl. Brit.* XIX. 534/1 *Portsmouth*, a municipal and parliamentary borough, seaport, and naval station of Hampshire.

†**b.** A place in a harbour for the reception of a vessel. *Obs.*

1630 *R. Johnson's Kingd. & Commw.* 561 The Turkish Arsenals for shipping are foure; the first . . containeth three and thirty docks or stations for so many Gallies.

c. A place or region to which a government ship or fleet is assigned for duty.

1666 in *Verney Mem.* (1907) II. 350 We shall have but 80 sayle this summer to fight the Dutch, the rest are designed for the western station. **1669** STURMY *Mariner's Mag.* I. ii. 18 Now we are in our Station, and a good Latitude. **1775** *Lond. Chron.* 14–16 Mar. 254/2 His Majesty's ship Coventry . . is under sailing orders for the East Indies, with dispatches for the Commander in Chief of his Majesty's ships on that station. **1813** SIR J. GRAHAM in C. S. Parker *Life & Lett.* (1907) I. 32, I hear from all the captains on the station that there cannot be a more promising youngster. **1912** *Times* 19 Dec. 11/1 She was fit for service on the Australasian Station.

d. The period for which a vessel is appointed to a particular station.

c **1784** NELSON in Mahan *Life* (1899) 54 To the end of the station his order was never repealed.

11. *Mil.* **a.** A place where soldiers are garrisoned, a military post.

In the first quot. (tr. L. *statio*) the body of men garrisoned.

[**1382** WYCLIF *1 Sam.* xiii. 23 The stacioun of Philistym wente out [Vulg. *egressa est statio Philisthiim*].] **1609** HOLLAND *Amm. Marcell.* XVI. i. 55 Marcellus Generall of the Horse, who abode then but in the next stations, drave off to aid him. **1665** MANLEY *Grotius' Low C. Wars* 253 Prince Maurice . . built a continuing Station for his Camp. **1769** *De Foe's Tour Gt. Brit.* (ed. 7) III. 295 Between Hornby Castle and Kirkby-Lonsdale . . stands Overborough, . . which was a famous Station of Antoninus, called Bremetonacum. **1802** C. JAMES *Milit. Dict., Post, in war*, a military station; any sort of ground, fortified or not, where a body of men can be in a condition of resisting the enemy. **1876** VOYLE & STEVENSON *Milit. Dict.* 402/1 *Station, Military*, a locality chosen for the garrisoning of troops.

b. In India, a place where the English officials of a district, or the officers of a garrison (not in a fortress) resided. Also the aggregate society of such a place. Now *Hist.*

1848 *Alfred in India* 12 There are also numbers in the civil service, and they reside at what are called *stations*. **1860** W. H. RUSSELL *Diary India* I. xii. 194 The small and great pecuniary relations between the station and the bazaar. **1866** TREVELYAN *Dawk Bungalow* I. in *Fraser's Mag.* LXXIII. 231 Who asked the Station to dinner, and allowed only one glass of simkin to each guest? **1914** in *Cornhill Mag.* Dec. 811 The ordinary desultory after-dinner conversation of a small mofussil station.

c. *Air Force.* An aerodrome where personnel are employed or garrisoned.

1911, etc. [see *air-station* s.v. AIR *sb.*[1] B. III. 7]. **1922** *Encycl. Brit.* XXXI. 85/1 At the outbreak of the World War the stations on the organized east coast system of aerial patrol were as follows:—Eastchurch, [etc.]. **1942** T. RATTIGAN *Flare Path* I. 5, I suppose you came to see someone up at the station. **1977** *Daily Tel.* 7 Nov. 2 The Service's Ground Branch is most seriously affected, with one in three group captains nominated for command making it known at pre-selection stage that they are not interested in taking over their own station.

12. a. The locality to which an official is appointed for the exercise of his functions.

1632 LITHGOW *Trav.* III. 116 Their . . Priests are bred here, and from hence dispersed to their seuerall stations. **1667** PEPYS *Diary* 14 June, I am glad my station is to be here, near my own home. **1788** *Massachusetts Spy* 31 July 3/2 The 12th of March, Col. James Robertson's son . . was killed at a sugar camp, within a few hundred yards of his father's station. **1802** J. BENSON in J. Macdonald *Mem.* (1822) 374 We have spent the four last days in preparing a draught of the stations of the Preachers. **1893** D. DAVIDSON *Mem. Long Life* viii. (ed. 2) 198 Tanna was his judicial station.

b. *pl.* The annual list of appointments of Methodist ministers.

1885 *Minutes Wesleyan Conf.* 43 Each of the places mentioned in these Stations . . is the head of a Circuit.

13. a. A place where men are stationed and apparatus set up for some particular kind of industrial work, scientific research, or the like. Often with defining word, as ***fishing, seismological, telegraph, zoological station.***

1823 W. SCORESBY *Jrnl.* p. xl, This colony, which subsequently increased to a number of stations, has been continued. **1842** *Penny Cycl.* XXIV. 154/1 Any means of telegraphic communication which depends upon the deciphering of signals exhibited at a distant station is necessarily dependent upon contingencies of weather. **1861** MRS. MEREDITH *Over the Straits* i. 7 At Maria Island, the rocky hills and other so-called 'probation-stations' . . the prisoners were used in tens and twenties. **1870** HUXLEY in L. Huxley *Life & Lett.* (1900) I. 332 How glad I shall be to see your plan for 'Stations' carried into effect. Nothing could have a greater influence upon the progress of zoology. **1883** GOODE *Fish. Industr. U.S.A.* (Fish. Exhib. Publ.) 68 The following is a list of the hatching stations operated by the United States Fish Commission in 1883. **1885** W. K. BROOKS in *Mem. Boston Soc. Nat. Hist.* III. 367 Their fruitful harvest furnishes one with the earliest evidences of the value of marine zoological stations. **1912** *Standard* 20 Sept. 6/7 It has been decided . . to establish a wireless telegraph station at Barfleur. **1913** *Nature* 14 Aug. 610/1 Milne's aim was to secure a great number of seismological stations, scattered as widely as possible over the globe.

b. = POLICE-STATION.

1889 *Pall Mall Gaz.* 4 Nov. 3/1 Proceeding to Leman-street police station . . Mr. Davis found the entrance to the station barricaded with several crossings of red tape. **1901** MARY L. HENDEE tr. *C. Wagner's Simple Life* v. 65 The officer, though he finally collar the thief, can only conduct him to the station, not along the right road.

c. *Sc.* = PREACHING STATION.

1904 R. SMALL *Hist. U.P. Congreg.* II. 402 The station was opened..on the first Sabbath of November.

d. A mission station; a mission (MISSION *sb.* 6).

1834 J. A. WILSON *Jrnl.* 2 Jan. in *Missionary Life & Work in N.Z.* (1889) I. 7 We are..satisfied with the central position of the station. The large tribes are within a circle of twenty miles. **1851** H. R. RICHMOND *Jrnl.* in *Richmond-Atkinson Papers* (1960) I. ii. 85 On Monday evening we arrived at Mr Ashwell's station at Tukapoto. **1883** C. F. WILDER *Sister Ridnour's Sacrifice* 229 The converts..have been for many weeks at the station. **1923** O. SCHREINER *Thoughts on S. Afr.* 16 A minister of the Dutch Reformed Church..came to spend a night at our station. The accommodation of an up-country mission house is limited.

e. *U.S.* A branch post office.

1896 *Ann. Rep. U.S. Postmaster General* 14 All detail matters relating to the establishment and discontinuance of post offices, the establishment of stations,..would be superintended personally by the district supervisors. **1939** J. L. FLOHERTY *Make Way for Mail* x. 158 Twenty-four sub-postal stations are connected by tube system with the general post office. **1960** E. K. MEADOR *Billion Dollar Pork Barrel* i. 20, I..was appointed a regular clerk..at the same station where I had been working as a sub-carrier. **1977** *Times Lit. Suppl.* 18 Feb. 187/4 (Advt.), P.O. Box 307, Times Square Station, New York.

f. A broadcasting station; an establishment or organization transmitting radio or television signals. Cf. *radio station* s.v. RADIO sb. 7; *television station* s.v. TELEVISION 3 c.

1912: see *radio station* s.v. RADIO *sb.* 7. [**1913** *Wireless World* Apr. 8 (*caption*) Aden Wireless Station.] **1922** *Science & Invention* Feb. 937/2 We amateurs and experimenters sit by our cozy fireside..and enjoy wireless telephone music sent out by the now famous Westinghouse broadcasting station at Newark, or from one of the dozen other stations. **1923** *Daily Mail* 13 May 8/2 You turn the handle a quarter of an inch, 'tuning'-in to the Cardiff station. **1944** S. S. MCKAY *W. Lee O'Daniel & Texas Politics, 1938–1942* i. 22 In addition to the WBAP programs the Doughboys were taken to Dublin every Wednesday night for a program over a small station there. **1959** A. WEBSTER *Roots* II. i. 37 She turns the radio on, turning the dial knob through all manner of stations and back again until she finds some very loud dance music. **1969** *Listener* 6 Feb. 177/2 The daily output of all these stations is remarkable considering their limited resources in money, staff and equipment. **1978** J. IRVING *World according to Garp* xix. 432 The Vermont station carried the game..from Philadelphia.

g. A location in an automated system (e.g. for data processing or a manufacturing process) where a particular operation takes place.

1948 *Math. Tables & Other Aids to Computation* III. 150 The card reading unit is similar to a standard IBM Reproducing Punch, except that a full reading station has been inserted ahead of the punching station. **1949** B. L. DAVIES *Technol. Plastics* xvii. 317 Each one of a number of moulds is placed at a station round the table and a cam device is provided for opening it and ejecting the moulding automatically as the table rotates. **1976** *Sci. Amer.* Feb. 77 (*caption*) The three components..are mounted on an underbody shuttle and carried rear end first past five welding stations in sequence.

h. *colloq.* The headquarters of an intelligence service.

1973 A. MANN *Tiara* vii. 57 Would you ask the station to let me know each day what they hear? **1975** N. LUARD *Robespierre Serial* iv. 18 A member of the Paris station, a young cypher clerk. **1978** R. CASSILIS *Winding Sheet* I. xiv. 44 He was a good man... A good Head of Station..who hadn't forgotten his tradecraft.

14. *Australia* and *N.Z.* (See quot. 1898.)

1822 J. DIXON *Voyage to N.S.W.* 47 There have, however, been instances of stock-keepers, at distant stations, having been murdered. **1833** STURT *S. Australia* I. Introd. p. I, They..will only be occupied as distant Stock Stations. **1840** *Sydney Herald* 3 Jan. 1/7 My Station on the Lachlan River..was robbed by three armed Bushrangers. **1845** W. DEANS *Let.* 25 Nov. in J. Deans *Pioneers of Canterbury* (1937) 100 There will be no stations so far inland here as there are in Australia. **1851** E. SHORTLAND *Southern Districts N.Z.* xiii. 245 We arrived early in the afternoon at the native station near Lake Wairewa. **1873** *Hobgoblins* 31 The impenetrable woods disappeared and they were soon in sight of the home Station. **1891** E. KINGLAKE *Australian* 116 His holding is called a 'station', never a sheep farm or cattle ranch, in spite of the English novelists. **1898** MORRIS *Austral Eng.* 436 *Station*, originally the house with the necessary buildings and home-premises of a sheep-run, and still used in that sense; but now more generally signifying the run and all that goes with it. **1930** [see HOMESTEAD *sb.* 2 b]. **1950** *N.Z. Jrnl. Agric.* May 463/1 Years previously, when the present farm was part of a large station.

** In figurative applications.

15. *gen.* A metaphorical standing-place or position, e.g. in a class or enumeration, in a scale of estimation or dignity; and the like.

1605 SHAKS. *Macb.* III. i. 102 If you haue a station in the file, Not i' th' worst ranke of Manhood. **1611** BIBLE *Isa.* xxii. 19, I will driue thee from thy station, and from thy state shall he pull thee downe. **1681–6** J. SCOTT *Chr. Life* (1747) III. 124 The Apostles were placed in a higher Station than any of the rest, as being authorized by Christ to superintend and preside over them. **1772** MACKENZIE *Man of World* I. iv. (1823) 430 And he shortly attained the station of experienced vice. **1781** COWPER *Charity* 336 He..wins mankind, as his attempts prevail, A prouder station on the gen'ral scale. **1848** DE QUINCEY *Poetry of Pope* Wks. 1890 XI. 53 For not only is much that takes a station in books not literature; but inversely, much that really *is* literature never reaches a station in books. **1863** KINGLAKE *Crimea* (1876) I. 5 The invasion of the Crimea so tried..the enduring power of the nations engaged, that..their relative stations in Europe were changed. **1874** DUNGLISON *Med. Dict.* (Cent.), Given as a tonic, but not worthy an officinal station.

16. A person's position in the world; a state of life as determined by outward circumstances or conditions; *spec.* a calling, office, employment. Now *rare* or *Obs.* exc. in *private station*, an unofficial position.

1675 OWEN *Indwelling Sin* vii. (1732) 70 When any Lust grows high and prevailing..it is from the peculiar Advantage that it hath in the natural Constitution, or the Station or Condition of the Person in the World. **1697** G. DALLAS *Syst. Stiles* I. Ded., Being perswaded by some persons of the greatest Quality in the Kingdom, and others in Publick Stations. *Ibid.* (89) King Charles..most deservedly Conferred upon your Lordship, not only Titles of Honour, but also several Eminent Stations. *a* **1700** EVELYN *Diary* 4 Feb. 1685, A Proclamation order'd to be publish'd, that all Officers should continue in their stations. *a* **1704** T. BROWN *Satire Marriage* Wks. 1730 I. 58 This pagan confinement, this damnable station, Suits no order, nor age, nor degree in thy nation. **1713** ADDISON *Cato* IV. iv, When vice prevails, and impious men bear sway The post of honour is a private station. **1725** DE FOE *Voy. round World* (1840) 276 It is easy to be placed in a station of life, where ..gold..would be of no value. **1726** SWIFT *Gulliver* I. vi, They believe that the common Size of Human Understandings is fitted to some Station or other. **1784** J. POTTER *Virtuous Vill.* II. 71 His sermon on Sunday se'nnight is to consist of some general observations concerning the marriage station. **1801** *Farmer's Mag.* Jan. 79 The soldiers and sailors employed, are unproductive branches of the community; and the stations formerly occupied by them, must one way or other be filled up by others. **1815** W. H. IRELAND *Scribbleomania* 82 The station of groom to a lanky-ear'd Neddy. **1819** SHELLEY *Peter Bell 3rd* VI. xii, It is a dangerous invasion When poets criticize; their station Is to delight, not pose. **1822** SCOTT *Nigel* x, George Heriot, with the formality belonging to his station, observed, that [etc.]. **1833** HT. MARTINEAU *Vanderput* ix. 134 God appoints his servants their station. **1837** CARLYLE *Fr. Rev.* I. II. v, Great in a private station, Necker looks on from the distance; abiding his time. **1842** DICKENS *Amer. Notes* iv. (1850) 47/2 It is their station to work. And they *do* work.

17. a. Position in the social scale, as higher or lower.

1682 SIR T. BROWNE *Chr. Mor.* I. xxvii, Content may dwell in all Stations. **1693** EVELYN *De La Quint. Compl. Gard.* I. 12 Not affecting to be dress'd or adorn'd above the common Station of a Gard'ner. **1742** SHERLOCK *Let.* in G. Harris *Life Ld. Hardwicke* (1847) II. 27 Your lordship's great character & station place you out of the reach of any little service I am able to doe. **1783** BURKE *Rep. Affairs of India* Wks. 1842 II. 45 The reasons, assigned by Mr. Barwell..seem to your committee to be..not very fit to be urged by a man in his station. **1803** *Edin. Rev.* Jan. 289 We are well off to have got so much from a man of this Lord's station, who does not live in a garret, but 'has the sway' of Newstead Abbey. **1837** LOCKHART *Scott* I. v. 156 If the club consisted chiefly of persons..somewhat inferior to Scott in birth and station. **1849** MACAULAY *Hist. Eng.* vii. II. 197 These were the highest in station among the proselytes of James. **1851** DIXON *W. Penn* xiv. (1872) 121 A young girl of great beauty and spirit,..and of his own station in society. **1862** STANLEY *Jewish Ch.* (1877) I. vii. 137 The prophets.. were confined to no family or caste, station or sex.

b. *spec.* Elevated position, high social rank.

1731 SWIFT *On Death of Dr. Swift* 352 He never courted men in station. **1781** COWPER *Table Talk* 354 Such men are rais'd to station and command, When Providence means mercy to a land. **1824** W. IRVING *T. Trav.* (1848) 181 The villains could not sympathize with the delicate feelings of a man in station. **1832** HT. MARTINEAU *Ireland* vi. 91 Many other gentlemen of station and fortune. **1861** BROUGHAM *Brit. Const.* xx. 384 The army is officered by men of station and influence in the country.

III. A stopping-place.

18. A stopping place on a journey; a place of temporary abode in a course of migration.

1585 FETHERSTONE tr. *Calvin on Acts* xiii. 13. 299 Here is set downe another of Paul's stations. **1609** HOLLAND *Amm. Marcell.* XXVIII. xv. 349 Thinking with himselfe, what a deale of criminall matters he had brewed, in a certaine station [*marg.* or baiting towne]. **1796** H. HUNTER tr. *St. Pierre's Study Nat.* (1799) II. 500 My landlord, in another of my stations, has lived a very different life. **1825** SCOTT *Talism.* i, He joyfully hailed the sight of two or three palm-trees, which arose beside the well which was assigned for his mid-day station. **1837** CARLYLE *Fr. Rev.* II. VI. iii, They roll through the streets, with stern-sounding music,..pausing at set stations.

19. a. A regular stopping place on a road. Chiefly *U.S.*, a place on a coach route where a stop was made for change of horses and for meals.

1797 F. BAILY *Tour* (1856) 193 About half past nine we came to Graham station on the Kentucky shore; it may contain about twenty houses. **1834** J. HALL *Kentucky* II. 3 And every here and there a station—a rude block-house, surrounded with palisades, afforded shelter to the traveller, and refuge, in time of danger, to all within its reach. **1867** A. D. RICHARDSON *Beyond Mississippi* xxviii. 330 (Funk) The ranches forty or fifty miles apart where passengers take meals, are termed 'home stations'; those where the coach only stops to exchange teams, 'swing stations'. **1872** 'MARK TWAIN' *Roughing It* iv. (1882) 18 Then the rattling of the coach..awoke to a louder and stronger emphasis, and we went sweeping down on the station at our smartest speed.

b. *transf.*

1899 *Allbutt's Syst. Med.* VI. 808 Many of these nuclei are stations in long commissural fibre systems.

20. a. (More explicitly *railway station*.) A place where railway trains regularly stop for taking up and setting down passengers or for receiving goods for transport. Also, and more frequently, a building or group of buildings erected at such a place for purposes connnected with the transport of passengers and goods. Also with defining word, *passenger*, *goods station*.

In English the word is applied not only to an intermediate stopping-place (like the F. *station*), but also to a terminus (= F. *gare*). In recent use, a stopping-place not provided with buildings is called a 'halt'.

1830 BOOTH *L'pool & Manch. Railw.* 46 This Railway will cost above £800,000 including the charge for stations and depots at each end. **1838** *Times* 5 June 5/1 Here there is a 'station' for supplying coals, water, &c. to the engine, and for the embarking and disembarking of passengers. **1840** F. WHISHAW *Railw. Gt. Brit. & Irel.* 128 [Grand Junction Railway]. Besides the terminal stations, there are the following intermediate stations. **1847** HELPS *Friends in C.* I. iii. 33 As Milverton was driving me from the station through Durley Wood, there was [etc.]. **1886** *Encycl. Brit.* XX. 234/2 Railway stations are either 'terminal' or 'intermediate'. A terminal station embraces (1) the passenger station; (2) the goods station. **1891** MEREDITH *One of our Conq.* xxv, The former was requested to meet her at Penshurst station at noon.

b. *station-to-station* attrib. phr., used with reference to traffic between neighbouring stations.

1878 F. S. WILLIAMS *Mid. Railw.* 424 A piece of ground ..has been laid out for a stone, mineral, and station-to-station traffic. **1903** *Daily Chron.* 18 Dec. 6/3 They were asking Parliament to abolish some of the low station-to-station rates.

IV. Ecclesiastical uses.

21. *Hist.* A service at which the clergy of the city of Rome assembled at one of a certain number of churches within the city, each of which had its fixed day in the year for this celebration.

c **1410** LYDG. *Lyf Our Lady* lxii. (1484) i vj b, In a chirche whiche men of custome calle Sancta sanctorum..The same day there the prestys alle Solempnely make a stacion. **1483** CAXTON *Golden Leg.* 143 b/1 The pope ordeyned a stacion in that chyrche euery yere on ester day. *a* **1502** in *Arnolde's Chron.* (1811) 154 In the circumsicion of our Lorde is stacions to Saint Mari Transtiberine.

22. Each of a number of holy places visited by pilgrims in fixed succession; esp. each of those churches in the city of Rome at which 'stations' (see 21) were held, and to the visiting of which on certain days indulgences were attached. Also, a visit to such a holy place, or an assembly held there for purposes of devotion on the appointed day.

c **1380** WYCLIF *Wks.* (1880) 80 þei techen men þat for staciones of rome..þei schullen haue þousandis of ȝeris of pardon. *a* **1400** *Stac. Rome* (Vernon MS.) 230 And pardon in Rome þat is grete. þe Stacions þer men hit clepe Pope Bonefas confermed alle. *c* **1450** *MS. Ashm.* 61 lf. 128 The stasyons of Jerusalem. **1513** BRADSHAW *St. Werburge* I. 2412 So dyd Offa..Deuoutly to vysyte all the hole stacyons of the cytee of Rome. **1528** ROY *Rede me* (Arb.) 106 Hathe Englond soche stacions Of devoute peregrinacions As are in Fraunce and Italy? **1546** LANGLEY tr. *Pol. Verg. de Invent.* VIII. i. 147 Gregory..named the pompous sacrifices stacions bycause thei wer celebrated on certain daies limited and prescribed by statute. **1547** BOORDE *Introd. Knowl.* xxxix. (1870) 220 Forasmuch as ther be many that hath wrytten of the Holy Lande, of the stacyons, & of the Iurney or way. **1826** T. COLEMAN *Indulgences* etc. *Order Mt. Carmel* 18 When..we give the name of Stations to the visits we pay the churches or other places appointed by the Popes to pray there, we understand so many intervals of rest to gain the indulgences granted to those places. **1826** [J. R. BEST] *Transalpine Mem.* I. 130, I shall now transcribe..the account given in the 'Diario Romano'..of the ceremonies to be performed in Holy week... April 11th. Palm Sunday. Station at S. Gio. in Laterano.

23. *Stations* (*of the Cross*): the series of images or pictures (usually fourteen in number) representing successive incidents of the Passion, placed in a church (or sometimes in the open air) to be visited in order for meditation and prayer; the series of devotional exercises appointed to be used on this occasion.

1553 BECON *Reliques of Rome* (1563) 185 b, Pope Alexander the sixt assigned the Iubile and Stations to be had in sundrie prouinces and countreis. **1837** J. E. MURRAY *Summer in Pyrenees* II. 113 Numbers of devotees may be seen..kneeling and repeating the prescribed Pater and Ave at the various stations, or chapels. **1863** [MARG. ROBERTS] *Denise* I. 141 A station (one of those little chapels commemorating the different incidents of the Passion of our Lord). **1881** *Parochial Hymn-bk.* [R.C.] §xxxvii. 701 The Franciscan Fathers erected Calvaries,..surrounded them with Stations (or pictures representing the chief circumstances of our Lord's last painful journey)... The Sovereign Pontiffs, who had already granted..Indulgences to the *real* Stations of our Lord's Passion, did not hesitate to extend the same to these representations of them.

24. Phrases. *to go, make, perform one's* (or *the*) *stations, to go on* or *for stations*: to perform the prescribed acts of devotion in succession at certain holy places, or at the Stations of the Cross.

a **1445** ? GASCOIGN *Life St. Bridget* in *Myrr. our Ladye* (1873) p. lii, When she was at Rome..she wente euery daye the Stacyons ordeyned by the churche. *c* **1461** *Bale's Chron.* in *Town Chron.* (1911) 141 A generall remission and pardon to assoille all þoo that hadde made any avowe to goo the Stacions of Jerusalem or to Room. **1485** *Digby Myst.* (1882) III. 1911, I have gon þe stacyones by and by. **1509** FISHER *Funeral Serm. C'tess. Richmond* Wks. (1876) 295 After dyner full truely she wolde goe her Statyons, to thre Aulters dayly. *a* **1540** J. HEYWOOD *Four P.* A j, Yet haue I been at Rome also And gone the stacions all arowe. **1574** HELLOWES *Gueuara's Epist.* (1584) 173 There was alwaies in the temple one priest alone..and those that went thither on stations, they might only kisse yᵉ walls. **1687** A. LOVELL tr. *Thevenot's Trav.* I. 182 They made us perform the Stations at three Altars. **1702** MARWOOD *Diary* in *Cath. Rec. Soc. Publ.* VII. 119 Mond. 23 [Jan.]. In Classe the Esqʳ was a little Indisposed but Stayᵈ it out, & held well all day after, but did not go for his Stations. *Ibid.* Wed. 25. He went his Stations in ye Morn... Thursd. 26... We were at my Lᵈ W.[aldegrave] & at even made Station wᵗʰ him. **1753** CHALLONER *Cath. Chr. Instr.* 220 And where there are many Churches the Faithful make their Stations to visit our Lord in these Sepulchres, and meditate on the different Stages of his Passion. **1815** MRS. SCHIMMELPENNINCK *Demol. Port Royal* III. 283 When he had finished his stations, he returned to his beloved solitude.

25. A special service held at a holy place.

1447 BOKENAM *Seyntys, Elisabeth* 335 And eek at stacyowns wher sermons shuld be, She nold ben among þe statys hy, But among þe wummen of porest degre She alwey wold syttyn. **1554** tr. *Doctr. Masse Bk.* B vij b, The halowing of the fyre on Easter Euen. ¶ This wyse let there be a station vnto the fyre. Let the priest stand by the fyre,..and let yᵉ deacon stand on his lefte hand, [etc.]. *a* **1843** in *Southey's Comm.-pl. Bk.* Ser. II. (1849) 8, I attended the stations that are performed in the chapels on Sunday evenings. *Ibid.* 9, I went to the Lough, and performed the station according to order, but found no ease to my troubled mind thereby. **1847** W. REEVES *Eccl. Antiq.* 301 A holy well where the Roman Catholics of old held stations at midsummer. **1890** J. HEALY *Insula Sanct.* 210 The Wedder's well..is still regarded as a holy well by the people who hold a station there on the feast of Brendan.

26. *Hist.* The bi-weekly fast (on Wednesday and Friday) anciently observed.

1637 GILLESPIE *Eng. Pop. Cerem.* III. iv. 78 No man taketh the Stations to have beene occasionall, but only set fasts. **1673** CAVE *Prim. Chr.* I. vii. 180 These fasts [weekly fasts kept on Wednesdays and Fridays] they called their stations—not because they stood all the while but by an allusion to the Military Stations and Keeping their Guards. *a* **1711** KEN *Urania* Poet. Wks. 1721 IV. 451 She sacred Fasts and Stations strictly keeps, And for the publick Provocations weeps. **1909** C. BIGG *Orig. Chr.* xv. 191 They fasted commonly upon the 'Stations', that is to say, on all Wednesdays and Fridays.

27. *Ireland.* A visit of a Roman Catholic parish priest and his curate to the house of a parishioner on a weekday, to give to those living in the neighbourhood the opportunity of confession.

1830 CARLETON *Traits Ir. Peasantry* (1843) I. 145 [The parish priest says] 'Take notice, that the Stations for the following week will be held as follows:—On Monday, in Jack Gallagher's,' [etc.]. **1844** *Min. Proc. & Evid. Athlone Election Petit.* 26 What do you mean by a station?—The priest goes to the house to hear the family their duties and confessions.

V. Combinations.

28. Obvious combinations: in sense 20, as ***station announcer, buffet, -building, -clerk, -door, -foreman, hotel, †-keeper, manager, platform, -porter, -yard***; in sense 14, as ***station hack, holder, horse, manager, owner, property, stock; station-bred*** adj.; in sense 19, as ***station-boss, -building***; in senses 23–26, as ***station-chapel, -vigil***; in sense 11c, 13b, as ***station commander***; in sense 13f, as ***station director, manager, operation***; in sense 13h, as ***station chief***.

1964 'J. H. ROBERTS' *'Q' Document* (1965) ii. 54 The blaring voice of the *station announcer calling the trains. **1872** 'MARK TWAIN' *Roughing It* iv. (1882) 22 The *station-boss stopped dead still, and glared at me, speechless. **1890** 'R. BOLDREWOOD' *Col. Reformer* (1891) 223 Quiet *station-bred cattle. **1939** N. COWARD *To step Aside* 61, I had some tea with her in the *station buffet at Dieppe. **1941** J. D. CARR *Case of Constant Suicides* i. 15 Drinking slopped tea..in a steamy station-buffet. **1978** D. KYLE *Black Camelot* viii. 119 He went into the station buffet and bought a cup of tea and a Banbury cake. **1872** 'MARK TWAIN' *Roughing It* iv. (1882) 19 The *station buildings were long low huts, made of sun-dried, mud-coloured bricks. **1898** *Engineering Mag.* XVI. 77 One range of station buildings suffices for the travellers by all the trains. **1890** A. J. C. HARE *S.E. France* 575 Seven *station-chapels rise..amongst the wormwood and lavender on the tufa rocks. **1974** W. GARNER *Big Enough Wreath* iv. 41, I have a *station chief in London. **1858** SIMMONDS *Dict. Trade*, **Station-clerk*, a railway clerk. **1943** C. H. WARD-JACKSON *It's a Piece of Cake* 8 We've a new *Station Commander who is keen on physical training, and life is one long parade from six in the morning till ten at night. **1972** *Police Rev.* 1 Dec. 1569/2 Why should not the station commander himself take action? **1978** R. V. JONES *Most Secret War* xliv. 419 The Station Commander told Hartley that he had been watching all three squadrons. **1923** J. REITH *Diary* 25 Oct. (1975) ii. 132 Very busy on new regulations for SB... I am leaving it more to the *station directors. **1860** W. COLLINS *Woman in White* xiv, She set them down outside the *station-door. **1901** *Westm. Gaz.* 24 Dec. 7/2 *Station foreman. **1890** 'R. BOLDREWOOD' *Col. Reformer* (1891) 101 The ordinary *station-hacks. **1878** E. S. ELWELL *Boy Colonists* 27 When the men..wanted any of these articles for *personal use*..the *station-holder sold them to them. **1911** C. E. W. BEAN *'Dreadnought' of Darling* vii. 75 Leagues away even from the homestead cows or the *station horses. **1966** 'J. HACKSTON' *Father clears Out* 14 No station horse of any standing would have approved of our little farm. **1862** *Bailey's Mag.* Sept. 156 Never for many years had York been so full before; and at the *station hotels Lords were as plentiful as partridges in Norfolk. **1846** *Commerc. Mag.* Oct. 134 He quitted the first-class carriage on reaching Rugby..desiring the *station-keeper to inform the directors, that [etc.]. **1911** C. E. W. BEAN *'Dreadnought' of Darling* xvii. 167 One *station manager told us that he had found scores of them [*sc.* rabbits] dead around their burrows. **1962** *B.B.C. Handbk.* 30 The station managers must aim to build a partnership between the broadcaster and the community. **1965** *Guardian* 11 Feb. 16/4 Stationmasters in the London-Midland region of British Rail..would be replaced by station managers, who would have wider powers. **1977** D. L. ALTHEIDE in Douglas & Johnson *Existential Sociol.* iv. 142 Secondly, there is the relation of the news to the overall *station operation, including sales, production, and programming. **1911** E. M. CLOWES *On Wallaby* iii. 69 A *station-owner's life, even in these days, is not all beer and skittles. **1968** K. WEATHERLY *Roo Shooter* 42 Three weeks later it rained... The station owners smiled. **1886** KIPLING *Plain Tales from Hills* (1888) 117 Nobody ever dreamed of seeing him handcuffed on a *station platform. **1907** J. H. PATTERSON *Man-Eaters of Tsavo* vii. 75 The 'boy'..informed me that..an enormous lion was standing on the station platform. **1886** W. J. TUCKER *E. Europe* 384 The station-master..filling the posts as he did of *station-porter, station-master, and chief of the postal and telegraphic department. **1890** *Golden South* 96 We invested ours in a large *station property. **1880** *Town & Country Jrnl.* (N.S.W.) 14 Feb. 314/4 The *station stock seldom feed near the road. **1898** BAYLAY tr. *Batiffol's Hist. Rom. Breviary* 14 Sunday vigils, *station vigils, vigils in cemeteries, each comprising a triple office. **1854** MRS. STOWE *Sunny Mem.* II. 184 We made a descent like an avalanche into the *station yard. **1886** *Encycl. Brit.* XX. 234/2 In laying out the approaches and station-yard of passenger stations ample width and space should be provided.

29. Special combinations: **station agent,** (*a*) chiefly *U.S.*, a person in charge of a stage-coach or railway station; (*b*) a person working for an intelligence service; **station-bill** *Naut.* (see quot.); **station break** *U.S.*, a break (BREAK *sb.*[1] 8k) between radio or television items or programmes, during which the station identifies or advertises itself; **station-day** † (*a*) in Ireland, the day of some municipal ceremony (sense 4b); (*b*) *Eccl.* the day of a station or special service (see 21, 25); also, the day of the ancient bi-weekly fast (see 26); **station-distance** *Surveying* (see quot.); **station-finder** = *station-pointer*; **station hand** *Austral.* and *N.Z.*, a man employed on a station; **station head,** the chief of an intelligence service headquarters; **station hospital,** a hospital attached to a military station; **station-indicator** (see quot. 1884); **station-jack** *Austral.*, a kind of meat pudding used in the bush; **station-keeping** *Naut.*, the maintenance of the proper relative position of ships in a moving squadron; also *transf.* and as *ppl. a.*; **station-line,** (*a*) *Perspective*, the vertical line drawn through the point of sight (see also quot. 1704); (*b*) *Surveying* (see quot. 1875); **stationman,** (*a*) a person employed on the (underground) railways, as a platform attendant, porter, etc.; (*b*) = *station hand*; **station meter** *Gas-making* (see quot. 1844); **station-point,** (*a*) *Perspective* (see quot. 1859); (*b*) *Surveying*, a station or the point on a plan corresponding to a station; **station-pointer** *Surveying* (see quot. 1876); **station-pole** *Surveying*, a pole set up at a station; **station-rod** = *station-staff*; **station-sergeant,** the police sergeant in charge of a station; † **station ship,** a patrol vessel appointed to a particular station; **station-staff** *Surveying* (see quot. 1701); **station time** *Eccl.*, the time when a station is celebrated.

1857 *Trans. Illinois Agric. Soc.* II. 25 The active co-operation of this company, through its *station agents...in bringing forward an interesting show. **1879** E. J. SIMMONS *Mem. Station Master* (1974) ix. 131 The Long and Narrow Railway paid their station-agent better than the Great Smash Company. **1910** J. HART *Vigilante Girl* xv. 203 He stopped at the stage station... When the station agent looked to see what the man had written [etc.]. **1948** *Westerners Brand Bk.* (Denver Posse) 21 Louis J. F. Jaeger ..was the Butterfield station agent at Fort Yuma. **1974** J. GRADY *Six Days of Condor* 109 Who do you suppose was station agent out of Taiwan? **1815** *Falconer's Dict. Marine* (ed. Burney), **Station Bill* (*rôle de postes*, Fr.) a list containing the appointed posts of the ship's-company, when navigating the ship. **1949** *Consumer Rep.* May 236/2 A '*station-break' can..be inserted between the close of one commercial program and the opening of the next. **1971** D. E. WESTLAKE *I gave at Office* (1972) 133 I've been in this business long enough to know a lead-in for a station break when I see one, and that finish was a natural, so I took a station break. **1560** in Sir J. T. Gilbert *Cal. Anc. Rec. Dublin* (1891) II. 9 Fremen..shall attende upon the Maior..at all *stacion daies, and not to depart tyll the stacion be done. **1563–83** FOXE *A. & M.* 1402/1 (Canon of Mass), In the city of Rome they sayd them [*sc.* collects] ouer the people collected together in the station day. **1637** GILLESPIE *Eng. Pop. Cerem.* III. iv. 78 Their set dayes of 150 fasting, which were called Station dayes. **1898** W. BRIGHT *Some Aspects Prim. Ch. Life* iii. 118 Wednesdays and Fridays [were] called 'Station-days' apparently by adaptation of a term used for military duty. **1798** HUTTON *Course Math.* (1807) II. 67 measure the distances from station to station... And in measuring any of these *station-distances, mark accurately where [etc.]. **1875** W. PATERSON *Notes Milit. Surv.* (ed. 3) 38 *Station-Distance*, measurements entered in the centre column of the field-book which are taken upon the station-lines from each station. **1888** W. H. RICHARDS *Milit. Topogr.* 115 The problem is seldom used except for finding a ship's place with regard to points on the coast, which are shown on the chart; an instrument called a '*station finder' is generally used for the purpose. **1885** RAE *Chirps Austral. Sparrow* 99 Some *station hands had been in jail. **1894** H. NISBET *Bush Girl's Rom.* xxix. 271 The station hands, who have to go out at daybreak, generally have their main feed then. **1930** L. G. D. ACLAND *Early Canterbury Runs* 1st Ser. i. 8 When an old fashioned squatter or station hand used the word 'homestead' he used it to signify the owner's residence. **1974** J. GRADY *Six Days of Condor* 108 He worked his way..from special field agent to *station head. **1901** *Empire Rev.* I. 435 The details of management of *station hospitals. **1884** KNIGHT *Dict. Mech.* Suppl. 853 **Station indicator*, an indicator operating in connection with the driving-wheels to exhibit automatically the name of the station or street immediately preparatory to arrival. **1895** *Daily News* 28 Nov. 5/4 The station indicator has been in experimental running on this Company's Hounslow branch for many months past. **1853** *Emigrant's Guide Australia* 112 Take.. the flour and work it into a paste; then put the beef into it, boil it, and you will have a very nice pudding, known in the bush as '*Station-jack'. **1886** *Pall Mall Gaz.* 19 Aug. 2/1 Giving me my first introduction to the mysteries of *station-keeping. **1898** KIPLING in *Morn. Post* 5 Nov. 5/1 The ships haven't worked together, and station-keeping isn't as easy as it looks. **1962** *Punch* 18 Apr. 597/3 A British scheme 'envisages'..'twelve station-keeping active-relay satellites'. **1971** *Daily Tel.* 14 Sept. 2/6 The 'station-keeping' device would be useful in fog..to indicate the correct distance behind the vehicle in front. **1704** J. HARRIS *Lex. Techn.* I, **Station-Line.* See *Line of Station. Line of Station*, in Perspective, according to some Writers, is the common Section of the Vertical and Geometrial Planes. Others, as Lamy, mean by it the perpendicular Height of the Eye above the Geometrick Plane. Others, a Line drawn on that Plane, and perpendicular to the Line expressing the Height of the Eye. *c* **1791** *Encycl. Brit.* (ed. 3) VII. 679/1 The distances taken by the off-set staff, on either side of the station-line, are to be entered into columns on either side of the middle column. **1798** HUTTON *Course Math.* (1828) II. 68 As you go along any main station-line, take offsets to the ends of all hedges [etc.]. **1859** RUSKIN *Perspective* Introd. 9 From S let fall a perpendicular line SR, to the bottom of the paper, and call this line the Station-line. This represents the line on which the observer stands at a greater or less distance from the picture. **1875** W. PATERSON *Notes Milit. Surv.* (ed. 3) 38 *Station-line*, the one the surveyor walks along in measuring from one station to another, and from which he takes his angles, distances, and off-sets. **1952** *Britannica Bk. of Year* 667/1 **Stationman*,..a platform attendant of the London Transport (Underground) railways. **1963** *Times* 24 May (London Underground Centenary Suppl.) p. vii/4 Passengers refused to leave trains at the haughty ordering of stationmen who refused to give any explanation of why the journey could not continue. **1966** 'J. HACKSTON' *Father clears Out* 174 Fearfully I looked round as if at that moment one of the station men would come riding up and find me with the dead sheep. **1968** *Daily Tel.* (Colour Suppl.) 13 Dec. 14/1 The wild adventures of train controllers and station men, or signalmen and porters as they used to be called in the dull old days. **1974** P. WRIGHT *Lang. Brit. Industry* i. 19 Notice that on the London tubes, the 'degrading' rank of *porter* has been engulfed in *stationman.* **1844** *E. A. Parnell's Appl. Chem.* I. 145 A large meter, called the *station meter, is placed at the gas-works between the purifier and the gasometers, to ascertain at pleasure the quantity of gas made during any given period. **1859** RUSKIN *Perspective* Introd. 10 On this line [the Station-line] mark the distance ST, at your pleasure, for the distance at which you wish your picture to be seen, and call the point T the *Station-point. **1880** L. D'A. JACKSON *Aids Surv.-Pract.* 96 Some recorders use alphabetical letters to designate station-points. **1774** M. MACKENZIE *Marit. Surv.* 24 Such an Instrument as this may be called a *Station-pointer. **1804** *Nicholson's Jrnl.* VII. 1 Description and Use of the Station Pointer; an Instrument for readily ascertaining the Situation of the Observer after having determined the angular Position of three known Objects. **1876** *Catal. Loan Collect. Sci. Apparatus S. Kens. Mus.* (1877) 733 Station Pointer, 6-inch. For placing the observer's position on the chart from angles taken between three objects, the relative positions of which are known. **1880** L. D'A. JACKSON *Aids Surv.-Pract.* 112 The *station poles used as survey marks. **1835** *Lond. Jrnl. Arts & Sci.* Conj. Ser. VI. 329 The graduated *station rods or staffs..placed perpendicularly .., the glass vessel at the lower station must be slidden up its rod [etc.]. **1890** *Daily News* 5 Dec. 7/1 The old term *station-sergeant will be substituted in lieu of sub-inspector. The pay of station-sergeants will commence at 45s. per week, as at present. **1901** *Essex Weekly News* 13 Sept. 6/5 Station-Sergeant George Card was found in the station shot through the heart. **1758** *Memoirs of Last War* 20 Being favoured therein by the casual Absence of the Canso *Station Ship, omitted to be sent that Year, as was likewise the usual Station Ship to Boston. **1658** PHILLIPS, **Station-staff*, an instrument used in Surveying, being a streight pole divided into feet, inches, and parts of inches, from the bottom upward. **1701** MOXON *Math. Instr.* 19 *Station-staff*, made of 2 Rulers that slide to ten Foot, divided into Feet and Inches, with a moving Vein or sight, two of which are used with a Leavel, and on the edges we divide the Links of Gunter's Chain: used in Surveying for the more easie taking off Sets. **1708** *Brit. Apollo* No. 32. 2/1, 2 Station-Staves, with Moveable Vanes. **1842** *Penny Cycl.* XXII. 359/2 Direct the object-end of the telescope successively to the station-staves held up on the different pickets. **1387** TREVISA *Higden* (Rolls) VII. 77 Þere þe pope syngeþ þe masse þre Sondayes in þe ȝere in þe *stacioun tyme. **1643** in *10th Rep. Hist. MSS. Comm.* App. v. 494 We.. doe order that all Assemblies and station tymes that all the aforesaid persons respectivelie shall take their places as is aforesaid sett downe.

station (ˈsteɪʃən), *v.* [f. STATION *sb.* Cf. F. *stationner* (1606 in Hatz.-Darm.), Pg. *estacionar*.]

1. *trans.* To assign a post, position or station to (a person, troops, ships, etc.); to place or post (a sentinel, etc.) in a station.

1748 SMOLLETT *Rod. Rand.* xxix, I was not a whit more exposed than those who were stationed about me. **1760** *Inform. Dk. Gordon* v. *Earls Murray & Fife* 11 The bay which the river forms at its mouth in which ships are stationed. *a* **1781** WATSON *Philip III* (1839) 91 Some companies of Scotch troops, which had been stationed in Cadsant. **1786** BURNS *Tam Samson* iv, Wha will they [the Curlers] station at the cock, Tam Samson's dead? **1809**

Lond. Chron. 29 July 101/2 Some sheep, which he had stationed upon a very deep declivity near the rocks. **1823** SCOTT *Quentin D.* xvii, Upon knocking gently at the gate, a brother, considerately stationed for that purpose by the Prior, opened it. **1842** LD. ABERDEEN in *Excheq. Rep.* II. 182 The laudable practice of stationing cruisers off slave-factory stations. **1849** MACAULAY *Hist. Eng.* i. I. 142 The troops stationed near London. **1867** SMYTH *Sailor's Word-bk.*, *Stationing a Ship's Company*, arranging the crew for the ready execution of the evolutionary duties of a ship. **1892** BIERCE *In Midst of Life* 108 Before stationing his men the young officer..had [etc.]. **1903** *Union Mag.* Jan. 16/1 He was at that time 'stationed' in the Brixton Hill circuit in London.

transf. **1837** LYTTON *E. Maltravers* I. i, He kept his eyes stationed on the door.

b. To place in a certain position in a list.

1865 *Nat. Hist. Rev.* 313 At the head of the order Dr. Günther stations the Typhlopidæ, Tortricidæ, [etc.].

c. *refl.* To take up one's station, post oneself. Also in *passive* with reflexive notion. Said occas. of a thing.

1780 *Mirror* No. 103 There is a.. merry-looking dog of a sailor..stationed at the corner of the street where I live. **1826** F. REYNOLDS *Life & T.* II. 56 Stationing himself at the side,..he said, 'There!' **1829** *Chapters Phys. Sci.* 343 According to the motions which the object makes, the image touches it or stations itself by its side. **1838** LYTTON *Alice* I. viii, Lady Vargrave was stationed by the open window. **1889** W. LOCKHART *Ch. Scot. 13th C.* vii. 79 The bishop stationed himself at the left corner of the church towards the east.

d. In *passive*, of a plant: To have a certain station or position of growth.

1837 P. KEITH *Bot. Lex.* 323 Such species as have their barren and fertile flowers on distinct plants, do not perfect their fruit except where individuals of both sorts are stationed in the vicinity of one another.

2. *Shipbuilding.* To determine the proper position for (timbers).

1797 *Encycl. Brit.* (ed. 3) XVII. 406/2 In stationing the timbers upon the keel for a boat, there must [etc.]. **1869** E. J. REED *Shipbuild.* viii. 148 There was no necessity for stationing every beam at a frame.

stational ('steɪʃənəl), *a.* [ad. L. *stațiōnālis*, f. *statiōn-em* STATION *sb.*: see -AL[1]. Cf. F. *stationnal* (in eccl. sense), Sp. *estacional* seasonable.] Of or pertaining to a station or stations, in any sense of the sb. *stational mass*: see quot. 1905.

1610 FOLKINGHAM *Feudigr.* II. vi. 57 Now describe a Circle vpon this stationall point. **1620** —— *Brachigr.* iv, The Puncts in the Paralels imply the fiue Vowels respectiuely sutable to their stationall Regions and priorities in vulgar enumeration. **1826** T. COLEMAN *Indulgences*, etc. *Order Mt. Carmel* 49 It is to be observed, that except on the above named days, there is no Stational Indulgence at Rome. **1863** FLOR. NIGHTINGALE (*title*), The stational reports..on the Sanitary State of the Army in India. **1902** J. K. MANN *Hist. Popes* I. I. 284 This part gives the ceremonies to be observed in the celebration of a *stational* Mass by the Pope. **1905** ATCHLEY *Ordo Rom. Primus* 32 A stational mass or station was one whereat the whole local Church was present (or represented), from the bishop to the layfolk. *Ibid.* 33 Preceded..by the stational cross. *Ibid.* 119 The stational church.

stationar ('steɪʃənə(r)). *Eccl.* [ad. med.L. use of late L. *statiōnārius*: see STATIONARY *sb.*]

†**1.** Used to render G. *stationirer*, mendicant friar.

c **1640** H. BELL *Luther's Colloq. Mens.* (1652) 285 It will ere long com to that pass in Germanie (said Luther) as it is in Spain and in France, where no Preachers are, but onely Runners up and down, as in former time with us the Stationars were.

2. (See quot.)

1868 WALCOTT *Sacred Archæol.* 554 The Roman churches in which the Pontiff officiates on stated days are called churches of the stations or mansionary, and the assistant clergy are spoken of as stationars.

stationarily ('steɪʃənərɪlɪ), *adv.* [f. STATIONARY *a.* + -LY[2].] In a stationary manner.

1778 [W. MARSHALL] *Minutes Agric., Observ.* 158 *note*, The Barometer remaining stationarily heavy. **1872** ELLACOMBE *Ch. Bells Devon*, etc. 535 The usual way of mounting this 'chime' is to make the tenor swing, for occasional ringing, all the others being stationarily hung from trusses.

stationariness ('steɪʃənərɪnɪs). [+ -NESS.] The condition or quality of being stationary.

1727 BAILEY vol. II, *Stationariness*, Settledness in a Place. **1797** GODWIN *Enquirer* II. v. 231 All..depended upon the perennial stationariness of his understanding. **1803** MALTHUS *Popul.* III. ii. (1806) II. 119 On this happiness or degree of misery depends principally the increase, stationariness, or decrease of population. **1882** FARRAR *Early Chr.* II. 9 When once settled in that city, St. James, with the natural stationariness of the Oriental, seems never to have left it.

stationarity (ˌsteɪʃəˈnærɪtɪ). [f. STATIONARY *a.* + -ITY.] The condition of stationary motion. More widely, the state of being stationary or unvarying; stationariness; constancy.

1901 *Nature* 11 Apr. 573/2 Signor Levi-Civita..is of opinion that Routh's definition of stationarity should be completed by adding the proviso that [etc.]. **1955** M. LOÈVE *Probability Theory* ix. 418 In the integral stationarity case, the basic ergodic inequality takes very simple forms. **1972** *Nature* 8 Dec. 338/1 Hot spots have been hypothetically identified as mantle plumes and their stationarity with respect to the Earth's spin axis demonstrated. **1973** *Sci. Amer.* July 8/2 The demographic behavior of these nations is pointing in the direction of a rough equilibrium of deaths and births, that is, stationarity. **1973** *Animal Behaviour* XXI. 181/1 The assumption of stationarity of the processes in equation (7) seems justified if one bears in mind that the animals observed lived under constant conditions.

stationary ('steɪʃənərɪ), *a.* and *sb.* Also 5 **stacionarye**, *Sc.* **stationeir**, 6 **stationarie**. [ad. L. *statiōnārius*, in classical Latin 'belonging to a military station', f. *statiōn-em* STATION *sb.*: see -ARY. Cf. F. *stationnaire*, It. *stazionario*, Sp. *estacionario*.]

A. *adj.*

1. Having a fixed station or place.

a. Residing or established in one place; not itinerant or migratory.

1670 R. COKE *Disc. Trade* 15 As sundry Laws provided against wandring Beggers..so this Law provides for, and relieves stationary Beggers. **1768** BLACKSTONE *Comm.* III. iv. 38 The court being thus rendered fixed and stationary. **1796** MME. D'ARBLAY *Camilla* I. i, A passion for field sports had, with equal constancy, kept his brother stationary. **1815** JANE AUSTEN *Emma* xxxvi, She has now been a longer time stationary there than she ever was before. **1831** SCOTT *Cast. Dang.* ii, We..scorn to be chased from our supper, or cheated out of our share of it by a dozen Scotchmen, whether stationary or strollers. **1851** MAYHEW *Lond. Labour* I. 388 The stationary lace sellers, for the most part, display their goods on stalls. **1866** GEO. ELIOT *F. Holt* ii. I. 67, I suppose I know the state of Europe as well as if I'd been stationary at Little Treby for the last fifteen years. **1870** SPENCER *Princ. Psychol.* I. IV. v. 437 Instead of a stationary creature, suppose the creature contemplated to be one that habitually moves about in the water. **1900** *Daily News* 17 May 3/2 A field hospital is a very different affair from a stationary base hospital.

b. Standing still; not moving.

stationary air, the amount of air which remains constantly in the lungs in ordinary respiration.

1784 COWPER *Task* IV. 147 No stationary steeds Cough their own knell. **1794** MRS. RADCLIFFE *Myst. Udolpho* xxviii, It was still stationary, and she began to doubt, whether it was really animated. **1826** *Art of Brewing* (ed. 2) 48 The thermometer was stationary more than 30 hours. **1832** BREWSTER *Nat. Magic* iv. 65 So that the image may remain stationary. **1839** DICKENS *Nich. Nick.* ii, The clerk calmly remained in a stationary position. **1862** STANLEY *Jew. Ch.* (1877) I. xi. 211 The sun, being stationary, could not be said to stand still or to move. **1878** H. N. MARTIN in *Jrnl. Physiol.* I. 149 When..the lungs are emptied, some of this pure air must be left in the mouth, and, in the immediately succeeding inspiration, will be sent into the lungs as a sort of 'tidal air' with some of the air just expelled from them, which will correspond to the 'stationary air' of the mammal.

c. *Astr.* Said of planets at the portions of their orbits in which they have no apparent motion. (Cf. STATION *sb.* 5.) Hence *stationary point* = 'point of station'.

1426 LYDG. *De Guil. Pilgr.* 12353 And cause hem [the Planets] in the ffyrmament Ther tabyde stacionarye. *c* **1480** HENRYSON *Mor. Fab.* IV. (*Fox's Confess.*) iii, The planeitis.. Sum retrograde, and sum stationeir. **1665** *Phil. Trans.* I. 105 The star becomes stationary. **1700** MOXON *Math. Dict.* (1701) s.v., Hence a Planet is said to be Stationary, when he is about either of these his Stations. **1812** WOODHOUSE *Astron.* xxiii. 249 When a planet is stationary, the fact of observation is, that [etc.]. **1852** HIND *Astron. Vocab.*, *Stationary Points* of a planet's orbit are those in which as viewed from the earth, it appears to have no motion amongst the stars. **1901** *Athenæum* 27 July 131/2 Jupiter and Saturn ....are approaching their stationary points.

d. Having a fixed position; not movable. Of a machine or part of a machine: That remains in one spot when in operation. *stationary bicycle*, *bike* (N. Amer.), a fixed machine, resembling a bicycle, used in fitness exercises.

1648 WILKINS *Math. Magick* II. iv. 172 Thus much of those Automata, which were said to be fixed and stationary. **1815** J. SMITH *Panorama Sci. & Art* II. 115 The forcing pump is furnished with two valves, which are both stationary. **1821** CRAIG *Lect. Drawing*, etc. ii. 96 By making everything in the scenery whether stationary or adventitious, darker than any part of the sky. **1825** J. NICHOLSON *Oper. Mech.* 661 The low pressure engines used in vessels, which are made twice as strong as stationary engines. **1840** H. S. TANNER *Canals & Rail Roads U.S.* 260 *Stationary engines* are used for effecting the ascent and descent of carriages along inclined planes. *Stationary plane*, a plane worked by a stationary engine and rope. **1869** RANKINE *Machine & Hand-tools* Pl. P 5, Looking on the stationary-rivet end of the machine. **1881** *Nature* 29 Sept. 514/2 The instrument thus provides a stationary solar star-disk for continuous observation. **1889** G. FINDLAY *Eng. Railway* 5 Steam [in 1804]..had been applied to the working of stationary engines. **1962** E. LUCIA *Klondike Kate* ii. 53 And pedalled for hours on the stationary bicycle to keep her figure. **1969** *Sears Catal.* Spring/Summer 400/2 Stationary Bike... Pedal for miles without leaving the comfort of your own home. Chain-driven pedal action gives you the same exercise as regular bicycle. **1976** *Woman's Day* (U.S.) Nov. 154/2 If you don't want to be on public display, try a stationary bicycle or running in place in your bedroom.

e. *Physics. stationary motion*: see quot. 1870. *stationary wave* = *standing wave* s.v. STANDING *ppl. a.* 11 e.

1856 D. LARDNER *Hand-bk. Nat. Philos.* IV. IV. i. 350 (*heading*) Stationary waves. **1867** J. TYNDALL *Sound* 101 The step of a water-carrier is sometimes so timed as to throw the surface of the water in his vessel into stationary waves, which may augment in height until the water splashes over the brim. **1870** tr. *Clausius* in *Lond.*, etc. *Philos. Mag.* Aug. 123 By stationary motion I mean one in which the points do not continually remove further and further from their original position, and the velocities do not alter continuously in the same direction, but the points move within a limited space, and the velocities only fluctuate within certain limits. **1877** E. J. ROUTH *Dynamics Rigid Bodies* (ed. 3) 283 The first result is clear, since in stationary motion $\Sigma X = 0$, &c. **1905** *Brit. Pat. 8200* In consequence of the interference of the impressed and reflected oscillations, the phenomenon of 'stationary waves'..is produced. **1962** WALSHAW & JOBSON *Mechanics of Fluids* xii. 387 By passing light through the divergent part of a supersonic nozzle, the existence of stationary waves inclined to the stream at the appropriate Mach angle may be confirmed on a shadowgraph.

†**f.** Of a battle: Fought without change of place. *Obs.*

1737 WHISTON *Josephus* II. *Jew. War* VI. ii. 927 This fight was, for the most part, a stationary one.

g. Of an artificial satellite: geostationary.

1970 *Gloss. Aeronaut. & Astronaut. Terms* (*B.S.I.*) XVIII. 3 *Stationary satellite*, a synchronous satellite in a circular, equatorial orbit, moving in the direction of rotation of the primary body. **1979** *Sci. Amer.* Feb. 58/1 Data on the expanses not accounted for by the World Weather Watch are provided by five geosynchronous ('stationary') weather satellites, [etc.].

2. *transf.* **a.** Remaining unchanged in condition, quality, or quantity; neither advancing nor retrograding.

1628 WOTTON *Let.* Reliq. W. (1685) 565 Mine own businesses stand as they did: And..they are rather stationary then retrograde. **1646** SIR T. BROWNE *Pseud. Ep.* VI. xi. 332 By this way likewise the Moores escape the curse of deformity, there concurring no stationary colour, and sometimes not any unto Beauty. **1776** ADAM SMITH *W.N.* I. viii. I. 87 Though the wealth of a country should be very great, yet if it has been long stationary, we must not expect to find the wages of labour very high in it. **1789** A. CRAWFORD in *Med. Commun.* II. 336 The ulcer..appeared to become stationary. **1801** *Med. Jrnl.* V. 64 He was discharged as cured by his physician, even at a time when his emaciation was stationary. **1848** MILL *Pol. Econ.* IV. vi. §1 (1876) 452 At the end of what they term the progressive state lies the stationary state..all progress in wealth is but a postponement of this. **1856** FROUDE *Hist. Eng.* (1858) I. i. 53 Such laws could be enforced only..when production and population remained..nearly stationary. **1858** LD. ACTON in Gasquet *Ld. Acton & his Circle* (1906) 25 Theology is not a stationary science. **1872** BAGEHOT *Physics & Pol.* (1876) 211 As a rule a stationary state is by far the most frequent condition of man. **1892** WESTCOTT *Gospel of Life* 288 A revelation which deals with man not as a stationary being but as advancing with a continuous growth. **1898** 'MERRIMAN' *Roden's Corner* ii. 16 It would never do if the world remained stationary.

b. *stationary state* (Physics), a steady state; *spec.* any of the stable orbits of the electrons in the Bohr model of the atom.

1900 *Rep. Brit. Assoc. Adv. Sci.* 634 If we are given the probability that the coordinates of the system may be between given limits, then a condition for the stationary state is that the mean values of the accelerations of $\frac{1}{2}mv^2$, $\frac{1}{2}mv^2$, $\frac{1}{2}mv^2$ are zero. **1913** N. BOHR in *Phil. Mag.* XXVI. 7 The dynamical equilibrium of the systems in the stationary states can be discussed by help of the ordinary mechanics, while the passing of the systems between different stationary states cannot be treated on that basis. **1932** *Jrnl. Chem. Soc.* 359 Each spectral term, multiplied by Planck's constant, may be taken to represent, for the corresponding stationary state of the atom, the work necessary to remove the electron to an infinite distance from the proton. **1974** G. REECE tr. *Hund's Hist. Quantum Theory* v. 67 Bohr now sums up his results as follows: in the 'stationary states' classical mechanics is used. **1977** I. M. CAMPBELL *Energy & Atmosphere* iv. 65 Under normal conditions, E:C* will be the type of reactive intermediate to which the Stationary State Approximation can be applied, i.e. $d[E{:}C^*]/dt = 0$.

c. *Math.* That is not instantaneously changing; associated with a derivative whose value is zero.

1901 G. A. GIBSON *Elem. Treat. Calculus* vi. 105 Since $f'(x)$ measures the rate of change of the function it is usual to class those values of the function for which $f'(x)$ is zero as stationary values. **1902** SNYDER & HUTCHINSON *Differential & Integral Calculus* xiii. 153 A point at which the direction of bending changes from positive to negative, or *vice versa*..is called a point of inflexion, and the tangent at such a point is called a stationary tangent. **1954** H. R. COOLEY *First Course Calculus* v. 89 Points at which the derivative is equal to 0 are sometimes called stationary points. They are points at which, if a particle were progressing along a curve from left to right, its vertical motion would be momentarily stopped. **1978** K. AHMAD *Trad. & Mod. Math.* 83 A stationary point is a point at which $dy/dx = 0$. Maxima, minima and points of inflection are stationary points.

d. *Statistics.* Applied to a series of observations that has attained equilibrium, so that the expected value of any function of a section of it is independent of the time for which it has been running.

1938 H. WOLD *Stud. in Analysis of Stationary Time Series* 1 Observational series which describe phenomena changing with time may be roughly classified in two broad categories, viz. evolutive and stationary. *Ibid.*, Stationary time series are unchanging in respect to their general structure. The fluctuations up and down in such a series may seem random or show tendencies to regularity—in any case, the character of the series is, on the whole, the same in different sections. **1968** P. A. P. MORAN *Introd. Probability Theory* iii. 151 A set of numbers, p_i, $i = 0, 1, \ldots$, such that $p_i \geqslant 0$, $\Sigma p_i = 1$, $p_i = \sum_j p_{ij} p_j$, will be called a 'stationary distribution' of the process. **1975** *Nature* 11 Dec. 490/1 Two assumptions are commonly made about earthquakes: first, that their occurrence has a stationary random Poisson distribution.

†**3.** Standing, in contradistinction to sitting. *Obs.*

1659 H. L'ESTRANGE *Alliance Div. Off.* 120 The stationary posture is most significant.

4. Of or belonging to a station or stations.

†**a.** *Surveying.* (Cf. *station-distance, -line.*)

1571 DIGGES *Pantom.* I. xxiii. G iij b, Draw an arcke rising from the same line that representeth your stationarie distance. **1610** HOPTON *Baculum Geodæt.* II. i. 19 That your stationary line, or line that you measure, be not too short.

†**b.** Of or pertaining to a military post. *Obs.*

1609 HOLLAND *Amm. Marcell.* 179 The stationarie or garrison souldiors. **1691** NORRIS *Pract. Disc.* 331 The Stationary Angels that wait upon the throne of God. **1781** GIBBON *Decl. & F.* xviii. II. 105 The stationary troops of Singara retired on the approach of Sapor.

c. *Eccl.*

1626 DONNE *Serm.* lxviii. (1640) 688 When we shut our doores, and observe our stationary houres for private prayer in our Chamber. **1693** W. W[OTTON] *Dupin's Hist. Eccl. Writers* I. II. 94 The Stationary days, that is to say, those days when several of the Faithful continued in Prayer and Fasting till Three a Clock in the Afternoon. **1872** SHIPLEY *Gloss. Eccl. Terms* s.v. *Acolyte*, In Rome acolytes were of four kinds: 1. Palatial..2. Stationary, who served in the church where a station was made.

5. ***stationary fever***: see quot. 1855.

A rendering of mod.L. *febris stationaria* (Sydenham).

1696 PECHEY *Sydenham's Wks.* I. ii. (1729) 5 Therefore I call these Fevers Stationary. **1742** J. SWAN *Sydenham's Wks.* I. ii. (1753) 5 *marg.*, Stationary fevers defined. **1855** DUNGLISON *Med. Lex.*, *Stationary*, a name given by Sydenham and Stoll to certain diseases, which depend upon a particular state of the atmosphere; and which prevail in a district for a certain number of years, and then give way to others.

†**6.** 'Belonging to a stationer' (T.). *Obs.*

In the first quot. with reference to exposure in the shop of a 'stationer' or bookseller.

1630 I. CRAVEN *God's Tribunal* (1631) Ep. Ded. A2, Consciousnesse of mine owne meanenesse and withall the great disparity twixt a liuely voice, and breathlesse lines, haue easily disswaded me hitherto from appearing in Stationary view. **1679–88**, **1689**, **1716**, etc. [see STATIONERY 2].

B. *sb.*

†**1.** App. the title of an officer of the royal household: cf. STATIONER 1. *Obs.*

1485 *Rolls of Parlt.* VI. 375/2 Lettres Patents made under oure greate Seale to Piers Actores, of the Office of oure Stationary.

2. = STATIONAR 2.

1868 WALCOTT *Sacred Archæol.* 558 [Three orders of acolytes] Palatines..; stationaries, those connected with the arrangement of stations and processions; and regionaries.

3. Elliptical uses of the adj.

†**a.** A planet when stationary. *Obs. rare*$^{-1}$.

1601 HOLLAND *Pliny* II. xvi. I. 11 As also, that then they [[the planets] are Stationaries in their houses which be in the middle points of the latitudes, which they cal eclipticks.

†**b.** An indulgence for attending a station. *Obs. rare*$^{-1}$. [See note under MANUARY *sb.*]

1537 tr. *Latimer's Serm. Convoc.* ii. Dj b, How some brought forth..pardons, & these of wonderful varietie, some Stationaries, some Iubilaryes.

c. One of a force of permanent or stationary troops. *Obs.* exc. *Rom. Hist.* (= L. *stationarius*), a member of a kind of military constabulary.

1698 FRYER *Acc. E. India & P.* 359 Besides 80000 Stationaries to and again in Garisons. **1727** H. HERBERT tr. *Fleury's Eccl. Hist.* I. 544, I will read the information given in by the Stationary concerning these persons here present. *Ibid.* 545 Since..you have not obeyed the stationaries and chief soldiers who sollicited you to renounce Jesus Christ in writing. **1853** KINGSLEY *Hypatia* xx, The stationaries are mine already. So are the soldiery all the way up the Nile.

d. A politician hostile to progress. Also *transf.* (*nonce-use*), one who does not wish to go forward.

1831 *Examiner* 225/1 'The lame and impotent conclusion' which the Stationaries are desirous of putting to the Revolution of July. **1852** MRS. P. SINNETT tr. *Huc's Trav.* xv. 234 The caravan became henceforth divided between the party of movement and that of resistance—the progressives and the stationaries.

stationed ('steɪʃənd), *ppl. a.* [f. STATION *v.* + -ED[1].] In senses of the verb.

1735 SOMERVILE *Chase* III. 438 T'employ his station'd Legions in the Works of Peace. **1791** *Ann. Reg., Hist.* 187 Firing their broadsides on each hand with great spirit and effect upon the stationed ships. **1811** in *Rep. Comm. Publ. Rec. Irel.* (1815) 68 The two stationed copying Clerks. **1812** BYRON *Ch. Har.* I. li, The station'd bands, the never-vacant watch. **1900** G. J. HOLYOAKE *Sixty Yrs. Agitator's Life* I. xxi. 111 While I was a stationed lecturer in Sheffield, he lived in my house.

stationer[1] ('steɪʃənə(r)). Also 4 **statiner**, 5 **stacyener, stacyonere**, 5–6 **stacioner**, 6 **stacyoner**. [ad. L. *statiōnārius* (see STATIONARY), in med.L. used subst. for a tradesman (chiefly, a bookseller) who has a station or shop, as distinguished from an itinerant vendor. Cf. early Sp. *estacionario* bookseller, It. †*stazioniere* shopkeeper.

The direct adoption of the Latin word is accounted for by the fact that in the Middle Ages booksellers with a regular 'station' or shop were rare except at the universities; the typical example of such a trader was the *stationarius* licensed and controlled by the academic authorities, whom he was sworn to obey.]

1. †**a.** A bookseller; in wider sense, one engaged in any of the trades connected with books (cf. quot. 1625). *Obs.*

†***flying, running stationer***: see the ppl. adjs.

[**1262** *Memoranda Roll 45 & 46 Hen. III*, m. 9b, Mandatum est vicecomiti quod venire [faciat].. Reginaldum stacionarium Oxoniensem ad respondendum Ricardo Brun de Rowell', clerico de scaccario, de I codice precii .xx. s. quem ei debet, et iniuste detinet, vt dicit.] **1393–4** *Rolls of Parlt.* III. 326/1 Statiners & Bokebynders del dit Universite [of Cambridge]. *c* **1440** *Jacob's Well* 27 And alle þo, þat makyn statutys agens þe fredam of holy cherch, & alle wryteres of swyche statutes, & stacionerys. *c* **1440** *Promp. Parv.* 471/2 Stacyonere, or he þat sellythe bokys, *stacionarius, bibliopola.* **1479–81** *Rec. St. Mary at Hill* (1905) 101 Item, payd to a Stacioner for the grete Antyphoner, and for a quayer of clene stuffe sette into the same [etc.], xxij s. ij d. **1496–7** *Ibid.* 226 Item, to the Stacyener for settyng of all the new feestes in to the bookes that lakkyd them. **1529** J. TAVERNER in Arber *Transcr. Stationers' Reg.* (1875) II. 8 Item I gyue and bequeth vnto my crafte of Stacioners vj s. viij d. **1560** DAUS tr. *Sleidane's Comm.* 33 b, He commaundeth also his Bokes should be brent, appoyntynge a greate penaltie herafter for the Stationers [orig. *librariis*]. **1572** in Feuillerat *Revels Q. Eliz.* (1908) 161 To the stacyoner for a lidger booke. **1612** ROWLANDS *Knaue of Harts* 29, I grieue thou hast a groate to buy this Booke:..I hate the Printer if he haue done well, And Stationer, that doth these humours sell. **1625** WITHER *Scholars Purg.* 116 An honest Stationer is he that exercizeth his Mystery (whether it be in printing, bynding or selling of Bookes) with more respect to the glory of God..then to his owne commodity. **1626** F. MORYSON *Shakespeare's Europe* v. i. (1903) 429 This one Vniversity [*sc.* Bologna] indeede hath two Academies, one of the nations beyonde the mountaynes, the other of those on that syde the Alpes... The Stationers are Chosen by three Citramontans, and three Vltramontans. **1679–88** *Moneys Secr. Serv. Chas. II & Jas. II* (Camden) 98 To Anne, relict and ex'trix of Samuel Mearne, dece'd, King Charles the 2[d]'s stationer, in part of 862[li] 3[s] 4[d] for Church Bibles, Com'on Prayer Books, and other books, ..215 10 o. *a* **1680** BUTLER *Rem.* (1759) I. 90 Thy Works..never have been known to stand in need Of Stationer to sell, or Sot to read. **1705** DUNTON *Life & Err.* (1818) I. vii. 254 He was the first stationer I ever dealt with. **1727** SWIFT *Poisoning of E. Curll* Misc. 1732 III. 19 Yet was it plain by the Pangs this unhappy Stationer felt soon after, that some poisonous Drug had been secretly infused therein. **1895** RASHDALL *Univ. Europe* I. iv. §4. 191 [Bologna] The Stationer's primary business was to let out books on hire to scholars. *Ibid.* I. v. §3. 416 [Paris] All Stationers and Booksellers were sworn to obey the University and were required to give security.

†**b.** A publishing bookseller, publisher. *Obs.*

1541 COPLAND *Guydon's Quest. Cyrurg.* To Rdrs., A certayne yonge gentyll man..moued the ryght honest persone Henry Dabbe bybliopolyst & stacyoner to haue it translated in to englysshe. **1615** W. LAWSON *New Orchard* Pref. (1623), The Stationer hath..bestowed much cost and care in hauing the Knots and Models by the best Artizan cut in great varietie. **1657** *Brome's Queenes Exch.*, The Stationer to the Readers. **1659** BP. WALTON *Consid. Considered* 21 The Prolegomena..came to his hands after he had finished his Treatise of the Scripture, and was ready to give it to the Stationer. *a* **1661** FULLER *Worthies, Gen.* xxv. (1662) 74, I have passed my promise..to my former Stationer, that I will write nothing for the future, which was in my former Books, so considerable, as may make them Inter-fere one with another to his Prejudice. **1673** OLEY *Jackson's Wks.* I. Pref. (d) 1 b, I..here set down all such particulars as may..contribute to the benefit..of the Reader, to the credit or caution of the Stationer.

†**c.** A scribe, copyist. *Obs. rare.*

1583 FULKE *Def.* iv. 138 The other translatours..left out that title altogither, as being no part of the text and word of God, but an addition of the stationers or writers.

d. A tradesman who sells writing materials and similar articles. Cf. LAW-STATIONER.

The sale of parchment, paper, pens, ink, etc. was originally a regular branch of the business of the 'stationer' or bookseller. The restriction of the term *stationer* to the dealer in these articles is first evidenced in quot. 1656; it had probably been in vogue in accurate mercantile parlance some time before, but was not established in ordinary use until the 18th century. Phillips (ed. Kersey 1706) s.v. *Stationers*, has the term ***paper-stationer***.

1656 BLOUNT *Glossogr.*, *Stationer*..is often confounded with Book-seller, and sometimes with Book-binder; whereas they are three several Trades; the Stationer sells Paper and Paper-Books, Ink, Wax, etc. The Book-seller deals onely in printed Books, ready bound; and the Book-binder binds them, but sells not. Yet all three are of the Company of Stationers. **1755** JOHNSON, *Stationer*,..2. A seller of paper. **1796** PEGGE *Anonym.* (1809) 155 A Stationer is now one that sells writing-paper, pens, &c. but formerly meant any one that kept a station or shop. **1812** H. & J. SMITH *Horace in Lond.* 164 My paper boasts no edge of gold; My stationer is Henry Hase. **1859** (*title*) The Stationers' Hand-book; and Guide to the Paper Trade. **1880** *Print. Trades Jrnl.* xxx. 35 The exhibition..will be intended more particularly for Printers, Paper Makers, Stationers, and kindred traders.

e. Possessive combinations: **stationer's knot, stationer's rule** (see quots.).

1870 *Routledge's Ev. Boy's Ann.* 601 The model tie of tradesmen is the Stationer's Knot. **1866** W. F. STANLEY *Math. Instrum.* 211 The Stationer's, or Cutting rule, is a piece of hard wood..with the edges covered with brass.

f. ***the Company of Stationers*** (or ***the Stationers' Company***): one of the Livery Companies of the City of London, founded in 1556, comprising booksellers, printers, bookbinders, and dealers in writing materials, etc. ***Stationers' Hall***: the hall of the Stationer's Company, at which a register of copyrights is kept. (The Copyright Act of 1842 provided that no action for breach of copyright could be brought unless the work had been entered in this register. The Copyright Act of 1911 abolished this rule.)

The charter of 1556 (ed. 1741, p. 6) is thus worded: 'Volumus, damus, et concedimus..Thomæ Dockwray..[*names of the Wardens and Freemen*] Liberis Hominibus Misteræ sive Artis Stationarii Civitatis Nostre Londinensis ....quod de cetero sint..Unum Corpus de se in perpetuum [etc]'.

An earlier guild of stationers is said to have been established in London in 1403: see quot. 1529 in 1.

1566 *Star Chamber Decree* in Arber *Transcr. Stationers' Reg.* (1875) I. 322 All Bookes to be so forfaited, shall be brought into the Stationers hall in London. **1709** *Act 8 Anne* c. 21 §2 Before such Publication be entred in the Register Book of the Company of Stationers. **1765** *Bickerstaff's Maid of Mill* Advt., This Opera is entered at Stationers Hall, and whoever presumes to Print the Songs, or any Part of them, will be prosecuted by the Proprietors. **1790** J. FISHER *Poems*, back of title, Entered in Stationers' Hall, according to Act of Parliament. **1859** *Stationers' Hand-bk.* back of title, Entered at Stationers' Hall. **1864** *Chamb. Jrnl.* 19 Nov. 748/2 'Almanac-day' at Stationers' Hall.

†**2.** One who has a stall at a market. *Obs. rare.*

1616 SHELDON *Surv. Miracles Ch. Rome* 174 Standing Stationers and Assistants at your miracle markets and miracle forges, are for most part of lewdest life.

stationer[2] ('steɪʃənə(r)). *Naut. rare*$^{-1}$. [f. STATION *sb.* + -ER[1].] (See quot.)

1867 SMYTH *Sailor's Word-bk.*, *Stationer*, one who has had experience, or who has been some time on a particular station.

stationery ('steɪʃənərɪ). Also 8–9 **-ary.** [f. STATIONER[1] + -Y.

The word seems to have been evolved from or suggested by combinations like *stationary ware*, where the first word was originally adj. (see STATIONARY *a.* 6), but was naturally taken as a sb. used attributively.]

1. The articles sold by a stationer; writing materials, writing-table appurtenances, etc. (see quot. 1887). (Not in Johnson or in Todd 1818.)

1727 BAILEY vol. II, *Stationary*, Stationers Wares. **1809** *Parl. Paper* (*title*), An Estimate of the Charge for Printing, Stationary etc...for Dublin Castle. **1828–32** WEBSTER. **1837** HALLAM *Lit. Europe* I. I. iii. §145 They sold parchment and other materials of writing, which with us have retained the name of stationery. **1857** DICKENS *Dorrit* II. viii, To make a curious calculation of the amount of stationery consumed in it [*i.e.* the Circumlocution Office]. **1880** *Print. Trades Jrnl.* xxx. 35 A special exhibition of Printing Machinery, Paper, and Stationery is to be held. **1887** *Encycl. Brit.* XXII. 460/2 Under the name of stationery are embraced all writing materials and implements, together with the numerous appliances of the desk and of mercantile and commercial offices. In addition to these, the term fancy stationery covers a miscellaneous assemblage of leather and other goods, such as pocket books, purses, bags, card-cases [etc.]. **1894** J. RUSSELL *Remin. Yarrow* vi. 125 A rush was generally made to the desk where the stationery was kept.

2. *attrib.* as in ***stationery business, trade, ware***; **stationery literature**, ballads, chap-books, etc., hawked about the streets; **Stationery Office**, an office in London through which government offices are supplied with stationery, and which issues the reports, etc. published by the government.

1679–88 *Moneys Secr. Serv. Chas. II & Jas. II* (Camden) 153 To Marg[t] Royston..in satisfacc'on of so much money due to her for stationery wares supplied by her husband to the Earle of Middleton, ..133 11 o. **1689** *Order in Council* 24 Oct. in *Lond. Gaz.* No. 2500/1 Stationary Ware. **1716** *Lond. Gaz.* No. 5438/3 Proposals..for furnishing the Custom-House with Stationary Wares. **1798** *Rep. Comm. Ho. Comm.* (1803) XIII. 427 Stationary Office. This Office was established in 1786..with a view to the saving of Expenses, ...and to guard against Abuses in the application of the Stationary necessary for carrying on the business of Government. **1851** MAYHEW *Lond. Labour* I. 205 The street trade in stationery literature. **1859** *Stationers' Hand-bk.* 1 The Stationery trade. *Ibid.* 2 A stationery business.

stationette (steɪʃə'nɛt). [f. STATION *sb.* + -ETTE.] A small station.

1893 BURRELL & CUTHELL *Indian Mem.* 213 A..railway.. conveys the traveller..to a stationette at the very foot of the mighty mountains.

station-house.

1. The house provided for a coastguardsman at his station. *rare.*

1833 HT. MARTINEAU *Loom & Lugger* I. v. 89 If they sent an order to all us Preventive people to vacate our station-houses and march off.

2. The lock-up attached to a police-station; the police-station itself. Now chiefly *U.S.*

1836 DICKENS *Sk. Boz, Visit to Newgate*, Tell them of hunger and the streets,..the station-house, and the pawn-broker's, and they will understand you. **1854** *John Bull* 1 July 411 Whallor was actually taken by a policeman to the station-house, the real criminal accompanying them, as witness. **1867** AUGUSTA WILSON *Vashti* xxxiv, Watchman McDonough..picked up, on the sidewalk, the insensible body of Maurice Carlyle, who showed some signs of returning animation after his removal to Station House No. ——. **1870** *Galaxy* Feb. 272 An headquarters of police ...is called in New York a station-house, though in many other places this word is more correctly used to indicate a stopping house on railroads. **1931** H. F. PRINGLE *Theodore Roosevelt* I. xi. 138 He arrived..at a station house in the lower part of the city, and interrupted the meditations of the sergeant. **1963** *Listener* 4 Apr. 585/1, I began my police career in June, 1951. After three months' training I was assigned to the W. 54th Street station house. **1979** *Honolulu Advertiser* 8 Jan. D-1/4 2,000 Hasidic Jews stormed a Brooklyn police station-house.

3. A railway station; now only, a small country station.

1838 *Times* 5 June 5/1 The station-house close to Maidenhead shows the terminus. **1846** MRS. GORE *Engl. Char.* 320 How different from the flashy gaudiness of a station-house albergo! **1850** HAWTHORNE *Amer. Note-bks.* (1868) II. 199 It [the train] dashes along in front of the station-house, and comes to a pause. **1891** 'J. S. WINTER' *Lumley* ii, When Jock Airlie and the painter came out of the little station-house, they found [etc.].

4. A building at which travellers halt in crossing the desert. ? *nonce-use.*

1856 STANLEY *Sinai & Pal.* i. (1858) One solitary station-house and fort marks this wilderness [the Desert of the Tih.]

5. *Austral.* and *N.Z.* The house belonging to a station.

1888 A. MCKAY in *Bull. N.Z. Geol. Survey* No. 1. 4 The station-house was so far wrecked. **1894** H. NISBET *Bush Girl's Rom.* 234 Uncle Timothy, the sole representative of the nobler sex who could keep these ladies company at the deserted station-house. **1933** L. G. D. ACLAND in *Press* (Christchurch) 4 Nov. 15/7 *Men's hut,* house where the station hands live. On some stations it is called the *station house.*

stationing ('steɪʃənɪŋ), *vbl. sb.* [f. STATION *v.* + -ING[1].] The action of the vb. STATION.

1801 J. BENSON in J. Macdonald *Mem.* (1822) 366 We have completed . . the Plan for the stationing the preachers. *a* **1821** KEATS *Notes on 'Parad. Lost'* Wks. 1883 III. 28 But in no instance is this sort of perseverance more exemplified, than in what may be called his [Milton's] stationing or statuary. **1851** *Butler, Wine-dealer,* etc. 104 The stationing of many servants for due efficiency without confusion requires much judgment. **1914** *Eng. Hist. Rev.* July 474 Matters having to do principally with the stationing of troops and commanders in the West Indies.

attrib. **1822** J. MACDONALD *Mem. J. Benson* 321 The four following days he was fully engaged as a member of the Stationing Committee. **1902** *Daily Chron.* 4 Aug. 4/2 The Wesleyan Stationing Committee has issued a revised list of ministerial stations.

† '**stationize**, *v. Obs.*$^{-0}$ [f. STATION *sb.* + -IZE.] *trans.* = STATION *v.*

1598 FLORIO, *Instazzonare,* to stationize.

stationmaster ('steɪʃən,mɑːstə(r)). [f. STATION *sb.* (sense 20) + MASTER *sb.*] The official who has the control of a railway station.

1857 W. COLLINS *Dead Secr.* III. vi, Did the station-master issue the tickets for that train? **1866** DICKENS, etc. *Mugby Junction, No. 5 Branch Line,* Then the guard's whistle shrilled out, and the station-master made his last bow. **1889** G. FINDLAY *Engl. Railway* 15 The 'Station-master', attends to the passenger work.

So '**stationmistress**.

1897 *N. & Q.* 18 Dec. 485/2 Her husband was killed in the service of the company, and she succeeded as stationmistress.

stationnaire (steɪʃə'nɛə(r)). *Obs.* exc. *Hist.* [Fr.] A naval guard-ship, stationed at a foreign port for the use of an ambassador.

1895 *F.O. 64/1351* (Public Record Office) No. 284 He feared the arrival of the second stationnaires would inevitably excite ill-feeling amongst the Mahomedans. **1914** R. RANKIN *Inner Hist. Balkan War* xii. 364 As yet no warships were at hand except the weakly-armed 'stationnaires' or European guard-ships which at all times lie in the Bosphorus for the use of the Ambassadors. **1922** *Glasgow Herald* 21 Dec. 9/3 As regards the Foreign Embassy stationnaires, Lord Curzon said that he had never thought they could be detrimental to Turkey's sovreignty. **1958** M. BUCHANAN *Ambassador's Daughter* vi. 68 Ambassadors accredited to the Sublime Porte before the Turkish Revolution . . were given a summer residence on the shores of the Bosphorus, . . with an armed sloop or *stationnaire* always anchored in the vicinity in case of a rising of the Turks.

station-wagon. Also station wagon, (-)waggon.

†**1.** *U.S.* **a.** A type of horse-drawn covered carriage, used for conveying passengers. *Obs.*

1894 *Hub News* 23 May 77/1 Business has been fairly good this spring. . . Traps are in most demand, next come buggies, cutunders, and business rockaways or station wagons. **1901** *Varnish* 15 July 253/1 Then we would all know the difference between a cabriolet and an extension-top phaeton; a station wagon and a rockaway.

b. A similar type of motorized carriage.

1904 *Motor World* 21 Jan. 680/2 The station wagon is a new model exhibited the first time this year. **1904** *Sci. Amer.* 30 Jan. 99/1 Manufacturers of Electric Broughams, Landaus, . . Station Wagons, Surreys.

2. orig. *U.S.* An estate car; a saloon motor car with a rear door or doors, and capable of carrying goods as well as passengers.

1929 *N.Y. Times* 6 Jan. XI. 1/5 The Ford Motor Company is having its own exhibition. . . The three new models added to the line are on display there. These are the town sedan, the convertible cabriolet, and the station wagon. **1930** *Amer. Speech* V. 276 The other commercial bodies have usually retained old names—*delivery wagon, station wagon.* **1942** *E. African Ann. 1941–2* 11/1 *Safari* cars . . have box-bodies, of the station-wagon model. **1949** F. MACLEAN *Eastern Approaches* II. iii. 200 This was a new cut-down Ford station waggon, with room in it for six people and a certain amount of kit. **1951** 'J. WYNDHAM' *Day of Triffids* v. 88 We kept on foot for a while, looking out for a suitable car. After a mile or so we found it—a station-waggon. **1969** *Sydney Morning Herald* 24 May 55/4 (Advt.), Datsun station waggon. **1976** *Encounter* June 9/2 They advanced, the distinguished party, . . down the steps, into Halpert's Dodge station wagon, where, along with two sacks of lawn fertiliser, they fitted comfortably.

statiscope, erron. form of STATOSCOPE.

statism ('steɪtɪz(ə)m). [f. STATE *sb.* + -ISM.]

†**1.** Subservience to political expediency in religious matters. *Obs. rare.*

1609 [W. BARLOW] *Answ. Nameless Cath.* 370 Religion turned into Statisme, will soone prooue Atheisme. **1626** R. BERNARD *Isle of Man* II. (1627) 137 The Billes of Inditement framed by those false Informers beforementioned, . . Machiauilian Statisme [etc.] . . against Christian Conference . . , and the rest. *c* **1660** SOUTH *Serm.* (1715) 150 Hence it is, that the Enemies of God take Occasion to blaspheme, and call our Religion Statism.

†**2.** ? Political science, statecraft. *Obs. rare.*

1620 E. BLOUNT *Horæ Subsec.* 40 Such as professe to read Theorie of Statisme.

3. a. Government of a country by the state, as opposed to anarchy. *rare.*

1880 *Echo* 2 Jan. 4/1 The Nihilists do not believe in Communism, which is as bad as Statism, and equally deserving of suppression.

b. = ÉTATISME.

1919 *Sociol. Rev.* XI. 62 Traditional phrases such as 'The Appeal to Democracy', 'Freedom for Little Nations', etc., . . have been used so often, with so poor a result during the past century, in which all the time 'individualism' and 'statism' have been struggling together for supremacy and power under their cover. **1940** *Sun* (Baltimore) 5 Nov. 5/7 Republican Senator Charles L. McNary concluded his Vice-Presidential campaign tonight with the charge the New Deal is 'taking deeper and deeper refuge in paternalism and statism'. **1945** A. HUXLEY *Let.* 8 Aug. (1969) 531 Men and women . . brought up under Statism . . have been taught to believe that the State is more important than the individual. **1962** *Times Lit. Suppl.* 23 Nov. 919/1 Anarchic egocentricity thus tugs against a Mum-providing statism. This has caused schizophrenia in British Labour. **1970** *Daily Tel.* 1 Dec. 9/4 In South America today . . various forms of Marxist-inspired Statism are establishing themselves. **1979** *Time* 2 Apr. 52/2 The shortfall itself is rooted in policies that have led to too much statism and not enough private initiative.

statist ('steɪtɪst), *sb.*[1] and *a.* [f. L. *stat-us* STATE *sb.*: see -IST. Cf. It. *statista* (in Florio 1611), F. †*statiste* (17th c.), Sp., Pg. *estadista,* G. *statist* (from 17th c.), Sw. *statist.*

The word probably originated in Italian, though evidence of its earlier currency in that lang. is wanting.]

A. *sb.* **1.** One skilled in state affairs, one having political knowledge, power, or influence; a politician, statesman. Very common in 17th c. Now *arch.*

1584 SIDNEY in A. Collins *S. Lett.* (1746) I. 1. 63 When he plais the Statist, wringing veri unlukkili some of Machiavels Axiomes to serve his Purpos then indeed; then he tryumphes. *c* **1590** *Sir T. More* (Malone Soc.) 772 Hees great in studie, thats the statists grace that gaines more reuerence then the outward place. **1600** W. WATSON *Decacordon* (1602) 222 Thereby shall be seene . . whether the seculars or Iesuits are greater statists: that is, intermedlers in state affairs. **1602** SHAKS. *Ham.* v. ii. 33. **1641** MILTON *Reform.* 10 They suffer'd themselvs to be the common stales to countenance with their prostituted Gravities every Politick Fetch that was then on foot, as oft as the Potent Statists pleas'd to employ them. **1643** SIR T. BROWNE *Relig. Med.* II. xiii, Statists that labour to contrive a Commonwealth without poverty, take away the object of charity. **1691** [S. BETHEL] *Provid. God* (1694) 29 This Government of ours has been by our late Kings carried on by Tricks, which our Statists valued themselves upon, as the Effect of their great Wisdom. **1799** WORDSW. *Poet's Epitaph* i Art thou a Statist in the van Of public conflicts trained and bred? **1850** HANNAY *Singleton Fontenoy* IV. ii, There was a statist in embryo; there was a leading-article man. **1875** BROWNING *Aristoph. Apol.* 17 To lift along the athlete and ensure A second wreath, proposed by fools for first, The statist's olive as the poet's bay.

2. One who deals with statistics, a statistician.

1803 *Edin. Rev.* II. 304 If Mr. Catteau's authority is called in question we are ready to corroborate it by the testimony of more than one dozen German statists. **1846** *Times* 18 Aug. 6/3 A statist is a student of statistics, i.e. a man who computes and analyses everything that relates to the visible state or condition of man. **1863** KINGLAKE *Crimea* (1880) VI. viii. 181 With these numbers before him . . a Statist will quickly educe what he calls the 'percentages'. **1802** *Daily News* 29 Jan. 5/5 The Government Statist of the Colony of Victoria.

3. (With capital initial.) A member of a conservative Belgian nationalist party which sought to maintain the power of the provincial assemblies or States in the late eighteenth century.

1909 *Cambr. Mod. Hist.* VI. xviii. 653 Only a short time was, however, to elapse before they [*sc.* States General] split asunder into two irreconcilable parties—the Statists of van der Noot . . and the Democrats of Vonck. **1921** E. CAMMAERTS *Belgium* 11 'Statists' and 'Vonckists'. **1966** V. R. LORWIN in R. A. Dahl *Pol. Oppositions in Western Democracies* v. 149 The Statists, or Van der Nootists, opposed the reforms of Joseph II; they sought to maintain the customs and privileges of the established Catholic Church and the narrowly based oligarchy of landowners, masters of urban crafts, and nobles who dominated the sclerosed provincial assemblies or Estates. **1974** *Encycl. Brit. Macropædia* XI. 157/1 Van Der Noot made a triumphant entry into Brussels, where he and his 'Statists' were supported by the Estates of Brabant.

4. A supporter of statism.

1976 *National Observer* (U.S.) 24 Apr. 17/2 So much for rent control, just one of many well-meant disasters visited upon us by the statists. **1979** *N.Y. Rev. Bks.* 25 Oct. 49/1 McCagg sees Stalin as a 'statist', more interested, that is, in building the Soviet state than in the Communist Party.

B. *adj.* Of, pertaining to, advocating, or based on statism.

1960 *New Statesman* 9 Jan. 26/2 Tory propagandists and Labour re-thinkers share in the admiration of the new 'statist' economic system we have in Britain. **1960** *New Left Rev.* May–June 6/2 Communist and Labour fundamentalists of the 'statist' variety. **1973** *Advocate-News* (Barbados) 8 May 3/2 In other systems, the cooperatives has been the peripheral to the main sector, whether capitalist or statist. **1976** K. JOSEPH *Monetarism is not Enough* 17 But the whole economy is not private. Nearly two-thirds is statist, and insensitive in itself to contraction of the money supply. **1977** *N.Y. Rev. Bks.* 27 Oct. 26/3 They include not only members of the intelligentsia but also working people who have experienced statist authoritarianism, rigidity, narrowness, and felt impelled to speak up, however discreetly. **1979** *New Society* 9 Aug. 295/2 The commitment to democracy was real in the later Marcuse—including a commitment to defend existing democratic liberties against statist and fascist incursions.

†**statist,** *sb.*[2] *Obs. rare*$^{-1}$. [a. G. *statist,* app. f. L. *stat-us* standing (see STATE *sb.*) + -IST.] A supernumerary actor on the stage who simply poses or stands by.

1807 *Goede's Trav. Eng.* 264 The theatre at Paris possesses a far greater number of excellent dancers of both sexes than that of London; and its statists and figurants are comparatively more skilful than on the latter.

†**sta'tistial,** *a. Obs. rare.* [f. STATIST *sb.*[1] + -(I)AL. (But perh. a misprint for STATISTICAL, which occurs in the same book.)] Political.

1600 W. WATSON *Decacordon* (1602) 11 Continually disswading from all such statistial affaires. *Ibid.* 349 Statistiall deuises.

statistic (stə'tɪstɪk), *a.* and *sb.* [ad. G. *statistik* sb. *statistisch* adj., F. *statistique* adj. and fem. sb., ad. mod.L. *statisticus,* f. **statista* (It. *statista*) STATIST. Cf. It. *statistico* adj., *statistica* sb., Sp., Pg. *estadístico* adj., *estadística* sb.

The earliest known occurrence of the word seems to be in the title of the satirical work *Microscopium Statisticum,* by 'Helenus Politanus', Frankfort (?), 1672. Here the sense is prob. 'pertaining to statists or to statecraft' (cf. STATISTICAL *a.* 1). The earliest use of the adj. in anything resembling its present meaning is found in mod.L. *statisticum collegium,* said to have been used by Martin Schmeizel (professor at Jena, died 1747) for a course of lectures on the constitutions, resources, and policy of the various States of the world. The G. *statistik* was used as a name for this department of knowledge by G. Achenwall in his *Vorbereitung zur Staatswissenschaft* (1748); the context shows that he did not regard the term as novel. The F. *statistique* sb. is cited by Littré from Bachaumont (died 1771); Fr. writers of the 18th c. refer to Achenwall as having brought the word into use. The sense-development of the word may have been influenced by the notion that it was a direct derivative of L. *status* STATE *sb.*]

A. *adj.*

1. = STATISTICAL 2. Now *rare.*

1789 *Polit. Geog.; Introd. Statist. Tables Europe* 17 With a view to facilitate the study of the Statistic science. **1802–12** BENTHAM *Ration. Judic. Evid.* (1827) II. 597 The sort of collateral use thus capable of being derived from any article of official evidence, may be termed the statistic use. **1851** MRS. BROWNING *Casa Guidi Wind.* I. 892 The poet who neglects pure truth to prove Statistic fact.

†**2.** Political. *Obs. rare.*

1824 SOUTHEY *Bk. Ch.* (1841) 298 The religious and the statistic measures must not be confounded.

3. Of or pertaining to status.

1871 POSTE tr. *Instit. Gaius* IV. §6. Comm. 404 Their title is a breach of contract or the violation of some real right, statistic, primordial, or proprietary.

B. *sb.*

1. a. = STATISTICS 1. *rare.*

1796 MORSE *Amer. Geog.* II. 228 (Germany) Academical sciences . . under the name of Technology, Economy, Science of Finances, and Statistic. **1864** KINGSLEY *Rom. & Teut.* ix. 232 Till that point is reached, the history of the masses will be mere statistic concerning their physical well-being or ill-being.

b. A quantitative fact or statement.

1880 'MARK TWAIN' *Tramp Abroad* xvi. 148 There is not a statistic wanting. It is as succinct as an invoice. This is what a translation ought to be. **1928** H. BELLOC *Hist. England* III. iii. 244 Before the siege-piece had been developed as a fairly reliable arm, a city or a castle wall was attacked in one of five ways. . . There was direct attack. . . There was a starving out of the garrison. . . Probably, if a statistic could be made, the latter would be found the most commonly successful method of the true Middle Ages. **1934** *Punch* 14 Mar. 292/2 Few citizens realise that there *is* any river traffic other than the boat race. Let me give them a statistic:—At least 3,000 craft of all sizes pass under Waterloo Bridge every week. **1949** E. HYAMS *Not in our Stars* xvi. 198 Although the first dead was a horror and a tragedy, the ten thousandth was a statistic. **1973** *Times* 24 Apr. 12/2 The statistic of 22·2 unemployed to every notified vacancy in Scotland. **1975** *Nature* 11 Sept. 81/1 A more pertinent statistic is that about 98% of all trips taken with second family cars, lie within the 50-mile range of present battery technology.

c. *Statistics.* Any of the numerical characteristics of a sample (as opposed to one of the population from which it is drawn). Cf. PARAMETER 2 f.

1922, etc. [see PARAMETER 2 f]. **1925** R. A. FISHER *Statistical Methods for Research Workers* iii. 43 The utility of any particular statistic, and the nature of its distribution, both depend on the original distribution. **1976** *Biometrika* LXIII. 438 The sample sizes are enormous, the smallest being 23517, so that under the null hypothesis this statistic should be distributed as a χ^2 variate with $x_0 - 3$ degrees of freedom.

2. = STATISTICIAN.

1804 SOUTHEY *Let. to W. Taylor* 1 July in Robberds *Mem. Taylor* (1843) I. 508 Henley said you were the best statistic in Europe. **1898** *Westm. Gaz.* 22 Sept. 3/2 It is the province of the statistic to upset fixed notions, to compare the actual with the accepted.

statistical (stəˈtɪstɪkəl), *a.* [Two formations: in sense 1 f. STATIST + -IC + -AL[1]; in senses 2 and 3 f. STATISTIC + -AL[1].]

†**1.** Political. *Obs. rare.*

1600 W. WATSON *Decacordon* (1602) 228 There are a hundred twise told of the like statisticall principles and practises.

2. a. Of or pertaining to statistics, consisting of or founded on collections of numerical facts, esp. with reference to economic, sanitary, and vital conditions.

1787 *Crit. Rev.* LXIV. 188 The work [by Zimmermann] before us is properly statistical. It consists of different tables, containing a general comparative view of the forces, the government, the extent and population of the different kingdoms of Europe. **1790** SIR J. SINCLAIR *Let.* in *Statist. Acc. Scot.* (1798) XX. App. p. xix, In many parts of the Continent, more particularly in Germany, Statistical Inquiries, as they are called, have been carried to a very great extent. **1841** W. SPALDING *Italy* I. 75 The most prominent moral and statistical features of the period now to be considered must not..be passed over in silence. **1871** MAXWELL *Theory of Heat* xxii. 288 If however, we adopt a statistical view of the system, and distribute the molecules into groups, according to the velocity with which at a given instant they happen to be moving, we shall observe [etc.].

b. Of a writer, etc.: Dealing with statistics.

1787 ZIMMERMANN *Polit. Surv. Europe* Pref. 5 Some respectable statistical writers. **1845** MᶜCULLOCH *Literature Pol. Econ.* 222 In 1832, a Statistical Department was organised in the Board of Trade for preparing, classifying, and publishing..information respecting the statistics of the United Kingdom and its dependencies, and also respecting foreign states.

c. ***statistical significance*** = SIGNIFICANCE 3.

1938 *Jrnl. Parapsychol.* II. 210 The primary requirement of statistical significance is met by the results of this investigation. **1971** *Jrnl. Gen. Psychol.* LXXXV. 68 None of the..interactions reached statistical significance. **1974** *Jrnl. Dental Res.* LIII. 763/2 Whether to use the standard test for statistical significance or the Bechhofer test depends on the problem that is studied.

d. Of a branch of science, or a physical process or condition: not absolutely precise but dependent on the probable outcome of a large number of small events, and so predictable; ***statistical mechanics***, the description of physical phenomena in terms of a statistical treatment of the behaviour of large numbers of atoms, molecules, etc., esp. as regards the distribution of energy among them; hence ***statistical-mechanical*** adj.

1885 J. W. GIBBS in *Proc. Amer. Assoc. Adv. Sci.* XXXIII. 57 (*heading*) On the fundamental formula of statistical mechanics, with applications to astronomy and thermodynamics. **1900** *Rep. Brit. Assoc. Adv. Sci.* 617 The statistical dynamics of the distribution of the molecules. **1902** J. W. GIBBS (*title*) Elementary principles in statistical mechanics. **1917** *Proc. K. Akad. van Wetensch. te Amsterdam* XIX. 578 The statistical mechanical explanation Boltzmann gave of it [*sc.* the second law of thermodynamics] rests on statistical foundations which are destroyed by the introduction of the quanta. **1927** [see FERMI-DIRAC]. **1945** H. D. SMYTH *Gen. Acct. Devel. Atomic Energy Mil. Purposes* ix. 102 Such effects are used in six 'statistical' separation methods: (1) gaseous diffusion (2) distillation... In all these 'statistical' methods the separation factor is small so that many stages are required. **1955** H. B. G. CASIMIR in W. Pauli *Niels Bohr* 132 As long as this phenomenon [*sc.* superconductivity] is not understood an essential element is lacking in our comprehension of statistical mechanics and of the nature of the solid state. **1955** FRIEDMAN & WEISSKOPF in *Ibid.* 138 The statistical method of determining the yield of nuclear reactions gives a reasonable account of their most important features. **1956** E. H. HUTTEN *Lang. Mod. Physics* iv. 149 This H-function may be taken as the statistical-mechanical analogue of entropy, since it exhibits a one-sided change in time. **1962** J. RIORDAN *Stochastic Service Systems* iii. 28 The system is said to be in statistical equilibrium... It is not without changes, for probabilities are still in question, but the probabilistic description of its behavior in time is invariant with time. **1964** J. D. BERNAL in *Proc. R. Soc.* A. CCLXXX. 302, I found..that we did not know much about heaps and that to understand heaps we had to open a new subject, that of statistical geometry. *Ibid.* 307 It would be very well worth while to examine the purely geometrical properties of random close-packed aggregates without holes, particularly in relation to kinds of lines that can be drawn through neighbouring points. This should be one of the first tasks of the proposed statistical geometry. **1971** *Nature* 13 Aug. 450/1, I believe that the most widespread opinion is that quantum mechanics can be 'grafted' onto the classical statistical mechanics of Boltzmann and Gibbs and that therefore quantum mechanics does not require anything essentially new. **1974** G. REECE tr. *Hund's Hist. Quantum Theory* i. 14 The great achievement of statistical physics was that of deriving thermodynamics from mechanical principles. *Ibid.* iii. 46 In the years 1902–7 Einstein completed a basis for statistical thermodynamics.

¶**3.** *Gram.* Misused for STATIVE *a.* 3.

1846 D. FORBES *Hindústání Gram.* 132 From the present participle is formed the compound verb called *statistical*, by using the masculine inflection of the participle together with some verb of motion. *Ibid.* 65 From the present participle are formed..Statisticals, *gáte ánā*, 'to come singing'; *rote daurnā* 'to run crying'.

statistically (stəˈtɪstɪkəlɪ), *adv.* [f. STATISTICAL *a.* + -LY[2].] In a statistical manner, according to or by means of statistics, from a statistical point of view. ***statistically significant***: see SIGNIFICANT *a.* 5.

1821 W. TAYLOR in *Monthly Rev.* XCV. 18 A considerable condensation might yet be accomplished by mapping the country more statistically. **1860** MOTLEY *Netherlands* (1868) I. ii. 29 It was what would now be considered statistically speaking, a rather petty power. **1879** *Cassell's Techn. Educ.* II. 168/2 If it can be proved statistically that [etc.]. **1885** *Manch. Exam.* 17 Feb. 4/4 While cotton was firm and statistically strong, the Indian exchanges again came lower.

statistician (stætɪˈstɪʃən). [f. STATISTIC + -IAN; cf. F. *statisticien.*] One versed in or engaged in collecting and tabulating statistics.

1825 MᶜCULLOCH *Pol. Econ.* I. 59 The object of the statistician is to describe the condition of a particular country at a particular period. **1879** *Cassell's Techn. Educ.* IV. 355/1 The domestic consumption has been estimated by statisticians, at twenty-two pounds per head.

Hence **statiˈsticianly** *adv.*, in the manner of a statistician.

1882 *Blackw. Mag.* Nov. 630/2 The vulgar criticism which concerns itself maliciously, not statisticianly,..with the question of feminine *taille.*

statisticize (stəˈtɪstɪsaɪz), *v.* [f. STATISTIC(S + -IZE.] *trans.* To arrange in the form of statistics. Also *intr.*, to collect or employ statistics. Hence **staˈtisticized** *ppl. a.*; **staˈtisticizing** *vbl. sb.*

1879 *St. George's Hosp. Rep.* IX. 216 The 210 statisticised cases correspond to 202 patients. **1927** *Sunday Express* 17 July 11 Miss Inderrieden has reduced desertions to a percentage basis. She says that the wife is to blame in fifty percent. of desertions... This is a dreadful specimen of statisticising. It means absolutely nothing. **1971** *Nature* 30 Apr. 602/3 The objective..is not to help budding statisticians to statisticize but to help experimental scientists to experiment properly.

statistics (stəˈtɪstɪks). Pl. of STATISTIC.

1. a. Construed as *sing.* In early use, that branch of political science dealing with the collection, classification, and discussion of facts (especially of a numerical kind) bearing on the condition of a state or community. In recent use, the department of study that has for its object the collection and arrangement of numerical facts or data, whether relating to human affairs or to natural phenomena.

1770 W. HOOPER tr. *Bielfeld's Elem. Universal Educ.* III. xiii. 269 The science, that is called statistics, teaches us what is the political arrangement of all the modern states of the known world. **1787** ZIMMERMANN *Polit. Surv. Europe* Pref. 2 This science, distinguished by the newly-coined name of Statistics, is become a favourite study in Germany. **1797** *Encycl. Brit.* (ed. 3) XVII. 731/2 *Statistics*, a word lately introduced to express a view or survey of any kingdom, county, or parish. **1798** SIR J. SINCLAIR *Statist. Acc. Scot.* XX. App. p. xiii, In 1786, I found, that in Germany they were engaged in a species of political inquiry, to which they had given the name of Statistics; and though I apply a different idea to that word, for by Statistical is meant in Germany, an inquiry for the purpose of ascertaining the political strength of a country, or questions respecting matters of state; whereas, the idea I annex to the term, is an inquiry into the state of a country, for the purpose of ascertaining the quantum of happiness enjoyed by its inhabitants, and the means of its future improvement; yet, as I thought that a new word might attract more public attention, I resolved on adopting it. **1838** *Lond. & Westm. Rev.* XXIX. 70 Statistics..is merely a form of knowledge—a mode of arranging and stating facts which belong to various sciences. **1839** CARLYLE *Chartism* xi. 115 Statistics is a most important science. **1895** MAYO-SMITH *Statist. & Sociol.* 9 Statistics consists in the observation of phenomena which can be counted or expressed in figures.

b. With defining word. Chiefly in ***vital statistics***, see VITAL *a.* 4 d.

1829 F. B. HAWKINS *Elem. Med. Statistics* 2 A combination of these scattered features forms Medical Statistics... We may perhaps define it, in a few words, to be the application of numbers to illustrate the natural history of man in health and disease. **1845** NEISON (*title*) Contributions to Vital Statistics. **1889** A. NEWSHOLME (*title*) The Elements of Vital Statistics.

2. a. Construed as *plural.* Numerical facts or data collected and classified.

1837 HT. MARTINEAU *Soc. Amer.* II. 292 There is great virtue in figures, dull as they are to all but the few who love statistics for the sake of what they indicate. **1838** *Lond. & Westm. Rev.* XXIX. 58 The valuelessness of all prior statistics of crime. **1844** KINGLAKE *Eothen* Pref., From all useful statistics..the volume is thoroughly free. **1859** *Westm. Rev.* Oct. 593 The statistics of suicide are striking. **1868** G. DUFF *Pol. Surv.* 6 To collect on the spot masses of statistics. **1881** HOOPER in *Jrnl. Statist. Soc.* XLIV. 44 We all know what we mean by 'statistics of pig iron,' 'statistics of coffee,' 'population statistics,' or 'revenue statistics.' We mean actual concrete figures relating to a particular set of phenomena.

b. = *vital statistics* (*b*) s.v. VITAL *a.* 4 d. Also *transf. colloq.*

1958 *Times* 24 Feb. 11/3 It is a pretty thought to contemplate all those statistics hipping and swaying and shimmering. *Ibid.* 13 Nov. 9/4 To-day, except for the slightly high waist-lines and one or two modified trapezes, feminine statistics were where nature intended them to be. **1960** *Punch* 3 Aug. 148/2 An enticing girl with yellow hair and sound statistics. **1978** O. WHITE *Silent Reach* vi. 61 Next time you get into position, try squeezing her statistics.

c. *Comb.* (in sing. form). Cf. STATISTIC *sb.* 1 b.

1855 THACKERAY *Charac. Sk., Capt. Rook*, The statistic-mongers and dealers in geography have calculated to a nicety how many quartern loaves..are consumed. **1902** S. COLERIDGE *Open Let. to Registrar-General* 6 The impertinences of a mere statistic-collector.

3. *Physics.* The statistical description appropriate to the behaviour and properties of an ensemble of many atoms, molecules, etc., esp. as regards the distribution of energy among them; *spec.* = *quantum statistics* s.v. QUANTUM 7 a.

[**1873** J. C. MAXWELL in *Nature* 25 Sept. 440/1 The modern atomists have therefore adopted a method which is I believe new in the department of mathematical physics, though it has long been in use in the Section of Statistics.] **1900** *Phil. Mag.* XLIX. 114 In the case of a gas, of which the statistics are assumed to be regular, the potential energy remains approximately constant. **1903** *Nature* 12 Mar. 453/2 The new Lucasian professor will next term lecture on 'The Theory of Gases and the Molecular Statistics of Energy.' **1909** *Proc. R. Soc.* A. LXXXIII. 86 The general thesis of which a development is here attempted is thus the molecular statistics of distributions of energy. **1927** [see FERMI]. **1928** [see BOSE-EINSTEIN]. **1950** W. J. MOORE *Physical Chem.* xii. 356 In deriving the Boltzmann statistics, we assumed that the individual particles were distinguishable and that any number of particles could be assigned to one energy level. **1979** *Sci. Amer.* Feb. 89/1 Two fundamental categories of particles, the fermions and the bosons. These categories are distinguished by the intrinsic angular momentum, or spin, of the particles, and by their statistics, or behavior in groups.

statistology (stætɪˈstɒlədʒɪ). *rare.* [f. STATIST-ICS + -(O)LOGY.] 'A discourse on statistics.' (Worcester 1860, citing *West. Rev.*)

stative (ˈsteɪtɪv), *a.* and *sb.* [ad. L. *statīv-us*, f. *stat-* ppl. stem of *stāre* to stand. Cf. F. †*statif* (16–17th c.), also G. *stativ* sb., stand for a telescope, etc.] **A.** *adj.*

1. Stationary, fixed, having a permanent situation, a fixed recurring date, or the like. Now only *Rom. Ant.* in ***stative camp***, etc.

a **1631** [SIR R. COTTON] *Disc. Power Peers*, etc. (1640) 2 In the Rolles of Henry the 3. It [Generale Placitum apud London] is not stative, but summoned by Proclamation. **1631** R. BYFIELD *Doctr. Sabb.* 81 Macrobius saith, there are foure kindes of publike holy-dayes.., Stative, Conceptive, [etc.]. **1816** SCOTT *Antiq.* iv, They are stative forts, whereas this was only an occasional encampment. **1856** MERIVALE *Rom. Emp.* xlv. (1865) V. 338 Rome was the proper sphere of his business and duty,..the stative camp of the warrior nation.

†**2.** That stands or continues in a certain state. *Obs.*

1643 R. O. *Man's Mortality* vi. 47 It incur'd this Absurditie, that the Soules of the Damned shall not perish, but stand as well as the Stative Angels.

3. Orig. (in *Hebr. Gram.*) an epithet of verbs which express a state or condition. [= mod.L. *verba stativa.*] Now also applied to languages other than Hebrew, to sentences, and to words other than verbs.

1874 A. B. DAVIDSON *Introd. Hebr. Gram.* 47 The term stative verbs, i.e. verbs of state, is used by some grammarians. *Ibid.*, The class of stative verbs is very numerous. **1913** C. T. WOOD & LANCHESTER *Hebr. Gram.* 69 Stative Verbs are a class of verbs, usually intransitive, which express a state or condition. **1930** F. R. BLAKE in J. T. Hatfield et al. *Curme Vol. Linguistic Stud.* 38 All temporal and locative relations have theoretically three aspects, a stative indicating existence or rest at a time or place (time when, place where), an ablative indicating continuance or motion from a time or place.., and a terminal indicating continuance or motion to a time or place. **1939** L. H. GRAY *Foundations of Lang.* vii. 202 The stative verb expresses 'the state of being in a certain condition'. **1964** *Language* XL. 78 Stative verbs occur with the nasal simulfix and typically with stative prefixes. **1967** FENN & TEWKSBURY *Speak Mandarin* 3 The stative sentence consists of a subject and a stative verb. **1970** *Language* XLVI. 830 English adjectives, much like English verbs, seem to divide into *stative* and *active* ones. **1979** *Trans. Philol. Soc.* 230 A fundamental distinction exists in Abkhaz between stative and non-stative (or dynamic) verbs.

B. *sb.* Orig. (in *Hebr. Gram.*) a stative verb. Now also applied to languages other than Hebrew, and to words other than verbs.

1874 DRIVER *Tenses Hebr.* §11. 12 To the verbs already cited may be added..the following, which are selected from the list given by Böttcher..: by this grammarian they are not inaptly termed *verba stativa* or 'statives'. **1913** C. T. WOOD & LANCHESTER *Hebr. Gram.* 67 Chapter xv. A. Tenses—Perfect Qal—Statives. **1966** J. E. BUSE in C. E. Bazell *In Memory of J. R. Firth* 54 These constraints may be used to divide full-words into the four sub-classes of verb, stative, noun and negative. **1973** *Canad. Jrnl. Linguistics* XVIII. 103 In order to explain the possessive function of statives and the limitations of this function in Sechelt, it is necessary to consider a cross-section of occurrences of this verbal aspect and to define its semantic range.

Hence **staˈtivity** *nonce-wd.*

1871 CAYLEY *Math. Papers* (1895) VIII. 213 What may be termed the 'stativity' of the curve.

†**statiˈzation.** *Obs.* [f. STATIZE *v.* + -ATION.] The action of the verb STATIZE; an instance of this.

1600 W. WATSON *Decacordon* (1602) 349 Any difference.. betwixt the secular priests, and Iesuites, in points of statization and medling of matters not belonging to our professions. *Ibid.* 353 [The Jesuits are] right Puritanes in al these statizations.

†**statize**, *v.* *Obs.* [f. STATE *sb.* + -IZE. Cf. STATIST.] *intr.* In depreciative sense: To meddle in state-affairs.

1600 W. WATSON *Decacordon* (1602) 224 In these..cases may seculars statize, that is, deale in state affaires how to preuent mischieuous statizers, of their purpose and practises. **1612** T. JAMES *Iesuites Downefall* 21 According to their doctrine of statizing, they must be stirring, tamporing, temporizing, and statizing like martiall men..in all temporal, mundane, and stratagematicall affaires. **1651** *Mr. Love's Case* 37 That he must needs suffer for the Word and Conscience, and not for statizing out of his Sphær.

Hence †**statizing** *vbl. sb.* and *ppl. a.*

1600 W. WATSON *Decacordon* (1602) 134 [They voided] their thoughts of all temporizing, statizing, and seditious medlings with the affaires of Prince or Peer. **1615–16** BOYS *Wks.* (1622) 160 The bloudy practises of turbulent and statizing Iesuites. *Ibid.* 224 So the Iesuite is a statizing Priest, a Court-rabbi. *Ibid.* 458 Statising worldlings on the contrarie thinke that Preacher of the word [etc.] **1630** *R. Johnson's Kingd. & Commw.* 18 By this people the rudiments of civill behaviour, of Lawes, good Customes, Statizing, Merchandizing, Oratorie, and Dialect, have beene bettered, if not invented. **1655** FULLER *Ch. Hist.* IX. xvi. 233 By his statizing, and dangerous activity, he had so incensed the Queens Councill, that [etc.]. **1657** PURCHAS *Pol. Flying-Ins.* II. 325 The upstart broode of perverted statising Loyalists.

†**statizer**. *Obs.* [f. STATIZE *v.* + -ER.]

1. One who meddles in state-affairs.

1600 W. WATSON *Decacordon* (1602) 222 The party must ..be holden for a statiser in a sense detestable. *Ibid.* 352 Puritanes, and such like factious statisers.

2. ? A partisan.

1616 J. LANE *Contn. Sqr.'s T.* VIII. 229 The verie names of Ethel and Canac causd the fregiliens allmost leese the place, had not Algarsife's statizers rann in, to putt some hope, wheare no hope was to winn.

stato- (stætəʊ), repr. Gr. στατό-ς standing, used (mainly as virtual combining form of STATIC, STATICS) in scientific words, chiefly *Biol.*, as ˌ**stato-a'coustic** *a.* *Anat.*, pertaining to the senses or faculties of both equilibration and hearing; *spec.* the epithet of the eighth cranial nerve (the vestibulo-cochlear nerve). '**stato-blast**, a reproductive gemmule developed in some Polyzoa and Sponges and liberated after the death of the parent organism; hence ˌ**stato'blastic** *a.* '**statocone** [Gr. κονία dust], each of the large number of granules in the statocyst of some animals, similar to a statolith, but smaller; also, an otolith in a vertebrate; also **stato'conia** *sb. pl.* '**statocyst, -cyte**, each of the cells or cysts containing statoliths. ˌ**stato'gen-esis, sta'togeny**, the (theoretical) origin of organic structures from static conditions (opposed to KINETOGENESIS); hence ˌ**statoge'n-etic** *a.*, ˌ**statoge'netically** *adv.* '**statolith**, a calcareous body found in some locomotor invertebrates, and supposed to be a means of orientation; hence applied to a starch-grain found in the cell-sap of some plant-cells (see quots.); also, an otolith in a vertebrate. **sta'tometer**, an instrument for measuring the degree of exophthalmos (*Syd. Soc. Lex.* 1898). '**statoplast** (see quot.). '**statorhabd** [Gr. ῥάβδος rod] = TENTACULOCYST. '**statoscope**, a form of aneroid barometer adapted for recording minute variations of atmospheric pressure. '**statosphere, 'statospore** (see quots.).

1958 *Gray's Anat.* (ed. 32) 144 The ganglia of the vagus, glossopharyngeal, *stato-acoustic (in part), facial and trigeminal nerves are derived from the ganglion-crest, but they migrate ventrally and soon come to lie on the ventrilateral aspect of the hind-brain. **1964** J. Z. YOUNG *Model of Brain* vii. 122 There is thus the possibility of correct interaction of visual and stato-acoustic information, these being the two chief systems that project to the mid-brain roof. **1974** D. & M. WEBSTER *Compar. Vertebr. Morphol.* xi. 255 (*caption*) Cross section through a mammalian upper myelencephalon, just behind the cerebellum, showing the relationships of the abducens, facial, and statoacoustic cranial nerves. **1855** ALLMAN in *Rep. Brit. Assoc.* II. 118 To the bodies in question, the author proposed to give the name of **statoblasts*. **1882** *Cassell's Nat. Hist.* VI. 327 Statoblasts of Spongilla. **1898** *Syd. Soc. Lex.*, **Statoblastic*. **1910** PARKER & HASWELL *Text-bk. Zool.* I. XII. 707 Each statocyst [in molluscs] may contain a number of minute *statocones or, more usually, a single, larger statolith. **1963** *Biol. Bull.* CXXV. 441 In the labyrinth of teleosts there are generally three large statoliths. .. Most other vertebrates, however, have otolith masses consisting of a very great number of small *statoconia held more or less firmly together by an organic gel. **1979** *Nature* 30 Aug. 832/1 Inner ear sensory surfaces from the Pacific herring..were prepared... After removal of the statoconia (otoliths) the tissues were dehydrated. **1980** *Gray's Anat.* (ed. 36) 1205/1 The gelatinous mass into which the cilia project is flatter and is termed an otolithic membrane.., because it contains numerous minute crystalline bodies called otoliths, otoconia, or statoconia. **1904** F. DARWIN in *Nature* 8 Sept. 468/1 In the Crustacean Palæmon the sense of verticality depends on the pressure of heavy bodies on the inside of cavities now known as *statocysts, and formerly believed to be organs of hearing. **1900** E. A. MINCHIN in *Ray Lankester's Treat. Zool.* II. *Sponges* 60 Gemmule cells or **statocytes*, such as compose the gemmule in *Spongilla*. **1894** E. D. COPE in *Amer. Naturalist* XXVIII. 213 *Statogenesis is work done in the construction of tissues like those of the parent and without interference. **1893** J. A. RYDER in *Proc. Amer. Philos. Soc.* XXXI. 198 In so far [as] the figure of a developing being is disturbed or modified by statical agencies its figure may be said to be subject to *statogenetic influences. *Ibid.* 194 Any formal modification thus caused and maintained would be developed *statogenetically. *Ibid.*, This general term ergogeny, will include not only kinetogeny, but also its antithesis, *statogeny. **1903** F. DARWIN in *Nature* 16 Apr. 571/2 The *Statolith Theory of Geotropism. **1955** *Sci. News* XXXVI. 92 Even plants which have no statoliths respond to gravitational stimuli. **1962** D. NICHOLS *Echinoderms* vi. 83 These are tiny fluid-filled spheres containing calcareous statoliths, the differential movement of which is registered in special nerves. **1969** *Nature* 28 June 1229/1 Starch statoliths are mobile starch grains found in almost all plant organs that respond to gravity. **1975** *Ibid.* 2 Oct. 380/2 Statoliths of at least one species of cephalopod are composed of aragonite, a stable form of calcium carbonate. **1904** *Ibid.* 8 Sept. 468/2 *note*, I would suggest the word *statoplast in place of the cumbersome expression movable starch-grains. **1910** *Encycl. Brit.* XIV. 143/2 In the Trachylinæ the simplest condition of the otocyst is a freely projecting club, a so-called *statorhabd. **1908** *Daily Chron.* 3 Feb. 6/3 We smashed all our instruments, the first crash quite settling the *statoscope. **1898** *Syd. Soc. Lex.*, **Statosphere*, the envelope of the statoblast of fresh-water Sponges and Bryozoans. **Statospore*, a resting spore, or hypnospore.

statocracy (steɪ'tɒkrəsɪ). [f. STATE *sb.* + -(O)CRACY.] Government or rule by the state alone, uncontrolled by ecclesiastical power.

1864 in WEBSTER (*citing* O. A. Brownson).

sta'tolatry. *rare.* [f. STATE *sb.* + -(O)LATRY.] Idolizing of the state.

1853 *Brownson's Q. Rev.* Apr. 188 In these days of statolatry, carnal Judaism, and political atheism.

statolon ('stætəlɒn). *Biochem.* Also *erron.* **statalon.** [Prob. a blend of mod.L. *stoloniferum* (see below and STOLONIFEROUS *a.*) and -STATIC.] A complex polysaccharide obtained from the mould *Penicillium stoloniferum*, now known to contain a fungal virus which is an antiviral agent, stimulating the release of interferon.

1961 PROBST & KLEINSCHMIDT in *Federation Proc.* XX. 441/2 A fermentation broth of *Pen. stoloniferium* [sic] prophylactically inhibits a number of viruses both in animals and in tissue culture... The active principle, designated as statolon, has been subjected to a variety of purification procedures. **1964** *Proc. Nat. Acad. Sci.* LII. 741 Statolon is a complex anionic polysaccharide with a relatively high content of galacturonic acid. **1967** *New Scientist* 10 Aug. 300/2 W. J. Kleinschmidt and L. F. Ellis have now refined the technique of fractionating statalon, and have discovered, to their surprise, that one of the active fractions contained numerous virus-like hexagonal particles... They have confirmed that..it is these particles that are responsible for stimulating interferon activity in mice. **1971** *Sci. Amer.* July 28/2 Eli Lilly and Company demonstrated the presence of a fungal virus in statalon, an extract of another penicillium species. **1976** P. COLLARD *Devel. Microbiol.* v. 64 There are a number of compounds that either stimulate the production of interferon in the host cells, as does Statolon, originally believed to be a fungal product but now shown to be a virus, or release interferon which is already pre-formed in the cells. **1978** *Nature* 29 June 760/1 Tilorone, statolon and Newcastle disease virus (NDV), all potent inducers of interferon in mice, induced a marked increase in spleen cell cytotoxicity.

‖**stator**[1] ('steɪtɔ(r)). *rare.* [L., sustainer, supporter (primarily an epithet of Jupiter), agent-n. f. **sta-, sistĕre* to cause to stand.] (See quots.)

1657 CLEVELAND *Rustic Rampant* Wks. 514 He was the Stator, the Saviour of the Nation.

stator[2] ('steɪtə(r)). [a. L. *stator*, agent-n. f. *sta-, stāre* to stand.]

1. *Electr.* The stationary portion of an electric generator or motor, esp. of an induction motor.

1895 S. P. THOMPSON *Polyphase Electr. Currents* v. 113 In describing the parts of polyphase motors..[we] shall call the rotating part the rotor, and the stationary part the stator. **1902** S. SHELDON & H. MASON *Altern.-Current Machines* 142 The stationary part of an induction motor is called the *stator*, and the moving part is called the *rotor*. **1903** *Nature* 23 Apr. 588/2 The high pressure current is taken only to the stators of the high tension motors. **1903** [see ROTOR 2].

2. The casing enclosing the revolving blades of a steam turbine. More widely, an immovable part of any turbine; *spec.* a stator blade (see sense 3 below), or a row of such blades.

1911 *Encycl. Brit.* XXV. 846/1 The tips [of the blades] are fined down..so that in the event of contact taking place.. between the 'rotor' or revolving part, and the 'stator' or case, they may grind without being stripped off. **1916** J. W. M. SOTHERN *Marine Steam Turbine* (ed. 4) VIII. 424 The turbine consists of two principal parts, the rotor or moving part, and the cylinder (sometimes called the 'stator') or stationary part. **1951** COHEN & ROGERS *Gas Turbine Theory* vi. 133 Each stage will consist of one rotating row followed by a stator but it is usual to provide an additional stator row at entry to guide the air correctly into the first rotor. **1962** F. I. ORDWAY et al. *Basic Astronautics* x. 404 The rotor turns within the stator, which is a series of blades arranged in a circle around the inside wall of the compressor housing. **1967** N. E. BORDEN *Jet-Engine Fundamentals* 80 The first four stages of the high-pressure compressor are provided with variable stators, automatically positioned by hydraulic actuators. **1971** P. J. MCMAHON *Aircraft Propulsion* iv. 124 Figure 4.2 shows a view in the radial direction of the blading of a compressor stage—rotor plus stator—with the stators of the previous stage included for completeness.

3. *attrib.* and *Comb.*, as ***stator coil, winding***; **stator blade**, a small stationary aerofoil fixed to the casing of an axial-flow turbine, rows of which are positioned between the rows of rotor blades.

1946 G. G. SMITH *Gas Turbine & Jet Propulsion* (ed. 4) iv. 58 Stator blades to direct the air flow between stages will also be of either steel or light alloy. **1977** J. L. KERREBROCK *Aircraft Engines & Gas Turbines* v. 120 There are normally three types of blade row in an axial compressor: the inlet guide vanes, the rotor blades, and the stator blades. **1904** W. R. BOWKER *Dynamo, Motor & Switchboard Circuits* 102 The 'stator' coils are arranged in a six-pole grouping. **1895** S. P. THOMPSON *Polyphase Electr. Currents* v. 113 The stator winding is usually the primary, the rotor winding secondary.

statory, erron. form of STATARY.

stats (stæts). Colloq. abbrev. of STATISTICS.

1. (With capital initial.) A department responsible for collecting or recording numerical facts or data.

1942 N. BALCHIN *Darkness falls from Air* vi. 102 Why not give Stats. a new man and leave Giles where he is? **1953** D. PARRY *Going up—going Down* iv. 130 He visited the Stats. Branch. **1966** M. WOODHOUSE *Tree Frog* i. 2 Do you know what we pay those girls in Stats?

2. = STATISTICS 2 a.

1962 L. DEIGHTON *Ipcress File* x. 64, I am not a statistician... I was getting pretty fed up with his housebreaking stats. **1974** Cleveland (Ohio) *Plain Dealer* 26 Oct. 4-D/1 The positon statistics have been impressive even though individual stats for many have not shocked anyone. **1975** *New Yorker* 14 Apr. 90/1 Drove to Fort Lauderdale.., found the ballpark, parked, climbed to the press box, said hello, picked up stats and a scorecard, took the last empty seat, filled out my card. **1981** J. WAINWRIGHT *Tainted Man* 169 The bumpf... This never-ending paper crap. Stolen cars, crime stats.

3. = STATISTICS 1 a.

1970 *Guardian* 15 Jan. 13/3, I..went on to stress the importance of what..I have decided to dub stats education. .. It's..vital that people should know more about statistics.

†'**statua.** *Obs.* Pl. 6–7 statuas, 7 statuaes, statua's. [a. L. *statua*: see STATUE *sb.*]

In mod. edd. of Shaks. the following passages have *statua* (or pl. *statuas*) where the reading of the early edd. is *statue* (or *statues*): *Rich. III*, III. vii. 25, *Jul. C.* II. ii. 76, III. ii. 192, *2 Hen. VI*, III. ii. 80. The emendation is prob. right, as a trisyllable is required, and there is no evidence of trisyllabic pronunciation of *statue*.

= STATUE *sb.*

c **1400** *Pilgr. Sowle* IV. xxix. (1859) 61 This word statua, whiche that we transumen in to Englysshe, that is to mene an Image. **1451** CAPGRAVE *Life St. Aug.* 19 Whech man for grete sciens had a statua rered to his liknesse in þe markette at Rome. **1599** HAKLUYT *Voy.* II. Ep. Ded. *2 b, With the same intention that the old Romans set vp in wax in their palaces the Statuas or images of their worthy ancestors. **1605** BACON *Adv. Learn.* I. viii. §6. 44 b, It is not possible to haue the true pictures or statuaes of Cyrus, Alexander, Cæsar..; for the originals cannot last. *Ibid.* II. i. §2. 7 b, Without which the History of the world seemeth to me, to be as the Statua of Polyphemus with his eye out. **1625** —— *Ess., Building* (Arb.) 552 And let there be a Fountaine, or some faire Worke of Statua's, in the Middest of this Court. **1646** G. DANIEL *Poems* Wks. 1878 I. 12, I stood A verie Statua, dull as my owne Mudde. **1691** WOOD *Ath. Oxon.* I. 117 A fair Table Monument..with their statua's from head to foot laying thereon. *Ibid.* 264 Over his Grave was..the Statua or Bust of the Defunct to the middle part of his body.

†'**statual,** *a.* *Obs. rare*[−1]. [ad. med.L. *statuālis*, f. L. *statu-s* standing, stature, etc. (see STATE *sb.*).] (See quot.)

1825 FOSBROKE *Encycl. Antiq.* 698 These offerings of wax ..appear to be, in some instances, tapers of the stature or height of the person, and are called, in the Miracles of Simon the Hermit, Statual Tapers.

†'**statuarism.** *Obs. nonce-wd.* [f. STATUAR-Y + -ISM.] Partisanship for the art of sculpture.

1791 H. WALPOLE *Let. Miss Berry* 12 May, Madrid and the Escurial she owns have gained her a proselyte to painting, which her statuarism had totally engrossed.

statuarist ('stætjuːərɪst). Now *rare.* [f. STATUAR-Y + -IST.] = STATUARY A. 1.

1679 BP. CROFT *Let. Popish Idol.* 22 An excellent Painter and Statuarist, as well as Physician. **1760** RHYS *Tour Spain & Portugal* 110 That famous Roman Statuarist Giovanni Batista Moreli. **1847** J. WILSON *Lands of Bible* I. iv. 86 The Cyclopean statuarists of old. **1887** SMILES *Life & Labour* 221 The four Stones were statuarists,—father and three sons.

statuary ('stætjuːərɪ), *sb.* and *a.* [ad. L. *statuārius* adj. (also absol. as sb. masc., sculptor, and ellipt. fem. *statuāria* sc. ars, art of sculpture), f. *statua* STATUE *sb.* Cf. F. *statuaire* adj. and sb. masc. and fem. (sb. masc. from 14th c.), It. *statuario* adj. and sb. masc., *statuaria* sb. fem. (similarly Sp., Pg. *estatuário, -ária*).]

A. *sb.* **1.** One who practises the art of making statues, a sculptor of statues.

1581 MULCASTER *Positions* v. 35 If I..should seeme to contemne that principle, which brought forth..so many statuaries, so many architectes. **1607** CHAPMAN *Bussy d'Ambois* I. i. 7 Vnskilfull statuaries, who suppose (In forging a Colossus) if they make him Straddle enough.. Their worke is goodly. **1631** MASSINGER *Emperor East* II. i, If Statuaries could By the foote of Hercules set downe punctually His whole dimensions. **1777** JOHNSON *Let. to Mrs. Lucy Porter* 20 Nov., in *Boswell* (1831) IV. 63 Mr. Nollikens, the statuary, has had my direction to send you a cast of my head. **1814** SCOTT *Diary* 25 Aug. in *Lockhart* III. vii. 237, I think a statuary might catch beautiful hints from the fanciful and romantic disposition of the stalactites. **1864** TENNYSON *Boadicea* 64 Burn the palaces, break the works of the statuary. **1890** *Daily News* 21 Mar. 5/4 Other cracks.. may easily be discovered, and the statuary should be called in before the damage gets more serious.

2. Sculpture composed of statues, statues collectively. †Also pl., works of sculpture.

1673 [R. LEIGH] *Transp. Reh.* 97 The image of episcopacy, like the statuaries in Pallas target. **1701** in *Cath. Rec. Soc. Publ.* VII. 106 We were.. to see yᵉ fine antient pieces of Statuary, of which there are several of the Passion. **1848** H. ROGERS *Ess.* I. vi. 305 The persons of the drama stand out in their appropriate characteristics as distinctly as the various forms in a group of Greek statuary.

3. The art of making statues, sculpture.

1563 SHUTE *Archit.* B iij b, Neither in painting like Apelles nor Plastes, or Stattuary like vnto Miron or Policrates. **1704** ADDISON *Italy* Pref., The noblest productions of statuary and architecture. **1776** JOHNSON in *Boswell* 19 Mar., The value of statuary is owing to its difficulty. You would not value the finest head cut upon a carrot. **1839** URE *Dict. Arts* 1009 It was he [Wedgewood] who first erected magnificent factories, where every resource of.. science was made to co-operate with the arts of painting, sculpture, and statuary. **1840** HOOD *Up Rhine* 55 A painted wooden figure of a Dutchman... This wooden statuary is, timberly speaking, quite a branch of the Dutch fine arts. **1846** ELLIS *Elgin Marbles* I. 110 Statuary, or the art of making complete figures.

4. *Comb.*

1875 KNIGHT *Dict. Mech.*, Statuary-casting. **1914** *Daily News* 15 Jan. 12, I was admitted to the inner sanctum of the statuary-makers' haunts.

B. *adj.*

1. Of or pertaining to the making of statues.

1627 HAKEWILL *Apol.* III. v. §3. 198 And therefore Plato banished Poets from his common-wealth; and Moses,.. both painting and the statuary Art. *a* **1700** EVELYN *Diary* 16 June 1683, Nor doubt I at all that he will prove as greate a master in the statuary art.

2. Consisting of statues or a statue; sculptured.

1629 MAXWELL tr. *Herodian* (1635) 120 He.. presented them also to publicke view, in Statuarie Representations. **1654** H. L'ESTRANGE *Chas. I* (1655) 64 Sir Francis Bacon.. hath there a fair statuary monument erected for him of white Marble. *a* **1718** PENN *Tracts* Wks. 1726 I. 542 Which shows he [Orpheus] meant no Statuary Deity, but God that made the Heavens and the Earth. **1753** in Picton *L'pool. Munic. Rec.* (1886) II. 159 The statuary work by him executed. **1892** *Daily News* 13 May 3/1 When Cato was offered statuary honours, he refused them on the ground that he would rather people asked why there was not a statue of Cato than why there was one.

†**3.** *fig.* Resembling that of a statue; statuesque.

1759 GOLDSM. *Bee* No. 2 *On our Theatres* ⁋1 Actresses.. who have.. what connoisseurs call statuary grace, by which is meant elegance unconnected with motion.

4. Of materials: Suitable for statues or statuary work; esp. ***statuary marble*** (see quot. 1909), hence ***statuary vein***, a variety of statuary marble (see quot. 1909).

1815 W. BAKEWELL *Introd. Geol.* 87 The crystalline translucent qualities of statuary marble. **1823** W. PHILLIPS *Introd. Min.* (ed. 3) 152 Statuary Marble. The most celebrated statuary marble was found in the island of Paros, thence termed Parian marble. **1875** KNIGHT *Dict. Mech.*, *Statuary-brass*, an alloy of copper, zinc, and tin, used for statuary, generally known as bronze. **1909** RENWICK *Marble* 218 *Statuary*, a general name given to pure white marble, free from markings, but generally understood as meaning the best quality of Italian white marble. *Ibid.*, *Statuary Vein*, white Italian marble having a statuary ground and fine blue veins traversing the formation.

attrib. **1881** W. S. GILBERT *Foggerty's Fairy* (1892) 26 A handsome statuary marble mantelpiece.

statue (ˈstætjuː), *sb.* Also 6 *Sc.* statw. [a. F. *statue* (12th c.), a. L. *statua*, f. *sta-*, root of *stāre* to stand. Cf. It. *statua*, Sp., Pg. *estátua*.]

1. a. A representation in the round of a living being, sculptured, moulded or cast in marble, metal, plaster or the like materials; esp. a figure of a deity, allegorical personage, or eminent person, usually of life-size proportions. Also *transf.* and *similative*, as a type of silence or absence of movement or feeling.

For *colossal*, *equestrian statue*, etc. see the adjs.

13.. *E.E. Allit. P.* B. 995 For his make [Lot's wife] was myst, þat on þe mount lenged In a stonen statue þat salt sauor habbes. *c* **1386** CHAUCER *Monk's T.* 169 This proude kyng leet maken a statue of gold.. To which ymage he bothe yonge and oold Comanded to loute. **1471** CAXTON *Recuyell* (Sommer) 223 And that they myght no more lifte theyr swerdes than myght statues or ymages. **1576** FLEMING *Panopl. Epist.* 283 In buying statuies [*sic*] or standing images, they spend their substance. **1606**, **1691** [see RELIEF³ 1]. **1608** SHAKS. *Per.* II. 10 And to remember what he does, Build his Statue to make him glorious. **1611** —— *Wint. T.* v. iii. 10 We saw not That which my Daughter came to looke vpon, The Statue of her Mother. **1622** [see ROUND *sb.*¹ 4 a]. **1628** COKE *On Litt.* Pref. ⁋4 b, The bodie of our Author is honourably interred.. vnder a faire Tombe of Marble, with his statue or portrature vpon it. **1634** MILTON *Comus* 661 If I but wave this wand, Your nerves are all chain'd up in Alabaster, And you a statue. *a* **1700** EVELYN *Diary* 4 Feb. 1644, In the middle.. stands on a noble pedestal, a brazen Statue of Lewis XIII. **1730–46** THOMSON *Autumn* 138 The statue seemed to breathe And soften into flesh beneath the touch Of forming art. **1794** GODWIN *Cal. Williams* 128 He looked the statue of despair. **1823** BYRON *Island* III. iv. 7 Still as a statue.. He stood. **1833** TENNYSON *Pal. Art* 37 And high on every peak a statue seem'd To hang on tiptoe. **1860** —— *Sea Dreams* 217 Ever when it broke The statues, king or saint, or founder fell. **1886** *Encycl. Brit.* XXI. 571 For the execution of a marble statue the sculptor first models a preliminary sketch on a small scale in clay or wax.

¶**b.** App. loosely used for: Image, effigy.

c **1386** CHAUCER *Knt.'s T.* 117 The rede statue of Mars with spere and targe So shyneth in his white baner large. **1513** DOUGLAS *Æneis* IV. xi. 112 To.. birn ȝon Troians statw in flamb funerall. *a* **1547** SURREY *Æneid* IV. (1557) G j b, And Troian statue throw into the flame. **1615** E. HOWES *Stow's Ann.* 815 [Q. Eliz. funeral] And when they beheld her statue or picture lying vppon the coffin.. hauing a Crowne vppon the head thereof, and a ball and scepter in either hand: there was such a generall.. weeping, as the like hath not beene seene. **1632** MASSINGER *City Madam* v. iii, *S[ir] Jo[hn].* Your Neeces.. crave humbly Though absent in their bodys, they may take leave Of their late suitors statues... *Luke.* There they hang.

c. *pl.* The name of various children's games which involve the players standing still in different postures.

1906 *Dialect Notes* III. 158 *Statues, n.*, the name of a game in which children pose. **1916** N. DOUGLAS *London Street Games* 41 Catch-in-the-Rope is also for boys and girls, and so is.. Statues... When you play this game you have to line yourselves up against a wall or a house; then the judge comes along and pulls one of you forwards and in that moment you have to make a posture and a face.. and pretend to be a statue. **1935** E. FARJEON *Nursery in Nineties* v. 240 She quickly suggests a game, Magical Music, or Forfeits, or Statues. She.. thumps the only tune to which Statues can be played. **1950** B. PYM *Some Tame Gazelle* xxi. 236 When they realized that a prayer was being said, they stood stiffly with the urn, like children playing a game of 'statues'. **1981** L. DEIGHTON *XPD* xliv. 356 'You're moving,' called Stein loudly. It was a good-natured complaint of the sort that children might use when playing the game of 'statues'.

2. attrib. and Comb., as ***statue-†craft***, ***-lantern***, ***-marble***, ***-portrait***; ***statues game***; objective and obj. genitive, as ***statue-hewing***, ***-maker***, ***-turning***, ***worshipper***; instrumental, as ***statue-bordered*** adj.; similative, as ***statue-blind*** adj., ***statue-like*** adj. and adv.; **statue-dress** *Theat.*, 'a dress for the body and legs, made in one piece, worn in representations of statuary' (*Cent. Dict.* 1891).

1844 MRS. BROWNING *Vis. Poets* xxxvi, And Shelley, in his white ideal, All *statue-blind. **1835** TALFOURD *Ion* IV. iii, These *statue-border'd walks. **1634** PEACHAM *Compl. Gentl.* xii. (1906) 110 Such as are well seene in *statue-craft. **1975** 'D. JORDAN' *Black Account* II. xxxv. 175 Guy stood by the door like a child playing the *statues game. **1850** C. BRONTE *Pref. to E. Bronte's Wuthering Heights* p. xxiv, It sets to work on *statue-hewing, and you have a Pluto or a Jove. **1904** R. J. FARRER *Gard. Asia* xiii. 117 From this [court] one passes through others,.. each forested with high toro or *statue-lanterns. **1822** BYRON *Juan* VI. lxviii, A fourth as marble, *statue-like and still, Lay in a breathless, hush'd, and stony sleep. **1828** MISS MITFORD *Village* III. 38 Her long straight hair, parted on the forehead and twisted into a thick knot behind, gave a statue-like grace to her head. **1850** R. G. CUMMING *Hunter's Life S. Afr.* xxviii. II. 233 The elephant .. stood statue-like beside the fountain. **1635** JACKSON *Creed* VIII. xxvii. 305 The vulgar Latine hath it.. *ad Statuarium*, to the *Statue-maker. **1861** L. L. NOBLE *Icebergs* 170 Frozen under enormous pressure,.. it.. resembles.. freshly broken *statue-marble. **1872** HEAD *Sel. Grk. Coins in Electrotype Brit. Mus.* 18 Thistetradrachm.. may give us the traits of the *statue-portrait by Lysippos, or the gem-portrait by Pyrgoteles. **1832** BREWSTER *Nat. Magic* xi. 287 The *statue-turning machine of Mr. Watt. **1678** CUDWORTH *Intell. Syst.* I. iv. 473 The Image and *Statue-worshippers among the Pagans.

Hence **'statueless**.

1860–3 THACKERAY *Round. Papers* xix. 303 In the spirit I am walking.. round the Place Vendôme, where the *drapeau blanc* is floating from the statueless column.

statue (ˈstætjuː), *v.* [f. STATUE *sb.*]

1. *trans.* To represent in a statue or in statuary; to honour (a person) by erecting a statue of him. Now only as *nonce-use*.

?**1607** DAY *Parl. Bees* viii. (1641) F 2 b, At the foure corners of this Chariot Ile have the foure windes statued. **1611** FLORIO, *Statuare*, to statue, to image. **1628** FELTHAM *Resolves* II. xv. 42 He did not feare to lose his head,.. for if he did, the Athenians would give him one immortall. He should be Statued, in the treasury of eternall fame. **1672** EACHARD *Hobbes' St. Nat. Consid.* 64 It is great pity but that you should be entomb'd at Westminster, and statued up at Gresham Colledge for the great moral discoverer of the Age. **1895** W. WRIGHT *Zenobia & Palmyra* x. 107 Another citizen erected seven columns.. and he was 'statued' in March 179 A.D.

†**2.** To turn into a statue. *Obs. rare.*

1628 FELTHAM *Resolves* II. xxxvi. 111 The eye is dimme, in the discoloured face; and the whole man becomes as if statued into stone and earth.

statued (ˈstætjuːd), *ppl. a.* [f. STATUE *v.* and *sb.* + -ED.]

1. Furnished or ornamented with statues or statuary.

1806 W. TAYLOR in Robberds *Mem.* II. 144 The stately yew-hedge walks, and vased and statued terraces. **1855** TENNYSON *Daisy* xvi, I stood among the silent statues, And statued pinnacles, mute as they. **1870** DISRAELI *Lothair* lxix, An arcadian square flooded with light and resonant with the fall of statued fountains.

2. Represented in a statue or in statuary.

1731 L. THEOBALD *Orestes* IV. iii. 57 The Statued Goddess born in solemn Pomp, Guarded, as 'twere the Spoils of hostile Bands? **1839** BAILEY *Festus* (1852) 243 The statued satyrs seemed to grin and jibber 'neath her eye. **1850** BLACKIE *Æschylus* I. 31 And the statued forms that look from their seats With a cold smile serenely. **1875** BROWNING *Aristoph. Apol.* 338 Free to stand Pedestaled mid the Muses' temple-throng, A statued service, laureled, lyre in hand.

3. Statue-like.

1820 J. H. WIFFEN *Aonian Hours* (ed. 2) 108 The statued clouds scarce err Over the marbled skies.

statuefy (ˈstætjuːfaɪ), *v. rare.* Also **statufy**. [f. STATUE *sb.* + -FY.] *trans.* **a.** To turn into a statue. **b.** To erect a statue to.

1868 HELPS *Realmah* viii. 232 There were 27 degrees of frost that day. As we sat on our horses.. we were nearly statuefied. **1903** *Pilot* 17 Oct. 372/2 The occasion was the erection of a statue to Vercingetorix—statufied everywhere except his native district.

statuesque (ˌstætjuːˈɛsk), *a.* [f. STATUE *sb.* + -ESQUE, after *picturesque*.] Having the qualities of a statue or of sculpture.

a **1834** COLERIDGE *Notes & Lect.* (1849) I. 71 Their productions were, if the expression may be allowed, statuesque, whilst those of the moderns are picturesque. **1849** THACKERAY *Pendennis* xvii, An image of statuesque piety and rigid devotion. **1855** SMEDLEY *H. Coverdale* xlvii, He had always admitted her statuesque grace. **1858** CARLYLE *Fredk. Gt.* v. ii. (1872) II. 71 Statuesque immovability of posture. **1891** *N. & Q.* Ser. VII. XII. 99 The more reserved and statuesque formulæ of the Western Churches. **1905** SIR F. TREVES *Other Side of Lantern* II. xxx. (1906) 190 The statuesque native soldiers who stand as sentries.

Hence **statu'esquely** *adv.*, **statu'esqueness**.

1833 COLERIDGE *Table-t.* 1 July, Euripides.. embraces within the scope of the tragic poet many passions.. which Sophocles seems to have considered as incongruous with the ideal statuesqueness of the tragic drama. **1868** BROWNING *Ring & Bk.* IX. 802 Hold, as it were, a deprecating hand, Statuesquely, in the Medicean mode. **1886** G. ALLEN *Maimie's Sake* xxiii, He had never before seen her.. look so .. statuesquely beautiful. **1888** *Harper's Mag.* Aug. 330 Each lithe figure.. has a statuesqueness and a luminosity impossible to paint in words.

statuette (ˌstætjuːˈɛt). [a. F. *statuette* dim. of *statue*; see STATUE *sb.* and -ETTE.] A small statue; a statue less than life-size.

1843 *Fraser's Mag.* XXVIII. 103 In every space.. stood a little statuette of marble. **1863** SIR G. SCOTT *Glean. Westm. Abb.* (ed. 2) 64 These niches contained thirty statuettes of different personages. **1906** PETRIE *Relig. Anc. Egypt* xiii. 83 Little statuettes of gods of glazed pottery, and often of bronze, silver, and even of gold.

attrib. **1866** *Reader* 19 May 500 'The Chase'.. is life size, but 'The Stag at Bay'.. is little more than statuette size.

†**'statuist.** *Obs. rare*⁻¹. [f. STATUE *sb.* + -IST.] A statuary, sculptor.

1620 E. BLOUNT *Horæ Subs.* 365 The most famous Painter and Statuist in the world, Michael Angelo.

statuit, obs. form of STATUTE.

†**'statuize**, *v. nonce-wd.* [f. STATUE *sb.* + -IZE.] *trans.* To make a statue of, to commemorate by means of a statue.

1719 OZELL tr. *Misson's Trav. Eng.* 309 James II. did also statuize himself [orig. *s'est aussi fait Statuër*] in Copper, in one of the Courts of White-hall.

†**sta'tuminate**, *v. Obs.* [f. L. *statūmināt-*, ppl. stem of *statūmināre*, f. *statūmin-*, *statūmen* prop, support, f. *statu-ĕre* to set up: see STATUTE.] *trans.* To support, establish.

a **1628** F. GREVIL *Sidney* i. (1652) 6 Those eminent Plants .. which blast, or bite not, but rather statuminate, and refresh the Vines.. or whatsoever groweth under their shaddows. **1631** B. JONSON *New Inn* II. vi, I will statuminate and vnderprop thee. *a* **1676** HALE *Prim. Orig. Man.* IV. vi. (1677) 346 A miraculous interposition in all the ordinary procedures of things already fully setled and statuminated by the first Divine Efficiency.

Hence †**sta'tuminated** *ppl. a.* Also †**statumi'nation**.

1658 PHILLIPS, *Statumination*, an underpropping or setting up. **1674** HALE *Diffic. Nugæ* (1675) 238 The God of Nature, whose standing and statuminated Law Nature is, hath so ordered it.

ˌstatuo'mania. *nonce-wd.* [f. STATUE *sb.* + -MANIA.] A mania for the erection of statues.

1882 *Contemp. Rev.* Oct. 656 The rage for statues, now being erected all over France, seems to be degenerating into a statuomania.

ˌstatu-'quoism. *nonce-wd.* [f. L. phrase (*in*) *statū quō* (see IN *Latin prep.* 29) + -ISM.] Partisanship of the existing condition of things. So also **statu-quo-ite**, whence **statuquoitism**.

1816 T. L. PEACOCK *Headlong Hall* i, These four persons were, Mr. Foster, the perfectibilian; Mr. Escot, the deteriorationist; Mr. Jenkison, the statu-quo-ite; and the Reverend Doctor Gaster. **1826** H. N. COLERIDGE *Six Months in W. Ind.* (1832) 184 There is so much statuquoitism in the old colonies. **1848** STEINMETZ *Hist. Jesuits* III. 388 Another peculiarity of the Chinese was *statu-quo-ism*, their imitative faculties having from time immemorial completely palsied the inventive.

statural (ˈstætjʊərəl), *a. rare*⁻¹. [f. STATURE *sb.* + -AL¹.] Of or pertaining to stature.

1868 H. BUSHNELL *Serm. Living Subj.* xxi. (1872) 426 The human soul is overborne.. by the statural dimensions of God.

stature ('stætjʊə(r)), *sb.* Forms: 3–6 statur, 5 statour(e, 6 statyre, 4– stature. [a. OF. *stature*, *estature* (mod.F. *stature*) ad. L. *statūra* f. *sta-*, *stāre* to stand: see -TURE. Cf. It. *statura*, Sp., Pg. *estatura*.]

1. The height of an animal body in its normal standing position. **a.** esp. of a human body.

a **1300** *Cursor M.* 22321 [þis king Constans was] a mikel man, o statur hei. **1340** HAMPOLE *Pr. Consc.* 73 God..man last made Til hys lyknes and semely stature. **1382** WYCLIF *Matt.* vi. 27 Sothely who of ȝou thenkinge may putte to to his stature oo cubite? *a* **1400–50** *Wars Alex.* 1702 Darius.. Askis þam of sir Alexander all at he cuthe, Bathe of his statoure & his strenth. *c* **1440** *Alphabet of Tales* ccclxxii. 256 He was so febull & of so little a statur. **1551** T. WILSON *Logic* C j b, Stature or brodenes cannot be taken from man. **1591** SHAKS. *Two Gent.* IV. iv. 163 *Sil.* How tall was she? *Jul.* About my stature. **1597** —— *2 Hen. IV*, III. ii. 277 Care I for the Limbe, the Thewes, the stature, bulke, and bigge assemblance of a man? giue me the spirit. **1625** N. CARPENTER *Geogr. Del.* II. xiv. (1635) 224 Hippocrates pronounced the people of the North to be..of a small and dwarfish stature. **1710** STEELE *Tatler* No. 75 ¶5 He was low of Stature... But he was more prudent than Men of that Height usually are. **1726** POPE *Odyss.* XVIII. 258 Thy riper days no growing worth impart, A man in stature, still a boy in heart! **1839** FR. A. KEMBLE *Resid. Georgia* (1863) 38 Her stature..must have been..five feet seven or eight. **1847** TENNYSON *Princess* Prol. 40 Her stature more than mortal in the burst Of sunrise. **1860** TYNDALL *Glac.* I. xvi. 104 A remarkable-looking man,..of middle stature.

†**b.** of a beast or a fish. *Obs.*

1390 GOWER *Conf. A.* III. 117 The ferste..is cleped Aries, Which lich a wether of stature Resembled is in his figure. *a* **1505** in Kingsford *Chron. Lond.* (1905) 255 The later ende of ffebruary was taken..a ffishe of greate statur. **1600** J. PORY tr. *Leo's Africa* IX. 341 It is..shaped like a ramme, and of the stature of an asse. **1774** GOLDSM. *Nat. Hist.* (1776) IV. 216 These [monkeys]..are all small in stature.

c. *transf.* esp. of a tree.

1633 T. JOHNSON *Gerarde's Herbal* II. clxxxiii. §8. 593 This [Dwarfe Mountaine Pinke] for his stature may iustly take the next place. **1707** MORTIMER *Husb.* (1721) II. 26 In transplanting..be very sparing of the Roots, that is, for such Trees as are of Stature. **1742** SHENSTONE *School-mistress* xviii, Their books, of stature small, they take in hand. *a* **1767** M. BRUCE *Lochleven* 79 Poems (1796) 73 The stately ash Rear'd high his nervous stature. **1796** C. MARSHALL *Gardening* Contents *note*, Those trees, shrubs, and flowers ..must be looked for in this Section; where is mentioned their stature,..nature, and propagation. **1830** J. G. STRUTT *Sylva Brit.* 89 The lives and stature of trees, like those of animals, must vary with the situations in which they are placed. **1898** 'MERRIMAN' *Roden's Corner* vi. 61 There are quiet nooks..where the trees have grown to a quite respectable stature.

d. put for: Standard of height.

1781 GIBBON *Decl. & F.* xvii. (1787) II. 48 Yet, although the stature was lowered,..the insurmountable difficulty of procuring a regular..supply of volunteers, obliged the emperors to adopt..more effectual and coercive methods.

e. *fig.*

1834 NEWMAN *Par. Serm.* I. xii. 186 Not making matters worse than they are, or showing our whole Christian stature ..when we need but put out a hand..or give a glance. **1850** S. DOBELL *Roman* vii. Poet. Wks. 1875 I. 117 You do mistake The stature of your courtesy for that Of my desert. **1857** H. REED *Lect. Brit. Poets* iv. 125 The language had gradually reached its full stature. **1868** E. EDWARDS *Ralegh* I. xxiii. 530 A leading mark of Ralegh's mental stature. **1875** STUBBS *Const. Hist.* (1896) II. xvi. 323 The men are of meaner moral stature.

†**2.** Bodily form, build. *Obs.*

c **1385** CHAUCER *L.G.W.* 2446 And lyk his fadyr of face & of stature And fals of loue. **1387** TREVISA *Higden* (Rolls) III. 469 þe stature of þe body of mankynde is made of þe elementes i-medled to-gidres. **1526** *Pilgr. Perf.* (W. de W. 1531) 3 And aboue yᵉ myddle he was the moost amiable stature of a man. **1626** T. H. tr. *Caussin's Holy Court* 45 Nicephorus relateth certaine lineaments of his [the Saviour's] stature, colour and proportion of his members, which he drew out of antiquity.

†**3.** An effigy, statue. *Obs.* [So F. *stature* in 15th c.]

1390 GOWER *Conf.* III. 52 And while he slepte..Him thoghte he syh a stature evene. *c* **1400** *Destr. Troy* 11654 Lelly, the lett, þat vs long taries, Is a statur full strong of a stith god [*sc.* the Palladium]. *Ibid.* 11698. **1513** DOUGLAS *Æneis* VI. xv. 3 The peple of vdyr realmis..Bene moyr expert..To forge and carve lyflyk staturis of bras. *Ibid.* VII. iv. 31 And Janus statur eik with double face. **1583** MELBANCKE *Philotimus* K iij, Parrhasius painted an erected statyre, and on the top thereof a Partridge, so liuely, that [etc.]. **1585** T. WASHINGTON tr. *Nicholay's Voy.* II. iii. 33 The stature of a woman cloathed after the Grecian fashion. *Ibid.* II. xiv. 49 b, The stature of a dragon of the length of 120. foote. **1592** R. JOHNSON *Nine Worthies* C 2, [Fame] vowed to erect his stature where..it should stande immoveable. **1596** WARNER *Alb. Eng.* XII. lxxiii. (1612) 301 The statures huge, of Porphyrie and costlier matters made. **1653** tr. *Carmeni's Nissena* 142 An alter was raised trampled on by a stature of Pallace.

†**4.** State, condition. *Obs.*

? *a* **1500** *Chester Plays* i. 86, I haue forbyd that yow ne sholde, but kepe yow well in this stature, the same Covenant, I charge yow, hold. **1500–20** DUNBAR *Poems* xiv. 41 Sic vant of wostouris with hairtis in sinfull staturis.. Within this land was nevir hard nor sene.

5. The posture of standing. In quot. *fig. rare.*

1742 YOUNG *Nt. Th.* VII. 1441 And what is reason?.. Reason is upright stature in the soul.

stature ('stætjʊə(r)), *v. rare* exc. in pa. pple. [f. STATURE *sb.*] *trans.* To give stature to. (Some of the examples quoted may belong to STATURED *a.*)

c **1440** *Pallad. on Husb.* XIII. 24 Ypomelides Beth appultreen,..A commyn tre statured dout[e]lees, With whitly flour coloured. **1609** HEYWOOD *Brit. Troy* XI. xvi, Their growth is strange, whom I compare aright, Vnto the Mush-roome, statur'd in a night. **1635** QUARLES *Embl.* II. vi, Were thy dimension but a stride, Nay, wert thou statur'd but a span. **1638** MAYNE *Lucian* (1664) 260 But if they will appeare alike statured, the taller is to stoope, and depresse himselfe. *a* **1661** FULLER *Worthies, Essex* (1662) 334, I match him [Tusser] with Thomas Church-yard, they being mark'd alike in their Poeticall parts, living in the same time, and statur'd alike in their Estates, both low enough I assure you. **1872** TENNYSON *Gareth & Lynette* 277 Old Master, reverence thine own beard That..seems Wellnigh as long as thou art statured tall!

statured ('stætjʊəd), *a.* [f. STATURE *sb.* + -ED².] Having (a certain kind of) stature. Chiefly in parasynthetic formations, as ***fair-***, ***low-***, ***full-statured***; also †***well statured***.

1610 HEALEY *St. Aug. Citie of God* XV. xxiii. 562 As though that we haue no such extraordinary huge statured creatures euen in these our times. **1635** [see LOW *a.* 21]. **1647** J. HALL *Poems* 93 How doth the Giant Honour seeme Well statur'd in my fond esteeme. **1691, 1844** [see FULL *a.* 12 c]. **1801** SOUTHEY *Thalaba* II. xiii, Man, fair-statured as the stately palm.

status ('steɪtəs). Pl. (*rare*) **status** ('steɪtjuːs) now usu. **statuses** ('steɪtəsɪz). [a. L. *status* (*u* stem), f. *sta-* root of *stāre* to stand. Cf. the adopted form STATE *sb.*]

‖**1.** *Path.* **a.** The height or acme of a disease: cf. STATE *sb.* 7 and STATION *sb.* 6. Now *rare* or *Obs.*

[**1693** tr. *Blancard's Phys. Dict.* (ed. 2) *Status Morbi*, see *Acme*. (Cf. 1706 PHILLIPS, *Acme*..among Physicians the height of a Disease.)]

transf. **1671** EVELYN *Let. to Sir T. Clifford* 31 Aug., Diary & Corr. (1906) 646 The third and last period includes the *status* or height of the war..to the conclusion of it in the Treaty at Breda, 1667.

b. Used (with the sense 'state, condition') in many mod.L. combinations with adj., as ***status arthriticus***, ***epilepticus***, ***lymphaticus***, ***nervosus***: see *Dorland's Illustr. Med. Dict.* 1913. ***status asthmaticus***, the condition of a patient during a prolonged severe asthmatic attack; also *ellipt.*, = status epilepticus.

a **1883** FAGGE *Princ. & Pract. Med.* (1886) I. 684 There is ..a special modification of the disease in which the fits follow one another in rapid succession... This has by modern French physicians been called the *état de mal épileptique*, and in England some writers have made use of the equivalent expression, *status epilepticus*. **1898** *Syd. Soc. Lex.*, *Status* (L.),..A stage in which the disease having reached its height, it remains for a time before convalescence begins. **1899** *Allbutt's Syst. Med.* VI. 323 Epilepsy with 'status' [i.e. *status epilepticus*] or complications. **1909** *Daily Mail* 5 Aug. 5/6 The exact causation of the status lymphaticus was unknown. **1947** DORLAND & MILLER *Med. Dict.* (ed. 21) 1392/1 Status asthmaticus. **1962** J. H. BURN *Drugs, Med. & Man* xviii. 179 Sometimes the attacks (asthma) follow one another so steadily that the patient's life is in danger. He is then said to be in 'status asthmaticus' and in the past patients have often died. **1971** *Where* Dec. 360/1 There was no sign of epilepsy until she was two and a half, when she went into status (a condition where the fits follow one another without pause).

2. a. *Law.* The legal standing or position of a person as determined by his membership of some class of persons legally enjoying certain rights or subject to certain limitations; condition in respect, e.g., of liberty or servitude, marriage or celibacy, infancy or majority.

1791 BOSWELL *Johnson* an. 1777 (1904) II. 156 To abolish a *status*, which in all ages God has sanctioned, and man has continued, would..be extreme cruelty to the African Savages. **1813** *Edin. Rev.* Oct. XXII. 24 The forfeiture of condition, or *status*, is a class of great extent theoretically speaking. **1832** AUSTIN *Jurispr.* (1869) I. Outline 41 The rights, duties, capacities, or incapacities, which determine a given person to any of these classes, constitute a condition or *status* which the person occupies, or with which the person is invested. **1865** H. W. FISHER *Consid. Amer. War* 84 Therefore his *status* as free or slave depended on the laws of Missouri. **1888** BRYCE *Amer. Commw.* I. xxiv. 351 But the majority of the court..delivered a variety of *dicta* on various other points touching the legal status of negroes. **1904** TALLENTYRE *Voltaire* II. xliii. 295 The man who for sixty years had not ceased to try to improve the civil status of actors. **1910** M. GASTER in *Encycl. Brit.* XII. 40/1 The history of the legal status of the Gipsies..would form a remarkable chapter in the history of modern civilization.

b. *transf.*

1897 D. W. FORREST *Christ of Hist. & Exper.* 442 Notes, He says that the status and the spirit of sonship 'are not only distinguishable but separable'.

c. In application to things.

1914 *Daily News* 6 Nov. 1 The Sultan of Turkey not having ratified the Convention relating to the status of enemy merchant vessels. **1914** *Contemp. Rev.* Dec. 729 The status of Egypt cannot continue what it now is.

3. a. Position or standing in society, a profession, and the like. Also *social status*.

1820 SCOTT *Monast.* Introd. Ep., The shopkeeper..stood indeed pretty much at his ease behind his counter,..but still he enjoyed his *status*, as the Bailie calls it, upon condition of tumbling all the wares in his booth over and over, when any one chose to want a yard of muslin. **1848** MILL *Pol. Econ.* I. 383 The status of a day labourer has no charm for infusing forethought, frugality or self-restraint into a people devoid of them. **1852** MILL *Pol. Econ.* (ed. 3) II. IV. vii. 331 As to civil and social *status*, in framing a new reform bill..the opportunity was not taken. **1859** LEVER *Dav. Dunn* iv. 35 On the one side he had..a sure status in society. **1873** C. M. DAVIES *Unorth. Lond.* (1876) 60 As..the sect grew in social status as well as in numbers, gradually the miraculous tongues fell into silence. **1883** S. C. HALL *Retrospect* II. 248 As an actress, [she] took a professional status amongst the highest. **1901** G. B. SHAW *Socialism for Millionaires* in *Fabian Tract* No. 107. 15 A millionaire does not really care whether his money does good or not, provided he finds his conscience eased and his social status improved by giving it away. **1936** R. LINTON *Study of Man* viii. 114 There are no rôles without statuses or statuses without rôles. **1946** D. L. SAYERS *Unpopular Opinions* 120 The commercial middle classes acquired the plutocratic and aristocratic notion that the keeping of an idle woman was a badge of superior social status. **1955** T. H. PEAR *English Social Differences* i. 25 Each individual..can have many statuses. **1960** D. POTTER *Glittering Coffin* iv. 54 The links between job and social status..are too often taken for granted. **1970** C. T. RESTREPO in I. L. Horowitz *Masses in Lat. Amer.* xiv. 517 Cultural ascent in society refers to the acquisition of those cultural forms corresponding to a higher class or social status. **1977** R. HOLLAND *Self & Social Context* v. 89 Occupants of similar statuses may support each other against threats from members of a role-set, as when teachers support each other against parents of their students.

b. *transf.* of a thing.

1885 J. MARTINEAU *Types Eth. Theory* I. I. II. ii. §8. 201 Of this Ego, or soul, of ours,..how is it possible, after thus setting it up as a known separate entity, to cancel its status and hand over its contents to another subject? **1890** *Hardwicke's Science-Gossip* XXVI. 154 The medical status of ivory was based on its alkaline properties.

4. a. Condition of things.

1860 MAURY *Phys. Geog. Sea* IV. §236 Diligent, therefore, in their offices must the agents be which have been appointed to maintain the chemical status of the atmosphere. **1889** *Anthony's Photogr. Bull.* II. Pref., The illustrations give a good idea of the present status of the art in the various methods of printing.

b. *Finance.* A particular grouping of the conditions bearing on the continuance of an annuity.

1838 DEMORGAN *Ess. Probab.* 190 This status may be simple or complicated... For instance, A is to enjoy an annuity to the end of his life, unless B should die before C, in which case it is to cease. This annuity will be enjoyed as long as either of the following status exist. A, B, and C all living. A and B living, and C dead. A living, and B and C dead, C having died first. **1862** WATERSTON *Man. Commerce* 303 *Status of an Annuity*, the state of things during the continuance of which the annuity is to be paid. A *compound status* is one which exists as long as either of two or more status remain.

c. *Sc. Comm.* Position (of a trader) in respect of solvency and credit. In quot. *attrib.*

1901 *Scotsman* 8 Mar. 5/6 [Aberdeen] The status enquiries numbered 2054 during the year.

5. a. *attrib.* or as *adj.* That confers prestige on its possessor; having a high social status; superior.

1950 M. MEAD *Male & Female* xiii. 266 A caustic critic has labelled the one child of middle-class families as a 'status child', a child that merely gives the parents the status of *having had* a child. **1956** C. W. MILLS *Power Elite* iv. 79 As a status model the debutante declined. **1960** S. KAUFFMANN *If it be Love* I. viii. 113 A status-car, matched to your income, and a station wagon. **1961** A. SMITH *East-Enders* vii. 122 One of the status cafés on the edge of the East End, beautifully kept. **1964** A. HUNTER *Gently Sahib* iv. 33 The locals had taken him a room at the Angel Inn, the status hotel in Abbotsham. **1977** D. MORRIS *Manwatching* 125 What the rapist wants is..the total, abject subjection of his victim... This is Status Sex, and it is not by any means an exclusively human pattern of activity.

b. *Comb.*, as (sense 3) ***status-conscious***, ***-dissenting***, ***-ridden*** adjs.; **status anxiety**, anxiety about one's social status, esp. the fear of losing it; **status group(ing)**, any group of people who have similar social standing (see quot. 1978); **status-seeker**, one who is concerned with improving or demonstrating his social status; hence **status-seeking** *vbl. sb.* and *ppl. a.*; **status symbol**, a possession or asset sought or acquired as a symbol of social prestige; hence **status-symbolism**; **status system**, a social structure or organization in which status derives from one's position or achievement in some aspect of the group's activity; **status-trophy** *rare* = *status symbol* above.

1959 *Encounter* Sept. 58/1 The political conflicts of the 'fifties..were..explained by sociological concepts such as '*status anxiety'. **1971** HALSEY & TROW *Brit. Academics* xiii. 329 This may be due to the status anxiety associated with marked social mobility. **1959** V. PACKARD *Status Seekers* (1960) i. 6 Wives..tend to be more *status conscious than their husbands. **1974** tr. *Wertheim's Evolution & Revolution* 234 Asian peasants are generally status conscious and..the more prosperous ones often recognize mutual social obligations only towards those whom they consider to be their peers. **1956** J. M. MOGEY *Family & Neighbourhood* viii. 140 The remainder of St. Ebbe's people we may call, by contrast, *status-dissenting. **1965** *New Society* 4 Feb. 26/3 On the newer suburban housing estates..a new species has developed, the *status dissenting* working class person. **1910** HADDON *Races of Man* 61 The Mahrattas form the higher *status group of this people. **1978** *Listener* 19 Jan. 77/3 Status groups—for example, peers of the realm or vagrants —are social networks of those who share similar social prestige. **1964** *Punch* 29 July 172/2 We hear a lot about *status-groupings in the US. **1953** *Observer* 16 Aug. 7/5 Miss Thurburn can move us to admiring recognition when she deals with..the *status-ridden society. **1962** *Guardian* 14 Aug. 5/3 The prestige notions of a Pakistani civil servant are almost as inflexible as those found in our own status-ridden society. **1959** V. PACKARD *Status Seekers* (1960) i. 7 The *status seekers..are people who are continually straining to surround themselves with visible evidence of the superior rank they are claiming. **1979** *United States 1980/81* (Penguin Travel Guides) 214 There are no phone calls to take, except for those status-seekers foolish enough to have telephones in their cars. **1951** R. R. Sears in Parsons & Shils *Toward General Theory of Action* 477 Secondary motivational systems..between mother and child... include aggression, dependency, self-reliance..and *status-seeking. **1960** *Guardian* 23 Dec. 6/6 The status-seeking educational system. **1962** *Punch* 31 Jan. 227/3 Status-seeking, broken marriages, intrigue among research staff of Midland firm. **1962** E. Snow *Red China Today* (1963) xl. 300 It should not be supposed that they are any less outer-directed than the status-seeking sons of Madison Avenue. **1976** J. Wainwright *Who goes Next?* 52 This over-expensive, status-seeking building. **1955** *Status symbol [see *sign-vehicle* s.v. sign *sb.* 12 b]. **1957** *Wall St. Jrnl.* 29 Oct. 1/1 The most common sources of interoffice rivalry over status symbols involve such obvious executive trappings as the size of the desk, the quality of drapes and carpets in private offices, [etc.]. **1965** G. Maxwell *House of Elrig* v. 77, I was singled out as a target for jealousy by those whose parents would have liked 'a handle to their names' and whose status-symbol cars compared spectacularly with the modest and practical conveyances my mother chose. **1981** *Church Times* 23 Oct. 10/2 A fragment of the true Cross —a status symbol if ever there was one. **1957** *Wall St. Jrnl.* 29 Oct. 9/2 In their place he introduced a highly formalized system of *status symbolism. **1968** *Punch* 7 Aug. 183/2 The main design criteria [*sic*] of motor-manufacture is now neither comfort nor status-symbolism, but simple safety. **1942** Warner & Lunt *Status System Mod. Community* ii. 16 We shall hereafter refer to the eighty-nine behavioral situations (or statuses) as social positions or statuses, and the total social system of Yankee City as the positional or *status system. **1978** *Listener* 12 Jan. 35/2 Our Martian would quickly conceptualise pair-bonding in what we call marriage, scientific organisations in the social relations of discovery, status systems in the relations of dominance and submission, and so on. **1964** Auden in *Listener* 1 Oct. 525/2 This unpopular art which cannot be..hung as a *status-trophy by rising executives.

Hence **'statusless** *a.*, without status.

1905 W. O'Brien *Recoll.* ix. 186 The reporting profession was still in the statusless condition in which [etc.].

statusful ('steɪtəsfʊl), *a.* [f. status + -ful.] Having or conferring (high) social status or distinction.

1969 *Daily Tel.* (Colour Suppl.) 17 Oct. 57/1 Ordering a 22-carat Dunebuggy with ocelot seats and rhinestone headlamps in a bid for statusful individuality. **1975** *Times* 22 Aug. 10/1 'Statusful speakers', like BBC newsreaders. **1977** J. A. Fishman in H. Glass *Lang., Ethnicity & Intergroup Relations* i. 37 It is not ethnicity *per se* that is of concern to it but the recrudescence of less statusful, narrower, 'peripheral' identities. **1978** *Amer. Speech* LIII. 14 Its use implies the user's special familiarity..with that less statusful or less responsible class of people who have such special familiarity and use the term.

‖**status quo** ('steɪtəs kwəʊ). [L.: 'state in which'. Cf. *in statu quo* (see in *Latin prep.* 29).] The existing state of affairs. ***status quo ante***: the state of affairs previously existing (also *absol.*).

1833 *Edin. Rev.* LVI. 436 The *status quo* was to be maintained in Luxemburg during negotiations respecting that duchy. **1853** Ld. J. Russell *Let. to Ld. Cowley* 28 Jan., in H. Paul *Hist. Mod. Eng.* (1904) I. xvii. 301 The Ambassador of France was the first to disturb the *status quo*. **1864** *Spectator* 439 The country gentlemen can be satisfied with the *status quo* as a principle. **1877** L. W. M. Lockhart *Mine is Thine* xxxv. (1879) 300 His autumn plans were in the *status quo ante*. **1884** tr. *Lotze's Logic* 403 The desire to protect that particular *status quo* on principle against all innovation. **1951** W. Stevens *Let.* 9 Mar. (1967) 709 Everything is now proceeding in status quo ante. **1965** H. Kahn *On Escalation* xiii. 244 It is normal that *status quo* nations will tend to be crisis-avoiding nations. **1967** *Listener* 27 July 103/1 Supposing that Israel withdrew, and that the Arabs were re-supplied with arms, we should be back at a sort of status quo ante. **1971** *Guardian* 6 Dec. 13/8 The TUC puts its money firmly on the need for a 'status quo' declaration by the employer. In other words, the unions insist that the employer must..abandon his authority to change a work practice or agreement without the blessing of his employees... Workers can be expected to observe procedures only if they contain a 'status quo' clause and the employer observes it. **1976** *New Yorker* 24 May 115/2 There is a great move to the status quo ante. **1978** R. Lewis *Inevitable Fatality* vi. 163 The attempts by Sir Henry Monroe to return QWARTA [*sc.* a company] to a *status quo* position.

statusy ('steɪtəsɪ), *a. colloq.* [f. status + -y¹.] Possessing, indicating, or imparting a high status.

1962 *Guardian* 29 Nov. 7/1 No matter how many irrelevant if statusy pieces the 'New Yorker' publishes. **1964** *Punch* 22 Jan. 112/2 As statusy a combination as you can get. **1969** *Time* 26 Sept. 72/2 Pretty soon about 85% of the kids smoked. It got to be a really statusy thing. **1971** *Daily Colonist* (Victoria, B.C.) 3 Sept. 21/6 Katherine Gibbs, who in 1911 founded the statusy secretarial school that bears her name.

statutable ('stætjuːtəb(ə)l), *a.* [f. statute *sb.* + -able.]

1. Prescribed, authorized, or permitted by statute.

1636 Featly *Clavis Myst.* viii. 99, I have no commission ..to make privie search for concealed Idols, or vailed Impudency, or statuable Usurie. **1713** *Guardian* No. 108 ¶2 Five Foot..is the statutable Measure of that Club. **1723** Swift *Argt. agst. Power Bishops* Wks. 1761 III. 260 There is but one instance in the memory of man of a bishop's lease being broken upon the plea of not being statutable. **1798** Evelyn *Weights & Meas.* in *Phil. Trans.* LXXXVIII. 167 Although they do not carry with them..any statuteable authority. **1868** Milman *St. Paul's* xi. 260 How were they in the custody of the Archdeacon, not of the Treasurer, their statutable guardian? **1870** W. R. Greg *Polit. Problems* 299 On an average, the family of the labourer will comprise three members above the statutable age—frequently more.

2. Conformed to the requirements of the statutes as to quality, size, or amount. †Also *transf.*, of regular or standard quality; that will pass muster.

a **1661** Fuller *Worthies, Essex* (1662) 318 Hops..being adjudged wholesome, if Statuable and unmixed with any powder, dust, dross, [etc.]. **1664** Evelyn *Sylva* xxviii. §8 (1679) 149 Statutable Billet should hold three foot in length [etc.]. **1667** Dryden *Sir M. Mar-all* Prol. 6 Fops in the Town more easily will pass; One story makes a statutable Ass: But such in Plays must be much thicker sown. **1676** Mace *Musick's Mon.* 28 Those Ancient (former denominated) Statutable Wages of 8, 10, or 12 l. a year. **1742–3** Bp. Sherlock in *Johnson's Debates* (1787) II. 448 So every part of the kingdom will be equally debauched, and no place will be without a vender of Statutable poison. **1758** Borlase *Nat. Hist. Cornw.* 88 Twenty bushels of wheat..on one statutable acre of ground. **1762** Sterne *Tr. Shandy* V. xxvii, My father put on his spectacles, looked,—took them off,—put them into the case,—all in less than a statutable minute. **1774** Pennant *Tour Scot. in 1772*, 321 A cooper examines if they are statutable and good. **1800** Marq. Wellesley in Owen *Desp.* (1877) 702 The conveyance..of such goods..beyond the amount of the statutable tonnage of 3,000 tons. **1856** Froude *Hist. Eng.* (1858) I. i. 26 Persons ..were punishable if they refused to work at the statutable rate of payment.

b. In university use: Satisfying the requirements of the university statutes.

1687 Bp. Cartwright in *Magd. Coll.* (O.H.S.) 122 Was he a statutable person? *a* **1715** Burnet *Own Time* iv. (1724) I. 699 The Fellows..did upon this choose Dr. Hough,.. who..was in all respects a statutable man. **1794** in *Burke's Corr.* (1844) IV. 240 Nothing could be more unseasonable.. than to appoint to the provostship any man who is not..a statutable, academical character. **1868** M. Pattison *Academ. Org.* iv. 88 No college can undertake to say what is or is not now statutable. **1880** Fowler *Locke* i. 9 The statutable time of taking both degrees was anticipated. **1882** *Nature* XXVII. 47 Mr. Minty..being over the statutable age, was not eligible for a scholarship.

3. Of an offence: Recognized by statute; legally punishable.

1792 W. Roberts *Looker-On* No. 3 (1794) I. 29 Though nonsense is not statutable among us, yet we are not afraid of its going to any great lengths under the evident disadvantages of order and tranquillity. **1864** *Daily Tel.* 8 June, Hoaxing is not a statutable offence.

Hence **'statutableness**.

1687 Dr. Hough in *Magd. Coll.* (O.H.S.) 127 The legality and Statutableness of my Election. **1727** Bailey vol. II., *Statutableness*, the being according to the Statute, relating to the Matter.

statutably ('stætjuːtəblɪ), *adv.* [f. statutable *a.* + -ly².] In a statutable manner; by the operation of a statute or statutes; in accordance with the requirements of the statutes.

a **1661** Fuller *Worthies, Westminster* (1662) 243 Beniamin Johnson..was Statutably admitted into Saint Johns-college in Cambridge. *a* **1683** Oldham *Art of Poetry* (1686) 24 Others by this conceit have been misled So much that they're grown statutably mad. **1691** *Case of Exeter-Coll.* 30 Unless it was made appear that Mr. Colmer was not Statutably Expell'd. **1705** Hearne *Collect.* 17 Nov. (O.H.S.) I. 84 He was..statutably qualified. **1872** *Contemp. Rev.* XX. 546 By courts statutably imposed upon the Establishment. **1879** H. Hardcastle *Statutory Law* 290 Appendix. Certain words and expressions, used in statutes, which have been judicially or statutably construed. **1885** M. Pattison *Mem.* 175 Stanley, not being statutably eligible, could not have come in, unless he had been invited to do so.

†**'statutary**, *a.* [f. statute *sb.* + -ary.] = statutory.

1647 Ward *Simple Cobler* 13 That all Christian States, ought to disavow and deny all such Errours, by some peremptory Statutary Act. **1776** Adam Smith *W.N.* i. ix. 110 All these different statutary regulations seem to have been made with great propriety.

statute ('stætjuːt), *sb.* Forms: 3, 5–6 **statuit**, 4 **statout**, 4–7 **statut**, 6 **statuytt**, 4– **statute**. (Also estatute 1514–1610.) *Pl.* 3–4 **statuz** (*z* = *ts*), 4 **statutz**, 5 **statutez**, **statuitz**, 6 **statewes**, 9 *dial.* (sense 6) **stattice**, **stattits**. [a. F. *statut* (OF. also *estatut*, whence estatute), ad. late L. *statūtum* decree, decision, law, subst. use of neut. pa. pple. of *statuĕre* to set up, establish, decree, f. *sta-* root of *stāre* to stand. Cf. Pr. *statut-s*, Sp., Pg. *estatuto*, It. *statuto*.]

I. 1. a. A law or decree made by a sovereign or a legislative authority. Now *rare* or *Obs.* in general sense.

c **1290** *Beket* 759 in *S. Eng. Leg.* 128, I not ȝwat is þe newe statuit þat þu þencst forth to drawe. **13..** *Cursor M.* 13613 (Gött.) þe Iuus..had mad..A statute again iesus crist, If ani wold him leue or loute, þair synagoge suld be put vte. *c* **1325** *Song Flemish Insurr.* in *Pol. Songs* (1839) 188 The Kyng of Fraunce made statut newe In the lond of Flaundres. **1387** Trevisa *Higden* (Rolls) III. 365 [Aristotle] made statutes to iustefie þe citees of Grees [orig. *justificationes urbium Graecarum*]. *c* **1391** Chaucer *Astrol.* i. §10. 6 The names of thise Monthes were cleped in Arabycus, somme for hir propretes, & some by statutz of lordes, some by other lordes of Rome. *c* **1400** *Pilgr. Sowle* iv. xxix. (1859) 61 Ordynaunces of pryuate lawes in Reames..ben cleped statutes, for they sholde be stabelly kepte. **1520** *Caxton's Chron. Eng.* iii. 20 b, They made this statut that 2 consules sholde be chosen, and they sholde governe the cyte and the people. **1526** *Pilgr. Perf.* (W. de W. 1531) 222 b, To this article also perteyneth the decrees, counseyles & statutes of the chirche. **1535** Coverdale *Dan.* vi. 13 Daniel..(O kynge) regardeth nether the ner thy statute, that thou hast made. **1593** Shaks. *Rich. II*, iv. i. 213 All Pompe and Maiestie I doe forsweare:..My Acts, Decrees, and Statutes I denie. *c* **1670** Hobbes *Dial. Com. Laws* (1681) 30 The Positive Laws of all places are Statutes. **1725** Pope *Odyss.* ix. 127 By these no statutes and no rights are known. **1764** Goldsm. *Trav.* 385 When I behold..Each wanton judge new penal statutes draw.

b. Applied to an ordinance or decree of God, a deity, fate, etc.

c **1381** Chaucer *Parl. Foules* 387 Ȝe knowe wel how seynt volantynys day By myn statute..ȝe come for to cheese ..ȝoure makis. *c* **1393** —— *Envoy to Scogan* 1 To-brokene ben þe statutis in heuene þat creat were eternally to dure. **1513** Douglas *Æneis* xii. xiii. 72 Quhilk, weill I wait, is Na wys include in statutis of the fatis. **1535** Coverdale *Ps.* cxviii. 12 Praysed be thou O Lorde, O teach me thy statutes. *a* **1631** Donne *Holy Sonn.* xvi, Men argue yet, Whether a man those statutes can fulfill. **1707** Watts *Hymns*, '*How honourable is the Place*' iii, Enter ye Nations that obey The Statutes of our King.

c. A law made by a guild or corporation for the conduct of its members; a by-law of a borough; a provision in a municipal charter.

1389 in *Eng. Gilds* (1870) 100 These been ye statuz of ye gylde of ye holy prophete Seynt Jon baptist. **1429** *Rolls of Parlt.* IV. 346/2 In the Statuitz of the honourable Ordre of the Gartier. **1509** in *Star Chamber Cases* (Selden Soc.) I. 277 They bothe offendid the statute of the Cyte thervppon made. **1538** Latimer in Ellis *Orig. Lett.* Ser. iii. III. 204 Hytt were gode you wolde sum tyme sende for Masters of Collegis in Cambryge and Oxforde with there Statuytts, ande yf the Statuytts be natt god and to the furtherance of god lettres, change them. **1546** in J. Bulloch *Pynours* (1887) 64 Tha chesit Johne Vodman and Hungre Jok decanis of the said craft to causs this present Statut to be obseruit. **1590** Shaks. *Com. Err.* i. ii. 6 This very day a Syracusian Marchant Is apprehended..And not being able to buy out his life, According to the statute of the towne, Dies ere the wearie sunne set in the West. **1641** in *Verney Mem.* (1907) I. 204 Local statutes to appoint sermons almost every day. **1702** Charlett in *Pepys' Diary* (1879) VI. 251 At a weekly meeting, which by our statutes is every Monday, consisting of the V.C., Heads of Colleges and Halls, and the two Proctors, I moved [etc.]. **1785** Paley *Mor. Philos.* iii. i. xxi, The statutes of some colleges forbid the speaking of any language but Latin within the walls. **1808** Scott *Marm.* ii. xix, The statutes of whose order strict On iron table lay. **1856** Emerson *Eng. Traits, Universities* Wks. (Bohn) II. 90 Oxford..is still governed by the statutes of Archbishop Laud.

†**d.** *gen.* An authoritative rule or direction.

c **1391** Chaucer *Astrol.* Prol. 3/68 The .5. partie shal ben an introductorie aftur the statutz of owre doctours. *Ibid.* ii. §4. 18/10 After the statutz of Astrologiens. **1605** A. Warren *Poor Man's Pass.* B 1 b, And I shall die vntested in my death, Doubting least mine Executors refuse The statute of my Testament to vse.

2. a. An enactment, containing one or more legislative provisions, made by the legislature of a country at one time, and expressed in a formal document; the document in which such an enactment is expressed.

In England, Scotland, and Ireland, *statute* is in general synonymous with 'Act of Parliament' (see, however, quot. 1765), but the designation is applied also to certain early enactments by the king and his council before the rise of regular parliaments.

c **1386** Chaucer *Prol.* 327 Euery statut koude he pleyn by rote. **1386** *Rolls of Parlt.* III. 226/1 The Statut ordeigned and made bi Parlement. **1434** *Ibid.* V. 438/2 Lawes, custumes and Statutes of his Reaume. *a* **1475** Ashby *Active Policy* 522 Aftur the statutes autorised By noble Kynges your progenitours. **1532** *Dial. on Laws Eng.* ii. xlvi. 116 b, Sometyme in diuers statutes penalles they yᵗ be ignoraunt be excused. **1552** *Bury Wills* (Camden) 142 Yᵉ booke of yᵉ Kings Statuts. **1556** *Ir. Act 3 & 4 Ph. & Mary* c. 14 The moost auncynt statuits of this realme. **1597** Hooker *Eccl. Pol.* v. lxxxi. §16 A testimonie vpon the credite whereof sundry statutes of the Realme are built. *c* **1645** Howell *Lett.* (1655) IV. xlix. 117 To Dye once is that uncancell'd debt Which Nature claymes, and raiseth by Eschet On all Mankind by an old Statute past *Primo Adami*. **1683** *Col. Rec. Pennsylv.* I. 21 Other duties by any law or statute due to vs. **1765** Blackstone *Comm.* i. Introd. §3. 85 *note*, All the acts of one session of parliament taken together make properly but one statute; and therefore when two sessions have been held in one year, we usually mention stat. 1. or 2. Thus the bill of rights is cited, as 1 W. & M. st. 2. c. 2. **1790** Burke *Fr. Rev.* 44 The famous statute, called the Declaration of Right. **1817** Selwyn *Law Nisi Prius* (ed. 4) II. 795 But (after argument) it was holden, that the case was not within the statute. **1856** Emerson *Eng. Traits, Ability* Wks. (Bohn) II. 43 Their social classes are made by statute. **1858** Ld. St. Leonards *Handy-Bk. Prop. Law* xiii. 80 A remedy is afforded by statute. **1871** C. Davies *Metric Syst.* iii. 116 By this statute the ale gallon was expressly declared to be the eighth part of the measure of the bushel. *Ibid.* 230 Rhode Island has no statute on the subject. **1875** Stubbs *Const. Hist.* II. xvii. 585 The statute is a law or an amendment of law, enacted by the king in parliament, and enrolled in the statute roll. **1910** J. Dowden *Medieval Ch. Scot.* ii. 27 In 1390 another Act was passed by Parliament strengthening the earlier statute.

†**b.** ***by*** (†***the***) ***statute***: according to the measure, price, or rate appointed by statute. Hence, by fixed rule, strictly. *Obs.*

c **1450** *Bk. Curtasye* 377 in *Babees Bk.*, Be statut he schalle take þat on þe day. **1523–34** Fitzherb. *Husb.* §12 An acre of grounde, by the statute, that is to say xvi. fote and a half to the perche or pole. *a* **1630** J. Taylor (Water P.) *Wks.* ii.

174/2 Hee will pay him by the Statute. **1642** MILTON *Apol. Smect.* 4 One who makes sentences by the Statute, as if all above three inches long were confiscat. **1781** COWPER *Table-T.* 72 Nor judge by statute a believer's hope.

c. With identifying designation.

Certain early statutes are currently designated from the place at which the parliament was held, as *Statute of Acton Burnell, Statute of Lincoln, Statute of Westminster*, etc. Others are named from their subject, as *Statute of Labourers, of Limitations, of Provisors, of Treasons of Uses*, etc. (see those words).

Bloody Statute: a popular name for the Act 31 Hen. VIII. c. 4, called the *Law of the Six Articles*, imposing severe penalties on all who disputed certain articles of faith (see SIX *a.* 1 d).

a **1325** tr. *Hengham Parva* MS. Rawl. B. 520 lf. 70 b, Seche þe auctorite in þe furste statut of Westmunstre. *a* **1648** LD. HERBERT *Hen. VIII* (1649) 446 The Six Articles, called by some the Bloody Statute, were also enacted this Parliament [1539]. **1766** BLACKSTONE *Comm.* II. xx. 324 The statute of frauds 29 Car. II. **1860** FORSTER *Gr. Remonstr.* 41 The long and remarkable reign of Edward the First's grandson is the date of the Statute of Treasons, one of the greatest gains to constitutional freedom. **1902** W. T. S. HEWETT *Terms & Phr. Eng. Hist.* 34 *Statute of Fines...* (4 Henry VII).. intended to put a check on suits for the recovery of lands... *Statute of Grace.* A Bill of Indemnity for all political offences, passed in 1690 (William and Mary)... *Statute of Kilkenny.* This statute, passed in 1366 (Edward III), forbade the adoption of the Irish language, name or dress by any man of English blood.

3. In international law, [= F. *statut personnel, réel*] ***personal statute***: the system of law to which an alien party to a process is personally subject, as distinguished from ***real statute***, the system of law to which the particular transaction is otherwise subject.

1907 E. J. SCHUSTER *Princ. Ger. Civ. Law* 26 The question as to what law is to be applied for the determination of any particular crime frequently depends upon the so-called 'personal statute' of one of the parties. **1907** *Parl. Papers, Rep. Egypt & Soudan* 20 The foreigner resident in Egypt is fully entitled to retain his Consular Court as a Court of Personal Statute. **1907** E. H. YOUNG in *Law Q. Rev.* XXIII. 155 The true province of the 'real statute' and of the 'personal statute'.

II. Uses originating in ellipsis.

†**4.** Applied to certain legal instruments or procedures based on the authority of a statute. **a.** A STATUTE MERCHANT or STATUTE STAPLE; a bond or recognizance by which the creditor had the power of holding the debtor's lands in case of default. **b.** ***statute of bankrupt, statute of lunacy***: the process by which a person was declared a bankrupt or a lunatic. *Obs.*

a. 1475 *Rolls of Parlt.* VI. 120/2 By any statut or recouvere extended. **1596** BACON *Maxims Com. Law* i. (1636) 2 If I be bound to enter into a statute before the Mayor of the Staple at such a day. **1598** CHAPMAN *Blinde Begger* C 3 b, He onely did agree that paying him foure thousand pound at the day I should receiue my statute safely. *c* **1600** SHAKS. *Sonn.* cxxxiv. 9. **1602** —— *Ham.* v. i. 113 This fellow might be in's time a great buyer of Land, with his Statutes, his Recognizances, his Fines. *a* **1625** FLETCHER *Noble Gent.* I. i, Take up at any Use, give Band, or Land, Or mighty Statutes, able by their strength, To tye up Sampson. **1668** SIR J. DENHAM in *Wills from Doctor's Comm.* (Camden) 121 Three judgments or statuts which I have upon the manor of Thorpe. **1678** BUTLER *Lady's Answ.* 88 What tender Sigh and Trickling tear, Longs for a Thousand Pound a year. And Languishing Transports, are Fond Of Statute, Mortgage, Bill and Bond. **1701** SEDLEY *Mulberry Gard.* v. 1, He that marries her shall give the other a statute upon his estate for two thousand pounds.

b. 1707 HEARNE *Collect.* 7 June (O.H.S.) II. 19 A Statute of Bankrupt was out against him. **1742** C. YORKE in G. Harris *Life Ld. Hardwicke* (1847) II. 20 Dean Swift has had a statute of lunacy taken out against him.

†**5.** A kind of cloth, of breadth fixed by statute. Cf. *statute-galloon, -lace* in 8 b.

1466 *Mann. & Househ. Exp.* (Roxb.) 328 For xxij. narow clothes called statutes. **1545** *Rates Custom Ho.* d ij, vi. Statutes for a clothe. **1583** *Ibid.* G ij, Rates for clothes... Statewes. **1599** HAKLUYT *Voy.* II. I. 96 Certaine clothes called Statutes, and others called Cardinal-whites.

6. (*sing.* and *pl.*) [Short for †*statute-sessions*: see 9.] A fair or gathering held annually in certain towns and villages for the hiring of servants. Also called *statute-fair, -hiring* (see 9).

a **1600** DELONEY *Thomas of Reading* Wks. (1912) 223, I heare that at the Statute, folkes do come of purpose to hire seruants. **1656** BLOUNT *Glossogr., Statutes* is also used in our vulgar talk, for the petit Sessions, which are yearly kept for the disposing of Servants in service, by the Statutes of 1, and 5 Eliz. cap. 4. **1668** O. HEYWOOD *Diaries* (1883) III. 101, 14 persons were going over the boate to Normanton statutes. **1763** BICKERSTAFF *Love in Village* I. vi, You must know there is a statute, a fair for hiring servants, held upon my green to-day. **1770** C. JENNER *Placid Man* IV. vii, What then are we to hire lovers at a statute? **1821** CLARE *Vill. Minstr.* I. 33 Statute and feast his village yearly knew. **1847** T. MILLER *Pict. Country Life* 157 A Country Statute (or 'Stattice', as it is always pronounced by the villagers) is a rural feast or wake, where farmers hire their assistants,..held both in villages and small market towns. **1859** GEO. ELIOT *A. Bede* vi, I hired you at Treddles'on stattits, without a bit o' character. **1897** *Sheffield Chron.* 16 Dec. 9 Ashbourne Statutes.—The Annual Statutes fair for hiring farm servants was held yesterday.

III. 7. Misused for STATUE *sb.*

Now only an illiterate blunder; in some early instances the confusion may have been helped by the knowledge of the literal sense of L. *statutum*, 'something set up'.

a **1400-50** *Wars Alex.* 5641 With ilk a statute þat þar stude stoutely enarmed. *c* **1440** *Gesta Rom.* x. 25 This Virgilie made by his crafte an ymage or a statute. **1615** A. STAFFORD *Heavenly Dogge* 89 Suffer not sycophants to perswade thee to the erecting of thy statutes. **1649** *Fabric Rolls York Minster* (Surtees) 334 A statute of brasse. **1650** EARL MONM. tr. *Senault's Man bec. Guilty* 345 They..put their trust in Gods made of clay and wood, and consulted with statutes. **1719** D'URFEY *Pills* (1872) IV. 277 Their statutes with garlands adorning. [**1880** TENNYSON *Village Wife* vii, An' 'e bowt little statutes all-naäkt an' which was a shaame to be seen.]

IV. *attrib.* and *Comb.*

8. a. quasi-*adj.*, with the senses 'fixed by statute', 'recognized by statute', 'statutory'. Also *transf.* of what is prescribed by custom.

1643 SIR T. BROWNE *Relig. Med.* I. §46 Not only convincible and statute madnesse, but also manifest impiety. **1650** BULWER *Anthropomet.* 91 These Nations are well ring'd for rooting, and enjoy the Statute beauty of our Swine. *a* **1687** PETTY *Polit. Arith.* (1690) Pref. a 3, Those who can give good Security, may have Money under the Statute-Interest. **1831** W. L. BOWLES *Life Bp. Ken* II. 229 *note*, Informator is the statute-name of the head-master [of Winchester]. **1856** EMERSON *Eng. Traits, Result* Wks. (Bohn) II. 134 At home they have a certain statute hospitality.

b. designating a unit of measure or weight as fixed by statute, as in ***statute acre, mile, perch, pole, ton***; articles of merchandise of size regulated by statute, as † ***statute brick***, †***fringe***, †***galloon***, † ***lace***, † ***yarn***.

1590 LUCAR *Lucarsolace* I. ii. 8 *marg.*, A *statute acar of land doth contain..4840 square yardes. **1861** *Times* 16 Oct., More than 6*l.* per statute acre. **1703** T. N. *City & C. Purchaser* 43 *Statute-bricks. **1771** *Encycl. Brit.* I. 676/1 Statute bricks, or small common bricks. **1594** in *Archæol. Cant.* (1886) XVI. 191 For 6 oz. and ½ *statute fringe, ijs. ijd. **1882** CAULFEILD & SAWARD *Dict. Needlework* 460/2 **Statute galloon.* These are narrow cotton or silk ribbons, employed for the binding of flannels. **1590** in *Antiquary* XXXII. 118, xij yeards *stattute lace, xii d. **1592** *Wills & Inv. N.C.* (Surtees) II. 211, ij grose of statute lace 12*s.* **1612** W. PARKES *Curtaine-Drawer* (1876) 23 A Curtaine..and that a gawdy one, imbrodred with Statute-lace. *a* **1652** BROME *Queen & Concubine* IV. i. (1659) 76 And can you handle the Bobbins well, good Woman? Make statute-Lace? **1610** HOPTON *Baculum Geodæt.* VI. lii. 263 To reduce *Statute measure into customary measure. **1889** SKRINE *Mem. Thring* 122 The statute measures of things were startlingly discredited. **1862** ANSTED *Channel Isl.* I. v. 92 It is about eleven *statute miles in length. **1590** LUCAR *Lucarsolace* I. ii. 8, 5 meating yards and ½ meating yeard make a *statute pearch. **1766** *Complete Farmer* s.v. *Surveying* 7 F 1 b/1 Four *statute-poles or perches. **1883** *Encycl. Brit.* XVI. 457/1, 418 *statute tons. **1598** FLORIO, *Accia*,..spinning cruell or *statute yearne.

c. objective, as ***statute-breaker, -drawer***.

a **1831** BENTHAM *Nomogr.* iii. Wks. 1843 III. 242 The productions of an official statute-drawer. **1909** *Q. Rev.* Oct. 386 A statute-breaker is but little oppressed with a sense of moral guilt.

9. Special comb.: **statute-barred** *a.*, (of debts, claims) barred by the statute of limitations; †**statute-cap**, the woollen cap ordered by the Act of 13 Eliz. c. 19 (1571) to be worn on Sundays and holy days by all persons not of a certain social or official rank; †**statute congregation**, a separatist designation for a congregation of the established church; **statute duty** = *statute-labour*; **statute-execution**, the summary execution of a statute-merchant (see 4 a); **statute fair, statute hiring** = sense 6; †**statute hall**, a building open at the 'statutes' (see 6) for hiring of servants; **statute labour**, a definite amount of labour on works of public utility, formerly required by statute to be performed by the residents in the district interested (also *attrib.*); so ***statute labourer***; **statute law**, a law contained in a statute; also in generalized sense, the system of law contained in statutes, as distinguished from common law; **statute money**, money paid as commutation for statute labour; †**statute-Protestant** (see quot. *a* 1591); **statute-roll**, the roll on which the statutes are engrossed; often = STATUTE-BOOK 2; †**statute-sessions** = sense 6 (see quot. 1607); **statute-work** = *statute labour*.

1905 *Daily Chron.* 8 Aug. 2/7 A desire to liquidate debts that were *statute-barred. **1588** SHAKS. *L.L.L.* v. ii. 281 Better wits haue worne plain *statute caps. **1594** HOOKER *Eccl. Pol.* Pref. viii. §1 [The separatists say:] we thinke the *statute-congregations in Englande to be no true Christian Churches. *c* **1830** *Pract. Treat. Roads* 25 in *Libr. Usef. Knowl., Husb.* III, The system of *statute-duty naturally induces a larger outlay to take place in horse labour, than would otherwise occur. **1766** BLACKSTONE *Comm.* II. xxxi. 487 It hath also been held, that under a commission of bankrupt, which is in the nature of a *statute-execution, the landlord shall be allowed his arrears of rent..in preference to other creditors. **1826** HOR. SMITH *Tor Hill* (1838) I. 89 The *statute-fair had a few days before completely exhausted their little hoards of half-pence and farthings. **1863** MRS. GASKELL *Sylvia's Lovers* i, Many a rustic went to a statute fair or 'mop', and never came home to tell of his hiring. **1772** *Town & Country Mag.* 33 She..resolved..to repair to one of the *Statute-halls, in order to obtain a place in quality of servants. **1878** J. H. GRAY *China* I. x. 240 For these servants there are what in England are termed *statute hirings. **1800** *Local Act 39 & 40 Geo. III*, c. xxxii, An Act for levying a Conversion Money in lieu of the *Statute Labour [on roads]. **1831** M. O'BRIEN *Jrnl.* 16 Feb. (1968) xvi. 155 We shall have a share as the statute labour employed on the Street will then come upon the side lines. **1845** W. PAGAN *Road Reform* III. 208 There is an excellent statute labour road diverging at Leslie. **1847** *Jrnl. Agric.* 1847–49, 65 The 8th and 9th Vict. c. 41 (the general statute labour act,) which §9 enacts [etc.]. **1895** W. ELKINGTON *Five Years in Canada* vi. 52 Every person owning property is required to put in a certain amount of work every year on Government roads or fireguards; it is called Statute Labour. **1968** E. RUSSENHOLT *Heart of Continent* IV. xii. 223 The Council of Assiniboia for 1901..abolishes statute labor, that time-honored method of doing road-work. **1612** R. DABORNE *Christian turn'd Turke* 886 He would haue me a cuckold by law forsooth, by *statute law. *a* **1637** B. JONSON *Discov., Poesis*, There is no Statute Law of the Kingdome bidds you bee a Poet, against your will. *a* **1653** SIR R. FILMER *Patriarcha* iii. §11 (1680) 115 What is hitherto affirmed of the Dependency and Subjection of the Common Law to the Soveraign Prince, the same may be said as well of all Statute Laws. **1818** HALLAM *Mid. Ages* viii. III. (1819) III. 225 Though the statute law is full of authorities in their favour. **1863** COX *Instit.* I. ii. 10 The system of jurisprudence..is in a great measure independent of statute-law. **1799** J. ROBERTSON *Agric. Perth* 363 That the commissioners of supply, as public bodies in separate counties,..should borrow money, upon the credit of the *statute money. *a* **1591** H. SMITH *Serm.* (1622) 544 *Statute-Protestants, which goe to the Church and heare an Homily, and receiue once a yeere. **1818** HALLAM *Mid. Ages* viii. III. (1819) III. 71 These petitions..were..entered upon the *statute-roll. **1875** STUBBS *Const. Hist.* III. xviii. 274 His statute-roll contains no acts for securing or increasing public liberties. **1607** COWEL *Interpr.*, *Statute sessions..are a meeting in every hundred..vnto the which the constables doe repaire, and others both householders and seruants, for the debating of differences between masters and their seruants, the rating of seruants wages, and the bestowing of such people in seruice, as being fit to serue, either refuse to seeke, or cannot get Masters. **1726** in Picton *L'pool Munic. Rec.* (1886) II. 63 The roads..cannot be sufficiently repair'd by the *statute work. **1807** *Beverley & Kexby Road Act* 7 All persons who by law are or shall be liable to do Statute Work.

†**'statute,** *v.*[1] Chiefly *Sc. Obs.* Pa. pple. often †**statut(e (statuit).** [f. L. *statūt-*, ppl. stem of *statuĕre*: see STATUTE *sb.*]

1. *trans.* To ordain, decree. Chiefly with clause as obj.

c **1435** in *Three 15th Cent. Chron.* (Camden) 91 It was enactyd, statuted, and decrede by all the hole counsel of the saide cite. *c* **1470** HENRY *Wallace* IV. 133 Than statute thai, in ilk steide of the west, In thar boundis Wallace suld haiff no rest. *c* **1500** *Lancelot* 2527 The day that vas Y-statut and ordanit for to bee. **1513** in W. H. Turner *Select. Rec. Oxford* (1880) 10 It was enacted, established and statuted. *c* **1530** L. Cox *Rhet.* (1899) 46 Superyours whiche haue power to make, or statute, lawes to the inferiours. **1560-1** *1st & 2nd Bks. Discipl. Ch. Scot.* (1621) 18 For better execution of the said Act, It is statute, that [etc.]. **1594** in *Maitl. Club Misc.* I. 67 The presbiterie of Glasgow statutis and ordenis, that [etc.]. **1629** *Descr. S'hertogenbosh* 7 The Burgers..began to statute Lawes, and to make a Magistrate. **1640-1** *Kirkcudbr. War-Comm. Min. Bk.* (1855) 151 The said Committie of Estates..have, be thir presents, fund and resolvit, statuit and ordainit, that [etc.]. **1661** *Sc. Acts Parlt.* (1814) VII. 235 It is heirby statute that the Commissioners shall be releived of the pryces therof. **1678** SIR G. MACKENZIE *Crim. Laws Scot.* I. xiv. §v. (1699) 79 Seing this pain is only statuted in the case of Paracide. **1698** in R. M. Fergusson *Logie* (1905) II. 300 The Session..statuts and appoints all these in the Congregation who hath pipers or fiddlers at their weddings to lose their Dollars. **1730** KAMES *Decis. Crt. Sess. 1730–52* (1799) 5 An Act..which statutes, That the acting [etc.]. **1756** AMORY *Buncle* (1770) III. 53 He..statuted that men should maintain the dignity of the conjugal state. **1880** SKENE *Celtic Scot.* III. 241 In another law the King statutes that if any [etc.].

2. To appoint (a term, time of payment, etc.).

1557 KNOX *Let.* Sel. Writ. (1845) 350 Statuted it is to all men once to die. **1560** *Maitl. Club Misc.* III. 221 In the terme statut to ansuer to the said Williames petitioun Compered Elizabeth. **1563** *Ibid.* III. 315 The superintendent statutis wednesdaye nixt to cum to pronunc in presens of Jhon & decernis his summondis to summond Barbara yarto.

3. To set in order (a kingdom, country).

c **1470** HENRY *Wallace* IV. 13 A gret consell was sett..Off Inglis lordis, to statute this cuntre. *Ibid.* VIII. 1594 Scotlande atour, fra Ross till Soloway sand, He raid it thrys, and statut all the land.

Hence **'statuted** *ppl. a.*, **'statuting** *vbl. sb.*

1755 AMORY *Mem.* (1769) I. 284 The statuted appointment of mercy rejoices us. **1843** CARLYLE *Past & Pr.* ii. 13 Enforce it by never such statuting, three readings, royal assents,..it will not stand. **1891** F. THOMPSON *Sister-Songs* (1895) 39 [The soul] ripe for kingship, yet must be Captive in statuted minority!

†**'statute,** *v.*[2] [f. STATUTE *sb.*] *trans.* To include in the scope of a 'statute' or bond (see STATUTE *sb.* 4).

1681 T. FLATMAN *Heraclitus Ridens* No. 10. (1713) I. 63 He has nothing to shew for his Money but an Order of a Committee, and that's Statuted too.

statute-book.

†**1.** A book containing an Act of Parliament. *Obs.*

1593 R. HOLTBY in J. Morris *Troubles Cath. Forefathers* (1877) 223 Some of the jury required the statute book, that they might proceed the more assuredly.

2. The book containing the statutes of a nation or state; usually (*sing.*, occas. *pl.*) the whole series of volumes forming the official record of the statutes. Phrase, ***on the statute-book***.

a **1648** LD. HERBERT *Hen. VIII* (1649) 368 In which many Acts pass'd, the most materiall whereof, I have set down briefly, not alwaies according to the order observed in the Statute-Book, but rather according to the matters handled. **1675** BAXTER *Cath. Theol.* VIII. II. 175 They searched the whole Scripture, read over the Statute-Book, and all the Common Law-Books and Cases, that they could get. **1705** ADDISON *Italy, St. Marino* 133, I saw in their Statute-Book a Law against such as speak disrespectfully of him. **1765** BLACKSTONE *Comm.* I. Introd. §3. 85 The oldest of these now extant, and printed in our statute books, is the famous *magna carta.* **1815** J. SMITH *Panorama Sci. & Art* II. 585 If the game-laws were only a dead letter on our statute-books. **1825** SYD. SMITH *Sp.* Wks. 1859 II. 200/2, I should have said, that the disabling laws against the Catholics were a disgrace to the statute-book. **1827** HALLAM *Const. Hist.* xvii. (1876) III. 310 We must not look to the statute-book of Scotland for many limitations of monarchy. **1863** FAWCETT *Pol. Econ.* II. viii. (1876) 223 Our own statute-book proves that the attempt has frequently been made to regulate wages by law. **1871** C. DAVIES *Metric Syst.* III. 85 In England..the statute-books are filled with ineffectual attempts of the legislature to establish uniformity. **1934** G. B. SHAW *On Rocks* II. 253 You will have to wait two years and go through the whole job again before you can get your Bill on the statute book as an Act of Parliament. **1972** *Times* 2 Feb. 16/6 His Lordship thought as the Act was already on the statute book the judge was fully entitled to have regard to it.

fig. **1831** CARLYLE *Sartor Res.* III. viii, Those same unalterable rules, forming the complete Statute-Book of Nature.

statute merchant. *Law.* Now only *Hist.* [STATUTE *sb.* + MERCHANT *a.*

An elliptical use of the designation of the *Statute of Merchants* of 1285, (Anglo-L. *statutum de mercatoribus*, also *statutum mercatorium*, AFr. *estatut marchand*) whence the powers of summary execution of this kind of instrument were derived.]

A bond of record, acknowledged before the chief magistrate of a trading town, giving to the obligee power of seizure of the land of the obligor if he failed to pay his debt at the appointed time.

[**1347-8** *Rolls of Parlt.* II. 211/2 Robert Lok, & Walter de Norton furent tenutz & obligetz a dit Everard en centz & vintz livrez d'esterlings par Estatu Marchaund a paier a certein jour.] **1442** *Calverley Charters* (Thoresby Soc. 1904) 253 Walter shall fynd sufficiant surety, boundon in statute marchant, in D marc' to the saide Sir John. **1456** in *Sel. Cases Chanc.* (Selden Soc.) 139 A statut marchant of ccc.li. specyfied yn the sayde bylle. **1463** *Mann. & Househ. Exp.* (Roxb.) 180 An oblygasyon of statew marchend. cc. marke. **1592** GREENE *Black Book's Messenger* Wks. (Grosart) XI. 30 The welthy Gentleman..lends him money, and takes a faire Statute marchant of his Lands before a Iudge. **1592** NASHE *P. Penilesse* Wks. (Grosart) II. 15 The Diuel..would let one for a neede, haue a thousand poundes vppon a Statute Merchaunt of his soule. **1766** BLACKSTONE *Comm.* II. x. 160 During such time as the creditor so holds the lands, he is tenant by statute merchant or statute staple. **1825** OWEN & BLAKEWAY *Shrewsbury* I. 541 The Clerk of the Statute Merchant. **1855** MACAULAY *Hist. Eng.* xii. III. 211 How much money had proprietors borrowed on mortgage, on statute merchant, on statute staple!

statute staple. *Law.* Now only *Hist.* Also **statute of the staple.** [An elliptical use of *statute of the staple* as the name of the ordinance of 1353 (see STAPLE *sb.*^{2} 1); cf. STATUTE MERCHANT. (The shortened form *statute staple* is on the analogy of *statute merchant.*)] A bond of record, acknowledged before the mayor of the staple, conveying powers similar to those given by the statute merchant.

1444 *Rolls of Parlt.* V. 106/2 A reconisaunce to him made of the seid somme.., in a Statute of the Staple. **1472-3** *Ibid.* VI. 6/2 By force of eny execution, by Statuit of Staple, Estatuit Marchaunt, or any Jugement yeven in any of the Kynges Courtes. **1576** GASCOIGNE *Steele Gl.* (Arb.) 71 To stay their steps by statute Staples staffe. **1581** LAMBARDE *Eiren.* II. ii. (1588) 111 Such bonds shall be of the nature of a Statute Staple. **1586** [see STAPLE *a.* 3]. **1587** FLEMING *Contn. Holinshed* III. 1956/2 The cooke of the Temple was arrested in London, and in execution vpon a statute of the staple. **1592** GREENE *Def. Conny Catching* Wks. (Grosart) XI. 55 The gentleman..promised to acknowledge a statute staple to him, with letters of defeysance. **1607** MIDDLETON *Fam. Love* I. iii. 86 There is not one gentleman amongst twenty but his land be engaged in twenty statutes staple. **1613** SIR R. BOYLE in *Lismore Papers* (1886) I. 21 Cormech M^{c}dermott of Blarney forfeited to me his statute staple of 2000^{li}. **1726** AYLIFFE *Parergon* 188 Nor can his Body be taken in Execution on a Recognizance upon a Statute-Staple. **1766** BLACKSTONE *Comm.* II. x. 160 The recognizance in the nature of a statute staple.

statutorily ('stætju:tərɪlɪ), *adv.* [f. next + -LY^2.] In a statutory manner; by statutory enactment; in accordance with the provisions of the statutes.

1886 *Pall Mall Gaz.* 12 Apr. 4/2 These rents had been statutorily fixed. **1892** tr. *Schäffle's Impossibility Soc. Democracy* 221 It would be quite possible, if it were not statutorily provided against. **1893** J. MORLEY in *Standard* 11 Mar. 2/3 An increase of the 'free' force was not statutorily possible.

statutory ('stætjʊtərɪ), *a.* and *sb.* [ad. assumed L. type **statūtōrius*, f. *statuĕre* to decree, enact; see STATUTE *sb.* and -ORY. In later use f. STATUTE *sb.* + -ORY. Cf. STATUTARY.]

A. *adj.*

†**1.** Of a clause, etc.: Enacting. *Sc. Obs.*

1717 WODROW *Corr.* (1843) II. 331 The statutory part of that act. **1742** KAMES *Decis. Crt. Sess. 1730–52* (1799) 56 The statutory clause is in the following words: 'Statutes and ordains, That [etc.].

2. a. Pertaining to or consisting in statutes; enacted, appointed, or created by statute; conformable to the provisions of a statute.

1766 JOHNSON in *Boswell* (1791) I. 277 In the formulary and statutory part of law, a plodding block-head may excel. **1776** ADAM SMITH *W.N.* I. I. ix. 93 All these different statutory regulations. **1808** TOLLER *Law Tithes* ix. (1816) 236 A defendant in such case may set up a customary payment to protect himself against the claim of the statutory tithes. **1818** SCOTT *Br. Lamm.* xxi, The statutory penalties. **1845** M^{c}CULLOCH *Taxation* III. ii. (1852) 441 The statutory rate of interest..was six per cent. **1863** H. COX *Instit.* I. vi. 33 The prerogative of the Crown..is now subject to statutory and constitutional limitations. **1879** H. HARDCASTLE *Statutory Law* 141 *note*, A corporation created by statute for a particular purpose is called a statutory corporation, to distinguish it from a corporation at common law. **1893** *Law Times* XCV. 26/1 It is high time that this branch of the law should be thrown into statutory shape. **1911** *Act 1 & 2 Geo. V*, c. 16 §3 (2) It shall be a statutory condition for the receipt of an old age pension by any person, that [etc.].

b. ***statutory company***, a company created by statute, as distinguished from a chartered company or a joint-stock company; also, any company other than one incorporated by royal charter; ***statutory declaration***: a declaration in accordance with the provisions of the Statutory Declaration Act (1835), which substituted simple affirmations for the oaths or solemn affirmations formerly required on certain occasions; ***statutory holiday***, a holiday established by statute; ***statutory instrument***, a common type of subordinate legislation (see quot. 1946); ***statutory meeting***, a general meeting of the members of a company, held in accordance with a statute; *spec.* the first such meeting, held between one and three months after the company is entitled to commence business; ***statutory rape*** (*U.S.*), sexual intercourse with a female who is below the age of consent (whether it occurs against her will or not); ***statutory tenant***, a person who is legally entitled to remain in possession of premises although his tenancy of them has expired; so ***statutory tenancy***; ***statutory treason***: an offence made treasonable by statute.

1915 *Act 5 & 6 Geo. V* c. 44 §2 The expression '*statutory company' means any railway company, canal company, dock company, water company, or other company incorporated by special Act, who are for the time being authorised under such an Act to construct, work, own, or carry on any railway, canal, dock, water, or other public undertaking, and includes any person or body of persons so authorised. **1970** M. GREENER *Penguin Dict. Commerce* 108 Certain contracts are not binding unless made by deed. These are: (1) gratuitous promises, (2) transfers of *shares* in statutory *companies* [etc.]. **1890** F. A. STRINGER *Oaths & Affirm.* 76 A *statutory declaration cannot be filed in the Supreme Court in lieu of an affidavit or affirmation. **1911** *Daily Colonist* (Victoria, B.C.) 18 Apr. (Mag. section) 7/3 Yesterday [*sc.* Easter Monday] was a *statutory holiday and many Victorians took advantage of the fact to drop their daily business cares. **1975** *Globe & Mail* (Toronto) 2 June 5/7 He also increased to double time-and-a-half, the pay for policemen working on statutory holidays. **1976** *Alyn & Deeside Observer* 10 Dec. 28/4 (Advt.), Refuse Collection... Due to the incidence of Christmas and New Year statutory holidays it has been necessary to rearrange certain collection days. **1946** *Act 9 & 10 Geo. VI* c. 36 §1 (1) Where by this Act or any Act passed after the commencement of this Act power to make, confirm or approve orders, rules, regulations or other subordinate legislation is conferred on His Majesty in Council or on any Minister of the Crown then, if the power is expressed—(a) in the case of a power conferred on His Majesty, to be exercisable by Order in Council; (b) in the case of a power conferred on a Minister of the Crown, to be exercisable by *statutory instrument, any document by which that power is exercised shall be known as a 'statutory instrument'. *a* **1974** R. CROSSMAN *Diaries* (1976) II. 549 The issue the journalists were raising concerned a statutory instrument. **1851** *Bradshaw's Railway Directory, Shareholder's Guide, Manual, & Almanack* 164 The *statutory meetings held in March and September. **1900** *Act 63 & 64 Vict.* c. 48 §12 Every company limited by shares and registered after the commencement of this Act shall, within a period of not less than one month nor more than three months from the date at which the company is entitled to commence business, hold a general meeting of the members of the company, which shall be called the statutory meeting. **1970** M. GREENER *Penguin Dict. Commerce* 313 The report should be certified by the auditors, if any, and must be delivered to the Registrar of Companies. It must also be sent to each member fourteen days before the statutory meeting. **1898** *Northwestern Reporter* LXXV. 439 The respondent was convicted of *statutory rape. **1959** *Time* 26 Oct. (Canadian ed.) 99/2 His taste for young flesh led to three statutory rape scandals..but the older he got, the more he [*sc.* Errol Flynn] seemed a cardboard sinner. **1977** I. SHAW *Beggarman, Thief* I. iv. 54 They jailed him on the charge of statutory rape. **1920** *Act 10 & 11 Geo. V* c. 17 §15 Conditions of *statutory tenancy. **1928** *Daily Mail* 25 July 7/3 Mr. Hunt's case was that he owned the freehold of 294, Upper Richmond-road and occupied two rooms. Mr. Sullivan was the *statutory tenant. **1972** *N.Y. Law Jrnl.* 10 Oct. 19/2 The parties concede that the defendants' occupancy of the apartment after the expiration of the lease was that of 'statutory tenants', since the premises were rent controlled under the City Rent and Rehabilitation Law. **1973** *Country Life* 3 May (Suppl.) 17 (Advt.), 3-bedroomed flat let unfurnished to statutory tenant. **1804** M. LAING *Hist. Scot.* IV. 377 The former iniquitous trials in Scotland appeared indisputably to have proceeded from the accumulation of *statutory treasons.

3. *transf.* **a.** Obligatory by custom; regular.

1822 SCOTT *Nigel* vi, The board displayed beef and pudding, the statutory dainties of old England.

b. Required for the sake of appearances; having only token significance. Used esp. with reference to the formal inclusion of women in male-dominated areas of activity.

1968 *Guardian* 31 July 1/6 Lord Conesford..was protesting against the cold and abstract 'statutory woman'. **1970** *Listener* 19 Nov. 707/2 Mary Stocks..was in great demand as a Statutory Woman, serving on one government committee and commission after another. **1977** *Observer* 1 May (Colour Suppl.) 12/4 I've noticed that most committees nowadays have a statutory woman on them.

B. *sb.* A member of the 'statutory' branch of the Indian Civil Service.

1892 W. DIGBY in *Pall Mall Gaz.* 26 Apr. 7/1 In 1886 or 1887 it was discovered that the rules were not working well, and the 'Statutories' (as the nominees under the Act of 1870 were called) were declared not to be a success.

statuvolence (stə'tju:vələns). [f. next: see -ENCE.] = STATUVOLISM.

1891 in *Century Dict.*

statuvolent (stə'tju:vələnt), *a.* [f. L. *stātu-s* STATE *sb.* + *volent-em*, *volens* pr. pple. of *velle* to will.] Inducing or affected by statuvolism.

1891 in *Century Dict.*

statuvolism (stə'tju:vəlɪz(ə)m). [f. STATUVOLENT + -ISM.] (See quots.) So **statu'volic** *a.*, pertaining to statuvolism; **sta'tuvolize** *v.*, to produce statuvolism in (a patient).

1871 W. B. FAHNESTOCK (*title*) Statuvolism; or, artificial somnambulism, hitherto called mesmerism; or animal magnetism, etc. **1883** MISS C. L. HUNT *Priv. Instr. Org. Magnetism* 54 Dr. W. Baker Fahenstock's [*sic*] system of what he terms Statuvolism. *Ibid.* 56 You will recognise that Statuvolism is a slow form of Auto-Magnetisation. *Ibid.*, Statuvolising would be more easily recognised, as a kind of weak-minded, indolent, though tedious, method of Magnetising by persuasion.

staulande, obs. form of STALLION.

staule, obs. f. STALE *v.*^{2}, STALL *sbs.* and *v.*^{1}

staull, obs. form of STALL *sb.*^{1}

staum, variant of STAM *sb.*^{3} *dial.*

staumrel ('stɑmrəl), *a.* and *sb.* *Sc.* Also **staumeral, stammrel.** [f. *staumer*, dial. var. of STAMMER *v.* + -EL.] **a.** *adj.* Stupid, half-witted. **b.** *sb.* A stupid, halfwitted person.

1787 BURNS *Brigs of Ayr* 170 Staumrel, corky-headed, graceless Gentry. *a* **1801** R. GALL *Poems* (1819) 31 Habby Graeme the haflins fool,..An' staumrel Willy Gray the Smith. **1802** SIBBALD *Chron. Sc. P.* IV. Gloss., *Staumrel*,.. one who is incapable of expressing his meaning. **1835** D. WEBSTER *Sc. Rhymes* 163 (E.D.D.) My stupid auld muse often lurks o' the gait, But goes staumering about like a staumeral gowk. **1868** SHELLEY *Flowers* 207 (E.D.D.) The stammrel gaed stampin right through the buss.

staunch, stanch (stɔ:nʃ, stɑ:nʃ, -æ-), *a.* Forms: (5 **stawnche, staunche**), 6–7 **stanche**, (6 **stantche**), 5– **stanch**, 7– **staunch.** [a. OF. *estanche* fem. of *estanc* (mod.F. *étanche* of both genders) corresp. to Sp. *estanco*, Pg. *estanque* water-tight, It. *stanco* exhausted, weary, f. Com. Rom. **stancare*: see STANCH *v.*

The spelling *staunch* and the associated pronunciation are in British use much the more common for the adj., while for the related verb the form STANCH (stɑ:nʃ, -æ-) is preferred.]

1. Impervious to water, not leaking; water-tight. Also occas. air-tight.

1412-20 LYDG. *Chron. Troy* I. 652 Þe schip..was so stawnche it myȝt no water lade. *c* **1440** *Pallad. on Husb.* XII. 305 In bechen baskettis men saue also This fruyt, so they [with cley] be staunche ywrie. **1531** *Charterparty* in R. G. Marsden *Sel. Pl. Crt. Adm.* (1894) 37 The sayd owner shall warrant the sayd shypp stronge stanche well and sufficientlye vitalled. **1569** *Southampton Court Leet Rec.* (1905-6) I. 57 The seastron in gossling Lane..is not stantche for that the water breaketh oute. **1633** T. JAMES *Voy.* 7 We sayed the pumps, and found her stanch. **1660** BOYLE *New Exp. Phys. Mech.* xv. 102 What we endeavored in vaine, may be performed by..some other Virtuoso that shall have stancher Vessells then we had. **1667** —— in *Phil. Trans.* II. 584 We found all had not continued so stanch, but that some small portion of Air had insinuated it self into the Receiver. **1726** SWIFT *Gulliver* II. i, Our Ship was staunch, and our Crew all in good Health. **1776** G. SEMPLE *Building in Water* 46 Our Coffer-dam..which we began to despair of ever getting made even tolerably staunch. **1856** KANE *Arctic Expl.* II. xxix. 296 The Mariane, a stanch but antiquated little barque. **1870** BRYANT *Iliad* I. III. 82 Crossing the deep in thy stanch ships.

†**b.** *fig.* (Cf. the phrase *to hold water.*)

1606 SHAKS. *Ant. & Cl.* II. ii. 117 Yet if I knew, What Hoope should hold vs staunch[,] from edge to edge Ath' world I would persue it. *a* **1641** BP. MOUNTAGU *Acts & Mon.* (1642) 100 Which [interpretation] cannot hold stanch possibly, as in termes it is proposed by him.

†**2.** Of blood: Not flowing out. *Obs. rare.*

1673 *Phil. Trans.* VIII. 6052 The pledgets being then thrown off, the blood continued staunch, and the mouths of the Arteries remained close.

3. Of strong or firm construction, in good or firm condition, substantial.

1455-6 *Cal. Anc. Rec. Dublin* (1889) I. 290 The sayd Jhon shall repeyre sayd towyr..and so to kepe hite up styf and stanch duryng the terme forsayde. **1644** MILTON *Areop.* (Arb.) 64 Doubtles a stanch and solid peece of framework, as any January could freeze together. **1692** RAY *Discourses* I. iii. (1693) 19 The foresaid new-raised Mountain..hath stood firm and staunch, without the least sinking or subsidency, for above an hundred and fifty years. *a* **1706** EVELYN *Diary* 23 July 1679, The house a stanch good old building. *Ibid.*, One of the closetts is parquetted with plaine deale, set in diamond, exceeding stanch and pretty. **1864** SKEAT tr. *Uhland's Poems* 357 'Gainst whom is shivered the staunchest brand. **1870** HAWTHORNE *Eng. Note-Bks.* (1879) II. 36 The wall of the tower is still stanch and strong.

†**4.** Restrained in behaviour, guarded, reserved.

[**1623**: see STAUNCHNESS.] *a* **1677** BARROW *Serm.* (1687) I. xiii. 186 Commonly such as are greatly staunch in other enjoyments of pleasure, are enormously intemperate in speaking, and very incontinent of their Tongue. *Ibid.* I. xxi. 296 It is good to be very staunch and cautious of talking about other men and their concernments.

†**b.** quasi-*adv.* ? Strictly. *Obs.*

1693 LOCKE *Educ.* §107 (1699) 186 This is to be kept very stanch, and carefully to be watched.

5. Of a sporting dog: That may be trusted to find or follow the scent, or to mark the game; dependable.

1576 TURBERV. *Venerie* xl. (1908) 112 Vntill they haue rowzed or founde him againe with their bloudhounde, or with some other stanche old hounde of the kenell. **1616** BULLOKAR, *Stanchhound*, an old hound well experienced. **1668** DAVENANT *Rivals* IV, The Dogs..by that silence soon their fault confess'd, Most of e'm were Stanch-Hounds. **1677** N. COX *Gentl. Recreat.* (ed. 2) 110 Let such as you cast off at first be old staunch-Hounds, which are sure. **1735** SOMERVILLE *Chase* IV. 125 With these consort The stanch and steddy Sages of thy Pack. **1810** SCOTT *Lady of L.* I. vii, For, scarce a spear's length from his haunch, Vindictive toil'd the bloodhounds stanch. **1842** J. WILSON *Chr. North* (1857) I. 151 Two excellent double-barrelled guns, and three staunch pointers. **1883** *Century Mag.* Aug. 492 A dog that..is stanch on a covey.

transf. **1686** BLOME *Gentl. Recreat.* II. 29 Old staunch Hawks should have more rest. **1835** W. IRVING *Tour Prairies* 290 Our half-breeds displayed that quickness of eye, in following up a track, for which Indians are so noted. Beatte, especially, was staunch as a veteran hound.

6. Of a person: Standing firm and true to one's principles or purpose, not to be turned aside, determined.

1623 MASSINGER *Bondman* I. iii, Yet, tho' he obserue, and waste his state vpon vs, If he be stanch and bid not for the stocke That we were borne to traffick with; the truth is We care not for his company. **1678** DRYDEN *All for Love* III. i, O, he's the coolest Murderer, so stanch, He kills, and keeps his temper. **1678** PHILLIPS (ed. 4), s.v., So a man of Credit and Reputation, and well to pass in the World, is usually called a Stanch-man. **1689** PRIOR *Ep. Fleetwood Shephard* 133 In Politicks, I hear, you'r stanch. **1710** HEARNE *Collect.* 24 Feb. (O.H.S.) II. 348 He is a stanch Whigg. **1742** BLAIR *Grave* 364 The Foe, Like a stanch Murth'rer steady to his Purpose, Pursues her close through ev'ry Lane of Life. **1784** COWPER *Tiroc.* 492 And you are staunch indeed in learning's cause. **1824** W. IRVING *T. Trav.* II. vii. (1848) 143 He was stanch, however, to church and king. *a* **1839** PRAED *Poems* (1864) 11 My tried staunch friend, Sir Matthew Chase. **1841** DICKENS *Barn. Rudge* vi, You, who from a girl have had a strong mind and a staunch heart. **1868** E. EDWARDS *Ralegh* I. x. 182 The toil..began..to wear down the strength if not the spirit of the stanchest. **1879** FROUDE *Cæsar* xv. 249 Those who ought to have been staunch have fallen away.

b. Of personal qualities, actions, etc.: Showing determination or resolution, unwavering.

1690 R. LUCAS *Humane Life* 239 Riper years..should bring on naturally wiser and stancher thoughts. **1818** SCOTT *Hrt. Midl.* vii, The vengeance they had prosecuted with such stanch and sagacious activity. **1823** —— *Q. Durward* xxxvii, De la Marck might have effected his escape..but for the stanch pursuit of Quentin. **1883** A. FORBES in *19th Cent.* Oct. 720 Their devotion to their sovereign is staunch.

7. *Comb.*, as ***staunch-hearted*** adj.

1838 DICKENS *O. Twist* iii, There ain't a stauncher-hearted gal.

Hence **'staunchly**, **'stanchly** *adv.*; **'staunchness**, **'stanchness**.

1825 COBBETT *Rur. Rides* 291, I had him a puppy, and he never had any breaking, but he pointed staunchly at once. **1848** DICKENS *Dombey* xx, There never was a man who stood by a friend more staunchly than the Major. **1862** THORNBURY *Turner* II. 142 The terms once made, he was true, undeviating, and stanchly honest. **1899** F. T. BULLEN *Log Sea-waif* 252 She must have been staunchly built.

1623 CONWAY in *Hacket's Life Abp. Williams* (1693) I. 157 His Majesty would not that you should press him for a Note of his Hand for Secresie and Stanchness. **1669** BOYLE *Contn. New Exp.* I. i. 3 Having once, to try the stanchnesse of the viol, blown in so much Air..that [etc.]. **1702** S. PARKER tr. *Cicero's De Finibus* I. 11 As to the Truth and Stanchness of his Affections I cannot suppose you'll pretend to dispute it. **1776** G. SEMPLE *Building in Water* 46 We made the first Trial of our Coffer-dam..and proved its Stanchness several Times. **1826** in *Sheridaniana* 308 The extraordinary staunchness of a cross-bred setter. **1865** M. ARNOLD *Ess. Crit.* iv. (1875) 165 The stanchness which the religious aspirant needs.

staunch, *sb.* and *v.*: see STANCH.

stauncheon, -(i)on, var. ff. STANCHION.

staung(e, **staunk(e**, obs. ff. STANK, STANCH.

Staunton ('stɔːntən). The name of Howard *Staunton* (1810–74), English chess-player and writer, used *attrib.* and *absol.* to designate chessmen of a design now accepted as standard.

[**1891** R. B. SWINTON *Chess for Beginners* ii. 5 A chessboard and a set of men are necessary. The latter alone are to be purchased at all prices, from sets in 'African ivory', after Staunton's pattern, down to flimsy wooden pieces. *Ibid.* 7 Your wooden men..will..be easily identified with the drawings of Staunton's men which form headpieces to the..chapters.] **1898** *Dict. Nat. Biogr.* LIV. 117/1 Staunton's name was conferred on the set of chessmen which are recognised as the standard type among English-speaking peoples. His 'Chess Player's Text-book' was issued in 1849, without date, to be sold with the Staunton chessmen. **1913** H. J. MURRAY *Hist. Chess* II. x. 773 Chessmen of fanciful shapes and forms are often made as curiosities. For actual play, most players would prefer to use the 'Staunton chessmen', the pattern of which Howard Staunton designed in 1849. **1951** G. FRANKAU *Oliver Trenton* ix. 77 The set of ivory Stauntons I won from him. **1959** L. BARDEN *Chess* ii. 14 The pieces of a 'Staunton design' are..the most popular nowadays... The photograph shows what they look like in your Staunton-type set. **1977** M. KELLY in D. Marcus *Best Irish Short Stories* II. 66 The Staunton with its austere lack of pretension. **1979** P. ALEXANDER *Show me Hero* iv. 55 A chess-board and one of the earliest Staunton sets.

staup (stɔːp), *sb. north.* [f. STAUP *v.*] (See quot. 1825.)

1825 JAMIESON *Suppl.*, *Staup* 1. A long awkward step, Roxb. 2. A tall awkward person; as 'Haud aff me, ye muckle lang staup', ibid. **1897** E. W. HAMILTON *Outlaws of Marches* xvii. 185, I was..Never a happer-hippit staup of a thing like yourself.

staup (stɔːp), *v. north.* Also **stoep**. [? Altered from STEP *v.*, with vowel symbolic of awkward movement.] (See quot. 1788.)

1788 W. H. MARSHALL *Yorksh.* II. 356 To *Staup*; to lift the feet high, and tread heavily in walking. *a* **1857** J. RAYSON *Misc. Poems* (1858) 55 They stoep i' their walking, leyke stegs amang heather.

staup, variant of STAP *sb.* stave of a cask.

staupings ('stɔːpɪŋz), *sb. pl. north.* [? f. STAUP *v.* + -ING^1.] (See quot. 1847.)

1847 HALLIWELL, *Staupings*, the holes made by the feet of horses and cattle in miry highways, and other places. *North.* **1857** C. B. ROBINSON *Best's Farm. Bks.* (Surtees) Gloss., Saddened. Dried or hardened. Otherwise the action of the feet on the wet ground would make 'staupings'.

'stauracin. *Antiq.* *rare*$^{-0}$. [ad. late L. *stauracinus* (also *stauracium* and *stauracin* indecl.).

According to Du Cange s.v. *Storax*, the correct form is *storacinus*, an adj. meaning 'of the colour of storax'; see the quot. from Papias (11th c.) *ibid.* The explanation cited below, based on a supposed derivation from Gr. *σταυράκιον dim. of σταυρός cross, was proposed by the Bollandists, but rejected by the Benedictine editors of Du Cange.

The word has app. no real existence in English, but an attempt has been made to thrust it into the text of Marlowe *Faustus* 369 (iv. 17) as an 'emendation' for *staues acre.*]

'A silken stuff figured with small crosses.'

1876 ROCK *Textile Fabrics* v. 36.

stauro- ('stɔːrəʊ, stɒ'rɒ), before a vowel **staur-**, combining form of Gr. σταυρός cross, employed in several terms, chiefly scientific. **stauractin(e** [Gr. ἀκτιν-, ἀκτίς ray], 'hexactinellid spicules of the dermal sponge-layer in which two of the arms are atrophied, leaving the remaining four in the form of a cross' (*Cent. Dict.* Suppl. 1909). **stauro-baryte** *Min.*, an obsolete synonym of HARMOTOME (Chester *Dict. Min.* 1896). **staurology** *nonce-wd.*, a science or doctrine of the cross. **stauro-microscope** (see quots.). **staurotypous** *a. Min.* [Gr. τύπος TYPE *sb.*; cf. eccl. Gr. σταυρότυπος marked with the sign of the cross], 'having mackles or spots in the form of a cross' (Ogilvie 1850).

1905 *Jrnl. R. Micros. Soc.* Apr. 190 The earliest regular form of spicule was the *stauractine. **1893** C. T. CRUTTWELL *Hist. Early Christianity* I. 53 Justin, who presses nearly every allusion to a tree or a piece of wood into the service of a mechanical *Staurology. **1879** RUTLEY *Stud. Rocks* ix. 75 For the purpose of investigating the optical properties of minerals various instruments, such as..the stauroscope,.. Rosenbusch's *stauro-microscope, &c., have from time to time been devised. **1843** CHAPMAN *Pract. Min.* 190 *Staurotypous kouphone spar.

†**stau'rolatry.** *Obs. rare.* [ad. late L. *staurolatrīa* (Tertullian), f. Gr. σταυρό-ς cross + λατρεία worship: see -LATRY.] The worship of the Cross. Hence †**staurolatrian**, one who worships the Cross.

1600 O. E. [M. SUTCLIFFE] *Repl. Libel* I. v. 100 With the Staurolatrians they worship the crosse, & crucifixe, giuing to the same diuine worship. **1649** J. OWEN *Shaking Heaven & Earth* 26 They..will not hearken to the Angels preaching the everlasting Gospel, that men should worship..the God of heaven..in opposition to all their Iconolatry,.. Staurolatry, and Masse abominations. **1684** I. MATHER *Ess. Rec. Providences* viii. 272 Satans design in advancing staurolatry to the destruction of thousands of Souls.

staurolite ('stɔːrəʊlaɪt). *Min.* [a. F. *staurolite* (Delamétherie 1792): see STAURO- and -LITE.]

†**1.** = HARMOTOME. *Obs.*

1796 KIRWAN *Elem. Min.* (ed. 2) I. 282 Staurolite, or cross stone of St. Andreasberg in the Hartz. **1837** DANA *Min.* 277 Harmotome, *Vulcanus gemellus*... Staurolite.

2. Silicate of aluminium and iron, of yellowish brown to dark brown colour, found frequently in cruciform twins.

1815 AIKIN *Min.* (ed. 2) 189. **1888** RUTLEY *Rock-Forming Min.* 163 Staurolite occurs chiefly in the crystalline schists.

attrib. and *Comb.* **1879** RUTLEY *Stud. Rocks* xiv. 292 Staurolite slate is a dark micaceous slate containing crystals of staurolite. **1888** —— *Rock-forming Min.* 201 The staurolite-bearing schists of Brittany.

Hence **stauro'litic** *a.*

1880 DANA *Man. Geol.* (ed. 3) 237 Staurolitic mica schist.

staurolith ('stɔːrəʊlɪθ). *Min.* [f. STAURO- + -LITH.] = STAUROLITE 2.

1815 AIKIN *Min.* (ed. 2) 189.

stauroscope ('stɔːrəʊskəʊp). [f. Gr. σταυρός cross (see STAURO-) + -SCOPE.] An instrument used for the microscopic examination of rocks (see quot. 1879). Also *attrib.*

1875 KNIGHT *Dict. Mech.* **1877** *Catal. Special Collect. Sci. Apparatus S. Kens. Mus.* (ed. 3) 220 Stauroscope, according to the design of F. von Kobell, executed by Wiedemann. **1879** RUTLEY *Stud. Rocks* ix. 81 The determination of the crystallographic system to which a mineral belongs, and the exact position of the planes of vibration and of the axes of elasticity, are best effected by means of the stauroscope. **1888** —— *Rock-Forming Min.* 48 The most perfect arrangement yet devised for this purpose is Bertrand's stauroscope eye-piece.

Hence ˌ**stauro'scopic** *a.*, of, pertaining to or made by means of the stauroscope. ˌ**stauro'scopically** *adv.*, by means of the stauroscope.

1879 RUTLEY *Stud. Rocks* vii. 56 A small plate of calcspar for making stauroscopic measurements. *Ibid.* ix. 81 The stauroscopic examination of thin sections of minerals. *Ibid.* ix. 84 The different crystallographic systems may be determined stauroscopically in the following way.

staurotide ('stɔːrəʊtaɪd). *Min.* [a. F. *staurotide* (Haüy 1801), app. f. Gr. σταυρωτός cruciform, f. σταυρός cross.] = STAUROLITE 2.

1802 T. THOMSON *Syst. Chem.* III. 459 Granatite. Staurotide of Hauy. **1804** R. JAMESON *Min.* I. 76 Grenatite. .. Staurotide. **1837** DANA *Min.* 356 Staurotide is very abundant throughout the mica slate of New England. **1881** *Church Times* 669/2 Staurotides, cruciform crystals of basalt probably supposed to bring good to the possessor.

stauroti'diferous. [-FEROUS.] Containing staurotide.

1863 DANA *Man. Geol.* 71.

‖**staurus** ('stɔːrəs). *Zool.* [mod.L., ad. Gr. σταυρός cross.] A type of sponge spicule of the form of a cross.

1887 SOLLAS in *Encycl. Brit.* XXII. 417/1 (*Sponge*) The suppression of both proximal and distal rays [of a sexradiate spicule] gives the staurus.

staval(l, **stavel**, dial. ff. STADDLE (*sb.* 3 b).

1669 Reek-staval [see RICK *sb.*^{1} 2 b]. **1707** MORTIMER *Husb.* 246 As for the making of Stavalls, Graneries, Barns, &c... I have already given you directions how to make them. **1794** Stavel barn [see STADDLE *sb.* 8].

stave (steɪv), *sb.*^{1} [A back-formation from *staves* pl. of STAFF *sb.*]

I. A stick of wood (and senses thence derived).

1. a. Each of the thin, narrow, shaped pieces of wood which, when placed together side by side and hooped, collectively form the side of a cask, tub or similar vessel. (Cf. STAFF *sb.*^{1} 14 f.)

1398 TREVISA *Barth. De P.R.* XIX. cxxviii. (1495) 934 A tonne is an holowe vessel made of many bordes and tonne staues craftly bounde togyder. *c* **1580** in *Eng. Hist. Rev.* July (1914) 518 For..pipestaves and hoghed staves. **1613** SIR R. BOYLE in *Lismore Papers* (1886) I. 26 Butt staves and hogshead staves. **1687** PETTY *Pol. Arith.* (1690) 79 All sorts of Timber, Plank, and Staves for Cask. **1769** E. BANCROFT *Nat. Hist. Guiana* 85 This quality renders it suitable for staves for sugar hogsheads. **1837** CARLYLE *Fr. Rev.* III. I. i, One Citoyen has wrought out the scheme of a wooden cannon... It is to be made of staves, by the coopers. **1844** H. STEPHENS *Bk. of Farm* III. 900 [The milking-pail] is made light, of thin oak staves bound with iron hoops. **1906** T. SINTON *Poetry of Badenoch* 21 Presenting him with the milk-cog, she assured him that so long as a stave of it remained [etc.].

b. Phrases. ***to ding in staves***: to break in pieces. ***to fall into staves***: to fall to pieces. ***to take a stave out of one's cog*** (cf. COGUE 1).

1786 BURNS *Author's Cry* ix, To see his poor, auld Mither's pot, Thus dung in staves. **1889** H. JOHNSTON *Chron. Glenbuckie* xvi. 179, I must either get my income augmented or take a 'stave out of my cog', as the saying is. **1895** W. C. FRASER *Whaups of Durley* ii. 17 'A dune man', the villagers said, 'fa'in into staves', and become quite unable to control a herd of boisterous children.

2. A rod, bar, pole or the like.

a. A rung (of a ladder); a cross-bar to the legs of a chair. Now *dial.* (Cf. STAFF *sb.*^{1} 14 a, b.)

c **1175** *Twelfth Cent. Hom.* (E.E.T.S.) 80 He bið ilic þam men þe..asithð..uppon þære læddrestæfæ..& wule þonne stiȝan ufor butan stafæ [= Ælfric *Saints' Lives* I. 12 Be þære hlæddre stapum..buton stapum]. *a* **1825** FORBY *Voc. E. Anglia*, *Stave*, a step or round of a ladder.

†**b.** A pump-rod. (Cf. STAFF *sb.*^{1} 9 b.) *Obs.*

1750 BLANCKLEY *Naval Expos.* 124 Stave or Spear (Pump Hand) is a long Rod of Iron with an Eye at the upper End, which Hooks to the Brake.

c. A bar or pin (of a trundle).

1834–6 BARLOW in *Encycl. Metrop.* (1845) VIII. 102/1 The teeth of pinions are also distinguished by the term leaves, and those of the trundle by staves or rounds. *Ibid.* 102/2 The centre of the stave A..half the diameter of the stave. **1869** Rankine *Machinery & Millwork* 137 When two wheels gear together, and one of them has cylindrical pins (called staves) for teeth. *Ibid.*, Draw curves parallel to and within the epicycloids, at a distance from them equal to the radius of a stave.

d. (See quot.)

1823 P. Nicholson *Pract. Builder* 372 The laths [for plastering] generally used in London are made of fir, imported from Norway, the Baltic, and America, in pieces, called staves.

e. A graduated rod used in levelling. (Cf. staff *sb.*[1] 10.)

1838 *Rep. 8th Meeting of Brit. Assoc.* Notices 154 Description of an Improved Leveling Stave, for Subterranean as well as Surface Leveling. By Thomas Sopwith.

†**f.** *U.S.* ? A pig (of lead).

1864 C. H. Hunt *Life E. Livingston* i. 7 [For land purchased from the Indians R. Livingston agreed] to pay to the said Owners these following Goods..; Six Guns, fifty pounds of Powder, Fifty staves of Lead [etc.].

g. The shaft of a lance: = staff *sb.*[1] 3 a.

1873 Dixon *Two Queens* III. xiii. viii. 43 Stave after stave was broken, but the unknown knights still challenged every one to ride his best.

h. = bowstaff. *arch.*

1891 Doyle *White Company* xv, 'Tis the master-bowyer's rede:..Every stave well nocked. Every string well locked.

i. [Cf. Norw. *stav.*] A vertical wooden post forming part of the framework of a building, usu. a stave church (see sense 8 c below); also, a plank used in the walls of such a construction.

1915 H. G. Leach *Scandinavia of Scandinavians* ii. xiii. 162 In architecture, the most distinctive survivals from the Middle Ages in Norway are the so-called 'stave' churches, tepee-like structures, built of wooden staves, rising roof above roof. *Ibid.*, Stave churches often contain elaborate wooden carvings which have served as models for modern Norwegian decoration... This is especially true of the church of Urnaes.., one of the earliest existing stave structures, with its intricate animal and vegetable motives. **1974** *Encycl. Brit. Micropædia* IX. 539/1 The stone foundation of the stave church supports four horizontal wooden beams, from which rise four corner posts, or staves.

II. A bundle (of certain things).

3. A bundle of teasel-heads. = staff *sb.*[1] 16.

1707 Mortimer *Husb.* 147 The common Produce is about 160 Bundles or Staves upon an Acre, which they sell for about one Shilling a Stave. **1805** R. W. Dickson *Pract. Agric.* II. 785 By some, before forming them into packs, they are done up into what are termed *staves*, by means of split sticks.

4. ? *Anglo-Irish.* (See quot.) *rare*$^{-1}$.

1861 O Curry *Lect. MS. Materials* 13 The next book..is that called *Cin Droma Snechta*... The word Cin..is explained in our ancient Glossaries as signifying a stave of five sheets of vellum. *Ibid.* 196 The workmen..carried off several loose leaves, and even whole staves of the book.

III. (Cf. staff *sb.* II.)

5. a. A 'verse' or stanza of a poem, song, etc. = staff *sb.*[1] 19 c.

1659 J. C[aryl] *Peter's Pattern* (1680) 3 After they had sang the two first Staves of the Tenth Hymn of Larners Twelve Songs of Sion. **1709** Hearne *Collect.* 24 Dec. (O.H.S.) II. 331 In most of the Churches..the 3 first Staves of the 64th Psalm were sung. **1757** Mrs. Griffith *Lett. Henry & Frances* (1767) IV. 233 That Posterity may bless us, should be one of the Staves of the Litany. **1784** Cowper *Task* vi. 662 The simple clerk, but loyal, did announce, And eke did roar right merrily, two staves, Sung to the praise and glory of King George! **1805** Scott *Last Minstr.* v. end, Last, o'er the warrior's closing grave, Rung the full choir in choral stave. **1823** Byron *Island* ii. v, One long-cherish'd ballad's simple stave. **1841** Dickens *Barn. Rudge* xxxix, 'Cheer up, captain!' cried Hugh, when they had roared themselves out of breath. 'Another stave!' **1858** Merivale *Rom. Emp.* (1865) VI. lii. 285 Britannicus chanted a lyric stave on the sorrows of the discrowned and disinherited. **1875** Lowell *Spenser* Prose Wks. 1890 IV. 305 *note*, Spenser's innovation lies..in valuing the stave more than any of the single verses that compose it.

b. Phrase. *to tip* (one) *a stave*: to sing a song to (one); *jocularly*, to send a line to. Cf. tip *v.*[4] 1.

1838 Haliburton *Clockm.* Ser. ii. xxiii, Jist tip a stave to the Governor of Nova Scotia, order him to inquire out the author. **1886** Stevenson *Treas. Isl.* ii. x, 'Now, Barbecue, tip us a stave', cried one voice.

6. *Mus.* A set of lines for musical notation: = staff *sb.*[1] 20.

c **1800** Busby *Dict. Mus.* (1811). **1842**, **1873** [see staff *sb.*[1] 20]. **1875** Stainer & Barrett *Dict. Mus. Terms.*

7. a. quasi-*arch.* An alphabetic letter. (Cf. runestave and staff *sb.*[1] 18.)

1866–7 G. Stephens *Runic Mon.* I. Introd. p. x, Many staves are more or less the same in both [Runic and Roman]. **1896** A. Austin *Eng. Darling* iv. i, Ask them that read the staves. This crimson-dawn, The beechen slips on the white cloth spelled out The runes of death.

b. An alliterating letter in a line of Old English verse. Also ***head-stave.*** Cf. G. *stab, hauptstab.*

1894 H. Sweet *Anglo-Saxon Reader* (ed. 7) p. lxxxv, In our texts..the letters or staves are in italics. *Ibid.*, We denote the first and second verse of each line by I and II respectively. II..has only one stave called the head-stave, while I has either one or two called under-staves. **1959** R. B. Le Page in *Jrnl. Eng. & Gmc. Philol.* LVIII. 434 The two alliterating staves, one in each half-line, have a definite structural function. **1962** K. Malone *Widsith* 67 Grammatically *fela ic monna* makes a unit but because of the m-stave that binds the two halves of the line together the on-verse must be classified as D in spite of the f-stave.

IV. 8. *attrib.* and *Comb.*: **a.** simple attrib., as ***stave-hole, teeth***; ***stave-wise*** adv.; **b.** objective, as ***stave-cutting, -making***; **c.** special comb.: **stave bolt**, a log for cutting into staves; **stave church** [tr. Norw. (Bokmål) *stavkirke*], a church built with walls of upright planks or staves, of a type mainly built in Norway from the eleventh to the thirteenth century; **stave mill** *N. Amer.*, a mill making cask-staves; **stave-rime** [cf. G. *stabreim*], alliteration; an alliterating word in a line of alliterative poetry; **staverow** *rare*, an alphabet; **stavesman**, an official bearing a stave or wand; **stave-tankard**, an antique tankard formed of staves of wood (*Cent. Dict.* 1891); **stave-wood**, a name given to several trees furnishing wood suitable for cask-staves (see quots.).

1878 *Lumberman's Gaz.* 26 Jan., Large quantities of *stave bolts are being hauled in. **1915**, etc. *Stave church [see sense 2 i above.] **1933** F. Lingstrom *This is Norway* facing p. 12 (*caption*) Borgund Stave Church in Laerdal. **1936** A. W. Clapham *Romanesque Archit.* viii. 189 A highly remarkable class of building in timber, which includes the celebrated mast or stave-churches of Norway. **1968** G. Jones *Hist. Vikings* ii. iii. 116 An oak-built stave church at some time destroyed by fire. **1840** *Mechanics' Mag.* XXXIII. 497 Taylor's Improved *Stave-cutting Machine. **1901** *J. Black's Carp. & Builder, Scaffolding* 34 The sides..in which the points for centre of *stave-holes [of a ladder] are shown. **1874** *Spons' Dict. Engin.* viii. 2917 Stave-making and Cask Machinery. **1937** R. Flannagan *County Court* 188 Widowed five years before by an automobile accident, she had held on to her late husband's chain of *stave-mills and had prospered. **1957** *Daily Progress* (Charlottesville, Va.) 7 May 15/8 Blake and other stave mill operators say they will remain in business as long as it is profitable. **1968** E. R. Buckler *Ox Bells & Fireflies* vi. 102 If there was urgent need of ready money..you worked off and on in the stave mill. **1888** *Academy* 14 Jan. 27/1 The law of the alliterative verse does not require us to adopt the reading of the Dublin MS., as three *stave-rimes are a sufficient number for a line. **1866–7** G. Stephens *Runic Mon.* I. Introd. p. x, These particular staves died out, and assumed other forms in the later Runic *staverow. **1786** J. Smith in *Mem. J. E. Smith* (1832) I. 172 The area of the square [on election-day] was crowded with *stavesmen and spectators: the candidates rode as usual. **1834–6** Barlow in *Encycl. Metrop.* (1845) VIII. 103/2 Draw the line AB, joining the centres of the *stave teeth. **1659** Torriano *Dict. Ital. & Eng.*, *A-fusóne*, adv., made *stave-wise. **1778** W. Wright in *Trans. Roy. Soc. Edin.* (1790) II. 76 *Quassia Simaruba*... This tree is known in Jamaica by the names of Mountain Damson, Bitter Damson and *Stave-wood. **1864** Grisebach *Flora W. Ind. Islands* 788 Stave-wood, *Simaruba amara.* **1889** Maiden *Usef. Pl. Austral.* 542 *Flindersia Schottiana*.. Stavewood. **1889** *Century Dict.*, *Stavewood*,..a tall stout tree, *Sterculia fœtida*, of the East Indies, eastern Africa, and Australia.

†**stave**, *sb.*[2] *Obs. rare*$^{-1}$. [? For *staven*, var. of stam *sb.*[1]] ? The stem of a ship.

13.. *Coer de L.* 64 All it [a ship] was whyt of huel-bon, And every nayl with gold begrave: Off pure gold was the stave.

stave (steɪv), *sb.*[3] *north.* [f. stave *v.*[1]]

1. A crushing blow, a heavy stroke.

1819 [Rennie] *St. Patrick* I. xv. 220 Our bit curragh's no that rackle sin it got a stave..on the Partan-rock. **1867** [J. P. Morris] *T'Lebby Beck Dobby* 5 (E.D.D.) T'roof fair rang again wi' sic like staves as thissan.

2. A sprain. *Sc.*

1900 *Brit. Med. Jrnl.* 5 May 1076/2 The so-called 'stave of thumb,' or Bennett's fracture.

stave (steɪv), *v.* Pa. t. and pa. pple. **staved**; also (chiefly *Naut.*), 8–9 **stove**. [f. stave *sb.*[1]]

1. *trans.* To break up (a cask) into staves; to break into and let out the contents.

c **1595** Capt. Wyatt *R. Dudley's Voy. W. Ind.* (Hakl. Soc.) 10 A bark..beinge forst to cast overborde all..theire fish and to stave theire caske in the which theire fresh water was. **1627** Capt. Smith *Sea Gram.* ii. 9 They..staue the Caske to make more roome. **1679** *Lond. Gaz.* No. 1433/4 Yesterday 7 Hogsheads of French wine..were publickly staved by the Officers of the Custom House. **1771** Smollett *Humph. Cl.* 8 June, In an action at law, laid against a carman for having staved a cask of port. **1841** Dickens *Barn. Rudge* lxvii, They..could see them..broaching the casks, staving the great vats,..and lying down to drink at the channels of strong spirits.

b. To destroy (wine, etc.) by breaking up the cask.

1615 G. Sandys *Trav.* i. (1621) 66 Diuers times all the wine in the Citie hath bene staued. **1633** T. James *Voy.* 32, I made all the water in hold to be stau'd: and set some to the pumpes to pumpe it out. **1694** Echard *Plautus* 168 He's a plaguy hard custom-master and staves all prohibited goods. **1733** P. Lindsay *Interest Scot.* 139 That all seiz'd Brandies should be either staved or exported. **1758** *Ann. Reg., Chron.* 85/1 They..stove all the beer in the cellar. **1768** *Ibid.*, *Hist. Europe* 33/1 Wine was forbid..; and all those who were possessed of any quantities of it were obliged to stave it. **1827** Southey *Hist. Penins. War* II. 310 They had..staved all the liquor which they could not drink.

fig. **1700** Dryden *Fables* Pref. *A2, If the Searchers find any [irreverent expressions, etc.] in the Cargo, let them be stav'd or forfeited, like Counterbanded Goods.

c. *intr.* Of a barrel: To fall to pieces. *rare.*

1797 Mrs. A. M. Bennett *Beggar Girl* (1813) III. 20 One fair day the old barrel staved, over her poor dear tipped, and broke his neck.

2. *trans.* To break a hole in (a boat); to break *to pieces*; also, to break (a hole in a boat). ***to stave in***, to crush inwards, make a hole in.

1628 Digby *Voy. Mediterr.* (Camden) 65 The man swimming well he saued himselfe with much difficultie, the boate being staued in many peeces. **1668** *Lond. Gaz.* No. 324/1 The 17th instant was driven on shoar..a vessel.. where by the violence of the winds and waves, she was staved to pieces. **1719** De Foe *Crusoe* i. (Globe) 263 The first Thing we had to do, was to stave the Boat..and..leave her so far useless as not to be fit to swim. **1748** *Anson's Voy.* i. viii. 81 A sea..stove in the quarter gallery, and rushed into the ship like a deluge. *Ibid.* iii. v. 334 The loss of our long-boat, which was staved against our poop,..put us to great inconveniences. *a* **1779** Cook *Voy. Pacific* (1784) I. ii. i. 174 The attempt could not be made..unless at the risk of having our boats..staved to pieces. **1819** Byron *Juan* ii. xlviii, The other boats, the yawl and pinnace, had Been stove in the beginning of the gale. **1823** Scoresby *Jrnl.* 458 Our ship was driven against the corner of a floe, and her starboard-bow completely stove. **1834** Marryat *P. Simple* xi, He was forced to place sentries in the chains with cold shot, to stave the boats if they came alongside. **1884** *Manch. Exam.* 7 Oct. 5/1 The captain..ordered the boats to be lowered, but the sea stove in two of them. **1897** Mary Kingsley *W. Africa* 496 C...fetches up on a floating stump in the river, and staves a hole you could put your head in, in the bow of the said canoe.

b. *intr.* for *refl.* of a boat: To break up; hence *trans.* to break a hole in.

1743 Bulkeley & Cummins *Voy. S. Seas* 147 Otherwise she must have stove to pieces, the Ground being very foul. **1794** Morse *Amer. Geog.* 71 During the storm, one of the Indian canoes stove, and became unfit for service. **1820** J. Oxley *Jrnl. Exped. N.S. Wales* 225 The large boat struck on a sharp rock, and with such violence as to stave her bottom. **1839** Longf. *Hesperus* xix, Like a vessel of glass, she stove and sank. **1856** Kane *Arct. Expl.* II. xxvi. 264 The Hope stove her bottom.

3. *transf.* trans. To burst in, crush inwards. Chiefly with *in.*

1716 Church *Philip's War* (1865) i. 24 There Philip had staved all his Drums, and conveyed all his Canoo's to the East-side of Metapoiset-River. **1753** *Scots Mag.* Mar. 109/1 To break open and stave trunks and chests. **1822** A. Clarke in *Life* x. (1834) 253, I found two of the maids..pushing.. against the shutters, as the windows themselves had been stove in by the tempest. **1862** Trollope *Orley Farm* xxix, He had..broken his right arm, which had been twisted under him as the horse rolled, and two of his ribs had been staved in by the pommel of his saddle. **1862** Burton *Bk. Hunter* (1863) 327 The doors staved in, the wainscoating pulled down. **1879** J. Long *Virgil's Æneid* x. 557 He staves The face of Thoas with a rock—a mass Of bones and blood and brains outspattering.

4. To renew the staves of (a bucket); to put together the staves of (a cask, etc.).

1627 Capt. Smith *Sea Gram.* viii. 36 The Cooper is..to staue or repaire the buckets. **1842** Browning *Pied Piper* vii, A bulky sugar-puncheon, All ready staved.

5. To fit with a staff or handle.

1542 in *Rutland MSS.* (1905) IV. 335 Item payd..for the mackyng off leyden malles for archers, the yerne warcke, the lede and casteng, with the staweng off them at [blank] the pece. **1611** Florio, *Alberáre*,..to shaft or stave any weapon as a holberd.

6. To drive off or beat with a staff or stave; esp. in *to stave off*, to beat off (a dog in Bear- or Bull-baiting; also *transf.* a human combatant); to keep back (a crowd). Now only *arch.*

c **1624** Dekker etc. *Witch Edmonton* v. i, But you must play fair, you should be stav'd off else. **1633** T. Adams *Exp. 2 Peter* ii. 4. 521 He is like an old bitten curre, that being fleshed to the game, will not be stav'd off. **1658** Ussher *Ann.* 717 He went abroad with the rods..and staving the young gamsters when they had contended as long as he thought good, parted them. **1671** tr. *Frejus' Voy. Mauritania* 73 Others, who with Clubs, and other weapons in their hands, staved off the Croud of People. **1820** Scott *Monast.* xxxvii, 'Stave the miller off him', said Murray, 'or he will worry him dead.' **1878** Tennyson *Q. Mary* i. iii, Stave off the crowd upon the Spaniard there.

b. *fig.* and in fig. context.

1609 B. Jonson *Sil. Woman* iii. i, For gods sake, let's goe staue her off him [*i.e.* Mistress Otter from Captain Otter, who are quarrelling]. **1611** Beaum. & Fl. *Tri. Time* i, I.. found him in a young Lords ear so busie..: I pulled him..; spoke unto him, His answer still was, By the Lord, sweet Lord,..Nothing could stave him off. **1627** Sanderson *Serm. ad Magistr.* i. §25 (1632) 175 And as for Courage to execute justice..whether it be..that a faire word whistleth him off; or that a great mans letter staveth him off;..sure we are, the Magistrate too often letteth the wicked carry away the spoyle, without breaking a Iaw of him. **1647** Trapp *Comm. 1 Thess.* iii. 6 God stints him [the devil], and staves him off, when he would worry his poor lambs. **1649** Earl Monm. tr. *Senault's Use Passions* vi. iii. 467 Other Passions are in a perpetuall motion; and..they never fix themselves so strongly on an Object, but they may be staved off. **1884** Tennyson *Becket* Prol., And this Becket, her father's friend, like enough staved us from her.

c. Phrase. ***to stave and tail***: see tail *v.*[1] 2. Also *transf.* and *fig.*

1663 [see tail *v.*[1] 2]. **1668** R. L'Estrange *Vis. Quev.* (1708) 68 As they were Staving and Tayling, you might have had more Manners (cry'd one) than to give such Language to your Betters. *a* **1697** J. Aubrey *Countrey Revell* ii. iii. in *Brief Lives* (1898) II. 334 Yesterday we Cheshire gentlemen mett at a barrell of ale at the bull-ring where we sufficiently bayted both bull and barrell; and having well dranke there, staved and tayled. *Ibid.* 335 The Justice and I..parted em, and, with something more trouble then staving and tayling dog and bull. **1823** Scott *Quentin D.* xxxiii, They seized him, pulled him down, and would probably soon have throttled him, had not the Duke called out—'Stave and tail!—stave and tail!—Take them off him!' **1829** —— *Let.* 30 Jan. in *Croker Papers* (1884) II. 31 Jamie then set to staving and tailing between his father and the philosopher, and.. reduced the debate to more order.

d. (See quot.)

1867 Smyth *Sailor's Word-bk.* s.v., *To stave off*, to boom off; to push anything off with a pole.

7. *fig.* Chiefly *to stave off.*

†**a.** To keep (a person) away or at a distance; to repel. *Obs.*

1631 LENTON *Charact.* C 8 b, Hee aspiers sometimes to his Masters daughter, but being stau'd off there, hee choppes vpon the Chambermaid, and there stickes fast. **1636** HEYLIN *Sabbath* II. vi. 185 To allure the people thither, being before staved off by a former Synod, it was provided that [etc.]. **1641** LD. BROOKE *Disc. Nat. Episc.* II. vi. 88 Heresies distract our soules, dismember our Churches, stave off Iew and Gentile, who know not whether part to believe. **1667** SOUTH *12 Serm.* (1697) II. 60 The Condition of a Servant staves him off to a distance; but the Gospel speaks nothing but Allurement.

†**b.** To keep (a person) *from* (doing something); to divert *from* (an object, practice, or course of action). *Obs.*

1630 *R. Johnson's Kingd. & Commw.* 329 This makes them..to put themselves under the protection of the Spaniard, the feare of whose power staves off the Duke from attempting upon that State. **1636** B. JONSON *Discov., Nil gratius*, How can they escape the contagion of the Writings, whom the virulency of the calumnies hath not stav'd off from reading? **1641** QUARLES *Enchyridion* III. xvii. (Grosart) 31/2 Divert the course of the vulgar humor, by devulging.. some..novelty, which may..stave their tongues from off thy worried name. *Ibid.* III. xxviii. 32/2 If he be given to lavish Company, endeavour to stave him off with lawfull Recreations. **1646** GAULE *Cases Consc.* 86 And there's no staving them off their owne conceited way of Tryall. **1651** N. BACON *Disc. Govt. Eng.* II. vi. (1739) 27 It was the policy of these times..to carry a benign Aspect to the Pope, so far only as to stave him off from being an enemy. **1654** OWEN *Doctr. Saints' Persev.* xii. §59. 297 This dread and terrour [used] for the hedging up their wayes from folly, and staving them off from any Actuall evill. **1658** HEYLIN *Stumbling-block* iii. §4. 81 Enough of conscience to have staved them from the prosecution, but that they had it in design, and resolved to carry it. **1668** OWEN *Expos. 130th Ps.* 111 What staves off these hungry creatures [*sc.* souls] from their proper food? **1684** H. MORE *Answer* xiii. 95 By this sharp reproof they may be the more effectually staved off from committing Idolatry.

c. To put off as importune or inopportune; to treat with evasion.

1646 J. HALL *Horæ Vac.* 4 Columbus..had beene stav'd off by severall Christian Princes, yet..He gained the assistance of the King and Queene of Castile. *a* **1656** HALES *Gold. Rem.* I. (1673) 43 God himself in the Book of Psalms, staves them off with a *Quid tu ut enarres mea?* etc. **1680** N. LEE *Cæsar Borgia* III. i, But speak, thou stav'st me off. **1723** WATERLAND *2nd Vind. Christ's Divin.* ii. 66 But it is high Time now to come to Antiquity; which has been so long staved off, and yet must make a great part of our Discourse. **1843** A. BETHUNE *Scott. Peasant's Fireside* 79 The poor lad was staved off from time to time, wi' ae excuse after anither, till he grew impatient. **1887** HAGGARD *Jess* xxxiv, This staved the fellows off for a while.

d. To ward off (something undesirable or hurtful); to prevent the occurrence or event of; to keep back, delay. Also (rarely), *to stave away.*

1662 J. WILSON *Cheats* v. iii, Had you but mist me now, I should have ventur'd that, and perhaps stav'd, That misery, which alwayes follows rashness. **1664** —— *A. Commenius* II. iii, 'Tis seal'd, and done: Nor shall the fate, or fortune of the Empire Stave it off longer. **1684** tr. *Bonet's Merc. Compit.* VI. 170 The Powder being given again, the fit is staved off. **1691** *d'Emiliane's Frauds Rom. Monks* 397 They..earnestly entreated him, to make use of all his Credit with the Pope, to stave off this fatal Blow from them. **1759** *Ann. Reg.* 6/2 New methods were devised, which might stave off the entire ruin of their finances. **1837** CARLYLE *Fr. Rev.* II. VI. iv, Insurrection will come; but likewise will it not be met? Staved off, one may hope, till Brunswick arrive? **1849** W. IRVING *Goldsmith* xxxii. 278 He had obtained an advance of money from Newbery to stave off some pressing debts. **1859** TENNYSON *Geraint & Enid* 352 But Enid.. answer'd with such craft as women use, Guilty or guiltless, to stave off a chance That breaks upon them perilously. **1865** CARLYLE *Fredk. Gt.* XX. vii. IX. 140 One huge peril handsomely staved away, though so many others impend. **1879** DIXON *Windsor* III. xxiii. 231 A little fish sufficed to stave off hunger. **1884** CHURCH *Bacon* vi. 129 The proposed conference was staved off by management for a day or two; but it could not be averted.

8. *intr.* To fight with staves.

1663 BUTLER *Hud.* I. iii. 88 He..stav'd it out, Disdaining to lay down his arms.

9. *trans.* To drive with a heavy blow. *U.S.*

1837 *Knickerbocker Mag.* Nov. X. 408 (Thornton *Amer. Gloss.*), [He had] stove two of his front teeth down his throat. **1837** J. C. NEAL *Charcoal Sketches* (Bartlett *Dict. Amer.*), I'll stave my fist right through you, and carry you on my elbow, as easily as if you were an empty market-basket.

10. *intr.* To go with a rush or dash; to 'drive'. *Sc.* and *U.S.*

1819 [RENNIE] *St. Patrick* III. xi. 265 The puir lads..ha'e been a' night stavin' at ane anither, and struislin' i' the dark. **1825** J. NEAL *Bro. Jonathan* II. xxiii. 303 'Hold in!'..cried out a long, slab-sided Virginian, as our adventurers went, staving through Broadway, in Mr. Ashley's go-cart. **1836** *Phila. Public Ledger* 5 Oct. (Thornton *Amer. Gloss.*), He stove about in every direction, like a mad bull. **1880** 'MARK TWAIN' *Tramp Abroad* ii, Other pedestrians went staving by us with vigorous strides. **1886** STEVENSON *Kidnapped* xxvi, If we seek to creep round..it's..there that they'll be looking to lay hands on us. But if we stave on straight to the auld Brig of Stirling, I'll lay my sword they let us pass unchallenged. **1894** P. H. HUNTER *James Inwick* iii. (1900) 37 He was staivin doon the street.

11. *Forging.* To thicken (bar-iron) by heating and hammering, to UPSET; also *to stave up.* Also *absol.* **b.** *intr.* Of the iron: To undergo staving; also *to stave up.*

1906 J. WATSON *Tables for Blacksm. & Forgers* Pref., The information required is generally about allowances for staving and drawing down. *Ibid.* 9 To stave up out of a bar 6″ wide by 4″ thick a part 7″ wide by $4\frac{1}{2}$″ thick by 9″ long. *Ibid.*, So that 12″ long of 6″ wide by 4″ thick staves up to 9″ long of 7″ wide by $4\frac{1}{2}$″ thick. *Ibid.* 15 A 4″ diameter bar is to have a length of 2″ at 5″ diameter staved on one end, and a part drawn down to $3\frac{1}{4}$″ diameter by 10″ long. *Ibid.* 23 A bar $1\frac{1}{4}$″ round is to be staved to $1\frac{1}{2}$″ square by $1\frac{1}{2}$″ long: what length of $1\frac{1}{4}$″ round is required?

c. *transf.* (See quot.)

1850 OGILVIE, *Stave*, v...6. To make firm by compression. The term is applied to the compressing of lead by a hammer or a blunt chisel, after it has been run in to secure a joining, such as the socket joints of pipes.

12. To sprain (one's thumb, etc.) *Sc.*

1887 *Jamieson's Sc. Dict.* Suppl. 228/1 He steved his wrist and staved my thumb.

stave, variant of STEEVE *v. Naut.*

staved (steɪvd), *ppl. a.* [f. STAVE *v.* + -ED[1].

In some uses prob. f. STAVE *sb.*[1] or *staves* pl. of STAFF *sb.*[1]]

1. Furnished with a stave or staves. †**a.** Having a handle or a supporting stem. *Obs.*

1481–90 *Howard Househ. Bks.* (Roxb.) 333 My Lord paied to I. Gravele uppon vj. bylles staved, and v. unstaved iij.s. iiij.d. **1599** in *15th Rep. Hist. MSS. Comm.* App. v. 72 Waddhookes staved, twelve. **1628** FELTHAM *Resolves* II. xv. 45 The same fire may be in the waxen Taper, which is in the staued Torch, but 'tis not equall either in quantity, or advancement.

b. Of a ladder: Furnished with rungs.

1603 KNOLLES *Hist. Turks* (1621) 635 But climing too fast up the evill staved ladder of ambition, suddenly fell. **1769** *Ann. Reg., Nat. Hist.* 101/1 You pass thirty ladders, some half broken, other not half staved.

c. *Arch.* Of a column: Having a round convex moulding or bead in the lower part of the fluting. (Cf. CABLE *v.* 2 and RUDENTURE.)

1664 EVELYN *Freart's Archit.* 130 Sometimes we find the Striges [by our Workmen call'd Flutings and Groeves] to be fill'd up with a swelling, a third part from the Base, and these we call stav'd, or Cabl'd-Columns.

†**2.** Beaten with a stave or staff. *Obs.*

a **1625** FLETCHER *Knt. Malta* IV. ii, Thou art a dogge, I will make thee sweare, a dog stav'd.

3. Broken; also *staved in.*

1699 GARTH *Dispensary* v. (1730) 53 Each Combatant his Adversary mauls, With batter'd Bed-pans, and stav'd Urinals. **1727** BAILEY vol. II, *Staved* (of the Staves of a Cask), beat to Pieces. **1913** *Daily News* 4 Feb. 11 The staved-in barrels, and the lidless boxes that everywhere met the eye.

4. *Forging.* Thickened by hammering.

1906 J. WATSON *Tables for Blacksm. & Forgers* 15 The staved part [of an iron bar].

staveless (ˈsteɪvlɪs), *a.* [f. STAVE *sb.*[1] + -LESS.]

a. Of a rune: Having no upright stem. *rare.* **b.** Of a barrel: Having no staves.

1866–7 G. STEPHENS *Runic Mon.* I. Introd. 135 We may even have the side-stroke alone, the stave being absent; thus' is A in the staveless Helsing-runes. **1892** *Daily News* 6 Aug. 6/2 His system of making staveless barrels from one sheet of wood, instead of from a number of staves.

staver (ˈsteɪvə(r)), *sb.*[1] *dial.* and *Sc.* In 6 stavir. [? f. STAVE *sb.*[1]]

1. A rung (of a ladder). Also, 'one of the bars of a hay-rack' (*N.W. Linc. Gloss.*); 'a stake for a hedge, etc.' (*Sheffield Gloss.*).

1534 *Eng. Ch. Furniture* (Peacock 1866) 190 Item in the whete chamber a ladder of viij stavirs. **1866** BROGDEN *Prov. Lincs., Stavers*, the staves or rounds of a ladder.

2. A stave (of a cask).

1891 'HUGH HALIBURTON' (J. L. Robertson) *Ochil Idylls* 89 'Maist like an auld cask dung to stavers.

staver (ˈsteɪvə(r)), *sb.*[2] *dial.* and *U.S.* [f. STAVE *v.* + -ER[1].] One who is continually 'staving' about; an active, energetic person.

1860 J. G. HOLLAND *Miss Gilbert's Career* xii. (1881) 146 Oh! she's right, I tell you, and she's got one of the mothers —regular staver. **1869** MRS. STOWE *Oldtown Folks* x. (1870) 105 She was spoken of with applause under such titles as 'a staver', 'a pealer,' 'a roarer to work'. **1880** *W. Cornw. Gloss., Staver*, a fussy, noisy person. 'She's a regular staver; she staves about from morning to night.'

staver (ˈstævə(r)), *sb.*[3] [f. STAVER *v.*] In pl. (const. as sing.) The staggers = STAGGER *sb.*[1] 2.

1597 [implied in *staverwort*: see below]. **1639** DE GRAY *Compl. Horsem.* 30 This preventeth yellowes, stavers, and such like diseases. *c* **1720** W. GIBSON *Farrier's Guide* II. xv. (1738) 56 That Distemper which Farriers call the Stavers, or Staggers. **1749** *Lond. Mag.* 277 A disease called the staggers, or stavers, in horses.

b. Comb.: **staverwort**, the plant *Senecio Jacobæa*, ragwort.

1597 GERARDE *Herbal* II. xxvi. 219 *Jacobea*... The countrey people do call it Stagger woort, and Stauerwoort. **1707** MORTIMER *Husb.* 187 Take [of]..Staverwort..a handful. **1866** *Treas. Bot.* 1093/2 Staverwort, *Senecio Jacobæa*.

staver (ˈsteɪvə(r)), *v.* Chiefly *Sc.* Also 9 staiver. [? Alteration of STAGGER *v.*, after *daver.*] *intr.* **a.** To stagger (*lit.* and *fig.*). **b.** To wander about aimlessly or in a restless manner.

c **1425** WYNTOUN *Cron.* III. v. 797 (Cott.) Þus in seige a sote to se,..Sal ger standande statis stauer. *Ibid.* IV. vii. 816 Al þus in wodnes as thai waueryde And stekyt sa withe stokys staweride [*v.r.* stauerit]. **1755** R. FORBES *Ajax' Sp., Jrnl. fr. Lond. to Portsmouth* 30, I was lyin tawin an' wamlin ..like..a stirkie that had staver'd into a well-eye. *Ibid.* 50 Key, Staver'd [=] Stagger'd. **1776** C. KEITH *Farmer's Ha'* xxxii, [The ganger] gangs just staivering about In quest o' prey. **1820** *Blackw. Mag.* Nov. 203 So out I stavers, for rest I could na' within. **1864** LATTO *Tam. Bodkin* xix. (1894) 199, I staivered awa in, an' tauld my story. **1884** FROUDE *Carlyle's Life in Lond.* I. iii. 69 He slept badly from overwork, 'gaeing stavering aboot the hoose at night', as the Scotch maid said, restless alike in mind and body.

stavesacre (ˈsteɪvˌzeɪkə(r)). Forms: 4 **scafisage**, 5 **staphisagrie**, 5–6 **-agre**, (5 **stafi-sagre**, **scapysagre**, 6 **stafesagre**, **stavysagre**, **-acre**, **stavis akre**), 6–8 **stavesaker**, (7 **stav-aker**, **stassaker**, **stavis-acre**), 6–7, 9 **staphisacre**, 7–8 **-ager**, 8 **stave-acre**, (**staves-ager**), 6– **stavesacre**. [ad. L. *staphisagria*, a. Gr. σταφὶς ἀγρία lit. wild raisin (σταφίς raisin, ἀγρία fem. of ἄγριος wild).] A plant of the species *Delphinium Staphisagria* (N.O. *Ranunculaceæ*), native in southern Europe and Asia Minor; the seeds of this plant, used to destroy vermin, and formerly as an emetic.

a **1400** *Stockholm Med. MS.* 156 Scafisage *scafisagia.* *c* **1400** *Lanfranc's Cirurg.* 184 Herof we moun do þerto sal gemme, sulphuris, euforbij ana ʒ.ij. staphisagrie, cantaridarum ana ʒj. **14..** *Bk. Hawking* (MS. Harl. 2340) in *Rel. Ant.* (1841) I. 297 Take a greyn of staphisagre, and put under her [a hawk's] tong, and she shall caste. *Ibid.* 300 Take scapysagre, and sethe it in water. *c* **1440** *Pallad. on Husb.* I. 596 As staphisagre, minget in theire mete Wol hele her tong. **1460–70** *Bk. Quintessence* II. 20 Medle it wiþ a good quantite of poudre of stafi-sagre. **1538** TURNER *Libellus, Staphis agria* Stauesacre. **1547** BOORDE *Brev. Health* (1870) 87 Take..of Stauysacre made in fyne pouder, halfe an vnce. **1578** LYTE *Dodoens* III. xxxix. 372 Staphisacre, especially the seede, is hoate almost in the fourth degree. **1599** NASHE *Lenten Stuffe* Ep. Ded. A 2 b, Looke how much Tobacco wee carry with vs to expell cold, the like quantitie of Staues-aker wee must prouide vs of to kill lice in that rugged countrey of rebels. **1611–12** *Shuttleworths' Acc.* (Chetham Soc.) 198 For stassaker to John Leighe, ij[d]. **1630** J. TAYLOR (Water P.) *Taylor's Goose* 85 Wks. I. 105/1 Mix'd with Stauesacre, and *Argentum viue*, It will not leaue a man a Lowse aliue. **1682** G. WHELER *Journ. Greece* IV. 290 *Staphys agria*, or Staves-acre. **1731** MILLER *Gard. Dict.* s.v. *Delphinium*, Larkspur with a Plane-Tree Leaf, commonly call'd Stavesacre, or Lousewort. **1736** BAILEY *Houshold Dict.* 330 Pound burnt cummin and staphisager of each equal quantities and mix it with wine. **1757** DYER *Fleece* I. 288 Th' infectious scab..is by water cur'd Of lime, or sodden stave-acre. **1822–29** *Good's Study Med.* (ed. 3) V. 660 The most fatal poisons to all these vermin are the mercurial oxydes, staphisacre, [etc.]. **1838** T. THOMSON *Chem. Org. Bodies* 246 A pound of stavesacre furnishes from 55 to 60 grains of delphina. **1876** J. HARLEY *Royle's Mat. Med.* (ed. 6) 769 Stavesacre is a native of the South of Europe, and of the Mediterranean islands.

attrib. **1688** HOLME *Armoury* II. 90/1 He beareth Argent, a Stavesacre slip. **1837** *Penny Cycl.* VIII. 375/1 Stavesacre seeds are not now used internally. **1899** *Allbutt's Syst. Med.* VIII. 866 For infants..stavesacre or weak balsam of Peru ointment may be substituted for the sulphur.

stavies, var. STOVIES *sb. pl.*

staving (ˈsteɪvɪŋ), *vbl. sb.* Also 4 *Sc.* **staffing.** [f. STAVE *v.* and *sb.* + -ING[1].]

1. The action of the verb STAVE. Chiefly with advs. *off, in.*

1633 W. WATTS in T. James *Voy.* S, He..does like the Ship here spoken of, runne against a Rocke, endanger his owne bulge, and the stauing of his vessell. **1666** TEMPLE *Let. Ld. Arlington* Wks. 1731 II. 14 Neither the Emperor nor Spain will contribute any thing towards the Bishop's Assistance, nor so much as the staving off Enemies. **1815** COLERIDGE *Let. W. Money* Lett. (1895) II. 651 The staving off of pain is no pleasure. **1852** *Bentley's Misc.* XXXI. 57 Talk of fun, there never wos any like that which followed the staving-in of the heads of them barrels.

†**2. a.** The action of striking with staves. *Obs.* **b.** The action of setting up defensive or protective stakes or staves. *Obs.*

c **1375** BARBOUR *Bruce* XVII. 785 With staffing, stoking, and striking Thar maid thai sturdy defending. *c* **1543** *Plumpton Corr.* (Camden) 245 The Kings Majesties oficeres requireth of you and of me..to be contributors to the charges and staving of the watters of Ancotes.

3. Staves collectively. **a.** The staves of a trundle (see TRUNDLE *sb.* 2). **b.** (See quot. 1875.)

1491 in *Reg. S., Cant. Cath. Libr.* 368 b, The Priorie & Conuent shall repair the seid two watirmylles Except coggyng and stavyng, which shalbe at the costes of the seid John John & Thomas. **1875** KNIGHT *Dict. Mech., Staving*, a casing of staves or planks which forms a curb around a turbine or similar water-wheel.

staving (ˈsteɪvɪŋ), *ppl. a.* [? f. STAVE *v.* + -ING.]

†**1.** ? Addicted to fighting with staves, quarrelsome. *Obs.*

But possibly a misprint for *staring.*

1621 FLETCHER *Pilgr.* II. ii, *Rod...* What have you brought me Souldiers? *Lop.* We know not wel what: a strange staving fellow, Sullen enough I am sure.

2. *U.S. colloq.* As an intensive: Very strong, excessive. [Cf. STAVE *v.* 10.]

c **1850** *Cincinnati Times* (Farmer citing Bartlett), A staving dram put him in better humour. **1882** LUDLOW *Nick Hardy* 111, I've got a staving long lesson.

Stavka (ˈstafkə, ˈstɑːvkə). [Russ., f. *stavit'* to put, place.] The general headquarters of the Russian army.

1928 *Daily Express* 16 July 8 The actual relations between the Stavka (G.H.Q.) and the Duma are revealed clearly for the first time. **1931** W. S. CHURCHILL *World Crisis* VI. ix. 142 By August 6 the Russian General Headquarters—in future called the Stavka—learned definitely that the German main forces..were entraining for the French front.

1949 I. DEUTSCHER *Stalin* 466 The *Stavka*, the Red Army's G.H.Q., was in his offices in the Kremlin. **1963** P. FLEMING *Kolchak* xiv. 158 The swollen Stavka, besides embodying all the worst technical vices of Russian military bureaucracy, was rotten to the core with dishonesty, nepotism and intrigue.

stavy ('steɪvɪ), *a. U.S.* [f. STAVE *sb.*[1] + -Y.] Of butter: Tasting of the staves or cask.

1888 *Voice* (N.Y.) 23 Feb., Stavy or woody butter [comes] from tubs made of green wood.

staw, Sc. and dial. form of STALL *sb.*[1] and *v.*

staw(e, obs. pa. t. of STEAL and STY.

stawbote, variant of STALL BOAT. *Obs.*

1536 in *Hist. MSS. Comm., Var. Collect.* (1904) IV. 262 [His] stawbote, [anchors, cocks, ropes, nets, &c.,..to be sold.]

stawk, -er, obs. Sc. ff. STALK, STALKER.

stawl(e, -ling, stawll: see STALL, -ING.

stawnche, obs. form of STANCH *v.*

stawyll, obs. form of STALL *sb.*[1]

‖**staxis** ('stæksɪs). *Path.* [mod.L., a. Gr. στάξις a dripping, f. στάζειν to drop, drip.] 'Slight defluxion of any humour, as nasal hæmorrhage' (*Syd. Soc. Lex.*).

1745 R. JAMES *Med. Dict.* III. s.v., A Staxis, in the Doctrine of Crises, is justly condemned as indicating a Weakness and Decay of Strength in Nature.

stay (steɪ), *sb.*[1] Also 4–5 **stey(e**, 5 **stye**, 5–6 **staie**, 6 **staye**. [OE. *stæȝ* (? neut.) corresp. to Du. *stag* neut. and fem., *staag* neut., WFris. *staech*, LG. *stach* (16th c.), *stag(g* (E. Friesland), G. *stag* neut., ON. *stag* neut. (Da., Sw., Norw. *stag*, Icel. *stag* stay, clothes-line):—OTeut. **stago-*, f. Teut. root **stah-*: *stag-* to be firm (in **stahlo-* STEEL *sb.*, ON. *stagl* the rack, Norw. *stagle* pole):—pre-Teut. **stak-* or **stok-*. The Teut. word has been adopted in the Rom. langs.: OF. (12th c.) *estai* (mod.F. *étai*), Sp., Pg. *estay*.]

1. *Naut.* A large rope used to support a mast, and leading from its head down to some other mast or spar, or to some part of the ship.

The stays which lead forward are called fore and aft stays; and those which lead down to the vessel's sides backstays (see BACKSTAY). The stays have also special names according to the mast to which they are attached: see FORESTAY, MAINSTAY, MIZEN-STAY.

a **1100** *Ags. Voc.* in Wr.-Wülcker 288/26 [*De Nave et Partibus eius.*] *Safo*, stæȝ. [Cf. '*safon*, stæþ', *Suppl. Ælfric's Gloss*, ibid. 182/27; '*scaphon*, funis in prora positus' (Isidore).] **1296** *MS. Acc. Exch. K.R.* 5/20 m. 4b, Capiuntur..ad vsum Galee..octo Copule Cord[orum] Capital[ium] .j. Stay, ij. Schetes, ij. Huppeteyes, j. Boye. **1307–8** *Ibid.* 14/14 In .ij. hupteghes. vj. couplis de hauedropes et .ij. Steyes..pro masta dicte Bargie..xxviij.s. **1336** *Ibid.* 19/31 m. 4 In xxx petris cordis de canabo..pro tribus steyes inde faciendis. **1417** in *For. Acc. 8 Hen. V*, D/2 In v peciis de ropes pro styes j. Couple Bakstyes ij hailers ij vpties. **1420** in *For. Acc. 3 Hen. VI*, G/2 De j. cathena ferri vocata lichechine ad seruiendum pro le Steye dicte Carrac'. **1485** *Naval Acc. Hen. VII* (1896) 40 Sherhokes for the stay ..ij. *Ibid.* 48 For shrowdes.. vj, ffor staies..j. **1496** *Ibid.* 177 The Steyes for the Mayne maste. **1620** J. TAYLOR (Water P.) *Praise Hempseed* Wks. (1630) III. 66/2 Your mastlines, ropeyarnes, gaskets, and your stayes. **1626** CAPT. SMITH *Accid. Yng. Seamen* 30 A stay, a halyard, sheats. **1627** —— *Sea Gram.* v. 19 The vse of those staies are to keepe the Masts from falling aftwards, or too much forwards. **1719** DE FOE *Crusoe* I. (Globe) 232, I was near two Months..rigging and fitting my Mast and Sails; for I finish'd them very compleat, making a small Stay, and a Sail, or Foresail to it. **1748** *Anson's Voy.* III. v. 341 The mast itself is supported.. by the shrowd..and by two stays. **1750** BLANCKLEY *Naval Expos.* s.v. *Cordage*, Stays are Cablelaid, but made with four Strands as Cables are with three, with an Addition of an Heart which goes through the Center of them. **1850** LONGF. *Build. Ship* 225 Each tall..mast is swung into its place; shrouds and stays holding it firm and fast! **1864** BOUTELL *Her. Hist. & Pop.* xvii. (ed. 3) 261 A Rudder sa., the tiller and stays or. **1877** BRYANT *Odyss.* v. 313 And, rigging her with cords, and ropes, and stays, Heaved her with levers into the great deep.

b. *transf.* (*a*) A guy or rope supporting a flag-staff, or a pole of any kind. (*b*) A supporting wire or cable on an aircraft.

a **1533** BERNERS *Huon* cxiii. 393 They..strake and cut asonder the cordys and stayes so that many tentis fell to the erth. **1642** H. BOND *Boatswain's Art* 2, 1 Maine Flag-staffe stay. *Ibid.* 7, 1 Lanniard of the fore Topmast stay. *Ibid.* 8, 1 Maine Topgallant mast Stay. **1875** KNIGHT *Dict. Mech.* 2317 *Stay*, a guy supporting the mast of a derrick, etc. **1876** PREECE & SIVEWRIGHT *Telegr.* 202 For this purpose stays and struts are employed. By a stay is meant whatever takes the pull or tension of the forces acting upon the pole. **1884** *Act 47 & 48 Vict.* c. 76 §20 A post, pole, standard, stay, strut, or other above ground contrivance for carrying, suspending or supporting a telegraph. **1892** *Pall Mall Gaz.* 8 Aug. 5/2 At an early hour the wire stays which supported one of the semaphores were cut preparatory to removing the post. **1894** O. CHANUTE *Progress in Flying Machines* 237 This main aeroplane..is trussed and stiffened in every direction by wire stays. **1908** H. G. WELLS *War in Air* x. 317 It had taken only an hour or so to substitute wing stays from the second flying machine and to replace the nuts he had himself removed. **1919** S. CAMM *Aeroplane Construction* xiii. 108 The various wires used in construction may be classified into four distinct types: the solid wire stay, the straining cord or cable used for stay wires, the extra flexible cable used for controls, and the swaged tie rods in plane or streamline form.

2. Nautical phrases.

a. †*at stays* (obs.), *on, upon* (*the*) *stays* = ABACKSTAYS. *in stays*: said of a ship when her head is being turned to windward for the purpose of tacking.

a **1586** SIDNEY *Arcadia* I. i. (1912) 11 And now they were alreadie come upon the staies; when [etc.]. *c* **1595** CAPT. WYATT *R. Dudley's Voy. W. Ind.* (Hakl. Soc.) 9 Our Generall, to the intent they might with more ease fett us up, caused great draggs to be hanged over borde, oftentimes comminge on the staies, of purpose for them. *a* **1599** J. LOCKE in Hakluyt *Voy.* II. I. 106 And all this while the shippe lay on staies. **1606** *Adm. Ct. Exam.* 38, 1 Apr., Fell on his stayes and cast about. **1626** CAPT. SMITH *Accid. Yng. Seamen* 29 Ware yawning, the ships at stayes, at backestayes. *a* **1642** SIR W. MONSON *Naval Tracts* II. (1704) 253/2 There are so few Sailors to tackle their Ships, that they will be taken upon the Stays. **1706** PHILLIPS (ed. Kersey) s.v. *Stay*, *To bring a Ship upon the Stays* or *To stay her*, is to manage her Tackle and sails so that she cannot make any way forward. **1823** W. SCORESBY *Jrnl.* 91 With the aid of a few observations taken 'in stays' the remaining twelve points were likewise determined. **1797** S. JAMES *Narr. Voy.* 31 The ship being put in stays before the sail was half furled, the wind blew the body of the sail with great force flat against the Crosstrees. **1830** MARRYAT *King's Own* xvi, As he was in stays, a raking shot entered the cabin windows. **1846** A. YOUNG *Naut. Dict.* 296 A vessel in the act of tacking is said to be in stays, or to be hove in stays: if she work slowly in tacking, she is said to be slack in stays. **1861** *Times* 16 Aug., Christabel was sailed the freeest,..and was remarkably quick in stays.

b. *to miss, lose stays*: of a ship, to fail in the attempt to go about.

1758 *Ann. Reg.* 83 The Invincible..of 74 guns,..missed her stays, and run upon a flat. **1770** *Ibid.* 166 The pilot-boat ..losing her stays, was driven upon Hoyle's Bank. **1847** LEVER *Knt. Gwynne* lxxiv, In a last endeavour to clear the head-lands of Clare, she missed stays. **1873** G. C. DAVIES *Mount. & Mere* xvi. 142 Hesitating a little in his management of the helm, the yacht missed stays.

c. (*at*) *a long, short stay* (*stay apeak, stay-peak*): see quots.

1846 A. YOUNG *Naut. Dict.* 16 The anchor is a-stay when, in heaving it, the cable forms an acute angle with the water's edge. This is called a long stay-peak or a short stay-peak according as the anchor is farther from or nearer to the ship. **1862** *Catal. Internat. Exhib.* II. XII. 25 Elasticity of form, which enables it to sustain sudden strains or jerks at short stay-peak. **1867** SMYTH *Sailor's Word-bk.* 46 A ship drawn directly over the anchor is *apeek*; when the fore-stay and cable form a line, it is *short stay apeek*; when in a line with the main-stay, *long stay apeek*. **1875** BEDFORD *Sailor's Pocket Bk.* vi. (ed. 2) 223 In being towed by a vessel, if alongside, contrive to have the rope from as far forward as possible, so as to avoid riding at a short stay. **1882** NARES *Seamanship* (ed. 6) 198 Heave in to a short stay (when the amount of cable out is a little more than the depth of water).

3. *Comb.*, **stay-block**, a block buried in the ground as an attachment for the stay of a telegraph pole; **stay-hole** (see quot.); **stay-light**, a riding light (*Cent. Dict.* 1891); †**stay-nail**, a nail for securing a stay; **stay-peak** (see 2c); **stay-rope**, = sense 1; **stay-tackle** (see quot. 1815); **stay-wire**, (*a*) a wire forming part of a stay for a telegraph pole; (*b*) a supporting wire on an aircraft. Also STAY-SAIL.

1876 PREECE & SIVEWRIGHT *Telegr.* 204 The hole for the *stay-block should be under-cut in the manner shown in fig. 119. **1794** *Rigging & Seamanship* I. 89 **Stay-holes.* Holes made through staysails, at certain distances along the hoist, through which they are seized to the hanks on the stay. **1875** KNIGHT *Dict. Mech.*, Stay-hole. **1296** *MS. Acc. Exch. K.R.* 5/20 m. 4b, In vna petra ferri yspannie ad *staynayl faciendum iiij.d. *c* **1515** *Cocke Lorell's B.* 12 Some the *stay rope suerly byndes. **1815** *Falconer's Dict. Marine* (ed. Burney) **Stay-Tackle*, a large tackle, attached by means of a pendant to the main stay. It is used to hoist heavy bodies ..in and out of the ship or out of the holds. **1836** MARRYAT *Pirate* xiii, Their yards and stay-tackles are up, all ready for hoisting out the long-boat. **1876** PREECE & SIVEWRIGHT *Telegr.* 206 The *stay-wires should be at least three inches distant from the line wire nearest to them. **1919** [see sense 1 b above]. **1969** K. MUNSON *Pioneer Aircraft 1903–14* 9 The superposed horizontal surfaces, A, formed by stretching cloth upon frames of wood and wire, constitute the 'wings' or supporting part of the apparatus. They are connected to each other through hinge-joints by upright standards and lateral stay-wires.

stay (steɪ), *sb.*[2] Also 6 **staigh(e**, **stey(e**, 6–7 **staie**, **staye**, 8 *pl.* **steas**. [Prob. f. STAY *v.*[2]; but in sense 1 perh. in part ad. OF. *estaye* fem. (mod.F. *étai* masc.), vbl. noun f. *estayer* STAY *v.*[2]

The early mod. Flemish *staede*, *staeye*, 'fulcrum, sustentaculum, columen' (only in Kilian), which is usually given as the source of the Fr. words, is prob. ad. OF. *estaye*, the spelling *staede* being due to false etymology.]

1. a. Something that supports or steadies something else; esp. an appliance for holding up or securing in position some part of a structure; a prop, pedestal, buttress, bracket, or the like. † Also (*rarely*), something to lay hold upon.

c **1515** in Willis & Clark *Cambridge* (1886) I. 484 Glewe nayles broddes and Stayes. *c* **1535** in Gutch *Coll. Cur.* I. 205 Item for two stays for the vane of the said griffin. **1541** COPLAND *Guydon's Quest. Cyrurg.* O j, Take a lytell candell of waxe and gyue it a lytel stey belowe that it may holde ryght upon the flesshe. **1544** BETHAM *Precepts War* I. cxiv. F vj b, Longe berdes and longe heere,..in battayle be troublesome... For they be good stayes, to holde a man hard and fast. Wherfore it shalbe good to clap them shorte. **1573** BARET *Alv.* B. 1004 A Bragget or staie cut out of stone or timber in building to beare vp the sommer or other part, ..*mutulus*. **1576** GASCOIGNE *Philomene* Wks. 1910 II. 204 At last: my staffe (which was mine onely stay) Did slippe. **1602** *Churchw. Acc. Pittington* (Surtees) 51 Item given to John Scotte for settinge a stay to the Steple. *c* **1610** *Women Saints* 115 Withoute pillow or any like supporting staye. **1617** MORYSON *Itin.* III. 166 Their said shirt bands..hung upon their shoulders, notwithstanding they had staies to beare them up. *a* **1618** *Rates of Merchandizes* E 4, Deskes or staies for bookes the dozen, ij. s. **1658** A. FOX *Wurtz' Surg.* II. xxv. 164 Let not his Heel [in leg fracture] be without a stay and rest. **1680** MOXON *Mech. Exerc.* xi. 201 So that a Tool held steddy on any part of the Stay..will describe and cut a Screw. *c* **1680** BEVERIDGE *Serm.* (1729) II. 49 An anchor that is fixed in firm ground, is reckon'd a sure stay for the ship in all weathers. **1713** DERHAM *Phys.-Theol.* VI. ii. 360 A Part of the Cerebell is on each side fenced with the *Os petrosum*; so that by this double Stay, its whole Mass is firmly contained within the Skull. **1827** FARADAY *Chem. Manip.* xiv. (1842) 309 It will be proper to introduce a stay or two, pieces of black lead tube, for instance, as supporters to the lute. **1834–6** BARLOW in *Encycl. Metrop.* (1845) VIII. 105/2 Face wheels..have sometimes stays or braces proceeding from the back of the rim to some distance along the shaft. **1836** THIRLWALL *Greece* xvi. II. 361 The scarcity became such that they were driven to boil and eat the leathern stays of their bedding. **1842** GWILT *Archit.* Gloss., *Stay*, a piece performing the office of a brace, to prevent the swerving of the piece to which it is applied. **1886** C. E. PASCOE *Lond. T-day* xxxiv. (ed. 3) 310 A tree..propped up by iron stays.

b. *fig.* A thing or a person that affords support; an object of reliance.

Exceedingly common in the second half of the 16th century. In modern use the word, though not uncommon even colloquially, has often a suggestion of archaism.

a **1542** WYATT *Ps.* cxxx. 24 Thi holly word off eterne excellence thi mercys promesse..have bene my stay my piller & pretence. **1553** *Respublica* 457 What marvaile then yf I, wanting a perfecte staigh From mooste flourishing welth bee falen in decaye? **1560** BIBLE (Geneva) *2 Sam.* xxii. 19 The Lord was my stay. *Ibid.*, *Isa.* iii. 1 For lo, the Lord God of hostes wil take away from Ierusalem and from Iudah the stay and the strength: euen all the stay of bread, and all the stay of water. **1563** *Homilies* II. xviii. *Matrimony* X xxxiv, For there is no stronger defence and staye in all our lyfe, then is prayer. **1583** STUBBES *Anat. Abus.* II. (1882) 27 Commons and moores which were woont to be the onely staie of the poore. **1641** J. JACKSON *True Evang. T.* III. 190 Surely that is a very aery soule, whose chiefe rest and stay is not his Religion. **1719** DE FOE *Crusoe* (1840) II. i. 7 She was ..the stay of all my affairs. **1802** WORDSW. *Resolution & Indep.* 139 'God', said I, 'be my help and stay secure'. **1821** SCOTT *Kenilw.* viii, His daughter, who should be the stay of his age. **1836** T. KELLY *Hymn*, '*Speed thy Servants*' ii, As their stay thy promise taking. **1849** C. BRONTE *Shirley* xii, She was still such a stay, such a counsellor. **1861** READE *Cloister & H.* iv. (1896) 21 From that hour Gerard was looked upon as the stay of the family. **1884** *Congregational Year Bk.* 70 Make a legal statute the stay of religion, and you repeal religion. **1885** 'MRS. ALEXANDER' *At Bay* vii, His finery, however, was no stay to his self-esteem, for his..face had an uneasy, crestfallen expression. **1909** *Expositor* Jan. 55 The Temple was in his experience the centre and stay of Hebrew worship.

c. In abstract sense: Support. Also, †reliance. †*to make stay upon*: to rely on.

c **1530** COX *Rhet.* (1899) 77 That what maketh for the accuser, euermore the contrary is sure staye for the defender. **1542** UDALL *Erasm. Apoph.* Erasm. Pref., Wee putte not our whole trust and staigh in thynges external. **1561** HOLLYBUSH *Hom. Apoth.* 44b, Let him walke..wyth the staye of other. **1593** CHURCHYARD *Shore's Wife* liv, When weake Shore's wife had lost her staffe of stay. **1615** CHAPMAN *Odyss.* IV. 171 She tooke her State-chaire; and a foot-stooles stay Had for her feete. **1618** in Foster *Eng. Factories India* (1906) 7, I am very glad of your stay and allowance. **1648** W. MOUNTAGU in *Buccleuch MSS.* (Hist. MSS. Comm.) I. 309 The sad news of my mother's death is to me a very great affliction, that had so great a stay by her. **1651** C. CARTWRIGHT *Cert. Relig.* II. 44 The Popes not erring was but an opinion of policy, and not of Theologie; to give stay to the Laity. **1682** BUNYAN *Holy War* (1905) 324 But for that you must wholly and solely have recourse to, and make stay upon his Doctrine, that is your teacher after the first order. **1866** SEELEY *Ecce Homo* ii. (ed. 8) 11 We see the good man..deprived of the stay of all precedent or example.

2. *spec.* **a.** A support for a climbing plant. ?*Obs.*

1577 GOOGE *Heresbach's Husb.* I. (1586) 33 This amongest all other Pulse groweth in height without any stay. **1601** HOLLAND *Pliny* XVII. xxiii. I. 538 If a Vine bee to climbe trees that are of any great height, there would bee staies and appuies set to it, whereupon it may take hold. *a* **1682** SIR T. BROWNE *Tracts* i. (1683) 33 In many places out of Italy Vines do grow without any stay or support. **1697** DRYDEN *Virg. Past.* III. 16 When I..Cut Micon's tender Vines, and stole the Stays. **1705** ADDISON *Italy*, *Brescia* 60 The Trees themselves serve, at the same time, as so many Stays for their Vines.

†**b.** The arm or back of a chair. *Obs.*

1560 BIBLE (Geneva) *1 Kings* x. 19 There were stayes on ether side on the place of the throne. **1656** W. DU GARD tr. *Comenius' Gate Lat. unl.* §470. 135 For the more commodious sitting are stools and chairs, with staies [*cum fulcris*].

†**c.** = *stay-bar* (see 5b (*b*)). *Obs.*

1669 in Willis & Clark *Cambridge* (1886) II. 558 There shalbe..iron Stayes for all the said casements.

†**d.** One of the strings holding up the brim of a shovel-hat. Also a cap-string passing under the chin. *Obs.*

With regard to the sense in quot. 1601 cf. Cooper 1565: '*Spira*,..a bande or lace aboute a cappe, or hatte.'

1601 HOLLAND *Pliny* XXXIII. iii. II. 462 But say that women may be allowed to weare as much gold as they will, ..in carkanets about their necks, in earings pendant at their ears, in staies, wreaths, & chinbands [L. *collo, auribus, spiris*]. **1720** SWIFT *Right of Preced. betw. Physicians &*

Civilians 21, I know no Reason..that a White Wig should lower to hoary Hair, or a brush'd Beaver strike to a Carolina-Hat with Stays. **1775** R. CHANDLER *Trav. Greece* (1825) II. 156 The head-dress is a skull-cap, red or green, with pearls; a stay under the chin.

e. *Weaving.* = THRUM *sb.* 1.

1697 DRYDEN *Virg. Georg.* I. 381 Then, Weavers, stretch your Stays upon the Weft [orig. *licia telæ addere*].

f. A transverse piece in a link of a chain.

1831 J. HOLLAND *Manuf. Metal* I. 185 Any advantage supposed to be derived from stays or bars inserted in the direction of the shorter axis of the link. **1859** F. A. GRIFFITHS *Artil. Man.* (1862) 310 The stay across the link of a chain increases its strength about one-sixth.

†**g.** A maulstick. *Obs.*

1672 [see MAULSTICK].

h. In various applications: see quots.

1841 W. TEMPLETON *Locomot. Engine* 13 The stays..are generally of ⅞ths round copper,..being for the purpose of rendering the flat surfaces of the fire box capable of withstanding the force of the steam. **1860** *Engl. & For. Mining Gloss.* (ed. 2) 44 *Stays*, pieces of wood to secure the pumps in the engine-shaft. **1867** SMYTH *Sailor's Word-bk.*, *Stay of a steamer*, an iron bar between the two knees which secure the paddle-beams. **1871** WIGRAM *Change-Ringing* 2 From the top of the stock there rises a strong, upright piece of wood, or sometimes of iron, called the 'stay'; and immediately below the bell's mouth, fixed to the frame, is the 'slider', or sliding-rest..by which the stay is caught when the bell is thrown mouth uppermost. **1875** KNIGHT *Dict. Mech.* 2317 *Stay* (steam), *a.* a rod, bar, bolt, or gusset in a boiler, to hold two parts together against the pressure of steam...*b.* sling-rods (sling-stays) connecting the locomotive boiler to its frame. *c.* Rods beneath the boiler supporting the inside bearings of the crank-axle of an English locomotive.

i. ? A gate-post. ? *dial.*

1869 BLACKMORE *Lorna D.* ii, I leaned back on the stay of the gate.

3. a. *pl.* (Also ***a pair of stays.***) A laced underbodice, stiffened by the insertion of strips of whale-bone (sometimes of metal or wood) worn by women (sometimes by men) to give shape and support to the figure: = CORSET 2.

The use of the plural is due to the fact that stays were originally (as they still are usually) made in two pieces laced together.

1608 MIDDLETON *Trick to catch Old One* I. i. 50 Stay (a thing few women can do..therefore they had need wear stays). **1682** *Lond. Gaz.* No. 1762/4 A pair of hair-coloured Sattin Stays. **1697** VANBRUGH *Prov. Wife* II. i, With nothing on but her Stays, and her under scanty quilted Petticoat. **1706–7** FARQUHAR *Beaux' Strat.* III. i, Come unlace your Steas. **1713** GAY *Poems, Araminta* 18 The rich Stays her Taper Shape confine. **1831** *Ann. Reg., Chron.* 26 Apr. 67/1 The Jury..returned a verdict, 'that the deceased died of apoplexy, produced by her stays being too tightly laced.' **1843** MRS. CARLYLE *Lett.* I. 231 Her improved appearance in a pair of stays and a gown. **1846** FAIRHOLT *Costume* 267 The men's custom of sometimes wearing stays. **1848** DICKENS *Dombey* iii, Susan..had suddenly become so very upright that she seemed to have put an additional bone in her stays. **1867** J. HATTON *Tallants* iv, His enemies said he wore stays and slept in gloves. **1885** *Truth* 28 May 850/2 The stays..displace the bust, pushing the bosom up almost to the neck.

in figurative context. **1824** BYRON *Juan* XV. lxxxv, But Virtue's self, with all her tightest laces, Has not the natural stays of strict old age. **1826** SCOTT *Jrnl.* 28 Oct., Beauvais is called the *Pucelle*, yet..she wears no stays—I mean, has no fortifications. **1842** TENNYSON *Talking Oak* 60 The slight she-slips of loyal blood,..Strait-laced, but all-too-full in bud For puritanic stays.

b. *sing. rare.*

1731 *Gentl. Mag.* I. 289 The stay he has an invincible aversion to, as giving a stiffness that is void of all grace. **1795** WOLCOT (P. Pindar) *Pindariana* Wks. 1812 IV. 188 Long, very long, was Mistress Dinah's waist; The stiff stay high before. **1848** THACKERAY *Van. Fair* iii, He had tried, in order to give himself a waist, every girth, stay, and waistband then invented. **1871** *Figure Training* 97 My figure when unlaced would scarcely betray the fact that I had ever worn a stay.

†**c.** (See quot.) *Obs.*

1688 HOLME *Armoury* III. 94/1 In a Womans Gown there are..the Stayes, which is the body of the Gown before the Sleeves are put too, or covered with the outward stuff.

†**4.** ? A bag for applying a poultice. *Obs.*

1685 J. COOKE *Marrow Chirurg.* VI. §2. ix. (ed. 4) 215 As for the Throat, a Saffron-Stay, or a *Millipedes* sowed up in a Stay, which is reputed excellent. **1728** E. SMITH *Compl. Housew.* (ed. 2) 249 A Stay to prevent a sore Throat... Take Rue,..mix it with Honey [etc.]..sew it up in a Linen Stay, and apply it.

5. *attrib.* and *Comb.* **a.** Obvious combinations, as (sense 3) ***stay-binding, -busk, -cord, -maker, -making, -stitcher, -wearer, -worker.***

1882 CAULFEILD & SAWARD *Dict. Needlework* 460 **Stay Bindings*..are of twilled cotton, and may be had in white, grey, drab,..and buff colour. **1858** SIMMONDS *Dict. Trade*, **Stay-busk*, a stiff piece of wood, steel, or whalebone for the front support of a woman's stays. **1882** CAULFEILD & SAWARD *Dict. Needlework* 460 **Stay Cord*..is to be had made of cotton and of linen, for the purpose of lacing stays. **1730** BERKELEY *Let.* Wks. 1871 IV. 172 One of Mrs. Van Homrigh's creditors (I think a *stay-maker) was in France. **1791** BOSWELL *Johnson* an. 1737, At the house of Mr. Norris, a staymaker. **1864** D. ALLAN *Hist. Sk. Kirriemuir* 15 He also wove cloth for staymakers. **1843** DICKENS *Let.* 2 Nov. (1974) III. 589 Trades... I think of..*stay-making [etc.]. **1888** *Pall Mall Gaz.* 4 June 10/1 The parties conducted a large stay-making and ladies' underclothing business. **1723** *Lond. Gaz.* No. 6192/9 Elizabeth Beker,..*Stay-stitcher. **1871** *Figure-Training* 51 As a *stay-wearer of a quarter of a century, you will, perhaps, allow me to [etc.]. **1879** *St. George's Hosp. Rep.* IX. 141 *Stay-worker.

b. Special comb.: **stay-band** *Sc.*, an iron rod serving to keep one leaf of a folding door in position; **stay-bar,** (*a*) *Arch.* (see quot. 1836); (*b*) a bar for keeping a casement window open at a certain angle; (*c*) = *stay-rod*; †**stay-bobbin,** cord used for lacing stays; **stay-bolt,** a bolt connecting plates of a boiler, to secure them against internal pressure; **stay braid,** a kind of braid used in ornamenting stays (1775 in Ash); **stay-end** (see quot.); **stay-goods,** the materials of which stays are made (Ash); **stayhold** *nonce-word*, a firm foothold; **stay-hook,** (see quot. 1860); **stay-irons,** (*a*) (see quot. 1833); (*b*) (see quot. 1876); **stay-rod,** a rod serving to give support, or to connect two parts of a machine or structure to prevent displacement; **stay-slot** *Sc.*, a diagonal bar of a hurdle; **stay-tube,** in a multitubular boiler, each of a number of tubes that are made stronger than the rest, and fitted with nuts so as to serve as stays between the tube-plate and the front of the boiler; **stayword** *rare*, a saying or maxim that gives support.

1844 H. STEPHENS *Bk. Farm* I. 199 The upper-barn door, of two vertical leaves, requires an iron *stay-band to fasten it with. **1399** *MS. Acc. Exch. K.R.* 473/11 m. 2, .j. *staybarre .v. transonbarrez. **1503–4** *Rec. St. Mary at Hill* (1905) 252 Payd for a stay bar of yerryn to stay the Nev pevys [= pews] in to þe vavtt. **1532–3** in E. Law *Hampton Crt. Pal.* (1885) 348 Payd to John à Guylders, smythe, for 170 lockketts, 25 staybarres. **1836** PARKER *Gloss. Archit.* (1850) I. 445 *Stay bar*: the horizontal iron bar which extends in one piece along the top of the mullions of a traceried window. **1839** *Civil Engin. & Arch. Jrnl.* II. 361/1 One of the most universally useful of these is a window fastening, or staybar. **1846** [see *stay-rod*]. **1775** ASH, **Stay-bobbin*, a kind of bobbin used for stays. **1839** R. S. ROBINSON *Naut. Steam Eng.* 118 Strong *stay bolts, rivetted at each end, secure the flues to each other, and to the sides of the boiler. **1759** *Newport* (Rhode I.) *Mercury* 26 June 4/3 To be sold by Jacob Richardson,..Stay Braid and Cord. **1884** KNIGHT *Dict. Mech.* Suppl., **Stay end*, the end of a back-stay in a carriage. Stay-ends are sold separately as pieces of carriage hardware. **1851** SIR F. PALGRAVE *Norm. & Eng.* I. 619 He was sliding down a precipice seeming to offer some narrow ridge giving *stayhold to his feet. **1743** *Boston Gaz.* in *Alice M. Earle's Costume Col. Times* (1894) 240 Silver'd *Stayhooks. **1771** SMOLLETT *Humphry Cl.* 21 Apr. (1815) 29 She pretended she was cheapening a stay-hook. **1860** FAIRHOLT *Costume* (ed. 2) 591 *Stay-hook*, a small hook stuck in front of the boddice for hanging a watch or etui upon. **1833** LOUDON *Encycl. Archit.* §84 Cast-iron casements, made to open with strong hinges, latches and spring *stay-irons (irons to keep the window open). **1876** VOYLE & STEVENSON *Milit. Dict.* 402/1 *Stay-irons*, in artillery carriages, the iron rods which connect the ends of the axle-bed to the splinter-bar. **1844** H. STEPHENS *Bk. Farm* II. 542 Two iron *stay-rods pass from the end frames to the shafts as an additional support to the latter. **1846** A. YOUNG *Naut. Dict.* 310 Each engine has two of these frames, the whole supported by strong malleable iron stay-bars or stay-rods. *a* **1844** MAIN in *H. Stephens' Bk. Farm* II. 70 The 2 *stay-slots are cut with a bend at the bottom, and rather sharply pointed. **1887** *Encycl. Brit.* XXII. 499/1 (*Steam-Engine*), There are 127 tubes at each end, 46 of which are *stay-tubes. **1897** *Westm. Gaz.* 16 June 10/1 The Prince of Wales naturally finds in the motto of his crest a *stayword.

stay (steɪ), *sb.*³ Also 6 stey, staie, staye. [f. STAY *v.*¹]

1. The action of stopping or bringing to a stand or pause; the fact of being brought to a stand or delayed; a stoppage, arrest, or suspension of action; a check, set-back.

1537 HEN. VIII in *St. Papers* (1834) II. Sithens the first stey of the violence of the late rebellion of the said Thomas Fytzgarald. **1550** CROWLEY *Last Trumpet* 283 As men that woulde never fynde stay, Tyll all the earth were in theyr hand. **1551** ROBINSON tr. *More's Utopia* II. vi. (1895) 214 In lesse than iii yeres space their was nothing in the Grek tonge that they lackede. They were able to reade good authors wythout anny staye [L. *inoffense*]. **1594** SPENSER *Epithal.* 250 Poure out the wine without restraint or stay. **1594** KYD *Cornelia* II. 351 Fraile men..Had neuer power to practise stayes Of this celestiall influence. **1625** BACON *Ess., Vicissitude* (Arb.) 572 As farre, as the Weaknesse of Humane Iudgement, can giue stay to so great Reuolutions. **1628** DIGBY *Voy. Mediterr.* (Camden) 2 To protect the skipper from a like stay againe if he should meete with other men of warre in his iorney to London. **1640** in Rushworth *Hist. Coll.* III. (1692) I. 164 That there be a stay of committing any waste in the felling of any Wood. **1810** SCOTT *Lady of L.* V. xxi, Whose fiery steeds ill brooked the stay Of the steep street and crowded way. **1842** MACAULAY *Horatius* lxiii, But for this stay, ere close of day We should have sacked the town. **1862** BORROW *Wild Wales* III. 99 A conqueror who no stay will brook. **1886** *Pall Mall Gaz.* 9 Sept. 12/1 It is hard to see what decent case Mr. Parnell will be able to make out for that stay upon the right of eviction which forms a provision of his bill. **1898** *Daily News* 22 Sept. 4/5 Our Special Correspondent suggests as a practicable minimum the stay of armaments for five years.

b. *Law.* Suspension of a judicial proceeding.

1542 in *Vicary's Anat.* (1888) App. III. i. 125 The Wardeyns of the Surgeons..to be here the next Court day..for the Stey of theyr sute in the Escheker. *c* **1590** *Sir T. More* (Malone Soc.) 603 Some of the Benche Sir, think it very fit that stay be made, and giue it out abroade the execution is deferd till morning. **1617** EARL OF WORCESTER in *Buccleuch MSS.* (Hist. MSS. Comm.) I. 208 There was a letter..for the stay of a suit depending in the Chancery. **1621** ELSING *Debates Ho. Lords* (Camden) 31 Whether Yelverton made a stay of the last patent, and the reason why he past yt? **1743** KAMES *Decis. Crt. Sess. 1730–52* (1799) 67 This..makes it necessary for the charger to get the stay to his diligence removed. **1752** J. LOUTHIAN *Form of Process* (ed. 2) 214 And then asks her, What she can say for herself in stay of Execution. **1769** BLACKSTONE *Comm.* IV. viii. 115 To obtain any stay of proceedings, other than by arrest of judgment or writ of error,..is likewise a *praemunire*. **1856** *Ann. Reg., Chron.* 65/2 The prisoner's counsel then moved for a stay of execution. **1875** MAINE *Hist. Instit.* x. 281 The Distress when seized was in certain cases liable to a Stay.

†**c.** ***to make stay of***: to put a stop to (an action); to arrest (a person); to intercept (goods, etc.) in transit; to stop the circulation of (a book).

1572 in *13th Rep. Hist. MSS. Comm.* App. IV. 12 To make staie of suche frebutters, rovers and men of warre with their shipes and boates. **1586** F. GREVIL *Let.* in Arber *Garner* I. 488, I think fit there be made stay of that mercenary book. **1633** T. STAFFORD *Pac. Hib.* I. xxi. 119 Whereupon hee wrote unto the Lord Deputie this ensuing Letter, making stay of the Lord Awdley untill he should receiue answer thereof. **1642** *Declar. Lds. & Comm. conc. Necess. Kingd.* 7 Jan. 3 Stay is made of their Cole-ships. **1647** MAY *Hist. Parlt.* II. iv. 73 They should take special care to make stay of all Arms and Ammunition carrying towards York. **1648** HEYLIN *Relat. & Observ.* I. 121 Major Generall Lambert had made stay of a Scotish Gentleman. **1654** E. JOHNSON *Wonder-working Provid.* 12 He will ease you of your burden by making stay of any farther resort unto you.

†**d.** *concr.* An appliance for stopping. *Obs.*

1523–34 FITZHERB. *Husb.* §3 The plough-fote..is a staye to order of what depenes the ploughe shall go.

†**2.** Control; restraint; self-control. *Obs.*

1556 J. HEYWOOD *Spider & F.* xiii. 15 Stey in him selfe he toke. **1561** NORTON & SACKV. *Gorboduc* I. ii. 307 That they, restreyned by the awe of you, May liue in compasse of well tempred staye. **1596** DANETT tr. *Comines* (1614) 218 Yet was it much that hee had such stay of himselfe. **1622** BACON *Hen. VII*, 14 Well shewing and fore-tokening the wisdome, stay, and moderation of the Kings spirit of Gouernment.

3. A coming to a stand; a cessation of progress or action; a stop, pause, halt. Phr. ***to make*** (***a***) ***stay.***

c **1530** *Jyl of Brentford's Test.* (1871) 14 Now hold your hand, and make a stay there. **1585** T. WASHINGTON tr. *Nicholay's Voy.* III. viii. 82 b, Trauailing both day and night without any rest or stay. **1586** *Let. to Earl Leycester* 6 She might by the stay thereof, procure the heauie displeasure of Almightie God. **1590** SHAKS. *Mids. N.* V. i. 428 Trip away, make no stay. **1598** FLORIO, *Falchi*, are staies when a horse doth rest vpon his hinder parts. **1609** HOLLAND *Amm. Marcell.* 262 Among whome there was now no hoe nor stay at all of their hands. **1609** BIBLE (Douay) *Josh.* x. 12 *marg.*, Josue did thinke if the moone moued the sunne also must necessarily moue so he obtained the stay of both. **1616** R. C. *Times' Whistle* (1871) 76 Yet fond man Runnes in this gulfe of sinne without all stay. **1633** G. HERBERT *Temple, Pulley* ii, When almost all was out, God made a stay. *a* **1637** SPOTTISWOODE *Hist. Ch. Scot.* (1851) II. 62 It was night before they came thither..because of the stays she made by the way. **1641** J. TAYLOR (Water P.) *Last Voy.* A 6, With many stops, stayes, and taking leaves, wee gat to Oatlands at night. *a* **1648** LD. HERBERT *Hen. VIII* (1683) 43 At last he commands a stay. **1659** HAMMOND *On Psalms* cx. 7. 566 Souldiers..that are thirsty, but will not make stay at an Inne. *a* **1721** PRIOR *Epigr. Bp. Atterbury* i, Without stop or stay,..make the best of your way. **1805** WORDSW. *Waggoner* I. 36 And up the craggy hill ascending Many a stop and stay he makes. **1843** RUSKIN *Mod. Painters* I. II. III. i. §8 We can plunge far and farther, and without stay or end, into the profundity of space.

†**b.** A cessation of hostility or dissension. Also, a means of reconciliation. *Obs.*

1563 *Homilies* II. xii *Nativity* A aaa j, A Messias, or mediatour,..whiche shoulde make intercession, and put him selfe as a staye betwene both partes, to pacifie the wrath and indignation conceaued agaynst sinne, and [etc.]. **1599** SANDYS *Europæ Spec.* (1632) 172 If any stay or agreement could bee taken with the Turke, all Germany were in daunger to bee in uprore within it selfe by intestine dissention.

†**c.** *Astr.* ***stay of the sun*** = SOLSTICE. *Obs.*

1538 ELYOT *Dict.*, *Solstitium*, the stay of the sonne, whan he can not be eyther hygher or lower. **1555** EDEN *Decades* I. II. (Arb.) 72 In no place towarde the stay of the sonne (cauled *Solsticium*) can the night be equall with the day.

†**d.** *Mus.* = PAUSE *sb.* 3 b. *Obs.*

1667 C. SIMPSON *Compend. Pract. Mus.* 25 This Mark or Arch 𝄐..is also set..over certain particular Notes in the middle of Songs, when (for humour) we are to insist or stay a little upon the said Notes; and thereupon it is called a *Stay*, or *Hold*.

†**e.** A stop, sign in punctuation; the pause indicated by a stop. *Obs.*

1596 COOTE *Engl. School-m.* v. (1627) 26 Those which we do call points or stayes in writing, as this marke (,)..noteth a small stay; two pricks thus (:) makes a longer stay; and one prick thus (·) is put for a ful stay.

†**4.** Delay, postponement, waiting. ***to make stay of***: to withhold for a time; to postpone. *Obs.*

1530 CROMWELL in Merriman *Life & Lett.* (1902) I. 329 Your chauncelour shall do the semblable in another request made by his Maiestie unto him without staye tract or further stycking. **1586** A. DAY *Eng. Secretary* I. (1625) 103 If it shall notwithstanding seeme further convenient unto your L. to make stay of his acceptance. *a* **1592** GREENE *Jas. IV*, IV. v. 1998, I like no stay; go write, and I will signe. **1599** B. JONSON *Cynthia's Rev.* v. iii [viii], Bounty forbids to paull our thankes with stay. **1605** CHAPMAN *All Fooles* v. i. H 4, Hast, for the matter will abide no staye. **1611** SIR P. BARTY in *Buccleuch MSS.* (Hist. MSS. Comm.) I. 103 To make stay of the money lately agreed to be paid. **1627** J. WARE in *Lett. Lit. Men* (Camden) 135, I have now, after almost a yeare's stay, returned unto you (by this bearer) the MS. Life of St. Modwen. **1633** T. STAFFORD *Pac. Hib.* I. viii. 56 Her cause of stay was, the danger of the way. **1650** S. CLARKE *Eccl. Hist.* I. (1654) 50 Peace will come, albeit there be a little stay for a while. **1671** MILTON *Samson* 1536 A little stay will bring some notice hither. **1707** MORTIMER *Husb.* 423 There is no Stock you can have Money in that will turn to better account, tho' you stay long for it; nor any thing that it can be better secured in, which I think will make amends for the Stay.

†**5.** A cause of stoppage; an obstacle, hindrance.

a **1533** BERNERS *Gold. Bk. M. Aurel.* (1546) T vij b, I shall not drede the staies of Fortune. **1548** UDALL *Erasm. Par. Matt.* iii 7–10 That mennes pronitie to naughtynes, beynge compassed in with these stayes, myght be refreyned from fallyng into farther inconuenyence. **1551** ROBINSON *More's Utopia* Ep. to P. Giles (1895) 3 Seynge all theyes cares, stayes and lettes were taken awaye. **1563** GOOGE *Eglogs*, etc. (Arb.) 119 Whom yf your Grace do not repuls and fynde some present staye, Vndoubtedly he wyll wyn this Realme and take vs all awaye. **1596** SPENSER *State Irel.* Wks. (Globe) 666 The presence of the Governour is..a great stay and bridle unto them that are ill disposed. **1598** R. BERNARD tr. *Terence, Andria* III. i, *In mora illi est*, Hee is a stay, hindrance, or let to him. **1631** GOUGE *God's Arrows* I. §20. 26 Good Iosiah was a stay of those judgements which God had threatned. **1633** G. HERBERT *Temple, Ch. Porch* iii, Not grudging, that thy lust hath bounds and staies. **1665** DRYDEN *Ind. Queen* IV. i, My Rage, like dam'd-up Streams swell'd by some stay, Shall from this Opposition get new force.

†**b.** A demur, hesitation, scruple. *Obs.*

1550 CROWLEY *Epigr.* 1254 We counte hym not wyse, That seketh not by all meanes that he canne devise To take offices togither wythoute any staye. **1566** FECKENHAM (*title*) The declaration of suche Scruples, and staies of Conscience, touchinge the Othe of the Supremacy. **1567** JEWEL *Def. Apol.* 72 If they be al Heretiques, and Schismatiques, and Despisers of Christe,..that make staie at it, or cannot receiue it, then [etc.].

6. The action or fact of staying or remaining in a place, continued presence; an instance of this, a period of temporary residence or continuance in a place, a sojourn.

1538 LONDON in Ellis *Orig. Lett.* Ser. III. III. 215 We went to every place of them, and toke suche a vew and stay among them as the tyme wolde permytt. **1577–87** HARRISON *England* II. v. (1877) I. 120 As a testimonie of his presence and staies from time to time as he did trauell. **1596** SHAKS. *Merch. V.* III. ii. 328 Till I come againe, No bed shall ere be guilty of my stay. *a* **1601** ? MARSTON *Pasquil & Kath.* I. 165 Daughter, lay your expresse commandement vpon the stay of Master Mamon. **1601** HOLLAND *Pliny* XXXI. iii. II. 408 Low grounds where there is a settling or stay of raine water fallen from higher places. **1619** in Foster *Eng. Factories India* (1906) 143 Having..lymited the commander 15 dayes stay there. **1635** in *Verney Mem.* (1907) I. 86, I do not intend to make a long stay there. **1664** D. FLEMING in *Extr. St. Papers rel. Friends* Ser. II. (1911) 191 The Trainband horse ..are to continue here dureing the Judges stay. **1667** MILTON *P.L.* IV. 898 Let him surer barr His Iron Gates, if he intends our stay In that dark durance. **1670** W. CLARKE *Nat. Hist. Nitre* 34 Lots Wife was only by looking Back, so small a stay, overtaken by this Artillery of Heaven. **1755** CHATHAM *Lett. to Nephew T. Pitt* xiii. (1805) 72, I have delayed writing to you in expectation of hearing farther from you upon the subject of your stay at college. **1789** MRS. PIOZZI *Journ. France* I. 17 Her stay in London was longer than mine in Paris. **1797** HT. LEE *Canterb. T., Old Woman's T.* (1799) I. 370 St. Aubert..strenuously urged his stay. **1845** BUDD *Dis. Liver* 270 Because the bile, during its stay in the bladder, becomes concentrated. **1878** BOSW. SMITH *Carthage* 108 As though their stay was not going to be a short one. **1884** CHURCH *Bacon* viii. 206 It was one of man's first duties to arrange for his stay on earth according to the real laws which he could find out if he only sought for them. **1897** *Westm. Gaz.* 1 Sept. 3/1 Every year has added to the stay of children at school.

†**b.** A place of sojourn; a fixed abode. *Obs.*

1566 DRANT *Hor. Sat.* I. v. D i b, As nowe I am, I coulde not wyshe almoste a better staye. *c* **1586** C'TESS PEMBROKE *Ps.* LXXX. iv, O God, retorne, and from thy starry stay Review this vyne. **1592** KYD *Sol. & Pers.* II. i. 266 Whether shall I go? If into any stay adioyning Rhodes, They will betray me. **1894** A. LAING *Misc. Poems* 108 (E.D.D.) If we sud hae nae ither stay Than hell beyond the tomb.

†**c.** Continuance in a state, duration. *Obs.*

1595 SPENSER *Col. Clout* 98 Record to vs that louely lay againe: The staie whereof shall nought these eares annoy. *c* **1600** SHAKS. *Sonn.* xv. 9 When I consider euery thing that growes Holds in perfection but a little moment:.. Then the conceit of this inconstant stay Sets you most rich in youth before my sight. *a* **1680** GLANVILL *Saddücismus* I. (1682) 122 For there can be no perception of the external Object, unless the Object that is to be perceived act with some stay upon that which perceiveth. **1700** DRYDEN *Cock & Fox* 675 Alas, what stay is there in human state.

d. Staying power; power of endurance; strength; power of resistance. Now somewhat *rare*.

1586 T. B. *La Primaud. Fr. Acad.* (1589) 49 Prudence, Magnanimitie, and Justice are ankers of greatest stay. **1590** SPENSER *F.Q.* IV. xi. 25 But Thame was stronger, and of better stay. **1890** SPURGEON in *Voice* (N.Y.) 21 Aug. 7/2 Some men are always great at beginnings; but they have no stay in them.

7. A stationary condition, a standstill; a state of neither advance nor retrogression. Chiefly in phrases, ***at*** or ***in a*** or ***one stay***, rarely ***at stay***.

Now somewhat *arch.*, chiefly in echoes of the Prayer-book phrase in quot. 1549.

1525 BERNERS *Froiss.* II. cxxxvi. [cxxxii.] 379 Then the duke stode in a staye, and toke counsayle what was beste to do. **1542** in *Tytler's Hist. Scot.* (1864) III. 6 *note*, This busyness..whiche, at this present, is at such a staye, that [etc.]. **1546** PHAER *Bk. Childr.* (1553) T vij b, The pulse is incertayn, and neuer at one stay. **1549** *Bk. Comm. Prayer, Burial of Dead*, Man that is borne of a woman..neuer continueth in one staye. **1553** BRENDE *Q. Curtius* II. 9 b, The king in yᵉ meane season stode at a staye. **1556** J. HEYWOOD *Spider & F.* ix. 36 Here stoode they both, a while in silent stay. **1560** GRESHAM in Burgon *Life* (1839) I. 292 So that now the Quene's Majestie's credit ys at a whole steye. **1579** FULKE *Heskins' Parl.* 159 Then is he at a staye, he can go no further. **1595** HUNNIS *Life & Death Joseph* 54 But Jacob yet amased was, and stood in doubtful stay. **1598** R. BERNARD tr. *Terence, Phormio* V. viii, I am brought to such a stay that I knowe not what to doe with him. **1600** SURFLET *Country Farm* VII. xviii. 830 [Oaks have] one hundred years to growe, one hundred to stande at a staie, and one hundred to decline and fall away. **1611** BIBLE *Lev.* xiii. 5 And beholde, if the plague in his sight be at a stay, and the plague spread not in the skinne, then [etc.]. **1681** W. ROBERTSON *Phraseol. Gen.* 1168/2, I am brought to that stay, that [etc.]. **1758** BINNELL *Descr. Thames* 181 A River Pike grows fast till he arrives at twenty-four..Inches in length; then he stands a little more at stay. **1851** MEREDITH *Love in Valley* ii, Swifter she seems in her stay than in her flight. **1875** MANNING *Mission Holy Ghost* iv. 106 We are never in one stay. **1876** BRIDGES *Growth of Love* xxvi, True only should the swift life stand at stay. **1880** FROUDE *Bunyan* ix. 151 In this world of change the point of view alters fast, and never continues in one stay.

†**b.** A permanent state or condition. Chiefly in phrase in ***good*** (***quiet***, etc.) ***stay***. *Obs.*

1536 in Furnivall *Ballads fr. MSS.* I. 311 Then they together xuld, or this tyme, a brought Inglond in-to a better stey then it is now. **1542** *Lam. & Piteous Treat.* in *Harl. Misc.* (1745) IV. 509/2 All Thynges beynge in good Ordre and Staye. **1544** BETHAM *Precepts War* I. civ. F iij, My counsayl is, to set all thynges in quyet staye, and brynge them [soldiers at variance] agayne to concorde. **1553** *Respublica* 735 Ye know it is no small weorke from so greate decaie..to sett all in good staighe. **1563–83** FOXE *A. & M.* 852/1 Moreouer..the world nowe was at another stay, then when the beleuers were all of one hart and soule. **1566** CHAMBRELAYNE in *Strype's Ann. Ref.* (1709) I. 489 Where he, with his Father and Mother,..had lately repaired unto him; and were in some good Stay. **1570** BUCHANAN *Chamæleon* Wks. (1892) 49 Be ye diligence and wisdom of ye regent the cuntre wes brocht to sum stay. **1575** *Gammer Gurton* I. i, Aske them what they ayle, or who brought them in this staye? **1580–3** GREENE *Mamillia* Wks. (Grosart) II. 207 Hath she not promised to chaunge..the state of a Curtizan into the staie of a matron. **1616** HEALEY tr. *Theophrastus* 90 The State is at an euill stay, where more then one the Scepter sway.

†**c.** ***to set in*** or ***at stay***: to reduce to order or quiet; to settle. Also ***to set a stay***, ***to set stays***: to settle matters. *Obs.*

1538 in *Lett. Suppress. Monasteries* (Camden) 193 But in all thes placys I have sett steys by indenturys making, and the common sealys sequestering, so that [etc.]. **1542** *Lam. & Piteous Treat.* in *Harl. Misc.* (1745) IV. 505/1 Themperour beyng in Allmeigney, to Thentent to appease and set a staye in the Controuersyes and Dyssencyons, which are amonge the Allmeignes in Matters of Religion. **1555** PHAER *Æneid* I. (1558) A ij b, But first is best the fluddes to set in staie [L. *sed motos praestat componere fluctus*]. **1561** NORTON & SACKV. *Gorboduc* III. i. 56 So shall you force Them to agree, and holde the lande in stay. **1568** GRAFTON *Chron.* II. 8 He would first set such a stay in his Duchy of Normandie, that [etc.]. **1575** CHURCHYARD *Chippes* (1817) 187 Such falshood raignde, and raged in the land... But by my friendes, I set these thinges in staye. **1615** *Liber Depos. Archd. Colch.* (MS.) 74 Finding him very weake and sicke, he asked him [the said Testator] whether he had sett things at a staye.

8. Combinations: **stay-law** *U.S.* a legislative enactment establishing a general moratorium; †**stay-liquor** *Salt-making*, sea-water left by the tide, exposed in feeding-ponds for partial evaporation; **stay-maker** *nonce-wd.*, one who makes a long stay; †**stay-rig** *Sc.* (see quot.).

1880 T. M. COOLEY *Const. Law U.S.A.* 311 The withdrawal of the remedy for a time by *stay laws is an impairment of the obligation of contracts. **1682** J. COLLINS *Salt & Fishery* 19 This Liquor..is called *Stay-Liquor. **1897** W. C. HAZLITT *Four Generations* II. 145 Meadows was a desperate *staymaker. **1591** in *A. Maxwell's Hist. Old Dundee* (1884) 242 At the tails of all their rigs to make ane *stayrig upon the auld bounds of the said acres [*footn.* A cross ridge to stay the plough].

stay (steɪ), *v.*[1] Pa. t. and pa. pple. **stayed** (steɪd). Forms: 5 **steyyn**, 6 **stee**, **stai**, 6–7 **staye**, **staie**, **stey(e**, 7 **steaye**, 5– **stay**. *Pa. t. and pple.* 5–8 **stayd**, 6 *Sc.* **stayit**, **-et**, **steyit**, 6–7 **stayde**, **staied**, **staide**, 6–9 **staid**, 6– **stayed**. [Prob. a. OF. (*e*)*stai-*, (*e*)*stei-*, flexional stem of *ester* (:—L. *stāre*) to stand. Cf. the earlier RESTAY *v.*

In AF. the regular form of the pres. sing. indic. was *estais*, *estait*; an inf. **esteier*, **estaier* may have existed in colloquial use, but has not been found; the gerund *esteaunt* (three-syllables) occurs in *Boeve de Haumtone* (ed. Stimming) 2244. Eastern and North-eastern dialects of OF. have an inf. form *esteir*. Other North-eastern forms cited by Godefroy are *staieiz* (2 pl. pres.), *stairont* (3 pl. fut.).

The view adopted by Skeat, that the original sense was to support (see STAY *v.*[2]), and that from this the other senses were developed in the order 'to hold, retain, delay, abide', cannot be said to involve any abstract improbability, but the chronology of the appearance of the senses in English is strongly unfavourable to it.]

I. *intr.* * To cease moving, halt.

†**1.** To cease going forward; to stop, halt; to arrest one's course and stand still. *Obs.* (exc. as in b.)

c **1440** *Promp. Parv.* 473/1 Steyyn or steppyn of gate (*v.r.* stoppyn), *restito*, *obsto*. **1576** GASCOIGNE *Philomene* (Arb.) 90 She came apace, and stately did she stay. **1578** LYTE *Dodoens* III. xxxix. 372 Whosoeuer hath receiued of this seede [stavesacre], must walke without staying. **1594** SHAKS. *Rich. III*, I. ii. 33 Stay you that beare the Coarse, & set it down. **1601** HOLLAND *Pliny* viii. xl. I. 219 The dogges which be neere unto Nilus, lap of the riuer, running still and never stay while they are drinking, because they will give no vantage at all to be a prey unto the greedie Crocodiles. **1611** BIBLE *Josh.* x. 13 And the Sunne stood still, and the Moone stayed, vntill the people had auenged themselues vpon their enemies. **1640** tr. *Verdere's Rom. of Rom.* I. xxii. 96 Their Bark staying at an Island,..they went on shore. **1777** SIR W. JONES *Caissa* 135 With radiant feet he pierc'd the clouds nor stay'd Till in the woods he saw the beauteous maid.

b. To stop, halt, pause *and* (do somewhat), or in order *to* (do something). Now somewhat *rare*.

1577 HARRISON *England* III. iv. 103 in *Holinshed*, His gromes and gentlemen passed by it as disdaining to stoupe & take vp such a trifle: but he knowing yᵉ owner commaunded one of them to staye & take it vp. **1600** SHAKS. *A.Y.L.* II. i. 54 Anon a carelesse Heard..iumps along by him And neuer staies to greet him. **1750** GRAY *Long Story* 55 The Heroines..Rap'd at the door, nor stay'd to ask, But bounce into the parlour enter'd. **1794** MRS. RADCLIFFE *Myst. Udolpho* xxviii, Emily scarcely stayed to thank him for it. **1865** VISCT. MILTON & W. B. CHEADLE *N.-W. Passage by Land* viii. (1867) 120 When we stayed to camp, [we] shivered and shook as we essayed to light a fire.

2. To cease or desist from some specified activity. Const. *from*. *Obs.* or *arch.*

1576 FLEMING *Panopl. Epist.* 86 This is the purpose and meaning of them all, in generall: not to stay, till they haue procured the slaughter of Cæsar. **1590** SPENSER *F.Q.* I. vii. 15 He hearkned, and did stay from further harmes. **1611** BIBLE *2 Kings* xiii. 18 And he smote thrise, and stayed. **1611** B. JONSON *Catiline* I. i, He that, building, stayes at one Floore, or the second, hath erected none. **1654** Z. COKE *Logick* 77 In Etymologies we must not go on without End, but must stay in some that is first. **1864** AMELIA B. EDWARDS *Barbara's Hist.* lix, I wept, and could not stay from weeping.

†**b.** To cease speaking, break off one's discourse; to pause, stop or hesitate before speaking. Said also of a discourse. *Obs.*

1551 T. WILSON *Logic* II. K ij, Aesope coulde not vtter his minde at large, but dyd stammer, and staye muche in his speche. **1555** EDEN *Decades* (Arb.) 286 And here steyinge a whyle, he began to speake ageyne and sayde. **1571** GRINDAL *Injunct.* B iv b, Nor the Minister shall pawse or stay betweene the morning prayer, Letanie and Communion. **1600** *Chester Pl.* Proem 168 And after those ended, yet doth not the storie staye. **1665** HOOKE *Microgr.* 25, I cannot here stay..to examine the particular Reasons of it. **1671** MILTON *P.R.* IV. 485 So talk'd he, while the Son of God went on And staid not, but in brief him answer'd thus.

c. In *imper.* used as an injunction to pause, arrest one's course, not to go on doing something. Hence often = give me time to consider, decide, etc.; wait for me to make some remark or give some order.

1590 SHAKS. *Com. Err.* V. i. 364 Stay, stand apart, I know not which is which. **1598** —— *Merry W.* V. v. 84 But stay, I smell a man of middle earth. **1598** B. JONSON *Ev. Man in Hum.* (1601) L 4, *Cle.* Stay now let me see, oh signior Snowliuer I had almost forgotten him. **1749** FIELDING *Tom Jones* XIV. vii, If you knew my father, you would never think of obtaining his consent—Stay, there is one way. **1823** SCOTT *Quentin D.* xxxiii, And begone!—Yet stay. **1873** B. HARTE *Caldwell of Springfield* in *Fiddletown*, etc. 81 Nothing more did I say? Stay one moment; you've heard [etc.].

3. Of an action, activity, process, etc.: To be arrested, to stop or cease at a certain point, not to progress or go forward. *Obs.* or *arch.*

1563 in *Vicary's Anat.* (1888) App. III. 164 The same courte..shall stey & cease vntyll the xv.th daye of September next commynge. **1570–6** LAMBARDE *Peramb. Kent* (1826) 291 Neither did the matter stay here. **1593** SHAKS. *2 Hen. VI*, II. iv. 76 And't please your Grace, here my Commission stayes. **1671** MILTON *P.R.* IV. 421 Nor yet staid the terror there. **1820** KEATS *Hyperion* I. 295 Therefore the operations of the dawn Stay'd in their birth.

†**b.** Of a line: To cease being prolonged, to terminate (*at* a point). *Obs.*

1563 SHUTE *Archit.* D j b, The vprighte line, which staieth at the ouerthwart line. **1660** H. BLOOME *Archit.* D d 1, Turne another halfe Circle, which shall stay at the place.

** To remain stationary.

4. To remain in a place or in others' company (as opposed to going on or going away).

1575 GASCOIGNE *Glasse Govt.* V. ii. Wks. 1910 II. 74 *Fidus.* Stay a while good fellowe... *Nuntius.* Yea but I may not long tary. **1591** SHAKS. *Two Gent.* II. vii. 62 If you thinke so, then stay at home, and go not. **1600** PORY tr. *Leo's Africa* IX. 334 In rainie weather it so increaseth, that trauellers..are constrained to staie two or three daies by the riuers side till it be decreased. **1615** HEYWOOD *Foure Prentises* I. B 3 b, If I knew where to go to warre, I would not stay in London one houre longer. **1700** T. BROWN *Amusem. Ser. & Com.* 19 Those that won't take the Pains to follow us, may stay where they are. **1702** SIR D. HUME *Diary Parl. Scot.* (Bannatyne Club) 82 As to the transporting the Forces, she [the Queen] signifies her inclinations it be done, unless there be an absolute necessity for their staying. **1726** SWIFT *Gulliver* I. i, I grew weary of the sea, and intended to stay at home with my wife and family. **1753** RICHARDSON *Grandison* (1754) I. l. 398 He comes for half an hour, and stays an hour. **1757** GRAY *Bard* 101 Stay, oh stay! nor thus forlorn Leave me unbless'd. **1832** HT. MARTINEAU *Homes Abroad* i. 18 His wife seemed utterly indifferent whether she went or staid. **1849** M. ARNOLD *Forsaken Merman* 20 Mother dear, we cannot stay! **1897** HALL CAINE *Christian* x, If you're badly bored we'll not stay long.

b. *contextually*. To be allowed to remain; to be left in (undisturbed) residence or tenancy.

1765 BICKERSTAFF *Maid of Mill* II. ii. 27, I am determined farmer Giles shall not stay a moment on my estate, after next quarter day.

c. To remain *and* (do something).

1596 SHAKS. *1 Hen. IV*, V. iv. 47 Stay, and breath awhile. **1601** *2nd Pt. Return fr. Parnass.* V. iv. 2237 Nay stay a while and helpe me to content. **1833** T. HOOK *Parson's Dau.* I. ii, 'You will stay and take some tea, Mr. Sheringham,' said Lovell. **1885** 'MRS. ALEXANDER' *Valerie's Fate* v, 'I need not go, I suppose?' 'No! I wish you would stay and talk.'

d. With inf.: To remain or tarry in order *to* (do something). Also ***to stay to*** (dinner, etc.).

1591 SHAKS. *Two Gent.* IV. iv. 66 Away, I say: stayest thou to vexe me here. **1663** PATRICK *Pilgrim* xxii. (1687) 229 If you mean to finish your journey, stay not to listen to their tales. **1706** E. Ward *Wooden World Diss.* (1708) 31 The Ale-Wives tickle him in the Gills with the Title of Captain, which makes him oft-times stay to get drunk in their Houses, out of pure Joy and Gratitude. **1812** Byron *Ch. Har.* II. xcv, Thou hast ceased to be! Nor stay'd to welcome here thy wanderer home. **1819** Scott *Ivanhoe* xxvii, Some hilding fellow he must be, who dared not stay to assert his claim to the tourney prize which chance had assigned him. **1908** S. E. White *Riverman* viii, Your friend seems a nice-appearing young man... Wouldn't he stay to dinner?

e. with advs., as ***to stay away, behind, down, in, on, out, up.*** Also ***to stay over*** (orig. *U.S.*): to stop overnight.

1594 Shaks. *Rich. III*, II. ii. 154 Towards Ludlow then, for we will not stay behinde. **1622** J. Taylor (Water P.) *Shilling* B 5, Whilst all the Drawers must stay vp and waite Vpon these fellowes be it ne're so late. **1664** in *Verney Mem.* (1907) II. 236 My fathar stais so long a wae. **1711** Addison *Spect.* No. 120 ¶14 In Winter..she grows more assiduous in her Attendance, and stays away but half the Time. **1847** Tennyson *Princess* Prol. 176 We seven stay'd at Christmas up to read. **1875** Jowett *Plato* (ed. 2) I. 341 They might come if they liked, and they might stay away if they liked. **1883** Brinsley-Richards *Seven Years at Eton* x. 98 Sometimes Blazes had a lazy fit, and put himself on the sick list for a day. This was called 'stay-out', for the reason that one had to stay in. *Ibid.*, One day it happened that I was 'staying out' on the same day as Blazes. **1884**, etc. [see over *adv.* 9b]. **1885** 'Mrs. Alexander' *Valerie's Fate* vi, I *must* go with you. I feel as if I could not bear to stay behind! **1895** Kipling *Day's Work* (1898) 175 She had 'stayed down three hot weathers', as the saying is, because her brother..could not afford the expense of her keep at even a cheap hill-station. **1901** *Athenæum* 27 July 121/1 The habit of frequent 'staying out,' Etonian for staying *in*, on the score of feeble health. **1904** E. H. Coleridge *Life & Corr. Ld. Coleridge* I. iv. 58 Friends..who wrote to him during the vacations and when he was obliged to 'stay down', owing to prolonged ill-health. **1911** A. Plummer *Churches Brit. bef. A.D. 1000* I. iv. 122 Wilfrid made the grave mistake of staying on in Gaul. **1981** E. A. Taylor *Cable Car Murder* (1983) xviii. 130 We had a satisfying visit. I stayed over, and she took me to the train the next morning.

f. *U.S.* (See quot.)

1889 Farmer *Americanisms* s.v., Lovers *stay with* one another when courting.

5. Of a thing: To remain (in a place or position); to remain (as opposed to being lost, changing its nature, etc.). Now somewhat *rare* exc. in ***to stay with***: to remain in the mind or memory.

1593 *Tell-Trothes N.Y. Gift* (1876) 5 A lesson learned with stroakes, staies with the scholler. **1639** G. Plattes *Discov. Subterr. Treas.* 29 No royall Mettall will stay in the Cinder, but sinke down into the Lead, through an attractiue vertue betwixt them. **1663** Patrick *Pilgrim* xxviii. ¶1 Having at last overcome the excess of it [*sc.* his joy], and dissembled it also while it staid as well as he could. *a* **1827** Wordsw. *Somnamb.* 62 Delightful blossoms for the May Of absence! but they will not stay, Born only to depart. **1942** A. Woollcott *Let.* 26 May (1946) 260, I want to tell you that seldom has anything I have heard stayed with me like your reading of that first poem in the *Spoon River Anthology*. **1973** *Christian Science Monitor* 12 July 19/4 On the way home that stayed with me, 'The whole world needs mothering'.

b. Of food, etc.: To be retained by the stomach after swallowing. Also (*U.S. colloq.*) to give lasting satisfaction to hunger.

1643 Steer tr. *Exp. Chyrurg.* ix. 43 By reason of the Childs unpatience I could not make the Medicine stay. **1719** De Foe *Crusoe* II. (Globe) 472, I took a Draught of Water without Sugar, and that stay'd with me. **1894** Fiske *Holiday Stor.* (1900) 128 'No,' replied the boy... 'No; stew's good, but they don't stay wid yer. Kin I have some-think solid?'

†**c.** To remain adhering *to*. *Obs. rare*$^{-1}$.

1684 R. Waller *Nat. Exper.* 45 We apply'd it to several pieces of Straw, which in the Descent of the Mercury stayed to the sides of the Glass.

6. With predicative extension: To remain in the specified condition.

1573–80 Tusser *Husb.* (1878) 11 To staie amis, not hauing this. **1600** Shaks. *A.Y.L.* III. ii. 348 Ile tel you..who Time gallops withal, and who he stands stil withall... Who staies it stil withal? **1600** Pory tr. *Leo's Africa* I. 20 That this their meate may not stay long vndigested in their stomackes, they sup off the foresaid broth. **1640** Suckling *Ballade upon Wedding* 38 Her finger was so small, the Ring Would not stay on which he did bring, It was too wide a Peck. **1855** Lynch *Rivulet* LVII. vi, No heart that desponds Desponding need stay. **1865** Ruskin *Eth. Dust* iv. (1883) 70, I can bend them up and down and they stay bent. **1871** B. Taylor *Faust* (1875) II. II. iii. 121 She grows not old, stays ever young and warm.

b. ***to stay put***: to remain where or as placed; to remain fixed or steady; also *fig.* (of persons, etc.). *colloq.* (orig. *U.S.*).

1843 *New Mirror* 23 Sept. 385/2 And now we have put her in black and white, where she will 'stay put'. **1848** Bartlett *Dict. Amer.* s.v. *Put, To stay put*, to remain in order; not to be disturbed. A vulgar expression. **1864** Maria S. Cummins *Haunted Hearts* I. iv. 46 This curl sticks right out straight; couldn't you put this pin in for me, so that it would stay put? **1870** Lowell *Study Wind.* 248 He has a prodigious talent, to use our Yankee phrase, of *staying put*. **1891** 'L. Malet' *Wages of Sin* IV. v. 217 It takes a lot of latent strength to sit, either mentally or physically, really still. Not to fidget. To 'stay put', in short. **1924** J. Buchan *Three Hostages* vii. 102 He's able enough; but he won't stay put, and that makes him pretty well useless. **1936** F. Clune *Roaming round Darling* xv. 139 Here, for the time being, Sturt must 'stay put', while the Poet and I begin rolling down the Darling. **1959** *Globe & Mail* (Toronto) 17 Aug. 3/8 Fire Chief Dawson told him to stay put until the car could be pulled away safely. **1978** R. Busby *Garvey's Code* xii. 159, I keep the gun. And you stay put.

†**c.** To remain without specific definition *in* a general class. *Obs.* (*nonce-use.*)

1592 West *1st Pt. Symbol.* I. xii. (1594) A 3 b, Named Contracts, be those which haue a cause by law defined, and they are called by proper names. The same also be termed certain... Besides these all the reste are vncertaine, as steying in that their generall appellation or name.

7. With emphasis or contextual colouring: **a.** To tarry or linger where one is; to delay (as opposed to going on). Chiefly with negative. Cf. sense 4 d.

? *a* **1500** *London Lyckpeny* ii. (MS. Harl. 367) Yet for all that I stayd not longe, Tyll to the kynges bench I was come. **1585** Washington tr. *Nicholay's Voy.* I. vi. 4 b, [He] was again sent..to the King to aduertise him of our arriual, who stayed not, but straightwayes ther came with him diuers other Chiaous, captaines and Ianissaries to receiue the Ambassadour. **1611** Bible *Josh.* x. 19 And stay you not, but pursue after your enemies. *Ibid.*, *1 Sam.* xx. 38 And Ionathan cryed after the ladde, Make speed, haste, stay not. **1616** W. Browne *Brit. Past.* II. v. 112 His eye deceiued mingles his colours wrong, There strikes too little, and here stayes too long. **1871** R. Ellis *Catullus* lxi. 196 Husband, stay not [*Jam licet venias*]: a bride within Coucheth ready.

b. To stand one's ground, stand firm (as opposed to fleeing or budging). Now *rare*.

1593 Shaks. *3 Hen. VI*, II. iii. 50 And giue them leaue to flye, that will not stay. **1597** Lok *Sundry Chr. Pass.* I. liii, But yet (in hope of grace from thee) I stay, And do not yeeld, although my courage quaile. **1851** Mrs. Browning *Casa Guidi Wind.* I. 1082 Who, born the fair side of the Alps, will budge, When Dante stays, when Ariosto stays, When Petrarch stays for ever?

†**c.** Of a thing: To linger, be long in coming or beginning. *Obs.*

1602 Marston *Antonio's Rev.* IV. iii, Why staies the doome of death? **1639** Du Verger tr. *Camus' Admir. Events* 355 If the good theeves helpe had stay'd a little longer, it is likely that it had come too late.

8. To reside or sojourn in a place for a longer or shorter period; to sojourn or put up *with* a person as his guest.

1554 in Tytler *Eng. Edw. VI & Mary* (1839) II. 410 From Villa Franca unto St. James,..where he stayeth about two days. **1617** *Acct. Bk. W. Wray* in *Antiquary* XXXII. 214 He stayed at Rippon one night. **1666** H. Jackson in *Extr. S.P. rel. Friends* Ser. III. (1912) 248, I travailed Seaven miles that morneing, and then stayed at a friends house, intending in a short time, to have passed on my journey. **1674** *Essex Papers* (Camden) I. 288, I will come over post and stay a month wth Essex. **1823** A. Clarke *Mem. Wesley Fam.* 514 While she staid with her uncle. **1831** *Society* I. 287 She had hoped a very lovely girl staying in the house, would be a counter-charm to the other. **1847** Helps *Friends in C.* I. viii. 121 It was arranged..that Ellesmere should come and stay a day or two with me. **1883** Ruskin *Art of Eng.* 24 Two English ladies..were staying at the same hotel. **1905** Elin. Glyn *Viciss. Evangeline* 162, I don't think Park Street is the place for you to stay.

b. To dwell, lodge, reside (permanently or regularly). *Sc., S.Afr., India,* and *U.S.*

1754 E. Burt *Lett. N. Scot.* (1818) I. 20, I was told that I must..inquire for such a *launde* (or building), where the gentleman *stayd*, at the *third stair*, that is, three stories high. **1800** *Monthly Mag.* I. 322 [Scotticisms], He stays in the Canongate, means, He lives in that suburb. *a* **1915** *Mod.* (Sc.) Mr. A. moved last Whitsunday; I don't know where he stays now. *Mod.* (Cape Colony: communicated.) *Englishman.* Who lived in that house last? *Colonial.* Oh, Mr. Brown stayed there. **1951** *Amer. Speech* XXVI. 75/1 'Do you stay here?' In common Negro parlance *stay* is used for 'live' but is heard otherwise. **1959** A. Fullerton *Yellow Ford* v. 45 'Would you care to stay round here, man?' I had not caught on, at first, to her meaning: the verb 'stay' is used in South Africa when in England we'd say 'live'. **1962** W. Faulkner *Reivers* i. 13 Mr Wimbush stays a solid eight miles from town. **1980** D. Moraes *Mrs Gandhi* p. xiii, In March 1977..my wife..and I went to see her in New Delhi, at 1 Safdarjang Road, the house where she had stayed since she first became Prime Minister in 1966.

c. ***to come to stay***: To become permanent or established, to come into regular use or recognition; to assume a secure position in public favour or as meeting a public need. *colloq.* Similarly, ***to be here to stay***.

1863 A. Lincoln *Let. to Conkling* 26 Aug. in E. McPherson *Polit. Hist. U.S. Rebell.* (1864) 336, I hope it [*sc.* peace] will come soon, and come to stay. **1894** *Westm. Gaz.* 9 May 2/1 Those dreadful [advertisement] boards—their dimensions are 18 ft. by 6 ft.—have, as the Yankees put it, 'come to stay.' **1901** *Athenæum* 13 Apr. 455/1 The issue..of Byron's letters will leave very little doubt..that Lord Byron as a letter-writer has 'come to stay'. **1936** M. Mitchell *Gone with Wind* xli. 739 Everyone knew hard times were here to stay. **1947** [see *post-industrial* s.v. post- B. 1 b]. **1966** *Listener* 5 May 661/3 It's a small question, though, when viewed against the more important fact that Mahler is indubitably here, and here to stay. **1969** *Ibid.* 31 July 135/1 In all the present uncertainties about the future of radio, one thing seems certain: local radio is here to stay, and we shall have more of it. **1971** J. Wainwright *Dig Grave* 85 'I don't go for them [*sc.* automatic gears]. They'll kill real driving.' .. 'They're here to stay, mate, whether you go for 'em, or not.' **1976** *Guardian* 17 Apr. 13/8 Multinationals are here to stay.

9. To remain inactive or quiet; to wait (without doing anything or making progress); to put off action (*until*). Cf. *stay for*, 14 b. ? *Obs.*

a **1550** *Image Ipocr.* III. 27 in *Skelton's Wks.* (1843) II. 433 Some be still and stey, And hope to haue a daye. **1560** Daus tr. *Sleidane's Comm.* xvi. 216 All the which thinges they haue eager to theyr powers resisted, and ofte desired the Archebishop, that he woulde staye vntyll the counsell. **1591** Shaks. *Two Gent.* I. ii. 131 Madam: dinner is ready, and your father staies. **1621** Elsing *Debates Ho. Lords* (Camden) 125 The booke of the Collecciones of the presidents not yett bounde. Whether you wyll use the booke as yt is, or staye untill to-morrowe? **1625** Bacon *Ess., Delays*, Fortune is like the Market; where many times, if you can stay a little, the Price will fall. **1640** Suckling *Let.* Fragm. Aur. (1648) 91 Nor must he stay to act till his people desire. *a* **1703** Burkitt *On N.T., Luke* ii. 28 Though God stays long before he fulfils his promises, he certainly comes at last with a double reward for our expectation. **1751** Chesterf. *Lett.* III. ccliv. 166, I told you in a former letter..that I should stay till I received the patterns pitched upon by your ladies.

†**10.** Of a business or other matter: To be deferred or postponed for a season; to be kept waiting, be allowed to wait. *Obs.*

1642 tr. *Perkins' Prof. Bk.* v. §335. 148 Execution shall stay during the Terme of yeares. **1680** Otway *Orphan* I. iv, The time has been When business might have stay'd and I been heard. **1728** Swift *Jrnl. Modern Lady* 93 The footman, in his usual phrase, Comes up with 'Madam, dinner stays.'

†**11. a.** To scruple, be in doubt, raise difficulties (*at*). **b.** To delay *in* (doing something). **c.** To hesitate, delay, be slow, scruple *to* (do something). **d.** To refrain *from*. *Obs.*

1533 More *Apol.* xxii. 135 b, At some of them [prelates proposed to be replaced by laymen] they stayed and stakered. **1539** Cromwell in Merriman *Life & Lett.* (1902) II. 174 It is not to be doubted, but whenne all the rest shulde be agreed, no man wold styck nor staye for any parte concerning her beautie and goodnes but rather haue more then contentement. **1551** R. Robinson tr. *More's Utopia* I. (1895) 83 Whyles they all staye at the chyefeste dowte of all, what to doo in the meane tyme with England. **1553** Brende *Q. Curtius* IX. 192 Whye doest thou staye in riddyng me quickelye out of this payne? **1583** Babington *Commandm.* (1590) 287 Their bolde speaking is not euer sounde proouing, and therefore wee stay to beleeue them. **1599** Porter *Angry Wom. Abingt.* (1841) 34 *Mal.* Do you heare, mother? would you stay from pleasure When yee haue minde to it?.. *Mis. Bar.* Well, lustie guts, I meane to make ye stay, And set some rubbes in your mindes smothest way. *c* **1605** Rowley *Birth Merl.* v. ii. 46 Why do we stay to binde those Princely browes With this Imperial Honor? **1644** Milton *Areop.* (Arb.) 31 Which though I stay not to confesse ere any ask.

12. *Sport.* To last, hold out, exhibit powers of endurance in a race or run. Also, to hold out for (a specified distance). [? Derived from sense 7 b.]

1834 Darvill *Race Horse* (1846) II. 44 If he finds that his horses can go faster and stay longer at the pace by being drawn fine. **1860** Rous in *Baily's Mag.* I. 18 There is another popular notion that our horses cannot now stay four miles. **1871** M. Collins *Marq. & Merch.* III. iv. 114 Such a galloper—and can't he stay! **1874** *Slang Dict.* 309 *Stay*, to exhibit powers of endurance at walking, running, rowing, etc. **1889** *The Pauline* VIII. 39 The Indian Civil boat made a good race of it for half the course but could not stay. **1897** *Allbutt's Syst. Med.* II. 841 [Alcohol] may enable a man 'to spurt' but not 'to stay'.

b. To keep up *with* (a competitor in a game, a race, etc.). *colloq.* (orig. *U.S.*). Also *fig.*, to concentrate on, to apply oneself to, to continue with.

1887 F. Francis Jun. *Saddle & Mocassin* 145 Sam'll 'stay with em as long as he's got a check. *Ibid.* 177 But they couldn't bluff the old man off; he stayed with them. **1894** *Outing* XXIV. 342/2, I determined upon a course which would in the end enable me to score my elk, and that was simply to 'stay with it.' **1956** H. Kurnitz *Invasion of Privacy* i. 12 I gave you an order. Stay with it. **1961** 'A. A. Fair' *Stop at Red Light* (1962) vii. 108 That adds up, Donald. Stay with it. You're doing fine. **1969** *Guardian* 15 July 7/1 These astronauts..have an amazing capability to stay with their tasks. **1976** 'J. Ross' *I know what it's like to Die* xxv. 158 I've got to stay with it [*sc.* a police inquiry]. I can't just drop it. **1982** *Times* 6 Feb. 15 (*heading*) Fed stays with its tight money policy.

13. *Poker.* 'To come in when an ante has been raised' (*Cent. Dict.*); also ***to stay in. to stay out***, to go out of the game.

1882 *Poker; How to play it* 8 If a number of players have gone in, it is best generally for the ante-man to make good and go in, even with a poor hand, because half his stake is already up, and he can therefore stay in for half as much as the others have had to put up. *Ibid.* 12 Everybody stayed out except one man. **1897** R. F. Foster *Compl. Hoyle* 183 (Poker) Suppose there has been no straddle, and that all conclude to *stay*, as it is called.

14. to stay for ——. **a.** To remain or wait in a place for (a person or thing); to remain and take part in or witness (a meal, ceremony, etc.); to await the coming of.

1554 in Tytler *Eng. Edw. VI & Mary* (1839) II. 410 And so to the Groyne..where he will stay only for a good wind. **1591** Shaks. *Two Gent.* III. i. 382 Thy Master staies for thee at the North gate. **1628** Digby *Voy. Mediterr.* (Camden) 9 But they steyed for us and made readie for fight. **1763** Bickerstaff *Love in Village* II. ix, Well, sir, will you read this letter,..it is just brought by a servant, who stays for an answer. **1796** Mrs. Robinson *Angelina* I. 270 We shall stay for you in the wilderness. **1833** T. Hook *Parson's Dau.* II. ix, 'Come, Doctor,' said Lady Frances, 'stay for coffee.'

†**b.** To wait or tarry for (a person or thing) before doing or beginning to do something. Sometimes contextually, to be compelled to wait for. *Obs.*

1598 Shaks. *Merry W.* I. i. 314 Come, gentle M. Slender, come; we stay for you. **1625** Bacon *Ess., Truth* (Arb.) 499 What is Truth; said jesting Pilate; and would not stay for an Answer. **1651** Hobbes *Leviathan* II. xxvi. 150 The Civill Law takes away that Liberty, in all cases where the protection of the Law may be safely stayd for. **1704** Cibber *Careless Husb.* II. i. 22 Dinner's serv'd, and the Ladies stay for us. **1705** H. Blackwell *Engl. Fencing-Master* 16 If the Hand stays for the Foot, the Thrust is much slower. **1738**

SWIFT *Pol. Conversat.* 126 You see, sir John, we stay'd for you, as one Horse does for another.

†**c.** *contextually.* (To be forced) to wait for (something one wishes or hopes to get). *Obs.*

1592 *Murther J. Brewen* in *Kyd's Wks.* (1901) 288 [He] requested that he might haue his gifts againe, to whom disdainfully she made answere that he should stay for it. **1780** JOHNSON *Let. to Mrs. Thrale* 10 July, For all this I must stay, but life will not stay.

†**d.** said of a thing. *Obs.*

1601 B. JONSON *Poetaster* II. ii. Wks. (1616) 291 There's a slight banquet staies within for you. **1603** DEKKER *Wonderf. Yeare* F 4, Another poore wretch..throwne..into a graue vpon a heape of carcases, that stayd for their complement. **1662** J. DIXON in *Extr. S.P. rel. Friends* Ser. II. (1911) 144 You are desired to seend your Collecttion yt was for London with speed for it steayes for youres and mosdals.

†**15. to stay of ——.** To be delayed by, be kept waiting by, have to wait for (a person or thing). *Obs.* [Cf. midl. dial. 'to wait of' = *to wait for.*]

1681 W. ROBERTSON *Phraseol. Gen.* 1168/2, I stay of this; *Hoc mihi moræ est. Ibid.*, Fetch the Midwife that we may not stay of her; *Obstetricem accerse, ne in mora nobis fiet. Ibid.* 1169/1, I will tell them they shall not stay of us; *Illis dicam nullam esse in nobis moram.*

16. to stay on, upon ——. †**a.** To wait for (a person); to await, await the issue of (an event, circumstance); to attend on, be subject to (a person's will or pleasure, etc.). *Obs.*

1540 PALSGR. *Acolastus* Ep. to King b iij, Where as nowe the scholers..haue no maner remedy, but vtterly and holly to staye vpon theyr maysters mouth. **1590** SHAKS. *Com. Err.* v. i. 20 You haue done wrong to this my honest friend, Who but for staying on our Controuersie, Had hoisted saile, and put to sea to day. **1601** —— *All's Well* III. v. 48, I thanke you, and will stay vpon your leisure. **1603** —— *Meas. for M.* IV. i. 47, I haue a Seruant comes with me along That staies vpon me. *c* **1611** CHAPMAN *Iliad* XIV. 308 We little need to stay On his assistance, if we would our owne strengths call to field.

†**b.** To dwell upon (a topic, subject); to sustain or stress (a note in singing). Of the eye: To rest upon, be arrested by (an object of vision). *Obs.*

c **1580** LODGE *Repl. Gosson's Sch. Abuse* 24 But other matter call [*sic*] me and I must not staye vpon this onely. **1601** SHAKS. *Twel. N.* II. iv. 24 My life vpon't, yong though thou art, thine eye Hath staid vpon some fauour that it loues. **1605** BACON *Adv. Learn.* II. xxiii. §22. 97, I haue staied the longer vpon this precept..because it is a maine part by it selfe. **1667** [see STAY *sb.*3 3 d].

II. quasi-*trans.* and *trans.* uses derived from I.

17. quasi-*trans.* To remain for, to remain and participate in or assist at (a meal, ceremony, prayers, etc.); to remain throughout or during (a period of time). = *stay for*, 14 a.

1570 in Kempe *Losely MSS.* (1836) 234 At the tyme poynted he cam and stayd the service, from the beginning to th'end. **1599** HAYWARD *1st Pt. Life Hen. IV*, 26 The rest of the lords departed, except the Earle of Darby, who stayed supper with the King. **1661** P. HENRY *Diaries & Lett.* (1882) 85, I stay'd ye sermon. *a* **1700** EVELYN *Diary* 29 Nov. 1661, My Lord Mordaunt, with whom I staid the night. **1778** MISS BURNEY *Evelina* (1791) I. xx. 87 We intended to stay the farce. **1786** —— *Diary* 27 July (1842–6) III. 37 At the dessert I was very agreeably surprised by the entrance of Sir Richard Jebb, who stayed coffee. **1808** JANE AUSTEN *Lett.* (1884) I. 357 She stayed the Sacrament, I remember, the last time that you and I did. **1832** MOORE *Mem.* (1854) VI. 244 Went to Bowood, and stayed prayers. **1862** CARLYLE *Fredk. Gt.* XI. iii. (1872) IV. 51 A certain Colonel..contrives to get invited to stay dinner. **1888** G. GISSING *Life's Morning* II. xi. 135 I'm obliged to ask them to stay tea.

b. *to stay the course*: to hold out to the end of a race. Freq. *fig.*

1885 *Daily Tel.* 11 Nov. 3/7 Doubts are also entertained.. concerning her [*sc.* a horse's] ability to stay the course. **1916** *Times* 8 May 9/1 If we are to 'stay the course' set before us, other sections must be prepared for greater sacrifices. **1939** A. HUXLEY *After Many a Summer* I. viii. 103 'Do you suppose you'd still be a scholar and a gentleman?'.. 'One will certainly have stopped being a gentleman,' he answered. 'One's begun to stop even now, thank heaven.' 'But the scholar will stay the course?' **1966** *Listener* 10 Mar. 365/3 There was much to be learnt from this programme—about metal fatigue, for instance—for those who could stay the course. **1983** *Verbatim* IX. IV. 16/2 When President Reagan exhorted Senators and Congressmen to stay the course, the actual meaning of his words was the opposite of his intended meaning.

18. quasi-*trans.* with *out.* **a.** To remain to the end of; to remain and witness the end of. Also, to remain beyond the limit of, outstay.

1639 FULLER *Holy War* IV. xxi. 206 By this time Lewis in Syria had stayed out the death and buriall of all his hopes to receive succour from his own countrey. **1768** LADY M. COKE *Jrnl.* 27 Feb., Went to the new Opera:..upon the whole dull —not that I staid it out. **1858** HAWTHORNE *Fr. & It. Note-bks.* (1872) I. 2 It seemed as if we had stayed our English welcome out.

b. To remain longer than (another), outstay.

1749 FIELDING *Tom Jones* XIII. iv, The company had now staid so long, that Mrs. Fitzpatrick plainly perceived they all designed to stay out each other.

19. *trans.* To wait for, await (a person, his coming, an event, etc.); to wait upon, serve (a person's leisure); to abide, sustain (a question, onset). Now *arch.* (= *stay for* 14 a, b, *stay upon* 16 a).

a **1586** SIDNEY *Arcadia* III. xviii. §6 Never staying either judge, trumpet, or his owne launce, [he] drew out his sword. **1590** SPENSER *F.Q.* II. iv. 40 Ne thou for better hope, if thou his presence stay. **1590** SHAKS. *Mids. N.* II. i. 235, I will not stay thy questions, let me go. **1592** —— *Ven. & Ad.* 894 They basely flie and dare not stay the field. *a* **1625** FLETCHER *Elder Bro.* II. i, Like a blushing Rose that staies the pulling. *a* **1625** —— *M. Thomas* v. ii, Get you afore and stay me at the Chapel. **1638** JUNIUS *Paint. Ancients* 22 Neither doe they stay our leisure to let us take a full view of them. **1705** tr. *Bosman's Guinea* 472, I was..desired to stay the arrival of their King. **1811** *Spirit Publ. Jrnls.* (1813) XVI. 7 They would not stay our arrival; for, the moment they saw us, they made off. **1864** *Realm* 8 June 1 The overhurry of the messenger (who had stayed no question) induced suspicion. **1888** STEVENSON *Black Arrow* 6 There is a fight toward,..and my lord stays a reinforcement.

b. = to stay to make or offer. *poet.*

1588 SHAKS. *L.L.L.* II. i. 193, I cannot stay thanks-giuing. *Ibid.* IV. ii. 147 Stay not thy complement, I forgiue thy duetie, adue.

III. *trans.* To stop, arrest, check.

20. To detain, hold back, stop (a person or thing); to check or arrest the progress of, bring to a halt; to hinder from going on or going away; to keep in a fixed place or position. Now only *literary.*

[*c* **1440** ? see 1.] **1532** CROMWELL in Merriman *Life & Lett.* (1902) I. 351 Ye lytell Regarding the kynges auctoryte and Commyssyon have stayed dyuers masons and woorkmen abowte you. **1560** BIBLE (Geneva) *Job* xxxviii. 11 And here shal it staye thy proud waues. **1560** DAUS tr. *Sleidane's Comm.* 136 Than the tounes men..stayed the reste that would lykewise have invaded. **1562** GRESHAM in Burgon *Life* (1839) II. 9 To wryte me your pleasure whether I shall send you Doctor Mount's letters in post, or to stey them bye me till the ordinary post goeth. **1576** FLEMING *Panopl. Epist.* 310 A running streame is stayed by weedes and shallownesse. **1627** *Lisander & Calista* II. 31 While the rain stayes you here. **1635** R. N. *Camden's Hist. Eliz.* I. 20 An infinite masse of money being stayed at home, which was wont to be exported daily to Rome. **1654** BRAMHALL *Just Vind.* ii. (1661) 25 They..are like men running down a steep hill that cannot stay themselves. **1686** tr. *Chardin's Trav. Persia* 255 He stay'd me to dine with him. *a* **1700** EVELYN *Diary* 14 Nov. 1672, This businesse staide me in London almost a weeke. **1768** STERNE *Sent. Journ.*, *Fille de Chambre* (1778) II. 3 As I had nothing to stay me in the shop, we both walk'd out. **1782** COWPER *John Gilpin* 37 So three doors off the chaise was stay'd. **1810** SCOTT *Lady of L.* III. xiv, The plough was in mid-furrow staid. **1830** TENNYSON *Poems* 96 Thou shalt not wander hence to-night, I'll stay thee with my kisses. **1873** HELPS *Anim. & Mast.* vi. 152 Among the reeds, where, at the moment, we had stayed the boat. **1902** *Munsey's Mag.* XXVI. 596/1 Attacking and withdrawing again before any force could be mobilized to stay him.

b. const. *from.*

1591 H. SMITH *Serm., Restitut. Nebuchad.* 15 Therefore when he knew this, nothing could stay him from his kingdome, no more then they could stay him in his kingdome before. **1605** BACON *Adv. Learn.* II. vii. §7. 32 b, They are indeed but *Remoraes* and hinderances to stay and slugge the Shippe from furder sayling. **1618** W. LAWSON *Orch. & Gard.* ii. (1623) 4 Make Trenches by degrees,..so as the Water may be staied from passage. **1703** EVELYN *Diary* 21 Nov., The wet and uncomfortable weather staying us from church this morning. **1850** TENNYSON *In Mem.* lxxxiii, O sweet new-year delaying long..What stays thee from the clouded noons?

†**c.** *refl.* To abide (in a place); to take up a settled residence. Similarly in *passive. Obs.*

1558 PHAER *Æneid* VIII. (1562) Bb iiij, Than at Etruria sore affright did settling stay them selues, & in ye field their camp haue pight. **1563** *Homilies* II. *Place & Time of Prayer* I. 139 b, They were not stayed in any place, but were in a continuall peregrination and wandering. **1579–80** NORTH *Plutarch, Romulus* (1595) 20 Some thinke that the Pelasgians ..in the end did stay themselues in that place where it [Rome] was new builded. **1590** SPENSER *F.Q.* III. i. 67 For nothing would she lenger there be stayd, Where so loose life ..Was vsd of Knights and Ladies seeming gent.

d. *poet.* To take prisoner; to hold in confinement or captivity.

1590 SPENSER *F.Q.* I. x. 40 And captiues to redeeme with price of bras From Turkes and Sarazins, which them had stayd. **1872** TENNYSON *Gareth & Lynette* 600 Three knights Defend the passings,..and a fourth..holds her stay'd In her own castle.

21. To render motionless or keep immovable; to fix, hold fast.

1627 MAY *Lucan* II. (1631) C8, Each Galley doe foure anchors stay. **1669** STURMY *Mariner's Mag.* I. ii. 8 Bring the Index of the Moon to the West-by-North Point, staying it there. **1811** WORDSW. *Misc. Sonn.* I. ix, I Praised be the Art whose subtle power could stay Yon cloud, and fix it in that glorious shape. **1855** TENNYSON *Daisy* 23 Till, in a narrow street and dim, I stay'd the wheels at Cogoletto. **1868** —— *Lucretius* 257 My golden work in which I told a truth That stays the rolling Ixionian wheel.

†**b.** To cause to rest or remain *on* something; to rest or fix (the eyes) *on* an object. *Obs.*

a **1586** SIDNEY *Ps.* XXX. xi, Lord, heare, lett mercy thine be staid On me. **1633** G. HERBERT *Temple, Elixer* iii, A man that looks on glasse, On it may stay his eye; Or if he pleaseth, through it passe, And then the heav'n espie. **1674** PLAYFORD *Skill Mus.* II. 102 Your second and third Fingers staid upon the Hair, by which you may poise and keep up your Bow.

22. a. To detain or delay (a reader).

1578 TIMME *Calvin on Gen.* 261 To the end the disordered division of the Chapters may not trouble or stay the readers. **1653** H. MORE *Conject. Cabbal.* 93 Not to stay you with too tedious a Prologue to the matter in hand. **1690** LOCKE *Hum. Und.* III. v. §16, I was willing to stay my Reader on an Argument, that appears to me new.

b. To arrest (the attention).

1639 DU VERGER tr. *Camus' Admir. Events* 193 His consideration was no lesse stayed by her vertue, then his sences charmed by her beauty.

†**c.** To stop the course of, terminate (a line).

1563 SHUTE *Archit.* ciij, The vpright line..which stayeth that lyne which is drawen ouerthwart the pillor.

23. To prevent, hinder, stop (a person or thing) from doing something; to check, restrain. Const. *from*, †*of* a course of action, etc.); †*to* (with inf.); †*but that.* Now *rare* or *poet.*

1560 DAUS tr. *Sleidane's Comm.* 123 b, Kynge Ferdinando ..commaunded the lawe to cease..but that woulde not staye them. **1562** T. COOPER *Answ. Def. Truth* xii. 85 b, If that would haue stayed you from wrytinge. **1566** *Acts Gen. Assemb. Kirk Scot.* (Maitland Club) I. 86 Diverse of our deirest brethren..by you are stayed to promote the kingdome of Chryst. **1574** A. L. *Calvin's Foure Serm.* i, Nothing staied him but that he set up the true and pure religion. **1574** in *Maitl. Club Misc.* I. 104 Sene the tyme that thai war steyit of thair said pretendit mariage. **1585** HIGINS *Junius' Nomencl.* 191/2 *Repagulum*,..the barre which staieth horses from running. **1611** BIBLE *Haggai* i. 10 Therefore the heauen ouer you is stayed from dew, and the earth is staied from her fruite. *a* **1628** PRESTON *New Covt.* (1630) 87 When he stayed himselfe, and did it not, how did the Lord bring it to passe with out him? **1630** PAGITT *Christianogr.* I. ii. (1636) 73 This made St. Augustine..to write his bookes.. to stay his countriemen from Idolatrie. **1846** H. G. ROBINSON *Odes of Horace* II. viii, Lest your bewitching air should stay Their husbands from their duty. **1852** M. ARNOLD *Empedocles* I. ii. 125 Rivers are dried, winds stay'd.

†**b.** *refl.* To check oneself; to desist from something one is doing or intending to do; to cease speaking, writing, etc. *Obs.*

1560 BIBLE (Geneva) *Haggai* i. 10 Therefore the heauen ouer you staied it self from dewe. **1561** CLOUGH in *Burgon's Life Gresham* (1889) I. 410 Herein I am somwatt tedyus: desyryng you to pardone me, for beyng ownse enteryd into the matter, I collde nott stee myselffe. **1598** R. BERNARD tr. *Terence, Adelph.* IV. iv, Neuerthelesse I staied my selfe, least I should vtter any thing of my brother to that babler.

c. with object a limb or activity of the body, a weapon, etc.; esp. *to stay* (one's own or another's) *hand* (chiefly *fig.*, to cease or cause to cease from attack or working). Now somewhat *arch.*

1560 BIBLE (Geneva) *Dan.* iv. 35 And none can stay his hand, nor say vnto him, What doest thou? **1579** GOSSON *Apol. Sch. Abuse* (Arb.) 75 But I stay my handes till I see his booke. **1581** A. HALL *Iliad* IV. 65 The golden buckle of my belt..hath surely stayde the blow. **1591** SHAKS. *1 Hen. VI*, I. ii. 104 Stay, stay thy hands, thou art an Amazon. *a* **1600** *Flodden F.* iii. (1664) 25 Himself set forth in seemly aray, And neither stint nor staid his foot. **1800** WORDSW. *Pet Lamb* 16 But ere ten yards were gone her footsteps did she stay. **1877** TYNDALL in *Daily News* 2 Oct. 2/5 That power did not work with delusions, nor will it stay its hand when such are removed. **1880** R. G. WHITE *Every-Day Eng.* xx. 303 My tongue is tied and my hand is stayed.

†**d.** To cause (a bell) to cease ringing. *Obs.*

a **1593** MARLOWE *Massacre at Paris* 452 And now stay That bel that to ye deuils mattins rings. **1655** F. RAWORTH *Jacob's Ladder* 35 But Satan, stay the bels.

24. †**a.** *Law.* To hold back, refuse to release or cancel (a bond). *Obs.*

1578 WHETSTONE *2nd Pt. Promos & Cass.* II. v, Nay mary, the same I would gladly pay, But my bonde for the forfeyt he doth stay.

†**b.** To keep back or withhold (a person) temporarily *from* (something due). *Obs.*

1643 BAKER *Chron., Hen. VII*, 153 His brother Henry Duke of Yorke was stayed from the title of Prince of Wales, the space of halfe a yeer, till to women it might appear, whether the Lady Katherine, the Relict of Prince Arthur, were with childe, or no.

25. To stop, arrest, delay, prevent (an action or process, something which is begun or intended). Freq. in legal parlance.

1525 *St. Papers Hen. VIII*, VI. 513 On the morow..Your Highnes letters..arryvyd here, whiche stayde our goyng to thEmperour, unto we had perused them over. **1542–3** *Act 34 & 35 Hen. VIII*, c. 27 §114 Item that no execucion of any iudgement geuen..be staied or deferred. **1579** LYLY *Euphues* (Arb.) 114 Neither lette rayne nor thunder..stay thy iourney. **1597** SHAKS. *2 Hen. IV*, IV. iii. 78 Retreat is made, and Execution stay'd. **1665** HOWARD & DRYDEN *Ind. Queen* III. i, If you would have this Sentence staid. **1690** DRYDEN *Amphitryon* IV. i, You had best stay dinner, till he has proved himself to be Amphitryon in form of law. **1768** BLACKSTONE *Comm.* III. xiv. 227 The courts of equity..will grant an injunction or order to stay waste, until the defendant shall have put in his answer. **1796** BURKE *Regic. Peace* i. Wks. 1808 VIII. 186 When a neighbour sees a new erection, in the nature of a nuisance, set up at his door,..the judge..has a right to order the work to be staid. **1855** PRESCOTT *Philip II*, I. i. ix. 141 He marched against the Turks and stayed the tide of Ottoman inroad in Hungary. **1856** in *Hurlstone & Norman's Exch. Rep.* (1857) I. 494, I do order..that until such indemnity be given all further proceedings be stayed. **1861** GEN. P. THOMPSON *Audi Alt.* III. clxiii. 179 To stay printing, there-fore, is the object of all who object to the knowledge it is to dispense. **1913** D. BRAY *Life-Hist. Brahui* iv. 53 A death in the household.. will stay a wedding forty days.

b. To arrest the course or growth of (a disease, something noxious or destructive).

1563 T. GALE *Antidot.* I. i. 1 We staye by them [*sc.* medicines] the fluxe of humours in their beginning. **1598** BASTARD *Chrestol.* VII. xx. 169 So in fayre faces moulds somtimes arise, Which serue to stay the surfeyte of our eyes. **1611** BIBLE *2 Sam.* xxiv. 21 That the plague may be stayed from the people. **1653** T. BRUGIS *Vade Mecum* (ed. 2) 61 It stayeth the cough. **1873** SYMONDS *Grk. Poets* vii. 195 When the righteous man appears, who performs an act of retributive justice, then the curse is stayed. **1913** *Standard* 14 July 12/1 He was the first to help Jessop to stay the 'rot' that had set in on Thursday.

26. To leave off, cease, discontinue (doing something, an activity of one's own). Also to delay, withhold (one's good opinion, thanks). Now *rare* or *Obs.*

1538 ELYOT *Dict.*, *Supprimere iter*, to stay or omitte a iourney. *c* **1550** J. CHEKE *Let.* in *Athenæum* (1909) 28 Aug. 237/2 As a man often..deceived with your promises, I will stay my good opinion. **1579** W. WILKINSON *Confut. Fam. Love* Brief Descr. ☛ iij, If Sathan there had stayd his rage. *c* **1610** *Women Saints* 199 Not intermitting or staying his talke of sublime things for his bodies infirmitie. **1611** SHAKS. *Wint. T.* I. ii. 9 Stay your Thanks a while, And pay them when you part. **1628** PRYNNE *Censure Cozens* 44 There is as much hope of making the restlesse Sunne to stay its motion. **1685** LADY R. RUSSELL *Lett.* I. xxvii. 72, I had not stayed supplying you with new French papers, but that I was doubtful how the last got to you. **1820** KEATS *Isabella* xlvii, Then 'gan she work again; nor stay'd her care, But to throw back at times her veiling hair.

b. To cease *to* (do something). *poet. rare*−¹.

1894 BRIDGES *Shorter P.* v. *Palm Willow* 2 The birds have stayed to sing.

†**27.** To defend, guard (a place) against entry or incursion. Const. *from*. *Obs.*

1575 CHURCHYARD *Chips* 44 b, *marg.*, Sir Thomas Manners..was sent before to stay the gates. **1576** GASCOIGNE *Steele Gl.* (Arb.) 70 Demosthenes in Athens vsde his arte..stil to stay the towne from deepe deceite Of Philips wyles, which had besieged it.

28. To appease, allay (strife, tumult); †to reduce to order, bring under control (rebellious elements); †to compose (a disturbed district). †Also *refl.* to compose oneself, control one's emotions. Now *rare*.

1537 R. ASKE in Ellis *Orig. Lett.* Ser. III. III. 59, I prey your Lordship to stay your quarters, as I have doon thes parts. *a* **1548** HALL *Chron., Rich. III*, 26 b, To putte some to execucion, and staie the countree, or els no small mischiefe had ensued. **1577** KENDALL *Flowers of Epigr., Trifles* 2 b, Seke still to staie the stormes of sturdie strife. **1588** SHAKS. *L.L.L.* III. i. 99 The Foxe, the Ape, and the Humble-Bee, Were still at oddes, being but three. *Arm.* Vntill the Goose came out of doore, Staying the oddes by adding foure. *a* **1593** MARLOWE *Massacre at Paris* 439, I haue done what I could to stay this broile. **1603** KNOLLES *Hist. Turks* (1621) 688 Auria somewhat troubled with this sudden comming out of the enemie,..yet notably staied him-self. *a* **1648** LD. HERBERT *Hen. VIII* (1683) 477 This alone yet could not have stayed the Rebels. **1810** SCOTT *Lady of L.* v. xxix, Old men..Bless'd him who staid the civil strife. **1877** TENNYSON *Harold* I. ii, Should not England Love Aldwyth, if she stay the feuds that part The sons of Godwin from the sons of Alfgar By such a marrying?

29. *to stay the stomach*: to appease its cravings, stave off hunger; to quiet the appetite temporarily. Similarly *to stay one's longing, hunger, the appetite*, etc. Also *fig.*

1608 SHAKS. *Per.* v. iii. 83 Lord Cerimon, wee doe our longing stay To heare the rest vntolde. **1610** B. JONSON *Alchemist* III. v, A piece of ginger-bread, to be merry withall, And stay your stomack, lest you faint with fasting. **1655** FULLER *Ch. Hist.* VII. 419 All this Income rather stayed the stomack, than satisfied the hunger of the Kings Exchequer. **1684** tr. *Bonet's Merc. Compit.* I. 23 Fat and clammy things stay too great hunger. **1739** H. WALPOLE *Let. to R. West* 18 June, To stay your stomach, I will send you one of the vaudevilles or ballads. *a* **1853** ROBERTSON *Serm.* Ser. III. xx. 258 A thing which when chewed will stay the appetite. **1877** SPURGEON *Serm.* XXIII. 495 Present mercies are a sip by the way—a morsel eaten to stay the stomach. **1879** STEVENSON *Trav. Cevennes* 89 Father Michael..gave me a glass of liqueur to stay me till dinner. **1888** *Sat. Rev.* 20 Oct. 453/1 It would appear that the fight at the Jalapla has..stayed the stomach of the Lamas for fighting.

IV. *Combinations.*

30. Combinations of the vb. + object: **stay-plough** = REST-HARROW (Prior *Plant-n.* 1863); **stay-stomach**, a snack to stay the stomach or appetite; also *fig.*; †**stay-time** *nonce-wd.*, ?something to arrest the flight of time. Also STAY-SHIP.

1800 BENTHAM *Wks.* (1843) X. 356 The accompanying forgery papers I send you for a *stay stomach, to keep you in good humour. **1825** COBBETT *Rur. Rides* (1885) II. 24 We had some bits of bread and meat in our pockets..which were merely intended as stay-stomachs. **1891** *Ch. Times* 328/4 The cross bun on Good Friday..was the only stay-stomach permissible till 3 p.m. **1713** M. HENRY *Catech. Youth* Wks. 1857 II. 162/2 We have more need of *stay-times than pastimes.

31. Combinations of the vb. + adv. or advb. phrase, as **stay-ashore**, one who stays ashore; **stay-away**, (*a*) one who stays away; (*b*) an act or process of staying away, esp. from work; also as *adj.*; **stay-a-while** *Austral.*, the shrub *Acacia colletioides*, from the difficulty of penetrating a tract covered with it; **stay-down** *a.*, of, pertaining to, or designating a strike staged by miners staying down a mine; **stay-in** *a.*, of, pertaining to, or designating a strike in which the strikers remain in their place of work; also *absol.* as *sb.*, (one who participates in) a strike of this kind; **stay-on** *adj.*, intended for guests who 'stay on' after an earlier function; **stay over**, a waiting at a port of transhipment when the regular connexion has been missed; **stay-up** *a.*, of stockings: remaining in place without garters or suspenders; also *absol.* as *sb.* Also STAY-AT-HOME.

1884 *Pall Mall Gaz.* 24 July 2/1 On landing the crew were severely censured by the *stay-ashores for 'lack of courage'. **1867** *Ch. & St. Rev.* 2 Feb. 99 The intolerable dulness of the sermons, and the want of sympathy evinced by the sermonisers with the political aspirations of the *stayaways, were the reasons given. **1940** *Sun* (Baltimore) 10 Sept. 7/2 A 'stay-away' strike by hundreds of Allegany county school children continued into its second week today, with parents' support. Students said the 'stay away' was a protest against the consolidation program of the Allegany County Board of Education. **1963** *Listener* 28 Feb. 363/1 The calls for general work-stoppages during recent years have been 'stay-aways' directed against political and urban restrictions rather than against employers. **1976** *Times* 24 Aug. 1/4 Thousands of people in Soweto heeded a call not to go to work... Whether the mass stay-away..reflected widespread support for the strike call is unclear. **1898** MORRIS *Austral Eng.* 436 **Stay-a-while*, a tangled bush; sometimes called *Wait-a-while*. **1948** *Sun* (Baltimore) 11 Feb. 3/1 (*heading*) '*Stay-down' strikers occupy British mine. *Ibid.*, Three hundred miners are staging a 'stay-down' strike in the Waleswood mine. **1948** *Times* 23 Feb. 3/1 More than 400 delegates from all parts of the South Wales coalfield at Cardiff on Saturday discussed measures to stop the wave of stay-down strikes. **1980** *Listener* 29 May 686/2 Miners in Hungary were winning themselves better conditions with a new tactic, the stay-down hunger strike. **1915** *Political Q.* May 95 The Withdrawal of Labour Committee..advised the men..to adopt the '*stay-in' strike. **1926** *Times* 29 Apr. 5/7 (*heading*) Lock-out of 'stay-in' strikers. **1937** *Amer. Speech* XII. 32 When this type of action takes place during working hours ..it is a *sit-down, folded arms* or *crossed arms* strike. When it is prolonged beyond that period, it becomes, in addition, a *stay-in*. **1944** *Time* 12 June 14/1 Some of the stay-ins crowded out on to the balconies. **1950** MILLIS & BROWN *Wagner Act to Taft-Hartley* viii. 278 In the 'stay-in' strike.. management was locked out and kept off the job. **1968** *Amer. Speech* XLIII. 63 Drop-outs and stay-ins have been noted. **1900** 'J. S. WINTER' *Married Miss Binks* 79 They sent out invitations for a sort of garden party with a *stay-on cold dinner and a dance to follow. **1898** M. DAVITT *Life & Progr. Austral.* 2 One of the most interesting experiences in a '*stay over' at this unsavoury place is that of watching the Arab porters coaling a ship. **1949** *Sun* (Baltimore) 20 July 4 No roll—*stay up tops. **1953** *Ibid.* 20 July (E ed.) 3 No supporters are necessary for they have their own stay-up tops! **1969** J. GARDNER *Complete State of Death* ix. 174 Her woollen kaftan riding up to display the dark elasticized top of her stay-up stockings. **1973** *Nation* (Barbados) 25 Nov. 3 (Advt.), Nylon Stay-ups 99 c.

32. The verb-stem used *attrib.*, as **stay-bit**, a snack before a meal.

1833 *Fraser's Mag.* VII. 686 Which might peradventure serve as a stay-bit to a ravenous public.

stay (steɪ), *v.*² Pa. t. and pa. pple. **stayed** (steɪd). Also 6 **stey, staie, staye.** [a. OF. *estayer* (mod.F. *étayer*) to prop up, prob. an extended use of the nautical verb *estayer* (mod.F. *étayer*) = STAY *v.*³]

1. *trans.* To support, sustain, hold up (a person or thing). Const. *on*, *upon*, †*unto*. Now somewhat rare exc. in technical use (see 4).

1548 COOPER *Elyot's Dict., Canalicula & Canaliculus*, a littell pype, or a lyttell splente to staie a broken fynger. **1550** T. LEVER *Serm.* (Arb.) 135 Beware therefore that ye staye not your selfe vnto a bryttell staffe. **1572** MASCALL *Plant. & Graff.* (1592) 35 When those Cions shall put foorth a fayre wood, ye must binde and staye them in the middest..with small wands. **1576** FLEMING *Panopl. Epist.* 150 The common wealth leaneth and stayeth it selfe vpon your shoulders. **1578** BANISTER *Hist. Man* IV. 47 Moreouer they [the muscles] are mad to stay the eyes. **1590** SPENSER *F.Q.* I. vi. 35 And in his hand a Iacobs staffe, to stay His wearie limbes vpon. **1607** ROWLANDS *Famous Hist.* 69 He sits him sadly down, And on his bending knees his elbow stays. *a* **1630** J. TAYLOR (Water P.) *Wks.* II. 175/2 A Water-man many times hath his Soueraigne by the hand, to stay him in and out the Barge. **1697** DRYDEN *Virg. Georg.* II. 575 Sallows and Reeds..for Vineyards useful found, To stay thy Vines, and fence thy fruitful Ground. **1817** KEATS *'I stood tip-toe'* 73 Where swarms of minnows show their little heads, Staying their wavy bodies 'gainst the streams. **1837** CARLYLE *Fr. Rev.* I. I. ii, On this younger strength it would fain stay its decrepitude. **1870** BRYANT *Iliad* XVIII. 703 The vines were stayed on rows of silver stakes. **1871** H. YULE tr. *Marco Polo* I. lxi. I. 264 He has another Palace built of cane. .. It is stayed on gilt and lackered columns. **1891** KIPLING *Barrack-room Ball., Eng. Flag* 48 Because on the bones of the English the English Flag is stayed.

b. *transf.* and *fig.* To support, sustain, strengthen, comfort. Now *arch.* (Biblical).

1526 *Pilgr. Perf.* (W. de W. 1531) 32 Thus these holy gyftes stayeth yᵉ soule of man. **1558** BP. WATSON *Sev. Sacram.* vi. 33 That our courage & strength maye bee stayed and directed to the right ende. **1560** BIBLE (Geneva) *Song Sol.* ii. 5 Stay me with flagons, comfort me with apples. **1573–80** TUSSER *Husb.* (1878) 9 Though countrie health long staid me. **1590** SPENSER *F.Q.* III. xi. 23 Neither may This fire be quencht by any wit or might,..So mighty be th' enchauntments, which the same do stay. **1612** T. TAYLOR *Comm. Titus* i. 7 (1619) 158 Whereby Iacob in want staied his minde. *a* **1720** SEWEL *Hist. Quakers* (1722) 13 Yet he was stayed by a secret Belief. **1872** O. W. HOLMES *Poet Breakf.-t.* vii, The trust that stayed the hearts of those we loved who have gone before us. **1913** D. BRAY *Life-Hist. Brahui* iv. 64 At her side sits some old dame, staying her with wise words of comfort.

c. with *up*. Now *rare* (*arch.*). Also †*to stay upright*.

1526 TINDALE *Matt.* iv. 6 With there handes they shall stey the vpp. **1535** COVERDALE *Exod.* xvii. 12 And Aaron & Hur stayed vp his handes. **1569** UNDERDOWNE *Heliodorus* VIII. 110 b, Cariclia..beganne to staie her vprighte. **1577** GOOGE *Heresbach's Husb.* II. 79 b, The Vines that are yoked, or stayed vp with proppes. **1611** BIBLE *1 Kings* xxii. 35 The king was stayed vp in his charet against the Syrians. **1646** GATAKER *Mistake Removed* 25 As a bruised staf of reed or cane, that is..unable to stay a man up and support him. **1842** MANNING *Serm.* I. xix. (1848) 283 He stayed them up even against themselves.

2. *fig.* To cause to rest *on*, *upon* or *in* (a firm support, base or ground); to base or ground *upon*, to fix or set firmly *in*.

1565 SHACKLOCK tr. *Hosius' Treat. Heresies* 51 *marg.*, What scriptures Stenckfeld stayeth his sect vpon. **1565** J. PHILLIP *Patient Grissell* Pref. (Malone Soc.) 2 Historians oft in Hystories, their hole delightes haue staid To pen & paynt forth painfully, the modest liues of those, That [etc.]. **1569** SPENSER *Sonets* i. 14 So I..In God alone do stay my confidence. **1611** BIBLE *Isa.* xxvi. 3 Thou wilt keepe him in perfect peace, whose minde is stayed on thee. **1850** TENNYSON *In Mem.* lxxx. 8 A grief as deep as life or thought, But stay'd in peace with God and man.

†**b.** *refl.* with *upon*: To rely or build upon, take one's stand upon, rest or act upon; to abide by; to content oneself with. *Obs.*

1550 CROWLEY *Last Trumpet* 69 Stay thou thi selfe therfore vpon These examples comfortable. **1560** BIBLE (Geneva) *Isa.* xlviii. 2 They..staie them selues vpon the God of Israel. **1570–6** LAMBARDE *Peramb. Kent* (1826) 333 But staying my selfe upon this generall note, I will proceede with the treatise of the place that I have taken in hand. **1576** FLEMING *Panopl. Epist.* Epit. Precepts A ij, The principalls of ech Prouince, stayed themselues vpon his determination. **1709** STRYPE *Ann. Ref.* I. v. 93 Their Adversaries stayed them-selves most upon Old Councils, and the Writings of Doctors and Fathers.

†**c.** To settle in a strong position or secure tenure; to establish. *Obs.*

1560 DAUS tr. *Sleidane's Comm.* 394 b, Wishing, that either nation with their forces joyned together, might so stay them selves, that they should nead to be afraid of no man. **1574** *Wills Northern C.* (Surtees) I. 398, I will that my trewe servant will'm pateson shalbe hynd of the too hous..vnto such tym as he be stayed wᵗʰ a fermhold.

3. *intr.* (for *refl.*) **to stay on, upon** ——.

†**a.** To lean upon, support oneself by (a staff, etc.). Of a thing: To rest upon, be supported by.

1585 HIGINS *Junius' Nomencl.* 208/2 *Columnæ*,..the vpright postes bearing vp the windbeame, and staying vpon the transains. **1598** R. BERNARD tr. *Terence, Andria* III. v. 65 Lo, what a sure speare I haue of thee, what a sure staffe to stay vpon. **1603** KNOLLES *Hist. Turks* (1621) 69 The aforesaid undermined towre, with some part of the wall (the timber whereon it staied soon burnt) fell downe. **1681** W. ROBERTSON *Phraseol. Gen.* 1168/1 To stay or lean upon; *niti, inniti, insistere*.

†**b.** To rely upon, trust to, have confidence in; to look to for help or support. Of a thing: To depend on, be vested in. *Obs.*

1560 BIBLE (Geneva) *Isa.* xxxi. 1 Wo vnto them that..stay vpon horses, and trust in charettes. **1587** FLEMING *Contin. Holinshed* III. 976/1 The letter was to be followed, the message not to be staied on. **1596** SHAKS. *Merch. V.* IV. i. 242, I stay heere on my bond. **1600** ROWLANDS *Lett. Humours Blood* (1874) 59 He hath a stocke whereon his lyuing stayes, And they are Fullams and Bard quarter-trayes. **1682** BUNYAN *Holy War* (1905) 324 You must not dwell in, nor stay upon any thing of that which he hath in Commission to teach you. **1722** DE FOE *Plague* (1840) 107 My heart smote me, suggesting how much better this poor man's foundation was, on which he stayed in the danger, than mine.

4. *trans.* (*spec.* and *techn.*) To support, strengthen or secure with stays. Also with *up*.

1556 *Fabric Rolls York Minster* (Surtees) 355 To Wm. Bellow and his ij workemen, in staying of the crosse & wallyng & settynge of the staires abowtt the said crosse, 10s. For staying of the owtshottis, etc. 7s. 8d. **1568–9** *Ibid.* 114 To Brian Daragon for making ij stayes to beare and stay uppe a gutter, 4d. **1580–1** *Ibid.* 118 For two longe yron gaddes for stayinge of a pynnacle of the churche, 11s. **1838** F. W. SIMMS *Publ. Wks. Gt. Brit.* 70 The roof and sides of the box shall be stayed with copper bolts. **1849** RUSKIN *Sev. Lamps* vi. §19. 181 Watch an old building with anxious care ..stay it with timber where it declines. **1869** RANKINE *Machine & Hand-tools* Pl. K 1, This machine consists of two very strong cast-iron plates, well stayed and bolted together. **1887** *Encycl. Brit.* XXII. 498/2 The front tube-plate in which the tubes terminate..is stayed to the back tube-plate by the tubes themselves. *Ibid.* 499/2 The steam-dome is a cylinder 2½ feet in diameter and 8 feet long, stayed by a central 3½-inch rod of steel. **1898** *Daily News* 10 May 6/7 It did not matter to you whether the building was stayed up or not?

stay, *v.*³ *Naut.* Pa. t. and pa. pple. **stayed** (steɪd). [f. STAY *sb.*¹ Cf. OF. *estayer* (mod.F. *étayer*).]

1. *trans.* To secure or steady by means of stays; to incline (forward, aft, or to one side) by means of stays.

1627 CAPT. SMITH *Sea Gram.* v. 19 Those staies doe helpe to stay the Boulspret. **1644** MANWAYRING *Seamans Dict.* 101 The foremast and masts belonging to it are in the same manner stayed at the bolt-sprit, and sprit-saile-top-mast. **1793** SMEATON *Edystone L.* §300 Our shears and tackle were so well lashed down and stayed. **1846** A. YOUNG *Naut. Dict.* 296 A mast is said to be stayed forward, or to rake aft, according as it inclines forward or aft. **1894** *Westm. Gaz.* 22 Feb. 5/1 The funnel had to be stayed.

2. To put (a ship) 'in stays' (see STAY *sb.*¹ 2 a); to put on the other tack.

a **1625** *Nomenclator Navalis* (Harl. MS. 2301) To Stay or bring a Ship a Stay. **1633** T. JAMES *Voy.* 93 We turned amongst this Ice, staying the Ship sometimes within her length, of great pieces. **1644** MANWAYRING *Seamans Dict.*, *To Stay, or, bring a Ship a-stay.* When we tack the ship, before the ship can be ready to be tacked; she must come a-stayes or a back-stayes, that is, when wind comes in at the bowe which was the lee-bowe before, and so drives all the sailes backward, against the shrowds and masts, so that the ship hath no way, but drives with the broad-side: the manner of doing it is, [etc.]. **1706** PHILLIPS (ed. Kersey), To *Bring a Ship upon the Stays* or *To stay her*, is to manage her Tackle, and sails so that she cannot make any way forward, which is done in order to her Tacking. **1895** *Daily News* 8 July 8/6 The Prince's cutter made a strong bid for the weather berth by crossing on the wrong tack, but Ailsa was stayed, and Carter's game was spoiled.

3. *intr.* To go about in stays; to turn to windward in order to tack.

a **1613** RALEGH *Let.* Sceptick etc. (1651) 130 The extream length of a Ship makes her unapt to stay. **1628** DIGBY *Voy.*

Mediterr. (Camden) 5 Wee..made all hast wee could to tacke about after them, but the sea went so high that it was long before we could make our shippe stay. **1769** FALCONER *Dict. Marine* II. (1780), *Refuser*, to fall off again, when in stays; expressed of a ship that will not go about, or stay. **1836** E. HOWARD *R. Reefer* xxxi, She has stayed within her own length. **1891** *Daily News* 19 Oct. 6/7 The helm was put up, but the ship refused to stay.

'stay-at-,home, *a.* and *sb.* [f. STAY *v.*[1]]

A. *adj.* That stays at home, not given to travelling or to gadding abroad; hence untravelled. Also *spec.* avoiding going abroad on military service.

1806 G. PINCKARD *Tour W. Indies* III. 342 The extravagant alarm pictured by the fearful imaginations of stay-at-home travellers. **1814** JANE AUSTEN *Mansf. Park* v, A talking pretty young woman like Miss Crawford is always pleasant society to an indolent, stay-at-home man. **1819** in *Lady Morgan's Autobiog.* (1859) 326, I went to bed most depressed, and in admiration of your stay-at-home wisdom. **1861** O. W. HOLMES *Sweet Little Man* 35 In the brigade of the Stay-at-Home Rangers Marches my corps. **1902** CORNISH *Naturalist Thames* 152 It is in the woods that the stay-at-home birds are most in evidence in winter. **1946** W. S. CHURCHILL *Victory* 78 You hear all this talk by the stay-at-home Left Wing *intelligentsia* that the soldiers will hold us guilty if we do not have a new world waiting for them on their return.

B. *sb.* **a.** One who stays at home, one not given to travelling or gadding abroad; *spec.* one who avoids going abroad on military service. Also *transf.*

1836 DICKENS *Let.* ? 27 Nov. (1965) I. 200 Mrs. Dickens is a great stay-at-home just now. **1841** DICKENS *Barn. Rudge* i, Sixty-six years ago a vast number both of travellers and stay-at-homes were in this condition. **1855** KINGSLEY *Westw. Ho!* xv, If some of you young gentlemen would..go forth to find us stay-at-homes new markets for our ware. **1883** A. PINKERTON *Spy of Rebellion* xxv. 499 Extravagant ideas of a struggle which should be 'short, sharp and decisive', were the only ones entertained by the great army of 'stay at homes'. **1918** *Nation* (N.Y.) 7 Feb. 131/1 Students..accused as stay-at-homes, unwilling to fight and suffer for the Fatherland. **1949** E. HYAMS *Grape Vine in England* 143 Not by any means all the root-dwelling insects change into winged insects. The stay-at-homes winter among the roots of the vines. **1981** A. COOKE in *N.Y. Times Mag.* 19 July 6/4 We..sent in 'technicians' and followed them up with a blood sacrifice, but burdened the stay-at-homes with no extra taxes.

b. A staying at home, *spec.* a strike.

1959 [see *neon world* s.v. NEON 3 a]. **1960** *Guardian* 20 Apr. 18/1 They disagreed on whether the stay-at-home should be for a day or a week. **1976** *Times* 24 Aug. 1/4 If today's stay-at-home is maintained..the organizers will have demonstrated that they are capable of arranging mass protests among urban blacks.

So also (nonce-words) **stay-at-homeative-ness, -itiveness** (mimicking phrenological terms), **stay-at-homeishness.**

1818 T. L. PEACOCK *Maid Marian* i, Domesticity, or as learned doctors call it—the faculty of stayathomeitiveness. **1826** *Westm. Rev.* VI. 327 Their un-Italianized countrymen, who are endowed with Spurzheim's bump, denominated stayathomeativeness. **1880** *Daily Tel.* 22 Sept., Our national tendency towards 'stay-at-homeishness'.

Staybrite ('steɪbraɪt). [f. STAY *v.*[1] + an arbitrary respelling of BRIGHT *a.*] A proprietary name for a make of stainless steel.

1925 *Metallurgist* I. 153/2 Dr. Westgren..prepared photograms of this chromium-nickel steel—known as 'Staybrite'—in both the fully quenched and softened condition. **1930** *Engineering* 11 Apr. 486/1 Some trouble had been experienced with Staybrite jackets. **1937** G. FRANKAU *More of Us* ii. 26 In hall of nearest-marble, gay With Staybrite, stood old Dorkins, butler hoary. **1937** *Trade Marks Jrnl.* 7 July 820 *Staybrite*... Stainless steels. Firth-Vickers Stainless Steels Ltd.,..Sheffield. **1964** BIRD & HALLOWS *Rolls-Royce Motor-Car* II. 244 Staybrite radiator shell, single-point suspension and pressure radiator cap.

stayed (steɪd), *a.* [f. STAY *sb.*[2] + -ED[2].] Provided with stays. Also **stayed-up.**

1819 *Metropolis* III. 174 A fourth stayed, and, perhaps, painted, male, smiles. **1884** *Pall Mall Gaz.* 16 Feb. 5/1 A stayed-up woman affected their impressionable and well-educated eyes as something monstrously ugly and absurd. Japanese dress is beautiful and so easy.

stayed (steɪd), *ppl. a.*[1] *rare.* [f. STAY *v.*[1] + -ED[2].] In senses of the verb.

c **1586** C'TESS PEMBROKE *Ps.* LXXVIII. ix, The raked sparkes in flame began t'appeare, And staied choller fresh againe to move.

stayed (steɪd), *ppl. a.*[2] See also STAID *a.* [f. STAY *v.*[2] + -ED[1].] In senses of the verb. Hence **stayedness** ('steɪɪdnɪs).

1845 J. J. GURNEY in *Mem.* (1854) II. 455 The soul is stayed on him, and finds a sure shelter. Somewhat of this blessed stayedness, this sweet shelter, has, I hope, been experienced. **1860** PUSEY *Min. Proph.* 416 Since this stayedness of faith is in everything the source of the life of the righteous.

stayer[1] ('steɪə(r)). [f. STAY *v.*[1] + -ER[1].]

1. One who stays or remains. Chiefly with advb. phrase, as in *stayer at home.*

1591 R. TURNBULL *St. James* 121 He that meeteth a wayfairing man, farre from al path or highway, wandring; and saith, go aright: yet teacheth not which hand he must turne on,..helpeth the staier nothing towardes his proposed iourney. **1729** SWIFT *Direct. Serv.*, *Gen.* (1745) 11 The Stayer at home may be comforted by a Visit from a Sweetheart. **1788** COWPER *Let. to Mrs. King* 28 Aug., I found you out to be sedentary, at least much a stayer within doors. **1805** W. TAYLOR in Robberds *Mem.* (1813) II. 72 My father is not very fond of long stayers, and I have more than once been obliged to interrupt the visits of friends of mine. **1851** HELPS *Comp. Solit.* viii. (1874) 144 A dignity such as the stayers at home never attained. **1853** R. S. SURTEES *Sponge's Sp. Tour* (1893) 235 He seemed to think that, being a stayer, he was a superior being to the mere dinner-comers.

b. *Sport.* A person or animal having great 'staying power'.

1862 *Sporting Mag.* May 381 Asteroid proved to be another of the Stockwell stayers. **1874** *Slang Dict.* 309 *Stayer*, one likely to persevere, one not easily discouraged. **1887** SHEARMAN *Athletics* 137 He could have beaten the [walking] record for seven miles, as he was a fine stayer.

2. One who or something which stops or restrains.

1597 MONTGOMERIE *Cherrie & Slae* 697 For they ar the stayer Of vs, alsweill as he. *c* **1610** SIR J. MELVIL *Mem.* (Bannatyne Club) 350 Sa that they wha past betwen mycht appear to be..stayers of bludscheding. **1722, 1840** [see STAYER[2] b]. **1876** MORRIS *Sigurd* IV. 378 No stirrer nor stayer of strife.

stayer[2] ('steɪə(r)). [f. STAY *v.*[2] + -ER[1].] One who stays or supports.

1579–80 NORTH *Plutarch, Theseus* (1595) 19 Gæiochus.. by interpretation doth signifie..the stayer of the earth.

b. With reference to the title of Jupiter Stator.

In quots. 1722 and 1840 interpreted as STAYER[1] 2.

1611 B. JONSON *Catiline* IV. ii, Thou Iupiter, whom we do call the Stayer Both of this Citie, and this Empire. [**1722** A. PHILIPS *Briton* I. i, May Jove, the Guardian of the Capitol, He, the great Stayer of our Troops in Rout, Fulfill your Hopes. **1840** ARNOLD *Hist. Rome* xxxiii. II. 349 The consul vowed to build a temple to Jove the stayer of flight.]

stayer, obs. form of STAIR.

stayes, obs. pl. form of STAITHE.

1613 [STANDISH] *New Direct. Planting* 16 Especially in the Riuer of Owes, where the maintaining of Stayes and Bankes, costeth the Bishops of Durham at least a hundred Marke a yeare.

staying ('steɪɪŋ), *vbl. sb.*[1] [f. STAY *v.*[1] + -ING[1].] The action of STAY *v.*[1]

1. In various intransitive senses: Coming to a stand, waiting, continuing in a place or a condition; †hesitating, delaying.

1546 J. HEYWOOD *Prov.* II. viii. (1867) 73 Whiche foreseene in this woman wisely waiyng, That meete was to staie somwhat for hir staiyng. **1576** FLEMING *Panopl. Epist.* A ij, There is a degree in growing, a stint or staying, and a diminishing. **1593** SHAKS. *2 Hen. VI*, IV. viii. 62 Heere is no staying. **1632** LITHGOW *Trav.* II. 52 In the time of my fiue dayes staying there. **1748** *Anson's Voy.* II. vi. 199 The cause of his staying behind. **1786** G. FRAZER *Dove's Flight* 59 It is our perverse wills that are the cause of our staying away from Christ. **1891** *Sat. Rev.* 28 Mar. 383/1 *Staying* may merely mean, as it sometimes does on the Turf, not being able to go fast enough to tire themselves.

†**b.** *staying of the sun*: = SOLSTICE. Cf. STAY *sb.*[3] 3 c. *Obs.*

[**1552** HULOET, Stayinge course or standinge of the sunne at the highest and lowest.] **1555** EDEN *Decades* (Arb.) 167 The steyinges & conuersyons of the soonne (cauled *Solstitia*).

c. Holding out in a race, etc.

1862 H. H. DIXON *Scott & Sebright* iii. 207 His staying arose rather from the fact that his speed was so tremendous that no horse could get him out, than from innate gameness.

2. Stopping, arresting, preventing.

1563 in *Vicary's Anat.* (1888) App. III. 165 The proclamacion devysed for the steyinge of thowneres of thinfected mansyon howses..from the lettynge of the same. **1620** in *10th Rep. Hist. MSS. Comm.* App. I. 45, I fear it prouffe ane improfitable work..bot there is no staying of him. **1654** J. OWEN *Doctr. Saints Persev.* xii. 287 The staying of the Mariners from going out of the ship, was a meanes that Paul was kept a live.

3. *attrib.* and *Comb.*, as *staying-place*; **staying power**, in a race or other contest (hence also *gen.*), power to 'stay' or continue in action for a long time; power of persistent effort; so *staying qualities.*

1870 MORRIS *Earthly Par.* II. III. 16 No middle, no beginning, and no end; No *staying place. **1859** H. H. DIXON *Silk & Scarlet* iii. 250 His stock..rather inherit his fine dash of speed, than his *staying powers. **1875** *Punch* 13 Mar. 115/2 Steddie has deteriorated, but his back is fairly straight, and his staying power is good. **1880** G. DUFF in *19th Cent.* No. 38. 661 The Greek is no doubt the higher civilisation, but the Bulgarian has more 'staying power.' **1887** SHEARMAN *Athletics* 112 The good steeplechaser must, of course, be a long-distance runner, as no one without staying powers can hope to last the distance. **1856** H. H. DIXON *Post & Paddock* ii. 38 The *staying qualities of the Hetmans. **1888** BRYCE *Amer. Commw.* III. lxxxix. 218 Its candidates, when elected, often betrayed it and went over to the regulars, who, they foresaw, had more staying qualities.

staying ('steɪɪŋ), *vbl. sb.*[2] [f. STAY *v.*[2] + -ING[1].] The action of STAY *v.*[2]; propping up, supporting. Also, †supporting oneself, leaning.

1428–9 *Rec. St. Mary at Hill* (1905) 70 For iron werk & nayles for stayeng of þe crosse iiijs jd. **1580–1** *Fabric Rolls York Minster* (Surtees) 118 For two longe yron gaddes for stayinge of a pynnacle of the churche, 11s. **1648** HEXHAM II, *Een leninge*, a Leaning or a Staying against any place.

b. *attrib.* †**staying staff**, a staff to lean upon.

1563 CHURCHYARD *Mirr. Mag.*, *Shore's Wife* lxxiii, A staying staffe and wallet therewithall I bare about as witnesse of my fall. **1577** KENDALL *Flowers of Epigr.* 68 b, A sachell and a staiyng staff..Were acceptable to the life, of wise Diogenes.

staying ('steɪɪŋ), *vbl. sb.*[3] [f. STAY *v.*[3] + -ING[1].] The action of STAY *v.*[3]

a **1618** RALEGH *Invent. Shipping* 29 Which may be chosen .., by reason of their ready staying and turning. *c* **1635** CAPT. N. BOTELER *Dialogues Sea Services* (1685), Staying of masts. **1830** MARRYAT *King's Own* xxiv, A boat..had been lowered down..to examine the staying of the masts.

staying ('steɪɪŋ), *ppl. a.* [f. STAY *v.*[1] + -ING[2].] That stays.

1. In intransitive senses. †**a.** With complement, as *staying silent. Obs.* **b.** Continuing in a place.

1570 ASCHAM *Scholem.* II. (Arb.) 115 Those that haue ye inuentiuest heades..and roundest tonges..(except they learne and vse this good lesson of *Epitome*) commit commonlie greater faultes, than dull, staying silent men do. **1853** R. S. SURTEES *Sponge's Sp. Tour* xli. (1893) 217 The staying guests could not do much for the good things set out. **1865** FLOR. MARRYAT *Love's Conflict* I. xiv. 225 In some cases it is *not* the staying horse who wins.

2. In transitive senses: Arresting.

1902 *Daily Chron.* 2 Sept. 5/1 There is yet time for a staying hand, which would preserve some plain brickwork in the interior.

Hence **'stayingly** *adv. rare*[−0].

1648 HEXHAM II, *Blijvelick*, Durable, or Stayingly.

staylace ('steɪleɪs), *sb.* [f. STAY *sb.*[2] + LACE *sb.*] A lace or cord used to draw together a woman's stays or bodice.

1720 SWIFT *Proposal Use Irish Manuf.* Misc. 1735 V. 204, I should rejoice to see a Stay-Lace from England be thought scandalous, and become a Topick for Censure. **1851** MAYHEW *Lond. Labour* I. 323 Pins and needles, stay-laces, and such small articles as are light to carry. **1882** CAULFEILD & SAWARD *Dict. Needlework* 460/2 *Stay laces*..are otherwise called Stay-cord, and are made of both cotton and linen.

Comb. **1889** HARDY *Mayor Casterbr.* i, A buxom staylace dealer.

'staylace, *v.* [f. STAYLACE *sb.*] *trans.* To lace up with staylaces. Hence **'staylaced** *ppl. a.*

1824 *Blackw. Mag.* XV. 368 The stay-laced dandy. **1832** J. C. H[ARE] in *Philol. Mus.* I. 678 Every departure from idiom, every attempt to staylace the language of polisht conversation, renders our phraseology inelegant and clumsy.

stayle, obs. form of STALL *sb.*[1]

stayless ('steɪlɪs), *a.*[1] Also 6 stailes, 6–7 **stailesse.** [f. STAY *sb.*[3] + -LESS.]

1. Not to be stayed or stopped, ever-moving, unceasing, ceaseless.

1578 BLENNERHASSET *Mirr. Mag.*, *Carassus* ix, They fled the fielde: They made me muse, to see how fast they striude, With staylesse steppes, eche one his life to shielde. **1590** C'TESS PEMBROKE *Antonie* 486 And neuer can our weaknes turne awry The stailes course of powerfull destenie. **1611** J. DAVIES (Heref.) *Sco. Folly* cxlvii. (Grosart) 25 That's staylesse time, which he doth precious hold. **1825** HOGG *Q. Hynde* 24 Onward he drove with stayless shock. *a* **1851** MOIR *Poet. Wks.* (1852) II. 341 Though years in stayless current roll. **1867** G. MACDONALD *Poems* 109 Stayless of foot, he turned not from the sea.

2. Without stay or permanence, ever-changing, unsettled.

c **1572** GASCOIGNE *Fruites Warre* lxxiii, In meane while yet hopeth to aduaunce His staylesse state, by sworde, by speare, by shielde. *c* **1586** C'TESS PEMBROKE *Ps.* LXXVIII. iv, A waiward, stubborn, stailesse, faithlesse race. **1590** L. ANDREWES *96 Serm.*, *Lent* ii. (1629) 277 We are but let see the wandring and staylesse estate we were in, till God vouchsafed to send us this gracious conduct. **1813** HOGG *Queen's Wake* 290 She leaned to the lee, and she girdled the wave; Aloft on the stayless verge she hung. **1881** G. MACDONALD *Mary Marston* II. 20 The bond between them was an eternal one, yet were they separated by a gulf of unrelation. Not a mountain range, but a stayless nothingness parted them.

'stayless, *a.*[2] [f. STAY *sb.*[2] + -LESS.]

1. Without stay or support, unsupported.

1587 HIGGINS *Mirr. Mag.*, *Pinnar* Lenuoye ii, If hee vnstatelike stammer out the same, With staylesse staggering footed verse, by ame. *c* **1590** *Faire Em* I. ii. 33 Although our outward pomp be thus abased, And thralde to drudging, staylesse of the world. **1590** LODGE *Euphues Gold. Leg.* F 2 b, Oh staylesse youth, by errour so misguided. **1607** J. DAVIES (Heref.) *Summa Totalis* (Grosart) 19/2 It was his will, That man, made stailesse, so should fall, and rise. *c* **1817** HOGG *Tales & Sk.* I. 291 Left helpless and stayless.

2. Unsupported by stays or corsets.

1880 MRS. LYNN LINTON *Rebel of Family* iii, The girl's slender, loose and stayless waist. **1883** *Philad. Press* 7 June 9 A stayless waist with divided underskirts.

Hence **'staylessness.**

1883 *Philad. Press* 7 June 9 Staylessness..is not by itself sufficient unto salvation in this matter, nor is the divided skirt by itself sufficient.

Stayman ('steɪmən). The name of Samuel M. *Stayman* (b. 1909), an American authority on contract bridge, used *attrib.* and *absol.* to designate a convention used in bidding at contract bridge.

1952 S. M. STAYMAN *Expert Bidding at Contract Bridge* vi. 53 The bidding method that has become known as the 'Stayman' Convention was not named by me. I was the first to describe it in print (in.. 1945), and bridge players.. called it by my name. **1955** —— *Compl. Stayman System of Contract Bidding* viii. 83 The Stayman System takes a position in the centre of the two popular standards. **1962** *Times* 4 Apr. 6/7 The use of artificial 'asking' bids such as the Neapolitan One Club, the Stayman Two Clubs and the Blackwood conventions. **1972** *Guardian* 26 June 12/4 When asked if I play Stayman, I find it difficult to answer. There are many versions of this convention. **1976** *National Observer* (U.S.) 10 July 15/1 The partnership also was playing 'double barrel' Stayman in which two clubs shows a weak hand and two diamonds forces to game.

stay-put ('steɪpʊt), *sb.* and *a. colloq.* Also **stay put, stayput.** [f. vbl. phr. *to stay put*: see STAY *v.*[1] 6 b.] **A.** *sb.* **a.** A refraining from movement or travel. (Stress variable.)

1941 KOESTLER *Scum of Earth* 194 It is a sort of general stay put. *Ibid.* 204 Crowd of smart civilians queuing up to get petrol for their cars—and actually getting it in spite of stay-put order.

b. One who refuses to move, one who stays at home. Chiefly *Austral.*

1967 PARTRIDGE *Dict. Slang* Suppl. 1388/2 *Stay-put*, one who holds his ground ('stays put'): coll., esp. Australian: since ca. 1950. **1977** C. MCCULLOUGH *Thorn Birds* vi. 120 Things were more amicable between vagabonds and stay-puts.

B. *adj.* Remaining where or as placed; during which one remains in one place. Also, refusing to move, refraining from travel.

1962 *N.Y. Times Mag.* 9 Sept. 77/1 (Advt.), Other important details you'll like: the grow-feature for extra long wear, our new stay-put moccasin foot. **1963** *Guardian* 13 July 4/5 A stay-put holiday at one resort. **1968** *Daily Tel.* (Colour Suppl.) 13 Dec. 31/1 In the United States, a mobile home can have two bedrooms... Some cost almost as much as a stay-put house of comparable size. **1969** *Sears Catal.* Spring/Summer 22 Fashion-back jeans and shorts with soil release... Bar tacked. Stay-put zipper. Band waist, belt loops. **1973** *Times* 13 Jan. 12/8 A centre for touring as well as for stayput holidaymakers. **1977** *Borneo Bull.* 7 May 2/1 Thirty four of Miri's stay-put squatter families who have been defying eviction deadlines for two years have won their battle for land.

stay-'putter. *colloq.* [f. as prec. + -ER[1].] One who refrains from moving.

1927 J. ADAMS *Errors in School* ii. 41 Leaving this suggestion of a restricted meaning of the term *idea* to the tender mercies of the stay-putters. **1971** 'E. FENWICK' *Impeccable People* xix. 105, I don't understand you stay-putters, but you're probably wise people.

staysail ('steɪseɪl, 'steɪs(ə)l). *Naut.* [f. STAY *sb.*[1]] A triangular sail hoisted upon a stay. Often with defining word prefixed.

1669 STURMY *Mariner's Mag.* I. ii. 18 Hoise up Main Staysail, and Mizen Stay-sail. **1748** *Anson's Voy.* II. iv. 163 Their top-gallant sails and stay-sails all fluttering in the wind. **1806** A. DUNCAN *Life Nelson* 124 The Foudroyant's ..stay-sails..were all in tatters. **1899** F. T. BULLEN *Log Sea-waif* 46 Some of the fore and afters had actually got staysails set, with the sheets hauled flat aft.

b. *attrib.*

1857 DUFFERIN *Lett. High Lat.* (ed. 3) 300 The staysail sheet is let go. **1863** A. YOUNG *Naut. Dict.* 369 *Staysail-netting*, the netting above a vessel's bowsprit, for stowing away the fore-topmast staysail. **1867** SMYTH *Sailor's Wordbk.*, *Staysail-Stay*, the stay on which a staysail is set.

stay-ship ('steɪʃɪp). [f. STAY *v.*[1]] = REMORA.

1567, 1601 [see REMORA 1]. **1585** HIGINS *Junius' Nomencl.* 66 *Echeneis, remora*, ..a stay ship, because it will cleaue close and fast to the keele of yͤ ship, and hinder it in course. **1884** GOODE *Nat. Hist. Aquat. Anim.* 355 Several species of 'stay-ships' or 'remoras' occur on our coast.

stay-tape ('steɪteɪp). [f. STAY *sb.*[2]] A staylace, often used by tailors, etc. as a binding to a fabric. †Also *slang* (see quot. 1785).

1698 E. WARD *Lond. Spy* IV. (1706) 91 To find Canvas, Stay-Tape, and Buckram in a Taylors Bill. **1709** [W. KING] *Usef. Trans. Philos.* Jan. & Feb. 24, I discours'd to him of the Nature..of Staytape, Stifning, and Grogram. **1785** GROSE *Dict. Vulgar T.*, *Staytape*, a taylor; from that article and its coadjutor buckram, which makes no small figure in the bills of those knights of the needle. **1801** tr. *Gabrielli's Mysterious Husb.* II. 72 The coat alone had cost upwards of eight-and-twenty shillings, what with staytape, and buckram, and the other et cæteras. **1817** COLERIDGE *Biog. Lit.* II. xxi. 130 The pin-papers, and stay-tapes, which might have been among the wares of his pack. **1882** CAULFEILD & SAWARD *Dict. Needlework* 461 *Stay Tape*..is more properly called *Stay Binding*.

stchi: see SHCHI.

stead (stɛd), *sb.* Forms: 1 stede, styd(d, styde, steyde, 2–6 stede, 2–5 stude, 4–5 stud, stide, stad, 3, 6 stidde, 3–7, 8 *arch.* sted, 3, 5–6 stedd, 6 stedde, 4 steode, stode, stade, (stayd), 4–7 *Sc.* steid, 4, 6 styde, (5 steyde), 6 *Sc.* steide, steyd, 4–5, 8 stid, 5 styd, stydd, stydde, 7 stidd, 4–7 steede, 6–7 steed, steade, 5– stead. [Com. Teut.: OE. *stęde* masc., corresp. to OFris. *stede, stidi* (NFris. *städ*, WFris. *stêd* town), OS. *stad* (?), *stedi* masc. and fem., place (MLG. *stad, stede* fem., place, town), MDu. *stat, stēde* fem., place, town (mod.Du. *stad* fem., town, *stede, stee* place), OHG. *stat* fem., place (MHG. *stat, stete* fem., place, town, mod.G. *statt* place, stead, *stätte* place, site, *stadt* town), ON. *staðr* masc., place (Sw., Da. *stad*, with the sense 'town' from G.), Goth. *staþ-s* masc., place:—OTeut. **staði-z*:—pre-Teut. **stəti-s* (cf. Skr. *sthiti* standing, position, Gr. *στάσις* standing, stoppage, L. *statim* advb. accus., immediately, *statio* STATION *sb.*), f. wk.-grade of **stā-* to STAND.

A parallel form, OTeut. **stadō(n)-* fem., occurs in OHG. *stata* condition, opportunity, proper time or place (MHG. *state*, mod.G. *statt* in certain uses), MLG., Du. *stade* opportunity, help, ON. *staða* standing, position, condition. Some of the uses of *stead* closely approach those of MLG. *stade*, and may possibly be due to influence from MLG.]

†**I. 1.** Standing still, as opposed to movement; stoppage, delay. *Obs. rare.*

c **1000** ÆLFRIC *Hom.* I. 156 Hwæt is þæs Hælendes stede, oððe hwæt is his fær? *Ibid.* I. 490 Sceawiað eac æfter ðisum, þæt nan stede nis ures lichaman: cildhad ȝewit to cnihthade, and cnihthad to ȝeðungenum wæstme. *c* **1400** *Destr. Troy* 4654 All turnyt þaire tacle with trussyng of sailes, And stird hom full streight withouten stad more Into Awlida þe yle.

II. A point or tract in space. Cf. PLACE *sb.* I.

†**2.** A particular part of the earth's surface, or of space generally, considered as defined by its situation; a locality: = PLACE *sb.* 3. *Obs.*

†**a.** with descriptive adj. *Obs.*

c **975** *Rushw. Gosp.* Mark i. 35 Ðona eode in westiȝe stowe *vel* steyde & ðær ȝebæd. *c* **1050** *Suppl. Ælfric's Gloss.* in Wr.-Wülcker 187 *Circumlutus locus*, mid wæter ymbtyrnd stede. *c* **1200** *Trin. Coll. Hom.* 85 Ðenne þe iuele gost..wandreð ouer al, fro driȝe stede to oder sechende reste. *c* **1290** *St. Mɪhel* 599 in *S. Eng. Leg.* 316 Novþe is þare uppe in þe ufte a swyþe cold stude, i-wis. **1390** GOWER *Conf.* II. 388 Now se, mi Sone, which a sinne Is Sacrilege in holy stede. *c* **1400** tr. *Secreta Secret., Gov. Lordsh.* lviii. 79 þat wyn whos grape ..growys in playn and moyst valeyes, and stedys shadwyd. **1567** DRANT *Horace Ep., Art Poet.* Bij, Of hills and dales and secret steades he feanes him to be fayne. **1590** SPENSER *F.Q.* I. xi. 46 Great God it planted in that blessed sted With his almightie hand.

†**b.** defined by dependent genitive, or by relative clause. *Obs.*

c **1000** ÆLFRIC *Joshua* v. 16 For þam þe se stede ys haliȝ, þe þu on stenst. *a* **1300** *Cursor M.* 22963 þe stede o dome quar all sal mete. **13..** *K. Alis.* 2548 (Laud MS.), Hij wendeþ to þe batailes stede And fyndeþ nouȝth bot bodies dede. *c* **1470** HARDING *Chron.* CXXI. iii. 6 Whiche Abbaye is in Sussex, in that stede Where the batayle was. **1483** CAXTON *Golden Leg.* 160/1 And al sodeynly the stones opened and shewed to alle the peple the place and stede where the holy body restyd. **1590** SPENSER *F.Q.* II. xii. 30 And now they nigh approched to the sted, Where as those Mermayds dwelt: it was a still And calmy bay. **1596** DALRYMPLE tr. *Leslie's Hist. Scot.* I. v. 261 Perceiueng.. how Scopulous, stenddirrie, or stanie, was the stedd, quhairon thay than stude.

†**c.** indeterminately. Often coupled with *time.* ***in every stead***: everywhere; similarly ***in any, no stead.*** *Obs.*

a **1067** *Charter of Eadweard* in Kemble *Cod. Dipl.* IV. 209 Wiðinne burhe and wiðuten and on æloe styde, be lande and be strande. *a* **1225** *Ancr. R.* 316 Abuten sunne ligggeð six þinges þet hit helieð;..persone, stude, time, manere, tale, cause. *c* **1230** *Hali Meid.* 22 Flih..þe stude & te time, þe mahten bringe þe on mis forte donne. **1303** R. BRUNNE *Handl. Synne* 2029 Yn stedys sere. **1340** HAMPOLE *Pr. Consc.* 1701 For dedely syn and þe devell and he In a stede may noght to-gyder be. *c* **1380** WYCLIF *Wks.* (1880) 318 So þise ordris holden not cristis rewle neþer in tyme ne in stide for crist preyede..bi hym self vndir the cope of heuene. **1390** GOWER *Conf.* I. 359 This Pilour,..A famous man in sondri stede Was of the werkes which he dede. *c* **1400** tr. *Secreta Secret., Gov. Lordsh.* xlvii. 75 Slepyng aftyr eityng vpon soft beddes & wele sauorand, in steydes & tymes couenable. *c* **1420** *Sir Amadace* (Camden) viii. 9 Seche a stinke as I had thare..had I neuyr are No quere in no stid. *c* **1460** *Towneley Myst.* i. 38 Waters, that so wyde ben spred, be gedered to geder in to one stede. **1513** DOUGLAS *Æneis* XII. ii. 39 Or quhar the schene lilleis in ony steid War pulderit wyth the vermel rosis reid. **1552–3** in Feuillerat *Revels Edw. VI* (1914) 109 As the same was neadfully behoveable to be occupied from tyme to time at sondry steades. **1557** NORTH *Gueuara's Diall Pr.* 122 Ought I, by wishe, to live in any stedde But closde with him together in the grave? **1566** DRANT *Horace, Wail. Hieremie* ii. Kiiij b, Ofte cryed they..Lyke wounded wightes throughout the streetes, they sounded in eche stede. **1596** SPENSER *F.Q.* VI. i. 42 Next that ye Ladies ayde in euery stead and stound.

†**d.** The place designated by the context. ***in, on (the, that) stead***, on the spot, there. *Obs.*

c **1000** ÆLFRIC *Joshua* x. 12 Ne stira þu sunne of þam stede furðor onȝean Gabaon. *Ibid.* x. 13 þa stod seo sunne on þam stede faste. *a* **1175** in Napier *Holy Rood-tree* 22 Ne mihte heom nan mon of þam stude awæcgan. *c* **1205** LAY. 6370 A-nan se he wes wrað wid eni i þan stude he hine wolde slæn. *c* **1220** *Bestiary* 404 [The fox] goð o felde to a furȝ and..Ne stereð ȝe noȝt of ðe stede a god stund deies. *a* **1225** *Leg. Kath.* 2453, I þat ilke stude, anan, iwurðen twa wundres. **13..** *Bonaventura's Medit.* 135 To a logher place þey gunne þan to go... He made hem sytte downe yn þat stede. **1390** GOWER *Conf.* II. 272 Bot the goddesse..appiereth in the stede, And hath..forbede That thei the children nocht ne sle. *c* **1400** *Destr. Troy* 8627 He stode þus in stid, starit hym vpon. *c* **1450** *Mirour Saluacioun* 1759 This hors and the two men than vanyst out of the stede. **1590** SPENSER *F.Q.* II. ii. 21 He ran Vnto that stead, their strife to vnderstond.

†**e.** ***on, in stead and stall***: see STALL *sb.*[1] 1 *note.*

1042 in Thorpe *Charters* (1865) 348 Nu bidde ic ealle Godes freond..þæt hi for Godes eiȝe næfre ne beon on stede ne on stealle þær æfre undon worðe þæt..we nu ȝeunnen habben into þæt haliȝe minstre. *c* **1220** *Bestiary* 489 Ðis wirm bitokneð ðe man ðat oðer biswikeð on stede er on stalle. *c* **1440** *Rule St. Benet* (Verse) Prol. 146 þat to hys neghburs dose no noy In stede ne stayll, þaire staite to stroy.

†**f.** ***to give stead = to give place***: see PLACE *sb.* 23, GIVE *v.* 47 a, b. *Obs.*

c **1340** HAMPOLE *Prose Tr.* 19 Bot if þe þinke it oþer-wyse, or elles any oþer man sauour by grace þe contrarye here-to, I leue þe saying and gyfe stede to hym. *c* **1375** *Sc. Leg. Saints* iv. (*Jacobus*) 267 And þe stane, quhen he lad was þer, wex nesch as it wax war, and gaf sic sted to þat body, as It a grave had bene, in hy. **138.** WYCLIF *Sel. Wks.* I. 41 Sitte not in þe first place, lest..þe lord of þe feste bidde þee ȝiue þis man stede. **1450–1530** *Myrr. our Ladye* 322 Waylynge gyueth stede to ioye. **1483** *Cath. Angl.* 155/2 To Giffe stede, *cedere, locum dare.*

†**g.** *abstr.* Situation. *Obs. rare.*

1387 TREVISA *Higden* (Rolls) I. 329 þerfore first me schall telle of [þe] place and stede of þat lond [L. *de situ terræ locali*], how greet and what manere lond it is.

†**3. a.** An inhabited place; a city, town, village, hamlet, etc.; occas. a country, land. *Obs.*

c **1250** *Gen. & Ex.* 1114 For men ðor sinne un-kinde deden, so for-sanc and brente ðat steden [Sodom]. **1297** R. GLOUC. (Rolls) 1520, & hei duc of al þulke stude he clupede þen toun iwis After his name gloucestre. *a* **1300** *Havelok* 744 And for þat Grim þat place aute, þe stede of Grim þe name laute. *c* **1320** *Sir Tristr.* 1163 A winde to wil him bare To a stede þer him was boun Neiȝe hand: Deluelin hiȝt þe toun. *c* **1375** *Sc. Leg. Saints* iii. (*Andrew*) 253 He met men bringand of þe sted a ȝonge man, þat wes ded. *c* **1400** *Destr. Troy* 9712 His body to britton, & his burgh take; All his stid to distroy, and his stith holdis. **1577** HARRISON *England* III. i. [II. vi.] 96/2 in *Holinshed*, These 2. [drinks] are very common in Kent, Worcester, & other steedes, where these kindes of fruites doe abounde.

†**b. the Steads** [= MLG. *de Steden*]: 'the Cities' of the Hanseatic League; the Hanse Towns. Also, the corporation of Hanse merchants in London. *Obs.*

15.. *Droichis Part of Play* 106 in *Dunbar's Poems* 318 Swadrik, Denmark, and Norraway, Nor in the Steiddis I dar nocht ga. **1533** *St. Papers Hen. VIII*, I. 414 The Cytees of Lubeke, Danske, Hamburgh, Bromeswyke, and all other the Stedes of the Haunse Tutonyk. **1552** in *Acts Privy Counc.* (N.S.) IV. 141 The Merchauntes of the Steedes, commonly called the Merchauntes of the Stilliarde. **1557** *Ibid.* VI. 73 The said Merchauntes..have alleadged..that the Steades have byn so letted by greate busynes as they coulde not sende thiere Agentes for the going forwarde with the said Diet. **1558** *Ibid.* 315 The returne home into their cuntreys of the lxxvj hulkes of the Steades presently at Portesmouthe. **1558** GRESHAM in Burgon *Life* (1839) I. 484 Thatt you neavir restore the steydes called the Stillyarde againe to ther privelydge.

†**4. a.** A definite spot on a surface, esp. on the surface of the body. *Obs.*

c **1000** *Sax. Leechd.* I. 74 Lecge on ðone stede þe se spring on ȝesittan wolde. *a* **1225** *Ancr. R.* 136 Bihold ofte þeron [the crucifix], & cus þe wunde studen. *c* **1300** *Seyn Julian* 57 (Ashm. MS.) Fram þe necke to þe fot ech stude it þoruȝ soutȝe. *a* **1375** *Joseph Arim.* 578 [He] wolde ha striken Seraphe at a stude derne, vppon an hole of his helm. *c* **1440** *Pallad. on Husb.* I. 204 Thy vyne in oon stede alway, thou ne bynde. **1470–85** MALORY *Arthur* VII. xii. 230 Thus they fought two houres..& in many stedys they were wounded.

b. *Sc.* A mark, imprint, vestige. Chiefly *pl.*

1513 DOUGLAS *Æneis* III. iv. 71 The pray half ettin behind thame lat thay ly, With fute steidis vile and laith to se. **1596** DALRYMPLE tr. *Leslie's Hist. Scot.* I. II. 170 The reliques or stedis thairof [Adrian's Wall] this day ar seine, ȝit named the Vale of Adrian. **1710** RUDDIMAN *Gloss. Virgil's Æneis* s.v. *Stede, Fute stedis*, foot steps, tract or print of the feet: For Stead Scot. is commonly taken for the foundation or ground on which a house or such like stands, or the tract or impression made in the Earth, and appearing when they are taken away. **1826** GALT *Last of Lairds* iv. 32 He nippit my twa lugs till he eft the stedt o' his fingers as plainly upon them as [etc.]. **1896** CROCKETT *Grey Man* v. 35 On the trampled clay and mud, there were the steads of naked feet.

5. Chiefly with *possessive.* **a.** The place assigned to, belonging to or normally occupied by a thing; appointed or natural place. *Obs.* exc. *arch.*

c **888** ÆLFRED *Boeth.* xxxiii. §5 Ac þæs fyres aȝen stede is ofer eallum woruldȝesceaftum ȝesewenlicum. *c* **1250** *Gen. & Ex.* 117 God bi-quuad watres here stede. *c* **1384** CHAUCER *H. Fame* 731 Thou wost..That euery kyndely thynge that is Hath a kyndely stede ther he May best in hyt conserued be. *c* **1450** *Mirk's Festial* 2 The fyrst day, as Saynt Jerom sayth, þe see schall aryse vp yn hyr styd. **1887** MORRIS *Odyss.* XII. 402 The mast in its stead we 'stablished and hauled the sails in air.

†**b.** A space or place assigned to or occupied by a person; a seat. *Obs.*

c **960** *Rule St. Benet* xliii. 68 (Schröer) Ne stande he on chore on his stede and endebyrdnesse, ac stande he ealra ytemest. **1303** R. BRUNNE *Handl. Synne* 1418 þe soþe myght y neuer wytte, who shuld yn þo stedys sytte. *c* **1400** LOVE *Bonavent. Mirr.* (1907) 106 Sitte and take thy stede in the lowest place. *c* **1400** *Gamelyn* 851 Whan Gamelyn was i-set in the justices stede. **1590** SPENSER *F.Q.* I. ix. 41 The soldier may not moue from watchfull sted, Nor leaue his stand, vntill his Captaine bed. **1633** P. FLETCHER *Purple Isl.* VII. iii, Where glorious Cities stood,..There shrieching Satyres fill the peoples emptie steads. **1751** G. WEST *Educ.* xci, Fir'd with th' Idea of her future Fame She rose majestick from her lowly sted.

†**c.** The place where a body of soldiers is stationed, a military position. *Obs.*

c **1330** R. BRUNNE *Chron. Wace* (Rolls) 5085 He did sette in wardes [*v.r.* stedes] seers, Knyghte to wachem, & squiers. **1577** HOLINSHED *Hist. Eng.* I. 39/1 Being returned into Gallia, [he] placed his souldiors in steeds to soiourne there for the winter season. *Ibid.* 49/1 Plautius..placed garrisons in steedes, where neede required, to keepe those places whiche hee had gotten. **1627** DRAYTON *Agincourt* 53 A vast Route..Had for their safety..Got in their flight into so strong a stead, So fortifi'd by nature..They might not thence, but with much blood be brought.

6. A property or estate in land; a farm; also †a portion of an estate.

1338 R. BRUNNE *Chron.* (1725) 247 þe dettes þat men þam auht, þer stedes & þer wonyng, Wer taxed. **1452** in P. F. Tytler *Hist. Scot.* (1864) II. 387 All the tenants..except them that occupies the grangis and steids whilk war in the hands of the said Earle William. **1487** *Exch. Rolls Scot.* IX. 470 *note*, All and hale our stedis of Catslak [etc.] with aucht hundreith scheip..apon the said stedis. **1508** KENNEDIE *Flyting w. Dunbar* 365 Thow has a tome purs, I haue stedis and takkis. **1535** STEWART *Cron. Scot.* II. 532 And mony ane out of his awin hous chaist, And mony sted wnpleneist lyand waist. **1579** SPENSER *Sheph. Cal.* May 43 Thilke same bene shepeheards for the Deuils stedde. **1594–5** *Durham Wills* (Surtees) II. 255 A farme or stead, worthe 20 l. **1825** BROCKETT *N.C. Gloss., Stead, Sted, Stid,* a place, a farm house and offices. **1887** STOKES tr. *Tripartite Life of Patrick* 139 On the water is a stead, Buale Patraic ('Patrick's Byre') is its name. **1889** RIDER HAGGARD *Allan's Wife* vii, I took a Hottentot..who lived on the stead, into my confidence.

7. A site for a building; the land on which a building stands; also, an enclosure attached to a building, a yard. (Cf. *farmstead, homestead, mowstead.*)

1246–68 *Cockersand Chartul.* (Chetham) III. I. 843 Quamdam partem terræ in Caton jacentem subtus le Walkemilnestude infra has divisas, scilicet [etc.]. **1534** *Munim. de Melros* (Bannatyne Club) 629 Giff it sall happyn ws..till byg..ane walk myll on þe said myll sted within þe saidis landis. **1546** *Yorkshire Chantry Surv.* (Surtees) 181 A barne stede j garden stede. **1610** *Reg. Mag. Sig. Scot.* 80 Lie teind-barne et teind-barne yaird, cum lie peithous-steid. **1634** *Ibid.* 103, 2 terras husb. et 3 terras cott. et lie grasteid. **1773** *East Cottingwith Incl. Act* 7 Messuage steads and cottage steads. **1894** R. S. FERGUSON *Hist. Westmorland* 165 The 'steads' or sites of many disused 'walk mills' or fulling mills.

†8. The framework which supports the bedding of a bed. *Obs.* Cf. BEDSTEAD.

a **1400–50** *Bk. Curtasye* 517 in *Babees Bk.*, Þen..the vssher..Brynges hym in bed where he shalle wynke; In strong styd on palet he lay. **1625** QUARLES *Sion's Sonn.* xi. iii, The Bridall bed of Princely Solomon,..Was but of Cedar; and her Sted of gold. **1697** DRYDEN *Virg. Georg.* II. 726 With Wars and Taxes others waste their own,..To loll on Couches, rich with Cytron steds. **1799** E. DU BOIS *Piece Family Biog.* III. 102 The valance or curtain that hangs round the tester and stead of the bed. **1858** SIMMONDS *Dict. Trade, Stead,* the frame of a bed.

III. Metaphorical and idiomatic uses.

†9. In various rare or occasional uses. **a.** Abiding-place (of hope, passions, etc.). **b.** *to take stead*: to take effect. **c.** *in good* (etc.) *stead*: in good (etc.) circumstances. **d.** A space of time. *Obs.*

a. *c* **1200** *Vices & Virtues* 95 Ðe faste hope hafð hire stede up an heih. **1395** HYLTON *Scala Perf.* (W. de W. 1494) I. lxx, In thyn herte where the stede of loue is thou sholde mow haue parte of suche loue to thyn euen crysten. *c* **1412** HOCCLEVE *De Reg. Princ.* 3403 Wengeance, in þis good lord, hadde no stide.

b. *c* **1200** ORMIN 10101 Hiss spell toc mikell stēde i þa þatt herrdenn whatt he seȝȝde. *a* **1300** *Cursor M.* 19266 And custom it es..Quen lagh es mad bituix þam neu At þe biginning for to be redd, þat dred mai do þe lagh ta sted. *Ibid.* 29274 On þam þis cursing stede first takes.

c. *c* **13..** R. GLOUC. (Rolls) App. H. 30 Whanne he was out of wrapþe and was in god stad. *c* **1375** *Sc. Leg. Saints* xxviii. (*Margaret*) 91 Ʒet, þo scho wes in pouir stede & nocht with hyr fadir cane be fede, nocht-þane [etc.]. **1596** SPENSER *F.Q.* V. xii. 23 With the souse thereof full sore aghast, He staggered to and fro in doubtfull sted.

d. **1596** SPENSER *F.Q.* VI. vii. 40 [He] though she were with wearinesse nigh dead, Yet would not let her lite, nor rest a little stead.

†10. a. A place or passage in Scripture or other writing. **b.** A point in order of progression. *Obs.*

a. *c* **1175** *Lamb. Hom.* 73 On oðer stude of rihte ileue spec þe apostle and seið..*Inpossibile* [etc.]. *a* **1200** *Vices & Virtues* 81 An oðer stede he seið, godd: *Ve qui ridetis* [etc.]. *a* **1225** *Ancr. R.* 144 Vor wecche is ine holi write i monie studen ipreised. *Ibid.* 410, I-writen on oðer stude. **1377** LANGL. *P. Pl.* B. XIV. 131 As dauid seith in þe sauter..; And in an other stede also *velud* [etc.]. **1390** GOWER *Conf.* II. 264 Ful many an other thing sche dede, Which is noght writen in this stede. *c* **1520** M. NISBET *N.T. in Scots* Acts xiii. 35 And tharfor on an vthir stede he sais, Thou sal nocht geue thi hali to se corruptioun. **1557** CARD. POLE in Strype *Eccl. Mem.* (1822) III. II. App. lxviii. 507 And what is the benedictyon of this stede of almesse, the prophete Esaias shewethe in that same place.

b. *c* **1370** *Lay Folks Mass Bk.* (MS. B.) 454 When þou has made þis orison, þen shal þow with deuocion Make þi prayeres in þat stede for alle þi frendes, þat are dede.

†11. An office or position assigned to or held by a person. *Obs.*

c **1000** ÆLFRIC *Hom.* in Sweet *Sel. Hom. Ælfr.* 9 Þu ȝeearnast..þone stede þe se deofol of afeoll þurh ungehyrsumnysse. *c* **1205** LAY. 239 Asscanius þe kene þe wes i kinges stude four & þritti winter he heold þat lond. *a* **1225** *Leg. Kath.* 3 Constantin & Maxence weren, on ane time, as in keiseres stude hehest i Rome. *a* **1300** *Fall & Passion* 17, 18 in *E.E.P.* (1862) 13 Har [Lucifer & his angels] stides for to ful fille þat wer i-falle for prude an hore, god makid adam to is wille to fille har stides þat wer ilor. *c* **1450** in Aungier *Syon* (1840) 363 When..any is absente, they that be present schal fulfylle ther stedes. *c* **1600** in *Trans. Roy. Hist. Soc.* (1902) XVI. 46 [They] shall continue in the said office place Roome and Stead of Assistants till [etc.].

12. The place, 'room', 'lieu', or function (of a person or thing) as held by a substitute or a successor. Only in certain phrases.

†a. *to keep* (a person's) *stead*: to be (his) deputy, act on (his) behalf. So *to commit one's stead to* (another). *Obs.*

c **1450** *Godstow Reg.* 72 He committid his stede to eueriche of hem, with þe powere of lawful constreininge. *Ibid.* 131 Whenne Ralph, prior of wircetur, kepid þe stede of Roger, bisshoppe of wircetur. *Ibid.* 350 A-fore þ[e] prior of walingeforde, principall iugge, & the chaunter of walingeforde, kepynge the stedys of the abbottes of Abendon & of dorchester.

b. *to* †*do* (obs.), *fill, serve, supply the stead of*, to serve as a substitute for. Now *rare.*

1558 BP. WATSON *Sev. Sacram.* iii. 13 Martyrdome..dothe supplye the steede of Babtysme,..when onely necessitie..excludeth the Sacrament. **1601** DANIEL *Civ. Wars* VII. lviii, Conducting their fresh troupes against their King (Who leaves a woman to supply his steed). **1611** W. SCLATER *Key* (1629) 244 Suffering sometimes doth the steed of baptisme. **1837** C. LOFFT *Self-form.* I. 199 They may serve the stead of presence of mind, to a certain point at least. **1888** GOODE *Amer. Fishes* 2 The allied *Percichthys* replaces it in temperate South America,..while in northern China *Siniperca* fills its stead.

c. *in the stead of*: (*a*) in the room of, in succession to (one who has died, has retired from or is superseded in an office); †(*b*) as the deputy or representative of (*obs.*); †(*c*) in lieu of, instead of (a person or thing that might more naturally have been chosen, have happened, etc.) (*obs.*); (*d*) in lieu of, in exchange for (something given up); (*e*) predicatively, *to be in the stead of* (also, ? nonce-use, †*to be in stead for*), to make up for the want of. Now somewhat *arch.*

(*a*) *c* **1250** *Gen. & Ex.* 425 Ðan bor ghe seht in ðe stede Of caym ðat abel for-dede. **1558** *Cal. Anc. Rec. Dublin* (1889) 481 Mr. Thomas Fynen is elected Alderman in the styde of Mr. John Nangle. **1784** *Acts & Laws Connecticut* 159 Such Select-men and Committees as shall from Time to Time succeed, and come in the Room and Stead of others removed by Death. **1786** W. THOMSON *Watson's Philip III* (1839) 255 Matthias II. being raised to the imperial throne in the stead of his deceased brother.

(*b*) *c* **1380** WYCLIF *Wks.* (1880) 55 Siþ prelatis & prestis ordeyned of god comen in þe stede of postlis & disciples, þei ben alle bounden..to preche þus þe gospel.

(*c*) *c* **1400** *Apol. Loll.* 6 Þat þe peple..worschip not..þe fend in þe sted of Crist. **1422** tr. *Secreta Secret., Priv. Priv.* xviii. 146, I putte lateyn in the stydde of Englyshe. **1460–70** *Bk. Quintessence* II. 16 If ȝe haue non preparate redy..þanne take in þe stide þerof fyn brennynge watir. **1544** BETHAM *Precepts War* I. xxv. Cij b, For whych cause a capitayne..wyll cause false tales..to be sparpled abrode, in the stede and place of true tydynges. **1654** R. CODRINGTON tr. *Justine* xx. 289 They brought home comfort to their distressed Army in the stead of help. **1734** WATTS *Relig. Juv.* (1789) 35 Sometimes they shew a painted idol in the stead of him [God].

(*d*) *a* **1761** LAW *Comf. Weary Pilgrim* (1809) 101 It was human nature..that had lost its first heavenly life and got a bestial, diabolical life in the stead of it. **1874** GREEN *Short Hist.* x. §3. 775 A Constitution..was accepted by Lewis the Sixteenth in the stead of his old despotic power.

(*e*) **1596** SPENSER *F.Q.* IV. vii. 7 A tall young oake he bore, Whose knottie snags were sharpned all afore, And beath'd in fire for steele to be in sted. **1839** DE QUINCEY *Recoll. Lakes* Wks. 1862 II. 193 This pleasure was to him in the stead of many libraries.

d. *in his stead* (or with any other possessive): (*a*) as a successor in his room (cf. 12 c (*a*)); (*b*) as his deputy or representative (*arch.*), also †*predicatively*; †(*c*) as a substitute in the place occupied by him (*obs.*); (*d*) instead of him (cf. 12 c (*c*)).

Now only *literary*. Formerly the plural *steads* was often used when preceded by a plural possessive.

(*a*) *c* **1320** *Seuyn Sag.* (W.) 1207 Thai sschal..Put the out of thi kinges sete, And sette him stede inne thine. **1362** LANGL. *P. Pl.* A. v. 39 Leste þe kyng and his Counseil ȝor Comunes apeire, And beo stiward in oure stude. *c* **1375** *Sc. Leg. Saints* Prol. 161 Mathias wes chosin in his stede. *c* **1400** *Rom. Rose* 4862 Whanne fader or moder arn in grave, Hir children shulde..Ful diligent ben, in her steede. **1603** OWEN *Pembrokeshire* ii. (1891) 31 Chancerye and Eschequer were cleene abolished..and newe Courtes errected in theire steedes by the saied Statute. **1696** *Churchw. Acc. Pittington,* etc. (Surtees) 260 A new saxton to be chosen in his roome or steed.

(*b*) *c* **1400** *Rule St. Benet* (Prose) lxiii. 41 Þabbesse, for sho es in godis stede, sal be callid 'dame'. **1417** in *Proc. Privy Council* (1834) II. 238 Charjng the captens and cunstables to take other in hor styddes. **1500–20** DUNBAR *Poems* xliii. 27 Send in ȝour steid, Ʒour ladeis grathit vp gay. **1560** BIBLE (Geneva) *Gen.* xxx. 2 Am I in Gods stede, which hathe withholden from thee the frute of the wombe? **1577** HANMER *Anc. Eccl. Hist., Socrates* II. xxxi. 288 In their steede which were absent, their readers and Deacons subscribed. *a* **1629** HINDE *J. Bruen* vii. (1641) 24 Acknowledging that he was unto him in Gods stead.

(*c*) **1590** GREENE *Never too late* II. (1600) Q4, The seedes of shame I from my hart remoue, And in their steades I set downe plants of grace. **1612** COVERTE *Voy.* 5 Which sheepe we tooke with vs and left sixe beasts or bullocks in their steads. **1676** HALE *Contempl.* I. 109 Thou..wert willing to put thy soul in our souls stead. **1728** POPE *Dunc.* I. 180 Or quite unravel all the reas'ning thread, And hang some curious cobweb in its stead. **1774** CHESTERF. *Lett.* I. viii. 21 Diana put a hind in her [Iphigeneia's] stead. **1823** SCOTT *Peveril* xlix, Zarah..admitted that she had deranged the project.., by placing the dwarf in her own stead.

(*d*) *c* **1230** *Hali Meid.* 10 For under weole, i wunnes stude þu hauest her ofte helle. **1589** PUTTENHAM *Eng. Poesie* III. x. (Arb.) 172 Some busie carpers will scorne at my new deuised termes: *auricular* and *sensable*, saying that I might with better warrant haue vsed in their steads these words, *orthographicall* or *syntacticall*. **1735** POPE *Prol. Sat.* 304 A lash like mine no honest man shall dread, But all such babbling blockheads in his stead. **1784** COWPER *Task* III. 769 Down falls the venerable pile... Springs a palace in its stead But in a distant spot. **1813** SCOTT *Rokeby* I. iii, Terror reigns in sorrow's stead. **1852** H. ROGERS *Eclipse of Faith* (1862) 210 Each seemed to substitute in its stead something he liked better. **1856** LONGF. *Golden Leg.* II, *Gottlieb.* Or unless Some maiden..Offers her life for that of her lord, And is willing to die in his stead. **1871** MISS YONGE *Cameos* II. viii. 103 He begged the King to choose in his stead, one of the numerous royal princes.

†e. *in stead of*: see INSTEAD. *Obs.*

f. *stead of* = instead of. (See INSTEAD.) Now only *dial.* and *colloq.*, and usu. considered (also as *'stead*) to represent INSTEAD *phrasal comb.*

1430–40 LYDG. *Bochas* IX. xxix. (1494) Gij, Sabath desyrous to succede Stede of his brother the kingdom to possede. **14..** *Pol. Rel. & L. Poems* 76 The whyche..Songe a balad stede of the masse. **1612** R. DABORNE *Chr. turn'd Turke* 1180 [He] who adiudged to death By his heads losse, should craue (stead of one stroke) To dye a lingring torment on the racke. **1791** NAIRNE *Poems* 131 And backwards, 'sted of forwards, walk. **1818** SCOTT *Br. Lamm.* ix, Or if, stead o' that, ye wad but dine wi' them at the change-house. **1903** K. D. WIGGIN *Rebecca of Sunnybrook Farm* xxvi. 279 Rebecca's fifty dollars had to be swallowed up in a mortgage, 'stead of goin' towards school expenses. **1916** G. B. SHAW *Pygmalion* II. 121, I want to be a lady in a flower shop stead of selling at the corner of Tottenham Court Road. **1939** JOYCE *Finnegans Wake* 283 They ought to told you every last word first stead of trying every which way to kinder smear it out poison long. **1971** *Black World* Oct. 62/1 The sweet-potato bread was a dollar quarter this time stead of dollar regular. **1978** J. THOMSON *Question of Identity* x. 100 He'd've been all right with me... 'Stead of which..he marries her.

†g. *in the stead*: instead of it, as a substitute.

c **1450** HOLLAND *Howlat* 777 He couth cary the cowpe of the kingis dess, Syne leve in the sted Bot a blak bunwed. **1567** *Gude & Godlie Ball.* 145 All Ire and malice thow put vs fra, Thy seruandis gouerne in the steid. **1615** HEYWOOD *Four Prentises* I. I 2 b, Stage-dir., Guy and Eustace..beate the Pagans, take away the Crownes on their heads and in the stead hang vp the contrary Shields. **1708** SWIFT *Abol. Chr.* Wks. 1755 II. I. 93 Altering the constitution of the church established, and setting up presbytery in the stead.

h. *to stand in stead of, instead of, in the stead of*: see STAND *v.* 49.

c **1350** *Will. Palerne* 3521 He..seide to þe quene, þat..he wold in hire sones stede stand euer at nede.

IV. 13. a. Advantage, avail, profit, service, support; esp. in *to stand in stead*, also †*to stand to stead*, †*to stand stead* (see STAND *v.* 48); *to do*, †*make*, †*render stead*. Now only *arch.*

a **1300** [see STAND *v.* 48]. *c* **1425** tr. *Arderne's Treat. Fistula*, etc. 66 Bot þis haþe no stede bot to so streyt a wounde þat þe been may take within his extremitez þe extremitez of þe wounde. **1513** DOUGLAS *Æneis* x. vi. 61 The giltyn mailȝeis makis hym na steyd, For in the coist he tholis dynt of deyd. **1524** *Reg. Aberdon.* (Maitland Club) I. 389 Ane precept of seysing without charter or ony oþer euident followand þerapoune suld do nane steide nor be of effect. **1524** *St. Papers Hen. VIII*, IV. 112 To rendre all hert, lefull service, steide, and pleasure, that lyeth in our power. **1524** WOLSEY *Ibid.* IV. 139 [They] may and shal do grete stede in advertising the Kinges Grace from tyme to tyme..of the procedinges. **1542** *Ibid.* XI. 272 And now last of all what a stede His Highnes entryng in to the warre was to Him. **1546** *Reg. Privy Council Scot.* I. 47 Thai ar contentit to do steid and service to the said Schir Neill. **1551** P'CESS MARY in Ellis *Orig. Lett.* Ser. I. II. 165 Of my good wyll and prayour to do you stede or pleasur, you shalbe ever duryng my lief assured. **1625** in Foster *Eng. Factories India* (1909) III. 113 He..assured him by passed experience what stead your language was to us in the time of our imprisonment. **1634** MILTON *Comus* 611 But here thy sword can do thee little stead. **1643** *Orkney Witch Trial* in *Abbotsford Club Misc.* I. 175, I was about the loch with Jonet Sklateris,..but it is for no stead, it will never mend hir. *a* **1670** SPALDING *Troub. Chas. I* (Bannatyne Club) I. 294 And sic [beasts] as wold not call thay hocht and slew, that thay sould never mak steed. **1823** E. MOOR *Suffolk Words, Stead,* aid, assistance, usefulness. **1873** BROWNING *Red Cott. Nt.-cap C.* 321 The two grey points that did him stead And passed their eagle-owner to the front.

†b. *to serve* (one) *in some, no stead*, to be of some, no advantage or profit to (one). *Obs.*

1601 HOLLAND *Pliny* VIII. xv. I. 200 His hornes bend so inward..that they serve him in no steed at all for fight. **1662** [see SERVE *v.*[1] 19]. **1678** *Trans. Crt. Spain* 170 What stead would the Queens word then serve me in. **1680** BURNET *Rochester* (1692) 46, I told him all his speculations of Philosophy would not serve him in any stead. **1712** ARBUTHNOT *John Bull* IV. vii, I am glad I have made the Experiment, it may serve me in some stead.

V. 14. *Comb.*: †**steads bearing**, †**stead holder** [cf. STADHOLDER], †**stead-holding** *Sc.*, a 'locum tenens', substitute, deputy; **stead-horse** *dial.* (see quot. 1894); †**stead-man** = *steadward*; **steadsman** *dial.*, a substitute, deputy; †**stead mother** *nonce-wd.* (see quot.); †**stead-stathelfastness** = STEADFASTNESS; †**steadward** (see quot.).

c **1460** *Oseney Reg.* 92 By þ[e] vicare of Cudelynton or his *stedys beryng [orig. *vel eius vices gerentem*]. **1456** SIR G. HAYE *Law Arms* (S.T.S.) 111 Verray vicare and *stede haldare till our lord Jhesu Crist. *c* **1375** *Sc. Leg. Saints* xxi. (*Clement*) 647 Bot opunyonys ware sere, quhethyr þire twa papis were, or þe papis *sted-haldande. **1708** J. C. *Compl. Collier* (1843) 37 The Banck's-Man..leads his *Stead-Horse away with the Loaden Corfe. **1894** *Northumb. Gloss.* s.v. *Steed*, A 'steed (or stead) horse' is a horse employed upon a pit heap-steed. **1613** R. C. *Table Alph.* (ed. 3), *Steward*, *steed-man, the keeper of the place. **1897** F. S. ELLIS *Reynard* 283 A farm in old speech was a stead, And to the stead-man's name oft wed. **1876** *Whitby Gloss.*, *Steeadsman, a substitute for another person. **1591** H. SMITH *Prepar. Marriage* 106 A stepmother dooth signifie a *stedmother, that is, one mother dyeth, and another commeth in her stead. *a* **1225** *Ancren R.* 6 Non ancre bi mine read ne schal..bihoten..bute þreo þinges, þet is, obedience, chastete, & *studestaþeluestnesse. **1876** *Whitby Gloss.*, **Steeadward*, the keeper of the stead or place; a steward. Old local document.

stead (stɛd), *v.* Forms: 2 stude, 4 stede, 5 stedde, 6–7 steed(e, *Sc.* steid, 6–7 sted, 7– stead. *Pa. t.* and *pa. pple.* 3 stedde, 4 stedd, 3–5 stad, 4 stadde, staad, 3–6 staid, 4–8 sted, 6–9 stead; 4 stedyd, *Sc.*

-it, -yt, 4–5 sted(d)ede, (4 stadded), 7 steeded, 7–9 **steaded.** [Early ME. *stude* (ü), *stede*, f. *stude*, *stede* STEAD *sb.* The pa. t. and pa. pple. form *stad* is a. ON. *stadde* (pa. t.), *stadd-r* (pa. pple.) of *steðja* vb. to make to stand, stop, place, f. *stað-r* = OE. *stęde* STEAD *sb.*

The ON. verb is 'little used exc. in pa. pple.' (Vigfusson); the pres.-stem was therefore not adopted in Eng., its place being taken by the pres.-stem of the cognate native verb. The form *stad* of the pa. t. and pa. pple. is almost confined to the senses of Scandinavian origin (branch II); for an exception see quot. *c* 1400 in 1 a.]

I. To stand in stead.

1. *trans.* (The obj. was prob. orig. *dative.*)

a. *impers.* or with subj. a clause, inf., or noun of action: To avail, profit, be of use to (a person); †to help (a person) *to do* something. Also *absol.* Now *arch.*

c **1175** *Lamb. Hom.* 77 Men þet..nulleð heore sunnen forleten boð on þe doules on-walde, and þet hwile ne studed hom nawiht þet ho singe pater noster. *c* **1400** *Destr. Troy* 4681 Þai with stode hom a stoure, but it stad litle. **1590** SPENSER *F.Q.* II. ix. 9 Perhaps my succour, or aduizement meete Mote stead you much your purpose to subdew. **1591** SHAKS. *Two Gent.* II. i. 119 So it steed you, I will write..a thousand times as much. **1592** —— *Rom. & Jul.* II. iii. 54 (2nd Qo.) My intercession likewise steads my foe. **1619** DRAYTON *Idea* xv. Minor Poems (1907) 52 Since to obtaine thee nothing me will sted, I haue a Med'cine that shall cure my Loue. **1661** GLANVILL *Van. Dogm.* 31 The concession of which will only steed us as a Refuge for Ignorance. **1832** MISS MITFORD in T. A. Trollope *What I Remember* (1887) II. 339 Your answering these questions will stead me much. **1837** CARLYLE *Fr. Rev.* I. III. ix, It steads not the doomed man that he have interviews with the King. **1838** EMERSON *Addr. Lit. Ethics* Wks. (Bohn) II. 212 Translate, collate, distil all the systems, it steads you nothing. **1879** E. ARNOLD *Lt. Asia* IV. 274 How hath it steaded man to pray.

b. Of a thing: To be useful or advantageous to. Also *absol.* Now *arch.* (*rare.*)

1594 DANIEL *Compl. Rosamond* (ed. 2) lxxxvii, All these teares you shed will nothing steed. **1598** SYLVESTER *Du Bartas* II. ii. IV. *Columnes* 236 Here-by, a Crane shall steed in building more Then hundred Porters' busie pains before. **1598** GRENEWEY *Tacitus, Ann.* VI. viii. (1604) 134 The Sarmates laying aside their bowes which steeded them but a short time, ran in to the enemie with their swords and launces. **1600** HOLLAND *Livy* IX. xxiv. 331 The place will steed you, I know. **1601** SHAKS. *All's Well* V. iii. 87 Had you that craft to reaue her Of what should stead her most? **1610** —— *Temp.* I. ii. 165 Rich garments, linnens, stuffs, and necessaries Which since haue steeded much. **1608** TOPSELL *Serpents* 273 It is cleere that they [spiders] were made to serue and stead vs to many excellent vses. **1623** WHITBOURNE *Newfoundland* 54 Which fish is in all those parts in great request, and steeds them greatly. **1635** J. HAYWARD tr. *Biondi's Banish'd Virg.* 79 Arrowes, speares, and javelings to steede them in occasions of boording. **1841** BROWNING *Pippa Passes* III. Poems (1905) 182 But guess not how the qualities required For such an office..Would little stead me, otherwise employed. **1891** M. MURIEL DOWIE *Girl in Karp.* 254 No adjectives would stead me.

c. With subj. a person: To succour, help, render service to. Now *rare.*

1582 T. MATHEW in Nicolas *Mem. Sir C. Hatton* (1847) 300 Knowing how much you have steaded me therein from time to time. **1600** HOLLAND *Livy* XXII. xxxii. 452 If they could haue bethought themselues of any other meanes besides, wherein they might steed and befriend them. **1604** SHAKS. *Oth.* I. iii. 344, I could neuer better steed thee then now. **1611** SPEED *Hist. Gt. Brit.* Concl. §2 They [the Britons] steeded the Romanes in most of their Conquests. **1625** W. B. *True Sch. Warre* 15 The Sea of Rome in times past was for the most part wont to steede it selfe with the endeauours of the Minor obseruant Fryers. *c* **1645** HOWELL *Lett.* (1655) II. xxxiii. 44, I shall be glad to steed you in any thing that may tend to your advantage. **1818** SCOTT *Rob Roy* xxiii, It's like I may pleasure you, and stead your father in his extremity. **1834** SIR H. TAYLOR *Artevelde* II. III. ii, Alas! Would I could stead you more than with the prayers Of such a sinful creature! **1888** G. GISSING *Life's Morning* II. 147 The consciousness of what was before her killed her power to stead him in his misery.

†**d.** To serve (one's turn), minister to (necessities, desires). *Obs.*

1571 GOLDING *Calvin on Ps.* lxxii. 1. 269 If kings had ynough in themselves too stede their turnes withall. **1573** —— *Calvin on Job* xxxi. 16–23. 535 True it is that wee cannot steade all the necessities that we see. **1603–26** BRETON *Mad World* (Grosart) 9/1 If in either my aduise or better meanes, I may stead your desire, you shall [etc.]. **1605** A. WARREN *Poor Man's Pass.* etc. E 4 b, So Competence Necessities may steede.

†**e.** To supply *with* something helpful. Also const. *of. Obs.*

1587 GOLDING *De Mornay* xxxiiii. 552 He sendeth vs pardone, and steadeth vs of a Suertie that is able to pay our debts: this Surety is the Messias. **1592** BABINGTON *Notes Gen.* ii. 9 The great power of God to furnish and steede himselfe euer with meanes to effect his wyll. **1648** BP. HALL *Select Th.* lxxii. 207 Thou..thoughtst fit to stead him with such a society as might make his life comfortable to him.

†**f.** To suffice for, serve the needs of. Also *absol. Sc. Obs.*

1497 *Acc. Ld. High Treas. Scot.* I. 335 Item,..for ane cabil tow to stede the well of Dunbar quhen it was red. *Ibid.* 357 Item, to Schir Andro, to steid the pur folk for vij owkis, xxj lib. **1519** *Extracts Burgh Rec. Edin.* (1869) I. 190 That na maner of persouns..by ony meill in greitt, mair nor will steid his awin hous honestly quhill Michaelmes nixttocum. **1535** STEWART *Cron. Scot.* II. 71 Victuall als to steid for fourtie dais. **1557** TUSSER *100 Points Husb.* xix, Thy saffron plot..shal stede both thine own house, and next neighbour too.

g. *dial.* In passive: see quots.

1823 E. MOOR *Suffolk Words, Stedded*, suited—engaged. 'I can't git no work—the farmers are all stedded.' *a* **1825** FORBY *Voc. E. Anglia, Stead*, to supply a place left vacant. 'I am at last steaded with a servant.'

†**2.** To serve (a person) *for. Obs.*

1563 WINȜET tr. *Vincent Lirin.* Ded., Wks. (S.T.S.) II. 6 A litle..instrument that may suffice ws..for a speir or a spade..; and with that also may sted for a bricht lantern. *a* **1652** BROME *Queene's Exch.* IV. i, You have yet a Brother May stead you for a Father, Husband, Friend.

†**3.** *to stead up*: to fulfil in the stead of another.

1603 SHAKS. *Meas. for M.* III. i. 260 Wee shall aduise this wronged maid to steed vp your appointment, goe in your place.

II. To place.

4. To establish, fix, place. Chiefly *passive*, to be situated, stand. *Obs.*

a **1300** *E.E. Psalter* lxxxvii[i]. 8 Over me es þi wreth stedde [Vulg. *confirmata*]. *a* **1300** *Cursor M.* 1045 Now es adam in erth stad [*Gött.* stad, *Fairf.* stadde]. *Ibid.* 1442 He moght wel thinc his stund to strang þat in þat sted ware staid sa lang. *c* **1325** *Poem temp. Edw. II* (Percy) 6 Whan the ȝong persoun Is stedyd in hys cherch. **1340** HAMPOLE *Pr. Consc.* v. 6170 And whan saw we þe seke and in prison sted. **13..** *E.E. Allit. P.* B. 983 Ones ho bluschet to þe burȝe, bot bod ho no lenger, þat ho nas stadde a stiffe ston. *c* **1375** *Sc. Leg. Saints* xxxvi. (*Baptist*) 585 Þe quhilk sancte tecle with hir tuke,..& stedit it honorably in þe kirk of marytany. *c* **1400** *Sc. Trojan War* II. 508 A brassynge horse..In whome may weille a thousande knyghtes Be steddede. *c* **1400** *Sege Jerusalem* (E.E.T.S.) 33/589 [Þey] broȝten þe bishup & alle his bew clerkes þer þe standard stode & stadded hem þer. **14..** *Sir Amadace* (Robson) xlii. 9 In stid quere thou art stadde. *c* **1440** *York Myst.* xvii. 28 That..stedde yone sterne to stand stone stille. *a* **1450** *Bk. Curtasye* 231 in *Babees Bk.*, Ȝif þou be stad in strange contre, Enserche no fyr þen falles to the. **1473** *Rental Bk. Cupar-Angus* (1879) I 177 Ȝif tha thynk that tha ma sted tham bettyr in vthir placis tha sal haue our fre licens. **1500** *Caldwell Papers* (Maitland Club) I. 52 The quhilk tenands ye said lord erle promitte to steid in uthir place. **1618** W. LAWSON *Orch. & Gard.* ix. (1623) 25 Stead them on the North side of your other Apples. **1821** KEATS *Isabella* xx, But it is done..To honour thee..To stead thee as a verse in English tongue.

†**5.** To put into a certain condition, to settle. *Obs.*

c **1470** HENRY *Wallace* IX. 1893 For thai traistyt, and Scotland war weill stad, Wallace wald cum, as he thaim promyst had. *Ibid.* x. 748 Thus in gud pece Scotland with rycht he stad.

†**b.** *refl.* To apply oneself. *Obs.*

c **1425** *Non-Cycle Myst. Plays* (1909) 47 Onto my warke I must me stede.

†**c.** To treat, deal with. *Obs.*

c **1460** J. RUSSELL *Bk. Nurture* 614 in *Babees Bk.*, The bak of þe Crevise, þus he must be sted: array hym as ye dothe þe crabbe.

†**6.** *pass.* To be placed *in* a certain (evil or difficult) plight or condition; to be burdened *with* (sickness), beset *with* (enemies, etc.). *Obs.*

a **1300** *Cursor M.* 674 In mikul blis þan was he staad. *Ibid.* 13787 Bot sua wit seckenes am i stadd þat i ne mai to water win. *c* **1375** *Sc. Leg. Saints* ii. (*Paul*) 26 And sailand in Italy In parelis wes he stad sindry. **14..** *Burgh Lawis* xcv. in *Anc. Laws Scot.* (Burgh Rec. Soc.) 46 Gif..and eftirwart he that tuk the lande in nede is stadd it to sell. *c* **1440** *York Myst.* xlviii. 289 In harde presse whan I was stedde, Of my paynes ȝe hadde pitee. *c* **1450** *St. Cuthbert* (Surtees) 5586 In sorow was he stadd. *c* **1470** *Rauf Coilȝear* 136 Sa troublit with stormis was I neuer stad. *c* **1470** HENRY *Wallace* IX. 901 Sen we ar stad with enemys on ilk syd. *c* **1480** HENRYSON *Test. Cress.* 542 Now is my breist with stormie stoundis stad. **1535** STEWART *Cron. Scot.* II. 47 Honorious of Rome the empriouré, That tyme with seiknes staid wes in ane stour.

†**b.** With adverb, *to be hard* (*straitly, stiffly*, etc.) *stead*: to be hard put to it, to be beset with difficulties or perils. Cf. BESTED *pa. pple.*

a **1300** *Cursor M.* 3470 Þe leuedi was ful ferli drad Als womman þat ful hard was stad. **1375** BARBOUR *Bruce* III. 204 Men redys off mony men that war Fer hardar stad then we yhet ar. *Ibid.* VI. 664 They wend I wes stratly stad. *c* **1375** *Sc. Leg. Saints* vii. (*James Less*) 650 Full hard in þat towne þai war sted. *c* **1400** *Rowland & O.* 1528 There were oure folkes full styffely stadde. *a* **1440** *Sir Eglam.* 459 Thou haste byn strongly stadd. *c* **1440** *York Myst.* xlv. 137 Men þat are stedde stiffely in stormes or in see. *a* **1450** ? LYDG. *To Sov. Lady* 109 Therfore I love no labour that ye lese Whan, in longing, sorest ye be stadde. ?*c* **1470** *What shall I do?* 10 in *Q. Eliz. Acad.* 86 Thus am I sted ful heuely. *a* **1500** *Ratis Raving* I. 461 Quhen þow art stad ocht narowly With Irous wyll and gluttony. **1535** STEWART *Cron. Scot.* III. 125 He circulit him sone efter at ane seig, Into ane place quhair he wes sted rycht herd. **1605** *1st Pt. Jeronimo* III. ii. 91 O me, ill stead, valliant Rogero slaine. **1818** SCOTT *Hrt. Midl.* xix, O father, we are cruelly sted between God's laws and man's laws.

†**7.** *intr.* **a.** To stay, tarry. **b.** To stop, come to a stand. **c.** To stand, consist. *Obs.*

13.. *K. Alis.* 4146 Alisaunder to him cometh, and nought stet. *c* **1420** *Avow. Arth.* xliii. 13 The knyȝte stedit and stode. *c* **1420** *Anturs of Arth.* xxxii. 4 (Ireland MS.) Tell me ..Quy thou stedis in that stid, and stondus so stille? *c* **1440** *York Myst.* xlvi. 94, I schall nott stedde in no stede but in stall and in strete. *c* **1460** *Towneley Myst.* vii. 206 For soth, my lord, I shall not sted till I haue theym theder led. *c* **1500** *Sc. Poem on Her.* 170 in *Q. Eliz. Acad.* 100 In quhat metallis or colouris that thai sted.

Hence †**'steaded** *ppl. a.*, ? placed in position. *Obs.*

1609 *Ev. Woman in Hum.* II. i. C 4, Let your faire hand be beame vnto the ballance, And with a stedded peyze, lift vp that beame.

stead, obs. form of STEED.

†**'steadable**, *a. Sc. Obs.* Also 5–7 stedable, 6 stedabyl, steddabill, 7 stedibill, steedable, steidable, stedible. [f. STEAD *v.* + -ABLE.] Serviceable, helpful.

1467 *Aberdeen Reg.* (1844) I. 27 The saide Thomas sall be stedable to the saide Willam in all thingis that he has ado. **1524** *Q. Marg.* in *St. Papers Hen. VIII*, IV. 116 This wilbe ..steddabill to His Grace. **1624** *Aberdeen Reg.* (1848) II. 394 The bigging of ane brig ower the water of Bogye..wilbe most stedibill to the haill cuntrie. **1635** J. HAYWARD tr. *Biondi's Banish'd Virg.* 113 The taking it away would prove a service very steedable to Bramac. **1637** WARISTON *Diary* (S.H.S.) 287 On that feareth the Lord and may be steidable to me. **1648** CHAS. I *Let.* 28 Oct. in Carte *Collect. Lett.* (1735) III. 589, I am sure, all things considered, it is fittest for my service, and I am confident will prove as steadible to him. **1653** URQUHART *Rabelais* I. xi, He shoo'd the Geese, kept a self-tickling to make himself laugh, and was very stedable in the Kitchen. **1656** J. FERGUSSON *On Coloss.* 130 The meanest haue somewhat whereby they may prove steadable to the best.

steade, obs. form of STEED.

steadfast ('stɛdfɑːst, -fæst, -fəst), *a.* (*adv.*) and *sb.* Forms: 1, 3 stedefæst, 1 stydefæst, 2–5 stedefast (3 *Ormin* -fasst), 3 stedevast, 4 **stedefaste**, 3–4 **studefast**, 3 **studevast**, **-vest**, 4 **studfaste**, 4–5 **stid(e)fast**, **stydfast(e**, (4 **steddfast**, 5 **steddefaste**), 5–6 *Sc.* **steidfast**, 6–7 **steedfast**, 4–6 **stedfaste**, (5 **stedfasst**), 4–9 **stedfast**, 8– **steadfast.** [OE. *stędefæst*, f. *stęde* (see STEAD *sb.*) + *fæst* FAST *a.* Cf. MLG. *stedevast* (mod.G. †*stattfest*), ON. *staðfast-r.*] **A.** *adj.*

1. Fixed or secure in position. **a.** Of a person, esp. a soldier in battle: Maintaining his ground. (Now with mixture of sense 2.) †Also, of a battle: Fought without change of position.

993 *Battle of Maldon* 127 (Gr.) Stodon stædefæste: stihte hi Byrhtnoð. *Ibid.* 249 Ne þurfon me embe Sturmere stedefæste hæleð wordum ætwitan. **1623** BINGHAM *Xenophon* 67 Armed..sufficiently to skip vp and downe, and run away, but not to come to hands in a stedfast fight. **1821** SHELLEY *Hellas* 375 Victor myriads, formed in hollow square With rough and steadfast front.

†**b.** Fixed in abode. *Obs. rare.*

a **1272** *Luue Ron* 18 in *O.E. Misc.*, Nis no mon iboren o lyue, þat her may beon studeuest.

c. Of a thing, e.g. a pillar, a foundation: Firmly fixed, not to be moved or displaced. Also in fig. context. *Obs.* exc. in rhetorical language (of the earth, etc.).

c **1000** *Instit. Polity* x. in Thorpe *Anc. Laws* (1840) II. 318 *note*, Wislic wærscipe & steðe-fæst [*sic* (*MS. G.* styde-)] mod-staðol..biþ witena ȝehwilcum weorðlicre micle. *a* **1225** *St. Juliana* 75 (Bodl. MS.) Lokið þet te heouenliche lauerd beo grund wal of al þat ȝe wurcheð, for þat stont studeuest, falle þat falle. *a* **1300** *Cursor M.* 8483 Stedefast stode þe marbel stan on ferr þe golden letters scan. *c* **1330** R. BRUNNE *Chron. Wace* (Rolls) 15562 Manie skiles forþ were cast, How hit [River Douglas] mighte be mad studefast. *c* **1480** HENRYSON *Mor. Fab.* II. (*Town & C. Mouse*) vi, Ane sillie scheill vnder ane steidfast stane. **1577** GOOGE *Heresbach's Husb.* III. (1586) 148 Into that vessel they powred in milke, and set it where it might stande stedfast. **1590** BARROUGH *Meth. Physick* II. x. (1639) 87 Let them sit in open aire, having a stedfast bed, and of a good height. **1625** N. CARPENTER *Geogr. Del.* I. vii. (1635) 179 The finding out of the Centers where the sted-fast foot of the compasse ought to be fixed in drawing of each circle. **1667** MILTON *P.L.* II. 927 These Elements In mutinie had from her Axle torn The stedfast Earth. *Ibid.* VI. 833 Under his burning Wheeles The stedfast Empyrean shook throughout. **1781** COWPER *Retirem.* 534 The rising waves..Thunder and flash upon the stedfast shores. **1822–56** DE QUINCEY *Conf.* Wks. 1862 I. 102 What was it?..Earth-quake was it? convulsion of the steadfast earth?

†**d.** Of the hands: Steady, not tremulous. Also of shooting: Steady. *Obs.*

1535 COVERDALE *Exod.* xvii. 12 So his handes were sted-fast. **1541** R. COPLAND *Guydon's Quest. Chirurg.* Bij, A stedfast hande without shakynge. **1545** ASCHAM *Toxoph.* II. (Arb.) 127 To make the ende compasse heauy with the fethers in fliyng, for the stedfaster shotyng.

†**e.** Of a pain: Not changing its position. *Obs.*

1398 TREVISA *Barth. De P.R.* VIII. lv. (1495) 268 The ache of the reynes is stable and stedfaste.

†**f.** Solid; firm in substance. *Obs.*

1477 NORTON *Ord. Alch.* iv. in Ashm. (1652) 47 Stedfast to stedfast will it selfe combinde. **1545** RAYNALDE *Byrth Mankynde* I. xv. (1552) 43 The sede is of a more faste, compacte, and stedfaste substaunce.

†**g.** Unshaken in health. *Obs.*

a **1300** *Cursor M.* 1024 He suld in eild be ai stedfast, Sekenes suld he neuer drei. **1387** TREVISA *Higden* (Rolls) IV. 167 He..fauȝt wiþ hem somtyme forto make his body stedefast by use in tra[ua]ylle forto dure.

†**h.** *steadfast land*: the mainland, as opposed to an island. *Obs.* [Cf. G. *festland.*]

a **1470** TIPTOFT *Cæsar's Comm.* i. (1530) 2 They also of the Isle of Britayn had no knowledge of no parte of the stedfaste londe.

2. Of persons: Unshaken, immoveable in faith, resolution, friendship, etc. Also said of belief, purpose or affection. Occas. const. *to.*

c **1200** *Vices & Virtues* (1888) 135 Nis ðe hierte nauht ȝiet stedefast. *c* **1200** ORMIN 1597 Ȝiff þin heorrte iss harrd & starrc, & stedefasst o Criste. *c* **1220** *Bestiary* 374 Oc eurilc luuen oðer, also he were his broder, Wurðen stedefast his wine. *c* **1290** *Beket* 171 in *S. Eng. Leg.* 111 Þare was i-sene þat heo was treowe and of studefast mod! **1340** HAMPOLE *Pr. Consc.* 2139 To serve hym and his werkes to wyrk In stedfast trouthe of haly kyrk. *c* **1369** CHAUCER *Dethe Blaunche* 1227 And swore and gan hir hertely hete Ever to be stedfast and trewe. *c* **1450** LOVELICH *Merlin* 12321 Stedfast sche was to hire Lord. **1472–3** *Rolls of Parlt.* VI. 32/2 Your true

Liegeman and moost obeisaunt and stedfast Subgiet. **1526** *Pilgr. Perf.* (W. de W. 1531) 8 b, Stande stedfast in the fayth & hope of god. **1535** COVERDALE *Prov.* xii. 4 A stedfast woman is a crowne vnto hir huszbonde. **1549** *Bk. Comm. Prayer, Commun.* Collect, Whom thou doest bryng vp in thy stedfast loue. **1667** MILTON *P.L.* I. 58 Huge affliction and dismay Mixt with obdurate pride and stedfast hate. **1693** *Col. Rec. Pennsylv.* I. 405 You shall alwayes find me stedfast to what I promise you. **1738** WESLEY *Psalms* XXXVI. iii, Above the Clouds thy Mercies rise, Stedfast thy Truth and Faithfulness. **1837–9** HALLAM *Hist. Lit.* II. II. ii. §2. 59 It would have required all their stedfast faith in the arm of Providence to anticipate. **1867** SMILES *Huguenots Eng.* vi. (1880) 106 Elizabeth..proved herself the steadfast friend and protector of the Protestant exiles. **1895** DENNEY *Stud. Theol.* vi. (ed. 3) 144 It is His steadfast faithful purpose freely to impart His own character to men.

†**b.** Applied to God: Unchanging. *Obs.*

a **1400** *Relig. Pieces fr. Thornton MS.* 3 The toþer es, þat þe heghe ffadir of Heuen es stedfaste and sothefaste Godde Almyghtyn. *c* **1440** *Lay-Folks Mass Bk.* (MS. E.) 180 In þe name of the fadur and þe sonne and þe holy goste, On stydfast [*other texts* sothfast] god. **1611** BIBLE *Dan.* vi. 26 For he is the liuing God, and stedfast for euer.

†**c.** In bad sense: Confirmed, incorrigible. *Obs.*

1644 MILTON *Areop.* (Arb.) 58 To be common stedfast dunce will be the only pleasant life.

3. Of a law, a treaty, an institution, a condition of things: Firmly settled, established, unchangeable.

1258 *Proclam. Hen. III* (Ellis) 19 Stedefæst and ilestinde in alle þinge abuten ænde. *c* **1290** *St. Dunstan* 47 in *S. Eng. Leg.* 20 Sone he was Abbot of þe hous..He makede þare godes seruise studefast and stable i-novȝ. **1387** TREVISA *Higden* (Rolls) IV. 333 þe dome of hem schulde stonde stedefast and nouȝt be i-chaunged. **1390** GOWER *Conf.* III. 115 Seid is that he hath his aspect Upon the holi lond so cast, That there is no pes stedefast. *c* **1460** *Osney Reg.* 109 This my ȝifte that hit þe moor surer and stedfaster here-after may be, I maade hit in þe presente of lorde John of Constances, Archedecun. **1535** COVERDALE *Heb.* ii. 2 For yf the worde which was spoken by angels, was stedfast, [etc.]. **1607** DEKKER *Sir T. Wyatt* F 3 b, A stedfast silence doth possesse the place. **1742** GRAY *Propertius* II. 17 Who taught this vast machine its steadfast laws. **1877** E. R. CONDER *Basis Faith* iv. 188 The stedfast regularity of phenomena tells with no doubtful significance of a corresponding permanence of the causes on which they depend.

†**b.** Of a language: Settled. *Obs.*

1422 YONGE tr. *Secreta Secret.* 146 Lateyn is the moste stydfaste langage.

4. Of sight, the eye (occas. of the mind): Steadily directed.

a **1300** *Cursor M.* 27999 If þou..woud hir wit wordes slight, Or loked wit ouur stedfast sight [? *read with MS. Galba* sleghe..eghe]. *c* **1430** *Prymer* (1895) 38 Y schal make stidefast myn iȝen on þee. *a* **1593** MARLOWE *Edw. II*, v. v. 2526 That euen then when I shall lose my life, My minde may be more stedfast on my God. **1593** SHAKS. *Lucr.* 1339 The homelie villaine..blushing on her with a stedfast eye, Receaues the scroll without or yea or no. **1629** MILTON *Hymn Nativ.* 70 The Stars with deep amaze Stand fixt in stedfast gaze. **1817** SHELLEY *Rev. Islam* I. ix, The [serpent's] neck..Sustained a crested head, which warily Shifted and glanced before the Eagle's steadfast eye.

†**5.** *adv.* = STEADFASTLY. *Obs.*

a **1300** *Cursor M.* 2874 If þou a brand þar-in [*sc.* into the Dead Sea] wil cast þe fire it haldes þar stedfast. **13..** *Minor Poems fr. Vernon MS.* xlix. 87 In herte loke þou holde stedefast þe benfet þat þou ones hast. **1398** TREVISA *Barth. De P.R.* v. xxxvi. (Bodl. MS.), Blood is ipiȝt in þe lunges, but he is more stedefast ipight in þe herte. *c* **1580** *Sat. Poems Reform.* xliv. 92 Sathan led men steid fast be the mane. **1756** TOLDERVY *Hist. 2 Orphans* IV. 21 Duroy now looking more stedfast found this to be very identical only son of Sir Gilbert Goosley. **1887** MORRIS *Odyss.* XII. 437 So I held on steadfast [to the tree].

†**B.** *sb.* The castor-oil plant, *Ricinus communis.*

1597 GERARDE *Herbal* Suppl., Stedfast is *Palma Christi.* **1665** LOVELL *Herbal* (ed. 2) 416 Sted fast, see Palma Christi.

†**'steadfast,** *v. Obs.* Forms: 5 stefast, 5–6 stedfast(e. [f. STEADFAST *a.* Cf. ON. *staðfesta* to give a fixed abode to (Sw. *stadfästa*, Da. *stadfæste* to confirm, establish).] *trans.* To make steadfast; to confirm, establish.

c **1450** *Brut.* II. (1908) 296 King Edward..ordeyned & stefastyd þe day of þe forsaide Rounde Table to be holde þer at Wyndissore in Whitesen-wike euermore after erly. *c* **1450** tr. *De Imitatione* III. xv. (1893) 84 He..þat sted-fastiþ [*firmavit*] all his hope in god. **1545** RAYNALDE *Byrth Mankynde* III. i. 110 To confirme, stedfaste, and to defende the body from noysome thynges.

†**'steadfasthead.** *Obs. rare*$^{-1}$. [-HEAD.] Steadfastness.

c **1400** *Solomon's Bk. Wisdom* 286 Many men schullen turne to yuel, men may drede, ffor on erþe men may se to liþer stedfast hede.

steadfastly ('stɛdfɑːstlɪ, -fæst-, -fəst-), *adv.* [f. STEADFAST *a.* + -LY^2.]

1. In physical sense: Steadily, firmly, so as not to be shaken or displaced. *rare.*

a **1300** *Cursor M.* 6430 Vr held up, and als aaron, His handes..Vnder aiþer hand was an þat held þam stedfastli als stan. **1635** HEYWOOD *Hierarchy* 177 To whom his father [Neptune] gaue that vertue, to walk as stedfastly vpon the sea, as the land. **1817** SHELLEY *Marianne's Dream* vii, Each mighty rock Stood on its basis steadfastly.

†**2.** With reference to a command or bequest: Securely, bindingly. *Obs.*

a **1200** *Charter of Athelstan A.D. 939* in Kemble *Cod. Dipl.* V. 236 And ich stedeuastliche hote and bebeode in Gode almiȝties heȝe name..ðæt [etc.]. **1388** WYCLIF *1 Sam.* xxx. 25 *marg.* This was ordeyened stidefastliere bi Dauyth.. that it schulde be kept aftirward outirly. *c* **1450** *Godstow Reg.* 343 This yifte of hym I-made stedfastly he had, and with his seale impressed, confermed.

3. Constantly, persistently; with firm resolve, fidelity, belief, etc.

a **1225** *Ancren R.* 162 Beo stille, & wune studeuestliche i sume stude, ut of monne sihðe. *c* **1250** *Kent. Serm.* in *O.E. Misc.* 28 Be-leue we stede-fast-liche þet he is fader and sune and holy gost. **1258** *Proclam. Hen. III* (Ellis) 19 þæt heo stedefæstliche healden and swerien to healden and to werien þo isetnesses þæt beon imakede. **1303** R. BRUNNE *Handl. Synne* 313 Stedfastlych þey preyd a-none Tyl þat woke were alle gone. *c* **1386** CHAUCER *Clerk's T.* 1038 Youre woful mooder wende stedfastly That crueel houndes or som foul vermyne Hadde eten yow. *c* **1450** *Merlin* i. 8 Of hem that in hym stadfastly beleve. **1568** GRAFTON *Chron.* II. 706 She stedfastlye blamed and accused her painefull labor. **1631** GOUGE *God's Arrows* III. §80. 333 We are wont to believe more stedfastly that which is confirmed by an oath. **1712** STEELE *Spect.* No. 423 ⁋2 You will be very steadfastly my Rival. **1867** RUSKIN *Time & Tide* iii. §12 That is what I would steadfastly say again. **1877** C. GEIKIE *Christ* lvii. (1879) 691 They steadfastly refused to accept him.

4. With steadfast gaze.

13.. *K. Alis.* 219 (Laud MS.) In hir he loked stedfastlyk. *a* **1450** *Knt. de la Tour Landry* (1868) 58 Therfor, doughtres, be ware of youre lokes, whereon ye sette hem stedfastly. **1592** SHAKS. *Ven. & Ad.* 1063 Vpon his hurt she lookes so stedfastly, That her sight dazling, makes the wound seem three. **1648** BOYLE *Seraph. Love* xii. (1700) 64 They that gaze steadfastliest on the noondays Sun can least of all discern what it is. **1871** AINSWORTH *Tower Hill* I. xv, He gazed at her steadfastly for a moment, bowed, and retired.

steadfastness ('stɛdfæstnɪs). [f. STEADFAST *a.* + -NESS.] The quality of being steadfast.

1. Constancy or fixity in purpose, belief, fidelity, affection, etc.

a **1000** *Rit. Dunelm.* (Surtees) 50 *Virtute constantiæ*, mægne stydfæstnis. *c* **1220** *Bestiary* 182 Feste ðe of stedefastnesse, and ful of ðewes. *c* **1397** CHAUCER *Lack Stedf.* 7 Al is loste for lac of stedfastnesse. **1508** DUNBAR *Gold. Targe* 164 Scho led wyth hir Nurture and Lawlynes, Contenence, Pacience Gude Fame and Stedfastnes. **1526** TINDALE *2 Pet.* iii. 17 Beware lest ye..fall from youre owne stedfastnes. **1631** GOUGE *God's Arrows* III. §23. 225 He would with the best stedfastnesse of faith that he could pray for them. **1707** *Lond. Gaz.* No. 4308/1 His Steadfastness in their Interest might be depended on. **1855** MACAULAY *Hist. Eng.* xx. IV. 389 Middleton adhered to the cause of hereditary monarchy with a stedfastness which [etc.]. **1876** MISS BRADDON *J. Haggard's Dau.* x. II. 21 The man who is without steadfastness will neither do good to others nor to himself.

†**2.** Established or permanent condition. *Obs.*

c **1450** *Godstow Reg.* 343 We, grauntyng and in stedfastnesse havyng, and our forseid present of witnesse, conferme and strengthe the yifte which we have I-made. **1568** GRAFTON *Chron.* II. 819 The Duke and the Bishop declared what thing was deuised..for to set the realme in a quiet stedfastnesse.

3. In physical sense: Fixity in position. *arch.*

a **1542** WYATT *Ps.* xxxviii. 14 Nor in my bonis there is no stedfastnes. **1787** SMEATON in *Phil. Trans.* LXXVII. 320 A stand of such solidity and steadfastness that the telescope might preserve the position in which it was placed. **1827** STEUART *Planter's G.* (1828) 65 The steadfastness of the plants, in consequence of their fastenings..almost precluded contingency. **1868** MORRIS *Earthly Par.* I. I. 267 And forward did the mighty waters press As though they loved the green earth's steadfastness.

4. Steadiness or fixity (of gaze).

1567 MAPLET *Gr. Forest* 84 Hee taketh his yong when as they be yong and tender, and haue not ful stedfastnesse in their eies. **1647** FULLER *Good Th. Worse T.* 50 For our Saviour glancing his Eyes at the Peoples instruction, did no whit hinder the steadfastnesse of his lookes, lifted up to his Father. **1847** C. BRONTË *Jane Eyre* xxx, There was..a decided steadfastness in his gaze now.

†**'steadfastship.** *Obs.* [-SHIP.] = prec.

c **1320** *Cast. Love* 282 Of on wille heo weoren bo, And of on studefastschipe also.

†**'steadful,** *a. Sc.* and *north. Obs. rare.* [f. STEAD *sb.* + -FUL.] Serviceable.

1585–6 *Reg. Privy Council Scot.* IV. 52 The settling of a steidfull and continewing ordour of the ministeris stipendis. *a* **1600** *Flodden F.* vii. (1664) 67 Yet they such stedful faiths did bear.

†**'steadful,** *v. Obs. rare*$^{-1}$. [f. STEAD *sb.* + FULL *a.*] *trans.* (An etymological rendering of *locuplētāre* to enrich.)

a **1300** *E.E. Psalter* lxiv. 10 Þou soght þe land, and dronkened it yhite; Þou mani-falded to stedful ite [Vulg. *multiplicasti locupletare*].

steadie: see STITHY anvil.

steadier ('stɛdɪə(r)). [f. STEADY *v.* + -ER^1.] Something which steadies.

1864 *Reader* 5 Mar. 301/1 The peroneus longus muscle [in the chimpanzee]..instead of being a steadier of the leg from a fixed point below, becomes [etc.]. **1899** E. PHILLPOTTS *Human Boy* 25 Mathers..fancied tobacco was probably a fine steadier for the nerves before a football match.

steadily ('stɛdɪlɪ), *adv.* [f. STEADY *a.* + -LY^2.] In a steady manner (see senses of the adj.); firmly, unwaveringly, steadfastly, uniformly, etc.

1540 PALSGR. *Acolastus* III. iii. P ij, Seyng that she [fortune] is but a wandrer, that strayeth from place to place like a vacabunde .i. dothe nothyng stedyly or certainly. **1565** COOPER *Thesaurus* s.v. *Pressus, Presso gradu incedere*, to goe steedily and surely. **1678** BUNYAN *Pilgr.* I. (ed. 2) 202 The remembrance..made their hand shake; by means of which impediment, they could not look steddily through the Glass. **1794** MRS. RADCLIFFE *Myst. Udolpho* xli, Dorothee, however, steadily refused to do this. **1827** FARADAY *Chem. Manip.* iii. (1842) 81 When the jars to be graduated are such as cannot stand steadily upon their own bases. **1886** *Field* 4 Sept. 347/2 The pack, working steadily on his [the stag's] line, ran right up to him. **1909** J. MCCABE *Decay Ch. Rome* xii. 268 The Catholics have steadily lost ground.

Comb. **1891** *Hardwicke's Science-Gossip* XXVI. 1/2 A small but steadily-increasing distance.

steadiment ('stɛdɪmənt). *rare.* [f. STEADY *v.* + -MENT.] A means of steadying; also, the condition of being steadied.

1810 BENTHAM *Offic. Apt. Maximized, Def. Econ.* (1830) 67 Instrument attempted to be made for the 'fixing himself in power', Burke's East India Bill: a steadiment, containing in it a sort of pump, contrived for drawing from the East Indies the matter of wealth... His grand instrument of steadiment and 'fixation' having failed. **1878** SIR G. SCOTT *Lect. Archit.* I. vi. 227 Its footing on the capital..requires as much steadiment as possible. *Ibid.*, To give greater steadiment to the foot of the arch. **1894** ADM. ELLIOT in *Morn. Post* 15 May, The wonderful steadiment produced by the clutch of the side keels of Hodgetts' patent form of vessel.

steadiness ('stɛdɪnɪs). [f. STEADY *a.* + -NESS.]

†**1.** The condition or quality of standing fast, permanence, stability. *Obs.*

1530 PALSGR. 275/2 Stedynesse, *estableté, permanableté.* **1653** H. MORE *Def. Cabbala* App. viii. (1713) 184 Which word *μένειν* he often uses in setting out the steddiness and immutableness of the Matter.

2. Freedom from rocking, swaying, tottering, or other irregular movement.

a **1586** SIDNEY *Arcadia* II. (Sommer) 122 Himself [*sc.* a horseman]..shewing at one instant both steadines & nimblenes. **1651** HOBBES *Leviath.* I. x. 44 Like the steddinesse of a Ship laden with Merchandise. **1765** *Museum Rust.* IV. 167 The breadth of the wheels gives a steadiness to the whole machine. **1872** TYNDALL *Forms of Water* §17 ⁋136 Here perfect steadiness of foot is necessary—a slip would be death. **1910** *Encycl. Brit.* III. 271/1 To allow for the superior centering of the shot.., Bashforth introduces a factor σ, called the coefficient of steadiness. This steadiness may vary during the flight of the projectile.

3. Freedom from wavering or indecision; constancy or persistence in resolve, attachment, or conduct.

1663 PATRICK *Pilgrim* xxiii. (1687) 248 So you will be conducted..in paths..of setledness and steadiness of mind. *a* **1715** BURNET *Own Time* II. iv. (1897) I. 266 The presbyterians, who were quite dispirited by the steadiness of his conduct, would take heart again. **1874** GREEN *Short Hist.* iii. §7. 149 There is the same steadiness of will and purpose in his patriotism. **1893** *Speaker* 20 May 553/1 The steadiness with which all sections of the Ministerialists have clung to their posts.

b. Freedom from perturbation in mind or demeanour. ? *Obs.*

1642 FULLER *Holy & Prof. St.* IV. xvi. 323 It is inconsistent with the steddinesse of his gravity to be startled with a wonder. **1647** CLARENDON *Hist. Reb.* I. §46 He answered the articles with great steadiness and unconcernedness.

c. Of troops: Firmness in *moral.*

1666 DK. ORMONDE in *11th Rep. Hist. MSS. Comm.* App. v. 13 It has given mee good proof of the steadynesse of the Regiment. *a* **1859** MACAULAY *Hist. Eng.* xxiii. V. 13 Everything must then be staked on the steadiness of the militia.

d. Of a horse: Freedom from skittishness or nervousness.

1835 [SIR G. STEPHEN] *Adv. in Search of Horse* ix. 125 Steadiness is a great virtue in a gig-horse.

4. Uniformity of action, maintenance of an even rate of progress or level of quality, amount, and the like.

1638 JUNIUS *Paint. Ancients* I. v. §4. 74 The learned.. understand the reason of Art, the unlearned feele the pleasure..: softnesse doth take them both, and forciblenesse doth stirre them both alike; both approve of steadinesse.. and loathe all manner of excessivenesse. **1776** ADAM SMITH *W.N.* I. I. xi. 263 The durableness of metals is the foundation of this extraordinary steadiness of price. **1882** *Jrnl. Fabrics* 12 Feb. 68/2 Linen.—Trade has presented a fair degree of steadiness during the whole month. **1884** *Law Times* 13 Sept. 331/2 The electric light was turned on, but refused to burn with any kind of steadiness.

5. Sobriety or regularity of living.

1864 SMILES *Stephenson* iii. 32 He had contrived, by thrift, steadiness, and industry to save..money.

steading ('stɛdɪŋ). *Sc.* and *north.* Also 6 steding, stedding, steiding, steden. [f. STEAD *sb.* + -ING^1.]

1. A farm-house and outbuildings; often, the outbuildings in contrast to the farm-house.

1472 *Munim. de Melros* (Bannatyne Club) 591 Thare Kirkis takkis teyndis stedingis malingis manaris [etc.]. **1541** *Acc. Ld. High Treas. Scot.* VIII. 31 Item, gevin to Alexander Kempt to help him to plenys ane steding,..x li. **1549** *Compl. Scot.* xv. 123, I am exilit fra my takkis and fra my steddyngis. **1555** *Wills & Inv. N.C.* (Surtees 1860) 146, I geue to my son Thomas Rede all my steden in the hould toune. **1682** *Lond. Gaz.* No. 1682/1 [The Earl of Argyle] to have forfault [*printed* for Fault]..all and Sundry his Lands, ..Tackes, Steadings [etc.]..to our Sovereign Lord. **1799** J. ROBERTSON *Agric. Perth* 482 Here is the most elegant and the most compleat steading of offices in that part at least of the county. **1818** SCOTT in Lockhart *Life* (1839) V. 289, I should like to convert the present steading at Beechland into a little hamlet of labourers. **1861** STEPHENS & BURN *Farm-buildings* 5 The farmhouse should be situated so as to command a view of the fields of the farm, and also be near the steading. **1901** *Scotsman* 28 Feb. 6/2 The steading at the farm..was completely destroyed by fire.

2. A site for a building.
1822 GALT *Provost* vi. 40 His wife's brother, with whom he had entered into a plea, concerning the moieté of a steading at the town-head. **1824** MACTAGGART *Gallovid. Encycl.* s.v. *Sted, Stedding o' houses*, the ground on which an onset is built.

steadite ('stɛdaɪt). [f. the name of J. E. *Stead* (1851–1923), English metallurgist + -ITE[1].]
1. *Metallurgy.* A constituent of phosphorus-rich irons and steels which is a eutectic of austenite and iron phosphide (and sometimes also cementite) and contains dissolved phosphorus.
1902 *Jrnl. Iron & Steel Inst.* LXI. 118 Mr. A. Sauveur (Boston)..suggested [in correspondence]..'Steadite', to designate the eutectic alloy of iron and the phosphide Fe_3P formed in iron rich in phosphorus. **1925** *Machinery* XXVI. 501/1 Steadite is distributed throughout the metal and gives the abrasive action previously mentioned. **1964** S. H. AVNER *Introd. Physical Metall.* xi. 327 Steadite is relatively brittle, and with high phosphorus content, the steadite areas tend to form a continuous network outlining the primary austenite dendrites. **1975** *Brit. Foundryman* LXVIII. 106/1 Phosphorus..segregates in the last portion to solidify, known as steadite, which is composed of iron, iron carbide and iron phosphide.
2. *Min.* A siliceous variety of apatite, usu. containing iron, found as yellowish needles in basic slag.
1911 V. A. KROLL in *Jrnl. Iron & Steel Inst.* LXXXIV. 130 In the new mineral, which..he [*sc.* the author] distinguishes by the name of Steadite, measurement of the angles reveals the occurrence of the hexagonal system. **1950** *Mineral. Mag.* XXIX. 184 Steadite is frequently a late constituent to crystallize; its crystals are the commonest in the vugs of basic slags. **1951** *Science* 29 June 755/2 Metallographic studies..prove the presence of cohenite, steadite, and schreibersite, as well as troilite. The percentage of nickel is about double that of the meteorite fragments found in the same area.

†**'steadless**, *a. Obs. rare.* [f. STEAD *sb.* + -LESS. OE. had *stędeléas* without support, unsteady.] Having no place or position in space.
c **1425** WYNTOUN *Cron.* v. 5249 Þe dewil said..; Sa, qwhar was God..Befor þat hewyn and erde was wroucht? Sancte Serf said: In hym selff stedles, Hys godheide hamprede neuir wes.

†**'steadship.** *Obs. rare*[−1]. In 4 stedship. [f. STEAD *sb.* + -SHIP.] ? Security of position.
1387 T. USK *Test. Love* I. iv. (Skeat) 40 In vayne travayle men to cacche any stedship, but-if ye, lady, first the locke unshet.

steady ('stɛdɪ), *sb.* [f. STEADY *a.* and *v.*]
1. [absol. use of the adj.] **a.** Something which is steady. *spec.* in Newfoundland, a part of a river which has little or no perceptible current.
1792 G. CARTWRIGHT *Jrnl. Labrador* I. Gloss. p. xv, *Steady in a River*, a part where the bed widens, inclining to a pond, and there is no perceptible stream. **1842** J. B. JUKES *Excursions in & about Newfoundland* II. 241, I understood from a salmon-fisher, the only person inhabiting the neighbourhood, that a succession of 'steadies', with occasional rapids, may be met with for twelve miles farther. **1907** J. G. MILLAIS *Newfoundland* xi. 206 At noon we entered a beautiful 'steady'. **1969** H. HORWOOD *Newfoundland* i. 4 The canoe..bounced joyously past the white water into the still and foam-flecked steady below.
b. A regular boyfriend or girlfriend. *colloq.* (orig. *U.S.*).
1897 F. MOSS *Amer. Metropolis* III. ix. 172 Her 'steady' is Jim Clarke. **1927** *Vanity Fair* Nov. 132/3 His steady has quit him for another or he is lonesome for her. **1950** 'N. SHUTE' *Town like Alice* 313, I suppose he's turning into Rose's steady. **1960** AUDEN *Homage to Clio* 56 You won't find a steady in *that* museum Unless you prefer Tea with a shapeless angel to bedtime With a lovely monster. **1978** *Daily Mirror* 12 Jan. 3/4 Meanwhile Rod was flying off to Rio—with a farewell kiss for his latest 'steady', 23-year-old model Bebe Bluell.
2. [From the vb.] **a.** Something which steadies.
1899 M. COBBETT *Bottled Holidays* viii. 141 Two officials fulfilled the awkward duties of being rounding posts [in a skating match], the competitors generally catching hold of them for a steady as they made the turns.
b. *spec.* A device for holding steady an object in process of being fashioned. (Cf. *steady-rest*, STEADY *a.* 9 b.)
1885 [HORNER] *Pattern Making* 106 Make a steady, shaped roughly to fit the bed of the lathe and to take the diameter of the pipe. **1911** *Encycl. Brit.* XXVII. 26/1 [Lathes.] Of devices for this purpose..some are fixed,..and others are bolted to the carriage of the slide-rest and move along with it—travelling steadies.

steady ('stɛdɪ), *a.* (and *adv.*) Forms: 6 stedy(e, 6–7 steddie, steedie, steadie, 6–8 steddy, 7 stydie, -y, study, studdie (*Sc.*), steedy, 7– steady. [First in Palsgrave 1530; app. f. STEAD *sb.* + -Y.
Perh. the formation may have been suggested by MLG., MDu. *stâdig, stêdig*, steady, stable, constant = OHG. *stâtîc* (MHG. *stætig*, mod.G. *stetig* constant, perpetual):—WGer. **stâdigo-* f. the synonymous **stâdjo-* (MLG., MDu. *stâde, stêde*, OHG. *stâti*, MHG. *stæte*, mod.G. *stet*), f. OTeut. **stæ-* (:*sta-*) root of STAND *v.*
Closely similar in meaning, and from the same ultimate root, are ON. *stǫðug-r* steady, stable (Norw. *stødug*), and OE. *stæððiʒ, ʒestæððiʒ*, grave, serious.
OE. had *stędiʒ* (app. f. *stęde* STEAD *sb.*) with the sense 'barren', corresponding to G. *stätig*, in dial. use 'barren' (said of animals), in general use 'restive, stubborn' (= LG. *stedich*, Du. *stedig, steeg*).]
A. *adj.*
†**1. a.** Fixed or immovable in position; not liable to give way or become displaced. Also *fig. Obs.*
1530 PALSGR. 325/2 Stedye stedfast, *ferme*. **1540** —— *Acolastus* I. i. C iv, Wherof I myght promysse to my selfe an euerlastyng and very stedy ioye [L. *gaudium perpetuum & bene stabile*]. **1591** SYLVESTER *Du Bartas* I. vii. 95 The dull Earth's prop-less massie Ball Stands steddy still. **1594** T. B. *La Primand. Fr. Acad.* II. 596 For if we would moue one of our feete, the other must abide steddie and firme. *a* **1677** BARROW *Serm.* Wks. 1716 I. 3 The fool building his choice ..not upon the steddy warrant of good reason. **1680** MOXON *Mech. Exerc.* x. 175 Any Substance..pitcht steddy upon two points..and moved about on that Axis... And an Edg-Tool set steddy to that part. *a* **1683** SIDNEY *Disc. Govt.* iii. §30. (1704) 362 This being built upon the steddy Foundation of Law, History, and Reason, is not to be remov'd.
b. Of affairs: Stable. Of a rule, etc.: Settled, established. ? *Obs.*
1571 CAMPION *Hist. Irel.* I. xi. (1633) 34 From this time forward the amity waxed steddy. **1627** DRAYTON *Agincourt* 2 When presently a Parliament is calld To sett things steddy. **1690** LOCKE *Hum. Und.* II. xxviii [xxix]. §10. 165 By what has been said, we may observe how much Names, as supposed steady signs of Things..are the occasion of denominating Ideas distinct or confused. **1704** HEARNE *Duct. Hist.* (1714) I. 13 It was a steady Rule, that the Moon wherein the Vernal Equinox happens should be the Month Nisan. **1818** SCOTT *Hrt. Midl.* ix, It became at length understood..that their union should be deferred no longer than until Butler should obtain some steady means of support.
2. a. Firm in standing or movement; not tottering, rocking, or shaking; that is in stable equilibrium.
1574 HYLL *Art Gard., Ord. Bees, Husb. Conject.* i. 48 If any washeth the handes with snowe, it doth then make them steddie. **1593** SHAKS. *2 Hen. VI*, IV. vii. 101 *Cade.* Nay, he noddes at vs, as who should say, Ile be euen with you. Ile see if his head will stand steddier on a pole, or no. **1621** SANDERSON *Serm., Ad Pop.* iv. §3. (1637) 356 Othersome.. like a young unbroken thing that hath mettall..would be.. guided with a steddy and skilfull hand. **1624** *Ibid.* v. §20. 434 The colours..are yet so thin: that a steddy eye, not bleered by prejudice, may discerne the lye through them. **1770** LUCKOMBE *Hist. Printing* 319 Justifiers of wood..to wedge it tight and steddy in its place. **1785** BURNS *Jolly Beggars* Air II. vi, But whilst with both hands I can hold the glass steady Here's to thee, my hero, my sodger laddie! **1851** *Butler, Wine-dealer*, etc. 9 The stands [for casks] should be fixed perfectly steady. **1865** J. B. HARWOOD *Lady Flavia* xiv, The hand that held the candle was as steady as a rock. **1892** *Photogr. Ann.* II. 471 The bottom of the lamp being loaded, it is perfectly steady.
b. Said of things held with a firm hand.
1590 SPENSER *F.Q.* I. xi. 16 The knight gan fairely couch his steadie speare. **1711** SHAFTESB. *Misc. Refl.* Charac. III. 37 So this high and noble affection..requires a steddy rein and strict hand over it.
c. Of movements or actions: Free from tremulousness or faltering.
1777 POTTER *Æschylus, Agamem.* 281 With steddy step I trace foul deeds that smell above the earth. **1845** J. COULTER *Adv. in Pacific* xiii. 182, I determined to do justice to the gun, took a steady aim, and broke the pearl shell to pieces.
3. a. Of a person or his mind: Not easily perturbed or discomposed; balanced. Of the head: Free from giddiness. Of the eye: Not diverted from its object; unwavering.
1602 MARSTON *Ant. & Mel.* I. B 4 b, Giue me a husband ..Of steddie iudgement, quicke and nimble sense. **1642** FULLER *Holy & Prof. St.* IV. v. 264 They need to have steddy heads who can dive into these gulfs of policy. **1672–5** COMBER *Comp. Temple* (1702) 19 No man can pray with a truly devout and steddy mind, without a known form. *a* **1710** BP. BULL *Serm.* (1713) I. v. 210 Few Men have such steddy Heads as to be able to stand upon the Spires and Pinnacles of Glory without Giddiness. **1819** SHELLEY *Mask of Anarchy* 344 With folded arms and steady eyes.
b. Of troops, their attributes or actions: Firm, disciplined; not liable to panic or loss of self-control. Also *ellipt.* = 'be steady'.
1670 MILTON *Hist. Eng.* II. 37 Whereby at length all the Foot..with a more steddy charge put the Britans to flight. **1759** GARRICK *Song, Hearts of Oak* refrain, Steady, boys, steady! We'll fight and we'll conquer again and again. **1769** ROBERTSON *Chas. V*, VII. III. 32 The steddy and disciplined valour of the Spanish infantry. **1821** BYRON *Sardanap.* III. i. 115 Our troops were steady. **1823** SCOTT *Quentin D.* xxx, The knaves are numerous and steady—Can they not hold out their town against him? **1837** LEVER *H. Lorrequer* i, They're coming up: steady, boys; steady now. **1878** *N. Amer. Rev.* CXXVI. 252 But they [soldiers] were as steady as clocks and chirpy as crickets.
c. Of a hound: Not easily diverted from the scent. Of a horse: Not nervous, skittish, or excitable; also (cf. 4), that travels at a moderate and even pace.
steady from hare: (of a foxhound) trained to disregard a hare. Cf. quot. 1901 in STEADY *v.* 2 c.
1735 SOMERVILLE *Chase* IV. 125 With these consort The Stanch, and steddy Sages of thy Pack. **1826** J. COOK *Foxhunting* 107 And to do him [the hound] justice, he was a good finder, steady from hare. **1835** [SIR G. STEPHEN] *Adv. in Search of Horse* ix. 129 They [mares] may be temperate and steady for months,..and yet when the season arrives, will kick your chaise to pieces. **1852** BURN *Naval & Mil. Techn. Dict.* II. (1863) s.v., Horse steady to fire, *cheval fait, dressé, sage au feu.* **1886** RUSKIN *Præterita* I. vi. 182 As a rule, there were four steady horses and a good driver, rarely drunk.
4. a. Regular in operation or intensity; that is maintained at an even rate of action, output, or the like; uniform, equable.
1548 *Elyot's Dict.* s.v. *Pressus, Presso gradu incedere*, to go a rounde and stedy pase. **1644** MILTON *Educ.* 6 In which methodicall course..they must proceed by the steddy pace of learning onward. **1766** JOHNSON in *Boswell* (1791) I. 274 Dryden's horses are either galloping or stumbling: Pope's go at a steady even trot. **1817** SHELLEY *Rev. Islam* II. xii, My spirit onward past Beneath truth's steady beams upon its tumult cast. **1836** MARRYAT *Midsh. Easy* xxiii, A steady pull, my lads, and not too much exertion. **1855** *Poultry Chron.* III. 431 There was a steady trade in all descriptions of barley. **1873** MAXWELL *Electr. & Magn.* (1881) I. 327 The most convenient method of producing a steady current is by means of the Voltaic Battery. **1874** GREEN *Short Hist.* vi. §5. 320 The steady rise in the price of wool was..giving a fresh impulse to the agrarian changes.
b. spec. ***steady motion*** (see quots.).
1877 E. J. ROUTH *Stabil. Given State of Motion* 2 We may therefore define a steady motion to be such that the same change of motion follows from the same initial disturbance at whatever instant the disturbance is communicated to the system. **1882** G. M. MINCHIN *Unipl. Kinemat.* 140 If..all the particles..pass through it with the same velocities and accelerations (both in magnitude and in direction), the record of the motion at *P* becomes constant, and there is said to be *steady motion* at *P*.
c. Of wind, a gale: That blows equably in force and direction.
1612 COVERTE *Voy.* 7 From the 22. day..wee could haue no steedy gale of wind to carry vs forward, vntill the 25. day. **1726** SHELVOCKE *Voy. round World* (1757) 255 Whilst you are in this road, it is impossible you should have the wind steady in any quarter. **1867** SMYTH *Sailor's Word-bk., Steady-Gale*, a fresh breeze pretty uniform in force and direction.
d. Of weather, temperature: Free from sudden changes, settled. Of climate: Having little variation of temperature. Hence said of an instrument for recording variations of weather.
a **1700** EVELYN *Diary* July 1694, Glorious steady weather. **1806** G. PINCKARD *West Indies* III. xiv. 176 This climate is perhaps one of the most steady in the world, the range of the thermometer..being only from 11 to 15 degrees. **1869** PHILLIPS *Vesuv.* iii. 94 The barometer during all the eruption was steady.
e. *Commerce.* Of prices: Free from sudden rise or fall; hence of the market, goods, shares, etc.
1857 A. MATHEWS *Tea-Table Talk* II. 343 Ceylon coffee, heretofore steady and pressing for immediate sale, is now inactive. **1889** *Textile News* 29 Mar. 1/2 Subsequently the market became quieter and then declined, prices remaining steady. **1896** *Daily News* 9 Dec. 10/7 Corn opened steady and unchanged. **1898** 'H. S. MERRIMAN' *Roden's Corner* vii. 68 The paper markets of the world began to settle down again, and steadier prices ruled. **1912** *Times* 19 Dec. 16/5 Rubber shares were comparatively steady.
f. *Cricket.* Of a batsman or his play: consistent, safe, cautious.
1826 S. MAUNDER in R. Dagley *Death's Doings* 54 A steady Player, careful of his fame, May have a *good long Innings*. **1833** *New Sporting Mag.* V. (Cricketers' Reg.) 13 This style [of bowling] Pilch met by steady play. **1857** T. HUGHES *Tom Brown's School Days* II. viii. 398 To the suggestions that Winter is the best bat left, Tom only replies, 'Arthur is the steadiest, and Johnson will make the runs if the wicket is only kept up.' **1890** J. LILLYWHITE *Cricketers' Annual* 143 W. G. Turnbull: A steady bat, but lacking power; should hit more at loose balls. **1924** H. DE SÉLINCOURT *Cricket Match* iv. 104 As a matter of sad fact there was no steady and reliable batsman upon the side. *Ibid.* v. 159 He felt a batsman, pure and simple; and decided that he was..in for a good, steady display of batting.
5. *Naut.* Of a ship: That moves without deviation (in her course); hence, applied to the helm and the steersman.
1626 CAPT. SMITH *Accid. Yng. Seamen* 18 He stands right a-head; out with all your sayles, a stydy man to the helme, sit close to keep her stydie. **1815** SHELLEY *Alastor* 333 The Poet sate Holding the steady helm.
6. a. Persistent, unwavering in resolution, attachment, or in a course of action; persistently devoted *to* a cause, resolution, etc.
1602 MARSTON *Antonio's Rev.* IV. v. I 1 b. We must be stiffe and steddie in resolue. **1697** DRYDEN *Æneid* Postscr. 621 Yet steady to my Principles, and not dispirited with my Afflictions, I have..overcome all difficulties. **1749** SMOLLETT *Regicide* III. viii, A trusty counsellor and steady friend. **1797** HT. LEE *Canterb. T., Frenchm. T.* (1799) I. 274 Steady to honour and to feeling, there was yet one point on which his reason obstinately wandered. **1819** SCOTT *Leg. Montrose* Introd., He was a steady jacobite. **1849** MACAULAY *Hist. Eng.* ii. I. 182 It was only in retirement that any person could long keep the character either of a steady royalist or of a steady republican. *Ibid.* vii. II. 226 The influence of the Hampdens..kept him steady to the cause of the constitution. **1871** R. ELLIS *Catullus* cii. 2 A friend whose soul steady to honour abides.
b. of attributes, actions, etc.
1647 CLARENDON *Hist. Reb.* VI. §407 His person was not less acceptable to those of steady and uncorrupted principles than to those of depraved inclinations. **1667** MILTON *P.L.* XII. 377 Now clear I understand What oft my steddiest thoughts have searcht in vain. **1698** NORRIS *Pract. Disc.* IV. 51 The steddy View, or rather Possession they have of the other World gives them..a daily Triumph over this. **1710** SHAFTESB. *Soliloquy* II. ii. 81 The mean genius..endeavours by the best outward Gloss and dazling Shew, to turn the Eye from a direct and steddy Survey of his Piece. **1754** SHERLOCK *Disc.* (1759) I. vii. 225 A constant and steddy Belief..in the Resurrection of the Dead. **1818** HALLAM *Mid. Ages* viii. II. (1819) III. 235 Their own serious and steady attachment to the laws. **1891** *Law Times* XCII. 96/1 A convict who gains by steady industry the maximum number of marks.

c. Of a boyfriend or girlfriend: regular or constant. *colloq.* (orig. *U.S.*).

1887 *Lantern* (New Orleans) 23 July 2/2, I expect my steady company at the house this evening. **1922** S. BENSON *Poor Man* v. 127 She had just mislaid her last steady beau, so she was at the moment a little susceptible. **1932** J. DOS PASSOS *1919* 43 Della let Joe kiss her when they said good night and he began kinder planning that she'd be his steady girl. **1975** D. LODGE *Changing Places* iii. 126 She's become Charles Boon's steady girl friend. **1977** *Rolling Stone* 5 May 47/4 He has no steady girl.

7. Not given to frivolity; staid.

1759 FRANKLIN *Ess.* Wks. 1840 III. 236 They were too wise and too steady to be amused. **1818** T. MOORE *Diary* 26 Oct. *Mem.* (1853) II. 175 Which disconcerted the latter (who, strange to say, is a very grave, steady person) considerably.

8. Regular in habits; not given to dissipation or looseness in conduct.

1832 HT. MARTINEAU *Life in Wilds* vi. 79, I wondered.. what made Robertson steal away into the wood so often, so steady a workman as he is. **1857** SMILES *Stephenson* iv. 24 At Callerton, Stephenson—habitually sober and steady—was a standing example of character to the other workmen. **1889** 'R. BOLDREWOOD' *Robbery under Arms* xlvii, He'd always been as steady as a rock.

9. *Comb.*, as ***steady-looking*** adj.; parasynthetic, as ***steady-eyed, -footed, -handed, -headed, -minded, nerved*** adjs.

1901 FRANCES CAMPBELL *Love* 307 *Steady-eyed, muscular men. **1611** COTGR. s.v. *Ferré, Ferré à glace*, ..*Steadie-footed, sure of foot. *Ibid.* s.v. *Main, Avoir la main seure*, to be *steadie handed. **1897** 'SARAH TYTLER' *Lady Jean's Son* xv. 258 *Steady-headed as the young man was. **1826** MRS. ANNE GRANT *Mem. & Corr.* (1844) III. 105 A plain, *steady-looking man who..is sober and regular. **1818** SCOTT *Hrt. Midl.* xliii, Whatever David felt, he was too proud and too *steady-minded to show any unpleasant surprise. **1865** E. BURRITT *Walk to Land's End* 4 Even men called brave and *steady-nerved waited for company to make the journey.

b. Special combinations and collocations: **steady-fast** (see quot.); **steady pin**, a pin or each of several pins used to secure the relative positions of two adjoining surfaces or to prevent them from sliding upon each other; **steady quaker**, a kind of moth (see quot.); **steady-rest** *Turning*, = *back rest*, BACK- IV B.

1867 SMYTH *Sailor's Word-bk.*, **Steady-Fast*, a hawser carried out to some fixed object to keep a vessel steady in a tide-way, or in preparation for making sail from a fast. **1791** SMEATON *Edystone L.* §229 The Lewis Holes, each being filled with an extuberance of mortar, which, when hard, would in effect become a *steady pin. **1825** J. NICHOLSON *Oper. Mech.* 513 The piece..is screwed to the side of the plate..and made firm by small pins..; these pins are called steady-pins. **1875** KNIGHT *Dict. Mech.*, *Steady-pin* 1. (*Founding.*) One of the pins—generally three or four, in one flask—which, by fitting into holes in the lugs of another, enable the two parts to be restored to their original position after the pattern is drawn. **1884** F. J. BRITTEN *Watch & Clockm.* 247 *Steady Pin*,..a pin used to secure the relative positions of two pieces of metal. **1832** J. RENNIE *Consp. Butterfl. & Moths* 58 The *Steady Quaker (*Orthosia stabilis*, Ochsenheimer). **1882** OGILVIE, **Steady-rest*. Same as Back-rest. **1884** KNIGHT *Dict. Mech. Suppl.*

B. *adv.* **a.** In a steady manner, steadily. Chiefly *Naut.*: see A 5. Also *to go steady colloq.* (orig. *U.S.*), to keep regular company (*with* someone) as a boyfriend or girlfriend.

a **1605** MONTGOMERIE *Misc. Poems* xlviii. 151 Steir studdie, mate. **1626** CAPT. SMITH *Accid. Yng. Seamen* 27 Steare study before the wind. **1639** FULLER *Holy War* II. vii. (1647) 52 Learning doth accomplish a Prince, and maketh him sway his sceptre the steadier. **1653** T. BRUGIS *Vade Mecum* (ed. 2) 157 With..your little finger leaning upon the arme, to rest your whole hand the more steddier, gently thrust in your Lancet. **1815** SCOTT *Guy M.* xxxiii, Ay, but I have a notion that I could make you go steady about, and try the old course again. **1822** *Cobbett's Weekly Reg.* 9 Mar. 634 The Yankee Captain..stood upon the deck, calling out ..'Steady she goes, my boys!' **1905** E. WHARTON *House of Mirth* II. xiii. 493, I thought we were to be married: he'd gone steady with me six months and given me his mother's wedding ring. **1923** *Saucy Stories* 1 Mar. 78/1 Puzzled, she asked him, Well, wasn't we... Didn't you go with me steady? **1946** *Coast to Coast 1945* 136 Are you going steady with anyone, Billy? **1962** M. URQUHART *Frail on North Circular* xii. 70 Noticing a huge, cheap ring on Joan's finger. 'Where'd you get that?' 'It's a going steady ring.' **1978** F. WELDON *Praxis* xx. 163 I'm going steady with one of the young doctors.

b. *ellipt.* Orig. *Naut.* = 'steer steady': cf. STEADY *v.* 3. Also in sporting contexts, or *gen.*, or *transf.* Freq. in colloq. phrases expressing caution, as ***steady as she goes, steady on*** (*with* something), ***steady there***, etc.; ***steady the Buffs*** (BUFF *sb.*[2] 6), hold on! keep calm! be careful!

1620 J. TAYLOR (Water P.) *Praise Hemp-seed* (1623) 12 Cleere, cleere the boighrope, stedy, well steer'd, so. **1669** STURMY *Mariner's Mag.* I. ii. 17 The Ship wears bravely, study, she is before it. *a* **1699** TEMPLE *Mem. 1672–9* Wks. 1770 II. 462 The prince..said..Will the King never learn a word that I shall never forget since my last passage, when ..the captain was all night crying out to the man at the helm, Steady, Steady, Steady?' **1769** FALCONER *Dict. Marine* (1780), *Steddy*, the command given by the pilot, &c. to the helmsman..to steer the ship according to the line on which she advances at that instant. **1825** H. WILSON *Mem.* II. 162 Here the men, forgetful of the caution..began to draw [their swords]. Steady there!! Never a finger or a high to move. **1836** MARRYAT *Midsh. Easy* xix, Steady—port it is—port. —Steer small, for your life, Easy. Steady now. **1853** C. BRONTË *Villette* I. ix. 168 She was going to bestow on me a kiss..but I said, 'Steady! Let us be steady, and know what we are about.' **1888** KIPLING *Story of Gadsbys* 6 I'd like to see Mr Khan being rude to that girl! Hullo! Steady the Buffs! **1893** *Illustr. London News* 18 Feb. 222/2 (Advt.), Steady there, Spencer with the milk, Rosebery here has not had a drop yet. **1895** MANSON *Sporting Dict.*, *Steady*, the order to dogs at work to be cautious. **1900** G. SWIFT *Somerley* 87 Women are jolly ready to stop men when they're going too far,..but, if a man says 'steady' to a girl, she thinks she's been insulted. **1903** G. B. SHAW *Man & Superman* II. 70 Here! mister! arf a mo! steady on! **1936** A. RANSOME *Pigeon Post* xiii. 140 'Sorry,' sobbed Titty. 'Awfully sorry. I didn't mean to.'..'All right, Titty... All right... Steady on.' **1953** N. JACOB *Morning will Come* xiii. 241 He was growing nervous, and kept saying, 'Steady, Charles, steady the Buffs!' **1959** J. VERNEY *Friday's Tunnel* i. 12 Here, steady on with the sugar, greedy guts. **1971** *Time* 30 Aug. 4/2 No changes were contemplated in the Administration's approach. 'Steady as she goes was the watchword,' said Shultz. **1972** J. WAINWRIGHT *Night is Time to Die* 155 Steady the Buffs! (thought Ripley). He's goading you. **1976** in R. Crossman *Diaries* II. 307 The 'steady as she goes' budget was welcomed by foreign bankers. **1976** *Shooting Times & Country Mag.* 18 Nov. 28/2 Opening gates, and holding them open without a hound rushing into the field, at the words 'steady there!' **1979** A. WILLIAMSON *Funeral March for Siegfried* xxxiii. 167 'She had last year been Andersson's mistress—' 'Here, steady on!' cried Von Wolstenholm..purple with indignation.

c. Comb. as ***steady-goer***; ***steady-going*** adj.

1837 DICKENS *Pickw.* xviii, Always the vay vith these here old 'uns hows'ever, as is such *steady goers to look at. **1825** T. HOOK *Sayings* Ser. II. *Sutherl.* I. 4 The *steady-going devotion which he paid to Miss Grace Lazenby. **1889** J. S. WINTER' *Mrs. Bob* i, Those who do stay are the steady-going unambitious ones of the flock.

steady ('stɛdɪ), *v.* [f. STEADY *a.*

OE. had *ȝestędeȝian* (once) to bring to a standstill.]

1. a. *trans.* To keep from rocking, shaking, tottering, or similar movement.

1530 PALSGR. 734/1, I stedye, I sattell, or set faste a thing, *je me arreste*. **1541** R. COPLAND *Guydon's Quest. Chirurg.* L j, And vnder them is the bone of the hele, of the whiche all the fote is stedyed. **1745** P. THOMAS *Jrnl. Anson's Voy.* 156 They..carried out a Cable and Anchor to steddy the Ship. **1791** SMEATON *Edystone L.* §226 These stones being fixed.. by a pair of wedges on each side.., and still further steadied by joint wedges at the head of the dovetails. **1828–32** WEBSTER s.v., Steddy my hand. **1850** *New Monthly Mag.* Aug. 420 He..brought him again to the surface, turning him on his back..and steadying the floating body with one hand. **1899** *Allbutt's Syst. Med.* VIII. 26 The chronic drunkard, who takes a glass of spirits to 'steady the hand'. **1901** T. J. ALLDRIDGE *Sherbro* xx. 202 So strained do one's muscles become that one's legs shake violently, and it is impossible to steady them.

b. To support upon the feet, to keep from falling.

1848 *New Monthly Mag.* Oct. 159 Steadying her between us,..we handed her along as well as we could to the platform. **1851** MRS. BROWNING *Casa Guidi Wind.* I. 12 A little child, too, who not long had been By mother's finger steadied on his feet.

refl. **1853** MRS. GASKELL *Ruth* xxiv, They walked apart, he back to the inn,..she to steady herself along till she reached the little path. **1914** W. W. JACOBS *Night Watches* 113 Then, steadying herself by the wall, she tottered into the front room.

c. *intr.* for *refl.*

1849 FROUDE *Nemesis of Faith* 163 If he could only have been permitted some few months or years of further silent communing with himself, the reeling rocking body might have steadied into a more constant motion. **1876** G. M. HOPKINS *Wreck of Deutschland* iv, in *Poems* (1967) 52, I steady as a water in a well, to a poise, to a pane. **1910** *Encycl. Brit.* III. 271/1 The shot may be unsteady for some distance after leaving the muzzle, afterwards steadying down, like a spinning-top.

2. a. *trans.* To settle (one's mind, thoughts, etc.).

1530 PALSGR. 734/1, I love nat this waveryngе mynde of yours, I wolde have you stedye your mynde upon somwhat. **1866** R. W. DALE *Disc. Spec. Occas.* i. 3 It is hard to steady our thoughts.

b. To bring (troops) to a steady condition.

1901 'LINESMAN' *Words by Eyewitness* viii. 169 The Wakkerstroom commando..stayed the demoralised..men, ..and a formidable force was soon steadied on the already prepared position.

c. To make (hounds) steady *from hare*, etc. (Cf. STEADY *a.* 3 c.)

1901 *Westm. Gaz.* 4 Jan. 4/3 The eighteenth century was well advanced before hounds were finally steadied from deer or hare and trained to hunt fox.

3. *Naut.* **a.** To keep (a vessel) to the direct line of her course. Also *absol.* (From the word of command *Steady!* See STEADY *adv.* b.)

1627 CAPT. SMITH *Sea Gram.* ix. 37 Steady, that is, to keepe her right vpon that point you steare by. **1858** *Merc. Mar. Mag.* V. 82 *The Corsair*..put her helm to port, and then steadied. **1875** F. T. BUCKLAND *Log-Book* 348 The bow of the boat well steadied towards the advancing wave.

b. *intr.* for *refl.*

1798 COLERIDGE *Anc. Mariner* III. v, She doth not tack from side to side..Withouten wind, withouten tide She steddies with upright keel.

c. *to steady the helm*: to keep it in the position in which it has been put.

1875 BEDFORD *Sailor's Pocket Bk.* x. (ed. 2) 354 Steady the helm.

4. To cause to go at a less impetuous pace; to bring to a more regular rate of progress. Also *intr.* for *refl.*

1812 *Sporting Mag.* XXXIX. 267 All horses in their career require to be steadied by a pull. **1849** CUPPLES *Green Hand* xvi. (1856) 157 As the tide steadied, this said creek proved to be a smaller river. **1861** TROLLOPE *Orley F.* II. x. 75 He turned his horse, and without giving the beast time to steady himself he rammed him at the fence. **1892** RIDER HAGGARD *Nada* 210 See! he steadies his pace, he gathers himself together, and now he leaps!

5. To keep (a person) from irregularity of conduct; to make sober in habit. Also *intr.* for *refl.*, and with *down* or *up*.

1848 *Q. Rev.* Sept. 360 He breaks off..from folly;..he steadies down..and lives in usefulness and repute. **1861** PYCROFT *Agony Point* xviii. I. 283 He was being steadied by increasing responsibilities. **1877** *Chamb. Jrnl.* 21 Apr. 241/1 But though his wife was a quiet and respectable young woman, his marriage does not appear to have steadied him. **1878** SUSAN PHILLIPS *On Seaboard* 34 But she steadied when she married Bill. **1932** E. WAUGH *Black Mischief* iii. 104 When you're convinced he's steadied up a bit, let him have chambers of his own in one of the Inns of Court. **1963** *Times* 2 Feb. 5/1 The port's Trawler Officers' Guild asked the owners to co-operate in steadying up the men who go on board from the public houses and take bottles with them on late-night sailing.

6. *Comm.* intr. To become more free from fluctuation; also with *up*.

1913 *Times* 9 Aug. 19/5 Wheat..after fluctuating narrowly, but with a downward tendency, steadied up slightly near the end.

Hence **'steadying** *vbl. sb.* (also *concr.* and *attrib.*); **'steadying, 'steadied** *ppl. adjs.*

1736 HAWKSMOOR *Lond. Bridge* 12 For placing the Grand Pier in the Middle of London-Bridge;..I am of Opinion, he did it..To be a Steadying for the whole Machine. **1827** FARADAY *Chem. Manip.* xix. (1842) 525 Placing a block..at such a distance..that the back of the blow-pipe may bear slightly against it. If these steadying-blocks be formed [etc.]. **1860** H. STUART *Seaman's Catech.* 7 See the.. steadying lines fast. **1862** *Catal. Internat. Exhib.* II. xi. 25 The sling is attached to the scroll or steadying-piece placed behind the guard. **1876** HARDY *Ethelberta* xvii. I. 176 My dear mother, you will be necessary as a steadying power— a flywheel, in short, to the concern. **1883** *Manch. Guardian* 22 Oct. 5/3 It has worked..with a steadying influence on the balance of political power. **1884** *St. James's Gaz.* 10 May 6/2 Look for instance at the gulls..: how those that are going into the picture, battle against the breeze, while those that come out sweep on with steadied wings. **1890** GLADSTONE in Morley *Life* x. iv. (1903) III. 422, I derived from him what I thought very valuable and steadying knowledge. **1905** *Daily News* 10 Oct. 2/4 Gold shares displayed some irregularity..but showed finally a more favourable disposition, which produced a steadying effect on markets generally.

steady: see STITHY anvil.

steadyish ('stɛdɪɪʃ), *a.* [f. STEADY *a.* + -ISH.] Moderately or fairly steady.

1833 T. HOOK *Parson's Dau.* III. ii, He....stepped out with a steadyish step, but a fluttering heart. **1924** H. DE SÉLINCOURT *Cricket Match* iv. 104 Gauvinier tried to arrange for a steadyish man to go in at No. 7.

steady state. [f. STEADY *a.* + STATE *sb.*]

1. An unvarying condition; a state of equilibrium.

1885 *Electrician* 10 Jan. 180/1 With special arrangements (solenoidal) of impressed force, there is no transmission of energy in the steady state. **1905** *Nature* 27 July 293/2 His [*sc.* Planck's] ensemble of systems has not yet reached a statistical 'steady state'. **1930** RUARK & UREY *Atoms, Molecules & Quanta* ix. 272 These five quantum numbers may be taken as those required to fix the steady states of an atom in a strong magnetic field. **1963** *Wall St. Jrnl.* 19 Aug., It long had been held by many scientists that the universe is in a steady state, that, in its general features, it is the same now as it always has been. **1971** *Nature* 8 Jan. 75/1 If present patterns..continue, the annual death rate from lung cancer will increase from about 15,000 to more than 45,000 in the steady state that will be attained in the 1980s. **1977** *Lancet* 3 Sept. 509/2 Plasma-carbamazepine concentrations were in steady state in all patients.

2. *attrib.* (freq. with hyphen). **a.** *gen.*

1909 *Phil. Mag.* XVII. 251 There is no *a priori* reason why there should not be different 'steady state' formulæ corresponding to different kinds of matter. **1942** *Jrnl. Appl. Physics* XIII. 710/2 The steady state current is then the difference of the expressions for the total current and for the transient current. **1965** H. I. ANSOFF *Corporate Strategy* iii. 32 The microeconomic theory of the firm..is basically a steady-state theory concerned with successive equilibrium conditions. **1970** J. EARL *Tuners & Amplifiers* iii. 66 For good quality listening we should not go in for anything less than..8W steady-state power per channel. **1976** *Conservation News* Nov./Dec. 22/1 The author is sceptical that steady-state economics will ever find practical application, since people's desires for consumption show no evidence of having a reasonable upper limit. **1977** A. HALLAM *Planet Earth* 296 Hutton and Lyell were postulating a steadystate Earth—ceaseless piecemeal local change was occurring. But the consequence of such change was to maintain from the indefinite past to the indefinite future an overall, constant equilibrium in the terrestrial economy. **1978** P. MARSH et. al. *Rules of Disorder* iv. 112 Evidence for the existence of a 'steady-state' system of rules and a sense of social propriety.

b. *Astr.* Used with reference to any cosmological theory which embraces the principle that on a large scale the universe is essentially unchanging in time and space; *spec.* the theory propounded by Bondi, Gold, and Hoyle of an isotropic universe expanding at a constant rate, with matter being continuously created so that mean density of the universe remains constant.

1948 BONDI & GOLD in *Monthly Notices R. Astron. Soc.* CVIII. 252 (*heading*) The steady-state theory of the expanding universe. **1955** *Sci. News* XXXVII. 22 The steady-state theory was designed to overcome a difficulty in the world-models of general relativity which no longer exists. Until a few years ago it was thought that these gave a value for the age of the universe..which was too small to satisfy other astrophysical evidence. **1969** *Times* 23 June 6/7 The steady state theory..says that the universe looks roughly the same from any position and at any time in the past, present or future. **1971** J. Z. YOUNG *Introd. Study Man* xxvi. 363 There are other versions of steady-state cosmologies according to which new galaxies are continuously being formed by newly created matter. **1973** [see RADIO ASTRONOMY]. **1977** J. NARLIKAR *Struct. Universe* iv. 132 With the help of the PCP [Perfect Cosmological Principle], Bondi and Gold were able to deduce a number of important properties of the steady-state Universe. As we shall see.., they were able to deduce that such a Universe must continually expand. **1978** PASACHOFF & KUTNER *University Astron.* xxix. 732 If we have indeed discovered radiation from the big bang itself then clearly the steady state theory is discredited.

Hence **steady-stater**, an advocate of a steady-state theory of the universe.

1966 *Time* 11 Mar. 51 As the galaxies move farther away from each other, steady-staters believe, new galaxies are constantly being formed. **1973** 'D. HALLIDAY' *Dolly & Starry Bird* xiii. 188 Black holes..according to theory are nonluminous stars..concealing whole galaxies..to the satisfaction of all the Steady Staters.

steak (steɪk). Forms: 5 **steike, steyke, styke**, 5–6 **steke**, 6 **steake**, 7–8 **stake**, 7– **steak**. [a. ON. *steik* fem. (Sw. *stek*, Da. *steg*), cogn. w. *steikja* to roast on a spit, *stikna* to be roasted.]

1. a. A thick slice or strip of meat cut for roasting by grilling or frying, sometimes used in a pie or pudding; esp. a piece cut from the hind quarters of the animal; when used without qualification = BEEF-STEAK; also with qualifying word indicating the part from which it is cut, as ***rump, sirloin steak***, or specifying how it should be cooked, as ***stewing steak*** (meat from a less tender cut: see STEWING *vbl. sb.* b).

14.. *King & Hermit* 373 in Hazlitt *E.P.P.* (1864) I. 27 Fyll this eft, and late us lyke, And between rost us a styke. *c* **1420** *Two Cookery Bks.* 3 To make stekys of venysoun or Beef. **1426** LYDG. *De Guil. Pilgr.* 12802 Now to ffrye, now steykës make, And many other soteltes. *c* **1450** *Douce MS.* 55 xvij, Take feyre moton of the buttes & kutt it in maner of stekes. **1530** PALSGR. 275/2 Steke of flesshe, *charbonnee*. **1646** QUARLES *Sheph. Oracles* IV. 39 You can convert a dish Of Steakes to Roots. **1735** DYCHE & PARDON *Dict., Stake*,.. a small Slice of Meat to be broiled before or on the Fire, when a Person cannot or will not stay till a regular Joint is boiled or roasted, &c. **1747** MRS. GLASSE *Cookery* i. 6 To Broil Steaks... Take fine Rump Steaks about Half an Inch thick [etc.]. *Ibid.*, As to Mutton and Pork Steaks, you must keep them turning quick on the Gridiron. *Ibid.* ii. 16 Cut a Neck of Veal into Steaks. **1842** TENNYSON *Will Waterproof* 148 How out of place she makes The violet of a legend blow Among the chops and steaks! **1848** DICKENS *Dombey* iv, Uncle Sol and his nephew were speedily engaged on a fried sole with a prospect of steak to follow.

b. A thick slice (of cod, salmon, halibut, or hake).

1883 *Standard* 30 Nov. 2/2 'G. S. C.'s' Fishmonger charged 10*d.* per lb. for his best cod steaks.

c. *transf.* and *fig.* Now *rare* or *Obs.*

1607 MIDDLETON *Five Gallants* IV. v. F4b, *Bun.* You must not thinke to tread ath ground when you come there. —*Go.* No, how then? *Bun.* Why vpon paths made of fig-frailes, & white blankets cut out in steakes. **1607** —— *Phœnix* I. v. C3b, Is that your Lackey yonder, in the steakes of veluet. *a* **1616** BEAUM. & FL. *Maid in Mill* IV. ii, *Bust.* Safe? do you hear? take notice what plight you find me in, if there want but a collop or steak o' me, look to't. **1641** MILTON *Reform.* II. 44 Their Malvezzi that can cut Tacitus into slivers and steaks. **1694** MOTTEUX *Rabelais* v. xvi. 73 With this he lugg'd out his slashing Cutlas..to cut the cousening Varlets into Stakes.

2. Similative uses.

†**a.** *sea steak.* (See quot.) *Obs.* [Cf. STICK *sb.*]

1798 *Rep. Herring Fisheries* in *Rep. Committees Ho. Comm.* (1803) X. 215/2 Sea Steaks, which mean Herrings in their first state of being barrelled.

b. ***two-eyed steak*** slang: see quot. 1894.

1893 FARMER *Slang*, s.v. *Glasgow Magistrate*, Two-eye'd steak. **1894** *Daily News* 4 Sept. 5/2 Mr. George Augustus Sala writes to say 'a two-eyed steak' is a red herring or bloater cut open—otherwise a 'kippered' herring.

c. ***Hamburg steak***: a dish composed of flat balls of meat like fillets, made of chopped lean beef, mixed with beaten eggs, chopped onions and seasoning, and fried. Cf. HAMBURGER 2.

1884 *Boston Jrnl.* 16 Feb. 2/2 We take a chicken and boil it. When it is cold we cut it up as they do meat to make Hamburg steak. **1892** *Encycl. Cookery* I. 117/2 Fried Hamburg Steak served with Russian Sauce. **1951** *Good Housek. Home Encycl.* 502/2 *Hamburg steak*, a fried or baked flat cake of freshly minced seasoned steak, very popular in the United States.

3. *attrib.* and *Comb.*, as ***steak dinner, -meat, pie, piece, pudding, sandwich***; in names of implements for beating raw steak to make it tender, as ***steak-beater*** (Simmonds *Dict. Trade* 1858), ***-crusher, hammer, -masher*** (Knight *Dict. Mech.* 1875); in names of restaurants or other eating-places serving mainly beefsteak, as ***steak bar, house, restaurant***; **steak and kidney**, used *attrib.* to designate a pie or pudding containing a mixture of beefsteak and kidney; also *ellipt.*; **steak au poivre** (‖o pwavr), beefsteak flavoured with coarsely crushed peppercorns before cooking; = *pepper steak* s.v. PEPPER *sb.* 7; **steak broiler** (see quot.); **steak Diane** (‖dian), a dish consisting of thin slices of beefsteak fried with seasonings, esp. Worcestershire sauce; **steak fish**, cod of a size suitable for cutting into steaks; **steak knife**, (*a*) a butcher's knife; (*b*) a serrated table knife; **steak tartare**, a dish consisting of raw minced beefsteak mixed with egg and seasonings; **steak-tongs** (see quot. 1858).

1910 *Steak and kidney [see SAY *v.*[1] B. 1 a]. **1930** H. BURKE *Cookery Bk.* 103 Steak and kidney pudding... Put in the beef and kidney (see Steak and Kidney Pie recipe). **1960** I. JEFFERIES *Dignity & Purity* iv. 59 Cobb..spirited us off to a nearby pub for steak and kidney pud. **1965** L. SANDS *Something to Hide* ix. 154 The sight of the steak-and-kidney glistening succulently between them. **1977** C. MCCULLOUGH *Thorn Birds* ix. 206 The seven of them sat in the small dining room eating steak-and-kidney pie. **1953** BEARD & WATT *Paris Cuisine* 132 *Steak au poivre. **1976** 'F. CLIFFORD' *Drummer in Dark* iv. 17 Avocado vinaigrette and steak au poivre... Choosing didn't take long. **1971** *Guardian* 10 June 7/8 Fire damaged a kitchen, restaurant, and *steak bar in..Hull yesterday. **1858** SIMMONDS *Dict. Trade*, **Steak-broiler*, a gridiron which catches the gravy from the steak. **1957** *Gourmet Cookbk.* II. 270 (*heading*) *Steak Diane. **1974** W. GARNER *Big Enough Wreath* viii. 103 The waiter [was] serving his steak Diane. *a* **1964** C. WHITNEY in D. Macarthur *Reminiscences* VIII. 271 We were seated and served a *steak dinner. **1979** *Tuscon* (Arizona) *Citizen* 20 Sept. 8c/1 About 2,000 steak dinners will be served. **1894** *Outing* (U.S.) XXIII. 404/1 *Steak fish are cod measuring twenty-two inches or more in length. **1934** WEBSTER, *Steak hammer. **1974** *Habitat Catal.* 81/3 Wooden steak hammer with a square toothed head knocks coarser cuts of steak into succulent shape. **1762** J. BOSWELL *Jrnl.* 15 Dec. (1950) 86, I went into the City to Dolly's *Steak-house in Paternoster Row and swallowed my dinner by myself. **1954** I. LEVIN *Kiss before Dying* III. v. 178 They went to a steak house on Fifty-second street. **1977** B. ROUECHÉ *Fago* (1978) II. iii. 101 There was a steakhouse restaurant across the street. **1895** *Montgomery Ward Catal.* Spring & Summer 447/2 *Steak knives,..12 inch blade... No butcher shop would be without them after a trial. **1951** *Catal. of Exhibits, South Bank Exhib., Festival of Britain* 59/2 Steak knife, hollow-ground blade. **1959** L. SMITH *One Hour* xxv. 321 Even now, I see those steak knives cutting through the meat. **1979** N. HYND *False Flags* v. 43 The barman gave Mason a steak knife. The sandwich arrived. **1901** *Westm. Gaz.* 27 Dec. 2/3 We bought..a pound of beef (it must be *steak meat) for our black eyes. **1723** J. NOTT *Cook's & Confectioner's Dict.* sig. Kk2, To make a *Stake-Pye. **1791** J. WOODFORDE *Diary* 8 Aug. (1927) III. 291 We did our best and gave them some Beans and Bacon..Stake Pye and a Codlin Pudding. **1930** H. BURKE *Cookery Bk.* 103 Steak Pie. Follow the Steak and Kidney Pie recipe, omitting the kidney. **1981** 'M. YORKE' *Hand of Death* xiv. 121 He went home to the steak pie Nancy had prepared. **1844** H. STEPHENS *Bk. Farm* II. 171 The plan of cutting the line between..the rump and aitch-bone in the hind quarter, lays open the *steak-pieces to better advantage. **1747** MRS. GLASSE *Cookery* vi. 69 A *Stake-Pudding. **1970** J. UPDIKE *Bech: a Book* 199 We..made all those *steak restaurants in the East Fifties light up like seraglios under bombardment. **1941** B. SCHULBERG *What makes Sammy Run?* v. 85 Sammy had his mouth full of..*steak sandwich? **1979** J. VAN DE WETERING *Maine Massacre* ix. 123 Would you like a sandwich? A steak sandwich? **1911** A. FILIPPINI *Internat. Cook Bk.* 676 (*heading*) *Steaks, Tartare. **1958** *Observer* 26 Jan. 5/6 A steak tartare. **1969** 'M. UNDERWOOD' *Shadow Game* ii. 22 Peacock was having Steak Tartare...rather appropriate food for one who dwelt in a ruthless world of sophisticated gangsterism. Raw meat! **1845** E. ACTON *Mod. Cookery* (ed. 3) vii. 161 If..it should be necessary, for want of *steak-tongs, to use a fork, it should be passed through the outer skin..of the steak. **1858** SIMMONDS *Dict. Trade*, *Steak-tongs*, small tongs for turning chops or steaks when broiling on a gridiron.

steak(e: see STEEK *v.*[1] and *v.*[2]

steak raid. *Sc. Hist.* Also 8 **stike**. [repr. Gael. *staoig rathaid* (*staoig* collop, a. Eng. *steak* or ON. *steik*; *rathaid* genit. of *rathad* road.] (See quots.)

1775 L. SHAW *Hist. Moray* 219 MacIntosh, then [an. 1454] residing in the Island of Moy, sent to ask a Stike Raide, or Stike Criech, *i.e.* a Road Collup; a custom among the Highlanders, that when a party drove any spoil of cattle through a Gentleman's land, they should give him part of the spoil. **1814** SCOTT *Wav.* xxiii, I take what the people of old used to call 'a steakraid,' that is, a 'collop of the foray,' or, in plainer words, a portion of the robber's booty, paid by him to the Laird, or Chief, through whose grounds he drove his prey.

steal (stiːl), *sb.*[1] *Obs.* exc. *dial.* Forms: 1 **stela, steola, stæla**, 4–7, 9 **stele**, 5–6 **stile**, 5, 7 **steele**, 6 **style, steyle**, 6–7 **steile**, 6–9 **steale**, 7, 9 **steel**, 9 **steil, steyl**, 8–9 **stell, steal**. [OE. *stela* wk. masc., f. OTeut. **stel-* (cf. Gr. στελεός, -όν handle), ablaut-var. of **stal-* whence STALE *sb.*[2] (The OHG. *stil*, mod.G. *stiel*, handle, is prob. unconnected).

For the difficulty of distinguishing the forms of the synonymous *steal* and *stale*, see STALE *sb.*[2]]

1. The stalk or stem of a plant, leaf, flower or fruit.

c **700** *Epinal Gloss.* 215 *Caulem*, stela. *c* **1000** *Sax. Leechd.* I. 154 Mædere..bið ȝefrætewud mid feower readum stælum [*v.r.* stelum, L. *cauliculis*]. **13..** *Liber regum Angliæ* (Auchinleck MS.) in Scott *Minstrelsy* (1810) II. 261 Dansimond ȝede and gadred frut, For sothe were plommes white, The steles he puld out everichon, Puisoun he dede therin anon, And sett the steles al ogen, That the gile schuld nought be sen. **13..** *Propr. Sanct.* (Vernon MS.) in *Archiv Stud. neu. Spr.* LXXXI. 83 þis whete-corn..þat furst stod on a luytel stele. *c* **1440** *Pallad. on Husb.* XII. 77 But forto hede hem gret, trede doun the stele [*Sicapitatum facere volueris, ubi cœperit caulis prodire, proculca*]. **1562** TURNER *Herbal* II. 23b, The floures..stand..vpon theyr stiles or foot stalkes. **1577** GOOGE *Heresbach's Husb.* I. 28 Rye... The stalke or steale thereof, is smaller then the Wheate stalke. **1601** HOLLAND *Pliny* XIII. vi. I. 389 The steles of the leaves grow contrarie one against the other. **1611** COTGR., *Queue*, ..the staulke, or steale, of fruits. **1639** HORN & ROB. *Gate Lang. Unl.* xi. §119 A cherry hangeth by somewhat a long stalk, a bullace on somewhat a short stele. **1818** WILBRAHAM *Chesh. Gloss., Stele*, or *Steal*, the stalk of a flower. **1865** BANKS *Prov. Words Wakefield* 68 A 'musheram steil'.

†**b.** ? The trunk of a tree. *Obs.*

c **1440** *Pallad. on Husb.* III. 770 Ther is also graffyng in trees seer, As..asshes, quynce; & punyk, cleef his stile [*et punico, sed fisso ligno*].

†**2.** ? A supporting post or pillar. *Obs.*

c **1000** ÆLFRIC *De Novo Testamento* 20 (Gr.) Se cinestol stynt on þisum þrim stelum: *laboratores, bellatores, oratores.* **1547–8** in Swayne *Churchw. Acc. Sarum* (1896) 275 For breakynge downe of the steles of the ymages in the churche, xxij d.

†**3.** An upright side of a ladder; in later use, a rung or step of a ladder: = STALE *sb.*[2] 1. *Obs.*

13.. *E.E. Allit. P.* C. 513 Wymmen vnwytte þat wale ne couþe þat on hande fro þat oþer, for alle þis hyȝe worlde, Bitwene þe stele & þe stayre disserne noȝt cunen. **1395** HYLTON *Scala Perf.* (W. de W. 1494) II. xvii, A man that woll clymbe vpon a ladder hye & setteth his fote vpon the lowest stele. *c* **1400** *Rule St. Benet* (Prose) vii. 11 þe stiȝe hauis tua tres... þe stelis bytuixe bitakins oure gude dedis. *c* **1440** *York Myst.* xxxiv. 91 Sties..With stalworthe steeles.., Bothe some schorte and some lang. **1621** J. MAYER *Engl. Catech.* 364 Euery steale of the ladder [is] a part of the ladder.

4. The handle of a tool or utensil (e.g. a hammer, axe, pot, spoon).

13.. *Gaw. & Gr. Knt.* 2230 þe gome..Sette þe stele to the stone, & stalked bysyde. **1377** LANGL. *P. Pl.* B. XIX. 274 Lerned men a ladel bugge with a longe stele. *c* **1386** CHAUCER *Miller's T.* 599 And caughte the kultour by the colde stele. *c* **1440** *Promp. Parv.* 473/2 Stele, or stert of a vesselle, *ansa.* **1498** in *Somerset Med. Wills* (1901) 365 A posnet with a stele and broken feete. *c* **1520** in Gutch *Collect. Cur.* (1781) II. 297 Item oone Sponne with a flat Steyle. **1570–80** *Fabric Rolls York Minster* (Surtees Soc.) 117 For mendinge the mason's towles in ther worke and for style to them, 4s. 3d. **1596** SPENSER *F.Q.* v. xii. 14 An huge Polaxe ..Whose steale was yron studded, but not long. **1625** in Rymer *Fœdera* XVIII. 239/2 Item a Lookeing Glass sett in Goulde,..the Steele of Aggott. **1631** GOUGE *God's Arrows* I. §25. 35 The Censer was..made..of gold..with a steele or handle to hold it by. **1788** VALLANCEY *Voc. Bargie* in *Trans. R. Irish Acad.* II. 33 *Stell*, the handle of a thing. **1802** SIBBALD *Chron. Sc. P.* IV. Gloss. s.v., *Steils of a barrow* or *plough*, the handles. **1894** *Northumb. Gloss.* s.v., The tiller or handle of a rudder was formerly called a *steel* or 'start'.

Proverb. phr. **1402** HOCCLEVE *Lett. Cupid* 50 And whann this man the pot hath be the stele, and fully is in his possessyon. *c* **1412** —— *De Reg. Princ.* 5247 Thei hadden bi þe stele Prosperite.

b. *esp.* A long straight handle, e.g. of a rake or broom.

c **1386**, *c* **1440** Rake stele [see RAKE *sb.*[1] 5]. **1523–34** FITZHERB. *Husb.* §24 If the rake be made of grene woode, the heed wyll not abyde vppon the stele. **1597** BP. HALL *Sat.* III. vii. 66 Like a broad shak-forke with a slender steale. **1765** *Lond. Chron.* 6 July 18 He then went into the pond with a rake-steale in his hand. **1796** [R. WALKER] *Plebeian Politics* (1801) 5 Hee took th' mop stele, an b'eet it eawt again. **1839** SIR G. C. LEWIS *Gloss. Heref.*, *Stele*, the wooden handle of a rake or pitchfork. **1879** JEFFERIES *Wild Life in S. Co.* 70 The peculiar broad-headed nail which fastens the mop to the stout ashen 'steale' or handle.

†**c.** The shank of a candlestick; the long neck of a matrass or retort. *Obs.*

1585 HIGINS *Junius' Nomencl.* 245/2 *Candelabri scapus*,.. the shanke of steile of the candlesticke. **1594** PLAT *Jewell-ho.* III. 44 A bolt glasse, hauing a long steale.

d. The stem of a tobacco-pipe.

1672 JOSSELYN *New-Eng. Rarities* 72 The Roots are..of the bigness of the steel of a Tobacco Pipe. **1866** [R. HALLAM] *Wadsley Jack* xi. (E.D.D.), [He] shuv'd a poipe steil i't foire.

†**5.** The shaft or stem of an arrow or spear; = STALE *sb.*[2] 4. *Obs.*

1530 PALSGR. 275/2 Steale of a shaft, *fust.* *Ibid.* 548/2, I fether a shafte, I put fethers upon a steale, *jempenne.* **1545** ASCHAM *Toxoph.* II. (Arb.) 123 A shaft hath three principall partes, the stele, the fethers, and the head. **1609** HOLLAND *Amm. Marcell.* XXIII. iii. 223 An arrow made of a cane, betwixt the head and the steile. **1611** COTGR., *Fust*..the steale of a dart, or iauelin.

steal (stiːl), *sb.*[2] [f. STEAL *v.*]

1. a. The act, or an act, of stealing; a theft; the thing stolen or purloined. Chiefly *U.S. colloq.*

[In the first quot. the word is prob. of different formation; if not an error for or variant of STALE *sb.*[1], it may represent an OE. **stæl* f. OTeut. **stæl-* ablaut-var. of **stel-* STEAL *v.*]

c **1200** *Trin. Coll. Hom.* 79 Gif þe unfele man..teð him to unwrenches, to stele, oðer refloc, oðer swikedom [etc.]. **1825** JAMIESON, *Steal*. 1. A theft. *Aberd.* 2. The thing stolen. *Ibid.* **1890** *Sat. Rev.* 26 July 110/1 This is an audacious steal from 'In a Gondola'! **1891** KIPLING *Light that failed* iii. 'Yes, it is rather a cold-blooded steal,' said Torpenhow critically.

b. *N. Amer.* A piece of dishonesty or fraud on a large scale; a corrupt or fraudulent transaction in politics.

1872 *Daily Gaz.* (Little Rock, Arkansas) 1 Apr., Of all the swindles and steals that have ever been proposed or carried out in our State, this is the largest and boldest. **1884** *Reading* (Pa.) *Morn. Herald* 15 Apr., When the makers of the constitution of the United States put in that apparently harmless clause giving Congress the power to legislate for the 'general welfare', they little thought what jobs and steals it would ultimately be made the excuse for. **1888** BRYCE *Amer. Commw.* III. lxiv. II. 471 Rings are the cause of both peculation and jobbery, although St. Louis has had no 'big steal'. **1891** *Weekly Empire* (Toronto) 3 Sept. 4/2 The late gigantic steal.

c. *colloq.* (orig. *U.S.*). A bargain.

1942 Berrey & Van den Bark *Amer. Thes. Slang.* §546/2 Advantageous purchase; a bargain, .. *steal.* **1951** *N.Y. Herald-Tribune* 14 Dec. 6 The asking price is $45,000, but I'm pretty sure you could get it for 43,000, and at that price it's a *steal.* **1960** *News Chron.* 2 May 3/1 At £30,000 it was a steal. I think it's worth £75,000. **1969** C. Drummond *Odds on Death* vi. 142 A car like this .. is a steal at three thousand quid. **1979** *Fortune* 15 Jan. 67 A sentimental gesture, but it was a steal—a quarter of a million acres for less than $10 an acre!

†**2.** An act of going furtively. *Obs. rare*$^{-1}$.

1590 *Tarlton's News Purgatory* 29 The vickar .. forbad it openly: yet it was not so deepely inveighed against, but that diuerse Sundayes they would make a steale thither to breakefast.

3. a. *Golf* (see quot. 1897.)

1842 G. F. Carnegie *Golfiana* in *Golfiana Misc.* (1887) 81 A most disgusting steal. **1867** *Poems on Golf* 53 Though such long steals are now but rarely done. **1897** *Encycl. Sport* I. 473/2 (Golf) *Steal*, a long putt holed unexpectedly.

b. *Base-ball.* A stolen run from one base to another.

1867 *Chicago Times* 26 July 5/2 Norton made first base, but, on essaying Berthrong's steal, he was similarly ousted. **1891** N. Crane *Base-ball* iv. 36 The runner .. must, therefore, look out for an exceptional chance to make the steal. **1908** [see run down *sb.* 1]. **1949** *Oregonian* (Portland) 10 Aug. III. 4/1 Davis overthrew second in an attempt to nail Hale on a steal. **1976** *National Observer* (U.S.) 12 June 14/3 Don't worry. I give the steal sign, and if you're thrown out, I'll take the blame. **1976** *Washington Post* 19 Apr. D4/4 Washington's glamour boy also struck out when he labeled the Yanks' Roy White 'an excellent steal man, 15 for 16 last year' only to correct himself a minute later by giving White 16 steals in 31 attempts last season.

c. *Basketball.* An act of obtaining possession of the ball from an opponent.

1974 *State* (Columbia S. Carolina) 15 Feb. 3-B/4 Then, on a steal, Iona tied it up 62-62.

steal (sti:l), *v.*[1] Forms: 1 (ȝe)stelan, 3 stelin, steolin, 3-4 stelen, 3-7 stele, 4 stel(le, steln, 4-5 steele, 4-6 *Sc.* steile, steyle, 5 stelyn, steyl(l, 5-6 *Sc.* steill, 6 staile, steel, stell, 6-7 steale, *Sc.* steil, 6- steal. *Pa. t.* 1-2 stæl, (*pl.* stǽlon), 3 *pl.* stalen, 3-4 stel, 3-6 stal, 4 *pl.* stelyn, stolen, 4-5 staal(e, 4-6 stall, 4-7 stale, 4-8 *Sc.* staw, 5 staall(e, stele, *Sc.* sta, stawe, 6 stalle, *Sc.* staill, 4- stole. Also (weak forms) 7, 9 *dial.* stealed, 6 stolled, 9 *dial.* stoalt. *Pa. pple.* 1 (ȝe)stolen, 2 istolen, 3-4 i-stole, 4 stollyn, stoolen, ystole, *Sc.* stowine, 4-5 stoll(e, stolyn, 4- 7 stollen, stolne, 4-8 stole, stoln, 5 ystolne, *Sc.* stone, stowyn, 5-7 stollin, stollyne, -yng, *Sc.* stoune, stowin, stowne, 6 *north.* stowen, 8 *Sc.* sta'en, 8-9 *Sc.* and *dial* stown, 3- stolen. Also (weak forms) 6 stolled, stollyd, 6, 9 *dial.* stealed. [A Com. Teut. strong verb: OE. *stelan*, pa. t. *stæl*, pl. *stǽlon*, pa. pple. *stolen*, corresponds to OFris. *stela*, OS. *stelan*, Du. *stelen*, OHG. *stelan* (MHG. *steln*, mod.G. *stehlen*), ON. *stela* (Sw. *stjäla*, Da. *stjæle*), Goth. *stilan*, f. OTeut. **stel-* (:*stal-*: *stǣl-*: *stul-*). Outside Teut. no certain cognates are known.

In the 14th c. the regular form *stal* of the pa. t. began to be superseded by *stole* (after the pa. pple.), which has been the accepted form since the 17th c. The Bible of 1611 has in two places *stale* (but mod. reprints *stole*), and in four places *stole*. The weak forms *stealed*, and the mixed forms *stolled*, *stoald*, appear in the 16th c. and in modern dialects, but have never been general.]

I. To take dishonestly or secretly.

1. a. *trans.* To take away dishonestly (portable property, cattle, etc., belonging to another); *esp.* to do this secretly or unobserved by the owner or the person in charge. Const. *from* (earlier *dative*).

The notion of secrecy (cf. stealth) seems to be part of the original meaning of the vb., which, however, is also employed in a generic sense applicable to open as well as secret acts of theft. In mod. use it takes the place of reave *v.*[1] 5, rob *v.* 5, and of combinations like 'to steal and reave'.

c **1000** Ælfric *Gen.* xliv. 8 Wenst þu, þæt we þines hlafordes gold oððe his seolfor stælon? *a* **1250** *Prov. Ælfred* B. 665 He wole stelin þin haite & keren, & listeliche onsuerren. *c* **1290** *Beket* 816 in *S. Eng. Leg.* 130 'Bel ami, þou hast', quad þe king: 'i-stole me muchel guod'. *a* **1300** *Cursor M.* 4936 Quils i sald þam o mi sede þai stall mi cupe a-wai to lede. **1338** R. Brunne *Chron.* (1725) 77 þe Normans did it alle in þe guyse of theft, þe godes þerof stal. *c* **1375** *Sc. Leg. Saints* xxiii. (*Seven Sleepers*) 311 Be lauty þu tellis ws now .. quhare þat þu has stowine þis tresoure ore reft. **1387** Trevisa *Higden* (Rolls) VII. 65 Oon of þis secounde Richard his knyȝtes staal a spone, and leyde it to wedde among oþer þinges. **1400** in *Roy. & Hist. Lett. Hen. IV* (Rolls) 38 Thu knowlechest .. that thy men hath stolle our horsen out of our parke. *c* **1450** *Mirk's Festial* 14 When þys Jew was comen home and fonde hys good ystolne, he was wod wroth wyt Saynt Nycholas. *a* **1500** *Bernard. de cura rei fam.* (E.E.T.S.) iii. 3 Now has a boy stone þe brydylle of his blonke hede, agayne he buske shulde. *a* **1500** *Ratis Raving* III. 302 He is a theif rycht as he stald. **1546** J. Heywood *Prov.* I. xi. (1867) 35 As dyd the pure penitent that stale a goose And stack downe a fether. **1595** W. W[arner] *Plautus' Menæcmi* v. (1779) 141 Even now thou deniedst that thou stolest it [the cloak] from me, and now thou bringest it home openly in my sight. **1677** in *12th Rep. Hist. MSS. Comm.* App. v. 37 Some mischievous persons to dishonour my Lord Chancellour crept through a window of his house .. and stole the Mace and the two purses. **1738** Wesley *Wks.* (1872) I. 121 Both my books were stole. **1787** Burns *Banks o' Doon* v, And my fause luver staw the rose, But left the thorn wi' me. **1875** Jowett *Plato* (ed. 2) V. 512 He who steals a little steals with the same wish as he who steals much. **1891** Farrar *Darkn. & Dawn* xlviii Yes; I stole money from Philemon, my beloved master. **1909** J. G. Frazer *Psyche's Task* iii. 23 Whoever steals sticks from the fence will have a swollen head.

†**b.** with *of* used partitively. *Obs.*

a **1300** *Cursor M.* 4904 He þat has yow don socur Stoln haue yee of his tresur. *c* **1400** *Rule St. Benet* 569 Of oþer mens we sal not steyl Ne couet here no wordly wele. **1483** Caxton *Golden Leg.* 112/2 Judas .. bare the purse .. and stale of that whiche was gyuen to cryst.

c. with *away*, †*out*, †*over*.

c **1375** *Sc. Leg. Saints* xl. (*Ninian*) 448 þefis .. in þe circle þane but dout ȝed, for to steile þe catel owte. **1471** Caxton *Recuyell* (Sommer) 440 How Cacus stale away the Oxen & kyen longyng to hercules. **1530** Palsgr. 734/2, I steale awaye a thing by thefte, *je emble.* **1565** Jewel *Reply Harding* (1611) 370 The people of Israel, by his Commande-ment, stale away the Egyptians goods, without breach of the Law. **1576** J. Dee *Gen. & Rare Memor.* 23 *marg.*, Though of Late in the .. Low Country Trublesome disorders, Some Few (by Stealing ouer of vittayles, and other things, from this Common Wealth) haue made them selues priuatly rich. *c* **1610** *Women Saints* 48 They stale away the coffins and reliques. **1711** Steele *Spect.* No. 78 ¶5 A Pickpocket, who during his kissing her stole away all his Money. **1883** Tylor in *Encycl. Brit.* XV. 199/2 The sorcerer has other means of attacking his victim: .. he can steal away his kidney fat.

d. In wider sense: To take or appropriate dishonestly (anything belonging to another, whether material or immaterial).

c **1275** *Sinners Beware!* 153 in *O.E. Misc.* 77 In helle he may adrynke If he steleþ cristes theoþinge. *a* **1300** *Cursor M.* 3516 How yonger o þir tua þe blissing stal his broþer fra. *Ibid.* 3988, I stal him fra his benisun. **1340** *Ayenb.* 26 þo byeþ ypocrites .. steleþ þe dingnetes and þe baylyes. **1477** Norton *Ord. Alch.* ii. in Ashm. (1652) 34 For when I had my warke well wrought, Such stale it away and left me nought. **1643** Baker *Chron., Hen. VI*, 67 Affirming that deceitfully .. he had stolne many Cities and places of importance belonging to the Crown of England. *a* **1704** T. Brown *Dial. Dead, Belgic Hero* Wks. 1711 IV. 67 By which [treaty] he was obliged to vomit up numberless Provinces and Towns, which he had dishonourably stolen from their true Proprietors. **1824** Scott *St. Ronan's* xxvii, You not only steal my ideas, .. but [etc.] .. No man like you for stealing other men's inventions.

e. *esp.* To plagiarize; to pass off (another's work) as one's own; to 'borrow' improperly (words, expressions). Also *absol.*

1544 Betham *Precepts War* Ep. Ded. Avjb, All translatours ought to vse the vsuall termes of our englyshe tounge .. and not to breke .. in to the boundes of the latyn tounge, to steale termes of it. **1590** *Tarlton's News Purgatory* 21 His Motto is stolne out of Tully, *Non solum pro nobis.* **1620** J. Taylor (Water P.) *Praise Hemp-seed* (1623) 36, I haue not stolne a Sillable, or Letter From any man, to make my booke seeme better. **1655** Stanley *Hist. Philos., Xenophon* vii. (1687) 115/2 When he might have stollen the writings of Thucydides .. he chose rather to publish them with honour. **1716** Hearne *Collect.* (O.H.S.) V. 331 He steals unmercifully, and amongst the Rest from Naunton's. **1841** W. Spalding *Italy & It. Isl.* I. 201 It was stolen as genius steals from genius, it was stolen as Phidias stole from Homer.

f. To derive obscurely and dishonourably. *nonce-use.*

1693 Stepney in *Dryden's Juvenal* viii. (1697) 193 Who know not from what Corner of the Earth The obscure Wretch, who got you, stole his Birth.

g. With a person as quasi-obj., in phr. *to steal* (someone) *blind*, to rob or cheat (someone) totally or mercilessly. *colloq.* (orig. *N. Amer.*).

1974 *Times* 28 Feb. 9/5 Mr. Howard Hughes, the eccentric multimillionaire .. replied: 'Because he's a no-good, dishonest son of a bitch, and he stole me blind.' **1975** *Citizen* (Ottawa) 29 Oct. 21/2 Trustee Dalton McGuinty .. said there was no other way to keep students from 'stealing us blind'. **1977** I. Shaw *Beggarman, Thief* I. ii. 21 We'd've been stolen blind without him. **1978** D. Bagley *Flyaway* xxi. 182 These people are Fulani... We're not staying here—they'd steal us blind.

2. *absol.* and *intr.* To commit or practise theft. †Const. *dat.* of person.

c **725** *Corpus Gloss.* C 859 *Conpilat*, stilith. *c* **950** *Lindisf. Gosp.* John x. 10 Ðeaf ne cymes buta þætte ȝestele & eteð & losað. *a* **1000** *Laws of Æthelb.* ix, Ðif friȝman freum stelþ. *c* **1175** *Lamb. Hom.* 31 Seodðan bisechen milce et þan ilke monne þe he haueð er istolen oðer oðer-weis wa idon. *a* **1200** *Vices & Virtues* 67 Ne sleih, ne ne stel, ne reaue. *c* **1375** *Sc. Leg. Saints* xii. (*Matthias*) 246 þo he wes thefe & ay wald steyle. **1390** Gower *Conf.* II. 134 For every thief upon richesse Awaiteth forto robbe and stele. **1483** Caxton *Golden Leg.* 286/3 Ther was a theef that ofte stale. **1568** Grafton *Chron.* II. 45 The Souldiour's stale, extorted, and spoyled vpon both parties. **1610** Shaks. *Temp.* iv. i. 239 We steale by lyne and leuell. *c* **1660** in *10th Rep. Hist. MSS. Comm.* App. iv. 100 About 80 torres .. doe continually robe and stele. **1684** Burnet tr. *More's Utopia* 16 By which every Man might .. so be preserved from the fatal necessity of stealing. **1815** Elphinstone *Acc. Caubul* (1842) II. 53 They plunder weak travellers, and steal from those who are too strong to be plundered. **1871** R. W. Dale *Commandm.* viii. 208 To give short weight or measure, is to steal.

3. a. *trans.* To take away by stratagem or by eluding observation (something that is in the possession or keeping of another).

c **950** *Lindisf. Gosp.* Matt. xxviii. 13 Cuoðað ȝie þætte ðeȝnas his on næht cuomun & .. stelende weron hine. **13..** *Seuyn Sag.* (W.) 2652 He priked to the galewes with his fole, And fond that a thef was i-stole. *c* **1440** *Alphabet of Tales* 281 þe aungell stale þe syluer copp at þai dranke of. *c* **1450** Capgrave *St. Augustine* ix. 14 þei pulled up sail & stale þe schip from hir. **1638** Sir T. Herbert *Trav.* (ed. 2) 14 Lyons, (which usually steale Beefe out of the water when Ships are here). **1749** Lavington *Enthus. Meth. & Papists* II. (1754) Pref. p. xxi, You have climbed up and stole the Sacred Fire from Heaven. **1830** Tennyson *Ode to Mem.* 1 Thou who stealest fire From the fountains of the past.

b. with *away*; rarely with other advs., as †*down*, †*over*.

c **1375** *Sc. Leg. Saints* ii. (*Paul*) 401 Men .. stall a-way be mycht þe twa bodis of mekill mycht of petir and paule, fra quhare þai lay. **1470-85** Malory *Arthur* IV. xiv. 137 She alyghte of her hors & thoughte for to stele awey Excalibur his swerd. **1535** W. Stewart *Cron. Scot.* (Rolls) II. 392 Quietlie awa the heid tha stall. *a* **1586** Sidney *Astroph. & Stella* xiv, Vpon whose breast a fiercer Gripe doth tire Then did on him who first stale down the fire. **1587** Higgins *Mirr. Mag., Nero* xii, (Letter) And bad them say, that his disciples stale his corps away. **1602** Chettle *Hoffmann* I. (1631) B 2 b, This is Hannce Hoffmans sonne, that stole downe his fathers Anotamy from the gallowes. **1629** Ford *Lover's Mel.* II. ii. E 4, Shall I fetch a Barbour to steale away his rough beard, whiles he sleepes? **1816** J. Wilson *City of Plague* II. iv. 160 Many look With tears of sorrow on a mortal creature Whom death may steal away.

c. Of an impersonal agent.

1844 A. B. Welby *Poems* (1867) 60 The wind! that for no creature careth, Yet stealeth sweets from every thing. **1878** Huxley *Physiogr.* 72 The heat of the sun which quietly steals vapour from every exposed piece of water.

d. To carry off (young animals) from the dam.

13.. *K. Alis.* 1890 The tiger, that fynt y-stole Hire weolp from hire hole. *c* **1386** Chaucer *Knt.'s T.* 1769 Ther nas no Tygre .. Whan þat hir whelpe is stole whan it is lite So crueel on the hunte as is Arcite. **1398** Trevisa *Barth. De P.R.* XVIII. cxiii. (1495) 854 The female beer is moost cruell beest whanne her whelpys ben stollen. *c* **1480** Henryson *Mor. Fab., Fox & Wolf* 738 Fra the Gait he stall ane lytil Kid.

e. To carry off, abduct, kidnap (a person) secretly. Now *rare.*

c **1386** Chaucer *Doctor's T.* 184 My seruant .. Which fro myn hous was stole vp-on a nyght. *c* **1400** *Destr. Troy* 13197 þat onone in the night, þat noble he stale Fro the souerain hir Syre. *c* **1475** Henryson *Poems, Bludy Serk* 19 Stollin he hes the lady ȝing. **1513** Douglas *Æneis* I. x. 45 Him sall I sownd slepand staile away. **1560** Phaer *Æneid* x. (1562) F f iij, Was it by my conduct, thaduoutrer stale the Sparta quene? **1592** *Soliman & Pers.* IV. ii. 72 O wicked Turque, for to steale her hence. *a* **1700** Evelyn *Diary* 26 Dec. 1690, Executed .. for being an accomplice with Campbell .. in stealing a young heiress. **1710** W. King *Heathen Gods & Heroes* xv. (1722) 63 She [Proserpine] was stole away by Aidoneus. **1769** Blackstone *Comm.* IV. xv. 208 Their forcible abduction and marriage; which is vulgarly called stealing an heiress. **1788** Mrs. Inchbald *Child Nat.* IV. ii. 51 Amanthis is lost, gone, stole from me! **1815** Scott *Guy M.* xi, The young Laird was stown away by a randy gipsy woman. **1837** Carlyle *Fr. Rev.* II. III. v, Intent on stealing Majesty to Metz.

†**f.** To capture (a fortress, a military position) by surprise. *Obs.*

13.. *E.E. Allit. P.* B. 1778 þay .. Lyfte laddres ful longe & vpon lofte wonen, Stelen stylly þe toun er any steuen rysed. *c* **1450** *Brut* II. 424 This Erle of Gascoigne .. come be nyght, and stale the toune of Pounteyse of the Frensshe men, and drof hem oute. **1623** Bingham *Xenophon* 73 It is better therefore to endeuour priuily, to steale, if we can, and to lay hold of .. a peece of the void mountaine, than [etc.].

g. *dial.* To catch (wild-fowl). ? *Obs.*

1698 M. Martin *Voy. St. Kilda* (1749) 57 Some thousands being catched, or, as they term it, Stolen every March.

4. In various applications with immaterial obj.

a. To cause the loss of, take away (something valued, e.g. happiness, a person's life, etc.).

c **1374** Chaucer *Troylus* III. 1451 O crueel day accusour of þe Ioye That nyght and loue han stole and faste y-wryen. **1570** *Sat. Poems Reform.* xxi. 18 Thay Renigats .. Hes stollin our Regentis lyfe. **1631** Milton *Sonn.* ii. 2 How soon hath Time the suttle theef of youth Stoln on his wing my three and twentith yeer! *a* **1721** Prior *Pastoral to Dr. Turner* 4 Why dost thou .. steal from life the needful hours of rest? **1777** Sir W. Jones *Palace Fortune* 24 A sudden cloud his senses stole. **1793** Burns *Bonie Jean* iii, Her heart was tint, her peace was stown. **1806** G. Pinckard *Notes W. Indies* III. 269 Which .. frequently causes us to steal another hour from the already too shortened day.

b. To take without permission (esp. a kiss). †Also (cf. sense 6) to give (a kiss) *to* a person.

1390 Gower *Conf.* II. 348 If thou hast stolen eny cuss Or other thing which therto longeth. *a* **1400-50** *Wars Alex.* 5385 Scho .. stelis to him cussis. **1584** Lodge *Forb. & Tris.* (Shaks. Soc.) 99 Her pleasant kisse where she might steale a touch. **1592** Shaks. *Ven. & Ad.* 726 Lest she should steale a kisse and die forsworne. **1598** Bastard *Chrestol.* II. ii. 28 And yet a second course he vndertakes. And steeling leaue for gayne which is so deare, A third and fourth aduenture yet he makes. *a* **1796** Burns *Delia* 15 O let me steal one liquid kiss! **1838** *Times* 14 Apr. 7/3 Mr. John Cunningham .. appeared to answer the charge of stealing a sly kiss from the lips of .. the pretty wife of a young tonsor.

†**c.** To conceal improperly. (Cf. 5.) *Obs.*

1303 R. Brunne *Handl. Synne* 3691 No pryde ne may be stole, No yn shryfte be forhole.

†**d.** To gain by secret or unobtrusive means. *Obs.*

1426 Audelay *Poems* 53 Sum men ther ben that stelon heven, With penans, prayers, and poverte. **1605** Chapman *Al Fooles* II. i. 371, 378 That hath stolne By his meere industry, and that by spurts Such qualities as no wit else can match With plodding at perfection every houre... I meane, besides his dycing and his wenching, He has stolne languages, th'Italian, Spanish, [etc.].

e. To take (time) by contrivance *from* its ordinary employment, sleep, etc. to devote to some other purpose.

1526 *Pilgr. Perf.* (W. de W. 1531) 59 Be euer diligent.. whan thou hast done all thy dutyes..to stele tyme wherin thou mayst giue thy selfe all hoolly to prayer. **1712** SWIFT *Jrnl. to Stella* 18 Nov., This makes me sometimes steal a week from the exactness I used to write to MD. **1758** S. HAYWARD *Serm.* xvii. 515 They must frequently steal an hour to converse with him [Christ] whom they love. **1849** MACAULAY *Hist. Eng.* iii. I. 409 Both Chief Justice Hale and Lord Keeper Guildford stole some hours from the business of their courts to write on hydrostatics.

f. To gain possession of, or to entice away from another (a person's heart, affections, etc.).

1526 *Pilgr. Perf.* (W. de W. 1531) 34 b, Wherby he steleth many a soule fro god. **1587** D. FENNER *Song of Songs* iv. 9 Sister, my spouse, my hart thou hast stole with one eye Myne hart thou hast stole, with one chayne which on thy necke doeth lye. **1590** SPENSER *F.Q.* III. i. 37 So did she steale his heedlesse hart away. **1596** SIR J. DAVIES *Orchestra* lxxxvi, And they who first Religion did ordaine, By dauncing first the peoples harts did steale. **1605** *1st Pt. Jeronimo* II. v. 40 in *Kyd's Wks.* (1901) 322 Intending, as it seemed, by that sly shift, To steale away her troth. **1667** FLAVEL *Saint Indeed* (1754) 146 Take heed..lest thy shop steal away thy heart from thy closet. *a* **1678** CHALKHILL *Thealma & Clearchus* 108 Or hath some worthier Love Stole your Affections? **1720** OZELL tr. *Vertot's Rom. Rep.* II. VIII. 28 His expression [was]..so moving, that he stole away the Assent of all that heard him. **1720** J. WELWOOD *Pref. to Rowe's Lucan* p. xxxix, The Muses had stoln away his heart from his infancy. *a* **1797** BURNS *Song, 'Hark the Mavis'* v, Thou hast stown my very heart. **1835** JAMES *Gipsy* i, How many would steal from one the affection of one's mistress or wife!

†**g.** To adopt or 'borrow' (what belongs to another art). *Obs.*

1581 SIDNEY *Apol. Poetrie* (Arb.) 22 Both he [*sc.* Herodotus] and all the rest that followed him, either stole or vsurped of Poetrie, their passionate describing of passions [etc.].

h. *to steal* (*the*) *picture, scene, show*: (*colloq.* (orig. *U.S.*)) in theatrical contexts, to outshine unexpectedly the rest of the cast; also *transf.*, to become or make oneself the centre of attention; *to steal* (one's) *thunder*: see THUNDER *sb.* 3 c.

1928 *Amer. Speech* III. 368 If a 'part' actor leaves a better impression on the audience and critics than the 'star',..the 'part' actor or actress 'steals' the picture. **1934** *Everyman* 24 Aug. 201/2 (*caption*) It seems we've stolen the show, Aussie. **1937** H. G. WELLS *Brynhild* ix. 143 He appeared in bright new flannels,..the best-looking author in the bunch. He stole the picture. **1941** F. SCOTT FITZGERALD *Last Tycoon* iii. 37 'Somebody been catching flies on him?' she asked—a phrase for stealing scenes. **1942** E. WAUGH *Put out More Flags* iii. 189 They came to the little party.., and stole the scene. **1963** AUDEN *Dyer's Hand* 185 Short of cutting him [*sc.* Falstaff] out of the play altogether, no producer can prevent him from stealing the show. **1979** *Tucson Mag.* Jan. 55/3 Kate Gardiner could well steal the show in the delectable role of Dorine.

5. a. To effect or accomplish clandestinely or unperceived; to get opportunity for (an action) by contrivance.

1625 BACON *Ess., Of Gt. Place* (Arb.) 289 Alwayes, when thou changest thine Opinion, or Course, professe it plainly and declare it..; And doe not thinke to steale it. **1681** H. MORE *Expos. Dan.* 53 He might spring up with them and amongst them, but in such an occult manner, and so unawares, as if he had stoln his growth behind them. **1682** N. O. *Boileau's Lutrin* IV. 31 What a mad coil you keep here, That people cannot steal a Nap, or sleep here? **1758** MRS. LENNOX *Henrietta* v. ix. (1761) II. 267, I will make you no apology for stealing a visit to her. **1826** HOOD *Recipe for Civiliz.* 86 When their force Can't take a town by open courage They steal an entry with its forage. **1857** J. HAMILTON *Less. Gt. Biog.* 264 He did not steal an interview [with Jesus], nor come, like Nicodemus, disguised.

†**b.** With complementary adj. or adv. *to steal oneself drunk*: to get drunk secretly. *to steal down* (Sc.): to cause to fall, ruin, by secret means.

1570 *Sat. Poems Reform.* xvii. 101 Thy poysoun did doun steill Not only him quhom wofully thow woundit; Bot [etc.]. **1596** DALRYMPLE tr. *Leslie's Hist. Scot.* II. VII. 22 Machabie deuyses to cal Bancho and Fleanch..till a banket, that he sik a trayne quyetlie he may steil thame doune. **1670** T. BROOKS *Wks.* (1867) VI. 67 So accordingly he stole himself drunk. **1719** LONDON & WISE *Compl. Gard.* 41 The difference of hot or cold Summers does steal more considerably forward, or set back the same Fruits, of one and the same Climate and Season.

c. To direct (a look), breathe (a sigh) furtively.

a **1586** SIDNEY *Arcadia* I. (Sommer) 62 b, As I..stale a look on her. **1697** DRYDEN *Alexander's Feast* 87 And, now and then, a Sigh he stole. **1711** ADDISON *Spect.* No. 106 ¶1, I have observed them stealing a Sight of me over an Hedge. **1794** MRS. RADCLIFFE *Myst. Udolpho* xxxi, She stole a glance at them. **1866** G. MACDONALD *Ann. Q. Neighb.* iii. (1878) 33 He stole a shy pleased look at me.

†**d.** *to steal a marriage*: to get married secretly. *Obs.* [Cf. Gr. γάμον κλέπτειν.]

c **1450** *Merlin* ii. 363 This mariage wolde he haue stole hadde no Merlin I-be. **1562** *Child-Marr.* 189 They did steale a mariage without banes askinge. **1711** STEELE *Spect.* No. 133 ¶7 A story I had heard of his intending to steal a marriage without the privity of us his intimate friends. **1731-8** SWIFT *Pol. Conversat.* 130 You have stolen a Wedding it seems... How does your Lady unknown? **1782** MISS BURNEY *Cecilia* x. vi, 'Your daughter..has made a little change in her situation, which she was anxious you should hear from myself.' 'Ha! ha! stolen a match upon you I warrant!' cried the facetious Mr. Hobson. *a* **1797** H. WALPOLE *Mem. Reign Geo. III* (1845) III. x. 326 He..had stolen a marriage with an idiot sister of the Spanish Charles Townshend. *c* **1820** S. ROGERS *Italy, Marguerite de Tours* 45 They stole a match and fled.

e. *to steal a march*: in military sense, to succeed in moving troops without the knowledge of the enemy; hence *gen.* to get a secret advantage over a rival or opponent. Const. *on, upon,* †*of*.

1716 *Addr. Edinb.* 27 Mar. in *Lond. Gaz.* No. 5422/2 We saw him..steal a March for our Preservation. **1740** CIBBER *Apol.* (1756) I. 143 After we had stolen some few days march upon them. **1771** SMOLLETT *Humph. Cl.* 6 May (1815) 73 She yesterday wanted to steal a march of poor Liddy. **1834** MARRYAT *P. Simple* xxiii, We must be off early to-morrow, while these good people are in bed, and steal a long march upon them. **1855** MACAULAY *Hist. Eng.* xv. III. 519 Those who had intended to gain the victory by stealing a march now disclaimed that intention. **1856** READE *Never too Late* xxii, Happening to awake earlier than usual, he stole a march on his nurses, and..walked out and tottered into the jail. **1885** 'F. ANSTEY' *Tinted Venus* 100 He shan't have the chance: we'll steal a march on him this time.

†**f.** To get a hasty glance at. *Obs.*

1731 FIELDING *Letter Writers* I. ii. 7 Will you go steal an Act or two of the new Tragedy? *Rak.* Not I—I go to no Tragedy.

g. In various games, esp. Cricket, Golf, Baseball, Basketball, and Ice Hockey (see quots.). Also *fig.* Also *intr.* (in Baseball), esp. in *to steal home*.

1836 *New Sporting Mag.* Oct. 361 [The batsmen's scores] added to the byes they stole, and the wide balls bowled, sufficed to make a hands of eighty-six runs. **1851** J. PYCROFT *Cricket Field* x. 196 A sharp runner..will often try a long-stop's temper by stealing runs. **1857** HUGHES *Tom Brown* II. viii, He has stolen three byes in the first ten minutes. **1862** *Sunday Mercury* (N.Y.) 13 July 6/2 Creighton..made his base by a missed fly-catch of Sawyer's; Brainard and Young getting their runs by stealing in on the pitcher and catcher. **1874** CHADWICK *Base Ball Man.* 47 If he [the batsman] steal home on the catcher or pitcher. **1881** FORGAN *Golfer's Handbk.* 35 *Steal*, to hole an unlikely 'put' from a distance. **1882** *Daily Tel.* 24 June, He next took Ramsay round to the leg boundary, and shortly stole a single off him also. **1891** N. CRANE *Baseball* iv. 32 His antics in trying to deceive the fielders and steal a base excite great amusement among the ..spectators. **1895** MANSON *Sporting Dict., Stealing a Base.* When a base runner makes his next base by leading off and then running while the ball is being thrown by the pitcher to the catcher. **1895** *Times* 19 Feb. 11/4 The Englishmen were able to steal many runs. **1897** *Encycl. Sport* I. 247/1 (Cricket) *Steal runs*, to get a run for a hit, when no run seems reasonably possible. **1936** *Philadelphia Rec.* 31 July 15/1 No Landon speech is likely to startle anybody. You know in advance that he will never take a full cut at the ball, try to steal a base or catch a line drive with one hand. **1938** M. DUTTON *Hockey* vi. 110 It is hard enough to steal the puck in your own end zone, without trying to regain a lost puck in the other fellow's. **1942** C. BEE *Basketball Library* IV. ii. 7 An attempt to 'steal' the ball from a good dribbler often leaves the defensive player out of position. **1968** *Globe & Mail* (Toronto) 5 Feb. 18/3 Ballantyne was ahead 5-3 going into the sixth end, but Lawrie tied it up in the seventh and stole one in each of eighth and ninth for the victory. **1978** *Boston Globe* 4 Jan. 42/2 Hollins stole the ball with seven seconds to play and scored.

6. a. To place, move, or convey stealthily. Now somewhat *rare*. †*to steal on*: to put on (one's clothes, etc.) hastily, so as not to be observed (*obs.*). *to steal* (some one or something) *in*: to smuggle in, procure secret entrance for.

a **1300** *Cursor M.* 3872 Bot þar [Laban] did a trecheri, For þan [Jacob] had may rachell wedd, Lia he stall vn-til his bed. *c* **1555** J. BRADFORD in Coverdale *Godly Lett. Martyrs* (1564) 470 Pray Walshe to steale you in, as I hope he will doe. *a* **1620** WEBSTER *Appius & Virg.* IV. i, Thy violent Lust shall like the biting of the invenom'd Aspick, steal thee to hell. **1633** G. HERBERT *Temple, Love-unknown* 43, I bath'd it often, ev'n with holy bloud, Which at a board, while many drunk base wine, A friend did steal into my cup for good. **1648** J. BEAUMONT *Psyche* VI. xlvi, Know'st thou why He gathers up his Tail's ashamed Train, And steals it round about his scaly thigh? **1649** DAVENANT *Love & Hon.* IV. i. 65 Steale on this funerall habit. **1654-66** EARL ORRERY *Parthen.* (1676) 641, I stole the Letter into Monyma's hand. *a* **1685** R. NORTH *Autobiog.* i. (1887) 3 But there was another use made of this botle, for our Mother would steal into it slices of Rubarb, and..this way, it was stole upon us, and not tainted with aversions. **1710** [BEDFORD] *Vind. Ch. Eng.* 179 The Words..were..stol'n into the..Article. *a* **1712** FOUNTAINHALL *Decis.* (1759) I. 292 The Merchants did undersel them, by stealing in English cloth that was prohibit. **1712** STEELE *Spectator* No. 354 ¶3 The Prentice speaks his Disrespect by an extended Finger, and the Porter by stealing out his Tongue. **1718** PRIOR *Solomon* II. 428, I.. from beneath his Head, at dawning Day, With softest Care have stol'n my Arm away. *c* **1730** RAMSAY *For Sake Somebody* iii, I'll..steal on linens fair and clean. **1752** H. WALPOLE *Let. to Mann* 28 Oct., [Lord Coventry] coursed his wife round the table, on suspecting that she had stolen on a little red, seized her, scrubbed it off by force with a napkin, and then told her, that [etc.]. **1760-72** H. BROOKE *Fool of Qual.* (1809) III. 17 He stole a bill for 16*ol.* into his hand, saying..there is what I owe you. **1779** JOHNSON *L.P., Savage* III. 367 Nor [did he] ever read his verses without stealing his eyes from the page, to discover, in the faces of his audience, how they were affected. **1792** S. ROGERS *Pleas. Mem.* II. 10 Whose constant vigils chase the chilling damp Oblivion steals upon her vestal lamp. **1817** MOORE *Lalla Rookh* (ed. 2) 165 If the sweet hours of intercourse so imprudently allowed them should have stolen into his heart the same fatal fascination as into hers. **1818** SCOTT *Hrt. Midl.* xxx, The hag..now unclosed her hand, stole it away from the weapon, and suffered it to fall by her side. **1821** CLARE *Vill. Minstr.* I. 199 Slily steal thy bonnet on,..And wander out with me. **1824** T. JEFFERSON *Writ.* (1830) IV. 397 It may amuse you, to show when, and by what means, they stole this law in upon us. **1883** D. C. MURRAY *Joseph's Coat* xxxiv, It was noticed that the silent two had stolen each a hand towards the other's and thus..they sat handed.

†**b.** To fire (a gun) stealthily. *Obs.*

1794 NELSON in *Sotheby's Catal.* (1900) 26 Feb. 118 Except one general discharge and a gun now and then stole at us, we have had no opposition.

c. Of a hen: To make (her nest) in a concealed place. Also *US.* of a ewe: To bring forth (lambs) out of season.

1743 W. ELLIS *Mod. Husbandman* July xvi. 77 One of my Hen Pheasants..got Abroad, and stole her Nest. **1854** *Poultry Chron.* I. 436 Turkey hens generally steal their nests, but do not readily forsake them, unless scared. **1859** ALLEN *New Amer. Farm Bk.* (1883) 417 If young ewes have stolen lambs, they should be taken away from them immediately after yeaning. **1881** YOUNG *Ev. Man his own Mechanic* §979. 466 When laying every hen likes extreme privacy. This is why fowls when at liberty 'steal' their nests as it is called.

7. *techn.* To omit or suppress (some out of a usual number of parts of a structure). **a.** *Naut.* (See quot.) **b.** *Netting.* (? Implied in STOLEN *ppl. a.*)

1711 W. SUTHERLAND *Shipbuild. Assist.* 47 It's therefore very customary in many Ships to drop, or steal, as they term it, some Strakes short of the Stern.

II. To go secretly or quietly.

†**8.** *refl.* To withdraw oneself secretly or quietly. Chiefly with *away*. *Obs. rare.*

[So ON. *stela-sk*. For the development of meaning cf. F. *dérober* to steal, *se dérober* to hide oneself.]

a **1300** *Cursor M.* 3918 Laban o leue þam nicked nai, And þai bi night þam stal a way. *c* **1386** CHAUCER *Pard T.* 282 For which as soone as it myghte be He stal hym hoom agayn to his contree. *c* **1489** CAXTON *Sonnes of Aymon* xvi. 381 Whan the spye had wel vnderstonde all the conclucion, he stele hymself fro the company. *Ibid.* xxviii. 590 Alas, ye stale awaye yourself by nyghte. **1725** POPE *Odyss.* XI. 165 So peaceful shalt thou end thy blissful days, And steal thy self from life, by slow decays.

9. a. *intr.* To depart or withdraw secretly or surreptitiously from a place. Chiefly with adv., as *away*, †*forth*, *off*, *out*, or const. *from*, *out of*.

1154 *O.E. Chron.* an. 1140, & te æorl stæl ut & ferde efter Rodbert eorl of Gloucestre. *c* **1205** LAY. 15019 Heo swiþe stille stelen ut of buruwe. *c* **1290** *Magdalene* 540 in *S.E. Leg.* 477 Marie..stal a-wey from hire kunne. **1487** *Cely Papers* (Camden) 171 Diversse of them stelyth dayly aweye and goyth to Myddelborow. **1530** PALSGR. 734/2, I steale awaye, I convaye my selfe prively out of syght, or out of company. **1535** W. STEWART *Cron. Scot.* (Rolls) II. 178 How Wortigerne for Dreid of Hungest staw in the Walis. **1561** NORTON & SACKV. *Gorboduc* V. ii. 40 And other sort..Stale home by silence of the secret night. *a* **1578** LINDESAY (Pitscottie) *Chron. Scot* (S.T.S.) I. 294 The Earle of Angus was stowin quyitlie out of his ludging. **1580** STOW *Chron.* 533 (an. 1399), But when they saw the King came not, they stealed away, and left the Earle of Salisburie in manner alone. **1596** in *Spalding Club Misc.* I. 86 Thow was apprehendit..steilling furth of the said..Adam Mairis yard, at twa houris in the morning, greyn growand bear. **1617** MORYSON *Itin.* II. 57 The Lord Deputie..received advertisement..that Tyrone..was stolne out of Mounster with sixe hundred in his company. **1639** FULLER *Holy War* III. xvi. (1640) 135 Other Captains secretly stole home. **1667** DRYDEN *Ind. Emperor* IV. iv, The gods are good; I'le leave her to their care, Steal from my Post, and in the Plunder share. **1704** CIBBER *Careless Husb.* v. 47 My Lady Graveairs had an Eye upon me, as I stole off. **1761** HUME *Hist. Eng.* xxvii. II. 131 Many of them had stolen from the camp, and retired homewards. *a* **1774** GOLDSM. tr. *Scarron's Com. Romance* (1775) II. 251 She had stole out in order to acquaint me with this. **1786** MME. D'ARBLAY *Diary* 18 July, The sub-governess stole from her charges, and came to the window. **1867** MORRIS *Jason* II. 583 But made him think of some beast from his lair Stolen forth at the beginning of the night. **1869** TOZER *Highl. Turkey* II. 267 Maria stole off to the honey. **1881** JOWETT *Thucyd.* I. 232 The inhabitants had stolen away and taken up a position on the top of the hills.

b. with advb. accusative, *to steal one's way* (†in early use = to steal away). Now *rare*.

c **1385** CHAUCER *L.G.W.* 2174 He..as a traytour stal his wey. **1432-50** tr. *Higden* (Rolls) VII. 101 That Edricus seenge the Danes to be inclynede, stale his weye from the hoste. *c* **1500** *Three Kings' Sons* 152 Some stale their wey, and lefte the places allone. **1847** MRS. A. KERR tr. *Ranke's Hist. Servia* 182 During the night, he, with his Momkes, stole his way into the midst of their camp. **1884** W. COLLINS *I say No* ix, Steal your way into that poor little fool's heart.

c. Hunting. *to steal away*. Of a hunted animal: To leave its lair unperceived and gain a start of the pursuers.

c **1369** CHAUCER *Dethe Blaunche* 381 And so, at the laste, This hert Rused and staale away Fro alle the houndes a prevy way. *c* **1400** *Master of Game* (MS. Digby 182) xxxiii, To se if þe deer þat is herbowrede wolde sterte and steele away or þe lymer meved hym. **1711** BUDGELL *Spect.* No. 116 ¶5 That 'twas a Wonder they had not lost all their Sport, for want of the silent Gentleman's crying Stole Away. **1756** FOOTE *Engl. fr. Paris* II. Wks. 1799 I. 111 Hola, Sir Toby, Stole away! **1818** SCOTT *Rob Roy* vi, I..soon heard, far behind, the 'hey whoop! stole away! stole away!' of my baffled pursuers. **1872** T. PEARCE *Idstone Papers* ii. 19 Just then..there was a rustle amongst the long grass, and a fine dog fox..stole away.

†**d.** *fig.* of things. *Obs.* (Distinct from 11.)

a **1366** CHAUCER *Rom. Rose* 371 The tyme that..steleth from vs so priuely. *c* **1412** HOCCLEVE *De Reg. Princ.* 5248 But it [prosperity] a-way gan stele Whan þei him drough to profyte singuler.

10. a. To go or come secretly or stealthily; to walk or creep softly so as to avoid observation.

a **1300** *Cursor M.* 12524 Iosep..sent him to þe yerd..For to gedir þam sum cale; And iesus still him efter stal. *c* **1374** CHAUCER *Troylus* I. 81 And to þe Grekes ost ful pryely He stal a noon. *c* **1475** HENRYSON *Orpheus* 142 And Orpheus atour his [*sc.* Cerberus'] wame in stall, And nethir mare he went. **1544** BETHAM *Precepts War* II. vii. K ij, Yf he steale into the campe, by walles or ditches, dryuen by no great feare, he is worthye the same punyshment. **1577–87** HARRISON *England* II. xiii. (1877) 246 Such of Belgie as stale over hither from the maine. *a* **1586** SIDNEY *Arcadia* III. i. (1912) 356 [He] stale up into Pamelaes chamber. **1589** GREENE *Menaphon* (Arb.) 39 Affection is like the Snayle, which stealeth to the top of the lance by minutes. **1596** RALEIGH *Discov. Guiana* 4 The same evening there stale also abord vs in a small Canoa two Indians. **1640** SUCKLING *Ballade upon Wedding* 44 Her feet beneath her Petticoat, Like little mice stole in and out. **1695** BLACKMORE *Pr. Arthur* II. 947 The timorous Hare steals from the Brakes. **1710** SWIFT *Jrnl. to Stella* 2 Sept., I have stole here again to finish this letter. **1778** MISS BURNEY *Evelina* (1791) I. xxxiii. 168 Madame Duval.. stole softly down stairs, desiring me to follow her. **1799** CAMPBELL *Pleas. Hope* I. 325 On Erie's banks, where tigers steal along. **1833** HT. MARTINEAU *Manch. Strike* iii. 33 They steal to one another's houses when they think we are asleep. **1837** CARLYLE *Fr. Rev.* I. III. iii, At nightfall, President Lamoignon steals over to the Controller's. **1852** MRS. STOWE *Uncle Tom's C.* xxvii, There were.. soft whisperings and foot-falls in the chamber, as one after another stole in, to look at the dead. **1859** FITZGERALD *Omar* xlii, And lately,.. Came stealing through the Dusk an Angel Shape Bearing a Vessel on his Shoulder. **1877** BLACK *Green Past.* ii, The Lady Sylvia.. dressed and stole noiselessly down the stairs.

b. *fig.*

1592 GREENE *Upst. Courtier* C 4, Such vpstarts.. wil at last steale by degrees into some credit by their double diligence. **1599** SANDYS *Europæ Spec.* Pref. (1632) 3 Yet, neverthelesse, since that time; there hath beene another Impression of the same stolne into the world. **1679** C. NESSE *Antichrist* 213 It stole into the world.. unsensibly, and at unawares. **1763** CHURCHILL *Night* 188 Calm, independent, let me steal thro' life. **1875** JOWETT *Plato* (ed. 2) III. 342 The child of which he is the father, if it steals into life.

†**c.** With *to* adv. *Obs.*

c **1250** *Owl & Night.* 1432 An go to him bi daies lihte þat er stal to bi þeostre nihte. *c* **1290** *Barnabas* 98 in *S. Eng. Leg.* 29 Ake cristine Men þat weren bi-side stelen to bi niȝte.

d. To come stealthily *on* or *upon* a person for the purpose of attack or injury.

13.. *King Alis.* (Laud MS.) 3989 For þou hast demed þi self here þoo þou.. stale byhynden on oure kyng. *c* **1369** CHAUCER *Dethe Blaunche* 654 At the chesse.. She staale on me and toke my fers. **1393** LANGL. *P. Pl.* C. VII. 106 'Ich am wratthe', quaþ þat wye, 'wol gladliche smyte Boþe with ston and with staf, and stele vp-on myn enemy.' **1399** —— *R. Redeles* III. 21 Þo schrewed wormes, þat steleth on þe stedis to stynge hem to deth. *c* **1450** *Brut* II. 379 And aftir come þer tydynges.. þat þere was a new Batayle of Frenschmen ordeyned, redy to stele on hem, and comyn towarde hym. **1508** STANBRIDGE *Vulgaria* (W. de W.) B iij b, He came stelynge vpon me, *Adortus est me.* **1530** PALSGR. 734/2, I steale upon one, I come prively upon hym, *je viens a lemblée.* **1577** GOOGE *Heresbach's Husb.* III. (1586) 156 b, The catte.. stealing suddenly and swiftly vpon the mouse. **1598** T. ROGERS *Celest. Elegies* C 4 b in *Lamport Garl.* (Roxb.), Death stole vppon her with his Eben darte. **1680** *Debates Ho. Commons* (1681) 115, I believe it was only to quiet our Thoughts, while Popery steals on upon us. **1684** *Contempl. St. Man* I. vii. (1699) 77 Death steals treacherously upon us, when we least look for it. **1704** ROWE *Ulysses* II. i. 569 The God of Sleep Insensible and soft, had stole upon me. **1788** BURNS *Bonie Moor-hen* Chorus, Tak' some on the wing, and some as they spring, But cannily steal on a bonie moor-hen. **1821** SCOTT *Kenilw.* xxix, With the stealthy step.. of the cat that steals on her prey.

11. Of things. **a.** Of time (with *on*, *away*): to come or go unobserved.

1590 SHAKS. *Com. Err.* IV. i. 52 The houre steales on, I pray you sir dispatch. **1592** KYD *Span. Trag.* III. xi. 46 Then time steales on, And steales, and steales. **1600** E. BLOUNT tr. *Conestaggio* 19 But in the meane space time steales away. **1773** HAN. MORE *Search Happ.* ii. 143 No plan e'er mark'd the duties of the day, Which stole in tasteless apathy away. **1885** 'MRS. ALEXANDER' *At Bay* xi, As years stole on, and he didn't care to move about much.

b. Of a condition, esp. sleep, insensibility, infirmities, etc.: To come insensibly *over* or *on* a person.

14.. *Pol. Rel. & L. Poems* (1903) 279 ȝif any sterynge on me stele. **1562** WINȜET *Cert. Tractates* iii. Wks. (S.T.S.) I. 27 That be the proces of tyme vnthankful forȝetfulnes steil not vpon us. **1660** DRYDEN *Astræa Reaux* 129 So on us stole our blessed change; while we Th'effect did feel but scarce the manner see. **1807–8** IRVING *Salmag.* (1824) 332 Infirmities had stolen upon him. **1812** CRABBE *Tales* xix. 166 He began to feel Some self-approval on his bosom steal. **1827–54** DE QUINCEY *Last Days Kant* Wks. III. 123 The infirmities of age now began to steal upon Kant. **1834** *Life Adam Clarke* iv. 101 Mr. Clarke.. began to feel a sense of drowsiness steal over him. **1847** C. BRONTË *Jane Eyre* xxviii, A kind of pleasant stupor was stealing over me.

c. Of a stream, tears, a body of vapour, a ship, etc.: To glide, or move gently and almost imperceptibly. Also with adv., *along*, *on*, *out*.

1626 BACON *Sylva* §919 The Vapour of Char-Coale.. is the more dangerous, because it commeth without any Ill Smell; But stealeth on by little and little. *a* **1678** CHALKHILL *Thealma & Cl.* 93 Anon she drops a tear That stole along her cheeks. **1709** POPE *Ess. Crit.* 379 Now sighs steal out, and tears begin to flow. **1737** [S. BERINGTON] *G. de Lucca's Mem.* (1738) 62 With Tears stealing down his Cheeks. **1786** BURNS *Vision* I. xiv, Auld, hermit Aire staw thro' his woods, On to the shore. **1849** HELPS *Friends in C.* II. ii. (1854) I. 283 Look at that ungainly puppy trying to catch the thistle-down as it steals up the hill. **1874** LADY BARKER *Station Life N. Zealand* xvii. 135 The faint wreath of smoke stealing up through the calm air. **1896** 'H. S. MERRIMAN' *Flotsam* i. 1 The Hooghly was stealing past the quiet bungalow built on the bank. **1898** BRIDGES *Hymn Nat.* Poems (1912) 404 The white ships swim, And steal to havens far.

d. Of sound, fragrance, light: To become gradually perceptible. Const. *on*, *upon*, (the sense).

1634 MILTON *Comus* 557 At last a soft and solemn breathing sound Rose like a steam of rich distill'd Perfumes, And stole upon the Air, that even Silence Was took e're she was ware. **1777** POTTER *Æschylus, Prometh. Chain'd* 12 Ah me! what sound, what softly-breathing odour Steals on my sense? **1785** BURNS *Winter Nt.* 36 When on my ear this plaintive strain, Slow, solemn, stole. *c* **1790** W. L. BOWLES *Sonn.*, '*As one who long*', With such delight, o'er all my heart I feel, Sweet Hope! thy fragrance pure and healing incense steal. **1822** LAMB *Elia* Ser. I. *Some old Actors*, You could see the first dawn of an idea stealing slowly over his countenance.

†**e.** To insinuate itself, find acceptance in disguise. Also, to gain influence by imperceptible degrees. Const. *on*. *Obs.*

1581 SIDNEY *Apol. Poetrie* (Arb.) 35 Whose pretty Allegories, stealing vnder the formall tales of Beastes, make many.. begin to heare the sound of vertue. **1648** J. BEAUMONT *Psyche* XX. cclxxxvi, The Art of charming Sanctity can steal upon The coldest bosom. *a* **1661** FULLER *Worthies, Brecknock* (1662) 23 With a smooth stream.. his matter by a lawful and laudable felony, did steal secretly into the hearts of his hearers. **1805** EMILY CLARK *Banks of Douro* I. 259 The society of Montague;.. insensibly stole on her esteem.

†**f.** To operate by insensible degrees *upon*. *Obs.*

1639 G. PLATTES *Discov. Subterr. Treas.* 19 When you use them [*sc.* the new pots] set them in the fire at the first kindling: and so let the Fire steale upon them till they be red hot.

†**g.** *to steal off*: to diverge in an inconspicuous way. *nonce-use.*

1793 [EARL DUNDONALD] *Descr. Est. Culross* 30 From the .. main lay of the Coal.. a leader of Coal steals off as it were.

†**h.** To develop by insensible degrees *from*; to pass or change insensibly *into*, *to* something else.

1660 DRYDEN *Astræa Redux* 127 As wise Artists mix their Colours so That by degrees they from each other go, Black steals unheeded from the neighb'ring white. *a* **1759** COLLINS *Epist. to Hanmer* 114 Chaste and subdued the modest lights decay, Steal into shades, and mildly melt away. **1821** CLARE *Vill. Minstr.* II. 34 Buds to blossoms softly steal. **1826** DISRAELI *V. Grey* V. iii, A bright sun-shiny afternoon was stealing into twilight.

i. Of an event, a proposal: To come *upon* a person without attracting attention.

1798 SOPHIA LEE *Canterb. T., Young Lady's T.* II. 336 Day had unobserved stolen upon them. **1819** J. MARSHALL *Constit. Opin.* (1839) 161 The bill.. did not steal upon an unsuspecting legislature.

III. 12. The verb-stem in combination: **steal-clothes**, **steal-coat** (see quots.); †**steal-counter**, ? a gamester who cheats by stealing counters (in quot. *fig.*); †**steal-placard**, one who has stolen a 'placard' or begging licence; †**steal-truth**, a heresy.

1809 *Edin. Rev.* XIV. 143 '*Wadds.*' This youthful amusement.. is called, on the Borders, by the very appropriate name of *Scotch and English.* In the south of England, it has the blunter appellation of **steal-clothes.* [**1825** BROCKETT *N.C. Gloss.*, *Stealy-clothes*, or *Watch-webs*, a game.] **1816** *Gentl. Mag.* July 36/1 In Lancashire we have a game, for which I can procure no other name than *Steal Coat. **1588** *Hay any Work* 6 That olde *stealecounter masse priest, John O Glossester. **1601** DEACON & WALKER *Answ. Darel* 79 You are now (like a steale-counter) thus couertly creeping vnto their supposed dispossessions by prayer and fasting. **1592** NASHE *Saffron-Walden* N 1 b, Pigmey Dicke.. is such another Venerian *steale Placard as Iohn was. **1628** H. LYNDE *Via tuta* 48 By which publique notice, the *steale-truth was discouered.

steal (sti:l), *v.*[2] Now *dial.* [f. STEAL *sb.*[1]] *trans.* To furnish with a handle.

1543 *Fabric Rolls York Minster* (Surtees) 356 Payd to viij masons, every of them, for stelyng of ther ger, 12d. To ij prentec' for thir stelyng sylver, 2s. **1570–80** *Ibid.* 117 For mendinge and styling four chesells. **1573** in *Rep. MSS. Ld. Middleton* (Hist. MSS. Comm.) 434 For steeling an axe for John Dune.. xij d. **1580** *Nottingham Rec.* IV. 194 For mendyng and stelyng of a pycke iij s. vj d.

steal, obs. form of STALL *sb.*[1]

stealable ('sti:ləb(ə)l), *a.* [f. STEAL *v.*[1] + -ABLE.] That can be stolen.

1827 *Hone's Every-day Bk.* II. 814 The fruit.. is not yet stealable.. by boys. **1885** *Church Times* 3 July 511/2 If all the stealable property of the Church were stolen.

stealage ('sti:lɪdʒ). [f. STEAL *v.*[1] + -AGE.] **a.** Losses due to stealing. **b.** *nonce-use.* The right of stealing.

1769 J. WEDGWOOD *Let.* 7 Apr. (1965) 72 On calculating the expence, breakage, and stealage by Sea, and comparing it with Land Carriage, I find there is about half saved. **1865** S. HUGHES *Gas-works* (ed. 2) 249 Mr. Croll.. estimated that one-sixth of the whole gas sent out would be absorbed by leakage and stealage. **1884** H. GEORGE *Soc. Probl.* ii. 25 [A man] who would administer the government of these municipalities for fifty per cent. of present waste and stealage! **1888** J. A. MORGAN *Bankside Shaks.* I. Introd. 16 Did Shakespeare sell the stealage as well the stage-right of his plays?

stealed, *a.* [f. STEAL *sb.*[1] + -ED[2]] Having a 'steal' or handle. Only in *long-stealed.*

1530 PALSGR. 756/1, I throw a darte or any longe stealed weapen, *Je darde.*

†**stealed**, *ppl. a. Obs. rare.* [f. STEAL *v.*[1] + -ED[1].] = STOLEN.

1577 GRANGE *Golden Aphrod.* etc. R j, I stryde the streetes both long and wyde, A stealed sight of hir to haue. **1883** C. STEWART *David Blythe* 22 Wattie.. saw his ain stealed beast quietly grazing close at hand.

stealer[1] ('sti:lə(r)). [f. STEAL *v.*[1] + -ER.] One who steals; a thief; now only, one who steals something specified.

1500–20 DUNBAR *Poems* xxvii. 11 Off stomok steillaris and clayth takkaris, A graceless garisoun. **1508** *Reg. Privy Seal Scot.* I. 283/1 He dredis that the stelaris of it [a seal] hes fenȝeit and maid fals lettrez.. on his behalff. **1538** ELYOT *Dict.*, *Plagiarius*,.. also a stealer of bokes. **1547–64** BALDWIN *Mor. Philos.* 60 Cut off stealers hands. Hang up theeves and robbers. **1583** BABINGTON *Commandm.* 338 The cause why the stealer stole was want of labouring in his calling. **1585** HIGINS *Junius' Nomencl.* 528/1 *Mango*,.. a stealer away of mens children of seruants that selleth and buyeth them. **1649** J. OWEN *Serm. H. of C.*, *Of Toleration* 44 If so, why doe Adulterers unmolested, behold the violent death of Stealers. **1769** COOK *1st Voy.* I. xv. in Hawkesw. *Voy.* (1773) II. 157 A Chief.. whose father's name was Pahairedo, the stealer of boats. **1829** BENTHAM *Justice & Cod. Petit.* 29 The authority, from which the power was thus filched, was.. that of some judge or judges, co-ordinate with that of the stealers. **1878** B. TAYLOR *Pr. Deukalion* I. v. 45 Older than thou, the stealer of the fire!

b. slang. ***the ten stealers***: the fingers.

[**1603** SHAKS. *Ham.* III. ii. 349 By these pickers and stealers.] *a* **1639** R. DAVENPORT *K. John & Matilda* III. i, Since they have neither eaten bit nor drunk drop, nor by these ten stealers shall not, till I heare againe from my Lord.

stealer[2] ('sti:lə(r)). *Naut.* Also steeler. [The same word as prec.: cf. STEAL *v.*[1] 7.] (See quots.)

1805 *Shipwright's Vade-M.* 201 It is therefore customary to work, in the bow of such ships, a steeler next under the wale. **1815** *Falconer's Dict. Marine* (ed. Burney), *Steeler*, in ship-building, the foremost or aftmost plank in a strake, which is dropped short of the stem of stern-post. **1852** FINCHAM *Ship Build.* II. (ed. 3) 26 These planks are called steelers. **1874** THEARLE *Nav. Archit.* 50 The last plank of the strake which does not extend right forward or aft, as the case may be, is termed a 'stealer'.

stealewurðe, variant of STALWORTH *a.*

stealing ('sti:lɪŋ), *vbl. sb.* [-ING[1].] The action of STEAL *v.*[1] in its various senses. Also *Comb.* with advs., as ***stealing-forth***, ***-in***.

13.. *Seuyn Sages* (W.) 1275 Thef of steling wil nowt blinne Til he honge bi the chinne. **1526** *Pilgr. Perf.* (W. de W. 1531) 238 By rape, pykyng, estorcyon, sacrilege, or ony other maner of stelyng. **1568** GRAFTON *Chron.* II. 170 By the strength of those Castelles, they were kept from their olde accustomed rauynes and stealings. **1581** A. HALL *Iliad* IX. 165 No groome perceiues my stealing forth, nor tooke thereof regarde. **1596** DALRYMPLE tr. *Leslie's Hist. Scot.* I. 97 Be steiling and reif, thay raþer seik thair meit. **1612** BRINSLEY *Lud. Lit.* 155 For preuenting of stealing, or any helpe by the Latine booke.. you may both cause them to write in your presence, and also make choise of such places which they know not where to find. **1669** BOYLE *Contn. New Exp.* I. 171 But the Stealing in of any Air, before the water was let in, is mentioned but as a Suspicion. **1690** LOCKE *Hum. Und.* II. xxvii [xxviii]. §16 Thus the taking from another what is his, without his Knowledge or Allowance, is properly called Stealing. **1887** BROWNING *Parleyings, B. de Mandeville* v. 37 If, at first stealing-forth of life in stalk And leaflet-promise, quick His spud should baulk Evil from budding foliage, bearing fruit.

b. *concr.* in *plural.* Gains made by stealing.

1839 MARRYAT *Diary Amer.* Ser. I. I. 195, I asked how much his office was worth, and his answer was six hundred dollars, besides stealings.

stealing ('sti:lɪŋ), *ppl. a.* [f. STEAL *v.*[1] + -ING[2].] That steals or moves stealthily; that eludes observation; that glides or creeps softly along; that comes on imperceptibly. Early use chiefly in ***stealing step***, ***pace*** (very common in the 16th c.; now *rare*).

1574 HIGGINS *Mirr. Mag.*, *Q. Cordila* xxxv, Eke nearer still to mee with stealing steps shee drewe. **1576** GASCOIGNE *Steele Gl.* (Arb.) 69 Nor heare the trampling of his stealing steppes. **1617** HIERON *Penance Sin* xxvii. Wks. 1619 II. 380 Sinne.. maketh boldnesse and security in a stealing and dangerous manner to encrease. **1629** GAULE *Holy Madn.* 324 With a learing Looke,.. stealing Pace, squeaking Voice. **1633** P. FLETCHER *Purple Isl.* VI. lxxvii, But see, the stealing night with softly pace,.. creeps up the East. **1748** COLLINS *Ode Death Thomson* 2 In yonder grave a Druid lies Where slowly winds the stealing wave! **1794** MRS. RADCLIFFE *Myst. Udolpho* xxxiii, He turned to the light, and proceeded with the same stealing steps towards Emily's apartment. **1813** BYRON *Corsair* I. vii, They watch his glance with many a stealing look. **1853** R. S. SURTEES *Sponge's Sp. Tour* (1893) 60 His [a horse's] easy stealing way of going, compared to the bounding elasticity of Hercules. **1892** *Welsh Rev.* I. 767, I.. followed her silently until we stood face to face in the stealing darkness. **1897** W. J. COURTHOPE *Longest Reign* iii, Not.. for Thee hath stealing Age, Sovereign Lady,.. Dimmed the glory of Thy golden prime.

b. *Comb.*, as ***stealing-wise*** adv.; **stealing-strake** *Naut.* = STEALER[2].

1632 J. HAYWARD tr. *Biondi's Eromena* 2 Seeing the fierce beast make stealing-wise towards him. **1830** HEDDERWICK *Mar. Archit.* 120 *Steeling-strake* or *plank*, one that does not run all the way to the stem or stern post.

Hence '**stealingly** *adv.*, stealthily, furtively, so as to elude observation. (Very common in the 16th and 17th c.; now *rare.*)

13.. *K. Alis.* 5080 Many of his men.. Agein kyng Alisaunder hestes, Stelendelich dronken of this lake. *c* **1400** *Ragman Roll* 62 in Hazl. *E.P.P.* (1864) I. 72 And now cometh age, foo to your beauté, And stelyngly it wastyth stownde-mele. *c* **1440** *Promp. Parv.* 473/2 Stelyngly, or theefly, *furtive, latrocinaliter.* **1502** *Ord. Crysten Men* (W. de W. 1506) IV. ix. 191 Whan ony clerke receyueth holy ordres stelyngely. **1596** R. L[INCHE] *Diella* (1877) 81 And stealingly there glides with heauy pace A Riuolet of Pearle along her face. **1603** DEKKER etc. *Patient Grissill* IV. i. 1719 Enter Grissill, stealingly. **1630** LENNARD tr. *Charron's Wisd.* III. iii. §7 (1670) 360 And in this case likewise he must proceed as it were stealingly, sweetly and slowly, by little and little, and almost insensibly. **1693** W. BATES *Serm.* viii. 278 A Disease neglected at first, that stealingly slips into the Habit of the Body,.. becomes a last uncontroulable and incurable. *a* **1843** SOUTHEY in *Fraser's Mag.* (1868) LXXVII. 731 The means wherewith he would stealingly attempt this change.

stealth ('stɛlθ). Forms: 3–4 **stalðe**, 4–6 **stelthe**, 4–7 **stelth**, 5 **stalth**, 6 **stilth**, 6– **stealth**. [Early ME. *stalðe, stelthe*; the fluctuation of vowel points to an OE. **stǽlþ*, f. OTeut. **stǽl-* ablaut- var. of **stel-*: see STEAL *v.* and -TH[1]. Cf. ON. *stulþ-r*, Icel. *stuld-r*, theft, STOUTH, from the weak-grade of the same root.]

†**1.** The action or practice of stealing or taking secretly and wrongfully; theft. *Obs.*

c **1250** *Gen. & Ex.* 1767 Stalðe ic for-sake. **1357** *Lay Folks Catech.* T. 513 Als be sacrilege, or be symonie, Stalthe, falshede, or oker. **1390** GOWER *Conf.* II. 346 With Covoitise yit I finde A Servant of the same kinde, Which Stelthe is hote. *c* **1412** HOCCLEVE *De Reg. Princ.* 1809 And stelthes [*printed* steltles] guerdon is swich paiëment, þat neuer thynke I his wages disserue. **1563** *Homilies* II. *Rogat. Wk.* II. 240 The man in his nede, woulde not relieue his want by stealth. **1599** R. GREENHAM *Short Form Catech.* 416 Thou shalt not steale. How many euils are herein forbidden? 1 First, all those outward acts are forbidden, whereby stealth is committed... all inward stealth of the heart is forbidden. **1607** SHAKS. *Timon* III. iv. 27. **1608** WILLET *Hexapla Exod.* 407 The stealing of men.. that kind of stealth. **1638** SIR T. HERBERT *Trav.* (ed. 2) 163 Safeguarded from sand and stealth, by a defensive wall. **1639** *Act* in *Arch. Maryland* (1883) I. 71 Stealth of ones self which is the unlawfull departure of a Servant out of service or out of the Colony. **1693** LUTTRELL *Brief Rel.* (1857) III. 159 This day was published their majesties proclamation for the preventing of the stealth and imbezilment of their majesties stores of war. **1781** COWPER *Expost.* 371 A despot big with pow'r obtain'd by wealth, And that obtain'd by rapine and by stealth.

¶ Contrasted with *force* or *violence*. *Obs.*

1651 HOBBES *Leviath.* II. xxvii. 157 If.. he take the food by force, or stealth, which he cannot obtaine for mony, [etc.]. **1779** JOHNSON *L.P.*, *Pope* Wks. 1787 IV. 16 Lord Petre cut off a lock of Mrs. Arabella Fermor's hair. This, whether stealth or violence, was so much resented [etc.].

†**b.** An instance of stealing; a theft. *Obs.*

1402 HOCCLEVE *Lett. Cupid* 362 And thus was mannes helthe beraft him by the fende ryght in a stelthe. **1444** *Rolls of Parlt.* V. 107/1 No such stelthe nor felony was comitted. *a* **1550** *Vox Populi Vox Dei* iii. in *Skelton's Wks.* (1843) II. 403 Vnto a comonwealthe This ys a very stealthe. **1596** SPENSER *State Irel.* Wks. (Globe) 620/1 A stealth being made by a rebell,.. the stollen goodes are convayed to some husbandman. **1613** T. CAMPION *Relat. Ld. Knowles' Entert.* C 3, [Prometheus] These heau'n borne Starres, Who by my stealth are become Sublunars. **1648** *Art. Peace Irel.* xxxii. in *Milton's Wks.* (1851) IV. 540 To hear and determin all Murders, Manslaughters, Rapes, Stealths,.. and other Offences. **1694** *Lond. Gaz.* No. 3038/3 Whereas Dermot Leary, and divers others.., have.. committed several Murders, Burglaries, Robberies, and Stealths. **1701** SEDLEY *Ant. & Cl.* IV. iv, Lovers, like misers, cannot bear the stealth Of the least trifle from their endless wealth. *a* **1704** T. BROWN *Sat. on Quack* Wks. 1730 I. 63 I'th' face of day, thou robb'st us of our health, And yet art never question'd for the stealth. **1797** SHERIDAN *Pizarro* II. i, A mother's love for her sweet babe is not a stealth from the dear father's store.

†**c.** Plagiarism. *Obs.*

a **1568** ASCHAM *Scholem.* II. (Arb.) 122 For the matter, it is whole Aristotles.. both Catulus and Crassus do oft and pleasantly lay that stelth to Antonius charge. **1627** HAKEWILL *Apol.* (1630) 29 One collected his [Virgil's] faults, another his stealths, as Donatus in his life hath observed. **1637** SUCKLING *Acc. Relig.* Fragm. Aurea (1648) 107 For all before were but little stealths from Moses works. **1653** MILTON *Hirelings* Wks. 1851 V. 367 The unskilful and immethodical teaching of thir Pastor, teaching.. at random.. as his ease or fansie, and oft-times as his stealth guides him.

†**d.** Cunning thievishness. *Obs.*

1605 SHAKS. *Lear* III. iv. 96 Hog in sloth, Foxe in stealth, Wolfe in greedinesse.

†**2.** Something stolen; something to steal; plunder. *Obs.*

1426 LYDG. *De Guil. Pilgr.* 13252 Forth with hym hys stelthe he bar. **1560** PHAER *Æneid* IX. (1562) C iij, Aye watching lyke some Wolfe, y[t].. about mens deiries houling trotts at midnight seking stealth. **1596** SPENSER *State Irel.* Wks. (Globe) 620/1 By which meanes the theeves are greatly encouraged to steale, and theyr mayntayners emboldened to receave theyr stealths. **1617** MORYSON *Itin.* II. 9 That none of the Countrey receive any stelths from Neighbour-Countreys. **1634** MILTON *Comus* 503, I came not here.. to pursue the stealth Of pilfering Woolf. **1638** MAYNE *Lucian* (1664) 344 Next morning he was apprehended with his stealths about him. **1655** FULLER *Ch. Hist.* VII. 419 More were concealed by parties not detectable, so cunningly they carried their stealths.

fig. **1567** PAINTER *Pal. Pleas.* II. 407 Ye I say, that pursue the secrete stelths of loue.

†**3.** The action of stealing or going furtively into or out of a place; the action of stealing or gliding along unperceived. *Obs.*

1590 SHAKS. *Mids. N.* III. ii. 310, I told him of your stealth vnto this wood. *c* **1600** —— *Sonn.* lxxvii, Thou by thy dyals shady stealth maist know, Times theeuish progress to eternitie. **1601** —— *Twel. N.* I. v. 316 Methinkes I feele this youths perfections With an inuisible, and subtle stealth To creepe in at mine eyes. **1614** RALEGH *Hist. World* II. xxviii. §6. 650 By this secret subterrane vault Zedechias making his stealth, recouered.. the plaines or deserts of Iericho. **1638** JUNIUS *Paint. Ancients* 281 A quiet and insensible induction, deceiving the eye with a strange stealth of change. **1788** T. WARTON *On H.M. Birth-day* 51 And many a fane he rear'd, that still sublime In massy pomp has mock'd the stealth of time.

†**b.** A stealing or coming by surprise *upon* a person. *Obs.*

1611 SPEED *Hist. Gt. Brit.* IX. xii. (1623) 698 Skulking surprises and vnder-hand stealthes. **1614** RALEGH *Hist. World* I. viii. §13. 166 So doe I thinke, that neither the Sabæi on the Red Sea, nor those toward the Persian Sea, could by any meanes execute the stealth vpon Job.

†**4.** Furtive or underhand action, an act accomplished by eluding observation or discovery. *Obs.*

1297 R. GLOUC. (Rolls) 4057 Vor hii ne mowe no3t segge þat wiþ treson oþer stalþe it were ydo. **1603** SHAKS. *Meas. for M.* I. ii. 158 The stealth of our most mutuall entertainment With Character too grosse, is writ on Iuliet. **1605** —— *Lear* I. ii. 11 Base, Base? Who in the lustie stealth of Nature, take More composition, and fierce qualitie, Then [etc.]. **1615** DANIEL *Hymen's Tri.* I. i, And hence it grew that gaue us both our fears, That made our Meeting Stealth, our Parting Tears. **1621** G. SANDYS *Ovid's Met.* I. (1626) 16 Iuno.. For her mist Husband searcheth Heauen: as one, To whom his stealths so often had beene knowne. **1668** P. M. *Charleton's Ephes. & Cimm Matrons* II. 23 No eye can.. be able to trace them in their amorous stealths. **1797** COLERIDGE *Christabel* I. 120 But we will move as if in stealth.

5. *by stealth.* †**a.** With reference to taking or appropriating: By an act of theft; secretly and without right or permission. Also, in wider sense, with reference to wrongful or forbidden acts generally. *Obs.* **b.** In modern use, the phrase has ordinarily no conscious association with *steal* vb. or sense 1 of the sb., and has the neutral sense: Secretly, clandestinely.

1390 GOWER *Conf.* I. 63 [He] hath his pourpos ofte achieved.. of worldes welthe, And takth it, as who seith, be stelthe. **1398** TREVISA *Barth. De P.R.* XVIII. lv. (1495) 814 The dranes.. vneth they ben suffryd to ete of ony, but as moche as they ete it is by stelthe. **1454** *Rolls of Parlt.* V. 274/2 Grete habundaunce of Wolles as welle by stalth as by licence is uttred into the parties beyond the See. **1480** *Cov. Leet Bk.* (1908) 459 [They] ffysshen be nyght & day the seid pole.. be staith. *c* **1530** *Crt. of Love* 1362 And who come late he pressed in by stelth. **1592** *Arden of Feversham* I. 138 And, Mosbie, thou that comes to me by stelth, Shalt [etc.]. **1611** BIBLE *2 Sam.* xix. 3 The people gate them by stealth that day into the citie, as people beeing ashamed steale away when they flee in battell. **1617** MORYSON *Itin.* III. 134 The English bring into France.. sheep skinnes, and by stealth other Hides, forbidden to be exported. **1697** DRYDEN *Virg., Georg.* IV. 352 Lurking Lizards often lodge, by Stealth, Within the Suburbs, and purloin their Wealth. **1738** POPE *Epil. Sat.* I. 136 Let humble Allen.. Do good by stealth, and blush to find it Fame. **1762–71** H. WALPOLE *Vertue's Anecd. Paint.* (1786) V. 261 He had been privately engaged to draw by stealth the portrait of old Mr. Thomas Baker. **1775** HARRIS *Philos. Arrangem.* Wks. (1841) 248 Marcus Antoninus.. still persisted in.. committing his thoughts to writing, during moments gained by stealth from the hurry of courts and campaigns. **1784** COWPER *Task* VI. 995 So life glides smoothly and by stealth away. **1849** MACAULAY *Hist. Eng.* vii. II. 220 Congregations which had hitherto met only by stealth and in darkness. **1875** JOWETT *Plato* (ed. 2) I. 135 He did enter by stealth into the common workshop of Athene and Hephaestus.

6. *Comb.* (nonce-words) as ***stealth-like*** adj., ***stealth-wise*** adv., ***stealth-won*** adj.

1800 COLERIDGE *Death Wallenstein* I. xii, What import these silent nods and gestures Which stealthwise thou exchangest with her? **1807** WORDSW. *White Doe* VII. 1650 A little while it stayed;.. And then advanced with stealth-like pace. **1893** F. THOMPSON *Poems* 3 As lovers, banished from their lady's face,.. Fondly adore Some stealth-won cast attire she wore, A kerchief, or a glove.

stealthful ('stɛlθfʊl), *a. poet.* [f. STEALTH + -FUL.] Stealthy. Hence **'stealthfully** *adv.*; †**'stealthfulness.** *Obs. rare*[−0].

c **1624** CHAPMAN *Hymn to Hermes* 378 And no such stealth-full ill Her light hath showne me. **1796** J. BIDLAKE in *New Ann. Reg.* 155 Almeria.. wip'd in haste, a stealthful tear unseen. **1822** MILMAN *Martyr of Antioch* 26 Evening darkens round my stealthful steps. **1828** WEBSTER, *Stealthfully, Stealthfulness.* *a* **1838** A. LAING in D. H. Edwards *Edzell & Glenesk* (1908) 59 Till Peathaugh, stealthfully, Hamstrung M[c]Gregor unawares.

stealthily ('stɛlθɪlɪ), *adv.* [f. STEALTHY *a.* + -LY[2].] In a stealthy manner.

1806–31 A. KNOX *Rem.* (1844) I. 59 They effected this, without doubt, stealthily, and to appearance, by the minutest alteration. **1837** W. IRVING *Capt. Bonneville* I. 261 The enemy crept stealthily along under cover of the river bank. **1848** THACKERAY *Van. Fair* xxiv, They went upstairs quietly, Mr. Bullock accompanying them stealthily on his creaking shoes. **1890** BRIDGES *Lond. Snow* Poems (1912) 265 Stealthily and perpetually settling and loosely lying.

Comb. **1856** KANE *Arctic Expl.* II. vi. 74 He appeared troubled, and had several stealthily-whispered interviews with John. **1897** F. T. BULLEN *Cruise 'Cachalot'* xxv. (1901) 333, I was watching a few stealthily-gliding barracouta sneaking about over the plainly visible bottom.

stealthy ('stɛlθɪ), *a.* [f. STEALTH + -Y.] Of movement or action: Taking place by stealth; calculated to elude observation; proceeding by imperceptible degrees; furtive. Of persons or things: Moving or acting by stealth or secretly; furtive in movement or action; stealing on by imperceptible degrees.

1605 SHAKS. *Macb.* II. i. 54 Wither'd Murder.. With his stealthy pace.. towards his designe Moues like a Ghost. **1728–46** THOMSON *Spring* 689 With stealthy wing.. Amid a neighbouring bush they silent drop. **1841** DICKENS *Barn. Rudge* lxxi, There was much stealthy going in and out. **1856** FROUDE *Hist. Eng.* II. 240 The stealthy evil crept on irresistibly. **1865** KINGSLEY *Herew.* xiii, Casting stealthy glances at the fen, to see if the mysterious mare was still there. **1876** FREEMAN *Norm. Conq.* V. xxiv. 461 A series of gradual and stealthy encroachments on the rights of the people. **1907** J. H. PATTERSON *Man-Eaters of Tsavo* xv. 169, I saw a jackal come up on its trail.. not even rustling a fallen leaf in its stealthy advance on the poor little antelope. **1910** *Solitary Summer* 76 Turning my head to watch a stealthy cat.

Comb. **1839–52** BAILEY *Festus* 320 The dashing dog, and stealthy-stepping cat.

Hence **'stealthiness.**

1837 CARLYLE *Fr. Rev.* III. I. vii, Dumouriez.. started from brief slumber at Sedan,.. with stealthiness, with promptitude, audacity. **1869** SPURGEON *Treas. Dav.* Ps. x. 9 I. 126 The cunning of the lion, and of the huntsman, as well as the stealthiness of the robber.

steam (stiːm), *sb.* Forms: 1 **stéam, stém, stíem**, 4 **stem**, 4–5 **steme**, 5–7 **steeme**, 5–8 **steem**, 6–7 **steame**, 7– **steam**. [OE. *stéam* = WFris. *steam*, Du. *stoom*:—OTeut. type **staumo-z*, of obscure origin.]

I. 1. a. A vapour or fume given out by a substance when heated or burned.

In this and following senses the word was freq. used in the pl. down to *c* 1800.

c **1000** *Sax. Leechd.* II. 284 Man pintreow bærne to gledum.. and onfo ðam steme. **1660** BOYLE *New Exp. Phys.-Mech.* xi. 80 The stifling steames of the Coals. **1668** CULPEPER & COLE *Barthol. Anat.* II. ix. 119 The steam of newly whited Walls. **1669** BEALE in *Phil. Trans.* IV. 1113 The steames of the Mercury in some hot Summer. **1704** F. FULLER *Med. Gymn.* (1705) 165 The Steam of their inflammable Parts is of Use. **1794** M[c]PHAIL *Treat. Cucumber* 92 The heat of the cucumber bed began to rise; a little air was given to it to let the steam pass off. **1845** G. MILLS *Treat. Cucumber* (ed. 2) 29 The steam which arose from the well-prepared manure of the bed. **1859** TENNYSON *Enid* 1451 And all the hall was dim with steam of flesh.

b. *spec.* An odorous exhalation or fume.

a **1000** *Panther* 45 (Gr.) Æfter þære stefne stenc ut cymeð of þam wongstede, wynsumra steam swettra & swiþra swæcca ʒehwylcum. **1589** GREENE *Menaphon* (Arb.) 87 Thy breath is like the steeme of apple pies. **1608** MIDDLETON *Five Gallants* IV. viii, A fellow of several scents and steams. **1616** B. JONSON *Devil an Ass* V. vii, Fough! what a steeme of brimstone Is here? **1644** JESSOP *Angel of Ephesus* 27, I will not cause the Reader to stop his nose at those putrid steemes which would arise if that puddle were stirred. **1667** MILTON *P.L.* XI. 442 His Offring soon propitious Fire from Heav'n Consum'd with nimble glance, and grateful steame. **1781** COWPER *Conversat.* 262 [Tobacco] Thy thirst-creating steams. **1827** T. HAMILTON *Cyril Thornton* (1845) 75 The savoury steams of roast and stew,.. pervaded the mansion. **1835** WILLIS *Pencillings* I. 61 The steams of sulphur, as we approached the summit, were all but intolerable.

fig. **1599** B. JONSON *Cynthia's Rev.* I. iii, I do neither see, nor feele, nor taste, nor savour the least steame, or fume of a reason, that should invite this foolish fastidious Nymph, so peevishly to abandon me.

†**2. a.** A vapour or exhalation produced as an 'excrement' of the body, e.g. hot breath, perspiration, the infectious effluvium of a disease. *Obs.*

c **1000** ÆLFRIC *Hom.* I. 86 Him stod stincende steam of ðam muðe. **1303** R. BRUNNE *Handl. Synne* 2526 Þe steme stode oute of hys mouþ brennand. *c* **1330** —— *Chron. Wace* (Rolls) 1818 Oft aboute ilk oþer þrew, þe stem stod vp, so þey blew. *c* **1400** *Song Roland* 836 Kene knyghtis cry and crossen helmes,.. out flow the stemes. **1592** SHAKS. *Ven. & Ad.* 63 Panting he lies, and breatheth in her face. She feedeth on the steame, as on a pray. **1670** COVEL in *Early Voy. Levant* (Hakl. Soc.) 116 These [insects] never stir out of their holes and lurking-places till the steam and perspiration of your bodyes invite them. **1722** DE FOE *Plague* (1884) 160 The Effluvia or Infectious Steams of Bodies infected. **1731** SWIFT *Strephon & Chloe* 11 No humours gross, or frowzy steams,.. Could from her taintless body flow.

†**b.** A noxious vapour generated in the digestive system; the 'fume' supposed to ascend to the brain as a result of drinking alcoholic liquor. *Obs.*

c **1000** *Sax. Leechd.* II. 226 Fleo þa mettas þa þe him dylsta & forbærnunga & stiem on Innan wyrcen. **1602** MARSTON *Antonio's Rev.* V. iii, Pieros lips reake steame of wine. **1605** *Trag. End Sir J. Fites* (1860) 12 She avoyded further perill of death, which hee in his steame of wine, had bin likely to have offered unto her.

c. Close and hot air arising from persons crowded together. *arch.*

1609 HOLLAND *Amm. Marcell.* XXIX. ii. 352 When as neither the common goales.. nor privat mens houses could now hold the number of them that were committed to ward, as being thronged and thrust close together with a hot steame among them. **1625** BACON *Ess.*, *Masques*, Some Sweet Odours, suddenly comming forth, without any drops falling, are, in such a Company, as there is Steame and Heate, Things of great Pleasure and Refreshment. **1793** T. BEDDOES *Observ. Calculus*, etc. 141 The steams abounding in [a crowded] room.. may be injurious to consumptive persons. **1850** TENNYSON *In Mem.* lxxxix. 8 The dust and din and steam of town.

†**d.** *fig. Obs.*

1602 MARSTON *Antonio's Rev.* III. v, Looke how I smoake in blood, reeking the steame Of foming vengeance. **1672** OWEN *Disc. Evang. Love* i. 19 For the most part they [the outcries on account of schism] are nothing but the steam of

Interest and Party. **1677** GILPIN *Dæmonol.* (1867) 46 Sometimes he reaps a large harvest where he had sown little, and from one temptation not only wounds the soul of him that committed it, but endeavours to diffuse the venom and poisonous steam of it to the infection of others.

†**3.** A ray or beam of light; a flame. *Obs.*

c **1300** *Havelok* 591 Of hise mouth it stod a stem, Als it were a sunnebem. *c* **1440** *Promp. Parv.* 473/2 Steem, or lowe of fyre, *flamma*.

4. An exhalation or watery vapour rising from the earth or sea.

1612 DRAYTON *Poly-olb.* vii. 104 It is your foggie steame The powerfull Sunne exhales. **1695** WOODWARD *Nat. Hist. Earth* (1702) 209 The Steams and Damps of Mines are detrimental to Health. **1748** *Anson's Voy.* II. v. 183 The equability and duration of the tropical heat contribute to impregnate the air with a multitude of steams and vapours from the soil and water. **1774** GOLDSM. *Nat. Hist.* (1776) I. 371 The assemblage of the rays darting upon the water.. will cause it to rise in a light thin steam above the surface. **1859** TENNYSON *Guinev.* 593 She saw, Wet with the mists and smitten by the lights, The Dragon of the great Pendragonship Blaze, making all the night a steam of fire. **1906** 'BARONESS ORCZY' *Son of People* xvi. (1908) 175 [The sun's] noonday rays drew a warm steam from the wet earth.

†**5.** Used as a scientific term for: Matter in the state of gas or vapour; any impalpable emanation or effluvium. *Obs.*

1662 BOYLE *Def. Doctr. Spring of Air* III. xviii. 81 Glass.. is impervious to the subtilest steams that are. **1670** BEALE in *Phil. Trans.* V. 1154 The changes of Heat and Cold, with other unknown Steames. **1684** R. WALLER *Nat. Exper.* 18 The Liquor.. will fall down.. like Dew separated from that fine steame of Air contained in the froth. *a* **1704** LOCKE *Elem. Nat. Phil.* vi. (1754) 21 Besides the springy particles of pure air, the atmosphere is made up of several steams or minute particles of several sorts, rising from the earth and the waters, and floating in the air.

6. a. The vapour into which water is converted when heated. In popular language, applied to the visible vapour which floats in the air in the form of a white cloud or mist, and which consists of minute globules or vesicles of liquid water suspended in a mixture of gaseous water and air. (Also sometimes applied to the vapour arising from other liquids when heated.) In modern scientific and technical language, applied only to water in the form of an invisible gas.

The invisible 'steam', in the modern scientific sense, is, when its temperature is lowered, converted into the white vapour called 'steam' in popular language, and this under continued cooling, becomes 'water' in the liquid form.

dry steam, in Steam-engine working, steam containing no suspended vesicles of water: opposed to *wet steam*.

c **1440** *Promp. Parv.* 473/2 Steem [*Winch. MS.* Steme] of hothe lycure, *vapor.* **1631** B. JONSON *New Inn* II. vi, We shall ..send you downe to the dresser, and the dishes... *Pru.* Commit you to the steem! *Lad.* [*Lady F.*] Or els condemn you to the bottles. *a* **1682** SIR T. BROWNE *Tracts* (1683) 113 The steam or vapour of artificial and natural baths. **1697** DAMPIER *Voy.* I. 480 They cover the mouth of the Pot with leaves, to keep in the steam, while it boils. **1712** ADDISON *Spect.* No. 403 ¶3 A Knot of Theorists, who sat in the inner Room, within the Steams of the Coffee-Pot. **1781** GIBBON *Decl. & F.* xviii. II. 85 The adulteress was suffocated by the steam of a bath, which, for that purpose, had been heated to an extraordinary degree. **1785** PRIESTLEY in *Phil. Trans.* LXXV. 305 Having transmitted steam, or the vapour of water, through a copper tube. **1815** J. SMITH *Panorama Sci. & Art* II. 505 The steam of alcohol at 174° is equal to that of water at 212°. **1839** *Civil Engin. & Arch. Jrnl.* II. 287, 7 lbs. of coal are required to convert 1 cubic foot of water at 40° into atmospheric steam. **1847** TENNYSON *Princess* Prol. 73 A dozen angry models jetted steam. **1878** HUXLEY *Physiogr.* 39 The steam, or watery vapour, when pure and uncondensed, is.. transparent. **1884** DUTTON in *4th Ann. Rep. U.S. Geol. Surv.* 110 Condensed steam floating away in the form of white vapor. **1894** *Times* 15 Aug. 12/2 A boiler which supplies wet steam is a bad boiler, because wet steam is prejudicial to the efficiency of the engine. **1895** *Model Steam Eng.* 51 The purpose of the steam-dome is to collect the steam in as dry a condition as possible.

b. The visible vesicles produced by the condensation of watery vapour, as drops forming on a surface, e.g. a mirror or window-pane.

1615 CROOKE *Body of Man* 88 When a Vessell of boyling water is couered, though the couer be hot, yet the vapour of the water turneth into a steame vppon it, and will stand in drops. **1699** tr. *H. de Blancourt's Art of Glass* 350 You must keep these [steel] Mirrours from the Moistness of the Air, and Steams.

7. a. The vapour of boiling water used, by confinement in specially contrived engines, for the generation of mechanical power. Hence, the mechanical power thus generated.

1699 *Phil. Trans.* XXI. 228 [Savery's 'fire-engine'.] Two Cocks which convey the Steam by turns, to the Vessels D. **1765** WATT in Muirhead *Invent. Watt* (1854) I. 3 Mine ought to raise water to 44 feet with the same quantity of steam that theirs does to 32. **1788** J. RUMSEY (*title*) A short Treatise on Steam, whereby is clearly shewn.. that steam may be applied to propel Boats or Vessels of any burthen. **1825** HONE *Every-day Bk.* I. 1535 *The Times*.. of Tuesday, November the 29th, 1814, was the first newspaper printed by steam. **1848** DICKENS *Dombey* xxxv, Do steam, tide, wind, and horses, all abate their speed? **1872** BUCKLE *Misc. Wks.* I. 250 By the application of steam, we have diminished space.

b. *fig.* Energy, 'go', driving power, and the like.

1826 DISRAELI *Viv. Grey* II. ii, Has not your Lordship treasure? There is your moral steam which can work the world. **1875** BLAKE-HUMFREY *Eton Boating Bk.* 60 The Etonians had not steam enough. At Hammersmith, Westminster was two lengths ahead. **1898** *Daily News* 24 Nov. 7/3 Corbett now appeared a trifle weary.. and was lacking in steam. **1900** *Westm. Gaz.* 23 Oct. 9/2 All the steam has gone out of American Railroad shares.

c. Phr. ***by steam***, (to travel) by steamer. ***under steam***, worked by steam (as opposed to *under sail*).

1829 SCOTT *Jrnl.* (1890) II. 305 To-morrow I expect Sophia and her family by steam. **1839** CARD. WISEMAN in W. Ward *Life* (1897) I. ix. 313, I shall travel.. by the mail direct to Marseilles,.. and so by steam to Civitá Vecchia. **1875** BEDFORD *Sailor's Pocket Bk.* iii. (ed. 2) 61 In the following Rules every steam ship which is under sail and not under steam, is to be considered a sailing ship.

d. In phrases descriptive of the working of a steam-engine, esp. of a locomotive; often used *fig.*; e.g. ***(at) full (half,*** etc.) ***steam***; ***with full*** or ***all one's steam on***; ***to have*** (all, much, etc.) ***steam on***; ***to get up, put on steam***; ***to blow off, shut off, turn off steam***; ***under steam, with steam up, in steam***, with the engine working or ready to start working; ***under one's own steam***; ***like steam*** (*Austral.*), furiously; ***to let off steam***: freq. *fig.*, to relieve one's pent-up energy by vigorous activity; to give vent to one's feelings, esp. harmlessly; ***to run out of steam***: see RUN *v.* 66 c.

1768 WATT in Muirhead *Invent. Watt* (1854) I. 18, I am now getting an apparatus ready for setting it [the engine] wholly in steam as before. **1824** [see SHUT *v.* 16 a]. **1831** *Rep. Sel. Comm. Steam Carriages* 20 Are you frequently obliged to let off steam? **1832–83** [see GET *v.* 80 q]. **1837** [see BLOW *v.*[1] 10]. **1837** DICKENS *Pickw.* xlviii, Get on a little faster; put a little more steam on, ma'am, pray. **1857** HUGHES *Tom Brown* II. ii, Now jumping the old ironbound tables,.. then joining in some chorus of merry voices; in fact, blowing off his steam, as we should now call it. **1860** *Merc. Marine Mag.* VII. 216 Orders were given.. to let the ship go under easy steam. **1863** *Blackw. Mag.* Feb. 249/1 This is a free country, and a few eloquent or blustering Radicals serve to 'let off the steam' of their class. **1869** H. JAMES *Let.* 16 Apr. in J. Strouse *Alice James* (1980) viii. 138, I feel an irresistible need to let off steam periodically & to confide to a sympathetic ear the impressions which the week has generated in my soul. **1870** *Remin. Amer.* 203 Their steam fire-engines.. are always kept in readiness with steam up and the horses harnessed. **1873** *Routledge's Young Gentlem. Mag.* June 392/2 The *Forward* was under steam, ready to seize the first opening to make her exit. **1878** KINGSTON *Three Admirals* xviii. 416 Full steam was put on. *Ibid.* 417 The engineer having thoughtfully turned off the steam to prevent the boilers from exploding. **1881** M. REYNOLDS *Engine-driving Life* 112 Of course his engine is in steam. All is done for him. **1887** F. FRANCIS Jun. *Saddle & Mocassin* 107 'And he [the bull] came for you?' 'When he'd got up steam he did.' **1894** ASTLEY *50 Years Life* I. 82, I naturally went to grass through having too much steam on to be able to pull up in time. **1896** KIPLING *Seven Seas, Three Sealers* ad fin., Half-steam ahead by guess and lead, for the sun is mostly veiled. **1899** *Allbutt's Syst. Med.* VIII. 147 A result of some previous shutting off of nervous steam. **1905** H. LAWSON *Coll. Verse* (1968) II. 4 We was draftin' 'em out for the homeward track and sharin' 'em round like steam. **1912** CONRAD in *English Rev.* XI. 311 We are not allowed to bring them in under their own steam. **1916** H. J. LASKI in *Holmes-Laski Lett.* (1953) I. 25, I intend to write you a weekly letter to Washington—for I must let off steam somewhere. **1949** J. SYMONS *Bland Beginnings* 142 'Would you be kind enough to.. see Miss Cleverly home.' 'That's not necessary... I can move under my own steam.' **1976** J. I. M. STEWART *Young Pattullo* iii. 72 It's just a dining club letting off steam. **1979** B. HARDY *World owes Me Nothing* 102, I hammered at the door like steam and over he came and opened it.

e. *transf.* Cheap wine laced with methylated spirits; methylated spirits as an intoxicant. *Austral.* and *N.Z. slang.*

1941 BAKER *Dict. Austral. Slang* 71 *Steam*, cheap wine, esp. laced with methylated spirits. **1963** A. LUBBOCK *Austral. Roundabout* 59 To my regret, I never got a chance to sample either 'plonk', or 'steam'! **1966** J. K. BAXTER *Pig Island Lett.* 36 I'd give old Rose the go-by For a bottle of steam tonight.

8. a. Short for *steam-coal* (see 17).

1897 *Daily News* 25 Jan. 9/3 Best qualities steam are now up to 11s 3d per ton. **1903** *Times* 1 Dec. 3/5 Steams remain dull and generally slow of sale, owing to the poor trade prevailing among steam users generally.

b. Short for *steam radio*, sense 17 below.

1959 C. MACINNES *Absolute Beginners* 112, I heard one of your arias on the steam, last evening. **1960** *Spectator* 15 July 103 John Arlott over on steam is still the best of the commentators. **1973** G. TALBOT *Ten Seconds from Now* (1974) v. 83 Frank Gillard.. crowned his Corporation career by becoming Managing Director of Radio, our 'Head of Steam'.

9. [f. STEAM *v.*] A trip by steamer. *colloq.*

1854 KINGSLEY in *Life* (1877) I. 419 Had a charming steam across the Firth of Forth. **1905** *Daily Chron.* 16 Sept. 4/4 He saw before him a few hours' steam to Caen.

10. [f. STEAM *v.*] A dish cooked by steaming. *colloq.*

1900 *Soc. Life Brit. Army* 98 Apart from soup, the cooking arrangements will only allow of Tommy being given his choice between a bake and a steam. A steam resembles what we have been taught to call Irish stew.

II. *attrib.* and *Comb.*

11. simple *attrib.* = of or pertaining to steam; consisting of steam.

1831 *Rep. Sel. Comm. Steam Carriages* 25 The comparative expense between Horse and Steam Power for drawing Carriages on common roads. **1838** TREDGOLD *Steam Eng.* 416 The force of the draught produced by the steam-blast is so great that cinders are drawn through the tubes. **1869** E. A. PARKES *Pract. Hygiene* (ed. 3) 145 The moving agent here is the force of the steam-jet. **1879** GEO. ELIOT *Theo. Such* II. 49 The white steam-pennon flies along it. **1881** JUDD *Volcanoes* 23 The roaring of the steam-jets may be heard for many miles around. **1897** GEIKIE *Anc. Volcanoes Gt. Brit.* I. 16 The steam-cavities of lavas.

12. With reference to heating, cooking, or washing by steam, and in the names of implements and apparatus used in these processes, as ***steam-bakery, -bath, -box, -chamber, -chest, -coil, -kiln, -kitchen, -laundry, -oven, -pan, -pipe, †-pot, radiator, -table, -tank, -tube***, etc.

1725 *Bradley's Family Dict.* s.v. *Gooseberry-wine*, When it is thoroughly cold it is put into a Steam-Pot. **1794** J. B. S. MORRITT *Let.* 24 June (1914) ii. 47 After a violent steam bath, they would run out and roll in the snow. **1797** *Encycl. Brit.* (ed. 3) XVII. 772/2 Steam-Kitchen. **1827** FARADAY *Chem. Manip.* iv. (1842) 134 The figure represents an arrangement in which a saucepan is converted into a temporary steam chamber. **1828** DUPPA *Trav. Italy*, etc. 142 The steam-baths of Dædalus.. consist of several sudorific grottos. **1832** *Boston* (Lincs.) *Herald* 20 Nov. 4/3 A new patent steam-oven for baking bread. **1856** KANE *Arct. Expl.* I. xxxi. 421 We have passed wooden steam-tubes through the deck-house to carry off the vapors of our cooking-stove. **1857** MILLER *Elem. Chem., Org.* 672 Heat, furnished by steam-pipes. **1862** *Catal. Internat. Exhib.* II. XXXI. 7 Steam Table for dishing up. *Ibid.* 8 Steam Kettles of copper or block tin, for boiling meat, vegetables, puddings, &c. **1868** *Rep. U.S. Commissioner Agric.* (1869) 427 The food is cooked in a large steam-box. **1879** *Bradstreet's* 22 Nov. 2/1 In close rooms close stoves are better than steam radiators. **1897** HOWELLS *Landlord at Lion's Head* 142 The reeking steam-table, with its great tanks of soup and vegetables. **1903** ADE *In Babel* 29 For ten years it had braced itself against the onsweeping rush of big machine-shops and steam-bakeries. **1962** A. LURIE *Love & Friendship* xii. 228 That.. asthma kind of like a steam radiator. **1977** C. MCCULLOUGH *Thorn Birds* xi. 251 Hot nights in Gilly were bearable compared to this steam bath.

13. In the names of the various contrivances for containing, conveying, or regulating the steam in a steam-engine, as ***steam-box, -case, -chamber, -chest, -cock, †-course, -cylinder, -dome, -gauge, -pipe, -port, -stack, trap, -valve, -way***, etc.

1765 WATT in Muirhead *Invent. Watt* (1854) I. 4 The moment the steam-cock was opened, the piston descended with rapidity. **1769** *Ibid.* 53 To-day I stopped the neck of the steam-pipe where it enters the cylinder. *Ibid.* 73 The size of the steam-valve is six square inches. **1797** J. CURR *Coal Viewer* 41 A steam chest [in a fire-engine] upon a good construction, (*a*) being the steam valve. **1825** J. NICHOLSON *Oper. Mech.* 181 C, the steam-gauge. *Ibid.* 207 Fans.. opening and closing the steam-course. **1838** *Civil Engin. & Arch. Jrnl.* I. 139/2 The jacket of an 80-inch steam cylinder. **1839** R. S. ROBINSON *Naut. Steam Eng.* 51 Sliding the valve up or down will permit this steam to enter the cylinder, either by the upper or lower steam port. **1873** G. E. WEBSTER *Steam Eng. & Steam* I. 61 The Steam Dome serves the purpose of drying the steam. **1875** KNIGHT *Dict. Mech.*, *Steam-way*, a passage leading from the steam-port of a valve to the cylinder. **1877** Steam trap [see TRAP *sb.*[1] 8 b]. **1935** JOYCE *Let.* 28 Aug. (1957) 381, I would also like a pleasure yacht with a steamstack. **1955** *Times* 12 July 1/6 Before ordering any steam trap ask for its expectation of life. It is no use saving on steam equipment to pay it out later servicing traps.

14. In the names of implements, machines, processes, etc. operated by steam or by a steam-engine, as ***steam-crane, dredge, dredger, drill, -dryer, elevator, †-gun, -hammer, -mill, -milling, -plough, -ploughing, press, -pump, shovel*** (hence ***-shovelful***), ***-thresher, -threshing, trowel, -trumpet, -whim, -winch***, etc.

1801 *Phil. Trans.* XCI. 160 It.. has now four fire-engines and two steam-whims on it. **1804** *Nicholson's Jrnl.* VII. 161 Description of a new Steam Digester for Philosophic Researches. **1812** *Ann. Reg., Chron.* 79 They entered into a solemn obligation to destroy steam-looms, [etc.]. **1815** D. DRAKE *Nat. & Statist. View Cincinnati* iii. 137 The most capacious.. building in this place is the Steam Mill. **1824** *Reg. Arts & Sci.* II. 105 Perkins's 'Steam Gun'. **1843** NASMYTH in *Civil Engin. & Arch. Jrnl.* VI. 41/2 With a view to relieve all these defects, I have contrived my direct action steam hammer. **1844** DICKENS *Martin Chuz.* xi, A greater number.. than the steam-gun can discharge balls in a minute. **1847** *Mech. Mag.* 30 Jan. 98 Mr. Osborn's patent system of steam ploughing. **1861** *Mitchell's Maritime Reg.* 1651/3 The launch of the Ancona, a very fine steam dredger, of 300 tons, recently took place at Southampton. **1865** RUSKIN *Sesame* i. 35 The Word of God.. cannot be.. sown on any wayside by help either of steam plough or steam press. **1873** H. JAMES *Let.* 25 Apr. (1974) I. v. 373 It was once a goodly old palace and though pitifully inconvenient as a hotel, is charminger to stay in than if it had a steam elevator. **1877** *Encycl. Brit.* VII. 464/1 The construction of large river steam dredges is now carried on by many engineering firms. **1879** R. J. BURDETTE *Hawk-Eyes* 25 The depot policeman looked in to say to him that if he was tired out, he would send in a section hand or the steam shovel to give him a spell. **1880** *Harper's Mag.* Aug. 344/2 The grist from it [*sc.* the tide mill] is said to be of a better quality than from the steam-mills, as being less heated in the process. **1884** *Leisure Hour* Sept. 533/2 With one blow from a steam-riveter.. they are securely fixed. **1889** 'F. ANSTEY' *Pariah* VI. i, They're putting up swings and a steam-circus and tents. **1891** HARDY *Tess* xlviii, I have told the farmer that he has no right to employ women at steam-threshing. **1891** *Argus* (Melbourne) 7 Nov. 13/4 Occasionally.. a British India liner rouses the echoes with the hoarse call of its steam siren. **1898** 'MERRIMAN' *Roden's Corner* v. 45 Presently the jerk and clink of the steam-winch told that the anchor was being got home. **1904** *Jrnl. Inst. Electr. Engin.* XXXIII. 965 Steam-dryers are fitted in the flues of two of the boilers.

1906 T. ROOSEVELT *Let.* 20 Nov. (1919) 182 There the huge steam-shovels are hard at it; scooping huge masses of rock and gravel and dirt. **1906** W. DE MORGAN *Joseph Vance* xli. 367 He told how she and he were awakened by the sudden stoppage of the screw, followed by the roar of the steam-trumpet. **1907** J. H. PATTERSON *Man-Eaters of Tsavo* xvii. 187 My heart was thumping like a steam hammer. **1925** L. R. HARRIS in *Messenger* VII. 387/1 A so-called 'steam-drill'..guaranteed to drill a hole faster than any ten men could drill one in the old way with sledge hammer and steel. **1928** *Observer* 15 Apr. 5/4 The people in the restaurants shovel food into their mouths as the steam-trowel takes up its load of earth. **1937** *Discovery* Dec. 362/2 All advances in technique such as the steam press and the linotype, had been developed by the news-printer and later used by the book-printer. **1966** T. PYNCHON *Crying of Lot 49* iii. 65 A wildcat transistor outfit that..was underselling even the Japanese and hauling in loot by the steamshovelful. **1972** J. MOSEDALE *Football* vii. 95 After a trip through the steam presses, caps and uniforms were either too large or too small. **1978** J. IRVING *World according to Garp* iv. 79 His mouth still reminded Garp of a steam shovel's power.

15. With reference to locomotion by steam-power, and in names of vehicles and vessels propelled by steam, as ***steam barge, bus, -ferry, ferry-boat, -flat, -frigate, hopper*** (HOPPER[1] 6), ***-launch, lawn-mower, locomotion, locomotive, lorry, -navigation, -navy, -omnibus, -packet, railway, -ram, schooner, -train, -tram, -trawler, -trawling, -whaler, -yacht***, etc. See also *steam-car, -carriage, -tug*, etc. in 17, and the main-words STEAM-BOAT, etc.

1812 in *Mech. Mag.* (1847) XLVI. 21/1 Steam passage boat, The Comet, Between Glasgow, Greenock, and Helensburgh. **1814** *Niles' Wkly. Reg.* 128/2 The steam frigate Fulton the First was launched at New York October 31. **1819** [*title*] The Thanet Itinerary, or Steam-Yacht Companion. **1819** *N.Y. Even. Post* 4 Jan. 2/5 Steam sch[oone]r Ramapo, Reid, New Orleans. **1821** CROKER *Diary* 29 Aug., Sailed in the steampacket, the wind quite against us. **1831** *Jrnls. Ho. Comm.* LXXXVI. 827/2 The frequent calamities by Steam Navigation. **1834** J. B. PURCELL *Jrnl.* 21 Mar. in *Catholic Hist. Rev.* (1919) V. 253 Mr. Mtgomery an hour & ½ in crossing the River in Steam-ferry boat. **1842** J. MCDONOUGH *Papers* (1898) 65 The steam ferry which runs from one side of the river to the other lands a short distance below my house. **1849** [EMILY C. AGNEW] *Rome & the Abbey* v. 47 They entered the steam-train for Bruges. **1849** *Jrnls. Ho. Comm.* CIV. 87/2 The practicability of providing, by means of the Commerical Steam Marine of the Country, a reserve Steam Navy, available for the National Defence when required. **1860** *Ann. Reg.* 202 Our government were urged to adopt the scheme of steam-rams. **1866** *Mitchell's Maritime Reg.* 18 Aug. 1033/3 Messrs. C. and W. Earle launched from their yard a steam barge [named *Lion*] the first of its class built in Hull. **1869** *Bradshaw's Railway Man.* XXI. 34 A steam ferry across the river Severn. **1872** F. TREVITHICK *Life Richard Trevithick* II. xxi. 207 Cast-iron wheels were ordered with a view to steam locomotion in the Cordilleras. *Ibid.* xvii. 26 The high-pressure steam-puffer..moved.. towards the broken mass..and..changing its powers from steam-crane to steam-locomotive, conveyed it to the port. **1877** *Encycl. Brit.* VII. 464/2 The steam hoppers employed to receive and remove the dredgings carry about 500 tons of excavations. **1878** C. SCHREIBER *Jrnl.* 30 June (1911) II. 155 The Embassy steam launch met us. **1879** *Encycl. Brit.* (ed. 9) IX. 250/2 Steam trawling. **1884** J. HATTON in *Harper's Mag.* Feb. 344/2 The steam-launch is the snob of the Thames. **1890** G. MEREDITH *Let.* 14 Apr. (1970) II. 997, I am promised a steam-yacht to take me up at Oban. **1902** H. C. MOORE *Omnibuses & Cabs* I. iv. 38 The first real steam omnibuses, the 'Era' and 'Autopsy', were invented by Walter Hancock, of Stratford, and placed on the London roads in 1833. **1892** *Speaker* 3 Sept. 289/2 The high road, with its shrieking steam-tram. **1915** *Naut. Gaz.* 31 Mar. 4/1 The Panama Canal has brought us the steam schooner and other Pacific curiosities. **1916** *Law Rep. I King's Bench* 148 The defendants, who were brewers, used a Steam lorry weighing five tons, for the purpose of delivering beer from their premises to various public-houses served by them. **1923** *Blackw. Mag.* Nov. 681/1 In the harbour..there were lying odd craft... The one romance of life for these steam-hoppers..had been quenched. **1928** J. MASON *Before Mast in Sailing Ships* 174 He was picked up by a steam barge which happened to be passing. **1933** V. SOMMERFIELD *London's Buses* 5 (*caption*) Three of Hancock's Steam Buses, 1832 to 1836. **1946** G. FOREMAN *Last Trek of Indians* 116 A steam ferryboat was in service. **1946** NOBLE & JUNNER *Vital to Life of Nation* vi. 88 Sumner..began experimenting in the design of a steam wagon in 1889, a year or two later producing a steam lawn mower. *Ibid.* 96 (*caption*) A London steam omnibus of 1902. **1958** *Listener* 11 Sept. 379/2 He was knocked down and killed by a steam lorry. **1965** D. ARUNDELL *Sadler's Wells* xi. 144 Mrs. Warner and Phelps were shown arriving..in a first-class steam-railway carriage. **1970** F. MCKENNA *Gloss. Railwaymen's Talk* 1 Most steam locomotive depots in England are embedded in the older parts of our towns and cities. **1971** *Sat. Rev.* (U.S.) 6 Nov. 86/3 The purpose of the California steam-bus project is to demostrate how effectively city buses can operate at low levels of exhaust emission. **1977** D. JACK *Leyland Bus* i. 11 The back-bone of the business was production of steam lawn-mowers selling with 30-inch roller at £85 each. **1977** H. FAST *Immigrants* I. 72, I got two steam schooners, wooden ships, six hundred tons each. **1980** *Times* 25 June 4/2 The inaugural voyage of the National Trust's restored 1859 steam yacht the Gondola took place on Coniston Water yesterday.

16. Instrumental, with ppl. adjs., as ***steam-bent, -driven, -going, -hauled, -heated, -operated, -ridden*** (fig.), ***-set, -wrought***; ***steam-like*** adj. Also with vbl. sbs., as ***steam-bending, cleaning, -heating***; and vbs., as ***steam-bend, -clean*** (trans.).

1835 URE *Philos. Manuf.* 381 Attendants on steam-going looms. **1845** S. JUDD *Margaret* I. xvii, A steam-like vapour arose from the frozen river. **1852** HOSKYNS *Talpa* 183 A steam-driven cultivator can be brought to bear. **1868** JOYNSON *Metals* 54 A steam-wrought hammer. *a* **1884** KNIGHT *Dict. Mech.* Suppl. 861/1 In Campbell & Pryor's method of steam heating for dwellings, the steam boiler and radiators are inclosed in a heating room in the cellar. **1885** G. ALLEN *Babylon* xiii, This steam-ridden nineteenth century. **1890** *Harper's Mag.* Sept. 576/1 The Kents lived in a steam-heated flat. **1901** *Scotsman* 4 Sept. 7/8 Instead of a steam-driven train every two hours they might have an electrically-driven train every half-hour. **1917** S. GRAHAM *Priest of Ideal* iv. 53 This mansion, with its good roof and closed windows and doors, and probably steam-heating to keep out the damp. **1934** *Discovery* Nov. 314/1 In 1934 the German railways made some striking accelerations in the schedules of their steam-hauled expresses. **1936** *Ibid.* Nov. 357/1 Accelerations of steam-operated trains in Great Britain continues. **1946** *Nature* 5 Oct. 474/1 This at once prompted Rudall to examine the effect of 50 per cent urea on steam-set β-keratin. **1949** *Sun* (Baltimore) 14 Dec. 5/2 Already, automobile 'laundries' and firms that steam-clean buildings have been told to cease operation. **1956** *Handbk. Hardwoods* (Forest Prod. Res. Lab.) 2 Classification of timbers according to their steam-bending properties is.. based mainly on the minimum bending radius of sound, clear specimens 1 in. thick at a moisture content of about 25 per cent. **1956** *Amer. Speech* XXXI. 86 Advertisement of Adelaide Steam Cleaning Service. **1962** J. T. MARSH *Self-Smoothing Fabrics* ix. 122 It is not necessary to employ a special chamber for curing, but only the usual steam-heated cylinders or a stenter. *Ibid.* ii. 9 The steam-set fabric has a pleasant handle, and good crease recovery. **1966** A. W. LEWIS *Gloss. Woodworking Terms* 106 *Oak, Japanese*..easier to work than European oak. Steam-bends excellently. **1973** *Times* 4 Oct. 24/5 The chair is demountable and consists of eight wooden staves..steam-bent into a soft, flowing outline. **1977** *Modern Railways* Dec. 493/3 Steam-hauled excursions would be operated over this short length. **1978** *Detroit Free Press* 2 Apr. 2F/4 The natives claim 'the diggers', which is even more impolite than calling them Aussies, come to this spectacular thermal display to get their suits steam-cleaned for free.

b. Objective, as ***steam-raising***.

1923 *Engineering* 26 Jan. 101/2 The boilers, furnaces.. economisers, coal bunkers and other details of the steam-raising equipment are carried by the steel framework of the building. **1979** *Improved Energy Efficiency* (Shell Internat. Petroleum Co.) 5 Substantial savings are possible in steam-raising.

17. Special comb.: **steam age**, the era when trains were drawn by steam locomotives; also, *attrib.* or as *adj.*, belonging to this era; *fig.* out-of-date; **steam beer**, a Californian effervescent beer; **steam-boiler**, a vessel in which water is heated to generate steam, esp. for working a steam-engine (BOILER *sb.* 2 b); **steam-bomb** = *candle-bomb* (CANDLE *sb.* 7); **steam calliope** *U.S.* = *steam organ*; **steam-car**, a car driven or drawn by steam, e.g. a motor-car worked by steam instead of petrol; *U.S.* a railway-carriage; †**steam-carriage**, a carriage driven or drawn by steam (*a*) on a railroad or tramway, (*b*) on common roads; †**steam-chaise**, a chaise driven by steam; †**steam-coach** = *steam-carriage*; **steam-coal**, coal suitable for heating water in steam-boilers; **steam-colour** *Calico-printing*, a colour developed and fixed in the cloth by steaming; **steam cracking**, the thermal cracking of petroleum using steam as an inert diluent which reduces polymerization and increases the yield of olefins; hence **steam-cracked** *a.*; **steam cracker**, an installation for this process; **steam curing**, the curing or hardening of a material by treatment with steam; hence **steam-cure** *v. trans.*; **steam-cured** *ppl. a.*; **steam distillation** *Physical Chem.*, distillation of a liquid in a current of steam, used esp. to purify at temperatures below their normal boiling points liquids that are not very volatile and are immiscible with water; hence (as a back-formation) **steam-distil** *v. trans.* and *intr.*; †**steam-doctor**, one who treats diseases by vapour-baths; **steamfitter**, one who installs the pipes of a steam-heating system; a steam-heating engineer; **steam fly**, the small brown cockroach, *Blattella germanica*, commonly found in kitchens and bathrooms; **steam heat**, heat produced by steam; now *spec.* (the heat produced by) a steam-generating central heating system, used in passenger trains and buildings; hence ***steam heater, heating***; †**steam-horse**, a kind of traction-engine; **steam-iron**, an electric iron containing water which is heated and emitted as steam from its flat surface to assist in the pressing of clothes; **steam-jacket**, a jacket or casing filled with steam in order to preserve the heat of the vessel round which it is placed; hence **steam-jacketed** *pa. pple.* and *adj.*, **steam-jacketing** *vbl. sb.*; †**steam-kettle**, a kettle used in sick-rooms to create a moist warm atmosphere (*obs.*); **steam line**, a line in a phase diagram representing the conditions of temperature and pressure at which water and water vapour are in equilibrium in the absence of ice; **steam-navvy**, a machine for digging or excavating by steam; **steam nigger** *U.S.* the long cylinder with piston and rod by which the log is forced up to the saw in a sawing mill; **steam-organ** = CALLIOPE; **steam point**, (*a*) a temperature at which liquid water and water vapour are in equilibrium; *spec.* the boiling point of water under standard atmospheric pressure; (*b*) *N. Amer.*, a metal pipe which is driven into frozen earth and down which steam can be passed in order to thaw the ground for mining; **steam radio**, colloq. name for sound radio, considered outmoded by television; hence, a radio receiver; **steam-raiser**, a person employed in an engine shed to light the fires of locomotives and raise steam; **steam-road**, a road prepared for steam-traction; *U.S.* a railroad; **steam-room**, (*a*) *steam-space* below; (*b*) *U.S.*, a vapour bath; **steam-space**, the space above the water-level in a steam-boiler; **steam table** *U.S.*, a table in a cafeteria, etc., slotted to hold containers of cooked food kept hot by steam circulating beneath them; **steam-tight** *a.*, tight enough to resist the ingress or egress of steam; also quasi-*adv.*; **steam-tug**, a steam-boat specially constructed for towing vessels; †applied jocularly to a railway-engine; **steam turbine**: see TURBINE 1 b; †**steam-wagon**, a wagon drawn by steam on a railway or on a common road; †**steam-wheel**, the rotary steam-engine; also *fig.*

1941 AUDEN *New Year Letter* III. 66 The genius of the loud *Steam Age. **1961** *Spectator* 4 Aug. 181 The jet-age author gets the same sort of romance out of beaten-up old Dakotas..as steam-age Robert Louis Stevenson did from a schooner. **1978** W. GARNER *Möbius Trip* (1979) I. i. 34 Suppose you're..a bullion dealer. You're not happy with your present security. It's a little bit steam age. **1898** *Western Brewer* XXVIII. 278/1 *Steam beer..is bottom fermenting... The steam beer mash is made according to the English downward mashing method. **1941** *American Neptune* Oct. 402 Claus Spreckels is the reputed inventor of the great San Francisco speciality, steam beer. **1959** *San Francisco Chron.* 28 June 1 There won't be a drop of steam beer in Northern California after a few more days. **1974** W. R. HUNT *North of 53°* xv. 102 Many saloons served the 'choicest goods' and steam beer at two bits a glass. **1805** R. W. DICKSON *Pract. Agric.* I. 66 *Steam-Boilers [for boiling meat]. **1815** *Ann. Reg., Chron.* 91 A new steam boiler, worked by what is called a pressure engine. **1847** *Mech. Mag.* 2 Jan. 23/2 Dr. Ritterbrandt's Process for Preventing the Incrustation of Steam-boilers. **1895** *Model Steam Eng.* 14 Candle or *Steam Bombs. **1868** *Daily Territorial Enterprise* (Virginia City, Nevada) 29 Aug. 3/1 Even a *steam calliope would not cause our firm nerves to tremble as vigorously as this worst of all combinations of unsweet tones. **1936** J. DOS PASSOS *Big Money* 164 The clanking roar of the rollercoaster and the steam-calliope. **1976** *St. Louis Post-Dispatch* 16 Sept. 1/2 A steam calliope is the ransom for the return of Nipper. **1833** *Amer. Rail Road Jrnl.* II. 225/2 The *Steam Car accomplished the distance. **1875** KNIGHT *Dict. Mech., Steam-car*, a car drawn by steam-power. **1877** *Rep. Sel. Comm. Tramways* 105 Steam cars might be very safely used, perhaps in Whitechapel. **1886** WINCHELL *Geol. Talks* 11 There, in the distance, flies the train of steam-cars. **1888** BRYCE *Amer. Commw.* IV. lxxxi. III. 69 When you meet them in the steam cars (*i.e.* on a railway journey). **1900** [see PETROL 3]. **1903** J. FOX *Little Shepherd of Kingdom Come* v. 65 'Steam cars!' they cried. **1962** E. LUCIA *Klondike Kate* 7 They clambered aboard..the steam cars. **1969** *Listener* 3 July 31/3 Mr Donald Healey, developer of Austin-Healey sports cars, is rumoured to be building..a 140 m.p.h. steam car... The current spate of steam-car development projects. **1788** in *Rep. U.S. Comm. Patents 1849* (1850) 581 If any person..shall make..any elevator, hopper-boy, or any *steam-carriage..without the consent of the said Oliver Evans. **1824** T. G. CUMMING (*title*) Illustrations of the origin and progress of Rail and Tram Roads, and Steam Carriages, or locomotive Engines. **1831** *Rep. Sel. Comm. Steam Carriages* 17 Are you [Mr. G. Gurney] the proprietor of a Steam Carriage used on public roads? **1844** *Queen's Regul. Army* 211 Officers thus circumstanced are likewise to proceed by Steam-Carriages upon Railroads. **1769** DR. SMALL in Muirhead *Invent. Watt* (1854) I. 52 A linen-draper at London, one Moore, has taken out a patent for moving wheel-carriages by steam... However, if you will come hither soon, I will..buy a *steam-chaise of you and not of Moore. **1825** J. NICHOLSON *Oper. Mech.* 661 A *steam-coach for the conveyance of passengers [on a railroad]. **1828** *Sporting Mag.* XXI. 267, I hear it is intended in good earnest to start a steam-coach from London to Southampton. **1834** L. RITCHIE *Wand. by Seine* 177 We saw a steam-coach which had stopped at the door of the public house. **1850** ANSTED *Elem. Geol., Min.* etc. 414 There is a third..condition of coal now known as '*steam-coal', and admirably adapted for the use of the steam-navy. **1883** GRESLEY *Gloss. Coal-mining* 238 The finest steam coals of South Wales are towards Hirwain, and almost smokeless. **1844** *E. A. Parnell's Appl. Chem.* I. 368 *Steam colours. **1962** MURPHREE & CIPRIOS in *Mod. Petroleum Technol.* (ed. 3) ix. 318 The octane number of this *steam-cracked naphtha ranges from about 80 to 100 research method (unleaded). **1968** *Economist* 2 Nov. 73/1 When finished, the plant will include a new *steam cracker, with a production capacity of 340,000 tons a year of ethylene, 200,000 tons of propylene, [etc.]. **1959** *Petroleum Times* 25 Sept. 602/1 No. 3 olefine plant is..based on the *steam cracking process. **1962** MURPHREE & CIPRIOS in *Mod. Petroleum Technol.* (ed. 3) ix. 318 Although the primary purpose of steam cracking is the production of light hydrocarbons, the process also produces material in the gasoline boiling range. **1977** *Shell in Base Chemicals* (Shell Internat. Petroleum Co.) 4 Benzene, toluene and mixed xylenes coming from oil are extracted in special plants from reformate and pyrolysis gasoline, formed when lower olefins are manufactured by the steam-cracking of liquid feedstocks. **1910** *Cement Era* VIII. 169/1 Blocks of 1 part cement to 8 parts sand and [*sic*] *steam cured at 80 pounds pressure showed a crusting strength of 2,100 pounds per square inch. **1962** J. T. MARSH *Self-Smoothing Fabrics* xi. 177 It sometimes happens that, with cotton goods which have been steam-cured, the crease recovery is very slightly below that obtained in an atmosphere free from steam. **1909** *Chem. Abstr.* III. 1210 *Steam-cured blocks may be made all winter. **1962** J. T. MARSH *Self-Smoothing Fabrics* xi. 176 It was possible to show a linear relation between the improvement in resistance to abrasion of steam-cured fabrics over dry-cured fabrics and the amount of steam present. **1907** *Engin. News* 5 Sept. 249/1 (*heading*) Effect of *steam curing on the crushing strength of concrete. **1921** HATT & VOSS *Concrete Work* I. viii. 181 Steam curing is accomplished in curing tunnels with a roof of such a shape that it will drain the condensed moisture to the sides of the tunnel. **1967** M. CHANDLER *Ceramics in Mod. World* iv. 128 The whole assembly is..put into a steam-curing cabinet. **1923** W. M. CUMMING et. al. *Systematic Org. Chem.* ii. 24 When the liquid to be *steam-distilled is lighter than water, the small glass tube E is extended to the bottom of the receiver. **1964** *Oceanogr. & Marine Biol.* II. 152 The compound is reduced to trimethylamine with $TiCl_3$, which is then steam-distilled into an excess of standardized acid. **1974** ROSSER & WILLIAMS *Mod. Org. Chem. for 'A' Level* xiii. 253 If care is not taken to dry organic liquids thoroughly, the water/liquid mixture will often steam-distil over at a temperature lower than the actual boiling point of the pure liquid. **1904** *Analyst* XXIX. 385 (*heading*) Laboratory apparatus for *steam distillation. **1954** *Thorpe's Dict. Appl. Chem.* (ed. 4) XI. 85/2 The chief advantage offered by steam distillation is that a substance of fairly low volatility can be separated from non-volatile impurities at a temperature much below its normal boiling-point. **1972** P. R. S. MURRAY *Princ. Org. Chem.* ix. 58 Steam distillation is most effective when one of the components to be separated..has a high molecular weight. **1830** *Cincinnati Chron.* 6 Feb. 2/3 The Mayor was induced ..to issue his warrant for the apprehension of a black man calling himself Caesar Gimsoun, and practising in this city as a *'steam doctor.* **1855** DUNGLISON *Med. Lex.*, *Steam-doctor*, a term applied to one who treats all or most diseases by steam. **1860** [see THOMSONIAN 1]. **1906** *Daily Colonist* (Victoria, B.C.) 12 Jan. 7/7 (Advt.), To plumbers, *steam fitters etc. We have just received two carloads of iron pipes in all sizes. **1977** J. CROSBY *Company of Friends* xvii. 114 They both laughed...talking about the problems of the trade like steamfitters discussing occupational hazards. **1933** M. LOWRY *Ultramarine* iv. 184 'You shuffle them—' '—King of the *steam-flies, eh—'. **1944** *Jrnl. R. Army Med. Corps* LXXXIII. 188 The steam fly or German cockroach. **1962** *New Scientist* 11 Oct. 75/1 The German cockroach, commonly referred to as 'the steam fly', is dark brown to tan in colour and is also very widely distributed. **1822–7** GOOD *Study Med.* (1829) II. 594 The extract of hemlock or of hyoscyamus, prepared in a *steam-heat. **1904** *Railway Mag.* XIV. 169/2 Since the general introduction of steam-heat.. it appears to be an easy matter for the guard to simply turn a valve to supply sufficient steam to heat the cars comfortably. **1941** J. MASEFIELD *In Mill* 36 The winter steam-heat made it impossible to wear a coat while at work. **1974** *Times* 1 Apr. 14/5 Hugh Lawson, deputy city engineer of Nottingham, gave a speedy talk on his city's steam-heat system. *a* **1884** KNIGHT *Dict. Mech.* Suppl. 861/1 **Steam Heater*,..a low pressure *steam-heating apparatus. **1967** G. F. FIENNES *I tried to run Railway* ii. 7 The second [mistake was] to report myself for pulling off the steam-heater pipe. **1815** *Specif. De Baader's Patent* No. 3959. 7 Those complicated..machines called locomotive engines or *steam horses. **1855** *Pract. Mechanics' Jrnl.* Sept. 139 Mr. Boydell's 'steam horse,' or 'traction engine,' was put upon the brake in order to test its power. **1951** *Good Housek. Home Encycl.* 154/2 Electronic *steam irons are now available, but ..are not always so effective as they might appear. **1962** *Which?* Sept. 270/1 If you want to avoid using a damp cloth or damping the clothes, then your choice may well be a steam iron. **1972** *Guardian* 30 Aug. 9/5 The opening for filling steam irons with distilled water is usually mingy, and the thing overflows. **1838** *Civil Engin. & Arch. Jrnl.* I. 139/2 The best engines in Cornwall have the *steam jackets supplied from a pipe communicating directly with the boiler. **1883** R. HALDANE *Workshop Rec.* Ser. II. 35/1 Wrought-iron cylinders..provided with a steam-jacket to control their temperatures. **1876** *S. Kens. Mus. Catalog.* No. 2152, The cylinders of the engines are *steam jacketed. **1904** *Windsor Mag.* Jan. 275/1 Six steam-jacketed boilers. **1870** *Jrnl. Franklin Inst.* LXXXIX. 21 In a paper upon *steam jacketting. **1890** F. TAYLOR *Man. Pract. Med.* (1891) 356 In the intervals, the largyngitis is to be treated by a moist warm atmosphere (*steam-kettle) and mild opiates as in other cases. **1879** *Steam line [see HOAR-FROST b]. **1937** M. W. ZEMANSKY *Heat & Thermodynamics* xi. 175 In the particular case of water..the vaporization curve is called the steam line. **1881** *Spon's Dict. Engin.* Suppl. III. 1107 A *steam navvy..consisting of a rectangular truck, supported on four wheels, carrying the engine and boiler. **1795** MASON *Ch. Mus.* i. 36 And who knows but a certain noble Mechanic.. may place a *Steam Organ upon the Poop and play *ça ira* upon it. **1841** *Civil Engin. & Arch. Jrnl.* IV. 247 M. Lax, jun., has just invented a steam organ, which can be heard through the extent of a whole province. **1910** 'I. HAY' in *Granta* 11 June 12 Even the *steam organs seemed to have stopped of their own accord. **1962** L. DAVIDSON *Rose of Tibet* vi. 106 It was as though he had been pushed into a steam organ at a fair. The stupefying blare of sound. **1895** *Jrnl. Chem. Soc.* LXVII. 196 It is absolutely necessary that the surface of the pyrometer should be free from all soluble salts when the *steam point is being taken. **1909** *Yukon Territory* (Canada Dept. Interior) iv. 38 A steam point is an iron pipe of about 5½ feet in length,..connected to a boiler supplying the steam... The miner drives the steam point into the ground, where it is left..until a hole is thawed. **1965** *Jrnl. Chem. Physics* XLII. 274/2 In 1954 the size of the Kelvin degree was fixed by assigning the value 273·16°K to the triple point of water, so that the value of the steam point is now subject to experimental determination. **1974** W. R. HUNT *North of 53°* iv. 15 Steam points replaced wood fires for thawing and this greatly speeded the mining work. **1957** V. GIELGUD *Brit. Radio Drama 1922–1956* The flight from '*steam-radio' to television has become an admitted rout. **1961** *Radio Times* 6 Apr. 41/4, I am the proud possessor of 'square eyeballs', but still feel that the good old 'steam' radio has a winner in the *Scrapbook* series. **1976** J. SNOW *Cricket Rebel* 7 Overseas tours were followed equally avidly on the old 'steam' radio in the lounge. **1925** PATERSON & WEBSTER *Man. Locomotive Running Shed Management* viii. 114 The usual method is for the *steam raiser to 'line' the grate along the firebox sides and well into the corners with coal, leaving the centre of the grate bare. **1947** H. WEBSTER *Locomotive Running Shed Pract.* 177 Following an interval of 30 minutes or so the fire is inspected by the steam-raiser who breaks it up and adds fresh fuel. **1837** W. B. ADAMS *Carriages* 291 To make a *steam-road is more costly than an animal road, because it imperatively requires a more exact level. **1911** H. S. HARRISON *Queed* xv. 174 The cars are steam-road size. **1875** KNIGHT *Dict. Mech.*, **Steam-room*, the capacity for steam over the surface of the water in the boiler. **1972** *Village Voice* (N.Y.) 1 June 73/1 A steamroom in which vapors rise and good men fall. **1861** *Steam table [see *hot plate* s.v. HOT *a.* 12 c]. **1944** S. BELLOW *Dangling Man* 32, I looked around at the steam tables and the posters of foundering ships. **1976** M. MACHLIN *Pipeline* xiii. 154 Next to the sandwiches was a steam table with several containers of soggy-looking breaded veal cutlets. **1867–72** BURGH *Mod. Marine Engin.* 371/2 Lowness of the *steam space above the water line in the boiler. **1765** WATT in Muirhead *Invent. Watt* (1854) I. 8, I..have not got the piston *steam-tight yet. **1856** DEMPSEY *Locomotive Eng.* 40 The passage is closed completely steam-tight. **1892** LOW *Machine Draw.* 118 A steam-tight joint. **1835** MARRYAT *Olla Podr.* vi, Three *steam tugs, whose names are the Stephenson, the Arrow, and the Elephant, are to drag to Malines..all his majesty's ministers. **1891** KIPLING *Light that Failed* viii. (1900) 134 A steam-tug on the river hooted as she towed her barges to wharf. **1821** T. GRAY *Observ. Iron Rail-way* (ed. 2) 5 Conveyance of all merchandise as well as persons, by *steam waggons and coaches. *a* **1876** M. COLLINS *Pen Sk.* (1879) I. 245 This perturbed period of the steam-wagon and the lightning-wire. **1797** *Encycl. Brit.* (ed. 3) XVII. 744/1 A project of a *steam-wheel, where the impulsive force of the vapour was employed. **1820** SHELLEY *Lett. Maria Gisborne* 108 The self-impelling steam-wheels of the mind. **1841** BREES *Gloss. Civil Engin.* 218 Rotary, Rotatory, or Concentric Engine (sometimes called a steam-wheel).

steam (stiːm), *v.* [OE. *stéman*, *stýman* :—prehist. **staumjan*, f. **staum-* STEAM *sb.*]

I. *intr.*

†**1.** To emit a scent or odour. Of a scent: To be emitted or exhaled. Also with advs., as *out*, *up*. *Obs.* as a specific use: merged in 4.

a **1000** *Phœnix* 213 Will-sele styméð swetum swæccum. *c* **1000** ÆLFRIC *Saints' Lives* xxvii. 110 Wynsum bræð stemde of þære halȝan rode. **1667** *Phil. Trans.* II. 547 Laying open the hollow of the Thorax, there steam'd out at first a very offensive smell. **1847** PRESCOTT *Peru* III. iv. (1850) II. 94 They found themselves in a small and obscure apartment..from the floor and sides of which steamed up the most offensive odours, like those of a slaughter-house.

†**2.** To emit flame, glow. *Obs.*

c **1386** CHAUCER *Prol.* 202 Hise eyen stepe, and rollynge in his heed, That stemed as a forneys of a leed. *c* **1440** *Promp. Parv.* 473/2 Stemyn, or lowyn vp, *flammo.*

3. a. Of vapour, etc.: To be emitted or exhaled; to rise or issue in the form of steam. Also with *away*, *up*, etc.

1582 STANYHURST *Æneis* III. (Arb.) 76 And smoak swift steamd to the skyward. **1590** SPENSER *F.Q.* I. xii. 2 When the last deadly smoke aloft did steeme. **1661** BOYLE *Cert. Physiol. Ess.* (1669) 66 The dissolved Amber..swimming like a thin film upon the surface of the Liquour, whence little by little it steamed away into the air. **1683** SNAPE *Anat. Horse* I. xxvi. (1686) 55 From which Seed a certain air or spirit steams through the Trumpets to the Testicles. **1697** DRYDEN *Virg. Georg.* II. 479 The Water..thus imbib'd, returns in misty Dews, And steaming up, the rising Plant renews. **1699** POMFRET *Love Triumphant* 166 The Water round it gave a Nauseous Smell, Like Vapours Steeming from a Sulph'rous Cell. **1820** SHELLEY *Sensit. Plant* III. 104 Then there steamed up a freezing dew. **1859** DICKENS *T. Two Cities* I. ii, The reek of the labouring horses steamed into it.

b. *fig.*

1590 SPENSER *F.Q.* III. i. 55 Which she misconstruing, thereby esteemd That from like inward fire that outward smoke had steemd. **1692** E. WALKER tr. *Epictetus' Mor.* x, A waking Dream, Such as from ill-digested Thoughts doth steam. **1833** TENNYSON *Lotus-Eaters* 163 They find a music centred in a doleful song Steaming up, a lamentation and an ancient tale of wrong.

4. To emit, give off, exhale steam or vapour.

1614 GORGES *Lucan* VII. 285 The swords are cold on Pompeys part But Cæsars steeme in bloody mart. **1667** DRYDEN *Ind. Emp.* III. iii, See, see, my Brother's Ghost hangs hovering there, O're his warm Blood, that steems into the Air. **1708** J. PHILIPS *Cyder* II. 140 Nor let the crude Humors dance In heated Brass, steaming with Fire intense. **1820** SCOTT *Monast.* xxxvii, Censers steaming with incense. **1842** DICKENS *Amer. Notes* ix, Several damp gentlemen, whose clothes, on their drawing round the stove, began to steam again. **1860** TYNDALL *Glac.* I. xxvii. 206 The glacier ..steaming under the influence of the sun. **1865** DICKENS *Mut. Fr.* I. v, On the hob, a kettle steamed. **1913** *Engl. Rev.* Apr. 45 My eye glanced at the laboratory where the madder-vats were steaming.

5. Of a surface: To become covered or bedewed with condensed vapour.

1892 *Photogr. Ann.* II. p. cxlvii, Ventilation Apertures to prevent Condensing Lenses steaming during exhibition.

6. To generate or produce steam for mechanical purposes: said of an engine or boiler. *to steam up*, to turn on steam or set it working; hence *fig.*

1860 *What shall I be?* (U.S.A.) 95 Not so fast, Mr. Spitfire; You needn't steam up so fast. I'm as good company as you'll find here. **1877** M. REYNOLDS *Loco.-Eng. Driving* 88 Some engines steam best with a low fire. **1897** *Pall Mall Mag.* Sept. 81 The engines steam splendidly, and haul without assistance a train of 250 tons. **1911** WEBSTER, *Steam* v. i. 4. To generate steam; as, the boiler steams well.

7. To move or travel by the agency of steam: **a.** of a ship or its passengers. Also *to steam it*. Also with advs., as *away*.

1831 MRS. TROLLOPE *Domest. Manners Amer.* (1832) I. 255 Even were all the parties strangers to each other [on long river excursions], the knowledge that they were to eat, to drink, and steam away together for a week or fortnight, would induce something like a social feeling in any other country. **1832** R. H. FROUDE *Rem.* (1838) I. 306 We shall.. see Avignon and Nismes, and then steam it up the Rhone to Lyons. **1837** *Civil Engin. & Arch. Jrnl.* I. 28/1 She [a ship] will either steam or sail. **1844** W. H. MAXWELL *Sports & Adv. Scot.* ii. (1855) 33 Every mile we steamed, the lake assumed a new character. **1878** KINGSTON *Three Admirals* xix. 437 The *Bellona* accordingly steamed on towards the entrance of the harbour. **1886** *Law Times Rep.* LIII. 726/1 When the tug was completed it was found that she could only steam ten or eleven knots an hour. **1888** *Poor Nellie* 388 The young lady had steamed over from America.

b. of a railway-engine, the train or its passengers.

1863 MRS. H. WOOD *Verner's Pride* xi, The train was steaming into the station. **1899** GRATTON *Memory's Harkback* 196 Now you can rail there, unconscious as to the beauties through which you have steamed.

c. *fig.* (*colloq.*)

1842 C. FOX *Jrnl.* 29 May (1882) viii. 156 Steamed away to London Bridge and saw the Maurices. **1849** *Ibid.* 13 June xv. 244 Steamed to Chelsea, and paid Mrs. Carlyle a humane little visit. **1857** HUGHES *Tom Brown* I. vii, Young Brooke..then steams away for the run in, in which he's sure to be first. **1911** *Concise Oxf. Dict.*, *Steam v.*..(colloq.) work vigorously, make great progress, esp. *s. ahead*, *away*.

II. *trans.*

8. a. To exhale (steam or other vapour); to emit, send out in the form of vapour. Also with advs., as *forth*, *away*, *up*.

1666 BP. S. PARKER *Free Censure* (1667) 208 The Earth may steam forth vapours grosse enough to cloud the Sun. **1730–46** THOMSON *Autumn* 514 The mighty bowl, Swelled high with fiery juice, steams liberal round A potent gale. **1833** TENNYSON *Pal. Art* 39 Tossing up A cloud of incense of all odour steam'd From out a golden cup. **1862** DICKENS *Somebody's Luggage, His Umbrella* 14/2 The gingham article that lay open before me, steaming away its moisture. **1871** G. MACDONALD *Pict. Songs* I., *Wks. Fancy & Imag.* III. 39 The moorland pond is steaming A mist of gray and blue.

†**b.** *fig.* (Cf. *evaporate.*)

1590 SPENSER *F.Q.* II. vi. 27 How ill did him beseeme In slouthfull sleepe his molten hart to steme.

9. a. To apply steam to, expose to the action of steam; to treat with steam for the purpose of softening, cooking, heating, disinfecting, etc.

1798 *Trans. Soc. Arts* XVI. 208 Potatoes that are either broiled or steamed. **1840** *Mechanics' Mag.* XXXIII. 498/1 The wood to be operated on, is first steamed, until it acquires such softness and pliancy, that it can be cut or blocked..into the different forms required. **1842** LOUDON *Suburban Hort.* 210 A pipe..by which, whenever the water boils, the house may be steamed. **1844** *E. A. Parnell's Appl. Chem.* I. 370 [Calico-printing.] The cotton requires to be steamed about thirty minutes. **1899** *Allbutt's Syst. Med.* VIII. 757 It is usually recommended to steam the face over hot water.

b. To expose (a gummed packet) to the action of steam in order to soften the gum. *to steam open*, to open by this method. Similarly, *to steam* (a postage stamp, label, etc.) *off*.

1899 BURGIN *Bread of Tears* I. ii. 35 He had steamed it over a jar of hot water, read the contents, and reclosed the letter. **1911** MAX BEERBOHM *Zuleika Dobson* xiv. 212 She might easily steam open the envelope and master its contents. **1920** M. WEBB *House in Dormer Forest* xvi. 214 The kettle having complied, she began to steam the letter open. **1944** R. LEHMANN *Ballad & Source* I. vi. 49 She used to send us postcards... We steamed the stamps off. **1979** 'J. LE CARRÉ' *Smiley's People* (1980) xix. 242, I can still tap your phone, steam open your mail.

c. To fill with 'steam' or warm odour.

1861 *Two Cosmos* v. viii. II. 191 Chops, steaks, toasted cheese, and almost all descriptions of drink steamed the whole apartment.

d. To bedew (a surface) with vesicles of condensed vapour.

1860 *All Year Round* No. 42. 362 Glass, already opaquely steamed with youthful breath.

e. *calico-printing.* To fix (colours) by the steam-process.

1862 C. O'NEILL *Dict. Calico Printing* s.v. *Steam colours*, The process of steaming colours.

10. To convey on a steam-vessel. *colloq.*

1891 CONST. MACEWEN *Three Women One Boat* xv. 115 We will just..let him steam us back.

11. Colloq. with *up*. **a.** To stir up or rouse (ardour, etc.). *rare.*

1919 F. HURST *Humoresque* 97 Ed says he'd never get him to steam up his nerve enough to call at a girl's house after her. **1931** *Daily Express* 21 Sept. 19/2 He was trying to steam up interest in the contest.

b. To rouse or excite (a person), esp. to anger; to agitate, upset.

1922 H. C. WITWER in *Collier's* 17 June 22/4 Are you asking me to go with you so's to steam Rags Dempster up? **1964** WODEHOUSE *Frozen Assets* iii. 61 She's one of those calm, quiet girls you'd think nothing would steam up. *a* **1974** R. CROSSMAN *Diaries* (1977) III. 366 The Department have steamed me up into the idea that I have got a terrible series of difficulties here.

12. With *up*: *Agric.*, to subject (an animal) to steaming up (see STEAMING *vbl. sb.* 5).

1947 V. C. FISHWICK *Dairy Farming* II. 164 We steam-up our heifers and cows, and feed a balanced milk-production ration during the lactation period. **1959** *Observer* 15 Nov. 3/1 There are no special hazards in artificial twinning provided that the cow is generously fed—steamed up as it is called in farming language—before calving. **1969** N. W. Pirie *Food Resources* iii. 104 The extreme case is the process known as 'steaming up' or 'flushing' ewes before mating. The extra food given..increases the probability of conception.

'steamboat. A boat propelled by steam; esp. a coasting or river steamer of considerable size, carrying either passengers or goods. Also *attrib.*

1787 M. Cutler in *Life*, etc. (1888) II. 399 In all probability, steamboats will be found to do infinite service in all our extensive river navigation. **1814** Scott *Diary* 8 Sept. in *Lockhart*, Embarked in the steam-boat for Glasgow. **1817–8** Cobbett *Resid. U.S.* (1822) 268 We are now frequently met and passed by large, fine steam-boats, plying up and down the river. **1821** *Deb. Congress U.S.* 28 Dec. (1855) 44 The jurisdiction had only embraced steamboat navigation. **1847** [see *raft-man* s.v. raft *sb.*[1] 6]. **1866** Lowell *Study Wind.*, *Swinburne's Trag.* (1871) 162 A Mississippi steamboat captain. **1906** *Tribune* 5 Dec. 6/3 The Thames steamboat service.

b. *fig.*

1823 Byron *Juan* ix. lxxiv, I needs must rhyme with dove, That good old steam-boat which keeps verses moving 'Gainst reason. **1854** Mrs. Stowe *Sunny Mem.* I. xvi. 296 If he [Abp. Whately] had been born in our latitude..the natives would have..said he was a real steamboat on an argument. **1859** Bartlett *Dict. Amer.* (ed. 2) 449 *Steam-boat*, a term used at the West to denote a dashing, go-a-head character.

c. *Comb.*, as **steamboat Gothic** *adj. phr.* (*U.S.*), used to designate an ornamented style of architecture typical of houses built by retired steamboat captains in the mid-nineteenth century.

1962 W. Faulkner *Reivers* viii. 166 The big rambling multigalleried multistoried steamboat-gothic hotel where the overalled aficionados..gathered..each February. **1970** K. Platt *Pushbutton Butterfly* (1971) iv. 43 The beautiful old mansions with their bay windows, ornate Steamboat Gothic cornices and mouldings.

Hence **'steamboating** *vbl. sb.* (*a*) travelling by steamboat; the business of working on or operating a steamboat; (*b*) *fig.* (see quots. 1875, 1891); also **steamboatman** *U.S.*, one who works on a steamboat, esp. a steamboat owner or captain.

1826 Malthus *Diary* 7 July (1966) 263 Dr Brown said that the introduction of Steam boating had quite altered the habits of the people of Glasgow. **1828** Mrs. B. Hall *Let.* 7 June in *Aristocratic Journey* (1931) xxii. 288 Two nights more and we shall have done with it and have no more steamboating in this country. **1834** Lady Granville *Lett.* 9 Sept. (1894) II. 162 Having enjoyed our steamboating on the Rhone so much. **1856** Lever *Martins of Cro' M.* lxv. 601 That rattling, noisy steam-boating up the Rhine. **1875** Knight *Dict. Mech.*, *Steamboating* (Bookbinding), cutting simultaneously a pile of books which are as yet uncovered, that is, are *out of boards*. **1875** 'Mark Twain' in *Atlantic Monthly* Jan. 69/1 When I was a boy, there was but one permanent ambition among my comrades... That was, to be a steamboatman. **1883** *Athenæum* 2 June 694/3 They treat of a time when steamboating was a great industry [on the Mississippi]. **1891** *Century Dict.*, *Steamboating* 2. Undue hurrying and slighting of work. (Colloq.) **1910** D. W. Bone *Brassbounder* 251 Sailormen walk fore and aft; steamboat men, athwart. **1929** G. L. Eskew *Pageant of Packets* ii. 101 All the steamboatmen when in New Orleans did their banking at the Banque des Citoyens.

steamed (sti:md), *ppl. a.* [f. steam *v.*]

1. In the simple senses of the vb.

1802 Willich *Dom. Encycl.* II. 133 Steamed potatoes are always more wholesome and nutritious than such as are boiled in water. **1868** *Rep. U.S. Commissioner Agric.* (1869) 427 The horses..receive four quarts of corn each per day, sprinkled on the steamed food. **1876** *Encycl. Brit.* IV. 691/2 The waggons for receiving the steamed fabrics. **1884** N. Lake *Menus made Easy* viii. 149 *Pouding soufflé*—a very light steamed pudding. *Ibid.* viii. 150 *Pouding à la Snowdon*—a steamed pudding of suet, breadcrumbs, brown sugar and marmalade. **1945** *ABC of Cookery* (Ministry of Food) xvii. 61 Most modern steamed puddings are made by one or other of the cake-mixing methods already described. **1978** K. Webber *Bk. Winter Cooking* 93 Boiled or steamed puddings can be stodgy.

2. With *up*. **a.** Excited or roused, esp. to anger; agitated, upset. Freq. in phr. ***all steamed up***. Rarely without *up*. *colloq.*

1923 H. C. Witwer in *Cosmopolitan* Sept. 72/2, I was a bit steamed up about her making my popular sex ridiculous by going boy-crazy at fifty. **1935** J. Hargan *Gloss. Prison Lang.* 8 *Steamed*, envious, angry. **1936** M. H. Bradley *Five-Minute Girl* v. 79 If she was all steamed up like this over embroidery silks, he thought, what would she be when he told his news? **1943** P. Cheyney *You can always Duck* vi. 101, I reckon he's a bit steamed up over my allure. **1953** K. Amis *Lucky Jim* xiv. 148 People get themselves all steamed up about whether they're in love or not. **1965** M. Bradbury *Stepping Westward* vii. 330 People live naked in this country [*sc.* the USA]. If you get steamed up you let everyone know. **1979** G. F. Newman *List* ii. 22 They sounded pretty steamed with him. **1980** D. Bogarde *Gentle Occupation* ii. 44 The General insists it is sent to all the Brigades. He's getting very steamed up about the bloody little thing.

b. Drunk, intoxicated. Rarely without *up*. *slang.*

1929 M. A. Gill *Underworld Slang* 10/2 *Steamed up*, drunk. **1950** *Landfall* June 126 Little Spike is six foot two and has a reputation for being a hard case when he is steamed-up. **1971** J. Terrell *Bunkhouse Papers* xii. 156 A cowman sat next to the houseman, and he was steamed with liquor so that he slumped a little to one side.

3. With *up*. Of a glass surface, etc.: covered or bedewed with condensed vapour.

1972 G. Lyall *Blame the Dead* xv. 106, I went along to the buffet car..and stared at the steamed-up window.

'steam-,engine. An engine in which the mechanical force of steam is made available as a motive power for driving machinery, etc.

Earlier names were *fire-engine* (see fire-engine 2) and *atmospheric engine* (Newcomen). The ordinary (stationary) engine is due to James Watt (patented 1769).

1751 F. Blake in *Phil. Trans.* XLVII. 197 The fire-engine, or (to term it more properly) the steam-engine, for draining of mines, is a master-piece of machinery. **1757** K. Fitzgerald *Ibid.* L. 54 A small boiler,..made in the shape of those commonly used in steam-engines. **1766** Watt in Muirhead *Invent. Watt* (1854) I. 14, I have thought on a simpler circular steam-engine than what I mentioned to you. **1821** Scott *Pirate* xvii, The monster..blew, with a noise resembling the explosion of a steam-engine, a huge shower of water into the air. **1856** Emerson *Eng. Traits* v, The rapid doubling of the population dates from Watt's steam-engine.

b. A locomotive engine propelled by steam.

1815 [see locomotive A. 2 d]. **1821** T. Gray *Observ. Iron Rlwy.* i. 12 The canal boats might be towed by steam-engines running on a rail-way along the canal. **1823** Byron *Juan* x. ii, Full soon Steam-engines will conduct him to the moon. **1934** *Railway Wonders of World* I. 309/1 There is one factor, however, where the steam engine will probably always score, and that is in its greater length of useful life and lower maintenance costs. **1970** F. McKenna *Gloss. Railwaymen's Talk* p. iii, The crash of the coal hopper..and the noise of steam engines preparing for their journeys no longer disturb the peaceful inhabitants of Mortimer Terrace and Highgate Road.

c. Often in hyperbolic or jocular comparisons.

1833 Nyren *Yng. Cricketer's Tutor* (1902) 101 Neither he nor Quiddington ever had to stand against such steam-engine bowling as Brett's. *c* **1840** Syd. Smith in Lady Holland *Mem.* (1855) I. 267 Daniel Webster struck me much like a steam-engine in trousers. **1865** M. Arnold *Ess. Crit.* i. 15 When your party talks this language like a steam engine.

Hence **steamengineing** *vbl. sb.* (*nonce-wd.*).

1839 Carlyle *Chartism* viii. (1840) 87 The Saxon kindred burst forth into..steamengining, railwaying, commercing.

steamer ('sti:mə(r)). [f. steam *v.* and *sb.* + -er[1].]

1. One who steams; a person employed in some process of steaming.

1832 *Min. Evid. Comm. Factories Bill* 27 You say you were taken to be a steamer: are not very stout and healthy youths usually selected for that purpose?—Yes. **1881** *Instr. Census Clerks* (1885) 64 Woollen Cloth Manuf., Steamer. *Ibid.* 69 Calico, Steamer. **1902** *Brit. Med. Jrnl.* 15 Feb. 380/1 Hatting Operatives..Proofers, including 'stovers'..and 'steamers'.

2. a. An apparatus for steaming (in various technical processes); a vessel in which articles are subjected to the action of steam, as in washing, cookery, etc.

1814 *Sporting Mag.* XLIII. 275 Stew-pans, hot dressers, steamers, digesters. **1846** Soyer *Cookery* 605 Place them in a vegetable steamer, and steam them well for half an hour. **1846** A. Young *Naut. Dict.* 177 Kiln, Stove, or Steamer. **1858** Simmonds *Dict. Trade*, *Steamer*, a spare top fitting on a saucepan, with holes at the bottom, for cooking potatoes by steam. **1895** *Arnold & Sons' Catal. Surg. Instrum.* 777 Steamer, Copper, with spirit lamp and tray, for softening poroplastic jackets, etc. **1897** *Allbutt's Syst. Med.* II. 551 If bales of dry wools and hairs were placed in steamers—as is done in the melange printing process.

b. Applied to a boiler in respect to its power of generating steam.

1891 *Century Dict.* s.v., The boiler is an excellent steamer.

†**3.** *slang.* A tobacco-pipe. *Obs.*

1811 *Lex. Balatr.*, *Steamer*, a pipe. A swell steamer; a long pipe, such as is used by gentlemen to smoke. **1823** 'Jon Bee' *Dict. Turf* s.v., 'Keep up the steam or steamer,' to smoke indefatigably.

†**4.** *Austral.* A dish of stewed kangaroo. *Obs.*

1820 C. Jeffreys *Van Dieman's Land* 70 **1827** P. Cunningham *Two Yrs. New South Wales* I. 309. **1861** Whyte Melville *Good for Nothing* xxvi.

5. a. A vessel propelled by steam; a steamboat, steamship.

1825 T. Hook *Sayings* Ser. ii. *Man of Many Fr.* II. 46 The Brighton Steamer to Dieppe. **1828** Scott *Let.* 18 July in Mrs. Hughes *Lett. & Recoll.* vii, Though not afraid of a breeze in a good sea-boat I should not relish it much in a *steamer*, for if any part of the machinery goes wrong [etc.]. **1847** Bentinck in *Croker Papers* (1884) III. xxv. 143 We had five war steamers lying in the Tagus and Douro. **1890** 'R. Boldrewood' *Col. Reformer* xiv, A stately ocean steamer. **1897** *Daily News* 23 Sept. 5/3 The word 'steamer' still suggests to most people a vessel with a pair of funnels and a pair of paddles.

b. *attrib.*, as ***steamer rug***, ***trunk***, etc.; **steamer-chair**, a lounge-chair such as is used on the deck of a steamer.

1839 [Miss Maitland] *Lett. fr. Madras* (1843) 283, I have a whole steamer-load of things to say, and I scarcely know where to begin. **1886** Mrs. Burnett *Little Ld. Fauntleroy* iv, The people who had been sea-sick had..come on deck to recline in their steamer-chairs and enjoy themselves. **1886** in *New Canaan Hist. Soc. Ann.* (1959) 19/1 A steamer trunk I believe they call them; something to hold necessary articles on their voyage. **1890** S. Hale *Let.* 22 Dec. (1919) 253 It is ..so cold..that we are sitting close up to the grate..and all wound about with the heaviest steamer rug! **1895** R. W. Chambers *King in Yellow*, *Street of Our Lady of Fields* ii, He ..had not yet unpacked his steamer-trunk. **1977** H. Fast *Immigrants* vi. 365 They were covered by a big steamer rug.

6. a. A steam-propelled road-locomotive, traction-engine or the like. *rare.* **b.** A motor-car driven by steam.

1837 W. B. Adams *Carriages* 202 The steamers on the railroad can carry their own materials, which the steamers on common roads cannot so conveniently do. **1870** *Pall Mall Gaz.* 9 Aug. 4 The reports on Thomson's 'road steamer' made to the War Department. **1900** *Daily News* 14 Nov. 6/3 Trevithick constructed a road steamer that made its appearance upon the Cornish highways on the Christmas Eve of 1801. **1901** *Morn. Leader* 18 Dec. 6/4 The War Office has again been testing motor transport vehicles, mostly steamers.

c. A steam locomotive engine or train.

1837 W. Tayler *Diary* 22 Sept. (1962) 51 We passed the Southampton rail road and was just in time to see the steamer go past, with about forty cars fastened to it full of gravel.

1961 *Times* 16 Aug. 9/4 This strong feeling, stimulated in this decade by the departure of the 'steamer', has served to produce something of a golden age in railway literature. **1972** *Times Lit. Suppl.* 10 Nov. 1377/3 All over Britain people are banding together to buy, restore and, they hope, run a steamer. **1975** 'J. Lymington' *Spider in Bath* ix. 156, I meant a real locomotive. A steamer. **1981** *Railway Mag.* Mar. 115/3 No. 765 is the first main-line steamer of the decade to be returned to active duty.

7. a. A fire-engine the pumps of which are worked by steam.

1870 *Daily News* 15 Oct. 7/4 Alarming Fire at the Gaiety Restaurant... The 'call' for engines was rapidly responded to, no fewer than eight steamers being soon present. **1876** E. M. Shaw *Fire Protection* 63 The proper course would be.. to remove the hose to the steamer, and attach the steamer's suction-pipe to the hydrant. **1886** *Manch. Exam.* 8 Jan. 6/1 Steamers and manuals from all parts of the metropolis arrived at the fire.

b. A steam thrashing-machine.

1898 Rider Haggard *Farmer's Yr.* Feb. (1899) 104 The steamer began to work at the All Hallows Farm on the little stack of barley. **1900** 'H. Lawson' *On Track* 75 He reaped it by hand, had it thrashed by travelling 'steamer' (portable steam engine and machine).

8. a. (*transf.* from sense 5.) The duck *Tachyeres* (or *Micropterus*) *cinereus* (or *brachypterus*) of the Falkland Islands; the loggerhead or race-horse. Also ***steamer-duck***.

1827 P. P. King *Voy. Adventure & Beagle* I. 35 Here we saw, for the first time, that most remarkable bird the Steamer-duck. *Ibid.* 36, I am averse to altering names..; but in this case I do think the name of 'steamer' much more appropriate and descriptive of the swift paddling motion of these birds, than that of 'race-horse'. **1845** Darwin *Voy. Nat.* ix. (1873) 200 These ducks from their extraordinary manner of paddling and splashing upon the water..are now called steamers. **1895** Lydekker *Roy. Nat. Hist.* IV. 357 The steamer-duck (*Tachyeres cinereus*) of the Falkland Islands and Patagonia.

b. = *long-neck clam* s.v. long-neck 2 b, freq. eaten as a delicacy. Also ***steamer clam***.

1909 *Rep. Mollusk Fisheries Mass.* (Mass. Comm. Fisheries) 179 Small clams, or 'steamers', are shipped in the shell. **1947** P. A. Morris *Field Guide Shells of our Atlantic Coast* 89 *Mya arenaria*... Known by such names as 'long clam', 'soft-shelled clam', 'steamer clam', and 'long-necked clam', it lives in the muds and gravels between the tides. **1960** J. J. Rowlands *Spindrift* 84 The delicious steamer clam of the North Atlantic is becoming scarce. **1977** [see quahaug, quahog].

9. *local.* (See quot.)

1865 J. T. F. Turner *Slate Quarries* 8 If the stone to be raised be large, a chain with hooks is sent down in lieu of the wagon, and the stone is named a 'steamer'.

†**10.** The name of a back-stroke in swimming (see quots.). *Obs.*

1861 'R. Harrington' *Swimming* 10 The 'steamer'.. consists in striking the water violently with the foot, raising each leg alternately out of the water to do so. **1879** *Boy's Own Ann.* I. 415/3 The Steamer... Lie on the back, point your feet as much as possible, and then strike them alternately into the water, the knees being kept quite stiff.

11. *Rhyming slang.* [Abbrev. of *steam tug* = 'mug'.] = mug *sb.*[5] 1; also *spec.* a male homosexual, esp. one who seeks passive partners.

1932 G. S. Moncrieff *Café Bar* vii. 63 The mug became pleasanter... 'I'm a porter, at some service flats in Victoria ..What's your friend do?' the steamer asked genially. **1936** J. Curtis *Gilt Kid* xxxvi 258 If you think I'm going to make a steamer of myself and let you hang about half a dozen more charges on me, you're mistaken. **1958** *Times Lit. Suppl.* 2 May 237/4 Terry..spending his time..among the young homosexuals and their 'steamers' **1968** G. J. Barrett *Guilty, be Damned!* viii. 95 You might get yourself caught. The Police are a lot sharper than steamers give them credit for being. **1978** M. Puzo *Fools Die* iv. 48 The third player at the table was a 'steamer', a bad gambler who chased losing bets.

Hence **'steamer** *v.*, to travel by steamboat; so **'steamering** *vbl. sb.* **'steamerful**, a steamboat-load. **'steamerless** *a.*, without a steamer or steamers.

1866 R. W. Church *Lett.* 21 Sept. in *Life* (1894) 175 Tuesday we steamered up the lake to Villeneuve. **1883** Carlyle in *Mrs. Carlyle's Lett.* I. 95 This autumn [1838], after lectures,..I steamered to Kirkcaldy. **1886** Froude *Oceana* 316 On certain days he threw open house and grounds to excursion parties from Auckland. A steamerful would come. **1895** *Punch* 28 Sept. 148/1 Capital boating and fishing—likewise plenty of steamering. **1900** *Truth* 3 May 1057 A steamerless Thames.

steamie (ˈstiːmɪ). *Sc.* Also **steamy**. [f. STEAM *sb.* + -IE.] A public wash-house.

1926 *Glasgow Herald* 19 Oct. 8 The perambulator holds much besides..the baby... In the poorer parts of the city the washing is conveyed to and from the 'steamy' thereon. **1935** *Scottish Educ. Jrnl.* 8 Mar. Suppl. p. vi/2 Modern sanitation has..caused the coining of 'steamie' (the public wash-house). **1958** *3rd Statistical Acct. Scotl.* V. III. xvii. 560 Attendances at the 'steamies' in the year were just short of 1,800,000. **1969** *Dumfries & Galloway Standard* 29 Oct. 1 There was still a need for the 'steamie' as launderettes were not as cheap as the council maintained. **1978** *Times* 18 May 24/1 It was the talk of the steamie, so to speak. It was a topic of conversation at the company.

steamily, steaminess: see after STEAMY *a.*

steaming (ˈstiːmɪŋ), *vbl. sb.* [-ING¹.] The action of the verb STEAM, in various senses.

1. †**a.** The exhaling of odour. †**b.** The glowing of flame. **c.** Emission of vapour, fuming (in quots. *fig.*).

a **1100** *Aldhelm. Glosses* 3490 (Napier) *Fraglantiam* .i. *odorem*, steminge. *c* **1440** *Promp. Parv.* 474/1 Stemynge, or leemynge of fyyr, *flammacio*. **1675** J. OWEN *Indwelling Sin* vii. (1732) 77 It [sin] darkens the Mind..through the steaming of the Affections, heated with the noisom Lusts that have laid hold on them. **1819** R. L. SHEIL *Evadne* IV. ii. 64 You wonder That tears are dropping from my flaming eyelids, But 'tis the steaming of a burning heart.

2. The process of subjecting to the action of steam.

1812 SIR J. SINCLAIR *Syst. Husb. Scot.* I. 117 The practice of steaming [potatoes] was not known in those days. **1862** C. O'NEILL *Dict. Calico Printing* s.v. *Steam colours*, The damper the steam the sooner will the steaming be done. **1868** *Rep. U.S. Commissioner Agric.* (1869) 427 Steaming is done only twice a week, the food keeping warm three or four days in the box.

attrib. **1745** *De Coetlogon's Hist. Arts & Sci.* II. 106/2 A Steaming-Bason [used in hat-making]. **1832** *Min. Evid. Comm. Factories Bill* 29 They all had 4*s.* that worked at Mr. Noble's steaming-mill.

3. The production of steam in a boiler. Also *attrib.*

1874 RAYMOND *6th Rep. Mines* 39 The Mount Diablo coal is used to a very great extent for steaming. **1875** BEDFORD *Sailor's Pocket Bk.* v. (ed. 2) 146 Whether wood can be procured in quantity sufficient for steaming purposes.

4. a. Travelling by steamboat or steamship.

1836 *Southern Lit. Messenger* II. 696 Steaming from Washington to Baltimore is an improvement upon that route at least. **1853** HAWTHORNE *Eng. Note-Bks.* (1883) I. 416, I went over to the Royal Rock Hotel, about fifteen or twenty minutes' steaming from this side of the river. **1883** F. M. CRAWFORD *Dr. Claudius* viii, Miss Skeat also thought sailing much more poetic than steaming. **1913** J. H. MORRISON *On Track Pioneers* xxi. 98 Eight hundred miles of swift steaming down the Coromandel Coast brings us to Madras.

attrib. **1889** *Pall Mall Gaz.* 9 May 5/1 The *City of Paris*.. arrived at New York yesterday, her steaming time from Queenstown to Sandy Hook being 5 days 23 hours 7 minutes.

b. *Comb.*, as **steaming light**, a white light carried on the masthead of a steamship under way at sea by night.

1909 *Man. Seamanship* (Admiralty) II. i. 29 *Navigation lights*,..oil ones..consist of steaming light, in charge of 2nd captain of forecastle, who is responsible for placing it; after steaming light..; starboard bow light..; and port bow light. **1947** *Sea Breezes* IV. 139/2 A steamer appeared, also carrying steaming lights.

5. With *up*. In *Agric.*, the provision of extra food to farm animals as preparation for reproduction.

1943 R. BOUTFLOUR in *Agriculture* L. 306 It is now over twenty years since I coined the expression 'steaming up'; the reason for its choice was to imply that a definite preparation was required. **1947** V. C. FISHWICK *Dairy Farming* II. 156, I believe in steaming-up and preparation for calving. This is how you get the milk. **1953** K. RUSSELL *Princ. Dairy Farming* xiii. 153 The amount of steaming-up ration to be fed as concentrates is then decided by two factors—the condition of the cow or heifer and her probable milking capacity. **1960** *Farmer & Stockbreeder* 19 Jan. 122/3 Cows require 'steaming up' prior to calving.

ˈsteaming, *ppl. a.* [-ING².] That steams.

†**1.** Glowing, flaming. *Obs.*

a **1541** WYATT *Of meane & sure Estate* 53 Under a stole she spied two stemyng eyes In a rounde head. **1583** MELBANCKE *Philotimus* 66 A cat in seing with her steeming eies.

2. a. That emits steam or vapour.

a **1637** B. JONSON *Praises Country Life* 66 To view..The wealthy houshold swarme of bondmen met, And 'bout the steeming Chimney set! **1667** MILTON *P.L.* v. 186 Ye Mists and Exhalations that now rise From Hill or steaming Lake. **1697** DRYDEN *Virg. Georg.* IV. 68 Nor near the steaming Stench of muddy Ground. **1735** SOMERVILLE *Chase* I. 321 Soon the sagacious Brute..the steaming Vapour snuffs Inquisitive. **1799** WORDSW. *Two Apr. Mornings* 10 Through the grass, And by the steaming rills. **1860** DICKENS, etc. *Message fr. Sea* iii. *Christm. Stor.* (1874) 164 At the upper end of this room stood long stoves like metal counters, laden with steaming pans. **1865** LE FANU *Guy Deverell* vii. I. 96 He..pulled up his steaming horse by the station. **1883** STEVENSON *Treas. Isl.* xiv, The sun still shining mercilessly on the steaming marsh. **1899** E. PHILLPOTTS *Human Boy* 28 A steaming glass of hot grog is what you want.

b. quasi-*adv.* in phr. ***steaming hot.***

1686 E. VERNEY in *V. Mem.* (1899) IV. 381 For fear..you should catch harm, for as I did once coming out of the Theatre at a publick Act when it was very full and stiaming-hot [*sic*], and walkin a Broad in the cold. **1815** SCOTT *Ld. of Isles* v. xxxiii, Then on the board his sword he toss'd, Yet steaming hot. **1907** J. H. PATTERSON *Man-Eaters of Tsavo* xiii. 150 A cup of steaming hot coffee.

3. Used as a substitute for a strong expletive: consummate, 'blithering'. *slang.*

1962 *Listener* 13 Dec. 1024/3 A cautionary tale concerning a real steaming nit of a British civilian. **1965** A. GARNER *Elidor* xix. 147 Roland! You great steaming chudd! Come back!

steamless (ˈstiːmlɪs), *a.* [f. STEAM *sb.* + -LESS.] Without steam; that has run out of steam or is not propelled by steam. Also of a railway: not carrying steam-engines.

1920 *Blackw. Mag.* Apr. 573/2 The N.T.O. insisted on placing the skipper of the steamless tug under arrest. **1967** *Gloss. Sanitation Terms* (*B.S.I.*) 49 *Steamless inlet*, a device to reduce the amount of steam produced in filling a bath with hot water. **1970** *Railway Mag.* Oct. 544/2 My old room facing the now steamless railway.

steam-roller (ˈstiːm,rəʊlə(r), formerly ,stiːm ˈrəʊlə(r)), *sb.* **a.** A heavy locomotive engine with wide wheels used for crushing road-metal and levelling roads.

1866 *Engineering* 18 May 318/3 The Ballaison steam roller ..may now be seen at all hours of the day crushing smooth the granite of the new boulevards of Paris. **1877** PHILIPSON in *Q. Rev.* CXLIV. 424 There, too, six-horse rollers are found to do the work of setting a roadway far more effectually than our steam-rollers.

b. *fig.* (*colloq.*) A crushing power or force. Also *attrib.*

Russian steam-roller: with reference to Russian military capacity in the war of 1914–18.

1896 LLOYD GEORGE *Let.* 6 Aug. (1973) 106 One of them [*sc.* M.P.s] threatened to pass a steamroller over me yesterday... Killed the Military Lands Bill. Just heard from Balfour. That's their steamroller. **1902** *Munsey's Mag.* XXVI. 489/1 She [Russia] sought to achieve her end by means of the 'steam roller' of the concert of Europe. **1902** *Blackw. Mag.* Dec. 731/1 At last Kitchener..set his steam-roller in motion and rolled the enemy flat. **1906** *Westm. Gaz.* 16 June 15/1 In the Caucasus, as in Finland, she [*sc.* Russia] has adopted the steam-roller policy, and by crushing national aspirations has estranged possible loyalists. **1912** *Chicago Tribune* 3 June 2/2 The Roosevelt adherents.. expect through publicity to prevent the operation of the steam-roller. **1916** G. B. SHAW in *N.Y. Times* 9 Apr. VI. 1/3 A combination of the British fleet, the French Army, and the Russian steam roller. **1934** J. HILTON *Goodbye, Mr. Chips* xiii. 89 The Battle of the Marne, the Russian steam-roller, Kitchener. **1952** *Sun* (Baltimore) 7 July 2/4 Meanwhile Taft's men proceed on the lines slammed down by Elihu Root's steamroller. **1976** *Listener* 5 Feb. 132/3 The Soviet military doctrine of the so-called 'steamroller approach'—huge numbers of well-disciplined, fit and adequately trained privates, as distinguished from the élitist concept of an all-volunteer army, like Britain's.

Hence **steam-roll,** (also **steamroll**, stress variable) *v. trans.*, (*a*) to crush or level with a steam-roller; (*b*) *fig.*; also, to force or drive in a given direction (cf. STEAM-ROLLER *v.* 2); **ˈsteam-,rolling** (formerly *,steam-ˈrolling*) *vbl. sb.*

1879 T. CODRINGTON *Macadamised Roads* 99 The cost of steam rolling, when there is constant work for the machine, is far less than that of horse rolling. **1900** *Daily News* 26 Dec. 6/3 The usual plan..is to finish off the laid road metal with gravel, which is well watered and steam rolled. **1914** *Times* 29 Aug. 6/2 Our task is stonewalling, and that of the Russians is steamrolling. **1915** F. M. HUEFFER *Good Soldier* IV. v. 274 So Edward and Nancy found themselves steam-rolled out and Leonora survives. **1955** *Times* 15 Aug. 5/4 The big screen, Vistavision, the Hollywood technique, and all the rest of it will steamroll the lightness and gaiety of the original idea out of all recognition. **1975** *Times* 21 July 1/8 The ruling party..will steamroll the endorsement through. **1976** *Conservation News* Sept./Oct. 22/1 The main TV companies have made *some* attempt to cover the most excessive speculation and steamrolling of community rights.

ˈsteam-roller, *v.* Also as one word. [f. the sb.]

1. *trans.* To crush or level with a steam-roller; to force with a steam-roller.

1913 *New Statesman* 26 July 497/2 To attempt to get through his poems in Classical Prosody is like trying to ride a bicycle over miles of newly-stoned road not yet steam-rollered. **1940** V. BRITTAIN *Testament of Friendship* xix. 361 What had happened..to the mortal remnants of those slaughtered thousands?.. Had they been ploughed, exploded and steam-rollered into the soil?

2. *fig.* **a.** To crush or break down, as with a steam-roller; to ride roughshod over; to overwhelm or squash. Freq. in *Pol.* contexts.

1912 *Chicago Daily Tribune* 7 June 1/4 They [*sc.* the Taft men] assent..that they will 'steam roller' the Roosevelt contests with a vengeance. **1918** G. B. SHAW in *Daily Chron.* 12 Jan. 5/2 He hammered poor Mr Walsh with trenchant repetitions of his chivalrous Christian phrase, and steamrollered him amid thunderous plaudits. **1921** *Round Table* June 651 His block majority, with which, if necessary, he could steam-roller opposition. **1930** G. B. SHAW *What I really wrote about War* xi. 283 An Ally [*sc.* Russia] on whom we had depended to steamroller our enemies on their eastern front. **1953** *Manch. Guardian Weekly* 3 Dec. 4/1 It would be a tragedy if the personal intimate side of British elections was steam-rollered into a flat monotony. **1982** *N. & Q.* Apr. 174/2 The book seems..to be an example of that kind of academic system-building where the subtleties of a text are 'steamrollered' in the interests of interpretative 'schemes'.

b. To push (a measure or bill) *through* (a legislative assembly, committee, etc.) by forcibly overriding opposition.

1947 A. W. GRANTHAM in *Hong Kong Hansard* 31 July 257 It is too readily assumed that because there is a majority of Officials the slightest wish of Government is 'steam-rollered' through this Council. **1960** *Times* 1 Mar. 12/3 Certainly, each measure is steam-rollered through. **1964** *Daily Tel.* 27 Feb. 1/1 They accused him..of having 'steam-rollered the Bill through the Cabinet'.

c. To force (someone) *into* (a course of action, situation, etc.).

1959 *Economist* 18 Apr. 212/2 If the Government is steamrollered into granting a flat rate increase for all these pensioners right across the board, this will be the third successive general election which has been immediately preceded by such a step. **1959** P. BULL *I know Face* ii. 42 Luckily Robert and I..were not steam-rollered into a phoney romance to appease the fans and newshawks.

3. *intr.* With *adv.* or *prep.* To proceed (esp. to continue speaking), regardless of opposition or interruption.

1969 D. FRANCIS *Enquiry* I. iii. 38 Gowery steamrollered on. 'You found certain objects.' **1970** J. PORTER *Rather a Common Sort of Crime* iii. 31 The Hon. Con steam-rollered happily through the interruption. **1977** *Evening Gaz.* (Middlesbrough) 11 Jan. 13/8 Walker steam-rollered in with a 4–3 finish to win 16–15!

ˈsteamship. A ship propelled by steam. Also *attrib.*

1819 SHELLEY *Lett.* Prose Wks. 1888 II. 311 Every body here is talking of a steam-ship which is building at Leghorn. **1821** SCOTT *Fam. Lett.* 6 July (1894) II. xvii. 121 We can now make the journey in the steam-ship within sixty hours. **1866** 'MARK TWAIN' *Lett. from Hawaii* (1967) 24 The permanent establishment of a San Francisco and Honolulu steamship line. **1884** *List of Subscribers* (London & Globe Telephone Co.) 11 Culliford & Clark Steam Ship Brokers. **1901** HALL & OSBORNE *Sunshine & Surf* i. 1 You were just now bewailing..that there was such a beastly sameness about steamship travelling. **1909** *Gt. Central Rlwy. Rep.* 6 Aug. 5 Steamship receipts show a heavy decline.

ˈsteam-vessel.

†**1.** A vessel for holding steam; *esp.* one in which steam is condensed for working an engine. *Obs.*

1769 DR. SMALL in Muirhead *Invent. Watt* (1854) I. 37 The vessels mentioned in this paragraph you call *steam-vessels*. **1798** CT. RUMFORD in *Phil. Trans.* LXXXVIII. 464 The phial..was exposed one hour to the heat of boiling water in a steam-vessel. **1804** A. WOOLF in *Repert. Arts* etc. Ser. II. VI. 88 The smaller steam vessel, or cylinder, must be a measure for the larger. **1843** *Penny Cycl.* XXVII. 69 Surface of steam-pipe, or other steam-vessel, heated to 200°.

2. A steamboat or steamship.

1825 *Gentl. Mag.* XCV. I. 163 In the ports of Brest and Bordeaux six steam-vessels are building of an extraordinary size. **1844** LD. BROUGHAM *Brit. Const.* xx. (1862) 393 Most of the steam-vessels now used in our trade could be converted easily into men-of-war. **1863** H. COX *Instit.* III. v. 658 River steam-vessels.

ˈsteam-whistle.

A powerful whistle worked by a jet of steam (usually from a steam-boiler): used as a signal.

1840 H. S. TANNER *Canals & Rail Roads U.S.* 261 *Steam whistle*, a device for warning people when the engine is approaching. **1856** EMERSON *Eng. Traits* xiv, The voice of their modern muse has a slight hint of the steam-whistle. **1899** T. M. ELLIS *Three Cat's-eye Rings* 123 A bullet.. shrieked past Clayside's ear like a steam-whistle.

attrib. **1870** RUSKIN *Let.* in *Athenæum* (1905) 30 Sept. 428/3 Dickens was a pure modernist—a leader of the steam-whistle party *par excellence*. **1887** F. HUME *Myst. Hansom Cab* viii, Let us go outside, for I see your father has got that girl with the steam-whistle voice to sing.

Hence **steam-whistling** *vbl. sb.*

1866 RUSKIN *Crown of Wild Olive* iv. §152 Steam-piston labour on the earth, and the harvest of it brought forth with steam-whistling.

steamy (ˈstiːmɪ), *a.* [f. STEAM *sb.* + -Y.]

1. Consisting of, abounding in, or emitting steam; resembling steam.

1644 DIGBY *Nat. Bodies* xxvii. §7. 247 Were they not continually stuffed and clogged with grosse vapours of steamy meates. **1785** COWPER *Task* IV. 39 While the bubbling and loud-hissing urn Throws up a steamy column. **1818** MILMAN *Samor* 97 So they bravely strove For the bleak freedom of their steamy moors. **1866** LIVINGSTONE *Last Jrnls.* (1874) I. 21 The steamy, smothering air. **1899** *Edin. Rev.* Oct. 288 The climate is steamy and enervating.

fig. **1841** CARLYLE *Ess., Baillie* (1857) IV. 232 Baillie is the true newspaper; he is to be used and studied like one. Taken up in this way, his steamy indistinctness abates.

2. Covered with condensed vapour. (Cf. STEAM *v.* 5 and 9d.) *Path.* Of the cornea: Covered or apparently covered with condensed vapour.

1869 G. LAWSON *Dis. Eye* (1874) 30 The cornea grows dull and steamy. **1879** *St. George's Hosp. Rep.* IX. 488 Both corneæ continued steamy.

3. *fig.* Salacious; lustful, sexy, 'torrid'. Cf. HOT *a.* 6c.

1970 *Daily Tel.* 19 June 7/4 Making Marilyn Roberts semi-nude curiously lessens the eroticism of one originally steamy scene. **1976** M. MACHLIN *Pipeline* xii. 139 Once he remembered a steamy necking session out in the middle of a field of oats. **1980** R. MCINERNY *Second Vespers* (1981) xv. 108 It was a moral outlook, one that had never..been disturbed by the steamy fiction that was her steady diet.

Hence **ˈsteamily** *adv.*; **ˈsteaminess.**

1857 LIVINGSTONE *Trav. S. Africa* xxviii. 578, I myself felt an oppressive steaminess in the atmosphere. **1880** MISS BIRD *Japan* I. 128 The temperature is from 72° to 86°, and in the steaminess, needles rust. **1909** *English Rev.* Mar. 734, I became steamily hot.

steamy, var. STEAMIE.

stean (stiːn). Forms: 1 stǽne, 3-6 stene, 4, 6, 8- steen, 5 steene, 6-7 steane, (8 stein), 7- stean. [OE. *stǽne* wk. fem. (only once, inflected *stǽnan*) = OHG. *steinna* stone jug:—OTeut. type **stainjōn-*, f. **staino-* (OE. *stán*): see STONE *sb.*] A vessel for liquids (or, in later use, for bread, meat, fish, etc.), usually made of clay, with two handles or ears; a jar, pitcher, pot, urn. Now only *dial.* and *arch.*

c **1050** *Voc.* in Wr.-Wülcker 415/18 *Gillone*, stænan. *c* **1275** *Wom. Samaria* 15 in *O.E. Misc.*, Ase he þer reste ..þar com gon o wymmon,..myd hire stene [= Vulg. *hydria*, John iv. 28]. **1382** WYCLIF *1 Kings* vii. 50 And Salomon made..the..stenys [1388 pottis]..of moost pure gold. *Ibid.* xvii. 12, I haue not breed, but as myche as an handful may take of mele in a stene [1388 pot; Vulg. *in hydria*]. **1387** TREVISA *Higden* (Rolls) II. 207 þese beeþ þe names of þe signes: þe Wether,..þe Steen [*printed* Sceen; repr. L. *Aquarius*], the Fisshe. *c* **1440** *Pallad. on Husb.* III. 1165 Of that they do Viij cotuls in a stene of wynes trie [*per amphoram uini*]. *Ibid.* IV. 666 Whan they beth bake, al hoot into a stene Let hem be pressed. *a* **1500** *Medulla Gram.*, *Anfora*, a steene or a canne with two eerys. **1542** UDALL *Erasm. Apoph.* 74 Plato sent hym a whole stene or pitcher full [orig. *lagœnam.*] **1562** J. HEYWOOD *Prov. & Epigr.* (1867) 147 That doth diligently: Attend the tappes of stande and steane: To moyst thy lippes full dry. *a* **1599** SPENSER *F.Q.* VII. vii. 42 Vpon an huge great Earth-pot steane he stood; From whose wide mouth, there flowed forth the Romane floud. **1662** J. DAVIES tr. *Olearius' Voy. Ambass.* 261 The Pots..are very much esteem'd, especially the Steans, or great Pitchers. **1728** E. SMITH *Compl. Housew.* (ed. 2) 202 Strip them into an earthen Stean that has a cover to it. **1750** *Ibid.* 236 Put them into an earthen stein that has a saucer. **1742** *Lond. & Country Brew.* I. (ed. 4) 48 The Ale ..is drank while it is fermenting in earthen Steens. **1746** *Gentl. Mag.* XVI. 407 (Exmoor Vocab.) *Steyan* or *Stean*, an earthen pot, like a jar. **1880** *E. Cornw. Gloss.*, *Stean*, an earthenware pot such as meat or fish is cured in. **1888** DOUGHTY *Arabia Deserta* I. xvi. 450 If the thing fall to them for which they vowed [at the wishing-place], they will..lay up a new stean in a little cave. **1908** A. BENNETT *Old Wives' Tale* I. iii. 34 In the corner nearest the kitchen was a great steen in which the bread was kept.

attrib. *c* **1450** *Mirk's Festial* 293 A grete tode was in þe stene bothom. **1728** E. SMITH *Compl. Housew.* (ed. 2) 203 Put into a Stean-pot two pounds of Raisins stoned.

stean(e: see STAIN *v.*, STEEN *v.*, STONE.

steap(e: see STEEP, STEP.

steaple, obs. f. STEEPLE.

steapsin (stiːˈæpsɪn). *Physiological Chem.* [f. Gr. στέα-ρ fat, after PEPSIN.] A ferment of the pancreatic juice which saponifies fat (*Syd. Soc. Lex.* 1898).

1896 *Allbutt's Syst. Med.* I. 175 Whether it [*i.e.* fat necrosis] be due to a change produced by the steapsin on the fat..is not decided. **1897** *Ibid.* III. 723 The ferments of the pancreas, especially the fat-transforming steapsin, may be searched for.

stear: see STAIR, STARE *sb.*[1], STEER, STIR.

stearate (ˈstiːəreɪt). *Chem.* [Formed as STEAR-IC + -ATE.] A salt or ester of stearic acid.

1841 BRANDE *Man. Chem.* (ed. 5) 1139 Stearate of Baryta is formed by mixing hot solution of stearate of potassa with nitrate of baryta:..Stearate of Lead. **1897** *Allbutt's Syst. Med.* III. 297 The other fatty constituents of the bile consist of saponifiable fats, especially the oleates and stearates. **1899** *Jrnl. Chem. Soc.* LXXV. 358 (*table*) [Amylic] *n*-stearate. **1904** *Ibid.* LXXXVI. I. 284 *iso*Amyl stearate is a neutral, white solid melting at 21°. **1950** KIRK & OTHMER *Encycl. Chem. Technol.* V. 845 *n*-Butyl stearate..is a colorless liquid... It is of value in compounding lubricating oils and as a lubricant for the textile and molding trade, in special lacquers, and as a waterproofing agent. **1976** [see SORBITAN].

stearerin (stiːəˈrɛrɪn). *Chem.* [f. Gr. στέαρ fat (see STEARIC) + ἔρ-ος (Ionic εἶρος) wool + -IN.] A fatty substance analogous to stearin found in the oil of sheep's wool. So **stearerate** [-ATE[4]], a salt derived from stearerin.

1868 WATTS *Dict. Chem.* V. 412 The fat contained in the wool of Merino sheep is..a mixture of more liquid fat, elaerin, and a more solid fat, stearerin... When treated with strong potash-ley, it yields a salt, stearerate of potassium.

stearic (stiːˈærɪk), *a.* [ad. F. *stéarique* (Chevreul *c* 1819) f. Gr. στέαρ fat, tallow: see -IC.]

a. *Chem.* Derived from or containing stearin. ***stearic acid*** ($C_{18}H_{36}O_2$), an organic acid found mixed with palmitin and olein in most tallows. ***stearic ether***, a compound of stearic acid with the alcohol radicals. **b.** ***stearic candle***: the trade name of a kind of candle made of the 'stearine' of commerce.

1831 T. P. JONES *New Convers. Chem.* xxx. 304 In the conversion of suet into soap, a third acid, called stearic, has also been detected. **1836-9** BRANDE in *Todd's Cycl. Anat.* II. 233/2 The stearic portion of train oil..concretes..at a temperature between 70° and 80°. **1838** R. D. THOMSON in *Brit. Annual* 348 Stearic ether. **1852** ROYLE in *Lect. Gt. Exhib.* 485 The wax candles from Patna, and the stearic candles..from Calcutta. **1898** *Allbutt's Syst. Med.* V. 35 Fatty crystals (palmitic and stearic)..are also found.

stearidge, obs. form of STEERAGE.

steariform (ˈstiːərɪfɔːm), *a.* [f. STEARIN + -FORM.] Resembling stearin, or hard fat.

1860 MAYNE *Expos. Lex.* **1911** *Webster's Dict.*

stearin (ˈstiːərɪn). Also -ine. [ad. F. *stéarine* (Chevreul), f. Gr. στέαρ stiff fat, tallow, suet: see -IN.]

1. *Chem.* A general name for the three glycerids (monostearin, distearin, tristearin) formed by the combination of stearic acid and glycerine; chiefly applied to tristearin, which is the chief constituent of tallow or suet.

1817 T. THOMSON *Syst. Chem.* (ed. 5) II. 371 Stearin.. was first described by Chevreul in 1814. **1819** BRANDE *Man. Chem.* 374 A dry, concrete, fatty matter is obtained, which Chevreul has called stearine. **1819** J. G. CHILDREN *Chem. Anal.* 310 Stearin..somewhat resembles wax. **1845** TODD & BOWMAN *Phys. Anat.* I. 43 Stearine exists but sparingly, or not at all, in human fat. **1869** ROSCOE *Chem.* 386 The Stearic ..Ethers of Glycerin, or Stearins..may be prepared artificially by heating glycerin with stearic acid.

Comb. **1873** C. H. RALFE *Outl. Phys. Chem.* 21 Stearic acid unites with glycerine to form stearin glycerin.

2. The solid portion of any fixed oil or fat, in contradistinction to OLEIN 2.

1910 *Encycl. Brit.* VI. 635/2 By boiling the livers at a somewhat high temperature, 'unracked' cod oil is obtained, containing a considerable quantity of 'stearine', this fat, which separates on cooling, is sold as 'fish-stearine' for soap-making.

3. (Chiefly spelt *stearine.*) The commercial name of a preparation consisting of purified fatty acids, used for making candles, and formerly also as a material for statuettes.

1839 URE *Dict. Arts* 248 In June, 1825, M. Gay Lussac obtained a patent in England for making candles from margaric and stearic acids, improperly called stearine. **1870** *Illustr. Lond. News* 1 Oct. 359 Casts in stearine from two busts of Prince Leopold and Princess Amelie. **1879** *Cassell's Techn. Educ.* II. 74/2 Every one is now familiar with those [candles] made of stearine or stearic acid. **1887** *Encycl. Brit.* XXII. 527/1 Stearine, in commerce, designates a solid mixture of fatty acids (chiefly palmitic and stearic) which is being produced industrially from animal fats and used largely for the making of candles.

b. *attrib.*

1848 J. BURNET *Ess. Fine Arts* iv. 130 His pictures possess that peculiar stearine substance found in the works of Watteau. **1844** *E.A. Parnell's Appl. Chem.* II. 303 Stearine candles, when properly made, are white and inodorous. **1878** A. H. MARKHAM *Gt. Frozen Sea* xix. 267 A stearine lamp.

ˈstearinery. *rare.* [f. STEARIN + -ERY. Cf. F. *stéarinerie*, factory in which stearine is made.] The manufacture of stearine or stearine products.

1875 KNIGHT *Dict. Mech.* 2362/2 The next step made in stearinery was the decomposition of the fats by water.

†**stearing.** *Obs. rare*⁻¹. (See quot.)

1769 COOK *Jrnl.* 23 Mar. (1893) 53 There are also Birds in Newfoundland called Stearings.

stearne, obs. f. STERN.

stearo- (stiːərəʊ), used as combining form of STEARIC or STEARIN in many names of chemical compounds containing or derived from stearin, e.g. *stearochlorhydrin*, *stearoglucose*, *stearolaurin* (see Watts *Dict. Chem.*).

1873 C. H. RALFE *Outl. Phys. Chem.* 21 Stearo-cholesterin. **1911** *Encycl. Brit.* XX. 44/1 Examples of such glycerides are..stearo-palmito-olein [etc.].

stearoid (ˈstiːərɔɪd). [f. STEAR-IN + -OID.] A stearin substance.

1882 T. TWINING *Food & Nutrition* 30 Non-nitrogenous constituents of food. The stearoids or fats.

stearone (ˈstiːərəʊn). *Chem.* Also -on. [f. STEAR-IN + -ONE.] A ketone obtained from stearic acid.

1836 BRANDE *Man. Chem.* (ed. 4) 962 Stearone.—When stearic acid is distilled with a fourth-part of quicklime, a substance is obtained sparingly soluble in ether and alcohol. **1842** *Penny Cycl.* XXIII. 1/2 Stearon.

stearoptene (stiːəˈrɒptiːn). Also -en, -ine. [ad. mod.L. type *stearoptēnum* (Herberger 18..), f. Gr. στέαρ solid fat (cf. STEARIN) + πτηνό-ς winged (taken to represent 'volatile'). Cf. F. *stéaroptène*. Both this and the parallel ELÆOPTENE are bad formations, and do not express the intended meaning.]

The solid crystalline component of a volatile oil, in contradistinction to the liquid part or *elæoptene*; a camphor.

1836 *Penny Cycl.* VI. 204 Camphor is the stearopten, or one of the principles arising from the separation of the volatile oil of [etc.]. **1846** LINDLEY *Veg. Kingd.* 537 The Camphor of commerce..is a kind of Stearoptine. **1887** BENTLEY *Man. Bot.* (ed. 5) 642 The stearoptene called menthol..is said to be derived from *Mentha arvensis*.

†**stearrhœa** (stiːəˈriːə). *Med. Obs.* [a. G. *stearrhœa* (J. H. L. Kunzmaun (or C. W. Hufeland) 1824, in *Jrnl. d. pract. Heilkunde* LIX. 45), f. Gr. στέαρ (see STEATO-) + ῥοία flux.] = STEATORRHŒA.

1842 W. J. E. WILSON *Pract. & Theoret. Treat. Dis. Skin* xiv. 290 (*heading*) Augmentation of secretion. Stearrhoea. **1913** *Q. Jrnl. Med.* VI. 242 The term stearrhoea, or steatorrhoea, has had an unfortunate history. It was originally employed..to designate passage of liquid fat with the stools, but was applied later, by Erasmus Wilson, to the disease of the skin commonly known as seborrhoea.

stearyl (ˈstiːərɪl). [f. STEAR-IN + -YL.] The radical of stearic acid.

1868 WATS *Dict Chem.* V. 426.

steaschist (ˈstiːəʃɪst). *Min.* [f. Gr. στέα-ρ tallow + SCHIST. Cf. F. *stéaschiste.*] A laminated variety of talc.

1833-4 J. PHILLIPS *Geol.* in *Encycl. Metrop.* (1845) VI. 764/2 The limestone is in thin tortuous beds, and as it were dissolved with the shining slate and steaschist. **1874** BIRCH *1st & 2nd Egypt. Rooms Brit. Mus.* 74 The greater number [of these scarabæi] are of a white steaschist or steatite.

steath, obs. form of STAITHE.

steath, steathing: see STOOTH, STOOTHING *north.* and *Sc.*

steatite (ˈstiːətaɪt). *Min.* Also 7-9 in L. form steatites. [ad. L. *steatītis* or *-ītēs* (Pliny), a. Gr. *στεατῖτις, -ίτης (λίθος), a stone resembling tallow, f. στεατ-, στέαρ tallow, suet: see -ITE.] A massive variety of talc, commonly of a grey or greyish green colour, with an unctuous or soapy feel; soap-stone.

α. [**1601** HOLLAND *Pliny* XXXVII. xi. II. 630 Some [precious stones] there be which bear the names of certain members of the body; as for example, Hepatites, of the liuer; Steatites, of the sundry sorts of fat, grease or tallow.] **1758** BORLASE *Nat. Hist. Cornw.* 66 There is a white steatites, in the parish of Guenap, of a more indurated Earth than the former. **1806** *Gazetteer Scot.* (ed. 2) 236 There are several beds of steatites or rock-soap. **1816** PARKES *Chem. Catech.* (ed. 7) 533 *Steatites*, a kind of stone composed of silex, iron, and magnesia. Also called French chalk.

β. **1794** SCHMEISSER *Syst. Min.* I. 192 Steatite Soap Stone. **1803** MALTHUS *Popul.* I. v. 62 In New Caledonia, the inhabitants..are sometimes reduced to eat great pieces of steatite. **1879** RUTLEY *Stud. Rocks* x. 127 Serpentine, steatite, and limonite are probably the most common of these alteration-products of British eruptive rocks.

b. *attrib.*

1839 DE LA BECHE *Rep. Geol. Cornwall*, etc. iii. 97 Steatite veins are found traversing the serpentine. **1851** *Catal. Gt. Exhib.* 1421/1 Two carved steatite ornaments [from China]. **1911** PETRIE *Revol. Civilisation* iii. 54 The splendid steatite vases with reliefs of figures. **1911** *Encycl. Brit.* XXVI. 369/1 In Burma steatite pencils are used for writing on black paper.

Hence **steatitic** (stiːəˈtɪtɪk), † **steaˈtitical** *adjs.*, of or composed of steatite, of the nature of steatite.

1795 J. HUTTON *Th. Earth* I. 616, I have a specimen of steatetical [*sic*] whinstone or basaltes from some part of Cumberland. **1796** KIRWAN *Elem. Min.* (ed. 2) I. 109 A steatitic rock. **1811** PINKERTON *Petral.* II. 235 Basalt, in which the chrysolite is become very steatitical through decay. **1879** RUTLEY *Stud. Rocks* iii. 30 Giving rise to steatitic matter.

steatitous (ˈstiːətaɪtəs), *a.* [ad. F. *stéatiteux*, f. *stéatite*: see STEATITE and -OUS.] = STEATITIC.

1853 TH. ROSS tr. *Humboldt's Trav.* III. xxxii. 386 Green steatitous slate mixed with amphibole.

steatization (ˌstiːətaɪˈzeɪʃən). *Min.* [f. STEAT-ITE + -IZE + -ATION.] (See quot.)

1911 *Encycl. Brit.* XXI. 869/1 There is often extensive 'steatisation', or the deposit of talc and steatite in place of the original minerals of the rock.

steato- (stiːətəʊ), used as combining form of Gr. στεατ-, στέαρ stiff fat, tallow, suet, in many scientific terms, chiefly Medical. **steˈatocele** [a. Gr. στεατοκήλη], a fatty tumour in the scrotum. **steˈatogene, -ˈogenous** *adjs.*, tending to produce steatosis. **steatoˈgenic** *a.* [-GENIC], tending to produce steatosis. **steaˈtolysis** [Gr. λύσις solution] (see quot.); hence **steatoˈlytic** *a.* (see quot.). **steaˈtopathy** [Gr. πάθος disease], disease of the sebaceous glands (Dorland *Med. Dict.* 1913); hence ˌ**steatoˈpathic** *a.*, pertaining to steatopathy.

1693 tr. *Blancard's Phys. Dict.* (ed. 2), **Steatocele*, a Rupture or Tumor in the *Scrotum*, of a Fatty or Suet-like Consistence. **1849-52** *Todd's Cycl. Anat.* V. 1013/1 Collections of fat in the scrotum have been known from the time of Galen by the term steatocele. **1893** E. S. D'ODIARDI *Med. Electr.* 55 Generators of fat, called *steatogene poisons. **1956** *Nature* 14 Jan. 75/1 Experiments on phosphorus poisoning and *steathogenic [*sic*] (Handler) diets in which thioctic acid normalizes the fat content of the liver. **1980** *European Jrnl. Cell Biol.* XXII. 567 After 7 days, steatosis developed in all animals on steatogenic diet alone. **1899** *Allbutt's Syst. Med.* VIII. 741 The *steatogenous functions of the sweat-glands. **1898** *Syd. Soc. Lex.*, **Steatolysis*, the emulsifying process by means of which fats are prepared for absorption and assimilation. **1891** W. D. HALLIBURTON *Text-bk. Chem. Physiol.* 158 Steatolytic [ferments]: those which split fats into fatty acids and glycerine. **1876** DUNGLISON *Med. Lex.*, **Steatopathic*.

steatoid (ˈstiːətɔɪd). *Min.* [Named by E. F. Glocker 1839, from its resemblance to STEATITE:

see -OID.] A name given to the serpentine pseudomorphs found at Snarum, in Norway.

1877 *Watt's Dict. Chem.* V. 426.

‖**steatoma** (stiːə'təʊmə). *Path.* Also anglicized **steatom(e.** [L. *steatōma*, a. Gr. στεάτωμα, f. στεατοῦσθαι to be converted into fat, f. στεατ-, στέαρ fat, tallow. Cf. F. *stéatôme.*] An encysted fatty tumour.

α. **1599** A. M. tr. *Gabelhouer's Bk. Physicke* 18/4 The vlceration Steatoma, a kinde of fatte matter, like suet. **1674** tr. *Barbette's Chirurg.* (ed. 2) 323 Steatoma's and other Abscesses, are often generated in the Caul. **1763** *Phil. Trans.* LIII. 233 The glands of the mesentery..represented small and distinct steatomas. **1854** C. H. JONES *Path. Anat.* iv. 166 A steatoma..is a fatty tumour, with a preponderating excess of areolar tissue.

β. **1737** JAMIESON in *Med. Ess. Edinb.* (ed. 2) III. 354 A large Steatom passing with the Oesophagus from the Thorax into the Abdomen. **1829** *Good's Study Med.* (ed. 3) V. 324 The steatome grows to a larger size, than any of the rest. **1835–6** *Todd's Cycl. Anat.* I. 63/2 Small steatoms are not unfrequent in the eyelids and in the scalp.

steatomatous (stiːə'tɒmətəs), *a. Path.* [f. Gr. στεατωματ-, στέατωμα (see prec.) + -OUS.] Of the nature of or resembling a steatoma.

1681 E. TYSON in *Phil. Coll.* No. 2. 14 In a thin pale Lympha or Serum, there did swim in several..pieces a steatomatous or cruddy Matter. **1772** *Phil. Trans.* LXI. 131 [A] Steatomatous Tumour. **1849–52** *Todd's Cycl. Anat.* IV. 1355/2 The limbs [of the Hottentot] are slight; the buttocks, however, frequently present a steatomatous appearance.

‖**steatopyga** (ˌstiːətəʊ'paɪgə). *Phys.* [mod.L., f. Gr. στεατ-, στέαρ fat, tallow + πυγή rump, buttocks.] A protuberance of the buttocks, due to an abnormal accumulation of fat in and behind the hips and thighs, found (more markedly in women than in men) as a racial characteristic of certain peoples, esp. the Hottentots and Bushmen of South Africa.

1822 W. J. BURCHELL *Trav. S. Afr.* I. xi. 216 *note*, It is not a fact, that the whole of the Hottentot race are thus formed; neither is there any particular tribe to which this *steätopyga*, as it may be called, is peculiar. **1873** ELLEN E. FREWER tr. *Schweinfurth's Heart of Africa* I. vii. 296 Shapes developed to this magnitude..I saw..among the Bongo, and they may well demand to be technically described as 'Steatopyga'.

So ‖**steatopygia** (-'pɪdʒɪə), anglicized **steatopygy** (stiːə'tɒpɪdʒɪ), the condition of having a steatopyga; also *transf.* in *Archæol.* with reference to figurines that display steatopygy; also **steato'pygial** *a.*, **steato'pygism** (both *rare*); **steatopygous** (stiːə'tɒpɪgəs, stiːətəʊ'paɪgəs), *a.*, pertaining to or characterized by a steatopyga; ˌ**steato'pygic** *a.* = prec.

1871 DARWIN *Desc. Man* II. xix. 345 With many Hottentot women the posterior part of the body projects in a wonderful manner; they are steatopygous. **1879** tr. *De Quatrefages' Hum. Species* 52 This steatopygia reappears however in certain tribes situated much further north than the Houzouana races. **1889** *Athenæum* 13 Apr. 475/3 Dr. Topinard has been considering the probable cause of the steatopygy of Hottentot women. **1900** DENIKER *Races of Man* ii. (ed. 2) 93 Steatopygia is characteristic of the Bushman race. **1900** *Jrnl. Anthrol. Inst.* XXX. 253 In..the figure from Adalia..the steatopygia is by no means so pronounced, and is further concealed by the rudeness of the workmanship,..and the abbreviated treatment of the lower limbs. **1901** W. RIDGEWAY *Early Age of Greece* I. i. 66 In the graves females figurines have been found, some steatopygous, one of the slighter type and tattooed. **1910** M. C. HARRISON tr. *Mosso's Dawn of Mediterranean Civilization* ix. 150 *(caption)* Neolithic steatopygic figure, Knossos. **1912** *19th Cent.* Dec. 1219 Hideous autochthonoi of the Upper Nile, whose mis-shapen, steatopygic nudity amazed Old Egypt. **1912** WACE & THOMPSON *Prehist. Thessaly* xii. 225 The..statuettes reported to have been found at Sparta..are clearly of the mainland..type. The legs are short and stumpy, the heads are round, and the steatopygy is most marked. **1923** A. HUXLEY *Antic Hay* ii. 24 Gumbril's Patent Small-Clothes... A comfort to all travellers, civilization's substitute for steatopygism, indispensable to first-nighters. **1932** J. G. D. CLARK *Mesolithic Age in Brit.* iii. 48 Resting on the living rock was found a curious object of shale, thought by the Abbé Breuil to partake of the nature of a phallus or a degenerate steatopygic figurine. **1966** J. MELLAART *Chalcolithic & Early Bronze Ages in Near East & Anatolia* ii. 28 The figurines, both male and female.., show naked or near-naked persons with hands at the waist... The women are slender with small breasts, and exaggerated stomach, enormous navel and a strongly marked pubic triangle, but no steatopygy. **1971** *Ann. Brit. School at Athens* LXI. 66 This figurine..is almost flat, and it is significant that..about half of those from Crete are steatopygous only when viewed from front or rear; from the side they are seen to be almost flat. **1973** F. GARVIE tr. *Buchholz's Prehistoric Greece & Cyprus* 99/2 Thera. Crudely formed, ill-proportioned female clay statuette, with steatopygia, moulded breasts and disc eyes. **1978** J. UPDIKE *Coup* (1979) v. 182 The steatopygial silhouettes of naked mortals.

‖**steatornis** (stiːə'tɔːnɪs). [mod.L. (Humboldt 1814), f. Gr. στεατ-, στέαρ fat + ὄρνις bird.] A bird of the species *Steatornis caripensis*, the type and only representative of the family *Steatornithidæ*; the GUACHARO or oil-bird of South America.

1818 HELEN M. WILLIAMS tr. *Humboldt's Trav.* III. III. vii. 125 The guacharo is of the size of our fowls... I have noted it under the name of steatornis. **1895** *Pop. Sci. Monthly* Apr. 776 Steatornis breeds by the hundreds in the vast gloomy caves.

steatorrhœa (stiːətəʊ'riːə). *Med.* Also **-rrhea.** [Alteration of STEARRHŒA: see STEATO-.] **1.** The excretion of fat with the stools.

1859 R. G. MAYNE *Expos. Lex. Med. Sci.* (1860) 1202/2 *Steatorrhœa*, term for a fatty dejection. **1903** E. L. OPIE *Dis. Pancreas* xiii. 315 In some cases of pancreatic disease..fat is discharged with the fæ ces as an oily, yellow fluid, and the condition may be designated a true steatorrhœa. **1923** A. E. GARROD *Inborn Errors of Metabolism* (ed. 2) ix. 167 Apart from the steatorrhœa there was nothing to suggest disease of the pancreas in either case. **1956** *Nature* 4 Feb. 237/1 These organisms were obtained from a patient with steatorrhœa.., it would appear that fat synthesis of this type [of bacterium] might make a significant contribution to fæcal fat. **1974** R. M. KIRK et al. *Surgery* vi. 100 The stones may occlude the orifice of the pancreatic duct, preventing exocrine..secretions from reaching the bowel, resulting in steatorrhoea.

2. = SEBORRHŒA. Now *rare* or *Obs.*

1878 W. J. E. WILSON *Lect. Dermatol.* 1876–8 259 Steatorrhœa in its commonest form, namely, steatorrhœa simplex or steatorrhœa oleosa..is illustrated by the model No. 571, which affords a striking example of this affection. **1899** *Allbutt's Syst. Med.* VIII. 759 The name seborrhœa (more correctly steatorrhœa) is not a satisfactory one.

‖**steatosis** (stiːə'təʊsɪs). *Path.* [mod.L., ad. assumed Gr. *στεάτωσις, f. στεατοῦσθαι: see STEATOMA and -OSIS.] Fatty degeneration.

1860 MAYNE *Expos. Lex.* **1880** *Med. Temp. Jrnl.* Oct. 5 They are of two kinds, steatosis and cirrhosis. **1897** *Allbutt's Syst. Med.* II. 860 Extensive fatty changes (steatosis) are common in drinkers apart from cirrhosis.

steave, steaven, var. ff. STEEVE, STEVEN.

stecados(e: see STECHADOS.

†**ste'ccado**[1]. *Obs.* Also 7 **steccato, stecata.** [ad. It. *steccada*, mod.It. *steccata* palisade, lists to fight in: see -ADO.]

1. Lists to fight or joust in.

1600 O. E. [M. SUTCLIFFE] *Repl. Libel* Ep. Ded. 9 It shall not be long, before I come into the steccato, and buckle with you againe. *Ibid.* I. vii. 184 A foolish challenger, that euen in the midst of danger conueieth himselfe out of the steccato. **1617** MINSHEU *Ductor.* **1656** BLOUNT *Glossogr.*

2. A palisade of stakes, stockade.

1652 EARL MONM. tr. *Bentivoglio's Hist. Relat.* 29 He master'd the River of Schelde with his famous Stecata. **1654** —— tr. *Bentivoglio's Warrs Flanders* 225 Divers rowes of great Piles of Trees..closed together overthwart with divers others..; they were called Steccadoes... The Steccado of Callo advanced about 120 usual paces.

†**ste'ccado**[2]. *Obs. rare*[−1]. [erron. form of STOCCADO.] A thrust with a rapier.

c **1600** *Distracted Emp.* IV. ii. in Bullen *Old Pl.* (1884) III. 233 Favorytts are not without their steccados, imbrocados and pun[to]-reversos.

stech, stegh (stɛx), *v. Sc.* and *north.* [Of obscure origin.] *trans.* To fill (the stomach) to repletion; to cram (food) into (the stomach). Also *fig.* Also *intr.* for *refl.*

1724 RAMSAY *Tea-t. Misc.* (1775) II. 131 How sair I sweat, To stegh your guts, ye sot. **1725** —— *Gentle Sheph.* III. iv, His father steght his fortune in his wame. *a* **1774** FERGUSON *Election* Wks. (1807) 293 They stech and connach sae the meat Their teeth mak mair than tongue haste. **1786** BURNS *Twa Dogs* 61 An' tho' the gentry first are steghan, Yet ev'n the ha' folk fill their peghan. **1819** W. TENNANT *Papistry Storm'd* (1827) 216 Gae, get Deaf Meg and Crookit Mou'; Stech their how hungry stammachs fou.

†**stechados.** *Obs.* Forms: α. 4, 6 **sticados,** 6 **stycados, stichados;** β. 6–7 **stechados,** 7 **stœ-, stæchados, stæ-, stecados, stecadose;** 6 **stechado, steckado,** 7 **-doe.** See also STICKADOVE, STICKADOOR. [a. med.L. *sticados, stecados* etc., corrupt forms of L. *stœchados* genit. of *stœchas* STŒCHAS.] French Lavender, *Lavandula stœchas*.

α. **1516** *Gt. Herbal* cccxc. (1529) X iv b, Sticados citrine is called barba iouis.., and hercules grasse. De stycados Arabyke. Sticad[o]s arabyke is an herbe that groweth in sharpe places & hylles. **1542** BOORDE *Dyetary* (1870) 288 Mayden-heere, and stycados. *Ibid.* 289 Sticados. **1562** TURNER *Herbal* II. 148 The broth of stichados..is profitable and good for the diseases of the breste.

β. **1578** LYTE *Dodoens* I. lxi. 89 Golde floure Motheworte, or Golden Stechados. **1591** PERCIVALL *Sp. Dict.*, *Cantuesso*, stechado. **1597, 1611** Steckado [see STICKADOVE]. **1621** BURTON *Anat. Mel.* II. iv. I. v. 448 Camomile, Stæchados, ..&c. to be vsed after bathing. **1639** O. WOOD *Alph. Bk. Secrets* 3 Wherein infuse some Stœchados. *Ibid.* 26 The flowers of Stæcados. *Ibid.* 227 Stecadose, or French Lavender, opens all stoppings in body. **1641** FRENCH *Distill.* ii. (1651) 57 The flowers of Stechados.

stechiometry, obs. form of STOICHEIOMETRY.

Stechkin ('stɛtʃkɪn). [The name of Igor Yakovlevich *Stechkin*, Soviet engineer, its designer.] A Soviet 9mm automatic or semi-automatic machine pistol. Also *attrib.*

1962 *Guns Rev.* May 23/2 The Soviets..in 1961 produce[d] an article ostensibly similar in function if not in cyclic rate, to the egregious Star of 1934. It is known as the Stechkin Machine Pistol or 'APS' in Russian notation. **1974** 'J. GRAHAM' *Bloody Passage* v. 82 A Stechkin..A true machine pistol. Best I've seen since the Mauser. **1979** K. BONFIGLIOLI *After You with Pistol* xv. 109 The owner of the tan-coloured hand was grasping a large, crude Stechkin automatic pistol... The Stechkin is by no means a lady's handbag-gun. **1981** J. TRENHAILE *Kyril* i. 4 'You have the gun?' In answer Yevchenko pressed a Stechkin into Stanov's hand.

steck, variant of STEEK *v.*[1]

†**steckle.** *Obs. rare.* Also 5 **stekill.** [? repr. ONorthumb. **stecel* (:—**steklo-*), f. **stecan* STEEK *v.*[1]] The bar of a door.

a **1300** *Cursor M.* 17414 Bot yee him mist þar alsun, Als your steckles war vndon. ? *a* **1500** *Peblis to the Play* xxii, And oure doure hes na stekill.

sted, stedame: see STEAD, STEED, STEPDAME.

steddie, -y, stedding, steddle, stede: see STEADY, STITHY, STEADING, STADDLE, STEAD, STEED.

†'**stedill**, *v. Obs. rare*[−1]. [? f. *stede* STEAD *sb.* Cf. STATHEL, STIGHTLE *vbs.*] *trans.* To array (soldiers), draw up in order.

a **1400–50** *Wars Alex.* 3977 Forþi lat stedill all oure stoure & stedd þam esoundire.

Stedman ('stɛdmən). The name of Fabian *Stedman* (*fl.* 1670), used *attrib.* and in the possessive to designate a method of change-ringing devised by him. Also *absol.*

1731 *Norwich Gaz.* 11 Sept. 4/1 That most noted and harmonious Peal on 7 Bells called Stedman's Triples. **1813** W. SHIPWAY *Campanologia* I. 98 Let a ringer choose what method he will, it must still be on Stedman's principle. **1814** *Ibid.* II. 187 Doubles, or, as commonly called, a Stedman Grandsire, is completed by two singles. **1903** C. D. P. DAVIES *Stedman* 1 Throughout the whole province of Change Ringing, there is no more delightful method than Stedman. **1931** E. MORRIS *Hist. & Art Change Ringing* 78 The Norwich ringers performed a 'touch' of Stedman Cinques. **1957** *Encycl. Brit.* III. 375/2 Stedman's principle, which is *sui generis*, consists in the three front bells ringing their six possible changes, while the remaining pair or pairs of bells dodge. **1975** *Islander* (Victoria, B.C.) 16 Mar. 13/1 They rang a quarter peal of Stedman's triples for Canada's Centennial year.

stedulle, obs. forms of STUDDLE.

stedy(e, stee, var. ff. STEADY, STITHY, STY.

steeboy, steboy, var. ff. STABOY *int.*

steed (stiːd). Forms: 1 **stéda,** 2–6 **stede,** 4 *Sc.* 5 *north.* **sted,** 4–6 **steede,** 4–7 *Sc.* **steid,** (4 **stiede,** 6–7 **stead,** 7 **steade, stied),** 5– **steed.** [OE. *stéda* wk. masc., a stud-horse, stallion:—OTeut. type **stōdjon-*, f. **stōdō* (OE. *stód*) STUD *sb.* Cf. ON. *stedda* mare.

The G. *stute* and Sw. *sto*, mare, seem to be shortened from compounds of OHG. *stuot* and Sw. *sto* (MSw. *stoþ*) = STUD *sb.*]

1. †**a.** In OE., a stud-horse, stallion. *Obs.* †**b.** In ME. and early mod.Eng., a high-mettled horse used on state occasions, in war, or in the lists; a great horse, as distinguished from a palfrey. *Obs.* **c.** From the 16th c. used only *poet.* or *rhetorically* for: A horse, usually one for riding; often with eulogistic adjs. (Also sometimes slightly jocular, as being a rather grandiloquent word.)

a **900** tr. *Bæda's Hist.* II. x. [xiii.] (1890) 138 Ond þone cyning bæd þæt he him wæpen sealde & stodhors..þa..nom his spere on hond & hleop on þæs cyninges stedan [L. *emissarium*]. *c* **1000** ÆLFRIC *Hom.* I. 210 Ne het Crist him to lædan modiᵹne stedan..ac þone wacan assan he ᵹeceas him to byrðre. *c* **1175** *Lamb. Hom.* 5 He mihte ridan ᵹif he walde on riche stede and palefrai. *c* **1200** *Trin. Coll. Hom.* 89 He..bed hem bringen a wig one te riden, noðer stede ne palefrei, ne fair mule. *c* **1205** LAY. 26519 He wende his stede & to him gon ride. *Ibid.* 31405 Nim an hundred steden. *c* **1380** *Sir Ferumb.* 3810 An hors þat is worþ many a toun, No-war nys such a stede. *c* **1385** CHAUCER *L.G.W.* 1115 There was courser wel I-brydelid non Ne stede for to iuste wel to gon. *c* **1400** MAUNDEV. (Roxb.) xxv. 118 Foure whyte stedez..drawez þis chariot. *c* **1430** *Syr Gener.* (Roxb.) 3792 Here Palfreys tho thei forsoke, And to here stedes thei hem toke. *c* **1440** *Promp. Parv.* 473/1 Steede, hors, *dextrarius, gradarius, sonipes.* **1470–85** MALORY *Arthur* VII. xv. 236 Thenne they broughte hym a rede spere and a rede stede. **1593** SHAKS. *Rich. II*, v. ii. 8 Mounted vpon a hot and fierie Steed. **1623** COCKERAM I, *Steed*, a lustie horse. **1667** MILTON *P.L.* IV. 858 The Fiend repli'd not..But like a proud Steed rein'd went hautie on, Chaumping his iron curb. *Ibid.* VI. 17 Chariots and flaming Armes, and fierie Steeds Reflecting blaze on blaze. **1733** POPE *Ess. Man* III. 35 The bounding steed you pompously bestride. **1740** SOMERVILLE *Hobbinol* II. 218 He spur'd his sober Steed, grizled with Age, and venerably dull. **1817** BYRON *Mazeppa* ix, 'Bring forth the horse!'—the horse was brought; In truth, he was a noble steed. **1836** W. IRVING *Astoria* III. 14 Mr. Stuart and his little band mounted their steeds and took a farewell of their fellow travellers. **1841** BORROW *Zincali* I. vii. II. 335 There was one steed which he particularly cherished, the finest horse in Spain. **1852** TENNYSON *Ode Wellington* 55 And a reverent people behold The towering car, the sable steeds. **1894** BARING-GOULD *Deserts S. France* II. 256 He was fanciful about his steed, and always rode choice horses.

d. *transf.* of other animals used for riding.

c **1450** *Mirour Saluacioun* 4121 Ane asse on palmesondaye was his stede certeynly. **1900** POLLOK & THOM *Sports Burma* iii. 77 Neither steed [*sc.* elephant] would budge an inch.

e. Applied to a bicycle.

1877 H. H. Griffin *Bicycles of the Year* 8 The makers relying on the adopted and favourite types whereon to build a good steed.

2. *attrib.* and *Comb.*, as ***steed-subduing*** adj., ***steed-like*** adj. and adv.; † **steed-back** in phr. ***on steed-back***, on horseback; **steed-horse** † (*a*) *Sc.*, a stud-horse, stallion (*obs.*); (*b*) ? *U.S.* a riding-horse; **steid-meir** *Sc.* = stud-mare; † **steed shroud**, the trappings of a horse; † **steed-yoke**, a two-horsed car or chariot.

c **1400–25** Langl. *P. Pl.* C. vii. 43 (MS.F), [Strengest vp-on] *stede-bac. **1766–80** *Hugh Spencer* xxv. in Child *Ballads* III. 280 Now I am on that steede-back that I could not ride. *c* **1425** Wyntoun *Cron.* i. 1030 Þe *steid hors gais in pasture gude, .. þe meris ar wiþin þar sicht. **1842** J. F. Watson *Ann. Philad. & Pennsylv.* (1877) I. 275 He mounted a very fine steed horse. **1818** Milman *Samor* 238 The proud *steedlike tossing of his crest. **1839** Bailey *Festus* xxvii. (1848) 324 The steed-like world stands ready. Mount for life. **1582** *Reg. Mag. Sig. Scot.* 127/2 Unius *steid-meir. *a* **1300** *Cursor M.* 25464 Nu ask i noþer gra ne grene, Ne *stede scrud [*a* 1300–1400 Stede schrud (Gött.); *c* **1375** purtraied stede (Fairf.)]. **1818** Shelley *Homer's Castor & Pollux* 6 *Steed-subduing Castor. **1582** Stanyhurst *Æneis* ii. (Arb.) 52 Hector .. Harryed in *steedyocks [L. *bigis*] as of earst.

steeded (ˈstiːdɪd), *a.* *nonce-wd.* [f. steed + -ed.] With steeds.

1905 R. Garnett *Shaks.* 32 Reading to our rapt silence histories Of steeled and steeded war.

steedless (ˈstiːdlɪs), *a.* [f. steed + -less.] Without a steed.

1795 Anna Seward *Lett.* (1811) IV. 93 When the horses have drawn us to the ocean's brim, they are taken off, and we pursue our needleworks in the steedless vehicle. **1841** Whittier *Norsemen* 20 The .. rapid jar Of the fire-winged and steedless car. **1867** *Chronicle* No. 39. 926/1 Here I linger spearless, steedless.

Hence ˈ**steedlessly** *adv.*

1865 S. Evans *Bro. Fabian's MS.* 118 Shiplessly, steedlessly, Takes he his journey.

steegh, obs. form of sty *v.*

† **steek**, *sb.*[1] *Sc. Obs. rare.* Also steik. [a. Flemish or LG. *stuk*, *stik* piece (= G. *stück*).] = piece *sb.* in certain commercial uses: **a.** a cask of wine; **b.** a coin of specified value; a 'piece' of work (cf. *maisterstik* s.v. masterpiece).

1468 *Extracts Burgh Rec. Edin.* (1869) I. 23 Of Rynche wyne becaus of greitt steikes of ilk crowne ijd. **1573** *Sat. Poems Reform.* xxxix. 207 Sum gat thair handfull of thir half mark steikis. **1581** *Ibid.* xliv. 15 That maisters of ane euil steik of vark Sould ay detest the godlie, vpricht lyf.

steek (stiːk), *sb.*[2] *Sc.* Also steik. [Northern ME. **stīk*(*e*, **stēk*(*e*:—OE. *stice* masc., stitch *sb.*]

1. A stitch (in needlework or knitting).

1737 Ramsay *Sc. Prov.* 30 For want of a steek a shoe may be tint. **1786** Burns *Twa Dogs* 57 A bonie, silken purse .. whare thro' the steeks, The yellow letter'd Geordie keeks. **1823** Galt *Entail* I. iv. 31 With the help of a steek or twa of darning .. it would do very well. **1900** R. J. Muir *Myst. Muncraig* iii. 46 Ye maun e'idently watch every turn o' the shears and every steek o' the needle.

fig. phrase. **1822** Galt *Sir A. Wylie* ii, I hope ye'll allow me to gie her an opportunity to tak up the steik in her stocking. **1834–5** M. Scott *Cruise Midge* xi, When the steek in my father's purse, let down by my mother's spiritual propensities, was taken up.

b. ***every steek***: every 'stitch' (of clothing, etc.).

1820 Scott *Monast.* xxxv, They would tirl every steek of claithes from our back. **1894** Crockett *Raiders* x, We could see the king's ship coming .. wi' every steek o' canvas set.

c. Phr. ***to keep steeks with***; to keep pace or time with.

a **1801** R. Gall *Tint Quey* 39 Poems (1819) 27 Then wi' her hands her tongue kept steeks. **1896** Crockett *Grey Man* vi. 42 The wearers of the butcher's colours had enough to do to keep steeks with us.

2. A strenuous spell or turn of an occupation.

1895 Crockett *Men of Moss-Hags* xxv. 185, I had given up all thought of escape, and was putting in hard steeks at the praying. **1912** A. Reid *Forfar Worthies* 86 Aff I ran at a fine steek.

steek (stiːk), *sb.*[3] *north.* Also 8 stick. [? f. steek *v.*[1]] A strike (of workmen).

α. **1768** *Ann. Reg.* 92/2 The keelmen of Sunderland made a stick, refusing to work. **1825** Brockett *N.C. Gloss.*, *Stick*, or *Strike*, a stand or combination among workmen.

β. **1844** M. A. Richardson *Local Hist. Table Bk.*, Leg. Div II. 2 A somewhat serious disagreement between the keelmen of the Tyne and their employers, which ended in a steek of long continuance. **1862** Smiles *Engineers* III. 10 They were .. hard workers, but very wild and uncouth; much given to 'steeks', or strikes.

steek (stiːk), *v.*[1] Chiefly (now only) *Sc.* and *north.* Forms: 2–5 **steken**, (2 *Ormin* **stekenn**), 4–5 **stekye**, 4–7 **steke**, (5 **stek**), 5–9 *Sc.* **steik**, (6 **steike**), 8–9 *north.* **steck**; *Sc.* and *north.* 6–9 **steak**, 7, 9 **steick**, 7– **steek**; *Pa. t.* 3, 5 **stake**, 4 **stac**, 5 **stak**, 4–5 **stoke**; 5 **steked**, 7 **steek't**, 9 *north.* **steak'd**; *Sc.* 4 **stekyte**, **stekit**, **-yt**, **steikit**, 7 **steeked**, 9 **stieket**, **steekit**; *Pa. pple.* 3–4 **isteke**, 4–5 **y-steke**, **steke**, 5 *Sc.* **stek**, 3–6 **stoken**, (4 **stokin**), 5 **stokyn**, (4 *Sc.* **stekine**), 4–5 **i-stoke**, **y-stoke**, **stoke**; 4–5 **ystekyd**, (4 **isteked**, 5 **stekid**, **steked**); *Sc.* 4 **stekyt**, 4, 6 **stekit**, 6 **steikket**, **steikit**, **steiked**, 8–9 **steekit**, 9 **steeked**. [Early ME. *steken* str. vb., prob. repr. an unrecorded OE. **stecan* (**stæc*, **stǣcon*, **stecen*). This can hardly be anything else than a developed use of the formally identical verb **stecan* to thrust, stab, prick, pierce (see next), but the manner of evolution of the sense 'to shut' is not clear; possibly it may have arisen from the notion of fastening with a pin or bolt. Cf. ME. bisteke *v.*; Sweet gives an OE. *bestecan* 'close, bar (door)', which we are unable to verify.]

1. *trans.* To shut up, enclose, imprison (a person *in* a place); also with *up*. Also *refl.*

c **1200** Ormin 8087, & he toc iwhillc hæfedd mann .. & let hemm stekenn inn an hus, & haldenn swiþe fasste. *a* **1350** *Child. Jesu* 257 Þe false ymages bi gunne to breke þat þe feondes weren inne i steke. **13..** *K. Alis.* 1132 Ac yet heo is in prison stoke. *a* **1400** *Minor Poems fr. Vernon MS.* xxiii. 111 Crist .. Called us fro deþ þer we weore stoke. *c* **1400** *Destr. Troy* 13844 Telamocus he toke, .. Stake hym in a stith house. **1412** *26 Pol. Poems* xi. 5 Oure enemys .. þat hadde vs in cheynes stoken. *a* **1450** Lovelich *Grail* l. 202 In strong presoun they scholen ben stoke. **1816** Scott *Antiq.* xxxvii, If they steek me up here, my friends are like eneugh to forget me.

b. To enclose, shut *up* (a thing *in* a place).

c **1330** *Assump. Virg.* 848 (Add. MS.) That floure was manna yclepid; Hit was in þe tumbe ystekyd. **13..** *E.E. Allit. P.* B. 1524 Goddes .. Þat were of stokkes & stones .. Neuer steuen hem astel, so stoken is hor tonge. *c* **1400** *Destr. Troy* Prol. 11 Sothe stories ben stoken vp, & straught out of mynde. **1401** *26 Pol. Poems* iii. 93 In euyl soule no grace is stoken, ffor wikked soule is graceles. *c* **1421** *Ibid.* xxiii. 65 While obley in yrnes, or boyst ys stoken, Hit nys but bred. **1837** R. Nicoll *Poems* (1843) 144 An' ahint the door o' cauld disdain My heart I canna steek.

† **c.** ? To keep back (the truth). *Obs.*

c **1400** *Cato's Morals* 17 in *Cursor M.* App. iv. 1669 Fainteli for to speke, and þe soþ for to steke, is falsid and blame.

d. To shut out, exclude (a person or thing); to shut (a person) *out* (of doors).

c **1375** *Sc. Leg. Saints* ii. (*Paulus*) 900 Gregor sais .. þat nothir stekis fra godis mercy Of þe fel syne þe quantite Na 3et þe gret ennormyte. **1390** Gower *Conf.* II. 21 That what as evere I [Forgetfulness] thoghte have spoken, It is out fro myn herte stoken. **1402** *Pol. Poems* (Rolls) II. 97 Crist .. hadde noon harborow, to resten in his owne heed, and steken out the stormes. *c* **1412** Hoccleve *De Reg. Princ.* 3469 And wratthe & irous tene Out of þe herte for to spere and steke. **1595** Duncan *App. Etym.* (E.D.S.), *Discludo, secludo*, to steike out. *Ibid.*, *Excludo*, to steik out, to cleck. *Ibid.*, *Secludo*, to steak out. **1792** A. Wilson *Watty & Meg* 183 That ye'll .. Never out at e'ening steek me. **1816** Scott *Antiquary* xxxii, What for are ye steeking them out?—let them come in.

2. To shut up (a place), to close securely, to lock *up*.

a **1225** *Ancr. R.* 50 Lokeð þ te parlurs beon euer ueste .. & eke wel istekene. **1390** Gower *Conf.* III. 314 This Cofre .. thei finde faste stoke, Bot thei with craft it have unloke. *c* **1440** *York Myst.* xxxvii. 193 Þis steede [Hell] schall stonde no lenger stoken, Opynne vppe and latte my pepul passe. **1561** *Maitl. Club Misc.* III. 289 Papisticall jurisdictione aboleschad furth of ye same ye consistorie hows dischergit and stekyt vp. **1563** *Reason. betw. Crosraguel & Knox* A iii b, Wo be vnto you Scribes and Pharises .. for ye steak the kingdome of heauen before men: .. suche as wold enter ye suffer not. **1597** *Skene's Acts Parl. Scot.* Table s.v. *Tavernes*, Tavernes suld be steiked at nine houres, and na person suld be found therein.

fig. *a* **1500** *Lancelot* 316 This process (now) mot closine ben and stek; And furth I wil one to my matter go.

3. To shut, fasten (a door, window, etc.). Also †with *to*, *up* advs.

a **1225** *Ancr. R.* 62 Ase men wolden steken veste euerich þurl .. þat heo muhten bisteken deað þer vte. *c* **1290** *Becket* 689 in *S. Eng. Leg.* 126 In þe Eueninge he bad is knaue to steken þe dore faste. *c* **1380** Wyclif *Wks.* (1880) 341 Summe .. vndurstonden bodily keyȝes, by whiche heuen ȝates shulden be openid and stokune. **1387** Trevisa *Higden* (Rolls) I. 65 Martianus seiþ þat þe ȝates of Caspij beeþ i-steke wiþ yren barres. *c* **1425** *Seven Sag.* (P.) 1352 He ros .. And stoke to the dore anoone. *c* **1440** *Gesta Rom.* xlix. 220 Afterward the knyȝt come home, & he fonde the yate of his castell stoken. **1523–34** Fitzherb. *Husb.* §40 And whan the shepe are in the greate folde, .. steke the gate. **1582** *Reg. Privy Council Scot.* III. 470 The provest and baillies .. hes steikit up thair buith durris. **1728** Ramsay *Monk & Miller's Wife* 57 He knock'd, for Doors were steekit. **1816** Scott *Bl. Dwarf* ix, Will ye gie me your word .. that I am free to come and free to gae, with five minutes to open the grate, and five minutes to steek it and to draw the bolts? **1828** Carr *Craven Gloss.* s.v., Steck the door and come in. **1879** G. Macdonald *Sir Gibbie* xxxiii, And gien 't war a fine simmer nicht 'at a body cud lie thereoot .. I wad steek the door i' yer face.

b. To close, stop *up* (a hole, way, etc.).

13.. *E.E. Allit. P.* B. 439 Þen he stac vp þe stangez, stoped þe wellez. **1375** Barbour *Bruce* xix. 687 We ar the fox & thai the fischer That stekis forouth ws the way. *c* **1380** *Sir Ferumb.* 5189 Ac þys lordes .. habbeþ .. þat hole aȝayn y-stoken. *a* **1774** R. Fergusson *King's Birthday*, The Muse maun also now implore Auld wives to steek ilk hole and bore.

c. *intr.* of a door, also *rarely* of a book.

14.. *Burgh Lawis* xxvi. in *Anc. Laws Scot.* (Burgh Rec. Soc.) 14 He sall suere at he wate neuer whare the dure opynnis na stekis of hym fra wham he bocht that ilke forsayde thyng. **1683** G. Meriton *Yorksh. Dial.* 51 Ile Swear 't upon all Beauks, that opens and steeks. **1737** Ramsay *Sc. Prov.* (1750) 109 When ae door steeks anither opens.

4. *trans.* To shut (the mouth, eyes, ears, heart). ***to steek one's gab***: see gab *sb.*[3]

1303 R. Brunne *Handl. Synne* 11224 But leuer ys me my mouþe to steke Þan y spak oȝt oute of skorne. *a* **1400** *Relig. Pieces fr. Thornton MS.* 51 Steke thyn eghne fro fowle syghtes, thyn heres fro foule herynges, thy mouthe fro foule speche. **1421** *26 Pol. Poems* xviii. 130 Fro wordis of vanyte, ȝoure lippes steke. *a* **1500** *Lancelot* 1651 For qwho his eris frome the puple stekith, .. His dom sall be ful grewous. **16..** *Gude & Godlie Ball.* (S.T.S.) 238 Thow steik thy Ene fra warldis vanitie. **1723** Ramsay *Fair Assembly* xiv, These lips she ne'er should steek. **1786** Burns *Earnest Cry & Prayer* xxx, Sages their solemn een may steek. **1818** Scott *Rob Roy* xxix, I redd ye keep your mouth better steekit, if ye hope to speed. **1893** Stevenson *Catriona* xv, The hand of him aye cawed the shuttle, but his een was steeked.

5. *absol.* To close a place, lock a door.

a **1400** *Relig. Pieces fr. Thornton MS.* 51 It es callede 'cloyster' for it closys and steskys [? *read* stekys], and warely sall be lokkede. *c* **1400** *Apol. Loll.* (Camden) 34 No man is worþi .. noiþer to lowse þat he byndiþ, ne to bynd þat he lowsiþ, befor þat he ȝeuiþ þe key, and kenniþ to opun and to steyke. *a* **1500** *Ratis Raving* I. 466 Wertews .. That beris the ȝettis of thi resone Tyll opin and stek with discreccione.

Hence **steeked**, ˈ**steeking** *ppl. adjs.*

1710 Ruddiman *Gloss. Douglas' Æneis* s.v. *Steik*, As we say Scot. .. a steeked neive. **1732** J. Louthian *Process Crt. Justiciary Scot.* (1752) 137 And also, that ye make steiked and lock-fast Gates .. open. **1790** J. Fisher *Poems* 68 Then cam' he to a steeking slap, Fu cannily he shot it back. **1897** N. Munro *John Splendid* i, The burghers of Inneraora .. slept, stark and sound, behind their steeked shutters.

steek, *v.*[2] *Obs.* exc. *dial.* Forms: 4–6 **steke**, 5–6 *Sc.* **steik**, 6 **steek(e**, 6, 9 *north.* **steak**. *Pa. t.* 4–6 **stak**, 4–5 **stakk**, 5 **stake**, (*Sc.* **stakke**), 4 **stoke**; 4 **stekede**, 4–5 *Sc.* **stekit**, **-yt**, 5 **stekyd**, **stekid**. *Pa. pple.* 4–5 **steke**, 6 **steek**; 4 **stoken**, 4–5 **stokyn**, 6 *Sc.* **stokin**, 5 **stoke**; 4 **i-stekid**, **-yd**, **stekid**, 5 **stekede**, 7 **steaked**, 4–6 *Sc.* **stekit**; 6 *Sc.* **stokit**. [ME. *steke* (pa. t. *stak*, pa. pple. *steke*, *stoken*); recorded only from 14th c., but prob. repr. OE. **stecan* (pa. t. **stæc*, **stǣcon*, pa. pple. **stecen*) = OFris. *steka*, OS. *stekan* (LG., Du. *steken*), OHG. *stehhan* (MHG., mod.G. *stechen*); the WGer. root **stek-* (: **stak-*) is an alteration of OTeut. **stik-*: see stick *v.*[1]

As the ME. *stike* (:—OE. *stician*: see stick *v.*[1]) would normally become *stēke* in certain northern dialects (cf. *prēke* prick *v.*), it is probable that some of the examples below may strictly belong to stick *v.*[1] In ME. the two cognate and partly synonymous vbs. were confused together; the originally strong vb. *steke* was often conjugated weak, and on the other hand its strong pa. t. and pa. pple. ultimately came to be associated with the originally weak stick *v.*[1]]

1. *trans.* To pierce, stab; to transfix. Also, to thrust (a spear, etc.) *through*. Also *fig.*

c **1320** *Sir Tristr.* 2999 Mine hert hye haþ y steke, Brengwain briȝt and fre, þat frende. *c* **1330** R. Brunne *Chron. Wace* (Rolls) 13047 Helmes bowed, & þorow were steke. **1375** Barbour *Bruce* x. 416 [He] stekit him vpward vith ane knyff. *c* **1386** Chaucer *Knt.'s T.* 707 (Camb. MS.) Loue hath hese fery darte so brennyngely I-stekid þour myn trewe carful herte. *c* **1386** —— *Frankl. T.* 748 (Camb. MS.), I hadde wel leuere I-stekyd for to be. **1387** Trevisa *Higden* (Rolls) VII. 121 For overmoche sorwe the herte is stoken and spered. *c* **1440** *Promp. Parv.* 111/2 Daggare, to steke wythe men, *pugio*. **1455** in *Paston Lett.* I. 336 Hit was seyd .. that Harpere and ij. other of the Kynges chamber were confedered to have steked the Deuk York in the Kynges chamber. *c* **1470** Henry *Wallace* I. 197 To cutt his throit, or steik hym sodanlye, He wayndyt nocht. **1596** Dalrymple tr. *Leslie's Hist. Scot.* II. 46 Robert Grahames hand, quhilk sa cruellie stak the king.

absol. *a* **1613** [see snick or snee 1].

2. To fix (a thing) by thrusting in its point or the point of an attached pin, etc.; also, to fix (a thing) upon a point.

c **1374** Chaucer *Troylus* iii. 1372 A broche .. Criseyde hym yaf and stak it on his sherte. **1387** Trevisa *Higden* (Rolls) VI. 427 Uppon grete plates of gold was i-steked [L. *figebatur*] on [of] þe foure irene nayles þat Crist was i-nayled with to þe rode. *c* **1440** *Pallad. on Husb.* iv. 625 Another seith the rootis shal be bored, A wegge in euery boore ek shal he steke. **14..** *Sir Beues* (O.) 2539 The dragons hede he smote of ryght, And stake it vpon his spere. **1513** Douglas *Æneis* iv. xii. 40 Thairwith, gan hir seruandis behald Hir fallin and stekit on the irn cald.

b. To fasten in position. (Without the notion of penetration.)

c **1385** Chaucer *L.G.W.* 2202 Hire couerchif vp-on a pole stekede she. *c* **1440** *Anc. Cookery* in *Househ. Ord.* (1790) 430 Take the greynes of pomogarnard and steke therin. *c* **1450** *Mirk's Festial* 128 Fyue pepynce of encens ben steked in þe paschall lyke to þe crosse. **1513** Douglas *Æneis* vi. x. 21 At the entre, in hy The goldin branche he steikis wp fair and weill. **1843** T. Wilson *Pitman's Pay*, etc. 109 Ahint their lugs, the Customs' sparks Ye see ne langer steekin' Their idle pens.

c. *fig.*

13.. *Guy Warw.* (1891) 418 So michel sorwe is on me steke, þat min hert it wil to-breke. *a* **1400** *Minor Poems fr. Vernon MS.* xlix. 134 An arwe in an houndes buttoke And counseil in a foles herte istoke A-cordeþ wel. *c* **1475** *Partenay* 3538 At hys hert gret noysaunce gan he steke.

3. To set (oneself) in position.

c **1400** *Sc. Trojan War* ii. 210 Ande rytht besyd the hye altere .. Stakke þe seluen in þe walle. **1891** C. Rigby *From Mids. to Martinmas* iii. 24 Ye needn't be steakin' yoursell down on a seat; thear yon Mr. Hazelden int' house, been waitin' an hour on ye.

4. To set or garnish *with* things attached.

c **1385** Chaucer *L.G.W.* 161 A garlond .. Stekid al with lylye floures newe. *c* **1450** *Bk. Curtasye* 509 in *Babees Bk.*, Tho chambur dore stekes þo vssher thenne, With preket and tortes þat conne brenne.

5. To fill *full* of something.

c **1440** *Pallad. on Husb.* vi. 32 Se whether drie or weet, or playn or rowe Hit be, or ful of bosh, or stones steke. *c* **1475**

Partenay 3955 So with fumy smoke Was the caue Anon full As myght be stoke.

6. *intr.* To pierce and remain fixed (in something); to be fixed by or as by piercing.

1340 HAMPOLE *Pr. Consc.* 5602 Þe nayles þat in his hend and fete stak. **13..** *Bonaventura's Medit.* 910 Þe nayles stokyn so fast yn þe tre. *a* **1400–50** *Wars Alex.* 683 Quat sterne is it at ȝe stody on quare stekis it in heuyn? *c* **1400** MAUNDEV. (Roxb.) xiii. 58 Þe whilk brand efterwardes hitt on þe erthe and stakk still þerin and growed. *c* **1450** LOVELICH *Merlin* 7241 This swerd to me is good tokenyng. For this same stak Jn the ston. **1533** BELLENDEN *Livy* II. v. (S.T.S.) I. 146 Þir dartis fast stekand in his targe.

7. To remain fixed where placed, to adhere.

?*a* **1366** CHAUCER *Rom. Rose* 458 She nadde on but a streit old sak, And many a clout on it ther stak. **13..** *Propr. Sanct.* (Vernon MS.) in *Archiv. Stud. neu. Spr.* LXXXI. 89/178 What bond in eorþe þou breke, In heuene beo hit no lengore steke. *Ibid.* 112/90 As heore schip wolde to-breke, And neuer a pece wiþ oþur steke. *c* **1412** HOCCLEVE *De Reg. Princ.* 2573 And as he heng & stak Vppon þe croys, þus to þe kyng he spak.

8. Of thoughts, memories, etc.: To remain fixed and immovable in one's mind, heart, etc.

c **1407** LYDG. *Reson & Sens.* 2088 Declaringe myn oppinion..As hyt stake ryght in my thought. *c* **1412** HOCCLEVE *De Reg. Princ.* 2048 The tendir loue..Vnto his herte stak and satte so nere, That..his counseill yave he clere Vnto his lord. **1412–20** LYDG. *Chron. Troy* IV. 2627 He gan compasse..To be venged of his woundis smerte Vp-on Troylus, þat stak ay in his mynde. **1469** MARG. PASTON in *P. Lett.* II. 364 He woost welle that her demenyng had stekyd soor at our harts. *c* **1485** *Digby Myst.* III. 1256 Thys Iesu.. was put to dethe.., Wheche mater stekytt In my thowth. **1596** DALRYMPLE tr. *Leslie's Hist. Scot.* II. VIII. 127 Quhilk [answer] to him was the mair acceptable, that of a sinceir mynd it proceidet, and quhilk afor stak fast in his awne mynd.

9. To be hindered from proceeding.

c **1330** R. BRUNNE *Chron. Wace* (Rolls) 1453 So ar þo Nykeres faste aboute To brynge schipmen þer hit ys doute, To som swelw to turne or steke. *c* **1386** CHAUCER *Man of Law's T.* 411 (Camb. MS.) For in northumbyrlond the wawis hire caste And in þe se hire schip steked so faste. **1513** DOUGLAS *Æneis* II. xii. 27 Speik mycht I nocht, the voce in my hals sa stak. **1533** BELLENDEN *Livy* II. ii. (S.T.S.) I. 136 This multitude of quhete discending throw tiber abaid and stak stil in þe schald wattir þareof. **1535** JOYE *Apol. Tindale* (Arb.) 20 Thei..so corrupted the boke that the simple reder might ofte tymes be taryed and steek. **1583** *Leg. Bp. St. Androis* 162 in *Sat. Poems Reform.* 358 His schip come never on the schalde, But stak still on the ancker halde. **1603** J. DAVIES (Heref.) *Microcosmos* (Grosart) 13/2 So, thoughts in them, so one another woo To be out first, and so the same doe seeke, That in the Portall of the minde they steeke.

10. To project, stick *out*.

c **1400** *Destr. Troy* 3758 Stokyn ene out stepe with a streught loke.

11. Of a person: To cling tenaciously *to*.

1535 JOYE *Apol. Tindale* (Arb.) 39 Here thou seist whother Tindale is brought for so supersticyously steking to onely one significaccion of this worde *Resurrectio*.

12. To demur, hesitate.

1478 J. PASTON in *P. Lett.* III. 219, I comend with my brodyr..of syche maters as ye wold have amendyd in the bylle that he sent on to yow, and he stake not gretly at it. **1573** G. HARVEY *Letter Bk.* (Camden) 2 As thei them selues have sinc not steekid to tel me. **1579** *Ibid.* 60, I will not steeke to bestowe so mutch in exhibition uppon the University.

steek (stiːk), *v.*[3] *Sc.* and *north.* Forms: 6 steke, styk, stike, steik, stick, 9 steek. [f. STEEK *sb.*[1]]

1. *trans.* To stitch.

1502 *Acc. Ld. High Treas. Scot.* II. 198 For i pund cottoune to it [ane doublat] to steik it with, iij s. **1513** DOUGLAS *Æneis* IV. v. 163 Ane purpour claith..Fetisly stekit with prynnit goldin thredis. **1540** *Acc. Ld. High Treas. Scot.* VII. 389 To be ane doublate to the Kingis grace cuttit and stekit upoun caddes, thre elnis blak sating. **1552** *Ibid.* X. 123 Item, v unce Paris silk to styk the samin [cloik]. **1597** SKENE *De Verb. Sign.* s.v. *Actilia*, Stuffed with caddes, and stiked verie thick with threid. **1886** WILLOCK *Rosetty Ends* (1887) 148 Wi' a stockin' needle an' a bit worsit he steekit it on the inside o' the collar.

2. *intr.* To sew.

1865 JANET HAMILTON *Poems* (1870) 183 An' four bonnie lassies were needlin' an' steekin'. **1871** SARAH S. JONES *Northumbld.* 20/2 Sae I gaed on, aye steek steekin.

Hence **steeked** *ppl. a.*

1503 *Acc. Ld. High Treas. Scot.* II. 204 Item, for ij elne iij quartaris satin, to be ane steikit doublat to the King. **1531** *Ibid.* VI. 17 Ane stikkit doublet. **1541–2** *Ibid.* VIII. 63 Item, gevin to the tapescher for ane stekit matt to hir, xxxvs. **1578** *Invent R. Wardr. Scot.* (1815) 211 Twa steikit coveringis of beddis of holane claith. *Ibid.*, Ane auld stickit covering of grene taffetie.

‖**steekgras** ('stɪəkxras). *S. Afr.* Also †stick-grass; steek-grass. [Afrikaans, f. *steek* to prick + *gras* GRASS *sb.*[1]] Any of several grasses of the genus *Aristida* or *Andropogon*, having spiky awns which damage the fleeces of sheep.

1838 J. ALEXANDER *Exped. Discovery Interior Africa* I. ix. 237 The Boschmans have a peculiar mode of fishing in the 'Oup river; they make conical baskets of stick grass, which is as thick and hard as quills. **1893** W. SPILHAUS in J. Noble *Illustr. Official Handbk. Cape & S. Afr.* (rev. ed.) xiv. 314 A year or two ago the Colony was troubled with a particularly obnoxious seed, that of the 'steekgrass' (*Andropogon contortus*, Ness, and *Aristida congesta*, R. and T.). **1896** R. WALLACE *Farming Industries Cape Colony* v. 99 'Steekgrass' is the colonial name applied to a number of species..having long sharp awns attached to their seeds. **1913** C. PETTMAN *Africanderisms* 474 *Andropogon contortus*..is also a steekgras, but it is not the common one. **1954** D. D'EWES *Mydorp* vii. 57 The seeds of the *steekgras* struck in our stockings and bored relentlessly through to prick the skin. **1975** *Stand. Encycl. S. Afr.* XI. 382/1 Stick-grass or steekgras (*Aristida congesta*) is a biennial pioneer grass.

steeking ('stiːkɪŋ), *vbl. sb.*[1] *dial.* [f. STEEK *v.*[1] + -ING[1].]

1. The action of the verb.

1544 *Acc. Ld. High. Treas. Scot.* VIII. 319 Item, for steking of ane slang put in the *Lyoun* at hir departing witht the ambassatourris,..lvj s.

†**2.** *concr.* A fastening, lock. *Obs.*

c **1375** *Sc. Leg. Saints* vii. (*Jacobus minor*) 785 Bot Ihesus ..come bodyly..&, al vnsterynge þe stekyne of þe presone ..owte of þe cawe þan can me ta. *c* **1400** *Sc. Trojan War* II. 517 Thys horse..In þe which mayd he sere stekynges.

†'**steeking**, *vbl. sb.*[2] *Obs.* [f. STEEK *v.*[2] + -ING[1].] The action of the verb; stabbing.

c **1470** HENRY *Wallace* VIII. 225 The fers steking, maid mony grewous wound.

steeking ('stiːkɪŋ), *vbl. sb.*[3] *dial.* [f. STEEK *v.*[3] + -ING[1].]

1. The action of the verb; stitching; also *concr.* and *attrib.*

1561 *Invent. R. Wardr.* (1815) 140 With a cordoun of gold upoun the sticking maid in broderie. **1568** in G. Chalmers *Mary Q. Scots* (1818) I. 285 *note*, 2 lb. wgt. of fyne steiking silk £12. 16. 0. **18..** *Gay Goss-Hawk* xx. in Aytoun *Sc. Ballads* (1858) I. 180 The claith of it was satin fine, The steeking silken wark.

2. *transf.* in *Mining.* = STICKING *vbl. sb.*

1789 J. WILLIAMS *Min. Kingd.* I. 301 A thin strake or seam of clay betwixt the rider and the side or sides of the vein, which miners call a steeking. **1894** *Northumbld. Gloss.*, *Steekin o' clay*, a thin strake or infiltration of clay in a rock fissure.

‖**steekkan** ('stikkan). Also 8 stekan, stakan, 8–9 steekan, steckan, 9 stechkanne. [Du. *steekkan*, f. *steke-n* to broach, tap (= STEEK *v.*[2]) + *kan* CAN *sb.*] A Dutch liquid measure containing half an anker or about 5¼ gallons English measure.

1728 CHAMBERS *Cycl.* s.v. *Measure* 517/1 Dutch Liquid Measures... The Mingle is divided into two Pints... The Stekan, or Stekamen, contains sixteen Mingles. **1753** Stakan [see ANKER 1]. **1797** *Encycl. Brit.* (ed. 3) X. 718/2 The aume is reckoned at Amsterdam for 8 steckans. **1834** MCCULLOCH *Dict. Comm.* (ed. 2) 34 s.v. *Amsterdam*, The *aam* liquid measure = 4 ankers = 8 steckans. **1847–54** in WEBSTER; and in some later Dicts. **1858** SIMMONDS *Dict. Trade*, *Steekkan*, *Stechkanne*, a Dutch liquid-measure, the 12th part of a barrel.

steel (stiːl), *sb.*[1] Forms: 1 stǽli, steeli, stéli, stýle, 3–4 stel (3 *pl.* stelen), 3–5 stiel, 3–6 stele, 4 styl, *Sc.* steile, 4–5 steell, style, 4–6 stile, *Sc.* steill, 5 steille, stelle, steyle, stiell, 5–6 stell, steyll, still, 6 steelle, steil, stiele, (steiele,) 6–7 steele, 4– steel. [OE. *stýle* neut., earlier *stǽli* = OS. *stehli* (Gallée), OFris. **stêl* (whence *stêlen* made of steel; WFris. *stiel*, NFris. *stel*, *stial*):—OTeut. type **staχljo-m* (literally, something made of steel, but in OE. also used for the metal itself, as in late L. *aciārium* superseded *aciēs*):—f. OTeut. **staχlo-* steel, represented by MLG. *stâl*, MDu. *stael* (mod.Du. *staal* neut.), OHG. *stahal* (MHG. *stahel* neut., masc., mod.G. *stahl* masc.), ON. *stál* neut. (Sw. *stål*; Da. *staal*). Outside Teut. no corresponding word has been found; the OPrussian *stakla* steel is prob. adopted from Teut. with sound-substitution. The root appears to be Teut. **staχ-*: **stag-* (:—pre-Teut. **stak-*) to be firm or rigid: see STAY *sb.*[1]]

I. 1. a. A general name for certain artificially produced varieties of iron, distinguished from those known as 'iron' by certain physical properties, esp. greater hardness and elasticity, which render them suitable as material for cutting instruments, and for various other industrial purposes.

Chemically steel is a nearly pure iron, the proportion of other substances varying from less than 1 to 3 per cent. Formerly 'steel' could be defined as containing more carbon than wrought iron, and less than cast iron; but since about 1860 the name has been extended to certain products containing very little carbon. With a few exceptions the term is now usu. restricted to iron alloys containing not more than 1·7% carbon.

Beowulf 985 Wæs steda nægla ȝehwylc style ȝelicost. *c* **725** *Corpus Gloss.* 1431 *Ocearium* stæli. *c* **825** *Epinal Gloss.* 49 *Accearium* steeli. *c* **1205** LAY. 25814 Hælm an his hafde hehne of stele. *a* **1225** *Ancr. R.* 160 Vor ne beo neuer so briht gold, ne seoluer, ne iren, ne stel, þet hit ne schal drawen rust of on þet is irusted. *c* **1290** *S. Eng. Leg.* 460/130 Wit strongue dores of Ire and stiel. ?*a* **1366** CHAUCER *Rom. Rose* 946 Iren was ther noon ne steell For al was golde. *c* **1380** *Sir Ferumb.* 3313 Grete slabbes of styl & yre to þe walles þo wern y-slente. **1436** *Libel Eng. Policy* in *Pol. Poems* (Rolls) II. 171 Now bere and bacon bene fro Pruse ibroughte Into Fflaundres,..Osmonde, coppre, bow-staffes, stile, and wex. **1526** *Pilgr. Perf.* (W. de W. 1531) 232 b, An hammer of golde is..more worth than is a hammer of stele, yet ye hammer of steile is more profytable. *a* **1548** HALL *Chron.*, *Hen. VI*, 118 He now doubteth not but to find you..as sure to hym as the Adamant to the stele. **1549** *Acc. Ld. High Treas. Scot.* IX. 347 Item, for foure punde steill deliverit to Schir Williame Makdougall, price of the punde xx d.; summa vj s. vij d. **1561** HOLLYBUSH *Hom. Apoth.* 34 b, Take two flynt stones and a pece of stile. **1583** *Rates Custom Ho.* D ij, Looking glasses of Steel. **1601** HOLLAND *Pliny* XXXIV. xiv. II. 514 The purest part thereof [*sc.* of iron ore] which in Latine is called *Nucleus ferri*, *i.* the kernell or heart of the yron (and it is that which we call steele). **1611** BIBLE *Jer.* xv. 12 Shall yron breake the Northren yron, and the steele? **1626** BACON *Sylva* §874 A Looking-Glasse with the Steele behinde, looketh Whiter, than Glasse Simple. *a* **1661** FULLER *Worthies*, *Glouc.* (1662) 349 Steele..is Eldest Brother of Iron, extracted from the same Oare, differing from it not in kind, but degree of purity, as being the first running thereof. It is more hard and brittle (whilest Iron is softer and tougher). **1680** MOXON *Mech. Exerc.* x. 179 Its point is made of tempered Steel. **1812** SIR H. DAVY *Chem. Philos.* 390 Steel is usually made by a process called cementation, which consists in keeping bars of iron in contact with powdered charcoal in a state of ignition for 10 to 12 days. **1823** W. PHILLIPS *Min.* (ed. 3) 214 It is also said that pseudo-volcanic steel..was found a league and a half from Neiss. **1866** G. EDE *Managem. Steel* (ed. 4) ii. 15 Steel is a compound of iron and carbon... The carbon rarely exceeds two per cent. **1870** YEATS *Nat. Hist. Comm.* 355 Spathose pig-iron can be converted into steel without any intermediate processes. **1890** *Nature* 20 Nov. 51 The old definition of steel, i.e. a compound of iron and carbon, is as true as ever, when applied..to tools with cutting edges &c. .. The Bessemer product cannot in this sense be termed steel at all. **1895** E. L. RHEAD *Metallurgy* xi. 137 Steel proper contains from 0·5 to 1·5 or 1·7 per cent. of carbon. **1946** *Thorpe's Dict. Appl. Chem.* (ed. 4) VII. 47/1 Steel may be roughly defined as an alloy of iron and carbon containing up to 1·7% carbon, all of the carbon being in the combined condition. A second definition, distinguishing it from cast or wrought iron, is that it has been produced in the molten condition, and a third states that steel can be hardened by quenching from a suitably high temperature. There are.. certain exceptions to all these definitions. **1967** A. H. COTTRELL *Introd. Metall.* xi. 135 At present, about 80 per cent of steel in Britain is made by the open hearth process. **1976** *Sci. Amer.* July 68/2 For the iron to be made into steel (defined as iron with a carefully controlled carbon content of 1·7 percent or less) the sulfur, the silicon and the excess carbon must be removed. **1983** *Steel Times* Aug. 424/1 Even in the mildest of mild steels, with a carbon content of not more than 0·2% carbon, some other elements are present.

b. A particular variety or sort of steel.

1839 URE *Dict. Arts* 1172 The bars are exposed to two or three successive processes of cementation, and are hence said to be twice or thrice converted into steels. **1891** *Daily News* 14 Dec. 2/6 Fair orders for self-hardening and other special steels are coming in. **1898** *Ibid.* 25 Apr. 9/4 A steady business is being done in all kinds of Swedish steels.

c. with defining attribute: see also BESSEMER-, BLISTER- (*sb.* 4), CAST (*ppl. a.* 8), TOOL- (*sb.* 5) *steel*; SHEAR-STEEL.

1812 SIR H. DAVY *Chem. Philos.* 390 Cemented steel is made into the substance called cast steel by being fused in a close crucible with a mixture of powdered glass and charcoal. **1822** IMISON *Sci. & Art* II. 107 Steel of cementation. *Ibid.*, Natural steel is made by keeping cast iron in a state of fusion in a furnace. **1858** GREENER *Gunnery* 129 Mr. Armstrong may..lay claim to being an originator of wrought steel cannon;..to Mr. Krupp is due the honour of first introducing cast steel cannon to the notice of our Government. **1876** VOYLE & STEVENSON *Milit. Dict.* 406/1 *Firth's Steel*, the steel used in the manufacture of the tube of British rifled guns. **1892** GREENER *Breech-loader* 12 The alloys of iron, manganese steel, nickel steel, aluminium steel, ..are not yet made of such uniform quality as will admit of their adoption by gun-makers of reputation. **1900** *Engineering Mag.* XIX. 766/1 The use of concrete and of concrete steel for dry-dock work. **1902** *Westm. Gaz.* 24 July 8/1 The hull..is built of chrome steel.

¶**d.** Applied (after It. *acciaio*; cf. STEEL GLASS 2) to: An alloy of tin and copper used for making optical 'spheres'. *Obs. rare.*

1662 MERRETT *Neri's Art Glass* cxiii. 166.

e. The name of a cold shade of grey resembling the colour of steel; steel-grey. Also as *adj.*

1851 E. RUSKIN *Let.* 28 Dec. in M. Lutyens *Effie in Venice* (1965) II. 236 Falkenhayn gave..to Jane a steel glacé silk dress. **1881** [see BURGUNDY 2d]. **1895** *Montgomery Ward Catal.* Spring & Summer 9/2 Chambray mixtures in steel or blue with narrow white stripes. **1914** [see BEAVER[1] 2c]. **1925** in M. & N. Ward *Home in Twenties & Thirties* (1978) 39 Maids' morning dresses of strong washing gingham..in blue, grey, butcher, or steel.

2. a. Similative and figurative uses, in which steel is taken as the type of hardness.

c **1205** LAY. 25879 Þe alle þine leomen wule to-draȝen þeh þu weore stel al. **1297** R. GLOUC. (Rolls) 3956 Þey my tonge were of stel, me ssolde noȝt dure þer to. *a* **1300** *Cursor M.* 4297 Þof his hert al stillen were, Hert o stele and bodi o brass. *c* **1375** *Sc. Leg. Saints* xvi. (*Magd.*) 408 Weman..with wordis cane rycht wele our-cum mene hard as stele. **1606** SHAKS. *Ant. & Cl.* IV. iv. 33 Like a man of Steele. **1633** G. HERBERT *Temple*, *Sacrifice* liii, He would not cease to kneel, Till all were melted, though he were all steel. **1772** *Gentl. Mag.* Mar. 149/2 A lawless set of levellers in the North of Ireland, called *Hearts of Steel*, attacked the house of Richard Johnson, Esq. **1849** ROBERTSON *Serm.* Ser. I. xiii. (1866) 216 The heart of steel which beat beneath the Roman's robe. **1853** *Ibid.* Ser. IV. xvii. (1876) 222 We have steel and nerve enough in our hearts to dare anything.

b. Phrase, ***true as steel*** (said of persons, rarely of things, statements, etc.). Also, † ***steel to the (very) back***: thoroughly robust; thoroughly trustworthy.

a **1300** *Siriz* 95 in *Anecd. Lit.* (1844) 5 Oure love is also trewe as stel, Withouten wou. *c* **1330** R. BRUNNE *Chron. Wace* (Rolls) 4864 Tristiloker þan ony stel. *c* **1385** CHAUCER *L.G.W.* 334 That ben as trewe as euer was any steel. **1589** NASHE *Martin Marprelate* Wks. (Grosart) I. 174 Report it of my word; for it is as true as steele. **1599** PORTER *Angry Wom. Abington* (Percy Soc.) 41, I promise ye, maister Philip, you haue spoken as true as steele. **1705** DUNTON *Life & Err.* 244 He's as true as Steell to his Word. **1862** MRS. HOUSTON *Recomm. Mercy* iv, True as steel to the man to whom she had sworn to be faithful unto death.

1588 SHAKS. *Tit. A.* IV. iii. 47 We are.. No big-bon'd men, fram'd of the Cyclops size, But mettall Marcus, steele to the very backe. **1600** HOLLAND *Livy* XXXIX. xl. 1050 His bodie was steele to the verie backe [L. *ferrei prope corporis*]. **1603** CHETTLE etc. *Grissill* II. C 1 b, Hee's Steele to the backe you see, for he writes Challenges. **1635** HEYWOOD *Philocoth.* 44 One that is steele to the backe. [Here euphemistically of a drunkard.]

c. *Sport.* Power of endurance or sustained effort.

1850 SMEDLEY *Frank Fairlegh* xxxi. 256 The horses are in first-rate condition.. till they've done about ten miles; that takes the steel out of them a bit. **1891** *Daily News* 8 July 8/3 The Oxonians struggled on pluckily, but the steel was taken all out of them by this time. **1897** W. H. THORNTON *Reminisc. W.-Co. Clergyman* vii. 233 All the steel and energy had left me.

3. a. Steel in the form of weapons or cutting tools (occas. spurs, a trap, etc.). Hence in particularized use, †a sword, lance, bayonet, or the like.

a **1000** *Riddles* xciii. 18 Blod ut ne com, heolfor of hreþre, þeah mec heard bite stiðecȝ style. *c* **1205** LAY. 9799 Helmes þer gullen stercliche to-stopen mid steles egge. *Ibid.* 19503 Mid bitele stelen. *c* **1250** *Owl & Night.* 1030 For heom ne may halter ne bridel Bringe from here wode wyse, Ne mon mid stele ne mid ire. **1581** A. HALL *Iliad* VIII. 143 He with these words doth plucke his bow, & sends his piercing steele, To Hector straight. **1593** SHAKS. *Rich. II*, III. ii. 59 Euery man that Bullingbroke hath prest, To lift shrewd steele against our Golden Crowne. **1597** J. PAYNE *Royal Exch.* 23 Yt ys as a rustie cancker eatinge throw without recoverie by eyther gentle oyle or the hard steele. **1602** tr. *Guarini's Pastor Fido* IV. iii. L 2 b, Mirtillo.. throwes his Dart, thinking to wound Nicander: And had the steele hit as he did direct, Nicander had been slaine. **1712** SHAFTESB. *Charac.* (1733) III. 115 But who wou'd dream that out of abundant Charity and Brotherly Love shou'd come Steel, Fire, Gibbets, Rods. **1735** SOMERVILLE *Chase* III. 206 By th' indented Steel With Gripe tenacious held, the Felon grins, And struggles, but in vain. **1764** *Oxf. Sausage* 59 Or Groom invade me.. whose emaciate Steeds.. Had panted oft beneath my goring Steel. **1784** COWPER *Task* III. 414 No meaner hand may discipline the shoots, None but his steel approach them. **1810** SCOTT *Lady of L.* V. x, The stern joy which warriors feel In foe-men worthy of their steel. **1815** BYRON *Hebr. Melodies, Song Saul* 4 Bury your steel in the bosoms of Gath! **1892** KIPLING *Barrack-room Ballads* 139 Grapple her stern and bow. They have asked for the steel. They shall have it now; Out cutlasses and board! **1896** *Harper's Mag.* XCII. 708/1 He trained his soldiers to trust the steel.

b. *cold steel*: cutting or thrusting weapons.

[Cf. G. *kalter stahl*; also *cold iron* (COLD *a.* 1 b, IRON *sb.* 6 a) = ON. *kalt járn*].

1816 [see COLD *a.* 1 b]. **1896** BADEN-POWELL *Matabele Campaign* vi, Nor do they wait for their bayonets:.. for though fond of administering cold steel, it is the last thing they wish to meet with themselves.

c. *U.S.* ***to draw one's steel***: to use one's pistol.

1902 WISTER *Virginian* ii, He has handed Trampas the choice to back down or draw his steel.

d. Used for: Steel shot.

1898 *Westm. Gaz.* 1 June 5/1 The crews at the port batteries were pumping steel at the enemy.

4. Steel as the material of defensive armour.

c **1320** *Sir Tristr.* 3324 Þai gun hem boþe armi In iren and stiel þat tide. *a* **1400-50** *Wars Alex.* 1378 Þan Alexander all his ane an-ane he ascendis, Closid all in clere stele. *c* **1450** in Kingsford *Chron. London* (1905) 120 Stedes þ[er] stumbelyd in þ[t] stownde þ[t] stood stere stuffed vnder stele. *c* **1470** *Gol. & Gaw.* 200 Weill stuffit in steill, on thair stout stedis. **1500-20** DUNBAR *Poems* xxvii. 81 So stern he wes in steill. **1602** SHAKS. *Ham.* I. iv. 52 In compleat steele. **1667** MILTON *P.L.* II. 569 Or arm th' obdured brest With stubborn patience as with triple steel. **1842** TENNYSON *Galahad* 6 The hard brands shiver on the steel.

fig. **1634** MILTON *Comus* 421 She that has that [chastity], is clad in compleat steel. **1817** SHELLEY *Rev. Islam* VIII. vii. 9 Though truth and virtue arm their hearts with tenfold steel.

5. As a material for plates engraved with drawings or designs to be reproduced by printing. Hence, as a trade term: A steel engraving.

1843 J. BALLANTINE (*title*) The Gaberlunzie's Wallet. With numerous illustrations on steel and wood. **1887** *Athenæum* 11 June 779/1 A re-issue of the Examples of the Architecture of Venice. By John Ruskin... With the Text, and the 16 Plates (10 Steels and 6 Lithographs) as originally published.

6. a. Iron as used medicinally; chalybeate medicine.

In early practice iron or steel filings were sometimes administered internally; another mode of exhibition was to give the water in which iron or steel had been quenched when red hot, or had been allowed to remain for some days. The ordinary notion was that 'iron' and 'steel' were different medicines, with similar but not identical therapeutic effect. '*Steel* is now used in untechnical lang. for any chalybeate medicine, perh. especially iron chloride' (*N.E.D.*).

1647 HAMMOND *Serm.* x. Wks. 1683 IV. 535 A stronger physick is now necessary, perhaps a whole course of steel: A physick, God knows, that this Kingdom hath been under five or six years. **1675** G. HARVEY *Dis. Lond.* xxiii. 249 Medicines prepared of Steel have their particular uses. **1699** GARTH *Dispens.* IV. 58 Some fell by Laudanum, and some by Steel, And Death in ambush lay in ev'ry Pill. **1702** J. PURCELL *Cholick* (1714) 159 The only Addition.. to be made, is the use of gentle Steel. Strong Steel.. will heat too much. **1704** J. HARRIS *Lex. Techn.* I, *Steel* is not so good as Iron for Medicinal Operation. **1706** WATTS *Horæ Lyricæ* II. 146 When bark and steel play well their game To save our sinking breath. **1712** SWIFT *Jrnl. to Stella* 18 Sept., The doctor tells me I must go into a course of steel, though I have not the spleen. **1801** *Med. Jrnl.* V. 212 Dropsy.. yielded to the stimulus and invigorating powers of steel combined with diuretics. **1866** P'CESS ALICE *Mem.* (1884) 158, I.. am really only kept alive by steel. **1898** *Hutchinson's Arch. Surg.* IX. 303 At first iodide of potassium was given, but subsequently steel.

b. † ***salt of steel***: usually, iron chloride (but used also for the sulphate or other salts of iron). ***flowers of steel***: iron chloride prepared by heating steel filings, etc. with sal-ammoniac. † ***sugar of steel***: see SUGAR *sb.* 3 a. ***tincture of steel***: tincture of iron chloride.

1704 J. HARRIS *Lex. Techn.* I, *Vitriol of Mars*, or Salt of Steel, is made by dissolving Steel in some proper Acid Menstruum, then Evaporating [etc.]. **1758** [R. DOSSIE] *Elaboratory laid open* 291 Ens veneris, or flowers of steel. Take, of washed colcothar of green vitriol, or steel filings, one pound, of sal ammoniacum, two pounds [etc.]. **1758** E. WRIGHT in *Phil. Trans.* L. 598 Salt of steel, taken internally, must retain its astringency until it be precipitated. **1765** A. DICKSON *Treat. Agric.* (ed. 2) 45 Plants of barley were poisoned.. by salt of steel. **1797** *Encycl. Brit.* (ed. 3) IV. 465/1 These [crystals] are named *salt of steel*, and are used in medicine; but for the salt made with the pure acid and iron, the common copperas is commonly substituted. **1818** S. F. GRAY *Suppl. Pharmacop.* 267 Tincture of Steel.

7. The steel part of anything.

c **1450** *Merlin* vi. 98 The archebisshop lowted to the swerde, and sawgh letteres of golde in the stiel. *Ibid.* xiv. 222 The stiell of the speres stynte at the haubrekes. **1471** CAXTON *Recuyell* (Sommer) 160 Employeng the steell of his swerd the most best wyse that in hym was possible. **1561** EDEN tr. *Cortes' Art Navig.* III. iv. 63 Whiche shalbe the marke for the settynge of the Irens and Stieles [in making a mariner's compass]. **1816** BYRON *Siege Cor.* xxvi, Many a hand's on a richer hilt, But none on a steel more ruddily gilt. **1895** *Daily News* 22 Aug. 6/2 It is far longer in the steel than a common salmon hook, and is a double hook.

8. As the name of various instruments made of steel. **a.** A piece of steel shaped for the purpose of striking fire with a flint. †In a pistol or firelock, the piece of steel which is struck by the 'cock' carrying the flint.

c **1220** *Bestiary* 535 Of ston mid stel in ðe tunder wel to brennen one ðis wunder. **1589** [see FLINT *sb.* 2]. **1590** SIR J. SMYTH *Disc. Weapons* 47 Or vpon the hammers or steeles, if they be Snap-hances. **1619** H. HUTTON *Follies Anat.* B 2 b, Where's your Tobacco box, your steele and touch? **1660** BOYLE *New Exper. Phys.-Mech.* xiv. 89 The Cock falling with its wonted violence upon the Steel. **1701** *Lond. Gaz.* No. 3708/3 The Hammer, a Bag, a Pick-Ax, a false Key, and a Steel, were left by the said Murderers. **1833** *Reg. Instr. Cavalry* I. 99 Bring the Carbine.. to the priming position, the thumb before the steel. **1837** CARLYLE *Fr. Rev.* II. VI. vii, Nor will the steel-and-flint answer, though they try it.

b. A rod of steel, fluted or plain, fitted with a handle, used for sharpening table or butchers' knives.

1541 *Extracts Aberdeen Reg.* (1844) I. 176 The steill to scherp the schawing jrne. **1580** HOLLYBAND *Treas. Fr. Tong, Vn Fusil*.. the stile of a butcher wherewith he whetteth or sharpeneth his kniues. **1688** HOLME *Armoury* III. 292/2 The Butchers Steel.. is his only badg of being a Slaughter-Man. **1758** JOHNSON *Idler* No. 67 ¶5 A man whose steel by his side declared him a butcher. **1851** MAYHEW *Lond. Labour* I. 177/1 A butcher's knife, 1*s.*; a steel, 1*s.* 6*d.* **1894** HALL CAINE *Manxman* 186 Cæsar sharpened the carving-knife on the steel.

†c. A steel mirror. *Obs.* (? *nonce-use.*)

a **1643** CARTWRIGHT *Lady Errant* V. iv, The Steels you see your faces in.

d. A flat-iron. *Obs.* exc. *dial.*

1638 J. TAYLOR (Water P.) *Bull, Bear & Horse* (1876) 39 One of them having occasion to use a Steele, smoothing Iron, or some such kinde of Laundry Instrument. **1873** *Exhibition* 67 (E.D.D.) Weth a iron flat, what they do iron clooas weth, called a still.

e. A needle; a knitting-needle. *dial.*

[**1784** COWPER *Task* IV. 165 The threaded steel.. Flies swiftly.] **1839** M[c]DOWALL *Poems* 87 (E.D.D.) 'Twere better she had steek'd her gab Wi' steel an' thread. **1901** 'ZACK' *Dunstable Weir* 133 At that mother would pick up her knitting and clack the needles together till the stitches fair tumbled from the steels.

†f. A stylet, a stylus. *Obs.*

1799 G. SMITH *Laboratory* I. 230 With a pointed steel, or needle, draw or write on it what you please.

g. ***the steels*** = skates.

1875 *Field* 2 Jan. 1/3 The ladies, whenever they can, are acquiring the use of the steels. **1895** *Outing* XXVII. 201/1 Considerable skill on the steels.

9. *Dress.* **a.** A strip of steel used to give stiffness or support, or to expand a dress.

1608 MACHIN *Dumb Knt.* I. i, I haue a ruffe is a quarter deep, measured by the yard... You haue a pretty set too, how big is the steele you set with? **1885** *Pall Mall Gaz.* 11 May 4/1 Creatures with 16-inch waists, and a weight of steels, horse-hair, and drapery depending therefrom. **1891** *Eng. Illustr. Mag.* Dec. 198 A semi-tubular arrangement of steels, that gave a peculiar swinging motion to the train of the dress. **1904** *Daily Chron.* 22 Feb. 5/4, I suppose the bullet must have struck the steels in my corsets.

b. A dress trimming made of steel beads or ornaments.

1899 *Daily News* 26 Jan. 6/3 A trailing skirt embroidered in what is termed fine steel.

10. *pl.* (*Finance.*) Shares in steel-manufacturing companies.

1912 *Times* 19 Dec. 19/4 Steels lost ½ in the Common and 1 point in the Preferred stock at 35¾ and 64 respectively. **1913** *Ibid.* 13 Sept. 17/3 Industrials were generally good, with Steels prominent on trade advices.

II. *attrib.* and *Comb.*

11. *attrib.*, passing into *adj.* Made or consisting of steel.

Such combinations are sometimes hyphened or formed into one word (e.g. *steel-filings, steelwork*) in order to indicate their specific character.

c **1400** *Laud Troy Bk.* 4679 Coffres grete with stele barrelles. **1497** *Naval Acc. Hen. VII* (1896) 108 Stele spades.. vj. **1537** *Bury Wills* (Camden) 130 My stell pan and my lyttell huche on the soller. **1542** *Invent. R. Wardr. Scot.* (1815) 63 Item ane steill mirrour set in silver. **1607** B. BARNES *Divils Charter* V. i. K 2, He shall haue two steele bullets strongly charg'd. *a* **1618** *Rates of Merchandizes* L 4, Steele Wire. **1681** GREW *Musæum* I. §7. ii. 169 The under parts blew, exactly like that colour which Watch-Makers and others give to their Steel-Works. **1697** —— *Epsom Waters* 46 Take, of Steell-Filings powder'd, ten Grains. **1760-72** H. BROOKE *Fool of Qual.* (1809) IV. 117 As steel-dust rushes to adamant. **1771** *Encycl. Brit.* III. 511/2 A slender sharp-pointed steel-bodkin. **1854** EMERSON *Lett. & Soc. Aims, Poet. & Imag.* Wks. (Bohn) III. 143 As when a boy finds that his pocket knife will attract steel filings. **1890** W. J. GORDON *Foundry* 63 All the steelwork of the ship is made in the shop except the fore and aft posts. **1944** M. LASKI *Love on Supertax* xi. 103 A tall steel-mesh gate. **1976** J. WHEELER-BENNETT *Friends, Enemies & Sovereigns* v. 156 King Peter attributed his father's, King Alexander's, death to the fact that.. he had not worn his steel-mesh bullet-proof shirt.

b. often of weapons and armour.

1340-70 *Alisaunder* 416 Strained in stel ger [*MS.* stelger] on steedes of might. **13..** *Gaw. & Gr. Knt.* 260 Þy burȝ & þy burnes best ar holden, Stifest vnder stel-gere on stedes to ryde. *c* **1400** *Destr. Troy* 9634 Mony stoute þere was storuen vnder stel wedis. *c* **1460** *Towneley Myst.* xvi. 107, I shuld with this steyll brand Byrkyn all his bonys. **1549** *Compl. Scot.* xix. 163 In steil iakkis and in cotis of mailȝe. **1551** *Acc. Ld. High Treas. Scot.* X. 18 My lord governouris steill bonett. **1588** *Shuttleworths' Acc.* (Chetham Soc.) 44 Sixtene hundrethe and a halffe of plates to be a stiell cote, ix[s] vj[d]. **1632** W. LITHGOW *Trav.* III. 89 On his head he weareth a bare steele cap. **1814** SCOTT *Ld. of Isles* VI. xxxii, Stirrup, steel-boot, and cuish gave way. **1829** —— *Anne of G.* xxvi, I will grasp the mountain-hedgehog, prickles and all, with my steel-gauntlet. **1868** MORRIS *Earthly Par., Man born to be King* 1259 Raise up the steel-cap from thine head.

c. in poetical or rhetorical allusion to the use of steel for armour or weapons.

1604 SHAKS. *Oth.* I. iii. 231 (Qo.) The tyrant custome.. Hath made the flinty and steele Cooch of warre My thrice driuen bed of downe. **1815** SCOTT *Field of Waterloo* xi, Steel-gleams broke Like lightning through the rolling smoke. **1837** CARLYLE *Fr. Rev.* I. III. ix, So, however, with steel-besom, Rascality is brushed back into its dim depths.

12. Indicating medicaments, etc. containing iron, as ***steel drops, lozenge, pill, water, wine.***

1652 FRENCH *Yorksh. Spa* x. 92 To mix some Sugar of steel, or steel wine with the first glass. **1675** G. HARVEY *Dis. Lond.* xxiv. 264, I have found a singular Virtue in Steel drops, præpared after my Mode. **1712-13** SWIFT *Jrnl. to Stella* 17 Feb., I.. take some nasty steel drops, and my head has been better. **1713** *Phil. Trans.* XXVIII. 248 Our English Steel-Waters at Tunbridge. *a* **1734** NORTH *Exam.* III. ix. §7 (1740) 653 Let the Author reflect upon the Need he hath of such a Steel Course as this. **1818** S. F. GRAY *Suppl. Pharmacop.* 308 Steel lozenges. **1858** SIMMONDS *Dict. Trade, Steel-wine*, sherry wine in which steel filings have been placed for some time. **1865** *Morn. Star* 23 June, A box of steel pills. **1900** *Allbutt's Syst. Med.* V. 620 Cod-liver oil and steel wine are useful in the later stages.

13. Of or belonging to steel as a product or an article of commerce, as ***steel man, mine, plant, town, trade, works.***

1601 HOLLAND *Pliny* VII. lvi. I. 188 The discoverie of the yron and steele mines. **1837** CARLYLE *Fr. Rev.* III. v. vi, From their new dungeons at Chantilly, Aristocrats may hear the rustle of our new steel furnace there. **1842** *Penny Cycl.* XXIII. 2/2 The usual operation in large steel-works is first to cut the bar-iron into certain lengths. **1869** RANKINE *Machine & Hand-tools* Pl. E 1, The Plate represents the steel plant at the Langley Mill Steel and Iron Works. **1890** W. J. GORDON *Foundry* 111 Let us cross to the steel-sheds again. **1905** F. HARRISON *Chatham* vi. 106 The toilers in those mines and steel-yards [of Pittsburg]. **1921** *Daily Colonist* (Victoria, B.C.) 1 Oct. 9/3 Mr. Fraser outlined the benefits that would come.. from the erection of a steel plant here. **1922** L. MUMFORD in H. E. Stearns *Civilizations in U.S.* 10 The steel towns of the Ohio [River]. **1961** *Universe* 27 Jan. 2/4 Steelmen There. Pope John on Monday received members of the council of the European coal and steel authority. **1976** *National Observer* (U.S.) 24 Jan. 1/1 East Chicago, Ind., a smoky Lake Michigan steel town that isn't exactly famous for its esthetic splendor even when the sun shines. **1977** *Times* 19 Dec. 13/3 Sound arguments have been put forward by many respected steelmen for moving away from the large integrated coastal works. **1979** *Steel Times Internat.* Sept. 91/2 The building of a new steelplant.

14. = engraved on steel.

1880 'MARK TWAIN' in *Mark Twain Let. Writer* (1932) iii. 48 The best picture I have had yet is the steel frontis-piece to my new book. **1884** *Athenæum* 19 July 83 The volume will contain a steel portrait of the author.

15. a. With the sense 'resembling steel' (in colour, hardness, etc.), as ***steel gloss; steel-bright, -hard, -sharp, -straight, -strong, -thin,*** adjs.; esp. with names of colour, as ***steel-black, -blue, -grey, -green*** adjs. and sbs.

1560 PHAER *Æneid* x. (1562) G gj, Wher neuer cessing soyle doth steelebright stuff send out from mines. **1817** STEPHENS in *Shaw's Gen. Zool.* X. I. 88 Steel-blue Swallow. *Ibid.* 93 Top of the head.. shining steel-black. *Ibid.* 97 Upper parts of the plumage black, with a steel gloss. **1833** JARDINE *Humming-Birds* 146 On the throat is a patch of the clearest violet-blue, shading off to steel-blue on the sides. **1842** PARNELL *Chem. Anal.* (1845) 273 A steel-gray crust of metallic arsenic. **1882** CROOKES *Dyeing & Tissue-Printing* 197 Dark Steel Greens on Half Woollens. **1899** A. H. EVANS *Birds* 548 *Manucodia atra* is steel-green and black. **1916** A. HUXLEY *Burning Wheel* 8 The adamant core and the steel-hard chain. **1920** E. SITWELL *Wooden Pegasus* 32 Dusty voice that throbs with heat, Hoping with its steel-thin beat To put stitches in my mind. **1921** J. BUCHAN *Path of King* i. 9 The world put on a new dress, all steel-blue and misty green... Spring had fairly come. **1923** D. H. LAWRENCE

Birds, Beasts & Flowers 29 Sit beside the steel-straight arms of your fair women. *Ibid.* 177 Steered and propelled by that steel-strong snake of a tail. **1944** BLUNDEN *Shells by Stream* 4 Steel-sharp might Which blows the babe and nurse to atoms in the night. **1944** A. L. ROWSE *English Spirit* xiii. 105 Narrow temples and steel-grey eyes. **1954** L. MACNEICE *Autumn Sequel* 95 She ascends where steelbright rays impinge. **1976** 'Z. STONE' *Modigliani Scandal* II. i. 69 A steel-blue Mercedes coupé. **1977** A. GIDDENS *Stud. in Social & Polit. Theory* 23 His sombre characterization of the 'steel-hard cage' of the modern social order. **1978** 'M. M. KAYE' *Far Pavilions* iv. 73 The steel-grey curtain of the rain.

b. *fig.* = as hard as steel, steely.

1600 SHAKS. *Sonn.* cxxxiii. 9 Prison my heart in thy steele bosomes warde. **1602** CHETTLE *Hoffman* v. (1631) I 3, My heart is steele Nor can it suffer more then it doth feele. *a* **1618** E. BOLTON *Hypercritica* ii. §3 This steel Rule whosoever honestly follows may perhaps write incommodiously for some momentany Purposes, but [etc.]. **1847** TENNYSON *Princess* VI. 215 Not one word? not one? Whence drew you this steel temper? **1899** BRIDGES *Septuagesima* ii. Poems (1912) 340 Steel is the ice.

16. Objective, with agent-nouns, as ***steel-erector, -maker, -worker***; with vbl. sbs. and ppl. adjs., as ***steel-making, -piercing, -rolling, -using***.

1624 QUARLES *Job Milit.* xviii. 58 That Steele-digesting Bird. **1815** J. SMITH *Panorama Sci. & Art* I. 4 The steel-making process. **1839** URE *Dict. Arts* 1171 G, is the door by which the steel-maker enters. **1858** SIMMONDS *Dict. Trade, Steel-roller*, the cylinder of a mill for rolling out steel into sheets. **1881** *Nature* XXIII. 568 The commotion among steel-users caused by the total failure of the steel plates. **1884** *Pall Mall Gaz.* 8 Jan. 9/1 A Glasgow telegram states that 2,000 steelworkers.. refused to resume work to-day. **1903** *Daily Chron.* 17 Mar. 9/2 An elderly retired steel smelter. **1932** AUDEN *Orators* III. 102 Our steel-piercing bullet, our burglar-proof safe. **1959** *Daily Tel.* 12 Dec. 1/2 Loss of work because of steel shortages in car and other steel-using industries. **1960** *Times* 22 Mar. 12/1 The site of many industries and the country's largest steel-rolling mill. **1974** 'J. ROSS' *Burning of Billy Toober* xi. 100 Almost permanently unemployed but registered as a steel-erector. **1977** *Whitaker's Almanack 1978* 757/1 Some of the country's [*sc.* Nigeria's] more important industrial installations include a steel-rolling mill. **1977** *Time* 19 Sept. 48/3 The relatively brisk pace of the economy is boosting demand in many steel-using industries.

17. Instrumental and parasynthetic, as ***steel-born, -bound, -clad, -girt, -graven, -lined, -shod; steel-barred, -bosomed, -coloured, -grated, -hilted, -lined, -nerved, -pointed, -rimmed, -shafted, -studded, -tempered, -tipped, -topped***, etc.

a **1400-50** *Wars Alex.* 284, vij stele-grauyn stanys. **1591** SYLVESTER *Du Bartas* I. vi. 324 Whose thorny sides are hedged round about With stiff steel-pointed quills. **1596** DRAYTON *Mortimer.* 39 In steele bound locks he safely lodg'd the Guard. **1597** —— *Heroic. Ep., Brandon to Q. Mary* 143 His steele-tempered blade. **1642** H. MORE *Song of Soul* III. iii. 45 Steel-coloured clouds with rattling thunder knocks. **1682** N. O. *Boileau's Lutrin* IV. 183 Come, Girot! Come, my trusty steel-edg'd friend. **1687** *Lond. Gaz.* No. 2202/4 A little Steel Hilted French Sword. **1751** WARTON *Poems* (1777) 61 Our steel-clad steeds. **1805** SCOTT *Last Minstr.* II. ix, A steel-clenched postern door. **1875** J. W. BENSON *Time & T.-tellers* (1902) 40 The watch being only silver gilt, and steel-faced. **1900** ELWORTHY *Horns of Honour* ii. 124 Steel-framed spectacles. **1909** *Westm. Gaz.* 11 Nov. 5/2 A new steel-studded tyre. **1924** W. J. LOCKE *Coming of Amos* xvi. 211 What kind of steel-nerved wisp of a woman are you? **1926** 'C. BARRY' *Detective's Holiday* vii. 66 A pair of steel-rimmed spectacles. **1929** L. MACNEICE *Blind Fireworks* 8 The steel-bosomed siren calling bitterly. **1930** BLUNDEN *Poems* 139 But steel-born bees, birds, beams invade. **1935** KIPLING in *Times* 17 July 19/4 In the steel-grated prisons where I cast him. **1947** DYLAN THOMAS *Let.* 12 Apr. (1966) 302 In steel-barred rooms, where Mussolini personally had.. interrogated. **1950** *Times* 22 May 4/3 Four golfers and a caddy.. were carrying steel-shafted clubs. **1954** L. MACNEICE *Autumn Sequel* 94 The steel-clad troops begin arriving from the rear to rally or harry their humble fellows. **1972** P. BUCKLAND *Irish Unionism* I. viii. 215 Armed raiders who had removed the steel-lined shutters from the windows. **1973** M. RUSSELL *Double Hit* xx. 149, I just don't believe that an accidental swipe with a squash racket, even a steel-shafted one, would have killed a man. **1974** J. AIKEN *Midnight is a Place* x. 290 The duels.. which the men.. fought, using no weapons but the steel-tipped clogs on their feet. **1978** R. LUDLUM *Holcroft Covenant* xv. 174 The face was strong, the eyes behind the steel-rimmed spectacles alert.

18. Special comb.: **steel band**, (*a*) *Mus.*, a band composed of musicians who play (chiefly calypso-style) music on steel drums; so **steel bandsman**, a musician in a steel band; (*b*) *Austral.* [BAND *sb.*[2] 12], 'hard thin stratum of ferruginous and siliceous material lying below the sandstone roof and above the opal dirt' (J. S. Gunn *Opal Terminol.* (1971)); **steel bar** *slang*, a needle; † **steel beetle**, some American beetle; **steel bender** (see quot. 1921); **steel-bow(ed)** *a. U.S.*, (of spectacles) having steel frames; † **steel-browed** *a.*, shameless; **steel driver** *U.S.*, who have makes holes for explosive charges, using a steel stake and a sledgehammer; **steel drum** *Mus.*, a percussion instrument originating in the West Indies, made out of an oil drum with one end beaten down and divided into grooved sections to give different notes; hence **steel drummer**; **steel engraving**, the art of engraving upon a steel plate; a print or impression from such a plate; similarly **steel-engraved** *a.*, **-engraver**; **steel-facing**, the process of covering an engraved metal plate with a film of steel to increase its durability; hence **steel-faced** *a.*; (as back formation) **steel-face** *v. trans.*; **steel fall** *local*, [FALL *sb.*[2]] = *steel trap*; **steel finch** (see quot.); **steel fixer**, a skilled steel worker in the construction industries; **steel frame**, a framework, esp. of a building, made of steel; also *fig.*; freq. *attrib.*; hence **steel-framed** *a.*; also **steel framework**; **steel grain**, a granular texture like that of steel; **steel-grained** *a.*, having a steel grain; **steel guitar** = *Hawaiian guitar* s.v. HAWAIIAN *a.* and *sb.* II.; **steel-hardened** *a.*, case-hardened (in quot. *fig.*); **steel iron**, (*a*) a native iron resembling steel; (*b*) iron suitable for converting into steel; (*c*) (see quot. 1883); **steel lustre**, a composition used for ornamenting pottery; **steel marl**: see MARL *sb.*[1] 1 b; **steel master**, a manufacturer of steel; † **steel-nose**, app. a slang name for some kind of strong drink; **steel orchestra** = *steel band* above; † **steel-ore**, (*a*) an ore of lead with a 'steel-grain'; (*b*) siderite or native ferrous carbonate; **steel pan** = PAN *sb.*[1] 1 f; † **steel saddle**, ? a saddle with a steel frame; **steel tape**, (*a*) a measuring tape made of steel; † (*b*) tape made of steel for use as a recording medium (*obs.*); **steel trap**, (*a*) a trap with jaws and spring of steel; (*b*) *fig.* (chiefly in *attrib.* use) and in U.S. phr. ***smart as a steel trap*** and varr.; † **steel wasp** (see quot.); **steel wool**, fine strands of steel matted together, used as an abrasive, esp. for scouring.

1949 *Caribbean Quarterly* I. I. 30 The audience was introduced to.. Trinidad's own *steel band. **1950** *Bull. Austral. Bur. Mineral Resources* No. 17. 27 The first or upper level is indicated by the presence of a very thin and hard band of siliceous sandstone known as the 'Steel Band'. **1960** *Times* 17 Sept. 7/6 The steelband competition of the Trinidad music festival. **1967** *Sunday Mail Mag.* (Brisbane) 8 Jan. 6/7 Then comes eight to twelve feet of quartzite.. and often after that, a layer of hard siliceous sandstone known as the 'steelband'. **1974** E. AMBLER *Dr. Frigo* I. 15 He had collapsed while listening to the steel band. **1948** *Trinidad Guardian* 16 June 5/6 (*heading*) Judge advises *steel bandsman to mend ways. **1967** *Listener* 31 Aug. 277/2 The steel bandsmen can play anything well: without a conductor and from memory. **1785** GROSE *Dict. Vulg. T.*, **Steel bar*, a needle; a steel bar flinger, a taylor, staymaker, or any other person, using a needle. *c* **1711** PETIVER *Gazophyl.* VIII. lxxi, Small Carolina *Steel-Beetle with a yellow girdled Back and Neck. **1921** *Dict. Occupational Terms* (1927) §279 **Steel bender*,.. bends steel rods and girders in hand operated or power press, into required shape, to form framework for concrete. **1939** M. SPRING RICE *Working-Class Wives* iii. 53 An unemployed steel-bender in Newcastle. **1963** *Times* 10 June 8/1 The accent on industrialized building and the increasing development over recent years in concreting have created a great new demand for new skilled labour such as scaffolders, concreters, steelbenders and fixers. **1834** in *Proc. Mass. Hist. Soc.* (1924) LVII. 258 Appears to be a pleasant fellow, with frightful whiskers and *steel bow spectacles. **1932** *Steel-bowed [see *notion-peddler* s.v. NOTION 9 c]. **1950** W. FAULKNER *Lo* in *Coll. Stories* III. 390 From the pocket of his dressing gown he took a pair of steel-bowed spectacles. **1600** O. E. ? [M. SUTCLIFFE] *Repl. Libel* I. iv. 91 If he had not beene both *steelebrowed, and beetilbrowed, yea and beetilheaded, he woulde neuer haue beene so bolde. **1916** in *Jrnl. Amer. Folk-Lore* (1919) XXXII. 505 He [John Henry] was a *steel driver and was famous in the beginning of the building of the C & O Railroad. **1973** A. DUNDES *Mother Wit* 586 The story of John Henry is powerful whether there was an actual steel-driver named John Henry or.. not. **1952** *Holiday* Feb. 94/2 Rainbow-uniformed dandies parade and compete in making music on tuned *steel drums from oilcans. **1971** *West Indian World* 12 Nov. 7/1 Trinidad.. known.. for its calypso singers and steel-drum bands. **1978** *New York* 3 Apr. 31 (Advt.), A cool drink slakes your thirst, steel drums stir your blood. **1960** *Times* 17 Sept. 7/6 This influenced the *steeldrummers to discard their tubes and bars and to use tops of oil-drums hung from the neck. **1975** R. L. SIMON *Wild Turkey* (1976) x. 60 The reggae band.. had a steel drummer who could go day and night and enough dope to turn on a rock festival. **1823** J. BADCOCK *Dom. Amusem.* 136 *Steel Engraved Bank Note Plates. **1842** *Penny Cycl.* XXIII. 6/2 The early *steel engravers. **1824** *Encycl. Brit.* Suppl. VI. 547/2 *marg.*, *Steel-Engraving. **1842** *Penny Cycl.* XXIII. 6/1 The application of steel engraving to matters of fine art. **1879** (*title*) The Works of Sir Edwin Landseer, R.A. Illustrated by forty-four steel engravings and about two hundred woodcuts. **1884** J. S. HODSON *Guide to Art Illustration* II. iii. 213 The proper thickness of copper having been deposited in the mould, the shell is filed or ground flat on the back, and the face coated with a deposit of iron,—a process commonly called *steel facing. **1897** SINGER & STRANG *Etching, Engraving* iii. 61 Steel-faced it may be printed over and over again.., for as soon as the steel face should wear off, the plate can be again immersed in the electrotyper's bath [etc.]. **1937** *Discovery* Mar. 76/2 The burr [in drypoint] being raised, will quickly wear, owing to the rubbing and the pressure it receives in printing. To overcome this a fine film of iron is deposited by an electric process on the plate. This is called steel-facing. An unfaced drypoint will yield only four or five-class impressions before the burr starts to wear. A steel-faced plate will give as many as fifty. **1961** WEBSTER, Steel-face, v. **1965** ZIGROSSER & GAEHDE *Guide Coll. Orig. Prints* iii. 26 An invention of the mid-nineteenth century.. steel-facing... The reason steel-faced prints have acquired a bad name is that they have often been printed on a slipshod manner. *Ibid.* v. 86 It used to be standard practice among professional etchers to steel-face the copperplate. **1895** P. H. EMERSON *Birds* etc. *Norf. Broadland* 290 The iniquitous '*steel-fall' or common steel rat-trap. **1869-73** T. R. JONES *Cassell's Bk. Birds* I. 163 The *Steel Finch (*Hypochera ultramarina*) frequents the banks of the Nile. **1936** *Record* Apr. 219/3 There is an awakening of interest amongst another section of building trade workers, namely, the *steel benders and fixers. **1949** *Transport & General Workers' Record* June 26/3 (*heading*) Steel fixers and tubular scaffolders. **1974** Steel fixer [see PRECASTING *vbl. sb.*]. **1898** *Engineering* 8 July 39/3 An architect is made responsible for the general arrangement of the building.. while the *steel frame or skeleton is the work of a skilful engineer experienced in such matters. **1906** G. A. T. MIDDLETON *Mod. Buildings* IV. xiv. 134/2 Probably the most thorough example of steel-frame construction yet erected in England is that of the Ritz Hotel, Piccadilly. **1922** LLOYD GEORGE in *Hansard Commons* 2 Aug. 1513, I can see no period when they can dispense with the guidance and the assistance of this small nucleus of the British Civil Service, of British officials in India—this 1,200 in a population of 315,000,000... They are the steel frame of the whole structure. **1928** M. MUGGERIDGE in *Young Men of India* XL. 624 There is that amount of truth in the contention of the Die-hard as against that of the sentimental liberal—it must be a steel frame or nothing. **1948** O. BONDY in E. de Maré *New Ways of Building* 70 It was not until the 1890's that the first complete steel-frame buildings were erected in the U.S.A. **1980** J. BOYD-CARPENTER *Way of Life* v. 59 To this day they [*sc.* the *Carabinieri*] are, I believe, the steel frame of the distracted Italian Republic. **1906** G. A. T. MIDDLETON *Mod. Buildings* IV. xiv. 134/2 A steel frame-work may often be used with considerable economy, as is evidenced by the number of *steel-framed structures that are now springing up. **1974** D. SEAMAN *Bomb that could Lip-Read* iii. 23 His steel-framed grey suitcase. **1906** *Steel framework [see *steel-framed* adj. above]. **1940** *Engineering* 1 Nov. 343/3 The steel framework.. embedded in the concrete. *a* **1728** WOODWARD *Fossils* (1729) I. 211 [Lead-]Ore of the finest *Steel-Grain. *Ibid.*, *Steel-grain'd Lead-Ore. **1841** *Civil Engin. & Arch. Jrnl.* IV. 262/2 Steel-grained cast-iron, or crude steel. **1925** *Glasgow Herald* 19 Mar. 8/7 Those two seductive Hawaiian instruments, the ukulele and the *steel guitar. **1974** V. GIELGUD *In such a Night* ix. 90 The nerve-battering provided by invisible steel guitars. **1834** MEDWIN *Angler in Wales* II. 255 His muscles were *steel-hardened by service. **1980** *Guardian Weekly* 13 July 1/2 It has all the grisly mod military cons: an isolated water supply, a purified air system, steel-hardened concrete. **1839** URE *Dict. Arts* 681 Native *steel-iron. This substance has all the characters of cast-steel. *c* **1840** MUSHET in *Greener's Gunnery* (1858) 150 We humbly feel our dependence on two foreign markets for the supply of that steel-iron, without which the beauty, the utility, and extent of our hardware manufactures would be essentially injured and abridged. **1840** —— *Papers Iron and Steel* 751 Steel iron and steel have since been manufactured to some extent near Ulverston. **1883** *Science* I. 46/1 M. Keil has succeeded in producing a welded metal which is stated to possess the characters of both iron and steel... This so called steel-iron is said to have been prepared in five ways. **1829** S. SHAW *Staffordsh. Potteries* x. 227 The *Steel Lustre employs oxide of Platinum. **1885** *Daily Tel.* 28 Sept. (Cassell) Iron-masters, *steel-masters, iron-consumers. **1901** *Daily News* 22 Jan. 10/5 A leading Staffordshire steel master and blast furnace owner. **1654** WHITLOCK *Zootomia* 459 They can tell you whose Pudding hath Sewet in it, and whose not; who drinks Rot-gut, and who *Steele-nose. **1952** S. SELVON *Brighter Sun* xii. 233 Crowds jumped up to the music of *steel orchestras. **1971** *News-Advocate* (Barbados) 20 Mar. 7/1 (Advt.), Dancing to the rhythmic beats of the.. Elk Owls steel orchestra. **1661** BOYLE *Ess. Unsuccessf. Exper.* i. (1668) 52 Lead.. so like Steel and so unlike common Lead-Oar, that the workmen upon that account are pleased to call it *Steel-Oar. **1789** J. WILLIAMS *Min. Kingd.* I. 410 Steel ore, or steel grained lead ore. **1796** KIRWAN *Elem. Min.* (ed. 2) II. 192 Calcareous, or Sparry Iron Ore.. affords.. the best Steel... Hence it is generally called Steel Ore. **1973** *Nation* (Barbados) 23 Dec. 8 Trinidad's famed *steel pans [will] be produced in masse in England. **1983** *Times* 7 Jan. 2/1 [He] was employed for several years by the local education authority to teach steel pan playing in schools. **1503** *Acc. Ld. High Treas. Scot.* II. 205 Ane haknay sadill, and ane *steil sadill. **1596** DALRYMPLE tr. *Leslie's Hist. Scot.* II. 129 Certane horssis plesand and fayr with steil sadles. **1900** *Steel tape [see TAPE *sb.*[1] 2 a]. **1901** *Electrician* 26 Apr. 7/2 The next [electromagnet] is connected to a microphone circuit to convey the record to the steel tape. **1949** S. J. BEGUN *Magnetic Recording* i. 10 A recording made on steel tape.. has been played more than 100,000 times with no measurable deterioration after a slight initial falling off in output level. **1977** J. F. FIXX *Compl. Bk. Running* vii. 90 Measure off a half-mile with a steel tape. **1735** SOMERVILE *Chase* III. Argt., The *Steel-Trap described. **1775** [see SPRING-GUN 1]. **1827** *Hone's Every-day Bk.* II. 906 The stranger.. is in jeopardy of falling into the.. fangs of a steel-trap. **1872** MRS. STOWE *Oldtown Fireside Stories* 57 She was a little thin woman, but tough as Inger rubber, and smart as a steel trap. **1899** A. M. BINSTEAD *Gal's Gossip* 127 He posted sentinel, bright and ready as a new steel-trap. **1921** D. H. LAWRENCE *Tortoises* 32 Little old man, Scuffling beside her.. Parting his steel-trap face, so suddenly and seizing her scaly ankle. **1937** E. S. GARDNER *Case of Dangerous Dowager* i. 8 You're going up against a crook who is smart as a steel trap. **1972** *Publisher's Weekly* 17 Apr. 19/1 He's rather amused by what he calls his steeltrap memory. 'I have a tight grip on things in inverse proportion to their importance.' *c* **1711** PETIVER *Gazophyl.* VI. lviii, Shining Cape *Steel Wasp... The Wings shine like polisht Steel. **1896** *Iron Age* 9 Apr. 871/2 The interesting product '*steel wool' is intended for use in all cases where sandpaper, emery paper, pumice stone and materials of a kindred nature are employed. **1947** J. C. RICH *Materials & Methods of Sculpture* vi. 169 'Fire-skin' may be removed by rubbing the work with steel wool, which is available in several grades, varying from very coarse to very fine. **1958** *Listener* 16 Oct. 627/1 Scour round the inside with a steel wool soap-pad. **1977** C. MCCULLOUGH *Thorn Birds* xvii. 444 His thick mane of hair was exactly the color of steel wool.

steel (stiːl), *sb.*[2] [A shortened form of BASTILE.] (See quots.)

1811 *Lex. Balatr.*, *Steel*, the house of correction. **1812** J. H. VAUX *Flash Dict.*, *Bastile*, generally called for shortnes, *the steel* a cant name for the House of Correction, Cold-

Bath-Fields, London. **1839** in 'Ducange Anglicus' *Vulgar T.* (1857) 35 *The steel*, the tread-mill. **1877** *Five Yrs. Penal Serv.* i. 5 A series of rapid inquiries as to who I was,..had I ever been in the 'steel,' a slang name for one of the large metropolitan prisons, as the 'Gate' is for Newgate.

steel (stiːl), *v.* Also 3–5 stele, 6–7 steele. [f. STEEL *sb.*[1] Cf. MHG. *stæhelen* (mod.G. *stählen*), ON. *stǽla*; also (without umlaut) MLG. *stâlen*, Du. *stalen*.]

1. a. *trans.* To overlay, point or edge with steel. Often in passive *to be* (*well*) *steeled.*

[*a* **900**: see STEELED *ppl. a.*] *a* **1240** *Sawles Warde* in *Cott. Hom.* 253 Hure þolien ant a beoren hare unirude duntes wið mealles istelet. *c* **1320** *Cast. Love* 1248 A swerd..þat wel i-steled and kene were. *a* **1440** *Sir Degrev.* 1043 Hys helme shal be wel steled. **1581** A. HALL *Iliad* IV. 63 An arrow he out of his quiuer cought, Sure steelde at end with piercing head. **1650** BULWER *Anthropomet.* 215 Performed with a sharp cutting stone, and not with any knife of iron steeled. **1693** LISTER in *Phil. Trans.* XVII. 865 With a Guess at the way the Ancients used to Steel their Picks for the cutting or hewing of Porphyry. **1776** G. SEMPLE *Building in Water* 18 The Chissell or Piercer, was well steeled, with a drill Point. **1805** R. W. DICKSON *Pract. Agric.* I. Plate xxxvii, The teeth are one foot in length..steeled at the point. **1831** J. HOLLAND *Manuf. Metal* I. 220 It was the common notion..that the art of steeling tools in the highest degree of perfection was certainly lost to the moderns. **1864** G. L. M. STRAUSS etc. *Engl. Workshops* 93 The former process is technically termed steeling in the centre, the latter steeling on the face. **1911** J. WARD *Roman Era Brit.* xi. 195 The face of the hammer was 'steeled' by a plate of steel welded to it.

fig. **1594** SHAKS. *Rich. III*, I. i. 148 Ile in to vrge his hatred more to Clarence, With Lyes well steel'd with weighty Arguments. **1614** W. B. *Philos. Banquet* (ed. 2) 114 He euer steeled the forefront of his armie with men of hiest spirit. **1651** JER. TAYLOR *Serm. Golden-Grove, Summer* xix. 248 When God..draws aside his curtain, and shows his arsenal and his armory, full of arrows steeled with wrath.

†**b.** To back (a mirror) with steel. *Obs.*

1625 DONNE *Serm.* (1649) II. xxxiii. 302 Nay, a Crystall glasse will not show a man his face, except it be steeled, except it be darkned on the backside. **1630** MASSINGER *Renegado* I. iii, Here is a mirror Steelde so exactely, neither taking from Nor flattering the obiect it returnes To the beholder.

c. To cover (an engraved metal plate) with a film of iron by electrolysis to render it more durable.

1880 HAMERTON *Etching* (ed. 3) 342 *note*, My large dry-point,..called *Two Stumps of Driftwood*, gave 1000 copies (after being steeled) without perceptible wearing. **1887** RUSKIN in Spielmann *Mem.* (1900) 195 Now that everybody can..engrave the photograph, and steel the copper, and print piles and piles of the thing by steam.

2. To cause to resemble steel in some quality.

a. *fig.* To make hard, unbending, or strong as steel, to render insensible to impression, to make determined or obdurate, to nerve or strengthen; also to fortify *against*.

1581 A. HALL *Iliad* VI. 110 But stil he was so steelde With heart so good, as victor he dead left them in the field. **1592** SHAKS. *Ven. & Ad.* 375, 376 Giue me my heart..O giue it me lest thy hard heart do steele it, And being steeld, soft sighes can neuer graue it. **1654** WHITLOCK *Zootomia* 443 With this Position let us..steele our Resolves. **1720** WATERLAND *Eight Serm.* 97 Let any man..that..is not steel'd against Conviction, be left to draw the Conclusion. **1796** MME. D'ARBLAY *Camilla* II. 370 Steel yourself, then, firmly to withstand attacks from the cruel and unfeeling. **1822** LAMB *Elia* Ser. I. *Decay of Beggars*, It is possible I could have steeled my purse against him. **1826** SCOTT *Woodst.* v, I..was steeled by honour against the charms of my friend's Chloe. **1882** FARRAR *Early Chr.* II. 380 The rich experience of a long life steeled in the victorious struggle with every unchristian element. **1884** *Leisure Hour* Sept. 545/2 The air and exercise had steeled my nerves completely.

b. To make like steel in appearance. *rare.*

1807 WORDSW. *Sonn. Nat. Indep. & Liberty* II. v, And lo! those waters, steeled By breezeless air to smoothest polish, yield A vivid repetition of the stars.

†**3.** *to steel it*: ? to use steel, strike with the sword. *Obs.* or *nonce-use.* (The sense is disputed.)

a **1593** MARLOWE *Edw. II*, III. ii. 1333 We haue beene..Too kinde to them, but now haue drawne our sword, And if they send me not my Gaueston, Weele steele it on their crest, and powle their tops.

†**4.** To impregnate (a liquid) with steel. *Obs.*

1657 J. COOKE *Hall's Cures englisht* 117 She drunk her drink steeled, with which she was cured.

5. To convert (iron) into steel: = STEELIFY *v.*

1853 in *Jrnl. Franklin Inst.* (1888) CXXV. 303 By passing an electric current thus through the bars the operation of steeling is much hastened. **1977** *Sci. Amer.* May 61/3 Iron that has been 'steeled' with that much carbon will not deform under stresses of less than 140,000 p.s.i. *Ibid.* Oct. 127/1 It seems evident that by the beginning of the 10th century B.C. blacksmiths were intentionally steeling iron.

6. To sharpen (a knife) with the steel.

1888 *Berksh. Gloss.*

7. *dial.* To iron (clothes).

1746 *Exmoor Scolding* 273 Tha hasn't tha Sense to stile thy own Dressing. **1837** J. F. PALMER *Gloss. to Mrs. Palmer's Devon Dial.* 85.

steel, obs. form of STEAL *v.*, STILE.

†**'steelback.** *Obs.* [f. STEEL *v.* + BACK *sb.*] A name for Alicant wine, from its supposed property of strengthening the back.

[**1609** *Pimlyco* C 4 b, The fat lecherous Alligant, Whose Iuice repaires what Backes doe want.] **1633** C. FAREWELL *East-Ind. Colation* 48 Raysin Wine, almost of the colour of Alicant, or steelebacke.

†**steel-bow**[1], **'steel bow.** *Obs.* [BOW *sb.*[1]]

1. ? A stirrup.

c **1205** LAY. 23899 Arður stop a stel boȝe And leop an his blancke. *a* **1400–50** *Wars Alex.* 778 Ilk a hathill to hors hiȝis him be-lyue, Stridis into stele-bowe, stertis apon loft.

2. A bow made of steel; a cross-bow.

[**1535** COVERDALE *Job* xx. 23 Yf he fle the yron weapens, he shall be shott with the stele bowe. **1545** ASCHAM *Toxoph.* II. (Arb.) 112 Iron bowes, and style bowes, haue bene of longe tyme, and also nowe are vsed among the Turkes.] **1607** DEKKER & WEBSTER *Sir T. Wyat* E 1 b, *Norf.* Yonder the Traitor marcheth with a steele-bowe Bent on his Souereigne, and his kingdomes peace. **1671** MILTON *P.R.* III. 305 Steel Bows, and Shafts their arms Of equal dread in flight, or in pursuit.

3. A part of a lathe. *Obs.*

1680 MOXON *Mech. Exerc.* xiv. 236 There is a strong Steel Bow..fastned about its middle part to the further side of the Puppet... And to the ends of this Steel Bow is fastned a strong String of Gut.

Hence †**'steelbowman**, a crossbowman.

1585 HIGINS *Junius' Nomencl.* 484/1 *Balistarij*,..the crossebow or steelebowmen.

steelbow[2] ('stiːlbəʊ). *Sc. Law. Obs.* exc. *Hist.* Forms: 5–6 steil-, 6 stele-, 7 steelbow. [f. STEEL *sb.*[1] + BOW[3].

It corresponds to the F. *cheptel de fer* (see Littré), lit. 'iron farm-stock', and to early mod.G. *stählin vieh*, *eisern vieh* (in German Law Latin *pecora chalybea*, *ferrea*), and obs. Da. *jernfæ*. These terms denote the quantity of live stock which a farming tenant receives from his landlord on entering, under a contract to restore the same quantity and value at the end of his tenancy. This is precisely the sense of *steelbow*, exc. that the Sc. term seems to have been extended to apply to dead as well as live stock. The F. *cheptel de fer* is also used, like *steelbow*, for the species of tenure or contract under which cattle are so held by a tenant. In early mod.Ger. there were other legal terms containing the adjs. *stählin* 'made of steel', *eisern* 'made of iron', in the figurative sense 'rigidly fixed in amount': e.g. *stähline gült*, a fixed regular payment or income: *stähline pfründe*, a church living subject to no deductions. The figure of speech doubtless comes down from very early Germanic legal formulæ; but evidence is wanting. See Schilter *Glossarium*, s.v. *Stal*; also Grimm *Deutsche Rechtsaltertümer* (ed. 4, 1899) II. 131.]

a. A quantity of farming stock, which a tenant received from his landlord on entering, and which he was bound to render up undiminished at the close of his tenancy. Also *attrib.*, as ***steelbow goods***. **b.** The kind of tenancy or contract by which farming stock is hired on the condition that the tenant renders up on the expiration of his tenancy the same quantity and value that he received; esp. in phrase ***in steelbow***. Also *attrib.*, as ***steelbow lease***, ***rent***, ***tenant***, ***tenancy***.

1434 *Exch. Rolls Scot.* IV. 596 Pro herbagio 96 vaccarum domini regis, locatarum in steilbow infra domin[i]um de Stewartoun. **1507** *Reg. Privy Seal Scot.* I. 221/1 His ground and Manys of Dunbar, quhilk the said reverend fader had in tak and stelebow of him hienes. **1532** in *Pitcairn's Crim. Trials* I. 162* Havand in his possessioune ane hundreth punds worth of gudis, steilbow and ferm of þat ȝere alanerlie except. **1565** *Reg. Privy Council Scot.* I. 410 The cornis cattell and gudis being upoun the landis of Baddinhaith, steilbow and utheris. **1566** *Reg. Mag. Sig. Scot.* 431/1 Prius dicti monast. bonis lie steilbow-gudis occupatas. **1640** in *Black Bk. Taymouth* (Bannatyne Club) 351 Thair is presentlie on the landis..of steilbow corne, sexteine chalders small aittis; and of steilbow beir, fyve chalders; and of strenth silver and steilbow horss on the forsaids lands [etc.]. **1733** in W. R. Mackintosh *Glimpses Kirkwall* (1887) 126 And beside there is a steilbow upon the lands of Yairsay of horses, oats, and bear. **1754** ERSKINE *Princ. Sc. Law* II. vi. (1870) 173 Steel-bow goods, i.e. corns, straw, cattle, or instruments of tillage, delivered by a landlord to the tenant upon his entry. **1805** FORSYTH *Beauties Scot.* II. 443 The rent was frequently paid in kind, or in what was called half-labour, by the steel-bow tenants, like the metayers of France. **1844** H. STEPHENS *Bk. Farm* III. 1321 In such a case the straw and dung are said to be held in steelbow. **1911** A. W. RENTON in *Encycl. Brit.* XXIII. 104/2 Up to 1848 or 1850 there existed in Scotland 'Steelbow' leases..the tenant ..paying in addition to the ordinary rent a steel-bow rent of 5% on the value of the stock.

Hence **steelbowed** *pa. pple.*

1606 BIRNIE *Kirk-Buriall* Ded. (1833), For as..Gods Altarmens trauels in his own trueth ought to be steil-bowed.

Steel boy. *Irish Hist.* A member of a body of insurgents, calling themselves 'The Hearts of Steel', who committed agrarian outrages in 1772–4. See quot. 1772 in STEEL *sb.*[1] 2; cf. *oak-boy*, OAK 8.

1772 *Lond. Chron.* 18–21 Apr. 378/1 The Steel Boys came and fired into the house. **1780** A. YOUNG *Tour Irel.* 112 The rising of the steel boys was owing, as they said, to the increase of rents, and complaints of general oppression. **1844** THACKERAY *Barry Lyndon* xvi, The kingdom of Ireland was at this period [*c* 1772] ravaged by various parties of banditti:..under the name of Whiteboys, Oakboys, Steelboys.

steeled (stiːld), *ppl. a.* [f. STEEL *sb.*[1] or *v.* + -ED.]

1. Made of steel, or with the outer surface, edge or point of steel.

a **900** *Cynewulf's Christ* 679 Sum mæȝ styled sweord wæpen ȝewyrcan. *a* **1225** *Juliana* 58 Ha bigon to breoken al as þat istelet irn to limede hire. *c* **1350** *Lybeaus Disc.* (Kaluza) 976 Wiþ coronals stif and stelde, Eiþer smitte oþer in þe scheld, Wiþ well greet envie. ? *a* **1400** in *Rel. Ant.* I. 240 Stark strokes thei stryken on a stelyd stokke. **1513** DOUGLAS *Æneis* VII. xi. 79 Al instrumentis of pleuch graith, irnit or stelit. **1591** SHAKS. *1 Hen. VI*, I. i. 85 Giue me my steeled Coat. Ile fight for France. **1639** DU VERGER tr. *Camus' Admir. Events* 35 He seeks to end his dayes..another time by poison, againe by some steeled weapon. **1747** HOOSON *Miner's Dict.* E 2 b, This sort will wear a new steel'd pick off in three or four times Sharping. **1751** LABELYE *Piers Westm. Bridge* 4 Sharp and well steel'd Drills. **1841** *Civil Engin. & Arch. Jrnl.* IV. 29/1 By the use of steeled tires these evils are henceforth to be avoided.

b. (See STEEL *v.* 1 c.)

1890 *Pall Mall Gaz.* 26 Apr. 3/1 Practically all the artist's proofs which find their way into the market are taken from these 'steeled' plates.

2. Of a man, army, etc.: Armed or protected with steel.

1596 *Edw. III*, III. iii. 219 Then thus our steelde Battailes shall be rainged. **1672** DRYDEN *1st Pt. Conq. Granada* I. i, On their steel'd Heads their demy-Lances wore Small Pennons which their Ladies Colours bore. **1819** KEATS *Otho* I. iii. 67 Amid a camp whose steeled swarms I dar'd But yesterday.

3. Of wine, etc.: Containing an infusion of steel.

1640 PARKINSON *Theat. Bot.* 444 Being drunk in steeled or red wine. **1694** SALMON *Bate's Dispens.* (1713) 594/2 The Chalybeated or Steeled Syrup.

4. Wearing a 'steel' for sharpening knives. *nonce-use.*

1827 HONE *Every-day Bk.* II. 132 A 'steeled' butcher..carries the flag.

5. Of a person, his attributes, etc.: Hardened like steel, insensible to impression, inflexible.

1599 SHAKS. *Hen. V*, II. ii. 36 So seruice shall with steeled sinewes toyle. **1603** —— *Meas. for M.* IV. ii. 90 This is a gentle Prouost, sildome when The steeled Gaoler is the friend of men. **1624** A. H. in *J. Davies' (Heref.) Scourge Paper-Persecutors* 1. 5 What steeled patience could behold those Dawes Præuaricate the Muses sacred Lawes. **1713** TICKELL *Prosp. Peace* 133 Let the steel'd Turk be deaf to Matrons Cries. **1810** SHELLEY *Zastrozzi* ii. Pr. Wks. 1888 I. 11 His steeled soul persisted in its scheme. **1826** DISRAELI *Viv. Grey* III. v, This last specimen of Mrs. Felix Lorraine was somewhat too much even for the steeled nerves of Vivian Grey.

†**'steelen,** *a. Obs.* Forms: 1 stýlen, 2 stælen, 2–4 stelene, (3 -ane, stillen), 3–5 stelen, 4–5 -yn, (5 -in, -un, stilen), 7 steelen. [OE. *stýlen* (*stǽlen*, **stíelen*) = OFris. *stêlen* (WFris. *stielen*), MLG. *stelen*, MHG. *stehelîn* (mod.G. †*stählen*) :—WGer. **stahalîn-*, f. OTeut. **stahlo-*: see STEEL *sb.*[1] The MLG. *stalen*, MDu. *staelen* (mod.Du. *stalen*) are independently f. the sb.]

1. Made of steel; also, having a steel point.

a **1175** in Napier *Holy Rood-tree* 26 Ða wearð hit swa head swylce hit stælen wære. *c* **1175** *Lamb. Hom.* 131 He to-þruste þa stelene gate and to brec þe irene barren of helle. *c* **1205** LAY. 7634 Wæs þe stelene brond swiðe brad & swið e long. *c* **1350** *Will. Palerne* 3535 Was non so stif stelen wede þat with-stod his wepen. *c* **1475** *Partenay* 256 With the stilen swerde there tho made entre. **1629** QUARLES *Argalus & P.* III. 122 With that the little angry god did bend His steelen Bow.

2. Hard as steel, steely.

a **1000** *Sal. & Sat.* 504 Ne meahte ic of ðære heortan heardne aðringan stylenne stan. *a* **1300** *Cursor M.* 4296 Strengh o luu..nan mai stere, þof his hert al stilen were. **1659** *Commw. Ballads* (Percy Soc.) 138 From steelen heroes that rule us with rods..Libera nos, Domine.

†**steelet.** *Obs. rare*[−1]. [Anglicized form of F. *stylet*, stiletto.]

1616 (*title*) A Proclamation against Steelets, Pocket Daggers, Pocket Dagges, and Pistols.

steeletto, obs. form of STILETTO.

†**steel glass.** *Obs.*

1. A mirror made of polished steel, whether an ordinary looking-glass or an optical instrument of some special construction.

1530 [see GLASS *sb.*[1] 8 b]. **1542** in *Archæol. Jrnl.* XVIII. 139 Item oone square Loking stele glasse sett in crymsen vellat. **1553** T. WILSON *Rhet.* 78 b, With that he offered him at his commynge a stele glasse to loke in. **1579** LYLY *Euphues* (Arb.) 71 A woman,..the onely steele glasse for man to beholde hys infirmities, by comparinge them wyth woemens perfections. **1614** BP. HALL *Recoll. Treat.* 901 As some steel-glasses, wherein the Sun looks and shewes his face in the variety of those colours which he hath not. **1677** SIR T. HERBERT *Trav.* 120 Near which is hung a Mirrour or steel-Glass.

2. (See quot. 1753.)

1662 MERRETT *Neri's Art Glass* Notes 342 Cardan. l. 2. [= XI] de variet. c. 57. Glasses call'd Steel-Glasses [orig. *Specula chalibea uocata*] are made of three parts of Brass, of one part of Tin and Silver, and an 18th part of Antimony. **1675** BOYLE in *Phil. Trans.* X. 348 Those metalline *Specula*, whether plain or concave, that are call'd Steel-glasses. **1753** *Chambers' Cycl.* Suppl., *Steel glasses*, a name given by some authors to the metalline spheres used in optics.

steel-head, *a.* and *sb.* Also steelhead.

A. *adj.* Having a head of steel. *poet.*

1590 SPENSER *F.Q.* II. vi. 40 With that he stiffely shooke his steelehead dart. **1609** HEYWOOD *Brit. Troy.* XI. lvi. 243 The steel-head Lance.

B. *sb.*

1. The rainbow trout of N. America, *Salmo irideus* or *S. Gairdneri*. Also *attrib.*, as ***steelhead trout***.

1882 JORDAN & GILBERT *Syn. Fishes N. Amer.* 313 *Salmo gairdneri*, Steel-head; Hard-head; Salmon Trout. **1911** *Rep. U.S. Comm. Fisheries 1908* 317/2 *Salmo* is represented by.. the steelhead trout. **1946** [see CUTTHROAT 5 b]. **1968** *Times* 22 Oct. 3/3 Another species of trout, the steelhead, has been found to suffer from a vascular disease. **1976** *Vernon* (B.C.) *Daily News* 21 June 20A/5 Sea-going Rainbow are known as *steelhead* trout.

2. The ruddy duck, *Erismatura rubida*. *U.S.* (local).

1888 G. TRUMBULL *Names & Portraits of Birds* 112 William Wagner, a well known Washington gunner, tells of hearing it called Water-Partridge and Steel-head. **1917** T. G. PEARSON *Birds Amer.* I. 153/1 They are extremely tough, hardy little birds and gunners know them by such names as Tough-head, Hard-head, Steel-head, etc.

steel-headed, *a.* Having a head, tip or top of steel.

1590 SPENSER *F.Q.* II. iii. 29 A bow and quiver gay, Stuft with steele-headed dartes. **1606** SYLVESTER *Du Bartas* II. iv. II. *Magnif.* 1110 Steel-headed Cones. **1825** SCOTT *Talism.* i, The long steel-headed lance. **1875** KNIGHT *Dict. Mech.* 2367 *Steel-headed rail*, a railway rail having an upper surface or tread of steel welded on to a body of iron.

steelheader (ˈstiːlhɛdə(r)). *N. Amer.* [f. STEEL-HEAD *sb.* + -ER[1].] One who fishes for steelhead trout. Hence **ˈsteelheading** *vbl. sb.*

1948 *Game Trails in Canada* Feb. 25 The average steelheader that lands one in three seems quite content. **1954** *Daily Progress* (Charlottesville, Va.) 5 Nov. 13/1 They had gone out steelheading that morning. **1964** *Vancouver Province* 14 Feb. 18/1 The Gold River has blanked many a good steelheader. **1971** *Islander* (Victoria, B.C.) 24 Jan. 3/1 She had learned to avoid the cardinal sins of steelheading. **1972** *Daily Colonist* (Victoria, B.C.) 1 Jan. 21/3 April is the awakening month, when.. steelheaders shift to trout fishing.

steel-hearted, *a.*

1. Stout-hearted, courageous.

1571 GOLDING *Calvin on Ps.* iv. 2. 10 Dauid was not so steeleharted [L. *ferreus*], but that his aduersitie dyd cast hym intoo piteowse anguish of mynd. **1833** NYREN *Yng. Cricketer's Tutor* (1902) 78 A handful of steel-hearted soldiers.

2. Hard-hearted; cruel, unfeeling; obdurate, inflexible.

1571 GOLDING *Calvin on Ps.* viii. 3. 23 Against the steeleharted despysers of God [L. *contra ferreos Dei contemptores*]. **1692** WASHINGTON tr. *Milton's Def. People* Pref. 11 As for those fierce, those steel hearted men [L. *istos feros ac ferreos*]. **1818** COBBETT *Pol. Reg.* XXXIII. 378 Experienced and well-tried and steel-hearted men whom they call Judges. **1897** E. CONYBEARE *Hist. Cambridgesh.* 128 Who could be so steel-hearted that that woman could not bend him to her wishes?

steel ˈhelmet. [f. STEEL *sb.*[1] + HELMET *sb.*]

1. A helmet made of steel (or other metal), worn as a form of protection in conditions of war.

1916 R. ASQUITH *Let.* 23 May (1980) IV. 263 One fearful addition to the honours of War since I have been away is the steel helmet which we all have to wear now, when in the shell area. **1940** *War Illustr.* 5 Jan. 563/1 It was not until February 1916 that the first steel helmets were issued to the British troops in the last war, but in this war they are an essential part not only of the soldiers' equipment but of that of the police, the A.F.S. and A.R.P. workers. **1978** A. PRICE *'44 Vintage* v. 52 Knitted cap-comforters instead of berets or steel helmets.

2. (With capital initials.) [tr. G. STAHLHELM.] An organization, founded in 1918 by F. Seldte, of German ex-service men (and others, from 1924) drawn mainly from the Nationalist Party and having a strong conservative bias; a member of this.

The organization was dissolved in 1935, and refounded under the Federal Republic in 1951.

1925 *Spectator* 28 Mar. 487/1 How could he really fail to stand for monarchy when he is championed by such societies as the 'Steel Helmet League' and the 'Front Fighters'? **1926** *Times* 25 May 14/3 The Nationalist 'Steel Helmet' organization. *Ibid.*, Most of the 'Steel Helmets' wore iron crosses. **1932** H. R. KNICKERBOCKER *Germany —Fascist or Soviet?* 137 The four militant organizations are the Republican Reichsbanner, the National Socialist Storm Troops, the Conservative Steel Helmets, and the Communist Red Front. **1933** E. A. MOWRER *Germany puts Clock Back* 94 The Steel Helmet, or Confederation of Front-line Soldiers, the most respectable of the private armies, was founded on Christmas Day, 1918. **1983** C. MCCARRY *Last Supper* 32 A Steel Helmet, wearing two Iron Crosses on his civilian jacket.. seized the weedy young man.

Hence **steel-ˈhelmeted** *a.*, wearing a steel helmet.

1926 *British Worker* 10 May 1/3 Thus all the display of steel-helmeted troops, all the tearing about of motor-cars filled with special constables.. have failed of their object. **1977** N. SAHGAL *Situation in New Delhi* xvi. 159 One of the students informed him it was the police or perhaps the army —many were steel-helmeted and the boy could not tell.

†**steel hemp.** *Obs.* [First element uncertain: possibly STEAL *sb.*[1]] ? = CARL HEMP.

a **1618** *Rates of Merchandizes* H 3, Hempe vocat. Cullen and Steele Hemp. **1657** *Acts of Interregn.* (1911) II. 1211 Hemp called Cullen and Steel Hemp, and all other sorts of drest Hemp. **1666** MERRETT *Pinax* 19 *Cannabis mas*, male or steel hemp. **1667** *Pat. Office* 155, 1 Ordering, workeing and makeing 'Certayne sort of Hempe called Steele Hempe.'

steelification (stiːlɪfɪˈkeɪʃən). *rare.* [f. STEELIFY *v.*: see -FICATION.] The action of the verb STEELIFY; the process of converting iron into steel.

1875 *Ure's Dict. Arts* (ed. 7) III. 899 In the production of natural steel, the molecules of metal which compose the mass are *per se* charged with a certain percentage of carbon necessary for their steelification. **1888** *Jrnl. Franklin Inst.* CXXV. 304 The steelification is so equalized throughout the mass that [etc.].

steelify (ˈstiːlɪfaɪ), *v.* [f. STEEL *sb.* + -(I)FY.]

†**1.** *trans.* To add steel to, imbue with the properties of steel. *Obs.*

1662 J. CHANDLER *Van Helmont's Oriat.* 227 In the mean time, very many Clisters of Whey steelified,.. were injected, and all in vain.

2. To convert into steel.

1807 G. GREGORY *Dict. Arts & Sci.* I. 344/3 Cast iron contains too great a quantity of carbonaceous substance: it may be called steel too much steelified. **1860** *Repert. Patent Invent.* Apr. 305 A.. Process for Cementing, Converting, Refining, Strengthening and Steelifying Iron. **1888** *Jrnl. Frankl. Inst.* CXXV. 304 Another process for the formation of steel from iron consists in connecting the mass to be steelified with an electric source.

Hence **ˈsteelified** *ppl. a.*; **ˈsteelifying** *vbl. sb.* (also *attrib.*); **steeˈlifying** *ppl. a.*

1843 HOLTZAPFFEL *Turning* I. 262 The time occupied in this steelifying process, is sometimes only minutes instead of hours and days. **1860** *Ure's Dict. Arts* (ed. 5) III. 761 The workman has to judge.. of the amount of carbon which he has retained from the pig iron;.. if too little, he obtains only a steelified iron. **1875** KNIGHT *Dict. Mech.* 2365/2 The substitution of phosphorus for carbon as a 'steelifying agent'.

steeliness (ˈstiːlɪnɪs). [f. STEELY *a.* + -NESS.] The quality or condition of being steely.

1571 GOLDING *Calvin on Ps.* viii. 3. 23 Theis oneeyed Gyants.. endeuer with their steelynesse [L. *sua duritie*] to breake open euen heauen it self. **1675** J. SMITH *Chr. Relig. Appeal* I. 70 Their Nurture and Education in the soft and warm bosom of that pacifick Age, had so far temper'd the natural Steeliness of their Mettal, as it turn'd Edge. **1856** *Leisure Hour* V. 812/1 Demonstrating the goodness or steeliness of our knife-blades. **1909** RIDER HAGGARD *Yellow God* 49 There was something in her voice.. of steeliness and defiance.

steeling (ˈstiːlɪŋ), *vbl. sb.* [f. STEEL *v.* + -ING[1].]

†**1.** The action of stiffening (a bodice, etc.) with steel. *Obs.*

1601 DENT *Plain Man's Pathw.* (1617) 43 It was neuer a good world, since starching and steeling, buskes and whale-bones.. came to bee in vse.

2. The giving a steel edge or point to iron, etc.

a **1819** REES *Cycl.*, *Steeling*, in Cutlery, the laying on a piece of steel upon a larger mass of iron, to make that part which is to receive the edge harder than the rest.

3. Conversion into steel.

1860 *Repert. Patent Invent.* Oct. 317 These processes offer considerable advantages over those ordinarily employed for effecting the 'steeling' or the conversion of objects made of wrought or of cast iron into steel. *Ibid.* 318 The conversion into steel or the 'steeling' of iron or of cast iron. **1977** *Sci. Amer.* Oct. 125/1 If bloomery iron is treated in a certain way, it can be transformed into an alloy that is for most purposes far superior to bronze. That treatment is steeling, and its initial discovery was probably accidental.

4. In *Engraving*, the process of covering a metal plate with steel to render it more durable.

1871 HAMERTON *Etcher's Handbk.* 41 Since the invention of steeling (protecting the copper by means of an infinitesimally thin coat of steel applied by galvanism) a dry point will yield larger editions than an etching would formerly. **1887** *Athenæum* 24 Sept. 412/2 It will be retorted that, in these days of steeling, stamped proofs of etchings, line or mezzotint engravings, are in many cases.. little better than ordinary prints.

5. The steel part of a machine.

1869 RANKINE *Machine & Hand-tools* Pl. K 3, The bottom steeling on which iron is placed when it is being cut [by the shears]. *Ibid.* Pl. K 11, The steelings [of a guillotine plate shears] are 6 feet 6 inches long.

6. *attrib.* **steeling-box**, ? a box-iron (cf. STEEL *v.* 7).

a **1680** GLANVILL *Sadducismus* II. (1681) 152 That she hurt Dorothy the Wife of George Vining, by giving an Iron slate to put into her steeling Box.

steeling (ˈstiːlɪŋ), *ppl. a.* [-ING[2].] That steels, in quot. hardening, stiffening.

1849 STOVEL *Canne's Necess. Introd.* p. x, He had already sustained the steeling influence of 'seventeen years' spent in banishment.

steeling, obs. var STILLING, stand for a cask.

steelle, obs. form of STILE.

steelless (ˈstiːllɪs), *a.* [f. STEEL *sb.*[1] + -LESS.] Of an article: Containing no steel.

1831 J. HOLLAND *Manuf. Metal* I. 143 The steelless articles already noticed.

steel mill.

†**1.** A device for producing a stream of sparks by the rapid revolution of a steel disc in contact with a flint; used for light in coal-mines before the invention of the safety-lamp. *Obs.*

1772 PENNANT *Tour Scot.* (1774) 49 The colliers.. have invented.. what they call a steel-mill, consisting of a small wheel and a handle; this they turn with vast rapidity against a flint. **1844** *Civil Engin. & Arch. Jrnl.* VII. 235/1 A shower of sparks from a steel-mill, turned by a boy, was the only light by which he dare work.

2. A mill or factory where steel is rolled into sheets.

1858 SIMMONDS *Dict. Trade*, *Steel-mill maker*, a manufacturer of forge tilts, or rolling mills, for hammering steel into bars, or rolling it into sheets.

3. (See quot.)

1875 KNIGHT *Dict. Mech.*, *Steel-mill*, a mill with metallic grinding-surfaces, usually of steel... Coffee and spice mills are instances.

steel pen.

1. A pen made of steel, split at the tip like a quill. (In quot. 1636 *transf.*)

1636 MASSINGER *Bashful Lover* I. i, With this Steel-pen [*sc.* his sword] I'll write on Florence helm, how much I can and dare do for you. [**1657** a Pen of steele: see PEN *sb.*[2] 4.] ? **1678** *Hatton Corr.* (Camden) 169 It comes in my mind to ask you if you have, in England, stel penns. **1700–1** NORTH *Let.* 8 Mar. in *Lives* (1890) III. App. 247 You will hardly tell by what you see, that I write with a steel pen. It is a device come out of France. **1777** MME. D'ARBLAY *Early Diary* Mar., I am now writing with a Steel Pen, which Mr. Cutler .. has just sent me. **1834** MRS. CARLYLE *Lett.* (1883) I. 12, I write with a steel pen. **1892** 'MARK TWAIN' *Amer. Claimant* vii. 71 Steel pens on his table with the ink-bottle. **1922** JOYCE *Ulysses* 8 He fears the lancet of my art as I fear that of his. The cold steelpen. **1975** *Islander* (Victoria, B.C.) 16 Feb. 10/3 By 1803 producers could no longer keep pace with the consumption of quills and the first steel pen came into use. **1983** *Daily Tel.* 10 Mar. 14/4 The steel-pen writing is brisk and persuasive.

2. *colloq.* Applied to the 'swallow-tail' or evening-dress tail-coat.

1873 LELAND *Egypt. Sketch-Bk.* 257 The steel-pen coat, as Tom Hood, junior, calls it. **1882** SALA *Amer. Revis.* xiii. (1883) 164 The swallow-tail,.. from its caudal bisection, is more appropriately designated by Americans the 'claw-hammer' or 'steel-pen' coat.

steel plate. A plate of steel used for engraving, for the armour of warships, etc. Also *attrib.*

1680 MOXON *Mech. Exerc.* xiv. 241 A Steel Plate, about half a quarter of an Inch thick. **1806** J. PERKINS (*title*) The permanent stereotype steel plate. **1824** *Encycl. Brit.* Suppl. VI. 547/1 *marg.*, Steel-Plate Engraving. *Ibid.* 548/1 Notes, with ornamental borders, printed from steel plates. **1880** *Print. Trades Jrnl.* xxx. 34 Copper and steel-plate printing machines.

Also **steel-plated** *a.*, **-plater**, **-plating.**

1819 SCOTT *Ivanhoe* xxxi, His triangular steel-plated shield. **1825** —— *Talism.* xx, A broad pavesse, or buckler,.. covered with steel-plating. **1882** *Standard* 13 Oct. 2/3 The dispute originated with the frame benders and steel platers. **1898** *Daily News* 19 Oct. 5/6 Five steel-plated vessels.

steel spring. A spring made of steel (see SPRING *sb.*[1] 22). Also *transf.* and *fig.*

1680 MOXON *Mech. Exerc.* xiv. 242 Two strong Steel Springs. **1855** GEO. ELIOT *Ess.* (1884) 194 All these natural muscles and fibres are to be torn away and replaced by a patent steel-spring, anxiety for the 'glory of God'. **1899** WERNER *Captain of Locusts* 3 Even as you looked, those wonderful steel-springs [a locust's hind legs] would bend, and send the creature forward.

Hence **steel-spring** *v. trans.*, to fit with a steel spring.

1778 MICKLE tr. *Camoens' Lusiad* IX. (ed. 2) 392 Some store the quiver, some steel-spring the bow.

steely (ˈstiːlɪ), *a.* Also 6 **stely**. [f. STEEL *sb.*[1] + -Y.]

1. a. Of or belonging to steel, made or consisting of steel.

c **1586** C'TESS PEMBROKE *Ps.* CV. v, His soule was clog'd with steely boultes of care. **1590** SPENSER *F.Q.* I. xi. 22 The steely head stucke fast still in his flesh. **1672** NEWTON in *Phil. Trans.* VII. 4032 If the steely matter imployed.. be more strongly reflective than this which I have used. **1726** POPE *Odyss.* XXII. 300 Again the foe discharge the steely show'r. **1765** A. TUCKER *Lt. Nat.* (1834) II. 557 The flowers of rhetoric, when aptly fitted on, like the feathers to an arrow, give force to the steely points of argumentation. **1807** CRABBE *Par. Reg.* I. 748 Steel, through opposing plates, the magnet draws, And steelly atoms culls from dust and straws. **1861** [LYTTON & FANE] *Tannhäuser* 58 For every sword Flash'd bare upon a sudden; and over these.. the sinking sun Stream'd lurid, lighting up that steely sea.

†**b.** Of a blow: Given with a sword or spear.

1562 LEGH *Armory* (1597) 114 Such as with steelie strokes haue stablished stout stomackes. **1647** N. WARD *Simple Cobler* 69 Break not with Steely blows, what oyle should melt.

2. a. Resembling steel in appearance, colour, hardness, or some other quality.

1596 *Edw. III*, III. v. 68 The boystrous sea Of warres deuouring gulphes and steely rocks. **1601** SHAKS. *All's Well* I. i. 114 When Vertues steely bones Lookes bleake i'th cold wind. **1824** HOOD *Two Swans* 239 When fiercely drops adown that cruel Snake—His steely scales a fearful rustling make. **1874** SYMONDS *Sk. Italy & Greece* (1898) I. i. 21 The hill-tops standing hard against the steely heavens.

b. Of iron: see quots.

1839 URE *Dict. Arts* 681 Native iron of three kinds: pure, nickeliferous, and steely. **1869** RANKINE *Machine & Hand-tools* App. 57 The term 'steely iron' or 'semi-steel', may be applied to compounds of iron with less than 0·5 per cent. of carbon.

c. Of corn, esp. barley: Very hard and brittle.

1580 TUSSER *Husb.* (1878) 48 Wheat somtime is steelie or burnt as it growes. **1742** *Lond. & Country Brewer* I. (ed. 4) 5 The smooth plump corn imbibing the Water more kindly, when the lean and steely Barley will not naturally. **1817** KEATINGE *Trav.* II. 30 The wheat here is of a very dry quality, nearly approaching to what our millers term steely. **1891** *Times* 27 Oct. 12/2 It was a bit unripe and 'steely', having been probably harvested in too great a hurry. **1897** *Jrnl. Roy. Agric. Soc.* Mar. 75 Above all it [this barley] is invariably 'steely', that is to say, when cut transversely it shows a yellow or flinty rather than a white and mealy surface to the fracture.

†**3.** Of a liquid: Having an infusion of steel. *Obs.*

1580 FRAMPTON *Monardes' Joyf. News, Dial. Iron* II. 151 b, Aliabas..doeth say that the water that hath quenched hot steele is hot and dry... Auicen..saith that the steelie water doth resolue.

4. Of a person, his qualities, etc.: **a.** Hard and cold as steel, unimpressionable, inflexible, obdurate.

1509 FISHER *Seven Penit. Ps.* cii. Wks. (1876) 187 O tough & stely hertes, o herte more hard than flynt or other stone. *a* **1586** SIDNEY *Arcadia* II. iii. (1912) 164 That she would unarme her hart of that steely resistance against the sweet blowes of Love. **1748** RICHARDSON *Clarissa* (1811) VIII. 398 The steely forehead and flinty heart of such a libertine. **1788** JOHNSON *Lett.* I. cxiv. 239 But you never mind him nor me, till time forces conviction into your steely bosom. **1865** AMELIA B. EDWARDS *Half a Million* xxx, The steely light so rarely seen there, flashed into Abel Keckwitch's eyes. **1868** FARRAR *Seekers* I. x. (1875) 115 This awful giant-shape of steely feminine cruelty.

b. In physical sense: Strong as steel.

1648 J. BEAUMONT *Psyche* XV. xxxiv, Or heav'n-commanding Joshua earth become, Or steely Sampson turn to rotten Clay. **1894** F. M. CRAWFORD *Ralstons* (1897) 117 He's handsome, too, and straight, and steely, and formidable. **1898** 'H. S. MERRIMAN' *Roden's Corner* xix. 205 He was long and lithe, of a steely strength which he had never tried.

5. *Comb.* **a.** with names of colours, as *steely-blue*, etc. **b.** in parasynthetic formations, as *steely-eyed, -hearted, †-stomached, -tongued* adjs.

1867 MORRIS *Jason* I. 381 The piled up crowd [of clouds] Began to turn from *steely blue to grey. **1878** SMILES *Robt. Dick* iv. 27 The black or steely-blue eyes of the Celts. **1964** D. F. DOWD in I. L. Horowitz *New Sociology* 60 *Steely-eyed, if amiable, technicians. **1976** *Saturday Night* Mar. 82/3 A haughty Trudeau is seated at a press conference giving some questioner that familiar steely-eyed look of his. **1884** *Bazaar* 24 Dec. 675/2 The rest of the plumage is *steely grey. **1571** GOLDING *Calvin on Ps.* xxx. 12. 111 He was not so blockish or *steely harted [L. *ferreum*], but that hee moorned in heauinesse and sorow. **1876** FARRAR *Marlb. Serm.* v. 49 Even the steely-hearted murderess in the splendid tragedy..loves her aged father. **1604** T. WRIGHT *Passions* v. 184 A *steelie stomackt boore. **1828** P. CUNNINGHAM *N.S. Wales* II. 9 Some of the most *steely-tongued will sometimes halloo in at the window. **1903** *Daily Chron.* 25 Nov. 6/6 The flash being *steely-white and very subdued.

6. quasi-*adv.* In a steely manner. Also in *Comb.*

1621 BP. MOUNTAGU *Diatribæ* 147 It is more than stony or steely hard, to say that his substance was at all Tithed. **1871** G. MACDONALD *Songs of Winter Days* 11, *Wks. Fancy & Imag.* III. 83 Heed not the winds that steely blow. **1922** JOYCE *Ulysses* 252 Bronze By Gold Heard The Hoofirons, Steelyringing.

steelyard[1] ('sti:ljɑ:d). *Hist.* Forms: α. (5 stileyerd, stil-, styliarde, -ierd, -ȝerd), 6 stiliard, (stuliard, -yard), 6-7 stilyard, (6 stwyl-, stylyarde), stilliard(e, (6 stylliarde, 7 styllard, stilliart, stillyart, stilliyard), 6-7, 9 stillyard (6 -yarde). β. 6 stel(e)yard(e, 6-7, 9 steelyard, 7-9 steel-yard. [f. STEEL *sb.*[1] + YARD *sb.*[1]; a mistranslation of MLG. *stâlhof* (whence G. *stahlhof* in historical use), f. *stâl* sample, pattern + *hof* courtyard. The word *stâl*, pattern, being homophonous with the word for steel, the meaning of the compound was misunderstood.]

1. The place on the north bank of the Thames above London Bridge where the Merchants of the Hanse had their establishment. Also, the merchants collectively.

[**1394** in *N. & Q.* Ser. x. VI. 413/2 In civitate Londonia ..in Curia Calibis.] **1474** in Rymer *Foedera* (1710) XI. 796/1 Quandam Curiam Londoniæ sitam vocatam Staelhoeff aliàs Stylgerd [? *read* Stylȝerd]. **1475** *Rolls of Parlt.* VI. 123/1 The said Merchauntes of the Hanze, shuld have a certeyn place within the Citee of London, called the Stylehof, otherwise called the Stileyerd. *Ibid.*, Where the Maire and Communaltie of the Cite of London, be seased in their demeane as in fee, of the said place called the Stilehof, otherwise called the Stileyerd. **1493** WRIOTHESLEY *Chron.* (Camden) I. 3 This yeare was a risinge of yonge men agaynste the Stiliarde. **1546** *Acts Privy Council* N.S. I. 360 Bernarde Emeke and Symonde Percevall, merchauntes of the Stwylyarde. **1551-2** EDW. VI *Jrnl.* (Roxb.) 390 This day the stiliard put in their aunswere to a certen complaint that they merchauntis adventurers laid against them. **1610** J. MORE in *Buccleuch MSS.* (Hist. MSS. Comm.) 90 Such.. of their goods as remains in the Styllard and other places of this town. *a* **1648** LD. HERBERT *Hen. VIII* (1649) 320 Which Act yet was not extended to the Merchants of the Stillyart. **1752** CARTE *Hist. Eng.* III. 266 The merchants of the Hanse or (as they were commonly called from their house in an open place where steel had been formerly sold) of the steel-yard. **1885** *Pall Mall Gaz.* 13 June 5 To the midst of the present century, when the last stillyard was converted into a London railway terminus.

b. A similar establishment in a provincial town.

1474 in Rymer *Foedera* (1710) XI. 796/1 Item, in Villa de Boston Curiam de Staelhoeff, aliàs dictam Stylierd. **1601** in P. Thompson *Hist. Boston* (1856) 247 [An acre of land] at the Steelyards. **1676** J. LOGAN in *Guillim's Her.* (1679) II. 178 Leaving us its large Vaults, Ware-houses, Cellarages, Drapery, Steel-yard, and public Halls, as indications of its [*sc.* Coventry's] former opulency and splendour. **1856** P. THOMPSON *Hist. Boston* 339 The ancient custom-house at Boston was called the 'Stylyard's House'. **1890** GROSS *Gild Merch.* I. 154 *note*, It is said that there were German Hanse societies or 'steelyards' in Hull, York, Newcastle, Boston, and Lynn.

c. A tavern within the precincts of the Steelyard where 'Rhenish wine' was sold.

1592 NASHE *P. Penilesse Supplic.* F i b, Men, when they are idle, and know not what to do, saith one, let vs goe to the Stilliard, and drinke Rhenish wine. **1607** B. BARNES *Divils Charter* III. v. F 3, Till they transported..By Charon, Ferriman of Black Auerne, Fall Anchor at the Stilliard Tauerne. **1636** J. TAYLOR (Water P.) *Trav. through Signes Zodiack* D 7, There are foure Houses in London that doe sell Rhennish Wine, inhabited onely by Dutchmen; namely. The Stilliyard [etc.].

2. *attrib.* and *Comb.* with the sense 'of or pertaining to the Steelyard,' 'produced in or distributed through the Steelyard'.

1551-2 EDW. VI *Lit. Rem.* (Roxb.) 509 It were good the Stiliard men ware for this time gentelly aunswerid. *a* **1552** LELAND *Itin.* VIII. 59 The staple and the stiliard houses yet there [*sc.* Boston] remayne. **1593** A. CHUTE in *G. Harvey's Pierces Super.* G g 2, The Rhennish furie of thy braine, Incenst with hot fume of a Stilliard Clime. **1593** G. HARVEY *Ibid.* D d 1, His Stilliard hatt in his drousie eyes. **1611** COTGR. s.v. *Coquillé, Pain coquillé*, a fashion of an hard-crusted loafe, somewhat like our Stillyard Bunne. **1657** *Burton's Diary* (1828) I. 181 We make no distinction of Hambrough or stillyard merchants.

steelyard[2] ('sti:ljɑ:d). Forms: α. 7-8 stiliard, -yard, stilliard, (7 stilard), 8 still-yard. β. 7 steeleyard, 8- steelyard, steel-yard. [f. STEEL *sb.*[1] + YARD *sb.*[2]; the formation was prob. suggested by the existence of STEELYARD[1].

The following passage has been supposed to be an example of this word:

1531 in *Lett. & Papers For. & Dom. Hen. VIII*, V. 104/2 [The beam of] le Hanzes Hangis, [called] the Stilliarde Beme.

But prob. 'Stilliarde Beme' means the public weighing scales kept at the Steelyard. The relation to the older word STELLEER, which rests ultimately on the sole authority of Cotgrave, is obscure.]

A balance consisting of a lever with unequal arms, which moves on a fulcrum; the article to be weighed is suspended from the shorter arm, and a counterpoise is caused to slide upon the longer arm until equilibrium is produced, its place on this arm (which is notched or graduated) showing the weight: = *Roman balance* (ROMAN *a.*[1] 15 a). Also *pl.* and *a pair of steelyards.*

1639 *Act in Arch. Maryland* (1883) I. 79 No more shall be demanded for sealing of a pair of Steeleyards..then the fee ..for sealing of a measure. **1650** B. *Discolliminium* 16 It must be weighed..at the most just..beam the State hath,.. not at every Souldiers petty Stilliards. **1682-90** HOOKE *Posth. Wks.* (1705) 565 If on a Stilyard a weight of thirty Pound be hung at thirty times the distance from the Center that a weight of nine hundred Pounds is hung, the Stilyard shall remain in æquilibrio. *a* **1790** WARTON *Prol. Old Winch. Playhouse* 23 Hither your steelyards, Butchers, bring, to weigh The pound of flesh, Anthonio's bond must pay! **1849** LONGF. *Kavanagh* xi. Pr. Wks, 1886 II. 322 He likewise weighed all the babies. There was hardly a child in town that had not hung beneath his steelyards. **1872** YEATS *Techn. Hist. Comm.* 349 Railway luggage is weighed by means of a strong iron steelyard.

attrib. **1777** *Birmingham Directory* 5 Beach, Thomas, Stilliard maker.

†**steem,** *sb. Obs.* Also 6 steeme. [Aphetic var. of ESTEEM *sb.* Cf. next.

It is noteworthy that the first two examples are much earlier than any known instance of the fuller form.]

Estimation, value.

c **1330** R. BRUNNE *Chron. Wace* (Rolls) 98 Þat may þou here in sir Tristrem; ouer gestes it has þe steem, Ouer alle that is or was. *a* **1380** *St. Ambrose* 893 in Horstm. *Altengl. Leg.* (1878) 22 Þou schuldest þenke bi good steem þou nart but riht as on of hem. **1588** GREENE *Alcida* (1617) E 4, Of little steeme is Crystall being crackt.

†**steem,** *v.*[1] *Obs.* [Aphetic var. of ESTEEM *v.*] *trans.* To estimate, value.

1590 GREENE *Never too late* II. Wks. (Grosart) VIII. 120 The more it workes, the quicker is the wit; The more it writes, the better to be steem'd. **1592** DANIEL *Sonn. Delia* iv, Wks. (Grosart) I. 39 These lines I vse, t' vnburthen mine owne hart; My loue affects no fame, nor steemes of Art. **1596** SPENSER *F.Q.* IV. v. 3 Whilome it was..Dame Venus girdle, by her steemed deare, What time she vsd to liue in wiuely sort. **1642** H. MORE *Song of Soul* I. ii. 134 Is Honesty in such unruly fit That it's held in no rank? they 'steem it not awhit.

steem (sti:m), *v.*[2] *dial.* (Yorks.) [variant of STEVEN *v.*] *trans.* To obtain (goods) on credit; to order in advance, bespeak. Also, to pay a deposit upon goods bought.

1674 in *Depos. York Castle* (Surtees) 210 Thy father went to John Walker's to steime a pare of shooes, and he would not let him have them without he had money in his hand... Likewise he went to George Coppley's to steime a wastcoate cloth. **1674** RAY *N.C. Words*, To *Steem*: to bespeak a thing. **1862** C. C. ROBINSON *Dial. Leeds*, *Steim*, to bespeak. 'Steimed a plaace fur t' meeting'.

steem, obs. form of STEAM.

steen (sti:n), *v.* Forms: 1 stǽnan, 2 stænen, 3-5 stene, 3 steane, 5 steyn(e, 8-9 steen, stein, 9 stean, steyn(e. [OE. *stǽnan* = OHG. (MHG., mod.G.) *steinen*, Goth. *stainjan*, f. OTeut. **staino-z* STONE *sb.*

In certain northern dialects this and STONE *v.* are formally coincident.]

†**1.** *trans.* To stone (a person); to put to death by stoning. *Obs.*

c **950** *Lindisf. Gosp.* Matt. xxiii. 37 Ðu stænas [*c* **975** *Rushw.* stænest] hia ðaðe to ðe ȝesendet sint. *a* **1225** *Ancr. R.* 122 Seint Stefne þet te stones þet me stenede him mide [etc.]. *a* **1225** *Juliana* 41 And ich hit am þet makede sein iuhan þe baptiste beon heafdes bicoruen & seinte stephene isteanet. **1340** *Ayenb.* 213 God..made ane man to stene to-uore al þe uolke uor þet he [etc.]. **1387** TREVISA *Higden* (Rolls) VI. 31 Þey schulde þrowe out stones þorow holes of þe walles, as it were for to stene the devel. *c* **1440** *Gesta Rom.* 178 Jerusalem! that sleist prophites, & steynist hem that bethe I-sent to the. *c* **1450** *Mirk's Festial* 28 Þay drowen hym out of þe cyte, forto stenen hym to dethe.

2. To line (a well or other excavation) with stone, brick or other material. Also with *up.*

1723 *Phil. Trans.* XXXVI. 192 We..artificially steen'd the whole Depth [of the well] with circular Portland Stone. **1797** *Ibid.* LXXXVII. 325 The well was sunk and steined to the bottom. **1833** LOUDON *Encycl. Archit.* §234 To dig a cesspool..and steen it with four-inch brick-work. **1838** HOLLOWAY *Prov. Dict.* s.v., To line a well with stones or bricks is to Stean it. **1839** *Civil Engin. & Arch. Jrnl.* II. 245/2 The excavation was..steined with 9 inch brickwork in cement. **1877** *Fraser's Mag.* XV. 422 The original plan of steyning the banks, or lining them with stones, must..be resorted to. **1886** *W. Somerset Word-bk.*, *Steen*, to line..., without mortar the circular wall of a well... 'I've a-got good stones, I'll steen un up well'. **1891** *Antiquary* Nov. 208 The lower part of this was steined with oak boards.

b. *dial.* (See quot.)

1886 *W. Somerset Word-bk.*, *Steen*,..2. To put fresh metal on a road.

Hence **steened** *ppl. a.*

1721 MORTIMER *Husb.* (ed. 5) II. 283 He had several times seen at the pulling up of such old [ox] Stalls, some that have had a well steen'd Channel under the Planks, leading to a large steined Receptacle without the Stall. **1863** *Archæol. Cantiana* V. 15, I found another steined grave of Caen stone.

steen, obs. form of STEAN.

‖**steenbok** ('ste:nbɔk). Also steenboc(k, -buck, steinboc(k, -bok, -buck, stembok. [Du. *steenbok*, f. *steen* STONE *sb.* + *bok* BUCK *sb.*[1] Cf. STEINBOCK.] A small South African antelope, *Rhaphiceros campestris.*

1775 MASSON *Journ. Cape* in *Phil. Trans.* LXVI. 295 Some had the skin of a steenbock hung over their breast. **1850** R. G. CUMMING *Hunter's Life S. Afr.* (1902) 157/2 Returning..I shot a steinbok. **1893** F. C. SELOUS *Trav. S.E. Africa* 431 He has shot every kind of game in Africa, from a steinbuck to an elephant. **1894** LYDEKKER *Roy. Nat. Hist.* II. 307 Although the name steinbok is properly restricted to a single species of antelope, it will be found [etc.]. **1913** C. PETTMAN *Africanderisms*, Steenbok... *Raphicerus campestris*. The word is frequently corrupted to Stembok.

‖**steenbras(s** ('ste:nbras). *S. Afr.* Also 8 steenbras(s)en, 9 -brassem, steembras. [Cape Du., f. Du. *steen* stone + *brasem* bream.] Any of several marine fishes of the family Sparidæ, esp. the red steenbras, *Petrus rupestris*, the silver steenbras, *Sparodon durbanensis*, or the white steenbras, *Lithognathus lithognathus.*

1791 tr. *Le Vaillant's Trav.* I. 22 There are plenty of fish at the Cape. Among those most valued..are the *rooman*.., *steenbrasen*..and some others. **1801** J. BARROW *Trav. S. Afr.* I. i. 30 Next to the Roman are the red and the white *Steenbrassems*. **1893** [see KINGKLIP]. **1910** *Encycl. Brit.* V. 230/2 [Cape Colony.] The steenbrass and geelbeck are common in the estuaries and bays. **1914** *19th Cent.* Sept. 591 [Walfish Bay.] Other fish are harders (grey mullet), steembras, and barbers. **1931** *Times Lit. Suppl.* 16 Apr. 301/2 Many of the Cape fish, such as the geelbek,..the steenbras. **1958** *Cape Times* 20 May 2/2 Fishermen have been bringing in some fine, big red-steenbras... Anglers on the rocks have..had good hauls of smaller fish including white stumpnose, galjoen and white steenbras. **1973** [see KABELJOU].

steene, obs. form of STEAN.

steening ('sti:nɪŋ), *vbl. sb.* Also steaning, steining, steyning. [f. STEEN *v.* + -ING[1].]

1. *concr.* The lining of a well or other excavation.

1767 *Ann. Reg., Chron.* 56/1 The steining [of the well] fel in upon him and inclosed him at the bottom. **1783** *Phil. Trans.* LXXIV. 13 A brick steening, of two bricks thick in tarris, [was] raised gradually towards the top of the well. **1898** F. DAVIS *Silchester* 40 They [the wells] were mostly lined with a flint steining as far as the water. **1926** T. E. LAWRENCE *Seven Pillars* (1935) I. x. 80 The well was old, and broad, with a good stone steyning, and a strong coping round the top. **1939** *Oxoniensia* IV. 94 They might have been stones used to edge or pave the mouth of the well, as similar fragments of stone occurred in most wells, but they could not be taken as steyning.

2. *dial.* **a.** A paved ford across a river.

1838 HOLLOWAY *Prov. Dict.*, *Steaning*. **1887** S. H. A. HERVEY in *Wedmore Chron.* I. 288 (E.D.D.) Here I suppose was once a stream; and they crossed it by a stenning.

b. (See quot.)

1886 *W. Somerset Word-bk.*, *Steening*,..2. The metal fresh laid on a road.

steenkirk, steinkirk ('sti:nkɜ:k). *Hist.* Also 8 stinkirk. [a. F. (*cravate à la*) *Steinkerke*, *Steinkerque*, from the victory of Steenkerke

(Belgium) gained by the French over the English and their allies on 3 Aug. 1692.

It has long been common to give the names of victories to new patterns of attire etc. introduced about the time of the battle. It is said that in France the designation *à la Steinkerke* had a great temporary vogue as applied to clothing, jewellery, cosmetics, and the like. According to Voltaire, the original *cravate à la Steinkerke* simulated the appearance of negligence, in allusion to the disordered dress of the French nobles when hastily summoned to the battle.]

A kind of neckcloth (worn both by men and women), having long laced ends hanging down or twisted together, and passed through a loop or ring.

1694 D'URFEY *Don Quixote* I. Prol., The Modish Spark may Paint, and lie in Paste, Wear a huge Steinkirk twisted to his Waste. *a* **1695** HALIFAX *Wks.* (1912) 162 If the Judges upon the Bench should.. be Cloathed like the Jockeys at New-Market, or wear Jack-Boots and Steenkirks. **1695** CONGREVE *Love for L.* I. xiii. [xiv], There are huge Proportion'd Criticks, with long Wigs, Lac'd Coats, Steinkerk Cravats, and terrible Faces. **1697** DRYDEN *Virg. Past.* Pref. **** 2 b, The Beau presses into their Dressing-Room,.. to adjust his own Steenzkirk [*sic*] and Peruke. **1704** CIBBER *Careless Husb.* v. 54 Stage-dir., Takes her Steinkirk from her Neck, and lays it gently over his Head. **1707** MRS. CENTLIVRE *Platonick Lady* III. i, *Milliner.* And a long Neck and a hollow Breast, first made use of the Stinkirk. **1711** ADDISON *Spect.* No. 128 ¶ 11 A Fashion makes its Progress much slower into Cumberland than into Cornwall... The Steenkirk arrived but two months ago in Newcastle.

1818 SCOTT *Rob Roy* xxxi, I had yielded up my cravat (a smart Steinkirk,.. and richly laced). **1854** AINSWORTH *Jack Sheppard* III. xiii, [He wore] a muslin cravat, or steenkirk, as it was termed, edged with the finest point lace. **1869** MRS. PALLISER *Lace* xxv. 300 These old-fashioned articles of jewellery were worn to fasten.. the lace Steinkirk.

steenstrupine ('sti:nstru:pi:n). *Min.* [f. the name of Knud J. V. *Steenstrup* (1842–1913), Danish geologist + -INE[5].] A silicate and phosphate of rare-earth and other elements (chiefly cerium, sodium, calcium, iron, and manganese), found as dark brown or black rhombohedral crystals. Also (*rare*) **'steenstrupite**.

1882 J. LORENZEN in *Mineral. Mag.* V. 67 The analysis of this mineral has shown it to be a new species, and, as suggested by Prof. Johnstrup, I have therefore given it the name of *Steenstrupine*, after Mr. *Steenstrup*, who.. first found the mineral. **1901** *Meddelelser om Grønland* XXIV. 204 The steenstrupite is found partly in pegmatitic veins and partly embedded in grained albite. **1943** *Mineral. Abstr.* VIII. 369 The unit-cell dimensions of steenstrupine.. show a similarity to those of apatite. **1977** *Jrnl. R. Soc. Arts* CXXV. 406/2 The peralkaline nepheline syenites of Ilimaussaq in south Greenland, where the main mineral is steenstrupine (silicate and phosphate of rare earths, sodium, niobium, tantalum, thorium and uranium).

steentjie ('stɪəncɪ). *S. Afr.* Also **steen(t)je**. [Afrikaans, dim. of Du. *steen* stone.] Either of two small marine fishes of the family Sparidæ, *Spondyliosoma emarginatum* or *Sarpa salpa* (= STREPIE).

1893 H. A. BRYDEN *Gun & Camera S. Afr.* xx. 448 We caught also.. steenje, another small fish, which we cut up principally for bait. **1913** W. W. THOMPSON *Sea Fisheries Cape Col.* 154 *Cantharus emarginatus*.. Steentje. **1930** C. L. BIDEN *Sea-Angling Fishes of Cape* ix. 166 The men.. caught many steentjies which were scaled and pulped with a baton and baited whole on the big lines. **1957** S. SCHOEMAN *Strike!* iii. 88 There are two species of fish commonly referred to as steentjies, namely the common steentjie.. alias strepie,.. and the blue or bank steentjie.

steep (sti:p), *sb.*[1] Forms: (5 stipe), 6 stepe, (steppe), 6–7 steepe, (8 stip, stiep), 7– steep. [f. STEEP *v.*]

1. The process of steeping or soaking; the state of being steeped, esp. in phr. (*to lay*) †*a steep* (obs.), †*in a steep* (obs.), *in steep*.

c **1430** *Two Cookery-bks.* I. 16 Take þe brothe, þe pouches & þe lyuerys wer sodoun in, in a stipe or on fayre brede. **1516** *Gt. Herbal* ccccxvii. (1529) Y v b, And let the fylynge lay a stepe a day and a nyght in vynegyre. **1563** T. GALE *Antidot.* II. 25 Let all these be beaten together and layed in stepe in Rose water. **1601** HOLLAND *Pliny* XXXII. vii. II. 439 The same ought first to be cut or shred small, and then to lie infused or in steepe a whole day and a night in water or vinegre. **1707** MORTIMER *Husb.* 175 Take Plantain, Rue, [etc.].. of each an handful,.. lay them in steep in a Pint of old wash. **1709** LADY G. BAILLIE *Household Bk.* (1911) 74 For makeing 2 stip of mallt.. £6.0.0. **1765** *Museum Rust.* III. 220 If barley is left too long on the steep in the same water, the water will grow slimy. **1800** *Act 41 Geo. III*, c. 6 (*title*) For shortening.. the Time of keeping in Steep for malting, Barley damaged by Rain. **1851** A. MARSHALL in H. Schroeder *Ann. Yorksh.* (1851) I. 419 Turning the beets inside out for the second steep. **1876** *Encycl. Brit.* IV. 267/2, 81½ bushels of good dry barley will, after forty-eight hours steep, swell to exactly 100 bushels. **1893** W. R. MACKINTOSH *Around Orkney Peat Fires* II. (1905) 126 A farmer.. had just taken his malt out of steep, when two excisemen paid him a visit.

b. *fig.*

1592 NASHE *P. Penilesse* 18 b, I haue tearmes (if I be vext) laid in steepe in *Aqua fortis*. **1615** CHAPMAN *Odyss.* II. 29 She.. sweete sleepe Powr'd on each wooer; which so laid in steepe Their drowsie temples, that each brow did nod. **1627** SANDERSON *Serm. ad Pop.* vi. §21. (1632) 523 He.. doth but lay more rods in steepe for his own back. **1895** 'IAN MACLAREN' *Briar Bush* 255 Man [doctor], ye 'ill need tae pit yir brains in steep. Is she clean beyond ye?

†**2.** *the steep*: the midday plunge taken by a stag in hot weather.

1486 *Bk. St. Albans* e iij b, To the stepe then thay goon yche hote day at noon... The cause of the steepe is to weere hym fro the flee. **1576** TURBERV. *Venerie* xxxvii. 100 A Hart goeth to the steepe at noone in the heate of the day to keepe him from the flye. *Ibid.* 244 He goeth to the Steppe.

†**3.** ? A steeping vessel. *Obs. rare*[−1].

1614 in W. S. Gibson *Hist. Monast. Tynemouth* (1846) II. 122 Repayring the Malthowse, Host and Steep, lx.s.

4. The liquid in which a thing is placed to undergo soaking or maceration; a prepared liquor used as a dyeing bath or cleansing wash; in *Agric.* a wash for seeds; often with qualifying word, as *alum, bran, lime steep*, etc.

1759 tr. *Duhamel's Husb.* I. xvi. (1762) 102 Steeps were brought very early into use in husbandry. **1805** R. W. DICKSON *Pract. Agric.* I. 446 Steeps or pickles of these kinds appear to have been principally made use of for preparing wheat, in order to prevent it from being affected with disease. **1839** URE *Dict. Arts* 600 The manufacturer.. is.. careful to ensure their purification by subjecting them to a weak lime steep. **1882** CROOKES *Dyeing & Tissue-Printing* 134 The second peachwood beck may be saved and used for the first peachwood steep of the next lot. **1897** W. G. SMITH tr. *Von Tubeuf's Dis. Plants* 65 Sterilization of the seed.. is chiefly carried out by the use of 'steeps', which kill the smut-spores adherent to the seed.

5. = RENNET *sb.*[1]

1688 HOLME *Armoury* III. 244/1 Bad Cheese.. made of Burnt Milk, and of stinking and bad Runnet or Steep. **1769** MRS. RAFFALD *Eng. Housekpr.* (1778) 255 To make Cream Cheese. Put one large spoonful of steep to five quarts of afterings. **1845** *Jrnl. R. Agric. Soc.* VI. I. 108 The rennet, or steep as it is commonly called, is next added. **1895** E. RYDINGS *Manx Tales* 65 And, Mrs. Kelly, I'll be sendin' you a boddle of steep.

b. *Sc.* The plant *Ranunculus flammula*.

1894 J. SHAW in R. Wallace *Country Schoolm.* (1899) 354 *Steep*, Ranunculus flammula, from its acting like rennet.

steep (sti:p), *a.*, *sb.*[2] and *adv.* Forms: 1 stéap, 3 steap, stæp, 3–6 stepe, (4 steppe), 4–7 steepe, 5 steype, 6 stipe, stype, stiepe, 6–7 *Sc.* steip, 7 stiep, 7– steep. [OE. *stéap*, corresp. to OFris. *stâp*, MHG. *stouf (as sb. with the sense 'steep, declivity', in the proper name *Hohenstaufen*) :—OTeut. type **staupo*-, f. Teut. root **steup*-: *staup*-: *stūp*-: see STOOP *v.*]

A. *adj.*

†**1. a.** Extending to a great height; elevated, lofty.

Beowulf 222 (Gr.) Beorȝas steape. *a* **1000** *Riddles* iv. 10 (Gr.) Weallas beofiað steape ofer stiwitum. *c* **1205** LAY. 19815 [They] mid eorðe & mid stanen stepne hul makede. **13..** *E.E. Allit. P.* B. 1396, & Baltazar vpon bench was busked to sete, Stepe stayred stones of his stoute throne. *a* **1400–50** *Wars Alex.* 4828 A cliffe at to þe cloudis semed, þat was so staire & so stepe. *c* **1440** *Promp. Parv.* 474/1 Steepe, nowt lowe, *elevatus, ascendens*. **1615** CHAPMAN *Odyss.* I. 200 To a roome they came, Steepe, and of state. **1667** MILTON *P.L.* IV. 135 Where delicious Paradise,.. Crowns with her enclosure green,.. the champain head Of a steep wilderness. **1738** WESLEY *Hymn, 'Eternal Wisdom'* ix, Thy Breath can raise the Billows steep, Or sink them to the Sand.

†**b.** = 'High' in certain transferred uses. Of warriors or their attributes: Of high courage, noble. Of a voice: High, loud. *Obs.*

c **1205** LAY. 1532 þer wes moni steap mon mid stele to-swngen. *Ibid.* 1541 Cuð nu þine strengða & þina steapa main. *Ibid.* 5879 And make we.. auer alche hæpe hertoȝe stæpne. **13..** *Coer de L.* 5985 Kyng Richard.. cryyd on hym with voys ful stepe, 'Home, schrewe!'

2. †**a.** Of eyes: Projecting, prominent (also *steep-out*); staring; glaring with passion.

c **1000** ÆLFRIC *Hom.* I. 456 He hæfð steape eaȝan [= L. 'oculi grandes', *Pass. S. Bartholomæi*]. *a* **1225** *Leg. Kath.* 307 þe keiser bistarede hire wið swiðe steape ehnen hwil þat ha spek þus. *c* **1320** *Sir Beues* 685 Wiþ stepe eiȝen & rowe bren So loþeliche he gan on hem sen,.. þai were aferde. *c* **1386** CHAUCER *Prol.* 201 His heed was balled.. Hise eyen stepe, and rollynge in his heed. **1397** TREVISA *Barth. De P.R.* III. xvii. (1495) 64 Grete and stepe eyen [L. *oculus eminens*].. se not well aferre: but depe eyen se wel aferre. *c* **1400** *Destr. Troy* 3758 Crispe herit was the kyng,.. Stokyn ene out stepe with a streught loke. *Ibid.* 7724 His Ene [were] leuenaund with light as a low fyn, With stremys full stithe in his stepe loke. *c* **1400** tr. *Secreta Secret., Gov. Lordsh.* 115 He þat hauys steepe-owt eghen [L. *oculos extensos*] ys malicious & feloun. *a* **1450** LOVELICH *Grail* xiii. 651 With grete stepe Eyen In his hed Also. **1555** WATREMAN *Fardle Facions* II. x. 212 The Tartares are very deformed,.. hauying great stiepe eyes.

†**b.** Of jewels, eyes, stars: Brilliant. In later use only of eyes, in the poetical phrase *steep and gray*. *Obs.*

a **1000** *Gnomic Verses* i. 23 (Gr.) Ðim sceal on hringe standan steap & ȝeap. *a* **1000** *Sal. & Sat.* 284 (Gr.) Ne mæȝ hit steorra ne stan ne se steapa ȝimm.. wihte beswican. *a* **1225** *Leg. Kath.* 1647 A deorewurðe wal, schininde, & schenre, of ȝimstanes steapre þen is eni steorre. *a* **1225** *St. Marher.* 9 His twa ehnen steappre þene steorren ant þene ȝimstanes ant brad as bascins. *c* **1330** *King of Tars* 15 Eyyen stepe and graye. **13..** *E.E. Allit. P.B.* 583 By-þenk þe sumtyme, Wheþer he þat stykked vche a stare in vche steppe yȝe, 3if hym self be bore blynde hit is a brod wonder. *a* **1529** SKELTON *P. Sparowe* 1014 Her eyen gray and stepe Causeth myne hert to lepe. **1577** GRANGE *Golden Aphrod.* G j b, Hir twinckling eyne bothe steepe and grey, they seeme like Christall cleare.

3. a. Of a hill, mountain, cliff: Having an almost perpendicular face or slope, precipitous. Of a gradient or slope, a staircase, etc.: High-pitched.

The sense prob. goes back to OE., but is difficult to authenticate, as when applied to mountains, cliffs, etc. the word prob. expressed a mixed notion of senses 1 and 3.

c **1200** ORMIN 11379 & ȝet to deofell.. brohhte himm onn an lawe þatt wass well swiþe stæp & heh. **13..** *K. Alis.* 7041 Theo path on mount was narwe and stepe, In valeys, dark and deope. **1533** ELYOT *Cast. Helthe* (1539) 50 b, Stronge or violente exercises be these.. clymmyng or walkyng against a stipe vpright hyll. **1549** THOMAS *Hist. Italie* 161, I thynke the stipe descent of the hill causeth, that they haue not roome enough to make theyr stretes large. **1588** SHAKS. *L.L.L.* IV. I. 2 Was that the King that spurd his horse so hard, Against the steepe vprising of the hill? **1605** VERSTEGAN *Dec. Intell.* iv. 98 These clifs.. are.. as it were cut of stiep or straight down, from the top to the bottom. **1610** HOLLAND *Camden's Brit.* 344 A mighty ridge of steepe high Cliffs [L. *cautium eminentia*].. runneth for seaven miles or there about, as far as to Dover. **1611** BIBLE *Matt.* viii. 32 The whole herd of swine ranne violently downe a steepe place into the Sea. **1667** MILTON *P.L.* II. 71 The way seems difficult and steep to scale With upright wing against a higher foe. *a* **1700** EVELYN *Diary* 28 Aug. 1670, Those huge steepe stayres ascending to it. **1718** LADY M. W. MONTAGU *Let. to Mrs. T——* 25 Sept., The descent is.. steep and slippery. **1796** H. HUNTER tr. *St.-Pierre's Stud. Nat.* (1799) I. 137 The declivity of the bason of the Sea is much steeper than that of the bounding lands. **1813** SHELLEY *Q. Mab* ix. 218 Again the burning wheels inflame The steep descent of Heaven's untrodden way. **1838** ARNOLD *Hist. Rome* I. 32 The hills of Rome are.. low in height but with steep and rocky sides. **1876** MISS BRADDON *J. Haggard's Dau.* II. 17 The narrow path.. had been cut into steps where the slope was steepest. **1884** [see GRADIENT *sb.* 1].

b. *transf.* of movement. *poet.*

1603 DRAYTON *Barons' Wars* VI. xxii, That slippery way Where the most worldly prouident doe slide, Feeling the steepe fall threatning sure decay. **1667** MILTON *P.L.* III. 741 [He] Throws his steep flight in many an Aerie wheele. **1818** SHELLEY *Homer's Hymn to Sun* 22 His rapid steeds soon bear him to the West; Where their steep flight his hands divine arrest.

†**c.** Of a ditch, cave or the like: Having precipitous sides or entrance. *Obs.*

1568 GRAFTON *Chron.* II. 974 With diuers fortresses in the ditches, which were so broade and so plumme steepe that was wonder to beholde. **1598** *Extracts Burgh Rec. Glasgow* (1876) 189 His steip trocht and wolt biggit be him. **1601** *Ibid.*, Ane steip troche. **1608** TOPSELL *Serpents* 10 Ouid writeth: Longo caput extulit antro Cæruleus serpens,.. That is—The greenish Serpent extolld her head from denne so steepe.

†**d.** Of a forehead: Upright, high. *Obs. rare*[−1].

1509 HAWES *Past. Pleas.* xxx. (Percy Soc.) 146 Her forehead stepe, with fayre browes ybent.

†**e.** Of water: Having a headlong course, flowing precipitously. Of rain (*Sc.*): Pouring. *Obs.*

c **1330** *Arth. & Merl.* 1450 Her vnder is a ȝerde depe A water, boþe swift & stepe. **1634** MILTON *Comus* 97 And the gilded Car of Day, His glowing Axle doth allay In the steep Atlantick stream. *c* **1655** —— *Ps. lxxxi.* 31, I tri'd thee at the water steep of Meriba renown'd. **1659** A. HAY *Diary* (S.H.S.) 149 Mr Rot Broun and I cam away from Lanerick in a very steep raine.

f. *Coal-mining.* Of a seam or measure: Having a high inclination.

1883 GRESLEY *Gloss. Coal-mining* 239 Steep seams [of coal]. **1892** *Labour Commission Gloss.*, *Steep Measures*, a description of the seams of coal on the South crop.. in South Wales, which are highly inclined.

g. *steepest descent*(*s*) (Math.), used with reference to a method of finding a minimum of a function of two or more variables by repeatedly evaluating it at a point displaced from the previous point in the direction that locally involved the greatest drop in its value.

1939 *Proc. R. Soc.* A. CLXIX. 484 In the method of steepest descents the displacement affects all co-ordinates and affects them in the ratio of their residual forces. **1943** *Bull. Amer. Math. Soc.* XLIX. 18 We now choose the line along which the motion proceeds so that the descent is as steep as possible (lines of steepest descent). **1974** ADBY & DEMPSTER *Introd. Optimization Methods* iii. 57 The steepest descent method uses the Jacobian gradient g to determine a suitable direction of movement.

4. In occasional figurative uses. (Very common in Milton). **a.** Of an aim, an undertaking, etc.: Arduous, full of difficulty, ambitious.

1598 BASTARD *Chrestol.* IV. xii. 85 His heedlesse good and steepe presumptuousnesse. **1816** BYRON *Ch. Har.* III. cv. They were gigantic minds, and their steep aim Was, Titan-like, on daring doubts to pile Thoughts which [etc.].

†**b.** Of a difficulty: Hard to surmount. *Obs.*

1644 MILTON *Areop.* (Arb.) 32 To which [bound of civill liberty].. wee are already in good part arriv'd, and yet from such a steepe disadvantage of tyranny and superstition grounded into our principles as was [etc.].

†**c.** = HEADLONG *a.* 4. *Obs.*

1616 B. JONSON *Forest* xi, Who.. Would, at suggestion of a steepe desire, Cast himselfe from the spire Of all his happiness? **1649** MILTON *Eikon.* 42 The stay and support of all things from that steep ruin to which he had nigh brought them. **1653** —— *Ps. vii.* 60 With ruine steep. **1667** —— *P.L.* VI. 324 It met The sword of Satan with steep force to smite Descending.

d. Of inequalities, contrasts: Violent, extreme.

1856 EMERSON *Eng. Traits, Result* Wks. (Bohn) II. 136 The feudal system survives in the steep inequality of property and privilege. *Ibid.*, *Manners* ibid. II. 51 The range of nations from which London draws, and the steep contrasts of condition, create the picturesque in society.

5. *slang.* Excessive, extravagant, 'stiff', 'tall'. Of a price, an amount: Exorbitant. Of a story, etc.: Exaggerated, incredible.

1856 *Knick. Mag.* Apr. XLVII. 362 (Thornton *Amer. Gloss.*) He's too steep in his price, anyway. **1857** *Chicago Tribune* 17 Oct. (Bartlett), One hundred and ten Winnebago Indians, wearing their blankets, voted the Democratic ticket; but the agent thought this was rather steep, so he afterwards crossed that number from the list. **1895** *Westm. Gaz.* 22 Apr. 4/3 This is rather a steep statement, even for a party that exists on credit. **1901** *Munsey's Mag.* XXIV. 441/1 Forty thousand marks..is a pretty steep price even for a royal motor carriage.

6. attrib. and Comb., as ***steep-grade*** adj.; chiefly parasynthetic, as ***steep-backed, -faced, -fronted, -gabled, -pitched, -pointed, -roofed, -scarped, -sided, -streeted***; †**steepward** *adv.* ? on a steep slope. Also STEEP-DOWN, STEEP-TO, STEEP-UP, STEEPWISE.

1889 F. COWPER *Captain of Wight* 227 The old man once more turned to climb the *steep-backed hill. **1894** J. C. ATKINSON *Old Whitby* 60 The *steep-faced cliff. **1936** *Nature* 21 Mar. 491/2 The test piece is flashed over with a *steep-fronted impulse in about a microsecond or less. **1915** *Blackw. Mag.* Jan. 124/2 A *steep-gabled house. **1896** *Daily News* 25 Feb. 5/4 The..*steep-grade tramway. **1885** WARREN & CLEVERLY *Wand. Beetle* 140 We swung under the bridge, and ran in to the *steep-pitched landing. **1912** 'GUY THORNE' *Great Acceptance* x. (1915) 255 Turrets with *steep-pointed roofs. **1814** SCOTT *Wav.* viii, The house, which seemed to consist of two or three high, narrow, and *steep-roofed buildings. **1878** RAMSAY *Phys. Geog.* xviii. 296 The *steep-scarped front..faces to the north-west. **1856** KANE *Arct. Expl.* I. ix. 93 Large gorges..generally *steep-sided. **1872** M. COLLINS *Plunges for Pearl* I. vi. 116 The *steep-streeted little town of Silveroar. **1588** KYD *Househ. Philos.* Wks. (1901) 270 Whether it lie *steepeward downe the hyls, vneasie and painful to be past.

B. *sb.*

1. a. The declivity or slope of a mountain, hill, cliff; a steep or precipitous place.

1555 EDEN *Decades* (Arb.) 133 Ryuers..wherwith al suche trees as are planted on the stiepe or foote of the mountaynes, as vines..are watered. **1590** SHAKS. *Mids. N.* II. i. 69 Why art thou heere Come from the farthest steepe [Qo. 1 steppe] of India? **1615** G. SANDYS *Trav.* 27 Having climbed the mountaine steepe towards the sea. **1667** MILTON *P.L.* IV. 680 How often from the steep Of echoing Hill..have we heard Celestial voices. **1721** DE FOE *Mem. Cavalier* (1840) 76 On the steep of the rock was a bastion. **1791** W. BARTRAM *Carolina* 341 They then pass on rapidly to a high perpendicular steep of rocks. **1801** CAMPBELL *Ye Mariners* 22 Britannia needs no bulwarks, No towers along the steep. **1861** M. ARNOLD *Southern Night* 23 There, where Gibraltar's cannon'd steep O'erfrowns the wave. **1883** MRS. RITCHIE *Bk. Sibyls* i. 2 The old..highroad..winds its way resolutely up the steep. **1899** *Daily News* 24 Oct. 5/4 He broke and fell back, being driven pell mell over the steeps to the rear of his position.

transf. **1860** DICKENS etc. *Message fr. Sea* iv. *Christm. Stor.* (1874) 182 Having..launched the boat down the steep of the deck, into the water.

b. *poet.* of the sky.

1697 DRYDEN *Virg. Georg.* I. 602 The setting Sun survey, When down the steep of Heav'n he drives the Day. **1837** CARLYLE *Fr. Rev.* I. II. i, Behold the new morning glittering down the eastern steeps. **1850** S. DOBELL *Roman* ii. 26 Let me breathe thee round the base Of the celestial steep. **1878** JOAQUIN MILLER *Songs of Italy* 87, I have looked to the steeps of the starry sky.

c. *fig.*

1742 YOUNG *Nt. Th.* VII. 705 By straining up the steep of excellent What gains she? **1780** J. ADAMS in *Fam. Lett.* (1876) 380 Hercules marches here in full view of the steeps of virtue on one hand and the flowery paths of pleasure on the other. **1877** L. MORRIS *Epic of Hades* III. 32 For Knowledge is a steep which few may climb, While Duty is a path which all may tread. **1883** S. C. HALL *Retrospect* II. 132 His first wife helped him up the steep, cheered him on the way [etc.]. **1910** W. JAMES *Mem. & Stud.* 275 The notion of a sheep's paradise like that revolts, they say, our higher imagination. Where then would be the steeps of life?

†**2.** ***a steep*** (advb. phr.), steeply sloping. *Obs.*

1573–80 TUSSER *Husb.* (1878) 98 Some maketh a hollownes, halfe a foot deepe, with fower sets in it, set slant wise a steepe.

C. *adv.*

1. With a steep slope, abruptly.

1548 THOMAS *Ital. Dict.* (1550), *Rattezza*, quickenesse, or the goyng stype vp hyll. **1548** *Elyot's Dict.*, *Prærupté*, stype without any bendying.

2. ***to run steep = to run high*** (HIGH *adv.* 9).

1894 *Outing* (U.S.) XXIV. 475/2 Others..are never so happy as when enjoying a glorious thresh to windward, with ..the sea running steep.

†**3.** With the eyes wide open. *Obs.*

14.. *Guy Warw.* 7730 He lokyd vp steype starande.

4. *Comb.* with pres. and pa. pples., as ***steep-ascending, -bending, -cut, -descending, -hanging, -rising, -yawning***.

1727–46 THOMSON *Summer* 608 The *steep-ascending eagle soars With upward pinions through the flood of day. **1538** ELYOT *Dict.*, *Accliue*, *stepe bendynge. **1888** KIPLING *Lett. Marque* (1891) xv. 115 Up rough banks..down *steep-cut dips. **1901** *Harper's Mag.* CII. 741/2 They found themselves on top of a steep-cut bluff. **1728** THOMSON *Spring* Seasons (1730) 41 The trembling Steed..*steep-descending stems The headlong Torrents foaming down the Hills. **1591** SYLVESTER *Du Bartas* I. vii. 26 Here from a craggy Rock's *steep-hanging boss..A silver Brook in broken streams doth gush. *Ibid.* II. iii. III. *Law* 659 Can we (like Birds) with still-*steep-rising flight Surmount these Mountains? **1725** ARMSTRONG *Imit. Shaks.* 177 Misc. Wks. 1770 I. 157 A gulph that swallows vision, with wide mouth *Steep-yawning to receive them.

steep (stiːp), *v.*[1] Forms: 5–6 **stepe, stipe,** 5–7 **steepe,** 6 **stiep(e, stype, (steyp),** *pa. pple.* **stept,** 6–7 **steap,** 6– **steep.** [Of difficult etymology. On the assumption that (notwithstanding the late date at which it is recorded) the vb. represents an OE. **stīepan*, **stēpan*, it would be the formal equivalent of Sw. *stöpa*, Da. *støbe*, Norw. *støypa*, to steep (seeds, barley for malting):—OTeut. type **staupjan*, perhaps f. **staupo-m* (OE. *stéap*, ON. *staup*, STOUP) vessel for liquor. Cf. Norw. *setja korn i staup* = to put corn in steep (see STEEP *sb.*[1]).

The mod. Scandinavian words cited coincide in form with a verb meaning to cast down, to cast (metals), to run (candles, etc.) into a mould, which descends from ON. *støypa* of the same meaning, a causative of ON. *stú pa* (once), Sw. *stupa* to STOOP. It is phonologically impossible that, as is usually supposed, the Eng. word can be a. ON. *støypa*: and even if it be referred to an OE. **stīepan* corresponding to the ON. vb., the development of sense appears less natural on this view than on that suggested above.]

1. *trans.* To soak in water or other liquid; chiefly, to do so for the purpose of softening, altering in properties, cleansing, or the like, or for that of extracting some constituent. Const. *in*, rarely *with*.

c **1400** MAUNDEV. (Roxb.) xviii. 84 Þai take alde peper and stepez it and strewez apon it spume of siluer. *c* **1420** *Liber Cocorum* (1862) 46 Fyrst sethe þy mustuls..In water,..þer in þou stepe white brede fayre. *c* **1440** *Pallad. on Husb.* XII. 545 Elite olyues xl dayes stepe In oil barm. **1530** PALSGR. 734/2, I stepe, I laye in water, or lay a stepe any salte meate to take out the brine, *je destrempe*. Stepe this salt fysshe. **1533** ELYOT *Cast. Helthe* (1539) 41 Also wyne..wherin rootes of perseley or fenel be stieped. **1561** HOLLYBUSH *Hom. Apoth.* 34 b, A slyce of bread styped in colde water. **1565** JEWEL *Def. Apol.* (1611) 463 The Priests..vsed to dip or to stipe the Sacred Body of our Lord vnder forme of Bread in the consecrated Blood and so to giue it to the people. **1577** HARRISON *England* I. II. vi. (1877) 156 Our Mault is made of the best Barley, which is steeped in a cysterne..vntyll it be thorowlye soked. **1587** GREENE *Tritameron* II. I 1 b, Hanniball..stieped poyson in a cuppe of drinke. **1594** *Gd. Huswifes Handmaid Kitchin* 43 Take faire bread and Vinigar, & steep the bread with some of the same broth. **1611** SHAKS. *Wint. T.* II. i. 40 There may be in the Cup A Spider steep'd. **1617** MORYSON *Itin.* I. 114 Into the foresaid Lake they cast flax, which will be steeped in that water in 14 houres. **1697** DRYDEN *Virg. Georg.* I. 280 Some steep their Seed, and some in Cauldrons boil. **1769** MRS. RAFFALD *Eng. Housekpr.* (1778) 69 Steep your ham all night in water. **1800** G. ROSE *Diaries* (1860) I. 284 The distillers steep their malt a fortnight before they can use it. **1815** J. SMITH *Panorama Sci. & Art* II. 823 When he steeped seeds ..in a strong solution of liver of sulphur, he never lost a seed by vermin. **1844** G. DODD *Textile Manuf.* v. 148 The [flax] plants are then..steeped, a very important operation. **1849** BALFOUR *Man. Bot.* §248 Some have advocated a system of steeping seeds and grains in certain solutions before sowing them. **1890** *Hardwicke's Sci.-Gossip* XXVI. 53 The Hottentots..use the leaves steeped in brandy for all sorts of complaints.

b. *absol.* To soak barley or malt.

1390–1 *Earl Derby's Exped.* (Camden) 74 Pro ij fattes.. pro stepyng yn. **1468** *Cov. Leet-bk.* 338 Þat noman..fech watir þens to brue nor to stepe with, vp þe peyn of iiij d.

c. To plunge or bathe (one's face, eyes, limbs, etc.) in water. Somewhat *rare*.

1579 SPENSER *Sheph. Cal.* Mar. 116 But see the Welkin thicks apace, And stouping Phebus steepes his face. **1708** N. BLUNDELL *Diary* (1895) 62, I Steeped my Feet in hot Whey ..to make my Cornes come out. **1865** DICKENS *Mut. Fr.* III. xv, I have steeped my eyes in cold water. **1893** STEVENSON *Catriona* vii, I sat by the lake side.., and there steeped my wrists and laved my temples.

transf. **1817** SHELLEY *Rev. Islam* I. li, The wingless boat paused where an ivory stair Its fretwork in the crystal sea did steep.

d. *transf.* Of mist, vapour, smoke, light: To 'bathe', envelop like a flood.

1798 COLERIDGE *Anc. Mariner* VI. xvii, The moonlight steeped in silentness The steady weathercock. **1817** SHELLEY *Rev. Islam* I. ii, Long trains of tremulous mist began to..steep The orient sun in shadow. **1860** TYNDALL *Glac.* I. v. 37 The Glacier..was also steeped for a time in the same purple light. **1887** MISS BRADDON *Like & Unlike* x, Every room was steeped in tobacco. **1890** BRIDGES *Shorter Poems* I. ii. 1 A river-mist is steeping The trees.

2. To soak, saturate, thoroughly moisten. Const. *in*, rarely *with* (water, blood, dye, etc.); also *simply* in *passive* (now *dial.*), to be wet through.

1590 SPENSER *F.Q.* II. vi. 18 Then she with liquors strong his eyes did steepe, That nothing should him hastily awake. *Ibid.* III. i. 65 Drops of purple bloud..Which did her lilly smock with staines of vermeil steepe. **1593** SHAKS. *3 Hen. VI*, II. i. 62 A Napkin, steeped in the harmlesse blood Of sweet young Rutland. **1633** LD. WARRISTON *Diary* (S.H.S.) 185 Evin so that with tears my naipkin was lyk on steaped in walter [*sic*]. **1717** POPE *Iliad* XI. 729 His Coursers steep'd in Sweat, and stain'd with Gore. **1720** *Ibid.* XVII. 415 A sanguine Torrent steeps the reeking Ground. **1768** STERNE *Sent. Journ.* (1778) II. 177 (*Maria*) My handkerchief..was steep'd too much already to be of use. **1812** J. WILSON *Isle of Palms* I. 303 Oh! must those eyes be steep'd in tears. **1849** AYTOUN *Lays Scott. Cavaliers* (ed. 2) 20 Never yet was royal banner Steeped in such a costly dye. **1892** *Verney Mem.* I. 5 There was probably little or no glass in the house of Henry VII.'s time; linen steeped in oil was the substitute. **1898** *Shetld. News* 27 Aug. (E.D.D.) My claes wis dat wye steepid 'at da watter ran doon ower my hide.

fig. **1595** SHAKS. *John* III. iv. 147 For he that steepes his safetie in true blood, Shall finde but bloodie safety. **1607** DEKKER & WEBSTER *Sir T. Wyat* B j b, See, on my knees I humbly take my leaue, And steep my wordes with teares.

b. To soak or imbrue (a weapon, etc.) *in* blood, poison, etc.

1594 KYD *Cornelia* II. 283 Would Death had steept his dart in Lernas blood. **1594** CHAPMAN *Shadow of Nt.* C j, No pen can any thing eternall wright, That is not steept in humor of the Night. **1602** SHAKS. *Ham.* II. ii. 533 With tongue in Venome steep'd. **1817** SHELLEY *Rev. Islam* VII. i, Time, though he wield the darts of death and sleep, And those thrice mortal barbs in his own poison steep.

c. *hyperbolically.* To 'soak' in alcoholic liquor: with reference to constant or excessive drinking; chiefly in *passive*. Also, to deaden, stupefy (one's memory, senses), to drown (grief, etc.) *in* liquor.

a **1592** GREENE *Jas. IV*, 1735 Our iolly horsekeeper, being well stept in licor, confessed to me the stealing of my maisters writings. **1601** B. JONSON *Poetaster* III. v, And liue like them, That..euery eu'en, with neat wine steeped be. **1649** LOVELACE *Poems* 97 When thirsty griefe in Wine we steepe. **1746** FRANCIS tr. *Hor., Sat.* II. i. 10 Swim o'er the Tiber, if you want to sleep, Or the dull Sense in t' other Bottle steep. **1821** SCOTT *Kenilw.* iii, Unless my memory fails me, (for I did steep it somewhat too deeply in the sack-butt). **1839** W. CARLETON *Fardorougha* xiv. 201 'He is afeard if he got drunk that he might n't be able to keep his own secret.' 'Ah, thin be the holy Nelly, we'll steep him yet.' **1856** EMERSON *Eng. Traits, Race* Wks. (Bohn) II. 31 A wealthy, juicy, broad-chested creature, steeped in ale and good cheer. **1862** MISS BRADDON *Lady Audley* xxxiii, He was steeped to the very lips in alcohol.

d. *fig.* (*jocular*) To 'wet', initiate or celebrate by a drink.

1765 STERNE *Tr. Shandy* VIII. xxviii, Here's a crown, corporal, to begin with, to steep thy commisssion.

3. In various metaphorical applications.

a. To 'bathe' (the heart, head, limbs, etc.) in slumber or rest.

1591 SPENSER *Virg. Gnat* 245 Sleep; Which..In quiet rest his molten heart did steep. **1635** QUARLES *Embl.* I. vii, Is this a time to steepe Thy braines in wastfull slumbers? **1697** DRYDEN *Virg. Georg.* IV. 278 When once in Beds their weary Limbs they steep, No buzzing Sounds disturb their Golden Sleep. **1827** KEBLE *Chr.-Y., Sun of my soul* ii, When the soft dews of kindly sleep My wearied eyelids gently steep. **1833** TENNYSON *Lotos-Eaters* 66 We only toil..Nor steep our brows in slumber's holy balm.

b. To soak and stupefy or deaden (grief, the senses) *in* (sleep, etc.).

1597 SHAKS. *2 Hen. IV*, III. i. 8 O Sleepe,..thou no more wilt weigh my eye-lids downe, And steepe my Sences in Forgetfulnesse. **1602** MARSTON *Antonio's Rev.* I. iii, My sense was steep't in horrid dreames. **1790** COWPER *Mother's Pict.* 19 Fancy..Shall steep me in Elysian reverie. **1822** LAMB *Elia* Ser. II. *Detached Thoughts on Books*, She has snatched an hour..to steep her cares, as in some Lethean cup, in spelling out their enchanting contents. **1856** MERIVALE *Rom. Emp.* l. V. 534 Messalina..steeped the senses of her consort in brutal indulgences. **1882** B. HARTE *Flip* ii, He awoke with the aroma of the woods still steeping his senses.

c. To involve deeply in a state or condition; to imbue or permeate thoroughly (with some quality); to make profoundly acquainted (with a subject of study); to absorb *in* (a pursuit). Const. *in*. Chiefly in *passive*; often, ***to be steeped to the lips***.

1603 CHETTLE etc. *Grissill* A 4, All his words and deedes are like his birth, Steept in true honor. **1604** SHAKS. *Oth.* IV. ii. 50 Had they..Steep'd me in pouertie to the very lippes. **1663** PATRICK *Parab. Pilgrim* xxvii. (1687) 293 He seldom departed from meditation, but..with..his whole heart steeped in new sweetness. **1833** TENNYSON *Two Voices* 47 Thou art so steeped in misery. **1837** CARLYLE *Fr. Rev.* III. II. viii, Roland, so long steeped to the lips in disgust and chagrin, sends in his demission. **1850** W. IRVING *Goldsmith* xiv. 172 Langton..was still the..enthusiastic scholar, steeped to the lips in Greek. **1855** DICKENS *Lett.* (1880) I. 402, I am steeped in my story. **1856** KINGSLEY *Misc.* (1860) II. 130 But Milton had steeped his whole soul in romance. **1868** MORRIS *Earthly Par.* I. I. 304 Until the Golden Age seemed there to be, So steeped the land was in felicity. **1870** HUXLEY *Lay Serm.* vi. (1874) 117 The whole of modern thought is steeped in science. **1882** MISS BRADDON *Mt. Royal* iii, She has been steeped to the lips in worldliness and vanity. **1908** J. O. DYKES *Chr. Minister* xiii. 142 There is a language of devotion in which the minister does well to steep himself.

4. *intr.* To undergo the process of soaking in liquor.

c **1412** HOCCLEVE *De Reg. Princ.* 1126 Men Yerne and desiren after muk so sore, Þat they good fame han leyd a watir yore, And rekken neuer how longe it þer stipe. *c* **1440** *Pallad. on Husb.* II. 281 A day afore her settyng hem [*sc.* almonds] to stepe In meth is good. **1598** *Epulario* B ij b, Lay it to steepe in a little red wine. **1648** J. BEAUMONT *Psyche* II. cvii, He having steeping, in a box of Jett, A blacker Liquor. **1769** MRS. RAFFALD *Eng. Housekpr.* (1778) 323 Put one ounce of isinglass to steep in cyder. **1808** SCOTT *Marm.* I. xxx, The midnight draught of sleep, Where wine and spices richly steep, In massive bowl. **1809** PARKINS *Culpepper's Eng. Physician* 383 Then let them all steep ten days in the aquavitæ. **1913** *Daily Graphic* 24 Mar. 13/4 Basins of water in which salt cod was steeping so that it might be ready for cooking.

b. *transf.* and *fig.*

1577 GRANGE *Golden Aphrod.* E ij, As one whose browes had Morpheus bound and layde to stiepe ouer head and eares in the snowe of Tygetus. **1600** FAIRFAX *Tasso* XX. cxliii, The camp was wonne, and all in blood doth steepe. **1849** CUPPLES *Green Hand* xvi. (1856) 157 A huge lake, fringed in by a confused hazy bluish outline steeping in the heat. **1914** *Blackw. Mag.* Feb. 231/1 In a loch at Moy the stars were steeping.

5. Comb.: chiefly in the names of vessels used in steeping malt, flesh, etc. (cf. STEEPING *vbl. sb.*[1]

4), as ***steep cistern***, †***fat***, (FAT *sb.*[1] 2), †***lead*** (LEAD *sb.*[1] 5 a), †-***stone*** (*Sc.* and *north.*), ***tub***; **steep-grass, -weed, -wort,** *Pinguicula vulgaris*, so called from its property of curdling milk; **steep-skin** *dial.* (see quot.); **steep-water** = STEEP *sb.*[1] 4.

1839 URE *Dict. Arts* 93 [Malting] More barley is successively emptied into the *steep cistern. **1483** *Cath. Angl.* 361/2 A *Stepe fatte, *ptipsanarium.* **1550** *N.C. Wills* (Surtees 1908) 210 A stepffat of leyd. **1777** J. LIGHTFOOT *Flora Scotica* II. 1131 *Pinguicula vulgaris*... *Steep-grass. **1418** *Mem. Ripon* (Surtees) III. 142 Item j *stepelede 24*s.* **1582** *Wills & Inv. N.C.* (Surtees 1860) 88 Item in the kilne a lardge and new steapeleade. **1887** *S. Chesh. Gloss.*, *Bagskin*, the stomach of a calf salted, so as to be used as rennet in cheese-making. Also called *Steep-skin. *c* **1475** *Cath. Angl.* 361/2 (Addit. MS.) A *Stepstane or fatt. **1599** *Reg. Mag. Sig. Scot.* 317/1 Commisit dictis fratribus potestatem horrea, hortos, lie killis, cobillis, steip-stanis, granaria [etc.]. **1627** CAPT. SMITH *Sea Gram.* ix. 37 The *steepe Tubs in the chains to shift their Beefe, Porke, or Fish in salt water. **1867** SMYTH *Sailor's Word-bk.*, *Steep-tub*, a large tub in which salt provisions are soaked previous to being cooked. **1838** T. THOMSON *Chem. Org. Bodies* 1012 The *steep-water gradually acquires a yellow colour. **1876** *Encycl. Brit.* IV. 267/2 The steep-water should then be changed. **1886** BRITTEN & HOLLAND *Plant-n.*, Steep-grass, *Steep-weed, or *Steep-wort, *Pinguicula vulgaris*, L.

Hence **steeped** *ppl. a.*

1599 DRAYTON *Heroical Ep.*, *Geraldine to H. Howard* (ed. 3) 95 b, That honey-steeped gall, We oft are sayd to bayte our Loues withall. **1639** T. DE GRAY *Compl. Horsem.* 348 Give him one of the steeped egges. **1648** HEXHAM II, *Gerot Vlas*, Rotten or Steeped Flaxe. **1710** N. BLUNDELL *Diary* (1895) 83, I Rosted my Steeped Wheat to make Coffy on.

steep (stiːp), *v.*[2] [f. STEEP *a.*]

1. *trans.* To place in a sloping position. Now only *dial.*, to tilt (a cask). Cf. STOOP *v.*

1613–16 W. BROWNE *Brit. Past.* I. i. 20 Then did the God her body forwards steepe, And cast her for a while into a sleepe. **1837** J. F. PALMER *Gloss. to Mrs. Palmer's Dialogue Devon Dial.*, To *Steep*, to tilt or give an inclination to a barrel which is nearly run out. **1886** *W. Somerset Word-bk.*

2. To make a slope on the top or side of (*a*) a hedge; (*b*) a stack. (See quots.) *dial.*

(*a*) **1741** in *Hartland* (Devon) *Gloss.* s.v. *Steep*, Shall not cut shrid lop or steep any hedge or hedges. **1837** J. F. PALMER *Gloss. to Mrs. Palmer's Dialogue Devon Dial.*, To *Steep*,.. to dress or trim a hedge. **1856** MORTON *Cycl. Agric.* II. 724/1 (Devon.), to *lade* and *steep* hedges is to lay them down and bank up with earth.

(*b*) **1854** MISS BAKER *Northampt. Gloss.*, *Steep*, to top up or make up a rick. **1887** *Kentish Gloss.* s.v., To steep a stack, is to make the sides smooth and even, and to slope it up to the point of the roof.

3. *intr.* Of a cliff: To form a steep; to 'drop'. Also of the sea: To slope.

1890 CLARK RUSSELL *Ocean Trag.* I. iii. 46 He might just get a glimpse of green shore with a tremble of water.. steeping to it. **1911** *Nation* 16 Dec. 469/2 A huge hammer of mountains eight thousand feet high and steeping sheer into the sea.

steep-down, *a. Obs.* exc. *poet.* [f. STEEP *a.* + DOWN *adv.* Cf. STEEP-UP.] Precipitous.

1530 PALSGR. 827/1 Stepe downe, *tout bas en droycte lygne.* **1545** ELYOT *Dict.*, *Cliuosus*,.. pitching doune, or stiepe doune. **1560** BIBLE (Geneva) *Matt.* viii. 32 The whole herd of swine was caryed with violence from a stiepe downe place into the sea. **1584–7** GREENE *Carde of Fancie* Wks. (Grosart) IV. 74 The cliffes so steep-downe and fearefull, as to descend was no lesse daunger then death it selfe. **1604** SHAKS. *Oth.* v. ii. 280 Whip me ye Diuels..: Wash me in steepe-downe gulfes of Liquid fire. **1648** J. BEAUMONT *Psyche* III. xiv, You see Him till into the steep-down West He throws his course. **1828** TENNYSON *Lover's Tale* 390 Steep-down walls of battlemented rock.

†**b.** Of a shower. *Obs.*

1601 W. WATSON *Import. Consid.* (1831) 30 A steep-down shower of stormy sorrows.

steeped (stiːpt), *a.* [f. STEEP *v.*[2] + -ED[1].] Of a rock, rampart: Having a precipitous face or side. *Obs.* exc. in ***steeped-to*** = STEEP-TO.

1596 SIR F. VERE *Comm.* ii. (1657) 38 A massy rampier, with two round half bulwarks,.. not steeped and scarped: so as it was very mountable. **1686** PLOT *Staffordsh.* 173 The sides steeped and so hanging over, that it sometimes preserves Snow all the Summer. **1858** *Merc. Mar. Mag.* V. 361 The islet is.. steeped to on all sides.

steepen ('stiːp(ə)n), *v.* [f. STEEP *a.* + -EN[5].]

1. *intr.* To become steep or steeper.

1847 H. MILLER *First Impr.* ix. 153 As the way steepened ..I could detect..some traces of the old path. **1883** STEVENSON *Treas. Isl.* xxxi, But by little and little the hill began to steepen.

2. *trans. fig.* To increase, 'pile on', 'heap up'; also with *up*.

1909 LD. ROSEBERY in *Times* 11 Sept. 7/5 These death duties..have been constantly steepened up. **1914** *Q. Rev.* Apr. 458 The financial demands made upon under-writing members have been very much steepened of recent years.

Hence **'steepening** *vbl. sb.* and *ppl. a.*

1868 GLADSTONE in Morley *Life* (1903) II. v. xvi. 256, I ascend a steepening path with a burden ever gathering weight. **1909** LD. ROSEBERY in *Times* 11 Sept. 7/5 An argument for the steepening of the death duties was that [etc.].

steeper[1] ('stiːpə(r)). [f. STEEP *v.*[1] + -ER[1].]

1. One who steeps; *spec.* one who carries out the operation of steeping flax, wool, etc.

1611 COTGR., *Trempeur*, a dipper;..soaker, steeper. **1837** *Flemish Husb.* ix. (Libr. Useful Knowl.) 45 The best and most experienced steepers.. prefer the clear soft water of the river Lys. **1904** *Eng. Dial. Dict.*, *Steeper*, a wool-combing term: a man who steeps the wool before washing. w. Yks.

2. A vessel used in steeping or infusing; esp. a vat in which the indigo-plant is macerated.

1737 MILLER *Gard. Dict.* (ed. 3) s.v. *Anil*, The first, largest, and highest of these [Indigo] Vats is called the Steeper or Rot. **1839** URE *Dict. Arts* 666 (*Indigo*) The uppermost is called the fermenting vat, or the steeper. **1886** *Cornhill Mag.* July 51 The would-be drinker is then expected to seize the burning hot steeper [for tea].

3. *dial.* A soaking rain; also, a soaking with rain.

1878 E. WAUGH *Hermit Cobbler* vii, It's a steeper, and nought else. It's th' weetest back-end we'n had this ten-year. **1898** *Leeds Merc. Suppl.* 7 May (E.D.D.) T'rain com dahn i' buckets an' it gae me a steeper an' reight, tu.

steeper[2] ('stiːpə(r)). *dial.* [f. STEEP *v.*[2] + -ER[1].] (See quot. 1837.)

1815 *Sporting Mag.* XLV. 110 One may be placed about nine inches above the steepers of a hedge. **1837** J. F. PALMER *Gloss. to Mrs. Palmer's Dialogue Devon Dial.*, *Steepers*, in trimming hedges, the central branches, cut half through and laid lengthways.

†**'steepful,** *a. nonce-wd.* [f. STEEP *a.* or *sb.*[2] + -FUL.] Abounding in steeps, steep.

1605 SYLVESTER *Du Bartas* II. iii. I. *Vocation* 828 Anon he stalks about a steepfull Rock.

'steephead. *U.S.* (orig. *local*). *Physical Geogr.* [f. STEEP *a.* + HEAD *sb.*] A nearly vertical slope, from the base of which springs emerge, at the head of a pocket valley (see POCKET *sb.* 13).

1918 *10th & 11th Ann. Rep. Florida Geol. Survey* 27 A characteristic feature of this topography is the development of what is [*sic*] known locally as 'steepheads'. *Ibid.*, The depth of the steephead from the plateau is usually from 50 to 60 or more feet. **1942** O. D. VON ENGELN *Geomorphol.* xxii. 569 Pocket valleys of similar origin are also of widespread occurrence in northwestern Florida where they are known as steep-heads. **1971** [see *pocket valley* s.v. POCKET *sb.* 13].

steepil(l, obs. forms of STEEPLE *sb.*[1]

†**'steepiness.** *Obs.* [f. STEEPY *a.* + -NESS.] The condition of being 'steepy'; steepness.

Freely used by writers in the 17th c.

1612 [W. BIDDULPH] *Trav. four English Men* 90 The mountaine..somewhat steepy..: we rode so farre as we could for steepinesse and then..tooke vpon vs to clamber vp on foote. **1642** HOWELL *For. Trav.* (Arb.) 51 The cragginesse and steepinesse of places up and down is a great advantage to the dwellers. **1771** GOLDSM. *Hist. Eng.* IV. 398 The steepiness of the ground such as hardly to be surmounted.

steeping ('stiːpɪŋ), *vbl. sb.*[1] [f. STEEP *v.*[1] + -ING[1].]

1. The action or process of STEEP *v.*[1]; an instance of this.

c **1440** *Promp. Parv.* 474/2 Stepynge, yn lycure, *infusio, illiqueacio.* **14..** *MS. Sloane 73* lf. 201 Whanne it haþ leye þerynne a nyȝt on steping. **1548** *Act 2 & 3 Edw. VI*, c. 10 §2 That the same [barly malt] shall have in makinge thereof, that ys to saye, in the fatt flower stepinge..of the same Malte, thre wekes at the leste. **1626** BACON *Sylva* §500 The third [means of making plants medicinable] is, the Steeping of the Seed or Kernell in some Liquour, wherein the Medicine is Infused. **1790** *Act 30 Geo. III*, c. 3 §12 The Produce of Two or more Steepings of Corn or Grain. **1888** *Daily News* 7 July 2/7 The rains which have recently fallen should provide in all parts of Ireland ample water for steeping.

2. A liquor in which grain, etc. is steeped.

1585 HIGINS *Junius' Nomencl.* 465/2 *Infusio*,..a steeping or any liquor wherein graine or such like is layde to steepe. **1626** BACON *Sylva* §402 It may be some Steeping will agree best with some Seeds. **1842** LANCE *Cottage Farmer* 9 Salt-petre is the best steeping that corn can have.

3. A liquor obtained by steeping; an infusion.

1898 *Westm. Gaz.* 27 Jan. 2/1 His drink for the day is restricted to the milk of eighty cows and the steeping of seventy-five parcels of tea.

4. *attrib.* and *Comb.*, as ***steeping place, pool***; esp. in the names of utensils (cf. STEEP *v.*[1] 5), as ***steeping back*** (BACK *sb.*[2]), ***barrel***, †***fat*** (FAT *sb.*[1]), ***lead*** (LEAD *sb.*[1] 5), ***tub, vat.***

1820 W. SCORESBY *Acc. Arctic Reg.* II. 400 *Steeping-backs. **1480–1** *Durham Acc. Rolls* (Surtees) 97 *Lardar. piscium.* Quinque Stepyngtubbez,..ij *stepyngbarellez. **1459–60** *Ibid.* 89 Item in le fleshlardar..v *stepyngfattez. **1574** *Richmond Wills* (Surtees) 253 In the kylne..one steaping fatt of stone. **1395–6** *Durham Acc. Rolls* (Surtees) 136 In empcione j *Stepynglede. **1766** *Complete Farmer* s.v. *Hemp* 4 A 1/1 To make a small stream of water pass through the *steeping places, thereby to change the water. **1871** CARLYLE in *Mrs. Carlyle's Lett.* (1883) I. 76 Like flax thrown into the *steeping pool. **1480–1** *Stepyngtubbes [see above]. **1633** T. JAMES *Voy.* 93 They would steale our meate out of the steeping tubs. **1731** MILLER *Gard. Dict.* s.v. *Anil* N/2 The first [fraud] is the Beating the Plant too much in the *Steeping-Vat. **1861** *Chamb. Encycl.* II. 149/2 The cloth is immersed for about four hours in a steeping vat.

steeping ('stiːpɪŋ), *vbl. sb.*[2] [f. STEEP *v.*[2] + -ING[1].] The action or process of tilting or giving an (upward) inclination to the plough in ploughing.

1844 H. STEPHENS *Bk. Farm* I. 400 The remedy for this error is..to press harder upon the stilts..and..bring the sock nearer the surface of the ground, and this is called 'steeping'.

steeping ('stiːpɪŋ), *ppl. a.*[1] [f. STEEP *v.*[1] + -ING[2].] That steeps. Of rain: Soaking. *dial.*

1778 [W. MARSHALL] *Minutes Agric.* 27 July 1774, The hay is not much worse for the steeping rain of last night. **1877** *N.W. Linc. Gloss.* s.v., Well, this hes been a steepin' rain.

steeping ('stiːpɪŋ), *ppl. a.*[2] [f. STEEP *v.*[2] + -ING[2].]

†**1.** That slopes precipitously, steep. *Obs.*

a **1470** TIPTOFT *Cæsar* v. (1530) 8 Theyr horses ronne in placys slope steepyng. **1587** FLEMING *Contn. Holinshed* III. 1018/2 The citie..is set vpon a little hill, and lieth verie steeping towards two of the gates.

2. *Naut.* Of the surface of the sea: Sloping to the horizon.

1890 CLARK RUSSELL *Ocean Trag.* II. xv. 45 Never in all my time did so profound a sense of desolation..possess me as I stood bringing my eyes from the huge steeping plain of the sea [etc.].

steepish ('stiːpɪʃ), *a.* [f. STEEP *a.* + -ISH.] Somewhat steep, rather precipitous.

1814 JANE AUSTEN *Mansf. Park* xxv, I was suddenly, upon turning the corner of a steepish downy field, in the midst of a retired little village. **1881** *Jrnl. Linn. Soc.* XV. 422 Outer lip thin, with a flattened convex curve, which is steepish at the shoulder. **1890** 'R. BOLDREWOOD' *Robbery under Arms* 168 The driver's walking his horses up a steepish hill.

steeple ('stiːp(ə)l), *sb.*[1] Forms: 1 **stépel, stípel, stýpel,** 2–5 **stepel,** 4–5 **stepyl,** 4–7 **steple,** 5 **steepill, stepil, -yll(e, -ul, styple, styppyl,** 5–6 **stepell, -ull(e,** 5–7 **stepill,** 6 **steaple, steepil, stepelle, stypell,** *Sc.* **steipell, -il(l, steiple,** 6–7 **stiple,** 7 *Sc.* **steippell,** 6– **steeple.** [OE. *stépel, stýpel* masc.:—prehist. **staupil*, f. **staup-* STEEP *a.*]

†**I. 1.** A tall tower; a building of great altitude in proportion to its length and breadth. *Obs.*

c **1000** *Ags. Gosp.* Matt. xxi. 23 [He] ȝetimbrode anne stypel [L. *turrim ædificavit*]. *c* **1000** ÆLFRIC *Gen.* xi. 5 þæt he ȝesawe..þone stipel, þe Adames bearn ȝetimbrodon. **10..** *Lambeth Ps.* lx. 4 *Turris fortitudinis*, Stepel strænсðe. *c* **1175** *Lamb. Hom.* 93 Eontas walden areran ane buruh and anne stepel swa hehne, þet [etc.]. *c* **1290** *St. Michael* 539 in *S. Eng. Leg.* 315 Ʒif here were an heiȝ stepel; and a man a-boue sete. ? *a* **1400** *Morte Arth.* 3040 Stone [s]tepelles fulle styffe in þe strete ligges. *a* **1660** *Contemp. Hist. Irel.* (Ir. Archæol. Soc.) I. 60 An ould almost ruyned stiple extant in the ruynes of the said nunry temple. **1847** W. REEVES *Eccl. Antiq.* 63 *note*, The noble Round Tower, commonly called the Steeple [near Antrim].

2. a. A lofty tower forming part of a church, temple, or other public edifice (often serving to contain the bells); such a tower together with the spire or other superstructure by which it is surmounted.

1154 *O.E. Chron.* (C.) an. 1036, Hine man byriġde..æt þam west-ende þam styple ful ȝehende. **1297** R. GLOUC. (Rolls) 10860 In to þe stepel of oseneye þe legat fleu vor fere. *c* **1325** *Lai le Freine* 152 A chirche, with stepel fair and heighe. **1387** *Charters* etc. *Edin.* (1871) 35 The grete pyler of the stepyl. *c* **1440** *Promp. Parv.* 148/2 Fane of a stepylle, or oþer lyke, *cherucus.* *c* **1481** CAXTON *Dialogues* 40 Lamfroy the couerar of tyles Couerd the steple [Fr. *couury le belfroy*]. **1553** in Daniel-Tyssen *Surrey Ch. Goods* (1869) 107 Item in the stypell ij belles and a littell bell. **1561** T. HOBY tr. *Castiglione's Courtyer* II. (1577) M vij b, A place where was a steeple that stood by himselfe alone seuered from the Church. **1591** SHAKS. *Two Gent.* II. i. 142 Inuisible, As a nose on a man's face, or a Wethercocke on a steeple. *c* **1605** *Acc. Bk. W. Wray* in *Antiquary* XXXII. 212 This yeare [1593]..was the great spere of St. Wilfrides steple..sett on fire. **1610** HOLLAND *Camden's Brit.* (1637) 505 Thirty Steeples with Spires or square Towres within view at once. **1625** *Peebles Charters* etc. (1872) 414 Gewine to John Frank for schiwting of the tua goineis in the steippell. **1634** SIR T. HERBERT *Trav.* 155 When they [Persians] heare the Boy cry aloud vpon the Steeple, they fall to prayer. *a* **1701** MAUNDRELL *Journ. Jerus.* (1721) 122 It is thick set with Mosques and Steeples, the usual ornaments of the Turkish Cities. **1765** STERNE *Tr. Shandy* VII. v, The steeple, which has a spire to it, is placed in the middle of the church. **1795** BURNS *Song*, '*Does haughty Gaul*' iv, Who will not sing, 'God save the King,' Shall hang as high's the steeple. **1812** EDM. TURNOR *MS. Let.*, An Elevation of the west end of Great Ponton Church, to show the steeple. [Here a square tower.] **1842** GWILT *Archit.* Gloss. 1037 *Steeple*, a lofty erection attached to a church, chiefly intended to contain its bells. The word..applies to every appendage of this nature, whether tower or spire, or a combination of the two. **1852** HOOK *Ch. Dict.* (1871) 725 A steeple is the tower of a Church with all its appendages, as turret, octagon, and spire. It is often incorrectly confounded with the spire.

†**b.** Used by metonymy for church. In nonce-phrases: ***the sign of the steeple*** (referring to monastic hospitality); ***bigamy of steeples***, plurality of church livings. *Obs.*

1555 EDEN *Decades* (Arb.) 54 Sence the signe of the steeple, the poore mans Inne was pulled downe in all places. **1641** R. WILD in *Roxb. Ballads* (1888) VI. 456 Bigamy of Steeples is no laughing matter.

†**c.** ***to hunt the steeple***: see quot. *Obs.*

1785 *Edin. Advertiser* 15 Apr. 236 His Lordship and another gentleman determined to hunt the steeple. This is a common amusement among people of fashion, and consists in the horsemen riding helter skelter towards the first steeple that may catch their eye, and he that is first in is the best man.

3. a. A spire on the top of the tower or roof of a church or similar edifice. Also, more definitely, ***spire steeple, broach steeple.***

1473–4 in Swayne *Sarum Churchw. Acc.* (1896) 15 The castyng and laying iiij^{xx} xv^{c} of new and olde Led to the steple. **1548** *Elyot's Dict.*, *Pyramis*,..a stiple. **1551** TURNER *Herbal* I. N iij b, The tre..hath the figure of a steple, that is great beneth, and the hygher vp the smaller it is. **1578** BANISTER *Hist. Man.* VII. 93 The figure of this [right] auricle is like a poynted steeple pillour or other buildyng, whose brodest part is the bottome. **1582** BATMAN *Barth. De P.R.* III. xvii. 18 b, Out of the eye commeth a small appearaunce, that is shapen as a steeple or a top. **1595** DUNCAN *App. Etym.* (E.D.S.), *Pyramis*, a steiple or lyk building. **1607** WALKINGTON *Opt. Glass* 41 His head was made like a broch steeple, sharpe. **1610** HOLLAND *Camden's Brit.* (1637) 425 A mighty bigge and lofty Towre, upon which stood a Spire Steeple covered with Leade. **1766** ENTICK *London* IV. 283 The steeple is a spire.., raised upon a solid..tower. ?**1780** COWPER *Transl. Bourne, Jackdaw* 7 Above the steeple shines a plate, That turns and turns, to indicate From what point blows the weather. **1872** DE VERE *Americanisms* 233 With the Yankee, the meeting-house with its steeple—the word 'spire' is hardly ever heard in America—has found its way to every part of the Union. **1896** SWAYNE *Sarum Churchw. Acc.* p. xxvi, There were battlements..at the top of the tower, and above rose the steeple.

b. In wider sense (see quots.).

1816 J. SMITH *Panorama Sci. & Art* I. 131 Any building above the roof may be called a steeple. **1823** J. F. COOPER *Pioneers* viii, The 'steeple' was a little cupola, reared on the very centre of the roof.

†**4.** A steeple-shaped ornament on the cover of a censer or other vessel. *Obs.*

1517 *Archæologia* LXI. 87 A sencer of silver the stepull and the swages gilt.

5. *transf.* A steeple-shaped formation of the two hands, with the palms facing and the extended fingers rising to meet at the tips.

1940 *Detective Fiction Weekly* 26 Oct. 9/1, I..waited for him to begin. He made a steeple of his hands. 'Now it is a very simple matter.' **1972** T. P. MCMAHON *Issue of Bishop's Blood* (1973) iii. 35 He was sighting at me carefully along the top of the steeple made by his manicured fingers. **1978** G. VIDAL *Kalki* ii. 33 When I put out my hand, she made a steeple with her hands, and bowed. This was my first experience with the Hindu pranam, or greeting.

II. *attrib.* and *Comb.*

6. Obvious combinations: **a.** simple attributive, as ***steeple battlement, -bell, -chime, -door, -height, -spire, -stairs, -tower, -vane, window, work.*** **b.** objective, as ***steeple-climbing, -keeper***; also ***steeple-loving*** adj. **c.** similative, as ***steeple-form, -high, -like, -shaped*** adjs.; also in designations of headgear having a 'steeple-crown' (see 7), as ***steeple-cap, hat, head-dress, headgear, tire.*** **d.** instrumental, as ***steeple-shadowed, -studded*** adjs.

1525-6 *Rec. St. Mary at Hill* (1905) 332 Paid to a Mason, for a day, to mende þe *steple batilment, viij d. **1837** CARLYLE *Fr. Rev.* II. VI. vi, So go the *steeple-bells. **1642** H. MORE *Song of Soul* I. i. 25 By stealth her *steeple-cap she [*sc.* Night] doth assay To whelm on th' earth. *a* **1821** KEATS *Song of Opposites* 11 Funeral and *steeple-chime. **1483** in C. Welch *Churchw. Acc. All-hallows, Lond. Wall* (1912) 25 Payed for a lokke and a key to the *Stepill dor, iiij[d]. **1551** RECORDE *Pathw. Knowl.* I. Defin. Cj, Or els it is called a rounde spire, or *stiple fourme. **1629** GAULE *Holy Madn.* 329 His *steeple Hat hath harboured many a Thousand. **1841** T. H. WHITE *Fragm. Italy & Rhineland* 2 The noble countenance of the Spaniard, shadowed by his black steeple hat. **1877** *Encycl. Brit.* VI. 470 Fig. 39 '*Steeple' Head-dress. **1655** MARQ. WORCESTER *Cent. Inv.* §24 To shoot..an hundred pound weight a *Steeple-height. **1633** T. NASH *Quaternio* 35 Being mounted aloft, *steeple-high. **1692** [see SQUAB *adv.*]. **1663** GERBIER *Counsel* 11 And *Steeple-like to hang Bells in. **1800** HURDIS *Fav. Village* 111 Homeward returns the *steeple-loving daw. **1896** HOUSMAN *Shropshire Lad* lxi, And *steeple-shadowed slumber The slayers of themselves. **1859** W. S. COLEMAN *Our Woodlands* 34 [Form of fir-trees.] Conical or *steeple-shaped. **1664** COTTON *Scarron.* IV. 103 And if I ever do forget ye,..Let me be hang'd as high, or higher Then top of Carthage *Steeple Spire. **1817** COLERIDGE *Biog. Lit., Satyrane's Lett.* i. II. 202 A profusion of steeple-spires. **1559-60** *Ludlow Churchw. Acc.* (Camden) 97 Paid for the makynge clene of the *stepulle steyrez, iiij d. **1886** A. G. BUTLER in *Harold* etc. (1892) 151 The ghost-like city, *steeple-studded, Slumbering grey in a mist of green. **1603-26** BRETON *Poste Mad Lett.* (Grosart) 41/1 For your *steeple tire, it is like the gaud of a Maid-Marion. *c* **1842** WORDSW. *Eccl. Sonn.* III. xvii, Her Spires, her *Steeple-towers with glittering vanes. **1845** HIRST *Poems* 71 The roofs, the spires, the *steeple-vanes Seemed swimming in the silver mist. **1512** in *Archæologia* XLVI. 202 Paid for the frethyng of the *Stepyll wyndows iiij d. **1426** *E.E. Wills* (1882) 76 Also I bequeth to þe *stepul werk of seint Alpheies by Crepulgate, x mark.

7. a. Special comb.: **steeple clock,** (*a*) a clock fixed to a steeple; (*b*) *U.S.*, an antique mantel or shelf clock (see quot. 1959); **steeple-clocked** *a.*, having steeple-shaped clocks (CLOCK *sb.*[2] 1); †**steeple cream** *Confectionery*, a cream (CREAM *sb.*[1] 2) fashioned into a form pointed at the top; **steeple-crown,** a crown of a hat rising to a point in the middle; also a hat with a steeple-crown; hence ***steeple-crowned*** adj.; **steeple-cup** (see quot.); **steeple engine,** a kind of steam-engine used on river boats (see quot. 1873); †**steeple head,** the top of a tower or steeple; **steeple-hoofed** *a.*, having the hoof too upright; †**steeple hunt, hunter, -hunting** = STEEPLECHASE *sb.*, -CHASER, -CHASING; **steeple jack,** a man who climbs steeples or tall chimneys to repair them; †**steeple-moulded** *a.*, (of a hat) steeple-shaped; †**steeple-music** = bell-ringing; **steeple race, racing,** = STEEPLECHASE, -CHASING; **steeple-roofed** *a.*, having very high roofs; †**steeple running** = STEEPLECHASING; **steeple sugar-loaf,** a sugar-loaf shaped like a steeple; **steeple-top,** (*a*) the top of a steeple; (*b*) the bowhead, or great polar whale (*Balæna mysticetus*), so called from the spout-holes terminating in a sort of cone (*Cent. Dict.* 1891).

1830 CARLYLE *Richter Again* Ess. 1840 II. 372 The down-rolling wheels of the *steeple-clock, which was striking eleven, had awakened me. **1923** W. I. MILHAM *Time & Timekeepers* xx. 368 There are two kinds of clocks, however, which came into vogue shortly after 1850 and are usually classed among 'antiques' and not among the endless varieties of modern clocks. These are the small, spring-driven, brass shelf clock often in a rose-wood veneer case and the steeple clock, sometimes called the 'Sharp Gothic'. **1959** L. GROSS *Housewives' Guide to Antiques* viii. 114 The steeple clock of the mid-nineteenth century was another popular mantel clock. It takes its name from the steeple-like appearance of its case. **1976** R. B. PARKER *Promised Land* (1977) xvi. 97 There was an old steeple clock with brass works on the mantle. **1776** ANSTEY *Election Ballads* (1808) 229 With a shoe like a sauce boat and *steeple-clock'd hose. **1747** MRS. GLASSE *Cookery* 143 To make *Steeple Cream. **1769** MRS. RAFFALD *Eng. Housekpr.* (1778) 231 They are pretty with either steeple cream, any kind of flummeries, or [etc.]. **1684** *Roxb. Ballads* (1891) VII. 475 There came up a Lass from a Country Town..In *steeple-crown Hat. **1706** [E. WARD] *Hudibras Rediv.* (Nares), The good old dames.. were..drest In stiffen-body'd russet gowns, And on their heads old steeple-crowns. **1710** *Tatler* No. 257 ⁋3 The most remarkable Parts of her Dress, were the Beaver with the Steeple Crown, [etc.]. **1804** *Europ. Mag.* XLV. 411/1 *Steeple-crowned hats. **1900** CROCKETT *Love Idylls* (1901) 33 An ancient steeple-crowned Puritan hat. **1909** *Century Dict.*, **Steeple-cup*, a silver standing cup having on its cover a pyramidal, steeple-like crest. **1839** R. S. ROBINSON *Naut. Steam Eng.* 177 This engine, common on the Clyde, is called a *steeple engine, but it is unfitted for the open sea. **1873** G. E. WEBSTER *Steam Eng. & Steam* II. 187 Steeple Engines derive their name from the high erections on deck required by the guide to the connecting-rod which works the crank. **1572** *Diurn. Occur. Scot.* (Bannatyne Club) 307 The haill artailʒerie in Edinburgh, about the wallis, on the *steipill heid of Sanctgeill and Kirk of feild, wer tane to the castell of Edinburgh. **1823** PURSGLOVE *Pract. Farriery* 226 It will give great relief to the animal if his heels are lowered as much as possible, to prevent him from being what is termed *steeple-hoofed. **1831** YOUATT *Horse* iv. 57 The *Steeple Hunt is a relic of ancient foolhardiness and cruelty. **1830** *Examiner* 531/1 She bolts at the object of her aim with the ardour of a *steeple hunter. **1772** GILPIN *Observ. Picturesque Beauty* (1786) II. 251 *Steeple-hunting. **1851** CARLYLE *Sterling* I. v. 53, I have known few creatures whom it was more wasteful..to set to steeple-hunting, instead of running on highways! **1881** *Instr. Census Clerks* (1885) 52 Builder ..*Steeple Jack. **1894** *Bye-Gones* 14 Feb. 277/1 For some time past steeplejacks have been engaged in repairing the spire. **1710** *Pict. of Malice* 8 The good Women of Derbyshire..ought to appear in the Churches with their *Steeple-mol'd Hats, and lay aside their Hats of Straw. **1732** *Tricks of Town* 33 He had..paid the three Guineas for the *Steeple-Musick. **1809** *Sporting Mag.* XXXIII. 187 A match..to ride a *steeple race. **1840** BLAINE *Rural Sports* §1280 The popularity of *steeple racing from this time increased. *c* **1870** BROWNING *Miniature* 2 In the bright Touraine, In a high-turreted, *steeple-roofed town. **1818** 'W. H. SCOTT' *Brit. Field Sports* 299 In *Steeple Running and matching their Horses to run Train-Scents. **1649** DK. NEWCASTLE *Country Capt.* I. i. 4 No *steeple sugar-loaues to sweeten his Neighbours at Christmas. *c* **1440** *Alphabet of Tales* 497 Þe clerk saw þe preste bodie oft sithis born vp to þe *steple topp with strenth of fendis. **1805** SOUTHEY *Madoc* I. xv, David would hang thee on thy steeple top.

b. In names of plants: **steeple bells, steeple bell-flower,** *Campanula pyramidalis*; **steeple-bush** = HARDHACK.

1597 GERARDE *Herbal* II. cxi. 366 Of Peach bels, and *Steeple bels. *Ibid.* 367 fig. 2 *Campanula lactescens pyramidalis* Steeple milkie Bell flower. **1611** COTGR., *Campanette*,..the Peach-bell, or Steeple-bell flower. **1812** *New Bot. Gard.* I. 121 The plants of the steeple bell-flower. **1847** DARLINGTON *Amer. Weeds* 120 *Spirea tomentosa*.. Hardhack. *Steeple Bush.

steeple ('stiːp(ə)l), *sb.*[2] [Altered form of STAPLE *sb.*[1], perh. influenced by prec.]

1. = STAPLE *sb.*[1] 2.

1722 W. HAMILTON *Wallace* 57 Wallace..with a furious shock The Bar and Steeple all in Flinders Broke, Then open drave the Gate. **1825** JAMIESON *Dict.*, *Steepil*, the staple or bolt of a hinge. Ettr. For. **1867** J. K. HUNTER *Retrospect Artist's Life* viii. (1902) 76 A steeple at the corner. **1894** CROCKETT *Lilac Sunbonnet* 84 A sharp noise as of one clicking in the 'steeple' or brace of the front door.

2. *Shetland.* [Cf. Du. *stapel* heap.] = PACK *sb.*[1] 9.

1822 HIBBERT *Desc. Shetl. Isl.* 519 They [fish] are afterwards built into a large stack named a steeple. **18..** [see PACK *sb.*[1] 9].

steeple ('stiːp(ə)l), *v.* [f. STEEPLE *sb.*[1]]

1. *trans.* To place (a bell) in a steeple.

1644 S. KEM *Messengers Prepar.* 18 Like a Bell, which whilst it lyeth on the ground, can make no musick; but when steepled, then it sounds loud.

2. To imprison in a steeple.

1881 G. MACGREGOR *Hist. Glasgow* xvii. 149 The keeper was forbidden to allow any of those who had been 'steepled' to have other than prison fare.

3. *intr.* To rise or tower like a steeple.

1892 [implied at *steepling ppl. adj.* below]. **1922** BLUNDEN *Shepherd* 81 The cornel steepling up in white shall know The two friends passing by.

4. *trans.* To place (the fingers or hands) together in the shape of a steeple.

1968 A. MACLEAN *Force 10 from Navarone* iv. 59 The German captain leaned back in his chair and steepled his fingers. **1975** W. SAFIRE *Before Fall* VI. vi. 446 Nixon..was relaxed when seated, steepling or folding his hands. **1977** G. SCOTT *Hot Pursuit* ii. 18 He steepled his fingers and looked wisely at me across the desk-top.

Hence '**steepling** *ppl. a.*, rising up like a steeple; also *fig.*

1892 *Harper's Mag.* Feb. 427/1 They have adopted what they call 'the Chicago method' in putting up these steepling hives. **1955** *Times* 28 June 3/2 He struck a steepling blow, but he fell into Kenyon's hands just inside the ropes beneath the Nursery Clock Tower. **1977** *Guardian Weekly* 17 July 24/2 McCosker hooked at it and sent a steepling catch to Underwood at mid-on. **1982** *Daily Tel.* 20 Aug. 9/4 The steepling rises in standing charges.

'**steeplechase,** *sb.* [f. STEEPLE *sb.*[1] + CHASE. Cf. *to hunt the steeple, steeple-hunting*, STEEPLE *sb.*[1] 2 c 7.]

1. A horse-race across country or on a made course with artificial fences, water-jumps, and other obstacles. Formerly, a race having a church steeple in view as goal, in which all intervening obstacles had to be cleared.

1793 *Sporting Mag.* Apr. 57/2 The Hon. Mr. O'Hea and Captain Magrath ran a Steeple-chace, near Galloway. **1803** W. TAPLIN *Sporting Dict. & Repository* II. 486 This kind of chase [*sc.* Wild-Goose chase]..was long since changed to a *train scent*, (that is, a drag across the country;) better known by the denomination of a *steeple chase*. **1818** 'W. H. SCOTT' *Brit. Field Sports* 433 A late Steeple Chase. **1848** THACKERAY *Van. Fair* xvii, Tom Cinqbars, who was going to ride the steeplechase. **1884** A. E. T. WATSON in *Longman's Mag.* Apr. 606 In these days steeples had something to do with steeple-chases.

attrib. **1839** *Sporting Mag.* Apr. 472 Men who make a profession of Steeple-chase riding. *Ibid.* 473 Ground.. called in requisition to form part of the Steeple-chase course. **1853** R. S. SURTEES *Sponge's Sp. Tour* (1893) 54 Caingey..was now hoisted on to the renowned steeple-chase horse again. **1862** *Catal. Internat. Exhib., Brit.* II. No. 4694, Hunting saddles, steeple-chase saddle. **1897** *Badminton Mag.* IV. 393, I won the regimental steeplechase cup with her last April.

fig. *c* **1865** J. WYLDE in *Circ. Sci.* I. 394/2 Expending considerable time in a chemical steeple-chase. **1898** *16th Cent.* Apr. 523 Evidently all that is the result of this steeplechase of colonial aggrandisement.

2. *transf.* A foot-race across country or over a course furnished with hurdles, ditches, and other obstacles.

1864 *Jackson's Oxf. Jrnl.* 12 Mar. 5/4 Oxford & Cambridge Athletic Sports... Steeple Chase, over about two miles of fair hunting country. **1897** *Encycl. Sport* I. 58/1 (Athletics) Steeplechasing. For many years past no athletic sports programme has been considered quite complete without a steeplechase.

3. A parlour game played on a board representing a steeplechase course, each player having a metal figure of a horse, the movements of which are regulated by the casting of dice and by the nature of the obstacles supposed to be encountered.

1892-3 *T. Eaton & Co. Catal.* Fall & Winter 67/1 Games ..errand boy, steeplechase, yacht race [etc.]. **1895** *Stores' Price List*, Race, or Steeplechase Game. **1911** *Encycl. Brit.* XXV. 868/2 Steeplechase.

'**steeplechase,** *v.* [f. STEEPLECHASE *sb.*] *intr.* To ride or run in a steeplechase; to practise riding in steeplechases. Also *transf.* and *fig.* So '**steeple-chasing** *vbl. sb.*

1816 in *Racing & Steeple-chasing* (Badm. Libr. 1900) 283 Steeple-chasing. **1856** 'STONEHENGE' *Brit. Rural Sports* II. II. ii. 379 Steeplechasing... This once fashionable amusement was brought into notice about 25 years ago, avowedly for [etc.]. **1866** BALLANTYNE *Shifting Winds* viii. (1881) 74 That is more arduous work than steeple-chasing! **1883** PENNELL-ELMHIRST *Cream Leicestersh.* 233 Over fence after fence they steeplechased. **1887** H. SMART *Cleverly won* xi. 96 There's a good deal of uncertainty about steeplechasing. **1887** M. SHEARMAN *Athletics & Football* 114 Steeplechasing is quite unknown at athletic meetings at the Universities. **1895** *Westm. Gaz.* 2 Nov. 3/3 He has steeplechased for twenty-nine years in England, Ireland, and India. **1905** *Daily Chron.* 16 Feb. 4/5, I..steeplechased over benches and iron bars, until I reached the best position in the Albert Hall.

'**steeplechaser.**

1. One who rides in a steeplechase.

1837 SIR G. STEPHEN *Search of Horse* (1841) p. xxvi, I am neither a horse-breaker, nor a steeple-chacer. **1862** G. A. LAWRENCE *Barren Honour* xix, The great stock-breeder and steeple-chaser. **1905** A. R. WALLACE *My Life* xiv. 215 At fairs they may be seen racing like steeple-chasers.

b. One who runs in a steeplechase.

1887 M. SHEARMAN *Athletics & Football* 112 The good steeplechaser must, of course, be a long-distance runner..; he must be a good jumper as well.

2. A horse trained for steeplechasing.

1839 *Sporting Mag.* Jan. 261 [It] applies as equally to the proprietor of a steeple-chaser as to the owner of a hunter. **1898** T. HAYDON *Sporting Reminisc.* 62 A steeple-chaser called Peter Osbeck, a horse imported from New Zealand, where he had won a few good races.

steepled ('stiːp(ə)ld), *ppl. a.* [f. STEEPLE *sb.*[1] + -ED[2].]

†**1.** Having the form of a steeple. *Obs.*

1600 FAIRFAX *Tasso* IX. viii, A steepled Turbant on her head she wore. **1604** T. WRIGHT *Passions* VI. 332 The like I might say of long steepled hattes.

2. Of a building: Having a steeple or steeples.

1711 *Dissent. Teachers' Addr. agst. Bill building Fifty new Churches* 10 And shall this be done for a few ungodly steepled Ædifices? **1884** W. C. SMITH *Kildrostan* I. i. 10 Why tolls the bell from the steepled kirk?

3. Of a town, etc.: Having many steeples; conspicuous for its steeple or steeples.

1837 CARLYLE *Fr. Rev.* I. I. i, On green field and steepled city, the May sun shines out. **1893** K. L. BATES *Eng. Relig. Drama* 117 This steepled town [Coventry] was famous for its Corpus Christi pageants. **1896** HOUSMAN *Shropshire Lad* xxviii, The bridges from the steepled crest Cross the water east and west.

4. Crowned as if with steeples.

1861 L. L. NOBLE *Icebergs* 223 It was only a fair field for the steepled icebergs, a vast metropolis in ice.

5. Of the fingers or hands: brought together in the form of a steeple.

1971 P. O'DONNELL *Impossible Virgin* x. 212 Tapping the tips of his steepled fingers together. **1981** 'L. EGAN' *Miser* (1982) ii. 26 'Not much criminal practice,' said Jesse, brooding over his steepled hands.

†steeple fair. *Obs.* In sarcastic use, an imaginary fair or market for church livings.

The definition 'a common fair or mart' given in some Dicts. is based on a misunderstanding of quot. 1622.

1597 BP. HALL *Sat.* II. v. 8 Thou seruile Foole: why couldst thou not repaire To buy a Benefice at Steeple-Faire? **1602** *2nd Pt. Return fr. Parnass.* IV. ii. 1764 Are not you the yong drouer of liuings..that haunts steeple faires. **1622** J. TAYLOR (Water-P.) *Water-Cormorant* E 2 b, These youths [*i.e.* the 'penny clarks' of a 'symonicall patron'], in Art, purse, and attire most bare Giue their attendance, at each steeple faire. **1624** BP. MOUNTAGU *Immed. Addr.* 44 To buy a Bishopricke, or Office, and dye soone after: or some other Preferment at Steeple-faire.

steeple-house. A building with a steeple.

1. Used by the early Quakers (and, before them, sometimes by other scrupulous persons) instead of 'church', on the ground that that word ought not to be applied to a building.

1644 QUARLES *Whipper Whipt* Wks. (Grosart) I. 161/2 It was first used when Steeplehouses, or Meeting-places were built, which Papists call Churches. **1654** WHITLOCK *Zootomia* 161 Steeple houses (as Churches are styled in our new Childrens Dictionary). **1664** G. FOX *For All Bps. & Priests* (1674) 31 Paul..had no Monastry nor Abbey, nor great Steeple house to preach in then. **1710** C. SHADWELL *Fair Quaker Deal* I. i. 11, I suppose the Fortune my Father left thee will be thrown into the Arms of one of the lewd Pillars of thy Steeple-house. **1785** GROSE *Dict. Vulgar T., Steeple house*, a name given to the church by Dissenters. **1877** WHITTIER *In the Old South* 41 There are steeple-houses on every hand, And pulpits that bless and ban.

attrib. **1681** S. FELL in *Jrnl. Friends' Hist. Soc.* (1912) July 136 Unrighteous demands touchinge the Preists wages, and Steeplehouse Repaires, etc. **1710** O. SANSOM *Acc. Life* 33, I was Excommunicated..for not Paying the Steeple-house Tax.

2. *gen.* ? *nonce-use.*

1807 SIR R. C. HOARE *Tour Irel.* 279 Round Towers... Peter Walsh supposes them to have been erected first by the Danes as watch-towers against the natives, and appropriated afterwards to holy uses, as Steeple-houses, and belfries.

steepleless ('sti:p(ə)llɪs), *a.* *nonce-word.* [f. STEEPLE *sb.*[1] + -LESS.] Having no steeple.

1849 THOREAU *Week on Concord* Tues. (1889) 187 The humble village of Litchfield, with its steepleless meeting-house.

steepler ('sti:plə(r)). *Cricket.* [f. STEEPLE *v.* + -ER[1].] = SKYER, esp. one from which the batsman is caught out.

1959 *Times* 7 Aug. 4/2 He was caught and bowled off a steepler. **1963** *Times* 5 Feb. 3/6 Parfitt at long-on judged a steepler well to end the innings. **1976** *Cricketer Internat.* Sept. 35/2 Crockham Hill caught everything, including two stupendous steeplers in the last over.

'steeplet. *rare*[−1]. [-ET[1].] A small steeple.

1891 R. B. S. KNOWLES *Glencoonoge* I. 166, I saw the pretty steeplet of his church.

'steeplewise, *adv.* [f. STEEPLE *sb.*[1] + -WISE.] After the manner of a steeple; in a conical or pyramidal form. Also, † ***after a steeple wise.***

1545 RAYNALDE *Byrth Mankynde* I. ix. 17 [Veins] enlargynge them selfe lytell and lytyll stepel wyse not fully rounde but flattyshe before and behynde. **1545** ELYOT *Dict., Pyramidatus*, made steeple wise brode beneth, and small and sharpe vpward. **1582** BATMAN *Barth. de P.R.* III. xvii. 18 Not onelie the lykenesse of the thinge seene commeth to the sight after a steeple wise [*Trevisa* shelde wise], but also [etc.]. **1637** HEYWOOD *Dialogues* ii. 26 His crowne Picked, made steeple-wise. *a* **1661** FULLER *Worthies, Chester* (1662) 192 He erected a seemly Waterwork built Steeplewise at the Bridgegate. **1725** *Bradley's Family Dict.* s.v. *Pears*, When they serve them up, they range them handsomly upon a Dish Roseways, and mount them one upon another Steeple-wise.

steeplish ('sti:plɪʃ), *a.* *nonce-wd.* [f. STEEPLE *sb.*[1] + -ISH.] Somewhat like the form of a steeple.

1856 *Chamb. Jrnl.* 18 Oct. 251/1 A felt-hat, broadish in the brim, and steeplish in the crown.

†'steeply, *a.* *Obs.* *rare*[−1]. In 6 steply. [f. STEEPLE *sb.*[1] + -Y.] Having the form of a steeple.

1551 TURNER *Herbal* I. N iij b, Pliny maketh two kynde of Cypres trees, one wyth sharp steply top, whyche is called the female.

steeply ('sti:plɪ), *adv.* [f. STEEP *a.* + -LY[2].] In a steep manner.

1772 PENNANT *Tours Scot.* (1774) 328 An amazing mountain steeply sloping. **1816** BYRON *Ch. Har.* III. lv. 2 Many a rock which steeply lowers. **1860** H. F. TOZER in Galton *Vac. Tourists* (1861) 407 We..after ascending steeply through a fine gorge, found ourselves in a green upland valley.

b. quasi-*Comb.* with adj. or ppl. adj.

1793 ANNA SEWARD *Lett.* (1811) III. 261 That steeply-sloping field at Eyam. **1905** W. J. SOLLAS *Age of Earth* x. 296 The Carboniferous beds..in the steeply-folded form they now present. **1912** KEITH *Human Body* xiv. 221 Hence the races with short feet, high insteps and steeply set heels, have large calves.

steepness ('sti:pnɪs). [f. STEEP *a.* + -NESS.]

1. The quality or condition of being steep.

c **1440** *Promp. Parv.* 474/2 Stepnesse, or sydenesse of a roof (*P.* stopnesse), *elevacio.* **1530** PALSGR. 276/1 Stepnesse of a hyll, *cliuité.* **1538** ELYOT *Dict.* Addit., *Abruptum*, that whiche hath suche a fall or stepenesse downe, that no man maye passe by it, but onely fall downe. **1615** CHAPMAN *Odyss.* VI. 408 Whose Towres you see ascend To such a steepnesse. **1756–7** tr. *Keysler's Trav.* (1760) I. 29 In a niche in the mountain of Zurl, which also from its perpendicular steepness is called St. Martin's wall. **1861** W. FROUDE *Rolling of Ships* (1862) 54 Assuming a smaller degree of steepness in the wave. **1892** K. PEARSON *Gram. Sci.* vi. §10. 257 If we examine the time-chart we see that there is a considerable difference in its steepness at different points.

2. *concr.* A steep part or slope of a hill, etc.

1585 HIGINS *Junius' Nomencl.* 379/2 *Dorsum montis*,..the side, hanging or steepenesse of an hill. **1602** CHETTLE *Hoffman* v. (1631) H 4 b, I did perceiue her..Clambring vpon the steepenes of the rocke. **1887** HALL CAINE *Deemster* xl, A hut built against a steepness of rugged land from which stones had sometimes been quarried. **1904** *Westm. Gaz.* 24 Aug. 2/1 Under the steepnesses ending in that dolomite crag which [etc.].

steep-to, *a.* *Naut.* [f. STEEP *a.* + TO *adv.*] (See quot. 1815.)

1748 *Anson's Voy.* II. iii. 139 The coast was very high and steep to. *Ibid.* 141 This Island towards the harbour is steep to, and has six fathom water close to the shore. **1815** *Falconer's Dict. Marine* (ed. Burney) s.v., *A Shore Steep-to* ..is said of a shore when it descends almost perpendicularly into the water. **1897** F. T. BULLEN *Cruise of 'Cachalot'* 24 These islands have long been a nursery for whale-fishers, because the cachalot loves their steep-to shores.

steep-up, *a.* *arch.* [f. STEEP *a.* + UP *adv.* Cf. STEEP-DOWN.] Precipitous; perpendicular.

1565 COOPER *Thesaurus* s.v. *Assurgo, Assurgit clementer & molliter collis*, riseth by littel and littell, and is not stipe vp. **1571** DIGGES *Pantom.* I. xxv. H j b, If the hill or turret be steepe vp, so that the foote be visible lying perpendicularly vnder the top. *c* **1600** SHAKS. *Sonn.* vii. 5 And hauing climb'd the steepe-vp heauenly hill. **1847** TENNYSON *Princess* Prol. 63 The fountain of the moment, playing, now A..steep-up spout whereon the gilded ball Danced like a wisp. **1878** —— *Q. Mary* III. iv, And on the steep-up track of the true faith Your lapses are far seen.

†'steepwise, *adv.* (and *a.*). *Obs.* [f. STEEP *a.* + -WISE.] **a.** *adv.* In a steep manner, with a steep inclination or slope. **b.** *adj.* Steep.

1545 ELYOT *Dict., Accliue*, stepe wise, bendyng wise. **1572** HULOET (ed. Higins), Stypewyse, pitching, or hanging downe, *cliuosus.* **1577** HANMER *Anc. Eccl. Hist.* 313 His shoulders..lay flatte or stipe wise. *Ibid.* 426 This temple lyeth from Bosphorus litle more then two furlonges situated in a very pleasaunt soyle, rising vpwarde steepe wise.

steepy ('sti:pɪ), *a.* *Obs.* exc. *arch.* Also 6 stipye, ste(i)pie, 7 steepie, ? steppie. [f. STEEP *a.* + -Y.] Steep; full of steep places; precipitous.

1565 STAPLETON tr. *Bede's Hist. Ch. Eng.* 147 Stipye and craggie hylles. *c* **1590** *Marlowe's Faustus* (1616) 1268 (Brooke) This Traytor flies vnto some steepie rocke. **1632** J. HAYWARD tr. *Biondi's Eromena* 52 A steepie and rockie dale. **1735** SOMERVILLE *Chase* III. 98 So Ships in Winter-Seas now sliding sink Adown the steepy Wave. **1774** GOLDSM. *Nat. Hist.* (1862) I. vi. 30 The banks of rivers, or steepy sea-shores. **1812** BYRON *Ch. Har.* II. xxii, Through Calpe's straits survey the steepy shore. **1872** HOWELLS *Wedd. Journ.* (1892) 285 That huge rock, base and steepy flank and crest.

Comb. **1638** BRATHWAIT *Barnabees Jrnl.* I. (1818) 33 Thence to Kighley, where are mountaines Steepy-threatning. **1672** DRYDEN *2nd Pt. Conq. Granada* III. iv. 130, I..found th' eternal fence so steepy high.

b. *fig.*

1600 SHAKS. *Sonn.* lxiii. 5 When his youthfull morne Hath trauaild on to Ages steepie night. **1603** FLORIO *Montaigne* I. xix. 36 The leape from an ill beeing, vnto a not beeing is not so dangerous or steepie; as it is from a delightfull and flowrishing beeing, vnto a painefull and sorrowfull condition. *a* **1614** DONNE *Βιαθανατος* (1644) 216 Because the limits are obscure, and steepy, and slippery, and narrow. **1616** W. DRUMMOND OF HAWTH. *Sonn.* *'Ah burning Thoughts'*, What though I trace not right Heauens steppie Wayes?

c. of movement.

1681 DRYDEN *Abs. & Achit.* 860 Now take thy steepy flight from Heav'n, and see If thou canst find on Earth another He. **1697** —— *Æneis* III. 670 The Night..view'd with equal Face Her steepy rise, and her declining Race. **1756** P. BROWNE *Jamaica* 1 Large currents flow from different parts of the main ridge, and continue their winding steepy courses to the sea.

steer (stɪə(r)), *sb.*[1] Forms: 1 stéor, 3 steore, 4, 6 ster, 4–7 stere, steere, 5 steyr, sterre, 6 sterr, styre, stiere, (sthere), 6–7 steare, 8 stear, 4– steer. [OE. *stéor* masc. = MLG. *stêr*, MDu., Du. *stier*, OHG. *stior* (MHG., mod.G. *stier*), Goth. *stiur*:—OTeut. type **steuro-z*:—pre-Teut. *(*s*)*teuro-s*, f. Indogermanic root **st*(*h*)*eu-* to be fixed or rigid; the form without *s* is represented by ON. *þjór-r* (Sw. *tjur*, Da. *tyr*).

According to some the word goes back to an Indogermanic **sthewəro-* (Skr. *sthavira*) stout. Connexion with Gr. ταῦρος, L. *taurus*, and their cognates is doubtful.]

1. a. A young ox, esp. one which has been castrated.

In the United States, Australia, etc., applied to male beef-cattle of any age.

a **700** *Epinal Gloss.* 596 *Ludarius*, steor. *c* **1290** *S. James* 182 in *S. Eng. Leg.* 39 þe Bollokes and þe ȝoungue steores. *c* **1340** *Nominale* (Skeat) 723 *Boef bouet et ienyce*, Oxe stere and hefere. *c* **1386** CHAUCER *Knt.'s T.* 1291 Aboute his Chaar ther wenten white Alauntz, Twenty and mo, as grete as any steer. **1463–4** *Compota Domest.* (Abbotsford Club 1836) 48 In x bouiculis vocatis steres emptis. **1500** *Ortus Vocab., Buculus*, a stote or a sterre. **1549** *N.C. Wills* (Surtees 1908) 204 A pied stere of foure yeres. **1590** SPENSER *F.Q.* III. xi. 42 And Aeolus faire daughter Arne hight, For whom he turnd him selfe into a Steare. **1597** SHAKS. *2 Hen. IV*, IV. ii. 103 Like youthfull Steeres, vnyoak'd. **1638** tr. *Bacon's Hist. Life & D.* (Mosley) 38 Old spent Oxen being put into fresh pastures, recover new tender flesh, and as sweete as if it were of a Steere. *a* **1722** LISLE *Husb.* (1757) 222 Steers will not be beef till four or five years old. **1808** SCOTT *Marm.* v. iii, Or musing, who would guide his steer To till the fallow land. **1830** *Hobart Town Almanack* 105 Mr. Lord's men..had been compelled to ride after a small herd, and to shoot a steer at random on the plain. **1854** MISS BAKER *Northampt. Gloss., Steer*, a bullock, after it is one year old, till it enters its fourth year, when it is termed an ox. **1898** RIDER HAGGARD *Farmer's Yr.* (1899) 64 There are four red-poll steers tied up fatting in a shed.

b. *attrib.*

1537 *Bury Wills* (Camden) 132 A rede stere calfe. **1620** VENNER *Via Recta* iii. 51 The flesh of Steeres, which we commonly call Steere-beefe. **1676** *Lond. Gaz.* No. 1126/4 Stolen or strayed.., two Steer Runts. **1817–8** COBBETT *Resid. U.S.* (1822) 175 Steer-beef is not nearly so good as ox-beef. **1846** J. BAXTER *Libr. Pract. Agric.* (ed. 4) II. 106 Eight of the best steer calves should be brought into work when three years old.

2. *Comb.* Designating events or participants in a rodeo, as ***steer roper, wrestler; steer bull-dogging, roping, wrestling.***

1910 *Oregon Daily Jrnl.* 30 Sept. 18/5 Steer roping contest for championship of the northwest. **1912** *Oregon Sunday Jrnl.* 18 Sept. 2/1 Among the many events to be featured at the Round-Up this year is the world's championship wild steer bull-dogging contest. **1914** *World's Work* (N.Y.) Feb. 445/2 It by no means follows that a good steer roper is a good calf roper. **1922** *N.Y. Times* 12 Nov. I. 5/2 One of the conditions of the steer-wrestling contests is that the contestants will suffer a 'ten-second fine' for 'loosening or knocking off horns'. **1923** *Ibid.* 11 Aug. 16/4 Steer Wrestlers Here. Twenty-three contestants in the 'steer-wrestling' or 'bull-dogging' competitions..arrived in New York yesterday. **1924** *Glasgow Herald* 17 June 9 The 'steer-roping', which at Saturday's display met with some public disapproval, was withdrawn. **1968** R. F. ADAMS *Western Words* (rev. ed.) 305/1 *Steer wrestling*, one of the five standard rodeo events; also called *bulldogging*. The contestant rides alongside a running steer, jumps from his saddle to the steer's head, stops it, and twists it to the ground with its head and all four feet pointing in the same direction. **1976** *Billings* (Montana) *Gaz.* 16 June 1-c/3 University of Wyoming steer wrestler Shawn Madden took an early lead in the second go-round of steer wrestling, throwing his animal in 3.67 seconds. **1979** *Sunset* Apr. 6/3 Horses will compete in 36 classes, including calf and steer-roping events.

b. Special combination. **steerhide** *N. Amer.*, the hide of a steer; *spec.* leather made from this or from the hide of a similar beast.

1921 *Jrnl. Amer. Leather Chemists Assoc.* May 295 (*heading*) On certain characteristics of fresh steer hide. **1925** J. R. ARNOLD *Hides & Skins* ii. 32 The thickest part of a steer hide is over the rump. **1948** H. G. KATES *Luggage & Leather Cards Manual* 184 Steerhide leather is extensively used because of its adaptability to tooling. **1979** *PN Rev.* IX. 39/1 All winter your brute shoulders strained against collars, padding and steerhide over the ash hames.

steer, *sb.*[2] *Obs.* exc. in *Comb.* Forms: 1 stéor, stýr, 2 steore, 2–5 ster, 2–6 stere, 4 stiere, 4–6 *Sc.* steir, 6 *Sc.* steyr, 6–7 steare, 7 stear, 4–7 steere, 5–7 steer. [OE. *stéor* (also *stýr*) str. fem., action of guiding or governing (also, correction, punishment); a neut. **stéor* rudder is inferred from the comb. *stéoresman* STEERSMAN. The immediate Teut. cognates are: OFris. *stiure*, MLG. *stûre* (whence late MHG. *stiure*, mod.G. *steuer*), MDu. *stûre, stiere* (mod.Du. *stuur*), ON. *stýri* neut., rudder, stern (:—OTeut. type **steurjo-m*); OHG. *stiura* str. fem., rudder, stern, also (and prob. originally) staff (:—OTeut. type **steurjō*); a different ablaut grade of the root (**steu-*) is found in ON. *staur-r* pole, stake (cf. Gr. σταυρός cross).]

1. The action of directing or governing; guidance, control, rule, government. Phr. ***to have, take the steer*** (*of* a country, etc.).

Of the presumed literal sense, action of steering, no example is known. In 15–16th c. senses 1 and 2 b are not easy to distinguish.

a **900** *Bæda's Hist.* IV. v. (1890) 278 þætte nænig biscop oðres biscopes scire inswoge, ac þætte he þoncful sy steore [*v.r.* styre] him þæs bibodenan folces [*sed contentus sit gubernatione creditae sibi plebis*]. *c* **1000** ÆLFRIC in *O.E. Hom.* I. 304 Fela beoð stuntnyssa þær nan steor [*c* **1175** *Lamb. Hom.* 117 steore] ne bið. *c* **1250** *Gen. & Ex.* 3418 Ilc of ðe .v. steres-men Vnder hem welden in stere tgen. **1423** JAS. I *Kingis Q.* 130 Tak him before In all thy gouernance, That in his hand the stere has of ȝou all. **1501** DOUGLAS *Pal. Hon.* II.

xii, Calliope..scho of nobill fatis hes the steir, To write thair worschip, victorie and prowes. **1513** —— *Æneis* VIII. viii. 127 My son Pallas..Exhort I wald to tak the steyr on hand. **1558** *Extracts Burgh Rec. Edin.* (1873) III. 21 To haue the steir reull and gouernance of the toun. **1596** DALRYMPLE tr. *Leslie's Hist. Scot.* II. 179 How sune he began to tak the steir of the Realme.

2. A rudder, helm.

Not in OE.; Anglo-Fr. had *estiere*, presumably from English, early in the 13th c. (Marie de France, *Eliduc* 866).

c **1290** *S. Mary Magd.* 175 in *S. Eng. Leg.* 467 Huy weren in .A. schip i-pult with-outen ster and ore. *c* **1305** *Land Cokayne* 154 Þe ȝung nunnes takith a bote And doth ham forth in that riuer Bothe with oris and with stere. **1377** LANGL. *P. Pl.* B. VIII. 35 For ȝif he ne arise þe rather and rauȝte to þe stiere, þe wynde wolde wyth þe water þe bote ouerthrowe. *c* **1385** CHAUCER *L.G.W.* 2416 And with a wawe brostyn was his stere. *c* **1430** *Pilgr. Lyf Manhode* IV. vi. (1869) 178 In swimmynge he streccheth his wynge and maketh þer of a seil and a steere. **1530** PALSGR. 276/1 Stere or roder in a shyp, *gouernail*. *a* **1568** *Bannatyne MS.* (Hunter. Club) 290 We sailit in storme, but steir, gyde or glas, To Paradice. *a* **1625** *Nomenclator Navalis* (Harl. MS. 2301) Steare.

b. *fig.* or in fig. context.

c **1200** ORMIN 15258 Forr itt iss sett her att te ster To sterenn baþe þoþre. *c* **1386** CHAUCER *Man of Law's T.* 735 In hym triste I, and in his mooder deere, That is to me my seyl, and eek my steere. **1390** GOWER *Conf.* I. 60 For whanne I may my lady hiere, Mi wit with that hath lost his Stiere. **1500–20** DUNBAR *Poems, Memento, homo* 46 Thy Ransonner, with woundis fyve, Mak thy plycht anker and thy steiris. **1621** BURTON *Anat. Mel.* I. ii. III. xv. 183 They commonly respect their own ends, commodity is the steer of all their actions. **1640** REYNOLDS *Passions* xxxix. 516 Judgement is the Ballace to Poise, and the Steere to guide the course.

c. Put by synecdoche for: Ship, boat.

a **1300** *K. Horn* 101 Þaruore þu most to stere..To schupe schulle ȝe funde. *Ibid.* 1373 Hi comen vt of stere.

d. *on, in steer*: astern.

c **1374** CHAUCER *Troylus* v. 641 Toward my deth with wynd in stere I sayle. *c* **1470** HENRY *Wallace* IX. 110 With out tary than mon yhe stryk on ster.

3. A plough-handle. (Cf. *steer-tree* b.)

1552 HULOET, Stere for the ploughe, *trio*.

4. *Comb.*: **steer-oar**, an oar used at the stern for steering a boat; †**steer-staff**, a tiller; **steer-tree**, †(*a*) a tiller; (*b*) a plough-handle (now *dial.*). See also STARBOARD *sb.*, STEER-MAN.

1802 *Naval Chron.* IX. 293 To take the *steer-oar. **1882** NARES *Seamanship* (ed. 6) 162 A steer oar must be used to steer the boat. **1382** WYCLIF *Prov.* xxiii. 34 Thou shalt ben ..as the steris man al forslept, the *steer staf lost [*amisso clavo*]. *c* **1460** *Towneley Myst.* iii. 433 Wife, tent the *stere-tre, and I shall asay The depnes of the see that we bere, if I may. **1483** *Cath. Angl.* 361/2 A Stere tre, *stiua, regimen.* **1562** *Wills & Invent. N.C.* (Surtees 1835) I. 207, x pleughe heads, vj plewe sheares, ij steretres.

†**steer**, *sb.*[3] *Obs.* Forms: 1 stéora, stíora, stíera, 3–5 stere, 4–6 steere, 6 *Sc.* steir. [OE. *stéora* wk. masc. = OHG. *stiuro* (MHG. *stiure*, *stûre*):—OTeut. type **steurjon-*, related to prec. sb.] A steersman, helmsman; *transf.* a ruler or controller.

c **897** ÆLFRED *Gregory's Past. C.* lvi. 431 Swelce se stiora slepe on midre sæ, & forlure ðæt stiorroður. *c* **1250** *Gen. & Ex.* 3413 Al bi ðhusenz ðis folc was told, Ilc ðhusent adde a meister wold; And vnder ðis tgen steres ben, Ilc here on hundred to bi-sen. *c* **1386** CHAUCER *Man of Law's T.* 350 He that is lord of Fortune be thy steere. *c* **1500** *Lancelot* 1020 She is here, That of thi lyue and of thi deith is stere.

a **1568** A. SCOTT *Poems* xv. 25 Sweit maistres,..Steir, rewll, and gyder of my senssis richt.

steer, *sb.*[4] *rare.* [Origin unknown; perh. some error.] ? A pile (of wood).

The word is not used in the corresponding passage of the earlier Acts, 7 & 8 Geo. IV. c. 30 §17 and 9 Geo. IV. c. 56 §18.

1837 *Act 1 Vict.* c. 89 §10 Whosoever shall unlawfully and maliciously set fire to any Stack of Corn, Grain,..Charcoal or Wood, or any Steer of Wood, shall be guilty of Felony. **1861** *Act 24 & 25 Vict.* c. 97 §17 Any steer of Wood or Bark.

steer (stiːə(r)), *sb.*[5] *slang* (orig. *U.S.*). [f. STEER *v.*[1]] A piece of advice or information; a tip, a lead. (See also quot. 1970.)

1899 C. H. HOYT *Texas Steer* (typescript) IV. 21 You're going back to Texas to give the voters of my district a steer. What's that steer to be? **1924**, etc. [see BUM *a.*]. **1926** *Flynr's* 16 Jan. 638/2 An' divvy with th' crooked barkeep for a steer or some kind of a tip if th' stunt panned out ok. **1935** L. E. LAWES *Cell 202, Sing Sing* ix. 553 You're both on the wrong steer..thinkin' about the devil when all the while it's the man himself deserves your attention. **1959** 'M. M. KAYE' *House of Shade* x. 127 All I've done is to give you a wrong steer, and make bad worse. **1970** D. FRANCIS *Rat Race* vi. 79 I'd have to go round the Luton complex...could probably get a steer home from there, from the twenty-four hour radar. **1982** *Times* 21 Apr. 16/1 Steers from Smiths Industries on its financial performance are obviously worth listening to.

steer (stɪə(r)), *a.* *Obs.* exc. *Sc.* and *dial.* (see E.D.D.). Forms: 3–5, 9 stere, 4 ster, ? sterre, 5, 9 steer, 7 steare. [App. repr. OE. **stére* (EWS. **stíere*) = OHG. *stiuri*, *stûri* strong, proud, MLG. *stûr* stiff, severe, stern:—OTeut. type **steurjo-*, usually referred to the Indogermanic root **st(h)eu-* to be fixed or rigid: cf. STEER *sb.*[1] and *sb.*[2]]

1. Strong, stout.

13.. *Ipotis* 440 (Vernon MS.) in Horstm. *Altengl. Leg.* (1881) 346 Beten wiþ scourges stronge and ster. *c* **1415** *Pol. Poems* (Rolls) II. 125 Stedes ther stumbelyd in that stownde, That stod stere stuffed under stele. *c* **1425** *Non-Cycle Myst. Plays* 19 With storms both stiff and steer. *c* **1450** *Guy Warw.* 662 Then came the dewke Raynere, An hardy knyght and a stere. **1641** BEST *Farm. Bks.* (Surtees) 51 Wheare the oates have beene steare, and much scattered.

†**2.** ? Staunch, steadfast in affection (*to* another).

a **1300** *K. Horn* 1344 (Camb.) He luueþ him so dere, & is him so stere.

steer (stɪə(r)), *v.*[1] Forms: 1 stíeran, (ȝe)stéoran, stéran, stíoran, stíran, stýran, 2 isteoran, -en, stieran, 3 ste(o)ren, *Orm.* ste(o)renn, 3–7 stere, 4 stiere, steir, (sture), *Sc.* steyr, 4–5 ster, 4–7 steere, 4–8 *Sc.* steir, 5 steare, 5–6 styre, 6 stir(e, 6–7 stirre, stear (6 *arch.* ysteare), 7 sterre, 5– steer. *Pa. t.* 2 stierde, 3 steorede, 4 sterd, steryd, 5 stered, *Sc.* sterit, 6–7 steard, 8 steird. *Pa. pple.* 1 ȝestíored, 4 steerid, sterede, stierd, 4–5 stered, 6 *Sc.* steirt. [Com. Teut.: OE. *stíeran* = OFris. *stiura*, MLG. *stûren*, (M)Du. *sturen*, *stíeren*, OHG., MHG. *stiuren* (mod.G. *steuern*), ON. *stýra* (Sw., Norw. *styra*, Da. *styre*):—OTeut. **steurjan*, f. **steurō* rudder, STEER *sb.*[2]

A verb of identical form, OTeut. **steurjan* f. **steurjo-* strong, rigid (see STEER *a.*), appears in Goth. *stiurjan* to establish, to affirm. It is possible that the OE. sense 'to rebuke' may belong to a verb f. the Teut. adj.]

1. *trans.* To guide the course of (a vessel) by means of a rudder, or of an oar or paddle used like a rudder.

Now occas. in wider sense, to guide (a vessel) by other mechanical means, e.g. by a propeller or arrangement of sails.

a **1122** *O.E. Chron.* (Laud MS.) an. 1046, Up þæs cynges scipe þe Harold eorl ær steorde. *a* **1200** *Vices & Virtues* 43 [Noe] hie [*sc.* ða arche] swa stierde on ðe muchele wilde flode ..ðat [etc.]. *c* **1330** R. BRUNNE *Chron. Wace* (Rolls) 14099 To þer schipes þey gaf þer tent To stere þem boþe fer & hende. **1390** GOWER *Conf.* I. 59 Thei conne noght here Schipes stiere, So besiliche upon the note Thei herkne. **1400** *26 Polit. Poems* i. 65 Whanne a fool stereth a barge, Hym self and al the folke is shent. **1598** FLORIO *Ital. Dict.* To Rdr. 9 They were many to steere a passage-boate. *a* **1647** PETTE in *Archæologia* XII. 268 The ship wrought exceeding well and was so yare of conduct that a foot of helm would steer her. **1748** *Anson's Voy.* III. v. 342 The proa generally carries six or seven Indians; two of which are placed in the head and stern, who steer the vessel alternately with a paddle according to the tack she goes on. **1815** J. SMITH *Panorama Sci. & Art* II. 183 In steering a vessel, it has been usual for the helmsman to have one compass, and the captain in his cabin to have another. **1853** MISS YONGE *Heir of Redclyffe* xxiii, Martin had best steer it; he knows the rocks. **1909** *Edin. Rev.* July 219 No less impossible than to steer a boat without taking a seat in it.

In figurative context. *c* **1200** ORMIN 15259 Forr itt iss sett her att te ster To sterenn baþe þoþre. **1390** GOWER *Conf.* I. 11 Lo, thus was Petres barge stiered Of hem that thilke tyme were. *a* **1529** SKELTON *Bouge of Court* 107 She that styreth the shyp, make her your frende. **1577** GOSSON in *Kirton's Mirr. Mans Lyfe* K viij, The prime of youth, whose greene vnmellowd yeres..sets vp saile, and sternlesse ships ysteares. *c* **1645** HOWELL *Lett.* (1655) I. VI. lviii. 305 Unless wisdom sit at the Helm and steer the motions of his Will. **1663** BUTLER *Hud.* I. i. 874 For whatsoe're we perpetrate, We do but row, we're steer'd by Fate. **1911** SIR H. CRAIK *Life Clarendon* I. ii. 60 He steered his bark through the dangerous eddies with consummate skill.

b. *transf.* Of animals.

1398 TREVISA *Barth. De P.R.* v. liv. (1495) 171 In foules wyth clouen fete the fote is nedefull to ledynge, styrynge and rulynge in waters. **1657** tr. *Jonstonus' Wond. Things Nat.* 233 He [the squirrel] takes the bark of a Tree..and sets it on the water, sitting in it, and stears it with his Tail lifted up, and so the wind carries him over. **1873** TRISTRAM *Moab* vii. 131 Without a perceptible movement of their wings, only their long tails gently steering them in and out.

c. To guide (a vessel) to a specified point or in a specified direction.

1470–85 MALORY *Arthur* XVIII. xix. 760 Lete me be putte within a barget & but one man with me suche as ye trust to stere me thyder. **1574** W. BOURNE *Regiment for Sea* (1580) 78 Nowe for to set any course to stirre the ship vpon any place appoynted. **1781** COWPER *Charity* 25 When Cook.. Steer'd Britain's oak into a world unknown. **1850** TENNYSON *In Mem.* ciii, We steer'd her toward a crimson cloud. **1876** J. G. HOLLAND *Seven Oaks* x. 133 Jim steered his boat around a little bend and in a moment it was running in shallow water.

†**d.** To work (the rudder). *Obs.*

c **1570** *Sat. Poems Reform.* xxx. 57 In trublous time yow micht haif steirt ye ruther. **1609** HOLLAND *Amm. Marcell.* XXVI. i. 284 For tenne dayes space there was none to steere the helm of the Empire.

e. *to steer a, one's course*: (*a*) *lit.* of a helmsman or a navigator, to guide a vessel along a certain course; also of the vessel (cf. 2 d); (*b*) *transf.* and *fig.*

1602 MARSTON *Antonio's Rev.* IV. i, He beares an unturned sayle with every winde: Blowe east, blowe west, he stirs his course alike. **1644** in *Verney Mem.* (1907) I. 325 Those particulars that first induced me to steere this course. **1650** HUBBERT *Pill Formality* 193 If they have not Christ Jesus for their Pilot to steere their course for them, they must certainly sinke. **1660** F. BROOKE tr. *Le Blanc's Trav.* 248 Intending to take ship at Alexandria, and steer the course for Italy. **1709** T. ROBINSON *Vind. Mosaick Syst.* 49 The Magnet..which guides him to steer his Course through these vast Expansions of Water. **1748** *Anson's Voy.* III. i. 302 It blew from the S.W, and consequently was directly opposed to the course we wanted to steer. **1756** C. LUCAS *Ess. Waters* III. 174 Let us learn to steer the middle course. **1764** HARMER *Observ.* ii. 59 Deserts where the Arabs alone know how to steer their course. **1822** HAZLITT *Men & Mann.* Ser. II. v. (1869) 113 You must steer a middle course. **1867** SMYTH *Sailor's Word-bk.*, *Steer her course*, going with the wind fair enough to lay her course. **1873** BLACK *Pr. Thule* xxii. 358 To see that the boat was steering her right course.

†**f.** *refl.* = to steer one's course. Also in *passive*, to be guided (*by* the compass, etc.) in steering.

1399 LANGL. *Rich. Redeles* IV. 80 Ne had þei striked a strake and sterid hem þe better,..þey had be þrowe ouere þe borde backewarde ichonne. **1651** J. C[LEVELAND] *Poems* 35 The Card by which the Mariners are stear'd.

2. *absol.* and *intr.* To guide a vessel by means of a rudder or the like.

c **897** ÆLFRED *Gregory's Past. C.* ix. 59 Swiðe eaðe mæȝ on smyltre sæ unȝelæred scipstiera ȝenoh ryhte stieran. **1390** GOWER *Conf.* I. 312 He that behinde sat to stiere Mai noght the forestempne hiere. *c* **1515** *Cocke Lorell's B.* 12 Some stered at the helme behynde, Some whysteled after the wynde. **1587** *Mirr. Mag.*, *Severus* viii, Who takes to raygne the scepter in his hand, Is like to him, in sterne to stirre that sits. **1613** PURCHAS *Pilgrimage* (1614) 745 Some of their men were starued, the rest all so weake, that onely one could lie along vpon the Helm and sterre. **1762** FALCONER *Shipwr.* II. 395 Two skilful helmsmen on the poop to steer. **1839** MALCOM *Trav.* (1840) 45/1 Boats lie before the town, literally in thousands... The wife steers, while the husband rows. **1883** *Century Mag.* Sept. 655 Even the men whose work lies ashore..can steer and reef on a pinch.

In figurative context. **1596** DALRYMPLE tr. *Leslie's Hist. Scot.* II. 155 The Prior of S. Androis elected Bischop.. intendis in thair contrare to steir and row, with diligens. **1681** FLAVEL *Right Man's Ref.* 202 Let God steer for you in a storm.

b. *intr.* in passive sense. Of a ship: To admit of being steered; to answer the helm (well or ill).

1627 CAPT. SMITH *Sea Gram.* ix. 40 Foundering is when she will neither veere nor steare. **1669** STURMY *Mariner's Mag.* I. ii. 18 The Ship will Stear the better when you sit all quiet. **1692** *J. Smith's Seaman's Gram.* I. xvi. 83 The Ship ..does not steer steddy. **1829** *Ann. Reg., Chron.* 127/1 She pulls six oars; has two lug sails; steers either with a scull or rudder. **1880** *Times* 25 Dec. 7/4 The ship..Steers well under all circumstances.

c. Of a navigator: To guide a vessel in a certain direction; to sail or row towards a specified place.

1340–70 *Alex. & Dind.* 185 Þanne whitli þe weiht ouur þe watur sterus, And þe lettrus to his lord ledus ful sone. *c* **1614** SIR W. MURE *Wks.* I. 64 The Ile no sooner to their eyes appear'd, Till thither Palinure their pilote steir'd. **1667** MILTON *P.L.* II. 1020 Or when Ulysses on the Larbord shunnd Charybdis, and by th' other whirlpool steard. **1669** STURMY *Mariner's Mag.* II. vi. 67 You may estimate the Min. but you cannot Steer by a whole Deg. **1687** A. LOVELL tr. *Thevenot's Trav.* I. 270 We steered South-west till Sunday. **1743** BULKELEY & CUMMINS *Voy. S. Seas* 116 We came to sail, and steer'd out of the Lagoon West. **1781** GIBBON *Decl. & F.* l. III. 128 They steered by the guidance of the stars. **1797** *Encycl. Brit.* (ed. 3) III. 599/2 But failing of this, they steered to Jamaica. **1799** *Monthly Rev.* XXX. 134 *note*, They seized a canoe, and steered along shore. **1840** THIRLWALL *Hist. Greece* lix. VII. 325 He set sail from Ephesus..and steered direct for Athens. **1871** B. TAYLOR *Faust* II. II. iii. 146 They have left the place, Steering away to Samothrace. **1874** GREEN *Short Hist.* vii. §6. 407 The daring adventurer steered undauntedly for the Moluccas.

fig. *a* **1639** T. CAREW *To Her in Absence* 10 Love is the Pilot, but o'r-come with fear Of your displeasure, dares not homewards stear. *c* **1655** MILTON *2nd Sonn. to Cyriack Skinner* 8 Yet I..still bear vp and steer Right onward. **1674** TEMPLE *Let.* Wks. 1731 II. 297, I knew he was a great Man, but could not tell yet, to what Points of the Compass he intended to steer. **1675** LD. DANBY in *Essex Papers* (Camden) 22 Though itt bee very difficult to steere amongst so many rocks of faction, without striking upon some.

d. Of a ship: To be guided by the helm in a certain direction.

1667 MILTON *P.L.* IX. 515 As when a Ship..where the Wind Veres oft, as oft so steers, and shifts her Saile. **1669** STURMY *Mariner's Mag.* I. ii. 18 You have the Ship as at first, steering under all her Canvas. **1720** RAMSAY *Prosp. Plenty* 156 Vers'd in the critic seasons o' the year, When to ilk bay the fishing-bush should steer. **1748** *Anson's Voy.* II. x. 247 The galeon..steers for the latitude of 13° or 14°. **1839** MARRYAT *Phant. Ship* xii, The *Batavia* steered into the roads. **1885** *Law Times Rep.* LIII. 60/1 The *Chusan* was steering E. by S., and proceeding at the rate of about ten knots.

e. *to steer large, small*: see quot. 1867.

1834 M. SCOTT *Cruise Midge* ix, The frigate was steering large, about a mile on our lee-bow. **1846** A. YOUNG *Naut. Dict.* 319 *To steer small*, means to steer steadily without putting the helm too much to either side. To steer large, is the reverse. **1867** SMYTH *Sailor's Word-bk.*, *Steer Large*, to go free, off the wind. Also, to steer loosely. *Ibid.*, *Steer Small*, to steer well and within small compass, not dragging the tiller over from side to side.

f. *to steer clear of*: chiefly *fig.*, to avoid completely.

1723 DE FOE *Col. Jack* (1840) 69 We would have steered clear of them, and cared not to have them see us, if we could help it, but they did see us, and cried, Who comes there? **1789** BELSHAM *Ess.* I. xviii. 338 Of tame acquiescence in vulgar opinion..Walpole..has steered perfectly clear. **1804** *Med. Jrnl.* XII. 415 It is incumbent on them..whilst they steer clear of Scylla, to beware they do not fall into Charybdis. **1809** MALKIN *Gil Blas* III. vii. ¶5, I steered clear of Hortensia. **1838** PRESCOTT *Ferd. & Is.* I. xviii. (1842) II. 160 Columbus..had been instructed..to steer clear of all Portuguese settlements on the African coast. **1884** *Manch. Exam.* 11 June 5/5 Mr. Marshall spoke with good humour, and steered clear alike of levity and acerbity. **1893** HODGES *Elem. Photogr.* (1907) 68 Enabling him to steer clear of some of these [difficulties].

3. *trans.* In extended sense, to guide something that is in motion. In various applications. **a.** To guide (a chariot, a horse, cattle, etc.).

In mod. racing parlance the sense is a new development from sense 1.

c **888** ÆLFRED *Boeth.* xxxvi. §iii, Se stiorð þam hrædwæne eallra ȝesceafta. **1375** BARBOUR *Bruce* VI. 334 Thar may no man haf worthy hede, Bot he haf wit to steir his stede. *a* **1568** *Wyf of Auchtermuchty* 100 in *Bannatyne MS.* (Hunter. Club) 345 Scho..stowtly steird the stottis abowt. **1590** SPENSER *F.Q.* III. viii. 30 His charet swift in haste he thither steard. **1844** KINGLAKE *Eothen* xxi, I steered my dromedary close up alongside of the mounted Bedouin. **1850** R. G. CUMMING *Hunter's Life S. Africa* (1902) 105/2 The native who led the long team..suddenly turned the leading oxen short towards the river's bank, thus rendering it impossible for the driver to steer his after-oxen. **1884** *Longman's Mag.* Apr. 605 It may be that he is going to steer his own animal in the race for which it is being prepared. **1890** D. DAVIDSON *Mem. Long Life* iv. 92 Tapp was the jockey..and 'steered him to victory'.

b. To guide (a plough).

c **1480** HENRYSON *Mor. Fab.* 2224 Thair wes ane Husband, quhilk had ane pleuch to steir. **1724** RAMSAY *Tea-t. Misc.* (1733) I. 29 Twa good stilts to the pleugh And ye your sell maun steer. **1758** AKENSIDE *Odes* II. xi. 9 The conquerors..fed Calabrian flocks, and steer'd the Sabine plough. **1914** *Daily News* 25 Feb. 2 He feeds the pigs and steers the plough.

c. To guide the course of (a vehicle, a bicycle, a balloon, etc.) by mechanical means; to guide (a floating object) by taking advantage of a current.

1756–7 tr. *Keysler's Trav.* (1760) I. 233 These sledges hold only two, the traveller and the guide, who sits forward steering with a stick. **1788** COWPER *Dog & Water Lily* 18 With cane extended far I sought To steer it close to land. **1873** G. C. DAVIES *Mount. & Mere* xi. 91 A plague of gnats ..doubly unpleasant when steering a bicycle along rutty lanes. **1910** *Encycl. Brit.* I. 269/2 Santos Dumont..won the Deutsch prize by steering a balloon from St. Cloud round the Eiffel Tower and back in half an hour.

d. To guide, lead, 'pilot' (a person) through a crowd, along an intricate path, etc. Also *absol.* Also (*U.S. slang*) to manœuvre or decoy (a person) to a place, or into doing something.

1859 *Habits of Gd. Society* v. 210 It is the gentleman's duty to *steer*, and in crowded rooms nothing is more trying. **1889** *Century Dict.*, *Bunko-steerer*, that one of the swindlers called bunko-men who allures or steers strangers to the bunko-joint or rendezvous. **1891** C. ROBERTS *Adrift Amer.* 159, I don't thank you very much for steering me up against such a job. **1911** C. F. HAMILTON in *United Empire* June 383 There is little or no suggestion that he is sent to 'steer' us, as an American would say. **1915** *Sketch* 16 June 227/1, I.. shook hands with old Lemann, and steered him into the smoking-room.

4. *intr.* To shape one's course (on land, in the air). Also *trans.* with cognate object.

c **1500** *Lancelot* (S.T.S.) 3428 And brandymagus chargit he to stere Efter hyme, within a lytill space. **1629** MILTON *Ode Nativ.* 146 Mercy..With radiant feet the tissued clouds down stearing. **1633** C. FAREWELL *East-Ind. Colation* 45 [The elephant] steeres like a hulke, stifnecked, almost all of one peice. **1667** MILTON *P.L.* I. 225 Then with expanded wings he stears his flight Aloft. *Ibid.* VII. 430 So stears the prudent Crane Her annual Voiage. ?*c* **1670** *Hist. Tom Thumb* III. 104 in Hazl. *E.P.P.* II. 237 But Tom cry'd in a merry mood: Unto the King we'll steer. **1700** T. BROWN *Amusem. Ser. & Com.* 11 Let's Steer for the Court, for that's the Region which will furnish us with the finest Lessons. *a* **1701** MAUNDRELL *Journ. Jerus.* (1732) 134 Here steering Northerly directly up the Valley. **1725** RAMSAY *Gentle Sheph.* I. ii, Driven frae house and hald, where will ye steer? **1774** GOLDSM. *Nat. Hist.* (1776) V. 32 The quails..steer their flight back to enjoy in Egypt the temperate air. **1792** BURNS *My ain kind Dearie* iii, At noon the fisher seeks the glen, Along the burn to steer. **1807** WORDSW. *White Doe* v. 32 She..oft her steps had hither steered. **1828** LYTTON *Pelham* xxix, The Frenchman..bowed, and drew himself aside. Vincent steered by. **1837** W. IRVING *Capt. Bonneville* I. 111 He was bravely steering his way across the continent. **1887** J. BALL *Nat. in S. Amer.* 128 Passing the houses, I at once steered for the rocky slopes behind. **1896** BADEN-POWELL *Matabele Campaign* xvi, I steered by moon and time until I thought I was near Enkeldoorn.

b. Of an inanimate thing: To travel in a set course.

1692 BENTLEY *Boyle Lect.* viii. 25 The Winter of the Year, when the Sun was the nearest of all, and steer'd directly over mens heads. **1830** MARRYAT *King's Own* xxii, The moon.. was high in the heavens, steering for the zenith in all her beauty. **1861** CLOUGH *Ess. Class. Metres, Elegiacs* i. 5 Thou busy sunny river;..Through woodlands steering, with branches waving above thee.

†**c.** *trans.* To direct one's course towards (a place). *Obs.* (? nonce-use.)

1667 MILTON *P.L.* x. 328 Satan..Betwixt the Centaure and the Scorpion stearing His Zenith.

†**5.** To check, restrain, control. In OE. also: To rebuke. (In OE. the obj. is in the dative.) *Obs.*

c **950** *Lindisf. Gosp.* Mark viii. 30 Forbead *vel* stiorde *vel* stiorend wæs him [Vulg. *comminatus est eis*]. **971** *Blickl. Hom.* 19/5 Seo meniȝo styrde þæm blindan þæt he cleopode. *c* **1000** *Sax. Leechd.* II. 192 Wið maȝan bryne & þurste; wlaco wæter menge wið þone selestan ele, sele drincan, þæt styrð þam þurste. *a* **1225** *St. Marher.* 9 þu steorest te sea stream þæt hit fleden ne mot fir þan þu markedest. *a* **1300** *K. Horn* (Camb. MS.) 434 'Lemman' he sede 'dere, þin herte nu þu stere'. *a* **1300** *Cursor M.* 4295 Thoru strengh o luue þat nan mai stere. **13..** *E.E. Allit. P.* C. 27 þay ar happen also þat con her hert stere. *c* **1385** CHAUCER *L.G.W.* 935 And fyr so wod it myȝ te nat been steerid In al the noble toure of ylioun. **1390** GOWER *Conf.* I. 122 So that thou myht thi tunge stiere. **1423** JAS. I *Kingis Q.* 194 His tong for to reule[n] and to stere. *c* **1440** *Bone Flor.* 825 The lady swowned, and was full woo, Ther myght no man hur stere. *a* **1500** *Frere & Boy* (*c* 1512) A ij b, All that may the pype here Shall not themselfe stere But laugh and lepe aboute. *c* **1640** R. DAVENPORT *Surv. Sci.* Wks. (1890) 325 Rhethorick ..whose sweete tongue Can steere the stubborn'st hart.

†**6.** To guide (a person, his conduct) by admonition or counsel. *Obs.*

a **1000** ÆLFRIC *Hom.* I. 320 He nolde mid his to-cyme ða synfullan fordeman,..Ærest he wolde us mid liðnysse styran [*c* **1175** *Lamb. Hom.* 95 isteoren] þæt he siððan mihte on his dome us ȝehealdan. *c* **1200** ORMIN 14705 To wurrþenn herrsumm..Till alle þa þatt hafenn þe To ȝemenn & to sterenn. *a* **1225** *Juliana* 30 Festne mi bileaue steor me ant streng me. **12..** *Prayer to Virgin* 30 in *O.E. Misc.*, Bricht and scene quen of storre..in þis false fikele world so me led and steore. **1362** LANGL. *P. Pl.* A. IX. 42 He strengþeþ þe to stonde he stureþ þi soule. **1655** STANLEY *Hist. Philos.* III. xvii. (1687) 94/2 Euripides is steer'd by Socrates.

†**b.** *to steer off*: to guide away *from* some opinion. *Obs.*

1662 H. MORE *Antid. Ath.* I. i. (1712) 9 The attempt of endeavouring to steer them off from Atheism. **1681** —— *Expos. Dan.* Pref. p. xv, When men see so palpable a correspondency..they will be steared off from conceiving any such sense.

†**c.** To conduct (one's life). Also *refl.*

a **1250** *Prov. Alfred* 562 ȝif..þu ne moȝe mid strenghe þeselwen steren. *a* **1300** *Cursor M.* 19822 Fott him to þe, he sal þe lere, Al o þi lijf, hu þu sal stere. **1673** CAVE *Prim. Chr.* I. ix. 271 He..by Letters gave them [his sons] counsels for the steering themselves. **1699** T. C[OCKMAN] tr. *Tully's Offices* (1706) 117 By whose Counsel and Direction they may steer their Lives.

†**d.** Of reasons, indications, influences: To guide. *Obs.*

1649 *Nicholas Papers* (Camden) 135, I am confident..his fathers last desires and commands will steere our yong King right. *a* **1652** J. SMITH *Sel. Disc.* i. 21 Their life being steered by nothing else but opinion and imagination. **1653** BLITH *Engl. Improver Impr.* 63 Therefore in every new work some triall would be made of all materials, and therein thou must be steered by those the very place affords, whether Stone, Chalk, Wood, or Earth, or all. *a* **1683** OWEN *Holy Spirit* (1693) 262 So as to be steered thereby in his Work.

e. *intr.* To direct one's course of action (*by* guiding indications). Often, to find a safe course *between* two evils or two extremes.

1658 SIR T. BROWNE *Hydriot.* 18 If we steer by the conjecture of many and Septuagint expression; some trace thereof [burial of treasures] may be found. **1670** TEMPLE *Let.* Wks. 1731 II. 224 By his Advice his Highness resolves to steer in the Course of his Affairs and Motions relating to England. **1697** DRYDEN *Æneis* Ded. (e) 4 b, I thought fit to steer betwixt the two extreams, of Paraphrase, and literal Translation. *a* **1718** PRIOR *Paulo Purg.* 57 Her Prudence did so justly steer Between the Gay and the Severe. *c* **1721** in *10th Rep. Hist. MSS. Comm.* App. I. 198, I have been now two years on this side [of the water] but still steer'd snugg and clear that I might preserve my credit and safety at home. **1722** WOLLASTON *Relig. Nat.* iii. 51 Rational animals should use their reason, and steer by it. **1769** ROBERTSON *Chas. V*, III. VIII. 103 Now he should steer in that difficult and arduous conjuncture. **1818** HALLAM *Mid. Ages* viii. III. (1819) III. 294 The rolls of parliament, by whose light we have hitherto steered. **1858** GREENER *Gunnery* 309, I am quite satisfied to steer between extremes.

†**7.** To govern, rule. *Obs.* exc. as conscious metaphor (figurative use of sense 1).

to have to steer: to have under one's command.

a **900** *Bæda's Hist.* IV. xii. (1890) 300 Tweȝen biscopas [wæron] on his stowe ȝesette..þæt wæs Boosa, se styrde [*v.r.* steorde] Dera mæȝðe, & Eata Beornicea. *c* **1200** ORMIN 3679 He þatt all þiss weorelld shop & alle shaffte stereþþ. *a* **1300** *E.E. Psalter* ii. 9 In yherde irened salt þou stere þa. **1375** BARBOUR *Bruce* I. 38 Alexander the King..That Scotland haid to steyr and leid. *a* **1400** *Launfal* 684 Be god, that all may stere. *c* **1430** *Syr Gener.* (Roxb.) 117 Thre thousand knightes he had to stere. *c* **1470** HENRY *Wallace* v. 920 Off kyn he was, and Wallace modyr ner, Off Craufurd syd that mydward had to ster. *c* **1480** HENRYSON *Mor. Fab.* 1571 To reule and steir the land, and Iustice keip. **1500–20** DUNBAR *Poems* xi. 14 All are gone At will of God that all thing steiris. **1601** LAMBARDE *Dict. Angl. Top.* (1730) 42 One of the most wise..Princes that ever stered this common Weale. **1633** FORD *Broken H.* v. ii. K 1, Neuer liu'd Gentleman of greater merit, Hope, or abiliment to steere a kingdome. **1678** CUDWORTH *Intell. Syst.* 878 Some will from hence be apt to infer, That there is no God at all, but that blind Chance and Fortune steer all.

†**b.** To manage, administer (government); to conduct (business, negotiations, etc.). *Obs.*

c **888** ÆLFRED *Boeth.* xvii, þæt ic..ȝerisenlice mihte steoran & reccan þone anwald þe me befæst wæs. *a* **1225** *Leg. Kath.* 10 Maxence steorede þe refschipe in Rome. **1456** SIR G. HAYE *Law Arms* (S.T.S.) 62 The quhilk sterit ane Emperouris estate in his tyme. **1647** CLARENDON *Hist. Reb.* I. §157 The great persons who steered the public affairs.

†**c.** To keep in order (a crowd). *Obs.*

1616 J. LANE *Contn. Sqr.'s T.* XI. 248 For whome large space was made by th' marshallers, gardantes, and tipp staves, which the people stears.

†**d.** *intr.* To have charge *of*. *Obs.*

13.. *Seuen Sages* 894 In that forest woned an herd, That of bestes loked an sterd.

steer (stɪə(r)), *v.*² *rare.* [f. STEER *sb.*¹] *trans.* To make a steer of, castrate (a calf).

1886 *Daily Tel.* 18 Oct. (Cassell), The male calves are steered and converted to beef.

steer, obs. and dial. var. STAIR, STIR.

steerable ('stɪərəb(ə)l), *a.* and *sb.* [f. STEER *v.*¹ + -ABLE.]

A. *adj.* That may be steered or guided, dirigible.

1836 L. HUNT in *New Monthly Mag.* XLVIII. 60 Balloons shall be equally safe and guidable, steerable against the wind. **1884** *Pall Mall Gaz.* 1 Oct. 7/2 A steerable balloon. **1899** *Westm. Gaz.* 30 May 10/2 A steerable torpedo.

B. *sb.* A dirigible balloon. *rare.*

1908 *Daily News* 25 Dec. 5 Between the German steerable, the 'Zeppelin,' and the French craft..there are some important differences.

Hence ˌsteeraˈbility.

1907 *Westm. Gaz.* 4 Dec. 10/1 'La Patrie', the French airship..gave a marvellous exhibition of its steerability.

steerage ('stɪərɪdʒ). Forms: 5–7 **sterage**, 6–7 **stirrage**, 7 **stearage**, **-idge**, (**styrage**, **stieridge**), 7–8 **steeridge**, (7 **-edge**, 8 **-adge**), 6– **steerage**. [f. STEER *v.*¹ + -AGE.]

1. The action, practice or method of steering a boat or ship; the guidance of a balloon or airship, *rarely* of a carriage.

c **1450** *Brut* II. 435 The foreseide barge, thorough mysgouernaunce of sterage, fill vpon the pilis. **1599** HAKLUYT *Voy.* I. 602 The English shippes vsing their prerogatiue of nimble stirrage..came often times very neere vpon the Spaniards. **1654** J. P. *Tyrants & Protectors* 33 These Pilots by their ill steerage did split their Vessels. **1719** DE FOE *Crusoe* I. (Globe) 193 Having a strong Steerage with my Paddle, I went at a great Rate, directly for the Wreck. **1791** SMEATON *Edystone L.* §93 The carriages..[having] a draught-tree for steerage and yoking the cattle to. **1805** LD. COLLINGWOOD in Nicolas *Disp. Nelson* (1846) VII. 242 Had we to pass them from the leeward, it would have been still more difficult, as it required nice steerage. **1914** *Q. Rev.* Apr. 346 He discussed the problems of the propulsion and the steerage of such a body [*sc.* a balloon].

b. *transf.* of an animal or person.

1599 T. M[OUFET] *Silkewormes* 73 When afterward..The Flies haue bor'd a passage through their clewes, Obserue their gate and steerage al along. **1774** *Ann. Reg., Misc.* 193/1 If I am not very accurate in my steerage, I am sure to tumble over a pail.

c. Phrase. (*to be, stand*) *at the steerage.* lit. and fig.

1688 *Lond. Gaz.* No. 2322/3 The Grand Signior went..in a Barge of 28 Oars,..the Bostangi Bachi..being..at the Steerage. **1731** SWIFT *On Death Swift* 413 While they who at the steerage stood, And reap'd the profit, sought his blood. **1733** —— *On Poetry* 456 You raise the honour of the peerage, Proud to attend you at the steerage.

d. Of a ship: The action, method or ability of answering to the helm.

1653 *Fight Legorn-Road* 16 Likewise was the Dutch Admiral singled out, and to the weatherward (which was occasioned by loss of her Stearidge, having her Rudder shot, as I heard). **1745** P. THOMAS *Jrnl. Anson's Voy.* 146 She.. roll'd very much, and made bad Steerage. **1769** FALCONER *Dict. Marine* (1776), *Steerage* is also used to express the effort of the helm; and hence Steerage-way is [etc.].

2. †**a.** Management (of goods). *Obs.*

1487 *Sc. Acts Parlt.* (1814) II. 178/2 Na man sale in the saidis partis in the way of merchandice bot..men haifand.. half a last of gudis or samekle in sterage and gouernance.

b. The direction or government of affairs, the State, one's life. (Often with conscious metaphor.)

1592 SHAKS. *Rom. & Jul.* I. iv. 112 But he that hath the stirrage of my course, Direct my sute [1597 Qo. saile]. **1636** E. DACRES tr. *Machiavel's Disc. Livy* Ep. Ded., Your Grace may doe well to inable your selfe for the service of your Prince and Country, that being cald for into the steerage in turbulent times, not favour onely may give you a place there. **1688** BP. THOMAS in Gutch *Coll. Cur.* I. 332, I pray God direct and prosper his steerage of the Church of England in these tempestuous times. **1783** COWPER *Let. J. Newton* 15 Dec., Wks. 1837 XV. 142 But now we float..as the wind drives us; for want of..that steerage which invention..may be expected to supply. **1808** SCOTT *Marmion* I. Introd. 116 [He] With dying hand the rudder held, Till, in his fall, with fateful sway, The steerage of the realm gave way! **1831** W. L. BOWLES *Life Bp. Ken* II. xi. 190 Under the firm steerage of Walpole..the vessel of state held its way through all the storms of faction.

c. A course held or steered, esp. a course of conduct.

?*a* **1625** WEBSTER & ROWLEY *Cure for Cuckold* IV. ii, He bore his steerage true in every part, Led by the Compass of a noble heart. **1645** MILTON *Tetrach.* 41 If we marke the steerage of his words, what course they hold. **1789** *Triumphs Fortitude* I. 45, I would wish always to keep a steerage, rather than to be carried away by the stream of dissipation. **1827** B'NESS BUNSEN in Hare *Life* I. viii. 296 There are no rocks, no shoals, for him whose steerage is ever regulated according to the true compass of the soul.

3. The steering apparatus **a.** of a boat.

1857 P. COLQUHOUN *Comp. Oarsman's Guide* 30 The term steerage includes yoke-lines, yoke, and rudder. **1869** R. H. BLAKE-HUMFREY *Eton Boating Bk.* (1875) 45 *note*, This year [1845]..Silver Oars and Steerage [were given] to the winners of the Pulling.

b. of an agricultural machine. In quot. *attrib.*

1884 *West Sussex Gaz.* 25 Sept., Capital front-steerage 13-coulter seed and corn drill,..steerage horse hoe.

c. *steerage of his wings*: Dryden's rendering of L. *remigium alarum*, meaning wings viewed as instruments of rowing.

1697 DRYDEN *Æneis* VI. 24 Dedalus..here alighting, built this costly Frame. Inscrib'd to Phœbus, here he hung on high The steerage of his Wings. **1700** —— *Ceyx & Alcyone*

351. **1870** JEAN INGELOW *Four Sonnets* iv, When.. Down the steep slope of a long sunbeam brought, He[*i.e.* the eagle] stirs the wheat with the steerage of his wings.

4. That division of the after part of a ship which is immediately in front of the chief cabin; the second cabin. Also called † ***steerage room***.

In the 16th and 17th c. this was the place from which the ship was steered. Early in the 18th c. the wheel was placed on the open deck, so that the vessel was no longer steered from the 'steerage', which, however, retained its name.

1612 COVERTE *Voy.* 24 The Merchants had some 10000 l. lying betweene the maine Maste and the Stearidge. **1627** CAPT. SMITH *Sea Gram.* ii. 11 The Stearage. The Stearage roome, is before the great Cabin, where he that steareth the Ship doth alwaies stand. **1644** MANWAYRING *Seamans Dict.*, The Stieridge is the place where they Steere, out of which they may see the leech of the sailes. **1726** SHELVOCKE *Voy. round World* 25 This insolence being carried on in the steeradge. **1769** FALCONER *Dict. Marine* (1780), *Steerage*, an apartment without the great cabin of a ship, from which it is separated by a thin partition. In large ships of war it is used as a hall through which it is necessary to pass, to arrive at, or depart from the great cabin. In merchant-ships it is generally the habitation of the inferior officers and ship's crew. **1834** MARRYAT *P. Simple* xvi, I went down into the most solitary place in the steerage, that I might enjoy it [a letter] without interruption. **1840** R. H. DANA *Bef. Mast* xxiii. 71 The mate came down into the steerage, in fine trim for fun. **1864** SEMMES *Cruise Alabama & Sumter* I. 269 Passing through the ward-room, the visitor entered the gun-room, or 'steerage', allotted on the starboard side to the midshipmen, and on the port to the engineers. **1867** SMYTH *Sailor's Word-bk.*, *Steerage*,.. that part of the ship next below the quarter-deck, immediately before the bulkhead of the great cabin in most ships of war. The portion of the 'tween-decks just before the gun-room bulkhead.

5. The part of a passenger ship allotted to those passengers who travel at the cheapest rate. Also quasi-advb. in *to go, travel steerage*.

The steerage is now usually in the bow and on a lower deck.

1804 W. IRVING *Life & Lett.* (1864) I. 94 They sleep in the steerage, and leave the cabin to myself. **1816** R. BUCHANAN *Propelling Vessels by Steam* 24 Before the engine is the steerage or second cabin. **1822** J. FLINT *Lett. fr. America* 287 There were twelve cabin passengers.. and about an equal number of persons in the steerage. **1844** DICKENS *Mart. Chuz.* xvii, It being necessary for me to observe strict economy, I took my passage in the steerage. **1892** E. REEVES *Homeward Bound* 124 In the steerage we are told the thermometer reaches 109° in the shade. In our saloon 90° to 100° is the highest. **1906** *Westm. Gaz.* 20 June 4/2 He travelled steerage with a ship of emigrants.

6. *attrib.* and *Comb.*, as ***steerage door, -hole, -house, passage, -power***; **steerage country** *U.S.*, the open space in the middle of the steerage of a man-of-war, not occupied by berths or state-rooms (*Cent. Dict.*); **steerage mess, steerage officer** *U.S.* (see quots.); **steerage-passenger**, one who occupies a berth in the steerage (sense 5) of a passenger-vessel; † **steerage room** = sense 4; **steerage-way**, a way or motion sufficient for the helm to have effect; also *fig.*

a **1625** N. ROBERTS in Purchas *Pilgrims* II. 1578 Putting his foot against the *Steeredge doore. **1855** BROWNING *Bp. Blougram's Apol.* 357 Though you proved me doomed To a viler berth still, to the *steerage-hole. **1842** DICKENS *Amer. Notes* xi. (1850) 108/2 There is no visible deck, even: nothing but a long, black, ugly roof..; above which tower two iron chimneys.. and a glass *steerage-house. **1891** H. PATTERSON *Naut. Dict.* 364 **Steerage Mess.* This mess is composed of midshipmen, ensigns, clerks and mates. *Ibid.* 386 **Steerage Officers*, midshipmen, cadet midshipmen, mates, cadet engineers, and ensigns when they do not perform duty as regular watch officers. **1849** LEVER *Con Cregan* xix. I. 298, I took a *steerage passage. **1822** J. FLINT *Lett. fr. America* 91 A *steerage passenger pays only about half the freight that is charged for a passage in the cabin of a ship. **1840** HOOD *Up the Rhine* 50 The deck of a steamer is supposed to be divided amidships by an imaginary line, aft of which the steerage passengers are expected not to intrude. **1869** *Chamb. Jrnl.* 29 May 338/1 By making the paddle-wheels revolve in opposite directions.. perfect *steerage-power is obtained. **1626** CAPT. SMITH *Accid. Yng. Seamen* 11 In the *stearage roome, the whip, the bittakell, the trauas boord, the Compasse. **1769** FALCONER *Dict. Marine* (1780) Z 3 b, A.. ship.. in a very light wind, and scarcely having *steerage-way. **1868** LOWELL *Among my Bks.* Ser. I. *Shaks. once more* (1870) 211 Hamlet.. never keeps on one tack long enough to get steerage-way.

steere-board, -boord, obs. ff. STARBOARD.

steerer ('stɪərə(r)). Also 4 styrer, 5 sterer, 6 stirrer, 7 stearer. [f. STEER *v.*[1] + -ER[1].]

† **1. a.** A rudder. *Obs.*

1398 TREVISA *Barth. De P.R.* XII. xi. (1535) 169/2 And in swymmynge he [the swan] vseth that one fote in stede of an oore, and the other in stede of a styrer [*pro gubernaculo*], and ruleth hym selfe therwith. **1633** DRUMM. OF HAWTH. *Entert. K. Chas.* Sp. Caledonia i. 58 Being to themselves Oares, Steerers, ship and all.

b. 'A machine for controlling the rudder of a boat or yacht' (*Cent. Dict.* Suppl. 1909).

c. (See quot.)

1895 HEADLEY *Struct. Birds* vi. 153 The large tail feathers are called rectrices or steerers.

2. One who steers, a steersman; a coxswain (of a rowing boat).

1585 HIGINS *Junius' Nomencl.* 515/1 *Gubernator*,.. the gouernor, director, or pilot of the ship: the sterneman or stirrer. **1675** HOBBES *Odyss.* (1677) 153 A sudden blast.. breaks the cordage that upheld the mast; Which falling down beats out the steerers brains. **1868** *Field* 28 Nov. 445/2 Though repeatedly urged by his steerer, he [the oarsman] seemed quite unable to quicken. **1887** J. THOMSON in J. B. Thomson *Mem.* ix. (1896) 198 But when contrary or violent winds rise then the steerer is helpless.

fig. **1659** PEARSON *Creed* i. 36 Thus appears the Maker to be the steerer of this great ship [the world]. **1730** SWIFT *Ep. Ld. Carteret* 59 There's not a better Steerer in the Realm, I hope, my Lord, you'll call him to the Helm.

3. *U.S. slang.* A swindler whose business it is to lead his victims to the rendezvous. Also, see quot. 1910.

1873 'J. MORRIS' *Wanderings of Vagabond* xix. 210 Let us now take a peep into the brace room, while the steerer and his victim are on their way to it. **1883** [cf. *bunko-steerers* s.v. BUNCO]. **1889** *Columbus* (Ohio) *Dispatch* 6 Sept., The [gambling-] place was full of players, who got there by means of 'steerers' sent out for the purpose. **1905** *Blackw. Mag.* Jan. 137/1 'Steerers' and 'boosters' [of gambling-hells] were always on the look-out for 'suckers' whom they encountered at the railway-stations, at the hotels, or even in the streets. **1910** *N.Y. Evening Post* 10 Jan. (Thornton *Amer. Gloss.*), A steerer is the go-between of the shyster and prisoner; by wile and guile he brings clients to the lawyer.

4. That directs its course: **a.** of a ship with adj. referring to its power of answering to the helm or rudder.

1887 *Times* (weekly ed.) 19 Aug. 4/1 The ship is a bad steerer and her speed is not very great. **1901** *Daily Tel.* 18 Mar. 7/4 Dr. Warre's model [of a rowing boat].. is also a very quick steerer, for her rudder is not 7 inches long.

b. of a cycle, with prefix indicating the position of its steering-wheel.

1882 *Wheel World* Mar. 185 [Tricycles.] Two rear-steerers... A front-steerer. **1888** *Encycl. Brit.* XXIII. 559/2.

steering ('stɪərɪŋ), *vbl. sb.* [f. STEER *v.*[1] + -ING[1].]

1. a. The action of the verb, in various senses.

c **1220** *Bestiary* 574 Sipmen here steringe forgeten for hire [the siren's] stefninge. **1375** BARBOUR *Bruce* IX. 510 Thai twa the land had in stering. **1387-8** T. USK *Test. Love* II. iii. (Skeat) 107 Shal fyr ben blamed for it brende a foole naturelly, by his own stulty witte in steringe? **1599** SANDYS *Europæ Spec.* (1632) 89 The persons defiled with it [were] of so eminent a place in the steering and upholding of their church. **1769** FALCONER *Dict. Marine* (1780) s.v., The perfection of steering consists in a vigilant attention to the motion of the ship's head. **1855** MACAULAY *Hist. Eng.* xxi. IV. 641 But now came a crisis which required the most skilful steering. **1875** *Encycl. Brit.* III. 665/1 Steering.. is managed by a transverse handle attached to the driving-wheel [of a bicycle]. **1911** *Daily Mail* 19 June 8/4 Major Wodehouse.. has been.. devising means for the safe steering of the tremendous crowds.

b. *Meteorol.* The process by which pressure systems, precipitation belts, etc., are moved by temperature gradients or winds.

1919, etc. [see *steering line*, sense 3 b below]. **1944** HEWSON & LONGLEY *Meteorol. Theoret. & Appl.* xxiv. 428 The changes in pressure at the earth's surface are controlled by atmospheric movements at levels of 4 km and higher, the process whereby this occurs being known as 'steering'. **1956** S. PETTERSSEN *Weather Analysis & Forecasting* (ed. 2) I. xiii. 277 From the point of view of theory it is difficult to make any distinction between the steering and the blocking of the movement of sea-level cyclones. **1959** R. E. HUSCHKE *Gloss. Meteorol.* (Amer. Meterol. Soc.) 541 *Steering*, in meteorology, loosely used for any influence upon the direction of movement of an atmospheric disturbance exerted by another aspect of the state of the atmosphere.

c. *Electronics.* The switching of pulses from one part of a circuit to another.

1956, etc. [see *steering circuit, diode*, sense 3 a below]. **1962** SIMPSON & RICHARDS *Physical Princ. Junction Transistors* xvi. 410 In many bistable circuits,.. trigger pulses of opposite polarity must be used alternately.. or pulses of one polarity must alternately be switched from one collector or base to another. The latter process, which is usually performed by diodes or auxiliary transistors, is called steering. **1969** J. J. SPARKES *Transistor Switching* v. 122 Two quite distinct methods of controlling the penetration of pulses to the transistor are available, namely pulse steering by applying logic voltages to S_A or R_A, or pulse gating via additional diodes at the pulse inputs.

2. Short for *steering-gear*.

1877 H. H. GRIFFIN *Bicycles of the Year* 12 He makes the Eureka, which is a very fair machine (Spider), Stanley steering, cone bearings, &c. *Ibid.* 16 The steering is either the Stanley or Rudder plan. **1970** K. BALL *Fiat 600, 600D Autobook* ix. 103/2 The first step in dismantling the steering is to remove the steering wheel. **1977** *Western Morning News* 30 Aug. 8/2 (Advt.), Austin 2200. Blue. Power-assisted steering.

3. *attrib.* and *Comb.*: **a.** simple attrib., as ***steering-apparatus, -fan, -fork, -gear, -handle***; (sense 1 a) ***steering-bridge***; (sense 1 b) ***steering principle***; (sense 1 c) ***steering circuit, diode***; (sense 2) ***steering angle, arm, axle, circle, knuckle, lever, linkage, rod***.

1936 *Proc. Inst. Automobile Engineers* XXX. 757 The angle of the front wheels or '*steering angle' is particularly important. **1846** A. YOUNG *Naut. Dict.* 319 A *Steering Apparatus.. consists of an endless screw [etc.]. **1902** A. C. HARMSWORTH et. al. *Motors & Motor-Driving* 216 With a broken *steering arm.. a car.. may be hurled into a ditch. **1978** D. CLARKE *Car* 84/1 All but the last type of box require a system of linkages to take the movement created by the drop arm.. to the steering arms on the wheels. **1912** *Motor Man.* 87 Details of *steering axle with steering arms and connecting bar. **1902** *Chamber's Jrnl.* Oct. 739/1 He left the bridge, roused all hands, and arraigned them on the *steering-bridge. **1912** *Motor Man.* 88 Whichever wheel is on the inside of the steering circle turns through a wider angle than the outer wheel does. **1970** K. BALL *Fiat 600, 600D Autobook* ix. 108/2 The *steering circle diameter on the Multipla is 28 feet 10 inches. **1956** L. P. HUNTER *Handbk. Semiconductor Electronics* xv. 23 In order to operate the trigger in a binary fashion, it is necessary to provide *steering circuits. **1971** J. H. SMITH *Digital Logic* iv. 58 Steering circuits.. control the operation of the gates. **1957** R. F. SHEA *Circuit Engin.* x. 337 (*caption*) Bistable multi-vibrator with *steering diodes for high-speed triggering. **1962** SIMPSON & RICHARDS *Physical Princ. Junction Transistors* xvi. 410 Steering diodes may be used in a similar way at other electrodes and for other circuits than the simple bistable one. **1903** *Westm. Gaz.* 2 Nov. 9/1 There is a propeller in front and a *steering-fan in the rear [of an airship]. **1869** *Routledge's Ev. Boy's Ann.* 375 The vertical *steering-fork of the vehicle [*i.e.* a bicycle]. **1869** SIR E. REED *Iron-Clad Ships* i. 6 The rudder-head and *steering-gear were exposed to shot within thin iron sides. **1907** H. WYNDHAM *Flare of Footlights* ii, The chauffeur.. fumbling stupidly with the steering-gear. **1868** *Routledge's Ev. Boy's Ann.* 477 The *Steering-Handle [of a bicycle] may be made of any fancy curve. **1906** *Westm. Gaz.* 20 July 8/3 In the collision.. the stout steering-handle [of a motor car] being bent nearly double. **1904** *Sci. Amer. Suppl.* 27 Aug. 23953/2 The front axle is provided with ball-bearing *steering knuckles. **1970** K. BALL *Fiat 600, 600D Autobook* viii. 98/2 Remove the upper end shaft retaining nut from the steering knuckle and the two washers. **1866** *Eng. Mech.* 6 Apr. 33/1 Velocipede. SL is the *steering lever. **1915** *Autocar Handbk.* (ed. 6) xv. 219 This steering lever is mounted upon a short spindle or shaft which is carried in bearings in the steering gear box. **1970** K. BALL *Fiat 600, 600D Autobook* viii. 97/2 The *steering linkage also differs from that on the Sedan. **1945** F. A. BERRY et. al. *Handbk. Meteorol.* x. 818 Guiding of surface systems by the upper-level flow has been referred to as the *steering principle. **1963** *Meteorol. Gloss.* (Met. Office) (ed. 4) 254 Application of the steering principle is most successful in the type of situation.. in which almost straight thickness lines intersect a well marked pattern of surface vorticity. **1909** R. W. A. BREWER *Motor Car* xv. 148 The transverse arm on the off side is connected to the *steering rod, generally by means of a knuckle joint. **1977** 'J. GASH' *Judas Pair* ix. 106 She twisted something near the steering-rod. The engine muted instantly into a deep, steady thrum.

b. Special comb: **steering box**, a housing attached to the body of a motor vehicle that encloses the end of the steering column and the gearing that transmits its motion to the next members; **steering column**, a columnar assembly in a motor vehicle or motor bicycle carrying at its top the steering wheel or handle-bars and transmitting their motion to the rest of the steering gear; **steering compass**, the compass by which a ship is steered as distinguished from the variation compass (see COMPASS *sb.*[1] 12 d); **steering line** *Meteorol.* (see quot. 1959); **steering lock**, (*a*) the turning movement of the wheels of a motor-vehicle (see LOCK *sb.*[2] 15); (*b*) an appliance fitted to some bicycles by means of which the front wheel may be prevented from turning from side to side; also, a similar mechanism fitted to the steering assembly of a motor vehicle, as an anti-theft device; **steering-oar**, an oar used as a steering-scull (q.v.); † **steering pillar** = *steering column* above (*obs.*); **steering post** = prec.; on early motor vehicles (see also quot. 1904); **steering sail** *Naut.* = STUDDING SAIL; also *attrib.*; † **steering scull** = SCULL *sb.*[1] 1 a; **steering wheel**, (*a*) *Naut.*, a vertical wheel by which motion is communicated to the rudder through the medium of a tiller-rope or other device; (*b*) a hand-wheel for guiding a traction engine, motor-car or other heavy vehicle; (*c*) the wheel of a cycle by which steerage is effected; also, a road wheel of a motor vehicle by which steerage is effected.

1913 W. E. DOMMETT *Motor Car Mechanism* xiii. 118 The method of mounting the *steering box and column is clearly shown. **1970** K. BALL *Fiat 600, 600D Autobook* ix. 103/1 The linkage between the steering box and wheels is via a pair of symmetrical track rods and a central link rod connecting the pitman arm to a relay level. **1903** *Motor* 27 May 348/1 The *steering column of the motor-bicycle is.. a vitally important part. **1931** D. L. SAYERS *Five Red Herrings* xxiii. 262, I was jammed up behind the steering-column. **1976** *Derbyshire Times* (Peak ed.) 3 Sept. 20/5 The single steering column stalk that operates lights, wipers, washers and flasher has too much to do. **1669** STURMY *Mariner's Mag.* II. vi. 67 To shew you the difference between the true Compass and the *Steering Compass. **1919** J. BJERKNES in *Geofysiske Publ.* I. II. 1 As the line thus gives the momentaneous direction of the cyclone, it may, for practical purposes, be called the *steering line. **1923** N. SHAW *Forecasting Weather* v. 155 The dividing line of the cyclone from the centre towards the eastern or advancing side is called the steering line or more recently, warm front. **1959** R. E. HUSCHKE *Gloss. Meteorol.* (Amer. Meteorol. Soc.) 541 *Steering line*, according to Bjerknes' cyclone model, the line of convergence (corresponding to the warm front of a wave cyclone) which tends to be parallel to the direction of motion of the cyclone at the line's point of juncture with the cyclone center. **1897** *Encycl. Sport* I. 274/1 (Cycling), *Steering Locks are valuable.. for preventing the machine from moving when resting against a wall. **1955** *Times* 10 May 7/6 The greatest asset in this connexion.. is the admirable steering lock, with which the car can be turned in 37ft. and can be driven into small parking spaces. **1960** O. GREGORY tr. *Spoerl's Living with Car* 212 Various devices.., some of which lock ignition and steering simultaneously... These locks are by no means impossible for a thief to cope with. However, if he has to choose between a car with one of the steering locks and one without he is likely to choose the one without. **1971** A. PRICE *Alamut Ambush* ix. 104 The new Triumph has a steering lock—it would be a verra difficult car to move. **1816** H. KER *Travels* 30 In endeavouring to run the outside of a sawyer, I ran with my stem athwart it, and unshipped my *steering oar, which I lost. **1840** R. H. Dana *Bef. Mast* ix, The officer using his utmost strength, with his steering-oar, to keep her stern on. **1938** B. L. Burman *Blow for Landing* 298 The black lifted the steering oar... The rafts began to speed down the water. **1904** A. C. Harmsworth et. al. *Motors & Motor-Driving* 218 Looseness between steering wheel and end of *steering pillar can be found at any time. **1921** W. H. Berry *Mod. Motor Car Practice* xvi. 324 A long chassis with a large engine involves a steering pillar of considerable length. **1904** A. B. F. Young *Compl. Motorist* iv. 118 The *steering post, being situated in the middle of the car, and the steering tiller available on either side, it is possible for the driver to sit either on the right-hand or left-hand side of the car. **1969** J. Gores in *Ellery Queen's Mystery Mag.* Dec. 145/2 He was impaled on the steering post. **1669** Sturmy *Mariner's Mag.* I. ii. 16 The Lee *steering Sails of Main-sail, and Main-top sail. **1805** in Nicolas *Disp. Nelson* (1846) VII. 144 *note*, Wore Ship and made Sail—set the royal and top-gallant steering-sails. **1420** in *For. Acc. 3 Hen. VI*, F/2, j. Remus grossus vocatus *Sterynge skulle. **1750** Blanckley *Naval Expos.* 160 To guide or govern a Ship by the Helm or *Steering Wheel. **1888** *Encycl. Brit.* XXIII. 559/2 In early days the steering wheel [of the tricycle] was made small to save weight. **1902** A. C. Harmsworth et. al. *Motors & Motor-Driving* 217 The free or direct gear moves with the impulse or pressure brought against the steering wheels or one of them by any ruts or obstructions on the road. **1907** R. W. Whitman *Motor-Car Princ.* x. 159 The irreversible type is used for all but the lightest cars, and..it prevents any movement from being transmitted from the wheels to the steering wheel or lever. **1912** *Motor Man.* 231 A weakened [tyre] cover will, as a general rule, give a considerable period of further service mounted on a steering wheel. **1915** *Autocar Handbk.* (ed. 6) xv. 220 It is very important..that the steering road wheels should be easily movable by means of the hand steering wheel... If a car is travelling on a much-rutted road the steering wheels tend to fall into the ruts. **1970** K. Ball *Fiat 600, 600D Autobook* ix. 103/2 Pry off the horn button from the steering wheel with a screwdriver.

steering ('stɪərɪŋ), *ppl. a.* [f. steer *v.*[1] + -ing[2].] ***steering committee.*** (orig. *U.S.*): a committee set up to determine the order of business for another body, or to manage the general course of an operation. Also ***steering group, sub-committee.***

1887 *Courier-Jrnl.* (Louisville, Kentucky) 6 Feb. 2/2 A steering committee upon the order of business for the remainder of the session was appointed. **1918** H. W. Dodds *Procedure in State Legislatures* iv. 56 Just as the power of standing committees developed when the number of bills introduced had become too large for consideration by the whole house, so the steering committee emerged when measures approved by the standing committees increased until a further selective agency became an irresistible temptation. **1955** *Times* 19 July 6/4 The steering committee making arrangements for the conference of Ministers on further European integration met to-day in Brussels. **1966** N. Johnson *Parliament & Administration* i. 22 The Chairman of the Estimates Committees presides over sub-committee A (now called the Steering sub-committee). **1974** 'E. Lathen' *Sweet & Low* ii. 20 Only three people are really important..the members of the steering committee. **1977** *Wandsworth Borough News* 7 Oct. 14/5 The Steering Group officially recognised by the Council's Recreation Committee at that meeting has met regularly and has discussed such matters as management, development, and use of the building. **1979** 'D. Meiring' *Foreign Body* v. 57 We have all read the Steering Committee's exhaustive report.

steering, Sc. variant of stirring.

†'**steerish**, *a. Obs.* [f. steer *sb.*[1] + -ish[1].]

1. Having the qualities of a steer; brutish.

c **1411** Hoccleve *De Reg. Princ.* 604 The cause why men oghten þider gon, Nat conceyue can his wylde steerissh heed.

2. *dial.* (See quots.)

1789 W. H. Marshall *Glouc.* I. 332 *Steerish*: spoken of a young, raw, growing ox; not 'oxey'. **1851** *Glouc. Gloss.*, *Steerish*, young.

†'**steerless**, *a. Obs.* [OE. *stéorléas*: see steer *sb.*[2] and -less.]

1. Not amenable to guidance or control, ungovernable, unrestrained.

c **888** Ælfred *Boeth.* v. §3 þa ðu wendest ðætte stiorlease men & recelease wæren ȝesælie & wealdendas þisse worulde. *c* **1175** *Lamb. Hom.* 117 Gif þu uuel were iwend þe from uuele þi les þe ðu steorles losie on ende.

2. Without a rudder. *lit.* and *fig.*

c **1374** Chaucer *Troylus* I. 416 Al sterles with-Inne a bot am I. *c* **1386** —— *Man of Law's T.* 341 In a ship all steerelees. **1423** Jas. I *Kingis Q.* 15 As the schip that sailith stereles Vpon the rok(kis) most to harmes hye. *a* **1547** Surrey *Eccles.* iii. 1 Like to the steereles boote that swerues with euery wynde. *a* **1565** in *Q. Eliz. Boeth.* App. 156 We men, with Fortunes waves are tosste and cast In steerles Shipp. *a* **1639** T. Carew *Answ. Eleg. Lett.* 62 A troope of deities came down to guide Our steerelesse barkes.

steerling ('stɪəlɪŋ). [f. steer *sb.*[1] + -ling.] A young steer.

1648 Herrick *Hesper., Beucolick* (1915) 244 To get thy Steerling once again, I'le play thee such another strain; That [etc.]. **1743** Francis *Horace, Odes* iv. ii. 54 While I, with pious Care, one Steerling feed.

steerling, obs. form of starling *sb.*[2]

steerman ('stɪəmən). Now *rare.* Forms: 1–2 **stéorman, 3 steoreman, 5 ster man, stereman, 6** *Sc.* **steirman, 7 steereman, 7– steerman.** [f. steer *sb.*[2] + man *sb.* Cf. Du. *stuurman*, MLG. *stûreman*, MHG. *stiurman* (mod.G. *steuermann*), ON. *stýrimað-r*, (Sw. *styrman*, Da. *styrmand*). The Teut. word was adopted in OF. as *esturman*, *estrumant*.] A steersman.

c **1000** Ælfric *Hom.* II. 560 Hera ðone steorman ac na swa-ðeah ærðan ðe he become ȝesundful to þære hyðe. *c* **1205** Lay. 28436 And nom alle þa scipen..and þa steormen alle to þan scipen neodde. *c* **1470** Henry *Wallace* ix. 121 Bathe schip maistir, and the ster man also, In the holl, but baid, he gert thaim go. **1586** *Reg. Privy Council Scot.* IV. 79 The foirsaidis personis furnissand steirmen thairto thameselffis. **1663** Gerbier *Counsel* d4b, My Steerman found the Ebb and Flood all along the Coast of America. **1725** Pope *Odyss.* xiv. 287 Safe through the level seas we sweep our way; The steer-man governs, and the ships obey. **1892** Stevenson & L. Osborne *Wrecker* xii, Suppose the steerman's eye to have wandered.

fig. *c* **1460** *Towneley Myst.* iii. 427 Help, god, in this nede! As thou art stere-man..best, as I rede. **1591** Sylvester *Du Bartas* I. i. 117 Their Star the Bible, Steer-man th' holy Ghost. **1638** Sir T. Herbert *Trav.* (ed. 2) 206 No sooner was old Abbas by bold death struck from the helme of Persia; and young Soffy his Grand-sonne made the royall Stear-man, but [etc.].

†'**steermost**, *a. Obs. rare*[−1]. [f. steer *sb.*[2] + -most.] Sternmost, rearmost.

1667 *Lond. Gaz.* No. 160/4 The Vice Admiral being steermost of the squadron,..intended then to cross the Hause.

steerne, obs. form of stern *a.*

steersman ('stɪəzmən). Forms: 1 **stéoresman,** 2, 4 **stieresman(n,** 3 **steores-man, -mon,** (*Ormin* **steoressmann**), 3–5 **steresman,** 4–6 **sterisman,** 5–6 **sterysman(n,** (5 **stersman,** 6 **stirsman**), 6–7 **stear(e)sman,** 7 **steeresman,** 6– **steersman.** [OE. *stéoresman*, f. *stéores-* genit. of *stéor* steer *sb.*[2] + man *sb.* Cf. steerman.

The word was early adopted into Irish in the form *stiursuman*; an example occurs in *3 Fragm. Irish Annals* 116 (early 11th c.).]

1. a. One who steers a boat or ship; one who sits at the stern of a canoe and steers (*N. Amer.*).

c **1000** *Ags. Laws, Ethelred* §4 in *Liebermann* (1898) I. 222/1 Ðyf man beo æt his æhtan bereafod, & he wite of hwilcum scipe, aȝyfe steoresman ða æhta. *a* **1200** *Vices & Virtues* 43 Ðe gastliche hierdes..folȝið Noe ðane gode stieresmann. *c* **1200** Ormin 2135 Forr all swa summ þe steoressmann Aȝȝ lokeþþ till an steorrne. *c* **1330** R. Brunne *Chron. Wace* (Rolls) 13092 Namore þan schip or barge can [keep its course], þere hym wanteþ a steres man. *c* **1450** *St. Cuthbert* (Surtees) 4728 þe sterys man toke þe helme in hande. **1577** Bullinger *Decades* (1592) 638 As a boate destitute of a stirsman, is with contrarie windes tossed to and fro. **1667** Milton *P.L.* ix. 513 As when a Ship by skilful Stearsman wrought.., where the Wind Veres oft, as oft so steers, and shifts her Saile. **1774** Hearne & Turnor *Jrnls.* (1934) 122 The Pataroon or Steersman of each Cannoe has 50£ pr annom. **1791** W. Bartram *Trav.* 108 The steersman paddles softly, and proceeds slowly along shore. **1801** [see middleman 5 c]. **1889** Welch *Text Bk. Naval Archit.* xiii. 140 The steersman moves his wheel in the required direction. **1897** E. Coues *New Light Early Hist. Greater Northwest* I. 29 The steersman, finding himself within reach of the shore, jumped upon the rock with one of the midmen. **1968** [see bowsman].

b. *fig.*

a **1200** *Vices & Virtues* 43 Swa scule ða gastliche stieresmenn steren ða arche of ðe hali cherche. *c* **1440** *Towneley Myst.* xix. 259 Farwell! stersman to theym that ar sted In stormes, or in desese lyse! **1579** W. Wilkinson *Confut. Fam. Love* 40 From them [the Vniuersityes] come the most skilfull stearesmen to gouerne, both the state ecclesiasticall, and ciuill. **1650** H. Brooke *Conserv. Health* 221 Their Steersman is Reason. **1809–10** Coleridge *Friend* (1865) 48 The great merit of Buonaparte has been that of a skilful steersman. *a* **1894** Stevenson in G. Balfour *Life* vi. (1911) 74 There stood at the wheel that unknown steersman whom we call God.

c. *transf.* One who drives and guides a machine.

1828 Sir H. Steuart *Planter's Guide* (ed. 2) 250 The Machiner seizes the end of the pole-rope, in order to act as Steersman [of a machine for transplanting trees]. **1906** *Westm. Gaz.* 26 June 5/1 The Hotchkiss..overturned at Saint Calais, but fortunately without injury to the steersman [in a motor-car race].

†**2.** A ruler or governor (of a certain number of people). *Obs. rare.*

c **1250** *Gen. & Ex.* 3417 Ilc of ðe .v. steres-men Vnder hem welden in stere tgen. *Ibid.* 3429.

Hence '**steersmanship**.

1818 Bentham *Ch. Eng.* Introd. 187 It is truly edifying to observe the steersmanship displayed by the Reverend Secretary in his passage through these straits. **1840** J. W. Bowden *Gregory VII*, II. 43 We feel ourselves unable to save, by any steersmanship, the church, which seems almost foundering before our eyes.

†'**steersmate.** *Obs. rare.* [f. *steers-* in steersman + mate *sb.*] A steersman.

a **1575** Gascoigne *Posies* (1907) 356 Aloofe, aloofe, then cried the Maister out, The Stearesmate strives to sende us from the shore. **1671** Milton *Samson* 1045 What Pilot so expert but needs must wreck Embarq'd with such a Stearsmate at the Helm?

'**steerswoman.** *rare.* [Formed as steersman + woman *sb.*] A woman who steers.

1815 W. H. Ireland *Scribbleomania* 148 As females can manage their lords in this realm, I shall station, as steerswoman, famous Ma'am Helme. **1884** May Crommelin *Brown-Eyes* v. 55 None for her age was so quick and brave a steerswoman.

'**steery, 'steerie,** *sb.* and *a. Sc.* [f. *steer*, Sc. form of stir *sb.* + -y.]

A. *sb.* A commotion, disturbance, stir.

a **1776** *Herd's Sc. Songs* II. 217 But when the bedding came at e'en Wow, but the house was in a steery. **1816** Scott *Antiq.* ix, Indeed, brother, amang a' the steery, Maria..set away to the Halket-craig-head.

B. *adj.* Busy, full of bustle and stir.

1866 J. Smith *Merry Bridal* 190 See ye the toun, a' sae steery an' thrang?

steeve (stiːv), *sb.*[1] *Naut.* Also 8–9 **stive,** 9 **steve.** [f. steeve *v.*[1]] (See quot. 1852.)

1794 *Rigging & Seamanship* I. 31 The stive of the bowsprit. **1809** *Naval Chron.* XXI. 27 The bowsprit..has not so much stove [*read* steve] as is usual. **1846** A. Young *Naut. Dict.* 320 The Steeve is the angle which it makes with the horizon. **1852** J. Fincham *Ship Building* iv. (ed. 3) 110 *Stive*, the angle upwards that any timber, &c. makes with the horizon, or its elevation above a horizontal line, as the stive of the cathead, bowsprit, &c. **1888** W. C. Russell *Death Ship* I. xi. 124 Look hard, and you'll mark the steeve of her bowsprit. **1901** *Munsey's Mag.* XXIV. 461/1 A gradual diminution of the steve of the bowsprit.

steeve (stiːv), *sb.*[2] *U.S. Naut.* [? f. steeve *v.*[2] But cf. Sp. *esteba* of the same meaning.] A long derrick or spar, with a block at one end, used in stowing cargo. (*Cent. Dict.*)

1840 R. H. Dana *Bef. Mast* xxix, Two long, sharp spars, called steeves..were placed with their wedge ends into the inside of the hide.

steeve (stiːv), *a.* and *adv.* Now *Sc.* and *dial.* Forms: 4 **stef** (inflected and as adv. **steve**), 6, 9 **steve,** 6 **steif,** 7 **steave,** 8–9 **sti(e)ve,** 9 **steive,** 8– **steeve.** [ME. *stef* (inflected *steve*), of uncertain etymology; connexion with the synonymous stiff *a.* is doubtful. Cf. Du. and LG. *stevig* of the same meaning; by some referred to the root of staff *sb.*[1]] **a.** *adj.* Firm, unyielding, strong, †rigid, stiff (as in death). **b.** *adv.* Firmly, unyieldingly.

c **1300** *Leg. Gregory* (Schulz) 574 Gregorij was feir of teyle, Strong and stef in eueri liþ. *a* **1320** *Sir Tristr.* 3079 Bifore was stef on stede Tristrem and ganhardine. **1330** *Otuel* 447 þei riden to-gedere wiþ speres kene, þat were steue & nouȝt longe. *c* **1330** *Arth. & Merl.* 7116 He to grounde plat þere, Al so he stef & stan-ded were. **13..** *Guy Warw.* 438 Loue me doþ to grounde falle, þat y ne may stond stef wiþ alle. *c* **1350** *Will. Palerne* 2894 Was non so stef him wiþ-stod so sternli he wrouȝt. *Ibid.* 3600 He dede þen his stef stede stert a god spede. *c* **1375** Wyclif *Sel. Wks.* I. 286 Bodi of Crist þat was stable and stef in al his temptaciouns. **1382** —— *Deut.* ix. 14 Y shal set thee vpon folk that is more and strenger [*v.r.* steuere; Vulg. *fortior*] than this. *Ibid., Jer.* xxxi. 9 Y shal lede them bi stef stremes of watris [Vulg. *per torrentes aquarum*]. **1581** *Sat. Poems Reform.* xliv. 177 Vnder the schaddou lat Louson fut it steue, Scurgar of Christ, quhilk is ane odius thing. **1594** A. Hume *Hymnes* ii. 113 The earth, quhilk of it selfe, is stable, firme, and steif. **1637** Ld. Wariston *Diary* (S.H.S.) 251 The roots of my haire..stood al steave. *a* **1774** R. Fergusson *Hallowfair* xiii. Wks. (1805) 141 It's gude, as lang's a canny chiel' Can staun steeve in his shoon. **1786** Burns *To Auld Mare* iii, A filly buirdly, steeve an' swank. *a* **1801** H. Macneill *To C.L.* Poet. Wks. II. 46 Wi' crack—and joke—and steeve rum toddy. **1819** Tennant *Papistry Storm'd* (1827) 119 Doth by this mou' o' mine defy The steevest o' your host. **1829** Brockett *N.C. Gloss.* (ed. 2), *Stive*, strong, muscular. **1870** J. Nicholson *Idylls* 114 We're a' grown steeve abstainers noo.

Hence †'**stefhede** [see -head], firmness; †'**stefnes** [see -ness], rigidity.

1340 *Ayenb.* 263 Bote yef þe ilke uaderes stefhede hise strayny and ordayny. *c* **1530** *Judic. Urines* II. xii. 41 Grete swellyng & betyng & stefnes at yᵉ breste.

steeve (stiːv), *v.*[1] *Naut.* Also 7 **steve,** 8 **steave, stive,** 9 **stave.** [Of obscure origin.

Usually explained as f. steeve *a.*, on the ground that a tilted bowsprit is 'steeve' or incapable of motion; but this seems unlikely. A connexion with OF. *estive* ploughtail (:—L. *stiva*) would not be improbable with regard to the sense.]

intr. Of a bowsprit, etc.: To incline upwards at an angle instead of lying horizontally. Also *trans.* to set (a bowsprit) at a certain upward inclination.

1644 Manwayring *Seamans Dict.* 102 To *Steve* or *Steving.* Wee say the bold-sprit, or beake-head Steves, when it stands too upright, and not straight forward enough. **1711** W. Sutherland *Shipbuild. Assist.* 74 Catheads..To steave in every Foot..2 inches. *Ibid.* 164 Steaving; when a Part rises from a horizontal Position, as in the Cathead, Bowsprit, and Knee of the Head. **1794** *Act 34 Geo. III*, c. 50 §7 The said Bowsprit to be steaved or elevated at least two Inches in every Foot from the straight Line of the Range of the Deck. **1794** *Rigging & Seamanship* I. 31 Set off what the bowsprit stives. **1839** Marryat *Phant. Ship* viii, The bowsprit staved very much, and was to appearance almost as a fourth mast. **1897** Kipling *Capt. Cour.* iii, That yaller, dirty packet with her bowsprit steeved that way, she's the *Hope of Prague.*

transf. **1791** Smeaton *Edystone L.* §34 The rock stives from E. to W. 10 feet 11 inches in 24 feet.

Hence '**steeving** *vbl. sb.*[1] and *ppl. a.*

1664 E. Bushnell *Compl. Ship-wright* iii. 8 Then for the steeving of him, and rounding the Knee, a regard must be had to the lying of the Boltspreet. **1769** Falconer *Dict. Marine* (1780), *Steeving*, the elevation of a ship's bowsprit above the stem, or the angle which it makes with the horizon. **1791** Smeaton *Edystone L.* §6 The sloping (or stiving of the rocks as it is technically called). *c* **1850** *Rudim. Navig.* (Weale) 153 *Stiving*, the elevation of a ship's cathead or bowsprit; or the angle which either makes with the horizon. **1893** F. M. CRAWFORD *Childr. King* I. 6 The martinganes flatten in their jibs along their high steeving bowsprits and jib-booms.

steeve (stiːv), *v.*[2] Chiefly *Naut.* Also 8 steave, *Sc.* stieve, 9 steve. [a. F. *estiver* or its source, Pr. *estibar*, Catal. *stibar*, Sp., Pg. *estivar*, corresp. to It. *stivare* to crowd, pack tightly:—L. *stīpāre*. Cf. the variant STIVE *v.*] *trans.* To compress and stow (wool, cotton or other cargo) in a ship's hold, etc.; also to pack tightly. Hence **'steeving** *vbl. sb.*[2]

1482 *Grant* 30 Apr. in *Cal. Patent Rolls* (1901) 300 [An occupation called 'le pressing' or 'stenyng' (*read* steuyng = stevyng) of wools]. **1644** MANWAYRING *Seamans Dict.* 102 Also the Merchants call the stowing of their Cottons (which they force in with skrewes so much that the Decks will rise 6, or 8, inches) Steveing of Cottons. **1669** STURMY *Mariner's Mag., Penalties & Forfeit.* 5 [To] put, press, or steeve Wooll or Woollen Yarn into any Pipe, But, or Hogshead. **1709** M. BRUCE *Soul Confirm.* 20 (Jam.), I am even like a sojourner with his knapsack on his back... I stieved the knapsack well. **1711** W. SUTHERLAND *Shipbuild. Assist.* 89 As in Stowing (term'd Steaving) a Ship with Wool. **1840** R. H. DANA *Bef. Mast* xxix, Each morning we went ashore, and.. brought off as many hides as we could steeve in the course of the day.

absol. **1840** R. H. DANA *Bef. Mast* xxix, All hands were called aboard to steeve.

steeve (stiːv), *v.*[3] *Sc.* In 6 steve, 9 steave. [f. STEEVE *a.*] *trans.* To make 'steeve' or firm; to strengthen, fix, secure.

1554 *Extracts Burgh Rec. Edin.* (1871) II. 206 The bigging of the Tolbuith and steving of the geistis of the over hous thairof. **1877** W. WATSON *Unco Bit Want* iii, (Jam. *Suppl.*) I steave up my temper-string gayly, An' whiles a bit verse I do chant.

steevely ('stiːvlɪ), *adv.* Now only *Sc.* Forms: see STEEVE *a.* [f. STEEVE *a.* + -LY[2].] Firmly, unyieldingly.

1340 *Ayenb.* 258 [If] to moche bysy agrayþinge ne were zenne: oure lhorde ne sayde nazt zuo stefliche ine his spelle a-ye þe queade riche þet [etc.]. ?*c* **1450** *Polit. Poems* (Rolls) II. 239 Usure and rapyne stefly dothe stande. **1647** in D. M'Naught *Kilmaurs* (1912) 151 [He was] stievly and sharplie rebukit. **1684** J. ERSKINE *Jrnl.* (S.H.S.) 29 Mr. Morison.. owned the Covenant stievely before the Justice Court. **1790** A. WILSON *Poems & Lit. Prose* (1876) II. 90 I'm now stively on my feet. **1816** SCOTT *Bl. Dwarf* i, 'Your father believed it unco stievely, though,' said the old man. **1880** A. RALEIGH *Way to City* xxv. 315 Our firm-set creeds —stievely, staunchly built, like boats with oaken planks—sail the waters in vain. **1899** LUMSDEN *Edin. Poems* 317 And steevely thou thy posts did fill aye!

steeven, variant of STEVEN.

‖**steever** ('stiːvə(r)), *sb.* *Jewish.* Also **stever**, **shtibbur**. [Yiddish pronunciation of LG. *stüver* = G. *stüber*, Du. *stuiver*.] = STIVER.

1892 ZANGWILL *Childr. Ghetto* xxii, A *Shtibbur* (penny) for a poor blind man! *Ibid.*, Fourteen *Shtibbur's* a lot of *Gelt*! **1899** BINSTEAD *Houndsditch* 78 'Not a steever', returned the son; 'your money was not on last night'. **1905** —— *Mop Fair* 91 While one is not winning a single steever.

stef, obs. form of STEEVE *a.*

Stefan ('stɛfæn). *Physics.* The name of Josef *Stefan* (1835–93), Austrian physicist, used *attrib.* and in the possessive with reference to a law discovered by him (see J. Stefan 1879, in *Sitzungsber. der Österreich. Akad. der Wissensch. in Wien* LXXIX. 391), as **Stefan('s) constant, law** = *Stefan-Boltzmann constant, law* (see next).

1898 *Sci. Abstr.* I. 391 The author's attempt to realise Kirchhoff's conception of an equivalent to an absolutely black body in the shape of a uniformly heated hollow space with a small opening, and test Stefan's law, which maintains that the radiation of such a body is proportional to the 4th power of its absolute temperature. **1923** GLAZEBROOK *Dict. Appl. Physics* III. 711/1 By the Stefan-Boltzmann law.., and a knowledge of Stefan's constant, the whole radiation from the blackened surface is known. *Ibid.* IV. 569/1 Apart from this constant Stefan's law leads straight to Maxwell's law of radiation pressure. **1962** *Newnes Conc. Encycl. Electr. Engin.* 718/1 Here ϵ is the Stefan or total-radiation constant. **1966** [see *Planck('s) equation* s.v. PLANCK]. **1979** T. B. AKRILL et. al. *Physics* xxviii. 377/2 For a non-black or 'grey' body we can apply Stefan's law in the form $P_{tot} = \epsilon\sigma AT^4$, where ϵ is called the total emissivity of the body and is a number always less than 1.

Stefan-Boltzmann ('stɛfæn 'bəʊltsmən). *Physics.* The names of Josef *Stefan* (see prec.) and Ludwig Eduard *Boltzmann* (1844–1906), Austrian physicists, used *attrib.* with reference to a law independently discovered by them (L. E. Boltzmann 1884, in *Ann. der Physik u. Chemie* XXII. 291; see also prec.), as **Stefan-Boltzmann constant**, the constant in the Stefan-Boltzmann law, equal to $5{\cdot}67 \times 10^{-8}$ $J\,m^{-2}\,s^{-1}\,K^{-4}$; **Stefan-Boltzmann law**, the law which states that the total radiation emitted by a black body is proportional to the fourth power of its absolute temperature.

1898 *Sci. Abstr.* I. 391 The Stefan-Boltzmann law is confirmed to within 3 to 8%. **1915** R. A. HOUSTOUN *Treat. Light* xxv. 448 By considering such a cycle Boltzmann proved that the total radiation from a black body was proportional to the fourth power of its absolute temperature. This law had been stated previously but erroneously by Stefan as holding good for all bodies, and as the amended version was due to Boltzmann, it is very often referred to as the Stefan-Boltzmann law. **1954** [see LANGLEY]. **1958** CONDON & ODISHAW *Handbk. Physics* VI. i. 15/1 The total radiation crossing unit area in unit time in all directions in one hemisphere is usually written σT^4, where σ is called the Stefan-Boltzmann constant. **1977** I. M. CAMPBELL *Energy & Atmosphere* i. 13 This is related to T through the Stefan-Boltzmann law: $E(T) = \sigma T^4$ where σ is known as the Stefan- Boltzmann constant and has value $5{\cdot}672 \times 10^{-8}$ for T in Kelvin and $E(T)$ in Wm^{-2}.

stef(f)ne, stefninge: see STEVEN, STEVENING.

stefhede, stefnes: see after STEEVE *a.*

steg (stɛg). Now *dial.* Also 5 stegg(e, 6 steyg, 9 stegg, stag, staig. [a. ON. *steggi*, *stegg-r* masc., male bird (Norw. *stegg*, mod.Icel. *steggur*; in Icel. also tom-cat); prob. cogn. w. STAG *sb.*]

1. A gander; also, a clumsy or stupid person. For later examples see *Eng. Dial. Dict.*

1483 *Cath. Angl.* 361/1 A Stegge, *ancer.* **1570** *Richmond Wills* (Surtees) 229 Inventorie.. vij geyse and steygs. **1691** RAY *N.C. Words* 69 A Steg; a Gander. **1790** ANN WHEELER *Westmorld. Dial.* ii. 53 Will yee preia sell me a Goos... A fearful fine Stegg yea hev for sure. *a* **1823** in *Mactaggart's Gallovid. Encycl.* 440 Ye come, led by your chosen king, Some champion steg wha heads your string. **1873** HARLAND & WILKINSON *Lanc. Leg.* v. 201 He who will have a full flock Must have an old stagge (gander) and a young cock.

2. *Comb.*: †**steggander** = sense 1; **steg-month**, = *gander-month* (GANDER *sb.* 4).

1570 LEVINS *Manip.* 53/25 A steggander, *anser.* **1828** CARR *Craven Gloss.*, *Steg-month*, the month or period of a woman's confinement. **1857** DUNGLISON *Med. Lex.* s.v. *Parturient*, The period from parturition to perfect recovery, which is usually a month. In the north of England this is called the *steg-month.*

steganography (stɛgə'nɒgrəfɪ). *Obs.* exc. *Hist.* [ad. mod.L. *steganographia* (Trithemius 1500), a. assumed Gr. *στεγανογραφία, f. στεγανό-ς covered + γράφ-ειν to write: see -GRAPHY. Cf. F. *stéganographie* (1567 in Hatz.-Darm.).] The art of secret writing; cryptography. Also, cryptographic script, cipher.

1569 J. SANFORD tr. *Agrippa's Van. Artes* 97b, Steganographie a marueilous kinde of writinge but not commonlye knowne. **1591** WOTTON *Let. to Zouch* Rel. W. (1685) 647 Concerning the Steganography I can by none of those means that I advertis'd this last Week of, pass further than I have. **1593** R. HARVEY *Philadelphus* 56 The Histories were written in some strange kind of polygraphy and steganography. **1602** [J. WILLIS] *Art Stenogr.* title-p., Where-vnto is annexed a very easie direction for Steganographie, or, Secret Writing. **1677** *Phil. Trans.* XII. 862 *Steganography*, (which word imports the Art of signifying ones mind to another by an occult or secret way of writing). **1780** tr. *Von Troil's Iceland* 299, I afterwards found the same kind of steganography mentioned in a little work ascribed to Rhabanus Maurus. **1823** 'S. COLLET' *Relics Lit.* 112 Steganography.

So **'steganogram**, a cryptogram; **stega'nographer, stega'nographist**, one expert in steganography, a cryptographer; **stegano'graphical** *a.*, pertaining to steganography.

1562 LEGH *Armory* 227b, This Herehaught is no Steganographer. **1588** J. HARVEY *Disc. Probl.* 29 Whose mightie and wonderfull proceedings no Poligrapher can expresse, or Steganographer decipher. *Ibid.* 53 Facing it out with a certaine learned tincture, that should require as well a Steganographicall decipherer, as a logicall, or philosophicall interpreter. **1727** BAILEY vol. II, *Steganographist*, an Artist in private Writing. **1753** CHESTERF. in *World* No. 24 I. 213 One of them being already in possession (to speak in their own style) of a more brachygraphical, cryptographical and steganographical secret in writing their warrants. **1780** tr. *Von Troil's Iceland* 299 Another hand has patched in a steganographical writing. **1904** *Sat. Rev.* 23 July 114/2 Colonel Hime.. has elucidated a steganogram contained in his [Roger Bacon's] 'Epistola de secretis operibus' which is decisive.

steganopod ('stɛgənəʊpɒd), *sb.* and *a.* *Ornith.* [ad. mod.L. *Steganopodes*, pl. (Illiger 1811), a. Gr. στεγανοποδ-, -όπους (Aristotle), web-footed, f. στεγανό-ς covered + ποδ-, πούς foot.] **a.** *sb.* A bird belonging to the group *Steganopodes*, which comprises the pelicans, cormorants, frigate-birds, gannets, tropic-birds, and snake birds (Newton *Dict. Ornith.* 904). **b.** *adj.* Of a bird: Belonging to the group *Steganopodes*.

Somewhat *rare*, the mod.L. form being usual for the sb. pl.

1842 BRANDE *Dict. Sci.* etc., *Steganopods.*

So **stega'nopodan, stega'nopodous** *adjs.*, belonging to the group *Steganopodes*.

1887 NEWTON in *Encycl. Brit.* XXII. 188/2 Eggs with the white chalky shell that is so characteristic of most Steganopodous birds.

stegh: see STECH *v.*

stegh, obs. f. STY, ladder; var. and pa. t. of STY *v.*

†**steg'notic**, *a.* and *sb.* *Med.* *Obs.* [ad. mod.L. *stegnōticus*, ad. Gr. στεγνωτικός, f. στεγνοῦν to render costive, to stop bleeding, f. στεγνός watertight, costive, f. στέγ-ειν to cover.]

a. *adj.* Of a medicine: Adapted to arrest diarrhœa, flow of blood, or other discharges; astringent, styptic. **b.** *sb.* A 'stegnotic' medicine.

1674 SALMON *Lond. Disp.* (1678) 47/1 Clematis, vinca pervinca... Periwinkle, is Segnotick [*sic*] and Vulnerary, stops the Bloody Flux. **1684** tr. *Bonet's Merc. Compit.* III. 78 Applying Lint dipt in a Stegnotick. **1710** *Brit. Apollo* III. No. 21. 2/2 We bid you consider all matter, either as Lyptyntic, Segnotic [*sic*], or Balsamic. Now.. the Segnotic is Styptic... So that.. Segnotics may be very proper in the Case. **1727** BAILEY vol. II, *Stegnotick*, binding, rendering costive.

stego- (stɛgəʊ), used as combining form of Gr. root στεγ- of στέγειν to cover, στέγη covering, στέγος (neut.) roof, in certain modern scientific terms. **stego'carpous** *a.* [Gr. καρπός fruit], epithet of certain mosses, forming the division *Stegocarpi*, characterized by having an operculate capsule. **stegocephalian** (-sɪ'fæliən) *a.* [Gr. κεφαλή head] = STEGOCEPHALOUS; *sb.* a member of the order *Stegocephala* of fossil Batrachians, characterized by having the skull protected by bony plates. **stegocephalous** (-'sɛfələs) *a.*, pertaining to, or having the characteristics of the order *Stegocephala*. **stegocrotaphous** (-'krɒtəfəs) *a.* [Gr. κρόταφος, side of the forehead, temple], having the side of the skull protected by bony plates. **stegodon** ('stɛgədɒn) [Gr. ὀδοντ-, ὀδούς tooth], a fossil genus or subgenus of elephants, having 'ridged' teeth; an elephant of this genus. **'stegodont** *a.*, belonging to or having the characteristics of the genus *Stegodon*. ‖**Stego'saurus** [Gr. σαῦρος lizard], a genus of dinosaurs, characterized by the completeness of their armour; an animal of this genus; also **'stegosaur**; hence ‖**Stego'sauria** *pl.*, the order of which this genus is typical; **stego'saurian** *a.* and *sb.*

1884 K. E. GOEBEL in *Encycl. Brit.* XVII. 73/2 The *stegocarpous Mosses. **1891** *Amer. Naturalist* Dec. 1123 A *Stegocephalian Skull from the Kilkenny Coal Measures. **1900** *Nature* 12 July 254/2 The extinct labyrinthodonts or stegocephalians. **1895** *Information* 6 July 3/1 The *Stegocephalous Batrachians (primitive Salamanders) of the coal period. **1901** H. GADOW *Amphibia* etc. (Camb. Nat. Hist.) 78 The incipient Reptilia which have sprung from some members of this Stegocephalous stock. **1907** WILLISTON in *Proc. U.S. Nat. Mus.* XXXII. 488 The turtles have a *stegocrotaphous skull. **1857** H. FALCONER in *Q. Jrnl. Geol. Soc.* XIII. 314 To this group we have assigned the subgeneric name of **Stegodon*... The Stegodons constitute the intermediate group of the Proboscidea from which the other species diverge through their dental characters, on the one side into the Mastodons, and on the other into the typical Elephants. **1894** LYDEKKER *Roy. Nat. Hist.* II. 555 The so-called *stegodont elephants. **1901** *Westm. Gaz.* 1 Oct. 10/2 The *stegosaur was the most remarkable of the sauropods. **1877** O. C. MARSH in *Amer. Jrnl. Sci.* Ser. III. XIV. 513 A new order, which may be termed **Stegosauria*, from the typical genus here described. **1905** A. S. WOODWARD *Guide Fossil Rept.* etc. *Brit. Mus.* (ed. 8) 21 Another Wealden *Stegosaurian. **1912** *Return Brit. Mus.* 168 The Stegosaurian Dinosaurs. **1892** *Daily News* 28 Dec. 3/6 The *stegosaurus, a huge torpid reptile about 20 feet in length.

stegoid ('stɛgɔɪd), *a.* *Craniometry.* [f. Gr. στέγ- (see STEGO-) + -OID.] (See quot.)

1894 tr. *Sergi's Var. Hum. Species* 52 There are stegoid varieties also, that is, with a roof-like arch, not very high.

stegomyia (stɛgəʊ'maɪə). [mod.L. (F. V. Theobald 1901, in *Jrnl. Trop. Med. & Hygiene* IV. 235/1), f. STEGO- + Gr. μυῖα fly.] A mosquito of the genus formerly so called, now usually regarded as a sub-division of the genus *Aedes*, which includes tropical and subtropical species responsible for the transmission of yellow fever.

1911 A. ALCOCK *Entomol. for Med. Officers* v. 96 (*heading*) Genera of the Stegomyia type. **1915** G. B. SHAW in *New Statesman* 10 July 326/2 The same result could have been obtained by inoculation with anopheles vaccine and stegomyia emulsion. **1920** *Glasgow Herald* 6 July 6/4 The success of General Gorgas's methods can be gauged.. after a campaign extending over eight years against the stegomyia. **1932** *Discovery* Oct. 326/2, I [*sc.* Robert Ross] then examined a small *Stegomyia*. **1971** J. D. GILLETT *Mosquitos* iii. 46 Other *Stegomyia* also at times glide through the water head-first.

steiar, steick: see STAIR, STEEK *v.*[1]

steid, steier: see STEAD, STEED, STAIR.

steif, obs. form of STEEVE *a.*

‖**steifkin, stiebkin.** *Obs. rare*$^{-1}$. [app. meant for G. *stäufchen*, LG. *stöpken*, dim. of G. *stauf*, LG. *stop*, can: see STOUP.] (See quot.)

1617 MORYSON *Itin.* I. 39 At Breme I paied halfe a Doller for dinner, supper and breakfast, and a stiebkin or measure of wine extraordinary. *Ibid.* 56 At Stode I paid.. for a steifkin or measure of Rhenish wine, halfe a doller.

steigerite ('staɪgəraɪt). *Min.* [f. the name of George Steiger (1869–1944), U.S. chemist + -ITE[1].] A monoclinic hydrated aluminium

vanadate, $AlVO_4.3H_2O$, found as a canary-yellow powdery coating on vanadium-containing concretions.
1935 E. P. HENDERSON in *Amer. Mineralogist* XX. 769 A new yellow, hydrous aluminum vanadate, $Al_2O_3·V_2O_5·6·5H_2O$, which has been named steigerite, is here descibed. **1959** *Amer. Mineralogist* XLIV. 336 Electron micrographs of steigerite from Gypsum Valley, Colorado..show that the material is composed of thin, poorly developed laths and angular flakes.

steik(e: see STEEK, STICK.

steil(l(e, obs. forms of STEAL, STEEL, STILE.

steimming, variant of STAMIN *Obs.*

steimy, variant of STYMIE.

‖**stein** (ʃtaɪn). [G. *stein*, lit. 'stone'.] 'An earthenware mug, esp. for beer, commonly holding about a pint; also the quantity of beer which a stein holds' (W.).
1855 *Trans. Hist. Soc. Lancs. & Cheshire* VII. 190 The 'Moss Pottery'..was..confined to the making of common red-clay ware, for domestic use, as jowls, steins, flower-pots, &c. **1897** [see PRETZEL, BRETZEL 1]. **1901** W. CHURCHILL *Crisis* II. x. 206 They clattered their steins on the table and sang wonderful Jena songs. **1908** *Daily Chron.* 15 Feb. 4/6 Bismarck..loved to pour into a huge stein a bottle of champagne and then a bottle of porter. **1909** *Westm. Gaz.* 21 Aug. 13/2 Small earthenware steins with metal tops..not more than 4.80 marks in value. **1915** *Sat. Even. Post* 13 Feb. 52/3 So I sat down and et with 'em and had a few steins of beer. **1976** *Billings* (Montana) *Gaz.* 27 June 1-c/6 Beer was flowing at 50 cents a stein—three for $1. **1981** *West Lancs. Even. Gaz.* 18 July 8/4 A night on the town turned sour when a 22 year-old man hit a glass collector in the face with a beer stein.

stein, rare obs. form of STEAN.

Steinberger (ˈʃtaɪnbɜːgə(r)). [Ger., f. the name *Steinberg* (also used) of the vineyard where the wine is produced.] A white wine produced near Hattenheim in the Rheingau.
1833 C. REDDING *Hist. & Descr. Mod. Wines* vii. 205 The Steinberger..takes rank after the Schloss-Johannesberger among these wines. It has the greatest strength, and yet is one of the most delicate, and even sweetly flavoured. **1894** J. L. W. THUDICHUM *Treat. Wines* 201 The *Johannisberg* is the only rival of the Steinberg. **1907** *Hatch, Mansfield Price List* Jan. 18 (Advt.), *Steinberg*, magnificent wine, with great body. **1926** M. SHAND *Bk. Wine* vi. 187 The number of classified districts in the Rheingau, from one or other of which all but three of its wines (Steinberger, Markobrunnen, and Schloss Vollrads) take their first name. **1951** *Good Housek. Home Encycl.* 508/2 The best Hock, which is sold under a number of well-known names, e.g. Johannisberger, Steinberger. **1965** O. A. MENDELSOHN *Dict. Drink & Drinking* 322 Starting at simple Steinberger and ending at the almost hallowed Steinberg Kabinett.

steinboc, -bok, -buck, var. ff. STEENBOK.

steinbock (ˈstaɪnbɒk). Also **steinboc**, (7 **steinbokt**). [a. G. *steinbock* wild goat, f. *stein* STONE *sb.* + *bock* BUCK *sb.*[1] Cf. STEENBOK.] A wild goat of the genus *Ibex*; the Alpine Ibex (*Capra Ibex*).
1683-4 ROBINSON in *Phil. Trans.* XXIX. 482 In passing the high Alps, I had a View of the Ibex or Steinbock. **1695** tr. *Misson's Voy. to Italy* I. 106 We dined..at Steertzingen, where they gave us..some Flesh of a certain Beast called Steinbokt. **1776** [see IBEX]. **1859** WOOD *Illustr. Nat. Hist.* I. 668 Of the genus Capra,..the Ibex or Steinbock is a familiar ..example. **1881** *Encycl. Brit.* XII. 605/2 The European ibex or steinboc (*Capra ibex*) abounded during the Middle Ages among the higher mountain ranges of Germany, Switzerland, and the Ural.

steinch, obs. f. STANCH *v.*
1573-5 GASCOIGNE *Adv. Mr. F. J.* Wks. 1907 I. 391 Hir bleeding was throughly steinched.

†**ˈsteinchek.** *Obs. rare*[−1]. [f. *stein* repr. northern form of STONE *sb.* + CHECK *sb.*[4] Cf. STONE-CHACKER, STONECHAT.] A name for the Wheatear or the Stonechat.
1544 TURNER *Avium Præcip.* (1903) 52 De Cœrvleone... Anglicè, a clotburd, a smatche, an arlyng, a steinchek.

steine, obs. form of STAIN.

Steiner (ˈʃtaɪnə(r)). *Math.* The name of Jakob *Steiner* (1796–1863), Swiss geometer, used *attrib.* and in the possessive to designate various mathematical concepts suggested by him: **a.** ***Steiner triple*** or ***triplet system*** (see quot. 1939); so ***Steiner triplet***; also ***Steiner system***, a generalization of the triple system to other numbers (see quot. 1974). [Steiner first described such systems in *Jrnl. f. d. reine u. angewandte Math.* (1853) XLV. 181.]
1939 R. C. BOSE in *Annals Eugenics* IX. 354 Steiner (1853) proposed the problem of arranging *N* things in triplets, such that every pair occurs in just one and only one triplet. Such an arrangement may be called a simple triple system or a Steiner's triplet system. **1963** H. J. RYSER *Combinatorial Math.* viii. 100 The Steiner triple system of order 7 is the same as the projective plane of order 2 in the preceding chapter. **1966** *Annali di Matematica* LXXI. 199 The *Steiner* system $S(5, 8, 24)$ is an arrangement of 24 elements in sets of 8, such that any 5 of the elements belong to exactly one set. **1974** I. ANDERSON *First Course Combinatorial Math.* vii. 102 A Steiner system $S(l, m, n)$ is a collection of m-element subsets of an n element set B such that every l-element subset of B lies in exactly one of the m-element sets. *Ibid.*, A Steiner triple system is an $S(2, 3, n)$ for some n. **1980** *Sci. Amer.* May 14/2 Since Steiner triplets are not ordered, the solution is of course unique.
b. Used with reference to the problem of finding the set of line segments of minimum total length needed to connect a given set of points in a metric space.
1941 COURANT & ROBBINS *What is Math.?* vii. 359 In Steiner's problem three fixed points A, B, C are given. It is natural to generalize this problem to the case of n given points. *Ibid.* 360 To find the really significant extension of Steiner's problem we must abandon the search for a single point P... Given n points..to find a connected system of straight line segments of shortest total length such that any two of the given points can be joined by a polygon consisting of segments of the system. **1961** *Canad. Math. Bull.* IV. 143 Given a triangle T with the vertices a_1, a_2, a_3, to find in the plane of T the point p which minimizes the sum of the distances $|pa_1| + |pa_2| + |pa_3|$. p, called the Steiner point of T, is unique. **1968** *SIAM Jrnl. Appl. Math.* XVI. 1 A Steiner minimal tree for given points $A_1, .., An$ in the plane is a tree which interconnects these points using lines of shortest possible total length. In order to achieve minimum length the Steiner minimal tree may contain other vertices (Steiner points) beside $A_1, ..An$. **1979** *Sci. Amer.* Apr. 37/1 First is the Steiner problem of the shortest roads linking many cities.

Steinerian (staɪˈnɪərɪən), *a.* and *sb. Math.* [f. *Steiner* (see prec.) + -IAN.] **a.** *adj.* Pertaining to the discoveries of Jakob Steiner. ***Steinerian polygon***, a figure composed of a number of vertices with connecting lines. **b.** *sb.* The locus of points whose first polars with respect to a given curve have double points.
1873 SALMON *Higher Plane Curves* (1879) 57 This locus we shall call after the geometer Steiner, the Steinerian of *U*. *Ibid.* 363 To any point *P*, then, on the Steinerian corresponds a point *Q* on the Hessian.

Steinert (ˈʃtaɪnət). *Path.* [The name of H. G. W. *Steinert* (b. 1875), German physician, who described the disease in 1909 (*Deutsche Zeitschr. f. Nervenheilkunde* XXXVII. 58).] ***Steinert's disease*** = ***myotonia atrophica*** s.v. MYOTONIA 2 b.
1932 *Index Medicus* XII. 429/1 (*heading*) Cachetic form of myotonia atrophica (Steinert's disease). **1948** F. B. CARLSEN tr. *Thomasen's Myotonia* vii. 94 Steinert's disease invariably set in in later life, generally between the ages of twenty and thirty. **1963** [see MYOTONIA 2 b].

steing, obs. variant of STING *sb.*

steingall: see STANIEL etymol. note.

Steinhäger (ˈʃtaɪnhɛːgə(r)). Also **-haeger**, (*erron.*) **-hager**. [Ger., f. the name *Steinhagen* of the town, in Westphalia, where it is produced.] A spirit made from juniper-berries; a measure or glassful of this.
1959 M. CROSLAND tr. *Rovan's Germany* 180 Many fine spirits are made in Germany..a white *eau-de-vie* in Westphalia called *Steinhäger*. **1964** L. DEIGHTON *Funeral in Berlin* xl. 239 Coffee, doughnuts and tiny glasses of Steinhager. **1966** R. THOMAS *Cold War Swap* i. 9 Steinhaeger is best when drunk ice cold and washed down with a liter or so of beer. **1968** 'J. LE CARRÉ' *Small Town in Germany* xvii. 273 He drank a Steinhager from the tray. The mat stuck to the stem of the glass. **1976** R. PERRY *One Good Death* xi. 172, I handed him the flask of Steinhager... Muller took a generous swig.

Steinheim (ˈʃtaɪnhaɪm). The name of a village twelve miles north of Stuttgart, West Germany, used *absol.* or *attrib.* in **Steinheim skull** to designate a Middle Pleistocene fossil hominid known from a skull found there in 1933 by Karl Sigrist and described as *Homo steinheimensis* by F. Berckhemer in 1936 (*Forschungen & Fortschritte* XII. 349/2).
1946 F. E. ZEUNER *Dating Past* ix. 296 If the geological age of the Steinheim Skull were settled..we should at least know whether he, or his ancestor, lived in the middle Pleistocene. **1973** B. J. WILLIAMS *Evolution & Human Origins* x. 170/1 The Steinheim skull also comes from a gravel pit. *Ibid.* 170/2 In facial features Steinheim could indeed be a good ancestor for the later Neandertals.

steining, variant of STEENING.

steinkirk: see STEENKIRK.

Stein-Leventhal (ʃtaɪn ˈlɛvəntɑːl). *Path.* [The names of I. F. *Stein* (1887–1976) and M. L. *Leventhal* (1901–71), U.S. gynæcologists, who described the condition in 1935 (*Amer. Jrnl. Obstetrics & Gynecol.* XXIX. 181–91).] ***Stein-Leventhal syndrome***: a hormonal abnormality in women characterized by enlarged polycystic ovaries, infertility, and oligomenorrhœa, often with hirsutism.
1950 F. A. SIMMONS in Meigs & Sturgis *Progr. in Gynecol.* II. 334 These curves are common in the 'Stein–Leventhal syndrome', a condition wherein poor or nonovulatory cycles are thought to be caused by polycystic ovaries. **1972** *Brit. Med. Jrnl.* 20 May 457/2 A second ovarian cause of amenorrhoea is the Stein–Leventhal Syndrome.

Steinmann (ˈʃtaɪnmən). *Surg.* The name of Fritz *Steinmann* (1872–1932), Swiss surgeon, who described the device in 1907 (*Zentralbl. Chir.* XXXIV. 939), used in the possessive and *attrib.* to designate a surgical pin that may be passed through one end of a major bone for traction or setting.
1916 ROBERTS & KELLY *Treatm. Fractures* i. 77 (*heading*) Technic of application of Steinmann's nails. **1925** WILSON & COCHRANE *Fractures & Dislocations* xv. 546 Steinmann's pin has now been largely superseded in general use by the calipers, or ice-tongs, which grasp, but do not penetrate the bone. **1933** P. B. MAGNUSON *Fractures* iii. 25 The use of the Steinmann pin is not advisable except in skilled hands. **1974** A. HENRY in R. M. Kirk et al. *Surgery* xvi. 370 A Thomas's splint is fitted, and skeletal traction set up through a Steinmann's pin..in the proximal tibia.

steinmannite (ˈstaɪnmænaɪt). *Min.* [Named (*steinmannit*) by Zippe 1833 after Prof. J. J. *Steinmann*: see -ITE.] A variety of galenite, containing arsenic and antimony.
1849 J. NICOL *Man. Min.* 483 Steinmannite..occurs at Przibram in Bohemia. **1850** ANSTED *Elem. Geol., Min.* etc. 214.

Steinway (ˈstaɪnweɪ). The name of Henry Engelhard *Steinway* (1797–1871), celebrated German piano-builder, used *attrib.* or *absol.* to designate a piano manufactured by him or by the firm which he founded in New York in 1853.
1875 T. YELVERTON *Teresina in Amer.* ii. 181 In the latter there was one of the best pianos (a Steinway) that I touched in America, where good pianos are by no means rare. **1889** G. B. SHAW in *Star* 13 July 4/4 She was presented with a Steinway Grand. **1905** A. BENNETT *Sacred & Profane Love* III. v. 260 The piano, a Steinway in a hundred Steinways. **1933** E. WHARTON *Human Nature* 172, I always knew fashionable people could barely distinguish a barrel-organ from a Steinway. **1965** J. M. CAIN *Magician's Wife* (1966) ii. 18 At one end of the room was a Steinway baby grand. **1977** *New Yorker* 19 Sept. 64/2, I pictured a sea of Steinways to choose from in Juillard's basement. **1981** J. JOHNSTON *Christmas Tree* 130 There was a piano, a beautiful Steinway concert grand... The only reality was the room with the Steinway.

Steinwein (ˈʃtaɪnvaɪn). [Ger.] The name of a dry white wine produced in the Steinmantel vineyards, near Würzburg, Bavaria, and sold in special bottles called Bocksbeutel.
1833 C. REDDING *Hist. & Descr. Mod. Wines* vii. 206 The Steinwein of 1748, brought in 1832 seventy pounds the ahm. This may serve to show how much these wines gain by age. **1843** *Penny Cycl.* XXVII. 456/2 The Steinwein must not be confounded with the Steinberger wine of the Rhine. **1920** G. SAINTSBURY *Notes on Cellar-Bk.* xii. 177 The popular form seems to have been..the *bocksbeutel* flasks of Steinwein. **1966** H. YOXALL *Fashion of Life* xxiii. 212 At Würzburg..a dinner with salmon and *Steinwein*. **1980** *Times* 9 Aug. 8/7 The Steinburg vineyard, whose fame caused Franconian wines to be referred to as 'Steinwein'.

steinzie, obs. Sc. form of STAIN.

steip, obs. Sc. form of STEEP *a.*

steipell, -il(l, etc., obs. forms of STEEPLE.

steir(e, obs. Sc. forms of STEER, STIR *vbs.*

steirne, obs. form of STERN.

steiryr, ? obs. Sc. form of STIRRER.

stek(e, variant forms of STICK *sb.*[3]

steke, obs. f. STICK *sb.*[2]; variant of STEEK *v.*[1]

stekelyng, stel, obs. ff. STICKLING, STALL *sb.*[1]

‖**stela** (ˈstiːlə). Pl. **stelæ** (ˈstiːliː), *rarely* **stelas**. [L. *stēla*, ad. Gr. στήλη: see STELE.] = STELE 1.
1776 R. CHANDLER *Trav. Greece* viii. 35 In the courts of the houses lie many round stelæ, or pillars, once placed on the graves of the Athenians. **1837** WILKINSON *Mann. & Cust. Anc. Egypt.* ii. (1841) I. 101 He erected a stela, with an inscription in the sacred character, to commemorate his successes. **1876** S. MANNING *Land of Pharaohs* 203 The upright blocks or stelas are among the most curious parts of the present ruin. **1893** BUDGE *Mummy* 30 Thothmes I. set up two stelæ near the Euphrates.

stelar (ˈstiːlə(r)), *a. Bot.* [f. mod.L. *stēla* STELE 2 + -AR.] Pertaining to a stele or steles.
1901 *Ann. Bot.* XV. 404 Stelar structure.

Stelazine (ˈstɛləziːn). *Pharm.* Also **stelazine**. [f. *Stel-*, of unkn. origin + AZINE.] A proprietary name for trifluoperazine.
1958 *Brit. Med. Jrnl.* 12 July 91/1 A short pilot trial of the drug stelazine was undertaken with 25 chronic psychotic patients. **1958** *Trade Marks Jrnl.* 23 July 738/1 *Stelazine* 772,994. Azine chemical compounds for use in medicine and pharmacy. Smith, Kline & French Laboratories Ltd., London. Manufacturing Chemists.—9th January, 1958. **1965** *Nursing Times* 5 Feb. 187/2 In hospital the phenothiazine tranquilizers seem most useful for relieving the fear and tension prominent at this stage. Stelazine (trifluoperazine) seems particularly useful. **1976** H. FERGUSON *Confessions of Long Distance Acid Head* 45 This hospital did not even stock the drug Stelazine which had, apparently, cured me when I had my first nervous breakdown.

stele (stiːl, ‖stiːliː). *Antiq.* [As a disyllable, repr. Gr. στήλη standing block or slab, f. Indogermanic root **stā-* to stand. As a monosyllable, anglicized form of the Gr. word; cf. F. *stèle.*

It is not always possible to decide which of the two pronunciations was intended by a writer using the word. The form *stele* is generally preferred for the singular, and *stelæ* (which belongs formally to *stela*) in the plural.]

1. a. An upright slab bearing sculptured designs or inscriptions. Sometimes loosely applied to any prepared surface on the face of a building, a rock, etc., covered with an inscription.

1820 T. S. HUGHES *Trav. Sicily* I. x. 303 A superior class of members..had their names inscribed upon a marble stélé or column. **1825** FOSBROKE *Encycl. Antiq.* 70 It appears, that when any one of the family died, a stelè to his memory was added to the tomb. **1833** SIR H. ELLIS *Elgin Marbles* (1846) II. 169 A large sepulchral stele. **1847** LEITCH tr. *C. O. Müller's Anc. Art* §224. 193 In Egypt they [obelisks] belonged to the class of steles (commemorative pillars). **1873** *Contemp. Rev.* XXI. 568 With inscriptions either on steles or columns, or on tablets. **1877** MISS A. B. EDWARDS *Up Nile* vi. 143 Two large hieroglyphed steles incised upon the face of a projecting mass of boldly rounded cliff. **1882** CHEYNE *Isaiah* xvi. 12 *note*, The Stele of Mesha..was found in a depression between the two hillocks. **1884** A. LANG *Custom & Myth* 285 The Australian stele, or grave-pillar.

b. *Arch.* (See quot.)

a **1840** HOSKING *Archit.* in *Encycl. Brit.* (ed. 7) III. 470 *Stele.* The ornaments on the ridge of a Greek temple, answering to the antefixæ on the summit of the flank entablatures, are thus designated.

2. *Bot.* [ad. F. *stèle* (Van Tieghem & Douliot 1886, in *Bull. de la Soc. bot. de France* XXXIII. 216).] The axial cylinder in the stems and roots of vascular plants, developed from the plerome.

1895 [see TETRARCH *sb.*[2]]. **1898** H. C. PORTER tr. *Strasburger* etc. *Text-bk. Bot.* 109 The so-called central cylinder, for which Van Tieghem has proposed the name stele (column).

stele, obs. f. STEAL *v.*, STEEL, STILE.

†**ˈstelechite.** *Obs.* [ad. Gr. στελεχίτης (sense 1), f. στέλεχος crown of a root, trunk: see -ITE.]

1. One of the kinds of storax enumerated by Dioscorides.

In recent Dicts.

2. Used (after Aldrovandus) for ENTROCHITE.

1681 GREW *Musæum* III. §i. ii. 270 The Stelentrochite. By some, called Stelechites. **1695** WOODWARD *Nat. Hist. Earth* IV. 181 The Selenites, Belemnites, Stelechites.

†**steˈlentrochite.** *Obs.* [? f. Gr. στήλη (see STELE) or στέλ(εχος) + ENTROCHITE.] = prec.

1681 [see STELECHITE 2].

†**steletic,** app. a blunder for next.

1653 GAUDEN *Hierasp.* 385 By spiritlesse Prefacings, to lead on their ruder steleticks and declaimings against the Order..of the Church of England.

Steliteutic (stɛlɪˈtjuːtɪk). *rare.* [ad. Gr. στηλιτευτικός (*sc.* λόγος), f. στηλιτεύειν to post or placard publicly, f. στηλίτης one who is placarded as an offender, f. στήλη: see STELE.] An invective discourse. (Only as the title of certain orations of St. Gregory Nazianzen.)

1751 LAVINGTON *Enthus. Meth. & Papists* III. (1754) 235 As Gregory Nazianzen hath it in his First Steliteutic. **1824** WATT *Bibl. Brit.* II. 835 Savile, Sir Henry..Nazianzen's Steliteutics. 1610.

stelk (stɛlk). *Anglo-Ir.* [Prob. ad. Ir. *stailc* stubbornness, sulkiness, (in Co. Donegal) starch: cf. STALK *sb.*[1]] A cooked vegetable dish made with onions, mashed potatoes, and butter, or other ingredients.

1844 W. CARLETON *Traits & Stories Ir. Peasantry* (new ed.) II. 167 Norah..sent you a crock of her own lard. When you're makin'..*sthilk*.., if you slip in a lump of this, it'll save you the price of butther. *Ibid.*, *Sthilk* is made by bruising a quantity of boiled potatoes and beans together. The potatoes, having first been reduced to a pulpy state, the beans are but partially broken. It is then put into a dish, and a pound of butter or rendered lard thrust into the middle of it. **1890** D. A. SIMMONS *List Words & Phr. S. Donegal* 16 *Stelk*, champ, food made of pounded potatoes. **1949** 'M. INNES' *Journeying Boy* xiii. 162, I greatly fear that for dinner now we shall have to fall back upon stelk. **1971** *Guardian* 10 July 9/6 Stelk..is alternatively known as champ and consists of spring onions simmered in milk.

stell (stɛl), *sb.*[1] *Sc.* and *north.* Also 2 stelle, 4, 7 stel-, 6–7 steill, staill, 8 stale, 7–9 still. [app. repr. OE. (Northumb.) *stællo* catching of fish, prob. from the root of *steall* place (STALL *sb.*[1]), *stęllan* to place.] A place in a river provided with arrangements for spreading salmon-nets. In Cumberland, 'a barrier placed across a river' (*Eng. Dial. Dict.*).

1099–1128 *Charter* in *Feodarium Prior. Dunelm.* (Surtees) 98 *note*, And haliware stelle ic habbe ʒetyðed Sc̄e cuhtberht his aʒen into his cyrce. **1467** *Dunfermline Reg.* (Bannatyne Club) 358 Inquisicion..langand þe merchis..betwix þe fischingis of þe ald stell pertening to þe Abbot..and [etc.]. **1574** *Rec. Monast. Kinloss* (1872) 158 The remanent fischeingis of the yardis and stellis upoun the watter of Findorne. **1583** *Reg. Mag. Sig. Scot.* 186/1 Salmonum piscaries de lie staillis et Yairis super aquam de Fyndhorne. **1595** *Ibid.* 77/2 Fretum de Kessok et piscariam ejusdem vocatam the Steill. **1707** FOUNTAINHALL *Decis.* (1759) II. 363 The said stells..are deep ponds, pools and ditches in the river, where the salmon haunting are taken in nets spread beneath them. **1783** *Ann. Reg., Chron.* 215 An action was brought against the corporation of Carlisle, for having a stell across the river Eden. **1794** W. HUTCHINSON *Hist. Cumberld.* II. 522 The river produces..excellent salmon (which are taken in draw-nets since the destruction of the stell at King-garth). **1874** A. HISLOP *Scot. Anecd.* 542 A still means space in which to extend a net, and sweep round with a view to enclose fish.

b. Comb., as ***stell (salmon) fishery, fishing***; **stell-net** [cf. WFlem. *stelnet* and STELL *v.*], (see quot. 1870); † **stell yair**, a 'yair' or fish-lock built at the issue of a 'stell'.

1792 *Statist. Acc. Scot.* III. 4 There is belonging to the public good of Dingwall, a *stell salmon fishery on Conan. **1798** *Surv. Moray* 188 Mr. Brodie of Brodie has a still-fishery on the east side of the river. **1707** FOUNTAINHALL *Decis.* (1759) II. 363 Five *stell salmond fishings in the river of Findhorn. **1794** *Statist. Acc. Scot.* XII. 270 The herrings are the only fish caught in this coast, except a few salmon caught at Stale fishing. **1806** MORISON *Decis.* XXXIII. 14258 The stell fishing in the ferry of Kessoch..is properly a sea fishing. *c* **1303** *Reg. Pal. Dunelm.* (Rolls) III. 40 Quatuor *stelnettes, duo rednettes. **1564** in *Reg. Mag. Sig. Scot.* 1584, 213/1 Cum piscationibus salmonum lie steill nettis, in dominio de Lorne. **1602** *Ibid.* 484/2 Piscationes salmonum vocatas lie Steill-nett of the Priore-schottis on the water mouth of Aw..cum piscatione vocata Staill-nett de Keanlochtive. **1792** *Statist. Acc. Scot.* IV. 557 A still net has been tried on the lake with some success. **1845** *New Statist. Acc. Scot.* XIV. II. 206 Salmon Fishery... The fish are chiefly caught with the stell-net. **1870** *Law Rep., Comm. Pl.* V. 695 A stell net, that is, a net fastened to stakes across the whole bed of the river. **1900** *Law Rep., App. Cases* 406 It is denied that toot and haul nets, or stell nets, or either of them, are fixed engines. **1600** *Reg. Mag. Sig. Scot.* 341/1 Terras de Culmoir, cum lie *stel-yair, halecum et salmonum piscationibus [etc.].

†**stell**, *sb.*[2] *Obs.* [? a. Du. *stel.*] A stand for a barrel.

a **1658** CLEVELAND *Sing-song* xiv. Poems (1659) 157 Her brests..Like swelling Buts of lively Wine Upon their ivory stells did shine. **1854** MISS BAKER *Northampt. Gloss.*, *Stell*, a stand or stall for beer barrels. **1881** *Leicester Gloss.*, *Stell*, a stand or frame to support barrels.

stell (stɛl), *sb.*[3] *dial.* [Of obscure origin: perh. a use of OE. *stęll* (*stiell, styll*) a leap, related to *stęllan* to leap, jump.] An open ditch or brook.

1651 in *N. Riding Rec.* V. 76 The inhabitants of Pottoe ..[are presented] for not scouring their proportion of Traineham Stell. *c* **1783** *Roxb. Ballads* (1890) VII. 94 When fully intending to lead the whole field, A damn'd Stell held 'em both 'till the Fox he was kill'd. **1825** BROCKETT *N.C. Gloss.*, *Stell*, a large open drain in a marsh. **1825** *Sporting Mag.* XVI. 14 *note*, A stell is the Durham name for a brook whose banks are not firm. **1827** *Ibid.* XXI. 33 We shall never get over that stell. **1878** SUSAN PHILLIPS *On Seaboard* 164 Where Tees sweeps into the Northern main, And the glittering 'stells,' and the link's long range. **1885** *Manch. City News* 31 Jan. 2/4, I came upon a lane with a tiny brook crossing it, which in Yorkshire is called a stell. **1886** W. H. BURNETT *Old Cleveland* 126 This stable was built on an open stell, which rose and fell with the tide.

stell (stɛl), *sb.*[4] *Sc.* [Presumably related to STELL *v.*] An enclosure for giving shelter to sheep or cattle, usually circular, smaller than a 'fold' and with higher walls. Also a ring of trees serving as a shelter for sheep or cattle.

1766 *State of Proc., Dk. Roxburghe* v. *Pringle* 10 At replacing the Cauld, the Workers did take Stones from a Stell the Deponent had built. **1829** BROCKETT *N.C. Gloss.* (ed. 2), *Stell*, a fold or small enclosure for cattle. **1844** H. STEPHENS *Bk. Farm* II. 58 A stell may be formed of planting or high stone-wall. Either will afford shelter. **1886** C. SCOTT *Sheep Farming* 126 'Stells' were erected at various parts of the hills for sheltering the sheep.

‖**stell** (stɛl), *sb.*[5] *South African.* [Du. *stel.*] A trap for wild animals.

1801 J. BARROW *Trav. Interior S. Afr.* I. vi. 360 The animal had been shot through the body by a *stell-roar* or trap-gun, set by a Hottentot. **1852** BARTER *Dorp & Veld* viii. 116 As soon as he [the wolf] has seized the bait.., he tightens the string, releases the trigger, and if the *stel* is properly set, receives the bullet in his head. **1863** W. C. BALDWIN *Afr. Hunting* ix. 377 The lions had killed two zebras..and I set a stell (a spring gun) for them by the remains of one of the zebras. *Ibid.* 381 The Masaras set these spears (stells) for rhinoceros and other game. **1895** J. G. MILLAIS *Breath fr. Veldt* (1899) 264 A 'still'..is formed by two rifles fixed to trees or posts.

†**stell**, *sb.*[6] *Obs. rare*$^{-1}$. In 7 *pl.* stels. [Cf. STELL *v.* 3.] ? An outline.

1657 LIGON *Barbadoes* 82 So as the outmost stels, or profile of the figure, may be perfectly discerned.

[**stell**, *sb.*[7], a spurious word in Nares and subsequent Dicts., explained as 'place, station', is due to a misprint for *castell* (= castle) in Danett tr. *Comines* (ed. 1, 1596), corrected in later edd.]

stell (stɛl), *v.* Forms: 1 stellan (3 sing. pres. **steleþ**, pa. t. -stelidæ, -stealde, -stalde), 3 stellen (pa. t. stalde, stolde, pa. pple. isteald), 5 stell. [OE. *stęllan, stiellan, styllan* (also in combs. *á-stęllan* ASTELL *v.*, *on-stęllan* ONSTELL *v.*) = OS. *stellian*, (M)Du. *stellen*, OHG., MHG., mod.G. *stellen*:—WGer. **stalljan*, f. OTeut. **stallo-* place, STALL *sb.*]

†**1.** *trans.* To set (an example); to establish (a law). *Obs.*

c **893** ÆLFRED *Orosius* II. ii. §1 Hwelce bisena he ðær stellende wæs. *c* **897** —— *Gregory's Past. C.* xxviii. 191 Ðonne he oðrum yfele bisene steleþ. *a* **1225** *Ancr. R.* 6 þe vttre riwle..nis for noþing elles istald bute forte seruie ðe inre. *Ibid.* 8 þeos..ne beoð nout monnes fundles, ne riwle þet mon stolde. *c* **1230** *Hali Meid.* 19 Wedlac ham ikepte þat ilke lahe þat godd haueð istald for þe unstronge. *c* **1275** *Serving Christ* 60 in *O.E. Misc.* 92 He wolde þe lawe leoflyche holde As god..i þis world stolde.

2. *Sc.* To fix, post, place; chiefly, to station (oneself, troops), to place (cannon) in position.

c **1470** HENRY *Wallace* IV. 430 In a dern woode thai stellit thaim full law. *Ibid.* VII. 868 Heich in Cragmor he maid it [a decapitated head] for to stand, Steild on a stayne for honour of Ireland. **1559** *Aberdeen Reg.* (1844) I. 327 To desist and ceiss fra forther stelling and stenting of their netts athort the water. **1573** BIRREL *Diary* (1798) 20 The Englisch cannone ..began to shoute at ye castell of Edinburghe, being steillit at foure several places, viz. 5 at Egers hous [etc.]. *a* **1578** LINDESAY (Pitscottie) *Chron. Scot.* (S.T.S.) II. 251 Thai.. had with thame twa small cairted peices and stylled thame vpone the craigheid abone leith wynd. **1596** DALRYMPLE tr. *Leslie's Hist. Scot.* II. 298 The Jnglismen..raiset thair camp, to stel cannounes, and thair feild peices, at the hil of the place namet Pinkincleuch. **17..** *Lads of Wamphray* vii. in Child *Ballads* III. 459 Twixt the Staywood Buss and Langside Hill, They stelld the broked cow and branded bull. **1819** SCOTT *Leg. Montrose* x, Yonder round hillock.. whereon an enemy might stell such a battery of cannon as would make ye glad to beat a chamade within forty-eight hours. **1901** G. DOUGLAS *Ho. Green Shutters* 7 On the slope the horses were..forced to stell themselves back against the heavy propulsion of the carts behind.

b. To fix (one's eyes). Also *pass.* and *intr.* of the eyes: To have a fixed stare, to set rigidly.

c **1817** HOGG *Tales & Sk.* IV. 57 John's eyes stelled in his head. **1888** A. WARDROP *Poems & Sk.* 201 Dinna stell yer een sae, but jest sit doon there. **1890** *Blackw. Mag.* Sept. 325 He tell't us aboot the deid man wi the glowerin' e'en —they were stell't in his heed.

3. To portray, delineate. *Obs.* exc. *arch.*

1598 HAYDOCKE tr. *Lomazzo* I. 16 Before you begin to Stell, delineat and tricke out the proportion of a man [It. *prima che delinei, e disegni un' huomo*], you ought to know his true quantity and stature. *c* **1600** SHAKS. *Sonn.* xxiv, Mine eye hath play'd the painter and hath steeld [*sic*; *rime* held] Thy beauties forme in table of my heart. **1657** R. LIGON *Barbadoes* Ded., Rough drawn, and unproportionably stell'd, though it be, I here present it. **1880** BRIDGES *Portr. Grandfather* Poems (1912) 390 If truly A painter had stell'd thee there, with thy lips ready to speak.

stell, obs. f. STEAL, STEEL, STILL.

‖**stella** (ˈstɛlə). Pl. stellæ. [L., *lit.* star.]

1. a. *Zool.* A star-shaped projection on the surface of a coralline; also, a star-shaped sponge-spicule.

1828 STARK *Elem. Nat. Hist.* II. 431 Surface rough with elevated pyramidal stellæ; stars conical, with a solid central axis.

b. *Crystallogr.* A stellate crystal.

1844 G. BIRD *Urin. Deposits* (1857) 238 The octohedra of oxalate may be readily detected mixed with the prisms or stellæ of the former [*sc.* phosphate of magnesia and ammonia].

†**steˈllaceous,** *a. Obs.* [f. mod.L. **stellāce-us* (f. *stella* star): see -ACEOUS.] Star-shaped.

1657 TOMLINSON *Renou's Disp.* 247 Coronated with Flowers..but longer, white and stellaceous.

stellacyanin (stɛləˈsaɪənɪn). *Biochem.* [f. the name *Estelle* (see quot. 1967) after PLASTOCYANIN.] An intensely blue copper-containing protein found in the latex of the Japanese lac tree, *Rhus vernicifera.*

1966 W. G. LEVINE in J. Peisach et al. *Biochem. of Copper* 377 Omura,..in the course of purifying *Rhus* laccase.., separated a second, blue, copper protein which Peisach later named stellacyanin. **1967** J. PEISACH et al. in *Biochem. Jrnl.* CCXLII. 2857/2 The authors would like to thank..Dr. Tsuneo Omura, whose permission was kindly given to name stellacyanin after Mrs. Estelle Peisach. **1976** *Nature* 27 May 346/1 Stellacyanin..and umecyanin have about 110 and 130 amino acids with a single cysteine residue plus one disulphide bridge.

‖**Stella Maris** (ˈstɛlə ˈmærɪs). [L., lit. 'star of the sea'.] A title given to the Virgin Mary (see SEA-STAR 1), used allusively of a protectress or a guiding spirit.

1876 GEO. ELIOT *Dan. Der.* III. v. xxxvii. 113 If a man could paint the woman he loves..as the *Stella Maris* to put courage into the sailors..so much the more honour to her. **1897** O. WILDE *Let.* 31 May (1962) 583 Even for the sheep who has no shepherd there is a Stella Maris to guide it home. **1913** W. J. LOCKE *Stella Maris* i. 1 Stella Maris—Star of the Sea! That was not her real name. No one could have christened an innocent babe so absurdly. *Ibid.* 2 Walter Herold.., one night of storm and dashing spray, seeing the light, burning steadily like a star.., cried: 'Stella Maris! What a name for her!'

stellar (ˈstɛlə(r)), *a.* [ad. late L. *stellāris*, f. L. *stella* star: see -AR. Cf. F. *stellaire*, It. *stellare*, Sp. *estrellar.*]

1. Pertaining to the stars or a star; of the nature of a star.

1656 BLOUNT *Glossogr.*, *Stellar*..starry, pertaining to a star. *Bac.* **1667** MILTON *P.L.* IV. 671 These soft fires..shed down Thir stellar vertue on all kinds that grow On Earth. **1669** FLAMSTEED in *Phil. Trans.* IV. 1109 At the middle of this Stellar Eclipse the Moons Center is but 20 sec. more to the South than the Star. *c* **1786** BURNS *To Miss Cruickshank* 7 Never baleful stellar lights, Taint thee with untimely blights! **1833** SIR J. HERSCHEL *Treat. Astron.* (1839) 404 They present the appearance of a dull and blotted star, or of a star with a slight burr round it, in which case they are called stellar nebulæ. **1840** CARLYLE *Heroes* iii. (1841) 165 Not a leaf rotting on the highway but is indissoluble portion of solar and stellar systems. **1858** SEARS *Athan.* 7 Localities somewhere among the planetary and stellar spaces. **1868** ROSCOE *Elem. Chem.* 10 Within the last few years the foundations of a solar and stellar chemistry have, however, been laid. **1869** M. PATTISON *Serm.* (1885) 179 The stellar worlds, this earth included. **1875** WHITNEY *Life Lang.* vi. 99 A mishap due to a baleful stellar aspect. **1888** *Times* (weekly ed.) 14 Sept. 3/2 This stellar origin of totemism goes far to account for the widespread character of the institution. **1975** *Physics Bull.* Nov. 484/3 Astrophysicists use the term white dwarfs to describe objects which are stellar, that is to say luminous by themselves, but with a low luminosity and a small radius.

2. Star-shaped, stellate. Chiefly of crystals; also *Arch.* in ***stellar vault*** (see quot. 1835), ***stellar groining***.

1670 *Phil. Trans.* V. 1199 The Stellar Fish described in Numb. 57. **1835** R. WILLIS *Archit. Mid. Ages* vii. 85, I would call this class of decorated vaults Stellar vaults, from the regular stellate form they assume on the plan. **1841** *Civil Engin. & Arch. Jrnl.* IV. 286/1 The vaulting immediately preceding fan groining,.. designated as stellar groining. **1844** H. STEPHENS *Bk. Farm* II. 383 It may be advisable to make a clump of planting of a stellar form. **1845** G. E. DAY tr. *Simon's Anim. Chem.* (1846) I. 55 Urate of soda.. occasionally constitutes a very peculiar stellar form of deposit in the urine. **1851** E. SHARPE *Seven Periods Archit.* 36 The plans of these vaultings are very various; some are called Fan-tracery vaults, and others Stellar vaults, terms which explain themselves. **1897** *Allbutt's Syst. Med.* IV. 299 Occasionally stellar phosphate—that is dicalcic phosphate—is thrown down when the acidity of the urine is diminished.

3. Having the quality of a star (STAR *sb.*[1] 5); leading, outstanding. So **'stellardom**, stardom. orig. and chiefly *U.S.*

1883 *N.Y. Mercury* 3 Nov. 2/2 Effie Ellsler's dramatic stellardom is at an end and the supporting cast will be disbanded. **1883** *Sunday Mercury* (N.Y.) 4 Nov. 7/3 A fine specialty performance will be given by selected stellar artists. **1912** M. B. LEAVITT *Fifty Years Theatr. Managem.* xxx. 464 In those days a theatrical star was obliged to work his way up to the rungs of the legitimate ladder until he was found worthy of ranking in stellardom... It made good actors,.. who have since taken their places as leaders in the stellar ranks. **1932** KAUFMAN & RYSKUD *Of Thee I Sing* I. iv. 75 The two centre chairs are conspicuously empty, obviously waiting for the stellar pair. **1950** J. DEMPSEY *Championship Fighting* 26 It is only in.. 'partial' punches that the body-weight does not play a stellar role. **1958** WODEHOUSE *Cocktail Time* xviii. 156 A man of regular habits, he would normally have shrunk from playing a stellar role in an E. Phillips Oppenheim story. **1964** W. C. PUTNAM *Geol.* ix. 215/1 Second of the factors is the nature of the ground. San Francisco, 1906, and Long Beach, 1933, both [earthquakes] in California, are stellar examples of the importance of this control. **1976** *Times Lit. Suppl.* 25 June 804/5 The most spectacular book sale held this spring... The stellar attraction was the whole Book of Daniel, twelve leaves, from the Trier copy of the 42-line or Gutenberg Bible, 1455. **1977** *Amer. N. & Q.* XV. 94/1 He has eschewed the glitter of Hollywood which has lured and made stellar personalities out of so many of his fellow novelists.

stellarator ('stɛləreɪtə(r)). *Physics.* [f. STELLAR *a.* (see quot. 1951) + L. *-ātor* (see -OR 2 and cf. Eng. *generator*).] One kind of toroidal apparatus for producing controlled fusion reactions in a hot plasma, distinguished by the fact that all the controlling magnetic fields inside it are produced by external windings.

1951 L. SPITZER *Proposed Stellarator* (U.S. Atomic Energy Commission NYO-993) 4 Since the proposed system generates power and neutrons by reactions similar to those occurring in the stars, the device analyzed below is called a 'Stellarator'. **1967** CONDON & ODISHAW *Handbk. Physics* (ed. 2) IV. xi. 209/2 The feature that distinguishes a stellarator from a torus with solenoidal windings alone is the presence of helical windings around the channel which cause the magnetic-field lines to be twisted in such a way that as the particles drift they are constantly turned back toward the channel center. **1980** *Ann. Rep. U.K. Atomic Energy Authority 1979–80* 32/1 Another type of toroidal magnetic trap studied at Culham is the stellarator. **1981** *Nature* 19 Feb. 625/1 The tokamak must create the longitudinal current in the plasma by a transformer effect, and so must be pulsed. The stellarator, on the other hand, can in principle be run statically.

‖**Stellaria** (stɛ'lɛərɪə). *Bot.* [mod.L. *stellāria* (1517 in Diefenbach; the present application is due to Linnæus 1753), f. L. *stella* star: see -ARY.] A genus of caryophyllaceous plants, of which several species (known as 'chickweed', 'stitchwort', 'starwort', etc.) are common in Great Britain and the U.S.; also, a plant of this genus.

1785 MARTYN *Lett. Bot.* xix. (1794) 273 Arenaria and Stellaria have a capsule of one cell. **1806** *Med. Jrnl.* XV. 264 Common chickweed... This species of stellaria is a notable instance of what is called the sleep of plants. **1863** *Life in South* II. 229 Flights of pigeons were whirling over head, violets and stellarias were sprouting beneath the feet, and such was the January of Savannah.

†**'stellary**, *a. Obs.* [irreg. ad. late L. *stellāris*: see prec. and -ARY.] = STELLAR *a.*

1623 COCKERAM I, *Stellary*, starrie. **1658** SIR T. BROWNE *Gard. Cyrus* iii. 46 Could we have any light, why the stellary part of the first masse, separated into this order, that the Girdle of Orion should ever maintain its line. **1731–9** TULL *Horse-hoeing Husb.* (1822) 76 Astronomers take notice of those parts of plants alone which exist within that element where they are accustomed to make their stellary observations. **1763** STUKELEY *Paleogr. Sacr.* 43 An infinite infinity of such groups of stellary orbs. **1790** in *Ann. Reg. 1817, Chron.* 390 Should you shine throughout the intellectual and stellary universe.

†**'stellascope.** *Obs.* (? *nonce-wd.*) [f. L. *stella* star + -SCOPE. (? An intentional perversion of *telescope.*)] An astronomical telescope.

1661 MORGAN *Sph. Gentry* I. 44 Though the stellascope doth discover a seeming hole, or spot in the body of the planet Mars.

stellate ('stɛlət), *a.* and *sb.* [ad. L. *stellātus*, f. *stella* star: see -ATE[2].]

A. *adj.* **1.** Of the sky: Studded with stars. *poet.*

c **1500** KENNEDY *Poems* (Schipper) iv. 27 Þe hevyne stellat, planetis, montanis and fellis, War fair perchiament, and all as Virgillis dyte.

†**2.** Pertaining to or proceeding from the stars.

1658 FRANCK *North. Mem.* Ded. Virtuosos (1694) p. xi, There you may see the Operation of Elements and stellate Influences.

3. a. Star-shaped; arranged or grouped in the form of a conventional star or stars; (chiefly in scientific use) radiating from a centre like the rays of a star.

1661 LOVELL *Hist. Anim. & Min.* 228 The Stellate Raie is lesse hard.. than the Smooth. **1661** BOYLE *Cert. Physiol. Ess.* (1669) 56 Several Stellate Regulusses of both Antimony and Mars. **1704** J. HARRIS *Lex. Techn.* I, *Stellate Plants*, are by the Botanists called such Plants as have their Leaves growing on the Stalks at certain Intervals or Distances, in the form of a Radiant Star. **1752** tr. *Heister's Surg.* (1768) II. 363 *marg.*, The Stellate Bandage. **1755** *Phil. Trans.* XLIX. 17 The uniform stellate form of snow is very remarkable. **1832** LINDLEY *Introd. Bot.* I. ii. 40 In many plants the hairs grow in clusters,.. and are occasionally united at their base: such are called stellate. **1857** MILLER *Elem. Chem., Org.* 272 The Sulphate.. crystallizes in stellate groups of silky needles. **1872** H. A. NICHOLSON *Palæont.* 111 In their form the Star-fishes differ considerably, though in most the figure is markedly stellate. **1876** DUNGLISON *Med. Lex.*, *Stellate Ligament*, a name given to the anterior costo-vertebral ligament, from its shape. **1880** SOLLAS in *Ann. & Mag. Nat. Hist.* Ser. v. V. 257 The stellate spicules.. are produced within the interior of cells.

b. *Comb. Esp.* in *Anat.*, as ***stellate cell***, any of various types of cell with long processes, as a Langerhans cell, a Kupffer cell, or an astrocyte (sense a); ***stellate ganglion***, the lowest of the three cervical ganglia of the sympathetic trunk; ***stellate reticulum***, a layer of cells with long processes within the enamel organ of a developing tooth.

1870 HOOKER *Stud. Flora* 32 Draba muralis, suberect or prostrate, stellate-hispid. **1884** BOWER & SCOTT *De Bary's Phaner.* 130 Stellate-branched fibres occur in the foliage-leaf of Sciadopitys. **1890**, etc. [see LANGERHANS]. **1895** A. H. SMITH *Dental Microsc.* p. xvii, Stellate reticulum of enamel organ. **1899** *Allbutt's Syst. Med.* VI. 300 The patches, examined microscopically, are found to consist of embryonic round cells, spindle and stellate cells arranged in layers. **1901**, etc. [see KUPFFER]. **1918** *Gray's Anat.* (ed. 20) 935 The accelerator fibres of the heart leave mainly through the second and third thoracic nerves and pass to the stellate ganglion. **1921** TILNEY & RILEY *Form & Function Central Nervous Syst.* xli. 749 Immediately beneath the layers of large and medium-sized pyramidal cells is a stratum containing a number of small monopolar stellate cells belonging exclusively to the Golgi type II. **1945** [see ASTROCYTE]. **1969** W. A. BERESFORD *Lect. Notes Histol.* xxiv. 169 'Mesectoderm' cells.. induce overlying ectodermal lamina to separate into tooth germs and provide for each an enamel organ with its pulp/stellate reticulum and inner and outer epithelia. **1980** *Gray's Anat.* (ed. 36) 1129/1 The cervicothoracic (stellate) ganglion is.. much larger than the middle cervical ganglion, being probably formed by the coalescence of the lower two cervical segmented ganglia with the first thoracic.

B. *sb.* A stellate sponge-spicule.

1880 SOLLAS in *Ann. & Mag. Nat. Hist.* Ser. v. V. 132 *Stelletta*... The skeleton consists of long-shafted spicules, minute hair-like spicules, and stellates. **1887** —— in *Encycl. Brit.* XXII. 417/2 (*Sponge*) By reduction of the spire the spiraster passes into the stellate or aster.

Hence **'stellately** *adv.*

1847 W. E. STEELE *Field Bot.* 106 Leaves plane, lanceolate, stellately hairy. **1848** DANA *Zooph.* 283 Surface lamello-striate, and usually stellately so, stars not circumscribed. **1884** BOWER & SCOTT *De Bary's Phaner.* 58 One may, for instance, call the flat horizontal appendages of the Elæagneæ,.. stellately branched, multicellular hairs.

stellate ('stɛleɪt), *v.* [f. L. *stellāt-*, ppl. stem of *stellāre* f. *stella* star.] *trans.* To make stellate or star-shaped.

1859 CAYLEY *Math. Papers* (1891) IV. 82 Each face is formed by stellating a face of the great dodecahedron. **1948** [see STELLATION 7].

stellated ('stɛleɪtɪd), *a.* [f. STELLATE *a.* + -ED[1].]

1. a. = STELLATE *a.* 3.

1661 BOYLE *Cert. Physiol. Ess.* (1669) 57 My own Laboratory has afforded me divers such parcels of Regulus without Mars (some of which I have yet by me very fairly stellated). *c* **1711** PETIVER *Gazophyl.* IX. xc, Its yellow stellated Flowers adhere to the middle rib of a jagged Membrane. **1785** MARTYN *Lett. Bot.* xv. (1794) 163 This class comprises another natural order of plants, entitled Stellated, from the manner in which the leaves grow upon the stem. **1788** BLAGDEN in *Phil. Trans.* LXXVIII. 281 When these stellated crystals once began to form. **1804** SHAW *Gen. Zool.* V. 378 Stellated Sturgeon.. head subtetragonal and roughened with stellated marks and tubercles. **1821** W. P. C. BARTON *Flora N. Amer.* I. 87 Stem and branches.. densely beset with stellated hairs. **1859** CAYLEY *Math. Papers* (1891) IV. 81 The great stellated dodecahedron. **1892** CROOKES *Wagner's Man. Chem. Technol.* 203 That stellated crystalline surface which is preferred in trade.

b. *Geom.* Of a polygon, polyhedron, or polytope: capable of being generated from a convex polygon, etc., by extending the edges, etc., until they once more meet at a new set of vertices, etc. [The sense is due to L. Poinsot, who used F. *étoilé* in *Jrnl. de l'École Polytechn.* (1810) IV. 41.)]

1859 A. CAYLEY in *Phil. Mag.* XVII. 123 It is shown by Poinsot.. that, besides the regular polyhedrons of ordinary geometry, there are (of course in an extended signification of the term) four new regular polyhedrons, viz. an icosahedron, which I will call the great icosahedron.., and three dodecahedrons, which I will call the great dodecahedron.., the great stellated dodecahedron.., and the small stellated dodecahedron. **1931** *Proc. Cambr. Philos. Soc.* XXVII. 206 Consider.. the 'small stellated dodecahedron' {, 5}, bounded by pentagrams. **1952** CUNDY & ROLLETT *Math. Models* iii. 83 These four beautiful solids were unknown to the ancient world and were not discovered until modern times. The two with star faces—the two stellated dodecahedra—were found by Kepler (1571–1630); the others with regular faces and star vertices—the great icosahedron and dodecahedron—by Poinsot (1777–1859). **1976** I. LAKATOS *Proofs & Refutations* i. 62 Take for instance the 'great stellated dodecahedron' (fig. 15). It consists, like the 'small stellated dodecahedron' of pentagrams, but differently arranged. It has 12 faces, 30 edges and 20 vertices, so that $V - E + F = 2$.

2. Studded with stars.

1755 B. MARTIN *Mag. Arts & Sci.* 88 The Stellated Planetarium: shewing the Inferior Planets. **1824** J. JOHNSON *Typogr.* I. 490 The back-ground is black, thickly stellated.

Hence **ste'llatedly** *adv.*

1833 HOOKER in *Smith's Eng. Flora* V. I. 119 Stem.. stellatedly branched.

stellation (stɛ'leɪʃən). [Noun of action f. L. *stellāre* to diversify with stars, to place among the stars, etc., f. *stella* star: see -ATION.]

†**1.** Blighting or blasting of trees (attributed to starry influence): = SIDERATION 1. *Obs.*[−0]

1623 [see SIDERATION 1]. **1656** BLOUNT *Glossogr.*, *Stellation*, a blasting.

†**2.** ? = CONSTELLATION. *Obs. rare*[−1].

a **1629** T. ADAMS *Serm.* Wks. 158 Some haue thought that these Magi, hauing so profound skill in Astrologie, might by calculation of times, composition of Starres, and Stellations of the Heauens, foreknow the birth of the Messias.

†**3.** Placing among the stars; stellification. *Obs.*

1635 HEYWOOD *Hierarchy* III. 138 The cause of it's [*sc.* the Scorpion's] stellation to enquire,.. Comes next in course.

†**4.** (See quot. 1661.) *Obs.*[−0]

1661 BLOUNT *Glossogr.* (ed. 2), *Stellation*, a making star-like, or adorning with stars. **1721** BAILEY, *Stellation*, an Adorning with Stars.

†**5.** (See quot.) *Obs.*[−0]

1755 JOHNSON *Stellation*, emission of light as from a star.

6. Each of the 'stars' composing a stellate tissue.

1859 TOMES *Dental Surg.* 44 Below the epithelium comes a thick layer of stellate areolar tissue... Nuclei are present in the centres of the stellations.

7. The making or being stellate.

1859 CAYLEY *Math. Papers* (1891) IV. 83 On account of the stellation $e = 2$. **1938** H. S. M. COXETER et al. *Fifty-Nine Icosahedra* i. 1 We enumerate and describe the polyhedra that can be five Platonic solids by stellation, *i.e.*, by extending or 'producing' the faces until they meet again, always preserving the rotational symmetry of the original solid. **1948** —— *Regular Polytopes* xiv. 264 The first stellation of {5, 3, 3} is constructed by stellating the 720 pentagons into {$\frac{5}{2}$}'s, and the 120 dodecahedra into {$\frac{5}{2}$, 5}'s. The result is {$\frac{5}{2}$, 5, 3}. **1971** *Sci. Amer.* Dec. 114/2 The five Platonic solids are complete of their symmetrical kind. By mixing regular polygon faces, however, Archimedes made 13 more solids. These can be variously extended by putting cells on faces, called stellation, or by cutting away cells whenever that process can reveal new regular polygon faces within.

stellato- (stɛ'leɪtəʊ). *Biol.* Used as combining form of STELLATE *a.*

1866 *Treas. Bot.* 1094/1 *Stellato-pilose*, having hairs formed in a stellate manner. **1871** W. A. LEIGHTON *Lichen-flora* 3 Thallus stellato-orbicular. *Ibid.* 5 Thallus minute, stellato-divided. *Ibid.* 10 Perithecia several, stellato-congregate. *Ibid.* 32 Stellato-laciniate.

stellatour, obs. Sc. var. STILLATORY.

†**'stellature.** *Roman Law. Obs.* [ad. late L. *stellātūra*, of uncertain origin.] Some kind of fraud practised by tribunes in the supply of provisions to soldiers.

1608 TOPSELL *Serpents* 277 When the Tribunes did withdraw from the Souldiours their prouision of victuall and Corne, it is said, *Tribunos qui per Stellaturas Militibus aliquid abstulissent, capitali pœna affecit.* And therefore Budæus relateth a history of two Tribunes, who for this stellature were worthilie stoned to death. *a* **1629** T. ADAMS

Serm. Wks. 896 Extortion and Cousenage is prouerbially called, *Crimen Stellionatus*, the sinne of Stellature.

stelle, obs. f. STEAL *v.*, STEEL, STILL.

'stelled, *a. Obs.* exc. *poet.* [f. L. *stella* star + -ED[1]: cf. STELLATE *a.*] **a.** ? Formed into stars; stellar. **b.** Studded with stars, starred.

1605 SHAKS. *Lear* III. vii. 61 The Sea..Would have buoy'd vp, And quench'd the Stelled fires. **1628** FELTHAM *Resolves* I. viii. 18 Open Rebukes are for Magistrates, and Courts of Iustice: for Stelled Chambers, and for Scarlets, in the thronged Hall. **1656** BLOUNT *Glossogr.*, *Stelled*, full of, or garnished with stars. **1949** BLUNDEN *After Bombing* 41 Thence the eye soon travelled over much green plain, Swathed with plats blush-dyed, with blue meres stelled.

†**stelleer(e.** *Obs. rare.* [Of obscure origin. (Cotgr. is prob. the only real authority for the word).] A steelyard.

1611 COTGR., *Crochet*,..also, a Roman beame, a Stelleere. *Ibid.*, *Romaine*, a Roman beame, a Stelleere. **1678** J. PHILLIPS tr. *Tavernier's Trav.* II. 9 Acc. Money of Asia, The Chineses..carry their weights always along with them, being like a Roman Beam, or a Stelleer [orig. *une petite romaine*], about eight Inches long, with which they weigh all the Gold and Silver which they receive. **1727** BAILEY vol. II, *Stelleer.*

Stellenbosch ('stɛlənbɒʃ), *v. Milit. slang.* [f. *Stellenbosch*, a town and a division of Cape Province.] (See quot. 1913.)

1900 KIPLING in *Daily Express* 16 June 4/6 'After all', said one cheerily..'what does it matter, old man? You're bound to be Stellenbosched in three days'. **1900** *Daily Tel.* 2 Oct. 6/1, I heard..that he had been 'Stellenbosched'... I must inform the uninitiated that Stellenbosch..was formerly the place selected for command by officers who had failed in Kaffir wars; and to be 'Stellenbosched' is the equivalent of being superseded without formal disgrace. **1900** *Ibid.* 20 Oct. 7/1 It is a gross injustice to Stellenbosch any doctor because some nurse does not get her own way, and has influence in high quarters. **1913** PETTMAN *Africanderisms* 475 *Stellenboshed* [sic], *To be*, to be relegated, as the result of incompetence, to a position in which little harm can be done.

Steller ('stɛlə(r)). The name of Georg Wilhelm *Steller* (see STELLERITE), used *attrib.* or in the possessive to designate certain animals associated with his explorations, as ***Steller's (eider) (duck)***, a black and white duck with reddish underparts, *Polysticta stelleri*, found in Siberia, Alaska, and Canada; ***Steller('s) jay***, a blue jay with a dark crest, *Cyanocitta stelleri*, found in western North America; ***Steller's sea-cow***, an extinct sirenian, *Hydrodamalis stelleri*, once found in the Bering Sea; ***Steller('s) sea-lion***, a large sea-lion, *Eumetopias jubata*, found in the northern Pacific. Cf. STELLERINE.

1814 tr. *G. H. von Langsdorff's Voyages & Travels* II. i. 23 My curiosity was particularly directed to..Steller's sea-cow. **1828** C. L. BONAPARTE *Amer. Ornithol.* II. 44 The Steller's Jay is one of those obsolete species alluded to in the preface to this volume. **1884** *Bull. U.S. Nat. Mus.* No. 27. 162 Steller's Duck..Arctic and subarctic coasts. **1902** *Bull. Amer. Mus. Nat. Hist.* XVI. 111 The northern and southern Sea Lions, often known respectively as Steller's Sea Lion and Forster's Sea Lion. **1917** Steller's jay [see *mountain jay* s.v. MOUNTAIN 9c]. **1938** P. A. TAVERNER *Birds of Canada* 104 Steller's Eider... The smallest and the least eider-like of any of the birds known under that name. **1947** L. G. INGLES *Mammals California* 88 Steller Sea Lion bulls weigh up to 1,800 pounds. **1948** *Pacific Discovery* Jan. 14/2 Steller jays, bald eagles, mountains of wild geraniums,..these are the Teton country. **1957** P. J. DARLINGTON *Zoogeography* vi. 400 Steller's Sea Cow..was hunted to extinction. **1963** *Times* 11 Feb. 14/4 One of these was an account of Steller's Eider Duck. **1968** G. MAXWELL *Raven seek thy Brother* viii. 103 No one had ever proved whether or not the..beautiful little duck called Steller's Eider..actually bred in Varanger Fjord. **1972** *Village Voice* (N.Y.) 1 June 75/2 In the dense fir forests you can hear..the scream of the steller's jay. **1972** L. HANCOCK *There's a Seal in my Sleeping Bag* vii. 145 The rocky shores..are used by the Steller sea-lions as hauling-out grounds. **1975** *Islander* (Victoria, B.C.) 27 Apr. 3/1 He has been studying California and Steller's sea lions in Barkley Sound. **1976** *Ibid.* 27 June 2/2 When the potatoes were small, many Steller jays came to rob the patch.

Stellerid ('stɛlərɪd). *Zool.* [ad. F. *stelléride* (Lamarck) app. irreg. f. L. *stella* star. (See -ID[3].)] A star-fish. Also **ste'lleridan** [see -IDAN], †**stelliridean, -ian.**

1835 KIRBY *Hab. & Inst.* I. vi. 201 Lamarck..has divided it [the order of Echinoderms] into three sections, the Stelleridans, Echinidans, and Fistulidans. **1836** BUCKLAND *Geol. & Min.* (1869) I. 348 No fossil Stelleridans have yet been noticed in strata more ancient than the Muschelkalk. **1837** *Penny Cycl.* IX. 262/2 Lamarck made his *Radiaires Echinodermes* consist of three sections. 1st, the Stellirideans (star-fishes). **1842** *Ibid.* XXIII. 17/2 Agassiz also divides the Stelliridians into three families. **1882** *Cassell's Nat. Hist.* VI. 271 The bases of the lateral tentacular branches which they give off open into large ambulacral vesicles, just as in the Stellerids. **1896** *Q. Jrnl. Microsc. Sci.* XXXVIII. 389 *note*, A paper on the 'Organogeny of Stellerids'.

Stellerine ('stɛlərɪn). [f. name of G. W. *Steller*, a German traveller (*died* 1745), who first described the species.] The arctic or Steller's sea-cow, *Rhytina stelleri.*

1854 A. ADAMS etc. *Man. Nat. Hist.* 20.

stellerite ('stɛləraɪt). *Min.* [ad. G. *stellerit* (J. Morozewicz 1909, in *Bull. internat. de l'Acad. des Sci. de Cracovie* (Math.-Nat. Classe) II. 350). f. the name of Georg Wilhelm *Steller* (1709–46), German naturalist and explorer of the Komandorski Islands in the Bering Sea where the first samples were found: see -ITE[1].] A zeolite, $CaAl_2Si_7O_{18}.7H_2O$, found as tabular orthorhombic crystals.

1909 *Jrnl. Chem. Soc.* XCVI. II. 1028 A new zeolite, stellerite, has been found at the N.W. Cape of Copper Island, one of the Komandorski islands in the Aleutian Group. **1968** *Amer. Mineralogist* LIII. 511 *Stellerite*, a valid orthorhombic end member of a continuous series with monoclinic stilbite. **1973** *Lithos* VI. 85 The walls of large cavities and fractures are lined with polycrystal aggregates of stellerite.

stelleroid ('stɛlərɔɪd). *Zool.* [f. mod.L. *Stelleroidea* (J. W. Gregory in E. R. Lankester *Treat. Zool.* (1900) III. xiv. 237), f. F. *stelléride* (J. B. P. A. de Lamarck *Hist. Nat. Animaux sans Vertèbres* (1816) II. 527): see STELLERID and -OID.] A star-fish or a similar invertebrate belonging to the class Stelleroidea.

1900 J. W. GREGORY in E. R. Lankester *Treat. Zool.* III. xiv. 237 This list of characters is quite sufficient to mark off the Stelleroids from all other Echinoderms. **1935** TWENHOFEL & SHROCK *Invertebr. Paleontol.* vi. 190 Stelleroidea—..referring to the starlike appearance of the stelleroid. **1962** D. NICHOLS *Echinoderms* iv. 62 They were burrowers, and, like some recent stelleroids, sat in the substratum with only the arm-tips exposed above the surface. **1970** R. M. BLACK *Elements Palaeontol.* ix. 105 The stelleroids, too, are vagrant.

stellettid (stɛ'lɛtɪd). *Zool.* [f. mod.L. *Stelletta* + -ID[3].] A sponge resembling the genus *Stelletta.*

1888 W. J. SOLLAS in *Challenger Rep.* XXV. p. cxii, Were it [this spicule] absent the Sponge would become a Stellettid. *Ibid.*, The Stellettid type.

stelletto, obs. form of STILETTO.

‖**'stellifer.** *Obs.* [L., f. *stella* star + *-fer* bearing.] A knight or friar of the Teutonic order (*Stelliferi Hospitalarii*), who bore a red star above a cross.

a **1550** *Image Hypocr.* IV. 217 Some be Stellifers.

†**ste'lliferal**, *a. Obs. rare*[−1]. [f. L. *stellifer* (see prec.) + -AL[1].] = STELLIFEROUS.

c **1495** *Epit. Dk. Bedford* in *Skelton's Wks.* (1843) II. 396 And than moste craftely dyd combyne Another heuen, called cristalline, So the thyrde stellyferal to shyne Aboue the skye.

†**ste'lliferant**, *a. Obs. rare*[−1]. [a. OF. *stelliferant*, f. L. *stellifer* (see prec.).] = next.

1490 CAXTON *Eneydos* xxvii. 95 The cours celestiall & regyon stellyferaunt.

stelliferous (stɛ'lɪfərəs), *a.* [f. L. *stellifer*: see STELLIFER and -FEROUS.] Bearing stars. **a.** Said of the vault of heaven; *loosely*, †of the beams of the sun. **b.** *Biol.* Having star-shaped markings.

1583 STUBBES *Anat. Abuses* (1877) 79 The stelliferous beames of the glistering Sun. **1616** J. LANE *Contn. Sqr.'s T.* III. 285 Th' whole forme to bee as round as globe edight,.. its vault stelliferous. **1822** J. PARKINSON *Outl. Oryctol.* 76 *Agaricia*—A stony polypifer,..the upper surfaces only having stelliferous grooves. **1828** STARK *Elem. Nat. Hist.* II. 430 Fixed, stony, developing a free foliaceous membrane, waved and sublobed, with one stelliferous face. **1849** H. MILLER *Footpr. Creat.* iii. (1874) 23 Its true scales..were not stelliferous.

stellification (stɛlɪfɪ'keɪʃən). [f. med.L. *stellificāre* STELLIFY *v.*: see -ATION.] The action of stellifying or placing among the stars.

1650 J. REYNOLDS *Flower Fidelity* 1 The..no lesse rejoycing of his..joyful Subjects; who in stellification of their young Prince his nativity, so sumptuously solemnized his Birth with Heroical triumphs, that [etc.]. **1660** A. BRETT *Threnodia* 19 Stellification, fancy is, And so is Metem-psychosis. **1906** A. CLARK in *Essex Rev.* XV. 90 The conclusion is the stellification of Mansfield's wig: Sudden it mounted to the starry skies. **1907** *Expositor* Apr. 378 The nearest approach to stellification that the somewhat prosaic Northern mythology allows.

stellified ('stɛlɪfaɪd), *ppl. a.* [f. STELLIFY *v.* + -ED[1].] In senses of the verb.

1611 PENUEN *Ambit. Scourge* C 1 b, Will not yon christall stellified gate Ope, and with milde aspect adorne my Fate? **1694** SALMON *Bate's Dispens.* (1713) 417/1 Mercury seven times sublimed from the stellified Regulus Martis.

stelliform ('stɛlɪfɔːm), *a.* [ad. mod.L. *stelliformis*, f. L. *stella* star: see -FORM. Cf. F. *stelliforme.*] Shaped like a star; existing in the form of star-shaped crystals.

1796 KIRWAN *Elem. Min.* (ed. 2) I. 14 Jargonia..forms.. stelliform crystals. *Ibid.* 102 A radiated stelliform limestone (Sternspath). **1836** *Todd's Cycl. Anat.* II. 32/1 They were named stelliform processes by Tiedemann. **1868** tr. *Figuier's Ocean World* vii. 152 The animals belonging to this group, which may be characterised as stelliform or star-like, are very abundant in every sea. **1875** GRINDON *Life* xxv. 327 Radiate flowers, and other stelliform products of plants.

Hence **'stelliformly** *adv.*

1822 J. PARKINSON *Outl. Oryctol.* 73 The base pointed, the terminating cell stelliformly lamellated.

stellify ('stɛlɪfaɪ), *v.* [a. OF. *stellifier*, ad. med.L. *stellificāre*, f. *stella* star: see -FY.]

1. *trans.* To transform (a person or thing) into a star or a constellation; to place among the stars.

c **1384** CHAUCER *H. Fame* 1002 When thou redest poetrie How goddes gonne stellifye Briddes, fisshe, best, or him or here. *c* **1403** LYDG. *Temple of Glas* 136 Hou þat she,..I-weddit was to god of eloquence,..And with hir song hov she was magnified With Iubiter to bein Istellified. **1423** JAS. I *Kingis Q.* 52 O venus clere! of goddis stellifyit! **1426** LYDG. *De Guil. Pilgr.* 18835 [He] is in heuene stelleffyed, And with seyntis gloreffyed. **1530** PALSGR. 734/2 The olde panymes for a vayn glory dyd stellyfye their kynges. *a* **1562** G. CAVENDISH *Poems* (1825) II. 44 O lady most excellent, by vertue stellefied, Assendyng the hevyns, where thou raynest aye. **1563–87** FOXE *A. & M.* (1596) 278/2 The bishop of Rome..which for his abhominable pride is fallen from heauen..thinketh..to stellifie againe himselfe there from whense he fell. *a* **1630** J. TAYLOR (Water P.) *Dog of War* C 2 b, Thou shalt be Stellifide by me, I'le make the Dog-star wayte on thee, And in his roome I'le seate thee. **1873** RUSKIN *Fors Clav.* xxv. III. 12 The great Charles..therefore deserves to be stellified by British astronomers.

†**b.** *fig.* To extol. *Obs.*

1523 SKELTON *Garl. Laurel* 963, I wyll my selfe applye,.. Yow for to stellyfye. **1595** E. C. *Emaricdulfe* Sonn, xxxix. in *Lamport Garl.* (Roxb.), Thy name, thy honour, and loues puritie, With Stanzas, Layes and Hymnes Ile stellifie. **1644** J. TAYLOR (Water P.) *No Merc. Aulicus* 3 You did most audaciously stellifie the head fire-brand of this Kingdome Iohn Pym. **1721** D'URFEY *Operas* etc. 230 This Lady you have stellify'd, Is my Acquaintance.

†**c.** To compare to stars. *Obs.*

1628 SHIRLEY *Witty Fair One* I. (1633) B 3 b, I ha' knowne him..stellifie their eyes.

†**2.** To set with stars, or with something compared to stars. *Obs.*

1426 LYDG. *De Guil. Pilgr.* 21174 Thys lasse world ys stellefyed Lych hevene, and as the ffyrmament. **1608** PLAT *Gard. Eden* (1653) 173 The physicall use of this fire is to divide a *Cœlum terræ*, and then to stellifie the same with any animall or vegetable starre. **1616** DRUMM. OF HAWTH. *Sonn.* '*Then is She gone*', With Roses here Shee stellified the Ground. **1650** T. BLOUNT *Estienne's Art Devises* etc. 86 Sir James Mongomery..had another Devise wherein was depainted the Skie stellified. **1658** PHILLIPS s.v. *Orbe*, That without stars is the Primum Mobile, the other are all stellified, either with fixed Stars or Planets.

Hence **'stellifying** *vbl. sb.*

a **1612** HARINGTON *Epigr.* I. (1633) 68 They cald this sparing diet, Stellifying. **1634** T. CAREW *Coelum Brit.* (1640) 258 In the firmament about him, was a troope of fifteene stars, expressing the stellifying of our Brittish Heroes. **1640** W. CRABTRIE in *Phil. Trans.* XXVII. 280, I must acknowledge you say more for the stellifying of these Solar Obscurities, than I have heard before.

†**ste'lligerate**, *a. Obs. rare*[−1]. [f. L. *stelliger*, star-bearing, starry (f. *stella* star + *-ger* bearing) + -ATE.] ? Exalted to the heavens.

c **1450** METHAM *Wks.* 10/274 (E.E.T.S.) The gloryus chyualry stellygerat In qwemyng off Venus and Mars.

stelling ('stɛlɪŋ), *sb. Guyana.* [a. Du. *stelling* scaffolding, landing-stage, f. *stellen* to place.] A wooden pier or landing-stage.

1862 *List Contrib. Br. Guiana to Lond. Exhib.* in Veness *El Dorado* (1866) App. 139 Portion of the Fender Cap of the ferry steamer stelling, Demarara river. **1879** J. W. B. WHETHAM *Roraima* xiii. 135 The wharf—or stelling, as the wooden pier is called—presented an animated scene. **1898** H. KIRKE 25 *Yrs. Brit. Guiana* 102 At 7 a.m. we cast off from the stelling, and were soon steaming down the muddy waters of the Demerara River.

stelling ('stɛlɪŋ), *vbl. sb. Sc.* and *north.* [f. STELL *v.* + -ING[1].]

1. The action of placing in position.

1560 *Aberdeen Reg.* (1844) I. 327 To desist and ceiss fra forther stelling and stenting of thair netts athort the water.

2. A place of shelter; now = STELL *sb.*[4] Also †*stelling-place.*

1513 DOUGLAS *Æneis* XI. x. 95 It is a stelling place and sovir harbry. **1828** CARR *Craven Gloss.*, *Stelling*, a place where cattle retire to in hot weather.

‖**Stellio** ('stɛlɪəʊ). [Latin form of next.] = next. Now only *Zool.* as generic name.

1388 WYCLIF *Lev.* xi. 30 Mygal, camelion, and stellio. **1535** COVERDALE *Lev.* xi. 30 These shalbe vncleane..the Hedge-hogge, the Stellio, the Lacerte, [etc.]. **1601** CHESTER *Love's Mart.* etc. (1878) 112 The Stellio is a beast that.. liueth by the deaw thats heauenly. **1658** ROWLAND tr. *Moufet's Theat. Ins.* 1052 A Scorpion..doth not hurt a Stellio, an Ascalabotes, a Crab, a Hawk. **1834** MᶜMURTRIE *Cuvier's Anim. Kingd.* 175 The *Agamæ* bear a great resemblance to the common Stellios. **1863** WOOD *Illustr. Nat. Hist.* III. 88 The Stellio..is a well-known Lizard inhabiting Northern Africa, Syria and Greece.

stellion ('stɛlɪən). Forms: 4 stellioun, (6 *erron.* stelon), 6– stellion. [ad. L. *stelliōnem* (*stellio*); according to Pliny f. *stella* star. Cf. F. *stellion.*] In early use, a kind of lizard with star-like spots, mentioned by ancient writers. In modern use, a lizard of the genus *Stellio* or family *Stellionidæ*, native in Southern Europe and Asia.

1382 WYCLIF *Lev.* xi. 30 A stellioun, that is a werme depeyntid as with sterris. **1572** BOSSEWELL *Armorie* II. 62 b, The fielde is Argente, a Stellion proper. **1592** LODGE *Euphues Shadow* N 4, Stelon vnlesse it encounter the Toade is of no proofe. **1600** SURFLET *Country Farm* II. lxii. 405 Neither the venemous stellion, nor the villanous beetle.. shall possibly enter to rob the hiues. **1609** BIBLE (Douay)

Prov. xxx. 28 The stellion stayeth on his handes, and tarieth in kings houses. **1621** G. SANDYS *Ovid's Met.* v. Argt., Th' ill-nurtur'd Boy a spotted Stellion growes. **1661** LOVELL *Hist. Anim. & Min.* 282 Stamped they help the poyson of the Stellion. **1688** HOLME *Armory* II. 206/2 A Stellion proper; or a Stellion Serpent, to distinguish it from the Stellion-Horse. **1840** *Cuvier's Anim. Kingd.* 275 The Stellions. **1845** J. E. GRAY *Catal. Lizards Brit. Mus.* 255 The Stellion or Hardun. *Stellio Cordylina.* *Ibid.*, The Caucasian Stellion. *Stellio caucasicus.*

stellionate ('stɛlɪənət). *Civil Law.* Also 7 **-at.** [ad. L. *stelliōnātus* (*u* stem), f. *stelliōn-em*, a fraudulent person, perh. a transf. use of *stelliōn-em* a kind of lizard (see STELLION). See -ATE[1].] (See quot. 1754.)

1622 BACON *Hen. VII*, 64 This Court of Star-chamber.. discerneth also principally of foure kinds of Causes; Forces, Frauds, Crimes various of Stellionate, and the Inchoations or middle Acts towards Crimes Capitall, or hainous, not actually committed. **1637** BASTWICK *Litany* I. 13 As if I were guilty of crimes of stellionate or maluersation. **1678** SIR G. MACKENZIE *Crim. Laws Scot.* I. xxviii. §1 (1699) 144 Legislators were forced to invent this general name of Stellionat; under which they might range all Cheats, and thence sprung that Maxime. **1754** ERSKINE *Princ. Sc. Law* (1809) 519 The crime of stellionate..includes every fraud which is not distinguished by a special name; but is chiefly applied to conveyances of the same numerical right, granted by the proprietor to different disponees. **1861** *Two Cosmos* III. iii. I. 300 'Art and part stealing an heiress, and for aught I see stellionate and stouthrieff!' said he.

Hence †'**stellionated** *a.* *Obs.* *rare*$^{-1}$, fraudulent.

1672 G. THOMSON *Let. to H. Stubbe* 25 To discover their Stellionated and counterfeit Devices, in making the World believe, that they are the onely true Chymists.

'**stelliscript.** *nonce-wd.* [f. L. *stella* star + *scriptum* a writing, SCRIPT.] A writing in the stars.

1835 SOUTHEY *Doctor* xcv. (1848) 215 One important rule is to be observed in perusing this great stelliscript.

Stellite ('stɛlaɪt), *sb.* Also **stellite.** [? f. L. *stell-a* star + -ITE[1].] Any of various cobalt-based alloys that usu. contain chromium and small amounts of tungsten and molybdenum and are used for their great hardness and their resistance to heat.

A proprietary name in the U.S.

1913 *Engin. Mag.* XLV. 840/2 It is an alloy of cobalt, chromium, and tungsten and has been called 'Stellite' by its inventor, Mr. Elwood Haynes. **1916** *Official Gaz.* (U.S. Patent Office) 3 Oct. 267/2 The Haynes Stellite Co.... *Stellite*... Metal alloys. **1937** *Jrnl. R. Aeronaut. Soc.* XLI. 330 The mean thermal expansion coefficients of the stellities were obtained between 20°C and a higher temperature ranging from 100°C to 850°C. **1975** BRAM & DOWNS *Manuf. Technol.* iii. 79 Stellite can be purchased in bars of round or square section for manufacturing cutting tools. **1980** *Daily Tel.* 11 Sept. 7 (Advt.), The new 1300cc 'A' Plus unit with stellite faced valves.

Hence '**stellite** *v. trans.*, to coat with Stellite; '**stellited** *ppl. a.*, '**stelliting** *vbl. sb.*

1934 *Jrnl. R. Aeronaut. Soc.* XXXVIII. 329 If only one part is to be 'stellited' it is better to treat the valve. *Ibid.*, The 'stelliting' of the valve stem and neck..would also be beneficial. **1937** *Ibid.* XLI. 330 The cracking of stellited steels is attributed to this difference in expansion. **1959** *Engineering* 9 Jan. 49/2 The journal portions of extension shafts on the vanes are Stellited and ground to provide a wear resistant bearing surface.

stellium ('stɛlɪəm). *Astrol.* [mod.L., f. L. *stella* star.] (See quot.)

1819 J. WILSON *Dict. Astrol.* 380 *Stellium*, a crowd of planets in an angle... So far as my observation extends, a stellium of 4 or 5 planets in any part of the radix always produces in the course of the native's existence some tremendous catastrophe.

stell-net: see STELL *sb.*[1] b.

stellular ('stɛljʊlə(r)), *a.* [f. late L. *stellula*, dim. of *stella* star + -AR.] Having the form of a small star or small stars.

1796 KIRWAN *Elem. Min.* (ed. 2) II. 169 Fracture coarse, ..but commonly stellular. **1805–17** JAMESON *Char. Min.* (ed. 3) 238 Stellular diverging, when the fibres diverge in all directions, like the radii of a circle, as in brown hematite. **1833** MANTELL *Wonders Geol.* (1838) II. 477 The Red Coral ..consists of a bright red, stony axis, invested with a.. gelatinous substance..which is studded over with stellular polypi. **1857** A. GRAY *First Less. Bot.* 232 *Stellate, stellular*, starry or star-like. **1885** *Harper's Mag.* Dec. 141/2 Here and there an isolated stellular light illumined the snow.

Hence '**stellularly** *adv.*

1796 KIRWAN *Elem. Min.* (ed. 2) II. 278 Acicular prisms, concentrically or stellularly arranged. **1821** JAMESON *Man. Min.* 5 Crystals, which are scopiformly or stellularly aggregated.

Stellwag ('stɛlvæg). *Med.* [The name of Carl *Stellwag* von Carion (1823–1904), Austrian ophthalmologist.] ***Stellwag's sign***: orig., retraction of the upper eyelid in thyrotoxicosis (called also Dalrymple's sign); now often applied to the diminished blinking that normally accompanies it.

1887 *Brit. Med. Jrnl.* 26 Mar. 680/1 A married woman, aged 32, with marked retraction of the left upper eyelid (Stellwag's sign), no proptosis, and no goitre. **1907** *Practitioner* Nov. 733 [In exophthalmic goitre] the margins of the eyelids are unduly separated (Dalrymple's sign); the upper lid tardily follows the eyeball in its downward movements (von Graef[e]'s sign); there is diminished frequency of winking (Stellwag's sign). **1950** R. I. PRITIKIN *Essent. Ophthalm.* vii. 321 Stellwag's sign—infrequent winking. **1973** R. S. DILLON *Handbk. Endocrinol.* vi. 248/1 'Stellwag's sign' is retraction of the upper eyelids producing apparent widening of the palpebral opening associated with infrequent and incomplete blinking.

stelography (stiː'lɒgrəfɪ). *rare*$^{-0}$. [ad. late Gr. *στηλογραφία*, f. *στήλη* STELE + *-γραφία* writing: see -GRAPHY.] An inscription on a stele; the practice of placing commemorative inscriptions on steles, tablets, or pillars.

Todd gives a quot. from Stackhouse, where the correct reading is *stylography*.

1727 BAILEY vol. II, *Stelography*, an Inscription or Writing on a Pillar, &c. **1775** ASH, *Stellography* [*sic*].

stelth(e, obs. forms of STEALTH.

stem (stɛm), *sb.*[1] Forms: 1 **stefn, stemn,** 6–7 **stemme,** 7 **steame, stemm,** 4– **stem.** [OE. *stęmn*, *stęfn* str. masc. (for the corresponding forms in continental Teut. see STEM *sb.*[2]):—OTeut. **stamni-z*; a parallel and synonymous OTeut. formation (**stamno-z*) is represented by (M)LG., (M)Du., OHG., MHG. *stam* (mod.G. *stamm*) masc., trunk or stem of a tree (so Sw. *stam*, Da. *stamme*, from German); also by OS. *stamn* (? masc.), ON. *stamn*, *stafn* neut., which are recorded only in the derived sense = STEM *sb.*[2] The word is prob. f. the root **sta-* to STAND + *-mn-* suffix; cf. Gr. *στάμνος* earthen jar (? lit. 'standing vessel'). The ON. and OE. *stofn* (see STOVEN) tree-stump is prob. unconnected.

It is remarkable that between the OE. period and the 16th c. only a single instance of the word has been found (quot. 1338 in sense 1 b).]

1. a. The main body (usually more or less cylindrical) of the portion above ground of a tree, shrub, or other plant; a trunk, stock, stalk. (Ordinarily implying a greater degree of slenderness than *stock* or *trunk*.)

c **888** ÆLFRED *Boeth.* xxxiv. §10 He onȝinð of þæm wyrtrumum & swa upweardes grewð oð ðone stemn. *a* **1000** *Sal. & Sat.* 296 (Gr.) Beam heo abreoteð..astyreð standendne stefn on siðe. **1538** ELYOT *Dict.*, *Caulis*, a stalke or stem of an herbe or tree. **1585** HIGINS *Junius' Nomencl.* 111/1 *Scapus*,..the stocke, or stemme. **1688** HOLME *Armoury* II. 84/2 The Stem, or Trunk, is the body of the tree to the branches. **1697** DRYDEN *Virg. Georg.* IV. 393 From one Root the rising Stem bestows A Wood of Leaves, and Vi'let-purple Boughs. **1712** tr. *Pomet's Hist. Drugs* I. 36 Cinquefoil..produces its Leaves,..on a Stem or Wire. **1773** MRS. BARBAULD *Hymn, 'Praise to God'* 22 Should rising whirl-winds tear From its stem the ripening ear. **1796** WITHERING *Brit. Plants* (ed. 3) I. 84 *Stem* (stipes) formerly called the pillar, which supports the pileus of some of the Fungi. **1818** SHELLEY *Rosal. & Helen* 1292 When the living stem Is cankered in its heart, the tree must fall. **1831** MACGILLIVRAY tr. *A. Richard's Elem. Bot.* ii. 103 Many herbaceous stems are employed as food for man and animals. **1833** TENNYSON *Lotos-Eaters* 28 Branches they bore of that enchanted stem, Laden with flower and fruit. **1850** MISS PRATT *Comm. Things Sea-side* i. 18 The sea eryngo (*Eryngium maritimum*) has a stem about a foot high. **1909** G. W. YOUNG in *Contemp. Rev.* Apr., Suppl. 2 The dark solemn stems in dim-seen lines Stand sentinel.

b. *fig.*

c **888** ÆLFRED *Boeth.* xxxiv. §5 Þeah is an God; se is stemn & staðol eallra goda. **1338** R. BRUNNE *Chron.* (1810) 296 Þe bisshop of Durham trauailed day & nyght, Of strife to felle þe stem. **1611** SPEED *Hist. Gt. Brit.* IX. xvii. §56 King Edward..thought it no policy long to delay, lest Henry should take growth to a bigger steame. **1659** W. CHAMBERLAYNE *Pharonnida* IV. 94 That short stem of nature, life.

c. *Bot.* The ascending axis (whether above or below ground) of a plant, in contradistinction to the descending axis or root. (The various kinds of subterraneous stem, the bulb, rhizome, tuber, etc., are popularly regarded as 'roots.')

1807 J. E. SMITH *Phys. Bot.* 116 The Stem is either simple, as in the White Lily, or branched, as in most instances. **1855** MISS PRATT *Flower. Plants* VI. 140 The true stem of the fern..from its resemblance to a root is termed the rhizoma.

†**d.** Occasionally, a branch or shoot, in contradistinction to the *stock*. *Obs.*

1584 GREENE *Arbasto* Wks. (Grosart) III. 205 We think he little fauoreth the stems that cutteth downe the olde stocke.

2. a. The stalk supporting a leaf, flower, or fruit; a peduncle, pedicel or petiole.

1590 SHAKS. *Mids. N.* III. ii. 211 Two louely berries molded on one stem. **1667** MILTON *P.L.* VII. 337 Each Plant of the field, which e're it was in the Earth God made, and every Herb, before it grew On the green stemm. **1781** COWPER *Retirement* 179 The fruits that hang on pleasure's flow'ry stem. **1820** SHELLEY *Sensit. Plant* III. 40 Till they [weeds] clung round many a sweet flower's stem.

b. *transf.* in *Anat.* and *Path.*

1861 PRITCHARD *Hist. Infusoria* (ed. 4) 586 *Vorticella*.. Body bell-shaped,..supported on a highly contractile, unbranched pedicle or stem. **1862** W. THOMSON in *Phil. Trans.* CLV. 536 The mature Antedon has no true stem. **1898** J. HUTCHINSON in *Arch. Surg.* IX. 372 A dilated arteriole always enters the stem of a wart. **1912** KEITH *Human Body* ii. 26 When they [the cerebral hemispheres] are raised from the floor or base of the skull we see a great stem—the brain stem—issuing from them.

c. (See quot.)

1905 *Dundee Advertiser* 15 July 6 The stem, to give the banana its trade name.

3. a. The stock of a family; the main line of descent from which the 'branches' of a family are offshoots; the descendants of a particular ancestor. Also *abstr.*, ancestry, pedigree.

In the 16th and 17th c. commonly associated with L. *stemma*, in pl. a genealogical tree, pedigree: see STEMMA.

c **1540** tr. *Pol. Verg. Eng. Hist.* VIII. (Camden 36) 279 The regall stemme and pedegree was allmost utterlie extinguished. **1586** FERNE *Blaz. Gentrie* 2 To intreate of the honours, dignities, stemmes, and atchieuments, of certaine personages, nobly discended in England and France. **1586** HOOKER *Giraldus' Irish Hist.* 17/2 in *Holinshed*, Dardanus the sonne of Jupiter, from whom is deriued vnto vs not onlie the stemme of ancient nobilitie, but also [etc.]. *a* **1599** SPENSER *F.Q.* VII. vi. 2 Whom, though high Ioue of kingdome did depriue, Yet many of their stemme long after did surviue. *c* **1610** *Women Saints* 80 This happie branch of that vertuous stemme. **1611** BIBLE *Isa.* xi. 1 There shall come forth a rod out of the stemme of Iesse. **1640** HOWELL *Dodona's Grove* 72 The Imperiall diademe..hath continued these two Ages and more yeares in that stemme which is now so much spoken of. *a* **1645** MILTON *Arcades* 82 Where ye may all that are of noble stemm Approach. **1652** HEYLIN *Cosmogr.* III. 155 Jarres..of brothers..not only in private families, but in the stems of Princes. **1697** EVELYN *Numism.* viii. 290 Stems and Genealogies of the most Renowned Princes of Germany. **1763** CHURCHILL *Confer.* 15 Recent men who came From stems unknown, and sires without a name. **1781** COWPER *Expost.* 460 The rich, the produce of a nobler stem, Are more intelligent at least. **1818** SHELLEY *Hymn Venus* 52 Mortal offspring from a deathless stem. **1827** SCOTT *Highl. Widow* v, Allan Breack is a wise man and a kind one, and comes of a good stem.

b. An ethnic stock, a race.

c **1540** tr. *Pol. Verg. Eng. Hist.* VII. (Camden 36) 258 Emonge whome the Danishe governement beganne longe beefore to bee verie tedius and hatefull, as a thinge moste exitiall and pestilent to the Englishe name and stemme. **1613–16** W. BROWNE *Brit. Past* II. v, Cannot I dye but like that brutish stem Which have their best belov'd to die with them. **1856** EMERSON *Eng. Traits* iv. Wks. (Bohn) II. 22 Neither do this people appear to be of one stem; but collectively a better race than any from which they are derived. **1861** PEARSON *Early & Mid. Ages* 90 The trial of strength which would certainly have taken place had all the invading people been of one stem. **1868** GLADSTONE *Juv. Mundi* ii. (1870) 32 The relation between this older race and the Hellenic tribes leads to the conclusion that both alike were derived from the Aryan stem.

†**c.** The primal ancestor or founder of a family.

1604 E. G[RIMSTONE] *D'Acosta's Hist. Indies* VI. xx. 474 The first whom they make the head and steame of this family, was called *Ingaroca*. **1780** *Mirror* No. 103 The stem of it..was a Norman baron, who came over with the Conqueror.

†**d.** [fig. use of 1 d.] A branch or offshoot of a family. *Obs.*

1591 SHAKS. *1 Hen. VI*, II. v. 41 And now declare sweet Stem from Yorkes great Stock, Why didst thou [etc.]. **1599** —— *Hen. V*, II. iv. 62 This is a Stem Of that Victorious Stock. **1610** HOLLAND *Camden's Brit.* (1637) 365 Coberley, a seat of a stem of Barkeleies. **1634** W. WOOD *New Eng. Prosp.* Ded. Note, Blessings..be multiplied upon your selfe, your vertuous Consort, my very good Lady, together with all the Stemmes of your Noble family.

4. Applied to various objects resembling the stem of a plant or of a flower, etc. (Cf. STALK *sb.*[1] 4, 5.)

a. *Calligraphy* and *Printing*. The upright stroke of a letter.

1676 MOXON *Print Letters* 6 The Stem is the straight fat stroke of the Letter; as in B the upright stroke on the left hand is the Stem. **1685** MATLOCK *Fax Nova Artis Scrib.* 25 The Length of the tallest Stemms [in Court-Hand], *viz.* of [b, h, k, l, and w] be One Fourth of an Inch. **1790** W. NICHOLSON in *Repert. Arts* (1796) V. 147 Instead of leaving a space in the mould for the stem of one letter only. **1899** DE VINNE *Pract. Typogr.* (1902) 30 The body mark, or stem, is the thick line of the face which most clearly indicates the character and the height of the letter. It is better known among printers as the thick-stroke.

b. *Mus.* The vertical line forming part of a minim, crotchet, quaver, etc.

1806 CALCOTT *Mus. Gram.* i. 2 The Notes of Music consist generally of the parts, a Head and a Stem. **1873** H. C. BANISTER *Music* 256 When other notes than semibreves are used, the stems, on each stave, should be turned contrary ways.

c. The long cylindrical body of an instrument, etc., as distinguished from the 'head', or from branches or projections; the tube of a thermometer or similar instrument; the tube of a tobacco-pipe.

1815 J. SMITH *Panorama Sci. & Art* II. 89 When the stem in Fahrenheit's hydrometer is long, the weight put in the dish at the top, will sometimes render the instrument unsteady. **1827** FARADAY *Chem. Manip.* iv. (1842) 136 Thermometers are generally graduated by having two points marked upon their stems, corresponding to the melting temperature of ice and the boiling temperature of pure water. **1843** HOLTZAPFFEL *Turning* I. 213 A piece of bolt-iron of five-eighths of an inch diameter, or of the size of the stem of the bolt, is cut off somewhat longer than the intended length. **1843** DICKENS *Chr. Carol* iv. 131 The old man..having trimmed his smoky lamp..with the stem of his pipe. **1851** in *Abridgm. Specif. Patents Locks* etc. (1873) 87 The convenience offered by thus having the 'bit' of the key separate from the stem. **1869** RANKINE *Machine & Hand-tools* Pl. P 22, On the lower end of this boss is formed the socket, S, for the reception of the stem, T, of the pick, U. **1875** KNIGHT *Dict. Mech.* 2373 *Stem* (*Valve*), the projecting-rod which guides a valve in its reciprocations. *Ibid.*, *Stem* (*Vehicle*), the bar to which the bow of a falling hood is hinged. **1892** *Photogr. Ann.* II. 83 A cork, bored with two holes, through one of which passes the stem of a globular funnel.

d. The upright cylindrical support of a cup, a wineglass, or other vessel.

1835 DICKENS *Sk. Boz, Publ. Dinners*, Several gentlemen knock the stems off their wine-glasses, in the vehemence of their approbation. **1850** J. MARRYAT *Pottery & Porcelain* 288 *Stem. Culot, Fr.*, that portion of a vase which unites the body to the base, and is simple, elongated, shortened, or variously fashioned. **1883** H. J. POWELL *Princ. Glass-Making* 61 Wine-glasses or goblets are classified by the nature of their stems, or by the nature of their feet. **1870** F. R. WILSON *Ch. Lindisf.* 90 The stem [of the font] is composed of a portion of a Saxon cross.

e. *Arch.* (See quot.)

1835 R. WILLIS *Archit. Mid. Ages* vii. 108 Where a pier is made up of four cylindrical shafts attached to a nucleus or stem, this nucleus and the lateral shafts carry the longitudinal arches.

f. *dial.* (See quot.)

1796 W. H. MARSHALL *W. Eng.* I. 330 *Stem*, the handle of a fork. **1838** HOLLOWAY *Prov. Dict.*, *Stem*, a long round shaft used as a handle for various tools.

g. *Watchmaking.* The pendant-shank of a watch.

1866 in *Abridgm. Specif. Patents, Watches*, etc. (1871) 157 Instead of the push piece consisting of a rod passing up the centre of the pendant stem. **1871** *Ibid.* 156 The pendant is so arranged that the bow or stem cannot be wrenched off by torsion. **1881** F. J. BRITTEN *Watch & Clockm. Handbk.* (ed. 4) 73 The part of the winding stem below the bevelled pinion is square. **1885** D. GLASGOW *Watch & Clock Making* 262 The stem is fitted easy in the pendant.

h. The SHAFT of a hair, of a feather.

1845 *Encycl. Metropol.* VII. 197/2 The Hair-shaft, Stem or Cylinder, *caulis, filamentum, truncus pili*, is that part commonly called the hair. *Ibid.* 205/1 The Shaft or Stem [of a feather], *rachis*, though usually described as distinct, might not improperly be considered as a continuation of the barrel.

i. *pl.* The legs. *slang.*

1860 HOTTEN *Dict. Slang* (ed. 2) 227 *Stems*, the legs. **1927** *Vanity Fair* XXIX. 67/2 Among some of Conway's more famous expressions are:..'Stems' and 'Gambs' (legs). **1970** C. MAJOR *Dict. Afro-Amer. Slang* 109 *Stems*, the legs.

j. More fully ***drill stem***: (*a*) (also ***auger stem***) in percussion drilling, a heavy metal rod above the bit in a string of tools, used to provide added weight; (*b*) in rotary drilling, = *grief stem* below; also, the entire drilling column; ***grief stem***: in rotary drilling, the rod at the top of the drilling column, having a square cross-section so that it fits in and is turned by the rotary table; = KELLY *sb.*[2] 4.

drill-stem test: a test of the potential of a well in which a sample of the oil or gas is allowed to run into the drill pipe for a short time before the hole is completed, the flow being measured and the fluid recovered; so ***drill-stem testing*** vbl. sb.

1880 J. F. CARLL *Geol. Oil Regions Warren, Venango, Clarion & Butler Counties* III. xxviii. 300 On the down stroke the auger-stem falls 20 inches, while the sinker-bar goes down 24 inches. **1907** *Internat. Libr. Technol.: Rock Boring* 13 The tools consist of a rope socket, sinker bar, jars, stem, and bit. *Ibid.* 15 Auger or Drill Stem.—This part of the string of tools.. is made about 30 feet long in some cases. **1922** B. REDWOOD *Petroleum* (ed. 4) II. 402 The lower end of the drilling-rod or casing with the bit is passed through the rotary table provided with grip rings or square 'grief' stem and clamped tight enough to cause it to revolve. **1938** D. HAGER *Practical Oil Geol.* (ed. 5) viii. 252 After drilling into an oil stratum, some idea of productivity may be gained by making a drill-stem test. **1939** —— *Fund. Petroleum Industry* ix. 210 When the kelly is deep enough for a joint of drill stem, the kelly and bit are pulled out. **1951** K. K. LANDES *Petroleum Geol.* ii. 51 The string of tools consists of the bit..; the stem, into which the bit fits; the jars; and the socket. **1962** E. J. LYNCH *Formation Evaluation* viii. 291 Drill stem testing is the most hazardous of all drilling operations. **1965** E. LEHNER et al. in G. J. Williams *Econ. Geol. N.Z.* xix. 350/2 Both the Taramakau and Arahura wells..encountered faint traces of oil in the Brunner Sandstone at 5,700 ft and 5,030 ft respectively, but drill-stem tests of these zones yielded only salt water. **1973** J. W. JENNER in Hobson & Pohl *Mod. Petroleum Technol.* (ed. 4) iv. 108 A drilling bit..is attached to a heavy drill stem suspended by a cable from a cantilever arm, the Walking Beam, at the surface. **1976** L. ST. CLAIR *Fortune in Death* i. 8 The drill stem had snapped... 'Stem crystalize?' 'Yep. Damned basalt is hard as the drill.'

k. Similarly, a drill used by a burglar or safe-breaker. *U.S. Criminals' slang.*

1914 JACKSON & HELLYER *Vocab. Criminal Slang* 81 *Stem, noun.* Current among yeggs. A steel drill. **1926** J. BLACK *You can't Win* x. 133 Get the 'dan' and 'stems' (drills), and put them safely away. **1935** *Flynn's* 16 Mar. 102/1, I was inserting a 'stem' (drill) in a brace when I heard a most peculiar noise.

5. *Philol.* †**a.** The primary word from which a derivative is formed. *Obs.*

a **1653** GOUGE *Comm. Hebr.* viii. 6 The noun (λειτουργία) translated 'ministry' is derived from the same stemme that 'minister' (λειτουργός) was.

b. That part of an inflected word that remains unchanged (except for euphonic variations) in the process of inflexion; the theme of a word (or of a particular group of its cases or tenses), to which the flexional suffixes are attached.

1851 T. H. KEY in *Trans. Philol. Soc.* 93 We refer to such stems as ..βα and βαν of ἐβησα and βαινω. **1865** MALDEN *Ibid.* 169 All first perfects, except those in which the suffix κα is attached to a stem ending in a vowel. **1871** [see *present-stem*, PRESENT *sb.*[1] 3 c].

c. Applied to a Semitic triliteral 'root'. Also *attrib.*

1874 DAVIDSON *Hebr. Gram.* xvi. 31 Stems in Hebrew are considered to contain three consonantal letters. The noun may be regarded as expressing the stem idea in rest.

6. a. A principal railway line, from which other tracks may branch; = MAIN STEM.

1832 [see MAIN STEM]. **1869** *Bradshaw's Railway Man.* XXI. 426 *Assets.* Main Stem..Lebanon Branch extension ..Richmond Branch. **1934** in *Amer. Ballads & Folk Songs* i. 24 The manifest freight Pulled out on the stem behind the mail.

b. A street, esp. one frequented by beggars and tramps (see also quot. 1923); also, = MAIN STREET a; *transf.*, an act of begging. *U.S. slang.*

1914 [see MOOCH *v.* 6]. **1923** N. ANDERSON *Hobo* i. 4 Every large city has its district into which these homeless types gravitate. In the parlance of the 'road' such a section is known as the 'stem' or the 'main drag'. **1929** *Amer. Speech* IV. 345 *Stem*, act of begging; also a street where one begs. **1931** 'D. STIFF' *Milk & Honey Route* v. 59 The hobo also damns the hash houses along the stem. **1936** *New Republic* 15 July 289/1 The appearance of the applicant is perhaps not so important as in the case of private residences or on the 'stem'. **1955** D. W. MAURER in *Publ. Amer. Dialect Soc.* xxiv. 133 This is all done on the *stem* or street.

7. Short for *stem-stitch* (see 9).

1882 CAULFEILD & SAWARD *Dict. Needlework* 461 To work *Beginner's Stem*: This stitch is used to form the stalks of leaves, or [etc.]. *Ibid.*, Buckle Stem differs from Stem Stitch by being worked with a Plain Edge upon both sides, [etc.].

8. *attrib.* and *Comb.*: (sense 1) ***stem-bark, -climber, -fruiting, -growth, -leaf, -like*** adj., ***-node, -selecting*** adj., ***-sucker, -tendril, -wood***; (sense 2 b) ***stem-joint, process***; (sense 5 b) ***stem-form, -formant, -suffix, -vowel***; ***stem-final, -formative, -initial*** adjs. (all also *absol.* as sb.); ***stem-forming*** adj.

1832 *Planting* 7 in *Lib. Usef. Kn., Husb.* III, During this conversion of the *stem-bark to that of the root the plant advances but little. **1875** *Stem-climbers [see TENDRIL *sb.* 3]. **1949** E. A. NIDA *Morphology* (ed. 2) ii. 34 All *stem-final vowels before vowel suffixes are lost. **1965** *Canad. Jrnl. Linguistics* X. 130 It seems that Chipewyan and Navaho treat it as a stem final, while Mattole treats it as a stem initial. **1973** A. H. SOMMERSTEIN *Sound Pattern Anc. Greek* ii. 17 There is a large class of nouns ending, in the nominative singular, in -εύς [-éws]..which have a stem-final [w] when a consonant follows. **1928** O. JESPERSEN *Internat. Lang.* II. 97 The bare *stem-form of many adjectives would not be euphonious enough. **1966** *English Studies* XLVII. 53 These genetive [*sic*] 'causative' objects disappear in early ME and give place to objects in stem-form or prepositional types. **1935** G. K. ZIPF *Psycho-Biol. of Lang.* iv. 144 A *stem-formative (or stem-formant) is a morpheme added to the root either at the beginning (prefix) or at the end (suffix) or tucked inside (infix) to make the stem (root plus formant) to which endings are added. **1964** K. L. PIKE in D. Abercombie et al. *Daniel Jones* 428 The stem is made up of three monosyllabic roots plus three following stem-formative syllables. **1968** CHOMSKY & HALLE *Sound Pattern Eng.* 130 In short, there are '*stem-forming' vowels /i/ and /u/ which are deleted in final position..but which remain before certain affixes. **1978** *Language* LIV. 220 Most stem-forming suffixes consist of a single segment, and a certain amount of homophony results. **1821** S. F. GRAY *Brit. Plants* I. 43 *Stem-fruiting, *caulocarpæ*. The fruit growing on the stem. **1868** *Rep. U.S. Commissioner Agric.* (1869) 257 When the vertical *stem-growth is three or more inches in each sapling, the work may be reduced. **1949** E. A. NIDA *Morphology* (ed. 2) ii. 15 When *stem-initial consonants are aspirated, the reduplicated consonant has the same point of articulation, except that it is unaspirated. **1965** [see *stem-final* above]. **1977** *Word* 1972 XXVIII. 223 The inappropriate stem-initial consonants. **1862** W. THOMSON in *Phil. Trans.* CLV. 528 The sheaf-like calcareous cylinders which form the axes of the *stem-joints. **1796** WITHERING *Brit. Plants* (ed. 3) I. 84 **Stem-Leaves* (caulina) such as grow immediately upon the stem, without the intervention of branches. **1870** HOOKER *Stud. Flora* 32 Stem-leaves broadly ovate. **1611** SPEED *Hist. Gt. Brit.* VII. ix. 238 Whose *stemlike draught annexed, both in the marriages, issues, and collaterals, are therein branched as farre as any warrantable Records affordeth. **1855** *Orr's Circ. Sci., Inorg. Nat.* 87 A singular but very abundant stem-like fossil. **1882** VINES tr. *Sachs' Bot.* 293 Each leaf begins with a node (the basal node), by which it is united with the *stem-node. **1899** *Allbutt's Syst. Med.* VI. 521 The branches of the *stem process (neuraxon) of a neuron may offer a cross-section 370,000 times greater than that of the parent stem. **1837** P. KEITH *Bot. Lex.* 287 The false parasites, or *stem-selecting epiphytes, belong chiefly to the tribe of the Epidendra or Air-plants. **1842** LOUDON *Suburban Hort.* 279 The branches of a coniferous plant pegged down to force it to throw up a *stem-sucker as a leader. **1902** GREENOUGH & KITTREDGE *Words* 169 The exact nature of *stem-suffixes is far from certain. **1877** A. W. BENNETT *Thomé's Bot.* (1879) 109 According as they belong to the stem..or to the leaf.. they are called *stem- or leaf-tendrils. **1852** *Proc. Philol. Soc.* V. 197 The weakening of a strong *stem-vowel by virtue of a weak vowel in the suffix. **1884** BOWER & SCOTT *De Bary's Phaner.* 155 The differences between the wood of the root and that of the branches..are as regards the width of the tracheides even greater than in the case of the *stem-wood.

9. Special comb.: **stem analysis** *Forestry*, (an) investigation of the past growth of a tree by study of a series of cross-sections of its trunk taken at different heights; **stem-bed** *Geol.*, a stratum containing stems of trees; † **stem-book** [ad. G. *stammbuch*, Du. *stamboek*], an album; **stem borer**, an insect larva that bores into plant stems; **stem-bud** *Bot.* (see quot.); **stem-building** *Gram.* [tr. G. *stammbau*], the formation of stems from roots; **stem cell** *Biol.*, (*a*) a cell in the stem of an organism (*nonce-use*); (*b*) a cell of a multicellular organism which is capable of giving rise to indefinitely more cells of the same type and from which certain other kinds of cell arise by differentiation; **stem-clasping** *a.* (see quot.); **stem-composition** *Philol.*, composition of word-stems, as distinguished from syntactical combination of words; **stem-cup**, a Chinese porcelain goblet of a type with a wide shallow bowl mounted on a short base, first made in the Ming dynasty; **stem-eelworm**, a nematoid causing stem-sickness in certain plants; **stem-end**, that end of a fruit that is next to the stem; **stem family** *Sociol.* [tr. F. *famille-souche* (F. le Play *La Réforme Sociale en France* (1866) I. iii. 249)], a family unit in which property descends to a married son who remains within the household, other (esp. married) children achieving independence on receipt of an inheritance; **stem-father** [cf. G. *stammvater*], a tribal ancestor; **stemflow** *Forestry*, precipitation which reaches the ground after running down the branches and trunks of trees; **stem-fly** (see quot.); **stem ginger**, a superior grade of crystallized or preserved ginger; **stem-glass**, (*a*) a tall narrow glass vase for the display of a single flower or flowers; (*b*) a drinking-glass mounted on a stem; **stem-house** *nonce-wd.* [after G. *stammhaus*] the ancestral mansion of a family; **stem-line**, (*a*) the upright line (edge of a tablet, etc.) on which the strokes forming the Ogham alphabet are set; (*b*) a line of genealogical descent; (*c*) (**stemline**) *Med.*, the group of cells having a chromosome number that is (one of) the most frequent in a mixed population, esp. of tumour cells; **stem mother** *Ent.* = FUNDATRIX 2; **stem-muscle, pessary**, (see quots.); **stem root**, a root that develops from the stem of a plant, esp. on a lily from just above the top of the bulb; so **stem-rooting** *a.*, producing roots of this kind; **stem rust**, any of various fungus diseases of plants that produce spots on the stems; *esp.* that caused by *Puccinia graminis* on wheat and other cereals, marked by rows of black telia on the stems; **stem sawfly** (see quots.); **stem-setting** *a. U.S.*, (of a watch) that is set by rotation of a stem (1895 in *Funk's Stand. Dict.*); **stem-sick** *a.*, (of plants) having the stems affected by a malady produced by the eelworm; hence ***stem-sickness***; **stem stitch** *Needlework* (see quot. 1882); also used more widely in *Embroidery*; **stem succulent**, a plant chiefly native to dry regions, distinguished by a fleshy stem and often very small leaves or spines; **stemware**, stemmed glass drinking-vessels; **stem-wind** *a. U.S.* = *stem-winding a.*; **stem-winder** *U.S.* (*a*) a keyless watch; (*b*) a geared logging locomotive (Webster, 1911); (*c*) *slang*, a person or thing that is first-rate; also, an enterprising or energetic person; an impassioned talker or public speaker; (*d*) *slang*, a rousing speech; **stem-winding** *sb.* (see quot.); **stem-winding** *a. U.S.* (of a watch) that is wound up by means of a stem; also *transf.*

1895 W. SCHLICH *Man. Forestry* III. I. vi. 83 The investigation of the progress of increment throughout the life of a tree is called a *stem analysis. **1974** *Forest Sci.* XX. 75/2 In the comparisons to be discussed, three sets of stem analysis data were used, one for noble fir, one for Douglas-fir, and one for red alder. **1853** J. MORRIS in *Q. Jrnl. Geol. Soc.* IX. 338 Clays between the above [oyster-bed and marly rock] and the *stem-bed. **1592** MORYSON *Let.* in *Itin.* (1617) I. 38 Desiring to have the name of so famous a Divine, written in my *stemme-booke, with his Mott, after the Dutch fashion. **1921** H. T. FERNALD *Appl. Entom.* xxxiii. 340 Superfamily Tenthredinoidea (The Saw-flies and *Stem Borers). **1939** *Geogr. Jrnl.* XCIII. 140 The crop [of rice] would be destroyed by rats and stem-borers. **1972** J. MINIFIE *Homesteader* xv. 121 The Manitoba maple was subject to a stem-borer which destroyed its growing tips. **1877** A. W. BENNETT *Thomé's Bot.* (1879) 71 The *stem-bud, or plumule, is divided from the outset into stem and leaves. **1870** J. F. SMITH *Ewald's Introd. Hebr. Gram.* 91 *Stem-building I. Of Verbs. **1885** A. SEDGWICK tr. *Claus' Text-bk. Zool.* II. 79 Ctenostomata..*Stem-cells and root-filaments frequently occur. **1896** E. B. WILSON *Cell* iii. 111 In *Ascaris megalocephala univalens*..each of the first two cells receives two elongated chromosomes... In one of them, which is destined to produce only somatic cells, the thickened ends of each chromosome..degenerate... In the other cell, which may be called the stem-cell.., all the chromatin is preserved and the chromosomes do not segment into smaller pieces. **1959** W. ANDREW *Textbk. Compar. Histol.* vi. 234 The cells of this organ, while they include many lymphocytes, apparently serve as stem cells for all of the types of white corpuscles. **1970** *Sci. Jrnl.* June 32/3 The production of a continuous supply of spermatozoa from the testis is ensured by the continued existence of germ cells which form a reservoir of stem cells from which future spermatozoa are derived. **1796** WITHERING *Brit. Plants* (ed. 3) I. 84 **Stem-clasping* (amplexicaulis)..embracing the stem. **1866** *Treas. Bot.* 1094/1 *Stem clasping*, when the base of a leaf surrounds a stem. The same as *Amplexicaul.* **1902**

Greenough & Kittredge *Words* 177 By this process of *stem-composition a kind of rudimentary syntax arose. 1912 W. H. Stevenson in *Eng. Hist. Rev.* Jan. 22 The Old English dialects adhering to the older (Indo-Germanic) and more proper stem-composition. 1915 R. L. Hobson *Chinese Pottery & Porcelain* II. xii. 208 In the Bushell collection there are some beautiful reproductions of the Ch'êng Hua '*stem-cups'. 1942 *Burlington Mag.* June 151/2 The part of the base immediately below the stem-cup is a rather squat form of the Venetian bell base. 1980 *Catal. Fine Chinese Ceramics* (Sotheby, Hong Kong) 36 A *Longquan* (Lung Ch'üan) *Celadon stemcup* with plain circular bowl raised on a ribbed columnar foot. 1890 Miss Ormerod *Injur. Insects* (ed. 2) 51 *Stem eelworm. *Tylenchus devastatrix.* 1868 *Rep. U.S. Commissioner Agric.* (1869) 240 Cut, halved lengthwise, then across, *stem end. 1936 Zimmerman & Frampton *Family & Society* vii. 125 The *stem-family.. unites one married child to the paternal household, and supplies all the other offspring in a 'state of independence [with a dowry] which the patriarchal family does not give them'. 1947 P. H. Landis *Your Marriage & Family Living* i. 5 The stem family is about halfway between the great family of historic rural societies and the small, individualistic family of urban industrial societies. 1977 P. Laslett *Family Life & Illicit Love in Earlier Generations* v. 211 In certain eighteenth-century areas of Austria and Germany, where a stem family arrangement prevailed.. the old were allotted a familial situation which gave to retirement an institutional form. 1879 *Encycl. Brit.* IX. 75/1 The Leinster and Meath Fenians, consisting of the *Clanna Baiscné*, from a *stem-father *Bascné.* 1941 *Jrnl. Forestry* XXXIX. 521/1 *Stemflow, although apparently not related to crown-length density, tree height, basal area, or crown area, does tend to increase with excess or deficit of height of tree as compared with adjacent trees. 1967 M. E. Hale *Biol. Lichens* vii. 96 Stemflow on trees.. has been shown to be enriched, relative to throughflow, with potassium and calcium. 1980 Spurr & Barnes *Forest Ecol.* (ed. 3) ix. 230 Airborne dust, ash, and gaseous aerosols may also become attached to or impacted on tree surfaces and carried to the soil as throughfall and stem flow. 1844 H. Stephens *Bk. Farm* III. 951 The wheat *stem-fly, *Chlorops pumilionis*,.. derives its specific name,.. in consequence of the effects it produces on the plants it attacks. 1922 A. Ward *Encycl. Food* 224 Crystallized ginger is also made from the young roots. The best grades, selected for uniform size and appearance, are called '*stem ginger'. 1977 *Times* 2 Sept. 10/5 The menu offers.. bananas with stem ginger. 1922 Joyce *Ulysses* 224 He took a red carnation from the tall stem-glass. 1974 L. Deighton *Spy Story* xvii. 187 A stem glass from the ice-box, really cold Beefeater and.. seven per cent dry vermouth. 1979 B. Hines *Price of Coal* i. 14 He.. took down a tinted stem-glass.. [and] selected his favourite bloom. 1762 tr. *Busching's Syst. Geog.* IV. 408 Nesselrod, the *stem-house of the ancient noble family of Nesselrod. 1892 J. Anderson in J. R. Allen *Early Chr. Monum. Scot.* (1903) p. xx, The nose and the fore-leg of the stag cross and interrupt the *stem-line of the ogham inscription. 1914 Munro *Prehist. Britain* ii. 25 The progress of man's intellectuality, ever since he diverged from the common stem line from which he and the anthropoid apes have descended. 1953 Levan & Hauschka in *Jrnl. Nat. Cancer Inst.* XIV. 5 Chromosome numbers and the concept of 'stemline'... The chromosome class with the highest number of cells, and the adjacent classes, represent the types mainly responsible for growth and characterize the particular stemline of each tumour. 1962 *Lancet* 27 Jan. 218/2 Several cases of mosaicism in mongolism have been reported... Two of these cases were mosaics with three stemlines, 46, 47, and 48 chromosomes; and two with two stemlines, 46 and 47 chromosomes. 1972 *Science* 23 June 1340/3 The establishment of this pattern was based on the analysis of stemlines, sidelines, and single deviating cells in 80 primary and 20 metastatic tumors. 1878 *Entomologist's Monthly Mag.* XIV. 224 An enormous single egg, from which, undoubtedly, will come the *stem-mother. 1907, 1923 [see fundatrix 2]. 1979 *Vole* Dec. 40/2 Here the mated females [*sc.* grain aphides] hide the eggs that will come through the winter. These hatch in the late spring.., becoming 'stem mothers' that grow up to fly in quest of grain fields. 1870 H. A. Nicholson *Man. Zool.* I. 61 A spiral contractile fibre [in *Vorticella*], which is sometimes called the '*stem-muscle'. 1876 Dunglison *Med. Lex.*, *Pessary*, Intraüterine, *stem pessary,.. an instrument for rectifying uterine displacements—as [etc.]. 1901 G. Jekyll *Lilies for Eng. Gardens* iii. 8 It should be planted six to seven inches deep, as it forms *stem roots. 1978 B. Mathew *Larger Bulbs* 85 Some species [of *Lilium*] produce a tuft of roots from the stem just as it emerges from the bulb, these stem-roots partly acting as extra support. 1876 T. W. Sanders *Encycl. Gardening* (ed. 2) 19 *Artocarpus*... Propagation: By *stem-rooting firm shoots in Feb., March; suckers at any time. 1974 H. G. W. Fogg *Compl. Handbk. Bulbs* vii. 91/1 This stem-rooting lily should be planted at least 4 ins deep. 1899 M. A. Carleton *Cereal Rusts U.S.* 57 The *stem rust.. is not constant in occurrence, but will occasionally miss one or two years. 1923 *Jrnl. Agric. Res.* XXIV. 979 There are several biologic forms of stem rust of wheat. 1946 K. S. Chester *Nature & Prevention of Cereal Rusts* xiv. 199 Disproportionate emphasis.. has been laid on stem rust.. in wheat. 1979 Tanous & Rubinstein *Wheat Killing* (1980) ix. 57 There's some stem rust around... The black spores of the rust were clearly visible. 1895 D. Sharp *Insects* i. 504 Cephidae—*Stem Sawflies. 1896 Lydekker *Roy. Nat. Hist.* VI. 15 Stem Saw-flies.. pass their lives in the stems of plants or young shoots of trees. 1890 Miss Ormerod *Injur. Insects* (ed. 2) 54, I have notes of Clover plants *stem-sick from this Eelworm. *Ibid.* 52 'Stem-sickness'. 1873 *Young Englishwoman* June 299/1 The embroidery is worked.. in satin and *stem-stitch, and point-russe. 1882 Caulfeild & Saward *Dict. Needlework* 461 *Stem Stitch*.. is largely used to form the stems, tendrils, curves, and raised parts in Honiton and other Pillow Lace making. There are three kinds of Stem Stitch—Beginner's Stem, Buckle Stem, and Stem Stitch proper. 1897 J. C. Willis *Man. & Dict. Flowering Plants & Ferns* I. iii. 182 In the *stem-succulents the leaves are reduced to scales or thorns. 1966 E. Palmer *Plains of Camdeboo* xvi. 258 It is the stem-succulents.. that are the most typical of Cranemere—Euphorbias, Stapeliads, and other such.. most of them leafless, the work of the leaves being done by the stems and so protected from excessive transpiration; or bearing leaves for a short time only. 1929 *Sears Catal.* Fall 898/1 One of the newest creations in *stemware. 1966 H. Nielsen *After Midnight* (1967) xv. 194 A small, circular dinner table.. had been meticulously set with china, silver and stemware. 1900 *Westm. Gaz.* 17 Feb. 10/1 1,000 *stem-wind, brass, hunting-watch movements. 1875 Knight *Dict. Mech.* 2373/2 Some of the *stem-winders are so constructed that by pushing in the pendant it is [etc.]. 1892 Gunter *Miss Divid.* (1893) 68 'Ain't he a stem-winder, though?' goes on the boy. 'He was the most popular man on the line when it was built.' 1926 in J. F. Dobie *Rainbow in Morning* 85 He's a stemwinder and go-getter. 1942 Berrey & Van den Bark *Amer. Thes. Slang* §422/5 *Speech-maker*,.. stemwinder, vitalics, *a forceful talker*. 1973 T. H. White *Making of President 1972* (1974) viii. 210 After all the calls to unity,.. a stemwinder in the old tradition from Hubert Humphrey,.. appearances by Muskie and Kennedy, Sargent Shriver was formally nominated for Vice-President. 1977 *Time* 3 Jan. 55/2 The 1,008 cadres and 24 fraternal foreign delegations.. endured no fewer than 55 speeches, including an eight-hour stem-winder by Le Duan. 1884 F. J. Britten *Watch & Clockm.* 247 *Stem Winding.. [is] winding by means of a stem running through the pendant of a watch. The ordinary method of keyless winding. 1867 *Rep. Comm. Patents 1866* (U.S.) 1115 Either side of the case of the *stem-winding watch is opened by pressure upon the head of the winding arbor. 1875 Knight *Dict. Mech.* 2373 Stem-winding Watch. 1966 *Atlantic Monthly* Sept. 90 A stem-winding sermon by Reverend Cecil Todd.. can be obtained by sending one dollar to *Revival Fires* in Joplin, Missouri.

stem (stɛm), *sb.*[2] *Naut.* Forms: 1 stefn, stefna *or* -ne, stemn, 5–6 steme, 6–7 stemme, 7 stemb, 7–8 stemm, 6– stem. [OE. *stęmn*, *stęfn* str. masc. (also *stęfna* wk. masc. or *stęfne* wk. fem.), originally a specific application of stem *sb.*[1] in the sense 'tree-trunk'. The nautical use occurs (sometimes with differentiated form) in several Teut. langs.: OFris. *stevene* (WFris. *stjûwn*, NFris. *stēven*), Du., LG. *steven* (whence G. *steven*; MDu. had also *steve*), OS. *stamn*, ON. *stafn*, *stamn* masc. (whence ME. stam *sb.*[1]), Da. *stavn*, also (? from LG.) *stævn*, Sw. (? from LG.) *stäf*.

After the OE. period the native word does not occur in our quots. until late in the 15th c., though the 14th and 15th c. have several examples of stam (from the equivalent ON. form) and of the compound forestam. The native form must of course have been preserved in oral tradition alongside the Scandinavian form, which disappears in the 15th c. A few examples of steven are found in Sc. writers of the 16th c.; whether this descends from OE. *stefn*, or a late adoption from LG. or Du., cannot be determined.]

†**1.** The timber at either extremity of a vessel, to which the ends of the side-planks were fastened; the 'stem' (in the modern sense) or the stern-post. Hence, either extremity of a vessel, the prow or the stern. *Obs.*

Beowulf 212 Beornas on stefn stiʒon. *a* 1000 *Andreas* 495 Ic æfre ne ʒeseah æniʒne mann.. þe ʒelicne, steoran ofer stæfnan. 10.. *Voc.* in Wr.-Wülcker 288/1 *Puppis*, se æftera stemn. 1486 *Naval Acc. Hen. VII* (1896) 16 A plate of Irne for the steme of the same Cokke. 1497 *Ibid.* 291 The Shippe Kele with the ij stemys belongyng vnto the same.

2. The curved upright timber or piece of metal at the bow of a vessel, into which the planks of the bow are scarfed; = the earlier forestam. ***false stem***: see quot. 1627. ***main stem***: the 'stem' proper as distinguished from the 'false stem'.

1538 Elyot *Dict.*, *Rostrum*,.. also the stemme of a ship or boote. 1587 Marlowe *1st Pt. Tamburl.* i. ii, Christian Merchants that with Russian stems Plow vp huge furrowes in the Caspian Sea, Shall vaile to us. 1601 Holland *Pliny* vii. lvi. I. 190 Piseus the Tyrrhene.. armed the stemme and beake-head of the ship with sharpe tines and pikes of brasse. 1627 Capt. Smith *Sea Gram.* ii. 2 At the one end is skarfed into it the Stem, which is a great timber wrought compassing. *Ibid.* ix. 53 If her stem be too flat.. fix another stem before it, and that is called a false stem, which will make her rid more way and beare a better saile. 1652 Nedham tr. *Selden's Mare Cl.* 54 As far as Nereus doth, to Ashur's Land Plow out a passage with his stemm's and oars. 1668 *Lond. Gaz.* No. 236/1 But the Flyboat breaking her Stemm, sunk.. suddenly. 1748 *Anson's Voy.* iii. vii. 367 The joining of the stem where it was scarfed. 1797 *Encycl. Brit* (ed. 3) XVII. 377/2 The height and rake of the stem and sternpost. 1830 Hedderwick *Mar. Archit.* 246 From the foremost perpendicular, set off all the rakes of the stem inside and out. 1865 Kingsley *Herew.* vi, He rode back to the ship,.. and wondered at her carven stem and stern. 1869 Sir E. Reed *Shipbuild.* iii. 48 The stem of an iron ship.. is usually a prolongation of the keel. 1889 Welch *Text Bk. Naval Archit.* vii. 98 The stems of all ships complete, as it were, the framing at the fore part of the vessel.

b. Phrases. ***from stem to stern*** (†***from stern to stem***, †***from post to stem***): along the whole length of a ship. ***to give*** (a ship) ***the stem***: to ram. †***stem for stem***: (of ships) abreast, exactly alongside each other. ***stem on***: so as to strike with the stem. ***stem to stem***: (of ships) with their stems facing each other.

1548 Hall *Chron.*, *Hen. VIII* (1550) 21 b, Sir Henry Guilford and sir Charles Brandon.. beyng in the Souereigne,.. laied stemme to stemme to the Caricke. 1622 Sir R. Hawkins *Voy. S. Sea* xxxiii. 80 Wee had.. our shippe Calked from Post to Stemme. 1627 Capt. Smith *Sea Gram.* ii. 2 Pulling it from sterne to stem. *a* 1642 Sir W. Monson *Naval Tracts* vi. (1704) 535/1 The Ship gave Stem to a Whale that lay a sleep..; it was a Stem upon a Whale. 1644 Manwayring *Seamans Dict.* 102 To give a ship the Stem, that is to run right upon her with the Stem. 1667 *Lond. Gaz.* No. 120/1 Three Ulushing Men of War.. immediately came roundly up with us, Stemb to Stemb. 1670 Covel in *Early Voy. Levant* (Hakl. Soc.) 129 There were five great ships a Head, coming stem for stem towards us. 1697 Dryden *Æneis* i. 164 Orontes Barque.. From Stem to Stern, by Waves was overborn. 1836 Thirlwall *Greece* III. xxvi. 431 The Athenians.. would be forced to meet them.. stem to stem. 1842 Tennyson *Morte d' Arthur* 194 Then saw they how there hove a dusky barge, Dark as a funeral scarf from stem to stern. 1842 Lever *Jack Hinton* ii, The sea ran high, and swept the little craft from stem to stern. 1880 *Daily Tel.* 7 Sept., Steer her straight, good captain, stem on to the mark, and wear her round smart. 1884 *Manch. Exam.* 24 Nov. 6/1 My little boat.. has been driven full tilt, stem on, against a rock in mid-stream. 1885 *Daily Tel.* 21 May 5/3 The cry was, 'Give privateers the stem!' that is, run them down. 1885 *Law Times Rep.* LIII. 55/1 The *Earl of Beaconsfield* struck the *J. M. Stevens* on the port quarter stem on.

3. The prow, bows, or the whole forepart of a vessel.

1555 Eden *Decades* (Arb.) 195 Turnynge the stemmes or forpartes of their shyppes ageynst the streame. 1676 Wood *Jrnl.* in *Acc. Sev. Late Voy.* i. (1694) 187 So we lay South-south-west with the Stem. 1710 W. King *Heathen Gods & Heroes* xii. (1722) 49 Ships, which had Stemms and Decks that resembled Towers. 1711 W. Sutherland *Shipbuild. Assist.* 164. 1833 M. Scott *Tom Cringle* ii, The spray from the stem was flashing over me. 1878 *Masque of Poets* 122 While her stem peeled the scum as an apple. 1898 *Encycl. Sport* II. 298/1 (Rowing) *Stem*, the bows of a boat.

4. *attrib.* and *Comb.*, as in ***stem-end***, ***-head***; ***stem-beat*** adj.; ***stemwards*** adv. Also **stem-knee** (see quot.); †**stem-lock** (meaning obscure: cf. ON. *stafnlok* 'the locker in the stem' (Vigf.), and *stampneloker* s.v. stam *sb.*[1]); **stem-mould**, the mould (mould *sb.*[3] 1 b) for shaping the stem of a vessel; **stem-piece** (see quots.); **stem-post** = sense 2; †**stem-rudder**, ? a false stem.

1627 May *Lucan* ii. D 1 b, The *stemme beat sea with a vast murmur grones. 1611 Cotgr., *Piquant*,.. the nose, beake, or *stem-end of a ship. 1637 Heywood *Royall Ship* 40 Upon the *stemme-head there is Cupid,.. bestriding, and bridling a Lyon. 1884 *Daily News* 13 Nov. 5/1 They all clung to the stemhead, the only part of the lugger which kept above water. 1863 A. Young *Naut. Dict.* 388 **Stem-knees*, crooked pieces of timber, the bolting of which connects the keel with the stem. 1532 *Privy Purse Exp. Hen. VIII* (1827) 211 Paied to the said Carter for half a steme and for a *steme locke to the bote, iiij s. 1830 Hedderwick *Mar. Archit.* 257 Draw the inside and outside of the rabbet fair by the *stem-mould. *c* 1860 H. Stuart *Seaman's Catech.* 67 What is the *stem piece for? It lies between the knight heads, and strengthens that part of the ship which the bowsprit passes through. 1875 Knight *Dict. Mech.* 2373 *Stem-piece* (*Shipbuilding*), a piece in front of the stem, into which the main piece of the head is stepped. 1841 *Penny Cycl.* XXI. 393/1 At A and B, the extremities of the keel, the stern-post, and *stem-post are set up. 1664 E. Bushnell *Shipwright* 60 You may.. measure the content of the Keel and Post and *Stem-rudder, all of it that is without the Plank and under the water line. 1665 Hooke *Microgr.* 45 The mouth of it open from the *stemwards. 1892 *Illustr. Lond. News* 17 Dec. 774/3 His course, whether stemwards or sternwards, was steadily south.

stem (stɛm), *sb.*[3] Also 1 stemn, 4 stemme, stempne. [OE. *stemn* str. masc., var. of *stefn* steven *sb.*[2]]

†**1.** A fixed time; a period of time; a turn, vicissitude. *Obs.* Cf. steven *sb.*[2]

O.E. Chron. an. 894, Hie hæfdon þa heora stemn ʒesetenne,.. & wæs se cyng þa þiderweardes on fære. *a* 1300 *Cursor M.* 11225 Wel moght he ger witvten stemme, Maiden ber barn wit-vten wemme. 1387 Trevisa *Higden* (Rolls) III. 439 He deled þe tymes and stempnes of þe myʒtes among companyes of strompettes. *Ibid.* IV. 29 þey tweyne regnede by stempnes. 1398 —— *Barth. De P.R.* ii. ii. (1495) 28 In that he is a creature he hath stemnes of chaungynge. *Ibid.*, They ben not chaunged by dedely stempnes, nother they haue contraryousnesse of passybylite.

2. *Mining.* (See quots.)

1778 Pryce *Min. Cornub.* 179 Sometimes they are necessitated to work considerably longer than their stated hours; and then they are said to make a stem, or part of a stem, or to work a stem out of core. 1778 Pennat *Tour Wales* (1883) I. 65 The laborers worked by stems, relieving each other at stated times. 1868 *Tregellas' Cornish Tales* 191 Gloss., *Stem*, day's work. 1896 *Daily News* 10 Feb. 3/6 Newport... Stems are numerous at this and the adjoining ports.

attrib. *a* 1863 Tregellas *Cornish Tales* (1868) 17 And every stem-man lev un come.

3. *Fishing.* (See quots.)

1701 Brand *Descr. Orkney* etc. (1703) 151 Up the Water they cannot run, because of the larger Net, and neither down can they go, because of the Stem, or Stones laid together in form of a Wall. 1776 *Act 16 Geo. III*, c. 36 §1 The six several Stems or Stations for taking Fish within the said Bay of Saint Ives. 1879 *Encycl. Brit.* IX. 254/1 It is divided into six stations or 'stems', by marks or boundaries on the land.

stem (stɛm), *sb.*[4] *Sc.* [f. stem *v.*[2]] Resistance, opposition; a check.

c 1700 Mrs. Goodal in Tweedie *Sel. Biogr.* (Wodrow Soc.) II. 484 There is something of a stem lately risen in my heart. 1889 H. Morton in *Life* (1895) 189 The notice gave us a stem.. He did not seem to think he was dying.

†**stem**, *v.*[1] *Obs.* Also 4 stemm, steme, stempme. [? a. ON. *stemna*, *stefna* to summon, call before a tribunal (whence late OE. *stefnian* in *O.E. Chron.* ann. 1048, 1093), f. *stefna* = OE. *stefn* stem *sb.*[3]]

a. *trans.* To contend with. **b.** *intr.* ? To debate with oneself.

a 1300 *Cursor M.* 21135 þat folk ilkan wald oþer stemm [*Gött.* stem], Qua rin moght titest on his hemm. 13.. *Gaw. & Gr. Knt.* 230 He stemmed & con studie, Quo walt þer most renoun. *Ibid.* 1117 þay stoden, & stemed, & stylly speken. *a* **1400–50** *Wars Alex.* 2480 ȝe suld noȝt stody ne stem þe sternes for to handill. *Ibid.* 2960 He studis & he stuynes, he stemes [*MS. Dubl.* stempmys] with-in. *Ibid.* 5301 þan stemes he with þe stoute kyng, & stiggis with his name.

stem (stɛm), *v.*[2] Also 4, 7 **stemme**. [a. ON. *stemma* (Sw. *stämma*, Da. *stemme*) = OHG., MHG., mod.G. *stemmen* (? Du. *stempen* to stop the flow of):—OTeut. **stamjan*, f. **stam-* root of STAMMER *v.*]

†**1.** *intr.* ? To stop, delay. *Obs.*

a **1300** *Cursor M.* 24327 Speke we wald, might had we nan, For-þi we stemmed still als stan. **13..** *E.E. Allit. P.* B. 905 And loke ȝe stemme no stepe, bot strechez on faste. **1570** LEVINS *Manip.* 60/2 To stemme, *tutubare* [? for *titubare*].

2. *trans.* To stop, check; to dam up (a stream, or the like).

When used fig. in phrases like 'to stem the tide', this verb is sometimes confused with STEM *v.*[3], to make headway against.

c **1450** *St. Cuthbert* (Surtees) 4313 þere myght na thing thaim stem. **1713** STEELE *Englishm.* No. 28. 184 They were able to stem the proceedings of the Crown when they pleased. *a* **1806** H. K. WHITE *To Friend in Distress* 4 When from my downcast eye I chase the tear, and stem the rising sigh. **1840** DICKENS *Old C. Shop* xxi, Little Jacob stemmed the course of two tears. **1855** PALEY *Æschylus* (1861) Pref. p. xxxiii, Aristophanes evidently saw the tide that was setting strongly in favour of the new candidate for scenic supremacy, and he vainly tried to stem it by the barrier of his ridicule. **1860** GEO. ELIOT *Mill on Floss* I. xii, Mr. Glegg.. sat down to his milk-porridge, which it was his old frugal habit to stem his morning hunger with. **1883** FROUDE in *19th Cent.* XIII. 637 It was the Spanish power indisputably which stemmed the Reformation.

3. a. To set (one's limbs, hand) firmly.

1827 HONE *Every-day Bk.* II. 340 This they do, by stemming themselves with their haunches against the gates. The elephant.. stems his knees against the wheels. **1859** WRAXALL tr. *R. Houdin* ii. 9 And he stemmed his fist in his side while he held his head impudently high.

b. intr. *to stem back*: to resist being driven forwards.

1899 *N.B. Daily Mail* 12 Dec. 2 When these bullocks reached the threshold of the slaughter-house they stem'd back with their fore-feet... What made these bullocks stem back?

4. trans. *Mining.* To plug or tamp (a hole for blasting).

1791 SMEATON *Edystone L.* §223 *note*, The stemming a hole for blasting rocks with gunpowder. **1875** J. TAYLOR *Poems* etc. 35 Often a good shot of the powder well 'stemmed' would not remove a capfull of the rock. **1880** J. LOMAS *Man. Alkali Trade* 273 At the four corners.. a diamond is formed, and thoroughly stemmed with dry fireclay just moistened with tar [etc.]. *Ibid.* 305 The cover [of the still] is usually formed of segments of stone, and is let and stemmed into a ledge cut in the side stones.

5. a. To stop, to staunch (bleeding, etc.). *Sc.*

c **1470** HENRY *Wallace* x. 351 Be than he had stemmyt full weill his wound. *c* **1550** *Clariodus* I. 1021 He with diverse herbis vertewus Stemit his woundis, and stintit the bleiding. *a* **1835** HOGG *Tales & Sk.* (1837) VI. 10 John, nevertheless, did all that he could to bind up and stem his cousin's wounds. **1870** J. BRUCE *Gideon* ii. 29 So that the bleeding wound should be stemmed and bound up.

b. *intr.* Of bleeding: to become staunched.

1844 H. STEPHENS *Bk. Farm* II. 613 The tail sometimes bleeds for a long time.. though usually the bleeding soon stems.

6. *Skiing.* [ad. G. *stemmen.*] **a.** To decelerate (esp. before a turn) on a traverse descent by weighting the upper ski and angling its outer edge into the snow, causing the ski to turn downhill.

1904 E. C. RICHARDSON *Ski-Running* 41 (*caption*) *The proper way to stem...* A good stemming-spoor is at once known by the broad track of the braker. **1935** *Punch* 6 Feb. 164/3 *Stemming.*—Your ordinary straight running will lack the easy confidence.. it should have unless I first show you how to stem, which is the only legitimate way of applying the brake other than using complicated turns like the christiania or the telemark. **1948** H. INNES *Blue Ice* x. 249 Jill stopped then and I stemmed. We were standing at the end of the snowshed. **1970** N. FLEMING *Czech Point* i. 22, I sideslipped at first, grew tired of it, stemmed for a while and then had just started to take the slope straight when the shot was fired.

b. The vb. in Comb., as **stem-Christiania**, a turn made by stemming and lifting the lower ski parallel as the manœuvre is completed (less advanced than the full CHRISTIANIA); hence as colloq. abbrev. **stem-Christie** (also *v. intr.*, to turn in this manner); **stem turn**, an elementary turn made by stemming and then bringing the unweighted ski parallel in the new line; also *transf.* and as *v. intr.*, to make a stem turn or turns.

1922 V. CAULFEILD *Ski-ing Turns* xii. 228 The Stem-Christiania, like the Stem turn, is mainly used for down-hill turning on hard snow... A downhill turn can.. be made more sharply by the Stem-Christiania than by any other means except a jump. **1961** *Times* 7 Jan. 7/6 The tried and basic essentials of the snowplough and the stem-christiania in particular. **1936** *Sierra Club Bull.* Feb. 57, I soon began very short linked stem-christies with the aid of the inner pole. **1942** 'N. SHUTE' *Pied Piper* ii. 20 At each new slope of snow he thought to see John come hurting over the brow, stem-christie to a traverse, and vanish in a white flurry that sped down into the valley. **1972** 'M. YORKE' *Silent Witness* VI. iv. 141 They stem-christied inexpertly over the wide plateau. **1922** V. CAULFEILD *Ski-ing Turns* vii. 123 The Stem turn is impossible in heavy soft snow or breaking crust... There are two forms of the Stem turn... The Pure Stem turn is only possible on gentle slopes... The Lifted Stem Turn can be employed for down-hill turning on moderately steep slopes. **1938** [see CHRISTIE]. **1959** M. GILBERT *Blood & Judgement* ix. 98 Petrella.. started straight off down the pavement, did a stem turn at the corner... 'At least he can still walk,' said Borden. **1973** J. GOODFIELD *Courier to Peking* xiii. 171 They were moving downhill with the competence of an Olympic skier in a slalom race, stem-turning neatly at every snake-like twist of the road.

stem (stɛm), *v.*[3] Also 6 **steme, stemp**, 6–7 **stemme**. [f. STEM *sb.*[2]]

1. *trans.* Of a vessel, a navigator: To urge the stem against, make headway against (a tide, current, gale, etc.). Hence of a swimmer, a flying bird, and the like: To make headway against (water or wind), to breast (the waves, the air). Often in figurative context: see note to STEM *v.*[2] 2.

1593 SHAKS. *3 Hen. VI*, II. vi. 36 As doth a Saile, fill'd with a fretting Gust, Command an Argosie to stemme the Waues. **1613–16** W. BROWNE *Brit. Past.* I. iv. 68 Milke-white Swannes which stem the streames of Poe. **1619** DRAYTON *Heroical Epist., Lady Jane Gray* 77 The true-bred Eagle strongly stems [*earlier edd.* beares] the Wind. **1654** WHITLOCK *Zootomia* 27 He that would stemme the Tyde, had need of a good Gale. **1682** DRYDEN & TATE *Abs. & Achit.* II. 1132 This year did Ziloah Rule Jerusalem, And boldly all Sedition's Syrges stem. **1720** DE FOE *Capt. Singleton* v. (1840) 80 We stemmed the ebb easily. **1754** HUME *Hist. Gt. Brit., Chas. I*, iv. 249 Charles, in despair of being able to stem the torrent, at last resolved to yield to it. **1764** GOLDSM. *Trav.* 71 The naked negro, panting at the line,.. Basks in the glare, or stems the tepid wave. **1769** FALCONER *Dict. Marine* (1780) II, *Eviter à marée*, to stem the tide. *Eviter au vent*, to carry the head to windward, to stem the wind. **1815** *Falconer's Dict. Marine* (ed. Burney), *To Stem the Tide*, is to acquire a velocity in sailing against the tide equal to the force of the current. **1816** TUCKEY *Narr. Exped. R. Zaire* iii. (1818) 78 Though the current was running scarcely three miles an hour, she [the ship] at first barely stemmed it. **1816** SCOTT *Old Mort.* xxx, The prudence of Morton found sufficient occupation in stemming the furious current of these contending parties. **1861** BUCKLE *Civiliz.* (1869) III. v. 298 He opposed the tide which he was unable to stem. **1899** F. T. BULLEN *Log Sea-waif* 289 The swift ebb past us.. straining our cable out taut as if we were stemming a gale.

b. *transf.* and *fig.* To go counter to, make headway against (something compared to a stream); *rarely*, †to face, defy (a person).

1675 OTWAY *Alcibiades* I. i, I then.. Will bravely stem him, and with this bold Hand Revenge, or fall a Victim to your Flame. **1675** V. ALSOP *Anti-Sozzo* iii. §2. 161 Never was Man so confuted.. as he that stems the Experience of the whole World. **1759** JOHNSON *Rasselas* xlvii, Every one is not able to stem the temptations of public life. *a* **1844** CAMPBELL *Transl., Martial Elegy* 23 Leave not our sires to stem th' unequal fight. **1847** DE QUINCEY *Joan of Arc* Wks. 1890 V. 412 [This calumny] has a weight of contradicting testimony to stem. *a* **1853** ROBERTSON *Serm.* Ser. III. xxi. 272 We are now to ask how he will stem those seductions. **1888** F. COWPER *Caedwalla* 250 At a very slow pace.. the grey frocked monks.. stemmed the still hurrying bodies of fugitives.

c. *to stem one's course*: to make one's way against difficulties. *rare.*

1826 MRS. SHELLEY *Last Man* II. 36 Slowly and sadly I stemmed [*sic*] my course from among the heaps of slain.

d. To direct the head of (a vessel) *on* a place; to keep (a vessel) on a fixed course.

1594 J. DICKENSON *Arisbas* (1878) 85 The Pilot mistaking his course, stemmed the ship on a rock. **1653** HOLCROFT *Procopius, Goth. Wars* I. 31 No wind being able to stemme them up the Stream. **1684** tr. *Corn. Nepos* Ded. a 8 He is the Master of true Courage that all the time sedately stemms the Ship.

e. *intr.* Of a vessel or a navigator: To head in a certain direction, keep a certain course.

1375 BARBOUR *Bruce* v. 25 Thai na nedill had na stane, But rowit alwayis in-till ane, Stemmand alwayis apon the fyre, That thai saw byrnand. **1595** T. EDWARDS *Narcissus* (Roxb.) 53 Then like a cunning pilate making out, To gaine the Oceans currant stem I forward. *a* **1656** USSHER *Ann.* (1658) 153 Upon the sudden Alcibiades came stemming in with 18 fresh ships. **1667** MILTON *P.L.* II. 642 They on the trading Flood.. Ply stemming nightly toward the Pole. **1672** *Lond. Gaz.* No. 680/1 We got up with them on their weather Gage, they and we stemming up S by W. **1769** FALCONER *Dict. Marine* (1780) II. s.v. *Gouverne*, The order to steer the ship exactly as she stems, or carries her head. **1801** *Naval Chron.* VI. 12 The.. squadron.. found themselves stemming for the centre of the.. fleet. **1863** COWDEN CLARKE *Shaks. Char.* xx. 520 There it was, stemming away against wind and tide. **1908** L. BINYON *Lond. Visions* 88 Ships on far tracks are stemming through the night.

2. To dash against with the stem of a vessel; to ram. *Obs.*

c **1500** *Melusine* xxxvi. 269 They.. stemed the shippes of the sarasyns in suche manere that they were sparpylled. **1537** *Adm. Ct. Exemplif.* i. No. 174 [An English ship mistook another for a Spaniard and] stemped the foresaid Thomas. **1596** SPENSER *F.Q.* IV. II. 16 As when two war-like Brigandines.. Doe meete together.. They stemme ech other with so fell despight, That [etc.]. **1614** RALEGH *Hist. World* III. vi. §6. 68 Stemming the formost of their enemies, and chasing the rest. **1617** PURCHAS *Pilgrimage* v. vii. (ed. 3) 599 Their three smaller Ships had thought to haue Stemmed the Hope then riding at an Anchor. **1654** H. LESTRANGE *Chas. I* (1655) 95 When suddenly rose a violent storm which drave a greater vessel.. so forcibly upon them as stemm'd them. *a* **1670** HACKET *Abp. Williams* I. (1693) 132 And like two great Caraques in a foul Sea, they never met in Counsel, but they stemmed one another. **1810** *Naval Chron.* XXIII. 53 A beak of metal was fixed on their prows for the purpose of *stemming* the enemy's ships.

†**b.** *transf.* Used of natural agencies. *Obs.*

a **1592** GREENE & LODGE *Looking Gl.* (1598) F 2 b, Our Barke is battered by incountring stormes, And welny stemd by breaking of the floods.

†**c.** *to go stemming*: to ram a ship. *Obs.*

1644 MANWAYRING *Seamans Dict.* 102 To goe Stemming a-boord a ship, that is the same, as giving the ship the Stem.

†**3.** *intr.* To meet stem to stem *with*. *Obs.*

1697 DAMPIER *Voy.* I. 461 We stemm'd right with the middle of it [*sc.* the shoal], and stood within half a mile of the Rocks, and sounded; but found no ground.

†**4.** *trans.* To furnish (a ship) with a stem. *Obs.*

1585 HIGINS *Junius' Nomencl.* 219/2 *Nauis rostrata*,.. a ship stemmed, beaked, or pointed with brasse. *c* **1590** GREENE *Friar Bacon* 1057 (Grosart), Frigats bottomd with rich Sethin planks,.. Stemd and incast with burnisht Iuorie.

stem (stɛm), *v.*[4] Also 6 **steam**. [f. STEM *sb.*[1]]

†**1.** *intr.* To rise erect, mount upwards. Also with *up*. *Obs.*

1577 STANYHURST *Descr. Irel.* iii. 14 b in *Holinshed*, The greater part of the towne [Rosse] is steepe and steaming vpwarde. **1582** —— *Æneis* II. (Arb.) 43 Thee Greekish captayns.. Framd a steed of tymber, steaming lyk mounten in hudgnesse. **1609** [W. BARLOW] *Answ. Nameless Cath.* 107 Romulus his Iaueling, which hee darting from him, it immediately stemmed vp into a stately Cornell Tree. **1786** G. FRAZER *Dove's Flight* etc. 111 [He] suffered it to stem out until it became a tree of full growth.

†**2.** To produce a stem. *Obs.*

1631 CHAPMAN *Cæsar & Pompey* III. i. 16 All which hath growne still, as the time encrease [*sic*] In which twas gather'd, and with which it stemm'd. **1787** *Fam. Plants* I. 105 It seems distinguished from Androsace, by the habit, the plant stemming, with simple peduncles.

3. *trans.* **a.** *Tobacco-manuf.* To remove the stalk and midrib from tobacco-leaf. Cf. STRIP *v.*

In quot. 1724 the senses of *stem* and *strip* are confused (*D.A.E.*).

1724 H. JONES *Present State of Virginia* 40 It lies till they have Leisure or Occasion to *stem* it (that is pull the leaves from the Stalk) or *strip* it (that is to take out the great Fibres). **1797** G. IMLAY *Topogr. Descr. Western Terr. N. Amer.* (ed. 3) 248 This done, you stem the tobacco, or pull out the middle rib of the leaf. **1844** *Rep. Sel. Comm. Tobacco Trade, Min. Evid.* 103 In America, where there is no duty on tobacco, they stem the tobacco in a very rough kind of way, and a great deal of leaf adheres to the stalk. **1859** [see STEMMERY]. **1904** *Daily Chron.* 20 Apr. 8/3 The process of stemming or stripping the leaf.

b. To remove the stalk from (a leaf, fruit, etc.).

1873 *Trans. Illinois Dept. Agric.* X. 61 The grapes were pressed without stemming. **1907** KATE D. WIGGIN *New Chron. Rebecca* x. 308 Her aunt and her mother were stemming currants on the side porch. **1908** *Daily Chron.* 10 Apr. 7/4 To the chicken add one half pound of fresh mushrooms, peeled and stemmed.

4. To beg or 'panhandle' on the streets. Cf. STEM *sb.*[1] 6 b. *U.S. slang.*

1924 'DIGIT' *Confessions 20th Century Hobo* 12 *Stemming*, begging, cadging. **1931** 'D. STIFF' *Milk & Honey Route* viii. 84 Panhandling falls into two classes: the domestic type.. and a kind carried on in the streets and known as 'stemming'. **1937** *Lit. Digest* 10 Apr. 12/2 *Stemming*, panhandling in cities.

5. *fig.* **a.** To derive or take origin *from*; to spring from. (The principal modern sense.) orig. *U.S.*

1932 A. H. QUINN *Soul of Amer.* 131 The policy of vigorous intervention in the affairs of the nations bordering on the Caribbean Sea stems from Roosevelt's administration. **1937** R. S. MORTON *Woman Surgeon* i. 15, I realize now that my apparent indifference to suitors for marriage stemmed from my determination to study medicine. **1942** W. FAULKNER *Go down, Moses* 86 He knew what he had seen in his father's face.. something.. not stemming from any difference of race nor because one blood strain ran in them both. **1949** *Here & Now* (N.Z.) Nov. 27/1 From this stemmed a whole line of high-grade thrillers. **1952** B. SMALLEY *Study of Bible in Middle Ages* 358 Both literal and spiritual exposition stemmed from Origen. **1958** *Times* 11 Feb. 11/7 The whole of this trouble has stemmed entirely from your own behaviour. **1961** I. FLEMING *Thunderball* xviii. 194 The source of his wealth was unknown but did not stem from funds held in Italy. **1976** H. WILSON *Governance of Britain* x. 183 Bills normally stem from the legislative arm. **1979** J. GRIMOND *Memoirs* vi. 98, I believe that much that is wrong with attitudes and organisation in Britain stems from the war.

b. To extend *back to* in origin. Also, to arise *out of*.

1937 *Sun* (Baltimore) 24 Nov. 2/7 Wall Streeters said the controversy stemmed back to the annual report issued by Mr. Gay as president of the exchange last August. **1959** N. LOFTS *Heaven in your Hand* 99 The whole thing stemmed back to the beliefs in the African witch-doctors. **1965** *Listener* 11 Nov. 740/1 It is sometimes claimed that race antipathy stems out of the same order of cultural differences. **1974** *Times Lit. Suppl.* 26 Apr. 430/3 There is still doubt and conflict here, stemming back to the ancient world.

†**stem**, *v.*[5] *Obs.* (? *nonce-wd.*) [? f. L. *stemma*, garland.] *trans.* To encircle.

1596 SPENSER *F.Q.* VI. x. 12 The whilest the rest them round about did hemme, And like a girlond did in compasse stemme.

stem (stɛm), *v.*[6] *Coal-trade.* [Var. of STEVEN *v.*, STEEM *v.*[3]] *trans.* (See quot. 1903.)

1898 *Westm. Gaz.* 2 Apr. 1/3 Several contracts for boats stemmed on Admiralty orders were cancelled this morning. **1903** *Pitman's Business Man's Guide* 409 To stem a vessel means to load her, or arrange to load her, with coals, within a certain time. **1908** PAASCH *Keel to Truck* 732 *Stem, to* (a vessel). Term frequently used when booking a vessel for a turn in a dock, dry-dock, etc.

stemapod ('stɛməpɒd). *Ent.* [f. Gr. στῆμα filament + ποδ-, πούς foot.] One of the caudal filaments of the caterpillars of certain moths.

1893 DYAR in *Proc. Boston Soc. Nat. Hist.* XXVI. 158 Stemapods absent, their abbreviated bases rounded and held close together.

steming, variant of STAMIN.

stemless ('stɛmlɪs), *a.*[1] [f. STEM *sb.*[1] + -LESS.] Having no stem.

1796 WITHERING *Brit. Plants* (ed. 3) I. 374 The stemless Agarics and Boleti present similar appearances about the edge. **1834** *Penny Cycl.* II. 386/1 Little stemless herbs. **1870** HOOKER *Stud. Flora* 379 Convallaria, Lily of the Valley. A stemless herb. **1907** *Athenæum* 20 July 76/3 This handsome beaker, or stemless drinking cup.

stemless ('stɛmlɪs), *a.*[2] [f. STEM *v.*[2] + -LESS.] That cannot be stemmed.

a **1822** in H. Miller *Scenes & Leg. N. Scot.* (1850) 257 Till the life-blood, stemless gushing, Lays the plaided hero low. **1911** *Daily News* 14 Apr. 2 Time is an ebbless Tide, a stemless stream.

stemlet ('stɛmlɪt). [f. STEM *sb.*[1] + -LET.] A small stem.

1838 *Penny Cycl.* XII. 240/1 The third joint is short, and gives insertion to two multi-articulate stemlets (tigelles). **1900** B. D. JACKSON *Gloss. Bot. Terms* 253/1 *Stemlet*, a small stem, as the plumule.

† **'stemlings**, *adv. Obs.* Also 7 **stemlinge, stemlins**, 8 **stemlands**. [f. STEM *sb.*[2] + -LINGS.] *to run stemlings*: to run stem on, to stem.

1626 CAPT. SMITH *Accid. Yng. Seamen* 19 Lash fast your graplins and sheare off, then run stemlins the mid ships. **1626** *Adm. Ct. Exam.* 46 The Unity fetched up the Butterflye and ran stemlinge against the luffe beame of the Butterflye. **1712** *Ibid.* 84 f. 534 The Fredick run stemlands aboard the midships of the Felton.

‖**stemma** ('stɛmə). Pl. **stemmata** ('stɛmətə). [L., a. Gr. στέμμα garland, f. στέφειν to crown. In Latin chiefly a garland placed on an ancestral image, hence ancestry, pedigree, genealogical tree.

In the 17th c. a supposed literal sense 'STEM of a tree' was often wrongly inferred from the sense 'stem of a family'.]

1. a. *Rom. Ant.* The recorded genealogy of a family. **b.** A diagram showing genetic relationships, a genealogical tree.

[**1658** PHILLIPS *Stemma*, (Greek) the stalk of any herb or flower; also a stock, linage or pedigree.] **1879** *Encycl. Brit.* X. 144/1 In the case of plebeian families (whose stemmata in no case went farther back than 366 B.C.). **1904** W. SANDAY *Crit. Fourth Gosp.* viii. (1905) 239 If we were to construct a stemma, and draw lines from each of the authorities to a point *x*, representing the archetype, the lines would be long [etc.].

c. A diagram which represents a reconstruction on stemmatic principles of the position of the surviving witnesses in the tradition of the transmission of a text, esp. in manuscript form. Cf. STEMMATOLOGY.

1930 W. P. SHEPARD in *Mod. Philol.* XXVIII. 130 The claim that the Lachmannian method can deduce..the *ipsissima verba* of the author, takes no account of the fact that an author may change his mind...and the final and most telling objection to this method..is the fact that in practice it..leads to the establishment of a dichotomous 'stemma', a family tree. **1942** J. B. SEVERS in *English Institute Ann. 1941* 79 And so we deal with each of our families in turn, until the manuscripts in each family have been completely outlined. .. Thus we build up a complete stemma, or genealogical chart, for our whole body of manuscript. **1949** *Oxf. Classical Dict.* 889/1 Where one witness depends on two or more other witnesses, i.e. where the transmission is 'contaminated' and the stemma 'convergent', it is seldom possible to ascertain the type of interrelationship by stemmatics. **1962** E. J. DOBSON in Davis and Wrenn *English & Medieval Studies* 136 We thus arrive at the stemma shown by the unbroken lines in the diagram. **1982** *N. & Q.* Feb. 77/2 The meticulous detail of information is made clear by stemma diagrams. for those with the courage to penetrate the complexity.

2. *Zool.* A simple eye, or a single facet of the compound eye, in invertebrates.

1826 KIRBY & SP. *Entomol.* III. 504 A kind of auxiliary eyes with which a large portion of them [*sc.* insects] are gifted. These Linné, from his regarding them as a kind of coronet, called *Stemmata*. *Ibid.* 505 [Swammerdam] ascertained that the stemmata, as well as the compound eyes, were organs of vision. *c* **1865** *Wylde's Circ. Sci.* II. 34/1 Similar to the stemmata of some worms are what are called the simple eyes of insects. **1880** F. P. PASCOE *Zool. Classif.* (ed. 2) 285 *Ocelli* or *stemmata*, simple or supplementary eyes in insects and spiders. **1892** A. B. GRIFFITHS *Physiol. Invertebr.* 355 In the Myriapoda..each stemma has its retinal elements..so disposed..that [etc.].

ste'mmatic, *sb.* and *a.* [a. G. *stemmatik* (P. Maas in *Byzantinische Zeitschrift* (1937) XXXVII. 289), f. L. *stemma(t-)* STEMMA + -IC.]

A. *sb. pl.* **stemmatics** = STEMMATOLOGY.

1949 [see STEMMA 1 c]. **1958** B. FLOWER tr. *P. Maas' Text. Criticism* 42 Errors arising in the course of transcription are of decisive significance in the study of the interrelationships of manuscripts—I may be allowed to use the term 'stemmatics'. **1968** REYNOLDS & WILSON *Scribes & Scholars* v. 140 The classic statement of the theory of stemmatics is that of Paul Maas. **1975** *Times Lit. Suppl.* 15 Aug. 928/4 There has been a tendency to see stemmatics as something born in an instant. **1980** *Early Music Gaz.* Jan. 13/3 Source studies and stemmatics play an increasingly important role in musicology.

B. *adj.* Of or pertaining to a textual stemma or stemmata; concerning the reconstruction of the interrelationships between the readings of manuscripts of a text, esp. as ***stemmatic theory***.

1958 B. FLOWER tr. *P. Maas' Text. Criticism* 44 Such errors are so rare..that we cannot rely on being able to find one to establish every stemmatic relationship. **1968** REYNOLDS & WILSON *Scribes & Scholars* 140 In practice the stemmatic theory has serious limitations. **1980** *Early Music Gaz.* Jan. 13/3 Alejandro Planchart concluded that traditional stemmatic theory (after Paul Maas) best fits the text transmission of plainsong.

stemmatiform ('stɛmətɪfɔːm), *a. Zool.* [f. L. *stemmat-*, STEMMA + -FORM.] Having the form of stemmata.

1839–47 T. R. JONES in *Todd's Cycl. Anat.* III. 547/2 Scolopendra. Eyes 4-4, Stemmatiform.

stemmatology (stɛmə'tɒlədʒɪ). [f. L. *stemma(t-)* STEMMA: see -OLOGY.] The study which attempts to reconstruct the tradition of the transmission of a text or texts (esp. in manuscript form) on the basis of the relationships between the readings of the various surviving witnesses; this sphere of scholarship.

1942 *Essays & Studies* XXVII. 43 In what may be called stemmatology, the veterans..have done brilliant work. **1981** *N. & Q.* Feb. 1/2 Mr. Hamer..attempts a 'provisional' stemma. The darkness of conflicting and 'contaminated' evidence might have made a less brave man shrink from stemmatology.

stemmatous ('stɛmətəs), *a. Zool.* [f. L. *stemmat-*, STEMMA + -OUS.] Of the nature of a stemma.

In recent Dicts.

stemmed (stɛmd), *a.* [f. STEM *sb.*[1] + -ED[2].] Having a stem or stems.

1576 NEWTON *Lemnie's Complex.* I. viii. 62 Sondry Plantes and great stemmed hearbes. **1807** CRABBE *Par. Reg.* I. 151 Tulips tall-stemm'd..rise. **1897** A. HARTSHORNE *Old Engl. Glasses* 271 The opaque-twisted stemmed glasses.

stemmed (stɛmd), *ppl. a.* [f. STEM *v.*[4] + -ED[1].] Of tobacco leaf: Stripped of its stem.

1844 *Rep. Sel. Comm. Tobacco Trade, Min. Evid.* 234 As stemmed tobacco is only used for this country, if, [etc.]. **1883** KILLEBREW *Rep. Tobacco U.S.* 19 The larger consumption was of strips or stemmed tobacco.

stemmer[1] ('stɛmə(r)). *Mining.* [f. STEM *v.*[2] + -ER[1].] **a.** A metal bar used for stemming; a tamping bar. **b.** (See quot. 1909.)

1860 *Mining Gloss., Derbysh. Terms* 44 *Stemmer*, a piece of iron with which the clay is rammed into the shot holes to make them water tight. **1909** *N. Hawkins' Mech. Dict.*, *Stemmer*, in mining, a copper or bronze rod inserted into a powder charge, so as to leave a passage through the tamping for the fuse; a blasting needle.

stemmer[2] ('stɛmə(r)). Also **stemner**. [f. STEM *sb.*[2] + -ER[1].] (See quot. 1858.)

1858 *Jrnl. R. Agric. Soc.* XIX. I. 193 All trees are here [Sussex] cut down with the saw, and the stump, though quite level with the ground, is called the stem. This stem throws up shoots all round; the strongest is frequently left, and the rest cut off with the bill-hook. In time this shoot becomes a worthless tree, called a 'stemmer'. **1878** [see TILLER *sb.*[3] 2]. **1895** *Lease* (Surrey), All timber and other trees, tellers, stemners, already let to stand for timber and saplings.

stemmer[3] ('stɛmə(r)). [f. STEM *v.*[4] + -ER[1].]

1. In *Tobacco manuf.*, the workman who 'stems' tobacco-leaf; a stripper.

1895 *Funk's Stand. Dict.*

2. A machine for stemming grapes, etc.

1898 *Year-bk. U.S. Dept. Agric.* (1899) 558 Crushers and stemmers capable of working up 300 tons of grapes per day.

stemmery ('stɛmərɪ). [f. prec.: see -ERY.] (See quot. 1859.)

1859 BARTLETT *Dict. Amer.* (ed. 2) 450 *Stemmery*, a large building in which tobacco is stemmed, that is, in which the thin part of the leaf is stripped from the fibrous veins that run through it. **1897** KILLEBREW & MYRICK *Tobacco Leaf* 283 The work in the stemmeries goes on from November.. until June.

stemmet(t, variant forms of STAMMET.

stemminess ('stɛmɪnɪs). [f. STEMMY + -NESS.] The state or condition of being stemmy.

1827 STEUART *Planter's G.* I. (1848) 328 A striking poverty and stemminess usually offends the eye.

stemming ('stɛmɪŋ), *vbl. sb.*[1] [f. STEM *v.*[4] + -ING[1].] The action of the vb. STEM[4].

1703 *La Hontan's Voy. N. Amer.* I. 30, I found that the stemming of the Currents whether in towing of the Canows, or in setting them along with Poles, was equally laborious. **1796** MORSE *Amer. Geog.* II. 403 A current from the Atlantic .., and for the stemming of it a brisk gale is required. **1914** *Eng. Hist. Rev.* Jan. 137 The process of feudalization.. broke out again with great force under the Carolingians, after a brief stemming-back by the efforts of such princes as Charles Martel [etc.].

stemming ('stɛmɪŋ), *vbl. sb.*[2] *Mining.* [f. STEM *v.*[2] + -ING[1].]

1. = TAMPING 1 b.

1791 SMEATON *Edystone L.* §223 *note*, The efficacy of the gunpowder to split the stone, rather than to drive out the stemming or wad, is greatly owing to a further circumstance. **1851** GREENWELL *Coal-trade Terms, Northumb. & Durh.* 51 *Stemming*, Small coals or stones, with which a hole is tamped. **1898** *Colliery Guardian* 22 July 155 Tubed Cylinder Stemming for Boreholes. *Ibid.*, Clay stemming undoubtedly is the best, as it can be pressed directly upon the primer. **1908** *Times* 24 Mar. 10/3 The shot did its work, ..and all the stemming was driven from the stone.

2. *Skiing.* The action of STEM *v.*[2] 6 a.

1904, etc. [see SNOW-PLOUGHING *vbl. sb.*] **1935** P. FRANKAU *I find Four People* v. 311 We circled on our awkward attempts at stemming, frozen and undecided.

stemming, variant of STAMIN.

stemmy ('stɛmɪ), *a.* [f. STEM *sb.*[1] + -Y.]

1. Having long bare stems.

1552 HULOET, Stalkye or stemmye herbes which be no trees and yet growe in height. **1827** STEUART *Planter's G.* (1828) 299 Letting the principal members of your group be tall and stemmy. **1865** *Reader* No. 122. 477/3 Stemmy herbage and productive trees.

2. Of a root: Long and slender like a stem.

1728 CHAMBERS *Cycl.* s.v. *Root*, *Cauliformes*, i.e. Stemmy or Stalky, which shoot down deep directly, though often sending out Fibres and Strings from the great Stem.

3. Containing stems.

1863 *Jrnl. R. Agric. Soc.* XXIV. I. 134 The larger stemmy and leafy portions were thus separated. **1892** WALSH *Tea* 182 'Dusty' and 'stemmy' teas in particular.

stemmyng, variant of STAMIN.

stemplar ('stɛmplə(r)). = next 1.

1828 CARR *Craven Gloss.*, *Stemplar*, timber to support the roof of a mine.

stemple ('stɛmp(ə)l). *Mining.* Also **stempel**. [Of obscure origin; = MHG. *stempfel* (Lexer), mod.G. *stempel*; cf. MDu. *stympel* foot of a piece of furniture.]

1. ? A stull piece.

1653 [See BUNDING]. **1671** *Phil. Trans.* VI. 2107 We under-prop our Drifts with Stemples, and Wall-plates, placed much like a Carpenters square, on the one side, and over head. **1778** W. PRYCE *Min. Cornub.* 97 The adventurers have been often put to unnecessary expence in stemples and lock-pieces to secure the Mine from falling in. **1883** *Encycl. Brit.* XVI. 453/1 They put in strong pieces of timber from wall to wall, and cover these cross-pieces (*stempels, stull-pieces*) with boards or poles.

2. (See quots.)

1674 J. RAY *Coll. Words, Of smelting Silver* 118 The transverse pieces of wood they call stemples and upon these catching hold with their Hands and Feet they descend without using any rope. **1875** J. H. COLLINS *Metal Mining* 9 The native miners of Chili..continue..to carry the ore to the surface on their backs, mounting the 'stemples' which are driven into the wall of the lode to serve instead of ladders.

stempne, obs. form of STEM *sb.*[3]

stemson ('stɛmsən). *Naut.* [f. STEM *sb.*[2], after *keelson*, KELSON.] (See quot. 1769.)

1769 FALCONER *Dict. Marine* (1780), *Stemson*, an arching piece of timber fixed within the apron to reinforce the scarf thereof. **1849** LONGF. *Build. Ship* 178 Stemson and keelson and sternson-knee. **1886** *Encycl. Brit.* XXI. 819/1 The foremost end of the keelson scarphs to the stemson.

stemyng, variant of STAMIN.

Sten (stɛn). Also **sten**. [Acronym f. the initial letters of the surnames of the designers, R. V. *S*hepherd and H. J. *T*urpin + *En*field, Greater London (see quot. 1942[1]), after BREN.] More fully, ***Sten gun***. A type of light, rapid-fire, sub-machine-gun. Also *fig.* and *attrib.*

1942 *Times* 16 July 8/3 It [*sc.* the gun] was known as the Schmeisser gun, and the Sten was merely a slight modification of it... The Ministry of Supply was not justified in taking to itself high praise for the speed of production of the Sten, and in giving the country the false impression that 'Colonel S' and 'Major T' invented and designed the gun. **1942** 'G. ORWELL' *Diary* 7 Aug. in *Coll. Ess.* (1968) II. 442 Last night for the first time took a Sten gun to pieces. **1959** 'N. BLAKE' *Widow's Cruise* 99 He went off into a sten-gun burst of Greek. **1971** B. W. ALDISS *Soldier Erect* 255 It was bloody murder. I had shed the set, and went in firing the sten from the hip. *Ibid.* 261 In my ammo pouch, against the sten magazines, I had stuffed the picture of Hanuman. **1974** S. GULLIVER *Vulcan Bulletins* 18 Automatic weapons like Stens and Sterlings.

Hence **'Sten-gun** *v. trans.*, to shoot at or kill with a Sten gun; **'Sten-gunner**, one who operates a Sten gun.

1949 KOESTLER *Promise & Fulfilment* II. v. 280 There is.. no conceivable justification..for Sten-gunning the representative of an international body. **1961** *Times* 8 Mar. 13/6 The Tunisian stengunners outside the luxury hotel: the Hiberno-Scandinavian-Afro-Asian chatter in the café below United Nations headquarters.

stench (stɛnʃ), *sb.* Forms: α. 1 stenc, stengc, 3–6 stenche, 3, 4, 6– stench. β. 6 staunch, 7–8 stanch. γ. 2–4 stunch(e, 3 *Orm.* stinnch, 4, 5–7 stinche, 5–8 stinch, 4–6 stynch(e, (6 stintch, styntche). [The α and β forms represent OE. *stenc* masc. = OS. *stanc* (LG., Du. *stank*; Sw., Da. *stank* from

LG.), OHG. *stanch* (MHG. *stanc*, mod.G. *stank*):—OTeut. types **stankwi-z*, *-kwo-z*, f. **staŋkw-* ablaut-var. of **stiŋkw-* STINK *v.* The *y* forms are morphologically a distinct word, repr. OE. **stync* = OS. *stunc* masc.:—OTeut. type **stuŋkwi-z*, f. the weak-grade of the same root.]

† **1.** An odour, a smell (pleasant or unpleasant); also, the sense of smell. *OE.* only (very common).

a **900** *Bæda's Hist.* III. viii. (1890) 174 Swa micel swetnisse stenc. **971** *Blickl. Hom.* 59 Þa swetan stencas ȝestincað þara wuduwyrta. *c* **1000** ÆLFRIC *Hom.* II. 372/26 Ða fif andȝitu ures lichaman þæt sind ȝesihð, hlyst, swæcc, stenc, hrepung.

2. A foul, disgusting, or noisome smell, a disagreeable or offensive odour, a stink.

α. *c* **893** ÆLFRED *Oros.* v. 226 Eall forwearð..for þæm stence. *a* **900** *Bæda's Hist.* I. xiii. (1890) 48 Se wolberenda stenc þære lyfte. *a* **1225** *St. Marher.* 11 His fule stench. *a* **1240** *Ureisun* in *Cott. Hom.* 193 Þer ne schulen heo neuer karien ne swinken, Ne weopen ne murnen ne helle stenches stinken. **1387** TREVISA *Higden* (Rolls) IV. 119 Wormes come out of his body, and þe stenche of hym greved all þe oost. *c* **1450** *Mirk's Festial* 11 Anon þys fende vanechet away wyth an horrybull stenche. **1491** *Chast. Goddes Chyld.* 18 Wyckid sauours and fowle stenches. **1591** SHAKS. *1 Hen. VI*, I. v. 23 So..Doues with noysome stench, Are from their..Houses driuen away. **1697** DRYDEN *Virg. Georg.* III. 836 Nor cou'd Vulcanian Flame The Stench abolish, or the Savour tame. **1735** SOMERVILLE *Chase* III. 158 Plunging he wades besmear'd, and fondly hopes In a superior Stench to lose his own. **1828** COLERIDGE *Cologne* 4 In Köhln..I counted two and seventy stenches, All well defined, and several stinks! **1841** DICKENS *Barn. Rudge* lx, The air was perfumed with the stench of rotten leaves and faded fruit. **1883** STEVENSON *Treas. Isl.* xvi, The nasty stench of the place turned me sick.

β. **1652** FRENCH *Yorksh. Spa* xiv. 104, I shall the better make to appear the Cause of its stanch and bitterness. **1653** H. COGAN tr. *Pinto's Trav.* xlix. 190 The great stanch which proceeded from these dead bodies. *a* **1653** GOUGE *Comm. Heb.* ix. 19 The cleer sun is noysome to dunghils..by reason of the stanch in the dunghil. *a* **1711** KEN *Urania* Poet. Wks. 1721 IV. 473 Fear not the stanch nice Sense may meet.

γ. *c* **1200** ORMIN 1209 Sinness fule stinnch. *a* **1225** *Ancr. R.* 216, & he schal bidon ham & þinen ham mid eche stunche iðe pine of helle. *c* **1290** *Brendan* 491 in *S. Eng. Leg.* 233 Strong was þe stunch and þe smoke. **1422** YONGE tr. *Secreta Secret.* xlv. 208 By the noosthurles we haue knowlech of odeurs and stynches. **1477** NORTON *Ord. Alch.* v. in Ashm. (1652) 70 Stinch is a Vapour..Of things which of Evill Complexions be. *c* **1585** [R. BROWNE] *Answ. Cartwright* 6, I maruaile howe his penne coulde droppe downe such poyson, and he not smell the stinch thereof as he wrote it. **1643** BAKER *Chron., Hen. I*, 60 His Physitian that tooke out his braines, with the intolerable stinch shortly after died. **1765** J. BROWN *Chr. Jrnl.* 226 My candle is near wasted... Now extinguished, it goes out with a stinch.

3. without article. Evil-smelling quality or property, offensive odour, stink.

α. *c* **1200** *Trin. Coll. Hom.* 167 Þo ne mihte no man for stenche cumen him enden. *a* **1225** *Ancr. R.* 216 Stench stihð uppard. **1340** *Ayenb.* 248 Huerof ne may go out bote uelþe and stench. **1398** TREVISA *Barth. De P.R.* XIX. xl. (1495) 884 Stenche may be so stronge that it may be cause of soden deth. **1590** SPENSER *F.Q.* I. xi. 13 That all the ayre about with smoke and stench did fill. **1697** DRYDEN *Æneis* VIII. 638 Till choak'd with Stench..The ling'ring Wretches pin'd away, and dy'd. **1756** C. LUCAS *Ess. Waters* III. 317 Acids cause neither stench nor precipitation in the above solution. **1849** MACAULAY *Hist. Eng.* v. I. 652 In the dungeon below all was darkness, stench, lamentation, disease and death. **1859** DICKENS *T. Two Cities* I. v, A narrow winding street, full of offence and stench.

β. **1592** DANIEL *Epitaphium* Wks. (Grosart) I. 80 Fayre Rosamond..Who whilome sweetest smelt..Doth nowe wth deadly staunch infest ye nose.

γ. *c* **1175** *Lamb. Hom.* 43 Þe siste [uþe wes] smorð er þe seofeþe ful stunch. *c* **1300** *Beket* (Percy Soc.) 2306 Hit stonk so foule..That unethe myȝte eni man for stinche [*S.E. Leg.* line 2386 stunche] neȝ him beo. **13..** *Minor Poems of Vernon MS.* xxxvii. 970 Foul he stonk as stunch of helle. *c* **1440** *Jacob's Well* 147 Eueremore he brast out horryble stynch. *c* **1530** *Judic. Urines* II. xii. 40 W^t^ stynche or els w^t^ euyll sauor at ye nose. **1583** STUBBES *Anat. Abuses* (1877) 42 But inwardly is full of all stinche and lothsomnes. **1646** EARL MONM. tr. *Biondi's Civil Warres* IX. 227 From Filth and Mire, nothing but Pollution and Stinch can be expected.

4. Something that smells offensively.

1595 SHAKS. *John* III. iv. 26 Thou odoriferous stench, sound rottennesse. **1909** *Edin. Rev.* Oct. 292 Brayton has long been a stench in the nostrils of all decent citizens.

5. *attrib.* and *Comb.*, as ***stench-charged***, ***-involved*** adjs.; **stench-pipe**, an extension of a soil-pipe to a point above the roof of a house, to allow foul gases to escape; **stench-trap**, a device in a drain, etc. to prevent the upward passage of noxious gas; a stink-trap.

1899 *Daily News* 28 Dec. 6/3 A noisome loft, *stench-charged and drenched with moisture from the rotten..thatch. **1730–46** THOMSON *Autumn* 1204 A proud city..convulsive hurled Sheer from the black foundation, *stench-involved, Into a gulf of blue sulphureous flame. **1891** *Rutland Gloss.* s.v. *Crookle*, What you want is *stench-pipes. You run 'em up as high as your chimney, and they'll be no eyesore. **1833** LOUDON *Encycl. Archit.* §1803 The whole to enter into one drain in each area, where a proper *stench-trap and grate are to be formed.

stench (stɛnʃ), *v.* Also 6–7 stinch(e, 7 stanch. [OE. *stęncan* (Northumbrian):—prehistoric **staŋkwjan*, f. **staŋkwi-z* STENCH *sb.* In the 16th c. (sense 2) prob. a new formation on the sb.]

1. *intr.* To have an ill smell, to stink.

c **950** *Lindisf. Gosp. John* xi. 39 Uutudlice stenceð [Vulg. *fetet*]. **1297** R. GLOUC. (Rolls) 8401 Þe smoke þer of ssolde boþe stenche & blende. **1570** LEVINS *Manip.* 134/36 To stinche, *fœtere*.

2. *trans.* To cause to emit a stench, to make to stink, to render offensive. Also with *up*. ? *Obs.*

1577 GOOGE *Heresbach's Husb.* IV. 163 b, The Goose..stencheth the ground with her vnprofitable..dounging. **1596** HARINGTON *Apol.* Aa 7 b, This same companie hath so stencht vp his house, that he must be forced to lye at London tyll his house be made sweeter. *a* **1631** DONNE *Serm.* (1649) II. 203 But after a Goose that stanches the grasse they [*sc.* sheep] will not [feed]. **1655** MOUFET & BENNET *Healths Improv.* iii. 13 Is not Middleborough, Roterdam, Delf,..stinched every dry Autumn with infinite swarms of dead frogs, putrifying the aire worse then carrion? **1707** MORTIMER *Husb.* 227 'Tis the foulness of the Ponds only that stencheth the Water. **1762** YOUNG *Resign.* I. 96 Dead Bards stench every Coast. **1801** *Farmer's Mag.* Nov. 371 Taking the sheep off their feed to lodge in the night, we think of great use, as it prevents dropping their soil on the pasture (what our shepherds here term stenching their food). **1838** HOOD *To Mr. Izaac Walton* 10 'How dare you,' says I, 'for to stench the whole house by keeping that stinking liver?'

3. To subject to stenches.

1824 *Blackw. Mag.* XV. 473 The fullest impression that could be purchased by our being parched, passported,..starved and stenched, for 1200 miles.

Hence **'stenching** *ppl. a.*

1654 Z. COKE *Logick* 37 Smel. Simple. Sweet or Stinching. **1694** MOTTEUX *Rabelais* IV. l, As if..some divine Vertue could lye hid in a stenching ulcerated rotten Shank. **1905** *Dundee Advertiser* 1 Mar. 8 The villages are vile and stenching.

stench, obs. form of STANCH *v.*, STAUNCH *a.*

1659 *Lady Alimony* III. iii. F 4 b, And if thou canst not live so stench But thou must needs enjoy thy Wench.

†**'stenchall.** *Obs. rare.* Also **stainshall.** [Of obscure origin.] A tin receptacle containing oil in which painters' brushes are placed to keep them soft and workable.

1688 HOLME *Armoury* III. 145/1 Stainshall, of some called a Smuch Box. *Ibid.* 369/2 Stenchall.

stenchall, obs. form of STANCHEL².

†**'stenched**, *a. rare.* [? Alteration of **stanched*, f. OF. *estanche* STANCH *sb.*² + -ED².] Of a fish: ? Confined in a stank.

1621 LADY M. WROTH *Urania* 257 So little a place as a Garden being like fresh-water, comfortable to stenched fish: so this to a prisoner.

stenchel, -en, obs. ff. STANCHEL², STANCHION.

stencher, variant of STANCHER². *Sc. Obs.*

stenchful ('stɛnʃfʊl), *a.* [f. STENCH *sb.* + -FUL.] Full of stench, smelling offensively, stinking.

1615 T. ADAMS *Black Devil* 50 The smoake and stenchfull mistes ouer some populous Cities. **1628** FELTHAM *Resolves* I. xlvii. 139 The body..must once perish in a stenchfull nastinesse. **1872** TALMAGE *Serm.* 140 A sepulchre reeking and stenchful with corruption.

stenchil, var. STANCHEL¹.

1775 L. SHAW *Hist. Moray* III. 161 Hawkes, Gleds, Stenchils,..Magpies, &c. are numerous.

stenchy ('stɛnʃɪ), *a.* [f. STENCH *sb.* + -Y.] Emitting a stench, foul-smelling.

1757 DYER *Fleece* I. 661 In dusty towns, Where stenchy vapours often blot the sun. **1819** *Metropolis* II. 133 Gross and abusive as the stenchy Canongate of his native land. **1892** MEREDITH *Empty Purse* 21 No stenchy anathemas cast Upon Providence, women, the world.

stencil ('stɛnsɪl), *sb.* Also 8 stanesile, 9 † stensil. [In 18th c. *stanesile*, app. f. ME. *stansel* vb., to ornament with various colours: see STENCIL *v.* 1.]

1. A thin sheet of metal, cardboard, etc., in which one or more holes have been cut, of such shape that when a brush charged with pigment is passed over the back of the sheet, a desired pattern, letter, or figure is produced on the surface upon which the sheet is laid.

1707 *Phil. Trans.* XXV. 2398 They colour them [playing cards] by the help of several Patterns or Stanesiles, as they call them; they are Card Paper cut thro' with a Penknife, for every Colour, as Red, &c. **1816** SINGER *Hist. Cards* 75 *note*, Savary describes the Indian mode of printing cottons, which he says is by means of a perforated pattern, or stensil. **1848** CHATTO *Hist. Cards* 89 That those cards were depicted by means of a stencil is evident. **1868** W. SUTHERLAND *Pract. Guide Ho. Decoration* 16 When the pattern is very small and intricate, it is best to cut a separate stencil for each colour. **1884** *Harper's Mag.* Mar. 583/1 Fig. 6 is a treatment produced by three stencils.

2. A pattern or design produced by stencilling.

1899 KIPLING *Stalky* 105 He looked regretfully round the cosy study which M'Turk..had decorated with a dado, a stencil, and cretonne hangings.

3. The colouring matter used in stencilling. Also (*Ceramics*), a composition used in transfer-printing and enamelling, to protect from the oil those portions of the pattern that are to be left uncoloured.

1853 URE *Dict. Arts* II. 454 s.v. *Porcelain*, The stencil (generally a mixture of rose-pink, sugar, and water) is laid on in the form desired with a pencil. **1859** in *Abridgm. Specif. Patents, Printing* 397 The article is then fired with the stencil on. The stencil is rubbed off on its leaving the kiln.

4. *attrib.* and *Comb.*, as ***stencil alphabet***, ***design***, ***letter***, ***pattern***; **stencil-brush**, the brush used in stencilling; **stencil-cutter**, (*a*) a person who makes stencils; (*b*) a tool for cutting letters, etc. out of stencil-plates (Knight); **stencil-painting** *vbl. sb.*, decorating by means of stencils; **stencil-paper** = sense 1; **stencil-paste**, the composition used in stencilling; **stencil-plate** = sense 1.

1866 W. F. STANLEY *Math. Instrum.* 227 Plain *stencil alphabets. **1868** W. SUTHERLAND *Pract. Guide Ho. Decoration* 15 Now dip the *stencil brush into colour. **1858** SIMMONDS *Dict. Trade*, **Stencil-cutter*, a person who pierces patterns, letters, or ornaments, on thin metal plates, or on oil-cloth, etc. for the use of a stenciller. **1888** *Lady* 25 Oct. 374/2 Deepen the tint, and in dark red, wash in the *stencil designs. **1866** W. F. STANLEY *Math. Instrum.* 227 One of the most imperfect *stencil letters. **1845** G. DODD *Brit. Manuf.* IV. 133 The method of '*stencil-painting'. **1868** W. SUTHERLAND *Pract. Guide Ho. Decoration* 13 The *stencil paper being prepared, trace the design upon it. **1875** KNIGHT *Dict. Mech.* 2374/2 The ink used is known as *stencil-paste, and is essentially a water-color. **1868** W. SUTHERLAND *Pract. Guide Ho. Decoration* 12 *Stencil patterns play a very important part in house decoration. **1816** SINGER *Hist. Cards* 178 The artist is using a *stencil plate and broad flat brush. **1873** SPON *Workshop Rec.* Ser. I. 7/1 Copper is much better than brass for stencil plates.

stencil ('stɛnsɪl), *v.* Also 5 **stansel**, **stencel**. [In sense 1, a. OF. *estanceler*, *estenceler*, f. *estencele* (mod.F. *étincelle*):—popular L. **stincilla* metathesis of *scintilla* spark. In sense 2, a late derivative of STENCIL *sb.*, which appears to be f. the verb.]

† **1.** *trans.* To ornament with bright colours or pieces of precious metal. *Obs.*

a **1420** *Aunturs of Arth.* (Irel. MS.) xxxi. 2 In stele was he stuffut, that sterne on his stede, With his sternes of gold, stanseld on stray. **14..** *Sir Beues* (S.) 3777 + 7 Florysschyd [*v.r.* Stencelled] wiþ rosys off syluyr bryȝt.

2. a. To produce (an inscription, design, etc.) by using a stencil. ***to stencil out***, to blot out by stencilling.

1861 SALA *Dutch Pict.* xiv. 215 His Lordship's invitation ..printed upon placards, and stencilled on the walls. **1886** *Art Jrnl.* Apr. 107/2 Old English, Arabic, and other inscriptions may be stencilled as friezes in rooms. **1894** FISKE *Holiday Stor.* (1900) 108 The goods are probably shipped West and sold, the dealers' names and numbers being stencilled out.

b. To mark or paint (a surface) with an inscription or design by means of a stencil.

1833 LOUDON *Encycl. Archit.* §580. 278 A simple..mode of stencilling the walls of plain cottages. **1865** *Reader* 4 Feb. 130/3 The earliest cards were stencilled, the figures being produced by a brush passing over the stencil, in which the outlines were cut through.

Hence **'stencilled** *ppl. a.*

1853 R. S. SURTEES *Sponge's Sp. Tour* lxiii. 354 A fragment of glass nailed against the stencilled wall. **1881** YOUNG *Ev. Man his own Mechanic* §1409. 644 A..pale blue ground with a stencilled pattern in darker shades of blue.

stenciller ('stɛnsɪlə(r)). [f. STENCIL *v.* + -ER¹.] One who stencils or works with a stencil.

1832 THACKRAH *Effects Arts* etc. *on Health* (ed. 2) 55 Stencillers do not appear to suffer from the currents of cold air to which they are exposed by their employ. **1901** *Daily Chron.* 3 Dec. 10/7 [advt.], Colourer, good stenciller, female, wanted.

stencilling ('stɛnsɪlɪŋ), *vbl. sb.* [-ING¹.] The action of the vb. STENCIL. Also *attrib.*

1781 *Encycl. Brit.* (ed. 2) VIII. 5851/1 Stencilling is indeed a cheaper method of ridding coarse work than printing. **1865** *Reader* 4 Feb. 131/1 The colouring apparently imparted by the stencilling process. **1884** *Harper's Mag.* Mar. 583/1 Stencilling is the cheapest kind of decoration.

stend, *sb.*¹ *dial.* In 7 **stan.** [f. STEND *v.*¹] A stick used by butchers to hold open a carcase.

1481 *Durham Acc. Rolls* (Surtees) 97 Slaughterhous..j fleshaxe, j dresyng-knyfe, iij capistra, v stendez. **1688** HOLME *Armoury* III. 313/1 Butchers Instruments..A Stan. **1893** *Northumbld. Gloss.*, Stend.

stend (stɛnd), *sb.*² *Sc.* Also 8 **sten.** [f. STEND *v.*²] A leap, spring or bound. Also *fig.*

c **1425** WYNTOUN *Orig. Cron.* IV. iii. 236 Quhar stend for stend the coursere maid. **1513** DOUGLAS *Æneis* X. x. 72 [The horses] brak away with the cart to the schor, With stendis feyll. **15..** *Christ's Kirk* 46 in *Bannatyne MS.* 284 Than Stevin come stoppand in with stendis, No rynk mycht him arreist. *a* **1728** RAMSAY *Answ. to Somerville* 82 While Sauls stride Warlds at ilka Stend. **1788** BURNS '*O death! thou tyrant*' iv, Ye burnies..foaming, strang, wi' hasty stens Frae lin to lin. **1790** —— *Tam Glen* 22 My heart to my mou' gied a sten. **1816** SIR A. BOSWELL *Skeldon Haughs* Poet. Wks. (1871) 167 Forward, ye Crawfords wi' a stend. **1893** STEVENSON *Catriona* xv, There gaed a cauld stend o' fear into Tam's heart.

†**stend**, *v.*¹ *Obs.* [aphetic form of EXTEND *v.*]

1. *trans.* To assess: = EXTEND *v.* 10.

1402 *Pol. Poems* (Rolls) II. 80 Thus prelatis and persouns aftir her state, ben stended to paien what that nede askith.

2. To erect (a tent). = STENT *v.*¹ 1.

1594 *Batt. Balrinness* in *Scot. Poems 16th C.* II. 351 Besyd that castell, on a croft They stended pallionis ther.

stend (stɛnd), *v.*² *Sc.* Also 8 **sten** (9 **stenn**). [Of obscure origin; perh. identical with prec.] *intr.*

To leap, bound, spring up. Of an animal: To rear, be restive.

1560 ROLLAND *Seven Sages* 296 Incontinent thay stendit on thair steidis. **1567** *Gude & Godlie B.* (S.T.S.) 109 Quhat gart 3ow montanis lyke rammis stert and stend? *a* **1724** *Ramsay's Tea-t. Misc.* (1729) 16 The Lover he stended up in haste And gript her hard about the Waste. **1786** BURNS *To Auld Mare* xiv, Thou never lap, an' sten't, an' breastet. **1804** R. COUPER *Poetry* I. 112 Athort the field, wi' wildest pranks, Th' unwieldly oussen stenn. **1824** SCOTT *Redgauntlet* let. xi, The nag begin to spring, and flee, and stend, that my gudesire could hardly keep the saddle. **1890** SERVICE *Thir Notandums* xix. 124, I was like to reist and to sten' at the doctor's orders.

transf. and *fig.* **1721** RAMSAY *Concl.* 34 My Saul to higher Pitch cou'd sten. **1893** STEVENSON *Catriona* xv, The lassies were bits o' young things, wi' the reid life dinnling and stending in their members.

Stender ('stɛndə(r), 'ʃt-). *Biol.* and *Med.* Also stender. [The name of Wilhelm P. *Stender*, a manufacturer of Leipzig.] ***Stender dish***: a shallow glass dish.

1900 DORLAND *Med. Dict.* 637/1 Stender-dish. **1904** *Bot. Gaz.* XXXVII. 12 A simpler..method is to float a quantity of these spores on the surface of water half filling a stender dish. **1978** G. C. BROWN *Introd. Histotechnol.* xi. 174 Other items that should be stored at the staining bench in adequate quantities are:..Stender dishes for frozen sections.., in three sizes.

Stendhalian (stɑ̃'dɑːlɪən), *a.* and *sb.* [f. *Stendhal*, the nom-de-plume of the French writer Henri Beyle (1783–1842) + -IAN.]

A. *adj.* Characteristic or suggestive of the writings of Stendhal. **B.** *sb.* A follower or devotee of Stendhal or his works.

1907 G. B. SHAW *Mahor Barbara* Pref. 150 The sensation first came to me from Lever and may have come to him from Beyle, or at least out of the Stendhalian atmosphere. **1928** *Sunday Express* 8 Apr. 7/4 The Stendhalians are invariably cynics who delight in heartlessness and selfishness. **1937** WYNDHAM LEWIS *Blasting & Bombardiering* 53, I was not surprised, luckily, when I became a lion, to find this gilded tamer a tough customer. I began studying her ways with curiosity, this spoilt and cocksure goddess of the ocean wave. I filled a notebook with Stendhalian observations. **1950** *Essays & Studies* III. 86 In this sense the Stendhalian analogy of crystallization may be applied equally to the reasons of the intellect as to the reasons of the heart, of which reason itself comprehends nothing. **1968** E. HYAMS *Mischief Makers* vi. 99, I had gone flabby; no Stendhalian hero. **1980** A. ALPERS *Life Katherine Mansfield* ix. 163 Murry [was].. starting a huge Stendhalian novel.

stendirrie, obs. form of STANNERY *a.*

† **'stendle**, *v. Sc. Obs. rare*⁻⁰. [frequentative of STEND *v.*²: see -LE.] *intr.* To leap or bound frequently. Hence † **'stendling** *vbl. sb.*

1549 *Compl. Scot.* vi. 66 It vas ane celest recreation to behald ther lycht lopene, galmonding, stendling bakuart and forduart.

stene, obs. form of STEAN, STONE *v.*

stenelytrous (stɪ'nɛlɪtrəs), *a.* [f. mod.L. *Stenelytra* pl. (f. Gr. στεν-ός narrow + ἔλυτρον: see ELYTRON) + -OUS.] Of or pertaining to the *Stenelytra*, a family of Coleoptera having narrow elytra. So **ste'nelytran**, a beetle of this family.

1842 BRANDE *Dict. Sci.* etc., Stenelytrans. **1854** A. ADAMS etc. *Man. Nat. Hist.* 196 Stenelytrous-Beetles.

‖ **Steneosaurus** (stɛnɪə'sɔːrəs). Also anglicized **steneosaur**. [mod.L., badly formed (after *Teleosaurus*) on Gr. στενό-ς narrow + σαῦρος lizard.] A fossil genus of saurians characterized by a narrow beak. Hence **steneo'saurian** *a.*, belonging to this genus.

1836 BUCKLAND *Geol. & Min. consid.* (1837) I. 252 *note*, M. Geoffroy St. Hilaire has arranged the fossil Saurians with long and narrow beaks, like that of the Gavial, under the two new genera, Teleosaurus and Steneosaurus. **1869** HULKE in *Q. Jrnl. Geol. Soc.* XXVI. 168 Dr. Rolleston.. informs me that these bones are also shown in a cast of the Honfleur (Geneva) Steneosaur in the Oxford Museum, and that the relations of the bones in the upper surface of a Steneosaurian skull from Shotover exactly correspond with those figured in the 'Ossemens Fossiles'. **1896** H. WOODWARD *Guide Fossil Reptiles Brit. Mus.* 6 Teleosaurs and Steneosaurs.

steng, stengle: see STANG, STING, STINGLE.

stengah ('stɛŋə). Also **stingah**. [ad. Mal. *setengah* half.] A half measure of whisky with soda (sometimes water), popular amongst the British in Malaysia.

1899 *Munsey's Mag.* XXI. 697/1 The majority of young Englishmen and Germans fared equally well when they limited the numbers of whiskies and sodas (or 'stengahs') which they drank. **1903** W. DEL MAR *Around World through Japan* vii. 64 A 'peg' of whiskey and tonic-water, followed by a *stengah* (the Malay word for half, usually pronounced *stinger*) or split drink. **1927** *Blackw. Mag.* June 726/1 At this establishment we learn all about gin-slings and 'Stingahs'. **1948** M. LASKI *Tory Heaven* i. 14 Stewards..to bring him.. stengahs and pahits when-ever he wanted them. **1966** D. FORBES *Heart of Malaya* xiii. 156 Malays could not be seen publicly knocking back *stengahs*. **1975** 'G. BLACK' *Big Wind* i. 18 When I was a boy in Malaysia a whisky-soda was called a *stengah*. It hasn't been for twenty-five years.

stenke, obs. form of STINK.

stenlock ('stɛnlɒk), *Sc.* and *Anglo-Irish*. Also **stainloch**. [Of doubtful origin; found in recent Gaelic as *steinloch*.

A Scandinavian fish-name of similar sound is Sw. *stenlake* stickleback, app. f. *sten* stone + *lake* eelpout (also in MSw. and mod.Norw.); cf. Norw. *lakesild* (*sild* herring) a kind of whitefish. But connexion seems unlikely.]

The Coal-fish or Sillock, *Merlangus carbonarius*.

179. *Agric. Surv. Hebrides* 631 (Jam.) [The inhabitants of Islay] catch a number of stenlock..off the point of the Rinns of Islay. **1863** [W. F. CAMPBELL] *Life in Normandy* I. 283 It was some time before I knew that stainloch, greyfish..and poddly, were all one fish at different ages. **1864** *Rep. Sea Fisheries Comm.* (1865) II. 1190/2 Stenlock are caught in great abundance with the cod-nets.

attrib. **1893** N. MUNRO *Gilian the Dreamer* (1893) 167 A gross of stenlock hooks to grapple ye.

stenn, variant of STEND *v.*²

steno ('stɛnəʊ). Colloq. abbrev. of:

a. STENOGRAPHER (also *attrib.*), or abbrev. STENOGRAPHIC *a.* orig. and chiefly *U.S.*

1906 J. F. KELLY *Man with Grip* 36 This bright young lady was on the waiting list of a steno. agency. **1928** 'L. NORTH' *Parasites* ii. 34 (*heading*) 'Stalls' and stenos. *Ibid.* vii. 89 That Whispering Slim guy seems to be falling for that steno' of his. **1935** *Motion Picture* Nov. 40/2 Frances Dee.. skyrockets to new importance with an amazingly fine performance as a small town steno who wins a five-thousand-dollar lottery. **1958** E. BIRNEY *Turvey* v. 49 There was a good-lookin steno all alone. **1971** D. E. WESTLAKE *I gave at Office* (1972) 19 He led the unsuccessful attempt to ban miniskirts in the steno pool. **1978** P. BOARDMAN *Worlds of Patrick Geddes* ix. 342 A social workers' weekly..sent a stenotypist to take them [*sc.* lectures] down and a department editor to check up on the steno.

b. STENOGRAPHY. *U.S.*

1946 *N.Y. Times* 1 Apr. 42/3 (Advt.), Girl, genl office work, typ, some steno. **1954** *Los Angeles Times* 21 Mar. 3/2 (Advt.), Clerk—lite steno..$200 start. **1973** *N.Y. Law Jrnl.* 20 July 16/2 (Advt.), *Law secretary*...legal experience and excellent skills required, dictaphone and light steno.

steno- (stɛnəʊ), combining form of Gr. στενός narrow, occurring in many scientific terms, as **steno'bathic** *a. Biol.* [Gr. βάθ-ος depth], (of aquatic life) limited to or found at only a narrow range of depths. **stenobregmate** (-'brɛgmət), *a. Craniol.* [Gr. βρέγμα front of the head], having a narrow BREGMA; so **ˌstenobreg'matic** *a.* (Dorland *Med. Dict.* 1913). ‖ **stenocardia** (-'kɑːdɪə) *Path.* [Gr. καρδία heart], contraction of the heart or its orifices; also *angina pectoris* (see ANGINA 2); hence **steno'cardiac, steno'cardial** adjs. **stenocephalic** (-sɪ'fælɪk), *a. Craniol.* [Gr. κεφαλή head], (of a skull) characterized by abnormal or excessive narrowness; so **stenocephalous** (-'sɛfələs), *a.* = *stenocephalic* (Dorland). **stenocephaly** (-'sɛfəlɪ), excessive narrowness of the skull. **stenocoronine** (-kə'rəʊnɪn), *a.* [Gr. κορώνη crown], having narrow-crowned molar teeth (see quot.). **stenocranial** (-'kreɪnɪəl), *a. Craniol.* [CRANIAL], = *stenocephalic*. **stenocrotaphy, -krotaphy** (-'krɒtəfɪ) *Craniol.* [Gr. κρόταφος temple], excessive narrowness of the temporal region of the skull. **stenoderm** ('stɛnəʊdɜːm), a bat of the genus *Stenoderma* or of the family *Stenodermata*, the members of which are characterized by having a contracted wing-membrane; so **steno'dermatous** *a.*, belonging to the family *Stenodermata*, resembling a stenoderm. **steno'dermine** *a.* = *stenodermatous*; *sb.* a stenoderm. **stenohaline** (-'heɪlaɪn) *a. Biol.* [Gr. ἅλιν-ος of salt], (of aquatic life) adapted to only a narrow range of salinity. **steno'hydric** *a. Biol.* [HYDRO-], adapted to only a narrow range of humidities. **stenometer** (-'nɒmɪtə(r)), [-METER], a distance-measurer consisting of a small telescope with a divided object-glass and a micrometer-screw for moving the half-lenses (*Cent. Dict.* Suppl.). **stenopetalous** (-'pɛtələs), *a. Bot.* [PETALOUS], having narrow petals (Paxton *Bot. Dict.* 1840). **ste'nophagous** *a. Zool.* [-PHAGOUS] (see quot. 1926). **stenophyllism** (-'fɪlɪz(ə)m), **-phyllous** (-'fɪləs) *a.* [Gr. στενόφυλλος, f. φύλλον leaf] (see quots.). **steno'podium** *Zool.* [PODIUM], a narrow, two-branched crustacean limb the flexibility of which is provided by joints. **steno'rhynchous** *a.* [Gr. ῥύγχος beak] having a narrow beak. **steno'stomatous** *a.* [Gr. στόμα mouth], having a small mouth (*Syd. Soc. Lex.* 1898). **stenostomy** (-'ɒstəmɪ), the contraction of any mouth or aperture (*Ibid.*). **steno'thermal** *a.* [THERMAL], *Zool.* (of an animal) capable of living in only a small range of temperature. [ad. G. *stenotherm* (K. Möbius 1871, in *Jahresber. d. Commission z. wissensch. Untersuchung d. deutschen Meere in Kiel* (1873) I. 139)]; hence **'stenotherm**, **steno'thermic** *adjs.* **steno'topic** *a. Biol.* [Gr. τόπ-ος place] (see quot. 1949).

1902 *Stenobathic [see EURYBATHIC *a.*]. **1975** B. FELL *Introd. Marine Biol.* xi. 92 A deep-water stenobathic species, when brought too rapidly to the surface in a net, suffers disruption of the internal organs. **1813** PRICHARD *Phys. Hist. Man.* (1826) I. II. iii. 173, I propose to divide the varieties of the skull into three classes... 1...mesobregmate ..2. *Stenobregmate: the section of the vertex narrowed; the skull having the appearance of lateral compression,..3. Platybregmate. **1857** DUNGLISON *Med. Lex.*, **Stenocardia*. **1898** *Allbutt's Syst. Med.* V. 912 *note*, The symptoms [are] those of increasing 'stenocardia'. **1899** *Ibid.* VI. 54 *Stenocardiac and cardiac muscle failure. **1899** *Ibid.* VII. 754 Morphine may be given..if there is *stenocardial pain. **1866** J. A. MEIGS *Cranial Forms Amer. Aborig.* 36 Narrow Oval Form (*Stenocephalic). **1878** BARTLEY tr. *Topinard's Anthropol.* Index, *Stenocephaly. **1865** H. FALCONER in *Q. Jrnl. Geol. Soc.* XXI. 259, I propose therefore to substitute ..for the latter [Hippopotamine type] '*Stenocoronine' or narrow-crowned type. **1904** *Biometrika* Mar. & July 240 Brachycranial, *stenocranial and chamaecranial. **1884** J. E. LEE tr. *Römer's Bone Caves of Ojcow* 32 [In this scull] there is some *stenokrotaphy, the frontal margins are very smooth. **1871** *Cassell's Nat. Hist.* (1896) I. 336 The *Stenoderms have been divided..into several genera... The Spectacled Stenoderm is one of the best-known species of this group. *Ibid.* 337 The Jamaican Stenoderm..is very nearly allied. **1930** *Biol. Rev.* V. 350 Most *stenohaline marine invertebrates are poikilosmotic: their body fluids have an osmotic pressure which is the same as that of the external medium. **1973** P. A. COLINVAUX *Introd. Ecol.* xx. 278 When temperature or salinity may fluctuate widely without seriously affecting individuals, the species are called eurythermal or euryhaline; when slight changes of temperature or salinity are fatal to animals or plants, they are called stenothermal or stenohaline. **1953** E. P. ODUM *Fund. Ecol.* iii. 27 *Stenohydric—Euryhydric refers to water. **1974** *Ciba Foundation Symp.* XX. 56 In general, relative humidities below 60% (temperatures of 21–28°C) are deleterious for these stenohydric species. **1901** WALCOTT *22nd Ann. Rep. U.S. Geol. Surv.* I. 168 The rivers were meandered by using a prismatic compass for directions and a *stenometer for distances. **1926** A. S. PEARSE *Animal Ecol.* iii. 72 Animals that have a narrow range of foods are called *stenophagous and those that eat a wide variety are euryphagous. **1976** *Environmental Entomol.* V. 46/2, 21 (46%) of 46 identified species of phytophagous insects found associated with *A*[*mbrosia*] *dumosa* in southern California were stenophagous. **1904** GIGLIOLI & GUILLEMARD tr. *Beccari's Wand. Forests Borneo* xx. 305 The action of running water..has brought about a special adaptation in the leaves of many fluviatile plants. To the modification thus produced the term '*Stenophyllism,' or 'narrow-leavedness,' may be conveniently applied. **1880** WEBSTER *Suppl.*, **Stenophyllous*, having narrow leaves. **1904** GIGLIOLI & GUILLEMARD tr. *Beccari's Wand. Forests Borneo* App. 392 *Stenophyllous Plants*... I have adopted this term for certain plants growing on river banks, or in the beds of torrents, which have linear or else very narrow leaves. **1932** BORRADAILE & POTTS *Invertebrata* xii. 298 Since..the phyllopodium possesses the same two rami, and bears them, though not as a distal fork, yet in the same way as a great number of limbs of the first type, it is well not to use a name which might imply that there is a constant difference in respect of the rami between the limbs of the two types. We shall therefore call the first type the *stenopodium, referring to its usually slender form. **1967** P. A. MEGLITSCH *Invertebrate Zool.* xviii. 755/1 A good case can be made for thinking of stenopodia as the more primitive form of crustacean appendage. **1861** R. E. GRANT *Tabular View Rec. Zool.* 14 Vespertilionida... Anhistophorous, narrow-jawed (*stenorhynchous), long-headed (macrocephalous). **1888** *Stenotherm [see EURYTHERM *a.*]. **1964** *Oceanogr. & Marine Biol.* II. 284 Most stenosaline organisms live either in the ocean (polystenosaline forms) or in fresh water (oligostenosaline forms). These terms are analogous to steno- or eurytherm and just as relative in their meaning. **1881** SEMPER *Anim. Life* 105 We shall..do well..to designate animals, according to Möbius, the former as eurythermal, the latter as *stenothermal. **1937** *Brit. Birds* XXX. 247 It should be borne in mind that whereas the adult bird is stenothermal (warm-blooded), in the young the thermotaxic arrangements are undeveloped. **1973** P. A. COLINVAUX *Introd. Ecol.* xx. 279 Between about 55°C and 40°C the algal mats are largely made up of filamentous blue-green algae, but these plants are rather stenothermal and will not actively grow at temperatures below 40°C. **1926** A. S. PEARCE *Animal Ecol.* ii. 34 Animals are often classified into two groups: *stenothermic and eurythermic, the former being restricted to a narrow range of temperature changes and the latter having ability to live through a wide range. **1965** B. E. FREEMAN tr. *Vandel's Biospeleology* xxiii. 384 Summer cysts containing the adults of stenothermic species [of copepods] are formed during the warm season. **1949** J. H. KENNETH *Henderson's Dict. Sci. Terms* (ed. 4) **Stenotopic*, having a restricted range of geographical distribution. **1967** *Oceanogr. & Marine Biol.* V. 546 This species is also stenotopic; it needs exposed rocky shores, but where the wave-action is not too strong. **1976** *Nature* 24 June 695/1 A major terminal extinction event..will tend selectively to eliminate the larger, more specialised, more stenotopic species.

stenochromy ('stɛnəkrəʊmɪ). The art or process of printing a design composed of several colours at one impression. Hence **ˌsteno-chro'matic** *a.*, of or pertaining to stenochromy. **'stenochrome**, a print produced by stenochromy.

1876 *Jrnl. Soc. Arts* 15 Dec. 68/1 Stenochromy. A New Process for printing a Number of Colours at the Same Time. *Ibid.*, Before I show you any specimens produced by the stenochromatic process, I think it will be advisable to give a short outline..of the manner in which stenochromes are produced. *Ibid.* 68/2 Stenochromatic printing.

stenog (stɛ'nɒg). Also with full point. Colloq. abbrev. of STENOGRAPHER. So as *v. intr.*, to write in shorthand or type. orig. and chiefly *U.S.* Cf. STENO.

1905 'O. HENRY' in *N.Y. World Mag.* 2 Apr. 3/1 Not being able to stenog, she could not enter that bright galaxy of office talent. **1909** *Fra* (East Aurora, N.Y.) Mar. 82/1 The Stenog wanted a new set of curtains. **1912** WODEHOUSE *Prince & Betty* ix. 132 If I was good enough for him to marry when I was a stenog., he's good enough for me to marry when I'm a plute. **1941** B. SCHULBERG *What makes Sammy Run?* vi. 103 'Start typing up that last scene, Ellen,' Kit told the stenog. **1967** *Spectator* 20 Oct. 468/3 Julie Andrews, as tireless Millie the faithful stenog.

stenograph ('stɛnəgrɑːf, -æ-), *sb.* [f. Gr. στενό-ς narrow + -GRAPH. Cf. F. *sténographe* stenographer.]

1. A shorthand report. *rare.*

1856 EMERSON *Eng. Traits, The 'Times'* Wks. (Bohn) II. 118, I saw the reporters' room, in which they redact their hasty stenographs.

2. A shorthand typewriting machine.

1891 *Century Dict., Stenograph*, . . 2. A stenographic machine.

stenograph ('stɛnəgrɑːf, -æ-), *v.* [Back-formation from STENOGRAPHER; perh. after F. *sténographier.*] *trans.* To write in shorthand, to represent by stenography; also *absol.* Hence **stenographed** *ppl. a.*

1821 *Lives Scott. Poets* I. 62 The contracted, stenographed, blurred . . state in which their manuscripts have been consigned . . to Printer's Readers. **1865** *Morn. Star* 18 Jan., It is equally possible to stenograph by the pantelegraphic machine with marvellous rapidity. **1872** *Daily News* 31 July, The conversation of M. St. Hilaire might be stenographed straight off. **1903** R. D. SHAW *Pauline Epist.* IV. ii. 439 If Paul dictated the letters, then, to use Renan's phrase, we have a kind of 'stenographed conversation'.

stenographer (stɪ'nɒgrəfə(r)). [f. STENOGRAPH-Y + -ER[1].] A shorthand writer. Now also *spec.* a shorthand typist.

1809 W. IRVING *Knickerb.* VI. ii. (1820) 365 My predecessors, who were furnished, as I am told, with the speeches of all their heroes taken down in shorthand by the most accurate stenographers of the time. **1862** B. TAYLOR *Home & Abroad* 2nd Ser. vii. 449 A practised stenographer . . took down many of these communications as they were spoken. **1893** F. M. CRAWFORD *Marion Darche* I. v. 136 John had sent for his stenographer. **1921** *Dict. Occup. Terms* (1927) §939 *Stenographer*, . . shorthand typist; wholly engaged in taking down letters, . . etc., in shorthand from dictation of another, and in transcribing them on typewriter. **1978** A. MALING *Lucky Devil* xxx. 159 Taught herself stenotyping, and now she's a legal stenographer.

stenographic (stɛnəʊ'græfɪk), *a.* [f. STENOGRAPHY: see -GRAPHIC. Cf. F. *sténographique.*] Of, pertaining to, or expressed in stenography.

1681 COLVIL *Whigs Supplic.* (1710) 14 Greek, Syriack, or Arabick, Or Breviations Stenographick. **1775** ASH. **1837** PITMAN (*title*) Stenographic Sound-hand. **1888** STEVENSON *Some Gentlemen in Fiction* in *Scribner's Mag.* June 764/1 [My characters] turned their backs on me and walked off bodily; and from that time, my task was stenographic—it was they who spoke. **1907** G. SALMON *Human Element in Gosp.* 111 It is not imagined that the historian made use of stenographic reports.

Hence **steno'graphical** *a.*, (in the same sense). **steno'graphically** *adv.*, by means of shorthand.

1656 S. HOLLAND *Zara* II. v. 112 Reading his unalterable resolvs written (Stenographically) in his face. **1674** JEAKE *Arith.* (1696) 271 But as the Denominations are various, and therefore must be exprest; so the Stenographical Mantles in which they are wrapt up, are . . arbitrary. **1727** BAILEY vol. II, *Stenographical*, pertaining to secret writing. **1824** T. MOLINEUX (*title*) The Stenographical Copy-Book. **1906** *Daily Chron.* 22 Mar. 6/7 The staff that stenographically chronicles the House's doings from day to day.

ste'nographist. *rare.* [f. STENOGRAPH-Y + -IST.] A shorthand writer. = STENOGRAPHER.

1839 *Spirit of Times* 20 Apr. 74/2 Paris swarms with scribblers of indifferent merit, authors of well founded pretensions, editors, stenographists, vaudevillists, translators, compilers, and correctors of work. **1845** *Times* 19 Aug. 4/5 England alone has despatched 30 stenographists (short-hand writers). **1850** in OGILVIE. **1905** J. JOYCE *Let.* 28 Feb. (1966) II. 83 If I had . . a clever stenographist I could *certainly* write any of the novels I have read lately in seven or eight hours.

stenography (stɪ'nɒgrəfɪ). [f. Gr. στενός narrow + -GRAPHY. Cf. F. *sténographie* (1812 in Hatz.-Darm.).]

1. The art of writing in shorthand.

1602 [J. WILLIS] (*title*) The Art of Stenographie, teaching . . the way of compendious Writing. **1632** BROME *North. Lass* III. ii, Sure tis Stenography, every Character a word: and here and there one for a whole sentence. **1791** BOSWELL *Johnson* an. 1778, Although I did not write what is called stenography, or short-hand, in appropriated characters devised for the purpose, I had a method of my own of writing half-words, [etc.]. **1838** J. GRANT *Sk. Lond.* 264 A gentleman who was exceedingly fond of stenography previous to the derangement of his intellects, . . incessantly wrote short-hand to his own dictation, after he was placed in an asylum. **1908** *Q. Rev.* Oct. 528 Stenography has caused reporting to be more professional than in those days.

2. *transf.* and *fig.*

1647 CLEVELAND *Lond. Diurnal & Sel. Poems* 33 Oh the accurst Stenographie of fate! The Princely Eagle shrunke into a Bat. **1664** POWER *Exp. Philos.* Pref. 8 In these prety Engines . . by an Incomparable Stenography of Providence are lodged all the perfections of the largest Animals. **1837** DICKENS *Pickw.* vii, Mr. Pickwick was sufficiently versed in the stranger's system of stenography to infer from this rapid and disjointed communication that [etc.]. **1902** A. SYMONS in *Academy* 23 Aug. 200/1 A fine play is not the copy of an incident, or the stenography of a character. **1911** *Q. Rev.* July 229 The speech of the stage had become a mere stenography.

Hence †**ste'nography** *v.* [cf. STENOGRAPH *v.*]. *trans.*, in quot. *fig.*, to write or express in brief.

1652 E. BENLOWES *Theoph.* To my Fancie, Be Wit Stenography'd, yet free; 'Tis largest in Epitome.

stenol ('stiːnɒl). *Chem.* [f. ST(ER)OL, blended with inserted *en* (see -ENE); cf. STANOL.] Any sterol having one carbon-carbon double bond in its skeleton.

1949, **1958** [see STANOL]. **1968** *Lipids* III. 397/2 Derivatives of many Δ^{24}-stenols undergo loss of two nuclear hydrogen atoms together with the side chain. **1979** *Nature* 25 Jan. 287/2 Core 16 . . was analysed for its sterol (stenol + stanol), stanone, and sterene contents.

Stenonian (stɪ'nəʊnɪən), *a. Anat.* [ad. mod.L. (*ductus*) *Stenonian-us*, f. *Stenon-* (*Steno*) or *Stenoni-us*, latinized name of Nikolaus Stensen, Danish anatomist, who first described this structure.] *Stenonian duct*: the parotid duct; also called *Steno's* or *Stensen's duct.* So 'Stenonine [-INE].

1769 CROKER etc. *Dict. Arts & Sci.*, Stenonian Duct. **1845** G. J. E. DAY tr. *Simon's Anim. Chem.* II. 15 The stenonian duct of a sheep. **1848** *Quain's Anat.* (ed. 5) II. 1008 The parotid duct, named also the Stenonian duct, appears at the anterior border of the gland. **1884** COUES *N. Amer. Birds* 210 In woodpeckers, . . elaborate special salivary glands occur, having a . . special 'stenonine' duct.

stenopæic (,stɛnəʊ'piːɪk), *a. Ophthalmic Surgery.* Also **-opaic, -opeic.** [f. Gr. στεν-ός narrow + ὀπαῖ-ος perforated (f. ὀπή opening, hole) + -IC.] Of an eye-piece: Having only a narrow translucent aperture, designed to increase the accuracy of the sight by cutting off all obscurations. Hence of instruments, methods, etc.: Characterized by the use of a stenopæic eye-piece.

1864 W. D. MOORE tr. F. C. Donders *Anomalies in Accommod. & Refraction of the Eye* iv. 128 Stenopæic spectacles, stenopæic lorgnette, stenopæic apparatus. *Ibid.* 129 These reflexions on the injurious effect of obscurations led me to the application of stenopæic remedies. Their object is to cut off the light which should reach the obscurations. **1874** LAWSON *Dis. Eye* 55 Stenopaic spectacles may be tried. **1895** *Pop. Sci. Monthly* Aug. 470 A most useful appliance for viewing pictures is the so-called stenopaic slit.

stenosed (stɪ'nəʊst), *ppl. a. Path.* [f. STENOSIS + -ED[1].] Affected with stenosis or stricture.

1897 *Allbutt's Syst. Med.* II. 57 The mouth may become extremely stenosed and incapable of being opened. *Ibid.* III. 839 The stenosed bowel has been kinked or acutely bent upon itself and so closed.

stenosing (stɪ'nəʊsɪŋ), *a. Med.* [f. STENOS(IS + -ING[1].] Causing or characterized by stenosis.

1903 A. STENGEL tr. *Riegel's Dis. Stomach* II. 392 This condition . . closely resembles the stenosing gastritis described by Boas. **1971** *Brit. Med. Bull.* XXVII. 26/2 A stenosing ulcer of the small bowel.

stenosis (stɪ'nəʊsɪs). *Path.* Pl. **stenoses.** [mod.L., a. Gr. στένωσις narrowing, f. στενοῦν to narrow, f. στενός narrow.] The contraction or stricture of a passage, duct or canal.

1872 [see MITRAL *a.*]. **1879** *St. George's Hosp. Rep.* IX. 732 Cicatricial stenoses are frequent causes of constipation. **1880** M. MACKENZIE *Dis. Throat & Nose* I. 361 An infant . . died from acute stenosis of the larynx in about three weeks. **1880** A. FLINT *Princ. Med.* (ed. 4) 335 In mitral stenosis less blood than normal flows into the left ventricle.

stenotic (stɪ'nɒtɪk), *a.* [f. prec.: see -OTIC.] Pertaining to, characterized by or resulting from stenosis.

1897 *Allbutt's Syst. Med.* III. 539 Some authors speak also of . . a stenotic form [of gastric ulcer]. **1899** *Ibid.* VI. 262 Litten found in two cases systolic or systolic and diastolic stenotic murmurs in the first and second intercostal spaces.

stenotype ('stɛnəʊtaɪp). Also **-typ.** [f. *steno-* in STENOGRAPHY + TYPE.]

1. An ordinary type letter used to denote a shorthand character.

1891 *Century Dict.* (citing Munson *Dict. Phonogr.*).

2. = STENOTYPER. Also *stenotype machine.*

1913 *Chambers's Jrnl.* Feb. 189/2 An English device of this kind appeared upon the market—the stenotype. **1942** *Amer. Cinematographer* Apr. 190/1 A secretary sits over in one corner with a stenotype, faithfully recording, ad verbatim, everything that's said. **1946** A. HUXLEY *Let.* 27 Oct. (1969) 555 We have just sent her stenotype machine over. **1970** J. HANSEN *Fadeout* xix. 161 He left them with a fat young sergeant and a . . woman who ran a stenotype machine. **1976** *New Yorker* 5 Apr. 82/2 The stenotype machine, above which Gnusse could see the court reporter's fingers poised.

stenotypy ('stɛnəʊtaɪpɪ). [f. prec.: see -Y.]

1. A method of representing shorthand characters and outlines by ordinary type-letters.

1891 *Century Dict.*

2. a. The art of using the stenotyper. **b.** Typewritten shorthand.

1899 *Daily News* 19 July 7/3 To read stenotypy the eye must learn a new style of type. **1904** *Daily Record & Mail* 9 May 4 The London Chamber of Commerce (which has included stenotypy in its syllabus as a special subject).

So **'stenotyper**, a shorthand typewriting machine; **steno'typic** *a.*, of, pertaining to, or printed by stenotypy (*rare*); **steno'typing** *vbl. sb.*; **'steno,typist**, one skilled in stenotypy.

1889 *Cent. Dict.*, Stenotypic. **1898** *Business Lett. in Stenotypy* 2 Instructions for using the Stenotyper. *Ibid.* 19 A thoroughly capable Stenotypist and typist. **1908** *Chambers's Jrnl.* Oct. 765/1 A simple machine, the 'stenotyper', has been devised. *Ibid.* Oct. 766/1 One stenotypist can be retained . . solely for dictation purposes. **1946** *Nature* 17 Aug. 217/2 A judicious combination of this privilege [*sc.* emendation] with verbatim reporting by the new stenotypic method has resulted in a lively and informal record. **1951** *Catal. Exhibits, South Bank Exhib., Festival of Britain* p. liii, The only British system of stenotyping (machine shorthand). **1978** Stenotyping [see STENOGRAPHER]. **1979** 'A. HAILEY' *Overload* II. viii. 148 A male stenotypist, who was keeping the official commission record, flipped back through the folded tape of his notes. **1980** 'E. ANTHONY' *Defector* ix. 223 There was a stenotyper who recorded every word spoken.

Stensen ('stiːnsən, 'stɛnsən). *Anat.* Also (*erron.*) **Stenson.** The name of Niels *Stensen* (1638–86), Danish anatomist, used in the possessive and with *of* to designate structures investigated by him, as: **a.** *Stensen's duct*, the duct of the parotid gland. Cf. STENONIAN *a.*

[**1803** C. BELL *Anat. Human Body* III. II. ii. 463 The duct of this gland [*sc.* the parotid] was discovered by Needham, and afterwards by Steno: it is very often called Steno's duct.] **1867** W. SHARPEY et al. *Quain's Elem. Anat.* (ed. 7) II. 816 The parotid duct, named also Stenson's duct (d. Stenonianus), appears at the anterior border of the gland. **1977** G. D. ZUIDEMA *Johns Hopkins Atlas Human Functional Anat.* xiii. 56/2 Surrounding the [oral] cavity and exiting into it are the major salivary glands: the parotid (Stensen's duct), the submaxillary (Wharton's duct), and the sublingual glands.

b. Each of two (sometimes four) canals through the bony palate, running from just behind the incisor teeth to each half of the nasal cavity; also the orifices of these canals in the bony palate.

1867 W. SHARPEY et al. *Quain's Elem. Anat.* (ed. 7) I. 45 This aperture may be seen to be divided into four smaller foramina, two of which placed laterally are the incisor foramina, called also foramina of Stenson. **1871** Canals of Stenson [see JACOBSON]. **1893** Stenson's canal [see JACOBSONIAN *a.*]. **1936** L. B. AREY *Developmental Anat.* (ed. 3) vii. 182 Fusion between the median palatine processes and the palate is incomplete, so that in the midplane there is a gap, the incisive foramen, flanked by the incisive canals (of Stenson). These become covered with mucous membrane. **1969** G. N. C. CRAWFORD tr. *Donath's Anat. Dict.* 480 *Stenon's* (*Stensen's*) *foramen*, foramen incisivum: one of the inferior openings of the incisive canals.

stent (stɛnt), *sb.*[1] *Obs.* exc. *Sc.* Forms: α. 4–5 **stente**, (6 **steynte**, 5 *Sc.* **stenth**, 7 *Sc.* **staint**), 6– **stent.** β. 5–6 **stynte**, 6 **stynt(t**, 6–7 **stint.** [a. OF. *estente*: see EXTENT *sb.* (Cf. STINT *sb.*[1], with which this word seems to have been partly confused.)]

1. The valuation or assessment of property formerly made for purposes of taxation; the amount or value assessed, tax, impost, duty. = EXTENT *sb.* 1 a, b.

α. **138.** WYCLIF *Sel. Wks.* II. 422 Whanne a prelat dieþ þe pope wole have his stente of alle þat falliþ to his hous. *c* **1390–1400** in *R. Glouc.* (Rolls) 7678 [*MS. C has* stentes *for* rentes *in the following passage*: þe king willam . . Let enqueri þoru al engelonde . . þe rentes of ech toun]. *c* **1440** *Promp. Parv.* 474/1 Stente, or certeyne of valwe, or drede [*Winch.* dette], and oþer lyke, . . *taxacio.* **1502** ARNOLDE *Chron.* Contents, The valewe and steynte of the benyfice of seint magnus in london. **1535** *St. Papers Hen. VIII*, II. 249 Your Counsaill . . may foresee a new stent to be made of your revenewes. **1557** in Marwick *Edin. Guilds* (1909) 89 That na burges sonn . . salbe haldin to pay taxt, stent, walk or waird . . nocht haffing stob nor staik. **1581** W. STAFFORD *Exam. Compl.* ii. (1876) 35 And so as the pryce of your wares riseth; and yet I doe but keepe my land at the olde stent. **1642** in Row *Hist. Kirk* (Wodrow Soc.) Life J. Row 20 The presbitrye had sett down a stent on every kirk. **1657** *Kirk Sess. Rec.* in J. Campbell *Balmerino* (1899) 408 Ane staint of a hunder merkis laid upon the heritors. **1786** BURNS *Twa Dogs* 51 Our Laird gets in his racked rents, His coals, his kane, an' a' his stents. **1862** G. HENDERSON *S. Matt. in Lowl. Scotch* ix. 9 (E.D.D.) He saw a man sittin' at the resett o' stent. **1883** W. C. SMITH *N. Country Folk* 103 *Mad Earl* lxvii, And there are three old burghs too, paying him stents and dues.

β. **1470–85** MALORY *Arthur* I. xxiv. 72, I had leuer than the stynte of my land a yere that he were on lyue. *Ibid.* VII. xxxv. 269, I wold not for the stynte of my croune to be causar to withdrawe your hertes. *a* **1513** FABYAN *Chron.* VII. (1811) 363 To pay the .v. part of the stynte of theyr landes. **1538** STARKEY *England* II. i. 175 That al such rentys as be inhaunsyd by memory of man schold be rebatyd, and set to the old stynt of that tyme. **1568** GRAFTON *Chron.* II. 157 They should . . pay the fift part of the stint of their landes. **1577** V. LEIGH *Surv.* M ij b, That he maie thereby the better perceiue what euery Tenaunte commonly paieth for an acre . . after the stinte of his rente. **1740** *New Hist. Jamaica* 55 The Successors of Columbus . . used the utmost Severity in collecting the Stints which they imposed.

†**b.** ? Valuation. *Obs.*

c **1460** SIR R. ROS *La Belle Dame* 769 in *Pol. Rel. & L. Poems* (1903) 108, I can nat se but all is at o stent, þe good, þe yll, þe vyce, and eke vertu.

†**2.** *attrib.* and *Comb.*, as ***stent maker, making***; **stent oil**, ? the quantity of oil claimed as duty on the year's produce; **stent-roll**, assessment roll.

1613 *Extracts Burgh Rec. Glasgow* (1876) 337 Sindrie.. quha in tyme bygane haif blasphemit the *stent makeris. **1569** *Reg. Privy Council Scot.* I. 683 Anent the assisting, contributioun, and *stent making in tyme bipast. **1614** *Reg. Mag. Sig. Scot.* 486/1 Payand..for thrie leischepund 1½ merk *stent oylie 5 pundis 2s. 2d. **1633** *Ibid.* 740/2 Reddendo unum lie leispund de lie stent-oyllie. **1517** *Acc. Ld. High Treas. Scot.* V. 126 Item..for non-delivering of thair *stent row ij^s^. **1657** *Melrose Regality Rec.* (S.H.S.) I. 162 The whole elders of the parish..to collect and deliver to him the stent of their towns conforme to the stent-roll produced. **1723** WODROW *Corr.* (1843) III. 44 Some are threatened to have their stent-roll heightened in August next, if they come not in and vote.

†**stent**, *sb.*[2] *Sc. Obs. rare*$^{-1}$. [Of obscure origin; perh. an error.] ? A staple or hole to receive the end of a bar.

c **1470** HENRY *Wallace* IV. 238 Wallace..Be fors off handis it [a locked bar] raist out off the stent [*ed.* 1570 sprent].

stent (stɛnt), *sb.*[3] *Sc.* [f. STENT *v.*[1]] A stake for stretching fishing nets upon in a river. Also Comb. ***stent-net***.

a **1712** FOUNTAINHALL *Decis.* (1759) I. 293 There were two other points then found irregular in them, viz. their fishing with stent-nets. 2 *do*, Their [etc.]. **1797** in Morison *Decis.* (1806) XXXIII. 14283 [The Lords..prohibited the defenders] from using stent-nets or hang-nets of any sort. **1863** *MacQueen's Rep.* (1866) IV. 548 The right to put a stake or stents in the *alveus* of the river,..and the right to use the stakes when placed there for the purposes of fishing. **1900** LD. HALSBURY in *Law Rep., App. Cases* 418 The one end of the stent net being fixed by an anchor in the stream.

stent (stɛnt), *sb.*[4] Tin-mining rubble.

1778 W. PRYCE *Min. Cornub.* 133 Care is requisite to throw off the Stent or rubble from the tye to itself. **1902** BARING-GOULD *Book of West* II. v. 63 The rubbish thrown out of a mine is called stent.

stent (stɛnt), *sb.*[5] *Med.* Also **Stent**, **stint**. The name of Charles T. *Stent* (1807–85), English dentist. **a.** Used *attrib.*, *absol.*, and in the possessive to designate a substance invented by him for taking dental impressions; also, an impression or cast of a part or body cavity made of this or a similar substance, and used to maintain pressure on it so as to promote healing, esp. of a skin graft.

The form *Stents* is a proprietary name.

1878 [see *impression material* s.v. IMPRESSION *sb.* 9]. **1899** *Trade Marks Jrnl.* 15 Feb. 155 *Stents*... A composition, sold in tablet form, specially intended for taking impressions of the gums and for like dental purposes. Caroline Stent, 5, Coventry Street, London, W.C.; dentist and manufacturer of dental composition. **1920** H. D. GILLIES *Plastic Surgery of Face* i. 10 An impression of the Sulcus is taken with warm Stent. *Ibid.*, The dental composition used for this purpose is that put forward by Stent, and a mould composed of it is known as a 'Stent'. **1939** S. FOMON *Surgery of Injury & Plastic Repair* ii. 128 Over irregular areas and where the base lacks resistance, such as on the eyelids and neck, and in inaccessible areas, like the nose and mouth..the use of dental modeling compound, commonly referred to as stent, is invaluable, as it acts in the dual capacity of pressure dressing and splint. *Ibid.* xvii. 1268 All cicatricial tissue beneath the surface is removed to form a pocket into which a stent mold covered with a razor graft, raw side out, is buried and sutured in place. **1961** WEBSTER, *Stent*, also *stint*. **1961** *Brit. Med. Dict.* 1350/1 *Stent's composition*, a proprietary form of composition used in dentistry, and in skin grafting. **1964** R. BATTLE *Plastic Surgery* x. 234 An impression of the raw surface [of the eyelid] must be taken in Stent's wax.

b. A tube implanted temporarily in a vessel or part.

1964 *Jrnl. Prosthetic Dentistry* XIV. 1168 All stents must be removed daily and cleaned. A pipestem cleaner is effective in cleaning the tube. **1975** *Year Bk. Ear, Nose & Throat* 114 Packing consists of a rayon basket with cellulose sponges in the meatus. Sutures and packing are removed after 7 days. Stents are not used. **1978** *Sci. Amer.* Apr. 67/1 A soft Teflon tube called a stent is placed in the vessel to keep the lumen open and facilitate the suturing. **1980** D. M. MAHONEY in R. C. A. Weatherley-White *Plastic Surg. Female Breast* vii. 203/2 At the time of the surgery, the physician lacerates the common bile duct and the liver. Both are successfully repaired but the common bile duct, of course, requires a stint.

stent (stɛnt), *v.*[1] *Sc.* Also 5 **stynt**. [? Altered form of STEND *v.*[1], due to the influence of the pa. t. and pa. pple. *stent*.]

1. *trans.* To extend, stretch out or set (a tent, sail, curtain, net, etc.) in its proper position.

1375 BARBOUR *Bruce* XVI. 282 He..gert ane tent soyne stentit be. *c* **1430** *Pilgr. Lyf Manhode* IV. vi. (1869) 177 þe cordes þat þe wylde beste hadde stented [orig. *tendu*] in my wey. **1496** *Acc. Ld. High Treas. Scot.* I. 293 Giffin to xij pynouris to stent the Kingis pailȝounis, vij s. **1508** DUNBAR *Gold. Targe* 236 To schip thai went, And swyth vp saile vnto the top thai stent. *a* **1510** DOUGLAS *King Hart* 378 The courtinis all of gold about the bed Weill stentit was quhair fair Dame Plesance lay. **1513** —— *Æneis* III. iv. 111 The south wyndis stentis furth strait our schete. **1597** SKENE *De Verb. Sign.* s.v. *Particata*, But of the vulgar people there is but ane forme of metting vsed.., to wit,..be ane string or coard, of sex elnes lang, stented betwixt twa staues. **1651** D. CALDERWOOD *Hist. Kirk* (1843) II. 365 An ensigne was caried before her..stented betwixt two speeres. **1806** MORISON *Decis.* XXXIII. 14280 He..stented his nets across both the head and foot of another pool. **1815** W. FINLAYSON *Sc. Rhymes* 85 (E.D.D.) Your fiddle sweet, stent ilka string, An dinna spare 't. **1900** *Law Rep., App. Cases* 409 No net had ever been declared illegal that had not been fixed or stented.

†**b.** *transf.* To set *up*, erect (a tomb). *Obs.*

1513 DOUGLAS *Æneis* IX. iv. 120 And in my memor vp a tumbe to stent.

†**c.** To hang with curtains. *Obs.*

1512 *Acc. Ld. High Treas. Scot.* IV. 279 Item,..deliverit to Thome of Pebles to stent the wyndois of the Palace of Linlithgow.., xxxvj elnis Bertane claith.

†**2.** To extend (a person) *on*, *in* (an instrument of torture). Also with *out*. *Obs.*

c **1375** *Sc. Leg. Saints* xxxvii. (*Vincent*) 155 þar-for in a frame stent hyme in lynth & brede, lith & lyme. *Ibid.* xlviii. (*Juliana*) 157 A quhele þan he gert sone dycht,..& stent hir þar-one but hone with cordis. *c* **1500** KENNEDY *Passion of Christ* 783 Lord, my syn..Garis þe now ly stentit on þe tre. **1728** RAMSAY *Fables, Miser & Minos* 44 Should he..stented be on Ixion's wheel?

†**3.** To keep in place, stiffen (garments, etc.). *Obs.*

1488 *Acc. Ld. High Treas. Scot.* I. 139 Item, for thre elne of rownde braide clayth to stynt the saim thre dowblatis. **1501** *Ibid.* II. 26 Item, for xviij elne cammas to stent the samyn ruf, xviij s. **1504** *Ibid.* 293 Payit..for lynyng clath to stent the said cheseb on, iij s. **1552–3** *Ibid.* X. 164 Item, v. quarteris small canves to stent the same [doublat], iij s. ix d.

4. *transf.* To distend (the stomach). *Obs.*

1801 J. THOMSON *Poems Scot. Dial.* 51 As lang as we get meal and bread, And ither things to stent our wame.

Hence **ˈstented** *ppl. a.*

1513 DOUGLAS *Æneis* I. xi. 7 The quene was set at deis, Vndir hir glorius stentit capitale. **18..** *Burns' Mary Morrison* ii. in Whitelaw *Sc. Songs* (1844) 49 Yestreen, when to the stented string The dance gaed through the lichtit ha'.

†**stent**, *v.*[2] Chiefly *Sc. Obs.* Also 6 **stynt**, **stinte**. [f. STENT *sb.*[1], or aphetic var. of EXTENT *v.* (Cf. STINT *v.*, with which this word seems to have been to some extent confused.)]

1. *trans.* To assess, tax (a person, community, country).

c **1440** *Promp. Parv.* 474/1 Stentyd, *taxatus*. *a* **1513** FABYAN *Chron.* VII. (1811) 448 The warde of Algate was stynted or sessyd at .xxx.li. *Ibid.* 522 The lordis and gentylmen were stynted at certeyne men, after the value of theyr landys. **1557–8** *Acc. Ld. High Treas. Scot.* X. 334 To vesie and considder quha wes absent witht thair oxin stentit to carie the munitioun of Hume. *a* **1670** SPALDING *Troub. Chas. I* (Bannatyne Club) I. 92 Then they begane to stent the king's leidges within the shyre of Angus. **1725** RAMSAY *Gentle Sheph.* II. i, For never did he stent Us in our thriving, wi' a racket rent.

absol. **1569** *Reg. Privy Council Scot.* II. 12 That thai [our Soverane Lordis liegis, landit men] convene..and stent and contribute every man according to the avale of thair landis.

2. To assess and tax (land, goods).

1548–9 *Acc. Ld. High Treas. Scot.* IX. 278 Chargeing the Shereffis to gif up thair retoures of the landis withtin thair sherefdomes and ballieries for stenting of the punde landis, etc. **1570** FOXE *A. & M.* (ed. 2) 18/1 To prescribe hys lawes, to stinte his landes, and such other. **1654** *Kirk Sess. Rec.* in J. Campbell *Balmerino* (1899) 408 [Three elders appointed as] stentours..impartiallie to stent and sie what bolls of victuall everie heretor was. **1848** *Edin. Topogr. & Antiq. Mag.* Dec. 146 The lands and barony of Nevay, stented at £5 old, and £20 new extent.

3. To levy (a sum of money) as an assessment; to determine the amount of (an assessment).

1633 in A. M^c^Kay *Hist. Kilmarnock* (1880) 153 [Parliament passed an Act to establish a school in every parish in Scotland,] upon a sum to be stented upon every plough or husband land. **1687** *Rec. Elgin* (New Spalding Club) I. 341 The Counsell appoyntit Saturday next..for stenting the cess. **1720** in W. Cramond *Ann. Cullen* (1888) 80 For ale and brandy at stenting the Lambas cess 15s.

Hence **ˈstented** *ppl. a.*, **ˈstenting** *vbl. sb.*

c **1440** Stented [see sense 1]. **1587** *Sc. Acts Jas. VI* (1814) III. 508/2 Fra all taxationis..watching warding stenting and vtheris chargeis.

†**stent**, *ppl. a.*[1] *Sc. Obs.* [Pa. pple. of STENT *v.*[1]] Extended; distended; taut.

1513 DOUGLAS *Æneis* IX. vii. 31 The wod was large,..Of breris ful, and thyk thorn ronnis stent. **1789** D. DAVIDSON *Seasons* 120 Until her apron was sae stent [with gathered nuts], The strings in targets, flew. **1886** J. BARROWMAN *Sc. Mining Terms* 64 *Stent*, taut.

stent (stɛnt), *ppl. a.*[2] *Sc.* [Pa. pple. of STEND *v.*[1]] Assessed, taxed.

1544 in Leadam *Crt. Requests* (Selden Soc.) 122 The Lordes & ther offycers wolde not alow ther yeldyng stent fynes. **1679** *Spirit of Popery* 16, I judge it fit..to leave my Testimony against the stent taxation cess that hath been so unjustly imposed.

stent, variant of STINT *sb.* and *v.*

stenter (ˈstɛntə(r)), *sb.* Also 6 *Sc.* **-ar**. [f. STENT *v.*[1] + -ER[1].]

†**1.** One who sets up (tents). *Sc. Obs.*

1545 *Acc. Ld. High Treas. Scot.* VIII. 406 Jhonne Aichisoun,..stentar of the saidis pavillionis.

2. = TENTER *sb.*[1] Also *attrib.* In mod. use, a machine through which fabric is carried mechanically while under sideways tension.

1875 KNIGHT *Dict. Mech.*, *Stenter*, a tenter;..common in Scotland and in the North of England. **1880** *Spon's Encycl. Industr. Arts* etc. II. 504 The piece [of book-muslin] is now taken to be stretched and dried on the stenter frames. **1891** *Century Dict.*, *Stenter*, A machine or apparatus for stretching or stentering muslins and other thin fabrics. Also called *stenter-hook*. **1911** C. SALTER tr. *Polleyn's Dressings & Finishings for Textile Fabrics* xxii. 244 The stenter and drying machine has been greatly improved by the addition of the longitudinal stretching device. **1939** A. J. HALL tr. *Hünlich's Textile Fibres & Materials* iv. 152 The fabric may be dried and stretched simultaneously on a hot air stenter. **1962** J. T. MARSH *Self-Smoothing Fabrics* ii. 9 The alternative use of radiant heat units mounted over the stenter is also quite common. **1973** *Materials & Technol.* VI. vii. 458 By the time the fabric has travelled the 50 or 60 ft..which represents the length of the stenter, it is practically free from alkali and shows no further inclination to contract.

stenter (ˈstɛntə(r)), *v.* [f. STENTER *sb.*] 'To operate upon (thin cotton fabrics, as book-muslins, etc.) in a manner to impart to them a so-called elastic finish' (*Cent. Dict.* 1891). Cf. TENTER *v.* Also, to pass (fabric) through a stenter. Hence **ˈstentering** *vbl. sb.* (also *attrib.*)

1880 *Spon's Encycl. Industr. Arts* etc. II. 504 The continuous clip stentering machine. **1946** A. J. HALL *Stand. Handbk. Textiles* iv. 228 The modern machine undertakes both the drying and the stentering. **1962** J. T. MARSH *Self-Smoothing Fabrics* xi. 171 The water content of the fabric may be reduced to a figure which prevents any migration during stentering. **1973** *Materials & Technol.* VI. vii. 458 Cotton fabrics are treated with the caustic soda solution while they are in open width on a powerful 'stentering' machine in which the fabric is anchored by its edges as it travels through.

stenting (ˈstɛntɪŋ), *sb.* *Mining.* Also **stenton**. [Perh. the same word as next *vbl. sb.*; but the etymological notion is obscure.] (See quot. 1860.)

1812 J. HODGSON in J. Raine *Mem.* (1857) I. 95 The single black lines in the walls and stentings represent stoppings. **1839** URE *Dict. Arts* 987 The pillars or walls of coal, marked *e*, are called stenting walls. **1860** *Eng. & For. Mining Gloss.*, *Newcastle terms* (ed. 2), *Stenton*, a passage between two winning headways. *Stenton-wall*, the pillar of coal between two winning headways.

stenting (ˈstɛntɪŋ), *vbl. sb.* *Sc.* [f. STENT *v.*[1] + -ING[1].]

1. The action of the verb; extending, etc.

1507 *Acc. Ld. High Treas. Scot.* III. 397 Item, to Robert Stanelee, broudstair, for..pak threid for stenting. ix s. x d. **1533** BELLENDEN *Livy* (S.T.S.) I. 40 But ony stenting of palȝouns in the campis [L. *non castris positis*].

†**2.** *concr.* Stiffening for a doublet. *Obs.*

1488 *Acc. Ld. High Treas. Scot.* I. 164 Item, for flotin and stentin to thir saim doublettis xxvj s. viij d. **1647** *Caldwell Papers* (Maitland Club) I. 99 For vi. quarters of stenting at 10 ss ye elne. **1658** *Rec. Elgin* (New Spalding Club) I. 305 Tailyors..shall neither buy nor sell any merchandice except so much plaiding,..stenting, bleached or unbleached, threed [etc.].

3. *attrib.* and *Comb.*

1551 *Acc. Ld. High Treas. Scot.* X. 17 Item, for buttonis and stenting canves to the samyn [doublett], viij s. **1868** *Perthsh. Jrnl.* 18 June, Muir Commissioners... The meeting..agreed to allow Mr. Herdman to remove the wire-fence on the outside of the hedge to the inside of it, with an additional wire and stenting posts. **1886** J. BARROWMAN *Sc. Mining Terms* 64 *Stenting-bogie*, a wheeled waggon or bogie carrying a pulley round which the haulage rope is passed, tension of the haulage rope being secured by [etc.].

stentmaster (ˈstɛntˌmɑstər). *Sc.* [f. STENT *sb.*[1]] An official appointed to fix the amount of tax payable by the inhabitants of a town or parish.

1624 *Extracts Burgh Rec. Glasgow* (1876) 342 The said.. counsall haif electit Archibald Andersone [and sixteen others] stent maisteris for stenting of the inhabitants of this burgh. **1818** SCOTT *Rob Roy* xxiii, It might weigh down one provost's,..six deacons', besides stent-masters.

stentor[1] (ˈstɛntə(r)). *Sc. Obs.* exc. *Hist.* Also 6–7 **-ar**, 7 **-er**, **-our**. [f. STENT *v.*[2] + -OR.] An assessor of taxes, a STENTMASTER.

1574 *Reg. Privy Council Scot.* II. 413 The Provest, Baillies and Counsale..hes nominat certaine personis burgessis of the said burgh, Stentaris, be quhome thay have causit taxt and stent the inhabitantis thairof. **1622** in A. Maxwell *Hist. Old Dundee* (1844) 425 He wes stenter for the last taxation. **1624** *Ann. Banff* (New Spalding Club) I. 52 Electit stentaris of the taxatioun of the fourt termes payment. **1659** A. HAY *Diary* (S.H.S.) 127, I went to Skirling..to stent the parish for a schoole, but..I could not get a competent number of men to be stentours. **1897** J. WILLOCK *Shetl. Minister* 141 (E.D.D.) A quorum of the Heritors, Stentors of the town of Lerwick. **1906** J. PATTERSON *Wamphray* iv. 85 To appoint 'stentors' to lay on a tax to meet repairs where needed.

Stentor[2] (ˈstɛntɔː(r)). [Gr. Στέντωρ, Hom. *Il.* v. 785.]

1. The name of a Greek warrior in the Trojan war, 'whose voice was as powerful as fifty voices of other men'; applied allusively to a man of powerful voice.

1600 NASHE *Summer's Last Will* F 3 b, Those mountaines are the houses of great Lords, Where Stentor with his hundreth voices sounds A hundreth trumpes at once with rumor fild. **1609** B. JONSON *Sil. Wom.* IV. ii, Rogues, Hell-hounds, Stentors, out of my doores, you sonnes of noyse and tumult. *c* **1611** CHAPMAN *Iliad* To Rdr., Brutish noises.. Are bellow'd-out, and cracke the barbarous voices Of Turkish Stentors. **1748** SMOLLETT *Rod. Rand.* v, [He] bawled out, 'Murder! thieves!' with the voice of a Stentor. **1840** DICKENS *Old C. Shop* i, Laughing like a stentor, Kit gradually backed to the door, and roared himself out. **1870** R. BROUGH *Marston Lynch* x. 90 She roared the..words through her hands with the lungs of a stentor.

‖2. [mod.L.] A genus of Protozoa; an individual of this genus, a trumpet-shaped protozoan.

1863 Wood *Illustr. Nat. Hist.* III. 766 The second figure represents the Stentor, so called because its general shape bears some resemblance to that of a speaking-trumpet. **1875** *Hardwicke's Sci.-Gossip* XI. 160/2, I found it to consist of an immense assemblage of stentors, apparently *Stentor polymorpha*, imbedded in a mass of dirty-looking jelly.

3. A platyrrhine monkey of the South American genus *Mycetes*.

1891 *Century Dict.*

4. *attrib.* with the meaning 'stentorian'.

1837 Carlyle *Fr. Rev.* I. iii. iii, Where Mirabeau is now, with stentor-lungs, 'denouncing Agio.' *Ibid.* III. i. iv, 'Legislators!' so speaks the stentor-voice.

stentorial (stɛnˈtɔərɪəl), *a.* [Formed as next + -(i)al.] = next.

1754 A. Murphy *Gray's Inn Jrnl.* No. 98 ¶6 It is ushered in with a stentorial Voice enough to crack the Ceiling. **1846** *Blackw. Mag.* LX. 756 In the course of his stentorial and senatorial career he [John Bright] has more than once [etc.].

stentorian (stɛnˈtɔərɪən), *a.* [f. Stentor² + -ian. Cf. Gr. Στεντόρειος, L. *Stentoreus*.]

1. Of the voice: Loud, like that of Stentor (see Stentor² 1); very loud and far-reaching; hence, of uttered sounds, song, laughter and the like.

1605 Sylvester *Du Bartas* ii. iii. iii. *Law* 20 My Stentorian Song,..Shall brim be heard from India even to Spain. **1606** *Ibid.* ii. iv. ii. *Magnificence* 264 Whose Stentorian sound Doth far and wide o'r all the world rebound. **1623** Cockeram i, *Stentorian-voice*, a voice so loud and strong, as the voice of one hundred men. **1711** *Countrey-Man's Let. to Curat* 31 The Mighty Talkers..who Conjure down the whole Modest Part of the Creation with a Stentorian noise. **1865** Livingstone *Zambesi* vii. 169 An uproarious dance follows, accompanied with stentorian song. **1872** C. Gibbon *For the King* xxxviii, 'Hold' exclaimed the general, in stentorian tones.

fig. **1638** Featly *Strict. Lyndom.* ii. 77 What a lowd and Stentorian untruth is here uttered by a foule mouthed Iesuit?

2. That utters stentorian sounds.

stentorian trumpet = stentorophonic *trumpet*.

1690 *Pagan Prince* xli. 119 Setting a Stentorian Trumpet to his Mouth, [he] call'd out to the Belgians in a most Terrible and Astonishing Tone. **1875** F. T. Buckland *Log-Book* 27 An invitation issuing from stentorian lungs to 'Step hinside and see' [etc.]. **1878** H. W. Bates *Stanford's Compend. Geogr., Central Amer.* etc. 187 Here [Trinidad] we meet, among the monkey tribe, with..the stentorian Howlers (*Mycetes*).

Hence **stenˈtorianly** *adv.*

1880 Mrs. Compton Reade *Brown Hand & White* ix, 'We are going to smoke', [said she] stentorianly.

stentorin (ˈstɛntərɪn). [f. mod.L. *Stentor* (see stentor² 2) + -in.] (See quot.)

1873 Ray Lankester in *Q. Jrnl. Microsc. Sci.* XIII. 139 Blue Stentorin.—The Colouring Matter of Stentor cæruleus. *Ibid.* 140 Comparing the bands of stentorin, as we may term this blue pigment, with those of chlorophyll.

stentorious (stɛnˈtɔərɪəs), *a. rare.* Also 6 -eous. [f. stentor² + -ious.] = stentorian.

15.. Becon *Castle of Comfort* Wks. 1560 II. 104 b, These Papistes, whych cease not wyth theyr stentoreous voyces to speke euyll of the true preachers of Gods worde. **1622** Mabbe tr. *Aleman's Guzman d'Alf.* ii. 280 Will you haue them with a stentorious voyce to deliver an Oration *ex tempore*. **1655** Fuller *Ch. Hist.* x. xvii. 77 They will remember the loudness of his stentorious voice.

Hence **stenˈtoriously** *adv.*, **stenˈtoriousness**.

1656 Fuller *Notes Jonah* i. 2. 11 [They] who change the strength of matter into stentoriousnesse of voice. **1685** G. Sinclair *Satan's Invis. World* Postscr. ¶5 A great multitude of People, Stentoriously laughing and Gapping with Tahies of laughter. **1882** *Fraser's Mag.* XXV. 487 To whose convenient indefinity the porter stentoriously invites us.

stentoronic (stɛntəˈrɒnɪk), *a. rare.* [irreg. f. stentor².] = stentorian.

1762 Warburton *Doctr. Grace* ii. v. Wks. 1788 IV. 617 For thus he measures out his own Stentoronic voice. **1861** [F. W. Robinson] *Under Spell* I. vi. 199 Jemmy..threw open the door and bawled out their names in a stentoronic manner.

stentorophonic (ˌstɛntərəʊˈfɒnɪk), *a.* Also 7-8 -ick; blundered forms 7 **stentoreophonic**, 7-8 **stentrophonick**, 8 **stentonorophonic(k**. [ad. mod.L. *Stentorophōnicus* (f. Gr. Στεντορόφωνος having the voice of a Stentor, f. Στεντορ- (Στέντωρ) + φωνή voice), in *tuba Stentorophonica*, the name given by Sir S. Morland to the speaking-trumpet invented by him (also called *Stentorophonicon*).]

†1. *stentorophonic horn, trumpet, tube*: a speaking trumpet. *Obs.*

[**1671** Sir S. Morland (*title*), A description of the Tuba-stentoro-phonica. **1683-4** *Phil. Trans.* XIV. 481 For if the Stentoro-phonecon..does such great feats, what might be done [etc.]. **1698** Fryer *Acc. E. India & P.* 96 He has Loud Trumpets made as big, and like our Stentoro-Phonica, or speaking Trumpet.]

1685 *Phil. Trans.* XV. 1185 He writes of.. Stentoreophonic Tubes, the invention of which he justly ascribes to Sr Samuel Morland. *a* **1704** T. Brown *Walk round Lond., Quaker's-Meeting* (1709) 19 The spirit speaks in them, they are but the Stentonorophonic Tubes. **1710** Steele & Addison *Tatler* No. 257 ¶2 There was an Organ, ..a Stentorophonick-Trumpet. **1713** Derham *Phys.-Theol.* iv. iii. 130 Of this Stentorophonick Horn of Alexander, there is a Figure preserved in the Vatican. **1800** Vince *Hydrost.* xi. (1806) 113 Sound is conveyed to the greatest distance by a trumpet, called a speaking or stentorophonic trumpet. **1803** Cavallo *Elem. Nat. Philos.* II. 312 Hence arises the effect of the speaking trumpet, or stentorophonic tube. **1811-31** Bentham *Language* Wks. 1843 VIII. 313/2, 1. Instruments whereby increase is given to the diffusion of audible and evanescent signs:—1. Stentorophic [*sic*] tubes.

2. †Loud as a speaking-trumpet (*obs.*); in later use (echoed from Hudibras) = stentorian *a.* 1.

1678 Butler *Hud.* iii. i. 252, I heard a Formidable Noise Loud as the Stentrophonick Voice, That Roar'd far off, Despatch and Strip. **1682** T. Flatman *Heraclitus Ridens* No. 72 (1713) II. 193, I heard..a loud Stentorophonick Bawl, which presently was raised to a high Scream. **1704** D'Urfey *Hell beyond Hell* 72 Bawling with stentrophonick might. **1782** V. Knox *Ess.* No. 164 ¶13. II. 324 A stentorophonic voice is the fundamental excellence of your Fine Man. **1822** T. L. Peacock *Maid Marian* xii, Little John read aloud with a stentorophonic voice. **1914** C. Mackenzie *Sinister St.* II. iv. i. 834 The whirr of the ventilating fans, the stentorophonic orchestra, the red-faced raucous atom on the stage combined to irritate him beyond farther endurance.

So †**stentoroˈphonical** *a.* (in the same sense), †**stentoroˈphonically** *adv.*

1676 Shadwell *Virtuoso* ii. 36 *Sir Nic.* After dinner we.. will survey my Microscopes,..Stentrophonical Tubes, and the like. **1693** *Urquhart's Rabelais* iii. xxi, A fair White Cock ..crowed Stentoriphonically loud.

†**stentorphone** (ˈstɛntəfəʊn). *Obs.* [f. Stentor² + -phone.] An electrical device for reproducing sounds, esp. the human voice, with increased intensity.

1921 *Punch* 2 Feb. 86/1 At Oxford Circus I have known What townmen call the 'stentorphone'. **1927** *Dancing Times* June 357/1 *Al fresco* dancing under cover is provided, with stentorphone music.

ˈstentorship. *nonce-wd.* [f. stentor² + -ship.] The function of a stentor.

1817 Coleridge *Biog. Lit.* xxiii. (1882) 287 Whatever his sleep might have been his waking was perfectly natural, for lethargy itself could not withstand the scolding stentorship of Mr. Holland, the Prior.

†**ˈstentour.** *Sc. Obs.* [f. stent *v.*¹ (The suffix is uncertain: see -or 3 and 4.)] A stiffening for a doublet.

1502 *Acc. Ld. High Treas. Scot.* II. 289 For iij elne cammes to be stentouris and patrownis to him.

†**stentrel.** *Obs. rare*$^{-1}$. [ad. Sp. *estanterol*, 'the Mid part of the Galley, where the Captain stands in time of Fight' (Stevens).] ? The centre gangway of a galley.

1755 Smollett *Quix.* (1795) II. i. iv. xii. 189/2 Seizing the captain, who stood upon the stentrel,..they tossed him forwards from bench to bench.

steolin, obs. form of steal *v.*

steore, obs. form of star, steer, stir.

steorne, steorre, obs. forms of stern, star.

steovene, obs. form of steven *sb.*¹

steowe, obs. form of stow *sb.*

step (stɛp), *sb.*¹ Forms: α. 1 stæpe, 1-2 *pl.* stapas, 3-4 stape, (3 *pl.* stapen), 4-5 stap(pe, 6 stapp, *pl.* stapys, (7 stiape), 9 *Sc.* stap. β. 1 stępe, 2-3 steape, 3-5 stepe. γ. 1 *pl.* steppan, 3-7 stepp(e, (6 *pl.* steppen), 3- step. [OE. *stæpe, stępe* str. masc.:—OTeut. type **stapi-z*, f. root **stap-*: see step *v.* The precisely equivalent form is not found in continental Teut., but cognate and synonymous sbs. are (M)LG., (M)Du. *stap* (inflected *stapp-*), OHG. (MHG., rare mod.G.) *stapf*:—OTeut. type **stappo-z*; also OHG. *stapfo* wk. masc. (MHG. *stapfe* masc., fem., mod.G. *stapfe(n* masc., *stapfe* fem.):—OTeut. type **stappon-*. The mod. form of the sb. does not directly represent the OE. *stæpe, stępe*, but the rare OMercian *stęppe* or *stęppa*, which is influenced by the verb.]

I. Action of stepping.

1. a. An act of bodily motion consisting in raising the foot from the ground and bringing it down again in a fresh position; usually, an act of this kind as constituting by repetition the progressive motion of a human being or animal in walking, running, or climbing.

false step: see false *a.* 6. *hop, step, and jump*: see hop *sb.*² 3.

a **1023** Wulfstan *Hom.* (1883) 302 Ælc þæra stæpa and fotlæsta, þe we to cyricean weard..ȝestæppað. **1297** R. Glouc. (Rolls) 6942 Hire legges bare binеþe þe kne þat me miȝte ech stape ise. *a* **1300** *Cursor M.* 5194 Israel wit þis vplepp þat moght noght forwit strid a step. *c* **1380** *Sir Ferumb.* 3989 He prykeþ hem forþ wyþ such an eyr, þat at euery stape sprong out þat fyr þat þay made þanne. **1387** Trevisa *Higden* VII. 527 (MS. β) ȝif heo wole go barfot for hir silf foure stappes and for the bischop fyve stappes, continulich uppon nyne solow schares brennyng and fuyre hote. **1538** Elyot *Dict.*, *Gradior*, to go by steppes. **1574-1794** [see stealing *ppl. a.*]. **1617** Moryson *Itin.* i. 22 On this side the City they shew a stone, whence they say, the Saint called Aurelia passed the lake..at one step. **1667** Milton *P.L.* xii. 648 With wandring steps and slow. **1750** Gray *Elegy* 99 Brushing with hasty steps the dews away. **1784** Cowper *Task* vi. 564 An inadvertent step may crush the snail That crawls at ev'ning in the public path. **1825** Scott *Talism.* ii, What do you in the desert with an animal which sinks over the fetlock at every step? **1829** —— *Anne of G.* xxix, If you will walk a few steps this way. **1867** Augusta Wilson *Vashti* xxix, To-day her manner was excited, and her steps betrayed very unusual impatience.

b. *contextually.* A footstep or footfall considered in regard to its audibility.

1605 Shaks. *Macb.* ii. i. 57 Thou sowre and firme-set Earth Heare not my steps. **1797** Mrs. Radcliffe *Italian* xviii, The steps of travellers seldom broke upon the silence of these regions. **1816** Scott *Antiq.* x, Step after step Lovel could trace his host's retreat along the various passages. **1879** *Blackw. Mag.* Aug. 180 There were steps coming down the staircase, and voices talking. *Mod.* How did you know who it was, when you did not turn your head? I knew him by his step.

c. Manner of stepping or treading; one's stride.

a **1000** *Riddles* xciii. [lxxxviii.] 10 Strong on stæpe. *c* **1470** Henry *Wallace* ii. 407 With a rud step Wallace coud eftyr glide. **1677** N. Cox *Gentl. Rec.* i. (ed. 2) 68 All Harts which have a long step will stand up very long. **1686** Blome *Gentl. Recr.* ii. 78/2 When the Huntsman endeavoureth to find a Hart by the Slot, and then mind his Step to know whether he is great or long, then say, He is known by his Gate. **1736** Gray *Statius* ii. 2 With sturdy step and slow, Hippomedon. **1832** Lytton *Eugene A.* i. vi, There is no bound in our step. **1863** Geo. Eliot *Romola* xii, Tito walked along with a light step. **1870** E. Peacock *Ralf Skirl.* I. 13 His step was steady and his voice firm.

d. *Mil.* One of the various paces taught in drill; as *slow* or *quick step*.

1798 Washington *Lett.* Writ. 1893 XIV. 18 To train troops to the 'quick step'. **1802** C. James *Milit. Dict.* s.v., *Back Step*, a step taken to the rear from any position without any change of aspect. **1802-**: see quick step. **1806-**: see goose-step *sb.* **1833** Balance step [see balance *sb.* 22]. **1847** *Infantry Man.* (1854) 7 *Slow Step*... The recruit is to be taught to take 75 of these steps in a minute.

e. *Dancing.* Any one of the various paces taught by the master; esp. the gliding movement formerly used in the quadrille and other dances (see chassé *sb.*). Also, a person's individual manner of pacing in the dance.

1678 Gailhard *Complete Gentl.* ii. 49 A Master teaches the steps, but the grace, the carriage, and the free motion of the body must chiefly come from us. **1698** Farquhar *Love & Bottle* ii. ii, My Dancing-Master has forbid me any more, lest I should discompose my steps. **1717** Lady M. W. Montagu *Let. to Pope* 1 Apr., The steps are varied according to the pleasure of her that leads the dance. **1815** Scott *Guy M.* xxix, I have even taught her some of La Pique's steps. **1859** *Habits Gd. Society* v. 206 'Steps', as the *chasser* of the quadrille is called, belong to a past age, and even ladies are now content to walk through a quadrille. **1884** 'Edna Lyall' *We Two* ix, Captain Golightly had the most delicious step imaginable. **1885** W. J. Fitzpatrick *Life T. N. Burke* I. 16 They never saw him dance, though his small feet seemed naturally formed for 'steps'.

f. Chiefly *pl.* Any of various children's games (see quots.). Cf. *Grandmother's (Foot)steps* s.v. grandmother *sb.* 1 d.

1909 J. H. Bancroft *Games for Playground* 188 Step... The object of the game is for the players who are lined up in the rear to advance forward until they cross the line where the counter is stationed [etc.]. **1940** N. Marsh *Surfeit of Lampreys* (1941) ix. 127 The childish game of Steps in which, whenever the 'he' has his back turned, the players creep nearer. **1969** I. & P. Opie *Children's Games* vi. 189 'May I?' as the usual name, but sometimes the game is known as 'Steps', 'All Sorts', 'Walk to London', 'Variety', or 'Mother, May I?'.

2. *pl.* Progress by stepping or treading; a person's movements, his goings and comings, the course which he follows. In many phrases, as *to bend* or *direct* one's *steps* (to a place, etc.); *to retrace, tread back*, one's *steps* (see retrace *v.* 3, 3 b, tread *v.* 2 b); *to conduct, guide* a person's *steps*; *to attend, dog* (a person's) *steps*; all used both *lit.* and *fig.*

c **1000** *Ags. Ps.* xvi. 5 Ȝeriht, Drihten, mine stæpas on þine weȝas. *a* **1340** Hampole *Psalter* xvi. 6 þat my steppis be noght stirid. ? *a* **1500** *London Lyckpeny* i, To london once my stepps I bent. **1593** Shaks. *2 Hen. VI*, iii. ii. 304 Threefold Vengeance tend vpon your steps. **1596** —— *Tam. Shr.* iii. ii. 141 Were it not that my fellow schoolemaster Doth watch Bianca's steps so narrowly. **1598** Brandon *Octavia* iv. E 5 b, Honour attend thy steps. **1693** Dryden *Ovid's Met., Acis & Galatea* 56 A Pine..He wielded for a Staff; his steps to guide. **1742** Gray *Adversity* 29 Wisdom..And Melancholy ..Still on thy solemn steps attend. **1812** Brackenridge *Views Louisiana* (1814) 46 The river pursues a zig zag course for forty or fifty miles, constantly returning upon its steps. **1842** Tennyson '*Flow down, cold rivulet*' 3 No more by thee my steps shall be. **1856** Capern *Poems* (ed. 2) 151 And may no rude steps intrude On thy happy solitude. **1858** Trelawny *Shelley* etc. (1887) 184 Envy, malice and hatred bedogged his steps. **1885** 'Mrs. Alexander' *At Bay* ii, He directed his steps to the hotel.

3. *fig.* a. An action or movement which leads towards a result; a particular move or advance in a course of action; one of a series of proceedings or measures; also in phr. ***a step in the right direction***; ***a step up***, a rise in social status; a higher position on a ladder of success.

1549 Coverdale, etc. *Erasm. Par. 1 John* iii. 11-17 For in dede the hate of the neghbour is a step vnto murther. **1602** Chettle *Hoffman* i. (1631) B 4, The first step to reuenge, this seane is donne. **1605** Shaks. *Lear* i. i. 231 No vnchaste action or dishonoured step. **1656** in J. Simon *Ess. Irish Coins*

(1749) 125 The expedients and steps for this worke are many. **1663** Patrick *Pilgrim* xxiv. (1687) 266 How hard do most Men find the first step to any Science. **1719** De Foe *Crusoe* II. (Globe) 395 The Belief that the Savages were all kill'd, made our two Men come boldly out from the Tree before they had charg'd their Guns again, which was a wrong Step. **1722** Wollaston *Relig. Nat.* ix. 171 Every motion and step in life should be conducted by reason. **1827** Faraday *Chem. Manip.* vii. (1842) 200 The best preparatory step is to insure the cleanness and dryness of the retort. **1841** *Penny Cycl.* XXI. 181/2 That prince deprived the town of its municipal franchises, a step which much depressed it. **1849** R. Patterson *(title)* First steps to Zoology. **1860** Hook *Lives Abps.* II. ii. 144 The next step was to assert the royal supremacy. **1877** C. Reade *Woman-Hater* I. i. 190 A little money was given her for a bad purpose. She has used it for a frivolous one. That is 'a step in the right direction'—jargon of the day. **1879** *Cassell's Techn. Educ.* IV. 273/1 The first step in the preparation of cotton yarn. **1913** *Times* 7 Aug. 8/3 An anatomical prognosis that marked a great step forward. **1919** H. S. Walpole *Jeremy* xii. 294 Going to school..was a mixed business; but the balance was now greatly to the good. It was a step in the right direction towards liberty and freedom. **1926** N. Coward *Easy Virtue* II. 86, I don't consider my position in this house a step up... It's been.. the most demoralising experience. **1939** L. M. Montgomery *Anne of Ingleside* xxi. 137 'It'll be a step up for a Plummer if you marry a Mitchell,' Ma said. **1954** *Encounter* May 52/1 Eventually she became a model—a further step-up—and she received her first film-part in that capacity. **1974** J. Pope-Hennessy *R. L. Stevenson* i. 32 The Thomas Stevensons..made..a final move to..Heriot Row. This was in all senses a step up, for Heriot Row..was considered one of the most delectable residential streets in Edinburgh. **1976** *Glasgow Herald* 26 Nov. 6/1 Extensions of the fishing limits around our coasts to 200 miles..are a step in the right direction.

b. A stage in a gradual process.

1811 Pinkerton *Petral.* I. 151 The first step in the process of crystallisation is the formation of grains; the second is [etc.]. **1875** Jowett *Plato* (ed. 2) V. 14 The regularity with which the steps of the argument succeed one another.

c. *Astronautics.* = stage *sb.* 12 b.

1932 D. Lasser *Conquest of Space* vi. 103 Each step, as it is called, is a complete rocket motor, containing fuel, combustion chambers, exhausts, etc. **1956** *Spaceflight* I. 5/2 Each extra step multiplies the total weight by a factor of up to ten, so that..rockets of more than five stages are not often contemplated. **1966** H. O. Ruppe *Introd. Astronautics* I. ii. 35 There are cases when a two-step design can do the mission but a one-step rocket cannot.

4. a. In phrases which refer to the action of walking evenly with another, putting the right and left foot alternately forward at the same moment with the corresponding foot of the other person; as ***in step*** and its opposite ***out of step*** (***with***); ***step for step*** (***with***); ***to keep step*** (***with***; also ***to*** music, etc.); †***to tell steps with.*** Also *fig.*

1613 Shaks. *Hen. VIII*, I. ii. 43, I..front but in that File Where others tell steps with me. **1784** Cowper *Task* v. 18 The shapeless pair, As they design'd to mock me, at my side Take step for step. **1844** Mrs. Browning *Rhapsody Life's Progr.* viii. I could walk, step for step, with an angel beside, On the heaven-heights of truth. **1852** Thackeray *Esmond* I, v, The officer, who rode alongside him step for step. **1858** Lovejoy in *Congressional Globe* 18 Feb. 754/2 We hear about keeping step to the music of the Union. **1876–89** Bridges *Growth of Love* xxxvi, Wherefore my feet go out of step with time. **1896** Housman *Shropshire Lad* lviii, When I came last to Ludlow..Two friends kept step beside me. **1898** *Weekly Register* 15 Jan., We need not go in step with the Bishops over the whole ground exhaustively surveyed.

b. *Electr.* ***in step***: (of two or more alternating currents) having the same frequency and always in the same phase. Similarly ***out of step***.

1903 W. Rogers in *Electr. Engin.* 25 Dec. 965/2 The secondary voltages are always in step, owing to the primaries being excited off the same mains. **1961** *Listener* 9 Nov. 768/2 There is also the problem, with direct current lines, of providing what is called the reactive power—power where the current is out of step with the voltage—for the operation of converter equipment.

5. step by step. a. Moving one foot after the other continuously; *fig.* by successive degrees, by gradual and regular progress, with pauses at regular intervals.

1581 E. Campion in *Confer.* II. (1584) N iiij, That..bodie ..ascended vpward steppe by steppe. **1701** Norris *Ideal World* I. ii. 26 If a man does but think and reason on from one thing to another, step by step, in a methodical train. **1732** Berkeley *Alciphr.* i. §16, I have been drawn into it step by step through several preliminaries. **1870** Thornbury *Tour rd. Eng.* II. xxiii. 119 Step by step Wykeham rose to the highest dignities. **1875** Jowett *Plato* (ed. 2) III. 173 The revolution which human nature desires to effect step by step in many ages. **1885** 'F. Anstey' *Tinted Venus* iii. 32 He had retired step by step before her. **1893** [see sense 5 c]. **1966** *McGraw-Hill Encycl. Sci. & Technol.* XIII. 355/1 A shaft which can be driven step-by-step in a vertical direction and subsequently can be moved step-by-step in a rotary direction.

b. Keeping pace with another; at the same rate of progress. (Cf. *step for step* in 4.)

1565 Cooper *Thesaurus* s.v. *Confero*, *Gradum conferre*, to goe as faste as an other: to sette steppe by steppe. **1580** Tho. M. *Pref. Verses* 29 in *Baret's Alvearie*, Euen step, by step, in following of his feete, In rightest waies. **1610** Shaks. *Temp.* III. iii. 78 Lingring perdition..shall step by step attend You, and your wayes. **1766** H. Walpole *Let. to Selwyn* 31 Jan., I go step by step with the British Ambassador. **1802** Mar. Edgeworth *Moral T.*, *Forester* xiv, Whilst he followed him, step by step, through his instructive narrative. **1899** *Allbutt's Syst. Med.* VIII. 594 It [i.e. diarrhœa] disappeared step by step with the skin-trouble.

c. *attrib.* or quasi-*adj.* = that moves or advances step by step; *esp.* (of mechanisms and the like) moving with pauses at regular intervals; *spec.* in *Teleph.*, with reference to one type of automatic switching, in which successive switches establish contact by a step-by-step movement first in a vertical and then horizontally in a rotary direction.

1803 G. Ellis *Let.* in Lockhart *Scott* (1837) I. xi. 401, I am unable to guide my elephants in that quiet and decorous step-by-step march which the nature of such animals requires. **1813** *Examiner* 11 Jan. 19/2 We beg the reader to give them a calm...step-by-step perusal. **1845** *Brit. Pat. 10,838* 15 The Invention of causing the two elementary actions..to produce a step by step motion of an indicator in two contrary directions, for the purpose of giving signals. **1879** *Specifications of Patents* (U.S.) 9 Dec. 392/2 An electro-automatic central [station] for telephone exchanges provided with a step-by-step action. **1889** *Engineering* 4 Oct. 386/2 The step-by-step advance of the platen somewhat resembles that in the Caligraph. **1893** Sloane *Electr. Dict.*, *Step-by-step Telegraphy*, a system of telegraphy in which in the receiving instrument a hand is made to move step-by-step, with an escape movement around a dial. **1911** A. B. Smith *Mod. Amer. Telephony* xxvi. 700 Their devices were usually based on some step-by-step ratchet action. **1933** [see strowger]. **1938** G. H. Sewell *Amateur Film-Making* iv. 46 The apparatus available to the amateur printer is all of the step-by-step type. Here the films remain stationary for a fraction of time opposite the printing aperture while the exposure is made. **1973** [see strowger].

d. *fig.* Involving or comprising a series of distinct stages or operations, often devised to facilitate the accomplishment of something.

1918 C. I. Lewis *Survey of Symbolic Logic* ii. 134 This is a 'step by step' definition. **1937** Michell & Belz *Elem. Math. Analysis* II. x. 608 The elementary fractions are of the first type.., as we shall now demonstrate by the use of a step-by-step process. **1957** K. A. Wittfogel *Oriental Despotism* 284 The step-by-step rise of a new system of landed property. **1968** *Daily Tel.* 8 Nov. 17 Very clear instructions and step-by-step diagrams for making a glove puppet. **1980** 'R. B. Dominic' *Attending Physician* xx. 182 [He] had been subjecting Fournier's narrative to step-by-step dissection.

6. to make or **take a step. a.** To perform the act of moving the foot as in walking or climbing. Cf. F. *faire un pas*.

to make or ***take but one step*** (***from — to —***): to pass the interval in a single stride.

1532 More *Confut. Tindale* 138 As from ye shotte of a gonne a man were metely saufe, that had ere the gonne were losed, made a steppe asyde .xv. hundred myle from it. **1606** Shaks. *Tr. & Cr.* II. iii. 193 Weele consecrate the steps that Aiax makes, When they goe from Achilles. **1678** Bunyan *Pilgr.* I. 43 How many steps have I took in vain. **1687** A. Lovell tr. *Thevenot's Trav.* II. 60 They had hardly made one step, when they returned with all speed. **1746** G. Adams *Microgr. Illustr.* 142 A general Description of the common Steps a Polype makes in moving from Place to Place. **1748** Richardson *Clarissa* VI. 349 He had the insolence to lay hands on me: And I made him take but one step from the top to the bottom of a pair of stairs. **1798** Sophia Lee *Canterb. T.*, *Young Lady's T.* II. 503 He..made but one step from the door to the bed. **1842** Borrow *Bible in Spain* xxxii, Many is the weary step you will have to make before you reach Giyon and Oviedo. **1859** Tennyson *Elaine* 390 She stay'd a minute, Then made a sudden step to the gate.

†**b.** To make a short journey *to* (a place or person). *Obs.*

1670 Cotton *Espernon* I. IV. 144 Making a step into Gascony to Visit Madam de la Valette, his Mother. **1685** Evelyn *Mrs. Godolphin* (1888) 217 Often have I knowne her privately slipp away..to make a stepp to some miserable poor sick Creature. *a* **1701** Maundrell *Journ. Jerus.* (1732) 1 Intending to make only a short step that Evening. **1733** Swift *Let. to Lady B. Germain* 8 Jan., I..was resolved to take a step to Paris for my health.

†**c.** To perform a stage in a journey. *Obs.*

1695 tr. *Misson's Voy. Italy* II. 305, I..intend..only to run over the several Steps that we made in our Voyage. **1829** Scott *Anne of G.* xix, That good Christians may bestow their alms upon him, and so make a step on their road to Heaven.

d. fig. ***to take a step*** or ***steps***: to perform a move or moves in a course of action; to take action or measures towards attaining an end. Similarly ***to make a step*** or ***steps*** (now *rare*).

to take the necessary steps: often, to take the action prescribed by law as necessary to attain some implied object, e.g. the enforcement of a debt.

a **1628** Preston *New Covt.* (1634) 53 Thou takest not a steppe into any action..but it is ruled and over-ruled by the Lord. **1737** *Gentl. Mag.* VII. 150/1 These, Sire, are the principal Steps to be taken in order to reform your State. **1775** Sheridan *Duenna* III. i, How shall I entreat your pardon for the rash step I have taken? **1849** Macaulay *Hist. Eng.* vi. II. 44 James now took a step which greatly disconcerted the whole Anglican party. **1867** Trollope *Chron. Barset* II. xlvii. 33 He wishes that I should take some step in the matter. **1885** *Law Rep.*, *10 App. Cases* 386 The owner..has taken no steps to disabuse them of that belief. **1891** *Leeds Mercury* 2 May 6/5 Steps have already been taken to suppress this demoralising traffic.

1675 Temple *Wks.* (1731) II. 340 This must be the first open Step that can be made towards the Peace. *a* **1715** Burnet *Own Time* (1823) I. 333 To make some steps towards the bringing in of their new religion. **1849** Macaulay *Hist. Eng.* vii. II. 233 Every step which they made towards union increased the influence of him who was their comon head. **1888** Fergus Hume *Mme. Midas* Prol., Come, let us make the first step towards our wealth.

7. a. The space traversed by the movement of one foot beyond the other in walking or running; a pace. Hence as a measure of length or distance, sometimes vague, sometimes defined, as ***military step*** (see quot. 1862).

c **975** *Rushw. Gosp.* Matt. v. 41 *Mille passus*, þusend steppan [*c* **1000** stapa]. *c* **1000** Ælfric *Gloss.* in Wr.-Wülcker 147/23 *Passus*, stæpe. *c* **1250** *Owl & Night.* 1592 Vych stape hire þinkþ a Mile. *a* **1490** Botoner *Itin.* (1778) 123 Navis continet 36 steppys meos; et longitudo chori continet circa 60 steppys. *a* **1548** Hall *Chron.*, *Hen. VIII* 41 b, A lyttell brooke, called Sandyfforde, whyche is but a mans step ouer. **1663** Patrick *Pilgrim* (1687) 304, I remember once that I met with a Man that thought he wanted not above two or three steps of the Gate of Jerusalem. **1703** Cibber *She wou'd*, etc. IV. 56 Move but a step,..this Minute is thy last. **1711** Swift *Jrnl. to Stella* 15 May, It is two good miles, and just five thousand seven hundred and forty-eight steps. **1798** Wordsw. *We are seven* 39 Their graves are green, they may be seen,..Twelve steps or more from my mother's door. **1862** W. Paterson *Treat. Milit. Drawing & Surv.* 17 The military step of 30 inches, of which there are 2112 to a mile. **1887** Farrell *How he died* 39 Not another step, or I'll have to pot you!

fig. **1780** *Mirror* No. 74 What if I should go a step further, and say [etc.]? **1847** Yeowell *Anc. Brit. Ch.* iii. 23 Irenæus, who is but one step removed from St. John himself. **1856** *N. Brit. Rev.* XXVI. 49 This course of reasoning..might well have been pursued some steps further. **1869** Huxley in *Sci. Opinion* 5 May 505/2 There is a long step from the demonstration of a tendency to the estimation of the practical value of that tendency. **1870** E. Peacock *Ralf Skirl.* II. 147 The son went a step further than this.

b. With limitation or negative (expressed or implied): A very short distance; (only, even) the smallest distance.

c **1000** Ælfric *Josh.* x. 12 Ne gang þu mona onʒean Achialon anne stæpe furðor. *c* **1300** *Cursor M.* 17704 Ga þou noght o þi hus a stepe. **1535** Coverdale *1 Sam.* xx. 3 There is but one steppe betwene me & death. **1667** Milton *P.L.* IV. 22 For within him Hell He brings, and round about him, nor from Hell One step no more then from himself can fly By change of place. **1781** Cowper *Retirement* 491 'Tis such an easy walk..; A step if fair. **1784** —— *Ep. Joseph Hill* 26 'Tis but a step, sir, just at the street's end. **1815** Scott *Guy M.* xii, I'll slip on my hood and pattens, and gang to Mr. MacMorlan mysell..it's hardly a step. **1831** *Westm. Rev.* Jan. 232 There is but one step, said Napoleon, from the sublime to the ridiculous. **1845** Lady Dufferin *Irish Emigrant* 17 'Tis but a step down yonder lane, The little Church stands near. **1876** Smiles *Sc. Natur.* iv. 61 Edward did not know a step of the road.

c. ***a good, tidy,*** etc. ***step***: a considerable walking distance. *dial.*

1768 Sterne *Sent. Journ.*, *Fragm.* II. 128 He had brought the little print of butter..; and as..he had a good step to bring it, he had [etc.]. **1869** R. B. Peacock *Lonsdale Gloss.*, *Step*, a walking distance. **1888** *Berkshire Gloss.* s.v., 'A goodish step' means rather a long distance. **1894** Blackmore *Perlycross* 57 The field was a good step from the village.

†**d.** A square on a chess-board. *Obs. rare.*

1562 Rowbothum *Playe of Cheasts* A vj b, The king.. hath libertie to assault thre roumes or stepps as he listeth.

e. The movement through a fixed linear or angular distance made by a stepping device (see stepping *ppl. a.*) in response to an applied voltage pulse.

1957 *Control Engin.* Jan. 74/1 The simple rugged construction of this new unit leads to high reliability, speeds to 100,000 steps per minute. **1964** *IEEE Trans. Automatic Control* IX. 102/2 Several companies..offer step motors with maximum stepping rates in excess of 3000 steps per second. **1974** T. E. Beliny in B. C. Kuo *Theory & Applications of Step Motors* x. 209 Load torque may actually vary somewhat from step to step.

8. a. [Partly fig. use of sense 12.] A degree in an ascending scale; a remove in an upward process; a grade in rank or promotion. ***to get the*** or ***one's step*** (Mil.): to be promoted to the next higher grade.

In early writers often used where we should now say *grade* or *degree*.

c **1000** Ælfric *Gram.* v. (Z.) 15 *Positvus* is se forma stæpe. *c* **1000** —— *Hom.* II. 70 On Godes ʒelaðunge synd þry stæpas ʒecorenra manna. *a* **1300** *Cursor M.* 29134 þar es steps thrin þat man mai fall wit-all in sin, egging, liging [*Galba* lyking], and consent. **1340** *Ayenb.* 46 þe lecherie of herte zuo heþ vour stapes. **1577** Hanmer *Eusebius' Anc. Eccl. Hist.* III. xxxiii. 55 Obtayning the first stepp of Apostolical succession. **1594** Shaks. *Rich. III*, IV. iv. 301 They are as Children but one steppe below. **1601** Bp. W. Barlow *Serm. Paules Crosse* 30, I am not either a penny the richer or a steppe the higher for him. **1641** J. Jackson *True Evang. T.* iii. 168 A graduall expression, growing up to the height of its emphasis by foure steps. **1779** *Mirror* No. 25 This contempt of authority, and affectation of fashion, has gone a step lower in my household. **1781** Cowper *Retirem.* 722 One [friend]..Will stand advanc'd a step above the rest. **1801** G. Rose *Diaries* (1860) I. 348 It might be desirable to confer the..step in the peerage on Lord Nelson. **1821** Scott *Let.* in *Lockhart* (1839) VI. 316, I trusted you would get the step within the twelve months that the corps yet remains in Europe. **1829** J. Donovan tr. *Catech. Counc. Trent* II. vii, After first tonsure, the next step is to the order of Porter. *c* **1830** Mrs. Sherwood *Houlston Tracts* III. lxxxi. 4 The housemaid..had been at the head of the sweeping-department,..and..by her going Anne was to get a step. **1848** Thackeray *Van. Fair* xxviii, 'He and I were both shot in the same leg at Talavera.' 'Where you got your step,' said George, with a laugh. **1892** Bierce *In Midst of Life* 124 Each had taken two steps upward in rank. **1902** S. Sheldon & H. Mason *Altern.-Current Machines* 207 Take readings thus by steps of five degrees throughout one complete cycle.

b. Mus. A melodic interval of a single degree of the scale (i.e. a tone or semitone). Cf. leap *sb.*[1] 7. ***by step***: by progression through a single degree of the scale (i.e. a tone or semitone).

1889 E. PROUT *Harmony* (ed. 10) vi. §164 A second inversion may be approached either by leap..or by step.. from the root position of another chord. **1907** C. E. KITSON *Art of Counterpoint* iv. 50 If the..third and fourth crotchets are discordant with the C.F. the part must proceed in the same direction by step to the next concord. If the next step will not produce a concord, the passage must be rearranged. **1930** A. M. RICHARDSON *Helps to Fugue Writing* v. 27 If the two missing beats were supplied thus..the result would be impossible cacophony. The only thing to do is to transpose this last group a step lower. **1952** A. O. WARBURTON *Melody Writing & Analysis* I. 7 When a melodic part moves by step it is said to be 'conjunct'. When it moves by leap it is 'disjunct'. **1971** A. HOPKINS *Talking about Sonatas* iv. 58 The Exposition of the Hammerklavier ends with three giant steps.

9. a. The mark or impression made by the foot on the ground; a footprint.

c **1290** *S. Eng. Leg.* 6/182 Euerech stape þat we stepen forbarnde onder ore fet... For þe foule sunnes þat we duden ore stapen beoth euere i-sene. *c* **1385** CHAUCER *L.G.W.* 829 He sey the steppis brode of a lyoun. *c* **1400** *Master of Game* (MS. Digby 182) xxiv, He shall say the trace of an herte and eke of þe bucke,..and þat of þe stynkynge beestes, þat men calle vermynn, he shall clepe hem steppes. *c* **1400** *Ywaine & Gaw.* 2889 Lo her the steppes of his stede, Evyn unto him thai wil the lede. *c* **1450** *Mirk's Festial* 152 And þer [he] laft þe steppus of hys fete þroste downe into þe hard erth, þat euer sythen has ben sen. **1530** PALSGR. 276/1 Steppe a print of ones fote, *trac.* **1538** ELYOT *Dict.*, *Peda & Pedatura*, the steppe or token of a mannes foote. **1746** FRANCIS tr. *Horace, Epist.* I. i. 105 The Steps, that to thy Den Look forward all, but none return again.

†**b.** *fig.* A trace, vestige; mark or indication left by anything material or immaterial. *Obs.* (Cf. FOOTSTEP 3.)

1382 WYCLIF *Wisd.* ii. 3 Oure lif shal passe as the step of a cloude. **1388** —— *Gen.* xli. 21 Tho secounde ȝauen no steppe of fulnesse. *c* **1400** LOVE *Bonavent. Mirr.* lviii. (Gibbs MS.) 113 Oure lorde reserued in hys gloryouse body þe steppes of hys woundes. **1432-50** tr. *Higden* (Rolls) II. 35 As ȝitte the stappes of that famose dyche remayne. **1565** STAPLETON *Fortr. Faith* 132 Purging them from all steppes and tokens of Idolatry. **1578** J. FOXE in *Bk. Chr. Prayers* 26 Vnles among the far Ethiopians some old steps of Christianitie peraduenture doe yet remayn.

10. a. *to walk in* (or †*tread*) a person's *steps*, to follow him as he walks; usually *fig.*, follow his example. †Also in phrases of opposite sense, as *to swerve from, shun, refuse* one's *steps*. The phr. *to follow,* (†*sue,* †*pursue*) a person's *steps* is perhaps to be referred in part to sense 5.

a **1240** *Ureisun* in *O.E. Hom.* I. 187 He mot foleȝi þine steapes þurh sar and þurh sorewe. **1382** WYCLIF *Rom.* iv. 12 To hem that suen the steppis [**1534** TINDALE, walke in the steppes] of the feith of our fadir Abraham. **1432-50** tr. *Higden* (Rolls) II. 343 Which folowenge the stappes of an oxe made a place, namenge hit Boetia. *Ibid.* V. 431 The doȝhters of the seide Romilda not foloynge the stappes of theire moder, but lovynge chastite. *c* **1480** HENRYSON *Test. Cres.* 17 Thair fadirs steppis iustly to persewe. **1513** BRADSHAW *St. Werburge* II. 1508 This Matilde, clerely refusyng The steppes of Sara..And other good matrons. **1538** STARKEY *England* 145 In thys processe we wyl take nature for our exampul, and, as nere as we can, folow hyr steppys. **1560** DAUS tr. *Sleidane's Comm.* 169 b, Not to swarve from the steppes of the confession at Auspurge. **1577** B. GOOGE *Heresbach's Husb.* 18 A good token is it..of good ground, where the Crowe and the Pye folowe in great number the plowe, scraping in the steppes of the Plowman. **1579-1752** [see TREAD *v.* 2 b]. *a* **1586** SIDNEY *Ps.* XVII. iv, Ledd by thy word, the rav'ners stepps I shun. **1695** HICKERINGILL *Lay-Clergy* Wks. 1716 I. 322 Arch-bishop Laud did but Lackey it after those, and followed their steps. **1714** *Barrow's Euclid* Pref. 2 Whose Steps I was obliged closely to follow. **1788** GIBBON *Decl. & F.* lix. VI. 72 The jackall..is said to follow the steps, and devour the leavings, of the lion. **1881** ILLINGWORTH *Serm.* xi. 149 Thousands upon thousands..have taken courage from their example to follow in their steps.

b. *to watch* (or *mind*) *one's step*, to be careful about one's actions, to tread warily. (Chiefly admonitory.) *colloq.*

1934 'G. ORWELL' *Burmese Days* viii. 139 You watch your step. Tom Lackersteen may be a drunken sot, but he's not such a bloody fool that he wants a niece hanging round his neck for the rest of his life. **1935** D. L. SAYERS *Gaudy Night* vii. 154, I can have a word with her and tell her to mind her step. **1955** M. GILBERT *Sky High* xii. 168 The Inspector... Bit of an awkward mood... I'd mind my step, if I were you. **1977** P. D. JAMES *Death of Expert Witness* I. 23 He seems to be taking quite an interest in you... You'd better watch your step.

†**11.** The sole of the foot. Only as a rendering of L. *vestigium*. *Obs.*

1382 WYCLIF *2 Sam.* xiv. 25 Fro the stap of the foot [*a vestigio pedis*] vnto the top, there was not in hym eny spot. **1609** BIBLE (Douay) *Deut.* xxviii. 65 Neither shal there be resting for the steppe of thy foote.

II. Something on which to place the foot in ascending or descending.

12. a. A flat-topped structure, normally made of stone or wood and some six or seven inches high, used, singly or as one of a series, to facilitate a person's movement from one level to another.

c **825** *Vesp. Psalter* xliv. 9 *A gradibus eburneis*, from stepum elpanbaennum. *c* **1000** ÆLFRIC *Exod.* xx. 26 Ne ga þu on stapum to minum weofode. *a* **1300** *Cursor M.* 10589 Þis maiden..Was on þis grece..On þe neþermast stepp don. *c* **1320** *Cast. Love* 740 In þulke..tour þer stont a trone.. Seuene steppes þer beoþ þer-to. **1426-7** *Rec. St. Mary at Hill* (1905) 66 For a mason & his man..to make a stayer with iij stappes. **1538** ELYOT *Dict.*, *Scamnum*,..a step or grise, wherby a manne gothe vp vnto a high bedde. **1554** tr. *Doctr. Masse Bk.* A iv b, Let there be a benediction of Salt and Water..made by the Priest at the step of the Chauncell. **1567-8** *Fabric Rolls York Minster* (Surtees) 114 For amending and repayring the greases or steppes before the southe doore, 6s. **1637** *MS. Acc. St. John's Hosp., Canterb.*, For a great stone to make a stiape vj[d]. **1705** [E. WARD] *Hudibras Rediv.* IV. 16 That dwells in Allies, God knows where, Down seven Steps, and up one Stair. **1823** P. NICHOLSON *Pract. Build.* 184 Each riser and tread, when fixed together, is called a step. **1847** C. BRONTË *Jane Eyre* xvii, Adèle and I sat down on the top step of the stairs to listen. **1908** [MISS E. FOWLER] *Betw. Trent & Ancholme* 39 The steps down into the Fellows' garden.

fig. **1604** SHAKS. *Oth.* I. iii. 200 (Qo.), Let me..lay a sentence, Which as a greese or step may helpe these louers Into your fauour. **1605** —— *Macb.* I. iv. 48 The Prince of Cumberland! that is a step, On which I must fall downe, or else o're-leape, For in my way it lyes. **1642** FULLER *Holy & Prof. St.* II. xv. 106 Not like those Masters, who making their Colledges as steps to higher advancement will trample on them to raise up themselves.

b. The height or depth of this.

1662 J. DAVIES tr. *Olearius' Voy. Ambass.* 271 This Hall was rais'd three Steps from the Ground. **1877** JEFFERIES *Gamekeeper at H.* i. (1890) 5 Inside the door the floor of brick is a step below the level of the ground.

c. A foothold cut in a slope of earth or ice.

1860 TYNDALL *Glac.* I. xi. 69 Cutting steps in the ice wherever climbing was necessary. **1871** WHYMPER *Scrambles Alps* x. 230 He cut steps down one side of a *sérac*. **1892** DENT *Mountaineering* vi. 175 To cut traversing steps is harder than to cut steps down hill.

d. A flat projecting foot-piece, fixed or made to let down when wanted, for entering or alighting from a vehicle; also, a projecting bracket attached to a bicycle to rest the foot on when mounting.

1816 JANE AUSTEN *Emma* I. xiii. 240 They arrived, the carriage turned, the step was let down. **1837** DICKENS *Pickw.* iv, The fat boy..let down the steps, and held the carriage door invitingly open. **1841** THACKERAY *Gt. Hoggarty Diamond* iii, The carriage steps being let down. **1847** LEVER *Knt. Gwynne* xvii, The steps were up, the door banged to,.. and the next moment saw the chaise at the end of the street. **1852** THACKERAY *Esmond* I. iv, The young page..riding.. on the step of my lady's coach. **1877** H. H. GRIFFIN *Bicycles of Year* 8 The step is placed at a convenient distance from the ground, and at the portion of fork best suited to bear the rider's weight. **1882** 'EDNA LYALL' *Donovan* xxxi, By the time the newspaper boy had sprung down from the step [of a railway carriage].

e. *Fortif.* = BANQUETTE I.

1672 LACY tr. *Tacquet's Milit. Archit.* 18 The Step, or Banquet is built at the foot of all Brestworks on the inside, and is 3 feet thick or broad, and $1\frac{1}{2}$ feet high. **1834-47** J. S. MACAULAY *Field Fortif.* (1851) 303 To render the steps or traverses..available for the active, as well as passive defence.

f. *Eton Fives.* The shallow step which divides the court into an inner and outer part.

1890 A. C. AINGER *Fives* 463 The vertical face of the 'step' does not reckon as part of the floor of the court. **1897** [see HOLE *sb.* 4 e]. **1975** *Oxf. Compan. Sports & Games* 290/2 Running across the court is a shallow step 10 ft. (3·05 m.) from the front wall, dividing the court into an inner or upper court and an outer or lower court.

g. *to go up the steps*: to be committed or appear for trial at a higher court, esp. the Old Bailey. Also in related phrs. *slang.*

1931 [see BOTTLE *sb.*[2] 1 g (*a*)]. **1938** F. D. SHARPE *Sharpe of Flying Squad* 334 *Up the Steps*, being committed to the Sessions or Assizes. **1952** 'J. HENRY' *Who lie in Gaol* iv. 62 They think it's wonderful 'to go up the steps'—to be sent for trial at the Old Bailey. **1962** *John o' London's* 25 Jan. 82/1 You'll go up the steps.

13. a. A rung or stave of a ladder; each of the flat cross-pieces of a step-ladder.

c **1000** ÆLFRIC *Saints' Lives* i. 22 Þonne bið he þam men ȝelic þe..stihð be þære hlæddre stapum oðþæt he to ðæm ænde becume. **1375** BARBOUR *Bruce* x. 361 He gert Sym of the Ledowss..Of hempyn rapis ledderis ma, With treyn steppis bundin swa, That vald brek apon na kyn wiss. **1530** PALSGR. 276/1 Steppe or staffe of a lader, *eschellon.* **1548** *Elyot's Dict.*, *Climacter*, the rounde or step of a ladder. **1659** N. R. *Prov., Eng. Fr.* etc. 89 Step after step the Ladder's ascended. **1674** *Churchw. Acc. Pittington* etc. (Surtees) 236 A new ladder containing 31 stepps. *c* **1850** *Rudim. Navig.* (Weale) 153 Steps for the Ship's side. The pieces of quartering, with mouldings, nailed to the sides amidships, about 9 inches asunder, from the wale upwards, for the convenience of persons getting on board. **1902** J. OMAN *Vision & Authority* I. iv. 30 No step of the ladder by which man climbs equals the first.

b. *pl.* A step-ladder; also *a pair* or *set of steps*. *colloq.*

1693 EVELYN *De La Quint. Compl. Gard.* II. 17 If that Branch be too high, he must get upon something, either a Ladder, or Steps, to the end that he may Cut it with ease. **1730** *Inventory R. Woolley's Goods* (1732) 11 A Pair of wooden Steps. **1855** TROLLOPE *Warden* xiv. 221 A pretty portable set of steps in one corner of the room. **1861** F. W. ROBINSON *No Church* I. I. ii. 66 A hammer, and nails, and a pair of steps. *Ibid.* 67 Steps, nails and hammer were quickly at the disposal of the stranger. **1875** KNIGHT *Dict. Mech.*, *Steps*, a ladder for in-door use.

III. Transferred uses of sense 12.

14. *Geol.* A fault or dislocation of strata.

1789 J. WILLIAMS *Min. Kingd.* I. 23 The single slips, or steps, for they are known by both names, are of various degrees of magnitude. **1824** G. CHALMERS *Caledonia* III. ii. §3. 53 This bed [of coal]..when clear of steps and dikes, which frequently occur, at thirty yards' distance, dips one foot in twelve. **1839** URE *Dict. Arts* 965 Hitches are small and partial slips, where the dislocation does not exceed the thickness of the coal-seam; and they are correctly enough called steps by the miner. **1886** J. BARROWMAN *Sc. Mining Terms* 64 *Step*, a hitch or dislocation of the strata.

15. a. An offset or part resembling a step in outline, singly or in a series; e.g. in the bit of a key.

1674 HOOKE *Animadv. Machina Coelestis* etc. 71 Unscrew the Plates, and place them in such order, that the Teeth may gradually follow each other,..and with such steps, that the last Tooth of one Degree, may within one step answer to the first Tooth of the next Degree. **1808** in *Abridgm. Specif. Patents, Locks* etc. (1873) 17 The key..moves the horizontal tumbler or tumblers to certain limit or limits by a step or steps cut in the key nose. **1813** MAWE *Diamonds* (1823) 128 When cut in steps,..it [the peridot] will appear to the greatest advantage. **1815** *Falconer's Dict. Marine* (ed. Burney), *Step* or *Tongue*, for the tar-kettle, in rope-making, is made of three inch oak plank [etc.]. **1859** F. A. GRIFFITHS *Artill. Man.* Plate (1862) 112 Steps [of a gun-carriage]. **1862** *Catal. Internat. Exhib., Brit.* II. No. 6105, The 'bits' or steps on the 'web' of the key, that act on the levers inside the lock.

b. (See quot.)

1909 *N. Hawkins' Mech. Dict.*, *Step of Screw*, the distance between two adjacent threads, more commonly termed *the pitch of the screw.*

c. *Aeronaut.* An edge built across the float or hull of a seaplane or hydroplane, giving its outline the form of an inverted step and designed to facilitate its separation from the water; *on the step*, with the part of the hull forward of the step out of the water.

1911 *Flight* 25 Nov. 1026/1 Each hydroplane has two steps, the middle step being halfway back from the bow. **1913** *Aeroplane* 24 Apr. 482/1 The [flying] boat got up on its step in a few yards. **1934** W. NELSON *Seaplane Design* vi. 54 Floats without steps tend to cling to the water with a tenacity that requires abnormal power for the take-off. **1935** *Sun* (Baltimore) 10 Oct. 24/4 As the clipper reached Middle River its speed increased until it was flying over the water on the hydroplane step. **1936** J. GRIERSON *High Failure* v. 91 After about half a mile of almost imperceptible acceleration, [the seaplane] Robert Bruce 'got on to the step' and began to hydroplane. **1952** A. Y. BRAMBLE *Air-Plane Flight* xi. 167 The floats are curiously shaped on their under sides, having a sudden discontinuity of surface known as a 'step'. **1983** D. STINTON *Design of Aeroplane* ix. 359 It is necessary to break down the suction by ventilation..and this is done by making a step about half-way along the planing bottom, slightly aft of the aircraft CG.

16. *Naut.* The block in which is fixed the heel of a mast or capstan.

c **1000** in Cockayne *Shrine* (1864) 35/15 Hiȝ fæstniað þone stepe þurh þa þilinge. *c* **1440** *Promp. Parv.* 474/2 Step, where a mast stant yn a schyppe, *parastica.* **1532** [see HOUND *sb.*[2] 1]. **1644** MANWAYRING *Seamans Dict.* 102 A *Stepp.* They call that peece of timber, which is made fast to the Keelson, wherein the maine-mast doth stand, a Stepp: Also those places, and timber, wherein the missen-mast, fore-mast, and the capstaine doe stand, are called Stepps. **1719** DE FOE *Crusoe* I. (Globe) 139, I fix'd my Umbrella also in a Step at the Stern, like a Mast. *c* **1850** *Rudim. Navig.* (Weale) 152 *Steps for the Capstan.* Solid lumps of oak, fixed on the beams, in which the heels of the capstan work. **1912** *Blackw. Mag.* Sept. 342/2 Our mast suddenly gave out, and, breaking at the step, went overboard.

17. *Mech.* **a.** The lower bearing or block on which a vertical pivot, shaft or the like rotates.

1814 BUCHANAN *Millwork* (1823) 547 The bearings for pivots, at the lower extremity of upright shafts, are denominated steps. **1835** URE *Philos. Manuf.* 172 Their lower ends [of the spindles] are pointed conically, and turn in brass sockets called steps. **1841** BREES *Gloss. Civil Engin.*, *Steps* or *Bearings*, those parts which receive the lower gudgeons of upright shafts. **1860** *Burn's Gloss. Techn. Terms* 12 *Step*, a pedestal for carrying the brass or bush in which the lower end of a vertical shaft revolves.

b. The lower brass of a journal-box or pillow-block in which a horizontal shaft revolves; also, see quot. 1887.

1875 KNIGHT *Dict. Mech.* 1887 D. A. LOW *Machine Draw.* 30 The brass bush [of a pillow block]..is in halves, called brasses or steps.

18. A change in the value of some quantity, esp. voltage, occurring over a negligibly short interval of time. Freq. *attrib.*

1940 in *Chambers's Techn. Dict.* 806/1. **1958** W. G. HOLZBOCK *Autom. Control* iii. 20 Assume that Figure 3-3c represents the change in level seen in Figure 3-5 after a step change in valve position..closes the valve slightly. **1959** W. I. CALDWELL et al. *Frequency Response or Process Control* ii. 15 If the input to the controller undergoes a step change of 1 psi, then the controller output will be a step equal in magnitude to the setting of proportional gain. **1962** SIMPSON & RICHARDS *Physical f Princ. Junction Transistors* xv. 372 i_0 is the change of output current resulting from the application of a sudden step of input current. **1973** *Nature* 23 Nov. 220/1 Where *C* is membrane capacitance, *i* is membrane current and *V* is the magnitude of the applied voltage step. **1975** G. J. KING *Audio Handbk.* ii. 41 Although a perfect step-wave (i.e. one of zero rise time) cannot, of course, be produced, a good evaluation of amplifier rise time is possible.

IV. 19. *Comb.*: **step-bearing** = sense 17; **step-board**, the tread or flat part of a wooden step; **step-collar**, a collar with a V-shaped opening at the junction of the collar and lapel (cf. *step-roll* (*collar*) below); **step-cut** = TRAP-CUT; also as *adj.*; **step-cutter, cutting** (see 12 c); **step-dance**, a dance intended for the display of special steps by an individual performer; also as *v. intr.*; hence **step-dancer, -dancing; step-fashion** *adv.* = STEP-WISE; **step-fault** *Geol.*, one of a series of parallel faults with successive falls like steps; also, the compound fault comprising such a series; **step flaking** *Archæol.*, secondary flaking of a flint tool to produce a strong, ridged cutting edge; **step function** *Math.* and *Electronics*, a function that increases or decreases abruptly from one constant value to another; **step-gable** = *corbie-gable* s.v. CORBIE 3 (cf. STEPPED (*ppl.*) *a.*, quot. 1833); hence **step-gabled** *a.*; **step-girl**, a girl who goes out cleaning doorsteps; **step-grate**, a furnace-grate having the bars arranged step-wise, to promote completeness of combustion; **step iron**, an iron projection fixed into a wall or the like to serve as a support for the foot when ascending; **step-like** *a.*, like a step or a series of steps; **step motor**, a stepping motor (see STEPPING *ppl. a.*); **step pattern** *Art Hist.*, a simple geometric pattern progressing in steps; **step-plate**, (*a*) *Naut.*, in iron ships, a plate of iron upon which the mast-heel rests when fixed in position; (*b*) *Mech.*, a metal bearing; **step printer** *Cinemat.* (see quots.); hence (as back-formations) **step print** *v. trans.*, **step printing**; **step print** *sb.* (see quot.); **step-pyramid**, a monumental pyramid the faces of which are built so as to form a series of large steps; **step response**, the output of a device in response to a step input (STEP *sb.* 18); **step rocket**, a rocket of two or more stages; **step-roll (collar)**, a rolled step-collar (cf. ROLL-COLLAR); **step saver** *U.S.*, a kitchen designed to reduce the necessity of walking between units, etc.; also *attrib.*, as *step-saver kitchen*; hence **step-saving** *a*; **step-stile**, a stile formed by steps projecting from a wall; **step-stone**, (*a*) a stepping-stone; now *dial.*; (*b*) a stone forming a door-step; **step-stool**, a stool which can convert into a short stepladder; **step wedge** *Photogr.*, a line of contiguous rectangles each of a uniform neutral shade but getting progressively darker from white (or light grey) at one end to black (or dark grey) at the other; also *transf.*; **step-vein** (see quot.); † **step-ward**, the ward of a lock nearest the pin; also, the ward of a key nearest the pin or barrel; **step-way**, a way up or down a flight of steps; **step-wheel**, a wheel with an edge formed in twelve steps arranged spirally, used in striking-clocks.

1873 J. RICHARDS *Wood-working Factories* 149 The *step-bearings for these machines should be as long and nearly as large in diameter as the top bearings. **1885** [HORNER] *Pattern Making* 226 The guide-ring plate E, carries the step bearing of the turbine shaft. **1823** P. NICHOLSON *Pract. Build.* 191 Proceed with all the succeeding risers and *step-boards until the winders are complete. **1895** J. P. THORNTON *Sectional Syst. Cutting* 104 *Step collar vest. **1977** *Summit* (Austin Reed Mag.) Autumn 41 Step collar dress suit..with satin facings £69. **1865** EMANUEL *Diamonds* 98 The Trap or *Step Cut. **1905** C. DAVENPORT *Jewellery* i. 19 A step-cut diamond..the sides facetted in gradually decreasing sizes. **1884** *Pall Mall Gaz.* 10 June 11/2 Kauffman..is, I believe, generally admitted to be the fastest *step-cutter living. *Ibid.* 11/1 It was a very steep bit of *step cutting. **1898** *Encycl. Sport* II. 36/1 (Mountaineering) Ice-slopes and Step-cutting. **1887** KIPLING *Plain Tales from Hills* (1888) 103 Orth'ris began rowlin' his eyes an' crackin' his fingers an' dancin' a *step-dance for to impress the Headman. **1946** D. HAMSON *We fell among Greeks* xix. 204 The Bishop of Kozáni, who was in full regalia on the speaker's platform, executed a step-dance. **1950** A. CLARKE *Coll. Plays* (1963) 297 It was younger than the mayflies That step-danced above it. **1969** in Halpert & Story *Christmas Mumming in Newfoundland* 67 Sometimes janneys 'step-dance'. **1896** STUART & PARK *Variety Stage* iii. 42 The sentimental vocalist, the male impersonator..and the *step-dancer were familiar performers. **1969** in Halpert & Story *Christmas Mumming in Newfoundland* 214 True step-dancers in 'Coughlin Cove' have learned their art from their fathers or grandfathers. **1886** *St. James's Gaz.* 25 Sept. 6/2 Have they learned '*step-dancing'? **1748** RICHARDSON *Clarissa* VI. 2 Half a dozen..boys behind him, ranged *gradatim*, or *step-fashion, according to age and size. **1879** *Encycl. Brit.* X. 305/2 Section of strata cut by *step faults. **1884** PEACH & HORNE in *Nature* 13 Nov. 35/1 The very preservation of the Durness Basin is due to two normal step-faults. **1931** R. A. SMITH *Sturge Coll. Flints from Britain* 30 Implement of triangular section... There is some undercutting along both sides, sometimes called resolved flaking or *step flaking. **1959** J. D. CLARK *Prehist. Southern Afr.* vi. 146 The Fauresmith tools were made by using what is known as *step flaking*. **1971** *World Archaeol.* III. 161 Macroscopic inspection also revealed woodworking wear in the form of distinctive step-flaking (the result of progressive wear and resharpening of the working edge). **1946** H. CRAMÉR *Math. Methods Statistics* vi. 53 Any non-decreasing function..may be represented..as the sum of a *step-function and an everywhere continuous function, both non-decreasing and uniquely determined. **1947** R. LEE *Electronic Transformers & Circuits* iv. 99 It is obtained by applying a step function voltage to the series R_8L_8C circuit. **1967** *Oceanogr. & Marine Biol.* V. 32 Assuming the sea to be at rest at $t = 0$, elevations were found due to northerly stress fields, the stress magnitude varying in time either exponentially, or as a step-function, or as a single half sine wave. **1971** J. H. SMITH *Digital Logic* iv. 74 In the circuit described here the input signal is a step function. **1921** *Glasgow Herald* 8 Jan. 6 It is a whitewashed house, with *step-gables. **1937** *Times Lit. Suppl.* 18 Dec. 954/3 The *step-gabled houses at Llanedwen. **1978** R. FEDDEN et al. *Hughenden Manor* (1980) 8 Its delightful step-gabled entrance, wood-strutted to the yard. **1884** *All Yr. Round* 18 Oct. 32/1 It is not a pretty spectacle to see two girls—even *step-girls—toss off their hats and jackets, and 'go' for each other in pugilistic fashion. **1869** CROOKES & RÖHRIG *Kerl's Metallurgy* II. 372 Furnaces with *Step Grates. **1912** F. N. TAYLOR *Main Drainage of Towns* vii. 139 *Step irons are let into the walls of the shaft.., but sometimes a small wrought-iron ladder is substituted. **1973** R. D. SYMONS *Where Wagon Led* xvi. 260 The wagon was swept down at right angles to the team. My neighbour yelled for the rope, which I threw. He caught the loop and fastened it to the step-iron. **1822** J. PARKINSON *Outl. Oryctol.* 225 *Ostrea scalarina*:..with transverse,..*step-like rugæ. **1855** *Orr's Circ. Sci., Inorg. Nat.* 170 The high step-like terraces, by which one may descend nearly to the water's edge. **1961** E. M. GRABBE et al. *Handbk. Automation, Computation, & Control* III. xxii. 55 Small *step motors have three to six times as much stall torque as the same size a-c servo motor. **1974** B. C. KUO *Theory & Applications of Step Motors* i. 3 High-speed printers of up to 3000 lines per minute can be driven satisfactorily with step motors. **1908** *Encycl. Relig. & Ethics* I. 842/1 '*Step' patterns occur in the *cloisonné* settings of Teutonic jewels. **1959** E. A. FISHER *Anglo-Saxon Archit. & Sculpt.* 74 The simple *step pattern* also was common in Celtic art of the pagan period, though it was rare in Celtic Christian art and may have been an independent invention of the Celtic people. **1869** SIR E. REED *Shipbuild.* xv. 284 The mast steps of the new Indian troop-ships, in which the *step-plate has been worked directly upon the inner-skin plating. **1869** RANKINE *Machine & Hand-tools* Pl. I 5, The two worms are..each of them provided with a spherically shaped step-plate, to insure a perfect fit on the rubbing surfaces next to the worms. **1953** K. REISZ *Technique Film Editing* xiii. 207 Shot 32..was too short for the present film and had to be *step-printed to the needed length. **1960** O. SKILBECK *ABC of Film & TV* 125 *Step Print.* Most Positives are made on a continuous process machine in which they run in contact with the Negative; but for some purposes, *step printing, Frame by frame, is used. **1930** *Sel. Gloss. Motion Pict. Techn.* (Acad. Techn. Bureau Hollywood), **Step printer*, machine which prints a positive, a frame at a time. **1959** W. S. SHARPS *Dict. Cinematogr.* 120/1 *Step printer*, a printer in which the film to be printed and the raw stock are moved intermittently, and are stationary whilst being exposed one frame at a time. **1886** *Encycl. Brit.* XX. 124/1 The *step-pyramid or cumulative mastaba. **1959** ZIMMERMAN & MASON *Electronic Circuit Theory* viii. 368 (*caption*) Approximating the *step response of a linear *RC* coupling circuit including stray capacitances. **1967** *Electronics* 6 Mar. 9/1 (Advt.), Step response over the full 4½-inch span..is 40 milliseconds. **1932** D. LASSER *Conquest of Space* vi. 104 The *step-rocket will ascend to a far greater height than a unit rocket of the same weight. **1946** *Sun* (Baltimore) 23 Dec. 2/4 The 'Tiamat' is a 'step' rocket—that is, it has a rocket booster mounted on its tail. **1966** H. O. RUPPE *Introd. Astronautics* I. ii. 26 Optimization of step rockets poses some very interesting problems. **1881** *Record of Fashion* 27 July 178/2 *Step roll is the most suitable style for most of the goods now fashionable. **1901** P. N. HASLUCK *Tailoring* 99 Step-roll collar vest. **1967** *Boston Sunday Globe* 23 Apr. B59/3 The large kitchen..is a *stepsaver when the dining room is being used. **1974** *State* (Columbia, S. Carolina) 1 Apr. 9-B/8 (Advt.), Spanish style home includes 3 bedrooms, 2 full baths, cozy den, patio, step saver kitchen with built-ins, enclosed garage and central air. **1978** *Detroit Free Press* 16 Apr. F9/5 (Advt.), 4 bedroom Quad..featuring..*step-saving kitchen with all built-ins. **1904** J. DERRY *Across Derbysh. Moors* xii. (ed. 3) 116 A stone *step-stile crosses the wall on the right close beyond Stony Ford. **1605** *Shuttleworths' Acc.* (Chetham Soc.) 169 For xv *steppstonnes for the starres of the said stable (vij[d] the steppe) viij[s] ix[d]. **1868** M. H. SMITH *Sunsh. & Shadow N. York* 136 Ten men could not put her off that step-stone. **1966** J. POTTS *Footsteps on Stairs* (1967) iii. 38 Hazel had to laugh, just at the sight of him up there on the *step-stool. **1881** RAYMOND *Mining Gloss.*, **Step-vein*, a vein alternately cutting through the strata of country-rock, and running parallel with them. **1677** MOXON *Mech. Exerc.* ii. 22 In Fig. 3. AAAA the Cover-plate [of a spring-lock],..E the *Step ward, or Dap ward. In Fig. 4. A the Pin-hole [of a key], B the Step or Dap ward. **1797** *Encycl. Brit.* (ed. 3) X. 111/2 To the cover-plate belong the pin, main-ward, cross-ward, step-ward or dap-ward. **1810** *Hull Improv. Act* 51 Cellar-grate *step-way or hatch-way. **1906** H. G. WELLS *In Days Comet* I. i. 26 We walked together..up the stepway and the lanes towards Clayton Crest. **1931** *Phil. Trans. R. Soc.* A. CCXXX. 91 The intensities were estimated by covering part of the lines with a *step-wedge of aluminium foil..and making use of the known absorption-coefficient of aluminium for CuKα rays. **1936** F. R. NEWNES *Technique Colour Photogr.* (ed. 2) iii. 39 The print from the blue filter negative will show less contrast than the others... If the white end of the step wedge is white, then the black end will only be a dark grey. **1962** *Which?* May 135/1 A black and white film's characteristic curve can be obtained by photographing a grey step wedge..and measuring the densities of the grey steps in the picture in relation to their known real densities. **1971** *Jrnl. Oil & Colour Chemists' Assoc.* LIV. 881 A method of achieving this was evolved using a step-wedge produced by gradually increasing the exposure in strips across the film. *a* **1735** W. DERHAM *Artif. Clockm.* (1759) 7 The Snail or *Step-Wheel in Repeating-Clocks.

20. Combinations with an adv., as *step-back*, *-down*, *-up* = an act of stepping backwards, etc.

1603 FLORIO *Montaigne* III. xiii. 658, I begin to perceive a dimnes and weakenes in reading... Loe—heere a steppe-backe, and that very sensible. **1833** *Reg. Instr. Cavalry* I. 17 The 'Step Back' is performed in the slow time and length of pace, from the halt.

step, *sb.*[2] Colloq. abbrev. of *stepfather*, *-mother*, *-son*, etc. Cf. STEP- and the associated main entries.

1895 C. M. YONGE *Long Vacation* ii. 15 Anyone would have thought those poor boys were her steps, not good old Lamb's. **1913** ROWNTREE & KENDALL *How Labourer Lives* iii. 227 There are three 'steps', Mr. Hopwood's children by a former marriage. **1933** G. HEYER *Why shoot Butler?* ii. 23 'You should not encourage your friend to talk disloyally about her brother.'.. 'He's only a "step"'. **1939** A. THIRKELL *Before Lunch* ii. 43 She's an angel. Not a bit like a step. I really think she married father so that she could look after Denis and take me about a bit. **1954** E. EAGER *Half Magic* 155 *Step*,..short for *step-father*. **1971** O. NORTON *Corpse-Bird Cries* iv. 68 They're not her natural parents. They're both steps.

step (stɛp), *v.* Pa. t. and pa. pple. **stepped** (stɛpt). Forms: α. 1 **steppan**, *North.* **steppa**, **stepa**, 3 **steppen**, (**stepen**), 3–7 **steppe**, 3– **step**. β. 1 **stæppan**, 3–5 **stappe**, **stap**, 4–5 **stapp**, **stape**, 7– *Sc.* **stap**. *Pa. t.* α. 1 **stóp**, *pl.* **stópon**, 3–4 **stop**, *pl.* **stopen**. β. 3 **step**, **steap**, **steop**, *pl.* **stepen**, 3–4 **stepe**. γ. 3–5 **stap**, 5 **stappe**. δ. *weak forms.* 3–4 **stapte**, 4–5 **stapped**, **-id**, 6 **stepte**, 7 **step'd**, 7– **stepp'd**, 5– **stept**, **stepped**. *Pa. pple.* α. 1 (**be**)**stapen**, 4–5 **stape**(**n**. β. 4–5 **stope**(**n**, 6 **ystope**. γ. 6 **step**, **steppte**, 6– **stept**, **stepped**. [A Com. WGer. strong verb, with *j*- present-stem (cf. SHAPE *v.*). The original conjugation (OTeut. type **stapjan*, **stōp*-, **stapan*-) is completely evidenced only in English and Frisian: OE. *stæppan*, *steppan*, pa. t. *stóp*, pa. ppl. (*be*)*stapen*, corresponds to OFris. **steppa* (3rd sing. *stepth*, *stapth*, subj. *steppe*), pa. t. *stôp*, pa. pple. *stapen*. The present-stem is normally represented also in OHG. *stephen* (MHG. *stepfen*), and WFlem. *steppen*; the strong pa. t. in OS. *stôp* and in WFris. *stoep*, which is the only trace of the strong inflexion surviving in any mod.Teut. dialect. The continental WGer. langs. have a synonymous wk. vb. with *pp* and without umlaut, (M)LG., (M)Du. *stappen*, mod.Fris. *stappe*, OHG. *staphôn* (MHG., mod.G. *stapfen*):—WGer. **stappōjan*, where the doubled *p* appears to be due to derivation from the sb. WGer. **stappon*- (see STEP *sb.*[1]); in LG. and Du., however, the history of the form may be complicated with that of the original *j*-present.

In OE. the normal form *steppan* was Anglian, while WS. had the form *stæppan*, the anomalous vowel of which has not been satisfactorily accounted for. In ME. the forms with *a* are confined to certain southern writers (cf. mod.Somerset *staap*). The present Sc. *stap*, recorded from the 17th c., appears to be a late development.

The normal strong pa. t. and pa. pple. survive into the 14th and 15th centuries, but beside them appear two analogical formations: *steop*, *stepen*, app. modelled on the reduplicating verbs (cf. the similar development in MDu. *stiep* pa. t.); and *stap*, *stappe* of uncertain origin. Beside the regular *stapen* there is also a new pa. pple. *stopen*. Weak forms are found from the end of the 13th century, and from the 16th century are universal.

The affinities of the Teut. root **stap*- are uncertain. On the assumption that the form with single *p* has been altered by some analogy from **stapp*-, with *pp* representing Indogermanic *pn*, possible cognates are OSl. (and Russian) *stopa*, step, pace, *stepenĭ* step, degree.]

I. Intransitive.

1. a. To lift the foot and set it down again on the ground in a new position; to lift and set down the feet alternately in walking; to pace, tread. With adv.: To use a (specified) gait or motion of the feet (often of a horse: cf. 6).

to step short (Mil.): see quots. 1802, 1859.

a **1000** *Juliana* 374 Stepeð stronglice. *c* **1000** ÆLFRIC *Gram.* xxix. (Z.) 185 *Gradior*, ic stæppe. *c* **1205** LAY. 18420 Ac we scullen steppen [*c* **1275** stap] heom to, swa we stelen wolden. *c* **1220** *Bestiary* 10 in *O.E. Misc.*, Alle hise fet steppes After him he filleð, Draʒ eð dust wið his stert ðer he steppeð. **1377** LANGL. *P. Pl.* B. v. 352 He myȝte neither steppe [*C text* stappe] ne stonde er he his staffe hadde. *c* **1386** CHAUCER *Reeve's T.* 154 Stepe on thy feet, com out, man, al atanes! **1398** TREVISA *Barth. De P.R.* XVIII. xcvi. (1495) 843 Apes maye goo and steppe on two fete, for they haue soolys in theyr fete as a man hath. **1399** LANGL. *Rich. Redeles* III. 54 As sone as þey styffe and þat þey steppe kunne. **1570** LEVINS *Manip.* 70/7 To steppe, *gradi, gressus ponere.* **1727** H. BLAND *Milit. Discipl.* 45 Those who Faced step with their left Feet towards the Rear. **1802** C. JAMES *Milit. Dict.*, *To Step*, to move forward or backward, by a single change of the place of the foot... *To step short*..is to diminish or slacken your pace. **1821** CLARE *Vill. Minstr.* I. 8 Soft would he step lest they his tread should hear. **1829** LYTTON *Disowned* xxx, And now tell me all about your horse, does he step well? **1859** F. A. GRIFFITHS *Artill. Man.* (1862) 6 In slow or quick time the length of a pace is 30 inches,..in 'stepping short' 10.

b. with cognate obj. (*a step*, *stride*, etc.).

a **1023** WULFSTAN *Hom.* lviii. (1883) 302/27 Ælc þæra stæpa and fotlæsta, þe we to cyricean weard..gestæppað. *c* **1290** *S. Eng. Leg.* 6/182 Euerech stape þat we stepen for-barnde onder ore fet. **1802** G. COLMAN *Br. Grins, Elder Bro.* (1819) 125 He couldn't help, at every step he stepp'd, Grunting, and grumbling. **1821** SCOTT *Kenilw.* iii, Nay, without expecting either pleasure or profit, or both, I had not stepped a stride within this manor. **1893** KIPLING *Many Invent.* 209, I rose and stepped three paces into the *rukh*.

c. To move with measured paces in a dance. Also quasi-*trans.*, to go through the steps of, perform (a dance).

1698 E. Ward *Lond. Spy* II. (1706) 46 A Vintners Daughter, bred at the Dancing School,..steps a Minuet finely. 1864 Tennyson *Aylmer's F.* 207 A stiff brocade in which..she, Once with this kinsman..Stept thro' the stately minuet of those days. 1878 B. Taylor *Deukalion* III. i. 95 Step to the music of the song I gave, My Poet, homeward! 1893 *Chamb. Jrnl.* 19 Aug. 518/1 He stepped a minuet gravely and gracefully.

d. Phrase. ***as good*** (etc.) ***a man as ever stepped*** (***in shoe-leather***).

1818 [see shoe-leather]. 1834 *Westm. Rev.* XX. 495 Major Fancourt, as fine a young aristocrat as steps.

2. a. To move to a new position by extending the foot to a higher or lower level or across an intervening object or space (e.g. in entering or leaving a carriage or boat, ascending or descending stairs); with adv. or prep., as *across, in, into, off, out of, on* or *upon, over, up* (see also branches III and IV).

to step short, to make an insufficiently long stride, so that the foot fails to reach the intended position.

897 Ælfred *Gregory's Past. C.* xiii. 77 Ðylæs he ofer ðone ðerscold his endebyrdnesse stæppe. *c* 1205 Lay. 32035 He..somnede alle þa scipen..and þohte mid strengðe steppen to londe. *a* 1320 *Sir Tristr.* 2865 Her hors apolk stap in. *c* 1375 *Sc. Leg. Saints* xxxiii. (*George*) 259 He one horse gat stepande. 1706 Mrs. Centlivre *Love at Venture* I. i. 3 A Lady designing to Land at White-Hall Stairs, stepping short from the Boat, fell into the Water. 1801 J. Thomson *Poems Scot. Dial.* 149 They'll get for crossin' o' a street, Or stappin' up a stair, Five gude red guineas at a heat. 1823 Syd. Smith *Wks.* (1859) II. 21/2 A boat from shore reached the ship, and from it stepped a clerk of the Bank of England. 1860 Tyndall *Glac.* I. xi. 70 It was necessary to step from a projecting end of ice to a mass of soft snow. *Ibid.* xvii. 119 Retaining my boots [I] stepped upon the floating ice. 1886 C. E. Pascoe *Lond. To-day* xxxiv. (ed. 3) 302 He might..get to the Royal Exchange without once stepping off the pavement. 1890 Bridges *Shorter Poems* III. vii, And in our boat we stepped and took the stream.

fig. 1715 Pope *Iliad* I. Pref. D 3 b, Let them think..that they are stepping almost three thousand Years backward into the remotest Antiquity.

b. ***to step astray, awry,*** † ***beside***: to move from the straight or proper path (*lit.* and *fig.*). See also *step aside* in IV.

1297 R. Glouc. (Rolls) 6897 ȝif heo quakieþ Oþer stepþ biside. 1592 *Arden of Feversham* I. 373, I cannot speak or cast aside my eye, But he Imagines I haue stept awry. 1598 Bastard *Chrestol.* v. xxxiii. 124 He steps awrie, and fals in to Aiax. 1666 Dryden *Ann. Mirab.* cclxv, If my heedless Youth has stept astray.

c. Of an electromechanical device: to move a small, fixed distance in response to an input pulse.

1957 Goode & Machol *System Engin.* iv. 48 The switch steps up through the various banks, taking 0·1 sec to arrive at the first and 0·1 sec to go to each succeeding one. 1958 [see stepping *ppl. a.*]. 1964 *IEEE Trans. Automatic Control* IX. 98/1 The idea of mechanically stepping in angle goes as far back as the clock escapement. 1974 B. C. Kuo *Theory & Applications of Step Motors* i. 4 Many solenoid type motors can step only in one direction. 1978 [see stepper 4].

3. a. In a more general sense: To go or proceed on foot. Now chiefly, to go a 'step' or short distance for a particular purpose: often in polite formulas of request or direction to another person. The direction, etc. is indicated by an adv. or prepositional phr.: for further illustration of these see branches III and IV.

c 900 tr. *Bæda's Hist.* III. xiv. (1890) 196 Se cyning..stop ofostlice toforan [þam] biscope & feoll to his fotum. 1297 R. Glouc. (Rolls) 6293 Is armes he gan to caste & wiþ gret ernest step ner & asailede edmond vaste. *c* 1300 *K. Horn* 1392 (Laud MS.) Þe knyt to hem gan steppe. *a* 1400 *Octouian* 1435 Clement ner þe stede stapte. *c* 1400 *Beryn* 192 And sith to the dynerward they gan for to stappe. 1581 Marbeck *Bk. Notes* 287 S. Luke had before declared that the Apostles did not step from Hierusalem. 1594 Kyd *Cornelia* v. 324, I stept to him To haue embrac'd him. 1704 Cibber *Careless Husb.* v. 59 Step with this to my Lady Graveairs. [Seals the Letter and gives it to the Servant.] 1705 [E. Ward] *Hudibras Rediv.* IV. 12 Who should step by, but Doctor Trotter. 1709 Steele etc. *Tatler* No. 88 ¶ 12 The Gentlewoman of the next House begged me to step thither. 1722 Bp. Atterbury *Let. to Pope* 6 Apr., I may step to town to-morrow, to see how the work goes forward. 1794 Mrs. Inchbald *Wedd. Day* I. ii. 7 Your guardian is just stept home, to bring his wife to dine with us. 1835 Lieber *Stranger in Amer.* I. 262 Passengers who have not paid their passage, please to step to the captain's office! 1837 Carlyle *Fr. Rev.* I. v. v, Besenval, before retiring for the night, has stept over to old M. de Sombreuil, of the *Hôtel des Invalides* hard by. 1847 Tennyson *Princess* VI. (Song), Stole a maiden from her place, Lightly to the warrior stept. 1857 W. Collins *Dead Secret* III. iv, Will you step this way, and see her at once?

fig. 1882 Mrs. Oliphant *Lit. Hist. Eng.* I. 3 All is not absolute good or advantage to the human race; but yet the race is stepping onward.

b. with advb. accusative.

1885–94 Bridges *Eros & Psyche* Oct. i, [She] chose to step the most deserted ways. 1892 Meredith *Sage Enamoured* Poet. Wks. (1912) 382 She stepped her way benevolently grave.

c. ***to step and*** (do something). Now *rare*.

1704 Cibber *Careless Husb.* IV. 46 What say you Ladies, shall we step and see what's done at the Basset-Table? 1764 Foote *Patron* III. Wks. 1799 I. 353 My good girl, will you step, and take care that when any body comes the servants may not be out of the way. 1802 Mrs. E. Parsons *Myst. Visit* IV. 3, I shall step and visit my patient. 1853 Dickens *Bleak Ho.* xlv, Would you step and speak to Mr. Jarndyce?

†**d.** *fig.* To advance, proceed (in an action, argument, etc.). *Obs.*

1599 Hayward *1st Pt. Life Hen. IV*, 65 In priuate attempts a man may step and stope when he please. 1611 G. H. tr. *Anti-Coton* 7 In the Chapter following, hee steps yet one degree farther. 1616 *R. Johnson's Kingd. & Commw.* 177 Yet are they..maintainers of their Honours and Families; wherein they step so far as if true gentrie were incorporat with them. 1620 E. Blount *Horæ Subs.* 107 Liberality is a Vertue, and so is Parsimony within their seueral bounds, but the error is, when the one steps, or the other declines too neere the contrary. 1644 Milton *Divorce* II. xxi. 75 Thus farre by others is already well stept, to inform us that divorce is not a matter of Law but of Charity.

e. ***step-and-repeat*** adj. phr. In photographic printing, etc., involving or pertaining to a procedure in which performance of an operation and progressive movement of something involved in it occur alternately. Also *absol.*

1933 N. Montague in W. Atkins *Art & Pract. Printing* III. xii. 91 The second method consists of exposing a negative on to a coated plate, moving it a definite distance, exposing again and repeating the process... Thus by means of this 'step and repeat' method..one negative may be used for printing a large number of copies. 1954 J. Southward *Mod. Printing* (ed. 7) II. xxxv. 388 The key forme is now made up..for step and repeat. 1967 E. Chambers *Photolitho-Offset* vi. 65 Where multiple repeats are required with great precision step-and-repeat machines are necessary. These are most versatile, and can be used for multi-negative work for postage stamps, labels, cheque backgrounds and the like. 1977 J. Hedgecoe *Photographer's Handbk.* 256 (*heading*) Step-and-repeat images.

†**4.** In past pple. **a.** (***well, far,*** etc.) ***stepped in age, in*** or ***into years***: advanced in years, elderly.

c 1386 Chaucer *Nun's Pr. T.* 1 A poure wydwe, somdel stape [*v.r.* stope] in Age. *Ibid., Merch. T.* 270 And trewely it is an heigh corage Of any man that stapen [*v.r.* stopen] is in age To take a yong wyf. 1513 Douglas *Æneis* VI. v. 23 Allthocht he eildit was, or step in age. *c* 1530 *Crt. of Love* 281 This old, Thus fer y-stope in yeres. 1562 Legh *Armorie* 69 Certaine knyghtes..beynge sore brused, lamed, and well steppte into yeares. 1593 Nashe *Four Lett. Conf.* Wks. (Grosart) II. 253 Shores wife is yong, though you be stept in yeares. 1603 Holland *Plutarch's Mor.* 493 Hellanicus, a man very farre stept in age. 1629 Hobbes *Thucyd.* I. 4 Such of the Rich as were any thing stepped into yeeres. 1629 Maxwell tr. *Herodian* (1635) 112 He was now well stept in yeares.

†**b.** ***far stepped***: far advanced *in* (an action, attainment, etc.). *Obs.*

1594 Carew *Huarte's Exam. Wits* x. (1596) 145 Not so far stept in perfection as the former. 1596 Shaks. *Tam. Shr.* I. ii. 83 Since we are stept thus farre in, I will continue that I broach'd in iest. 1605 —— *Macb.* III. iv. 137, I am in blood Stept in so farre.

5. *colloq.* To go away, make off. Cf. 3 c. Also *to step it.*

c 1400 *Beryn* 2433 Beryn gan to stappe, he sparid for no cost. 1851–61 Mayhew *Lond. Labour* III. 198/1 After I had been with him about three months more I 'stept it' again. 1859 *Hotten's Slang Dict.* 102 *Step it*, to run away or make off. 1902 *Munsey's Mag.* XXIV. 851/2 Well, I must be stepping... It's getting late.

6. Of a horse: To go at a good pace. Also ocularly of persons. Cf. *step out*, 27 c.

1856 [H. H. Dixon] *Post & Paddock* x. 176 The gentler sex seem to step along quite as briskly as their companions. 1857 Hughes *Tom Brown* I. iv, How that ere cob did step! 1891 S. C. Scrivener *Our Fields & Cities* xii. 95 She could 'step' as well as dress herself, and we were very soon on the Hertford road.

7. *Naut.* and *Mech.* Of a mast or other upright: To be fixed *in* its step. Of other parts: To be fixed or jointed *in* or *into* (a groove, etc.); to rest securely *on* or *against* (a support).

1791 Smeaton *Edystone L.* §81 The lower end of the shores stepping against some hole or prominence of the rock. 1797 *Encycl. Brit.* (ed. 3) XVII. 395/2 The quarter-piece.., the heel of which must step on the after end of the middle stool. *Ibid.* 403/1 The partners on the lower deck, wherein the capstan steps. *c* 1850 *Rudim. Navig.* (Weale) 119 *Foot-space rail*, the rail..in which the balusters step. 1869 Sir E. Reed *Shipbuild.* iv. 61 The outer keel-plate..steps up into a rabbet in the side.

8. *colloq.* To clean doorsteps.

1884 *All Yr. Round* 18 Oct. 29/2 A housewife..who will habitually do her own stepping, sublimely regardless of what Mrs. Grundy may say. *Ibid.* 31/1 Or again..they 'step' for houses that are practically in a state of siege.

II. Transitive (causal, or by omission of prep.).

9. To move (the foot) forward or through a specified step. Chiefly with advs., as *down, in, across.* Phr. ***to step foot in*** (a place). Now only *U.S.*

1540 Palsgr. *Acolastus* v. v. A a iv b, Steppe not one foote forth of this place. *a* 1547 Surrey *Compl. Abs. Lover* 2 in *Tottel's Misc.* (Arb.) 19 Good Ladies,..Step in your foote, come take a place, and moorne with me a while. 1705 H. Blackwell *Engl. Fencing-Master* 51 Engage him in Carte, disingage in Tierce, stepping your Right-Foot a-cross at the same Time. 1849 Cupples *Green Hand* xiii. (1856) 130 Stepping one of his long trowser-legs down from over the quarterdeck awning. 1864 R. B. Kimball *Was he Successful?* II. i. 182 When Hiram stepped foot in the metropolis. 1880 S. G. W. Benjamin *Troy* I. iv. 26 (Funk) Calchas announced that the first man who stepped foot on the enemy's soil was doomed at once to die.

10. To measure (a distance) by stepping over it. Also with *off, out.*

1832 S. Warren *Diary Physic.* II. iii. 166 The work of loading being completed, and the distance—six paces—duly stepped out. 1842 Lover *Handy Andy* iii, I, that have stepped more ground and arranged more affairs [*sc.* duels] than any man in the country! 1856 Miss Yonge *Daisy Chain* II. xi. 456 'Hardly space enough I should say,' replied Dr. Spencer, stepping it out. 1859 Jephson *Brittany* xii. 210, I endeavoured to calculate its size by stepping it, and found that the capping-stone measured twelve of my strides. 1863 W. C. Baldwin *Afr. Hunting* ix. 439 To give myself a good idea in rifle-shooting at game, I have been for years constantly judging and stepping off distances.

11. *Naut.* and *Mech.* To fix (a mast or other upright) *in* or *into* its step; to fit (a piece) *into* (a groove, etc.); to fix securely *on* or *against* (a support).

1711 W. Sutherland *Shipbuild. Assist.* F 7 The most convenient Place for stepping every Mast. 1741 Woodroofe in *Hanway's Trav.* (1762) I. II. xvii. 75 We stept our masts and bowsprit. 1815 *Falconer's Dict. Marine* (ed. Burney), *To Step a Boat's Mast*, is to erect and secure it in readiness for setting sail. 1856 Kane *Arct. Expl.* II. xvi. 171 It [the mast] was stepped into an oaken thwart. 1874 Thearle *Naval Archit.* 196 It was customary to dispose the knight head, stem piece, and hawse timbers in a fore and aft plane, stepping their heels against the foremost canted frame that heeled against the deadwood. 1879 Jefferies *Wild Life in S. Co.* 195 These sheds are..supported..by a row of wooden pillars stepped on stones to keep them from rotting. 1892 *Daily News* 24 Oct. 2/6 The new flagstaff..at Windsor Castle was successfully stepped..on Saturday afternoon.

12. *Mech.* To cut steps in (a key); to arrange (the teeth of a toothed wheel or rack) stepwise.

1856 G. Price *Depositories, Locks & Keys* 798 Workmen, who have been stepping keys as they thought quite different from each other, have found that the keys passed each others' locks. 1869 Rankine *Machine & Hand-tools* Pl. M 2, To prevent jarring the teeth of the driving wheels..are stepped. 1895 *Funk's Stand. Dict., Step*,..to cut steps in or adjust tools for cutting steps in (keys or the like).

13. To cause to move or progress intermittently; to cause to assume successively larger or smaller values.

1960 *McGraw-Hill Encycl. Sci. & Technol.* XIII. 356/1 Magnets are provided to step the shaft by means of a pawl mechanism. 1971 *Sci. Amer.* June 85/1 If a series of adjacent loops is energized in sequence, a bubble will be stepped along from one loop to the next. 1977 *New Scientist* 7 Apr. 9/2 You can 'step' the laser from one frequency to another in this way, but cannot tune it continuously. 1977 *Offshore Engineer* Aug. 7/1 In the case of the larger Bass Strait fields ..price rises are likely to be stepped.

III. Intransitive uses with prepositions.

14. step between (or *betwixt*) —. To come between (two persons, a person and thing, etc.) by way of severance, interruption or interception.

1601 Shaks. *All's Well* v. iii. 319 Deadly diuorce step betweene me and you. 1605 *1st Pt. Jeronimo* III. ii. 157 O then stept heauen and I Betweene the stroke. 1615 Heywood *Four Prentices* D 4, Stage-dir., *Bell.* Stay Gentlemen. *Shee steps betweene them.* 1742 Gray *Propertius* II. 12 When..Age step 'twixt love and me, and intercept the joy. 1839 T. Mitchell *Frogs of Aristoph.* 201 *note*, We will no longer step between the reader and his mirth.

15. step into —. a. See sense 3 and into *prep.*

c 1000 Ælfric *Hom.* I. 60 Mid þam ðe se apostol Iohannes stop into ðære byriȝ Ephesum. *c* 1400 *Beryn* 309 He stappid in-to the tapstry wondir pryuely. 1598 Shaks. *Merry W.* IV. ii. 11 Step into th' chamber, Sir Iohn. *a* 1700 Evelyn *Diary* 21 Apr. 1657, I stept into Bedlame, where I saw several poore miserable creatures in chaines. 1732 Swift etc. *Poisoning Curll* Misc. III. 26 He desir'd his Wife to step into the Shop for a Common-Prayer-Book. 1765 Bickerstaff *Maid of Mill* III. ii. 57 But, stay and take a letter, which I am stepping into my study to write. 1832 S. Warren *Diary Physic.* II. ii. 95 Before leaving the house, I stepped into the parlour, to speak a few words to Miss E——.

b. To walk into (a place on a higher or lower level, e.g. a vehicle) by taking one or more steps up or down.

c 1380 *Sir Ferumb.* 5793 If þou wilt ben a crysteman, Mahoun þou most for-sake,..And suþþe stape in-to þis water clere. 1825 T. Hook *Sayings* Ser. II. *Passion & Princ.* xii. 294 The ladies having set all their finery in order,..the party stepped into the coach. 1862 Borrow *Wild Wales* II. x. 105 Your honour can..trifle away the minutes over your wine..till seven, when your honour can step into a first-class for Bangor.

c. To obtain possession of (an estate, a place or office) at a single step; to succeed at once to (the place of another person or thing).

1607 Shaks. *Timon* II. ii. 232 By whose death hee's stepp'd Into a great estate. 1609 Holland *Amm. Marcell.* xxx. viii. 389 Leo.., in case the other, now aloft, should once fall downe from the rocke, was readie to step into his Præfectship. 1671 Trenchfield *Cap Gray Hairs* (1688) 18 The Discourse of [Religious] Ceremonies hath brought things to this pass..that the Circumstances hath stept into the room of the Substance. 1766 Goldsm. *Vic. W.* xx, A gentleman in London who had just stepped into taste and a large fortune. 1802 C. James *Milit. Dict.* s.v., The guards..have the exclusive privilege of going over this intermediate rank, and stepping into a lieutenant-colonelcy at once. 1871 Freeman *Norm. Conq.* IV. xvii. 65 William in short had stepped into the place of those whom he had himself overcome. 1886 C. E. Pascoe *London To-day* xxiii. (ed. 3) 218 Until Button's Coffee-house stepped into the place of 'Will's'.

†**d.** To enter suddenly and incautiously into (a course of action, etc.). *Obs.*

1607 Shaks. *Timon* III. v. 12 A Friend of mine, who in hot blood Hath stept into the Law, which is past depth To those that (without heede) do plundge intoo't. 1648 Fanshawe *Il Pastor Fido*, etc. 304 In pursuance of this fury, about ten years after, Caius Gracchus stept into action (as the Irish call it) to play the second part of his Brother. 1656 in *Burton's Diary* (1828) I. 31, I know no reason for this speed; for we may offend as well in proceeding and sudden stepping into judgments.

16. step on or **upon —. a.** To put the foot down upon; to walk on or over; to tread on (something that lies in the way); *fig.* to come suddenly upon (a person or thing). Also, to set one's foot on (a position) from a higher or lower level or by striding across an intervening space.

a 1000 *Cædmon's Gen.* 1136 Siððan Adam stop on grene græs. a 1000 *Riddles* xxvii. 10 Fuʒles wyn..stop eft on mec. c 1205 LAY. 23861 He þat scip stronge scaf from þan londe and stop uppen þat æit-lond. a 1290 *S. Eustace* 113 in Horstm. *Altengl. Leg.* (1881) 213 Crist.. þat on erþe rod and stop. 1297 R. GLOUC. (Rolls) 6950 Heo stap vpe þis furi yre euerich stape al clene. c 1394 *P. Pl. Crede* 649 For stappyng on a too of a styncande frere. 1417 *E.E. Wills* 27/1 That my body be Beryed in the Chirchhey..as men goth ouer into þe church at þe South Syde, ryȝte as they mowe stappe on me. 1530 PALSGR. 734/2, I steppe upon a thyng, *je saulx par dessus. Ibid.* 735/1, I stepped upon hym or I was ware. 1601 SHAKS. *Twel. N.* III. iv. 306 He payes you as surely, as your feete hits the ground they step on. 1638 JUNIUS *Paint. Ancients* 61 The Poët stepping with Phaëton upon the waggon hath noted..every particular. 1901 ABP. TEMPLE in Sandford *Mem.* (1906) II. 702 The moment we begin to assign motives we are stepping on unsafe ground.

b. ***to step on the gas***: see GAS *sb.*[2] Also, ***to step on it*** (†*her*). *colloq.* (orig. *U.S.*).

1923 R. CROTHERS *Mary the Third* II. i. 53 This is life! Go on, Lynn! *Step on her!* (Lynn bends lower over the wheel.) 1926 MAINES & GRANT *Wise-Crack Dict.* 13/1 *Step on it*, hurry. 1930 F. L. PACKARD *Jimmie Dale & Blue Envelope Murder* xxii. 316 Then for heaven's sake step on it, old man! 1939 G. GREENE *Confidential Agent* IV. ii. 283 'Step on it, Joe.' They ricocheted down the rough path. 1957 'N. SHUTE' *On Beach* i. 27 Get up into it, and I'll step on it and show you how she goes. 1974 K. CLARK *Another Part of Wood* vi. 234 His aim was to complain to M. Jean Zay that he was not getting enough drink. 'Tell him to step on it' he repeated. 1981 C. LEOPOLD *Night Fishers of Antibes* lxxv. 201 All he had to do was to put the Citroën into second and step on it.

17. step out of —. See simple senses and OUT OF *prep.*

1489 CAXTON *Faytes of A.* I. xxiii. E iv, Dyuerse rowes.. full smothly renged and not steppyng out of place. 1588 SHAKS. *Tit. A.* I. i. 391 (Qo.) To step out of these drirrie dumps. 1691 HARTCLIFFE *Virtues* 45 When we step out of the way of Virtue. 1704 NORRIS *Ideal World* II. v. 279 No sooner do we step out of selves, but we launch out into a vast sea of intelligible objects, where we see no shore. 1785 MARTYN *Rousseau's Bot.* xxviii. (1794) 438 But here we are stepping out of our province.

18. step over —. To walk or stride across (an intervening space, cavity or obstacle); *fig.* to OVERSTEP, transgress; to 'skip', miss or neglect in passing; also *Mil.* to be promoted to a position above (another who is considered to have a prior claim).

1387 TREVISA *Higden* (Rolls) VII. 527 (MS. β) ʒif heo stapeth harmles over alle these stappes. c 1440 *Promp. Parv.* 474/2 Steppyn ovyr a thynge, *clunico.* 15.. *Droichis Part of Play* 86 in *Dunbar's Poems* 317 Or he of aige was ʒeiris thre, He wald step over the occiane sie. 1530 PALSGR. 735/1, I wil steppe over this brooke, I holde the a peny. 1546 J. HEYWOOD *Prov.* I. xi. (1867) 34 Where thou wilt not step ouer a straw, I thynke. 1592 SHAKS. *Rom. & Jul.* IV. ii. 27 Not stepping ore the bounds of modestie. 1687 A. LOVELL tr. *Thevenot's Trav.* I. 192 You must step over a great many people,..lying and tumbling confusedly in the Church. 1726 SWIFT *Gulliver* I. iv, I stept over the great western gate. 1746 WESLEY *Princ. Methodist* 39 Stop, Sir. You are stepping over one or two Points, which I have not done with. 1802 C. JAMES *Milit. Dict.*, *To step over*, to rise above another... As, young men of interest and connection frequently step over old soldiers. 1872 EARL OF PEMBROKE & G. H. KINGSLEY *S. Sea Bubbles* i. 23 We strolled about the gardens all the evening, stepping over or picking our way between the numerous babies that were scattered about the ground. 1885 E. GOSSE *Shakesp. to Pope* 146 An intellectual and fanciful..element, which really stepped over the Marinists, and linked the Elizabethans with the classical school.

19. step to —. †To address oneself vigorously to (a task, encounter, etc.). *Obs.*

1530 PALSGR. 734/2 Step to it, man, *hardyment a cela.* Steppe to it agayne and take better holde. 1540 —— *Acolastus* IV. iv. Vj, Let vs goo to it, or steppe to it (lyke men). *Ibid.* v. v. A a iij b, What yf I steppe to it, and diuise some humble prayer to my father.

IV. With adverbs.

20. step aside. *intr.* **a.** To go a little distance away from one's place or from the path one is following; to withdraw or retire for a short distance; to take one or more steps to one's right or left. Also *fig.*

1530 PALSGR. 734/2, I steppe a syde out of the way, *je me desmarche.* Let them lay to my charge what they lyste, I wyll never steppe a syde for it. 1560 DAUS tr. *Sleidane's Comm.* 316 b, He steppeth a side into the countrey by. 1592 SHAKS. *Rom. & Jul.* I. i. 162 See where he comes, so please you step aside. 1600 FAIRFAX *Tasso* XI. lxxx, He stept aside the furious blow to shunne. 1770 LANGHORNE *Plutarch, Timoleon* II. 215 Upon which Timoleon stepped aside, and stood weeping. 1859 *Musketry Instr.* 35 He will leave his rifle on the rest and step aside, in order that the instructor may take his place.

†**b.** To abscond. *Obs.*

1620 in *Crt. & Times Jas. I* (1848) II. 210 Sir John Samms is stept aside and gone for Bohemia,..being..ready to sink under the burthen of his debts. 1689 LUTTRELL *Brief Rel.* (1857) I. 595 The cook was sent to Newgate, but the lord Griffin himself, hearing of it, is stept aside. a 1715 BURNET *Own Time* (1823) II. 153 They did not know whether he might not have stepped aside for debt.

†**c.** To make a digression in discourse. *Obs.*

1653 GATAKER *Vind. Annot. Jer.* 125 Herodote made his History somewhat the more delightful, by stepping aside to tel a tale or two now and then. 1799 J. ROBERTSON *Agric. Perth* 190, I request the indulgence of the reader..while I step aside to give a few directions to the inhabitants of the Highland districts.

d. To deviate from the right path, err, go astray.

1786 BURNS *Addr. to Unco Guid* vii, To step aside is human.

21. step back. (*a*) To go back a little distance, to retire or withdraw a short distance to the rear. (*b*) To go one or more paces backwards without turning the body round. Also *fig.*

1538 ELYOT *Dict.*, *Resulto*, to..to leape or steppe backe. 1544 BETHAM *Precepts War* I. cxliii. G viij b. Whome we muste imbolden..that gladly they wyll marche forwarde, and not to steppe backe for anye ieopardyes. 1605 CHAPMAN *All Fooles* II. i. E 1 b, I stept me backe, and drawing my olde friend heere, Made to the midst of them. 1667 MILTON *P.L.* IV. 820 Back stept those two fair Angels half amaz'd. 1759 JOHNSON *Rasselas* xxxi, The favorite of the Princess, looking into the cavity, stepped back and trembled. 1802 C. JAMES *Milit. Dict.*, *Step Back, March*,..a word of command which is given when one or more men are ordered to take the back step according to regulation. 1857 MRS. GATTY *Parab. Nat.* Ser. II. 65 He stepped back again to the path. 1859 F. A. GRIFFITHS *Artil. Man.* (1862) 6 In stepping back the pace is 30 inches.

22. step down. a. To go from a higher level to a lower, esp. by treading on a step or stairway. Also, to go a short distance to a place which is, or is regarded as, lower. Also *fig.*, to withdraw or retire from office. orig. *U.S.*

a 1400 *St. Alexius* 503 (Trin.) Of here bedde hy sprong.. And hardeliche a-doun stap, þe folk alle among. 1526 TINDALE *John* v. 7 Another stoppeth [? *read* steppeth] doune before me. 1590 *Tarlton's News Purgatory* 33 So he stept downe out of the pulpit. 1818 SCOTT *Br. Lamm.* xxi, Pray, step down to the cellar, and fetch us up a bottle of the Burgundy. 1825 T. HOOK *Sayings* Ser. II. *Passion & Princ.* xi. III. 253, I wish, Macaddle, that to-morrow morning early, you would step down to the Tower, and see the Colonel. 1842 TENNYSON *Beggar Maid* 5 In robe and crown the king stept down. 1890 *Stock Grower & Farmer* 3 May 3/2 If the bureau cannot do this, let the members of it, the lunkheads, step down and resign. 1945 *Sun* (Baltimore) 22 Sept. 5-0/1 (*heading*) Henry Ford steps down: Grandson becomes president of motor company. 1983 *Times* 30 Aug. 1/2 Mr Menachim Begin has pledged to make a final announcement..abou..his intention to step down as Israel's sixth prime minister.

†**b.** To plant the foot firmly on the ground at each step. *Obs.*

1747 *Gentl. Mag.* XVII. 77 Such exercise is not much less salutiferous than riding, if the walker steps down firmly, so as to shake the intestines.

c. *trans.* in *Electr.* To reduce (the voltage of a supply); to reduce the voltage of (a supply).

1903 *Electr. World & Engin.* 8 Aug. 230 (Cent. Suppl.) The..transformers..step the pressure down to 2,000 volts. 1938 [see *scanning coil* s.v. SCANNING *vbl. sb.* 4]. 1978 *Gramophone* Jan. 1340/3 It is also very safe, since it uses only a 12-volt supply, stepped down by a small isolating mains transformer.

23. step forth. To advance a short distance from one's place or position; to come out to the front or into the midst, present oneself before the public; to advance with some immediate purpose in view. Also *fig.* of things.

c 1000 *Ags. Gosp.* John xi. 44 & sona stop forð se þe dead wæs. c 1205 LAY. 25819 Forð he gon steppen. a 1300 *Cursor M.* 10763 Son ilkan wit þair wand forth stepe. 1518 *Sel. Cases Star Chamber* (Selden Soc.) II. 140 Whan they [jurymen] wer callyd and ther namys redd, steppyd forth one Robert Edward and seyd [etc.] 1526 TINDALE *Acts* v. 20 Goo, steppe forthe, and speake in the temple to the people. 1588 SHAKS. *L.L.L.* IV. iii. 151 Now step I forth to whip hypocrisie. 1605 CHAPMAN *All Fooles* II. i. E 1 b, Steps me forth Their valiant fore-man, with the word, I rest you. 1667 MILTON *P.L.* VI. 128 From his armed Peers Forth stepping opposite, half way he met His daring foe. 1674 N. FAIRFAX *Bulk & Selv.* 188 Why might he not 10000 ages before the world was, give it its bidding to step forth? 1837 CARLYLE *Fr. Rev.* I. III. ix, Not for a century and half had Rascality ventured to step forth in this fashion. 1913 D. BRAY *Life-Hist. Brahui* iv. 62 Then those that can shoot a good shot step forth for a match.

24. step forward = *step forth.*

1793 [JOHNSON] *Consid. Coal in Scot.* 56 The gentlemen who, in this exigency, stepped forward to second the efforts of the Magistrates. 1799 HT. LEE *Canterb. T., Frenchm. T.* (ed. 2) I. 300 His comrade, stepping forward, remonstrated with some warmth. 1802 C. JAMES *Milit. Dict.*, *To step forth* or *forward*, to take an active part in any thing. Thus, when the circle was formed, the grenadiers stepped forward to beg off their comrade. 1845 GLADSTONE *Corr. Ch. & Relig.* (1910) I. 349 A rear-rank man steps forward when his front-rank man falls in battle. 1855 *Poultry Chron.* III. 162 Any one who could step forward in this time of no reports with a few facts, would be a public benefactor.

†**b.** To present oneself as the champion of a woman's reputation (with reference to duelling).

1796-7 JANE AUSTEN *Pride & Prej.* xlvii, Could he expect that her friends would not step forward? *Ibid.*, Lydia has no brothers to step forward.

c. *Wrestling.* = *step in*, 25 c.

1898 *Encycl. Sport* II. 547/2 (Wrestling) The hype. After securing a tight grip step forward with the left leg [etc.].

25. step in. a. To come or go indoors; to enter a house or apartment casually or for a short visit. Also, to enter a boat, vehicle, etc.

c 1000 ÆLFRIC *Judg.* iv. 21 Seo wifman..stop inn diʒollice. 1534 TINDALE *John* v. 4 Whosoever then fyrst after the steringe of the water, stepped in, was made whoale. 1622 FLETCHER *Span. Cur.* IV. vi, 'Pray ye let's step in, and see a friend of mine. a 1700 EVELYN *Diary* 19 Aug. 1641, As we returned, we stepped in to see the Spin-house. 1785 MRS. INCHBALD *I'll tell you what* I. i. (1787) 11 Do step in and take your chocolate with her. 1832 HT. MARTINEAU *Ella of Gar.* xi. 138 The little boat pushed off..the three boatmen..having waved their bonnets and cheered before they stept in, in honour of the spectators. 1837 CARLYLE *Fr. Rev.* I. v. viii, Such Deputation is on the point of setting out, —when lo, his Majesty himself, attended only by his two Brothers, steps in. 1898 GIBBS *Cotswold Village* iii. 50 If he could get you to 'step in,' he would offer you gooseberry, ginger, cowslip, and currant wine.

b. To come forward and join in what is going on; to come to close quarters, enter the fray; to intervene in an affair, a dispute, etc. *lit.* and *fig.*

1474 CAXTON *Chesse* III. iii. (1883) 101 His frende..forthwyth stept in and sayde that he hymself was culpable of the deth of this man. 15.. *Christ's Kirk* I. vi, Then Steven cam steppand in with stendis. 1546 J. HEYWOOD *Prov.* I. iii. (1867) 7 While I at length debate and beate the bushe, There shall steppe in other men, and catch the burdes. 1604 SHAKS. *Oth.* II. iii. 229 This Gentleman Steppes in to Cassio, and entreats his pause. 1657 BILLINGSLY *Brachy-Martyrol.* II. i. 150 While they for the crown contended, In step'd the Romans, so the quarrel ended. 1702 ADDISON *Dial. Medals* i. (1726) 30 It is here therefore..that the old Poets step in to the assistance of the Medallist. 1774 GOLDSM. *Nat. Hist.* (1776) IV. 230 Just when, by long labour, the weasel..had removed the board, the monkey stept in, and..fastened it again in its place. 1867 FREEMAN *Norm. Conq.* I. vi. 497 Certain Bishops and other chief men stepped in to preserve peace. 1877 *Ibid.* (ed. 3) II. ix. 407 The three able statesmen who are represented as stepping in [*edd.* 1, 2 intervening] between him and his dangerous vassal.

c. In *Wrestling*, to bring one's leg round the opponent's. In *Cricket*, of a batsman: To advance a step to meet a ball.

1714 PARKYNS *Inn-Play* (ed. 2) 55 Step in with your left Leg the inside of his Right. *Ibid.* 56 At the same time he steps in with his other Leg to turn you. 1837 *New Sporting Mag.* XI. 197 Stepping in to meet the ball... In stepping in the hitter must get well over the ball. 1862 PYCROFT *Cricket Tutor* 35 As to forward play, with an over-pitched ball every first-rate player knows how to step in.

26. step off. a. *intr.* To take one or more steps down and away from a higher level.

1833 T. HOOK *Parson's Dau.* II. i, He [a would-be visitor at a house] stepped off, and turning down Grosvenor Street [etc.].

b. *Mil.* To begin to march at a prescribed pace.

1802 C. JAMES *Milit. Dict.*, *To step off*,..to take a prescribed pace from a halted position, in ordinary or quick time, in conformity to some given word of command or signal... In stepping off to music,..the word of command is the signal to lift up the left foot.

c. *trans.* To mark off by successive equal movements of a leg of the compasses. Cf. 27 d.

1895 ELEANOR ROWE *Chip-carving* 21 Divide the circle into three equal sectors, by stepping off the radius six times upon the circumference.

d. *intr.* To die. Cf. *step out*, sense 27 e below. *slang. rare.*

1926 E. WALLACE *Man from Morocco* iii. 21 There will only be the the bit of money I have when I—er—step off.

27. step out. a. *intr.* (Cf. sense 3.) To go or come out from a place, usually for a short distance or for a short time; esp. to leave the house, go out of doors. Also, to leave a boat or vehicle. Also, to move one or more paces away from one's position.

a 1533 BERNERS *Huon* cxxxiii. 494 He stepte out aparte to behold the batayle. 1576 GASCOIGNE *Kenelw. Castle* Wks. 1910 II. 91 Sibilla being placed in an arbor..did step out and pronounced as foloweth. c 1730 SWIFT *Direct. Serv.*, *General Rules*, When your master..wants a servant who happens to be abroad, your answer must be, that he had but just that minute stept out. 1753 RICHARDSON *Grandison* (1754) II. 4 Sir Charles, stepping out, brought in with him Miss Jervois. 1837 DICKENS *Pickw.* xiv, 'Never mind', said the one-eyed man, calling after the girl as she left the room. 'I'll step out by and by, Mary.' 1857 HUGHES *Tom Brown* II. viii, The first ball of the over Jack steps out and meets, swiping with all his force. 1880 MRS. R. O'REILLY *Sussex Stories* I. 276 Mother's stepped out, and I'm alone up here. *fig.* 1602 tr. *Guarini's Pastor Fido* IV. ii. K 4 b, At each of Siluioes actes My soule stept out, push't on with all her will.

b. *Mil.* To lengthen the pace in marching.

1802 C. JAMES *Milit. Dict.*, *To step out*, to lengthen your pace. 1833 *Reg. Instr. Cavalry* I. 17 On the word *Step out*, the recruit must be taught to lengthen his step to 33 inches.

c. To walk with a vigorous step or stride. Also *transf.* of a ship.

1806 J. DAVIS *Post-Captain* xii. 74 The sailors were making a run of the tackle-falls, and Mr. Hurricane..was heard to exclaim,..'Step out, men! step out! Walk away with him, cheerily!' 1842 *Penny Cycl.* XXIII. 214/1 The truly-bred Suffolk horses are active in their walk..They step out well. 1848 THACKERAY *Van. Fair* xxx, Jack or Donald marches away to glory..stepping out briskly to the tune of 'The Girl I left behind me'. 1859 JEPHSON *Brittany* ix. 140, I therefore stepped out hard, and at length..reached a town. 1867 SMYTH *Sailor's Word-bk.*, *Step out*, to move along simultaneously and cheerfullly with a tackle-fall, &c. 1884 H. COLLINGWOOD *Under Meteor Flag* 250 It was..the weather in which the little 'Vigilant' stepped out to the greatest advantage.

d. *trans.* Cf. *step off* 26 c.

1895 ELEANOR ROWE *Chip-carving* 68 Divide the circumference into six parts by stepping out the radius six times round the circumference.

e. To die; to disappear. *U.S. slang.* ? *Obs.*

1844 *Yale Lit. Mag.* IX. 381 Of the other pieces..some will be found in the present number..and the remainder have '*stept out*'. 1851 T. A. BURKE *Polly Peablossom's Wedding* 177 Ay, dead!—stepped out!—d—d—dead as

Tecumseh! **1903** A. D. McFaul *Ike Glidden* xxx. 277 He is the cause of my ruin. Yes, that is why he stepped out when he did.

f. To appear in company or society; *spec.* to accompany or walk out (*with* a person of the opposite sex); to consort (*with* a lover). *N. Amer. dial.* and *colloq.*

1907 'Mark Twain' in *Harper's Mag.* Dec. 44/2, I thought what a figure I should cut stepping out amongst the redeemed in such a rig. **1918** *Dialect Notes* V. 28 *To step* [*out*], vb. i. To go out with a jane. Usually with an unvirtuous intention. General, but especially college communities. **1934** T. E. Sullinger *Children of Divorce* 9 It affords the father an opportunity to find out how his former wife is spending his alimony, who she is 'stepping out with'. **1936** L. Lefko *Public Relations* 27 She must be cultured —none of those speak-easy belles you step out with will do. **1940** *Chatelaine* June 59/3 Sally's stepping out again! **1955** D. W. Maurer in *Publ. Amer. Dial. Soc.* xxiv. 190 [Support] will continue as long as she does not have anything to do with men; as soon as she 'steps out' and the fact becomes known, her support stops. **1977** *Detroit Free Press* 11 Dec. 11-b/1 Woodard believes Rae is stepping out with Frank.

g. To parachute *out* of a (disabled) aircraft. *R.A.F. slang.*

1942 B. J. Ellan *Spitfire* p. x, If you are unlucky enough to get shot down yourself, you..step out. **1953** R. Chisholm *Cover of Darkness* i. ii. 24 He climbed to ten thousand and he and his observer stepped out as we used to say.

h. *to step out of line*: see line *sb.*[2] 28 b.

28. step together. †**a.** Of two or more persons: To meet or engage in conflict. *Obs.* **b.** Of a pair of horses: To be well matched in pace and action. Also *fig.* of persons, to be in sympathy.

c **1205** Lay. 28408 Heo to-gadere stopen and sturnliche fuhten. **1866** Annie Thomas *Walter Goring* I. i. 5 They stepped together well in fact, and so defied censure. **1880** Miss Braddon *Just as I am* xxi, 'How well Morton and Fan step together!' said Beville, speaking of the dancers as if they were horses.

29. step up. a. *intr.* To go up from a lower position to a higher; to mount, ascend (also *fig.*); *spec.* to go up by treading on a step or stairway. Also, in later use, to go a short distance, or pay a short visit, to a place which is, or is regarded as, higher.

a **1000** *Riddles* xxii. 19 Hy stopan up on oþerne. *a* **1225** *Leg. Kath.* 713 & mid tet ilke step up, & steah to þe steorren. *a* **1240** *Lofsong* in *O.E. Hom.* I. 207 His up ariste do me stepen uwward in heie and holi þeawes. *a* **1400–50** *Wars Alex.* 1437 Sum stepis vp on sties to þe stane wallis. *c* **1400** *Destr. Troy* 351 To this soueravne Citie þat yet was olofte, Jason aioynid and his iust fferis, Steppit vp to a streite streght on his gate. **1758** Jortin *Erasmus* I. 35 He often stepped up to Town.

b. To mount a pulpit, rostrum, or the like.

1535 Coverdale *Acts* v. 20 Steppe vp and speake in the temple to the people. *a* **1700** Evelyn *Diary* 8 Nov. 1644, After him stepp'd up a child of 8 or 9 years old who pronounced an oration. *Ibid.* 4 Dec. 1653, Going this day to our Church I was surpriz'd to see a tradesman, a mechanic, step up.

c. To come forward for some purpose; to leave one's place and come close *to* (a person).

1660 F. Brooke tr. *Le Blanc's Trav.* 6 He..suddenly stept up to him, and..laid him dead at his feete. **1725** De Foe *Voy. round World* (1840) 88 One of our men stepped up to the fellow. **1764** in *R. S. Hawker's Footpr. Far Cornw.* (1870) 62, I made up my mind to..step up and ask his name right out. **1840** Thackeray *Barber Cox* Jan., 'A mighty wet day, sir,' says I to Mr. Hock, stepping up and making my bow.

†**d.** *fig.* To arise, come suddenly into prominence.

1577 Hanmer *Anc. Eccl. Hist., Socrates* ii. xxviii. 279 At Antioche in Syria there stept vp an other hereticke. **1610** Knolles *Hist. Turks* Induct. to Rdr., There stept vp among the Turks in Bythinia one Osman or Othoman.

e. *Wrestling.* To bring one's leg up (between the opponent's legs).

1714 Parkyns *Inn-Play* (ed. 2) 51 Step up with your left Leg betwixt his Legs.

f. *trans.* To bank up in steps.

1901 S. B. Miles in *Geogr. Jrnl.* (R.G.S.) XVIII. 480 The terraces being stepped up with revetments wherever the natural features of the ground had not availed, to maintain the earth in position.

g. *Electr.* To increase (the voltage of a supply) by means of a transformer; to increase the voltage of (a current).

1902 S. Sheldon & H. Mason *Altern.-Current Machines* 154 The autotransformer is used to step-up the voltage..to 500 volts. **1909** *Electrician* 2 July 463/1 By means of the three resonance relays..the telephone current was stepped up to 10^{-2} amperes and audible working obtained. **1912** *Nature* 21 Nov. 346/1 One method to obtain this is to step up by means of an E.H.T. transformer. **1956** A. H. Compton *Atomic Quest* i. 14 Step up the voltages used in our experiments with nuclei, and we should expect to produce interesting nuclear reactions. **1980** J. W. Hill *Intermediate Physics* xxi. 205 The transformer can step up or step down voltages.

h. *fig.* To raise to a higher level or standard, by a stage or stages. More widely, to advance gradually; to increase, intensify.

1920 *Glasgow Herald* 8 July 7 They would suggest that this increase..should be 'stepped up' over a period of years. **1931** *Amer. Speech* VII. verso rear cover (Advt.), Can you 'step-up' education to meet the new requirements of society? **1938** *Sun* (Baltimore) 5 Sept. 8/8 Soon after they had cleared the Hanover street bridge they stepped up their stroke. **1941** *Punch* 19 Feb. 173/2 People have..stepped their ideas up..about the telephone; I mean, nowadays very few of them actually brush their hair before answering. **1958** *Spectator* 18 July 117/1 The output..could be quickly stepped up. **1967** *Listener* 23 Mar. 390/2 An Aden nationalist leader says terrorist activity will be stepped up when U.N. mission arrives. **1978** K. Hudson *Jargon of Professions* ii. 50 The war in Vietnam was being stepped up. **1982** *Times* 25 Oct. 6/1 The Solidarity underground..stepped up its pressure this weekend on..the beleaguered Polish leader.

V. 30. The vb.-stem in combination with advbs. and preps. **step-on** *a. U.S.*, that may be operated by pressure of the foot. See also step-down, -in, -out, -up.

1945 *Richmond* (Va.) *Times-Dispatch* 9 Nov. 24 (Advt.), Step-on pail. **1978** *Detroit Free Press* 5 Mar. a 20 (Advt.), Powerful cleaner has..Convenient step-on switch, easy-change bag holder.

step, var. stap *Sc.* and *north.*, stave of a tub.

step-, OE. *stéop-* (earlier *stéup-*, Northumb. *stéap-*), corresponding to OFris. *stiap-*, *stiep-* (NFris. *stjap-*, *sjap-*, *stîp-*, WFris. *stiep-*), MLG. (irreg.) *stêf-* (mod. LG. *staif-*), (M)Du. (irreg.) *stief-*, OHG. *stiuf-* (MHG., mod.G. *stief-*), ON. *stjúp-*, (MSw. *stiup-*, *stiuf-*; mod.Sw. *stiuf-*, *styf-*; Da. *stif-*, *stiv-*, now superseded by *sted-*):—OTeut. **steupo-*; a Com. Teut. combining element (not recorded in Gothic), prefixed to terms of relationship (as son, father, brother) to form designations for the degrees of affinity resulting from the remarriage of a widowed parent. The primitive sense of the word is indicated by the use of OE. *stéopbearn*, *-cild* (stepbairn, stepchild) for 'orphan', and by the cognates, OE. *ástieped* bereaved, OHG. *stiufen* (also *ar-*, *bistiufen*) to bereave. Etymologically, *stepfather* (*stepmother*) might be rendered 'one who becomes a father (mother) to an orphan', and *stepson* (*stepdaughter*) 'an orphan who becomes a son (a daughter)' by the marriage of the surviving parent. It is uncertain which of these two applications of the prefix is the original one; all branches of Teut. (exc. Gothic) have both, and also the extended use in *stepbrother*, *stepsister*. ON. had shortened forms, *stjúpa* stepmother, *stjúp-r* (mod.Icel. *stjúpi*) stepson. In Du. and LG., and in later Scandinavian, the *p* of OTeut. **steupo-* is anomalously represented by *f* instead of *p*. This is prob. not due to HG. influence, but to assimilation to the following *f* in the compound *stepfather* (cf. the early ME. form *steffadyr*). A solitary OE. example of this anomaly occurs in the form *stéfdohtor* (quot. 912 s.v. stepdaughter). Occasional forms of the prefix in ME. are *stip-* (*styp-*), *sti-*, *ste-*, *stappe-*.

In 1755 Johnson says that *stepmother* is the only one of the compounds of *step-* that has survived in general use. At the present day *stepfather* is hardly less frequently used, and *stepson*, *-daughter*, *-child*, *-brother*, *-sister* are by no means rare, while *stepdame* occurs in somewhat archaistic language (chiefly *fig.*). In the 16th and 17th c. a few writers employed the prefix in nonce-formations which would now seem un-English, as *step-devil*, a term of abhorrence for a stepmother; *step-duchess*, the stepmother of a duke's children; *step-lord*, one who has the position of a lord without the true lord's affection for his subjects; *step-Tully*, one who assumes the function of a Cicero. New formations with the prefix, denoting actual relations of affinity, do not appear earlier than the 19th c.; in the latter part of the century they became somewhat common, chiefly as more or less jocular nonce-words, though one or two of them, as *step-nephew*, *-niece*, have obtained some currency in serious use.

The concept of orphanage has recently ceased to be essential to the meaning of the *step-* combinations. Consequently, the relationships of *step-brother*, *-sister*, etc., may be considered to refer reciprocally to children of a later as well as a former marriage: i.e. step-brother = half-brother, etc. A step-parent may be created by marriage to a divorced or a bereaved person.

The older compounds of *step-* are in this Dictionary treated as main words; the following examples illustrate the extended applications of the prefix from the 16th c. onwards.

1549 Latimer *1st Serm. bef. Edw. VI* (Arb.) 39 You landelordes, you rentreisers, I maye saye you steplordes, you vnnaturall lordes, you haue for your possessions yerely to much. **1593** G. Harvey *Pierce's Super.* Wks. (Grosart) II. 74 His betters will neuer pen such a peec of Latin, whosoeuer wer the Stepp-Tully. **1607** Tourneur *Rev. Trag.* i. ii, Was't euer knowne step-Dutchesse was so milde. **1633** *Costlie Whore* iv. iii. in Bullen *O. Pl.* IV. 283 Oh she was vertuous,..But this step-divell doth promise our fall. **1812** Miss L. M. Hawkins *C'tess & Gertrude* I. 244 Mr. Sterling, the step-uncle to the countess. **1825–9** Mrs. Sherwood *Lady of Manor* V. xxxii. 349 'And I am heartily glad of it,' said the old man... 'I am much mistaken, if, after all, the step-lady [*sc.* a stepmother] will not prove the best friend.' **1839** Burgon *Life Sir T. Gresham* II. vii. 400 Her maternal step-grandmother. **1852** Miss Sewell *Exp. Life* xi. (1858) 84 She is a step-niece of Major Colston. **1868** L. H. Morgan *Syst. Consanguinity* (1870) 482 Since the step-relationships are not discriminated. **1876** Mrs. Whitney *Sights & Insights* ii, She is also my cousin; that is, my step-cousin. **1893** 'Mark Twain' in *Century Mag.* Jan. 346/2 Yes; he's my steppapa, and the dearest one that ever was. **1895** Black *Briseis* ii, I never know what that excellent step-papa of mine may be up to. **1898** *Westm. Gaz.* 5 Sept. 8/2 Mrs. Neale, step-granddaughter of the wife of Lord Nelson. **1900** Mary E. Wilkins *Love of Parson Lord* 40 Richard Pierce, the squire's step-grandson. **1904** *Westm. Gaz.* 4 Jan. 3/2 The step-sisters and step-aunts. **1905** R. Bagot *Passport* vii. 69 It had amused him to address no small part of his conversation to his step-niece during these little dinners. **1924** G. B. Stern *Tents of Israel* vii. 105 Val,..the eldest step-grandchild..had returned from Vienna especially not to miss the occasion. **1936** M. Mitchell *Gone with Wind* xlvii. 844 Ah ain' gwine leave Miss Ellen's gran' chillun fer no trashy step-pa ter bring up. **1959** 'E. H. Clements' *High Tension* v. 83 His step-cousin's [neck] rose..from an open-necked shirt. **1960** M. Spark *Ballad Peckham Rye* vii. 130 Your step-dad's on about young Leslie. **1962** *Listener* 10 May 828/1 A comic private detective, besides step-mum and callous dad. **1974** D. Francis *Knock Down* xii. 146 My new step-mama will be able to maintain us in the style to which we are accustomed. **1980** M. McMullen *My Cousin Death* (1981) vii. 82 He's some kind of step-relative, and he's on his uppers. **1982** *Listener* 23—30 Dec. 12/1 Christmas for many will either be as desolate as an Oxford Street Santa's heart or so extended—what with the myriads of stepfathers, stepmothers, step-siblings, step-uncles and step-aunts—as to conjure up images of those family groupings which American family therapists love to gather for what they call 'working together'.

stepbairn ('stɛpbɛən), *sb.* [OE. *stéopbearn*: see step-. Cf. ON. *stjúpbarn* (Sw. *styfbarn*, Da. *stifbarn*) in sense 2.]

†**1.** An orphan. *Obs.*

c **1000** Ælfric *Saints' Lives* ix. 63 þæt mann.. steopbearnum ȝehelpe. *c* **1175** *Lamb. Hom.* 115 He scal biwerian widewan and steopbern. *a* **1340** Hampole *Psalter* ix. 38 Til stepbarn þou sall be helpere.

2. *Sc.* A stepson or stepdaughter; = stepchild 2.

1535 Stewart *Cron. Scot.* III. 402 Suppois scho wes bot hir stepbarne as than. **1631** Rutherford *Lett.* (1862) I. 76 And that if any were a Stepbairn, in respect of comfort and sense, it were rather myself than His poor bairns. **1721** J. Kelly *Sc. Prov.* 328 That's the piece the Step-Bairn never got. **1909** R. J. Drummond *Faith's Cert.* 329 There are no step-bairns in the family of God.

Hence †'**stepbairn** *v. Sc.*, *trans.* to treat as a step-child.

1606 Birnie *Kirk-Buriall* (1833) 34 Why doe they so partially step-barne the pursse-miserable poore from such a soul-helpe?

stepbrother ('stɛpbrʌðə(r)). [See step-. Cf. MHG. *stiefbruoder* (mod.G. *stiefbruder*).] A son, by a former marriage, of one's stepfather or stepmother.

1440 *Promp. Parv.* 474/1 Stepbrothyr, of the fadyrs syde, *victrigenus*. Stepbroder, on the modyrs syde, *novercatus*. **1530** Palsgr. 276/1 Stepbrother, *beau frere*. **1828** in Webster. **1868** L. H. Morgan *Syst. Consanguinity* (1870) 482 These are step-brothers and step-sisters to the children of their mother's sisters. **1869** J. Eadie *Galatians* 89 If, then, the theory of step-brethren or cousins be surrounded with difficulties. **1882** Farrar *Early Chr.* I. 510 Whether he [*sc.* St. James] were a half-brother or only a step-brother of Jesus.

Hence '**stepbrotherhood**.

1869 J. Eadie *Galat.* 78 For the theory of step-brotherhood, there is no explicit evidence in Scripture.

stepchild ('stɛptʃaɪld). [OE. *stéopcild*: see step-. Cf. OHG. *stiufchint* (MHG. *stiefkint*, mod.G. *-kind*).]

†**1.** An orphan. *Obs.*

971 *Blickl. Hom.* 45 þonne sæȝde Sanctus Paulus þæt se biscop nære miltsiende wydewum, ne steopcildum, ne nanum Godes þearfan. *c* **1000** *Ags. Gosp.* John xiv. 18 Ne læte ic eow steopcild. *a* **1300** *E.E. Psalter* xciii. 6 Widow and comeling slogh þai, And stepchildre þai drape al dai.

2. A stepson or stepdaughter.

c **1350** *Will. Palerne* 131 þan studied sche stifly, as step-moderes wol alle, To do dernly a despit to here stepchilderen. **1631** [see stepfather]. **1868** L. H. Morgan *Syst. Consanguinity* (1870) 482 Their children by other wives would be my step-children. **1889** S. Walpole *Ld. John Russell* I. xiii. 340 Lord John went down with his children and step-children to Buckhurst.

b. *transf.* and *fig.*

1407–10 Hoccleve *Min. Poems* (1892) 58 Let me no step-chyld been for I am he That hope haue in yow, confort & gladnesse. *c* **1450** Lovelich *Grail* xlviii. 385 Whiles that ȝe to God diden take, thanne was he to ȝow fadyr ful kynde.. and sethen that stepchildren that ȝe ben, he hath ȝow forȝeten ful Clen. **1774** Goldsm. *Nat. Hist.* V. 266 It parts good friends, the step-child [*sc.* the young cuckoo] seldom offering any violence to its nurse. **1911** *Q. Rev.* Jan. 150 The navy has been the step-child of both parliaments.

stepdame ('stɛpdeɪm). Now *arch.* Also 4 **stedame**. [f. step- + dame (sense 8).] A stepmother.

1387 Trevisa *Higden* (Rolls) V. 273 Vortymerus deide, þoruȝ venym of his stedame Rowen. *c* **1400** Maundev. (Roxb.) xxv. 120 þai wedd..þaire stepdames efter þe deed of þaire faders. **1590** Spenser *F.Q.* i. v. 39 His cruell step-dame. **1667** Milton *P.L.* iv. 279 Where old Cham..Hid Amalthea and her Florid Son, Young Bacchus, from his Stepdame Rhea's eye. **1697** Dryden *Virg. Past.* iii. 48 A Step-dame too I have, a cursed she, Who rules my Hen-peck'd Sire, and orders me. **1818** Scott *Hrt. Midl.* ix, Other stepdames have tried less laudable means for clearing the way to the succession of their own children. **1894** Lowell tr. *Kalevala* in *Century Mag.* May 27/2 Small and weak my mother left me..In the keeping of the stepdame.

b. *fig.*

1387 Trevisa *Higden* (Rolls) I. 5 Forȝetingnes all wey kypinge þe craft of a stepdamme, he is enmy of mynde. **1395** Purvey *Remonstr.* (1851) 137 Necligence is stepdame of lernynge. **1447** Bokenam *Seyntys, Marg.* 942 To eschewyn prolixyte, Stepdam of fauour. **1563-87** FOXE *A. & M.* (1596) 257/2 The church of Rome, which of a mother is become a stepdame. **1598** BARRET *Theor. Warres* v. ii. 131 An ouer commaunding mount is a stepdame to a fortresse. **1646** EARL MONM. tr. *Biondi's Civil Wars* VI. 8 Vertue the mother of courage..when it meets with desperation the step-dame of courage. **1730** T. BOSTON *Mem.* xii. 512 The world hath been a step dame to me. **1866** CARLYLE *Remin.* (1881) I. 219 What a tragic, treacherous stepdame is vulgar Fortune to her children!

c. *attrib.*

1800 CAMPBELL *Lines Grave Suicide* 13 To feel the step-dame buffetings of fate. **1827** HEBER *Europe* 99 And dread the step-dame sway of unaccustom'd war. **1837** CARLYLE *Fr. Rev.* I. VI. v, Did Nature..fling thee forth, stepdame-like, a Distraction into this distracted Eighteenth Century?

stepdaughter (ˈstɛpdɔːtə(r)). [OE. *stéopdohtor*: see STEP-. Cf. MLG. *stêfdochter*, Du. *stiefdochter*, MHG., mod.G. *stieftochter*, ON. *stjúpdóttir* (Sw. *styfdotter*, Da. *stifdatter*).] A daughter, by a former marriage, of one's husband or wife.

a **850** *Kentish Glosses* in Wr.-Wülcker 88/20 *Filiaster*, steopdohtor. **912** *MS. Vesp. D xiv.* lf. 170 *Prouigna*, stefdohtor. **1387** TREVISA *Higden* (Rolls) V. 103 Theodora þe step-douȝter [**1432-50** tr. *Higden* stappe-doȝhter] of Herculeus Maximianus. **14..** *Lat.-Eng. Voc.* in Wr.-Wülcker 605 *Pri-vigna*, a stypdowtur. **1581** PETTIE tr. *Guazzo's Civ. Conv.* III. (1586) 121 In families there are.. the step Mother, and the steppe Daughter, the Coosins and Allies. **1681** FOUNTAINHALL *Hist. Notices* (Bannatyne Club) I. 343 Lady Sophia Lindsay, his stepdaughter. **1791** BOSWELL *Johnson* an. 1776, Next morning he introduced me to Mrs. Lucy Porter, his step-daughter. **1913** C. READ in *Eng. Hist. Rev.* Jan. 48 Leicester was planning to marry his step-daughter to James.

Hence **ˈstepdaughtership**.

1876 MRS. WHITNEY *Sights & Insights* xiii, She was keenly delicate of her step-daughtership.

ˈstep-down, *a.* and *sb.* [f. vbl. phr. to *step down*: see STEP *v.* 22.] **A.** *attrib.* or as *adj.*

1. In sense 22c of the vb.: causing or pertaining to a reduction in voltage or some other quantity.

1893 SLOANE *Electr. Dict.*, *Step-down* adj...applied to a converter or transformer in the alternating current distribution, indicating that it lowers potential difference and increases current from the secondary. **1929** *Exper. Wireless* VI. 307/2 This reduces the step down ratio required in the potentiometer. **1947** R. LEE *Electronic Transformers & Circuits* vi. 172 Driver transformers are usually step-down because the grid potentials are relatively low. **1959** *Motor Man.* (ed. 36) 95 It has a stepdown gear which reduces the speed of the propeller shaft in a ratio which is usually between 5 to 1 and 4 to 1. **1961** *Wall St. Jrnl.* (Eastern ed.) 14 Nov. 10 (Advt.), With Con Edison's step-down rates, the more electricity you use, the less it costs per kilowatt-hour. **1981** *Daily Tel.* 22 July 12/6 For really rough going there is a 1·96:1 step-down ratio for four-wheel-drive.

2. In sense 22a of the vb. Esp. from or in which one steps to a lower level. Chiefly *U.S.*

1949 *Newsweek* 28 Nov. 56 (*caption*) Hudson enters lower-priced field with smaller version of step-down car. **1954** *Sun* (Baltimore) 8 Mar. 20/1 Dr. Clifford M. Witcher..calls his device a 'step-down detector'. When the user approaches a curb, a flight of steps or the edge of a sub-way platform, the detector buzzes a warning. **1966** A. R. BELLAMY in *Biochim. & Biophys. Acta* CXXIII. 102 (*title*) RNA synthesis in exponentially growing tobacco cells subjected to a step-down nutritional shift. **1976** *Billings* (Montana) *Gaz.* 27 June 5-D/4 (Advt.), Three bedrooms, step-down living room, and main floor family room with fireplace.

B. *sb.* **1.** A reduction or decrease.

1922 [see REGENERATIVE *a.* (and *sb.*) 2 b]. **1962** A. NISBETT *Technique Sound Studio* ix. 165 The result is a sudden step-down in volume and quality just before the second signal appears on the tape.

2. The act of stepping down or withdrawing from a position.

1973 *Guardian* 7 June 2/4 In a cleverly disguised step-down from the position that these controversial logs would never be released, Mr Nixon's spokesman said today that.. the documents would now be turned over.

stepe, obs. form of STEEP.

stepell(e, stepende: see STEEPLE, STIPEND.

stepfather (ˈstɛpfɑːðə(r)). Forms: 1 stéupfædær, stéopfæder, 4 stifader, -dre, steffader; 4- step- (see FATHER *sb.*). [OE. *stéopfæder* (see STEP-) = OFris. *stiapfeder* (NFris. *stjåpfader*, *sjapfar*, WFris. *stiepfader*), MLG. *stēfvadere*, Du. *stiefvader*, OHG. *stiuffater* (MHG., mod.G. *stiefvater*), ON. *stjúpfaðer* (Sw. *styffader*, Da. *stiffader*).] A man who has married one's mother after one's father's death or divorce.

c **825** *Epinal Gloss.* 1070 *Vitricius*, steupfaedaer. *c* **893** ÆLFRED *Oros.* I. viii. 42 Adipsus [i.e. Oedipus]..æȝþer ofsloh ȝe..his steopfæder, ȝe his steopsunu. **13..** *Sir Beues* 464 Beten ichaue me stifadre Wiþ me mace. **1387** TREVISA *Higden* (Rolls) I. 93 Medus..folowed þe dedes of Iason þat was his owne stepfader. *c* **1489** CAXTON *Sonnes of Aymon* iii. 83 It is no loue of a natureill fader, but it is rigoure of a stepfader. **1538** ELYOT *Dict.*, *Vitricus*, a father in lawe or steppefather. **1631** ANCHORAN *Comenius' Gate Tongues* 123 A stepfather, & stepmother, loue not very well their steppe sonnes, or steppe children. **1737** *Gentl. Mag.* VII. 30/2, I am not your own Child, but was adopted by one of your former Husbands; who..proved an excellent Step-Father to me. **1874** STUBBS *Const. Hist.* II. xiv. 46 He was the stepfather of Arthur of Brittany.

b. *transf.* and *fig.*

c **1325** *Metr. Hom.* 123 Hir [*sc.* the Church's] steffader cal I the Fend, For igain hir es he unhende. **1380** WYCLIF *Sel. Wks.* III. 335 þis weiward steffadris of mennus soulis. **1628** WITHER *Brit. Rememb.* v. 128 Who but Stepfathers to their Poemes be. **1705** HICKERINGILL *Priest-cr.* II. viii. 86 Kings, if they be Wise for themselves will be Nursing Fathers,.. not Stepfathers. **1865** KINGSLEY *Herew.* xv, 'Dare we resist the Holy Father?' 'Holy step-father, you mean.' **1888** BRYCE *Amer. Commw.* liii. II. 327 [Washington] was commonly called by them 'The stepfather of his country.'

¶ **c.** A father-in-law. (? A conscious misuse.)

a **1625** FLETCHER *Double Marr.* IV. i, *Pand.* [to Juliana, his daughter-in-law] A word or two of a kind step-father I'll have put in.

Hence **ˈstepfatherly** *a.*

1912 *Nation* 23 Mar. 1012/1 His step-fatherly rule does not kill even his own officialism.

‖**stephane** (ˈstɛfæniː). *Antiq.* [Gr. στεφάνη, related to στέφανος crown.] A kind of diadem or coronet, represented in statuary as worn by the goddess Here and other deities; also worn by military commanders.

1847 LEITCH tr. *C. O. Müller's Anc. Art* §425. 505 The three figures on vases with high stephane (ὄγκος?) seem to be statues in the stage costume of Hercules, Hermes and a third. **1858** BIRCH *Anc. Pottery* I. 407 Hera is adorned with the stephane, or diadem. **1875** F. HUEFFER tr. *Guhl & Koner's Life Greeks & Romans* 235 The helmets of the common soldiers were generally without ornaments, those of the officers only being decorated with figures or patterns; the cap, visor, and stephane were frequently covered with these.

stephanial (stɪˈfeɪnɪəl), *a.* [f. STEPHANION + -AL[1].] Of or pertaining to the stephanion.

1891 *Century Dict.* A stephanial point.

Stephanian (stɪˈfeɪnɪən), *a.* *Geol.* [ad. F. *stéphanien* (A. de Lapparent *Traité de Géol.* (ed. 3, 1893) 819), f. *Stephan-us*, latinized form of Saint-*Etienne*, name of a city in central France where it is represented: see -IAN.] Of, pertaining to, or designating the uppermost division of the Carboniferous in Europe, especially where represented by coalbearing formations. Also *absol.*

1901 *Jrnl. Geol.* IX. 196 The flora of the Caradons stage contains a mingling of uppermost Westphalian species with Stephanian types. **1903** A. GEIKIE *Text-bk. Geol.* (ed. 4) II. 1051 Stephanian. **1912** A. J. JUKES-BROWN *Student's Handbk. Stratigr. Geol.* (ed. 2) x. 317 A few small tracts of Stephanian measures occur in Brittany and Normandy... The most northern of these is at Littry.., the Coal-measures here..being conformably overlain by Permian Beds, and they belong, therefore, to the latest phase of the Stephanian. **1931** GREGORY & BARRETT *Gen. Stratigr.* vii. 118 The Stephanian is absent from the N. of France and Westphalia, and is present in numerous coalfields preserved in basins in the pre-Palaeozoic rocks of the Central Plateau of France. **1959** [see DINANTIAN *a.*]. **1963** [see SAKMARIAN *a.*].

stephanic (stɪˈfænɪk), *a.* *Craniometry.* [a. F. *stéphanique*: see STEPHANION and -IC.] Pertaining to the stephanion.

1878 BARTLEY tr. *Topinard's Anthrop.* II. ii. 249 The superior and maximum frontal or stephanic diameter upon the temporal ridge. **1884** J. G. GARSON in *Jrnl. Anthrop. Inst.* XIV. 129 Viewed from the *norma frontalis*, the arch of the top of the cranium is markedly flat, giving the stephanic region a somewhat angular appearance.

‖**stephanion** (stɪˈfeɪnɪən). *Craniometry.* Pl. -ia, -ions. [mod.L. use of Gr. στεφάνιον, dim. of στέφανος crown.] The point where the coronal suture crosses the temporal ridge.

1878 BARTLEY tr. *Topinard's Anthrop.* II. ii. 248 Whose two measuring points are the stephanions at the union of the temporal ridge and the coronal suture. **1886** A. MACALISTER in *Jrnl. Anthrop. Inst.* XVI. 22 A transverse green band of staining crosses the bone above the frontal eminences from stephanion to stephanion. **1902** DUCKWORTH *Ibid.* XXXII. 142 In the coronal suture on each side at and below the stephania.

stephanite (ˈstɛfənaɪt). *Min.* [ad. G. *stephanit* (Haidinger, 1845), named after the Archduke Stephan of Austria: see -ITE.] Sulphantimonide of silver, black in colour and very brittle.

1849 J. NICOL *Man. Min.* 493. **1877** RAYMOND *Statist. Mines & Mining* 195 A 50-foot quartz-vein, carrying disseminated stephanite.

stephanome (ˈstɛfənəʊm). [irreg. f. Gr. στέφανο-ς crown (taken in the sense of CORONA 1) + -νόμος distributor.] An instrument for measuring the angular dimensions of fog-bows, halos, etc.

1889 *Times* 21 Mar. 3/3 The stephanome..is used for measuring the angular size of halos, fog-bows, and glories at the Ben Nevis Observatory. **1890** *Lond.* etc. *Philos. Mag.* Ser. v. XXIX. 454 *note*, A stephanome, consists of a graduated bar, at one end of which the eye is placed, and in which slides a cross-bar carrying certain projections. With its aid faint objects, for which a sextant would be useless, may be measured to within 5′.

†**stephanophore.** *Obs. rare*[−1]. [ad. Gr. στεφανοφόρος wearing a crown, f. στέφανο-ς crown + -φόρος (related to φέρειν to bear).] (See quot.)

1624 DARCIE *Birth of Heresies* xii. 51 The Herculean Pontifes, called for this reason Stephanophores, as wearing a Crowne vpon their heads.

stephanotis (stɛfəˈnəʊtɪs). [mod.L. (L. M. A. A. Dupetit-Thouars *Genera Nova Madagascariensia* (1806) 11), a. Gr. στεφανωτίς fem. adj., fit for a crown or wreath, f. στέφανος crown.]

1. ‖**a.** *Bot.* A genus of tropical asclepiadaceous twining shrubs having fragrant white flowers. **b.** A plant of this genus; a flower of such a plant.

1843 *Curtis's Bot. Mag.* LXX. 4058 (*heading*) Copious-flowering Stephanotis. **1869** S. R. HOLE *Bk. about Roses* iii. 41 The stove, truly, is a gladness and refreshment—gay.. with the golden Allamandas,..the bridal Stephanotis. **1870** DISRAELI *Lothair* xxxi, The voice was as sweet as the stephanotis. **1882** *Cornh. Mag.* Apr. 390 With a sprig of stephanotis in his buttonhole.

2. A perfume said to be prepared from the flowers of *Stephanotis floribunda*.

1895 *Army & Navy Co-op. Soc. Price List* 716/1 A new fragrant Toilet Water in Jockey Club, White Rose, Stephanotis, [etc.]. **1907** H. WYNDHAM *Flare of Footlights* xvii, A sickly odour of stephanotis arose from it [the letter]. **1980** M. FORSTER *Bride of Lowther Fell* xvi. 244 The perfume was..stephanotis, faint and unbelievably fragrant.

Stephen: see *even Stephen* s.v. EVEN *a.* 14d.

stephne, obs. form of STEVEN *sb.*[1]

stepil(l, obs. forms of STEEPLE.

stepille, obs. Sc. form of STAPLE *sb.*[1]

1597 in *Spalding Club Misc.* I. Pref. 53 Joggis, Stepillis, and Lockis.

ˈstep-in, *sb.* and *a.* [f. vbl. phr. *to step in*: see STEP *v.* 25.]

A. *sb.* A garment or shoe put on by stepping into it; *spec.* in *pl.*, loose drawers (more recently, brief panties) for women (chiefly *U.S.*).

1922 *Woman's Home Compan.* June 70 (*caption*) The children like to wear step-ins. **1928** *Sunday Dispatch* 15 July 16 The same *couturière* is all for 'step ins' for swimmers. **1934** [see SCANTY *sb.*]. **1939** M. B. PICKEN *Lang. Fashion* 131/1 *Step-in*, shoe with no obvious method of fastening, usually held on snugly by an elastic gore. **1946** WODEHOUSE *Money in Bank* xxvii. 234 A bottle of brandy which she.. kept stowed away..in a drawer underneath her step-ins. **1958** S. ELLIN *Eighth Circle* (1959) II. xx. 208 Her brassière and step-ins plastered wetly to her body. **1964** P. WHITE *Burnt Ones* 86 Eileen began to pull. Her step-ins had eaten into her. **1975** J. GORES *Hammett* (1976) xxii. 153 The upended torcher wore no step-ins under her tight red sequins.

B. *attrib.* or as *adj.* Designating a garment or shoe of this type.

1923 *Weekly Dispatch* 18 Feb. 12 Step-in cami-knickers. **1960** *Amer. Speech* XXXV. 79 These dresses were listed variously as..'a step-in sundress of acetate', and 'a step-in charmer'. **1975** *Times* 3 May 8/2 The 'step-in' dress with buttons down the front, which permitted a woman to step into a dress instead of pulling it over her head.

Stepin Fetchit (ˈstɛp(ə)n ˈfɛtʃɪt). *U.S.* Also Steppin Fetchit. [*Stepin Fetchit*, the stage-name of Lincoln Theodore Perry (b. 1902), a popular Black vaudeville actor noted for playing a series of fawning characters in Hollywood films of the 1920s and 1930s. For earlier uses of the sb. phr. *step and fetch it* applied to persons, see *Eng. Dial. Dict.*, *Dialect Notes* (1903) II. 301, (1914) IV. 113.] A type of a shuffling, obsequious, Black servant. Hence, any servile Black man; an Uncle Tom. Also *attrib.*

1940 F. SCOTT FITZGERALD *Let.* 1 Feb. (1964) 597 This way of looking at war gives great scope for comedy without bringing in Stepin Fetchit and Hattie McDaniel as faithful negro slaves. **1951** MCWHINEY & SIMKINS in A. Dundes *Mother Wit* (1973) 588/1 The mere mention of a ghost makes him shake as actively as Step'in Fetch'it under the influence of an Arctic breeze. **1967** P. WELLES *Babyhip* xvii. 121 He shrugged his shoulders in his phoney Steppin Fetchit pose and went home leaving a perfectly groovy [chess] strategy unfinished. **1968** *N.Y. Times* 21 Feb. 56/3 He talks disparagingly of comics and other artists who don't fill the role of rebel. Among these he lists Danny Thomas, Jack Benny, Woody Allen and 'Stepin Fetchit Negroes doing the same thing under a new veneer'.

step-ladder. [STEP *sb.*[1]] A ladder which has flat steps instead of rungs.

1751 *Hist. Acc. New Forest* etc. 49 Step Ladders were fixed against the Wall of the Park [Richmond] in divers Parts. **1795** HELEN M. WILLIAMS *Lett. France* II. 12 (Jod.) One of the secrets of Robespierre's government was to employ as the step-ladders of his ambition, men whose characters were marked with opprobrium. **1830** MISS MITFORD *Village* Ser. IV. 239 The staircase..is as much like a step-ladder in a dark corner as any thing well can be. **1904** MAY SINCLAIR *Div. Fire* 22 Standing on a step-ladder and fumbling in the darkness for a copy of Demosthenes.

b. *attrib.*

1908 *Daily Graphic* 21 Mar. 13/2 The chemise and step-ladder patterns [of sleeve] are the two..most insistent applicants for our favour. *Ibid.*, Step-ladder sleeves are distant relatives of the Kimono.

steple, obs. form of STEEPLE.

stepless ('stɛplɪs), *a.* [f. STEP *sb.*¹ + -LESS.]

1. Having no step or steps.

1827 DARLEY *Sylvia* 20 You might as well climb the stepless air and catch that voice..as overtake my Sylvia.

2. Continuously variable; capable of being given any value within a certain range.

1969 *Jane's Freight Containers 1968–69* 23 adv., Speed control is through the Wessex Carbon Pile, providing smooth, stepless acceleration. **1971** *Engineering* Apr. 111/2 (Advt.), This equipment provides stepless current adjustment over the full range of the..generator. **1973** *Physics Bull.* Feb. 110/1 The instruments in this range produce stepless DC voltage outputs. **1978** *Amateur Photographer* 2 Aug. 6/2 Stepless shutter speed range of 1/1000th to 4 seconds + B.

Hence **'steplessly** *adv.*

1958 *Times Rev. Industry* Oct. 67/3 The rate of travel.. can be varied steplessly by a knob on the body. **1977** *Design Engin.* July 73/2 Frequency and amplitude can be steplessly varied during operation.

steply, variant of STEEPLY *a.*

stepmother ('stɛpmʌðə(r)), *sb.* Also 1 stéop-, 4 stip-, 5 stappe-, *Caxton* styfe- (after Du.). [OE. *stéopmódor*: see STEP-. Cf. OFris. *stiepmoder* (NFris. *stjap-*, WFris. *stiep-*), MLG. *stēfmoder*, Du. *stiefmoeder*, OHG. *stiufmuoter* (MHG. *stiefmuoter*, mod.G. *-mutter*), Sw. *styfmoder*, Da. *stifmoder*.]

1. A woman who has married one's father after one's mother's death or divorce.

c **725** *Corpus Gloss.* (Hessels) N 167 *Nouerca*, steopmoder. *c* **893** ÆLFRED *Oros.* III. vii. §2 Heo wæs Philippuses steopmodor. *c* **1205** LAY. 222 He ȝef heo his stepmoder For þon lofe of his broþer. *Ibid.* 14421 Heore steopmoder. *c* **1290** *S. Eng. Leg.* 47/8 Stepmoder is selde guod. *c* **1305** *St. Swithin* in *E.E.P.* (1862) 45 Seint Edwardes fader was þat his stipmoder a-slouȝ. **1390** GOWER *Conf.* I. 104 My Stepmoder for an hate, Which toward me sche hath begonne, Forschop me. **1432–50** tr. *Higden* (Rolls) V. 273 His stappemodyr. **1471** CAXTON *Recuyell* (Sommer) 83 His styfemoder. **1562** J. HEYWOOD *Prov. & Epigr.* (1867) 195 Thy fathers second wife, thy steppe mother. **1598** BERNARD tr. *Terence's Hecyra* II. i, With one consent all stepmothers hate their daughters in law. **1611** SHAKS. *Cymb.* I. i. 71 You shall not finde me (Daughter) After the slander of most Step-mothers, Euill-ey'd vnto you. *a* **1692** SHADWELL *Volunteers* I. ii, What is that Fathers Wife of kin to you? *Clara.* My true Stepmother. **1865** LE FANU *Guy Deverell* iv. I. 51 His mother indeed she was not; but only the stepmother of his deceased wife. **1914** J. MACKAY *Ch. in Highlands* ii. 49 A man might marry his stepmother.

b. *transf.* Said of a bird that hatches another bird's eggs.

1567 MAPLET *Gr. Forest* 97 b, So soone as those yong can heare but their..Natiue Dams note, they leaue their Stepmother or Nurses [the Partridge's] foode by and by. **1711** ADDISON *Spect.* No. 121 ¶1 The young, upon the sight of a pond, immediately ran into it; while the step-mother, with all imaginable anxiety, hovered about the borders of it. **1815** STEPHENS in *Shaw's Gen. Zool.* IX. I. 76 The bird often proves a mother and step-mother at the same time, by bringing into life the whole brood.

c. *fig.*

1387–8 T. USK *Test. Love* III. ix. (Skeat) 86 My dul wit is hindred by stepmother of foryeting. [Cf. Higden *Polychr.* (Rolls) I. 5 *Novercante oblivione*.] **1396–7** in *Eng. Hist. Rev.* (1907) XXII. 296 Qwan þe chirche of Yngelond began to dote in temporalte aftir her stepmodir þe grete chirche of Rome. *a* **1400** *Relig. Pieces fr. Thornton MS.* (1867) 13 Ydillnes es..stepmodire and stameryngе agaynes gude thewes. **1426** LYDG. *De Guil. Pilgr.* 15985 The Step-moder off vertu, And ful enmy to cryst ihesu, Wych callyd ys 'Prosperyte'. **1430–40** —— *Bochas* II. ii. (1554) 44 Flattery Which is a stepmother called..To all vertue. **1646** J. HALL *Horæ Vac.* 15 He seem'd to carry Reason along with him, who called Nature Step-mother, in that she gives us so small a portion of Time. **1659** N. R. *Prov., Eng. Fr.* etc. 32 Fortune to one is a mother, another a step-mother. **1664** EVELYN *Sylva* (1679) 18 All sort of Clay, is held but a step-mother to Trees. *c* **1695** J. MILLER *Descr. New York* (1843) 10 New York, in these [necessaries], is not unkind; but though a stepmother to those who come from England, yet furnishes them..plentifully. **1705** HICKERINGILL *Priest-cr.* II. v. 56 Happy we, that Her Majesty does not behave Her self like a Step-mother to the Moderate Party. **1913** *Contemp. Rev.* June 827 The monastery had got the credit of founding a school, but had really been a stepmother to it.

quasi-adj. **1715** CHAPPELOW *Right Way to be Rich* (1717) 81 Turn'd naked into a frowning step-mother world.

d. *attrib.* as *stepmother dole*, † *shive* (with reference to the stinginess ascribed to stepmothers). Also Comb. *stepmother-in-law*.

1483 *Cath. Angl.* 361/2 A Stepmoder schyfe, *colirida*. **1847** C. BRONTË *Jane Eyre* xxxi, Nature..forgetting her usual stinted stepmother dole of gifts, had endowed this, her darling, with a granddame's bounty. **1904** *Verney Mem.* II. 133 Eleanor, Countess of Warwick..stepmother-in-law to the Protector's daughter.

2. *dial.* **a.** More fully, *stepmother's blessing*: an agnail.

1818 WILBRAHAM *Chesh. Gloss.*, *Stepmother's Blessing*, a little reverted skin about the nail, often called a back friend. **1862** C. C. ROBINSON *Dial. Leeds* 421 *Stepmothers*, hang-nails.

b. (See quot.)

1828 CARR *Craven Gloss.*, *Step-mother*, the name given to the flowers of the violet in general, but more particularly to those of the *viola tricolor*, pansies or hearts-ease, etc.

Hence **'stepmother** *v. trans.*, (*a*) to provide with a stepmother; (*b*) to behave as a stepmother to. **'stepmotherly** *a.*, pertaining to or characteristic of a stepmother; hence **'stepmotherliness**.

1848 [M. W. SAVAGE] *Bachelor of Albany* 210 [The cook] obliged her barbarous mistress to abandon..her stepmotherly designs. **1860** WRAXALL *Life in Sea* viii. 192 The Acephala have not been treated by her [Nature] in such a step-motherly fashion as might be supposed from their headless condition. **1887** AUGUSTA WILSON *At Mercy of Tiberius* vii, When I want my children step-mothered I will let you know. **1894** KATE K. IDE in *Advance* (Chicago) 22 Mar., A good grandmother, whose grandchildren had become step-mothered. **1892** JANE BARLOW *Irish Idylls* iii. 41 He knows what ills forthwith await him, what step-motherliness of barren earth. **1896** E. A. KING *Ital. Highways* 63 Alma Mater is but step-motherly to her daughters in our own country.

Stepney ('stɛpnɪ). Also **stepney**. [f. the name of *Stepney* Street, Llanelli, the place of manufacture.] **1.** A spare wheel for a motor vehicle, comprising a ready-inflated tyre on a spokeless metal rim, which could be clamped temporarily over a punctured wheel. Also *stepney wheel*. Now *Hist.* exc. in Bangladesh, India, and Malta, where = any spare wheel.

1907 *Westm. Gaz.* 3 Dec. 4/3 The popularity of the Stepney Wheel has never been more clearly demonstrated than at the Olympia Show. **1910** G. K. CHESTERTON *Alarms & Discursions* 179 Then he said, 'And I left the Stepney behind.' **1911** *Daily Chron.* 5 Jan. 4/7 Wales claims the origin of the 'stepney', the spare wheel and tyre. **1928** *Evening News* 7 Aug. 9/2 None of your detachable wheels, rims, or Stepneys! **1929** H. NICOLSON *Let.* 22 July in J. Lees-Milne *Harold Nicolson* (1980) xvi. 376 [In Berlin he was like] a stepney wheel of a car that is seldom taken out of the garage. **1937** *Autocar Handbk.* (ed. 13) xi. 196 With the introduction of pneumatic tyres came the puncture, and soon the 'Stepney' appeared: a spare rim and tyre fitted with clamps. **1971** *Listener* 11 Nov. 653/1 After jacking up the car, one of them turned to me and said: 'Have you a Stepney?' 'Yes, in the boot,' I answered... It takes an old Edwardian like me to know that a Stepney was an attachable wheel-rim, which came in about 1907 and went out about ten years later. You wouldn't hear the term in England now, but in Malta it is the *ordinary* word for a spare wheel. **1973** *Opinion* (Bombay) July 31 It helps to have a few holes in the roof of the car and to go about without a Stepney. **1975** J. DAY *Bosch Bk. Motor Car* 178 An early attempt to make puncture mending less troublesome was the Stepney spare wheel of T. M. and W. Davies in 1904. **1977** *Navbharat Times* (Bombay) 2 June (Advt.), Yezdi stepney wheel complete with tyre, tube, hub and bearings. **1980** L. LEWIS *Private Life of Country House* iii. 35 About 1920 we bought a secondhand T model Ford... In case of punctures there was a Stepney wheel to be clamped on to the rim to get you home.

2. *fig.*

1928 E. SUTTON tr. *A. Londres's Road to Buenos Ayres* ii. 18, I told her I had a woman already in Buenos Ayres, that she could only be my little sweetheart, as we say, or my 'stepney', if you like that better. **1929** E. LINKLATER *Poet's Pub* xxvi. 282 Redemption being carried as a kind of stepney on the best of all possible worlds. **1979** P. NIHALANI et al. *Indian & Brit. Eng.* 1. 167 Dr X may not be able to give his talk—we'd better arrange for a stepney.

† **'stepony.** *Obs.* Also 7 stepponi, -ony, stipone, stiponie, stipony, 8 steponey, stepany, stepney. [Of obscure origin; possibly a use of *Stepney*, the name of a parish in the East of London (cf. quot. 1656).] A kind of raisin-wine, made from raisins with lemon-juice and sugar added.

1656 BLOUNT *Glossogr.*, *Stipone*, a kind of sweet compound liquor, drunk in some places of London in the summer time. **1664** ETHEREDGE *Comical Rev.* v. iv, Do not you understand the mystery of Stiponie, Jenny? **1669** *Sir K. Digby's Closet Opened* 124 To make Stepponi. **1672** HANNAH WOOLLEY *Queen-like Closet* I. (1684) 29 To make Raisin-Wine or Stepony. **1676** *Poor Robin's Intell.* 11–18 Apr. 2/2 Then comes in the faculty of spunging Stipony, and of enflaming the reckoning as occasion shall require. *a* **1700** B. E. *Dict. Cant. Crew*, *Steppony*, a Decoction of Raisins of the Sun, and Lemons in Conduit-water, sweetned with Sugar and Bottled up. **1717** *Poor Robin* July B 2 b, They drink..Chocolate,..Stepany, Tea. **1726** *Dict. Rust.* (ed. 3), *Wine-Raisin* or Stepony may be thus made [etc.]. **1785** GROSE *Dict. Vulgar T.*, Stepney.

'step-out. *Oil Industry*. [f. vbl. phr. *to step out*: see STEP *v.* 27.] In full *step-out well*. A well drilled beyond the established area of an oil or gas field to find out if it extends further.

1948 *Bull. Amer. Assoc. Petroleum Geologists* XXXIII. 1082 Step-out well No. 55, 1 kilometer east of No. 26, is now drilling. **1955** *N.Y. Times* 28 Aug. I. 72 Common practice is to drill 'step outs' at specified distances in all four directions from a discovery well. **1962** F. E. WELLINGS in M. J. Wells *Oil Industry Tomorrow* 32 Step-out wells make [*sic*] the usual division between exploratory wells and development wells. In development wells, if they are intelligently done, the percentage of success is very high,..but less so for the step-out wells. **1977** *Offshore Engineer* Aug. 19/3 Well 3/8-3, south of Ninian, found a hydrocarbon accumulation which has been extended into block 3/7 to the west with a step-out. **1979** *Jrnl. R. Soc. Arts* CXXVII. 407/1 The Gas Council.. have indicated a wish to sink step-out wells on the Goathorn Peninsula and on the Studland Peninsula.

steppage ('stɛpɪdʒ). *Path.* [a. F. *steppage* (Charcot), f. *stepper* to step (racing term), ad. E. STEP *v.*: see -AGE.] A peculiar high-stepping gait characteristic of certain nervous diseases.

1898 *Syd. Soc. Lex.* **1900** CHURCH & PETERSON *Nervous & Mental Dis.* (ed. 2) 300.

steppe (stɛp). Also 7–9 step. [a. Russian *step'*. Cf. F., G. *steppe*.]

1. One of the vast comparatively level and treeless plains of south-eastern Europe and Siberia.

1671 [S. COLLINS] *Pres. St. Russia* xviii. 81 Going towards the more Southern parts of Syberia, you shall see a Wilderness called the Step. **1710** WHITWORTH *Acc. Russia* (1758) 119 The place being on the *step*, or desert. **1762** tr. *Busching's Syst. Geog.* I. 478 The Steppe, or wide desert plain of Astracan,..is a dreary waste. **1830** LYELL *Princ. Geol.* I. 319 The great steppe of Tartary..is unexplored. **1876** BURNABY *Ride to Khiva* xxvi. 240 The Turkomans and other nomad races in the steppes often attribute a disease or illness to the devil.

2. *transf.* An extensive plain, usually treeless.

1837 W. IRVING *Capt. Bonneville* (1849) 61 These great steppes, which range along the feet of the Rocky Mountains. **1842** LOUDON *Suburban Hort.* 43 *Saline steppes*, where the soil is impregnated with salt, but where the foliage is not influenced by a saline atmosphere. **1878** A. K. JOHNSTON *Africa* ii. 20 These rocky steppes possess but few streams. **1903** W. R. FISHER tr. *Schimper's Plant Geog.* 551 The steppe of the Hungarian plain exhibits close climatic similarity to that of South Russia.

3. *attrib.* and *Comb.*, as *steppe bird*, *country*, *district*, *fauna*, *horse*, *lake*, *land*, *-travelling*; **steppe cat**, the manul (*Felis manul* or *caudatus*); **steppe-murrain** = RINDERPEST; **steppe rue**, the plant *Peganum Harmala*, the seeds of which are sometimes eaten as a narcotic.

1884 H. SEEBOHM *Hist. Brit. Birds* II. 234 Richard's Pipit is essentially a *steppe bird. **1885** *Riverside Nat. Hist.* (1888) V. 462 The *Steppe Cat..of Bokhara. **1911** MARETT *Anthrop.* iv. 106 A belt of grassland or *steppe-country. **1903** W. R. FISHER tr. *Schimper's Plant Geog.* 594 *Steppe districts. **1898** *Archæol. Jrnl.* Ser. II. V. 284 The Tundra fauna [had] given place to the *Steppe fauna. **1877** C. GEIKIE *Christ* xxv. (1879) 272 Their lean and untiring *steppe horses. **1901** *Geogr. Jrnl.* (R.G.S.) XVIII. 92 A typical *steppe-lake. **1901** *Wide World Mag.* VI. 444/1 The *steppe lands..in Western Siberia. **1865** *Athenæum* 7 Oct. 473/2 Pulmonary and *steppe murrain. **1881** *Spon's Encycl. Industr. Arts* etc. IV. 1324 Syrian or *Steppe Rue. **1890** 'R. BOLDREWOOD' *Col. Reformer* xvi, The monotony of Australian *steppe-travelling.

Hence **steppe-ful** *nonce-wd.*

1857 DUFFERIN *Lett. High Lat.* 37 [He] could let me have a steppe-ful of horses if I desired.

steppe: see STEEP *a.*, STAP *sb.*

stepped (stɛpt), (*ppl.*) *a.* [f. STEP *sb.*¹ and + -ED.]

1. Having a step or steps; formed in a series of steps (see STEP *v.* 12); *spec.* of the float or hull of a seaplane or hydroplane. Cf. STEP *sb.* 15 c.

1833 LOUDON *Encycl. Archit.* §1890 In this style we have the simple gable of two lines..and the stepped gable. **1861** BERESF. HOPE *Engl. Cathedr.* v. 155 The more grandiose yet theatrical form of the stepped bema. **1869** RANKINE *Mach. & Millwork* iv. §150 Stepped Teeth... A wheel with stepped teeth. **1875** MCILWRAITH *Guide Wigtownsh.* 62 The stepped path on the cliff. **1875** KNIGHT *Dict. Mech.* 2376/1 *Stepped Gage*, one having a series of notches which may fit varying sizes of holes. *Ibid.*, The stepped key was shown in Rountree's lock, English patent, 1790. **1881** E. WILSON *Egypt of Past* 24 The stepped pyramid. **1893** J. A. R. MUNRO in *Athenæum* 4 Nov. 632/2 The inscribed field of the architrave..occupies the top of the blocks above a stepped surface. **1898** M. HEWLETT *Forest Lovers* xiv, There are three ravines about it, with a stepped path through each to the Castle. **1911** *Flight* 9 Dec. 1074/2 The float consists of a three-stepped hydroplane. **1951** [see *hard chine* s.v. HARD *a.* (*sb.*) 22].

2. Carried out or occurring in stages or with pauses, rather than continuously.

1935 *Proc. R. Soc.* A. CLII. 597 The prolific branching of the main part of the first stroke of a series arises solely from downward branching in the stepped leader which precedes it. **1944** *Jrnl. Iron & Steel Inst.* CL. 128A, The causes of the distortion of steel parts during heat treatment are analysed and methods of preventing it, including austempering and other forms of stepped quenching, are discussed. **1977** J. HEDGECOE *Photographer's Handbk.* 125 If you project a transparency using a zoom lens, you get a similar effect to stepped zoom. **1981** *Sci. Amer.* Mar. 28/1 Subsequent leaders..move an order of magnitude faster than the first stepped leader in the freshly ionized gas.

3. With *up*. Raised by degree to a higher standard or level; increased, intensified.

1933 *Sun* (Baltimore) 22 Nov. 20/2 Demands were being made on brewers for a 'stepped-up' beverage, whereas the normally brewed beer runs about four per cent. **1941** *Battle of Britain Aug.–Oct. 1940* (Ministry of Information) 26 Twenty Dornier 215's were encountered over the London Docks flying in a diamond formation escorted by Me 109's 'stepped up' to 22,000 feet. **1955** *Times* 22 Aug. 9/6 Mr. Sinclair Weeks, Secretary of Commerce, to-day announced 'a stepped up programme' to make public as quickly as possible non-classified research reports of industrial significance by the Atomic Energy Commission. **1963** P. FLEMING *Kolchak* xx. 212 They themselves were frightened men, and this combined with the necessarily stepped-up tempo of the interrogation to make them hectoring and exigent. **1976** *National Observer* (U.S.) 23 Oct. 4/4 But he concedes that post officials are 'a little concerned' about handling the stepped-up volume of business over the Christmas season if the strike continues.

stepper ('stɛpə(r)). [f. STEP *v.* + -ER¹.]

1. A horse with good paces and showy action. Often with adj., *good*, *sure*, etc.; cf. HIGH-STEPPER.

1835 SIR G. STEPHEN *Search of Horse* ii. 32 If he is 'a beautiful stepper', you will find that he has the action of a peacock. **1850** SMEDLEY *Frank Fairlegh* xl. 330 'By Jove! what splendid steppers!' was Lawless's exclamation, as I drove up. **1908** A. KINROSS *Joan of Garioch* x. (1911) 44 A quiet closed brougham passed by drawn by two fiery Hungarian steppers.

2. *slang.* †**a.** The treadmill. *Obs.* **b.** *pl.* The feet.

1846 *Swell's Night Guide* 59, I does the safe, if they cops me it's nix; six veeks, a fly at the stepper and turn up. **1851–61** MAYHEW *Lond. Labour* III. 380 These thoughts used to come over me when I was 'on the stepper', that is, on the wheel. **1853** *Househ. Words* VIII. 75 The feet are steppers. **1874** *Slang Dict.* 309 *Stepper*, the treadmill. **1891** 'F. W. CAREW' *No.* 747 xvi. 188 Toiling under our heavy burdens up that everlasting staircase—as Tony Klism said, it was ever so much worse than 'the stepper'.

3. *colloq.* = *step-girl* (STEP *sb.*[1] 18).

1884 *All Yr. Round* 18 Oct. 29/2 Door-step cleaners—known among themselves and their own class as steppers.

4. In full ***stepper motor***. A stepping motor (see STEPPING *ppl. a.*).

1961 *Control Engin.* May 116/1 Applications employing interlocked steppers are ballistic missile prelaunching exercises, reconnaissance drone control, and precise positioning of radioactive fuel elements. *Ibid.* Nov. 103/1A, Stepper motor resembles the conventional ac servomotor except that its winding is excited by a stream of pulses from a multivibrator. **1976** NASAR & BOLDEA *Linear Motion Electric Machines* ix. 255 Some of the advantages of linear stepper motors are ease of control..and locking force. **1978** R. P. HUNGER *Automated Process Control Systems* xiv. 328 The VR stepper requires its windings to be energized in the proper sequence for predictable operation. Also, it can be made to step bidirectionally.

steppie, obs. variant of STEEPY *a.*

stepping ('stɛpɪŋ), *vbl. sb.* [f. STEP *v.* + -ING[1].]

1. a. The action of STEP *v.*; an instance of this.

c **1394** *P. Pl. Crede* 649 þer is no waspe in þis werlde þat will wilfulloker styngen For stappyng [*v.r.* stamping] on a too of a styncande frere. **1580** HOLLYBAND *Treas. Fr. Tong, Marchemenet plus oultre*, a stepping forward. **1663** J. SPENCER *Prodigies* (1665) 130 Nature's voluntary errors and steppings out of her more common road of Operation. **1835** T. MITCHELL *Acharn. of Aristoph.* 198 *note*, The Homeric word πλίσσοντο, which in the Odyssey..is applied to the stepping of mules. **1875** M. ARNOLD *God & Bible* 72 Existence, again, means a stepping forth.

†**b.** *pl.* Footsteps, footprints. *Obs.*

1575 GASCOIGNE *Posies, Jocasta* v. v, Leade the waye Into the stonie rockes and highest hilles, Where fewest trackes of steppings may be spyde. **1583** MELBANCKE *Philotimus* T ij, It is a custome of purloining burglairers, to strew pepper in the tract of their steppings. **1647** H. MORE *Song of Soul* I. ii. 82 Though short he fall of old Corvino's age, His steppings with the other footsteps fit.

†**c.** *pl.* Gradual advances. *Obs.*

1651–3 JER. TAYLOR *Serm. for Year* (1678) 54 Still the Flood crept by little steppings, and invaded more by his progressions than he lost by his retreat.

d. Places on which to step. *rare.*

1854 MILLER *Sch. & Schm.* xvii. (1858) 370 That common sense..which enables men to pick their stepping prudently through the journey of life.

e. With *up*. The action of STEP *v.* 29 h.

1958 *Listener* 24 July 112/1 This would involve a stepping-up of supplies from Persia and from Venezuela. **1965** D. FRANCIS *For Kicks* i. 8 There were trials and prison sentences..and a stepping-up of regular saliva and urine tests.

f. The step-by-step movement of a stepping device (see STEPPING *ppl. a.*).

1960 *McGraw-Hill Encycl. Sci. & Technol.* XIII. 356/2 These selectors may be arranged for..absorbing the digit pulsed without any stepping of the switch. **1964** [see STEP *sb.* 7 e]. **1974** B. C. KUO *Theory & Applications of Step Motors* i. 4 There are many different versions of switches and actuators which give stepping motion through the principle of solenoid action. **1977** *Engin. Materials & Design* Aug. 41/1 Medium power switching types provide operating voltage ranges from 6 to 110V dc and 6 to 220V ac, with latching and stepping facilities in selected items.

2. *concr.* †**a.** *pl.* Steps, stairs. Also, stone for making steps. *Obs.*

1608 WILLET *Hexapla Exod.* 453 All steppings vp [to the altar] being forbidden. **1676** in Willis & Clark *Cambridge* (1886) II. 144 Item for Steppings 70 and ½ foot at seven shillings per foot.

b. *pl.* = STEPPING-STONES. *dial.*

1796 W. H. MARSHALL *Yorksh.* (ed. 2) II. 347.

c. *Naut.* A rabbet taken out of the deadwood, for the heels of the timbers to step on.

1805 *Shipwright's Vade-M.* 135. **1874** THEARLE *Naval Archit.* 195 At present, however, the cants are heeled against the keel and deadwood without any such stepping.

3. *Surveying.* A method of ascertaining the horizontal measure of a slope by extending the chain horizontally in a series of successive positions resembling a flight of steps.

1888 B. H. BROUGH *Mine-Surv.* 15 The process is called *stepping*, and, on steep ground, may be carried on by half-chains, or even shorter distances.

4. *attrib.*, as ***stepping-board, -line, -piece, -place, -wheel***; ***stepping-off place*** *jocular*, the place at the end of the world, whence one steps off into vacancy; ***stepping-stile*** = *step-stile.*

1843 *Penny Cycl.* XXV. 150/1 The tread-wheel is similar to a common water-wheel. Upon its circumference are *stepping-boards. **1846** A. YOUNG *Naut. Dict.* 30 *Bearding-line*,..often called the *stepping-line. **1893** MRS. CUSTER *Tenting on Plains* 21 In my mind, Texas then seemed the *stepping-off place. **1879** *Cassell's Techn. Educ.* III. 83 [Ship-building.] It is usual..to fit a '*stepping piece'. **1824** SCOTT *Redgauntlet* xiii, By knowing exactly where certain *stepping-places and holdfasts were placed. **1791** CHARLOTTE SMITH *Celestina* (ed. 2) II. 209 She then went into the park over the *stepping stile. **1872** JENKINSON *Guide Engl. Lakes* (1879) 143 A stepping-stile leads into the field. **1884** A. GRIFFITHS *Chron. Newgate* II. iv. 168 The newly-invented tread-wheels, or *stepping wheels, as they were at first called.

stepping ('stɛpɪŋ), *ppl. a.* [f. STEP *v.* + -ING[2].] Of an electric motor or other electromechanical device: designed to make a rapid succession of small, equal movements in response to a pulsed input, each pulse causing one movement.

1957 GOODE & MACHOL *System Engin.* iv. 48 Consider a stepping switch acting as a line finder in a telephone system. **1958** J. G. TRUXAL *Control Engineers' Handbk.* v. 69 Besides stepping relays and the Ledex rotary solenoid, few digital devices are available that can step from one point to another rapidly enough to be useful as a control-system output actuator. **1975** *Physics Bull.* July 319/3 The precision divided tables may be fitted with calibrated hand wheels or driven by either stepping motors or DC gear motors. **1979** *Nature* 12 July 121/1 The electrodes were advanced through the brain with a stepping microdrive..until a cell or process was penetrated.

stepping-stone. Also 4 stoppyngston, 7 *Sc.* stopping stane, stapping ston. [STEPPING *vbl. sb.*]

1. A stone for stepping upon. **a.** A stone placed in the bed of a stream or on muddy or swampy ground, to facilitate crossing on foot. Chiefly *plural*, referring to a row or line of such stones.

c **1325** *Gloss. W. de Bibbesw.* in Wright *Voc.* 159 S[t]eping-stones *passueres*. *c* **1340** *Nominale* (Skeat) 515 *Caliow fusil et passuer*. Flynt firehiron stoppyngston. **1550** [see SIKET]. **1579** *Nottingham Rec.* IV. 189 Steppingstones to be sett be tweene Frear Poole. **1603** *Reg. Mag. Sig. Scot.* 506/1 Passand to ane grene dyk besouth the stopping stanes of the Ile-ark. **1655** LAMONT *Diary* (Maitl. Club) 91 The water.. ran away some of the stapping stons at Nether Largo. **1682** O. HEYWOOD *Diaries* (1881) II. 303 Going over stepping stones at a brook. **1733** SWIFT *On Poetry* 169 Like stepping Stones to save a Stride, In Streets where Kennels are too wide. **1815** SCOTT *Guy M.* viii, Once he [the Dominie] fell into the brook crossing at the stepping-stones. **1833** TENNYSON *Miller's Dau.* 54 The tall flag-flower that sprung Beside the noisy steppingstones. **1852** E. W. BENSON in *Life* (1899) I. iii. 110, I reached the Abbey by the stepping-stones. **1899** CROCKETT *Kit Kennedy* 189 Kit crossed the brook at the stepping-stones.

b. A raised stone on which the foot can be placed to facilitate a climb or ascent; *spec.* 'a horse-block' (Halliwell). *rare* in literal sense: see 2.

1837 DICKENS *Pickw.* xxviii, The stile..was full three feet high, and had only a couple of stepping-stones. **1841** JAMES *Brigand* xi, He sat down on one of the stepping-stones placed to aid travellers in mounting their horses.

c. *transf.* A place for a break of journey.

1849 NOAD *Electricity* (ed. 3 104) The intermediate clouds serving as intermediate conductors, or stepping-stones as it were for the electric fluid. **1856** STANLEY *Sinai & Pal.* xii. 398 'Chittim' thus became the first stepping-stone to the isles of the West. **1880** A. R. WALLACE *Isl. Life* 274 Some islands may have intervened between them [the Galapagos] and the coast, and have served as stepping-stones by which the passage to them of various organisms would be greatly facilitated.

2. *fig.* Something that is used as a means of rising in the world, or of making progress towards some object; often, a position, office, or the like, that serves to afford opportunity for further advancement.

1653 BAXTER *Christian Concord* 47 Some Ministers lately put in, are young, weak, and indiscreet, and fit matter for them to contemn, and modestly to make stepping stones to their own reputation. **1715** CHAPPELOW *Right Way to be Rich* (1717) 165 She has..made them stepping-stones to her own grandeur. **1773** W. EDEN in Jesse *Selwyn & Contemp.* (1844) III. 59 His office..would suit our friend Hare exactly, as an introduction or stepping-stone to something better. **1806** G. ROSE *Diaries* (1860) II. 248 [They] would see through it too clearly to allow themselves to be made stepping-stones for their Lordships to mount into power by. **1850** TENNYSON *In. Mem.* i, I held it truth..That men may rise on stepping-stones Of their dead selves to higher things. **1855** MACAULAY *Hist. Eng.* xi. III. 49 Those obstacles his genius had turned into stepping stones. **1884** H. SWEET in *13th Addr. Philol. Soc.* 83 Such a shorthand would serve as a stepping-stone from the ordinary Roman alphabet to such a one as Bell's Visible Speech. **1891** *Speaker* 11 July 36/1 A type of snobbery which regards the established religion as a stepping-stone to respectability. **1898** R. B. O'BRIEN *Parnell* I. viii. 168 Agrarian revolution was to be made the stepping-stone to separation from England.

'steppy, *a. rare.* [f. STEP *sb.*[1] + -Y.] Full of steps.

1882 MRS. B. M. CROKER *Proper Pride* I. ii. 25 The narrow, sun-scorched, steppy streets of Valetta.

†**'stepsire.** *Obs. rare.* = STEPFATHER.

13.. *Sir Beues* 3464 Alse glad he was of hire, Of his damme, ase of is stipsire. **1581** STUDLEY *Seneca's Hercules Œtæus* II. 193 b, His former Stepsiers stocke heereby the overthrow shall haue.

stepsister ('stɛpsɪstə(r)). [See STEP-. Cf. Du. *stiefzuster*, MHG., mod.G. *stiefschwester*, Sw. *styfsyster*, Da. *stifsøster*.] A daughter of one's stepfather or stepmother.

c **1440** *Promp. Parv.* 474/1 Stepsystyr. **1530** PALSGR. 276/1 Step sustre, *belle seur.* **1828** in WEBSTER. **1868** [see STEPBROTHER]. **1883** MISS M. BETHAM-EDWARDS *Disarmed* xxx, Throwing his arms round his step-sister's neck. **1910** C. N. & A. M. WILLIAMSON *Love & Spy* I. i. 10 Di and I are only step-sisters.

stepson ('stɛpsʌn). Also 1 stéop-, 5 styp-. [OE. *stéopsunu*: see STEP-. Cf. Du. *stiefzoon*, MLG. *stēfsone*, OHG. *stiufsun* (MHG. *stiefsun*, G. *-sohn*), ON. *stjúpsonr* (Sw. *styfson*, Da. *stifsøn*).] A son, by a former marriage, of one's husband or wife.

c **725** *Corpus Gloss.* (Hessels) F 210 *Filiaster*, steopsunu. *c* **893** [see STEPFATHER]. *c* **1150** *Voc.* in Wr.-Wülcker 538/5 *Priuiuignus* [sic], stepsune. *c* **1205** LAY. 32138 Yuor wes his step-sune. **1297** R. GLOUC. (Rolls) 1412 Tibery is stepsone after him com. **14..** *Lat.-Eng. Voc.* in Wr.-Wülcker 605/4 *Privignus*, a stypsone. **1490** CAXTON *Eneydos* lxv. 164 Lauyne..retourned..to her stepsone ascanius. **1570** LEVINS *Manip.* 164/26 A step son, *priuignus*. **1631** WEEVER *Anc. Funeral Mon.* 210 This Queene [Joan] endured some troubles in the raigne of her Stepsonne King Henry the fift. **1797** HOLCROFT tr. *Stolberg's Trav.* (ed. 2) II. xlvii. 119 The stepson of Sylla. **1870** FREEMAN *Norm. Conq.* (ed. 2) I. vi. 452 Where his banished step-sons were being brought up as his possible rivals. **1872** MORLEY *Voltaire* 2 Calvin, again, like some stern and austere step-son of the Christian God.

stepull(e, stepyl(l(e, obs. ff. STEEPLE *sb.*[1]

'step-up, *a.* and *sb.* [f. vbl. phr. *to step up*: see STEP *v.* 29.] **A.** *attrib.* or as *adj.* **1.** Causing or pertaining to an increase in voltage.

1893 SLOANE *Electr. Dict.*, *Step-up* adj., the reverse of step-down. **1903** C. H. SEWALL *Wireless Telegr.* IV. 149 The transmitter of the DeForest system uses..a step-up transformer to increase the voltage. **1947** R. LEE *Electronic Transformers & Circuits* v. 142 Input Transformer,.. Step-up ratio 1:20. *Ibid.* 188 If the transformer is step-up, C_1 = [etc.]. **1977** *Gramophone* Oct. 744/2 A particular criticism levelled towards moving-coil cartridges is that their output is so low as to require a step-up transformer.

2. Furnished with a step to a higher level. Also, of a room with such a feature.

1958 J. MYERSCOUGH *Procession of Lancs. Martyrs & Confessors* xix. 260 A typical example of the 'step-up' chapel provided for Catholics in the days of persecution may be seen..in Alston Lane, Grimsargh. **1979** *Arizona Daily Star* 5 Aug. (Advt. Section) 13/1, 2 bdrms., 2 full baths, step-up dining area.

B. *sb.* **1.** An increase in rate or quantity; an intensification.

1922 GLAZEBROOK *Dict. Appl. Physics* II. 889/1 The amplifying action of a valve is usually more a question of potential step-up than of ratio of power output to power input. **1944** *Times* 26 May 2/1 We should probably finish the war with very nearly the same step-up in engine power over the present war period as occurred between 1914–18. **1972** *Newsweek* 10 Jan. 14/3 Coupled with the increasingly hard line adopted by both negotiating teams in recent weeks, the step-up in the air war might even jeopardize the continuation of the talks themselves.

2. Chiefly *pl.* A step taken on to a platform (such as a bench, etc.) and back again, repeated as a fitness exercise.

1973 *Observer* 7 Oct. 28/1 A middle-aged actor keeping his paunch at bay with weights and interminable step-ups. **1978** *Kingston* (Ontario) *Whig-Standard* 15 July 15/2 Stations 5–9 include such exercises as..chin-ups and step-ups.

stepwise ('stɛpwaɪz), *adv.* and *a.* Also with hyphen. [f. STEP *sb.* + WISE *sb.*[1] II.] **A.** *adv.*

1. Like or in a series of steps.

1888 WIDGERY *Teaching Lang.* 53 A note-book cut step-wise into an alphabet. **1902** *Jrnl. R. Inst. Brit. Architects* 20 Dec. 101 The balustrade of its upper flight rising step-wise, and showing at intervals the sockets of its colonnade. **1950** *Jrnl. Neurophysiol.* XIII. 193 The response builds either step-wise or abruptly to a complex series of peaks at 5–8 msec.

2. *Mus.* = *by step* s.v. STEP *sb.* 8 b.

1955 G. ABRAHAM in H. Van Thal *Fanfare for E. Newman* ii. 12 A purely harmonic cadence, the separate parts moving stepwise, even chromatically, with a much less decisive cadential effect rhythmically.

3. In a series of distinct or separate stages; with intermittent pauses, not continuously.

1971 J. Z. YOUNG *Introd. Study Man* iii. 55 It may be that the new mRNA is synthesized stepwise in the nucleus. **1972** *Science* 2 June 1014/2 The details of..whether the velocities increase smoothly or stepwise..cannot be resolved without additional data.

B. *adj.* **1.** *Mus.* Of musical progression, etc.: occurring or arranged regularly in steps (STEP *sb.* 8 b).

1920 S. MACPHERSON *Melody & Harmony* i. 4 In the above extracts there is a considerable amount of 'conjunct' (i.e. step-wise) movement. **1930** A. M. RICHARDSON *Helps to Fugue Writing* vii. 37 A progression like the following does not look interesting..but by supplying embellishments it can be made much more effective... The thirds need not be stepwise. **1949** W. PISTON *Counterpoint* (rev. ed.) i. 20 In the Corelli example the upward octave skip is both preceded and followed by a downward stepwise movement. **1952** A. O. WARBURTON *Melody Writing & Analysis* I. 7 After stepwise movement it is usually wise to leap in the opposite direction. **1979** *Early Music* Jan. 138/2 The manuscripts.. specify 'clarinet' on the title-page, and include stepwise movement in their lower register.

2. = *step-by-step* attrib. or quasi-adj. s.v. STEP *sb.* 5 c.

1934 *Jrnl. Amer. Chem. Soc.* LVI. 913/1 The development of a complex polymer must require a series of consecutive reactions... It is necessary to assume that the first-formed polymers possess an ordinary double bond and are capable of being isolated. This scheme will be called 'stepwise'. **1954** [see DEGRADATION[1] 4 c]. **1960** KOESTLER *Lotus & Robot* I. i. 43 The result of this step-wise dismantling of reality is that consciousness alone remains. **1975** N. CHOMSKY *Logical Struct. Linguistic Theory* x. 469 Transformational analysis permits the stepwise formation of complex phrases from already constructed simple phrases. **1980** *Jrnl. R. Soc. Arts* May 348/2 Step-wise mutations in the bacterium..are shown to produce corresponding changes in the synthesized amidase.

ster, obs. form of STAR, STEER, STIR.

-ster, *suffix*. Forms: 1 **-istræ, -estre,** later **-ystre, -istre,** 2–4 **-estre,** 4–5 **-estir,** 5 **-ister,** 4–7 **-star(e,** 4–5 **-estere, -stere,** 4– **-ster.** [Corresponding to MLG. *-(e)ster*, (M)Du. and mod.Fris. *-ster*, it represents a WGer. type *-strjōn-*, forming feminine agent-nouns, prob. a derivative of the OTeut. *-stro-* forming nouns of action, as in ON. *bakstr* masc., act of baking, OHG. *galstar* neut., incantation.

The existence of the suffix is not attested for High German, OS. or OFris.; the supposed examples sometimes cited, OHG. *wagastria* lance, *agalastra* (OS. *agastria*) magpie, OS. *hamstra* marmot, *ramestra* some plant, are very doubtful; even if the suffix be formally identical with the agential suffix, it has not the same function. In Du. *-ster* regularly forms feminine agent-nouns corresponding to masculines in *-er*, e.g. *schrijfster* fem. of *schrijver* a writer. In MLG., and in mod.Fris., although most of the nouns in *-ster* are fem., several occur as masc., e.g. MLG. *bedriegster* deceiver, NFris. *grewster* gravedigger, *wäwster* weaver.

In the original types of the formation the suffix was prob. preceded by the thematic vowel of the word to which it was attached, thus becoming *-astrjōn-*, *-istrjōn*, ? *-ustrjōn-*. In the historical forms, however, there is no evidence of this (unless in the OE. *byrdistræ*: see below); in Du. and Fris. the suffix is *-ster* without prefixed vowel; in MLG. usually *-ster*, sometimes *-ester*, app. merely for euphony. In OE. it is *-estre*, which does not produce umlaut, though it is often added to a stem containing an umlaut-vowel.]

In OE. *-estre* was freely used to form fem. agent-nouns, in exactly the same manner in which *-ere* (-ER[1]) was used to form masc. agent-nouns. Thus it was appended to the pres.-stems of verbs, as in *lǽrestre* female teacher, *hoppestre* female dancer, and to certain monosyllabic nouns of action as in *sangestre* songstress, *séamestre* sempstress, *lybbestre* female poisoner or witch. In a few instances fem. agent-nouns were formed by the substitution of *-estre* for the masc. suffix *-a* (:—*-jon-*), as in *bigengestre* fem. of *bigenga* cultivator, worshipper, *webestre* (WEBSTER) beside *webbe* as fem. of *webba* weaver. *Lattéow*, leader, functionally an agent-n. though without agential suffix, gave rise to a fem. *lættewestre*. An anomalous formation is *huntigestre* (instead of **huntestre*) huntress which occurs once as a variant reading for *hunticge*.

In OE. the suffix may be said to have retained its original function, for the few instances in which it is used as a masculine are renderings of Latin designations of men exercising functions which among the English were peculiar to women, as *byrdistræ* embroiderer (gl. *blaciarius*, *primicularius*), *bæcestre* baker (gl. *pistor*), *séamestre* tailor (gl. *sartor*), *wæscestre* washer (gl. *fullo*).

In northern ME., however, perh. owing to the frequent adoption by men of trades like weaving, baking, tailoring, etc., the suffix came very early to be used, indiscriminately with -ER[1], as an agential ending irrespective of gender; thus in the *Cursor Mundi* (*a* 1300) *demestre* (see DEMPSTER) appears instead of *demere* (DEEMER), a judge, *bemestre* instead of *bemer* a trumpeter. It is probable that *-ster* was often preferred to *-er* as more unambiguously referring to the holder of a professional function, as distinguished from the doer of an occasional act. In Scotland, *baxter* and *webster* survived as masculines down to the 19th c. The only word of this formation that in Scotland has remained exclusively feminine is SEWSTER.

In the south the suffix continued to be predominantly feminine throughout the ME. period. The OE. formations, *baxter*, *seamster*, *tapster*, were in southern English usually feminine before 1500; many new designations of occupation, originally feminine, arose in ME. as *bellringestre*, *hordestre* treasurer (*Winteney Rule St. Benet*, 13th c.), *hotestre* fem. of *hotere* commander (Ayenbite), *brewster*, *dyester*, *litster*, *throwster*, *huckster*; also *spinster*, which alone of the group has survived (though with change of sense) solely as a feminine. A few feminines in *-estere* were formed to correspond to masculines in *-er(e* of French origin: *fruitestere*, *tumbestere*, *tumblestere*, *wafrestere*. As a feminine suffix of purely agential import, *-ster* was in the 14th c. still used for new formations by some writers, but was generally replaced by the French *-eresse*. Thus MS. Bodl. 277 of the Wyclif Bible has *chesister*, *daunster*, *dwelster*, *weilster*, where other copies have *cheseresse*, *daunseresse* (*leperesse*), *dwelleresse*, *weileresse*.

From the 16th c. onwards the older words in *-ster*, so far as they survived, have been regarded as masculines, and several of them have given rise to feminines in *-ess*, as *backstress*, *seamstress*, *songstress*, *huckstress*. In the modern English period the suffix has been very productive, but it is doubtful whether any of the new formations are really derived from verbs; in every instance in which this would be formally possible there is a sb. of the same form as the vb., and the derivative is (in present feeling at least) associated rather with the sb. than the vb. so in *gamester*, *rhymester* (late 16th c.), *drugster* (1611; but cf. *druggister*), and the much later *dabster*, *jokester*, *punster*, *trickster*, *tipster*. The formation here imitates that of trade designations; hence the disparaging sense, e.g. in *rhymester*, *jokester*, as compared with *rhymer*, *joker*. An anomalous use is that in *rubster* (17th c.) something used to rub with.

In the 16th c. two formations on adjs. occur: *youngster* (after which *oldster* was formed later) and *lewdster*.

†**'steracle.** *Obs.* Forms: 5 **staracle,** 6 **sterakel, sterracle, stiracle,** 5–6 **steracle.** [Of obscure origin: possibly f. STARE *v.*, after *spectacle*.] A spectacle, show. Also with play on *miracle*.

c **1440** *Jacob's Well* 105 To gon to wakys & to wrestlynges, to daunsynges & to steraclys. **14..** *Pain Evil Marr.* in *Mapes' Poems* (Camden) 297 At staracles to sitte on high stages. **1540** PALSGR. *Acolastus* IV. iv. T iij b, Why whippest thou it about, or playest thou thy steracles. *c* **1550** BALE *K. Johan* 996 With ymages and rellyckes he shall wurke sterracles. **1563** BECON *Acts of Christ* Wks. III. 416 b, But to pray at..places..where the deuil worketh stiracles, I would say, miracles,..this passeth al.

steradian (stəˈreɪdɪən). *Geom.* [f. Gr. στερεός solid + RADIAN *sb.*] A unit of measurement of solid angles (see quot. 1881).

1881 HALSTED *Mensuration* 78 A steradian is the angle subtended at the center by that part of every sphere equal to the square of the radius. **1883** W. THOMSON in *Encycl. Brit.* XVI. 25/2 Number of Steradians in an Angle. **1885** A. MACFARLANE *Phys. Arith.* 87 The unit-rate S per (L radius)^2 is sometimes called a steradian, that is, a solid radian.

sterage, obs. f. STEERAGE; var. STIRRAGE.

sterane (ˈstɪəreɪn, ˈstɛreɪn). *Min.* and *Chem.* [f. STER(OID + -ANE.] Any of a class of saturated hydrocarbons with a steroid structure which are found in crude oils and derived from the sterols of ancient organisms; orig., †the compound whose molecule consists of the saturated nucleus only.

1951 *Jrnl. Chem. Soc.* 3527 The substance (II) shall be named gonane (preferred) or sterane (alternative). **1969** *Geochim. & Cosmochim. Acta* XXXIII. 1307 The C_{27}, C_{28} and C_{29} steranes are present in the bitumen from the Green River oil shale and..they were derived from cholesterol, ergosterol, stigmasterol or related sterols. **1973** *Nature* 27 Apr. 603/1 These steranes and terpanes represent the complete reduction of naturally occurring steroids or terpenoids to relatively stable fossil molecules which preserve intact the complete molecular skeleton and stereochemistry of their precursors. Steranes..provided convincing proof for the biological origins of petroleums.

sterap, obs. Sc. form of STIRRUP.

sterc, sterch, obs. ff. STARK *a.*

stercobilin (ˌstɜːkəʊˈbaɪlɪn). [irreg. f. L. *sterc-us* (*stercor-*) dung + *bīl-is* BILE + -IN.] The colouring matter of the fæces.

1880 J. W. LEGG *Bile* 32 Vanlair and Masius describe another derivative found in abundance in the fæces,..which they name sterco-bilin. **1900** A. E. GARROD in *Lancet* 10 Nov. 1323/2 The urobilin of urine and the stercobilin of fæces are identical in composition.

stercolith (ˈstɜːkəʊlɪθ). *Med.* [f. L. *sterc-us* dung + -O + -LITH.] A piece of hardened fæces which has become the centre of a concretion.

1910 *Practitioner* July 106 We came upon another abscess cavity, from which a typical appendicular stercolith was dislodged. **1973** EARNEST & SLEISENGER in Sleisenger & Fordtran *Gastrointestinal Dis.* cxii. 1531/1 A smaller, rounded, smooth hard mass of stool which cannot be expelled is called a stercolith or enterolith.

stercoraceous (stɜːkəˈreɪʃəs), *a.* [f. L. *stercorāce-us*, f. *stercor-*, *stercus* dung: see -ACEOUS.]

1. Consisting of, containing, or pertaining to fæces.

1731 ARBUTHNOT *Nat. Aliments* i. (1735) 11 A putrid stercoraceous Taste and Odour. **1759** MILLS tr. *Duhamel's Husb.* I. viii. (1762) 19 The stercoraceous salts of the dung. **1787** [see STERCORARIOUS, 1785 quot.]. **1834** *Rep. Sel. Comm. Metrop. Sewers* 115 Pumping of stercoraceous filth is practised sometimes every night. **1876** BRISTOWE *Th. & Pract. Med.* (1878) 662 This discharge of 'stercoraceous' matter by the mouth is due..to the fact that [etc.].

fig. **1832** *Westm. Rev.* XVII. 522 A sneaking stercoraceous policy.

b. *Path.* Of vomiting: Consisting of fæces, fæcal.

1754–64 SMELLIE *Midwifery* III. 516 The Child had that night Stercoraceous vomitings. **1898** ROSE & CARLESS *Man. Surg.* 931 This shock..is..followed by vomiting, at first gastric, then bilious, and finally stercoraceous or fæcal.

2. *Ent.* Of certain beetles, flies, etc.: Frequenting or feeding on dung.

1891 *Century Dict.*

Hence **sterco'raceously** *adv.*

1894 J. M. WALSH *Coffee* 142 The appreciation of such stercoraceously deposited beans by the natives being an undoubted fact.

‖**stercoræmia** (stɜːkəˈriːmɪə). *Path.* Also **-emia.** [mod.L. f. L. *stercor-*, *stercus* dung, fæces + Gr. αἷμα blood.] Contamination of the blood by absorption from retained fæces.

1890 BILLINGS *Nat. Med. Dict.* II. 588 *Stercoræmia.* Name proposed by Bouchard for systemic poisoning due to alkaloids absorbed from the intestines. **1898** *Syd. Soc. Lex.*, *Steroræmia*, *Stercoremia.*

stercoral (ˈstɜːkərəl), *a.* [f. L. *stercor-*, *stercus* dung + -AL[1].]

1. *Path.* = STERCORACEOUS. ***stercoral ulcer***, an ulcer produced by the pressure of fæcal matter.

1758 J. S. *Le Dran's Observ. Surg.* (1771) 198 Which..would inundate the Cavity of the Abdomen with stercoral Matter. **1817** COLERIDGE *Ess. Own Times* (1850) III. 957 Some Hottentots..having publicly abjured the uric and stercoral faith of their grandmothers. **1894** *Athenæum* 10 Feb. 184/1 The posterior end of the intestine is dilated into a large stercoral pouch which is part of the midgut. **1898** ROSE & CARLESS *Man. Surg.* 930 Fæcal material..gives rise..occasionally to stercoral ulcers.

2. *Bot.* (See quot.)

1889 WAGSTAFFE *Mayne's Med. Voc.*, *Stercoral*,..*Bot.* Applied to plants that grow upon excrements or dung.

stercoranism (ˈstɜːkərənɪz(ə)m). *Eccl. Hist.* Also incorrectly **ster'corianism.** [Formed as next + -ISM.] The beliefs of the Stercoranists.

1728 CHAMBERS *Cycl.* s.v. *Stercorarians*, Which Opinion he imagined led directly into Stercoranism. **1758** MACLAINE tr. *Mosheim's Eccl. Hist.* II. 156 That imaginary heresy, that..was branded with the title of Stercoranism. **1798** HEY *Lect. Divinity* IV. IV. xxviii. 340 *note*, This might be held, in order to avoid the charge of Stercorianism. **1847–54** WEBSTER, *Stercorianism.* **1882** OGILVIE, *Stercoranism*, *Stercorianism.*

stercoranist (ˈstɜːkərənɪst). *Eccl. Hist.* Also incorrectly **stercorianist.** [ad. med.L. *stercoranista*, irreg. f. L. *stercor-*, *stercus* dung: see -IST.] A nickname given to one who holds that the consecrated elements in the Eucharist undergo digestion in, and evacuation from, the body of the recipient.

1686 W. HOPKINS tr. *Ratramnus* Dissert. v. (1688) 98 The first I can learn of the Name, is, that Humbertus Bishop of Sylva Candida calls Nicetas Stercoranist. **1721** in BAILEY. **1844** *Cranmer's Lord's Supper* 55 *marg.*, A sect reproved that were called Stercoranists. **1891** *Century Dict.*, Stercorianist. **1893** RICKABY in *Month* May 28 Delaying his answer to the Stercoranists, as they are called.

†**'stercoranite.** *Obs. rare.* [See -ITE.] = STERCORANIST.

1579 W. FULKE *Heskin's Parl.* 41 Hee chargeth, I knowe not what Stercoranites of our time, to affirme that the fleshe of Christ, passeth through the bodie as other meates.

sterco'rarian, *sb.* and *adj.* [f. L. *stercorāri-us* (see STERCORARY) + -OUS.]

†**A.** *sb.* **1.** A derisive appellation for a physician following obsolete methods of practice. *Obs. rare.*

1651 N. BIGGS *New Dispens.* ¶ 11 The old stercorarian and snaile-creeper, the Galenist.

2. = STERCORANIST. *Obs. rare.*

1728 CHAMBERS *Cycl.*, *Stercorarians*, or *Stercoranists.*

B. *adj. Biol.* [f. mod.L. *Stercoraria*, name of a section of the genus *Trypanosoma* (C. A. Hoare 1964, in *Jrnl. Protozool.* XI. 203/1).] Used to designate those species of *Trypanosoma* which occur in the digestive tract of the secondary host, and are transmitted in its fæces. Cf. SALIVARIAN *a.*

1964 C. A. HOARE in *Jrnl. Protozool.* XI. 203/2 It must be admitted that not all Stercorarian trypanosomes can be fitted with certainty into the above subgenera,..since the life cycle of many of them is still unknown. **1971**, **1977** [see SALIVARIAN *a.*].

stercorarious (ˌstɜːkəˈrɛərɪəs), *a.* [f. L. *stercorāri-us* (see STERCORARY) + -OUS.]

1. = STERCORACEOUS 1.

1656 BLOUNT *Glossogr.*, *Stercorean* or *Stercorarious.* **1752** STACK in *Phil. Trans.*, XLVII. 344 Without the least mixture of a stercorarious stench. **1785** COWPER *Task* III. 463 The stable yields a stercorarious [ed. 3, 1787 stercoraceous] heap. **1816** KIRBY & SP. *Entomol.* xxi. (ed. 2) II. 261 They can elevate or drop their stercorarious parasol so as most effectually to shelter or shade them.

2. *Ent.* Of beetles, etc.: Living in dung.

1826 KIRBY & SP. *Entomol.* xliv. IV. 227 They..may often be seen..prowling in search of the stercorarious beetles.

stercorary ('stɜːkərərɪ), *a.* and *sb.* [ad. L. *stercorārius*, f. *stercor-*, *stercus* dung: see -ARY.]

A. *adj.* Of or pertaining to dung. Of insects: Living in or feeding on dung.

1664 POWER *Exp. Philos.* I. 6 The Stercorary or Yellow Flyes that feed upon Cow-dung. **1669** W. SIMPSON *Hydrol. Chym.* 78 Innate and connatural to the place like the stercorary ferment to the *cæcum.* **1765** *Universal Mag.* XXXVII. 130/1 The stercorary beetle is seen at fig. 5. **1864** D. G. MITCHELL *Wet Days* 17 (Cent.). **1869** tr. *Hugo's By King's Command* III. i. (1875) 114 The stercorary tribe which, like the envious, are addicted to defiling high places.

B. *sb.* A place where manure is stored, a dungheap. Now *rare* or *Obs.*

1759 MILLS tr. *Duhamel's Husb.* I. viii. (1762) 29 Mud, or the product of your stercorary. **1792** WASHINGTON *Let.* 14 Oct., Writ. 1891 XII. 239 That lately sown in Lucern from the stercorary to the river fence. **1828–32** WEBSTER, *Stercorary*, a place properly secured from the weather for containing dung. **1851** *Rural Cycl.* IV. 338 *Stercorary*, a collection of putrescent manure in a position of security from injury by the weather.

stercorate ('stɜːkəreɪt), *v.* [f. L. *stercorāt-*, ppl. stem of *stercorāre*, f. *stercor-*, *stercus* dung.]

trans. To manure or dung.

1623 COKERAM I, *Stercorat*, to empt dung. **1657** TOMLINSON *Renou's Disp.* 242 If it be transplanted into a soyl well stercorated. **1665** HAVERS *P. della Valle's Trav. E. India* 112 The Houses whose pavements are thus stercorated, are good against the Plague. **1672** G. THOMSON *Let. to H. Stubbe* 17 Those Baconical Ignoramus's, if they catch this Brazen-face within their Precincts, will.. Stercorate such a durty person, that he may fructifie the better hereafter. **1727** BAILEY vol. II, *Stercorated*, dunged, manured with Dung. **1821** SCOTT *Pirate* iv, It savoured of the earth..to have a man's mind always grovelling in mould, stercorated or unstercorated.

stercoration (stɜːkə'reɪʃən). [ad. L. *stercorātiōn-em*, f. *stercorāre*: see prec. and -ATION. Cf. F. *stercoration.*]

1. The action or an act of manuring with dung.

1605 TIMME *Quersit.* II. i. 103 What..maketh the earth fatte..but a certaine stercoration, and spreading of dung and of urine which commeth from cattle? **1626** BACON *Sylva* §595 The first and most Ordinary Helpe is Stercoration. **1696** EVELYN *Let. to Wotton* 28 Oct., They tooke great care indeede of their vines and olives, stercorations, ingraftings. **1707** *Curios. Husb. & Gard.* 121 A Field might be sown every year; if we restor'd to it by Stercoration, what we take from it in the Harvest. *a* **1849** H. COLERIDGE *Ess.* (1851) II. 23 When there was a god Sterquilinius, an agricultural poet might be allowed to sing of stercoration.

†**2.** Dung, manure. *Obs.*

1694 MOTTEUX *Rabelais* IV. lxvii, Do you call this.. Excrement, Stercoration, Sir-reverence, Ordure? **1733** TULL *Horse-hoeing Husb.* vii. (8°ed.) 55 When the Saliva and Ferment of the Stomach have served for Stercoration to it.

†**3.** *nonce-use.* A disgusting utterance. *Obs.*

1702 C. MATHER *Magn. Chr.* VII. App. (1852) 652 Another ..publickly held forth in one of his late stercorations, that [etc.].

stercorean (stɜː'kɔːriːən), *a.* [f. L. *stercore-us* (f. *stercor-*, *stercus* dung) + -AN.] = STERCORACEOUS.

1656 BLOUNT *Glossogr.* **1875** MCILWRAITH *Guide Wigtownsh.* 33 It was found impossible..to clear the ground of its vast stercorean encumbrance.

stercoreous (stɜː'kɔːriːəs), *a. rare.* [f. L. *stercore-us* (see prec.) + -OUS.] = STERCORACEOUS.

1659 H. MORE *Immort. Soul* II. ix. (1713) 99 A Receptacle of Stercoreous excrement. **1753** DODSLEY *Agric.* II. 70 From stercoreous fumes of rottenness and filth, can sweetness spring? **1862** WRAXALL tr. *Hugo's Les Misérables* V. xix. (1877) 12 The stercoreous trench of a great city.

stercoricolous (stɜːkə'rɪkələs), *a.* [f. L. *stercor(i)-*, *stercus* dung + *col-ĕre* to inhabit + -OUS.] Living in dung or excrement.

1885 RAY LANKESTER in *Encycl. Brit.* XIX. 842/2 Parasitic and stercoricolous forms.

stercorin ('stɜːkərɪn). [a. F. *stercorine* (see quot. 1868), f. *stercor-*, *stercus* dung: see -IN.] A fæcal extractive resembling biliary cholesterin.

[**1868** A. FLINT, Jr. *Recherches expérim. sur une nouvelle fonction du Foie* 67 Trouvant cette substance en si grande quantité dans les matières fécales, nous l'avons désignée sous le nom de stercorine.] **1873** RALFE *Phys. Chem.* 21 *Stercorin.* Under this name Dr. Austin Flint has described a substance which, if not identical with serolin, resembles it closely in its physical and chemical characters. **1881** MIVART *Cat* 188 Their nutritious matter being re-absorbed and their refuse driven on as excretin, stercorin [etc.].

'stercorist. [a. F. *stercoriste*, f. L. *stercor-*, *stercus* dung: see -IST.] = STERCORANIST.

1872 MORLEY *Voltaire* v. 239 Writers like Sanchez or the stercorists, who had opened frivolous and unbecoming questions that could hardly be exposed with gravity.

stercorite ('stɜːkəraɪt). *Min.* [f. L. *stercorāre* to manure with dung, f. *stercus* dung + -ITE[1].] A hydrated acid phosphate of sodium and ammonium, $Na(NH_4)HPO_4.4H_2O$, occurring as colourless triclinic crystals; microcosmic salt.

1850 T. J. HERAPATH in *Q. Jrnl. Chem. Soc.* II. 73 This being the first instance in which the ammonio-phosphate of soda has been met with as a natural production, I propose to class it amongst our minerals under the name of 'Stercorite'. **1975** *Mineral. Abstr.* XXVI. 125/2 The X-ray powder data of stercorite from Chincha Islands, Peru, prove that the mineral corresponds with [*sic*] the synthetic $Na(NH_4)HPO_4.4H_2O$.

stercorolith ('stɜːkərəlɪθ). *Path.* [f. L. *stercor-*, *stercus* dung + *-lith.*] = STERCOLITH.

1901 R. MORISON in *Lancet* 23 Feb. 537/2 A stercorolith in the cavity of the abscess is usually lying close to a perforation in the appendix.

†**stercorose,** *a. Obs.* [ad. L. *stercorōs-us*, f. *stercor-*, *stercus* dung: see -OSE.] = STERCOROUS.

1727 BAILEY, vol. II, *Stercorose*, full of Dung, &c.

stercorous ('stɜːkərəs), *a.* Also 6 -us. [ad. L. *stercorōs-us*, f. *stercor-*, *stercus* dung: see -OUS.] Stercoraceous, excrementitious.

1542 BOORDE *Dyetary* xvi. (1870) 272 A swyne..with stercorus matter doth fede in Englande. **1880** SWINBURNE in *Fortn. Rev.* Dec. 719 Unlike Dante, he never permitted the too fetid contact of their stercorous feculence to befoul the sandal of his Muse.

†**'stercory.** *Obs. rare.* Also stercorry. [irreg. f. L. *stercor-*, *stercus* dung.] Excrement, filth.

c **1495** *Epit. Dk. Bedford* in *Skelton's Wks.* (1843) II. 394 Man is but duste, stercorye, and fylthe. *a* **1529** SKELTON *K. Edw. IV*, 75 Sainct Bernard..Seyth a man is but a sack of stercorry, And shall returne vnto wormis mete.

stercovorous (stɜː'kɒvərəs), *a. Ent.* [irreg. f. L. *sterc-us* dung + -VOROUS.] Of certain insects: Feeding on dung or excrement.

1845 DARWIN *Voy. Nat.* xxi. (ed. 2) 490 *note*, These stercovorous insects. *Ibid.*, In England the greater number of stercovorous beetles are confined in their appetites.

‖**sterculia** (stɜː'kjuːlɪə). [mod.L., f. *Sterculius* the god of manuring, f. *stercus* dung.]

1. *Bot.* A genus of polypetalous plants (typical of the N.O. *Sterculiaceæ*); a plant of this genus.

Most of the species are trees, and all contain mucilaginous gum; some have a fetid odour, whence the name.

1771 *Encycl. Brit.* III. 627 *Sterculia.* **1857** LIVINGSTONE *Trav. S. Africa* xxvi. 534 A kind of sterculia, which is the most common tree at Loanda. **1866** *Treas. Bot.* 1098/1 All the Sterculias contain mucilage.

2. *Ent.* A beetle of the family *Xantholinidæ.*

1874 J. G. WOOD *Insects Abr.* vi. 77 The Sterculias are readily known by their very peculiar shape.

Hence **sterculi'aceous** *a. Bot.* pertaining to the *Sterculiaceæ*; **ster'culiad**, a sterculiaceous plant.

1846 LINDLEY *Veg. Kingd.* 361 Sterculiads..are chiefly remarkable for the abundance of mucilage they contain. **1866** *Treas. Bot.* s.v. *Bombax*, A genus of large soft-wooded trees belonging to the order of Sterculiads. **1885** *Athenæum* 26 Dec. 846/2 This sterculaceous [*sic*] tree is a native of the tropics. **1898** *Syd. Soc. Lex.*, Sterculiaceous.

sterd, obs. pa. t. of STEER *v.*

stere, ‖**stère** (stɪə(r), ‖stɛr), *sb.* [Fr. *stère*, f. Gr. στερεός solid.] The unit of the metric system for solid measures; a cubic metre, equal to about 35·3 English cubic feet.

1798 *Tilloch's Philos. Mag.* I. 248 Measures for Fire wood. *Stere*, a quantity equal to a cubic metre. By giving the length of a metre to billets, nothing more will be necessary, in order to obtain the stere, than to range them within a square frame (*chassis*), each side of which is equal to a metre. **1837** J. T. SMITH tr. *Vicat's Mortars* 17 Every cubic metre of lime consumes (on an average) 1.66 steres in fire-wood, 22.00 steres in faggots, and 30 steres in fascines. **1885** A. MACFARLANE *Phys. Arith.* 93 In the metric system we have three series of units of volume. The stere and its derivatives are for solid measure.

†**stere,** *v. Obs.* In 3 steoren. [OE. *stéran*, *stýran*:—**stórjan*, f. *stór* incense: see STOR.]

1. *intr.* To burn or offer incense.

c **1000** ÆLFRIC *Num.* xvi. 47 Aaron þa ardlice arn to þam folce and sterde mid thimiama.

2. *trans.* To perfume with or as with incense.

c **1000** *Sax. Leechd.* I. 98 Ster [*v.r.* styr] hyne mid pære wyrte þe man aristolochiam nemneð. *a* **1240** *Ureisun* 45 in *O.E. Hom.* I. 193 þer me schal ham steoren mid guldene chelle.

stere, obs. form of STAR, STEER, STIR.

steregon ('stɛrɪgɒn). *Solid Geom.* [irreg. f. Gr. στερε-ός solid + γωνία angle.] (See quot. 1881.)

1881 HALSTED *Mensuration* 78 A *steregon*, the natural unit of solid angle, is the whole amount of solid angle about a point in space. **1883** W. THOMSON in *Encycl. Brit.* XVI. 25/2 [Adopts the word from Halstead, but uses it for 'a plane solid angle', i.e. the amount of solid angle at the centre which is subtended by the hemisphere].

sterel'minthan. *Zool. rare.* [Formed as next + -AN.] A sterelminthous worm.

1842 BRANDE *Dict. Sci.* etc., Sterelminthans.

sterelminthous (stɛrɛl'mɪnθəs), *a. Zool.* [f. mod.L. *Sterelmintha* (irreg. f. Gr. στερ-εός solid + ἑλμινθ-, ἕλμινς intestinal worm) + -OUS.] Of or pertaining to the *Sterelmintha*, Owen's name for a division of the Entozoa comprising the endoparasitic worms having a solid body with no visceral cavity. So **sterel'minthic** *a.* (in recent Dicts.).

a **1843** *Encycl. Metrop.* (1845) VII. 268/2 The Sterelminthous Order..have no distinct cavity for their alimentary apparatus. **1870** ROLLESTON *Anim. Life* 138 *note*, Neither are the Hirudineae truly 'parenchymatous' or 'sterelminthous' Vermes in the same sense.

steren, obs. form of STERN *a.*

sterenchyma (stə'rɛŋkɪmə). *Bot. rare.* [irreg. f. Gr. στερ-εός solid + ἔγχυμα infusion, after *parenchyma.*] = SCLERENCHYMA 2.

1856 GRIFFITH & HENFREY *Microgr. Dict.* 642 *Sterenchyma*, a name which might be used to distinguish the bony cellular tissue of shells, stones of fruit, &c. **1861** BENTLEY *Man. Bot.* 28 When..parenchymatous cells become much thickened by..secondary deposits,..if the secondary deposits are of bony hardness, as in the stones of fruits, &c., Henfrey has proposed the term sterenchyma.

stereo ('stɛriːəʊ, 'stɪəriːəʊ), *sb.*[1] abbreviation of STEREOTYPE (*lit.* and *fig.*); also *attrib.*, as ***stereo forme, -matter, -metal***, etc.

1823 'JON BEE' *Dict. Turf* 166 *Stereo*, abbreviated from *stereotype*, one of the cheap-and-nasty manufactures in this country, the pages being usually left incorrect and blunderous, in pursuance of the saving plan which first suggested casting them in stereo. **1880** F. J. F. WILSON *Stereotyping & Electrotyping* 49 Small Stereo Foundries. **1880** *Q. Rev.* CL. 533 Firms which deal in stereo-matter. **1883** *Athenæum* 22 Dec. 811/1 We have not compared the two issues line for line together; but on a cursory examination they appear to owe their origin to the same set of stereos. **1886** *Pall Mall Gaz.* 23 Nov. 2 It is printed on the flat, from six stereo formes. **1888** JACOBI *Printers' Vocab.* 132–3. **1896** G. B SHAW in *Sat. Rev.* 18 Apr. 397/2 The best part of the entertainment is Mr. Osmond Carr's music—mere stereo, no doubt, much of it, but smart, appropriate stereo. **1897** TILDEN *Man. Chem.* 531 Stereo-metal is also a mixture of lead, tin, and antimony. **1901** *Daily Chron.* 13 Dec. 4/5 The old, hammered 'stereos' of the cricket reporter.

stereo ('stɛriːəʊ, 'stɪəriːəʊ), *sb.*[2] and *a.*[1] abbreviation of STEREOSCOPE, STEREOSCOPIC. **stereo card**, a card on which are mounted a pair of stereoscopic photographs; **stereo pair**, a pair of photographs showing the same scene from slightly different points of view, so that when viewed appropriately a single stereoscopic image is seen.

1876 *Nature* 12 Oct. 525/2 A stereo-slide to which it was appended was sketched by myself in January last. **1892** *Photogr. Ann.* II. p. cli, Single Stereo Lenses. *Ibid.* 309 A camera..specially constructed for stereo work. **1897** *Pop. Sci. Monthly* Dec. 187 Stereo views can be shown upon a screen. **1943** H. T. U. SMITH *Aerial Photographs* iii. 79 Ink marks..detract seriously from the effectiveness of depth perception, particularly when on only one photo of a stereo pair. **1966** [see *photo-interpretation* s.v. PHOTO- 2]. **1975** *New Yorker* 26 May 11/3 (Advt.), Also on view are such items as a glass-plate camera from the period and stereo cards mounted in hand-operated viewers. **1976** *Church Times* 3 Dec. 6/5 Two handsome books contain, respectively, a stereoscopic viewer with facsimiles of old stereocards, and a lively illustrated history of stereographic photography. **1977** J. HEDGECOE *Photographer's Handbk.* 299 One reason why stereo cameras have gone out of favour is that you can easily make stereo-pairs with an ordinary camera.

stereo ('stɛriːəʊ, 'stɪəriːəʊ), *a.*[2] and *sb.*[3] *colloq.* [Abbrev. of STEREOPHONIC *a.*, STEREOPHONY.]

A. *adj.* = STEREOPHONIC *a.*

1954 *Wireless World* Jan. 7/1 The first full-length stereophonic film to be released was Walt Disney's 'Fantasia',.. with stereo sound photographically recorded on four tracks on a separate sound film. **1958** *Times* 20 Jan. 10/4 What stereo discs have achieved is to combine these two channels in one groove traced by one stylus. *Ibid.*, When the B.B.C. establishes stereo broadcasts..it may give a new lease of life to radio manufacturers. **1960** *Practical Wireless* XXXVI. 299/2 A variety of instrumental, choral and solo recordings, both monaural and binaural (stereo). **1963** *Which?* Jan. 3/1 Equipment for reproducing stereo records is more elaborate than for mono, and relatively few stereo record players are sold. **1976** 'A. YORK' *Dark Passage* xii. 144 The stereo cassette recorder was switched on. **1977** G. SCOTT *Hot Pursuit* xv. 147 My heartbeat began to pound as though stereo headphones had been clamped to my head.

B. *sb.* **1.** = STEREOPHONY.

1956 *Radio & Television News* Aug. 35/1 (*heading*) What should stereo do? **1957** *Audio* Jan. 12/2 Tape is the only logical medium for stereo. **1958** *Observer* 20 Apr. 10/5 In adding another dimension to our listening, stereo represents a most significant advance in the quest for concert-hall realism. **1961** *John o' London's* 5 Oct. 396/4 The new Decca issue..presents both works in first-class stereo. **1970** *Jrnl. Audio Engin. Soc.* XVIII. 624 The transmission of four-channel stereo by means of FM-multiplier techniques. **1972** *Daily Tel.* 9 Aug. 13/1 The BBC is to start programmes in stereo on Radios 1 and 2 from the end of September.

2. Any stereophonic apparatus for playing records or tapes. Cf. STEREOGRAM[2].

1964 *House & Garden* Nov. 62/2 (*caption*) The wall unit houses the stereo. **1971** *Daily Tel.* 24 Sept. 12, I am unable to understand pop words seated 3ft away from a high quality stereo. **1976** P. CAVE *High Flying Birds* iv. 52 Lorna showed us into the villa and put some low, slow background music on the stereo. **1980** J. GARDNER *Garden of Weapons* I. iii. 37 You got full sound in the Charlton house? And a stereo? I can't live without music.

stereo- ('stɛriːəʊ, 'stɪəriːəʊ-), before a vowel properly **stere-**, combining form repr. Gr. στερεός solid, in various (chiefly recent) scientific and technical terms; for the more important of these see their alphabetical places. (In some instances referring to the use or principle of the stereoscope, and thus practically serving as combining form of *stereoscope* or *stereoscopic*: cf. STEREO *sb.*) **ˌstereo-aˈcuity**, the sharpness of the eyes in discerning separation along the line of sight. **ˈstereo-camera**, a camera for simultaneously taking two photographs of the same thing from adjacent viewpoints, so that they will form a stereoscopic pair. **ˌstereoˈcentric** (-ˈsɛntrɪk) *a.*, *Chem.*, applied to a formula indicating a hypothetical direction of the bonds of certain atoms in a molecule towards a common centre (cf. *stereo-isomer* below, and STEREOCHEMISTRY). **stereo-ˈcilium** *Anat.*, an immotile cell process of certain epithelial cells of the male reproductive tract and the labyrinth of the ear, similar to a cilium at low magnifications only; hence **stereo-ˈciliary** *a.* **ˌstereo-ˈcomparator** [COMPARATOR], an instrument enabling two different photographs of the same region to be seen simultaneously, one by each eye, either to detect any change (in the case of photographs of the night sky taken at different times) or to make measurements of the area depicted in stereoscopic photographs. **ˌstereocon'trol** *sb. Chem.*, the control of a synthesis by the choice of reagents and reaction conditions so as to produce a product with a desired stereochemical conformation; also as *v. trans.*, to control thus; **ˌstereoconˈtrolled** *ppl. a.* **ˈstereodiagram**, a diagram intended to show the three-dimensional structure of something. †**ˌstereo-eˈlectric** *a.*, applied to a (thermo-electric) current produced by contact of solids (opp. to HYDRO-ELECTRIC 1). **ˌstereoelecˈtronic** *a. Chem.*, pertaining to the relative positions of the electron orbitals in reacting molecules; hence **ˌstereoelecˈtronically** *adv.* **ˌstereofluoˈroscopy** *Med.*, the production of X-ray images which can be interpreted in three dimensions; = *stereoradiography* below; hence **stereoˈfluoroscope**, an instrument for producing such images; **ˌstereofluoroˈscopic** *a.* **ˈstereoglyph** *v.* [Gr. γλύφ-ειν to engrave: cf. GLYPH] = STEREOMOULD *v.* **stereoˈgnosis** [Gr. γνῶσις means of knowing], the stereognostic sense or faculty. **ˌstereoˈgnostic** *a.* [Gr. γνωστικός: see GNOSTIC], pertaining to the mental apprehension of the forms of solid objects by touch. **ˌstereo-ˈisomer** (-ˈaɪsəmə(r)), *Chem.*, one of two or more isomeric compounds which are held to differ by virtue of a difference in the spatial arrangement (not in the order of connexion) of the atoms in the molecule; so **ˌstereo-isoˈmeric** *a.*, **-iˈsomeride** (= *-isomer*; now *obs.*), **-iˈsomerism**. **ˌstereoisomeriˈzation** *Chem.*, the conversion of one stereoisomer into another; hence (as back-formations) **ˌstereoiˈsomerize** *v. intr.*, to undergo stereoisomerization; *trans.*, to cause the stereoisomerization of (a compound); **ˌstereoiˈsomerized** *ppl. a.*, **-isomerizing** *vbl. sb.* **ˈstereomer**, **ˌstereoˈmeric** *a.*, **stereˈomerism**, *Chem.* [after ISOMER, etc.] = *stereo-isomer*, *-isomeric*, *-isomerism*. **stereoˈmicrograph**, a micrograph that conveys a vivid impression of depth, such as one obtained with a scanning electron microscope. **stereoˈmicroscope**, a binocular microscope that gives a stereoscopic view of the subject. **ˌstereoˈmonoscope** [see MONO- and -SCOPE], an instrument invented by A. F. Claudet in 1858, with two lenses by which an image of an object is projected upon a screen of ground glass so as to appear solid, as in a stereoscope. **ˌstereomuˈtation** *Chem.*, the conversion of a *cis*- to a *trans*-isomer or vice versa. **ˌstereophanˈtasmascope**, **-phantascope** [Gr. φάντασμα appearance, PHANTASM + -SCOPE], a form of kinetoscope giving a stereoscopic effect. **stereo-photo** *a.*, abbrev. of *stereophotographic* adj.; also as *sb.*, a stereophotograph. **ˌstereophotoˈgrammetry**, photogrammetry by means of stereophotography; hence **ˌstereophotograˈmmetric** *a.* **ˌstereo-ˈphotograph**, a stereoscopic photograph; so **ˌstereophotoˈgraphic** *a.*, pertaining to or involving the use of **ˌstereophoˈtography**, the making of stereoscopic photographs. **ˌstereo-ˌphotoˈmicrograph**, a photomicrograph taken with a stereoscopic camera. **stereoˈplanigraph** *Cartography* [a. G. *stereo-planigraph*], a machine which plots a map of an area semi-automatically under the guidance of the operator as he views a stereoscopic pair of aerial photographs of it. **ˈstereoˌplasm** [Gr. πλάσμα: see PLASMA], (*a*) *Biol.* Nägeli's term for the denser or more solid part of protoplasm (distinguished from HYGROPLASM); (*b*) *Zool.* an endothecal structure in corals, enveloping or connecting the septa, or forming a mass in the interior; hence **ˌstereoˈplasmic** *a.*, consisting of or of the nature of stereoplasm (*Cent. Dict.*, 1891). **ˈstereoplotter**, an instrument used for plotting maps of an area from stereoscopic aerial photographs that are projected on to the plotting table. **ˌstereo-ˈplotting** *a.* that is a stereo-plotter. **stereoˈradiograph**, a stereoscopic radiograph; so **ˌstereoradioˈgraphic** *a.*, **-ˈgraphically** *adv.* **ˌstereoradiˈography** = *stereofluoroscopy* above. **ˈStereoscan**, **ˈstereoscan**, a proprietary name for a scanning electron microscope; hence (as *stereoscan*), a picture obtained with a scanning electron microscope. **ˌstereoˈspondylous** *a. Zool.* [Gr. σπόνδυλος vertebra], characterized by completely ossified vertebræ, as the suborder *Stereospondyli* of amphibians. **ˌstereoˈstatic** *a.*, *Mech.* [see STATIC], applied to an arch constructed to sustain the pressure of a mass of solid matter, as a geostatic arch. **ˌstereoˈstatics**, the statics of solid bodies. **ˌstereoteˈlemeter** [TELEMETER], a stereotelescope with a scale or other contrivance for measuring the distance between objects viewed. **ˌstereoˈtelescope**, a binocular telescope with the objectives a considerable distance apart (variable at pleasure), used in military operations, etc. **ˈstereoˌtrope**, a form of thaumatrope or zoetrope fitted with a stereoscope, so that the figures appear solid and in motion. **stereˈotropism**, *Biol.* [see TROPISM], the growth or movement of an organism in a particular direction under the stimulus of contact with a solid body: so **ˌstereoˈtropic** *a.*, pertaining to stereotropism. **ˈstereoviewing** *vbl. sb.*, stereoscopic viewing.

1942 *Summary Progress Rep. Tests of Stereoscopic Vision* (Harvard Univ. Psycho-Educational Clinic, Publ. Bd. No. 55797) 1 The objects of this investigation were: (1) to appraise tests of *stereo-acuity in current use. **1974** *Nature* 13 Sept. 141/1 Stereoacuity falls in the region of the resolution of the Calcomp plotter, so it could not be measured. **1959** *Observer* 7 June 3/4, I have had a *stereo-camera for five years now and the range of new experiences it can offer is constantly widening. You can photograph people and they are three-dimensional people, frozen in a moment of time. **1961** *New Scientist* 19 Oct. 173/2 The Japanese workers used a stereocamera to record the contours of waves generated by the model. **1977** Stereo-camera [see *stereo pair* s.v. STEREO²]. **1902** *Nature* 3 July 238/1 Chemical Society, June 18... A discussion of the various possible space formulæ of benzene and a reply to Graebe's objections to the *stereocentric representation. **1979** *Nature* 30 Aug. 832/2 The *stereociliary array [in the herring utricle] consists of rows of stereocilia which decrease in height the further away they are from the kinocilium. **1933** *Stereocilium [see *kinocilium* s.v. KINO-]. **1950** A. W. HAM *Histol.* xxviii. 659/2 The epithelium [of the epididymis] is tall and regular, and tufts of large nonmotile stereocilia.. project toward the lumen from the free margins of the cells. **1970** J. BABEL et al. *Ultrastructure Peripheral Nerv. System* 270 Every vestibular sensory cell carries 80–100 stereocilia.. and one kinocilium... The stereocilia of the hair cells of the cristae are exceedingly long. **1901** *Observatory* Dec. 471 A new instrument called a '*Stereocomparator',.. described by Dr. Max Wolf in *Astr. Nach.* No. 3749. **1903** *Daily Chron.* 1 Dec. 7/7 The object of the stereo-comparator is.. to detect at a glance any unusual objects, such as new stars, variable stars, or small planets. **1908** Stereocomparator [see *stereoplotter* below]. **1939** *Geogr. Jrnl.* XCIII. 240 An improved stereocomparator for air triangulation. **1950** *Jrnl. R. Aeronaut. Soc.* LIV. 619/2 In cases where co-ordinate measurements are made in a precise stereocomparator, the prints are made on a non-distorting surface such as sensitised aluminium foil. **1975** J. B. HARLEY *O.S. Maps* i. 11 By means of self-recording stereocomparators precise pairs of measurements of co-ordinates are made on pairs of overlapping aerial photographs. **1970** *Jrnl. Macromol. Sci.: Chem.* A. IV. 1014 A very useful technique for the exploration of the *stereocontrol of ionic polymerizations. **1979** *Tetrahedron Lett.* Oct. 3805 Unique stereocontrol in aldolization at C6 of penicillanates through modification of solvent and cation has been observed. **1959** *Stereocontrol *v.* [see STEREOREGULATE *v.*]. **1969** *Jrnl. Amer. Chem. Soc.* XCI. 5675 (*heading*) *Stereo-controlled synthesis of prostaglandins F_{2a} and E_2 (*dl*). **1975** *Ibid.* XCVII. 5873 Formylation followed by acidic treatment effects cyclobutyl ring cleavage to an enol lactone which constitutes a net stereocontrolled geminal alkylation with introduction of a one-carbon and a three-carbon chain differentially functionalized. **1945** M. F. GLAESSNER *Princ. Micropalaeont.* v. 96 (*caption*) *Stereodiagram of a segment of *Loftusia persica* Brady. **1979** *Nature* 13 Dec. 681/2 (*caption*) Stereodiagram of three molecules in the crystal lattice as they are stacked along the *c* axis in what looks like a continuous double helix. **1832** *Nat. Philos., Magnetism* xiii. §cccv. 93 (U.K.S.) The term *Stereo-electric current has.. been applied to the former [the Thermo-electric],.. to mark its being produced in systems formed of solid bodies alone. **1956** *Jrnl. Amer. Chem. Soc.* LXXVIII. 6273/1 The tendency of bromine to adopt the axial orientation in the bromination of an enol would seem to indicate that *stereoelectronic control is unusually large in this case since the opposing steric effect is certainly quite large. **1972** *Ibid.* XCIV. 3657/1 It is expected that σ-π conjugation would have similar stereoelectronic requirements to p-π conjugation. **1956** *Ibid.* LXXVIII. 6272/2 Addition reactions to the Δ^6-double bond.. take place predominantly from the α- rather than the β- direction despite the fact that these are *stereoelectronically controlled. **1978** *Further Perspectives Org. Chem.* (CIBA Found. Symp. New Ser. No. 53) 94 The cyclization step is likely to be stereoelectronically impeded. **1932** *Lancet* 2 Jan. 47/2 The perfection of a *stereofluoroscope for use in hospitals is reported. **1942** *Radiology* XXXVIII. 392/1 Stereofluoroscopes continue to gather dust, or go to the junk heap. **1928** *Lancet* 3 Mar. 442/2 The latest development in *stereofluoroscopic work. *Ibid.*, The law governing *stereofluoroscopy has not been fully recognised. The law stated simply is that angles of vision which the X rays make with the body should be identical with those made by the vision of the observer of the body... Early in the days of X rays the tubes were of a size which rendered stereofluoroscopy impossible. **1964** *Radiology* LXXXII. 125 A test of depth perception in 62 subjects strongly suggested that binocular stereofluoroscopy provided an advantage in the perception of depth over the clues available from motion parallax alone. **1857** *Athenæum* 6 June 720 The tables before us are calculated, and *stereoglyphed. **1862** *Catal. Internat. Exhib., Brit.* II. No. 3006 Tables calculated and stereoglyphed by the Swedish calculating machine. **1900** DORLAND *Med. Dict.* 637/2 *Stereognosis. **1905** A. W. CAMPBELL *Histol. Stud. Localisation Cerebral Function* viii. 205 Damage to this part of the brain is attended by disorder of high and combined forms of sensation, such as the muscle sense and that of stereognosis. **1980** D. JENSEN *Human Nerv. System* xiv. 212/2 Faulty stereognosis provides an early indication of cortical damage. **1894** GOULD *Illustr. Dict. Med.*, **Stereognostic*, pertaining to the cognition of solidity, or tri-dimensional forms. **1898** C. L. DANA *Nervous Dis.* (ed. 4) 54 *note*, The stereognostic sense. **1899** *Brit. Med. Jrnl.* 9 Dec. 1600 This condition [of inability to recognise objects by the tactile sense] has been described as 'touch paralysis' or loss of the stereognostic sense. **1894** *Stereo-isomer [see HEXONIC *a.*]. **1903** SLOSSON in *Amer. Chem. Jrnl.* Apr. 294 My work on these bodies was chiefly directed towards the preparation of stereoisomers. **1906** *Athenæum* 28 Apr. 519/2 The two different lactic acids.. are supposed to be stereo-isomers of one another. **1897** *Jrnl. Chem. Soc.* Abstr. II. 129 *Stereo-isomeric compounds. **1907** A. W. STEWART *Stereochem.* 270 The stereo-isomeric cobalt salts. **1893** *Jrnl. Chem. Soc.* Abstr. I. 681 Determination of *Stereoisomerides. **1938** *Biochem. Jrnl.* XXXII. 1627 The pentose phosphoric acid most readily attacked.. is not the *d*-arabinose-5-phosphoric acid.. but is the stereoisomeride *d*-ribose-5-phosphoric acid. **1894** *Jrnl. Chem. Soc.* 393 *Stereoisomerism. **1907** A. W. STEWART *Stereochem.* 135 Stereoisomerism without optical activity. **1943** *Jrnl. Amer. Chem. Soc.* LXV. 1524/2 Oxidation.. was the only reasonable interpretation six years ago when the *stereoisomerization of carotenoids was still unexplored. **1977** *Jrnl. Organometallic Chem.* CXXV. 185 This approach has enabled us to determine the lowest energy (threshold) rearrangement mode occurring in the stereoisomerization of these [β-diketonate] complexes. **1952** *Jrnl. Gen. Physiol.* XXXVI. 306 Some of the [*sc.* carotenoids] *stereoisomerize even at room temperature. *Ibid.*, A general procedure for stereoisomerizing carotenoids is to heat them in solution. **1962** L. ZECHMEISTER *Cis-Trans Isomeric Carotenoids* v. 56 An attempt to stereoisomerize β-carotene epoxides.. did not afford *cis* compounds but furanoid oxides. *Ibid.* 51 The following ratios of unchanged to stereoisomerized starting material were found in the recovered pigment. **1952** *Jrnl. Gen. Physiol.* XXXVI. 306 The possibility that there exists a *stereoisomerizing enzyme—a vitamin A or retinene isomerase. **1898** EILOART tr. *van't Hoff's Arrangemt. Atoms* 81 The isomers.. in the cases we have been considering, may be called *stereomers. *Ibid.* 194 *Stereomeric compounds of dyad platinum. *Ibid.* 195 Certain cases of *stereomerism. **1956** *Nature* 17 Mar. 516/2 Electron micrographs and *stereomicrographs showing the surface characteristics and microfibrillar texture of keratin fibres were exhibited. **1975** J. G. EVANS *Environment Early Man Brit. Isles* i. 10 (*caption*) Stereomicrograph of pollen grains of *Fraxinus excelsior*, ash, × 2570. **1962** *Radiology* LXXIX. 31/1 The image on the output phosphor was viewed through a low-power *stereomicroscope. **1978** FRIEDMAN & SANDERS *Princ. Sedimentol.* xiii. 417/2 Cuttings from cable-tool drilling are.. examined with a stereomicroscope. **1858** *Proc. Roy. Soc.* IX. 194 On the *Stereomonoscope: a new Instrument by which an apparently Single Picture produces the Stereoscopic Illusion. **1876** *Encycl. Brit.* V. 815/1 In 1858 he [*sc.* A. F. Claudet] produced the stereo-monoscope, in reply to a challenge from Sir David Brewster. **1955** *Jrnl. Chem. Soc.* 3446 The *cis*-nitro-acid.. on reduction gives about equal quantities of *cis*- and *trans*-amino acid, thus indicating that some *stereomutation occurs during reduction. **1975** *Jrnl. Amer. Chem. Soc.* XCVII. 238/2 Pyrolysis of cyclopropane or its substituted derivatives causes.. stereomutation (e.g., *trans* → *cis-cyclopropane*-1,2-d_2). **1865** *Brit. Jrnl. Photogr.* 15 Sept. 473/1 The *Stereo-phantasmascope. **1890** BILLINGS *Nat. Med. Dict.* II. 588/2 *Stereophantascope.. or Bioscope. **1901** J. MAREY in *Smithsonian Rep.* 318 *note*, An apparatus devised in America about 1861.. was called a 'stereophantascope'. **1908** *Geogr. Jrnl.* (R.G.S.) XXXI. 534 *Stereo-photo Surveying. By F. Vivian Thompson, Lieut. R.E. **1972** *Science* 9 June 1116/2 Turnbull's contribution consists chiefly of figuring the Field Museum's Trinity (Albian Cretaceous) mammal teeth by means of stereophotos. **1930** *Geogr. Jrnl.* LXXV. 159 *Stereo-photogrammetric methods. **1936** *Ibid.* LXXXVII. 99 To carry out a stereo-photogrammetric examination of the northern aspect and valleys of Mount Everest. **1913** *Engin. News* 27 Mar. 604/2 A method by which the troubles arising in photogrammetric surveys are eliminated is based on the principle of making the necessary measurements on stereoscopic pictures, and is called *stereophotogrammetry. **1950** *Engineering* 14 July 28/3 The application of aerial photography and stereo-photogrammetry to large-scale railway surveys. **1980** I. NEWTON in K. B. Atkinson *Devel. Close Range Photogrammetry* I. vi. 129 Stereophotogrammetry has made it possible to analyse the size and shape of the palate in far greater detail than hitherto. **1865** H. SIDGWICK *Let.* Apr. in A. & E. M. Sidgwick *Henry Sidgwick* (1906) iii. 129, I got your *stereo-photograph (what is the short for it?) at 113 Rue de Sebastopol. **1902** *Year Bk. Photogr. 1902* 162 The effect described will be at once apparent in the stereo-photograph. **1959** *Observer* 7 June 3/4 To look at your first stereo-photograph can be an experience as climactic as seeing the Mediterranean for the first time. **1980** I. NEWTON in K. B.

Atkinson *Devel. Close Range Photogrammetry* I. vi. 127 An analysis of surgically corrected abnormal faces had been undertaken in the USA from stereophotographs taken pre- and post-operatively. **1908** *Geogr. Jrnl.* (R.G.S.) XXXI. 537 *Stereo-Photographic Surveying. **1903** *Nature* 8 Oct. 546/1 *Stereophotography is the subject which concludes Col. Laussedat's review of instruments and methods. **1907** *Nature* 14 Nov. 46/2 Mr. Taverner exhibited a number of *stereo-photomicrographs of water mites, taken with a stop behind the objective. **1906** J. A. FLEMER *Elem. Treat. Phototopographic Methods* x. 309 Dr. Pulfrich has devised a *stereoplanigraph which is being made by the Carl Zeiss firm in Jena. **1974** P. R. WOLF *Elements of Photogrammetry* xiv. 320 Each projector of the C-8 stereoplanigraph has the customary three angular rotations, but translations are introduced as movements of the reference mirrors. **1889** *Hardwicke's Science-Gossip* XXV. 246 Naegeli..considers protoplasm to be compounded of a fluid hygroplasm and a solid *stereoplasm. **1897** J. S. GARDINER in *Proc. Zool. Soc.* 949 The corallites..are almost completely filled up below by stereoplasm. **1908** *Geogr. Jrnl.* XXXI. 544 An instrument..which makes the plotting of points and the reading of heights nearly automatic. To distinguish it from the stereo-comparator it has been called a *stereo-plotter, as it combines the offices of the stereo-comparator and plotting board. **1979** *Photogrammetric Engin. & Remote Sensing* XLV. 802/1 Systemhouse has developed a universal analytical stereoplotter system with the primary theory of operation of an analytical stereoplotter being applied to its fullest extent. **1927** *Geogr. Jrnl.* LXX. 358 (*heading*) An attempt to describe Mr. Wild's *stereo-plotting machine—the Autograph. **1975** J. B. HARLEY *O.S. Maps* i. 11 With the 1:10 000 series control points are plotted on a stable plastic sheet... A stereo-plotting machine is then used to derive map and contours, with the operator plotting the detail..in relation to the control points. **1945** *Light Metals* VIII. 269/2 The *stereo radiograph, corresponding to a multiplicity of shots from different angles, is produced on a single film, an important economic advantage. **1965** D. N. & M. O. CHESNEY *Radiographic Photogr.* xiii. 319 In order to have perception of depth, various methods are available for viewing stereoradiographs. **1975** *Radiology* CXV. 455/1 Stereo radiographs usually eliminate the problem of matching sources, since the two views are more similar, but they do not always permit accurate 3-D reconstruction. **1936** *Amer. Rev. Tuberculosis* XXXIV. 517 *Stereoradiographic examination of the chest on the same day revealed a widely disseminated infiltrative process throughout the right lung field. **1965** D. N. & M. O. CHESNEY *Radiographic Photogr.* xiii. 319 The anteroposterior projection of the sacro-iliac joints made *stereoradiographically. *Ibid.* 317 In *stereoradiography a pair of radiographs is taken. **1968** *Official Gaz.* (U.S. Patent Office) 12 Mar. TM 69/2 Cambridge Instrument Company Limited, London... **Stereoscan* for electron microscopes and parts and fittings therefor... First use on or about Mar. 31, 1966. **1970** AMBROSE & EASTY *Cell Biol.* xi. 377 The form of the ruffles is clearly seen in the Stereoscan picture. *Ibid.*, The Stereoscan allows us to see these contacts directly. **1970** *New Scientist* 27 Aug. 419/2 We were able to confirm using the stereoscan microscope that, as skin ages, the amount of extension possible in the fibre network is progressively limited. **1973** *Trade Marks Jrnl.* 11 Apr. 701/2 *Stereoscan*... Stereoscopic scanning electron microscopes and parts and fittings therefore included in Class 9. Cambridge Instrument Company Limited..; manufacturers. **1974** *Physics Bull.* Mar. 103/1 Many types of instrument are discussed, from the earliest use of a single lens to the present day field-ion and stereoscan electron microscopes. **1979** *Nature* 1 Mar. 102/2 Plates, including stereoscans, of pollen grains and spores. **1901** H. GADOW *Amphibia*, etc. (Camb. Nat. Hist.) 79 The vertebræ exhibit three types... 1. Lepospondylous and pseudocentrous... 2 a. Temnospondylous... 2 b. *Stereospondylous.—The three component units fuse by co-ossification into a solid, amphicœlous vertebra. **1875** KNIGHT *Dict. Mech.* 2378 *Stereostatic arch. **1830** HERSCHEL *Study Nat. Phil.* 228 Pneumatics, hydrostatics, and what might, without impropriety, be termed *stereostatics. **1893** *Nation* (N.Y.) 2 Feb. 90/2 This mathematical part might well be called stereostatics. **1861** *Proc. Roy. Soc.* XI. 70 A new Optical Instrument called the '*Stereotrope'. **1900** J. LOEB *Compar. Physiol. Brain* xiii. (1901) 184 Many plants and animals are forced to orient their bodies in a certain way toward solid bodies with which they come in contact. I have given this kind of irritability the name *stereotropism... There is..a positive and negative stereotropism, and there are also *stereotropic curvations. **1968** *Times* 1 Nov. 6/8 The idea is to carry automated photographic mapping to the full extent possible and to use *stereoviewing for interpretation. **1973** *Nature* 17 Aug. 413/1 Recently, direct stereoviewing has been developed for use in the scanning microscope.

stereobate ('stɛriːəʊbeɪt). *Arch.* [= F. *stéréobate*, It. *stereobate*, ad. L. *stereobata*, ad. Gr. *στερεοβάτης, f. στερεός solid + -βάτης as in στυλοβάτης STYLOBATE] A solid mass of masonry serving as a base for a wall or a row of columns. (See also quots.)

The term occurs only once in ancient use (Vitruvius III. iii). Vitruvius explains it as a massive wall built from the ground as a support for a row of columns. Modern writers (Latin in the 15–16th c., Italian, French, and English) have used it in various applications. According to some, *stereobate* is the generic term for a basement either under a wall or a row of columns, and a 'stylobate' is a stereobate of which the superstructure is columnar. Others restrict *stereobate* to the basement of a wall, as distinguished from *stylobate*, a basement under a row of columns. Others, again, use *stereobate* for the whole basement, and *stylobate* for the upper portion of this, which is added when there are columns.

1836 PARKER *Gloss. Archit.* (1840) 206 *Stylobate, Stereobate*, the basement or substructure of a temple below the columns. *a* **1840** HOSKING *Archit.* in *Encycl. Brit.* (ed. 7) III. 470 *Stereobate*, a basement. It is sought to make a distinction between this term and *Stylobate* q.v., by restricting the latter to its real import, and applying stereobate to a basement in the absence of columns. **1875** *Encycl. Brit.* II. 441/1 [Italian Architecture.] A basement is either a low stereobate or a lofty story, according as it is intended to support a single ordinance [etc.].

Hence **stereo'batic** *a.*, pertaining to or having the character of a stereobate.

1875 *Encycl. Brit.* II. 408/1 A stereobatic dado raised on the stylobate and antæ-base mouldings.

'stereoblock. *Chem.* [ad. It. *stereoblocchi* (G. Natta et al. 1957, in *Chim. e Industr.* XXXIX. 276/2): see STEREO- and BLOCK *sb.*] A segment of a polymer chain possessing stereoregularity. Also *attrib.*, as ***stereoblock polymer***, a polymer the chains of which contain such segments.

1957 *Chem. Abstr.* LI. 12536 New linear high polymers of α-olefins are described which are distinguished by the presence within the macromol. of chain portions of different steric configurations. Designated 'stereoblock' polymers.., these differ from the block copolymers in that the former are obtained by polymerization of a single type of monomer. **1959** GAYLORD & MARK *Linear & Stereoregular Addition Polymers* 483 As originally defined by Natta, stereoblock polymers of α-olefins are polymers consisting of macromolecules containing crystallizable segments having isotactic structure and noncrystallizable segments. Actually, these macromolecules may consist either of both isotactic and atactic segments or of adjacent isotactic segments having different steric configuration... In practice, amorphous polymers, considered as atactic, may contain very short stereoblocks. **1979** C. H. BAMFORD in R. N. Haward *Developments in Polymerisation* II. 253 The 'hopping' of a propagating chain from an isotactic to a syndiotactic matrix (or vice versa) could give rise to a stereoblock daughter polymer. **1980** *Jrnl. Polymer Sci.: Polymer Physics Ed.* XVIII. 630 The length and the type of junctions between isotactic stereoblocks affects the crystallization of polypropylene.

stereochemistry (ˌstɛriːəʊ'kɛmɪstrɪ). [f. STEREO- + CHEMISTRY, after G. *stereochemie* (V. Meyer 1890, in *Ber. d. Deut. Chem. Ges.* XXIII. 568), *stereochemisch* adj. (Auwers & Meyer 1888, in *Ibid.* XXI. 789).] That department of chemistry which deals with theoretical differences in the relative position in space of atoms in a molecule, in relation to differences in the optical and chemical properties of the substances. Also, the stereochemical properties *of* something; a stereochemical configuration or arrangement.

1890 V. MEYER in *Smithsonian Rep.* 366 Le Bel and van't Hoff..considering those substances which turn the plane of polarization of light, arrived at..a conception of the aggregation of the atoms within the molecules in space. Thus a field of study was created which van't Hoff called '*la chimie dans l'espace*' and which we now call Stereochemistry. **1899** *Dublin Rev.* Oct. 340 This is called Geometrical Isomerism or Stereochemistry. **1905** *Rep. Brit. Assoc. Adv. Sci. 1904* 169 The stereochemistry of nitrogen has..attracted considerable attention. **1969** *Jrnl. Leeds Univ. Union Chem. Soc.* XI. 43 The important stereochemistries are octahedral.., tetrahedral.., and square planar. **1972** *Nature* 21 Jan. 180/3 Nyholm's researches in transition metal chemistry..were particularly concerned with metal carbonyl, metal-metal bonded systems, unusual stereochemistries and..the reactivity of coordinated organic groups. **1972** DEPUY & CHAPMAN *Molec. Reactions & Photochem.* vi. 84 It is often observed that related thermal and photochemical processes, while both stereospecific, give products with differing stereochemistry.

Hence ˌ**stereo-'chemical** *a.*, pertaining to stereochemistry; **stereo'chemically** *adv.*, as regards the relative spatial positions of atoms; **stereo'chemist**, an expert or specialist in stereochemistry.

1890 V. MEYER in *Smithsonian Rep.* 366 Numerous cases of isomerism..were regarded as stereo-chemical ones. **1890** *Jrnl. Chem. Soc.* LVIII. II. 970 The authors regard the existence of stereochemically isomeric azo-compounds as doubtful. **1907** A. W. STEWART *Stereochem.* 314 Stereochemical problems into which isomerism does not enter. **1935** TIPSON & STILLER in Harrow & Sherwin *Textbk. Biochem.* ii. 84 Where the two monoses are not identical, four stereochemically different disaccharides are theoretically capable of existence. **1937** *Nature* 10 July 49/2 The stereochemist is catered for in the precise directions given for the synthesis and complete optical resolution of that useful stereochemical agent, α-phenylethylamine. **1963** *Times* 23 Jan. 15/1 From there he went in 1905 to the University of Zurich to work with Alfred Werner, the distinguished stereochemist. **1974** GILL & WILLIS *Pericyclic Reactions* iii. 75 The stereochemically distinguishable modes of addition on a single olefin component.

stereochrome ('stɛriːəkrəʊm). [a. G. *stereochrom* (v. Fuchs), f. Gr. στερ-εός solid + χρῶμα colour.]

1. = STEREOCHROMY. Also, a picture produced by stereochromy. Also *attrib.*

1854 *Chem. Gaz.* XII. 219 The Stereochrome of Fuchs... The stereochrome is essentially the process of fresco secco invested with the capability of receiving and perpetuating works of the highest artistic character. **1896** *Westm. Gaz.* 28 May 7/3 The two great stereochrome pictures by Maclise in the Royal Gallery.

2. (See quot.)

1875 *Ure's Dict. Arts* (ed. 7) III. 911 *Stereochrome.* A name given to a process of stereotyping, the printing of which is effected in colours.

stereochromy ('stɛriːəʊˌkrəʊmɪ). [ad. G. *stereochromie*, formed as prec.: see -Y.] A process of mural painting in which water-glass is used as a preservative against atmospheric influences.

1845 *Builder* 6 Sept. 422/3 Stereochromy. A new method of architectural painting, by Dr. Fuchs and Professor Schlotthauer in Munich. **1851** ANNA M. HOWITT *Art-Stud. Munich* (1853) I. 239 *Sterrio-chromie* [sic] is the discovery of the celebrated chemist..von Fuchs of Munich. **1887** *Encycl. Brit.* XXII. 54/1 In this process of 'stereochromy', ..the more immediate basis for the painting consists of a thin layer of..cement made up of powdered marble, dolomite, quartz, and air-worn quicklime with water glass. On it the colours are laid with plain water.

So ˌ**stereochro'matic**, **-'chromic** *adjs.*, pertaining to or executed by stereochromy; ˌ**stereochro'matically** *adv.*; ˌ**stereo'chromatize** *v.*, *trans.* ? to treat with water-glass as in stereochromy.

1859 R. HUNT *Guide Mus. Pract. Geol.* (ed. 2) 33 A *stereo-chromatic painting on baked clay. **1845** *Builder* 6 Sept. 423/1 The picture executed *stereochromatically on this coat is fixed (after its completion) in a very particular way. **1907** *Athenæum* 23 Nov. 660/1 Burrows's figurines were carefully kept from the air when they were dug up, and were as soon as possible *stereochromatized. **1845** *Builder* 6 Sept. 423/2 For testing these qualities, *stereochromic paintings have been subjected to the most severe trials. **1887** *Encycl. Brit.* (ed. 9) XXII. 54/1 A stereochromic painting (unlike one made by the old fresco process) is practically proof against atmospheric influences.

stereogram[1] ('stɛriːəʊgræm). [f. STEREO- + -GRAM.]

1. A diagram representing a solid object on a plane; esp. a drawing in which the inequalities or curvature of a surface is indicated by contour lines or shading.

1868 J. C. MAXWELL *Sci. Papers* (1890) II. 101 The Construction of Stereograms of Surfaces. **1877** *Catal. Spec. Collect. Sci. Apparatus S. Kens. Mus.* (ed. 3) 40 Stereograms of the Lines of Curvature of Surfaces.

2. A stereoscopic picture: = STEREOGRAPH 1. Also *fig.*

1866 J. SHANKS *Elgin & Cathedr.* 103 Shakespeare's plays stand out by themselves, from all others, beyond all comparison, a stupendous intellectual stereogram. **1872** PROCTOR *Ess. Astron.* iv. 60 He had exhibited..some beautiful stereograms of this globe [*sc.* Mars].

stereogram[2] ('stɛriːəʊ-, 'stɪəriːəʊgræm). [f. STEREO *a.* + RADIO)GRAM[2].] An instrument for stereophonic reproduction of sound combining a radio and gramophone in a single cabinet; a stereo radiogram. Cf. STEREO *sb.*[3] 2.

1958 *Daily Mail* 27 Aug. 3/5 Some stereograms have both amplifiers and speakers inside one cabinet. **1976** *Gramophone* Nov. 914/1 Continuing their tradition of manufacturing single-unit stereograms, Thorn Consumer Electronics have just announced the latest in the line. **1977** M. JANCATH *Seatag* II. xi. 122 The stereogram in the corner stopped.

stereograph ('stɛriːəʊˌgrɑːf, -æ-), *sb.* [f. STEREO- + -GRAPH.]

1. A picture (or pair of pictures) representing the object so that it appears (or may be made to appear) solid, a stereoscopic photograph.

1859 *Atlantic Monthly* June 743 We have now obtained the double-eyed or twin pictures, or Stereograph, if we may coin a name. **1859** JEPHSON *Brittany* i. 6 Making stereographs of any object of interest. **1862** *Weldon's Reg.* Nov. 165/1 The stereographs of the full moon taken by Mr. Delarue show that our satellite deviates very considerably from the spherical form. *a* **1876** M. COLLINS *Pen Sk.* (1879) II. 96 His [Borrow's] vivid style seems to act on common-place objects as the stereoscope on the stereograph; it gives them a solidness and reality.

2. An instrument for making projections or geometrical drawings of skulls or similar solid objects.

1877 *Catal. Spec. Collect. Sci. Apparatus S. Kens. Mus.* (ed. 3) 956 Craniograph, by M. Broca. Stereograph, by M. Broca. **1878** BARTLEY tr. *Topinard's Anthrop.* II. iii. 268 The stereograph..gives..all the visible details, as well as some inaccessible to the eye, and is applied to each of the five surfaces of the skull which it is useful to reproduce.

3. An apparatus for making embossed points in metal plates in a system of printing for the blind.

1896 *Living Topics Mag.* (N.Y.) Feb. 131 Mr. Wait..brought out in 1894..the stereograph, by which they [the blind] can emboss metal plates for printing in embossed characters.

Hence **'stereoˌgraph** *v.*, *trans.*, to take a stereograph or stereoscopic photograph of.

1860 O. W. HOLMES *Prof. Breakfast-t.* viii, Having been photographed, and stereographed.

stereographic (ˌstɛriːəʊ'græfɪk), *a.* [ad. mod.L. *stereographicus*, f. Gr. στερεό-ς solid + -γραφικός: see -GRAPHIC. Cf. F. *stéréographique*, It. *stereografico*.]

1. Delineating or representing a solid body on a plane; applied *spec.* to a kind of projection used in maps, etc., in which the centre of projection is a point on the surface of the sphere, and the whole sphere is represented once on an infinite plane, circles being represented as circles, and the angles being retained.

1704 J. HARRIS *Lex. Techn.* I, Stereographick Projection. **1706** W. JONES *Palm. Math.* A4b, The Laws of the..Stereographic..Projection of the Sphere. **1730**

GREENWOOD in *Phil. Trans.* XXXVII. 68 In the Figures I have attempted the Stereographic Projection of the most considerable Scenes. **1737** *Gentl. Mag.* VII. 611 In those Stereographic Maps, where a..Hemisphere is projected upon a Plan parallel to a Meridian. **1863** HARBORD *Gloss., Navig.*, s.v., The stereographic projection of the sphere is a natural projection of the concavity of the sphere, on a diametral plane as primitive, the eye being placed on the surface at the opposite extremity of the diameter perpendicular to the primitive. **1872** PROCTOR *Ess. Astron.* iv. 62 A..chart of Mars on the stereographic projection. **1879** SIR A. R. CLARKE in *Encycl. Brit.* X. 203 Notwithstanding the facility of construction, the stereographic projection is not much used in map-making.

†**2.** Used to designate the 'stereotype steel plates' used for reproducing copper-plate engravings. *Obs.*

1810 in *Abridgm. Specif. Patents, Printing* (1859) 122 Plates thus constructed are what I call Perkins' 'steriographic [*sic*] steel plates,' one of which will serve to give as many impressions as would wear out a great number of copper-plates.

3. Pertaining to stereoscopic photography.

1859 *Atlantic Monthly* June 748 To render comparison of similar objects, or of any that we may wish to see side by side, easy, there should be a stereographic *metre* or fixed standard of focal length for the camera lens. *Ibid.*, Already a workman has been travelling about the country with stereographic views of furniture.

4. Pertaining to the use of the stereograph in craniometry. (See STEREOGRAPH 2.)

1886 *Buck's Handbk. Med. Sci.* II. 26/1 Particular methods of craniometric projections, diverse stereographic proceedings [etc.]..cannot here be mentioned in detail.

ˌstereo'graphical, *a.* Now *rare.* [f. as prec. + -AL[1].] = prec.

1675 SHERBURNE *Sphere of Manilius* c 2 b, This and All other Stereographical Projections. **1738** J. HAMILTON *Stereogr.* I. 13 The different ways of describing Objects on a Plane by Mathematical Rules are two, Geometrical and Stereographical. **1797** *Month. Mag.* III. 41 Useful in the practice of stereographical projection. **1805** *Gentl. Mag.* Mar. 251/1 All the sterographical plates are to be made according to the improved process described by Earl Stanhope. **1884** *Health Exhib. Catal.* 137/1 Geological and Stereographical Maps of the British Isles.

ˌstereo'graphically, *adv.* [f. prec. + -LY[2].] In a stereographic manner; by stereographic projection.

1679 *Phil. Collect.* XII. 44 A Representation of the Heavens in two large Hemispheres..Stereographically projected. **1708** *Brit. Apollo* No. 14. 4/1 To Project Stereographically a Spherical Triangle. **1890** GREENHILL in *Messenger Math.* XX. 16 Suppose we project the terrestrial meridians and parallels stereographically with respect to a pole on the equator,..we obtain a system of dipolar circles.

stereography (stɛriː'ɒgrəfɪ). [ad. mod.L. *stereographia*, f. Gr. στερεό-ς solid + -γραφία: see -GRAPHY. Cf. F. *stéréographie.*]

1. The art of delineating or representing the forms of solid bodies on a plane, as in perspective; in quot. 1860, stereoscopic photography.

1700 MOXON *Math. Dict.*, *Steriography*, or the Description or Drawing the Forms of Solids upon a Plain. **1738** J. HAMILTON (*title*) Stereography; or a compleat body of perspective in all its branches. **1842** GWILT *Archit.* Gloss., *Stereography*, that branch of solid geometry which demonstrates the properties and shows the construction of all regularly defined solids. **1860** MRS. BYRNE *Undercurrents* I. 240 The animadversions of this journal are directed against the abuse of photography and stereography.

2. See quot. (Cf. STEREOGRAPH 2.)

1886 *Buck's Handbk. Med. Sci.* II. 25/2 Graphic representation of the skull, or stereography, is a branch of craniometry by which the forms of the diverse curves of the head are traced, after measurement, on paper, or otherwise figured.

stereology (stɛriː-, stɪəriː'ɒlədʒɪ). [f. STEREO- + -LOGY.] The science of the reconstruction of three-dimensional structures from two-dimensional sections of them.

1963 *1st Internat. Congr. Stereology* ii. 2 With the aid of a Greek pocket dictionary we [*sc.* Hennig & Elias] coined the word Stereology. **1967** *Proc. 2nd Internat. Congr. Stereology* 1 Stereology is three-dimensional interpretation of flat images or extrapolation from two to three-dimensional space. *Ibid.* 2 An announcement in a few journals brought 11 scientists together on the Feldberg Mountain in the Black Forest 11–12 May, 1961. The word stereology was then coined and the International Society for Stereology was founded. **1974** *Nature* 29 Nov. 412/1 Stereology has revealed that there is a continuous increase in mitochondrial volume during the cycle. **1977** N. T. JAMES in Meek & Elder *Analytical & Quantitative Methods Microsc.* 20 An absolute requirement of stereology is that the test samples should be representative of the test tissue.

Hence **stereo'logical** *a.*, of, pertaining to, or by stereology; **stereo'logically** *adv.*; **stere'ologist**, one skilled in stereology.

1963 *1st Internat. Congr. Stereology* v. 3 The..arithmetical and geometrical principles which I now assume to be those generally employed by nature and therefore of common interest to stereologists. *Ibid.* vi. 21 The stereological field includes all the investigations in respect to the three-dimensional structures. **1972** *Science* 12 May 655/1 Like all stereology..stereological shape determination is a matter of geometrical probability. *Ibid.*, Simple shapes can be identified stereologically by measuring the length and width of each profile of a feature in section, classifying the quotients length/width of many profiles, and applying mathematical rules elaborated by the reviewer. **1975** *Nature* 10 July 151/2 Articles on high resolution, dark-field microscopy, in-focus phase contrast and stereological techniques. **1981** *McGraw-Hill Yearbk. Sci. & Technol.* 376/2 This relationship has been defined stereologically by Eq. (5).

stereome ('stɛriːəʊm). Also (after Ger.) -om. [ad. Gr. στερέωμα solid body or part, firmament, f. στερεοῦν to make solid, strengthen, f. στερεός solid.] **a.** *Bot.* Schwendener's term for those elements of a fibro-vascular bundle which contribute to its strength or stability; 'mechanical' tissue: cf. MESTOME. **b.** *Zool.* A proposed general term for the hard strengthening or skeletal tissues of animals in general, including invertebrates: see quot. 1891.

1885 GOODALE *Physiol. Bot.* 191 To the elements which impart strength to a bundle Schwendener has given the name stereom. **1887** HILLHOUSE *Strasburger's Handbk. Pract. Bot.* 88 The system of mechanical tissue, the Stereome. **1891** F. A. BATHER in *Nature* 12 Feb. 345/1 Among wants long felt..is some word that shall express for Invertebrata the idea that the word *bone* expresses for Vertebrata... I..venture to suggest the adoption of the word *Stereom*... This word..may..be thus defined: any hard calcareous tissue forming skeletal structures in Metazoa Invertebrata, and in Protozoa. **1898** H. C. PORTER tr. *Strasburger* etc. *Text-bk. Bot.* 169 Mechanical Tissues (Stereome).

†**stere'ometer**[1]. *Obs.* [f. Gr. στερεό-ς solid + -μέτρης measurer.] One versed in stereometry.

1608 R. NORTON *Stevin's Disme* B 3 b, To Land-meaters, Measurers of Tapistry, Stereometers in generall.

stereometer[2] (stɛriː'ɒmɪtə(r)). [a. F. *stéréomètre*, f. Gr. στερεό-ς solid + -μέτρον: see -METER.]

1. An instrument for measuring the specific gravity of porous or pulverulent bodies, invented by Say, a French officer of engineers, in 1797. Also *attrib.*

1801 *Encycl. Brit.* Suppl. II. 525/2 *Stereometer*, an instrument lately invented in France for measuring the volume of a body, however irregular, without plunging it in any liquid. **1856** W. H. MILLER in *Phil. Trans.* CXLVI. 799 To construct an instrument on the principle of the Stereometer invented by M. Say for the purpose of determining the specific gravity of gunpowder. *Ibid.* 801 The stereometer was mounted in a room..at the Mint, September 12, 1843. *Ibid.* 877 Stereometer observations. **1876** *Cat. Sci. Appar. S. Kens.* 30 Stereometer for ascertaining the density of bodies by determining their volume.

2. An apparatus consisting of a frame of bars and columns with sliding rods and wires, for illustrating problems in solid geometry.

1884 KNIGHT *Dict. Mech.* Suppl.

3. *Cartography.* Any of various instruments for measuring the parallax of a feature depicted in a stereoscopic pair of aerial photographs.

1911 *Encycl. Brit.* XXV. 900/1 The stereometer may be regarded as a modification of the stereocomparator. **1940** C. A. HART *Air Photogr.* vi. 178 In order that the stereometer may be moved easily while maintaining a direction parallel to the base-line of the pair of photographs, a parallel-guidance mechanism is often fitted. **1974** P. R. WOLF *Elem. Photogrammetry* viii. 150 Parallaxes of points may be measured stereoscopically. This method employs a stereoscope in conjunction with an instrument called a parallax bar and also..a stereometer.

†**ˌstereo'metrian.** *Obs. rare*[−1]. [f. STEREOMETRY + -AN.] = STEREOMETER[1].

1608 R. NORTON *Stevin's Disme* D 4, The Stereometrian shall vse the measure of the towne or place, as the Yard, Ell, &c.

stereometric (ˌstɛriːəʊ'mɛtrɪk), *a.* [ad. mod.L. *stereometricus* (Freigius 1583), f. *stereometria* STEREOMETRY.] Pertaining to stereometry or solid geometry; relating to or existing in three dimensions of space. Hence **stereo'metrically** *adv.*

1862 *Jrnl. Franklin Inst.* June 416 Mr. John Warner submitted to the meeting his Stereometric Tablet. *Ibid.* 417 The Stereometric Tablet is intended to assist computation of earthwork by the method of Transverse Ground-Slopes. **1875** *H. Vogel's Chem. Light & Photogr.* xiii. 137 If the flat figure is parallel to the retina,..by well-known stereometric laws the representation is like the original. **1890** V. MEYER in *Smithsonian Rep.* 366 The stereometric forms of a few simple molecules. **1890** *Stereometric* in WEBSTER. **1928** B. J. LEGGETT *Theory & Practice Radiol.* III. ix. 430 If..we radiograph this pelvis stereometrically and then reconstruct the pelvis in space by the method above, we are in a position to directly and accurately measure this diameter by means of suitable orthographic apparatus. **1972** *Science* 9 June 1136/1 The relative volume of extracellular space was estimated stereometrically.

ˌstereo'metrical, *a.* Now *rare.* [f. as prec. + -AL[1].] = prec.

1656 W. DU GARD tr. *Comenius' Gate Lat. Unl.* §527. 155 A Gage, whereon stereometrical numbers are inscribed. **1673** J. SMITH *Stereom.* Synopsis, The Stereometrical Problems, &c. in this Book. **1727** BAILEY vol. II, *Stereometrical*, pertaining to the Art of Stereometry.

stereometry (stɛriː'ɒmɪtrɪ). Now *rare.* [ad. mod.L. *stereometria*, a. Gr. στερεομετρία, f. στερεό-ς solid + -μετρία: see -METRY. Cf. F. *stéréométrie* (1560 in Hatz.-Darm.).]

1. The art or science of measuring solids; that branch of geometry which deals with solid figures, solid geometry; the practical application of this to the measurement of solid bodies.

1570 DEE *Math. Pref.* a iij b, The generall name of these Solide measures, is Stereometrie. **1594** R. ASHLEY tr. *Loys le Roy* 128 Plato affirmeth, that Geometrie was vnperfect in his time, and that Stereometrie, and the Cubike wanted. **1608** R. NORTON *Stevin's Disme* D 4, Gaudgerie is Stereometrie..but all Stereometrie is not Gaudgerie. **1673** J. SMITH (*title*), Stereometrie; or the Art of Practical Gauging. **1674** *Phil. Trans.* IX. 88 In Stereometry, or Measuring of Solids as a tapering Timber. **1683** T. EVERARD (*title*), Stereometry made easie, or The description and use of a new Gauging rod, or Sliding rule. **1795** T. MAURICE *Hindostan* I. xii. (1820) I. 439 From planimetry, or the mensuration of surfaces, they..proceeded to..stereometry, or the mensuration of solids. **1827** GUTTERIDGE (*title*), A New System of Stereometry. **1874** *Edin. Rev.* July 175 The text [of Dürer]..is full of detailed measurements, and calculations of the stereometry, or solid contents, of the several limbs.

2. The art of measuring specific gravities with a STEREOMETER (sense 1).

In recent Dicts.

stereomould ('stɛriːəʊˌməʊld), *v.* [f. STEREO- + MOULD *v.*, after *stereotype*: cf. STEREO *sb.*] *trans.* To stereotype by casting in a mould. So **'stereomould** *sb.*, 'a mould used in stereotyping' (*Cent. Dict.* 1891).

1857 G. & E. SCHEUTZ (*title*), Specimens of Tables, Calculated, Stereomoulded and Printed by Machinery. *Ibid.* Pref. p. xvi, By turning the handle..the whole table required is calculated and stereomoulded in the lead. By this expression is meant that the strip of lead is made into a beautiful stereotype mould.

stereophonic (stɛriːəʊ-, stɪəriːəʊ'fɒnɪk), *a.* [f. STEREO- + PHONIC *a.* (*sb.*).] Giving the impression of a spatial distribution in reproduced sound; *spec.* employing two or more channels of transmission and reproduction so that the sound may seem to reach the listener from any of a range of directions.

1927 *Wireless World* 26 Jan. 117/2 A marked improvement in quality of reproduction will be noticed, due to the phase-difference introduced by the distance between loud-speaker and phones. This phase-difference also varies with the frequency of the sounds reproduced, and thus a constantly varying difference in phase produces the stereophonic effect so superior to ordinary reproduction. **1940** *Nature* 3 Aug. 174/1 Demonstrations of the stereophonic reproduction of music and speech were given at the Carnegie Hall. **1953** *Sun* (Baltimore) 3 Aug. 16/7 Many picture men believe in the long-range possibilities of theater TV, but they also think that standardization of stereoscopic, stereophonic, wide screen equipment will have to come first. **1957** *Observer* 8 Sept. 10/2 An incredibly lush stereophonic music score exploits all the Hollywood clichés and adds some of its own. **1958** *Times* 14 Jan. 8/3 The B.B.C. last night carried out an experiment in the London area in stereophonic sound transmission. **1958** *Listener* 16 Oct. 605/1 Recently stereophonic disks have been introduced which have brought 'stereo' within reach of a much wider public. **1969** *Islander* (Victoria, B.C.) 6 July 5/2 Travellers enjoy a movie and stereophonic music through individual ear phones. **1977** *Rep. Comm. Future of Broadcasting* 13 in *Parl. Papers* 1967–77 (Cmnd. 6753) VI. 1 The BBC..introduced stereophonic broadcasting in 1966. Stereo was also provided by the IBA's radio VHF transmissions.

Hence **stereo'phonically** *adv.*, in a stereophonic manner; as regards, or by means of, stereophony.

1940 *Nature* 3 Aug. 174/1 A symphony concert produced in Philadelphia was transmitted over telephone wires to Washington and there reproduced stereophonically. **1958** *Times* 4 Aug. 10/2 After a fly has been buzzing stereophonically round her..a flash-back considerately takes over the task of explanation. **1969** *Amateur Photographer* 16 July 75/1 Testing for stereo should be done with recordings which have been proved to be satisfactory themselves stereophonically. **1972** K. BONFIGLIOLI *Don't point that Thing at Me* ii. 16 Martland..busied himself coaxing a few more decibels out of the stereo equipment... The Flying Scotsman whooped stereophonically for a level-crossing. **1977** *Gramophone* Sept. 504/2 You cannot distinguish the players stereophonically but quality and playing are excellent.

stereo'phonics, *sb. pl.* [f. prec.: see -IC 2.] Stereophonic techniques; stereophonic sound.

1958 *Punch* 22 Jan. 153/1 As yet there has been no talk of marrying these clever stereophonics with the echo-chamber, but it is bound to come. **1973** D. FRANCIS *Slay-Ride* v. 65 Arne..switched Beethoven on again fortissimo... I sat resignedly..while the stereophonics shook the foundations. **1975** *Listener* 2 Oct. 448/1 Getting your ears in phase with different sound sources, otherwise called stereophonics.

stereophony (stɛriː-, stɪəriː'ɒfənɪ). [f. as prec.: see -Y[3].] Stereophonic reproduction; stereophonic sound.

1950 *Wireless World* Sept. 327/1 The first broadcast of stereophony, the system in which sources of sound are restored to their relative positions in space, took place in France on June 19th, 1950. **1958** *Manch. Guardian* 30 June 5/3 Even on monaural discs the equipment..gives a remarkable impression of stereophony. **1972** *Daily Tel.* 31 Jan. 7/5 The BBC started experiments with stereophony in 1926.

stereopsis (stɛriː-, stɪəriːˈɒpsɪs). [f. Gr. στερε-ός solid (see STEREO-) + ὄψις power of sight.] The ability to perceive depth and relief by stereoscopic vision.

1911 STEDMAN *Med. Dict.* 826/1 *Stereopsis*, stereoscopic vision. **1920** *Arch. Opthalmol.* XLIX. 64 When the facts are known it is quite possible that visual tests will not stop with measuring the acuity of each eye and the color sense, but that a certain standard of stereopsis will be required. **1961** *Lancet* 22 July 168/2 No stereopsis has been demonstrated in any of these patients. **1972** *Sci. Amer.* Aug. 86/3 By providing very precise localization of objects in visual space, stereopsis can be regarded as the *raison d'être* of binocular vision.

Hence **stere'optic** *a.*; **stere'optically** *adv.*, with an appearance of depth; stereoscopically.

1931 *Arch. Ophthalmol.* VI. 139 Stereoptic reactions of a grade above the lowest are observable in ordinary fishes, but the lowest grade is probably not represented in any surviving species. **1972** *Sci. Amer.* Apr. 65/3 One can also feed the three-dimensional coordinates into a computer and obtain simple ball-and-stick drawings that can be viewed stereoptically, enabling one to visualize the folded chain of the protein in three dimensions. *Ibid.* Aug. 120/2 No one believes that the anatomical retina could possibly be given information on any large scale from the mind; there are few, if any, outgoing pathways. Therefore, Julesz conjectures, the eidetic image is formed later than the image on the retina but earlier than the stereoptic image, perhaps much earlier. **1976** *Billings* (Montana) *Gaz.* 24 June 16-A/1 More pictures were taken Wednesday on Viking's fourth pass over the site, Chryse, by Viking's twin cameras. They were lined up to photograph overlapping strips which can be viewed stereoptically for a three-dimensional effect.

stereopticon (stɛriːˈɒptɪkən). [f. Gr. στερε-ός solid + ὀπτικόν, neut. of ὀπτικός OPTIC.] A double magic lantern arranged to combine two images of the same object or scene upon a screen, so as to produce the appearance of solidity as in a stereoscope; also used to cause the image of one object or scene to pass gradually into that of another with dissolving effect. Also *attrib.*

1875 KNIGHT *Dict. Mech.* 2376. **1878** E. W. CLARK *Life in Japan* 171 The fame of the stereopticon reached the palace. *Ibid.*, Splendid stereopticon pictures. *Ibid.* 178 After the stereopticon entertainment. **1894** *Outing* Sept. 449/1 The stately Nelson Column,..just as I had seen it projected by a stereopticon lantern fifteen years before.

stereoregular (stɛriːəʊ-, stɪəriːəʊˈrɛgjʊlə(r)), *a. Chem.* Also **stereo-regular**. [f. STEREO- + REGULAR *a.*] Of a polymer: having each substituent atom or group on the main polymer chain oriented in the same manner on the chain with respect to the neighbouring atoms or groups. Of a reaction: giving rise to such a polymer.

1959 GAYLORD & MARK *Linear & Stereoregular Addition Polymers* 473 The most significant new developments have involved the successful preparation of stereoregular polymers from monomers..which previously had only yielded atactic polymers. **1961** *Industr. Chemist* Feb. 74/2 Although stereoregular polymers prepared with Ziegler-type catalysts are now of considerable commercial interest, research is continuing in attempts to obtain stereo-specific polymers by other, and perhaps less complex, catalysts. **1962** *Engineering* 12 Jan. 57/1 The increasing commercial availability of the 'stereo-regular' synthetic rubbers. **1971** *Sci. Amer.* Dec. 50/3 One striking example of the ability of catalysts to perform highly selective molecular alterations is the stereoregular polymerization of olefins pioneered by Karl Ziegler and Giulio Natta. **1979** C. H. BAMFORD in R. N. Haward *Developments in Polymerisation* II. 251 Stereoregular poly(methylmethacrylate) can function, under suitable conditions, as a template for the polymerisation of the monomer.

Hence ˌ**stereoreguˈlarity**.

1959 *Jrnl. Polymer Sci.* XLI. 80 A decrease in polymerization temperature could result in increased regularity as a result of a simultaneous improvement in stereoregularity, linearity, and head-to-tail structure. **1964** *Ibid.* II. A. 4642 Stereoregularity was noticed in acetaldehyde polymerization only when solid borontrifluoride-etherate was used as the initiator. **1976** *Makromol. Chemie* CLXXVII. 1475 The four catalyst systems employed for the *cis* polymerization..give polymers with a different degree of stereoregularity. This could depend on a different stereoregulating power of the catalysts. **1979** *Jrnl. Polymer Sci.: Polymer Chem. Ed.* XVII. 2022 There was no significant difference between the stereoregularities of the polymers obtained with cesium naphthalene and fluorenylcesium as catalyst. This result indicates that the difference in initiator anions..did not affect stereoregulation.

stereoregulate (stɛriːəʊ-, stɪəriːəʊˈrɛgjʊleɪt), *v. Chem.* [f. STEREO- + REGULATE *v.*] *trans.* To cause (a polymerization or its product) to be stereoregular. So ˌ**stereoˈregulated** *ppl. a.*, **-ˈregulating** *vbl. sb.* and *ppl. a.*; ˌ**stereoreguˈlation**.

1959 GAYLORD & MARK *Linear & Stereoregular Addition Polymers* 476 Even the application of free radicals as initiators does not rule out the formation of stereoregulated addition polymers. *Ibid.* 478 The propagation reaction will be stereoregulated or stereocontrolled and the polymer will be tactic, which means that the individual monomers in the chain will overwhelmingly be added in one of the different possible ways and the resulting macromolecule will display stereospecificity, i.e., a high degree of internal orderliness. *Ibid.*, Experience..has shown that stereoregulating effects are strongest in the case of Ziegler-type catalysts. *Ibid.* 479 It appears that a methyl group at the alpha carbon atom is favorable for stereoregulation. **1961** *Industr. Chemist* Feb. 73/1 (*heading*) Nature of the stereoregulating catalysts. **1962** E. L. ELIEL *Stereochem. Carbon Compounds* xv. 448 The 'stereoregulated' (i.e. isotactic or syndiotactic) polymers have higher densities, higher melting points, and lower solubility than the atactic polymers. **1976**, **1979** Stereo-regulating, -regulation [see STEREOREGULARITY]. **1979** C. H. BAMFORD in R. N. Haward *Developments in Polymerisation* II. 249 The stereoregulating influence of added prepolymers has been shown to be more pronounced at lower temperatures.

stereoscope (ˈstɛriːəʊskəʊp, *often* ˈstɪəriːəʊ-). [f. Gr. στερεό-ς solid + -SCOPE.]

1. An instrument for obtaining, from two pictures (usually photographs) of an object, taken from slightly different points of view (corresponding to the positions of the two eyes), a single image giving the impression of solidity or relief, as in ordinary vision of the object itself.

In the original form of the instrument (***reflecting stereoscope***), invented by Wheatstone, the images were combined by means of mirrors placed at a suitable angle; the common form (***refracting*** or ***lenticular stereoscope***), invented afterwards by Brewster, has two tubes each containing a lens, through which the two pictures are viewed by the corresponding eyes.

1838 C. WHEATSTONE in *Phil. Trans.* CXXVIII. 374, I.. propose that it be called a Stereoscope, to indicate its property of representing solid figures. **1849** *Rep. Brit. Assoc.* II. 6 The most generally useful of these forms is the Lenticular Stereoscope. **1856** *Mech. Mag.* 12 Jan. 36 The Cosmorama Stereoscope. **1858** *Edin. Rev.* Oct. 453 The books of Mr. Newman, the well-known philosophical-instrument-maker supply..evidence of his having constructed stereo-scopes for Professor Wheatstone in..the year 1832. **1861** SIR D. BREWSTER in Mrs. Gordon *Home Life* (1869) 346, I am not the discoverer of the Stereoscope. I am only the inventor of the Lenticular Stereoscope now in universal use. **1863** FAWCETT *Pol. Econ.* I. v. (1876) 59 The stereoscope has now become a drawing-room toy.

2. *Surg.* An instrument resembling a catheter, for detecting solid foreign bodies, as calculi. *rare.*

1857 DUNGLISON *Med. Lex.*, *Stereoscope*..., an instrument for detecting a calculus in the bladder, and foreign bodies in the soft parts.

stereoscopic (ˌstɛriːəʊˈskɒpɪk), *a.* [f. prec. + -IC.] Of, pertaining to, or adapted to the stereoscope; having an appearance of solidity or relief like an object viewed in a stereoscope.

1855 *Jrnl. Franklin Inst.* Feb. 143 A stereoscopic locket,.. so arranged that the two pictures, with the appropriate lenses, are contained in a medallion of ordinary size. **1859** *All Year Round* 19 Nov. 79/1 Those stereoscopic slides which look so curiously like life. **1862** *Catal. Internat. Exhib., Brit.* II. No. 2958, Stereotrope or stereoscopic thaumatrope. **1879** H. GRUBB in *Proc. Royal Dubl. Soc.* 182 This arrangement..causes the images to coalesce, and produces the stereoscopic effect.

fig. **1909** G. K. CHESTERTON *Orthodoxy* ii. 47 His spiritual sight is stereoscopic like his physical sight.

ˌ**stereoˈscopically**, *adv.* [f. prec. + -AL[1] + -LY[2]: see -ICALLY.] In a stereoscopic manner; by or as by means of the stereoscope; with an appearance of solidity as in a stereoscope; also *fig.*

1856 *Mech. Mag.* 12 Jan. 36 By using larger lenses of proper focal length, pictures of any dimensions may be viewed stereoscopically. **1860** O. W. HOLMES *Prof. Breakfast-t.* vi, If we will..look at them stereoscopically, with both eyes instead of one. **1868** LOCKYER *Guillemin's Heavens* (ed. 3) 57 He combines Sun-pictures stereoscopically, and shews the faculæ to be above, and the spots below the general surface.

stereoscopism (stɛriːˈɒskəpɪz(ə)m). *nonce-wd.* [f. STEREOSCOPE + -ISM.] Appearance of solidity, as of an object viewed in a stereoscope; stereoscopic effect.

1892 E. M. NELSON in *Jrnl. Quekett Micros. Club* July 54 Stereoscopism, or 'solid view', can be obtained by one eye, ..but solidity is better and more perfectly seen with two eyes.

stereoscopist (stɛriːˈɒskəpɪst). [f. as prec. + -IST.] One skilled in the use of the stereoscope; a maker of stereoscopes.

1875 *H. Vogel's Chem. Light & Photogr.* x. 102 Stereoscopists must have glasses that can be shifted, in order that persons may adapt the position of the image to the eye.

stereoscopy (stɛriːˈɒskəpɪ). [f. as prec. + -Y: cf. *microscopy.*] The art or practice of using the stereoscope.

1861 *Once a Week* 30 Mar. 371 Ocular stereoscopy. **1913** *Engl. Rev.* Mar. 670 It is more than photography, it is more than stereoscopy.

stereoselective (ˌstɛriːəʊ-, ˌstɪəriːəʊsɪˈlɛktɪv), *a. Chem.* [f. STEREO- + SELECTIVE *a.*] Of a reaction: producing a particular stereoisomeric form of the product preferentially, irrespective of the configuration of the reactant; = STEREOSPECIFIC *a.* 1 a.

Orig. (quot. 1957) = STEREOSPECIFIC *a.* 2.

1957 *Jrnl. Amer. Chem. Soc.* LXXIX. 1595/2 Comparable *trans* eliminations in open-chain systems are stereoselective. **1959** *Ibid.* LXXXI. 110/1 A stereospecific process is one in which the configuration of the product is related to that of the reactant... A stereoselective process is one in which there is no relationship between the configuration of the reactant and that of product but one in which there is a definite driving force for forming one of the possible stereoisomeric products. **1962** E. L. ELIEL *Stereochem. Carbon Compounds* xv. 436 All stereospecific processes are stereoselective, but not all stereoselective processes are stereospecific. For example, the low-temperature free-radical addition of hydrogen bromide to the 2-bromo-2-butenes..is both stereospecific and stereo-selective in that the cis olefin gives *meso*-2,3-dibromobutane whereas the trans olefin gives the *dl*-dibromide. At higher temperature the reaction is still stereoselective (formation of 75% *dl* isomer to 25% meso isomer) but no longer stereospecific; both olefins now give the same product mixture. **1968** [see STEREOSPECIFIC *a.* 2]. **1979** *Canad. Jrnl. Chem.* LVII. 646/1 Our synthesis [of sucrose] was predicated upon the stereoselective methoxybromination of the diene 8.

Hence ˌ**stereoseˈlectively** *adv.*; ˌ**stereoseˈlection**, ˌ**stereoselecˈtivity**, the property or fact of being stereoselective.

1956 *Jrnl. Amer. Chem. Soc.* LXXVIII. 1171/1 The decreased stereoselectivity of ketonization..in the 2-methyl-3-phenylindanone system as compared with the 1-phenyl-2-benzoylcyclohexane situation. **1957** *Ibid.* LXXIX. 1594/2 The fact that eliminations from I and II.. occur stereoselectively rules out the possibility of an intermediate carbanion of any but very short half-life. **1968** S. I. MILLER in V. Gold *Adv. in Physical Org. Chem.* VI. 186 We shall then describe a number of causes of stereoselection associated with bonding, steric, thermodynamic [etc.] factors. **1974** GILL & WILLIS *Pericyclic Reactions* vi. 191 Likewise the *trans*-alkene is formed in the other processes with fairly high stereoselectivity. **1979** *Tetrahedron Lett.* 4867 (*heading*) Stereoselection in the $AlCl_3$-catalysed ene additions of chloral to 1,2-dialkyl ethylenes. **1979** *Canad. Jrnl. Chem.* LVII. 646/1 A new synthesis of sucrose in which all of the steps involved proceeded with complete stereoselectivity. **1980** *Chem. in Brit.* XVI. 518/1 He was able to put one of the carbon-carbon bonds in place stereoselectively creating two of the six contiguous chiral centres on the left hand side of the molecule.

stereospecific (ˌstɛriːəʊ-, ˌstɪəriːəʊspɪˈsɪfɪk), *a. Chem.* Also **stereo-specific**. [f. STEREO- + SPECIFIC *a.*] **1. a.** Of a reaction: = STEREOSELECTIVE *a.* Also of a catalyst: causing a reaction to be (more) stereoselective.

1949 *Jrnl. Amer. Chem. Soc.* LXXI. 3866/2 The reaction giving rise to the acetates was at least 90% stereospecific since the ratio of the yield of the acid phthalate of racemate I to the yield of the acid phthalates of other alcohols was ten to one. Stereospecificity of even a higher degree was found in the II series. **1957** [see ATACTIC *a.* 3]. **1958** *Chem. Abstr.* LII. 1106 (*heading*) Isotactic and other stereospecific polymers. **1959** *Times Rev. Industry* Feb. 57/1 Using the stereospecific catalysts developed in Germany by K. Ziegler, Professor Natta in Milan had succeeded in producing, from propylene gas, useful polymers which he characterized as isotactic. **1960** *Times* 19 July (Royal Soc. Tercentenary Suppl.) p. xiv/3 The past decade has seen the emergence of various stereospecific syntheses. **1966** *Petroleum Handbk.* (ed. 5) 215/2 There are two possibilities in building up the polymer chain [of propylene]; the methyl groups can be situated either at random on both sides of the chain or on one side of the chain only (stereospecific polymerization). **1968** [see sense 2 below]. **1978** J. A. BRYDSON *Rubber Chem.* i. 8 Stereospecific catalyst systems ..led to the availability of..rubbers with a much more controlled molecular architecture than had been obtained before. **1979** *Jrnl. Org. Chem.* XLIV. 3374 The determination of the configuration at C-24 of the revised structure of oogoniol..was accomplished by the stereospecific synthesis of the model compounds..which contain the oogoniol side chain.

b. Of a polymer, esp. rubber: = STEREOREGULAR *a.*

1959 *Times* 27 Apr. (Rubber Industry Suppl.) p. ii/7 Polymer chemists have long yearned to synthetize such stereo-specific polymers found to occur so prevalently in Nature. **1961** [see STEREOREGULAR *a.*]. **1966** *Petroleum Handbk.* (ed. 5) 224/1 In the last few years..a new family of synthetic rubbers—the stereospecific rubbers—have been developed. **1974** J. FORD-SMITH tr. *Heinisch's Dict. Rubber* 447/1 Examples of stereospecific polymers are cis-1:4-polyisoprene and cis-1:4-polybutadiene.

2. Of a reaction or process: yielding a product, or having a rate, that depends on the particular stereoisomeric form of the starting material.

1959, **1962** [see STEREOSELECTIVE *a.*]. **1968** I. L. FINAR *Org. Chem.* (ed. 4). II iv. 126 The term stereospecific reaction has been used in the same sense as stereoselective reaction, but now the tendency is to restrict the use of stereospecific to a reaction in which different stereoisomers produce different products or act at different rates. **1970** J. H. QUASTEL in Ehrenpreis & Solnitsky *Neurosci. Res.* III. 15 Stereospecific effects are also observed in cerebral amino acid exchange reactions; for example, elevated cerebral L-lysine is more effective than elevated cerebral D-lysine in increasing L-lysine exchange. **1978** *Biochem. Pharmacol.* XXVII. 653/1 The finding that the R-enantiomer of gliflumide binds less strongly [than the S-enantiomer] indicates that antidiabetic drugs are bound to plasma by a stereospecific process.

Hence ˌ**stereospeˈcifically** *adv.*, in a stereospecific manner: ˌ**stereospeciˈficity**, the property or state of being stereospecific.

1949 Stereospecificity [see sense 1 a above]. **1955** *Jrnl. Amer. Chem. Soc.* LXXVII. 4567/1 *cis*-Propenyllithium prepared from *cis*-2-bromopropene with lithium in ether.. reacts stereospecifically with benzaldehyde..to give..the alcohol with the same configuration as that of the starting bromide. **1965** PHILLIPS & WILLIAMS *Inorg. Chem.* I. x. 383 Other monomers can be stereo-specifically polymerized. **1970** *Jrnl. Polymer Sci.* A. VIII. 988 The stereospecificity of these catalysts is remarkable since they yield polybutadienes with a very high 1,4 content. **1970** J. H. QUASTEL in Ehrenpreis & Solnitsky *Neurosci. Res.* III. 15 Studies of the stereospecificity of amino acid uptake in vivo have shown.. that the L-amino acid usually penetrates the brain to a greater extent than the corresponding D-isomer. **1979** *Jrnl.*

Chem. Soc.: Chem. Comm. 918/2 Oxidation of labelled hexa-1, 5-dienes with permanganate generages four new chiral centres with complete stereospecificity. *Ibid.* 920/2 The oxidative cycloaddition constitutes a method for the formation, stereospecifically, and in a single step, of four chiral centres from an archiral, acyclic reactant.

stereotactic (stɛriːəʊ-, stɪəriːəʊˈtæktɪk), *a.* [f. STEREO- + TACTIC *a.*[2] (*sb.*[2]).]

†**1.** *Biol.* = THIGMOTACTIC *a. Obs. rare.*

1902 *Q. Jrnl. Microsc. Sci.* XLVI. 171 There appear to me to be yet two possible explanations of the penetration [of sperm into the egg]: (1) it is due to reaction to a stereotactic stimulus; (2) it is purely mechanical.

2. *Biol.* and *Med.* = STEREOTAXIC *a.*

1954 *Amer. Jrnl. Roentgenol.* LXXI. 441/2 A new type of stereotactic instrument for use in man. **1961** *Lancet* 2 Sept. 552/1 Stereotactic operations for parkinsonism. **1976** *New Scientist* 26 Feb. 427/2 Some of the patients will undergo stereotactic brain surgery, which enables lesions to be placed very precisely in the required parts of the brain.

Hence **stereoˈtactically** *adv.*

1934 in WEBSTER. **1949** *Jrnl. Neurophysiol.* XII. 371 Electrolytic lesions were made..at a site determined stereotactically. **1966** *Arch. Neurol.* XIV. 334/2 Cross and Green, utilizing microelectrodes placed stereotactically in the hypothalamus of rabbits, studied the activity of single units, presumably single cells.

stereotaxic (stɛriːəʊ-, stɪəriːəʊˈtæksɪk), *a. Biol.* and *Med.* [f. STEREO- + TAX(IS + -IC.] Involving or designed for the accurate three-dimensional positioning and movement of objects inside the brain.

1908 HORSLEY & CLARKE in *Brain* XXXI. 63 The foundation of the stereotaxic instrument is a rigid quadrilateral rectangular frame..the ends of which..can be approximated by joints which slide on the lateral bars. **1919** S. PAGET *Sir V. Horsley* 189 R. H. Clarke..also devised a stereotaxic apparatus, probably the most complex of all the mathematical instruments of physiology. **1935** *Arch. Neurol. & Psychiatry* XXXIV. 162 With the aid of the Horsley-Clarke stereotaxic instrument, lesions were placed in..the hypothalamus in forty adult cats. **1969** *New Scientist* 30 Jan. 230/1 The stereotaxic..procedure reaches deep areas of the brain. **1971** *Nature* 8 Jan. 131/1 The brain was exposed from above and a fine knife lowered between the two hemispheres until the blade was at the correct stereotaxic setting for the supraoptic commissure. **1971** 'D. HALLIDAY' *Dolly & Doctor Bird* xvi. 247 Nothing short of stereotaxic surgery will ever obliterate the events of..that night.

Hence **stereoˈtaxically** *adv.*

1964 *Jrnl. Neurophysiol.* XXVII. 754 Electrolytic lesions produced by passing 3-mA anodal d.c. for 10 sec. through a stereotaxically guided stainless steel electrode with 1 mm. bared at the tip. **1979** *Nature* 4 Jan. 52/1 I.c. cannulae (o.d. 0·6 mm) were implanted stereotaxically in male Wistar rats.

stereotaxis (stɛriːəʊ-, stɪəriːəʊˈtæksɪs). *Biol.* [f. STEREO- + TAXIS.] †**1.** *Biol.* = THIGMOTAXIS. *Obs. rare.*

1897 C. B. DAVENPORT *Exper. Morphol.* I. iv. 105 (*heading*) Effect of molar agents in determining the direction of locomotion—thigmotaxis (stereotaxis) and rheotaxis. **1902** *Q. Jrnl. Microsc. Sci.* XLVI. 175 The passage of the spermatozoa through the gelatinous coat..is more or less in a radial direction as regards the egg... The phenomenon is possibly due to stereotaxis, but a purely mechanical explanation seems to the author more probable.

2. *Biol.* and *Med.* Also **ˈstereotaxy**. Stereotaxic surgery.

1959 SCHALTENBRAND & BAILEY (*title*) Einführung in die stereotaktischen Operationen. Introduction to stereotaxis. **1959** L. V. AMADOR et al. in *Ibid.* I. 5/2 Most of the childrens [*sic*] brains were discarded because at the present stage stereotaxy will most likely be applied to adults only. **1974** C. B. T. ADAMS in R. M. Kirk et al. *Surgery* xiv. 284 This may be done by 'bimedial leucotomy' cutting the white matter under direct vision from above or by undercutting the orbital part of the frontal cortex from below (by open operation or by stereotaxis). **1974** *Lancet* 13 July 106/1 (*heading*) Stereotaxy for obesity.

stereotomy (stɛrɪˈɒtəmɪ). [ad. F. *stéréotomie*, f. Gr. στερεό-ς solid + -τομία: see -TOMY.] The science or art of cutting, or making sections of, solids; that department of geometry which deals with sections of solid figures; the art of cutting stone or other solid bodies into measured forms, as in masonry.

1728 CHAMBERS *Cycl.* **1801** J. JONES tr. *Bugge's Trav. Fr. Rep.* v. 101 Stereotomy,..in the scientific language of the Polytechnic School, signifies that part of stone-cutting, on which Frezier and De la Rue have written so much. The theory and rules of projection are first studied. **1843** *Blackw. Mag.* LIII. 618 A division of the cube, or, as he [De Lisle] called it, the stereotomy of the cube. **1843** *Civil Engin. & Arch. Jrnl.* VI. 99/1 His stereotomy, profile, proportion, and composition are admirable. **1903** *Nature* 12 Mar. 439/1 Stereotomy. By A. W. French..and H. C. Ives... This is another text-book for the student in civil engineering, and treats of masonry work.

Hence **stereotomic** (ˌstɛriːəʊˈtɒmɪk), **-ical** *adjs.*, pertaining to stereotomy; **stereˈotomist**, one skilled in stereotomy.

1828 WEBSTER, Stereotomical. **1860** WORCESTER, Stereotomic. *c* **1900** MRS. SCHUYLER VAN RENSSELAER *Handbk. Eng. Cathedrals* 32 (Cent. Suppl.) Gothic architects were wonderfully skilful stereotomists.

stereotype (ˈstɛriːəʊtaɪp, ˈstɪəriːəʊ-), *sb.* and *a.* [a. F. *stéréotype* adj., f. Gr. στερεό-ς solid + τύπος TYPE *sb.*

In Fr. the word has only the original adjectival use, and the subst. use = *édition stéréotype.*]

A. *sb.*

1. The method or process of printing in which a solid plate or type-metal, cast from a papier-mâché or plaster mould taken from the surface of a forme of type, is used for printing from instead of the forme itself.

1798 *Ann. Reg. Chron.* 22 The celebrated Didot, the French printer, with a German, named Herman, have announced a new discovery in printing, which they term stereotype. **1809** *Europ. Mag.* LV. 19 The prospectus of almost every work informs us, that the thing will be done in stereotype. **1816** *Q. Rev.* XV. 345 The introducer of that mode of printing called Stereotype. **1824** J. JOHNSON *Typogr.* II. xxii. 657 The invention of Stereotype, like that of Printing, is somewhat involved in mystery.

2. a. A stereotype plate. (In quot. 1817 used *transf.*)

1817 *Gentl. Mag.* Dec. 500 *note*, An obelisk with engraved heiroglyphics upon it—a wooden or copper plate—a medal—are stereotpyes. *a* **1823** HUTTON *Course Math.* (1827) I. 150 [They] are printed with what are called stereotypes, the types in each page being soldered together into a solid mass. **1858** SIMMONDS *Dict. Trade, Stereotype*, a solid page of metal cast from the letter-press. **1888** *Times* 7 Jan. 7/1 He seized the stereotypes and withdrew.

b. In generalized sense.

1823 *Encycl. Brit.* Suppl. VI. 378/1 The mode of casting stereotype is sufficiently simple. *Ibid.* A plate of stereotype does not require to be more than the seventh or eighth part of the thickness or height of the ordinary types.

3. *fig.* **a.** Something continued or constantly repeated without change; a stereotyped phrase, formula, etc.; stereotyped diction or usage.

1850 PRESCOTT in Ticknor *Life* (1864) 337, I told the Queen of the pleasure I had in finding myself in a land of friends instead of foreigners,—a sort of stereotype with me. **1877** MORLEY *Crit. Misc.* Ser. II. 91 The growth of brighter ideals..will go on, leaving even further and further behind them your dwarfed finality and leaden moveless stereotype. **1908** *Q. Rev.* July 5 The stereotype of school, newspaper and department prevails.

b. A preconceived and oversimplified idea of the characteristics which typify a person, situation, etc.; an attitude based on such a preconception. Also, a person who appears to conform closely to the idea of a type.

1922 W. LIPPMAN *Public Opinion* vi. 93 A stereotype may be so consistently and authoritatively transmitted in each generation from parent to child that it seems almost like a biological fact. **1935** G. W. ALLPORT in C. Murchison *Handbk. Social Psychol.* xvii. 809 Attitudes which result in gross oversimplifications of experience and in prejudgements...are commonly called biases, prejudices, or stereotypes. **1948** KRECH & CRUTCHFIELD *Theory & Probl. Social Psychol.* II. v. 171 The concept of stereotype..refers to two different things. (1)..a tendency for a given belief to be widespread in a society... (2)..a tendency for a belief to be oversimplified in content and unresponsive to the objective facts. **1960** T. HUGHES *Lupercal* 42 Who lived at the top end of our street Was a Mafeking stereotype, ageing. **1968** W. E. LAMBERT et al. in J. A. Fishman *Readings Sociol. of Lang.* 487 American students of English-speaking backgrounds who are in the process of studying the French language have a generally negative set of stereotypes about the basic personality characteristics of French-speaking people. **1974** *Howard Jrnl.* XIV. 102 The stereotypes which society has of the offender, are quickly matched by stereotypes which many offenders create of society. **1981** *Church Times* 23 Oct. 9/1 The neatly dressed unmarried lady (never without handbag)..is definitely not the narrow stereotype our media would have us think she is.

c. *Zool.* A stereotyped action or series of actions performed by an animal (see STEREOTYPED *ppl. a.* c).

1966 R. A. HINDE *Animal Behaviour* xxiii. 389 In captivity animals often develop behaviour stereotypes or tics which are repeated monotonously. **1971** *Sci. Amer.* June 117/1 Although subordinate males had no chance to mate with hens at the display grounds, they did perform mock matings... Mounting a pile of dry cow manure or a log or simply squatting on the ground, they would go through the stereotype of mating actions: treading the object, fluttering their wings, lowering their tail and even in some cases ejaculating.

4. *attrib.* and *Comb.*, as ***stereotype art, metal, office, plate; stereotype-founder, manufacturer, printer***; **stereotype-block**, (*a*) a stereotype plate; (*b*) a block of iron or wood on which a stereotype plate is fixed; **stereotype-press**, (*a*) a press for shaping and drying the mould in which a stereotype is cast; (*b*) a printing-press in which stereotypes are used.

1801 *Tilloch's Philos. Mag.* X. 277 If there would be an advantage in applying the *stereotype art to books of rapid sale. **1859** R. HUNT *Guide Mus. Pract. Geol.* (ed. 2) 188 *Stereotype Blocks of Fusible Metal. **1875** KNIGHT *Dict. Mech., Stereotype-block*, a block on which a stereotype is mounted to make it type-high. **1813** A. WILSON in *Trans. Soc. Arts* XXVIII. 321 Having resolved to unite the business of a *Stereotype Bookseller to those of a Stereotype Manufacturer and Printer, I propose that [etc.]. **1843** HOLTZAPFFEL *Turning* I. 325 The *stereotype-cast is nearly as sharp as the original type. *Ibid.*, The *stereotype-founder takes a copy of the entire mass of type in plaster of Paris. **1813** *Stereotype manufacturer [see *stereotype bookseller*]. **1839** URE *Dict. Arts* 51 The alloys called type metal, *stereotype metal. **1875** KNIGHT *Dict. Mech.*, Stereotype-metal. **1804** tr. *Freylinghausen's Abstr. Chr. Relig.* before title, Standing Rules of The *Stereotype Office. **1807** *Monthly Mag.* May 372/2 The expence of *Stereotype plates..is not 20 l. per cent. of that of moveable type pages. **1872** YEATS *Techn. Hist. Comm.* 339 A compound of tin and bismuth is employed in stereotype plates. **1805** *Gentl. Mag.* Mar. 250/2 The first production of the new *stereotype press. **1875** KNIGHT *Dict. Mech., Stereotype-press*, a small press for use in the clay process [of stereotyping]. **1813** *Stereotype printer [see *stereotype bookseller*]. **1820** T. HODGSON *Ess. Stereotype Printing* 119 As a stereotype printer Mr. Wilson must ever rank amongst the most eminent.

B. *adj.* (Often undistinguishable from the attrib. use of the sb.)

1. *lit.* Of an edition: Printed by the process described above in A. 1. Also used as an epithet of the process.

1801 *Tilloch's Philos. Mag.* X. 268 The processes connected with letter-press-plate or stereotype printing. **1817** *Gentl. Mag.* Dec. 500 *note*, At the present Epoch (1800), the art of Printing is become rather retrograde; or we should not hear so much of Stereotype editions. **1820** MILNER *Suppl. Mem. Eng. Cath.* 243 A small stereotype edition of the New Testament. **1861** SMILES *Engineers* II. 142 Earl Stanhope..also made important improvements in the process of stereotype printing.

2. *fig.* = STEREOTYPED b. Now somewhat *rare.*

1824 MORIER *Hajji Baba* I. Introd. Ep. p. xxxiv, It is an ingenious expression which I owe to you, sir, that the manners of the East are as it were stereotype. **1837** CARLYLE *Fr. Rev.* II. III. iii, Cartels by the hundred: which he..answers now always with a kind of stereotype formula. **1846** *Hints on Husband-Catching* 20 This same stereotype smile. **1848** CURWEN *Singing* Introd. p. xx, Thus is..singing made almost a hopeless thing by the stereotype faults of the Old Notation. **1895** *Oracle Encycl.* I. 561/1 The style began to assume a stereotype character. **1899** A. GUDEMAN in *Class. Rev.* XIII. 216/1 A veritable mosaic of stereotype ideas.

ˈstereotype (ˈstɛriːəʊtaɪp, ˈstɪəriːəʊ-), *v.* [ad. F. *stéréotyper*, f. *stéréotype*: see prec.]

1. *trans.* To cast a stereotype plate from (a forme of type); to prepare (literary matter) for printing by means of stereotypes. Also *absol.*

1804 tr. *Freylinghausen's Abstr. Chr. Relig.* title-p., The first book stereotyped by the new Process. **1818** TODD (citing *Entick*). **1835** W. IRVING *Life & Lett.* (1866) III. 74, I have nearly stereotyped the third volume of my Miscellanies. **1855** DORAN *Hanov. Queens* II. x. 169 Early in 1798,..the first book was stereotyped in England. **1877** H. SPENCER in *Min. Evid. Copyright Comm.* (1878) 258, I was sanguine enough when I began this series of books, to stereotype.

2. *fig.* To fix or perpetuate in an unchanging form.

a **1819** REES *Cycl.* s.v. *Engraving*, Vosterman..may be said at once to have successfully translated and stereotyped the great originals of those..painters [*sc.* Rubens and Vandyke]. **1841** MIALL in *Nonconf.* I. 401 The state-church stereotypes a system of faith. **1846** *Engl. Rev.* Sept. 150 Yet he proposes a measure which would stereotype heresy and schism for ever. **1874** SAYCE *Compar. Philol.* ii. 73 Shakespeare and the Bible have stereotyped English. **1888** TANSLEY in *Hardwicke's Sci.-Gossip* XXIV. 121/2 In flowers the colours are stereotyped and perpetuated by insect selection.

ˈstereotyped (-taɪpt), *ppl. a.* [f. prec. + -ED[1].]

a. *lit.* Cast in the form of, or prepared for printing by means of, stereotype. *rare.*

1820 T. HODGSON *Ess. Stereotype Printing* 57 Hoffmann ..announced a stereotyped (or in his phrase a polytyped) book..which appeared in 1787. *Ibid.* 95 They engaged to sell stereotyped plates.

b. Usually *fig.* Fixed or perpetuated in an unchanging form. (Most commonly of phrases or formulas of speech, or the like; rarely of persons.) Also *spec.* in *Psychol.* (see quot. 1934).

1849 *Knife & Fork* 29 That common, every-day love, that contents itself with stereotyped epithets of endearment. **1854** MRS. GASKELL *North & South* xii, Uttering..stereotyped commonplaces. **1862** THACKERAY *Philip* iii, Phil's father..entered the dining-room..with his stereotyped smile. **1900** A. CHURCH & PETERSON *Nervous & Mental Dis.* (ed. 2) 663 A single motion of the arm or body may be reiterated for hours (stereotyped movements). **1912** *Throne* 7 Aug. 213/3 The stereotyped business man who thinks a successful commercial career must begin with the sweeping out of a draper's shop. **1934** H. C. WARREN *Dict. Psychol.* 262/2 *Stereotyped* (*responses*), characterizing certain responses which are always performed in substantially the same manner. **1950** T. WIESENGRUND-ADORNO et al. *Authoritarian Personality* IV. xvi. 627 He..personalizes his own stereotyped hostility. **1957** [see CONSUMMATORY *a.* 2]. **1968** A. STORR *Human Aggression* ii. 11 This mechanism is easily set off, and, like other emotional responses, it is stereotyped and, in this sense, 'instinctive'.

c. *Zool.* Of an animal's action or behaviour: repeated though serving no obvious purpose.

1934 E. S. RUSSELL *Behaviour of Animals* i. 8 Their [*sc.* chaffinches'] behaviour is mainly instinctive, independent of previous experience, and to a considerable extent stereotyped and invariable. **1950** G. SIRCOM tr. *Hediger's Wild Animals in Captivity* viii. 88 M. Holtzapfel..was able ..to remove a long standing stereotyped movement in an armadillo..kept on a slippery and therefore unbiological floor, by providing a layer of earth ten inches deep. **1970** R. A. & B. M. MAIER *Compar. Animal Behavior* xvii. 356 Stereotyped movements displayed during courtship can evolve out of general movement patterns.

Hence **ˈstereotypedness**, the quality or state of being stereotyped.

1977 *Spare Rib* June 37/1 The visual equivalents tend to have a journalistic stereotypedness about them. **1979** *Trans. Philol. Soc.* 140 We also learn a good deal about..live Old Persian speech, many features of which, owing to the wretchedly small number of OP inscriptions and the stereotypedness of most of them, have remained hitherto well beyond our reach.

'stereo,typer. [f. STEREOTYPE *v.* + -ER[1]. Cf. F. *stéréotypeur*.] One who stereotypes.

1. One who makes stereotype plates.

1818 TODD (citing *Entick*). **1841** *Civil Engin. & Arch. Jrnl.* IV. 56/2 Fresh burnt plaster..is always adopted by the cunning stereotypers, for they state that if it simply stands a fortnight, the casts will not be so good. **1882** *Daily News* 29 Nov. 6/5 Wanted,..experienced Stereotyper for Daily and Weekly Newspaper.

2. *fig.* One who fixes unchangingly.

1890 C. MARTYN *W. Phillips, Agitator* 519 A propounder of truth—not a stereotyper of it into statutes.

So **'stereo,typery**, (*a*) the business of making stereotypes; (*b*) a place where stereotypes are made, a stereotype-foundry.

In recent Dicts.

stereotypic (,stɛriːəʊ'tɪpɪk), *a. rare.* [f. STEREOTYPE *sb.* + -IC.] Pertaining to or having the character of a stereotype. †**a.** *lit.*, as in *stereotypic plate* = stereotype plate. *Obs.* **b.** *fig.* Fixed, unchanging: = STEREOTYPE *sb.* 3 b, STEREOTYPED b.

1801 J. JONES tr. *Bugge's Trav. Fr. Rep.* xvi. 392 The newly invented stereotypic plates. **1802** *Monthly Rev.* XXXVIII. 498 The stereotypic art, as it is practised in the printing of books. **1884** GRONLUND *Co-op. Commonw.* i. 28 That other stereotypic definition of Capital..'accumulated Labor'. **1887** W. M. TAYLOR *Scott. Pulpit* 144 There is no need of adhering in that matter to any Quaker-like, stereotypic anachronism.

stereotypical (stɛriːəʊ-, stɪəriːəʊ'tɪpɪkəl), *a.* [f. STEREOTYPE *sb.* + -ICAL.] Of, pertaining to, or resembling a stereotype (sense 3 b). Also *spec.* in *Psychol.*, designating behaviour which is repeated without variation irrespective of the particular circumstances. Cf. STEREOTYPIC *a.*

1949 *Commentary* July 41/2 The stereotypical Negro, the unstinting giver. **1950** T. WIESENGRUND-ADORNO et al. *Authoritarian Personality* IV. xix. 747 Only by identifying stereotypical traits in modern humans..can the pernicious tendency towards all-pervasive classification..be challenged. **1957** P. LAFITTE *Person in Psychol.* v. 50 Co-operation on a ground of stereotypical distrust is not the same as co-operation on a ground of confidence. **1968** S. STUCKEY in A. Chapman *New Black Voices* (1972) 439 Small wonder we have been saddled with so many stereotypical treatments of slave thought and behavior. **1975** *Nature* 25 Dec. 750/1 Furthermore, a similar class of stereotypical behaviour is elicited by the DA agonist apomorphine. **1981** *Times Lit. Suppl.* 29 May 602/1 It boasts some fine performances and some stereotypical Allen dialogue.

stereotypically, *adv.* [f. as prec. + -AL[1] + -LY[2].] †**a.** By means of stereotypes (*obs.*). **b.** By a stereotyped phrase, etc. **c.** So as to constitute a stereotype (sense 3 b); in a stereotypical manner. **d.** *Zool.* As a stereotyped action.

1802 *Sk. Paris* II. lxvi. 357 The French tables of Logarithms, printed stereotypically. **1864** W. J. FITZPATRICK *Mem. Abp. Whately* I. 332 'What is the laziest letter in the alphabet?' His neighbour..responded stereotypically, 'Give it up!' **1950** T. WIESENGRUND-ADORNO et al. *Authoritarian Personality* I. iii. 98 The inner conflict is replaced by a new conflict between groups: the stereotypically moral 'we' and the stereotypically immoral 'they'. **1950** G. SIRCOM tr. *Hediger's Wild Animals in Captivity* viii. 76 The path stereotypically followed by a dingo. **1975** *Daily Tel.* 19 Nov. 14/3 Do all minority faces look stereotypically alike or are they depicted as genuine individuals? **1977** *Time* 26 Dec. 40/1 A throughly Episcopal church in Darien, Conn., an almost stereotypically proper and affluent Northeastern suburb. **1980** *Times* 3 June 11/6 The Nordic countries, which we might stereotypically expect to be sober and/or tormented, are just that.

'stereo,typing, *vbl. sb.* [f. STEREOTYPE *v.* + -ING[1].]

1. The action or process of making stereotype plates for printing. Also *attrib.*

1807 *Monthly Mag.* May 372/2 The wear of moveable types, in Stereotyping, does not exceed 5l. per cent. of the heavy expence incurred by the old method of printing. **1820** T. HODGSON *Ess. Stereotype Printing* 87 A plate was then obtained from the matrice by means of the stereotyping, or striking, machine. **1904** H. SPENCER *Autobiog.* II. 164 The cost of composition and stereotyping.

2. *fig.* The action of fixing or perpetuating in an unchanging form.

1888 BULMAN in *Hardwicke's Sci.-Gossip* XXIV. 231/2 The 'stereotyping' of the developed colours by insect selection. **1903** MORLEY *Gladstone* IX. vii. III. 331 There ought to be no stereotyping of our minds against modifications. **1914** J. PATRICK *Clement of Alexandria* vi. 220 An illustration of a familiar experience—the stereotyping of an error, not recognised as an error in the mind of a writer.

3. *Zool.* = STEREOTYPY 3.

1950 G. SIRCOM tr. *Hediger's Wild Animals in Captivity* viii. 76 This stereotyping is not serious, yet it shows clearly enough that the animal's surroundings need enrichment. **1967** *Animal Behaviour* XV. 64 There were no significant differences between any of the groups in spot-picking, route-tracing, or total stereotyping.

stereotypist ('stɛriːəʊ,taɪpɪst). [f. STEREOTYPE *sb.* + -IST.] One whose business is the making of stereotypes; a stereotyper.

In recent Dicts.

,stereoty'pographer. *rare*$^{-0}$. One who prints from stereotypes. So **,stereoty'pography**, printing from stereotypes.

1818 TODD (citing *Entick*). **1841** E. SCUDAMORE *Nomenclator, Stereotypography*, the art of printing from stereotypes.

stereotypy ('stɛriːəʊ,taɪpɪ). [ad. F. *stéréotypie*, f. *stéréotype* STEREOTYPE *a.*]

1. The process of making stereotype plates; stereotyping.

1891 in *Century Dict.*

2. *Path.* Persistence of a fixed or stereotyped idea, mode of action, etc., in cases of insanity.

1909 C. L. DANA *Nervous Dis.* (ed. 7) 686 Stereotypy is shown in two ways. **1912** B. HART *Psychol. Insanity* Index 176. **1934** H. C. WARREN *Dict. Psychol.* 262/2 *Stereotypy*, a pathological phenomenon consisting in the endless repetition of fragmentary or apparently senseless words, apparently useless movements, or of certain postures. **1948** [see CATATONIC *a.*]. **1976** M. HAMILTON *Fish's Schizophrenia* (ed. 2) iii. 58 A stereotypy is a movement which is not goal-directed and which is carried out in a uniform way, but some mannerisms which are abnormal exaggerations of expressive movements may be confused with stereotypies; however they are not executed in such a rigid way.

3. *Zool.* The frequent repetition by an animal of an action that serves no obvious purpose.

1934 E. S. RUSSELL *Behaviour of Animals* v. 98 Examples of this stereotypy or rigidity of instinctive behaviour. **1967** *Animal Behaviour* XV. 63/2 In this stereotypy, a bird would repeatedly touch the tip or side of the bill to a particular spot. **1981** *Ibid.* XXIX. 4/1 Inappropriate and often perseverant stereotypy can be elicited in many animals by raising them in abnormal and restricted environments.

4. *gen.* The state or quality of being stereotyped (sense b).

1950 T. WIESENGRUND-ADORNO et al. *Authoritarian Personality* I. iii. 94 One striking characteristic of the imagery in anti-Semitic ideology is its *stereotypy*. **1973** O. SACKS *Awakenings* i. 36 Witty and precise in her speech without significant stereotypy or stickiness of thought. **1976** *Word 1971* XXVII. 128 This stereotypy of semantic relations of nouns reported by Bowerman decreases as mean sentence length increases.

sterep, sterer, obs. ff. STIRRUP, STIRRER.

stereynge, obs. form of STIRRING.

sterhydraulic (stɜːhaɪ'drɔːlɪk), *a.* [ad. F. *stérhydraulique*, irreg. f. Gr. στερεός solid + F. *hydraulique* HYDRAULIC.] Applied to a form of hydraulic press in which pressure is generated by displacement of the contained liquid by a solid body, as a rod, screw, or rope, introduced with a continuous movement through a packed opening.

1866 *Mechanics' Mag.* 4 May 279/2 The Sterhydraulic Press..is the name given to the new hydraulic press, invented by MM. Desgoffe and Olivier, civil engineers. **1875** KNIGHT *Dict. Mech.* 2382.

steri, obs. form of STIR *v.*

steric ('stɛrɪk), *a. Chem.* [irreg. f. Gr. στερεός solid + -IC: cf. STEREOCHEMISTRY.] Pertaining or relating to the arrangement in space of the atoms in a molecule.

steric hindrance, hindrance of a reaction, held to be due to the spatial arrangement of the atoms in the molecules of one of the reacting compounds.

1898 H. N. STOKES in *Smithsonian Rep.* 301 Stereochemical formulas are..more than reaction formulas, and the steric conception of the so-called double and triple union asserts that these actually exist. **1905** A. W. STEWART in *Jrnl. Chem. Soc., Trans.* LXXXVII. 185 Angeli.. suggested that steric hindrance played a part in the reactions involving the addition of metallic hydrogen sulphites [etc.] ..to carbonyl groups.

Hence **'sterically** *adv.*, by, or as regards, the three-dimensional arrangement of atoms.

1918 *Jrnl. Chem. Soc.* CXIV. I. 127 If only one group is sterically hindered, then reactions can take place at both tertiary amino-groups. **1959** *New Scientist* 19 Feb. 399/1 Propylene,..using a Natta catalyst, can be turned into straight chains of polypropylene molecules, with all the arms or side groups projecting in the same direction: that is to say, they are sterically oriented. **1974** GILL & WILLIS *Pericyclic Reactions* v. 130 The face to face interaction of the two π-systems is the only mode that is geometrically and sterically feasible.

stericks, vulgar aphetic form of *hysterics* (see HYSTERIC B. 3).

1765 FOOTE *Commissary* III. (1782) 64 *Fun.* Fye upon you! you have thrown the old gentlewoman into the stericks. **1859** C. BRAY *Let.* 26 June in *Geo. Eliot Lett.* (1954) III. 94 We had Sara in strong stericks all the way home, because she had missed her final chance of explanation and advice from you.

sterie, obs. form of STIR *v.*

‖**sterigma** (stə'rɪgmə). *Bot.* Pl. **-ata.** [mod.L., a. Gr. στήριγμα prop, support, f. στηρίζειν to set fast, support.] **a.** A ridge extending down a stem below the point of attachment of a decurrent leaf. **b.** In fungi, a stalk or filament bearing a spore; often a branch or outgrowth of a basidium.

1866 *Treas. Bot.* 1098/2 *Sterigmata*, the elevated lines or plates upon stems produced by the bases of decurrent leaves. **1874** COOKE *Fungi* 21 Each spore is borne upon a slender stalk or sterigma. **1879** *Encycl. Brit.* IX. 832/1 From the hymenium rise the basidia, at the apex of which are usually four sterigmata bearing the spores.

Hence **sterigmatic** (stɛrɪg'mætɪk) *a.*, pertaining to or of the nature of a sterigma.

1882 *Encycl. Brit.* XIV. 555/1 The spermatia..at first appear as minute protrusions on the apices of the sterigmatic cells.

†**'steril.** *Obs.*$^{-1}$ [Cf. STARE *sb.*[3]] Some foreign measure of capacity.

c **1645** HOWELL *Lett.* (1655) I. III. xvii. 129 To lade so many thousand Sterils or measures of corn out of Sardinia and Sicily custom-free.

sterilant ('stɛrɪlənt). [f. STERIL(IZE *v.* + -ANT[1].] A sterilizing agent. **a.** An agent used to make something free of plant life or micro-organisms; a herbicide or disinfectant.

1955 *Proc. 12th Ann. North Central Weed Control Conf.* 45/1 The estimated erodibility of the soil treated with various sterilants..is shown in Table 3. **1960** *Farmer & Stockbreeder* 12 Jan. 71/1 In the dairy, a mobile washing-up trough on castors is filled with 30 gallons of hot water with added detergent and sterilant. **1960** *Agronomy Jrnl.* LII. 707/2 The best way to relieve the erosion hazard is to eliminate the weeds with soil sterilants so that crops can be produced that will leave a protective cover. **1973** *Nature* 20 Oct. 455/2 Leaflets were..surface sterilized in 1·5% sodium hypochlorite solution (10 min). The sterilant was removed by 8 successive washes with sterile water. **1979** *Arizona Daily Star* 8 Apr. A1/2 The formula containing 2,4,5-T is used as a sterilant on driveways and brick walks to prevent plant growth.

b. An agent used to render an organism incapable of producing offspring.

1961 *Jrnl. Economic Entomol.* LIV. 688/1 Tests were made to determine the effect of the sterilant on copulation by treated males and on zygote formation in females inseminated by them. **1973** J. J. MCKELVEY *Man against Tsetse* iii. 197 When the flies are released, they can transmit this sterilant venereally to their mates and again shatter the potential of the fly to increase in numbers. **1978** *Times* 4 Sept. 13/4 There is no problem in producing sterilization substances; the difficulty lies in finding a sterilant that does not have side effects and in persuading wild animals to take it regularly.

sterile ('stɛraɪl, 'stɛrɪl), *a.* Also 6 steryl(e, -yll, 6–7 stirrill, sterill, 6–9 steril, 7 sterrile, sterrill, stirrile. [ad. L. *sterilis*, cogn. w. Skr. *starī*, barren cow, Gr. στεῖρα barren cow, στέριφος barren, Goth. *stairō* fem. adj., barren. Cf. F. *stérile*, It. *sterile*, Sp. *esteril*.] Barren; not producing fruit or offspring.

1. In undetermined sense.

1552 HULOET, Steryll, barayne, or fruiteles, *sterilis*. **1570** LEVINS *Manip.* 129/11 Steril, *sterilis*.

2. Of soil, a country, occas. of a period of time: Unproductive of vegetation.

1572 HULOET (ed. Higgins), Sterill, or barrayne grounde, *terra ieiuna*. **1597** SHAKS. *2 Hen. IV*, IV. iii. 129 Like leane, stirrill, and bare Land. **1600** FAIRFAX *Tasso* XV. xv, The sterill coastes of barren Rinoceere They past. **1626** BACON *Sylva* §525 It is certaine, that in very Sterile Yeares, Corne sowne will grow to an Other Kinde. **1635** BRERETON *Trav.* (Chetham Soc.) 119 This country..now..is so sterile of corn as they are constrained to forsake it. **1784** COWPER *Task* I. 710 With nice incision..She ploughs a brazen field, and clothes a soil So sterile with what charms soe'er she will. **1796** MORSE *Amer. Geog.* II. 100 No country has a smaller proportion of land absolutely steril and incapable of culture. **1806** *Gazetteer Scot.* (ed. 2) 337 Owing to the too copious use of marl,..some farms have been rendered perfectly sterile. **1828** NAPIER *Penins. War* I. iv. (1878) I. 22 Catalonia, the most warlike, rugged, and sterile portion of Spain. **1836** MACGILLIVRAY *Trav. Humboldt* xxv. 376 Causing many places to be improved which would otherwise have remained steril. **1845** DARWIN *Voy. Nat.* i. (1879) 2 The novel aspect of an utterly sterile land possesses a grandeur which more vegetation might spoil. **1890** SWINBURNE *Stud. Prose* (1894) 223 A ghastly and hardly accessible wilderness of salt marshes, with interludes of sterile meadow and unprofitable vineyard.

fig. **1720** WELTON *Suffer. Son of God* II. xxiii. 639 Procure me some few Drops of those Celestial Waters, to bedew this Barren Clay, this Dry and Steril Heart. **1794** LD. AUCKLAND *Corr.* (1862) III. 229 Though the times are sterile in some respects, you see they have produced a plentiful crop of peers. **1855** BROWNING *Old Pict. Florence* xxxiv, Contrast the fructuous and sterile eras.

3. a. Producing no offspring; incapable of producing offspring. (Chiefly said of females.)

1558 [cf. STERILENESS]. **1612** *Benvenuto's Passenger* I. ii. 111 The pouder thereof is excellent for all cold infirmities of the head or ioynts, it makes the sterile plentifull. **1741** CHAMBERS *Cycl.* s.v. *Sterility*, Women frequently become sterile after a miscarriage. **1828** STARK *Elem. Nat. Hist.* I. 147 The adult males and sterile females shed their horns in winter. **1878** BROWNING *Poets Croisic* 26 Anne of Austria, Twenty-three years long sterile, scarce could look For issue. **1889** J. M. DUNCAN *Clin. Lect. Dis. Women* xxi. (ed. 4) 168 A woman may be sterile with this man and fecund with another. **1890** *Hardwicke's Sci.-Gossip* XXVI. 122/2 Sterile workers constitute the vast majority of the commonwealth [of bees].

fig. **1659** PEARSON *Creed* 271 We must not look upon the divine nature as steril, but rather acknowledge and admire the fecundity and communicability of it self, upon which the creation of the world dependeth. **1678** CUDWORTH *Intell. Syst.* I. iv. 546 Affirming that..Christians did not..make God a Solitary and Steril Being, before the Creation neither, as the Jews did.

†**b.** *transf.* Producing nothing living. *Obs.*

1602 WARNER *Alb. Eng.* XI. lxiii. (1612) 275 The sterile Lake where Heauen-fir'd Sodom was.

†**c.** Causing sterility. *Obs.*

1601 SHAKS. *Jul. C.* I. ii. 9 Our Elders say, The Barren touched in this holy chace, Shake off their sterrile curse.

4. Of a plant: Not bearing fruit.

1626 BACON *Sylva* §620 Those Things, which are knowne to comfort other Plants, did make that more Sterill. **1842** LOUDON *Suburban Hort.* 575 In all plantations of this variety a number of sterile plants will be found. **1845** LINDLEY *Sch. Bot.* (1862) 60 *b*, *Potentilla Fragaria* (Sterile Strawberry).

5. a. Mentally or spiritually barren. Also, unproductive of results; fruitless; barren *in* or *of* (something sought or desired).

1642 H. MORE *Song of Soul* II. I. ii. 52 Die they again? draw they in any breath? Or be they sterill? **1665** J. WEBB *Stone-Heng* (1725) 93 He seems..to be very steril of Invention. **1665** EVELYN *Let. to Sir P. Wyche* 20 June, For our language is in some places sterile and barren. **1803** W. GODWIN *Life Chaucer* I. Pref. p. x, Antiquities have too generally been regarded as the province of men of cold tempers and sterile imaginations. **1848** GALLENGA *Italy* I. Introd. p. xxvii, Meanwhile, the land was sterile of events. **1849** MURCHISON *Siluria* viii. 183 These deposits..are necessarily sterile in organic remains. **1878** JEVONS *Primer Pol. Econ.* 97 It has been objected to commerce that it is sterile and produces no new goods. **1879** R. K. DOUGLAS *Confucianism* iii. 84 Confucius perceived that the..ancients had for their object the worship of the one God, but he allowed this knowledge to remain sterile. **1914** *Daily News* 23 Oct. 4/2 His adventures in search of victory are uniformly sterile.

b. *nonce-use* as *sb.* A sterile person.

1870 [see IMPRACTICABLE B.].

6. *Biol.* **a.** Of an organ or structure that would normally contain reproductive elements: Barren, infertile.

Said, e.g., in *Botany* of a flower with only male organs, a stamen without an anther, a seed without an embryo, a frond without sori.

1646 SIR T. BROWNE *Pseud. Ep.* IV. vi. 194 This is also a way to separate seeds, whereof such as are corrupted and sterill swim. **1753** *Chambers' Cycl.* Suppl. s.v. *Sicyoides*, Some of the flowers on this plant are steril, or male-flowers, having no embryo. **1777** ROBSON *Brit. Flora* 30 *Sterile*, without antheræ, as in Rupturewort. *Ibid.* 215 *Herniaria*.. five antheræ, five sterile chives. **1842** BRANDE *Dict. Sci.* etc., *Lepals*, a term invented to denote stamens that are sterile. It is very rarely used. **1849** BALFOUR *Man. Bot.* §649 Flowers having stamens only, are staminiferous, staminal, or sterile.

b. Of cells, etc. Not capable of reproduction.

1856 W. CLARK *Van der Hoeven's Zool.* I. 76 The terminal cells sterile, the axillary oviferous. **1882** VINES tr. *Sachs' Bot.* 306 The fructification of a Fungus consists of..a sterile portion,..and of a fertile portion.

7. Free from micro-organisms. Now often of surgical instruments, etc. = STERILIZED.

1877 TYNDALL *Ess. Floating Matter Air* (1881) 215 The three tubes remained perfectly sterile. **1898** R. T. HEWLETT *Man. Bacteriol.* 98 Blood may be obtained..by pricking the finger..with a sterile needle or lancet. **1899** *Allbutt's Syst. Med.* VII. 550 The diplococcus was present in all except one case, which proved sterile. **1907** M. H. GORDON *Abel's Labor. Handbk. Bacteriol.* 160 The finger..is then rubbed with sterile wool soaked in..alcohol and ether.

8. *Comb.* **sterile-male** *Biol.*, used *attrib.* to designate the technique of controlling a natural population by releasing large numbers of sterile males into it, so that females that mate only with these do not reproduce. **sterile-wood**, a shrub, *Coprosma fœtidissima* (N.O. *Rubiaceæ*), native of New Zealand.

1874 *Treas. Bot.* Suppl. 1344/1. [**1955** E. F. KNIPLING in *Jrnl. Econ. Entomol.* XLVIII. 459/1 The purpose of this paper is to consider the possibility of controlling insects by releasing sexually sterile males among the existing population.] **1959** *Science* 9 Oct. 903/1 The possibility of controlling animal populations by the sterile-male method is not necessarily limited to insects. **1975** *Nigerian Jrnl. Entomol.* I. 181 Because of the ease of preparation, good-keeping quality and reuseability of the [bat's wing] membrane, it..may have a very important role in the control of tsetse flies in Africa by the use of the sterile male technique. **1980** *Adv. Vet. Sci. & Compar. Med.* XXIV. 166 Screwworm populations subjected to autocidal control by the sterile-male technique.

Hence **ˈsterilely** *adv.*, **ˈsterileness**.

1558 W. FORREST *Grysilde Seconde* (Roxb.) 54 They laide to good Grysilde her sterylenes, Whiche she cowlde not helpe: God sendeth all increase. *Ibid.* 84 Consernynge the sterylnes layde vnto her. **1727** BAILEY vol. II, *Sterilness*, Barrenness. **1886** HOWELLS in *Century Mag.* XXXIII. 191 Many men might go through life harmlessly without realizing this, perhaps, but sterilely.

ˌsteriliˈfidianism. *nonce-wd.* [f. L. *sterili-s* STERILE *a.*: see SOLIFIDIAN.] Belief in the sufficiency of a 'barren' faith.

1833 COLERIDGE *Lit. Rem.* (1838) III. 410 Antinomian-Solifidianism, more properly named Sterilifidianism.

sterility (stəˈrɪlɪtɪ). [ad. L. *sterilitās*, f. *sterili-s* STERILE *a.* Cf. F. *stérilité*, It. *sterilità*.] The quality of being sterile, barrenness.

1. Unproductiveness of the earth.

1426 LYDG. *De Guil. Pilgr.* 23780 Afterward..Vij yeres of Sterylite folwed on,..wherof Ioseph took good hed long a-forn. **1483** CAXTON *Golden Leg.* 283/2 There by his merytes he chaced awey the Sterylyte and barrynes that was in that Countre. **1580** *Reg. Privy Council Scot.* III. 294 The barrennes and sterilitie of the ground. **1653** RAMESEY *Astrol. Restored* 216 From whence you are to inquire of the fertility and sterility of the Earth. **1676** HALE *Prim. Orig. Man.* (1677) 225 There have been great Devastations and Decrements of Mankind by..Plagues and Epidemical Diseases, Famines, and Sterilities of great parts of the World. **1750** JOHNSON *Rambler* No. 33 ¶5, I will teach you to remedy the sterility of the earth. **1813** SIR H. DAVY *Agric. Chem.* viii. (1814) 359 Sicily was the granary of Italy and the quantity of corn carried off from it by the Romans is probably a chief cause of its present sterility. **1841** ELPHINSTONE *Hist. India* II. 149 Máldeó, rája of that country,..derived additional strength from the sterility of his territory. **1865** GEIKIE *Scen. & Geol. Scot.* viii. 211 One looks in vain for a tree or field or patch of green, to relieve the sterility of these lonely shores.

2. Incapacity for producing offspring (chiefly said of the female).

1535 STEWART *Cron. Scot.* II. 250 His wyffe ay in sterilitie, All his dais scho wes withoutin cheild. **1568** GRAFTON *Chron.* II. 837 He complayned..of the infortunate sterylitie and barennesse of hys wyfe. **1605** SHAKS. *Lear* I. iv. 300 Heare Nature,..Into her Wombe conuey stirrility. **1708** W. KING *Cookery* Let. ix. 149 Varro, the great Roman Antiquary, tells us how to do it by burning of their Spurs; which occasioning their Sterility, makes them Capons in effect. **1876** GROSS *Dis. Urin. Bladder* 271 Impotence and Sterility..are very rare after lateral lithotomy. **1883** H. DRUMMOND *Nat. Law in Spir. W.* (ed. 2) Pref. p. xiii, Inappropriate Hybridism is checked by the Law of Sterility.

†**b.** Of water: Unproductiveness of anything living. *Obs.*

1707 *Curios. Husb. & Gard.* 171 The horrible Sterility of the Sea of Sodom... No Animal can live in it.

c. Of plants: Incapacity of reproduction.

1837 P. KEITH *Bot. Lex.* 205 The cause of the sterility of hybrids is not well known. **1866** *Treas. Bot.* 1098/2 Far more frequently, however, sterility arises from outward agents, from the effect of long-continued drought or moisture, [etc.].

3. *fig.* Mental or spiritual barrenness; unproductiveness of results.

1665 GLANVILL *Scepsis Sci.* xxi. 133 Its experienced sterility through so many hundred years, drives hope to desperation. *a* **1678** WOODHEAD *Holy Living* (1688) 194 Yet where is a sterility in thinking on any subject, there is a necessity to change it. **1716** POPE *Iliad* II. *Ess. Homer's Battles* 323 Yet one cannot ascribe this to any Sterility of Expression, but to the Genius of his Times, that delighted in those reiterated Verses. **1782** V. KNOX *Ess.* lx. (1819) II. 16 Such has been the sterility of epigrammatic genius in our country. **1846** GROTE *Greece* (1862) II. 13 Sterility of intellect. **1891** *Speaker* 11 July 36/2 The fear is..that public life may be stricken with sterility in consequence of this veto.

4. The state of being free from micro-organisms.

1877 TYNDALL *Ess. Floating Matter Air* (1881) 133 The observed sterility was not due to any lack of nutritive power in the infusion. **1899** *Allbutt's Syst. Med.* VII. 550 The sterility in this case was probably due to the fact that death occurred nearly four months after the onset of the disease.

sterilizable (ˈstɛrɪˌlaɪzəb(ə)l), *a.* [f. STERILIZE *v.* + -ABLE.] Capable of being sterilized. Hence **ˌsterilizaˈbility**.

1904 *Lancet* 25 June 1782/1 Some of the earliest electric sigmoidoscopes were not sterilisable, as the electric light and connexions were an integral part of the tube. **1903** *Jrnl. R. Microsc. Soc.* Oct. 680 Simplicity, cheapness, and easy sterilisability are claimed for the syringe.

sterilization (ˌstɛrɪlaɪˈzeɪʃən). [f. STERILIZE *v.* + -ATION.] The action of sterilizing. Also *fig.*, esp. in *Econ.* (cf. sense 6 of STERILIZE *vb.*).

1874 W. ROBERTS in *Phil. Trans.* CLXIV. 458 On the sterilization by heat of organic liquids and mixtures. **1885** LD. NAPIER & ETTRICK in *Comm. Housing Working Cl.* V. 113/2 The formation of deer forests and sterilization of land in all parts of Scotland. **1900** *Nature* 1 Mar. 422/1 The thorough sterilisation of the syringe in every case. **1905** *Brit. Med. Jrnl.* 26 Aug. 443 Treat every man after the deserts of his grandfathers and who should scape sterilization? **1910** R. R. RENTOUL in *Brit. Health Rev.* Feb. 74 In 1903 I publicly advocated the sterilisation of the insane. **1938** *Times* 15 Feb. 14/2 'Sterilization' is the word used to describe the Treasury's policy of limiting the expansion of credit which would follow if the imports of gold were used as a basis for the expansion of the note issue or bank credits. **1942** *Sun* (Baltimore) 20 Jan. 10/2 The fall or 'sterilization' of Singapore could contribute to a clearing of the way for Japanese naval debouchment into the Indian Ocean. **1955** *Times* 3 Aug. 12/2 The Swiss authorities would be the first to admit that the sterilization of deposits..cannot be held to promise a solution of the problem posed by the existence of too much money and lack of sufficient opportunities for investing it. **1968** R. A. MUNDELL *International Econ.* xviii. 256 Sterilization (or neutralization) policy is a specific combination of monetary and exchange policy. When the central bank buys or sells foreign exchange the money supply increases or decreases. The purpose of sterilization policy is to offset this effect. **1974** A. K. SWOBODA in Johnson & Nobay *Issues in Monetary Econ.* 66 Keeping the money supply at its initial level involves a lower rate of sterilization operations when non-trade goods are present.

steriliˈzator. [ad. F. *stérilisateur*, f. *stériliser* to STERILIZE.] = STERILIZER 2.

1898 *Syd. Soc. Lex.*

sterilize (ˈstɛrɪlaɪz), *v.* [f. STERILE *a.* + -IZE. Cf. F. *stériliser*.]

1. *trans.* To cause to be unfruitful; to destroy the fertility of.

1695 WOODWARD *Nat. Hist. Earth* II. 101 Why therefore may we not as well suppose the other part of the Sentence, the Sterilizing the Earth, was also suspended? **1737** SAVAGE *Of Publ. Spirit* 204 No, no—such wars do thou, Ambition, wage! Go, sterilize the fertile with thy rage! Whole nations to depopulate is thine. **1810** SOUTHEY in *Edin. Ann. Reg.* I. I. 147 An experiment to sterilize the country for one year. **1891** *Spectator* 4 Apr., Gambia is worth far more to the French than the French right to sterilise the French shore of Newfoundland is to the English.

absol. **1910** MARGOLIOUTH in *Expositor* Mar. 216 The practice of sowing with salt, in order to sterilize, is alluded to in the Old Testament.

2. To deprive of fecundity; to render incapable of producing offspring.

1828 in WEBSTER. **1905, 1910** [implied in STERILIZATION].

3. *Biol.* To render (organs) sterile.

1891 *Hardwicke's Sci.-Gossip* XXVII. 77/1 Its ray-florets ..besides doubling or semi-sterilising themselves, have attained a broad stripe of yellowish white up each strap-shaped corolla.

4. *fig.* To make mentally or spiritually barren; to render unproductive, unprofitable or useless; to deprive of result; to render harmless.

1880 J. A. SYMONDS in H. F. Brown *Biog.* (1895) II. 168 Men who might have written excellent books are sterilised by starting with fastidious conceits. **1887** *Chamb. Jrnl.* 19 Feb. 114/1 That prodigious find of 1882 seems to have almost sterilised 1883 so far as treasure-trove is concerned. **1911** F. HARRISON *Autob. Mem.* II. xxiii. 60 M. Grévy being sterilised by office,..power fell to M. Gambetta. **1939** *Economist* 8 July 64/2 The Reich Government..is evidently thinking a good deal more of its own commercial ambitions in East Europe and..of ways and means of breaking up the embryonic 'Peace Front' by sterilising Poland as an anti-German military power.

5. To render free from micro-organisms.

1878 TYNDALL *Fragm. Sci.* (1879) II. 297 Schwann.. sterilised the flask by boiling. **1899** *Allbutt's Syst. Med.* VIII. 69 The milk should be sterilised.

absol. **1877** TYNDALL *Ess. Floating Matter Air* (1881) 229 In the one case five minutes' action completely sterilizes.

6. *Econ.* To inhibit the use of resources in order to exercise control over the economy, esp. to control the balance of payments by taking offsetting action to hold down the money supply.

1930 *Economist* 3 May 1007/2 The directors conclude a somewhat discursive report with remarks upon the wastefulness of sterilised gold, which they regard as one of the principal causes of the fall in commodity prices. **1935** A. D. GAYER *Monetary Policy & Econ. Stabilization* ii. 32 By the consistent utilization of the devices of 'offsetting' and 'sterilising'..the total media of payments were regulated independently of her [*sc.* America's] resources. **1936** *Sun* (Baltimore) 6 June 16/1 Such action would be aimed primarily at sterilizing the mobile gold received from abroad. **1938** *Times* 15 Feb. 14/2 No more gold will be 'sterilized' by the Treasury. **1942** *Sun* (Baltimore) 11 Feb. 1/3 Such a technique would 'sterilize' the money..; that is, keep it from building up the nation's purchasing power. **1944** *Ibid.* 3 Apr. 9/3 WPB suggested..that legislation be proposed to 'sterilize' such reserves to keep them from affecting the economy. **1968** R. A. MUNDELL *International Econ.* x. 149 The practice of 'sterilizing' the monetary effects of foreign exchange (or gold) purchases and sales has become widespread as countries look for means of adjusting the balance of payments other than that implicit in price level (or interest rate) adjustments. **1977** C. & D. S. AMMER *Dict. Business & Econ.* 180 Even though the United States is no longer on the gold standard, the term [*sc.* sterilization] continues to be used with the understanding that not gold but other reserves..are being sterilized.

7. *Town Planning.* To preserve (a piece of land) from building or other development.

1935 A. P. HERBERT *What a Word!* i. 18 The Townplanners and Green-Belters, when they propose to 'sterilize' a given area, mean that it shall *not* be sterile, that it shall produce *nothing* but vegetation and natural life, as opposed to buildings. **1937** *Times* 27 July 11/2 The council have also accepted offers to sterilize, free of compensation, the attractive Duncombe Farm estate at Ivinghoe, comprising 64 acres, on the understanding that there will be no building on the adjoining land. **1942** *Rep. Comm. Land Utilisation in Rural Areas* 71 in *Parl. Papers* (Cmd. 6378) IV. 497 The term 'green belt'..has come..to mean a belt of open land..to be 'preserved' from building (or, as is often said, 'sterilised'). **1973** *Town & Country Planning* Nov. 495 Any urban growth entailing the phased development of land would become impossible under site-value rating, except given some action to sterilize the land concerned, which would be precisely contrary to the aim of stimulating development.

Hence **ˈsterilized** *ppl. a.*; **ˈsterilizing** *vbl. sb.* and *ppl. a.*

1846 *Blackw. Mag.* LX. 13 The sudden sterilizing of districts previously fruitful. **1847** H. MILLER *First Impr. Eng.* xi. (1857) 177 New crops of them..appear as fast as the surface is relieved from its sterilizing burden. **1866** ALGER *Solit. Nat. & Man* III. 155 Nothing is so sterilizing as retirement, when [etc.]. **1877** TYNDALL *Ess. Floating Matter Air* (1881) 133 A sterilized infusion..remained sterile. **1880** 'VERNON LEE' *Stud. Italy* IV. i. 146 He had the intense, blind, sterilising love of antiquity of the men of the fifteenth century. **1888** *Sat. Rev.* 2 June 641 The chief certain result ..was the sterilizing..of French political capacity. **1891** G. S. WOODHEAD *Bacteria* 399 Sterilized vessels for the reception of various media.

sterilizer (ˈstɛrɪlaɪzə(r)). [f. STERILIZE *v.* + -ER[1].] One who, or something which, sterilizes.

1. A substance that renders soil sterile.

1839 URE *Dict. Arts* 793 [Lime from magnesian limestone] has been unfairly denounced by Mr. Tennent and Sir H. Davy, as a sterilizer.

2. An apparatus for destroying micro-organisms.

1891 G. S. WOODHEAD *Bacteria* 398 Steam Sterilizer. **1895** *Arnold & Sons' Catal. Surg. Instrum.* 716 Sterilizer for Ligatures. **1898** EVA C. E. LÜCKES *Gen. Nursing* xi. 144 Schimmelbusch's sterilizer is the one most used for the sterilization of instruments.

sterin, stering, obs. ff. STERN *a.*, STIRRING.

sterisol (ˈstɛrɪsɒl). *Pharmacy.* Also steresol. [contr. of *sterilizing solution.*] (See quot. 1898.)

1896 *Westm. Gaz.* 24 Sept. 8/2 In hitherto unknown solutions—holzin, holzinol, and sterisol. **1898** *Syd. Soc. Lex.*, *Steresol*, (Not official), an antiseptic benzoinated collodion.

sterk(e, obs. forms of STARK *a.*, STIRK.

sterks, sturks (stɜːks). *Austral. slang. rare.* [? abbrev. f. STERCORACEOUS *a.*] A fit of depression, irritation, annoyance. Also **'sterky** *a.*, having loose bowels from fear.

1941 BAKER *Dict. Austral. Slang* 71 *Sterks, give one the*, to infuriate, annoy, depress. **1944** J. DEVANNY *By Tropic, Sea & Jungle* 162 The croc disappears, and there's Ernest, standing up to his waist in the water..scared as hell, but too game to come out... So my dad goes in. He's a bit sterky too. **1959** D. FORREST *Last Blue Sea* 24 He just gives me the sturks.

sterlet[1] (ˈstɛːlɪt). Also 6 sterledey, 7 sterledy, 8 starlett, sterled, -ett, -id, (? *pl.* sterlitz), 8–9 sterlit, (9 sterelet). [a. Russ. *sterlyadi*. Cf. G. and F. *sterlet.*] A small species of sturgeon, *Acipenser ruthenus*, found in Russia.

1591 G. FLETCHER *Russe Commw.* (Hakl. Soc.) 12 Of ickary or cavery, a great quantitie is made..out of..the severiga, and the sterledey. **1698** *New Descr. Moscovy* 22 The Severinga or Sterledy, somewhat in fashion and tast like a Sturgeon, but not so thick nor long. **1698** A. BRAND *Embassy fr. Muscovy into China* 126 Among the Fish, the Sterlet is counted one of the most delicious in Russia. **1753** HANWAY *Trav.* (1762) I. II. xix. 83 The principal sorts are sturgeon, starlett, beluga and assotra. **1762** tr. *Busching's Syst. Geog.* I. 380 The Kosteri has rougher scales than the Sturgeon or the Sterled. **1782** P. H. BRUCE *Mem.* IV. 112 Some vessels going for Petersburgh, with live fish, called sterlit,..were beat to pieces. **1796** MORSE *Amer. Geog.* II. 74 Different sorts of sturgeon..viz. the common sturgeon, the beluga, the sterlid, &c. **1881** *Cassell's Nat. Hist.* V. 46 The best isinglass is yielded by the Sterlet and by *Acipenser huso.* **1883** *Fisheries Exhib. Catal.* 340 Hatched sterlit preserved in spirits. **1915** B. DIGBY in *Travel* July 23 Sterelet, one of the numerous kinds of fishes found in Baikal, is usually smoked and eaten raw.

attrib. **1860** WRAXALL *Life in Sea* v. 124 Prince Potemkin is said to have frequently paid three hundred roubles for a Sterlet soup.

'sterlet[2]. [? For **sternlet*, dim. of STERN *sb.*[1]; cf. STERNET.] ? The Lesser Tern, *Sterna minuta.*

1703 *La Hontan's Voy. N. Amer.* I. 240 The Seamews, Grelans, and Sterlets, are fowls that fly incessantly over Seas, Lakes, and Rivers.

sterling (ˈstɜːlɪŋ), *sb.*[1] and *a.* Forms: α. 3–6 sterlinge, -ynge, 4 sterlyngge, 4–6 starlinge, -yng(e, 4, 6–8 starling, 5–6 sterlyng, 7 sterlin, 8 sterline, 3– sterling. β. *Sc.* 5 strivilin, 6 stirveling, stirviling, striveling, striviling, strivling, 6–7 stirling, 7 stirlin, stirvlin. [Early ME. *sterling*, whence OF. *esterlin*, med.L. *esterlingus*, *sterlingus*, *sterlinus*, MHG. *sterlinc*, It. *sterlino.* Of uncertain origin, but probably a late OE. formation in -LING[1].

The earliest known example (in the Fr. form *esterlin*) is believed to occur in a charter of the Norman abbey of Préaux (Round *Cal. Documents, France*, p. 111). The date is supposed to be either 1085 or 1104, on the evidence of the golden number, but so far as this is concerned it might be later by 19 years or a multiple of 19; the cartulary is of the 13th c. Ordericus Vitalis (*a* 1145) has in Latin *libræ sterilensium*, and *libræ sterilensis monetæ*, as if he took the word for an *-ing* derivative of a place-name. The Anglo-Latin *sterlingus* is cited by Ducange from the year 1180. Continental examples are frequent in the 13th c., the excellence of the English penny having procured for it extensive currency in foreign countries; in Oct. 1202, Baldwin Count of Flanders contracts to pay to certain Venetian nobles 'the sum of 121 ounces in marks sterling (marcas sterlinorum) at the rate of 13 "solidi" and 4 "denarii" for each silver mark' (Rawdon Brown, *Cal. State Papers, Venice* I. 1).

The word, if of English origin, presumably was descriptive of some peculiar characteristic of the new Norman penny. The most plausible explanation is that it represents a late OE. **steorling*, 'coin with a star' (f. *steorra* star), some of the early Norman pennies having on them a small star. An old conjecture is that the word is derived from *stær* a starling (STARE *sb.*[1]), and alludes to the four birds (usually called 'martlets') on some coins of Edward the Confessor; but if this were so the early form would normally have been *starling.* Until recently, the prevailing view was that the word was a shortening of EASTERLING. Walter de Pinchebek (*c* 1300) gives this explanation, saying that the coin was originally made by Easterling moneyers; but the stressed first syllable would not have been dropped.

In Scotland the word was confused with the name of the town of Stirling, anciently *Strivelin*; hence the β forms common in the 15th and 16th centuries.]

A. *sb.*

1. a. The English silver penny of the Norman and subsequent dynasties. Often in ***pound of sterlings***, originally a pound weight of silver pennies, afterwards a name for the English pound (240 pence) as a money of account. Also in ***mark, shilling,*** etc. ***of sterlings.*** *Obs.* exc. *Hist.*

1297 R. GLOUC. (Rolls) 5949 He ȝef hem atten ende Four þousend pound of sterlynges. *Ibid.* 11840 þe king..eche ȝer him sende A certein summe of sterlinges to is liues ende. *c* **1300** *Fleta* II. xii. (1647) 72 Per denar' Angliæ qui sterling' appellatur, et fit rotundus, qui debet ponderare triginta duo grana frumenti mediocria. *a* **1330** *Syr Degarre* 297 The ten pound of starlings Were i-spended in his fostrings. **1377** LANGL. *P. Pl.* B. xv. 342 As in lussheborwes is a lyther alay and ȝet loketh he lyke a sterlynge. *c* **1386** CHAUCER *Pard. T.* 579 Myn hooly pardon may yow alle warice So þat ye offre nobles, or sterlynges, Or elles siluer broches [etc.]. **1387** TREVISA *Higden* (Rolls) VIII. 167 Þ e kyng..ȝaf hym an hondred schillynges of sterlynges. **1418** *E.E. Wills* (1882) 32, I bequethe to Ionet my wyfe..xl. li of Sterlinges. **1423** *Rolls of Parlt.* IV. 256/2 Silver..beyng as gode of alay as the sterlyng. *a* **1500** *Brome Bk.* (1886) 149, xx s. of starlynges. **1598** STOW *Surv.* vii. (1603) 52 Paid in starlings which were pence so called. **1861** *Numism. Chron.* I. 56 English and Foreign Sterlings found in Scotland. **1868** MISS YONGE *Cameos* (1877) I. xxiii. 179 Your words smell of English sterlings.

b. *Sc.* Applied to the Scottish penny.

This use is sometimes erroneously said to go back to the 12th c., on the ground of its occurrence in the so-called 'Assize of David I', which is a compilation of later date.

1387 *Charters* etc. *Edin.* (1871) 36, vi^c mark of sterlyngis of the payment of Scotlande. ? *a* **1600** tr. *Assisa de Mensuris* in *Sc. Acts* (1844) I. 674 King David ordanyt at þe sterlyng [orig. (? 15th c.) *sterlingus*] suld wey xxxij cornys of gude and round quhete. **1609** SKENE *Reg. Maj.*, *Stat. Robt. II* 56 b, The stirlin in the time of..king David, did wey threttie twa graines of gude and round quheat: Bot now it is otherwaies, be reason of the minoration of the money. **1884** *Encycl. Brit.* XVII. 656/2 The oldest pieces are silver pennies or sterlings, resembling the contemporary English money, of the beginning of the 12th century.

†**c.** With ellipsis of *of*, in ***pound, mark,*** etc. ***sterlings.*** *Obs.*

Chiefly with the plurals *pounds*, *marks*, etc., and hence in later use prob. apprehended as an adj. with plural inflexion.

1433 *E.E. Wills* (1882) 95 Y bequethe to litill Watkyn, my Godsone..x markes sterlynges. **1464** *Rolls of Parlt.* V. 530/1 An annuall rent of xl li. Sterlinges. *c* **1483** CAXTON *Dialogues* 51/22 A pound sterlings. **1486** *Rec. St. Mary at Hill* (1905) 11, vj marc sterlynges. **1528** *Sel. Cases Star Chamber* (Selden Soc.) II. 20 As moche wood as ys woorth iiij powndes sterlynges. **1542** UDALL *Erasm. Apoph.* 248 b, The thousande pieces wer muche about the summe of twentie nobles sterlynges.

†**2. a.** = PENNYWEIGHT. *Obs.*

1474 *Stat. Winch.* in *Cov. Leet Bk.* 396, xxxij graynes of whete take out of the mydens of the Ere makith a sterling oþer-wyse called a peny; & xx sterling makith an Ounce. **1496–7** *Act 12 Hen. VII* c. 5 Every unce [shall] conteyn xx sterlinges, and every sterling be of the weight of xxxij cornes of whete that growe in the myddes of the Eare of the whete. **1611** COTGR. s.v. *Carat*, For eight of them [carrats] make but one sterlin, and a sterlin is the 24 part of an ounce. **1776** ENTICK *London* I. 160 A penny, weighing two sterlings.

†**b.** attrib. ***sterling weight.*** *Obs.*

In the Table 'sterling weight' is stated in pounds, shillings, and pence; the lb. avoirdupois = 1lb. 2oz. 10dwt. troy, £1. 1s. 2d. sterling.

1612 W. COLSON *Gen. Tresury* H hij, A Table to finde Auerdupois weight reduced to Troy weight, and sterling weight.

3. Money of the quality of the sterling or standard silver penny; genuine English money. †In the 17th c. occas. used rhetorically for: Money.

1565 COOPER *Thesaurus*, *Centussis*..A rate of Romaine money conteynyng..10. Denarios, that is .x. grotes of olde sterlynge, when .viii. grotes went to an ownce. **1583** GREENE *Mamillia* II. (1593) L 2, It is..so hard to descrie the true sterling from the counterfeit coyne. **1602** DEKKER *Satirom.* D 2, Drop the ten shillings into this Bason... So, ist right Iacke? ist sterling? **1605** A. WARREN *Poor Man's Pass.* E 3, Whose coffers with Commodities abound So full, that they no sterling more may hold. *a* **1635** RANDOLPH *Poems* (1640) 113 Hexameter's no sterling, and I feare What the brain coines goes scarce for currant there. **1699** GARTH *Dispens.* 19 By useful Observations he can tell The Sacred Charms that in true Sterling dwell, How Gold makes a Patrician of a Slave [etc.]. **1707** NORRIS *Humility* vii. 320 To see a rich man that has nothing else to recommend him..but pure naked sterling, to grow proud and haughty upon a full purse ..nothing can be more ridiculous.

fig. **1584** GREENE *Mirror Modestie* Wks. (Grosart) III. 25 And seeing we haue you here alone, your stearne lookes shall stande for no sterling. **1584** —— *Tritameron* I. B iv, Your censure is no sentence, neither can this broken coine stande for sterlyng. **1602** SHAKS. *Ham.* I. iii. 107 You haue tane his tenders for true pay, Which are not starling.

4. a. English money as distinguished from foreign money. Formerly often in contrast to *currency*, i.e. the depreciated pounds, shillings, and pence of certain colonies.

1601 in *Stafford's Pac. Hib.* II. iv. (1633) 157 Monies of this new Standard of Ireland..being brought back againe to the Exchange to be converted in sterling. **1724** SWIFT *Drapier's Lett.* i. (1730) 17 The Tenants are obliged by their Leases to pay Sterling, which is Lawful Current Money of England. **1834** J. D. LANG *Hist. Acc. N.S. Wales* (1837) I. 206 The debts of the small settlers had all been contracted in sterling, and the price they received for their wheat..was in currency. **1890** *Daily News* 2 July 3/6 The lay treasurer of the society, who said that for a long time he had been opposed to the payments in India being made in sterling. **1892** *Ibid.* 19 Dec. 3/3 The effort has been made here to draw bills on America with the notion of selling at once for sterling, and using depreciated currency to pay the bills when due. **1900** *Westm. Gaz.* 8 Nov. 5/2 Sterling rose as promptly as it fell during last week's chaotic Money market. (New York.)

b. *fig.* in Australian use. (See quots.)

1827 P. CUNNINGHAM *Two Yrs. N.S. Wales* II. 53 Our colonial-born brethren are best known here by the name of Currency, in contradistinction to Sterling or those born in the mother-country. **1834** J. D. LANG *Hist. Acc. N.S. Wales* (1837) I. 220 Contests..between the colonial youth and natives of England, or, to use the phrase of the colony, between currency and sterling. **1837**, **1892** [see CURRENCY 4 b. *fig.*].

c. *attrib.* with the sense: Related to or payable in sterling. **sterling area**, the group of countries (chiefly of the British Commonwealth, from 1947 officially known as *scheduled territories*: see SCHEDULED *ppl. a.* b) that from 1931 to 1972 pegged their exchange rates to sterling, or kept their reserves in sterling and not in gold or dollars, and transferred money freely amongst themselves; also ***sterling bloc(k), group***; **sterling balances**, deposits in sterling which are held in British banks by overseas creditors (see also quot. 1948).

1894 H. BELL *Rlwy. Policy India* 81 A new contract.. granting a sterling guarantee of 3½ per cent on the capital expended. *Ibid.* 244 The sterling interest charges now payable on Indian railways..are equivalent to a payment of interest of over 7·6 per cent..if converted into rupees at par. **1898** W. J. GREENWOOD *Commerc. Corresp.* (ed. 2) 108 This sterling invoice was sent to Hamburg. **1903** *Pitman's Business Man's Guide* 409 *Sterling Bonds*, the bonds of certain American railroad companies which have been issued in the United Kingdom and are payable in English currency, and not in that of the United States. **1912** *Times* 19 Dec. 16/3 Sterling exchange was irregular. **1932** B. BLACKETT in *Times* 23 Jan. 12/4 What I have called the sterling area is sufficiently large and diversified to enable it to be to a very large extent self-contained. **1935** *Economist* 5 Jan. 1/2 The devaluation of the dollar and of the currencies of the sterling group..means that the currency value of the world's existing gold supply has immensely increased. *Ibid.* 26 Jan. 216/2 They might reasonably hope for a moderate increase in trade during the coming year, particularly, between countries within the 'sterling *bloc*'. **1937** A. HUXLEY *Ends & Means* v. 41 This has already been done in the case of the Sterling Bloc, which is composed of countries whose rulers have decided that it is worth while to co-ordinate their separate national plans so that they shall not interfere with one another. **1948** G. CROWTHER *Outline of Money* (ed. 2) v. 170 Overseas countries, especially those of the Commonwealth, were content during the war to sell more to Britain than they bought from her, and to take bank deposits in London..in payment of the difference. These were the famous 'sterling balances'. **1949** KOESTLER *Promise & Fulfilment* xv. 166 On February 22, 1948, Palestine was at short notice expulsed from the Sterling Block. **1956** R. S. SAYERS *Financial Policy* viii. 235 The Sterling Area became a legal entity, an area inside which payment in sterling was unrestricted. **1977** *Time* 24 Jan. 14/1 In the past three decades, few remnants of that empire have bedeviled the British more than the 'sterling balances'—deposits from governments and private parties abroad that are kept in British banks and government bonds. **1979** H. WILSON *Final Term* 3 The Sterling Area was dismantled at a stroke.

†**5.** Standard degree of fineness. *Obs.*

The sense was prob. evolved from traditional expressions like 'as good as the sterling' (see quot. 1423 in sense 1).

1696–7 *Act 8 & 9 Will. III*, c. 8 §8 Plate of finer Siluer then the Sterling or Standard ordained for the Moneys of this Realme. **1724** SWIFT *Drapier's Lett.* ii. (1730) 55 Gold and Silver of the Right Sterling and Standard.

B. *adj.* (Formerly often abbreviated ***ster.***, ***sterl.***)

1. In ***pound*** etc. ***sterling***, altered from the older ***pound*** etc. (***of***) ***sterlings*** (see A 1, 1 b), and originally used in the same sense. Hence, in later use, appended to the statement of a sum of money, to indicate that English money is meant.

α. **1444** *Rolls of Parlt.* V. 115/1 That the Seneschall..and other Officers..forfete M. marks sterlyng. **1523** *Act 14 & 15 Hen. VIII*, c. 12 §1 They shall stryke..as many halfe grotes..as shall amount to the somme of .xx. li. sterlyng. **1535** JOYE *Apol. Tindale* 22, iiij pense halpeny starling. **1665** LAMONT *Diary* (Maitl. Club) 176 He was dew..of excyse,.. ane thowsande lib. sterl. **1673** TEMPLE *Observ. United Prov.* ii. 86 Above Sixteen hundred thousand pounds Sterling a year. **1689** in *Acts Parlt. Scot.* (1875) XII. 60/1 þat they retaine 25 lib. starling of the excyse. **1713** J. WATSON *Hist. Printing* Publ. Pref. 16 For which he was to have a Salary of 100 lib. Sterl. per Annum. **1717** in *Nairne Peerage Evid.* (1874) 31 Between seven and eight hundred pound sterline yearly. **1724** SWIFT *Drapier's Lett.* ii. (1730) 62 England gets a Million Sterl. by this Nation. **1727** A. HAMILTON *New Acc. E. Ind.* I. xxi. 249 A Xerapheen is worth about sixteen Pence half Peny Ster. **1806** *Gazetteer Scot.* (ed. 2) p. xxv, The shilling Scots is the 12th part of a shilling Sterling, or one penny Sterling; the pound Scots..is equal to one shilling and eightpence Sterling. **1838** DE MORGAN *Ess. Probab.* 18 Concerns which now employ many millions sterling. **1849** LYELL *2nd Visit U.S.* II. 167 The value of the whole..amounting to 350,000 dollars, or 73,500*l.* sterling. **1856** EMERSON *Eng. Traits, Relig.* Wks. (Bohn) II. 100 The religion of England..believes in a Providence which does not treat with levity a pound sterling.

β. *a* **1578** LINDESAY (Pitscottie) *Chron. Scot.* (S.T.S.) I. 236 Ane hundreith thowsand pound striuiling. **1589** *Exch. Rolls Scot.* XXII. 17 Fra the scheref of Selkirk, 6d. strivling ..fra the scheref of Drumfreis, 3s. money, 1d. striviling. **1596** DALRYMPLE tr. *Leslie's Hist. Scot.* I. 333 He was redeimet with a ransoune of ane hunder libs stirling. *Ibid.* II. 355/20 [He] suld pay xx shilling Stirueling for his offence. **1611** SPEED *Hist. Gt. Brit.* IX. xii. §119 His [David II's] ransome was one hundreth thousand markes striueling. **1613–18** DANIEL *Coll. Hist. Eng.* Wks. (Grosart) V. 261 The ransome of a hundreth thousand Markes stirulin.

2. a. Prefixed as the distinctive epithet of lawful English money or coin. Now *rare.* †Also, in early Sc. use, of lawful Scots money.

α. *c* **1400** *Brut* clxiii. 182 The Kyng [Edw. I] ordeynede þat þe sterlinge halfpeny and ferthinge shulde go þrouȝ-out his lande. **1482** *Cely Papers* (Camden) 100 The sowdeers hath leiver to be payd here at xxvj s viij d. than hawe in Yngland sterlyng money. *c* **1483** CAXTON *Dialogues* 17/35 Ryallis nobles of englond,..Olde sterlingis pens. **1561** NORTON tr. *Calvin's Inst.* IV. xviii. 146 *marg.*, The common price of a Masse in fraunce is .iii. Karolus.. about the value of a sterling grote. **1565** COOPER *Thesaurus* s.v. *Census equestris*, 400 Sestertia, of olde sterlyng money 2000 poundes. **1590** WEBBE *Trav.* (Arb.) 27 A pennie loafe of Breade (of English starling money) was worth a crowne of gold. **1597** SHAKS. *2 Hen. IV*, II. i. 131. **1651** MARIUS *Adv. conc. Bills Exch.* 69 How to bring French Crownes into Starling Money. **1634** PEACHAM *Compl. Gentl.* xii. (1906) 122 *Libra* or *Pondo*..was worth of sterlin money three pounds. **1755** in *Nairne Peerage Evid.* (1874) 36 Eighteen pounds eighteen shillings ster[l] money. **1816** SCOTT *Antiq.* i, Three shillings of sterling money of this realm. **1837** CARLYLE *Fr. Rev.* I. III. iii, And, say, in sterling money, three hundred thousand a year.

β. **1488** in *Acta Dom. Concil.* (1839) 98/2 Twa vnces of striuilin pennyis. **1535** STEWART *Cron. Scot.* III. 382 Fiftie thousand of stirling mony gude To pay in hand. **1588** *Exch. Rolls Scot.* XXI. 391 The comptar dischargis him of striviling money..extending to 32d. **1609** SKENE *Reg. Maj.*, *Stat. Dav. II*, 44 It is statute that the kings money, that is, stirlin money, sall not be caried furth of the Realme.

b. Phrase, *to pass for* (later as) *sterling*. Chiefly *fig.* Also, *to allow, mark for sterling*.

1641 MILTON *Animadv.* 21 Setting aside the odde coinage of your phrase, which no mintmaister of language would allow for sterling. **1651** CULPEPPER *Astrol. Judgem. Dis.* (1658) 154 If the credit of Hippocrates may passe for starling, he protests that [etc.]. **1727** DE FOE *Eng. Tradesman* (1732) I. xviii. 248 What are they but washing over a brass shilling to make it pass for sterling? **1780** BURKE *Sp. Bristol* Wks. 1842 I. 257 If our member's conduct can bear this touch, mark it for sterling. **1817** JAS. MILL *Brit. India* III. i. 30 Such are the inconsistencies of a speech, which yet appears to have passed as sterling in the assembly to which it was addressed.

†**c.** *fig.* That has course or currency. *Obs.*

a **1568** ASCHAM *Scholem.* II. (Arb.) 96 This waie of exercise was..reiected iustlie by Crassus and Cicero: yet allowed and made sterling agayne by M. Quintilian. **1593** SHAKS. *Rich. II*, IV. 264 If my word be Sterling yet in England, Let it command a Mirror hither straight.

3. a. Of silver: †Having the same degree of purity as the penny. (*obs.*) Hence, in later use: Of standard quality. *sterling mark, stamp*: the hallmark guaranteeing sterling quality.

With the first quot. cf. quot. 1423 in A 1.

1488–9 *Act 4 Hen. VII*, c. 2 All suche fyne silver..shall be ..made soo fyne that it may bere xij. peny weyght of alaye in a pound wight, And yet it be as good as sterlynge and rather better than worse. **1551** SIR J. WILLIAMS *Accompte* (Abbotsf. Club 1836) 86 In grotes stricken w[t] harpes, the some of M[l]M[l] li, converted and made..of M[l]DCXXV li sterlinge siluer. **1676** W. B. *Touchst. Gold & Silver* (1677) 35 If it [plate] be worse then Starling it will appear Yellowish. **1681** *Lond. Gaz.* No. 1632/4 Five Silver-Hilted Swords, the Hilts of which are found upon the Tryal, more then one Shilling in every Ounce worse than the Sterling. **1684** ROSCOMMON *Ess. Transl. Verse* 310 Before the Radiant Sun, a Glimmering Lamp; Adult'rate Mettals to the Sterling Stamp, Appear not meaner, than mere humane Lines, Compar'd with those whose Inspiration shines. **1723** *Lond. Gaz.* No. 6134/4 Silver..Shoe-Clasps, mark'd Old Sterling. **1743** TINDAL tr. *Rapin's Hist.* II. XVII. 157 A pound of old Sterling Silver [was coined] into Half-Shillings, [etc.]. **1776** ADAM SMITH *W.N.* I. I. x. 129 The sterling mark upon plate, and the stamps on..cloth, give the purchaser much greater security.

b. In figurative context. (Passing into sense 4.)

1689 J. COLLIER *Misc.* ii. (1694) 73 There is another Profession, which possibly does not glitter altogether so much upon the Sense, but for all that, if you touch it, 'twill prove right Sterling. **1767** HARTE *T. à Kempis, Medit.* 72 True faith, like gold into the furnace cast, Maintains its sterling pureness to the last. **1784** COWPER *Task* v. 358 Were kingship as true treasure as it seems, Sterling, and worthy of a wise man's wish, I would not [etc.]. *Ibid.* VI. 990 What is base No polish can make sterling.

c. *absol.* Sterling silver tableware.

1974 *State* (Columbia, S. Carolina) 3 & 4 Mar. G2/1 Sterling promises to grow both more valuable, and more beautiful, with time. Its luminous beauty..is destined to take on the soft, lustrous patina..prized by so many collectors of antique silver. **1977** 'E. MCBAIN' *Long Time no See* iv. 48 The women cleaned house for other women, soaping fine china and polishing heavy sterling.

4. Of character, principles, qualities, occas. of persons: Thoroughly excellent, capable of standing every test.

c **1645** HOWELL *Lett.* (1650) II. 122 Twas your judgment, which all the world holds to be sound and sterling, induced me heerunto. **1755** YOUNG *Centaur* v. Wks. 1757 IV. 219 This love, supposing it sterling, I (*stultus ego!*) returned in kind. **1781** COWPER *Table-T.* 638 Then decent pleasantry and sterling sense..Whipp'd out of sight, with satire just and keen, The puppy pack that had defil'd the scene. **1789** WOLCOT (P. Pindar) *Subj. Painters* Wks. 1816 II. 20 The Dev'l's a fellow of much sterling humour. **1815** W. H. IRELAND *Scribbleomania* 70, I..advise this nobleman to apply his abilities to some more sterling and lasting theme. **1824** MISS L. M. HAWKINS *Annaline* I. 248, I know the sterling qualities you have. **1828** W. SEWELL *Dom. Virtues Greeks & Romans* 33 They derived from their Celtic origin ..many sound and sterling principles of conduct. **1832** W. IRVING *Alhambra* I. 83 The nephew..is a young man of sterling worth, and Spanish gravity. **1876** MOZLEY *Univ. Serm.* iv. (1877) 74 Gospel prophecy would not only develope what was sincere and sterling in man, but what was counterfeit in him too. **1891** C. ROBERTS *Adrift Amer.* 147 Her husband also was one of the most sterling good-hearted men I ever knew. **1896** HOUSMAN *Shropshire Lad* lxii, Then the world seemed none so bad, And I myself a sterling lad.

Comb. **1807–8** W. IRVING *Salmag.* (1824) 196 A knot of sterling-hearted associates.

Sterling ('stɜːlɪŋ), *sb.*[2] The proprietary name of a sub-machine gun made by the Sterling Armament Company Limited.

1958 J. BOLAND *League of Gentlemen* v. 100 Orderly piles of automatic weapons of all types—Stens, Brens, and Sterlings—were on the racks. **1969** M. PUGH *Last Place Left* vii. 46 One of them ran his torch up and down me, while a second man held the tip of his Sterling into the light. **1971** J. WAINWRIGHT *Last Buccaneer* II. 237 He hefted the Sterling sub-machine gun. **1974** S. GULLIVER *Vulcan Bulletins* 18 Automatic weapons like Stens and Sterlings. **1975** *Trade Marks Jrnl.* 21 May 1034/2 Sterling 976,708. Sub-machine guns; and parts and fittings included in Class 13, sold in kits for modifying the calibre of rifles. Sterling Armament Company Limited, 9 Berkeley St., London. Manufacturers and Merchants.—22nd June 1971.

sterling(e, obs. ff. STARLING[1] and [2].

'sterlingly ('stɜːlɪŋlɪ), *adv.* [f. STERLING *a.* + -LY[2].] In a sterling manner.

1883 JOLLY *Life J. Duncan* xxxix. 478 So sterlingly honest was he.

sterlingness ('stɜːlɪŋnɪs). [f. STERLING *a.* + -NESS.] Sterling quality.

1816 J. SCOTT *Vis. Paris* (ed. 5) 223 It will not be denied that they fairly try the sterlingness of the dramatic taste of the people. **1844** H. STEPHENS *Bk. Farm* I. 11 To judge of their lucubrations by the sterlingness of their practical worth.

sterlit, variant of STERLET[1].

stern (stɜːn), *sb.*[1] Forms: 1 **stearn, stearno, stærn, stern;** 7 **sterne,** 9 **stern,** 9 *dial.* **starn.** [OE. *stearn*, glossing L. *beacita, fida, gavia* and also *sturnus*. Cf. Fris. *stern (steern)*; *stern-k*; *stern-s (stirn-s, starn-s)* sea-swallow, tern. The mod.E. vowel, if genuine, is probably the result of lengthening before *-rn*.

ME. examples are wanting, but W. Turner *Avium præcipuarum historia*, 1544, art. *Gavia*, speaks of a species 'nostrati lingua *sterna* vocata'. The word was taken up by Gesner and other writers, whence probably it found its way into the Douay Bible. It was later adopted by Linnæus as the name of a genus *Sterna*; hence F. *sterne*.

The meaning 'starling', implied by early glosses to *sturnus (stronus)*, seems to be found in mod. Somerset dial. (see Eng. Dial. Dict. s.v. *Starn* sb.[4]); but the two names might easily be confused.]

A sea-bird; the tern, esp. the black tern (*Hydrochelidon nigra*).

c **800** *Erfurt Gloss.* 1116 *Gavia, avis qui dicitur*: stern *saxonice.* *a* **950** *Seafarer* 23 (Gr.) Stormas þær stanclifu beotan þær him stearn oncwæð isigfeþera. **1609** BIBLE (Douay) *Lev.* xi. 16 Of birdes these are they which you must not eate..the ostrich, and the owle, and the sterne, and the hauke. **1813** MONTAGU *Ornith.* Suppl. *Tern, black*.. Provincial. Stern. Car-Swallow. **1896** NEWTON *Dict. Birds* 955 *note*, *Starn* was used in Norfolk in the middle of this century for the bird known by the book-name of Black Tern.

stern, starn (starn), *sb.*[2] Now only *Sc.* Forms: *α.* 3 (*Orm.*) **steorrne, sterrne,** 4–6 **sterne,** 4–6, 9 **stern;** *β.* 4–6 **starne,** 6–9 **starn.** [a. ON. *stjarna*: see STAR *sb.*[1]] = STAR *sb.*[1]

α. *c* **1200** ORMIN 3646, & teȝȝre steorrne wass wiþþ hemm To ledenn hemm þe weȝȝe. *Ibid.* 7112 New sterrne & all unncuþ wass wrohht. *a* **1300** *Cursor M.* 375 Þe firmament.. wit sterns, gret and smale. *c* **1300** *Havelok* 1809 Was non of hem þat his hernes Ne lay þer-ute ageyn þe sternes. *c* **1330** R. BRUNNE *Chron. Wace* (Rolls) 9031 Þen ros a sterne ..'Comete' ys cald in astronomye. **1375** BARBOUR *Bruce* IV. 711 Thouch a man..Studeit swa in astrology, That on the sternis his hed he brak. **1456** SIR G. HAYE *Law Arms* (S.T.S.) 17 Thare fell a grete stern out of the hevin. **1508** DUNBAR *Golden Targe* 1 Ryght as the stern of day begonth to schyne. **1599** A. HUME *Hymns* ii. 121 Strange tailed sterns appeiris. **1818** SCOTT *Hrt. Midl.* xvii, There's a heaven aboon us a',..and a bonny moon, and sterns in it forby. **1819** W. TENNANT *Papistry Storm'd* (1827) 42 The sterns are blindet wi' the licht.

β. *c* **1375** *Sc. Leg. Saints* xl. (*Ninian*) 167 Sancte martyne, ..þat as a starne clerly schane. *c* **1460** *Towneley Myst.* xiv. 98 To wyt what this starne may mene. **1581** DERRICKE *Image Irel.* (1883) 86 A passyng starne, to guide mans shipp aright. **1596** DALRYMPLE tr. *Leslie's Hist. Scot.* II. 90/4 The Pleiades called the 7 starnis. **1725** RAMSAY *Gentle Sheph.* III. iii, Kiss, kiss! we'll kiss the sun and starns away. **1790** BURNS *'O death! thou tyrant'* iii, Ye hills, near neebors o' the starns. **1835** CARRICK *Laird of Logan* (1841) 185 No a starn was to be seen i' the lift.

b. In transferred uses (see STAR *sb.*[1]).

c **1400** *Anturs of Arth.* xxxi, With his sternes of gold, stanseld on stray. *c* **1450** *Reg. Vestments* etc. *St. Andrews* in *Maitl. Club Misc.* III. 205 Item thre gret sternis of brace for the kyrk. *c* **1450** *St. Cuthbert* 405 Þe calf is rede I vndertake, With a white sterne in þe fronte. **1454** *Test. Ebor.* (Surtees) II. 176 Rede cape with starnes of gold. **1569–70** G. CONYERS *Will* in *Fabric Rolls York Minster* (Surtees) Gloss., A blacke stagge with a starne in his forehead. **1814** W. NICHOLSON *Tales in Verse* 145 The lairdy langs for titles braw, For ribbons an' for starns.

c. *attrib.* as †*stern-leam*, †**stern-shot**, a shooting star (cf. STAR-SHOT); †**stern-slime**, nostoc (cf. STAR *sb.*[1] 22 b).

c **1200** ORMIN 7276 Forr Crist sellf iss þatt sterrnelem þatt all mannkinn birrþ follȝhenn. **1483** *Cath. Angl.* 362/2 A Sterne slyme, *assub.* **1513** DOUGLAS *Æneis* v. ix. 69 As dois oft sterne schot falling fra the hevin Drawand thair-efter a taile of fyrie levin.

stern (stɜːn), *sb.*[3] Forms: *α.* 4–8 **sterne,** 4 **steorne,** 5–6 **steerne,** 6 **stierne,** 6–7 **stearne,** 4– **stern.** *β.* 6, 9 **starn** *dial.*, 7 **starne** *dial.* *γ.* 6 **storne.** [Probably a. ON. *stjórn* fem. steering; an abstract formation with *-nō* suffix from OTeut. **steurjan*, ON. *stýra*, OE. *stíeran*: see STEER *v.* Cf. OFris. *stiarne, stioerne* stern, rudder.

This etymology accords with the scanty evidence of early distribution. But the earliest sense recorded in English, 'hinder part of a ship', appears in OFris. and not in ON., and a native origin is not impossible. Evidence is, however, lacking for the supposed OE. **stéorn*.]

†**1. a.** The steering gear of a ship, the rudder and helm together; but often applied to the rudder only, less commonly to the helm only. *Obs.*

13.. *E.E. Allit. P.* C. 149 Þe bur ber to hit baft þat braste alle her gere, Þen hurled on a hepe þe helme & þe sterne. **1387–8** T. USK *Test. Love* I. i. (Skeat) 35 How shulde a ship, withouten a sterne, in the grete see be governed. *c* **1430** *Pilgr. Lyf Manhode* II. xc. (1869) 108 Þilke þat maketh þe gouernour slepe amiddes þe ship vnder þe mast, whan he hath lost oþer broken þe steerne. **1471** CAXTON *Recuyell* (Sommer) 171 A tempest..bare many shyppys wyth theyr apparayll vnder water, brake theyr sternes and helmes [etc.]. **1607** R. WILKINSON *Merchant Royall* 11 A ship..is yet commanded by the helme or sterne, a small peece of wood. **1610** HOLLAND *Camden's Brit.* (1637) 657 This Beaver.. having a long taile..which in his floting he useth in lieu of a sterne. **1640** HABINGTON *Q. Arragon* v. H 2, A storme Ore tooke the ship, so powerfull that the Pilot Gave up the Sterne to th'ordering of the waves. **1671** tr. *Palafox's Conq. China by Tartars* xxiv. 414 They..made them content to bring ashore all their great Guns.., nay the very Sails and Sterns from off their Ships.

†**b.** *transf.* An apparatus which controls a horse, machine, etc. as a rudder controls a ship. *Obs.*

1607 MARKHAM *Caval.* II. (1617) 213, I discommended them [sharp cavezans] vtterly as the first instruments or釋 sternes wherewith to gouerne a Colt at his first backing. **1660** MARQ. WORCESTER *Exact Def.* 15 The [Water-Commanding] Engine consisteth of..5. A Helm or Stern with Bitt and Reins, wherewith a Child may guide, order, and controul the whole Operation.

†**c.** *fig.* That which guides or controls affairs, actions, etc.; also, from (the metaphor of the ship of state), government, rule. *Obs.*

1577 tr. *Bullinger's Decades* 1001 Whiche is the healme.. and stearne of the Euangelists and Apostles doctrine. *a* **1586** SIDNEY *Arcadia* III. (1598) 361 The turning of Zelmanes eye was a strong sterne enough to all their motions. **1591** SYLVESTER *Du Bartas* I. vii. 233 His envious brethren's trecherous drift, Him to the Stern of Memphian State had lift. **1597** BEARD *Theatre God's Judgem.* (1612) Pref., There is a God aboue that guideth the sterne of the world. **1602** FULBECKE *2nd Pt. Parall.* 15 Of both these riseth an action triable wel enough by the Canon Law: for in this matter the Canon is the sterne and motiue of our iudgements. *c* **1618** MORYSON *Itin.* IV. I. vii. (1903) 111 To the hands of these 28 Familyes, the Stern of the Commonwealth was committed.

†**d.** In various phrases, with literal or figurative meaning. *to be, sit, at the stern, to stand to stern, to conduct, guide, hold, keep, possess, rule, steer, turn the stern*: to steer, govern, control, to occupy the seat of government. *to take in hand the stern*, to assume the government. *Obs.*

1401 *Pol. Poems* (Rolls) II. 109 Ne were God the giour, and kept the stern,..al schulde wende to wrak. *c* **1500** *Three Kings' Sons* 60 Some [shippes]..had neither saile ne maste, nor noman so hardy that durst conduyte the steerne. **1513** BRADSHAW *St. Werburge* II. 1183 Kynge Edgare kept the storne as most principall, Eche prince had an ore to labour with-all. *a* **1542** WYATT *Poems*, *'So feeble is the thread'* 83 Those handes..y[t]..rule the sterne of my pore lyff. **1542** UDALL *Erasm. Apoph.* 6 Fye on hym that would take vpon hym to sitte and holde the stierne in a shyppe, hauyng none experience in y[e] feate of marinershyp. *a* **1547** SURREY *Poems*, *'Girt in my guiltless gown'* 6 How som to guyd a shyppe in stormes styckes not to take the stearne. **1553** *Respublica* 278, I shall tell Respublica ye can beste governe: bee not ye than skeymishe to take in hand the stern. *a* **1568** ASCHAM *Scholem.* I. (Arb.) 48 The father held the sterne of his whole obedience. **1576** FLEMING *Panopl. Epist.* 152 Wee satt at y[e] sterne, and had the weale publique in our rule and gouernement. **1577–87** HOLINSHED *Hist. Scot.* 356/1 The male line..descended from the women, haue sometime possessed the sterne of Scotland. **1580** GREENE *Mamillia* I. (1583) 6 b, Construe al thinges to the best, turne the stearne the best waye. **1583** *Ibid.* II. (1593) D 3, Pilot..if thou hadst no greater cunning in stirring of the stearne. **1591** SHAKS. *1 Hen. VI*, I. i. 177, I intend to..sit at chiefest Sterne of publique Weal. **1593** CHURCHYARD *Challenge* 6 In greatest stormes, I stoutly stood to sterne, And turnd about, the shippe to winne the winde. **1604** T. WRIGHT *Passions* VI. 338 He that guideth by his providence the sterne of mens soules. **1625** *Deb. Commons* (Camden, 1873) 87 He that was then at the sterne fetch't many sighes before he fetch' it aboute. *a* **1708** BEVERIDGE *Thes. Theol.* III. 323 We are in a more special manner to pray for such as sit at the stern, and are in authority.

2. a. The hind part of a ship or boat (as distinguished from the bow and midships); in restricted sense, the external rear part of a ship's hull; also *spec.* in vessels of ordinary type, the overhanging portion of the hull abaft the sternpost. Often in collocation with STEM, HEAD. Also, the rear part of an aircraft.

c **1300** *K. Horn* 935 Þe hondes gonnen at erne In to þe schypes sterne. *Ibid.* 1412 He comen out of scyp sterne. *c* **1440** *Promp. Parv.* 474/2 Sterne, of a schyppe, *puppis.* **1526** TINDALE *Mark* iv. 38 He was in the sterne a slepe on a pelowe. **1555** EDEN *Decades* (Arb.) 86 Beholdinge the foreshippe & the sterne. **1608** SHAKS. *Per.* IV. i. 64 And with a dropping industrie they skip from sterne to sterne. **1622** R. HAWKINS *Voy. S. Sea* xliv. 104 Our Shippe..coming aground in the sterne. **1626** CAPT. SMITH *Accid. Yng. Seamen* 8 First lay the Keele, the Stemme, and Starne, in a dry docke. **1773** HAWKESWORTH *Cook's 1st Voy.* II. x. III. 462 The ornament at the stern was fixed upon that end, as the stern-post of a ship is upon her keel. **1817** SHELLEY *Revolt Islam* IX. ii. 5 The stern and prow Were canopied with blooming boughs. **1835** SIR J. ROSS *Narr. 2nd Voy. N.-W. Passage* v. 59 It would be necessary.. to moor the ship both head and stern. **1867** SMYTH *Sailor's Word-bk.*, *Stern*, the after-part of a ship, ending in the taffarel above and the counters below. **1915** *Morning Post* 9 Dec. 6/6 The *Severn* was anchored head and stern. **1931**, etc. [see STERN-POST]. **1942** *R.A.F. Jrnl.* 16 May 17 There is..a turret in the extreme stern.

transf. **1878** STEVENSON *New Arab. Nts.* (1882) II. 146 The round stern of a chapel, with a fringe of flying buttresses.

b. Phrases with preps.: ***on stern, a stern***, ? also ***stern*** adv.: see ASTERN. ***at stern, to stern***: behind, in the rear of a ship; ***at (the) stern***, used of a boat towed behind. ***(down) by the stern***: see BY A. 9 and quots. ***under the stern***: under the overhanging part technically called the stern.

c **1500** *Melusine* xxxvi. 271 He lefte the Ermayns..at sterne. **1562** J. SHUTE tr. *Cambini's Turk. Wars* 34b, Wherupon they tawed the palandre after them at the storne of some of their galleys. **1574** W. BOURNE *Regiment for Sea* xiv. (1577) 40b, The one place must be thwart of you, the other must be a head or stern of you. **1616** CAPT. SMITH *Descr. New Eng.* 53 This examinate fell on sterne. **1633** T. JAMES *Voy.* 7 Our long Boate..we were faine to Towe at Sterne. *a* **1779** COOK *3rd Voy.* II. vi, Towards noon, a large sailing canoe came under our stern. **1806** A. DUNCAN *Life Nelson* 70 She might anchor by the stern. **1846** A. YOUNG *Naut. Dict.* 56 If her stern be lower in the water than her head, she is by the stern.

c. ***stern-foremost***: backwards, with the stern (senses 2, 3) first; also *fig.* ***stern on***: with the stern presented.

1840 MARRYAT *Poor Jack* xxxi, The man..backs out, stern foremost. **1852** HAWTHORNE *Blithedale Rom.* viii, Few of our seeds ever came up at all, or, if they did come up, it was stern-foremost. **1865** DICKENS *Mut. Fr.* I. i, The boat.. drove stern foremost before it [the tide]. **1900** *Jrnl. Sch. Geog.* (U.S.) June 231 [The ship] thus runs..the risk..of getting stern-on to the heavy sea. **1907** 'Q.' (Quiller-Couch) *Poison Isl.* xxv. 244 After a stroke or two I easied and let her back stern-foremost.

3. (Arising out of a figurative use of sense 2.) The buttocks of a man (chiefly humorous and vulgar) or beast; the hinder part of any creature.

1614 B. JONSON *Bart. Fair* Induct., A Punque set vnder [a pump] vpon her head, with her Sterne vpward. **1830** MARRYAT *King's Own* xxvi, When it was a kitten, they had cut off his tail close to its starn. **1836** —— *Midsh. Easy* xix, I was obliged to come up the side without my trousers, and show my bare stern to the whole ship's company. **1854** *Poultry Chron.* I. 455 With, in the hens especially, a well-rounded stern. **1863** W. C. BALDWIN *Afr. Hunting* vi. 179 Firing from the saddle, and giving the giraffe the ball in the stern. **1869** FURNIVALL *Forewords to Q. Eliz. Acad.* p. xxiii, We don't want to..fancy them cherubs without sterns. **1913** *Engl. Rev.* May 201 [The ducks] point their sterns into the air, and stick their heads under water.

4. The tail of an animal, esp. of a sporting-dog or a wolf. Also, †the fleshy part of a horse's tail; †the tail feathers of a hawk.

1575 TURBERV. *Faulconrie* 190 Fasten a bell upon the two couert feathers of your hawkes Stearne or trayne. **1576** —— *Venerie* 243 The tayle of a Wolfe is to be called his Stearne. **1590** SPENSER *F.Q.* I. i. 18 Tho wrapping vp her wrethed sterne arownd, Lept fierce vpon his shield, and her huge traine All suddenly about his body wound. **1607** MARKHAM *Caval.* I. (1617) 27 Others approue a Horses age in this sort: take him with your finger and your thumbe by the sterne of the tayle, close at the setting on of the buttocke. *Ibid.* II. 9 His taile long and hairie..the sterne whereof, small and strong, and close coutched betwixt his buttockes. **1618** CHAPMAN *Hesiod's Georg.* II. 223 Wilde beasts abhor him, and run clapping close Their stern's betwixt their thighes. **1677** N. COX *Gentl. Recreat.* (ed. 2) 149 The benefit of cutting off the tip of a Spaniel's Tail or Stern. **1682** *Lond. Gaz.* No. 1684/4 Lost..a Fallow Greyhound Bitch, with a white spot at the end of her Sterne. **1725** *Bradley's Family Dict.* s.v. *Entering of Hounds*, Some [hounds]..will prick up their Ears a little, and either Bark or wag their Stern or Ear. **1881** V. SHAW *Bk. Dog* x. 91 The stern or tail [of the Bull-dog]..must be short and very fine. *Ibid.* xliv. 372 The Stern or Flag [of the Setter]. **1890** S. W. BAKER *Wild Beasts & Ways* II. 317 When he spoke..with stern erect and nose to the ground, there was a general rush by every dog.

†**5.** Used *gen.* for: Rear, latter end. *Obs.*

1623 HEXHAM *Tongue-Combat* 48 You need not in the sterne of your Discourse recapitulate the notable pieces which you have proued.

¶**6.** Misused by Stubbes for: An ensign, flag.

1583 STUBBES *Anat. Abuses* I. (1877) 51 An other sort..are content with no kind of Hatt without a great bunche of feathers..peaking on toppe of their heades..as sternes of pride and ensigns of vanitie. *Ibid.* 68 It [curling etc. of the hair] is the ensigne of Pride, and the stern [*v.r.* 1595 standerd] of wantonnes to all that behould it.

7. *attrib.* (all locative, referring to sense 2) as ***stern-anchor, -balcony, -beam, -becket, -davits, deck, -gun, -paddle*** (also *attrib.*), ***-plate*** (also *attrib.*), ***-sheave, -sling-bolt, -turret, -window***.

1633 T. JAMES *Voy.* 82 Ice..brought home our *Sterne-Anker. **1904** HARDY *Dynasts* I. II. ii. 66 White sea-birds, which alight on the *stern-balcony of Villeneuve's ship. **1878** CUYLER *Pointed Papers* 45 He lies down to slumber on the *stern-beam of the boat. **1897** KIPLING *Capt. Cour.* ii. 35 He..caught Dan's tackle, hooked it to the *stern-becket, and clambered into the schooner. **1863** A. YOUNG *Naut. Dict.* 389 **Stern-davits*, pieces of iron or timber projecting from a vessel's stern to hoist boats up to. **1913** SIR H. JOHNSTON *Pioneers Austral.* iii. 99 They were received by the king on the *stern deck of a very large prau or native vessel. **1892** KIPLING *Barrack-r. Ballads* 137 And the great *stern-gun shot fair and true, With the heave of the ship, to the stainless blue, And the great *stern-turret stuck. **1849** W. S. MAYO *Kaloolah* vi. (1850) 50 The savage wielding the *stern paddle of the foremost canoe. **1905** A. R. WALLACE *My Life* II. xxxi. 139 We saw one of the old-fashioned stern-paddle steamboats. **1890** W. J. GORDON *Foundry* 70 The tip only of the *stern-plate rivets is heated. **1890** *Pall Mall Gaz.* 4 Oct. 7/1 It was astonishing to see the..cable..bob under the dynamometer, and up over the *stern-sheave, and finally dive into the water. **1875** BEDFORD *Sailor's Pocket Bk.* vi. (ed. 2) 216 Take the tow-line to the after thwart or foremost *stern-sling bolt. **1834** MARRYAT *P. Simple* xxxii, Brigs having no *stern-windows, of course she could not see my manœuvre.

8. Special comb.: †**stern-bearer**, a rudder-bearer, ship; **stern-boat**, (*a*) a boat hanging at a ship's stern; (*b*) an attendant boat following astern; **sterndrive** [DRIVE *sb.* 6] *Naut.* (chiefly *N. Amer.*), an inboard engine connected to an outboard drive unit at the rear of a powerboat; **stern-frame**, (*a*) the framework of a ship's stern; (*b*) (see quot. 1908); **stern-gallery** (see GALLERY 2 d); **stern-knee**, = STERNSON; **stern-ladder** (see quots.); **stern-line**, = STERNFAST; **stern-locker** (see LOCKER *sb.*[1] III.); **stern-notch**, a notch cut in the topmost plank of a boat's stern to receive an oar used in sculling or steering; **stern-ornament**, (*a*) an ornament on a vessel's stern; (*b*) *jocularly*, the tail of an animal; **stern-piece**, †(*a*) a gun mounted in the stern; (*b*) a flat piece of wood to which the side planks of a ship or boat are brought, so that it terminates the hull behind; **stern-port**, a port or window in the stern of a vessel; **stern-race**, a race in which one boat closely follows another without being able to overtake it; **stern-rail**, (*a*) an ornamental moulding on a ship's stern; (*b*) the rail placed about the deck at the stern; **stern-rudder**, the rudder at the stern, as distinguished from the *bow-rudder* with which some craft are fitted; **stern sea**, a sea which beats upon a ship's stern; a following sea; **stern shot**, a shot at the buttocks of a fleeing animal; **stern speed**, the speed of a vessel travelling stern-foremost with engines reversed; **stern-timber** (see quots.); **stern-trawler**, a trawler whose nets are operated from the stern of the vessel; **stern tube**, (*a*) the tube in which the propeller-shaft works; (*b*) a tube fitted in the stern of a warship from which torpedoes are discharged; **stern-wager** = *stern-race*; **stern-walk** (see quot. 1867); **stern-way**, the movement of a ship going stern-foremost; also *transf.*; **sternways** *adv.*, in a position or direction facing to the stern; **stern-works**, *jocularly*, the buttocks. Also STERN-BOARD, -CHASE, -CHASER, -FAST, -MAN, -POST, -SHEET, -WHEEL.

1599 NASHE *Lenten Stuff* 20 In M. Hackluits English discoueries I haue not come in ken of one..mediteranean *sternebearer sente from her [Yarmouth's] Zenith or Meridian. **1837** CARLYLE *Fr. Rev.* II. IV. v, Huge leathern vehicle:—huge Argosy, let us say, or Acapulco-ship; with its heavy *stern-boat of Chaise-and-pair. **1846** A. YOUNG *Naut. Dict.* 40 The jolly-boat..is very commonly called the stern-boat, if hung to davits over the ship's stern. **1968** *N.Y. Times* 9 Feb. 31 When they appeared on the water about eight years ago, they looked like outboards with the power head sawed off... Variously called *stern drives, inboard-outwards, [etc.] .., they are one of the hottest items in recreational boating. **1976–7** *Sea Spray* (N.Z.) Dec./Jan. 94/1 'Best way to beat the opposition is to join 'em' would seem to be the philosophy behind a decision by C. W. F. Hamilton Marine Ltd to offer OMC, MerCruiser and Volvo sterndrives through its dealers. **1815** *Falconer's Dict. Marine* (ed. Burney), **Stern-frame*, in ship-building, is that frame of timber which is composed of the stern-post-transoms and fashion-pieces. **1880** *Times* 17 Dec. 5/6 The Persian Monarch..is reported..to be leaking slightly; supposed around the stern frame. **1908** PAASCH *From Keel to Truck* 123 *Stern-frame*..forming in single-screw steamers stern-post, propeller-post, and the connections between them. **1842** DICKENS *Amer. Notes* xi. (1850) 111/1 All this I see as I sit in the little *stern-gallery. **1846** A. YOUNG *Naut. Dict.* 322 *Sternson*, or **Stern-knee*, a piece of compass timber forming a continuation of a vessel's keelson. **1794** *Rigging & Seamanship* I. 234 **Stern-ladders* are made of cable-laid rope. **1867** SMYTH *Sailor's Word-bk.*, *Stern-ladder*, made of ropes with wooden steps, for getting in and out of the boats astern. **1880** 'MARK TWAIN' *Tramp Abroad* xvii. 157 Lay her in shore and stand by to jump with the *stern-line the moment she touches. **1898** *Jrnl. Sch. Geog.* (U.S.) Oct. 306 The vessels..are secured with double bow anchors and usually two stern lines. **1849** CUPPLES *Green Hand* xvi. (1856) 159 [The bird] was stowed away..into the *stern-locker. **1907** 'Q.' (Quiller-Couch) *Poison Isl.* xxv. 240 Slipping a paddle into the *stern-notch, [I] sculled gently for shore. **1885** RIDER HAGGARD *K. Solomon's Mines* iii, As though nature had..stuck the *stern ornaments of a lot of prize bulldogs on to the rumps of the oxen. **1908** PAASCH *From Keel to Truck* 98 Stern ornament. **1622** R. HAWKINS *Voy. S. Sea* liii. 127 Our *stearne peeces were vnprimed. **1626** CAPT. SMITH *Accid. Yng. Seamen* 19 Giue him your stern peeces. **1895** *Outing* XXVI. 382/1 Her [the yacht's] stern-piece is elliptical. **1591** RALEGH in *Last Fight Revenge* (Arb.) 19 Besides those of her *Sterne portes. **1834** MARRYAT *P. Simple* viii, One of them ere midshipmites has thrown a red hot tater out of the stern-port. **1903** CONRAD & HUEFFER *Romance* II. iv. 83 The stern-ports, glazed in small panes, were black and gleaming in a white framework. **1883** BRINSLEY-RICHARDS *Seven Yrs. Eton* xi. 106 Ricardo and Campbell were gamely rowing a good *stern-race, but no more. **1846** A. YOUNG *Naut. Dict.* 322 **Stern-rails*,.. narrow pieces of projecting plank on which mouldings are raised,—arranged on a vessel's stern and counter in various forms. **1914** *Blackw. Mag.* Feb. 248/2 The finest sight in all the East—Bombay seen over the stern-rail of a P. & O. steamer. **1889** WELCH *Text Bk. Naval Archit.* xiii. 136 The following remarks..will be confined to *stern rudders and the gear for actuating them. **1745** P. THOMAS *Jrnl. Anson's Voy.* 156 A very great *stern Sea, which staved the Long-boat against the Stern. **1863** W. C. BALDWIN *Afr. Hunting* v. 130 He [the rhinoceros] suddenly made right off, and I had only a *stern shot left me. **1904** *Westm. Gaz.* 26 Sept. 6/2 For moderate speeds astern a reversing turbine was adequate, but for high *stern speeds a reciprocating engine was preferable. **1797** *Encycl. Brit.* (ed. 3) XVII. 398/2 A curve described through the several points thus set off will be the representative of the *stern timber. **1846** A. YOUNG *Naut. Dict.* 342 *Stern-timbers*, a general name given to all the timbers in the stern-frame. **1961** *Times* 9 Aug. 5/2 A large *stern-trawler..has been ordered by J. Marr and Son, of Hull. **1977** *Grimsby Even. Tel.* 5 May 8/3 A new French stern trawler landed over 1,700 kits of blue ling on Grimsby Fish Docks this week. **1982** *Daily Tel.* 29 July 2/4 The last modern stern trawler fleet in Britain was being forced into an increasingly nomadic existence. **1883** CLARK RUSSELL *Sailor's Lang.*, **Stern-tube*, a cylinder in the after peak of a steamer in which the propeller shaft works. **1912** *Times* 19 Dec. 20/2 Portuguese s. *Beira*..with propeller shaft port engine broken and stern tube cracked or broken. **1914** DOMVILLE-FIFE *Submarine in War* 144 The submarine might..then fire her stern tubes at close range. **1852** J. F. BATEMAN *Aquatic Notes* 74 The Cambridge men..rowed a very plucky *stern-wager. **1867** SMYTH *Sailor's Word-bk.*, **Stern-walk*, the old galleries formerly used to line-of-battle ships. **1893** *Daily News* 18 July 6/1 Looking out of a stern port into the stern walk. **1915** 'BARTIMEUS' *Naval Occas.* 161 While under the stern-walk a flock of gulls screeched and quarrelled. **1769** FALCONER *Dict. Marine* (1780) s.v. *Aback*, The sails..are laid aback,..to give the ship *stern-way. **1865** *Daily Tel.* 16 Oct. 4/4 The steers-men of the public schools perceived that they were making stern-way; the age was overhauling them. **1875** BEDFORD *Sailor's Pocket Bk.* vi. 179 Before going alongside a vessel.., observe if she have head or sternway. **1872** EARL OF PEMBROKE & G. H. KINGSLEY *S. Sea Bubbles* i. 8 Some [fish]..swimming or floating frontways, *sternways, sideways, with apparently equal ease and partiality. **1879** STEVENSON *Trav. Cevennes* (1886) 17 Plucking a switch out of a thicket, he began to lace Modestine about the *stern-works.

stern (stɜːrn), *a.* (*sb.*[4] and *adv.*) Forms: *α.* 1 styrne, 3–5 sturne, 3 stuyrne, 4–5 stuerne, 5 stourne; 4 sturen, 5 sturun; *β.* 3 *Orm.* stirne, 5 styrn; 5 stirrun; *γ.* 2 *Kent.* stiarne; *δ.* 3 stearne, 4–5 steerne, styerne, stierne(e, steirne; 4–5 steren(e, -in, -yn(e, -ynne; 6 stearne, 3–7 sterne, 4– stern. [OE. (WS.) *styrne*, earlier **stierne* evidenced by *stiernlīce*; see STERNLY *adv.* The ME. forms, particularly Ormin's *stirne* (cf. *hirde* from Anglian *hiorde*), point to an OTeut. type **sternjo-*, which is represented only in English.

The Indogermanic root **ster-*: **stor-* is represented in several words with the sense 'hard, rigid,' or the like, e.g. Gr. στερεός solid, G. starr stiff, rigid; cf. STARE *v.*]

A. *adj.*

1. Of persons and things personified, their dispositions and temper: Severe, strict, inflexible; rigorous in punishment or condemnation; not inclined to leniency.

a **1000** *Cædmon's Gen.* (Gr.) 60 Hæfde styrne mod ȝegremod grymme. *a* **1122** *O.E. Chron.* (Laud MS.) an. 1070, He wæs swiðe styrne man. *a* **1225** *Ancr. R.* 268 Rihtwisnesse, he seið, mot beon nede sturne. *Ibid.* 366 Ase þe moder þet is reouðful deð hire bitweonen hire childe & þe wroðe sturne ueder, hwon he wule beaten. **1340** *Ayenb.* 130 þou sselt uinde þane domes man zuo sterne and zuo stout and zuo strayt an zuo miȝtuol. *c* **1386** CHAUCER *Pars. T.* 170 Then shal the stierne and wrothe Iuge sitte aboue. *c* **1475** *Partenay* 5730 Both stourne men & meke. **1607** SHAKS. *Cor.* IV. i. 24 My (sometime) Generall, I haue seene the sterne. **1776** GIBBON *Decl. & Fall* xiv. I. 401 The stern temper of Galerius was cast in a very different mould; and while he commanded the esteem of his subjects, he seldom condescended to solicit their affections. **1781** COWPER *Conversat.* 850 As stern Elijah said of old. **1841** W. SPALDING *Italy & Ital. Isl.* II. 341 A characteristic likeness of the stern, ambitious, military old bishop.

absol. **1820** SHELLEY *Prometh. Unb.* I. i. 537 The spell Which must bend the Invincible, The stern of thought. **1850** TENNYSON *In Mem.* cx. 9 The stern were mild when thou wert by.

b. Const. *with, to, towards.* (OE. dative.)

a **1023** WULFSTAN *Hom.* (1883) 267/1 And æȝðer he sceal beon mid rihte ȝe milde ȝe reðe, milde þam godum and styrne þam yfelum. *c* **1205** LAY. 3228 Hire fader hire wes sturne. *Ibid.* 6586 Wið þa goden he wes duhti and sturne [*c* **1275** sterne] wið þa dusie. **1297** R. GLOUC. (Rolls) 4951 King cadwal to him to sturne verst nas. *a* **1547** SURREY *Æneis* II. Cijb, Achilles was to Priam not so stern. **1847** PRESCOTT *Peru* (1850) II. 72 He was..towards his own people stern even to severity. **1900** *New Cent. Rev.* VII. 401 They have to be stern with applicants who have grown up under a lax system.

c. Rigorous in morals or principles; uncompromising, austere.

c **1374** CHAUCER *Boeth.* II. met. vii. (1868) 60 What is now brutus or stiern Caton [L. *rigidus Cato*]? **1703** ROWE *Ulyss.* IV. i. 1438 Honour stern, impatient of Neglect. **1742** BLAIR *Grave* 538 The supple Statesman, and the Patriot stern. *a* **1835** HOGG *Tales & Sk.* (1837) VI. 12 Lord Nithsdale, who was a stern Catholic. **1837** WORDSW. *Cuckoo at Laverna* 34 A few Monks, a stern society, Dead to the world and scorning earth-born joys. **1911** *Contemp. Rev.* May 577 He was a stern moralist.

d. Of personal attributes, actions, utterances, feelings, etc.: Severe, strict, hard, grim, harsh.

a **1225** *Ancr. R.* 428 Uor swuch ouh wummone lore to beon—luuelich & liðe, and seldhwonne sturne. *c* **1380** WYCLIF *Sel. Wks.* III. 434 Not for his lordship ne his sterne power. **1687** DRYDEN *Hind & P.* II. 506 But when the stern conditions were declar'd, A mournful whisper through the host was heard. **1777** POTTER *Æschylus, Prometh. Chain'd* 14 Is there a god, whose sullen soul Feels a stern joy in thy despair? **1814** WORDSW. *Laodamia* 55 But thou, though capable of sternest deed, Wert kind as resolute. **1820** W. IRVING *Sketch Bk.* I. 143 Even his enemies lamented the stern policy that dictated his execution. **1856** KANE *Arctic Expl.* II. viii. 90 Desertion, or the attempt to desert, shall be met at once by the sternest penalty. **1892** *Verney Mem.* I. 343 The stern solemnity of the speakers.

†**2.** Resolute in battle, steadfast, fiercely brave, bold. *Obs.*

c **1205** LAY. 31471 Ah Oswi wes cniht sturne. *a* **1300** *K. Horn* 877 (Camb. MS.) Þe paens þat er were so sturne, Hi gunne awei vrne. *c* **1350** *Will. Palerne* 3409 A ful breme bataile bi-gan þat ilk time, Whan eþer sides a-sembled of þo segges sturne. ? *a* **1400** *Morte Arth.* 157 Take kepe to thoos lordez, To styghtylle tha steryne mene as theire statte askys. *c* **1400** *Destr. Troy* 3960 Polidamas.. A full strong man in stoure, sturnyst in Armys. *c* **1450** HOLLAND *Howlat* 652 Thar was.. Stanchalis, steropis strecht to thai stern lordis.

b. Of battle, debate and the like: Stubbornly-contested, fierce, hard.

c **1205** LAY. 20774 Þer gode cnihtes cumeð to sturne fihte. *c* **1395** *Plowman's Tale* I in *Polit. Poems* (Rolls) I. 304 A sterne strife is stirred newe. **1422** YONGE tr. *Secreta Secret.* 174 Steryn battaill he yaue. **1579** SPENSER *Sheph. Cal.* Feb. 149 Stirring vp sterne strife. **1607** CHAPMAN *Bussy d'Ambois* II. i. 32 His friends and enemies; whose stern fight I saw. **1777** POTTER *Æschylus, Prometh. Chained* 16 When stern debate amongst the gods appear'd And discord in the courts of heav'n was rous'd. **1876** BLACKIE *Songs Relig.* 182, I must go and do stern battle With herds of stiff-necked human cattle.

c. In alliterative verse and phrases, often with sense weakened, or influenced by the words with which it is coupled; as † ***stern on steed***, † ***stern in steel***, † ***stern in stour***; † ***stern of slate***, high in rank; † ***stern and stout***; † ***a stern steed***, a fiery steed.

c **1300** *Leg. Gregory* (Schulz) 883 Þe housbond was stern and stout. **13..** *Sir Beues* 4500 He armede him in yrene wede And lep vpon a sterne stede. **1340–70** *Alex. & Dind.* 429 Non is sternere of stat ne stouter þan oþir. *c* **1386** CHAUCER *Knt.'s T.* 1296 Armed ful wel, with hertes stierne and stoute. ? *a* **1400** *Morte Arth.* 3872 He was the sterynneste in stoure that euer stele werryde. *c* **1400** *Aunturs of Arth.* 391 (Thornton MS.) In stele was he stuffede, þat steryne was one stede. *c* **1420** *Avow. Arth.* xii, He had drede, and doute, Of him that was stirrun, and stowte. *a* **1500–20** DUNBAR *Poems* xxvii. 81 He went agane to bene bespewit, So stern he wes in steill. **1576** GASCOIGNE *Philomene* Wks. 1910 II. 194 Or if (quoth she) there bee Some other meane more sure, More stearne, more stoute, than naked sword.

†**3.** In a bad sense: Merciless, cruel. *Obs.*

c **1205** LAY. 25840 He wende to finden þene feond sturne. *c* **1290** *St. Kenelm* 202 in *S. Eng. Leg.* 351 And bi-cam stuyrne and bi-ladde hire men harde with muche wrechhede. *c* **1374** CHAUCER *Troylus* IV. 94 O sterne and cruwel fader þat I was. **1387** TREVISA *Higden* (Rolls) III. 71 For drede of lyouns þat were cruel and sterne. *c* **1400** *Brut* xxx. 29 Artogaile.. bicome so wickede and so sterne, þat þe Britons wolde nouȝt suffre hym to bene kyng. **1555** WATREMAN *Fardle Facions* I. iii. 35 Thei ware sterne, and vnruly, and bruteshely liued. **1590** SHAKS. *Mids. N.* III. ii. 59 Pierst through the heart with your stearne cruelty. **1593** —— *2 Hen. VI*, III. ii. 213 Thy Mother tooke into her blamefull Bed Some sterne vntutur'd Churle. **1600** —— *Sonn.* xcvi, How many Lambs might the sterne Wolfe betray.

4. Of looks, bearing, gait: Indicating a stern disposition or mood; expressing grave displeasure; resolute, austere, gloomy.

1390 GOWER *Conf.* III. 289 The king declareth him the cas With sturne lok and sturdi chiere. **1400–20** LYDG. *Thebes* 2118 And in despit who that was lief or loth, A sterne pas thorgh the halle he goth. *c* **1470** *Gol. & Gaw.* 616 On twa stedis thai straid, with ane sterne schiere. **1581** A. HALL *Iliad* VII. 127 His countenaunce stout, his sterne martch, when they saw in such sort,.. they doe beginne to ioye. **1591** LODGE *Catharos* B 1 b, The still streame is deepest, & the stearne looke doublest. **1600** SHAKS. *A.Y.L.* IV. iii. 9 As I guesse By the sterne brow and waspish action.. It beares an angry tenure. **1634** MILTON *Comus* 446 Gods and men Fear'd her stern frown. **1770** GOLDSM. *Des. Vill.* 197 A man severe he was, and stern to view. **1818** SHELLEY *Rosal. & Helen* 330 With the stern step of vanquished will. **1881** LADY HERBERT *Edith* i. 18 Graver and sterner grew Mr. Gordon's face. **1890** DOYLE *White Company* vi, The soldier stood in front of them with stern eyes, checking off their several packages.

†**b.** Terrible or threatening in aspect. *Obs.*

c **1205** LAY. 17873 Com of þan steore a leome swiðe sturne. *c* **1440** *Promp. Parv.* 474/2 Sterne, or dredeful in syghte, *terribilis, horribilis*. *c* **1450** *Merlin* iii. 43 He come to hem like a begger,.. and hadde a grym berde and steirne loke. **1573** BARET *Alv.* S. 758 Sterne, cruell & sturdie in lookes, grimme, terrible, fell, *toruus*.

c. *transf.* Of a building: Severe in style; gloomy or forbidding in aspect. Cf. 7.

1822 SCOTT *Peveril* xxxvi, Julian, who was led along the same stern passages which he had traversed upon his entrance, to the gate of the prison. **1833** WORDSW. *Lowther* 3 Lowther! in thy majestic Pile are seen Cathedral pomp and grace, in apt accord With the baronial castle's sterner mien. **1871** FREEMAN *Norm. Conq.* (1876) IV. xix. 395 Paul.. reared the vastest and sternest temple of his age.

5. Of the voice: Expressive of a stern disposition or mood. (Cf. 6 c.)

c **1330** *Spec. Gy de Warw.* 446 Wid sterne voiz and wid heie. *a* **1400–50** *Wars Alex.* 611 His steuen stiffe was [and] steryn þat stonayd many. **1817** SCOTT *Harold Dauntless* II. vii, Stern accents made his pleasure known, Though then he used his gentlest tone. **1820** —— *Monast.* xix, Father Eustace.. addressing Halbert in a stern and severe voice.

6. Of things, in various transferred uses.

†**a.** Of blows, weapons: Inflicting severe pain or injury. *Obs.*

c **1025** in Napier *OE. Glosses* 56/112 *Asperis* (*uerberibus seu liuidis*), styr[num] *vel* tear[tum]. *a* **1175** *Cott. Hom.* 231 Mid gode repples and stiarne swepen. *Ibid.* 239 Þe wereȝede gastes þe hine uniredlice underfangeð mid stiarne swupen. *a* **1400** *Leg. Rood* 184 Þe hamur bothe sterne and gret þe drof þe nayles þorow hond and fete. **1615** CHAPMAN *Odyss.* XIV. 375 About whom Mischiefe stood And with his stern steele, drew in streames the blood. **1805** SCOTT *Last Minstr.* III. vi, Stern was the dint The Borderer lent!

b. Of grief or pain: Oppressive, hard to bear.

c **1300** *Leg. Gregory* (Schulz) 174 Hir sorwe was strong and sterne. **1811** SHELLEY *Bereav.* I How stern are the woes of the desolate mourner.

†**c.** Of sound: Harsh, menacing (cf. 5). *Obs.*

13.. *E.E. Allit. P.* B. 1402 Sturnen [? *read* sturne] trumpen strake steuen in halle. **1390** GOWER *Conf.* I. 113 A trompe with a sterne breth, Which cleped was the Trompe of death.

†**d.** Of the weather: Severe, causing hardship.

c **1449** PECOCK *Repr.* II. ii. 146 To couere him fro reyne and fro othir sturne wedris. **1605** SHAKS. *Lear* III. vii. 63 If Wolues had at thy Gate howl'd that stern time, Thou should'st haue said, good Porter turne the Key. *c* **1611** CHAPMAN *Iliad* XXIV. 332 In this so sterne a Time Of night, and danger.

†**e.** Of a stream, a wind: Strong, violent. *Obs.*

13.. *Guy Warw.* 5840 He com to a water sterne. *c* **1374** CHAUCER *Troylus* III. 743 The sterne wynd so lowde gan to route That no wight oþer noyse myghte here. **1426** LYDG. *De Guil. Pilgr.* 55 Lyk a Ryuer sterne, and of gret myght, He restyth nat nouther day nor nyght.

†**f.** Formidable in bulk, massive. *Obs.*

13.. *Gaw & Gr. Knt.* 143 For of bak & of brest al were his bodi sturne, Bot his wombe & his wast were worthily smale. *c* **1394** *P. Pl. Crede* 214 And all strong ston wall sterne opon heiþe.

7. Of a country, or its physical features, the soil, etc. (with fig. notion of senses 1 and 4): Unkindly, inhospitable; destitute of amenity; forbidding in aspect, frowning, gloomy.

1812 BYRON *Ch. Har.* II. xlii, Stern Albania's hills. **1814** WORDSW. *Excurs.* II. 92 Mountains stern and desolate. **1836** W. IRVING *Astoria* I. vii. 116 The Tonquin ploughed her course towards the sterner regions of the Pacific. **1869** TOZER *Highl. Turkey* I. 196 The wild stern regions of European Turkey. **1884** P'CESS ALICE *Mem.* 5 The sterner scenery of the Scotch Highlands. *a* **1894** STEVENSON *In South Seas* II. ii. (1900) 154 The coco-palm in particular luxuriates in that stern *solum*.

8. Of circumstances and conditions, oppressive, compelling, hard, inexorable; esp. in the phrases ***stern necessity***, ***stern reality***.

1830 CARLYLE *Richter Again* Ess. 1840 II. 309 Poverty of a sterner sort than this would have been a light matter to him. **1849** MACAULAY *Hist. Eng.* vii. II. 193 The great enterprise to which a stern necessity afterwards drove him. **1854** *Poultry Chron.* I. 92 It is useless to deny the stern fact, that [etc.]. **1856** FROUDE *Hist. Eng.* (1858) II. vii. 174 The times were too stern to admit of nice distinctions. **1912** *Standard* 20 Sept. 7/3 This is no flight of imagination; it is stern reality.

9. *Comb.* **a.** parasynthetic formations, as ***stern-browed***, ***-eyed***, ***-faced***, ***-featured***, ***-gated***, ***-lipped***, ***-visaged*** adjs.; **b.** complemental, as ***stern-born***, ***-issuing***, ***-looking***, ***-sounding*** adjs.

1594 KYD *Cornelia* IV. i. 167 Braue Romaine Soldiers, sterne-borne sons of Mars. **1597** DRAYTON *Heroical Ep.*, *Mortimer to Q. Isab.* 87 And we will turne sterne-visag'd Furie backe. **1648** J. BEAUMONT *Psyche* XVII. xlvi, The bold impetuousness Of stern-fac'd Mamalukes. **1725** POPE *Odyss.* VIII. 564 He sung the Greeks stern-issuing from the steed. **1776** MICKLE *Lusiad* III. (1778) 99 The stern-brow'd tyrant roars and tears the ground. **1787** POLWHELE *Engl. Orator* II. 4 A Warrior-Brood Stern-featur'd. **1825** J. NEAL *Bro. Jonathan* I. 151 Six evangelical, stern-looking men. **1837** CARLYLE *Fr. Rev.* II. VI. iii, They roll through the streets, with stern-sounding music. **1870** BRYANT *Iliad* xx. 50 Vulcan.. Strong and stern-eyed. *a* **1900** S. CRANE *Gt. Battles* (1901) 206 That curious stern-lipped stupidity.

†**B.** *sb.* In alliterative verse: A stern or bold man. *Obs.*

13.. *Gaw. & Gr. Knt.* 214 Þe stele of a stif staf þe sturne hit bi-grypte. *c* **1400** *Destr. Troy* 567 Ye may strive with no stuerne but of your strength nobill. *c* **1400** *Aunturs of Arth.* 532 (Douce MS.) Þe sturne strikes one stray. *c* **1470** *Gol. & Gaw.* 19 Mony sterne our the streit stertis on stray.

C. *adv.* or *quasi-adv.* Sternly, resolutely, severely, harshly.

a **1175** *Cott. Hom.* 231 Ȝief he fend were, me sceolden anon eter [= et þer] gat ȝemete.. and stiarne hine besie. *c* **1200** ORMIN 15514 He þratte stirne wind o sæ & itt warrþ stille & liþe. *c* **1250** *Owl & Night.* 112 Þe faukun.. lude yal and sturne chidde. **1377** LANGL. *P. Pl.* B. xv. 248 Noyther he.. Lakketh, ne loseth ne loketh vp sterne. *c* **1450** *Mirk's Festial* 300 God lokud so sterne on hym. **1581** A. HALL *Iliad* I. 12 Thereby displeasing Agamemn, himselfe so gloriously And sterne who beares. **16..** in *Peasants' Rising* (1899) 49 The said maior beareth him so sterne and hawty. **1637** MILTON *Lycidas* 112 He shook his Miter'd locks, and stern bespake.

Comb. **1727** BROOME *Poems* 223 The dreadful Brotherhood stern-frowning stands. **1912** *Contemp. Rev.* Nov. 688 His stern-set, deep-lined mouth.

Stern (stɜːn), *sb.*[5] The name of Avraham *Stern* (1907–42), used *attrib.* in ***Stern gang*** or ***group*** to designate a militant Zionist organization (officially *Loḥame Ḥerut Yisra'el* Fighters for the Freedom of Israel) founded by him in 1940.

1944 *Nation* 2 Dec. 685/1 The so-called Stern gang, with 150 active members. **1947**, etc. [see IRGUN]. **1959** I. JEFFERIES *Thirteen Days* iv. 51 One of the two terrorist groups was called the Stern Gang. **1963** D. LEITCH in Sissons & French *Age of Austerity* iii. 64 The Stern Gang was responsible for the murder of Lord Moyne, Minister resident in Cairo, in November 1944. **1978** L. HEREN *Growing up on The Times* iii. 86 The Stern Gang was a savage organisation which even Koestler could not defend despite his theory that ruthlessness was essential for human progress.

Hence **'Sternist** *a.* and *sb.*

1944 *Nation* 2 Dec. 685/2 Nathan Friedman-Yellin, the thirty-one-year-old Sternist chief. *Ibid.* 686/1 The Sternists' chief weapon is murder. **1949** KOESTLER *Promise & Fulfilment* I. viii. 92 The Sternists were believers in unrestricted and indiscriminate terror. *Ibid.* II. v. 279 Then a Sternist girl came in who once made international news. **1978** L. HEREN *Growing up on The Times* iii. 83 Goldschmidt .. assumed that the Sternist philosophy, which was never made clear to me, would prevail.

stern (stɜːn), *v.*[1] [f. STERN *sb.*[3]; cf. ON. *stjórna.*]

†**1.** *trans.* and *intr.* To steer, govern. *Obs.*

14.. *Lat.-Eng. Voc.* in Wr.-Wülcker 605/27 *Proreto*, to sterne or to stere out. **1577–86** STANYHURST *Descr. Irel.* iii. 26/1 in *Holinshed*, A castell.. which is a notable marke for pilots, in directing them which waie to sterne their ships. **1615** I. BARGRAVE *Serm.* E 2, There was need of a skilfull pilot to rule and sterne the ship of State. **1648** *Royalist's Def.* 86 Suppose three single persons had jointly the Soveraigne power of government, no man can imagine, but that they would.. sterne severall wayes.

2. *trans.* To propel a boat stern foremost; also *intr.* to go stern foremost.

In this sense developed from the whaling term ***stern all***, the order to back off after an harpoon has been entered, where *stern* originally = ASTERN.

[**1823** J. F. COOPER *Pilot* xvii, 'Starn all!' 'Stern all!' echoed Barnstable. *Ibid.*, 'Starn off, sir, starn off! the creater's in his flurry.'] **1845** J. COULTER *Adv. Pacific* vii. 86 In I darted both irons with all my force—'stern all—and stern they did quickly enough. **1892** F. M. CRAWFORD *Childr. King* (1893) I. 70 The dingy came rapidly back and the sailor sterned her to the rock for the boys to get in. **1904** F. T. BULLEN *Creatures of Sea* xix. 270 He [the swordfish] sterns clear, describes a great circle and.. again buries his weapon deep in its vitals.

3. To place astern, in the phrase ***stern the buoy*** (see quot.).

1711 *Milit. & Sea Dict.* s.v. *Buoy*, *Stern the Buoy*; that is, before they let the Anchor fall, whilst the Ship has Way, they put the Buoy into the Water, so that the Buoy-Rope may be stretch'd out strait, that so the Anchor may fall clear from entangling it self with the Buoy-Rope.

4. To cut off the tail of (a dog); see STERN *sb.*[3] 4.

1858 LEWIS in *Youatt's Dog* (N.Y.) v. 170 The often absurd fancy of cropping and sterning dogs.

Hence †**'sterning** *vbl. sb.* steering, guidance. Also †**'sterner**, pilot, director.

a **1634** R. CLERKE *Serm.* ii. (1637) 15 He that is *Regens Sidera*,.. the Sterner of the Starres. **1638** R. BAKER tr. *Balzac's Lett.* (vol. III.) 230, I leave you liberty.. to saile with the wind. Nothing but good success can be expected from your sterning.

†**stern**, *v.*[2] *Obs. rare*[−1]. [app. ad. L. *sternĕre.*] *trans.* To cast down.

1599 A. HUME *Poems* ii. 168 All things beneth the voult of heuin are sterned vnder feit.

stern, *v.*[3] *rare*[−1]. [f. STERN *a.*] *trans.* To make stern.

1722 W. HAMILTON *Wallace* 77 Wallace stern'd his Brow and cry'd My Life alone shall the long Strife decide.

sterna, plural of STERNUM.

sternad ('stɜːnæd), *adv. Anat.* [f. STERN-UM + *-ad*: see DEXTRAD.] Towards the sternum or the sternal aspect.

1803 J. BARCLAY *New Anat. Nomencl.* 166 Sternad [will signify] towards the sternal [aspect]. **1808** —— *Muscular Motions* 237 This vein.. advances sternad, sinistrad, and sacrad. *Ibid.* 333 The dorsal muscles are more numerous, more powerful.. than their antagonists which are situated sternad. **1814** J. H. WISHART tr. *Scarpa's Treat. Hernia* Mem. I. 19 The aponeurosis.. attached anteriorly [*note* Sternad] to the *linea alba*.

†**'sternage**, *sb. rare*[−1]. [f. STERN *sb.*[3] + -AGE.] The sterns of a fleet collectively.

1599 SHAKS. *Hen. V*, III. Prol. 18 Follow, follow: Grapple your minds to sternage of this Nauie.

sternal ('stɜːnəl), *a.* (*sb.*) *Anat.* and *Zool.* [ad. mod.L. *sternālis*, f. STERN-UM: see -AL[1]. Cf. F. *sternal.*] **A.** *adj.*

1. Of, pertaining to, or connected with the sternum or breast-bone.

1756 G. DOUGLAS tr. *Winslow's Struct. Hum. Body* (ed. 4) I. 234 The Sternal Portion passes foremost and covers the Clavicular. **1833** MANTELL *Geol. S.E. Eng.* 307 A small sternal bone has been discovered. **1835–6** *Todd's Cycl. Anat.* I. 201/2 This sternal plastron is distinctly shewn. **1890** COUES *Ornithol.* 212 Birds offer two leading types of sternal structure, the ratite and the carinate.

2. Situated on the same side as the sternum; anterior (in man) or inferior (in other animals); ventral; hæmal. (Opposed to *dorsal*, *tergal*, or *neural*.)

1803 J. BARCLAY *New Anat. Nomencl.* 120 Instead of Anterior and Posterior, we might adopt Sternal and Dorsal. **1814** J. H. WISHART tr. *Scarpa's Treat. Hernia* Mem. I. 34 The anterior surface [*note*, Sternal Aspect] of the abdomen.

3. Of or pertaining to a sternum or sternite in Arthropoda; sternitic. (Often coinciding with 2.)

1835 KIRBY *Habits & Inst. Anim.* II. xvi. 89 A bilobed organ which Savigny calls a sternal tongue. **1852** DANA *Crustacea* I. 20 Each of these rings consists normally of eight parts or segments,—two below, called sternal, two above, called dorsal, [etc.]. **1880** HUXLEY *Cray-Fish* 20 Its under, or what is better called its sternal surface.

B. as *sb.* A sternal bone.

1901 HATCHER in *Mem. Carnegie Mus.* I. I. 40 Taken together the sternals of *Diplodocus* would thus form a shallow raft-like sternum.

sternalgia: see STERNO-.

sternbergite (ˈstɜːnbɜːgaɪt). *Min.* [Named by Haidinger in honour of Count Caspar *Sternberg*: see -ITE.] A native sulphide of silver and iron, occurring in brown flexible laminæ with metallic lustre.

1826 HAIDINGER in *Edin. Jrnl. Sci.* (1827) VII. 242. **1850** ANSTED *Elem. Geol., Min. etc.* 226 *Sternbergite*, Sulphuret of silver and iron ($Ag\ S_2 + 4\ FS$).

ˈstern-ˈboard[1]. [f. STERN *sb.*[3] + BOARD *sb.*[1]]

1. A board forming the flat part of the stern of a small vessel, punt, etc.

1849 CUPPLES *Green Hand* xvi. (1856) 160 The stern-board of some small vessel or other. **1863** ATKINSON *Stanton Grange* (1864) 104 Working the stern-board in was the worst piece of the whole work to do.

b. *transf.* The tail-board of a cart.

1887 HALL CAINE *Deemster* xxxvi, Carts were tipped up in corners, and their stores.. were guarded by a boy.., who sat on the sternboard.

2. *Naut.* In phrase ***to make a stern-board***, to go backwards as the result of tacking; also, to force a ship astern with the sails.

1815 *Falconer's Dict. Marine* (ed. Burney) s.v. *Board, To make a stern Board*, (*faire culer*, Fr.), is when, by a current, or any other accident, the vessel has fallen back from the point she has gained on the last tack, instead of having advanced beyond it. **1883** *Man. Seamanship* (1886) 147 *Making a stern board.* It is effected by throwing the sails aback. **1897** ANSTED *Dict. Sea Terms* 271 Her next course must be in a direction W.S.W....which is actually going backwards, or in other words, she then makes a stern board.

ˈsternboard[2]. *Obs.* In 6 sterneborde. [Prob. an alteration of *stereborde* STARBOARD after STERN *sb.*[3] The coincidence with ON. *stjórnborðe* starboard is prob. accidental.] ? = STARBOARD.

In quot. a mistranslation; the original has *a la proa del navio*, to the prow of the ship.

1588 PARKE tr. *Mendoza's Hist. China* 343 There was a marriner commanded by the captaine of the ship, to keepe the sterneborde side.

ˈstern-ˈchase. *Naut.* [f. STERN *sb.*[3] + CHASE *sb.*[1]]

1. A chase in which the pursuing ship follows directly in the wake of the pursued.

1627 CAPT. SMITH *Sea Gram.* xii. 57 If he be right a-head of you, that is called a Stern-chase. **1722** DE FOE *Col. Jack* (1840) 298 We gave them [the other ships] what they call a stern chase, and they worked hard to come up with us. **1915** *Land & Water* 14 Aug. 36*/2 The German battle-cruisers.. had a fourteen-miles start of the British squadron, and Admiral Beatty settled down at once to a stern chase at top speed.

Proverb. **1849** LEVER *Con Cregan* I. xx. 331 The sailor's adage says 'that a stern chase is a long chase,' and so it is.

b. *transf.*

1863 W. C. BALDWIN *Afr. Hunting* vi. 182 Swartz and Kleinboy were soon in the saddle, and the former killed a fat cow [giraffe], after a very long stern chase.

2. The chase (CHASE *sb.*[1] 6) or chase-guns arming the stern of a war-ship. ? *Obs.*

1679 *Observ. Last Dutch Wars* 10 Let us keep our Stern chace out against another Enemy. **1748** *Anson's Voy.* III. viii. 501 The galeon returned the fire with two of her stern-chace. **1798** in Nicolas *Disp. Nelson* (1846) VII. p. clx, The Tonnant firing into her [the Majestic's] quarter with her stern chase raked her with great effect.

attrib. **1790** BEATSON *Nav. & Milit. Mem.* II. 317 Captain Jekyl.. was obliged to fire from both broadsides and stern-chase guns at the same time.

ˈstern-ˌchaser. *Naut.*

1. A gun belonging to the STERN-CHASE (sense 2).

1815 SCOTT *Guy M.* ix, They saw a lugger.. closely pursued by a sloop of war, that kept firing upon the chase from her bows, which the lugger returned with her stern-chasers. **1833** M. SCOTT *Tom Cringle* xv. (1842) 380 He worked his two stern chasers with great determination.

b. *jocularly.* A firearm discharged at a pursuer.

1835 W. IRVING *Tour Prairies* xxx. 283 The worthy Commissioner.. drew his sole pistol from his holster, fired it off as a stern-chaser, shot the buffalo full in the breast, [etc.].

2. The hindmost vessel in a race.

1883 *Times* 27 Aug. 8/2 The Lorna [yacht].. was weathered again by the little craft and was sternchaser.

‖**sternebra** (ˈstɜːnɪbrə). *Anat.* Pl. **-æ** (-iː). [mod.L. f. STERN-UM, with ending of VERTEBRA.] Any one of the segments of the sternum or breastbone, each corresponding to a pair of ribs. Also (in some recent Dicts.) in anglicized form **sterneber.**

1881 MIVART *Cat* 50 It.. consists of a chain of eight bones, called sternebræ. **1888** ROLLESTON & JACKSON *Forms Anim. Life* 362 The last sternebra.. sometimes.. giving attachment to more than one pair of ribs.

Hence **ˈsternebral** *a.*, pertaining to or constituting a sternebra.

In recent Dicts.

†**sterned,** *a.*[1] *Obs.* Also 6 *Sc.* **sternit.** [f. STERN *sb.*[2] + -ED[2].] = STARRED.

1340 HAMPOLE *Pr. Consc.* 7571 Ane es þat we þe sterned heven calle, þare þe planetes and þe sternes er alle. **1513** DOUGLAS *Æneis* v. xiv. 22 The sternit hevin.

sterned (stɜːnd), *a.*[2] [f. STERN *sb.*[3] + -ED[2].] Having a stern. Only as second element in parasynthetic formations like ***black-sterned***, PINK-STERNED.

c **1611** CHAPMAN *Iliad* XI. 740 But take me to thy blacke sternd ship. **1711** W. SUTHERLAND *Shipbuild. Assist.* 6 In Square Stern'd Ships.

sterner: see under STERN *v.*[1]

†**ˈsternet,** *sb. rare*[−1]. [f. STERN *sb.*[1] + -ET[1].] Some species of stern or tern.

1638 W. LISLE *Heliodorus* I. 8 The Swan both swimming there, and flying freely, The loftie Sternet crying t'Ely, t'Ely.

stern-fast. *Naut.* [f. STERN *sb.*[3] + FAST *sb.*[2]] A rope by which a vessel's stern is moored.

c **1569** [see HEADFAST]. **1627** CAPT. SMITH *Sea Gram.* vii. 30 A Brest-fast is a rope which is fastened to some part of the Ship forward on, to hold her head to a wharfe or any thing, and a Sterne-fast is the same in the Sterne. **1797** S. JAMES *Narr. Voy.* 131 The man.. at the time the painter broke, called for another rope, or sternfast. **1835** MARRYAT *Olla Podr.* iii, The stern-fast was thrown on the quay. **1911** *Contemp. Rev.* Mar. 283 The boats are either jambed up against her up-stream side or tailing off from their painters and stern-fasts on the down.

sternful (ˈstɜːnfʊl), *a.* [f. STERN *a.* + -FUL.] Full of sternness, severe, bold. *Obs.* or *arch.*

? *a* **1400** *Morte Arth.* 2692 Thane stirttes to his sterape sterynfulle Knyghttez. *Ibid.* 3822 He stekys stedis in stoure, and sterenfulle Knyghttes. *a* **1500** *Medulla Gram.*, *Austerus*, smert or sternfull. **1849** J. A. CAMERON *Monks of Grange* I Brave warders all, with sword and lance That guard it round with sternful glance.

Hence †**ˈsternfully** *adv. rare*[−1], fiercely.

1582 STANYHURST *Æneis* etc. (Arb.) 138 For Mars they be sternfulye flayling Hudge spoaks and chariots.

†**ˈsternhead.** *Obs. rare.* [f. STERN *a.* + -HEAD.] Sternness, severity.

1297 R. GLOUC. (Rolls) 2806 Rome ssal is sturnede Douty & quaky þeruore. *Ibid.* 7603 Ac to men þat him wiþsede to alle sturnhede he drou.

sterniform (ˈstɜːnɪfɔːm), *a. Ent.* [f. STERN-UM + -(I)FORM.] Having the form of a sternum or sternite; applied to a process (***sterniform process*** or ***horn***) of the first ventral segment of the abdomen in insects, also called *intercoxal process*.

1826 KIRBY & SP. *Entomol.* xxxvi. III. 709 A sharp sterniform conical horn.

sternine (ˈstɜːnaɪn), *a. Ornith.* [ad. mod.L. *Sterninus*, f. *Sterna*.] Belonging to or having the characters of the *Sterninæ* or terns, a subfamily of *Laridæ*, typified by the genus *Sterna*.

1874 COUES *Birds N.W.* 656 Bill.. much compressed, very slender and sternine.

sternite (ˈstɜːnaɪt). *Zool.* and *Comp. Anat.* [f. STERN-UM + -ITE.] **a.** The under or ventral part of each somite or segment of the body of an insect or other arthropod: correlated with *tergite* and *pleurite*. **b.** = STERNEBRA. *rare*[−0]. (In recent Dicts.)

1868 PACKARD *Guide Study Insects* 9 The typical ring or segment.. consists of an upper (tergite), a side (pleurite), and an under piece (sternite). **1882** *Athenæum* 14 Jan. 60/2 The chilaria of Limulus.. are regarded as metathoracic sternites.

Hence **sternitic** (stɜːˈnɪtɪk) *a.*, pertaining to a sternite.

In recent Dicts.

†**ˈsternless,** *a. Obs.* [f. STERN *sb.*[3] + -LESS. Cf. STEERLESS.] That has no rudder. Also *fig.*

c **1412** HOCCLEVE *Compl. Virg.* xxxii, (Egerton MS.) And right as that a schippe, or barge or boot Among the wawes dryveth sterneles [*v.r.* steerelees]. **1576** GOSSON *Sch. Abuse* etc. (Arb.) 76 The prime of youth.. settes up sayle, and sternlesse ship ysteares. **1628** FELTHAM *Resolves* I. lxxxiv. 239 Drunkennesse, arising from the Grape, is the floating of the sternelesse Sences in a Sea.

sternly (ˈstɜːnlɪ), *adv.* Forms: see STERN *a.* and -LY[2]. In a stern manner (see the senses of the adj.); with sternness of temper, aspect, utterance, etc.; severely, harshly, unbendingly; †fiercely, cruelly; †loudly.

c **897** ÆLFRED *Gregory's Past. C.* xxviii. 197 Ac he him sona ondwyrde, & him suiðe stiernlice stierde. *c* **1205** LAY. 25240 þa wes Arðures hired sturneliche awraððed. **1377** LANGL. *P. Pl.* B. Prol. 183 A mous.. Stroke forth sternly and stode biforn hem alle. *c* **1384** CHAUCER *H. Fame* III. 408 (Pepys MS.) A piler.. Of yren wrought full sternely [*Bodl.* sturnelye, *Fairf.* sturmely]. *c* **1385** —— *L.G.W.* 239 For sternely on me he gan beholde. **1398** TREVISA *Barth. De P.R.* XV. xii. (Tollemache MS.) þese Goothes were sternely [1495 cruelly] killid. ? *a* **1400** *Morte Arth.* 745 Sterynly thay songene [said of the sailors of a fleet]. **1590** SPENSER *F.Q.* II. xi. 37 He.. strooke at him so sternely, that he made An open passage through his riven brest. **1615** CHAPMAN *Odyss.* IX. 402 No mountaine Lion tore Two Lambs so sternly. **1671** MILTON *P.R.* I. 406 To whom our Saviour sternly thus replied. *a* **1771** GRAY *Dante* 56 Father, why, why do you gaze so sternly? **1835** HAWTHORNE *Tales & Sk., Dr. Bullivant* (1879) 136 We see the mountains rising sternly and with frozen summits up to heaven. **1846** MACAULAY *Hist. Eng.* vi. II. 147 He was sternly told that his defence was not satisfactory. **1855** KINGSLEY *Westw. Ho!* xxv, I must be just, and sternly just, to myself, even if God be indulgent. **1911** *Q. Rev.* July 123 The Mildmay household was sternly Puritan.

Comb. **1608** SYLVESTER *Du Bartas* II. iv. IV. *Decay* 1114 Sternly-valiant to the stubborn-stout. **1808** WORDSW. *George & Sarah Green* 17 Those sternly-featured hills. **1814** —— *Excurs.* VI. 853 A sternly-broken vow.

ˈsternman. Also 7 sternsman. [f. STERN *sb.*[3] + MAN. Cf. STEERMAN, STEERSMAN.]

†**1.** A steersman, pilot; cf. STERN *sb.*[3] I. *Obs.*

1582 BATMAN *Barth. De P.R.* XI. xii. 163 b, The sternman doubteth, and cannot know whetherward he shall stir the ship a right. **1608** WILLET *Hexapla Exod.* 50 God as the sternesman that directeth and guideth all. **1625** K. LONG tr. *Barclay's Argenis* III. xxi. 217 The rash Sterneman split her dangerously against a hidden Rocke. **1627** W. SCLATER *Exp. 2 Thess.* (1629) 147 Before hee hath described the Sternsman, a man of sinne.

2. A man posted in the stern of a boat.

1894 *Outing* XXIV. 189/2 The sternman sits on the gun-wale of the extreme end of the craft.

sternmost (ˈstɜːnməʊst, -məst), *a.* [f. STERN *sb.*[3] + -MOST.]

1. Farthest in the rear, last in a line of ships.

1622 R. HAWKINS *Voy. S. Sea* iv. 9 The Vice-admirall that should haue beene starnmost of all, was the headmost. **1727** A. HAMILTON *New Acc. E. Ind.* II. l. 226, I kept in the headmost Jonk, and a good Officer in the sternmost. **1838** SOUTHEY in *Q. Rev.* LXII. 7 Under a press of sail, he came alongside the sternmost ship.

2. Nearest the stern.

1838 *Civil Engin. & Arch. Jrnl.* I. 341/2 Mr. Abbinet, with a magazine of 200 lbs. of powder, blew off about 30 feet of the sternmost part of the wreck. **1914** *Glasgow Herald* 31 Aug. 7 The sternmost funnel was shot clean away.

sternness (ˈstɜːnnɪs). Forms: α. 4–6 **steernesse, stiernesse,釘sternesse,** 5 **sturnesse;** β. 4–5 **sturnenesse, sternenysse,** 7 **sternenes;** 6 **sternnesse,** 7– **sternness.** [f. STERN *a.* + -NESS.]

1. Severity of disposition or mood; rigour in punishment or condemnation; an instance of this; hardness, harshness, obduracy, †fierceness.

1382 WYCLIF *Ezek.* xxxiv. 4 Bot with steernesse [1388 sturnenesse] ȝe comaundide to hem, and with power. *c* **1400** *Sege Jerus.* (E.E.T.S.) 29/517 Noþer grounded in god, ne on his grace tristen, Bot alle in sterymnes [*v.r.* sternenysse] of stour & in strengþ one. **1483** *Cath. Angl.* 363/1 Sternesse, *pertinacia*. *a* **1500** *Medulla Gram.*, *Austeritas*, steernesse or felnesse. **1540–1** ELYOT *Image Gov.* 22 That grauitee and sternesse, whiche is in you, as it were by nature ingenerate. **1692** DRYDEN *Cleomenes* I. i. 7, I have sternness in my Soul enough To hear of Murders, Rapes, and Sacrilege. **1741** RICHARDSON *Pamela* I. 35 She was a little too much frighted, as she owned afterwards, at his Sternness. **1844** MRS. BROWNING *Lay Brown Rosary* I. vi, But his mother was wroth. In a sternness quoth she, 'As thou play'st at the ball, art thou playing with me?' **1885** *Manch. Exam.* 26 Jan. 5/3 It is found compatible with the strictest discipline, and indeed with rhadamanthine sternness. **1914** *Edin. Rev.* Oct. 320 A typical Frenchman.. bland and gracious, but with a capacity for sternness.

b. quasi-*concr.*, applied to a goddess.

a **1616** BEAUM. & FL. *Bonduca* III. i, Thou sure-steel'd sternnesse, give us this day good hearts, good enemies.

†**2.** Rigour, inclemency (of climate). *Obs.*

1387 TREVISA *Higden* (Rolls) I. 51 And for þe sturnesse of heuene [L. *inclementia caeli*] he haþ þe more wildernes.

3. Of aspect: Severity, formidableness.

1590 SPENSER *F.Q.* II. x. 7 Of stature huge, and eke of courage bold, That sonnes of men amazd their sternnesse to behold. **1611** SHAKS. *Wint. T.* IV. iv. 24 How Should I.. behold The sternnesse of his presence. **1794** MRS. RADCLIFFE *Myst. Udolpho* xxxix, Emily was terrified by the sternness of his look.

b. Of scenery, buildings, etc.: Severity; harshness in nature or aspect.

1812 J. WILSON *Isle of Palms* II. 387 The sternness of this dismal Isle Is soften'd by thy saintly smile. **1860** TYNDALL *Glac.* I. xxvii. 197, I.. enjoyed for a time the sternness of the surrounding scene.

Sterno (ˈstɜːnəʊ). *U.S.* A proprietary name for solidified alcohol supplied in containers for use as fuel for cooking stoves, etc.

1915 *Official Gaz.* (U.S. Patent Office) 11 May 672/1 *Sterno.* S. Sternau & Co., New York, N.Y. Filed Mar. 24, 1915.... Solid fuel composed mainly of alcohol. Claims use since Jan. 12, 1915. **1935** Z. N. HURSTON *Mules & Men* I. ix. 186 Somebody had squeezed the alcohol out of several cans of Sterno and added sugar, water and boiled-off spirits of nitre and called it wine. **1958** *Washington Post* 1 Nov. 1/3 They drink stuff like.. Sterno (liquefied and strained 'canned heat'). **1969** *Trade Marks Jrnl.* 30 July 1237/2 *Sterno*.... Solid fuels consisting mainly of alcohol. Colgate-Palmolive Company,.. New York, State of New York 10022, United States of America; Manufacturers. **1978** R.

DOLINER *On Edge* (1979) xvii. 223 There was no electricity. . . . He cooked his meals over a can of Sterno. **1979** P. THEROUX *Old Patagonian Express* i. 16 Survival techniques at home . . cooking on Sterno stoves and the like.

sterno- (stɜːnəʊ), before a vowel **stern-**, combining form repr. Gr. στέρνον or L. STERNUM, occurring in several terms, chiefly of anatomy, usually denoting muscles, etc. connected with the sternum and some other part. (Many of these are found in Fr.: see Littré.) ‖**sternalgia** (-ˈældʒɪə); [Gr. ἄλγος pain], pain in the region of the sternum; *spec.* a synonym for *angina pectoris*; hence **sterˈnalgic** *a.*, pertaining to or affected with sternalgia. ˌ**sternoclaˈvicular** *a.*, pertaining to or connecting the sternum and clavicle. **sternocleidoˈmastoid** *a.* [Gr. κλειδ-, κλείς key, clavicle + MASTOID], connecting the sternum, the clavicle, and the mastoid process of the temporal bone; applied to each of two muscles of the neck which serve to turn and nod the head; also as *sb.* (Also in L. form **-oideus**, pl. **-oidei**.) **sternoˈcostal** *a.* [L. *costa* rib], pertaining to or connecting the sternum and the ribs. **sternoˈglossal** *a.* [Gr. γλῶσσα tongue], pertaining to or connecting the sternum and the tongue, as the long retractor muscle of the tongue in the great ant-eater; also as *sb.* **sternoˈhyoid** *a.*, pertaining to or connecting the sternum and the hyoid bone; name of each of two muscles serving to depress the larynx; also as *sb.* †ˈ**sternomancy** [-MANCY; cf. F. *sternomantie* (Rabelais)], divination by the breast-bone. †**sternoˈmastic** *a.* = next. **sternoˈmastoid** *a.*, pertaining to or connecting the sternum and the mastoid process of the temporal bone; applied to the sternocleidomastoid muscle, or the part of it connected with the sternum (cf. CLEIDOMASTOID); also to an artery supplying this muscle; also as *sb.* (*sc.* muscle). ˌ**sternomaˈxillary** *a.* [L. *maxilla* jaw], pertaining to or connecting the sternum and lower jaw-bone, as the sternomastoid muscle in the horse. ˌ**sternoˈnuchal** *a.*, pertaining to the sternum and the nape of the neck. ˌ**sternoperiˈcardiac, -al** *adjs.*, pertaining to or connecting the sternum and the pericardium. **sternoˈpleuron** (also **-pleurum**, †**-pleura**; pl. **-pleura**) *Ent.*, in flies, each of the two hard plates of the body wall to which the middle two legs are attached, protecting parts of the sides and parts of the underside; so **sternoˈpleural** *a.*, of or pertaining to the sternopleuron, or to the sternum and the pleura. ˈ**sternothere** (-θɪə(r)), *Zool.*, a tortoise of the genus *Sternothærus* [Gr. θαιρός hinge], characterized by a hinged plastron. **sternoˈthyroid** *a.*, pertaining to or connecting the sternum and the thyroid cartilage (also †**sternothyroˈeidal**); also as *sb.* (*sc.* muscle). ˈ**sternotribe** *a. Bot.* [Gr. τρίβειν to rub], applied to flowers adapted for cross-fertilization by insects, in which the stamens and styles are so arranged as to touch the breast of the insect. **sterno-ˈvertebral** *a.*, connected with the sternum and the vertebrae.

1822–29 *Good's Study Med.* (ed. 3) I. 660, I have . . been under the necessity of giving it a new denomination . ., hence the above name of *Sternalgia. *Ibid.* II. 443 The pain and struggle . . sometimes resemble the signs of sternalgia or angina pectoris. **1840** OWEN in *Penny Cycl.* XVIII. 257/2 For what purpose . . were *sterno-clavicular and coracoid arches assigned to the Ichthyosaurus? **1887** *Brit. Med. Jrnl.* I. 279 The angle of the right jaw rested on the sterno-clavicular notch. **1826** S. COOPER *First Lines Surg.* (ed. 5) 408 A rigid contraction of one of the *sterno-cleido-mastoidei. **1831** R. KNOX *Cloquet's Anat.* 27 The aponeuroses of the large pectoral and sterno-cleido-mastoid muscles. **1899** *Allbutt's Syst. Med.* VIII. 41 The muscles of the tongue, the masseters, and sterno-cleido-mastoids. **1785** CULLEN *Instit. Med.* I. (ed. 3) 142 The *sterno-costal and infra-costal muscles. **1862** H. W. FULLER *Dis. Chest* 5 The second sterno-costal articulation. **1891** *Century Dict.*, *Sternoglossal. [**1693** tr. *Blancard's Phys. Dict.* (ed. 2), Sternohyoides. **1843** WILKINSON tr. *Swedenborg's Anim. Kingd.* I. i. 20 The sterno-hyoideus.] **1872** MIVART *Elem. Anat.* 287 The *sterno-hyoid muscle is a long band which springs from within the sternum or clavicle, and goes to the basi-hyoid. **1875** W. TURNER in *Encycl. Brit.* I. 836/2 The hyoid bone and larynx . . can be . . drawn downwards by the action of the sterno-hyoids, [etc.]. **1652** GAULE *Magastrom.* xix. 165 *Sternomancy. **1693** *Urquhart's Rabelais* III. xxv, Sternomancy . . maketh nothing for thy Advantage, for thou has an ill proportion'd Stomach. **1745** *Gentl. Mag.* XV. 312/1 Behind the *sternomastic muscles. **1835–6** *Todd's Cycl. Anat.* I. 746/1 The *sterno-mastoid and splenius muscles. **1846** BRITTAN tr. *Malgaigne's Man. Oper. Surg.* 114 The anterior surface of this [*sc.* the mastoid] process and the corresponding border of the sterno-mastoid should be grazed. **1880** BARWELL *Aneurism* 72 The sternal and clavicular portions of both sterno-mastoids were widely separated. *Ibid.* 106 The right sterno-mastoid muscle. **1871** HUXLEY *Anat. Vert. Anim.* 353 The anterior portion of the sternomastoid is fixed to the mandible, and thus becomes '*sternomaxillary'. **1899** *Allbutt's Syst. Med.* VI. 865 Sterno-nuchal or 4th cervical area. **1877** W. TURNER *Introd. Hum. Anat.* II. 396 The *sterno-pericardiac ligaments of Luschka. **1901** DORLAND *Med. Dict.* (ed. 2), *Sternopericardial. **1884** C. R. OSTEN-SACKEN in *Trans. Entomol. Soc. London* 503 **Sternopleura*; it is that portion of the mesosternum which, from its position, forms a part of the pleura. . . It is convenient to have a separate name for it. **1925** A. D. IMMS *Gen. Textbk. Entomol.* III. 600 The sternopleuron is situated below suture 2 and above the anterior coxa [of the thorax of Diptera]. *Ibid.*, The mesopleuron is the area in front of the root of the wing between the noto- and sterno-pleural sutures. **1961** J. E. COLLIN *Brit. Flies* VI. 108 Sternopleura with a bare polished patch. **1975** *Nature* 25 Dec. 668/1 The distribution of small bristles on the ventral part of the sternopleurum. **1884** C. R. OSTEN-SACKEN in *Trans. Entomol. Soc. London* 503 *Sternopleural suture*, horizontal suture below the dorsopleural and parallel to it; separates the mesopleura from the mesosternum. *Ibid.* 510 Sternopleural bristles. **1975** *Nature* 25 Dec. 666/2 Studies of polygenes affecting sternopleural bristle number in *Drosophila melanogaster*. **1876** *Nature* XIV. 17/2 Four Blackish *Sternotheres (*Sternotherus subniger*) from Madagascar. [**1693** tr. *Blancard's Phys. Dict.* (ed. 2), **Sternothuroeides*, a pair of Muscles of the *Cartilago Scutiformis*, which draw it downward: They arise from the uppermost and inward part of the Breast-Bone.] **1840** E. WILSON *Anat. Vade M.* (1842) 111 The sterno-thyroid muscles. **1872** HUMPHRY *Myology* 111 Occasional inscriptions in the sterno-hyoid and sterno-thyroid. **1681** tr. *Willis' Rem. Med. Wks.* Vocab., *Sternothyroeidal muscle. **1861** R. E. GRANT *Tabular View Rec. Zool.* 18 False ribs anterior to the *sterno-vertebral ribs.

†ˈ**sternon.** *Obs.* [mod.L., a. Gr. στέρνον: see STERNUM. Cf. F. †*sternon.*] = STERNUM 1.

1597 A. M. tr. *Guillemeau's Fr. Chirurg.* 7/3 In the middle of anye ribbe or in the sternon. **1676** WISEMAN *Chirurg. Treat.* VII. iv. 485 Another having by accident of a Fall in wrastling, started the end of the Clavicle from the Sternon. **1682** *Phil. Collect.* XII. 149 He hath . . a broad Breast, and a large, firm Sternon.

ˈ**stern-post.** *Naut.* [f. STERN *sb.*³ + POST *sb.*¹]

a. A more or less upright beam, rising from the after end of the keel of a boat and supporting the rudder; an analogous part in an aircraft (see quot. 1969).

1580 H. SMITH in *Hakluyt's Voy.* (1599) I. 448 The William had her sterne post broken. **1627** CAPT. SMITH *Sea Gram.* ii. 2 The Sterne post is another great timber, which is let into the keele . . somewhat sloping. **1753** HANWAY *Trav.* (1762) I. III. xxv. 107 The punishment . . was to be nailed by the ear to the stern-post of a ship. **1805** SOUTHEY *Madoc* II. xxv. 11 They . . Lay down the keel, the stern-post rear, and fix The strong-curved timbers. **1873** *Act 36 & 37 Vict.* c. 85 §3 A scale of feet denoting her draught of water shall be marked on each side of her stem and of her stern post. **1931** *Flight* 10 Apr. 324/2 Cases have occurred of the raised flange on plate NA 507, which secures the sternpost to the top longeron, bending and cracking in way of the taper pin. **1939** C. H. L. NEEDHAM *Aircraft Design* II. ix. 157 Where tail-plane supporting members attach to the fin stern post, the resultant compressive load should be taken into account. **1969** *Gloss. Aeronaut. & Astronaut. Terms* (*B.S.I.*) III. 5 *Stern post*, a single member terminating a fuselage, hull or float. **1979** D. B. THURSTON *Design for Flying* xv. 233 The afterbody sternpost and deadrise angles requires for a stable hull are set forth. . . These data are based upon actual water handling characteristics of many seaplanes.

†**b.** *jocularly.* The buttocks. *Obs.*

1810 *Naval Chron.* XXIV. 369 Come, Sir, bring him . . along; point your sword in his stern-post.

c. *attrib.*, as ***sternpost-knee*** (= STERNSON), ***tub***.

1845 J. COULTER *Adv. in Pacific* vii. 72 The other [end of the line] . . is left hanging out of the sternpost tub. **1881** HAMERSLY *Nav. Encycl.*, Sternpost-knee.

ˈ**stern-sheet.** *Naut.* [f. STERN *sb.*³ + SHEET *sb.*²; cf. next.

The parallel of FORE-SHEET, which is however comparatively late, suggests that sense 1 is original, and senses 2, 3 secondary with the general signification 'the place from which the mizen-sheets are controlled'. But historical evidence is lacking, and it is not impossible that some other meaning of OE. *scéat* is the basis of senses 2, 3.]

†**1.** *pl.* The ropes controlling the mizen-sail. *Obs.*

1626 CAPT. SMITH *Accid. Yng. Seamen* 15 The misen sheats, are called the starne sheats.

2. *sing.* and *pl.* The internal stern portion of a boat; *spec.* that part abaft the hindmost thwart.

1481 *Cely Papers* (Camden) 71, j pack lyeth yn the sterne shete. **1568** *Adm. Crt. Oyer & Ter.* 75 He was in the said catche [ketch] sittinge in the sterne sheates thereof. *a* **1625** *Nomenclator Navalis* (Harl. MS. 2301) 71 That part with in bord abaft in yᵉ Run of the Shipp is called the Sterne sheats [[cf. SHEET *sb.*² 3 quot. 1644.] **1766** SMOLLETT *Trav.* II. 5 There is a tilt over the stern sheets [of the feluca], where the passengers sit. **1875** BEDFORD *Sailor's Pocket Bk.* vi. (ed. 2) 226 A similar locker to be built in the after part of the stern sheet for the officers. **1905** QUILLER-COUCH *Shining Ferry* vii, The party settled themselves in the stern sheets.

3. *pl.* **a.** The flooring boards in the after portion of a boat or small ship.

1644, 1898 [see SHEET *sb.*² 3]. **1706** PHILLIPS (ed. Kersey) s.v. *Sheats, Stern-Sheats*, the Planks that are within board abaft in the Run of the Ship.

b. The seats with which the after portion of a boat is furnished.

1912 'G. A. BIRMINGHAM' *Inviolable Sanctuary* xviii. 280 She herself pulled a spinnaker from beneath the stern-sheets.

stern-shoots, *sb. pl. Obs.* exc. *dial.* Forms: 7 sterne-shootes, 9 *dial.* stern-shuts. [f. STERN *sb.*¹ + SHOOT *sb.*²] = STERN-SHEET 2.

1633 T. JAMES *Voy.* 70 The lower hole which we had cut in the Sterne-Shootes. **1904** *Eng. Dial. Dict.*, *Stern-shuts*, the place aft in a 'keel' where the 'huddock' is placed.

sternsman: see STERNMAN 1.

sternson (ˈstɜːnsən). *Naut.* [An English formation from STERN *sb.*³ on the analogy of KELSON, KEELSON. For the second element *-son*, see the etymological note *s.v.* KELSON.

Falconer *Dict. Marine* (1769–1815) explains and uses *stemson*, but does not recognize *sternson* as a term for the sternpost knee.]

In a wooden vessel, the knee-shaped timber fitted into the angle formed by the junction of stern-post and kelson in order to secure the joint.

1846 A. YOUNG *Naut. Dict.* 322 *Sternson*, or *Stern knee*, a piece of compass timber forming a continuation of a vessel's keelson, and extending over the deadwood to the stern-post, which is secured to it by bolts. *c* **1860** H. STUART *Seaman's Catech.* 66 The 'sternson', or 'inner post' . . bears the same relation to the stern post that the stemson does the stem.

b. sternson-knee (in the same sense).

1849 LONGF. *Build. Ship* 178 Stemson and keelson and sternson-knee.

sternum (ˈstɜːnəm). *Anat.* and *Zool.* Pl. **sterna** or **sternums**. See also STERNON. [mod.L., ad. Gr. στέρνον chest, breast. Cf. F. *sternum.*]

1. The breast-bone; a long bone or series of bones, occurring in most vertebrates except snakes and fishes, extending along the middle line of the front or ventral aspect of the trunk, usually articulating with some of the ribs, and with them completing the wall of the thorax.

Occasionally applied to the plastron of a turtle.

1667 *Phil. Trans.* II. 544 Thrust it in about an Inch, directing the end of it toward the Sternum. **1681** GREW *Musæum* I. §2. iii. 43 The fore part of the Sternum [of a Crocodile] is plainly bony. **1793** T. BEDDOES *Lett. to Darwin* 48 She had very acute pain under the sternum. **1801** [C. STEWART] *Elem. Nat. Hist.* I. 272 *Testudo* . . 3. The land species . .; shell convex, joined to the sternum with bony commissures. **1831** R. KNOX *Cloquet's Anat.* 27 The Sternum is composed of three bones placed one above another. These bones are in the adult most commonly joined together. **1890** COUES *Ornithol.* 211 The Avian Sternum . . is highly specialised; its extensive development is peculiar to the class of birds.

2. In Arthropoda: The ventral part of the body, or more usually of each somite or segment of the body (= STERNITE); opp. to *tergum*.

1835 J. DUNCAN *Beetles* (Nat. Lib.) 107 The inferior portion of the thorax is composed of a single piece named the sternum, or breastbone. It is much developed in certain tribes, particularly water-beetles. **1881** PACKARD *Zool.* (ed. 3) 329 These parts are respectively called tergite, pleurite, and sternite, while the upper region of the body is called the tergum, the lateral the pleurum, and the ventral or under portion the sternum. **1887** C. L. MORGAN *Anim. Biol.* 263 Ten terga and nine sterna can be made out in the male [cockroach].

†**sternutament.** *Obs. rare*⁻¹. [ad. L. *sternūtāmentum*, f. *sternūtāre*: see next.] = next.

1677 GALE *Crt. Gentiles* III. I. iii. 65 Casaubon . . saith that they received Sternutament with Adoration.

sternutation (stɜːnjuːˈteɪʃən). [ad. L. *sternūtātiōnem*, n. of action f. *sternūtāre*, frequentative f. *sternuĕre* to sneeze, cogn. w. Gr. πτάρνυσθαι (:—**pstrnu-*) of the same meaning.] The action of sneezing; a sneeze. (Chiefly *Med.* and *Path.*; otherwise, in mod. use, *affected* or *humorous*.)

1545 RAYNALDE *Byrth Mankynde* 124 Infantes . . troubled . . . . with often sternutation and sneesynge. **1646** SIR T. BROWNE *Pseud. Ep.* IV. ix. 199 The custome of saluting or blessing upon that motion . . is . . beleeved to derive its originall from a disease, wherein Sternutation proved mortall. **1713** POPE *Frenzy John Dennis* Misc. 1732 III. 6, I hope you have upon no Account promoted Sternutation by Helle-bore. **1842** BORROW *Bible in Spain* xlvii, His words . . were stifled . . by a sudden sternutation which escaped him. **1872** COHEN *Dis. Throat* 106 The secretions are viscid and acrid, inducing spasms of sternutation.

†**b.** Loosely used for STERNUTATORY *sb. Obs.*

1547 BOORDE *Brev. Health* cxix. (1557) 45 Let them . . vse dyuers tymes sternutacions with gargaryces. **1684** tr. *Bonet's Merc. Compit.* x. 349 If the Disease [Lethargy] continue, . . the use of Sternutations is very proper.

sternutative (stɜːˈnjuːtətɪv), *a.* and *sb.* Now *rare.* [f. L. *sternūtāt-*, *sternūtāre*: see prec. and -IVE.] = STERNUTATORY.

1666 BOGHURST *Loimogr.* (1894) 83 Use sternutatives, if they [patients] doe not sneeze of themselves. **1786** *Pogonologia* v. 63 This sternutative powder [snuff]. **1859** FAIRHOLT *Tobacco* (1876) 78 Such as used it as a sternutative.

Hence **sternutativeness**. *rare*⁻⁰.

1727 BAILEY vol. II, *Sternutativeness*, aptness to cause Sneezing.

sternutator (ˈstɜːnjuːteɪtə(r)). [f. *sternutat-* (in STERNUTATORY *a.* and *sb.*, etc.) + -OR.] A substance that causes nasal irritation; *esp.* a poison gas that causes irritation of the nose and eyes, pain in the chest, and nausea.

1922 *Encycl. Brit.* XXXII. 111/2 The sternutators were originally considered from the point of view of putting a man temporarily out of action by a violent fit of sneezing. **1951** KIRK & OTHMER *Encycl. Chem. Technol.* VII. 136 The introduction of sternutators in the form of aerosols as a gas warfare agent was a deliberate attempt by the Germans in World War I to penetrate the gas-mask canister and thus force demasking. **1971** [see JUGLONE].

sternutatory (stɜːˈnjuːtətərɪ), *a.* and *sb.* [ad. med.L. *sternūtātōrius* (neut. *-um* as sb.), f. L. *sternūtāt*, *sternūtāre*: see STERNUTATION and -ORY.]

A. *adj.*

1. Causing or tending to cause sneezing.

1616 T. ADAMS *Dis. Soul* 11 For the curing of this bodily infirmity, many remedies are prescribed..with scarification, gargarismes and sternutatory things. **1710** T. FULLER *Pharm. Extemp.* 394 Sternutatory Powder. **1829** LANDOR *Imag. Conv.*, *Chaucer, Boccaccio, & Petrarca* Wks. 1853 I. 404/2 He had about him a powder of sternutatory quality.

2. Of or pertaining to sneezing. (In quots. humorously pedantic.)

1842 THACKERAY *Fitz-Boodle Papers* Pref., He..was seized with a violent fit of sneezing—(sternutatory paroxysm he called it). **1858** LEWES in *Chamb. Jrnl.* 19 June 399/2 The showers of snuff which had too often attacked my sternutatory muscles. **1859** F. E. PAGET *Curate Cumberworth* 329 Miss Martha replied by a sneeze. A terror seizing me lest this sternutatory conclusion might be a preliminary to another fit of hysterics, I immediately took my leave.

B. *sb.* A substance that causes sneezing; *esp.* a drug, usually in the form of powder, used to excite sneezing; an errhine.

1634 T. JOHNSON *Parey's Wks.* XXVI. XXXV. (1678) 654 Drie Errhines that are termed sternutatories, for that they cause sneezing, are made of powders onely. **1646** SIR T. BROWNE *Pseud. Ep.* IV. ix. 200 Physitians..in persons neere death doe use Sternutatories, or such as provoke unto sneezing. **1722** QUINCY *Lex. Physico-Med.* (ed. 2) 15 Vomits and Sternutatories. **1811** A. T. THOMSON *Lond. Disp.* (1818) 273 Tobacco is chiefly employed as a sternutatory, and is the basis of all the kinds of snuff generally used. **1876** tr. *Wagner's Gen. Pathol.* 29 Muscular irritability is excited..by powerful light, by sternutatories, [etc.].

sternutory (ˈstɜːnjuːtərɪ), contracted or erroneous form of STERNUTATORY.

a **1425** tr. *Anderne's Treat. Fistula* etc. 102 Put vinegre or mustard in his nose... And giffe hym som oþer sternutoriez. **1705** *Phil. Trans.* XXV. 1802 'Tis not to be imagined, how Worms seated at the Basis of the Brain,..should be expelled by sternutories. **1842** PRITCHARD in *Penny Cycl.* XXIII. 46/2 Sternutories are chiefly employed..either to restore suspended respiration,..or to dislodge some foreign body. **1876** DUNGLISON *Med. Lex.*

sternward, sternwards (ˈstɜːnwəd, -wədz), *adv.* [See -WARD, -WARDS.] Towards or in the direction of the stern. Also of position, astern.

1832 J. P. KENNEDY *Swallow Barn* (1860) 16, I gazed upon the receding headlands far sternward. **1892** HARDY *Well-beloved* III. vi. (1897) 309 Their course, whether sternwards or sternwards, was steadily south. **1904** *Blackw. Mag.* July 134 The Admiral glanced sternwards. **1913** *Daily News* 5 Jan. 6 Logs of trees drifted past us sternward.

b. *from the sternward*: in a direction from the stern: see -WARD.

1866 NEALE *Sequences & Hymns* 38 The shipmen..Cast four anchors from the sternward.

'stern-wheel, *sb.* [STERN *sb.*[3]] A paddle-wheel placed at the stern of a small river or lake steamer.

1816 *U.S. Patent* (John L. Sullivan) 10 Dec., Double stern wheel for boats. **1896** MARKHAM in *Geog. Jrnl.* VII. 188 [The steam-launch] is propelled by a stern wheel.

attrib. **1856** OLMSTED *Slave States* 368 The boat I was in ..was a stern-wheel craft. **1882** *Harper's Mag.* Dec. 3/2 Our stern-wheel boat creeps along up stream. **1884** *Pall Mall Gaz.* 3 Oct. 8/2 A new stern-wheel steamboat for the Nile expedition.

b. *transf.* in jocular use (*U.S.*).

1859 BARTLETT *Dict. Amer.* (ed. 2) 450 The term is applied to any thing small, petty; as, a 'stern-wheel church'.

Hence **'sternwheel** *v. intr.*, to move by the agency of a stern-wheel. **sternwheeler**, a boat propelled by a stern-wheel.

1807 in *Tennessee Hist. Mag.* (1919) V. 62 Struck a large and stubborn sawyer, two or three feet below the surface of the water in a rapid current—stern wheeled with rapidity. **1859** BARTLETT *Dict. Amer.* (ed. 2) 450 *Stern-wheeler*, a steamboat fitted up with a stern-wheel. **1905** *Blackw. Mag.* Apr. 345/1 The *Amka*..stern-wheels slowly from the murky flood into the green water. **1906** *Macm. Mag.* Oct. 939 Our little neat stern-wheeler emerges from the last great lock of the Assouan dam.

'sterny, 'starny, *a. Sc.* [f. STERN *sb.*[2] + -Y.] Starry.

a **1500** *Chaucer's Parl. Foules* 43 (MS. Arch. Seld. B 24).. A sterny [*other MSS.* sterry] place. **1552** LYNDESAY *Monarche* 6045 Boith sterny heuin and Christellyng. **1599** A. HUME *Poems* viii. 10 Quhen darkenes hes the heauen revest, Bot ather Moone or Starnie light. **1858** M. PORTEOUS *Souter Johnny* 31 But I maun stop—its no in verse Your starny travels to rehearse.

steroid (ˈstɪərɔɪd, ˈstɛrɔɪd). *Biochem.* [f. STER(OL + -OID.] Any of a large class of naturally occurring or synthetic organic compounds characterized by a nucleus of 17 carbon atoms in the form of four fused rings (three containing six carbon atoms and one containing five) and with varying substituents and degrees of unsaturation, the members of which include sterols, many sex and adrenocortical hormones, insect hormones, bile acids and alcohols, cardiac-active glycones, and some sapogenins and alkaloids, and many of which have important pharmacological uses. Freq. *attrib.* or as *adj.*, as *steroid chemistry, hormone.*

anabolic steroid, a steroid whose anabolic effects predominate over the masculinizing ones.

1936 CALLOW & YOUNG in *Proc. R. Soc.* A. CLVII. 194 The term 'steroids' is proposed as generic name for the group of compounds comprising the sterols, bile acids, heart poisons, saponins and sex hormones. **1956** *Nature* 28 Jan. 188/2 We have observed the effects on wool growth of treating sheep with adrenocorticotrophic hormone and with cortical steroids. **1959** S. DUKE-ELDER *Parsons' Dis. Eye* (ed. 13) xiv. 151 In ophthalmology, these steroids may be administered locally or ststemically. **1960** [see PROGESTATIONAL *a.*]. **1961** *Nature* 30 Sept. 1368/1 New anabolic steroids with low androgenic activity. **1969** *Times* 16 Jan. 4/8 Steroid hormones, which are excreted in the urine, are one of the many body chemicals that follow a daily fluctuation. **1969** J. A. VIDA *Androgens & Anabolic Agents* i. 2 Since anabolic steroids promote protein synthesis in the muscular system, these drugs find important application in clinical medicine to speed up healing of wounds. **1971** *Brit. Med. Bull.* XXVII. 26/1 The amount of oestrogen in steroid contraceptives influences the hazard of thrombo-embolism. **1972** *Nature* 21 Jan. 125/1 Steroids are small and rather simple molecules which nevertheless elicit a complex array of biochemical responses in their target tissues, often leading to profound changes in growth and differentiation. **1974** M. C. GERALD *Pharmacol.* xix. 355 Anabolic steroids.. have been used by football players, weight lifters, and athletes. *Ibid.* xxi. 384 Digitalis glycosides consist of an aglycone fraction that has a steroid nucleus. **1977** *Daily News* (Perth. Austral.) 19 Jan. 49 The British National Racehorse Trainers' Federation has officially admitted that anabolic steroids have been in common use throughout the training profession for several years.

Hence **ste'roidal** *a.*, possessing the structure of, or pertaining to, a steroid.

1938 *Jrnl. Amer. Chem. Soc.* LX. 1736/2 Arguments are advanced to indicate that the steroidal hormones and bile acids do not originate from cholesterol. **1957** *Ibid.* LXXIX. 3222/1 Bromination of the steroidal sapogenin side chain. **1963** KATZMAN & ELLIOTT in Florkin & Stotz *Comprehensive Biochem.* X. iii. 72 A number of methods have been developed for the quantitative estimation of the steroidal estrogens. **1972** *Lancet* 22 Sept. 611/1 Little is known about the growth and steroidal activity of the human ovarian follicle. **1977** *Listener* 18 Aug. 208/2 The wild yam, the source of steroidal compounds used as the starting material for oral contraceptives.

steroidogenesis (stɪəˌrɔɪd-, stɛˌrɔɪdəʊˈdʒɛnɪsɪs). *Biochem.* [f. STEROID + -O + -GENESIS.] The biosynthesis of steroids.

1951 *Recent Progress Hormone Res.* VI. 220 We have investigated the effects of several variables on the ACTH-controlled steroidogenesis of the isolated adrenal. **1970** *Nature* 28 Nov. 885/1 This second monograph..deals with the pathways of steroidogenesis of the ovary and testis. **1979** *Experientia* XXXV. 159/2 The cyclic AMP-dependent protein kinase may be involved in the processes of spermatogenesis and steroidogenesis as animals reach sexual maturity.

Hence **steˌroido'genic** *a.*, pertaining to or having the property of steroidogenesis.

1951 *Recent Progress Hormone Res.* VI. 240 Our data suggest the possibility that steroidogenic organs should be visualized as assembly-line processing plants, where specific groups are introduced in a highly specialized way. **1959** *Endocrinology* LXV. 29 Saline extracts of beef diencephalon were assayed in the decerebrate dog for steroidogenic activity. **1974** D. & M. WEBSTER *Compar. Vertebr. Morphol.* xiii. 313 In amphibians the chromaffin tissue is embedded in the ventral portion of the kidney along with steroidogenic tissue.

sterol (ˈstɪərɒl, ˈstɛrɒl). *Biochem.* [The ending of CHOLESTEROL, ERGOSTEROL, etc., used substantively.] Any of a class of solid, unsaturated steroid alcohols that occur naturally both free and in combination as esters or glycosides and are classified according to their origin as mycosterols, phytosterols, zoosterols, and marine sterols.

1913 *Biochem. Jrnl.* VII. 617 It is now proposed to limit the terms zoo- and phyto-sterol to sterols which are found as tissue constituents of animals and plants respectively. **1939** A. HUXLEY *After Many a Summer* I. v. 65 Those sterols!.. Always linked up with senility. The most obvious case, of course, was cholesterol. **1959** L. F. & M. FIESER *Steroids* xi. 358 The characteristic sterol fraction from freshwater green algae (*Chlorophyceae*) is the common sitosterol mixture of higher plants. **1975** *Lipids* X. 542/1 Sterols have been isolated from both adult and juvenile ivy in free and esterified form. Stigmasterol..is the main component. **1979** *Jrnl. Org. Chem.* XLIV. 3378/1 Algae and fungi produce sterols with 24β configurations, while most higher plants produce sterols with 24α configurations.

-sterol (stərɒl), *suffix. Biochem.* [f. CHOLE)STEROL.] A formative element in the names of many sterols, as in ERGOSTEROL, PHYTOSTEROL.

-sterone, formative element in the names of some steroids, as in ANDROSTERONE, PROGESTERONE. [ad. G. *-steron*, f. *ster*(*ol* STEROL + *ket*)*on* KETONE. App. first used in G. *androsteron* (*Zeitschr. f. phys. Chem.* (1934) CCXXIX. 167) and *luteosteron* (*Ber. d. Deut. Chem. Ges.* (1934) LXVII. 1271).]

sterop(e, -oppe, obs. forms of STIRRUP.

†**sterqui'linian,** *a. Obs. rare*[−1]. [Formed as next + -AN.] = next.

1772 [COURTENAY, etc.] *Batchelor* (1773) III. 170 One of those *novi homines*, whom I despise, (men generally of sterqualinian [*sic*] extraction).

†**sterqui'linious,** *a. Obs. rare*[−1]. [f. L. *sterquilīni-um* dunghill (f. *stercus* dung) + -OUS.] Of or belonging to the dunghill.

c **1645** HOWELL *Lett.* (1655) II. xlix. 58 It is just so now, that any triobolary pasquiller,..any sterquilinious rascal, is licenc'd to throw dirt in the faces of Soveraign Princes in open printed language. **1656** BLOUNT *Glossogr.* [**1818** TODD (erron.) *Sterquilinous.* (So in later Dicts.)]

sterracle, variant of STERACLE.

sterraster (stəˈræstə(r)). *Zool.* [f. Gr. στερρ-ός stiff, solid + ἀστήρ star.] A stellate sponge-spicule having very numerous rays soldered together for the greater part of their length.

1887 SOLLAS in *Encycl. Brit.* XXII. 417/2 Connective tissue fibres by which adjacent sterrasters are united together. **1888** —— in *Challenger Rep.* XXV. p. lxiv.

Hence **ste'rrastral** *a.*, pertaining to, or composed of, sterrasters.

1888 SOLLAS in *Challenger Rep.* XXV. p. cxliv, Thus a strong tough composite sclerose and fibrous layer results, which we shall term the 'sterrastral layer'. **1900** *Proc. Zool. Soc.* 130 When a bud is detached, a shallow circular depression remains, the sterrastral crust here being thin.

sterre, obs. f. STAR *sb.*[1], STEER *v.*, STIR *v.*

sterred, -id, -it, obs. forms of STARRED.

sterrep, obs. form of STIRRUP.

sterrettite (ˈstɛrətaɪt). *Min.* [See quot. 1940 and -ITE[1].] A hydrous basic phosphate of scandium occurring as transparent, usually colourless, orthorhombic crystals, and now identified with kolbeckite (eggonite).

1940 LARSEN & MONTGOMERY in *Amer. Mineralogist* XXV. 513 A few specimens contain orthorhombic crystals distinct from any previously described mineral... The mineral is named sterrettite in honor of Dr. Douglas B. Sterrett who was one of the first investigators of the Utah and Nevada variscite deposits. **1959** *Bull. Geol. Soc. Amer.* LXX. 1648 Powder patterns of sterrettite and kolbeckite showed that their cell sizes are identical with that of synthetic $Sc(PO_4).2H_2O$.., indicating that the major cation might be scandium rather than aluminum. **1968** *Amer. Mineralogist* LIII. 1227 In the course of this work, the supposed Al phosphate sterrettite..was identified..to be scandium phosphate, $Sc(PO_4).2H_2O$, identical with kolbeckite.

sterrile, -ill, obs. forms of STERILE.

sterro-metal. [Gr. στερρό-ς stiff, hard.] An alloy of copper and zinc, with a small amount of iron and tin. Also shortened *sterro.*

1865 *Sci. Rev.* Nov. 133/2 Sterrometal. **1869** *Spons' Dict. Engin.* I. 177 Sterro-metal. **1881** TRIPPLIN & RIGG *Saunier's Watchmakers' Handbk.* 74 Sterro..is an alloy containing 56 per cent. copper, 41 zinc, 2 tin, and 1 iron. **1884** C. G. W. LOCK *Workshop Rec.* Ser. III. 42/1 *Sterro-metal*..is a very strong and elastic alloy used by Austrian engineers for hydraulic press pumps.

sterrop, -up, obs. forms of STIRRUP.

stert(e, obs. forms of START.

stertel, stertle, obs. forms of STARTLE.

‖**stertor** (ˈstɜːtɔː(r)). [mod.L., f. L. *stertĕre* to snore. Cf. F. *sterteur.*] A heavy snoring sound accompanying inspiration in profound unconsciousness (*Syd. Soc. Lex.*). **a.** *Path.*

1804 *Med. Jrnl.* XII. 110 A profound sleep, attended with a stertor resembling that of apoplexy. **1845** BUDD *Dis. Liver* 198 The delirium passed into complete coma, with dilated pupils and stertor. **1901** R. L. BOWLES in *Lancet* 6 July 1/1 Mucous stertor is a term which may be given to the bubbling of air through mucus or fluids in the trachea or larger air-tubes.

b. *gen.*

1849 *Blackw. Mag.* LXVI. 99 Listening..to the loud nose of a distant comrade, lest its fitful stertor should startle another pair of nostrils. **1856** ALB. SMITH *Mr. Ledbury* I. v. 31 The stertor of intoxication.

ster'torious, -ness = STERTOROUS, -NESS.

1803 *Med. Jrnl.* X. 246 The sickness had considerably abated, his respiration less stertorious. *a* **1849** POE *Facts Case M. Valdemar* Wks. 1865 I. 125 The stertorious breathing ceased—that is to say, its stertoriousness was no longer apparent.

stertorous (ˈstɜːtərəs), *a.* [f. STERTOR + -OUS. Cf. F. *stertoreux.*] Characterized by, of the nature of, stertor or snoring: **a.** *Path.*

1802 *Med. Jrnl.* VIII. 80 The stertorous breathing [in apoplexy]. **1863** READE *Hard Cash* xxi, The stertorous breathing recommenced. **1884** M. MACKENZIE *Dis. Throat*

& *Nose* II. 176 He passed through an..attack of delirium tremens, falling into a deep stertorous sleep.

b. *gen.*

1842 F. E. PAGET *Milford Malvoisin* 98 The snortings and stertorous breathings which proceeded from Mr. Blote's pew. **1877–8** HENLEY in *Ballades & Rondeaus* (Canterb. Poets) 172 A stertorous after-dinner doze.

Hence **'stertorously** *adv.*, **'stertorousness.**

1832 WARREN *Diary Late Physic.* II. vi. 272 He lay in a state of profound stupor, breathing stertorously. **1845** POE *Facts of Mr. Valdemar's Case* in *Amer. Rev.* Dec. 563/1 The stertorous breathing ceased—that is to say, its stertorousness was no longer apparent. **1853** DICKENS *Bleak Ho.* xx, They find Krook still sleeping like one o'clock; that is to say, breathing stertorously with his chin upon his breast. **1876** BRISTOWE *Th. & Pract. Med.* (1878) 117 In coma..the patient breathes slowly, irregularly, and stertorously. **1898** *Syd. Soc. Lex.*, *Stertorousness.* **1910** *Blackw. Mag.* Nov. 606/1 The driver continued to slumber stertorously.

stertylle, sterve, obs. ff. STARTLE, STARVE.

steryn(e, -ynne, obs. forms of STERN *a.*

stet (stɛt). *Printing.* [3rd sing. pres. subjunct. of L. *stāre* to stand.] 'Let it stand'; a direction in the margin of a proof or MS. that matter which has been altered or struck out is to remain uncorrected. The direction occasionally signifies that a non-standard or irregular form should be retained. Cf. SIC *adv.*

1755 J. SMITH *Printer's Gram.* xi. 277 Where words are struck out that are afterwards again approved of, they mark dots under such words, and write in the Margin, *Stet.* **1821** DIBDIN *Bibliogr.* etc. *Tour* I. 129, I could discover..that..he wished me to..leave him to his *deles* and *stets*! *a* **1966** 'M. NA GOPALEEN' *Best of Myles* (1968) 295 A colossal imposition who will..cause your heart to beat like a sledge-hammer (*stet*).

Hence as *v. trans.*, to cancel a correction or deletion of (words in a proof or MS.) by writing 'stet' in the margin and underlining the words with a series of dots; to write 'stet' against (an accidental deletion, miscorrection, etc.).

1875 SOUTHWARD *Dict. Typogr.* s.v. **1895** G. B. SHAW *Let.* 16 Dec. (1965) I. 581 If you disagree with my deletions, you can dot them under and 'stet' them. **1968** K. MARTIN *Editor* i. 19 On the same line I had 'stetted' another word which had been accidentally crossed out. **1975** J. BUTCHER *Copy-Editing* iii. 26 Stet American and all unusual spellings that are to be retained.

stetch: see STITCH *sb. dial.*

†**stete,** *v. Obs.* Only in pa. t. and pa. pple. **stet,** stett, (? stite). [Perh. repr. OE. **stíetan* = OFris. *stêta* (EFris. *stête*, NFris. *stiate*, WFris. *stjitte*), ON. *støyta* (Sw. *stöta*, Da. *støde*):—prehistoric **stautjan*, related to the str. vb. Goth. *stautan*, Du. *stooten*, OHG. *stôzzan* (MHG. *stôzen*, mod.G. *stossen*), to push.]

1. *trans.* To push, shove, kick; to throw or fling violently.

c **1330** *Arth. & Merl.* 5255 Galathin wit fot him stett, Out of his sadel he him pett. *Ibid.* 9096 Þo þat in his way he met, Doun riȝt of hors he hem stett.

2. *intr.* To go quickly or suddenly; to start or rush *forth*; to hurl oneself *on* or *against*; to come *together* with a violent collision; to fall violently; to spring or jump *down*.

c **1330** *Arth. & Merl.* 3270 Wiþ so gret ire to gider þai mett, þat her bodis to gider stet. *Ibid.* 3312 To gider wiþ bodis þai metten, þat boþe to grounde þai stetten. *Ibid.* 3807 Þis spies anon forþ stetten. *Ibid.* 6360 Saphiran wiþ king Arthour mett, Wiþ miȝt gret on him stett. *Ibid.* 8479 Þe heþen swain sone doun stett. *Ibid.* 9020, & hadde þer of his heued ysmite, Nadde Adragenis to him stite.

stethi(e, obs. forms of STITHY.

stetho- (stɛθəʊ), before a vowel **steth-**, combining form repr. Gr. στῆθος breast, chest, occurring in medical terms. **ˌstetho-'cardiograph**, an instrument for automatically recording at once the movements of the lungs and of the heart (cf. STETHOGRAPH, CARDIOGRAPH). **ste'thendoscope** [Gr. ἔνδον within + -SCOPE], an instrument for examining the inside of the chest by means of Röntgen rays. **ˌstethogoni'ometer** [Gr. γωνία angle + -METER], an instrument for measuring the angles and determining the configuration of the chest. (See also following words.)

1876 A. RANSOME *Stethometry* iii. 35 Dr. Burdon Sanderson's *stetho-cardiograph is essentially a pair of callipers provided with similar drums. **1899** *Lancet* 12 Aug. 438/2 Dr. Walsham..showed his *stethendoscope for the examination of the chest. **1858** S. S. ALISON *Phys. Exam. Chest* (1861) 367 The *stetho-goniometer..is intended to measure the angles at which the planes of different parts of the thorax are inclined to each other.

stethogram ('stɛθəgræm). [f. STETHO- + -GRAM.] A stethographic tracing.

1900 W. S. HALL *Text-bk. Physiol.* Fig. 125 Normal stethogram of dorso-ventral diameter in nipple plane.

stethograph ('stɛθəgrɑːf, -æ-). [f. STETHO- + -GRAPH.] An instrument for automatically recording the movements of the chest in breathing; a recording stethometer; also called *pneumograph*.

1876 tr. *von Ziemssen's Cycl. Pract. Med.* IV. 352 The results..that I [*sc.* Riegel] have obtained by means of the graphic method of investigation, undertaken with my simple and double stethograph. **1900** W. S. HALL *Text-bk. Physiol.* 200 The Stethograph. *Ibid.* Fig. 124 Stethograph tambour.

So **stethographic** (-'græfɪk), *a.*, pertaining to or made by the stethograph; **stethography** (stɪ'θɒgrəfɪ), the action or use of the stethograph.

1875 tr. *von Ziemssen's Cycl. Med.* IV. 284 Stethography, introduced by myself [i.e. Riegel], elicits results..not altogether insignificant. **1890** *Nature* 9 Oct. 581/2 A paper on stethographic tracings of..respiratory movements.

stethometer (stɪ'θɒmɪtə(r)). [f. STETHO- + -METER. Cf. F. *stéthomètre* (? from Eng.)] An instrument for measuring the extent of the movement of the walls of the chest in breathing.

1850 QUAIN in *Lond. Jrnl. Med.* II. 927 *note*, The instrument..must have a name, and I have therefore called it a Stethometer. **1861** S. S. ALISON *Phys. Exam. Chest* 341 Dr. Quain's stethometer..resembles a watch, having a dial and index. **1877** M. FOSTER *Physiol.* II. ii. (1878) 256 The movements of the chest walls may be recorded by means of the recording stethometer of Burdon Sanderson.

So **stetho'metric** *a.*, pertaining to or obtained by means of the stethometer; **stethometry** (stɪ'θɒmɪtrɪ), measurement by a stethometer, the use of the stethometer.

1876 A. RANSOME *Stethometry* vii. 137 The stethometric register in June 1872 was as under. *Ibid.* 138 Stethometry is..sometimes of use in supplementing the examination of the chest by other methods.

stethophone ('stɛθəfəʊn). [f. STETHO- + *-phone* as in TELEPHONE.] A name given independently to two improved forms of stethoscope: see quots.

1858 S. S. ALISON in *Proc. Roy. Soc.* IX. 197 An instrument which I have invented..and which, as it is specially adapted for the auscultation of differences in the sounds of different parts of the chest, I have named the Differential Stethoscope, or Stethophone. **1897** *Canadian Engin.* Mar. 329 [Instrument invented by Rev. D. B. Marsh, Hamilton, Ont. (Canadian patent 24 Nov. 1896)].

stethoscope ('stɛθəskəʊp), *sb.* Also 9 *erron.* **stethescope.** [a. F. *stéthoscope* (Laennec, the inventor, *c* 1819), f. Gr. στῆθος chest + σκοπ-εῖν to look at, observe: see -SCOPE.] An instrument used for examining the chest or other part by auscultation, the sounds of the heart, lungs, or other internal organs being conveyed by means of it to the ear of the observer.

1820 *Med. Jrnl.* XLIII. 165 The instrument used by M. Laennec, and to which he has applied the term stethoscope. **1824** J. FORBES (*title*) Original Cases, with Dissections and Observations illustrating the use of the Stethoscope and Percussion. **1828–32** WEBSTER, *Stethescope.* **1861** *Brit. & For. Med.-Chirurg. Rev.* XXVIII. 147 Bin-aural stethoscopes,..meant to intensify the sound..by conveying it simultaneously to both the ears of the auscultator. **1861** ALB. SMITH *Lond. Med. Stud.* 13 A stethescope—a curious instrument, something like a sixpenny toy-trumpet.

fig. **1861** *Sat. Rev.* 7 Sept. 238 The stethoscope which will record..the true state of the financial health of the States will be afforded by the market rates of Federal securities.

Hence **'stethoscope** *v. trans.*, to apply a stethoscope to, examine with a stethoscope. **stethoscopic** (-'skɒpɪk) [= F. *stéthoscopique*], **-scopical** *adjs.*, pertaining to, of the nature of, observed or obtained by a stethoscope. **stetho'scopically** *adv.*, by means of the stethoscope. **stethoscopist** (stɪ'θɒskəpɪst), one who uses a stethoscope. **ste'thoscopy** [= F. *stéthoscopie*], examination of the chest or other part with a stethoscope; the use of the stethoscope.

1840 A. EWING in A. J. Ross *Mem.* (1877) 66 He would be much better able to judge if I would allow him to *stethoscope me. **1865** *Spectator* 30 Sept. 1084 He has been repeatedly stethescoped, and his lungs pronounced perfectly sound. **1828** *Lancet* 23 Feb. 755/1 A *stethoscopic examination performed by a student. **1861** S. S. ALISON *Phys. Exam. Chest* 336 The hydrophone..is more an acoustic than a stethoscopic instrument. **1867** E. YATES *Forlorn Hope* x, The *stethoscopical examination, and the prescription-writing. **1876** BRISTOWE *Th. & Pract. Med.* (1878) 374 Many so-called dull sounds become obviously musical when tested *stethoscopically. **1828** *Lancet* 23 Feb. 755/1 The minute scrutiny of the attentive and accurate *stethoscopist. **1859** G. WILSON *Mem. E. Forbes* iv. 132 The skill which has characterized the Edinburgh stethoscopists. **1855** DUNGLISON *Med. Lex.* s.v. *Stethoscope*, This mode of examining affections of the chest, *Stethoscopy..is what Laënnec terms *Auscultation médiate.*

‖**'stethva.** *Obs. rare*$^{-1}$. Corrupt form of EISTEDDFOD.

1612 DRAYTON *Poly-olb.* iv. 177 That at the Stethva oft obtain'd a Victors praise, Had wonne the Siluer Harpe, and worne Apollos Bayes.

stethy, obs. form of STITHY.

‖**stet pro'cessus.** *Law.* [L. = let process be stayed.] (See quot. 1840.)

1840 LUSH *Pract. Superior Courts* 773 A *stet processus* is an entry on the roll in the nature of a judgment, that by consent of the parties all further proceedings be stayed. **1897** *Daily News* 3 Feb. 7/4 Baron Pollock ordered a stet processus to be entered and the record to be withdrawn.

Stetson ('stɛtsən). Also **stetson.** The name of John Batterson *Stetson* (1830–1906), American hat manufacturer, used *attrib.* and *absol.* to designate hats made by the company founded by him, esp. one with a broad brim and high crown associated with cowboys of the western U.S. Also applied *loosely* to other hats in this style.

A proprietary term in the U.S.

[**1895** *Montgomery Ward Catal.* Spring & Summer 274/1 Cow Boys' sombrero hats... J. B. Stetson's 'Boss of the Plains'. **1897** *Sears, Roebuck Catal.* 234/1 The world famous J. B. Stetson sombrero hat..crown 4½ inch; brim 4 inch.] *c* **1900** in *Amer. Mail Order Fashions* (1961) 27 Every railroad man knows that the Stetson hat is just the right style and shape for his business. **1903** *Everybody's Mag.* Dec. 739/2 'Send for me if you want me again,' says Redruth, and hoists his Stetson and walks off. **1906** *Official Gaz.* (U.S. Patent Office) 6 Mar. 290/1 *Stetson.* Hats and caps. John B. Stetson Company, Philadelphia, Pa. Filed Apr. 14, 1905. Used ten years. The name 'Stetson'. **1924** *Westm. Gaz.* 26 Aug. 5/5 The modern coster wants to wear a Stetson hat. **1940** W. FAULKNER *Hamlet* I. ii. 38 Pat Stamper..standing there at the gate to his rope stock pen, with that Stetson cocked and his thumbs still hooked in the top of his pants. **1953** D. CUSHMAN *Stay away, Joe* 19 He had donned for the occasion a new flame-red shirt and a thirty-dollar Stetson hat. **1967** *Telegraph* (Brisbane) 17 Apr. 4/1 He was amused at the surprise that greeted his announcement that the hat he was wearing—a snappy, small-brimmed business model—was also a Stetson... 'Stetson is a brand name. We make all kinds of men's hats.' **1970** *Guardian* 31 Dec. 2/7 His [*sc.* J. B. Stetson's] first hat was a 10-gallon Western, an ancestor of the stetsons worn by President Lyndon Johnson. **1978** D. BLOODWORTH *Crosstalk* II. xxi. 164 Idi Amin..went around twice talking to the hijacked passengers..wearing..a big stetson hat.

Hence **'Stetsoned** *a.*, wearing a Stetson.

1935 A. G. MACDONELL *Visit to America* xiii. 235 Fort Worth, overgrown village of spurred and Stetsoned cowpunchers. **1969** *Time* 8 Aug. 55/1 John Wayne as a pistoled and Stetsoned Captain Bligh. **1972** D. A. PAILIN in Cox & Dyson *20th-Cent. Mind* III. iv. 120, I remember a stetsoned rancher arriving at a Texas seminary. **1976** *National Observer* (U.S.) 1 May 7/3 They're often joined by Russian trawlermen or Stetsoned Oklahomans.

steuard, -art, obs. forms of STEWARD.

Steuben (st(j)uː'bɛn, 'st(j)uːbən). The name of the *Steuben* Glass Works at Corning, N.Y., founded in 1903, used *attrib.* to designate fine glassware made there, esp. the decorative engraved crystal produced since 1933. Also *absol.*

1920 *Official Gaz.* (U.S. Patent Office) 16 Mar. 529/2 *Steuben.* Corning Glass Works, Corning, N.Y. Filed Nov. 19, 1919. No claim being made to the exclusive use of the word 'Steuben' apart from the mark as shown in the drawing. *Particular description of goods.*—Cut Glass and Artistic Glassware. *Claims use* since about Jan. 1, 1904. **1941** G. S. & H. MCKEARIN *American Glass* ix. 422 A small, well formed vase blown from gold-ruby glass..is an opaque pink. It may also be a Steuben piece. **1948** J. S. PLAUT *Steuben Glass* ii. 9 Steuben glass is made by the so-called 'off-hand' process. **1958** 'S. MARLOWE' *Second Longest Night* I. iii. 19 He was carrying a cocktail glass, expensive Steuben, in his right hand. **1967** 'R. FOLEY' *Fear of Stranger* (1968) viii. 89 Her Steuben bud vase held an assortment of brushes. **1968** L. J. BRAUN *Cat who turned on & Off* ii. 23 Oh, what a lovely shop... She's got some old Steuben... Look at this decanter! **1979** *United States 1980/81* (Penguin Travel Guides) 556 Corning Glass Center, Corning, New York: An area has been set aside for visitors where the fine Steuben glass is hand-formed and engraved.

steuch, variant of STEW *v.*³ *Sc.*

steudiant, steure, obs. ff. STUDENT¹, STIR *v.*

stevedorage ('stiːvɪdɔərɪdʒ). *rare.* [f. STEVEDORE *sb.* + -AGE.] The charge for loading and unloading cargoes.

1860 *Merc. Mar. Mag.* VII. 73 Stevedorage,..8d per box.

stevedore ('stiːvɪdɔə(r)), *sb.* Also 8 **stowadore,** 9 (Dicts.) **stivadore.** [a. Sp. *estivador*, agent-n. f. *estivar* to stow a cargo: see STEEVE *v.*², STIVE *v.*

A med.L. *stivator* in the same sense, together with the verb *stivare*, occurs A.D. 1263 in Mas Latrie *Traités de Paix* (1868) Docum., 39, 40.]

A workman employed either as overseer or labourer in loading and unloading the cargoes of merchant vessels.

1788 *Massachusetts Spy* 10 July 2/3 Stowadores. **1828–32** WEBSTER, *Stevedore*, one whose occupation is to stow goods, packages, &c. in a ship's hold. *New York.* **1850** *Blackw. Mag.* July 54/1 Up mounted four or five..stevedores [Cape Town]. **1856** KANE *Arct. Expl.* II. xvii. 181 We scrambled off over the ice together, much like a gang of stevedores going to work over a quayful of broken cargo. **1870** *Standard* 17 Nov., The plaintiff was employed by Kennedy, a stevedore, in unloading the steam ship Sutherland. **1899** F. T. BULLEN *Log of Sea-waif* 6 The litter of cases, bales, etc., about the deck was fast disappearing under the strenuous exertions of the stevedores.

fig. **1867** F. H. LUDLOW *Little Brother* etc. 257 These stevedores of learning, the schoolmasters.

attrib. **1898** *Daily News* 16 Apr. 2/7 He was foreman of stevedore labourers. **1909** *Suppl. E. Essex Advertiser* 21 Aug. 4/3 One of the largest stevedore contractors.

stevedore ('stiːvɪdɔə(r)), *v.* [f. prec. sb.] *trans.* **a.** To stow (cargo) in a ship's hold. Cf. STEEVE *v.*² **b.** To load or unload the cargo of (a ship).

1862 *U.S. Congress* in De Vere *Americanisms* (1872) 637 Sugar.. not stevedored. **1877** *Law Rep., 4 App. Cases* 678 A contract that the Defendant would not stevedore any ship which by the agreement is allotted to the Plaintiff.

Hence **'stevedoring** *vbl. sb.*, the action of the verb; also the charge for handling cargo.

1879 *Law Rep., 4 App. Cases* 675 The stevedoring of all ships not consigned to any of such firms should be undertaken by the parties.. in turn. **1892** *Pall Mall Gaz.* 11 Oct. 7/1 Four or five shillings, without any freight or tonnage, or pilotage or stevedoring,.. is simply prohibitive.

steven (stɛv(ə)n), *sb.*[1] *Obs.* exc. *dial.* Forms: 1 stefn, stæfn, stemn, 2 steffne (*Ormin*), 3 stefne, stevne, stevone, 2–4 stephne, 3–5 stevene, 4 steovene, 4–6 stevyn, (4 *Sc.* stewyn(e, stewin, 6 *Sc.* stevyne), 5–6 stevin, (5 stevenne, 6 steeven), 6–7 steaven, 8–9 *dial.* stevvon, 2– steven. [OE. *stefn, stemn* fem. corresponds to OFris. *stifne*, OS. *stemna*, also *stemnia* (MLG. *stemne, stevene*), MDu. *stemme* (mod.Du. *stem*), OHG. *stimna, stimma* (MHG., mod.G. *stimme*), Goth. *stibna*; not in ON. (the Sw. *stämma*, Da. *stemme* are prob. from LG.). It is uncertain whether the Teut. root is **stem-* or **steƀ-*.]

1. = VOICE in various applications. In mod. dial. use chiefly: A loud voice (cf. 5).

a **900** tr. *Bæda's Hist.* IV. xxvi. [xxv.] (1890) 354 Ond swa swa he cuþre stefne wæs to me sprecende: Wel ðu dest, cwæð he, þæt [etc.]. *c* **1000** ÆLFRIC *Gen.* xxvii. 22 Witodlice seo stemn ys Iacobes stefn. *a* **1122** *O.E. Chron.* (Laud MS.) an. 656 Þa stod seo kyning up to foren ealle his ðægna & cwæd luddor stefne Ðancod wurð hit [etc.]. *c* **1175** *Lamb. Hom.* 45 Þa onswerede him drihten mildere steuene, Aris nu paul aris. *c* **1200** ORMIN 10680. & tær wass herrd an steffne anan. *c* **1250** *Gen. & Ex.* 355 After ðis dede a steuone cam, 'ðu, nu, quor art, adam, adam?' *a* **1300** *Havelok* 1275 Þanne she hauede herd the steuene Of þe angel ut of heuene, She was so fele siþes bliþe, Þat [etc.]. *c* **1300** *Leg. Gregory* (Schulz) 298 Þat child þan bigan to scriche Wiþ steuen, as it were a grome. **13..** *Gaw. & Gr. Knt.* 2008 Bi vch kok þat crue, he knwe wel þe steuen. *c* **1375** *Sc. Leg. Saints* xxviii. (*Margaret*) 685 As þe puple herd þis stewine And þe thonir þat hydwis was, Þai fel flatlingis on þare face. *c* **1385** CHAUCER *L.G.W.* 2328 Sche cryeth 'systyr' with ful loude a steuene. *c* **1450** *Mirk's Festial* 302 An so a steven comme and tolde þe Emperour þat [etc.]. **1513** DOUGLAS *Æneis* III. iii. 54 And strekand wp my handis towart hevin, Myne orisone I maid with devoit stevin. **1575** LANEHAM *Let.* (1871) 41 A doouty Dwarf.. With steeuen full stoout amids all the preas, Said 'hail, syr king'. **1768** ROSS *Helenore* III. 113 Quo Jean, my steven, sir, is blunted sair, An' singing frae me frighted aff wi' care. **1819** R. GALL *Poems* 93 Then could her Sangsters loud their steven raise. **1865** W. S. BANKS *Provinc. Words Wakefield* s.v., Thah's a rare stevven, lad. *a* **1886** G. E. MACKAY *Love Lett. Violinist* (1895) 197 He.. lifted up his steven To keep the bulwarks of his faith secure.

†**b.** *with one steven*, with one voice, in accord.

c **1320** R. BRUNNE *Medit.* 382 For ȝow we preyd alle with o steuene. *a* **1450** *Le Morte Arth.* 2584 All they sayd with one steuen: 'Lordyngis, how longe wolle ye chyde?

†**c.** Voice in petition; cry, petition, prayer. *Obs.*

c **1200** *Trin. Coll. Hom.* 43 On diepe wosiðes ich clupe to þe hlouerd, hlouerd her mine stefne. *c* **1275** *Anthem St. Thomas* 8 in *O.E. Misc.* 90 Haly thomas.. Vre stephne vnderstonde. **13..** *K. Alis.* 6846 For, byhold, up thy steovene Ys y-herd into the heovene. *a* **1400** *Pistill of Susan* 268 Lord, herteliche tak hede, and herkne my steuene So Fre. *c* **1460** *Towneley Myst.* ii. 175 *Abell.* God that shope both erth and heuen, I pray to the thou here my steven. **1589** LODGE *Scillaes Metam.* etc. E 2, Father of light.. Bring to effect this my desired steauen.

†**d.** Used for: Right of speaking. *Obs.*

c **1175** *Lamb. Hom.* 83 Mon hefde uorloren efre stephne bi-uore gode.

†**2.** Speech, speaking; language, tongue. *Obs.*

c **1386** CHAUCER *Sqr.'s T.* 150 Ther is no fowel þat fleeth vnder heuene That she ne shal wel vnderstonde his steuene. **14..** *Pol. Rel. & L. Poems* 245 'Superbia' ys the most prinsipall [sin], 'pryde pertly' in englysshe steven.

†**3.** Fame, report. *Obs.*

c **1374** CHAUCER *Troylus* III. 1723 Þat swych a voys was of hym and a steuene Thorugh-out þe world of honour and largesse.

†**4.** Sound, noise (of singing, music, laughter). *Obs.*

13.. *E.E. Allit. P.* A. 1125 Al songe to loue þat gay Iuelle, Þe steuen moȝt stryke þurȝ þe vrþe to helle. *c* **1369** CHAUCER *Dethe Blaunche* 307 Some of hem [birds] songe lowe Some hygh and al of one accorde.. Was neuer herde so swete a steuen. *c* **1400** *Sowdone Bab.* 2258 Dame Floripe lough with loude steven. *a* **1460** *Play Sacrament* 80 Now mynstrell blow up w[t] a mery stevyn.

5. Outcry, noise, tumult, din.

13.. *E.E. Allit. P.* B. 1402 Sturne [*MS.* sturnen] trumpen strake steuen in halle. *c* **1385** CHAUCER *L.G.W.* 1219 The thundyr rorede with a gresely steuene. **1500–20** DUNBAR *Poems* xxi. 69 Pitt obscure, Quhair youlis ar hard with horreble stevin. **1555** PHAER *Æneid* III. (1558) G j b, And from the skyes the lightning fyers do flashe w[t] grisly steauen. **1579** SPENSER *Sheph. Cal.* Sept. 224 And had not Roffy renne to the steuen [*gloss* Noyse], Lowder had be slaine. *a* **1586** MAITLAND in *Sat. Poems Reform.* xxxvii. 18 As furious fluidis w[t] gritter force ay flowis, And starkar stevin, quhene stoppit ar þe stremis. **1625** LISLE *Du Bartas, Noe* 25 Before some thunder-steaven For warrant of his act gave oracle from Heaven. **1826** HOGG *Q. Hynde* VI. Poems (1865) 262 All nature roar'd in one dire steven; Heaven cried to earth, and earth to heaven. **1876** *Whitby Gloss.* s.v., Your clock strikes with a desperate stevvon.

¶**6.** Used by Middleton with obscure application. [Prob. by some misunderstanding.]

1597 MIDDLETON *Wisd. Par.* v. 17–20 G 2 b, His shield is victories immortall steauen. *Ibid.* vii. 29–30 K 2, [Wisdom] Guilding her selfe with her selfe-changing steau'n. *Ibid.* xviii. 14–16 Y 3 b, And brought thy precept, as a burning steauen, Reaching from heauen to earth, from earth to heauen.

†**'steven,** *sb.*[2] *Obs.* Forms: 1 stefn, 4–5 stevene, 5 stevyn, (steywyne), 6 stevin, stewin, 4–6, 8–9 *north.* steven. See also STEM *sb.*[3] [OE. *stefn* masc. (also *stemn* STEM *sb.*[3]), cogn. with ON. *stef* fixed time, summons, *stefna* (see next). The Teut. root appears to be **steƀ-*.]

1. A time, turn, vicissitude, occasion. *niwan stefne* (OE.), afresh, anew. *to change (by) stevens* (= L. *mutare vices*), to take turns.

Beowulf 2594 Hyrte hyne hordweard,.. niwan stefne nearo þrowode fyre befongen, se ðe ær folce weold. **1398** TREVISA *Barth. De P.R.* VIII. x. (Tollemache MS.) For as a weþer in lyinge up on on side turneþ and chaungeþ by euen steuines: so þe sonne beynge in.. aries makeþ euenesse of day and nyȝte. *Ibid.* XII. Introd., And þey [cranes] ordeyne wacches, and in wakynge chaungen steuines. **1590** *Cobler of Canterb.* 50 [Descr. Scholar.] Mickle could he say at each steuen Of the liberall Arts seuen.

2. A set or appointed time; a date fixed for a meeting or a payment.

In ME. chiefly in the phrases *to set a steven*, to appoint a time; *at set steven*, at the or a fixed time; *at unset steven*, by chance, unpreparedly; *to break one's steven*, to fail to keep an appointment.

a **1225** *Juliana* 7 Ant efter lutle stounde wið ute long steuene wes him seolf sonde to Affrican. *c* **1374** CHAUCER *Compl. Mars* 52 That by her bothe assent was set a steuen That Mars shal entre. **13..** *Gaw. & Gr. Knt.* 1060 Þer was stabled bi statut a steuen vus by-twene. *Ibid.* 2213 Who stiȝtles in þis sted, me steuen to holde? *c* **1386** CHAUCER *Knt.'s T.* 666 For al day meeteth men at vnset steuene. **1390** GOWER *Conf.* II. 30 Wher was ther evere such a knyht, That so.. Of Slowthe and of foryetelnesse Agein his trowthe brak his stevene? *c* **1460** *Towneley Myst.* xxviii. 125 Me dere fader of heuen.. ffrom ded to lif at set stevyn rasid me. **1470–85** MALORY *Arthur* II. xiv. 92 Yf I slee hym here I shall not scape. And yf I leue hym now perauentur I shalle neuer mete with hym ageyne at suche a steuen. **1543** *St. Papers Hen. VIII*, V. 287 The Cardinal.. will sodenly, ere he be ware, prevent hym, and take hym at such unsett stevin, as he nor all the frendes he hath shall not be able to relief hym. *Ibid.* X. 723 And, as it chaunced, we met even at on steven, before the tent. **1555** WATREMAN *Fardle of Facions* App. 345 That.. ye maie haue wholesome remedies, when nede is, and not be driuen to sieke remedie at vnsette steuin. *a* **1600** *Robin Hood & Guy of Gisb.* xxvii. in Child *Ballads* III. 93/1 Wee may chance mee[t] with Robin Hoode Att some vnsett steven.

b. A convened assembly.

1481 BOTONER *Tulle of Old Age* (Caxton) When I am in my village.. I make every day meetings stevyns, and assemblies of my neighbours.

3. Comb.: †**steven-free**, some kind of right enjoyed by certain tenants with regard to the use of the lord's mill; ? exemption from restriction to particular times.

1316 *Covenant at Bishop's Castle, Salop* (Addit. Chart. 40846) Concessit etiam dictus Rogerus.. predicto Philippo.. Steuenefreo in dicto molendino suo.

†**'steven,** *sb.*[3] *Obs.* Forms: 1 stefn (?), 4 stevin, steven(e, 5 steyvyne, *Sc.* stewyn. [Late OE. *stefn* (pl. *stefna*) a. ON. *stefna*, f. *stefna* to fix a time, summon: see STEVEN *v.*[1] (sense 3).] A citation, summons; bidding, command.

c **1100** *O.E. Chron.* (MS. D.) an. 1052, Ðerædon þa þat man sealde ȝislas betweonan, & setton stefna ut to Lundene, & man bead þa folce [etc.]. **13..** *Gosp. Nicod.* 162 Þe men þat wight and willy ware said: to þi steuin we stand. **13..** *E.E. Allit. P.* B. 360 Now Noe neuer stystez [*margin* ? styntez].. Er al wer stawed & stoken, as þe steuen wolde. *Ibid.* B. 463 [The raven sent out from the ark] Fallez on þe foule flesch.. & sone ȝederly for-ȝete ȝister-day steuen. *a* **1400** *Isumbras* 299 And alle salle bowe hir to fote and hande, And noghte withstande hir stevene. *c* **1440** *York Myst.* ix. 6 Thre semely sonnes and a worthy wiffe I haue euer at my steven to stande. *c* **1470** HENRY *Wallace* VII. 232 Grantyt wes fra God in the gret hewyn, Sa ordand he that law suld be thair stewyn.

†**'steven,** *sb.*[4] *Sc. Obs.* Forms: 6 stewin, -yn, 6–7 steven. [Either repr. OE. *stefn* var. of *stemn* STEM *sb.*[2], or a. the equivalent Du. or LG. *steven*.] = STEM *sb.*[2] I.

1512–13 *Acc. Ld. High Treas. Scot.* IV. 473 Item,.. ane [dracht] fra Newbotill of stewmnys to boittis. **1513** DOUGLAS *Æneis* I. i. 65 With bent saill ful, richt merely saland, Thair stewinnis stowrand fast throw the salt fame. *Ibid.* I. iii. 19 The schippis stewyn frawart hir went can writhe. *Ibid.* v. iv. 137 Stevenis. **1673** D. WEDDERBURN *Vocab.* 22 (Jam.) *Prora*, the steven of a ship, or the fore castle.

'steven ('stɛv(ə)n), *sb.*[5] *slang.* Money.

1812 J. H. VAUX *Flash Dict., Steven*, money. **1812** *Sporting Mag.* XL. 131 The steven (meaning money in the language of a fighting ring). **1834** AINSWORTH *Rookwood* IV. ii, It plays the dickens with the steven.

†**'steven,** *v.*[1] *Obs.* [OE. *stefnan, stæfnan*, f. *stefn*, STEVEN *sb.*[2] Cf. ON. *stefna*.]

1. *intr.* In OE.: To alternate, take turns. Cf. STEVEN *sb.*[2] I.

c **725** *Corpus Gloss.* 126 *Alternantium* staefnendra.

2. *trans.* To appoint, constitute.

a **1000** *Cædmon's Gen.* 160 Frea engla heht þurh his word wesan wæter ȝemæne, þa nu under roderum heora ryne healdað stowe ȝestefnde. *a* **1225** *Ancr. R.* 310 'Pepigimus cum morte fedus, et cum inferno pactum iniuimus:' þet is, we habbeð trouðe ipluht deaðe, & foreward istefned mid helle. *c* **1440** *York Myst.* xxiii. 64 Lord God! I loue þe.. Þat me, thy poure prophett Hely, Haue steuened me in þis stede to stande.

3. To summon. [After ON. *stefna*.]

a **1122** *O.E. Chron.* (Laud MS.) an. 1048, Þa hi þider ut comon þa stefnede heom man to ȝe mote. *Ibid.* an. 1093, And se cing Willelm him steofnode to Gloweceastre.

4. To specify, state.

c **1425** ? LYDG. *Assembly of Gods* 824 A crane on hys hede stood, hys crest for to steuyn. *c* **1440** *Pol. Rel. & L. Poems* (1903) 143 In Rome Y shall ȝou steuene An honþred kyrkes fowrty and seuen.

5. *dial.* (See quots.)

1674 RAY *N.C. Words*, To Stein or steven; idem [i.e. to bespeak a thing]. **1828** CARR *Craven Gloss., Stevven*, to order, to bespeak.

Hence †**stevening** *vbl. sb.*, appointment.

13.. in Wright *Lyric P.* xiv. 46 Of treuthe nis the trechour noht Bote he habbe is wille ywroht At stevenyng umbestounde.

steven ('stɛv(ə)n) *v.*[2] Now *dial.* [f. STEVEN *sb.*[1]] **a.** *intr.* To make an uproar, shout. **b.** *trans.* To deafen with noise. Hence **'stevening** *vbl. sb.*

c **1220** *Bestiary* 575 Sipmen here steringe forgeten for hire stefninge. *c* **1440** *York Myst.* xxxii. 6 Ȝe stynte of youre steuenyng so stowte. **1855** ROBINSON *Whitby Gloss.*, To *Stevvon*, to shout with great strength of voice. **1862** —— *Dial. Leeds* Gloss. *s.v.*, Mak a less o' thee din, wi' tuh! it's fit to stevvon onnybody. **1873** *Swaledale Gloss., Stevin*,.. to rant.

†**steven,** *v.*[3] *Obs.* Also 5 stevyn, 6 stevin. [a. ON. *stefna*, to sail in a certain direction; to aim (at something), f. *stafn* stem of a ship.] *intr.* To direct one's course.

c **1440** *Alphabet of Tales* 302, & furthwith, evyn at he say, þis layser stevend vp vnto hevyn. *c* **1460** *Towneley Myst.* xx. 546 That childe.. rasyd hym self apon the thryd day, And stenen [? *read* steuen] to heuen. *Ibid.* xxvi. 594 *Ihesus.* Nay, mary, neghe thou not me, ffor to my fader, tell I the, yit stevynd I noght. *Ibid.* xxix. 336 When he stevynd vp so sodanly To his fader in maieste. **1513** DOUGLAS *Æneis* v. i. 57 This being said, towart the port thai stevin.

†**'stevened,** *a. Obs.* Forms: 5 stevynd, stevynyd, stevenyd, stevend. [OE. *ȝestefned, -od*, pa. pple. of *ȝestefn(i)an*, perh. to alternate, diversify, f. *stefn* STEVEN *sb.*[2]] ? Embroidered.

It is possible that there may sometimes have been confusion between this word and *steynyd* STAINED *ppl. a.*

a **1000** *Aldhelm Glosses* in Napier *OE. Glosses* i. 5323 *Manicæ sericis clauatæ*, handstocu mid godewebbum ȝestefnede. **1452–3** *Test. Ebor.* (Surtees) III. 135 De xv s de pret. iij costers, steuynd cum angelis. *c* **1474** *Invent.* in *Paston Lett.* III. 408 Item, stevynyd clothe. *c* **1475** *Cath. Angl.* 363 (Addit. MS.) A Stevenyd clothe, *polimitus*. **1479** *Test. Ebor.* (Surtees) III. 246 To.. my servaunt, a halling of white stevend with vij warkes of mercy. **1499** *Wills & Inv. N.C.* (Surtees) I. 104 A stevynd clath vj[d].

†**stevenet,** *v. Obs. rare*[−1]. [repr. OE. **stefnettan*, var. of *stemnęttan*, f. *stefn, stemn* STEVEN *sb.*[2]] *intr.* ? To stop.

a **1225** *Leg. Kath.* 1265 Hwi studgi ȝe nu, & steuentið se stille?

Stevengraph ('stiːvəngrɑːf, -æ-). [Proprietary term, f. the name of the inventor Thomas *Stevens* (1828–88), a ribbon weaver of Coventry + -GRAPH.] A type of coloured woven silk picture produced during the late 19th century by the firm founded by Stevens.

1879 *Bookseller* 2 June 510/1 Mr. Stevens, of Coventry, has produced two interesting 'Stevengraphs'—one the four-horse Mail Coach.. the other the Railway Locomotive. **1928** *Trade Marks Jrnl.* 4 July 1075 Stevengraph... Woven labels of cotton, or in which cotton predominates. Thomas Stevens (Coventry) Limited, Stevengraph Works,.. Coventry. **1957** W. S. LE VAN BAKER *Silk Pictures of Thomas Stevens* I. i. 15 An amazing third-dimensional effect is achieved in the tiny woven silk pictures known as 'Stevengraphs'. **1964** A. ADBURGHAM *Shops & Shopping* xix. 226 The weaving of dress labels was a development from the Stevengraphs... Many other ribbon firms copied the idea of Stevengraphs to see them through the depression. **1967** *Daily Tel.* 21 Oct. 13/1 A pair of Stevengraphs, illustrating Columbus leaving Spain and arriving in the New World made £105 (Hicks). **1971** G. A. GODDEN *Stevengraphs* i. 13 The.. decorative silkwood pictures known as Stevengraphs were first introduced.. as a gimmick at the York Exhibition which was opened on 7 May 1879. **1980** *Daily Tel.* 8 Dec. 7/1 (Advt.), Wednesday 10 December 12 noon Baxter Prints & Stevengraphs. Viewing: Day Prior and Morning of Sale until 11 am.

stevensite ('stiːvənzaɪt). *Min.* [f. the name of Edwin A. *Stevens* (1795–1868), U.S. inventor and businessman and founder of the Stevens Institute of Technology in Hoboken, New Jersey: see -ITE[1].] A brown, pink, or white magnesium-containing mineral of the montmorillonite group.

1889 A. E. FOOTE in *Naturalist's Leisure Hour* XIII. 31/1 Stevensite 5c to 1·50. **1896** A. H. CHESTER *Dict. Names Minerals* 257 Stevensite... This name was suggested in 1873, at a meeting of the N.Y. Lyceum of Natural History, but not published, though soon after used on labels. **1916** *Amer. Mineralogist* I. 44 In the old Hartshorn quarry, in Springfield Township, Essex County, New Jersey, Mr. Louis Reamer.. discovered a single vein of a peculiar mineral, called by the quarrymen 'magnesium' (= talc?)... It proved to be essentially identical with the hitherto imperfectly known stevensite. **1962** W. A. Deer et al. *Rock-Forming Minerals* III. 231 Brindley (1955) described stevensite as a talc-saponite interlayered mineral, whereas Faust and Murata (1953) and Faust *et al.* (1959) regard it as a smectite with a defect structure in which a small proportion of layers with the 'attributes of talc' play only a minor role. **1979** *Sci. Amer.* Apr. 81/2 A good example is the alkaline chemical sedimentation that deposits limestones, cherts, phosphates and magnesium-based clay minerals, including attapulgites, sepiolites and stevensites.

Stevenson ('stiːvənsən). *Meteorol.* [The name of Thomas *Stevenson* (1818–87), Scottish engineer and meteorologist (and father of R. L. Stevenson), who devised it (*Jrnl. Scottish Meteorol. Soc.* (1864) I. 122).] *Stevenson* (formerly *Stevenson's*) *screen*: a wooden box supported on a stand above the ground and made with doubly louvred sides and a double top with ventilation holes, so that thermometers or other instruments mounted inside it are sheltered from sunlight and precipitation and effectively register properties of the outside air.

1881 W. Marriott *Hints Meteorol. Observers* 10 The thermometers must be mounted in the Stevenson's screen. **1884** *Bull. Philos. Soc. Washington* VI. 24 The Stevenson screen and the double louvre screens in general. **1923** Glazebrook *Dict. Appl. Physics* III. 491/1 Owing to the intense solar radiation experienced in the tropics, it has been held..that the ordinary Stevenson screen is unsuitable for use in low latitudes. **1970** J. P. Glasgow in H. W. Mulligan *African Trypanosomiases* xv. 355 Meanwhile maximum temperatures (in a Stevenson screen four feet above the ground) rose to 41°.

Stevensonian (stiːvən'səʊnɪən), *a.* (and *sb.*) [f. the name of the writer Robert Louis *Stevenson* (1850–94) + -ian.] Of, pertaining to, or characteristic of R. L. Stevenson or his writings. Also as *sb.*, an admirer of R. L. Stevenson or of his writings.

1897 T. Davidson *Let.* 29 Mar. in R. B. Perry *Thought & Char. of W. James* (1935) I. 756 Nothing but a happy-go-lucky Stevensonian adventuresomeness. **1900** *Fortn. Rev.* Jan. 97 He did not underrate *Kidnapped* as a whole. 'By far the most human of my labours hitherto,' is his verdict, anticipating that of all the true Stevensonians. **1913** *Smart Set* No. 3. 45/1 That polished peanut style that passes for Stevensonian English in the 'culture' clubs. **1923** G. K. Chesterton in *Illustr. London News* 22 Sept. 512/2 It was.. the essence of the Stevensonian spirit that the melancholy was not incurable even if the misfortune was incurable. **1928** *Observer* 22 Jan. 15/1 Bouvet Island is a Stevensonian treasure island, bare, uninhabited, bleak. **1939** *John o' London's Weekly* 9 June 363/2 A new detective novelist.. whose equipment includes..a good homespun prose with Stevensonian echoes. **1974** J. Pope-Hennessy *R. L. Stevenson* vi. 118 Meredith did..start off on a portrait of Louis Stevenson, in the guise of 'Gower Woodseer' [in] ..*The Amazing Marriage* [but] the Woodseer of the later part..is not consistent with the Stevensonian youth we encounter at the beginning.

stevin, stevne, stevon(e, etc.: see steven.

stevioside ('stiːvɪəʊsaɪd). *Chem.* [ad. F. *stévioside* (Bridel & Lavieille 1931, in *Jrnl. de Pharm. et de Chim.* XIV. 105), f. mod.L. *Stevi-a*, f. the name of P. J. Esteve (d. 1566), Spanish botanist + -ia[1]: see -oside.] A glycoside, $C_{38}H_{60}O_{18}$, present in the leaves of a Paraguayan herb (*Stevia rebaudiana*) and comparable in sweetness to saccharin.

1931 *Chem. Abstr.* XXV. 4553 Dieterich named the principle eupatirin, which B[ridel] and R. [Lavieille] changed to stevioside. **1968** *Times* 3 Dec. 10/8 The weed, known to botanists as Stevia rebaudiana.., grows up to 1½ ft. high. Its leaves have a surprisingly sweet taste, the active principle being known as stevioside. **1978** *Nature* 9 Feb. 495/1 Stevioside, a triterpene glycoside, which is readily extracted from the leaves of *S. rebaudiana*, is being produced on a commercial scale in Japan... Stevioside, which is approximately 300 times sweeter than sucrose, is not a permitted food additive elsewhere.

stew (stjuː), *sb.*[1] Forms: 4 stuwe, (?) stuy, 4–7 **stewe, stue,** 5 **stiewe, stwe, styuye, stywe, stywye,** 5– **stew.** [a. OF. *estui* (mod.F. *étui* case, sheath, also tub for keeping fish in a boat), verbal noun f. *estuier* to shut up, keep in reserve.

Godefroy has an instance (dated 1396) of OF. *estui* in the sense of the Eng. word, although he explains it wrongly.]

†**1.** In the phrase *in stew* [= OF. *en estui*], said of fish kept in confinement, to be ready for the table.

c **1386** Chaucer *Prol.* 350 Ful many a fat partrich hadde he in Muwe, And many a Breem, and many a luce in Stuwe. **14..** *Piers of Fullham* in Hartshorne *Anc. Metr. T.* (1829) 119 They to fisshyng goon wyth envy,..And wayte in waraynes all the nyght,..To bribe and bere away the best. That soiourne and kept bien in stiewe For store that nothyng shulde hym remewe. **1573** Tusser *Husb.* (1878) 33 Thy ponds renew, put eeles in stew, To leeue till Lent.

2. A pond or tank in which fish are kept until needed for the table.

1387 in *E.E. Wills* (1882) 2 Þe sesterne þat longeþ to the stuys. **139.** *Earl Derby's Exped.* (Camden) 74 Cuidam valetto custodienti le Stewe manerii Episcopi, vs. pr. *c* **1400** *Pilgr. Sowle* v. xiv. (1859) 80 The Apostles were the fysshers whiche that Crist found in this worldly see; whiche fisshes he putte in the stewe of his loued chirche. *c* **1450** *Godstow Reg.* 665 Stywys, dichis and briggis. **1539** *Act 31 Hen. VIII*, c. 2 All manner of fisshinges with any nettes [etc.]..in any severall ponde stewe or mote withe an intent to steale fisshe out of the same. **1677** Plot *Oxfordsh.* 234 A contrivance for Fish-ponds,..where the stews not only feed one another,.. and may be sewed by letting the water of the upper Ponds out into the lower. **1755** Cambridge in *World* No. 123 ⁋2 It would be a noble employment for the lovers of antiquity, to study to restore those infallible resources of luxury, the salt-water stews of the Romans. **1774** T. West *Antiq. Furness* 95 Their mills, kilns, ovens, and stews for receiving their fish. **1862** Ansted *Channel Isl.* ii. ix. (1865) 213 A somewhat remarkable natural stew or pond exists in Jersey, in the manor of St. Ouen. **1888** Goode *Amer. Fishes* 24 The young fish may advantageously be confined in 'stews' or artificial enclosures.

†**b.** *transf.* A pond of any kind; also, a moat.

c **1440** *Pallad. on Husb.* i. 769 Let make a stewe With rayn watir, thyn herbis to renewe. **1592** Wyrley *Armorie, Capitall de Buz* 139 This castle was inuironde with deep stew.

3. An artificial oyster-bed.

1610 Holland *Camden's Brit.* (1637) 335 Oisters, (whereof there are many pits, or stewes). **1624** Middleton *Game Chess* v. iii, He that inuented the first stewes, for Oysters, And other Sea-fish. **1817** J. Evans *Excurs. Windsor*, etc. 452 At Colchester, Milton, &c., stews or layers of Oysters are formed in places which nature had never allotted for them. **1881** Ingersoll *Oyster-Industr.* (Fish. Industr. U.S.) 249 Stew, an artificial bed of oysters. Applied to the old Roman, and also to the modern methods of fattening (English).

4. A breeding place for pheasants.

1888 *Cassell's Encycl. Dict.*

5. *attrib.*, as † *stew-pool, stew-pond*.

1623 *Althorp MS.* in Simpkinson *Washingtons* (1860) App. p. l, To Martin 3 daies at the stue poole..00 02 02... To Browne 6 daies raming the stue poole heade..00 03 00. **1797** Jane Austen *Sense & Sensib.* xxx, There is a dovecote, some delightful stewponds, and a very pretty canal. **1865** G. F. Berkeley *Life & Recoll.* II. 314 In a stew-pond you may tame a fish to a certain extent.

stew (stjuː), *sb.*[2] Forms: 4 **stu, stuwe, stuyue, styue,** 4–5 **stwe,** 5 **stw, stywe,** 4–6 **stue,** 4–7 **stewe,** 5 **styewe,** 6 **stuue,** *pl.* **stuse,** 6– **stew.** [a. OF. *estuve* (mod.F. *étuve*), a Com. Romanic word, represented by Pr. *estuba*, Sp., Pg. *estufa*, It. *stufa*; the discrepant forms seem to proceed from the two vulgar Latin forms, *stūpha* (*stūfa*) and *stŭpa*, both which are recorded in med.Latin. The ulterior etymology is obscure: some regard the word as a verbal noun f. a vulgar L. vb. **extūfāre*, f. **tūfus* (It. *tufo*) vapour, a. Gr. τῦφος. Connexion of some kind no doubt exists between the Rom. word and the Teut. root **stub-* in OE. *stuf-bæþ* hot-air bath, *stofa* masc. bath (mod.Eng. stove sb.), MDu. *stove*, mod.Du. *stoof* fem. stove, footwarmer, Du. *stoven* to stew, OHG. *stuba* fem. heated room, bath-room (MHG., mod.G. *stube* room), ON. *stufa, stofa* wk. fem. room with a fireplace (Sw. *stufva, stuga* cottage, Da. *stue* room).

The It. *stufa* was in the 17th c. adopted as stufe.]

I. A stove, heated room.

†**1. a.** A vessel for boiling, a caldron. *Obs.*

c **1305** *Land Cokaygne* 109 Þe leuerokes..Liȝtiþ adun to man is muþ Idiȝt in stu ful swiþe wel Pudrid wiþ gilofre and canel. **1590** Spenser *F.Q.* i. xi. 44 As burning Aetna from his boyling stew Doth belch out flames, and rockes in peeces broke. **1603** Shaks. *Meas. for M.* v. 321 Here in Vienna, Where I haue seene corruption boyle and bubble, Till it ore-run the Stew.

†**b.** A furnace for heating rooms by flues. *Obs.*

1688 Holme *Armoury* iii. 424/1 A Stew or Stove... This is a thing by which Rooms are made warm, for Sick and Crazy Bodies, which cannot approach near a Fire.

†**2. a.** A heated room; a room with a fireplace.

c **1374** Chaucer *Troylus* iii. 601 Troylus..myght it se Thurgh out a lytel wyndowe in a stuwe, Ther he by-shet syn myd-nyght was [in] mewe. *c* **1400** Maundev. (1839) xi. 131 It fresethe more strongly in tho Contrees than on this half; and therfore hathe every man Stewes in his Hous, and in tho Stewes thei eten and don here Occupatiouns. **1572** R. H tr. *Lavater's Gosts & Spir.* (1596) 165 They heard a knife falling from the upper part, or flore of the stewe, wherein they were, yet sawe they nothing.

†**b.** 'A hatter's drying room.' *Obs.* or *spurious*; the F. *étuve* has this sense.

1847 Halliwell.

3. A heated room used for hot air or vapour baths; hence, a hot bath. *Obs.* exc. *Hist.* or *arch.*

1390 Gower *Conf.* III. 291 The bathes and the stwes bothe Thei schetten in be every weie. *c* **1400** *Lanfranc's Cirurg.* 192 His bodi schal be wel frotid in þe baþ ouþer in a stewe. *c* **1440** *Promp. Parv.* 481/1 Stwe, bathe, *stupha, terme*. **1460–70** *Bk. Quintessence* 16 Þe paralitik man schal be hool..if ȝe make him a stewe hoot and moist with herbis, þat is to seye, eerbe yue [etc.]. *c* **1483** Caxton *Dialogues* 42 Natalye the wyf of the stewes Kepeth a good styewe,..They goon thedyr to be stewed Alle the strangers. **1540–1** Elyot *Image Gov.* 84 After his exercise..he entred into a baine or stew not hotte, where he taried sometyme by the space of one houre. *c* **1550** H. Lloyd *Treas. Health* lxiii. (Copland) U ij, Then put the pacient in a stewe or hote house. **1648** Gage *West Ind.* 142 There is scarce any house which hath not also in the yard a stew, wherein they bath themselves with hot water. **1656** W. Du Gard *Comenius' Gate Lat. Unl.* §467. 135 Being entred into a stew or hot-hous, we get up into the sweating-tub, and draw out the sweat. **1799** Tooke *View Russian Emp.* I. 357 A messuage consists of a dwelling-house, a few little store-rooms, stables, and a stew or hot-bath, by which the yard is inclosed. *c* **1800** Canning *Poet Wks.* (1827) 39 Oh! where is the great Doctor Dominicetti, With his stews and his flues, and his vapours to sweat ye? **1809** A. Henry *Trav.* 301 Stews, sudatories, or sweating-houses, are resorted to for cure of sickness, for pleasure, or [etc.]. **1855** Dunglison *Med. Lex.*, *Stove*..is used for drying various substances, as plants, extracts, conserves, &c. or for taking vapour baths. In this case the *stew* or *stove* is said to be wet or humid; in the opposite case, it is said to be dry. **1865** *Pall Mall Gaz.* 23 Sept. 6/2 Above the vaults the original Turkish bath, or 'stew,' remains in good preservation.

4. A brothel. (Developed from sense 3, on account of the frequent use of the public hot-air bath-houses for immoral purposes. Cf. bagnio.) **a.** In plural (chiefly *collect.*; sometimes, a quarter occupied by houses of ill-fame).

1362 Langl. *P. Pl.* A. vii. 65 Iacke þe Iogelour And Ionete of þe stuyues. *c* **1386** Chaucer *Friar's T.* 34 So been wommen of the styves,..yput out of my cure. **1436** *Rolls of Parlt.* IV. 511/1 No person that had dwelled at the comone Stywes. *c* **1450** Capgrave *St. Aug.* vi. 8 He used tauernes and stewis and swech sory gouernauns as [etc.]. *c* **1460** *Towneley Myst.* xxx. 350 Ye Ianettys of the stewys, and lychoures on lofte. *c* **1520** Skelton *Magnyf.* 1226 Some of them renneth straynght to the stuse. **1550** Crowley *Epigr.* 281 The bawdes of the stues be turned all out. **1581** Pettie tr. *Guazzo's Civ. Conv.* ii. (1586) 90 b, Many Gentlemen.. thinke it no lesse shame to be seene in yᵉ companie of yᵉ baser sort, than to be taken in the common stewes. **1593** Nashe *Christ's T.* 77 London, what are thy Suburbes but licensed Stewes? **1621** Burton *Anat. Mel.* iii. ii. ii. i. (1624) 367 In Italy and Spaine, they haue their stewes in every great Citty. **1655** Fuller *Ch. Hist.* v. 239 At this time also, by the King's command, were the Stewes suppressed. **1681** [D'Urfey] *Progr. Honesty* iv. 4 Tickets from the Beldame of the Stews. **1709** Steele *Tatler* No. 33 ⁋9 All Affectation by any other Arts to please the Eyes of Men, would be banished to the Stews for ever. **1791** Boswell *Johnson* an. 1776, 5 Apr., He strongly censured the licensed stews at Rome. **1838** Dickens *O. Twist* xl, Among the most noisome of the stews and dens of London. **1865** J. Hatton *Bitter Sweets* xxxvi, He frequented the dens and fashionable stews of the metropolis. **1873** Dixon *Two Queens* iii. i. I. 118 Their ranks were filled by rogues and scare-crows from the styes and stews.

fig. **1657** Trapp *Comm. Job* iv. 13. II. 43 Carnall hearts are ..stewes of unclean thoughts.

¶ Erroneous explanation.

1836 S. Cooper *Pract. Surg.* (ed. 6) 332 (Cassell) In the borough of Southwark..there were places called stews, where prostitutes were confined, and received the benefits of surgical assistance. **1888** *Cassell's Encycl. Dict.*, *Stew*..an early form of lock hospital.

†**b.** in plural form construed as sing. *Obs.*

1530 Tindale *Answ. More* iv. ii. Wks. (1573) 320/1 His setting vp in Rome a stues not of women onely, but of the male kynde also agaynst nature, and a thousand abhominations to grosse for a Turke, are tokens good inough that he is yᵉ right Antichrist. **1572** R. T. *Discourse* 33 b, Hee deflowred Maydes and straungers: made Lateranense (that holy Pallace) a Stewes, and brothall house. **1611** Cotgr., *Huleu*, the name of a Stewes in Paris. **1632** Lithgow *Trav.* ix. 406 A playne Stewes or Brothel house. **1650** W. Brough *Sacr. Princ.* (1659) 230 Lasciviousness..is sacrilegiously to make the Body (God's Temple) a Stewes. **1691** *d'Emiliane's Frauds Rom. Monks* 61 A Monk..very scandalously kept a publick Stews.

†**c.** in sing. *Obs.*

c **1384** Chaucer *H. Fame* 26 By abstinence, or by sekenesse, Prison, stewe, or grete distresse. **1554** Bale *Declar. Bonner's Articles* 43 Hys house was nothing elles but a common stewe. **1611** Shaks. *Cymb.* i. vi. 152 To Mart As in a Romish Stew. **1634** Canne *Necess. Separ.* (1849) 145 For the glory of God, that it may appear his house to be no cage of unclean birds, no sty of swine, no den of thieves, no stew or brothel-house. **1640** *Depos.* 5 Mar. in *Glouc. Dioc. Reg.*, The breeding of the said Judith Ansley was noe better then in a Stewe or whorehouse. **1790** *Bystander* 373 Father and son may, with propriety, be seen together at the same stew. **1809** Kendall *Trav.* I. xiii. 155 Dost thou suppose, villain, I am acquainted with bad houses? What dost thou want of a stew?

†**d.** (sing. and pl.) A bawd or prostitute. *Obs.*

1552 Huloet, Stew, bavde, or marchaunt of whores, *leno*. **1578** Whetstone *1st Pt. Promos & Cass.* iv. iii, Shall Cassandra now be termed, in common speeche, a stewes? **1639** Mayne *City Match* v. v, I have matcht a Stewes; The notedst woman oth' Towne. **1650** Sir A. Weldon *Crt. King James* 146 Instead of that beauty he had a notorious Stew sent him.

II. Senses derived from stew *v.*[2]

5. a. A preparation of meat slowly boiled in a stew-pan, generally containing vegetables, rice, etc.

1756 Mrs. Calderwood in *Coltness Collect.* (Maitl. Club) 252 They can dress..upon this stove, a roast, a boill, a fry, a stew and a bake. **1817** Byron *Beppo* vii, Because they have no sauces to their stews. **1840** Dickens *Old C. Shop* xviii, It's a stew of tripe..and cow-heel..and bacon..and peas, cauliflowers, new potatoes, and sparrow-grass, all working up together in one delicious gravy. **1873** 'Ouida' *Pascarel* I. 53 Mariuccia poured her stew into a dish.

fig. **1859** Dickens *T. Two Cities* ii. iv, The last sediment of the human stew that had been boiling there all day.

b. Irish stew: a dish composed of pieces of mutton, potatoes, and onions stewed together.

1814 Byron *Devil's Drive* i, The Devil..dined on..a rebel or so in an Irish stew. **1826** in *Sheridaniana* 253 An Irish stew was that on which he particularly plumed himself. **1891** *Spectator* 14 Nov. 669/2 A recipe for Irish stew.

6. A state of excitement, esp. of great alarm or anxiety.

1806 J. Beresford *Miseries Hum. Life* i. Introd., Our perplexities and alarms, at which they presume to sneer under the nick-names of rubs, bores, stews, takings, &c. **1809** Lady Lyttelton *Corr.* (1912) 85 Poor Mr. Allen is in a stew about his sermon. **1817–8** Cobbett *Resid. U.S.* (1822) 18 What a stew a man would be in, in England, if he had his grain lying about out of doors in this way! **1825**

BROCKETT *N.C. Gloss.* s.v., In a sad stew, in a state of great perplexity. **1849** E. E. NAPIER *Excurs. S. Africa* II. 248 As you may readily fancy, I was all the time in a most confounded stew, lest the tender, pulpy branches should give way. **1884** *Sword & Trowel* Jan. 41 As to France..she is in an everlasting stew.

7. *colloq.* A state of being overheated or bathed in perspiration. Cf. STEW *v.* 3 a, d.

1892 A. M. FAIRBAIRN in W. B. Selbie *Life* (1914) ix. 330, I never was in such a stew, as it were confined in a stove within stoves. **1911** WEBSTER.

III. 8. *attrib.*, as (sense 2) † *stew-door*; (sense 4) † *stew-holder*, *stew instructed* adj.; (sense 5) *stewgravy*, *-jar*; also **stew-bum** *U.S. slang*, a tramp, *spec.* one who is habitually drunk (cf. BUM *sb.*[4] 1). † **stew-hole**, a hole in the floor of a kitchen to serve as a cooking fireplace; † **stew-side**, a quarter occupied by stews or brothels; **stew-stove**, a cooking stove. Also STEW-HOUSE.

1902 *Bookman* (N.Y.) Aug. 541/2 The dictum of the ordinary tramp (the 'gay-cat' and *stew-bum). **1918** [see DINGBAT 1]. **1952** B. HARWIN *Home is Upriver* xiii. 127 How come you to be a drunk damn' stew-bum when I found you? **1922** JOYCE *Ulysses* 167 Scoffing up *stewgravy with sopping sippets of bread. *c* **1374** CHAUCER *Troylus* III. 698 He..gan þe *stewe dore al soft vn-pynne. *c* **1430** in *Phil. Trans.* XXX. 842 That no *Stew-holder keep noo Woman wythin his Hous that hath any Sycknesse of Brenning. **1598** STOW *Surv.* 331 In a Parliament holden at Westminster the 8. of Henry the second, it was ordayned..That no stewholder or his wife should let or stay any single woman to go and come freely at all times. **1780** YOUNG *Tour Irel.* I. 100 The *stew hole in his kitchen. **1633** FORD *Love's Sacrif.* IV. i, Her *stewe-instructed Art. **1913** D. H. LAWRENCE *Sons & Lovers* 79 The *stew-jar was in the oven. **1552** HULOET, *Stewside or place for whores, *suburrana regio.* **1727** [E. DORRINGTON] *Philip Quarll* (1816) 56 He cut a hole in the ground.., after the manner of *stew-stoves in noblemen's kitchens.

stew (stjuː), *sb.*[3] *Sc.* and *north.* [Of obscure etymology.

The sense history of STEW *sb.*[2] and the related vb. seems to exclude the possibility of connexion with those words. From the similarity of sense, the word has been supposed to be cognate with (M)Du., LG. *stof*, OHG. *stoup* (mod.G. *staub*), Da. *støv*, dust; but the phonological possibility of this has not been shown.]

Suffocating vapour, stench, or clouds of dust.

1375 BARBOUR *Bruce* XI. 614 Sic ane stew raiss owth thame then Of aynding, bath of hors and men. **1513** DOUGLAS *Æneis* II. x. 88 With stew, puldir, and dust mixt on this wise. **1571** H. CHARTERIS *Lyndesay's Wks.* Pref. A iv b, Fra that fyre rais sic ane stew, quhilk struik sic sturt to thair stomokis, that thay rewit it euer efter. **1781** J. HUTTON *Tour to Caves* (ed. 2) Gloss. 96 *Stew*, when the air is full of dust, smoke, or steam. **1828** CARR *Craven Gloss.*, *Stew*, vapour, dust, an offensive smell. **1867** *Goodwife at Home* xxiv. 9, I fear ye'll sconfice wi' the reek, An a' the stoor an' stew.

stew (stuː, stjuː), *sb.*[4] *U.S.* colloq. abbrev. of STEWARDESS c.

1970 D. HARPER *Hijacked* (1971) 23 If a stew flies five years, she'll keep on as long as the company lets her. **1975** B. MEGGS *Matter of Paradise* (1976) v. iii. 122 She had been with Pan Am herself as a 'stew'. **1979** S. BARLAY *Crash Course* I. 6 I'm Mara. I used to be a stew myself.

† **stew**, *v.*[1] *Obs.* Also 3 steowien. [Early ME. *steowi*, *stewe* (the compound *wiðstewe* occurs *c* 1175 *Lamb. Hom.* 15), perh. repr. OE. **steowan*:—WGer. **stawwjan* (3 sing. **stawiþ*), whence MLG., MHG. *stöuwen*, *stauwen* to check, restrain, hinder, mod.G. *stauen* to dam up.] *trans.* To check, restrain.

c **1205** LAY. 6266 And he sette stronge lawen to steowien his folke. *a* **1225** *Leg. Kath.* 374 Stille beo þu þenne & stew swuche wordes. *Ibid.* 658 Meistre ham swa þt ha beon mid alle istewet & stille. *Ibid.* 1529 Stew þe, & stille þine wordes. *c* **1250** *Prayer to our Lady* 34 in *O.E. Misc.* 193 Moder ful of milce..læte me steowi mi flesc. ? *a* **1400** *Morte Arth.* 1489 Thay..alle stewede wyth strenghe, that stode theme agaynes. *c* **1400** *Sege Jerus.* 48/841 (E.E.T.S.) Waspasian stynteþ of þe stour, steweþ his burnes, þat wer for-beten & bled.

stew (stjuː), *v.*[2] Forms: 5 **stiwe, stuwe, stewyn, stuwyn, stuyn,** 5–6 **stewe,** 5–7 **stue,** 5– **stew.** *Pa. pple.* 5 **stewid, -yde, y-stwyde, -yed,** 6 **stuyd,** 7 **stewd.** [a. OF. *estuver* (mod.F. *étuver*), related to *estuve* STEW *sb.*[2] Cf. Pr. *estubar*, Sp., Pg. *estufar*, It. *stufare*.]

† **1.** *trans.* To bathe in a hot bath or a vapour bath.

c **1400** tr. *Secreta Secret.*, *Gov. Lordsh.* 69 Aftir þat stewe þe with stewynge couenable to þe tyme, for þat mekyl profytes. *c* **1400** *Lanfranc's Cirurg.* 192 At morowe he schal be stewid, and whanne he swetiþ his bodi schal be frotid wiþ vinegre. *c* **1430** *Pilgr. Lyf Manhode* II. xxxii. (1869) 87 Oon day thou chaufest him the bath, and sithe stiwest [orig. *estuues*] him. *c* **1440** *Gesta Rom.* (Addit. MS.) lxv. 381 Then seide the precidente, 'steweth hyme, ande than shalle he speke'. *c* **1440** *Promp. Parv.* 481/2 Stuwyn menn, or bathyn (*v.r.* stuyn in a stw), *balneo*. *a* **1533** BERNERS *Huon* cxlv. 543 And the lady had iiii ladyes to serue her and she was baynyd and stuyd, and aparaylyd. **1541** COPLAND *Guydon's Form.* X iij b, It were behouefull to bath or stewe the membre with the infusyon of a pyece of yren. **1599** A. M. tr. *Gabelhouer's Bk. Physicke* 2/1 For ach in the heade. Seeth Wormewoode in water... Some there are which boyle the same in vinegar, and soe stue therwithe their head. **1665** SIR T. HERBERT *Trav.* (1677) 39 The sweat dropt from us no otherwise than if we had been stew'd in Stoves or hot Baths.

2. *Cooking.* **a.** *trans.* To boil slowly in a close vessel; to cook (meat, fruit, etc.) in a liquid kept at the simmering-point.

c **1420** *Liber Cocorum* (1862) 14 Stue thy peions thus thou schalle. *c* **1430** *Two Cookery-bks.* I. 9 Pertrich stewyde. *Ibid.*, Smale Byrdys y-stwyde. *c* **1440** *Promp. Parv.* 481/2 Stuwyn mete (*v.r.* stuyn) *stupho*. **1530** PALSGR. 735/2, I stewe wardens, or any frutes, or meates, *je esteuue*. **1594** *Gd. Huswifes Handmaid Kitchin* 15 b, To stue a Neates foote. **1598** SHAKS. *Merry W.* III. v. 121 And in the height of this Bath when I was more then halfe stew'd in grease (like a Dutch-dish) to be throwne into the Thames. **1606** —— *Ant. & Cl.* II. v. 65 Thou shalt be whipt with Wyer, and stew'd in brine. **1632** SHERWOOD, To stew meate, *cuire, ou bouillir la chair entre deux plats.* **1669** *Sir K. Digby's Closet opened* 178 To stew a Breast of Veal. **1688** HOLME *Armoury* III. 82/2 To Hash is to stew any Meat that is cold. **1769** MRS. RAFFALD *Engl. Housekpr.* (1805) 121 To stew a Turkey brown. *c* **1770** MRS. GLASSE *Compl. Confectioner* 22 Pour it on your pippins, and stew them till they are quite tender. **1816** TUCKEY *Narr. Exped. R. Zaire* iii. (1818) 122 Earthen pots..in which they boil or stew their meats. **1828** SCOTT *F.M. Perth* xxviii, Pits, wrought in the hill-side and lined with heated stones, served for stewing immense quantities of beef, mutton, and venison. **1873** 'OUIDA' *Pascarel* II. 6 We saw the food stewed and fried ere it came to us.

b. *intr.* Of meat, fruit, etc.: To undergo stewing; to be cooked by slow boiling in a closed vessel. Also (of an infusion of tea, etc.), to 'stand' on the leaves, etc. Also *transf.*, of the pot containing it.

1594 *Gd. Huswifes Handmaid Kitchin* 1 Let them [Turneps, etc.] stew till they be verie tender. **1701** *Compl. Caterer* 79 Let them all Stew well together. *c* **1770** MRS. GLASSE *Compl. Confectioner* 25 Let them [pears] stew over a slow fire for half an hour. **1842** LOUDON *Suburban Hort.* 548 Catillac [pear]... Large, broadly turbinate, brownish-yellow, and red, stews a good colour. **1906** *Rep. Brit. Assoc. Adv. Sci.* 783 There is found in tea and coffee an astringent substance which gives the well-known bitter taste to the infusions when they are allowed to 'stew'. **1942** *R.A.F. Jrnl.* 3 Oct. 25 An imposing enamel teapot stands on top, quietly stewing. **1979** W. H. CANAWAY *Solid Gold Buddha* xxiv. 158 The tea stewed for fifteen minutes or so.

c. In fig. phrases, with the sense: To be left to suffer the natural consequences of one's own actions; as *to leave to* (or *let*) *stew in one's own juice*. Cf. FRY *v.*[1] 3, and F. *cuire dans son jus*. Also in the senses: To be left to one's own devices, to be kept in a state of uneasy suspense, and *ellipt.*, as *to leave* (one) *to stew, to let* (one) *stew*.

1656 EARL MONM. tr. *Boccalini's Advts. Parnass.* II. liii. (1674) 204 [He] could not better discover Hypocrites, than by suffering them (like Oysters) to stew in their own water. **1885** *Times* 21 May 8/3, I have held that it would be possible ..with some reservations, to allow the Soudan to 'stew in its own grease'. **1885** SIR W. HARCOURT *Sp. at Lowestoft* 14 Dec., Liberals must not be in a hurry to turn the Tories out. He would let them for a few months stew in their own Parnellite juice. **1901** *Scotsman* 7 Mar. 7/4 Abyssinian soldiers are to be withdrawn, and the Tigreans are to be left to stew in their own juice. **1921** GALSWORTHY *To Let* II. vii. 184 'Please don't let me bother you if you've got people.' 'Not at all... I want to let them stew in their own juice for a bit.' **1928** W. S. MAUGHAM *Ashenden* vii. 116, I left her to stew in her own juice for a week before I went to see her. She was in a very pretty state of nerves by then. **1934** 'G. ORWELL' *Burmese Days* ii. 38 Office babus are the real rulers of this country now... Best thing we can do is to shut up shop and let 'em stew in their own juice. **1961** B. FERGUSSON *Watery Maze* xv. 378 The Japanese in Tenasserim could safely be left to stew in their own juice once we had Rangoon. **1976** W. GREATOREX *Crossover* 182 'It was me,' Calder said. 'I made up the story.' Calder let them stew in the silence. **1980** *Church Times* 3 Oct. 9/2 After letting us stew for three months, the Lord served up a miracle in the form of a perfect house for us in Berkeley.

3. *transf.* † **a.** *trans.* To bathe in perspiration.

1605 SHAKS. *Lear* II. iv. 31 Came there a reeking Poste, Stew'd in his haste, halfe breathlesse, painting forth From Gonerill his Mistris, salutations. **1620** J. TAYLOR (Water P.) *Praise Hemp-seed* (1623) 31 Drencht with the swassing waues, and stewd in sweat. **1673** R. HEAD *Canting Acad.* 133 The expectation of..punishment had stew'd him in a cold sweat. **1686** tr. *Chardin's Trav. Persia* 226 We did not feel the Coldness of the Weather: For the Crowd of People.. almost stew'd us before we got out. **1687** A. LOVELL tr. *Thevenot's Trav.* II. 49 We encamped close by this Castle, all scorched with the Sun, and stewed in Sweat.

† **b.** *fig.* To soak, steep, imbue. *Obs.*

1602 SHAKS. *Ham.* III. iv. 93 To liue In the ranke sweat of an enseamed bed, Stew'd in corruption. *c* **1630** QUARLES *Solomons Recant.* Solil. ii, Wks. (Grosart) II. 174/2 Stue thy heart in mirth, And crush the childe of sorrow in her birth. **1635** BROME *Sparagus Gard.* v. xiii, His conscience is stewd in Bribes. **1822** HAZLITT *Table-t.* Ser. II. (1869) 223 An opinion is vulgar that is stewed in the rank breath of the rabble.

c. To confine in close or ill-ventilated quarters. Chiefly with *up*.

1590 GREENE *Mourn. Garm.* (1616) 5 If Aristotle had still, like a Micher, been stewed vp in Stagyra, he had neuer written his workes. **1698** FRYER *Acc. E. India & P.* 92 The Rich Banyans..stew themselves out of a penurious humour, crowding Three or Four Families together into a Hovel. **1714** MACKY *Journ. Eng.* (1729) II. 38 Formerly the Country Ladies were stewed up in their Fathers old Mansion Houses, and seldom saw Company. **1812** SIR J. SINCLAIR *Syst. Husb. Scot.* I. 17 Cattle suffer much from being huddled together, and stewed close up in a low-roofed cow-house in winter.

d. *intr.* To stay excessively long in bed. Also, to remain in a heated or stifling atmosphere; hence *slang*, to study hard.

1671 TUKE *Adv. Five Hours* I. (ed. 3) 15 Sir, they have certain Niches in their Walls, Where they climb up a Nights, and there they stew, In their own Grease, till Morning. **1705** VANBRUGH *Confederacy* II. i, Abroad, abroad, abroad already? why, she uses to be stewing in her bed three hours after this time. **1832** WARREN *Diary Late Physic.* II. iv. 219 What a gloomy man that Dr. —— is..! he keeps one stewing in bed for a week, if one has but a common cold. **1866** *Routledge's Ev. Boy's Ann.* 706 Cooper was stewing over his books. **1870** MISS BRIDGMAN *R. Lynne* I. vi. 81 The sea-breezes will freshen me up, after stewing in this hole. **1897** MARY KINGSLEY *W. Africa* 576, I had been stewing for nine months and more in tropic and equatorial swamps. **1906** *Westm. Gaz.* 17 Sept. 4/1 Should the charms of his book lure him to sleep,..the string tied to his tuft of hair would instantly remind him of the..necessity to 'stew' for the ensuing examination.

e. To fret; to suffer anxiety or suspense; to be in an agitated state.

1917 S. LEWIS *Innocents* xviii. 208, I was suspicious of these fellows that are always petting and stewing over their wives in public. **1930** E. B. WHITE *Lett.* (1976) 91 White has been stewing around for two days now, a little bit worried. **1932** 'A. BRIDGE' *Peking Picnic* iii. 31 He seemed to be stewing, so I told him to come over and have a cocktail later on. **1949** E. POUND *Pisan Cantos* lxxx. 92 Stewing with rage Concerning the landlady's *doings* with a lodger unnamed. **1956** W. H. WHYTE *Organization Man* x. 129 They don't want a man to fret and stew about his work. **1974** R. HARRIS *Double Snare* xviii. 133, I wouldn't let them go to life imprisonment... Why shouldn't they stew a little? **1979** *Tucson Mag.* Mar. 23/1 City planners don't just sit around and stew over traffic congestion.

stew, *v.*[3] *Sc.* Also 9 **steuch.** [f. STEW *sb.*[3]] *intr.* To stink, emit a stench.

1563 WINȜET tr. *Vincent. Lirin.* xxxi. Wks. (S.T.S.) II. 64 Thai knaw thair stink to na man almaist haistelie to be plesand, gif it stewit and reikit out naikit and plane. **1891** J. J. H. BURGESS *Rasmie's Büddie* 63 Da stink o brimstin in a bizz Cam steuchin but.

stewable ('stjuːəb(ə)l). [f. STEW *v.*[2] + -ABLE.] Capable of being stewed.

1873 RUSKIN *Fors Clav.* xxvii. 19 Probably stewable in your modern stoves with better effect.

steward ('stjuːəd), *sb.* Forms: 1 **stiȝweard, stíweard;** 1–5 **stiward,** 3 **stiwærd,** 4–5 **stiwarde,** 4–6 **styward(e,** 5 **styeward;** 4–5 **steiward;** 3–7 **stuard(e,** 5 **stwarde,** 5–6 **stuerd(e,** 4–6 **stuward(e;** 4–5 **steuard,** 5 **stewer(e)de,** 4–6 **steward(e,** 4– **steward.** *β. Sc.* and *north.* 5 **stewarte,** 5 **stwart;** 7–8 **stuart;** 5–8 **steuart,** 4– **stewart.** [OE. *stíweard*, *stiȝweard*, f. *stiȝ* of uncertain meaning + *weard* keeper, WARD *sb.*

The word is not found in any MS. earlier than the 11th c., and the form *stiȝweard*, though certainly the original, is recorded only in a late transcript. The first element is most probably OE. *stiȝ* a house or some part of a house (cf. *stiȝwita* house-dweller); this is doubtless cogn. with *stiȝu* STY *sb.* and *stiȝan* to climb (STY *v.*), but there is no ground for the assumption that *stiȝweard* originally meant 'keeper of the pig-sties'.

The Eng. title is quoted by Froissart in the OF. form *estuard*. The rare ON. *stívarðr* is adopted from OE.

Since the 16th c. the definitions of the word have often been influenced by the supposed etymologies *stead* + *ward* and *stow* + *ward*.]

1. a. An official who controls the domestic affairs of a household, supervising the service of his master's table, directing the domestics, and regulating household expenditure; a major-domo. *Obs.* exc. *Hist.*

c **1000** *Gloss.* in Wr.-Wülcker 223/7 *Discoforus*, *discifer*, *uel* stiweard. *c* **1000** ÆLFRIC *Gloss.* ibid. 129/13 *Economus*, stiward. *c* **1290** *St. Eustace* 144 in *S.E. Leg.* 397 þis kniȝtes þoȝte wonþer gret þat a such heiward Of so quinte seruise was as he were eny stuard. **1393** LANGL. *P. Pl.* C. XVI. 40 Reson stod and stihlede as for stywarde of halle. **14..** *Bk. Curtasye* 535 in *Babees Bk.*, At countyng stuarde schalle ben. *c* **1470** HENRY *Wallace* IV. 383 Hys stwart Kerlye brocht thaim in fusioun Gude thing eneuch quhat was in to the toun. **1590** SPENSER *F.Q.* I. x. 37 The first of them,..Of all the house had charge and gouernement, As Guardian and Steward of the rest. **1601** SHAKS. *Twel. N.* II. v. 169 If not, let me see thee a steward still, the fellow of seruants. **1623** WEBSTER *Duchess Malfi* Dram. Pers., Antonio Bologna, steward of the household to the Duchess. **1651** J. WHITE *Rich Cabinet* (1677) 171 A Steward comeing to buy fruit for his Lady, bought all the apples they had at 7 a peny.

transf. and *fig.* **1697** DE FOE *Ess. Projects* 302, I cannot think that God Almighty ever made them so delicate, so glorious Creatures..and all to be only Stewards of our Houses, Cooks, and Slaves.

b. A member of a college who supervises the catering or presides at table.

1749 POINTER *Oxon. Acad.* 23 'Tis a custom for one of these scholars to take it by turns to be steward every week, whose office it is to cater for the rest of the society. **1893** FOWLER *Hist. C.C.C.* (O.H.S.) 51 The Steward of the Hall was one of the graduate-Fellows appointed, from week to week, to assist the Bursars in the commisariat and internal expenditure of the College. **1899** B. W. HENDERSON *Merton Coll.* 249 To each Undergraduate table one member is appointed as steward. Forty years ago the Postmasters elected their own steward.

c. A servant of a college who is charged with the duty of catering. Also, the head servant of a club or similar institution, who has control of the other servants.

1518 in Willis & Clark *Cambridge* (1886) III. 473, iiij *li* shalbe delyeurd yerly to the stuward of the said Collegge. **1717** E. MILLER *Acc. Univ. Camb.* 106 The 7th Statute concerning the Steward..appoints him to go with the Cook to the Shambles, to see the Victuals bought; and to demand from the Fellows, &c. all Monies due for Commons, and sizeings at the end of every Moneth, &c. **1861** [TREVELYAN] *Horace at Univ. Athens* (1862) 19 The steward and the cook have done me brown. **1914** *Kelly's Oxf. Directory* 125 Worcester [College]. Steward & Head Cook.

d. An officer in a ship who, under the direction of the captain or the purser, keeps the stores and arranges for the serving of meals; now applied to any attendant who waits upon the passengers, often with defining word indicating rank or special function, as ***bath-, cabin-, deck-, table-steward***; ***captain's steward, chief steward, paymaster's steward***, etc.

In comic literature there are many allusions to the steward's function of attending to sea-sick passengers.

c **1450** *Pilgrims Sea-Voy.* 38 'Hale in the wartake!' 'hit shal be done.' 'Steward! couer the boorde anone.' **1496** *Naval Acc. Hen. VII* (1896) 166 John Swynborne styward—viij[s]. John Gylpyn coke—x[s]. **1585** T. WASHINGTON tr. *Nicholay's Voy.* III. iv. 76 Their daily prouision..is prepared by a steward & a cooke. **1626** CAPT. SMITH *Accid. Yng. Seamen* 5 The Steward is to deliuer out the victuall, according to the Captaines directions. **1694** MOTTEUX *Rabelais* IV. xviii. 76 Poor Panurge..sat on the Deck all in a heap,..and..bawl'd out frightfully, Steward, *Maistre d'Hostel*,..pr'ythee let's have a piece of Powder'd Beef or Pork. **1836** MARRYAT *Midsh. Easy* ix, But a cup of tea, and ship's biscuit and butter I can desire the steward to get ready for you. **1865** DICKENS *Mut. Fr.* IV. xii, Talk of trades,..who wouldn't know your brother to be a Steward! There's..an air of reliability about him in case you wanted a basin, which points out the steward! **1883** W. CLARK RUSSELL *Sailors' Lang.* 139 *Steward*, a saloon waiter. One who has charge of the stores. Those under him are called under-stewards. **1897** *Punch* 23 Jan. 37/1 *Mr. Dibbles* (*en route for Paris. Sea choppy*). Channel Tunnel not a bad idea... Steward! [*Goes below.*]

e. One employed on a train to serve meals, drinks, etc., to passengers and to attend to other needs. Also, one with similar duties on a motor coach or aeroplane.

1906 *Railway Epicurean* July 9 Harvey's chefs and stewards have the food products of a continent at their command. **1915** *Proc. Amer. Assoc. Dining Car Superintendents* xv. 44 Instead of the steward asking, 'All on one check?' we instruct our stewards to, in a quiet way, get around to one of the party and ascertain whether one or more checks are desired. **1928** *Lit. Digest* 13 Oct. 70/3 The 'Nitecoach' carries a crew of three, driver, steward, and porter. **1931** *Sci. Amer.* Oct. 236/3 The steward, who now becomes the [airline] passenger's guide on land, is trained to supply any desired information. **1939** [see *air hostess* s.v. AIR *sb.*[1] B. III. 4]. **1955** F. O'CONNOR *Wise Blood* i. 15 There was a steward beckoning people to places and handing out menus. **1975** *Economist* 11 Jan. 20/2 The £100,000 placed in the plane at Heathrow was recovered and the only damage, to a luckless steward, was one police dog-bite. **1979** P. THEROUX *Old Patagonian Express* iii. 59 It was the steward from the dining car... 'Lunch!' he yelled. 'First call for lunch!'

2. As the title of an officer of a royal household.

a. *gen.* Originally, an officer with similar functions to the 'steward' of an ordinary household (see sense 1). After the Norman Conquest, the title was the Eng. equivalent of the OF. *seneschal*, med.L. *senescallus*, *dapifer*, which, in England as on the Continent, had come to designate an office in the royal household held only by a great noble of the realm. *Obs.* exc. *Hist.*

?*a* **955** *K. Eadred's Will* in Birch *Cartul. Sax.* III. 75 And ælcan ȝesettan discðeȝne and ȝesettan hræȝlðene and ȝesettan biriele hundeahtatiȝ mancusa goldis... And ælcan ȝesettan stiȝweard þritiȝ mancusa goldes. *a* **1122** *O.E. Chron.* an. 1120, Swyðe maneȝa of þæs cynges hired, stiwardas, & burþenas, & byrlas. *c* **1205** LAY. 7422 He hæfde ene stiwarde þene wisseste mon of al þis ærde. *c* **1330** R. BRUNNE *Chron. Wace* (Rolls) 13602 Neuere styward ne botyler þat serued kyng ne kayser, So wel halp at here power. *a* **1350** *S. Thomas* 194 in Horstm. *Altengl. Leg.* (1881) 22 þe kinges steward and als þe quene To Cristes law conuertid he clene. *c* **1350** *Will. Palerne* 3378 A stif man & a stern þat was þe Kinges stiward & cheueteyn was chose þat eschel to lede. *c* **1450** *Merlin* vi. 102, I will praye yow, that yef ye be kynge, that ye make my sone Kay youre stywarde. **1535** COVERDALE *2 Kings* xviii. 18 Eliachim the sonne of Helchias the stewarde [Vulg. *præpositus domus*]. **1756–7** tr. *Keysler's Trav.* (1760) III. 310 Charles Maximilian Von Thurn, steward of the houshold to the empress-dowager Eleanora.

b. (Lord) Steward of the King's Household. A peer whose nominal duty it is to control the King's household above stairs, and to preside at the Board of Green Cloth (see GREEN CLOTH). In early times he exercised important judicial functions.

[*c* **1400** FROISSART *Chron.* Œuvres 1872 XVI. 23 Messire Thomas de Persy avoit esté ung grant temps souverain estuard de l'ostel du roy, c'est-à-dire en franchois maistre et sèneschal.] **1428** in Nicolas *Proc. Privy Counc.* (1834) III. 286 John Lord Typtot an off Powys sthuard off þe Kynges howse. **1532** *Act 24 Hen. VIII*, c. 13 §1 The same Licence to be declared in writing by the Kinges Highnese, or the Lorde Stewarde of his most honorable Houshold. **1554** *Act 1 Mary* c. 4 It hathe now pleased the Quenes Majestie to.. chaunge the name of the Greate Maister of her Highnes most honourable Houshold..into the name of the sayd Lorde Stuarde of her most honourable Householde. **1613** SHAKS. *Hen. VIII*, IV. i. 18 The Duke of Suffolke is the first, and claimes To be high Steward. **1710** J. CHAMBERLAYNE *St. Gt. Brit.* I. II. (ed. 23) 108 For the Civil Governement of the King's Court, the chief officer is Lord Steward.

3. a. (Lord High) Steward or †**Great Steward of England.** Recorded since the 15th cent. as: The title of a high officer of state, the earlier *senescallus Angliae*. Since the accession of Henry IV this officer has been appointed only on the occasion of a coronation, at which he presides, or for the trial of a peer, which takes place in the ***Court of the Lord High Steward*** if Parliament be not sitting.

Originally this office seems to have carried little more than the privilege of waiting on the king's table, especially on state occasions. But it soon became hereditary in the earls of Leicester, and powers similar to those of the French *seneschal* were claimed for it by Simon de Montfort. This development was checked by the attainder of Simon, and the office finally fell in to the crown by the accession of its holder Henry IV.

1454 *Rolls of Parlt.* V. 249/2 Thomas erle of Devonshire, uppon an enditement of high treasons..afore Humfrey Duc of Bukingham, steward of Englond for that tyme assigned. **1522–3** *Act 14 & 15 Hen. VIII*, c. 20 §1 Before Thomas Duke of Norffolk for that tyme oonely beyng greate Stuarde of Englande by the Kynges lettres patentis. *a* **1700** EVELYN *Diary* 15 Jan. 1641, The E. of Arundell and Surrey..was made High Steward. **1710** J. CHAMBERLAYNE *St. Gt. Brit.* I. II. (ed. 23) 83 The Lord High Steward of England or Vice-Roy. **1769** BLACKSTONE *Comm.* IV. xix. 257 They usually (in case of an impeachment of a peer for treason) address the crown to appoint a lord high steward. **1842** J. G. NICHOLS in *Gentl. Mag.* May 485/2 To the high office of Steward of England the Duke of Lancaster became entitled in right of his wife, on the death of his father in law Henry Duke of Lancaster in 1361. **1907** HARCOURT *His Grace the Steward* 379 We may regard the Southampton trial as the true source of the court of the lord high steward.

b. (Lord High) Steward of Scotland. *Hist.* The first officer of the Scottish King in early times; he had control of the royal household, great administrative powers, and the privilege of leading the army into battle. The office, described as *senescallatus Scotiae* in a charter of Malcolm IV, 1158, fell in to the crown upon the accession of Robert the Steward as Robert II, whence the name of the royal house of Stuart; but the title was given to the heir-apparent until the Union. ***Great Steward of Scotland*** is now a title of the Prince of Wales.

1507 *Reg. Privy Seal Scot.* I. 210 His derest son James, prince and stewart of Scotland. **1710** J. CHAMBERLAYNE *St. Gt. Brit.* II. II. (ed. 23) 411 The Lord High Steward of Scotland..was..in the old Charters, placed before the Constable and Mareschal. *a* **1768** ERSKINE *Inst. Law Scot.* I. iv. §10 (1773) 57 We may here..add a few words concerning the office of Steward of Scotland. **1845** *New Statist. Acc. Scot.* X. 497 Subsequently to his [*sc.* Malcolm's] time, we find the antiquated title of Abthane giving way to that of Steward of Scotland. **1875** MAINE *Hist. Inst.* 139 The blood of the Steward of Scotland runs in the veins of the Kings of England.

†**4.** A deputy-governor, vice-gerent. *Obs.*

c **1205** LAY. 11789 Sende ich wulle to Aðionærd þe is min aȝene stiward... For him ich habbe wel bi-tæht Brutlond to witene. *c* **1300** *Havelok* 666 þe wicke traitour godard, þat was denema[r]k a stiward. **1387** TREVISA *Higden* (Rolls) III. 435 Zephiron, Alisaundre his styward [L. *præfectus Alexandri*]. *Ibid.* IV. 425 He..ordeynede stywardes [L. *præsides*] to governe þese londes. *c* **1450** *Merlin* ii. 24 The barons chosen Vortiger to be stywarde.

fig. ?**1436** *Pol. Rel. & L. Poems* (1903) 12 Souden of all Surry, Emperour of Babilon, Steward of Helle. *Ibid.*, And whi þat I am Stiward of Helle: I lete you wite I haue alle gouernaunce of wicked mawmentries & wicked spirites. **1645** BALL *Sphere Gov.* 7 A King of England is but in nature of an high Steward of the Kingdome by inheritance.

5. a. One who manages the affairs of an estate on behalf of his employer.

a **1386** CHAUCER *Prol.* 579 Worthy to been stywardes of rente and lond Of any lord that is in Engelond. *c* **1420** *Sir Amadace* (Camden) i, The stuard sayd, Sir, ȝe awe wele more Thenne ȝe may of ȝour londus rere, In faythe this seuyn ȝere. **1488** *Maldon* (Essex) *Liber B.* fol. 39 Robert Plomer,..chefe Styward of landis on-to lord Henry, Erle of Essex. **1577** GOOGE tr. *Heresbach's Husb.* I. 11 Ouer my Gate I haue laide my Steward, from whence he may looke into the Court..and oversee his neighbour the Bayly. **1741** MIDDLETON *Cicero* I. vi. 456 The principal manager or steward of all his affairs. **1821** D'OYLY *Life Sancroft* I. 468 On the following day, the servants of his establishment were dismissed by the steward. **1846** M[c]CULLOCH *Acc. Brit. Emp.* (1854) I. 451 We believe that the stewards of England, though inferior, perhaps, to the factors of Scotland, are a.. useful body of men. **1892** LADY VERNEY *Verney Mem.* I. 14 The estate had been so long without a head, under the management of the steward. **1910** C. SHORTER *Highw. & Byways Buckingh.* xvi. 177 The present Manor House..has long been given over to the Duke of Bedford's steward.

b. ***steward of the manor***: one who transacts the financial and legal business of a manor on behalf of the lord; he holds the manor-court in the lord's absence, and keeps a copy of its rolls, whence the name ***steward of copyhold***. ***steward of the leet, steward of the hundred, steward of the haven-court***, an official with similar functions in the leet, hundred, and haven courts.

1303 R. BRUNNE *Handl. Synne* 5421 Stywardes..þat lordynges courtys holde. **1377** LANGL. *P. Pl.* B. Prol. 96 Some..in stede of stuwardes sytten and demen. **1425** *Rolls of Parlt.* IV. 306/2 Stuardus of Letus and Hundredis. **1531** *Star Chamber Cases* (Selden Soc.) II. 186 William Marchall gentleman than being Steward of the seid Manour. *c* **1537** in W. Rye *Cromer* (1889) 52 Henry Erle of Surrey High Stuard of the Kyngs Haven Courts in Cromer. **1577** LEIGH *Surv.* Gjb, Yerely Fees to any Receiuour..high Stewarde, or vnder Stewarde..to bee goyng out of a Mannour,..are called Reprises. *c* **1600** *Mannor & Crt. Baron* (1909) 200 The Stewarde ys an offycer named by the Lorde, and his offyce ys to directe the sewtors by order of lawe to recorde and regester the plees and Judgements of the Courte... And he is not Judge there but Recorder or clerke as shalbe sayde for he cannot quash an Essoin nor doe any other thinge withoute the assente of the Sewtors. **1791** RITSON *Jurisd. Crt.-Leet* Introd. p. viii, The Leet is a court of record... It is held before the Steward..of the Lord. **1864** MISS S. P. FOX *Kingsbridge Estuary* 3 The Manor of Kingsbridge belongs to John Scobell, Esq...whose Steward holds a Court Leet and Court Baron here. **1897** E. HOWLETT in *W. Andrews' Legal Lore* 93 The steward also usually presides at the copyhold courts of the manor.

c. The title of: The administrator, often with merely nominal duties, of certain estates of the Crown, as ***Steward of Blackburn Hundred***, † ***the Duchy of Lancaster***. For *Steward of the Chiltern Hundreds*, see CHILTERN 1.

1444 *Rolls of Parlt.* V. 106/1 The Styward of the Duche of Lancastre. *c* **1472** *Plumpton Corr.* (Camden) 26 To our right trustie & welbeloved Sir William Plompton, knight, Stuard of the lordshipp of Spofford. **1499** *N. Riding Rec.* N.S. (1894) I. 130 To..Sir Ric[d] Chomley, Stuard of oure lordship of Pykeryng. **1600** in *Cath. Rec. Soc. Publ.* V. 383 Out of Blacborne hundreth, whereof y[r] maiestie haith made him the stuarde.

d. In Scotland: A magistrate originally appointed by the king to administer the crown lands forming a STEWARTRY, *q.v.*; see quot. 1754. ***principal stewart***, such an official as distinguished from the ***stewart-depute***, to whom part of the duties were usually delegated. *Obs.* exc. *Hist.*

1432 *Sc. Acts Jas. I* (1814) II. 21 þe lorde of þe Regalite or his stewart or balȝe. **1473–4** *Acc. Ld. High Treas. Scot.* I. 10 Item of the Stewarte of Kirkcudbrith lx li. *c* **1575** BALFOUR *Practicks* (1754) 16 Stewartis and Stewartreis. Stratherne, Lord Drummond. **1678** SIR G. MACKENZIE *Crim. Laws Scot.* I. xxvii. §x. (1699) 143 The Sheriffs, Lords of Regalities, and Stewarts, are declared Judges competent to this Crime. *a* **1688** J. WALLACE *Descr. Orkney* (1693) 88 The Government of the Stewart is in the Kings Bounds, the Manner and Procedure of his Jurisdiction is after the form of Sheriffship, the Title only differing. **1708** *Procl.* 18 Aug. in *Lond. Gaz.* No. 4464/4 We..ordain.. Our Solicitor to Dispatch Copies thereof to the Sheriffs of the several Shires, Stewarts of Stewartries. **1754** ERSKINE *Princ. Sc. Law* (1809) 38 The stewart was the magistrate appointed by the King over such regality lands as happened to fall to the Crown by forfeiture, &c.; and therefore the stewart's jurisdiction was equal to that of a regality. *a* **1768** —— *Inst. Law Scot.* I. iv. §10 (1773) 56 Regality-deputes were sometimes called stewards; but steward, in the strict sense, signified a magistrate appointed by the King over special lands belonging to himself. **1901** R. DE B. TROTTER *Galloway Gossip* 236 Davie..summons't the laird for the price o' the hooses, but he made naething o't, for the Steward said he had nae writins on't. **1912** A. PORTEOUS *Hist. Crieff* ii. 32 The office of dapifer, seneschal, or steward, of Strathearn.

e. ***Steward of the High Peak***: see quot. 1851.

1653 MANLOVE *Cust. Lead-mines* 199 (E.D.S.) The Dutchie Court..may appoint a Steward, that may try The Cause again upon the minery. **1851** *Act 14 & 15 Vict.* c. 94 §3 To be called the Steward of the High Peak Barmote Courts, and such Steward shall hold his Office during the Will and Pleasure of Her Majesty.

6. *fig.* (From senses 1 and 5.) An administrator and dispenser of wealth, favours, etc.; esp. one regarded as the servant of God or of the people.

Partly after Biblical uses, in which the word represents Gr. οἰκονόμος, L. *dispensator.*

?*c* **900** *Solil. Augustine* in Cockayne *Shrine* (1864) 176 Me þincð betere þæt ic forlete þa ȝyfe and folȝyȝe þam ȝyfan ðe me eȝðer ys stiward ȝe ðas welan ȝe eac hys freonscypes. *a* **1225** *Ancr. R.* 386 Luue is heouene stiward. *c* **1430** *How Good Wyf tauȝte Douȝ.* 21 in *Babees Bk.*, þeue of þin owne good, and be not to hard, For seelden is þat hous poore þere god is steward. **1539** BIBLE (Great) *1 Cor.* iv. 1 Let a man thys wyse esteme vs, euen as ye minysters of Christ, and stewardes of the secretes of God. **1575–85** ABP. SANDYS *Serm.* x. 167 God hath made him rich, that he as a faithful steward might bestowe those riche blessings vpon the familie..of God. **1594** A. HUME *Poems* (S.T.S.) 147 The Lord is a wise and discreet stewurt, and dispensator of his benefits. **1597** SHAKS. *2 Hen. IV*, V. iii. 137 Master Shallow, my Lord Shallow, be what thou wilt, I am Fortunes Steward. **1615** G. SANDYS *Trav.* I. 32 Luxury being the steward, and the treasure vnexhaustible. **1765** BLACKSTONE *Comm.* I. vii. 257 He [the king] is the steward of the public, to dispense it [justice] to whom it is due. **1769** HARTE *Eulogius* 203 Just steward of the bounty he receiv'd, And dying poorer than the poor reliev'd! **1849** MACAULAY *Hist. Eng.* vi. II. 19 A man of business and a vigilant steward of the public money.

7. a. An officer in a gild, usually ranking next to the alderman; also *Hist.* often as a rendering of L. *senescallus*, ONF. *eskevein*: see SKEVIN.

10.. in Kemble *Cod. Dipl.* IV. 278, & ȝyf he on neawyste forðfaren sy warniȝe man þone stiwerd to hwylcere stowe þæt lic sceole & se stiwerd warniȝe syððan ða ȝeȝyldan. **1432** in F. A. Hibbert *Orig. Eng. Gilds* (1891) 46 The Stywardes and Maistres of the saide Crafte. **1494** in *Eng. Gilds* (1870) 188 The Stuarde off the Gilde for the tyme beyng shall truly countrolle them y[t] ben absente. **1870** TOULMIN SMITH *English Gilds* Introd. p. ciii, There was an alderman at the head of the Gild, and often stewards by his side as assistants.

b. In certain City companies: One of two or more officers, who are charged with the arrangements for the annual dinner. Cf. sense 10.

1614 in W. M. Williams *Ann. Founders' Co.* (1867) 90 That..Master Wardens, Assistants, and Livery should pay to the Stewards for the providing of dynner on the day of the Master's Feast the some of Two Shillings each. *a* **1700**

EVELYN *Diary* 21 Sept. 1671, I din'd..at the fraternity feast in Yron-mongers Hall, where the 4 stewards chose their successors. **1796** in W. M. Williams *Ann. Founders' Co.* (1867) 165 That as two stewards, properly enabled to serve the office, cannot be immediately fixed upon, the annual dinner, on Lord Mayor's day, be omitted.

c. In various societies, the title of certain officers forming an executive committee. Cf. sense 10.

1831 in *J. C. Whyte's Hist. Brit. Turf* (1840) I. 145 At a meeting of the Stewards and Members of the Jockey Club, it was stated that [etc.]. **1910** *Encycl. Brit.* (ed. 11) XIII. 732/2 Sport is carried on under the auspices of the Jockey Club... Three stewards, one of whom retires each year,.. govern the..work of the club... The stewards of the Jockey Club are *ex officio* stewards of Ascot, Epsom, Goodwood and Doncaster. All other meetings are controlled by stewards, usually well-known patrons of the Turf invited to act by the projectors of the fixture.

8. A corporation official, whose rank and duties vary widely in different muncipalities; often with a defining word, as ***capital steward, city steward, town steward.***

1433 *Rolls of Parlt.* IV. 477/1 The Styward of the seid Town. **1835** *App. Munic. Corpor. Rep.* I. 188 The Steward [of Cardiff]..is required to be learned in the law. *Ibid.* 613 The Capital Steward [of South Molton]..has neither duties nor emoluments. *Ibid.* II. 1275 The Town Steward [of Dorchester] is the treasurer of the corporation. *Ibid.* III. 1741 Previous to the year 1714, the city steward [of York] was appointed by the upper house.

9. high steward (see also 3).

a. In the Universities of Oxford and Cambridge, the title (in academic Latin *seneschallus*) of a judicial officer, in whom is vested the jurisdiction belonging to the university in causes of treason and felony.

1459 in *Munim. Acad.* (Rolls) I. 345 If the same prisoner be claymed by the said Chaunceller or his styward..within iv. wykes next after his takyng and imprisonyng in the common prison of the town. *c* **1674** WOOD *Fasti Oxon.* (1790) 180 The Office of Steward in this University concerning the capital and chief causes of Scholars and privileged persons, King Henry IV..did institute. **1714** AYLIFFE *Ant. & Pres. St. Univ. Oxf.* II. 166 The Lord High Steward..is to hold and keep the University Court-Leet.. either by himself, or his Under-Steward,..and on account of this Office, the High Steward receives the yearly Fee of five Pounds from the University. **1797** *Encycl. Brit.* (ed. 3) XVIII. 684 The trial of treason, felony, and mayhem, by a particular charter, is committed to the university jurisdiction in..the court of the lord high steward of the university. **1824** *Encycl. Metrop.* (1845) XVI. 184 art. *Cambridge* [Officers of the University] 2 A High Steward, who has special power to take the trial of scholars impeached of felony, and to hold and keep a court-leet within the university. **1845** G. R. M. WARD tr. *Oxf. Univ. Statutes* I. 178 The office of High Steward or Deputy High Steward of the University. **1895** RASHDALL *Universities* II. II. 409 Henry IV [in 1406] gave the University [of Oxford] the right to claim the surrender of 'privileged persons' indicted for felony, who were thereupon to be tried by a newly-constituted officer of the University, the Seneschal or Steward, to be appointed by the Chancellor. *Ibid.* 790 The jurisdiction of the Court of the High Steward of the University [of Oxford]..remains intact, but the privilege has never been claimed for a century or more.

†**b.** An official having at the inthronization of an archbishop ceremonial functions similar to those of the Lord High Steward at a coronation. *Obs.*

15.. in Dugdale *Monast.* (1817) I. 118/1 He shoulde be the hye stewarde of the sayde archbyshop, and of his successors, at their great feast, when it shoulde fortune the sayde archbyshoppe to be intronizated.

c. In certain English cities, a municipal title of dignity, usually borne by a nobleman or royal prince.

1563 in W. H. Turner *Select Rec. Oxford* (1880) 306 Sir Francis Knollis, Knyght, was chosen stuarde of this Cytie of Oxford this the third day of February, 1563. **1582** *Nottingham Rec.* IV. 199 The Earle of Rutland beinge Highe Steward. **1835** *App. Munic. Corpor. Rep.* I. 59 The present lord high steward [of Gloucester] is His Royal Highness the Duke of Gloucester. **1914** *Kelly's Oxf. Directory* 142 High Steward [of the city of Oxford], the Right Hon. the Earl of Jersey.

10. A person appointed to supervise the arrangements or maintain order at a race meeting, exhibition, dinner, ball, concert, public gathering, etc.

1703 *Lond. Gaz.* No. 3949/4 The Horses to be shewn at the George in Amsbury.., and to be entred by the Steward. **1709** BP. ATTERBURY *Serm. Sons of Clergy* Ded., To the Worshipful Mr. John Tenison [and others] Stewards for the Late Feast of the Sons of the Clergy. **1751** *Laws of Mus. Soc. at Castle-Tavern, Pater-noster-row* 13 The Stewards shall observe the Directions herein after mentioned..for preserving good Order at the Concerts. **1812** *Examiner* 24 Aug. 542/1 He himself was one of the Stewards of that dinner! **1841** ORDERSON *Creoleana* vi. 62 It was customary for the stewards..to arrange the order of the minuets. **1854** *Poultry Chron.* II. 330/2 Fill up the delivery order, stating how the birds are to be returned. The stewards will pack them after the show. **1910** [see 7 c]. **1915** *Morn. Post* 7 Dec. 4/3 The meeting was perfectly quiet..until one or two of the stewards..attempted to remove four or five Colonial soldiers.

11. An overseer of workmen. In mod. use, the 'underlooker' of a colliery, 'who receives his orders from the manager, and to whom the overmen and deputies report upon the state of the mine' (Gresley *Gloss. Coal-mining*, 1883); also, in Scotland, the foreman of a workshop. Also occas. = *shop steward* s.v. SHOP *sb.* 9 d.

a **1300** *Cursor M.* 5525 On þam þe king sett sere stuward [*magistros operum*] To hald þam in-to werkes hard. **1708** J. C. *Compleat Collier* (1845) 38 Six Pence per Corfe,.. which is Deducted..by the Steward or Pay-Master. **1916** *Observer* 9 Jan. 12/2 The fact that Logan had strong trades union views is nothing exceptional for a shop's steward. **1943** *Sun* (Baltimore) 13 Oct. 8/4 Union local stewards..voted to end their stoppage. **1977** *Times* 6 May 1/6 The stewards are also pointing out that they are at one with management.

12. Among Methodists, a layman appointed to manage the financial affairs of a congregation (***society*** or ***chapel steward***) or of a circuit (***circuit steward***). Also ***book steward***, the manager of the Book-room or publication department of the Wesleyan Methodist Society; ***poor steward***, a person appointed in a congregation to administer the funds collected for the poor.

1741 WESLEY *Jrnl.* 23 May (1749) 85 The Stewards of the Society (who receive and expend what is contributed weekly). **1771** —— *Jrnl.* 31 Mar. (1777) 22 In the Methodist discipline, the wheels regularly stand thus: the assistant, the preachers, the stewards, the leaders, the people. **1896** *Daily News* 10 Mar. 5/3 The Rev. C. H. Kelly, the book steward, who is still prosecuting his searches in the Archives of the Wesleyan Book Room. **1904** *Daily Chron.* 15 Feb. 3/5 Mr. Slack is an active member of the Wesleyan Methodist body. .. He is circuit-steward of the West London Mission.

13. *attrib.* and *Comb.*, as (sense 5 d) ***steward-clerk***; also **steward boy**, = *house-boy* s.v. HOUSE *sb.*[1] 24; †**stewart-compt**, *Sc.* the statement of the accounts of a stewartry; **stewart-, steward-court**, *Sc.* the court having jurisdiction within a stewartry; also *attrib.*; **steward-depute**, see 5 d; **steward's mate**, the assistant of a ship's steward; **steward's room, steward-room**, see quots.; **steward's table** (see quot.).

1897 MARY KINGSLEY *W. Africa* 613 Assisting Idabea and the *steward boys in chivying this pig. **1962** *Sat. Even. Post* 5 May 80/3 Her evening spent in helping Fossey's old stewardboy to beat carpets. **1977** *Daily Times* (Lagos) 25 Feb. 22/4 (Advt.), Driver, Steward boy, Houseboy, wanted. **1912** A. PORTEOUS *Hist. Crieff* ii. 48 Other officials connected with the Steward Court were: the Judge or Judex, the Steward Depute, the *Steward Clerk, the Doomster or Deemster. **1580** *Exch. Rolls Scot.* XXI. 549, I am restand awand in my *stewart compt of Menteyth the sowme of 32 pundis. **1475** in *3rd Rep. Hist. MSS. Comm.* 418/1 Vylȝam reyd, dempstar of the *stewart curt of Stratherne. *a* **1600** in W. Nicolson *Leges Marchiarum* (1705) 202 First that he.. charge him within the Stewart-Court Book. **1752** J. LOUTHIAN *Form of Process* (ed. 2) 287 The several Officers in the Sheriff or Stewart-courts are prohibited to take..any other or higher Fees. *a* **1600** in W. Nicolson *Leges Marchiarum* (1705) 202 Ane wise and famous Gentleman,.. to be *Stewart Deput. **1824** G. CHALMERS *Caledonia* III. III. v. 247 In 1747 this stewartry was placed under a stewart-depute. **1708** *Lond. Gaz.* No. 4440/1 The..*Stewards Mate, Cooks Mate,..and Marine-Soldiers, two Eighth Parts. **1627** CAPT. SMITH *Sea Gram.* ii. 13 The *Stewards roome. **1644** MANWAYRING *Seamans Dict.* 102 *Stewards-Roome*, is that part of the Howlde, wherein the Victuals are Stowed. *c* **1850** *Rudim. Navig.* (Weale) 153 *Steward's room*, an apartment built on the larboard side of the after platform, whence the purser's steward issues the provisions to the ship's company, and where he makes up his accounts. **1758** (*title*) Treatise on the Use and Abuse of the Second, commonly called the *Steward's Table, in Families of the First Rank.

steward ('stjuːəd), *v.* [f. STEWARD *sb.*]

1. *trans.* To manage, administer.

1621 BP. H. KING *Serm.* 25 Nov. To Rdr. L 3 b, Whether I haue vprightly stewarded his honour, and my owne faith, I leaue to the strict iudgement of any who are able to.. discerne Truth from Imposture. **1626** J. YATES *Ibis ad Cæsarem* I. To Rdr., The Athenian Commander,.. having ill stewarded the Treasury of the Commonwealth. **1639** FULLER *Holy War* II. xxxi. (1640) 85 Did he thus requite his mothers care in stewarding the State? **1905** *Daily Chron.* 22 Sept. 4/5 A race..who may..steward aright the mighty heritage which is passing into their hands.

2. *intr.* To do the duties of a steward.

1897 J. CHALMERS in R. Lovett *Autobiog. & Lett.* (1902) 434 We have with us two boys to cook and stward for us.

Hence '**stewarding** *vbl. sb.*

1548 UDALL *Erasm. Par. Luke* vi. 17–19 To whom the dispensacion & stewardyng of goddes woorde is to be committed. **1602** *Archpriest Controv.* (Camden) I. 232 Every baker or brewer, for stewarding and treasuringe.. must, by this newe device, be made equall with you. **1865** DICKENS *Mut. Fr.* IV. xii, As for stewarding, I think it's time my brother gave that up.

stewardess ('stjuːədɪs). [f. STEWARD *sb.* + -ESS[1].]

a. A female who performs the duties of a steward; also *fig.*

1631 *Celestina* xxi. 198 O variable fortune..thou Ministresse and high Stewardesse of all temporal happinesse. **1827** CARLYLE *Germ. Rom.* III. 212 She was his ..Castle-Stewardess. **1865** GLADSTONE in Morley *Life* v. x. (1903) II. 160 Her [*sc.* the church's] high office as stewardess of divine truth.

b. A female attendant on a ship whose duty it is to wait on the women passengers.

1837 HT. MARTINEAU *Soc. Amer.* II. 2 Mrs. F. and I were the only ladies on board; and there was no stewardess. **1885** *Times* 21 Sept. 10/1 There were five females among the passengers, including the stewardess.

c. A female attendant on a passenger aircraft who attends to the needs and comfort of the passengers; = *air hostess* s.v. AIR *sb.*[1] B. III. 4. Also, a similar attendant on other kinds of passenger transport.

1931 *United Airlines News* Aug. 5/2 (*caption*) Uniformed stewardesses employed on the Chicago-San Diego divisions of United. The picture shows the original group of stewardesses employed. **1937** *Sun* (Baltimore) 22 Apr. 6/1 (Advt.), America's *first* railroad adds another to its long list of *firsts*... A uniformed Stewardess who is also a graduate nurse! She looks after your comfort en route [etc.]. **1958** 'CASTLE' & 'HAILEY' *Flight into Danger* i. 12 He ducked into the aircraft..joined shortly by a stewardess..who smiled at him and made fast the door. **1968** M. WOODHOUSE *Rock Baby* x. 104 The stewardess announced our landing. **1978** R. LUDLUM *Holcroft Covenant* iii. 40 In two chairs against the wall sat the captain of the 747 and the stewardess assigned to its first-class lounge. **1981** *Christian Sci. Monitor* 28 July 6/1 Rooms at the St. James's club, a luxury bus with two stewardesses, and a special room overlooking the Strand.

stewardly ('stjuːədlɪ), *a.* [f. STEWARD *sb.* + -LY[1].]

†**1.** Pertaining to or administered by a steward; of the nature of a stewardship. *Obs.*

1642 BRIDGE *Wound. Consc. Cured* iv. 26 If abused that he do not perform his Stewardly trust as hee should, the people ..are to looke to it. **1643** J. COTTON *Doctr. Ch.* 2 The Government of his Kingdome is not Lordly, but Stewardly and Ministeriall. *a* **1683** OWEN *Holy Spirit* (1693) 256 They are sufficient of themselves for the Stewardly Dispensation of the Mysteries of the Gospel.

2. *dial.* Skilled in household management.

1746 *Exmoor Courtship* 569 Tha stewardlest vittest Wanch that comath on tha' Stones o' Moulton. *c* **1750** *Mrs. Palmer's Devon. Dial.* i. (1839) 11 A notable, thorough-paced stewardly body. **1874** MISS S. P. FOX *Kingsbridge* (E.D.D.) A good stewardly wife.

stewardly ('stjuːədlɪ), *adv. rare.* [+ -LY[2].] Like a steward; with the care of a steward.

1604 TOOKER *Fabric of Ch.* iv. 48 Euery dispensation..is to be stewaredly dispensed not wastfully spent or powred vpon euery ones head or altogether.

stewardry, variant of STEWARTRY.

stewardship ('stjuːədʃɪp). [f. STEWARD *sb.* + -SHIP.]

1. The office of steward; also *fig.*

1465 *Mann. & Househ. Exp.* (Roxb.) 178 Item, the bayly off Hadley owyth hym ffor hys ffe off the stewardsheppe off the same town. **1491** *Act 7 Hen. VII*, c. 20 §8 Any Stiward-shippes offices fees wages or annuities..to him graunted. **1593** SHAKS. *Rich. II*, III. iii. 78 Shew vs the Hand of God, That hath dismiss'd vs from our Stewardship. **1601** [? MARSTON] *Jack Drums Entert.* I. A 4 b, No, I do loue my Girles should wish me liue, Which fewe do wish that haue a greedy Syre: But still expect and gape with hungry lip, When heele giue vp his gowtie stewardship. **1709** BP. ATTERBURY *Serm. Sons Clergy* Ded., There are, I believe, Two hundred Persons now living, who have gone before You in the Stewardship. **1839** *John Bull* 11 Aug. 382/2 A new writ was..issued for Perth, in the room of Mr. Kinnaird, who vacated by accepting a stewardship of the Chiltern Hundreds. **1862** GOULBURN *Pers. Relig.* I. iv. (1871) 41 Each one of us has a stewardship somewhere in the great social system. **1886** *Manch. Exam.* 1 Oct. 5/3 At a meeting of the Jockey Club..H. W. Fitzwilliam was appointed as successor in the stewardship to the Marquis of Londonderry. **1907** *Outlook* 19 Jan. 91/1 The origin and development of the Stewardship of England.

2. a. Conduct of the office of steward; administration, management, control.

1526 TINDALE *Luke* xvi. 2 Geve a comptes off thy steward-shippe. **1684** NORRIS *Poems* etc. 46 Among all the Talents which are committed to our Stewardship, Time..is the most precious. **1791** COWPER *Iliad* XIX. 52 Those who held In stewardship the food. **1915** *Morn. Post* 22 Dec. 4/4 We want further such a stewardship of the economic resources of the country as will enable us to lift and to carry the financial burden.

b. *Eccl.* The responsible use of resources, esp. money, time, and talents, in the service of God; *spec.* the organized pledging of specific amounts of money etc. to be given regularly to the Church. Also *attrib.*

1899 C. M. SHELDON (*title*) His brother's keeper; or, Christian stewardship. **1931** D. W. P. STRANG *Studies in Christian Stewardship* i. 4 The philosophy of Stewardship can claim no less an authorship than that of our Lord Himself. **1938** H. GERLINGER *Money Raising* vi. 98 This lack of development of a social consciousness on the part of students is clearly due to the fact that practically no systematic effort is made to implant the idea of stewardship in undergraduates. **1950** *Christian Cent.* 22 Nov. 1392/2 There is only one legitimate answer to the financial problem ..to..teach our people to practice Christian stewardship. **1951** *National Council Outlook* May 12/1 The delegates asked for consolidation of stewardship and fund-raising efforts in the Council. **1959** *Christian Stewardship of Money* i. 5 The movement..has broadened out into an attempt to recover and to teach the principles of the right Christian attitude towards the use of money. For want of a less archaic word this attitude is called 'Stewardship'. **1980** *Oxf. Diocesan Mag.* May 15/3 The book deals with man's attitude to the natural world in general and his Christian stewardship in relation to its resources.

attrib. **1931** D. W. P. STRANG *Studies in Christian Stewardship* i. 5 The Stewardship movement has.. developed momentum mainly in the New World. **1942** *Christian Cent.* 1 July 829/1 (*heading*) United stewardship campaign might go even further. **1962** P. FERRIS *Church of England* ix. 175 Stewardship advisers..were soon appointed in most dioceses. **1979** *Oxf. Diocesan Mag.* Dec. 9/2 Stewardship campaigns are essentially teaching missions. *Ibid.* 10/1 Pastoral reorganisation and the stewardship movement have worked together to foster a sense of responsibility in parishes.

†**3.** Used for STEWARTRY 1. *Obs.*

1796 MORSE *Amer. Geog.* II. 97 Scotland is divided into 31 shires and two stewardships.

stewart: see STEWARD.

stewartite ('stju:ətaɪt). *Min.* [f. the name of the *Stewart* mine, Pala, San Diego County, California, where it was found + -ITE[1].] A hydrous basic phosphate of manganese and ferric iron, $MnFe_2(PO_4)_2(OH)_2.8H_2O$, found as pleochroic orange-yellow to colourless triclinic crystals.

1912 W. T. SCHALLER in *Jrnl. Washington Acad. Sci.* II. 143 Stewartite. Probably triclinic. A hydrous manganese phosphate from the Stewart Mine, after which it is named. **1975** *Neues Jahrb. für Mineralogie: Abhandl.* CXXIII. 148 Laueite, pseudolaueite, and stewartite occur in a similar paragenesis which is confined to the late stage hydrothermal leaching and oxidation of primary triphylite-lithiophilite, $Li(Fe,Mn)[PO_4]$, in granitic pegmatites.

stewartry, stewardry ('stju:ətrɪ, 'stju:ədrɪ). Chiefly *Sc.* [See STEWARD *sb.* and -RY.]

1. A former territorial division of Scotland under the jurisdiction of a steward: see STEWARD 5 d.

Two of the stewartries, that of Orkney and Shetland and that of Kirkcudbright, were identical with the present counties, and the term was used instead of *county* as the official designation of these districts. Elsewhere the stewartry was of smaller extent than the county. As an administrative division, the stewartry was abolished in 1748.

α. **1473–4** *Acc. Ld. High Treas. Scot.* I. 5 His landis of Barnagehane within the Stewartry of Kirkcudbrith. **1491** in *Acta Dom. Concil.* (1839) 199/2 Landis..liand in the stewartry of straitherne. **1685** *Sc. Procl.* 28 Apr. in *Lond. Gaz.* No. 2032/2 All the Heretors, Liferenters, Feuars and Wodsetters in the Shires of Air, Renfrew, Clidsdale, Wigtoun, Dumfreis, and Stewartries and Bailliaries within the same. **1747** *Act 20 Geo. II*, c. 43 §4 All Stewartries not hereby before taken away and extinguished. **1806** *Gazetteer Scot.* (ed. 2) 140 Dumfries-shire..comprehends 3 districts or stewartries, viz. Annandale, Eskdale or Wauchopedale, and Nithsdale. **1837** *Act 7 Will. IV & 1 Vict.* c. 39 The Words..'Shire', 'Sheriffdom', and 'County' [shall be deemed] to comprehend and apply to any Stewartry in Scotland. **1884** *Manch. Exam.* 9 Dec. 5/6 Sir John proposes to..add to it.. the stewartry of Kirkcudbright.

attrib. **1792** *Copper-Plate Mag.* No. ix, The stewartry (or county) courts are held at this place [Kirkcudbright].

β. **1495–6** *Acc. Ld. High Treas. Scot.* I. 219 Vmquhill McLelane of Garrochcragow wythin the steuardry of Kirkcowbrycht. **1708** *Lond. Gaz.* No. 4434/1 The Barons, Free-holders and Gentlemen of the Stewardry of Kirkcudbright. **1862** J. GRANT *Capt. Guard* xix, Sir Herbert Herries..had large possessions in the stewardry.

2. The office of steward in such a territory.

1483 in *Acts Parlt. Scot.* (1875) XII. 33/1 þe office of the steuartry of Kirkcwbrich with þe keping of þe castel of þe treif. **1563** *Ibid.* 44/2 þe said office of stewartrie of Menteith with all feis and dewities pertening thairto. **1711** in *Nairne Peerage Evid.* (1874) 142 To use and exerce the said office of steuartrie. **1746–7** *Act 20 Geo. II*, c. 43 §2 The possessors of the seid heretable baillieries, stewartries, or constabularies.

3. = STEWARDSHIP 3.

a **1763** BYROM *Poet. Version Let. Earl of Essex* 37 You have them [*sc.* Talents], not as Things your own..; But as an human Stewartry, or Trust, Of which Account is to be giv'n, and just. **1877** BLACKIE *Wise Men* 341 The statesman.. skilled by faithful stewartry to give Increase to money wisely husbanded.

stewarty ('stju:ətɪ). *Sc.* Also 8 **stuarty**. [f. *stewart*, STEWARD *sb.* + -Y.] = STEWARTRY.

Chiefly used by English writers, though one or two Scottish examples are found.

1610 HOLLAND *Camden's Brit.* II. 6 Counties which they cal Shiriffdomes, Seneschalsies commonly Stewarties and Bailiwickes. **1708** *Lond. Gaz.* No. 4473/1 The Head Burghs of the several Shires and Stuarties in Scotland. **1747** *Gentl. Mag.* XVII. 556 These jurisdictions are either regalities, justiciaries, sheriffalties, stewarties, bailliaries. **1752** J. LOUTHIAN *Form of Process* (ed. 2) 171 The Sheriffs or Stewarts of the Shires or Stewarties. **1796** MORSE *Amer. Geog.* II. 97 Caithness, and the two stewarties.

†**stewat.** *Sc. Obs.* [app. f. STEW *v.*[3] + *-art*, -ARD.] A stinker, stinkard.

1535 LYNDESAY *Satyre* 2486 Thou art ane stewat, I stand foird. *Ibid.* 2489 Thir stewats stinks as thay war Broks.

stewdyent, obs. form of STUDENT[1].

stewed (stju:d), *ppl. a.*[1] Also 5 stwed, 6 stude, stued(e, stuyd, 6–7 stewd, 7 stu'd. [f. STEW *v.*[2] + -ED[1].] **a.** Of meat, fruit, vegetables: Cooked by slow boiling in a closed vessel. Of tea: Made strong and bitter by being kept too long in the pot.

c **1450** *Two Cookery-bks.* II. 72 Stwed Beef..Stwed Mutton. **1538** ELYOT *Dict.*, *Offella*,..also a potage made with pieces of flesshe, as stuyd brothe or forced gruell. **1555** in W. H. Turner *Select. Rec. Oxford* (1880) 230 Item, stude meate..x[d]. *c* **1596** HENSLOWE *Diary* (1904) I. 32 Then take a stewed pryne and plucke owt the stone. **1664** F. HAWKINS *Youths Behav.* II. 178 A dish of stu'd Oysters. **1747** MRS. GLASSE *Cookery* ii. 48 A stewed Pheasant. **1816** TUCKEY *Narr. Exped. R. Zaire* iv. (1818) 138 A repast..consisting of a stewed fowl, a dish of stewed beans, and cassava bread named Coanga. **1908** A. BENNETT *Old Wives' Tale* IV. iii. 509 The lounge tea, which in any case would have been undrinkably stewed. **1915** *Blackw. Mag.* May 600/2 We had a great meal off lunch-tongue, bread, wine and stewed pears. **1924** KIPLING *Debits & Credits* (1926) 309 Drinking stewed tea with your meat four times a day. **1977** M. HINXMAN *One-Way Cemetery* i. 7 The old man poured some stewed tea into a couple of mugs.

absol. **1861** [TREVELYAN] *Horace at Univ. Athens* (1862) 24 I'm..tightly filled With roast, and boiled, and stewed, and pulled, and grilled.

b. Comb. †**stewed-pot**, a stew of various ingredients (cf. STEWPOT 2); **stewed quaker** *U.S.* (See quot. 1890).

1596 NASHE *Saffron Walden* S 2 b, Neither are these parts seuerally distinguished in his order of handling, but, like a Dutch stewd-pot iumbled altogether. **1785** GROSE *Dict. Vulgar T.*, *Stewed quaker*, burned rum with a piece of butter, an American remedy for a cold. **1890** *Century Dict.* s.v. *Quaker*, *Stewed Quaker*, a posset of molasses or honey, stewed with butter and vinegar, and taken hot as a remedy for colds. (Colloq.)

¶**c.** With pun on STEWED *ppl. a.*[2]

1596 SHAKS. *1 Hen. IV*, III. iii. 128 There's no more faith in thee then in a stu'de Prune. So **1597–1603** —— *2 Hen. IV*, II. iv. 158, *Merry W.* I. i. 296, *Meas. for M.* II. i. 92. **1606** —— *Tr. & Cr.* III. i. 44 Sodden businesse, there's a stewed phrase indeede. **1609** DEKKER *Gull's Horn-bk.* v. 25 When your Knight is vpon his stewed Mutton, be you presently.. in the bosome of your goose.

d. *slang* (orig. *U.S.*). Drunk. Also in phr. ***stewed to the ears*** (***eyebrows***, ***gills***, etc.). Cf. PICKLED *ppl. a.*[1] 2.

1737 *Pennsylvania Gaz.* 6 Jan. 2 The Drinkers Dictionary... Stew'd. **1871** A. A. WRIGHT *Diary* in J. Wright *Generations of Men* (1959) v. 63 A very jolly party.. we kept it up till daylight. I got pretty well stewed. **1912** *Pedagogical Seminary* Mar. 97 [expressions denoting] *Intoxication*..'half stewed'. **1922** S. LEWIS *Babbitt* xxix. 347 He saw you out the other night with a gang of totties, all stewed to the gills. **1925** WODEHOUSE *Sam the Sudden* iii. 29 'My opinion is that he was as tight as an owl'. 'Stewed to the eyebrows'. **1930** J. DOS PASSOS *42nd Parallel* 9 They're a bunch o bums and hypocrytes, stewed to the ears most of em already. **1945** B. MACDONALD *Egg & I* (1946) IV. xvi. 176 Yewgene got stewed and run into a tree. **1958** P. DE VRIES *Mackerel Plaza* vi. 82 A casual observer not familiar with him would have thought he was stewed to the gills as he rose and wobbled over to join me. **1978** J. CARROLL *Mortal Friends* V. ii. 522 He wondered if Cushing had collected himself. He wondered if Cushing was stewed.

†**stewed**, *ppl. a.*[2] *Obs.* [f. **stew* vb. (f. STEW *sb.*[2]) + -ED[1].] Belonging to the stews. ***stewed whore***, ***strumpet***: vaguely used as opprobrious epithets imputing unchastity.

1532 MORE *Confut. Tindale* Wks. 722/2 This good scholer of Tindalle..findeth in his heart written by the spirit of God, y[t] freres & monkes..may..vnder the name of weddyng, make stewed strumpettes of nunnes. **1532** *Lett. & Pap. Hen. VIII*, V. 425 The King's grace was ruled by one common stued huer, Anne Bullan. **1549** LATIMER *3rd Serm. bef. Edw. VI* (Arb.) 82 There is more open whoredome more stuede whoredome then euer was before. **1556** OLDE *Antichrist* 140 b, That Sodomitical stewed state. **1575** *Gamm. Gurton* III. iii, Where is the strong stued hore?

stewfe, variant of STUFE *Obs.*, hot bath.

†**stew-house.** *Obs.* [STEW *sb.*[2]] A stews.

1436 *Rolls of Parlt.* IV. 511/1 Other strange persones.. have set up Stywehouses, and houses of Bordell. **1572** R. T. *Discourse* 49 Sixtus the fourth pope of that name builded stuehouses of both the kindes. **1651** J. F[REAKE] *Agrippa's Occ. Philos.* 96 To hide them in a stew house.

stewin, variant of STEVEN.

stewing ('stju:ɪŋ), *vbl. sb.* [f. STEW *v.*[2] + -ING[1].]

a. The action of the vb. STEW in various senses; an instance of this.

1398 TREVISA *Barth. De P.R.* VII. lviii. (1495) 272 The pacyent shall haue stewynges and bamynges and oynementes hote other colde. **1618** J. TAYLOR (Water P.) *Pennyles Pilgr.* F 2, Such Baking, Boyling, Rosting, and Stewing. **1778** COOK *3rd Voy.* III. xii. (1784) II. 235 We met with no utensil there that could be applied to the purpose of stewing or boiling. **1877** *Encycl. Brit.* VI. 333/2 The lid of a vessel used for stewing should be removed as little as possible. **1899** *Allbutt's Syst. Med.* VIII. 497 Remembering to warn him against heated rooms, violent changes of temperature, stewing in bed, and any possible irritation by vestments.

b. *attrib.* and *Comb.*

1726 J. GAY *Let.* in *Corresp. J. Swift* (1963) III. 168 Take a knuckle of Veal... In a Stewing pan put it. **1833** LOUDON *Encycl. Archit.* §1484 The fundamental principles of the construction of stewing-hearths. **1837** *Civil Engin. & Arch. Jrnl.* I. 60/1 The kitchen..containing an oven, stewing-stoves, &c. **1860** HOGG *Fruit Man.* 156 A stewing pear, in season from November to April. **1921** *Daily Colonist* (Victoria, B.C.) 25 Oct. 6/1 (Advt.), Boneless Stewing Beef, per lb. 12½c. **1948** *Good Housek. Cookery Bk.* II. 159 Stewing steak is commonly used, but other meats (kidney and liver) may be made into a brown stew. **1969** M. KELLY *Write on Both Sides* xxiii. 102 He took out the shopping list... Stewing steak, mushrooms, onions. **1978** E. MALPASS *Wind brings up Rain* xiv. 149 She'd got stewing beef in the oven.

stewing ('stju:ɪŋ), *ppl. a.* [f. STEW *v.*[2] + -ING[2].] That stews; very hot.

1856 EMERSON *Eng. Traits, Voy. Eng.*, Wks. (Bohn) II. 12 Nobody likes to be treated ignominiously,..rolled over, suffocated with bilge, mephitis, and stewing oil. **1911** J. MASEFIELD *Everlasting Mercy* (1912) 24 Jane brought the bowl of stewing gin And poured the egg and lemon in.

b. *Comb.* **stewing-hot** *a.*

1711 SWIFT *Jrnl. to Stella* 7 June, 'Tis stewing hot, but I must rise and go to town between fire and water. **1897** MARY KINGSLEY *W. Africa* 684 The sudden fall of temperature that occurs after a tornado coming at the end of a stewing-hot day, is sure to tell on any one.

†'**stewish**, *a.* *Obs.* [f. STEW *sb.*[2] + -ISH.] Of or pertaining to the stews.

a **1555** R. TAYLOR in Foxe *A. & M.* (1583) 1528/1 This Babylonicall stewish spirituall whoredome. **1597** BP. HALL *Sat.* I. ix, Rymed in rules of Stewish ribaldry. **1609** SIR E. HOBY *Let. to T. H[iggons]* 91 Your..Reliques,..Stewish Pardons, Indulgences.

stewpan ('stju:pæn). [f. STEW *sb.*[2] or *v.*[2] + PAN *sb.* Cf. Du. *stoofpan*.] A saucepan for stewing (see quot. 1858).

1651 T. BARKER *Art of Angling* (1820) 14 Taken out of the stew-pan and dished. **1674** *Engl. & Fr. Cook* 2 Put him [the Carp] in a Stew-pan with a quart of White-wine. **1747** MRS. GLASSE *Cookery* ii. 14 Then butter your Stew-pan, and shake some Flour into it. **1853** SOYER *Pantropheon* 66 Each piece was well washed before putting it into the stewpan. **1858** SIMMONDS *Dict. Trade*, *Stew-pan*, a shallow sauce-pan of iron, copper, or block tin. **1915** *Daily Tel.* 14 Aug. 10/2 Next lay the prepared fish..in a large, deep stewpan.

b. *transf.* and *fig.*

1771 SMOLLETT *Humph. Cl.* 5 May (1815) 66 To lead a weary life in this stewpan of idleness and insignificance. **1863** G. H. KINGSLEY *Sport & Trav.* (1900) 397 That tideless stewpan of a harbour can be little less unwholesome than that of Naples.

c. *attrib.*

1839 *Mag. Dom. Econ.* IV. 174 When onions are fried as a flavouring substance in stewpan-cookery. **1846** SOYER *Cookery* 545 Turn it over upon the bottom of a stewpan-lid.

stewpot ('stju:pɒt). [f. as prec. + POT *sb.*]

1. A covered pot for stewing meat, etc.

1628 FORD *Lover's Mel.* IV. ii, He chafes hugely, fumes like a stew-pot. **1806** *Culina* 236 Put these into a stew-pot. **1883** 'ANNIE THOMAS' *Mod. Housewife* 108 She is a venerable bird, and would have become the stew-pot better than the spit.

fig. **1899** *Westm. Gaz.* 5 Apr. 2/3 The very air, damp with the pestilential steam from the fever stew-pots of the slimy swamps and lagoons, is poison.

†**2.** A dish of meat cooked in a stewpot; a stew. (Cf. *stewed-pot*.) *Obs.*

1542 BOORDE *Dyetary* xii. (1870) 263 Sewe and stewpottes, and grewell made with otmell..can do lytel displeasure. **1605** ROWLANDS *Hell's broke loose* To Rdr., They were constrayned to frie..Bootes in Steakes, and Stew-pottes of old Shoes.

¶**b.** *allusively.* (See STEW *sb.*[2]) A prostitute.

a **1613** OVERBURY *Characters, Sargeant* (1618) N 7, Vpon one of the Sheriffs custards he is not so greedy, nor so sharp set, as at such a stew-pot.

†**3.** (See quot.) *Obs.*

1688 HOLME *Armoury* III. 424/1 A Stew or Stove or Stew pot covered... This is a Vessel made of either Brass, Iron, or Copper; with high Feet and Rings on the sides by which it is removed..from place to place; in which a Fire is put.. by which Rooms are made warm.

stewth, variant of STOUTH.

stewy ('stju:ɪ), *a.* [f. STEW *v.*[2] + -Y.] Suggestive of being stewed; having a stewed flavour; resembling stew.

1895 *Pall Mall Gaz.* 30 Dec. 4/3 The beverage she doles out is too frequently repellantly cold and detestably stewy. **1967** [see *gas-stove* s.v. GAS *sb.*[1] 7].

stewyn(e, variant forms of STEVEN.

stey (steɪ), *a.* *Sc.* Forms: 4– stay, 6– stey, 9 *erron.* steigh. [? repr. OE. **stǽʒe* (:—prehistoric **staiʒjo-*), f. OTeut. **staiʒ-*: **stiʒ-* to climb: see STY *v.* Cf. OE. *stǽʒel* steep.]

1. Of a mountain, cliff, etc.: Approaching the perpendicular, difficult of ascent, steep.

1375 BARBOUR *Bruce* x. 25 On the owthir half ane montane was So cumrouss, and ek so stay, That it wes hard to pas that way. *c* **1375** *Sc. Leg. Saints* xvi. (*Magdalene*) 813 þat roche hey & stay. **1513** DOUGLAS *Æneis* III. viii. 56 A port thair is, ..With rochis set forgane the streme full stay. **1533** BELLENDEN *Livy* II. 214/24 þai mycht þe more eselie be dung doun agane be þe stay brayis þareof. *c* **1590** J. STEWART *Poems* (S.T.S.) II. 208 The entres is so strait and stay, Quhilk leeds to lyf. **1597** MONTGOMERIE *Cherrie & Slae* 357 The craige was vgly, stay and dreich. **1710** RUDDIMAN *Gloss. Douglas' Æneis*, *Stay*,..steep: As we say Scot. a stay brae. **1721** KELLY *Sc. Prov.* 287 Set a stout Heart to a stay Brea. **1786** BURNS *To Auld Mare* xiv, The steyest brae thou wad hae fac't it. **1826** J. WILSON *Noct. Ambr.* Wks. 1855 I. 250 They gang swinging up the stey streets without sweetin. **1893** STEVENSON *Catriona* xv. 168 There was he hingin' by a line an' speldering on the craig face, whaur it's hieest and steighest.

†**2.** *transf.* Unbending, upright. Also of a person: Reserved, haughty. *Obs.*

a **1586** *Sat. Poems Reform.* xxxvii. 47 Gif ȝe beir strange, þai ȝow esteme our stay. *a* **1605** MONTGOMERIE *Misc. Poems* xxvii. 36 Nou I must rot, vha some tym stoud so stay. *a* **1605** —— *Sonn.* xxxii. 2, I love the lillie as the first of flours, Vhose staitly stalk so streight vp is and stay. **1632** LITHGOW *Trav.* x. 503 This Patrones Crescent stands so stay.

stey(e, obs. forms of STAY, STY.

steyer, steyg: see STAIR, STEG.

steyl(e, steyll, obs. ff. STEAL, STEEL, STILE.

steylling, obs. form of STILLING.

steyme, Sc. form of STIME.

steyn(e, var. forms of STAIN *v.*, STEEN *v.*

steynch, obs. form of STANCH *v.*

1573-5 GASCOIGNE *Adv. Mr. F. J.* Wks. 1907 I. 391 Yᵉ Lady..felt hir bleeding began to steynch. *Ibid.* 395 For that you have so clerkly steynched my bleeding.

steyp(e, steyr, obs. ff. STEEP, STEER.

Steyr (ʃtaɪə(r)). The name of a town in Upper Austria used *attrib.* and *absol.* to designate a kind of automatic pistol made there.

1920 H. B. C. POLLARD *Automatic Pistols* iii. 24 The latest product of the Steyr factory, the celebrated armoury of the Mannlicher firm, is the 1916 *Steyr Mannlicher* pistol. *Ibid.* 26 Taking the Steyr in comparison with the Parabellum, it is less complicated than the latter, but not so well designed or easy to shoot with. **1934** G. BURRARD *Identification of Firearms & Forensic Ballistics* vii. 144 The rifling used in revolvers and self-loading pistols may be divided conveniently into the following..types: *Steyr type,* four grooves; right-hand twist; grooves and lands of equal width. Used in all earlier self-loading pistols, such as the Borchardt. **1972** R. GADNEY *Seduction of Tall Man* II. v. 154 This is a Steyr pistol, made in Austria... Fixed barrel, detachable seven shot magazine. **1974** A. PRICE *Other Paths to Glory* II. viii. 211 The battered remains of an Austrian Steyr which he had bought.

steyre, obs. form of STAIR, STIR.

steyvyne, -wyne: see STEVEN *sb.*³, *sb.*²

St. Foin(e, St. Foyne, obs. forms of SAINFOIN.

‖**sthenia.** *Path. Obs.* [mod.L. (Brown) irreg. f. Gr. σθέν-ος strength, after ASTHENIA.] Used by Brown (see next) for: Normal or excessive 'excitability' or vital power. Opposed to *asthenia.*

1788 J. BROWN tr. *Elem. Med.* II. 43 In every sthenia, in all sthenic diseases,..an universal criterion is encreased excitement over the whole system. **1833** *Cycl. Pract. Med.* II. 702/1 [Dr. Brown] maintained..that both sthenia and asthenia could never exist together in the same individual.

sthenic (ˈsθɛnɪk), *a. Path.* [ad. mod.L. *sthenic-us* (Brown), f. Gr. σθέν-ος strength: after *asthenicus* ASTHENIC *a.*] Applied by Dr. John Brown (1735–88) and his followers to diseases characterized by a normal or excessive accumulation of 'excitability' or vital power in the system. Similarly in later use, of diseases, symptoms, etc.: Marked by normal or excessive vital or nervous energy. Opposed to *asthenic.*

1788 J. BROWN tr. *Elem. Med.* I. Pref. p. xii *note,* Sthenic diseases..are such as depend upon an excessive application of the several powers that otherwise produce health. **1793** T. BEDDOES *Let. Darwin* 49 It had before occurred to me that air of a reduced standard would be extremely beneficial in sthenic inflammation. **1874** MAUDSLEY *Mental Dis.* iii. 83 Idiopathic insanity divisible into two varieties,—sthenic and asthenic, according to the strong or feeble condition of the bodily health. **1877** F. T. ROBERTS *Handbk. Med.* (ed. 3) I. 6 The sanguineous temperament is believed to predispose to fevers of a sthenic type. **1880** BARWELL *Aneurism* 94 When the too sthenic symptoms are somewhat subdued, a dry diet is preferable.

b. In extended sense: Belonging to, tending to produce, vital or nervous energy.

1797 *Monthly Mag.* III. 350/2 M. Humboldt concludes his letter with some observations on the sthenic or asthenic virtue of chemical agents, that is to say, their ability or impotence to produce irritation. **1899** *Allbutt's Syst. Med.* VII. 372 The cerebellum normally exerts on the apparatus of movement, a sthenic, tonic, and static influence.

sthreal, sthreel, varr. STREEL *sb.*

sti, stian: see STY, STYAN.

‖**stiacciato** (stiatˈtʃato). *Sculpture.* Also schiacciato. [It. *schiacciato,* (Tuscan) *stiacciato,* pa. ppl. of *schiacciare* (*stiacciare*) to flatten.] Very low relief. In full ***stiacciato-relievo*** or ***relievo stiacciato.*** Also *attrib.*

1862 J. C. ROBINSON *Ital. Sculpture of Middle Ages* 26 To him [*sc.* Donatello] is..due the invention of that..method of low relief, which is often..called the 'Donatello style'... the ancient Florentine writers on art designated this style 'relievo stiacciato', (flattened relief)..but..it has become obsolete even in Italy. **1899** R. GLAZIER *Man. Historic Ornament* 51 Donatello also carried the art of low flat relief called '*Stiacciato*' to the greatest perfection. **1940** *Burlington Mag.* Mar. 76/1 The design of the buildings in lowest relief in the background is hardly imaginable without the precedent of Donatello's *stiacciato* reliefs. **1947** J. C. RICH *Materials & Methods of Sculpture* i. 8 Flat relief, *stiacciato-relievo,* is the lowest possible true relief. In this form, the effects are achieved by means of contour outlines and finely incised lines. The projection is very slight and there are no undercuts in this type of relief. **1957** H. W. JANSON *Sculpture of Donatello* II. 31/1 A *schiacciato* panel 'reads' more like a picture than like a conventional relief.

stiarne, obs. form of STERN *a.*

stib-, used in *Chem.* as combining form of STIBIUM, before both a vowel and a consonant: see quots. Cf. STIBIO-.

1852 *Fownes' Chem.* (ed. 4) 438 A curious substance, which MM. Loewig and Schweizer have described under the name of stibethyl. **1857** MILLER *Elem. Chem., Org.* 226 Stibethyl, or Stibiotriethyl. **1863** WATTS *Dict. Chem.* I. 339 Anti-monides of Amyl, or Stibamyls..Stibdiamyl.. Stibtriamyl. *Ibid.* 341 Stibtriethyl.., commonly called Stibethyl. *Ibid.* 344 Stibtrimethyl. **1865** MANSFIELD *Salts* 317 The compounds called Stibmethyl and Stibethyl.

stibadium (stɪˈbeɪdɪəm). *rare*⁻¹. [a. L. *stibadium* a. Gr. στιβάδιον, dim. of στιβάς bed of straw.] A semicircular couch.

1840 BROWNING *Sordello* v. 174 He that sprawls On aught but a stibadium suffers... goose, Puttest our lustral vase to such an use?

stibble, Sc. form of STUBBLE.

†ˈ**stibbler.** *Sc. Obs.* Also 8 stibler. [Of obscure origin; for suggestions see Jamieson.] A licensed probationer who has not yet received a call to a settled ministerial charge.

1721 RAMSAY *Morning Interview* 211 Not the long 'tending stibler, at his call;..E'er knew such raptures as this joyful swain. **1815** SCOTT *Guy M.* xlvi, Ye sticket stibbler [addressed to Dominie Sampson]. **1865** R. PAUL in B. Bell *Mem.* (1872) 335 Mr. Burns..is away for six weeks, and only a set of young stibblers in his place.

†ˈ**stibial,** *a. Obs. rare*⁻¹. [ad. mod.L. *stibiāl-is*: see STIBI-UM and -AL¹.] Having the qualities of antimony, antimonial.

1666 G. HARVEY *Morbus Angl.* xv. (1672) 33 An adust Stibial or Æruginous Sulphur.

stibialism (ˈstɪbɪəlɪz(ə)m). *Med. rare*⁻⁰. [f. prec. + -ISM.] (See quot.)

1857 DUNGLISON *Med. Lex., Stibialism,* the aggregate phenomena produced by antimonials, when given in large quantities:—antimonial intoxication or poisoning.

†**stibiˈarian.** *Obs. rare*⁻¹. [f. STIBI-UM + *-arian,* denoting an adherent of a doctrine or practice.] One who administers antimony (as an emetic); in quot. *fig.*

1635 F. WHITE *Sabbath-day* Ep. Ded. 3 This Stibiarian.. tendereth a bitter pill of sacriledge and cruelty: but when the same was rejected because it was violent, then he presents his Antimonian potion, to the States of the Kingdome.

†ˈ**stibiate,** *a. Obs.* [ad. mod.L. *stibiāt-us*: see STIBI-UM and -ATE².] Impregnated or combined with antimony.

1625 HART *Anat. Ur.* II. ix. 113 Strong stibiate vomits are vsed. **1684** tr. *Bonet's Merc. Compit.* XIV. 487 They place the chief stress of the Cure in Stibiate Emeticks. **1754** HUXHAM *Antimony* in *Phil. Trans.* XLVIII. 853 'Tis also of some consequence how long the stibiate lixivium stands before the acid is poured on. *Ibid.* 868 As stibiate medicines are now so much in vogue.

ˈ**stibiated,** *a. rare*⁻⁰. [f. prec. + -ED.] = prec.

1828-32 in WEBSTER; and in later Dicts.

stibic (ˈstɪbɪk), *a. rare.* [f. STIB-IUM + -IC.] Of or belonging to antimony; antimonic.

† *stibic stone,* 'black antimony': see STIBIUM.

1609 BIBLE (Douay) *2 Kings* ix. 30 Jezebel..paynted her face with stibike stone [Vulg. *depinxit oculos suos stibio*]. **1839** *Hooper's Lex. Med.* (ed. 7) 1221 *Stibic Acid,* Berzelius's name for the yellow oxide of antimony.

stibiconite (ˈstɪbɪkənaɪt). *Min.* [f. STIBI-UM + Gr. κόν-ις dust + -ITE. Originally named *stibiconise* (Beudant 1832).] A hydrous oxide of antimony, sometimes found in a pulverulent form. Cf. STIBLITE.

1843 E. J. CHAPMAN *Pract. Min.* 70 Stibiconise. **1868** DANA *Min.* (ed. 5) 188 Stibiconite.

†**stibie.** *Obs.* Anglicized form of STIBIUM.

1548 UDALL *Erasm. Par. Luke* vii. 36–39 Hir iyes..she was woont..to payncte with Stibie.

stibilite: see STIBLITE.

stibine (ˈstɪbaɪn). [f. STIB-IUM + -INE.]

1. *Min.* = STIBNITE. (Named by Beudant 1832.)

1843 E. J. CHAPMAN *Pract. Min.* 124. **1860** PIESSE *Lab. Chem. Wonders* 2 Native sulphuret of antimony or stibine.

2. *Chem.* Any of the antimony-compounds on the type of ammonia, SbH_3.

1852 *Fownes' Chem.* (ed. 4) 568 Triethylstibin. **1878** ABNEY *Photogr.* (1881) 34 Antimoniuretted hydrogen or stibine. **1878** TIDY *Mod. Chem.* 667 Stibines. Trimethyl stibine Sb $(CH_3)_3$. Triethyl stibine (Stibethyl) $Sb(C_2H_5)_3$.

stibio- (ˈstɪbɪəʊ), combining form of STIBIUM, used in *Chem.* and *Min.* (see quots.). Cf. STIB-. **stibioˈpalladinite** *Min.*, a palladium antimonide, approximately Pd_5Sb_2, occurring as white or grey hexagonal crystals; **stibioˈtantalite** *Min.*, an oxide of antimony and tantalum, $SbTaO_4$, occurring as transparent brown or yellowish orthorhombic crystals in which niobium replaces some of the tantalum.

1874 *Amer. Jrnl. Sci.* Ser. III. VII. 152 Stibioferrite from Santa Clara Co., California. **1868** DANA *Min.* (ed. 5) 591 Stibiogalenite. **1929** P. A. WAGNER *Platinum Deposits & Mines S. Afr.* i. 12 The other [mineral], a palladium antimonide, described by H. R. Adam.., from the pegmatitic ore of Tweefontein,..it is proposed..to name stibiopalladinite. **1976** *Amer. Mineralogist* LXI. 1249 Stibiopalladinite from the type locality, Farm Tweefontein, near Potgietersrust, Transvaal, South Africa, is considered to have a composition between Pd_5Sb_2 and Pd_8Sb_3. **1893** G. A. GOYDER in *Proc. Chem. Soc.* IX. 184 (*heading*) Stibiotantalite: a new mineral. **1973** *Canad. Mineralogist* XII. 77/2 Sb, Bi, and As are characteristic trace elements in many well-differentiated Li-rich pegmatites... Stibiotantalite is presently known from about 10 localities in the world, all of them of this type. **1857** MILLER *Elem. Chem., Org.* 225 The radicles stibiotrimethyl and stibiotriethyl.

ˈ**stibious,** *a. rare*⁻⁰. [f. STIBI-UM + -OUS.] Of or belonging to antimony; antimonious.

1839 *Hooper's Lex. Med.* (ed. 7) 1221 *Stibious,* antimonial. *Stibious Acid.* So Berzelius calls the white oxide of antimony.

stibium (ˈstɪbɪəm). Also 6 stebium, 7 stybium. [a. L. *stibium* (also *stibi, stimmi* = Gr. στίβι, στίμμι).] 'Black antimony', i.e. trisulphide of antimony calcined and powdered, used as a cosmetic for blackening the eyelids and eyebrows. †Formerly used also for metallic antimony or any of its salts, esp. as a poison or an emetic.

1398 TREVISA *Barth. De P.R.* XIX. xxxv. (1495) 879 *Stibium* is a feyned colour made of Cerusa and of other thynges medlyd therwyth, wymmen paynted theyr faces therwyth. *c* **1596** HENSLOWE *Diary* (1904) I. 32 Take stebium & beate yt in powder verey fine. **1612** WEBSTER *White Devil* II. i. 281, I will compound a medicine out of their two heads, stronger then garlick, deadlier then stibium. **1633** T. ADAMS *Exp. 2 Peter* ii. 22. 1094 Sinne, like *Stibium,* will tarry with no body: up it must, either here by a humble confession, or hereafter by a wretched confusion. **1634** W. WOOD *New Eng. Prosp.* II. vi. 67 Their belly-timbers, which I suppose would be but *stibium* to weake stomacks as they cooke it, though never so good of it selfe. **1660** J. H. *Basil Valentine's Tri. Chariot of Antimony* 81 The Antimony thus melted in the Crucible, Take a plain and broad dish..; poure in the stibium by litle and litle. **1699** GARTH *Dispens.* v. 122 Of temper'd Stibium the bright Shield was cast. **1842** BONAR & M'CHEYNE *Narr. Mission to Jews* ii. (1843) 59 Their eyes painted with stibium. **1874** BIRCH *1st & 2nd Egypt. Rooms Brit. Mus.* 27 Vase for holding stibium,..called by the Arabs *kohl.*

stibler, variant of STIBBLER.

ˈ**stiblite.** *Min.* Also stibi(o)lite. [f. STIB-IUM + -LITE.] Obsolete synonym of STIBICONITE.

1854 DANA *Min.* (ed. 4) II. 142 Stiblite. **1858** GREG & LETTSOM *Man. Min.* 372 Stiblite.

stibnite (ˈstɪbnaɪt). *Min.* [f. STIBINE + -ITE.] Native trisulphide of antimony, 'gray antimony', the most common ore of the metal.

1854 DANA *Min.* (ed. 4) II. 33. **1878** TIDY *Mod. Chem.* 388.

stibocaptate (stɪbəʊˈkæpteɪt). *Pharm.* [f. STIB- + -O + *-capt-* in 'antimony dimer*capto*succinate', a chemical name for the substance (see MERCAPTAN) + -ATE⁴.] An antimony-containing drug used in the treatment of schistosomiasis and administered by intramuscular injection.

1962 *Trop. Dis. Bull.* LIX. 1281/1 (Index), Stibo-captate. **1967** *Lancet* 21 Jan. 130/2 Monthly intramuscular injections of stibocaptate 10 mg. per kg. body-weight proved to be the best treatment for Zanzibari schoolboys infected with *Schistosoma hæmatobium.* **1977** *Proc. R. Soc. Med.* LXX. 762/2 Stibocaptate (Astiban)..is the only antimonial used for schistosomiasis in the United Kingdom. **1978** *Nature* 22 June 628/1 Stibocaptate (antimony dimercaptosuccinate, Astiban), one of the more than 10,000 antimonials that have been synthesised, is still on the WHO list as a complementary drug.

stibogram (ˈstɪbəgræm). *rare*⁻⁰. [f. Gr. στίβο-ς footprint + γράμμα written character: see -GRAM.] A graphic record of footprints.

1891 *Century Dict.* **1898** *Syd. Soc. Lex.*

stibophen (ˈstɪbəfɛn). *Pharm.* [f. STIB- + -O + PHEN(-.]

The compound pentasodium antimonybis-(catechol-3, 5-disulphonate) heptahydrate, which is used principally in the treatment of schistosomiasis, and is administered by intramuscular or intravenous injection.

1941 *Brit. Pharmacopœia 1932* Add. III. 22 (*heading*) Stibophen. **1941** *Q. Jrnl. Pharmacy & Pharmacol.* XIV. 43 A further study of the effect of pH on the stability of stibophen solutions is being made. **1950** *Amer. Jrnl. Trop. Med.* XXX. 266 Fuadin, also known as 'stibophen', another trivalent [antimony] compound, which contains 13·6 per cent antimony, was introduced in 1929 for the treatment of Egyptian schistosomiasis. **1977** *Brit. Jrnl. Dermatol.* XCVII. 308 The patient was treated with 25 injections of stibophen..2 ml intramuscularly on alternate days.

stiborn(e, -ourne, -urn(e, obs. ff. STUBBORN.

stica: see STYCA.

sticados, variant of STECHADOS *Obs.*

stiˈccado. *Mus.* Also -ato. [? ad. It. *steccato.*] A kind of xylophone (see quot. 1875).

1776 BURNEY *Hist. Mus.* (1789) I. ii. 33 A kind of Sticcado, consisting of bars of wood of different lengths as sonorous as if they had been of metal. **1794** MRS. RADCLIFFE *Myst. Udolpho* xxxii, If I can but steal out into the woods, and play upon my sticcado, I forget it all directly. **1811** BUSBY *Dict. Mus.* (ed. 3) Sticcado. **1875** STAINER & BARRETT *Dict. Mus. Terms, Sticcado* or *Sticcato,* an instrument composed of pieces of wood of graduated lengths, flat at the bottom and rounded at the top, resting on the edges of an open box, and tuned to a diatonic scale. The tone is produced by striking the pieces of wood with small hard balls at the end of a flexible stick.

sticche, obs. form of STITCH *sb.* and *v.*

stich (stɪk). [ad. Gr. στίχ-ος row, line, verse, or the collateral form στίχ-ες (pl.).] A portion or division of prose or verse writing, of a measured or average length; a line, verse.

1723 S. MATHER *Vind. Holy Bible* 67 In some ancient Greek New Testaments, at the close of the epistles, there were some numeral letters added, signifying how many Stichs were in the epistle... The Jewish and Christian writers have computed these Stichs in scripture books, and added them at the end of each book. **1883** SCHAFF *Encycl. Relig. Knowl.* III. 1955 Trying whether these pauses have a like or symmetrically correspondent number of stichs.

stich(e, obs. forms of STITCH.

stichados, variant of STECHADOS *Obs.*

ˈstichering, *vbl. sb. dial.* [Of obscure origin.] A method of catching eels. **ˈsticherer**, one who catches eels by this method. (See quot. 1885.)

1867 F. FRANCIS *Angling* iii. (1880) 92 Stichering is yet another method of catching eels... An unskilful sticherer will sometimes chop off his neighbour's ear. **1885** *Sat. Rev.* 21 Nov. 673/1 'Stichering', a Hampshire method, is perhaps one of the most amusing... The only apparatus used is an old sickle,.. tied firmly on a light pole about 12 ft. long. The object of the sticherer is to thrust the sickle under the eel's body, and, with a sudden hoist, to land him on the bank.

stichewort, -wurt, obs. ff. STITCHWORT.

stichic (ˈstɪkɪk), *a.* [ad. Gr. στιχικ-ός, f. στίχος: see STICH, STICHOS.]

1. Pertaining to or consisting of verses or lines.

1864 WEBSTER. **1883** JEBB *Œdipus Tyr.* p. lxxii, Two rhythmical sentences of equal length..form a 'stichic' period. **1897** W. H. STEVENSON in *Eng. Hist. Rev.* XII. 490 Coote completed Palgrave's stichic re-arrangement of the text.

2. *Prosody.* Consisting of successive lines of the same metrical form.

1886 *Amer. Jrnl. Philol.* VII. 399 The stichic portions of the cantica of Terence are divided into strophes. **1900** H. W. SMYTH *Grk. Melic Poets* 219 Lesser Asclepiads in stichic arrangement.

So **ˈstichical** *a.* = prec. 1.

1787 A. GEDDES *Let. Bp. London* 43 No one will..assert the same of any stichical version made from the Hebrew.

stichid (ˈstɪkɪd). Anglicized form of next.

1891 *Century Dict.*

stichidium (stɪˈkɪdɪəm). *Bot.* Pl. **stichidia** (-ɪə). [mod.L. f. Gr. στίχ-ος STICHOS + dim. suffix *-idium* (= Gr. -ίδιον).] A pod-like receptacle for tetraspores in some rose-spored Algæ.

1855 OGILVIE *Suppl.* **1857** HENFREY *Elem. Bot.* §337 Transformed branches containing imbedded tetraspores are called *stichidia*.

stichle (ˈstɪx(ə)l), *v. Sc. intr.* To rustle, make a rustling sound. Hence **ˈstichling** *vbl. sb.*

1500-20 DUNBAR *Poems* xlii. 78 Sik straikis and stychling wes on steir. **1501** DOUGLAS *Pal. Hon.* I. xx, The stichling of a mouse out of presence. **1788** PICKEN *Poems* 166 Ithers dose, While, stichlan, whis'les through their nose The eldritch snore.

stichochrome (ˈstɪkəʊkrəʊm). *Phys.* [f. Gr. στίχο-ς STICHOS + χρῶμα colour.] 'Any nerve-cell having the stainable substance (chromophilic bodies) arranged in more or less regular striæ or layers' (*Dorland's Med. Dict.* 1913). Also *attrib.*

1899 *Allbutt's Syst. Med.* VII. 261 The stichochrome granules disappear from the cells, to reappear once more when the animal recovers. **1901** *Jrnl. Exper. Med.* I Oct. 552 Nissl..recognizes three subgroups [of nerve cells]:.. Stichochromes or cells in which the chromatic substance is arranged in more or less distinctly parallel rows.

stichoi, pl. of STICHOS.

stichology (stɪˈkɒlədʒɪ). *rare.* [ad. Gr. *στιχολογία, f. στίχος: see STICHOS and -LOGY.] The science or theory of poetic metres.

1737 E. MANWARING (*title*) Stichology: or, a recovery of the Latin, Greek and Hebrew numbers. **1895** LAMBROS in *Athenæum* 6 July 16/3 His exact acquaintance with Byzantine melody and the Neo-Hellenic stichology.

ˈstichomancy. *rare*⁻¹. [a. F. *stichomantie* (Rabelais), f. Gr. στίχο-ς STICHOS + -MANCY.] Divination by lines of verse in books taken at hazard.

a **1693** *Urquhart's Rabelais* III. xxv. 209 By A Sibylline Stichomancy.

stichometric (stɪkəʊˈmɛtrɪk), *a.* [f. STICHOMETR-Y + -IC.] = next.

1881 *Scribner's Monthly* Feb. 614 Euthalius..published portions of the New Testament, broken up into longer or shorter clauses, for the convenience of the reader, and to avoid the use of punctuation. The clauses terminated at the more important pauses. Manuscripts written in this style are called 'stichometric'. **1883** J. R. HARRIS in *Schaff's Encycl. Relig. Knowl.* III. 2245 The actual number of lines in the manuscripts never tallies with the stichometric record. **1883** —— in *Amer. Jrnl. Philol.* IV. 134 [*heading*] Nature of Stichometric data.

stichometrical (stɪkəʊˈmɛtrɪkəl), *a.* [f. prec. + -AL[1].] Of or pertaining to stichometry; characterized by measurement by *stichoi* or lines.

1845 W. WRIGHT in Kitto *Cycl. Bibl. Lit.* s.v. *Vulgate* (1849) II. 926/1 The beautiful Lindisfarne book of the Gospels (Nero D. 4) is a stichometrical uncial MS. of the seventh century. **1885** G. SALMON *Introd. N.T.* xxi. 537 *note*, Then follows a stichometrical catalogue of the books both of Old and New Testament. **1904** M. RULE in *Athenæum* 9 Apr. 464/3, I find..upon making a careful stichometrical analysis of the Libellus, that it resolves itself into thirty-eight sections. **1909** *Times Lit. Suppl.* 11 Feb. 52/2 The stichometrical note in the margin of Frag. 58.

Hence **sticho'metrically** *adv.*

1871 G. V. SMITH *Bible & Pop. Theol.* App. 320 The six clauses may be arranged stichometrically. **1882** G. C. MACAULAY in *19th Cent.* Dec. 908 Passages from this preface have been introduced word for word, or with insignificant changes, into subsequently published poems, being divided stichometrically into lines by the natural pauses of the sentence. **1882** SCHAFF *Encycl. Relig. Knowl.* I. 268 Written *stichometrically*, i.e., in single lines containing only so many words as could be read, consistently with the sense, at a single inspiration.

stichometry (stɪˈkɒmɪtrɪ). *Palæography.* [ad. late Gr. στιχομετρία, f. στίχο-ς STICHOS + -μετρ ία -METRY.] **a.** The measurement of a manuscript text by *stichoi* or lines of fixed or average length into which the text is divided. Also, a list or appendix stating this measurement. **b.** Occas. used for: The practice of writing a prose text in lines of nearly equal length corresponding to divisions in the sense. Also, *stichoi* collectively.

a. 1754 N. LARDNER *Credib. Gosp. Hist.* II. XI. 248 A Stichometrie is a Catalogue of books of sacred Scripture, to which is added the number of the verses, which each book contains. This Stichometrie [of Nicephorus] contains a Catalogue of the books of the Old and New Testament. **1855** WESTCOTT *Canon N.T.* 522 *note*, Credner has examined the Stichometry of Nicephorus in connexion with the Festal Letter of Athanasius. **1883** J. R. HARRIS in *Schaff's Encycl. Relig. Knowl.* III. 2245 The data of stichometry consist chiefly of subscriptions at the close of manuscripts, expressing the number of lines which are contained in the book..copied. **1884** D. HUNTER *Reuss's Hist. Canon* ix. 159 The Codex Claromontanus..presents at the end of the text the copy of an old complete list of the books of the Old and New Testaments, with the number of lines in each book, what was then called a stichometry. **1885** G. SALMON *Introd. N.T.* xxv. 617 *note*, It appears from the Claromontane stichometry, as well as from that of Nicephorus, that in length this Apocalypse was less than a quarter of that of St. John.

b. 1875 W. R. SMITH in *Encycl. Brit.* III. 645/2 Another system was to write the text in short lines (στίχοι) accommodated to the sense. The author of this stichometry was Euthalius of Alexandria in the second half of the 5th century, who applied it to the epistles and Acts. **1875** SCRIVENER *Lect. Text N.T.* 69 Stichometry, that is, the division of prose sentences into lines of about equal length corresponding as nearly as possible to the sense. *Ibid.* 71 Another manuscript in which the prose text..is broken up into stichometry. **1881** *Scribner's Monthly* Feb. 614 Stichometry was really nothing but a cumbrous substitute for punctuation.

‖**stichomythia** (stɪkəʊˈmɪθɪə). Also *rarely* **stichomuthia** (-ˈmjuːθɪə). [mod.L. a. Gr. στιχομυθία, f. στίχο-ς STICHOS + μῦθ-ος speech, talk.] In classical Greek Drama, dialogue in alternate lines, employed in sharp disputation, and characterized by antithesis and rhetorical repetition or taking up of the opponent's words. Also applied to modern imitations of this.

1861 PALEY *Æschylus* (ed. 2) *Prometh.* 640 It is not unlikely that a verse has been lost, which preserved the continuity of the stichomythia. **1914** *Blackw. Mag.* June 855/1 Take..the passage of dialogue between Richard and Queen Elizabeth in 'Richard III,' as vivid a piece of *stichomuthia* as the English drama has to show.

stichomythic (stɪkəʊˈmɪθɪk), *a.* [f. prec. + -IC.] Of the nature of stichomythia.

1866 FELTON *Anc. & Mod. Gr.* I. xii. 222 This is shown particularly in those parts called stichomythic or line for line dialogues, responding like alternate strokes of hammers on the anvil. **1908** SAINTSBURY *Engl. Prosody* II. 14 Much of it [the *Comedy of Errors*]..is devoted to..stichomythic bandying of speech.

‖**stichos** (ˈstɪkɒs). Pl. **stichoi** (ˈstɪkɔɪ). [a. Gr. στίχος row, line, verse. Cf. STICH.]

1. In the Greek Church, a verse or versicle.

1863 LITTLEDALE *Offices East. Ch.* 248 At the Praises, we recite six stichoi. **1868** WALCOTT *Sacred Archæol.* 555 *Stichos*, a short varying versicle and response in the Greek liturgy... The koinonikon is a sacramental hymn and stichos, sung a little before the Communion.

2. *Palæography.* A line of a stichometrically written text; a line of average length assumed in measuring the contents of a text or codex.

1885 G. SALMON *Introd. N.T.* xi. 236 *note*, According to the Stichometry of Nicephorus, it [this Gospel] contained 1300 stichoi. **1911** *Jrnl. Manch. Oriental Soc.* 2 The amount assigned to a stichos is determined, as in all the old inscriptions, by the sense.

sticht, pa. t. of STY *v.*

stichtite (ˈstɪtʃtaɪt). *Min.* [f. the name of R. C. *Sticht* (1856–1922), of Australia + -ITE[1].] A hydrated carbonate of magnesium and chromium, $Mg_6Cr_2(OH)_{16}CO_3.4H_2O$, occurring as trigonal crystals of a pink, lilac, or purple colour.

1910 W. F. PETTERD in *Papers & Proc. R. Soc. Tasmania* 167 Stichtite... This is beyond doubt an unrecorded mineral species which has hitherto been known under the name of kammererite... The writer has great pleasure in dedicating this new mineral species to Mr. Robert Sticht, the..general manager of the Mt. Lyell Mining and Railway Company. **1977** *Austral. Gemmologist* XIII. 103/1 Stichtite ..occurs as a deep purple to rose pink soft waxy mineral as knots and veins in serpentine.

stichwort(e, obs. forms of STITCHWORT.

stick (stɪk), *sb.*[1] Forms: 1 sticca, 3-7 sticke, 3-5 stikke, 4-5 stykke, 4-6 stik, styke, 5 stike, 5-6 styk, stycke, 6 styck, stykk, 6- stick. [OE. *sticca* masc. = ? OS. *stekko* (Gallée), MDu. *stecke* masc., fem. also *stec* masc., neut. (mod.Du. *stek* fem.), OHG. *stecko* (MHG. *stecke*, mod.G. *stecken*):—OTeut. type **stikkon-* (a synonymous **stikon-* is represented by the parallel forms OHG. *stehho*, MHG. *steche* masc.; cf. also ON. *stika* fem., stick, yardstick, *kerta-stika* candlestick, MSw. *stikka*, mod.Sw. *sticka* fem. stick, chip), f. Teut. root **stik-* to pierce, prick: see STICK *v.*]

I. A rod or staff of wood.

1. a. A short piece of wood, esp. a piece cut and shaped for a special purpose, usually with defining word indicating its use, as in *bung-stick*, POTSTICK, SETTING-STICK, *tooth-stick*, etc.

In OE. also in the specific applications 'tent-peg' and 'pointer of a dial': see Bosworth-Toller.

c **1000** *Sax. Leechd.* I. 386 ðenim twegen..sticcan federecgede & writ on ægðerne sticcan..an pater noster. *c* **1450** *Bk. Curtasye* 94 in *Babees Bk.* (1868) 180 Clense not thi tethe at mete sittande, Withe knyfe ne stre, styk ne wande. **1707** MORTIMER *Husb.* (1721) I. 334 The next Morning pluck out the Bung-stick or Plug. **1913** M. W. H. BEECH in *Man* XIII. 5 [It] can be used as either the female, i.e., the passive stick of the fire drill or for the male or active stick.

†**b.** A piece of wood used as a tally. Also WHITE STICK. *Obs.* as specific sense.

c **1380**, *c* **1400** [see WHITE STICK]. **1500** *God Speed Plough* (E.E.T.S.) 30 And to the kyngis courte we moste it lede, And our payment shalbe a styk of A bough. **1523-34** FITZHERB. *Husb.* §141 Yf he [the husbandman] canne not wryte, let hym nycke the defautes vppon a stycke, and shewe his bayely. **1664** MARQ. NEWCASTLE in M'ness Newcastle *Sociable Lett.* To Author, Each Tavern-token, Nick'd Sticks for Merchants [etc.]. **1737** POPE *Hor. Epist.* I. i. 84 To him who notches sticks at Westminster. **1784** COWPER *Tiroc.* 559 Th' indented stick, that loses day by day Notch after notch. **1846-8** LOWELL *Biglow P.* Ser. I. ix. 61 Wy, into Bellers's we notched the votes down on three sticks.

c. *Mining.* (See quot. 1899.)

1708 J. C. *Compl. Collier* (1845) 37 The..chief Banck's-Man..takes an Account..by Sticks or Pieces of Wood. **1797** J. CURR *Coal Viewer* 20 Nogs and boxes for mottys, or sticks, to distinguish the Corf, o. o. 6. **1899** DICKINSON & PREVOST *Cumbld. Gloss.*, *Stick*, the wooden token whereon was branded the distinguishing number of the hewer in the coal pit.

d. *the* (*sixty* or *sixty-four*) *sticks of fate*: the apparatus employed in a Chinese method of divination.

?*c* **1850** LADY DUFFERIN (*title of poem*) Consulting the 'Sticks of Fate'. **1860** COBBOLD *Pict. Chinese* 14. **1884** FRIEND *Flowers & Flower-lore* I. 268.

2. a. A slender branch or twig of a tree or shrub esp. when cut or broken off. Now *rare.*

c **1000** *Sax. Leechd.* II. 142 Læt yrnan þat blod on grennne [*sic*] sticcan hæslenne. *c* **1200** *Vices & Virtues* 135 Ne lat hie nawht ðe hande pleiȝende mid stikke, ne mid strawe—nis þat non god tocne of ripe manne. **13..** *K. Alis.* 4425 (Laud MS.), Þe speres crakeþ also þicke So on hegge sere stykke. *c* **1369** CHAUCER *Dethe Blaunche* 423 So grete trees..of.. fourty fifty fedme lengthe Clene withoute bowgh or stikke. *c* **1400** MAUNDEV. (Roxb.) vii. 25 Þe preste..lays þerapon spiceries..and stikkes of þe iunipre tree. **1593** SHAKS. *2 Hen. VI*, I. ii. 33 He that breakes a sticke of Glosters groue, Shall loose his head for his presumption. **1620** QUARLES *Feast for Worms* K 4, Thou, in whose distrustfull brest Despayre hath brought in sticks to build her nest. **1735** *Dict. Polygraph.* s.v. *Verdegris*, This [crystallised verdegrease] commonly comes from Holland..on sticks in form like our sugar-candy. To be good, these crystals must be..as free from sticks as possible.

b. *pl.* Pieces of cut or broken branches, also pieces of cut and chopped wood, used as fuel.

c **1200** ORMIN 8651, & her I gaddre stikkess twa..To ȝarrkenn þatt to fode. *c* **1300** *Havelok* 914 Stickes kan ich breken and kraken, And kindlen ful wel a fyr. **1382** WYCLIF *Numb.* xv. 32 Thei fonden a man gederynge stikkis in the holi day. *c* **1450** *St. Cuthbert* (Surtees) 807 Stikkes to a fyre þai gadird fast. **1653** WALTON *Angler* xi[xvi]. 209 Come, Hostis,..lay a few more sticks on the fire. **1737** POPE *Hor. Epist.* II. ii. 242 Such large-acred men..Buy every stick of wood that lends them heat. **1821** CLARE *Vill. Minstr.* II. 117 Seeking..her harmless sticks from hedges hung with rime. **1902** A. SYMONS *Stud. Prose & Verse* (1904) 251 Mr. Phillips has laid the paper, the sticks, and the coals neatly in the grate.

†**c.** A piece of wood from the hearth, a brand. *stick of fire*, a firebrand. *Obs.*

1538 ELYOT *Dict.*, *Torris*, a stycke of fyre. **1607** DEKKER *Jests to make Merry* 33 Your Glimerer, shees vp in the morning betweene 5 or 6 of the clock..and with a black brand in her hand... If she but perceiue a light..she desires to haue leaue to kindle her stick.

d. A twiggy bough or long rod stuck in the ground for a plant to 'run' upon, more definitely ***bean-stick, pea-stick.***

1577 GOOGE tr. *Heresbach's Husb.* 33 There are two sortes of Pease, the one sort..runneth vp vppon stickes. **1741** MILLER *Gard. Dict.* s.v. *Phaseolus*, [The Scarlet Bean] being supported either with Sticks or Strings, grows up to a good Height.

3. a. A stem or thick branch of a tree cut and trimmed and used as timber for building, fencing, etc.; a stave, stake. Also *fig.* Cf. sense 6.

c **1386** CHAUCER *Nun's Pr. T.* 28 A yeerd she hadde, enclosed al aboute With stikkes. **1577** GOOGE tr. *Heresbach's Husb.* 41 b, They vse a greater Sythe with a long Suath, and fenced with a crooked frame of stickes, wherwith with both their hands they cut downe the Corne, and laye it in Swathes. **1644** [see HEDGE *sb.* 6]. **1707** FOUNTAINHALL *Decis.* (1761) II. 408 The pursuer had no inclosure..neither was their a stick of planting or hedging therein.

b. ***every stick***, the whole materials of a building: used (sometimes *advb.*) to emphasize total destruction or ruin. Also negatively: ***(to leave) not a stick.***

1338 R. BRUNNE *Chron.* (1725) 113 Carro, Lodelow toun, ..Dunford & Maltone, Steuen wan þam ilk a stik. *a* **1400–50** *Wars Alex.* 1311 Þus þe strenth [of Alexander's towers] ilk stike was in a stounde wasted. *c* **1450** *Brut* 577 Thai brake vp al þe lede of the halle and of þe toures, and brent vp euery stykke. **1557–71** A. JENKINSON *Voy. & Trav.* (Hakl. Soc.) II. 339 One of ye dukes howses..was consomed with fyer and not one stick left. **1596** SPENSER *State Irel.* Wks. (Globe) 616/2 Of all townes, castels, fortes, bridges, and habitations, they left not any stick standing. **1625** in Foster *Eng. Factories India* (1909) III. 80 The Sultan suffaringe not a sticke to bee puld downe out of aney house.

c. Similarly in alliterative expressions, esp. ***(every, both) stick and stone, stick and stour*** dial., ***stick and stow*** Sc. and north. (cf. *stab and stow*, STAB *sb.*[2]), ***stick and stock.***

c **1436** *Brut* 583 Þe Calisers..bare lxiii clene away, Euery stikke & stone, & lafte not ther one log. **1459** SIR J. FASTOLF *Will* in *Paston Lett.* I. 462 That thanne the said John Paston shulde doo poule down the said mansion and every stone and stikke therof. **1542** UDALL *Erasm. Apoph.* 232 b, [He] to declare hym selfe [free from the assumption of kingly power], was fain to pul down his hous sticke and stone euen to yᵉ plain grounde. **1600** FAIRFAX *Tasso* IX. ix, Godfrey meane-while to ruin sticke and stone Of this faire towne, with battrie sore, assaies. **1611** BEAUM. & FL. *Knt. Burn. Pestle* II. i, Shee swore, neuer to marry, But such a one, whose mighty arme could carry..Her bodily away through sticke and stone. **1792** WOLCOT (P. Pindar) *Lyric Ep. Ld. Macartney* xxxvii. Wks. 1816 II. 355 For troops..May, like wild meteors, pour into mine east, And leave my palace neither stick nor stone. **1904** *Athenæum* 27 Aug. 271/3 Every stick and stone of Beau Nash's Pump Room [at Bath] has long since passed away.

c **1450** *St. Cuthbert* (Surtees) 7177 Þe place was brynt, styk and stoure, Abbay and house. **1877** *N.W. Linc. Gloss., Stick and stour*,..Often used to signify all a person's goods and chattels. 'They've sell'd him up, stick an' stour'.

1786 BURNS *To W. Simpson* Postscr. ix, Folk thought them ruin'd stick-an-stowe. **1862** C. C. ROBINSON *Dial. Leeds* 422 A nasty, thratching hussey!—shoo wants bundiling art o't' street stick an' stow.

1880 BARING-GOULD *Mehalah* xii. (1884) 161 Cousin Charles is not the man to see his relatives sold up stick and stock.

d. ***stick and rag***: see quot.

1911 *Encycl. Brit.* XXI. 786/1 Fibrous plaster is given by plasterers the suggestive name 'stick and rag',..for it is composed of plaster laid upon a backing of canvas stretched on wood.

e. ***over the sticks***: in steeplechasing and hurdleracing.

1898 T. HAYDON *Sporting Reminisc.* 67 The quality of the competitors, both in flat races and 'over the sticks' was of the highest class.

4. a. A long and relatively slender piece of wood, whether in natural form or shaped with tools, cut or broken of a convenient length for handling.

cleft stick: see CLEFT *ppl. a.*

c **1386** CHAUCER *Can. Yeom. Prol. & T.* 712 In his hand he bar An holwe stikke..In the ende of which an Ounce..Of siluer lemaille put was as bifore. **1523–34** FITZHERB. *Husb.* §21 And in his other hande he hath a forked stycke a yarde longe, and with his forked stycke he putteth the wede from hym. **1526** *Pilgr. Perf.* (W. de W. 1531) 30 b, Whiche by theyr enchauntementes made serpentes of styckes. **1590** LUCAR *Lucarsolace* I. iv. 11 Take vp your Geometricall table, ..leauing an arrow or sticke set vpright in the point of grounde directly vnder B. **1662** STILLINGFL. *Orig. Sacræ* III. i. §17 So in the sight of a stick, when under water, the representation of it by the sense to imagination is as crooked. **1784** COWPER *Task* I. 561 A Kettle, slung Between two poles upon a stick transverse. **1889** DOYLE *Micah Clarke* v, Like the turnip on a stick at which we used to throw at the fairs.

b. A staff, club, cudgel used as a weapon. Proverbial phrases: *to be after* (someone) ***with a sharp stick***: (see quot. 1848); ***a stick to beat*** (someone or something) ***with*** (perh. with ref. to the proverb: see quot. 1782). Also contrasted with *carrot* (= reward): see CARROT *sb.* 2 a.

1377 LANGL. *P. Pl.* B. XII. 14 Al-þough þow stryke me with þi staffe with stikke or with ȝerde. **1547** BOORDE *Brev. Health* (1870) 84 For the Feuer lurden..Take me a stycke or wan[d] of a yerde of length and more..and with it anoynt the bake. **1605** SHAKS. *Lear* II. iv. 125 She knopt 'em o'th' coxcombs with a sticke, and cryed downe wantons, downe. **1664** in *Verney Mem.* (1904) II. 214 [If the] Whelps meddle with Sheepe, they must be..whipped soundly, but not beaten with Stickes. **1847** W. C. L. MARTIN *Ox* 139/2 Contusions, and the blows of cattle-drivers, merciless in the use of their sticks about the heads of the poor beasts. **1850** A. M'GILVRAY *Poems* 69 For he has laid, with their own sticks, The strongest watchmen down.

phrases. **1653** D. OSBORNE *Let.* 24 July (1903) 125 What reason had I to furnish you with a stick to beat myself withal? **1782** F. HOPKINSON *Misc. Essays* I. 266 A proverb ..naturally occurs on this occasion: It is easy to find a stick to beat a dog. **1848** BARTLETT *Dict. Amer., Sharp stick.* He's after him with a *sharp stick*; i.e. he's determined to have satisfaction or revenge. **1871** *Trenton State Sentinel* 26 May in Schele de Vere *Americanisms* 631 We are pleased to see that the New York Tribune is still after Senators Carpenter, Conkling and others, with a very sharp stick, for [etc.]. **1889** G. B. SHAW in *English Illustr. Mag.* Oct. 49 A few of us go to Bayreuth because it is a capital stick to beat a dog with. **1928** D. H. LAWRENCE in *Evening News* 8 May 8/4 The last stupid stick with which the old can beat the young. **1962** *Listener* 5 Apr. 597/2 Israel has sometimes been just another stick with which the Arabs beat each other. **1966** *Ibid.* 9 June 824/2 The Liberals had been glad to use the horror [at Turkish atrocities] felt by people in Britain as a stick with which to beat the Conservatives.

c. (Chiefly ***the stick.***) A beating with a stick. Hence (without article) *transf.*, severe physical handling, 'punishment'; *fig.* unfavourable criticism, censure, reproof. Usu. in phrases ***to come in for, get, give,*** or ***take stick. to eat stick***: see EAT *v.* 2 d.

1856 MISS YONGE *Daisy Chain* I. viii, Come in, ye bad girls, or I'll give you the stick. **1884** SIR S. ST. JOHN *Hayti* iii. 81 The productiveness of the north [of Hayti] was founded on the liberal application of the stick. **1886** 'MAXWELL GRAY' *Silence Dean Maitland* I. v. 125 He'll do what he is told now without the stick. **1892** MRS. H. WARD *David Grieve* I. iv, Mak her behave... She'll want a stick takken to her, soon, *I* can see. **1942** *E. African Ann. 1941–2* 115/1 The Italians nipped across from Diredawa, and, as the troops say, 'gave us stick'. **1956** *People* 13 May 14/8 As usual the Australians are getting plenty of stick from the armchair critics. **1967** J. BURKE *Till Death us do Part* vii. 116 He went out on the booze... She didn't half give him some stick when she found out. **1977** J. WAINWRIGHT *Nest of Rats* III. v. 205 We took some stick, and we gave some stick... I belted that face. **1980** *Daily Tel.* 11 Apr. 19/2, I told him that he could expect trouble from the branches... He will come in for some stick over this.

d. = WALKING-STICK.

1620 *E. Blount's Horæ Subs.* 33 Some had rather bee lame ..of a legge, then lose the grace of carrying a French sticke. **1792** CHARLOTTE SMITH *Desmond* II. 285, I tapped at the old, thick, carved door with my stick. **1892** RIDER HAGGARD *Nada the Lily* xviii. 145 We went on in silence, the king leaning on my shoulder as on a stick.

e. A rod of dignity or office, a baton; also the bearer of such a stick. Cf. GOLD STICK, WHITE STICK.

1688 *Lond. Gaz.* 22 Oct. 7 He had the Honour to be in Waiting upon the King with the Stick. **1833** HOOD *Publ. Dinner* 14 Twelve sticks come attending A stick of a Chairman. **1876** VOYLE & STEVENSON *Milit. Dict.* 409/2 *Stick, Silver*, the field officer of the life guards, when on duty, is called silver stick. **1892** HUXLEY in L. Huxley *Life* (1900) II. 328 Then waiting about while the various 'sticks' were delivered. **1897** *Westm. Gaz.* 25 June 4/1 One of the 'Sticks' now doing duty at Buckingham Palace.

f. *Basket-making.* (See quot. 1910.)

1907 *Jrnl. Soc. Arts* 11 Jan. 190/1 A dog or commander for straightening the sticks. **1910** *Encycl. Brit.* III. 482/1 Rods ..known as 'sticks', are used to form the rigid frame-work of the bottoms and lids of square work.

g. In *Candlemaking*, the rod to which the wicks are attached in order to be dipped: = BROACH *sb.*[1] 2 b. Hence, the candles made at one dipping.

1711 *Act 10 Anne* c. 26 §106 Every Chandler..shall.. declare..the Number of Sticks which he designs to make.. and also the Sizes of the Candles whereof each Stick is to consist. **1751** *Chambers' Cycl.* s.v. *Candle*, The workman.. takes two sticks [ed. 1727 rods], or broches, at a time, strung with the proper number of wicks.

h. The rod of a sky-rocket (see quot. 1886).

1651 J. WHITE *Rich Cabinet* (1677) 83 Rockets whose sticks are longer than the staffe. **1792** T. PAINE *Let. to Addressers Proclam.* 4 As he rose like a rocket, he fell like the stick. **1848** ALB. SMITH *Chr. Tadpole* xxiv. 218 You'll go off like a regular rocket—all stars and no stick. **1886** *Encycl. Brit.* XX. 136/2 The stick of the sky-rocket serves the purpose of guiding and balancing it in its flight.

i. A conductor's baton.

1849 *Hamilton's Celebrated Dict.* s.v. *Battre la mesure*, To mark the time by beating with the hand or with a stick etc. **1884** F. NIECKS *Dict. Mus. Terms* s.v. *Bâton*, A stick used for beating time. *Ibid.* s.v. *Taktstock*, a conducting stick. **1920** A. BOULT *Handbk. Technique Conducting* 7 The conductor has, therefore, had to learn to show his ideas on the interpretation of a work by means of his stick and hand. **1931** *Times Lit. Suppl.* 14 May 394/2 Stickless conducting.. may suffice in ordinary class-room teaching; but in the interests of festival work..it is better to accustom all singers to watch a stick and to train up a generation of conductors who know the technique of using it. **1955** *Times* 2 Feb. 6/3 There were moments when a loose movement of the stick gave away a little concentration in the quiet entries of the strings. **1978** *Gramophone* Feb. 1390/1 His mentor was band leader Joe Loss. 'When Loss used a stick the bounce and freedom within a beat was masterly.'

5. *spec.* in various games.

a. A staff used for striking or pushing, as in Hockey; also applied to a billiard cue, a golf club, or the like.

1674 COTTON *Compl. Gamester* (1680) 25 (Billiards) He that removes the Port with his Stick when he strikes his Ball, and thereby prevents his Adversaries Ball from passing, loseth an end. **1726** *Art & Myst. Mod. Gaming* 109 They had Drawers, with Lock and Key, made for each of them to put their Sticks into, in the Billiard Room... When *R* came afterwards to play with the Stick, *B* beat him. **1857** H. B. FARNIE *Golfer's Man.* in *Golfiana Misc.* (1887) 134 We shall, therefore, take the clubs *seriatim*..and explain, in each case, what constitutes a good stick. **1896–7** *Rules of Hockey* (ed. 12) 21 The sticks shall have no metal fittings whatever, and no sharp edges.

b. Hence in Hockey, ***sticks***, the word used by the umpire in declaring a breach of rule committed by improperly handling the stick; a breach of rule of this kind.

1896–7 *Rules of Hockey* (ed. 12) 26 Except so far as Rule 14 applies to 'sticks,' for which a 'bully' only to be allowed. *Ibid.* 33 'Sticks' should be given, if a player's stick is above his shoulder after hitting or missing the ball.

c. *Cricket.* pl. The stumps of a wicket, the wickets. *rare* in *sing.* unless with qualifying word, as ***middle stick.***

between the sticks, at the wickets, batting, 'in'. ***behind the sticks***, keeping the wicket or acting as wicket-keeper. ***in front of the sticks***: at the wicket, batting.

1840 J. C. W. in *Sporting Mag.* Aug. 333 (Cricketing Extraordinary) New *stumps* are wanted to the number of six, So, good Mr. Charon, pray lend us the *sticks*! **1862** *Baily's Mag.* Oct. 200 They were..ten hours between the sticks —averaging 1 hour at the wicket, and 50 runs per man. **1882** *Daily Tel.* 19 May, Having added a couple [of runs], his sticks were disturbed by Palmer. **1886** *Pall Mall Gaz.* 28 Apr. 11/2 It was curious to see Blackham anywhere in the field except behind the sticks. **1892** *Ibid.* 2 July 6/2 Jackson played across at a delivery..and had his stick disturbed. **1924** LAWRENCE & SKINNER *Boy in Bush* ii. 22, I was captain of the first football eleven... And not bad in front of the sticks.

d. *pl.* The staves used for throwing in the game of Aunt Sally; also used for the game itself.

184. D. JERROLD *Men of Char.* (1851) 273 Next, he must have at least a pennyworth of sticks: he may knock down a tobacco-box. **1850** THACKERAY *Pendennis* II. xx. 197 The splendid young dandies who were strolling about the course, and enjoying themselves at the noble diversion of Sticks.

e. *Assoc. Football.* Phr. ***between the sticks***: between the goal-posts, keeping goal.

1950 *Sport* 7–11 Apr. 14/3 Good news for Reading fans is that goalkeeper George Marks is expected to be back between the Elm Park sticks at the start of season 1950–1951. **1976** *Wymondham & Attleborough Express* 19 Nov. 23/4 Wortwell could not produce the form of recent weeks and crashed heavily to their hosts. David Loome took over between the 'sticks'.

6. A timber-tree, also a tree-trunk when cut for timber; more fully ***stick of timber.*** Cf. sense 3.

1748 *Anson's Voy.* I. v. 54 The Carpenters were sent into the woods, to endeavour to find a stick proper for a foremast. **1866** *Treas. Bot.* 220/2 [*Carapa guianensis*] Its timber ..is obtainable in sticks, fifty feet long by fifteen inches square. **1878** JEFFERIES *Gamekeeper at Home* 38 The edge of a fir plantation where lies a fallen 'stick' of timber.

7. *Naut.* A mast or portion of a mast; also a yard. ***the sticks***, the masts and yards. ***to up stick(s*** (slang), to set up a boat's mast; also *fig.* (usu. in form ***up sticks***), to prepare to move, pack up, get going; to pack up and go, remove oneself.

1802 *Naval Chron.* VIII. 517 She has not a stick standing. **1819** BYRON *Juan* II. xxxix, But with a leak, and not a stick of mast, Nor rag of canvas, what could they expect? **1833** MARRYAT *P. Simple* xlvi, A raking broadside..brought the sticks about their ears. **1839** *Knickerbocker* XIV. 141 Why, in the name of common sense, do you not up sticks and off? **1845** J. COULTER *Adv. Pacific* vii. 88 So we 'up stick', that is, shipped our mast, made sail, and..brought our..whale alongside the ship. **1854** [see UP *adv.*[1] 31]. **1859** D. BUNCE *Trav. with Dr. Leichhardt* ix. 141 The place was so muddy as to render it necessary to 'up sticks!' and start for another ..camping ground. *c* **1860** H. STUART *Seaman's Catech.* 76 Topsail yards..are made in one stick. **1877** *Harper's Mag.* Jan. 213/2 If any man tries hard words with me, I knocks him down, up sticks, and makes tracks. **1888** CLARK RUSSELL *Death Ship* I. 286 To have nothing to do with her or me, but to bear a hand and 'up sticks'. **1893** H. M. DOUGHTY *Wherry in Wendish Lands* 76 We could see the mast, a very strong stick, whip with the weight. **1920** C. A. W. MONCKTON *Some Experiences of New Guinea Resident Magistrate* xxii. 262 Up sticks and away for Port Moresby and Sir Francis Winter. **1958** P. SCOTT *Mark of Warrior* II. 168, 0700 we up sticks here and get well under cover a mile into the jungle. **1967** *Economist* 21 Oct. 306/1 If businesses can up-sticks from Quebec.., they are being tempted to do so. **1972** G. GREEN *Great Moments in Sport: Soccer* i. 28 Neil Franklin..upped sticks..and departed to Bogotá. **1978** *Guardian Weekly* 26 Mar. 21/2 What on earth impels a man ..suddenly to up sticks at 84 and come back to this distressful country?

II. Transferred uses.

8. A piece of material rolled, moulded, or cut for convenience of use into a long and slender form like that of a stick: **a.** of rolled cinnamon bark; **b.** of sweetstuff; **c.** of glass; **d.** of lac or sealing-wax; **e.** of bread, esp. as ***French stick***; cf. BATON *sb.* 1 c, ***bread-stick*** s.v. BREAD *sb.* 10, GRISSINO; **f.** of various other substances (see quots.).

a. *a* **1460** [see CINNAMON 1]. **1594** *Gd. Huswife's Handmaid Kitchin* 3 b, A litle sticke of Sinamon. **1615** MARKHAM *Eng. Housew.* 73 To make most Artificiall Cinamon stickes. *a* **1777** in *Jrnl. Friends' Hist. Soc.* (1914) Oct. 188 Put in a stick of Cinnamon.

b. **1611** [see LIQUORICE]. **1862** THACKERAY *Philip* xxviii, She bought pink sticks of barley-sugar for the young ones. **1913** *Little Bk. Confect.* 39 Cocoa Sticks... Cut into three inch sticks and bake.

c. **1683** *Digby's Chym. Secrets* 19 Stir the Matter well with a stick of Glass. **1879** *Encycl. Brit.* IX. 348/2 A young girl sits by a jet of flame, holding in her hand a stick of prepared glass.

d. **1662** J. Davies tr. *Mandelslo's Trav.* 27 The Indians give it [lacque] what colour they please, black, red, green, yellow, &c. And make it into sticks to seal Letters withall. **1746** *Phil. Trans.* XLIV. 28 A Stick of the best black Sealing-wax. **1839** Ure *Dict. Arts* 1097 In forming the round sticks of sealing-wax..[the pieces are] rolled out upon a warm marble slab... The oval sticks..are cast in moulds.

e. **1909** [see *bread-stick* s.v. bread *sb.* 10]. **1943** A. Simon *Conc. Encycl. Gastron.* IV. 59/2 (*heading*) Grissini or salt sticks. **1959** *Times* 9 Mar. (Britain's Food Suppl.) p. xii/5 Her French sister who shops three times a day for her French sticks in order to get them really fresh. **1962** *Woman* 8 Dec. 51/3 A stick of French bread. **1972** *House & Garden* Feb. 98/2 Swiss fondue... Seasame seed sticks..make a happy accompaniment. **1980** *Sunday Times* (Colour Suppl.) 20 Jan. 57/3 *French stick*, long thin load with thick golden crust.

f. **1753** Chambers *Cycl.* Suppl. s.v. *Lycium*, The Dutch.. form it into twisted sticks, which they sell to the painters in water colours. **1836** J. F. Davis *Chinese* II. 135 The extreme carelessness with which burning paper and lighted sticks of incense are left about their combustible dwellings. **1844** Fownes *Chem.* 131 A stick of phosphorus held in the air always appears to emit a whitish smoke. **1848** Ronalds & Richardson *Knapp's Chem. Technol.* I. 224 Producing consecutively..flowers of sulphur..and sticks of sulphur. **1862** Miller *Elem. Chem., Org.* 671 Sticks of potash. **1882** Christy *Joints* 184 A stick of the metal [solder] must be fused at the same time and allowed to drop upon them. **1884** Britten *Watch & Clockm.* 86 Dissolve a stick of nitrate of silver in..water. **1891** *Pall Mall Gaz.* 21 Dec. 1/3 'It is a kind of grease that we keep in sticks.' (*Aside, to an attendant*: 'Just go and get a stick of paint.')

9. The stem of a culinary plant when trimmed for use, e.g. a root-stem of horse-radish; a root of celery with its blanched leaf-stems; a leaf-stem of rhubarb; a young shoot of asparagus.

a **1756** Mrs. Haywood *New Present* (1771) 53 A stick of horse-radish. **1872** Calverley *Fly Leaves* (1903) 14 To watch bronzed men and maidens crunch The sounding celery-stick. **1877** S. Hibberd *Amateur's Kitchen Gard.* 159 A plentiful supply of early sticks [of rhubarb]. **1882** W. Early *Profit. Market Gard.* 95 A bundle of celery, from eight to sixteen sticks. **1884** *Sutton's Culture Veget. & Fl.* (1885) 8 [Asparagus.] It is a matter of management merely, whether the sticks be blanched to the very tip, or [etc.].

10. Applied to various implements, either of the shape of a stick, or serving purposes for which a stick was originally used.

†**a.** A spoon. *Obs.*

c **1000** *Sax. Leechd.* III. 4 Nim ðry sticcan fulle on niht nihstiȝ. *a* **1225** *Ancr. R.* 370 þe on ber ase þauh hit were a letuarie, þe oðer ber enne sticke of gode gold. Vre Lefdi nome mid te sticke & dude iðe ones muðe þerof.

†**b.** A utensil for sprinkling holy water; more fully *holy water stick*. = aspergillum.

1415, 1552 [see holy water 2]. *c* **1450** *Reg. Vestments* etc. *St. Andrews* in *Maitl. Club Misc.* III. 203 Item ane haly wattyr fat of siluer with ane stik of the same for solemnit festis. **1543** *Invent. R. Wardr. Scot.* (1815) 112 Item ane halie watter fate with the stik of silver.

c. A support for a candle, a candlestick.

c **1540** in *Trans. Lond. & M'sex Archæol. Soc.* IV. 372 One styke of syluer p'sell gilt for the holy candell. **1832** Disraeli *Cont. Fleming* I. xii. 118 Many tall white candles, in golden sticks, illuminated the sacred table. **1895** *Church Q. Rev.* Apr. 253 The candles standing straight in their sticks.

d. = *composing-stick*: see composing *vbl. sb.* 2. *stick of letter(s*, a stickful of type. Also, in *Journalism*, a measure of copy, corresponding to about two column-inches.

1683 Moxon *Mech. Exerc., Printing* xx. ¶3 The Face of a Stick of Letter. *Ibid.*, The whole Stick of Letters..are screwzed together. *Ibid.* xxii. 332 With a Riglet fitted to the Stick, he presses the Letter to keep it straight in Line. **1820** T. Hodgson *Ess. Stereotype Printing* 106 *note*, All types have one or more nicks in their body, to serve as a guide to the compositor when arranging them in his stick. **1898** *Scribner's Mag.* May 579/1 He talked amiably enough; he said nothing he ought not to have said, but Linton [*sc.* a reporter] got five sticks out of it (a half column). **1907** *Scott. Typogr. Circular* Feb. 215/2, I find that nowadays, unless I read my sticks, it is impossible [etc.]. **1932** G. Greene *Stamboul Train* II. i. 44 They've asked me for a quarter of a column, but they'll cut it down to a couple of sticks. **1966** —— in *New Statesman* 25 Feb. 254/1 The ceremony could not possibly rate more than a couple of sticks in tomorrow's paper.

e. The hammer or mallet with which a dulcimer or drum is struck. Hence *pl.*, a nickname for a drummer (*Naval slang*).

1538 Elyot *Dict.*, *Pecten*.., it is also the stickes wherewith a man stryketh doulcemers whan he doeth playe on them. **1589-** [see drumstick]. **1926** *Melody Maker* Sept. 56 The tambourine is..played with the sticks. **1933** *Metronome* Oct. 51/2 Playing with the sticks widely separated on the head of the snare drum is a common fault. **1977** *Gay News* 24 Mar. 32/3 Drummer Rat Scabies (also 19) is very fast with the sticks.

1909 J. R. Ware *Passing Eng.* 234/1 *Sticks*,..drummer. **1916** 'Taffrail' *Carry On* 27 A drummer goes by the name of *sticks*, from the implements with which he beats his drum. **1950** Kerr & James *Wavy Navy* 263 *Sticks*, the ship's drummer.

f. A violin bow, a fiddlestick. †*a stick of fiddles*: ? a fiddler.

a **1600** T. Preston *Cambyses* F I b, They be at hand sir with stick and fiddle. *a* **1625** Fletcher *Woman's Prize* II. vi, *Jaq.* They have got a stick of Fiddles, and they firke it In wondrous waies. **1667** H. More *Div. Dial.* II. xviii. (1713) 145 As in a Musical Instrument, whose Strings are good, and the Stick good.

g. The melody pipe of a Highland bagpipe = chanter[1] 5.

1861 Mayhew *Lond. Labour* III. 167/2 My old chanter has..lost its tone; for when a stick gets too sharp a sound, it's never any good. *Ibid.*, My great grandfather played on this stick when Charley Stuart..came over to Scotland.

h. *pl.* The thin pieces of ivory, bone or other material upon which the folding material of a fan is mounted.

1701 *Lond. Gaz.* No. 3704/4 Lost.., an Italian Fan with Ivory painted Sticks. **1760-2** Goldsm. *Cit. World* xli, That old woman..who sits groaning behind the long sticks of a mourning fan. **1879** *Encycl. Brit.* IX. 28/1 The sticks [18th c.] were made of mother-of-pearl or ivory, carved with extraordinary skill.

i. = *joy-stick* s.v. joy *sb.* 10. Also occas., a gear lever in a motor vehicle.

1914 H. Rosher *Let.* 11 Aug. in *In R.N.A.S.* (1916) 13 Mr. Strutt, our instructor.., controls the engine switch and covers your hand on the stick. **1927** C. A. Lindbergh *We* v. 76 Pulling the stick back to go up. **1929** *Daily Express* 7 Nov. 1/1 On two occasions the pilot had to pull his stick back sharply, and once we only just cleared the tree tops. **1948** W. Fortescue *Beauty for Ashes* xxvii. 210 From their demeanour and that of the pilot, who handed 'the stick' over to a friend while he came to see that I was comfortable, one might almost have thought that this was my own private bomber. **1971** R. Dentry *Encounter at Kharmel* iii. 42 Pepper threw the gear stick into neutral, applied the handbrake firmly, switched off... She..moved the stick back to first. **1977** *R.A.F. Yearbk.* 31/1 The Hawk is very docile in the stall and..control is immediately regained once the stick is moved forward.

j. The propeller of an aircraft (*rare*). *dead stick*: see dead *a.* D. 2.

1917 *Editor* 21 Apr. 358 The propeller itself is generally known as the 'prop' or 'stick'.

k. = *ski stick* s.v. ski *sb.* 2 b.

1961 Webster, *Stick rider*, a skier who makes excessive use of ski poles. **1963** *Amer. Speech* XXXVIII. 207 *Sticks*,. .. Slang for skis, and also for ski poles. **1972** 'M. Yorke' *Silent Witness* ii. 14 He stacked his skis and sticks in..the rack. **1977** C. Wood *James Bond, Spy who loved Me* ii. 15 He stamped hard into his skis..and stabbed at the snow with his sticks.

l. *Surfing.* A surfboard.

1967 J. Severson *Great Surfing* Gloss., *Stick*, a surfboard. **1967** *Internat. Surfing* III. III. 29 Because of the lack of length when changing to a shorter board, different techniques from surfing a longer board are required. Margo Godfrey and Mike Purpus offer some helpful advice on adjusting to the short stick.

11. *slang.* **a.** A pistol; more explicitly *shooting stick*.

1788 Grose *Dict. Vulgar T.* (ed. 2), *Sticks*, pops or pistols. Stow your sticks; hide your pistols. **1834** Ainsworth *Rookwood* III. v, See how he flashes his sticks. **1890** 'R. Boldrewood' *Miner's Right* xvi, I always carry a brace of 'shooting sticks'.

†**b.** A sermon. *Obs. rare.*

1759 T. Boucher *Let. J. James* 7 Aug. (MS.), What matter of a new stick, vamp them one for next Sunday. **1762** *Ibid.* 5 Aug. (MS.), At sea, I drew up I believe ½ a dozen sticks—originals.

c. *Thieves' slang.* A jemmy or crowbar.

1879 *Macmillan's Mag.* Oct. 503/1 'What tools will you want?'.. He said, 'We shall want some twirls and the stick (crowbar)'. **1887** Horsley *Jottings fr. Jail* 11 We shall want some twirls and the stick (crowbar). **1890** *Daily News* 14 July 2/8 [He] took from his inside coat pocket a powerful jemmy, saying 'I suppose you don't want my stick.' **1934** P. Savage *Savage of Scotland Yard* xxiii. 252 It's a fair cop. I'll go quiet, and here's my stick (jemmy). **1960** [see loid].

d. *pl.* Furniture, household goods; more fully *sticks of furniture*. Rarely *sing.* in *every stick*, every article of furniture (cf. 3 b).

1809 Malkin *Gil Blas* VII. vii. (Rtldg.) 11 The moveables, not excepting my own apparel, every stick and every thread, had been carried off. **1823** 'Jon Bee' *Dict. Turf* s.v., I lost all my sticks by that 'ere fire at Stepney. **1864** Blackmore *Clara Vaughan* xxvi. (1872) 84 Her strange biographies of every table, chair, and cushion—her 'sticks', as she delighted to call them. **1867** *All Year Round* 13 July 55/1 The breaking up of the home, [and] the selling of 'the few sticks of furniture'.

e. *pl.* Legs.

1830 Marryat *King's Own* xxvi, He was so weak that he couldn't get up on his sticks again.

f. (Now *U.S.* and *colonial.*) *with a stick in it*: said of tea, coffee, etc., with a dash of brandy.

1804 R. Anderson *Cumbld. Ball.* (1808) 175 A quart o' het yell, and a stick in't. **1890** Mrs. C. Praed *Rom. of Station* vi, Have a parting drink for good luck—coffee, if you like, with a 'stick' in it... The waiter brought in coffee and cognac. **1892** F. M. Crawford *Three Fates* xiv, But you really do look dreadfully. Have some tea—with a stick in it, as papa calls it.

g. *the sticks*: a remote, thinly populated, rural area; the backwoods; hence, in extended (freq. depreciatory) use, any area that is off the beaten track or thought to be provincial or unsophisticated; esp. in phr. *in the sticks*. orig. *U.S.*

1905 N. Davis *Northerner* 78 Billy is a cane-brake nigger; he'll take to the sticks like a duck to water when he's scared. **1914** R. Lardner in *Sat. Even. Post* 7 Mar. 8/1, I will have to slip you back to the sticks [i.e. the minor baseball leagues]. **1921** *Daily Colonist* (Victoria, B.C.) 22 Oct. 11/3 Judge Landis..has not yet consigned Babe Ruth to oblivion for.. playing in the sticks for exhibition money. **1926** Whiteman & McBride *Jazz* xiii. 254 They had..all the real New Yorker's prejudice against 'the sticks'. **1936** J. Dos Passos *Big Money* 61 Mighty nice of you to ask me. I been out in the sticks... It makes you feel good to see folks from the other side... This is the nearest thing to Paree I've seen for some time. **1941** W. C. Handy *Father of Blues* (1957) ix. 126, I continued..playing for dances, touring on the road and through the sticks and giving concerts. **1958** C. Koch *Boys in Island* 101 What can y' expect, way out here in the sticks? You would pick on a dame from back of beyond. **1968** J. Lock *Lady Policeman* ix. 79 Where's that? I know, it's somewhere in the sticks. **1971** *N.Z. Listener* 27 Sept. 3/2 The 'real' New Zealand..is out there in the sticks, under the open sky, where men have dirt on their elbows. **1974** *New Society* 7 Feb. 309/1 The idea of 'provincial' journalists working 'out in the sticks' has strong pejorative overtones. **1977** C. MacInnes *City of Spades* I. v. 28 ... **1977** *Daily Express* 29 Jan. 39/2 More fighting talk came from Swindon striker Dave Syrett. 'Most people regard us as a bunch of farmers from out in the sticks,' he said.

h. A cigarette or cigar; *spec.*, a cigarette made with marijuana; also *stick of tea, weed* (cf. tea *sb.* 7 c, weed *sb.*[1] 3 c). See also *cancer stick* s.v. cancer *sb.* 5, *Thai stick* s.v. Thai *a.*

1919 W. H. Downing *Digger Dialects* 17 *Consumption stick*, a cigarette. **1935** E. Farjeon *Nursery in Nineties* 348 Papa..smokes all day long, but only affords himself the cheapest..sticks, except when Aunt Mary Albery sends him a hundred Coronas for Christmas. **1938** [see Mary 1 d]. **1940** R. Chandler *Farewell, my Lovely* xiv. 68 Evidence of what? That a man occasionally smoked a stick of tea, a man who looked as if any touch of the exotic would appeal to him. **1957** C. MacInnes *City of Spades* I. v. 28 'I'll roll you a stick.'.. I lit up... 'Good stuff. And what do they make you pay for a stick here?' **1959** L. Lipton *Holy Barbarians* iii. 78 Rolling their sticks of 'tea', they looked like a ring of kindergarteners. **1965** W. Soyinka *Road* 24 Say Tokyo reaches out a stick of weed to him which he accepts behind his back. **1978** T. Williamson *Technicians of Death* xiv. 121 He got his first 'buzz' with a blend of Thai stick and opium.

12. **a.** Applied, with qualifying adj., to a person, orig. with figurative notion of sense 2 or 4, as *tough stick*; *crooked* (Sc. *thrawn*) *stick*, a perverse, cross-grained person.

1682 N. O. *Boileau's Lutrin* II. 164 That tough stick of Wood, Boirude the Sexton. **1785** *Span. Rivals* 8 He's a queer stick to make a thivel on. **1833** Hood *Publ. Dinner* 15 A stick of a Chairman, A little dark spare man. **1839** A. Gray *Lett.* (1893) 223 He is a queer stick altogether. **1846-8** Lowell *Biglow P.* Ser. I. ix. 35 So, ez I aint a crooked stick, ..I'll go back to my plough. **1859** *Hotten's Slang Dict.* 102 'A rum' or 'odd stick', a curious man. **1886** J. R. Rees *Pleas. Book-Worm* v. 178 Some disagreeable old stick has probably eaten an enormous dinner [etc.]. **1893** Crockett *Stickit Minister* 30 Tammas Carlyle, thrawn stick as he was. **1897** W. Dyke *Craiktrees* ii, He's nobbit twenty-two—young—a verra young stick.

b. A 'wooden' person; one lacking in capacity for his work, or in geniality of manner; *Theatr.* an indifferent actor.

1800 Miss Edgeworth *Belinda* xx, And you, out of patience,..will go and marry..some stick of a rival. **1801** W. Burton *Pasquinade* 11 He's not a bad actor, though they call him a stick. **1820** Byron *Blues* I. 89 *Tracy.* In Prose My talent is decent, as far as it goes; But in rhyme——. *Inkel.* You're a terrible stick, to be sure. **1820** L. Hunt *Indicator* No. 33 (1822) I. 257 A habit..of calling insipid things and persons sticks... A poor stick, a mere stick, a stick of a fellow. **1856** Olmsted *Slave States* 83 He had had to hire white men to help him, but they were poor sticks and would be half the time drunk. **1873** *Punch* 15 Nov. 202/1 Charles Kemble was rather a stick at first, and was made a great artist by..close study. **1883** M. Pattison *Mem.* i. (1885) 23 Though the tutors..were first class men, yet the tuition was not esteemed good... Tommy Churton I afterwards came to know as a 'stick'. **1899** Kernahan *Scoundrels & Co.* xxi, To a good fellow, the right hand of fellowship is readily extended. The 'stick' will find himself as readily cold-shouldered.

c. *U.S. slang.* = shill *sb.*

1926 Maines & Grant *Wise-Crack Dict.* 14/1 *Stick*, a confederate who wins or loses at dealer's will. **1931** G. Irwin *Amer. Tramp & Underworld Slang* 182 The cash the 'stick' wins is handed back to the operator of the game..and the stick never has enough of his employer's money to make it worth his while to decamp. **1966** E. V. Cunningham *Helen* (1967) ix. 129 A shill is also called a stick, and the role of the shill or stick is to make the customer relax and feel at ease.

†**13.** Some measure of land: ? = staff *sb.*

1664 *Terrier of Westborne, Sussex* (MS.), One other Plott ..which James Sowter renteth of him..conteyneth about half a Stick of Land. Item one other Plott of Land.. conteyneth about a quarter of a Stick of ground.

14. *Mil.* **a.** A number (usu. five or six) of bombs dropped in quick succession from an aircraft.

1940 *Illustr. London News* 18 May 669 (*caption*) A 'stick' of five bombs has just burst across her bows. **1940** *Times* 6 Dec. 4/1 Seeing a convoy in the road, we dropped a stick plumb in the centre of it. **1942** *Tee Emm* (Air Ministry) II. 100 If you, as bomb aimer..watch a stick of bombs on a town you'll notice that they appear to move outwards... When they hit they form a *curved* stick. **1956** W. Slim *Defeat into Victory* VI. xxi. 500 British officers, watching from the ground the fall of each stick of bombs. **1975** T. Allbeury *Special Collection* iv. 18 There were dull thuds as another stick of bombs was dropped.

b. A group of parachutists jumping in quick succession.

1943 *Combined Operations* (Min. of Information) ii. 19 They [*sc.* airborne troops] practise dropping from an aircraft, first in 'slow' then in 'quick' pairs, until they are proficient enough to drop in 'sticks'. **1949** F. Maclean *Eastern Approaches* III. ix. 414, I had decided to jump first with the others following in a 'stick'. **1955** J. Thomas *No Banners* xiv. 127 The despatcher yelled hysterically: 'Now, a nice stick of three!' **1974** C. Ryan *Bridge Too Far* III. iii. 156 As the pilot held it steady on course, Mitchell saw the entire stick of paratroopers jump right through the fire. **1982** *Times* 5 June 4/6 The 15 marines in our 'stick' jumped through the [helicopter] door..with weapons ready.

III. **15.** Figurative phrases of various origins. (Chiefly slang or colloquial.)

a. *to play a good stick*: said of a fiddler (see sense 10). In later use *gen.* to play one's part well. So *to fire a good stick* (Shooting).

1748 SMOLLETT *Rod. Rand.* ix, You hear he plays a good stick. **1809** T. DONALDSON *Poems* 183 He handl'd his Rammy so terribly quick The folks all declar'd that 'he play'd a good stick'. **1824** W. IRVING *Tales Trav., Bold Dragoon* (1848) 25 He could swear a good stick himself. **1842** BELLEW *Mem. Griffin* xx, The captain..fired a capital *good stick* nevertheless, and knocked the birds about, right and left, in great style. **1867** E. WAUGH *Tufts of Heather* Ser. I. (1893) 188 The hungry travellers sat down. For about half-an-hour every man of the three 'played a good stick', as the old saying goes.

†**b.** Slang. *to be high up the stick*: to stand high in one's profession.

1818 SIR C. MORGAN in Lady Morgan *Autobiog.* (1859) 295 All my acquaintance among the doctors are so high up the stick, they have no time to spare to answer inquiries.

c. *to beat* (rarely *knock*) *all to sticks*, to overcome or surpass completely. *to go to sticks*, more emphatically *to go to sticks and staves*, to be ruined.

1820 *Blackw. Mag.* VIII. 85 Which in the west country beats our stot-beef here all to sticks. **1824** MISS FERRIER *Inherit.* ix, She married a Highland drover, or tacksman, I can't tell which, and they went all to sticks and staves. **1840** THACKERAY *Barber Cox* Apr., When I came to know his game, I used to knock him all to sticks; or, at least, win six games to his four. *c* **1842** CARLYLE in A. Bain *Autobiog.* (1904) 126 All that I could gather was that the Church of Christ was going to sticks. **1859** LEVER *Dav. Dunn* lxxvi. 669 It's as good as a play to hear about this,..it beats Newmarket all to sticks.

d. Sporting slang. *to shoot for the stick*, i.e. for the total amount of game shot as distinguished from 'for sport'. (Cf. 1 b.)

1834 *New Monthly Mag.* XLI. 288 In a battue..the shooting is *for the stick*, as it is technically phrased—not for the pleasure, but the pride of the murderer of hecatombs.

e. (*to have* or *get*) *the right* or *the wrong end of the stick*: to have the advantage or the contrary in a bargain or a contest. Also, *to have got hold of the wrong end of the stick*: to have got a story wrong, not know the facts of the case. Also with other adjectives. (Sense 4.)

1846 *Swell's Night Guide* 49 Which of us had hold of the crappy..end of the stick? **1890** 'R. BOLDREWOOD' *Col. Reformer* (1891) 249 If you happen to have the arrangement of a bargain..with the rural Australian, you will rarely find that the apparently impassive countryman has 'got the wrong end of the stick'. **1897** BEATTY *Secretar* xiii. 100, I was more convinced than ever..that I had the right end of the stick. **1930** E. WAUGH *Vile Bodies* viii. 143 My private schoolmaster used to say, 'If a thing's worth doing at all, it's worth doing well.'.. But these young people have got hold of another end of the stick, and for all we know it may be the right one. They say, 'If a thing's not worth doing well, it's not worth doing at all.' **1934** C. DAY LEWIS *Hope for Poetry* vii. 42 Although Lewis's analysis convinces us..as being correct in detail, we are compelled to feel that Lawrence rather than Lewis had got hold of the right end of the stick. **1939** 'G. ORWELL' *Coming up for Air* IV. vii. 283 Listen, Hilda. You've got hold of the wrong end of the stick about this business. **1959** 'M. CRONIN' *Dead & done With* iv. 61 I've had the rough end of the stick ever since I got here. **1977** P. SCOTT *Staying On* (1978) i. 14 Always..I have the mucky end of the stick. But then I am only part of the fixtures and fittings.

f. *to hold the sticks to*, *to hold sticks with*: to compete on equal terms with.

a **1817** W. MUIR *Poems* (1818) 58 (E.D.D.) Nae kitten, fam'd for fun an' tricks, Can to the weasel ha'd the sticks. **1853** READE *Love me Little* I. viii. 232 If I began by despising my business..how should I ever hold sticks with my able competitors?

g. *to keep* (one) *at the stick's end*: to keep at a distance, treat with reserve.

1886 STEVENSON *Kidnapped* viii, The captain, though he kept me at the stick's end the most part of the time, would sometimes unbuckle a bit and tell me of the fine countries he had visited.

h. Used to give additional emphasis in several alliterative phrases, as *stick, stark, staring* = absolutely, completely, downright. Cf. 3 c.

1839 HOOD *Lost Heir* 23, I shall go stick stark staring wild! **1892** MRS. H. WARD *David Grieve* I. iv, Aunt Hannah 'll be stick stock mad wi' boath on us. **1909** W. J. LOCKE *Septimus* 330 Now he had gone stick, stark, staring, raving, biting mad.

i. *up the stick*: pregnant. *slang.* Cf. *up the pole* s.v. POLE *sb.*[1] 1 b.

1941 BAKER *Dict. Austral. Slang* 71 *Stick, up the*: (of a girl or woman) to be pregnant. **1958** [see BUN *sb.*[2] 1]. **1968** R. LAIT *Chance to Kill* i. 10 Mary up the stick; funny how everyone counts the months. **1976** J. I. M. STEWART *Memorial Service* ix. 160 Do you know what it's like, Cyril, to be a decent and penniless young man who isn't sure he hasn't got his girl up the stick?

j. *to cut one's stick*: see CUT *v.* 44; *more than you can shake a stick at*: see SHAKE *v.* 5 b.

IV. *attrib.* and *Comb.*

16. a. simple attrib., as *stick fire, point*; (sense 8) as *stick cinnamon, liquorice, metal, phosphorus, pomatum, rhubarb*; (sense 10) *microphone, mike*; **b.** objective, as *stick-cutting, -rubbing*; *stick-dresser, -maker*; instrumental, as *stick-blow*; *stick-built* adj.; similative, as *stick-like, -shaped* adjs.

1886 R. F. BURTON *Arab. Nts.* I. 242 *note*, They..cut off the ear-lobes, gave ten *stick-blows. **1841** *Penny Cycl.* XX. 148/2 The *stick-built nest contains four..eggs. **1668** G. HARTMAN *Digby's Receipts Physick* etc. 15, 5 pennyworth of *stick Cinnamon. **1883** F. M. PEARD *Contradictions* xviii, Leaving Gina to watch the progress of Jim's *stick-cutting. **1890** *Daily News* 22 Oct. 7/7 A *stick-dresser was committed for trial on a charge of wounding [etc.]. **1808** ELEANOR SLEATH *Bristol Heiress* IV. 12 Dame Jenkinson was sitting by the blaze of a *stick fire. **1831** TRELAWNY *Adv. Younger Son* III. 292 A stoical apathy of look, that..the most *stick-like lords..would have envied. **1806–7** J. BERESFORD *Miseries Hum. Life* (1826) Post. Groans No. 29 Some long-forgotten bonbon of your boyhood..*stick-liquorice,..&c. **1803** *Censor* 1 Apr. 39 Mr. Huntsmill, the *stick maker of Whitechapel. **1900** HASLUCK *Model! Engin. Handybk.* 67 This nut is best turned from a piece of *stick metal. **1961** C. WILLOCK *Death in Covert* xii. 212 The interviewer from ITN..was holding a *stick microphone. **1976** B. JACKSON *Flameout* (1977) IV. xii. 204 He saw him [*sc.* the pilot] speak into the stick microphone attached to his headset. **1961** *Listener* 19 Oct. 622/3 Uncle Dimbleby is seated (with *stick mike) among a 'representative cross-section' of the British public. **1849** D. CAMPBELL *Inorg. Chem.* 21 The sixth part of an inch of *stick phosphorus. **1905** A. T. SHEPPARD *Red Cravat* II. ii. 60 Tossing the clothes to one side of the room with her *stick-point. **1858** SIMMONDS *Dict. Trade*, *Bandoline*, a kind of *stick pomatum. **1840** PEREIRA *Mat. Med.* 814 *Stick rhubarb..is said..to be obtained from Rheum undulatum. **1841** *Penny Cycl.* XIX. 451/1 Stick rhubarb is sold in the herb shops, and is in long pieces. **1912** *Contemp. Rev.* June 900 Fire was obtained by *stick-rubbing. **1857** HENFREY *Bot.* 586 A kind of minute *stick-shaped corpuscle.

17. Special comb.: **stick-and-carrot** *adj. phr.* [see CARROT *sb.* 2 a], characterized by both the threat of punishment and the offer of reward; **stick-back** *a.*, designating a kind of wooden chair having a back formed by upright rods or sticks; **stickball** *U.S.*, a game played with stick and ball; *spec.* (*a*) improvised baseball played with a stick and soft ball; (*b*) an American Indian ball game resembling lacrosse, played by the Indians of the South-eastern U.S.; **stick bean**, a runner bean; **stick-bomb**, a bomb or grenade with a protruding rod or stick for firing or throwing (cf. also STICK *v.*[1] 35); **stick-bug** *U.S.* (*a*) = *stick-insect*; (*b*) a predaceous reduvioid bug, *Emesa longipes* (Cent. Dict. 1891); **stick-caterpillar**, a larva resembling a stick; **stick chair**, a sedan chair; **stick chimney** *U.S.*, a log-house chimney composed of sticks piled up crosswise and cemented with mud or clay; **stick-cover, -covert** (see quot. 1854); **stick-dam** (see quot.); **stick dance**, any of various kinds of folk-dance in which the dancer holds a stick and (in some dances) beats it against the sticks of other dancers; **stick-dressing**, the art of making shepherd's crooks (cf. *stick-dresser*, sense 16 b); **stick-fighting** *W. Indies*, a kind of martial art; hence **stick-fighter**; **stick-figure**, a matchstick figure (see *matchstick* (*c*) s.v. MATCH *sb.*[2] 5), a pin-man; **stick fixed** *Aeronaut.*, the control column of an air-craft held in one position; freq. *attrib.*; **stick-flour** (see quot.); **stick force** *Aeronaut.*, the force or effort needed to move the control column of an aircraft or hold it in position; **stick free** *Aeronaut.*, the control column of an aircraft allowed to move freely, unguided by the pilot; freq. *attrib.*; **stick (hand-)grenade**, a grenade with a handle; **stick-handling** *vbl. sb.* orig. and chiefly *N. Amer.*, the handling of one's stick in ice hockey (or occas. in other sports) (cf. *stick-work* (*a*)); also fig.; hence (as back-formation) **stick-handle** *v. intr.*, to control the puck (in ice hockey) with one's stick; also **stick-handler**; **stick-heap**, an artificial fox-covert made of sticks (cf. *stick-cover*); **stick-helmet**, a mask with additional guards for the forehead and head, used in cudgel-play (*Cent. Dict.*); **stick holder** (see quot.); **Stick Indian** *Canad. colloq.*, a member of the North American Indian peoples inhabiting the forests of British Columbia and the Yukon [properly a loan transl. of Chinook Jargon *stick siwash* forest Indian, a term used by the Coast Indians for those of the interior in this area.]; **stick-insect**, any insect of the family *Phasmidæ*, from its resemblance to the branches and twigs of the trees in which it is found; **stick loaf**: occas. used = *French stick*, sense 8 f above; **stick-man**, (*a*) *slang*, a pick-pocket's accomplice (cf. *stick slinger*); (*b*) *U.S. colloq.*, a croupier; (*c*) *W. Indies* = *stick-fighter* above; (*d*) *rare* = *stick-figure* above; **stick mounter**, a workman employed to affix the mounts of walking-sticks; **stick-net**, a small net run upon a ring fixed at the end of a stick; **stick-pile** †(*a*) = HERON'S BILL; (*b*) = *stick-heap*; **stick-play**, play with cudgel or single-stick; so also **stick-player**; **stick-pot** *U.S.*, a lobster-pot constructed of laths or narrow strips of wood; **stick-shaker** *Aeronaut. colloq.*, a device which causes the control column to vibrate when the aircraft is close to stalling; **stick shift** *N. Amer.*, a manually operated mechanism for changing gear; a gear lever; **stick-sling**, a sling in the form of a stick with a cleft at one end in which the stone to be thrown was placed; **stick slinger** *slang* (see quot.); **sticktail** *U.S.* (*Long Island*), the ruddy duck *Erismatura rubida*, characterized by having narrow and rigid tailfeathers; **stickwork**, (*a*) in various ball games, the management of the bat or club; (*b*) something made from, or fashioned by the use of, sticks. Also STICKLAC.

1963 *Times* 4 Mar. 11/7 President Ayub has..given himself *stick-and-carrot powers to deal with the 'Ebdonians'. **1977** 'J. LE CARRÉ' *Hon. Schoolboy* vi. 136 It's a stick and carrot job. If you don't play, the comic will blow the whistle on you... That's the *bad* news... The good news is five hundred US into your hot little hand. **1783** *Narragansett Hist. Reg.* (1884) II. 314 Three good large Windsor or *Stickback Chairs. **1923** *Heal & Son Catal: Kitchen Furniture* 2 Unpolished Stickback Windsor Small Chair..12/6. **1963** *Guardian* 21 Aug. 6/6 A pale oak gate-leg table is set off by six flame stick-back chairs. **1978** *Cornish Guardian* 27 Apr. 10/4 (Advt.), Swivel chairs,..wheel back and stick back chairs, easy chairs[, etc.]. **1824** *Nantucket Inquirer* 12 Jan. 3/5 No person shall play Foot-ball or Poke, *Stick-ball or Swinger, within the compact part of the Town of Nantucket. **1934** E. NEWHOUSE *You can't sleep Here* xii. 154 Two contending stickball teams left the gutter to see what was up. **1946** *Life* 11 Nov. 91/1 On the Cherokees' Qualla Indian Reservation in North Carolina..the Wolftown Wolves met the Wolftown Bears in a crucial game of stickball... The game of stickball, which is a primitive version of modern lacrosse, was centuries old when De Soto led a Spanish expedition through Cherokee territory in 1540. **1947** *Commentary* May 464/1 Sometimes we became so engrossed by a punchball or stickball game that night would fall without anyone's being aware of it. **1953** *Sun* (Baltimore) 1 Apr. (B. ed.) 12/1 Governor McKeldin can remember romping barefooted in the neighborhood, playing stickball. **1979** *United States 1980/81* (Penguin Travel Guides) 533 A recreation of an early-18th-century Cherokee Village, where Cherokees in costume dance, play at stickball, work at crafting baskets, [etc.]. **1981** *TV Picture Life* Mar. 32/1 A group of young black children playing stickball on the streets of New York. **1906** *Dialect Notes* III. 158 **Stick bean*,..pole bean. **1980** J. GARDAM *Sidmouth Lett.* 134 D'you want some beans?.. Stick beans? **1916** in C. F. S. Gamble *Story N. Sea Air Station* (1928) xiii. 222 The silent firing of projectiles varying in size from the Mills grenade to the 250-lb. *stick bomb. **1925** FRASER & GIBBONS *Soldier & Sailor Words* 270 *Stick-bomb*, a type of trench-mortar bomb attached to a hollow steel rod which passed down the bore of the projectile. **1940** *Illustr. London News* 10 Feb. 167/1 A charge with 'stick-bombs'—a form of hand grenade. *Ibid.* 167/2 (*caption*) The patrol reaches the enemy lines, overwhelming them with the threat of 'stick-bombs'. **1894** *Harper's Mag.* Feb. 456 'Witches' horses,'.. which in some other States are dubbed '*stick-bugs'.., our Diapheromera femorata. **1898** MORRIS *Austral Eng.* 349 The various species [of the family *Phasmidæ*] are known as Leaf-insects, Walking-leaves, *Stick-caterpillars [etc.]. **1908** MARY JOHNSTON *Lewis Rand* i. 11 Coach and chaise, curricle and *stick-chair, were encountered. **1846** MRS. KIRKLAND *West. Clearings* 7 The house was..of the roughest;..its *stick chimney, so like its owner's hat, open at the top, and jammed in at the sides. **1897** *Encycl. Sport* I. 550/2 (Hunting) *Stick covers and faggot covers [for foxes]. **1854** MISS BAKER *Northampt. Gloss.*, **Stick-covert*, a plat of ground stuck with thorns to make a fox-cover. **1897** *Encycl. Sport* I. 550/1 (Hunting) Foxes..found in gorse and stick coverts are often short runners. **1884** *Evang. Mag.* May 214 The other kind of [beaver's] dam is the '*stick-dam', consisting of sticks and poles. **1899** KIPLING *From Sea to Sea* II. xxv. 12 A Zanzibar *stick-dance, such as you see at Aden on the coal boats. **1907** SHARP & MACILWAINE *Morris Bk.* I. 39 In the Stick and Handkerchief dances, pairs.. stand near enough to clap hands or tap sticks with each other. **1950** BLESH & JANIS *They All played Ragtime* (1958) 13 The banjo-ragtime rhythms of dances like the buck and wing, the Virginia Essence, the stick and the sand dances, and the soft-shoe routines. **1982** N. PAINTING *Reluctant Archer* vii. 113, I was also roped in..to play the piano for rehearsals of the stick dance which David Raeburn had introduced into his production of *The Shoemaker's Holiday*. **1968** P. JENNINGS *Living Village* 187 *Stick-dressing..is the making of shepherds' crooks. A stick is dressed down, a ram's horn is put on top of it and the whole thing is polished. **1956** *Caribbean Q.* IV. III & IV. 194 Later this aristocrat's masque was adopted by batonyé or *stick fighters. **1968** E. LOVELACE *Schoolmaster* i. 12 'Who say that?' Miguel asked hotly, growing angry, and moving up and down like a stickfighter in a rage. **1956** *Caribbean Q.* IV. III. & IV. 192 Antagonisms are relaxed from time to time by fêtes, when the traditional pastimes of dancing, singing and *stick-fighting are enjoyed, with liquor and food. **1974** *Trinidad Guardian* 2 Nov. 5/2 (Advt.), African culture in all forms. Dance, Stick-fighting, Drumming, Calypso, [etc.]. **1965** I. A. RICHARDS in *Times Lit. Suppl.* 27 May 439/2 A *stick-figure man is very different from any man but *is* a little like his silhouette or his shadow on a screen. **1976** *New Yorker* 9 Feb. 94/3 Weiss projects no character, he remains a stick figure. **1978** S. SHELDON *Bloodline* xxiv. 259 He was like a stick figure drawn by a child, with angular arms and legs, and a dry, unfinished face sketched on top of his body. **1945** *Jrnl. R. Aeronaut. Soc.* XLIX. 617/2 The stick movements the pilot has to make to control the aircraft are related to the *stick fixed stability, while the stick forces he has to exert are related to the stick free stability. **1961** A. W. BABISTER *Aircraft Stability & Control* iii. 63 The stick fixed static margin is related to the elevator movement (or stick movement) to trim the aircraft. **1858** SIMMONDS *Dict. Trade*, **Stick-flour*, a Brazilian name for cassava meal. **1937** *Jrnl. R. Aeronaut. Soc.* XLI. 960 The *stick forces required to operate them [*sc.* flaps] increased too rapidly with speed. **1942** *Tee Emm* (Air Ministry) II. 85 The stick force needed, say, to take violent avoiding action may be much too great. **1961** A. W. BABISTER *Aircraft Stability & Control* iii. 63 We shall now derive the relation between the stick force the pilot has to apply to hold the aircraft in a glide and the stick free static margin. **1983** E. BROWN *Wings of Weird & Wonderful* xvi. 100 The latter aircraft was the less pleasant to fly as the stick continually hunted either side of neutral, and there was no build up in stick force with increase in speed. **1945** *Stick free [see *stick fixed* above]. **1961** Stick free [see *stick force* above]. **1918** E. S. FARROW *Dict. Mil. Terms* 586 **Stick grenade*, a grenade attached to a stick and thrown over short distances like a dart. **1979** O. SELA *Petrograd Consignment* 53 Boris..took out two stick grenades and a Mills bomb. **1923** *Stick hand-grenade [see HAIRBRUSH 2. **1929** *N.Y. Times* 10 Mar. XII. 8/1 Trottier staged a prize play when he *stickhandled his way through the entire American team. **1969** M. BRAITHWAITE *Never sleep Three in Bed* (1970) xv. 182 Back in 1926, he really couldn't skate very well, but he could stick-handle like a fiend. **1915** *Official Ice Hockey Guide* 17 Hill of Cornell..is very fast, a good *stick handler. **1958** *Rosetown* (Saskatchewan) *Eagle* 29 May 10/1 Dick.. Elliot, plugger type, stick handler, back-bone of the team. **1904** *Ice Hockey & Ice Polo Guide* 35 *Stick-handling, like confidence, coolness, strength and speed, is acquired by practice... The better you can handle your stick the more effective player you will be, because stick-handling is one of the essentials of the game. **1962** *Times* 28 Feb. 4/4 Cool lacrosse at Cambridge... Cambridge..played calmly, showing glimpses of..skilful stick-handling. **1976** *Ottawa Citizen* 24 Dec. 2/3 They did some nifty stickhandling through government red tape. **1898** *Westm. Gaz.* 28 Sept. 4/3 *Stick heaps..when judiciously placed..seldom fail to hold foxes. **1901** E. A. PRATT *Notable Masters* 44 [Josiah Mason] also did a large business in making cedar-wood pen-holders, or '*stick-holders'. [**1869** L. SMITH *Let.* 30 Oct. in *Rep. Indian Affairs 1969* (U.S.) (1870) 567 Twice a year most of the Indians make a trip up the Stikine River to Talyan, at which place the Stick tribe reside.] **1885** F. SCHWATKA *Rep. Mil. Reconn. Alaska 1883* 76 The so-called '*Stick' Indians of the interior are seen in the villages near the trading stores. **1887** G. M. DAWSON *Notes on Indian Tribes of Yukon* 14 They are classed with the 'Stick Indians', by the coast tribes. **1963** R. SYMONS *Many Trails* vii. 72 Snowshoes are known only as a strange accoutrement of the 'Stick Indians'. **1854** A. ADAMS etc. *Man. Nat. Hist.* 210 *Stick-Insects (Phasmidæ). **1882** *Cassell's Nat. Hist.* VI. 130 Most of them resemble sticks, either green, growing twigs, or brown and withered branches, and hence the names of Stick-insects and Walking-sticks. **1980** *Times* 15 Dec. 1/8 Britons returned home with..wines, *stick loaves and under-ripe Camemberts. **1861** J. BINNY in H. Mayhew *London Labour* Extra Vol. (1862) 282/2 While drinking at the bar, one of the women tries to rob him... A man who is called a '*stickman', an accomplice..of hers, comes to the bar... If they have by this time secured the booty, it is passed to the latter, who thereupon slips away. **1931** *Amer. Speech* VII. 116 *Stick-man*,..a croupier in a gambling joint. **1952** *Evening News* (Port of Spain, Trinidad) 28 Jan. 8/2 A Trinidad stickman held his stick at both ends when going into action. **1958** *Newark* (New Jersey) *Star-Ledger* 23 Mar. 102/4 Then the stickman rakes in the dice, picks them up, and tosses them back to the shooter. **1966** J. DOS PASSOS *Best Times* ii. 47, I sent Arthur a cartoon..of warmongers.. hanging from the arc lights on Fifth Avenue, while two stickmen..danced the carmagnole in the foreground. **1975** [see POGUE]. **1980** J. SCOTT *Hunted* i. 8 He shoved the counters forward and the stickman flicked them into place. **1895** *Daily Chron.* 28 Aug. 8/4 *Stick Mounters wanted. **1862** CARPENTER *Microscope* (ed. 3) §394 *a*. 640 Among other animals captured by the *stick net, the marine Zoologist will be not unlikely to meet with..the Tomopteris. **1597** GERARDE *Herbal* Suppl., *Stike pile is Storkes bil. **1895** *Leamington Spa Courier* 14 Mar., in Mordaunt & Verney *Ann. Warwicksh. Hunt* (1896) II. 289 The next resort was to the noted stick-pile at Napton, where a fox..was at home. **1891** *Century Dict.* *Stick-play. **1886** *Pall Mall Gaz.* 29 Dec. 2/2 The professional boxer, wrestler, or *stick-player. **1887** G. B. GOODE *Fish. Industr. U.S.* v. II. 666 Other names by which they [lobster traps] are known to the fishermen are..'*stick-pots', and 'lath-coops'. **1962** *Flight Internat.* LXXXI. 330/1 At 70 kt the *stick shaker rattled again, but there was still plenty of aileron control. **1979** *Daily Tel.* 9 Aug. 7/2 The F.A.A. has proposed that an additional 'stick-shaker' be installed to warn the pilot when the plane loses enough speed and lift to approach a stall. **1960** *Wall St. Jrnl.* 13 Oct. 26 (Advt.), 'Welcome back, standard transmission.'.. A great majority of those who buy sports cars specify the '*stick shift' for the fun of it. **1976** 'E. MCBAIN' *Guns* (1977) vii. 200 Bucket seats in beige leather, stick shift on the floor. **1872** J. EVANS *Anc. Stone Impl.* xviii. 375 This flat lenticular form [of stone] is better adapted for the *stick-sling than a pebble. **1856** MAYHEW *Gt. World London* 46 Thieves, who admit of being classified as follows:—..'bludgers' or '*stick slingers', who rob in company with low women. **1909** *Westm. Gaz.* 11 Jan. 12/4 The outstanding feature of the game was the wonderful ..*stickwork of the..outside right. **1923** KIPLING *Irish Guards in Great War* I. 164 They [*sc.* the trenches] had been French..and [were] riveted with strange French stickwork. **1929** B. OLIVER *Cottages of England* iii. 44 The pricked treatment.., as also the scratched patterns, were equally the common finish to cottage exteriors all over Suffolk and Essex. Nothing looks better than this delightful Essex 'stickwork'. **1933** B. RACKHAM *Guide to Ital. Maiolica* i. 5 Lead-glazed earthenware with decoration done..by scratching with a pointed instrument..through a surface layer of..'slip'... Wares of this kind are..called..*sgraffito*. .. The phrase *a stecco* ('stickwork') is generally used..in referring to this process. **1977** *Penguin Dict. Decorative Arts* 759/1 *Stickwork*. Small objects such as chess-men, egg-cups, snuff-boxes, etc. made from sticks of various types of wood assembled by the same technique as in Tunbridge ware and then turned on a lathe.

stick (stɪk), *sb.*[2] *Obs.* exc. *Hist.* Forms: 4 **styk(e**, 5 **steke**, 6 **sticke**, **stykke**, 7– **stick**. [First in the Anglo-L. forms *stica*, *sticha*, *sticka*, *estika*; it is not clear whether the word thus latinized was English (= STICK *sb.*[1]) or OF. **estike* from a continental form of the same word.

Cf. MLG. *sticke* in 'xx sticken anguillarum' (*Werden Tax Roll*). The use no doubt arose from the practice of carrying a number of eels on a stick passed through the gills.]

A measure of quantity in small eels (app. twenty-five or twenty-six). Also Comb. ***stick-eel***, an eel of small size.

1086 *Domesday Bk.* (1783) I. 1 In Linnuartlest in brisennei habet rex consuetudinem . scilicet . ii . caretas . & ii . sticas anguillarum. *Ibid.* 155 Piscator redd .xxx. stichas anguillarum. **1244** *Liberate Roll* Nov. 28, Quod..emi faciat ...x. milia stickarum anguillarum bone salicionis. **1290** in *Archæologia* XV. 352 Pro v. estik' anguill' ij[s]. **1390–1** *Earl Derby's Exped.* (Camden) 20 Et per manus Thome Fyssher pro xlviij styks anguillarum. *Ibid.* 29 Pro j styke di. anguillarum, xiiij d. **1343** *Durham Acc. Rolls* (Surtees) 39 In 260 Stykell et anguill. grossis, 3s. 6d. **1481–90** *Howard Househ. Bks.* (Roxb.) 143 For vj. stekes of smale elle xxvj. to the steke ij.s. vj.d. **1510–11** *Durham Acc. Rolls* (Surtees) 661 Preter 12 lupos aquaticos et duos stickes anguillarum. **1664** SPELMAN *Gloss.* s.v. *Brochus*, A stick of Eels. **1715** *B.N.C. Muniments* 20. 28, *Kent* (MS.), [Tenant to have] the yearly dues of days of work, sticks of eeles, eggs, hens, Cocks,..and plowsheards. *a* **1728** [see BIND *sb.* 5].

† **stick**, *sb.*[3] *Obs.* Forms: 5 **stic**, **styc**, 5–6 **stik**, (5 **styke**), 6–7 **stick**, (6 **styck**), 7 **sticke**; *Sc.* 5–7 **steik**, 5 **stek**, (**steke**, 6 **steyk**, **styk**). [a. Flem. *stik*, *stuk*, = Du. *stuk*, G. *stück* piece.]

1. The customary length (varying according to the material) of a 'piece' or roll of certain textile fabrics imported from Flanders.

1476 in *Acta Audit.* (1839) 55/2 Twa stikkis of blak schamlot. **1489** *Acc. Ld. High Treas. Scot.* I. 136 Item,..for a steik of black chamlot to be a galbert to the King, price vj li. **1493** in *Acta Audit.* (1839) 180/2 A stik of grene sating contenand xxvj elln. **1513** *Inventory* in *Archæologia* LXVI. 346 A Counterpoint of Verdure cont. xxx. flemisshe stickes. **1565–[66]** *Reg. Privy Council Scot.* I. 430 Ane half stik of say, four half stekis of lynning Holand clayth. **1614** in *Archæologia* XLII. 359 Fowre shorte carpettes of verdure.. at ij s. vj d. the sticke. **1670** in *12th Rep. Hist. MSS. Comm.* App. v. 15 Courser [hangings] then theise..Your Honour may be served with from Flanders, att 18*s.* per stick. **1694** E. CHAMBERLAYNE *Pres. St. Eng.* III. ii. (ed. 18) 388 A Dutch Ell or Stick, by which Tapestry is measured, is but ¾ of a Yard.

† **2.** ***le styc***, ***the stic*** = the piece. (Cf. PIECE *sb.* 4.)

1482 *Cely Papers* (Camden) 111 They wull hawe noo noder money than nenyng grotes at iiij d. ob le styc. *Ibid.* 114 He..made vj oblygaschons payabull at vj monthys and vj monthis the stic conteynyng v[c] marke.

3. See quot. (Cf. STEAK 2 a.)

1615 E. S. *Brit. Buss* in Arber *Garner* III. 636 This Yager ..comes to the said Buss..and buys all such herrings as she hath barrelled. Which barrels, upon the first packing, are called Sticks. And, in part of payment for her said Herring Sticks, delivers..salt [etc.].

stick (stɪk), *sb.*[4] [f. STICK *v.*[1]]

1. A temporary stoppage, a hitch in proceedings or progress; a boggle. *Obs.* exc. *arch.*

1646 R. BAILLIE *Anabaptism* (1647) 139 But the greatest stick is upon the antecedent, Baptismes succession to Circumcision. **1675** V. ALSOP *Anti-Sozzo* iii. 161 But all the stick lyes there, and we must enter a Friendly Debate with him upon the issue. **1684** BUNYAN *Pilgr.* II. (ed. 6, 1693) 104 When we came at the Hill Difficulty, he made no stick at that, nor did he much fear the Lyons. **1889** STEVENSON *Master of Ballantrae* viii, It is a strange thing that I should be at a stick for a date. **1893** —— *Catriona* iv, The Advocate appeared for a moment at a stick, sitting with pursed lips.

2. Something which causes hindrance or delay, a difficulty, obstacle to progress. *Obs.* exc. *arch.*

1657 CROMWELL *Sp.* 21 Apr., in *Carlyle* (1871) V. 31, I think you may well remember what the issue was of the last Conference..and what the stick then was. **1658–9** *Burton's Diary* (1828) IV. 116 To consider in what way you will address to his Highness, to acquaint him clearly what has been your stick. **1893** STEVENSON *Catriona* ii, It would be ill for me to find a conveyance, but that should be no stick to you.

3. The power of adhering or of causing a thing to adhere; adhesiveness. *lit.* and *fig.*

1853 LOWELL *Fireside Trav.* (1864) 113 Surveyors' names have no natural *stick* in them. They remind one of the epithets of poetasters, which peel off like a badly-gummed postage-stamp. **1892** KIPLING *Barrack-room Ballads*, *Screw-guns* 10 We'd climb up the side of a sign-board an' trust to the stick o' the paint.

b. Something which causes adhesion, a sticky substance.

1898 *Engineering Mag.* XVI. 128/1 The liquor..is reduced to the consistency of thick syrup and is called 'stick'.

4. *Cricket.* A batsman who remains a long time at the wicket, one not easily 'got out'.

1863 *Lillywhite's Cricket Scores* III. 242 Mr. Haygarth (always a great 'stick') in his first innings was in three hours. **1901** R. H. LYTTELTON *Outdoor Games* vi. 121 One of the curses of the present day is the stick who, by restraining every impulse to hit, cannot be got out on these perfect modern wickets. *Ibid.* 126 Therefore the brilliant hitter had to abandon his naturally-attractive game and become a stick.

5. A stab. (Cf. STICK-FREE *a.*)

1633 SHIRLEY *Young Admiral* IV. G 2, No circumstance must be forgot, To make him free from sticke and shot. **1818** in TODD; and in later Dicts.

Stick ('stɪk), *sb.*[5] Shortened form of STICKIE, STICKY.

1978 D. MURPHY *Place Apart* ii. 37 The Officials are also known as the Stickies (or Sticks). **1979** *An Phoblacht* 29 Sept. 3/5 In a typical pro-British statement..the Sticks' chairman in South Antrim, Kevin Smyth, accused the IRA of 'gross sectarianism' in bombing the Lisburn premises. **1979** [see STICKIE, STICKY].

stick (stɪk), *v.*[1] Pa. t. and pa. pple. **stuck** (stʌk). Forms: 1 **stician**, **stycian**, 3–6 **stike**, **stik**, (3 **stikie**), 4–6 **styke**, **stycke**, (4 **stiken**, **stic**), 5 **styk(k)yn**, 6 **stikk**, **styk(ke**, **styck**, 6–7 **sticke**, 6– **stick**. *Pa. t.* α. 1 **sticade**, **sticode**, 3–4 **stikede**, 4 **stikid(e**, 4–5 **stiked**, **styk(k)ed**, 5 **stickede**, **stykkit**, (**stikt**, **stickyd**), 5–6 **stycked**, 6 **styckyd**, (**stykkyd**), (*Sc.* **stiket**, **stikit**, **stikkit**), 6–7 **stickt**, 6–9 *Sc.* **sticket**, **-it**, 5–7, 9 *dial.* **sticked**; β. 5 (9 *Sc.*) **stak**, 5–7 **stacke**, 5–7, 8–9 *arch.* and *north.* **stack**; γ. 6 **stoke**, **stocke**, 7 **stooke**, 6–7 **stucke**, 6– **stuck**. *Pa. pple.* α. 1 **sticod**, 3–4 **ystiked**, 3–5 **stiked**, 4 **styked**, **istiked**, **ystikked**, **stikked**, **stiken**, **stickid**, 4–5 **stikid**, 4–6 **stycked**, 5–6 **sticked**, 6–7 **stickt**, 6 **stickte**, **stickyd**, *Sc.* **stikkit**, 6–9 *Sc.* **stickit**, **sticket**; β. 6 **stacke**, 9 *dial.* **stack**; γ. 6 **stoke(n**, 6–7 **stucke**, (6 *Sc.* **stukne**), 7 **stucken**, 7– **stuck**. [OE. *stician* wk. v., f. Teut. root **stik-* to pierce, be sharp (whence STICK, STITCH *sbs.*):—Indogermanic **stig-* (:**steig-*) found in Gr. στίζειν (:—**stigy-*) to prick, στιγμή, στίγμα prick, point (see STIGMA), L. *instīgāre* to spur on, INSTIGATE; also with nasal infix, in Goth. *stigqan* to thrust, L. *-stinguĕre* to prick (*distinguĕre* to distinguish); and without initial *s* in Skr. *tij-* to be sharp, *tigmá* sharp. The Teut. root chiefly appears in the altered form **stek-* (**stak-*: **stǣk-*), as in the Com. WGer. strong verb **stekan* to prick, thrust: see STEEK *v.* The formal equivalent of OE. **stician* (WGer. type **stikōjan*, **stekōjan*, prob. denominative) occurs in OHG. *stehhôn* to prick, stab, cut the throat of; a parallel formation (WGer. type **stikkjan*, also prob. denominative) is found as (M)Du., (M)LG. *stikken* to prick, pierce, stab, also to embroider (Sw. *sticka*, Da. *stikke* from LG.), OHG. *sticchen* in the same senses (MHG., mod.G. *sticken* to embroider).

It is impossible accurately to separate the history of this originally weak verb from that of the originally strong STEEK *v.*[2] The latter was from an early period sometimes conjugated weak, while on the other hand the strong inflexions of *steek* became associated with *stick*, which, moreover, in the 16th c. formed a new strong pa. t. and pa. pple. *stuck* (cf. *dig*, *dug*). It is therefore often doubtful to which verb forms like *stack*, *stoken*, should be referred. Further, in some northern dialects the ME. *stĭke* is normally represented by *stēke*, and therefore coincides (at least graphically) with STEEK *v.*[2] The wk. form *sticked* remained in somewhat common use until the 17th c., and still survives (in certain senses) in Sc. and various dialects (see *Eng. Dial. Dict.*).]

I. To pierce, thrust.

1. *trans.* To stab, pierce, or transfix with a thrust of a spear, sword, knife, or other sharp instrument; to kill by this means, more explicitly ***to stick to death***. Also *refl.* Not now in dignified use.

a **900** *O.E. Martyrol.* 15 Nov. 206 Þa he þæt nolde, þa stycodon hiȝ hyne myd hyra sperum. *a* **900** tr. *Bæda's Hist.* I. x. [xiii.] (1890) 48 Betwih him twam we þus tweofealdne deað þrowiað, oððe sticode beoð oððe on sæ adruncene. *c* **1205** LAY. 20659 Heo..stikeden & sloȝen al þat heo neh comen. *Ibid.* 20962 Alle þa gode wiues heo stikeden mid cnifes. *a* **1300** *Cursor M.* 21124 Men sais he stiked was wit suord. *c* **1330** R. BRUNNE *Chron. Wace* (Rolls) 3527 Syþen wiþ swerd & knyf þey met; Ilk oþer on ran ilk oþer to styke. **13..** *Will. Palerne* 3818 Many a stef stede [was] stiked þere to dethe. **1387** TREVISA *Higden* (Rolls) IV. 471 He ordeyned him..to cacche flyes, and styke hem wiþ a scharp poyntel. **1395** HYLTON *Scala Perf.* (W. de W. 1494) I. xxxv, The sharpe spere that stykked hym to the hert. **1422** YONGE tr. *Secreta Secret.* 153 Whan he apercewid that scappe he ne myght, he raane to a stake and hym Stickyd throw the body. **1529** RASTELL *Pastyme, Brit. Hist.* (1811) 285 The moost comyn tale was that he [Hen. VI] was stycked with a dagger, by y[e] handes of Rycharde, duke of Gloucester. **1556** OLDE *Antichrist* 90 b, He was taken and sticked to deathe. **1615** SYLVESTER *Job Triumph.* II. 319 With Vipers' tongues hee shall be deadly stuck. **1619** DRAYTON *Ballad Agincourt* 72 Like a Storme suddenly, The English Archery Stuck the French Horses. **1705** VANBRUGH *Confed.* IV. i. G 4 b, If I had let him stick himself, I shou'd have been envy'd by all the great Ladies in the Town. **1832** *Examiner* 98/1 Were he to draw his bayonet and stick the brawler. **1842** BORROW *Bible in Spain* xxvi, If I had my knife here I would stick him.

fig. *a* **1300** *Cursor M.* 11370 Þin aghen hert A sorful suerd sal stik ouerthuert. *Ibid.* 24100 On mi soru mai be nan end, It stikes me sua strang. **1600** SHAKS. *A.Y.L.* I. ii. 254 My Fathers rough and enuious disposition Sticks me at heart. **1606** —— *Tr. & Cr.* III. ii. 202 Yea, let them say, to sticke the heart of falsehood, As false as Cressid.

absol. **1530** TINDALE *Expos. Matt. v.–vii.* (? 1550) 99 b, The scrybes and pharyseyes had thruste vp the swerde of the worde of God into a scabard..that it coulde neither sticke nor cutte. **1822** SHELLEY *Faust* ii. 172 [*Chorus of Witches*] Stick with the prong, and scratch with the broom.

b. Of a horned animal: To pierce with the tusks, to impale with the horns; to gore. Also *absol.* Now *dial.*

c **893** ÆLFRED *Oros.* IV. I. §5 Þa, siþþan he irre wæs & ȝewundod, he..þa oþre elpendas sticade & gremede. *c* **1890** W. G. LYTTLE *Adv. Robin Gordon, Robin's Read.* II. 18 (E.D.D.) Tell't hir about the goat neer stickin' her.

c. To kill (an animal, esp. a pig) by thrusting a knife into its throat. Also *transf.*

13.. *Pol. Songs* (Camden) 190 Hue leyȝen y the stretes y-styked ase swyn. **1470–85** MALORY *Arthur* VII. v. 220 Hym bysemeth better to stycke a swyne than to sytte afore a damoysel of hyhe parage. **1591** SHAKS. *Two Gent.* I. i. 108. **1594** LYLY *Mother Bombie* v. iii, I had thought they had beene sticking of pigs, I heard such a squeaking. **1616** R. C. *Times Whistle* II. (1871) 25 For all thou lookest soe big, Thou never yet durst see a sillie pig Stucke to the heart. **1884** TENNYSON *Becket* I. iii, By God's death, thou shalt stick him like a calf!

d. *Sport.* To spear (a salmon). *to stick a pig* (in India): to hunt the wild boar with a spear. (Cf. PIGSTICKING, etc.)

1820 SCOTT *Monast.* Introd. Ep., I have seen the fundations [of the old drawbridge] when we were sticking saumon. **1848** THACKERAY *Van. Fair* lxiii, He wrote off to Chutney..that he was going to show his friend..how to stick a pig in the Indian fashion. **1891** 'LUCAS MALET' *Wages of Sin* II. ii, He had regarded India as an awfully jolly place where you shot tigers and stuck pigs and played polo.

e. To make holes in (something) with a pointed instrument. *rare.*

1769 MRS. RAFFALD *Eng. Housekpr.* (1805) 102 Stick your neck [of mutton] all over in little holes with a sharp penknife.

f. To inoculate, to give a hypodermic injection to; to introduce a hypodermic needle into (a person). *U.S. colloq.*

1946 *Sun* (Baltimore) 19 June 10/1 Though he [*sc.* the traveler] surely has been 'stuck' for every known disease, no telling how often he will be halted by health officers and cast into quarantine. **1963** *New Yorker* 25 May 42/2 'Fraid I've got to stick you once more. **1969** E. WELTY in *New Yorker* 15 Mar. 43/1 The floor nurse came in to feed Mr. Dalzell, then stick him with a needle.

2. To thrust (a dagger, a spear, a pointed instrument) *in, into, through.*

c **1386** CHAUCER *Knt.'s T.* 707 Loue hath his firy dart so brennyngly Ystiked thurgh my trewe careful herte. **1569** UNDERDOWN *Ovid's Invect. Ibis* L j, And that a shafte stoke in thy heart, may take thy life away. **1596** SHAKS. *Merch. V.* III. i. 115 Thou stick'st a dagger in me. **1607** CHAPMAN *Bussy d'Ambois* v. iii. 61 Or thou great Prince of shades where neuer sunne Stickes his far-darted beames. **1615** G. SANDYS *Trav.* I. 7 The Bride-groome entring the Church, sticks his dagger in the doore. **1872** A. S. PACKARD *Guide Study Insects* (ed. 3) 428 The pin should be stuck through the right elytron.

fig. *a* **1400** *Minor Poems fr. Vernon MS.* xliii. 254 And þat loue mote also faste In-to myn herte stykyd be, As was þe spere in-to þin herte.

†**b.** *to stick the point*: to prove conclusively.

1655 FULLER *Ch. Hist.* VI. 268 This Quaternion of Subscribers, have stick'n the point dead with me that all antient English Monks were Benedictines.

c. *to stick one's eyes in*: to subject to a piercing gaze. *Sc.* and *dial.*

1456 SIR G. HAY *Gov. Princes* Wks. (S.T.S.) II. 110 Scho stykkit hir eyne in a man as scho wald throu lukand perse him with her sycht. **1898** S. MACMANUS *Bend of Road* 218 Masther Whoriskey is sittin'..with his eyes stuck in poor Mary as if he wanted to overlook her.

d. *indirect passive.*

1869 TOZER *Highl. Turkey* II. 16 A huge lump..which he carried over his shoulder, stuck through with a pole.

3. To thrust, push forward, protrude (one's head, hand, etc.) *in, into, over* something. Also with *out.*

1627 MAY *Lucan* VI. L 2 b, She..from their orbes doth teare His congeal'd eyes, and stickes her knucles there. **1713** BERKELEY *Guardian* No. 39 ⁋2 Prejudice in the figure of a woman standing..with her eyes close shut, and her fore-fingers stuck in her ears. **1834** M. SCOTT *Cruise Midge* viii, A number of joyous faces were stuck over the hammock cloths reconnoitring us. **1892** *Photogr. Ann.* II. 43 Stick the ends of your fingers in this, and then lightly go over the glass. **1893** STEVENSON *Catriona* ii, And that's what makes me think so much of ye—you that's no Stewart—to stick your head so deep in Stewart business. **1907** LE FANU *Dragon Volant* i, A lean old gentleman..stuck his head out of the window. **1914** A. BENNETT *Price of Love* 207 She belonged to the middle class..the class that sticks its chin out and gets things done.

b. *intr.* To project, protrude. Now only const. *from, out of.* Cf. *stick out*, 32 a.

1580 BLUNDEVILE *Curing Horses Dis.* cxiii. 52 b, Thrust in one of the pinnes from aboue downeward, so as both ends may equallie sticke without the skin. **1837** CARLYLE *Fr. Rev.* II. III. v, Or what is this that sticks visible from the lapelle of Chevalier de Court? **1886** STEVENSON *Kidnapped* xv, I saw a steel butt of a pistol sticking from under the flap of his coat-pocket.

II. To remain fixed.

4. *intr.* Of a pointed instrument: To remain with its point imbedded; to be fixed by piercing. More explicitly *to stick fast* (†*still*).

c **1000** ÆLFRIC *Judges* iii. 23 He forlet þa þæt swurd stician on him. *c* **1175** *Lamb. Hom.* 23 Hu mei þe leche þe lechnien þa hwile þet iren sticat in þine wunde. *c* **1290** *St. Edmund* 47 in *S. Eng. Leg.* 298 þe Arewene stikeden on him ful þicke. **1470–85** MALORY *Arthur* I. iii. 40 Theryn stack a fayre swerd naked by the poynt. **1483** CAXTON *Golden Leg.* 173/3 His staffe sprange out of hys honde..and..styked faste in the erthe. **1523** BERNERS *Froiss.* (1812) I. ccclxxiv. 621 The spere brake, and the tronchion stacke styll in the squiers necke. **1538** in *Lett. Suppress. Monasteries* (Camden) 198 Sum [of them] feytynge so that the knyffe hathe stoken in the bone. **1593** SHAKS. *Lucr.* 317 By the light he spies Lucrecias gloue, wherein her needle sticks. *c* **1622** FORD etc. *Witch Edmonton* II. i. (1658) 19 A Burbolt, which sticks at this hour up to the Feathers in my heart. **1867** MORRIS *Jason* IV. 316 Bleeding from arm and back Wherein two huntsmen's arrows lightly stack. **1884** W. C. SMITH *Kildrostan* 36 Where the joints are there the arrow sticks.

fig. *a* **1225** *Ancr. R.* 60 Erest heo scheot þe earewen of þe liht eien, þat fleoð lichtliche uorð,..& stikeð iðe heorte. *c* **1386** CHAUCER *Doctor's T.* 211 Vpon hir humble face he gan biholde, With fadres pitee stikynge thurgh his herte. **1621** T. WILLIAMSON tr. *Goulart's Wise Vieillard* 154 When hee [the infernall serpent] first bit and stung our first mother Eue, leauing fast sticking in vs the sting of sinne. **1851** KINGSLEY *Misc.* (1859) I. 366 Phrases..which stick, like barbed arrows, in the memory of every reader.

†**b.** To be fastened (*in* something) by having its end thrust or driven in. *Obs.*

c **1386** CHAUCER *Sir Thopas* 196 Vp on his Creest He bar a tour And ther Inne stiked a lilie flour. **1515** BARCLAY *Egloges* I. Argt., In the side of his felte there stacke a spone of tree. **1595** SHAKS. *John* II. 317 There stucke no plume in any English Crest, That is remoued by a staffe of France.

†**5.** Of things: To be fastened in position; to be fixed in or as in a socket; to be attached. *Obs.*

c **888** ÆLFRED *Boeth.* xxxix. §7 Swa swa þa spacan sticiað oðer ende on þære felȝe o er on þære nafe. **13..** *E.E. Allit. P.* B. 1186 O perle, quod I..If hit be ueray & soth sermoun, þat þou so stykes in garlande gay, [etc.]. **1340** HAMPOLE *Pr. Consc.* 7633 Seven planetes er oboven us;..þai styk noght fast, als smale sternes dose. **1470–85** MALORY *Arthur* VII. xxii. 248 Dame Lynet..enoynted it..there as it was smyten of, and in the same wyse she dyd to the other parte there as the hede stak. And thenne she sette it to gyders and it stak as fast as euer it did. **1567** GOLDING *Ovid's Met.* III. 39 Three spirting tongues, three rowes of teeth within his head did sticke. *c* **1586** C'TESS PEMBROKE *Ps.* cxlii. I Lord, thou.. knowst each path where stick the toyls of danger. **1665** BUNYAN *Holy Citie* 173 We shall stick like Pearls in the Crowns of the twelve Apostles. **1673** GREW *Anat. Pl.* VI. iv. §9 The particles..of Salt stick in them, as the Spokes do in the Hub of a Wheel, or as the Quills in the Skin of a Porcupine.

b. In phrases with *full, close,* expressive of crowding to the utmost. [Cf. G. *stecken.*]

c **1400** *Brut* cv. 107 þai..made Archires to him shote with Arwes, til þat his body stickede alse ful of Arwes as an hirchone is ful of prickes. **1776** G. SEMPLE *Building in Water* 9 Make..a solid Foundation..of Piles..driven in as close together as ever they can stick. **1889** 'R. BOLDREWOOD' *Robbery under Arms* xxviii, She..was..as full of fun and games as she could stick.

6. Chiefly of persons: To continue or remain persistently in a place. Now only *colloq.*

c **888** ÆLFRED *Boeth.* iv, Sticiað ȝehydde beorhte cræftas. *a* **1225** *Ancr. R.* 214 þe ȝiure glutun is þes feondes manciple. Uor he stikeð euer iðe celere, oðer iðe kuchene. *c* **1290** *Miȝhel* 782 in *S. Eng. Leg.* 322 þulke [soul] þat halt ane Mannes lijf and stikez in þe heorte. **1537** *Original of Sectes* 2 So agayn may one be out of yᵉ world wᵗ his body, & styck myddes in yᵉ world wᵗ his harte. **1577** tr. *Bullinger's Decades* I. viii. (1592) 68/2 Our Lord died..but hee taried not, nor yet stack faste amonge the deed. **1638** W. HAIG in J. Russell *Haigs* viii. (1881) 219 The longer I stick here the more I consume myself in expense. **1844** *Lillywhite's Handbk. Cricket* 18 Whenever you find two batsmen sticking at their wickets.. try a change [of bowling]. **1876** HARDY *Ethelberta* xxviii, I'll stick where I am, for here I am safe as to food and shelter. **1882** E. A. FREEMAN *Let.* 18 Apr. (MS.) There I should like to stick.

b. *fig.* (Sometimes with mixture of sense 4; cf. also sense 8.) Of feelings, thoughts, etc.: To remain permanently in the mind.

a **1300** *Cursor M.* 26927 [The soul cannot be healed of sin] To-quils it stikand es þar-in. **1303** R. BRUNNE *Handl. Synne* 5166 No make no sorowe, ne myslyke, þ at wanhope In þyn herte styke. *c* **1430** *Chev. Assigne* 241 That [saying] styked styffe in here brestes þat wolde þe qwene brenne. **1535** STARKEY *Let.* 15 Feb., in *England* (1878) p. xiv, Yf euer any of thes..dow styke in your memory & mynd, I besech you let thes few wordys..be put in the nombur of them. **1606** SHAKS. *Ant. & Cl.* I. v. 41 *Alex.* His speech stickes in my heart. *Cleo.* Mine eare must plucke it thence. **1666** PEPYS *Diary* 17 Aug., It sticks in the memory of most merchants how the late King..was persuaded in a strait..to seize upon the money in the Tower. **1741** WATTS *Improv. Mind* I. xvii. (1801) 143 And a hundred proverbial sentences..are formed into rhyme or a verse, whereby they are made to stick upon the memory. **1891** MEREDITH *One of our Conq.* xxviii, But again, 'the meaning of it past date,' stuck in her memory.

†**c.** To linger, dwell on a point in discourse. Const. *in, upon. Obs.*

1547 J. HARRISON *Exhort. Scottes* 218 In which point I will not muche stycke. **1586** W. WEBBE *Eng. Poetrie* (Arb.) 91 Therefore this last kinde of errour is not to be stucke vppon. **1599** ROLLOCK *Serm.* vii. Wks. 1849 I. 380 Then ze see heir ane revelation be the Spreit. Mark it, I sall stick sum thing on the wordis. *a* **1646** BURROUGHES *Exp. Hosea* vi. 108 That principally which we must stick upon a while, which is intended here in the Text most of all.

†**d.** To stop, end one's discourse. *Obs.*

1563 *Homilies* II. *Rogation Week* i. Nnnniiij b, And this once pronounced, he stacke not styl at this poynt: but forth-with thervpon ioyned to these wordes. To hym be glory.. for euer. Amen. **1680** H. MORE *Apocal. Apoc.* 310 We are never the wiser what Empire certainly to pitch upon if the Angel stick here; and therefore he holds on.

e. *Vingt-et-un.* To decline the opportunity of adding to one's hand.

1931 W. V. TILSLEY *Other Ranks* 147 A little group in the centre of the room sprawled on their blankets, playing pontoon. 'I'll stick!' 'Twist one!' 'Busted!' **1950** [see BUST *v.*² f]. **1956** R. FULLER *Image of Society* vii. 188 'In other words the bank is sticking at sixteen,' said Cawsey, amused at his own turn of phrase. **1976** G. SIMS *End of Web* iii. 22 Hello, young Clive. Still sticking on seventeens?.. I'm coming round for another pontoon lesson shortly.

†**7.** To remain firm, continue steadfast, stand *fast*; to be determined *to do* something; to persist *in* (an opinion, etc.); to be persistently engaged *upon. Obs.* Cf. *stick to*, 26.

1447 *Shillingford Lett.* (Camden) 11 Apon this mene he stiked faste, and thoghte hit was resonable. *c* **1500** in W. Denton *Eng. in 15th C.* (1888) 319 Bott I meruell grettly that ye styke so sore to make thaym to gyffe more then othere men hase gyffen afore. **1526** *Pilgr. Perf.* (W. de W. 1531) 8 b, All persones that wyll not be counseyled..but stycke fast in theyr owne blynde fantasy. **1597** MORLEY *Introd. Mus.* I But he still sticking in his opinion, the two gentlemen requested mee to examine his reasons. **1607** TOURNEUR *Rev. Trag.* v. i. I 1 b, Could you not stick: see what confession doth? *c* **1698** LOCKE *Cond. Underst.* §25 Wks. 1714 III. 411 If the Matter be knotty, and the Sence lies deep, the Mind must stop and buckle to it, and stick upon it with Labour and Thought.

b. To keep persistently *at.*

1886 G. ALLEN *Maimie's Sake* xxii, We've stuck awfully close at this thing while we've been working at it. **1977** J. F. FIXX *Compl. Bk. Running* iv. 49 One must stick at one's sport if it is to continue doing any good.

c. *trans.* (*slang.*) To put up with, endure association with, tolerate (a person or thing). Also *to stick it,* to continue what one is doing without flinching.

1899 *Daily News* 26 Oct. 6/6 He got on all right with his wife, but he could not 'stick' his mother-in-law. **1900** *Ibid.* I Jan. 3/2 They're big men, and they look as if they can 'stick it'. **1905** *Macm. Mag.* Nov. 68 Sergeant Chambers shouted back, 'Go to hell!' and to his men he cried, 'Stick it!' **1907** *Ibid.* Feb. 320 Dick had pulled out for home because 'he couldn't stick that Mr. Jenkins.' **1907** J. M. SYNGE *Lett. to Molly* (1971) 172, I cannot 'stick' these plays any more. **1922** A. S. M. HUTCHINSON *This Freedom* IV. iii. 279, I couldn't stick the place. **1928** *Daily Tel.* 27 Mar. 9/1, I resigned.. because I could stick the chief's bullying no longer. **1960** D. STOREY *This Sporting Life* I. ii. 29, I couldn't stick the sight of him standing up there against the Batley skyline.

8. *intr.* Of things: To remain attached or fastened by adhesion, to adhere, hold, cleave. Const. *on, to, unto, in.* See also *stick together*, 33.

1558 WARDE tr. *Alexis' Secr.* 21 b, Take the flower, that sticketh on the bourdes and walles of a Mille. **1601** HOLLAND *Pliny* xxxv. vi. II. 528 As for Sinopis..That which stucke fast unto the rockes, excelleth all the rest. **1617** MORYSON *Itin.* I. 60 Sounding with our plummet, sand of Amber stuck thereto. **1679** MOXON *Mech. Exerc.* ix. 160 Should the Augure-hole be too wide, the Shank would be loose in it, and not stick strong enough in it. **1747** MRS. GLASSE *Cookery* ii. 14 Take care they don't stick to the Bottom of the Pan. **1759** R. BROWN *Compl. Farmer* 104 First wet both the bag and the press to keep the wax from sticking. **1855** BROWNING *The Twins* i, Do roses stick like burrs? **1861** LOWELL *Biglow P.* Ser. II. i. 73 We'll try ye fair, ole Grafted-leg, an' ef the tar wun't stick, Th' ain't not a juror [etc.]. **1868–70** MORRIS *Earthly Par.* I. i. 450 But when that he Gat hold of it [*sc.* a stone upon the floor], full fast it stack.

Proverbial. **1818** SCOTT *Rob Roy* xxiii, Hout tout, man! let that flee stick in the wa'..; when the dirt's dry it will rub out. **1911** *Concise Oxf. Dict.* s.v., If you throw mud enough, some of it will stick.

b. *to stick to* (occas. *in,* †*by,* †*on*) *a person's fingers*: said *fig.* of money dishonestly retained.

1576 [see TELLER 2]. **1660** MARQ. WORCESTER in Dircks *Life* xiv. (1865) 229 Nothing hath stuck to my fingers, in order to benefit or self-interest. **1809** MALKIN *Gil Blas* VII. xv. (Rtldg.) 11 Probably something still stuck by the fingers. **1826** LAMB *Pop. Fallacies* ii, Some portions of it [alienated Church property] somehow always stuck so fast, that the denunciators have been fain to postpone the prophecy. **1860** MOTLEY *Netherl.* x. II. 87 He was..a most infamous peculator. One-third of the money sent by the Queen for the soldiers stuck in his fingers.

c. *fig.* in various uses. Of a fact, a saying: To abide in one's memory. Of an imputation: To be fastened upon a person. Of opinions, feelings, habits: To be fixed, not to be shaken off. Of a criminal charge: to be substantiated, take effect. Of an order or decision made by a court of justice, legislature, or other authority: to be implemented or complied with. Hence with wider application, esp. in phr. *to make* (something) *stick,* to make (that thing) effective; to clinch; to substantiate.

1605 SHAKS. *Macb.* v. ii. 17 Now do's he feele His secret Murthers sticking on his hands. **1677** SIR C. WYCHE in *Essex Papers* (Camden) II. 140 My Lord Treasurer has cleared himself of those things which seemed to stick upon him in relation to the excise. **1751** CHESTERF. *Lett.* cclxx, It is commonly said..that ridicule is the best test of truth; for that it will not stick where it is not just. **1820** SCOTT *Monast.* Answ. Introd. Ep., For MacDuff's peculiarity sticks to your whole race. **1839** LONGF. *Life* (1891) I. 331, I quote him [Horace]; because his phrases stick. **1845** FORD *Handbk. Spain* I. 39 A bad character sticks to a country as well as to an individual. **1857** W. COLLINS *Dead Secret* VI. i, The same fear that she had all the way from this house, still sticks to her. **1932** [see RAP *sb.*¹ 4 e]. **1942** *Sun* (Baltimore) 12 June 1/7 A..program of cooperation designed (1) to hasten the defeat of Germany and (2) to make that defeat stick. **1944** *Ibid.* 7 Feb. 1/1 The Department of Labor..would be empowered to hand down decisions 'which will stick and not be vetoed by any other Federal agency'. **1951** E. PAUL *Springtime in Paris* xvi. 324 Every officer at the Commissariat of the 5th had been itching to get Oudin, on any charge at all that could be made to stick. **1963** 'S. WOODS' *Taste of Fears* xiv. 148 'They couldn't make it stick,' said his uncle, positively... 'No evidence.' **1971** A. PRICE *Alamut Ambush* xii. 147 God knows whether the Americans and the Russians can make the cease-fire stick. **1981** *Times Lit. Suppl.* 9 Jan. 25/1 Picasso now taught himself how to use a poetic, half-theatrical imagination to make his art 'stick', while at the same time..taking pains to avoid the illustrational.

†**9.** To be joined as an appendage *to. Obs.*

1631 WIDDOWES *Nat. Philos.* 61 The Stomacke is a part like perchment, sticking to the throat. **1650** HOWELL *Giraffi's Rev. Naples* I. 25 The Vice-King..remov'd himself ..to castelnuovo, which sticks to the Royall Palace, there being a bridge to passe between.

10. Of a living creature: To cling *to, on, upon.* *to stick on, to* (a horse), to keep one's seat on.

1596 DALRYMPLE tr. *Leslie's Hist. Scot.* I. 62 The hail peple..saw..mony thousandis of sik lytle foules stiking to the schip. **1664** POWER *Exp. Philos.* I. 2 [The flea's] feet are slit into claws or talons, that he might the better stick to what he lights upon. **1706** E. WARD *Wooden World Diss.* (1708) 54 He hoists himself..upon..a Horse, and sticks as close to him with his Thighs, as if he were got cross a Yard-Arm. **1774** GOLDSM. *Nat. Hist.* (1776) VII. 310 The..leeches.. stuck to her so close, that the poor creature expired from the quantity of blood which she lost. **1861** TENNYSON *Sailor Boy* iii, And on thy ribs the limpet sticks. **1872** *Routledge's Ev. Boy's Ann.* 38/2 To learn how to stick on a horse's back. **1881** A. C. GRANT *Bush Life Queensld.* ix. (1882) 82 He tried his hand at sticking to some of the more notorious youngsters [horses].

fig. **1843** CARLYLE *Past & Pr.* II. iv. 78 Every fresh Jew sticking on him like a fresh horse-leech.

absol. **1869** BLACKMORE *Lorna Doone* xi, I should have stuck on much longer, sir, if her [a pony's] sides had not been wet. **1872** BLACK *Adv. Phaeton* iv, His riding was not a masterly performance, but at all events he stuck on.

b. *trans.* To retain one's seat on (a horse).

1844 W. H. MAXWELL *Scotland* iii. (1855) 42, I'll never stick him bare-backed.

11. *intr.* To be set fast or entangled in sand, clay, mud, mire, and the like; similarly of a boat, to become fixed or grounded on sand, a rock, etc.; more explicitly *to stick fast.*

*c*888 ÆLFRED *Boeth.* xxxvii. §2 ðesihst þu nu..on hu þiostrum horoseaðe þara unðeawa ða yfelwillendan sticiað [L. *quanto in cœno probra volvantur*]. *c*1386 CHAUCER *Man of Law's T.* 411 And in the sond hir ship stiked so faste That thennes wolde it noght of al a tyde. **1513** DOUGLAS *Æneis* I. i. 80 Scho with a thuid stikkit on ane scharp roike. **1530** PALSGR. 735/2, I stycke fast in a myer or a maresse, *je me arreste.* **1590** *Acts Privy Council* (1899) XIX. 406 The Thames is soe shallowe in divers places as boates and barges doe sticke by the waie. **1611** BIBLE *Acts* xxvii. 41 They ranne the shippe a ground, and the forepart stucke fast. **1665** MANLEY *Grotius' Low-C. Warres* 514 Unpassable Marishes and Moors, which a man no sooner treads upon, but he sticks in the Mud and Dirt. **1748** *Anson's Voy.* III. vii. 354 At length the ship stuck fast in the mud. **1815** SCOTT *Guy M.* xiii, Mrs. Mac-Candlish's postilion..said aloud, 'If he had stuck by the way, I would have lent him a heezie. **1860** TYNDALL *Glac.* I. xxvii. 198 The carriage..had stuck in one of the ridges.

b. In fig. phrases *to stick in the briers, clay, mire* (now *rare* or *obs.*): to be involved in difficulties or trouble. *to stick in the mud*: now usually, to remain content in a mean or abject condition.

*c*1450 tr. *De Imitatione* III. xxii. 90 Haue mercy on me oute of þe clay, þat I stike not þerin. **1565** COOPER *Thesaurus* s.v. *Hæreo,* They beyng accused of extortion and pillage were in muche trouble, or stacke in the bryars. *c*1620 A. HUME *Brit. Tongue* Ded., Quhiles I stack in this claye, it pleased God to bring your Majestie hame to visit your aun Ida. **1898** J. ARCH *Life* xiv. 345 To teach a man to be content to stick in the mud is to teach a man to curse himself.

†**c.** To be involved *in* (some undesirable state or condition). *Obs.*

*c*1640 H. BELL *Luther's Colloq. Mens.* (1652) 309 And whoso blameth mee for giving way and yielding so much to the Pope at the first, let him consider in what darkness I still stuck at that time. **1666** BUNYAN *Grace Abound.* §201, I should still be as sticking in the jaws of desperation.

12. To become fixed or stationary in or on account of some obstruction, to be arrested or intercepted. Of a thing made to run, swing, or slide: To become unworkable, to jam.

1531 *Sel. Pleas Crt. Admiralty* (Selden Soc.) I. 58 It chaunced his nett to styck or fasten in the bend or knot of a cable. **1707** E. SMITH *Phædra & Hippol.* I. i, My Blood runs backward, and my fault'ring Tongue Sticks at the Sound. **1852** SEIDEL *Organ* 46 One of the keys in the pedal sticks, moving neither up nor down. **1855** TENNYSON *Brook* 85 The gate, Half-parted from a weak and scolding hinge, Stuck. **1886** C. H. *Fagge's Princ. Med.* I. 31 A strip of flannel had got between the drawer and its frame, and had made the drawer stick. **1899** *Allbutt's Syst. Med.* VII. 352 If..an embolus sticks in the vertebral, the basilar artery may become gradually thrombosed and blocked.

fig. **1642** D. ROGERS *Naaman* 24 Let us not wonder that our praiers sticke in their ascent.

b. Of food, etc.: To lodge (in the throat).

to stick in one's gizzard, stomach (fig.): see the sbs.

1553 T. WILSON *Rhet.* 117 b, An other speakes in his throte, as though a good Ale crumme stacke fast. **1727** DORRINGTON *Philip Quarll* (1816) 16 A phlegm sticking in my throat, I happened to hem pretty loud. **1825** T. HOOK *Sayings* Ser. II. *Passion & Princ.* x. III. 195 'How's your throat, child?'..'Oh, quite well, Pa,..it was a bit of the rind of the cheese that stuck'. **1895** P. HEMINGWAY *Out of Egypt* I. ii. 12 He..saw a plate of macaroni for his supper. He tried to eat some, but it stuck in his throat.

c. *to stick in one's throat,* † *teeth*: (*a*) of words, 'to resist emission' (J.); (*b*) of a statement, proposal, notion, belief, etc.: to be difficult to swallow, to be unacceptable.

1605 SHAKS. *Macb.* II. ii. 33 Amen stuck in my throat. **1634** HALL *Contempl., N.T.* IV. xxi. 219 How this suit sticks in her teeth; and dare not freely come forth. **1822** SCOTT *Nigel* xiv, 'My lord,'— said Richie, and then stopped to cough and hem, as if what he had to say stuck somewhat in his throat. **1843** DICKENS *Let.* 1 Feb. (1973) III. 434 Your dedication to Peel stuck in my throat. **1885** E. W. HAMILTON *Diary* 3 May (1972) II. 855 To luncheon..with F. Rothschild to talk over politics... What sticks in his throat is Chamberlain's programme—his quack remedies for the agricultural labourer, of whose real wants he has no experience. **1924** G. B. SHAW *St. Joan* Pref. p. li, The truth sticks in our throats with all the sauces it is served with. **1938** W. S. MAUGHAM *Summing Up* lxxvi. 310 This notion has long stuck in my gizzard. **1953** A. J. TOYNBEE *World & West* vi. 98 The new religions which were now being offered.. would have stuck in a philosopher's throat if the missionary had not sugared the strange pill for him. **1958** C. P. SNOW *Conscience of Rich* xxxi. 232, I didn't like refusing, but it stuck in my gullet to help that blasted group of reds. **1976** A. PRICE *War Game* II. i. 193 Weston would find the accident..sticking in his throat, a question much too sharp to be swallowed.

d. Of a weather-glass, the wind: To remain without fluctuation or variation.

13. Of a matter: To be at a stand, to suffer delay or hindrance. Const. *at, in, on, upon.*

1530 PALSGR. 735/2 It stycketh, as a mater stycketh and gothe nat forward, *il tient.* The mater stycketh nat in me, *la matiere ne tient pas a moy.* **1537** LATIMER *Let. Cromwell* in *Serm. & Rem.* (1845) 383 As touching your request concerning your friend,..it shall not stick on my behalf. **1619** WOTTON in *Eng. & Germ.* (Camden) 50, I finde..a good disposition there,..but I doubte it will sticke upon who shall beginne. **1676** EARL ANGLESEY in *Essex Papers* (Camden) II. 84 Our King hath the French promises the generall peace shall not stick for want of the surrender [of Sicily]. **1703** BARRETT *Analecta* 30 May not this excite and encourage thee to set about the Work, to consider how the Lord is beforehand with thee, that the Work is not like to stick at him. *a*1715 BURNET *Own Time* IV. (1724) I. 629 A rich widow..hearing at what his designs stuck,..furnished him with ten thousand pounds. **1893** STEVENSON *Catriona* iii, 'I believe I could indicate in two words where the thing sticks', said I.

b. Of a person or thing: To remain in a stationary condition, to be unable to make progress. Of a commodity etc.: Not to 'go off', to remain unsold (cf. STICKER 3 b).

1641 *Nicholas Papers* (Camden) 46 We stick wher we were for officers, yᵉ King uppon his declaration and yᵉ Parlement uppon ther two propositions made to him. **1687** MIEGE *Fr. Dict.* II. s.v., His mind sticks betwixt Hope and Fear. **1729** SWIFT *Poems, Soldier & Scholar* 3 This Hamilton's Bawn, while it sticks on my Hand, I lose by the House, what I get by the Land. **1741** WARBURTON *Div. Legat.* IV. v. II. 269 And there they [the contending parties] must have stuck, till Famine and Desertion had ended the Quarrel. **1872** BAGEHOT *Physics & Pol.* (1876) 158 How then did any civilisation become unfixed? No doubt most civilisations stuck where they first were; no doubt we see now why stagnation is the rule of the world, and why progress is the very rare exception.

†**c.** Of a person or his thoughts: To rest *in* some intermediate or subsidiary object. *Obs.*

1534 *Prymer* E, Teache vs deare father not to styck, steye, or ground our selues in our good workes or deseruynges, but to gyue & submitte our selfe..to thyn infynyte..mercy. **1579** FULKE *Heskins' Parl.* 55 Yᵉ Iewes so sticked in the figure, that they considered not the thing signified. *a*1628 PRESTON *New Covt.* (1630) 386 The Jewes..could not see Christ himselfe, the inward promises, but stucke in the outward barke and rinde of Ceremonies. **1690** LOCKE *Hum. Und.* IV. viii. §13 Where-ever the distinct Idea any Words stand for, is not known..there our Thoughts stick wholly in Sounds, and are able to attain no real Truth or Falshood.

14. To be in difficulty or trouble; to stop or stand in a state of perplexity; to be embarrassed, puzzled, or nonplussed.

1577 tr. *Bullinger's Decades* I. x. 94/1 It is requisite that we firste shewe who it is that is our neighbour, touching whiche I see some men to doubt and sticke vncertainely [L. *addubitare & hærere ancipites*]. **1609** HOLLAND *Amm. Marcell.* xv. iv. 36 Who having read the same, sticking and doubting a good while what this should meane..returneth the..missives. **1677** LOCKE in P. King *Life* (1830) II. 164 But when we begin to think of..the beginning of either, our understanding sticks and boggles, and knows not which way to turn. **1730** T. BOSTON *Mem.* xii. 433 Sitting down to my studies on Friday, the Lord withdrew and I stuck. **1741** WATTS *Improv. Mind* I. xvi. (1801) 126 If the chain of consequences be a little prolix, here they stick and are confounded.

b. To be unable to proceed in narration or speech, through lapse of memory or embarrassment.

1579 GOSSON *Sch. Abuse* (Arb.) 74 He stuck fast continually in the midst of his verse, and could goe no farther. **1612** BRINSLY *Lud. Lit.* 258 If those..haue their notes lying open before them, to cast their eye vpon them here or there where they sticke. **1820** W. IRVING *Sketch Bk.* (1859) 170 He always stuck in the middle, everybody recollecting the latter part excepting himself. **1823** SCOTT *Quentin D.* xxxvii, He was only able to pronounce the words, 'Saunders Souplejaw'—and then stuck fast.

15. To hesitate, scruple, be reluctant or unwilling. Const. *to* (do something). Only with negative. (Now *rare.*)

1532 G. HERVET tr. *Xenophon's Tr. Householde* 61 For marchant men..wyll not stycke for daunger to passe any see what so euer it be. **1575** *Gammer Gurton* v. ii. 165 Yea, but he that made one lie about your cock-stealing, Wil not sticke to make another. **1583** STUBBES *Anat. Abus.* II. 25 Some will not sticke to sell you siluer gilt for gold. **1613** SHAKS. *Hen. VIII,* II. ii. 127 They will not stick to say, you enuide him. **1648** J. BEAUMONT *Psyche* XX. xcviii, Though I be Queen, I stick not to submit. **1712** ADDISON *Spectator* No. 451 ¶6, I ..have not stuck to rank them with the Murderer and Assassin. **1827** DE QUINCEY *Murder* Wks. 1854 IV. 4, I do not stick to assert, that any man who deals in murder, must have very incorrect ways of thinking.

†**b.** To be grudging or stingy. Const. *for. Obs.*

1533 *Pardoner & Friar* B iij, Fye on couetise, sticke nat for a peny. **1573** BARET *Alv.* S. 761 They will sticke for no labour, *neque parcetur labori.* **1625** MASSINGER *New Way* I. i, *Tapwell.* True, but they..had a gift to pay for what they call'd for, And stucke not like your mastership.

16. Of a workman: To refuse to continue working, to strike. *local.*

1851 GREENWELL *Coal-trade Terms, Northumb. & Durh.* 52 *Stick,* to cease work, in order to obtain an increase, or prevent a reduction of wages, &c.

III. To fix, cause to adhere.

17. *trans.* To fasten (a thing) in position by thrusting in its point.

*c*1290 *Wolston* 180 in *S. Eng. Leg.* 76 He wende forth.. And nam þe croce wel mildeliche þare he stikede hire er so faste. *c*1391 CHAUCER *Astrol.* II. §38 In centre of the compas stike an euene pyn or a whir vp-riht. *c*1440 *Pallad. on Husb.* XII. 356 Ther cannes styke; on hem sarmentis plie. **1591** SHAKS. *Two Gent.* II. vii. 56 Vnlesse you haue a cod-peece to stick pins on. **1617** MORYSON *Itin.* I. 186 Cloth..wherein I sticked needles. **1731** MILLER *Gard. Dict.* s.v. *Pisum* 6 M 2/2 You should stick some rough Boughs, or brush Wood, into the Ground close to the Peas, for them to ramp upon. **1742** LEONI *Palladio's Archit.* I. 85 Having by Engines stuck these pieces in the bottom of the River. *a*1756 ELIZA HAYWOOD *New Pres.* (1771) 127 Then stick a skewer into it. **1842** LOUDON *Suburban Hort.* 374 Stick a nail in the wall in the centre. **1907** J. A. HODGES *Elem. Photogr.* (ed. 6) 113 Stick the iron shoes [of a tripod] well into three good bungs.

fig. **1640** FULLER *Joseph's Coat* etc. 95 The wicked..have onely a superficiall hold in grace, rather sticked than rooted in it.

b. To secure (a thing) by thrusting the end of it *in, into, behind, through* (a receptacle).

1664 BUTLER *Hud.* II. i. 774 Quoth she, I grieve to see your Leg Stuck in a hole here like a Peg. **1818** SCOTT *Rob Roy* ii, A habit of sticking his pen behind his ear before he spoke. **1863** GEO. ELIOT *Romola* II. xxii, A man..who had a small hatchet stuck in his belt. **1869** TROLLOPE *He knew* etc. xxv, He was sitting, with a short, black pipe stuck into his mouth.

c. To fasten by transfixion *to.*

1535 COVERDALE *1 Sam.* xviii. 11 And Saul had a iauelynge in his hande, and cast it, and thoughte: I wyll stycke Dauid fast to the wall.

d. To fix on a point.

*c*1320 *Sir Beues* 828 And þe bor is heued of smot, And on a tronsoun of is spere þat heued a stikede for to bere. **1577** HANMER *Anc. Eccl. Hist.* VIII. xxvi. 165 He commaunded.. their right eyes to be stickt on the point of a bodkine, the apple, eye lidde and all, to be quite digged out. **1596** DALRYMPLE tr. *Leslie's Hist. Scot.* I. v. 273 In this Battel is Alpin takne;..heidet: stukne on a stake and borne to Camelodun his heid. **1670** DRYDEN *Tyr. Love* III. i. 28 It first shall pierce my heart: We will be stuck together on his dart. **1755** JOHNSON, To *Stick,*..2 To fix upon a pointed body. **1790** BURKE *Fr. Rev.* (ed. 2) 106 Their heads were stuck upon spears, and led the procession.

e. To set (an entomological specimen) by transfixing (it) with a pin.

1830 DARWIN *Life & Lett.* I. 182, I have not stuck an insect this term.

18. *gen.* To fasten in position; also in weaker sense, to place, set, put. Now chiefly, to place obtrusively, inappropriately, or irregularly. Also with advs., *down, on,* etc.

13.. *E.E. Allit. P.* B. 157 Byndez byhynde,..boþe two his handez..; Stik hym stifly in stokez. *Ibid.* B. 583 Byþenk þe sum-tyme, Wheþer he þat stykked vche a stare in vche steppe yȝe, ȝif [etc.]. *c*1430 *Pilgr. Lyf Manhode* I. xcviii. (1869) 53 Lady, quod j, seyth me..of these belles..why thei ben thus tacched and stiked in the skrippe. **1531** TINDALE *Exp. 1 John* (1537) 30 Lyghtes were stycked before theyr memorials. **1546** J. HEYWOOD *Prov.* I. xi. (1867) 35 As dyd the pure penitent that stale a goose And stack downe a fether. **1578** LYTE *Dodoens* VI. xxix. 696 Some hold, that the branches or bowes of Rhamnus stickte at mens dores and windowes, do driue away Sorcerie. **1588** SHAKS. *L.L.L.* III. 199 A whitly wanton,..With two pitch bals sticke in her face for eyes. **1658** BROMHALL *Treat. Specters* I. 70 As though she..were sticked in the bottom of a River to be drowned. **1697** DRYDEN *Æneis* Ded. (e) 4 b, The Additions, I also hope, are easily deduc'd from Virgil's Sense. They will seem..not stuck into him, but growing out of him. **1819** SHELLEY *Oed. Tyr.* I. i. 301 Sticking cauliflowers Between the ears of the old ones. **1823** SCOTT *Quentin D.* xxviii, Trois-Eschelles stuck a torch against the wall to give them light. **1875** HELPS *Soc. Press.* i. 5 Now let him make grand that commonplace word..by sticking that forcible article before it with a capital letter. **1909** A. N. LYONS *Sixpenny Pieces* ii. 19 Do you mind just putting a match to the gas stove and sticking a kettle on?

b. To fasten as an adornment or garnishing. Also with advs., as *about, on, up.*

*c*1430 *Two Cookery-bks.* I. 31, & styke þer-on Clowis, Maces, & Quybibis. **1591** A. W. *Bk. Cookrye* 25 b, When you serue him [a pheasant] in, stick one of his fethers vpon his brest. **1648** GAGE *West Ind.* xii. 53 Many devout persons came and sticked in the dowy Image pretious stones. **1665** SIR T. HERBERT *Trav.* (1677) 126 Hung it was..with threads tripartite..and some Cyprus-branches stuck about. **1769** MRS. RAFFALD *Eng. Housekpr.* (1778) 291 Stick curled parsley in it. **1834** DICKENS *Sk. Boz, Steam Excurs.,* Planting immense bright bows on every part of a smart cap on which it was possible to stick one. **1850** LOWELL *Unhappy Mr. Knott* 56 [A house] With Lord-knows-whats of round and square Stuck on at random everywhere.

c. *Joinery.* To work (moulding, a bead) with a plane fashioned for that purpose. Cf. STRIKE *v.*

1769 FALCONER *Dict. Marine* (1780), *Rails,* are narrow planks..upon which there is a moulding stuck. **1833** LOUDON *Encycl. Archit.* §983 The sashes to be 1 inch and three-quarters, stuck (worked) with astragal and hollow. **1842** GWILT *Archit.* §2105 Mouldings..are generally wrought by hand; but when a plane is formed for them they are said to be stuck, and the operation is called sticking. *Ibid.* §2106 When a bead is stuck on the edge of a piece of stuff.. the edge is said to be beaded... The beads..are sometimes stuck double and triple. **1902** R. STURGIS *Dict. Archit. & Build., Stick,* to run, strike, or shape with a moulding plane; by extension, to shape,..by the moulding mill.

d. *imp.* (or in constructions with equivalent force) and followed by *up* as a coarse expression of contemptuous rejection. Also *ellipt.* Similarly euphem. phr. ***stick it in your ear*** (U.S.). Cf. SHOVE *v.*[1] 10 e, STUFF *v.*[1] 15 a.

1922 S. LEWIS *Babbitt* xix. 240 Bad luck, old dear, and you can stick your job up the sewer! **1939** R. STOUT *Some Buried*

Caesar xi. 153 All right. Take your name and stick it up your chimney and go to hell. **1941** BAKER *Dict. Austral. Slang* 71 *Stick it!*, a contemptuous ejaculation. **1948** D. BALLANTYNE *Cunninghams* xx. 105 He had a good mind to tell Basil Fisher to stick his run. **1960** WENTWORTH & FLEXNER *Dict. Amer. Slang.* 520/1 *Stick it* (*something*) *up your* (*one's*) *ass* (taboo), .. the strongest reply to the question, 'What shall I do with this?' **1971** P. DRISCOLL *White Lie Assignment* ii. 20 If you do earn your thousand pounds you can stick it, d'you hear? Stick it right up where it belongs. I don't want a penny of it. **1973** *Houston Chron.* 21 Oct. 12/7 Members of the House are suggesting to members of the Senate that they take this idea and stick it in their ears. **1977** *Daily Tel.* 22 June 17/8 After the hearing Mr Jeeves said: 'They can stick their cottage. I shall not move into it.'

19. To set (a surface) *with*, to furnish or adorn with on the surface, to cover or strew with. Also with advs., as *about*, *over*, *full*.

c **1300** *Seyn Julian* (1872) 142 Al were þe velion [of the wheel] aboute; wiþ rasours istiked faste. **1597** BEARD *Theatre God's Judgem.* (1612) 234 Who .. put him into a great Pipe stickt full of long nayles, and then rolled him downe. **1601** SHAKS. *Twel. N.* II. iv. 56 My shrowd of white, stuck all with Ew, O prepare it. **1664** POWER *Exp. Philos.* I. 5 The Common Fly... Her body is .. stuck all over with great black Bristles. **1687** DRYDEN *Hind & Panther* III. 1047 With Garden-Gods, and barking Deities, More thick than Ptolomey has stuck the Skies. **1722** DIAPER tr. *Oppian's Halieut.* I. 486 Sea-Urchins, who their native Armour boast, All stuck with Spikes, prefer the sandy Coast. **1780** *Mirror* No. 106 Not a walk but is stuck full of statues. **1867** LOWELL *FitzAdam's Story* 48 As these bring home .. Their hat-crowns stuck with bugs of curious make. **1890** MRS. KINGSCOTE *Tales of Sun* x. 125 She made a big ball of clay and stuck it over with what rice she had, so as to make it look like a ball of rice. **1893** *Wiltshire Gloss.*, *Stick*, to decorate with evergreens, &c. 'We allus sticks th' Church at Christmas'.

b. *Cookery.* To set with a garnish.

1530 PALSGR. 735/2 Stycke your shoulder of mouton with herbes. **1588** SHAKS. *L.L.L.* v. ii. 654 *Ber.* A Lemmon. *Lou.* Stucke with Cloues. **1611** BEAUM. & FL. *Knt. Burning Pestle* v. i, We will have .. a good piece of beef, stuck with Rosemary. **1673** DRYDEN *Amboyna* I. i, I would not let these English from this Isle have Cloves enough to stick an Orange with.

c. *fig.*

1596 SHAKS. *1 Hen. IV*, v. ii. 8 Supposition, all our liues, shall be stucke full of eyes. **1651** HOBBES *Leviath.* Rev. & Conclus. 395 It is many times with a fraudulent Designe that men stick their corrupt Doctrine with the Cloves of other mens Wit.

20. To cause to adhere; to fasten, fix, secure (a thing) *against*, *on*, *upon*, *to* (a surface) by means of an adhesive, pins, etc. Also said of the adhesive. Also *to stick down*.

stick no bills: the usual form of the notice placed on a building forbidding placards to be posted upon it. Cf. *bill-sticker*, *-sticking*.

c **1400** *Laud Troy Bk.* 18382 For on her houses thei hadde stiked Certayn signes that wele were knowen. *c* **1440** *Promp. Parv.* 475/1 *Stykyn*, or festyn a thynge to a walle or a noþer þynge, wha so hyt be, *figo*, *affigo*, *glutino*. **1653** WALTON *Compl. Angler* ii. 49 An honest Alehouse, where we shall find a cleanly room, .. and twenty Ballads stuck about the wall. **1777** CAVALLO *Electricity* 320 The innermost of these tubes has a spiral row of small round pieces of tin-foil, stuck upon its outside surface. **1807** *Med. Jrnl.* XVII. 356 It had bled a drop of blood, which coagulating, stuck his stocking to it. **1820** SHELLEY *Witch of Atlas* lxxiii, The priests would write an explanation full, .. and bid the herald stick The same against the temple doors. **1851** DICKENS *Bill-sticking* in *Househ. Words* 22 Mar. 604/2 The company had a watchman on duty night and day, to prevent us sticking bills upon the hoarding. **1862** MRS. H. WOOD *Channings* xix, He put the bank-note in [the letter], wet the gum, and stuck it down. **1897** *Allbutt's Syst. Med.* II. 4 After sticking the preparation on the cover-glass or slide.

b. *fig.* To fasten (one's choice, opinion, an imputation, a nickname, dishonour, etc.) *on*, *upon*.

1601 SHAKS. *All's Well* v. iii. 45 Admiringly my Liege, at first I stucke my choice vpon her. **1605** B. JONSON *Volpone* III. ii, These imputations are too common, Sir, And eas'ly stuck on vertue, when shee's poore. **1667** MILTON *P.L.* IX. 330 His foul esteeme Sticks no dishonor on our Front, but turns Foul on himself. **1842** LOVER *Handy Andy* i, The nickname the neighbours stuck upon him was Handy Andy.

†**c.** To post up (a notice or document). *Obs.*

1796 J. GUTCH *Wood's Hist. & Antiq. Univ. Oxf.* II. 164 Thomas Greenway of that College [Corpus Christi] resigning his Presidentship, a Citation was stuck for the election of another to succeed him.

†**d.** (? Hence,) Of a sheriff: To return (a jury). (See RETURN *v.* 16 b. Cf. STRIKE *v.*) *Obs. rare.*

1688 T. CLARGES in Gutch *Coll. Cur.* I. 359 It is sayd the Master of the Office will stick the Jury and will name eight and forty.

21. To bring to a stand, render unable to advance or retire. Chiefly in *passive. colloq.*

1829 SCOTT *Anne of G.* xxxii, Every man of us was at home among the crags, and Charles's men were stuck among them as thou wert. **1891** MORRIS in Mackail *Life* (1899) II. 265 Get Hooper to do the colophon before he goes off, as otherwise it might stick us. **1902** *Westm. Gaz.* 14 July 12/1 The way is easy to miss, and the climber may easily find himself 'stuck' on the face of a precipice.

b. *colloq.* To pose, nonplus.

1876 [see COLD *a.* 12 b]. **1884** *Literary Era* II. 158, I knew it all from beginning to end; you could not stick me on the hardest of them. **1893** STEVENSON *Catriona* vi, You must not suppose the Government .. will ever be stuck for want of evidence.

c. ***to be stuck for***: to be at a loss how to obtain; to be unable to think of. *colloq.*

1937 in PARTRIDGE *Dict. Slang.* **1963** 'J. LE CARRÉ' *Spy who came in from Cold* iv. 32 'Who's Mr. Ironside?' .. 'I don't think he exists... He's her big gun when she's stuck for an answer.' **1965** A. J. P. TAYLOR *Eng. Hist. 1914–45* viii. 267 The Conservatives were strong in resistance. They were stuck for a positive programme. **1969** *Guardian* 31 July 6/1 Any time you're stuck for a meal .. come around. **1977** D. BEATTY *Excellency* iv. 53 He might have discovered a snag .. got stuck for some spare.

22. *Sc.* To break down in (a speech, song, etc.); to fail to carry through (a business, etc.). Also, †to cause a breakdown of (a speech).

1715 PENNECUIK *Tweeddale* etc. Poems 34 A comely Body and a Face, Would make a Dominie stick the Grace. **1726** WODROW *Corr.* (1843) III. 254 Wilson .. said warmly that the Commission had betrayed the rights of the Christian people. This drew a cry upon him to call him to the bar, where he was once before... This sticked his speech. **1782** SIR J. SINCLAIR *Observ. Scot. Dial.* 25 To stick any thing; to spoil any thing in the execution. **1829** HOGG *Sheph. Cal.* xxi. II. 315, I disdained to stick the tune, and therefore was obliged to carry on in spite of the obstreperous accompaniment.

23. *slang* and *colloq.* **a.** To cheat (a person) out of his money, to cheat or take in in dealing; to 'saddle' *with* something counterfeit or worthless in purchase or exchange. Cf. STRIKE *v.* ***to be stuck with***: to be saddled with, unable to get rid of (an unwanted person or thing). orig. *U.S.*

1699 E. S——CY *Country Gentl. Vade M.* 56 And so they draw him on from one set to another and from little Bets to great Ones (till they have stuck him, as they call it). **1843** *Blackw. Mag.* LIII. 81 They think it ungentlemanly to cheat, or, as they call it, 'stick' any of their own set. **1848** BARTLETT *Dict. Amer.* 333 To take in; to impose upon; to cheat in trade. 'I'm stuck with a counterfeit note;' 'He went to a horse sale, and got stuck with a spavined horse.' **1851** MAYHEW *Lond. Labour* II. 20/1 The pawnbrokers have been so often 'stuck' (taken in) with inferior instruments, that it is difficult to pledge even a really good violin. *a* **1860** *Providence Jrnl.* in J. R. Bartlett *Dict. Americanisms* (ed. 3) 458 We got stuck with a bad lot of paper, and were obliged to stick it on to our readers. **1900** M. H. HAYES *Among Horses Russia* Introd. 19 Has he [a horse-dealer] ever stuck you with a wrong one? **1943** F. J. BELL *Condition Red* iv. 47 So it was our coal, and we were stuck with it. **1959** W. KENNEDY in M. Ross *Arts in Canada* 136/1 We architects of the mid-twentieth century seem to be stuck with the gods who made us—Gropius, Corbusier. **1962** E. O'BRIEN *Lonely Girl* iv. 36 He bought me a grey astrakhan with a red velvet collar, and a flared skirt. 'I'm stuck with you now,' he said .. while he surveyed the coat from behind. **1972** *Guardian* 22 Mar. 16/2 Westminster .. cannot apply a totally British solution to an Irish problem. But being stuck with it, the British Government has to try to muddle through. **1979** R. JAFFE *Class Reunion* (1980) 14 Emily hated being 'petite', which was a euphemism for getting stuck with all the short boys on blind dates.

b. To induce to incur an expense or loss; to 'let in' *for*.

1895 J. G. MILLAIS *Breath fr. Veldt* i. 2 [He] publishes his work (at his own expense) and sticks his friends for a copy. **1915** 'A. HOPE' *Young Man's Yr.* 272, I'm awfully sorry I stuck you for such a lot.

c. ***to stick it in*** or ***on***: to make extortionate charges.

1844 DICKENS *Martin Chuz.* xxvii, In short, my good fellow, we stick it into B., up hill and down dale, and make a devilish comfortable little property out of him. **1853** DICKENS etc. *Househ. Words* Christm. No. 1/1 How they do stick it into parents—particularly hair-cutting, and medical attendance. **1857** 'DUCANGE ANGLICUS' *Vulgar Tongue* 20 *Sticking it on*, deceiving or defrauding.

d. ***to be stuck on*** (*slang*, orig. *U.S.*): to have one's mind or fancy set on, to be captivated with; also *esp.*, to be fond of, enamoured of, in love with.

1886 *American* XIII. 14 The latter's family so ridiculed him for having been 'stuck' on the canvas that he put it away. **1886** *Lantern* (New Orleans) 20 Oct. 3/2 Poor Charles Ernest is so stuck on a fairy named Emma Brown, that she can make him do anything she wishes. **1887** F. FRANCIS Jun. *Saddle & Mocassin* 163 Turn 'em on to your range when the grass is green; .. they get stuck on it then, and stop there. **1897** KIPLING *Captains Courageous* x. 221 I'm not stuck on myself any just now—that's all. **1909** J. MASEFIELD *Tragedy of Nan* I. 9 'Er father, as she's so stuck on—'E was 'ung. **1938** G. GREENE *Brighton Rock* VII. ii. 295 I'd stake you a fiver she's straight. Why—you told me yourself—she's stuck on you. **1939** A. HUXLEY *After Many a Summer* II. iii. 207 You'd say she was kind of stuck on the fellow. **1967** P. SHAFFER *Black Comedy* 55, I don't mean that's why he popped the question... He's always been stuck on you. **1974** A. LURIE *War between Tates* (1977) vi. 128 Sandy, who was rather pathetically stuck on her for a while, took her to hear *The Magic Flute*.

e. ***to get stuck into***: to lay into, make a physical attack on (someone); to make a serious start on, get down to (a task, a meal, etc.). Hence ***to get stuck in***, to pitch in, get down to it. *colloq.* (orig. *Austral.*).

1941 BAKER *Dict. Austral. Slang* 31 *Get stuck into*, to engage a person in a bout of fisticuffs. To tackle a job with a will. **1942** G. CASEY *It's harder for Girls* 228 A bit o' peace .. after you an' Winch nearly getting stuck into each other at the pub. **1948** C. FRY *Thor with Angels* 3 You get stuck Into some work, you whitebellied weasel. **1958** I. CROSS *God Boy* xix. 160 Though arithmetic wasn't my best subject, I was quite glad at the idea of getting stuck into some figures. **1962** *Observer* 18 Feb. 23/4, I heard a terrific clanging downstairs and went down to see Pancho getting stuck into the gas meter with an iron bar. **1974** A. MORICE *Killing with Kindness* iii. 31 He reached out a hand and promptly got stuck into his beloved evening paper.

1948 S. MATTHEWS *Feet First* x. 57, I have no time for that 'get stuck in' policy that is sometimes advised in cup-ties or local derbys. Once one side starts tackling with too much vigour there is inevitable retaliation and loss of tempers. **1959** G. SLATTER *Gun in my Hand* v. 51 Gives us a hand sometimes on the mixer .. Gets into his old mocker and gets stuck in. **1961** B. CRUMP *Hang on a Minute, Mate* 158 Mrs Wagner brought in two plates of food .. and told them to get stuck in. **1971** *Where* Sept. 260/2 He flung out his arms like a Petticoat Lane trader, and got stuck in. In five minutes he had an audience.

IV. Intransitive uses with prepositions.

24. stick at —.

a. To scruple at; to hesitate to accept or believe, to demur to, take exception to, be deterred by. (Chiefly used negatively.) ***to stick at nothing***: to be unscrupulous. Cf. sense 15.

1525 ABP. WARHAM in Ellis *Orig. Lett.* Ser. III. I. 361 If they loved their Prince, they wold not sticke at this demaund. **1550** BP. DAY *Ibid.* Ser. III. III. 303, I answered .. that I stycked not att the alteration .. of the matter (as stone or wode) wherof the Altar was made. **1615** RALEGH *Prerog. Parl.* (1628) Ded. (end), It is loue which obeyes, .. which giues, which stickes at nothing. **1691** CONSET *Pract. Spir. Crts.* (1700) To Rdr., Such time serving Wretches, as stick at no Extortion or Oppression. **1737** in *10th Rep. Hist. MSS. Comm.* App. I. 486, I shall Never Stick at any expence tho' it puts me into a thousand difficulties. **1741** RICHARDSON *Pamela* III. 328 Who, she had too much reason to think, would stick at nothing to gain his Ends. **1868** FREEMAN *Norm. Conq.* (1876) II. viii. 174 He stuck at no injustice which was needed to carry out his purpose. **1884** FLOR. MARRYAT *Under the Lilies* xxvii, Such women .. who do not stick at telling a falsehood, will not hesitate to listen at a door. **1890** 'R. BOLDREWOOD' *Col. Reformer* xxii, A d—d scoundrel, who would stick at nothing in the way of villainy.

b. To be impeded or brought to a stand at (a difficulty). Cf. sense 14.

1620 MIDDLETON *Chaste Maid* IV. i, He was eight yeeres in his Grammer, and stucke horribly at a foolish place there call'd *Asse in presenti*. **1688** BUNYAN *Heavenly Footman* (1811) 6 They who will have heaven must not stick at any difficulties they meet with, but press, crowd, and thrust through all that may stand between heaven and their souls. *c* **1698** LOCKE *Cond. Underst.* §6 Wks. 1714 III. 397 Sometimes they [*sc.* young scholars] will stick a long time at a part of a Demonstration .. for want of perceiving the Connection of two Ideas. **1773** MONBODDO *Lang.* (1774) I. Pref. 9 This ingenious author .. had not prosecuted it far, having stuck at this difficulty.

25. stick by —.

a. To remain resolutely faithful to (a person) as a follower, partisan, or supporter.

1526 TINDALE *Luke* xix. 48 The hye prestes and the scrybes .. coulde nott fynde what to do for all the people stocke by hym And gave him audience. **1597** SHAKS. *2 Hen. IV*, v. iii. 70 *Shal.* I thanke thee: the knaue will sticke by thee. **1716** in *10th Rep. Hist. MSS. Comm.* App. I. 157 To stick to the last extremity by them who were so unanimously engaged in my cause. **1852** THACKERAY *Esmond* III. x, But Swift .. had this merit of a faithful partisan, that he .. stuck by Harley bravely in his fall.

†**b.** Of a thing: To remain with, cling to (a person); to remain in (a person's) memory. *Obs.*

1533 MORE *Apol.* xxxvi. 196 Wythout any greate hurte that afterwarde sholde stycke by them. **1628** PRYNNE *Love-Lockes* 52 This Beautie will sticke by vs, and continue with vs for all eternitie. **1678** BUNYAN *Pilgr.* I. 54 The remembrance of which will stick by me as long as I live. **1708** POPE *Let. H.C.* 18 Mar. *Lett.* (1735) 77 At present I am satisfy'd to trifle away my Time any Way, rather than let it stick by me; as Shop-keepers are glad to be rid of those Goods [etc.]. **1770** C. JENNER *Placid Man* I. I. vii. 42 Norris had met with some disappointment which stuck by him.

c. To keep resolutely to, hold to, be constant to (a principle, one's word). Now *rare.*

1646 R. BAILLIE *Lett. & Jrnls.* (1841) II. 371 We shall be honest, and sticke by our Covenant... Hitherto we have stucke by our principles in many great and long tentations. **1837** CARLYLE *Fr. Rev.* I. IV. iv, He sticks by the Washington-formula; and by that he will stick. **1848** THACKERAY *Van. Fair* xx, He knew what a savage, determined man Osborne was, and how he stuck by his word. **1869** TENNYSON *North. Farmer, New Style* xv, Thim's my noätions, Sammy, wheerby I means to stick.

†**d.** To keep persistently to, continue at (some business or operation). *Obs.*

1556 ROBINSON tr. *More's Utopia* (Arb.) 139 And therfore if the other part sticke so harde by it, that the battel come to their handes, it is fought with great slaughter and blodshed. **1821** SCOTT *Kenilw.* i, On Friday, he stuck by the salt beef and carrot, though there were .. good spitchcock'd eels. **1829** —— *Anne of G.* xiii, Have the peasant-clods .. stuck by the flask till cock-crow?

26. stick to —. (Also †*unto* —.)

†**a.** To cling to for support. *Obs.*

1534 *Goodly Prymer* N v b, They that stycke to the lord [*Vulg. qui confidunt in Domino*] shal neuer stacker. **1538** BALE *God's Promises* A iv, Pater cœlestis [to Adam]. Than wyll I tell the, what thu shalt stycke vnto, Lyfe to recouer. **1586–7** Q. ELIZ. in Scoones *Four C. Eng. Lett.* (1880) 31 My stable amitie; from wiche, my deare brother, let no sinistar whisperars .. persuade to leave your surest, and stike to unstable staies.

b. To remain resolutely faithful or attached to (a person or party), not to desert. Now chiefly *colloq.*

1535 COVERDALE *Prov.* xviii. 24 A frende .. doth a man more frendship, and sticketh faster vnto him then a brother. **1536** *Act 28 Hen. VIII*, c. 7 §9 And holly to styck to them, as true and faithfull subjectes ought to doo to their regall rulers. **1563** GRESHAM in Burgon *Life* (1839) II. 34 Praying you now (as my trust ys in God and you,) that you will stycke unto me. **1691** WOOD *Ath. Oxon.* II. 680 When the Kings Cause declined he stuck close to the said family. *a* **1715** BURNET *Own Time* II. (1724) I. 200 He promised to all the Earl of Midletouns friends that he would stick firm to him. **1867** FREEMAN *Norm. Conq.* (1876) I. iv. 209 Under Rolf, Normandy had stuck faithfully to the King. **1885** 'MRS.

Alexander' *Valerie's Fate* vi, But I should have stuck to him through thick and thin.

†c. To give one's adhesion to (a doctrine, cause, etc.). *Obs.*

1548 Udall, etc. *Erasm. Par. John* xi. 45–8 When they had seene so notable a miracle, they beleued yt Jesus was Messias, and stacke to his doctrine. 1644 Milton *Divorce* I. (ed. 2) 4 Many points..likely to remain intricate and hopelesse upon the suppositions commonly stuck to. 1665 Glanvill *Def. Van. Dogm.* To Albius (a 3), The way to bring men to stick to nothing, being confidently to perswade them, to swallow all things.

d. To adhere, keep or hold to (an argument, demand, resolve, opinion, bargain, covenant, and the like); to refuse to renounce or abandon; to persist in.

1525 Sampson in Ellis *Orig. Lett.* Ser. III. II. 26 Th' Emperor havyng his enemy in his hande made the best argument that could be, and to suche argument must he styk if he entende to get any thing. 1655 tr. *Sorel's Com. Hist. Francion* III. 67 Being a man that stuck to his resolves. a 1688 Bunyan *Israel's Hope Encour.* Wks. (1692) 220/2 The Word Redemption, therefore must be well understood, and close stuck to. 1712 Arbuthnot *John Bull* IV. vi, Let us stick to our point, and we will manage Bull, I'll warrant ye! 1822 Hazlitt *Men & Manners* Ser. II. vi. (1869) 135, I like a person who knows his own mind and sticks to it. 1887 Lang *Myth, Ritual & Relig.* I. vi. 179 The old men do not know... But they stick to it that 'that bed of reeds still exists.' 1887 E. A. Freeman in *Life and Lett.* (1895) II. 368, I stick tight to Gladstone's best proposal, to clear the Irishry out of Westminster.

e. To refuse to be enticed, led or turned from; to attend unremittingly to (an occupation, course of action, work, etc.).

a 1548 Hall *Chron. Hen. VII.* 10 The Iryshemen, although they foughte hardely and stucke to it valyauntly, yet..they were stryken downe and slayne. 1552 Latimer *Serm., Septuagesima* (1584) 327 b, And therefore let vs sticke hard vnto it, and bee content to forgoe all the pleasures and riches of this world for his sake. 1611 Shaks. *Cymb.* IV. ii. 10 Sticke to your Iournall course: the breach of Custome, Is breach of all. 1612 Brinsly *Lud. Lit.* 11 They being nuzled vp in play abroad, are very hardly reclaimed and weaned from it, to sticke to their bookes indeede. 1662 H. Newcome *Diary* (Chetham Soc.) 112 Fell to my studdy on Ecles. xii. 1, and stucke to it allmost all day. 1720 Mrs. Manley *Power of Love* (1741) IV. 279 She was obliged to stick close to her needle, and not stir out of her Chamber. 1821 J. W. Croker in *C. Papers* 5 June (1884) He..would advise him to stick to his law. 1874 Blackie *Self-Cult.* 76, I never knew a man good for anything in the world, who, when he got a piece of work to do, did not know how to stick to it. 1877 'H. A. Page' *De Quincy* II. xvi. 7 His incapacity to stick to work was increased by his nervous dread of putting others to inconvenience.

f. To keep exclusively to (a subject of discourse or study, an employment, etc.). Phr. ***to stick to one's text.*** Also ***to stick to one's last*** (with allusion to the proverb: see last *sb.*[1] 2 c).

1711 Addison *Spect.* No. 66 ¶5 The Boy I shall consider upon some other Occasion, and at present stick to the Girl. 1795 Burke *Let. Hussey* Corr. (1844) IV. 317 Lord Fitzwilliam sticks nobly to his text, and neither abandons his cause or his friends. 1880 Sala in *Illustr. Lond. News* 4 Dec. 539 Still I stick to my text as regards champagne and raki imbibing among the upper classes in Turkey. 1927 Galsworthy *Castles in Spain* 92 Conrad had always a great regard for..workmen who stuck to their last and did their own jobs well. 1939 A. Powell *What's become of Waring?* viii. 227, I don't know why he wanted to meddle with writing at all. It wasn't his avocation. He should stick to his last. 1956 A. Wilson *Anglo-Saxon Attitudes* I. i. 19 You're not a member of the University Press Syndic... Stick to your last.

g. To keep exclusively to the use of (a particular article, kind of food or the like).

1815 Scott *Guy M.* xxi, I must stick to the flageolet, for music is the only one of the fine arts which deigns to acknowledge me. 1879 F. W. Robinson *Coward Consc.* I. viii, Thank-you, I'll stick to the claret. 1907 J. A. Hodges *Elem. Photogr.* (ed. 6) 125 The beginner should select one particular make, and stick to it.

h. To remain by or in (a place, etc.); to refuse to desert or leave.

to stick to one's colours: see colour *sb.* 7 d. *to stick to one's guns*: see gun *sb.* 6 b.

1609 Holland *Amm. Marcell.* XXIV. vii. 249 The Persians sticking close to their walls,..assayed to checke..our deadly violence. 1719 De Foe *Crusoe* I. (Globe) 103 The rains came on, and made me stick close to my first Habitation. 1853 Reade *Love me Little* I. viii. 231 While she [a boat] floats they stick to her. 1898 F. D. How *Bp. Walsham How* xxii. 313 He felt that this was an additional reason for sticking to his post.

i. To follow closely (an original, etc.).

1548 Udall etc. *Erasm. Par. Mark* ii. 6–12 The vulgar people..who whyles they stacke harde to the litterall sence of Moses lawe, were farre from the spirite and true mening thereof. 1612 Brinsly *Lud. Lit.* 157 The sense & drift of the Latine Author is principally to be obserued, and not the phrase nor propriety of the tongue, to bee so much sought to bee expressed or stucken vnto. 1697 Vanbrugh *Æsop* Pref., For I confess in the Translation, I have not at all stuck to the Original.

j. To keep close to (in a pursuit or race). *lit.* and *fig.*

1863 W. C. Baldwin *Afr. Hunting* ii. 56, I..singled out the largest bull. Crafty and Billy stuck to him like leeches. 1865 Carlyle *Fredk. Gt.* XVIII. v. (1872) VII. 189 Our hussars stuck to him, chasing him into Ostritz. 1879 H. C. Powell *Amateur Athletic Ann.* 19 Crossley had all his work cut out to win, as A. S. Smith..stuck closely to him all the way.

k. To keep possession of, refuse to part with.

a 1660 *Contemp. Hist. Irel.* (Ir. Archæol. Soc.) II. 162 Major Charles..did call for Colonell Moore, bidinge him to leade that horse as proper colonell, which he did and left, Dungan stikinge onely to one or two troupes. 1704 Cibber *Careless Husb.* III. i. 22 *Sir Cha.* If you keep your Temper she's Undone. *L. Mo.* Provided she sticks to her Pride, I believe I may. 1867 Trollope *Chron. Barset* xxxvii, She'll stick to every shilling of it till she dies. 1884 *Chr. World* 12 June 442/5 A bishop of Antioch, deposed and excommunicated, chose to stick to the church-buildings. 1888 Bryce *Amer. Commw.* I. xx. 283 Congress..may request the President to dismiss him, but if his master stands by him and he sticks to his place, nothing more can be done.

27. stick with —.

†a. To side persistently with. *Obs.*

1523 Berners *Froiss.* (1812) I. clxxxv. 219 And ther he..promysed the duke to stycke with hym in good and yuell. 1542 Udall *Erasm. Apoph.* 281 Because thei had taken parte and sticked hard with the enemies of Sylla [L. *quod hostium partibus adhæsissent*].

†b. To persist in arguing with, haggle with. *Obs.*

1530 Tindale *Answ. More's Dial.* IV. xi. Wks. (1572) 332/2 He saith, 'it is euident..that a man..may geue..his body to burne for the name of Christ, & al without charitie.' Wel I will not sticke with hym: he may so do [etc.]. 1626 B. Jonson *Staple of N.* III. ii, *P. Iv.* For that I'll beare the charge: There's two Pieces. *Fit.* Come, do not stick with the gentleman. 1651 Baxter *Inf. Bapt.* 179, I will not stick with you for the phrase of Speech, when the thing is the same.

†c. To be incredible or unacceptable to. *Obs.*

1643 Prynne *Sov. Power Parlt.* III. 140 Because this objection stickes most with many Schollars,..I shall endeavour to give a satisfactory answer to it. 1719 Waterland *Vind. Christ's Div.* 216 The principal Thing which stuck with Him [*sc.* Arius], was..the strict Eternity or Co-eternity of the Son. 1816 Scott *Old Mort.* Concl., Lady Margaret was prevailed on to countenance Morton, although the old Covenanter, his father, stuck sorely with her for some time.

†d. To remain painfully in the memory of. *Obs.*

1626 Bacon *Sylva* §997 The Going away of that, which had staid so long, doth yet sticke with mee. 1666 Bunyan *Grace Abound.* §148 And this [fear of eternal damnation] stuck always with me.

e. To adhere to (an account, plan, etc.); to be faithful to, support.

1915 J. London *Jacket* iv. 28 Stick with it. Don't ever let'm know. 1958 M. L. King *Stride toward Freedom* vii. 127 We would stick with them through their difficulties. 'We must remain together,' we kept repeating. 1976 M. Machlin *Pipeline* xlviii. 505 'I've known all along it was a Goddamn fool plan.'.. 'Then why have you stuck with it so long?'

V. Idiomatic uses with adverbs.

Many of the intrans. uses below serve as more colloquial variants of the corresponding phrases of *stand*, sometimes with added notion of persistence, obtrusiveness, or the like.

28. stick around. *intr.* To wait, remain in the vicinity, not to go away. *colloq.* (orig. *N. Amer.*).

1912 J. Sandilands *Western Canad. Dict. & Phrasebk.*, *Stick around*, wait about, hang around, or loaf around. The Canadian sport will stick around in the expectation of meeting the boys and having a good time. 1915 S. Lewis *Trail of Hawk* iii. 28 Stick around, son, and sit in any time, and I'll learn you some pool. 1919 E. Jordan *Girl in Mirror* iv. 79 I'm going to 'stick around', and guide them for a few days. 1943 P. Cheyney *You can always Duck* vi. 99 'I'm givin' no guarantees,' I tell her. 'But maybe I'll stick around. We'll see. So long, honey.' 1959 'S. Ransome' *I'll die for You* ix. 109 You stick around, Mr. Fisher, where I can find you when I want you? 1979 A. Fox *Threat Warning Red* xvi. 248 You'll be asked to come over here next week..and you'll have to stick around for a day or two.

†29. stick away. *trans.* To hide away. *Obs.*

1575 *Gammer Gurton* I. iv. 4 For these and ill luck togather ..Haue stacke away my deare neele, and robd me of my ioye.

30. stick down. (See simple senses and down *adv.*) †*trans.* To fasten by its point; to plant (a spear, stake, etc.) by driving (its point) into the ground.

1581 A. Hall *Iliad* VI. 111 His iaueline right he sticketh down with words ful curteously, And friendly cheere he thus begins. 1609 Skene *Reg. Maj., Stat. William* c. 27. 7 Bot that battell may be swa remitted: that is, quhen they haue sticken downe their speres; the defender may grant the fault. 1691 T. H[ale] *Acc. New Invent.* Let. Marlborough 80 If..the Lord Mayor appoint his Water-Bailiff..to se a Stake stuck down, beyond which the Repairers of the Wharf shall not proceed.

31. stick in.

a. *trans.* To insert; *Sc.* to plant (a tree).

1818 Scott *Hrt. Midl.* viii, Jock, when ye hae naething else to do, ye may be aye sticking in a tree. 1842 Loudon *Suburban Hort.* 341 In order to point out the stools or stocks ..the stem of every tree may be stuck in within an inch or two of its root-stock.

b. *intr.* To remain obstinately in (an office, a community); to refuse to leave, go out, or resign.

1848 Newman *Loss & Gain* III. iv. 321 If they were [honest], then, as the Puseyites are becoming Catholics, so we should see old Brownside and his clique becoming Unitarians. But they mean to stick in. 1894 Labouchere in *Daily News* 21 Apr. 5/6, I have had..a sufficient experience of governments to know how they stick in.

c. *Sc.* To persevere.

1887 Annie S. Swan *Gates of Eden* iv, Yer wark's honest ..an' if ye stick in, ye're bound to dae weel. 1895 W. C. Fraser *Whaups of Durley* vi. 73 Stick in wi' your lessons.

32. stick off. *intr.* and *trans.* †To show to advantage. *Obs.*

1602 Shaks. *Ham.* v. ii. 168 Ile be your foile Laertes, in mine ignorance, Your Skill shall like a Starre i' th' darkest night, Sticke fiery off indeede. 1614 Chapman *Masque Inns of Court* A 3, The humble variety whereof [*sc.* of the torchbearers' habits], stucke off the more amplie, the Maskers high beauties.

33. stick out.

a. *intr.* To jut out, project, protrude.

1567 Golding *Ovid's Met.* III. 83 The Iaueling steale that sticked out. 1585 T. Washington tr. *Nicholay's Voy.* III. x. 86 Nose, eares, or any other part of the bodie sticking out. 1679 Shadwell *True Widow* I. i. 4 He changed his Taylor twice, because his Shoulder-Bone sticks out. 1815 J. Smith *Panorama Sci. & Art* II. 230 In which wire is a pointed short pin, sticking out horizontally. 1882 Caulfeild & Saward *Dict. Needlework* s.v. *Spines*, Long straight points that stick out from the edge of the Cordonnet. 1886 J. K. Jerome *Idle Thoughts* 5 What did it matter to him if his toes did stick out of his boots?

b. To be prominent or conspicuous. Also in various phrases, esp. ***to stick out a mile. to stick out like a sore thumb***: see sore *a.* 9 f. *colloq.*

1638 Junius *Paint. Ancients* 15 Though we cannot mount up to the highest top of perfection, yet it is something for all that to sticke out above the rest in the second and third place. 1902 *Daily Chron.* 9 Dec. 3/3 'Of her' is all very well now and then, but when it occurs too often it 'sticks out,' as Mr. Henry James would say. 1933 E. Waugh *Scoop* II. i. 119 'Have you noticed it?' 'Yes..it sticks out a mile.' 1949 [see *road sign* s.v. road *sb.* 9 b]. 1952 M. Allingham *Tiger in Smoke* i. 16 You couldn't miss him. He stuck out like a lighthouse. 1977 'H. Carmichael' *Grave for Two* iv. 48 'You're saying she's left him.'.. 'Sticks out a mile.'

c. To persist in resistance; to hold out; also, to remain out on strike. Also, ***to stick it out***, to endure something to the end (cf. 7 c). *colloq.*

1682 *Lond. Gaz.* No. 1741/3 When the design..is made publick, several others will contribute, and none..who wish well to the Town will stick out. 1818 Todd, *To stick out*, to refuse compliance. 1845 Disraeli *Sybil* VI. viii, As long as you can give us money, I don't care..how long we stick out. 1882 'Mark Twain' *Let.* 17 May (1917) I. 419, I have promised Osgood, and must stick it out. 1886 Stevenson *Dr. Jekyll* i, He would have clearly liked to stick out; but.. at last he struck. 1889 'Mark Twain' *Conn. Yank.* xxvi. 334 The properties required me to stick it out. 1901 'L. Malet' *Sir R. Calmady* VI. vii, It would be ridiculous to fly, so she must stick it out. 1914 G. B. Shaw *Misalliance* 17, I really couldnt stick it out with Jerry, mother. 1929 J. B. Priestley *Good Companions* III. ii. 509 If you went, I'm durned sure I couldn't stick it out another week. 1981 P. P. Read *Villa Golitsyn* I. vi. 41 He stuck it out for a week and then shinnied down a drainpipe.

d. To be a stickler *for. rare.* (Cf. *stick up*, 35 b.)

1862 Mrs. H. Wood *Channings* xlix, Nobody sticks out for politeness more than Carrick.

e. To maintain, persist in asserting (*that*). ***to stick one out***: to maintain against one; to persist in an opinion in spite of all one's argument. *colloq.*

1904 R. Hichens *Woman with Fan* iii, Do you stick out that Carey didn't love you? 1910 A. Bennett *Clayhanger* I. vii. 49 She would not hear a word about the toast being a little hard... Maggie..'stuck her out' that the toast was in fact hard. 1915 F. M. Hueffer *Good Soldier* IV. i. 224 That checked Florence a bit; but she fell back upon her 'heart' and stuck out that she had merely been conversing with Edward. 1916 A Bennett *Lion's Share* vii. 53, I knew he was going to be ill when I left him in the cabin, but he stuck me out he wasn't.

f. To persist in one's demand *for. colloq.*

1902 *Cornhill Mag.* July 55 Th' old leech was only sticking out for every brass farthing he could get. 1906 *Westm. Gaz.* 28 Dec. 2/1 It is to be hoped that when the new boundary is determined we shall 'stick out' (if the expression be permitted) for the whole of Ruwenzori.

g. *trans. Naut.* (See quot. 1815.)

1815 *Falconer's Dict. Marine* (ed. Burney), *Stick out the Cable!* the order to slacken and push it out at the hawse-hole, when the anchor is hauling up to the cat-head, &c. 1833 M. Scott *Tom Cringle* xii, Stick out the warp, let her swing to her anchor.

h. In *passive*, to be adorned too lavishly, 'tricked out' (with jewels).

1748 Richardson *Clarissa* VI. 53 They were richly dressed, and stuck out with jewels.

i. ***to stick one's neck out***: see neck *sb.*[1] 3 e.

34. stick together. *intr.*

a. Of things: to adhere one to another, to cleave or cling together.

1583 Melbancke *Philotimus* Cc iv b, Good counsell and affection agre like iron and clay, which by no meanes can be brought to sticke together. 1677 Miege *Dict. Eng. Fr.* s.v., To stick together like burs. 1687 *Ibid.* II. s.v., Atoms that stick together, and are as it were a continued Body. a 1732 Gay *Songs & Ball., New Song* xviii, Let us like burs together stick.

b. Of persons, etc.: to keep together; chiefly *fig.*, to make common cause.

1560 Pilkington *Expos. Aggeus* E ij, To teach vs..that they should loue & sticke together like brethren. 1595 Shaks. *John* III. iv. 67. 1619 Drayton *Ballad Agincourt* 80 None from his fellow starts, But..like true English hearts, Stuck close together. 1680 Sir J. Scot in *Reg. Privy Council Scot.* Ser. III. VI. 576 Let us..sticke togither and positively refuse and..it shall not carry. 1724 Swift *Drapier's Lett.* vii. Wks. 1755 V. II. 146 Nature hath instructed even a brood of goslings to stick together, while the kite is hovering over their heads. 1856 Kane *Arct. Expl.* II. iii. 46 While we live we will stick together: one fate shall belong to us all. 1883 Stevenson *Treas. Isl.* vi, Jim and I shall stick together in the meanwhile.

35. stick up.

a. *intr.* To stand out from a surface; to project. †Of the hair: to stand on end.

1422 Yonge tr. *Secreta Secret.* 230 Who-so hath the browes stikkynge vp anent the noose into the templis in euery syde, bene foolis:..tho wyche bene a-dred haue hare lokkis stickynge vp. **1611** MIDDLETON & DEKKER *Roaring Girl* IV. ii, Goshawke goes in a shag-ruffe band, with a face sticking vp in't, which showes like an agget set in a crampe ring. **1805** STOWER *Typogr. Marks* 7 Where a space sticks up between two words, it is noticed by a perpendicular line in the margin. **1902** VIOLET JACOB *Sheep-Stealers* xi, The toll-gate..had not yet been re-erected, and the bare posts stuck dismally up at the wayside.

b. *to stick up for*: to defend the cause of, to champion. *colloq.* (Cf. *stand up for* STAND *v.* 103 o.)

1837 LOWELL *Lett.* (1894) I. 20, I shall always like him [Whittier] the better for 'sticking up' for old New England. **1887** *Poor Nellie* (1888) 115 The 'Times' always does stick up for the moral of everything.

c. *dial.* To make love *to*.

c **1850** 'Dow Jr.' in Jerdan *Yankee Hum.* (1853) 85, I will ..stick up to them, so long as there is anything sticky in the first principles of love. **1858** A. MAYHEW *Paved with Gold* II. xvi, It soon became known to the ladies..that the captain 'was sticking up to "Miss"'. **1899** CAROLINE GEAREY *Rural Life* x. 237, I doan't like ter see..a boy of sixteen sticking up to a gal.

d. To offer resistance *to*. *colloq.*

1843 *Cracks abt. Kirk* I. 2 (E.D.D.), I am but a plain weaver, and no fit to argue wi' the Dominie, tho' I carena about stickin' up tae Will. **1889** *Contemp. Rev.* Feb. 173 No matter how excellent may be the original disposition of the head boy, if there is no one who dare stick up to him, he soon becomes intolerable.

e. To hold one's ground in argument. *colloq.*

1858 DARWIN *Life & Lett.* (1887) II. 110, I admired the way you stuck up about deduction and induction.

f. To claim or give oneself out *to be*. Cf. *set up* (SET *v.*[1] 154 nn). *colloq.*

1881 BLACKMORE *Christowell* xxxiv, I never knew any good come of those fellows who stick up to be everything wonderful.

†**g.** *trans.* To tuck up. *Obs.*

c **1330** *Amis. & Amil.* 988 He stiked vp his lappes tho; In his way he gan to go. *c* **1440** *Promp. Parv.* 475/1 Stykkyn, or tukkyn vp cloþys, *suffarcino, succingo. Ibid.* 504/2 Tukkyn vp, or stykkyn vp, *suffarcino*.

h. To set up in position, to set up (a stake, etc.) on its own point, or (a head, body) by impalement.

1530 TINDALE *Answ. More's Dial.* II. ix. Wks. (1572) 298/2 The Israelites..neither prayed to hym..nor sticked vppe candels before hym. **1535** COVERDALE *1 Chron.* x. 10 His weapens layed they in the house of their god, and styckte vp his heade vpon the house of Dagon. **1596** SHAKS. *Merch. V.* I. iii. 87 The skilfull shepheard pil'd me certaine wands,.. And stucke them vp before the fulsome Ewes. **1608** DOD & CLEAVER *Expos. Prov.* ix–x. 78 His heart is not as..a stake that is sticked up, which euery hand may plucke awry. **1657** BILLINGSLY *Brachy-Martyrol.* i. 3 With his keen javelin, spirit-haunted Saul Assay'd to stick up David 'gainst the wall. **1669** STURMY *Mariner's Mag.* VII. xiii. 21 Stick up in the Vertical Line two Pins of equal height. **1772** FOOTE *Nabob* II, [You] only wanted a wife to..stick up in your room, like any other fine piece of furniture? **1850** LOWELL *Unhappy Mr. Knott* 28 'The woodland I've attended to'; (He meant three pines stuck up askew). **1892** *Photogr. Ann.* II. 219 As most photographers never do anything but 'stick it up' and 'fire away.'

fig. **1766** GOLDSM. *Vicar* xxvii, We should then find that wretches, now stuck up for long tortures, lest luxury should feel a momentary pang, might..serve to sinew the state.

i. To affix or post (a sheet, bill, or the like).

1788 FRANKLIN *Autobiog.* Wks. 1840 I. 122 It was reprinted on a large sheet of paper, to be stuck up in houses. **1821** *Act 1 & 2 Geo. IV*, c. 44 § 65 The Company..shall.. affix and stick up..upon every Stop-gate..an Account or List of the several Rates of Tonnage. **1866** GEO. ELIOT *Felix Holt* xxviii, You should be on the look-out when Debarry's side have stuck up fresh bills, and go and paste yours over them.

j. *colloq.* To place (a charge) in a tavern-score; *gen.* to put down to one's debit in an account.

1865 *Chamb. Jrnl.* 11 Feb. 82/1 The means to get drunk, too, were obtained by all manner of contrivances. Some would 'stick it up' till Saturday night. **1874** *Slang Dict.* 310 Stick it up to me, i.e., give me credit for it.

k. orig. *Austral.* To stop and rob on the highway; also, simply, to rob (a station, bank, etc.). Also *transf.* to demand alms from (a person). Also, (*Criminals' slang*) of the police: to hold up (a suspect). Cf. *hold up* HOLD *v.* 44 e.

1846 J. L. STOKES *Discov. in Australia* II. xiii. 502 It was only the previous night that he had been 'stuck up', with a pistol at his head. **1881** A. C. GRANT *Bush Life Queensland* xi. (1882) 116 [The blacks] stuck up Wilson's station there, and murdered the man and woman in the kitchen. **1904** 'O. HENRY' *Cabbages & Kings* xvii. 302, I couldn't take it with me, not knowing but what the monkeys might stick me up. **1926** J. BLACK *You can't Win* vii. 81 Anyway we'll sure be stuck up and frisked at Evanston. **1971** *Black Scholar* Sept. 32/2 It was the night he, Shotgun and Big Daddy stuck up the policy clearing house. **1978** S. BRILL *Teamsters* iii. 76 They had served time for sticking up a variety store in Akron, Ohio.

l. *Austral.* To hinder from proceeding (on a journey, in work or in any proceeding); hence to puzzle, nonplus.

1863 S. BUTLER *First Yr. Canterb. Settlement* v. 68 At last we came to a waterfall... This 'stuck us up', as they say here concerning any difficulty. **1887** HORSLEY *Jottings fr. Jail* 11 Now don't stick me up (disappoint); meet me at six to-night. **1890** *Melbourne Argus* 7 June 4/2 We are stuck up for an hour or more, and can get a good feed over there. **1897** *Australasian* 2 Jan. 33/1 (Morris) The professor seems to have stuck up any number of candidates with the demand that they should construct [etc.]. **1915** 'A. HOPE' *Young Man's Yr.* 299 We were absolutely stuck up for the rest of the money—couldn't go on without it, and didn't know where to get it.

m. *Austral.* To bring (an animal) to bay.

1884 'R. BOLDREWOOD' *Old Melbourne Mem.* iii. (1896) 24 We heard Violet's bark... We knew then that she had 'stuck up' or brought to bay a large forester [kangaroo]. **1888** D. MACDONALD *Gum Boughs* 15 The fiercest fighter [kangaroo] I ever saw 'stuck up' against a red gum tree.

†**n.** *Cricket.* To put a batsman on the defensive. *Obs.*

1864 *Baily's Mag.* Sept. 297 Grundy and Wootton..put every batsman on the defensive, stuck them up, man after man, over after over,..and then sent each back to the Pavilion. **1891** W. G. GRACE *Cricket* ix. 243 There are some bowlers who, by their wonderful accuracy of length, stick up the batsmen and get wickets on the most perfect grounds. **1904** P. F. WARNER *How we recovered Ashes* v. 70 Rhodes stuck up all the batsmen, with the exception of Trumper.

o. In phr. *stick 'em up*: an (armed) robber's order to his victim to raise his hands above his head; = *hands up!* s.v. HAND *sb.* 55. Usu. imp. *slang* (orig. *U.S.*). (Cf. *put them* (or *'em*) *up* (ii) s.v. PUT *v.*[1] 53 a (e).)

1931 [see REACH *v.*[1] 12 c]. **1938** G. GREENE *Brighton Rock* v. iii. 203 The children were scouting among the rubble with pistols from Woolworth's... Someone said in a high treble: 'Stick 'em up.' **1972** WODEHOUSE *Pearls, Girls, & Monty Bodkin* vi. 76 Sequences of spine-chilling drama, with people telling other people to stick 'em up and prodding them in the stomach with pistols.

VI. 36. The verb-stem in combination: **stick-all**, a cement for mending all kinds of articles; also *spec.*, toffee; also *transf.*; **stick-bomb** = *sticky bomb* s.v. STICKY *a.*[2] 5 a; **stick-culture**, a bacterial culture made by thrusting a platinum needle into the culture-medium (*Cent. Dict.* 1891); †**stickdirt**, a term of abuse; **stick-fast** *sb.* † (*a*) = SIT-FAST *sb.* 1 (*obs.*); (*b*) an act of sticking in the mud, mire, etc.; (*c*) one who or something which becomes grounded; *adj.* that causes travellers to become mired; **stick-jaw** *colloq.*, a pudding or sweetmeat difficult of mastication; also *attrib.* and *transf.*; **stick-knife**, a butcher's sticking knife; also *dial.* a large pocket knife; **stick-pin** *U.S.*, any (ornamental) pin that is merely stuck in (as distinguished from a safety pin), esp. a tie-pin; also *attrib.*; hence **stick-pinned** *ppl. a.*; **stick-seed**, a plant of the genus *Echinospermum*, the seeds of which are furnished with hooked adhesive prickles; **stick-slip**, alternate movement and cessation of movement of one surface over another as a result of frictional forces; freq. *attrib.*; **sticktight**, (*a*) a composite weed, *Bidens frondosa*, whose flat achenia bear two barbed awns; also one of the seeds (*Cent. Dict.*); (*b*) in full, ***sticktight flea***; a small flea, *Echidnophaga gallinicea*, which infests poultry; **stickwater**, the liquid that is squeezed out when cooked fish are compressed during the manufacture of fish meal and fish oil; **stickweed** *U.S.*, the Ragweed, *Ambrosia artemisiæfolia* (Britton & Brown *Illustr. Flora North. U.S.*, 1898).

1880 *Spon's Encycl. Industr. Arts* etc. II. 628 '*Stick-all'.. is a solution of silicate of potash... It will securely unite fragments of stone, marble, wood, &c. **1943** J. H. FULLARTON *Troop Target* xxiv. 175 Along comes a Jerry tank. Kiwi goes in with *stick bombs. Jerry hops out with his shirt-tail alight. Kiwi shoots him. **1971** 'A. HALL' *Warsaw Document* viii. 89 The main doors breached with five stick-bombs. *a* **1585** MONTGOMERIE *Flyting w. Polwart* 117 False strydand *stickdirt, I's gar thee stincke. **1610** MARKHAM *Masterp.* II. xliii. 285 Of the *Stickfast, Hornes, or hard bones growing vnder the saddle. **1863** W. C. BALDWIN *Afr. Hunting* iv. 110 After..a couple of stick-fasts, got on to the missionaries. **1887** C. H. RICHARDS in Gladden *Parish Probl.* 312 But when the tide rises,..these stick-fasts and waverers are easily brought into the harbor. **1819** *Sporting Mag.* V. 93 And dash and plunge through Belvoir's *stick-fast vale. **1829** CAROLINE A. SOUTHEY *Chapters on Churchyards* II. 23 Their Saturdays commons of scrap-pie and *stick-jaw. **1894** R. WELLS *Toffy & Sweets* 14 Stick-jaw. **1894** *Sat. Rev.* 3 Mar. 234 There are plums to be found even in the most stickjaw pudding. **1932** L. GOLDING *Magnolia Street* II. v. 352 Hush, Annie, hush! Here's some stick-jaw! **1938** AUDEN & ISHERWOOD *On Frontier* III. ii. 108 Gone to a demonstration, I suppose, to shout stickjaw slogans with the rest. **1950** 'R. CROMPTON' *William—the Bold* i. 13 'Look! There's some real stick-jaw toffee,' said Henry. **1843** R. J. GRAVES *Syst. Clin. Med.* xxiv. 302 An old razor, not so decent-looking nor so sharp as a tolerably good *stick knife. **1869** *Lonsdale Gloss.*, *Stick-knife*, a large pocket-knife. **1895** *Montgomery Ward Catal.* Spring & Summer 172 Fine solid gold scarf and *stick pins. **1906** 'O. HENRY' in *N.Y. World Mag.* 18 Dec. 2/2 He wore his tie drawn through a topaz ring instead of fastened with a stick pin. **1928** 'S. S. VAN DINE' *Greene Murder Case* v. 64, I was only looking for that old emerald stick-pin you borrowed and never returned. **1973** M. CROWELL *Greener Pastures* 132 A dapper tree sparrow, dark stickpin spot on his soft gray breast. **1847** DARLINGTON *Amer. Weeds* 244 Echinospermum, *Swartz.* *Stickseed. **1939** *Proc. R. Soc.* A. CLXIX. 378 The friction is fluctuating violently, and the measurement again shows that the motion is proceeding by a process of '*stick-slip'. **1940** *Phil. Trans. R. Soc.* CCXXXIX. 1 Certain substances..are able to prevent this 'stick-slip' motion and allow continuous sliding to take place. **1958** *Engineering* 14 Mar. 339/2 The movement of the ram is completely free from 'stick-slip' phenomena because of the small but significant clearance between piston and cylinder. **1959** *Times* 13 Oct. 4/4 This 'stick-slip' as it is called can make the steering stiff to move initially. **1975** *McGraw-Hill Yearbk. Sci. & Technol.* 21/2 The jerky motion happens because—under the pressure and temperature conditions of the shallow part of the Earth's lithosphere—rock exhibits a property known as stick-slip. **1884** W. MILLER *Plant-n.* 11 Beggar Ticks, or *Stick-tight, *Bidens frondosa.* **1915** F. C. BISHOPP *Fleas as Pests* (U.S.D.A. Farmers Bull. 683) 7 The sticktight flea, or southern chicken flea,..the most important of our live-stock infesting species. **1955** W. W. DENLINGER *Compl. Boston* II. 77 These sticktights abound in neglected..chicken houses. **1962** GORDON & LAVOIPIERRE *Entomol. for Students of Med.* xxxv. 218 Another species of burrowing flea,..the so-called 'sticktight flea', on rare occasions attacks man. **1915** *Rep. U.S. Comm. Fisheries 1914* App. III. 25 An apparatus for evaporating the water which is separated from the oil and known as '*stick water' has recently been installed... The residue or 'stick' will average about 9 per cent ammonia. **1945** *Poultry Sci.* XXIV. 379/1 The stickwater from fish-meal manufacture added materially to the riboflavin potency of a feed. **1965** G. H. O. BURGESS et al. *Fish Handling & Processing* x. 237 Acidification of the dilute stickwater coagulates some of the fine suspended solids and these are sometimes recovered by further centrifuging. **1800** WEEMS *Life Washington* i. (1877) 6 He will drop his false foliage and fruit and stand forth confessed in native *stickweed sterility and worthlessness.

b. in phraseol. comb., as **stick-at-it** *colloq.*, a plodding conscientious person; **stick-at-nothing** *a.*, that will hesitate or stop at nothing in order to accomplish his purpose; **stick-to-it-iveness** *colloq.* (orig. *U.S.*), dogged perseverance. Also STICK-IN-THE-MUD.

1909 H. G. WELLS *Tono-Bungay* II. ii. 162 I'm a boiler-over, not a simmering stick-at-it. **1805** LAMB *Let. Hazlitt* 10 Nov., The stick-at-nothing, Herodias'-daughter kind of grace. **1841** DICKENS *Barn. Rudge* xxxix, Here's a new brother,..a credit to the cause; one of the stick-at-nothing sort. **1915** CONRAD *Victory* 118 A false, lying, swindling, underhand, stick-at-nothing brute. **1867** in E. B. Custer *Tenting on Plains* (1889) xvi. 520 With the stick-to-it-iveness of a fox-hound when once on a trail. **1908** *Daily Express* 15 May 1/4 Success..is mostly hard work. It's work and it's stick-to-it-iveness. You've got to keep at it all the time. **1934** J. A. LEE *Children of Poor* I. 19 With the irresponsibility of my..father and my mother's stick-to-itiveness, I can.. fashion an edifice and then..set the whole show toppling. **1979** *N.Y. Rev. Bks.* 8 Feb. 10/3 This man who made his million apparently more by stick-to-itiveness than brilliance.

c. stick-on *a.*, that sticks on or can be stuck on; adhesive.

1925 J. W. BIGGER *Handbk. Bacteriol.* 60 Stick-on labels may be used, but these must never be licked in a bacteriological laboratory. **1941** *Sun* (Baltimore) 13 Aug. 16/6 There also will be speakers on the stick-on spray..and other matters of interest to apple growers. **1962** L. DEIGHTON *Ipcress File* i. 13 In crude stick-on letters the film title said *Jay. Leeds.* **1967** *Punch* 22 Nov. 780/1 False eyelashes, interchangeable wigs, adhesive eyebrows, stick-on fingernails. **1972** *Guardian* 11 Aug. 9/6 Another story book you make yourself with stick-on shapes.

stick (stɪk), *v.*[2] Pa. t. and pa. pple. **sticked** (stɪkt); often *erron.* **stuck**. [f. STICK *sb.*[1]]

1. *trans.* To lay sticks between (pieces of timber) in stacking (it). ? *local.*

1573 TUSSER *Husb.* (1878) 42 Now sawe out thy timber,.. Bestowe it and stick it, and lay it aright. **1714** [see STICKED *ppl. a.*[2]]. **1877** in *Dict. Archit.* (Arch. Publ. Soc.) s.v. *Stick*, Deals sticked under sheds to season, with a stick between each board. *Ibid.* s.v. *Stacking*, Deals..have to be placed in a yard with due regard to the means of drying..; the top end resting against a rack (called sticking), the other end on the ground.

2. To furnish (a plant) with a stick as a support.

1636 *Min. Archdeaconry of Essex 1635–8* (MS.) fol. 53 b, For cuttinge bowes of a tree to sticke pease. **1766** *Complete Farmer* s.v. *Pease*, The chief trouble after sowing them is, to stick the larger sorts which require support. **1816** F. VANDERSTRAETEN *Improv. Agric.* 185 *note*, Growing twice as high as the ordinary flax, it must be sticked or supported. **1887** G. M. FENN *This Man's Wife* I. i, Going to stick those peas, are you?

3. To furnish (an artificial leaf or flower) with a stem or stalk.

1896 *Daily News* 9 June 9/6 Then they [artificial leaves] are carried off to be 'sticked' and papered.

4. To set up (type) in a composing stick.

1842 Implied in *type-sticker*: see TYPE *sb.*[1] 10. **1882** in OGILVIE.

5. *intr.* To pick up sticks for firewood.

Only in phr. *to go sticking*.

1870 *Brand's Pop. Antiq.* I. 126 In parts of Huntingdonshire, the poor people go 'sticking', or gathering sticks for fuel in Warboy's Wood on May Day. **1891** *Rutland Gloss.* s.v., I've been sticking all the morning.

6. *Croquet.* To hit the post or peg.

1897 *Encycl. Sport* I. 254/1 (Croquet) *Post*,..Also called *Peg* and *Stick*, the last two being sometimes used as verbs, for hitting the post.

7. To strike (a person) with a stick.

1937 PARTRIDGE *Dict. Slang* 830/1 *Sticked* (, *be*), (to be) caned. **1962** M. DUFFY *That's how it Was* iv. 44 The whole of 3A was sticked..Miss Wilkinson..smacking the outstretched palms. **1982** *Sunday Sun-Times* (Chicago) 17 Oct. 138/1 Edmonton's Ken 'The Rat' Linseman was suspended..for sticking Toronto's Russ Adam during an exhibition game [of hockey].

stick, variant of STEEK *sb.*[3]

stickability (stɪkəˈbɪlɪtɪ). *colloq.* [f. STICK *v.*[1] + ABILITY.] Capacity for endurance, persistence, perseverance, staying power.

1888 *Voice* (N.Y.) 10 May 7/3 Stickability..is the most important ability a farmer can possess. **1905** *British Weekly*

28 May 193/2 To be able to take rebuffs happily and still go on requires, to use a coined word, 'stickability'. **1922** *Chambers's Jrnl.* Sept. 634/2 The foreigner has supplanted the middle and lower class Chilian in nearly every branch of industry in which the quality best described as 'stickability' is required. **1962** *Daily Tel.* 17 Aug. 18/1 All too many lack any degree of 'stickability' and flit from job to job like butterflies. **1976** P. DONOVAN *Relig. Lang.* iv. 45 Those engaged in such activities get their stickability..from the quite reasonable assumption that unless someone persists.., there is little chance of any discovery being made.

'stickadove, 'stickadoor. *dial.* Forms: 6–7 stic(k)adoue, 7, 9 stickadove, (8 stick-a-door, 9 stickadore). [Altered forms of STECHADOS.] French Lavender, *Lavendula Stœchas.*

1597 GERARDE *Herbal* II. clxx. 469 Of French Lauander, or Stickadoue. **1629** PARKINSON *Parad.* 448 Stœchas, Sticadoue, Cassidony, or French Lauender. **1668** WILKINS *Real Char.* II. iv. §6. 91 French Lavender, Stickadove. **1753** *Chambers' Cycl.* Suppl., App., *Stick-a-door*, a name sometimes used for the *stoechas*. **1866** *Treas. Bot.* 1099/1 Stickadore, *Lavandula Stœchas.* **1901** *Lady's Realm* X. 654/2 We sought for stickadove, oak of Cappadocia, [etc.].

stickage ('stɪkɪdʒ). *rare.* [f. STICK *v.*[1] + -AGE.] Tendency to stick; adhesion or cohesion.

1734 J. T. DESAGULIERS *Course of Experimental Philos.* I. iii. 89 We are to have regard to..the Quantity of *Stickage* or Friction; which differ according to the..Nature of the Materials. **1764** J. FERGUSON *Lect.* iii. 39 The resistance arising from the cohesion or stickage of the wood. **1794** G. ADAMS *Nat. & Exp. Philos.* III. xxxi. 259 Percussion puts all the parts of the wood into a tremulous motion; which by disuniting them, lessens the stickage. **1961** *New Scientist* 27 July 216 Most metals tend to stick to other metals they touch in a deep vacuum. Bearings must be found to prevent such stickage. **1968** *Encycl. Polymer Sci. & Technol.* IX. 33 Too much waxing can lead to further stickage.

stické ('stɪki:). [From the ending of SPHAIRISTICKE (a. Gr. σφαιριστική art of ball-play), the name given in 1874 to the game which afterwards developed into lawn tennis.] A game combining some of the features of lawn tennis and rackets; also *attrib.*, as *stické court, player.*

1903 *Windsor Mag.* Sept. 381 The Game of Stické: its Evolution and Progress. *Ibid.* 382 There is a Stické-court in Halifax, N.S... Prior to the year 1891 only three Stické-courts were in existence in the United Kingdom. **1910** SIR D. O'CALLAGHAN in *Times* 14 Apr. 20/4 The Game of Stické. Sir,—Now that a 'stické' court has been duly inaugurated at the Queen's Club, it may interest [etc.].

sticked (stɪkt), *a. nonce-wd.* [f. STICK *sb.*[1] + -ED[2].] Furnished with (walking) sticks.

1820 L. HUNT *Indicator* No. 33 (1822) I. 259 The Cavaliers of Charles the First's time were a sticked race, as well as the apostolic divines and puritans, who appear to have carried staves because [etc.].

sticked (stɪkt), *ppl. a.*[1] *Obs.* exc. *north.* [f. STICK *v.*[1] + -ED[1].] In the senses of the verb.

1499 *Promp. Parv.* (Pynson) p v b, Stikkyd vp, *succinctus.* **1565** COOPER *Thesaurus, Confixus*,..Pricked: thrust through: sticked. **1606** BIRNIE *Kirk-Buriall* xiv. (1833) D 3, Affirming the corps of sticked Tarquin to be both bathed and balmed.

b. esp. of a pig: Killed by cutting its throat, stuck. *Obs.* exc. *north.*

a **1330** *Otuel* 1502 Otuwel..smot poidras of barbarin, þat þpere he lay as a stiked swin. *c* **1386** CHAUCER *Pard. T.* 228 Thou fallest as it were a styked swyn. **1876** T. FARRALL *Betty Wilson's Cummerl. T.* 77 (E.D.D.) Bled like a stick't pig.

sticked (stɪkt), *ppl. a.*[2] [f. STICK *v.*[2] + -ED[1].] In senses of the vb.

1714 S. SEWALL *Diary* 28 July (1882) III. 13 A fine Boy.. was playing with other children about a pile of Stick'd Boards, which fell down upon him.

sticker[1] ('stɪkə(r)). [f. STICK *v.*[1] + -ER.] One who or that which sticks, in the senses of the verb.

1. One who sticks or stabs, esp. one who kills swine by sticking.

a **1585** POLWART *Flyting w. Montgomerie* 787 Tyk stickar. **1833** HOOD *Sk. Road, Sudden Death* Wks. 1870 II. 248 Master Bardell the pig-butcher, and his foreman Samuel Slark, or, as he was more commonly called, Sam the Sticker. **1881** INGERSOLL *Oyster-Industr.* (Hist. Fish. Industr. U.S.) 249 *Sticker*, an oyster-opener who rests the oyster against the bench while he thrusts the knife between the valves.

2. A weapon used for piercing or stabbing as distinguished from cutting or slashing; esp. a sticking-knife, a fishing spear, an angler's gaff. Chiefly *colloq.*

1896 BARING-GOULD *Dartmoor Idylls* viii. 188 Go and ax the butcher to lend you his sticker. **1899** R. WHITEING *No. 5 John St.* iv, There warn't no time to square up to 'im when I see the sticker [pocket knife] in 'is 'and. **1901** *Munsey's Mag.* XXIV. 442/2 Swords or knives can be divided into two classes, the hackers and the stickers.

3. a. One who or something which adheres or remains attached; one who remains constant; one who persists in a task. Const. *to*, †*unto.*

1674 N. FAIRFAX *Bulk & Selv.* 133 Motion or going on by steps, is such a sticker unto body, that it can no more belong to Ghost, than thinking can to that. **1824** in *Spirit Publ. Jrnls.* (1825) 516 When wed she'll change, for Love's no sticker, And love her husband less than liquor? *a* **1849** H. COLERIDGE *Ess.* (1851) II. 75 The same class of fastidious wits who in France became Zoilists, in England were the stoutest stickers to Homer. **1869** M. ARNOLD *Cult. & Anarchy* Pref. 55 For we are fond stickers to no machinery, not even our own. **1895** *Westm. Gaz.* 30 Apr. 6/1 Experience proves that these are the best 'stickers', as, knowing the difficulties, they do not expect to strike gold immediately, but are content to search for the metal. **1916** *Anzac Bk.* 130 He was no 'sticker', and in the third year of his medical course he had side-tracked himself. **1967** C. FREMLIN *Prisoner's Base* xii. 84 Daphne did not believe in dropping things; she was, as she would have told you, a Sticker. **1979** N. HYND *False Flags* viii. 71 Bobby wasn't any quitter. He was a sticker.

b. A commodity which does not find a ready sale. Also *transf.* (see quot. 1887). *colloq.*

1824 DIBDIN *Libr. Comp.* 573, I fear it [the book] will be a sticker. **1887** G. R. SIMS *Mary Jane's Mem.* x. 128 Stickers are servants that the [registry] office finds it hard to get places for.

c. *Sporting.* A horse or a person with good staying power; a stayer.

1860 WHYTE MELVILLE *Mkt. Harb.* 18 He's too fast for us ....Only, to be sure, we have a vast of plough hereabout, and *I* never see such a sticker through dirt. **1890** 'R. BOLDREWOOD' *Colonial Reformer* x, You've got..an out-and-out good hack... I'll forfeit my month's wages if he ain't a sticker, as well.

d. *Cricket.* A batsman who scores slowly and is hard to get out. *colloq.*

1832 P. EGAN *Bk. Sports* xxii. 344/2 At the *bat* and the *bottle* they find him a *sticker.* **1855** F. LILLYWHITE *Guide to Cricketers* 56 A 'sticker' with 'confidence' was all that was required, to have turned the 'tide' in their favour. **1903** W. J. FORD in *Cricket* (ed. Hutchinson) vi. 190 Louis Hall (the pioneer of stickers). **1977** *Times* 12 July 10/1 When Chappell was adding 55 with O'Keeffe, who is well known as a sticker, there were visions of England having to make 175, perhaps 200, today.

e. A person who stays too long on a visit.

1903 FARMER *Slang, Sticker*, 4 (colloquial), a lingering guest.

f. *U.S. colloq.* A thorn or bur.

1889 H. H. MCCONNELL *Five Years a Cavalryman* iv. 35 The leaves when submitted to the action of fire in order to burn off the sharp stickers, are used as food for cattle. **1898** G. F. ATHERTON *Californians* 231 Trennahan..plucked the "stickers' from his trousers. **1899** M. GOING *Field, Forest, & Wayside Flowers* 350 When the 'stickers' are at last picked or rubbed off, they fall to the ground. **1945** B. MACDONALD *Egg & I* (1946) III. viii. 94 My hair and shoulders were full of twigs and stickers.

4. Something which causes a person to stick or to be at a nonplus; a poser. *colloq.*

1849 THACKERAY *Pendennis* xxv, That's what I call a sticker for Wagg. **1903** FARMER *Slang, Sticker*, a pointed question, an apt and startling comment or rejoinder, an embarrassing situation.

5. a. orig. *U.S.* An adhesive label: spec. (*a*) = PASTER 2; (*b*) a small adhesive notice designed to be stuck in a conspicuous place and used to publicize a cause, commodity, or place. Also *attrib.* in **sticker price** *N. Amer.*, the advertised price (of a commodity).

1872 DE VERE *Americanisms* 270. **1888** [see PASTER 2]. **1888** C. A. KNIGHT in *Voice* (N.Y.) July 5 Quotations..printed on one side of little slips of paper..to be gummed and used as 'stickers'..on newspaper wrappers, [etc.]. **1919** *Nation* (N.Y.) 117/2 Defendants..had printed millions of seditious "stickers'. **1934** J. M. CAIN *Postman always rings Twice* ii. 13 About three o'clock a guy came along that was all burned up because somebody had pasted a sticker on his wind wing. I had to go in the kitchen to steam it off for him. **1943** K. TENNANT *Ride on Stranger* xvii. 185 Plastering it [*sc.* a vessel] with stickers demanding the guest's release. **1955** W. GADDIS *Recognitions* I. v. 192, I left all my luggage there covered with the most adorable stickers from everywhere, my dears, every chic hotel you ever heard of. **1959** *Listener* 21 May 884/1 An English 'sticker' about Nuclear Disarmament on the door of..the students' canteen. **1962** E. GODFREY *Retail Selling & Organ.* ix. 91 Special delivery instructions..should be written clearly..on a special sticker attached to the despatch docket. **1967** [see BUMPER *sb.*[1] 5 c]. **1970** *Globe & Mail* (Toronto) 25 Sept. B4/7 The company said the sticker or suggested retail prices, which include federal excise taxes..are up an average of $136. **1976** J. I. M. STEWART *Memorial Service* xvi. 273 His magazine's supposed to be coming out tomorrow. Have you seen the stickers for it?

b. A postage stamp. *Criminals' slang.*

1904 'No. 1500' *Life in Sing Sing* 253/1 *Stickers*, postage stamps. **1926** J. BLACK *You can't Win* ix. 107 You're a cinch to get some coin and a bundle of stickers out of every 'P.O.' You can peddle the stamps anywhere.

6. a. *Organ-building.* (See quot. 1884.)

1845 G. DODD *Brit. Manuf.* IV. 160 The 'under-hammer' [[acts] on the 'sticker'. **1884** *Encycl. Brit.* XVII. 834 [Organ.] The connexion between the keys and their pallets is made by various mechanisms... Where pressure has to be transmitted instead of a pull, thin but broad slips of wood are used, having pins stuck into their ends to keep them in their places. These are stickers.

b. In the pianoforte: = MOPSTICK 2. Also *attrib.*

1870 [see MOPSTICK 2]. **1885** LOCK *Workshop Rec.* Ser. IV. 281/2 To repair a broken sticker hinge, unscrew the button [[etc.]. **1908** *Times* 19 Feb. 14/4 The first improvement.. was in the sticker action.

7. (See quot.) Cf. STICK *v.*[1] 18 c.

1909 *N. Hawkins' Mech. Dict.*, *Sticker*, a wood working machine, used on articles of small cross sectional area, such as picture frame moulding, etc.

8. *sticker up*: One who 'sticks up' *for* something. *colloq.*

1857 BORROW *Romany Rye* App. v, Ah! but some sticker-up for gentility will exclaim, 'The hero did not refuse' [etc.].

9. sticker-up. *Australian.* **a.** A bush method of cooking meat by spitting it and setting it to roast. Also *attrib.*

1830 *Hobart Town Almanack* 112 Steaks..which he cooked in the mode called in colonial phrase a sticker up. **1852** MRS. C. MEREDITH *My Home Tasmania* I. iv. 54 Here I was first initiated into the bush art of 'sticker-up' cookery.

b. A bushranger.

1879 W. J. BARRY *Up & Down* xx. 197 They..were the stickers-up, or highwaymen, mentioned by me before.

Hence **'sticker** *v. trans.*, to affix a sticker (sense 5 a) to; **'stickered** *ppl. a.*; **'stickering** *vbl. sb.*

1972 *Daily Colonist* (Victoria, B.C.) 3 Feb. 48/8 The system started in 1963 in Monterey Park, Calif., where 5,000 stickered homes had been broken into only 19 times and about 6,000 non-marked homes suffered more than 2,000 burglaries. **1976** *Publishers Weekly* 29 Mar. 41/1 The titles are produced by Dent in London. Dutton warehouses its inventory in this country and the titles are stickered for the U.S. market here. **1977** *Periodical* XL. 196 Nothing vexes me more than to go into a bookshop and find not just one price sticker on the book jacket, increasing the price, but sometimes two or more... The stickering is a burdensome business.

sticker[2] ('stɪkə(r)). [f. STICK *sb.*[1] or *v.*[2] + -ER.] One who gathers sticks for firewood.

From a misreading of quot. 1422, Cowel, followed by Todd and later Dicts., has a spurious word *stickler.*

1422 *Rolls of Parlt.* IV. 179/1 Un Homme appellee Stikker, coillant chescun jour Bois, deins mesmes le Park. **1821** CLARE *Vill. Minstr.* II. 24 The ragged plundering stickers have been there, And pilfer'd it [a wattled arbour] away.

†**stick-free,** *a.* and *sb. Obs.* [f. STICK *sb.*[4] + FREE *a.*, after Du. *steekvrij*, G. *stichfrei* adj.]

a. *adj.* Proof against injury by the thrust of a weapon. **b.** *sb.* One who is 'stick-free'.

1621 BURTON *Anat. Mel.* I. ii. I. iii. 72 [Witches] can make stick-free's, such as shall endure a rapiers point, or musket shot and neu'r be wounded. **1637** SHIRLEY *Yng. Admiral* IV. G 2 b, *Paz.* Would somebody would challenge mee to fight before her, if the Ladies knew I were sticke free they would teare me in peeces for my company. *Ibid.* H 3, *Paz.* Though I be sticke and shotfree, I may be beaten, and bruis'd as I remember. **1676** [see SPURN *sb.*[1] 3 b].

stickful ('stɪkfʊl). [f. STICK *sb.*[1] + -FUL.] As much type as a composing-stick will hold.

1683 MOXON *Mech. Exerc., Printing* xxii. 224 Therefore he Justifies his Stick-full just to the breadth of the Wooden Letter with Quadrats or Quotations. **1888** *Encycl. Brit.* XXIII. 700/2 Stickful after stickful of type is placed on the galley.

Stickie, Sticky ('stɪkɪ). *Ir. slang.* [f. STICK *v.*[1]: see -Y[6], -IE.] A member of the official I.R.A. or Sinn Fein. Usu. in *pl.* See also STICK *sb.*[5]

1972 *Times* 21 Aug. 10/3 Who'll stop the boys fighting with the stickies (official IRA)? **1978** F. BURTON *Politics of Legitimacy* 188 'Stickies' is the widespread term used to designate the Official IRA/Sinn Féin. I heard two accounts of the origin of the term and both were somewhat apocryphal. One referred to the fact that the Official IRA 'stuck' to the existing organization whereas the Provisionals broke away. The other explained the name by referring to the fact that the Provisional IRA Easter Lilies were pinned to their supporters' clothes whereas the Officials had theirs stuck on. **1978** D. MURPHY *Place Apart* vi. 110 Her son.. was 'executed' last year as a punishment for deserting from the Stickies. **1979** J. B. BELL *Secret Army* 446 The term Stickies or Sticks came from the Official Republican innovation of putting gum on the back of the Easter Lily commemoration badge while the Provos stuck to the conventional pin.

stickily ('stɪkɪlɪ), *adv.* [f. STICKY *a.*[2] + -LY[2].] In a sticky manner.

1908 KIPLING *Actions & Reactions* (1909) 102 The Hive was half hidden by smoke... They heard a frame crack stickily. **1937** *Times* 12 July 5/1 The game started rather stickily. **1942** 'A. BRIDGE' *Frontier Passage* iii. 39 'Is he dead?'.. 'Supposed to be—very stickily finished off by the Reds, when they caught him.' **1973** *Times Lit. Suppl.* 9 Mar. 257/2 The book manages, in fact, to make something stickily implausible out of several familiar conventions.

stick-in, *a.* [f. vbl. phrase *stick in*: see STICK *v.* 31.] That is inserted. *stick-in piece*: a small piece of metal sometimes inserted in the notched ends of bars when making a butt-joint.

1843 HOLTZAPFFEL *Turning* I. 221 The butt joint is materially strengthened, when..it is..notched in on three or four sides, and pieces called stick-in pieces, dowels, or charlins..are..laid in the notches.

stickiness[1] ('stɪkɪnɪs). [f. STICKY *a.*[2] + -NESS.] The quality of being sticky; adhesiveness, glutinousness; also *transf.*, hesitancy, stubbornness; awkwardness, unpleasantness.

1727 BAILEY vol. II, *Stickiness*, Aptness to stick to. **1755** JOHNSON, *Stickiness*, adhesive quality; viscosity; glutinousness; tenacity. **1800** *Gentl. Mag.* LXX. I. 45 Which is preferable, the stickiness of the honey, or the greasiness of the hair? **1897** *Allbutt's Syst. Med.* III. 601 In the case [of peritonitis] there may be merely some injection of polished surface, and in its place a general stickiness.

fig. **1864** *Athenæum* 14 May 683/3 [The picture] is almost free from over-sweetness, or 'stickiness', as some call it. *transf.* **1933** C. MACKENZIE *Water on Brain* viii. 115 Major Hunter-Hunt let his emotion over the stickiness of the Treasury evaporate in a deep sigh. **1947** 'N. BLAKE' *Minute for Murder* viii. 167 He had not imagined..that there was anything more in Billson's recalcitrance..than his usual official stickiness. **1948** WODEHOUSE *Spring Fever* xiii. 126 The intense stickiness of the situation. **1962** J. D. MACDONALD *Girl* xii. 186 You do seem to have involved her in some sort of stickiness.

stickiness[2] ('stɪkɪnɪs). [f. STICKY *a.*[1] + -NESS.] Stiffness, woodenness. (Chiefly with reference to athletics.)

1910 *Evening News* 12 Mar. 2/6 The rapid improvement of the Light Blues [i.e. the Cambridge boat crew], contrasted with the 'stickiness' of their rivals. **1911** MARETT *Anthrop.* v. 143 It would prove an endless task if I were to try here to illustrate at all extensively the stickiness, as one might almost call it, of primitive modes of speech. **1912** *World* 7 May Suppl. 2/2 For spectators the abolition of 'offside' means a game without any of the old 'stickiness'.

sticking ('stɪkɪŋ), *vbl. sb.*[1] [-ING[1].]

1. The action of STICK *v.*[1] **a.** The action of piercing or stabbing, or of thrusting (a weapon, tool, etc.) *into* or *through* something.

a **1400-50** *Wars Alex.* 2623 Þare was stomling of stedis, sticking of erles [etc.]. *c* **1440** *Promp. Parv.* 475/2 Stykynge in beestes, *jugulacio.* **1823** SCOTT *Quentin D.* xviii, Although the doing such a deed were as ignoble as the sticking of swine. **1896** *Harper's Mag.* Apr. 772/1 The enemy received our bayonet attack up to within three paces; then began the sticking.

b. Fixing or fastening in position. Also with *on*, etc.

c **1386** CHAUCER *Pars. T.* 954 A whit wal, al-though it ne brenne noght fully by stikynge of a candele, yet is the wal blak of the leyt. *c* **1440** *Promp. Parv.* 475/2 Stykynge, or festynge to, *confixio, fixura.*

c. The action of setting a surface with something; †garnishing (of meat); setting (of cotton or wool cards) with teeth.

1633 HART *Diet of Diseased* I. xxii. 101 The Clove..is very much used in the kitchin both for sauces, and sticking of meat. **1794** MORSE *Amer. Geog.* 332 [There] are made yearly about 7000 dozen of cotton and wool cards... The sticking of these cards employs not less than 1000 people.

d. The process or condition of adhering.

1591 PERCIVALL *Sp. Dict., Apegamiento*, sticking to, cleauing to, *adhaesio, conglutinatio.* **1683** MOXON *Mech. Exerc, Printing* xi. ¶23 They..try its consistence by sticking together of their Finger and Thumb. **1719** LONDON & WISE *Compl. Gard.* v. 86 As for the sticking to the Stone in Plumbs, 'tis not worth minding. **1876** GEO. ELIOT *Dan. Der.* lviii, To move, like the limpet, by an apparent sticking which after a good while is discerned to be a slight progression. **1910** *N. Hawkins' Electr. Dict., Sticking*, in telegraphy, a tendency of the relay to cling to the pole of its magnet after the current is broken.

e. Hesitation, scruple, delay; an instance of this; also a cause of hesitation or delay. Now *rare* or *Obs.*

1528 GARDINER in Pocock *Rec. Ref.* I. l. 104 To the intent we might the better discipher the very lett and sticking. **1578** T. P. *Knowl. Warres* 19 The Souldiour..must be tractable, and obedient to the commaundement of his Captayne, and that without stycking. *a* **1631** DONNE *Let.* v. Poems, etc. (1633) 364 And as to that life, all stickings and hesitations seeme stupid and stony, so to this [etc.]. **1725** WODROW *Corr.* (1843) III. 201 My landlord is reflected on for sticking; and I believe, if he had not been ill treated and fretted, all had been easy.

f. Coming to a stand; being unable to proceed.

1570 T. WILSON tr. *Demosthenes* Pref. **j b, That such as bee not learned, may the rather go thorow with the reading of these Orations without any sticking at all. **1730** T. BOSTON *Life* xii. (1908) 315 My matter coming to me as I wrote..: if at any time I walked, it was occasioned by my sticking.

g. Of a batsman: Continuance at the wicket or 'in' by means of ultra-defensive play.

1901 R. H. LYTTELTON *Outdoor Games* vi. 122 If the wicket is to be enlarged I should prefer it in this form, though 'sticking' would be even greater than it is now.

h. **sticking-up.** *Australian.* The action of stopping (a conveyance or person) on the highway for robbery. Also *attrib.*

1855 *Melbourne Argus* 18 Jan. 5/4 [Witness] said he was coming from Richmond on the night of the robbery, and saw a sticking-up case. **1893** MRS. C. PRAED *Outlaw & Lawm.* I. 28 The sticking-up of the Goondi coach.

2. *concr.* **a.** *Mining.* = SELVAGE 5.

1747 HOOSON *Miner's Dict.* U 1, All Scrins, and smaller Kind of Veins, that afford not Shoulder Room, their width between the Sides may be called the Sticking, and this is the common Name that we Miners give to all of that Size. **1789** T. WILLIAMS *Min. Kingd.* I. 13 A blackish soft sticking of clay, perhaps not above half an inch thick. **1875** J. H. COLLINS *Metal Mining* 26 The country on each side is frequently much altered, 'mineralised' as miners say. This altered band..is variously known as capel, stickings, selvage, and..other names.

b. *pl.* 'Coarse, bruised, inferior meat; spec. the portions damaged by the butcher's knife' (Farmer).

Cf. STICKING-PIECE; also *sticking-bit, -part*, in 3.

1851 MAYHEW *Lond. Labour* I. 196 The meat (for pies) is bought in 'pieces', of the same part as the sausage-makers purchase—the stickings. **1894** *West Sussex County Times* 17 Mar. 4/6 The Guardians are desirous of receiving Tenders ..for..Meat, Consisting of Beef (thick flanks, and clods, and stickings) free from bone.

3. *attrib.* and *Comb.*

1869 J. P. MORRIS *Furness Gloss.*, **Stickin'-bit*, the neck-end of mutton. **1875** *Carpentry & Join.* 6 *Sticking boards used in planing up sash bars. **1885** LOCK *Workshop Rec.* Ser. IV. 3/1 This [coat] is usually a different mixture.. and is called a '*sticking-coat', its object being to secure adhesion between the fabric and the rubber. **1688** HOLME *Armoury* III. 87/2 The *Sticking Draught, is a part of the Breast [of an ox] when it is cut long-ways, over cross the bones. **1495-6** in *Finchale Priory Charters* etc. (Surtees) p. cccxciv, iij *stekyngknyffze. **1909** *N. Hawkins' Mech. Dict.*, **Sticking Machine*, a woodworking machine, forming straight mouldings by means of rotary cutters. **1881** *Daily News* 3 Sept. 2/5 My father had in three fore-quarters of beef. When the officer came in I was trimming up the *sticking parts. **1733** W. ELLIS *Chiltern & Vale Farm.* 238 This sort of Ground by its *sticking Quality, will more easily fasten about and hold the Beans.

sticking, *vbl. sb.*[2] [f. STICK *v.*[2] + -ING[1].]

1. The action of STICK *v.*[2]

1828 CARLYLE *Let.* 10 June in Froude *Life* (1882) II. ii. 26 Alas! Jack, there is no sticking of peas for me at this hour.

2. In *plural.* Sticks (for peas); more explicitly ***pea-stickings.***

1800 *Parish Acc. Much Wenlock* 5 May in Miss Jackson *Shropsh. Word-bk.* (1879) s.v., Paid John Wall for Stickings, &c., 0-2-3. **1841** HARTSHORNE *Salop. Ant.* s.v. *Swite*, Switing pea-stickings.

sticking ('stɪkɪŋ), *ppl. a.* [f. STICK *v.*[1] + -ING[2].] That sticks, in the senses of the verb.

1. That pierces or pricks (*obs.*); *dial.* of an animal, that gores.

c **1230** *Hali Meid* 35 (MS. Titus) þat sar sorhfule angoise þat stronge & stikinde [*v.r.* stinkinde] stiche. **1577** KENDALL *Flowers of Epigr.* 89 b, By stickyng spurre doest seke to sturre thy steede. **1614** GORGES *Lucan* VII. 286 No sooner did their palfries feele, Within their brest the sticking steele, But [etc.]. **1843** *Richardson's Borderer's Table-bk., Leg. Div.* I. 106 Should the sticking bull o' the Stobbs com down amang the kye.

2. That adheres.

1651 BAXTER *Inf. Bapt.* 144 They say far more..then the most notorious scorners were wont to do; and that not in a bare scorn, which is less sticking, but in serious slanders. **1883** J. PARKER *Tyne Chylde* 86 It's a sticking leech you have laid on me. **1908** *Westm. Gaz.* 9 June 4/2 [The] Mercédès.. suffered from a sticking valve.

3. That projects. Only with advs. †*off, out, up.*

1834 C. M. YONGE *Let.* 4 July in C. Coleridge *Charlotte Mary Yonge* (1903) iv. 123 There were two great sticking-out boxes like pulpits. **1843** C. RIDLEY *Let.* Feb. in U. Ridley *Cecilia* (1958) x. 118 Really it will be tiresome if he grows up with large, sticking-off ears. **1848** CURZON *Visit. Monast.* IV. vii. (1897) 301 The sticking-up legs of the subverted table. **1892** C. M. YONGE *That Stick* I. ii. 32 She had such horrid sticking-out ears. **1902** R. BAGOT *Donna Diana* viii. 98 The women with their great feet..and sticking-out teeth!

4. Special collocations: **sticking-grass** = CLEAVERS; †**sticking medicine** (see quot.); **sticking silk** = COURT-PLASTER.

1671 SALMON *Syn. Med.* III. xxvii. 471 Dropax, is a sticking Medicine, so called from Pitch, used with other sticking ingredients. **1760-72** H. BROOKE *Fool of Qual.* (1809) I. 18 Having found the wound, she put a small bit of black sticking silk to the orifice. **1844** H. STEPHENS *Bk. Farm* III. 942 The seed of the sticking-grass, or cleavers.

'sticking-piece. [STICKING *vbl. sb.*] The lower part of the neck-piece of a carcass of beef.

1469 *Ord. R. Househ.* (1790) 96 The Bocherye. Item, No fee of the oxe, more than barely the hedde, the steckinge-piece, the gollette. **1802-12** BENTHAM *Ration. Judic. Evid.* (1827) IV. 438 Neck-beef and sticking-pieces are provided by the butcher for those who cannot come up to the price of ribs and sirloins. **1844** STEPHENS *Bk. Farm* II. 169 The sticking-piece is a great favourite with some epicures, on account of the pieces of rich fat in it. **1886** *W. Somerset Word-bk., Sticking-piece*, the part of the neck of a bullock near where the knife entered—usually discoloured with blood and sold for gravy-beef.

sticking-place. [STICKING *vbl. sb.*]

1. A place in which to stick (something). *rare.*

1578 T. PROCTOR *Gorg. Gallery* P iiij, Which flower, out of my hand shall neuer passe, But in my harte, shall haue a sticking place.

2. The place in which a thing stops and holds fast.

Only in echoes of the Shaks. example, in which the allusion seems to be to the screwing-up of the peg of a musical instrument until it becomes tightly fixed in the hole.

1605 SHAKS. *Macb.* I. vii. 60 But screw your courage to the sticking place, And wee'le not fayle. **1829** SOUTHEY *Sir T. More* (1831) II. 136 His rent having been already screwed to the sticking-place. **1883** *Fortn. Rev.* 1 Oct. 473 But she.. saw that she must keep him to the sticking-place.

3. The lower part of the neck, the JUGULUM. †**a.** of the human body (*obs.*). **b.** of a beast (see quot. 1886).

1615 CROOKE *Body of Man* 361 The trunke of the hollow vein from the heart to the Iugulum or Sticking-place. **1886** *W. Somerset Word-bk., Sticking-place*, the point in an animal's throat where the knife is stuck.

'sticking-plaster. [STICKING *ppl. a.*] A material for covering and closing superficial wounds, consisting of linen, silk, or other textile fabric, or of plastic, spread with an adhesive substance; a general name for COURT-PLASTER, LEAD-*plaster*, DIACHYLON-*plaster*, etc.

1655 CULPEPPER etc. *Riverius* I. ii. 12 They heal up the wound with a sticking Plaister. **1749** GATAKER tr. *Le Dran's Operat. Surg.* 438, I secure them [the flaps of the wound] in that situation with straps of sticking plaister. **1841** DICKENS *Barn. Rudge* xxiii, He was fixing a very small patch of sticking-plaster..near the corner of his mouth. **1861** HULME tr. *Moquin-Tandon* II. III. 184 Court or Black Sticking-plaster is made with a solution of isinglass and tincture of benzoin laid upon black sarsenet. **1882** J. ASHTON *Soc. Life Q. Anne* I. 169 In the reign of Charles I, when suns, moons, stars, and even coaches and four were cut out of sticking plaister, and stuck on the face.

b. attrib. ***sticking-plaster miniature***, a silhouette cut in black paper (resembling court-plaster).

1837 THACKERAY *Ravenswing* vii, Little cracked sticking-plaster miniatures. **1848** —— *Book of Snobs* xiv, A sticking-plaster portrait of Hugby.., in a cap and gown.

'sticking-point.

1. = STICKING-PLACE 2.

1826 *Sporting Mag.* XVIII. 213 Screwing our courage to the sticking point. **1887** BIRRELL *C. Brontë* i. 16 To rouse her aunt's enthusiasm to the sticking-point of lending her some money.

2. A point at which one sticks and beyond which one refuses to go; a subject upon which one will not yield or compromise; an obstacle.

1965 *Listener* 23 Sept. 441/1 As a politician he has been mild to the point of compromise. But one sticking point for him has been India's unity. **1970** *Globe & Mail* (Toronto) 25 Sept. 3/2 An early sticking point is expected to come when the Russians raise the question of reopening the Port of Vancouver to the supply ships. **1981** *Church Times* 27 Mar. 12/5 It is not the matter of women priests that is the main sticking point.

stick-in-the-mud. [f. vbl. phr. *to stick in the mud*: see STICK *v.*[1] 11 b.] Contemptuously used for: A helpless or unprogressive person; one who lacks resource or initiative.

1733 *Gen. Evening Post* 15-17 Nov. 2/1 George Fluster, *alias* Stick in the Mud, has made himself an Evidence, and impeached the above two Persons. **1733** *Country Jrnl.* 15 Dec. 2/1 James Baker, *alias* Stick in the Mud, and Francis Ogilby [were convicted]. **1861** HUGHES *Tom Brown at Oxf.* x, This rusty-coloured one is that respectable old stick-in-the-mud, Nicias. **1886** W. H. MALLOCK *Old Order Changes* I. 286 She is such an old stick-in-the-mud. *attrib.* **1880** *St. James's Gaz.* 23 Oct. 12 He was none of your humdrum, stick-in-the-mud, oldfashioned practitioners. **1886** STEVENSON *Kidnapped* v, What a pleasure it was to get on shore with money in his pocket.. and surprise what he called stick-in-the-mud boys.

Hence **stick-in-the-muddish** *a.*

1936 M. MITCHELL *Gone with Wind* xxviii. 481 It wasn't hidebound and stick-in-the-muddish like the older towns and it had a brash exuberance that matched her own. **1959** A. SALKEY *Quality of Violence* x. 158 He's slow and easy and a little 'stick-in-the-muddish'.

'stickish, *a. nonce-wd.* [f. STICK *sb.*[1] + -ISH.] Something of a stick (cf. STICK *sb.*[1] 12 b).

1810 SCOTT in *Lockhart* (1839) III. 220 Malcolm de Grey was tolerable but *stickish.*

stickit ('stɪkɪt), *a. Sc.* Also **sticket**. [Sc. form of STICKED *ppl. a.*]

1. Of a task, a product of labour: Imperfect or bungled, unfinished.

1787 W. TAYLOR *Scots Poems* 60 (E.D.D.) Dad force't her to marry Rob, Whilk surely maks a stickit job. **1818** SCOTT *Br. Lamm.* xxxv, But I'll uphaud it for nae stickit job.

2. Qualifying a personal designation of trade or profession: That has relinquished his intended calling from want of ability or means to pursue it.

1815 SCOTT *Guy M.* ii, Upon his first attempt, he [Sampson] became totally incapable of proceeding in his intended discourse,..and was ever after designated as a 'stickit minister'. **1837** HOGG *Tales & Sk.* III. 62, 'I canna get her keepit a minute', said Geordie, 'for that stickit shopkeeper'. **1871** W. ALEXANDER *Johnny Gibb* ix. 70 Sandy disappointed the hopes of his friends by changing his mind, and turning out a kind of 'sticket doctor'.

sticklac ('stɪklæk). [f. STICK *sb.*[1] + LAC[1].] Lac in its natural state of incrustation on twigs.

1704 *Lond. Gaz.* No. 4059/4 The following Goods, viz... Shellack,..Sticklack. **1815** KIRBY & SP. *Entomol.* x. (1818) I. 326 It is distinguished by the names stick-lac when in its native state unseparated from the twigs to which it adheres [etc.]. **1826** *Vintner's, Brewer's* etc. *Guide* 64 An extract made by boiling stick-lach in water. **1883** *Daily News* 3 Oct. 2/6 Shellac... Sticklac—50 cases Siam sold at 50s. to 50s. 6d.

stickle ('stɪk(ə)l), *sb.*[1] *s.w. dial.* [Ellipt. use of STICKLE *a.*] A place in a river where the bed slopes and the water is shallow and runs swiftly; a rapid.

1616 W. BROWNE *Brit. Past.* II. iv. 108 Patient Anglers standing all the day Neere to some shallow stickle or deepe bay. **1857** G. H. KINGSLEY *Sport & Trav.* (1900) 450, I.. rushed frantically through stickle and over stone. **1887** W. H. H. ROGERS *Mem. West* ii. 19 A kind of little bay among some reeds at the foot of a stickle. **1897** *Encycl. Sport* I. 583/2 (Hunting, otter) *Stickle*, West country term for a shallow.

stickle ('stɪk(ə)l), *sb.*[2] [f. STICKLE *v.*]

†**1.** Persistent activity or endeavour (*in* a cause).

1675 V. ALSOP *Anti-Sozzo* III. ii. 173 Thus the poor Gentiles, after all his zealous stickle in their Cause, are left in the lurch to shift for themselves as well as they can.

†**2.** Contention, strife. *Obs.*

1682 N. O. *Boileau's Lutrin* I. 77 Have I by secreet Arts, nourisht the Stickle Between the Church-men, and the Conventicle?

3. An agitated or bewildered state of mind; consternation or alarm; hurry or flurry. *dial.*

1744 MRS. ROBINSON in Mrs. Climenson *Eliz. Montagu* (1906) I. 176, I was very composed, never thinking there would be any need to put myself in a stickle. **1825** BROCKETT *N.C. Gloss., Stickle*, a hurry, a bustle. **1853** G. J. CAYLEY *Las Alforjas* I. 218 The old Moorish merchant, who was in a tremendous stickle to get his wheat to the market at Tangier. **1877** *Holderness Gloss., Stickle*, fuss; perplexity; embarrassment; bewilderment; excitement.

stickle ('stɪk(ə)l), *a.* *Obs.* exc. *dial.* Forms: 1 sticol, 5 stikill, -ell, 6 stykell, stikle, 7 *superl.* stickellest, 6- stickle. [OE. *sticol* lofty, steep, rough, difficult (of a road) = OS. *stecul* (Gallée), MLG. *stekel*, OHG. *stechal*, abrupt, steep, sharp, rough, f. Teut. root **stik-* (**stek-*): see STICK *v.*[1]]

1. Of a hill or incline: Steep, high-pitched. *s.w. dial.*

c **960** *Rule St. Benet* (Schröer) Prol. 5 Se [weȝ] is neara and sticol, þe to life and to heofona rice læt. *c* **1475** *Partenay* 5848 Thys mont.. narew and stikell to sight. **1519** HORMAN *Vulg.* 177 b, That grounde boweth beste: that is easely stykell [*qui leniter molliterque adsurgit*]. **1623** R. CARPENTER *Conscionable Chr.* 23 Admonishing vs to auoyd.. the thorny copse of couetousnesse, and the stickle path of pride. **1796** W. H. MARSHALL *W. Eng.* I. 330 *Stickle*, steep, as a road; or rapid, as a stream. **1894** W. RAYMOND *Love & Quiet Life* iii. 28 The cottage with the stickle roof.

†**2.** Of a storm: ? Sharp, severe. *Obs.*

a **1400-50** *Wars Alex.* 4186 And stint was all þe stikill stormes in a stand-quile.

3. Of running water: Rapid. *s.w. dial.*

1586 J. HOOKER *Hist. Irel.* 37/1 in *Holinshed*, They found the same to be so deepe and stikle, that they could not passe ouer the same. **1614** GORGES *Lucan* I. 23 Through stickle Rhene the boates to steare. **1796** [see 1]. **1894** BLACKMORE *Perlycross* xliv. 461 A mile of water.. bright with stickle runs.

4. Of the hair of an animal: Rough, bristly. Hence *stickle-haired* adj. Now *dial.* (Yorks.).

1615 G. SANDYS *Trav.* I. 76 Their dogs.. that serue for that purpose [hunting] are stickle haired, and not vnlike to the Irish grayhounds. **1737** BRACKEN *Farriery Impr.* (1756) I. 42 Horses which.. have their Coats staring and stickle, (as the Term is). **1868** J. C. ATKINSON *Cleveland Gloss.* 496 *Stickle-haired*, with the hair rough and bristling; of the coat of a neglected horse or colt.

Hence †'**stickleness**. *Obs.*

1586 J. HOOKER *Hist. Irel.* 37/1 in *Holinshed*, The stiklenesse and danger of the water. **1602** CAREW *Cornwall* II. 120 b, A path.. in many places, through his sticklenesse occasioning, and through his steepnesse threatning, the ruine of your life, with the failing of your foote.

stickle ('stɪk(ə)l), *v.* Forms: 6 styckyll, 7 stickell, sticle, stikle, 6- stickle. [app. identical with the earlier STIGHTLE *v.*, to set in order.

For the phonology cf. *pickle* as a variant of PIGHTLE.]

†**1.** *intr.* **a.** To act as an official regulator of a tournament, wrestling match, or the like, in order to ensure fair play. **b.** Hence, to act as a mediator or umpire, to interpose or intervene (*between* or *among* combatants or contending parties). *Obs.*

1530 PALSGR. 736/1, I styckyll betwene wrastellers, or any folkes that prove mastries to se that none do other wronge. **1598** DALLINGTON *Meth. Trav.* I 4 b, The.. Great Prouost.. of the Kings house... His Office is to stickle among the Seruants, Pages, Lacqueis, and *Filles de ioye*.., and to punish all offences in these people. **1613** HEYWOOD *Silver Age* K 2, Stay and forbeare your vp-rore, till our club Stickle amongst you. *a* **1643** W. CARTWRIGHT *Ordinary* III. v, There had been bloud-shed, if I had not stickled. **1692** DRYDEN *Juvenal* Ded. (1697) p. xvii, The same Angel.. when half of the Christians are already kill'd.. stickles betwixt the Remainders of God's Host, and the Race of Fiends.

†**2.** *trans.* To compose (a dispute, disputants); to stop, quell (a strife or contest). Also with *forth*. *Obs.*

1577 GOOGE *Heresbach's Husb.* IV. (1586) 181 b, Their fights, whether it be among themselues, or one Hiue with an other, are easely stickled. **1578** BIBLE (Genev.) Almanacke, 25 June, *note*, As on this day, was the conflict at Mersbrough, betweene the Emperour Henrie the fourth, and Rodolfe duke of Sueuia, stickled forth by the Pope, Anno. 1080. **1600** HOLLAND *Livy* VII. xiv. 258 So as now they had growne to a full skirmish and battaile indeed, had not the Centurions speedily stickled them, and ended the fray. **1612** DRAYTON *Poly-olb.* xi. 428 Heere, Weever.. to the Muse refers The hearing of the cause, to stickle all these stirs. **1630** ——*Muses Eliz.* Nimphall vi. 36 Betwixt which three a question grew, Who should the worthiest be, Which violently they pursue, Nor stickled would they be.

†**3.** *intr.* To be busy, stirring, or energetic; to strive or contend pertinaciously; to take an active part (*in* a cause, affair). *Obs.*

1566 DRANT *Hor. Sat.* I. i. A iij b, She [the ant] stickleth, and bestirres her selfe, She huswyfes it right well. **1570** LEVINS *Manip.* 122/4 To stickle in a matter, *contendere, litigare*. **1630** SANDERSON *21 Serm.* (1681) 254 Oh how we can stickle in our own causes! **1655** *Baily's Life Bp. Fisher* xvi. 119 My Lord of Rochester was the onely man that most stickled in this businesse. **1663** BUTLER *Hud.* I. ii. 437 Or Argument, in which b'ing valiant, He us'd to lay about and stickle, Like Ram or Bull, at Conventicle. **1690** DRYDEN *Amphitryon* I. i, Nay the very Goddesses wou'd stickle in the cause of Love. **1706** PHILLIPS (ed. Kersey), To *Stickle hard in a Business*, to strive earnestly about it.

†**b.** To strive or endeavour *to* (do something).

1613 *Crt. & Times Jas. I* (1849) I. 277 The Lord Coke doth so stickle and fence by all the means he can make not to remove. **1658-9** in *Burton's Diary* (1828) IV. 234 'Tis apparent, how hard they stickle to impeade all. **1680** H. MORE *Apocal. Apoc.* 119 The Devil.. will stickle to do as much mischief as he can among you. **1683** *Lond. Gaz.* No. 1835/2 And for that end in all Elections they stickled to Chuse the most disaffected into Offices of the greatest Trust in the Government. **1727** SWIFT *Let. to Sheridan* 13 May, I hear no news about your bishops, farther than that the lord lieutenant stickles to have them of Ireland. **1732** FIELDING *Miser* II. i, The broker was forced to stickle hard to get such good ones.

†**c.** To contend or strive, meddle or interfere *with* (a person, etc.). *Obs.*

1647 N. BACON *Disc. Govt. Eng.* I. lix. 179 The Pope having lately been blooded against a braue Emperour, made the lesse difficulty to stickle with a valiant King. **1664** BUTLER *Hud.* II. ii. Argt., The Knight and Squire in hot Dispute.. Are parted with a sudden fright Of strange Alarm, and stranger Sight; With which adventuring to stickle, They're sent away in nasty pickle.

†**d.** To contend *against*. *Obs.*

1659 HEYLIN *Exam. Hist.* I. 7 Our Author doth as mainly stickle against it. **1678** *Trans. Crt. Spain* 122 He stickled not against those [taxes] that were raised for the repairing of the Palace of Germany. **1709** STRYPE *Ann. Ref.* I. iii. 76 This also the Roman Prelates in the House did tooth and nail stickle against.

†**e.** With dependent clause: To contend or maintain *that*; to dispute *which*. *Obs.*

a **1661** FULLER *Worthies, Yorks.* (1662) 208 Although the Scotch Historians stickle with might and maine, that such Homage was performed onely for the County of Cumberland. **1678** BUTLER *Hud.* III. ii. 518 The Cause is in the lurch Between a right and mungrel Church, The Presbyter and Independent, That stickle which shall make an end on't.

4. stickle for —. a. To strive or contend for (a desired object, an issue, principle, etc.).

1642 FULLER *Holy & Prof. St.* III. xx. 208 Pride.. makes men stickle for their opinions to make them fundamentall. **1647** N. BACON *Disc. Govt. Eng.* I. lxvi. 226 They had courage enough.. to stickle both with King and people for their own liberties. *a* **1680** GLANVILL *Sadducismus* I. (1682) 150 Those that so stickle and sweat for the proving their Opinion. **1728** MORGAN *Algiers* I. iv. 93 Without any of those mighty advantages so sanguinely stickled for by each Pretender to a Superiority in Purity of Morals. **1869** GOULBOURN *Purs. Holiness* x. 95 Stickling for the letter while the spirit is disregarded. **1901** RASHDALL & RAIT *New College* 207 Scholars will no longer stickle for his [Lowth's] view that Hebrew was the language spoken in Paradise. **1905** *Athenæum* 10 June 713/3 The plot.. will.. please those who stickle for happy endings.

†**b.** To take the part of, stand up for, contend on behalf of (a person). Also with *up*. *Obs.*

1652 HEYLYN *Cosmogr.* I. 41 If Servilius and others.. had not stickled hard for him with the Souldiers. **1663** BUTLER *Hud.* I. iii. 516 When Fortune (as she's wont) turn'd fickle And for the foe began to stickle. **1719** *Col. Rec. Pennsylv.* III. 72 He was Mr. Penn's stiff Friend and had stickl'd for him tho' to no effect. **1703** MRS. CENTLIVRE *Love's Contriv.* IV. ii. 41 Come, come, Cousin, we never stickle up for the Person we don't care for. **1748** RICHARDSON *Clarissa* (1768) V. xiv. 152 The Widow Bevis indeed stickled hard for me.

5. To make difficulties, raise objections, haggle (*about*); to be tardy in giving one's acceptance or compliance; to hesitate, scruple, take offence (*at*). (? Partly arising from confusion with *stick*.)

1819 KEATS *Otho* IV. i. 103 Albert! he cannot stickle, chew the cud In such a fine extreme,—impossible! **1829** I. TAYLOR *Enthus.* x. 306 An exaggerated notion of the right and duty of Christians to stickle upon their individual opinions. **1837** CARLYLE *Fr. Rev.* II. IV. v, Flying for life, one does not stickle about his vehicle. **1851** GLADSTONE in Morley *Life* III. vii. (1903) I. 406 He came back with a fresh message to go at once, and hear what Stanley had to say. I did not like to stickle, and went. **1877** MISS YONGE *Cameos* III. 148 He did not stickle at Edward calling himself King of France and England. **1879** FARRAR *St. Paul* I. xxii. 417 His soul was too large to stickle about matters of no moment.

b. To scruple or hesitate *to* (do something). (? A pseudo-archaism. Cf. 3 b and STICK *v.*[1] 15.)

1840 BARHAM *Ingol. Leg.* Ser. I. *Leech of Folkestone*, Some.. stickle not to aver that you are cater-cousin with Beelzebub himself.

Hence '**stickling** *vbl. sb.* and *ppl. a.*

1611 COTGR., *Interposition*,.. an intermedling in, or stickling of, controuersies. **1658** GURNALL *Chr. in Armour* II. 43 A busie stickling and ambitious disputing about truth. **1679** *Establ. Test* 25 Several stickling Itinerant Teachers. **1682** H. MORE *Annot. Glanvil's Lux Or.* 153 Some stickling imbittered Grandees of the Church. **1710** HEARNE *Collect.* (O.H.S.) II. 348 Lancaster's stickling for Sir Thomas is a plain Confirmation of it. **1848** BARTLETT *Dict. Amer.* 333 *Stickling* hesitating; delaying.

stickleback ('stɪk(ə)lbæk). Forms: 5 stykylbak, 6 sticklebanke, -banck, 6-7 stickle bag(ge, 7 stit(t)le bag(ge, 8 stittle-back, 7-9 stickle-back, 7- stickleback. [f. OE. *sticel* prick, sting + BACK *sb.*[1] Cf. the synonymous *banstickle*, *stanstickle*, *stickling*, *tittlebat*, *prickleback*, *-bag* (N. Irel. *spricklebag*).] A small spiny-finned fish, of the genus *Gasterosteus* or family *Gasterosteidæ*. The common three-spined stickleback, *G. aculeatus*, is found in both fresh and salt water.

sea stickleback: see SEA *sb.* 23 d.

14.. *Burlesque* in *Relig. Antiq.* I. 85 The borbottus and the stykylbakys. **1552** HULOET, Sticklyng or stickle bagge fishe. **1599** NASHE *Lenten Stuff* B 1, The silliest millers thombe or contemptible stickle-banck. **1611** COTGR., *Artiere*, the Sharpling, Stickling, or Sticklebacke. *a* **1616** BEAUM. & FL. *Wit at Sev. Weapons* v. i, I have been seven mile in length, along the new River; I have seene a hundred stickle bags. **1647-60** HEXHAM, *Tobaes*,.. a kind of Prick-fish, or Stitle bagge. **1653** WALTON *Angler* iv. 97 A small Loch, or a Sticklebag. **1656** H. MORE *Enthus. Tri. Observ.* 139 No fish, not so much as a small Stittle-bag. **1706** PHILLIPS (ed. Kersey), *Stittle-back*. **1769** PENNANT *Brit. Zool.* III. 217. **1799** A. YOUNG *Agric. Linc.* 259 Manuring... Sticklebacks in the East and West fens [are] so numerous, that a man has made 4*s.* a day by selling them at a half-penny a bushel. **1896** LYDEKKER *Roy. Nat. Hist.* V. 403 The sticklebacks have the honour not only of representing a genus (*Gastrosteus*), but likewise a family by themselves.

stickler ('stɪklə(r)). Also 6 styckler, stiklar, stickeler, 7 sticler. [f. STICKLE *v.* + -ER[1]. Cf. the earlier STIFFLER, STIGHTLER.]

1. A moderator or umpire at a tournament, a wrestling or fencing match, etc., appointed to see fair play, and to part the combatants when they have fought enough (*obs.* exc. *s.w. dial.*). Hence, †one who intervenes as a mediator *between* combatants or disputants.

1538 ELYOT *Dict., Interpres*,.. also a styckler betwene two, whiche are at varyaunce. **1549** CHALONER *Erasm. on Folly* N iij b, Hereby it appeared that Jesus was the stickler or mediator. **1572** HULOET (ed. Higins), Stickeler in games, *Designator, Arbiter certaminis*. *a* **1586** SIDNEY *Arcadia* I. xvii. §1. (1912) 105 Basilius the Judge appointed sticklers, and trumpets, to whom the other should obey. *Ibid.* §5. 109 Basilius rising himselfe [came] to parte them, the sticklers authoritie scarslie able to perswade cholerike hearers. **1602** PARSONS *Warn-word* I. 14 Receauing for his gaine the first broken head as wrangling sticlers ar wont to do. **1613-18** DANIEL *Coll. Hist. Eng.* (1626) 99 Theobald Earle of Bloys, that famous Stickler betweene the Kings of England and France. *a* **1656** USSHER *Ann.* (1658) 722 He sent Octavia.. to her brother Cæsar, that she might be a stickler between them. **1659** DRYDEN *Death of Oliver* xi, Our former Chiefs, like Sticklers of the War, First sought t'inflame the Parties, then to poise. **1825** JENNINGS *Dial. W. Eng.* 72 *Stickler*, a person who presides at backsword or singlestick, to regulate the game. **1897** PHILLPOTTS *Lying Prophets* I. v. 50 You 'm like the stickler at a wras'lin' match,.. you sees fair play betwixt God an' man.

Comb. **1606** SHAKS. *Tr. & Cr.* v. viii. 18 The dragon wing of night ore-spreds the earth And stickler-like the Armies seperates.

†**b.** *fig.* of things. *Obs.*

1582 STANYHURST *Æneis*, etc. (Arb.) 145 Thy nose, as a stickler, toe toe long vs parteth a sunder. **1598** NORDEN *Spec. Brit., M'sex & Herts* II. 6 The Lea.. continuing her most milde course as stickler betweene Essex and Middlesex. **1618** BOLTON *Florus* III. x. (1636) 199 The tide withdrawing upon course during the skirmish, the Ocean might, as it were, seeme to have been stickler in the battell.

†**c.** A composer or reconciler *of* (strife). Cf. STICKLE *v.* 2. *Obs.*

1624 BP. HALL *No Peace with Rome* iii. Wks. (1634) 608 Those honest and good-natured men, which would needs undertake to bee the sticklers of these strifes.

†**2.** One who takes an active or busy part (*in* a contest, affair, cause, etc.); an active partisan; a (great, chief, etc.) agent, mover, or instigator.

1565 CALFHILL *Answ. Treat. Crosse*, Ep. to Martiall B j b, Erasmus a gret stickler in the crosse quarrell. **1619** DENISON *Heav. Banq.* 64 Andradius a principall stickler at the Councell of Trent, and a vehement defender thereof. **1643** *Decl. Commons* (Reb. Ireland) 22 The Queen with her Romish Priests.. have been principall Actours and Sticklers herein. **1663** PATRICK *Pilgrim* v. (1687) 16 [He] is generally decry'd by all parties, as no friend to Truth, because he is no great stickler about the Questions that have vexed our unhappy days. **1690** C. NESSE *O. & N.T.* I. 30 Oleaster, that grand stickler in the Spanish Inquisition. **1728** CHAMBERS *Cycl.* s.v. *Heracleonites*, They were so fond of these Mystic Interpretations, that Origen, tho' a Stickler that Way himself, was obliged to reproach Heracleon with his abusing Scripture by that Means.

†**b.** In unfavourable sense: A factious, seditious, or pragmatic contender; a wrangler, one who stirs up strife; a meddler, busybody. *Obs.*

1579, 1643: cf. *Jack-stickler*, JACK *sb.*[1] 36. **1641** QUARLES *Enchyridion* I. xlviii, True Religion is a Setler in a State, rather than a Stickler. **1692** R. L'ESTRANGE *Josephus, Wars* II. iii. (1733) 615 And for those Sticklers that Varus found to be least malicious, he order'd them to be kept in Custody. **1693** PENN *Some Fruits Solit.* I. §531 A devout Man is one Thing, a Stickler is quite another. **1696** PHILLIPS (ed. 5), *Stickler*, a Busie Body in Publick Business, a Promoter of Faction and Disturbance.

†**3.** One who fights or contends *against* (a person, cause, etc.); an opponent, antagonist; one who makes difficulties or raises objections. *Obs.*

1613 JACKSON *Creed* I. xv. 78 Diomedes (who was one of the greatest sticklers against Troy). **1718** F. HUTCHINSON *Witchcraft* 63 Where they might do what they would, without being controuled by Sticklers. **1735** BP. GIBSON in Fraser *Life Berkeley* (1871) vii. 238 The men of science.. are the greatest sticklers against revealed religion. **1825** COBBETT *Rur. Rides* 197 Sir Thomas Baring appears to have been the great stickler against Mr. Hollis. **1826** CREEVEY in *C. Papers* (1903) II. 100 If a good ultra-Tory Government could be made, Canning and Huskisson must inevitably be ruined by this daring step. You never heard such language as the old sticklers apply to them. **1846** LANDOR *Imag. Conv.* Wks. II. 42 There are nowhere such stiff sticklers against idolatry, at the present day, as those gentlemen.

4. With *for*: One who contends for, pertinaciously supports, or advocates (a cause, principle, person, party, etc.); one who insists on or stands out for (something established by rule or custom, a form, ceremony, etc.).

1644 D. FEATLEY *Levites Scourge* 6 A great stickler for the new Reformation. **1654** VILVAIN *Theorem Theol.* ii. 49 Dr. Ward, a stif Stickler for effectual Grace. **1660** J. DAVIES *Hist. Chas. II*, 68 Nor wanted there some sticklers for his Majesty. **1768–74** TUCKER *Lt. Nat.* (1834) I. 61 Your sticklers for indifferency of will. **1792** A. YOUNG *Trav. France* 110 He is one of the most zealous sticklers for the popular cause. **1820** BYRON *Mar. Fal.* III. ii. 191 A stickler for the Senate and 'the Forty'. **1829** CASSAN *Bps. Bath & Wells* 162 He was a stickler for the Hanover succession. **1838** DICKENS *Nickleby* xlv, She was a great stickler for dignity and ceremonies. **1848** THACKERAY *Van. Fair* ix, Sir Pitt was a stickler for his dignity while at home. **1879** DIXON *Windsor* I. xxiii. 241 Beaufort was no stickler for pedantic rules. **1887** *Poor Nellie* (1888) 294 His father, who was somewhat of a stickler for etiquette. **1898** G. W. E. RUSSELL *Collect. & Recoll.* xxxiv. 455 Mr. Gladstone, the stiffest of sticklers for official reticence. **1901** *Scotsman* 4 Mar. 7/5 The Great Duke was a stickler for the principle that the Sovereign is the real head of the army.

†**5.** A second or backer in a contest. *Obs.*

1672 G. THOMSON *Let. to H. Stubbe* 28 Stubbe, and the rest of the Galenical Tribe, with all their Sticklers. **1678** WOOD *Life* (O.H.S.) II. 418 One of the principall parishioners and sticklers to the bishop against Oats. **1705** HICKERINGILL *Priest-cr.* I. 14 Priests of all Religions .. are the Sticklers, and clap their Hands, and cry Hulloo; setting the mad and Priest-ridden Laity at work, to fight up to the Ears in Blood for them. **1711** in *10th Rep. Hist. MSS. Comm.* App. v. 177 Their fathers were honest men, and sticklers to their lawful Prince. **1716** HEARNE *Collect.* (O.H.S.) V. 266 One of his great sticklers for the Degree of Master of Arts was Dr. Hudson. **1755** JOHNSON, *Stickler*, a sidesman to fencers; a second to a duellist. **1828** SCOTT *F.M. Perth* vi, My ambition of distinction in arms, and my love of strife .. do not fight even-handed with my reason .. but have their patrons and sticklers to egg them on.

[**stickler**, erron. form (in Dicts.) of STICKER².]

stickling ('stɪklɪŋ). ? *Obs.* Also 4 **stikelinge**, 5 **styk(e)lyng(e**, **stekelyng**, 6 **styckelyng**, **sticklyng**. [ME. *stikeling(e* = (M)Du. *stekeling*, MHG. *stichelinc* (mod.G. *stichling*, *stechling*), f. WGer. **stikil*, **stekal* (see STICKLE *a.*) + -ING³.] = STICKLEBACK.

a **1387** *Sinon. Barthol.* (Anecd. Oxon.) 12 *Aspiatiles* [read *Aspratiles*], an. stikelinges. *c* **1440** *Promp. Parv.* 475/1 Stykelynge, fysche, *silurus*. *c* **1475** *Pict. Voc.* in Wr.-Wülcker 763/29 *Hic ganerius*, a stekelyng. **1530** PALSGR. 276/1 Styckelyng a maner of fysshe. **1552** HULOET, Sticklyng or stickle bagge fishe. **1611** COTGR., *Espinoche*, a Sharpling, Shaftling, stickling. **1881** DAY *Fishes Gt. Brit.* I. 241 The .. stickleback .. is known as .. stickling and Jack-bannell, Oxfordshire (Beesley).

stick-out, *a.* and *sb.* Also **stickout**. [f. vbl. phrase *stick out*: see STICK *v.* 33.]

A. *adj.* **1.** That projects.

1900 ELINOR GLYN *Visits Eliz.* (1906) 2 There is a woman I like, with stick-out teeth.

2. *U.S. slang.* Outstanding.

1948 *Daily Progress* (Charlottesville, Va.) 27 Jan. 9/1 After that, you have to scratch your head to think of another stickout box office attraction. **1958** *Washington Post* 19 June C1/6 Kramer's only hope for a stickout newcomer would be Australia's Mal Anderson against Gonzales.

B. *sb.* **1.** A strike (of employees).

1845 DISRAELI *Sybil* III. i, I've .. seen as great stick-outs as ever happened in this country.

2. *U.S. slang.* **a.** A horse that seems a certain winner. **b.** An outstanding sportsman.

1937 D. RUNYON in *Collier's* 11 Sept. 70/3 This mare Cara Mia is a stick-out. **1942** BERREY & VAN DEN BARK *Amer. Thes. Slang* §636/4 Good player, .. *stickout*. **1949** *Sun* (Baltimore) 2 July 9/1 A 'stickout' on paper, Nokomis was in front most of the way along the six-furlong route. **1951** *Daily Progress* (Charlottesville, Va.) 26 Sept. 13/8 His former players now coaching send stickouts in his direction. **1958** *Washington Post* 26 June C1/1 As for third base, ball players and fans alike have no range of choice. Frank Malzone of the Red Sox is a stickout.

†**'stickpenny.** *Obs.* [STICK *sb.*¹] (See quot.)

1601 in *N. & Q.* 10th Ser. (1905) III. 70/2 [In 1601 all the inhabitants of Cawston, Norfolk, .. might take heath, ling, flags, &c., on paying the queen 13s. 4d. a year, by the name of 'Stickpenny.' Elsewhere it is stated that they gave 10d. yearly for 'stick pence'.]

stickum ('stɪkəm). *N. Amer. colloq.* [f. STICK *v.*¹ + UM, 'UM.] A sticky or adhesive substance; gum, paste; pomade. Also *transf.* and *fig.*

1909 *Dialect Notes* III. 376 *Stickum*, .. mucilage, paste. **1936** *Christian Sci. Monitor* 14 Aug. 1/3 See that he is keeping the quality of his postage stamp stickum up to standard. **1963** C. D. SIMAK *They walked like Men* ix. 48 We used to shave them and give them facials and all of them wanted stickum on their hair. **1969** R. WILLIAMS in D. Knight *100 Yrs. Sci. Fiction* 303 The fact still remains, this machine makes every man self-sufficient, it takes the stickum right out of society. **1978** J. IRVING *World according to Garp* viii. 157 Wet with sweat and sweet with the lush stickum of sex. **1980** *Globe & Mail* (Toronto) 23 Aug. 1/1 (*heading*) Gaudaur strikes at stickum. Football commissioner Jake Gaudaur has instructed referees to rule ineligible players who use excessive amounts of adhesive on their hands.

stick-up, *a.* and *sb.* [f. vbl. phrase *stick up*: see STICK *v.* 35.]

A. *adj.* That sticks up; esp. of a collar = STAND-UP *a.* I.

1854 'C. BEDE' *Further Adventures of Mr. Verdant Green* ii. 5 A modest-looking young gentleman, who appeared to be .. ill at ease in his frock-coat and 'stick-up' collars. **1873** *Punch* 10 May 191/2 We wonder who invented chignons, corsets, stick-up collars, .. and high-heeled boots. **1891** KIPLING *Light that Failed* 7 Be careful with the cartridges; I don't like those jagged stick-up things on the rim.

B. *sb.* **1.** Something which sticks up.

a. A stand-up collar.

1857 *Hotten's Slang Dict.* 20 *Stick-ups*, shirt-collar. **1896** *Punch* 8 Aug. 64/1 What a big Garçon he'll be when he's out of Jackets and Turn-downs, and gets into Tails and Stick-ups!

b. (See quot.)

1881 INGERSOLL *Oyster-Industr.* (Hist. Fish. Industr. U.S.) 249 *Stickup*, a long, thin oyster, growing in mud, etc. (Dennis creek, New Jersey).

2. *slang* (orig. *Austral.*, now chiefly *U.S.*). **a.** = HOLD-UP 1 b.

[**1887** W. H. SUTTOR *Austral. Stories Retold* 41 A body of men, mostly armed, met us. We at first thought it was a case of 'stick up'.] **1904** 'O. HENRY' in *McClure's Mag.* Apr. 611/1 The first 'stick-up' I was ever in happened in 1890... It will explain how most train robbers start. **1910** H. LAWSON *Skyline Riders & Other Verses* 62 Scott that fired at Brummy Hughson, when the 'stick-ups' used to be. **1930** *Punch* 26 Feb. 236/1 He was reminded .. that he had worked on the Babylon stick-up, and consented to come clean. **1944** *Sun* (Baltimore) 18 Mar. 12/1 The bank manager told police that the bandit .. drew a gun and said: 'This is a stickup.' **1955** H. KURNITZ *Invasion of Privacy* (1956) vii. 53 Morley .. told him they wanted to fake a stick-up. Then he shoots .. the holdup man. **1972** [see PULL *v.* 20 f].

b. One who robs by 'sticking up' his victims; = HOLD-UP 1 a. ? *Obs.*

1905 *N.Y. Times* 2 Jan. 4/1 The 'stick-up' is always a powerful man, whose duties are to intimidate intruders and kill them if necessary, while the others are at work on a safe. **1936** [see BIMBO²].

c. *attrib.* = HOLD-UP 2; *esp.* in ***stick-up man***.

1905 *N.Y. Times* 2 Jan. 4/1 The man .. is declared to be a typical 'yeggman of the stick-up' class. **1909** G. R. CHESTER *Making of Bobby Burnit* xiv. 169 Our local Hicks would rather be robbed by a lot of friendly stick-up artists. **1924** G. C. HENDERSON *Keys to Crookdom* 396 *Assaulter*, rough guy, hard bird .. stick-up man, thug. **1930** [see COOL *v.* 3 e]. **1935** D. RUNYON in *Cosmopolitan* Jan. 63/3 A fast stick-up job without any foolishness about it, maybe leaving any parties we come across tied up good and tight. **1950** *Times* 7 Feb. 8/4 It was the story of a 'stick-up' plot being hatched. **1973** 'H. HOWARD' *Highway to Murder* vii. 80 The old man got knocked off by a stickup guy at the filling station where he worked. **1979** G. F. NEWMAN *List* i. 3 Any moron could get a gun and become a stickup man.

sticky ('stɪkɪ), *a.*¹ [f. STICK *sb.*¹ + -Y.]

1. Of plant-stems: Like a stick; woody.

1577 GOOGE *Heresbach's Husb.* I. 35 The best kinde hath a stickie stalke [*orig.* caule lignoso]. **1626** BACON *Sylva* §583 But Herbs draw a Weake Iuyce; and have a Soft Stalke; And therefore those amongst them which last longest, are Herbs of Strong Smell, and with a Sticky Stalke. **1677** W. HUBBARD *Narrative* 81 The Ground-nuts running up to seed in the summer, began to grow so sticky, as they were scarce eatable. **1765** *Museum Rust.* III. 186 If he leaves it [vetch] till the seeds are nearly ripe, the stalks harden, grow sticky, and are of far less value. **1805** R. W. DICKSON *Pract. Agric.* I. 570 The stem or blade becomes firm and sticky. **1882** *Garden* 4 Mar. 141/2 The Mezereon .. is so often starved, and sticky and poor.

2. *Painting.* Characterized by hardness of outline.

1753 HOGARTH *Anal. Beauty* x. 109 Fig. 66 .. was .. treated in a more dry, stiff, and what the painters call 'sticky' manner than the nature of flesh is ever capable of appearing in.

3. *colloq.* Of a person: Like a 'stick'; wanting in animation or grace; awkward.

1881 MRS. LYNN LINTON *My Love* I. xii. 220 A girl looks such a stick when she does not talk like the rest; and I hate sticky girls.

sticky ('stɪkɪ), *a.*² [f. STICK *v.*¹ + -Y.]

1. a. Having the property of sticking or adhering; adhesive; also, of a substance, viscid, glutinous. Also *fig.*

[**1727**: cf. STICKINESS¹.] **1735** DYCHE & PARDON *Dict.*, *Sticky*, of a clammy Nature, apt to cleave or adhere to any Thing. **1755** JOHNSON (with quot. from Bacon: see STICKY *a.*¹). **1823** J. BADCOCK *Dom. Amusem.* 31 A well-known sticky substance called putty. **1855** LONGF. *Life* (1891) II. 290 Everything sticky except postage-stamps. **1864** *Intell. Observer* V. 269 In like manner limpid fluids oppose less resistance than sticky ones. **1870** DICKENS *E. Drood* iii, I'm too sticky to be kissed. **1908** [MISS E. FOWLER] *Betw. Trent & Ancholme* 378 Smelling of sticky paint and varnish. **1909** G. STEIN *Three Lives* 27 The horses dragged the carriage slowly over the long road, sticky with brown clay. **1939** *Amer. Speech* XIV. 262 The listener often hears, .. if the subject is a thief, 'He has sticky fingers.' **1940** N. MITFORD *Pigeon Pie* v. 95 'I have just labelled a few little things of my own ..' she said, putting a sticky one firmly on to the giant radiogram. **1956** H. GOLD *Man who was not with It* (1965) i. 3 They were caught .. like the flies caught wriggling in sticky-paper. **1976** A. MILLER *Inside Outside* i. 16 To safeguard the money from the sticky fingers of some of the boys.

b. *Path.* Of sounds heard in auscultation: Resembling those produced in viscid substances.

1896 *Allbutt's Syst. Med.* I. 681 The posterior parts of the lungs are full of sharp, sticky rales of a quality quite peculiar to the disease. **1898** *Ibid.* V. 756 [Pericardial friction sound] has also been described as 'sticky'.

c. *Racing* and *Cricket.* Of a course, a wicket: Having a yielding surface owing to wet. Also *fig.*, esp. in phr. ***to bat*** (or ***be***) ***on a sticky wicket***: to contend with great difficulties (*colloq.*).

1882 *Bell's Life in London* 29 July 4/6 The ground .. was suffering from the effects of recent rain, and once more the Australians found themselves on a sticky wicket. **1888** *Pall Mall Gaz.* 14 Mar. 11/1 'Do you think the bowler suffers much under the present law?' 'Well, he does somewhat; but only on sticky wickets.' **1894** *Westm. Gaz.* 17 July 6/3 The hurdle race... Here again the time—16 2-5 sec.—on 'sticky' turf, was excellent. **1952** *National News-Let.* 24 Jan. 244 It must be clearly understood that Mr. Churchill was batting on a very sticky wicket in Washington. **1957** P. KEMP *Mine were of Trouble* ix. 177 Until substantial reinforcements could arrive we should be batting, in the language of Mr. Naunton Wayne, on a very sticky wicket. **1964** *Language* XL. 239 Enmeshed in these remarks, however, is a sticky wicket. **1971** *Cabinet Maker & Retail Furnisher* 24 Sept. 517 When it comes .. to moulded plastics of various kinds, then the timber producer is on a stickier wicket.

d. *fig.* Sickly, mawkish, sentimental, 'soppy'.

1864 [implied at STICKINESS¹]. **1915** R. FROST *Let.* 11 Nov. (1964) 17 He needn't go calling himself sticky names like Gayheart in public. **1925** N. COWARD *Fallen Angels* I. 16, I hope you're not .. hurt at our refusing to call you Jasmin? .. It's a sticky name, isn't it—for the house? *a* **1961** O. SITWELL in WEBSTER s.v., Invest childhood with a sticky but romantic gloss.

e. *colloq.* (orig. *U.S.*). Of the weather: humid, muggy.

1895 in *Funk's Stand. Dict.* *a* **1961** in WEBSTER, A hot and sticky hour or two on shore. **1977** *Washington Post* 30 June F2/4 Hot, sticky summer weather—the kind of weather that seems to attack the mind as well as the body with its oppressiveness. **1983** *National Trust* Spring 16/1 On one of those stifling, sticky days of this curious summer .. , at rehearsal, the Philharmonia Orchestra and Norman del Mar were all in shirt sleeves.

2. a. Of a horse: Apt to 'stick' at a fence, i.e. to pause before and after the leap.

1886 *St. Stephen's Rev.* 13 Mar. 11/2 He has one fatal fault for a Liverpool horse which is being sticky at his fences.

b. Of troops: Apt to hesitate in obeying commands.

1898 STEEVENS *With Kitchener to Khartum* 305 When they were told to bring out their arms and ammunition they became a bit sticky, as soldiers say. They looked like refusing [etc.]. **1902** *Macm. Mag.* Sept. 394 It was this sort of thing which earned for some troops the .. admirably descriptive title of *sticky*.

3. a. *Stock Exchange.* (See quot. 1901)

1901 *Times* 24 Oct. 7/5 [Local Loans Stock] is ceasing to be 'sticky', to use the Stock Exchange slang describing a security which cannot always be sold just when the holder chooses. **1937** *Sun* (Baltimore) 28 June 12/1 Several recent offerings have been described as 'sticky' by dealers—meaning only partially sold. **1960** *Wall St. Jrnl.* (Eastern ed.) 5 Dec. 7/2 Underwriters released two 'sticky' corporate debt issues to the free market.

b. *Econ.* Of prices, interest rates, wages, etc.: resistant to change, slow to respond to altered conditions.

1930 *Economist* 6 Sept. 453/1 In many cases the amount of available stock has been limited, and when a fair supply has been in sight prices have proved surprisingly 'sticky'. **1936** J. M. KEYNES *Gen. Theory Employment, Interest & Money* IV. xvii. 232 Wages tend to be sticky in terms of money, the money-wage being more stable than the real wage. **1939** G. MYRDAL *Monetary Equilibrium* vi. 136 When we talk about sticky and flexible prices we are already thinking in terms of indices of different price levels. **1971** D. C. HAGUE *Managerial Economics* iv. 94 The idea that the kinked demand curve is likely to be found where there is oligopoly has led to the widespread feeling that in oligopoly prices will be 'sticky'. **1978** *Daily Tel.* 18 Dec. 14/7 Building society rates tend to follow movements in market rates only rather erratically and usually with a time-lag. As economists say they tend to be 'sticky'.

4. *colloq.* **a.** Of a person: difficult to cope with, awkward, uncooperative; strait-laced, punctilious, particular, tending to make difficulties (*about* or *over* something).

1882 L. TROUBRIDGE *Life amongst Troubridges* (1966) 162 Rather a sticky audience who evidently thought it vulgar to laugh, and only sniggered into their pocket handkerchiefs. **1925** T. E. LAWRENCE *Let.* 3 Nov. (1938) 486 I've got too many subscribers, so am very sticky over these last copies. **1933** C. MACKENZIE *Water on Brain* viii. 115 Personally I've always advocated the spending of money. The only snag is the Treasury. They've been sticky lately. **1935** WODEHOUSE *Luck of the Bodkins* iii. 34 He didn't actually call me a waster .. but his manner was sticky. **1937** E. BOWEN in *New Statesman* 6 Nov. 727/2 Be a shade too punctilious and you are sticky; make a little too free and you are a pariah. **1940** GRAVES & HODGE *Long Week-End* ix. 135 Even the stickiest British families seemed ready to abandon their mistrust of the cinema, if the vulgar American scene could only be replaced by a wholesome British one. **1953** J. BINGHAM *Five Roundabouts to Heaven* iii. 26 Sometimes aunt Emily was a bit sticky about paying up. **1960** *Times* 15 Oct. 8/7 We had to be immaculately turned out... Father was very 'sticky' about this. **1972** J. PHILIPS *Vanishing Senator* (1973) III. ii. 127 Bernstein will tell you. If he acts sticky have him call me.

b. Of a situation, issue, period of time, etc.: awkward, presenting great difficulty, disagreeable owing to hardship or danger; of a social function: slow to start, stiff, uncomfortable.

1915 D. O. BARNETT *Lett.* 86 We had a rather sticky time in the trenches .. as the enemy's artillery and snipers showed 'a certain liveliness'. **1930** 'SAPPER' *Finger of Fate* 17 You have the alternative of a sticky five minutes with three savage Alsatians. **1930** V. SACKVILLE-WEST *Edwardians* i. 17 What was Miriam's party like, Lucy? Sticky, as usual? **1946** WODEHOUSE *Money in Bank* xix. 155 It is a human trait to keep on hoping, however sticky the outlook. **1955** *Times* 22 Aug. 2/7 The play became rather sticky and it looked like one or two fouls before the umpires blew on a B.A.O.R. player. **1958** *Listener* 16 Oct. 621/3 This medley of the fine arts and show business may be accommodated to a pleasant pattern later on: it made a sticky start. **1958** [see PATCH *sb.*¹ 5 b]. **1960** L. COOPER *Accomplices* I. ii. 17 It was the stickiest do I've ever been in and I thanked God I'd been taught to fight. **1976** *Lancs. Evening Post* 7 Dec. 1/5 Preston South Labour MP Mr Stan Thorne..faced the prospect of a sticky interview with Government whips. **1977** B. PYM *Quartet in Autumn* xv. 127 He was so used to sticky church occasions that a lunch with two former colleagues should have been well within his powers. **1979** *Nature* 7 June 461/2 The sticky issues, however, will be over the appropriate forms of accountability and responsibility.

c. Phr. *to come to a sticky end* (or occas. *finish*): to die or come to grief in violent or exceptionally unpleasant circumstances.

1915 H. ROSHER *In R.N.A.S.* (1916) 40, I wish we could get out to the front... I would much rather come to a sticky end out there than here. **1930** J. COLLIER *His Monkey Wife* xviii. 255 Even if our love affair did come to a horrible sticky end, yet there's so much between us. **1930** J. B. PRIESTLEY *Angel Pavement* xi. 566 Never mind, he'll come to a sticky finish before he's done. **1959** F. MACLEAN *Back to Bokhara* iii. 152 The reformers..have usually come to a sticky end. **1970** 'D. HALLIDAY' *Dolly & Cookie Bird* ix. 142 The heroines I've seen come to a sticky end because while the murderer's still running around no one calls in the police. **1980** *Church Times* 19 Dec. 12/3 Some cast away all chances of redemption till they come to a sticky end.

5. a. Special collocations: **sticky-back**, a small photograph or poster with a gummed back; also *attrib.* or as *adj.*; **sticky bomb**, an anti-tank grenade covered with an adhesive substance to make it stick to its target; **sticky dog** *Cricket colloq.*, a sticky wicket; **sticky end** *Genetics*, and end of a DNA double helix at which one strand extends a few nucleotides beyond the other, unpaired; **sticky-fingered** *a.*, apt to steal, light-fingered; **sticky tape** = *adhesive tape* s.v. ADHESIVE *a.* 1.

1913 A. H. DAWSON *Dict. Slang* 184 *Sticky-backs*, photographs about the size of a postage-stamp with gummed backs. **1922** JOYCE *Ulysses* 56 Stamps: sticky-back pictures. **1939** 'G. ORWELL' *Let.* 4 Jan. in *Coll. Essays* (1968) I. 378 The commonsense thing to do would be to accumulate the things we should need for the production of pamphlets, stickybacks etc. **1940** W. S. CHURCHILL *Let.* 6 June in *Second World War* (1949) II. I. viii. 149 It is of the utmost importance to find some projectile which can be fired from a rifle at a tank... The 'sticky' bomb seems to be useful for..this. **1962** L. DEIGHTON *Ipcress File* vi. 38 It was a sticky bomb about as big as two cans of soup end to end; on impact its very small explosive charge spread a sort of napalm through tank visors. **1925** D. J. KNIGHT in *Country Life* 18 July 95/1 If you..get a chance of bowling on one of these 'sticky dogs', as we call them. **1928** *Daily Express* 9 July 17/1 Should he bat first or should he put Somerset in and hope for a 'sticky-dog' wicket? **1982** P. TINNISWOOD *More Tales from Long Room* vii. 86 That great Groundsman in the sky has secured his covers... And when the sun appears again, as appear it always will, there will be no 'sticky dog' and play will be resumed on time. **1968** *New Scientist* 18 July 142/1 This [enzyme] can be used for linking up small nucleotide sequences by what Professor Khorana calls the 'sticky end' technique. **1976** *Sci. Amer.* Dec. 108 (*caption*) The circle of viral DNA replicates, producing multiple copies that are then cleaved by a specific viral enzyme to give rise to the linear form with 'sticky' ends. **1980** AYALA & KIGER *Mod. Genetics* ix. 327 The purified p184 DNA is mixed with purified DNA from another plasmid..also possessing *Eco* RI sites. The mixture is cleaved with pure *Eco* RI enzyme at a temperature that permits the sticky ends to come apart and reanneal..to form larger hybrid plasmids. **1890** BARRÈRE & LELAND *Dict. Slang* II. 305/2 *Sticky-fingered*.., thievish or covetous. **1932** D. ACLAND *Sticky Fingers* xxv. 314 What a crew we are—sticky-fingered, every one of us. **1982** *Daily Tel.* 23 July 30/3 Mr Steel announced menacingly that a list of sticky fingered policemen had been made available. **1958** *Times* 4 Aug. 9/1 What is the sense of combining the most obdurate kind of fastening (sticky tape, for instance) with the flimsiest of paper bags? **1973** R. PARKES *Guardians* ix. 162 The naked body had been strapped into the armchair with yards of sticky tape.

b. *Comb.* **sticky-out** *a. colloq.*, that protrudes or sticks out.

1928 D. L. SAYERS *Unpleasantness at Bellona Club* x. 118 She has a bad skin and rather sticky-out teeth. **1957** *Woman's Jrnl.* May 51/1 People who had bright red hair and sticky-out teeth and glasses weren't the sort..that any parents wanted to adopt.

sticky ('stɪkɪ), *sb.* [Ellipt. use of STICKY *a.*[2]]

1. *slang.* Something that is sticky, *spec.* (*a*) an adhesive material; (*b*) a sticky wicket.

1859 HOTTEN *Dict. Slang* 102 *Sticky*, wax. **1937** PARTRIDGE *Dict. Slang* 831/1 *Sticky*,..sticking-plaster: lower and lower-middle class coll. **1954** A. G. MOYES *Australian Batsmen* 184 Again, the 'sticky' provides plenty of excitement. **1966** I. JEFFERIES *House-Surgeon* viii. 154 Bring me some more sticky and that pint of blood in the fridge. **1967** PARTRIDGE *Dict. Slang* Suppl. 1390/2 *Sticky*,..since late 1940's, usu. cellulose tape (Sellotape, Scotch tape, etc.). **1975** *Daily Mail* 3 June 11/2 As well as cash, the thieves took 'stickies'—the slang term for postage, national insurance and TV licence stamps. **1982** *Private Eye* 13 Aug. 13/2 All you ever get in the Alps is some ghastly sticky made out of rotting Edelweiss.

2. A film of which the action is slow-moving. *nonce-wd.* (*humorously* after *movies*).

1936 E. M. FORSTER *Abinger Harvest* 51 British ladies and gentlemen turn the movies into the stickies for old Elstree's sake.

sticky ('stɪkɪ), *v. colloq.* [f. STICKY *a.*[2]] *trans.* To smear with something sticky.

1865 MRS. GASKELL *Wives & Daughters* xxxv, Cook wanted a jar of preserve,..I was sadly afraid of stickying my gloves. **1894** *Harper's Mag.* May 853/1 He's stickying all the velvet seat with his hands.

stickybeak ('stɪkɪbi:k). *Austral.* and *N.Z. colloq.* Also **sticky-beak.** [f. STICKY *a.*[2] + BEAK *sb.*[1]] An inquisitive person; one who sticks his nose into others' affairs, a Nosey Parker. Also *attrib.*

1920 B. CRONIN *Timber Wolves* ix. 159 I've told the girls to give out that we've gone fishing, if any stickybeaks get to asking why we ain't visible no more. **1934** *Bulletin* (Sydney) 7 Feb. 10/1 One objection to 'party' telephone lines is the stickybeak subscriber. **1936** M. FRANKLIN *All that Swagger* xlix. 442 Fortunately such 'sticky-beaks' were few. **1948** D. W. BALLANTYNE *Cunninghams* I. v. 24 He wasn't like those other stickybeak kids, he reckoned. **1965** R. MCKIE *Company of Animals* i. 30 Fire is a strange thing to a jungle elephant. It's foreign. And because it's foreign and he's a stickybeak, he investigates. **1970** K. BENTON *Sole Agent* vi. 69 She rang me up, she did, the stick-beak, the prying old cow!

Hence **'stickybeak, sticky-beak** *v. intr.*, to pry, to snoop; **'stickybeaking** *vbl. sb.*

1934 *Bulletin* (Sydney) 12 Sept. 20/2 Special traps were set outside for any crocs. that might stickybeak. **1945** L. GLASSOP *We were Rats* II. xi. 65 You deny me the right to think as I like... You must prod, and pry, and sticky-beak. **1966** P. CARLON *Running Woman* xv. 144, I paused on my way back, looking at those houses. Such a temptation..to sticky-beak. **1969** *Coast to Coast 1967–68* 9 Mind your own business... I don't have to put up with you and your stick-beaking into my affairs.

stictane ('stɪkteɪn). *Biochem.* [f. mod.L. *Stict-a* (f. Gr. *στικτός* spotted), a name of a genus of lichens + -ANE.] Any of a class of pentacyclic triterpanes, unsaturated derivatives of which occur in some lichens.

1973 W. J. CHIN et al. in *Jrnl. Chem. Soc.: Perkin Trans.* I. 1437 Ten new triterpenes, derived from a new triterpane system for which the name stictane is proposed, have been isolated from the hexane extractives of the lichens named in the title [sc. *Sticta coronata*, etc.]. **1976** *Ibid.* 857/1 Stictane ..and the related flavicane..have an 8α-methyl group and a boat structure for ring B rather than the usual 8β-methyl group and chair ring B, hitherto found in pentacyclic triterpenoids. **1979** *Org. Mass Spectrometry* XIV. 160/1 We present detailed analysis of the mass spectral fragmentations of ten stictane triterpenoids.

†**'stictic,** *a.*[1] *Obs. rare.* [ad. mod.L. *sticticus* (Paracelsus), of obscure origin.

A marginal note in *Paracelsi Opera* (1658) III. I. 20/1—'Sticticum emplastrum, alias pro punctura, Germ. *Ein Stichpflaster*'—apparently explains the word as derived from G. *stich*, a stab, puncture.]

Of a plaster: Serving to close up wounds.

1638 A. READ *Chirurg.* iii. 20 Paracelsus undoubtedly framed his stictick emplaster after this description.

stictic ('stɪktɪk), *a.*[2] *Chem.* [tr. G. *stictinsäure* stictic acid (Knop & Schnedermann 1846, in *Jrnl. f. prakt. Chemie* XXXIX. 367), f. as STICTANE: see -IC.] *stictic acid*: a depsidone, $C_{19}H_{14}O_9$, found in many lichens.

1868 WATTS *Dict. Chem.* V. 431 According to Knop and Schneedermann [*sic*]..the acid of *Sticta pulmonacea*, which they call stictic acid, is distinct from cetraric acid, though very much like it in composition and properties. **1935** *Jrnl. Chem. Soc.* 1380 We have now made a detailed comparison of the two acids..and found them to be identical in every way. Accordingly, since stictic acid was discovered and names first.., we propose that the name scopuloric acid should be abandoned. **1963** *New Scientist* 14 Mar. 588/1 The lichen synthesises appreciable amounts of the extra-cellular, water-soluble constituents of lichen acids, atranorin and stictic acid. **1979** *Lichenologist* XI. 321 Chemical examination of two similar specimens..showed stictic acid to be present in the squamulose specimens and absent from the others.

stiction ('stɪkʃən). [f. *st(atic fr)iction.*] = *static friction* s.v. STATIC *a.* 3 c.

1946 *Jrnl. R. Aeronaut. Soc.* L. 365/1 'Stiction' might be caused by foreign bodies silting up round these pistons. **1953** *Electronic Engin.* XXV. 11/2 Armature stiction due to residual magnetism in the iron circuit..is normally overcome by facing the pole piece or armature, or both, with some non-magnetic coating. **1976** *Gramophone* Nov. 905/2 The bearings use tiny ball-races and the 'stiction' is of a very low order, some five-thousandths of a gram in both planes.

stid(e, obs. forms of STEAD.

stiddy ('stɪdɪ), *adv. E. Anglian dial.* [f. STEAD *sb.*] Instead (*of*).

1946 J. W. DAY *Harvest Adventure* iv. 57 If they'd left the rabbits to the workin' man we'd ha' had 'em in our bellies stiddy of the poor things suffocatin' in their burrows. **1971** *Country Life* 11 Mar. 533/1 Owd Bob, he cut a slice or tew out of it [a stranded sturgeon] with a hatchet an' all the roe runned away. That's where he done wrong. If we'd a-kept that roe in we'd a-got four bob a pound for it... Stiddy o' that we only got fi'pun from the fishmonger in Ely.

stiddy, var. form of STITHY, anvil.

stidfastliche, obs. form of STEADFASTLY.

stidie, obs. variant of STUDY *v.*

†**'stidy,** *a. Obs. rare*[−1]. [Of obscure origin; app. related to STITHE *a.* (Ormin's spelling implies a long *ī*.)] Obstinate.

c **1200** *Ormin* 9885 For hæþendom..& hæþenn follkess herrte Iss..stunnt & stidiȝ, dill & slaw To sekenn sawless seollþe.

stie, obs. form of STY *sb.* and *v.*

stiebel, var. SHTIBL.

stiebkin: see STEIFKIN.

stied(e, stiek: see STEED, STEEK *v.*[1]

Stiegel ('sti:gəl). The name of Henry William *Stiegel* (1729–85), German-born American manufacturer of iron and glass, used *attrib.* and *absol.* to designate glassware made by him or resembling his work.

[**1773** *Pennsylvania Packet* 8 Mar. 3/2 An Elegant Assortment of Henry William Stiegle's Glass is to be Sold.] **1906** *Bull. Pennsylvania Museum* 5 Jan., The Stiegel glassware was of better quality than any produced elsewhere in the United States. **1922** *Country Life* May 49/2 I'd rather have it than any other piece of Stiegel I ever saw. **1949** *Hobbies* June 104/1 Until quite recently the majority of our collectors were in the habit of calling all old blown glass either Stiegel or Wistar. *Ibid.* 104/2 All can not be the proud possessors of Stiegel sugar bowls in sparkling cobalt, creamers in lovely shades of amethyst. **1961** E. M. ELVILLE *Collector's Dict. Glass* 18/2 Other factories followed the Stiegel fashion, especially in Ohio and Pittsburgh districts. **1974** J. GARDNER *Corner Men* viii. 64 Peter was..about to pour vodka into a Stiegel-type glass. **1977** FLEMING & HONOUR *Penguin Dict. Decorative Arts* 759/1 The term 'Stiegel glass' is commonly applied to most c18 American pattern-moulded wares.

stiel, obs. form of STEEL, STILL *sb.*[1]

stiele, -ll: see STEEL, STILE *sb.*[1]

Stieltjes integral ('sti:ltʃəz). *Math.* [Named after Thomas-Jan *Stieltjes* (1856–94), Dutch-born French mathematician, who first considered such integrals in 1894 (*Ann. de la Faculté des Sci. de Toulouse* VIII. J.2).] A definite integral in which the value of a function is summed, not uniformly over an interval, but in accordance with some other function which assigns weightings continuously or discontinuously within the interval.

[**1910** H. LEBESGUE in *Compt. Rend.* CL. 86 On dé signe sous le nom d'*integrale de Stieltjes*..l'opération fonctionnelle faisant correspondre à $f(x)$ un nombre défini de la façon suivante.] **1914** *Proc. London Math. Soc.* XIII. 131 The definition of the integral of a continuous function with respect to a monotone increasing function given by Stieltjes..is defined to be the Stieltjes integral. **1952** J. C. C. MCKINSEY *Introd. Theory Games* ix. 169 Since the Stieltjes integral is defined by means of a complicated limiting process, it should not be an occasion for surprise that it does not always exist. **1980** A. J. JONES *Game Theory* 276 Technically we are using Stieltjes integrals here.

stiep, obs. form of STEEP *sb.*[1], *a.*, *v.*[1]

stier(e: see STEER, STIR, STYER.

stieridge, stierk: see STEERAGE, STIRK.

stierne, stieve: see STERN, STEEVE.

stiewe, obs. form of STEW *sb.*[2]

stifado (stɪ'fɑ:dəʊ). Also **stifato, stiffado, stiphado, stuffado.** [a. mod.Gr. *στιφάδο*, presumably f. It. *stufato* stew; cf. STUFATA.] A Greek dish of meat stewed with onions and other vegetables, esp. tomatoes.

1950 E. DAVID *Bk. Mediterranean Food* 76 Stuffado (a Greek ragoût). Cut 2 lbs. of steak into large pieces. Brown them in oil with 3 lb of small onions and several cloves of garlic. Into the same pan put ½ pint of thick and highly seasoned tomato purée and a glass of red wine. Simmer slowly for 4 or 5 hours. **1952** M. LO PINTO *New York Cookbk.* ix. 145 (*heading*) Stifado (beef stew). **1962** M. SOPER *Encycl. European Cooking* 329 (*heading*) Greek beef stew. *Stiphado.* **1975** I. MURDOCH *Word Child* 210 'What's for din-dins at your place?' 'Smoked salmon. Stifados. Lime soufflé.' **1977** T. HEALD *Just Desserts* i. 16 I'd like the Fritto misto and then the Stiffado.

stife (staɪf). Chiefly *dial.* Also 9 *Sc.* **stoif.** A suffocating fume or vapour.

1636 *Patent Specif.* (1856) No. 98. 1 Which Seacoales soe Charked for that they Burne without Smoake, Stife, or other Annoyaunce. **1825** JAMIESON, *Stife, Stoif*, a close sulphureous smell, particularly that arising from the burning of drossy coals. **1912** W. W. GIBSON *Fires* II. 38 The stealthy stife And deadly fume of burning coke.

stiff (stɪf), *a.*, *sb.*, and *adv.* Forms: 1 **stíf,** 2– **stif** (2–4 *also inflected* **stive**), 3–4 **stijf,** 3–6 **styf,** 4–6 **styfe,** (5 **stuffe**), 4–6 **styffe,** 4–7 **stiffe,** 4– **stiff.** [OE. *stíf* (once only, in a gloss) corresponds to MLG. *stîf* (mod.LG. *stief*), (M)Du. *stijf*, MHG. (? from MLG.) *stîf* (mod.G. *steif*); NFris. has *styf*, *stif*, WFris. *stiif*, which may descend from OFris. **stîf*; the Sw. *styf*, Da. *stiv* (whence Icel. *stíf-ur*) are prob. adopted from LG. The OTeut. type **stīfo-*:—pre-Teut. **stīpo-* is cogn. w. L. *stīpāre* to crowd, *stīpes* stake, Lith. *stiprus* strong.

The long vowel of OE. *stíf*, corresponding with that of the continental Teut. forms, is evidenced by the ME. spelling *stijf*, and by the pronunciation current in some mod.Eng. dialects. The present standard Eng. form, however, is abnormal as representing OE. *stíf*; it is uncertain whether a shortening has taken place from some unknown cause, or whether OE. had beside *stíf* an ablaut variant *stif*:—OTeut. type **stifo-* or **stibo-*. On the latter supposition, ME. *stef*, STEEVE *a.*, may be a variant of this word.]

A. *adj.*

I. 1. Rigid; not flexible or pliant.

1000 *Prudentius Glosses* 272 in *Germania* N.S. XI. 394/1, *Rigentem* [*barbam*], stifne. *c* **1200** *Trin. Coll. Hom.* 139 Bare eorðe to bedde, and hard ston to bolstre, stiue here to shurte. **1398** TREVISA *Barth. De P.R.* XVII. cxliii. (1495) 700 A thyrde kynde of wylowes is meane bytwene the two fyrste.. for it is more plyaunt than the more: and more stiffe than the lesse. *c* **1440** *Promp. Parv.* 475/1 Styffe, or starke, *rigidus.* **1530** PALSGR. 325/2 Styffe as a thyng is that wyll nat bowe, *royde.* **1577** GOOGE *Heresbach's Husb.* I. 45 The time of cutting of it [grass] is when the Bent beginneth to fade and to waxe stiffe. **1590** SPENSER *F.Q.* III. xii. 36 Horror gan the virgins hart to perse, And her faire locks vp stared stiffe on end. *a* **1677** BARROW *Wks.* (1686) III. Serm. xvi. 189 As a stick, when once 'tis dry and stiff, you may break it, but you can never bend it into a streighter posture. **1697** DRYDEN *Virg. Georg.* III. 559 The Garment, stiff with Ice, at Hearths is thaw'd. **1717** PRIOR *Alma* II. 35 The Gown with stiff Embroid'ry shining. **1801** in Nicolas *Disp. Nelson* (1846) VII. p. ccxxvii*, With sleet and rain, ropes stiff, and sails half set, very squally, she works like a Cutter. **1842** TENNYSON *Morte d'Arthure* 64 The many-knotted waterflags, That whistled stiff and dry about the marge. **1887** FENN *Master Cerem.* ii, Isaac was in his striped jacket and the stiffest of white cravats. **1892** *Photogr. Ann.* II. 215 A narrow piece can now be nailed along the top to keep all stiff. **1913** *Standard* 14 July 4/6 An emulsion of paraffin and soft soap, applied.. with a stiff brush.

2. a. Of the body, limbs, joints, muscles, etc.: lacking suppleness, unable to move without pain (esp. owing to age, cold, injury, disease, exhaustion, etc.).

to have a stiff neck: to suffer from a rheumatic affection of the neck (usually caused by exposure to a draught) in which the head cannot be moved without pain.

c **1305** *St. Andrew* 95 in *E.E.P.* (1862) 101 Here armes whan hi vpward reiȝte bicome as stif as treo. **1538** ELYOT *Dict.*, *Obrigeo*, to be or waxe styffe for colde. **1581** MULCASTER *Positions* xxxiii. (1887) 122 The body.. withall is verie wearysome, and stif oftymes after. **1799** HT. LEE *Canterb. T.*, *Frenchm. T.* (ed. 2) I. 329 When I awoke, I found my limbs stiff at once with weariness and cold. **1840** THACKERAY *Barber Cox* Feb., You and I, ma'am, I think, are too stiff to dance. **1847** C. BRONTE *Jane Eyre* xxxiv, They were stiff with their long and jolting drive from Whitcross. **1865** W. PENNEFATHER in Braithwaite *Life & Lett.* (1878) 393, I am like a stiff Irish post-horse, which, after it has stood still for an hour or two in the stable, can hardly move a limb. **1873** F. T. ROBERTS *Theory & Pract. Med.* 247 Torticollis, wry-neck, or stiff-neck. **1902** ALICE TERTON *Lights & Shadows Hospital* xi. 180 He was already possessed of one stiff leg. **1911** *Encycl. Brit.* XV. 488/2 A stiff joint may remain as the result of long continued inflammation. **1915** 'F. ANSTEY' *Percy* 6, I'd a good deal sooner put up with a little stuffiness than a stiff neck!

transf. **1804** WORDSW. *Small Celandine* 19 Stiff in its members, withered, changed of hue.

b. Rigid in death. ***stiff and stark***: see STARK 4 b. ***stiff one, stiff 'un***, (*a*) a corpse (*slang*); (*b*) *slang*, a racehorse certain to lose or not to run at all (cf. sense 2 f below and STIFF *sb.* 3 b); (*c*) *slang*, a forged note or cheque (properly sense 1: cf. STIFF *sb.* 2).

a **1200** *Soul & Body* in Phillipps *Fragm. Ælfr. Gloss.* 5 He [*sc.* the dead man] biþ sone stif. **1297** R. GLOUC. (Rolls) 7030 Astrangled he was riȝt þer, & deide atte borde al stif. *c* **1450** tr. *De Imitatione* I. xxiii. 32 He falling from hye brake his nek, he in etinge sodenly waxid stif. **1526** *Pilgr. Perf.* (W. de W. 1531) 257 Those blessed armes.. whiche were so sore stretched on the crosse, now all starke & styffe. **1603** R. JOHNSON *Kingd. & Commw.* 146 You shall see.. many travellers brought into the townes sitting deade and stiffe.

1823 P. EGAN *Grose's Dict. Vulgar Tongue* (rev. ed.), *Stiff ones*, of no use, dead men. **1831** *Ann. Reg.*, *Law Cases* etc. (1832) 321/1 He wanted witness to fetch a stiff 'un, which witness believes meant a dead body. **1837** LADY WILLOUGHBY DE ERESBY in *C. K. Sharpe's Lett.* (1888) II. 498 He addrest him [his adversary in a duel]: 'Ah! you'll be a *stiff one* by to-morrow'. **1871** 'HAWK'S-EYE' *Turf Notes* 11 Most assuredly it is the bookmakers that profit by the 'safe uns', or 'stiff uns', as.. horses that have no chance of winning are called. **1890** BESANT *Demoniac* i. 17 If he hadn't been such an uncommon big man he would be a dead un, too —stiff un and dead! **1890** BARRÈRE & LELAND *Dict. Slang* II. 306/2 There are two bookmakers in Melbourne nicknamed 'the Undertakers', because of their fondness for laying against *stiff 'uns*, which, in this case, means horses that are certain not to run. **1895** A. GRIFFITHS *Criminals I have Known* 228 He had been 'took' with the 'stiff uns' on him, and was sent to the 'boat' (penal servitude). **1897** in Farmer & Henley *Slang & its Analogues* (1903) VI. 365/2 Do not invest money Until you read The Rialto. Never on stiff 'uns, wrong 'uns, or dead 'uns. **1953** *Sat. Even. Post* 4 Apr. 18/3 'I put over a couple of stiff ones,' is the way a paperhanger describes an operation.

c. In figurative context.

1535 COVERDALE *Ps.* lxxiv. 5 Speake not with a stiff necke. **1593** SHAKS. *2 Hen. VI*, III. i. 16 He.. passeth by with stiffe vnbowed Knee Disdaining dutie that to vs belongs.

d. Of machinery, etc.: Working with excessive friction; apt to stick, hard to move.

1848 MRS. GASKELL *Mary Barton* v, The plugs were stiff, and water could not be got.

e. Intoxicated, drunk. Cf. STIFF *sb.* 4 c. *U.S. slang. rare.*

1737 *Pennsylvania Gaz.* 6 Jan. 2/2 He's Stiff. **1900** *Dialect Notes* II. 65 *Stiff, adj.*,.. very drunk. **1957** N. ALGREN *Walk on Wild Side* I. 6 Getting stiff on the courthouse steps while denouncing the Roman Catholic clergy was a feat which regularly attracted scoffers and true believers alike. **1975** G. V. HIGGINS *City on Hill* i. 9, I always got stiff on the Fourth because it was the only way I could listen to all that crap.

f. *Sport.* Of a horse or athlete: certain (to win). Also of an event: certainly won, 'in one's pocket'. Cf. sense 2 b above. *slang.* ? *Obs.*

1890 BARRÈRE & LELAND *Dict. Slang* II. 306/2 *Stiff for*, (sporting Australian), certain for. The metaphor here is something that cannot be diverted (or averted). After the Melbourne Derby and Cup of 1880, Grand Flaneur was considered *stiff for* every race for which he was entered. **1912** *Punch* 21 Aug. 168/3 He ought to have this event absolutely stiff at the next Olympic Games.

g. Unlucky. *Austral. and N.Z. slang.*

1919 W. H. DOWNING *Digger Dialects* 47 *Stiff* (adj.), unlucky. **1922** A. WRIGHT *Colt from Country* 124 'On'y just got cut out of second place,' declared Knocker. 'Ain't a man stiff?' **1930** *Bulletin* (Sydney) 3 Dec. 22/3 ''Struth!' gasped Chips. 'If we're not stiff! Nothing doing for two days, Tommy.' **1958** *N.Z. Listener* 27 June 6/3 Then came the third Test... Maybe they were a bit stiff to lose that, but once again I think it was just that lack of solidity in the middle of the pack.

3. Rigid as the result of tension; taut. Now *rare* or *Obs.*

c **1386** CHAUCER *Sompn. T.* 559 Thanne shal this cherl with bely stif and toght As any Tabour, been hyder ybroght. *c* **1611** CHAPMAN *Iliad* VIII. 260 Another arrow forth from his stiffe string he sent. **1649** MILTON *Eikon.* xxvii. 216 We shall not have it unless his arbitrary voice will so farr slack'n the stiff curb of his Prerogative, as to grant it us. **1696** PHILLIPS (ed. 5) s.v. *Set*, To set taught the shrouds, in the Navigators Dialect, is to make them stiffer when they are too slack.

4. Of a semi-liquid substance: Thick or viscous, so as to flow with difficulty or to be capable of retaining a definite shape.

c **1430** *Two Cookery-bks.* I. 15 & let þe Sirippe be rennyng, & not to styf. *c* **1450** *Ibid.* II. 71 Grynde hem thorgh a Streynour into stuffe mylke. **1594** *Gd. Huswifes Handmaid Kitchin* 40 b, Set the pan in some colde place that it [the liquor] may be stiffe: and when it is stiffe, take a sharp knife and cut away the vppermost of the gellie. **168.** MOXON *Mech. Exerc.* (1703) 262 In Summer time use your Morter as soft as you can, but in the Winter time pretty stiff or hard. *c* **1770** MRS. GLASSE *Compl. Confectioner* 118 Then work it up into a stiff paste. **1827** FARADAY *Chem. Manip.* xix. (1842) 503 If the hot part be on the convex side, it yields.. much more than the stiffer glass on the cooler part. **1892** *Photogr. Ann.* II. 271 Stiff paste such as used by bookbinders.

5. Of soil: Heavy, dense; not porous or friable; difficult to work.

1523–34 FITZHERB. *Husb.* § 10 Bigge and styffe grounde, as cley. **1618** W. LAWSON *Orch. & Gard.* (1623) 4 A stiffe clay will not receiue the water. **1763** *Museum Rust.* I. 194 On some stiff spewy land I have, I sow my peas in ridges. **1866** ROGERS *Agric. & Prices* I. ii. 19 Stiff lands, on which water was apt to lie, were ridged. **1867** SMYTH *Sailor's Word-bk.*, *Stiff Bottom*, a clayey bottom.

6. Tight, closely packed. Now *hyperbolically* in colloquial use: Densely crowded (*with*). Also *fig.*

1683 [see JUSTIFY *v.* 9]. **1907** *Motor Boat* 19 Sept. 182/1 There seemed as many, if not more, yachts than ever, and the water was 'stiff' with masts and rigging. **1915** *Daily News* 16 Aug. 4, I shall never forget one of his picturesque phrases about the difficulty of entering a harbour 'stiff with craft' on a dark night. **1916** *Blackw. Mag.* Feb. 284/2 The salient is stiff with guns. **1939** F. THOMPSON *Lark Rise* ii. 42 Their talk was stiff with simile. **1977** B. PYM *Quartet in Autumn* iv. 34 That season of the year was stiff with festivals.

7. Of a ship: Offering a high resistance to deflection from the vertical or normal floating position; stable, not crank.

A ship is more or less stiff according as the height of the metacentre above the centre of gravity is greater or less.

1627 CAPT. SMITH *Sea Gram.* xii. 56 So stiffe, she should beare a stiffe saile and beare out her lower tier in any reasonable weather. **1708** MOTTEUX *Rabelais* IV. lxiii, Our.. Vessels might not.. be walt, but well trimmed, and stiff. **1837** HT. MARTINEAU *Soc. Amer.* II. 10 She [the ship] was a lovely creature, and as stiff as a church. **1889** WELCH *Text Bk. Naval Archit.* i. 21 In order that the ship may be *stiff* —i.e. difficult to incline by external forces such as wind pressure on sails.

8. *fig.* a. Inflexible of purpose, steadfast, resolute, firm, constant.

c **1205** LAY. 2110 Stif he wes on þonke. *c* **1300** *Beket* (Percy Soc.) 944 Somme of the Kinges conseillers to him ofte wende, And seide, bote he hulde him stif, al his lond he schende. **1548** HALL *Chron.*, *Edw. IV* (1550) 24 b, All the tounes round about were permanent and stiffe on the parte of kyng Henry, and could not be remoued. **1602** MARSTON *Antonio's Rev.* IV. v, We must be stiffe and steddie in resolve. **1719** *Col. Rec. Pennsylv.* III. 72 He was Mr. Penns stiff Friend. **1847** C. BRONTE *Jane Eyre* xxxvii, He asked me more than once [to marry him], and was as stiff about urging his point as ever you could be. **1884** *Pall Mall Gaz.* 4 Jan. 1/1 We shall have to be a great deal stiffer about the Soudan.

b. In an unfavourable sense: Obstinate, stubborn; not amenable to reason. Now *rare.*

1526 *Pilgr. Perf.* (W. de W. 1531) 304 Whan they shall be obstynate in malyce, & styffe as a drye stycke. **1530** PALSGR. 325/2 Styffe as ones herte is, *dur.* **1563** *Homilies* II. xviii. 255 These thynges must be considered of the man, that he be not to styffe, so that he ought to wynke at some thynges, and must gentilly expounde all thynges, and to forbeare. **1601** BP. W. BARLOW *Serm. Paules Crosse* 49 Two of thy principall, stiffe and open Papists. *a* **1677** BARROW *Wks.* (1686) III. Serm. xxxiv. 378 To be termed.. a clownish singularist,.. a stiff opiniatre [are opprobrious names]. **1681** DRYDEN *Abs. & Achit.* I. 547 Stiff in Opinions, always in the wrong. *a* **1715** BURNET *Own Time* III. (1724) I. 345 You know my brother long ago, that he is as stiff as a mule. **1725** T. THOMAS in *Portland MSS.* (Hist. MSS. Comm.) VI. 122 A civil well-behaved man though a stiff Presbyterian. **1838** HALIBURTON *Clockm.* Ser. II. vii. 104 Considerable stiff folks, in their way them quakers—you can't no more move 'em than a church steeple.

†c. *to stand stiff*: to stand firm; esp. *fig.* to be steadfast or obstinate. *Obs.*

a **1290** *S. Eustace* 24 in Horstm. *Altengl. Leg.* (1881) 212 He stod stiuest of alle. **1362** LANGL. *P. Pl.* A. IX. 28 For stonde he neuere so stif he stumbleþ in þe waggyng. **1535** COVERDALE *Prov.* xxviii. 1 The vngodly flyeth no man chasynge him, but the rightuous stondeth stiff as a lyon. **1556** T. HOBY tr. *Castiglione's Courtyer* I. (1561) C 2, Neither will I stand stiffe that mine is better then yours. *a* **1631** DONNE *Poems* (1650) 28 Small townes which stand stiffe, till great shot Enforce them. **1655** JER. TAYLOR *Guide Devot.* (1719) 50 It is a Shame to stand stiff in a foolish or weak Argument or Resolution.

d. Of a battle, debate, etc.: Stubbornly contested, hard.

c **1250** *Owl & Night.* 5 Þat plait was stif and starc and strong. *a* **1400–50** *Wars Alex.* 2050 So sture & styff was þe stoure. **1639** *Conceits, Clinches* etc. (1860) 29 One was holding a stiffe argument with a grocer concerning matters of trade. *a* **1661** FULLER *Worthies, Surrey* (1662) 77 There is a stiff contest betwixt the Dutch and Italians which should exceed in this Mystery. **1812** WELLINGTON in Gurw. *Desp.* (1837) VIII. 666 Marmont's troops are all ready for a start but I hope to be strong enough for a stiff affair with him and Soult. **1823** 'JON BEE' *Dict. Turf* 166 In the ring, 'tis called 'a stiff fight' when the men stand up well to each other, giving and taking. **1868** G. DUFF *Pol. Surv.* 132 He has been elected after a very stiff contest. **1916** J. BUCHAN *Hist. War* IX. lxx. 161 To withdraw through that area meant a stiff holding battle around Brest.

e. Severe, stern; angry.

1856 THACKERAY *Miscellanies* II. 272 The old gent cut up uncommon stiff. **1930** W. S. MAUGHAM *Cakes & Ale* viii. 104, I wrote a pretty stiff letter to the librarian.

f. *Cricket.* Of a batsman: tending to play stubbornly in a defensive manner.

1869 *Field* 28 Aug. 176/3 This lucky escape seemed to endow the 'stiff batsman' with more than ordinary vigour. **1877** C. BOX *English Game of Cricket* xxvi. 461 *Stiff bat*, usually applied to a batsman who stubbornly defends his wicket. **1885** R. H. LYTTELTON in *J. Lillywhite's Cricketers' Compan.* 16 Midwinter.. [was] a stiff and careful bat.

9. Formal, constrained, lacking ease or grace.

a. Of bearing, manners, etc.: Unbending (expressing pride, coldness, displeasure, awkwardness, and the like); not easy or gracious; haughty.

1608 MIDDLETON *Mad World* I. A 3, He.. thinkes himselfe neuer happier then when some stiffe L. or great Countesse alights, to make light his dishes. **1613** WOTTON *Reliq.* (1672) 409 It is conceived that the King hath a good while been much distasted with the said Gentleman.. for too stiff a carriage of his fortune. **1754** CHATHAM *Lett. to Nephew* v. 36 Ceremonious, formal compliments, stiff civilities, will never be politeness. **1820** SCOTT *Monast.* xxix, The knight.. thanked him with the stiff condescension of the court of Elizabeth. **1831** *Society* I. 196 Lord Glamorgan was stiff and cold in his manner to strangers. **1859** JEPHSON *Brittany* v. 57 The stiff respectabilities.. of an English country neighbourhood.

b. Of style, diction, etc.: Lacking ease and grace; laboured, formal pedantic.

1664 DRYDEN *Riv. Ladies* Prol. 20 Though his Plot's dull as can be well desir'd, Wit stiff as any you have e'r admir'd. **1710** FELTON *Diss. Classics* (1718) 114 Too scrupulous an Observation of Rules spoileth all sorts of Writings: It maketh them Stiff and Formal. **1849** MACAULAY *Hist. Eng.* vii. II. 247 He had enjoyed high fame as an orator, though his diction.. was, towards the close of his life, pronounced stiff and pedantic. **1898** GOSSE *Short Hist. Mod. Eng. Lit.* vii. 238 A mass of stiff blank verse.

c. Of artistic form or arrangement: Excessively regular; lacking grace of line.

1779 *Mirror* No. 61. 203 In his grounds you find stiff, rectangular walks. **1813** SARAH LADY LYTTELTON *Corr.* (1912) 160, I cannot accustom myself at all to the foreign stiff way of furnishing the rooms. **1870** F. R. WILSON *Ch. Lindisf.* 23 It was.. replaced by a similar stiff structure. **1912** J. L. MYRES *Dawn of Hist.* viii. 175 A limited stock of stiff geometrical designs.

d. Of handwriting: Lacking ease and freedom; not flowing. Cf. sense 2.

1818 SCOTT *Hrt. Midl.* xlviii, The manuscript was a fair Italian hand, though something stiff and constrained. **1885** 'MRS. ALEXANDER' *At Bay* viii, Several letters were brought to him, one, directed in a stiff, careful, unknown hand.

10. Of price, charges, rates, etc.: Unyielding, firm; having an upward tendency. Hence of a commodity or the dealers in it. Cf. sense 20.

1883 *Manch. Exam.* 14 Dec. 4/1 For three month's bills the terms were firm at 2⅝ per cent, but for January paper the rate was stiffer. **1886** *Cheshire Gloss.* s.v., A butcher will tell you 'You're very stiff this morning' if you will not come down at all in the price of a beast. **1888** *Daily News* 5 Nov. 7/2 Buyers.. find sellers stiff. **1893** *Ibid.* 14 July 3/7 The latest reports from London show that merinos are a little stiffer.

11. a. Colloquial phrases. ***stiff as a poker***; ***stiff in the back***, firm, resolute; ***to keep*** (***carry, have***) ***a stiff upper lip***, to be firm, unyielding; hence ***stiff-upper-lip*** adj.; also as *v. intr.* and *adv.*; also ***stiff-upper-lipped*** adj., ***stiff-upper-lippery***, ***stiff-upper-lippish*** adj., ***stiffupperlippishness***.

1798 G. COLMAN *Heir at Law* (1800) III. ii. 34 The last lord Duberly's father.. with a wig as wide as a wash-tub and stuck up as stiff as a poker. **1800** MRS. HERVEY *Mourtray Fam.* II. 251 Lady Elizabeth, as stiff as a poker, sat with her mouth pursed up, vexed to death. **1815** *Massachusetts Spy* 14 June 4/4, I kept a stiff upper lip, and bought [a] license to sell my goods. **1837** HALIBURTON *Clockm.* Ser. I. x. 77 Its a proper pity sich a clever woman should carry such a stiff upper lip. **1852** MRS. STOWE *Uncle Tom's C.* x, 'Well, good-by, Uncle Tom; keep a stiff upper lip,' said George. **1876** E. W. HEAP *Diary* 22 Mar. in *Publ. Amer. Dial. Soc.* (1969) LII. 55 Frozen as stiff as a poker last night. **1887** *Spectator* 17 Sept. 1241 The Financial Secretary, who, it is supposed, will have a stiff upper lip and tightly buttoned pockets. **1894** DU MAURIER *Trilby* v. 275 Each walked off.. stiff as pokers. **1897** 'A. HOPE' *Phroso* iv. (1905) 75 'Are you going to let him off?' demanded Denny, suspiciously. 'You never can be stiff in the back, Charley.' **1934** J. BUCHAN *Free Fishers* xviii. 297 Old Utterson is as stiff as a poker, and would keep us arguing till midnight.

1958 *Listener* 16 Oct. 621/3 She criticizes herself for being too stiff-upper-lipped about the tragedy that she faces. **1961** A. O. J. COCKSHUT *Imagination of Charles Dickens* viii. 116 He oscillated between indignation, self-pity, and reticence of the stiff-upper-lip English school. **1961** *John o' London's* 19 Oct. 447/2 The second film contains a firmly disciplined ..undercurrent of Miniverish stiff-upper-lippery. **1963** *Listener* 3 Jan. 42/1 It was all very improbable and too stiff-upper-lippish to have been written by anybody but an anglophile Frenchman. **1973** *New Society* 31 May 483/2 MPs, in praising stiffupperlippishness, used sex as a stalking horse. **1977** *Broadcast* 14 Nov. 10/3 The British are stiff upper-lipping through power cuts. **1978** W. F. BUCKLEY *Stained Glass* xv. 153 As you say, we must be stiff-upper-lip formal. **1979** *Verbatim* Autumn 14/2 Two of the men, an upper-class Indian and an English Colonel, share a British university education, and they have a private joke of using *pip-pip!*, *I say*, and *stiff upper lip* expressions to each other. **1979** *Evening News* 6 Feb. 7/4 With rakish Parker, Prince Philip found that he could relax from the strains of state business and stiff-upper-lippery. **1983** *Listener* 20 Jan. 33/1 Nigel Anthony is the stiff-upper-lipped adventurer.

b. In predicative use (cf. RIGID *a.* 1 d): to an extreme degree, as ***to bore*** (***scare***, etc.) ***stiff***.

1905 *McClure's Mag.* May 100/1 He was scared stiff to hear that Morrow was in town. **1918** W. J. LOCKE *Rough Road* ix. 107, I think I ought to tell you that you're boring Durdlebury stiff. **1923** R. D. PAINE *Comr. Rolling Ocean* ix. 150 When that crazy fireman broke loose just now, I was scared perfectly stiff. **1928** F. B. YOUNG *My Brother Jonathan* II. v. 284 She bores everybody she meets stiff with talking about him. **1933** [see FEED *v.* 6 h]. **1952** [see FRONT *sb.* (and *a.*) 3 b]. **1956** *English* Summer 46 Billy Temple, who announced in Westminster School Hall that 'the longer poems of Milton bored him stiff'. **1964** I. MURDOCH *Italian Girl* xii. 137, I was scared absolutely stiff of Otto finding out.

12. *Math.* Of a differential equation: having a solution that shows completely different behaviour over widely different scales of time (or other independent variable).

1952 CURTISS & HIRSCHFELDER in *Proc. Nat. Acad. Sci.* XXXVIII. 235 In the study of chemical kinetics, electrical circuit theory, and problems of missile guidance a type of differential equation arises which is exceedingly difficult to solve by ordinary numerical procedures. A very satisfactory method of solution of these equations is obtained by making use of a forward interpolation process... The differential equations to which this method applies are called 'stiff'. **1973** *Physics Bull.* June 340/2 'Stiff' differential equation problems also have been the principal reason for combined analogue-digital (hybrid computer) simulation. **1979** *Nature* 18 Jan. 201/2 It would be interesting to extend the present work to the case of Bianchi-type models filled with a perfect fluid of equation of state: $p = (\gamma - 1)\rho$, which covers Zel'dovich's stiff equation of state.

II. Strong.

13. a. Of living creatures: Stout, stalwart, sturdy (cf. sense 8); esp. in alliterative phrases as † ***stiff in stour***, † ***stiff on steed***. *Obs.* exc. *dial.* (see *Eng. Dial. Dict.*)

1297 R. GLOUC. (Rolls) 7732 So stif mon he was in armes, in ssoldren, & in leade, þat vnneþe enimon miȝte is bowe bende. *a* **1300** *Cursor M.* 2203 Nembrot..O babilon king stijf in stur. **13..** *E.E. Allit. P.* B. 255 þe styfest, þe stalworþest þat stod euer on fete. ? *a* **1366** CHAUCER *Rom. Rose* 1270 The knyght was faire and styf in stour. *a* **1400** *Sir Perc.* 19 He was doughty of dede, A styffe body one a stede. *c* **1435** *Torr. Portugal* 1494 It were two dragons stif and strong. **1544** BETHAM *Precepts War* I. xxxiii. C iv, Kepe thyne armye in rough and mountayne places, to make theyr bodies styffe and stronge. *a* **1677** BARROW *Wks.* (1686) III. Serm. xvi. 188 But in stout proficients the heart becometh hard and stony, the neck stiff and brawny.

†**b.** Of a drinker: 'Hard'. *Obs.*

1617 MORYSON *Itin.* III. 27 The Sweitzers are for the most part Souldiers, and stiffe drinkers. **1632** *Lyly's Mother Bombie* II. i. *Song*, We already are stiffe Drinkers. [**1635** HEYWOOD *Philocoth.* 44 To title a drunkard by, wee..strive to character him in a more mincing and modest phrase, as thus: He is a good fellow Or, A boone companion,..A stiffe Blade.]

†**14. a.** Of things inanimate: Strong; stoutly built; massive. *Obs.*

c **1400** *Destr. Troy* 1527 The styfe towne to Restore ..[Priam] Gate masons full mony. *c* **1400** *Land Troy Bk.* 2899 Ther stode a Castel a litel ther-by, Gret, and stiff, and ful strong. *c* **1440** *York Myst.* XXIX. 268 Our stiffe tempill, þat made is of stone.

†**b.** Of a weapon: Hard, stout, formidable. *Obs.*

c **1250** *Owl & Night.* 78 þi bile is stif & sarp & hoked. **13..** *K. Alis.* 2740 (Laud MS.), He groep on honde a styff spere. *c* **1470** HENRY *Wallace* IX. 1649 With a styff suerd to dede he has him dycht. **1607** SHAKS. *Cor.* I. i. 167 Make you ready your stiffe bats and clubs.

15. Of natural agencies:

a. Strong, violent (of wind); also applied to a steady wind of moderate force.

c **1290** *Brendan* 464 in *S. Eng. Leg.* 232 þe wynd was boþe strong and stif. **1340-70** *Alex. & Dind.* 487 Stiue stormus of þe wind stiren vp þe wawus. *c* **1425** *Noah's Ark* in *Non-Cycle Myst. Plays* 19 All mankind dead shall be With storms both stiff and steer. *c* **1565** JENKINSON in Hakluyt *Voy.* (1599) I. 345 The winde being contrary, and a stiffe gale. **1613** SHAKS. *Hen. VIII*, IV. i. 72 Such a noyse arose, As the shrowdes make at Sea, in a stiffe Tempest. **1665** G. HAVERS *P. della Valle's Trav. E. India* 2 We again spread our sails freely to the wind, which was pretty stiff. **1725** POPE *Odyss.* IV. 483 When the stiffer gales Rise on the poop, and fully stretch the sails. **1846** A. YOUNG *Naut. Dict.* 130 A fresh breeze, implies a wind in which a vessel may safely carry all her canvass; a stiff breeze, implies one somewhat stronger than this, but not so violent as a gale.

in fig. context. **1399** LANGL. *Rich. Redeles* III. 104 Many a styff storme with-stode ffor þe comunes. **1663** PATRICK *Parab. Pilgr.* i. 4 The gale proves so stiff, that our hearts are swelled therewith.

†**b.** Of a river: Flowing strongly. *Obs.*

13.. *K. Alis.* 3482 (Laud MS.) þe water was wel styf & colde. **13..** *E.E. Allit. P.* C. 234 Styffe stremes & streȝt hem strayned a whyle. ? *a* **1366** CHAUCER *Rom. Rose* 115 From an hill..Cam doun the streme ful stif and bold. *a* **1400-50** *Wars Alex.* 2589 þai saȝe þe streme so stife, it stonaid þam all.

†**c.** Of news: Formidable, grave. *Obs.*

1606 SHAKS. *Ant. & Cl.* I. ii. 104 Labienus (this is stiffe-newes), Hath with his Parthian Force Extended Asia.

†**16.** Of voice, sound: Powerful, loud. *Obs.*

1377 LANGL. *P. Pl.* B. xv. 584 [Christ] With styf voys hym called, *Lazare, veni foras.* *c* **1386** CHAUCER *Prol.* 673 This Somonour bar to hym a stif burdoun Was neuere trompe of half so greet a soun. *a* **1400-50** *Wars Alex.* 611 His steuyn stiffe was & steryn þat stonayd many.

17. In modern use, of liquors (mainly spirits): Strong, potent. Also of tea and *loosely*, denoting a generous measure.

1813 *Sporting Mag.* XLII. 131 Mr. Jenkins..to the last 'belted' his three bottles of stiff port after dinner. **1842** TENNYSON *Will Waterpr.* 78 But tho' the port surpasses praise, My nerves have dealt with stiffer. **1883** STEVENSON *Treas. Isl.* xix, Each had a good stiff glass of brandy grog. **1904** H. JAMES *Golden Bowl* I. xviii. 212 You must awfully want your tea..so let me give you a good stiff cup. **1919** WODEHOUSE *Coming of Bill* (1920) II. xi. 213 Mr. Penway's eyes..fell upon the bottle of Bourbon... He sprang at it and poured himself a stiff dose. **1929** T. WOLFE *Look Homeward, Angel* xxxv. 522 A stiff drink of gin. **1951** 'J. WYNDHAM' *Day of Triffids* i. 21, I was shaky again, and..could have done with a stiff drink. **1970** G. F. NEWMAN *Sir, You Bastard* vii. 192, I think you've earned a very stiff scotch. **1975** D. LODGE *Changing Places* ii. 67 'Wow,' said the woman. 'You mix a stiff drink.' **1977** K. O'HARA *Ghost of Thomas Penry* xv. 149 They went off and poured themselves a stiff one each.

III. Hard, difficult.

18. Of an ascent or descent: Steep so as to be difficult. In *Hunting*: Difficult (said of an obstacle or a tract of country presenting many obstacles).

1704 *Churchill's Collect. Voy. & Trav.* III. 81/1, I have seen them run up the stiffest and streightest Hills. **1715** *Leoni's Palladio's Archit.* (1721) I. 54 The Roof would be too stiff [Ital. *troppo ratta*]. **1817** *Sporting Mag.* L. 38 The ground gone over was through a stiff country. **1853** R. S. SURTEES *Sponge's Sp. Tour* xxiii. 124 His lordship charged a stiff flight of rails in the brick-fields. **1883** C. HOWARD *Roads Eng. & Wales* (ed. 3) 139 Easy going to Braunston,.. into which there is a long stiff descent. **1897** MARY KINGSLEY *W. Africa* 571/1 Owing to the world being on a stiff slant here-abouts, it takes time to make it stand straight. **1903** M. A. STEIN *Sand-Buried Ruins of Khotan* xiv. (1904) 224 The next day's climb proved a stiff one.

19. That requires considerable effort; severe; laborious, toilsome.

1862 CARLYLE *Fredk. Gt.* XIII. ii. III. 414 They are dreadfully stiff reading, those Despatches of Hyndford. **1865** DICKENS *Mut. Fr.* IV. i, Your working days must be stiff 'uns if these is your holidays. **1886** STUBBS *Lect. Med. & Mod. Hist.* ii. 31 More modest men..passed a stiff examination in the History School. **1890** 'R. BOLDREWOOD' *Col. Reformer* xix, He encouraged him to digest a certain daily quantity of 'stiff' or improving literature. **1898** *Daily News* 22 July, What do you call a stiff pace on a level road?

20. a. Of a price, charge, demand, etc.: Unusually high, excessive. Cf. sense 10.

1824 DIBDIN *Libr. Companion* (1825) 730 *note*, The Denham of 1709 brought the stiff sum of 1*l.* 1*s.*..but the Donne..produced..the far stiffer price of 4*l.* 4*s.* **1886** STEVENSON *Dr. Jekyll* i, The figure was stiff; but the signature was good for more than that, if it was only genuine. **1903** A. C. P. HAGGARD *Sport. Yarns* 225 He naturally thought 3s. an hour pretty stiff boat hire.

b. *Finance.* = TIGHT *a.* 10 c. Now *rare* or *Obs.*

1845 *Punch* 11 Oct. 164/2 Money's stiff they say. **1912** *Q. Rev.* July 103 Money is in such keen demand all the world over that the rates tend to become high, whereupon it is called 'stiff' or 'tight'.

IV. 21. *Comb.* and special collocations.

a. Special collocations with sbs.: **stiff-bit, stiff field** (see quots.); **stiff sea-adder**, a provincial name of the fish *Nerophis ophidion*.

1875 KNIGHT *Dict. Mech.*, *Stiff-bit*, a bit without a joint, like a snaffle; or branches, like a curb-bit. **1883** DAY *Fishes Gt. Brit.* II. 263 Stiff sea-adder. **1910** *N. Hawkins' Electr. Dict.*, *Stiff Field*, a term sometimes applied to an intense electromagnetic field.

b. Collocations forming phrases used *attrib.*, as ***stiff-arm***, ***-brim***, ***-clay***, ***-land***, ***-leg***, ***-mud***, ***-plate***.

1778 [W. MARSHALL] *Minutes Agric.*, *Observ.* 24, I will not manure a stiff-land Meadow in winter. **1884** C. T. DAVIS *Bricks, Tiles* etc. (1889) 184 Stiff-clay bricks, or stiff-mud bricks as they are generally termed. **1896** 'MARK TWAIN' in *Harper's Mag.* Aug. 356/1 It was the first season anybody wore that kind—a black stiff-brim stove-pipe. **1899** *Westm. Gaz.* 7 Mar. 11/1 The boiler in English locomotives is invariably carried on a stiff-plate frame. **1909** *Ibid.* 25 Aug. 4/2 It..is a sort of stiff-arm punch which returns the ball very close to the net. **1930** *Engineering* 10 Oct. 449/2 The material—sand and gravel—was..unloaded by means of a stiff-leg derrick. **1932** W. FAULKNER *Light in August* ii. 27 He wore a tie and a stiffbrim straw hat that was quite new. **1943** *Sun* (Baltimore) 26 Nov. 6/3 The tower was first welded together on the ground. It was then lifted into its foundation by heavy lines attached to two high especially built 'stiff-leg' cranes.

c. Combinations with sbs.: **stiff-arm** *v. trans.* (occas. *absol.*), to fend off or push with a stiff arm; hence *fig.*, to rebuff or reject; also as *sb.* (usu. *attrib.*) in Rugby and U.S. Football, the act of tackling or fending off a tackle with a stiff arm; †**stiffgut**, a glutton; **stiff-leaf** *Arch.*, the term applied to the foliage of conventional form, with stiff leaf-stems, characteristic as a decoration in the Early English style; **stiff-neck**, an obstinate, haughty or self-righteous person; cf. STIFF-NECKED *a.*; †**stiffrump** *slang*, an obstinate or haughty person; **stiff-stalk** (see quot.); †**stiff-stander**, one who makes an obstinate stand (*for*).

1927 G. S. LOWMAN *Pract. Football* vii. 85 In all *stiff arm and shifting have the body slightly inclined toward the tackler. *Ibid.* xii. 218 When playing in the line, the defensive center should stiff-arm his opponent back into the play. **1934** CRISLER & WIEMAN *Pract. Football* vii. 86 The ball carrier is more easily stopped in the hole than anywhere else, since he cannot dodge, sidestep, reverse or stiff-arm at that point. **1945** *Tee Emm* (Air Ministry) V. 50 Ward off attack by kicking or stiffarming the shark... Kick or stiff-arm a shark to push him away. **1950** *Sport* 24-30 Mar. 9/1 Vindictive hacking and 'stiff arm' jabs were the rule rather than the exception. **1968** *Listener* 8 Aug. 189/2 There had been the fury of the British backs meeting persistent stiff-arm and late tackling, although these almost automatic fouls were only occasionally penalised. **1973** [see PLACE *sb.*[1] 9 d]. **1974** A. A. THOMPSON *Swiss Legacy* xviii. 185 She tried to slam the door, but McAllister stiff-armed it violently against the wall. **1630** J. TAYLOR (Water P.) *Gt. Eater of Kent* Ded. 2 Though you are the absolutest man of mouth and the most renowned *stifgut in this westerne angle of the world, yet we haue as great or greater eaters then your selfe. **1851** T. H. TURNER *Dom. Archit.* I. ii. 39 The shafts in the jambs have round capitals with foliage approaching to what is technically called *stiff-leaf. **1921** *Blackw. Mag.* Feb. 251/1 The *stiff-necks of Victoria's entourage would have been painfully shocked. **1962** E. SNOW *Red China Today* (1963) i. 18 The young stiff-neck dismissed them angrily and told me I could do as I pleased about disposing of my excess but if I carried it I'd have to pay. **1975** *New Yorker* 28 Apr. 124/2 A repatriated American stiffneck who has been imprisoned by the North Vietnamese finds his particular solace in not budging an inch from the mindless chauvinism he set out with. **1709** STEELE & ADDISON *Tatler* No. 110 ¶4 Ha! Is that thy Wisdom, old *Stiffrump, ha? **1884** W. MILLER *Plant-n.* 130 Mexican *Stiff-stalk, *Rigidella flammea.* **1642** H. MORE *Song of Soul* II. III. iii. 5 O You *stiff-standers for ag'd Ptolemee.

d. Parasynthetic adjs., as ***stiff backed***, ***-bodied***, ***-boned***, ***-bosomed***, ***-elbowed***, † ***-hearted***, ***-jointed***, ***-kneed***, ***-leathered***, ***-leaved***, ***-legged***, ***-limbed***, ***-lipped***, † ***-minded***, ***-shirted***, ***-winged***, † ***-witted***, etc.; **stiff-arsed** *slang* (see quot. 1937); †**stiff-docked**, strong in the hind quarters; †**stiff-rumped** *fig.*, unbending, obstinate, proud; †**stiff-stomached**, hard-hearted; †**stiff streamed**, having a strong current.

1937 PARTRIDGE *Dict. Slang* 831/2 **Stiff-arsed*, haughty; supercilious. **1971** B. MALAMUD *Tenants* 70 If you think you ..are goint to be stiffassed and uptight by what I say, maybe we ought to call it off before we start? **1848** THACKERAY *Van. Fair* xx, The *stiff-backed prig, with his dandified airs and West End swagger. **1697** J. LEWIS *Mem. Dk. Glocester* (1789) 11 His *stiff-bodied coats were very troublesome to him in his military amusements. **1727** MRS. DELANY *Life & Corr.* (1861) I. 138 They were draped in stiff-bodied gowns of silver tissue. **1896** MRS. CAFFYN *Quaker Grandmother* 198 We're not *stiff-boned, stubborn things like men folk. **1925** WODEHOUSE *Carry On, Jeeves* ix. 238 Then lay out one of the gents' *stiff-bosomed [shirts]. **1942** W. FAULKNER *Go Down, Moses* 74 A white stiff-bosomed collarless shirt beneath a pique vest. **1898** MRS. WOODS in *19th Cent.* XLIV. 1000 This *stiff-collared hypocrite of a young Briton. **1523-34** FITZHERB. *Husb.* §76 The .iiii. properties of a lyon. The fyrste is, to haue a brode breste; the seconde, to be *styffe-docked. *Ibid.* §76 The .ix. propertyes of an hare. The fyrste is *styffe-eared. **1956** H. GOLD *Man who was not with It* (1965) vi. 50, I..walked imperfectly awake, *stiff-elbowed, thick-tongued, and dim-sighted. **1973** M. AMIS *Rachel Papers* 190 In this fashion, with twelve stiff-elbowed tugs, he has wanked into her head. **1552** ABP. HAMILTON *Catech.* (1884) 82 The sone quhilk was inobedient, *stifhartit and thrawart to his father and mother. **1560** BIBLE (Geneva) *Ezek.* ii. 4 Thei are impudent children, and stiffe hearted. **1743** W. ELLIS *Mod. Husbandman* Oct. i. 126 Its *stiff-jointed, high-coloured, long Straw. **1876** 'MARK TWAIN' *Tom Sawyer* xvi. 142 They felt rusty, and stiff-jointed, and a little homesick. **1804** W. BLAKE in A. G. B. Russell *Lett.* (1906) 156 My good woman..is still *stiff-kneed but well in other respects. **1576** NEWTON *Lemnie's Complex.* I. ix. 74 As hard and *styffe-leathered bootes y[e] haue lyen long vnoccupyed. **1822** *Hortus Angl.* II. 396 Aster Rigidus. *Stiff-leaved Star Wort. **1854** DICKENS *Hard Times* III. i. 263 In staggering over the universe with his rusty *stiff-legged compasses, he had meant to do great things. **1922** JOYCE *Ulysses* 428 Bloom..blunders stifflegged, out of the track. **1914** 'SAKI' *Beasts & Super-Beasts* 65 Old Shep, the white-nozzled, *stiff-limbed collie. **1973** M. AMIS *Rachel Papers* 23 In normal circumstances, with her embarrassment in any kind of pre-coital conversation, her unassumingly pretty face, the stiff-limbed movements: you were a plaything of her unease. **1896** *Tablet* 23 May 801 A little cowardice, or complacency to *stiff-lipped colleagues, and the old inequality will be perpetuated. **1552** HULOET, *Stiffe minded or of courage, *infractus animi.* **1910** *Spectator* 5 Nov. 740/2 They are too stiff-minded. **1835** WHEWELL *Archit. Notes* (1842) 291 *Stiff-pointed curled tufts of foliage. **1715** *Phil. Trans.* XXIX. 233 *Stif-rim'd Marygold. **1728** SOMERVILLE *Epist. to Ramsay* I. 91 Self-conceit, and *stiff-rumpt Pride. **1812** COLMAN *Br. Grins, Knt. & Friar* I. xxx, The stiff-rumped rascals [the friars] looked so sanctified. **1918** G. FRANKAU *One of Them* iv. 34 The patient lights of brougham or rarer car shine, Waiting *stiff-shirted squires and ladies fair. **1933** DYLAN THOMAS *Let.* Nov. (1966) 51 Please don't go all stiff-shirted on me. **1540** PALSGR. *Acolastus* v. ii. Y iij, He that is so *styffe stomaked, or so harde harted. **1632** LITHGOW *Trav.* IX. 380 The *stiffe stream'd Dolf. *c* **1875** *Cassell's Nat. Hist.* IV. 195 The last group of the Wild-fowl contains the *Stiff-tailed Ducks, which are recognisable by their extremely rigid tail-feathers. **1616** T. SCOT *Philomythie* etc. K 8, Where the *stiffe-vdder'd Cow long'd twice a day, To meet the merry milke-maide on the way. **1901** *Practitioner* Mar. 241 Why not an 'Epic of Malaria'?.. But such a theme would surely spur the *stiffest-winged Pegasus to empyrean flights. **1977** *Devon Wetlands* (Devon County Council) vii. 26 Fulmars..have a characteristic stiff-winged, gliding flight. **1599** SANDYS *Europæ Spec.* (1632) 75 Much like to a stout-hearted and *stiff-witted Captaine, who scornes to imitate any stratageme before used by the enemy.

B. *sb.*

†**1.** Some stiffened article of female attire. *Obs.*

1680 *Will of Frances Dobson* in *Bedfordsh. N. & Q.* (1889) II. 237, I give to my seruant..all my working day clothes of wollen or stuffe, and also 3 of my strongest stiffs and aprons.

2. *slang.* **a.** Paper; a document, esp. a promissory note or bill of exchange; a clandestine letter.

1823 EGAN *Grose's Dict. Vulgar T.* s.v., Giving a bill instead of money is denominated, in the mercantile world, taking 'the stiff'. **1855** THACKERAY *Newcomes* vi, I wish you'd do me a bit of stiff. **1889** *Pall Mall Gaz.* 14 Feb. 4/3 The 'stiff,' as a note is called in convict parlance. **1892** M. WILLIAMS *Round London* (1893) 62 A hawker's licence, which is known among the [London] brotherhood as a 'stiff'. **1904** A. GRIFFITHS *50 Yrs. Publ. Serv.* 152 Other 'stiffs'—the prison term for anonymous or clandestine letters—were scattered about.

Comb. **1823** 'JON BEE' *Dict. Turf* 166 *Stiff-dealer*, a dealer in stiff, a pseudo-merchant, or trader in moonshine paper.

b. Money.

1897 'OUIDA' *Massarenes* i. 6 They are astonishing—biggest income in the United States... Made their 'stiff' there, and come home to spend it. **1930** BELLOC *New Cautionary Tales* 58 He wrang his hands, exclaiming, 'If I only had a bit of Stiff How different would be my life!'

3. *slang.* **a.** A corpse (= *stiff 'un*, A. 2 b).

1859 BARTLETT *Dict. Amer.* (ed. 2) 450. **1871** HAY *Myst. Gilgal* 41 They piled the stiffs outside the door. **1915** *Morn. Post* 7 Aug. 5/4 'This cigarette is all right', I said. 'Where do they come from?' 'Off that German stiff', he answered.

b. A racehorse which is unikely to win; *spec.* one which is not intended to win. Cf. STIFF *a.* 2 b. *U.S. slang.*

a **1890** in Barrère & Leland *Dict. Slang.* (1890) II. 306/1 'What do they mean by a *stiff* in the race?' 'That means generally a horse that on public form should win the race, and that either the jockey, trainer, or horse has been 'fixed' so that he will not win.' **1935** D. RUNYON *Money from Home* 197 There is also a rumor that Follow You is a stiff in the race. **1944** *Sun* (Baltimore) 21 Sept. 17/5 We either get shut out or find we are on a stiff which won't run.

4. *slang.* **a.** A penniless man; a wastrel; a tramp; a migratory or unskilled worker.

1899 *Daily Chron.* 10 Aug. 5/7 'Stiffs,' that is, men who work their passage by attending to cattle. **1901**, etc. [see BINDLE[2] a]. **1909** *Daily Mail* 10 Aug. 4/5 England knows the tramp and the loafer,..but greater than these is the Johannesburg 'stiff'. **1915** *Truth* 20 Jan. 90/2 A hopeless shortage of the best labour on the one hand, and an unusual proportion of 'stiffs' on the other. **1927** W. EDGE *Main Stem* iii. 16 No stiff ever got information about a job through a telephone directory. **1963** H. GARNER in R. Weaver *Canad. Short Stories* (1968) 2nd Ser. 41 Who would listen to a harvest stiff in the middle of the tobacco country? **1976** E. WARD *Hanged Man* iii. 13 The driver..reached out to pull Burnett into the dusty cab. Construction stiff. A wandering freemasonry.

b. A mean, disagreeable, or contemptible person (freq. *big stiff*). Also joc. and *loosely*, a man, a fellow; *working stiff*, an ordinary working man. *slang* (orig. *U.S.*).

1882 in *Colorado Quarterly* (1956) Winter 271 Cap. Cline, that lonely old stiff..is now demonotized. **1896** G. ADE *Artie* ii. 17 There I set like a big stiff for five hours. *Ibid.* iv. 36, I do n't come in here to give coin to no such stiffs as you. **1914** [see NANNY-GOAT 3]. **1925** C. CONNOLLY *Let.* 28 Feb. in *Romantic Friendship* (1975) 61 He was described..as 'rather a stiff' which is true at present. **1930** *Punch* 26 Feb. 228/2 He said 'You big stiff!' in a very loud voice and went. **1930** J. DOS PASSOS *42nd Parallel* v. 403 Charley said that working stiffs ought to stick together for decent living conditions. **1936** WODEHOUSE *Laughing Gas* viii. 82 He had told me this man was a pretty good sort of old stiff. **1949** *Daily Ardmoreite* (Ardmore, Oklahoma) 23 Feb. 18/6 A select group of working stiffs in high government circles have run into 20 assorted kinds of complications. **1951** E. PAUL *Springtime in Paris* vii. 139 Hold your trap, you old stiff. **1967** *Sun* 23 Apr. 5/8 A bad customer..a stiff who orders the table d'hôte and nothing to drink. **1975** *N.Y. Times* 8 Jan. 35/1 And if a black man did buy a house, hey, we knocked on his door and said hello. If he was a nice guy, great. If he was a stiff, well, I know lots of white stiffs, too. **1977** *Guardian Weekly* 10 July 15/2 The idea of two young working stiffs [*sc.* Woodward and Bernstein] carrying off the prize is irresistible to youngsters with their careers before them.

c. A drunkard (see also quot. 1969). Cf. STIFF *a.* 2 e.

1907 J. LONDON *Road* 170 Robbing a drunken man they call 'rolling a stiff'. **1969** *Telegraph* (Brisbane) 3 Oct. 42/1 We get all types of no-hopers here—hoboes, bums, 'alcos', homosexuals and 'stiffs' (methylated spirits drinkers). **1976** N. THORNBURG *Cutter & Bone* vi. 135 It had taken a good part of the day just to locate the poor stiff.

d. *Football.* A member of a reserve team. Freq. in *pl. slang.*

1950 *Sport* 22–28 Sept. 4/1 On Saturday the Forest 'stiffs' romped home to a 5–1 victory over Halifax. **1967** M. PROCTER *Rogue Running* xxv. 164 He became one of the 'stiffs', a second-team man who only played for the first team when a better man was ill, or injured. **1970** *Sun* 5 Sept. 28/6 (*heading*) Gunners sign Metchick for stiffs.

C. *adv.* or *quasi-adv.*

1. Stiffly, firmly, tightly, hard, etc. Phrase, *to give it to someone* (*pretty*) *stiff*: to speak severely to, to rate.

1422 YONGE tr. *Secreta Secret.* 174 The course of the ryuer So stronge and So styfe rane. *c* **1450** *Pol. Rel. & L. Poems* (1903) 133 þe werlde, my flesch, þe fende, felly þai me besale both strange & styfe. **1525** tr. *Brunswyke's Handywork Surg.* lxxiii. P iij b, Take hede that ye bynde hym not to styfe. **1680** MOXON *Mech. Exerc.* x. 182 This piece of wood is fitted stiff into a square Hole. **1712** J. JAMES *Gardening* 81 [This] makes the Joint go stiffer, or slacker, at Pleasure. **1880** J. PAYN *Confid. Agent* xliii, Giving it to her..pretty stiff.

2. In comb. with ppl. adjs. **a.** Rigidly, tightly, obstinately, etc. as †*stiff-holden*, *-rustling*, *-swathed*. **b.** So as to be stiff, in various senses, as *stiff-bent*, *-built*, *-dressed*, etc. **c.** †**stiff-borne**, obstinately pursued; †**stiff-girt**, *fig.* inflexible, obstinate; †**stiff-thrown**, thrown with great force.

1581 A. HALL *Iliad* III. 45 With bow *stifbent, and with quiuer, and many a shaft therein. **1647** H. MORE *Song of Soul* II. App. xxxviii, Sent out from bow stiff-bent with even string. **1624** QUARLES *Job Militant* iii, His *stiffe-bolting haire: (Not much vnlike the pennes of Porcupines). **1598** SHAKS. *2 Hen. IV*, I. i. 177 None of this..could restraine The *stiffe-borne Action. **1861** MAYHEW *Lond. Labour* III. 272 Some vessels are so *stiff-built, that they can discharge the whole of their cargo without taking in any ballast at all. **1886** *Daily News* 13 Oct. 2/6 *Stiff-dressed nets are still dull of sale. **1659** GAUDEN *Tears Ch.* II. xxx. 246 He, *stiffe-girt and inexorable, went with a short turn out of the Church. **1596** *Edw. III*, III. iii. 129 Like *stiffe growen oakes [they] will stand immouable, When whirle wind quickly turnes vp yonger trese. **1533** FRITH *Disp. Purgat.* II. K j b, An heresye is a *styffe holden opinion repugnaunte vnto scrypture. **1818** KEATS *Endym.* II. 9 Stiff-holden shields, far-piercing spears, keen blades. **1605** SYLVESTER *Du Bartas* II. iii. I. *Vocation* 538 A gagged Usher that doth never wear *Stif-rustling silks. **1828** MISS MITFORD *Village* III. 32 A woman ..*stiff-starched and strait-laced. **1657** W. RAND tr. *Gassendi's Life Peiresc* II. 224 A great *stiff-stretched swelling arose upon the Region of his Bladder. **1666** DRYDEN *Ann. Mirab.* cxxi, The Dutch..Whose Navy like a stiff-stretch'd cord did show, Till he bore in, and bent them into flight. **1608** SYLVESTER *Du Bartas* II. iv. IV. *Decay* 795 A *stiff-throw'n Bowl, which running down a Hill, Meets in the way some stub.

stiff, *v.* [f. STIFF *a.* (Cf. ME. STIVE *v.*, OE. *stifian.*)]

†**1.** *intr.* To grow strong. *Obs.*

1399 LANGL. *Rich. Redeles* III. 54 But as sone as þey [*sc.* young partridges] styffe and þat þey steppe kunne.

†**2.** *trans.* To make stiff, stiffen. *Obs.*

1486 *Bk. St. Albans* a vij, If her goorge be wide and the bowell any thyng stiffid. **1582** STANYHURST *Æneis* IV. (Arb.) 118 But Dido affrighted, stift also in her obstinat onset,.. Too the inner quadrant runneth. **1648** HEXHAM II, *Stijven, als, doecken Stijven*, to Stiffe or to Starch linnen. **1652** W. BROUGH *Sacr. Princ.* (ed. 2) 219 Covetousnesse..Lames the Hand to good Works. Stiffs the Knees to the Holy Sacrament.

3. To cheat; to refuse to pay or tip (a person). *slang* (orig. and chiefly *U.S.*).

1950 *Sat. Even. Post.* 15 July 124/3 It was a signal for the waiter to hustle over and put the arm on the customer who was trying to stiff him. **1968** J. M. ULLMAN *Lady on Fire* (1969) vi. 85 He's still haggling over the bill..trying to stiff me for a thousand less than agreed on. **1978** *Detroit Free Press* 5 Mar. B 3/1 Some New York waiters will tell you that the wealthiest men stiff you on a tip. **1979** *Globe & Mail* (Toronto) 31 May 2/5 Agents are still going bankrupt, but now it means they are leaving debts with the wholesalers and airlines. They aren't stiffing the consumer. **1982** *Washington Post* 9 Jan. 21/2 What is McCarthy doing when he refuses to tip a waiter who has given good service?.. He may be cursed by the waiter he stiffs. *Ibid.* 21/3 Instead of stiffing his servers, McCarthy should be stiffing their employers.

4. To kill; to murder. Cf. STIFF *sb.* 3 a. *slang.*

1974 R. L. SIMON *Wild Turkey* (1976) xiv. 104 'The Japanese girl..was found stiffed in an air-conditioning duct.' 'Stiffed?' '*Asesinato*.' **1978** C. EGLETON *Mills Bomb* vii. 73 Did she blow their cover too? Is that how they got stiffed in Prague?

Hence †**stiffed** *ppl. a.*

1565 T. STAPLETON *Fortr. Faith* 112 b, O hard stiffed necke, o froward harte.

stiffen ('stɪf(ə)n), *v.* [f. STIFF *a.* + -EN[5].] To make or become stiff or stiffer.

1. *trans.* To make stiff or rigid, e.g. by means of starch (†also *absol.*), or by the addition of a lining or a support.

1622 in *Chron. Perth* etc. (Maitl. Club) 87 Margaret Melling apprehended for stiffning ruffs and overlays on a Sunday. **1624** J. TAYLOR (Water P.) *Praise Cl. Linen* Wks. (1630) II. 169/1 She wrings, she folds, she pleits, she smoothes, she starches, She stiffens, poakes, and sets and dryes againe. **1860** RUSKIN *Unto this Last* ii. §41 The sands of the Indus and adamant of Golconda may yet stiffen the housings of the charger. **1885** *Mag. of Art* Sept. 459/1 A circular plate of thin wrought bronze, stiffened round the edge by a beading. **1892** *Proc. Roy. Soc.* LII. 347 The strips have a great tendency to warp, and..may be stiffened by sheet brass let into a slot on the under side.

b. *Naut.* To increase the initial stability of a ship; to render less liable to heel. See STIFF *a.* 7.

1706 E. WARD *Wooden World Diss.* (1708) 22 Those strong unexpected Turnadoes..most certainly overset him, if he be not ready stiffen'd with Peru Ballast. **1861** MAYHEW *Lond. Labour* III. 272 Sixty tons of cargo will stiffen the most cranky vessel.

2. To render stiff in consistency; to thicken, coagulate.

1627 MAY *Lucan* III. E 6 b, Dy'd is the Ocean, And the waues stiffen'd with congealed blood. **1726** LEONI *Alberti's Archit.* I. 58*a*, Allow one part of Mortar to three of Rubbish ..; and when it is laid, the way to stiffen it, is to pound it heartily with the Rammer. *a* **1774** GOLDSM. *Surv. Exp. Philos.* (1776) I. 348 The polar oceans being almost continually stiffened into ice. **1869** TOZER *Highl. Turkey* II. 252 The plastic condition of the language..not as yet stiffened by conventional rules.

b. *intr.* To become stiff in consistency; to harden. Also *fig.* with constr. *into*: To assume a more definite or permanent form or character.

1697 DRYDEN *Virg. Past.* VI. 53 The tender Soil then stiffning by degrees, Shut from the bounded Earth, the bounding Seas. **1811** A. T. THOMSON *Lond. Disp.* (1818) 732 Stir until the mixture stiffens in cooling. **1856** FROUDE *Hist. Eng.* II. 35 These things which in their proper nature are but illustrations, stiffen into essential fact. **1876** FREEMAN *Norm. Conq.* V. xxiv. 410 The 'landsitting men' of Salisbury easily stiffened into the tenants-in-chief of the Great Charter. **1883** *Fortn. Rev.* Feb. 242 But gradually the favour will stiffen into a right.

3. *trans.* To make more steadfast, unyielding, or obstinate; *Mil.* to increase the fighting value of a force by the admixture of soldiers of better quality.

? *a* **1500** *Chester Pl., Emiss. Holy Ghost* (Shaks. Soc.) II. 130 Nowe will I sende..My ghoste to glade them graciously,..That the[y] maie stiffned be theirby. **1632** SANDERSON *Serm.* (1681) 26 He thus stiffneth mine enemies still against me. *a* **1677** BARROW *Wks.* (1686) III. Serm. xvi. 189 So doth the man become incorrigible, who is settled and stiffened in vice. **1716** M. DAVIES *Athen. Brit.* I. 221 His Confessor and Emissary, to plod about, for to stiffen others in the old Romish Superstitions. **1883** *Broad Arrow* xxxi. 609 Foreign levies have been 'stiffened' before now by volunteers from other countries. **1898** *Daily News* 22 Feb. 5/2 The Home Secretary wants stiffening, and the House of Commons ought to stiffen him.

b. *intr.* To become hard or unyielding in temper.

1732 NEAL *Hist. Purit.* I. Pref. p. vi, The Bishops stiffened in their behaviour,..and became too severe against their Dissenting brethren. **1914** *Daily News* 12 Jan. 8 Military opinion has..stiffened in the last three weeks.

4. *trans.* To make rigid; to take away the natural suppleness or mobility of (the limbs, joints, muscles, etc.). Also *fig.*; *slang* to make a corpse of, kill; *Horse-racing*, to prevent a horse from doing its best to win.

1599 SHAKS. *Hen. V*, III. i. 7 Stiffen the sinewes, commune [*sic*] vp the blood. *c* **1611** CHAPMAN *Iliad* IV. 172 The haire stood vp on end On Agamemnon,..And stifned with the like dismay, was Menelaus to. **1750** JOHNSON *Rambler* No. 177 ¶ 3, I began to find my mind contracted and stiffened by solitude. **1798** COLERIDGE *Recant.* 46 His legs were stiffen'd with dismay. **1883** *Manch. Exam.* 30 Nov. 5/3 Considerations so powerful as these tend to stiffen the backs of the Chinese. **1888** *Daily News* 23 Nov. 7/2 Mr. Burgess threatened to blow my brains out and to 'stiffen' me. **1900** *Westm. Gaz.* 19 Dec. 12/1 Many popular country race-courses have been given up almost entirely to card-sharpers, because the public know that the horses are stiffened.

b. *intr.* Of persons: To become stiff or rigid; also, to die. Also *fig.*

1714 YOUNG *Force Relig.* II. 130 Fix'd in benumbing care, They stiffen into statues of despair. **1820** J. H. REYNOLDS *Fancy* (1906) 24, I wish'd you'd *stiffen*—that I might enclose Your royal limbs, and measure to the toes. **1859** DICKENS *Christm. Stor., Haunted Ho.* i, She [a cataleptic] would stiffen,..on the most irrelevant occasions. **1912** J. L. MYRES *Dawn of Hist.* x. 221 An indigenous culture which had passed its prime and was already stiffening.

5. *trans.* To make (a person) formal, cold, or constrained in manner; to make (an artistic composition) pedantic, laboured, or overloaded.

1763 SHENSTONE *Let. to S. Davenport* Wks. 1777 III. 347 True taste will never stiffen or over-charge any performance: it will rather be employed to smoothe, simplify, and give that ease on which grace depends. **1781** COWPER *Table-T.* 125, I pity Kings..Whom Education stiffens into state. **1863** GLADSTONE in Morley *Life* v. vi. (1903) II. 103 The people are, one and all, very easy to get on with, and Windsor, I suppose, stiffens them a little.

b. *intr.* To become formal, cold, or constrained.

1864 TENNYSON *Aylmer's F.* 273 Sir Aylmer Aylmer slowly stiffening spoke.

6. **a.** *intr.* Of prices, rates of interest, the market, etc.: To become stiffer (see STIFF *a.* 10 and 19). **b.** *trans.* To render (prices, etc.) stiffer.

1855 *Poultry Chron.* III. 407 Barley stiffens in value. **1883** *Daily News* 1 Sept. 2/4 The efflux of gold..which would stiffen the short loan market. **1883** *Manch. Exam.* 8 Dec. 4/1 There was a good demand both for discounts and advances and the rates stiffened up very sensibly. **1898** *Daily News* 20 June 9/5 Prices both of coal and iron have been stiffened.

7. *intr.* Of wind: To increase in strength or violence.

1844 HOOD *Captain's Cow* 111 A breeze again began to rise, That stiffen'd to a gale.

8. Of an ascent: To become more steep or difficult.

1877 *Fraser's Mag.* XVI. 152 The ascent stiffened.

Hence '**stiffened** *ppl. a.*

1602 MARSTON *Antonio's Rev.* I. iii, The juice of life Creepes slowly through my stifned arteries. **1896** SARA J. DUNCAN *His Honor & a Lady* iii. 41 To lave his stiffened powers of artistic enjoyment in the beauties of the Parthenon.

†**stiffen-bodied**, *a. Obs.* [prob. for **stiffened-bodied*, 'having a stiffened body'; see STIFFENED *ppl. a.*] Having the body (see BODY *sb.* 6) stiffened with whalebone, etc. (said of a garment).

1706 [E. WARD] *Hudibras Rediv.* (Nares s.v. *Steeple-crown*), The good old dames..Were all most primitively drest In stiffen-body'd russet gowns. **1748** LADY LUXBOROUGH *Lett. to Shenstone* (1775) 12 The stiffen-bodied gown would not add charms..to a beautiful woman.

stiffener ('stɪf(ə)nə(r)). [f. STIFFEN *v.* + -ER[1].]

1. A workman who stiffens (cloth, hats, etc.).

1696 *MSS. Ho. Lords* (N.S.) II. 245 Petition of the Glazers and Buckram Stiffeners. **1892** *Labour Commission* Gloss., *Stiffener*, the person who, after the hat has been sewn, applies to it a stiffening of gelatine to make it firm and to allow it to be properly fitted to the required shape. **1915** *Morn. Post* 20 Dec. 9/4 Manglers and stiffeners, beetlers, driers and stovers.

2. a. Something serving to stiffen; *spec.* a card, such as a cigarette card, used to stiffen a packet, envelope, etc.

1842 *Civil Engin. & Arch. Jrnl.* V. 363/2 The truss acting only in this capacity of a stiffener to the rib. **1847** BRANDON *Anal. Goth. Archit.* 101 That [metalwork] which is spread over the doors of the Chapter House at York, is merely used as a stiffener. **1859** R. F. BURTON *Centr. Afr.* in *Jrnl. Geog. Soc.* XXIX. 133 A stout lath is fastened as a stiffener to the shield lengthwise. **1871** EARLE *Philol. Eng. Tongue* 557 Metre acts as a sort of stiffener to the rhythm. **1883** *Glasg. Weekly Herald* 8 Sept. 3/3 As a stiffener of fabrics algin is better than starch. **1889** WELCH *Text Bk. Naval Archit.* x. 118 The smaller bulkheads..have vertical angle-bar stiffeners 2 feet apart. **1926** *Chambers's Jrnl.* 10 July 497/2 'Stiffener', the name by which the cigarette-card has always been, and still is, known in the trade. **1967** A. DAVIS *Package & Print* 55 Cigarette cards..were originally intended as stiffeners (and always known in the trade by this name). The first printed stiffeners were produced in America in 1879. **1971** D. POTTER *Brit. Eliz. Stamps* x. 114 As an added attraction they include a stiffener—a card which reduces damage to the envelope in transit—with informative technical and background data.

b. A band of stiff material worn round the neck to keep a neck-cloth in place. *Obs.*

1818 *Blackw. Mag.* III. 404 No patent stiffeners,—no erect shirt collars. **1866** GEO. ELIOT *F. Holt* xvi, Other anomalies now obsolete, besides short-waisted coats and broad stiffeners. **1876** *Remin. Old Draper* 157 Stiffeners were sold of various degrees of height, to suit either a long-necked or a short-necked man.

3. A fortifying or reviving drink, *spec.* an alcoholic one. *slang.*

1928 D. L. SAYERS *Unpleasantness at Bellona Club* ii. 12 Dick Challoner..took the gasping Fentiman away into the deserted library for a stiffener. **1973** G. MITCHELL *Murder of Busy Lizzie* xiv. 161 I'll buy you a stiffener in the bar. **1978** J. PUDNEY *Thank Goodness for Cake* 128 Another visit to the loo for a stiffener... There are always drinks on the way home.

stiffening ('stɪf(ə)nɪŋ), *vbl. sb.* [f. STIFFEN *v.* + -ING[1].]

1. The action of the verb; the process of making or becoming stiff; *concr.* a stiffened substance.

1614 J. TAYLOR (Water P.) *Nipping Abuses* B 3 b, I cannot Item it [a tailor's bill]..For cutting, edging, stiffning and for lacing. **1653** JER. TAYLOR *Serm.* I. iv. 44 Like the joynts of a bulrush, not bendings, but consolidations and stiffenings. **1799** *Repert. Arts & Manuf.* X. 284 The fourth and last operation of hat-making; namely, stiffening. **1883** *Pall Mall Gaz.* 26 Oct. 12/1 The stiffening of the Egyptian army with a body of English volunteers. **1909** D. FULTON tr. *P. Cohnheim's Dis. Digest. Canal* 8 It is especially important to recognize abnormally increased peristalsis, the so-called 'stiffenings' of the stomach, small intestine or colon.

2. a. Something that serves to stiffen.

1620 J. TAYLOR (Water P.) *Praise Hemp-seed* (1623) 28 Being edgd with Items, stiffnings, facings, With Bumbast, Cottens, linings, and with lacings. **1758** BORLASE *Nat. Hist. Cornw.* 79 The solids were preadapted by the divine power to form the foundation, or the stiffnings (if I may so say) of the globe. **1857** MILLER *Elem. Chem., Org.* 505 Lac is extensively used as a stiffening for hats.

b. An admixture of soldiers of better quality.

1900 *Daily Mail* 3 May 6/6 The column..consisted chiefly of Yeomanry, with a stiffening of Cape Police. **1915** J. BUCHAN *Hist. War* VII. lix. 151 Only the German stiffening kept them [the Austrians] to their work.

c. *Naut.* Heavy goods taken on board ship as ballast (see quot. 1894). Cf. *stiffening order*, sense 3.

1894 H. PAASCH *From Keel to Truck* (ed. 2) 463/1 *Stiffening*, is the term given to any weighty substances taken on board a vessel for the purpose of making her 'Stiff', i.e. less crank. Stiffening (whether consisting of ballast or a portion of the outward cargo) is put in vessels which do not remain upright without having sufficient weight in the bottom. **1902** B. LUBBOCK *Round the Horn* 29 We are waiting now for our 'stiffening', as we dare not take our last 400 tons of coals out until we get a like weight of grain. **1924** R. CLEMENTS *Gipsy of Horn* vi. 115 We heard one morning that we were chartered, and proceeded to shift ship down to the coal-tips to take in our 'stiffening'—just sufficient coal, that is, to ballast the ship. **1975** *Islander* (Victoria, B.C.) 23 Feb. 6/3 The *Pamir* was taken in tow with a small amount of coal ballast aboard for stiffening.

3. *attrib.*, as ***stiffening-brush***, ***-girder***, ***-rib***; ***stiffening-order*** (see quot.).

1688 HOLME *Armoury* III. 386/1 A Felt makers *Stiffning Brush. **1875** KNIGHT *Dict. Mech.*, **Stiffening-girder*, a truss girder which distributes the weight of the platform and load upon the suspension-chain and prevents undulation. **1858** SIMMONDS *Dict. Trade*, **Stiffening-order*, a permission granted by the Customs' to take on board heavy goods, by way of ballast, to steady the ship. **1869** RANKINE *Machine & Hand-tools* App. 26 The distance between the *stiffening ribs measured on a slope of 45°.

stiffening ('stɪf(ə)nɪŋ), *ppl. a.* [f. STIFFEN *v.* + -ING[2].] That stiffens: **a.** That becomes stiff or stiffer; **b.** That makes stiff or stiffer.

1704 ROWE *Ulysses* IV. i. 1722 It freezes every stiff'ning limb to Marble. **1843** LYTTON *Last of Barons* I. iv, The place where he had lain was damp and red with stiffening blood. **1863** GLADSTONE in Morley *Life* v. vi. (1903) II. 97 Walked 24¾ miles. Found it rather too much for my stiffening limbs. **1898** *Educ. Rev.* XV. 456 The efforts..have usually resulted in a stiffening formalization.

†**'stiffing**, *vbl. sb. Obs.* Forms: 6–7 stiffin(e, 7 steiffing, 7 stiffing. [f. STIFF *v.* + -ING[1].] That which makes stiff: **a.** *Sc.* Starch. **b.** Material such as whalebone or canvas used to stiffen a garment.

1597 in *Halyburton's Ledger* (1867) Pref. p. cxiv, Stiffine callit Amedone [*printed* Amedoue]. **1611** in Heath *Grocers' Comp.* (1869) 93 None should wear..any body or sleeves of wire, whalebone, or with any other stiffing, saving canvass or buckram only. **1613** *Extracts Rec. Convent. Burghs Scot.* (1870) II. 395 Item, for lossing and careing ilk trie steiffing frome the skoute flote to the schip or hous iiij gritt. **1636** in *Aberd. Jrnl. Notes & Q.* (1910) III. 28/2 Nine puncheons ten tries of white stiffin.

stiffish ('stɪfɪʃ), *a.* [-ISH[1].] Rather stiff.

1733 W. ELLIS *Chiltern & Vale Farm.* 266 A stiffish, loamy, moist Soil. **1769** MRS. RAFFALD *Engl. Housekpr.* (1778) 245 Dip a lump of..sugar in water, boil it stiffish. **1840** HOOD *Open Question* 41 Some stiffish people think that smoking joints Are carnal sins 'twixt Saturday and Monday. **1890** 'R. BOLDREWOOD' *Col. Reformer* xxix, I'd given him [a horse] some stiffish days after the farthest out cattle. **1911** MARETT *Anthrop.* ii. 41 It is not far, though a stiffish pull, to Ash. **1915** LD. REDESDALE *Memories* I. 111, I quite admit that there ought to be a stiffish examination of the nominees.

†**'stiffler.** *Obs.* [Alteration of *stiȝtler* STIGHTLER, by substitution of (f) for (ç).] = STICKLER. **a.** A mediator or umpire; ? one who intervenes *between* combatants. **b.** One who is active or stirring (*in* a matter); a busybody; a wrangler.

1473 *Paston Lett.* III. 98 The Kyng ententyth..to be as bygge as they bothe, and to be a styffeler atweyn them. **1565–6** ABP. PARKER *Corr.* (P. Soc. 1853) 252 The drift was (as I judged) for Dethick to continue such stifflers in the College of his pupils, to win him in time, by hook or crook, the master's room. **1585** GREENE *Planetom.* E 1 b, Promising ..neuer to be a stifler in the like cause. *a* **1825** FORBY *Voc. E. Anglia*, *Stifler*, a stickler; one who is very busy and active in any matter; as it were raising a dust.

stiffly ('stɪflɪ), *adv.* [f. STIFF *a.* + -LY[2].] In a stiff manner; so as to be stiff; (in various senses of the adj.).

c **1290** *S. Eng. Leg.* 113 Swyþe wel bi-gan þis Ercedekne holi churche bi-lede, And stifliche heold op hire riȝte. *c* **1386** CHAUCER *Wife's Prol.* 380 Thus..Baar I stifly myne olde housbondes on honde, That thus they seyden in hir dronkenesse. *c* **1400** *Lay-Folks Mass-Bk.* App. III. 123 þat he may ben myche more stifeloker groundyd in goddis seruise. **1422** YONGE tr. *Secreta Secret.* 153 Nero of the fayrnys of the fire-blaas stifly hym reioiet. *c* **1425** *Thomas of Erceld.* 49 Hir sadille was of reuylle bone,..Stifly sette with precious stone. **1535** COVERDALE *Prov.* xxx. 29 There be thre thinges y^t^ go stiffly, but the goinge of the fourth is the goodliest of all. *a* **1555** LATIMER *Let.* in Foxe *A. & M.* (1583) 1756/1 You confesse your brothers cause wherein he so stiffely standeth, to be uniust. **1599** DALLAM in *Early Voy. Levant* (Hakl. Soc.) 85 Wheare did run a rever, so bige and stifly,..that we durste not adventur to rid over it. **1623** J. TAYLOR (Water P.) *Discov. Sea Lond. Salisb.* Wks. (1630) II. 22/1 At last by Ramsgates Peere we stiffly Rowed, The winde and tyde, against vs blow'd and flowed. **1678** MOXON *Mech. Exerc.* v. 75 The Handle..hath a Mortess in it, as long within a quarter of an Inch as the thin piece (called the Tongue) is broad, and stifly so wide as to contain the thickness of the Tongue. **1766** *Complete Farmer* s.v. *Surbating*, The signs of this defect are his halting on both fore-legs, going stiffly. **1824** SCOTT *St. Ronan's* vii, A bow was very stiffly exchanged between the ladies. **1885** *Manch. Exam.* 24 Jan. 5/4 The client, however, has to pay for this..more stiffly than he often imagines.

b. In comb. with pple. or adj.

1606 SYLVESTER *Du Bartas* II. iv. I. *Tropheis* 90 Whose harmfull point is headed stifly-straight With burnisht Brasse above an Anvil's weight. **1614** —— *Bethulia's Rescue* II. 79 Noble Palm-Trees, mounting stifly-straight. **1892** E. REEVES *Homeward Bound* 319 Gardens, which rise terrace above terrace of stiffly cut trees. **1908** *Nation* 26 Sept. 892/1 The stiffly-worded Anglo-Russian note.

stiff-necked ('stɪfnɛkt), *a.* [f. *stiff neck* + -ED[2]; after Gr. σκληροτράχηλος, Heb. *qᵉshēʰ ʿōref* 'hard of neck'.] Having a stiff neck. Chiefly *fig.* of persons, with Biblical reference: Obstinate, stubborn, inflexible, haughty (cf. NECK *sb.*[1] 3 b). †Also of a horse: That will not obey the rein. Also *transf.*

1526 TINDALE *Acts* vii. 51 Ye stiffenecked and of vncircumcised hertes and eares. *a* **1533** FRITH *Disp. Purgat.* II. I j, Yf they be so stifnecked that they wyl not bow to the truth. **1545** BRINKLOW *Lament.* (1874) 79 The greate parte of these inordinate riche styfnecked Cytezens will not haue in their howses that lyuely worde of our soules. *c* **1550** MARY BASSET in *More's Wks.* (1557) 1366/1 If after feyre handelyng, we drawe styll stubbernely backeward, and.. contynue yet vnreasonably styffe necked, lyke a Horse and Mule whiche haue no maner of vnderstandynge. **1565** COOPER *Thesaurus* s.v. *Equus*, A stiffe necked horse that wil not be ruled. **1625** K. LONG tr. *Barclay's Argenis* IV. xix. 310 Being stiffe-necked and stronger than the Bit with which he was held in, hee carryed him forceably into the enemies' camp. **1710** *Tatler* No. 214 ¶1, I shall therefore give up this stiff-necked Generation to their own Obstinacy. **1867** FREEMAN *Norm. Conq.* (1876) I. vi. 462 One is converted, while the other seemingly goes away stiffnecked in his old errors. **1898** GISSING in *Strand Mag.* XV. 28 The stiff-necked old aristocrat had gone to London. **1963** *Times* 23 Apr. 13/2 Fortunately the recent exchanges promise slightly less stiff-necked attitudes on both sides.

Hence **,stiff'neckedly** *adv.*, obstinately; **,stiff'neckedness**, obstinacy.

a **1555** LATIMER *Let.* in Foxe *A. & M.* (1583) 1756/1 It is no small iniquitie to keep any one poore man so long from his right and duetie so stiffeneckedly and obstinately. **1563–83** FOXE *A. & M.* 449/1 He alwayes wrote most commendable protestations agaynst obstinacye and stifneckednesse. **1663** J. WILSON *Cheats* II. iii, We are wilfully, stiff-neckedly blind. **1699** CLAGETT *17 Serm.* 216 There will be both inconstancy and stiffneckedness. **1857** MISS WINKWORTH *Tauler's Life & Serm.* 132 *note*, He were a heretic who, after much admonition, should stiffneckedly disobey the Word of God. **1861** J. G. SHEPPARD *Fall of Rome* xi. 572 A strength of will degenerating into stiff-neckedness and obstinacy.

stiffner, variant of STIFFENER.

stiffness ('stɪfnɪs). [f. STIFF *a.* + -NESS.] The state or quality of being stiff (in any sense).

1. a. Rigidity, inflexibility; viscosity (of liquids and semi-liquids); density, heaviness, compactness (of soil). Also *fig.*

1398 TREVISA *Barth. De P.R.* XVII. clxxv. (1495) 717 Somtyme a crokyd rodde is put in the fyre: and by hete of the fyre the styfnesse and hardnesse is tempred and made nesshe, and so the rodde is the more easely streyghted. *c* **1440** *Promp. Parv.* 475/1 Styfnesse, or starkenesse, *rigiditas, rigor.* **1577** GOOGE *Heresbach's Husb.* I. 24 b, Some grounde requireth more seede then other, as the grounde is of stiffenesse or lightnesse. **1639** O. WOOD *Alph. Bk. Secrets* 169 Incorporate all these in a morter with a pestle with oyle of white Rose, and Virgins waxe thin scraped to the stifnesse of a plaister. **1642** FULLER *Holy St.* III. xx. 206 The stiffnesse of the judgement is abated, and suppled with charity. **1726–31** WALDRON *Descr. Isle of Man* (1865) 59 A woman.. was saved by the stiffness of her hoop petticoat which kept her above water. **1869** RANKINE *Machinery & Millwork* 531 In all cases in which precision of movement is required, stiffness is essential both to the moving pieces and to the framework of a machine.

b. *spec.* (*a*) the force required to produce unit deflection or displacement of an object; (*b*) the maximum deflection of a beam divided by its span or length.

1710 J. CLARKE tr. *Rohault's Nat. Philos.* (1729) I. 133 The Property which is called Stiffness, and which Work-men call the Power of Springing. **1824** TREDGOLD *Ess. Cast Iron* 202 The stiffness of a body is its resistance at a given deflexion. **1893** H. T. BOVEY *Theory of Structures* iii. 190, $dP_1/dl = EA/L$, and EA/L is consequently a measure of the longitudinal stiffness of a bar. *Ibid.* vi. 389 If D is the maximum deflection of a girder of span l under a load W, then W/D, or more usually D/l, is a measure of the stiffness of the girder. **1922** GLAZEBROOK *Dict. Appl. Physics* I. 808/2 The stiffness of a beam is usually measured by the maximum deflection, when loaded, divided by the span. **1925** J. CASE *Strength of Materials* xxiv. 386 The 'stiffness' of a spring is the load required to produce unit deflection. **1969** C. O. RASPOR in W. R. R. Park *Plastics Film Technol.* iv. 88 The tensile modulus is often used as a measure of film stiffness. This quantity is obtained by calculating the ratio of a stress to strain at a certain point on a tensile stress–strain curve. **1978** *Sci. Amer.* Dec. 116 (*caption*) Stiffness of an isolated muscle (the change in the force developed by the muscle when it is stretched, divided by its change in length) increases as the muscle is stretched.

c. *Naut.* (See quots.)

1877 W. H. WHITE *Nav. Archit.* iii. 65 This method may be used in estimating the 'stiffness' of a ship, i.e. her power to resist inclination from the upright by the steady pressure of the wind on her sails. **1913** ATTWOOD *Modern Warship* 67 The metacentric height is a measure of the stiffness of the ship.

2. Lack of suppleness (in limbs, muscles, etc.); the name of certain diseases causing rigor of muscles, esp. tetanus. Also *fig.*

1552 HULOET, Stifnes of sinowes, that the membres ne may be bowed, *tetanicus morbus, tetanos.* **1581** MULCASTER *Positions* vi. (1887) 47 Where ioyntes be to bend,..there must needes be motion: or else stifnesse will follow. **1591** PERCIVALL *Sp. Dict.*, *Calambre*, stifnesse of the sinewes, the crampe, *Neruorum rigor, spasmus.* **1641** TATHAM *Distracted State* IV. i. (1651) 20 Whose knee dares own a stiffeness? whose Obeysance To Adulanter dare be wanting? **1791** BURKE *Corr.* (1844) III. 365 Your mother is, bating occasional stiffness, very well. **1862** W. HUNTER *Biggar & Ho. Fleming* iv. 45 The cattle are often attacked with a disease called the 'stiffness' or 'cripple'.

†**3.** Strength, sturdiness, stoutness; violence. *Obs.*

1399 LANGL. *Rich. Redeles* III. 251 Iche rewme..Sholde stable and stonde..By styffnesse and strengthe Of steeris well y-yokyd. *c* **1460** *Promp. Parv.* (Winch.) 436 Styfnesse, or strength, *fortitudo, robur.* **1596** SPENSER *F.Q.* IV. iv. 19 And him against Sir Blandamour did ride With all the strength and stifnesse that he can. **1623** BINGHAM *Xenophon, Lipsius' Compar.* V 3, They throw stones..with such stiffenesse and strength, that the blow seemeth to come from some Engine.

4. Inflexibility in purpose, opinion, or course of action; resolution, firmness; obstinacy; haughtiness.

1526 *Pilgr. Perf.* (W. de W. 1531) 92 Styfnes of mynde or obstinacy they haue, whyche frowardly wyll defende theyr errour. **1641** J. JACKSON *True Evang. T.* II. 161 Such as did seeke the Glory of Martyrs..out of stiffenesse of spirit. **1673** [R. LEIGH] *Transp. Reh.* 39 There has been a party of 'em in England..of such a pontifical stiffness, as if they were companions for none but princes. *a* **1677** BARROW *Serm.* Wks. 1716 II. 38 Where may we discern..that stoutness of courage and stiffness of patience which you talk of as the.. issues of faith? **1690** LOCKE *Hum. Und.* IV. xvi. §3 And yet these of all Men hold their Opinions with the greatest stiffness. **1741** C. MIDDLETON *Cicero* (1742) II. vi. 52 The other chiefs of the Aristocracy..whose stiffness had ruined their cause. **1887** RIDER HAGGARD *Allan Q.* xxi. 242 The.. forces give on every side, there is no stiffness left in them.

5. Formality; constraint; lack of ease or grace; coldness, aloofness (of manners and deportment); artificiality, excessive regularity, pedantry (of style).

1638 JUNIUS *Paint. Ancients* 27 All the statues before Dædalus his time, have had a most unpleasant stifnesse. **1710** FELTON *Diss. Classics* (1718) 70 Provided he..doth not make himself a Slave to his Rules; for that will introduce a Stiffness and Affectation, which are utterly abhorrent from all good Writing. **1717** LADY M. W. MONTAGU *Let. to C'tess Mar* 18 Apr., An air so majestic, yet free from stiffness or affectation. **1748** *Anson's Voy.* III. x. 412 There is a stiffness and minuteness in most of the Chinese productions. **1765** *Ann. Reg.* II. 56 The king,..laying aside all the stiffness of state,..enjoys himself with a few select friends. **1789** BURNEY *Hist. Mus.* III. 330 The two parts in one..discover no restraint or stiffness in the melody, which continues to move with the same freedom, as if no canon had existence. **1836** [J. GRANT] *Random Recoll. Ho. Lords* xiii. 299 Before he had spoken two or three sentences, it must have been apparent..that he had not yet got rid of the formality and stiffness of school. **1907** J. A. HODGES *Elem. Photogr.* (ed. 6) 118 Introducing an unnatural stiffness into the portrait.

stiffy ('stɪfɪ). *U.S. slang.* [f. STIFF *a.* or *sb.* + -Y[6].] **1.** A beggar who pretends to be paralysed.

1917 'A.-NO. 1' *Coast to Coast with Jack London* ii. 22 The fellow..was a hobo. He introduced himself as 'Stiffy Brandon'. His moniker indicated that for a beggar craft he had chosen the one which imposed upon the credulous..the awful affliction of the paralytic. **1956** S. HARRIS *Skid Row, U.S.A.* ii. 38 Red Bill was the best stiffy in New York.

2. A naïve or stupid person.

1965 *Liberator* (N.Y.) Aug. 23/1 'You a trick, Dan—a stiffy,' Herman said. 'You so square Little Orphan Annie could put game on you.' *Ibid.*, Stacked broads rushed in on the arms of stiffies straight from the cornfields; you know —them cats with the cowboy hats and ice-cream suits. Some stiffs. **1966** C. KEIL *Urban Blues* v. 118 Negro artists who find their way into white concert halls still find it necessary to 'hip' those 'stiffies' in the audience who insist on clapping their hands in a martial manner.

stifle ('staɪf(ə)l), *sb.*[1] Also 6–8 **stiffle**. [Of obscure origin.

Connection with STIFF *a.* is commonly assumed, but is very doubtful.]

1. The joint at the junction of the hind leg and the body (between the femur and the tibia) in a horse or other quadruped: corresponding anatomically to the knee in man.

c **1320** *Sir Tristr.* 487 [With reference to cutting up a deer.] To þe stifles he ȝede And euen ato hem schare. **1580** BLUNDEVIL *Curing Horses Dis.* cxxii. 55 b, If a Horse halt behind, the griefe must either be in the hippe, in the stiffle, in the hough [etc.]. **1726** *Dict. Rust.* (ed. 3), *Gascoin*, the hinder thigh of a Horse, which begins at the Stiffle. **1882** *Daily Tel.* 26 Oct. 3/6 Although kicked in the stifle..and badly lamed, Althotas repeated his Tuesday's victory. **1897** *Encycl. Sport* I. 329/2 (Dogs) *Stifle*, the joint in a dog's hind leg next to the buttock; the hip joint. **1907** *Q. Rev.* Jan. 204 The size of the bone at the ankles and stifles being particularly important [in the foxhound].

†**2.** Dislocation or sprain of the stifle-joint. *Obs.*

Quot. 1587 seems erroneous.

1580 BLUNDEVIL *Curing Horses Dis.* cxxiv. 56 b, The stiffle commeth by meanes of some side blowe, or some great straine, slipping, or sliding. **1587** MASCALL *2nd Bk. Cattell, Horses* (1596) 124 For a stiffle in the heele of a horse.

3. *Comb.* **stifle-bone, -cap, -pan,** the patella of a horse, the bone in front of the stifle-joint; **stifle-joint** = sense 1; **stifle-slip** (see quot.).

1610 MARKHAM *Masterp.* II. lxxii. 338 If the horse be stifled, the *stifle bone will sticke out more of the one side then of the other. **1678** *Lond. Gaz.* No. 1321/4 With a white speck on the stifle bone on the far side. **1908** *Stifle cap [see quot. for *stifle slip*]. **1580** BLUNDEVIL *Curing Horses Dis.* cxxii. 55 b, If the griefe be in the stiffle, then the Horse in his going will cast the *stiffle ioint outward. **1888** MACFADYEAN *Comp. Anat. Dom. Anim.* I. 197 The stifle joint corresponds to the knee of the human subject. The bones that enter into its formation are the femur, the tibia, and the patella. **1893** DUNMORE *Pamirs* II. 75, I..fired at the last ram, hitting him in the last leg, breaking it at the stifle joint. *c* **1720** W. GIBSON *Farrier's Guide* I. vi. (1738) 97 A small bone, somewhat round, called the Patella or *Stifle-pan. **1908** *Animal Managem.* 334 **Stifle slip*, dislocation of the *stifle cap.

stifle ('staɪf(ə)l), *sb.*[2] In 4 **styffle.** [f. STIFLE *v.*[1]]

†**1.** An asthmatic complaint, with difficulty in breathing. *Obs. rare*$^{-1}$.

1398 TREVISA *Barth. De P.R.* III. xv. (Tollemache MS.) As in hem þat haue þe pirre and styffles and ben pursyf and þikke breþid [L. *ut patet in asthmaticis et anhelosis*].

2. The fact of stifling or the condition of being stifled. *rare.*

1823 LAMB *Elia* Ser. II. *Amicus Rediv.*, Life meantime was ebbing fast away, amidst the stifle of conflicting judgments. **1825** COLERIDGE *Lett., Convers.* etc. (1836) II. 188, I was ever in a stifle of my reflected anxieties. **1904** *Westm. Gaz.* 2 Nov. 1/3 The smell of trodden sods mingles with the stifle of all these poor unwashed folk in the warm moist air.

3. (See quot.)

1886 BARROWMAN *Sc. Mining Terms* 64 *Stifle*, noxious gas resulting from an underground fire.

stifle ('staɪf(ə)l), *v.*[1] Forms: 4 **stuf(f)le,** 5–6 **stifil,** 6 **styfel, stiefle, stiffel,** 6–7 **styfle, stifel,** 6–8, 9 *dial.* **stiffle,** 6– **stifle.** [Of obscure origin.

The early forms *stufle, stuffle* suggest connexion of some kind with OF. *estouffer* to stifle, smother. Cf. also STIFE, and the early forms of STEW *v.*[2] The view that the word is from ON. *stífla* to dam up (water) appears untenable on the ground both of form and sense.]

1. *trans.* To kill by stopping respiration; to kill or deprive of consciousness (a person or animal) by covering the mouth and nose, by depriving of pure air or by introducing an irrespirable vapour into the throat and lungs; to suffocate. †Also with *up*.

1513 MORE *Rich. III* Wks. 68/2 So..keping down by force the..pillowes hard vnto their mouthes, that within a while smored and stifled, theyr breath failing, thei gaue vp to god their innocent soules. **1548** HALL *Chron., Hen. VI* (1550) 69 b, Other write, that he was stiffeled or smoldered betwene twoo fetherbeddes. **1570** LEVINS *Manip.* 127/35 To stifil, *suffocare.* **1582** N. LICHEFIELD tr. *Castanheda's Conq. E. Ind.* 65 There is no covering to defend the sunne, whereon with the same only men are stiffeled up. [*Marg.*] Men stifled with the Sunne onely. **1592** SHAKS. *Rom. & Jul.* IV. iii. 33 Shall I not then be stifled in the Vault? **1665** *Phil. Trans.* I. 44 Fearing to be stifled by the bad Air. **1707** MORTIMER *Husb.* (1721) I. 326 You may smoke or stifle them [wasps] if they are in a hollow Tree. **1756** GRAY *Let.* Poems (1775) 245 A dirty inconvenient lodging, where, perhaps, my nurse might stifle me with a pillow. **1834** CROKER in *C. Papers* (1884) 11 June, One poor little boy..was nearly stifled. **1867** FREEMAN *Norm. Conq.* (1876) I. App. 741 For fear of a tumult the King has Eadric at once stifled to death.

b. In hyperbolic or exaggerated use. Sometimes = to affect with difficulty of breathing, produce a choking sensation in.

c **1400** *Brut* 138 þere was grete hete...þat al stuffled himself was, & felle into a grete sikenesse. **1585** GREENE *Planetomachia* II. C 3, The Caspians fearinge to bee stiffled with sweet sauors, weare in their bosomes buds of Hemlock. **1592** *Arden of Feversham* IV. ii. 35, I am almost stifled with this fog. **1613** SHAKS. *Hen. VIII*, IV. i. 58, I am stifled With the meere ranknesse of their ioy. **1625** in Foster *Eng. Factories Ind.* (1909) III. 56 To pack and stiffle us togeather into close and aireles, unholsom corners. **1767** *Woman of Fashion* I. 41 Bundled up in a green Cloth Joseph, enough to stifle the poor Child in this warm Weather. **1824** MISS L. M. HAWKINS *Annaline* I. 87 They..found the Baronet nearly stifled with laughing. **1832** HT. MARTINEAU *Ireland* ii. 23 He almost stifled her with caresses.

c. *absol.*

1667 MILTON *P.L.* XI. 313 But prayer against his absolute Decree No more availes then breath against the winde, Blown stifling back on him that breaths it forth. **1864** TENNYSON *Aylmer's F.* 613 A breathless burthen of low-folded heavens Stifled and chill'd at once.

d. *fig.*

1579 LYLY *Euphues* Wks. (Bond) I. 248 When loue tickleth thee decline it lest it stiffle thee. **1642** FULLER *Holy & Prof. St.* v. xi. 398 The Anabaptists in like manner stifle Gods Church by crowding it into their corner. **1878** B. TAYLOR *Deukalion* II. iv. 79 Breathing high thoughts unconsciously as air; Without them stifled!

†**2.** To choke by compressing the windpipe; to strangle, throttle. *Obs.*

1548 *Elyot's Dict.*, *Oblido*,..to styfle, to kyll. **1585** T. WASHINGTON tr. *Nicholay's Voy.* I. vii, [Him] they condemned to be hanged & stifled vpon the maste of the gallie.

†**b.** ? To numb (a limb of the body) by arresting the circulation. *Obs.*

1548 [see STIFLING *vbl. sb.*[1]]. **1632** LITHGOW *Trav.* v. 205, I would often fetch a walke, to stretch my legs, that were stifled with a stumbling beast.

†**c.** To cause stricture or strangulation in (a part). *Obs.*

1578 [see STIFLING *vbl. sb.*[1]].

†**d.** To choke, crush the life out of (a plant). *Obs.*

1530 TINDALE *Pract. Prelates* C viij b, [The ivy] waxeth greate..and sucketh the moystoure so sore out of the tre and his braunches, that it choketh and stifleth them.

†**3.** To suffocate by immersion; to drown. Also to choke by pouring water down the throat. *Obs.*

1387 TREVISA *Higden* (Rolls) VI. 449 A monke..fil doun of a brigge into a water, and was i-stufled [*v.r.* y-stoffed; L. *suffocatus est*]. **1582** N. T. (Rhem.) *Mark* v. 13 The heard.. were stifled in the sea. **1601** HOLLAND *Pliny* XXX. iv. II. 377 The hony wherein a number of bees were stifled and killed. **1607** TOPSELL *Four-f. Beasts* 509 There are other kind of moustraps which do ketch mice aliue: and othersome which do kil them, either being..stifeld with water, or otherwise. **1624** *Relat. Cruel Proc. Amboyna* 11 Being a little recouered, they..poured in the water as before, eftsoones taking him downe as he seemed to be stifled. **1705** tr. *Bosman's Guinea* 346 She despairing threw her self into a deep Well, in which she was stifled.

4. To stop the passage of (the breath); to suppress, prevent the emission of, choke in the utterance (the voice, a cry, sob, cough, etc.). Also *poet.* with *up*. Also in figurative context.

c **1495** *Epit. Dk. Bedford* in *Skelton's Wks.* (1843) II. 391 Dredeful Deth..Ful dolorously his breth hath stifild. **1599** B. JONSON *Cynthia's Rev.* III. v, Then stifling a sigh or two, ..you aduance your selfe forward. **1601** MARSTON, etc. *Jack Drum's Entert.* I. A 4 b, I was not borne..To choake and stifle vp my pleasures breath. **1665** HOWARD *Ind. Queen* v. i, Name thy bold Love no more, lest that last Breath Which should forgive, I stifle with my Death. **1711** STEELE *Spect.* No. 158 ¶4 As if she would if possible stifle her Laughter. **1768** STERNE *Sent. Journ.* II. *Case of Delicacy*, I did not attempt to stifle my cough. *a* **1770** JORTIN *Serm.* (1771) II. iii. 47 Men..take pains to..stifle the reproofs of their conscience. **1837** DISRAELI *Venetia* I. xviii, Cadurcis tried to stifle a sob. **1868** MISS YONGE *Cameos* I. xl. 344 His last cry, ere the flames stifled his voice. **1885** *Manch. Exam.* 12 Sept. 5/2 He attempted to raise an alarm, but they stifled his cries. **1902** BUCHAN *Watcher by Threshold* 250 Stifling the voice of conscience.

†**b.** To repress, keep back, check the flow of (tears).

c **1677** SIR P. WARWICK *Mem.* (1701) 326, I never saw him shed tears but once,..but he recollected himselfe, and soon stifled them. **1797** MRS. INCHBALD *Wives as they were* I. i. 20 They'll suppose I have been more indiscreet [*stifling her tears*] than I really have.

c. To make mute or inaudible through intervening space or obstructing medium.

1833 HT. MARTINEAU *Charmed Sea* i. 4 Our voices were stifled in space. **1867** MORRIS *Jason* III. 247 The man whose shout the close Nemean trees Had stifled. **1891** KIPLING *Light that failed* v. 83 The fog..stifled the roar of the traffic of London beyond the railings.

5. In various figurative uses. **a.** To suppress, smother, keep from manifestation, expression, or activity (a feeling, passion, internal faculty, etc.).

1610 HOLLAND *Camden's Brit.* (1637) 428 Their former piety was after a manner stifled. **1654** JER. TAYLOR *Real Pres.* 26 It is an usual device amongst their writers to stifle their reason. **1788** GIBBON *Decl. & F.* xlviii. V. 26 In the mind of Irene, ambition had stifled every sentiment of humanity. **1849–50** ALISON *Hist. Europe* li. §52. VIII. 280 The discontent of Melzi..was stifled by the title of Duke of Lodi. **1876** MOZLEY *Univ. Serm.* xv. 258 The higher mind in us is stifled and gives way to the lower.

b. To destroy, crush, suppress, deprive of vitality, prevent the working or spreading of (a movement, activity, measure, etc.); †to silence (a person, objection).

1621 ELSING *Debates Ho. Lords* (Camden) 102 The proviso for the prynters styfles the proviso for corporacions. **1668** R. STEELE *Husbandm. Calling* v. (1672) 76 Let not your faith stifle your industry. **1693** J. E. EDWARDS *Author. O. & N. Test.* 410, I will stifle this cavelling objection. **1705** *Lond. Gaz.* No. 4168/2 This Insurrection was stifled in its very beginning. **1771** SMOLLETT *Humph. Cl.* 2 Apr. (1815) 7 As it was my duty to stifle this correspondence in its birth. **1857** BUCKLE *Civiliz.* I. xii. 671 It was a prolonged and systematic attempt to stifle all enquiry and punish all inquirers. *a* **1873** DEUTSCH *Lit. Rem.* (1874) 172 The Koran for a time seemed to stifle all literature. **1884** *L'pool Mercury* 22 Oct. 5/3 This ..is the very way to stifle all efforts.

c. To conceal, keep from becoming known, withhold from circulation or currency, suppress (a fact, report, truth, etc.; a document, letter).

1577 STANYHURST *Descr. Irel.* vii. 26 b/2 in *Holinshed*, When hys [*sc.* Plunket's] workes shall take the ayre, that now ..are wrongfully emprisoned, and in maner stiefled in shadowed cowches. **1662** STILLINGFL. *Orig. Sacræ* II. v. §2 The other rank of those which were left to Gods hand consisted of these. 1. He that stifles and smothers his own prophecy, as Jonas did. **1687** A. LOVELL tr. *Thevenot's Trav.* II. 103 When complaints are brought to Court against any *Chan*, he lets them come to the King's Ear if the *Chan* be his Enemy, or stiffles them if the *Chan* be his friend. **1700** CONGREVE *Way of World* v. ii, We stif'd the Letter before she read so far. **1712** HEARNE *Collect.* (O.H.S.) III. 383 That Dr. Mill made a Will, and that Langhorn, or some body else, stifled it. **1788** FRANKLIN *Autobiog.* Wks. 1840 I. 209 The papers, he thought of too much value to be stifled, and advised the printing of them. **1828** SCOTT *F.M. Perth* xv, The rumour may stifle the truth for a short time.

d. To cover *up* so as to conceal from view or prevent display. *poet.*

1820 KEATS *Hyperion* I. 245 The shady visions come to domineer, Insult, and blind, and stifle up my pomp.

6. To smother or extinguish (a flame).

1726 SWIFT *Gulliver* I. v, I might easily have stifled it [the flame] with my coat. **1851** HAZLITT tr. *Huc's Tartary* xvi. (1856) 401 All the travellers, armed with felt carpets, were endeavouring to stifle the flame. **1895** 'G. MORTIMER' *Tales West. Moors* 260 The smoke is choking and pungent, as it jets out through the damp, black earth that 'stiffles', or stifles, the flames.

†**b.** To extinguish or quench (a physical quality).

1725 *Bradley's Family Dict.* s.v. *Salt*, The Salt made White in this manner is not so salt as the Grey, because the Fire has stifled many of its Points.

†**7.** To choke up, impede the flow of (running water); to obstruct the passage of, absorb, quench (rays of light). *Obs.*

1629 H. C. *Disc. Drain. Fens* B 4, The riuers [being] stifled with weedes for want of a current. **1704** NEWTON *Optics* I. II. x (1721) 161 They [coloured bodies] stop and stifle in themselves the Rays which they do not reflect or transmit. **1785** IMISON *Sch. Arts* (1790) I. 194 Its back part is black, to stifle the rays that are reflected upon it. **1794** HERSCHEL in *Phil. Trans.* LXXXV. 54, I found, that by stifling a great part of the solar rays, my object speculum would bear a greater aperture.

†**8.** To choke up (an orifice). *Obs. rare*$^{-1}$.

1631 SHIRLEY *Traitor* III. i. (1635) E 2, Make fast the Chamber-doore, stiffle the keyhole and the crannies, I must discourse of secret matters.

†**9.** To slip (money) secretly or surreptitiously *in* (a person's hand). (? A jocular or cant use.) *Obs.*

1604 MIDDLETON *Ant & Night.* D 2, With that they stifeled two or three Angels in the lawyers right hand.

10. *intr.* To be or become suffocated; to perish by stoppage of breath. In weaker sense: To feel in danger of suffocation, to feel almost unable to breathe.

1594 T. B. *La Primaud. Fr. Acad.* II. 363 We cary about vs infinite causes and meanes, whereby we are euery houre in danger of stifling, and as it were of drowning. **1847** C. BRONTE *Jane Eyre* xv, I was just beginning to stifle with the fumes of conservatory flowers and sprinkled essences. **1857** J. HAMILTON *Less. Gt. Biogr.* (1859) 314 To feel the breath stifling and the heart-strings breaking. **1902** *Westm. Gaz.* 26 Mar. 2/1 Others cannot remain in an atmosphere that is not constantly replenished with fresh oxygen; they stifle.

†**b.** *fig.* Of a person or an immaterial thing.

1588 T. HUGHES *Arthur* I. i. 14 What though.. the shame thou suffredst for his lusts, Reboundeth backe, and stifeleth in his stocke? **1603** SHAKS. *Meas. for M.* II. iv. 158 My vnsoild Name [etc.] Will so your accusation ouer-weigh, That you shall stifle in your owne report.

stifle ('staɪf(ə)l), *v.*^{2} *Farriery.* Also 6–8 **stiffle.** [f. STIFLE *sb.*^{1}] *trans.* To affect (a horse, dog, etc.) with stifle or dislocation of the stifle-bone. Chiefly in *passive.* Hence '**stifled** *ppl. a.*

1580 BLUNDEVIL *Curing Horses Dis.* cxxiv. 56b, The Horse is said to be stiffled when the stiffling bone is remooued from the right place. But if it be not remooued nor losened, and yet the Horse halteth by meanes of some griefe there, then we say that the Horse is hurt in the stiffle, and not stiffled. **1607** MARKHAM *Cavel.* VII. lxxvi. 77 If hee halt behinde, he is hipped or stiffled, if he be hipped hee is past cure, if stifled [etc.]. **1639** T. DE GRAY *Compl. Horsem.* (1656) 595 Take a cord and fasten it to the pastern of the stifled legge. **1685** DANGERFIELD *Mem.* 7 Mar. 32, I went.. thence to Ashfield, where I Stifled my Horse. **1859** H. H. DIXON *Silk & Scarlet* 325 But we are forgetting Tarquin [a foxhound], who became stifled at Berkeley.

'**stifle-burn**, *v. Agric.* [f. STIFLE *v.*^{1} or *sb.*^{2} + BURN *v.*] *trans.* To burn (field-refuse and surface-soil) in heaps pressed down with small access of air. Also '**stifle-burning** *vbl. sb.*

1844 *Jrnl. R. Agric. Soc.* V. I. 169 Paring and Burning, or, as it is called in North Wilts, 'stifle-burning', is a system lately introduced into the south of the county. **1849** JOHNSTON *Exp. Agric.* 257 The burning should be slowly conducted, and with little access of air, a method which is well described by the epithet of stifle-burning. **1862** in *Morton's Farmer's Cal.* 166 A neighbour stifle-burned a clover lea from which a crop of hay was just cleared.

stifled ('staɪf(ə)ld), *ppl. a.* [f. STIFLE *v.*^{1} + -ED^1.]

†**1.** Strangled. *Obs.*

1562 COOPER *Answ. Def. Truth* iii. 9b, To make men forbeare stifled meates.

2. In the ordinary senses of the verb: Suffocated, smothered, suppressed, etc.

a **1643** W. CARTWRIGHT *To Lydia* iii. Poems (1651) 243, I hate a secret stifled flame, Let yours and mine have Voice, and Name. **1697** DRYDEN *Virg. Georg.* IV. 381 Such stifl'd Noise as the close Furnace hides. **1817** SHELLEY *Revolt Islam* VI. xii. 5 The blood.. Of the dead and dying.. Like stifled torrents, made a plashy fen Under the feet. **1820** BYRON *Mar. Fal.* IV. i, Turbulent mutterers of stifled treason. **1845** DISRAELI *Sybil* V. iv, 'Hah, hah!' said Morley, with a sort of stifled laugh.

3. Devoid of fresh air, close, stuffy.

1824 SCOTT *Redgauntlet* ch. xiii, In a stifled and subterranean atmosphere. **1863** HAWTHORNE *Our Old Home, Pilgr. Boston* (1879) 175 We were shown into a small, stifled parlor.

stifler ('staɪflə(r)). [f. STIFLE *v.*^{1} + -ER^1.] One who or something which stifles, suffocates, smothers, suppresses, etc.

1642 H. MORE *Song of Soul* II. iii. II. xv, You stiflers now be gone. Let fall that smoring mantle. **1829** SCOTT *Demonol.* 267 Lord-keeper Guildford was also a stifler of the proceedings against witches. **1840** DICKENS *Old C. Shop* viii, My best affections have experienced, this night, a stifler. **1879** GEO. ELIOT *Theo. Such* xviii. 347 We have to consider who are the stifled people and who the stiflers.

b. *Thieves' slang.* The gallows.

1818 SCOTT *Hrt. Midl.* xxiii, I think Handie Dandie and I may queer the stifler for all that is come and gone.

c. *Mil. slang.* = CAMOUFLET I.

1836 *Penny Cycl.* VI. 197/1 *Camouflet*, or *Stifler.* **1875** KNIGHT *Dict. Mech.*

stifling ('staɪflɪŋ), *vbl. sb.*^{1} [-ING^1.]

1. The action of STIFLE *v.*^{1}; suffocating, smothering, suppressing, etc.; †numbing; †strangulation.

1548 PATTEN *Exped. Scot.* Pref. cvjb *marg.*, Cast in a deadly slumber with a stifelinge, & benumminge of al partes. **1578** LYTE *Dodoens* V. xxxviii. 602 The seede of wilde Carrot.. is very good agaynst the suffocation and stiflinges of the Matrix. **1711** ADDISON *Spect.* No. 21 ¶7 Retainers to Physick, who.. amuse themselves with the stifling of Cats in an Air Pump. **1805** WORDSW. *Waggoner* i. 19 Now and then Comes a tired and sultry breeze With a haunting and a panting, Like the stifling of disease. **1882** *Garden* 18 Mar. 178/2 This hardy little plant cannot bear stifling or coddling in high heat and close air.

†**2.** *Farriery.* (See quot.) *Obs.*

1610 L. W. C. *Perf. Disc. Horse* (1624) B 4, For the paine in the Head, or Stifeling.

'**stifling**, *vbl. sb.*^{2} *Farriery.* ? *Obs.* Also 6–7 stifeling, 6–8 **stiffling.** [f. STIFLE *v.*^{2} + -ING^1.]

1. Dislocation or sprain of the stifle-joint.

1580 BLUNDEVIL *Curing Horses Dis.* cxxiv. 56b, Of stiffling, and hurtes in the stiffle. **1639** T. DE GRAY *Compl. Horsem.* (1656) 596 Take pitch.. and.. annoint the stifling.

2. *Comb.* **stifling-bone** = *stifle-bone* (STIFLE *sb.*^{1} 3); **stifling-place,** ? the region of the stifle-joint.

1580 BLUNDEVIL *Curing Horses Dis.* cxxiv. 56b, The Horse is said to be stiffled when the *stiffling bone is remooued from the right place. **1725** *Bradley's Family Dict.* s.v., Some Blow or Stroak.. which either puts out the Stiffling-Bone, or much hurts or strains the Joint. **1580** BLUNDEVIL *Curing Horses Dis.* cxxiv. 57 The *stiffling place is not so broad as the shoulder. **1701** *Lond. Gaz.* No. 3751/8 A Scar in the Stifling-place on the off Side.

stifling ('staɪflɪŋ), *ppl. a.* [f. STIFLE *v.*^{1} + -ING^2.] That stifles or tends to stifle; suffocating, smothering, choking.

a **1560** PHAER *Æneid* VIII. (1562) A a iiij b, A cloud of stifling stinkinge smoke. **1602** MARSTON *Antonio's Rev.* IV. iv, Then death, like to a stifling incubus, Lie on my bosome. **1633** P. FLETCHER *Purple Isl.* II. xl, When the Chanel's stopt with stifeling mire. **1795** SOUTHEY *Joan of Arc* VIII. 593 The soil, that trampled late By multitudes, sent up its stifling clouds Of dust. **1863** GEO. ELIOT *Romola* xxxvi, As a strong body struggles against fumes with the more violence when they begin to be stifling.

b. Of hot or close air, a close room, etc.: Producing the sensation of suffocation; in which one breathes with difficulty; oppressive to the lungs. †Also quasi-*adv.*, in *stifling hot.*

1737 [S. BERINGTON] *G. di Lucca's Mem.* (1738) 105 The Weather was stifling hot. **1748** *Anson's Voy.* II. v. 184 A most intense and stifling heat. **1832** HT. MARTINEAU *Ireland* 120 The heat was stifling, from many sleepers being collected within a small space. **1899** LADY M. VERNEY *Verney Mem.* IV. 281 A stifling cell in Newgate.

c. *fig.*

1584–7 GREENE *Carde of Fancie* (1593) C iij, The stiffeling stormes of vnbrideled fancie. **1649** MILTON *Eikon.* xxvii. 514 A stifling and obstructing evil that hath no vent. **1884** R. PATON *Scott. Ch.* x. 104 The stifling atmosphere of legend and myth. *c* **1900** BRIDGES *La Gloire de Voltaire* Poems (1912) 384 Let your unwholesome flattery flow ungrudged, And with ungrudging measure shall men pour Their stifling homage back.

†**d. stifling grass,** the Royal Fern, *Osmunda regalis.*

1692 A. SYMSON *Descr. Galloway* (1823) 78 They call this plant also by the name of stifling-grasse.

Hence '**stiflingly** *adv.*

1839 H. ROGERS *Ess.* (1860) II. 149 They forget that it is possible for perfumes to be as stiflingly strong as ill odours. **1887** RIDER HAGGARD *Jess* xxiii, The air was stiflingly hot.

stifner, variant of STIFFENER.

‖**stift.** *Obs.* [G., a bishopric.] The domain of a German prince-bishop.

1637 R. MONRO *Exped.* II. 76 He.. left the Duke of Anhalt as Stat-houlder; not only over the Towne, but also over the whole Stifft of Madeburg. **1678** PHILLIPS (ed. 4), *Stift*, a German word, which hath been lately used among us for the small division of a Region or Province. **1819** SCOTT *Leg. Montrose* ii, I have myself commanded the whole stift of Dunklespiel on the Lower Rhine.

†**stig,** *v. Obs. rare*$^{-1}$. [a. ON. *styggja-sk*, f. *stygg-r* shy, wary.] *intr.* To start in alarm.

a **1400–50** *Wars Alex.* 5301 þan stemes he with þe stoute kyng & stiggis with his name.

Stiggins ('stɪgɪnz). The surname of a character in Dickens's *Pickwick Papers* (1836–7), used as the type of the pious humbug.

1916 [see HOLY *a.* 4c]. **1931** A. HUXLEY *Let.* 25 Sept. (1969) 355 That horribly snuffling Stiggins tone! **1935** *Times* 5 Jan. 6/3, I do protest strongly at any attempt to revive the activities of the Prudes on the Prowl, the spying of the Stigginses, and the chortling of the Chadbands.

stigh(e, stighele: see STY, STILE.

†**stight,** *sb.*^{1} *Obs. rare*$^{-1}$. [? Corrupt form of *stiȝ* STY *sb.*] A path.

a **1340** HAMPOLE *Psalter* xvi. 5 Mak perfit my gates in þi stretis [*v.r.* stightes, *Vulg.* semitas].

†**stight,** *sb.*^{2} *Obs. rare*$^{-1}$. In 4 stycht. [f. STIGHT *v.*] Battle array.

1375 BARBOUR *Bruce* III. 658 Till god giff grace we be of mycht Agayne our fayis to hauld our stycht.

†**stight,** *v. Obs.* In 4 pa. t. **stiȝthed,** pa. pple. **stiȝt.** [OE. *stihtan, stihtian* = OLow Frankish *stihtan, stiftôn* (MLG., MDu. *stichten, stiften,* mod.Du. *stichten*), OHG. (MHG., mod.G.) *stiften*, ON. *stétta* (Sw. *stifta*, Da. *stifte*, Icel. *stipta*, are from LG.).] *trans.* To set in order, arrange, place.

c **825** *Vesp. Psalter* cxii. 5 Wynsum mon.. stihtað [L. *disponet*] word his in dome. *a* **1000** *Boeth. Metr.* xx. 178 þu .. on us sawle ȝesettest, & hi siððan eac styrest & stihtest. *a* **1122** *O.E. Chron.* (Laud MS.) an. 1086, On þam an & twentiȝan ȝeare þæs þe Willelm weolde & stihte Engle land swa him God uðe. *c* **1350** *Will. Palerne* 4425 þan rauȝt sche forþ a ring a riche & a nobul, þe ston þat þeren was stiȝt was of so stif vertu, þat [etc.]. *a* **1400–50** *Wars Alex.* 195 þai.. stallid him in a stoute stede & stiȝthed him faire. *Ibid.* 1543 A Mitre,.. Stiȝt [*Dubl. MS.* stight] stafful of stanes. *Ibid.* 2693 Be þis ser Dary.. deuysid his pistill þe kyng of kyngs was called.. þus, vndirstand I, was þe stile & stiȝt [*v.r.* styght] in þare-eftir, 'ȝour satrapaires' [etc.].

†**stightle,** *v. Obs.* Forms: 4 **stiȝ-, styȝtle, -tel,** (**stighle, stigle, stichle**), 4–5 **stiȝtil(l, stightill, -tel, stigh-, styghtle, styghtylle,** (**stighill, stihle, stihȝle, stiȝle, stithle, stithil**). See also STICKLE *v.* [ME. *stiȝtle*, frequentative f. *stiȝte* STIGHT *v.*]

1. *trans.* To dispose, arrange, set in order; to prepare, make ready; to control, rule, govern; to direct (a helm or rudder); to ordain, assign, appoint; to set or establish (in a place or position).

a **1300** *Cursor M.* 19425 (Edin.) Steuin stichlid him al bune, and þan bigan a grete sarmun. *Ibid.* 22093 Riȝt sua [sa]le þe fend him þisse Chesin stede of birþe I wisse þate beste es stiglid [*Gött.* stighlid, *Cott.* titeld] til his stalle. *c* **1350** *Will. Palerne* 1199 þat oþer was his stiward þat stiȝtled al his meyne. **13..** *E.E. Allit. P.* C. 402 If we.. stylle steppen in þe styȝe he [God] styȝtlez hym seluen. *a* **1400** *Minor Poems fr. Vernon MS.* xxix. iv. 20 Alle þe Iewes bi hemselue Were stihlet to wone in a strete. *a* **1400–50** *Wars Alex.* 589 Lat him as ayre.. enherit my landis, And stall we him in stede of þis to stiȝtill my rewme. *c* **1400** *Destr. Troy* 13282 Nowthir stightill þai stere, ne no stithe ropes.

absol. **1393** LANGL. *P. Pl.* C. XVI. 40 Reson stod and stihlede as for stywarde of halle.

b. With hostile notion: To 'dispose of', put down (an antagonist).

c **1350** *Will. Palerne* 2899 þe stoutest & þe sternest he stiȝtled sone after, þat he garte þe grettest to hire prison louȝ te. *c* **1400** *Destr. Troy* 2193 All þe Renkes of my rewme will þi red folowe, As storest of strenght to stightill thy foose.

2. *intr.* To bestir or exert oneself, put forth one's strength or energy; to strive, contend, fight.

c **1350** *Will. Palerne* 3281 Moche folk him folwed þat ferli to bi-hold, how sternli he & þe [stede] schold stiȝtli to-gadere. **13..** *Gaw. & Gr. Knt.* 104 þer-fore of face so fere, He stiȝtlez stif in stalle. *c* **1450** *Merlin* xx. 333 And so haue thei medled and styghtled till they haue founde the kynge Boors vpon foote. *c* **1470** *Gol. & Gaw.* 460 Schipmen our the streme thai stithil full straught.

3. ? To intervene as mediator or umpire.

c **1440** *York Myst.* XXXI. 75 *Rex.* What! and schall I rise nowe, in þe deuyllis name? To stighill amang straungeres in stales of a state.

Hence †'**stightling** *vbl. sb.*

c **1400** *Destr. Troy* 1997 Was no stightlyng with stere, ne no stithe ropes. *c* **1450** *Merlin* xxii. 408 Gawein.. made soche stightlynge a-monge hem that alle dide resorte bakke wheder thei wolde or noon.

†'**stightler.** *Obs.* In 5 styteler. [f. prec. + -ER^1.] = STICKLER.

c **1425** *Cast. Persev.* p. 76 (Plan) Lete nowth ouer many stytelerys be with Inne þe plase.

†'**stightly,** *adv. Obs. rare.* [f. STIGHT *sb.*^{2} + -LY^2.] ? In due order.

1340–70 *Alisaunder* 293 Stones stirred they þo & stightlich layde On hur engines full gist to ungome [? *read* unioine] þe walles. *c* **1400** *Destr. Troy* 6773 All the nobill anon.. Gird doun of the grekes vnto grym dethe, And stird hom in the stoure stightly vnfaire.

stigian, obs. form of STYGIAN.

stigma ('stɪgmə). Pl. **stigmata** ('stɪgmətə) or **stigmas** ('stɪgməz). See also STIGME. [a. L. *stigma*, a. Gr. στίγμα, mark made by a pointed instrument, brand, f. root **stig-* in στίζειν (:—**stigy-*) to prick, puncture: see STICK *v.*]

1. A mark made upon the skin by burning with a hot iron (rarely, by cutting or pricking), as a token of infamy or subjection; a brand. Also *fig.*

1596 HARINGTON *Metam. Ajax* C 2b, Circumcision.. impressing a painefull stigma, or caracter in Gods peculiar people. **1645** RUTHERFORD *Tryal & Tri. Faith* (1845) 256 When a burning iron is put on the face of a evil-doer, it leaveth behind it a brand, or a stigma. **1778** *Sk. Tabernacle Frames* 35 His flinty Front my Stigma shou'd retain. **1863** W. H. RUSSELL *Diary North & S.* I. 246 The advertisements for runaway negroes,.. the description of the stigmata on their persons—whippings and brandings, scars and cuts. **1879** FARRAR *St. Paul* (1883) 471 He was branded.. with the stigmata of the Lord Jesus [cf. Gal. vi. 17]. **1891** MEREDITH *One of Conq.* i, He.. thankfully received his runaway hat,.. making light of the muddy stigmas imprinted by the pavement.

2. *fig.* A mark of disgrace or infamy; a sign of severe censure or condemnation, regarded as impressed on a person or thing; a 'brand'.

a **1619** FOTHERBY *Atheom.* I. xvi. §4 (1622) 168 They set a stigma, and a note vpon all that impugne it. *a* **1623** BUCK *Rich. III,* II. (1646) 63 All such slaughters [were] from thence call'd Bartelmies.. in a perpetuall Stigma of that Butchery. **1777** CHATHAM *Sp. on Addr.* 18 Nov., I.. call upon your Lordships.. to stamp upon it an indelible stigma of the public abhorrence. **1809** R. K. PORTER *Trav. Sk. Russia & Sweden* (1813) II. 273 (Index) Houghton gallery, purchased by Catherine, and added to the collection at the Hermitage; a stigma on this country. **1855** MACAULAY *Hist. Eng.* xiv. III. 410 Moderate politicians.. were unwilling to put a stigma on a man.. distinguished both by his abilities and by his amiable qualities. **1882** J. H. BLUNT *Ref. Ch. Eng.* II. 172 Branded with the stigma of illegitimacy.

b. A distinguishing mark or characteristic (of a bad or objectionable kind); in *Path.* a sign of some specific disorder, as hysteria.

1859 SALA *Tw. round Clock* (1861) 116 Among a family of blooming girls one who already wears the stigmata of old maidenhood. **1897** *Allbutt's Syst. Med.* II. 889 The stigmas of a morphinist are plausibility and disorderliness. **1907** W. C. KRAUSS tr. *E. Mendel's Psychiatry* 84 Stigmata of Degeneration. **1916** A. BENNETT *These Twain* 38 His incorrigible vulgarity of a small manufacturer who displays everywhere the stigmata of petty commerce.

3. *pl.* Marks resembling the wounds on the crucified body of Christ, said to have been supernaturally impressed on the bodies of certain saints and other devout persons.

Sometimes extended to other marks, as crosses, sacred names, etc., supposed to be supernaturally impressed.

1632 LITHGOW *Trav.* I. 24 St. Frances with his inuisible Stigmata. *a* **1700** EVELYN *Diary* 5 Aug. 1670, Monsr Monconys..was by no means satisfied with ye stigmata of those Nunns, because they were so shy of letting him scrape the letters, which were Jesus, Maria, Joseph. **1841** EARL SHREWSBURY *Let. to A.L. Phillipps* 6 Her confessor then told us that she had the stigmata on her hands, feet, and side. **1880** AUGUSTA T. DRANE *St. Catherine of Siena* 369 During the lifetime of the Saint the stigmas remained invisible, but were not so after her death.

b. *nonce-use.* Ineffaceable stains of blood, supposed to remain on the floor of a room where a murder has been committed.

1828 SCOTT *F.M. Perth* Introd., If any Seneschal..had, by means of paint,..endeavoured to palm upon posterity supposititious stigmata,..the impostor would have chosen the Queen's cabinet and the bedroom for the scene of his trick.

4. *Path.* A morbid spot, dot, or point on the skin, esp. one which bleeds spontaneously.

1661 LOVELL *Hist. Anim. & Min.* 128 The eye [of a wolf] applied extenuats the glaucoma and stigma's. **1877** F. T. ROBERTS *Theory & Pract. Med.* (ed. 3) I. 37 Cutaneous hæmorrhages assume the form of..*stigmata*, or minute points, *petechiæ*, or rounded spots, and *vibices* or lines. **1897** *Allbutt's Syst. Med.* IV. 180 The distended capillaries on the cheek, the so-called 'venous stigmata,' which are attributable to alcoholic excess.

5. *Zool.* and *Anat.* **a.** Each of the respiratory openings or breathing-pores in insects and other invertebrates; a spiracle. Also applied to other small openings or pores, as that of the pneumatocyst in *Hydrozoa*. (Pl. usually *stigmata*.)

1747 *Gentl. Mag.* XVII. 122/1 Such as have need of respiration have tracheas and stigmas, which admit..as much air as is..needful for the insect. **1774** GOLDSM. *Nat. Hist.* VIII. 13 The stigmata, as they are called; or those holes on the sides of its body, through which the animal [*sc.* caterpillar] is supposed to breathe. **1832** GRIFFITH tr. *Cuvier* XIV. 3 *note*, In the crickets..and the libellulæ, the sides of the metathorax are each provided with a stigma. **1861–2** LE CONTE *Classif. Coleoptera N. Amer.* I. Introd. p. xviii, The prothoracic breathing pore or stigma or spiracle. **1888** ROLLESTON & JACKSON *Anim. Life* 103 Ascidian..The longitudinal vessels..inclose the stigmata or apertures which lead from the cavity of the pharynx to the peribranchial or atrial cavity.

b. The part of an ovisac or Graafian follicle where it ruptures to discharge the ovum.

1890 COUES *Ornithol.* 327 Such rupture of the Graafian follicle (ovisac)..occurs along a line where the..blood-vessels..upon its surface appear to be wanting, called the stigma.

c. A natural spot or mark, as one formed by enlargement of a nervure on the fore-wings of certain insects (*pterostigma*), or the pigment- or eye-spot of an infusorian.

1826 KIRBY & SP. *Entomol.* III. 377. **1871** STAVELEY *Brit. Insects* 153 On the front margin of the fore-wing [of Hymenoptera] is a thickened spot or *stigma*. **1895** D. SHARP *Insects* I. 534 The Proctotrypidae..frequently have a pigmented spot or stigma on the front wings.

6. *Bot.* That part of the pistil in flowering plants which receives the pollen in impregnation, of very various form, situated either directly on the ovary (sessile) or at the summit (more rarely the side) of the style. Also applied to an analogous structure in cryptogams. (Pl. usually *stigmas.*)

1753 *Chambers' Cycl.* Suppl. s.v. *Seseli*, The stigmata are obtuse. **1812** *New Bot. Gard.* I. 26 The styles acuminate, and the stigmas obtuse. **1862** DARWIN *Contriv. Orchids fertilised* ix. (1877) 249 The viscid secretion of the stigmas of some Orchids. **1882** VINES tr. *Sachs' Bot.* 343 The female organs [in Cryptogams]..called archegonia, are, when..capable of being fertilised, flask-shaped bodies..prolonged into a long neck... A row of cells..passes through the neck ..and is continued as far as the cells which form the so-called 'Stigma.'

7. In Ellis's Stigmatic Geometry, A point whose movement in a certain plane is determined by that of another point (the *index*) in the same plane.

1863 [see STIGMATIC B. 4]. **1864** *Rep. Brit. Assoc.* II. 2 If H and K be fixed stigmata. *Ibid.*, M is the index and P the stigma of a stigmatic straight line.

stigmal ('stɪgməl), *a.* [f. STIGM-A + -AL[1].] Pertaining to a stigma; stigmatic (in scientific senses).

a **1916** In recent Dicts. **1957** *Imms's Gen. Textbk. Entomol.* (ed. 9) 683 It runs along the front margin as the marginal vein and gives off a short stigmal vein. **1962** GORDON & LAVOIPIERRE *Entomol. for Students of Med.* xli. 246 The hard and the soft ticks..possess a pair of stigmata, surrounded by a rounded chitinised plate (known as the stigmal plate) on each side of the body.

‖**stigmaria** (stɪg'mɛərɪə). *Geol.* Pl. -æ. [mod.L., f. STIGMA, in reference to the marks or scars on the fossil: see below.] A former genus of fossil plants, whose remains are found abundantly in the coal-measures; they consist of branching bodies, covered with regularly arranged depressions or scars, and are now commonly believed to be the roots of *Sigillaria* and possibly other trees, the scars being the points of attachment of the rootlets. Also *attrib.*

1845 LYELL *Trav. N. Amer.* I. 84, I was curious to know whether the *Stigmariæ* would be found here in the under-clays. **1846** *Proc. Amer. Philos. Soc.* IV. 274 The fossil plant known as stigmaria was the root of a sigillaria. **1851** MANTELL *Petrifactions* i. §2. 37 fig., Erect stem of Sigillaria with Stigmaria-roots; in a coal-mine in Nova Scotia. **1885** GEIKIE *Text-Bk. Geol.* VI. II. iv. §1 (ed. 2) 728 There can be little doubt..that *Stigmaria* was a type of root common to more than one kind of tree.

Hence **stig'marian** *a.*, belonging to, or containing remains of, *Stigmaria*; **stig'marioid** *a.*, resembling *Stigmaria*.

1855 J. PHILLIPS *Man. Geol.* 218 This is the under-clay —the stigmarian bed. **1902** *Ann. Bot.* XVI. 559 The vascular branches of Stigmarian rootlets.

stigmasterol (stɪg'mæstərɒl). *Biochem.* [ad. G. *stigmasterin* (Windhaus & Hauth 1906, in *Ber. d. Deut. Chem. Ges.* XXXIX. 4380) f. PHYSO)-STIGMA: see -STEROL.] A phytosterol, $C_{29}H_{48}O$, present in Calabar beans (*Physostigma venenosum*) and soya beans.

1907 *Chem. Abstr.* I. 1002 The compound..from the tetrabromide is termed stigmasterol. **1940** *Industr. & Engin. Chem.* Aug. 1138/1 Because of its chemical structure, stigmasterol is an excellent material for the synthesis of the hormone progesterone. **1975** *Lipids* X. 544/2 Sterol patterns of adult and juvenile ivy leaf were essentially identical, with quantities of sterol per 100 g fresh leaf being:..stigmasterol, 9 mg.

stigmat ('stɪgmæt). *Photogr.* [? back-formation from STIGMATIC *a.*] A stigmatic lens or combination of lenses: see STIGMATIC A. 8.

1901 *Photo-miniature* Sept. 245 (Cent., Suppl.) 'Single' lenses, such as the elements forming Gray's Double Stigmat.

stigmat, variant of STIGMATE.

'**stigmatal**, *a. rare*$^{-0}$. [f. Gr. στιγματ- STIGMA + -AL[1].] = STIGMAL.

1859 *Ann. Rep. Smithsonian Instit.* 1858, 187 The lateral region is that between the sub-dorsal and stigmatal lines.

stigmate ('stɪgmət). Only in *plural.* Now *rare.* Also 4–5 **stygmate**, 7 **stigmatte**, 7–9 **stigmat**. [pl. *stigmates* ad. L. *stigmata* pl. of STIGMA. Cf. F. *stigmate.*]

1. = STIGMA 3.

1387 TREVISA *Higden* (Rolls) VIII. 525 She had the stygmates in her handes and feete and side. **1483** CAXTON *Golden Leg.* 314 b, Whan he hadde praid..Saynt frraunceis by his holy Signes and Stygmates he was..delyueryd of his payne. **1610** tr. *Bonaventure's Life St. Francis* xvi. 170 Graced and adorned with the Sacred Stigmattes of our Lord. **1686** AGLIONBY *Painting Illustr.* 141 A Saint Francis in Fresco, who receives the Stigmats upon his Knees. **1839** A. L. PHILLIPPS tr. *Montalembert's St. Eliz. Hungary* p. xxvii, Those five bright and glorious stigmats, which..he [St. Francis] had received.

b. A mark as of a wound or puncture, a scar.

1861 J. H. BENNET *Shores of Mediterr.* III. xv. (1875) 545 So severely bitten [by ants] that it took weeks to efface the stigmates.

†**2.** A mark of correction or annotation in a book or manuscript. *Obs.*

1583 FULKE *Def.* Answ. Pref. 73 The Bible printed at Antwerpe,..where the margents..be full of diuerse readings, obeliskes, asterisks, stigmates.

Hence '**stigmated** *a.*, marked with the stigmata.

1867 LADY HERBERT *Cradle L.* 158 The joy..with which those crossed and stigmated hands [in the badge of the Franciscan monasteries] are welcomed by the traveller.

stigmatic (stɪg'mætɪk), *a.* and *sb.* [ad. med.L. *stigmaticus* (occurring in some MSS. of Cic. *De Off.* ii. 7. 25, where the true reading is *stigmatias*), f. L. *stigmat-*: see STIGMA and -IC. Fr. has *stigmatique* in sense 6 (Littré).

In early use sometimes accented '*stigmatic*: cf. '*heretic*.]

A. *adj.*

1. Constituting or conveying a stigma; branding with infamy; ignominious; severely condemnatory.

1607 HEYWOOD *Wom. killed w. Kindn.* (1617) C 4, Print in my face The most stigmaticke title of a villaine. *a* **1631** DONNE *Ignat. Conclave* (1634) 17 Hee..imprinted the names of Antichrist, Iudas, and other stigmatique markes vpon the Emperour. **1870** SWINBURNE *Ess. & Stud.* (1875) 311 The application of any such stigmatic phrase to the work of Webster is absurd. **1876** —— *Note Eng. Repub.* 10 Cruelty in Ireland, cruelty in Jamaica, cruelty in the plantation, cruelty in the jail, each of these in turn has naturally provoked the stigmatic brand of his approbation.

†**2.** Marked with a 'stigma' or brand, branded.

In quot. 1602 app. humorously used in reference to an academic degree or distinction; cf. B. 1.

1602 *2nd Pt. Return fr. Parnass.* I. iv. 437 Any of those Stigmaticke maisters of arte, that abused vs in times past. **1628** COKE *On Litt.* 158 If the Iuror bee..adiudged..to be branded, or to be stigmatique.

†**3.** Marked with or having a deformity or blemish; deformed, ill-favoured, ugly. *Obs.* (or *rare arch.*)

1597 DRAYTON *Heroical Ep., John to Matilda* 116 Hospitalls..for the crook'd, the hault, the stigmatick. **1601** YARINGTON *Two Lament. Trag.* IV. vi. in Bullen *O. Pl.* IV. 73 A loathsome toade, A one eyde Cyclops, a stigmaticke brat. **1609** HEYWOOD *Brit. Troy* VIII. ix. 171 The Muse hath made him Stigmaticke and lame. **1637** —— *Dialogues* xvii. Annot. V 5, A Proverbe..*Thersite fœdior*, asperst upon any stigmatick, and crooked fellow. **1827** LAMB *Sir Jeffery Dunstan* in *Hone's Every-day Bk.* II. 843 But some little deviation from the precise line of rectitude might have been winked at in so tortuous and stigmatic a frame.

4. Pertaining to or accompanying the stigmata (see STIGMA 3).

1871 G. E. DAY in *Macm. Mag.* Apr. 490, I shall now take up the history of the stigmatic bleedings, which..occur every Friday. **1882–3** SCHAFF *Encycl. Relig. Knowl.* III. 2248 It may be said that 'stigmatic neuropathy' is a pathological condition..explicable by physical and mental conditions.

5. *Path.* Pertaining to or characterized by a stigma or stigmata (see STIGMA 4).

1898 *Syd. Soc. Lex.*

6. *Zool.* Pertaining to or having the nature of a stigma or breathing-pore.

1835 J. DUNCAN *Beetles* (Nat. Libr.) 133 In order to bring the stigmatic openings in contact with the air, they [water-beetles] are obliged from time to time to repair to the surface. **1877** HUXLEY *Anat. Inv. Anim.* vii. 435 The stigmatic openings are usually situated upon the side of the abdomen.

7. *Bot.* Pertaining to, constituting, or having the character of a stigma: see STIGMA 6. In quot. 1902, having a stigma, stigmatiferous.

1830 LINDLEY *Nat. Syst. Bot.* 19 The pollen..shed upon the stigmatic surface. **1882** VINES tr. *Sachs' Bot.* 351 Hepaticæ... The primary stigmatic cell divides into the five or six stigmatic cells of the neck. **1902** OLIVER tr. *Kerner's Nat. Hist. Plants* I. 741 If..the pollen should fall..to the ground, it would..be lost..and neither..winds nor.. insects would be able to carry it..to the stigmatic flowers.

8. *Geom.* Pertaining or relating to the points called stigmata: see STIGMA 7, and B. 4 below.

1863 [see B. 4]. **1875** T. HILL *True Order Studies* 53 Hamilton's Quaternions, and Ellis's Stigmatic Geometry.

9. [Back-formation from ASTIGMATIC by omission of the privative prefix: thus etymologically equivalent to *anastigmatic*, in which the prefix is repeated. Cf. STIGMAT.] Applied to a photographic lens or combination of lenses constructed so as to correct the astigmatic aberration.

1896 *Brit. Jrnl. Photogr.* 1 May 280 The simplest form of a stigmatic lens consists of a glass plate with parallel plane sides. **1902** *Encycl. Brit.* (ed. 10) XXXI. 696/1 A..new type of anastigmatic objective..was brought out..by Messrs. Dallmeyer, under the name of 'Stigmatic'. **1902** *Westm. Gaz.* 12 May 4/2 The various models of stigmatic lenses with which the photographer is becoming somewhat bewildered... In practical photography..a good rapid rectilinear lens answers the purpose..and in nine cases out of ten the fine points of a stigmatic are wasted.

B. *sb.* [ellipt. use of the adj.]

†**1.** A person branded as a criminal; a profligate, villain. *Obs.* (or *rare arch.*)

In quot. 1597 app. humorously used for a person marked with an academic distinction: cf. A. 2.

1597 *Pilgr. Parnass.* II. 217 An ould drousie Academicke, an old Stigmaticke, an ould sober Dromeder. **1600** *Sir J. Oldcastle* V. x. 112 Foule stigmatike, Thou venome of the country. **1642** *Consid. Duties Prince & People* 10 He himselfe the reproach of Soveraignty, and an infamous stigmatique to all posterity. **1856** C. R. KENNEDY *Demosthenes* III. 46 Some too that are slaves and stigmatics [Gr. μαστιγίας].

†**2.** A person marked with some physical deformity or blemish. *Obs.*

1594 *1st Pt. Contention* H 2, Foule Stigmaticke [said to Richard 'Crookback']. **1633** T. ADAMS *Comm. 2 Pet.* i. 4. 80 Be not then married to the world, its a mishapen stigmaticke.

3. A person marked with the stigmata (see STIGMA 3).

1885 *Times* 16 Dec. 5/2 He appeared at Paris.. accompanied by his sister, Patrocinio, the famous stigmatic.

4. *Geom.* The aggregate of the curves traced by the points called stigmata (STIGMA 7); in *pl.* stigmatic geometry: see quot.

1863 A. J. ELLIS in *Proc. Roy. Soc.* XII. 442 The theory of stigmatics. An index point, supposed to move from any origin into every point on a plane, is accompanied by one or more satellite points, termed stigmata... The locus of the stigmata, corresponding to each path of the index, forms a stigmatic curve. The aggregate of these curves constitutes a stigmatic. **1875** T. HILL *True Order Studies* 162 Elements of more modern inventions, quaternions, stigmatics, &c.

5. *Photogr.* A stigmatic lens or objective.

1902 [see A. 9].

†**stig'matical**, *a. Obs.* [f. prec. + -AL[1].]

1. Of the nature of a 'stigma' or brand; made or inflicted by branding.

1610 GUILLIM *Heraldry* III. xx. (1632) 223 The Gentiles ..vsed to..cut their flesh, and to scorch the same with stigmaticall markes. **1619** W. SCLATER *Exp. 1 Thess.* (1630) 26 *marg.*, This insolent Sectary hath..receiued..publike stigmaticall punishment.

2. = prec. A. 1.

1609 W. M. *Man in Moone* D 4 b, His Mandilion edged round about with the stigmaticall Latine word Fur. **1672** MARVELL *Reh. Transp.* I. 306 Several unnecessary additions were made, only because they knew they would be more ingrateful & stigmatical to the Nonconformists.

3. Branded, or deserving to be branded; infamous, villainous: cf. prec. A. 2.

1591 GREENE *Conny Catching* II. Wks. (Grosart) X. 90 One stigmaticall shamelesse companion amongst the rest. **1596** NASHE *Saffron Walden* Ep. Ded. 17 Some tall old sinckanter, or stigmaticall bearded Master of Arte. **1657** J.

BENTHAM *Two Treat.* 13 False reports hatched..in the breasts..of ale-bench haunters, and other Stygmaticall varlots.

4. = prec. A. 3.

1589 GREENE *Menaphon* G j b, Tamberlaine, after his wife Xenocrate (the worlds faire eye) passed out of..this mortall life, he chose stigmatical trulls to please his humorous fancie. **1590** SHAKS. *Com. Err.* IV. ii. 22 He is deformed, crooked,..Vicious, vngentle,..Stigmaticall in making, worse in minde. **1624** HEYWOOD *Gunaik.* VIII. 399 [Witches] are for the most part stigmaticall and ouglie. *a* **1640** J. DAY *Parl. Bees* i. i. (1881) 26 A Bee that has a looke Stigmaticall.

5. = prec. A. 4.

1613 PURCHAS *Pilgrimage* VIII. ii. 616 The flower of the *Granadille*..hath the marks of the Passion, Nailes, Pillar, Whippes, Thornes, Woundes, exceeding stigmaticall Francis.

Hence †**stig'matically** *adv.* *Obs.*, ill-favouredly, villanously. †**stig'maticalness.** *rare*$^{-0}$.

1622 J. TAYLOR (Water P.) *Sir Greg. Nonsence* Wks. (1630) II. 2/1 Giue me a Medler in a field of blue, Wrapt vp stigmatically in a dreame. *c* **1626** *Dick of Devon.* IV. i. in Bullen *Old Pl.* (1883) II. 61, I heard one of you talke most stigmatically in his sleepe—most horriferously. **1636** DEKKER *Wond. Kingd.* III. i. E 1, Any man that has a looke, Stigmatically drawne, like to a furies. **1727** BAILEY vol. II, *Stigmaticalness*, infamousness, a being branded with a Mark of Infamy.

stigmatiferous (stɪgmə'tɪfərəs), *a.* *Bot.* [f. L. *stigmat-* STIGMA + -(I)FEROUS.] Bearing a stigma.

1831 MACGILLIVRAY tr. *Richard's Elem. Bot.* 471 The style ....bears at its summit a variable number of stigmatiferous divisions. **1870** HOOKER *Stud. Flora* 295 Verbena,..style slender, 2-lobed, one lobe only stigmatiferous.

stigmatiform (stɪg'mætɪfɔːm), *a.* *Nat. Hist.* [f. L. *stigmat-* STIGMA + -(I)FORM.] Having the form of a stigma (in sense 5 a, 5 c, or 6).

1843 HUMPHREYS *Brit. Moths* I. 111 An ovate black stigmatiform mark. **1888** HENSLOW *Orig. Floral Struct.* 292 The apex of the petal was green and stigmatiform.

stigmatism ('stɪgmətɪz(ə)m). [f. assumed Gr. *στιγματισμός, f. στιγματίζειν to STIGMATIZE.]

†**1.** Branding; *collect.* marks made by branding, or by tattooing or the like. *Obs.*

1664 H. MORE *Myst. Iniq.* 360 No Pagan could buy nor sell, unless he had some such sacred Stigmatism upon his body.

2. *Path.* The condition of being affected with stigmata (see STIGMA 4).

1900–13 DORLAND *Med. Dict.*

3. Absence of astigmatism. [Cf. STIGMATIC A. 9.]

1890 G. M. GOULD *New Med. Dict.*, *Stigmatism*, a condition of the refractive media of the eye in which rays of light from a point are accurately brought to a point on the retina. Synonymous with emmetropia.

stigmatist ('stɪgmətɪst). [f. *stigmata*, pl. of STIGMA + -IST.] †**a.** = STIGMATIC B. 1. *Obs.* **b.** = STIGMATIC B. 3.

1607 B. BARNES *Divils Charter* III. v. F 3, I coniure thee.. By Nan Riuehomo that hote stigmatist. **1880** *Ch. Times* 28 May 343 Louise Lateau the Stigmatist.

stigmatization (ˌstɪgmətaɪ'zeɪʃən). [f. STIGMATIZE *v.* + -ATION.] The action of stigmatizing, or condition of being stigmatized. *lit.* and *fig.*

1841 EARL SHREWSBURY *Let. to A.L. Phillipps* 42 Catherine Emmerich... Her stigmatization. **1854** M. D. WYATT & WARING *Mediæval Crt. Crystal Palace* 26 The youth of St. Francis..his stigmatization. **1872** J. S. SHEPARD tr. *Lefebvre's Louise Lateau* 126 One of the Friday stigmatizations of Louise Lateau. **1895** *Dublin Rev.* Apr. 489 Dr. Gourbeyre..has collected..three hundred and twenty-one cases of stigmatisation. **1902** R. H. SHERARD *Oscar Wilde* xx. (1905) 244 How cruelly unjust was this stigmatisation.

stigmatize ('stɪgmətaɪz), *v.* [a. med.L. *stigmatizāre*, a. Gr. στιγματίζειν, f. στιγματ- STIGMA: see -IZE. Cf. F. *stigmatiser* (1552 in Hatz.-Darm.), It. *stigmatizzare*, Sp., Pg. *estigmatizar*.]

1. *trans.* To mark with a 'stigma' or brand; to brand; also to tattoo. Now *rare*.

Very frequent in the 17th c., with reference to the then common punishment of branding.

1585 T. WASHINGTON tr. *Nicholay's Voy.* IV. xxvi. 145 Amongst them [the Thracians] it was esteemed a faire and noble thing to haue the forhead stigmatized. **1637** *Brief Relat. Bastwick* etc. 15 Mr. Prynne to be stigmatized in the Cheekes with two Letters (S & L) for a Seditious Libeller. **1737** STACKHOUSE *Hist. Bible* I. iv. (1744) I. 132 God stigmatized him on the forehead with a letter of his own name. **1784** *Acts & Laws Connecticut* 8 Both of them shall be..stigmatized, or burnt on the Forehead with the Letter A, on a hot Iron. **1818** MAULE in *Misc. Scot.* I. 68 The Picts marked their skins with iron, and stigmatised them with pictures of divers animals. **1848** A. HERBERT in *Todd's Irish Nennius* Notes p. lxi, I..prefer the supposition, that [these persons] were..simply painted..and not stigmatized.

b. *transf.* To mark with a stain, scar, or blemish.

1632 B. JONSON *Magn. Lady* III. iii, But my clothes To be defac'd and stigmatiz'd so foulely! **1705** [E. WARD] *Hudibras Rediv.* II. 19 An ill-look'd, thin-jaw'd Calves-head Rabble, All stigmatiz'd with Looks like Jews. **1893** *Scribner's Mag.* Sept. 287 The crimson panes like blood-drops stigmatize The western floor.

c. *Path.* To mark or affect with stigmata; to produce stigmata upon: see STIGMA 4. (Chiefly in *pa. pple.*)

1822–29 *Good's Study Med.* V. 697 Freckles. Cuticle stigmatised with yellowish-brown dots. **1899** *Hutchinson's Arch. Surg.* X. 179 She..[was] freckled and stigmatised.

d. To mark with the stigmata: see STIGMA 3.

1844 FABER *Sir Lancelot* (1857) 97 Francis..stigmatized in fashion as his Lord. **1872** TUKE *Illustr. Infl. Mind upon Body* 83 M. Maury states that Ursula Aguir..experienced every Friday severe pain in the place where, in a vision, she had been *stigmatised*.

e. To imprint as a brand (*lit.* or *fig.*). *rare.*

1644 MILTON *Divorce* I. i. (ed. 2) 7 Not to suffer the ordinance of his goodnes and favour, through any error to be ser'd and stigmatiz'd upon his servants to their misery and thraldome. **1647** R. STAPYLTON *Juvenal* (1670) 267 Letters stigmatized in slaves foreheads. **1822–29** [implied in STIGMATIZED c].

2. *fig.* To set a stigma upon; to mark with a sign of disgrace or infamy; to 'brand'; *esp.* to call by a disgraceful or reproachful name; to characterize by a term implying severe censure or condemnation.

1619 J. TAYLOR (Water P.) *Kicksey Winsey* A 7, A second Edition..wherein I will Satyrize, Cauterize, and Stigmatize all the whole kennell of curres. **1668** COWLEY *Verses & Ess., Liberty* (1669) 82 They..stick not to commit actions, by which they are more shamefully and more lastingly stigmatized. **1750** JOHNSON *Rambler* No. 78 ¶ 12 One of the most striking passages..stigmatizes those as fools who complain that [etc.]. **1819** SCOTT *Leg. Montrose* xviii, We dare not stigmatize Argyle with poltroonery; for [etc.]. **1824** L. MURRAY *Engl. Gram.* (ed. 5) I. 532 These arts, by assisting..to stigmatize every improper idiom, tend to give greater precision..to our style. **1839–40** W. IRVING *Wolfert's R.* (1855) 149 As to their white wines, he stigmatizes them as mere substitutes for cider. **1875** JOWETT *Plato* (ed. 2) V. 261 He must be stigmatized as ignorant, even though he be skilful in calculation.

b. Said of the 'brand' or mark (cf. STIGMA 2 b).

1650 J. HALL *Paradoxes* 57 It was..the first brand that stigmatized them after their fall. **1651–1883** [see STIGMATIZING *ppl. a.*].

stigmatized ('stɪgmətaɪzd), *ppl. a.* [f. prec. + -ED[1].] Marked with a stigma (*lit.* or *fig.*); branded; marked with infamy, severely censured.

1621 BURTON *Anat. Mel.* I. ii. III. vi. 135 Let them be proued, perjured, stigmatized, convict roagues, theeues, traitors. **1657** BILLINGSLY *Brachy-Martyrol.* xi. 36 To multiply their fame, And not as markes of stigmatized shame. **1828** P. CUNNINGHAM *N.S. Wales* II. 124 Doomed to be, like the seed of Cain, a stigmatised race. **1850** MᶜCRIE *Mem. Sir A. Agnew* ii. 35 In these days sympathy with the slave was a rare and stigmatized thing.

b. Marked with the stigmata: see STIGMA 3.

1841 EARL SHREWSBURY *Let. to A. L. Phillipps* 44 The spiritual condition of stigmatized persons. **1872** TUKE *Illustr. Infl. Mind upon Body* 83 The flux of the Stigmata upon Fridays has been verified also in the case of..the Stigmatised of the Tyrol.

c. *Path.* Impressed as a stigma: see STIGMA 4.

1822–29 *Good's Study Med.* III. 27 The stigmatised and pathognomonic dots.

stigmatizing ('stɪgmətaɪzɪŋ), *vbl. sb.* [f. as prec. + -ING[1].] The action of the verb STIGMATIZE; branding (*lit.* or *fig.*).

1641 MILTON *Animadv.* 63 A punishment..for the lopping, and stigmatizing of so many free borne Christians. **1641** *Remonstr. Comm.* in *Rushworth's Hist. Coll.* III. (1692) I. 442 His Majesties Subjects have been oppressed, by grievous Fines, Imprisonments, Stigmatizings, Mutilations, [etc.]. **1653** CHISENHALE *Cath. Hist.* 507 He makes those marks..to become Brands and Stigmatizings of her errors. **1727** A. HAMILTON *New Acc. E. Ind.* II. lv. 306 For small Faults whipping and stigmatizing are common Punishments.

'stigmatizing, *ppl. a.* [f. as prec. + -ING[2].] That stigmatizes: see the verb.

1650 BULWER *Anthropomet.* Pref., Art with her bold Stigmatizing hand. **1651** J. C[LEVELAND] *Poems* 39 A stigmatizing brand of Infamy. **1809** CAMPBELL *Gert. Wyom.* III. viii, Thy beloved heart..Would feel like mine the stigmatising brand! **1883** J. PARKER *Apost. Life* II. 198, I am not going to..fasten upon you some stigmatising term.

†**stigma'tology.** *Obs. rare.* [f. Gr. στιγματ-, στίγμα (see STIGMA; here taken in the sense of στιγμή point) + -(O)LOGY.] The study or subject of the Hebrew accents.

1730 [see TAGHMICAL *a.*].

stigmatose ('stɪgmətəʊs), *a.* [ad. mod.L. type **stigmatōsus*, f. L. *stigmat-* STIGMA: see -OSE.]

1. *Bot.* Said of a style bearing the stigma on some specified part, as along the side instead of (as usual) at the summit.

1840 PAXTON *Bot. Dict.*, *Stigmatose*, when the stigma is long, lateral, or on one side of the style. **1870** HOOKER *Stud. Flora* 71 Malva..styles stigmatose on the inner surface.

2. *Path.* Covered or affected with stigmata.

1894 G. M. GOULD *Illustr. Dict. Med.* etc. *Stigmatose*, marked with stigmata.

stigmatypy ('stɪgmətaɪpɪ). [f. Gr. στίγμα (see STIGMA; here taken in the sense of στιγμή point, dot) + *-typy* after STEREOTYPY or similar words.] The art or process of printing portraits, etc. with small types bearing dots of different sizes, so as to produce an effect of light and shade.

1875 SOUTHWARD *Dict. Typogr.*, *Stigmatypy*, printing with points; the arrangement of points of various thicknesses to produce a picture.

†**stigme.** *Obs. rare.* Anglicized form of STIGMA: in quots., in senses 1 and 2.

c **1400** *Apol. Loll.* 92 ȝe schal not prik ȝor flesch, ne mak to ȝow ani figeris, ne stigmes, þat are woundis. *a* **1619** FOTHERBY *Atheom.* I. iv. §1 (1622) 20 None..haue.. branded any nation with the marke and stigme of Atheisme.

stigmergy ('stɪgmɜːdʒɪ). *Ent.* [ad. F. *stigmergie* (P.-P. Grassé 1959, in *Insectes Sociaux* VI. 62), f. Gr. στιγμ-ός pricking + ἔργ-ον work: see -Y[3].] The process by which the results of an insect's activity act as a stimulus to further activity.

1959 tr. P.-P. Grassé in *Insectes Sociaux* VI. 79 The stimulation of the workers by the very performances they have achieved is a significant one inducing accurate and adaptable response, and has been named stigmergy. **1965** *Symp. Zool. Soc. Lond.* XIV. 128 Experimental evidence would seem to be desirable before accepting stigmergy as the explanation of all co-ordinated constructional behaviour. **1981** *Atlantic Monthly* July 49 There is a similar phenomenon in entomology known as stigmergy.

Hence **stig'mergic** *a.*

1970 G. ORDISH tr. *R. Chauvin's World of Ants* i. 41 At some point there seems to be a brake on the stigmergic process when the stimulation has gone beyond a certain stage. **1971** E. O. WILSON *Insect Societies* xi. 229/2 Stigmergic responses are evidently major elements in nest construction by social insects.

stih, stiif, obs. ff. STY, path, STIFF.

‖**Stijl** (staɪl). [Du., = style.] The name of a movement in art and architecture associated with the Dutch periodical *De Stijl* (1917–32), founded by Theo van Doesburg and Piet Mondrian, and devoted to the principles of neo-plasticism. Freq. with article *de*. Also *attrib.* and as *adj.*

1934 [see NEO-PLASTICISM]. **1936** A. H. BARR *Cubism & Abstract Art* 142 In his *Volume construction* of 1918..the sculptor Vantongerloo applied the *Stijl* love of rectangles to sculpture. *Ibid.* 158 Other of Gropius' buildings at Dessau were even more *Stijl* in character. **1945** R. MOTHERWELL tr. *Mondrian's Plastic Art* 14 In 1915, Theo van Doesburg.. was making analogous researches. Together we formed a small group of artists and architects: the De Stijl Group. **1962** H. MYERS tr. *Pingaud's Holland* 168 The *De Stijl* ('The Style') group, founded in 1917, is dedicated to the fight for a geometric art. **1974** *Encycl. Brit. Macropædia* IX. 516/1 Whereas the Bauhaus offered freedom of expression.., de Stijl offered dogmatic straitjackets of verticals, horizontals, and primary colours.

stik, obs. form of STICK *sbs.* and *vb.*

[**stike,** explained in Nares as a form of STICH, is a misprint for SIKE *sb.*[2] in Sackville *Induct. Mirr. Mag.* xxi.]

†**'stikelunge,** *adv.* *Obs. rare*$^{-1}$. [f. STICK *v.*[1] + -LING[2]. The scribe of the Titus MS. app. took the word for a pple.] ? Piercingly, intently. Also ††**'stikelliche** *adv.* [as if f. STICKLE *a.*], in the same sense.

c **1230** *Hali Meid.* (Bodl. MS.) lf. 58 ȝef þu bihaldest ofte && stikelunge [*Titus* ofte stikelinde] on ei mon. **13..** *K. Alis.* 219 (Linc. Inn MS.), On hire he lokid stikelliche [*Laud MS.* stedfastlyk], And heo on him al outreliche.

stilb (stɪlb). *Physics.* [a. F. *stilb* (A. Blondel in *Recueil des Trav. & Compt. Rend. des Séances* (Internat. Commission on Illumination, 1923) V. 88), f. Gr. στίλβ-ειν to glitter.] A unit of luminance equal to one candela per square centimetre.

1940 in *Chambers's Techn. Dict.* **1942** *Jrnl. Optical Soc. Amer.* XXXII. 355/2 The names, *phot* and *stilb* were.. coined by Blondel (1921) and are in general use on the Continent. **1953** [see NIT *sb.*[4]]. **1963** VAN WIJK & UBING in W. R. van Wijk *Physics of Plant Environment* iii. 90 In photometry a black body at the temperature of melting platinum (2042·16°K) is used as a standard light source. It has by definition a surface brightness of 60 candelas per cm^2 or 60 stilb, when viewed in a direction perpendicular to the surface.

stilbamidine (stɪl'bæmɪdiːn). *Pharm.* [f. STILB(ENE + *amidine* (f. AMID(E + -INE[5]).] A diamidine derivative, $(H_2N)(HN)C{\cdot}C_6H_4{\cdot}CH{:}CH{\cdot}C_6H_4{\cdot}C(NH)(NH_2)$, of stilbene which has antiprotozoal properties and has been used, usu. in the form of its isethionate, in the treatment of trypanosomiasis and leishmaniasis.

1941 [see PENTAMIDINE]. **1958** J. H. BURN *Lect. Notes Pharmacol.* (ed. 5) 110 Stilbamidine is no longer used [in the treatment of leishmaniasis] because it is toxic to the 5th nerve. **1977** *Jrnl. Pharmacol. & Exper. Therapeutics* CCI. 555/1 Pentamidine, stilbamidine and their close analogs are known to interfere with nucleic acid and protein synthesis.

stilbene ('stɪlbiːn). *Chem.* [f. Gr. στίλβειν to glitter + -ENE.] A hydrocarbon produced by the action of heated lead oxide on toluene, and in various other ways: used in dye-stuffs. So **'stilbin** [see -IN] in the same sense.

1868 WATTS *Dict. Chem.* V. 431 Stilbene. *Ibid.* 432 Stilbin. Syn. with Stilbene. 1891 J. E. MARSH tr. *van 't Hoff's Chem. Space* 107 The attempts of Aronstein and Holleman to obtain two isomeric stilbenes.

stilbid ('stɪlbɪd). *Bot.* [f. mod.L. *Stilb-um*, the typical genus of the *Stilbeæ* (f. Gr. στίλβ-ειν to glitter) + -ID.] A fungus of the group *Stilbeæ* or *Stilbaceæ*.

1846 LINDLEY *Veg. Kingd.* 607 Stilbids can hardly be associated with any of the Orders hitherto suggested. 1854 A. ADAMS etc. *Man. Nat. Hist.* 421 Stilbids (Stilbaceæ).

stilbite ('stɪlbaɪt). *Min.* [a. F. *stilbite* (Haüy 1796), f. Gr. στίλβειν to glitter: see -ITE.] A hydrous silicate of aluminium and calcium, in oblique prismatic crystals with pearly lustre. Formerly not distinguished from HEULANDITE.

1815 AIKIN *Min.* (ed. 2) 209 Stilbite..occurs crystallized, lamelliform, massive, and in fasciculated acicular prisms. 1854 DANA *Syst. Min.* (ed. 4) II. 332 Stilbite, H[aüy].

stilbœstrol (stɪl'biːstrɒl, -'bɛstrɒl). *Pharm.* Also (*U.S.*) **stilbestrol**. [f. STILB(ENE + ŒSTR(US + -OL.] †**a.** A synthetic derivative, $HOC_6H_4 \cdot CH{:}CH \cdot C_6H_4OH$, of stilbene having slight œstrogenic properties; also, any derivative of this. *Obs.*

1938 E. C. DODDS et al. in *Nature* 5 Feb. 248/1 In view of the fact that 4:4'-dihydroxystilbene is the mother substance of a series of œstrogenic agents, we suggest that it may be termed stillbœstrol. 1938 *Nature* 2 July 34/1 (*heading*) Oestrogenic activity of alkylated stilbœstrols. 1943 *Vitamins & Hormones* III. 233 This substance..is known as diethylstilbestrol, the term stilbestrol being used for the parent substance.

b. A powerful synthetic nonsteroidal œstrogen, $HOC_6H_4 \cdot C(C_2H_5){:}C(C_2H_5) \cdot C_6H_4OH$, used, often in the form of its dipropionate, in hormone therapy, as a postcoital contraceptive, and as a growth-promoting agent esp. in cattle and sheep; = *diethylstilbœstrol* s.v. DIETHYL 2.

1939 *Lancet* 7 Oct. 788/1 Oral administration of the synthetic œstrogen, stilbœstrol, will inhibit implantation of the ovum in the rat and rabbit. 1943 *Vitamins & Hormones* III. 233 In Great Britain the substance is commonly known as stilbestrol, although it should, of course, be referred to as diethylstilbestrol. 1957 [ŒSTROGENIC *a.*]. 1959 *Times* 29 Apr. 12/6 Farmers were warned yesterday that breeding stock should not be implanted with stilbœstrol. 1976 SMYTHIES & CORBETT *Psychiatry* xi. 209 Stilboestrol given to men reduces libido.

||**stil de grain** (stil də grɛ̃). Also shortened **stil**. [Fr.; according to Hatz.-Darm. corruptly a. Du. *schijtgroen*, f. *schijt* excrement + *groen* green.] A yellow pigment (see quots.).

1769 CROKER etc. *Dict. Arts & Sci.*, *Stil de Grain*,..a composition used for painting..made by a decoction of the lycium or Avignon berry in alum-water, which is mixed with whiting into a paste, and formed into twisted sticks. 1835 G. FIELD *Chromatogr.* 84 The pigment called *Stil*, or *Stil de grain*. 1862 C. O'NEILL *Dict. Calico Printing* 20/1 The yellow lake extensively used by artists..called 'stil de grain', and manufactured in Holland, is made by preparing a decoction [etc.]. 1885 J. S. TAYLOR *Field's Chromatogr.* 162 Brown-Pink, or Stil-de-Grain, is generally prepared from Avignon berries,..or from Turkey and Persian berries.

stile (staɪl), *sb.*¹ Forms: 1 **stiȝel, stiȝol, stihl, stioȝol**, 4 **stighele**, 5 **steyl(e, style**, 6 **steelle, stele, styile, -ill, styll**, 7 **steele, steill, stiele**, 9 *dial.* **steel(e, stele**, 4- **stile**. [OE. *stiȝel* str. fem., corresponding to OHG. *stigilla* wk. fem. (MHG. *stiegele*), f. Teut. root **stiȝ-* to climb: see STY *v.*]

1. An arrangement of steps, rungs, or the like, contrived to allow passage over or through a fence to one person at a time, while forming a barrier to the passage of sheep or cattle. Cf. TURNSTILE.

church stile: the stile giving entrance to the churchyard. (Very frequently referred to in records, directions for funeral services, etc., from the 15th to the 17th c. See CHURCH *sb.* 16 c, KIRK *sb.* 4.)

c779 *Grant by Offa* in Birch *Cartul. Sax.* I. 326 Of þam seaðe in þa ealdan stihle. a900 WÆRFERTH *Gregory's Dial.* 24 Hi þa becomon to þære stiȝole, þær se þeof oferstah in ðone wyrttun. 1304 in *Catal. Anc. Deeds* (1894) II. 390 [Land called] Stothamstighele. c1386 CHAUCER *Pard. T.* 384 Right as they wolde han troden ouer a stile An oold man and a poure with hem mette. 1430-40 LYDG. *Bochas* VIII. Prol. (1558) I Halfe within and half ouer the stile. c1460 *Oseney Reg.* 116 Sauyng to þe same Roger and to his heyres A pathe þorowgh þe middull of þe same close fro þe stile of þþe forsaide church. 1470-85 MALORY *Arthur* I. iii-v. 41 So whan he cam to the chircheyard sir Arthur aliȝt & tayed his hors to the style. 1536 *MS. Acc. St. John's Hosp., Canterb.*, Payd..for makyng off a stele & a gate. 1573 TUSSER *Husb.* (1878) 105 Saue step for a stile, of the crotch of the bough. 1601 *Manch. Crt. Leet. Rec.* (1885) II. 168 Robert Langley shall..sett two steeles..in the syde of Asheley ffields. 1654 LAMONT *Diary* (Maitl. Club) 77 Money for the poore, that day, was gathered at the church steill and church doore. 1661 *Reg. Gt. Seal Scot.* 19/1 Going downe ane march balk betwixt Ernslaw and Swyntoun-mylne style till you come to the old trouch of Leit. 1726 SWIFT *Gulliver* II. i, There was a stile to pass from this field into the next. 1763 BICKERSTAFF *Love in Village* I. ix, Scene IX. A field with a stile. 1827 Hone's *Every-day Bk.* II. 905 Stiles and fieldpaths are vanishing everywhere. 1847 JAMES *Convict* iv, They soon reached the wall, over which they passed by a stone style. 1865 TROLLOPE *Belton Est.* iii. 37 Getting over stiles and through gates. 1898 J. PATON *Castlebraes* 28, I..set my foot upon a style to step over into the public roadway.

b. In figurative phrases.

a1352 MINOT *Poems* i. 88 All þai stumbilde at þat stile. 1546 J. HEYWOOD *Prov.* I. xi. (1867) 32 To helpe a dogge ouer a style. *Ibid.* II. ix. 80 Ye would be ouer the style, er ye come at it. 1574-5 ABP. PARKER *Let.* 18 Feb. in Strype *Life* (1711) App. 181 What is ment, but to goo over the Style, where it is lowest? 1598 FLORIO *Ital. Dict.* Ep. Ded. 4 The retainer doth some seruice, that now and then..lendes a hande ouer a stile. 1639 DU VERGER tr. *Camus' Admir. Events* 112 He resolved to leape that stile, and take her to his wife. 1659 in *Burton's Diary* (1828) IV. 316, I would have it understood whether we confirm it as a law, or help a lame dog over a stile. 1675 ALSOP *Anti-Sozzo* 302 He lifted him over the Style with this. 1692 *Christ Exalted* 105 Now to help him over this stile, he troubles the Bishop. 1857 KINGSLEY *Two Y. Ago* xxv, 'I can..help a lame dog over a stile' (which was Mark's phrase for doing a generous thing). 1884 *Manch. Exam.* 20 May 5/1 It is a mere working arrangement; a lift over the stile at a crisis of some importance to the party.

2. *attrib.* and *Comb.*, as **stile-board, -post, -step, -way; stile-boot** (see quot.).

1891 HARDY *Tess* xii, The lichened *stile-boards. 1828 CARR *Craven Gloss.*, **Steel-boot*, wood claimed of the Lord, by an owner of lands, within certain manors, for making a stile. 1750 W. ELLIS *Mod. Husb.* VI. i. 126 By spurring up a gate or *stile-post before they are quite damaged, he may [[etc.]. 1844 H. STEPHENS *Bk. Farm* II. 65 The stell is entered by *stile-steps over the wall. 1751 PALTOCK *Peter Wilkins* I. xii. 108 Leaving only a Door-way on one Side, between two Stems of a Tree, which, dividing in the Trunk, at about two Feet from the Ground, grew from thence, for the rest of its Height, as if the Branches were a Couple of Trees a little distant from one another, which made a Sort of **Stile-way to my Room.

stile (staɪl), *sb.*² *Carpentry.* Also 9 **style**. [Of uncertain origin; perh. a. Du. *stijl* pillar, prop, door-post.] Each of the vertical bars of a wainscot, sash, panel door, or other wooden framing.

1678 MOXON *Mech. Exerc.* v. 83 You must leave some stuff to pare away smooth to the struck line, that the Stile (that is, the upright Quarter) may make a close Joynt with the Rail (that is the lower Quarter). 1710 J. HARRIS *Lex. Techn.* II, *Stiles*, the upright pieces which go from the bottom to the top in any Wainscot, are by the Workmen called *Stiles*. 1768-74 TUCKER *Lt. Nat.* (1834) I. 290 When we look upon the wainscot of a room, where the panels are painted of a different colour from the stiles and mouldings. 1801 FELTON *Carriages* (ed. 2) II. 43 Two crests on the door-stiles 8s. 1825 J. NICHOLSON *Oper. Mech.* 326 His turning machine..the legs or stiles L, the puppets A, B, the cheeks *o, o*. *Ibid.* 593 The face of the pulley-stile of every sash-frame ought to project about three-eighths of an inch beyond the edge of the brick-work. 1825 *Greenhouse Comp.* I. 15 In the case of Grecian architecture, the mouldings of any of the orders are readily applied to the styles, rails and bars. 1844 *Civil Engin. & Arch. Jrnl.* VII. 114/2 In constructing the walls of houses, in the first instance, 'stiles' or pieces of timber are inserted at convenient distances. 1846 HOLTZAPFFEL *Turning* II. 715 In a rectangular frame..the tenons are commonly made on the shorter pieces, called the rails, and the mortises on the longer or the styles. 1869 BLACKMORE *Lorna D.* xxxviii, Making spars to keep for thatching, wall-crooks to drive into the cob, stiles for close sheep-hurdles, and handles for rakes. 1881 YOUNG *Ev. Man his own Mech.* §§709. 323 Nor should nails be driven into the styles of any door. 1883 M. P. BALE *Saw-mills* 336 *Stiles*, part of a window sash.

stile, see STEEL, STYLE.

||**stile antico** ('stile an'tiko). *Mus.* [It., lit. 'old style'.] The strict contrapuntal style of the sixteenth century, esp. as exemplified in the works of Palestrina.

1944 W. APEL *Harvard Dict. Mus.* 550/2 *Palestrina style*. .... As early as the 17th century this style, under names such as *stile antico*, *stile osservato*..had become 'classical' in the Roman school. 1959 *Collins Mus. Encycl.* 624/2 *Stile antico*, the contrapuntal style of the 16th cent. as practised by Italian composers and formulated by Italian theorists in the 17th and early 18th cent. 1968 *New Oxf. Hist. Music* IV. x. 521 This consciously conservative tendency among Catholic composers..resulted in the ultimate petrifaction of the Palestrinian *stile antico*, which artificially survived well into the eighteenth century. 1974 *Early Music* July 197/1 A dull *stile antico* section for 'Domine fili unigenite'. 1976 *Ibid.* July 274 Cavalli's final work, the Requiem, looks backwards also, but its use of the *stile antico* is not quite so remote as that in the psalms.

||**stile concitato** ('stile kontʃi'tato). *Mus.* [It., lit. 'excited style'.] A baroque style developed by Monteverdi, emphasizing dramatic expression and excitement.

1926 H. PRUNIÈRES *Monteverdi* III. v. 180 The semiquavers of the *stile concitato* express their terror at the menace of the god. 1940 *Music & Letters* Apr. 244 Monteverdi..claimed, in the preface to the volume in which the 'Combattimento' is printed, to have originated a new *stile concitato*. 1947 M. F. BUKOFZER *Mus. Baroque Era* (1948) ii. 38 Monteverdi enriched the *concertato* style by an important innovation: the *stile concitato* (style of agitation) in which he turned the measured tremolo of the *gorgia* to dramatic effect. 1959 *Listener* 16 Apr. 692/3 He admired the *stile concitato* of Monteverdi. 1967 *Ibid.* 18 May 665/2 These were part of Monteverdi's *stile concitato*, a style he cultivated ....to express wrath, anger, indignation.

||**stile rappresentativo** ('stile ˌrapprezenta'tivo). *Mus.* [It., lit. 'representative style'.] The vocal style of recitative used by Italian musicians of the early seventeenth century (see quot. 1938).

1886 F. PRAEGER tr. *E. Naumann's Hist. Mus.* I. xv. 525 At first the opera was variously styled according to the individuality of the composer... The style itself was generally called *Stile rappresentativo*. 1915 *Strad* Jan. 299/1 The so-called *stile rappresentativo* of Florence was claiming more and more adherents and ministers; Monteverde, likewise, was moved by the ever-expanding ripple. 1938 *Oxf. Compan. Mus.* 896/2 *Stile rappresentativo*... The term was used by the early Roman composer of oratorio, Cavalieri, and the contemporary Florentine composers of opera..to indicate the use of their invention of recitative..which aimed rather at *representing* the sense and the natural inflection of the speaking voice than at providing the enjoyment of pure musical beauty. 1947 M. F. BUKOFZER *Mus. Baroque Era* (1948) ii. 25 The emergence of the *stile rappresentativo* or recitative about the year 1600 has often been regarded as the most important turning point in the entire history of music. 1959 N. C. CARPENTER *Mus. in Medieval & Renaissance Universities* iv. 357 University learning..led such people as Vincenzo Galilei..to experiment in a new musical style based upon his concept of Greek music, the *stile rappresentativo*, with its close affinity between words and music. 1980 *Early Music* July 298/1 But we should not let the polemics of the day in favour of monody obscure the very close, though perhaps not immediately apparent, bond between the expressiveness of the *stile rappresentativo* and the concept of melody that pervades the fabric of many polyphonic works from the second half of the 16th century.

stilet: see STYLET.

†**stile'ttato.** *Obs.* In 7 stilletato. [a. It. *stilettata*, f. *stiletto*.] A thrust with a stiletto.

1651 tr. *Life Father Paul Sarpi* 116 He thought that at the two first stilletato's he felt like two blowes strucken with fire at one instant.

stilette (stɪ'lɛt), variant of STYLET (*Surg.*).

stiletto (stɪ'lɛtəʊ), *sb.* Pl. **-oes**. Also 7 **stilletta, stelletto, steeletto**, 7-8 **steletto, stilleto, stiletto**. [a. It. *stiletto*, dim. of *stilo* dagger, STYLUS: see -ET¹. Cf. STYLET.]

1. A short dagger with a blade thick in proportion to its breadth.

1611 CORYAT *Crudities* 275 They [the Venetian 'Braves'] wander abroad very late in the night..armed with a privy coat of maile,..and a little sharpe dagger called a stiletto. 1627 H. BURTON *Bait. Pope's Bull* 44 What is it but pistols, stellettoes, poysons, your vsuall weapons? 1629 QUARLES *Argalus & Parthenia* I. 12 A keene Steeletto in his trembling hand He rudely grip'd. 1674 COTTON *Fair One of Tunis* 136 He..would a thousand times have plunged his Steeletto into his own bosom, had not he had a design to have stab'd it into that of his Rival. 1711 PUCKLE *Club* (1817) 7 Some use their wits as Bravoes wear stelettoes, not for defence but mischief. 1736 B. HIGGONS *Rem. on Burnet* I. 59 As Dark-lanthorns and Stilettoes are unlawful Weapons to attack his Person. 1783 JUSTAMOND tr. *Raynal's Hist. Indies* V. 163 Besides these, the Turks have a dagger, and the Moors a stiletto. 1841 JAMES *Brigand* v, Employing the stiletto or the drug when it suited his purpose to get rid of trouble-some friends. 1864 *Reader* 18 June 771/1 She discovers a stiletto hidden in a pond.

transf. and *fig.* 1673 MARVELL *Reh. Transp.* II. 315 Your whole Book of Ecclesiastical Politie having been Writ not with a Pen but a Stilletto. 1749 BOLINGBROKE *Lett. Patriotism* 145 Simulation is a stiletto, not only an offensive, but an unlawful weapon. 1843 MACAULAY *Ess., Addison* (1897) 738 [Pope's] own life was one long series of tricks... He was all stiletto and mask. 1844 KINGLAKE *Eothen* xi, The fleas of all nations were there:—the wary, watchful 'pulce' with his poisoned stiletto [etc.]. 1872 LOWELL *Milton* Pr. Wks. 1890 IV. 85 But the thin stiletto of Macchiavelli is a more effective weapon than these fantastic arms of his [Milton's].

2. †**a.** Short for *stiletto beard* (see sense 5). *Obs. rare*$^{-1}$.

1638 FORD *Fancies* III. i, The very *he* that Wears a stiletto on his chin.

b. Short for *stiletto heel* (see sense 5).

1959 *New Statesman* 10 Oct. 464/3 She came..smooching forward, her walk made lopsided by the absence of one heel of the stilettos. 1960 *Guardian* 18 Mar. 10/6 Wearing stilettos, you are, of course, tiptoeing. 1967 O. WYND *Walk Softly, Men Praying* ii. 13 She wobbled slightly on worn-over stilettos.

†**3.** A surgical instrument: ? = STYLET. *Obs.*

1698 LISTER *Journ. Paris* (1699) 233 He boldly thrusts in a broad Lancet or Stilleto into the middle of the Muscle of the Thigh near the *Anus*.

4. *Needlework*, etc. A small pointed instrument for making eyelet-holes.

1828 WEBSTER, *Stiletto*, a pointed instrument for making eyelet holes in working muslin. 1862 *Catal. Internat. Exhib., Brit.* II. No. 6513, Button-hooks, nail files, corkscrews, stilettoes, tweezers, nut picks, &c. 1879 E. A. DAVIDSON *Pretty Arts* 148 This material..may with ease be penetrated by the stiletto or a strong needle.

5. *attrib.* and *Comb.*, as **stiletto blade, wound; stiletto-like** adj.; †**stiletto beard**, a pointed beard; so †*stiletto cut*, †*fashion*; **stiletto-fly** (see quot. 1895); **stiletto heel**, a very narrow, high heel on women's shoes, fashionable esp. in the 1950s; a shoe with such a heel; hence **stiletto-heeled** *a.*

1621 J. TAYLOR (Water P.) *Superbiæ Flagellum* C 8, Some [beards] sharpe Steletto fashion, dagger like. 1635 DAVENANT *Tri. Prince d'Amour* 4 Two..swaggering

Souldiers,..their Beards mishapen, with long whiskers of the Stilletto cut. *a* **1660** *Prince d' Amour* etc. 127 The Steeletto beard, O it makes me afraid It is so sharp beneath. **1821** SCOTT *Kenilw.* xxxvi, By using the three-cornered stiletto-blade as a wedge, he forced open the slender silver hinges of the casket. **1851** H. MELVILLE *Whale* xlix, With a stiletto-like cry..the negro yelled out. **1865** *Daily Tel.* 26 Oct. 2/1 There was a mean shrinking from a condemnation of Lord Palmerston's life and policy, and a stiletto-like smiting in the back. **1895** COMSTOCK *Man. Insects* 464 Family Therevidæ... The abdomen is long and tapering, suggesting the name stiletto-flies. **1911** *Daily News* 12 Jan. 2 The same day her husband's body was found on the seashore [of Naples] bearing the marks of many stiletto wounds. **1953** *Daily Tel.* 10 Sept. 8/4 One of the models.. in the..winter collection..has the new stiletto heel, 3½ in high and just large enough at the base to cover a sixpence. **1959** *Times* 13 May 10/7 The iniquitous effect of stiletto-heeled shoes on the modern woman's feet. **1973** M. AMIS *Rachel Papers* 124 At this kind of speed it was advisable to place the stiletto-heeled shoe, kept in a side-pocket for this purpose, over the gear-stick to prevent it jiggering like a pump-drill. **1981** M. HARDWICK *Chinese Detective* ix. 73 She was in black slip and stockings and four-inch stiletto heels.

stiletto (stɪˈlɛtəʊ), *v.* Inflected stilettoes, stilettoed (†stiletted). [f. STILETTO *sb.*]

1. *trans.* To stab, esp. mortally, with a stiletto.

1613-4 BACON *Charge agst. W. Talbot* Resusc. (1657) 55 This King [Hen. IV of France] likewise, stilletted, by a Rascal votary. **1751** CHESTERF. *Let. to Son* 30 June, An excellent and short book; for which, and some other treatises against the court of Rome, he [Fra Paolo] was stiletto'd. **1835** LYTTON *Rienzi* IV. ii, How many peaceful men have been stilettoed in the day-light.

2. *nonce-use.* To mark with a 'dagger' or obelus.

1841-57 DE QUINCEY *Homer* Wks. VI. 357 Aristarchus.. cancels and stilettoes the whole passage. *Ibid. foot-n.*, 'Stilettoes':—i.e., obelises, or places his autocratic *obelus* before the passage.

stiliard, obs. form of STEELYARD^1,^{2}.

†ˈ**stiling**, *vbl. sb. Obs.* [f. STILE *sb.*^{1} + -ING^1.] The making of stiles.

1509 *Reg. Mag. Sig. Scot.* 725/2 In pratis et pasturis, clausuris le stiling.

†ˈ**stilking.** *Obs.* Some part of the gear of a plough.

1523-34 FITZHERB. *Husb.* §5 Bvt or he begyn to plowe, he muste haue his ploughe,..his oxen or horses, and the geare that belongeth to them; that is to say, bowes, yokes, landes, stylkynges, wrethynge temes.

still (stɪl), *sb.*^{1} Also 6 styll, stil, 8 *Sc.* stiel, 8-9 *Sc.* stell. [f. STILL *v.*^{1}]

1. An apparatus for distillation, consisting essentially of a close vessel (alembic, retort, boiler) in which the substance to be distilled is subjected to the action of heat, and of arrangements for the condensation of the vapour produced. Also applied to the alembic or retort separately.

1562 BULLEIN *Bulwarke, Bk. Simples* (1579) 85b, A horned Still. Bagpipe Still... Pelican Still. **1563** T. GALE *Antidot.* II. 87 Then styll them in a common styll, and keepe thys water to your vse. **1577** B. GOOGE *Heresbach's Husb.* IV. 193 Yf you do it in Stils made of Glasse,..your water shal haue the very taste, sauour, and propertie of the hearbe. **1579** LYLY *Euphues* (Arb.) 91 Not unlike to the damaske Rose, which is sweeter in the Still then on the stalke. **1620** *Unton Inventories* (1841) 27 In the Still Howse. iiij stills, iij brasse panns, wth table and presse. **1655** CULPEPPER etc. *Riverius* I. i. 8 Put them in a Retort, or Still so called. **1731** ARBUTHNOT *Aliments* iii. (1735) 68 This fragrant Spirit is obtain'd from all Plants which are in the least aromatick, by a cold Still. **1785** BURNS *Scotch Drink* xix, Thae curst horse-leeches o' th' Excise, Wha mak the Whisky stells their prize! **1818** SCOTT *Hrt. Midl.* I, A charcoal fire, on which there was a still working. **1885** LOCK *Workshop Rec.* Ser. IV. 121/2 All ordinary distilling apparatus consists of 2 parts—one in which the heat is applied to the body to be distilled and vaporised (called the 'still'). **1899** E. J. PARRY *Chem. Essential Oils* 200 The herbs [*sc.* mint] are distilled in the green state... In England most of the stills used hold from 4 to 8 cwt. of herbs. **1901** BOLAS & LELAND *Perfumes* 14 None of the domestic stills sold for purifying water..are well suited for making perfumes.

fig. **1579** LYLY *Euphues* (Arb.) 101 And witte..beeing purified in the styll of wisdome. **1598** SYLVESTER *Du Bartas* II. i. II. *Impost.* 518 God's grace, whose Still Extracts from dross of thine audacious ill, Three unexpected goods. **1873** SPENCER *Stud. Sociol.* xi. 289 When the fermenting mass of political passions and beliefs is put into the electoral still, there distils [etc.].

b. ***small-still (whisky)*** Sc. and Anglo-Irish: 'whisky supposed to be of superior quality, because the product of a small still' (Jam.).

1822 [J. WILSON] *Lights & Shad. Scott. Life* 382 Taste the whisky, Mr. Gordon—it is sma' still, and will do harm to no man. **1835** CARRICK *Laird of Logan* (1841) 312 Anither class contented themsells with sma'-stell whisky, made intil toddy. **1839** *John Bull* 11 Aug. 381/1 Retiring with his 'Riverence' to discuss small-still and the claims of the 'parsecuted Clargy'. **1856** LEVER *Martins of Cro' M.* x. 87 That is 'poteen'... It's the small still that never paid the King a farthing. **1861** G. H. KINGSLEY *Sport & Trav.* (1900) 245 A couple of black bottles, which ought to contain whisky of the smallest still.

2. †**a.** = STILL-ROOM. *Obs.* **b.** A distillery.

1533 in *Froude's Hist. Eng.* (1870) I. 44 In the Still beside the Gate. Two old road saddles, one bridle, a horse-cloth. **1654** WHITLOCK *Zootomia* 351 Shee gives that [Physick] a nobler way; more from her Purse than still, or Closet. **1845** S. JUDD *Margaret* I. xv, He engaged his services as night-warden of the Still... The 'Still,' or distillery, was a smutty, clouded, suspicious-looking building.

3. A chamber or vessel for the preparation of bleaching-liquor by the action of hydrochloric acid on manganese dioxide, or for the preparation of chlorine, of alkalis, etc.

1853 in *Abridgm. Specif. Patents, Acids* etc. (1869) 377 Improved apparatus for manufacturing chlorine or chlorides. [This consists in substituting for the] common leaden or stone still [..an iron vessel or still, having a lining of fire-bricks or tiles, etc.]. **1880** J. LOMAS *Man. Alkali Trade* 272 The liquid hydrochloric acid obtained from the sulphate of soda process is run upon a known weight of manganese binoxide in a 'still.' The best form of still is shown in Figs. 188 and 189. **1880** LUNGE *Manuf. Sulphuric Acid & Alkali* III. 26 The stills, B, B^1, B^2, B^3 communicate with each other by a distributor C,..which permits any boiler to be isolated without interrupting the distillation in the others. **1910** *Encycl. Brit.* (ed. 11) I. 684/1 (art. *Alkali*) Both these reactions are carried out in tall cylindrical columns or 'stills,' consisting of a number of superposed cylinders, having perforated horizontal partitions, and provided with a steam-heating arrangement in the enlarged bottom portion.

4. *attrib.* and *Comb.*, as ***still-cabin, -cock, -fire, house, nose***; **still-bottoms**, 'what remains in the still after working the wash into low wines' (*Chambers' Cycl.* Suppl. s.v.); **still-hanger** (see quot.); **still-hunting**, the search for illicit stills; **still-liquor**, bleaching liquor made in a still (see 3); **still-man**, a workman employed to attend to a still; **still-pot**, a small still; **still-spirit** (see quot.); **still-tub**, the condensing vessel of a still. Also STILL-BURNT, STILL-HEAD, STILL-HOUSE, STILL-ROOM, STILL-WORM.

1753 *Chambers' Cycl.* Suppl. s.v. *Wine*, The *still-bottoms have many uses. The distillers scald and recover their musty casks with them, and [etc.]. **1841** S. C. HALL *Ireland* I. 117 The light curl of smoke issuing from the roof of some illicit *still-cabin. **1652** in W. M. Williams *Ann. Founders' Co.* (1867) 110 They found..at Evan Evens's other great *still Cockes filled with Lead and so basely wrought, that [etc.]. **1725** G. SMITH *Distilling* 68 You must have for your *Still-fire a large Poker, Fire-shovel, [etc.]. **1858** SIMMONDS *Dict. Trade*, *Still-hanger, an engineer or worker, who fixes the stills for making rum in the West Indies. **1821** SCOTT *Let.* in *Lockhart* (1839) VI. 313 Pray write soon, and give me the history of your *still-huntings. **1844** G. R. GLEIG *Light Dragoon* ii. (1855) 17 There is not one [duty] on which I now look back with more unmixed abhorrence than the operation of still-hunting. **1869** *Abridgm. Specif. Patents, Acids* etc. 997 *Still liquor or chloride of manganese obtained in any other way..is treated [etc.]. *a* **1864** GESNER *Coal, Petrol.* etc. (1865) 167 One superintendent, two engineers, four *still men, and four helpers. **1725** G. SMITH *Distilling* 71 The worm end, in which your *Still nose is luted. *a* **1824** in Maidment. *N.C. Garland* 54 A *stell-pat they gat, and they brew'd Highland whisky. **1839** URE *Dict. Arts* 624 This apparatus consists of only two still-pots of cast iron. **1832** *Trans. Prov. Med. & Surg. Assoc.* VI. II. 202 These [cider dregs] were formerly collected and distilled, thus yielding a coarse ardent spirit, vulgarly called '*still-spirits.' **1826** HENRY *Elem. Chem.* II. 600 This test is so delicate, that water condensed by the leaden worm of a *still-tub, is sensibly affected by it.

still (stɪl), *a.* and *sb.*^{2} Forms: 1 stille, stylle, 3-6 stille, stylle, 3-7 stil, 4 stell, style, 4-6 styl, 5-6 styll, 3- still. [Com. WGer.: OE. *stille* = OFris. *stille*, OS. *stilli* (MLG. *stille*, whence prob. Sw. *stilla*, *still*, Norw. *still*, Da. *stille*), MDu. *stille* (mod.Du. *stil*), OHG. *stilli* (MHG. *stille*, mod.G. *still*):—OTeut. type **stilljo-*, **stelljo-*, f. **stel-* to be fixed, stand: see STEAL *sb.*^{2}]

A. *adj.*

1. Motionless; not moving from one place, stationary; also, remaining in the same position or attitude, quiescent. **a.** as *predicate* or *complement*.

In *stand, sit, lie still* the word may be taken either as adj. or adv. In OE., however, there is evidence that in these collocations it was sometimes adv., and no evidence that it was ever adj., the constant form being *stille* (which always admits of being regarded as adv.), never *stillu*, which would be the proper form of the adj. when the subj. is fem. sing. or neut. pl. Further, in OS. and OHG. the adv. *stillo*, not the adj., is used with the verb 'to stand'. These phrases are therefore treated under STILL *adv.* I.

Beowulf 2830 Se widfloga wundum stille hreas on hrusan. *c* **888** ÆLFRED *Boeth.* xxxix. viii, He astereð þone rodor & þa tunglu, & þa eorðan gedeð stille. *c* **1205** LAY. 4516 Stille he wes isworen on his kine-stole. *c* **1374** CHAUCER *Anel. & Arc.* 54 Mars..ne rested neuer stille But throng now here now þere. *a* **1400-50** *Wars Alex.* 263 Quen he þire sawis had sayd he in his sege lened, In stody still as a stane & starid in hire face. **1604** SHAKS. *Oth.* v. ii. 94 Hah, no more moouing? Still as the Graue. **1732** in A. Clarke *Mem. Wesley Family* (1823) 264 They were as soon taught to be still at family prayers. **1816** J. WILSON *City of Plague* I. i. 79 There it hangs Still as a rainbow in the pathless sky. **1859** REEVE *Brittany* 51 One or two women..remained still long enough to be more defined in outline. **1889** BADEN-POWELL *Pigsticking* 170 It is easy enough for a man to keep still, but the difficulty is to make the horse do so. **1897** HALL CAINE *Christian* x, The dance is over, but she can't keep her feet still.

†**b.** Abstaining from action. Const. *of* (in OE., genitive). Phrase, ***to hold oneself still***. *Obs.*

c **1000** *Laws of Wihtræd* §6 Sio he stille his þeȝnungæ oþ biscopes dom. *a* **1300** *Cursor M.* 408 Þe seuend o werk he hild him still. *Ibid.* 10323 Þof godd vmquil be funden still, Al mai he wirk þou quat he will. *c* **1338** R. BRUNNE *Chron.* (1725) 47 Edmunde & the erle Uctred þat tyme held þam stille. **1340** HAMPOLE *Pr. Consc.* 3449 When þou..wille noght help bot haldes þe stylle. **138.** WYCLIF *De Eccl.* Sel. Wks. III. 346 A stiward..þat whanne many servauntis done amys, holdiþ stille, and bryngiþ in newe þat done werse. **1590** SHAKS. *Com. Err.* III. ii. 69 Hold you still: Ile fetch my sister to get her good will.

c. in attributive use. (In quot. *a* 1586: †Averse from moving about, sedentary.) Somewhat *rare*.

a **1586** SIDNEY *Arcadia* III. iv. (1912) 374 Therfore would he not employ the stil man to a shifting practise, nor the liberall man to be a dispenser of his victuals. **1798** COLERIDGE *Anc. Mar.* IV. xi, The charmed water burnt alway A still and awful red. **1817** SHELLEY *Rev. Islam* II. xii. 8 Even as a storm let loose beneath the ray Of the still moon. **1853** C. BRONTE *Villette* iii, In his absence she was a still personage, but with him the most officious, fidgetty little body possible. **1875** HUXLEY & MARTIN *Elem. Biol.* 12 The still condition of Protococcus, just described, is not the only state in which it exists. Under certain circumstances, a Protococcus becomes actively locomotive. **1897** *Encycl. Sport* I. 129/2 (Bowls), *Still bowl*, a bowl at rest.

d. Of wine or a soft drink: Not sparkling or effervescing.

Chiefly used to designate a variety of one of those wines which have also a 'sparkling' variety, as champagne, hock, moselle. Used also of soft drinks, to distinguish them from the carbonated variety.

1777 P. THICKNESSE *Year's Journey* I. v. 31 The difference between still Champaigne, and that which is *mousser*, is owing to..the time of year in which it is bottled. **1833** REDDING *Mod. Wines* v. 71 Champagne wines are divided into sparkling.., demi sparkling.., and still wines (*non mousseux*). **1858** HAWTHORNE *Fr. & It. Jrnls.* (1871) II. 254 Wine..somewhat resembling still champagne, but finer. **1911** *Encycl. Brit.* XXVII. 724/1 The white growths of the Loire..up to 1834 were used only as still wines. **1949** *Acct. Soft Drinks Industry in Brit.* 1942-48 iii. 37 A number of beverages essential for some purpose, such as health..were excluded from the general restrictions... The list of these drinks included..sugar-free drinks for diabetics..and still spa waters. **1981** *Soft Drinks Rep.* I. 2 *Mineral and Bottled Water.* This includes natural spring water products which are either still or naturally or artificially sparkling. *Ibid.* II. 9, 2·5 billion litres of diluted still drink was consumed in 1980.

2. Silent.

†**a.** Predicatively of a person. ***to be (hold oneself) still***: to hold one's peace, refrain from speaking (*of* something). Also, † ***still of noise***. *Obs.*

a **1000** *Ags. Gosp.* Matt. xxii. 34 Þæt he het þa saduceiscan stylle beon [Vulg. *quod silentium imposuisset Sadducæis*]. *a* **1200** *Moral Ode* 112 Þe ðe lest wat biseið ofte mest; þe hit al wat is stille. *c* **1200** *Vices & Virtues* 11 Ðus ðu dedest, and ic was stille. *a* **1225** *Ancr. R.* 116 Ich am stille of þe more [*i.e.* I do not speak of the greater (offence)]. *a* **1225** *Leg. Kath.* 373 Stille beo þu þenne & stew swuche wordes. *c* **1275** *Passion our Lord* 253 in *O.E. Misc.*, Ihesuc hym wes stille, nolde heo nowyht speke. *a* **1300** *Cursor M.* 19994 Fra nu forward i will O þe apostels hald me still. *c* **1305** *St. Christopher* 165 in *E.E.P.* (1862) 64 þu miȝt, quaþ þis oþer: as wel beo stille. **1340** HAMPOLE *Pr. Consc.* 1388 *Ne sileas* [etc.]..þat es to say, be noght swa stille, þat [etc.]. *c* **1375** *Sc. Leg. Saints* xl. (*Ninian*) 665 þai held þame stil, þo þai wa ware, nedly for þai mycht nomare. **1382** WYCLIF *Matt.* xx. 31 Forsothe the cumpanye blamyde hem, for to be stille [Vulg. *ut tacerent*]. *c* **1386** CHAUCER *Knt.'s T.* 1677 (Hengwrt MS.) And whan he say the peple of noyse al stille Thus shewed he the myghty dukes wille. **1387-8** T. USK *Test. Love* I. viii. (Skeat) l. 67 Lo eke an olde proverbe amonges many other: He that is stille semeth as he graunted. *c* **1400** *Rule St. Benet* i. 4 Better es to be stille þan for to speke of þair lif. *a* **1425** tr. *Arderne's Treat. Fistula*, etc. 6 3if þou had bene stille thou had bene holden a philosophre. *a* **1500-20** DUNBAR *Poems* xli. 15 Be nocht of langage quhair ȝe suld be still. **1518** H. WATSON *Hist. Oliver of Castile* (Roxb.) K i b, Wherfore she helde her styll and sayd nothynge. *a* **1533** BERNERS *Huon* lxviii. 236 Better it is to shew the trouthe then to be styll. **1535** COVERDALE *Zech.* ii. 13 Let all flesh be still before the Lorde, for he is rysen out of his holy place. **1568** GRAFTON *Chron.* II. 794 All were still and muete, and not one worde aunswered to. **1590** SHAKS. *Com. Err.* III. ii. 69 Oh soft sir, hold you still. **1604** —— *Oth.* v. ii. 46 Peace, and be still.

b. Habitually silent, taciturn. Phrase, ***to keep a still tongue in one's head***.

1729 G. ADAMS tr. *Sophocles, Antig.* IV. i. II. 61 Lead me home, that he may..know how to keep a stiller Tongue, and ever be of a better Mind than now he is. **1855** KINGSLEY *Westw. Ho!* xv, He was a very still man, much as a mass-priest might be. **1859** GEO. ELIOT *Adam Bede* xxiii, I'll tell you what I know, because I believe you can keep a still tongue in your head if you like. **1859** TENNYSON *Grandm.* 13 Strong on his hands, and strong on his legs, but still of his tongue! **1869** HAZLITT *Eng. Prov.* 35 A still tongue makes a wise head. **1870** E. PEACOCK *Ralf Skirl.* I. 112 I'm a strange still chap mysen. **1890** W. A. WALLACE *Only a Sister* 328 He was a rare man John, a rare still 'un.

†**c.** *Prov.* (Very common in 16-17th c.) *Obs.*

c **1200** *Prov.* in *MS. Rawlinson* C. 641 lf. 13b/1 Sistille suȝe fret þere grunninde mete. **1546** J. HEYWOOD *Prov.* (1867) 22 The still sowe eats vp all the draffe Ales. **1598** SHAKS. *Merry W.* IV. ii. 109 'Tis old, but true, Still Swine eats all the draugh. **1611** FLORIO, *Acqua queta*,..a close, slie, lurking knaue, a stil sow as we say.

3. a. Of a voice, sounds, utterances: Subdued, soft, not loud. Now *arch.* (Chiefly after *1 Kings* xix. 12.)

c **1000** ÆLFRIC *Hom.* II. 410 Ðine æhta mid stylre stemne wyllað þe wreȝan to ð inum Drihtne. *a* **1225** *Leg. Kath.* 2005 Heo..cleopede toward heouene,..wið stille steuene [etc.]. *a* **1300** *Floriz & Bl.* (Camb. MS.) 37 To hire louerd heo sede wiþ stille dreme, 'Sire,' [etc.]. **13..** *K. Alis.* 7458 (Laud MS.), Alisaunder makeþ a stille cry. **13..** *Coer de L.* 177 She answeryd with wordys stylle, 'Sere, I am at my faderys wylle.' **1502** ATKYNSON tr. *De Imitatione* III. i. 195 The eris that here the styll spekynge or rownynge of almyghty god. *a* **1500-20** DUNBAR *Poems* xlii. 47 Sayand till hir with wirdis still [etc.]. **1531** TINDALE *Exp. 1 John* (1537) 87 The preste prayeth in latyne and sayeth euermore a styll Masse, as we saye. 1535 COVERDALE *1 Kings* xix. 12 After the fyre came there a styll softe hyssinge [1611 a still small voice]. 1585 HIGINS *Junius' Nomencl.* 358/1 *Susurrus*,..a soft or still noise, as of waters, falling with a gentle streame, or of leaues from trees. 1607 TOPSELL *Four-f. Beasts* 138 The louder and shriller voice of a Dogge, is called barking, the lower and stiller is called whining, or fawning. 1675 J. SMITH *Chr. Relig. Appeal* 100 To tune the still voice of the Gospel to the shrill tones of the Law. *c* 1750 GRAY *Elegy* Omitted Stanza (Mason MS.), In still small Accents whisp'ring from the Ground A grateful Earnest of eternal Peace. 1769 —— *Ode for Music* 6 Sweeter yet The still small voice of Gratitude. *a* 1777 *Transl. & Paraphr.* XXIII. iii, Gentle and still shall be his voice. 1788 GIBBON *Decl. & F.* lxix. III. 524 The still voice of law and reason was seldom heard or obeyed. 1811 SHELLEY *St. Irvyne* III. ix. 5 And, from the black hill, Went a voice cold and still. 1847 C. BRONTË *Jane Eyre* II. iv. 101 Strong wind, earthquake, shock, and fire may pass by: I shall follow the guiding..of that still small voice which interprets the dictates of conscience. 1874 J. G. WHITTIER *Poet. Wks.* 458/1 Speak through the earthquake, wind and fire, O still, small voice of calm! 1918 L. STRACHEY *Eminent Victorians* 64 In such a situation the voice of self-abnegation must needs grow still and small indeed. 1953 P. C. BERG *Dict. New Words in English* 14 The still small voice of Professor Bryant..has a few good words to say in favour of these 'abominations'. 1983 *Daily Tel.* 25 Mar. 20/5 If it is not too late, may a still small voice be allowed to publicise a fact not yet revealed by either the protagonists or critics of the Budget?

†b. *esp.* of music; hence of instruments, performers, etc. *Obs.*

1541 in *Vicary's Anat.* (1888) App. XII. 242 To the stille minstrelles, in rewarde iiij li. 1575 GASCOIGNE *Jocasta* v. Order of last Dumb Shewe, First the Stillpipes sounded a very mournful melody. 1595 T. EDWARDS *Narcissus* (Roxb.) 40 Some with Still musicke, some with pleasing songes Some with coye smiles, [etc.]. 1600 SHAKS. *A.Y.L.* v. iv. 113 stage-dir., Enter Hymen, Rosalind and Celia. Still Musick. 1602 MARSTON *Antonio's Rev.* IV. iii. stage-dir., ¶The still flutes sound softly. *a* 1639 T. CAREW *A Rapture* Poems (1651) 66 The gentle blasts of Western winds shall..breath Still Musick. 1642 FULLER *Holy & Prof. St.* IV. xv. 318 Yet spake she very little to any, sighing out more then she said, and making still musick to God in her heart. *a* 1645 MILTON *Passion* 28 Me softer airs befit, and softer strings Of Lute, or Viol still. 1658 ROWLAND tr. *Moufet's Theat. Ins.* 931 As still musick is sweeter then the loud. 1738 WESLEY *Hymns* 'Hark, dull Soul, how every Thing' iv, All the Flowers that paint the Spring Hither their still Musick bring. 1816 SHELLEY *Hymn Intell. Beauty* 34 Music by the night-wind sent Through strings of some still instrument.

†c. Secret. *Obs.*

c 1205 LAY. 4496 Stille boc runen heo senden him to ræden. 1303 R. BRUNNE *Handl. Synne* 5958 Ȝyf þou boghtest of any seriaunt pryuyly, yn stylle cunnaunt, þyng þat þou wystyst wel was stole. *a* 1450 *Le Morte Arthur* 3860 The bysshope..shrove hym..Off All hys synnes loude and stylle. 1647 H. MORE *Song of Soul, Notes Psychozoia* 349 It is inconceivable that the least motions of the mind, or stillest thought should escape her.

4. Free from commotion.

a. Of water: Having an unruffled surface, without waves or violent current; motionless or flowing imperceptibly.

a 1000 *Riddles* iii. 14 þonne streamas eft stille weorþað. 1390 GOWER *Conf.* II. 102 A stille water for the nones Rennende upon the smale stones. 1610 HOLLAND *Camden's Brit.* (1637) 699 Wherf..becometh more still, and so gently intermingleth his water with Ouse. 1735 SOMERVILLE *Chase* IV. 381 Where ancient Alders shade The deep still Pool. 1784 COWPER *Task* VI. 929 Stillest streams Oft water fairest meadows. 1803 WORDSW. *Yarrow unvisited* 43 Let..The swan on still St. Mary's Lake Float double, swan and shadow. 1834 MRS. SOMERVILLE *Connex. Phys. Sci.* xiii. (1849) 110 A stone plunged into a pool of still water. 1847 H. MILLER *Test. Rocks* viii. (1857) 337 While other fresh water fishes, such as the tench and carp, are reared most successfully in still reedy ponds.

Prov. 1791 SCOTT *Let.* in *Lockhart* (1837) I. vi. 183 Though he makes no noise about feelings, yet still streams always run deepest. 1852 MRS. STOWE *Uncle Tom's C.* xxvii, '"Still waters run deepest," they used to tell me,' said Miss Ophelia oracularly. 1895 'G. PASTON' *Study in Prejudices* xiii, Hers was a case of 'Still waters run deep'.

b. Of the air, weather: Free from commotion, quiet. Of rain: Unattended by wind, gentle.

1390 GOWER *Conf.* I. 371 For the weder stille Men preise, and blame the tempestes. *c* 1500 *Melusine* xx. 107 Wel fole is he that fighteth ayenst the wynd, wenyng to make hym be styll. 1632 MILTON *Penseroso* 127 Or usher'd with a shower still, When the gust hath blown his fill. 1642 FULLER *Holy & Prof. St.* I. x. 24 But our widows sorrow is no storm but a still rain. 1795–6 WORDSW. *Borderers* II. 25 The moon shone clear, the air was still, so still The trees were silent as the graves beneath them. 1797 MRS. RADCLIFFE *Italian* xii, As it came upon the still air and descended towards the cloudless heavens. 1829 *Chapters Phys. Sci.* 296 When he has been walking in still weather on the brink of a lake. 1859 TENNYSON *Merlin & V.* 1 A storm was coming, but the winds were still. 1908 [Miss E. FOWLER] *Betw. Trent & Ancholme* 313 The air is strangely still.

†c. Quiet, gentle in disposition; meek. ***still and bold*** (absol.), men of whatever temper. *Obs.*

c 825 *Vesp. Psalter* lxxv. 10 Alle stille eorðan [Vulg. *omnes quietos terræ*]. *c* 1000 in *Sax. Leechd.* III. 430 Heo wæs..on eallum þingum eaðmod & stille. *c* 1200 ORMIN 1177 Forr shep iss all unnskaþefull & stille der & liþe. *c* 1300 *Havelok* 955 Him loueden alle, stille and bolde. *c* 1300 *Leg. Gregory* (Schulz) 173 þo sche held hir stille and milde, Hir sorwe was strong and sterne. *c* 1460 SIR R. ROS *La Belle Dame* 656 For þai be not rebell, bot still as stone.

d. Settled, unperturbed in mind. † Also, in mystical language, said of one that has attained to freedom from passion.

1340–70 *Alex. & Dind.* 940 Stoute is he, stedefast & stille of his herte. *a* 1400 *Minor Poems fr. Vernon MS.* xxiii. 651 Heil, whos deore sone stod In þe Synagoge of goddes And iuged þer wiþ stille mood Princis. 1741 WESLEY *Jrnl.* 12 Feb., Others..who had constantly affirmed 'That Mr. Charles Wesley was *still* already, and would come to London no more.' 1858 G. MACDONALD *Phantastes* xv. 196 My soul was not still enough for songs.

5. a. In mixed sense of 2 and 4. Of places, times, conditions: Characterized by absence of noise and movement; silent, quiet, calm.

c 1205 LAY. 25481 Ah al hit wes stille in hirede and in halle. 13.. *E.E. Allit. P.* B. 1203 þay stel out on a stylle nyȝt er any steuen rysed. 1525 tr. *Brunswyke's Handywork Surg.* lix. N iv, Then shall the pacyent be layde in a styl place where he may haue rest. 1585 HIGINS *Junius' Nomencl.* 375/1 The dead or stil time of the night. 1598 SHAKS. *Merry W.* IV. iv. 28 That Herne the Hunter..Doth..at still midnight Walke round about an Oake. 1611 —— *Cymb.* v. iv. 69 For this, from stiller Seats we came. 1632 MILTON *Penseroso* 78 Som still removed place will fit. 1667 —— *P.L.* IV. 598 Now came still Eevning on. *a* 1722 LISLE *Husb.* (1757) 29 It must be spread the first still day. 1770 G. WHITE *Selborne, Let. to Barrington* 8 Oct., Swallows and house-martins abound yet, induced to prolong their stay by this soft, still, dry season. 1794 MRS. RADCLIFFE *Myst. Udolpho* xv, And oft at midnight's stillest hour, When summer seas the vessel lave. 1816 SHELLEY *Mont Blanc* 44 In the still cave of the witch Poesy. 1816 BYRON *Ch. Har.* III. lxxxix, All heaven and earth are still—though not in sleep. 1849 FROUDE *Nemesis of Faith* 194 The room was deathly still; no sound but the heavy breathing of the child, [etc.]. 1855 TENNYSON *Maud* II. v. 70 She comes from another stiller world of the dead. 1884 W. C. SMITH *Kildrostan* 34 You've seen the Loch, on some still evening, Mirror each stone.

†b. Of a mode of life: Quiet, uneventful, dull.

1706 ADDISON *Epil. to Ld. Lansdowne's Brit. Enchanters* 14 Scenes of still Life, and Points for ever fix'd, A tedious Pleasure to the Mind bestow. 1710 FELTON *Diss. Classics* (1718) 223 The stiller Scenes of Life. 1748 RICHARDSON *Clarissa* VII. 327 What a cursed still-life this! 1781 COWPER *Retirem.* 746 Yet neither these delights, nor aught beside.. Can save us always from a tedious day, Or shine the dulness of still life away.

c. *contextually* (*poet.*) = That has become still; no longer active or audible.

c 1485 *E.E. Misc.* (Warton Club) 1 The byrd was go; my joy was stylle, For woo, alasse! myselffe I spylle. 1742 GRAY *Spring* 21 Still is the toiling hand of Care. 1822 SHELLEY tr. *Calderon's Mag. Prodig.* II. 95 Since the fury Of this earthquaking hurricane is still. 1842 TENNYSON *Break, Break* 12 O for the touch of a vanish'd hand, And the sound of a voice that is still!

†6. Of a child: Dead before birth. Cf. STILLBORN. *Obs. rare*$^{-1}$.

1607 TOPSELL *Four-f. Beasts* 433 The milk of a Mare being drunk..doth cause a still childe to bee cast forth.

†7. Constant, continual; continued until now.

1570 LEVINS *Manip.* 124/4 Stil, *iugis, continuus.* 1588 SHAKS. *Titus A.* III. ii. 45 But I (of these) will wrest an Alphabet, And by still practice, learne to know thy meaning. 1594 —— *Rich. III*, IV. iv. 229 But that still vse of greefe makes wilde greefe tame. 1615 CHAPMAN *Odyss.* XVII. 711 Of Vlysses (where the Thesprots dwell,..) Fame, he sayes, did tell The still suruiuall.

8. *Comb.* **still-air** *a.*, (*a*) *Aeronaut.*, applicable or calculated for a state of no wind; (*b*) not employing forced draught; **still-bait** *U.S.*, bait for still-baiting; **still-baiting** *U.S.* (see quot. 1859); **still-fishing** = *still-baiting*; **still-footed** *a.*, with silent tread; **still-vaulting**, vaulting without a run.

1913 *Captain* Sept. 1072/2 A machine with *still-air speed of 57 miles per hour was sent up to fight a gale for 400 yds. 1948 *Jrnl. R. Aeronaut. Soc.* LII. 600/2 We often read..of two aircraft of widely varying characteristics being compared over similar still-air ranges. 1951 'N. SHUTE' *Round Bend* vi. 177 She had tankage for twelve hundred gallons, giving her a still-air range of about two thousand miles. 1960 *Farmer & Stockbreeder* 19 Jan. 108/1 Game birds are not..easy to hatch..in the big cabinet..machines. .. Reasonably good results, on a small scale,..can be got from the more old-fashioned still-air machines. 1961 P. W. BROOKS *Mod. Airliner* iv. 100 A payload of 6,000 lb. was required for a still-air range of 3,500 miles. 1977 *Shooting Times & Country Mag.* 13–19 Jan. 26/2 Small incubators —those that take 100–200 pheasant eggs—are nearly always the 'still air' type and depend on convection currents for ensuring air movement. 1888 GOODE *Amer. Fishes* 58 The angler finds them at the proper seasons equally eager for fly-hook, trolling-spoon, or *still-bait. 1859 BARTLETT *Dict. Amer.* (ed. 2) 451 **Still-baiting*, fishing with a deep line in one spot, as distinguished from trolling. 1897 *Encycl. Sport* I. 82/2 (Bass) *Still-fishing. 1894 *Outing* XXIII. 395/1 The fox comes trotting, *still-footed, along this avenue. 1854 G. ROLAND *Gymnastics* 28 Every young person who has seen what is called '*still-vaulting' at Ducrow's.

B. *sb.*[2]

†1. A calm, *lit.* and *fig.* *Obs.*

a 1225 *Ancr. R.* 376 *Quia post tempestatem tranquillum facit*..þat is, iblesced beo þu, Louerd, þet makest stille efter storme. 1615 BACON *Charge agst. O. St. John* Wks. 1778 II. 588 There is no better sign of *omnia bene*, than when the court is in a still. *a* 1626 —— *Hen. VIII* in *Consid. War Spain* (1629) 164 He had neuer any the least..Difference.. with the King his Father, which might giue any occasion of altering Court or Counsell vpon the change; but all things passed in a Still. 1626 —— *Sylva* §193 The Vnequall Agitation of the Winds, and the like,..make them to be heard lesse Way, than in a Still.

2. Stillness, quiet. Now only *poet.* or *rhetorical.*

1608 TOPSELL *Serpents* 99 In the still of the night, when euery one besides were at rest. 1810 SCOTT *Lady of L.* III. xxvi, No murmur waked the solemn still, Save tinkling of a fountain rill. 1830 W. PHILLIPS *Mt. Sinai* I. 512 A still of limb and lip Hush'd all his brethren. 1900 N. MUNRO in *Blackw. Mag.* Oct. 449/2 His ear had not grown accustomed to the still of the valleys.

†3. A still pool. *Obs.*

1681 CHETHAM *Angler's Vade-m.* xxxiii. (1689) 179 You may Dib with the Green-drake both in Streams, and Stills.

4. *Shetland.* (See quot.) [Perh. f. STILL *v.*]

1844 W. H. MAXWELL *Scotland* xiii. (1855) 118 A brief lull occurs at high water, and is termed by Shetlanders 'the still.'

†5. *slang.* A still-born child; a still-birth. *Obs.*

1864 HOTTEN *Slang Dict.* 247 *Stills*, the undertaker's Slang term for still-born children. 1897 [see MISS *sb.*[4]].

6. a. An ordinary photograph, as distinguished from a motion picture; *spec.* a single shot from a film (or a specially posed photograph of a scene from it) for use in advertising. Freq. with defining word, as ***cinema still, film still***, etc.

1916 *Independent* 5 June 86 (*caption*) A striking 'still' from the film 'The Fall of a Nation'. 1922 *Glasgow Herald* 12 Oct. 6 Mr Johnson succeeded in exposing 25,000 feet of film and in taking some 1000 'stills'. 1938 *Archit. Rev.* LXXXIII. *caption facing* p. 72 Two aspects of a turbulent age are seen in 'The Temple of Janus',..wherein the figures of the Furies are attested as in a cinema 'still'. 1945 H. READ *Coat of Many Colours* xxix. 142 We may select 'stills' for their closed form—for their pictorial composition—but the film itself is essentially open form. 1957 *Times* 25 Nov. 11/3 The story of that enchanting film *The Red Balloon* illustrated with film stills and with a photographic cover in colour. 1962 E. SNOW *Red China Today* (1963) xv. 109 McDermott and I used our Canons taking stills. 1972 C. WESTON *Poor, Poor Ophelia* (1973) xxvi. 164 The photo was a standard publicity still. 1976 *Oxf. Compan. Film* 66/1 *Frame stills* are reproductions of single frames from the film itself... They convey the true feeling of a film more exactly than can a posed production still. 1978 'A. GARVE' *Counterstroke* I. 88 George had brought along a full-face 'still' of Lacy.

b. *attrib.* (as *sing.* or *pl.*).

1922 *Opportunities in Motion Picture Industry* (Photoplay Research Society) 47 Ask the first director you meet where you can find the still man. *Ibid.* 48 Still pictures are made for the publicity department. *Ibid.* 50 Seldom are the many lights placed for the movie camera exactly suited to the still camera. *Ibid.*, The still cameraman is of necessity a versatile flea. 1925 R. BEETHAM in E. F. Norton *Fight for Everest 1924* 324 His time was so fully taken up with cinema work that most of the still photography had to be done by other members of the party. 1928 [see *news-reel* s.v. NEWS *sb.* (*pl.*) 6 c]. 1963 *Movie* July/Aug. 27/4 The still pictures have greater effect than the newsreel shots. 1964 C. WILLOCK *Enormous Zoo* ix. 165 Roger spent one whole afternoon trying to get the moment of entry and exit from the sandstone burrow with a stills camera. 1964 M. MCLUHAN *Understanding Media* II. xx. 193 The physical and psychic *gestalts*, or 'still' shots, with which they [*sc.* Freud and Jung] worked were much owing to the posture world revealed by the photograph. 1974 *Times* 16 Nov. 10/6 It was through stills photographs that the public were first introduced..to the stars. *Ibid.* 10/7 The stills men would retouch the negative. 1974 M. TAYLOR tr. *Metz's Film Lang.* i. 12 Rudolf Arnheim recognises that..still photography produces an impression of reality much weaker than that of the cinema. 1981 *Gossip* (Holiday Special) 54/3, I met her on a film I did a while back. She was the still photographer.

7. *Naut.* An instruction to cease work and stand to attention conveyed to a ship's crew by the boatswain's pipe.

1933 'L. LUARD' *All Hands* 140 Pipe the still, Cox'un. 1963 [see PIPE-DOWN].

still (stɪl), *v.*[1] *Pa. t.* and *pa. pple.* **stilled** (stɪld). Forms: 1 **stillan, styllan**, 3–5 **stille**, 5–6 **stylle**, 5–7 **stil**, 6 **styll**, 4– **still**. [OE. *stillan*, cogn. w. OS. (*gi*)*stillian* trans., *stillon* intr. (LG., Du. *stillen*), OHG. *stillen* trans., *stillên* intr. (MHG., mod.G. *stillen* trans. and intr.), to make or become still, ON. *stilla* to soothe, calm, to temper, moderate, tune, *intr.* to walk with measured noiseless steps (Sw. *stilla*, Da. *stille*) related to WGer. **stilljo*- STILL *a.*] To make or become still. (Very common in 16–17th c.; now chiefly *poet.* and *rhetorical.*)

I. *trans.* (In OE. sometimes with dative.)

1. To quiet, calm (waves, winds, etc.).

a 1000 *Andreas* 451 Engla eadgifa yðum stilde. *a* 1175 *Cott. Hom.* 229 He ȝestilde windes mid his hesne. *c* 1425 *Eng. Conq. Ireland* xlix. 126 & so the grete tempeste of that weddyr hape yn lytel whyle was I-queynt & I-stylled. 1535 COVERDALE *Ps.* lxxxix. 9 Thou rulest the pryde of the see, thou stillest the wawes therof, when they arise. 1634 MILTON *Comus* 87 A Swaine..Who with his soft Pipe.. Well knows to still the wilde winds when they roar. *c* 1639 SIR W. MURE *Ps.* cvii. 30 He..brings them glade, (the tempest stild,) To their desyred heawen. 1720 POPE *Iliad* XVIII. 481 Wide with distorted Legs, oblique he goes, And stills the Bellows. 1782 PRIESTLEY *Corrupt. Chr.* I. IV. 398 Power..to still winds and tempests. 1839 LONGF. *Wreck Hesperus* 55 And she thought of Christ, who stilled the wave On the Lake of Galilee. 1856 ROSSETTI *Blessed Damozel* 4 Her eyes knew more of rest and shade Than waters still'd at even. 1871 R. ELLIS *Catullus* xlvi. 3 Now doth Zephyrus.. Still the boisterous equinoctial heaven. 1881 W. BLACK *Beautiful Wretch* I. 166 The hot sun had stilled the water.

b. In fig. context.

1786 MME. D'ARBLAY *Diary* 10 Aug., This undid all again, though my explanation had just stilled the hurricane. 1810 SHELLEY *Marg. Nicholson, Despair* 14 Awhile it stills the tide of agony. 1840 A. CARSON *Hist. Providence* 388 He suffers the fury of the enemy to swell against his cause, but he stills it at his pleasure. 1868 HELPS *Realmah* vi. (1876) 118 Whom they stood aloof from only to break and still the opposing waves of popular opinion. 1903 MORLEY *Gladstone* IX. i. III. 220 The surface was thus stilled for the moment, yet the waters ran very deep.

c. To subdue, allay (sedition, tumult).

1570 LEVINS *Manip.* 123/37 To stil a trouble, *quietare, sedare.* 1770 LANGHORNE *Plutarch* II. 253 But Timoleon stilled the tumult, by representing, That [etc.]. 1868

Nettleship Ess. Browning vi. 196 Who like Saturn stilled the tumult and took throne supreme.

2. To relieve (pain); to assuage, allay (an appetite, desire).

c 1000 Sax. Leechd. II. 59 þæt stilð þam sare. 1387–8 T. Usk Test. Love III. vii. (Skeat) l. 36 Thus have I stilled my disese; thus have I covered my care. 1657 Trapp Comm., Esther iii. 1 Honour is but..a glorious fancie, a rattle to still mens ambition. 1856 Trench Serm. Camb. ii. (1857) 43 He tries..to still, or at least to deaden, the undying pain of his spirit. 1876 Geo. Eliot Deronda liv, But what can still that hunger of the heart which sickens the eye for beauty..? 1882 Rep. Prec. Metals U.S. 539 This thirst for land being stilled, we may count upon a greater stability in the number of miners.

†3. To keep back, repress, desist or refrain from (words, tears); to keep (one's tongue) still. *Obs.*

a 1225 Leg. Kath. 1530 Stute nu þenne, & stew þe, & stille þine wordes. a 1225 Ancr. R. 186 Þet child is wel ipaied..& stilleð his teares. c 1374 Chaucer Troylus II. 230 Yet were it bet my tonge for to stille Than sey a soth þat were a-yens youre wylle. c 1400 Rule St. Benet (1902) 51 Proibe linguam tuam a malo—In þe begining, still þi tung, And spek no uyl of ald na ȝong. c 1430 Syr Gener. (Roxb.) 307 Sore weping he coud nat stil.

4. To quiet, calm (a person's mind); to subdue (agitation, emotion); †*refl.* to compose oneself.

c 1250 Gen. & Ex. 3924 And sente after balaam ðe prest, Wið riche men and giftes oc, for to stillen hise [vn-]eðe mod. 1382 Wyclif Gen. xliii. 31 He..stillide hym self [Vulg. continuit se]. 1390 Gower Conf. III. 363 Sche wolde noght hirselven stille, Bot deide only for drede of schame. c 1400 Beryn 2565 Stillith ȝewe, quod Geffrey. c 1475 Partenay 2969 Geffray thaim said, 'stil you, noght dismay'. 1610 Shaks. Temp. IV. 163 A turne or two, Ile walke To still my beating minde. 1818 Shelley Rosal. & Helen 874, I stilled the tingling of my blood. 1828 Lytton Pelham lxx, With this reflection, I stilled the beating of my heart.

b. To appease (anger).

c 1290 Beket 511 in S. Eng. Leg. 121 Þo..radden him wende to þe kinge is wraþþe for-to stille. 1535 Coverdale Esther vii. 10 Then was the kynges wrath styled. 1891 Farrar Darkn. & Dawn lxiv, Nero stood amazed—his wrath stilled before so majestic an indifference.

†5. To pacify, induce to desist from complaint or opposition. *Obs.*

a 1300 Cursor M. 13075 To sla him was he noght in will, Bot for þat wicked wijf to still. c 1489 Caxton Sonnes of Aymon xix. 408 Reynawde was wyse and well taughte for to stylle thus hys bretherne, to whome he sayd, [etc.]. 1534 Tindale Rom. Prol. 190 This fredome..ministreth that which the lawe requyreth, and where with the lawe is fulfilled, that is to vnderstond, luste and loue, where with the lawe is styllled and accuseth vs no moare. 1647 N. Bacon Disc. Govt. Eng. I. xlvii. 130 It was but a noise to still the Clergy.

†6. To lull, soothe (a child); to induce (a person) to cease from weeping. *Obs.*

c 1315 Shoreham Poems vi. 65 Ine þe hys god by-come a chyld;..þou hast y-tamed [hyt], and i-styld Wyþ melke of þy breste. a 1400 Isumbras 199 Nowther of tham myghte other stille, Thaire sorowe it was fulle ranke! c 1400 Pilgr. Sowle IV. i. (1483) 58 He wald styllen the child with some maner of comfortable myrthe of recreacion. c 1440 Bone Flor. 831 Allas, sche seyde, that y was borne!.. Ther myght no man hur stylle. 1530 Palsgr. 736/1 Go styll the chylde, nourice, you wyll be shente els. 1545 Ascham Toxoph. (Arb.) 42 Euen the little babes..are scarce so well stilled in suckyng theyr mothers pap, as in hearynge theyr mothers syng. 1599 Shaks. Much Ado III. iii. 70. 1660 F. Brooke tr. Le Blanc's Trav. 263 He..would still his Nephews when they cryed with plums.

7. To silence, cause (a sound) to cease. Also *fig.* to cause the cessation of (murmurs, complaints, etc.).

1390 Gower Conf. III. 138 The softe word the loude stilleth. c 1430 How Gd. Wife taught Dau. 37 in Babees Bk., A sclaundre reisid ille Is yuel for to stille. 1623 J. Taylor (Water P.) Honour Conceal'd Wks. (1630) III. 124/2 And therefore 'twas ordain'd that thou shouldst come To hang the Colours vp, and still the Drum. 1631 R. Bolton Comf. Affl. Consc. xvi. (1635) 314 Earthly pleasures may for the present still the noyse of an accusing conscience. 1663 Patrick Parab. Pilgrim (1687) 365 In this manner he quieted and still'd all its grumblings. 1671 Milton P.R. IV. 428 Morning..Who with her radiant finger still'd the roar Of thunder, chas'd the clouds, and laid the winds. 1690 W. Walker Idiomat. Anglo-Lat. 143, I'll still your din, i.e. make you hold your tongue. 1738 Wesley Psalms XCIII. iii, The Floods, O Lord, lift up their Voice,..But God above can still their Noise. 1820 Scott Monast. xxxvii, There was a deep and solemn pause. The monks stilled their chant. 1820 Keats Isabella xlvii, Those dainties made to still an infant's cries. 1821–30 Ld. Cockburn Mem. iv. (1874) 213 The murmur..used to be stilled when this image stuck its awful head through the lofty orifice. 1835 Lytton Rienzi II. iii, The murmurs of the people were stilled. 1887 J. Payn Holiday Tasks 206 We stilled our scruples by reflecting that it was very mean of the victim [etc.].

†b. To cause (a person) to be silent; to impose silence on (an assembly); to put to silence (an objector). *Obs.*

c 1400 Destr. Troy 3519 The kyng þen comaund to..fetur hir fast in a fre prisoune,..to still hir of noise. 1608 Willet Hexapla. Exod. 753 Aaron sinned..in not staying the people and stilling them. 1611 Bible Num. xiii. 30 And Caleb stilled the people before Moses. 1654 Whitlock Zootomia 211 But it may be, according to my Assertion, his Name will sooner still opposers than his Reasons. 1665 Brathwait Comm. Two Tales 199 Which Answer still'd this Censor, and justified the Author.

†8. To check the turbulence of (a person); to compel to cease. *Obs.*

1300–1400 R. Glouc. (Rolls) App. xx. 507 He gan to stryue To ȝenst his owene fadere, god stilde him in þis So þat raþer þane he ded he was ywis. c 1450 Lovelich Grail xlii. 345 Eche Oþer wold han slayn In that plas ȝif they ne hadde I-stilled be. 1602 tr. Guarini's Pastor Fido IV. vi. M 1 b, O glorious child of great Alcides race, That monsters stilst, and wild Beastes doth deface.

†b. To 'quiet' by killing or stunning. ? *slang.*

1778 Anburey Trav. (1789) II. 167 We will suppose, he only orders them to knock a man down, or to prick him, or still him.

9. In occasional uses: To stop the movement or activity of.

1850 Tennyson In Mem. VI. iii, O father,.. Who pledgest now thy gallant son; A shot, ere half thy draught be done, Hath still'd the life that beat from thee. 1861 Temple Bar III. 433 To disuse cotton wholly, to still the British cotton-factories. 1866 Mrs. H. Wood St. Martin's Eve i, She stilled her feet and stared at the speaker. 1867 Augusta Wilson Vashti xiv, [She] struggled to steady her voice and still the twitching tell-tale muscles about her mouth.

II. 10. *intr.* To become still or calm.

a 900 Martyrol. 11 Nov., Ða stylde se storm sona, and seo sæ wearð eft smylte. 1695 Sibbald Autobiog. (1834) 128 When I cryed and weept upon any occasion I stilled upon the giving me the Psalms of Buchanan. 1798 W. Taylor in Monthly Mag. VI. 366 Slow beams the blooming dawn as stills the strife. Hence, down the winding stairs. a 1851 Moir Ruined Nunnery ii, At length the winds began to still. a 1853 Robertson Lect. ii. (1858) 67 The surges stilled below him, and the last cloud drifted from the sky above. 1888 Harper's Mag. Apr. 737 The sea only swayed a little, and stilled again. 1898 H. Calderwood Hume viii. 153 The worst storm stills at length.

†b. To remain still or quiet; to keep silence.

c 1330 R. Brunne Chron. Wace (Rolls) 11749 When þei were stilled a party, ffirst spak sire Ohel. a 1340 Hampole Psalter xxvii. 1 Deus meus, ne sileas a me..my god still not fra me. Ibid. xxxi. 3 For i stilled eldid my banes. 1450 Paston Lett. I. 180 Heruppon the people peacyd, and stilled unto the tyme the shire was doone. 1483 Cath. Angl. 364/1 To Stil[l]e, tacere.

c. To sound softly.

1900 N. Munro Doom Castle x, A bagpipe stilled in the hall, a lute breathed a melody from a neighbouring room.

still (stɪl), *v.*² Forms: 5–6 stille, 5–7 styll(e, 6 styl, 6–7 stil, (*Pa. t.* and *pa. pple.* stild), 7 stile, 6– still. [Aphetic form of distil *v.*]

†1. *intr.* To trickle down or fall in minute drops: = distil *v.* 1. *Obs.*

a 1300 K. Horn 676 (Camb. MS.) For Rymenhild weop ille, & horn let þe tires stille. c 1407 Lydg. Reason & Sens. 6307 Eke her stremys cristallyn That fro her chekys stylle doun Kam al of deuocioun. c 1450 Burgh Secrees 1861 Watir is profitable..neer to Citees stillyng as perlys Rounde. c 1470 Henryson Mor. Fab. VIII. (Preach. Swallow) ix, With heit and moysture stilland frome the sky. 1526 R. Whytford Martiloge 114 b, Whan the abbot was buryed, oyle stylled out of his graue. 1534 Elyot Cast. Helthe II. xxvii. (1541) 43 b, So that he drinke not a greate glutte, but in a littell quantitee, let it stil downe softly into his stomacke, as he sitteth. 1549–62 Sternhold & H. Ps. cii. 9 And mingled haue [I] my drink with teares that fro mine eyes haue still. 1560 Bible (Geneva) Deut. xxxii. 2 My speache shal stil as doeth the dewe. 1590 Spenser F.Q. III. ii. 29 If that any drop of slombring rest Did chaunce to still into her weary spright. 1596 Lodge Wits Miserie P j b, Lying continually on my backe, water stilleth vpon mine eies, yet I for sloth sake forsake not my bed. c 1690 Archibald in Macfarlane's Geogr. Collect. (S.H.S.) III. 189 The Water stills down into the Pit, wherewith they then fill their Pans.

†b. Of a person: To melt *into* tears. *Obs.*

1412–20 Lydg. Troy Bk. IV. 3614 And in-to terys he gan stille and reyne, As he wolde for verray sorwe deye.

†2. *trans.* To exude, discharge, or give forth in minute drops. *Obs.*

1412–1530 Myrr. our Ladye (1873) 285 The braunches of the bawlme tree when they are cutte, they stylle moste vertuous and swete lyquore. 1526 Pilgr. Perf. (W. de W. 1531) 183 Whiche neuer ceased to styll the swete balme of mercy & pite. 1610 Heywood Golden Age III. i, With rage and fury fright pale Pity hence, And drown him in the sweat your bodies still. 1646 Crashaw Steps, Another on Death Herrys 35 Wet with teares still'd from the eyes Of the flinty Destinyes. a 1660 Contemp. Hist. Irel. (Ir. Archæol. Soc.) II. 60 More reason should perswade me to doe it, then Dido the queene dowager of Cartagh to stile continually waterie pearles from her charminge lookes for the absence of Eneas. 1693 Dryden Juvenal iii. 122 His once unkem'd, and horrid Locks, behold, Stilling sweet Oyl.

†b. To cause to distil or fall in drops. *Obs.*

1576 Baker Gesner's Jewell of Health 131 b, If you styll one drop into the water. 1598 Sylvester Du Bartas II. ii. IV. Columnes 703 For you my smoothest quill His sweetest hony on this Book should still. c 1611 Chapman Iliad XIX. 36 She, with her faire hand, still'd into, the nostrils of his friend, Red Nectar, and Ambrosia. 1624 Quarles Job Milit. xvii. N 2, He pricks the Clouds, stils downe the raine by drops. 1719 D'Urfey Pills IV. 74 A Morn of May, which drops of Dew down stilleth.

†c. *fig.* To instil. *Obs.*

1551 Udall Erasm. Par. Matt. iii. 1 That the thyng whiche euer should be beleued, might by lytle and lytle be stilled [1548 instylled] and put into the hartes of men.

3. To subject to the process of distillation: = distil *v.* 4. Now *rare* or *Obs.*

a 1400 Stockh. Med. MS. ii. 455 in Anglia XVIII. 318 Do stille þese erbes be hemselwe. c 1450 ME. Med. Bk. (Heinrich) 102 After stille hem in a stillatorye. 1573 Tusser Husb. (1878) 96 Herbes to still in Sommer. 1646 Quarles Judgem. & Mercy (1651) 1 My recreations shall be to still Pleasure into a Quintessence. 1647 R. Josselin Diary (Camden 1908) 42 Wee had plenty of roses; stilled some May 22. 1694 Crowne Married Beau IV. 52, I'll see.. Whether it be a Flower or a Weed, Which you are stilling in this Limbeck here. c 1770 Mrs. Glasse Compl. Confectioner 274 Then still them in a limbeck with a slow fire, and take care your still does not burn.

†b. *transf.* To extract the essence of (meat). Also *intr.* of the meat. *Obs.*

1584 Cogan Haven Health clvii. 133 When it hath stilled so many houres, then take out the earthen pot,..streine out the broth [etc.]. 1591 A. W. Bk. Cookrye 11 b, To still a cock for a weake body that is consumed. Take a red Cock that is not too olde, and beate him to death, and..fley him and quarter him in small peeces [etc.].

4. To extract or produce by distillation. *Obs.*

a 1400 Stockh. Med. MS. ii. 448 in Anglia XVIII. 318 To styllyn [þer]of water for eyne is good. 1483 Cath. Angl. 364/2 To Stille waters, stillare, distillare. 1530 Palsgr. 736/1 Stylle some Damaske water, for it is good. 1534 Elyot Cast. Helthe II. viii. (1541) 24 In al cholerike feuers, the decoction of this herbe, or the water therof stilled, is right expedient. 1587 Marlowe 1st Pt. Tamburl. V. ii. 1946 (Brooke), The heauenly Quintessence they still From their immortall flowers of Poesy. ? c 1600 Distr. Emperor II. i. in Bullen Old Pl. (1884) III. 186 All the poysons and sharpe corrosyves Styll'd in the lymbecke of damde pollycie. 1660 T. Watson in Spurgeon Treas. David (1874) IV. 459 When we give him the soul in a duty,..by a holy chemistry we still out the spirits. 1681 R. Knox Hist. Ceylon 146 Others stilled Rack to sell. 1706–7 Farquhar Beaux' Strat. II. i, Brewing of Diet-drinks, and stilling Rose-mary-Water.

†b. *to still away*: to remove or drive off by distillation. *Obs.*

1628 Donne Serm. (1649) II. 395 It is a miserable Alchimy and extracting of spirits, that stills away the spirit, the soule it selfe.

†c. *to still forth*: To yield when distilled. *Obs.*

1605 Timme Quersit. I. v. 21 Those saltes, being put into a retort..with a receiver, stilleth forth a volatile salt.

†d. intr. *to still out*: To issue from something that is being distilled. *Obs.*

1799 G. Smith Laboratory I. 436 Every drop of water, which may happen to be mixed with the wine, will still out.

†e. *absol.* To practise distillation. *Obs.*

? 1668 Lady Lyttelton in Hatton Corr. (Camden) 54, I want..a house keeper that can preserve and still well.

still (stɪl), *adv.* Forms: see still *a.* [OE. *stille* = OS., OHG. *stillo* (MDu., MHG., mod.G. *stille*, Du. *stil*, Sw. *stilla*, Da. *stille*):—OTeut. type **stillō*, related to **stilljo-* still *a.*]

†1. a. Without noise or commotion; quietly, silently; in a low voice, softly. *Obs.*

c 1205 Lay. 735 Riht al swo stille stelen swa we wolden. a 1225 Juliana (Royal MS.) 36 Heo..stille bute stefne þus to criste cleopede. a 1250 Prov. Ælfred 325 Wimmon weped.. lude and stille, for to vordrye hire wille. a 1275 Ibid. B. 653 Þe bicche bitit ille þau[h] [printed þan] he berke stille. a 1300 Havelok 2997 Seye a pater-noster stille, For him þat haueth þe rym[e] maked. c 1330 R. Brunne Chron. Wace (Rolls) 15852 Brian stirt forþ in hure weye, & stille seide þat he wolde seye. 1398 Trevisa Barth. De P.R. I. (1495) 2 Yf I played in felde other medes Stylle other wyth noys I prayed helpe in all my dedes. 1483 Caxton Golden Leg. 263 b/1 He sayd thus to hym self alle stylle. 1544 Betham Precepts War I. liv. D j b, By whyche meane, the streame beneth wyl ronne more gently and styll. 1560 Daus tr. Sleidane's Comm. 267 b, That they myght go styll and closely to their enemies campe.

†b. Secretly. *Obs.*

c 1250 Gen. & Ex. 2015 One and stille ðoȝt hire gamen wið ioseph speken and plaiȝen samen. Ibid. 2718 And moyses druȝ him to ðe strond, And stille he dalf him [in] ðe sond. a 1300 K. Horn 287 (Camb. MS.) Þu schalt wiþ me to bure gon, To speke wiþ Rymenhild stille. 1375 Barbour Bruce XVII. 71 [He] held the spek preue and still.

†c. *still and loud*: both in secret and openly; under all circumstances: = *loud and still*, loud *adv.* 1 b.

[a 1250: see 1.] c 1320 Cast. Love 944 Þat al he..mis-doþ his neiȝebours boþe stille and loud. c 1400 Rom. Rose 7532 Fair-Welcoming..That ofte hath pleyed with you..The fairest games..Withoute filthe, stille or loude. 1430–40 Lydg. Bochas III. v. (1554) 73 Among the people, both still and loude, He called was Tarquinius the proude.

2. At rest, motionless; without change of place or attitude. With certain verbs. (In ME. often in alliterative phrase *still as stone*, *stone still*; in mod.Eng. occas. *stock still*.)

For the justification for treating the word in this use as adv. rather than as adj. complement, see note to still *a.* 1.

a. *to stand still.* (Sometimes merely a more explicit synonym of the vb. stand in senses 4, 27, and 32.)

c 1000 Sax. Leechd. III. 262 Seo sunne stod stille. c 1200 Ormin 2137 All swa summ þe steoressmann Aȝȝ lokeþþ till an steorrne, þatt stannt aȝȝ still upp o þe lifft & swiþe brihhte shineþþ. a 1300 Cursor M. 8188 Þe strem all still began to stand. c 1300 Leg. Gregory (Schulz) 401 Gregorij stod stille so ston. c 1400 Maundev. (Roxb.) xii. 50 It rynnes noȝt, ne nowþer ebbez ne flowez, bot standez ay still. 1523–34 Fitzherb. Husb. §132 A tree hath a propertye to growe to a certayne heyght, and whan he commeth to that heyghte, he standeth styll. 1526 Tindale Matt. xx. 32 Then Iesus stode styll, and called them. 1533 More Answ. Poysoned Bk. Wks. 1062/1 How the running riuer of Jordane stode still. 1548 in Vicary's Anat. (1888) App. III. i. 134 Ye other ij Aldermen ..which then shall remayne and stond still in the seyd office. 1577 Kendall Flowers of Epigr., Trifles 10 b, The Bowe that bended standeth still, his strength will loose and lack. 1600 Shaks. Sonn. civ, So your sweete hew, which me thinkes still doth stand Hath motion, and mine eye may be deceaued. 1613 Purchas Pilgrimage (1614) 740 The Ship stood still, and neither stirred forward or backwards. 1662 Playford Skill Mus. III. (1672) 15 When your Bass standeth still (that is to say, hath two or more Notes together in one and the same place). 1668 R. Steele Husbandm. Calling iii. (1672) 30 If God's providence above, and his plough below stand still, we must all shortly beg or starve. 1711 Addison Spect. No. 129 ¶1 A Clock that stands still is sure to point right once in twelve Hours. 1712 Ibid. No. 407 ¶1 Our Preachers stand stock still in the Pulpit. 1766 Goldsm. Vicar x, One of the horses took it into his head to stand still. **1828** LYTTON *Pelham* lxiv, I paused, and my heart stood still. **1858** *Jrnl. R. Agric. Soc.* XIX. I. 193 This shoot becomes a worthless tree ..which after a few years' growth stands still. **1861** FLOR. NIGHTINGALE *Nursing* 32 Many people seem to think that the world stands still while they are away, or at dinner, or ill. **1877** MISS A. B. EDWARDS *Up Nile* xii. 317 Time seems to have stood as still as in that immortal palace where everything went to sleep for a hundred years.

b. *to sit, lie still*. (See the senses of the verbs.)

c **1000** ÆLFRIC *Hom.* II. 438 Hire swuster Maria sæt stille æt Drihtnes fotum. *c* **1200** ORMIN 5839 Forr leness whellp þæp þær itt iss Whellpedd, tær liþ itt stille. *c* **1205** LAY. 3060 þus seide þe mæiden..& seoððen set swþe stille. *c* **1250** *Owl & Night.* 282 Me is leof to habbe reste And sitte stille in myne neste. **1297** R. GLOUC. (Rolls) 243 To deþe he sset his owe fader þat he lai þer stille. *a* **1300** *Cursor M.* 20509 Sittes stell now mar and lesse, And hers now þes mirines. *c* **1386** CHAUCER *Sompn. T.* 492 The lady of the hous al stille sat, Til she had herd what the frere sayde. *c* **1460** METHAM *Wks.* (E.E.T.S.) 60/1617 But Cleopes for fere lay ston stylle. *c* **1470** HENRY *Wallace* I. 247 In that same hous thai socht him beselye; Bot he sat still, and span full conandly. **1530** PALSGR. 719/1, I syt styll, I remove nat, *je ne me bouge*. Let every man syt styll on payne of his lyfe. **1548** HALL *Chron., Hen. VI*, 171 Kyng Henry..perceyving that the duke of Yorke lay still, and made no open apparance, of assemble or commocion, returned. **1562** J. HEYWOOD *Prov. & Epigr.* (1867) 56 Folke saie, better syt styll than ryse and fall. **1611** BIBLE *Zech.* i. 11 And behold, all the earth sitteth still, and is at rest. **1671** MILTON *P.R.* III. 164 And think'st thou to regain Thy right by sitting still or thus retiring? **1688** BUNYAN *Heav. Footman* (1886) 182 He that backslideth, and he that sitteth still in sin. **1711** ADDISON *Spect.* No. 50 ⁋7 This lazy People sat still above three hours. **1859** MRS. CARLYLE *Lett.* III. 7, I rose at six, tired of lying still. **1901** SIR REDVERS BULLER in *Scotsman* 11 Oct. 5/8, I said..'He is a gallant fellow; he will sit still to the end.'

†**c.** With other verbs, as *abide*, *dwell*. *Obs.*

In the 15–16th c. quots. there is a transition to senses 3, 4.

1303 R. BRUNNE *Handl. Synne* 308 Dwelle ȝyt with me a woke stylle. **13..** *Seuyn Sages* (W.) 1533 The child bileft still in prisoun. **1340** HAMPOLE *Pr. Consc.* 2746 In purgatori saules dueles stille Until þai be clensed of alle ille. *c* **1393** CHAUCER *Scogan* 39 That rustyth in myn schede stylle in pes. **1393** *Regist. Aberbrothoc* (Bannatyne Club) II. 43 Of the xxxv marcis v marcis sal dwel style in the abbotis hand ..quhillys the quer be thekyt and alurryt al abowyt with stane. **1398** TREVISA *Barth. De P.R.* XII. xxxvi. (1495) 435 The vulture huntyth fro mydday to nyght and restyth styl fro the sonne rysinge to that tyme. *c* **1400** *Ywaine & Gaw.* 1960, I pray yow for to dwel her still. *a* **1425** tr. *Arderne's Treat. Fistula*, etc. 25 Be it [a bandage] festned fast to þe girdel vpon þe womb, and lat it abide so stille to þe tyme come þat it be eft-sones remoued. *c* **1430** *How Gd. Wife taught Dau.* 140 in *Babees Bk.*, Wheþer þat þei dwelle stille or þei wende awey. **1526** TINDALE *John* xi. 6 Then aboode he two dayes still in the same place where he was. **1554** *Interl. Youth* (Waley) B j b, Let him come if he will, He were better to bide styll. **1560** *Nice Wanton* (facs.) C ij, Where it groweth strong there wil it abide stil.

3. a. With reference to action or condition: Without change, interruption, or cessation; continually, constantly; on every occasion, invariably; always. *Obs.* exc. *poet.*

c **1297** R. GLOUC. (Rolls) 5645 He broȝte hom alle to is wille, And hor olde seruage made hom holde al stille. **1390** GOWER *Conf.* I. 337 In tokne..That sche schal duelle a maiden stille. *c* **1450** *Godstow Reg.* 649 Except candyl vppon candylmes day, the whyche the seyd mynchyns shul haue stylle. **1490** CAXTON *Eueydos* xv. 58 Fame..hath..tonges.. that speken stylle without ceasse. **1535** COVERDALE *Isa.* lx. 11 Thy gates shal stonde open still both day and night. **1535** —— *Eccl.* i. 4 One generacion passeth awaye, another commeth, but the earth abydeth still [1611 for ever]. **1542** UDALL *Erasm. Apoph.* 12 b, Delius..was called a cunnyng swymmer that could kepe hym selfe styll above water without perill of drounyng. **1544** BETHAM *Precepts War* II. lxviii. L vij b, It is not conuenient ne yet necessary to vse one espye styll. **1549** LATIMER *Ploughers* (Arb.) 21 That plough God woulde haue styll going. **1570** LEVINS *Manip.* 124/5 Stil, *iugiter*. **1581** PETTIE tr. *Guazzo's Civ. Conv.* III. (1586) 154 They learne to liue as if they were still at the point to dye. **1600** SHAKS. *Sonn.* cxxvi, She may detaine, but not still keepe her tresure! **1613** DAY *Festiv., Serm.* vii. (1615) 20 How beit the Maister cannot still be at home, the Mistresse may. **1617** BRATHWAIT *Smoking Age* 194 *marg.*, Thus haue I prov'd Tobacco good or ill; Good, if rare taken; Bad, if taken still. *a* **1643** W. CARTWRIGHT *Ordinary* I. ii. (1651) 6 Woman was Not made to be alone still. **1669** STURMY *Mariner's Mag.* V. v. 19, 48 Miles above the Earth..There is never no Rain, Dew, Hail, Snow, or Wind, but still a clear serenity. *c* **1680** BEVERIDGE *Serm.* (1729) I. 114 Thus it is that God still governs and orders every thing in the world. **1704** TRAPP *Abra-Mulé* II. i. 494 His past Reign, which still has been attended With one continu'd Series of Misfortunes. **1704** POPE *Disc. Past. Poetry* §10 Spenser's.. Stanza is not still the same, nor always well chosen. **1737** DODDRIDGE *Hymn*, Oh God of Bethel, by whose Hand Thine Israel still is fed. **1763** GOLDSM. *Introd. Nat. Hist.* Misc. Wks. (1837) II. 517 The rook, if undisturbed, would never leave its native wood, the blackbird still frequents its accustomed hedge. **1766** REID *Let.* in Wks. 1863 I. 44/1 But you must direct them [workmen] in everything, and be still over the work. **1781** BURNS *1st Ps.* 8 The man..Who..with humility and awe Still walks before his God. **1817** COLERIDGE *Biog. Lit.* xvii. (1882) 171 The un-meaning repetitions..which an unfurnished..understanding interposes at short intervals in order to keep hold of his subject, which is still slipping from him. **1819** SCOTT *Noble Moringer* xxii, God rest the Baron in his grave, he still was kind to me! **1864** ANSTER *2nd Pt. Faust* I. 23 You never can get fools to understand How luck and merit still go hand in hand. **1865** SWINBURNE *Atalanta* 30 Howbeit these.. Devise new things and good, not one thing still.

†**b.** *still still*: on every occasion; ever more and more. *Obs.*

1592 NASHE *Strange Newes* Observ. for Rdrs. M 2 b, I am ..constrained still still, before I am warme in any one vaine, to start away sodainely. **1593** —— *Christs T.* 39 b, With example thou first exalteth them, and still still liftes them vp, till thou hast lifted vp theyr heads on thy gates. **1594** —— *Terrors Nt.* Wks. 1904 I. 354 This slimie melancholy humor still still thickning as it stands still.

†**c.** *still apece* (*apese*, *apeese*; corruptly *off pees*, *a peace*), continuously. (See PIECE *sb.* 14 b.) *Obs.*

There are 24 examples in *Syr Generydes*; otherwise the phrase occurs in our quots. only twice.

c **1440** [see PIECE *sb.* 14 b]. *c* **1470** HENRY *Wallace* VIII. 933 Ȝeit still off pees the ost lugyt all nycht. **1555** Still a peace [see PIECE *sb.* 14 b].

†**d.** *still as*: whenever. *Obs.*

a **1656** HALES *Serm. Eton* iv. (1673) 60 A loose, but a rich fellow..was wont to walk the streets with a purse of money, and still as he met any man he would give him a box on the ear, and then a twelve-pence.

e. †*still and anon*, †*still an end* (obs.): constantly from time to time. So Sc. *still and on*: 'nevertheless, notwithstanding, yet' (*Eng. Dial. Dict.*).

1591 SHAKS. *Two Gent.* IV. iv. 67 A Slaue, that still an end, turnes me to shame. **1595** —— *John* IV. i. 47, I..like the watchfull minutes, to the houre, Still and anon cheer'd vp the heauy time. *a* **1894** STEVENSON in *Pall Mall Gaz.* (1895) 21 Jan. 2/3 O still ayont the muckle sea, Still are ye dear, and dear to me, Auld Reekie, still and on! **1910** N. MUNRO in *Blackw. Mag.* Feb. 221/1 'Still-and-on,' said pawky Jamie Birrell cheerily, 'one may have a turn of the raptures too, falling back on the affections when they're done.'

f. With words denoting increase or progress: Ever more and more.

1596 SPENSER *F.Q.* IV. vi. 18 Sir Arthegall renewed His strength still more, but she still more decrewed. **1605** SYLVESTER *Du Bartas* II. iii. I. *Vocat.* 235 All their Cattell proves, Still, still increasing like to Stares and Doves. *c* **1643** LD. HERBERT *Autobiog.* (1824) 74, I attended my studies seriously, the more I learnt out of my Books, adding still a desire to know more. **1682** SIR T. BROWNE *Chr. Mor.* III. §6 He who thus still advanceth in Iniquity deepneth his deformed hue. **1697** DRYDEN *Virg. Georg.* I. 289 All below, whether by Nature's Curse, Or Fate's Decree, degen'rate still to worse. **1703** POPE *Thebais* 527 Thus still his courage, with his toils encreas'd. **1779** JOHNSON *L.P., Dryden* Wks. II. 420 Whatever subjects employed his pen, he was still improving our measures &c. **1807** J. BARLOW *Columb.* I. 216 Its form unfolding as it still draws nigh. **1820** SHELLEY *Skylark* 10 Thou..singing still dost soar, and soaring ever singest.

4. Indicating the continuance of a previous action or condition.

a. Now (or at the time in question) as formerly.

1535 JOYE *Apol. Tindale* 38 But and if Tindale wil nedis saye styll that I mocke out the Resurreccion. **1542** UDALL *Erasm. Apoph.* 255 b, If he came to any commen plaies or open sightes, it is ye guise even yet still that reverence bee dooen to hym. **1587** in *Cath. Rec. Soc. Publ.* V. 140 They take priests and other Catholics still very often; and now they begin to persecute also the schismatics. **1600** SHAKS. *Sonn.* civ, For as you were when first your eye I eyde, Such seemes your beautie still. **1620** *Reg. Mag. Sig. Scot.* 783/1 Minerallis..quhilkis hithertill hes lyin and still lyis obscure and hid within the bowellis and centre of the earth. **1689** in *Acts Parlt. Scotl.* (1875) XII. 79/2 Wee are still of the same mind quhich we did express in our former letter. **1711** ADDISON *Spect.* No. 164 ⁋11 Their Tombs are still to be seen. **1760** JOHNSON *Idler* No. 100 ⁋1 There still remain many words among us undefined. **1763** J. BROWN *Poetry & Mus.* v. 52 But the reason is still to seek. **1778** MISS BURNEY *Evelina* xi. (1791) I. 27 Seeing me still very much flurried, he led me to a seat. **1797** *Encycl. Brit.* (ed. 3) VIII. 462/2 The naval or rostral crown is still used with coats-of-arms. **1837** WHEWELL *Hist. Induct. Sci.* III. iv. I. 207 Another writer on the same subject is Menelaus,..whose three books on Spherics still remain. **1849** MACAULAY *Hist. Eng.* v. I. 592 Bridgewater was one of the few towns which still had some Whig magistrates. **1857** BUCKLE *Civiliz.* I. xi. 626 One of those harmless prejudices that still linger round the person of the sovereign. **1893** *Law Times* XCIV. 559/2 In the deed the consideration was left blank, and for all I know it is blank still. **1899** *Allbutt's Syst. Med.* VIII. 558 The still vaguely defined and very multiform affection seborrhœa. **1906** E. V. LUCAS *Wand. Lond.* i. 14 When I first came to London, Piccadilly still had its goat.

¶ quasi-*adj.* That still is such. *rare.* Cf. NOW 16, THEN 9 b.

1879 TROLLOPE *Thackeray* 22 The then and still owners of that happy periodical.

b. *contextually*. Now (or at the time in question) in contrast to the future; at present, as yet.

1632 LITHGOW *Trav.* VII. 301 Hauing euer one Fruite ready to be plucked..and another comming forwards.., that as some Reape, some are growing greene, others budding forth, and some still in the floorish. **1641** J. JACKSON *True Evang. T.* I. 5 The Jews construe it [Isa. xi. 6–8], of Christ still to come, and of his temporall Monarchy. **1766** GOLDSM. *Vicar* ii, I wrote a similar epitaph for my wife, though still living. **1824** MISS FERRIER *Inher.* xliv, A few large old trees, and many young ones still in their cages. **1827** FARADAY *Chem. Manip.* xxiv. 640 By sealing up the contracted aperture of the tube whilst it is still hot. **1849** SIR G. C. LEWIS *Lett.* (1870) 213 This is still in fieri. **1864** MEREDITH *Emilia* lv, He had waxed precociously philosophic, when still a junior. **1874** GREEN *Short Hist.* ii. §1. 62 The greater part of English soil was still utterly uncultivated.

c. After as before some point of time; in future as up to the present; further. ? *Obs.*

1526 *Pilgr. Perf.* (W. de W. 1531) 9 And though you receyue it not at your owne wyll, knocke styll, call on and perseuer, and you shall not mysse. **1577** KENDALL *Flowers of Epigr.* 104 b, Poore haue I been, and poore I am, and poore still shall I bee. **1597–8** BACON *Ess., Regim. Health* (Arb.) 56 Discerne of the comming on of yeares, and thinke not to doe the same things still. **1611** BIBLE *Exod.* ix. 2 For if thou refuse to let them goe, and wilt hold them still, [etc.]. **1641** J. JACKSON *True Evang. T.* III. 216 If it flie from thee as swift as a Roe or Hinde, yet follow the chace still. **1702** ROWE *Tamerl.* IV. i. 1539 Oh! Death! thou gentle end of Human Sorrows Still must my weary Eyelids vainly wake In tedious Expectation of thy Peace.

†**d.** Continuously in the same direction as before; further. *Obs.*

1602 *Reg. Mag. Sig. Scot.* 456/2 Keipand the said dyke southeist throuch Henderstoun-burne, and thairfra still southeist keipand the said dyke till it cum to the merche. **1634** SIR T. HERBERT *Trav.* 182 Our course lay still from Swalley Road. *Ibid.* 186 Thence we sailed still South. **1725** DE FOE *Voy. round World* (1840) 173 To keep still on southing as well as East. **1769** *De Foe's Tour Gt. Brit.* (ed. 7) II. 365 Going still West, we came to Caermarthen.

e. In addition; after the apparent ending of a series; yet.

1790 COWPER *Let.* 27 Feb., P.S...Still another P.S. **1857** RUSKIN *Pol. Econ. Art* i. §27 There is one thought still, the saddest of all, bearing on this withholding of early help.

5. In a further degree. **a.** Used to emphasize a comparative; = yet.

1730 *Lett. to Sir W. Strickland rel. Coal Trade* 33 The Woodmongers Abuse..of a former Charter leaves still less Reason to fear they shou'd succeed. **1748** RICHARDSON *Clarissa* VII. 393 But the generosity of her mind..is what stings me most. And the more still, as it is now out of my power any way..to be even with her. **1774** GOLDSM. *Nat. Hist.* V. 50 The lower part of the neck..is covered with still smaller feathers than those on the belly and back. **1788** J. BROWN tr. *Elem. Med.* I. 159 The sthenic diathesis, taking place in a high degree over the whole body, but in a still higher in the vessels of the skin. **1830** CARLYLE *Richter Again* Ess. 1840 II. 321 The two households stood like concave mirrors reflecting one another's keen hunger into a still keener for both. **1832** BREWSTER *Nat. Magic* ix. 243 Returning to the spot next day, he heard the sound still louder than before. **1849** MACAULAY *Hist. Eng.* iv. I. 494 But already that feeling had been indicated by still stronger and more terrible signs. **1884** PENNINGTON *Wiclif* viii. 247 He expresses himself still more strongly in his unprinted writings. **1912** J. L. MYRES *Dawn of Hist.* viii. 174 The Late-Minoan period is more precisely dated still.

b. Sometimes used where the comparative notion is merely implied. Now *rare* or *Obs.*

1593 SHAKS. *Lucr.* 229 The guilt beeing great, the feare doth still exceede. **1697** *C'tess D'Aunoy's Trav.* (1706) 140 Their hands have no defect, they are little, white, and well shaped. Their large sleeves..still contribute to make them appear less. **1705** ADDISON *Italy* Ded., Whatever great Impressions an Englishman must have of Your Lordship, they who have been Conversant Abroad will find 'em still improv'd. **1710** STEELE *Tatler* No. 233 ⁋2 When thus much was obtained for him, their Minds still softened towards him. **1762** GOLDSM. *Nash* 47 Their mutton, butter, fish, and fowl, are all allowed to be excellent, and their cookery still exceeds their meat.

6. With adversative notion.

a. [Developed from sense 4.] After or at the same time with some event or condition implied to be adverse; even then.

a **1699** STILLINGFL. *Serm.* xxxvi. Wks. 1710 I. 564 If we ask, Cannot good Men differ about some things, and yet be good still? Yes. **1711** STEELE *Spect.* No. 27 ⁋1 While they pant after Shade and Covert, they still affect to appear in the most glittering Scenes of Life. **1770** GOLDSM. *Des. Vill.* 212 For e'en though vanquished, he could argue still. **1861** FLOR. NIGHTINGALE *Nursing* 22 Nothing can make such a room healthy. Ventilation would improve it, but still it would be unhealthy.

b. Quasi-*conj.* In spite of what has been stated or conceded; nevertheless, notwithstanding, yet. Sometimes preceded by *but*, or followed by *however*.

1722 DE FOE *Plague* (1754) 7 'Tis true, St. Giles's buried two and thirty, but still as there was but one of the Plague, People began to be easy. **1779** *Mirror* No. 66 Still, however, with all these precautions to introduce the thought in a familiar and easy manner, he is aware of her displeasure. **1816** J. WILSON *City of Plague* II. ii. 67, I know well That they who love their friends most tenderly Still bear their loss the best. **1820** MILNER *Suppl. Mem. Eng. Cath.* 14 It is the law of nature and of the gospel that we should obey the constituted authority of the state... Still this obedience has its limits. **1825** MACAULAY *Ess., Milton* ⁋40 Still, however, there was another extreme which, though far less dangerous, was also to be avoided. **1837** P. KEITH *Bot. Lex.* 368 The quadrupeds, whose look, though prone, is still well suited to their form and condition. **1847** C. BRONTE *Jane Eyre* xvii, The soul..has an interpreter—often an unconscious, but still a truthful interpreter—in the eye. **1865** SWINBURNE *Chastelard* I. ii. (1894) 23 The legend is writ small: Still one makes out this—*Cave*—if you look. **1885** 'MRS. ALEXANDER' *At Bay* vii, I confess I lost hope as she spoke, still I begged for an interview with the incoming teacher.

c. *still and all*: nevertheless, even so; after all. *colloq.*

1829 G. GRIFFIN *Collegians* I. vii. 140 Lord K..gave him a lease o' that farm... Still an' all, Myles do be poor, for he never knew how to keep a hoult o' the money. **1928** F. N. HART *Bellamy Trial* iv. 104 Still and all, I believe that he was there precisely when he said he was. **1942** G. MARX *Let.* 16 Dec. (1967) 32 Still and all, as Lardner would say, it's a very cozy little place. **1963** A. LUBBOCK *Austral. Roundabout* 77 'Still-and-all,' they said, 'it's no use worrying over things y' can't help, is it?' **1969** *Guardian* 18 Aug. 9/5 Still and all, it is surely time to desist in good grace. **1978** R. MOORE *Big Paddle* (1979) i. 4 Still and all, if you see something I haven't, let me know.

7. Comb. and quasi-Comb. When qualifying an attributive adj., the adv. is usually hyphened.

a. In sense 1, the hyphened collocations may be regarded as genuine combinations, but are rare.

1535 COVERDALE *Isa.* viii. 6 The people refuseth the stil-renninge water of Silo. **1897** *Standard* 2 Oct. 2/2 On the banks of the still-flowing Medway.

b. In sense 3, 'always', 'ever'.

Many instances of the quasi-combination resulting from the prefixing of the adv. to an adj. or ppl. adj. occur in Shakspere, though the hyphen is rarely used in the early edd. In the 17th and 18th c. the use was common, but confined to poetry; in the 19th c. it scarcely occurs, this sense of the adv. having become rare even in verse. See also STILL-GREEN *a.*

1593 SHAKS. *Lucr.* 84 In silent wonder of still gazing eyes. **1610** —— *Temp.* I. ii. 229 To fetch dewe From the still-vext Bermoothes. **1597** BP. HALL *Sat.* II. ii. 30 To consume in vaine In latter Euen,.. Ill-smelling oyles, or some still-watching lights. **1599** B. JONSON *Cynthia's Rev.* V. vi, Monthly, we spend our still-repaired shine, And not forbid our virgin-waxen torch To burne and blaze. **1603** J. DAVIES (Heref.) *Microcosmos* 231 That still-closed booke of secrets. **1605** SYLVESTER *Du Bartas* II. iii. *1 Vocat.* 553 On a still-rocking couch lies blear-ey'd Sleep. **1609** DANIEL *Civ. Wars* VIII. xcii. 226 His religious Confessor (who best Could cast, with what a violent accesse, This feuer of Ambition did molest His still-sick minde). **1615** CHAPMAN *Odyss.* XIII. 424 Thou still-wit-varying wretch! **1619** A. NEWMAN *Pleas. Vis.* C 4 b, My seruants haue.. Still-liuing honors, and lou'd Fame. **1727–46** THOMSON *Summer* 1641 The generous still-improving mind. **1742** YOUNG *Nt. Th.* VI. 9 Tardy pressure's still-increasing weight. **1761** GLOVER *Medea* II. vi. 36 The settled frown, The still-renew'd upbraiding? **1780** COWPER *Progr. Error* 550 His still refuted quirks he still repeats. **1783** CRABBE *Village* II. 164 To bid the still-recurring thoughts depart. **1875** BROWNING *Aristoph. Apol.* 77 Each prim stiff phrase Of each old play, my still-new laughing-stock, Had meaning.

c. In sense 4 a, 'now as before', quasi-combinations of this kind are still formed freely.

1609 J. DAVIES (Heref.) *Holy Roode* I 3, Thy still-fresh-bleeding Wounds. **1648** J. BEAUMONT *Psyche* VI. cciii, As for the bugbear Threat of Death, behold Its confutation in still-florid Me. **1732** *Belle Assemblée* II. 210 Kerme having seen his still-admir'd Leonora in the possession of what alone could make her happy. **1772** COWPER *Let. to J. Hill* 5 Nov., The only return I can make you, for your many acts of still-continued friendship. **1855** MILMAN *Lat. Chr.* XIV. x. (1864) IX. 355 It is believed by a still-diminishing few that [etc.]. **1864** PUSEY *Lect. Daniel* (1876) 323 Most of these Psalms lament over the still-continuing abandonment to the Heathen. **1890** GROSS *Gild Merch.* I. 132 The still-existing Company of Merchants of Carlisle.

still, obs. form of STYLE *v.*

†**sti'llado.** *Obs.*$^{-1}$? Erron. var. STILETTO.

1607 CHAPMAN *Bussy d'Ambois* III. ii. 465 With any friend of yours Ile lay This poore Stilladoe heere, gainst all the starres.. That you did neuer good, but to doe ill.

stillage ('stɪlɪdʒ), *sb.*[1] Also 7 stilladge, 9 *dial.* stillige. [app. a. Du. *stellagie*, *stellaedsie* (Kilian), now written *stellazje*, *stellaadje*, *stellage*, scaffold, stand, f. *stellen* to place + Fr. suffix *-age*: see -AGE.]

1. *Brewing.* A stand for casks. Cf. STILLING *sb.*[1], STILLION 1.

1596 *Lanc. Wills* (Chetham Soc.) III. 5 In yᵉ buttery.. a rounde old table and ij stillages for bier. **1688** HOLME *Armoury* III. xx. (Roxb.) 248/1 A stilladge in sellers, on which barrells are sett. **1800** *Trans. Soc. Arts* XVIII. 337 And the tubs placed.. upon a stillage, near to each other. **1883** *Lancs. Brewer's Price List*, Casks should be placed on stillage, bung downwards. **1889** W. WESTALL *Birch Dene* III. 28 In one corner several casks on stillages.

2. In various industries, a stool or stand for keeping something from the ground. Now *spec.* a pallet, frame, or similar structure used for storage of goods. Also *collect.*

1875 KNIGHT *Dict. Mech.*, *Stillage*, a low stool to keep cloths off the floor of a bleachery. **1963** K. HUDSON *Industrial Archaeol.* vii. 111 Old fittings and furnishings which might well remain *in situ* at old factories.. include.. wooden stillages. **1970** *Cabinet Maker & Retail Furnisher* 25 Sept. 629/1 Each stillage is 36 in × 24 in × 6 ft high, and provides storage for 150 headboards... Customers who take regular bulk deliveries are offered these stillages on loan. **1976** *Listener* 22 July, Stacking of components in wooden stillage instead of metal bins.

stillage ('stɪlɪdʒ), *sb.*[2] Chiefly *U.S.* [f. STILL *sb.*[1] + -AGE.] The residue remaining in a still after a fermentation, usu. of grain or molasses, and removal of the alcohol by distillation.

1940 *Sun* (Baltimore) 5 Apr. 11/7 The experiments.. were designed to determine the value of distillers' dry rye grains and stillage as substitutes for other grains in feeding cattle for the market. **1945** *Industr. & Engin. Chem.* June 534/1 Distilleries processing molasses are frequently confronted with the problem of disposing of stillage. **1963** *Agric. & Biol. Chem.* XXVII. A19/2 (*heading*) Nutritional studies on the utilization of distiller's stillage. **1979** *Nature* 6 Dec. 551/1 The total output of stillage in Brazil is equivalent in biological oxygen demand to the untreated sewage produced by a city of 200 million inhabitants.

stillage ('stɪlɪdʒ), *v. dial.* [f. STILLAGE *sb.*[1]] *trans.* To place (a barrel of ale, etc.) on a stand ready for use.

1854 BRIERLEY *Tales & Sk. Lancs. Life* (1866) II. 82 There was a barrel of ale ordered to be stillaged at the door of the Blue Elephant.

†**'stillant,** *a. Obs.* [ad. L. *stillantem*, pr. pple. of *stillāre* STILL *v.*[2]] Distilling, issuing in drops.

1610 W. FOLKINGHAM *Art of Survey* I. v. 10 The first is either Stagnant, as standing Pooles, Ponds, Lakes,..: Or Stillant, viz. Springing or bursting forth of the bowels of the earth, as Wels, Fountaines. **1654** GAYTON *Pleas. Notes* II. ii. 37 Our Dons in blood, and won't heed Sancho's rules, But rides about the field which is all gules From his eare stillant.

‖**sti'llatim,** *adv. Obs.* [L. *stillātim*, f. *stilla* a drop.] Drop by drop.

1668 EVELYN *Let. to Beale* 27 Aug., I.. cause aboundance of cold fountaine-water to be poured upon me *stillatim*, for a good halfe-hour together. **1846** in WORCESTER (citing FOSTER).

stillation (stɪ'leɪʃən). *rare*$^{-0}$. [ad. L. *stillātiōnem*, f. *stillāre* to distil, issue in drops, f. *stilla* drop.] (See quots.)

1623 COCKERAM I, *Stillation*, a dropping. **1898** *Syd. Soc. Lex.*, *Stillation*, passage of a liquid drop by drop.

stillatitious (stɪlə'tɪʃəs), *a.* [f. L. *stillātīci-us* falling in drops (f. *stillāre*: see prec. and -ITIOUS) + -OUS.]

1. Falling in drops; issuing by drops. Also, †produced by falling in drops, as stalactites.

1656 BLOUNT *Glossogr.*, *Stillatitious*, that drops or distils. **1758** BORLASE *Nat. Hist. Cornw.* 110 Near the Holy-well.. there are several stillatitious productions of a sparry kind. **1822–7** GOOD *Study Med.* (1829) V. 469 Strangury. Painful and stillatitious emission of urine.

†**2.** Produced by distillation. *Obs.*

1657 TOMLINSON *Renou's Disp.* II. xiv. 70 As when Gems or Metals are extinguished in Wine-vinegar, pure or stillatitious matter. **1666** BOYLE *Orig. Formes & Qual.* 230 The Saline Corpuscles of Stillatitious acid liquors. **1681** GREW *Musæum* IV. §i. 352 The Stillatitious Oil of Lawang Barque. **1704** J. HARRIS *Lex. Techn.* I, *Stillatitious Oils* in Chymistry, are such as are Extracted out of Mixts, by the Force of Fire.

Hence **stilla'titiously** *adv.*, by drops.

1822–7 GOOD *Study Med.* (1829) II. 532 The urine will flow stillatitiously, and without ceasing.

stillatory ('stɪlətərɪ), *sb.* Forms: 4–7 **stillatorie**, 5 **-tor**, 5–6 **styllatory**, 6 **stellatour**, **stelletore**, **stillatori**, **stillatour**, **-torye**, **stilletorie**, **stillitary**, **-torye**, **styllathre**, **-torie**, **stylletorie**, **-ye**, **styllytory**, **-tary**, 6–7 **stillitorie**, 6–8 **-tory**, 7 **stellatour**, **stillotorie**, 6– **stillatory**. [ad. med.L. *stillātōrium*, f. L. *stillāre* to drip, distil: see -ORY.]

I. 1. A still. *Obs.* exc. *Hist.* and *fig.*

c **1386** CHAUCER *Can. Yeom. Prol.* 27 His forhead dropped as a stillatorie Were ful of Plantayne and of Paritorie. **1460–70** *Bk. Quintessence* 11 Putte aȝen þe watir in þe stillatorie of circulacioun til ȝe brynge it to so myche swetnes .. as ȝe dide þe brennynge watir. **1491** in *Acta Dom. Concil.* (1839) 195/2 Ane stillator price xiij s. iiij d. **1508** *Acc. Ld. High Treas. Scot.* IV. 137 For making of ane bos hed to ane stellatour of silvir weyand [etc.]. **1530** in *Ancestor* (1904) XI. 182 Wynington beryth to his crest a styllytory siluer in a wreeth. **1557** *Richmond Wills* (Surtees) 91 Item iij barrells, one stelletore, xc. ȝards of hemppen cloth, xxˢ. **1566** DRANT *Jerem.* iii. K vij, Mine eye, lyke stillitorie runs, and weepes. **1657** *Knaresb. Wills* (Surtees) II. 223, 1 Stillotorie. **1688** HOLME *Armoury* III. xx. (Roxb.) 232 Doctor Crato his stillatory for the prepareing and drawing of water or oyle of Cynamon.

b. *fig.*

1579 TOMSON *Calvin's Serm. Tim.* 329/1 This is another stillitorie of his where through Christ must passe. This is a meruellous alchumiste. **1592** SHAKS. *Ven. & Ad.* 443 For from the stillitorie of thy face excelling, Coms breath perfumd that breedeth loue by smelling. **1652** BENLOWES *Theophila* To Ladies A 2, So, Stillatories be of Love; That, what was Vapour, may, by Virtue, Essence prove. **1879** MEREDITH *Egoist* I. Prelude 4 The remedy of your frightful affliction is here, through the stillatory of Comedy, and not in Science.

2. A place where distillery is carried on; a still-room; a still-house, distillery.

1602 PLAT *Delights Ladies* Epist. (1611) A 3, The Quince, Pomgranate,.. Are heere maintain'd,.. For Ladies closets and their stillatories. **1604** R. CAWDREY *Table Alph.*, *Stillatorie*, a distilling place. **1624** WOTTON *Elem. Archit.* I. 8 All Offices that require heat, as Kitchins, Stillatories.. or the like would be Meridionall. *c* **1710** CELIA FIENNES *Diary* (1888) 7 So many little buildings apart from each other.. one for a stillitory. **1796** *Stat. Acc. Scot.* XVII. 294 Here is a stillatory which pays to the revenue £729 per annum.

3. *attrib.*

1561–2 in *Rep. Middleton MSS.* (Hist. MSS. Comm. 1911) 417 Paied to the smythe for makynge and mendynge a locke for the styllytary howse dore. **1586** BRIGHT *Melanch.* xxvii. 156 Placed over the rest as a stillitorye helme ouer the bodie.

†**II. 4.** = STILLICIDE. *Obs.*

1777 GOSTLING *Walk Canterb.* (ed. 2) 189 Stillatory is the name our workmen give to spaces between buildings.. to receive the rain which runs from the roofs.

†**'stillatory,** *a. Obs.* [ad. med.L. **stillātōrius*, f. L. *stillāre*: see STILLATION and -ORY. Cf. F. *stillatoire* (Cotgr. 1611).] **a.** Used in distilling. **b.** (See quot. 1656.)

1579 *Lanc. Wills* (Chetham Soc.) II. 125 Plate and butre stuffe wᵗʰ glasses stillatory. **1656** BLOUNT *Glossogr.*, *Stillatory*, stilling, distilling, dropping.

still-birth. Also **stillbirth**. [f. STILL *a.* + BIRTH, after STILL-BORN *a.*]

1. Birth of a still-born child; an instance of this. Also *fig.* Also, formerly, birth of a child alive or with a beating heart, but not breathing.

1785 COWPER *Let. to J. Newton* 25 June, Dr. Johnson laughs at Savage for charging the still-birth of a poem of his upon the bookseller's delay. **1872** MORLEY *Voltaire* i. 6 None of it was ever the dreary still-birth of a mind of hearsays. **1880** *Brit. Med. Jrnl.* 9 Oct. 596/2 Stillbirth—Resuscitation after two hours and five minutes. **1889** A. NEWSHOLME *Elem. Vital Statistics* 61 Still-births are not registered in England. **1897** *Allbutt's Syst. Med.* II. 980 In other animals still-birth was a constant feature. **1913** R. W. JOHNSTONE *Text-bk. Midwifery* xxxvii. 397 The infant is born in a state of suspended animation—its heart continues to beat, but it makes no effort to breathe or to move. 'Still birth' is therefore not the same thing as the child's being born dead, although death may supervene if prompt treatment is not applied. **1920** O. ST. J. MOSES *Man. Obstetr.* xviii. 269 In the pale or white form of still-birth the chances of recovery are much less. **1940** BROWN & GILBERT *Midwifery* l. 468 In certain circumstances, the fœtus continues to live as a fœtus external to the mother for some time—10 to 20 minutes—and it may die as a fœtus and be counted as a still-birth. **1947** G. I. STRACHAN *Textbk. Obstetr.* VIII. 699 The term 'stillborn' is therefore applied when the fœtus fails to maintain an independent existence, although some authorities.. have attempted to make a division into (*a*) dead birth in which the fœtus is obviously dead and exhibits neither heart beat nor respiration, and (*b*) stillbirth in which the heart is beating but respiration is never established. It is simpler, however, to employ the term 'stillbirth' to cover both these states. **1971** *Reader's Digest Family Guide to Law* 197/2 Even a still-birth—where a child is born dead after at least 28 weeks of pregnancy—must be registered as a birth. **1972** S. G. CLAYTON et al. *Obstetrics by Ten Teachers* (ed. 12) liii. 642 If the heart is beating after delivery, even though there is no sign of respiration, the death of a child born after 28 weeks should not be included as a stillbirth but as a neonatal death.

2. A still-born child.

1963 BUTLER & BONHAM *Perinatal Mortality* 210 Only six of the 'stillbirths' weighed 1,000 grams or less and were born before 28 weeks gestation. **1969** M. M. GARREY et al. *Obstetrics Illustrated* 469/1 A stillbirth is a baby that does not breathe or show any other sign of life after being completely separated from its mother.

still-born, *a.* (and *sb.*) Also **stillborn**. [f. STILL *a.* + BORN *ppl. a.*]

A. *adj.* **1.** Born lifeless; dead at birth; abortive. Also, formerly, born alive but not breathing.

1607 R. C[AREW] tr. *Estienne's World Wond.* 348 Restoring children to life, which were stil borne. **1613** BP. HALL *Farew. Serm. Pr. Henry* Wks. (1625) 462 If a childe were heard cry, it is a lawfull proofe of his liuing: else if hee be dead, we say he is still-borne. **1622–3** in Swayne *Churchw. Acc. Sarum* (1896) 176, iiij still borne Children 4 d. **1773** *Gentl. Mag.* XLIII. 118 It is of importance that the still-born children, and those who die before baptism, should also be registered. **1855** *Poultry Chron.* II. 436, I have often revived apparently still-born ducklings with whisky and water. **1896** W. A. N. DORLAND *Man. Obstetr.* II. vi. 706 It is a very common occurrence for a child to be born with the respiratory functions in abeyance: such a child is said to be asphyxiated. If efforts at resuscitation prove ineffectual, it is said to have been stillborn. **1899** H. D. CHAPIN in C. Jewett *Practice of Obstetrics* xxviii. 617 Fœtal death must be distinguished from asphyxia... In the latter the heart is pulsating, reflexes are present, and there may be feeble attempts at respiration... The distinction between a dead born and a still born infant can usually be made by the rapid fall of rectal temperature in the former. **1911** *Act 1 & 2 Geo. V*, c. 6 § 4 If any person.. falsely pretends that any child born alive was still-born.. he shall be guilty of a misdemeanour. **1936** O'D. BROWNE *Man. Pract. Obstetr.* xix. 170 Technically, if an infant is born alive but never breathes, it is said to be stillborn; if the heart has ceased to beat after birth, deadborn. **1953** *Act 1 & 2 Eliz. II* c. 20 §41 'Still-born child' means a child which has issued forth from its mother after the twenty-eighth week of pregnancy and which did not at any time after being completely expelled from its mother breathe or show any other signs of life, and the expression 'still-birth' shall be construed accordingly. **1955** W. P. D. LOGAN in Holland & Bourne *Brit. Obstetr. & Gynæcol. Practice*: *Obstetrics* xxxix. 1140 In certain countries children born alive but dying within a stipulated number of days are registered as stillborn.

2. *fig.*

1597 SHAKS. *2 Hen. IV*, I. iii. 64 Grant that our hopes (yet likely of faire byrth) Should be still-borne. **1648** HERRICK *Hesper.*, *Comf. Lady* 6 Winds have their time to rage; but when they cease, The leavie-trees nod in a still-born peace. **1679** DRYDEN *Tr. & Cr.* I. ii. 4, I haue with mighty anguish of my Soul Just at the Birth stifled this still-born-sigh. **1709** *Tatler* No. 110 ¶7 Authors in Prose and Verse. Those of them who had produced any still-born Work. **1827** NEELE *Lit. Rem.* (1829) 22 It is a very common error to suppose that it ['Paradise Lost'] fell almost still-born from the press. **1830** MARRYAT *King's Own* xxxv, Those still-born quotations of our messmate Price are most tryingly annoying. **1858** GREENER *Gunnery* Pref. p. iii, The numerous patents taken out during the last few years, most of which have fallen still-born. **1894** JEAFFRESON *Bk. Recoll.* I. viii. 135 [His] works one and all fell still-born from the press.

B. as *sb.*, a still-born child. Also *fig.*

1913 J. LONDON *Let.* 30 Jan. (1966) 369 For goodness sake, don't let's have a still-born of it. **1977** *Lancet* 30 July 257/1 She gave birth to a pair of male twins, one of which was a stillborn with no malformations. The other boy is normal and healthy.

still-burnt, *a.* [f. STILL *sb.*[1] + BURNT *ppl. a.*] Of alcoholic spirits: Damaged by burning in the process of distillation. Hence (in Dicts.) **still-burn** *v.*

1766 SMOLLETT *Trav.* I. 44 All the brandy which I have seen in Boulogne is new, fiery, and still-burnt. **1831** T. P. JONES *New Convers. Chem.* xv. 153 Spirituous liquors which are still-burnt and otherwise badly flavoured.

stilled (stɪld), *ppl. a.*[1] [f. STILL *v.*[2] + -ED[1].] Made quiet; quietened; silent.

1614 GORGES *Lucan* I. 26 And being layd, the stilled maine Reclaimes her mounted waues againe. **1820** C. R. MATURIN *Melmoth* (1892) III. xxiv. 65 Murderers exchanging their stilled and midnight whispers. **1874** L. CARR *Jud. Gwynne* I.

i. 10 The sweet rhythmical music..came chiming through the stilled air. **1883** MEREDITH *Poems & Lyrics, Melampus* xi, He drew the Master of harmonies, voiced or stilled, To seek him.

stilled (stɪld), *ppl. a.*[2] [f. STILL *v.*[1] + -ED[1].] = DISTILLED *ppl. a.*

a **1400** *Stockh. Medical MS.* i. 76 in *Anglia* XVIII. 297 Quan alle þese gresys ben i-take Stillid water þer-of lat make. **1542** BOORDE *Dyetary* x. (1870) 253 Better it is to drynke with wyne stylled waters. **1601** HOLLAND *Pliny* XVI. xi. I. 464 Thereupon it is called Stilled pitch. **1633** HART *Diet of Diseased* I. xv. 53 The stilled water of the plant [Marigold]..is esteemed good for red eyes. **1728** E. S[MITH] *Compl. Housew.* (ed. 2) 173 Then put in two or three spoonfuls of the same Syrup or still'd Water.

† **'stilledly,** *adv. Obs. rare*$^{-1}$. [f. STILLED *ppl. a.*[1] + -LY[2].] In a stilled manner; quietly.

c **1205** LAY. 14101 Ofte heo stilledliche spæken & spilieð mid runen.

stillehede: see STILLHEAD. *Obs.*

stilleite ('ʃtɪləaɪt). *Min.* [ad. G. *stilleit* (P. Ramdohr in *Geotektonisches Symp. zu Ehren von H. Stille* (1956) 482), f. the name of Hans W. *Stille* (1876–1966), Ger. geologist: see -ITE[1].] Native zinc selenide, ZnSe, found as grey or black cubic crystals.

1957 *Amer. Mineralogist* XLII. 584 (*heading*) Stilleite. **1970** *Mineral. Abstr.* XXI. 316/1 Mix crystals of ZnSe.., known as the mineral stilleite, and CdSe..were synthesized at 800° to 1200°C.

stilleli, -lich(e, -like, obs. forms of STILLY.

stillen, var. STEELEN *a.*; obs. f. STILLING *sb.*

stiller[1] ('stɪlə(r)). [f. STILL *v.*[1] + -ER[1].]

1. One who or something which makes still.

1608 J. KING *Serm. St. Mary's, Oxf.* 27 The stiller of wars, and extinguisher of rebellions. **1845–6** TRENCH *Huls. Lect.* Ser. I. i. 157 The stiller of creation's groans. **1849** *Tait's Mag.* XVI. 292/1 That is your true stiller of tempests.

2. (See quots.)

1862 C. C. ROBINSON *Dial. Leeds* 422 *Stiller*, a piece of wood placed on the surface of water in a pail to steady it, when carried any distance. **1874** R. G. WHITE *Words & Uses* 213 Floating on the top of the water was a disc of wood a little less in diameter than the rim of the pail. 'What's that, my lass?' he asked. 'That?' (with surprise); 'why, that's a stiller.'

stiller[2] ('stɪlə(r)). [f. STILL *v.*[2] + -ER[1].] One who distils; a distiller.

1580 HOLLYBAND *Treas. Fr. Tong, Chapelier*,..a stiller. **1615** in *Issues of Exch.* (1836) 328 To the stiller for his ordinary allowances in stilling of waters. **1757** A. COOPER *Distiller* I. ii. (1760) 20 How far the fine Stiller may profit by it, well deserves his Attention. **1902** *Blackw. Mag.* Aug. 260/1 He was a poacher and a stiller of whisky of course.

† **'stillery.** *Obs.* Also 7 stillary. [f. STILL *v.*[2] + -ERY.]

1. ? A still. In quots. *fig.*

1595 CHAPMAN *Ovid's Banq. Sence* B 4 b, Thus should I be her notes, before they be; While in her blood they sitte with fierye wings Not vapord in her voyces stillerie. *a* **1618** SYLVESTER *Tobacco Battered* 445 Causing a moist Brain, by uncease supply Of Rheums still drawn to th' bodie's Stillary. **1624** HEYWOOD *Captives* II. ii. in Bullen *O. Pl.* IV. 142 That stillary of all infectious sinnes.

2. A distillery.

1762 tr. *Busching's Syst. Geog.* IV. 353 In it also the farm-buildings, together with the brewery and stillery. **1804** T. TROTTER *Ess. Drunkenness* i. 6 Abundance of corn, was again, for the sake of taxation, converted into poisonous spirits, by opening the stilleries.

stillet, obs. form of STYLET.

still-fishing, *vbl. sb. N. Amer.* [f. STILL *a.* + FISHING *vbl. sb.*[1]] The practice of fishing from one spot, esp. with a baited line.

1883 *Century Mag.* July 383/1 The Floridians..use a long rod or pole for still-fishing. **1902** J. TURNER-TURNER *Giant Fish Florida* iii. 49 Still-fishing, the old-fashioned method of angling, is practised under the lea of some islands only on days that do not permit of your getting out into the Pass. **1963** P. A. PARSONS *Compl. Bk. Freshwater Fishing* xxiii. 250 Crappies may be caught by drifting, trolling, still-fishing, and casting. **1971** *Islander* (Victoria, B.C.) 7 Nov. 13/2 Which method calls for the most skill—bait fishing (sometimes called still fishing) or artificial lure angling?

Hence (as back-formation) **still-fish** *v. intr.*

1903 *Outing* XLII. 716/1 We could..troll or cast or still-fish with light tackle. **1953** *Sunday Sun Mag.* (Baltimore) 25 Oct. 28/4 Whether you fish on a comfortable party boat..or simply sit on a piling and still-fish,..it's the best kind of relaxation there is. **1974** M. HOYT *Thirty Miles for Ice Cream* i. 4 We still-fished for perch.

† **still-green,** *a. Obs.* [f. STILL *adv.* + GREEN *a.*] = EVERGREEN *a.*

1591 SYLVESTER *Du Bartas* I. iii. 981 Still-green Laurel shall be still thy Lot. **1603** J. DAVIES (Heref.) *Microcosmos, Extasie* 249 A gloomy Bowre of stil-greene Baies. **1665** J. REA *Flora* 16 We will conclude with two other Greens, which in their beautiful still-green leaves much resemble them.

† **'stillhead.** *Obs. rare*$^{-1}$. In 4 stillehede. [f. STILL *a.* + -HEAD.] Quietness.

1340 *Ayenb.* 142 þous biginþ þe zaule to louie onhede and stillehede.

still-'head. [f. STILL *sb.*[1] + HEAD *sb.*]

1. The cap, helm, or upper compartment of a still or alembic.

1694 *Act 6 & 7 Will. & M.* c. 18 §1 Bottles..Called Rounds, Squares, Receivers, Retorts, Bolt-heads, Still-heads. *c* **1770** MRS. GLASSE *Compl. Confectioner* 282 Also lute the nose of the still-head to the worm. **1798** *Repert. Arts & Manuf.* (1799) X. 290 The improved patent still-head. **1856** *Debates Jamaica Assembly* I. 87 The still, the worm, the still-head,..[etc.] shall be forfeited. **1866** SIR T. SEATON *From Cadet to Col.* I. ix. 277 This was my still, and a smaller pot, whose mouth would just go inside the larger, formed the still-head.

b. *at the still-head*: an expression used with reference to the collection of the spirit duty before the spirit has left the distillery.

1743 *Johnson's Wks.* (1787) *Debates* II. 386 By the new Bill a small Duty per gallon was laid on at the Still-head. **1878** LECKY *Eng. in 18th C.* (1883) I. 480 Lowering the duty on..spirits to 1d. in the gallon, levied at the still-head.

attrib. **1850** *Direct. Rev. Off. N.W. Prov.* 224 Licensed venders, who are bound to pay the still-head duty on the quantity of liquor for which the license is granted.

2. *Comb.* **still-headsman,** a workman in charge of a still-head.

1887 *Scott. Leader* 17 Nov. 5 Peter Paris, still-headsman.

'still-house. [f. STILL *sb.*[1] + HOUSE *sb.*] A building in which distillation is carried on; a distillery. †See also quot. *a* 1734 (cf. STILL-ROOM b).

1558 in Feuillerat *Revels Q. Eliz.* (1908) 47 One Stylle-house in the passage leading to the garden. **1617** MORYSON *Itin.* I. 59 This Gentleman had a very faire Library, full of excellent bookes, and a like faire still-house. **1695** *Lond. Gaz.* No. 3048/4 At Chichester..is a convenient Still-house ready fitted with Stills, Coppers, Hogpenns, Mill and Mill-house,..to be Lett. *a* **1734** NORTH *Lives, Life J. North* (1744) 249 [The custom] was for the..Gentlemen Officers to meet every Morning in a Sort of Stil-house, where a good Woman provided them with their Liquors as they liked best; and this they called their Coffee-house. *a* **1812** J. BARLOW *Poem on Hasty Pudding* (Bartlett) Joys that the vineyard and the still-house bring. **1834** A. PIKE *Prose Sk. & Poems* 24 Our party reached the still house in the valley. **1884** 'C. E. CRADDOCK' *In Tennessee Mountains* II. 118 Josiah Tait had put his troubles in to soak at the still-house. **1927** *Greensboro* (N.C.) *Daily News* 24 Apr. II. 7/5 One time I was sent fur to bury a feller who had been found dead by a still house over yon side the Roan. **1976** *Lancet* 18 Dec. 1358/2 Mountaineers' distrust of government for the past half-century has had vastly more to do with the antisocial environmental, economic, and developmental policies of half a dozen Federal agencies..than with overturning mash barrels and knocking down stillhouses.

attrib. **1624** in *Archæologia* XLVIII. 151 In the still house chamber, one standing bedsteed. **1856** *Debates Jamaica Assembly* I. 87 The Hon. Gentleman himself..would not be eligible for the situation of a Still-house book keeper.

still hunt, *sb. U.S.* Also **still-hunt.** [f. STILL *a.* + HUNT *sb.*]

1. A pursuit for game in a stealthy manner or under cover; stalking.

1860 MAYNE REID *Hunter's Feast* xvii, It was to be a 'still' hunt, and we went afoot. **1861** G. F. BERKELEY *Eng. Sportsman* xiv. 261 They started to a still hunt.

2. *transf.* and *fig.* The pursuit of any object quietly and cautiously; *esp.* (see quot. 1890).

1828 M. S. BIDWELL *Let.* in *Toronto Publ. Libr. MSS* B104. 69 Under the guidance of Mackenzie, who did not conduct himself with the caution and reserve of a new member, the House went on a still hunt for grievances. **1876** *N.Y. Tribune* 28 Aug. 4/4 It will be well for the Republican managers to bear in mind that a 'still hunt' is Gov. Tilden's favorite campaign method. **1890** C. L. NORTON *Polit. Americanisms* 109 *Still Hunt*, originally a sporting term, but applied during the campaign of 1876 to political methods conducted in secret, or underhanded methods. **1893** *Lightning* 9 Feb. 89/2 We go on the 'still-hunt' principle. **1916** 'B. M. BOWER' *Phantom Herd* ii. 32 I'm out on a still hunt for some real boys. **1936** H. HAGEDORN *Brookings* ix. 131 He took to riding afternoons in Forest Park along the western edge of the city, on a persistent, still-hunt for a site. **1948** E. N. DICK *Dixie Frontier* 241 Sometimes a candidate ..slipped off and went on a 'still hunt'; that is, he visited the people house-to-house and attended small gatherings unheralded.

still-hunt, *v. U.S.* [Back-formation from STILL-HUNTING *vbl. sb.*]

1. *trans.* To hunt in a stealthy manner; to stalk.

1877 C. HALLOCK *Sportsman's Gazetteer* 81 (Cent.) The best time to still-hunt deer is just before sunset, when they come down from the hills to drink. **1885** ROOSEVELT *Hunting Trips* 327 (Cent.) The only way to get one [a grizzly] is to put on moccasins and still-hunt it in its own haunts.

2. *intr.* To hunt for game in a stealthy manner.

1858 *Harper's Mag.* Oct. 615/2 An old woodsman..had been, without success, still-hunting. **1863** E. H. WALSHE *Cedar Creek* 107 You see I'm often away trapping or still-hunting. **1881** *Scribner's Monthly* XXII. 859/1 On rainy days, we go out from camp, singly, and 'still-hunt' for deer. **1894** *Outing* XXIV. 261/1, I was not still-hunting, though I made but slight disturbance. **1942** W. FAULKNER *Go down, Moses* 149 Once, still-hunting with Walter Ewell's rifle, he saw it [*sc.* a bear] cross a long corridor of down timber where a tornado had passed.

still-hunter. *U.S.* [Formed as STILL-HUNT *v.*: see -ER[1].] One who hunts game in a quiet or stealthy manner; a stalker.

1831 AUDUBON *Ornith.* I. 335 We shall therefore suppose that we are now about to follow the *true hunter*, as the Still Hunter is also called. **1895** *Outing* XXVI. 64/2 He hated that weapon with all the unreasonable pertinacity of the old school of still-hunters. **1904** T. S. VAN DYKE (*title*) The Still-hunter.

still-hunting, *vbl. sb. U.S.* [f. STILL *a.* + HUNTING *vbl. sb.*] The practice of hunting game in a stealthy and noiseless manner.

1831 AUDUBON *Ornith.* I. 335 Still Hunting is followed as a kind of trade by most of our frontier men. **1847** RUXTON *Adv. Mexico* xxxii. 301 There are two methods of hunting buffalo—one on horseback,..the other by 'still hunting', that is, 'approaching,' or stalking, by taking advantage of the wind and any cover the ground affords. **1860** MAYNE REID *Hunters' Feast* xxiii, The simplest and most common is that which is termed 'still' hunting.

still-hunting: see STILL *sb.*[1] 4.

stilliard(e, obs. forms of STEELYARD[1], [2].

† **Stilliardois,** *pl. Obs. rare.* [f. *stilliard* STEELYARD[1] + F. suffix *-ois* = -ESE.] A name given to the Merchants of the Steelyard.

1552 *Acts Privy Council* N. S. IV. 98 A lettre to William Sydney, Customer of London, to suffer the Stilliardoys to lade for the parties of beyonde the sea certaine cloth.

stillic, stillich(e, obs. forms of STILLY.

stillicide ('stɪlɪsaɪd). Also 7 **stillicid.** [Anglicized form of STILLICIDIUM.]

1. A falling of water, etc. in drops; a succession of drops. Now *rare.*

1626 BACON *Sylva* §24 Wee see it also in the Stillicides of water, which if ther be water enough to follow, will Drawe themselues into a small thredd, because they will not discontinue. *a* **1651** CULVERWELL *Lt. Nat.* etc. II. vi. (1654) 161 Those fallings down of water, that thred and spin themselves into such slender stillicids. **1657** TOMLINSON *Renou's Disp.* 192 To Irrigation we may refer the Stillicide or Laver of medicated waters. **1898** HARDY *Wessex Poems* 156 In the mated measured note Of..a lone cave's stillicide.

2. *Civil and Scots Law.* The dropping of rain-water from the eaves of a house upon another's land or roof; the right or the servitude relating to this.

1656 BLOUNT *Glossogr.*, *Stillicide*, the dropping of the Eaves of an house. **1681** STAIR *Inst. Law Scot.* XVII. vii. 342 The next positive City-servitude is, of Stillicides or Sinks; Stillicide is the easing-drop which falleth off any house [etc.]. **1754** ERSKINE *Princ. Sc. Law* (1809) 222 No proprietor can build, so as to throw the rain water falling from his own house immediately upon his neighbour's ground, without a special servitude, which is called of stillicide.

stilli'cidious, *a.* ? *Obs. rare*$^{-1}$. [f. STILLICIDIUM + -OUS.] Produced by a falling in drops.

1646 SIR T. BROWNE *Pseud. Ep.* II. i. 56 Crystall is..in some places not much unlike the stirious or stillicidious dependencies of Ice. **1656** in BLOUNT *Glossogr.*

‖ **stilli'cidium** (stɪlɪ'sɪdɪəm). Pl. **-cidia.** [L., f. *stilla* drop + *cid-* weakened root of *cadĕre* to fall.]

1. *Civil Law.* = STILLICIDE.

1727 BAILEY vol. II, *Stillicidium*, the Droppings of the Eaves of an House. **1765–8** ERSKINE *Inst. Law Scot.* II. ix. 309. **1892** KATH. GOULD tr. *Convers. Döllinger* i. 5 The stillicidia of the Romans..did not interest me in the least.

2. *Path.* A morbid dropping or trickling.

1791 G. WALLIS *Motherby's Med. Dict.* (ed. 3) s.v. *Vagina*, They [polypous tumours in the vagina] are attended with perpetual stillicidium from the vagina. **1876** BARTHOLOW *Mat. Med.* (1879) 408 A constant stillicidium of semen. **1876** tr. *Wagner's Gen. Pathol.* 94 Stillicidium and catarrh of the lachrymal ducts.

† **stillie,** *a. Her. Obs.* [f. L. *stilla* drop, after BARRY, CHECKY, etc.] Besprinkled with drops.

1572 BOSSEWELL *Armorie* II. 88 b, The fielde is Verte, Stillie, d'Argente.

† **'stillified,** *ppl. a. Obs.* [f. STILL *v.*[2] + -(I)FY + -ED[1].] Distilled.

1608 ROWLANDS *Humors Looking Gl.* B 4 b, Tobacco's stillified stink.

stilliform ('stɪlɪfɔːm), *a.* [f. L. *stilla* a drop + -FORM.] Drop-shaped.

In recent Dicts.

stilling ('stɪlɪŋ), *sb.*[1] Also 7 **steeling(e, stillinge, styling,** 8 **stillen.** See also STILLION. [Perh. corruptly a. Du. *stelling* stand, scaffold, f. *stellen* to place. Cf. STILLAGE.] A stand for a cask, a gantry.

1604 *Ball. Coll. Oxf. Acc.* (MS.), Item, to Golidge [a carpenter] for makinge stillings for beare, and other worke, vi[s] i[d]. **1665** in Halliwell *Acc. Collect. Bills* etc. (1852) 17 In the strong Beere Seller. A styling. **1743** *Lond. & Country Brewer* III. (ed. 2) 235 They roll and tumble the Barrel backwards and forwards up and down on a Stilling. **1827** SIR J. BARRINGTON *Pers. Sk.* II. 49 Very like a beer barrel on its stilling. **1875** KNIGHT *Dict. Mech.*, *Stilling*, a stand for casks. A stillion.

stilling ('stɪlɪŋ), *sb.*[2] *Mining.* [Of obscure origin.] (See quots.)

1883 GRESLEY *Gloss. Coal-mining* 240 *Stilling*, the walling of a shaft within the tubbing above the stone head. **1899** BARING-GOULD *Bk. West* II. *Cornw.* v. 63 [Tin mining] The walling on each side of a *tye* or adit is called *stilling*.

Stilling ('ʃtɪlɪŋ), *sb.*[3] *Ophthalm.* The name of Jakob *Stilling* (1842–1915), German ophthalmologist, used *attrib.* and in the possessive with reference to a test for colour-blindness based on the use of pseudo-isochromatic plates which he devised (*Arch. Ophthalmol.* (1879) VIII. 164).

1896 J. E. JENNINGS *Color-Vision & Color-Blindness* vii. 75 Stilling's plates are of practical value, and should be used in conjunction with the worsted test. **1925** M. COLLINS *Colour-Blindness* iii. 59 These students were examined [for colour blindness] in the course of the ordinary laboratory period by means of Stilling's Tables, and some of them failed completely to pass the tests. **1935** *Discovery* Jan. 15/2 Colour blindness tests (such as the Edridge Green or Stilling tests) are not much use in choosing men for this work. **1954** S. DUKE-ELDER *Parsons' Dis. Eye* (ed. 12) xx. 345 Stilling's original tests have now been largely replaced by Ishihara's.

stilling (ˈstɪlɪŋ), *vbl. sb.*[1] [f. STILL *v.*[1] + -ING[1].] The action of making still; quietening; calming.

1530 PALSGR. 276/1 Styllyng or apeysing, *apeisement.* **1622** HAKEWILL *David's Vow* vii. 258 A deceit..which Nurses vse for the stilling of their Children. *c* **1698** LOCKE *Cond. Understand.* §xlv, Thus some trivial sentence, or a scrap of poetry, will sometimes get into men's heads, and make such a chiming there, that there is no stilling of it. **1792** MME. D'ARBLAY *Lett.* 20 Dec., The pretended friends of the people..wait but the stilling of the present ferment of royalty to come forth. **1846** TRENCH *Mirac.* xix. 310 They ..might pluck the ripe ears for the stilling of their present hunger. **1863** MISS WHATELY *Ragged Life in Egypt* 200 It is beautiful when the sun draws in his fiery shafts to watch the stilling of the air.

stilling (ˈstɪlɪŋ), *vbl. sb.*[2] Also 6 **steeling, steylling, stylling, -yng.** [f. STILL *v.*[2] + -ING[1].]

†**1.** The action of the verb STILL[2]; distillation.

1477 NORTON *Ordin. Alch.* v. in Ashm. (1652) 79 Liquor is in manie manners found..Some with stilling, as Waters be made. **1573-80** TUSSER *Husb.* (1878) 115 The knowledge of stilling is one pretie feat. **1683** TRYON *Way to Health* 554, I appeal to your selves, if your Wort would not have turned sower,..and of no use or virtue, except for Stilling.

attrib. **1545** in R. H. Lathbury *Denham, Bucks* (1904) 339 All the shelfes and formes that are in the stillinge house. **1573** in *Rep. Middleton MSS.* (Hist. MSS. Comm. 1911) 438 To the cater..for the exchaunge of a steeling pott, iiij s. **1596** in *Archæologia* LXIV. 375 For 1 dor in ye steylling house. **1600** SURFLET *Country Farm* III. lxiv. 578 The stilling vessels. **1840** *Liebig's Org. Chem. Relat. Agric.* 294 The wine in the stilling-casks.

b. *Ireland.* Illicit distillation of spirits.

1896 *Blackw. Mag.* Oct. 470/1 The Roman Catholic Bishop of Raphoe..has done more to stamp out 'stilling' than the R.I.C. could accomplish in a generation. **1912** *Ibid.* Dec. 787/2 Many parts of the Blue Ridge have long been notorious for the stilling which was carried on there, mostly on the illicit plan.

†**2.** Dropping or trickling. *Obs.*

1530 PALSGR. 276/1 Styllyng or droppyng of lycour, *distillation.* **1538** ELYOT *Dict., Catarrhus,* a rewme or styllynge downe of water or fleme from the heed. **1576** BAKER *Gesner's Jewell of Health* 4 The yelowe seedes within the Rose..boyled in Wyne and drunke, doth staye..the styllings downe to the Gummes.

stilling (ˈstɪlɪŋ), *ppl. a.*[1] [f. STILL *v.*[1] + -ING[2].] That makes still; quietening; calming.

1635 SIBBES *Serm. John* xiv. 1 (1636) 35 Thus faith becomes a quieting and a stilling grace. **1844** KINGLAKE *Eothen* ii. (1847) 18 More stilling than very silence. **1873** MISS BROUGHTON *Nancy* III. 126 There is something so stilling in the far placidity of the high stars. **1902** *Academy* 22 Mar. 324/1 The touch like a stilling finger, The whisper, the sigh.

†**ˈstilling,** *ppl. a.*[2] *Obs.* [f. STILL *v.*[2] + -ING[2].] Trickling or falling in drops; distilling.

a **1542** WYATT *Poems, 'Process of time'* 6 And yet an hert that sems so tender receveth no droppe of the stilling teres that [etc.]. **1565** GOLDING *Ovid's Met.* I. (1593) 9 And on his feathers and his breast a stilling dew did sticke.

stillion (ˈstɪlɪən). [? var. of STILLING *sb.*[1]]

1. A stand for a cask; a gantry. Also, a stand or frame on which pottery is placed in the drying kiln (Knight).

1803 *Ann. Reg., Chron.* 396/2 Mr. Madden..had water and beer butts thrown flat from the stillions. **1839** URE *Dict. Arts* 383 The casks are raised upon gawntrees or stillions. **1875** KNIGHT *Dict. Mech.* 2386 *Stillion,* a stand for casks. The rounds or cleansing vats of a brewery stand on stillions in a trough which conveys away the overflowing yeast.

2. (See quot. 1836.)

1826 *Art of Brewing* (ed. 2) 6 The beer..not suffered to remain in small quantities in the stillions or other utensils. **1836** *Penny Cycl.* V. 404/2 A trough or stillion to catch the yest. **1871** G. SCAMELL *Breweries & Maltings* xv. 74 The yeast finding its way the best way it can into the stillion beneath.

stillish (ˈstɪlɪʃ), *a.* [+ -ISH.] Somewhat still.

1648 HEXHAM II, *Stilachtigh, ofte een weynigh stil,* Stillish, or somewhat Still. **1894** C. L. MORGAN in *Nature* 6 Dec. 127/1 One [limpet] was observed to make a short excursion from and to return to its scar under stillish water.

stillitorie, -ory(e, obs. ff. STILLATORY.

still life. [f. STILL *a.* + LIFE *sb.,* after Du. *stilleven* (in the 17th c. also *stilstaand leven, stilliggend leven*). Cf. G. *stillleben,* in the 18th c. *stillliegende sachen* (Zedler 1744).

The Du. expressions have been found only in the sense explained below, but it is presumed that they were originally applied to representations not of inanimate objects but of living things portrayed in a state of rest.]

a. Inanimate objects, such as fruits, flowers, dead game, vessels, etc., as represented in painting. (For other uses see STILL *a.* 5 b.) Also *fig.*

1695 [R. GRAHAM] *Short Acc. Painters* in *Dryden's Dufresnoy's Art Paint.* 277 His peculiar happiness in expressing all sorts of Animals, Fruit, Flowers, and the Still-life. **1701** WANLEY in *Phil. Trans.* XXV. 2004 In the Still life indeed, the Eye is quickly deceiv'd. **1706** tr. *De Piles' Art Paint.* 440 Kneller..did also several Pieces in Still-Life exceedingly well. **1762-71** H. WALPOLE *Vertue's Anecd. Paint.* (1786) III. 19 He painted still-life, oranges and lemons, plate, damask curtains, cloths of gold, and that medley of familiar objects that strike the ignorant vulgar. *a* **1784** G. A. STEVENS *Let.* in T. Wilkinson *Mem.* (1790) IV. 196 My existence now cannot properly be called living, but what painters term *still life;* having since February 13, been confined in this town gaol for a London debt. **1859** GULLICK & TIMBS *Paint.* 51 Still-life is the exact imitation of immobile objects, such as fruit, flowers, and eatables.

attrib. **1821** P. EGAN *Life in London* II. i. 156 It was not the still-life Beauty of the Sculptor and the Artist. **1831** F. REYNOLDS *Playwright's Adventures* vii. 112 This still-life personage, devoting the whole of her mind and time to her pianoforte. **1867** *Contemp. Rev.* VI. 387 Landscapists and still-life painters ought to go through a course of real drawing. **1887** W. P. FRITH *Autobiog.* I. iv. 52 He still insisted that I should paint a composition of still-life objects. **1898** GOSSE *Short Hist. Mod. Engl. Lit.* vii. 236 But these pedestrian studies of nature had no passion in them; they were but passages of an inventory or a still-life painting.

b. A painting of such objects. Pl. *still lifes.*

1957 *Encycl. Brit.* XXI. 408/1 The first signed and dated pure still life..was painted in 1504. **1961** R. B. LONG *Sentence & its Parts* ix. 206 Sometimes regular plurals replace even firmly established native irregular plurals: for example, in *she does still lifes.* **1970** *Oxf. Compan. Art* 1097/1 The development of the typical still life took place mainly in the Netherlands. **1981** *Daily Tel.* 30 Dec. 10/3 After the war, the artist returned to his delicate, vague, surrealist landscapes and little still-lifes.

stillness (ˈstɪlnɪs). [OE. *stilnes, -nys,* f. *stille* adj. See STILL *a.* and -NESS. Cf. OHG. *stilnissi.*] The condition or quality of being still.

1. Absence of movement or physical disturbance; motionlessness.

c **1000** ÆLFRIC *Saints' Lives* xxxi. 1053 Heo oncneow sona þæt heo alysed wæs and læg aþenod ætforan his fotum onfangenre stilnysse. *c* **1440** *Promp. Parv.* 475/2 Stylnesse, wytheowt mevynge, *tranquillitas.* **1585** HIGINS *Junius' Nomencl.* 363/2 *Malacia,*..calmenesse or stillnesse of the sea. **1617** PURCHAS *Pilgrimage* IV. xviii. (ed. 3) 498 A pleasant Riuer of fresh water, if it may not rather be called a Lake for the stillnesse. **1650** FULLER *Pisgah* IV. ii. 20 They will admire as much at the stilness of our station, and dulness of our constant dwelling in one place. **1711** SWIFT *Cond. Allies* 10 If a House be on fire,..those at next Door may escape, by a Shower from Heaven, or the stillness of the Weather. **1845** MAURICE *Mor. Philos.* in *Encycl. Metrop.* II. 614/1 The capacity of health and sickness is the same; of stillness and movement; of being raised up and of falling down. **1876** GEO. ELIOT *Deronda* vii, The background of green and grey stillness. **1885** 'MRS. ALEXANDER' *At Bay* ii, She..would have been rather handsome but for her extreme stillness, coldness, and want of colour. **1898** FLOR. MONTGOMERY *Tony* 19 The stillness of his figure and his utter silence. **1908** [MISS E. FOWLER] *Betw. Trent & Ancholme* 12 The stillness often betokens rain.

2. Freedom from tumult, strife, or agitation; tranquillity.

c **888** ÆLFRED *Boeth.* vii. §1 Forðæm þu eart eac nu of þinre stilnesse ahworfen. *a* **1122** *O.E. Chron.* (MS. C.) an. 1065, Her wearð Harold eac to kynge ȝehalȝod & he lytle stillnesse þar on ȝebad þa hwile þe he rices weold. *c* **1175** *Lamb. Hom.* 115 He scal..beon on erfeðnesse anred and edmod on stilnesse. **1388** WYCLIF *Isa.* xxxii. 17 The tilthe of riȝtfulnesse schal be stilnesse and sikirnesse. **1663** PATRICK *Parab. Pilgrim* xvii. (1687) 166 Prayer is the silence of our Souls: the stilness and calm of all our Passions. **1807** WORDSW. *White Doe* IV. 150 On my Mind A passive stillness is enjoined. **1828** LYTTON *Pelham* xliii, That air of perfect repose—the stillness of a deep soul, which rests over their writings. **1885** 'MRS. ALEXANDER' *At Bay* i, I love quietness, stillness—being with a few people I like.

3. Silence; freedom from noise; abstinence from speech, taciturnity.

c **1050** in Assmann *Ags. Hom.* xii. 7 þæt we..mid micelre eadmodnysse & stilnysse us to urum drihtne ȝebiddan. *a* **1225** *Ancr. R.* 156 Of þisse stilnesse he spekeð þer biuoren lutel. *c* **1374** CHAUCER *Boeth.* II. pr. 1. l. 2 After that she hadde gadered by atempre stillenesse [*modesta taciturnitate*] myn attencioun. *c* **1440** *Promp. Parv.* 475/2 Stylnesse, nowt spekynge..*taciturnitas, silencium.* **1596** SHAKS. *Merch. V.* v. i. 56 Soft stilnes, and the night Become the tutches of sweet harmonie. **1663** PATRICK *Parab. Pilgr.* (1687) 177 Who all this while had been in a profound stilness. **1750** GRAY *Elegy* 6 All the air a solemn stillness holds. **1784** J. KING *Cook's 3rd Voy.* v. iv. III. 55 We afterward saw the natives flying, the boats retire from the shore, and passing and repassing, in great stillness, between the ships. **1796** MORSE *Amer. Geog.* I. 425 A certain stillness and gravity of manner, perhaps in some degree peculiar to commercial people. **1821** LAMB *Elia* Ser. I. *Quaker's Meeting,* What is the stillness of the desert, compared with this place? **1838** DICKENS *O. Twist* xii, The darkness and the deep stillness of the room were very solemn. **1843** RUSKIN *Arrows of Chace* (1880) I. 28 Wordsworth, read in the stillness of a mountain hollow, has the force of the mountain waters. **1892** KIPLING *Barrack-room Ballads* 174 They are lifting their heads in the stillness to yelp at the English flag!

†**b.** Secrecy. *Obs.*

a **1400** *Hymns Virgin* etc. (1895) 110 Stele þou nouȝt þi neiȝebors þing, Nouþur wiþ stillenes ne wiþ strif. *a* **1779** WARBURTON *Serm.* vi. Wks. 1788 V. 105 In all the depth and stillness of Politics.

4. Quietness of temper or behaviour; freedom from turbulence or self-assertion. (See also STILL *a.* 4 d.)

a **1225** *Ancr. R.* 414 Marie dole is stilnesse and reste of alle worldes noise. *c* **1412** HOCCLEVE *De Reg. Princ.* 1013 But we labour in trauaillous stilnesse. *a* **1564** BECON *Commonpl. Script.* Wks. III. 93 The goodman with stilnesse and pacience taryeth for y[e] health of the Lorde. **1599** SHAKS. *Hen. V,* III. i. 4 In Peace, there's nothing so becomes a man, As modest stillnesse, and humilitie. **1738** WESLEY *Hymns* 'Meek, patient Lamb of God' ii, Give me in Stillness to sustaine Whate'er thy Wisdom shall ordain. **1745** —— *Answ. Ch.* 19 Your Notion of True Stillness is, 'A patient waiting upon God'.

stillotorie, obs. f. STILLATORY.

ˈstill-room. [STILL *sb.*[1]] **a.** *Hist.* Originally, a room in a house in which a still was kept for the distillation of perfumes and cordials. **b.** In later use, a room in which preserves, cakes, liqueurs, etc. are kept, and tea, coffee, etc. are prepared. Also *attrib.* in ***still-room maid, window.***

c **1710** CELIA FIENNES *Diary* (1888) 299 On one side is a building, a summer parlour for a still room. **1810** MALONE *Let.* 30 Jan. in *Windham Papers* II. 367 Pray, what is the precise notion of a still-room..? I imagine it is a housekeeper's room, where china and stores are kept... I never once heard the word, till I heard it used by a lady, a few months ago. **1833** LOUDON *Encycl. Archit.* §1698 A door in the housekeeper's room should open into the still-room, in which the housekeeper, assisted by the still-room maid, would make preserves, cakes, &c. **1853** DICKENS etc. *Househ. Words* Christm. No. 2/2 She used to give him a good-humoured look out of her still-room window sometimes. **1858** THACKERAY *Virgin.* xlv, A hundred years ago, every lady in the country had her still-room, and her medicine-chest, her pills, powders, potions, for all the village round. **1862** *Draper & Clothier* III. 9/2 This agreeable lady..announced herself as 'Mrs. Brown, the still-room maid'... Mrs. Brown had to take charge of vast quantities of stores in daily use,—goods sent in from grocers, oilmen, chandlers, and tradesmen of that class. **1865** J. B. HARWOOD *Lady Flavia* xlvi, There was babbling in milliners' work-rooms, and in what are facetiously called the still-rooms of country mansions. **1901** *Daily Chron.* 10 Sept. 10/6 Still-room Maid..wanted immediately. **1906** *Westm. Gaz.* 7 June 12/1 The still-room of the House of Commons is badly situated, and has but a small window through which to pass supplies.

Still's disease (stɪlz). *Path.* [Named after Sir George Frederic *Still* (1868–1941), English physician, who first described the disease in 1896 (*Med.-Chir. Trans.* (1897) LXXX. 47).] A condition affecting children, characterized by arthritis and ankylosis and now believed to be a form of rheumatoid arthritis.

1905 *Lancet* 27 May 1424/2 Though Still's disease was of the nature of a multiple joint affection no changes in the bones or the cartilages were observed. **1936** W. SHELDON *Dis. Infancy & Childhood* xxiii. 596 In some children the changes in and around the joints make up almost the entire clinical picture, but more often there is an accompanying lymphatic reaction, as shown by enlargement of the superficial lymphatic glands and enlargement of the spleen (Still's disease). **1974** A. HENRY in R. M. Kirk et al. *Surgery* xv. 303 Rheumatoid arthritis occurring in childhood (Still's disease..) is probably not a separate entity.

†**stillsitting,** *vbl. sb. Obs.* [f. STILL *adv.* + SITTING *vbl. sb.*] Sitting still, inactivity. So †**stillsitting** *ppl. a.,* that sits still, sedentary.

1535 COVERDALE *Isa.* xxx. 15 With stilsittinge and rest shal ye be healed. **1597** A. M. tr. *Guillemeau's Fr. Chirurg.* 3/1 That man which laboureth [will be cured] easier then a stillsittinge and idle persone.

Stillson (ˈstɪlsən). Also **Stilson, stilson.** The name of Daniel Chapman *Stillson* (1830–99), used *attrib.* and *absol.* to designate an adjustable pipe wrench invented by him in 1869 and originally manufactured by his employers, the Walworth Company of New York.

1902 *Sears Catal.* 563/3 The Stillson Pipe wrench is too well known to require a lengthy description of same. **1903** *Sci. Amer.* 10 Oct. 266/1 Your kit is not complete unless it includes the famous Stillson wrench which is particularly adapted for turning out the best work without crushing the pipe in the least. **1945** *Walworth 1842–1942* (Walworth Company Inc.) 42 The sales of the Stillsons are highly sensitive to changes in economic conditions. **1960** E. L. DELMAR-MORGAN *Cruising Yacht Equipment & Navigation* xiv. 162 It used to be said by the old-time mechanics that refractory pipe joints suddenly made themselves loose when they saw you pick up a Stillson. **1961** J. SEYMOUR *Fat of Land* v. 67, I spend half the night..working in the blizzard or the deep frost with 'stilsons'..and other esoteric devices. **1971** F. HAMILTON *World Encycl. Dogs* 119 The undershot lower jaw [of a boxer]..gives a leverage similar to that of the plumber's Stilson wrench; once contact is made it cannot be broken; a pull just makes it tighter. **1978** J. GORES *Gone, no Forwarding* (1979) x. 62 Balland was out of his car, eight-inch Stillson wrench..in hand.

ˈstill-stand. Also **stillstand.** [f. STILL *a.* + STAND *sb.* So Du. *stilstand,* G. *stillstand.*]

1. a. A stand-still. *rare.* Also spec. in *Path.*

1597 SHAKS. *2 Hen. IV,* II. iii. 64 As with the Tyde, swell'd vp vnto his height, That makes a still-stand, running neyther way. **1837** CARLYLE *Fr. Rev.* I. III. i, And so, towards the end of 1783, matters threaten to come to a still-stand. **1878** M. FOSTER *Physiol.* III. v. §2 (ed. 2) 479 The lymph hearts remained in a (diastolic) still-stand. **1885** T. L. BRUNTON *Text-bk. Pharmacol.* etc. xxxiii. 912 The systolic stillstand is removed, and pulsation again recommences.

b. *Physical Geogr.* A condition in which there is no crustal movement in a region or no change in sea-level.

1896 *Bull. Geol. Soc. Amer.* VII. 393 The English School denies..the probability or even the possibility of a period of still-stand long enough for essentially complete subaerial denudation close to sea level, but assumes the possibility of a period of still-stand or of slight depression continuous and long enough to allow the sea waves to plane off the sinking lands. **1937** WOOLDRIDGE & MORGAN *Physical Basis Geogr.* xv. 218 The cycle [of erosion] can only move uninterruptedly to its close if it coincides with a period of still-stand, *i.e.* of unvarying base-level, unaffected by major climatic changes. **1966** J. WYCKOFF *Rock, Time, & Landforms* iv. 103 All believe that the reduction of vast, lofty highlands by erosion demands time spans of the order of 25 million years, during which there is virtual stillstand—that is lack of uplift. **1972** R. A. DAVIS *Princ. Oceanogr.* xx. 322 One of the most prevalent and significant types of evidence is the presence of terraces which were formed during still-stands of sea level.

†**2.** *spec.* [After G. (*waffen*)*stillstand*, Du. *stilstand* (*van wapenen*).] An armistice. *Obs.*

1637 R. MONRO *Exped.* I. 74 A still-stand or cessation of Armes was concluded on by both parties, for a fortnights time. **1819** SCOTT *Leg. Montrose* xi, During a still-stand of arms.

'still water. [f. STILL *a.* + WATER *sb.*]

1. = SLACK-WATER I.

1626 CAPT. SMITH *Accid. Yng. Seamen* 17 It flows quarter floud, high water, or a still water. **1791** SMEATON *Edystone L.* §3 The change of direction or time of Still Water. **1808** FORSYTH *Beauties Scot.* V. 33 According as it is new made, half run, or approaching to still water.

2. (See quots.)

1832 W. D. WILLIAMSON *Hist. Maine* I. 66 The Metawamkeag..has frequent falls and intervening still-waters. **1867** SMYTH *Sailor's Word-bk., Still Water*..is also used for water under the lee of headlands, or where there is neither tide nor current. **1896** *Trans. Roy. Soc. Canada* II. ii. 210 Stillwater... A smooth place in a stream which is usually rough.

3. *attrib.*

1758 *Descr. Thames* 187 The Tench is a Still-water Fish, and delights in Ponds more than Rivers. **1834** *Oxf. Univ. Mag.* I. 307 Artificial canals or rather still-water navigation. **1889** WELCH *Text Bk. Naval Archit.* iii. 60 If a ship happens to fall in with waves having a period twice that of her own natural or still-water period, she will infallibly capsize after the passage of a few waves.

stillwellite ('stɪlwɛlaɪt). *Min.* [f. the name of F. L. *Stillwell* (1888–1963), Austral. geologist + -ITE[1].] A borosilicate of lanthanons and calcium, $(Ln,Ca)BOSiO_4$, found as brown rhombohedral crystals.

1955 MCANDREW & SCOTT in *Nature* 10 Sept. 509/2 The presence of stillwellite was discovered in 1954 during a mineralogical investigation of radioactive ore..34 miles east of Mt. Isa in north-western Queensland. **1971** *Doklady Acad. Sci. U.S.S.R.: Earth Sci. Sections* CCI. 182/1 The above data on our synthesis of the lanthanum analogs of stillwellite indicate that this borosilicate may be more widespread in nature than was previously thought.

†**'stillworth,** *a. Obs.* [app. f. STILL *a.* + *-worth* after STALWORTH.] Peaceful.

c **1275** LAY. 12834 And stilleworþe [*c* 1205 þa æhte] wifmen wepmenne cloþes dude heom on.

stilly ('stɪlɪ), *a.* [f. STILL *a.* + -LY[1].

In the modern sense 2 the word may have been suggested by STILLY *adv.* It may, however, be a distinct word, f. STILL *a.* or STILL *sb.*[2] + -Y. Cf. PALY *a.*[1]]

†**1.** Secret. (Frequent in Layamon.) *Obs.*

c **1205** LAY. 2374 [He] mid stilliche ginne brohte Æstrild þer inne. *Ibid.* 17776 Forð wende þe swike..& spec wið his monnen mid stilleliche rune.

2. Characterized by stillness. Chiefly *poet.*

1776 MICKLE tr. *Camoens' Lusiad* 386 Not a blast may shake Its fluttering pinions o'er the stilly lake. **1795** COLERIDGE *Eolian Harp* 11 The stilly murmur of the distant Sea Tells us of silence. **1811** SHELLEY *St. Irvyne* iii. Pr. Wks. 1888 I. 153 The wind sighed moaningly along the stilly colonnades. **1815** MOORE *Nat. Airs,* Oft, in the stilly night, Ere Slumber's chain has bound me. **1816** BRACKENRIDGE *Jrnl.* 13 Several deer..seemed to move across this stilly scene, like the shadows of the phantasmagoria. **1830** TENNYSON *Recoll. Arab. Nts.* 103 Many a shadow-chequer'd lawn Full of the city's stilly sound. **1841** LEVER *O'Malley* lxxix, How the pale and stilly figure counts over the hours. **1865** W. G. PALGRAVE *Arabia* I. 305 This dry and stilly region. **1889** HISSEY *Tour Phaeton* 59 A stilly sheet of water.

stilly ('stɪlɪ), *adv.* Forms: 1 **stillíce,** 2 **stillice,** 3 **stilleliȝ, stillelike, stilliȝ,** 3–5 **stil(le)liche,** 4 **stilleli, stillic(h, styllyche,** 4–5 **stillelich, -ly, stilli,** 4–6 **stylly,** 5 **stillie, stylleche, styly,** 4– **stilly.** [OE. *stillíce*, f. *stille* STILL *a.* + *-líce* -LY[2].] In a still manner; silently, quietly; in a low voice; †secretly.

c **1000** *De Consuet. Monach.* 266 in *Anglia* XIII. 384 *Silenter*, stillice. *c* **1200** ORMIN 16618 He wollde lernenn All stilleliȝ summwhatt at himm. *c* **1205** LAY. 6706 Hæhten his drihliche folc stilleluker dremen. *a* **1225** *Ancr. R.* 82 þe neddre, seið Salomon, stingeð al stilliche. *a* **1300** *Cursor M.* 4948 þan spak ruben, þe eildest broiþer, Stilli menand til þas oþer. **1303** R. BRUNNE *Handl. Synne* 2432 ȝyf þou withdrawest a mannys ryȝt Styllyche. **13..** *K. Alis.* 1562 (Laud MS.), He com & seide to þe kyng Stillich bitwene his lyppe þat [etc.]. **1382** WYCLIF *Ecclus.* xxi. 23 The fool in laȝhing enhaunceth his vois; forsothe a wis man vnnethe stilleli shal laȝhen. *c* **1425** *Eng. Conq. Irel.* lxii. 150 Al the Iresshe..stylly sworne ham to-gyddyr ayeyns the Englysshe. *c* **1430** *Pilgr. Lyf Manhode* II. cxxxii. (1869) 126 And took me this knyf priueliche, whiche j bere stilleliche and in hideles. *c* **1440** *Life St. Kath.* (Halliw. 1848) 10 Ihesu Cryste they thanked moche And went ageyne full stylleche. **1598** BARRET *Theor. Warres* IV. ii. 105 In their conuersations to talke modestly, stilly, and with low voices. **1599** SHAKS. *Hen. V*, IV. Chorus 5 From Camp to Camp,..The Humme of eyther Army stilly sounds. **1621** LADY M. WROTH *Urania* 177 So stilly did she mooue,..as trees grow without sence of increase. **1802** H. MARTIN *Helen of Glenross* III. 186, I am very sad—quietly, stilly sad. **1810** SCOTT *Lady of L.* III. xiv, The rocks, the bosky thickets, sleep So stilly on thy bosom deep. **1832** R. H. FROUDE *Rem.* (1838) I. 276 We made the rest of our voyage to Malta stilly and quickly. **1865** ALLINGHAM *50 Mod. Poems, Angela,* Stilly she glided in.

†**still-yard.** *Obs.* App. = STILLION.

1725 G. SMITH *Distilling* 64 It will be necessary also to have a..Water-tub set upon a strong frame, or Still yard. *Ibid.* 66 A Still-yard or gun-tree. *Ibid.* 78 A Still-yard or pair of Gantrees.

stillyard(e, obs. forms of STEELYARD[1], [2].

‖**stilo novo.** *Obs.* [mod.L., abl. of *stilus novus* new style.] Appended to a date: = 'New Style', i.e. according to the reformed (or Gregorian) calendar: see STYLE. Also *fig.* or *allusive.*

Similarly *stilo vetere* (abbreviated *st. v.*) = 'Old Style'.

[**1589** DEE *Diary* (Camden) 31, Aug. 5th, novo stylo, Edmond Hilton went toward Stade.] **1619** W. YONGE *Diary* (Camden) 33 The 25th of December *stilo novo.* *a* **1625** FLETCHER *Woman's Prize* IV. iv, *Petru.* Now the Devill.. shoure his blessing Upon ye all: into whose custody—*Mar.* I do commit your Reformation, And so I leave you to your *Stilo novo.* **1636** MARMION *Antiquary* III. (1641) G 2, He sent me Letters beyond sea, dated *Stilo Novo.*

†**stilp.** *Obs. rare*$^{-1}$. [Cogn. w. (? or mistake for) *stulp*, STOOP *sb.*[1]] A post.

c **1380** *Sir Ferumb.* 4553 Ac he failede of ys stroke, & þe axe ful on a stilp of oke, þat bar vp ther a chayne.

stilpnomelane (stɪlp'nɒmɪleɪn). *Min.* [ad. G. *stilpnomelan* (Glocker 1827) f. Gr. στιλπνό-ς glittering + μελαν-, μέλας black.] A hydrous silicate of iron and aluminium, occurring in thin scales, or as a velvety coating, of a black or bronze colour.

1850 ANSTED *Elem. Geol., Min.* etc. 198. **1854** DANA *Syst. Min.* (ed. 4) II. 287.

stilpnosiderite (stɪlpnəʊ'sɪdəraɪt, -saɪ'dɪəraɪt). *Min.* [ad. G. *stilpnosiderit* (Ullmann 1814), f. Gr. στιλπνό-ς (see prec.) + σίδηρος iron: see -ITE.] 'An obsolete synonym of LIMONITE' (Chester).

1823 W. PHILLIPS *Min.* (ed. 3) 227 Stilpnosiderite..is described as occurring in oblique quadrangular prisms. **1866** LAWRENCE tr. *Cotta's Rocks Classified* (1878) 58.

stilt (stɪlt), *sb.* Also 4–6 **stilte,** 5–6 **stylt(e.** [ME. *stilte*, cogn. w. (M)LG., MDu. *stelte* (mod.LG. *stelte, stilte*, Du. *stelt*), OHG. *stelza* (MHG., mod.G. *stelze*), Sw. *stylta*, Da. *stylte*; also LG. *stelter*, Norw. *styltra*.

The relation between the forms is somewhat obscure; they apparently point to three OTeut. ablaut-types **steltjōn-*, **staltjōn-*, **stultjōn-*. The Teut. root **stelt-* (:—pre-Teut. **steld-*) conjectured to mean 'to walk stiffly', seems to be represented also in MHG. *stolzen* to limp, Sw. *stulta* to totter, stagger, and perh. (if the word be native Teut.) in OFris. *stult*, LG. *stolt*, HG. *stolz* stately, proud (see STOUT *a.*).]

1. The handle of a plough. Occas. also with reference to other farm implements. *dial.*

c **1340** *Nominale* (Skeat) 854 *Manuel et tenoun* Handle and stilte. **1523, 1581** [see PLOUGH-STILT]. **1653** BLITH *Engl. Improver Impr.* 190 For the Plough-handles, some call them Stilts, and some Hales, and some Staves. **1798** C. CRUTTWELL *Gazetteer* (1808) s.v. *Pomona,* The plough..is of singular construction, having only one stilt. **1829** SCOTT *Rob Roy* Introd. 2nd half, He..shot MacLaren when between the stilts of his plough. **1840** *Penny Cycl.* XVIII. 272/1 The stilts or handles, of which there may be one or two, direct the plough. **1880** [A. J. MUNBY] *Dorothy* 35 Driving her furrows so straight..Guiding the stilts with a grasp skilful and strong as a man's. **1957** E. E. EVANS *Irish Folk Ways* x. 129 The Irish were amazed when they first saw a ploughman with a Scots plough both driving the horses and holding the stilts. **1971** *Country Life* 20 May 1203/1, I take the 'stilts' of the big grass cutter and struggle behind it. **1973** *Ibid.* 22 Feb. 474/1 My going to the plough that morning wasn't the first occasion upon which I had set my hands to the stilts.

2. a. A crutch. *Obs.* exc. *dial.*

In quot. 1520 applied to a crutch-headed walking-stick as figured on a brass.

c **1320** *Sir Tristr.* 2956 On astilt he com þo Ful swiþe. *a* **1375** *Joseph Arim.* 335 Verely she was heled, and left her styltes thore, And on her fete went home resonably well. **14..** *Beryn* 2380 A Crepill he saw comyng..Oppon a stilt vndir his kne. **1520** *Brass in Ingoldmells Church,* Pray for the sowle of Wylliam Palmer wyth the stylt. *c* **1590** MARLOWE *Jew of Malta* II. 977 (Brooke) I haue laugh'd agood to see the cripples Goe limping home to Christendome on stilts. **1658** A. FOX tr. *Wurtz's Surg.* II. xxvi. 170 This party carried it [a recovered limb] as well as any did with a stilt. **1697** in *M'Kerlie's Hist. Lands Galloway* (1870) I. 245 You..did.. beatt her almost to death with the stilt wherewith she walked. *a* **1825** FORBY *Voc. E. Anglia, Stilts,* crutches.

†**b.** *gen.* A prop, support. In quot. *fig. Obs.*

1633 WARISTON *Diary* (S.H.S.) 34 God as it wer..up-halding the by three stilts of fayth love and hope.

3. a. Each of a pair of props, usually slender wooden poles with a foot-rest some distance above the lower end, for enabling a person to walk with the feet raised from the ground, as over a marshy place, a stream, etc., the upper end being held by the hand or under the arm, or (in a modified form) strapped to the legs, or formerly sometimes fastened beneath the feet. (The ordinary current sense.) Phrase, ***to walk on*** (formerly †*in*) ***stilts.***

c **1440** *Promp. Parv.* 475/2 Stylte, *calepodium, lignipodium.* *c* **1460** *Burlesque* in *Rel. Ant.* I. 86 Dore-bundys stalkyng one stylttus. **1519** HORMAN *Vulg.* 279 Let vs daunce patende, or with styltis. **1596** NASHE *Saffron Walden* V 4 b, To consume my bodie as slender as a stilt or a broome-staffe. **1610** HOLLAND *Camden's Brit.* I. 491 Fen-men..who stalking on high upon stilts, apply their mindes, to grasing, fishing and fowling. **1714** ADDISON *Spect.* No. 559 ¶6 One of these looked like a Man walking upon Stilts. **1852** THACKERAY *Esmond* I. Introd., The actors in the old tragedies,.. speaking from under a mask, and wearing stilts and a great head-dress. **1863** GEO. ELIOT *Romola* I. viii, Those mysterious giants were really men..balancing themselves on stilts.

b. *transf.* Applied to long slender legs, or other natural supports (quot. 1665), of an animal, esp. a bird (cf. sense 5).

1597 A. M. tr. *Guillemeau's Fr. Chirurg.* 50 b, Those which we saye to be hipped and legged, or have a payere of goode and stedfast stiltes vnder them. **1665** SIR T. HERBERT *Trav.* (1677) 26 This fish..wanting fins; in place whereof she is aided with two paps, which are not only suckles, but serve for stilts to creep a shoar upon. **1709** T. ROBINSON *Vindic. Mosaick Syst.* 66 Herns..walking by the Sides of shallow Rivulets upon long Stilts. **1835–6** OWEN in *Todd's Cycl. Anat.* I. 272/1 Birds that seek their food in water.. wade into rivers and marshes on elevated stilts, as in the Crane, &c.

c. *fig.* or in figurative expressions, usually with allusion to the artificially raised position or long strides of a person walking on stilts: cf. STILTED 2.

1734 tr. *Rollin's Anc. Hist.* (1827) I. 110 Æschylus..his muse seemed rather to walk in stilts than in the buskins of his own invention. **1751** FIELDING *Amelia* V. i, Booth offered to explain, but to no purpose; the colonel was got into his stilts. **1781** H. WALPOLE *Let. to W. Mason* 14 Apr., Hurlothrumbo talked plain English in comparison of this wight on stilts [Dr. Johnson]. **1818** HAZLITT *Engl. Poets* i. (1870) 13 When artists or connoisseurs talk on stilts about the poetry of painting. **1826** LANDOR *Imag. Conv., Ld. Brooke & Sidney* Wks. 1846 I. 6/1 Ambition is but Avarice on stilts and masked. **1861** C. BENSON in *Macm. Mag.* Feb. 275 The whole audience raised itself on the stilts of expectation. **1883** HALL CAINE *Cobw. Crit.* vii. 199 Lifting himself into notoriety on the stilts of blasphemy.

4. In various technical senses.

a. Each of a set of posts or piles on which a building (esp. of primitive construction) is raised from the ground, or which are fixed under water to support the pier of a bridge, etc. (In quot. 1697 *transf.*; cf. sense 3 b.)

1697 DAMPIER *Voy.* I. 54 Neither the black nor white Mangrove grow towering up from stilts or rising roots, as the red doth; but the body immediately out of the ground, like other Trees. **1712** E. COOKE *Voy. S. Sea* 315 The Houses are built with split Bamboes,..standing on Stilts, or Posts. **1739** LABELYE *Piers Westm. Bridge* 42 Which method is commonly called building upon stilts. **1772** C. HUTTON *Bridges* 100 *Stilts,* a set of piles driven into the space intended for the pier, whose tops being sawed level off about low-water mark, the pier is then raised on them. **1860** *Burn's Gloss. Techn. Terms* 4 *Stilts,* piles driven into a river at small intervals, and a surrounding row of piles driven closely together, and the interstices filled with stones, to form a foundation for a pier to be built upon. **1883** MRS. BISHOP *Golden Chersonese* 217 Below there is a village, with clusters of Chinese houses on the ground, and Malay houses on stilts, standing singly.

b. *Arch.* A vertical course of masonry placed beneath and continuous with an arch or vault so as to raise the springing of it above the general level, or for a similar purpose beneath or above a column. Cf. STILT *v.* 1 b, STILTED *ppl. a.* 1 b (*b*).

1835 R. WILLIS *Archit. Mid. Ages* vii. 77 The latter [*i.e.* clerestory or longitudinal arches] are raised upon stilts,..so as to throw their imposts considerably above those of the transverse arches. **1842** *Civil Engin. & Arch. Jrnl.* V. 80/1 The continuous stilt or too lofty stylobate of the College of Surgeons. **1908** LENA MILMAN *Sir Chr. Wren* 206 Corinthian pilasters, which, by a two-fold stilt above their capitals, reach to the great cornice.

†**c.** Some appendage to a bell. (Perh. = *stay*: see STAY *sb.*[2] 2 h, quot. 1871.) *Obs.*

1672 in W. O. Blunt *Ch. Chester-le-Street* (1884) 98 For cotterels, wedges, and for mending the stilt of the bell.

d. Part of a type-founder's 'lining-stick' or lining-gauge: see quot. 1688.

1683 MOXON *Mech. Exerc., Printing* xvii. 155 The Stilt is a thin flat piece of Brass-Plate about a Scaboard thick, and a Double-Pica broad. **1688** HOLME *Armoury* III. xxi. (Roxb.) 262/2 A Letter Founders Lining Stick;..whose seueralls are as followeth... The Stilt, a slender ledge set vnder the side, to tilt vp the fore edge, that letters lying on it may rest against the bottom ledge.

†**e.** A support for a cask. *Obs.*

1701 *Lond. Gaz.* No. 3721/3 Several Hogsheads of Claret being ready placed on Stilts,..the Claret was set running.

f. *Pottery.* A small piece of baked ware placed between pieces of biscuit ware to prevent their adhering to each other in the kiln.

1825 J. NICHOLSON *Oper. Mech.* 473 Pieces of clay..called stilts, cockspurs,..&c. are put to keep them apart. **1880** JANVIER *Pract. Keramics* 70 The pieces are supported and held apart by little fireclay instruments or props, which from their shape derive such names as pins or thimbles, watches, cock-spurs, triangles or stilts.

5. Any bird of the widely-distributed genus *Himantopus*, characterized by very long slender legs and slender sharp bills, and inhabiting marshes; a long-legged plover. Cf. TILT *sb.*[2] 9.

[Perh. short for *stilt-plover* or *stilt-bird* (see 6), or imitated from G. *stelze* short for *bachstelze* brook-'stilt', an alteration of the OHG. name *wazzerstelza* water-'stilt'.]

1831 *Montagu's Ornith. Dict.* (ed. Rennie) 496 Stilt (*Himantopus melanopterus*, Meyer). **1838** AUDUBON *Ornith.* IV. 247 Black-necked Stilt, *Himantopus nigricollis.* **1861** H. B. TRISTRAM *Gt. Sahara* iv. 62 The beautiful black-winged stilt, the tamest of waders. *c* **1875** *Cassell's Nat. Hist.* IV. 167 The Stilts have a straight bill, but in other respects they are not unlike the Avocets.

6. *attrib.* and *Comb.*, as ***stilt-maker, -vaulting***; ***stilt-legged, -like*** adjs.; **stilt-bird**, (*a*) = sense 5; (*b*) any long-legged wading bird, a grallatorial bird; †**stilt-bond**, ? a band by which a stilt is fastened to the leg or foot; **stilt-bug** (*U.S.*), any one of the long-legged plant-lice of the family *Berytidæ*; **stilt heel**, (a shoe with) a high heel; **stilt-heeled** *a.*, (of shoes) high-heeled; **stilt-man**, a man who walks on stilts; **stilt-petrel**, a petrel of the genus *Fregetta*, having long legs (also *stilt stormy petrel*); **stilt-plover** = sense 5; **stilt prolegs**, *Ent.*, the prolegs of a caterpillar when unusually long, so as to raise the body; **stilt-root**, an aerial root, arising from the trunk or lower branches of a tree, and acting to provide support; hence **stilt-rooted** *a.*; **stilt sandpiper**, a long-legged N. American species of sandpiper, *Micropalama himantopus*; **stilt-shank** = sense 5; **stilt-walker**, (*a*) a person who walks on stilts (also *transf.*); (*b*) = *stilt-bird* (*b*).

1835–6 OWEN in *Todd's Cycl. Anat.* I. 287/2 The *Stilt-bird and other Waders. **1870** GILLMORE tr. *Figuier's Reptiles & Birds* 294 The Stilt Birds..obtain their name from the excessive length of their legs. *c* **1475** *Pict. Voc.* in Wr.-Wülcker 775/14 *Hoc subligar*, a *styltbonde. **1895** COMSTOCK *Man. Insects* 143 Family Berytidæ. The *Stilt-bugs. **1973** R. RENDELL *Some lie & some Die* vi. 49 She was ..dressed..in..full, longish skirt, *stilt heels. **1772** NUGENT *Hist. Fr. Gerund* II. 437 On *Stilt-heel'd shoes Mounted she Struts. **1948** 'P. WENTWORTH' *Traveller Returns* xi. 64 The sheer black stockings, and the stilt-heeled shoes. **1980** 'L. EGAN' *Motive in Shadow* iii. 39 She was wearing..stilt-heeled black patent leather pumps. **1863** BATES *Nat. Amazon* ix. (1864) 247 Flocks of *stilt-legged water-fowl. **1889** *Hardwicke's Sci.-Gossip* XXV. 189/2 The curious postures assumed by the animal [a species of rotifer] upon its long *stilt-like toes. **1625** in J. P. Shawcross *Hist. Dagenham* (1904) 253 *Stilt-makers all, and tanners, shall complain of this disaster, For they will make each muddy lake for Essex Calves a pasture. **1898** *Westm. Gaz.* 27 Sept. 6/2 Stilt-makers disavow the intelligence that they are full of orders. **1552** HULOET, *Stylt man or goer on a stilte, *grallator.* **1586** *Acts Privy Counc.* N.S. XIV. 75 Providing.. of xij or xvj Scatchemen or Stiltmen in the countie of Lincolne, to be chosen of the best able and most experte men. **1890** E. H. BARKER *Wayfaring in France* 37 The stiltmen observed this little comedy with quiet wonder. **1779** G. WHITE *Selborne, To Barrington* 7 May, These birds are of the plover family, and might with propriety be called the *stilt-plovers. *c* **1875** *Cassell's Nat. Hist.* IV. 167 The Stilts, or Stilt plovers (*Himantopinæ*). **1826** KIRBY & SP. *Entomol.* IV. 354 *Stilt Prolegs. **1894** F. W. OLIVER tr. *Kerner's Nat. Hist. Plants* I. 756 Trees whose erect trunks are supported by tabular roots and those which are provided with *stilt-roots may at the same time develop columnar roots from their branches. **1930** *Discovery* Nov. 381/1 No account of jungle vegetation..is complete without some mention of the trees with the curious stilt roots and those with the even stranger buttress roots. **1974** H. MACINNES *Climb to Lost World* xii. 221, I pointed..at a *stilt-rooted tree which had grown up with stilts at least fifteen feet clear of the ground... Young stilt roots were growing into the swamp from its base. **1872** COUES *N. Amer. Birds* 253 *Micropalama*, *Stilt Sandpiper. **1852** MACGILLIVRAY *Brit. Birds* IV. 310 *Himantopus.* *Stilt-shank. **1884** COUES *N. Amer. Birds* (ed. 2) 782 *Fregetta*, *Stilt Stormy Petrels. **1861** MAYHEW *Lond. Labour* III. 151 Rope dancing and *stilt-vaulting. **1863** A. J. MUNBY *Diary* 20 May in D. Hudson *Munby* (1972) 162, I saw..two young female acrobats or *stiltwalkers..forlorn and pitiable in their satin shoes & spangles. **1869–73** T. R. JONES *Cassell's Bk. Birds* IV. 1 The Stilt-walkers (*Grallatores*). **1889** F. H. HERRICK in *Amer. Nat.* Nov. 943 A growth of tropical bush, in which we notice the mangrove, the stilt-walker of the tropical swamp. **1891** *Daily News* 3 Apr. 5/6 Sylvain Dornon, the stilt-walker, who is on a tour for a wager from Paris to Moscow.

stilt (stɪlt), *v.* [f. STILT *sb.*]

1. *trans.* To raise as on stilts; to elevate artificially (*lit.* or *fig.*).

1649 J. H. *Motion to Parlt.* 26 Some..by the foresaid means stilt themselves into some profession. **1802** ANNA SEWARD *Lett.* (1811) VI. 29 Southey told a friend of mine.. that it was the finest poetic work which had appeared these fifty years. So Johnson stilted up Blackmore. **1825** HONE *Every-day Bk.* I. 516 The Sole [is] adapted by the workman ..to stilt the foot. **1849** DANA *Geol.* ii. (1850) 55 The atoll usually seems to stand as if stilted up in a fathomless sea. **1882** *Pop. Sci. Monthly* XX. 389 In low water the boats often run aground on the sand-bars, and have to be stilted over them with timbers. **1884** TENNYSON *Becket* II. ii, That would stilt up York to twice himself.

b. *Arch.* To raise (an arch, vault, or other structure) above the ordinary level by a 'stilt' or course of masonry beneath (see STILT *sb.* 4 b).

1835 R. WILLIS *Archit. Mid. Ages* vii. 76 The problem of vaulting an unequally sided rectangle..had early presented itself to the Romans, who..were led to the discovery..of stilting the arches. **1845** PALEY *Gothic Mouldings* 66 Decorated bases are often stilted, or raised above the floor, ..by graduated stages or tables. *a* **1878** SIR G. SCOTT *Lect. Archit.* (1879) II. 163 The Roman builders solved the problem..by what is called stilting the narrower arch; that is, raising its springing till its crown becomes level with that of the wider arch.

c. *Book-binding.* To bind (a book) in projecting covers so as to make it uniform with a volume of a larger size.

1824 DIBDIN *Libr. Comp.* 597 The third volume is often stilted, to make it dress with its companions. **1895** *Bookseller's Catalogue*, In one vol., royal octavo (stilted to folio).

2. To fit (a plough) with a 'stilt'. *dial.*

a **1883** F. HARPER in *Mod. Scott. Poets* VI. 345 Twice forty years..Has passed awa' sin' 'Airchie Scott' First fixed thy ribs..An' stiltit thee, an' turned thee oot A noble ploo!

3. *intr.* To walk on stilts; *fig.* (of a horse) ? to lift the legs high in walking or running, to prance.

1785 BURNS *Epist. Davie* xi, My spavet Pegasus will limp, Till ance he's fairly het; And then he'll hilch, and stilt, and jump, An rin an unco fit. **1861** W. W. WEBB in *Med. Times* 29 June 680/1 Our young Blondins do stilt over the artificial Niagaras we construct for them.

stilted (ˈstɪltɪd), *ppl. a.* [f. STILT *sb.* and *v.* + -ED.]

1. Furnished with or having stilts (in quot. 1615, crutches); raised artificially as on stilts.

1615 BRATHWAIT *Loves Labyrinth* 27 Decrepit age, stilted for want of strength. **1742** YOUNG *Nt. Th.* VI. 355 Where dwarfs are often stilted, and betray A littleness of soul by worlds o'er-run, And nations laid in blood.

b. (*a*) Supported on props or posts so as to be raised above the ground. (*b*) *Arch.* Raised above the general level by a course of masonry beneath, as an arch, vault, or other structure.

1820 *Blackw. Mag.* VIII. 31 *note*, The appearance of these stilted ricks..gives a sort of peculiarity to the landscape. **1835** R. WILLIS *Archit. Mid. Ages* vii. 78 All the arches are pointed, except the central transverse rib.., which is semi-circular and stilted. **1883** MRS. BISHOP *Golden Chersonese* 168 It is a genuine Malay house on stilts... This stilted house is the barrack of eleven Malay constables. **1895** *Jrnl. R. Inst. Brit. Architects* 14 Mar. 347 Corinthian capitals, supporting stilted pointed arches.

c. Of animals, esp. birds: Having very long slender legs resembling stilts.

1869–73 T. R. JONES *Cassell's Bk. Birds* II. 162 The Stilted Fly-catchers (*Fluvicolæ*)..a group of South American birds. **1896** LYDEKKER *Roy. Nat. Hist.* V. 134 The stilted lizards.

2. *fig.* Of (or in reference to) language or style (or, *rarely*, manner or deportment): Artificially or affectedly lofty; unnaturally elevated; formally pompous. (The usual current sense.)

1820 BYRON *To Murray* 28 Sept., You are taken in by that false, stilted, trashy style. **1832** S. WARREN *Diary Late Physic.* II. iii. 134 One might wither that fellow with a word or two, the stilted noodle! **1874** GREEN *Short Hist.* x. (1878) 730 His [Pitt's] letters to his family..are stilted and unnatural in tone. **1909** RIDER HAGGARD *Yellow God* 55 It caused him to cease his stilted talk.

3. Of a plough: Having a stilt or stilts: in parasynthetic formations, as ***double-, single-stilted.***

1844 W. H. MAXWELL *Scot.* xvi. (1855) 149 A single-stilted plough. **1911** E. BEVERIDGE *North Uist* x. 315 Double-stilted ploughs.

Hence (in sense 2) **ˈstiltedly** *adv.*; **ˈstiltedness.**

1828 LYTTON *Pelham* lxvii, There is a stiffness and stiltedness in the dialogue and descriptions perfectly ridiculous. *c* **1886** KIPLING *Lucia* 49 What the later generation is pleased to call the stiltedness of the old-time verse. **1893** G. TRAVERS *Mona Maclean* III. 252 He began somewhat stiltedly.

stilter (ˈstɪltə(r)). [f. as prec. + -ER[1].]

1. A person who walks on stilts.

1845 D. COSTELLO *Tour Valley Meuse* 171 An edict of the 17th of December 1755 interdicted the Stilters from assembling in the market-place. **1898** *Strand Mag.* XV. 17 [Stilt-racing in France] There were medals offered by various towns *en route* for the first stilter to arrive there.

2. A long-legged wading bird, a grallatorial bird.

1845 KITTO *Cycl. Bibl. Lit.* s.v. *Unclean Birds*, All long-legged waders or stilters.

†**stilth.** *Obs.* In 3 **stilðe.** [f. STILL *a.* + -TH[1].] Stillness, quietness, tranquillity.

a **1225** *Ancr. R.* 156 Hwat oðer god cumeð of þisse onliche sittunge,..& of þisse seli stilðe. *c* **1230** *Hali Meid.* 41 Simplete of semblaunt & buhsumnesse & stilðe.

stiltified (ˈstɪltɪfaɪd), *a.* Not in dignified use. [f. STILT *sb.* or *v.* + -(I)FY + -ED[1].] = STILTED 2.

1820 BYRON *To Murray* 7 June, Mrs. Hemans is a poet.. too stiltified and apostrophic. **1830** *Fraser's Mag.* I. 241 High-wrought romance and stiltified language. **1887** C. C. R. *Minora Carmina* 249, I care not for tragedy's stiltified ways.

So **ˈstiltify** *v. trans.* = STILT *v.* 1.

1860 C. READE *Cloister & Hearth* lxv. (1896) 201 Skinny dwarfs..cushioned and stiltified into great fat giants.

ˈstiltiness. [f. STILTY + -NESS.] The quality of being 'stilty'.

1826 *Sporting Mag.* XVIII. 382 Many [horses], owing to the severity of their training on hard ground, shewed stiltiness in their action.

stilting (ˈstɪltɪŋ). [f. STILT *sb.* or *v.* + -ING[1].]

1. The action or sport of walking on stilts.

1809 *Sporting Mag.* XXXIII. 316 Stilting may possibly become as fashionable in these, as tilting formerly was in better times. **1906** J. PATERSON *Wamphray* vi. 165 It was not uncommon for an expert at stilting to carry a passenger across the water.

2. *Arch.* The placing of a 'stilt' (STILT *sb.* 4 b) beneath an arch, etc. so as to raise it; *concr.* = STILT *sb.* 4 b.

1835 R. WILLIS *Archit. Mid. Ages* vii. 74 Both the larger and smaller vaults are raised above the entablature by stilting. **1869** TOZER *Highl. Turkey* II. 77 The stilting above one of the pillars..is wholly out of the perpendicular.

stiltish (ˈstɪltɪʃ), *a. rare.* [f. STILT *sb.* + -ISH[1].] Characterized by stiltedness. Hence **ˈstiltishness.**

1824 MEDWIN *Conversat. Ld. Byron* I. 194 He looked the Roman so well, that even 'Cato', cold and stiltish as it is, had a run. **1824** *Examiner* 694/1 His general deportment, with the exception of a little occasional stiltishness, is correspondent.

Stilton (ˈstɪlt(ə)n). [Name of a village in Cambridgeshire (formerly Huntingdonshire, on the Great North Road from London): see below.]

a. ***Stilton cheese***: a rich quality of cheese made at various places in Leicestershire; so called from having been originally largely sold to travellers at a coaching inn at Stilton; orig. also applied to similar cheeses made elsewhere, but since 1969 restricted to that made in the counties of Leicester, Derby, and Nottingham by members of the Stilton Cheese Makers Association.

1736 BAILEY *Househ. Dict.* s.v. *Cheese*, Stilton Cheese. Take two Gallons of morning milk [etc.]. **1813** BYRON *Let.* 3 Oct., Pray accept a Stilton cheese from me. *a* **1864** J. CLARE in *Sel. Poems & Prose* (1967) 25 He..seldom got astride of a saddle save when he gave old Dobbin a holiday from the plough to carry his Dame to the Fair to sell her Stilton cheese. **1904** *Century Mag.* Feb. 534/2, I'll..show you brass that is brass, all green in the creases, like Stilton cheese. **1930** L. G. D. ACLAND *Early Canterbury Runs* 1st Ser. ii. 30 In the 'fifties and early 'sixties [in New Zealand] they got two shillings a pound for their butter, tenpence for cheese, and eighteen-pence for stilton cheese. **1969** *Trade Marks Jrnl.* 5 Feb. 234/1 Stilton 831,407 Class 29. Cheese. The Chairman, The Stilton Cheese Makers Association, Melton Mowbray, Leicestershire.—28th Feb. 1962. **1973** *Leicester Mercury* 24 Dec. 8/1 The public in the States is being..misled into purchasing the Purity brand of Stilton cheese in mistaken belief that it is the genuine product produced in England.

b. *ellipt.* as *sb.* = Stilton cheese. Also *fig.*

1826 E. CRAVEN *Mem. Margravine of Anspach* I. v. 190 The Margrave had at his table good cream, and Stilton, or Berkeley hundred, made under my direction. **1835** DICKENS *Sk. Boz, Parl. Sk.*, Mark the air with which he gloats over that Stilton. **1867** LOWELL *Study Wind., Gt. Publ. Character* (1871) 70 We prefer a full, old-fashioned meal, with its side-dishes of spicy gossip, and its last relish, the Stilton of scandal, so it be not too high. **1913** *Times* 9 Aug. 19/6 Cheese,..finest Cheshire and cheddar, 72s. to 74s.;.. Stiltons, 10d. to 1s. per lb.

slang. **1859** *Hotten's Slang Dict.* 102 'That's the stilton', or 'it is not the stilton', i.e. that is quite the thing, or that is not quite the thing;—polite rendering of 'that is not the cheese'.

c. *attrib.*

1966 *Daily Tel.* 15 Nov. 15/2 The Stilton recipe..goes back to the 18th century... In seeking the trade mark, Stilton makers expressed fears that the same fate would befall the Stilton..as happened to the Cheddar. **1969** *Ibid.* 11 Apr. 19/5 Yesterday,..the Stilton Cheesemakers Association..obtained their trademark. **1971** *Sunday Times* (Colour Suppl.) 28 Mar. 36/1 Much the best way of tackling the half cheese on the table is with a knife with a long sharp pointed blade—not a Stilton spoon. **1973** *Leicester Mercury* 24 Dec. 8/1 (*heading*) Stilton men up in arms over 'spurious cheese'.

stilty (ˈstɪltɪ), *a.* [f. STILT *sb.* + -Y.]

1. Resembling stilts; *esp.* in *Racing slang*, said of a horse's legs when long and stiff in action.

1826 [implied in STILTINESS]. **1828** *Edin. Rev.* XLVII. 433 The solemn and stilty tread of the Athenian buskin. **1863** *Sporting Mag.* Sept. 230 The odds on him were speedily reduced..for he turned out to be one of the stilty sort, with a pair of awful fore-legs.

2. *fig.* = STILTISH *a.*

1845 W. B. S. TAYLOR *Hist. Univ. Dublin* 339 The *stilty dignity* which is to be found in some other places. **1846** WORCESTER (cites *Q. Rev.*). **1873** WAGNER tr. *Teuffel's Hist. Rom. Lit.* II. 159 His stilty tone and artificial conciseness. **1889** GRETTON *Memory's Harkback* 317 Macready..I once accidentally met..at dinner... I remember..my impression of him was stilty.

stilus: variant of STYLUS.

‖**stilyaga** (stɪˈljaga). Also **stilyag.** Pl. **-gi.** [*Russ.* (*colloq.*), lit. 'stylish person'.] In the U.S.S.R.: a young person who affects stylish dress as an expression of rebellion, nonconformity, etc.

1955 H. HODGKINSON *Doubletalk* 55 The *stilyag* who goes in for 'style' in his clothes. **1959** *Listener* 5 Feb. 236/2 Soviet

Russia has her..'teddy-boys', who are there called *stilyagi*. *Ibid.*, The introspective, thoughtful, humble type has taken the place of the *stilyaga*. **1960** *Guardian* 25 Feb. 4/1 Young people in Russia..wear the 'stilyagi' clothes that mark them as non-conformists. **1965** 'A. BURGESS' in *Times Lit. Suppl.* 22 Apr. 317/2 A trip to Russia showed me that *stilyagi* behaved much like our own (as they were then) teddy-boys. **1973** T. ALLBEURY *Choice of Enemies* xxiv. 129, I had difficulty in changing the money because one of the 'stilyagi' recognised me.

stim, slang abbrev. of STIMULANT *sb.*

1882 *Society* 11 Nov. 22/2 Stop..the 'nips,' the 'stims,' the 'sherries and Angosturas.'

†**stime**, *v. Obs.*, var. STEEM *v.*[1], to estimate.

1535 in Ellis *Orig. Lett.* Ser. II. II. 71 Mr. Pole is continual in writing of his work... By al the next month I stime that his labor shal take end. **1543** *St. Papers Hen. VIII*, IX. 537 It is stimid that the Turke shold be of retorne in Constantinople.

stime (*Sc.* and *north.*): see STYME.

stimie, variant of STYMIE (*Golf*).

stimmer ('stɪmə(r)), *v.* ? *Obs. rare.* In 7 stymmer. [Of obscure origin; app. phonetically symbolic: cf. *shimmer*, *flimmer*.] *intr.* To move about irregularly.

1616 SURFLET & MARKHAM *Country Farm* III. li. 426 So soone as you perceiue the smoake to stymmer or runne about the edges of the panne. **1808** JAMIESON, To *Stimmer*, to go about in a confused manner.

‖**Stimmung** ('ʃtɪmʊŋ). Also **stimmung**. [Ger.] Mood, spirit, atmosphere, feeling.

1909 W. M. URBAN *Valuation* v. 123 We may cite certain impressionistic or symbolic styles where the general mood or *Stimmung* is almost palpable. **1923** R. FRY *Let.* 13 May (1972) II. 534 Words as you use them..give me more of what the Germans call *stimmung*..than painting can ever do. **1939** E. H. W. MEYERSTEIN *Let.* 4 Apr. (1959) 222 He [*sc.* Eliot] cannot keep the poetic *stimmung* up as long as Bridges can. **1948** WYNDHAM LEWIS *Let.* 18 Oct. 463, I could not help imbibing from my very American father much Stimmung, a certain sentiment, and a lot about the Civil War. **1961** *Times* 23 Mar. 16/6 The Riffelalp had its own *stimmung*. **1972** *Guardian* 12 Aug. 8 The 'Kaiserwalzer'..is..[an] emanation of the Viennese spirit, Stimmung. **1980** R. ADAMS *Girl in Swing* iv. 59 In memory the whole *Stimmung* changes and our recollections become like a story we have read before.

stimoceiver ('stɪməʊsiːvə(r)). [f. STIM(ULATE *v.* + -O + RE)CEIVER[1].] A radio transmitter and receiver implanted in the head which transmits information about the brain and receives signals which electrically stimulate the brain.

1967 *N.Y. Times* 22 Mar. 49/1 Dr. Delgado's laboratory is developing an instrument, called a 'stimoceiver', that takes advantage of the increasing sophistication of circuit technology and microminiaturization. **1968** J. M. R. DELGADO et al. in *Jrnl. Nerv. & Mental Dis.* CXLVII. 331/1 The integration of the three-channel units for radio stimulation and EEG telemetry constitutes the stimoceiver. *Ibid.* 338/2 A new instrument called 'stimoceiver' has been developed for the stimultaneous multichannel recording and stimulation of the brain by FM radio waves in completely unrestrained subjects. **1979** *Amer. Jrnl. Orthopsychiatry* XLIX. 367/2 The grim prospects of a burgeoning psychosurgical technology for widespread telemetric surveillance of behavior via transponders, stimoceivers, and brain pacemakers *à la* Schwitzgebel, Meyer, and Delgado are adumbrated.

stimpart ('stɪmpərt). *Sc.* Also **-ard.** [? Contracted from *saxteent* (sixteenth) *part* (sc. of a firlot). Cf. FORPIT.] **a.** A measure of capacity, the fourth part of a peck: = FORPIT, LIPPY. (Inaccurately glossed by Burns as 'the eighth part of a Winchester bushel'.) **b.** *transf.* The fourth part of a 'rig' or ridge of land (yielding a quarter of a peck of flax seed).

1786 BURNS *To Auld Mare* xvii, A heapet stimpart, I'll reserve ane Laid by for you. **1896** J. LAMB *Ann. W. Kilbride* ix. 227 The flax grown was only in small patches for family use, often a mere headrig yielding two or three stimpards. **1906** *Scott. Rev.* 22 Nov. 571/1 The usual order to the grocer ..was for a stimpart of oatmeal.

stimulable ('stɪmjʊləb(ə)l), *a. rare.* [as if ad. L. **stimulābilis*, f. *stimulāre*: see STIMULATE *v.* and -ABLE.] Capable of being stimulated. Hence **stimula'bility**.

1803 W. TAYLOR in *Monthly Mag.* XIV. 488 The organ of idealisation is alike stimulable by each specific class of sensations, whereas the organ of sense is only irritable to its appropriate stimulus. **1944** *Mind* LIII. 90 Most of the essayists, having a good deal of vitality themselves, are eminently stimulable. **1975** *Year Bk. Ear, Nose & Throat* 36 If nerve stimulability is lost.

stimulance ('stɪmjʊləns). *rare*[−1]. [Formed as next: see -ANCE.] Stimulating quality.

1856 SIMPSON *Covenanters of South* 277 So powerful was the stimulance of his avarice.

stimulancy ('stɪmjʊlənsɪ). Now *rare.* [f. STIMULANT *a*: see -ANCY.] Stimulating quality.

1799 W. TAYLOR in Robberds' *Mem.* I. 311 Hexameters.. are less favourable to..the highest stimulancy of style, than blank verse. **1824** *Blackw. Mag.* XVI. 3 The narrow-minded bigotry which sets up either Madeira or Sherry at the expense of the other's ancestral stimulancy. **1825** COLERIDGE *Aids Refl.* Addr. to Rdr., Let then its comparative merits and demerits, in respect of style and stimulancy, possess a proportional weight. **1851** T. T. LYNCH *Lett. Scattered* (1872) 175 Recollections and wit have had especial charm and stimulancy.

stimulant ('stɪmjʊlənt), *a.* and *sb.* [ad. L. *stimulantem*, pr. pple. of *stimulāre*: see STIMULATE *v.* Cf. F. *stimulant* (18th c. in Hatz.-Darm.), Sp. *estimulante*, It. *stimolante.*]

A. *adj.* Having the property of stimulating.

1. = STIMULATING 1. Now *rare.*

1803 SOUTHEY in *Ann. Rev.* I. 18 The adventurers had so much of what was stimulant as well as true to relate. **1837** CARLYLE *Fr. Rev.* III. IV. vi, This is the celebrated 'Law of the Forty Sous'; fiercely stimulant to Sansculottism. **1875** LOWELL *Wordsw.* Writ. 1890 IV. 354 Religious canticles stimulant of zeal.

2. *Phys.* and *Med.*

a. Exciting an organ, or the organism, to increased activity; quickening some vital function or process. Now more commonly expressed by STIMULATING (sense 2).

1772 W. FALCONER *Ess. Bath Waters* I. 399 Where the effects of the water, particularly the stimulant and astringent, are desired in their full extent. *Ibid.*, Yet their stimulant qualities may prove too violent a shock for a tender frame to endure. **1788** J. BROWN tr. *Elem. Med.* I. 13 *note*, Those who have been accustomed to more stimulant meals. **1836–41** BRANDE *Chem.* (ed. 5) 428 Ammonia is very pungent and acrid,..but when diluted by mixture with common air, agreeably stimulant. **1839** HALLAM *Hist. Lit.* II. vii. §44. II. 316 We are now so accustomed to a more stimulant diet in fiction, that few would read it through with pleasure. **1861** BENTLEY *Man. Bot.* 562 Aromatic, Carminative, Stimulant, and Tonic Umbelliferæ.

b. *spec.* Applied to alcoholic drinks. *rare.* (Cf. B. 2 b.)

1872 J. G. MURPHY *Comm. Lev.* x. 8–11 Abstinence from stimulant drinks.

c. Acting as a stimulus (see STIMULUS 3); exciting the functional activity of an organ. (Cf. B. 2 c.) *rare.*

1785 CULLEN *Instit. Med.* I. (ed. 3) 66 Whatever can excite the contraction of muscular fibres is called a Stimulus; and in general, the means of exciting contraction are called Stimulant Powers. **1788** J. BROWN tr. *Elem. Med.* I. 6 The same exciting powers..ought to be denominated stimulant, or stimuli.

B. *sb.* Something that stimulates.

1. Something that rouses or incites to action; an incentive, a stimulus. Now *rare* exc. with some figurative notion of sense 2.

1794 R. J. SULIVAN *View Nat.* I. 30 A powerful stimulant to others, to employ their invention and ability. **1847** G. HARRIS *Life Hardwicke* I. 354 The pecuniary remuneration in every office of this kind is the direct and immediate stimulant to exertion and enterprise. **1855** MACAULAY *Hist. Eng.* xiii. III. 283 Even now the stimulants which he applied to his torpid and feeble party produced some faint symptoms of returning animation. **1873** HAMERTON *Intell. Life* II. i. 44 The three intellectual pursuits—literature, science, and the fine arts—are all of them strong stimulants.

2. a. *Phys.* and *Med.* Something that temporarily quickens some vital process, or the function of some organ; a stimulant agent.

1728 CHAMBERS *Cycl.* s.v., Stimulants produce Pain, Heat, Redness. **1772** W. FALCONER *Ess. Bath Waters* I. 338 The Bath Waters are in general indicated as stimulants, in cases of languid motion. **1815** J. SMITH *Panorama Sci. & Art* II. 268 In disorders of an inflammatory nature, electricity, as it is a stimulant, should not be resorted to. **1831** J. DAVIES *Mat. Med.* 134 Diffusible or general stimulants... Such..stimulating remedies as do not appear to act..on a particular organ, but the exciting action of which is equally felt throughout the whole economy. **1832** BREWSTER *Nat. Magic* xiii. 347 The operation of this remarkable stimulant [nitrous oxide]. **1870** YEATS *Nat. Hist. Comm.* 148 Pepper is a warm carminative stimulant. **1875** H. C. WOOD *Therap.* (1879) 114 Cardiac stimulants.. increase the..force of the circulation. **1882** EDISON in A. A. Reade *Study & Stimulants* (1883) 45 When so engaged I almost invariably chew tobacco as a stimulant. **1882** A. J. ELLIS *Ibid.* 46, I never took tobacco in any shape or form. For twenty-five years I have taken no sort of stimulant, not even tea or coffee. **1885** DR. RANNEY in *Harper's Mag.* Mar. 641/2 The abuse of stimulants, in the form of alcohol, tobacco, tea, and coffee.

b. *spec.* Applied to alcoholic drinks.

1848 MILL *Pol. Econ.* II. v. vi. 425 Among luxuries of general consumption, taxation should by preference attach itself to stimulants. **1859** —— *Liberty* v. 180 To tax stimulants for the sole purpose of making them more difficult to be obtained, is a measure differing only in degree from their entire prohibition. **1865** LIVINGSTONE *Zambesi* xxi. 427 The..craving for stimulants. **1899** A. C. BENSON *Life Abp. Benson* I. i. 10 In one of his many serious illnesses he refused all stimulants.

c. Something that excites an organ to its functional activity. (Cf. A. 2 b.) *rare.*

1880 HUXLEY *Crayfish* iii. 116 Sonorous vibrations..act as the stimulants of a special nerve.

Hence **'stimulantly** *adv.*

1814 W. TAYLOR in *Monthly Rev.* LXXV. 161 Such sayings..when stimulantly expressed, are easily remembered.

stimulate ('stɪmjʊleɪt), *v.* [f. L. *stimulāt-*, ppl. stem of *stimulāre*, f. *stimulus*: see STIMULUS. Cf. F. *stimuler* (14th c.), Sp., Pg. *estimular*, It. *stimolare.*]

†**1.** *trans.* To prick, sting, afflict. *Obs. rare*[−1].

a **1548** HALL *Chron.*, *Hen. VII*, 57 Kyng Henry.. euer punched, stimulated and pricked with the scrupulous stynges of domesticall sedicion.

2. To rouse to action or exertion as by pricking or goading; to spur on; to incite (a person) *to do* something; to impart additional energy to (an activity, a process).

1619 HUTTON *Follie's Anat.* etc. D 6, My..distemperd thoughts, Do stimulate proud Silla's Ire. *a* **1700** EVELYN *Diary* 27 Feb. 1644–5, The 3 races of the Barbarie horses, that run..without riders, onely having spurrs so placed on their backs,..as by their motion to stimulate them. **1759** HUME *Hist. Eng., Hen. VIII*, iii. I. 147 Hearing of the pope's captivity, they were farther stimulated to undertake the war with vigour for the restoring his liberty. **1768–74** TUCKER *Lt. Nat.* (1834) II. 526 The pricks of conscience will not so much afflict and torment us, as stimulate our resolution and excite our diligence. **1817** JAS. MILL *Brit. India* v. ix. II. 694 They..stimulated and importuned him, to bring forward a scheme of improvement. **1832** HT. MARTINEAU *Hill & Valley* v. 77 To stimulate production by useful..labour. **1836** DICKENS *Sk. Boz, Black Veil*, To..stimulate him to fresh exertions. **1842** LEVER *J. Hinton* xviii, You have stimulated my curiosity. **1863** GEO. ELIOT *Romola* II. xxii, They..stimulated their prisoners to beg.

absol. **1789** J. MOORE *Zeluco* lxviii. (1797) II. 188 Contemptuous language may stimulate to..revenge. **1815** JANE AUSTEN *Emma* v, Where Miss Taylor failed to stimulate,..Harriet Smith will do nothing.

3. *Phys.* To act as a stimulus to (see STIMULUS 1, 3). **a.** To excite (an organ) to increased activity, to quicken the action or function of. Also with the action or function as obj.

1707 FLOYER *Physic. Pulse-Watch* 201 In general we use Medicines of the same Taste, as the secreted Humours, to stimulate their Excretion. **1798** R. JACKSON *Hist. & Cure Fever* 260 Wine, brandy and opium stimulate the system to increased action. **1809** *Med. Jrnl.* XXI. 103 Oxygen stimulates the pulmonic vessels, and..makes them propel their contents. **1843** R. J. GRAVES *Syst. Clin. Med.* xi. 119, I frequently prescribe small doses of hydrargyrum cum cretâ, with the view of gently stimulating the liver.

absol. **1662** J. DEGRAVERE *Thesaurus Remediorum* (ed. 2) 16 Signes indicating Purgation... A looseness or flux of humors stimulating to expulsion. **1732** ARBUTHNOT *Rules of Diet* in *Aliments*, etc. 261 Things which stimulate in the extreme Degree, excite pain. **1842** ABDY *Water Cure* 75 With bandages, put on tight to stimulate, upon the whole limb.

b. To excite (a tissue or structure) to its specific activity.

1878 ROY in *Jrnl. Physiol.* I. 475 When the muscle was stimulated directly by the induced current.

4. To administer stimulants to.

1905 *Brit. Med. Jrnl.* No. 2317. 1139 No one familiar with infectious diseases would systematically stimulate all cases.

b. *intr.* for *refl.* To indulge in (alcoholic) stimulants. Now only *colloq.* (? *U.S.*) Also in *passive*, To be affected by alcoholic drinks.

1800 *Med. Jrnl.* III. 50 Men of strong constitutions began to stimulate in excess very early in life. **1839** MARRYAT *Diary Amer.* Ser. I. II. 224 [Examples of American language.] He stimulates too much. **1882** O'DONOVAN *Merv Oasis* I. 449 A servant brought in a silver tray, upon which were large glasses of..arrack... We were all slightly stimulated before a move was made towards the dinner table. **1898** TALMAGE *Serm.* in *Chr. Herald* (N.Y.) 30 Mar. 268/4 Now he must brace himself up. Now he stimulates.

Hence **'stimulated** *ppl. a.*

1887 BURDON-SANDERSON, etc. *Transl. For. Biol. Mem.* I. 255 The tract of nerve lying between the stimulating electrodes I call the stimulated region. *Ibid.* 273 Electrical phenomena in stimulated nerves. **1900** W. S. HALL *Text-bk. Physiol.* 52 The action of stimuli is..transient, *i.e.* the stimulated organism returns..to its former state of rest.

stimulating ('stɪmjʊleɪtɪŋ), *ppl. a.* [f. STIMULATE *v.* + -ING[2].] That stimulates.

1. Rousing to action or exertion; spurring or urging on; inciting; *spec.* inciting to mental activity.

a **1732** GAY *Fables* II. xv. 87 Urg'd by the stimulating goad, I [the ox] drag the cumbrous waggon's load. **1828** P. CUNNINGHAM *N.S. Wales* (ed. 3) II. 132 Urged on by the stimulating excitement afforded by publicity. **1873** R. W. CHURCH *Influences Chr. Nat. Charact.* ii. 87 The sentences of Seneca are stimulating to the intellect. **1908** J. WELLS *Stewart of Lovedale* iv. 29 Admirable and stimulating as he was as a preacher, Mr. Stewart was even more stimulating as a teacher.

2. *Phys.* and *Med.* = STIMULANT A. 2 a, c.

1684 tr. *Bonet's Merc. Compit.* XIX. 694/2 Aphrodisiacks are either 1. strengthners..Or 2. stimulating. **1732** ARBUTHNOT *Rules of Diet* in *Aliments*, etc. 255 Salts which make it pungent and stimulating. **1793** T. BEDDOES *Calculus*, etc. 198 The stimulating quality of light upon plants. **1836** A. COMBE *Physiol. Digestion* 270 Quantities of stimulating animal food. **1842** LOUDON *Suburban Hort.* 57 Sea-weed is still more readily decomposed..and hence this manure is stimulating as well as enriching. **1898** *Allbutt's Syst. Med.* V. 284 A stimulating liniment containing turpentine and iodine.

b. *spec.* = STIMULANT A. 2 c. Now *rare.*

1840 MACAULAY *Ess., Clive* ¶37 Stimulating drugs were employed to aid the effect of religious zeal, and the besiegers, drunk with enthusiasm, drunk with bang, rushed furiously to the attack. **1872** J. G. MURPHY *Comm. Lev.* x. 10, 11 Abstinence..from stimulating drinks.

stimulation (stɪmjʊ'leɪʃən). [ad. L. *stimulātiōnem*, n. of action f. *stimulāre* to STIMULATE. Cf. F. *stimulation* (14–15th c. in Hatz.-Darm.), Sp. *estimulacion*, Pg. *estimulação*,

It. *stimolazione*.] The action of stimulating or condition of being stimulated.

1. A pricking, goading, or spurring on to action; incitement; †pricking or compunction of conscience (*obs.*).

1526 *Pilgr. Perf.* (W. de W. 1531) 263 Y^e stimulacyons of the flesshe. **1640** LD. DIGBY *Sp.* in Rushw. *Hist. Coll.* III. (1692) I. 171 The Danger, when either true, or pretended Stimulation of Conscience hath once given a multitude Agitation. **1751** JOHNSON *Rambler* No. 145 ¶5 That industry which the stimulations of necessity..enforce. **1860** MILL *Repr. Govt.* (1865) 27/2 To supply reasons to his understanding, and stimulation to his feeling. **1873** E. H. CLARKE *Sex in Educ.* 106 The same girls are apt to be quick, ..and need not stimulation, but repression.

2. *Phys.* and *Med.* The action of a stimulus. **a.** Excitation to increased activity, quickening of some vital function or process (cf. STIMULUS 1). In quot. 1733 *loosely*, stimulating property (cf. STIMULUS 1 b). **b.** Excitation of an organ or tissue to its specific activity (cf. STIMULUS 3).

1733 CHEYNE *Eng. Malady* II. vii. §2 (1734) 186 The Bile, by its natural Acrimony and Stimulation [etc.]. **1799** *Med. Jrnl.* II. 217 The vaccine poison..produces inflammation, a little tumour, and sometimes pustule, which are not the effects of the specific stimulation of the matter. **1834** J. FORBES *Laennec's Dis. Chest* (ed. 4) 373 The stimulation communicated to or subtracted from the brain by the light. **1843** R. J. GRAVES *Syst. Clin. Med.* xv. 183 We should resort to stimulation by wine. **1879** CARPENTER *Ment. Phys.* App. 719 Muscles..can be thrown into contraction by stimulation of these lower centres. **1900** W. S. HALL *Text-bk. Physiol.* 52 A muscle-cell responds to all stimuli by contracting, a gland-cell by secreting, while the stimulation of the optic nerve can only produce the sensation of light.

stimulative (ˈstɪmjʊlətɪv), *a.* and *sb.* [f. L. *stimulāre*: see STIMULATE *v.* and -ATIVE.]

A. *adj.* Having the property of stimulating; of a stimulating nature or character. Const. *of*, *to*.

1791 NEWTE *Tour Eng. & Scot.* 200 This would be like spreading the stimulative power of manure over large tracts of waste land. **1836** HOR. SMITH *Tin Trump.* (1876) 217 More stimulative of the risible faculties. **1854** MILMAN *Lat. Chr.* III. ii. I. 271 Ulphilas..left out the Books of Kings, as too congenial and too stimulative to their warlike propensities. **1906** E. A. ABBOTT *Silanus* xvi. 143 This belief I found also stimulative to well-doing.

B. *sb.* Something having a stimulating quality; a motive inciting to action; a stimulus, incentive. Now *rare* or *Obs.* (Common *c* 1750–1800.)

1747 RICHARDSON *Clarissa* (1811) I. xxxi. 225 There are so many stimulatives to such a spirit as mine in this affair, besides love. **1790** *Bystander* 297 Otherwise there could be no stimulative to industry, no encouragement to invention.

†**b.** = STIMULANT B. 2. *Obs. rare*⁻¹.

1808 *Ann. Reg., Charact.* 68 Coffee is not a favourite drink with the Spaniards; he needs no stimulative.

stimulator (ˈstɪmjʊleɪtə(r)). Also 7 -er. [a. L. *stimulātor*, f. *stimulāre*: see STIMULATE *v.* Cf. F. *stimulateur*, Sp., Pg. *estimulador*, It. *stimolatore*.]

1. *gen.* One who or something which stimulates.

1614 JACKSON *Creed* III. 208 *marg.*, See the stimulator. **1684** tr. *Bonet's Merc. Compit.* XIX. 694/2 Cantharides are the strongest amongst these stimulaters. **1717** L. HOWELL *Desiderius* 55 The Indulgence of the Body being too often the great Stimulater of the Soul to vile Practices. **1768–74** TUCKER *Lt. Nat.* (1834) II. 549 The appetites are the great stimulators of action. **1851** *Jrnl. R. Agric. Soc.* XII. II. 357 This great stimulator of a vegetable soil. **1890** *Ch. Times* 3 Jan. 9/1 A practical administrator and stimulator of work in his great diocese.

2. *spec.* In the psychological laboratory, an instrument for communicating a stimulus.

1905 E. B. TITCHENER *Exper. Psychol.* II. I. 153 For simple reactions to noise we may use the..Sound stimulator. *Ibid.* 157 Pressure stimulators (areal) for break and make. *Ibid.* 163 Make and break stimulators for taste.

3. *U.S.* One addicted to the use of stimulants.

1891 *Cycl. Temp. & Prohib.* 621/1 The stimulator then resorts to his old remedy.

stimulatory (ˈstɪmjʊlətərɪ), *a.* and *sb.* [f. L. *stimulāre*: see STIMULATE *v.* and -ORY. Cf. It. *stimolatorio*.] **a.** *adj.* = STIMULATIVE *a.* **b.** *sb.* = STIMULANT *sb.* 2. *rare.*

1758 *Herald* No. 27. II. 187 That policy which contrives gratification..so stimulatory of a military spirit. **1812** J. SMYTH *Pract. Customs* (1821) 32 The powdered root of this plant is used as a stimulatory. **1968** *Times* 21 Oct. 7/1 The buds exert a differential influence during the season, being inhibitory in winter and stimulatory in spring. **1975** *Nature* 7 Aug. 487/2 Either germinating seeds or soil may provide the substrates for growth of the stimulatory micro-organisms. **1981** *Times* 27 Aug. 9/2 Even with the stimulatory measures, however, the deficit does not seem likely to be excessive in the years to come.

stimulatress. *rare*⁻⁰. [f. STIMULATOR + -ESS.] A female stimulator; a woman (or something personified as female) that stimulates.

1846 WORCESTER, *Stimulatress* [citing SUMNER]. **1850** OGILVIE, *Stimulator*, *Stimulatress*, one who stimulates.

‖**stimuˈlatrix.** *Obs. rare.* [L., f. *stimulāre*: see STIMULATE *v.* and -TRIX.] = prec.

1611 COTGR., *Stimulatrice*, a stimulatrix, an instigatrix. **1796** BURNEY *Mem. Metastasio* III. 6 The violent efforts to which this troublesome stimulatrix has obliged us to have recourse.

†**stimule.** *Obs. rare*⁻¹. [Anglicized form of STIMULUS. Cf. F. *stimule* = STIMULUS 4.] A goad.

1583 STUBBES *Anat. Abus.* I. G vij b, Doth not y^e Lord.. as it were with a stimule, or prick by his mandat..stirre them vp to the same.

stimulose (ˈstɪmjʊləʊs), *a.* *Nat. Hist.* [ad. mod.L. *stimulōsus* f. STIMULUS: see -OSE. Cf. F. *stimuleux* in the same sense.

Late L. had *stimulōsus* in the sense 'stimulative'.]

Covered with stings or stinging hairs.

1866 *Treas. Bot.* 1100/2.

stimulus (ˈstɪmjʊləs). Pl. **stimuli** (ˈstɪmjʊlaɪ). [Originally a mod.L. use (in medical books) of L. *stimulus* goad, of doubtful origin; perh. f. root **sti-* in *stilus*: see STYLUS.

Cf. F. *stimulus* (Phys.), *stimule* (Bot.); Sp., Pg. *estimulo*, It. *stimulo*, *stimolo* (and popular forms in dialects, e.g. Milanese *stombol*, Veronese *stombio*, Sardinian *strumbula*), Rumanian *stramur*.

The following quot. exemplifies the mod.L. medical use: *a* **1614** PLATERUS *Observ. in Hominis Affectibus* I. (1641) 255 In Impotentia [etc.] Ad stimulum addendum, primum exterioribus illud tentare volui, jubens perinæi regionem.. calide inungere oleo nucum in quo Formica & Cantharides decoctæ fuerint.]

1. *Phys.* Something that acts as a 'goad' or 'spur' to a languid bodily organ; an agency or influence that stimulates, increases, or quickens organic activity.

1684 tr. *Bonet's Merc. Compit.* XIX. 694/2 The Indian Chocolad..both increases Seed and adds a *stimulus*. **1732** ARBUTHNOT *Rules of Diet* in *Aliments*, etc. 276 By weakening the force of any Stimulus. **1750** J. THEOBALD *App. Medulla Med. Univ.* 55 In all Cases where the Nerves want a Stimulus to help them to perform their destined Offices. **1821** SCOTT *Kenilw.* xx, One of those unfortunate persons, who, being once stirred with the vinous stimulus, do not fall asleep like other drunkards, but [etc.]. **1843** R. J. GRAVES *Syst. Clin. Med.* x. 115 An attack of pneumonia, coming on in fever, frequently acts as a stimulus to the economy. **1875** JOWETT *Plato* (ed. 2) V. 68 The physician..would tell us that you cannot restore strength by a stimulus.

b. Stimulating property, action, or effect; stimulation or quickening of organic activity.

1684 tr. *Bonet's Merc. Compit.* XIX. 695/1 That..such Medicines be made use of as comfort the vital faculty, and yet have a gentle Stimulus withal. **1758** E. WRIGHT in *Phil. Trans.* L. 598 This salt is not only astringent, and consequently a strengthener, but at the same time acts with a gentle stimulus. **1785** PALEY *Moral Philos.* IV. ii. (1818) II. 13 As the liquor loses its *stimulus*, the dose must be increased. **1841** A. COMBE *Physiol. Digestion* (ed. 3) 292 They are less stimulating... Indeed, from this very want of stimulus, they are apt to disagree with weak stomachs, unless seasoned. **1847** W. C. L. MARTIN *Ox* 178/2 Common salt as an aperient often acts well..perhaps from the stimulus it gives to the stomach. **1861** FLOR. NIGHTINGALE *Nursing* 73 It is not a sleeping dose he wants, but food or stimulus.

2. a. *gen.* An agency or influence that stimulates to action or (const. *to*) that quickens an activity or process.

1791 W. ENFIELD *Hist. Philos.* II. i. 18 Among the philosophical works of Cicero, we do not now find his *Hortentius*,..which Augustine confesses operated upon his mind, as a powerful *stimulus* to the pursuit of wisdom. **1793** *Brit. Critic* II. 362 We should expect even the voluntary productions of the pen, without this violent stimulus, to be sufficient to support the honour of the society. **1803** WINDHAM *Sp.* (1812) II. 154 Measures so chosen.., as to become a powerful stimulus to recruiting. **1830** MISS MITFORD *Village* Ser. IV. 80 *note*, A person of great..talent, who,..if she were prompted by either of those two powerful *stimuli*, want of money or want of admiration, to take due pains—would..become a clever writer. **1833** HT. MARTINEAU *Loom & Lugger* I. i. 12 There is no stimulus to improvement like fair competition. **1834** MARRYAT *P. Simple* xv, The ship..reminded me of a goaded and fiery horse, mad with the stimulus applied. **1863** FAWCETT *Pol. Econ.* I. v. (1876) 63 Gold may have been the primary stimulus of Australia's prosperity. **1873** SPENCER *Study Sociol.* viii. 194 The needs of defence and attack were the chief stimuli to the cultivation of arts.

b. A quickening impulse; also, in generalized sense, quickening influence, stimulation.

1794 *Brit. Critic* III. 518 Those young Academicans.. will receive from the perusal of his book a powerful stimulus to their ambition. **1833** HT. MARTINEAU *Vanderput & S.* vi. 99 The turn of exchange had given such a stimulus to importation. **1849** C. BRONTË *Shirley* i, Do you expect passion, and stimulus, and melodrama? **1856** KANE *Arctic Expl.* II. xviii. 189 Their health improved under the stimulus of a new mode of life. **1865** M. ARNOLD *Ess. Crit.*, *Joubert* (1875) 319 They become..a source of stimulus and progress for all of us. **1911** T. B. KILPATRICK *N.T. Evangelism* iii. 76 These questions will come to him with rebuke and stimulus.

3. a. *Phys.* Something that excites an organ or tissue to a specific activity or function; a material agency that produces a reaction in an organism.

Developed from the older physiological sense 1.

1793 T. BEDDOES *Calculus*, etc. 191 Those stimuli which ..act continually more or less upon the irritable fibre, are, heat, light, nourishment, air, the circulation of the blood, the stimulus of generation, and the nervous stimuli. **1837** P. KEITH *Bot. Lex.* 224 Life is that energy, or attribute, of organized structures which renders them capable of receiving and of obeying the impulse of stimuli. **1848** CARPENTER *Anim. Phys.* 19 Muscles..are composed of a tissue which has the power of contracting suddenly and forcibly, when peculiar stimuli are applied to it. **1880** C. & F. DARWIN *Movem. Pl.* 4 The tip is sensitive to various stimuli, especially to very slight pressure. **1900** W. S. HALL *Text-bk. Physiol.* 52 Stimuli classified. The following forms of energy act as stimuli for most cells: (i) Heat, (ii) Light, (iii) Electricity, (iv) Mechanical Stimuli, (v) Chemical Stimuli. *transf.* **1851** MILL *Dissert. & Discuss.*, *Enfranch. Women* (1859) II. 438 What makes intelligent beings is the power of thought; the stimuli which call forth that power are the interest and dignity of thought itself.

b. Influence or effect in calling forth some specific reaction of a tissue; irritation of a nerve or other sensitive structure.

1785 CULLEN *Instit. Med.* I. (ed. 3) 73 The force of contraction, or the vigour of muscular fibres, will be always as the force of stimulus, and the vigour of the animal, nervous, and inherent powers taken together. **1837** P. KEITH *Bot. Lex.* 327 Rest, which they thus obtain after having been exposed throughout the day to the stimulus of light. **1841** *Penny Cycl.* XXI. 181/2 The infusion of tobacco, and hydrocyanic acid, appear to destroy completely the sensibility of the heart, so that it no longer responds to the stimulus of the blood. **1872** HUXLEY *Physiol.* viii. 187 The great majority..of the movements of the body..are the effect of an influence (technically termed a stimulus or irritation) applied..to the ends of afferent nerves. **1882** GASKELL in *Jrnl. Physiol.* IV. 67 Since then the ventricle does not contract after the auricle because separate stimuli pass from the sinus to the ventricle along nerve fibres, but does contract [etc.]. **1900** W. S. HALL *Text-bk. Physiol.* 75 The following laws of electrical response may be formulated: Law I. The make stimulus is kathodic; the break stimulus is anodic.

c. *Psychol.* Any specific change in physical energy or an event (whether internal or external to the organism) which excites a nerve impulse and gives rise to a reaction.

1894 CREIGHTON & TITCHENER tr. *Wundt's Human & Animal Psychol.* 16 The processes of motion which, by their operation upon our senses, give rise to sensations, we commonly denominate *stimuli*, or more particularly *sense-stimuli*... Thus we regard the sound-waves of the air or the light-waves set up in surrounding space as stimuli corresponding to our sensations of sound and light. **1919** J. B. WATSON *Psychol.* i. 9 The goal of psychological study is the ascertaining of such data and laws that, given the stimulus, psychology can predict what the response will be; or..given the response, it can specify the nature of the effective stimulus. **1957** E. R. HILGARD *Introd. Psychol.* (ed. 2) 596/1 *Stimulus*, some specific physical energy impinging on a receptor sensitive to that kind of energy... Any objectively describable situation or event..that is the occasion for an organism's response. **1980** E. L. DECI in E. Staub *Personality* ii. 43 People do not respond to objective external stimuli; they respond to stimuli *as they perceive them*.

4. *Nat. Hist.* A sting, a stinging hair. *rare* (? only as Latin).

1760 J. LEE *Introd. Bot.* III. xviii. (1765) 213 *Stimuli*, Stings, keep off naked Animals by their venomous Punctures. **1764** BERKENHOUT *Clavis Angl. Bot.*, *Stimuli*, stings: a species of *Arma* growing upon some plants for their defence... Linnæus divides the *stimuli* into *pungentes* and *urentes*. **1796** WITHERING *Brit. Plants* (ed. 3) I. 84 *Stimuli*, stings. **1866** *Treas. Bot.* 1100/2. **1909** *Century Dict.* Suppl., *Stimulus*. 6. In *entom.*, a stinging-hair.

5. *attrib.* and *Comb.*, as (sense 3 c) ***stimulus-complex***, ***control***, ***-error***, ***intensity***, ***-object***, ***-pattern***, ***-situation***, ***-threshold***, ***-value***, ***-word***; **stimulus diffusion** (see quot. 1940); **stimulus generalization**, the fact that the response elicited by one stimulus can also be elicited by other stimuli associated with but not identical to the original; **stimulus-response**, abbrev. form of ***stimulus-and-response***, used *attrib.* or as *adj.* to denote this process, esp. when considered as the basic element in the study of sense preception, learning or behaviour modification; = S-R s.v. S 4 a.

1924 R. M. OGDEN tr. *Koffka's Growth of Mind* 87 Fine differences in the stimulus-complex may lead to opposite reactions. **1954** W. H. MELCHING in E. L. Wilkes *Secondary Reinforcement* (1966) II. ii. 143 The presence (or absence) of the buzzer during conditioning and extinction was assumed to be an important component of the stimulus complexes. **1956** *Psychol. Monogr.* LXX. v. 2/2 A method which involved a greater degree of stimulus control than has usually been achieved in research on discrimination. **1979** H. K. RODEWALD (*title*) Stimulus control of behavior. **1940** A. L. KROEBER in *Amer. Anthrop.* XLII. 1 (*title*) Stimulus diffusion. *Ibid.*, It is the idea of the complex or system which is accepted, but it remains for the receiving culture to develop a new content. This somewhat special process might therefore be called 'idea-diffusion' or 'stimulus diffusion'. **1978** *Language* LIV. 207 If diffusion is to be thought of as operating between the sub-areas, it can only be 'stimulus diffusion'. **1909** E. B. TITCHENER *Text-bk. Psychol.* I. §66.218 The observer tends to judge, not in terms of sensation, but in terms of stimulus... This error,..is known technically as the stimulus error. **1949** *Mind* LVIII. 452 The Stimulus-error and the Constancy Hypothesis are particular forms of this fallacy. **1943** C. L. HULL *Princ. Behavior* xii. 183 The reaction involved in the original conditioning becomes connected with a considerable zone of stimuli other than, but adjacent to, the stimulus conventionally involved in the original conditioning; this is called *stimulus generalization*. **1977** in Honig & Staddon *Handbk. Operant Behavior* xi. 316/2 Another possibility is that the mechanism underlying conditioned reinforcement is stimulus generalization. **1909** *Amer. Jrnl. Psychol.* XX. 4 A progression of stimulus intensities such that the differences of corresponding sensation between any consecutive pairs are equal to one another. **1933** *Psychol. Abstr.* VII. 538/1 The relationship between stimulus intensity and duration in the motor nerve of the frog. **1921** *Psychol. Rev.* XXVIII. 398 The dependence of a stimulus-object upon its setting is especially familiar in the case of contrasting colors or objects. **1970** *Jrnl. Gen. Psychol.* Apr. 151 The strength with which an unfamiliar stimulus-object elicits a particular mediational process. **1924** R. M. Ogden tr. *Koffka's Growth of Mind* iii. 137 The phenomenon corresponding to a given stimulus-pattern. **1950** *Mind* LIX. 187 A red shape presents a stimulus pattern that I react to immediately. **1921** *Psychol. Rev.* XXVIII. 390 The response member of a stimulus-response couple may consist of a group of reactions. **1927** L. L. Bernard *Introd. Social Psychol.* viii. 109 Tropism is not a stimulus-response process in the same sense that reflexes and instincts are. It makes use of stimulus-response mechanisms. **1957** E. R. Hilgard *Introd. Psychol.* (ed. 2) i. 21/1 Stimulus-response theory (or S-R theory, as it is commonly called) asserts that all behavior is in response to stimuli. **1964** E. A. Nida *Toward Sci. Transl.* iii. 40 In most actual instances of communication, verbal symbols enter into a chain of stimulus-response situations. **1980** *Dædalus* Spring 23 This evidence of central control over receptors..affected the picture of the stimulus-response relationship that had dominated psychology for decades. **1923** Ogden & Richards *Meaning of Meaning* iii. 139 The excitation of part of an engram complex, which is called up by a stimulus.. similar to a part only of the original stimulus-situation. **1977** A. Giddens *Stud. in Social & Polit. Theory* i. 76 All descriptive predicates, however 'theoretical', are learned in conjunction with definite stimulus-situations. **1897** C. H. Judd tr. *Wundt's Outl. Psychol.* 254 The stimulus from which the resulting psychical process, for example, a sensation, can be just apperceived, is called the *stimulus-threshold*. **1935** L. Bloomfield in C. Hockett *Bloomfield Anthol.* (1970) 310 His audience will respond only to the exact stimulus-value of his words. **1962** *Science Survey* XV. 251 Now the 'stimulus value' of a moving object depends not only on the actual capacity of the eye to detect and evaluate movement, but [etc.]. **1905** *Psychol. Bull.* II. 249 The influence of the grammatical form of the stimulus-word on the reaction is rather striking. **1971** *Jrnl. Gen. Psychol.* Apr. 281 Stimulus words were carefully selected in order to control for associative response frequencies.

stimy, variant of STYMIE (*Golf*).

stinch(e, obs. forms of STANCH *v.*, STENCH.

stinck(e, obs. ff. STINK *sb.* and *v.*

† **stine.** *Obs. rare*[−1]. ? Support.

c **1420** *Liber Cocorum* (1862) 34 Take floure and rere þo cofyns fyne, Wele standand withouten stine.

stine, variant of STYAN *dial.*

sting (stɪŋ), *sb.*[1] *Sc.* and *north.* Forms: 1 stæng, (-ncg), 1, 4 steng, (1 -ncg, -ngc, -nc, -gn); 5 steyng, 5–6 steing; 1, 5–6 styng, 5– sting. [OE. *stęng* masc.: see STANG *sb.*[1]]

1. a. A pole, staff.

c **725** *Corpus Gloss.* (Hessels) C 450 *Claua*, steng [*Epinal* stegn, *Erfurt* stęng]. *a* **900** *O.E. Martyrol.* 8 Aug. 142 þa het se dema hi nacode gebindan to anum stenge ond hi bærnan mid fyre. *c* **1375** *Sc. Leg. Saints* xxxvi. (*John Baptist*) 850 His harme..stud strekit þare a hyldry steng as it ware. **1508** Dunbar *Poems* vi. 100 Et duos rusticos de rure Berand a barell on a styng. **1513** Douglas *Æneis* III. ix. 87 With ane scharpit and brint sting of tre, Out did we boir and pyke his mekle E. **1571** *Wills & Inv. N.C.* (Surtees) I. 361, ij styngs for ye wayne xd. **1580** *Shipping List of Dundee* in *D. Wedderburne's Compt. Bk.* etc. (S.H.S.) 198 Sex thousand steingis. **1643** *Orkney Witch Trial* in *Abbotsf. Club Miscell.* I. 177 If it war the dead manis sting which trublit him, it wold cuir and heale him. **1703** in W. Maitland *Hist. Edin.* (1753) 329 Twentie four Sayes, and threttie sex Stings with Knags, whereof sex standing full of Water, and the Stings hanging by them, [etc.]. **1724** in Cramond *Ann. Banff* (1893) II. 219 For a sting to drive the oxen, 1s. Sc.

b. A pole or staff or club used as a weapon; the shaft of a pike or spear. Often ***staff and sting***.

a **900** *O.E. Martyrol.* 20 Jan. 27 þa het he hine mid stengum þyrscan. *c* **950** *Lindisf. Gosp.* Matt. xxvi. 47 *Fustibus*, stencgum [*c* **975** *Rushw.* stængum]. *a* **1300** *Cursor M.* 24029 (Edin.) þai draw him forþ e with staf and steng. *c* **1470** Henryson *Mor. Fab., Fox, Wolf & Cadger* 151 That had not in my hand sa mekle gude, As staf or sting, ȝone truker for to strike. *c* **1470** Henry *Wallace* II. 49 Vpon the hed ane with the steing hitt he. **1513** Douglas *Æneis* IX. viii. 126 The Troianis..dang thame down with pikkis and poyntit styngis. **1535** Stewart *Cron.* (Rolls) II. 96 With staf and sting syne slew richt mony ane. **1550** Lyndesay *Sqr. Meldrum* 254 Bot thair wes daylie skirmishing, Quhair men of armis brak monie sting. **1590–91** *Reg. Privy Council Scot.* IV. 587 With thair lance staffis and stingis [they] gave him divers bauch, blaa and bludie straikis.

c. (*to carry*) ***with*** or ***by sting and ling*** [? LINE *sb.*[2]]: with a rope suspended from a pole borne on two or more persons' shoulders. Also ***sting and ling*** (without prep.); also *fig.* = bodily, by force.

1571 R. Bannatyne *Jrnl.* (1806) 130 He..was borne up with sex workmen with sting and ling, and Mr. Robert Maitland haulding up his heid. **1615** *Chron. Perth* in R. Chambers *Dom. Ann. Scot.* (1858) I. 453 Upon Fasten's E'en there was twa puncheons of Bourdeaux wine carriet, sting and ling, on men's shoulders, on the ice, at the mids of the North Inch. **1816** Scott *Antiq.* xliv, He..never intended to look near the place again, unless he had been brought there sting and ling. **1883** Martine *Reminisc. Haddington* 143 Cut figures of two brewer's men, in antique dress, carrying a barrel of ale 'Sting and Ling'.

2. A pointed instrument used in thatching.

1808 Jamieson. **1815** *Notes to Pennecuik's Descr. Tweeddale* 88 (Jam.) The thatch..is thrust into holes previously made obliquely upwards in the divots by an iron-shod, dove-tailed-pointed hand instrument, called a sting. **1893–4** *Northumb. Gloss.*

3. *Aeronaut.* A rod-like support used in wind-tunnel testing (see quot. 1933).

1933 *Gloss. Aeronaut. Terms* (*B.S.I.*) III. 20 *Sting*, a light rod attached to and extending backwards from a body for convenience of mounting for test in a wind tunnel. **1948** *Jrnl. R. Aeronaut. Soc.* LII. 240/1 In this work the model was supported from the rear by means of a sting. **1959** *Engineering* 6 Feb. 188/1 The model support consists of a quadrant and sting.

4. *Comb.*, as **sting-burden**, **-*lift***, **-*man***, †**-*sowel***; † **stingis-dint**, a fine for an assault with a stick.

1701 in J. Bulloch *Pynours* (1887) 73 Crews for caryeing *sting burdens. **1153–95** *Carta Hugonis* in *Boldon Bk.* etc. (Surtees) p. xlii, In burgo non debet blodwite nec merchete nec heriot nec *stengesdint [*printed* -duit] exigi. **14..** *Burgh Lawis* xvii. in *Anc. Laws Scot.* (Burgh Rec. Soc.) 10 Quod infra burgum non debet exaudiri blodewit nec styngis-dynt nec merchet. **1701** in J. Bulloch *Pynours* (1887) 74 Each *Sting lift caried by two men is to pay the double of ane back burden. **1554** *Extracts Burgh Rec. Edin.* (1871) II. 313 To vj *stingmen of the town to beir thir foirsaids stanis furth of the querrellis viij[s]. **1583** *Ibid.* (1882) IV. 303 The persouns vnderwrittin to be polkmen and stingmen and metters vpoun the said schoir. **1235–52** *Rentalia Glaston.* (Somerset Rec. Soc.) 88, j palum quem vocant *sting soghles.

sting (stɪŋ), *sb.*[2] Forms: 1 stincg, 4 *Kent.* steng, 5–6 stynge, 5–7 stinge, 1, 5–6 styng, 1, 4, 6– sting. [f. STING *v.*[1]

It is possible that two words from the root of the vb. have coalesced: OE. *sting*:—prehist. **stingo-z* and OE. *styng* (Kentish ME. *steng*):—**stungi-z* (= OHG. *stung*). A dial. form *stinge* (stindʒ) appears to represent yet another formation, OE. **stenge* or **stęngea*. Cf. Norw. *styng* masc., prick, sting.]

1. a. The act of stinging. **b.** The fact or effect of being stung; the wound inflicted by the *aculeus* of an insect, the telson of a scorpion, the fang of an adder, etc.; the pain or smart of such a wound.

c **900** *Bæda's Hist.* II. ix. (1890) 123 Næfde he scyld æt honda, þæt he þone cyning mid scyldan meahte: sette þa his lichoman betweoh beforan þam stynge. *a* **950** *Guthlac* (Prose) xvi, þa besloh se þorn on þone fot, and swa strang wæs se sting þæs þornes, þæt he eode þurh þone fot. *c* **1000** *Sax. Leechd.* I. 272 Wið scorpiones stincg ȝenim þas ylcan wyrte..leȝe to ðam stinge. *c* **1315** Shoreham *Poems* iv. 86 þe wonde swelþ an akeþ, So doþ þe naddre steng. **1593** Shaks. *2 Hen. VI*, III. ii. 325 Their softest Touch, as smart as Lyzards stings. **1636** Marmion *Antiquary* IV. (1641) G 4, Why did you send this serpent to my bosome, To pierce me through with greater cruelty, Than Cleopatra felt from stings of Adders? **1748** *Anson's Voy.* II. viii. 217 A most mischievous serpent..whose sting they believed to be inevitable death. **1865** *Hardwicke's Sci.-Gossip* 1 July 166/1, I am told by fishermen that many instances are known of persons losing the use of a hand by this sting [*sc.* of the weever-fish]. **1875** Ruskin *Hort. Inclus.* (1887) 33 The pang of a nice deep wasp sting.

c. The smart or irritation produced by touching a nettle or similar plant.

1878 T. F. T. Dyer *Engl. Folk-lore* 172 To cure the sting of a nettle, the person stung must [etc.]. **1884** R. Folkard Jun. *Plant Lore* 313 It is a common practice..for anyone suffering from the stings of a Nettle to apply a cold Dock-leaf to the inflamed spot.

2. A sharp-pointed organ in certain insects and other animals (e.g. bees, wasps, scorpions) capable of inflicting a painful or dangerous wound. Applied also to the fang or venom-tooth (and erroneously to the forked tongue) of a poisonous serpent.

1398 Trevisa *Barth. De P.R.* XII. v. (1495) 414 Many males of been ben wythout stinges. **1523–34** Fitzherb. *Husb.* § 122 It is a sayenge that she [the drone] hath loste her stynge, and than she wyl not labour as the other do. **1530** Palsgr. 276/1 Styng of a serpent or any other venomous beest, *esguillon*. **1590** Spenser *F.Q.* I. i. 15 Her huge long taile..Pointed with mortall sting. *Ibid.* I. i. 23 A cloud of combrous gnattes do him molest, All striuing to infixe their feeble stings. *c* **1611** Chapman *Iliad* III. 32 A serpent..Her blew necke (swolne with poison) raisd, and her sting out. **1697** Dryden *Virg. Ecl.* III. 145 Beware the secret Snake that shoots a Sting. **1726** Swift *Gulliver* II. iii, I took out their stings, found them an inch and a half long, and as sharp as needles. **1861** Hulme tr. *Moquin-Tandon* II. v. ii. 276 When not in use, the sting [of the bee] is completely enclosed in the abdomen.

3. *Bot.* A stiff sharp-pointed tubular hair, which emits an irritating fluid when touched. †Also applied to a thorn.

1567 Maplet *Gr. Forest* 62 b, The Thorn tree is armed about with Dart and sting. **1578** Lyte *Dodoens* IV. lxiv. 526 White Cotton Thistel... The stalke is great & thicke set full of prickley stings. **1597** Middleton *Wisd. Solomon* iv. 4 The nettle hath a sting, the rose a thorn. **1857** Miss Pratt *Flower. Pl.* V. 23 The sting of the Nettle is a tubular hair.

4. A spike used for driving cattle.

1833 Tennyson *Palace of Art* 150 The people here, a beast of burden slow, Toil'd onward, prick'd with goads and stings.

5. a. In many *fig.* uses; e.g. an acute pain or sharp wound inflicted on the mind or heart; something which (or that element in anything which) inflicts acute pain; the 'point' of an epigram or sarcasm; something which goads to action or appetite, a sharp stimulus or incitement. Also in phr. ***a sting in the tail*** and varr.

c **1412** Hoccleve *De Reg. Princ.* 3909 Yf..fortunes stynge hym ouerthwerte. **1526** Tindale *1 Cor.* xv. 56 The stynge of death is synne. *a* **1586** Sidney *Arcadia* III. (1598) 367 The renewed sting of iealosie. **1600** Shaks. *A.Y.L.* II. vii. 188 Freize, freize, thou bitter skie..thy sting is not so sharpe, as freind remembred not. **1601** —— *All's Well* III. iv. 18 Ah what sharpe stings are in her mildest words! **1603** —— *Meas. for M.* I. iv. 59 One, who neuer feeles The wanton stings, and motions of the sence. *c* **1611** Chapman *Iliad* XIII. 233 Be assur'd, my spirite needs no stings To this hote conflict. **1657** in *Verney Mem.* (1907) II. 52 His letter to you I hope will be full of douceur with out a stinge at the tayle of it. **1697** Dryden *Virg. Georg.* III. 326 Too soon they must not feel the Stings of Love. **1713** Addison *Cato* I. i, Portius, no more! your words leave stings behind 'em. **1770** Langhorne *Plutarch*, *Marcellus* II. 399 This [result of an ambuscade] added stings to Marcellus's desire of an engagement. **1818** Hallam *Mid. Ages* (1872) I. 67 The sting of taxation is wastefulness. *c* **1820** Blake *On Homer's Poetry* in *Compl. Writings* (1972) 778 Those who will have Unity exclusively in Homer come out with a Moral like a sting in the tail. **1823** Lamb *Elia* Ser. II. *Pop. Fallacies* xii, The innocent prattle of his children takes out the sting of a man's poverty. **1842** Macaulay *Fredk. Gt.* Ess. 1851 II. 672 For that end it was necessary that Prussia should be all sting. **1849** —— *Hist. Eng.* vi. II. 129 They never worked till they felt the sting of hunger. **1926** *Times* 7 Sept. 17/5 The sting of this book is in its tail. **1952** A. Christie *They do it with Mirrors* 192 Don't say it. I'm suspicious of these village parallels. They've always got a sting in the tail. **1979** A. Williamson *Funeral March for Siegfried* xxxii. 165 He.. added a sting in the tail. 'Of course, if the murderer were one of you, an interloper would not be necessary.'

b. In generalized sense: Stinging quality, capacity to sting or hurt; a (specified) degree or amount of this. Freq. in phr. ***to take the sting out of*** (something).

1860 *Bailey's Mag.* Oct. 42 Hayward's..rare defence completely took the sting out of the Surrey bowling. **1863** *Lillywhite's Cricket Scores* III. 74 He..often took the 'sting' out of the bowling, by getting his runs remarkably slow. **1876** Trevelyan *Macaulay* vii. II. 4 This passage, as it now stands, has been deprived of half its sting. **1893** 'Q.' (Quiller-Couch) *Delect. Duchy* 342 The firemen..robbed the epigram of all its sting. **1896** *Daily News* 29 June 7/2 When once collared the Yorkshire bowling lacks sting. **1900** J. G. Frazer *Golden Bough* (ed. 2) III. 92 To give more sting to every blow the whip-lashes are knotted. **1942** *R.A.F. Jrnl.* 3 Oct. 24 It has taken the sting out of the Adjutant. **1956** B. Holiday *Lady sings Blues* (1973) xix. 157, I was so happy I cried. People like Lena took the sting out of other little people. **1977** *Jrnl. R. Soc. Arts* CXXV. 464/1 This defence consists in establishing..that the derogatory words—or at least their sting—were true.

c. *Austral. slang.* (*a*) Strong drink, 'stingo'; (*b*) a drug, *spec.* one administered to a racehorse in the form of an injection.

1929 K. S. Prichard *Coonardoo* 60 'Misses his three square meals a day and sting,' Bob explained. **1949** L. Glassop *Lucky Palmer* 36 They're going to give it the sting. They'll hit it with enough dope to win a Melbourne Cup. **1958** F. Hardy *Four-Legged Lottery* 173 The 'smarties' soon found stings that didn't show on a swab. **1972** J. de Hoog *Skid Row Dossier* 4 You can share a bottle of sting (methylated spirits) down a lane.

d. *slang* (chiefly *U.S.*, orig. *Criminals'*). (*a*) A burglary or other act of theft, fraud, etc., esp. one that is carefully planned in advance and swiftly executed; (*b*) a police undercover operation designed to ensnare criminals.

1930 *Liberty* 20 Sept. 77/1 The hustlers would sit around planning their stings and I guess about half of the jobs pulled in southern Ohio that year started in my parlor. **1955** *Publ. Amer. Dial. Soc.* XXIV. 76 The *sting* we described involved a wallet obviously *on its feet*. **1975** *Courier-Mail* (Brisbane) 11 Mar. 6/8 A transaction between a jewellery salesman and a professed buyer with $230,000 in his pocket was intercepted yesterday by a cab driver who made off with the cash. Investigators believe the theft was a set-up 'sting'. **1976** *National Observer* (U.S.) 13 Mar. 6/3 The Sting also produced leads to three murders and several other unsolved major crimes. **1977** *Tel.* (Brisbane) 24 Aug. 25/2 'Sting' officers operated in old warehouses and run-down storefronts, developed close contacts with loose-lipped thugs who believe they dealt with fellow criminals. **1982** *Sunday Times* 14 Nov. 15/2 The Miami 'sting' was so well set up that it survived a remarkable breach of security. **1983** *Observer* 30 Jan. 10/2 His second reaction was to inform the American authorities and get their approval for an elaborate and costly 'sting'.

6. The tapering point of a pointer's tail. Cf. *sting-tail* (*a*) in sense 8.

1872 T. Pearce *Dog* 119 The genuine sort [of Pointers] has a tail thick at the root, and gradually tapering to an absolute point or 'sting.' *Ibid.* 122 At last we have seen the sting of her fine stern above the rushes.

†**7.** *Mus.* = *sting-grace* in sense 8. *Obs.*

1676 Mace *Musicks Mon.* 109 The Sting, is another very Neat, and Pritty Grace; (But not Modish in These Days).

8. *Comb.*, as *sting-proof* adj.; **sting-bull**, the greater weever, *Trachinus draco*; **sting-fish**, (*a*) the lesser weever, *Trachinus vipera*; (*b*) the sea-scorpion, *Cottus scorpius*; † **sting-free** *a.*, exempt from, or proof against, being stung; † **sting-grace** *Mus.*, a particular tremolo effect in lute-playing; **sting-moth**, the Australian moth, *Doratifera vulnerans*, the larva of which is able to sting; **sting-nettle**, *Urtica dioica* and other species; **sting-tail**, (*a*) a tail tapering to a point, as in the pointer (cf. 6); (*b*) *U.S.* = STING-RAY; **sting-tailed** *a.*, having a sting in the tail (also *fig.*); **sting-winkle** (see quot.); † **sting-worm**, ? a worm supposed to sting cattle (cf. TAINT-WORM). Also STING RAY.

1836 Yarrell *Brit. Fishes* I. 20 The Great Weever, *Sting-bull, Sea Cat. *Ibid.* I. 25 Lesser Weever, Otter-pike, *Sting-fish. **1863** Couch *Fishes Brit. Isl.* II. 8 Sting-fish ..*Cottus Scorpius.* **1644** S. Kem *Messengers Prepar.* 27 Nothing can arme death to hurt us but sin, otherwise thou art hard, *sting-free. **1658** Rowland *Moufet's Theatr. Ins.* 907 If you would indeed resolve to go sting-free, or at least heal your self being stung. **1676** Mace *Musick's Mon.* 126 Those Three Notes also to have the *Sting-Grace. **1863**

WOOD *Illustr. Nat. Hist.* III. 537 *Sting-moth, *Doratifera vulnerans.* **1822–7** GOOD *Study Med.* (1829) V. 132 Both *sting-nettles and flagellations..are said to have worked wonders. **1869** BLACKMORE *Lorna D.* vii, I rubbed them [my toes] well with a sprout of young sting-nettle. **1886** H. P. WELLS *Amer. Salmon Fisherm.* 85 Kid gloves are *sting-proof. **1872** T. PEARCE *Idstone Papers* iii. 30 That pointer, with his graceful lines, *sting-tail, and polished coat. **1881** INGERSOLL *Oyster-Industr.* (Hist. Fish. Industr. U.S.) 249 Sting-tail.—The sting-ray, *Dasybatis centrura.* (New York.) **1611** SPEED *Hist. Gt. Brit.* IX. xxiv. §104 Those *sting-tailed Locusts, arising with foggy smoake from the bottomlesse pit. **1905** *Q. Rev.* Jan. 30 Sting-tailed witticisms. **1851** WOODWARD *Mollusca* 106 Murex Erinaceus..is called '*sting-winkle' by fishermen, who say it makes round holes in the other shell-fish with its beak. **1577** GOOGE *Heresbach's Husb.* III. 134b, If he [a bullock] swell of the Taint, or *Stingworme, geue him Vrine, Salt & Tryacle to drinke.

sting (stɪŋ), *v.*[1] Pa. t. and pa. pple. stung (stʌŋ). Forms: *Inf.* 1 **stingan, stincgan,** 3 **stincgen,** 3–6 **stingen,** 4–5 **styngen, -yn,** 3–6 **stinge,** 4–6 **stynge,** 5 **styngge,** 6 **styng,** 3– **sting.** *Imper. sing.* 3 **sting, stink.** *Pa. t.* 1–7, 8–9 *dial.* **stang,** 3–6 **stong,** (5 **stoong),** 6– **stung;** *pl.* 1 **stungon,** 2–3 *Orm.* **stungenn,** 3 **stounge(n,** 3–4 **stungen,** 3–5 **stonge, stongen;** *weak* 6–7, 9 *dial.* **stinged,** 9 *dial.* **stunged.** *Pa. Subj. 3rd sing.* 2–3 **stunge.** *Pa. pple.* 1–4 **stungen,** 2–3 **istungen,** *Orm.* **-stungenn,** 3 **istunge,** 4–5 **stungyn,** 4–6 **stunge,** 6– **stung;** 3–5 **ystonge(n, istonge,** (3 **istounge,** 4 **ystonnge, stoungen),** 3–6 **stongen,** (4 **stangen,** 5 **stonken),** 6 **stonge, stounge, stoung,** 6–7 **stong;** *weak* 5–6 **stynged, -yd,** 6–7, 9 *dial.* **stinged.** [OE. *stingan* str. vb. corresponds to ON. *stinga*, pa. t. *stakk*, pl. *stungu*, pa. pple. *stungenn* (Sw., Norw. *stinga*, Da. *stinge*) to stick, stab, pierce, f. Teut. root **steŋg-*: **staŋg-*: **stuŋg-* to pierce, whence STANG *sb.*[1] and *v.*[1] (A Gothic imperative ***us-stagg***, occurring only once, is commonly regarded as a mistake for ****us-stigg***, and as belonging to the verb = OE. *stingan*; this, however, is not certain, as the Goth. vb. may have been of the reduplicating conjugation, with pres.-stem from the *a* grade of the root.)

The pre-Teut. root **steŋgh-*, according to some scholars, is found in Gr. στάχυς (:—**stŋghus*) ear of corn.]

†**1.** *trans.* To pierce with a sharp-pointed weapon or instrument. (Cf. THROUGH-STING *v.*) *Phr.* ***to sting to death.*** *Obs.*

993 *Battle of Maldon* 128 He mid gare stang wlancne wicing. *c* **1205** LAY. 27597 Boccus mid his spere stronge Bedver hafde istunge. *a* **1300** *Cursor M.* 26018 Wit thorn, glaiue, nail,.. Wit quilk þat crist for us was stongen. *c* **1315** SHOREHAM II. 116 A kniȝt wyþ one scharpe spere Stang hyne iþe ryȝt syde. **13..** *K. Alis.* 3717 (Laud MS.), He..smyteþ a Duk arabian.. And to þe deþ haþ hym stunge. *c* **1394** *P. Pl. Crede* 553 þei ben y-sewed wiþ whiȝt silk & semes full queynte, Y-stongen wiþ stiches þat stareþ as siluer. *c* **1430** *Syr Gener.* (Roxb.) 5000 Thurgh the bodie he him stoong. *c* **1440** *Promp. Parv.* 290/2 Lawncyn, or stynge wythe a spere, or blode yryne, *lanceo.* **1470–85** MALORY *Arthur* XXI. x. 855 There was laementacyon as they had be stungyn wyth sperys.

2. a. 'To pierce or wound with a point darted out, as that of wasps or scorpions' (J.). Said also of venomous serpents and some other animals which inflict sharp or poisonous wounds. Phr. ***to sting to death;*** also ***to sting to the quick*** (now rare in literal sense: see 5).

c **888** ÆLFRED *Boeth.* xxxi. §2 Swa swa seo beo sceal losian þonne heo hwæt irringa stingð. **1200** ORMIN 17441 þa neddress þatt stungenn þe menn. *c* **1250** *Gen. & Ex.* 3896 Ðor-fore hem cam wrim-kin among, ðat hem wel bitterlike stong. *c* **1290** *S. Eng. Leg.* 206/232 þe Crapoudes.. stoungen heom þoruȝ heore heortene with heore foule wrottes grete. **13..** *Seuyn Sag.* (W.) 759 The adder so the grehound stang. **1470–85** MALORY *Arthur* XXI. iv. 845 An adder..stonge a knyght on the foot & whan the knyght felte hym stongen [etc.]. **1530** PALSGR. 736/1, I wene this adder hath styngyd me. **1578** LYTE *Dodoens* v. xxv. 584 Good to be dronken of them which are stongue with Bees and Waspes. **1587** R. CROMPTON *Short Decl. End Traytors* D iij b, Some times they were stinged to death, with fierie Serpents of straunge kind. **1630** *True Trav. John Smith* xxvii. 58 Stung neere to death with a most poysoned taile of a fish called Stingray. *c* **1662** in *Verney Mem.* (1907) II. 262 Little flyes which sting our hands and faces. **1726** [see QUICK *sb.*[1] 4.]. **1849** MRS. CARLYLE *Lett.* II. 76 Stung by a wasp. **1878** HARDY *Ret. Native* IV. vii, Stung by an adder.

absol. *a* **1225** *Ancr. R.* 206 þe scorpiun..stingeð mid te teile. *c* **1394** *P. Pl. Crede* 648 þer is no waspe in þis werlde þat will wilfulloker styngen. **1590** SHAKS. *Mids. N.* III. ii. 73 With doubler tongue Then thine (thou serpent) neuer Adder stung. **1895** P. HEMINGWAY *Out of Egypt* II. 188 He flung the truth from him as one might fling a viper that had stung.

b. To insert (venom) by stinging. *nonce-use.*

1648 WINYARD *Midsummer-Moon* 2 His skull is a meer nest of hornets, which sting into him their own waspishnesse.

c. *transf.* and *fig.* To inflict a sharp or mortal hurt upon. (Cf. sense 1.)

a **1400** *St. Alexius* 1017 (MS. Laud 622) Deþ! why nyltou me stynge? *c* **1495** *Epitaph Dk. Bedford* in *Skelton's Wks.* (1843) II. 392 Thou, dolorous Deth, to the herte hast him stynged [*rimes with* reuenged]. **1559** *Mirr. Mag., Henry Percy* iv, I had a son which so the Scottes did sting, That being yong, and but a very spring Syr Henry Hotspur they gaue him to name. *a* **1653** BINNING *Sinner's Sanct.* xxviii. Wks. (1735) 313 He suffered Death to sting him, and by this hath taken the Sting from it. **1878** JEFFERIES *Gamekeeper at Home* ix. 194 Two fired,..'stinging' one man in the leg. **1883** *Daily News* 20 Sept. 6/7 The little vessel..taking her chance of stinging or demoralising the enemy.

†**d.** *slang.* To rob or cheat. *Obs.*

1812 J. H. VAUX *Flash Dict.*, *Sting*, to rob or defraud a person or place is called *stinging* them, as, that *cove* is too *fly*; he has been *stung* before; meaning that man is upon his guard; he has already been trick'd. **1823** EGAN *Grose's Dict. Vulgar T.*

e. ***to sting*** (someone) ***for*** (something): to induce (someone) to give (money, etc.) by begging or borrowing in an exploitative manner. *slang* (orig. *U.S.*).

1903 *Kansas City Daily Star* 21 Apr. 6/7 An undergraduate is no longer 'stuck' for a dinner, a seat at a play, a railroad ticket; he is 'stung'. **1940** N. MARSH *Surfeit of Lampreys* (1941) ii. 34 We hope to sting Uncle G. for two thousand [pounds]. **1973** WODEHOUSE *Bachelors Anonymous* iii. 26 He wants to make a touch... He even stung me for a bit the other day. **1976** P. CAVE *High Flying Birds* iv. 46 You still letting that bum sting you for drinks?

f. To swindle or overcharge (someone); to involve (someone) in financial loss. Freq. in *pass.* Cf. sense 2 d. *slang* (orig. *U.S.*).

1905 [see BUNDLE *sb.* 2 h]. **1922** S. LEWIS *Babbitt* iii. 27 Guess I'll have to get down to the office now and sting a few clients. **1923** *Daily Mail* 22 Jan. 8 [He] told me..he stood to lose some enormous number of millions of marks if Germany went *phut*... He seemed hurt when I said I was very glad if he got stung for trading with the enemy. **1927** WODEHOUSE *Small Bachelor* vii. 121 'How much did you pay?' 'Three hundred dollars.' 'You were stung... The stock is so much waste paper.' **1943** K. TENNANT *Ride on Stranger* vii. 62 In this world you've got to sting or get stung. **1955** M. ALLINGHAM *Beckoning Lady* v. 82 You sting 'em when the time comes. **1974** 'E. LATHEN' *Sweet & Low* xi. 108 Big names do not like getting stung. **1981** *London Mag.* July 15 I've no idea how much her son pays her... I like to think she's really stinging her son.

3. a. Of certain plants, etc.: To produce by contact a kind of rash or inflammation, accompanied with a burning sensation and itching, in (a person's skin). Also *absol.* (cf. STINGING *ppl. a.*).

1548 *Elyot's Dict.* s.v. *Compungo*, Ye must beware that he bee not stounge with a nettle. **1565** COOPER *Thesaurus* s.v. *Compungo*, He is stinged with a nettel. **1583** MELBANCKE *Philotimus* C iij, Play with the nettle neuer soe nimbly & it will sting thee. **1665** G. HARVEY *Disc. Plague* (1673) 133 A pricking of the intire skin, as if stung with Nettles. **1845** DARWIN *Voy. Nat.* xx. (1879) 464, I was a good deal surprised by finding two species of coral..possessed of the power of stinging. **1882** J. SMITH *Dict. Pop. Names Plants* 392 Lobed leaves, covered..with stiff hairs,..which sting fearfully. **1898** EVA LÜCKES *Gen. Nursing* x. (1900) 129 The discomfort of the mustard stinging in little patches is thus prevented.

b. *refl.* To get stung. *colloq.*

1663 TUKE *Adv. Five Hours* I. 14 I've touch'd a Nettle, and have stung my self.

4. *transf.* To affect with a tingling pain, a burning sensation, or the like.

1615 CHAPMAN *Odyss.* XIII. 128 As..foure braue horse Before a Chariot, stung into their course With feruent lashes of the smarting Scourge. *a* **1628** F. GREVIL *Life Sidney* xii. (1652) 149 He judiciously observing the pangs his wound stang him with by fits. **1853** 'C. BEDE' *Verdant Green* I. xi, His whole person put in chancery, stung, bruised, [etc.]. **1878** C. STANFORD *Symb. Christ* vii. 186 When stung by a spark of fire we start in agony.

b. *absol.* (Cf. STINGING *ppl. a.*)

1735 SOMERVILLE *Chase* IV. 423 With quick Sensation now The fuming Vapour stings. **1881** MISS YONGE *Lads & Lasses Langley* ii. 64 'Well, it don't sting like the other,' said Frank,..as if he thought stinging a good quality in beer. **1891** FARRAR *Darkn. & Dawn* xxxix, He felt the curling lash ..come stinging round his body.

5. *fig.* To affect with a sudden sharp mental pain or an access of painful emotion or irritation; to drive *to* or *into* (rage, madness, etc.) by some sharp passion or vexation; to goad or stimulate *to* or *into* (action).

c **1386** CHAUCER *Pard. T.* 85 Thanne wol I stynge hym with my tonge smerte. *a* **1400–50** *Wars Alex.* 667 Oft storbis me þi statour & stingis me ȝerne þat þi personale proporcion sa party is to myne. **1537** STARKEY *Let. to the King* in *Life & Lett.* (1878) p. l, The dethe of them wych suffryd in the cause hathe so stonge hys hart. **1600** *Weakest goeth to Wall* B 4, I am so stung with this indignitie. *a* **1602** W. PERKINS *Cases Consc.* (1619) 64 Their great and capitall sins, that stinged and wounded their consciences. **1700** DRYDEN *Pal. & Arc.* 234 Scarce had he seen, but, seiz'd with sudden Smart, Stung to the Quick, he felt it at his Heart. **1726** [see QUICK *sb.*[1] 4]. **1766** GOLDSM. *Vic. W.* xxiv, Little villany can at any time get within the soul, and sting it into rage. **1769** *Junius Lett.* xxix. 133 A man may be quite indifferent about one part of a charge, yet severely stung with another. **1787** *Generous Attachment* I. 136 Mrs. Penelope..stung with curiosity, came in. **1836** *Penny Cycl.* V. 290/1 Stung to madness by defeat. **1837** CARLYLE *Fr. Rev.* II. v. vii, This poor Legislative, spurred and stung into action by a whole France. **1849** MACAULAY *Hist. Eng.* vii. II. 224 The jurymen themselves were stung by remorse when they thought over what they had done. **1864** BURTON *Scot Abr.* I. iv. 177 Mary stung the dowager occasionally with her sarcastic tongue. **1891** F. H. WILLIAMS *Atman* vi. 296 The torrent of his thoughts and fears..stinging him to effort.

absol. **1725** RAMSAY *Gentle Sheph.* IV. ii. (1769) 77 The spleen, tint honour, and affronted pride, Stang like the sharpest goads in gentry's side. **1748** JOHNSON *Van. Hum. Wishes* 119 Remember'd folly stings. **1859** BOYD *Recreat. Country Parson* vi. 211 Further brooding over the subject would only vex and sting and do no good.

6. *intr.* To feel sharp pain or distress; to smart. Of a wound or sore: To shoot or throb with pain.

1848 THACKERAY *Van. Fair* xxxi, The groans of a person stinging under defeat. **1856** P. THOMPSON *Hist. Boston* 725 *Stang*, or *Sting* (to), to throb, with great pain. **1912** *19th Cent.* Nov. 1015 The West [of U.S.A.] was stinging with want.

sting (stɪŋ), *v.*[2] *Sc.* and *north.* Also (*midland dial.*) **stinge** (stɪndʒ). [f. STING *sb.*[1]; the variation in pronunciation is normal, as the sb. has an umlaut-vowel.] *trans.* To thatch or repair thatch with a 'sting' or pointed tool.

1707 in *Lady G. Baillie's Househ. Bk.* (S.H.S.) p. lxiv, For 85 threve oat stra crop 1707 @ 6s. to sting the house, £2. 2s. 6d. **1710** *Ibid.* 238. **1815** *Pennecuik's Wks.* 89 (E.D.D.) Heath is neither sewed nor stinged. **1854** MISS BAKER *Northampt. Gloss.*, *Stinge*, to repair thatched buildings by driving up the old thatch, and pushing in the new halm by means of the stinger. **1876** *Whitby Gloss.*, *Sting in*, to tuck in with a 'stinging-prod' [defined as 'a long iron point']. **1881** *Leicester Gloss.*, Stinge. **1893–4** *Northumb. Gloss.*, *Sting.*

sting, obs. f. STINK *v.*

stingaree (ˌstɪŋgəˈriː, ˈstɪŋgəriː). *U.S.* and *Austral.* [Corrupt f. STING-RAY.] A sting-ray, esp. *Trygon centrura* (*Dasyatis centrurus*).

1838 *Papers Mirabeau Buonaparte Lamar* (1922) II. 87 To crown the whole Sergeant Bryant was cut on the foot with an oyster shell, and Mr. Edington was stung by a Stingaree. **1859** BARTLETT *Dict. Amer.* (ed. 2) 451. **1871** *Field* 25 Nov. 457/2 The spear of the stingaree. **1882** JORDAN & GILBERT *Syn. Fishes N. Amer.* 47 *Dasyatis centrurus*, Common Sting Ray; Clam Cracker; Stingaree. **1887** MRS. D. DALY *S. Australia* 330 Sharks, stingarees,..you see swimming about.

Hence **stingareeing** *vbl. sb.*, the sport of catching stingarees.

c **1870** G. H. KINGSLEY *Sport & Trav.* iii. (1900) 57, I confess that I love 'stingareeing' for its own sake, as a sport. **1871** *Field* 25 Nov. 457/2 Few [sports] beat our afternoon's stingareeing!

stinge (ˈstɪndʒ). [Back-formation from STINGY *a.*] A stingy person. Hence as *v. intr.* (*rare*), to behave in a stingy manner.

1914 'BARTIMEUS' *Naval Occasions* xxi. 185 Accustomed to tribute tendered with a lavish hand, Arabella decided that this must be a 'proper stinge'. **1937** *Boy's Own Paper* 3 Dec. 143/1 The barber can't stand stinges. **1937** V. SACKVILLE-WEST *Pepita* II. iii. 205, I couldn't see why a person ready to spend hundreds of pounds should be equally ready to stinge over a stamp or a ball of string. **1977** C. BOYLAN in D. Marcus *Best Irish Short Stories* II. 113 Elizabeth had got herself a job. 'Well, I had to... My, Morgan has become a stinge.'

stinged (stɪŋd), *a.* [f. STING *sb.*[2] + -ED[2].] Furnished or armed with a sting (*lit.* and *fig.*).

1552 HULOET, Prycked or stynged, *Aculeatus.* **1608** TOPSELL *Serpents* 88 You shall haue all those that lacke stinges presently come flying about you, which the stinged waspes neuer are seene to doe. **1782** J. BROWN *View Nat. & Revealed Relig.* v. ii. (1796) 355 Christ's death being stinged by the curse, he met it with agony and terror. **1858** W. R. PIRIE *Inq. Hum. Mind* vii. 348 The drones..are killed by the more numerous stinged masses. *a* **1882** CHRISTINA G. ROSSETTI *Ballad of Boding* 27 Stinged Worm meseemed loathly in his place.

†**stinged,** *ppl. a. Obs.* [Irregular weak pa. pple. of STING *v.*[1]] Wounded by stinging, stung.

1565 STAPLETON tr. *Bede's Hist. Ch. Eng.* 14 Forthwyth all the force of the venim was staynched, and the swelling of the stinged bodies vtterly asswaged. **1577** KENDALL *Flowers of Epigr., Trifles* 24b, At last with tinglyng stynged hande, he comes his mother to. **1682** OTWAY *Venice Preserved* v, When our sting'd hearts haue leap'd to meet each other.

stinger[1] (ˈstɪŋə(r)). [f. STING *v.*[1] + -ER[1].]

1. One who stings; applied *fig.* to Death. Also, one who goads or instigates; one who has a sharp tongue.

1552 HULOET, Prycker or stynger, *Stigator, stimulator.* **1577** KENDALL *Flowers of Epigr., Trifles* 13 To stingers suche a stingyng crowne, of Nettelles doeth belong. **1602** CHETTLE *Hoffman* III. (1631) F 1 b, Haue ye not heard I haue bin a stinger, a tickler, a wormer. **1611** COTGR., *Esguillonneur*, a pricker, stinger. **1612** *Benvenuto's Passenger* II. ii. 511 Pratlers, tatlers, stingers [Ital. *mordaci*]. *a* **1618** SYLVESTER *Triumph Faith* III. ii, Life of our life, our death's death, Stinger's sting. **1827** LAMB *Poems, Epicedium, Going or Gone* 5 Death, that last Stinger.

2. An animal or plant that stings.

1593 G. HARVEY *Pierce's Super.* 143 The gad-fly is a little creature; but some little creatures be stingers. **1602** [see VENGIBLE *a.* 2]. **1616** T. SCOT *Philomythie* B 1 b, He longs for hony, That mongst the angry Waspes thrusts his bold fingers, And from their neasts in Summer, hunts those stingers. **1862** T. W. HARRIS *Insects Injur. Vegetation* (ed. 3) 512 The insects of this order [Hymenoptera] may be divided into two groups, Stingers and Piercers. **1880** C. R. MARKHAM *Peruv. Bark* 293 The *Girardinia Leschenaultii*, or Nilgiri nettle, a most virulent stinger.

3. Something that stings or smarts; e.g. a sharp blow, or the hand that delivers it; something that causes sharp distress, a pungent speech or crushing argument; a sharp frost. Now *colloq.* Also *Austral.*, an exceptionally hot or cold period of time.

1576 GASCOIGNE *Grief of Joy* IV. xxiii, But that so sweete a synger Shoulde dye so sone: that sorrowe seemde a stynger. **1623** WEBSTER *Devil's Law-Case* IV. ii. I 2 b, *San.* That's a stinger, tis a good wench, be not daunted. **1823** 'JON BEE' *Dict. Turf*, *Stinger*, a sharp and rapid hit. **1853** R. S. SURTEES *Sponge's Sp. Tour* (1893) 355 My eyes, but we're in for a stinger! **1855** BROWNING *Fra Lippo* 90 Old Aunt

Lapaccia trussed me with one hand, (Its fellow was a stinger as I knew). **1861** DICKENS *Gt. Expect.* xxv, At nine o'clock ..the gun fires... And when you hear him go, I think you'll say he's a Stinger. **1899** 'S. RUDD' in Murdoch & Drake-Brockman *Austral. Short Stories* (1951) 103 My! it'll be a stinger to-night. **1900** UPWARD *Ebenezer Lobb* 46, I wrote him back a stinger which he will not soon forget. **1904** WELLS *Food of Gods* II. i. 166 One [button] hit me a regular stinger just 'ere, mum. **1942** E. LANGLEY *Pea Pickers* (1958) II. vii. 167 The next day was a stinger... It dawned sultry red.

4. A long structure attached to the stern of a pipe-laying barge which supports the pipe as it enters the water and prevents it from buckling.

1958 *Offshore Drilling* Oct. 11/2 The 'stinger' is final cradle [*sic*], submerged 85 feet off the stern of the lay barge, which holds the pipe to a 2500 ft. radius to prevent any undue strain during the process of lowering it into the underwater trench. **1966** M. J. LAMB in *Exploiting the Ocean* (Marine Technol. Soc.) 296 A 'stinger' is used in deep water to limit the sag in the pipe. **1969** [see OVERBEND *sb.*]. **1976** *Offshore Platforms & Pipelining* 6/3 Key changes include.. the addition of 160-ft truss-type stinger in place of the usual pontoon stinger.

stinger² ('stɪŋə(r), 'stɪndʒə(r)). *Sc.* and *dial.* [f. STING *v.*² + -ER¹.] A thatcher; a thatching-tool.

1808 JAMIESON *Stinger*, a mender of thatched roofs; so called, because he uses a sting or short pointed stick in doing his work. **1854** MISS BAKER *Northampt. Gloss.*, *Stincher* or *Stinger*, a tool, described under its synonyme *Battledore*. Used by thatchers when repairing a roof, but not.. when a whole building is newly thatched.

stinger³ ('stɪŋə(r)). Corruption of STENGAH. Also used as the name of various other mixed drinks or cocktails (see quots. 1973, 1976).

1901 *Scribner's Mag.* Jan. 106 Two 'stingers' were brought... A 'stinger'.. is a noggin of Scotch whiskey, enlivened by much or little, according to individual taste, of the local buzz-water. **1903** [see STENGAH]. **1916** H. L. WILSON *Somewhere in Red Gap* ix. 376, I found 'em in the palm grill, or whatever it's called, drinking stingers. **1928** [see ROUND *sb.*¹ 20 a]. **1942** D. POWELL *Time to be Born* (1943) x. 242 Have another daiquiri... Or change to a stinger. **1961** I. FLEMING *Thunderball* xv. 156 After they had had coffee and a stinger at the bar they separated and went to the [gaming] tables. **1973** *Sat. Rev. Society* (U.S.) May 45/1 B & B Stinger. 3 parts B & B Liqueur, 1 part White Creme de Menthe. **1976** *Scotsman* 24 Dec. (Weekend Suppl.) 3/7 A Stinger.. is a better drink, being creme de menthe well laced with brandy, and stronger.

†**sting-hum.** *Obs. slang.* (See quot.)

a **1700** B. E. *Dict. Cant. Crew*, *Sting-hum*, a Niggard.

stingily ('stɪndʒɪlɪ), *adv.* [f. STINGY *a.* + -LY².] In a stingy manner.

1682 *Dryden's Satyr to Muse* 194 As loud he roard 'gainst the Prerogative, As sharply blam'd as Stingily wou'd give. **1701** HOWE *Some Consid. Pref. Enquiry* 28 Such as are.. not so stingily bigotted to a Party as he. **1837** CARLYLE *Fr. Rev.* III. I. i, Nor are Patriotic Gifts wanting.. nor stingily given. **1865** HOLLAND *Plain Talk* vii. 255 One is a man of wealth, who hoards his money, or spends it stingily or selfishly.

stinginess ('stɪndʒɪnɪs). [-NESS.] The quality of being stingy; niggardliness, meanness.

1682 NORRIS *Hierocles* 100 In expence of Money, Profusion and Stinginess. **1700-5** in Noake *Monast. Worcester* (1866) 611 Good wine, poor soules, is so above 'em, Their stingienes won't that allow 'em. **1748** SMOLLETT *Rod. Random* xix, The stinginess of her father, who refused to part with a shilling to promote the match. **1876** CREIGHTON *Age Eliz.* IV. i. 124 Elizabeth.. learnt an economy which soon became habitual to her and degenerated into stinginess.

stinging ('stɪŋɪŋ), *vbl. sb.* Also 5-6 *erron.* **stynkyng(g)e.** [f. STING *v.*¹ + -ING¹.] The action of wounding with a sting; an instance of this.

1398 TREVISA *Barth. De P.R.* XIII. xxvi. (1495) 461 The juys of euery fysshe helpyth agaynst venemouse styngynges. *c* **1450** *M.E. Med. Bk.* (Heinrich) 184 Ageyns bytynnge or stynkyngge of scorpyons or of serpentes. **1538** ELYOT *Dict.* s.v. *Psylli*, They also do cure the styngynge and poysonynge of serpentes by soukynge the place whyche is venymed. **1658** ROWLAND tr. *Moufet's Theat. Ins.* 926 Physicians have found out many remedies against the stingings of Wasps. **1823** J. BADCOCK *Dom. Amusem.* 98 A good remedy for stinging of nettles. **1832** S. WARREN *Diary Physic.* II. ii. 77 Comparing the pain to that which might follow the incessant stinging of a wasp at the spinal marrow.

b. *transf.* and *fig.*

a **1300** *E.E. Psalter* lix. 3 Þou dranke vs with wine of stinginge [*vino compunctionis*]. *c* **1400** *Apol. Loll.* (Camden) 29 Bi for þat bats were made in religioun bi stinging of þe fend [*Diaboli instinctu*]. **1506** *Kal. Sheph.* (Sommer) 163 Swete wordis with a venemous stynkynge of the tayle. **1579** J. FIELDE *Calvin's 4 Serm.* i. 8 b, The prickes & stingings they haue in their consciences. *a* **1631** DONNE *Poems, 'Goe, and catch a falling starre'* 6 Teach me to heare Mermaides singing, Or to keep off envies stinging. *a* **1700** EVELYN *Diary* Sept. 1646, This night I felt such a stinging all about me that I could not sleepe. **1855** SINGLETON *Virgil* II. 440 Drances, whom the fame Of Turnus spurred with crooked jealousy, And bitter stingings.

c. stinging-cell *Zool.*, a nematocyst.

1885 PENNINGTON *Brit. Zoophytes* 138 The stinging or urticating cells, or nematocysts, contain the stinging threads. **1892** J. A. THOMSON *Outl. Zool.* x. 127 On the tentacles [of *Hydra*] especially, one can see.. numerous clumps of clear stinging-cells.

stinging ('stɪŋɪŋ), *ppl. a.* [+ -ING².]

1. That stings, that has power to sting; used (often as a specific designation) **a.** of animals. ***stinging lizard***, one of several North American lizards, esp. a spiny lizard of the genus *Sceloporus*, also called a scorpion.

a **1225** *Ancr. R.* 82 Iherest tu hu Salomon euened bacbitare to stinginde neddre? **1382** WYCLIF *Exod.* xxiii. 28 Stynggynge flies. **1569** SPENSER *Vis. Petrarch* 78 A stinging Serpent by the heele hir caught. **1588** SHAKS. *Tit. A.* v. i. 14 Like stinging Bees in hottest Sommers day. **1670** MILTON *Hist. Brit.* I. 21 Swarmes of stinging Flies, whereof men dy'd. **1854** A. ADAMS etc. *Man. Nat. Hist.* 228 Stinging-Ants (Myrmicidæ). **1862** T. W. HARRIS *Insects Injur. Vegetation* (ed. 3) 513 The stinging Hymenoptera. **1870** J. C. DUVAL *Adventures Big-Foot Wallace* xlv. 294 They chaw tobacco and drink whiskey even in the winter-time, when the 'cow-killers' and stinging-lizards are all frozen up. **1889** H. H. MCCONNELL *Five Years a Cavalryman* 77 The 'scorpion' or 'stinging lizard' abounds. **1892** J. A. THOMSON *Outl. Zool.* x. 121 Cœlenterata or Stinging-animals. **1926** J. K. STRECKER in J. F. Dobie *Rainbow in Morning* (1965) 61 The true scorpion is popularly called a 'stinging lizard', this misnomer being in common use throughout the state of Texas.

b. of plants.

1525 tr. *Brunswyke's Handywork Surg.* xcii. R ij b, With water of the styngynge nettylles. **1593** SHAKS. *Rich. II*, III. ii. 18 Yeeld stinging Nettles to mine Enemies. **1776** J. LEE *Introd. Bot.* Explan. Terms 380 *Urens*, stinging, armed with stings. **1845** DARWIN *Voy. Nat.* xx. (1852) 464 In the East Indian sea, a stinging sea-weed is said to be found. **1874** *Treas. Bot.* Suppl. 1344/2 Stinging-bush, *Jatropha stimulans.* **1887** HILLHOUSE *Strasburger's Handbk. Pract. Bot.* 77 The stinging hairs of the common stinging nettle (*Urtica dioica*). **1890** LUMHOLTZ *Cannibals* 252 The stinging-tree (*Laportea moroides*).

2. *transf.* That produces a sharp pain or tingling smart, a burning sensation, or the like. Said also of the pain or sensation.

13.. *E.E. Allit. P.* B. 225 Er þat styngande storme stynt ne myȝt. **1597** A. M. tr. *Guillemeau's Fr. Chirurg.* 3/4 He hath a verye prickinge and stinginge payne. **1610** SHAKS. *Temp.* I. ii. 329 Thou shalt be pinch'd As thicke as honycombe, each pinch more stinging Then Bees that made 'em. **1820** KEATS *Isabella* xiv, And many once proud-quiver'd loins did melt In blood from stinging whip. **1825** SCOTT *Betrothed* iii, 'Good ware,' he said, 'Master Butler, strong stinging ware.' **1839** LONGF. *Wreck of Hesperus* 34 He wrapped her warm in his seaman's coat Against the stinging blast. **1862** MILLER *Elem. Chem., Org.* (ed. 2) 333 A concentrated acid liquid, which produces a stinging sensation when applied to the skin. **1866** G. MACDONALD *Ann. Q. Neighb.* xxix. (1878) 505 Fierce showers of stinging hail. **1889** JESSOPP in *Dict. Nat. Biog.* XVII. 230/1 She gave Essex a good stinging blow on the face. **1899** *Allbutt's Syst. Med.* VIII. 393 Shooting, darting, or stinging pains.

3. *fig.* That causes sharp mental pain or irritation, poignant; that goads or stimulates. Of speech: Biting, pungent.

a **1225** *Ancr. R.* 294 þe delit of þe stincgende lust. *a* **1529** SKELTON *Agst. Venomous Tongues* Wks. I. 134 Malicious tunges.. Are sharper then swordes.., More stinging then scorpions. **1567** TURBERV. *Epit., Epigr.* etc. 35 b, Doe thy worst to mee thou stinging spite. **1600** tr. *Garzoni's Hosp. Inc. Fooles* 96 They studied quicke and stinging sayings, for the sharpning of their wits. **1647** J. HALL *Div. Poems* II. 82 How stinging are our sorrowes! *a* **1732** T. BOSTON *Crook in Lot* (1805) 31 How could he miss of a stinging remembrance of the cheat he had.. put upon his own father? **1855** MACAULAY *Hist. Eng.* xv. III. 541 Eloquent vituperation and stinging sarcasm. **1885** *Manch. Exam.* 8 May 5/1 Except a stinging rejoinder from Mr. Pember, nothing more was said.

†**4.** Mus. ***stinging grace*** = ***sting-grace***: see STING *sb.*² 7, 8. *Obs.*

1676 MACE *Musick's Mon.* 131 You must Pause, and use the Stinging Grace a Pritty while.

Hence **'stingingly** *adv.*, **'stingingness**.

1667 H. MORE *Div. Dial.* II. xvii. (1713) 142 A Grief.. set off more stingingly to us by the more flush and full representations of another's Happiness. **1727** BAILEY vol. II, *Stingingness*, stinging Quality. **1748** T. SMITH *Jrnl.* (1849) 270 Cold, and the year ends stingingly. **1873** LYTTON *K. Chillingly* I. viii, Not exactly in those words—more covertly, and therefore more stingingly. **1888** *Pall Mall Gaz.* 16 May 11/1 The Government.. was stingingly criticised from the Opposition benches.

†**'stingle.** *Obs. rare.* In 4 stengle, 5 styngill. [OE. **stęngel*, f. *stęng* STING *sb.*², the suffix denoting an implement: see -LE I.] = STING *sb.*² 2.

1398 TREVISA *Barth. De P.R.* XII. v. (Bodl. MS.) Been þat beþ vnbuxome to þe kinge.. deye wiþ þee wounde of heere strengþe of here stengles. **1422** YONGE tr. *Secreta Secret.* 181 The bee is a Passynge wrathfull beste and full of fyght, and for vengeaunce they lewyth thar Styngill in the wonde, but the kynge of bees Is wythout a styngill.

stingless ('stɪŋlɪs), *a.* [f. STING *sb.*² + -LESS.] Having no sting. *lit.* and *fig.*

1554 T. MARTIN *Marr. Priests* xiv. Mm ij b, [They] were nowe able.. to treade vnder fote the head of their lustes, as of a stingles serpent. **1601** SHAKS. *Jul. C.* v. i. 35. **1604** WEBSTER *Marston's Malcontent* Induct. A 3 b, There are a sort of discontented creatures that beare a stinglesse enuie to great ones. **1618** CHAPMAN *Hesiod's Georg.* I. 15 The slothfull man is like the sting-lesse Drone. **1724** DERHAM in *Phil. Trans.* XXXIII. 55 These sting-less Male Wasps. **1859** DARWIN *Orig. Spec.* iii. (1873) 59 In Australia the imported hive-bee is rapidly exterminating the small, stingless native bee. **1872** MINTO *Eng. Prose Lit.* I. i. 52 So playful and stingless is his humour.

stingo ('stɪŋgəʊ). *slang.* [f. STING *v.*¹ (in allusion to the sharp taste) + *-o*, perh. simulating a Sp. or Ital. ending.]

a. Strong ale or beer.

a **1635** RANDOLPH *Hey for Honesty* II. vi, Come, let's in, and drink a Cup of stingo. **1665** BRATHWAIT *Comment Two Tales* 32 Returning with a large Quart of mighty Ale, that might compare with Stingo, for it would cut a Feather. **1756** *Connoisseur* No. 105 He would give me a cup of the best Yorkshire Stingo. **1826** *Sporting Mag.* XVII. 375 A glass of his Lordship's old Shropshire stingo. **1891** N. GOULD *Double Event* 307 Host Barnes had tapped a barrel of double stingo for the occasion.

attrib. **1810** *Splendid Follies* II. 157 My stingo cup.. was the horn of a d——d fine buffalo. **1861** *Bentley's Misc.* XLIX. 171 In prose fiction, too, has Thomas Hood turned out some stingo samples of storm-brewing. **1870** DISRAELI *Lothair* xxvii, Tea-gardens and stingo houses.

b. *fig.* Vigour, energy, vim; *to give* (a person) ***hot stingo*** = *to give it hot* s.v. HOT *a.* 11 d. ? *Obs.*

1885 *Punch* 22 Aug. 86/3 It's rare fun, by Jingo! I give 'em hot stingo. **1927** *Daily Tel.* 19 July 15 To keep in good trim and add stingo to your efforts in sport. **1927** GALSWORTHY in A. A. Horn *Ivory Coast* Foreword 5 A gorgeous book.. full of sheer stingo. **1928** *Observer* 18 Mar. 23/3 Some shanties, sung by Raymond Newell and a chorus, are full of stingo.

sting ray. [STING *sb.*²]

Any fish of the genus *Trygon* or family *Trygonidæ*, esp. *Trygon pastinaca*. The long tapering tail is armed near the middle with a flattened sharp-pointed bony spine, serrated on both sides, capable of inflicting a severe wound.

1624 CAPT. SMITH *Virginia* II. 27 Stingraies, whose tailes are very dangerous. **1676** T. GLOVER *Acc. Virginia* in *Phil. Trans.* II. 625 There is also a fish called a Sting-ray, which much resembleth a Skate, only on one side of his tayl grows out a sharp bone like a bodkin about four or five inches long. **1881** *Cassell's Nat. Hist.* V. 43 The Sting Rays form a large family, about twenty-four species of the genus Trygon being known.

stingy ('stɪndʒɪ), *a.* Also 7 stingie. [Perh. f. STING *sb.*² or *v.*¹ + -Y.

On the assumption that the sb. represents OE. *styng*:—**stungi-*, the pronunciation ('stɪndʒɪ) is explicable. It is possible that some of the examples under sense 1 represent a distinct word, pronounced ('stɪŋɪ), which is still occasionally heard in colloquial use. For the current sense 4, cf. the dial. *skingy* of the same meaning (*Eng. Dial. Dict.*).]

1. a. Having a sting; stinging, sharp, virulent. Chiefly *fig.* of controversy, or the like. *Obs.*

c **1615** D'EWES *Jrnl.* (1783) 13 This discontent gave many satirical wits occasion to vent themselves into stingie libels, in which they spared neither [etc.]. **1654** TUCKNEY *Death disarmed* 41 But in particular would we not have our death too stingy, and its sting deadly. **1657** R. B[ADDILY] *Life Bp. Morton* (1669) 23 Those virulent and stingie Pamphlets. **1681** HICKERINGILL *News fr. Doctor's Comm.* 1 It is.. vulgarly known, that the Waspish Swarms in Doctors Commons, have been as stinging as stingy against Mr. Hickeringil. **1682** —— *Hist. Whiggism* I. 17, I know your meaning, Whigg, and your stingy Reflection and Innuendo. **1705** —— *Priest-cr.* I. 17 The Sting of a Scorpion is not more fatal, more incurable, and more venemous than a stingy and enraged Priest, especially.. when you meddle with the Craft by which he gets his Wealth.

Mod. colloq. Those are very stingy ('stɪŋɪ) nettles.

b. Of weather, etc.: Sharp, biting, cold. *dial.*

1823 E. MOOR *Suffolk Words* s.v., Sharp, unsettled weather, inclining to rain, would also be called stingy. **1893** in Cozens-Hardy *Broad Norf.* 14 'It dew fare wonerful stingy', says the rustic, when the wind is in the east.

2. Bad-tempered, irritable, peevish, cross. *dial.*

1781 J. WOODFORDE *Diary* 22 Feb. (1924) I. 302, I was very stingy this morning alias in a bad humour and made Nancy uneasy by my talking. **1787** [J. BEATTIE] *Scoticisms* 81 *Stingy*, in many parts of Scotland, conveys the notion of peevish, or captious. **1796** GROSE *Olio* 113 So, then stingy means peevish or touchy! *a* **1800** PEGGE *Suppl. Grose*, *Stingy*, cross, untoward. Norf. *c* **1800** *Earl of Boyn* xvii. in Child *Ballads* IV. 316 She turned her about wie a very stingy look. **1808** *Spec. Yorksh. Dial.* 30 My mam grows se stingy, she scauds, an' she fleghts. **1823** E. MOOR *Suffolk Words*, *Stingy*, snappish—waspish—unruly—ill-tempered—quarrelsome. **1828** CARR *Craven Gloss. Stingy*, crabbed, ill-humoured.

†**3.** ? Narrow-minded, illiberal. *Obs.*

1694 PENN *Acc. Rise & Progr. Quakers* ii. 53 These things .. rendered this People Stingy and Conceited in such Persons Opinions. **1701** HOWE *Some Consid. Pref. Enquiry* 32 'Tis not to be let pass, that you, or your Author, industriously represent the Primitive English Puritans.. as if they were generally of your stingy, narrow Spirit.

4. a. Of persons, actions, etc.: Niggardly, penurious, mean, close-fisted.

1659 T. PECKE *Parnassi Puerp.* 21 Courtiers I ask ye nothing: for ye are Stingy in giving. **1698** FRYER *Acc. E. India & P.* 162 He lavishes into Excesses not approved of by that stingy Tribe. **1707** HEARNE *Collect.* 27 Jan. (O.H.S.) I. 323 He was a stingy, niggardly Fellow. *a* **1770** JORTIN *Serm.* (1771) VII. xi. 213 Liberal in promises, and stingy in performances. **1838** LYTTON *Alice* IV. vi, Without being stingy, the admiral had a good deal of economy in his disposition. **1866** GEO. ELIOT *F. Holt* Introd. I. 12 He perhaps remembered the fathers of actual baronets, and knew stories of their extravagant or stingy housekeeping.

b. const. *of.*

1723 *Portland Papers* (Hist. MSS. Comm.) VI. 76 So very stingy and saving of their ground are these yeomen of Kent. **1771** N. NICHOLLS *Correspond. w. Gray* (1843) 121 If you knew the pleasure your letters give me, I think you would not be quite so stingy of them. **1885** MABEL COLLINS *Prettiest Woman* v, Who is she, to be so stingy of her smiles. **1893** J. A. SYMONDS *Michelangelo* I. ii. §8. 83 He was never stingy of cash.

c. Betokening meanness; doled out sparingly or grudgingly.

1849 D. G. MITCHELL *Battle Summer* (1852) 250 Workmen too proud to buy such stingy dinner, snuff the fumes wishfully. **1865** TROLLOPE *Belton Est.* xvii. 193 With stingy breakfasts and bad dinners for herself. **1878** T. CUYLER *Pointed Papers* 103 Christ is put off with a stingy hour or two on the Sunday.

d. Meagre, spare, circumscribed.

1927 E. M. FORSTER *Aspects of Novel* viii. 205 [James's] characters..are constructed on very stingy lines. They are incapable of fun, of rapid motion, of carnality.

5. Scanty, poor in quantity or amount.

1854 MISS BAKER *Northampt. Gloss.*, *Stingy*, thin, weak; applied to the hair of an animal. **1863** LONGF. *Wayside Inn, Birds of Killingworth*, When your teams Drag home the stingy harvest.

6. Of the brim of a hat: narrow. Also as *sb.*, a narrow-brimmed hat. *U.S.* (*Black English*).

1965 *Liberator* Aug. 23/2 He was neat from toe to stingy. **1969** N. COHN *AWopBopaLooBop* (1970) ix. 86 He wore Stingy Brim straw hats, tight pants, lurid shirts.

stink (stɪŋk), *sb.* Forms: 3–4 stinc, 4 stenke, stinck, stync, 4–5 stynke, 4–6 stynk, 4–7 stinke, 7 stincke, 4– stink. [f. the vb.

Perh. in some instances a dialectal variant of *stinch*: see STENCH *sb.* γ]

1. a. A foul, disgusting, or offensive smell: = STENCH *sb.* 2.

a **1300** *Cursor M.* 11860 þe roting þat him rennes vte, þe stinck þat ai es him a-bute, Ne mai na liueand man it thole. **1382** WYCLIF *Joel* ii. 20 The stynk of hym shal stye vp. *c* **1420** *Sir Amadace* (Camden) vi, Suche a stinke in the chapelle he hade, That dwelle ther he ne myȝte. **1562** TURNER *Herbal* II. 62 b, I am suere that the white laus tibi hath the stynk that Dioscorides speketh of. **1611** BIBLE *2 Macc.* ix. 10 And the man that thought a little afore he could reach to the starres of heauen, no man could endure to carry for his intollerable stinke. **1674** BOYLE *Excell. Theol.* II. iii. 150 Why the smell of Castor or Assa Fœtida produces in most persons that which they call a stink rather than a perfume. **1727** POPE *Thoughts Var. Subj.* lxxv, A little Whiff of it [ambergrise]..is very agreeable; but when a Man holds a whole Lump of it to your Nose, it is a Stink. **1857** HUGHES *Tom Brown* II. iii, He had been kicking up horrid stinks for some time in his study. **1897** *Allbutt's Syst. Med.* IV. 676 Hajek has detected in ozæna a short bacillus..which possesses the property of decomposing organic substances with the formation of a penetrating stink.

b. *fig.*

1673 BUNYAN *Differ. Judgm.* 8 The Persons..are now a stink, and reproach to religion.

c. A contemptible person, a stinkard. *slang.*

1916 JOYCE *Portrait of Artist as a Young Man* 8 Rody Kickham was a decent fellow but Nasty Roche was a stink. **1918** E. POUND *Let.* 4 June (1971) 137 Meredith is, to me, chiefly a stink. I should never write on him as I detest him too much ever to trust myself as critic of him. **1950** R. MOORE *Candlemas Bay* v. 281 And the rest of you little stinks, shut up, too! **1972** D. DEVINE *Three Green Bottles* 102 That stink, Celia Armitage, had somehow found out.

2. a. Evil-smelling quality, offensive odour: = STENCH *sb.* 3.

c **1250** *Gen. & Ex.* 2556 Summe he deden in vn-ðewed swinc, for it was fuȝel and ful o stinc. *c* **1366** CHAUCER *A.B.C.* 56 But if þou my socour bee To stink eterne he wole my gost exile. *c* **1440** *Alphabet of Tales* 171 Yitt sho mott not com att hur for stynk with-oute sho had at hur nece many wele-saueryng spycis. **1528** LYNDESAY *Dreme* 325 That myrke Mansioun is tapessit with stynk. **1608** ROWLANDS *Humors Looking Gl.* B 4 b, One of the damned crew that lives by drinke, And by Tobacco's stillified stink. **1745** SIR C. H. WILLIAMS in Jesse *Selwyn & Contemp.* (1843) I. 65 But when the first [cracker] went off she threw the rest on the tea-table, where, one after another, they all went off, with much noise and not a little stink. **1882** 'OUIDA' *In Maremma* I. 184 There is so much stink of oil and sickly smell of silkworms.

b. *fig.*

1303 R. BRUNNE *Handl. Synne* 6518 The syxte synne ys glotonye; þat ys a shameful vyleynye þat men doun of mete and drynk, For ouermoche ys abominable & stynk.

3. a. *slang.* (See quots. 1812 and 1851.) Also, a row or fuss; a furore. Now chiefly in phrs. *to raise* (*kick up, make*) *a stink*.

1812 J. H. VAUX *Flash Dict.* s.v., When any robbery of moment has been committed, which causes much alarm, or of which much is said in the daily papers, the family people will say, there is a great stink about it. **1851** MAYHEW *Lond. Labour* I. 250 The newspapers..had raised before the eye and mind of the public, what the 'patterers' of his class proverbially call a 'stink',—that is, had opened the eyes of the unwary to the movements of 'Chelsea George'. **1907** [see JIM-HICKEY]. **1913** KIPLING *Diversity of Creatures* (1917) 293 We *mustn't* be tried! It'll make an infernal international stink. **1942** *Tee Emm* (Air Ministry) II. 81 Do you do it merely because there's a stink if you don't? **1948** 'N. SHUTE' *No Highway* ii. 31, I remember the Russians kicking up a stink. **1959** 'M. CRONIN' *Dead & done With* iv. 56 The first thing he'd do when he got back was see his M.P. and kick up a stink. **1976** L. SANDERS *Hamlet Warning* (1977) iii. 31 [She] commanded a world press. She could raise a tremendous stink if she chose to do so.

b. *like stink*, furiously, intensely. Cf. LIKE *adv.* 1 b. *colloq.*

1929 R. C. SHERRIFF *Journey's End* I. 40 If you see a Minnie coming..you have to judge it and run like stink sometimes. **1938** M. ALLINGHAM *Fashion in Shrouds* xv. 240 It's raining like stink. **1945** 'P. WOODRUFF' *Call Next Witness* II. v. 114 He clapped in his heels and rode like stink. **1955** M. ALLINGHAM *Beckoning Lady* iii. 40 The telephone's here..and when it rings you have to run like stink before the caller gives up. **1972** D. DEVINE *Three Green Bottles* 11 She wasn't really clever, she just worked like stink.

c. In other colloq. phrases (parallel to the use of *hell* and similar words).

1942 *R.A.F. Jrnl.* 16 May 26, I bet they've been giving old Jerry stink this afternoon. **1977** I. SHAW *Beggarman, Thief* I. ii. 21 We'd've been in a stink of a mess without him.

4. *pl.* University and Public School slang for Natural Science (originally and now chiefly for Chemistry) as a subject of study or university examinations.

1869 'WAT. BRADWOOD' *O.V.H.* v, He had abandoned further classics in final schools, and was aiming sedulously at a class in 'stinks'. **1900** FARMER *Publ. Sch. Word-bk.*, *Stinks* subs. (general).—Chemistry. Also as a nickname for a lecturer thereon. **1902** *Daily Chron.* 12 Nov. 7/1 The old public schools..look on Mathematics as "tics' and Natural Science as 'stinks,' presumably from the days when Chemistry was the only branch of Natural Science taught. **1914** 'I. HAY' *Lighter Side School Life* iv. 116 Master Nixon ..had pointed out that it would be a good thing to enrol as a member some one who understood 'Chemistry and Stinks generally'. **1928** R. CULLUM *Myst. Barren Lands* xi. 107 You can't afford to use up the source that gives you a living so you can carry on with your stinks. **1945** 'R. CROMPTON' *William & Brains Trust* vii. 129 'English isn't bad, 'cause ole Sarky can't see what you're doin' at the back, an' Stinks isn't bad, 'cause you can get some jolly good bangs if you mix the wrong things together.' **1955** [see LAB *sb.*[2]]. **1961** A. WILSON *Old Men at Zoo* i. 37 Eventually..the laboratory work will be on a scale that will make this place look like a school stinks room.

5. *Comb.*: **stink-ball**, a missile contrived for the purpose of emitting a suffocating vapour when thrown among the enemy (see quot. 1802); **stink beetle** = *stink bug*; **stink berry** *U.S.*, the yellow buckthorn; **stink-bird**, the name in Guyana for the Hoactzin, *Opisthocomus cristatus*; **stink bomb**, a small hand-missile which emits a nauseating smell when broken, typically thrown by schoolboys; also *transf.*; **stink brand** = *stinking smut*; **stink-bug**, a shield bug of the family Pentatomidæ, which includes many species that feed on plants and eject a strong-smelling liquid if attacked; **stink bush**, (*a*) a species of star-anise (*Illicium floridanum*), a shrub growing in the southern United States (*Funk's Stand. Dict.* 1895); (*b*) *Austral.*, the rutaceous tree, *Zieria smithii*; **stink-cat** *S. African*, the zoril or mariput, *Zorilla striata*; **stinkfinger**: in coarse slang phr. *to play (at) stinkfinger* (see quot. 1903) (now *rare* or *obs.*); **stink-fish**, (*a*) *S. Afr.* = *bamboo-fish* s.v. BAMBOO *sb.* 2; (*b*) *Ghana* = *stinking fish* (*b*) s.v. STINKING *ppl. a.* 2 a; **stink-fly**, a fly belonging to the genus *Chrysopa*; **stink gland**, a gland in certain animals producing a fetid secretion; **stink grass**, an ill-scented grass, *Eragrostis major*; **stink pheasant** = *stink-bird*; **stink quartz**, a variety of quartz, which emits a fetid odour when struck; **stink-rat** *U.S.* = STINK-POT 4 (*Cent. Dict.*); **stink-shad**, the mud-shad, *Dorosoma cepedianum*; **stink-trap** = *stench-trap*, STENCH *sb.* 5; **stink-tree**; (*a*) some tree native in Sri Lanka, having a disgusting odour; (*b*) *dial.* the name in the Isle of Wight for the guelder rose; **stink-turtle** = STINK-POT 4; **stinkwort** *Austral.*, a plant of the genus *Scrophularia*.

1753 *Chambers' Cycl.* Suppl., s.v. *Ball*, *Stink-balls, those which yield a great stench when fired to annoy the enemy. **1802** C. JAMES *Milit. Dict.* s.v. *Ball*, *Stink-balls* are prepared by a composition of mealed powder,..assa-fœtida, seraphim-gum or ferula, and bug and stinking herbs. **1889** H. VAUGHAN-WILLIAMS *Visit to Lobengula* (1947) xxv. 162, I must mention the *stink beetles, as they are called. They all emit the most horrible stench when killed or even touched. You get them all over South Africa. **1979** *Jrnl. Arid Environments* II. 101 When stink-beetles of the genus *Eleodes* are placed in a bottle.., their fumes will kill other insects placed inside the bottle. **1869–73** T. R. JONES *Cassell's Bk. Birds* III. 281 The Hoactzin, or *Stink Bird. **1915** D. O. BARNETT *Let.* 26 June 192 It seems that the tobacco stores had amalgamated with a *stink-bomb dépôt. **1922** A. HADDON *Green Room Gossip* iv. 117 At this juncture there was a good deal of sneezing and coughing in the auditorium... Both stink bombs and 'electric snuff' were thrown from the gallery. **1958** 'J. BYROM' *Or be he Dead* xiii. 167 He lobbed this [conversational] grenade..as innocently as a child with a stinkbomb. **1974** D. RAMSAY *No Cause to Kill* I. 38, I used to sit in the library wishing I had a stink bomb to set off under her nose. **1877** BARTLETT *Dict. Americanisms* (ed. 4) 647 Squash-bug... A small yellow bug, injurious to the vines of squashes, melons, and cucumbers... In Connecticut, called a *stink-bug. **1891** *Century Dict.*, *Stink-bug*, any one of several malodorous bugs, particularly the common squash-bug, *Anasa tristis*, of the *Coreidæ*. **1902** L. O. HOWARD *Insect Bk.* 313 The stink-bugs and their allies. (Family *Pentatomidæ*.) **1899** RIDER HAGGARD *Swallow* 50, I have shammed dead like a *stink-cat when dogs are about. **1903** FARMER & HENLEY *Slang* VI. III. 369/1 *To play at *stinkfinger*,..to grope a woman. **1934** H. MILLER *Tropic of Cancer* 282, I had no Odette Champs-divers with whom to play stinkfinger. [**1902** *Marine Investigation in S. Afr.* I. 116 Bamboesvisch. Stinkvisch. Scarce in Cape Town market, but common in Saldanha Bay.] **1913** *Stink-fish [see *bamboo-fish* s.v. BAMBOO *sb.* 2]. **1962** C. BAETA *Prophetism in Ghana* ii. 17 Adherents of the Twelve Apostles Church..are not allowed to eat pork, stink-fish, shark's meat or snails. **1902** L. O. HOWARD *Insect Bk.* 222 *Chrysopidæ*,..sometimes..called *stink flies. **1887** F. G. HEATHCOTE in *Phil. Trans.* CLXXIX. II. 164 These organs..are the first pair of *stink glands. **1884** GOODE *Nat. Hist. Aquat. Anim.* 610 In the Chesapeake region it is known as the 'Mud-Shad', 'Winter Shad', or '*Stink Shad'. **1782** in *Abridgm. Specif. Patents, Drains & Sewers* (1874) 5 This machine or *stink trap is let into lead or any other sort of pipes. **1873** SPENCER *Study Sociol.* iii. (ed. 6) 67 Infecting gases that are kept out only so long as stink-traps are in good order. **1906** *Hasluck's Sanitary Conveniences & Drainage* xv. 151 A 'trap', or 'stink-trap', as it was formerly called, is [etc.]. **1795** *Thunberg's Trav.* IV. 234 The *stink-tree was called by the Dutch *Strunt-hout*,..on account of its disgusting odour, which resides especially in the thick stem and the larger branches. **1842** BROMFIELD in *Phytologist* (1848) III. 421 *Viburnum Opulus*..is sometimes called stink-tree in this island [Isle of Wight]. **1890** *Kapunda Herald* 25 July 2/5 The following letter was received from Mr. J. McDougall..regarding a sample of *stinkwort sent to him:—'This sample has been duly examined, and I am satisfied that it is useless as a raw material from which to make paper stock'. **1897** *Westm. Gaz.* 23 July 8/1 The Bill which has just been introduced into the New South Wales Parliament for the destruction of noxious weeds..has a scheduled list of weeds, including thistle, stinkwort, and several others.

stink (stɪŋk), *v.* Forms: 1 stincan, 3 stinke-n, 4 stenk, stinc, stynke-n (4–5 sting, styng, styngk), 4–6 stynk, 4–7 stinke, stynkkyn, 5–6 stynke, 6 styncke, 6–7 stincke, 4– stink. *Pa. t.* 1–4 stanc, stonc, 3–4 stonk, *pl.* stunken, 4–5 stonke, 4–7 stanke, 5 stongke, 6 stonck, stunck, 6–9 stunk, 7 stunke, 8– stank; weak forms 5 stynkid, 6 stinckett, stynked. *Pa. pple.* 5 stonken, 6 stuncke, 7– stunk; weak 5 stynked. [Com. WGer.: OE. *stincan* str. vb. = OFris. **stiunka* (WFris. *stjonke*), (M)Du., (M)LG. *stinken* (whence Sw. *stinka*, Da. *stinke*), OHG. *stinchan* (MHG., mod.G. *stinken*):—WGer. **stiŋkwan*, f. Teut. root **stiŋkw-* (:**staŋkw-*: **stuŋkw-*; see STENCH *sb.* and *v.*).

The root is coincident in form with that of Goth. *stiggqan* to come into collision, ON. *støkkva* str. vb. (MSw. *stinka*, *stiunka*) to spring, leap, fly off, and the causative form Goth. *gastagqjan* to collide with, ON. *støkkva* wk. vb. (MSw. *stänkia*, mod.Sw. *stänka*) to cause to spring, sprinkle, OE. *stęncan* to scatter, disperse. The identity of the root is possible, but in view of the great diversity in meaning it cannot be positively asserted.]

†**1.** *intr.* To emit a smell or vapour of any kind; to smell (sweetly or otherwise). *Obs.*

c **725** *Corpus Gloss.* 895 Flagrans, stincendi. *c* **1000** ÆLFRIC *Gram.* xxxvii. (Z.) 220 Ic stince swote. *c* **1200** ORMIN 8194 To strawwenn gode gresess þær, þatt stunnkenn swiþe swete.

2. a. To emit a strong offensive smell; to smell foully. (In early examples, a contextual use of sense 1.) Const. *of*.

Now implying violent disgust on the part of the speaker; in ordinary polite use avoided as unpleasantly forcible.

c **1000** *Sax. Leechd.* II. 236 Eal se lichoma stincð fule. *c* **1200** *Trin. Coll. Hom.* 37 Dis oref..stincð fule for his golnesse. *c* **1200** ORMIN 4781 & all he toc forrþrihht anan To rotenn & to stinnkenn. *a* **1225** *Ancr. R.* 326 Lazre þet stonc so long he hefde ileien i þer eorðe. *c* **1400** MAUNDEV. (Roxb.) ii. 5 þai trowed þat Cristez body schuld hafe stynked. *c* **1450** *Mirk's Festial* 84 How his brethe stinkyth. **1533** J. HEYWOOD *Johan* A j, I wolde bete her..that she shall stynke. **1535** COVERDALE *Exod.* viii. 14 The land stanke of them. **1590** SPENSER *F.Q.* I. i. 20 A floud of poyson..Which stunck so vildly, that it forst him slacke His grasping hold. *a* **1631** DONNE *Poems, Elegy* iii. 31 Waters stincke soone, if in one place they bide. **1717** PRIOR *Alma* I. 51 When Cabbage stinks, or Roses smell. **1769** G. WHITE *Selborne, Let. to Pennant* 30 Aug., I wish I had not forgot to mention the faculty that snakes have of stinking *se defendendo*. **1820** SHELLEY *Sensit. Pl.* III. 57 The dock, and henbane, and hemlock dank,..stifled the air till the dead wind stank. **1889** J. K. JEROME *Three Men* iv, The High Street stunk of oil. **1899** MARY KINGSLEY *W. Afr. Stud.* i. 3, I myself saw certainly not less than 70 crocodiles at one time, let alone smelling them, for they do swarm in places and stink always.

b. *fig.* To be offensive; to be abhorrent; to savour offensively *of* something. Phrases, to *stink in* (a person's) *nostrils*; also (*slang*) *to stink of* (or *with*) *money*: to be 'offensively' rich.

a **1225** *Ancr. R.* 138 Auh swuch sacrefise stinkeð to ure Louerd. **1303** R. BRUNNE *Handl. Synne* 8312 þese twey cytees, boþe þey sank, For þey hadde ioye at synne þat stank. *c* **1450** *Mirk's Festial* 68 For oure forme synne stanke soo yn Godys nase, þat [etc.]. **1535** COVERDALE *Prov.* x. 7 The name of the vngodly shal stynke. **1608** SHAKS. *Per.* IV. vi. 145 He makes our profession as it were to stincke afore the face of the gods. **1612** *Benvenuto's Passenger* I. ii. 141 A false wicked tongue stinckes of an hereticall conscience, but what then? **1674** in *Verney Mem.* (1907) II. 359 To make me stincke in the nostrills of my ould associates. **1867** GOLDW. SMITH in Brodrick *Ess. Reform* 230 Reputed renegades, whose names stank in the nostrils of the party which they had left. **1877** E. PEACOCK *N.W. Lincs. Gloss.* 239/2 A very proud man is said to '*stink* wi' pride', a very rich one to '*stink* o' brass'. **1886** STEVENSON *Dr. Jekyll* i, We told the man we could..make such a scandal out of this, as should make his name stink from one end of London to the other. **1922** JOYCE *Ulysses* 9 Touch him for a guinea. He's stinking with money. **1932** I. BROWN *Marine Parade* xii. 152 We must do our best. He stinks of money. Will you fix up about rooms and for God's sake let's have a decent dinner.

Prov. c **1386**, **1539** [see PROFFERED *ppl. a.*]

†**c.** *to stink out*: to go out with a stink. *Obs.*

a **1637** B. JONSON *Underwoods, Execr. Vulcan* 188 Or in the Bell-Mans Lanthorn, like a Spy, Burn to a Snuff, and then stink out and dye.

†**d.** *trans.* To smell offensively of. *Obs.*

a **1225** *Ancr. R.* 86 þus þe uale uikelare..wrieð hore fulðe so þæt heo hit ne muwen stinken... Vor ȝif heo hit stunken, ham wolde wlatien þer aȝean.

e. To exhibit or savour of moral (artistic, etc.) decay. Of persons: also, to be despicable or completely incompetent. Of actions, phenomena, etc.: also *spec.* in phr. ***to stink to (high) heaven.*** *colloq.*

1934 J. T. Farrell *Young Manhood of Studs Lonigan* viii. 121, I watched you guys go through signal practice. You stunk! **1956** H. Kurnitz *Invasion of Privacy* xv. 99 She regarded Zorn bleakly. 'You stink, Michael Zorn,' she said. **1963** 'D. Cory' *Hammerhead* iv. 61 Sofia was the actress of the family. I stink.

1936 *Metronome* Feb. 61/2 *Stinks*, what one pub thinks of another's tunes. **1940** 'N. Blake' *Malice in Wonderland* I. v. 61 Big Business does rather stink, doesn't it? **1959** H. Hobson *Mission House Murder* iii. 21 Rock an' Roll came in ..now that's out—that stinks too. **1963** C. D. Simak *They walked like Men* ix. 53 'How did you know that?' 'Just a guess,' I said. 'This whole thing stinks to heaven.' **1973** *Times* 23 May 16/4 The affairs of Lonrho stunk to high heaven. **1979** R. Jaffe *Class Reunion* (1980) II. ii. 196 Chris would make it be like the old days. But the old days had stunk too.

3. quasi-*trans.* with complement. ***to stink to death***, to kill by emitting a bad smell. Chiefly *hyperbolical.*

1624 Middleton *Game at Chess* v. iii, Hee would hazard to be stunk [*v.rr.* stung, strucke] to death. **1789** Mrs. Piozzi *France & Italy* I. 173 Chicken-coops, which stink one to death. **1835** Browning *Paracelsus* III. 443 Such a suffumigation as, once fixed, Had stunk the patient dead ere he could groan.

4. *trans.* To fill (an animal's earth) with suffocating fumes. Also, to drive (animals or persons) *out* of a place by stench or suffocating fumes.

1781 Beckford *Th. Hunting* (1802) 338 In open countries foxes, when they are much disturbed, will lie at earth. If you have difficulty in finding, stinking the earths will sometimes produce them again. *Ibid.*, Badgers..they may be caught by stinking them out of a great earth. **1860** Reade *Cloister & Hearth* xliii. (1896) 125 Then with his own hands he let down by a rope a bag of burning sulphur and pitch, and stunk them out. **1880** *Brit. Med. Jrnl.* 7 Aug. 207/2 Treatment..to stink the [Guinea] worm out.

5. a. To cause to stink.

a **1300** *Satire on Monks & People of Kildare* xiv, in F. J. Furnivall *Early Eng. Poems* (1862) 155 Daþeit ȝur curteisie, ȝe stinkeþ al þe strete. **1733** W. Ellis *Chiltern & Vale Farm.* 294 If its Leaf or Seed is rubbed, it will stink the Hands for four or five Hours. **1896** Flora A. Steel *Face of Waters* I. vi. (1903) 63 One dead fish stinks a whole tank.

b. With *up*. To cause (a place) to stink. Also *fig. colloq.* (orig. and chiefly *U.S.*).

1956 B. Holiday *Lady sings Blues* (1973) vii. 65 The manager got panicky and began to holler at me that I was stinking up his Grand Terrace. **1967** C. Drummond *Death at Furlong Post* xi. 140 Harassed fat women cooking *sauerbraten* and stinking up the place with the smell of vinegar. **1977** D. MacKenzie *Raven & Ratcatcher* iii. 44 A rumour..that..I was allowed to resign rather than stink-up the fair name of the Serious Crimes Squad. **1979** R. Jaffe *Class Reunion* (1980) III. iii. 319 He was sweet even though he did stink up her bedroom because he always forgot to open the window.

6. Comb. in phr. used subst., as **stink-alive**, the bib or pout, *Gadus luscus.*

1863 J. G. Wood *Illustr. Nat. Hist.* III. 306 The Pout is graphically termed by the fishermen the Stinkalive, because it becomes putrid so soon after death.

stinkard ('stɪŋkəd). Also 7 stinckard, -erd, stinkarde, 8 stincard. [f. stink *v.* + -ard.]

1. One who stinks. Formerly often used as a term of abuse. Now *rare* or *Obs.*

c **1600** *Timon* I. ii. (1842) 6 Out, out, thou stinckard, mans grand enemy. **1601** B. Jonson *Poetaster* IV. i, The Gods were a sort of Goslinges, when they suffred so sweete a breath to perfume the bed of a stinkard. **1612** Chapman *Widows' T.* I. i. C 3 b, Your vnapprehending Stinckerd is blest with the sole prerogatiue of his Wiues chamber. **1684** Otway *Atheist* I. i. 7 The most insufferable Stinkard living. **1700** Congreve *Way of World* IV. xi, Your Turks are infidels, and believe not in the grape: your Mahometan, your Mussulman is a dry Stinkard.

†**b.** See quot. 1777. Also *attrib. Obs.*

1777 Robertson *Hist. Amer.* IV. (1778) I. 344 Among the Natchez..Some families were reputed noble... The body of the people were considered as vile... The former were called Respectable; the latter the Stinkards. **1792** W. Bartram *Trav. Carolina* 464 Those numerous remnant bands or tribes..generally speak the Stincard language.

2. A name given to various ill-smelling animals.

1774 Goldsm. *Nat. Hist.* III. 380 The Stinkards. This is a name which our sailors give to one or two animals of the weasel kind, which are chiefly found in America. *Ibid.* IV. 80 [The musk rat] is denominated by them [the savages of Canada] the stinkard. **1822** Southey in *Q. Rev.* XXVI. 281 The stinkard, who it seems is a sure shot at five feet distance, retreated leisurely..and stopt when the unhappy Jesuit drew nigh. **1843** J. E. Gray *List Mammalia Brit. Mus.* 69 The Stinkard or Teledu. *Mydaus meliceps.* Java.

3. A shark of the genus *Mustelus.*

1883 Day *Fishes Gt. Brit.* II. 296 *Mustelus vulgaris*... Smooth-hound,..Stinkard, in Ireland, due to its colour.

4. = stinker 5, stink pot 3.

1850 Scoresby *Cheever's Whalem. Adv.* iii. (1858) 40 Gonies, stinkards, horse-birds..had all many a good morsel of blubber.

†**'stinkardly,** *a. Obs.* [f. stinkard + -ly[1].] Stinking, disgusting, contemptible.

1609 B. Jonson *Epicœne* IV. ii, You notorious stinkardly Beareward, do's my breath smell? **1618** Mynshul *Ess. & Charact. Prison* 31 A rabble of such stinkardly companions, with whom no man of any reasonable fashion, but would scorne to conuerse.

stinkaroo, var. stinkeroo.

stinker ('stɪŋkə(r)). [f. stink *v.* + -er[1].] One who or something which stinks.

1. = stinkard 1 (*low slang*). Also in weakened slang uses, esp. banteringly and in mock-contempt.

1607 Dekker & Webster *North-w. Hoe* IV. i. F 1 b, I smelt out my noble stincker Greensheild in his Chamber. **1622** Massinger & Dekker *Virg. Martyr* II. i. D i, This boone Bacchanalian stinker did I make legges to. **1898** *Daily News* 23 July 9/4 He had called her 'a stinker' and 'a stinking idiot.' **1911** Webster, *Stinker* (slang), one who is disgustingly contemptible, a stinkard. **1922** [see house *sb.*[1] 4 c]. **1936** M. Allingham *Death of Ghost* xx. 237, I will show that stinker! **1949** A. Huxley *Let.* 6 Mar. (1969) 593 Saying what a stinker he is, both in bed and out. *c* **1951** T. Roethke *Selected Lett.* (1968) 170 After your generous words, I feel a terrible stinker questioning everything. **1962** Wodehouse *Service with Smile* viii. 120 Is that you, Stinker? **1975** *Daily Mail* 30 May 3/6 A gang of 'real stinkers' have raided a top wartime air ace and stolen his most prized souvenir—a 6ft. German propellor.

†**2.** A pot or jar containing a disinfectant. *Obs.*

1665 G. Harvey *Disc. Plague* (1673) 154 The Air may be purified..by burning of Stinck pots or Stinckers, as they call them, in contagious Lanes.

3. Anything that emits an offensive smell. Also formerly, a rank cigar or cigarette. *slang.*

1834 *Proc. Geol. Soc.* II. 21 The greater part of the workings are only shallow pits, touching merely the sulphureous beds, locally called 'stinkers'. **1898** *Westm. Gaz.* 29 Oct. 6/3 These gas cars were locally although vulgarly called 'Stinkers.' **1907** *Daily Chron.* 13 Aug. 2/7 Suppose I am compelled to smoke a cigar, I may purchase a few nasty penny 'stinkers,' and keep within the order of the restaurant edict. **1924** N. Coward *Rat Trap* I. 11 There are cigarettes in that silver box, Keld; stinkers on one side, and opulent Turkish on the other. **1935** Wodehouse *Luck of Bodkins* iv. 42 Have you such a thing as a stinker?.. And a match? **1961** J. W. Anderson *Fur Trader's Story* iii. 23 At Moose Factory, I saw the last of the sulphur matches ('stinkers' we used to call them) which were in their day considered a great advance on the striking of flint on steel to make fire. **1970** B. Cartland *We danced All Night* vii. 198 Virginian cigarettes were first called 'stinkers', then 'gaspers', and were considered a little vulgar.

4. *pl.* (See quot. 1841.) *local.*

1841 Hartshorne *Salop. Ant.* Gloss., *Stinkers*, Stinking-coal, a very inferior kind of coal which bears its title from the disagreeable smell of sulphur which it emits in burning.

5. A sailor's name for the giant fulmar (*Ossifraga gigantea*) and other ill-smelling petrels.

1896 Newton *Dict. Birds*, *Stinkpot*, *Stinker*, sailors' names for some of the Petrels. **1906** W. L. Sclater *Stark's Birds S. Africa* IV. 475 *Majaqueus æquinoctialis*... 'Stinker' of Sealers and Whalers.

6. *fig.* **a.** A strongly-worded letter; a disagreeable review or other communication. *slang.*

1912 *World's Work* Apr. 509/1 The principal content of this mail proved to be, as usual, a very long and wordy 'stinker'. **1936** Wodehouse *Young Men in Spats* vi. 157 For weeks..Stiffy had been yearning to write an absolute stinker to old Wivelscombe, telling him exactly what he thought of him. **1945** L. Durrell *Spirit of Place* (1969) 81, I was afraid ..that you would write me a stinker calling me a peach fed sod. **1953** E. M. Forster *Hill of Devi* 228, I composed a stinker... H. H. supervised it and decried any attempt at moderation.

b. More widely, something repugnant because of its difficulty or unendurable nature. *colloq.*

1917 Kipling *Diversity of Creatures* 241 The second stanza..of that Ode is what is technically called a 'stinker'. **1941** S. J. Baker *Dict. Austral. Slang* 72 *Stinker*, a disagreeable, highly unpleasant and often humid day. **1947** *Penguin New Writing* XXIX. 100 During the war the standard [of films] was undeniably high, with the exception of a few frank stinkers such as *Half-Way House.* **1959** D. Hewett *Bobbin Up* 170 Already the sky was pale and smoky with the promise of 'another stinker'. **1967** *Listener* 9 Feb. 196/2 Stylistically, the Royal Victoria Hospital is indeed a stinker. **1979** H. R. F. Keating *Inspector Ghote draws Line* xv. 149 The headache..has become a real stinker now.

c. In phr. ***to come a stinker*** = ***to come a cropper*** s.v. cropper[3] (chiefly in the work of P. G. Wodehouse). *slang.*

1923 J. Manchon *Le Slang* 293 *To come a stinker*, ramasser une pelle. **1936** Wodehouse *Laughing Gas* iv. 41 And then..the engagement went and busted itself up. One moment, it was buzzing along like a two-year-old... The next, it had come a stinker. *a* **1975** —— *Sunset at Blandings* (1977) iii. 26 Lack of the stuff [*sc.* wealth] is always the rock on which the frail craft of love comes a stinker where Blandings is concerned.

stinkeroo (stɪŋkə'ruː). *slang* (orig. *U.S.*). Also **stinkaroo.** [f. stink *sb.* or *v.*: see -eroo.] Something of a very low standard; a very bad performance. Also, a furore or 'stink'.

1934 D. Runyon in *Collier's* 24 Nov. 8/3 The contest.. turns out to be something of a disappointment, and, in fact, it is a stinkeroo, because there is little skill and no science whatever in it. **1946** *Sun* (Baltimore) 21 June 16/4 The fight last night was a 'stinkeroo' and should be investigated. **1951** J. B. Priestley *Festival at Farbridge* ii. 54 They've sunk two-and-a-half million dollars in this new stinkeroo that opens tonight. **1958** B. Nichols *Sweet & Twenties* ix. 120 It caused an absolute stinkaroo in the women's colleges. **1973** *Daily Tel.* 24 Nov. 11/7 Many of the critics' notices [of the play] were unfavourable, referring to it as 'an antique', 'a puerile affair' and 'a stinkaroo'.

stink-horn ('stɪŋkhɔːn). [f. stink *sb.* + horn *sb.*] A name for various ill-smelling fungi.

1724 *Ray's Synopsis Meth. Stirpium Brit.* (ed. 3) 12 Fungus phalloides... This is known to all our Country People by the Name of Stinkhorns; *Dr. Richardson.* **1755** *Gentl. Mag.* XXV. 545 Being known in Yorkshire by the name of *Stink-horns.* **1882** J. Smith *Dict. Pop. Names Plants* 393 Stink-horn, or Stinking Polecat, *Phallus impudicus* and *P. fœtidus*, fungi of the Lycoperdaceæ alliance... An allied species is *Clathrus cancellatus*, the Lattice Stink-horn.

†**'stinkibus.** *slang. Obs.* Also -ubus. [f. stink *sb.* + *-ibus* Latin ending of dat. pl.; cf. *circumbendibus*, *recumbentibus*, *muckibus.*] Bad liquor, esp. adulterated spirits.

1706 E. Ward *Wooden World Diss.* (1708) 99 He shall gulp ye down the rankest Stinkibus with as good a Gusto, as a Teague does Usquebaugh. **1771** Smollett *Humph. Cl.*, 5 June, Let 'em have plenty of blankets, and stinkubus, and wampum. **1899** Baring-Gould *Bk. of West* II. 276 Such deteriorated spirits were known amongst the coast-guardsmen as 'stinkibus.'

stinking ('stɪŋkɪŋ), *vbl. sb.* [-ing[1].] The action of the verb stink; an instance of this.

a **1320** *Sir Tristr.* 1177 No man miȝt bi him stand For stinking of his wounde. *c* **1460** J. Russell *Bk. Nurture* 302 in *Babees Bk.*, þy tethe be not pikynge,..ne stynkynge of brethe on youre soueroyne castynge. **1617** Moryson *Itin.* I. 43 The waters dividing the streetes, slowly or not at all moved, are in this City..subject to stinking. **1822** Shelley *Scenes fr. Faust* ii. 213 What glimmering, spurting, stinking, burning.

stinking ('stɪŋkɪŋ), *ppl. a.* [-ing[2].]

1. a. That stinks; offensively smelling.

to cry stinking fish: see cry *v.* 5 b.

c **1000** Ælfric *Hom.* I. 86 Him stod stincende steam of ðam muðe. *c* **1200** Ormin 8195 To strawwenn gode gresess ..Biforenn þatt stinnkennde lic. **1338** R. Brunne *Chron.* (1725) 177 Richard was hastif, & ansuerd þat stund, Certes þou lies cheitif, & as a stinkand hund. *a* **1400** *Prymer* (1895) 69 Lord, þat reisidist stynkynge lazar fro his graue, graunte hem reste! **1532** *Psalter of Jesus* ✠✠ j b, Thy grace lorde,.. defende me fro the stynkynge aungell and the spyryte of pestylence. **1604** Jas. I *Counterbl. Tobacco* (Arb.) 101 The loathsome, and hurtfull vse of this stinking Antidote. **1777** Robertson *Hist. Amer.* IV. Wks. 1851 V. 348 A fire of stinking herbs is kindled underneath, so as he may..be involved in its smoke. **1899** *Allbutt's Syst. Med.* VII. 601 Large stinking cholesteatomatous cavity in mastoid. **1908** C. Bigg *Orig. Chr.* xiv. (1909) 178 Many other of the captives died in that sunless, stinking dungeon.

Comb. **1604** F. T. *Case is Altered* C 3, Gagge toothed, slandering tongue, foh, stinking breathed. **1756** Mrs. Calderwood in *Coltness Collect.* (Maitl. Club) 117, I think she is a pert, stinking-like husy.

b. said of an odour.

1611 Bible *Eccl.* x. 1 Dead flies cause the oyntment of the Apothecarie to send foorth a stinking sauour. **1621** Lodge *Summary Du Bartas* I. 261 He yeeldeth a stinking smell.

c. Used as a vague epithet connoting intense disgust and contempt. Now only *vulgar.*

Very common in 14th–17th c.

a **1225** *Ancr. R.* 164 Auh hit, anonde meidelure, mei loosen his holinesse mid a stinkinde wil. *c* **1380** Wyclif *Sel. Wks.* III. 101 Stynkynge pryde. *c* **1450** *Mirour Saluacioun* (Roxb.) 149 Wasshe me out of bandes of my stynking synne vile. *c* **1530** *Songs, Carols*, etc. (1907) 111 Thou stynkyng coward! *a* **1564** Becon *Supplic.* Wks. III. 29 b, Banyshe out of the congregation that most vile & stinckinge Idol the Masse. **1684** Otway *Atheist* I. i. Where I..got no Meat, but such as the old *Succubus* his Wife bought at a stinking Price. **1710** Hearne *Collect.* (O.H.S.) II. 351 A man of Parts, but a most vile, stinking Whigg. **1898** [see stinker 1].

†**d.** quasi-*adv. Obs. rare.*

1589 Nashe *Martin Marprelate* Wks. (Grosart) I. 164 Their iests be so stinking stale, as you must holde your nose while you reade them. *a* **1661** Holyday *Juvenal* (1673) 263 Half a silurus, which is now stinking-ripe.

Mod. Sc. (*vulgar*) I'd be stinkin' fond (to do something) = 'I should never think of it', 'I should certainly not'.

e. As an intensifier: 'offensively', in ***stinking drunk, rich*** (somewhat *derog.*); also *absol.* and const. *with*, having too much (money, etc.). Cf. sense 2 b of the vb. *colloq.*

1887 *Lantern* (New Orleans) 12 Feb. 3/1 Dey had four bottles er booze and got stinkin' 'fore two o'clock. **1926** L. H. Nason *Chevrons* iii. 96 He went off and got stinking drunk. **1934** E. Waugh *Handful of Dust* iii. 115 'Tight that night.' 'Stinking.' **1940** E. Pound *Cantos* lvi. 62 Sangko stinking with graft. **1945** E. S. Gardner *Case of Golddigger's Purse* ii. 9 Not only is he rich but he's *stinking* rich. **1956** A. Christie *Dead Man's Folly* ii. 27 Stinking with money—absolutely stinking! **1965** *New Statesman* 19 Mar. 462/2 The father meets old cronies and gets stinking drunk. **1978** N. Marsh *Grave Mistake* iv. 111 She was in affluent circumstances, stinking rich in fact. **1980** D. Bogarde *Gentle Occupation* i. 22 The only thing to do is to get absolutely stinking... It was the best thing in the world for despair: a good skin-full.

2. a. Special collocations: **stinking badger** = teledu (Cassell 1888); **stinking bird** = *stink-bird*; **stinking bug** = *stink-bug* (stink *sb.* 5); **stinking bunt** = *stinking smut* (*Cent. Dict.* 1891); **stinking coal** *dial.* = stinker 4; **stinking fish**, (*a*) in allusion to the phr. *to cry stinking fish* (sense 1 a): something worthless or rotten; (*b*) *Ghana* (see quot. 1973); **stinking ill**, a disease of sheep; **stinking pheasant** = *stink pheasant* (Webster 1911); **stinking polecat**, one of the skunks or *Mustelidæ*; **stinking rust, smut**, a fungoid disease of plants.

1862 in Veness *El Dorado* (1866) App. 154 Eggs of Opisthocomus cristatus *Stinking bird, or Canje Pheasant. **1815** KIRBY & SP. *Entomol.* viii. (1818) I. 231 Nothing can exceed the irritation caused by the *stinking bugs when they get into the hair or between the linen and the body. **1803** PLYMLEY *Agric. Shropsh.* 53 Brown rock, called the *stinking-coal rock. **1868** PARTON *Shropsh. Coal-Field* 4 The Stinking Coal, is noted for containing a great proportion of sulphuret of iron. **1935** E. R. EDDISON *Mistress* vi. 98 Have I not proof of 's loyal mind within reason: his refusing on't when Lessingham did offer it? Nay, 'twas but *stinking fish then: 'twas under suzerainty. **1968** J. ABRUQUAH *Torrent* ii. 29 You are treated nice when you are a stranger instead of having little bits of dried stinking fish and kenkey thrown at you. **1973** K. A. SEY *Ghanaian Eng.* vii. 90 *Stinking fish*, fish preserved with salt and used for seasoning 'soups' and 'stews'. **1981** N. J. CRISP *Festival* xi. 260 Vincent Consel said to his editor, 'I detect the faint aroma of stinking fish.' *a* **1807** A. DUNCAN in *Prize Ess. Highl. Soc.* III. 364 On opening the body, it emits a strong sulphureous smell, characteristic of the disease; hence it is sometimes called the *stinking ill. **1791** SMELLIE *Buffon's Nat. Hist.* VII. 295 The Mouffettes, or *Stinking Polecats. **1861** *Chamb. Encycl.* II. 155/1 The disease in wheat.. which is also called Smut-balls, Bunt, Pepper Brand, or *Stinking-Rust. **1891** *Century Dict.* s.v. *Smut*, The *stinking smut is caused by two species of fungus.

b. In many names of plants, as ***stinking camomile***, ***hellebore***, ***horehound***, ***iris***, ***maid-weed*** (***mayweed, maythe***), ***motherwort***, ***nightshade***, for which see the sbs. Also **stinking ash**, box elder (Webster 1911); **stinking bean trefoil** (see quot.); **stinking Billy** or **Willie**, the common ragwort, *Senecio Jacobæa* (Eng. Dial. Dict.); **stinking Bob**, herb Robert, *Geranium Robertianum* (ibid.); **stinking cedar**, any species of *Torreya*; **stinking Christopher**, various kinds of figwort, *Scrophularia* (E.D.D.); **stinking crane's bill** (see quot.); **stinking gladdon**, *Iris fœtidissima*; **stinking grass** = *stink grass*, STINK *sb.* 5 (W. 1911); **stinking gum**, an Australian gum tree (*Eucalyptus tereticornis*) whose leaves have a strong cimicine smell (ibid.); **stinking morel** = STINK-HORN; **stinking orach** = *stinking motherwort*; **stinking polecat** = STINK-HORN; **stinking Roger**, *Scrophularia* and other plants (E.D.D.); † **stinking tree** = *stink-tree* (*b*); **stinking trefoil** = *stinking bean trefoil*; **stinking weed**, (*a*) *Cassia occidentalis*; (*b*) *Senecio Jacobæa*; **stinking wood**, a name for various trees the timber of which has a fetid smell, esp. *Cassia occidentalis* and *Anagyris fœtida*; **stinking yew** = *stinking cedar*.

1816 T. GREEN *Univ. Herbal* I. 94/1 *Anagyris Fœtida*, *Stinking Bean Trefoil,..grows wild in France, Spain, [etc.]. **1866** *Treas. Bot.* s.v. *Cedar*, *Stinking Cedar, *Torreya taxifolia*. **1857** ANNE PRATT *Flower. Pl.* II. 40 *Geranium Robertianum* (*Stinking Crane's-bill or Herb Robert). **1597** GERARDE *Herbal* I. xxxvii. 53 *Stinking Gladdon hath long narrow leaues like Iris, but smaller. **1670** RAY *Catal. Plant. Angl.* 84 Cotula fœtida... *Stinking Mayweed or Maithes. **1777** J. LIGHTFOOT *Flora Scotica* II. 1044 *Phallus impudicus* ..*Stinking Morel. **1597** GERARDE *Herbal* II. xlii. 258 *Stinking Orach is called of Cordus *Garosmus*, bicause it smelleth like stinking fish. **1874** *Treas. Bot.* Suppl. 1344/2 *Stinking Polecat, *Phallus impudicus*. **1681** GREW *Musæum* II. §i. i. 180 Part of an Arm of the *Stinking-Tree. **1548** TURNER *Names Herbes* 12 Anagyris..maye be called *stynkynge trifoly in englishe, or beane tree. **1756** P. BROWNE *Jamaica* 224 *Stinking-weed. This plant is very common about Kingston. **1777** J. LIGHTFOOT *Flora Scot.* II. 1132 *Senecio Jacobea*.. The stinking weed. **1793** J. TRAPP tr. *Rochon's Voy. Madagascar* Prelim. Disc. p. xxviii, Tacamacca, *stinking-wood, and ever so many other valuable trees. **1862** E. BALFOUR *Timber Trees India* etc. 77 *Chee Neb* Burm. Stinking Wood. Eng. **1866** *Treas. Bot.*, *Torreya*, a genus of *Taxaceæ*, to which the name of *Stinking Yews has been given.

stinkingly ('stɪŋkɪŋlɪ), *adv.* [f. STINKING *ppl. a.* + -LY[2].]

1. In a stinking manner.

1545 ELYOT *Dict.*, *Rancide*, aduerbe, stynkyngly. **1603** SHAKS. *Meas. for M.* III. ii. 28 Canst thou beleeue thy liuing is a life, So stinkingly depending? **1667** H. MORE *Div. Dial.* II. xviii. (1713) All these would have infinitely a worse Scent to our Souls, that this which you say is so stinkingly evil can have to our Noses. **1727** BAILEY vol. II, *Fulsomly*, stinkingly, loathsomly, nastily.

2. Excessively, extraordinarily. Cf. STINKING *ppl. a.* 1 e. *colloq.*

1906 R. FRY *Let.* 14 Jan. (1972) I. 248 The Raphael..[is] stinkingly pretty and gives me no aesthetic pleasure. **1951** M. KENNEDY *Lucy Carmichael* II. i. 65 He is..frightfully good-looking..and stinkingly rich. **1957** J. BRAINE *Room at Top* xxvi. 207 We got really stinkingly sozzled... I don't believe that I've ever drunk so much before. **1979** N. FREELING *Widow* xxvi. 158 A bungalow, very large and super and stinkingly rich.

stinkingness ('stɪŋkɪŋnɪs). [f. STINKING *ppl. a.* + -NESS.] The quality of being stinking.

1382 WYCLIF *Lev.* xviii. 19 To the womman that suffreth flux of blood thow shalt not goo, ne opne the stynkyngnes of hir. **1631** *Celestina* ix. 106 This [wine] takes away the stinkingnesse of the breath. **1886** *United Ireland* 24 Apr. 4/6 The black, sticky, stinkingness of coal tar.

stinko ('stɪŋkəʊ), *predic. a. slang* (orig. *U.S.*). [f. STINK *v.* + -O[2].] **a.** Of a very low standard; very bad. Cf. STINKEROO. *rare.*

1924 F. SCOTT FITZGERALD *Let.* 20 Dec. (1964) 174, I thought *The White Monkey* was stinko.

b. Intoxicated; blind drunk. Also as quasi-advb., ***stinko drunk***, (joc.) ***paralytico***.

1927 *New Republic* 9 Mar. 72/1 The following is a partial list of words denoting drunkenness now in common use in the United States..stinko. **1936** P. G. WODEHOUSE *Laughing Gas* ix. 92 Are you really such a poor judge of form as to imagine that I am stinko? **1942** E. WAUGH *Put out More Flags* iii. 182 'Darling, she was plastered.' 'Are you sure?' 'My dear, stinko paralytico.' **1954** G. SMITH *Flaw in Crystal* 55 They generally come every night for a week and get stinko every night. **1960** S. H. COURTIER *Gently dust Corpse* ii. 21 We ought to be getting stinko together today. An anniversary, see. **1974** D. RAMSAY *No Cause to Kill* II. 132 Jessie's a lush. Stinko most of her waking time. **1976** *National Observer* (U.S.) 6 Nov. 12/6 Poor unfortunates who get stinko drunk every day on skid row.

c. Over-supplied (*with* money, etc.). *rare.*

1960 *Sunday Express* 28 Feb. 3/3, I should be a stockbroker or someone stinko with money.

† **Stinkomalee** (ˌstɪŋkəmə'liː). *Obs.* Also **Stinkomiles.** [Fanciful combination f. STINK *sb.* or *v.* + TRINCOMALEE.] A disrespectful sobriquet of London University. Hence ˌ**Stincoma'lean** *a.*

1825 T. HOOK in *John Bull* 25 Dec. 413/1 In consequence of the nature of the property [beside a stagnant pond] the first act of the Council has been to give a new and distinguishing name to the Institution—instead of the London College, or Carmarthen-street University, as heretofore, it is in future to be called—*Stinkomalee*! **1827** T. CREEVEY *Let.* 14 Apr. in J. Gore *Creevey Papers* (1963) xiii. 223 The enlightened moderns who are now founding Stinkomiles College at the end of Gower Street. **1844** A. H. CLOUGH *Let.* 24 Nov. (1957) I. 141 It would be far better to be at Stinkomalee (the London University acknowledges that agnomen,..does it not?). **1849** —— *Let.* 15 Feb. in *Ibid.* I. 242, I have accepted the Stincomalean position. **1851** T. ARNOLD *Let.* 14 Sept. (1966) 205, I saw..that you had been made Professor of English at University College, London. Do you still call that institution by the irreverent name of Stinkomalee?

'**stink-pot.** [f. STINK *sb.* + POT *sb.*, after Du. *stinkpot.*]

† **1.** = STINKER 2. *Obs.*

1665 [see STINKER 2].

2. A hand-missile charged with combustibles emitting a suffocating smoke, used in boarding a ship for effecting a diversion while the assailants gain the deck.

1669 STURMY *Mariner's Mag.* I. ii. 20 Ply your Hand-Granadoes and Stink-Pots. **1798** Z. MACAULAY in Visctess. Knutsford *Life & Lett.* (1900) 185 She was prepared with stink-pots for boarding. **1875** KNIGHT *Dict. Mech.*, *Stink-pot*, a vessel used by the Chinese and Malay pirates to throw on board a vessel to suffocate the crew. **1906** *Westm. Gaz.* 24 Mar. 10/2 A piratical fleet closed round her, threw a stinkpot into the engine-room, and overpowered the crew.

Comb. **1704** SWIFT *Batt. Bks.* Misc. (1711) 242 Paracelsus brought a Squadron of Stink-Pot-Flingers from the snowy Mountains of Rhœtia.

transf. **1748** SMOLLETT *Rod. Random* xi, I'll teach you to empty your stink-pots on me. **1913** J. G. FRAZER *Golden Bough* VI. *Scapegoat* iii. 133 The girls discharge their stink-pots in the faces of their adversaries.

fig. **1738** WARBURTON *Div. Legat.* I. Ded. p. xxii, Your Scurrilities, those Stink-pots of your offensive War. **1778** WARNER in Jesse *Selwyn & Contemp.* (1844) III. 317 Venice is a stink-pot, charged with the very virus of hell! **1807** J. KING (*title*) The Beauties of the Edinburgh Review, alias, the Stink-pot of Literature.

3. A sailor's name for a petrel. Cf. STINKER 5. Also, in S. Africa, applied to the Sooty Albatross, *Phœbetria fuliginosa*, and the Cape hen, *Majaqueus æquinoctialis* (Pettman *Africanderisms*).

1865 *Hardwicke's Sci.-Gossip* 1 Oct. 239/1 The Stink-pot of sailors is the Black Petrel (*Procellaria æquinoctialis*, L.).

4. A name given to the musk turtle, *Cinosternum odoratum* or *Aromochelys odorata*.

1844 J. E. GRAY *Catal. Tortoises* etc. *Brit. Mus.* 34 The Stink-Pot. Kinosternon odoratum. **1903** *Nature* 1 Oct. 531/2 Fourteen Stink-pot Terrapins.

5. a. A term of abuse for a person or (*rarely*) a thing. *slang.*

1854 T. WOOLNER *Let.* 4 Oct. in *Geo. Eliot Lett.* (1954) II. 176, I will not..display the filthy contaminations of these hideous satyrs and smirking moralists—..stink pots of humanity. **1916** JOYCE *Portrait of Artist* v. 230 Go away from here, he said rudely. Go away, you stink-pot. **1928** D. H. LAWRENCE *Let.* Aug. (1932) 744 Whether I shall have the strength to put my nose into that stink-pot of an island [*sc.* England], I don't know. **1948** D. BALLANTYNE *Cunninghams* xx. 267 They can call me miserable old stinkpot. **1959** I. & P. OPIE *Lore & Lang. Schoolch.* ix. 155 These syllables are used..to turn a verb or adjective into a descriptive noun, as: ..fuss-pot, stink-pot, [etc.]. **1973** R. LUDLUM *Matlock Paper* xii. 112 *Nowhere* does your signing this little stinkpot say you *agree* to retire from the scene.

b. A machine which emits foul exhaust fumes: esp. a truck or motor-boat. *slang.*

1972 B. GARFIELD *Line of Succession* (1974) II. 155 Mario had..a hatred of stinkpot powerboats. **1977** H. FAST *Immigrants* I. 55 They're gone now, all of them [*sc.* fishing-boats with sails]. Nothing but stinkpots—I'm sorry—oil burners. **1978** D. BAGLEY *Flyaway* xxi. 179 The truck broke through..and it killed them... Lousy stinkpots! Never have liked them except when I'm in a hurry.

'**stinkstone.** *Min.* [f. STINK *sb.* + STONE *sb.* After G. *stinkstein*, which is sometimes used in Eng.] A name given to various limestones which give out a fetid odour on being scratched or struck.

1804 R. JAMESON *Min.* I. 521 Stink Stone... Colour is wood brown. **1823** W. PHILLIPS *Introd. Min.* (ed. 3) 156 Swinestone, or Stinkstone,..gives out a strong fetid odour when scraped. [**1856** PAGE *Adv. Text-bk. Geol.* xii. 141 Others, when rubbed..emit a highly fetid odour, and are well known as 'stinksteins' and 'swinestones'.] **1859** BARTLETT *Dict. Amer.* (ed. 2) 451 *Stinkstone*, swinestone, a variety of carbonate of lime, which emits a fetid odor on being struck.

'**stinkweed.** [f. STINK *sb.* + WEED *sb.* Cf. WFlem. *stinkwied*, the stinking camomile.]

a. The cruciferous plant *Diplotaxis muralis*.

1793 in Britten *Old Country Words* (E.D.S.) 110 The farmers here [Kingsgate, Kent]..have, on account of its very offensive smell, given it the name of stink-weed. *a* **1824** HOLDICH *Ess. Weeds Agric.* (1825) 57 Sand Mustard, Isle of Thanet Stink-weed (*Sinapis muralis*). **1884** W. MILLER *Plant-n.* 130.

b. *U.S.* The Thorn Apple, *Datura Stramonium*.

1804 C. B. BROWN tr. *Volney's View Soil U.S.* 69 *note*, These banks, and all the slopes along the Ohio, abound with the stramoneum (stink-weed), which is said to have been brought hither accidentally from Virginia. **1859** BARTLETT *Dict. Amer.* (ed. 2) 219 Jamestown weed... The Thorn Apple (*Datura stramonium*). Its Northern name is Stinkweed.

c. Any of several other plants with an unpleasant smell.

1932 [see *khaki bos, bush* s.v. KHAKI D.]. **1954** *Sun* (Baltimore) 4 June 21/1 Due to the fact that its leaves, when crushed, are very disagreeable to get next to, the *ailanthus* is also known as 'stinkweed'. **1970** J. H. GRAY *Boy from Winnipeg* 153 My job was to graze the cattle slowly..keeping them out of the stinkweed which, I was warned, spoiled the butter.

'**stinkwood.** [f. STINK *sb.* + WOOD *sb.*, partly after Du. *stinkhout.*] A name given esp. in Australia and South Africa to various trees the wood of which has an unpleasant odour; the wood of any of these trees.

1731 MEDLEY *Kolben's Cape Gd. Hope* II. 260 The Stink-wood tree grows to the size of an oak. **1827** HELLYER in *Bischoff's Van Diemen's Land* (1832) 175 The timber in this district I found to be principally myrtle, sassafras, and stinkwood. **1866** *Treas. Bot.* 1100/2 *Stinkwood*, the useful wood of *Oreodaphne bullata*, which has a most unpleasant odour lasting for a long time. Also that of *Fœtidia mauritiana* and *Zieria macrophylla*. **1882** J. SMITH *Dict. Pop. Names Plants* 240 Laurel, Cape of Good Hope (*Laurus bullata*)..well known in the Cape Colony as Stinkwood. **1898** *Daily News* 13 May 7/3 From South Africa come feather Court dresses, a stinkwood walking stick [etc.]. **1898** MORRIS *Austral Eng.* 439 *Stinkwood*... In Tasmania..the timber of *Zieria smithii*, Andr., N.O. *Rutaceæ*.

stinky ('stɪŋkɪ), *a.* (*sb.*). [f. STINK *sb.* + -Y[1].] = STINKING *ppl. a.* Also as *sb.*

1888 KIPLING *Plain Tales* 238 Now we've got the [joss-]sticks mixed with a lot of glue, and they..smell stinky. **1949** N. R. NASH *Young & Fair* I. ii. 17 What if you had a stinky summer? **1958** S. A. GRAU *Hard Blue Sky* v. 317 'And he does smell,' she said, 'phew.'.. 'Go on, stinky,' Annie told him. **1966** L. KIRSTEIN *Rhymes & More Rhymes of PFC* 163 Stinky shorts, dead shoes, sodden shirt. **1972** D. RAMSAY *Little Murder Music* 190, I think human nature is pretty stinky. **1982** *Observer* 25 Apr. 7/6 To get where he is and stay there he must have had to do some pretty stinky things. His is a pretty stinky country, after all.

stint (stɪnt), *sb.*[1] Forms: α. 4–6 **stynt**, (5 **styntt**), 5–6 **stynte**, (6 **styntte**), 5–7 **stinte**, 4– **stint**. β. 4– **stent**. [f. STINT *v.* In certain senses this sb. seems to have coalesced with the etymologically unrelated STENT *sb.*[1] Cf. the similar confusion noted under STINT *v.*]

I. The action of the verb STINT.

† **1. a.** Cessation of action or motion, pause, stay. Phrase, ***to make a stint***: to stop. ***withouten stint***, ***but stint*** (*Sc.*): without stopping, unceasingly. *Obs.*

α. *a* **1300** *Cursor M.* 12977 þat warlau him in armes hint, And bar him forth wit-vten stint. *c* **1330** R. BRUNNE *Chron. Wace* (Rolls) 6815 Made þey neuere stynt ne stal Tyl þey come to þe Romayns wal. **1375** BARBOUR *Bruce* II. 140 And syne, for-owtyn langir stynt, The horss he sadylt hastely. **1430–40** LYDG. *Bochas* VI. i. (1554) 144 b, Whan Fortune had said her wil.. Made a stint, and sobrely stode still, Iohn Bochas sate & heard [etc.]. *c* **1470** HENRY *Wallace* x. 286 Fra forgyt steyll the fyr flew out but stynt. **1576** FLEMING *Panopl. Epist.* Epitome A ij, As of Trees,.. Birdes, Beastes, yea and Men, there is a degree in growing, a stint or staying, and a diminishing. **1594** MARLOWE *Dido* IV. ii, And I will.. drop out both mine eyes in drisling teares, Before my sorrowes tide haue any stint. **1613** JACKSON *Creed* I. 19 True Christian beliefe admits no stint of growth in this life, but still comes nearer and nearer to that euidencie of knowledge.

β. *a* **1300** *Cursor M.* 17700 And bi þe hand þan he me hent, And forth me broght, wit-vten stent. *c* **1400** *Sc. Trojan War* II. 578 After þe forme of sacrament Swore in old tyme wy^{t}-outen stent.

† **b.** *Hunting.* A check or stop in the running of hounds owing to the loss of the scent; chiefly in the phrases ***to be on (a) stint***, ***to fall upon stint***. *Obs.*

c **1400** *Master of Game* (MS. Digby 182) i, The other rennyth goynge aboute and then abideth, wherfore the houndes ben þe ofter on stint. *Ibid.* xxxiii, It were goode to assigne somme of þe horsemen amonge þe relayes to helpe þe more redely þe houndes, if þei falle vpon stynte. *Ibid.*, If so be þat þe houndes haue enboysed, or be ouershete, or þat þe be on a stynte be any oþer wyse, what hunter.. þat perceueth it first, shulde blowe þe stynte.

2. Limitation, restriction.

†**a.** with respect to mode of action. *Obs.*

1593 NASHE *Christ's T.* 47 Whereas God stinted him, what Trees and fruites he should eate on, and goe no further, hee [the Serpent] entist him to breake the bondes of that stint. **1610** BP. HALL *Apol. Brownists* xxxvii. 93 If stinting our prayers be a fault..it is well that the Lords prayer it selfe beareth vs company... To denie that it may be vsed intirely in our Sauiours wordes, is..a fanaticall curiousnesse: yeelde one and all; for if the matter be more diuine, yet the stint is no lesse faulty. **1614** —— *Contempl.* II. VII. 318 It had beene as easie for the Angell to strike Balaam, as to stand in his way ..: But euen the good Angels haue their stints, in their executions. **1633** HERBERT *Temple, Praise* (No. 3) iv. 152 Angels must have their joy, Devils their rod, the sea his shore, The windes their stint.

b. with reference to amount, quantity, or degree. ***without stint***: with no fixed limit of amount, unstintedly.

In this phrase the sb. now tends to be interpreted in sense 2c.

1651 HOBBES *Leviathan* I. xvi. 82 Every man..owning all the actions the Representer doth, in case they give him Authority without stint. **1675** —— *Odyss.* (1677) 120 The gods do call it moly, And gather it, who have no stint of might. **1797** BURKE *Regic. Peace* iii. Wks. 1808 VIII. 420 Its armies, its navies, are given to them without stint or restriction. **1844** DISRAELI *Coningsby* VII. ii, Each poured forth his mind without stint. **1876** J. G. HOLLAND *Seven Oaks* xix, His wife and children had money lavished on them without stint. **1888** BRYCE *Amer. Commw.* II. II. xlvii. 212 But in all Congress may exercise without stint its power to override the statutes passed by a Territorial legislature.

c. Excessive restriction in the supply of anything, esp. of the necessaries or comforts of life; the condition of being kept scantily supplied.

1820 SCOTT *Fam. Lett.* 26 July, It can never be my wish.. that you should feel any stint. **1843** LYTTON *Last Bar.* I. v, Of furniture there was a woeful stint. **1863** GEO. ELIOT *Romola* I. ix, He..to whom life had hitherto had some of the stint and subjection of a school. **1881** EMMA R. PITMAN *Mission Life in Greece* 285 There was no need for stint where supplies were always at hand.

3. The putting a mare to the stallion. Cf. STINT *v.*

1764 *Museum Rust.* II. lxxix. 276 Inn-keepers, or jockeys, who can..by publishing a high premium for a stint, make the horse in their possession very famous.

II. Limited or fixed amount.

4. a. An allotted amount or measure; a prescribed or customary portion; an allowance. Now *rare* or *Obs.* (exc. as in b). Cf. sense 7.

α. *c* **1485** *Digby Myst.* (1882) II. (*Mary Magd.*) 1807, I gyff yow be-syde yower styntt, Eche of yow a marke for yower wage. **1555** WATREMAN *Fardle Facions* I. vi. 84 Thei come to the Graues of their kyndreade, and there when they haue praied their stinte, laye them doune..to slepe. **1574** T. NEWTON *Health Mag.* Diij, So that the thyng it self be neither ouercharged with to much, nor yet debarred from that stinte and sufficiencie that is needefull. **1570–6** LAMBARDE *Peramb. Kent* 125 Fiue and twentie were continually to watche and warde within the Castell for their seuerall stintes of time. **1620** SHELTON *2nd Pt. Don Quix.* lix. 398 The Beasts hee carried to the Stable, and gaue them their stint. *a* **1623** FLETCHER *Love's Cure* II. i, Put me to a certain stint Sir, allow me but a red herring a day. **1633** BP. HALL *Hard Texts, O.T.* 15, I will therefore set him a stint of yeares, before his common destruction. **1663** PEPYS *Diary* 24 Dec., I hope before I go I shall set myself such a stint as I may not forget myself. **1690** DRYDEN *Amphitryon* II. ii, Take back your sev'nty years, (the stint of Life). **1704** SWIFT *T. Tub* v. 122 Forty or fifty Pages of Preface and Dedication, (which is the usual Modern Stint). **1791** COWPER *Odyss.* VIII. 477 Wisdom beyond the common stint I mark In this our guest. **1809** MALKIN *Gil Blas* VIII. v. (Rtldg.) 287 There was..a scanty breakfast set out,..I never knew what it was to exceed this stint during the day.

β. **1447** BOKENHAM *Seyntys, Eliz.* (Roxb.) 277 Thow she.. Constreynyd wer to bedde yet in no degre Tyl hyr stent wer seruyd [*sc.* the omitted orisons were said] she ne wolde slepe.

b. ***one's stint***: an amount which one has resolved not to exceed.

1603–26 BRETON *Poste Mad Lett.* (Grosart) 9/1 For aparell, I will keepe my stint, and care for no fond fashion. **1683** H. SAVILE *Let.* 3 *May* in M. Morrison *Catal. Autographs* (1892) VI. 80 There I lost last night my twenty guinnyes, wch is my stint. **1732** SWIFT *Let. to Gay* 4 May, My stint [of wine] in company is a pint at noon, and half as much as night. **1824** MISS MITFORD *Village* I. 230 Three rubbers were our stint; as we were often game and game in the last before victory declared itself. **1846** MRS. GORE *Eng. Char.* (1852) 60, I can't afford half-crowns every day. A shilling is my stint for such jobs.

†**c.** ***to live at stint***: to live at a fixed rate of expenditure. *Obs.*

1681 OTWAY *Soldiers Fortune* IV. i, I do not enjoy my self with that freedom I wou'd do, there is no more pleasure in living at stint, then there is in living alone.

5. a. A measure, rate, gauge of amount, price, size, etc. fixed by authority. Chiefly in the phrases ***to set***, etc. ***at one stint***, ***to appoint, set a stint***.

α. **1485** in *10th Rep. Hist. MSS. Comm.* App. v. 320 In case that hydes come to an heigher or a lougher price than they bene nowe, that then the Maire..shal sett the saide crafte att one stynte accordynge to rayson. **1568** GRAFTON *Chron.* II. 168 The standard of the ounce was euer at one stynt, although the valuation of coynes altered. *a* **1600** HOOKER *Eccl. Pol.* VII. xxiii. §11 Convenient it was to provide that there might be a moderate stint appointed to measure their expenses by. **1601** J. WHEELER *Treat. Comm.* 57 There is a stint, and reasonable proportion allotted, and set..what quantite..euery man may ship out. **1611** CORYAT *Crudities* 137 But belike there is a limitation of the summe that is owed; for that if the summe..be aboue the stint, he shall not be released. **1715** N. BLUNDELL *Diary* (1895) 133 Severall Stints were set for the better Regulating the Affairs of the Parish. **1794** A. YOUNG *Agric. Suffolk* 78 A child's stint..for braiding nets..is four-pence a day.

β. **1606** HOLLAND *Suetonius* 54 The number of Senatours growing still to a shameful and confused company..he reduced to the auncient stent [L. *modum*].

fig. **1534** MORE *Dial. agst. Trib.* I. Wks. 1152/2 Both for release and reward, tempored after such rate as his.. wysedome shal se conuenient for vs: wherof our blynde mortality can not here imagine nor deuyse the stynt. **1534** —— *Treat. Passion* Wks. 1290/2 God..limited of his owne wisedome and goodnes, after what rate and stynt, the commoditie therof shoulde be employed vppon vs.

†**b.** Usual or customary measure. *Obs.*

1664 POWER *Exp. Philos.* II. 90 The Quicksilver will fall down to its wonted pitch and stint of 29. inches. **1733** CHEYNE *Eng. Malady* III. iv. (1734) 354 My Appetite and Digestion return'd to their usual Stint towards my new Food. **1747** J. RELPH *Misc. P.* 121 The snow has left the fells and fled..And to their stint the becks are fawn.

6. a. The limited number of cattle, according to kind, allotted to each definite portion into which pasture or common land is divided, or to each person entitled to the right of common pasturage; also, the right of pasturage according to the fixed rate. Also, a portion of land allotted for pasturing a limited number of sheep or cattle.

α. **1569** in W. H. Turner *Select. Rec. Oxford* (1880) 327 Portemeade: Rate and Stynte of Cattell. *Ibid.*, Stynt to be kept for Cattell in Portmead... The Baillies..shall yerely oversee that every man shall kepe his stynt of beastes in Port meade. **1597** *Pain Roll of Manor of Scawby, Lincs.* (MS.), None within this Lordshippe shall keepe but for every Oxgange 40 sheepe..accordinge to the old Stinte, in paine of x^s^. **1687** in *Croke's Case of Otmoor* (1831) 37 And if any take in joicement sheep, they shall not exceed the number of their stint in the townships. **1785** *Woodmansey Inclosure Act* 2 Proprietors..enjoy common of pasture..by a certain determinate stint. **1844** *Min. Evid. Sel. Comm. Commons' Inclosure* 26 By a stint, I mean the right of pasturage for one animal, or for a certain number of animals, according to age, size, and capability of eating. **1849** *Gloss. Provincial Words Teesdale, Co. Durham* 125 *Stint*, a limited number of cattle gaits. **1869** *Spectator* 17 Apr. 472/1 It was desirable to utilize ..that portion of the soil of England which was lying unenclosed, and subject to all manner of rights of common, turbary, stints, and the like. **1904** in *Eng. Dial. Dict.* V. 768/1 The marshes of Skinburness, &c.,..were not enclosed in 1811 as were the commons, but were divided into stints, 400 being made out of 1,008 acres. **1954** M. BERESFORD *Lost Villages* vi. 204 Abandoned cornfields tumble first to grass and weed... The flocks which had been stinted could now have their stint enlarged. **1975** *Country Life* 11 Dec. 1676/2 As winter sets in, the salt marshes on the English side of the Solway will be grazed by..hill sheep from the Lake District. The 'stints' (pasturage for sheep and cattle) are owned by the Solway-side farmers.

β. **1437** *Dunfermline Reg.* (Bannatyne Club) 285 The land liand betuix the estir oxgang and the orchard..[be] comon to bath the partis. Alsua bath þe partis sel kepe lauchful stent and noth excede. **1842** *Q. Jrnl. Agric.* XII. 52 In the oldest plantations, his young cattle were going to four times the stents the land had ever kept before it was so planted.

b. *gen.* Any kind of limitation of right of pasturage.

1766 BLACKSTONE *Comm.* II. iii. 34 All these species, of pasturable common, may be and usually are limited as to number and time; but there are also commons without stint, and which last all the year.

7. a. An allotted portion of work; a definite task; a period of time spent on a particular job; a turn (at doing something). ***to work by stint*** (see quot. 1891).

α. *a* **1530** HEYWOOD *Weather* (Brandl) 447 No water haue we to grynde at any stynt. *c* **1566** *Merie Tales of Skelton* in *Skelton's Wks.* (1843) I. p. lxvi, They wanted of their mele, and complained..that they could not make their stint of breade. **1683** MOXON *Mech. Exerc., Printing* xxiv. ¶15 The First [Press-man] takes his choice to Pull or Beat the agreed stint first. **1749** BERKELEY in Fraser *Life* viii. (1871) 320 Their stint, on account of health, is an hour and half a day for painting. **1803** T. NETHERTON in *Naval Chron.* XV. 314 The Caulkers..are employed by stint on new work. **1866** CARLYLE *Remin.* (1881) I. 285 Here..I..took to doing 'German Romance' as my daily work, 'ten pages daily' my stint. **1891** *Labour Commission* Gloss. *s.v.*, If a man is engaged to work for eight hours, and a certain quantity of work given him to perform in that time, he is said to be working by stint. **1904** KIPLING *Traffics & Discov.* 369 They were letting in the water for the evening stint at Robert's Mill. **1955** S. WILSON *Man in Gray Flannel Suit* (1956) xxii. 170 After college had come a brief stint in the Army. **1957** *Economist* 21 Dec. 1073/1 No really outstanding executives for private business have ever been ready to take on a stint in the hardest jobs that industry in this country has to offer. **1965** *Listener* 24 June 933/2 This is the end of my stint for *The Listener*. **1976** H. WILSON *Governance of Britain* vii. 130 His three or four weeks' compulsory stint as 'Minister in Attendance' at Balmoral. **1978** S. BRILL *Teamsters* viii. 307 He..then served a stint as a railroad brakeman.

β. **1773** R. FERGUSSON *Farmer's Ingle* ix, Yet frae the russet lap the spindle plays Her e'ening stent reels she as weel's the lave. **1789** ROSS *Helenore* I. (ed. 3) 49 Their stent [1768 task] was mair than they cou'd well mak out. **1844** H. STEPHENS *Bk. Farm* III. 754 On shifting the workers from one stent to another. **1887** *Kentish Gloss.*, *Stent*, a word used by the oyster dredgers in North Kent, to denote that amount or number of oysters, fixed by the rules of their association, which they may dredge in one day. **1898** E. P. EVANS *Evol. Ethics* v. 176 Spinoza had to secure his subsistence by grinding his stent of lenses before he could gratify his love of philosophy.

b. *Mining.* (See quots.)

α. **1850** OGILVIE, *Stint*... In coal mines, a measure of work two yards long by one broad, which each miner clears before he removes to another place. **1883** GRESLEY *Gloss. Coal-mining, Stint.* 1. (Midland.) A measure of length by which colliers hole and cut coal... 2. (Gloucestershire.) A certain number of trams filled per man per day. 3. (South Staffordshire.) A collier's day's work. **1888** *Daily News* 5 Oct. 2/5 The minimum wages was fixed at 3s. 4d. per day or stint for thick-coal men.

β. **1864** *Daily Tel.* 26 Oct., What is termed a day does not represent a day's work..but a certain cubical quantity of coal known as a 'stent'.

†**c.** As advb. accusative: In fulfilment of an appointed task. *Obs.*

1618 R. BOLTON *Florus* II. vi. (1636) 98 That most dangerous Captaine having..markt..where..the Easterne winde blew stint as it were [L. *quasi ad constitutum*].

8. Prescribed, destined, or customary limit.

†**a.** of spatial extension or progress. Also, destination or goal of a journey. *Obs.*

α. **1601** HOLLAND *Pliny* v. ix. I. 98 The ordinarie heighth of it is sixteene cubites. Vnder that gage the waters overflow not all. Above that stint, they are a let and hinderance. **1618** RALEGH *Rem.* (1644) 114 You are now imbarked in your final voyage, and not far from the stint and period of your course. **1690** LOCKE *Hum. Und.* II. xiii. §5 This Power of repeating, or doubling any Idea we have of any distance,..without being ever able to come to any stop or stint.

β. **1509** BARCLAY *Shyp of Folys* 18 If thou be dampned, than art thou at thy stent. **1563** SACKVILLE *Induct. Mirr. Mag.* vi, Erythius that in the cart fyrste went Had euen nowe attaynde his iourneyes stent.

†**b.** of duration. *Obs.*

1587 T. HUGHES *Misfort. Arthur* I. ii. 75 *Fron.* How can you then attempt a fresh offence? *Guen.* Who can appoint a stint to her offence? **1596** SPENSER *Astrophel, Mourn. Thestylis* 51 No humble speech nor mone, may moue the fixed stint Of destinie or death. **1620** QUARLES *Feast for Worms* viii. G4b, The stint of Niniuey was forty dayes, To cry for grace, and turne from euill wayes. **1633** BP. HALL *Hard Texts, O.T.* 144 God keeps the stint of their life secret from them. *a* **1659** BP. BROWNRIG *Serm.* (1674) I. iv. 62 Satan set a stint to Job's suffering. **1693** EVELYN *De La Quint. Compl. Gard., Refl. Agric.* 68 Every Plant has a peculiar, determinate, certain, and infallible Stint or Term, for the Beginning and Duration of its Action.

†**c.** of expansion or increase. *Obs.*

1598–1603 STOW *Surv.* (1908) II. 205 The number of the Citizens..farre exceedeth proportion of Hippodamus, which appoynted 10000. and of others which haue set downe other numbers, as meete stintes in theyr opinions to bee well gouerned. **1606** BRYSKETT *Civil Life* 192 For that mans desires had their determinate stint, wheras Alexanders increased stil, the more he enlarged his dominions. **1645** MILTON *Colast.* 12 A man..puft up with no luck at all, above the stint of his capacity. **1729** BUTLER *Serm.* Wks. 1874 II. 140 Every one of our passions and affections hath its natural stint and bound.

9. (See quot.)

1792 G. CARTWRIGHT *Jrnl. Labrador* I. Gloss. p. xv, *Stint*, the dam made by beavers across a stream, to raise the water to a height convenient for their purpose.

10. *attrib.* and *Comb.*, as ***stint allowance***; **stintholder**, a holder of a stint of pasture; **stint-holer** *Mining* (see quot.); †**stint-key** (? *nonce-wd.*), a key which checks the supply (of ale); in quot. *fig.*

a **1814** *Sailor's Ret.* I. vii. in *New Brit. Theatre* II. 328 British sailors shall find there's no *stint allowance at Growl-Hall. **1894** *Carlisle Patriot* 4 May 3/7 (Cumbld. Gloss.) The annual meeting of *stintholders..was held at the Wheatsheaf Inn. **1891** *Labour Commission* Gloss., **Stint-holer*, the man who undercuts the coal by 'piece'. **1827** C. WEBBE *Harvest-Home* iv, And the quaint and jocund tale Takes the *stint-key from the ale.

stint (stɪnt), *sb.*[2] Also 5–6 stynt(e, 6 styntt. *β.* 6 stent. [Of obscure origin.] A common name for any of the smaller Sandpipers (genus *Tringa*), esp. the Dunlin. Also a provincial name for the Sanderling (*Calidris arenaria*).

α. **1466** *Introniz. Abp. Nevell* in Leland *Collect.* (1774) II. 6 Quayles and Styntes rost. **1519** in *Archæologia* XXV. 422, iij Plovers, iij Spowes, & iij Stynts. **1531–2** *Durh. Household Bk.* (Surtees) 129, 6 dd stynts, 12 d. 1½ dd dunlyngs, 6d. **1622** DRAYTON *Poly-olb.* xxv. 339 For near this batning Isle [Axholme], in me is to be seen..The Puet, Godwin, Stint, the palate that allure. **1688, 1774, 1837** [see PURRE[1]]. **1893** in Cozens-Hardy *Broad Norf.* 49 There's a rare mess of stints on Breydon sometimes. **1902** C. J. CORNISH *Naturalist on Thames* 245 Canvey Island... Stints..were flitting everywhere on the mud and ooze.

β. **1579** Stent [see STAMPINE].

b. With distinguishing prefix (see quots.).

1843 YARRELL *Brit. Birds* II. 643 The Little Sandpiper, or Little Stint..goes through seasonal changes of colour in its plumage. **1848** C. A. JOHNS *Week at Lizard* 331 Temminck's Stint (*Tringa Temminckii*).—Very rare. **1898** MORRIS *Austral Eng.* 439 The Australian species are Curlew Stint *Tringa subarquata*, Gmel. Little Stint *T. ruficollis*. Sharp-tailed Stint *T. acuminata*, Horsf.

stint (stɪnt), *v.* Forms: *α.* 1 **styntan**, 3 *Ormin* **stinntenn**, 3–5 **stunt**, (3 **stunte**, 5 **stonte**), 4–6 **stynte**, **stinte**, (4 **styntt**, 5 **stynttе**), 4–7 **stynt**, 3– **stint**; *β.* 3–7 **stente**, 4– **stent.** *Pa. t.* (contracted forms); *α.* 3 **stunte**, 4 **stinte**, 4– 5 **stynt(e**, **stint**; *β.* 3–5 **stent(e**. *Pa. pple.* (contracted forms); *α.* 3 **stint**, 4 **stunt**, **i-stint**, **y-stynt**, **i-stynt**, **stynte**, 4–6 **stynt**, 5 **stinte**; *β.* 5 **stente**. [OE. *styntan* to blunt, dull; the simple vb. occurs only once (in *Corpus Gl.*, rendering L. *hebetare*), but cf. the compounds *ástyntan*, to blunt, dull, to check, stop (ME. ASTINT *v.*), *ætstyntan* to blunt (teeth), make ineffective (ME. ATSTUNT *v.*), *forstyntan* to blunt. The OE. verb corresponds formally to OScandinavian **stynta* (MSw. *stynta*, OIcel. *stytta*) to shorten:—OTeut. type **stuntjan*, f. **stunto-* adj. (OE. *stunt* stupid, foolish, MHG. *stunz* stumpy, MSw. *stunt-er*, OIcel. *stutt-r* short, scanty: cf. STUNT *a.* and *v.*). It is uncertain whether the ME. and mod.E. senses of the vb. are developed from unrecorded senses in OE., or are due to Scandinavian influence.

In certain uses this vb. closely approaches in meaning the etymologically unrelated STENT *v.*[1] Apparently some confusion has taken place between the two verbs, and as the phonetic variants *stent*, *stint* are common to both, it is sometimes doubtful to which verb a particular use belongs.]

I. To cut short, cease, stop.

1. *intr.* To cease action; to leave off (doing something); to desist, forbear. Now only *arch.* and *dial.* Const. †*of*, *in* †*fro*, and *to* with inf.

α. *c* **1200** ORMIN 12844 þatt menn þa shollden blinnenn, & standdenn stille, & stinntenn þa To þewwtenn Godd tatt wise. *a* **1225** *Ancr. R.* 202 þe ueorðe hweolp is Idelnesse: þet is, hwo se stunt mid alle. *a* **1300** *Cursor M.* 1740 Of his precheing þan con he stint. *Ibid.* 26059 If he ne had of his folis stint. *c* **1305** *Land Cokayne* 99 þer beþ briddes.. þat stinteþ neuer by har miȝt Miri to sing dai and niȝt. **13..** *Bonaventura's Medit.* 878 Fro wepyng she ne myȝt stynte no stounde. *c* **1369** CHAUCER *Dethe Blaunche* 1213 With sorweful herte.. styntynge in my tale For ferde. *c* **1420** *Chron. Vilod.* 4096 Bot euer þey song & dauncede yliche fast & nolde not stonte þere for no-mone. *c* **1460** *Oseney Reg.* 12 That þat parte þe which my modur holdeth, whenne so euer she stynteth to holde hit, þat hit come in to þe lordeship of the church. **1470–85** MALORY *Arthur* I. xv. 56 He stynte not tyl he had slayne xx knyȝtes. *c* **1520** SKELTON *Magnyf.* 2188 Holde thy hande, dawe, of thy dagger, and stynt of thy dyn. **1536** BELLENDEN *Cron. Scot.* (1821) II. 423 Als sone as the Inglismen wer cumin to this hill, thay stintit of thair fleing. **1556** ROBINSON *More's Utopia* (1895) p. xcix, But I wil neuer stynte, nor rest, vntil I haue gotte the full and exacte knowledge hereof. **1576** GASCOIGNE *Steele Gl.* (Arb.) 67 Art thou a seruing man? then serue againe, And stint to steale as common souldiours do. **1592** SHAKS. *Rom. & Jul.* I. iii. 48 Pretty foole it stinted, and said I. *a* **1650** *K. John & Bishop* viii. in Child *Ballads* I. 411 And thirdly, tell mee or euer I stinte, What is the thing, bishopp, that I doe thinke. **1677** W. HUGHES *Man of Sin* II. ii. 25 The strange Amazing Proofs made use of by them! But it is flatly necessary, that I should bound myself:.. I will stint at Twelve. **1818** SCOTT *Hrt. Midl.* x, 'Whisht, Effie,' said her sister; 'our father's coming out o' the byre.'—The damsel stinted in her song. **1819** SHELLEY *Peter Bell* VI. xxiv. 3 Their fierce successors, who.. would neither stint nor stick Our flesh from off our bones to pick. **1869** BROWNING *Ring & Bk.* VIII. 240, I see him strain on tip-toe, soar and pour Eloquence out, nor stay, nor stint at all. **1881** *Leicestersh. Gloss.* s.v., Coom, yo' stint, or oi'll meek ye!

β. *a* **1300** *Cursor M.* 3842 Abute hir hals þan he hir hent, And thris he kyst hir ar he stent [*other texts* stint]. **13..** *Guy Warw.* 849 Of rideing wil þai neuer stent To þai com to þe turnament. *c* **1386** CHAUCER *Clerk's T.* 678 But nathelees, for ernest ne for game He of his crueel purpos nolde stente. *c* **1470** HARDING *Chron.* XXXIII. v, For whiche [his death] his people of wepyng coulde not stent. **1563** SACKVILLE *Induct. Mirr. Mag.* xxxii, To her selfe oft would she [Remorse] tell Her wretchednes, and cursing neuer stent To sob and sigh. *c* **1590** J. STEWART *Poems* (S.T.S.) II. 42 O gif thy luifers knew, thay vold not stent To giwe the ayde. **1785** R. FORBES *Ulysses Answ. Ajax* lxxiii, I.. Syne took his coach, an' milk-white staigs, 'Ere ever I wad stent.

†**b.** with pr. pple. *Obs.*

c **1430** *Pilgr. Lyf Manhode* III. xliii. (1869) 159 Whan the first hath stinte etinge.. that oother.. seith he wole ete also. **1518** H. WATSON *Hist. Oliver of Castile* (Roxb.) D 4, In suche sorowe he neuer stynted rydynge tyll that he came to a lytell vyllage. **1565** COOPER *Thesaurus* s.v. *Comprimo*, *Lachrymas comprimere*, to stint weepyng.

†**c.** To cease to speak *of*. *Obs.*

c **1450** *Merlin* x. 145 But now stenteth the tale of hem, and returneth to speke of the vij kynges. *Ibid.* xv. 253 Of hem I shall stinte, and tell of the parliament that kynge Brangue heilde.

†**2.** Of processes, conditions, impersonal agencies: To cease, abate, come to an end. *Obs.*

α. *c* **1205** LAY. 31891 þe quale gon to stunte. *a* **1300** *Cursor M.* 6026 þe tres it [the tempest] brake, þe gresse it brint, At þe land iessen it stint. **1340–70** *Alex. & Dind.* 91 Men sey wel þat þe see seseþ & stinteþ, But whan þe wind on þe watur þe wawus arereþ. *c* **1340** HAMPOLE *Pr. Consc.* 1630 Bot at þe last, when þair lyfe sall stynt, þan sall all ioy be fra þam tynt. *c* **1374** CHAUCER *Boeth.* II. pr. v. (1868) 45 Certis þan is þilke moneye precious, whan it.. styntep to ben had by vsage of large ȝeuyng. *c* **1375** *Cursor M.* 23172 (Fairf.) Ȝour sorou salle neuer stint. *c* **1400** *Pilgr. Sowle* (Caxton) II. lxv. (1859) 59 Hit is ful hye tyme, that the discencion of you bothe stynte, and take an ende. *c* **1460** *Towneley Myst.* i. 161 We mon haue payne that neuer shall stynt. **1589** GREENE *Menaphon* (Arb.) 28 Streaming teares that neuer stint. **1628** WITHER *Brit. Rememb.* II. 489 Nor can I finde a reason how it [the plague] stinted, Or how our totall ruine was prevented. **1681** W. ROBERTSON *Phraseol. Gen.* s.v. *Stint*, Weeping stinteth: *arescit lachryma*.

β. *c* **1374** CHAUCER *Troylus* III. 1238 Right so Criseyde whan hire drede stente, Opned hire herte and tolde hym hire entente. *c* **1384** —— *H. Fame* I. 221 Ther saw I how the tempest stent. *c* **1470** HENRY *Wallace* IX. 239 Weyll bruk thow it! all thus stentis our stryff. **1530** *Dial. betw. Gentl. & Husbandman* 452 (Arb.) 147 Their furious malice never stentyd till they had the lightes quenchyd. **1587** T. HUGHES *Misfort. Arthur* I. Chorus 23 In Brytain warres and discord will not stent: Till Vther's line and offspring quite be spent.

3. To cease moving, pause in a journey, to halt, stop, stand still. †Also, to turn aside from pursuit, to stay in conflict. *Obs.*

α. *c* **1290** *Becket* 1118 in *S. Eng. Leg.* 138 Fiue and twenti mile he wende.. Are he stunte in anie stude. *c* **1290** *Magdalene* 187 ibid. 467 In one olde porche hy stunten al þat nyȝht. *a* **1300** *Cursor M.* 4321 For bettur it es bi-time to stint þan folu þi prai þat es bot tint. *c* **1330** R. BRUNNE *Chron. Wace* (Rolls) 13025 Wilde he [Beofs] nere stynte ne ses Vntil he cam in to alle þe pres þer Petron was. **1338** —— *Chron.* (1725) 10 Hard was þe bataile, als þei togider stynt. **1362** LANGL. *P. Pl.* A. VI. 66 Twei stokkes þer stondeþ but stunt þou not þere. **1430–40** LYDG. *Bochas* I. vii. (1544) 9 b, He fond.. a place pleasant of larges wheras he stynt and gan a citie rayse. *c* **1475** HENRYSON *Poems* (S.T.S.) III. 39 For seik hir suth I sall, And noþer stynt nor stand for stok nor stone. **1513** DOUGLAS *Æneis* VI. v. 75 Anchises son tho stintis a litle stound, And baith his futsteppis fixit in the ground. *a* **1650** *Rising in North* xxxviii. in Child *Ballads* III. 406 Vntill they came to Yorke castle, I-wis they neuer stinted nor blan. *c* **1749** *Robin Hood & Allen a Dale* xv. ibid. 174 He hasted over the plain, He did neither stint nor lin, Vntil he came unto the church. **1768** ROSS *Helenore* 20 But I shall never stint, Till o' the truth the verity be kend; Tho' to the warld's end my race should be. **1818** SCOTT *Rob Roy* xxi, But come on, what stint ye for?

β. **13..** *Sir Beues* 4025 Ne stente neuer sire Saber, Til þat he in Ingelonde were. *c* **1400** *Pilgr. Sowle* (Caxton) II. lvii. (1859) 55 And so I stent a whyle to see what maner thyng hit was, that hadde suche a wykked sauour. *a* **1450** *Le Morte Arth.* 1844 The other All agayne than stente; Aftyr hym dorste folowe no moo. **1745** A. SKIRVING *Tranent Muir* i. in *Herd's Coll. Sc. Songs* (1776) I. 109 The Chevalier.. Did march up Brisle brae, man, And thro' Tranent, e'er he did stent.

†**b.** Of a thing: To cease moving, to come to a stop. *Obs.*

α. **1390** GOWER *Conf.* I. 197 Hire Schip goth in among hem alle, And stinte noght, er it be falle And [etc.]. *c* **1430** *Syr Gener.* (Roxb.) 161 The sheld he put vnto that dint, And in the sheld the stroke stint. **1533** BELLENDEN *Livy* I. xv. (S.T.S.) I. 85 Thir treis [*sc.* huge rafts of fire].. war inflammyt cruelly be þe violent wyndis, and styntit never quhil þai come.. to þe pillaris of þe brig.

β. *c* **1374** CHAUCER *Troylus* I. 273 þurgh þat rout his eye perceyvid and so depe hit went Til on Cryseyd hit smote & þer it stent. *a* **1420** *Aunters of Arthur* 579 (Douce MS.) He bronched him yne withe his bronde,.. þe swerd stent for no stuf, hit was so wel steled.

†**c.** Of a stream, blood: To cease flowing. *Obs.*

1340–70 *Alex. & Dind.* 530 Ȝe [with your thirsty armies] maken stinte of his strem a stronde ful huge, þat nilus.. named is wide. **1579–80** NORTH *Plutarch*, *Antonius* (1595) 1004 The wounde.. killed him not presently, for the bloud stinted a litle when he was layed. **1616** R. C. *Times Whistle* 2808 The springs of lust.. being drawne dry The lesser streames would stint immediatly. **1626** G. E. *Vicary's Englishm. Treasure* 68 Take.. Nettles and bruse them, and then lay them upon the wound.. and it will stynt presently.

†**d.** Of the sun: To stand still (in its apparent course) at the summer and winter solstice. *Obs.*

1387 TREVISA *Higden* (Rolls) I. 329 þe sonne stynteþ twyes a ȝere: ones a somer, whan he goþ no heiȝer; and eftsones a wynter, whanne he gooþ no lower.

†**e.** To turn *aside*, *backward*. *Obs.*

c **1330** R. BRUNNE *Chron. Wace* (Rolls) 7424 For þe Saxons did þem bakward stynt. *Ibid.* 10864, I trowe his stede a syde stynt.

†**4.** To abstain from moving, stand still; to remain in a place, to stay. *Obs.*

a **1340–70** *Alisaunder* 386 þei þat stint at hur stroke stirred no more. **1387** TREVISA *Higden* (Rolls) II. 309 And at þe meuynge and styntynge of þat boole þe Egipcians meued and stynte vp on þe erthe [*ad cujus motum seu stationem Ægyptii in terra movebantur seu stabant*]. *a* **1450** *Le Morte Arth.* 3947 Syr Ector tent not to hys stede, Whedyr he wold stynt or Renne Away. *c* **1470** HENRY *Wallace* XI. 628 Quhen twa was ded, the tothir wald nocht stynt, Maid thaim to fle.

β. *c* **1385** CHAUCER *L.G.W.* II. 116 Whan this was don no lengere sche ne stente. *a* **1450** *Le Morte Arth.* 3936 At the laste they myght no lenger stent.

†**5.** *trans.* To cause (a person) to cease action, to cause to desist. Const. *of*, *from*. *Obs.*

α. **1338** R. BRUNNE *Chron.* (1725) 220 Sir Gilbert herd say of þer dedes ille, Of non þe had ay to stynt ne hold þam stille. **13..** *Will. Palerne* 4056 þe king.. was so styf in a studie þat non him stint miȝt. **1387–8** T. USK *Test. Love* III. iv. (Skeat) 108 Tho liste me a litel to speke, and gan stinte my penne of my wryting, and sayde in this wyse. *c* **1450** *Brut* II. 331 þe King sent his lettres to þe Erle of Warwyk, chargyng hym.. þat he shulde stynt, redresse & amende the evel doers & brekers of his pees. *c* **1489** CAXTON *Blanchardyn* 149 The kynge byganne.. to wepe and so ded blanchardyn, so that Sadoyne nor Beatryx.. coude do no thynge to stynte them. **1653** MILTON *Ps. viii.* ii, Out of the mouths of babes and sucklings thou Hast founded strength because of all thy foes To stint th' enemy.

β. *c* **1386** CHAUCER *Knt.'s T.* 510 And if he herde song or Instrument, Thanne wolde he wepe he myghte nat be stent. **1819** TENNANT *Papistry Storm'd* (1827) 107 That frae nocturnal 'sault may stent Thir rybalds o' the Testament.

6. To discontinue (an action); to hold in check, restrain (one's own actions or organs of action). Now *arch.* and *dial.*

α. **13..** *Will. Palerne* 61 þe child com of þe caue & his criynge stint. *c* **1366** CHAUCER *Rom. Rose* 1441, I mote my tonge stynten nede. *c* **1386** —— *Miller's Prol.* 36 The Reue answerde and seyde 'stynt thy clappe'. **1423** JAS. I *Kingis Q.* 118 The lytill birdis smale Styntith thaire song. **1563** B. GOOGE *Eglogs* vii. (Arb.) 57, I neuer could as thou canst stynt, the teares of my complaynt. **1592** R. WILMOT *Tancred & Gismund* II. iii, He.. ere I scarce had My tale out tolde, praid me to stint my suite. **1613** SHAKS. *Hen. VIII*, I. ii. 76 We must not stint Our necessary actions, in the feare To cope malicious Censurers. **1618** ROWLANDS *Sacred Mem.* 37 Weepe not he said, but stint thy vse of teares. **1624** J. USHER in *Lett. Lit. Men* (Camden) 131 In continueing the History of the Brittish.. beyond the yeare 600 (where I purposed to stint my selfe). *a* **1633** AUSTIN *Medit.* (1635) 29 Cease, all Creatures; peace all Things;.. Stint your ever-humming noyce. **1839** BAILEY *Festus* (1852) 394 Stint your breath. **1868** MORRIS *Earthly Par.*, *Doom Acrisius* I. 266 The thin jackals waiting for the feast Stinted their hungry howls as he passed by. **1876** ROBINSON *Whitby Gloss.* s.v., 'Stint your hand,' withold it, as in the act of pouring. **1886** R. F. BURTON *Arab. Nts.* (abr. ed.) I. 127 They stinted not their going.. till all went down by the trap-door.

β. *c* **1420** *Chron. Vilod.* 4098 Bot þe parson.. badde hem þat þey shulde stent hurre song or ellus þens gone. *a* **1440** *Sir Degrev.* 206 His game wolt he never stent. **1590** SPENSER *F.Q.* II. iv. 12 Yet n'ould she stent Her bitter rayling. **1881** *Leicester Gloss.* s.v., Yo' stent yer nize!

†**b.** To stay or suspend (a lawsuit). Cf. ASTINT *v.* 1. *Obs.*

1491 *Churchw. Acc. St. Dunstan's*, *Canterb.* (MS.), Be the consent of the executores the ple was stentyd.

†**7.** To cause to cease, bring to an end, check, stop (an event or state of affairs, actions of others). *Obs.*

Often in alliterative phrase, *to stint the strife*.

α. *a* **1310** in Wright *Lyric P.* viii. 31 A stythye stunte hire sturne stryf, that ys in heovene hert in-hyde. *c* **1366** CHAUCER *A.B.C.* 63 þanne shalt þou boþe stinte al his greuaunce And make oure foo to failen of his praye. **1375** BARBOUR *Bruce* v. 184 And syne he drew him to the hicht, To stynt bettir his fais mycht. *c* **1402** LYDG. *Compl. Bl. Knt.* 256 And tonges false.. Han gonne a werre that wil not stinted be. **1544** BETHAM *Precepts War* I. clxiii. Hvj, To stint the weapynges and skrykes of women. **1588** SHAKS. *Tit. A.* IV. iv. 86 The Eagle suffers little Birds to sing,.. Knowing that with the shadow of his wings, He can at pleasure stint their melodie. **1613–16** W. BROWNE *Brit. Past.* I. ii. 43 She.. stints his cry With many a sweet and pleasing Lullaby. **1680** C. NESSE *Church Hist.* 160 Strife is easier stirred than stinted. **1763** *Brit. Mag.* IV. 495 Stinting flame by bating fuel.

β. *c* **1386** CHAUCER *Knt.'s T.* 2442 Swich strif ther is bigonne.. Bitwixe Venus.. And Mars.. That Iuppiter was bisy it to stente. **1548** UDALL, etc. *Erasm. Par. Acts* iv. 5–7 It was no common or smalle matter, whiche they so carefully labored to stente.

†**b.** To assuage, quench (grief, pain, appetite).

α. *c* **1374** CHAUCER *Troylus* v. 686 Yevinge him hope.. That she shal come, and stinten [MS. Harl. 2280 stenten] al his sorwe. **1533** ELYOT *Cast. Helthe* (1541) 81 b, The powrynge of cold water upon ones head hath stinted the reume. **1580** LYLY *Euphues* (Arb.) 107 Achilles speare could as wel heale as hurt; the scorpion though he sting, yet he stints the paine. **1583** MELBANCKE *Philotimus* T ij, If this construction be applied to your stomacke, it will be a good confection to stint your shameles loue. **1620** QUARLES *Feast for Worms* ii. D 2 To stint his griefe, He chuses death.

β. *c* **1374** Stenten [see α above]. **1601** HOLLAND *Pliny* XXIV. vi. II. 177 All the rest doe.. stent the inveterat cough. **1666** G. HARVEY *Morbus Angl.* vi. (1672) 15 But the other implyes a very difficult cure, not by restoring the Spermatick parts.. but onely by stenting and removing the Corruption of the forementioned Essentials.

†**c.** To stop (rain, tempest, fire, etc.). *Obs.*

α. *a* **1300** *Cursor M.* 9151 Helias, þat prophet,.. þat stint þe rain thoru his praiyer. **1538** ELYOT *Dict.*, *Restinguo*, to stint or put oute, or cesse, as fyre, lyght, and thurst. **1690** C. NESSE *Hist. & Myst. O. & N.T.* I. 127 God stinted and stilled the flood.

β. **1594** *Selimus* G 4, The god that vales [sic] the seas, And can alone this raging tempest stent.

†**d.** To cause (a thing) to leave off its action.

c **1440** *Promp. Parv.* 476/1 Styntyn or make a thynge to secyn of hys werke or mevynge, *obsto*. **1674** N. FAIRFAX *Bulk & Selv.* 127 A whole set or draught of springs,.. some bigning or growing, others barely stirring or twitching, and after all so long stinted and so often checkt.

†**e.** ? To deprive of force, make of none effect.

α. **1509** BARCLAY *Shyp of Folys* 258 b, Thou wretchyd lust dost stynt abate and swage The strength of man, and his audacyte. **1631** GOUGE *God's Arrows* III. §43. 258 Where faith hath failed, the divine power hath been stinted.

β. **1619** SIR A. GORGES tr. *Bacon's De Sap. Vet.* 127 As for simple bodies, their powers are not many, though certaine and violent, as existing without being weakned, diminished, or stented by mixture.

8. To cause (a fluid, etc.) to stop flowing or emanating; esp. to staunch (blood). *Obs.* exc. *dial.*

α. **1398** TREVISA *Barth. De P.R.* VII. lxx. (1495) 290 Some medycynes constreyne and stynten blode. *a* **1400** *Minor Poems fr. Vernon MS.* xxviii. 13 Heil sterre þat neuer stunteþ liht. **1470–85** MALORY *Arthur* VII. xviii. 241 The mayden Lynet.. vnarmed hym and serched his woundes and stynted his blood. **1528** PAYNEL *Salerne's Regim.* b iij b, The vtilite is to make thycke the thynne bloud, to stynte the superfluous runnynge therof. **1599** BRETON *Disc. Scholler & Souldiour* 30 A Cobweb and Salt.. will Stint a bleeding.

β. **1548** *Elyot's Dict.* s.v. *Sisto*, *Sistere sanguinem*, to stent bleedyng. **1601** HOLLAND *Pliny* XXVI. xiii. II. 263 The juice if it bee conveighed up into the nosthrils, stenteth bleeding at nose. **1657** BILLINGSLY *Brachy-Martyrol.* xxi. 76 Nor shall the opened vein be stented. **1891** *Hartland* (Devon) *Gloss.*, *Staint*, to stanch. Some people have the power of 'staintin' blid' by repeating a charm.

†**9.** To cause (a person, animal, oneself) to cease moving, to bring to a stand. *Obs.*

Stent survives *dial.* in Somerset and Devon in the sense 'to bring (a horse) to a stand' (said of difficulties or obstacles). See *Eng. Dial. Dict.*

α. *a* **1330** *Otuel* 1571 King karnifees him haueþ istunt. *c* **1400** *Song Roland* 460 Then he stintid his sted & stod still sone. *c* **1450** *Merlin* x. 154 For the kynges were stynted at the entre of the forest by a river. **1450–1530** *Myrr. our Ladye* 42 As a man that rennyth downewarde from an hye hyl: he may not stynte hymselfe,.. tyll he comethe to the vale. **1533** BELLENDEN *Livy* II. xxvi. (S.T.S.) I. 238 þe consul, seand þe place vnganand for batall, styntit his army. **1680** H. MORE *Apocal. Apoc.* 82 Nor were they stinted here, but won also a great part of Italy.

β. *c* **1450** *Cov. Myst.* (1841) 396 Go stent me yone body wyth youre stonys.

†**b.** To stop (a blow). *Obs.*

a **1330** *Otuel* 497 þat strok ich mente to þe, & now it is on þi stede istunt. *c* **1470** Henry *Wallace* vi. 567 Quhan euir thai hyt, na harnes mycht thaim stynt.

10. To check the growth of (an animal, plant); to arrest (growth); to force (a plant) *into* bloom by restricting its supply of nourishment. Cf. stunt *v.*

1735 Somerville *Chase* iv. 117 The laborious Chace Shall stint his [a young hound's] growth. **1789** E. Darwin *Bot. Gard.* (1791) I. iv. 478 Where cruder juices swell the leafy vein, Stint the young germ, [etc.]. **1844** H. Stephens *Bk. Farm* II. 698 Young pigs are very susceptible of cold, and if exposed to it..their growth will be..stinted. **1844** Ld. Brougham *Brit. Const.* xv. (1862) 234 The vices and the weaknesses, which peaceful times and regular government either nip in the bud, or stint in their growth. **1845** *Florist's Jrnl.* (1846) VI. 147 The plant..was stinted into a blooming condition.

II. To limit, apportion, or appoint definitely.

11. *trans.* To set bounds, ends, or limits to, to limit in extent or scope, to confine to certain limits. Now *rare.* Also, † to fix the maximum price of. Const. †*at, to.*

1513 Douglas *Æneis* iv. Prol. 260 To stint all thing salue thine awin appetite, So was in luif thi frawart destanie. **1591** Savile *Tacitus, Hist.* iv. xl. 199 To moderate and stint the public expenses. **1604** T. Wright *Passions* vi. 346 Those wise and godly men which every day allot themselves a certaine time, stinting their howers for meditation. **1621** T. Williamson tr. *Goulart's Wise Vieillard* 7 By him, who hath the houre glasse of our life in his hand, who hath stinted our dayes how long they shall runne. **1624** Capt. Smith *Virginia* iv. 165 Corne was stinted at two shillings six pence the bushell. **1640** Fuller *Joseph's Coat* etc. 59 The Passeover by God was stinted to bee used no oftner. **1643** Baker *Chron., Jas. I* 140 And to keep the Order from swarming, he stinted it within the number of onely 200. **1661** Power *Exp. Philos.* Pref. b j b, They..that..think the particles of Matter may be too little, and that nature is stinted at an Atom, and must have a *non ultra* of her subdivisions. **1727** Gay *Fables* xiv. 47 Stint not to truth the flow of wit, Be prompt to lye, whene'er 'tis fit. **1781** Cowper *Retirem.* 719 Friends (for I cannot stint..that name to one). **1813** Byron *Br. Abydos* I. xiv, Nor these [battlements] will rash intruder climb To list our words, or stint our time. **1863** Kinglake *Crimea* (1877) I. ii. 22 The law of nations does not stint the right of executing justice. **1870** J. H. Newman *Gram. Assent* ii. viii. 259 When words are substituted for symbols, it will be its aim to circumscribe and stint their import as much as possible.

†**b.** *intr.* Of a portion of land: To end, have its boundary or limit. *Obs.*

1613 *North Riding Rec.* (1886) IV. 143 Thone acre a brode wrangland, stinting att the strete.

12. *trans.* To limit (the pasturage of common land) to a certain number of cattle; also, to assign a limited right of pasturage to (a person).

14.. *Coventry Leet-bk.* 438 Item,..the Maister of S. Jones..to go vnstynted, and the Comons of the Cite be stynted, no man to passe his rate. **1523** Fitzherb. *Surv.* 3 b, In the whiche close euery man is stynted and sette to a certayntie howe many beestes he shall haue in the same. **1652** Blithe *Eng. Improv. Impr.* (ed. 3) App., That all Commons..may be stinted or limited to a set number of cattell. **1808** J. C. Curwen *Hints Econ. Feeding Stock* 51 A dry sheltered pasture..which had been so hard stinted as to afford them [the cows] little or no food. **1831** Croke *Case of Otmoor* 23 Otmoor was not a common without stint; but was liable to be stinted by Orders from the Moor Court. **1880** J. Williams *Rights of Common* 84 A frith man..was appointed by the cattle gate owners to take care that Bretherdale Bank was properly stinted.

†**b.** To hold a stint of. Also *absol. Obs.*

1686 *Grassmen's Acc.* (Surtees) 95 Every inhabitant which stints in yᵉ Common pasture shall send a mowder to scayle yᵉ sᵈ Common pasture. **1698** *Ibid.* 93 All and every person qualifyed to stint yᵉ sᵈ Moor shall pay Threepence per Gate yearly for each Gate they shall stint.

†**13.** To prescribe or appoint definitely (a course of action, an amount, place, time, etc.); to restrict (a person) to a particular course of action or the like. *Obs.*

a **1513**, **1586** [see stinted *ppl. a.* 1, 1 b]. **1590** J. Greenwood *Collect. Sclaund. Art.* B ij b, We wonder..that they dare be so bold as to set & stint the holy ghost, what, when, and howe manie words to vtter in prayer. **1610** [see stint *sb.*¹ 2 a].

absol. **1641** Milton *Animadv.* 19 *Remon.* And if the Lord's Prayer be an ordinary, and stinted form, why not others? *Ans.* Because there bee no other Lords that can stint with like authority.

†**b.** *intr.* To fix a time for something. *Obs.*

1656 in *Burton's Diary* (1828) I. 231 He fully stinted to have been in York that night.

14. *trans.* To restrict (a person, his share or right) with respect to quantity or number; to limit in amount of allowance or indulgence.

α. **1592** Nashe *P. Penilesse* E 4 b, Yron cups..with yron pinnes in them, to stinte euery man how much he should drinke. **1593** —— *Christ's T.* M 3, God stinted him, what Trees and fruites he should eate on. *a* **1617** Bayne *On Eph.* (1658) 84 He hath not stinted us to any certain degree of knowledge. **1639** Fuller *Holy War* iii. xiv. 132 Wives he might have kept sans number, but stinted himself to one or two. *a* **1692** Shadwell *Volunteers* i. i, *Eugen...* May you..live till you shall wish to dye... *Teres.* I vow, I wish you may live an Hundred Years... *M. G. Bl.* A Dod Wench, that's not so well, thou stint'st me. **1710** Addison *Tatler* No. 255 ¶2 We ought to stint our selves in our most lawful Satisfactions. **1855** Macaulay *Hist. Eng.* xv. III. 591 Had he been wise he would have..stinted himself to one bottle at a meal.

β. **1567** Maplet *Gr. Forest* 105 He, fearing the Female to lauish and to be no sparer of such vittailes as they haue,..stenteth the Female and giueth hir hir task. **1678** Sir G. Mackenzie *Crim. Laws Scot.* ii. xv. §vi. (1699) 214 The Justice Court has its Macers, in which they are not stented to a particular number. **1724** Ramsay *Tea-t. Misc.* (1733) I. 58 Baith I canna get To ane by law we're stented. **1842** J. Aiton *Dom. Econ.* (1857) 150 Set the jobs by the piece, and not by day's wages... Give the preference to the men of your own parish. Don't stent them too tightly. **1860–95** J. Nicholson *Kilwuddie* (ed. 4) 166 (E.D.D.) Though stented to twa meals a day. **1894** *Northumb. Gloss., Stent*,..to limit. 'Aa's stented tiv an oor at dinner.'

15. (Now the most frequent use.) To limit unduly in supply; to keep on short allowance, to scant. Const. *of.*

α. **1722** De Foe *Plague* (1754) 136 If you stint us, we shall make ourselves the better allowance. **1769** Goldsm. *Des. Vill.* 40 One only master grasps the whole domain, And half a tillage stints thy smiling plain. **1794** *Girlhood of M. J. Holroyd* (1896) 262 The Horse..has been stinted of his Oats ever since. **1812** Combe *Picturesque* xxii, A work like this must not be stinted, Two thousand copies shall be printed. **1842** A. Combe *Physiol. Digestion* (ed. 4) 254 It is no uncommon practice to stint the healthy appetites of the young. **1850** Mrs. Jameson *Leg. Monast. Ord.* (1863) 404 Of virtuous and religious parents who stinted themselves of necessary things. **1875** Swinburne *Ess. Chapman* 65 The double thread of the main plot is stinted of room to work in. **1885–6** Spurgeon *Treas. Dav.* Ps. cxxvii. 2 They stint themselves in their meals. **1907** J. H. Patterson *Man-Eaters of Tsavo* App. i. 324 But stint them of their rice, and they at once become sulky mutineers.

β. **1865** W. H. L. Tester *Poems* 166 (E.D.D.) Dinna stent us whan ye carve.

b. To limit (a supply) unduly; to give in scanty measure.

1838 Prescott *Ferd. & Is.* (1846) II. xviii. 156 They were not disposed to stint the measure of it when his deserts were once established. **1880** 'V. Lee' *Italy* iii. 108 The deputation of patricians..stinted neither trouble nor money to obtain first rate performers.

absol. **1878** Marie A. Brown *Nadeschda* 17 On the way pluck roses, do not stint.

c. *intr.* for *refl.* To 'pinch', go short. ? *dial.*

1848 Mrs. Gaskell *Mary Barton* xxxvii, But it's in things for show they cut short; while for such as me, it's in things for life we've to stint. **1865** —— *Wives & Dau.* xliii, I would have stinted and starved if mamma and I had got on.. happily together.

16. *dial.* To apportion a 'stint' of work to (a person); also, to fix upon a definite portion of work as a stint. (Cf. stint *sb.*¹ 7.)

1794 A. Young *Agric. Suffolk* 76 Boys spin hemp, stinted at six-pence a day, one with another. **1866** W. Gregor *Banff Gloss., Stent*, to appoint a certain work; as, 'They stentit thimsels wee thir spinnan.' **1883** Gresley *Gloss. Coal-mining* 241 *Stint*, to fix upon, or agree to, a certain number of trams being filled per stall per day.

b. To assign (a workman) *to* a definite task.

1844 H. Stephens *Bk. Farm* III. 753 The field-workers of the farm..are placed or *stented* to the work, as it is termed, at every 2 rows. *Ibid.* 1058.

17. *passive.* Of a mare: To be served (by a horse): see quot. 1856. Const. *to.* Also of a ewe: To conceive.

1823 'Jon Bee' *Dict. Turf* s.v., A mare which has received a horse is said to be stinted to him. **1856** 'Stonehenge' *Brit. Rural Sports* ii. i. vii. 343/1 It is usual after putting the mare to the horse to take her to him every nine days, until she refuses him, when she is considered 'stinted'. **1884** *West. Morn. News* 30 Aug. 1/6 Most of the ewes are stinted early in lamb.

stint, var. stent *sb.*⁵

stintage ('stɪntɪdʒ). [f. stint *sb.*¹ or *v.* + -age.]

1. a. = stinting *vbl. sb.* 2. **b.** The allotment of 'stints'. (Cf. stint *sb.*¹ 6.)

1641 Best *Farm. Bks.* (Surtees) 116 In the middle field beyond Keldiegate where the flatte runnes out, that is called the stintage, and that which is up towards the Spellowe heads is sayd to bee above the stintinge. **1894** *Carlisle Patriot* 4 May 3/7 (Cumbld. Gloss.) The old herds were re-appointed for the summer stintage.

2. Niggardly apportionment.

1882 J. Walker *Jaunt to Auld Reekie* 250 Thy mean penurious stintage O' earthly pleasure.

†'**stintance.** *Obs. rare*⁻¹. [f. stint *v.* + -ance.] Cessation, limitation.

1605 *Lond. Prodigal* i. i, Nay, I cannot weepe you extempory: mary, some two or three dayes hence, I shall weep without any stintance.

stintch, obs. f. stench.

stinted ('stɪntɪd), *ppl. a.* [f. stint *v.* + -ed¹.]

†**1.** Fixed or limited by authority or decree; appointed, set. *Obs.*

α. *a* **1513** Fabyan *Chron.* vii. (1533) 27/2 Where the mayre and comynaltye of the cytye, hadde by the kynges graunte the cytye to ferme..for astynted and ascertayned summe of money. *c* **1550** *Disc. Commw. Eng.* (1893) 86 And some other, as gentlemen,..servingmen, and all other livinge by anie rated and stinted rent or stipend, are greate loosers by it [*sc.* by the alteration of the coinage]. **1593** Nashe *Christ's T.* 28 The Earth left to be so fruitfull as it wont. No season but it exceeded hys stinted temprature. **1611** Coryat *Crudities* 569 If any should dare..to passe by any of these places, and not pay the stinted summe of Money. **1644** Milton *Divorce* ii. xiv. 58 Of popular vices those that may bee committed legally, will be more pernicious then those.. not under a stinted priviledge to sin orderly and regularly. *a* **1716** South *Serm.* (1744) XI. 226 The creatures also have their set and stinted times allotted them, beyond which they can do nothing with success.

β. **1786** *Har'st Rig* xxxii, Now when the stented time is past Which they're allowed to break their fast The master comes.

†**b.** In the controversies of the 17th c. freq. applied (echoing Barrowe's use: see quot. 1586) to set liturgical forms as opposed to 'free' prayer. *Obs.*

1586 Barrowe *Exam.* (1593) B j b, Quest. 2. Wither he thinketh that any Leitourgies, or prescript formes of prayer may be imposed vpon the church: and whither al read and stinted prayers be mere babling in Gods sight? Ans. I finde in the worde of God no..such stinted leitourgies prescribed. **1610** Bp. Hall *Apol. Brownists* xxxvii. 92 The Priest was appointed of old to vse a set forme vnder the law, ..so the people,..Both of them a stinted Psalme for the Sabboth. **1649** Milton *Eikon.* xvi. 151 He with sighs unutterable by any words, much less by a stinted Liturgie, dwelling in us, makes intercession for us. **1712** Ld. King *Primitive Ch.* ii. 33 Now these other prayers which made up a great part of Divine Service were not stinted and imposed forms.

2. Of pasture: Divided into or subject to rights of pasturage; limited to the pasturing of a definite number of cattle.

1690 *Andros Tracts* (1868) I. 97 The Proprietors of the stinted Pasture in Charlestown. **1700** *Mem. St. Giles's* (Surtees) 96 The many Whins that groweth on Gilligate Moor (or stainted Pasture) do very much damnifie the said moor. **1796** W. H. Marshall *W. England* II. 136 They were made from the unreclaimed forest state; without the intervention of common fields or stinted pastures. **1854** *Spec. Rep. Inclosure Comm.* 3 Wanwood stinted pasture. *Ibid.*, Common fields and lands, subject to stinted rights. **1892** M. C. F. Morris *Yorks. Folk-Talk* Gloss. *s.v.*, A stinted pasture is a pasture limited to carry so many sheep.

3. Limited in quantity, scanty.

1629 Gaule *Pract. Theories* 169 Mine owne Infinicie [*sic*] enlarges me to Wrath aboue their stinted Capacities. **1783** Crabbe *Village* i. 169 Nor mock the misery of a stinted meal —Homely, not wholesome; plain, not plenteous. **1819** Scott *Ivanhoe* xxvi, I would rather remain in this hall a week without food save the prisoner's stinted loaf. **1863** Kinglake *Crimea* (1876) I. xi. 168 This order..conferred but a narrow and stinted authority. **1864** Tennyson *Enoch Ard.* 823 He..help'd At lading and unlading the tall barks That brought the stinted commerce of those days. **1890** *Spectator* 15 Feb., [He] made an insufficient and stinted apology, when at last it became evident that an apology must be made.

b. Limited in scope, narrow.

1710 Berkeley *Princ. Hum. Knowl.* §81 My own few, stinted, narrow inlets of perception. **1760–72** H. Brooke *Fool of Qual.* (1809) IV. 148 [They] would have thrust me wholly from Christ, if I did not consent to receive him within their stinted pale.

4. Of a plant or animal: Checked in growth, undeveloped; hence, undersized. Cf. stunted.

1759 tr. *Duhamel's Husb.* i. xii. (1762) 63 When plants grow stinted or sickly in a poor soil. **1763** Mills *Pract. Husb.* IV. 320 If they make thriving shoots, which have not a ragged or stinted appearance. **1795** Burns *Destr. Drumlanrig Woods* iv, And scarce a stintit birk is left To shiver in the blast its lane. **1842** *Florist's Jrnl.* (1846) III. 83 If the situation is much exposed and the soil very poor, the dog-rose is very stinted, and soon ceases to grow.

transf. **1831** Carlyle *Sartor Res.* i. i, Perhaps it is proof of the stinted condition in which pure Science..languishes among us. **1864–8** Browning *J. Lee's Wife* viii. iii, Who art thou, with stinted soul And stunted body?

5. Of a mare or she-ass: In foal.

1847 Halliwell, *Stinted*, in foal, as a mare. *West.* **1884** *W. Sussex Gaz.* 25 Sept., A female donkey, stinted.

Hence '**stintedly** *adv.*, '**stintedness**.

1827 Carlyle *Misc., Richter* (1840) I. 21 It is..a nature in harmony with itself, reconciled to the world and its stintedness and contradiction. **1863** Geo. Eliot *Romola* xxxviii, He was content to lie hard, and live stintedly. **1892** Tennyson *Foresters* i. i, Now you know why we live so stintedly.

stinter ('stɪntə(r)). [+ -er¹.] One who or something which stints, in the senses of the verb.

1598 Sylvester *Du Bartas* ii. i. 1. *Eden* 140 If there..the Sun (the Season's stinter) Made no hot Summer, nor no hoary Winter. **1611** Cotgr., *Limiteur*, a limiter, bounder, stinter. **1701** *Mem. St. Giles's* (Surtees) 96 All these present Inhabitants..not booked as Stinters, or yᵗ have not paid for ..their Gates on our stinted Pasture..shall have no right there without paying..Six pounds in hand for their six Gates. *a* **1716** South *Serm.* (1727) II. 112 Let us now see whether a Set-form, or this Extemporary way, be the greater hinderer, and stinter of it [the Spirit of Prayer].

'**stintily**, *adv. nonce-wd.* [f. stinty *a.* + -ly².] In a stinted or niggardly manner.

1881 Count Orsi *Recoll.* 28 The inefficiency of the police, so badly organised, and composed of men stintily paid.

'**stinting**, *vbl. sb.* [f. stint *v.* + -ing¹.]

1. The action of the verb stint in various senses; †stopping, ceasing, coming or bringing to an end (*obs.*); limiting, apportioning within limits; undue limitation, scant supply.

1338 R. Brunne *Chron.* (1725) 1 Had þei no styntyng, bot þorgh alle þei ran. **1340** Hampole *Pr. Consc.* 7016 Right swa þe devels salle ay dyng On þe synfulle, with-outen styntyng. *c* **1420** *Prymer* (MS. Douce 275 lf. 6 b), To thee cherubyn and ceraphin crien with voice with outen stentinge. *c* **1470** Henry *Wallace* vi. 46 And thus began the styntyn off this stryff. **1508** Dunbar *Flyting* 5 Bot had thay maid of mannace ony mynting In speciall, sic stryfe sould ryse but stynting. **1656** Bramhall *Replic.* 37 They have no Liturgy at all, but account it a stinting of the Spirit. *a* **1692** Pollexfen *Disc. Trade* (1697) 59 It may occasion prejudicial Retaliations,..and if too much Practised, may prove a Stinting of Trade. **1839** Thackeray *Fatal Boots* Feb., I always was fond of good wine..and, by Jupiter! on this night I had my little skinful,—for there was no stinting.

1907 *Macm. Mag.* Jan. 235 There is absolutely no stinting of vivid impressions on first treading Indian soil.

†**b.** ***stinting of the sun*** = SOLSTICE. *Obs.*

1387 TREVISA *Higden* (Rolls) I. 327 In þe somer tyme aboute þe styntynge of þe sonne.

2. *concr.* (See quot. 1889.)

1641 [see STINTAGE 1]. **1669** *North Riding Rec.* IV. 169 That is to say, two lands and one gaire, part thereof lying on the west stintinge of the Wetlands of Thirske. **1889** *N.W. Linc. Gloss., Stinting,* a portion of the common meadow set apart for the use of one person... In an Amcotts rental of the sixteenth century, I have met with a place called the 'upper stinting'.

'stinting, *ppl. a.* [-ING².] That stints.

1867 *Morn. Star* 12 Mar., The..dilution..requires to be added with a stinting hand.

Hence **'stintingly** *adv.*

1857 GEO. ELIOT *Scenes Cler. Life* (1858) II. 176 He often ate his dinner stintingly, oppressed by the thought that there were men, women, and children, with no dinner to sit down to.

stintless ('stɪntlɪs), *a.* [f. STINT *sb.*¹ + -LESS.]

†**1.** That may not be stinted or caused to cease; that may not be assuaged or satisfied. *Obs.*

1587 T. HUGHES *Misfort. Arthur* Epil. 8 See heere..The lasting panges: the stintlesse greefes: the teares. **1598** ROWLANDS *Betray. Christ* G j b, His life was nothing els but stintlesse passion. **1657** S. PURCHAS *Pol. Flying-Ins.* 114 Only resolution can make them give back, give over, they will make many tedious and stintlesse onsets.

2. Supplied without stint.

1844 LD. BROUGHAM *A. Lunel* I. i. 22 But, oh heavens! how much besides of this ceaseless and stintless chatter passed through both ears without..reaching the mind. **1889** RUSKIN *Præterita* III. 18 The only constant form of pure religion [is] in useful work, faithful love, and stintless charity.

3. quasi-*adv.* Ceaselessly.

1598 ROWLANDS *Betray. Christ* G iv, The Virgine mother cheefe in mournefull teares, With holy Maries twaine that stintlesse wept.

stinty ('stɪntɪ), *a. rare*⁻¹. [f. STINT *sb.*¹ + -Y.] Stinted, meagre, niggardly.

1849 ROCK *Ch. of Fathers* II. vii. 327 Those endowments which our Anglo-Saxon forefathers made..were neither few nor stinty. **1876** *Whitby Gloss., Stinty,* niggardly.

stiony, variant of STYANY *dial.*

stip, stipand, obs. ff. STEEP *sb.*¹, STIPEND.

stipate ('staɪpət), *a. Bot.* [ad. L. *stīpātus,* pa. pple. of *stīpāre*: see next.] Crowded.

1871 W. A. LEIGHTON *Lichen-flora* 83 Smooth or longitudinally rugulose, dispersed or stipate.

†**stipate,** *v. Obs. rare.* [f. L. *stīpāt-,* ppl. stem of *stīpāre,* to crowd, to accompany in crowds.] In *passive,* To be attended by a crowd.

1587 FLEMING *Contin. Holinshed* III. 1013/2 The duches of Clarence, the lord Dineham,..and the baron of Carew,..came to this citie, being accompanied and stipated with a thousand fightingmen.

stipation (staɪ'peɪʃən). [ad. L. *stīpātiōnem,* f. *stīpāre*: see prec. and -ATION.]

†**1.** 'A guarding or enuironing about' (Cockeram 1623). *Obs.*⁻⁰

2. *Bot.* 'An accumulation in the tissues or cavities' (B. D. Jackson *Gloss. Bot. Terms,* 1900).

stipe¹ (staɪp). [a. F. *stipe,* ad. L. *stīpes* (*stīpit-*) log, post, tree-trunk (in mod.L. = sense 1).]

1. *Bot.* A footstalk; in various applications: the stalk which supports the pileus of a fungus; the leafstalk of a fern; the support of a gynæceum or a carpel; = STIPES 1.

1785 MARTYN *Lett. Bot.* xxxii. (1794) 499 From these arises a stipe or stem supporting hollow conical receptacles. **1821** SIR J. E. SMITH *Gram. Bot.* 8 *Stipes,* a Stipe, is the Stem of a Frond as in Ferns, where it is commonly scaly; or the stalk of a Fungus. **1837** P. KEITH *Bot. Lex.* 46 If the stipe of *Aspidium Filix-mas* is divided by a transverse section, the section will exhibit [etc.]. **1861** H. MACMILLAN *Footn. Page Nat.* 214 The tubercle rapidly increases, until at last it produces from its interior, a long, thick, fleshy stem or stipe, surmounted by a pileus.

Comb. **1873** E. BALFOUR *Cycl. India* (ed. 2) V. 571 Stipe-clasping brake, *Pteris amplexicaulis.*

2. *Anat.* 'A stem: applied to two branches, anterior and posterior, of the zygal or paroccipital fissure of the brain.'

1891 *Century Dict.* citing B. G. WILDER.

3. *Zool.* = STIPES.

1891 *Century Dict.*

stipe² (staɪp). *slang.* Also *rarely* **stip.** [Abbrev. of STIPENDIARY *a.* and *sb.*] **1.** A stipendiary magistrate.

1860 HOTTEN *Dict. Slang* (ed. 2), *Stipe,* a stipendiary magistrate. **1956** S. HOPE *Diggers' Paradise* xvi. 141 The 'stipe'..had failed to find a permanent job to his liking in Britain. **1966** F. SHAW et al. *Lern Yerself Scouse* 65 *De Stipe,* the Liverpool Stipendiary Magistrate. **1978** *New Society* 28 Sept. 710/1 Roberts devoted the remainder of his..speech to remembering odd little incidents in the early career of the senior 'stip'.

2. A stipendiary racing steward. Chiefly *Austral.*

1922 *Daily Mail* 13 Nov. 11 The *Daily Mail* scheme for invigorating turf supervision... The plea for 'stipes' is a newspaper stunt. **1930** *Bulletin* (Sydney) 8 Jan. 35/1 And all the stipes and vets. and docs. galore..Wouldn't change that. **1963** *Truth* (Wellington, N.Z.) 9 July, Stipe should have acted [at Trentham races]. **1969** D. FRANCIS *Enquiry* i. 13 Stipendiary Stewards, officials paid by the Jockey Club... The Stipe who had been acting at Oxford was notoriously the most difficult. **1977** *Australian* 15 Jan. 20 The racing page screamed Stipes Probe Jockey.

stipe, obs. form of STEEP *a.* and *v.*

†**stiped.** *Bot. Obs.* [f. STIPE¹ + -ED².] = STIPITATE *a.*

1785 MARTYN *Lett. Bot.* xxvi. (1794) 378 *note,* In others it [the down] is stiped or stipitate; that is, has a stem interposed between it and the seed.

stipel ('staɪpəl). *Bot.* Also 9 **stipelle.** [ad. F. *stipelle,* ad. mod.L. *stipella*: see next.] (See quots.)

1821 S. F. GRAY *Brit. Plants* I. 84 Stipelle. *Stipella,* a kind of stipule placed at the base of the leaflets on the common petiole. **1835** LINDLEY *Introd. Bot.* (1839) 144 In pinnated leaves there is often a pair of stipules at the base of each leaflet, as well as two at the base of the common petiole: stipules, under such circumstances, are called stipels.

‖**stipella** (stɪ'pɛlə). *Bot.* [mod.L., dim. of L. STIPULA.] = prec.

1832 LINDLEY *Introd. Bot.* 99 Stipulæ, under such circumstances, are called stipellæ. [Cf. prec., quot. 1835.] **1870** HOOKER *Stud. Flora* 3 Thalictrum minus... Various forms have sometimes stipellæ to the leaflets.

stipellate (stɪ'pɛlət), *a.* [ad. mod.L. *stipellātus,* f. *stipella*: see prec. and -ATE².] Furnished with stipels. Also †**sti'pellated** *a.*

1821 S. F. GRAY *Brit. Plants* I. 80 Leafstalks... Stipellated, *stipellati.* Secondary, &c. leafstalks furnished at their base with small stipules. **1845** A. GRAY *Bot. Text-bk.* (ed. 2) 123 Stipellate. **1870** HOOKER *Stud. Flora* 84 Leguminosæ..leaflets often stipellate.

stipend ('staɪpɛnd), *sb.* Forms: 5 **stipendy,** 5–6 **stipende,** 6 **stipound, stipent,** *Sc.* **stepende, stipand,** 6–8 **stypend(e,** 7 **stipen, stippyant,** *Sc.* **steipen,** 8 **stypand,** 6– **stipend.** [a. OF. *stipende, stipendie,* ad. L. *stīpendium,* for **stippendium,* f. *stip-em* (nom. *stips* only in glosses) money payment, wages, alms, f. *pendĕre* to weigh, hence to pay. Cf. It. *stipendio,* Sp., Pg. *estipendio.*]

1. The pay of a soldier. Now *rare.*

1432–50 tr. *Higden* (Rolls) III. 441 If the faders diede theire sonnes scholde haue theire stipendy. **1555** EDEN *Decades* (Arb.) 127 Many offered them selues to goo with him of theyr owne charges withowt the kynges stipende. **1582** N. T. (Rhem.) *Luke* iii. 14 And he said to them,..be content with your stipends. **1600** J. PORY tr. *Leo's Africa* III. 160 Neither had they any other weapons but hand-bowes.. vnto which attendants the King allowed a large stipend. **1653** JER. TAYLOR *Serm. Yr., Winter* iii. 35 It is the gift of God; a donative beyond the ὀψώνιον, the military stipend. **1670** MILTON *Hist. Brit.* III. 112 Others..were..entertain'd without suspicion on these terms, that they should bear the brunt of War against the Picts, receaving stipend and some place to inhabit. **1845** STEPHEN *Laws Eng.* I. 176 The temporary use of land was bestowed on the one hand, as the stipend for military service to be performed on the other. **1855** MACAULAY *Hist. Eng.* xxi. IV. 546 The citizen was heavily taxed for the purpose of paying to the soldier the largest military stipend known in Europe. **1875** MERIVALE *Gen. Hist. Rome* xxxi. (1877) 224 Cicero..earned under the auspices of Strabo his first and only 'stipend'.

†**b.** ***at one's own stipends,*** i.e. 'charges': cf. 1 Cor. ix. 7 (Vulg.), *Quis militat suis stipendiis unquam?*

1432–50 tr. *Higden* (Rolls) III. 189 The Romanes vsede this consuetude, that men vsenge batelles scholde lyve of theire propre stipendies and goodes [L. *ut bellatores militarent stipendiis propriis*]. **1596** DALRYMPLE tr. *Leslie's Hist. Scot.* I. 104 Baith the nobilitie and the haill peple fechtes vpon thair awne stipends.

†**c.** Military service. *Obs.*⁻¹ [A Latin use.]

1604 EDMONDS *Observ. Cæsar's Comm.* 2 The law required euery man to perfect the complete number of twentie yeares stipend.

2. A salary or fixed periodical payment, made (annually or at shorter intervals) to a clergyman, teacher, or public official, in requital of his services.

In Scotland practically confined to the payment received by a clergyman. In England it is the usual word for the pay of a curate or other clergyman remunerated at a fixed rate, of a superior schoolmaster, of a professor, of a judge. The official income of a minister of state, on the other hand, or that of a civil servant, is more commonly called *salary.*

1432–50 tr. *Higden* (Rolls) V. 403 The consuetudo of the churche of Rome is that iiij. porcions be made of every stipendy congruente; oon porcion to the bischoppe and to his howseholde; the seconde porcion to the clergy [etc.]. **1480** in *Bury Wills* (Camden) 61, I wole yᵗ the seid chauntry priest haue for his stipende yerely x. marc' of lawfull money. **1523** *Lincoln Wills* (1914) I. 118 To an honest prest..to his stipound the sowme of *vl.* **1545** BRINKLOW *Compl.* ix. (1874) 22 That all iudges and pleaters shuld lyue vpon a stypend, & cetera. **1553** *Respublica* III. vi. 860 This bag..is bribes above my stipende in offecis. **1564** *Reg. Privy Council Scot.* I. 287 The ministeris gettis na payment of thair appointit stipends. **1575** GASCOIGNE *Glasse of Govt.* Wks. 1910 II. 14 It shall nowe bee our partes to understand what stipend may content you [*sc.* tutors] for your paines. **1591–5** SPENSER *Col. Clout* 746 For Cynthia doth in sciences abound, And giues to their professors stipends large. **1599** *Shuttleworth's Acc.* (Chetham Soc.) 117 To Mr. Saunders, the late vicar of Bolton, being last of his half yeares stipend,..xxvˢ. **1643** BAKER *Chron., Jas. I,* 151 Edward Allin..founded a faire Hospitall at Dulwich..to have a Schoolemaster with dyet, and a convenient stipend. **1649** LAMONT *Diary* (Maitl. Club) 11 At his transportation, the steipen of the said parish was augmented by the Earle of Keelly. *c* **1730** RAMSAY *Vision* xiv, Will preists without their stypands preich? **1782** V. KNOX *Ess.* liii. I. 235 The stipends of the most useful part of the clergy, those who officiate, are often not greater than the earnings of a hireling mechanic. **1786** BURNS *Ordination* 39 That Stipend is a carnal weed He takes but for the fashion. **1818** SCOTT *Hrt. Midl.* viii, What have I been paying stipend and teind, parsonage and vicarage, for,..an I canna get a spell of a prayer for't? **1849** MACAULAY *Hist. Eng.* iii. I. 309 In fact, however, the stipends of the higher class of official men were as large as at present, and not seldom larger. **1861** [TREVELYAN] *Horace at Univ. Athens* (1862) 37, I shall make bold to take the college plate, And lay a tax of ninety-nine per cent On all the fellows' stipends and the rent. **1883** *Athenæum* 30 June 828/1 A superintendent of the workshops must be paid a stipend sufficient to secure a man combining scientific knowledge..and practical ability. **1883** BOSW. SMITH *Ld. Lawrence* I. xi. 309 The stipend of the teacher was precarious enough.

†**b.** In generalized sense. *Obs.*

1529 *Supplic. to King* (E.E.T.S.) 29 Suche which haue receyued lyuinge and stypende to be in their churches. **1539** *Act 31 Hen. VIII,* c. 9 Reders of Grece, Ebrewe, and Latten to have good stipend. **1559** BP. COX in Strype *Ann. Ref.* (1709) I. vi. 100 We fear God will not bear it well, That the Stipend of his holy Ministry should be diminished or impaired. **1579–80** NORTH *Plutarch, Alexander* (1612) 676 Philip..sent for Aristotle..to teach his son, vnto whom he gaue honourable stipend.

†**3.** *gen.* Payment for services, wages. *Obs.*

1514 BARCLAY *Cit. & Uplondyshm.* (Percy Soc.) 23 Some gladly borowe, and never paye agayne, Some kepe from servauntes the stipend of theyr payne. **1551** T. WILSON *Logic* 51 Noble men are desirous to haue a good horse-keeper that can keepe their horses well, and they spare not to giue great stipends to such. **1586** WARNER *Alb. Eng.* IV. xxii. (1592) 97 Yet, wot I, neuer Traytour did his Treasons Stypend mis. **1614** RALEGH *Hist. World* IV. vii. § 1. 294 The Generall consecrated a Temple to them [Castor and Pollux] as a stipend for their paines. **1621** BURTON *Anat. Mel.* II. ii. IV. 341 Many Gentlemen..will..voluntarily vndertake that to satisfie their pleasure, which a poore man for a good stipend would scarce be hired to vndergoe. **1637** MARMION *Cupid & Psyche* II. ii. K 3 b, And a poore man, though tyde serve, and the wind, If he no stipend bring, must stay behind. **1642** MILTON *Apol. Smect.* Wks. 1851 III. 315 How can we believe ye would refuse to take the stipend of Rome, when ye shame not to live upon the almes-basket of her prayers? **1825** W. IRVING *Wolfert's Roost* (1855) 175 The porter and his wife act as domestics..making their beds, arranging their rooms,..and doing other menial offices, for which they receive a monthly stipend. **1856** SIR B. BRODIE *Psychol. Inq.* (1862) II. v. 149 The boys are generally taken away from school as soon as they are able to earn some small stipend. **1863** *Confess. Ticket-of-Leave Man* 51 Every postman has his 'walk', as you know; and certain houses in the City pay their postman a stipend for the speedier delivery of their letters every morning.

†**b.** In 16–17th c. often in echoes of Rom. vi. 23 (Vulg.), *Stipendia enim peccati mors.*

1549 LATIMER *7th Serm. bef. Edw. VI* B b v, [Christ] toke vpon hym our synnes... I meane not so, not to do it, not to commit it, but to purge it, to cleanse it, to beare the stypende of it. ? **1554** COVERDALE *Hope of Faithful* xxv. 172 The.. bible..sayeth euidently: death is yᵉ stypende or rewarde of synne. **1575–85** ABP. SANDYS *Serm.* xix. 330 Seeing our sinne with the remembraunce of the stipende due for the same, wee [etc.]. **1620** QUARLES *Feast for Worms* Med. vi. F 3, Lo, Death is..The iust procured stipend of our sinne. **1629** R. HILL *Pathw. Piety* (repr.) II. 58 For the stipend and wages of sin is death.

4. A fixed periodical payment of any kind, e.g. a pension or allowance, †a tax. Also, †***to keep in stipend,*** to defray the maintenance of.

1545 ASCHAM *Toxoph.* II. (Arb.) 130 The Romaynes.. appoynted..the Censores to alow out of ye common hutche yearly stipendes for ye findinge of certayne Geese. **1555** EDEN *Decades* (Arb.) 290 A certeyne stypende in maner of almes. **1560** DAUS tr. *Sleidane's Comm.* 114 This annual stypende, called of the common people Peter pence. **1560** GRESHAM in Burgon *Life* (1839) I. 310 Most humblye desiring you to be so good Father unto hym..as to augment his stipend to one hundrethe crowns more by the yere;.. wherebye a maye meynteyne hymselfe somethinge like your eldest son. **1607** TOPSELL *Four-f. Beasts* 200 There was no meane prince in all India which was not Lord of many Elephants. The king of Palibotræ kept in stipend, eight thousand euery day. **1607** *B.N.C. Muniments* 23. 81 Received of the Renter-warden of the Skinner Company for a yearly Stippyant for a Scholler. *a* **1652** BROME *Queenes Exch.* I. ii. (1657) B 4, Allowing you That yearly stipen formerly I gave you. **1694** E. PHILLIPS tr. *Milton's Lett. State* 36 It is..most unjust that they [*sc.* guests and strangers] should be compell'd to pay publick Stipends in a Foreign Commonwealth to him from whom they are.. deliver'd at home. **1751** ELIZA HAYWOOD *Betsy Thoughtless* IV. 45 For I confess my self utterly unable to maintain a family, like our's, on the nigard stipend you have allotted for that purpose. **1766** BLACKSTONE *Comm.* II. xxx. 454 Hiring is always for a price, a stipend, or additional recompense; borrowing is merely gratuitous. **1783** BURKE *Rep. Affairs of India* Wks. 1842 II. 60 On the same complicated principles the subsequent resolution of the board professes to allow the nabob the management of his stipend and expences. **1838** DICKENS *Nich. Nick.* xxxiv, Mr. Mantalini waited,..to hear the amount of the proposed stipend. **1848** —— *Haunted Man* i. 24 His very picter..hangs in what used to be..afore our ten poor gentlemen commuted for an annual stipend in money, our great Dinner Hall.

†**b.** A dole or allowance in kind. *Obs. rare.*

1631 WEEVER *Anc. Funeral Mon.* 331 A weekly stipend of bread to the poore.

†**c.** Income. *Obs.*

1605 CHAPMAN *All Fooles* I. i. B 4, That knights competency you haue gotten With care and labour; he with lust and idlenesse Will bring into the stypend of a begger. **1612** W. PARKES *Curtaine-Dr.* (1876) 20 Yearely, or certaine stipend hath he none.

5. *attrib.* as †*stipend coin, wage(s.*

1531 *Test. Ebor.* (Surtees) VI. 23, v li. for his stipent wage. **1538** BALE *Bapt. Preach.* in *Harl. Misc.* (1744) I. 102 For your peynes ye haue appoynted by the emproure Your stypende wages. **1591** *1st Pt. Troubl. Raigne John* D 3, And here in mariage I doo giue with her..thirtie thousande markes of stipend coyne.

†**'stipend**, *v.* *Obs.* Also 7 stipen. [f. STIPEND *sb.* Cf. F. *stipendier* (15th c. in Hatz.-Darm.), Sp. *estipendiar*, It. *stipendiare*; also L. *stīpendiārī* to be in receipt of pay.]

1. *trans.* To pay as a reward. (In the Fr. orig. *stipendier* is used as in 2 below; Caxton has mistaken or altered the construction.)

1490 CAXTON *Eneydos* ix. 38 She wolde rewarde theym wyth suche guerdons as apperteyneth to grete and hie goddys to be stypended.

2. To provide with a stipend, salary, or pension.

1597 WARNER *Alb. Eng.* IX. liii. 240 Scarse will their Studies stipend them, their wiues and Children cote. **1601** in Foley *Rec. Eng. Prov. S.J.* (1880) VI. 735 He hath stipened one Allen, a soldier, a cunning fellow, for that purpose. **1620** SHELTON *2nd Pt. Quix.* xlvii. 306, I, Sir, am a Physician, and am stipended in this Iland to bee so to the Gouernours of it. **1636** *Direct. Cure of Plague* B 3 b, Three Chirurgions..are also to be stipended by the City. **1651** tr. *Life Father Paul Sarpi* (1676) 60 In Rome after they were secur'd and stipended for a time, it came after to a resolution of casting them into Prison.

†**stipendary**, *a.* and *sb.* *Obs.* Also 6 stypendare. [f. STIPEND *sb.* + -ARY.]

A. *adj.* = STIPENDIARY *a.*

1540 *Act 32 Hen. VIII*, c. 23 §3 All and singulier stipendary preestis. **1552–3** *Inv. Ch. Goods Stafford* 84 Rychard Forsett..solde the ornaments of a stypendare prest ther..for the sume of ijs. **1584** B. R. tr. *Herodotus* I. 23 The souldiers stipendary. **1591–2** in Swayne *Churchw. Acc. Sarum* (1896) 298 Curates stipendary nobles dew for two yeares..13s. 4d. **1604** EDMONDS *Observ. Cæsar's Comm.* 2 According to the proportion of their stipendary time, as the Equites were admitted Tribunes at fiue yeares, so were the legionarie footmen at ten. **1604** BANCROFT in *Neal's Hist. Puritans* (1754) I. 435 These are either stipendary curates, or stipendary lecturers, or men beneficed. **1612** R. FENTON *Usury* 92 Stipendarie maintenance was first the inuention of that Idolater Micha. **1619** T. MILLES tr. *Mexia's* etc. *Treas. Anc. & Mod. Times* II. 336/2 We haue distributed the people gouernd in common by the Cantons of Switzerland, into fiue stipendary Townes, [etc.].

B. *sb.* = STIPENDIARY *sb.*

1530–1 *Act 22 Hen. VIII*, c. 15 §1 All persones Vicars Curates Chauntrie Prestes Stypendaries. **1549** in *Eng. Gilds* (1870) 223 All the stipendaryes above wrytton have hadd.. ij.s. wekelye ffor theyr dyett. **1561** ABP. PARKER in Cardwell *Docum. Ann.* (1839) I. 272 Stipendaries, and curates, and all such beneficed men. **1584** B. R. tr. *Herodotus* II. 116 When as..Apryes on the one side with his stipendaries, and on the other side Amasis with an huge army of the Ægyptians were come into the City Memphis, they closed battaile. **1601** [? MARSTON] *Jack Drums Entert.* II. D 3, As if she knew you more then for a youth, A younger brother, and a stipendary. **1625** MASSINGER *New Way* I. i. (1633) B4, Money from thee? From a boy? a stipendary? one that liues At the deuotion of a stepmother. **1657** SPARROW *Bk. Com. Prayer* (1661) 89 By Curates here are not meant Stipendaries... But all..to whom the Bishop..hath committed the cure of souls. **1660** COKE *Justice Vind.* 49 Like a Mercenary stipendary to Lewis the 13...he makes neither King nor People judge of succession.

stipended, (*ppl.*) *a.* *rare.* [f. STIPEND *sb.* or *v.* + -ED.] That receives a stipend.

1613 F. ROBARTES *Revenue Gosp.* 137 When the stipended Minister is at his stint, and can get no further.

†**sti'pendial**, *a.* *Obs.*$^{-0}$ [f. L. *stīpendi-um* STIPEND *sb.* + -AL[1].] 'Belonging to wages or hire' (Blount *Glossogr.* 1656).

stipendi'arian, *a.* *rare.* [f. L. *stīpendiāri-us* STIPENDIARY + -AN.] Characteristic of a stipendiary or mercenary soldier.

1796 W. SEWARD *Anecd.* III. 382 Lord Chatham was obliged to call in to its aid the mercenary troops of other Nations... He never so completely saturated stipendiarian rapacity, that [etc.].

sti'pendiarist. *rare*$^{-1}$. [f. L. *stipendiāri-us* (see next) + -IST.] = STIPENDIARY B 1.

1834 COBBETT *Hist. Geo. IV*, II. x. 505 The poor stipendiarists who officiated were left with means inferior to those of journeymen tradesmen.

stipendiary (staɪ'pɛndɪərɪ), *a.* and *sb.* Also 7 *Sc.* stipendiar. [ad. L. *stīpendiārius*, f. *stīpendium*: see STIPEND *sb.* and -ARY.] **A.** *adj.*

1. That receives a stipend. Of a soldier (now *rare*): Serving for pay, mercenary.

stipendiary magistrate: in England, a salaried official exercising judicial functions similar to those exercised by the unpaid justices of the peace.

In quot. *c* 1545 the MS. may have had *stipendary*.

c **1545** in *Burnet's Hist. Ref.* (1681) II. II. Rec. I. xxvii. 152 Salaries, or Wages of Stipendiary Priests. **1611** SPEED *Hist. Gt. Brit.* IX. viii. 532 He makes it his first care to fasten to himself, by present largesse, and large promises of future fauours,..all the Stipendiarie Souldiers..of his deceased Brother. **1617** MORYSON *Itin.* III. 251 Five stipendiary Cities,..so-called, because they serve the Sweitzers in warre at their stipend. *c* **1620** *Ibid.* IV. (1903) 426 Sigonius the Popes stipendiary Professor of historyes in this Vniversity [Bologna]. **1625** HART *Anat. Ur.* I. i. 10 Each Citie..hath moe or fewer of those stipendiarie Physitians. **1665** *Surv. Affaires Netherlands* 169 The Ministers..being Poor, and stipendiary, being allowed seldom above £50 a year. **1813** *Hansard's Parl. Deb.* XXVI. 100 Sir Samuel Romilly was against the principle of the [Manchester Justices'] Bill, inasmuch as it went to introduce stipendiary magistrates in the place of that respectable class of magistrates, who in this county discharged the functions of magistracy gratuitously. **1817** M. SUTTON *Ibid.* XXXVI. 91 A bill 'to consolidate and amend the laws..for the support and maintenance of stipendiary curates in England'. **1818** HALLAM *Mid. Ages* viii. II. (1819) II. 428 William [I]..had always stipendiary soldiers at his command. **1839** *Act 2 & 3 Vict.* c. 15 §2 Any such Stipendiary Justice to sit and act as a Justice of the Peace of the said County [of Stafford]. **1850** DICKENS *Dav. Copp.* xxvi, My very carpet bag was an object of veneration to the stipendiary clerks. **1859** MEREDITH *R. Feverel* i, Adrian became stipendiary officer in his uncle's household. **1863** H. COX *Instit.* III. viii. 703 Stipendiary troops, both national and foreign. **1865** DICKENS *Mut. Fr.* II. i, Mr. Bradley Headstone, highly certificated stipendiary schoolmaster. **1868** *Stephens' Laws Eng.* (ed. 6) II. 685 *note*, In certain populous districts, viz., in the metropolis and elsewhere, it has become the practice to appoint paid (or stipendiary) magistrates, and generally with additional powers. **1875** STUBBS *Const. Hist.* II. xvii. 555 To make the king a mere stipendiary officer.

2. Pertaining to a stipend or stipends; of the nature of a stipend. Also, of services: Paid for by a stipend.

1659 MILTON *Hirelings* 104 That the magistrate..should take into his own power the stipendiarie maintenance of church-ministers,..can stand neither with the peoples right nor with Christian liberty. **1839** HALLAM *Lit. Europe* II. II. ii. §9. 63 Did they perceive an unjust prejudice against stipendiary instruction? they gave it gratuitously. **1844** H. H. WILSON *Brit. India* III. 366 The non-compliance of the Government with his application for an augmented stipendiary grant.

3. *Roman Law.* (See quot.)

1880 MUIRHEAD *Gaius* ii. §21 Stipendiary lands are those situated in provinces regarded as specially belonging to the Roman people; tributary those lying in provinces held to belong specially to the emperor.

B. *sb.*

1. One who receives a stipend; a salaried clergyman or teacher; †a pensioner.

In quot. *c* 1584 the MS. may have had *stipendaries*.

c **1584** ABP. LOFTUS in Nicolas *Life Sir C. Hatton* (1847) 358 In the mean season, the several cures of the incumbents of the church must be left to unlearned stipendiaries. **1636** *Direct. Cure Plague* B3, That these Doctors bee stipendiaries to the City for their liues. **1638** SIR T. HERBERT *Trav.* (ed. 2) 106 They..post to Lahore to apprehend Sheryar whom they heard was baffled by Godgee Abdul-Hassen once his stipendiary. *a* **1668** *Chron. Perth* (Maitl. Club) 5 He taucht on Sonday befoir none the 28 of September preceding in eodem anno, his executouris cravit ane an, bot gott nane, he was ane nakit stipendiar. **1737** GLOVER *Leonidas* v. 228 [VIII. 261] If thou be'st some fugitive, who, lost To liberty and virtue, art become A tyrant's vile stipendiary. **1817** COLERIDGE *Lay Serm.*, '*Blessed are ye*' 33 The agriculturalist, the manufacturer, or the trades-man (all in short but annuitants and fixed stipendiaries)..would shortly have [etc.]. **1845** SUMNER *True Grandeur Nations* (1846) 15 A little cheese and a few vegetables are all that can be afforded to the sick and wounded, those sacred stipendiaries upon human charity. **1849–50** ALISON *Hist. Europe* I. v. §34. 594, I know but three ways of living in society: you must be either a beggar, a robber, or a stipendiary. **1853** DICKENS *Bleak Ho.* xx, Mr. Guppy's two fellow-stipendiaries are away on leave.

†**b.** A stipendiary soldier, a mercenary. *Obs.*

1768 BOSWELL *Corsica* ii. (ed. 2) 109 It may well be believed, that venal stipendiaries..could not oppose an army of brave men. **1778** G. STUART *View Soc. Europe* 116 [The fines, etc. levied by the crown] were to produce, in every country of Europe, a multitude of stipendiaries. These forces were a mixture of all nations. **1817** G. CHALMERS *Churchyard's Chips* Pref. 26 Churchyard and the English stipendiaries, were under Captain Morgan at the siege of Tergues.

c. A stipendiary magistrate (see A 1).

1875 H. CROMPTON in *Fortn. Rev.* XXIV. 696 There has been among the stipendiaries as well as among the unpaid magistrates a most extraordinary laxity with reference to crimes of violence. **1881** W. S. SHIRLEY *Magisterial Law* 6 Stipendiaries and police magistrates are appointed not by the Lord Chancellor, but by the Home Secretary.

2. *Rom. Ant.* A tributary, tax-payer.

1627 MAGEOGHAGAN tr. *Ann. Clonmacnoise* (1896) 46 Julius Cæsar after that he had Conquered the Gales and Brittans..made the Brittans stypendiaries.

stipendiate (staɪ'pɛndɪeɪt), *v.* Now *rare* or *Obs.* [f. L. *stīpendiāt-*, ppl. stem of *stīpendiārī*: see STIPEND *v.*] *trans.* To pay a stipend to.

1656 HARRINGTON *Oceana* 82 The Emperours must long before this have found out some other way of support; and this was by Stipendiating the Gothes. *a* **1677** —— *Syst. Politics* Oceana etc. (1700) 507 A Clergy not well stipendiated is to absolute Monarchy or to Democracy as great an Infamy. *a* **1700** EVELYN *Diary* 14 Sept. 1644, All the sciences are taught in the vulgar French by Professors stipendiated by the greate Cardinal. **1860** I. TAYLOR *Ult. Civiliz.* 14 It is good to endow colleges, and to found chairs and to stipendiate professors.

†**sti'pendious**, *a.* *Obs.*$^{-0}$ [ad. L. *stīpendiōsus*, f. *stīpendi-um* STIPEND *sb.*] (See quot.)

1656 BLOUNT *Glossogr.*, *Stipendious*, that hath often been retained in wars, and served for wages.

stipendless ('staɪpɛndlɪs), *a.* [f. STIPEND *sb.* + -LESS.] That has no stipend.

c **1700** in *Maidment's Bk. Scott. Pasquils* (1868) 306 My heart, my heart, take this propyne, Sent by a stipendless divyne. **1892** *Daily News* 18 Feb. 3/3 The vicar was left stipendless.

'stiper. *Obs.* exc. *dial.* (see Eng. Dial. Dict.) [OE. *stipere*. Cogn. w. the synonymous LG., MDu., MHG. *stîper*, Flem. *stijper*.] A prop.

a **1000** ÆLFRIC *Gloss.* in Wr.-Wülcker 126/10 *Destina, uel postis, uel fulcimen*, stipere. *a* **1400** *Disp. Mary & Cross* 127 in *Minor Poems fr. Vernon MS.* 615 þe stipre [? *MS.* scipre] þat is vnder þe vyne set May not bringe forþ þe grape.

‖**stipes** ('staɪpiːz). Pl. **stipites** ('stɪpɪtiːz). Also anglicized as STIPE[1], q.v. [L. *stīpes* (stem *stīpit-*): see STIPE[1].]

1. *Bot.* A stalk, esp. of some special kind, other than an ordinary leaf- or flower-stalk; e.g. one supporting a carpel or other part of a flower, or the pappus of the 'seed' or fruit of some composites; that of the frond of a fern or seaweed (also, the stem or caudex of a tree-fern); that supporting the pileus or cap of certain fungi.

1760 J. LEE *Introd. Bot.* I. vii. (1765) 15 *Pappus*, a Down, ..a feathery or hairy Crown..connected with the seed by *Stipes*, a Trunk, which here signifies the Thread on which the Down is raised and supported. **1796** WITHERING *Brit. Plants* (ed. 3) I. 84 *Stipes*, a pillar, or pedicle. Also the stem of some kind of Fungi. **1797** *Encycl. Brit.* (ed. 3) XVII. 597 The *stipites* or younger branches are directed for use, and may be employed either fresh or dried. **1830** LINDLEY *Nat. Syst. Bot.* 307 The stipes of Ferns, composed only of the united bases of the leaves or fronds, is scarcely analogous to the trunk of Vascular plants. **1847** HENFREY *Outl. Bot.* 114 When the *indusium* is torn by the expansion of the *pileus* and the elongation of the *stipes* or stem. **1864** T. MOORE *Brit. Ferns* 10 The fronds of Ferns consist of two parts—the leafy portion; and the stalk, which latter is called the *stipes*. **1871** W. A. LEIGHTON *Lichen-flora* 41 Stipites and capitula cinereo-suffused. **1879** *Cassell's Techn. Educ.* I. 274/1 Morel,..one of the few fungi..which may be eaten with safety. The stipes or stalk is hollow.

2. *Zool.* A part or organ resembling a stalk; *esp.* the footstalk or second joint of the maxilla of an insect; also applied to certain parts of the mouth-appendages in myriapods.

1826 KIRBY & SP. *Entomol.* III. 357 *Stipes* (the Stalk). **1861–2** LE CONTE *Classif. Coleoptera N. Amer.* I. Introd. p. xii, The hind portion or base of the maxillæ is composed of two pieces; the one articulating with the head is called the *cardo*, the second piece the *stipes*; attached to the stipes are the appendages. **1877** HUXLEY *Anat. Inv. Anim.* vii. 429 The short and almost rudimentary palp is attached to the extremity of the stipes. **1895** D. SHARP *Insects* I. 95 The maxilla is a complex organ consisting of numerous pieces, viz. cardo, stipes, palpiger, galea, lacinia, palpus.

stiphado, var. STIFADO.

stipiform ('staɪpɪfɔːm), *a.* *Bot.* and *Zool.* [ad. mod.L. *stīpiformis*, f. L. *stīpi-* (nom. *stīps*) collateral form of *stīpit-* STIPES: see -FORM.] Having the form or character of a stipe: applied esp. to the stems of certain dicotyledonous trees, of simple structure like those of lower classes.

1821 S. F. GRAY *Brit. Plants* I. 55 Stem..Stipiform,.. growing like those of palm-trees; with a bunch of leaves at top, and bearing the marks where the old leaves have fallen off. **1866** *Treas. Bot.* 1101/1 *Stipiform*, having the appearance of the trunk of an endogenous tree; as the papaw and other simple-stemmed exogens.

†**'stipit.** *Obs.* *rare*$^{-1}$. [ad. It. *stipite*, a. L. *stīpitem*, STIPES.] A post, an upright.

1592 R. D. *Hypnerotomachia* 54 A frame of three feete.. To the which were three stypits [It. *Sopra elquale erano tre stipiti infixi*]. *Ibid.*, Betwixt one and other of the stypets, there hung [etc.].

stipitate ('stɪpɪteɪt), *a.* *Bot.* and *Zool.* [ad. mod.L. *stīpitātus*, f. L. *stīpit-* STIPES: see -ATE[2].] Having or furnished with a stipes or stipe; stalked.

1785 MARTYN *Lett. Bot.* xxvi. 381 Tragopogon or Goat's-beard is known by..its..feathered stipitate down. **1818** T. NUTTALL *Genera N. Amer. Plants* II. 73 Capsule siliquose, stipitate. **1837** P. KEITH *Bot. Lex.* 43 Of the Stipitate Fungi a great many are furnished with a sort of conical or flattened production surmounting the stipe,..[called] the cap or pileus. **1845** LINDLEY *Sch. Bot.* iv. (1858) 87 Pappus feathery, stipitate, or sessile. **1846** DANA *Zooph.* (1848) 157 Coralla..stipitate. **1866** *Treas. Bot.* 1101/1 *Stipitate*, elevated on a stalk which is neither a petiole nor a peduncle; as, for example, some kinds of carpels. **1870** HOOKER *Stud. Flora* 363 Iris..sepals large, stipitate, reflexed, stipes channelled; petals smaller, suberect stipitate, margins of stipes involute. **1882** H. J. CARTER in *Ann. & Mag. Nat. Hist.* Ser. v. IX. 283 *Fibularia ramosa*. Stipitate, subcylindrical, solid, [etc.].

Also †**stipitated** *a.* *Obs.* (in the same sense).

1822 J. PARKINSON *Outl. Oryctol.* 41 *Sessile calix*—Turbinated, stipitated.

stipites, pl. of STIPES.

stipitiform ('stɪpɪtɪfɔːm), *a.* *Bot.* and *Zool.* [ad. mod.L. *stīpitiformis*, f. L. *stīpit-* STIPES: see

-FORM.] Having the form of a stipes; stalk-shaped; stipiform.
1859 J. B. SANDERSON in *Todd's Cycl. Anat.* V. 228/1 Cylindrical bodies..borne each at the extremity of a stipitiform cell are named stylospores. **1874** R. BROWN *Man. Bot.* 613 *Stipitiform*, resembling a stalk or stem.

stiple, obs. form of STEEPLE.

stipone, -onie, -ony, var. ff. STEPONY *Obs.*

stipound, obs. f. STIPEND.

stipple (ˈstɪp(ə)l), *sb.* [In sense 1 prob. a. Du. *stippel*, dim. of *stip* point; in sense 2 f. STIPPLE *v.*]
†**1.** *pl.* Dots or small spots used in shading a painting, engraving, or other design. *Obs.*
1669 A. BROWNE *Ars Pict.* 96 How to draw with Indian Ink... Dash on your shadows very faintly, and deepen it by degrees,..then finish it with stipples.
2. a. The method of painting, engraving, etc. by means of dots or small spots, so as to produce gradations of tone; the effect so produced; dotted work done with the point of a brush, a pencil, or a graver. Also *transf.* applied to natural appearances resembling this.
1837 *Penny Cycl.* IX. 422/1 Engraving in stipple, as practised by Bartolozzi, Ryland, and others, in imitation of chalk drawings. **1843** RUSKIN *Mod. Paint.* I. II. II. v. §16. 198 The stipple of the miniature painter would be offensive on features of the life size. **1912** *Daily News* 17 Apr. 4 A hedge sprinkled with many kinds of green stipple.
b. An engraving produced by this method.
1864 BURTON *Scot Abr.* II. 248 Like the other engravings ..a meagre stipple. **1907** *Tregaskis' Catal.* 29 July 47 The extra illustrations comprise..a series of 100 stipples, printed in brown.
3. *attrib.* and *Comb.*, as ***stipple artist, engraver, engraving, plate, print, shading; stipple-engraved*** adj.; **stipple graver**, an engraving tool for stippling, having the point bent downwards; **stipple-paper**, drawing-paper with an embossed surface which can be scraped off so as to intensify the high lights of a picture.
1841 T. H. FIELDING *Art Engraving* 63 The process of stipple engraving is very simple. *Ibid.* 64 The lighter parts are laid in with the dry-point or stipple graver. **1880** *Printing Times* 15 May 96/1 Wanted, a young chromolitho stipple artist. **1886** W. WALKER in *R. A. M. Stevenson's Delaborde's Engrav.* 320 The stipple engraver William Walker. **1896** H. HOLIDAY *Stained Glass* i. 23 Stipple-shading..is in common use. **1908** A. M. HIND *Engraving & Etching* 299 The lighter kind of crayon and stipple prints. *Ibid.*, One of the pure stipple plates. **1936** [see *line-engraved* s.v. LINE *sb.*[2] 32]. **1961** E. M. ELVILLE *Collector's Dict. Glass* 77/1 A stipple engraved wineglass with the standing figure of a small boy with a bird on his wrist. **1973** *Country Life* 6 Dec. 1931 (Advt.), Stipple engraved goblet..circa 1785.

stipple (ˈstɪp(ə)l), *v.* Also 9 **stippule.** [a. Du. *stippelen*, freq. of *stippen* to prick, speckle, f. *stip*, a point.]
1. *trans.* To paint, engrave, or otherwise design in dots; to produce gradations of shade or colour in a design by means of dots or small spots. **a.** with the design, or object represented, as obj. Also with *up*.
1760–2 GOLDSM. *Cit. W.* xlviii, Don't you think..that eye-brow stippled very prettily? **1807** J. LANDSEER *Lect. Engraving* 125 Perceiving that it was peculiarly expressive of softness, Agostino Veneziano, and Boulanger sometimes stippled their flesh, and Julio Campagnola his back-grounds also. **1862** *Athenæum* 30 Aug. 281 To grind at the mechanical practice of statue-copying alone, until he gets the bone-polishing power of stippling up antique forms with chalk to the regulation pitch.
fig. **1879** MRS. A. EDWARDES *Vivian* xii. 208 [In amateur theatricals] Every point..ought to be laboured at, stippled up like a miniature. **1892** BARING-GOULD *Trag. Caesars* I. 232 The characteristics of the man..sketched by Tacitus and stippled by Suetonius.
b. with the pigment as obj. Also with *in*.
1840 THACKERAY *Pict. Rhapsody* Wks. 1900 XIII. 331 The painter has been touching up the figures..with.. orange-colour; and you may see how this is stippled in upon the faces and hands. **1871** B. TAYLOR *Faust* (1875) II. Pref. p. vi, The master hand is still recognized, trembling with age and stippling in the color with slow and painful touches. **1902** E. R. SUFFLING *Glass Painting* vi. 104 A thin mat of colour should be either badgered over the whole surface, or else finely stippled with a French stippler.
c. with the surface or substratum as obj.
1765 T. H. CROKER et al. *Compl. Dict. Arts & Sciences* II. s.v. *Miniature*, The whole appears as if strippled [*sic*] or wrought with points. **1852** *Beck's Florist* 265 In one of the large stoves formerly used as an Orchid-house,..the panes have..been..re-glazed, and painted on the outside, 'stippuled', to prevent the rays of the sun from injuring the leaves. **1882** *Hardwicke's Sci.-Gossip* Jan. 2/2 A portion of the field should be disclosed to be carefully stippled up to an even tone. **1890** W. J. GORDON *Foundry* xi. 215 A transparent plate is hatched or stippled in parallel lines.
d. *intr.* or *absol.*
1868 W. SUTHERLAND *Pract. Guide Ho. Decoration* 20 [House painting.] It is best to use the large round stippling brushes to stipple with.
2. *transf.* in reference to natural processes or effects resembling this kind of painting or engraving.
a **1774** GOLDSM. *Surv. Exp. Philos.* (1776) II. 316 That each ray be diffused upon the cornea, and from thence be converged into a point, which will help to stipple or point out the image..upon the back of the eye. **1839–52** BAILEY *Festus* 532 Like silver raindrops stippled in the ground. **1867–77** G. F. CHAMBERS *Astron.* I. I. 17 Minute pores or dots which stipple the Sun's surface. **1894** *Forum* (N.Y.) Oct. 211 The Virginia-creeper stipples the church walls with green in summer and..scarlet in winter.

stippled (ˈstɪp(ə)ld), *ppl. a.* [f. prec. + -ED[1].]
1. Painted, engraved, etc. with dots: see the verb.
1811 *Self Instructor* 525 An elegantly finished stippled engraving. **1849** H. MILLER *Footpr. Creator* x. 199 Dots that somewhat resemble the stippled markings of the miniature painter. **1884** *Harper's Mag.* Mar. 583/2 A stippled painted wall.
2. *transf.* Of natural objects: Having a dotted or minutely spotted appearance like stippled painting or engraving.
1876 J. G. JEFFREYS in *Ann. & Mag. Nat. Hist.* Ser. IV. XVIII. 496 Inside glossy and stippled, showing under the microscope traces of longitudinal striæ. **1876** HARDY *Ethelberta* xli. II. 152 Unexpected breezes..rasped the smooth bay in evanescent patches of stippled shade. **1899** CAGNEY tr. *von Jaksch's Clin. Diagn.* ii. (ed. 4) 104 Varieties of coating [of the tongue] distinguished as 'stippled', 'coated', 'plastered', 'furred', and 'encrusted'.

stippler (ˈstɪplə(r)). [f. STIPPLE *v.* + -ER[1].]
1. One who stipples; an artist who paints, engraves, etc. in stipple.
1875 BESANT & RICE *With Harp & Crown* xii. 112 A stippler of photographs. **1894** SALA *Lond. up to Date* 181 He is a 'stippler' engaged at a photographer's studio.
2. A brush or engraving-tool used for stippling.
1891 in *Century Dict.* **1902** [see STIPPLE *v.* 1 b].

stippling (ˈstɪp(ə)lɪŋ), *vbl. sb.* [f. STIPPLE *v.* + -ING[1].] The action of the verb STIPPLE; the process or art of painting, engraving, etc. in dots; the design or shading so produced; dotted work: = STIPPLE *sb.* 2.
1807 J. LANDSEER *Lect. Engraving* 124 Stippling is a mode of producing prints by means of combinations of dots. **1868** LOCKYER *Guillemin's Heavens* (ed. 3) 43 Darker..portions.. often pretty thickly covered with dark dots, like stippling with a soft lead pencil.
attrib. **1862** *Catal. Internat. Exhib., Brit.* II. No. 4582, Graining Tools,..stippling brushes.
b. *transf.* Applied to natural appearances resembling stippled painting or engraving.
1851 J. P. NICHOL *Archit. Heavens* 49 An exceedingly delicate and uniform dotting or stippling of the field of view. **1904** *Brit. Med. Jrnl.* 10 Sept. 599 A large cell..showing a uniform basophile stippling or granulation.

stipply (ˈstɪp(ə)lɪ), *a.* [f. STIPPLE *sb.* + -Y.] Having the character of or resembling stipple.
1892 G. S. LAYARD *C. Keene* xii. 376 Breaking up of the lines into infinitesimal curves and dots, which gave a lithographic or stipply appearance.

stippyant, obs. form of STIPEND.

stiptic, -ik, -ike, etc., obs. ff. STYPTIC, etc.

‖**stipula** (ˈstɪpjʊlə). Pl. **stipulæ**, also **stipulas.** [mod.L. use of L. *stipula*, straw, STUBBLE, app. a dim. formation cogn. w. *stīpes*: see STIPES.
The mod. botanical use of the L. word is due to Linnæus, who seems to have misunderstood (or perhaps intentionally given a new interpretation to) a definition which occurs in dictionaries of the 16th and 17th c., and goes back to Isidore *Etym.* XVII. iii. §18, 'Stipulæ sunt folia seu vaginæ, quibus culmus ambitur'. Cooper *Thes.* (1565) has '*Stipula*..the husk that closeth in the straw', and Fuchs *De Hist. Stirp. Comm.*, Vocum difficilium explicatio, 'Stipulæ folia sunt culmum ambientia', which could easily be mistaken for a loose expression of the Linnæan sense.]
= STIPULE *sb.* **a.** *Bot.* **b.** *Ornith.* (*Cent. Dict.* 1891.)
1762 SOLANDER *Gardenia* in *Phil. Trans.* LII. 655 The plant..must be very different from a Jasmine..from the unlikeness in its leaves and stipulas. **1793** MARTYN *Lang. Bot.*, *Stipula*, a Stipula or Stipule... A scale at the base of the nascent petioles—or peduncles. **1807** J. E. SMITH *Phys. Bot.* 219 The most..usual situation of the Stipulas is in pairs, one stipula on each side of the base of the foot-stalk.

stipulaceous (ˌstɪpjuːˈleɪʃəs), *a.* [f. mod.L. *stipulāce-us*, f. *stipula*: see prec. and -ACEOUS. Cf. F. *stipulacé, -ée.*] Of the nature of or composed of stipules: see also quot. 1900.
1760 J. LEE *Introd. Bot.* III. xv. (1765) 205 Stipulaceous Buds. **1777** J. LIGHTFOOT *Flora Scot.* II. 623 The plant [Frog-bit] increases by runners, furnished with pendulous gems... These gems consist of two stipulaceous scales, folded together. **1900** B. D. JACKSON *Gloss. Bot. Terms*, *Stipulaceous* (1) belonging to a stipule; (2) with large stipules.

stipulane (ˈstɪpjuːleɪn), *a. Bot. rare*$^{-0}$. [ad. mod.L. *stipulāneus*, f. STIPULA.] (See quot.)
1821 S. F. GRAY *Brit. Plants* I. 86 Stipulane, *stipulanea*. Formed of stipules.

stipulant (ˈstɪpjʊlənt). *Roman Law.* [ad. L. *stipulantem*, pr. pple. of *stipulāre* to STIPULATE.] = STIPULATOR 1.
1880 MUIRHEAD *Gaius* III. 100 If the obligation be made coincident with the last breath of the stipulant or promiser. *Ibid.* 105 The stipulant must hear the words of the promiser.

stipular (ˈstɪpjʊlə(r)), *a. Bot.* [ad. mod.L. *stipulāris*: see STIPULA and -AR. Cf. F. *stipulaire.*] Of, belonging to or furnished with stipules; situated on, near or in the place of a stipule.
1793 MARTYN *Lang. Bot.* s.v. *Stipularis*, A Stipular bud. Formed of stipules or scales. **1829** T. CASTLE *Introd. Bot.* 104 Thorns, according to attending peculiarities, are.. called cauline, terminal,..pericarpal, stipular, [etc.]. *Ibid.* 105 Stipular—situated on the stipule, as in the mimosa nilotica. **1872** OLIVER *Elem. Bot.* II. 277 Observe..the ligule, a scale-like stipular projection at the base of the blade of the leaf. **1887** BENTLEY *Man. Bot.* (ed. 5) 141 The leaf.. consists of three distinct parts; namely..the lamina, or blade;..the petiole or leaf-stalk; and of a third or stipular portion.

stipulary (ˈstɪpjʊlərɪ), *a. Bot.* [f. prec. + -Y.] (See quot. 1900.)
1830 LINDLEY *Nat. Syst. Bot.* 154 Leaves [of the Sundew tribe] alternate, with stipulary ciliæ. **1900** B. D. JACKSON *Gloss. Bot. Terms, Stipulary*, (1) occupying the place of stipules, as some tendrils; (2) formed of stipules (Crozier).

stipulate (ˈstɪpjʊlət), *a. Bot.* [ad. mod.L. *stipulāt-us*, f. STIPULA: see -ATE[2].] (See quot. 1900.)
1776 J. LEE *Introd. Bot.* Explan. Terms (ed. 3) 380 *Stipulatus*, stipulate, having stipula. **1830** LINDLEY *Nat. Syst. Bot.* 26 Alternate stipulate leaves. **1870** HOOKER *Stud. Flora* 326 Euphorbiaceæ..Leaves usually alternate, simple, often stipulate. **1900** B. D. JACKSON *Gloss. Bot. Terms, Stipulate* (1) having stipules, or conspicuously provided with them; (2) with scales which are degenerate stipules.
Hence †ˈ**stipulated** *a.* = STIPULED *a.*
1829 T. CASTLE *Introd. Bot.* 51 Stipulated—when they are furnished with stipules at the axilla of each leaf.

stipulate (ˈstɪpjuːleɪt), *v.* Pa. t. and pa. pple. **stipulated**; 8 *Sc.* pa. pple. **stipulate.** [f. L. *stipulāt-*, ppl. stem of *stipulārī* (deponent, with pa. pple. also in passive sense). Of doubtful origin; according to Paulus (*c* 200 A.D.), f. an Old Latin *stipul-us* firm. Cf. F. *stipuler*, Sp. *estipular*, It. *stipulare*.
The alleged L. *stipulus* adj., if genuine, is prob. f. the root **stīp-* to be firm; cf. *stīpes* log, trunk (see STIPES), *stīpāre* to pack tightly; also STIFF *a.*]
1. *intr.* **a.** *Roman Law.* To make an oral contract in the verbal form (of question and answer) necessary to give it legal validity. Said *spec.* of the party who asks the question.
1656 BLOUNT *Glossogr.*, *Stipulate*, to require and demand a thing to be given him, or done for him with ordinary words of the Law, to require by, or make a covenant, to promise effectually what he is required to do. **1728** CHAMBERS *Cycl.* s.v. *Stipulation*, By the ancient Roman Law, no Body could Stipulate, but for himself; but as the *Tabelliones* were publick Servants, they were allowed to Stipulate for their Masters. **1880** MUIRHEAD *Gaius* III. 105 That mutes can neither stipulate nor promise is quite plain.
†**b.** *gen.* To contract, make a bargain, settle terms, covenant (*with* a person or persons). *Obs.*
a **1624** LD. HERBERT *Autobiog.* (1886) 192 Henry the Fourth and the King my master had stipulated with each other, that whensoever anyone of them died, the survivor should take care of the other's child. *a* **1677** BARROW *Serm.* xxxii. Wks. 1687 I. 467 Could he present a sacrifice, or disburse a satisfaction to his own justice? Could God alone contract and stipulate with God in our behalf? **1785** PALEY *Mor. Philos.* VI. iii. 419 In all stipulations,..the parties stipulating must both possess the liberty of assent and refusal, and also be conscious of this liberty.
2. *trans.* Of an agreement, or of both contracting parties: To specify (something) as an essential part of the contract.
c **1645** HOWELL *Lett.* I. III. xx. (1650) 66 He desir'd a valuable caution for the performance of those Articles which were stipulated in their favor. **1711** SWIFT *Cond. Allies* 53 When Portugal came, as a Confederate into the Grand Alliance, it was stipulated, That [etc.]. **1727** —— *Poisoning E. Curll* Misc. (1732) 25 You shall have your third Share of the Court Poems, as was stipulated. **1751** JOHNSON *Rambler* No. 103 ¶14 He knows..the jointure stipulated by every contract. **1755** in *Nairne Peerage Evid.* (1874) 37 Before the term of payment of his patrimony became due as stipulate by the s[d] bond. **1788** GIBBON *Decl. & F.* l. V. 199 The marriage-contract..stipulates a dowry of twelve ounces of gold and twenty camels. **1791** BOSWELL *Johnson* an. 1747 (1904) I. 125 The booksellers who contracted with Johnson ..were Mr. Robert Dodsley, [etc.]... The price stipulated was fifteen hundred and seventy-five pounds. **1819** J. MARSHALL *Const. Opin.* (1839) 156 The time of payment stipulated in the contract was extended by law. **1847** MRS. A. KERR tr. *Ranke's Hist. Servia* 260 A secret article of that treaty stipulated that Turkey should be invited to join in the alliance against Russia. **1855** CARLYLE *Prinzenraub* Misc. 1857 IV. 355 So he..made the Treaty of Passau with him.. by which..many liberties were stipulated for the Protestants. **1909** FIRTH *Last Years Protectorate* I. vii. 202 He was not provided with the 2000 cavalry stipulated in the treaty.
3. Of one of the parties to an agreement, or a person making an offer: To require or insist upon (something) as an essential condition. Now only with clause or inf. as obj.
1685 CROWNE *Sir C. Nice* v. 54 Did not I stipulate upon the surrendry of my self to this House, to be kept from Women? *a* **1700** EVELYN *Diary* 29 Aug. 1678, The D. of Norfolk..sent to me to take charge of the bookes and remove them, onely stipulating that I would suffer..Sir William Dugdale, to have such of them as concern'd Herauldry. **1712** SWIFT *Rem. Barrier Treaty* 6 To undertake for a great deal more, without stipulating the least Advantage for Her self. **1781** GIBBON *Decl. & F.* xxv. (1787) II. 525 They stipulated only a safe and honourable retreat: and the condition was readily granted by the Roman general. **1781** COWPER *Hope* 334 The deed, by which his

love confirms The largess he bestows, prescribes the terms. .. He stipulates, indeed, but merely this—That man [etc.]. **1821** SCOTT *Kenilw.* xxiii, I did but stipulate he would remove his hateful presence, and I drank whatever he offered. **1827** —— *Surg. Dau.* iv, All I stipulate, is to know the day. **1857** H. MILLER *Test. Rocks* vi. 231 Cromwell, in commissioning a friend to send him a helmet, shrewdly stipulated that it should be a 'fluted pot.' **1862** HOOK *Lives of Abps.* II. ii. 95 He had stipulated.. that they should erect and endow two abbeys and four hospitals. **1886** H. D. TRAILL *Shaftesbury* i. 4 Old Sir Anthony Ashley..had stipulated with Sir John Cooper that the name of Ashley should go with the estates.

4. *intr.* To make an express demand *for* something as a condition of agreement.

1790 *Dallas' Rep.* I. 105 What do treaties stipulate for to guard against violence on the seas? **1794** MRS. RADCLIFFE *Myst. Udolpho* xxxiii, Her prudence..had saved her from mentioning the name of Valancourt to Montoni,..and of stipulating for his release. **1796** JANE AUSTEN *Sense & Sens.* ii, He did not stipulate for any particular sum, my dear Fanny; he only requested me, in general terms, to assist them. **1832** HT. MARTINEAU *Homes Abr.* iv, His wife was to be a domestic servant in the same farm where he was shepherd; and even little Susan was carefully stipulated for. **1844** H. H. WILSON *Brit. India* II. v. II. 209 That officer was directed..to enter into a preliminary engagement with the Nawab, which should stipulate at present for nothing more than military service. **1860** TYNDALL *Glac.* I. xvi. 113, I had stipulated for ten minutes' sleep on reaching the summit. **1913** R. LUCAS *Ld. North* I. ii. 35 Pitt stipulated for condemnation of the Stamp Act and general warrants.

5. *trans.* To promise, give surety for, guarantee. Now only (somewhat *rare*) with clause or inf. as obj.

1737 WATERLAND *Eucharist* Introd. 22 All which is solemnly entred into for the present, and stipulated for the future, by every sincere and devout Communicant. **1759** HUME *Hist. Eng. Tudors, Hen. VIII*, i. 80 He required, that John should stipulate a neutrality in the present war. **1771** GOLDSM. *Hist. Eng.* I. 286 He required the prisoner to be delivered up to him, and stipulated a large sum of money to the duke as a reward for this service. **1796** MORSE *Amer. Geog.* I. 150 Ceded to the French, who stipulated to erect no fortifications on these islands. **1839** THIRLWALL *Greece* xvii. III. 41 To recover the Athenian prisoners,..the Athenians stipulated to withdraw all their troops from Bœotia. **1858** LD. ST. LEONARDS *Handy Bk. Property Law* v. 28 You should not sign a contract for the purchase of the estate until your solicitor has seen and read the leases, unless the vendor will stipulate in writing that they contain such covenants only as are justified by the custom of the country.

†**b.** *absol.* To become surety or bail (*for* another). *Obs.*

1692 WOOD *Life* 18 Nov. (O.H.S.) III. 407, I appeared [in the vice-chancellor's court]—where Benjamin Wood stipulated for me in 40 *li.* **1829** SCOTT *Anne of G.* xvi, 'Insolent hind!' replied the Knight, 'dost thou stipulate? *thou* offer thy paltry word as a pledge betwixt the Duke of Burgundy and Archibald de Hagenbach?'

Hence **'stipulating** *ppl. a.*, stipulatory.

1737 WATERLAND *Eucharist* iv. 104 The Covenant-Charter, was given soon after the Fall, to Mankind in general, and has been carried on thro' successive Generations, by new stipulating-Acts in every Age.

stipulated ('stɪpjʊleɪtɪd), *ppl. a.* [f. STIPULATE *v.* + -ED[1].] That has been specified in the conditions of a contract or undertaking.

1742 KAMES *Decis. Crt. Sess. 1730–52* (1799) 41 The children are creditors and fiars of the stipulated sums. **1775** JOHNSON *Tax. no Tyr.* 59 After the expiration of the stipulated term. **1815** J. CORMACK *Abol. Fem. Infanticide Guzerat* viii. 130 Promises..always clogged with the stipulated condition, that the example should be first set by some nominated chief. **1845** McCULLOCH *Taxation* Introd. (1852) 3 Lands were held as fiefs of the crown, on condition of their possessors performing certain stipulated services. **1848** WHARTON *Law Lex.*, *Stipulated damage*, liquidated damage [i.e. as distinguished from a penalty, which is both uncertain and unascertained]. **1879** H. GEORGE *Progr. & Pov.* I. iii. (1881) 48 The men..are paid their stipulated wages in coin.

stipulation[1] (stɪpjuːˈleɪʃən). [a. L. *stipulātiōn-em*, agent-n. f. *stipulārī*: see STIPULATE *v.* and -ATION. Cf. F. *stipulation*, Sp. *estipulacion*, It. *stipulazione*.] The action or an act of stipulating, in various senses of the verb.

†**1.** An engagement or undertaking to do something. *Obs.*

1552 HULOET, *Stipulation*, bonde, bargayne, obligation, or promise to do, perfourme, & satisfye y[t] thinge for the whyche suche stipulation or bond is made, whether it be for paiment of any summe of mony, or other act to be performed,..*stipulatio.* **1560** DAUS tr. *Sleidane's Comm.* 264 b, The Emperour pardoned them al, taking stipulation of them, that they should no more weare armure against him [L. *accepta fide ne* etc.]. **1597** HOOKER *Eccl. Pol.* v. §64. 156 Because the answere which they make to the vsuall demaunds of stipulation proposed in baptisme is not their owne. *a* **1618** SYLVESTER *Honour's Farew.* 127 Wks. (Grosart) II. 288 To trust our Soule with such whose Stipulation Cannot repaire, cannot reprive, Damnation. **1624** DONNE *Serm.* xliii. (1640) 427 Thou art bound to live according to that stipulation and contract, made in thy behalfe, at thy receiving of that Sacrament [of Baptism]. **1660** R. COKE *Justice Vind.* 2 A Contract is the mutual stipulation of two or more, that they will do or give. **1674** OWEN *Holy Spirit* (1693) 94 The stipulation of Obedience on our part is consequential thereupon. **1719** W. WOOD *Surv. Trade* 294 We can have no Security that the Subjects of those Nations shall not clandestinely Trade to the South-Seas, notwithstanding such Stipulation to the contrary, if they find any Advantage therein.

†**2. a.** A contract, agreement, treaty. *Obs.*

1649 MILTON *Tenure Kings* 28 All which..bore witness that regal power was nothing else but a mutuall Covenant or stipulation between King and people. **1681–6** J. SCOTT *Chr. Life* II. vii. §9 Wks. 1718 I. 444 That which unites them is ..their being obliged together under the same Laws and Stipulations. **1711** SWIFT *Cond. Allies* 33 Which is the only Article that I can call to mind, in all our Treaties or Stipulations, with any view of Interest to this Kingdom. *Ibid.* 47 The Emperor..was by Stipulation to furnish Ninety thousand Men against the Common Enemy. **1818** CRUISE *Digest* (ed. 2) III. 24 He doubted..whether a covenant, that the mortgagee should present..was not void; being a stipulation for something more than the principal and interest.

b. *Roman Law.* The action of making a contract or agreement in the verbal forms legally binding; a contract or agreement so made.

a **1623** SWINBURNE *Spousals* (1686) 6 Concerning the Form, so precise were the ancient Romans in the observation thereof, that they did not for a long time admit any other manner of contracting Spousals, but by stipulation. **1681** STAIR *Inst. Law Scot.* x. viii. 116 Instead of the remeids of Stipulation, the inconveniences that rejected naked Paction among the Romans, are remeided with us by this means. **1837–9** HALLAM *Hist. Lit.* II. II. iv. §82 He dwells on the folly of keeping up the old forms of stipulation in contracts. **1871** POSTE *Gaius* 311 The dumb cannot stipulate or promise, nor can the deaf, for the promisee in stipulation must hear the answer, and the promisor must hear the question. **1880** W. A. HUNTER *Introd. Roman Law* 101 Although the validity of a stipulation depended upon its being made orally, there was nothing to prevent..the practice of recording the terms of the stipulation in writing.

c. *U.S. Law.* An agreement between opposing parties (or their counsels) relative to the course of a judicial proceeding; a requirement or condition of such an agreement.

1802 *South Carolina Rep.* (1817) II. 162 The Court opened a stipulation entered into between the insurers and the insured, by which it was agreed that one case should decide all others. **1828** *U.S. Supreme Court Rep.* XXVI. 448 The want of possession, if consistent with the stipulations of the parties,..has never been held to be, *per se*, a badge of fraud. **1876** *Ibid.* (1877) XCIV. 278 Stipulations between counsel relative to the course of proceeding in a cause pending in this court cannot be withdrawn by one party without the consent of the other. **1909** *Northeastern Reporter* LXXXVIII. 786/1 By that stipulation the defendants had the right of inspection before final acceptance of the goods. **1948** *Pacific Reporter* (1949) XCIX. 956/1 The contents of the proposed stipulation with reference to the repairs of the damage as to sidewalks, are merely instructions to workmen. **1977** *National Observer* (U.S.) 8 Jan. 18/1 Agreements to something he [*sc.* your counsel] calls 'stipulations' pour from his eager lips so thick and fast that soon a miasma of confusion covers you. Eventually you learn that a stipulation is a point or condition agreed upon between the litigants.

3. a. A giving security for the performance of an undertaking. (Cf. STIPULATE *v.* 5 b.)

Now only in the language of the Admiralty Courts, after quot. 1648.

1648 COKE *Instit.* IV. xxii. 135 Whereas time out of minde the Admirall Court hath used to take stipulations for appearance and performance of the Acts and Judgements of the same Court: It is now affirmed..that [etc.]. **1768** BLACKSTONE *Comm.* III. vii. 108 These courts [of Admiralty]..also take recognizances or stipulation of certain fidejussors in the nature of bail.

†**b.** The action of giving security for an assertion; asseveration, assurance. *Obs.*

1720 *Wodrow Corr.* (1843) II. 488 From this method of stipulation, by a solemn appeal to God's omniscience, with implied imprecations to him as a Judge. **1737** WATERLAND *Eucharist* Introd. 22 They are supposed, when worthily performed, to carry in them all dutiful Allegiance to God,.. a Stipulation of a good Conscience, and [etc.].

4. The action of specifying as one of the terms of a contract or agreement; a formulated term or condition of a contract or agreement.

1750 JOHNSON *Rambler* No. 75 ¶11, I have never discovered any lady who did not think wealth a title to some stipulations in her favour. **1766** BLACKSTONE *Comm.* II. xx. 299 Next follow the terms or stipulations..upon which the grant is made. *a* **1802** BP. S. HORSLEY *Serm.* (1816) III. xlii. 266 Hence, we may understand..with what equity and reason salvation is promised in Scripture to faith, without the express stipulation of any other condition. **1817** SELWYN *Law Nisi Prius* (ed. 4) II. 1063 In a case where there was a stipulation between three persons who appeared to the world as partners, that one of them should not participate in the profit and loss. **1844** H. H. WILSON *Brit. India* III. 155 The stipulation of the treaty of Yandabo providing for the permanent residence of a representative of the British Government, at the capital of Ava. **1889** S. WALPOLE *Life Ld. John Russell* II. xxviii. 313 The stipulations on which the two emperors had agreed at Villafranca.

5. The action of stipulating for or insisting on something as a condition of agreement; an instance of this, a condition stipulated for.

1792 *Anecd. Pitt* II. xxii. 40 Pensions were thrown about indiscriminately... The only stipulation was, 'Give us your vote.' **1845** DISRAELI *Sybil* v. xi, I did not preface it by a stipulation of confidence, because that is idle. **1878** BOSW. SMITH *Carthage* 275 The stipulation made by the ease-loving inhabitants and granted by Hannibal, that no Capuan citizen should be required to serve in his army.

stipulation[2] (ˌstɪpjuːˈleɪʃən). *Bot.* [ad. mod.L. *stipulātiōn-em*: see STIPULA and -ATION.] The arrangement of the stipules.

1760 J. LEE *Introd. Bot.* III. xvii. (1765) 209 By Stipulation is meant the Situation and Structure of the Stipulæ at the Base of the Leaves. **1830** LINDLEY *Nat. Syst. Bot.* 24 Their stipulation points out their affinity with Urticeæ.

stipulative ('stɪpjuːlətɪv), *a.* [f. STIPULATE *v.* + -IVE.] That stipulates or specifies as an essential condition. *spec.* in ***stipulative definition*** (Logic), the act of stipulating what a word, phrase, etc. shall be used to mean; a definition so stipulated.

1950 R. ROBINSON *Definition* ii. 19 By 'stipulative definition' I mean establishing or announcing or choosing one's own meaning for a word. **1956** J. HOSPERS *Introd. Philos. Anal.* i. 51 We are stating what *we* are going to mean by it... We are stipulating a meaning, and we have a stipulative definition. **1965** E. J. LEMMON *Beginning Logic* 33 A definition such as *Df* ↔ may be called a *stipulative* definition. **1976** A. R. LACEY *Dict. Philos.* 48 Stipulative definitions are *prescriptive* in that they prescribe how a word is to be used. **1981** P. A. ANGELES *Dict. Philos.* 59 When Norbert Wiener coined the word 'cybernetics' he gave it the stipulative definition: 'the science of communication and control systems'.

stipulator ('stɪpjʊleɪtə(r)). [a. L. *stipulātor*, agent-n. f. *stipulārī* to STIPULATE. Cf. F. †*stipulateur* (Cotgr.).]

1. *Roman Law.* (See quots. and STIPULATE *v.* 1.)

1611 COTGR., *Stipulateur*, a stipulator; he that intending to bind another by words, asketh him whether he will giue, or doe, such a thing or no. **1861** MAINE *Anc. Law* ix. (1876) 329 In speaking of a party to a contract, it is always the Stipulator, the person who asks the question, who is primarily alluded to.

†**2.** One who makes a formal promise or pledge on behalf of another; a sponsor, surety, bail. *Obs.*

1610 DONNE *Pseudo-martyr* 348 They which were our stipulators at the Font. **1716** *Case Dr. Ayliffe* 32 The Doctor..had not Time allow'd him that Day to prepare himself with a Proctor and Stipulator (which the Common Law calls Bail).

stipulatory ('stɪpjuːlətərɪ), *a.* Now *rare.* [ad. mod.L. *stipulātōrius*, f. *stipulārī*: see STIPULATE *v.* and -ORY.]

1. Of the nature of or characterized by stipulation, in various senses.

1658 J. R. *Christian Subject* vii. 101 A limited power, bounded in by Oaths, Laws, Couenants, and solemn Stipulatory acts, contracted betwixt the Magistrate and the Subjects. *a* **1662** SANDERSON *Cases Consc.* (1678) 14 Whereunto agree those forms so frequent in holy Scripture, in Oaths both assertory, and stipulatory. **1695** *Whether Parliament be not in Law dissolved* etc. 17 There is no Original Contract, nor Stipulatory Agreement. **1702** H. DODWELL *Apol.* §23 in S. Parker *Cicero's De Finibus*, This is implied in the Baptismal Stipulation, inasmuch as the Signs there used are stipulatory, and stipulatory on our part, as well as God's. **1704** in H. M. B. Reid *Cameronian Apostle* (1896) 236 That all compacts and covenants..are mutual and stipulatory, binding each party conditionally to the performance of what they have engaged. **1880** MUIRHEAD *Gaius* II. 38 You must..take from him a stipulatory engagement for the same debt.

2. Constituted by stipulation or agreement.

1762 tr. *Busching's Syst. Geog.* IV. 492 He bequeathed.. the county of Pyrmont to his cousins the Counts Christian and Wolrad of Waldeck, his stipulatory successors and cousins.

stipule ('stɪpjuːl), *sb. Nat. Hist.* [a. F. *stipule*, ad. mod.L. STIPULA. Cf. Sw. *stipel*.]

1. *Bot.* A lateral appendage (often resembling a small leaf or scale) borne in pairs upon the leaf-base of certain plants. Also applied to a similar appendage in Characeæ, and to the paraphyllum of mosses.

1793 MARTYN *Lang. Bot.*, *Stipula*, a Stipula or Stipule... A scale at the base of the nascent petioles. **1800** *Asiatic Ann. Reg.* 276/1 Stipules lateral, paired, ovate, acuminated. **1875** BENNETT & DYER *Sachs' Bot.* 192 Stipules may be considered as lateral branches of the leaves which arise at their very point of insertion;..each single stipule is usually bilaterally unsymmetrical, and its shape is therefore such that [etc.]. *Ibid.* 281 From the basal nodes of Chara other foliar structures also arise,..which Braun calls Stipules.

2. *Ornith.* A newly sprouted feather; a pin-feather. [So F. *stipule* (Littré).]

1891 *Century Dict.*

Hence †**'stipuleless** *a.*

1802 R. HALL *Elem. Bot.* Dict., Stipule-less, *exstipulatus*, without stipules.

†**'stipule**, *v. Obs. rare*$^{-1}$. [a. F. *stipuler*: see STIPULATE *v.*] *trans.* = STIPULATE *v.* 2.

1623 tr. *Favine's Theat. Hon.* I. i. 11 Among Masles, the eldest..ought to be acknowledged by his Fathers Armes: If he [*mistranslation for* it] be not otherwise stipuled by Contracts of marriage, of donation, or of substitution. [Orig. *s'il n'est autrement stipulé* [etc.].]

†**stipulean**, *a. Bot. Obs.*$^{-0}$ [ad. mod.L. *stipuleānus*, irreg. f. STIPULA.] (See quot.)

1821 S. F. GRAY *Brit. Plants* I. 90 Stipulean, *Aculei stipuleani.* Growing near the leaves, and appearing to rise from stipules changed. *Ibid.* 91 Tendrils... Stipulean, *stipuleani.* Resulting from the change of a stipule.

stipuled ('stɪpjuːld), *a. Bot.* [f. STIPULE *sb.* + -ED[2].] Furnished with stipules, stipulate.

1793 MARTYN *Lang. Bot.*, *Stipulatus caulis*, a Stipulate or stipuled stalk. Having stipules on it. **1833** HOOKER in *J. E. Smith's Eng. Flora* V. I. 109 The gemmiferous elongations alone stipuled. **1855** ANNE PRATT *Flower. Plants* V. 94 *Salix stipularis* (The Stipuled or Auricle-leaved Osier or Willow). **1866** *Treas. Bot.* 140/2 Trees..having alternate, simple, stipuled leaves.

stipu'liferous, *a. Bot.* [f. mod.L. *stipulifer*, f. STIPULA: see -FEROUS. Cf. F. *stipulifère*.] Bearing stipules.

1900 B. D. JACKSON *Gloss. Bot. Terms.*

stipuliform ('stɪpjʊlɪfɔːm), *a. Bot. rare.* Also **stipulæform.** [f. L. type *stipuliform-is*, f. STIPULA: see -FORM.] Having the form of a stipule.

1870 HOOKER *Stud. Flora* 26 Cardamine Impatiens... Petioles with stipuliform fringed auricles. **1900** B. D. JACKSON *Gloss. Bot. Terms, Stipulæform, stipuliform*, shaped as though a stipule.

stipulode ('stɪpjuːləʊd). *Bot.* [f. STIPULA + -ODE[1].] A stipular organ of one cell, in one or more rows subtending the branchlets in *Chara*.

1880 H. & J. GROVES in *Jrnl. Bot.* Apr. 100 Lower circle of stipulodes very short. **1881** *Ibid.* Jan. 2 It is usual among Charas for a correlation to exist between the stipulodes and the bract cells.

stipulose ('stɪpjuːləʊs), *a. Bot.* [ad. mod.L. *stipulōs-us*, f. *stipula*: see STIPULE and -OSE. Cf. F. *stipuleux, -euse*.] Having very large stipules.

1900 B. D. JACKSON *Gloss. Bot. Terms.*

stipye, obs. form of STEEPY.

stir (stɜː(r)), *sb.*[1] Forms: see STIR *v.* [f. the verb. ONorthumbrian had *ȝestir* (only once, glossing *actio* in *Rit. Dunelm.* 187). The cognate ON. *styr-r* masc. (see STIR *v.*) may possibly be in part the source of the Sc. and northern uses, which (in the *β* forms) are recorded from the 14th c.] The action or an act of stirring, in various senses.

1. Movement, considered in contrast to or as an interruption of rest or stillness; slight or momentary movement; movement of disturbance, agitation. (†In quot. 1589, motion in general.) ***on the stir*** (*rare*): astir, stirring.

α. **1562** J. HEYWOOD *Prov. & Epigr.* (1867) 100 At stur of euery mouse. **1589** PUTTENHAM *Eng. Poesie* II. iii. (Arb.) 81 Some [words] aske longer, some shorter time to be vttered in, and so, by the Philosophers definition, stirre is the true measure of time. **1660** SHARROCK *Vegetables* 92 Heterogeneous things, upon their meeting, ordinarily cause that stir which is thought..to have great influence upon vegetation. **1803** SOUTHEY *Inchcape Rock* I No stir in the air, no stir in the sea. **1805** WORDSW. *Waggoner* i. 22 Hush, there is some one on the stir! 'Tis Benjamin the Waggoner. *a* **1821** KEATS *Hyperion* I. 7 No stir of air was there. **1845** BROWNING *Time's Revenges* 58 The stir Of shadow round her mouth. **1885** STEVENSON *Child's Gard. Verses* 14 Not a stir of child or mouse. **1898** 'H. S. MERRIMAN' *Roden's Corner* iii. 32 Presently there was a stir at the door, and Cornish entered the large room.

β. *c* **1470** [see 4]. *c* **1480** HENRYSON *Mor. Fab., Fox, Wolf & Cadger* 116, I trow ȝe haif bene tussillit with sum tyke, That garris ȝow ly sa still withouttin steir.

2. Active or energetic movement of a number of persons (or animals); bustle, activity. (In some cases hardly distinguishable from 3.)

c **1586** C'TESS PEMBROKE *Ps.* I.XXXVIII. iii, As one who free from strife, And sturr of mortall life Among the dead at rest doth sitt. **1634** MILTON *Comus* 5 Above the smoak and stirr of this dim spot, Which men call Earth. **1712-13** SWIFT *Jrnl. to Stella* 21 Mar., Company will come, and a stir, and a clutter. **1784** COWPER *Task* III. 739 The stir of commerce. **1836** THIRLWALL *Greece* xxv. III. 375 The stir of preparation immediately began. **1863** GEO. ELIOT *Romola* x, By this time the stir of the Festa was felt even in the narrowest side-streets.

3. Commotion, disturbance, tumult; general excitement; fuss. Now usually with *a*; the plural, now rare, was formerly common, esp. in the sense 'publick disturbance, tumultuous disorder' (J.), riot, insurrection. Phrase, †***to keep a stir***.

α. sing. a **1547** SURREY *Æneis* IV. (1557) G ij, Her sister Anne, spritelesse for dread to heare This fearefull sturre, with nailes gan teare her face. **1549** in Ellis *Orig. Lett.* Ser. I. II. 168 If you forsake to come to this..peaxable agrement, ..the inconveniences which may ensue upon stirre must grow of yow. *a* **1557** MRS. M. BASSET tr. *More's Treat. Passion* M.'s Wks. 1390/1 Sundry matters as in such a sodain styrre very sore perplexed theim. **1579** J. FIELD tr. *Calvin's 4 Serm.* i. 8 But what a blundering and stirre keepe they heere? **1629** HOBBES *Thucyd.* II. 112 Being then at their wits end, they kept a stirre at Pericles. **1655** BAXTER *Quaker's Catech.* 19 Your Prater also made a stirre with me for calling the sacred Languages the Originall. **1671** TRENCHFIELD *Cap Gray Hairs* (1688) 17 There are many things we make no small stir about. **1732** BERKELEY *Minute Philos.* (1732) I. 56 Glaucus, who used to say, that Statesmen and Lawgivers may keep a stir about right and wrong, just and unjust, but that, in truth [etc.]. **1782** COWPER *Mut. Forb.* 21 For one slight trespass all this stir? **1802** WORDSW. *To Small Celandine* 15 I'm as great as they, I trow, Since the day I found thee out, Little Flower!—I'll make a stir, Like a sage astronomer. **1847** JAMES *Convict* xiv, The Chartists are making a great stir about here just now. **1885** 'MRS. ALEXANDER' *At Bay* viii, He always came to the front when there was any stir in the Lambert affair.

pl. **1555** EDEN *Decades* (Arb.) 86 The Leauetenaunt asked hym what al these sturres and tumultes ment. **1575-85** SANDYS *Serm.* v. 85 His Apostles are not breeders of stirs and mutinies, they are messengers sent to make peace. **1650** S. CLARKE *Eccl. Hist.* I. (1654) 26 They never intended any stirs or rebellions against the Empire. **1680** MORDEN *Geog. Rect., Modena* 209 Great Stirs between the Popes and the old Dukes of Ferrara. **1847** EMILY BRONTE *Wuthering H.* iv, He complained so seldom, indeed, of such stirs as these, that I really thought him not vindictive. **1876** FREEMAN *Norm. Conq.* IV. xx. 531 The stirs [ed. 1871 commotions] which were soon to arise on the side of Maine, Anjou, and Brittany. **1896** CROCKETT *Grey Man* xl. 268 Thrusting myself into all the stirs and quarrels.

β. **1375**, *c* **1375**, *a* **1568** [see 4]. *c* **1400** *Destr. Troy* 7398 The stere was full stithe; þere starf mony knightes. **1570** *Sat. Poems Reform.* x. 196 Brother, allace, had ȝe bene heir, I had not cum in all this sturt and steir. **1728** RAMSAY *Step-daughter* 8 My Step-dame..keeps the hale House in a steer. **1873** C. GIBBON *Lack of Gold* vi, Annie's grandmother, a bairn then, was in the thick of the steer. **1912** R. M. FERGUSSON *Ochil Fairy T.* 45 A terrible steer got up among the ponies, that began jumping about like mad beasts.

†**4.** ***on steer*** (cf. senses 1-3): astir, in motion; in a state of commotion or tumult. *Sc. Obs.* (see ASTEER *adv.*)

1375 BARBOUR *Bruce* VII. 344 Swa that the host wes all on steir. *c* **1375** *Sc. Leg. Saints* xi. (*Simon & J.*) 343 Nere al þe land of babylone one stere mad þai. *c* **1470** *Rauf Coilȝear* 411 He saw na thing on steir. *a* **1568** A. SCOTT *Poems* (S.T.S.) ii. 112 Syne eftir denner raiss the din, And all the toun on steir.

5. *fig.* Movement of feeling or thought; emotion; impulse; intellectual activity.

1563 J. MAN tr. *Musculus' Commpl.* 438b, Thys sayeth Lactance. By whyche wordes he dothe not take from God the commotion and sturre of anger, but that onelye whyche is ioyned with fault. **1611** SHAKS. *Cymb.* I. iii. 12 He did keepe The Decke, with Gloue, or Hat, or Handkerchife, Still wauing, as the fits and stirres of 's mind Could best expresse how slow his Soule sayl'd on. **1820** KEATS *Isabella* i, They could not in the self-same mansion dwell Without some stir of heart. **1849** MACAULAY *Hist. Eng.* iii. I. 409 In this, as in every great stir of the human mind. **1878** SPURGEON *Treas. Dav.* Ps. cxiv. 4 God's power of creating a stir in lethargic minds. **1899** BRIDGES *New Poems* viii. (1912) 339 Fair Thy dreams.. Yea, godlike when thou hast the skill To steal a stir of the heavenly thrill.

6. An act of stirring something, e.g. a liquid, etc.; a poke, jog; *fig.* a rousing.

1818 COBBETT *Pol. Reg.* XXXIII. 71 Public opinion had received a great stir. **1857** HUGHES *Tom Brown* II. viii, 'Eh, Arthur?' said Tom, giving him a stir with his foot. **1904** *Daily News* 2 Dec. 6 Each of the family took a stir... A Christmas pudding required much stirring.

stir, *sb.*[2] *Sc.* Vulgar corruption of SIR.

1784 BURNS '*There was a birkie born in Kyle*' vi, Guid faith, quo' she, I doubt you, Stir. **1816** SCOTT *Old Mort.* viii, Troth, stir,..neshessity, stir—I'm seeking for service, stir.

stir (stɜː(r)), *sb.*[3] *slang.* [Origin unknown.] **1.** A prison. Also without article, esp. in phr. ***in stir***.

1851 MAYHEW *Lond. Labour* I. 421 I was in Brummagem, and was seven days in the new 'stir' (prison). **1896** A. MORRISON *Child Jago* 313 A man has time to think things out, in stir. **1907** *Times* 2 July 15/3 The prisoner..said, 'It is all right. I'll go to stir (prison) over this lot. I did not intend to kill her.' **1926** [see JOLT *sb.* 4 b]. **1939** J. STEINBECK *Grapes of Wrath* ii. 19 When you been in stir a little while, you can smell a question comin' from hell to breakfast. **1970** G. F. NEWMAN *Sir, You Bastard* ii. 79 Tasting stir, Goldby suddenly realized he was the wrong side of thirty for acquiring the habit. **1977** 'E. CRISPIN' *Glimpses of Moon* xii. 250 You get better conditions than that in stir.

2. *Comb.* (Designating) a person deranged, etc., by long imprisonment, esp. as ***stir-crazy***. Also *fig. Criminals' slang* (chiefly *U.S.*).

1908 J. M. SULLIVAN *Criminal Slang* 24 *Stir crazy, prison crazy*, a man whose mind has become affected by serving long sentences. **1924** G. C. HENDERSON *Keys to Crookdom* 419 *Stir bugs*, prison crazy. **1925** *Flynn's* 18 Apr. 116/2 *Stir-bug*, one whose mentality has been broken by confinement in prison. **1926** *Clues* Nov. 162/2 *Stir-simple*, been in so long they are losing their mind. **1929** M. A. GILL *Underworld Slang* 10/2 *Stir nut*, convict effected [*sic*] by long confinement. *Ibid.*, *Stir simple*, convict effected by long confinement. **1932** 'SPINDRIFT' *Yankee Slang* 60 *Stir crazy*, nervous dread of free convicts who have served a long term and fear to return to prison. **1935** N. ERSINE *Underworld & Prison Slang* 72 *Stirnuts*, mentally hazy because of long imprisonment. **1939** J. STEINBECK *Grapes of Wrath* iv. 36, I wonder what the stir-bug I got for a cell-mate is doin'. *Ibid.* xvi. 241 Maybe I'm kinda stir-nuts. *Ibid.* xx. 342 If say a fella's goin' stir-bugs..why, you know it 'fore it happens. **1950** H. E. GOLDIN *Dict. Amer. Underworld Lingo* 212/2, I must be gettin' stir-bugs or blowing my top (going insane) altogether. **1950** PATTERSON & CONRAD *Scottsboro Boy* II. vii. 133 Howard was stir-crazy. He would go around the prison saying to anybody about anybody, 'I kill the sonofabitch, I sure kill the sonofabitch.' **1956** P. I. WELLMAN *Death on Prairie* xxiv. 225 The latter came back after two years in prison with his mind gone— 'stir simple' to use a modern slang phrase. **1960** *Washington Post* 29 Jan. A14 A Democratic President would go 'stir crazy' without a depression or war to occupy his time. **1972** J. WAMBAUGH *Blue Knight* v. 74 She's..an ex-con and stir crazy as hell... She's got a phobia about jails.

stir (stɜː(r)), *v.* Inflected stirred, stirring. Forms: *α.* 1 styrian, 2-4 sturie (4 styry), 3-5 sture, 3-8 stire, 4-6 styrre, 4-7 stirre, 5-6 sterre, 4-8 styre, 5-6 styr, 5-7 stur(re, 6-7 stirr, 4- stir. *β.* 3-7 stere, 4 steore, 4-5 steri(e, *Sc.* steyr(e, 4-6 ster, (4 *inf.* stern), 4-7 *Sc.* steir, 5 stear, steure, 5-6 stier(e, (*Sc.* steire), 5-9 (chiefly *Sc.* and *north.*) steer, 6 steere, 6-7 steare. *γ.* 3 storie, 5 storre, 5-6 store, 6 stoure, stowre, stoore. [OE. *styrian* corresponds to MSw. *styra* or *styria* (once; the reading is doubtful), Norw. *styrja* to make a disturbance (? Da. *for-styrre* to disturb, influenced by G. *verstören*):—OTeut. type **sturjan*, related to **sturi-z* masc., a stir, disturbance (ON. *styr-r*, Norw. *styr*); the same Teut. root, according to some scholars, appears in **sturmo-z* STORM *sb.* An ablaut-variant **staurjan* is believed to be represented in OFris. *to-stêra*, OS. *to-stôrian* to destroy (MDu., mod.Du. *storen* to disturb), OHG. *stôrren*, *stôran* (MHG. *stœren*, LG., mod.G. *stören* to disturb, whence Sw. *störa*).

For the phonology of the *β* forms (chiefly northern), cf. SPEER *v.*, where the northern form is the only one common in literary use, and is therefore adopted as the typical form in the Dictionary.]

I. Transitive senses.

1. To move, set in motion; *esp.* to give a slight or tremulous movement to; to move to and fro; to shake, agitate.

α. a **1023** WULFSTAN *Hom.* xlix. (1883) 255 Ic mine hearpan ȝenam and mine strengas styrian ongan. *c* **1220** *Bestiary* 520 Storm stireð al ðe se. *a* **1400** *King & Hermit* 477 The frere gaff hym a bow in hond... He myȝt oneth styre þe streng. *c* **1440** *Jacob's Well* 6 þe watyr in þe se is styred wyth þe wynde. **1536** *Stories & Proph. Scripture* M j, The earthe hath bene styrred and hath quaked. **1651** HOBBES *Leviath.* I. ii. 4 When a thing lies still, unlesse somewhat els stirre it, it will lye still for ever. **1817** SHELLEY *Rev. Islam* III. xxx, The shrill sea-wind, whose breath idly stirred My hair. **1847** JAMES *Convict* iv, A brisk gale stirring the air. **1887** F. FRANCIS Jun. *Saddle & Mocassin* 123 'Get up, or I'll beat the stuffing out of you!' he says mildly, stirring the reins at the same time.

β. c **1384** CHAUCER *H. Fame* 817 Euerych ayre other stereth More and more and speche vpbereth. *c* **1530** *Judic. Urines* II. viii. 34 Whan..the humours be moche Agitat and moued and stered in the vessels. **1567** GOLDING *Ovid's Met.* v. 431 Calliope..with hir thumbe gan steare The quiuering strings. **1615** CHAPMAN *Odyss.* XXI. 324 He warm'd and suppl'd it, yet could not stere To any draught, the string [of the bow], with all his Art.

b. To move (a limb or member); chiefly, now almost always, in negative or similar expressions: to make any or the slightest movement with.

to stir one's stumps: see STUMP *sb.* † ***to stir one's tail*** (Sc. obs.), to bestir oneself, make a disturbance.

α. c **1205** LAY. 17434 He..sturede his tunge alse he bede sunge. *a* **1225** *Ancr. R.* 130 Ase brid hwon hit wule vleon stureð his hwingen. **1388** WYCLIF *Ps.* xxi[i]. 8 Alle men seynge me scorneden me; thei..stiriden the heed. *c* **1440** *Alphabet of Tales* 96 He garte bynd hym þer so with rapis, þat he myght nowder stur hand nor fute. **1567** PALFREYMAN *Baldwin's Mor. Philos.* I. li. (1600) 31b, Socrates..vsed sometime through vehemencie of his communication to shake his hand, and stirre his finger. **1590** SPENSER *F.Q.* III. vii. 45 Unable to arise, or foote or hand to styre. **1676** C. HATTON in *H. Corr.* (Camden) I. 134 They..soe bruised his arme y[t] he wase never able to stirr it after. **1712** ADDISON *Spect.* No. 369 ¶9 The Gods..do not stir their Feet, nor proceed Step by Step. **1823** SCOTT *Quentin D.* xx, 'I will not stir a foot', said the Countess, obstinately. **1825** —— *Talism.* iii, Thy companion had been slain by thy side,..without thy stirring a finger in his aid. **1887** J. PAYN *Holiday Tasks* 65 Sometimes he would sign anything in the most obliging manner, and sometimes refuse to stir a finger.

β. **1377** LANGL. *P. Pl.* B. XVII. 54 He myȝte neither steppe ne stonde ne stere fote ne handes. *c* **1400** tr. *Secreta Secret., Gov. Lordsh.* 116 He þat..with spekyng sterys his hondes, he ys fowl, eloquent, and deceyuant. *a* **1572** KNOX *Hist. Ref.* IV. Wks. 1848 II. 331 Hir Uncles war begyning to steir thair taill [*v.r.* taills], and to truble the hoill Realme of France. *a* **1578** LINDESAY (Pitscottie) *Chron. Scot.* (S.T.S.) I. 412 Auchtorite nor power spreitwall..micht nocht that tyme prevaill quhan Dame Curia began to steir hir taill. **1609** SKENE *Reg. Maj., Baron Crts.* xv. 104b, The quhilk partie, sall say, in this maner incontinent, fra the dome be given or he steir his taes, quhere his heill stude.

†**c.** To move about (something held in or grasped by the hand); to wield (a weapon); to brandish, flourish; to actuate, manage, ply (an instrument or mechanical appliance). *Obs.*

c **1205** LAY. 2197 Heo stureden heora wepnan. **13..** *Gaw. & Gr. Knt.* 331 Now has Arthure his axe, & þe halme grypez, & sturnely sturez hit aboute. **1575** GASCOIGNE *Glasse of Govt.* Wks. 1910 II. 43 To stir an ore, in every forward boate. **1603** J. DAVIES (Heref.) *Microcosmos* 145 He ..left a Sonne..Who being yong, could not yet stirre the sterne. **1607** EARL STIRLING *Jul. Cæsar* II. i. S 1, Th' insolent..Stirre now their tongues, as we did then our swords.

†**d.** To send forth, utter, cause to be heard (a voice or sound); also, to make (a gesture). *Obs.*

a **1000** *Boeth. Metr.* xiii. 49 Þonne hi ȝeherað hleoðrum bræȝdan oðre fuȝelas, hi heora aȝne stefne styriað. *a* **1300** *Cursor M.* 24101 Mi steuen þat i was wont to stere, Vn-nethes moght i self it here. *c* **1614** SIR W. MURE *Dido & Æneas* II. 529 So still he stands, nor voyce nor gesture steirs.

†**e.** To cause to move along or away; to drive, convey, impel; also *fig. Obs.*

a **1300** *Cursor M.* 29546 Cursing..steres his cristendame fro, and liuers him to þe find his foo. *c* **1400** *Destr. Troy* 3709 A shippe, þat was stird with the storme streght out of warde. *c* **1410** *Sir Cleges* 150 Sche hym comforttyd..Hys sorowe away to stere. **1575** CHURCHYARD *Chippes* 93b, Your dealyngs rash, and wretched reuels rued With sticks did stoer, from hiue the quiet Bees.

f. To move (something) from its place; to shift, displace. Chiefly (now always) with negative or its equivalent (implying ineffectual effort): (to be unable) to move or shift in the slightest degree. ? Now *rare* or *Obs.*

α. a **1000** *Boeth. Metr.* vii. 25 Swa bioð anra ȝehwæs monna modsefan miclum aweȝede, of hiora stede styrede. *c* **1205** LAY. 17403 ȝif ȝe hine [*sc.* a stone] maȝen sturien. *c* **1330** *Arth. & Merl.* 2832 King Nanters..No miȝt it [*sc.* the sword] drawe out of þe ston, Ne no gentil man of priis No miȝt it ones stiren. *c* **1450** *Mirk's Festial* 274 He layde hond to Martyns body,..but he myght not sture hit by no craft þat he cowthe. *a* **1628** PRESTON *Breastpl. Faith* (1630) 57 If you take other metall than Iron, the Load-stone will not stirre it. **1693** MOXON *Mech. Exerc.* (1703) 283 Take away the Centre Rule, but stir not the Wainscot. **1719** DE FOE *Crusoe* I. (Globe) 123 A great Block of hard Wood..as big as I had Strength to stir. **1759** FRANKLIN *Ess.* Wks. 1840 III. 110 Laying heavy burdens on men's shoulders, which they themselves would not stir with a single finger.

β. a **1300** *Cursor M.* 16568 þeþen moght þai for na might it stere a fote o strete. **1382** WYCLIF *Wisd.* iv. 19 He shal..stern hem [Vulg. *commovebit*; 1388 moue hem] fro the foundemens. *c* **1470** HENRY *Wallace* v. 425 The Gask hall standand..With out harme, nocht sterd off it a stane. **1557** PHAER *Æneid* v. (1558) N j b, Your prises certayn ben, shall no man them from order stere.

g. To rouse or disturb with a push.

1590 SPENSER *F.Q.* II. v. 2 His steed..fomed yre, When with the maistring spur he did him roughly stire. *a* **1722** LISLE *Husb.* (1757) 323 The rams would keep moving and stirring the ewes all night in the fold. **1891** KIPLING *Light that Failed* ix. (1900) 165 Binkie turned over on his back on the hearth-rug, and Dick stirred him with a meditative foot.

2. *refl.* To move oneself or one's limbs; to move or walk about; to take bodily exercise; to move from one's place. (Rarely of inanimate things.) Now *rare* or *Obs.*; replaced by the intransitive use (11, 12).

c **888** ÆLFRED *Boeth.* xxxv. §7 þa stanas hi styredon for þy sweᵹe. *c* **1000** *Sax. Leechd.* I. 316 He sceal gan & hyne styrian. **13..** *Cursor M.* 5138 (Gött.) He miht noght stir him of þat sted. **1470–85** MALORY *Arthur* VIII. viii. 284 He myȝt not..vnnethe stere hym of his lymmes. **1561** HOLLYBUSH *Hom. Apoth.* 44 b, Let him walke and steare himself without ceasynge. **1704** FULLER *Med. Gymn.* (1711) 21 The more a Man stirs himself, the more Animal Spirits are made in the Brain. **1871** B. TAYLOR *Faust* (1875) II. II. iii. 114 Stir yourselves, ye whispering rushes.

3. To agitate with the hand or an implement so as to alter the relative position of the parts of:

a. a liquid, or a soft or semi-liquid mass; *esp.* to agitate with a more or less circular continuous movement, as with a spoon, so as to mix the particles or promote solution of solid matter; also (*rarely*) to 'trouble', render turbid. Also with adv., as *about*, *round*.

a. c **1000** *Sax. Leechd.* II. 76 Styre mid sticcan. *a* **1300** *Cursor M.* 8937 Ilk dai..þar lighted dun..Angels,..For to stir þe stang. *c* **1440** *Pallad. on Husb.* XII. 588 Let stire hit wel and aysel mynge into. **1523–34** FITZHERB. *Husb.* §44 Put all in-to the sayde panne, and styrre it aboute. **1561** tr. *Calvin's 4 Serm. Idol.* i. C j, But what nede we herin to stirre the truth, as yf we shuld bloundre and trouble a water that is pure and clear. **1579** GOSSON *Sch. Abuse* (Arb.) 21 Amplyfying that which the more it is stirred, the more it stinkes. **1640** T. BRUGIS *Marrow of Physicke* II. 151 Set them off the fire, and with the backe of a Spoone, stirre them. **1769** MRS. RAFFALD *Engl. Housekpr.* (1778) 205 Boil it and keep stirring it all the while. **1802** WORDSW. *Resol. & Indep.* xii, He the pond Stirred with his staff, and fixedly did look Upon the muddy water. **1905** R. BAGOT *Passport* xxi. 212 Idly stirring her little cup of black coffee. **1915** 'F. ANSTEY' *Percy* 121 To be home in time to stir our Christmas pudding.

β. **1375** in Horstmann *Altengl. Leg.* (1878) 138/1 God sente eche day an angel..And to þat tre he wente..þe water þanne sterede ful son. *c* **1400** tr. *Secreta Secret., Gov. Lordsh.* 85 Lat þe sethinge be steryd and strenyd to it bycome cleer. **1535** COVERDALE *Ezek.* xxxii. 12 The catell..shal come nomore vpon the waters: so that nether mans fote ner beastes clawe, shal stere them eny more. **1787** BURNS *Holy Fair* xx, Sit round the table,..An' steer about the toddy. **1878** 'SAXON' *Gallov. Gossip* 222 He had yin Micht a served for a spurtel for steerin his brose.

(*b*) To mix (*in*, *together*, etc.) by stirring.

c **1420** *Liber Cocorum* (1862) 30 Do wyne þerto and venegur gode, Sture hom wele togeder. **1599** A. M. *Gabelhouer's Bk. Physic* 180/1 Take..whyt leade, & stirr it therin. *Ibid.* 183/1 Then stirr them al together, & let it stand. *c* **1770** MRS. GLASSE *Compl. Confectioner* 17 Stir in the sugar by degrees. **1827** FARADAY *Chem. Manip.* vi. (1842) 174 More water should then be added, and the whole stirred together. **1915** 'F. ANSTEY' *Percy* 124 The tokens were bound to turn up, as I had stirred them well into the pudding with my own hand.

(*c*) *absol.*

1712 MOTTEUX *2nd Pt. Quix.* xii. (1749) III. 91 The more ye stir, the more 'twill stink. **1806** A. HUNTER *Culina* (ed. 3) 24 Taking care to stir, or shake, only one way. **1853** LYTTON *My Novel* (Hoppe), The more you stir in it the more it stinks.

b. a collection of solid bodies or particles; *esp.* to poke (burning coals, a fire) so as to promote combustion. †*to stir coals* (fig.): see COAL *sb.* 11.

a. c **1250** *Gen. & Ex.* 3580 He..dede ðat calf melten in fir, And stired it al to dust sir. *c* **1386** CHAUCER *Can. Yeom. Prol. & T.* 725 He stired the coles. *c* **1532** DU WES *Introd. Fr.* in *Palsgr.* 956 To styrre the fire, *tiser.* **1765** *Museum Rust.* IV. 467 The [flax] seed..must be stirred every two or three days. **1888** 'J. S. WINTER' *Bootle's Childr.* ii, Seizing the poker and stirring the fire vigorously.

β. **1557** PHAER *Æneid* v. (1558) O iij, He steres the sleping brandes, And Troian sacred fyer. *a* **1794** *Donocht-Head* 21 in *Burns' Wks.* (1809) IV. 176 I'll steer my fire, I'll make it bleeze a bonnie flame. **1806** R. JAMIESON *Pop. Ballads* I. 348 He steer'd the ingle, and dichtit his beik.

c. soil or earth, as with an agricultural implement; *spec.* to plough across the furrows made by a former ploughing.

a. **1483** *Cath. Angl.* 365/1 To Styr lande, *barectare.* **1523–34** FITZHERB. *Husb.* §141 He wolde haue his landes plowed, donged, sturred, or sowen. **1686** tr. *Chardin's Trav. Persia* 125 The Earth had been stirr'd. **1731–33** TULL *Horse-Hoeing Husb.* xx. 291 This Sort of Land must not be stirred, i.e. plowed the second time in wet Weather. **1842** LOUDON *Suburban Hort.* 127 There is no mode of stirring the soil, whether by picks, forks, or hoes, which may not be performed with this implement [spade].

β. **1523–34** FITZHERB. *Husb.* §16 The rayne shall beate the lande so flat, and bake it so hard to-gyther, that if a drye Maye come, it wyll be to harde to stere in the moneth of June. **1843** HARDY in *Proc. Berw. Nat. Club* II. No. 11. 63 The ground for the barley crop..required to be twice..ploughed; once in the back end, and again in spring,—the latter process being termed 'steering the barley seed.'

4. *fig.* To move from a fixed or quiet condition; to disturb, trouble, molest; to put into tumult or confusion, to upset. *Obs.* exc. *dial.*, or as merged in other senses.

a. c **950** *Lindisf. Gosp.* Mark v. 35 Huætd lengc styres ðu [Vulg. *vexas*] ðone laruu? **1154** *O.E. Chron.* (Laud MS.) an. 1140, þa was al Engle land styred mar þan ær wæs. *a* **1225** *Ancr. R.* 268 þu nouhst nout sturien ne trublen þine heorte. *a* **1340** HAMPOLE *Psalter* xii. 5 If þai stire vs fra stabilnes of thoght. *c* **1400** *Laud Troy Bk.* 4868 That the Gregeis vs not sterre, To take oure toun with arte and sclegt. **1599** B. JONSON *Ev. Man out of Hum.* Prol. 83, I will not stirre your patience. **1602** CHETTLE *Hoffman* I. (1631) B 2, Sweare..to ayd assist me, not to stirre Or contradict me in any enterprise. *c* **1620** *Hist. Feuds & Confl. Clans* (1818) 31 Angus Macconald,..did not stir the pledges [hostages], who were innocent of what was done unto his lands in his absence. **1634** MILTON *Comus* 371, I do not think my sister..so unprincipl'd..As that the single want of light and noise..Could stir the constant mood of her calm thoughts.

β. c **1374** CHAUCER *Troylus* I. 228 (Harl. 1239) He..wende nothyng had hade suche myght A-ȝen his wille that schulde his hert stere. *c* **1394** *P. Pl. Crede* 829 Studye þou nouȝt þeron ne stere þi wittes. **1456** SIR G. HAYE *Gov. Princis* (S.T.S.) II. 82 He that all steris and misgovernis. *c* **1480** HENRYSON *Mor. Fab., Trial Fox* 922 My micht is merciabill, And steiris nane that ar to me prostrait. *c* **1550** BALE *K. Johan* (Camden) 33, I pray the,..my pacyens no more stere. **1786** BURNS *Twa Dogs* 187 Nae cauld nor hunger e'er can steer them. **1816** SCOTT *Old Mort.* xlii, Nane durst steer me when he was in power.

5. To rouse from rest or inaction; to excite to movement or activity.

c **1200** ORMIN 5845 þurrh þatt te faderr gaþ þærto & stireþþ itt & waccneþþ. *c* **1550** *Battle of Otterburn* iii. in Child *Ballads* III. 295/1 Vpon Grene Lynton they lyghted dowyn, Styrande many a stage. **1596** SHAKS. *Tam. Shr.* I. i. 182 Nay, then tis time to stirre him fro his trance. **1607** TOPSELL *Four-f. Beasts* 585 The Leopard when he was stirred ranne too and fro distracted. **1816** SCOTT *Antiq.* xxxvi, He's steered the town to get awa an express to fetch his carriage. **1829** —— *Anne of G.* xxvi, Follow forth your own..objects, without stirring a nest of hornets.

†**b.** To excite to activity, to stimulate (a bodily function, 'humour', etc.): also with the person as obj. *Obs.*

c **1000** [see STIRRING *ppl. a.* 3 a]. *c* **1400** tr. *Secreta Secret., Gov. Lordsh.* 73 Somer tyme ys hoot and drye, and þanne þe rede colere ys steryd. *c* **1491** *Chast. Goddes Chyld.* 20 The wycked humours ben styred and make the stomocke replete. **1609** [see STIRRING *ppl. a.* 3 a]. **1686** tr. *Chardin's Trav. Persia* 235 The Remedy..that kills in one Country, does but only stir a Man in another.

†**c.** *to stir one's time*: to make vigorous use of one's opportunity. *Sc. Obs.*

a **1578** LINDESAY (Pitscottie) *Chron. Scot.* (S.T.S.) II. 30 Seing this devissioun amangis the nobilietie of Scotland, they steirit thair tyme and wssit thair weiris the mair scharpelie. **1591** R. BRUCE *Serm. Edin.* S 7 b, His enemies were aloft, sturring their time, rageing in murther, oppression and bloode.

†**6.** *refl.* To bestir oneself; to be active; to act briskly or energetically; in early use often, to fight valiantly. *Obs.* (replaced by *bestir*; see also 14).

a. c **1205** LAY. 10195 Heo ferde forð rihtes..& stureden heom seoluen. **1297** R. GLOUC. (Rolls) 3663 þe king adde er among þe scottes ystured him uol wel. *a* **1320** *Sir Tristr.* 1082 He stird him as a kniȝt. **1573** TUSSER *Husb.* (1878) 139 Good husbandrie lusteth himselfe for to stur.

β. a **1300** *Cursor M.* 23757 If we stitli all wil vs ster, crist help sal be us ner. *c* **1400** *Gamelyn* 515 Stere the, good Adam, and lat ther noon flee. **1456** SIR G. HAYE *Law Arms* (S.T.S.) 64 [He] sa stoutly sterit him amang thame..that thare durst nane cum on him allane. **1470–85** MALORY *Arthur* XVIII. xvii. 755 When he was vpon his hors he stered hym fyersly.

γ. a **1225** *St. Marher.* 14 Hwen..he letten me nawt, ne ne storið hamseolf,..ich leade ham..iþe ladliche lake of þe suti sunne. *c* **1275** LAY. 15254 Hahtliche ȝou storieþ.

b. To begin to act; to busy oneself *to do* something: = 14 b. *rare.*

a **1225** *Ancr. R.* 306 He ne der, uor fearlac, sturien him touward sunne. *c* **1425** *Engl. Conq. Irel.* (1896) 86 None Iresshe-man ne durst hym styrre, wer to begynne. **1870** BURTON *Hist. Scot.* lv. V. 341 The..French ambassador..stirred himself not only to keep this project alive, but to bring it to a practical conclusion.

7. To move to action, urge, incite, instigate, stimulate. Also formerly in weaker or more general sense: To prompt, induce, persuade.

a. c **897** ÆLFRED *Gregory's Past. C.* 175 S[u]a sceal æᵹhwelc lareow to anre lufan..mid mislicum manungum his hieremonna mod styrigean. *a* **1225** *Ancr. R.* 130 þe hwingen þet bereð ham upward, þet beoð gode þeauwes þet heo moten sturien into gode werkes. **1340** HAMPOLE *Pr. Consc.* Prol. 154 Som thyng..þat myght styrre þam to gude lyfyng. *Ibid.* 157 To knaw þat, myght þam stir and lede Til mekenes. **1388** WYCLIF *Deut.* xxxii. 11 As an egle stirynge his briddis to fle [Vulg. *provocans ad volandum pullos suos*]. **1474** CAXTON *Chesse* III. v. (1883) 122 To take away all the thynges that miht styre or meue his men to lecherye. **1553** T. WILSON *Rhet.* 8 b, The onely namyng of theim, will stirre honest hartes, to speake well of them. **1595** SHAKS. *John* II. i. 63 An Ate, stirring him to bloud and strife. **1781** COWPER *Charity* 118 He..Imports what others have invented well, And stirs his own to match them, or excel. **1821** SCOTT *Kenilw.* xii, Can ye not stir his mind to any pastimes? **1858** FROUDE *Hist. Eng.* III. xiii. 163 The untruth of the stories by which they had been stirred to rebellion. **1893** TRAILL *Soc. Eng.* Introd. p. xxxii, The Revival of Letters stirred the human mind into more vigorous activity.

β. **1303** R. BRUNNE *Handl. Synne* 5186 Hyt sterynþ a man hym self to slo. **138.** WYCLIF *Sel. Wks.* I. 149 Who ever stere men to yvel lyfe. *c* **1440** CAPGRAVE *Life St. Kath.* v. 1679 Men wil wene that thou be ny wood To sle th[is] puple..And lete me scape whiche stered hem alle. *c* **1470** in *Som. & Dorset N. & Q.* (1905) Sept. 303 [He] provokid and stered his saide Dogge to renne uppon youre saide Bysecher. **1513** DOUGLAS *Æneis* VI. i. 102 To ask ansueris Now is the tyme; lo, lo, the God me steris! **1549** COVERDALE etc. *Erasm. Par. 1 Pet.* i. 3–9 Being prouoked by no merites of ours but stiered frely of his owne mercye. **1657** in *Burton's Diary* (1828) I. 415, I hope, that neither the humour of..unwise people, nor yet..[etc.] shall steer me to give other than such an answer as may be ingenuous and thankful.

†**b.** To urge with a view to persuasion, try to persuade, exhort, entreat. *Obs.*

a. c **1380** WYCLIF *Wks.* (1880) 41, I conseile, amoneste, and stire my freris. *c* **1449** PECOCK *Repr.* II. vi. 17 Peter stireth tho same men for to haue pacience. **1534** BERNERS *Golden Bk. M. Aurel.* (1546) P viii, This younge manne,..was importunately stirred by his naturall friendes. **1560** INGELEND *Disob. Child* H j, You hearde that by Sentences auncient and olde He styred his Sonne as he best thought.

β. **1387–8** T. USK *Test. Love* I. viii. (Skeat) 1 Eft gan Love to sterne [*read* steren] me with these wordes. *c* **1440** *Gesta Rom.* xlii. 127 (Add. MS.) A man..sterid his sone to gete hym frendes. **1544** S. FISH *Supplic. Hen. VIII*, 24 The Holy Ghoste, which moueth & steareth vs euer to mortefye the fleshe.

8. To excite to feeling, emotion, or passion; to 'move', affect.

a. a **1225** *Ancr. R.* 296 O sihð þet tu isihst, oðer on elpi word þet tu mis-iherest ȝif hit out stureð þe, cwench hit mid teares of watere. *c* **1380** *Sir Ferumb.* 2795 Alas! loue, wo dost þou me, þov sturest al my blod. **1382** WYCLIF *Matt.* xxi. 10 Whan he had entrid in to Jerusalem, al the cite was stirid, seyinge, who is this? **1382** —— *Luke* xv. 20 Whanne he was ȝit fer, his fader syȝ him, and he was stirid [**1388** stirrid] by mercy. *c* **1400** MAUNDEV. (Roxb.) xiii. 58 A wikked man..kest a brynnand fyrebrand at oure Lord for to stirre him til ire. **1553** T. WILSON *Rhet.* 92 b, Anye one that myndeth by hys vtteraunce to stirre the hartes of menne. **1630** R. N. *Camden's Eliz.* I. 21 The Bishop of Rome..being now more stirred, commanded Sir Edward Carne..to lay down his Office of Embassadour. **1799** WORDSW. *Fountain* 30 My eyes are dim with childish tears, My heart is idly stirred. **1865** TROLLOPE *Belton Est.* ix. 99 Words..that really stir the soul, and bring true comfort to the listener. **1889** JESSOPP *Coming of Friars* iii. 113 The story of a great man's life still stirs the heart.

β. c **1375** *Sc. Leg. Saints* xvii. (*Martha*) 321 To compuncione þu [? *read* þe] suld steyre, þe instance of myn prayer sere. *a* **1400–50** *Wars Alex.* 4256 Leue ȝe noȝt we be to heȝe ne hauten of will..or sterid to enuy. **1481** CAXTON *Godfrey* clx. 235 By thyse wordes were the barons gretely stered and meuyd. **1530** PALSGR. 735/1 Beware thou stere him nat to anger. **1581** A. HALL *Iliad* IV. 66 Then Agamemn appeard No whit to yeelde,..or ought with feare was steard.

γ. c **1440** *Gesta Rom.* xlvi. 181 (Harl. MS.) Whenne Ionathas sawe hir, he was I-storid to an vnlawfull maner of love.

b. To affect with strong emotion; to move strongly (a person, his spirit, 'blood', etc.).

c **1489** CAXTON *Blanchardyn* ii. 15 That sore mouyd and styryd his noble and hyghe corage. *c* **1610** BEAUM. & FL. *Maid's Trag.* I. i, The musicke must be shrill and all confus'd That stirs my blood. **1822** BYRON *Juan* VIII. lv, So was his blood stirr'd while he found resistance. **1905** R. BAGOT *Passport* xxvi. 279 The news of Sor Beppe's dismissal from the office of *fattore* had stirred public opinion in and around Montefiano to its depths.

9. To excite, occasion.

a. To excite or provoke (passion); to prompt, evoke or occasion (anger, hatred, affection, suspicion, also †laughter, fear, etc.); formerly in wider use, †to occasion (an event, mental or bodily condition).

a. c **1000** ÆLFRIC *Hom.* II. 298 Ne dranc he wines drenc, ne nan ðæra wætena þe druncennysse styriað. *a* **1225** *Ancr. R.* 198 þeo..þet beoð of muchel speche ȝelpeð..gabbeð,..stureið leihtres. *c* **1430** in *Pol. Rel. & L. Poems* 197 To stire mi wraþþe þou wolt a-saye. *c* **1450** *Mirk's Festial* 158 Forto styre your deuocyon. **1538** ELYOT *Dict., Conflare inuidiam, inimicitias, odium,* to stire or procure enuy, hostilitie, hate. **1580** E. KNIGHT *Trial Truth* 15 b, This part of Scripture may iustly stirre a feare in vs. **1667** MILTON *P.L.* VIII. 308 Each Tree Load'n with fairest Fruit,..stirr'd in me sudden appetite To pluck and eate. **1760** LLOYD *Actor* 195 A fault which stirs the critic's rage. **1823** SCOTT *Quentin D.* xxvi, If nothing occurs to stir the rage of this vindictive madman, I am sure of victory. **1847** TENNYSON *Princess* IV. 11 Blissful palpitations in the blood, Stirring a sudden transport rose and fell. **1871** MORLEY *Voltaire* (1886) 5 Antipathy against Voltaire to a degree that..must now and then have even stirred a kind of reacting sympathy.

β. **1430–40** LYDG. *Bochas* V. i. (1554) 114 Husbandes..had in maner a suspeccion Stiered by the serpent of false gelousye Toward Spurina. *c* **1450** *St. Cuthbert* 6627 þat sight sterid his deuocioun. **1513** DOUGLAS *Æneis* I. x. 7 Within hir banis grene The hote fyir of luif to kendle and steir. *a* **1586** SIDNEY *Astr. & Stella* xxv, Vertue..with vertuous care to ster Loue of herselfe, tooke Stella's shape.

γ. **1558** W. FORREST *Grysilde Seconde* (Roxb.) 72 Synne, sore of Kyngis, stoorthe Goddys malediction.

†**b.** To instigate, set going, set on foot (strife, commotion, etc.). *Obs.*: cf. *stir up* 16 e.

a. a **1023** WULFSTAN *Hom.* xviii. (1883) 106 Saca and wraca he styrede ᵹelome. *c* **1175** *Lamb. Hom.* 113 He ne flit mid cheste ne he sake ne sturað. **1521** FISHER *Serm. agst. Luther* i. Wks. (1876) 312 In lyke maner..hathe rysen many a tyme some blacke clowde of heresy, & stered suche a tempest..that [etc.]. **1563–83** FOXE *A. & M.* 248/2 The French king..stirred warre in Normandy. *c* **1610** *Women Saints* 150 So that they stirre a greater tumult than euer the people had donne before. **1669** DRYDEN *Tyr. Love* III. i. (1670) 23 The Soldiers love her Brother's memory; And for her sake some Mutiny will stir.

β. 1390 Gower *Conf.* I. 284 So that thou miht the betre lere What mischief that this vice stereth. 1426 Audelay *Poems* 18 That steren stryf and wrath.

c. To provoke or 'needle' (someone); to tease. See 14 d. *Austral. colloq.*

1972 L. Irish *Time of Dolphins* iii. 33 She's damned well stirring you. 1974 in Buckley & Hamilton *Festival* 187 Stirring teachers was our favourite sport. 1978 B. St. A. Smith *Spirit beyond Psyche* 180 She..had often 'stirred' him about his pretty hair, but secretly she had been proud of him.

10. To bring into notice or debate; to move, raise, moot (a subject or question). Now *rare.*

α. *Beowulf* 873 Secȝ eft onȝan sið Beowulfes snyttrum styrian. 1390 Gower *Conf.* I. 174 Many envious tale is stered, Wher that it mai noght ben ansuered. c1400 tr. *Secreta Secret., Gov. Lordsh.* 55 To stirre doutablys questions, honestly to aske hem, and discretly answore hem. 1444 *Rolls of Parlt.* V. 122/1 Yef ther be eny mater or maters stirred, desired or moeved bi the Baillifs. 1580 Spenser *Three Proper Lett.* A iij, Little newes is here stirred. 1607–12 Bacon *Ess., Of Great Place* (Arb.) 286 Preserve the rightes of thie place, but stirre not questions of Iurisdiccion. a1676 Hale *Hist. Common Law* iii. (1713) 49 Many Cases.. wherein the Question was not stirred. 1785 Paley *Mor. Philos.* vi. viii. (1818) II. 246 That..a doubt once decided may be stirred no more. 1831 Scott *Cast. Dang.* iv, 'I shall not stir the question,' said the minstrel. 1890 C. Martyn *W. Phillips, Agitator* 202 To the petition he stirred,..the Committee returned a brutal denial.

β. c1374 Chaucer *Boeth.* iii. pr. xii. (1868) 106 But na-þeles yif I stered resouns þat ne ben nat taken fro wiþ oute þe compas of þe þinge of whiche we treten. a1548 Hall *Chron., Hen. VI*, 145 Who that..moued or stered the matter firste vnto your Lordeship, counsailed you neither for your worship nor profite.

†**b.** To bring forward as an example, to instance.

1340 *Ayenb.* 226 To loki þet stat of wodewehod one ssel sterie þe uorbisne of þe turle.

II. Intransitive senses. (See also 3 a (*c*).)

†**11.** To move (continuously, or in general sense); to be in motion; *spec.* to move as a living being. (Cf. the reflexive sense 2.) *Obs.*

α. a1000 Ælfric *Gen.* i. 26 Ealle þa creopende, þe stirað on eorðan. a1225 *Leg. Kath.* 361 Cleopest þeo þinges godes, þt nowðer sturien ne mahen ne steoren ham seoluen. a1225 *Ancr. R.* 422 Water þet ne stureð nout readliche stinkeð. 13.. *E.E. Allit. P.* B. 403 By forty dayez wern faren, on folde no flesch styryed. c1400 tr. *Secreta Secret., Gov. Lordsh.* 98 Fyssh of þe water, þat gooþ on foure feet, & þat stirrys vpon wombe. 1583 Melbancke *Philotimus* E j, He..that hath an ore stirringe in other mens boates. 1633 G. Herbert *Temple, Assurance* vi, While rocks stand, And rivers stirre.

β. c1384 Chaucer *H. Fame* 567 And here with alle I gan to stere And he me in his fete to bere. 1456 Sir G. Haye *Law Arms* (S.T.S.) 75 Thingis that ar corporale in this erde steris nocht..with the moving of it. 1538 Bale *God's Promises* ii. (facs.) B j b, I wyll destroye..all that on earthe do stere. 1587 Turberv. *Trag. T.* vi. 87 b, The winde so slender was To cause the ship to steare.

†**b.** To move or pass from one place to another; to come or go. *Obs.*

Some of the quots., esp. in β, may belong to steer *v.*¹ 4.

α. a1225 *Leg. Kath.* 796 Ȝe alles to strif beoð isturet hidere. a1300 *Cursor M.* 3252 Qua him sagh moght vnderstand He stird was of a riche land. c1400 *Destr. Troy* 959 Iason.. Busket to the bank and the bote tok, Stird ouer the streame streght to þe lond. 1581 W. S. *Compend. or Briefe Exam.* 8 Wee might sturre from on place to an other.

β. a1300 *Cursor M.* 4959 Nour-quider mai we stere. c1450 *Mirk's Festial* 145 Þis man steryd ynto anoþyr howse. c1470 *Rauf Coilȝear* 12 Mony stout man steiris Of town with the King. 1513 Douglas *Æneis* xii. viii. 12 Turnus.. Persauyt thame thus sterand throw the plane.

γ. 1513 Douglas *Æneis* i. i. 65 Thair stewinnis stowrand fast throw the salt fame. a1568 *Wyf Auchtermuchty* ix. in *Bannatyne MS.* (Hunter. Club) 344 Than to the kyrn that he did stoure.

12. To pass from rest to motion, to begin to move; to make a slight movement, to move lightly (esp. to and fro); to make any movement, to move at all or in the least (chiefly with negative); to leave one's place, to budge; not to remain still; *occas.* to show signs of life or consciousness (after sleep or a faint).

α. c950 *Lindisf. Gosp.* Matt. xi. 7 Ðerd *vel* puulsper from uinde styrende *vel* sceæcende. a1000 Ælfric *Josh.* x. 12 Ne stira þu sunne of þam stede. c1200 Ormin 2810 Min child tatt i min wambe lip..bigann..To stirenn & to buttenn. c1205 Lay. 17421 Beoð alle stille þæt na man þer ne sturie. c1220 *Bestiary* 18 Stille lið ðe leun, ne stireð he nout of slepe Til [etc.]. 1377 Langl. *P. Pl.* B. xx. 102 Lered ne lewed he let no man stonde, That he hitte euene þat euere stired after. c1400 Maundev. (Roxb.) iv. 12 Men may see þare þe erthe of þe toumbe..stirre and moue, as þer ware a qwikke thing under. 1470–85 Malory *Arthur* i. xiv. 53, I wold that..they stere not tyl ye and your knyghtes haue foughte with hem longe. 1577 B. Googe *Heresbach's Husb.* iii. 115 b, The eares must bee shorte, standing vpright, and stirring. 1601 R. Johnson *Kingd. & Commw.* (1603) 120 Diuers.. gentlemen..who neuer stirre from the side of the captaine Generall. 1602 Chettle *Hoffman* iv. (1631) H 2, Art sure she is a sleepe!..She stirs not, shee is fast. *Ibid.* H 2 b, She stirs, and when she wakes obserue me well. 1604 Shaks. *Ham.* i. i. 10 *Barn.* Haue you had quiet Guard? *Fran.* Not a Mouse stirring. 1660 F. Brooke tr. *Le Blanc's Trav.* 38 Whether they snore, or stir much in their sleepe. 1667 Dryden & Dk. Newcastle *Sir M. Mar-all* iii. i, [Lady has fainted away] *Rose.* Open her Mouth with a Dagger. 2 *Wom.* She stirs, she revives, merciful to us all. 1704 Cibber *Careless Husb.* iii. 35 Nay, you shan't stir a step. 1711 Addison *Spect.* No. 112 ¶5 Nobody presumes to stir till Sir Roger is gone out of the Church. 1717 Prior *Alma* iii. 116 From every leaf that stirs, she flies. 1765 Blackstone *Comm.* I. i. 125 Life..begins in contemplation of law as soon as an infant is able to stir in the mother's womb. 1829 Southey *All for Love* vii. xlviii, He stirr'd not from his station. 1855 Tennyson *Maud* i. xxii. iii, All night has the casement jessamine stirr'd To the dancers dancing in tune. 1863 Mrs. H. Wood *Verner's Pride* xlv, I was so took aback ..that I could neither stir nor speak. 1885 'Mrs. Alexander' *At Bay* x, She..stood for an instant..in silent, prayerful thought. Glynn waited till she stirred.

β. c1220 *Bestiary* 404 Ne stereð ȝe noȝt of ðe stede. a1400 *Minor Poems fr. Vernon MS.* 604 Þer water is most deope, þe lesse þer þen steres he. c1430 *Chev. Assigne* 147 They stoden alle stylle for stere þey ne durste. 1567 Golding *Ovid's Met.* v. 116 Downe he fell and could not after steare. 1616 J. Lane *Contn. Sqr.'s T.* vii. 480 While tonges well much maie talke, but no hand steare. 1786 *Har'st Rig* xiv, They vow they'll never steer Sae lang's he has a cut to shear, But bide wi' him till fields are clear.

γ. 14.. *Guy Warw.* 3869 Loke, ye store not of þat stedde. c1420 *Chron. Vilod.* 3108 Þe clothe þat honged vpone hurre tombe þere þo Meue ofte & store wondere fast. c1450 *Erle of Tolous* 755 He durst not store, nor make no mone, To make the lady afryght.

b. To go out (from a house or place of abode); usually with †*abroad*, †*forth*, *out*: almost always with negative. Rarely of inanimate things.

α. 1567 Maplet *Gr. Forest* 86 b, The Frog saith Aristotle liueth quietly all the time of cold weather, and neuer stirreth abrode. 1601 Shaks. *Jul. C.* ii. ii. 38 *Cæs.* What say the Augurers? *Ser.* They would not haue you to stirre forth to day. 1644 Milton *Areop.* (Arb.) 59 Unoffensive books must not stirre forth without a visible jaylor in thir title. 1713 Swift *Jrnl. to Stella* 4 Apr., I came home at seven, and have never stirred out. 1743 Bulkeley & Cummins *Voy. S. Seas* 217 [We] were told by the Captain, we must not stir out of the Ship. 1823 Scott *Quentin D.* xii, He dare not stir far from his own Forest of Ardennes. 1827 Pusey in Liddon *Life* (1893) I. vi. 118 These [MSS.] never stir out of the walls of the Bodleian. 1832 Ht. Martineau *Life in Wilds* iii. 33 They could not stir till they had provision for their journey.

γ. ?a1500 *Chester Pl., Purif.* 91 Yet storred I not out of this place.

†**c.** Of a voice: To sound. (Cf. 1 d.) *Obs.*

c1205 Lay. 28161 Þa umbe stunde stefne þer sturede.

d. Of a colour: To move, be affected.

1792 *Trans. Soc. Arts* X. 199 This manufacture improves every time it is washed; and the colours never stir by washing.

e. To show signs of growth; to bud. *rare*⁻¹.

1843 *Penny Cycl.* XXVII. 457/1 A northern aspect is thought best, as the vines do not stir so soon in spring.

f. *fig.* To begin to show signs of 'life' or activity (as an intellectual movement or the like).

1873–1909 [implied in stirring *vbl. sb.* 2 d].

13. To move about in a place, to 'be about'; chiefly in *pres. pple.* (often *spec.* = out of bed, up and about).

α. c1205 Lay. 23756 Þat hit dæi wes amarȝen duȝeðe gunne sturien [c1275 gan to storie]. c1374 Chaucer *Troylus* iii. 692 But boden go to bedde with myschaunce, If ony wight was steryinge ony where. a1533 Berners *Huon* lxi. 213 They coude se no man steryinge within the castell. 1606 Shaks. *Tr. & Cr.* i. ii. 52 *Cre.* Hector was gone but Hellen was not vp. *Pan.* E'ene so; Hector was stirring early. 1619 in Foster *Eng. Factories India* (1906) 99 If any stronge drinke be stirringe. 1702 Steele *Funeral* ii. 17 How often must I tell you my Lord is not stirring: His Lordship has not Slept well. 1748 *Anson's Voy.* ii. v. 176 Had any ships been stirring in these seas..we must have met with them. 1825 Scott *Betrothed* xiii, Notwithstanding there are now no Welsh knaves stirring, yet the marches are never free from robbers. 1848 Dickens *Dombey* xviii, When no one in the house was stirring, and the lights were all extinguished. 1884 Henley & Stevenson *Adm. Guinea* iv. i. (1892) 244 *Arethusa* (*listening*). St! my father stirring in his room!

γ. c1275 [see α]. 1555 Eden *Decades* (Arb.) 114 When he had contynued a whyle in the haven, and sawe noo man stouryinge.

b. *transf.* To be in circulation, be current; chiefly in *pres. pple.* Now somewhat *rare*: chiefly of news (cf. c).

1423 *Rolls of Parlt.* IV. 257/2 Be ther never so muche white moneye forged, that shall be but litell the more sturryngge among the poeple. 1608 Bp. Hall *Charact.* ii. 79 No newes can stir but by his doore. 1634 W. Tirwhyt tr. *Balzac's Lett.* (vol. I) 187 To let you know what newes is stirring. 1691 Wood *Life* (O.H.S.) III. 370 [The] University very empty and dead: and money but little stirring. 1711 Addison *Spect.* No. 10 ¶5 Asking..whether there was any News stirring? c1850 *Arab. Nts.* (Rtldg.) 646 He asked the host if there were any news stirring.

c. To go on, happen, take place; chiefly in *pres. pple.* = going on, 'on foot'.

1526 *Pilgr. Perf.* (W. de W. 1531) 35 Euery thyng that stereth by hym, or that he seeth or hereth, he iudgeth to be a reuelacyon. 1596 Shaks. *Merch. V.* iii. i. 99 No ill luck stirring but what lights a my shoulders. 1684 Otway *Atheist* i. i, What Sins are stirring in this noble metropolis. 1722 De Foe *Plague* 141 There's no Trade stirs now. 1882 Pebody *Engl. Journalism* xx. 152 Telegrams from every part of the world where there is anything stirring that is of the slightest interest to Englishmen.

14. To move briskly or energetically; to be on the move, be active, 'look alive', bestir oneself. Cf. the refl. use 6.

α. c1205 Lay. 9334 He..sturede i þon compe al se hit þe king weore. a1225 *Ancr. R.* 152 Vor þui mine leoue sustren, bi nihte, ase þe niht fuel þet ancre is to iefned, beoð ȝeorne sturiinde. 1573 Tusser *Husb.* (1878) 169 Make maide to be clenly,..and teach hir to stirre, when hir mistresse doth speake. 1602 Middleton *Blurt, Master-Constable* ii. ii. 3 Trivia, Simperina, stir, stir: one of you open the casements. 1608 Shaks. *Per.* ii. i. 16 Looke how thou stirr'st now! 1830 Gen. P. Thompson *Exerc.* (1842) I. 301 Every free man in the civilized world is put on his defence, and called upon to be stirring for the preservation of all that he may wish to keep. 1841 Thackeray *Gt. Hoggarty Diam.* xii, Her husband stirred and bustled about until the requisite leave was obtained. 1849 W. S. Mayo *Kaloolah* vi. (1850) 57 Let's stir round and do something. 1884 W. C. Smith *Kildrostan* 34 Ina, your heart is low, as one will be Who sits down in a mist instead of stirring To keep the blood warm.

β. c1400 *Gamelyn* 519 (Corpus MS.) Stere [*v.rr.* Bi-, Bystere] good adam and late þer none flee. c1400 *Beryn* 548 So she sterith aboute this house in a wood rese. c1400 *Ragman Roll* 134 in Hazl. *E.E.P.* (1864) I. 75 Joly and lyght is your complexicion, That steryn ay, and kunne nat stonde still. c1470 Henry *Wallace* v. 838 The hardy Scottis so steryt in that sted. c1470 *Gol. & Gaw.* 559 Wondir sternly thai steir on thair stent stedis. 1538 Starkey *England* (1878) 82 So in our commynalty, certayn partys ther be wych euer be mouyng and sterryng.

γ. c1275 Lay. 9334 He..storede in þan fihte.

b. *fig.* To be active or occupied *about* something; to move or bestir oneself *in* a matter, to begin to act.

α. c1205 Lay. 18845 On hir he scal streonen þat scal wide sturien. c1400 *Destr. Troy* 4047 Now wete yche..þat stares vpon stories, & stirs in bokys, þat [etc.]. 1618 in Foster *Eng. Factories India* (1906) 19 If it bee prooved Mogolls goods, and that the King stirr in yt, I know this people. 1620 [G. Brydges] *Horæ Subs.* 304 A mans nature is to stirre more for the recouery of a good, which they once enioyed, then for the acquisition of what they are ignorant of. 1622 Callis *Stat. Sewers* (1647) 152 Surely this point hath heretofore been much stirred in, and not without some cause. 1653 W. Ramesey *Astrol. Restored* 183 Neither is it safe for those Rebels to stirr when she [i.e. the Moon] is weak. 1709 Hearne *Collect.* (O.H.S.) II. 175 The writer..was..advis'd ..to stir for it. c1721 Marq. Tullibardine in *10th Rep. Hist. MSS. Comm.* App. i. 126, I pray the capacity of those who are most able to stir about your Majesty's concerns, be well employed in [etc.]. 1818 Scott *Br. Lamm.* xv, The improbability of the young Master of Ravenswood's finding friends in parliament, capable of stirring in so weighty an affair. 1871 Freeman *Norm. Conq.* (1876) IV. xviii. 144 While Exeter was in arms, York did not stir, and when York did stir, Exeter had no longer the power of stirring.

β. c1480 Henryson *Test. Cress.* 469 Fortoun is fikkill, quhen scho beginnis & steiris. a1560 Phaer *Æneid* ix. (1562) Dd ij b, Gods, gods, o countrey gods, in whose protection Troy still steeres. 1647 *Ded. Epist. to Earl Pembroke* in *Beaum. & Fletcher's Wks.*, But directed by the example of some, who once steered in our qualitie..we have presumed to offer to your Selfe, what before was never printed of these Authours. 1891 'H. Haliburton' *Ochil Idylls* 40 At fifty, wi' a conscience clear, The man that sits, as I do here, Haund-haill, an' neither slow to steer Nor quick to tire.

c. To make a disturbance, commotion, or tumult; to rise in revolt or insurrection. Now *rare* and merely contextual.

c1205 Lay. 10717 In Lundene stureden þa leoden. 1399 Langl. *Rich. Redeles* iii. 269 To strie strouters þat sterede aȝeine rithis. c1425 Wyntoun *Cron.* iii. i. (S.T.S.) II. 273 Þe kynge of Moab than, Eglon, Had vndyr hym in subieccion þe folk of Israel fourteyn ȝhere, Qwhil Ayot begouthe to steyr. 1502 *Ord. Crysten Men* (W. de W.) iv. iv. (1506) 173 Good werkes that ben done for the loue of god stere put and knocke at the gate of mercy dyuyne. a1550 *Lynn Chron.* in *Six Town Chron.* (1911) 185 In this yere the Skots begane to store and the deweke of glossytr was sent to them but he retorned wth out battell. 1570 Levins *Manip.* 190/25 To sturre, neutre, *tumultuare.* 1648 Gage *West Ind.* 71 The King..was quiet and peaceable, and stirred not against him. 1891 Farrar *Darkn. & Dawn* li, 'Is not your nation seditious and turbulent?' 'It is not,' answered Ishmael. 'We never stir unless we are wronged.'

d. To cause trouble, to provoke authority; to make a nuisance of oneself. See 9 c and stirrer 1 d. *colloq.* (chiefly *Austral.*).

1972 J. de Hoog *Skid Row Dossier* 110 Several youths went 'stirring' one day—riding up and down the lifts of large office blocks. 1980 E. R. Hall *Can you hear Me?* 128 There were radio members who would 'stir' mainly in an effort to get the 'System' to work for the individual. 1984 'K. Royce' *Crypto Man* x. 153 'It will get straight back to Clarke.' 'Maybe that won't be a bad thing. All we can do is stir.'

15. To be roused or excited, as feeling, passion, etc.

a1000 *Boeth. Metr.* xxii. 64 Mid þæm bisgum þe on breostum styreð. a1300 *Cursor M.* 5052 Joseph beheild þan beniamin, Him stird al his blod wit-in. 1558 Phaer *Æneid* ii. D iv b, Sometime when tyryd ben their harts their manful stomacks steres [L. *victis redit in præcordia virtus*] And down their conquerours they quell. 1575 Churchyard *Chippes* 2 b, Our rage was great,..Our stomackes storde, as we did this beholde. 1577–82 Breton *Toyes of an Idle Head* (Grosart) 39/1 And then doo what I can, alas, my Heart beginnes to sturre. 1596 Shaks. *1 Hen. IV*, i. iii. 190 The blood more stirres To rowze a Lyon, then to start a Hare. 1704 Cibber *Careless Husb.* i. i. 10 My Blood stirs at the very thought on't. 1841 Dickens *Barn. Rudge* lxxxi, His wrath so stirred within him, that he could have struck him dead. 1847 Tennyson *Princess* v. 258, I..felt the blind wildbeast of force..Stir in me as to strike.

III. 16. stir up.

a. *trans.* To set in motion, agitate; to push or poke so as to displace, disturb, or mix the parts of: cf. 1, 3.

to stir up with a long pole (humorous, with allusion to a wild-beast showman 'stirring up' his beasts): to rouse from rest or inaction, to provoke to activity: cf. d, also 5, 7.

1340–70 *Alex. & Dind.* 487 Stiue stormus of þe wind stiren vp þe wawus. 1535 Coverdale *Deut.* xxxii. 11 As an Aegle stereth vp hir nest, and flotereth ouer hir yonge. 1679 *Trials of Green etc. for Murder of Sir E. Godfrey* 39, I was in the Parlor and stirred up the fire. 1823 'Jon Bee' *Dict. Turf* 166 'Stir 'em up with a long pole, as the fellow does with the beestes,' alludes to the bellowings of these latter. 1816 J. Smith *Panorama Sci. & Art* II. 684 Stir up and dress the soil of flowers and shrubs in pots. 1827 Faraday *Chem. Manip.* xviii. (1842) 481 It is best..to effect the mixture.. by stirring up the mass lightly with a pointed stick or a fork. 1857 Hughes *Tom Brown* ii. ii, Stir him up with a long pole, Jack, and hear him swear like a drunken sailor! 1912 C. Johnston *Why World laughs* 2 Whenever the dance showed signs of flagging, the policeman stirred them up with a long pole.

†**b.** To rouse from sleep or rest, to wake up. (Cf. 5.) *Obs.*

1526 TINDALE *Acts* xii. 7 He smote Peter on the syde and steryd him uppe. **1533** MORE *Answ. Poysoned Bk.* Wks. 1092/2 He that eateth my fleshe and drynketh my bloude, hath life euerlasting, and I shall stere hym vp in the last day. **1611** BIBLE *Song Sol.* viii. 4, I charge you.. that ye stirre not vp, nor awake my loue vntill he please. **1683** SALMON *Doron* I. 146 [It] gently awakes, or stirrs them up.

†**c.** To 'raise up', call into being. *Obs.*

1526 TINDALE *Rom.* ix. 17 Even for thys same purpose haue I stered the uppe [Gr. ἐξήγειρά σε], to shewe my power on the. **1532** MORE *Confut. Tindale* 284 We saye also that god hath dayly stered vp & dayly doth sterre vp new prophetes in sundry partes of hys catholyke chyrche. **1535** COVERDALE *Deut.* xxv. 7 My kynsman refuseth to stere vp [Vulg. *suscitare*: Luther *erwecken*] a name vnto his brother in Israel and wyl not marye me. *a* **1548** HALL *Chron., Hen. VIII*, 198 b, The dispensacion by the lawe of Deuteronomi of styrryng vp the brothers sede. **1561** WINȜET *83 Quest.* Wks. (S.T.S.) I. 52 An wngodly and wickit peple sterit vp to be Godis scurge. **1564** tr. *P. Martyr's Comm. Judges* 200 b, When God decreed to sende any notable and excellent man, he verye often tymes styrred hym vp out of a barren woman.

d. To rouse to action, activity, or emotion; to rouse from indifference or sloth; to incite, instigate, stimulate: cf. 7.

α. **1545** BRINKLOW *Compl.* iii. (1874) 16 God shal sturre vp the hartys euen of his own fryndes agaynst him. **1590** SPENSER *F.Q.* II. iv. 42 His am I Atin, his in wrong and right, That.. stirre him up to strife and cruell fight. *a* **1591** H. SMITH *Serm.* (1594) 529 That all the world may take heede how they stirre vp the Lyon of Iudah. *a* **1644** QUARLES *Sol. Recant.* xii. 11 The wise mans words are like to Goads, that doe Stir up the drowzy, and spur up the slow. **1665** MANLEY *Grotius' Low C. Wars* 403 At which time.. they stirred him up to recover the Right and Title of Oneal. **1671** MILTON *Samson* 1251 He will.. with malitious counsel stir them up ..yet further to afflict thee. *a* **1720** SEWEL *Hist. Quakers* (1795) I. II. 129 The constable stirred up the rude people, and cried, Kill him [Cf. *Acts* vi. 12 etc.]. **1838** J. L. STEPHENS *Trav. Russia* 107/1 The French.. were always suspected of being political emissaries to stir up the Poles to revolution. **1885** 'MRS. ALEXANDER' *At Bay* v, I shall write to my lawyers to stir up our detectives. **1890** *Boston* (Mass.) *Jrnl.* 4 Aug. 1/8 The Pennsylvania Road has stirred up a hornet's nest. **1894** BRIDGES *Feast of Bacchus* I. 44 Stirring up your servants.

β. *a* **1500** *Prophecy* 34 in *Bernard. de cura rei fam.* 33 þe stepsonys of þe lyonne steryt vp at ones, þe leoperde sall þame stryke doune. **1526** *Pilgr. Perf.* (W. de W. 1531) 10 We ought the more to.. stere vp our hertes to deuocyon. **1549** *Bk. Com. Prayer* 97 b, *Collect 25th Sunday after Trinity*, Stiere vp we beseche thee, O Lord, the wylles of thy faythfull people. **1570** BUCHANAN *Admonitioun* Wks. (1892) 22 Nowther honour nor commoun weill sterit ȝow up than. **1641** *Sc. Acts Chas. I* (1817) V. 579/2 To give ordour to the seuerall ministeris.. to steir vp the peopill of thair particular parosches.. to extend þr liberalitie þrto.

γ. **1555** EDEN *Decades* (Arb.) 113 Vaschus Nunnez.. stoured vp certeyne lyght felowes ageynst Ancisus.

e. To excite, provoke, induce; to raise, set on foot (strife, disturbance, etc.); to arouse (feeling or emotion): cf. 9.

α. **1538** ELYOT *Dict.*, *Irrito*, to prouoke, to kendyl wrathe, to styrre vppe. **1544** BETHAM *Precepts War* I. iii. B iv, It is a lyght thyng to styre vp battayl, but to leaue of with glorye.. is an harde thyng. **1546** BP. GARDINER *Detect. Devil's Sophistrie* 16 Ye deuyll.. sturreth vp this abhominable heresy. **1622** L. DIGGES tr. *Cespedes' Gerardo* 2 The sad spectacle stirred vp the poore mens compassion. **1634** MILTON *Comus* 174 Merriment, Such as the jocond Flute.. Stirs up among the loose unleter'd Hinds. **1683** W. LLOYD in *Lett. Lit. Men* (Camden) 187 Such songs as are most apt to stir up devotion. **1711** ADDISON *Spect.* No. 163 ¶6 Authors who are apt to stir up Mirth in the Mind of the Readers. **1820** SCOTT *Monast.* vi, Whet the temporal sword if it be necessary, and stir up the courage and zeal of your loyal vassals. **1855** MACAULAY *Hist. Eng.* xiv. III. 464 He did not conceive that he was bound to be always stirring up sedition against them. **1891** FARRAR *Darkn. & Dawn* vii, Unless they stir up a riot at Rome I shall not trouble the Emperor by mentioning them.

β. *c* **1530** *Spirituall Counsayle* G j, That I myghte stere up in me a fresche remembraunce of thy moste blyssed deathe. **1549** COVERDALE *Erasm. Par. Rom.* xvi. 25–27 The misterie, whiche.. nowe is opened.. to stere vp obedience to the fayth published among all nacions. **1567** DRANT *Horace, Ep.* II. i. G vij, That poet on a stretched rope maye walke and neuer fall, That can stere vp my passions or quicke my sprytes at all.

γ. *a* **1555** PHILPOT *Exam.* etc. (Parker Soc.) 380 The Jews ..for the ceremonies of their country and rites eftsoons stoured up great controversies.

IV. 17. *Comb.* with sb. in obj. relation: **stir-passion**, something that stirs or excites passion; **stir-strife** *a.*, that stirs or excites strife. *nonce-wds.* See also STIRABOUT, STIR-UP.

1586 WARNER *Alb. Eng.* v. xxiii. (1589) 104 That heard the Pope, canonizing the stir-strife Priest a Saint. **1604** T. WRIGHT *Passions* v. 185 It were requisite for an excellent stir-passion to have in a readinesse all those places.

stirabout (ˈstɜːrəbaʊt). Also 9 stirrabout. [f. verbal phrase *stir about*: see STIR *v.* and ABOUT *adv.*]

1. a. Porridge made by stirring oatmeal (or occas. some other meal) in boiling water or milk. (Originally *Anglo-Irish.*)

1682 PIERS *Descr. West-Meath* (1770) 121 They.. have to their meal one formal dish,.. which some call, stirabout or hasty pudding, that is flour and milk boiled thick. **1708** W. KING *Art of Cookery* Let. ix. 149 Milk Porridge,.. Flumary, Stir about, and the like. **1812** MAR. EDGEWORTH *Absentee* xi, If your honour takes stirabout, an old hand will engage to make that to your liking, any way. **1838** DICKENS *Nich. Nick.* viii, The boys, having previously had their appetites thoroughly taken away by stir-about and potatoes. **1843** THACKERAY *Irish Sk.-bk.* xiv, Look at them.. over a bowl of stir-about. **1873** E. SMITH *Foods* 159 Maize.. is very commonly made into pudding... It is now known in Ireland as Stirrabout, and in Italy as Polenta. **1894** D. C. MURRAY *Making of Novelist* 102 One pint of stirabout made of Indian meal.

b. (See quot. 1828.)

1828 CARR *Craven Gloss.*, *Stir-about*, oatmeal and drippings stirr'd about in a frying pan. **1863** MRS. GASKELL *Sylvia's L.* xliv, I've made mysel' some stirabout for my supper.

c. *fig.* A bustle, a state of confusion.

1905 E. ARMSTRONG in *Eng. Hist. Rev.* Jan. 158 This *guazzabuglio*, this stirabout of republic within republic [*sc.* Siena]. **1915** *Times* 28 May 9 The formation of this new office [the Ministry of Munitions] is the one outstanding fact in the political stirabout.

2. A bustling person.

1870 J. NICHOLSON *Idylls* 54 She's sic a steer-about, sae fu' o' mirth an' fun. **1903** *Westm. Gaz.* 17 Sept. 3/2 The 'stir-about' is not a popular person with his masters.

attrib. **1837** T. HOOK *Jack Brag* i, Get a sensible, stir-about husband.

stirage, stirap: see STIRRAGE, STIRRUP.

stirdy, obs. form of STURDY.

stire (staɪə(r)). Also 8–9 styre, 9 stere. [Of obscure origin. Cf. the synonymous STIROM.] A kind of cider apple; also the cider made from it. Also *attrib.*

1699 in *Chesh. Gloss.* s.v., [The lessor] shall enjoy.. one measure of apples or crabs commonly called stires, [etc.]. **1743** *Lond. & Country Brew.* III. (ed. 2) 246 In bottling their Styre Cyder. **1754** *Compleat Cyder-man* 66 Others [said] that the Styre Apple makes the best Cyder. **1826** *Art of Brewing* (ed. 2) 167 Stire cider, in the same state, sells for £5. **1853** *Jrnl. R. Agric. Soc.* XIV. II. 446 Some sort of apples, as the 'stere' and 'Haglor crab', in very dry seasons will only yield 1 hogshead of juice to 3 of fruit.

stire, obs. form of STEER *v.*, STIR *v.*

stirepp, obs. form of STIRRUP.

stirer, stirhap, -hop: see STIRRER, STIRRUP.

ˈstir-fry, *v.* orig. *U.S.* [STIR *v.*] **a.** *trans.* Chiefly in Chinese cookery: to fry (meat, vegetables, etc.) rapidly on a high heat, while stirring and tossing them in the pan. Also *absol.*

1959 C. B. T. LEE *Chinese Cooking for Amer. Kitchens* 82 Add all ingredients except egg roll skin and beaten egg. Stir-fry for 3 minutes. *Ibid.* 102 Stir-fry onions for 2 minutes. **1969** *Guardian* 16 July 16/4 Stir-fry the vegetables. **1972** K. LO *Chinese Food* I. 11 After the vegetables have been stir-fried for a minute or two the meat is returned to the pan and stir-fried together with the vegetables. **1976** 'M. DELVING' *China Expert* viii. 93 'You were in trouble with police,' she said, stir-frying thin strips of beef and vegetables. **1982** *Daily Tel.* 14 Jan. 15/4 Draw in prepared beef and stir/fry for 10 mins.

b. The vbl. phr. used *attrib.*

1959 *House Beautiful* June 146/1 The nub of stir-fry cooking is the chopping, so that all ingredients are in uniformly small pieces. **1976** *Publishers Weekly* 19 Apr. 76/1 Soufflés, stir fry cookery, casseroles. **1981** J. MANN *Funeral Sites* xii. 77 Ian.. had spent some time making a Chinese stir-fry dinner.

Also **ˈstir-fried** *ppl. a.*; **stir-ˈfrying** *vbl. sb.*

1959 C. B. T. LEE *Chinese Cooking for Amer. Kitchens* 64 *Chow* (stir-frying). This is the most popular method of Chinese cooking and is called either stir-frying or sautéing at high heat. *Ibid.* 65 Do not try to attempt more than two stir-fried dishes at one meal. **1972** K. LO *Chinese Food* I. 45 All that quick-fried dishes require is a very short period of stir-frying over high heat with a couple of tablespoons of oil. **1980** *Redbook* Oct. 136/2 To save time and money in the kitchen, Denise does a lot of stir-frying and uses a slow cooker. **1981** *Sunday Tel.* 6 Dec. 13/5 Stir-fried shredded beef with bean sprouts and celery.

‖**ˈstiria.** *Obs.* Also *erron.* styria. Pl. stiriæ, stirias. [L. *stīria*, icicle.] A concretion (e.g. a stalactite, an efflorescence) resembling an icicle.

1666 BOYLE *Orig. Formes & Qual.* 267 The copious shining Styriæ [**1667** Stiriæ] that enoble the darker Body. **1681** COTTON *Wond. Peak* 9 By which the Stiria longer, bigger grows. *a* **1722** LISLE *Husb.* (1757) 8 The atoms of heterogeneous juices will sometimes shoot themselves up in different angular stirias.

†**ˈstiriate**, *a. Obs.*$^{-1}$. [f. L. *stīria* (see prec.) + -ATE².] Formed into 'stiriæ'. Hence **ˈstiriated** *a.* in the same sense.

1664 POWER *Exp. Philos.* I. 52 Like a diaphanous heap of Icycles or striated Niter. **1669** W. SIMPSON *Hydrol. Chym.* 53 What remained was a bright styriate floscule. **1681** GREW *Musæum* III. §ii. iii. 334 Styriated Antimony.. from Cornwall. **1712** J. MORTON *Nat. Hist. Northamptonsh.* 154, I observed several of the Striated Stalactitæ (or Sparry Icecyles) hanging down from the Bank-side.

†**ˈstiricide.** *Obs.*$^{-0}$ [ad. late L. *stīricidium*, f. *stīria* (see STIRIA) + *cid-*, *cadĕre* to fall.] (See quot.)

1656 BLOUNT *Glossogr.*, *Stiricide*, the dropping of a house with ice-sickles.

stiring, obs. form of STIRRING.

†**ˈstirious**, *a. Obs.* [f. STIRIA + -OUS.] Pertaining to or formed like an icicle or a 'stiria'.

1646 SIR T. BROWNE *Pseud. Ep.* II. i. 56 Crystall is.. not much unlike the stirious or stillicidious dependencies of Ice. **1656** BLOUNT *Glossogr.*, *Stirious*, pertaining to a drop of ice, or an Icesickle. **1670** E. BROWN in *Phil. Trans.* V. 1193 A third [salt], to be found of somewhat stirious or long shoots.

stiripe, stirippe, obs. ff. STIRRUP.

stirk (stɜːk). Forms: 1 stírc, stíorc, stýrc, stýric, 5 stirkke, styyrke, strike, 5–6 strik, 5–7 stirke, 5–9 styrk, 6 steirk, sterke, stierke, striack, stryk, styrke, 6–7 sturke, 7–9 sturk, 4– stirk. [OE. *stírc*, *stíorc*, *stýrc*, *stýric*, neut., app. a diminutive f. *stéor* STEER *sb.*¹ + *-ic*, a variant (not found elsewhere) of *-oc*, *-uc*: see -OCK. Cf. MLG. *sterke*, *starke* (mod.G. *sterke*, *stärke*, ? from LG.), MDu., mod.Du. dial. (Gelderland) *sterke*, early mod.Du. *stierick* (Kilian, who marks it 'Sicambrian', i.e. Gelderland, etc.), fem., a heifer, a cow that has not yet calved. Another diminutive formation is MDu. *stierken* bull-calf.

Kluge and Falk & Torp reject the connexion with OTeut. **steuro-* STEER *sb.*¹, and compare HG. dial. *sterch* ram or hog, OHG. *stero* (HG. dial. *ster*) ram, which they refer to the root **ster-* of Goth. *stairō* fem. adj., barren, L. *sterilis* STERILE *a.* But the relationship of these words is obscure.]

1. A young bullock or heifer, usually between one and two years old.

The mod. application varies in different localities. In the midland counties generally the word denotes only the female; in Scotland it is chiefly applied to the male; in northern England and Lincolnshire it is applied to either sex, often with defining word as *bull-stirk*, *cow-*, *heifer-*, or *quey-stirk*.

8.. *Kentish Glosses* in Wr.-Wülcker 70/12 *Quam ad uitulum saginatum*, ðonne to fettum stiorce. *a* **1000** *Voc.* ibid. 195/29 *Bucula*, *iuuenca*, *uitula*, stirc. *a* **1000** *Ags. Gosp.* Luke xv. 23 Bringað an fætt styric [Vulg. *vitulum*] & of-sleað. *c* **1000** ÆLFRIC *Lives Saints* xv. 183 þæt þridde [*sc.* the third evangelist] stod anum styrce ȝelic [*cf.* þæs celfes ȝelicnyss 192]. **10..** *Voc.* in Wr.-Wülcker 321/9 *Juuencus*, styrc. **1377** in *Test. Karleol.* (1893) 117 Lego.. Margarete del Hall unam vaccam bonam cum uno stirk. *c* **1425** *Voc.* in Wr.-Wülcker 669/9 *Hic bouiculus*, styrk. **1448–9** in *Finchale Priory Charters* etc. (Surtees) p. cclvii, Item xxviij twynters. Item xxxiii striks. **1484** in *Acta Dom. Concil.* (1839) 95*/1 Three ky,.. twa stirkis. **1513** DOUGLAS *Æneis* v. vi. 75 The stirkis for the sacrifice.. War newly brittnit [L. *cæsis..* *juvencis*]. **1601** in *Househ. Ord.* (1790) 288 All beeves, muttons, veales, sturkes [etc.]. **1669** CHAMBERLAYNE *Pres. St. Eng.* 298 Yearly was spent [at the King's tables].. 400 Sturks or young Biefes. **1724** *Ramsay's Tea-t. Misc.* (1733) II. 181 My bairn has tocher of her awin;.. A Stirk, a staig, and acre sawin. **1808** *Compl. Grazier* (ed. 3) 97 *note*, The bull.. when turned a year old.. is a stirk, or yearling-bull. **1858–61** RAMSAY *Remin.* ii. (1870) 28 A twa-year-auld stirk. **1880** W. H. PATTERSON *Gloss. Antrim & Down* 100 *Stirk*, *sb.* a cow one or two years old. 'A bull *stirk*,' a young bull. **1909** D. HOUSTON *'E Silkie Man* 4 Fan Kirsty tethered 'e stirk. **1949** *Scotsman* 17 May 8/7 130 Store cattle including 60 choice West of Ireland black polled bullocks and stirks,.. and 30 North of Ireland stirks. **1973** *Stirling Observer* 25 July 7/2 They had on offer 51 dairy cattle,.. 64 accredited calves, 49 non-accredited calves and 81 store cattle and stirks... Charolais heifer stirks sold to £148,.. Hereford heifer stirks sold to £107. **1978** *Morecambe Guardian* 14 Mar. 22 (Advt.), Rearing Calves and Stirks, Fat Cattle and Slaughter Cows. **1979** L. DERWENT *Border Bairn* i. 15 Her brother, the shepherd.. accepted me more or less as one of his flock. A yowe or a gimmer, a stirk or a stot.

Prov. **1721** J. KELLY *Sc. Prov.* 309 There was ay some Water where the Stirk drown'd.

2. Used as a term of abuse: a foolish person.

c **1590** MONTGOMERIE *Sonn.* lxx. 13 Thou art a stirk, for all thy staitly stylis. **1728** RAMSAY *Last Sp. Miser* xv, I took them a' for stirks That loo'd na money. **1788** BURNS *Calf* ii, I doubt na, Sir, but then we'll find, Ye're still as great a Stirk. **1847** LE FANU *T. O'Brien* 213 Sure he's never where he ought to be—the sturk. **1894** A. GORDON *Northw. Ho!* 303 What's the guid o' learnin' when it turns decent countra lads intae stirks an' asses?

3. *attrib.* and *Comb.*

c **1470** HENRYSON *Mor. Fab.* x. (*Fox & Wolf*) xvii, The deuill ane stirk taill thairfoir sall ye haif. **1567** in Picton *L'pool Munic. Rec.* (1883) I. 109 A stag or stirk buckskin jerkin. **1573** in *Lanc. & Cheshire Wills* (Chetham Soc.) II. 139 Item one cowe hede one striack skyne and one fole skyne, vijs. **1601** in *Househ. Ord.* (1790) 289 The Clerke [of the Accatry] hath for his fee all the calves skinnes, and stirk skinnes. **1651** *Manch. Crt. Leet Rec.* (1887) IV. 68 For sellinge a stirke beefe wch wee were informed had the turne. **1891** 'H. HALIBURTON' *Ochil Idylls* 134 The haflin wi' his stirk-like glowre.

Hence **ˈstirkie** (*Sc.*), †**ˈstirkin**, diminutive formations used in the same sense.

1559 *Will of W. Perchy* (Somerset Ho.) Styrkyns & hecfordes of ij yeres olde. **18..** *Prov.* in *Ramsay's Remin.* v. (1870) 153 There's aye water where the stirkie drouns.

stirk, obs. Sc. form of STRIKE *v.*

†**ˈstirket.** *north. Obs.* [f. STIRK + -ET¹.] ? A stirk.

1313 *Bolton Compotus* 270 b, Pro viij. stirkettes emptis de executoribus Magistri Ade de Herteford' et venditis xvj. s. **1348** *Durham Acc. Rolls* (Surtees) 42 In 3 styrket emp. in villa, 7s. 6d. **1411** in *Finchale Priory Charters* etc. (Surtees) p. clviii, iiij vaccæ j stot ij quioks, ij stirketts. **1485** *Inv.* in *Ripon Chapter Acts* (Surtees) 372, x stirkettes.

stirkin, stirlene: see STRICKEN, STARLING.

stirless ('stɜːlɪs), *a.* [f. STIR *sb.* and *v.* + -LESS.] Not stirring, motionless.

Frequent in Byron, Charlotte Bronte, and P. J. Bailey.
1816 BYRON *Pris. Chillon* ix, Silence, and a stirless breath Which neither was of life nor death. **1819** —— *Juan* II. cxliv, O'er him lay the calm and stirless air. **1824** CARLYLE in Froude *Life* (1882) I. 214, I delight to see these old mountains lying in the clear sleep of twilight, stirless as death. **1833** L. RITCHIE *Wand. Loire* 198 The river..in which the stirless trees on the banks were reflected. **1839–48** BAILEY *Festus* i. 4 Ye who stand Stirless. **1849** C. BRONTE *Shirley* xiii, She would spend a sunny afternoon in lying stirless on the turf. **1873** LE FANU *Willing to Die* 337 The boat was now three lengths away;..out on the bosom of the stirless water. **1896** CROCKETT *Grey Man* i. 2 It was a stirless night.

Hence **'stirlessly** *adv.*; **'stirlessness.**

1825 *Blackw. Mag.* XVIII. 447 On their orbs the light Smote and sate stirlessly. **1888** W. CLARK RUSSELL *Death Ship* xxiv, The captain..held his place with the entranced stirlessness I was now accustomed to see in him.

Stirling[1] ('stɜːlɪŋ). [The name of the Revd. Robert *Stirling* (1790–1878), Scottish minister and engineer.] ***Stirling*** (or †***Stirling's***) ***cycle***, the thermodynamic cycle on which an ideal Stirling engine would operate, consisting of an isothermal expansion, a drop in temperature at constant volume by giving up heat to a regenerator, an isothermal compression, and an increase in temperature at constant volume by gaining heat from the regenerator; ***Stirling*** (or †***Stirling's***) ***engine***, orig., an external-combustion air engine invented by Stirling (*Brit. Pat. 4081* (1816)); more widely, a mechanical device used to provide either power or refrigeration and operating on a closed regenerative cycle, the working fluid being cyclically compressed and expanded at different temperatures; also *ellipt.* as ***Stirling***.

1845 *Minutes Proc. Inst. Civil Engineers* IV. 348 (*heading*) Description of Stirling's improved air engine. *Ibid.* 359 In Mr. Stirling's engine the intense heat of the fire did not come into actual contact with the pistons. **1887** *Encycl. Brit.* XXII. 523/1 Stirling's cycle is theoretically perfect whatever the density of the working air. **1889** C. H. PEABODY *Thermodynamics of Steam-Engine* xi. 174 A recent hot-air engine made on the same principle as Stirling's hot-air engine. **1943** E. H. LEWITT *Thermodynamics Applied to Heat Engines* (ed. 3) iii. 57 The Stirling cycle is thermodynamically reversible owing to the action of the regenerator. **1963** *Engineer* CCXIV. 1063/1 A Stirling cycle machine operates on a closed regenerative thermodynamic cycle. **1973** *Sci. Amer.* Aug. 81/2 In practice Stirling engines do not work on the Stirling cycle. It is not possible to have isothermal (constant temperature) compression and expansion processes. **1980** *Times* 16 Oct. (Internat. Motor Show Suppl.) p. xiv/8 Most of the technology of the Stirling has been established since the Second World War,..but mainly for vehicle and industrial duties rather than aircraft.

Stirling[2]. The name of Allan *Stirling* (1844–1927), Scottish-born American engineer, used *attrib.* to designate a water-tube boiler invented and patented by him (*U.S. Pat. 381,595* (1888)), usu. consisting of three interconnected upper steam and water drums and one or two lower water drums, connected by banks of inclined water-tubes which are heated by combustion gases and bent to enter the drums radially.

1889 *Amer. Machinist* 23 May 12/1 (Advt.), The Stirling Water Tube Boilers have unusually large steam and water spaces and well-defined circulation. **1924** F. J. DROVER *Coal & Oil Fired Boilers* II. v. 143 For from 1,000 to 10,000 sq. ft. of heating surface the standard Stirling boiler consists of three steam drums and two mud drums. **1940** H. M. SPRING *Boiler Operator's Guide* iv. 117 The Stirling boiler..is one of the first types of bent-tube boiler to come into common use.

Stirling[3]. *Math.* The name of James *Stirling* (1692–1770), Scottish mathematician, used *attrib.* and in the possessive to designate concepts in the theory of numbers, as **Stirling('s) approximation** or **formula**, either of two functions of an integer *n* which are approximations for factorial *n* when *n* is large, viz. $n! \sim n^n/e^n$ and (more accurately) $n! \sim \surd(2\pi n)n^n/e^n$; **Stirling('s) number**, a member of either of two arrays used in combinatorics, first described by him (*Methodus Differentialis* (1730)), *spec.* (*a*) the number of ways of arranging the integers 1 to *m* in *n* disjoint non-empty ordered sets, the first element of each ordered set being the least; (a Stirling number of the first kind); (*b*) the number of ways of partitioning the integers 1 to *m* into *n* disjoint non-empty sets; (a Stirling number of the second kind).

1938 *Biometrika* XXX. 220 The first order term in Stirling's approximation to *m*! **1948** GLASSTONE *Textbk. Physical Chem.* (ed. 2) xi. 874 Since *N* is a large number, viz., the Avogadro number, it is possible to use the Stirling approximation and to replace ln*N*! by $N \ln N - N$. **1970** ASHBY & MILLER *Princ. Mod. Physics* ii. 35 We can obtain an approximate analytical expression..by using Stirling's approximation for the factorials: For large *n*, $\ln(n!) \cong \frac{1}{2}\ln(2\pi) + (n + \frac{1}{2})\ln(n) - n$. **1978** P. W. ATKINS *Physical Chem.* xx. 650 Stirling's approximation is that *x* large: $\ln x! \approx x\ln x - x$. **1908** T. J. I'A. BROMWICH *Introd. Theory Infinite Series* 461 (*heading*) Stirling's asymptotic formula for the gamma-function when *x* is real, large and positive. **1934** I. S. & E. S. SOKOLNIKOFF *Higher Math. for Engineers & Physicists* xiii. 383 The first term of this series bears the name of Stirling's formula and gives satisfactory results even for small values of *n*. **1940** GLASSTONE *Text-bk. Physical Chem.* x. 861 By Stirling's formula $1/N!$ is approximately equal to $(e/N)^N$ if *N* is large. **1962** W. J. MOORE *Physical Chem.* (ed. 4) vii. 233 This expression is evaluated by means of the Stirling formula, $\log N! = (N + \frac{1}{2})\log N - N + \frac{1}{2}\log 2\pi$. **1928** *Amer. Math. Monthly* XXXV. 77 The Stirling Numbers are characterized by many very beautiful properties. **1933** *Tôhoku Math. Jrnl.* XXXVII. 255 (*caption*) Table of Stirling's numbers of the first kind. *Ibid.* 277 The Stirling number of the second kind can be obtained by aid of a problem of probability. **1966** F. N. DAVID et al. *Symmetric Functions & Allied Tables* v. 226 Stirling's Numbers of the first kind...1 1 2 6 24 120 720... 1 3 11 50 274 1764... 1 6 35 225 1624... 1 10 85 735... 1 15 175...1 21...[etc.]. *Ibid.* 223 Stirling's Numbers of the second kind...1 1 1 1 1 1 ...1 3 7 15 31 63...1 6 25 90 301 ...1 10 65 350...1 15 140...1 21...[etc.].

stirling, Sc. form of STARLING.

†**'stirment.** *Obs.* [f. STIR *v.* + -MENT.] An incitement, provocation.

c **1460** *Promp. Parv.* (Winch.) 143 Egment, or styrment, *incitamentum*.

stirne, obs. form of STERN *a.*

†**'stirom.** *Obs.* [Of obscure origin.] A kind of apple, and the cider made from it: = STIRE.

1708 J. PHILIPS *Cyder* II. 351 Stirom, firmest Fruit, Embottled (long as Priameian Troy Withstood the Greeks) endures, e'er justly mild. **1740** SOMERVILLE *Hobbinol* I. (1749) 45 Slumb'ring secure, with Stirom well bedew'd, Fallacious cask.

sti'rometry, obs. f. STEREOMETRY.

1619 H. LYTE *Art of Tens* 21 Likewise may you finde the stirometrie or square of anie thing by the foresaid table.

stirop(e, -opp(e, obs. forms of STIRRUP.

stirp (stɜːp). Also 6 **styrpe**, 6–7 **stirpe**. Also in L. form STIRPS. [ad. L. *stirpem* (nom. *stirps, stirpes, stirpis*), stock, stem (lit. and fig.). = STEM *sb.*, STOCK *sb.*, in various figurative senses.]

1. The stock of a family; a line of descent; a race, clan, or sept; the descendants of a common ancestor. Also *abstr.*, pedigree, lineage. Now somewhat *rare*.

The word became obsolete in the 17th c., and reappears (in affected literary use) about the middle of the 19th c.

1502 ARNOLDE *Chron.* 60 b/1 Abdalazys Soldan of babilon,..emperor of the worlde and of yͤ feith of machamet,..lyuylly [*read* lynylly] descendid from the stirp of prophettis. *c* **1530** *Crt. of Love* 16 No termys digne unto her excellence, So is she sprong of noble stirpe and high. *a* **1548** HALL *Chron., Edw. IV*, 249 b, His sequele and lineal succession, as the verie Images and carnall portratures, of his stirpe, line and stemme, naturally discended. **1568** GRAFTON *Chron.* II. 911 The Lady Margaret liyng in Flaunders,..ioyfully receyued and welcommed mee, as the onely type and garland of her noble stirpe and linage. **1569** *Ir. Act 11 Eliz.* c. 4 (1621) 304 Fiue persons of the best and eldest of euerie stirpe or nation of the Irishrie..shall be bound to bring in..all idle persons of their surname. **1625** BACON *Ess., Nobility* (Arb.) 191 Democracies..are commonly more quiet..then where there are Stirps of Nobles. *a* **1626** —— *New Atl.* 25 They haue some few Stirps of Iewes, yet remaining amongst them, whom they leaue to their owne Religion. *a* **1635** NAUNTON *Fragm. Reg.* (Arb.) 14 Now leaving her stirp, I come to her Person. **1654** VILVAIN *Enchir. Epigr.* IV. xli. 71 b, Ther were two Kings of English stirp descended, Who when thos Danes died to the Throne ascended. **1665** J. WEBB *Stone-Heng* (1725) 152 People..of another Stirp. **1854** THOREAU *Walden* 283 Still grows the vivacious lilac.. the last of that stirp, sole survivor of that family. **1869** LOWELL *Under Willows* 141 Loved by some maid Of royal stirp. **1896** KIPLING *Seven Seas, Song of Cities* xiii, The northern stirp beneath the southern skies—I build a Nation for an Empire's need. **1906** C. MERCIER *Scheme of Educ. Comm. Care of Feeble Minded* 3 If the community is disposed, not only the individual, but the stirp is exterminated.

†**b.** Ancestral stock. *Obs.*

1573 LLOID *Pilgr. Princes* (1586) 76 Auerni boasted of their stirpe and stocke, the ancient Troians.

†**2.** A scion, member of a family. *Obs.*

1574 J. JONES *Nat. Beg. Growing & Living Things* 49 The worthy and famous Stirpe of your auncient, most honorable, and trustie Stock. **1629** L. O[WEN] *Speculum Iesuit.* 30 Another Alexander Farnesius a Cardinall of Rome, a wicked stirp of that stocke.

¶**3.** Used for: ? Chief representative. *Obs.*

1513 J. T. *Bradshaw's St. Werburge* Prol. 2 Alas, of Chestre ye monkes haue lost a treasure, Henry Bradsha the styrpe of eloquence!

4. *Eugenics.* (See quot.)

1875 GALTON in *Contemp. Rev.* XXVII. 81, I beg permission to use, in a special sense, the short word 'stirp',..to express the sum-total of the germs, gemmules, or whatever they may be called, which are to be found..in the newly fertilized ovum—that is, in the earliest pre-embryonic stage—from which time it receives nothing further from its parents, not even from its mother, than mere nutriment... This word 'stirp'..is equally applicable to the contents of buds. *Ibid.* 84 As the stirp whence the child sprang can only be half the size of the combined stirps of his two parents, it follows that [etc.]. **1910** *19th Cent.* Sept. 490 Certain variations in the quasi-independent 'stirp' or 'germ substance' of the reproductive egg-cells and sperm-cells.

Hence **'stirpal** *a.*, pertaining to a 'stirp' (sense 4).

1875 GALTON in *Contemp. Rev.* XXVII. 82 Organization wholly depends on the mutual affinities and repulsions of the separate germs; first in their stirpal, and subsequently during all the processes of development.

stirpiculture ('stɜːpɪˌkʌltjʊə(r)). [f. L. *stirpi-* (see STIRP, STIRPS) + *cultūra* CULTURE *sb.*] The production of pure races or stocks by careful breeding.

1870 J. H. NOYES *Sci. Propagation* 12 It is one thing to seek in any existing race the best animals we can find to breed from..; and it is another thing to start a distinct family and keep its blood pure by separation from the mass of its race. It is this last method that has produced the Ayrshires, the short-horns, and the Leicesters. It deserves a distinct name, and we will take the liberty to call it stirpiculture. **1883** in OGILVIE. **1891** *Amer. Naturalist* Oct. 932 Mrs. Anita Newcomb McGee read a paper entitled 'An Experiment in Human Stirpiculture'. **1904** GALTON in *Sociological Papers* I. 78 Mr. Wells spoke of 'stirpiculture' as a term that had been used by others and was preferable to 'eugenics'. I may be permitted to say that I myself coined that word and deliberately changed it for eugenics.

Hence **stirpi'cultural,** *a.*, pertaining to stirpiculture; **stirpi'culturist,** one who is interested in stirpiculture.

1891 *Amer. Naturalist* Oct. 932 Of the stirpicultural children only one has since died. **1903** A. J. MCLAUGHLIN in *Pop. Sci. Monthly* Jan. 231 (Cent. Suppl.) The stirpiculturist, noting the poor physique..of some of the immigrants, fears race degeneration.

stirpital ('stɜːpɪtəl), *a. Law.* [Badly f. L. *stirps* (see STIRPS); the correct form would be **stirpal*.] Pertaining to division *per stirpes*.

1886 PEARSON in *Law Rep., 31 Chanc. Div.* 689 A division of the proceeds of sale *per stirpes* is more in accordance than a division *per capita* with the original stirpital division of the income.

‖**stirps** (stɜːps). Pl. **stirpes** ('stɜːpiːz). [L. *stirps* stem, stock: see STIRP.]

1. *Law.* A branch of a family; the person who with his descendants forms a branch of a family. Chiefly in L. phrase ***per stirpes***: see PER *prep.* I. 10; also ***in stirpes***.

1681 STAIR *Inst. Law Scot.* XXVI. iv. 84 They would not succeed *in capita*, the whole Successors getting Equal Share, but *in stirpes*. *a* **1768** ERSKINE *Inst. Law Scot.* III. viii. §12. (1773) 547 Succession *in stirpes*, or by the stock, makes the partition..according to the number of the stocks or stirpes from whom these heirs derive right. **1771** *Encycl. Brit.* II. 937/2 The share belonging to their ascendent or *stirps*, whom they represent. **1862** BROUGHAM *Brit. Const.* App. iii. 430 His brothers succeed to the exclusion of his issue female, and each brother becomes a stirps.

2. *Zool.* Used variously (often vaguely) as a term of classification: a family, subfamily, group, etc.

1863 HUXLEY *Man's Place Nat.* II. 103 The..practically infinite divergence of the human from the Simian stirps.

3. *Bot.* (See quot.)

1866 *Treas. Bot.* 1101/1 *Stirps*, a race or permanent variety: as the Red Cabbage.

stirrage ('stɜːrɪdʒ). *dial.* Also 6 *Sc.* **sterage, stirage,** 9 *dial.* **stirridge,** etc. (see *Eng. Dial. Dict.*). [f. STIR *v.* + -AGE.] Stirring, movement, commotion.

1513 DOUGLAS *Æneis* II. xi. 82 And me..Ilk swouch of wynd, and every quhisper now, And alkyne sterage affrayit. **1535** STEWART *Cron. Scot.* (Rolls) II. 660 To remane.. Without sterage ay still as ony stone. *c* **1590** J. STEWART *Poems* (S.T.S.) II. 27 He stabill stands, And dois no stirage mak. **1621** GRANGER *Eccl.* xii. 4. 320 Old men..cannot sleepe soundly,..euery small stirrage waketh them. **1892** SARAH HEWETT *Peas. Sp. Devon* 128 My ivers, whot a stirridge yu make vur nort at awl!

stirrage, obs. form of STEERAGE.

stirrah ('stɛrə). *Sc.* Also 7 **stirrow.** [Perh. corruption of SIRRAH; cf. *stir* for *sir*, STIR *sb.*[2]]

1. A young fellow.

1665 SIR J. LAUDER (Ld. Fountainhall) *Jrnls.* (S.H.S.) 17 Being oftner in telling of his beads then both his other 2 companions fat-looged stirrows ware. **1768** ROSS *Helenore* 7 Ralph..A dainty stirrah had, twa years out gane. *a* **1779** D. GRAHAM *Jockey & Maggy* v. Writ. 1883 II. 41 She's born a bra wally thumping stirra. **1811** A. SCOTT *Poems* (ed. 2) 177 Here they dwalt, till Cain an' Abel, Twa fine stirrahs, blest their bour.

2. 'A term of contempt, apparently corrupted from *Sirrah*'. (Jam.)

1816 SCOTT *Antiq.* xv, Stirra, this is no the road to Monkbarns. *Ibid.* xxi, Ay, and then, when the dogs barked at the lone farm-stead, the gudewife wad cry, 'Whisht, stirra, that'll be auld Edie'. **1818** HOGG *Brownie*, etc. *Woolgatherer* II. 125 'My faith, stirra!' said she,..'My faith, man, but ye're soon begun to a braw trade!'

†**'stirrance.** *Obs. rare*[−1]. In 7 **sturrance.** [f. STIR *v.* + -ANCE.] Disturbance.

1623 MARKHAM *Cheap Husb.* (ed. 3) 11 If the Rider can.. giue as well directions for the preseruation of a horses health, and the auoidance of sturrance and sicknesse, as put in practise artfully euery violence to be vsed in his lessons.

stirrand, stirrap, obs. ff. STIRRING, STIRRUP.

stirre, obs. form of STEER *v.*[1]

stirred (stɜːd), *ppl. a.* [f. STIR *v.* + -ED[1].] Moved, agitated, excited, etc.: see the various senses of the verb. Also with *up*: see STIR *v.* 16.

1483 *Cath. Angl.* 365/1 Stird (*v.r.* Styrryde), *motus, agitatus.* **1538** ELYOT *Dict., Percitus*, styrred. **1545** *Ibid., Concitatus*, stered, prouoked, meued. **1577** KENDALL *Flowers of Epigr.* 65 Is this (at last quoth he) Of all your sturred strife the cause? **1593** Q. ELIZ. *Boeth.* II. met. ii. 24 Sandz such store by raging flawes as stured sea turnes vp. **1607** TOPSELL *Four-f. Beasts* 307 He inclined him [his horse] first of al to lay away his stirred and angry minde. **1707** MORTIMER *Husb.* 448 [Cabbages] may be..transplanted.. into a very rich and well stirred Mould. **1827** STEUART *Planter's Guide* (1828) 496 Let a trench then be..cut as deep nearly as the depth of the trenched ground, or stirred earth, of which the orchard-soil has been originally formed. **1860** ELLICOTT *Life Our Lord* iv. 187 A storm of wind bursts upon the lake, and the stirred-up waters beat in upon the boat. **1862** MEREDITH *Mod. Love* xlii. 74 Thoughts black as death, Like a stirr'd pool in sunshine break.

stirred, obs. form of STARRED *ppl. a.*

†'**stirree.** *dial. Obs.* [Irregularly f. STIR *v.*] A light cross furrow ploughing of a fallow. Also *attrib.* Hence †**stirree** *v. trans.*, to give a 'stirree' to (land).

1733 W. ELLIS *Chiltern & Vale Farm.* 55 A Fallow and a Stirree is enough for a Chalk. *Ibid.* 308 The more industrious Man will give his Wheat Land a Fallow in April, and two Stirrees between that and sowing time. *Ibid.* 319 This is the strongest and largest Plough..imployed at Fallow and Stirree Times. **1750** —— *Mod. Husb.* IV. i. 21 (E.D.D.) They stirree it at the beginning of this month.

stirrer ('stɜːrə(r)). Forms: see STIR *v.* Also 7 stirrier (sense 3 b). [f. STIR *v.* + -ER[1].] One who or something which stirs, in various senses.

1. a. One who or something which excites or provokes something, as strife, passion, etc., or incites a person to something; an inciter, instigator; †a promoter (*obs.*); †an exhorter (*obs.*).

1382 WYCLIF *2 Macc.* iv. 1 Symont..spake yuel of Onye, as..he hadde be stirer of yuels [Vulg. *incentor malorum*]. **1399** *Rolls of Parlt.* III. 451/2 The man..sayd, that he was noght controevour, ne fyrst doer, no styrer of the Bille. *c* **1449** PECOCK *Repr.* III. viii. 324 Bischopis and abbotis, whiche schulden be grete sterers to the lay partie into deedis of pitee. **1455** *Rolls of Parlt.* V. 282/1 Thaire Assistours, Helpours, Sturrers, Confortours, and Counseillours aforesaid. **1543** in W. H. Turner *Select. Rec. Oxford* (1880) 170 Itt appeared the Mayor to have ben a great sturrer of this garboyle. **1545** *King's Primer, Lauds, Hymn* C iij b, Christ the styrer of the hert. **1599** THYNNE *Animadv.* (1875) 74 This woorde 'Minoresse' sholde bee 'Moueresse,' signyfyinge 'a mover or styrrer to debate'. **1609** HOLLAND *Amm. Marcell.* XIV. ix. 21 The principall stirrers of those tumults and seditions. **1632** MARMION *Holland's Leaguer* II. ii. D 4, With Musicke, Songs, and dancing, such as are The stirrers of hot appetites. **1635** H. SYDENHAM *Serm.* (1637) 74 This is..the prime wheele and stirrer of all our turbulent motions. **1695** LOCKE *Reasonabl. Chr.* (1696) 178 A stirrer of Sedition against the Publick Peace. **1817** BYRON *Manfred* I. i. 101, I am the Rider of the Wind, The Stirrer of the storm. **1849** JAMES *Woodman* xix, This Morton is..the stirrer of every trouble in the realm. **1876** MORRIS *Sigurd* IV. 378 No stirrer nor stayer of strife. **1890** *Illustr. Lond. News* 6 Sept. 298/3 You a stirrer of passions—you a minstrel!

b. Often with *up*: cf. STIR *v.* 16.

1532 TINDALE *Exp. v–vii. Matt.* (? 1550) 19 Cursed be.. sterers [**1573** stirrers] vp of princes to batayle & warre. **1563–83** FOXE *A. & M.* 1257/2 He was a styrrer vp of sedition & commotion. **1596** DALRYMPLE tr. *Leslie's Hist. Scot.* II. 357 He was author, and steiryr vp of the first president of Orknay. **1603** KNOLLES *Hist. Turks* (1638) 57 The chiefe stirrer vp of the King vnto this war, was one Gerbert. **1605** A. WARREN *Poor Man's Pass.* E 2 b, Sedition-sowers, stirrers vp of strife. **1641** J. JACKSON *True Evang. T.* 37 Maximinus, the stirrer up of the sixt Persecution. **1716** ATTERBURY *Serm.* (1734) I. 222 There is scarce any Truth so bright and clear, but that an Industrious Stirrer up of Doubts may do somewhat towards clouding and darkning it. **1800** COLERIDGE *Piccolom.* I. xii. 66 That long-practised stirrer-up Of insurrection. **1908** *Academy* 6 June 853/2 Goethe was undoubtedly..a tireless stirrer-up of ideas.

†**c.** One who makes a commotion, or raises a tumult; an agitator. *Obs.*

c **1450** tr. *De Imitatione* III. xxviii. (1893) 97 Kepe þou þiself in gode pees, and lete þe stirer stire [L. *dimitte agitantem agitare*] as muche as he wol. **1577** tr. *Bullinger's Decades* III. ix. 449 These fellowes are seditious stirrers. **1610** CARLETON *Jurisd.* 125 These Pharises, he describeth to be seditious and intollerable stirrers in States. **1612** PAULE *Abp. Whitgift* 48 The afore-said stirrers, and seditious attempts of sundry persons in this our Archbishops time. *a* **1637** B. JONSON *Underwoods, To Mem. Sir L. Cary* 30 What did this Stirrer, but die late? *a* **1660** *Contemp. Hist. Irel.* (Ir. Archæol. Soc.) I. 101 This good man will not trust any bodie..but those religions that are inative styrers of the present and other faction.

d. One who stirs up trouble or discontent; an agitator, a trouble-maker. *colloq.* (chiefly *Austral.*).

1963 T. & P. MORRIS *Pentonville* xi. 247 Other prisoners described him as a *stirrer* rather than a leader in that he got others to do the dirty work for him. **1970** *Sunday Truth* (Brisbane) 28 June 4/3 He was no stirrer. He came quietly to Brisbane made the scene for six months or so then quietly drifted back a few weeks ago to his favorite haunts around Kings Cross. **1973** C. MASON *Hostage* vii. 104 'You're a born boat-rocker.' 'D'you think so? A stirrer, they'd call it at home.' **1977** *Sounds* 9 July 15/2 He's an absolute stirrer with very little concept of what our job is. **1982** *Observer* 13 June 16/1 Jessica Mitford is what Australians call a stirrer, meaning a person with a talent for causing trouble.

2. In physical sense: **a.** An instrument or appliance for stirring a liquid or the like.

c **1450** *Two Cookery Bks.* II. 107 Sterre it well with ij sturrers. **1600** SURFLET *Country Farm* V. xxiii. 725 Leauing the same for the space of an hower to drinke in this water: afterward they put the meale aside with their stirrers. **1688** HOLME *Armoury* III. xx. (Roxb.) 247/1 The Third, is called a Padle or Mundle..; some call it a sturer; which is to stire vp the Tallow and turn it about in the pan whilest it is in melting. **1803** *Phil. Trans.* XCIII. 122 The whole being well melted, was stirred with a large earthen stirrer. **1813** RUDGE *Agric. Surv. Glouc.* 222 The stirrer, reever, and shovel used in the process [of cider making]. **1827** FARADAY *Chem. Manip.* vi. (1842) 174 Besides these vessels, stirrers are frequently required in the progress of these operations. They should be made of solid glass rod. **1845** G. DODD *Brit. Manuf.* V. 67 (Vinegar.) The mash-tuns..are circular vessels with a central 'stirrer' or instrument for keeping in constant agitation the ingredients which may be in the tuns. **1852** MORFIT *Tanning & Currying* (1853) 163 To make a fresh vat, quicklime is thrown in, covered with water, and agitated with a stirrer. **1856** J. C. MORTON *Cycl. Agric.* s.v. *Plough*, The stirrer, or acting tine, has a chisel-edge with a sloping front, down the middle of which is a vertical tine. **1884** *Health Exhib. Catal.* 110/1 Model Steam Jam Boiling Pan, with Revolving Stirrer in action.

b. One who troubles (a stream).

1851 TRENCH *Poems, Leg. Alhambra* 36 How, rising from that watery floor, A Moorish maiden..stands before The stirrer of the stream.

3. a. One who moves about; *esp.* in ***early stirrer***, one who is up early.

1538 ELYOT *Dict., Ambulator*, a walker or styrer. *a* **1560** PHAER *Æneid* VIII. Z 1, Nor morning styrer lesse, Æneas then abroad was stalkt. **1597** SHAKS. *2 Hen. IV*, III. ii. 3 An early stirrer, by the Rood! **1607** DEKKER *Westw. Hoe* II. i. B 4, I had not thought..you had bin such an early stirrer. **1620** FLETCHER *Chances* I. iii, And longer to expect my friend may pull me Into suspition of too late a stirrer, Which all good Governments are jealous of. **1638** BAKER tr. *Balzac's Lett.* (vol. III.) 131 The Prince I speak of, is a stirrer, and makes no stay any where. ? **1828** COLERIDGE *Alice du Clos* 143 Two stirrers only met my eyes, Fair Alice, and one more. **1855** DICKENS *Dorrit* II. xxv, They both looked up at the sunny morning sky, into which..the breath and voices of a few early stirrers were peacefully rising.

b. A person or animal that moves briskly; one who bestirs himself, an active person. †Of a horse: see STIRRING *vbl. sb.* 3 b, STIRRING *ppl. a.* 2 b.

1573 TUSSER *Husb.* lxxiii. (1878) 164 As huswiues keepe home, and be stirrers about, So speedeth their winnings. ? **1575** BLUNDEVIL *Art of Riding* II. i. D vj, If your horse be nimble..you maye make him a sterer, by teachinge him to bounde aloft, and to yarke withall: to galloppe [etc.]. **1611** COTGR., s.v. *Reposer, Qui va, il leche; qui repose, il seiche*: Prov. The stirrer thriues, the lazie house-Doue pines. **1639** T. DE GRAY *Compl. Horsem.* 6 Instead of a stirrier or horse for mannage, you have bred him fit for nought. **1657** LIGON *Barbadoes* (1673) 58 For Hawkes, I never saw but two, and those the merriest stirrers that ever I saw fly.

stirrer, stirrile, -ill, obs. ff. STEERER, STERILE.

stirring ('stɜːrɪŋ), *vbl. sb.* [f. STIR *v.* + -ING[1].] The action of the verb STIR, in various senses.

1. The action of moving (in general sense); movement, motion. *Obs.* or *arch.*

c **888** ÆLFRED *Boeth.* xx, Ascirped mid þære styringe hire azenre frecennesse [L. *ipsius adversitatis exercitatione prudentem*]. *Ibid.* xxi, Ðara unstillena zesceafta styring ne mæz no weorðan zestilled. *c* **1055** *Byrhtferth's Handboc* in *Anglia* VIII. 318 Momentum, þæt ys styrung. *a* **1300** *Cursor M.* 23678 Sun and mone and stern and lift, þat ai wit stiring ar nu scift,..fra þat time stil sal þai stand. *c* **1375** *Sc. Leg. Saints* iv. (*James*) 76 Quhow his master be his slicht had rewit hym steringe & mycht. *c* **1400** *Secreta Secret., Gov. Lordsh.* 66 þe seconde partye [of Astronomye] ys of þe qualyte & of þe manere to knowe þe sterynge of þe firmament. *c* **1530** *Judic. Urines* II. vii. 30 Pulmo the lunges is a membre softe and tendre..hauynge..ii. meuynges, y[t] is to say, .ii. maner of sterynges. **1613** PURCHAS *Pilgrimage* (1614) 744 The sterne that with little locall stirring guideth so many Ships. **1674** N. FAIRFAX *Bulk & Selv.* Contents, Bearing is neither rest nor stirring, but the keeper or spring of stirring.

2. A beginning to move; a slight or momentary movement; (with negative) any or the least movement.

1340 HAMPOLE *Pr. Consc.* I. 822 His [*sc.* a dying man's] pouce es stille, with-outen styringes. *c* **1375** *Sc. Leg. Saints* xxix. (*Placidas*) 134 He..lay stil..but steryng of fut ore hand. *a* **1425** tr. *Arderne's Treat. Fistula*, etc. 24 þat it be noȝt hurt þruȝ..sodayn styrryng of þe pacient wiþ þe poynt of þe rasour or of þe launcette. **1548** HALL *Chron., Edw. IV*, 215 They made no stirryng, nor once shewed them selfe in sight. **1805** WORDSW. *Fidelity* 6 He..searches with his eyes ..And now at distance can discern A stirring in a brake of fern. **1871** BURR *Ad Fidem* xvi. 349 Subtle stirrings of the air, that show the coming cyclone. **1909** H. J. NEWBOLT *New June* lxvii, The spark..was but smouldering and creeping. .. The first stirring of the flame was close at hand.

b. The action of leaving one's place, or of going out of doors.

1698 FRYER *Acc. E. India & P.* 76 Here being no stirring out to Sea, or travelling in the Country. **1710–11** SWIFT *Jrnl. to Stella* 10 Jan., He had no thoughts of stirring till summer. **1755** ELISA YOUNG in *A. Young's Autobiog.* (1898) 15 We have had so much rain lately that there has been no stirring.

†**c.** *fig.* Change, alteration, variation. *Obs.*

a **1240** *Ureisun* in *O.E. Hom.* I. 189 [Crist] þet is euer ille wiþ-ute truchunge, þet halt euer anon wiþ-ute sturunge. *Ibid.* 203 Wið-ute sturiunge.

d. *fig.* Beginning of action or activity; esp. of mental faculties, intellectual movements, or the like.

1387–8 T. USK *Test. Love* I. Prol. (Skeat) 82 This book shal be of love, and the pryme causes of steringe in that doinge. **1711** ADDISON *Spect.* No. 257 ¶9 Those weak Stirrings and Tendencies of the Will. **1873** SYMONDS *Grk. Poets* v. 111 The very earliest stirrings of conscious art in Greece. **1909** *Edin. Rev.* July 154 The stirrings of an independent life in the..peoples.

†**3.** Active movement; bodily exercise. *Obs.*

c **1400** tr. *Secreta Secret., Gov. Lordsh.* 71 Stirynge before þe mete sterith þe hete of þe stomak. *a* **1400–50** *Wars Alex.* 781 Quat of stamping of stedis & stering of bernes, All dymed þe dale. **1561** HOLLYBUSH *Hom. Apoth.* 40 b, Let him use moderate walkinge or stearing. **1562** J. HEYWOOD *Prov. & Epigr.* (1867) 180 Great sturryng, small mouyng. **1626** BACON *Sylva* §62 Excesse of Meat, Excesse of Drinke, Extraordinary Fasting, Extraordinary Stirring. **1719** DE FOE *Crusoe* II. (Globe) 512 Stirring about, and Trading.. had..more Pleasure in it..than sitting still.

†**b.** Of a horse: The designation of a particular kind of pace. Cf. STIRRER 3 b, STIRRING *ppl. a.* 2 b.

1477 *Paston Lett.* III. 186 The gentyllest hors in trotting and sterying that is in Calis.

4. Violent movement, commotion.

a. In physical sense. ? *Obs.* (In early quots. contextual or lit. from L. *motus.*)

c **1000** *Ags. Gosp.* Matt. viii. 24 Ða wearð mycel styrung [Vulg. *motus*; *c* **1160** *Hatton* steriung] zeworden on þære sæ. *Ibid.* Matt. xxiv. 7 Eorþan styrunga [*c* **1160** *Hatton* eorðe steriunge; Vulg. *terræ motus*]. **1382** WYCLIF *Matt.* viii. 24 A grete steryng [**1388** stiring] was maad in the see.

b. Tumult, uproar; political disturbance, sedition; insurrection. *Obs.* or merged in other senses.

a **1154** *O.E. Chron.* (Laud MS.) an. 975, & com þa on þam eaftran zeare swiðe mycel hungor, & swyðe mænizfealde styrunga zeond Angel cyn. **1415** LD. SCROPE in *43rd Rep. Dep. Kpr. Publ. Rec.* 590 A gret stiring of Lolardis. **1529** RASTELL *Pastyme* (1811) 281 A newe styrrynge began in the northe contrey. **1665** *Clarke Papers* (Camden) III. 28 There is noe stirring in Wales, nor any in armes that wee know of except these in Dorsetshire. [**1828** CARR *Craven Gloss., Stirrings*, a bustle, a commotion.]

†**c.** Disturbance of mind or feelings. *Obs. rare*[−1]. (rendering L. *motus.*)

a **1400** in *Pol. Rel. & L. Poems* (1903) 256 Wiþ weopinge we comen, Wiþ weopinge we passun. Wiþ steriinge we byginnen, Wiþ steriinge we enden.

5. The action of setting in motion, agitation. Now *rare* or *Obs.*

c **1000** *Ags. Gosp.* John v. 4 Æfter þæs wæteres styrunge. **1665** *Phil. Trans.* I. 52 Almost any Ventilation and stirring of the Air doth refrigerate. **1712** M. HENRY *Daily Commun.* (1822) 328 The sick and sore in Bethesda's pool waited for the stirring of the water.

†**b.** Shaking (of the head). *Obs. rare.*

a **1225** *Ancr. R.* 188 Hore hefden sturiunge [*v.r.* schakinge] upon him. *a* **1300** *E.E. Psalter* xliii. [xliv.] 15 þou set us..Stiringe of heved [L. *commotionem capitis*] in folke to be. *a* **1325** *Prose Psalter* ibid., Stirieng of heued.

6. Agitation with the hand or an implement so as to shift or mix the parts:

a. of a liquid, of coals, etc.: see STIR *v.* 3 a, b.

1398 TREVISA *Barth. De P.R.* XIX. cxxviii. (1495) 935 Lebes is a vessell of brasse to sethe flesshe therin and taketh blaknesse of often brennynge and vnclennesse and nedeth therfore ofte styryng and wypynge. **1611** COTGR., *Patouil*,.. a making foule by much sturring. **1640** T. BRUGIS *Marrow of Physicke* II. 151 Boyle it with stirring. **1782** J. BROWN *Nat. & Revealed Religion* III. ii. 238 The stirring of a wasps' nest makes them rage and sting the more.

b. of soil; *spec.* a second ploughing (see STIR *v.* 3 c); also *concr.* land that has just been 'stirred'.

14.. *Lat.-Eng. Voc.* in Wr.-Wülcker 582/27 *Febrimacio*, sturrynge of londe. **1523–34** FITZHERB. *Husb.* §17 If it be layde vpon the sturrynge, at euery plowynge it shall medle the donge and the erthe togyder. **1577** GOOGE tr. *Heresbach's Husb.* I. 21 b, Through many stirringes, your Fallowe is brought to so fine a moulde, as it shall neede very little or no harrowing at all when you sowe it. **1677** PLOT *Oxfordsh.* 239 Some short time before the second tilth, which they call stirring. **1725** *Bradley's Family Dict.* s.v. *Fallow-Ground*, Fallowing is the first Ploughing for Barley, as Stirring is the second, and Sowing the third. **1805** R. W. DICKSON *Pract. Agric.* I. 9 In cross-ploughing or stirring, they [*sc.* the coulters] may be set three-fourths of an inch towards the land. **1865** *Chamb. Encycl.* VI. 347/2 Hoeing or other stirring of the soil is beneficial.

7. The action of rousing or exciting to activity or emotion; incitement, instigation, provocation; †prompting, suggestion, inducement, persuasion.

1399 *Rolls of Parlt.* III. 452/1 By waye of counseill and styryng. **1420–2** LYDG. *Siege Thebes* I. 235 Thorgh his styring, and exortacioun With hym they went. **1507** in *Sel. Cases Star Chamber* (Selden Soc.) I. 271 They wold haue it sold & so by thair assentes & steringes it was sold for xx li. **1530** PALSGR. 276/2 Styrryng to angre, *irritation.* **1568** GRAFTON *Chron.* II. 124 The cause of this warre..was made by the styryng of a Frenche man. **1656** J. HARRINGTON *Oceana* (1658) 155 What convenience is there for debate in a crowd, where there is nothing but jostling, treading upon one another, and stirring of blood? **1891** KIPLING *Light that Failed* x. 205 He..remembered to stir Bessie, who needed very little stirring, into a tremendous rage.

b. Also with *up*: cf. STIR *v.* 16 d, e.

? *c* **1580** [H. NICHOLAS] (*title*) The Fift Epistle: a stirring-vp of the Heart to the Humiliation or Following of Jesus. **1586** A. DAY *Eng. Secretorie* I. (1625) 47 In matter of exhortation or stirring vp to wel-doing. **1675** J. OWEN *Indwelling Sin* x. (1732) 127 Warnings, Calls, Excitations, or Stirrings up. **1857** J. D. BORTHWICK *Three Yrs. California* ii. 42 He was such a dreadfully crabbed old rascal that I thought the stirring-up he got was quite necessary to keep him sweet. **1914** *Evening Standard* 10 Nov. 6 Yesterday London got just what it wanted—a stirring up.

8. Inward prompting, suggestion, or incitement; impulse; in later use, inward movement of feeling or desire (cf. 2 d).

a **1225** *Ancr. R.* 294 Eadi is he.. þat.. to brekeð.. þe ereste sturunges hwon þet fleshs ariseð. *a* **1340** Hampole *Psalter* ii. 10 Wickid sterynge of pride ire enuye couaitis iolifte and oþer vices. *c* **1400** *Apol. Loll.* 67 Oft he [a judge] folowiþ his steringis [*suae voluntatis motus.. sequitur*], & not þe meritis of causis. **1636** Massinger *Bashful L.* iii. i, I.. begin To feel new stirrings, gallant thoughts. **1746** Wesley *Princ. Methodist* 21 He has Power over all the Stirrings and Motions of Sin, but not a total Freedom from them. **1864** Bryce *Holy Rom. Emp.* iv. (1875) 42 The lofty.. mind of Charles was not free from the stirrings of personal ambition. **1884** W. C. Smith *Kildrostan* 65, I Begin to feel a stirring in my veins, As if I must be off into the woods.

†**b.** An affection of the mind, an emotion. *Obs.*

1552 T. Wilson *Logic* 21 There be .iiii. stirringes [1551, perturbacions] principall.. in.. the mynd... *Libido, seu cupiditas.* Lust or desire. *Leticia.* Mirthe. *Egritudo.* Grief. *Metus.* Feare.

9. *attrib.* and *Comb.*: in sense 5 a ('used for stirring'), as ***stirring-apparatus, -bar, -buddle, -rod, -spoon***; in sense 5 b ('for stirring'), as ***stirring-time***.

1877 Raymond *Statist. Mines & Mining* 399 A convenient *stirring-apparatus consists of two oblique blades fixed to the base of a vertical shaft. **1839** Ure *Dict. Arts*, etc. 1025 The mixture is agitated.. by hand with the *stirring-bar. *Ibid.* 751 The *stirring buddle, or chest for freeing the schlamms or slimy stuff from clay. **1839** Ure *Dict. Arts* 1264 The capital should be provided with a stuffing-box, through which a *stirring-rod may pass down to the bottom of the still. **1895** *Arnold & Sons' Catal. Surg. Instrum.* 328 Stirring-rod. **1915** Tremearne *Bori Beliefs* in *Jrnl. R. Anthrop. Inst.* XLV. 34 Making a porridge of flour, and then scraping it off from the *stirring-spoon with her fingers. **1523–34** Fitzherb. *Husb.* §16 The wiedes shall take suche roote, er *sterynge-tyme comme, that they wylle not be cleane tourned vndernethe.

'stirring, *ppl. a.* [f. stir *v.* + -ing^{2}.] That stirs, in various senses of the verb.

1. Moving; that is in motion, or capable of motion; moving about or along; moving lightly or tremulously.

In quot. *c* 1440, loose, not fixed; in quot. 1597 *transf.* moving from one note to another.

c **950** *Lindisf. Gosp.* Matt. Introd. 6 Trewum styrendum *vel* cerrendum. *c* **1384** Chaucer *H. Fame* 478 Yf y kan See owghwhere any stiryng man. *c* **1400** Maundev. (1839) xv. 162 Thei be not sterynge ne mevable. *c* **1440** *Pallad. on Husb.* ii. 141 Stiryng stonys [L. *mobiles lapides*] Commyxt with mold. **1597** Morley *Introd. Mus.* 81 If your descant should be stirring in any place, it should bee in the note before the close. **1611** Cotgr., *Grouillis*, a stirring heape of wormes, or other vermine. **1819** Keats *Indolence* v, A lawn besprinkled o'er With flowers, and stirring shades.

†**b.** *fig.* Changeful, unstable, inconstant. *Obs.* (Cf. the quot. from the same poem under sense 2.)

c **1400** *Destr. Troy* 8057 Hit is a propertie.. To all wemen.. To be vnstable & not stidfast, styrond of wille.

2. Moving briskly, active, lively, agile; energetic in action; actively occupied, busy, bustling.

c **1400** tr. *Secreta Secret., Gov. Lordsh.* 104 Swyft and stirrand as goote. *c* **1400** *Destr. Troy* 3833 A stythe man of his stature, stirond of wille, Menyt [*? read* Meuyt] hym to mony thinges, & of mynde gode. **1588** Shaks. *L.L.L.* v. ii. 16 Such a merrie nimble stirring spirit. **1628** Feltham *Resolves* i. xxx. 96 Naturall heate does more actuate the stirring Genius of Man. *a* **1641** Bp. Mountagu *Acts & Mon.* (1642) 263 Watch [was] set upon her, lest she being a stirring woman, should raise a tumult. **1709** Steele *Tatler* No. 180 ¶1 He.. wanted a stirring Man to take upon him his Affairs. **1845** J. Coulter *Adv. in Pacific* xvii. 280 The missionaries, or stirring mercantile people, whose professions kept them moving quickly about. **1849** Macaulay *Hist. Eng.* ii. I. 182 No man could be a stirring and thriving politician who was not prepared to change with every change of fortune.

†**b.** ***stirring horse***: a courser. Cf. stirrer 3 b, stirring *vbl. sb.* 3 b.

1375 Barbour *Bruce* xi. 129 Mony ane sturdy sterand steid. *c* **1470** *Gol. & Gaw.* 588 On ane sterand steid, that sternly will stert. **1477** *Paston Lett.* III. 183 That he be well trottyng of his owne corage, with owte fors of sporis, and also a steryng hors. **1538** Elyot *Dict.*, *Sternax*, a steerynge or ploungynge horse. *a* **1548** Hall *Chron., Hen. VII*, 53, I omit farther the costly apparel.. the massy cheynes, the stirrynge horses. **1551–2** Edw. VI *Jrnl.* (Roxb.) 392 Tou genettes, a sturring horse, and tow litle moyles. **1598** Stow *Surv.* 76 Hench men twaine, vpon great stirring horses following him. **1614** Rich *Honestie of Age* (1615) 28 Fitter to ryde in a Curtizans Coach vp and downe the streets, then to bestride a stirring Horse in the Field.

c. Characterized by or full of stir or activity.

1647 Boyle in Birch *Life* (1744) 76 Qualities, that in this stirring and necessitous age.. make very unfrequent matches in the self-same person. **1800** Wordsw. *Michael* 81 She was a woman of a stirring life, Whose heart was in her house. **1849** Macaulay *Hist. Eng.* ix. II. 484 The stirring market town of Brixham. **1853** Lytton *My Novel* viii. vii, You come from London? Stirring times for you English. **1873** Mrs. Brookfield *Not a Heroine* I. 32, I want a more stirring occupation.

3. That excites or incites. †**a.** Physically stimulating, stimulant. *Obs. rare.*

c **1000** *Sax. Leechd.* II. 106 Sele him oft styrȝendne drenc. **1609** Dekker *Gull's Horn-bk.* viii. 34 Capon is a stirring meate sometime.

b. Inciting to action, or inducing emotion; rousing, stimulating, animating, inspiriting; exciting, moving, thrilling.

1421 Hoccleve *Minor Poems* xxiii. 519 But thogh thy wordes sharpe & stirynge seeme, To many a man profyten they but lyte. **1530** Palsgr. 325/2 Steryng or provokyng to do a thyng, *incitatif.* **1645** Rutherford *Tryall & Tri. Faith* xxii. 255 If God should withdraw his stirring and prædeterminating influence. **1873** Black *Pr. Thule* xxvi. 446 Cheerful and stirring music. **1888** Burgon *Lives 12 Gd. Men* II. vi. 77 Lives.. without stirring incidents.

stirringly ('stɜːrɪŋlɪ), *adv.* [f. prec. + -ly^{2}.] In a stirring manner.

1. So as to stir to action or emotion; rousingly, excitingly, movingly.

1382 Wyclif *Ps.* xciii. [xciv.] 4 Thei shul steringli seyn [1388 Thei schulen telle out; Vulg. *effabuntur*], and speke wickidnesse. **1866** *Reader* 26 May 524 It is in the portrayal of the more stirringly emotional that his dramatic genius is most at home. **1900** P. C. Simpson *Fact of Christ* vi. 185 We men to whom this life calls so stirringly and strongly.

2. With brisk movement, actively. *rare*$^{-1}$.

1889 *Hardwicke's Sci.-Gossip* XXV. 199, I.. found them stirringly busy; and in the nest were some sixty or seventy pupæ, and six or seven female ants.

stirrow, stirrun: see stirrah, stern *a.*

stirrup ('stɪrəp, 'stɛrəp), *sb.* Forms: 1 **stiȝráp, stíráp**, 2–7 **stirop**, 3–5 **stirap**, 3–6 **stirope**, 4 **stirhap, stroupe**, 4–6 **sterap, styrop(pe**, 5 **sterep, -opp, stiroppe, stirrap, storrope, styrope, -up**, 5–6 **sterop(pe, sturope, styrope**, 5–7 **sterope**, 6 **sterrep, stirepp, -hop, ip(p)e, stor(r)ap, -oppe, sturropp, styrrep(e, -op(p)e, -uppe**, 6–7 **styrrop**, 6–8 **stirrop**, 7 **sterrup, stiropp, stirropp(e, sturrop, styrrup**, 7–8 **stirup**, 8 **sterrop**, 4– **stirrup**. [OE. *stiȝráp*, f. *stiȝ-e* climb (f. wk. grade of *stíȝan* to climb: see sty *v.*) + *ráp* rope *sb.* Cf. OS. *stigerêp* (MLG. *stegerêp*), MDu. *stegereep* (WFlem. *steegreep* stirrup-leather, stirrup), OHG. *stegareif* (MHG. *stegereif*, mod.G. *stegreif*), ON. *stigreip*.

As the etymology shows, the original 'stirrup' must have been a looped rope. In some of the continental Teut. langs. the word has been used for the stirrup-leather, the stirrup itself having a special name, MDu. *böghel* (Du. *beugel*, *stijgbeugel*), whence mod.G. *bügel*, *steigbügel*, Sw. *stigbygel*, Da. *stigbøile*.]

1. a. A contrivance suspended from the side of a saddle to serve as a support for the foot of the rider; in modern times, an arched piece of metal (rarely of wood, leather, etc.) closed by a flat plate to receive the sole of the boot.

to lose one's stirrups [= F. *perdre les étriers*]: to let one's feet accidentally slip out of the stirrups (for the figurative use see c).

c **1000** Ælfric *Gloss.* in Wr.-Wülcker 120/2 *Scansile*, stirap. *a* **1100** *Voc.* ibid. 332/11 *Scansile*, stiȝrap. *c* **1175** *Soul & Body* in *Fragm. Ælfric's Gloss.*, etc. (1838) 6 On stirope stonden mid fotan. *c* **1290** *Beket* 248 in *S. Eng. Leg.* 113 His loreins weren al of seluer, stirapes and spores al-so. *a* **1320** *Sir Tristr.* 3261 His strops he made him tine, To grounde he him wrong. **1338** R. Brunne *Chron.* (1725) 190 He smote him in þe helm, bakward he bare his stroupe. **1375** Barbour *Bruce* iii. 143 The King, in full gret hy, Strak at the tothir wigorusly, That he eftir his sterap drew. *c* **1386** Chaucer *Shipm. Prol.* i Ovre Ost vppon his stiropes stood anoon And seide good men herkeneth euerychoon. *a* **1400–50** *Wars Alex.* 3615 He standis vp in his stereps in starand maylis. *c* **1435** *Torr. Portugal* 987 Torrent in the storrope stod And prayd to god, þat dyed on Rode. *c* **1450** *Merlin* x. 164 Ban.. ficched hym in the styropes so harde that the Iren bente. **1470–85** Malory *Arthur* x. xlvi. 487 There with alle sire Palomydes lost his steroppes and lay vp ryght on his horsbak. **1549** in *Archæologia* XXV. 555 P^{d}.. for the vernyshyng of a styrepe iiij^{d}. **1585** T. Washington tr. *Nicholay's Voy.* i. viii. 8, [I saw] Moores mounted on.. horses without saddel, bridle, stirrops or spurres. **1686** Plot *Staffordsh.* 377 Of Stirrups they also make these several sorts, the swivel, barr'd, Rippon, and plain stirrop. *a* **1700** Evelyn *Diary* Apr. 1646, Instead of stirrups we had ropes tied with a loope to put our feete in. **1728** Chambers *Cycl.* s.v., Stirrops are allowed a modern Invention: Menage observes, that St. Jerom is the first Author who mentions them. **1820** Scott *Monast.* ix, I am a rude man, bred to lance and stirrup, and not used to deal with book-learned men and priests. **1837** Carlyle *Fr. Rev.* I. ii. vi, Now no man on a level with his age but will trot *à l'Anglaise*, rising in the stirrups. **1845** Ford *Handbk. Spain* i. 57 The stirrups are the primitive Moorish, copper or iron boxes of a triangular shape, in which almost the whole foot rests. **1886** Hall Caine *Son of Hagar* i. i, So when I put my feet into the stirrups, there they stuck.

b. ***to hold the stirrup***: lit. in helping a person to mount, esp. as a manifestation of homage or reverence; hence *fig.* to be subservient.

Sometimes with allusion to the rendering of this act of homage by certain emperors to the pope.

a **1548** Hall *Chron., Hen. VII*, 52 When the kynge approched, the duke at his lightynge offred to holde his styrope. **1593** Shaks. *2 Hen. VI*, iv. i. 53 Hast thou not kist thy hand, and held my stirrop? **1601** Dent *Pathw. Heaven* 222 They doe but hold the stirrup to their owne destruction. **1636** Rutherford *Lett.* (1862) I. 179 It becometh not Christ to hold any man's stirrup. **1661** Glanvill *Van. Dogm.* 228 Opinions hold the stirrup, while vice mounts into the saddle. **1675** E. Wilson *Spadacrene Dunelm.* 34, I hold the stirrop to Pyrotechnical Philosophy. **1763** Churchill *Duellist* iii. 136 Who was so mean.. That he would.. hold a stirrup for the Devil. **1908** J. Gairdner *Lollardy* I. 49 The fiery Frederic Barbarossa held the stirrup of Pope Alexander III.

c. In various figurative expressions.

1601 W. Cornwallis *Ess.* ii. xl. Cc3, By Marius and Sylla, the Romaines state lost her sturrops; by Cæsar, and Pompey was cast out of the Saddle. **1642** Bridge *Serm. Norf. Volunteers* 22 Make use of your experience as a stirrup to get up your spirits to the promise. *a* **1647** Boyle *Wks.* 1772 I. *Life* p. xiii, It could not be unwelcome to be of a quality, that was a handsome stirrup to preferment. **1647** Trapp *Comm. 2 Pet.* ii. 12 Some men.. fall beneath the stirrop of reason. **1657** in *Burton's Diary* (1828) I. 412 The plaintiff will ride post with *Festina*, but *Lentè*, quoth the defendant, and puts the plaintiff's foot many times besides the stirrup by Essoins, Imparlances,.. or the like. **1690** C. Nesse *Hist. & Myst. O. & N. Test.* I. 125 Rebels against God fall below the stirrup of sense. **1727** P. Walker *Life R. Cameron* in *Biogr. Presbyt.* (1827) I. 287 He got a Dispensation from the Pope to make a Stirrup of our Covenants to mount the Throne of Britain. **1812** J. H. Vaux *Vocab. Flash Lang.* in *Mem.* (1964) 277 A man who is in swell street, that is, having plenty of money, is said to be up in the stirrups. **1866** Dickens *Boy at Mugby* Christm. Stor. (1874) 331 Excitement was up in the stirrups. Expectation stood a-tiptoe.

†**d.** ***yeoman, groom of the stirrup***: former officers in the Royal Household (Master of Horse's department). *Obs.*

1526 in *Househ. Ordin.* (1790) 203 The wages of the yeoman of the stirrup at 3d. per diem. *Ibid.* 204 Five Groomes of the Stirrop every of them at 2d. per day. **1538** Elyot *Dict.*, *Strator*, he that helpeth his mayster to horsebacke, yeman of the styrope. **1547** in *Lett. & Papers Hen. VIII* (1910) XXI. ii. 401 Belle, groom of the stirrup. **1647** Haward *Crown Revenue* 23 Yeoman of the Stirrup: Fee, *per diem* 9. d. **1692** *Lond. Gaz.* No. 2809/3 The Yeoman of the Stirrup.

2. Applied to various kinds of foot-rest analogous to the stirrup. **a.** *Antiq.* In a crossbow, a rest in which the foot is placed in order to steady the bow while it is being bent.

1371–3 *MS. Acc. Exch. K.R.* 397/10 m. 3, ij vicz ad tendendum balistas. xviij. strops pro balistis.

b. *Shoemaking.* (See quot. 1886.)

With quot. *c* 1820 cf. stirrup *v.* 3.

1597 Deloney *Gentle Craft* Wks. (1912) 89 The Stirrup holding fast while we sowe the Cow-hide. **1611** Cotgr., *Tire-pied*, a Shoomakers stirrup. **1735** Dyche & Pardon *Dict.*, *Stirrup*,.. also an Instrument used by Shoemakers to put over their Knee and under their Foot to hold their Work tight upon their Knee. *c* **1820** J. Kitto in Eadie *Life* (1857) 32 S——.. bids us, under pain of the stirrup, make a pair of shoes per diem. **1886** *W. Somerset Word-bk.*, *Stirrup*, a shoemaker's strap, with which he keeps the last firm upon his knee.

c. [= F. *étrier.*] A kind of footless stocking having a strap which passes underneath the foot; also, the strap itself; hence, a similar strap attached to women's stretch trousers or slacks. orig. *U.S.* in modern use.

An alleged example *c* 1530 *Hyckescorner* 799 is an error for *stertups*: see startup, a kind of boot.

1659 Howell *Lex. Tetragl.* ii. xxxiii, The stirrop of the hose, *l'estrier de la chaussette.* **1685** *Rec. Scott. Cloth Manuf. New Mills* (S.H.S.) 87 Noe more silk or worset stockens be made with stirups. **1714** *Fr. Bk. of Rates* 123 And to these Stockings or Stirrups of Silk, which shall be hereafter imported, his Majesty ordains, that [etc.]. **1746** *Gentl. Mag.* XVI. 407 (Exmoor Vocab.) *Stirrups*, a kind of buskins. **1955** *Sun* (Baltimore) 7 Jan. (B ed.) 15/1 [Baseball] The stockings, modeled after those of the Boston Red Sox. The stirrup—that cutaway portion which extends down into the shoe—will be orange. **1963** *Women's Wear Daily* 23 Sept. 15/1 Rayon/nylon twill stretch pants... hi rise, back zip, no stirrups. **1967** *Boston Sunday Herald* 26 Mar. (Advt. Section), Comfy elastic waist, neat stitched pleat, self-fabric stirrups. **1980** *Times* 19 Feb. 8/4 The major buyers have bought.. denims, dungarees, stirrup trousers (they used to be called ski pants) in the now obligatory stretch fabrics.

d. *Netting.* A contrivance consisting of a footboard suspended by ribbons, serving to keep the work in place.

1844 Mrs. H. Owen *Ladies' Bk. Needlework* (ed. 2) 2 A netting vice or stirrup. **1870** *Mag. for Young* 6 Her foot in a netting stirrup. **1882** Caulfeild & Saward *Dict. Needlework* 358/1 For ordinary Netting the plain Stirrup is the best, as the whole weight of the foot is upon it.

e. *Surg.* An appliance used in operations for extension. Also, each of a pair of supports for holding the legs of a female patient raised and apart, as during childbirth.

1884 W. Pye *Surgical Handicraft* 187 The use of the stirrup and weight, introduced first for extension in hip disease, was soon applied to fractures. **1896** *Allbutt's Syst. Med.* I. 426 If the nurse be desired to apply an extension in cases of hip-disease the ends of the stirrup must be well above the knee. **1936** H. J. Stander *Williams' Obstetrics* (ed. 7) xv. 406 In the hospital she is.. placed on a suitable delivery table,.. the legs held in position by adjustable stirrups. **1977** M. French *Women's Room* (1978) i. 69 The humiliation of being in stirrups and having people peer at her exposed genitals whenever they chose.

f. *nonce-use.* (See quot.)

1585 Higins *Junius' Nomencl.* 169/2 *Encentris*,.. an iron stirrup, or a shooe driuen full of iron nayles poynted, which they vse that goe vpon ice: an icespur.

g. *Mining.* (Cornwall.) A foot-rest attached to the rope by which men were let down and drawn up the shaft.

1602 Carew *Cornwall* i. 11 The workmen are let down and taken vp in a Stirrup, by two men who wind the rope. **1778** Pryce *Min. Cornub.* 158 From the axis hangs a sort of an iron stirrup.. by its two hooks.

h. A stirrup-like foot-rest for working a bellows.

1843 Holtzapffel *Turning* I. 436 The bellows are.. worked by the foot,..by a chain from the rocking-shaft terminating in a stirrup.

i. (See quot.)

1901 H. E. Bulwer *Gloss. Techn. Terms Ch. Bells* 5 *Stirrup*, a separate loop of rope, or leather, attachable to the end of a rope for chiming with the foot.

3. *Anat.* = stapes.

1615 Crooke *Body of Man* 592 The first is called ..*Malleolus* the Mallet or the Hammer. The second *Incus* the Anuill or the Stithy. The third *Stapes* the Stirrop. **1730** Chamberlayne *Relig. Philos.* I. xiii. §5 The Auditory Bones are four in Number, the Hammer, the Anvil, the Stirrup, and between the Anvil and Stirrup there lies a small Bone. **1879** G. Prescott *Sp. Telephone* 5 A mechanical apparatus of wonderful delicacy..consisting of a series of bones termed respectively the hammer, anvil and stirrup.

4. Something shaped like a stirrup. **a.** *gen.*

1684 R. Waller *Nat. Exper.* 110 To observe by the Sound the like Dilatation in a Stirrup of Glass. **1874** *Spons' Dict. Engin.* viii. 2938 Any part of a machine resembling in shape or in functions the stirrup of a saddle, is called the stirrup.

b. A U-shaped clamp or support.

c **1450** *Reg. Vestments* etc. *St. Andrews* in *Maitl. Club Misc.* III. 205 Item thre stirrapis for the lampys. **1496–7** *Rec. St. Mary at Hill* 224 To the Smythe for iij Stays and a litill Sterope and a forth Ri3ht dogge of Iryn for the Roode-lofte. **1507** in *Rokewode's Suff.* 150 (Promp. Parv. 202 *note*) For goions and colars, with ij stireppis for my bruge, weiyng 36½ lb. **1531** *Lett. & Pap. Hen. VIII*, V. 185 For a sterop for the drawe-brygge. **1536–7** in W. H. St. John Hope *Windsor Castle* (1913) I. 265 A great storrap for to bear the gutter of the leades over the steres. **1844** *Civil Engin. & Arch. Jrnl.* VII. 149/2 A stirrup..supporting the table. **1850** Denison *Clock & Watch-m.* 86 The old form of mercurial pendulum was that of a glass cylinder standing on a stirrup at the bottom of a rod. **1869** Rankine *Machine & Hand-tools* Pl. P 11 The smaller end of the taper mandril is supported in a movable bearing in the balanced lever, the upper end of which is secured by the stirrup. **1866** R. M. Ferguson *Electr.* (1870) 3 Let us suspend a magnet..by a stirrup of paper, hanging from a cocoon thread. **1875** Knight *Dict. Mech.*, *Stirrup*, a band or strap which is bent around one object and is secured to another by its tangs or branches. *Ibid.*, *Stirrup* (Carpentry), *a.* a device for holding a rafter-post or strut to a tie... *b.* an iron strap to support a beam. **1883** Gresley *Gloss. Coal-mining* 241 *Stirrups*, a screw joint suspended from the brake-staff or spring-pole, by which the boring rods are adjusted to the depth of the borehole. **1884** F. J. Britten *Watch & Clockm.* 189 The parts of the stirrup may with advantage be annealed after they are finished. **1894** Bottone *Elect. Instr. Making* 22 The wire or fibre which supports the 'stirrup' in which is placed the magnetic needle or insulating rod.

†**c.** Some kind of appendage to a bell. *Obs.*

1341–2 *Ely Sacr. Rolls* II. 118 In vj steropis et iiij bondes pro Baunse [*sc.* a bell so named] 10d. **1474** in T. North *Bells Northamptonsh.* (1878) 371 For makyng of a storop to the sayd bell, iijd. *c* **1520** in C. Welch *Churchw. Acc. All-hallows, Lond. Wall* (1912) 56 Item for a sterope for the gret bell, ij^{d} ob. **1683** *Churchw. Acc. Pittington* etc. (Surtees) 252 For one stirrup for the 2nd bell and altering another.

5. *Naut.* **a.** (See quot. 1867.)

1495 *Naval Acc. Hen. VII* (1896) 152 Boltes with rynges and Styroppes of dyuerse makynges. **1626** Capt. Smith *Accid. Yng. Seamen* 12 The boule spret, the pillow, the sturrop, the spret sayle. **1769** Falconer *Dict. Marine* (1780) s.v. *Horse*, It [*sc.* the horse] is usually suspended thereto [*i.e.* to the yard] at proper distances, by certain ropes called stirrups, which hang about two feet under the yard, having an eye in their lower ends through which the horse passes. **1834** Marryat *P. Simple* vi, 'Captain of the foretop,' said he, 'up on your horses, and take your stirrups up three inches.'—'Ay, ay, sir.' (I looked and looked, but I could see no horses.) **1867** Smyth *Sailor's Word-bk.*, *Stirrups*, ropes with eyes at their ends, through which the foot-ropes are rove, and by which they are supported.

b. (See quots.)

1627 Capt. Smith *Sea Gram.* xi. 53 When a Ship hath lost a peece of her Keele,..you must patch a new peece vnto it, and bind it with a stirrop, which is an iron comes round about it and the Keele. **1691** T. H[ale] *Acc. New Invent.* 49 New Stirrups put on to secure the false Keel. *c* **1850** *Rudim. Navig.* (Weale) 153 *Stirrup*, an iron or copper plate that turns upwards on each side of a ship's keel and dead-wood, at the fore-foot, or at her skeg, and bolts through all.

†**6.** ***false stirrup***: the mace carried by a knight.

It has been suggested that the mace was so called because it hung down from the side of the saddle.

14.. Sir G. Haye *Bk. Knychthede* vi. (S.T.S.) 47 Item, a masse is gevin him..the quhilk masse is lyknyt till a false sterap. *Ibid.*, Quhen he has implyde his spere, his lang suerd, his polax, his false sterap.

7. In reinforced concrete construction, each of the vertical or diagonal members which bind together the upper and lower reinforcement of a beam, etc.

1909 *Concrete & Constructional Engin.* IV. 250 When vertical stirrups are used they take little stress until a diagonal crack has formed.

8. *attrib.* and *Comb.* as ***stirrup-buckle, -holder; stirrup-shaped*** adj.; ***stirrup†-fashion, -wise*** advs.; †**stirrup-band** = sense 5 b; **stirrup-bar**, (*a*) each of the bars on a saddle-tree to which a stirrup-strap is attached; (*b*) the bar of a stirrup on which the foot rests; **stirrup-bone** = sense 3; **stirrup-dram** = stirrup-cup; **stirrup-fast** *a.* (nonce-wd.), having the feet secure in the stirrups; **stirrup-foot**, (*a*) the left forefoot of a horse; (*b*) the left foot, the foot used first in mounting a horse; **stirrup-glass** = stirrup-cup; †**stirrup-hose** = sense 2 c; **stirrup-ladder**, a thatcher's short ladder holding to the roof with spikes (Halliw.); **stirrup lantern**, (see quot.); †**stirrupman**, = *yeoman of the stirrup* (see 1 d); hence †**stirrup-manship**; †**stirrup money**, a fee or perquisite of a groom; **stirrup-piece**, (*a*) (see quot. 1850); (*b*) *nonce-use*, a poem relating to riding; **stirrup pump**, a portable hand pump held steady by a stirrup-like foot-plate and used, esp. in the war of 1939–45, for extinguishing small fires and incendiary bombs with water drawn from a bucket and directed by a hose; **stirrup side**, ? the left side of a horse (cf. *stirrup-foot*); **stirrup-stocking** = sense 2 c; **stirrup-stone**, ? a stone used for mounting a horse; **stirrup-strap**, a leather strap by which a stirrup is suspended; **stirrup-vase** *Archæol.* [misrendering of G. *bügelkanne*, formed after *bügeleisen* flat-iron], a 'pseudamphora' with a square-cut handle on either side of the false spout; **stirrup-verse**, a verse at parting; †**stirrup-way**, a bridle-path.

1407 *MS. Acc. Exch. K.R.* 44/11 (1) m. 4, ij ligaturis ferri vocatis *steropebandes. **1875** Knight *Dict. Mech.* 2012/2 (art. *Saddle-tree*) Two *stirrup-bars are added and iron staples for the valise. **1891** Kipling *Light that Failed* vi. 89 He has slipped his foot from the stirrup-bar. **1646** Sir T. Browne *Pseud. Ep.* v. xiii. 253 Concerning the invention of the stapes or *stirrop bone. **1884** Coues *N. Amer. Birds* 185 The stapes, or 'stirrup-bone.' *a* **1774** Goldsm. tr. *Scarron's Com. Romance* (1775) I. 288 The tongue of the *stirrup-buckle had torn his stockings. **1815** Scott *Guy M.* xxii, Tib Mumps will be out wi' the *stirrup-dram in a gliffing. **1612** *Benvenuto's Passenger* I. i. 15 Reache me my needleworke bootehose, or those of cloth made *stirrop fashion. **1827** Carlyle *Germ. Rom.* I. 308 The latter..with difficulty kept his saddle, and scarcely continued *stirrup-fast. **1753** *Chambers' Cycl.* Suppl., The *stirrup-foot is the near, or left foot before. **1823** Lockhart *Sp. Ball.*, *Escape of Gayferos* vi, The stirrup-foot and the hilt-hand see that ye sunder both. **1775** Ash, **Stirrupglass*, the glass drank on horseback at parting. **1818** *Brathwait's Barnabees Jrnl.* Introd. 18 Taking leave of his host at the Inn door..by having a stirrup glass. **1552** Huloet, *Stirope holder, or yoman of the stirope, *strator*. **1626** T. H[awkins] *Caussin's Holy Crt.* 79 How many tymes he hath made himselfe a stirrop-holder, or foot boy. **1659** Howell *Lex. Tetragl.* ii. xxxiii, *Stirrop-hose, *chaussettes à estrier*. **1664** *Tarif Fr. King & Council* (1713) 12 Two pair of stirrup Hose to pay as one. **1824** *Reg. Arts & Sci.* I. 122 The *Stirrup Lantern is a small square lantern, fixed at the bottom of a stirrup by means of two screw rings on each side. **1524** *Reg. Privy Seal Scot.* I. 492 Ane Letter to Robert Gib, of the gift of the service of *steropmanschip to the king..siclik as ony uthir *steropman to the king had of before. **1756–7** tr. *Keysler's Trav.* (1760) IV. 475 *Stirrup money for the grooms. **1850** Ogilvie, **Stirrup piece*, a name given to a piece of wood or iron in framing, by which any part is suspended; a vertical or inclined tie. **1875** Stedman *Victor. Poets* ix. 302 That superb stirrup-piece..'How they brought the good news'. [**1902** *Shand, Mason & Co.'s Portable Fire Appliances* 3b, This is another adaptation of the 'London Brigade' Hand Pump. The pump is..provided with a stirrup, by means of which it can be used with an ordinary house pail.] **1939** C. C. Ramsay *Fire-Fighting in Peace & War* vi. 41 The Home Office specification insists on a *stirrup pump with a 30-ft. length of ½-in. rubber tubing (hose). **1939** *Punch* 27 Sept. 342/1 The long day, with its stream of gas-masks, sandbags, stirrup-pumps, dugouts,..had drawn to a close. **1974** M. Gilbert *Flash Point* xx. 165 He..had a stirrup pump, a relic of the last war, ready primed in the hall. **1900** *Engineering Mag.* XIX. 755/1 Current is taken off the conductors by three *stirrup-shaped wires. **1663** Butler *Hud.* i. ii. 96 Rais'd upon his desperate foot On *stirrup side he gaz'd about. **1611** Cotgr., *Chaussettes à estrier*, *stirrup stockings. **1662** in *Verney Mem.* (1894) III. 382, 6 Pair thread stirrup stockings. **1748** Richardson *Clarissa* V. 10 He could let me have a pair of coarse, but clean stirrup-stockens, if I pleased. **1838** Lytton *Alice* iv. iii, The peacock, who, perched on an old *stirrup-stone, was sunning his gay plumage. **1775** Ash, **Stirrup-strap*..the strap of leather by which the stirrup is suspended. **1890** Doyle *White Company* xxxvii, Stooping down he loosened the stirrup-straps. **1905** A. J. Evans *Prehist. Tombs Knossos* in *Archæologia* LIX. 510 The *stirrup-vases or false-necked amphoras. **1680** [J. Speed] *Batt upon Batt* 12 No *stirrup-Verse at Grave before she go? **1736** J. Lewis *I. of Tenet* (ed. 2) 38 *Shire-way*, a Way or only Horse or Foot Passengers; a Bridle or *Stirrup-way. **1610** R. Vaughan *Water-workes* R 3 b, A Ring of ground..scituate *stirrope wise.

stirrup ('stɪrəp), *v.* [f. stirrup *sb.*]

1. *trans.* To supply with or as with stirrups.

1610 Guillim *Heraldry* iv. xv. (1611) 233 He beareth argent three saddles stirroped sable. **1684** *Rec. Scott. Cloth Manuf. New Mills* (S.H.S.) 64 Orders lykways the silk stocken striuped in the head be maid wydder in the topps.

†**2.** *refl.* To rise in the stirrups; in quot. *fig.* to pride oneself *upon* something. *Obs.* (? *nonce-use.*)

1672 Marvell *Reh. Transp.* i. (1673) 85 This is that man who insists so much and stirrops himself upon the Gravity of his Profession.

3. *trans.* To flog with a stirrup-leather or with a shoemaker's stirrup. *slang.*

1735 Dyche & Pardon *Dict.*, *Stirrup* v., to thrash or beat a Person with a Shoe-makers Stirrup.

4. *Naut.* To attach stirrups to.

1748 *Anson's Voy.* i. x. 104 We exerted ourselves..to stirrup our shrouds.

Hence **'stirruped** *ppl. a.*, provided with a stirrup; **'stirruping** *vbl. sb.*, a flogging with a stirrup-leather.

1685 *Rec. Scott. Cloth Manuf. New Mills* (S.H.S.) 87 That they may be made long and well marreilled and full in the top as if had striuped head. *c* **1820** J. Kitto in Eadie *Life* (1857) 32 [The beadle] gravely gave us a stirruping all round. **1878** Stevenson *Inland Voy.* 184 The stirrupped foot projects insolently from the frame.

stirrup-cup. [Cf. F. *le vin de l'étrier*, *le coup de l'étrier.*] A cup of wine or other drink handed to a man when already on horseback setting out for a journey; a parting glass.

1681 T. Flatman *Heraclitus Ridens* No. 29 (1713) I. 187 Let's have one Stirrop Cup of Character; it's the only modish Liquor now. **1683** G. Meriton *Praise York-sh. Ale* (1685) 27 Wee'l have with you, a merry Stirrup Cupp. **1808** Scott *Marm.* i. xxxi, Then came the stirrup-cup in course. **1899** Lady M. Verney in *Verney Mem.* IV. 328 Such guests were sure of a hearty welcome and a potent stirrup-cup.

¶**b.** Used for: A drink offered to an arriving guest before he has dismounted.

1869 Tozer *Highl. Turkey* II. 240 [She] goes out to meet him and offer him the stirrup-cup.

¶**c.** Applied to the drinking-vessel.

1865 Kingsley *Herew.* xv, Torfrida stood to welcome them, as fair as day a silver stirrup-cup in her hand.

stirrup-iron. Now somewhat *rare.*

1. The metal portion of a stirrup, the stirrup proper (in the modern sense) as distinguished from the strap supporting it.

1474 *Acc. Ld. High Treas. Scot.* I. 36, j quarter of blew vellus to couir the Qwenis stirrap irnis, price xv s. **1533** *Ibid.* VI. 88 For spurris, brydill bittis, sterap irnis, girth buklis. **1683** *Lond. Gaz.* No. 1810/4 New Stirrop-Leathers, old Stirrop-Irons. **1782** *Phil. Trans.* LXXII. 371 One of the stirrup-irons..exhibits some appearances of fusion on the arch through which the stirrup-leather passes. **1853** R. S. Surtees *Sponge's Sp. Tour* (1893) 318 As he dangled his spurs against his stirrup-irons. **1875** Whyte-Melville *Riding Recoll.* xii. (1879) 70 Till the welcome heather is brushing your stirrup-irons once more.

2. An iron strip to hold the end of a beam or girder.

1838 *Civil Engin. & Arch. Jrnl.* I. 178/2 The parts of the vertical timbers above the roadway are..secured by stirrup-irons, bolts, and wedges, to the main ribs.

stirrup-leather. The leather strap by which a stirrup hangs from the saddle.

139. *Earl Derby's Exped.* (Camden) 46 Pro j pare styrop., et styrop lethres, viij s. pr. **1394–5** *Durham Acc. Rolls* (Surtees) 599 In 2 par. de Stirhaplethirs et 1 pari de Stiraps, 18d. **1470** *York Memo. Bk.* (Surtees) I. 92 To make stirrop lethyrs of blak barked lethir. **1591** Greene *Conny Catching* ii. Wks. (Grosart) X. 77 Stirhops and stirhop leathers, so quaintly and artificially made that is may bee put in the slop of a mans hose. **1620** Shelton *2nd Pt. Quix.* xiv. 87 So he ran after his Master, laying hold vpon one of Rozinantes stirrup leathers. **1701** *Lond. Gaz.* No. 3717/4 He had on a plain Leathern Saddle with new Stirrup-Leathers. **1890** 'R. Boldrewood' *Col. Reformer* xvi, The length of the stirrup-leathers conveyed..the fact that the rider..was an individual of unusual length of limb. **1895** Sir H. Maxwell *Duke of Britain* xii. 171 Numidian lancers..riding with very short stirrup-leathers after the African custom.

attrib. **1653** Urquhart *Rabelais* i. xxxv, He most nimbly ..shifting his feet in the stirrup, performed the stirrup leather feat.

b. As an instrument for flogging.

1611 Cotgr., *Stafilade*, a lash, or thwacke with a stirrup-leather. **1652** J. Wright tr. *Camus' Nat. Paradox* ix. 226 The Souldiers..laced their shoulders so well with their stirrop-leathers, that they made them swim in their own blood. **1726** N. Blundell *Diary* (1895) 221, I had seaven Lads of this Town beaton at my Gate-Hous with a Sterrop-Leather. **1831** Scott *Cast. Dang.* xii, Flagellation with belts, stirrup-leathers, or surcingles.

stirrupless ('stɪrəp-, 'stɛrəplɪs), *a.* [f. stirrup *sb.* + -less.] Without stirrups.

c **1430** *Syr Gener.* (Roxb.) 7270 Ageyn dressed him [Generides] Without bridel and stiroples. **1613** J. Taylor (Water P.) *Laugh & be fat* Wks. (1630) ii. 70/2 Thy riding Stirroplesse. **1879** J. Beerbohm *Patagonia* 98, I had to ride stirrupless back to Santa Cruz.

stirrup-oil. *jocular.* [Cf. stirrup-leather b.] (See quots.)

1679 Coles *Eng.-Lat. Dict.* (ed. 2), To give one some Stirrup-oyl, *aliquem fustigare*. **1825** Hone *Every-day Bk.* I. 411 They send to a cobbler's for a pennyworth of the best 'stirrup-oil.' **1854** Miss Baker *Northampt. Gloss.* s.v., One of the old jokes practised on the 1st of April is the sending a raw lad to a saddler's or cobler's for a 'penn'orth of stirrup-oil,' when he is termed an April fool, and his ignorance enlightened by the application of a stirrup-leather across his shoulders.

'stir-up, *sb.* and *a.* [f. the verbal phrase *stir up*: see stir *v.* 16.]

A. *sb.* The action of stirring up, or condition of being stirred up; agitation, commotion.

18.. *New Monthly Mag.* (Flügel), The stir-up of the ashes. **1845** Browning *Flight of Duchess* xvii, How it gives the heart and soul a stir-up As if [etc.]. **1900** *Daily News* 17 Oct. 6/7 The stir up at Oxford afforded a lesson for the whole country. **1908** *Westm. Gaz.* 16 Dec. 14/3 The 'stir-up' is welcomed, however, as it will disturb the food on the rocky ground and sand-banks.

B. *adj.* or *attrib.*

1. Having the quality of stirring up; rousing.

1890 *My Curates* ii. (ed. 8) 12, I was aware of my own.. want of power to fulfil the office of a 'stir-up' preacher.

2. ***Stir-up Sunday*** (colloq.): the Sunday next before Advent: so called from the opening words of the Collect for the day.

The name is jocularly associated with the stirring of the Christmas mincemeat, which it was customary to begin making in that week.

a **1825** FORBY *Voc. E. Anglia, Stir-up-Sunday*, the last Sunday after Trinity. **1854** MISS BAKER *Northampt. Gloss., Stir-up Sunday*, the twenty-fifth or last Sunday after Trinity; on which day the Collect in the Book of Common Prayer commences with the words 'Stir up', from which this name has arisen. **1867** *Hurst Johnian Mag.* Dec. 308 Stir-up Sunday. The sermon on this day was preached by the Ven. the Archdeacon of Chichester. **1904** *Daily Chron.* 30 Nov. 8/4, I believe those who love Christmas most ardently are the boarding school boys and girls, who have just noted with a thrill of joy 'Stir-up Sunday!'

stirup, obs. form of STIRRUP.

stishovite ('stɪʃəvaɪt). *Min.* [f. the name of S. M. *Stishov*, Russian geochemist, who first synthesized it in 1961: see -ITE[1].] A dense, tetragonal polymorph of silica, formed at very high pressure and found in meteorite craters. Cf. COESITE.

1962 E. C. T. CHAO et al. in *Jrnl. Geophysical Res.* LXVII. 419/1 Stishov and Popova (1961) recently synthesized a high-density polymorph of SiO_2 at 1200°–1400°C and at a pressure reported to be above 160,000 atmospheres... In honor of the senior author of the paper announcing the synthesis of this new polymorph, we propose to name the new mineral stishovite. **1971** I. G. GASS et al. *Understanding Earth* i. 35/1 The diamonds occasionally contain minute inclusions of coesite..but do not contain stishovite, another polymorph forming at even higher pressures. **1978** *Nature* 20 Apr. 714/2 Stishovite is the highest pressure polymorph of silica. It possesses the rutile structure with a density of 4·28 g cm^{-3} and is characterised by sixfold coordination of silicon by oxygen.

stitch (stɪtʃ), *sb.*[1] Forms: 1 stice, 3–6 stiche, 4–6 stych(e, 5 steche, 5 stytche, 6–8 stich, 6–7 stitche, 6– stitch. See also STEEK *sb.* [OE. *stice* str. masc., corresp. to OFris. *steke* prick, stab, OS. *stiki* (Gallée), point, thrust (MLG. *steke*), OHG. *stih* (MHG., mod.G. *stich*) prick, sting, stab, stitch (Da. *stik*, Sw. *stick*, stab, stitch, prob. from LG.), Goth. *stik-s* point of time:—OTeut. **stiki-z*, f. **stik-* root of STICK *v.*]

I. A thrust, stab.

†**1.** A prick, puncture, or stab, inflicted by a pointed implement. Only OE.

c **897** ÆLFRED *Gregory's Past. C.* xxxvi. 261 Se ðe us ȝehæleð from ðæm stice urra synna [*a peccatorum nos punctionibus salvans*]. *c* **1000** *Ags. Laws Æthelb.* lxvii, Ȝif man þeoh ðurhstingþ, stice ȝ ehwilce. VI. scillingas.

2. a. A sharp sudden local pain, like that produced by the thrust of a pointed weapon; esp. (now only) an acute spasmodic pain in the intercostal muscles, called more fully ***a stitch in the side***. Also in generalized or collective sense.

c **1000** *Sax. Leechd.* II. 174 Wið miltewærce & stice. *a* **1225** *Ancr. R.* 282 Al so, on eðelich stiche oðer on eðelich eche makeð uorte understonden hwu lutel wurð is prude. *c* **1230** *Hali Meid.* 35 Stiches i þi lonke. *c* **1440** *Promp. Parv.* 475/1 Styche, peyne on þe syde, *telum.* **1490** CAXTON *Eneydos* xxviii. 110 The gowte or the poplesie, the stytches or the paralesye. *a* **1500** *Brut* 604 Aftyr þat, ther fylle a gret dissese in Engelond callyd þe styche, þat moche peeple deyde sodeynly þerof. **1533** ELYOT *Cast. Helth* (1541) 83 b, Stytches and grefes in the sides. **1561** HOLLYBUSH *Hom. Apoth.* 20 If a man hath a stiche about the hart. **1601** SHAKS. *Twel. N.* III. ii. 73 If you desire the spleene, and will laughe your selues into stitches, follow me. **1683** ASHMOLE *Diary* (1774) 366 A stitch took me at the setting on of my left hip. **1713** *Phil. Trans.* XXVIII. 122 Pains and Stitches behind the Ears. **1748** SMOLLETT *Rod. Rand.* xxvii, The third [patient] complained of a pleuritic stitch. **1886** STEVENSON *Kidnapped* xxiv, I had a painful stitch in my side, which never left me. **1898** P. MANSON *Trop. Diseases* xxiii. 354 Fuller inspiration is attended with stitch. **1898** *Allbutt's Syst. Med.* V. 198 The agonising stitch of pleurisy.

†**b.** *fig.*

a **1225** *Ancr. R.* 110 In his seli soule..he hefde þe stiche of sori & seoruhful pine. **1622** BACON *Hen. VII*, 182 Thinking now that hee should be cured of those priuie Stitches which hee had long had about his Heart. **1661** BURNEY *Κέρδ. Δῶρον* 128 The King hates bribes... These are stitches to the Prince's sides.

¶**c.** A stiff and affected carriage of the body has sometimes been jocularly compared to the effect of a stitch in the side.

1599 B. JONSON *Cynthia's Rev.* III. iv. (1601) F 2 b, One that..Salutes a friend, as if he had a stitch. **1865** DICKENS *Mut. Fr.* I. ix, Mrs. Wilfer, majestically faint, and with a condescending stitch in her side: which was her company manner.

d. *pl.* Fits of laughter; esp. in phr. (*to have*, etc., someone) ***in stitches***. Occas. *sing.* = LAUGH *sb.* 4 b. (See also sense 2 a, quot. 1601.)

1935 *Motion Picture* Nov. 41/1 A laugh festival that will have you in stitches from its opening scene to its ridiculous but uproarious climax. **1952** E. O'NEILL *Moon for Misbegotten* I. 65 Listen to Jim still in stitches. It's good to hear him laugh as if he meant it. **1968** A. DIMENT *Great Spy Race* ii. 18 The party's in a house right opposite. It'll be a stitch, Phil. You must come. **1969** O. BLAKESTON *For crying out Shroud* vi. 56 I've got some new gear that will give you stitches. **1981** D. M. THOMAS *White Hotel* IV. i. 139 She had them in stitches with her absurd—but true—anecdotes. **1983** *Listener* 20 Jan. 38/4 The sardonic puppets, C4s, had my anglophone family in stitches.

†**3.** *transf.* A contortion of the face, a grimace.

1619 FLETCHER *M. Thomas* II. ii. (1639) D 3, Leave your stiches. *a* **1625** —— *Captain* II. ii, If you talke Or pull your face into a stich againe.

†**4.** *fig.* A grudge, dislike, spite, ground of complaint. Chiefly in phr. ***to have*** or ***take a stitch against*** (rarely *at*) (a person). *Obs.*

a **1591** H. SMITH *Serm.* (1594) 224 Therefore his Maiestie hath a stitch against her, as Salomon had to Shimei. **1625** BP. MOUNTAGU *App. Cæsar* 121 Their whole stitch is against the Church Representative in a Generall Councell. *a* **1639** W. WHATELEY *Prototypes* II. xxx. (1640) 100 We sometimes take such a stitch and spleene against those whom nature hath tyed to us. **1652** HEYLYN *Cosmogr.* Introd. 19 The Princes of Italy, and the Florentines, have a stich at Venice. **1679** ALSOP *Melius Inq.* I. i. 94 Against these persons the Enquirer has a desperate stitch.

II. A movement in sewing or the like.

5. a. Each of the movements of a threaded needle in and out of a fabric which is being sewn. Also, the like movement with the awl in shoemaking.

c **1290** *St. Mark* 12 in *S. Eng. Leg.* 362 þe soutare atþe furste stiche fuel vuele is hond he piȝte. *a* **1542** WYATT *Poems*, '*Who hath heard*', She..wisshed eche stitche as she did sit & soo had prykt my hert. **1562–75** *Gammer Gurton* Prol. 1 As Gammer Gurton, with manye a wyde styche, Sat pesynge and patching of Hodg her mans briche. **1594** LYLY *Mother Bombie* I. iii, Euery stitch in her sampler is a pricking stitch at my heart. **1794** *Rigging & Seamanship* I. 92 In the merchant-service it is common to stick the seams with two rows of stitches, when the sail is half worn. **1840** THACKERAY *Shabby-genteel Story* v, She had not gone through many pages, or Becky advanced many stitches in the darning of that table-cloth. **1875** *Plain Needlework* 14 This causes the needle to go in slanting, and so making one half of the stitch wider than the other half. **1878** *Encycl. Brit.* VIII. 162/1 Probabilities forbid us from believing that Matilda and her waiting maids ever did a stitch on this canvas.

Prov. **1793** *Friendly Addr. Poor* 14 A stitch in time may save nine. **1855** BOHN *Handbk. Prov.* 301 A stitch in time saves nine.

b. The portion or loop of thread or yarn left in the fabric as a result of this movement, and forming (usually in a series) the material by which the parts of the sewn fabric are held together.

1394 *P. Pl. Crede* 553 þei ben y-sewed wiþ whiȝt silk & semes full queynte, Y-stongen wiþ stiches þat stareþ as siluer. **1399** *On K. Richard's Ministers* in *Pol. Poems* (Rolls) I. 363 Hit is so roton on ych a side, Ther nul no stych with odur abyde, to set theron a clout. *a* **1529** SKELTON *P. Sparowe* 212, I toke my sampler..To sowe with stytchis of sylke My sparow whyte as mylke. **1662** DRYDEN *Wild Gallant* I. i, The Stitches of thy Doublet are so far asunder, that it seems to hang together by the Teeth. **1768** STERNE *Sent. Journ., Temptation*, A stitch or two had broke out in the gathers of my stock. **1821** DIBDIN *Bibliogr. Tour* I. 379 (Bayeux Tapestry) The stitches, if they may be so called, are threads laid side by side—and bound down at intervals by cross stitches, or fastenings—upon rather a fine linen cloth. **1844** *Newton's Lond. Jrnl.* Conj. Ser. XXV. 247 When the stitch which fastens on the outer sole is passed through the strip of leather, it draws the strip over the stitches that unite the upper leather to the inner sole, thus concealing them. **1886** *Encycl. Brit.* XXI. 831/1 They [the soles] are stitched to the welt, about twelve stitches of strong waxed thread being made to the inch.

fig. *a* **1586** SIDNEY *Arcadia* III. xxi. §3 If in the mean time one of them did not pull out their il-wrought stiches of vnkindnes. **1593** NASHE *Four Lett. Conf.* (end), Finally, Printers haue many false stiches, which are thus to bee drawen vp.

c. In machine sewing, a single motion of a needle and shuttle carrying the thread through the fabric; or the loop or interlocked thread thus produced.

1844 *Newton's Lond. Jrnl.* Conj. Ser. XXV. 305 When the work has passed through the machine, it will be found that a running stitch has been produced. **1883** S. CHAPPEL *Sewing Machine* 23 The machine will now gather the work, and the longer stitch you have on the fuller the gathering will be.

d. Phr. ***stitch by stitch***: used to describe strong and careful sewing in which one stitch is performed at a time (as distinct from 'running'); also *fig.*

1566 T. STAPLETON *Ret. Untr. Jewel* Pref. ****2 b, But for one man to answer the whole, and that stitche by stitche (as the Replier requireth) bothe the time woulde be so longe, that many a soule in the meane might perish,..and also the booke woulde be so greate that [etc.]. *Ibid.* IV. 195 b, M. Iewelles whole Replie in these matters hath bene at longe and stitche by stitche confuted. **1880** [MRS. L. S. FLOYER] *Plain Hints Exam. Needlew.* 107 The slow stitch-by-stitch movement [run]..in good plain work.

e. In emphatic phrases with a negative or the like: A single movement with the needle; *fig.* a 'stroke' of work of any kind.

1581 PETTIE *Guazzo's Civ. Conv.* II. (1586) 116 b, The other would not worke a stitch, but goeth loytering up and downe all daie long. **1623** MIDDLETON *More Dissemblers* I. iv, I must either have the Song..or I'll not do a stitch of service for you from one weeks end to the other. **1768–74** TUCKER *Lt. Nat.* (1834) I. 648 If men knew what was just enough to carry them to heaven, they would not do a stitch more than absolutely necessary. *Ibid.* II. 528 The shoemaker earns enough in four days to maintain him the whole week, so he never will do a stitch of work before Wednesday morning.

6. *Surgery.* The movement of the needle through the edges of a wound when it is being sewn up; each loop of thread or other material fastened in the skin or flesh as a result of the operation.

royal stitch: see ROYAL *a.* 15. †***dry stitch*** (= mod.L. *sutura sicca*): an appliance of sticking plaster serving the purpose of a suture.

1525 tr. *Brunswyke's Handywork Surg.* xiii. C iij, Ye shall set the fyrst stiche in yᵉ myddis of the woundys lyppys, the other a fynger brode betwene euery .ii. stiches. **1674** tr. *G. Fabritius (Hildanus) Cista Milit.* 32 In wounds of the face I never use Needle, but that which is called the *dry stitch*. **1749** GATAKER tr. *Le Dran's Oper. Surg.* 35 If the wound has one or more hanging lips of an irregular figure, the first stitch must be made at the angle of each lip. **1894** *Lancet* 3 Nov. 1028/2 The serous surfaces were apposed by several Lembert's stitches. **1908** *Animal Managem.* (Vet. Departm., War Office) 327 Stitches should be..not drawn so taut as to cause any tension on the skin.

7. A single complete movement of the needle or other implement used in knitting, netting, crochet, embroidery, lace-making, etc.; the portion of the work produced by such a movement. Phr. ***to let down, drop, take up a stitch.***

1599 MINSHEU *Sp. Dict., Dial.* 2 Looke well if the stockings haue any stitches broken in them. **1620** SHELTON *2nd Pt. Quixote* xliv. 288 As he pulled off his stockings, there broke from him..some foure and twenty stitches and a halfe, that made his stocking looke like a Lettice-window. **1773** JOHNSON (ed. 4), *Stitch*,..a link of yarn in knitting. **1818** MRS. SHERWOOD *Fairchild Family* I. xxiv. (1829) 257 She had been knitting,..but she dropped several stitches. **1844** CORNELIA MEE *Comp. Work-table* 25 Knit 15 stitches plain. **1844** MRS. H. OWEN *Ladies' Bk. Needlework* (ed. 2) 2 Netting... The stitch is formed by taking the mesh in your left hand, [etc.]. **1881** *Encycl. Brit.* XII. 299/1 The stocking-frame,..which mechanically produces the looped stitch.

fig. **1837** F. D. MAURICE *Let.* Feb. in F. MAURICE *F. D. Maurice* (1884) I. xiv. 224, I consider..whether we ought to take up our stitches (not intentionally dropped) at the age of twenty-four [*i.e.* go to a university]. **1862** *Sat. Rev.* 8 Feb. 148 When a dropped stitch is taken up in the personal biography of one who..has influenced the religious life of millions, it is [etc.]. **1881** *Times* 16 July 11/2 The Committee ..will be enabled to take up the stitches dropped in the process [of examining the bill].

8. *Bookbinding.* A fastening of leaves, esp. those of pamphlets, with thread or wire drawn through a hole previously pierced. Cf. STITCH *v.* 5.

1835 HANNETT *Bibliopegia* II. (1865) 224 The third sheet having only one stitch.

9. A particular mode of using the needle or other implement, in sewing, knitting, embroidery, etc.; the kind or style of work thus produced.

See also BACK-, CHAIN-, CROSS-, FEATHER-, HEM-, WHIP-STITCH; BREDE *sb.*[2] 4, BUTTON-HOLE *sb.* 4, CORAL *sb.*[1] 9, DAMASK *sb.* 10, DOT *sb.*[1] 8, FLEMISH *a.* 3, GERMAN *a.*[2] 4, GOBELIN 1, HERRING-BONE *sb.* 2 a, HONEY-COMB *sb.* 6, IRISH *a.* 2 c, LOCK *sb.*[2] 20, QUEEN *sb.* 14, RIBBED *ppl. a.* 2 b, ROPE *sb.*[1] 9, RUSSIAN *a.* 2 d, SATIN *sb.* 9 a, SPIDER *sb.* 11, STEM *sb.*[1] 9, etc. For *true-stitch* (lit. and fig.) see TRUE *a.* D. 1 c.

1624 in *Archæologia* XLVIII. 144 A long cushion of Irish stitch. **1640** J. TAYLOR (Water P.) *Prayse of Needle* A 2, Fine Ferne-stitch, Finny-stitch, New-stitch, and Chain-stitch, Braue Bred-stitch, Fisher-stitch, Irish-stitch, and Queen-stitch, The Spanish-stitch, Rosemary-stitch, and Mowse-stitch. **1677** PLOT *Oxfordsh.* 259 He also represents in a most exquisite manner, both the Irish and Bredth stitch in Carpets and Screens. **1758** JOHNSON *Idler* No. 13 ¶7 When she is engaged in teaching them a new stitch. **1856** MRS. PULLAN *Lady's Dict. Needlework.* **1890** SARA J. DUNCAN *Social Depart.* 121 Upstairs there were no trivialities in Kensington stitch, or any other stitch.

fig. **1565** T. STAPLETON *Fortr. Faith* I. vii. 37 b, I will with an other stitche worke this matter againe.

10. A loop of thread or yarn as an ultimate constituent of a sewn or woven fabric; hence, any the least piece of fabric or clothing. ***every stitch***, all the clothes one is wearing; every available piece (of sail); *occas.* every part (of a structure); every 'inch' (of a person).

? *a* **1500** *Chester Pl.* iii. 75, I will goe to gather sliche, the ship for to cleane and piche; anoynted yt must be every stich, board, tree, and pyn. **1817** BYRON *Beppo* iv, You'd better walk about begirt with briars, Instead of coat and smallclothes, than put on A single stitch reflecting upon friars. **1837** DISRAELI *Venetia* VI. x, A boat,..with every stitch of canvas set. **1854** H. MILLER *Sch. & Schm.* (1858) 16 The master..gave instant orders to lighten every stitch of sail. **1883** CLELAND *Inchbracken* xi. 88 Ducking me in burns till I haven't a dry stitch on my back! **1885** MARQ. DUFFERIN in Lyall *Life* (1905) II. 74 A mass of human beings with scarcely a stitch on their bodies.

11. ***a good stitch***: a considerable distance (in walking). *dial.*

1684 BUNYAN *Pilgr.* II. 148 You have gone a good stitch, you may well be a weary; sit down. **1901** F. E. TAYLOR *Folk-Speech S. Lancs.* (E.D.D.), He's come a lung stitch.

12. *jocular.* A tailor. Also ***man of stitches.***

a **1700** B. E. *Dict. Cant. Crew, Stitch*, a Tayler. **1809** T. DONALDSON *Poems* 32 Had ye but tauk'd about the yarn, The needle, or the clout, Then Stitch an' I had try'd to learn To gien ye word about. *c* **1848** J. KEEGAN *Leg. & Poems* (1907) 466 There being no other rival 'stitch' in the neighbourhood, Dandy thought he might..'set up' in his defunct master's place. **1871** B. TAYLOR *Faust* (1875) I. v. 91 He called his man of stitches, The tailor came straightway.

III. **13.** *Comb.*, as ***stitch-hole***; ***stitch-like*** adj.; **stitch-bird**, *Pogonornis cincta* of New Zealand, the clicking note of which has a fancied resemblance to the word 'stitch'; †**stitch-broth**, some kind of mulled beverage (? for curing stitches); †**stitch-dropped** *a.*, said of knitted work in which one or more stitches have been dropped; similarly †**stitch-fallen** (in quot. *fig.*); **stitch-man**, a workman employed in stitching (now esp. shoes); **stitch welding**, a form of spot welding in which a series of overlapping spot welds is produced by a machine which makes each weld and advances the work automatically; hence (as back-formation) **stitch weld** *sb.* and *v. trans.*; **stitch-welded** *ppl. a.*; **stitch welder**, a machine that performs stitch welding; **stitch-wheel**, a toothed wheel used for marking equidistant holes for stitching leather; = PRICKER 4 b (*g*); **stitch-while**, in phr. ***every stitch-while***, every moment, at brief intervals (now *dial.*); **stitch-work**, embroidery, tapestry.

1873 W. L. BULLER *Birds New Zeal.* 98 *Pogonornis cincta.* (*Stitch-bird.) **1635** HEYWOOD *Philocoth.* 48 We have moreover.. *Stitch-broth brew'd with rose-water and Sugar, Burn'd Sacke, Burn'd Wine, Muld-Wine. **1834** *Tait's Mag.* I. 631/1 The *stitch-dropped stocking. **1693** DRYDEN *Juvenal* x. 309 A *stitch-fal'n Cheek, that hangs below the Jaw. **1898** J. T. FOWLER in *Durham Acc. Rolls* (Surtees) 114 A small membrane with *stitch-holes at the foot. **1897** *Allbutt's Syst. Med.* IV. 162 *Stitch-like pains in the right side of the chest. **1710** in *Jrnl. Brit. Archæol. Assoc.* (1868) XXIV. 331 *Stitch-men. [The name given to the association of tailors, mercers, drapers, cappers, hatters, glovers, and skinners of Ludlow.] **1844** *Mechanics' Mag.* XL. 42 (Shoemaking) The English workman, who, as a stitchman, is far superior to the French. **1894** *Daily News* 22 Sept. 6/7 The defendant was.. a stitch-man, of Northampton. **1951** *Trans. Inst. Welding* June 90/1 A seam weld is considered better than a *stitch weld, because of its more regular formation. **1958** *Times Rev. Industry* July 26/2 The components [of the gas turbine] are stitch-welded around the circumference. **1961** J. A. OAKES *Welding Engineer's Handbk.* xxiii. 243 (*caption*) Set-up for stitch welding a steel door. **1972** *Automobile Engineer* Jan. 12/1 The fuel tanks are stitch-welded to the sides of the chassis. **1934** *Welding Industry* Dec. 348/1 A development which is the logical consequence of the attempt to speed up the spot welding process is the so-called continuous spot or *stitch welder. **1946** *Philips Resistance Welding Handbk.* i. 18 Stitch welders, which have been described as the sewing machines of the resistance welding industry, are either pneumatically or mechanically driven to produce a very large number of spots in rapid succession. **1934** *Welding Industry* Aug. 223/1 A continuous spot welding machine is shown... This is often called *stitch welding. **1978** D. R. ANDREWS *Soldering, Brazing, Welding & Adhesives* iii. 65 For stitch welding the electrodes are automatically opened and closed between the making of consecutive welds and the work is moved while the electrodes are parted. **1875** KNIGHT *Dict. Mech.*, *Stitch-wheel. **1620** SHELTON *2nd Pt. Quix.* xi. 63 Rozinante .. perceiuing the libertie he had, stayed euery *stitch-while [*acada paso*] to feede vpon the greene grasse. **1896** *Warwicksh. Gloss.* s.v., It teks me every stitchwhile to keep them children's clothes tidy. **1848** LYTTON *Harold* IX. i, The notable '*stitchwork' of Matilda the Duchess. **1863** HAWTHORNE *Old Home, Civic Banq.* II. 247 They [*sc.* tapestry figures].. vanish drearily into the old stitch-work of their substance when you try to make them out.

†**stitch**, *sb.*[2] *Obs.* Forms: 1 stycce, sticce, (*Northumb.* stycgc, *pl.* stycas, stycgce), 2–3 stuc(c)he (ü), 3 sticche, stec(c)he, 4 *Kent.* stechche. [Com. Teut. (wanting in Gothic): OE. *stycce* str. neut. = OS. *stukki*, MDu. *stucke*, *stic* (mod.Du. *stuk*), OHG. *stucchi* (MHG. *stücke*, mod.G. *stück*), ON. *stykki* (Sw. *stycke*, Da. *stykke*):—OTeut. **stukkjo-m*, cogn. w. **stukko-z* STOCK *sb.*] A fragment, piece.

In ONorthumbrian applied to 'the widow's mite'.

c **825** *Vesp. Psalter* cxlvii. 17 *Frusta panis*, stycce hlafes. *c* **900** *Bæda's Hist.* III. vi. (1890) 166 Se cyning.. bebead, þæt mon þone disc tobræce to styccum [*v.rr.* sticcum, sticum]. *c* **950** *Lindisf. Gosp.* John xix. 23 [Hia] worhton feuoer dælo, eghuoelcum anum cempan dæl *vel* stycg [*Rushw.* stycce]. *a* **1200** *Moral Ode* 189 in *O.E. Hom.* I. 171 We ȝeueð uneðe for his luue a stuche of ure brede. *c* **1205** LAY. 16703 Samuel .. al to-swadde þene king in Jerusalemus chepping, & þa stucchen [*c* **1275** sticches] tarueden wide ȝeond þa straten. *a* **1225** *Leg. Kath.* 1992 Smit se smertliche herto, þat alle þeos fowr hweoles tohwiðeren to stucchen. **1340** *Ayenb.* 111 Þet is to zigge þet me ssel recordi zueteliche and smalliche be little stechches alle þe guodnesses of oure lhorde.

stitch (stɪtʃ), *sb.*[3] Now *dial.* Forms: α. 5–6 steche, 8 stech, steach, 8–9 stetch, steatch. β. 7 stich(e, stytch, 6–9 stitch. [Prob. orig. identical or cogn. w. STITCH *sb.*[1] Cf. WFlem. *steek*, Fris. *steke* in sense 1.]

†**1.** ? The act of cutting or dividing the earth with the share in ploughing; the (greater or lesser) depth to which the share is driven in making a furrow. Phr. ***to take stitch***, to drive the share into the soil.

1600 HOLLAND *Livy* XLII. ii. 1117 The clots of earth, that were turned with the plow as it took stitch and made furrow. **1601** —— *Pliny* XVII. iv. I. 503 In Syria, the husbandmen goe lightly over with their plough, and take no deeper stitch in making their furrowes. **1620** MARKHAM *Farew. Husb.* ii. 14 Taking a good stitch (as they call it in Husbandry). *Ibid.* ix. 65 You shall plow vp the ground againe with somewhat a better and deeper stytch then you did before. **1653** BLITHE *Eng. Improver Impr.* 101 Plow it.. of such a stitch or depth as the Land will bear.

2. A ridge or balk of land; esp. a strip of ploughed land between two water-furrows; also, a narrow ridge in which potatoes, etc. are grown.

α. **1493** *Will of Hilbrond, Cambridge* (Somerset Ho.) ij. stechys of my whete. **1576** *Hibaldstow Fine Roll* in *N.W. Linc. Gloss.* (1889) s.v. *Steche*, Robert Ponton for his son carrying ij hors tyed together up the steche ij[d]. **1764** *Museum Rust.* III. 321 Fourth ploughing, a clean earth; draw it on to the steach. **1780** *Lett. & Pap. Bath Soc.* I. 15 A whole field was sown, and set, in alternate stetches. **1794** A. YOUNG *Agric. Suffolk* 24 In some districts, six, eight, and ten feet steatches, a little arched, are used. **1852** J. CAIRD *Eng. Agric.* 153 (Suffolk) It is ploughed into 'stetches' about 8 feet 2 inches in width. **1910** *Essex Rev.* Apr. 59 The field was ploughed.. in stetches 16½ feet wide.

β. **1610** FOLKINGHAM *Feudigr.* II. i. 48 Small Ridges or Stitches are accomodated to cold and stiffe ground... These Stitches are common in Norfolke and Suffolke. *c* **1611** CHAPMAN *Iliad* XVIII. 495 Men at plow.. that draue earth here and there, And turnd vp stitches orderly. **1664** SPELMAN *Gloss.*, *Selio*,.. A stiche of lande. **1763** *Museum Rust.* I. 21 A method of mowing wheat that grows on high ridges, as [well as] that which grows on stitches and flat lands. **1764** *Ibid.* II. 4 For coleseed, I lay it in broad lands, the stitches being pretty high in the middle. **1813** A. YOUNG *Agric. Essex* I. 199 On the strong land in the maritime district, eights, as they call them, stitches of eight furrows are general. **1854** MISS BAKER *Northampt. Gloss.*, *Stitches*, balks, or portions of grass land in arable fields. **1893** in Cozens-Hardy *Broad Norf.* 3 *Rig*, *stitch* are both used to describe the space between two double furrows.

b. *attrib.*

1733 W. ELLIS *Chiltern & Vale Farm.* 324 Broad Land and stitch Ploughings. **1750** —— *Mod. Husb.* VI. i. 45 (E.D.S.) Wheat lying in the stitch-shape lies too high and dry. *Ibid.* 48 It lay in the stitch-posture.

stitch (stɪtʃ), *sb.*[4] Now *dial.* In 7 *pl.* stiches. [Of uncertain origin; identity with STITCH *sb.*[1] or *sb.*[2] is possible.] A shock of corn consisting of a number of sheaves set up together in the field.

1603 HOLLAND *Plutarch's Mor.* 462 When the corne was newly reaped and cut downe, seeing the shocks and sheaves, cocks and stiches rannged even and orderly,.. he rejoiced. **1838** HOLLOWAY *Prov. Dict.*, *Stitch*, ten sheaves of corn set up together in the field; a shock of corn. **1891** HARDY *Tess* xiv, Every one placing her sheaf on end against those of the rest, till a shock, or 'stitch' as it was here called, of ten or a dozen was formed.

†**stitch**, *sb.*[5] *Obs.* Short for STITCHBACK.

1742 *Lond. & Country Brew.* I. (ed. 4) 23 For brewing strong brown Ale called Stitch.

stitch (stɪtʃ), *v.*[1] Forms: 3 stic(c)hen, (*3rd sing.* stihð, *pa. t. sing.* stiȝte, *pl.* stihten, *pa. pple.* istihd), 6 sty(t)che, sti(t)che, stech(e, *Sc.* stik(e, 7–8 stich, 6– stitch. Also STEEK *v.*[3] [f. STITCH *sb.*[1]; cf. (M)LG., MDu. *sticken* (mod.Du. *stikken*), OHG. *sticchen* (mod.G. *sticken*).]

I. To prick, stab.

†**1. a.** *trans.* To stab, pierce; *transf.* to afflict with a 'stitch' or sharp sudden pain. Also *fig.* Also ***thorough-stitch***. *Obs.*

a **1225** *Ancr. R.* 272 Heo þuruh stihten Isboset adun into schere... þe ueond þuruh stihð þet scher hwon delit of lecherie þurleð þe heorte. *c* **1230** *Hali Meid.* 9 Nat tah na mon bute ham self hwat ham sticheð ofte. *c* **1250** *Hymn to Virgin* i. 53 in *Trin. Coll. Hom.* App. 257 Þe ne stiȝte, ne þe ne priȝte, in side, in lende, ne elles where. **1525** tr. *Brunswyke's Handywork Surg.* xl. I ij b, The mouth is somtyme hewen that the cheeke hangeth of,.. and somtyme it is stytched with a dagger, or with a spere. **1598** SYLVESTER *Du Bartas* II. i. III. *Furies* 604 And in the end stitcht full of stings he dies. *c* **1620** Z. BOYD *Zion's Flowers* (1855) 91, I must by and by, Stitcht full of stings With paine lye downe and dye.

†**b.** To make (a wound) by stabbing. *Obs.*

1527 ANDREW *Brunswyke's Distyll. Waters* F j b, The same water heleth very well all fresshe woundes where they be hewen or stytched.

2. ? To make (the 'eye' or hole in a mill-stone) by piercing with a pick.

c **1900** *Trade Circular, Millstone Tools*, Mill Picks for stitching eyes, peak stones, &c.

II. To fasten or adorn with stitches.

3. a. *trans.* To fasten together or join (pieces of textile material, leather, etc.) by stitches; to make or mend (a garment, etc.) by thus joining its parts. Also with *together*; for *stitch up* see 9 a.

a **1225** *Ancr. R.* 424 Hore hesmel beo heie istihd [*MS. C.* Hare cop beo hecȝe i-sticched]. **1525** tr. *Brunswyke's Handywork Surg.* xiii. C ij b, Whan y[e] cloutis be well drye, than sowe them or styche them togeder. **1530** PALSGR. 736/2, I stytche, as a taylour doth a garment. **1587** MASCALL *Cattle, Horses* (1596) 119 The Carter ought to haue skill how to mend his harnaise, to stitch and sow it when any part or parcell thereof decayeth. **1709** W. KING *Art of Love* VI. 784 Full many a feather With twine of thread he stitch'd together. **1709** T. BAKER *Mrs. Centlivre's Busy Body* Prol., Court Ladies will.. stitch a Gown, to pass the time away. **1791** COWPER *Iliad* XII. 359 The forger of that shield.. with thickest hides throughout Had lined it, stitch'd with circling wires of gold. **1819** BYRON *Juan* II. lxi, Two blankets stitch'd together, answering ill Instead of sail. **1850** *Mechanics' Mag.* LII. 195 The thread is passed through the eye of the needle, and the fabric to be stitched placed between the wheels, to which rotary motion is communicated. **1885** J. B. LENO *Boot & Shoemaking* 144 When stitching strong work, run a piece of rag to which soap or beeswax has been applied, round the welt.

fig. **1602** MARSTON *Ant. & Mel.* III. E 4 b, Honest musk-cod, twill not be so stitched together. **1629** WOTTON *Lett.* (1907) II. 318 Some think the Parliament doth yet hang upon a thread, and may be stitched again together. *c* **1862** E. DICKINSON in *Poems* (1955) I. 300, I saw no Way—The Heavens were stitched—I felt the Columns close. **1936** L. MACNEICE tr. *Aeschylus' Agamemnon* 68, *I* stitched this murder together; it was my title. **1961** *Daily Tel.* 16 Nov. 21/3 The precast concrete sections are 'stitched' together with 33 miles of 1⅛ in diameter high tensile steel strand. **1973** M. AMIS *Rachel Papers* 220 My father.. crossed his little legs and stitched his fingers.

b. *Shoemaking.* (See quot. 1895.)

1895 HASLUCK *Boot Making* 57 Shoemakers call all work sewn that is treated with a round awl; while stitching is only technically applied where the square awl is used.

4. *Surgery.* To unite the edges of (a wound) by drawing stitches through the flesh. See also 9 b.

1580 HESTER tr. *Fioravanti's Disc. Chirurg.* 12 The pleggits of Tow which is layd vpon woundes when they are first stitched. **1585** HIGINS *Junius' Nomencl.* 262/1 *Fibula*,.. a kind of instrument wherewith a wound is stitched and drawne together. **1676** WISEMAN *Chirurg. Treat.* V. viii. 372 It may be reasonable to lay open the Wound, and stitch the Gut with the Glovers Stitch.

5. *Bookbinding.* To fasten together (a number of sheets or sections) by passing the thread or wire through all the sheets at once. Occas. with *up*, *together*. Distinguished from *sew*: see SEW *v.*[1] 1 e.

1566 *Star Chamber Decree* in Arber *Transcr. Stationers' Reg.* (1875) I. 322 No person shall.. put to sale, bind, stitch, or sowe, anie such Bookes or Copies. *a* **1670** HACKET *Life Abp. Williams* I. (1693) 159 The Collection of all the precedent Passages were gathered by that Lord himself, and stitched up into one Book. **1712** ADDISON *Spect.* No. 529 ¶2 All Pamphlets, or Works that are only stitched. **1827** SCOTT *Surg. Dau.* Pref., As soon as I became possessed of my first volume, neatly stitched up and boarded. **1912** LADY F. BALFOUR *Life J. MacGregor* 270 His sermons were stitched .. by his own hands.

6. a. To fasten or attach (something) by sewing. Const. *to*; also *in*, *into*, *on*, *upon*. Also with adv., as *on*, *in*.

1530 PALSGR. 736/1, I stytche, I fastyn one thyng to another with stytches of nedyll and threde, *je affiche*. *Ibid.* 736/2 Stytche on thys claspe better, *affichez ceste agraffe mieulx*. **1687** A. LOVELL tr. *Thevenot's Trav.* I. 56 Within doors they cover their head with a Cap of red cloth,.. to the middle whereof they stitch a round of Pearles. **1833** [S. SMITH] *Lett. J. Downing* xxii. (1835) 131, I sot down behind him, and stitched on the button in three minits. **1857** RUSKIN *Pol. Econ. Art* i. 32 Those stupid tailors' 'prentices who are always stitching the sleeves in wrong way upwards. **1883** S. CHAPPEL *Sewing Machine* 20 It makes a very neat trimming which may afterwards be stitched on to any article as desired.

fig. **1589** *Pappe w. Hatchet* (1844) 35 Stitch charitie to thy faith, or rip faith from thy works. **1591** LYLY *Endimion* I. i, My thoughts Eumenides are stitched to the starres. **1610** HOLLAND *Camden's Brit.* (1637) 540 Unto his glorious exploits they stitched also ridiculous miracles. *a* **1637** B. JONSON *Horace's Art Poet.* 19 Ye have oft-times, that may o'er-shine the rest, A Scarlet Piece, or two, stitch'd in. **1818** SCOTT *Br. Lamm.* xii, I'se warrant he'll stitch our auld lands of Ravenswood to her petticoat tail. *a* **1901** F. W. H. MYERS *Human Personality* (1903) I. 11 Stitching the thread-bare metaphysical arguments into a more stable fabric.

b. To enclose *in* or *into* a cover or receptacle secured by stitching. Also with *away*. Cf. 9 c.

1848 THACKERAY *Van. Fair* xxxii, She stitched away the major part of her trinkets, bills, and bank-notes about her person. **1885** 'MRS. ALEXANDER' *At Bay* ix, I had nigh a thousand pounds' worth stitched in my belt.

7. To ornament with stitches; to embroider.

a **1529** SKELTON *E. Rummyng* 69 She.. gyrdeth in her gytes Stytched and pranked with pletes. **1535** in *Archæologia* IX. 248 Three cootys of grene clothe styched with grene silke. **1570** LEVINS *Manip.* 150/26 To stitche, *acu pingere*. **1641** *Invent. Goods C'tess Arundel* in *Burlington Mag.* (1912) Jan. 235/2 Seauen Peeces of Indian Twilt hangings stitcht. with Orenge Colo[e] silke. **1710** SIBBALD *Fife & Kinross* I. viii. 34 Wearing White Shirts, stitcht with Red Silk, upon their Armour. **1837** CARLYLE *Fr. Rev.* II. v. viii, Tricolor stitched by their own needle. **1905** R. BAGOT *Passport* i. 2 Its button-holes stitched with red.

8. *absol.* and *intr.* To make stitches; to work with a needle and thread. ***to stitch away***, to go on sewing energetically.

1697 DE FOE *Ess. Projects* 282 To teach them [Women] to Stitch and Sow, or make Bawbles. **1712** MOTTEUX *2nd Pt. Quix.* xliii. (1749) IV. 62 Go on, go on, friend, said Don Quixote, thread, tack, stitch on, heap proverb on proverb, out with 'em, man, spew them out. **1843** HOOD *Song of Shirt* i, Stitch! stitch! stitch! **1853** MOTLEY in O. W. Holmes *Life* (1878) 72 There is nothing for it but to penelopize, pull to pieces and stitch away again. **1853** MRS. GASKELL *Ruth* i, More than a dozen girls sat in the room.. stitching away as if for very life. **1865** FLOR. MARRYAT *Love's Confl.* I. viii. 128 She took her work and.. stitched in silence.

9. stitch up. *trans.* (See also 5.)

a. To make or put together by sewing; sometimes with implication of hasty or inferior work. Also *fig.*

1590 NASHE *Pasquil's Apol.* C 3 b, By the end I haue giuen the Welch-man to his *All*, he may stitch vp his *Euerie* when it pleaseth him. **1663** BUTLER *Hud.* I. ii. 724 Did no Committee sit, where he [the Devil] Might cut our journy-work for thee;.. To stitch up sale and sequestration? **1701** STEELE *Funeral* v. i, She has out of Impatience to see her self in her Weeds, order'd her Mantua-Woman to stich up any thing immediately.

b. To close (an orifice, a wound), to mend (a rent), by sewing the edges together. Also *fig.*

1580 HESTER tr. *Fioravanti's Disc. Chirurg.* 35 b, Then hee was caryed to a Chyrurgian, and hee stitched him vp. *a* **1586** SIDNEY *Arcadia* II. v. §6 (1912) 182 It is in your hand as well to stitch up his life againe, as it was before to rent it. **1643** BAKER *Chron., Stephen* 68 Seeking to stitch up the breaches which the violence of warre had made. **1657** *Penit. Conf.* xi. 307 Be sure of the Confessor, his mouth is stitched up. *a* **1677** BARROW *Serm.* Wks. 1716 I. 183 No thread can stitch up a good name torn by calumnious defamation. **1679** J. YONGE *Currus Triumph.* 79, I dressed him with hot Ol. Terebinth, which restraining the flux, gave me opportunity to stitch up the wound. **1712** MOTTEUX *Quix.* IV. iii. (1749) II. 29, I am sure he would rather have stitch'd up his lips, or bit off his tongue, than have spoken a word, that should make him incur your displeasure.

c. To enclose *in* a cover or receptacle and secure it by sewing. Also *fig.*

1589 R. HARVEY *Pl. Perc.* Ded., Peace stichd vp in a Gaberdine without pleat or wrinckle. **1853** KANE *Grinnell Exp.* xxix. (1856) 254, I had this journal of mine stitched up in its tarred canvas-bag.

d. To tighten or confine (a fabric) by sewing the parts closer together.

1704 SWIFT *T. Tub* xi. (ed. 3) 207 He hired a Taylor to stitch up the Collar so close, that it was ready to choak him.

e. ? To strengthen with extra stitches.

1794 *Rigging & Seamanship* I. 92 The seams of courses and topsails are stuck or stitched up, in the middle of the seams, along the whole length, with double seaming-twine.

f. Of a criminal, etc.: to cause (a person) to be convicted, esp. by informing or manufacturing evidence. Also *gen.*, to swindle, to overcharge exorbitantly.

1970 G. F. NEWMAN *Sir, You Bastard* v. 142 Your confederate has just about stitched you up. **1977** *New Society* 7 July 6/2 Both Sheila and Gary have many stories of being 'stitched up' by the police or fleeced. Gary says the Dip Squad—the special police patrol looking for pickpockets—are 'a bunch of wankers'. **1977** *Woman* 3 Sept. 30/3 After shelling out £1.50 for a fold-up version [of an umbrella] she found that she'd been stitched up... Two spokes were broken. **1978** F. BRANSTON *Sergeant Ritchie's Conscience* I. v. 69 Those [rivals] who wouldn't be frightened he stitched up, his favourite method being to sell an opponent some drugs, then inform on him to the police.

stitch (stɪtʃ), *v.*^{2} *dial.* [Goes with STITCH *sb.*^{3}] *trans.* To turn up (the ground) in ridges in order to cover or protect the roots of potatoes, etc.; to earth *up*. (See also quot. 1866.)

1805 *Trans. Soc. Arts* XXIII. 31 In June, they were run through with the potatoe harrow, and made quite flat before they could be stitched up again. **1828–32** WEBSTER, *Stitch*.. To form land into ridges. (N. England.) **1866** BROGDEN *Provinc. Words Lincs.* 196 *Stitch-up*, to plough very deeply. **1899** *Cumbld. Gloss.*, *Stitch*, to form the ridge on which potatoes or turnips are grown.

stitch (stɪtʃ), *v.*^{3} *dial.* Also stich(e, stych(e. [f. STITCH *sb.*^{4}] *trans.* To set up in 'stitches' or shocks. Also with *up*.

1674 FLAVEL *Husb. Spiritualized* xv. 129 After these follow the binders, who stitch it up. *Ibid.* 138 Down go the laden ears flat to the ground; Which those that follow having sticht and bound, It's carted home unto the Barn. **1794** WEDGE *Agric. Warw.* 23 For pease and beans styched, from 2s. 6d. to 5s. per acre. **1879** MISS JACKSON *Shropsh. Word-bk.* s.v. *Stiche*, Stiche up them beäns i' rucks. **1886** *W. Somerset Word-bk.* s.v., To *stitchy* is to set up the sheaves, when bound, in rows of stitches.

†**'stitchback.** *Obs.* [f. STITCH *v.*^{1} + BACK *sb.* Cf. STEELBACK.] A kind of strong ale.

1671 CHAMBERLAYNE *Pres. St. Eng.* I. ii. (ed. 5) 56 There are sold in London.. many sorts of Ales very different, as Cock, Stepony, Stich-Back, [etc.]. *a* **1700** B. E. *Dict. Cant. Crew*, *Stitch-back*, very strong Ale. **1719** D'URFEY *Pills* VI. 224 Here's stitch-Back that will please your Wives.

'stitchdown. [f. STITCH *v.*^{1} + DOWN *adv.*] A shoe or boot on which the lower edge of the upper is turned outward and stitched on to the sole; a veldt-shoe. Also ***stitchdown shoe***.

1840 E. STIFF *Texan Emigrant* vii. 95 During the intolerable hot weather in the summer of 1838, the same Kentucky jeans pants, the same pair of stitchdowns,.. adorned the tall and disproportioned outward man. **1916** F. PLUCKNETT *Introd. Boot & Shoe Manuf.* xxx. 258 The 'veldtschoen', or 'stitchdown', has passed through so many stages that no description of it would correctly describe its production in all factories. The principal idea is that the edge of the upper (except just around the heel) shall be turned outward instead of being folded over the edge of an insole, and that this projecting flap shall be attached to the sole with a vertical thread seam. **1940** *Chambers's Techn. Dict.* 888/2 *Veldtschoen*,.. a sandal-like form of shoe in which the upper is attached directly to the sole by a row of stitches near the edge. Also called *stitchdown shoes*. **1969** T. C. THORSTENSEN *Pract. Leather Technol.* xv. 248 The stitchdown shoe differs from the Littleway in that the insole is fastened to the upper by flairing the upper outward rather than inward.

stitched (stɪtʃt), *ppl. a.* [f. STITCH *v.*^{1} + -ED^1.] In senses of the verb: *esp.* **a.** Embroidered, worked with ornamental stitches.

1583 *Rates Custom Ho.* E vj b, Stiched cloth to woork on the elle, xx. d. **1598** MARSTON *Sco. Villanie* III. xi. 229 A sticht Taffata cloake. **1624** J. TAYLOR (Water P.) *Praise Cl. Linen* Wks. (1630) II. 168/1 Ruffes.. the plaine, the stich'd, the lac'd, and shagge. **1713** in Halliwell *Acc. Collect. Bills* etc. (1852) 37 Paid for a box and cord to send yᵉ stiched gowne and coate 00 01 02. **1886** W. J. TUCKER *E. Europe* 428 Table-cloths were adorned with stitched scrolls.

b. Of a book or pamphlet: Fastened with stitches; in early use = SEWED *ppl. a.*; in present use, fastened together by a thread or wire which passes through all the sections at once.

1658 WOOD *Life* (O.H.S.) I. 264 To Godwin for stitched bookes, 4s. *a* **1697** AUBREY *Lives* (1898) I. 131 He wrote a stich't treatise of mines. **1716** M. DAVIES *Athen. Brit.* I. Pref. 66 'Tis not much to be question'd but of all Modern Pamphlets,.. the English sticht Sermons to be the most Edifying, Useful and Instructive. **1716** POPE, etc. *Further Acc. E. Curll* ℙ 1 The author of a three-penny stitched book.

†**'stitchel**^{1}. *Obs.* Also 7 stichel, 9 *dial.* stichal(l, stetchel, -il. [Etymology unknown; perh. the same word as next.] A term of reproach applied to (*a*) a grown-up person, (*b*) a child.

1659 *Lady Alimony* v. iii. I 4 b, Barren Stichel! that shall not serve thy turn. **18..** *MS. Gloss. Lincs.* in *Halliwell* s.v. *Stichall*, This term, which in some places has *Bub* prefixed to it, appears to be a word of reproach, used to children principally by their parents.., e.g. 'Get out of the way, you bub-stichal'; and, 'what a young stichall he must be to bring such a message!' **1866** BROGDEN *Provinc. Words Lincs.* 196 *Stetchel, stitchel*, a troublesome child.

'stitchel^2. *local.* ? *Obs.* [Of obscure etymology. Cf. STICKLE *a.* 4 and Fris. *stikelich hier, stikelhierrich* adj.] A kind of hairy wool. Also ***stitchel hair***. Also **stitchy** (? *adj.*), in comb. ***stitchy-haired*** adj.

1775 *Essays Agric.* 342 Stitchel hair (in France *Jarre*) is a kind of short opaque white-like hair that grows up among the fleeces of some kinds of sheep. **1828–32** WEBSTER, *Stitchel*, a kind of hairy wool. (*Local.*) **1839** *Compl. Grazier* IV. iii. (1846) 215 The pelt, or coat [of the sheep], should always be attentively examined, in order to ascertain whether it is not *stitchy-haired*.

†**'stitchen.** *Obs.* In 3 **stucchen** (ü). [dim. of STITCH *sb.*^{2}: see -EN^1.] A small part or piece; *spec.* a division or section of a discourse.

a **1225** *Ancr. R.* 14, I þisse distinctiun beoð fif cheapitres alse vif stucchenes efter þe vif wittes. *Ibid.* 428 Ȝe ancren owen þis lutle laste stucchen reden to our wummen eueriche wike enes. *a* **1225** *Leg. Kath.* 2006 (MS. R.) Stucchenes [*pl.*; *the other MSS. have* stucchen *pl.*].

stitcher ('stɪtʃə(r)). [f. STITCH *v.*^{1} + -ER^1.]

1. One who stitches or sews. In literary use as a general term; in technical use, a person employed in some operation specifically called 'stitching' (e.g. in shoemaking, bookbinding). †Formerly also a contemptuous term for a tailor.

1589 NASHE *Anat. Absurd.* B 4 b, Some stitcher, Weauer, spendthrift, or Fidler. *a* **1613** OVERBURY *A Wife* etc. (1638) 258 Shee that sets the first quest of enquiry amongst her gossips for new fashions shall not refuse a stitcher for her second husband. **1805** *Mod. London* 443 Printers, engravers, stitchers, binders, type-founders. **1858** ADEL. A. PROCTER *Leg. & Lyrics* 212 Where the weary stitcher Toils for daily bread. **1878** SIMPSON *Sch. Shaks.* I. 142 The stitcher or binder.. confounded the previous confusion by misplacing several of the scenes. **1886** *Athenæum* 7 Aug. 180/3 The Sicilian stitchers.. who supplied models to the Venetians.. for needlework.

b. In combination with *to* adv. In quot. fig.

a **1637** B. JONSON *Under-woods, Epigr. to Counsellor* 8 The names.. Of Hirelings, Wranglers, Stitchers-to of strife.

2. A tool or machine used for stitching.

1862 *Times* 12 June 6/2 The blank sole-cutting machine will cut out 60 soles in a minute, and the stitcher will stitch them on.. at the rate of about 50 seconds for each shoe. **1901** *Munsey's Mag.* XXV. 439/2 Carrying the magic power of steam to stitchers and folders.

stitchery ('stɪtʃərɪ). [f. STITCH *v.*^{1} or STITCHER: see -ERY 2. (App. coined by Shaks.)] Needlework.

1607 SHAKS. *Cor.* I. iii. 75 Come, lay aside your stitchery. **1780** C. BURNEY in *Early Diary F. Burney* (1889) II. 289, I have really been so hard fag'd with stitchery in new rigging papa's old shifets (as Mrs. Market calls em). **1897** L. F. DAY *Windows* (1909) 145 As well might the needlewoman go to a glazier to design her stitchery.

stitching ('stɪtʃɪŋ), *vbl. sb.* [f. STITCH *v.*^{1} + -ING^1.] The action of the verb, in different senses.

†**1.** The feeling of a sharp sudden pain. *Obs.*

1561 HOLLYBUSH *Hom. Apoth.* 29 b, [He hath] great stichynge when the ague commeth vpon hym. **1599** A. M. tr. *Gabelhouer's Bk. Physicke* 2/2 Therwith annoyncte the place of the stitchinge.

2. The action of fastening or uniting by stitches. Also, ornamentation with stitches.

1521–2 *Rec. St. Mary at Hill* 314 Item, paid for new bandyng and stichyng of iij su[r]plyses x d. **1678** *Orders, Rules & Ordin. Stationers' Co.* 23 The Imprinting, Binding, Stitching, Publishing or Dispersing of any such Book. **1719** DE FOE *Crusoe* I. (Globe) 232 With a great deal of Pains, and awkward tedious stitching.. I at length made.. a Shoulder of Mutton Sail. **1857** RUSKIN *Pol. Econ. Art* ii. 161 If the sempstresses tried to break each other's needles, that each might get all the stitching to herself.

3. *concr.* **a.** Stitches collectively; i.e. the portions or loops of thread, etc. fastened in the material as the result of sewing. Also, a series of stitches.

1562 J. HEYWOOD *Prov. & Epigr.* (1867) 179 The barres of mens breeches haue such strong stitching. **1597** A. M. tr. *Guillemeau's Fr. Chirurg.* 15/1 Betwixt the which stitching, we lay as yet other. **1875** R. F. MARTIN tr. *Havrez' Winding Mach.* 60 This would be quite certain to wear out the stitching of the flat ropes. **1885** *Daily News* 7 May 5/2 Pearl-grey Derby gloves.. with three black stitchings. **1915** *Blackw. Mag.* 683/1 The stitching had given way.

b. The thread, silk, or other material of which stitches are made. Also *pl.*

1614 J. TAYLOR (Water P.) *Nipping Abuses* B 3 b, For bumbast, stitching, binding, or for buckram. **1826** *Haberdasher's Guide* 16 Stitchings, a strong white thread.

c. A bundle of sheets of paper stitched together.

1679 WOOD *Life* (O.H.S.) II. 471 Sent to Sir William Dugdale, three stitchings or bundells containing corrections of his baronagium; the 1 stitching containes 5 papers, the 2d, 7 papers; the 3d., 11 papers.

4. *attrib.*, as ***stitching-awl, needle, silk, thread***; †**stitching quill** *Surgery*, a tubular needle.

1552 *Acc. Ld. High Treas. Scot.* X. 71 Item for stiking silk and buttonis to the samyn coit xvj s. **1585** HIGINS *Junius' Nomencl.* 251/2 *Acus Babylonia*,.. a fine stitching needle. **1589** *Acc. Bk. W. Wray* in *Antiquary* XXXII. 78 A q' white stechinge silke, viij d. **1674** tr. *G. Fabritius (Hildanus) Cista Milit.* 22 A stitching Quill [L. *cannula fenestrata*], which is used in stitching Wounds. **1681** GREW *Musæum* I. §iv. i. 62 Thick as a Taylors Stitching-Thread. **1699** E. WARD *Lond. Spy* IV. 11 With here and there a Remnant of Basting-Thread and Stitching-Silk hanging upon his Coat. **1767** GOOCH *Treat. Wounds* I. 154 Which is a better method in general, than to use the stitching quill. **1895** HASLUCK *Boot Making* 57 The stitching-awl.. is a similar tool to the sewing-awl, with the exception of being flat.

stitching ('stɪtʃɪŋ), *ppl. a.* [f. STITCH *v.*^{1} + -ING^2.] † Of a pain, esp. in the ribs: Sharp and spasmodic, lancinating.

1699 ROKEBY in *Surtees Soc. Miscell.* (1861) 63, I fell so ill with violent stitching paines in my breast and back. **1790** MRS. WHEELER *Westmld. Dial.* (1821) 112 My deaam gat a bad stitchin pain in her side this summer wie forkin hay.

'stitchless, *a.* [f. STITCH *sb.*^{1} + -LESS.] Without stitches; *spec.* (formerly) of a tennis ball, put together without stitches or a stitched seam. Also, 'without a stitch', unclothed.

1927 *Daily Tel.* 22 Mar. 15/6 W. H. Powell.. was beaten... It was due.. to the fact that Powell is not yet used to the stitchless ball. **1939** JOYCE *Finnegans Wake* 451 I'd plant you ..on the electric ottoman in the lap of lechery, simpringly stitchless with admiracion. **1953** M. PEAKE *Mr. Pye* xvi. 128 She had left her clothes on a high rock... 'My child..' said Mr. Pye '.. my stitchless child.'

†**'stitchmeal,** *adv. Obs.* [OE. *stycce-, sticce-, sticmælum* (see Bosw.-Toller), f. *stycce*: see STITCH *sb.*^{2} and -MEAL.] In separated pieces; in 'stitches' of land. (In quot. 1602 with *by* prefixed; there is prob. a reference to STITCH *sb.*^{3})

c **1000** ÆLFRIC *Hom.* I. 508 Þæs muntes cnoll.. is sticmælum mid wuda oferwexen, and eft sticmælum mid grenum felda oferbræded. **1602** CAREW *Cornwall* I. 66 Their grounds lay all in common, or onely deuided by stitchmeale.

stitchwort ('stɪtʃwɜːt). [f. STITCH *sb.*^{1} + WORT (see quot. 1657).] A name for *Stellaria Holostea*. Also a book-name for the genus.

c **1265** *Voc. Plants* in Wr.-Wülcker 557/30 *Ualeriane*, stichwurt. *a* **1387** *Sinon. Barthol.* (Anecd. Oxon) 27 *Lingua avis*, i. stichewort i. pigle. *a* **1500** *MS. Bodl.* 536 lf. 33 Pygla maior i. pygyll or steche wort. **1516** *Gt. Herbal* lxiii. (1529) D v b, De lingua anseris. Goos byll, or stychewort. **1597** GERARDE *Herbal* I. xxxii. 42 Stitchwoort. **1657** COLES *Adam in Eden* cxlvi, It is called in English Stitch-wort, for its property in helping Stitches and pains in the sides. **1726** THRELKELD *Syn. Stirp. Hibern.*, *Holosteum vernum*,.. The greater Stitchwort. **1770** BERKENHOUT *Nat. Hist.* II. 44 *Sagina Erecta*. Least Stichwort. **1861** S. THOMSON *Wild Flowers* (ed. 4) III. 187 The stellarias, or stitchworts. **1876** 'ANNIE THOMAS' *Blotted out* xxix. 263 The great pure white, starlike blossoms of the stitchwort.

stitchy: see STITCHEL^2.

stith (stɪθ), *sb.* Forms: 4 stiþ(e, (steyth), 4–7 styth, 5 stethe, stede, 5–7 stythe, 6–7 stithe, 4– stith. [See STITHY.]

1. = STITHY *sb.* 1. *Obs.* exc. *north.*

c **1300** *Havelok* 1877 [They] beten on him so doth þe smith With þe hamer on þe stith. *c* **1386** CHAUCER *Knt.'s T.* 1168 The Smyth That forgeth sharpe swerdes on his Styth. **1426** LYDG. *De Guil. Pilgr.* 10973 Wyth-inne an hevy styth off stel, A ffethre sholde entre as wel As any doctryne.. Sholde entre in-to hys hed. **1465** in *Finchale Priory Charters* etc. (Surtees) p. ccxcix, ij stethes, ij foyrhamers [etc.]. **1494** *Acc. Ld. High Treas. Scot.* I. 250 Item, for tussen of the stede to the smede viij d. **1584–7** GREENE *Carde of Fancie* (1593) D 4 b, Valericus.. determined to strike on the Stith while the yron was hot. **1586** WHITNEY *Choice of Emblems* 192 For there with strengthe he strikes vppon the stithe [*rhyme-word* pith]. **1609** HEYWOOD *Brit. Troy* VIII. xxi. 174 Most thinke Lame Vulcan on the Styth first wrought. **1787** GROSE *Prov. Gloss.*, *Stith*, an anvil. **1823** E. MOOR *Suffolk Words*, *Stith*, a smith's anvil. **1866** W. HENDERSON *Folk Lore N.C.* i. 27 They placed a charge of gunpowder in the stith, or anvil of the blacksmith's shop, and fired it.

†**2.** = STITHY *sb.* 2. *Obs. rare*$^{-1}$.

1633 P. FLETCHER *Purple Isl.* v. xliii, The first [bone] an Hammer call'd, whose out-grown sides Lie on the drumme; but, with his swelling end Fixt in the hollow Stithe.

stith (staɪθ), *a. Obs.* exc. *Sc.* Forms: 1–3 **stið**, 4 **stiþ, styþ**, (3 **stitth**), 4–5 **styth**, 5 **stythe**, 5–7 **stithe**, (5 **steyth**), 3– **stith**; *Sc.* 8–9 **styth**, 9 **stythe**. [OE. *stið* = OFris. *stîth*, ON. *stinn-r* (MSw. *stinder*):—OTeut. **stenþo-* (a type **stenþjo-* appears in MLG. *stîde*, WFlem. *stijde, stide*).]

1. Of material things: Not bending or giving easily, unyielding, stout, strong. ? *Obs.* exc. *Sc.*

Beowulf 1533 (Gr.) Hit [a sword] on eorðan læg, stið and stylecg. *c* **1000** *Sax. Leechd.* I. 288 Ðeos wyrt.. hafað lange leaf & stiþe. **1375** *Sc. Leg. Saints* xii. (*Mathias*) 278 [He] went furtht & hyme-self can hynge with a cord bath styth & strange. **1375** BARBOUR *Bruce* x. 364 A cruk thai maid.. Of irn, that wes styth and square. *a* **1400–50** *Wars Alex.* 5461 And all þe strands of þe streme stode full of stith reedis. *c* **1400** *Destr. Troy* 1997 Was no stightlyng with stere, ne no stithe ropes, Ne no sayle, þat might serue for vnsound wedur. *Ibid.* 13282. **a 1420** *Aunters of Arthur* 591 Stiþe stapeles of stele þey strike done stiȝte. **c 1450** *St. Cuthbert* (Surtees) 5005 He was taken, And in to stithe fettirs schakyn. **1513** Douglas *Æneis* x. vi. 17 Bend vp ȝour ayris styth, and rays ȝour schippys. [**1871** P. H. Waddell *Psalms in Scottis* xxxi. 4 Redd me frae the girns they hae happit for me; for yerlane are my stoop sae styth.]

†**b.** Of a place of defence or confinement: Strong, stout; formidable, powerful. *Obs.*

c 1000 *Ags. Ps.* lx. 2 þu me ȝelæddest mid lufan hyhte, wære me stranga tor, stið wið feondum. **c 1320** *Sir Tristr.* 897 Tounes þai ȝold him skete And cites stiþe of stan. **1340–70** *Alisaunder* 91 They..turned tit to a towne þat Attanus hyght, A stiþ stede, & a strong. **c 1375** *Sc. Leg. Saints* xl. (*Ninian*) 946 [He was] put in pressone stith of stane. **c 1425** Wyntoun *Cron.* vii. 3202 þis Kynge..made hym for to duel In til Edynburgh þe stythe castel.

2. Inflexible, rigid, stiff.

†**a.** (*OE.* only.) Of the neck: = stiff *a.*

c 897 Ælfred *Gregory's Past C.* xxxiii. 228, & him ðone stiðan swioran [L. *rigida colla*] fortræde.

b. *Sc.* Rigid (in death). ? *Obs.*

1755 R. Forbes *Ajax' Sp., Jrnl. fr. Lond. to Portsmouth* 30 An' the horses tak a brattle now, they may..ding me yavil, an' as styth as gin I had been elf-shot. **1768** Ross *Helenore* 8 Up by the lambie's lying yonder styth. **1808** Jamieson s.v. *Stith* 3 Sheet styth, shot dead, Aberd.

c. *Sc.* Of a rope: Taut. ? *Obs.*

1825 Jamieson, *Stith, Styth*..3. Stiff, in consequence of being stretched; applied to a rope, Upp. Clydes.

†**3.** Hard, severe, stern, harsh, austere, cruel towards persons or things. *Obs.*

c 897 Ælfred *Gregory's Past. C.* xvii. 126 Sie ðær eac reðnes [in a ruler], næs ðeah to stið. **a 1000** *Cædmon's Gen.* 2848 (Gr.) Stiðum wordum, spræc him stefne to. **a 1122** *O.E. Chron.* (Laud MS.) an. 1086, Ac he wæs swa stið þat he ne rohte heora eallra nið. **c 1175** *Lamb. Hom.* 95 He demað stiðne dom þam forsunegede on his efter to-come.

†**4.** Inflexible of purpose, immovable, steadfast; also, obstinately firm, stubborn. *to stand stith*, to stand firm. *Obs.*

c 1000 *Ags. Ps.* cxlvii. 6 For andwlitan celes, þær æni ne mæȝ him standan, stiðe mode. **c 1205** Lay. 10083 þes wes ræh þes wes strong þes wes stið an þonke. **c 1250** *Gen. & Ex.* 1591 Esau wifuede us to dere Quan he..Toc of kin ðe canaan bi-gat, For-ði he maked him stið & strong. **a 1300** *Cursor M.* 61 (Cott.) He þat stitthest wenis at stand [*c* **1375** (Fairf.) stiþest to stande], Warre hym his fall is nexst his hand. **1338** R. Brunne *Chron.* (1725) 194 My broþer Safadyn Is riche of tenement, his sonnes strong & stith, þer wille wille not be went. **1375** Barbour *Bruce* viii. 384 A lord ..so veill bowrdand, And in battale so stith to stand.

5. Intense in degree or quality; not mild or weak; severe, violent, strong.

†**a.** of a conflict, contest, etc. *Obs.*

c 1000 *Battle of Maldon* 301 þær wæs stið ȝemot. **a 1300** *Cursor M.* 3461 þair strut it was vn-stern stith. **1375** Barbour *Bruce* ix. 343 Thar wes oft bikkyrring stith & stout. **c 1400** *Destr. Troy* 9679 The store was full stith.

b. of the weather, a storm, etc. ? *Obs.*

c 1100 *O.E. Chron.* (MS. D.) an. 1048, Her wæs se stiþa winter. *Ibid.* an. 1052, He..feng swa stið weder þat he uneaðe a wæiȝ com. **c 1250** *Gen. & Ex.* 3266 Đhunder, and leuene, and rein ðor-mong, God sente on ðat hird, stið and strong. **c 1400** *Sc. Trojan War* i. 413 And wedderis styth [wald] Baith ger fall rayn and haile. **c 1420** *Sir Amadace* (Camd.) xlviii, Stithe stormes me ore-drofe. **1801** W. Beattie *Fruits of Time Parings* (1871) 24 Perforce of endrift styth He is oblig'd to seek a lyth Amo' the byres.

†**c.** of a stream. *Obs.*

1375 Barbour *Bruce* x. 84 Ane vattir..That ran doun by the hillis syde, And wes rycht styth, bath deip & wyde. **1513** Douglas *Æneis* v. 64 Quhair that Ionium clepit is the see, And als forgane the stith stremis of Malee.

†**d.** of things affecting the taste or smell. *Obs.*

c 1000 *Sax. Leechd.* I. 156 Ðenim þysse wyrte sæd..ȝemenged mid stiþum ecede. **c 1400** *Destr. Troy* 932 Iason.. Dange on the deuyll..Tyll the stremys of stynke & of stythe venum Past out in the place pyne to be-holde. **1674** Ray *N.C. Words* 45 Stithe Cheese, i.e. strong Cheese.

†**e.** of the voice, a noise. *Obs.*

c 1000 *Ags. Ps.* liv. 17 þæt þu bliðe me, mine stefne, stiðe ȝehyre. **a 1300** *Cursor M.* 22527 All bestes..cri sal wit stiþer steuen þan nu mai do ten or elleuen, All for dred. **a 1400–50** *Wars Alex.* 1251 Sa stithe a steuyn..As it was semand to siȝt as all þe soyle trymblid.

†**6.** Stout, stalwart, valiant, mighty. *Obs.*

Chiefly in alliterative phrases in ME. poetry.

a 1300–1400 *Cursor M.* 18181 (Gött.) Sua stith [*Cott.* stijf] in sture, and king of bliss, Dede and alsua liuand [þou] es. **c 1320** *Sir Tristr.* 66 A turnament þai ches Wiþ kniȝtes stiþe on stede. **c 1325** *Metr. Hom.* (1862) 10 [John the Baptist] said a stither gom than I, Efter me sal com in hy. **c 1330** *Amis & Amil.* 1303 On stedes that were stithe and strong, Thai riden togider with schaftes long. **c 1400** *Rowland & Otuel* 485 þis was a stythe stroke of a knyghte, & no thynge of a childe! **c 1440** *Pallad. on Husb.* iv. 912 A staloun asse ybolked, brawny, sadde And large ylimed, stronge & steyth. **c 1450** Holland *Howlat* 697 In flesche tyme, quhen the fische war away flemyt, Quha was stewart bot the Stork, stallwart and styth. **c 1470** *Gol. & Gaw.* 678 Right styth, stuffit in steill, thai stotit na stynt, But buskit to battaille.

absol. **c 1400** *Destr. Troy* 21 But olde stories of stithe þat astate helde, May be solas to sum þat it segh neuer.

†**stith,** *adv. Obs.* Forms: 1–2 **stiðe,** 4 **stith(e, styth.** [OE. *stíðe*, f. *stíð* stith *a.*] Strongly, stoutly, firmly; violently; harshly, severely.

a 1000 *Cædmon's Gen.* xlii. 30 (Gr.) And hu stiðe se landhlaford spræc wið hiȝ. **a 1122** *O.E. Chron.* (Laud MS.) an. 1006, Forþan þe hi hæfdon ælce scire on West Sexum stiðe ȝe marcod mid bryne. **a 1310** in Wright *Lyric P.* 99 Bote er aȝeyn the [God] stith y stod, Er ant late, loude ant stille. **1325** *Metr. Hom.* (1862) 4 Hou thai mai..stithe stand igain the fend. **c 1340** Hampole *Pr. Consc.* 3173 He says..þat ay þe styther þat ilk man here Gyves his lykyng..Til veniel syns,..þe langer sal he pyned be In purgatory. **c 1380** *Sir Ferumb.* 631 Hure strokes fulle so styþ & sare þay schulde so doþ þe þonder.

b. *Comb.* In Layamon prefixed to adjs. of ppl. form, forming combs. equivalent to parasynthetic derivatives of stith *a.*: **stith-bewalled,** strongly walled; **stith-imained,** having a strong force; **stith-imoded** (cf. OE. *stíðmód*), stout-hearted.

c 1205 Lay. 25820 And forð he gon steppen stið imainede eorl. *Ibid.* 26022 Arður gon step vorð stið imoded kempe. *Ibid.* 30697 Eorð-hus heo hureden stið biwaled on eorðen.

†**stith,** *v. Sc. Obs.* [f. stith *a.* (OE. had *ȝestíðian* intr., to become strong).] *trans.* To set firmly, to cause to remain immovable.

c 1375 *Sc. Leg. Saints* xliv. (*Lucy*) 242 þe haly gast had sa stithit hire, þat nane of þai mycht of þat place a fute hire stere. *Ibid.* 270 It is of criste þe benyfice, þat stithis me on þis wyse.

stith, obs. form of stythe.

†**stithe.** *Obs. rare*[−1]. A sty in the eye.

1797 M. Underwood *Treat. Disorders Childhood* II. 43 The Stithe, or Stye. The stithe is a small inflamed tumour on the edge of the eye-lids.

stithe: see stith, stythe.

stithil, stithle, variants of stightle *v. Obs.*

†'**stithly,** *adv. Obs.* [f. stith *a.* + -ly[2].] Strongly, stoutly, valiantly, severely, etc. (see the senses of stith *a.*).

a 1300 *Cursor M.* 2291 A wygur was mad wit his red, And command stithli til his men Als god þai suld it knau and ken. *Ibid.* 18933 Langage þat þai suld haf of ful knaulage To stand ai stitli for þe fai. **c 1325** *Metr. Hom.* (1862) 83 Sa stithelic igain him ras The fend, that him feld in place. **c 1375** *Sc. Leg. Saints* xxxiii. (*George*) 940 Sa stythly Inuch can þai ficht. *Ibid.* xxxv. (*Thaddæus*) 55 þane til a chawmir stithly made,..quare-in al hyre tresoure wes. **c 1400** *Destr. Troy* 1240 He..stert vp stithly, straght out a swerde, And flange at the freike. **1513** Douglas *Æneis* v. vii. 110 Syne stithlie in the sandis wpstandis he.

stithy ('stɪðɪ), *sb.* Forms: α. 3–4 **steþi,** 4 **stethie,** 4–5 **stiþi,** 4 **stithi,** 4–7 **stithie,** 5–6 **stethy, stythy(e,** 6 **stythie,** (5 **styhthy,** 6 **stethye, stithye,** 7 **stythe),** 7– **stithy;** β. chiefly *Sc.* and *north.* 4–6 **stedy,** 5 **stedye,** 6 **steddye, -ie, stedee, steadie,** 9 **steddy, steady;** 6 **styd(d)y, styddie, stidhy,** 6, 9 **stiddie,** 7– **stiddy;** γ. only *Sc.* and *north.* 5–6, 8–9 **study,** 6, 8–9 **studdie,** 6–9 **studdy,** (6 **stude, studie,** 9 **stoddy).** [a. ON. *steði* wk. masc. (accus. *steðja*):—prehistoric **staþjan-*, f. Teut. root **sta-* to stand.

Normally the ON. *steði* should become **steþe* in ME. This is represented by stith *sb.*, most of the forms of which, however, show irregular vowel-change. The disyllable forms here may be compared with those of smithy from ON. *smiðja* wk. fem.]

1. An anvil.

α. **1295** *MS. Exch. Acc.* 5/8 Et viij d. in uno stithi et stithistok portando..usque ad placeam galee. **a 1300** *Cursor M.* 23237 Als it war dintes on a steþi þat smythes smittes in a smeþey. **c 1340** *Nominale* (Skeat) 507 *Tenailes enclume et fow*, tonges stethie and bely. **c 1375** *Sc. Leg. Saints* xxxviii. (*Adrian*) 454, 457 þe emperoure..gert bryng hyme a gret steþi. sone þai sanctis..to þe stedy brocht wes þane..& gert þar theis brokine be sa smal [etc.]. **c 1423** *Inv.* in Raine *Abps. York* (Rolls) III. 306 Pro j incude magna, vocata stethy, de ferro. **1483** Caxton *Golden Leg.* 288/4 He commanded to brynge forth an anuelt or a stythye. **1572** Bossewell *Armorie* ii. 123 b, The Anuild..is an auncient addycion of armory, and is called in ye Northerne tongue a Stethye. **1656** Trapp *Comm. Mark* vii. 33 The wise Lapidist brings not his softer stones to the stithy. **1662** Hibbert *Body Divinity* i. 108 Mans heart..like the stithy, is still the harder for beating. **1753** *Chambers' Cycl.* Suppl., App., Stithy, or Stuthy. **1812** Scott *Rokeby* i. xxxi, While on the stithy glows the steel. **1867** Carlyle *Remin.* (1881) II. 42 Well do I remember our return.., with the clink of Alick's stithy alone audible. **1870** *Good Words* Apr. 253/2 [A nail-shop] in which a..sharp young fellow..is shedding showers of ruddy sparks from his 'stithy', or small anvil. **1890** A. J. Armstrong *Ingleside Musings* 153 But hear the sang, the ringin' stithy sings.

fig. **1821** Scott *Kenilw.* xviii, 'Let me sleep on that hard point,' said Varney; 'I cannot else perfect the device I have on the stithy.' **1869** Lowell *Fam. Epist. Friend* 76 Let whoso likes be beat, poor fool, On life's hard stithy to a tool.

β. **c 1375** Stedy: see α. **c 1425** Wyntoun *Cron.* i. v. 227 Iwball..wes the first þat musik fand, Wiþ hameris clynkand on a stedye [*v.rr.* stythy, study]. **1513** Douglas *Æneis* vii. xi. 67 Five..citeis, Thar wapynnis to renew..Sett vp forgys and steyle stydyis fyne. **1565** Jewel *Repl. Harding* viii. 387 Job saithe, *Stetit cor eius sicut incus*: His harte stoode as a steadie. **1583** Melbancke *Philotimus* T ij, The more you strike iron vpon the stidhy, the harder & tougher yᵉ iron is. **1868** Atkinson *Cleveland Gloss.*, *Stiddy*, (often pr. stithy), an anvil. **1894** P. H. Hunter *James Inwick* x. 131 It was a waly hammer he swung, an'..whan he brocht it doun, he gart the stiddy dirl an' the sparks flee. **1902** Baring-Gould *Nebo* ii. 9 Each 'jack' has in it socket holes. Into one of these ..the 'steady' is inserted, a slip of steel, upon which the worker places the white-hot end of his rod, and hammers it into shape.

γ. **c 1425** Study: see β. **a 1500–20** Dunbar *Poems* xxxiii. 52 As blaksmyth bruikit was his pallatt, ffor battering at the study. **1583** *Rec. Elgin* (New Spalding Club 1903) I. 172 Ane battering studdy. **1688** Holme *Armoury* iii. 379/2 A Pewterers..Bossing Studdy, or Stiddy. **1785** Burns *Scotch Drink* xi, [He] Brings hard owrehip..The strong forehammer, Till block an' studdie ring an' reel. **1841** Hartshorne *Salop. Ant.* Gloss., *Study*, a small anvil used in manufacturing nails. **1864** J. Brown *Jeems the Doorkeeper* 18 You hear the ring of the blacksmith's study, you see the smoke of his forge. **1900** C. Murray *Hamewith* 17 But see him..in his smiddy, An' mark the thuds that shape the shoon, An' dint the very studdy.

b. *transf.*

c 1620 A. Hume *Brit. Tongue* i. iv, The hammeres are the nether lip, the top of the tongue, and the midle tongue. The stiddles the overlip, the outward teeth, the inward teeth, and the roofe of the mouth.

†**2.** *Anat.* The anvil bone of the ear = incus i. (Cf. anvil 3 b.) *Obs. rare.*

1578 Banister *Hist. Man* i. 11 This is the second Ossicle, called by the name of a stedy or anueld. **1615** Crooke *Body of Man* 592 Those two [bones of the ear] which are knowne by the names of the Anuill or the Stithy, and the Mallet or Hammer.

3. A forge, smithy.

α. **1602** Shaks. *Ham.* iii. ii. 89 (1604 Qo.) My imaginations are as foule As Vulcans stithy. **1850** James *Old Oak Chest* I. 149 On this green, detached from all other houses, stood the stithy. **1876** Morris *Sigurd* iii. 178 When the day of the smith is ended and the stithy's fire dies out.

β. **a 1661** Fuller *Worthies, Linc.* (1662) 169 James Yorke a Blacksmith of Lincolne..is a Servant as well of Apollo as Vulcan, turning his Stiddy into a Study, having lately set forth a Book of Heraldry. **1825** Brockett *N.C. Gloss.*, *Stiddy, Stithy*,..used sometimes..for the smith's shop.

†**4.** A disease incident to horses and oxen. *Obs.*

1600 Surflet *Country Farm* i. xxiii. 132 The stithie [orig. F. *l'encueur*] hapning to the oxe, being otherwise called a mallet or hammer, is knowen when the beast hath his haire standing vpright, [etc.]. **1611** Cotgr., *Encueur*, the Stithie; (a disease of horses, and cattell). *Ibid.*, *Marteau*, a hammer ..; also, the Stithie (a beasts disease). **1706** in Phillips; and in some later Dicts.

5. *attrib.* and *Comb.*: (sense 1) as *stithy-man, -work*; **stithy-stock,** the stock or base of an anvil.

1597 Bp. Hall *Sat.* ii. i. 27 The subtile *Stithy-man. **1295** *Stithistok [see 1]. **1585** Higins *Junius' Nomencl.* 305/2 *Acmotheta*,..the anuile or stithe stocke. **1888** *Sheffield Gloss.*, *Stiddy-stock*, a stand for an anvil. **1839** Carlyle *Chartism* viii. 158 He had learned metallurgy, *stithy-work in general.

Hence †'**stithy** *v. trans.*, to forge. *lit.* and *fig.*

c 1420 Wyclif *Josh.* Prol., Wite he me not in to repreuynge of oold men newe thingis to stithie [Vulg. *sciat me non in reprehensionem veterum nova cudere*]. **1606** Shaks. *Tr. & Cr.* iv. v. 255 But by the forge that stythied Mars his helme, Ile kill thee euery where.

stitic, stitical, obs. ff. styptic, styptical.

stitle bagge, obs. form of stickleback.

†'**stitling.** *Obs. rare.* Also 5 **stytlyng.** Corrupt form of stickling, a stickleback.

c 1425 *Voc.* in Wr.-Wülcker 641/28 *Hic scorpio*, stytlyng. **1823** *Dame Wiggins of Lee* in *Ruskin's Wks.* (1903) II. 521 To comply with their wish To spend all their play-time In learning to fish For stitlings.

stittle-back, -bag, obs. ff. stickleback.

†**stitty stitty,** *a. nonce-word.* A derisive epithet applied to a stammerer.

1600 *Look about You* [ix.] G 2 b, Come to the Buttery bar, stitty stitty stammerer,..we'll drinke tryliil Ifaith.

†**stive,** *sb.*[1] *Obs. rare*[−1]. In 4 **styue.** [Var. of stew *sb.*[1], a. OF. *estuve*.

The rhyme *styues*: *lyues* (sb. pl.) shows that the word is not merely a different spelling of *stue, stewe*.]

= stew *sb.*[1] 4.

c 1386 Chaucer *Friar's T.* 34 'They han of us no Iurisdiccioun, Ne neuer shullen, terme of alle hir lyues.' 'Peter! so been the wommen of the styues' Quod the Somnour, 'y-put out of my cure!'

†**stive,** *sb.*[2] *Obs. rare*[−1]. [Of obscure origin; perh. some error.] ? The eyeball or the pupil.

1641 Best *Farm. Bks.* (Surtees) 79 Whearby groweth (as it weare) a scumme over the stive of the eye.

†**stive,** *sb.*[3] *Obs.* [? f. stive *v.*[3] (sense 3 b).] (See quot.)

1688 Holme *Armoury* ii. 252/1 A Stive, or Stove, is a thing made of straw, almost after the manner of a Bee Hive, to put the Cock in, to keep him warm.

stive (staɪv), *sb.*[4] [a. Du. †*stuive* (given by Kilian as obs.), related to *stuiven* to rise as dust. Cf. mod.Du. *stuifmeel* floating dust of flour.

The word seems to have belonged orig. to Pembrokeshire, where there was a Flemish colony, and to E. Anglia, where words from Du. are frequent.]

Dust; esp. the floating dust of flour during the operation of grinding.

1793 *Gentl. Mag.* Dec. 1084 *Stive*, dust. Pembrokeshire. —Dust is there only used to signify *sawdust*. **a 1825** Forby *Voc. E. Anglia*, *Stive*, dust. We use the word in no other sense. **1853** Glynn *Power Water* 138 The dust, or 'stive,' as millers call it. **1907** *Times* 15 Feb. 3/1 The filtering medium, whatever it was, speedily got choked by the stive or dust.

b. *Comb.*

1907 *Times* 15 Feb. 3/1 The air passing out through the cone was by no means free from impurities, and a second apartment or stiveroom was required as a settling chamber.

†**stive,** *sb.*[5] *Obs.* [a. OF. *estive*, latinized *stīva*.] A kind of bagpipe. Cf. stivour.

c 1290 *St. Thomas* 80 in *S. Eng. Leg.* 379 Tabours and fiþele and symphanye, stiues and harpingue.

† **stive**, *sb.*[6] *Obs. rare*$^{-1}$. [ad. L. *stīva* (in the original passage).] A plough-tail.

1693 [N. TATE] tr. *Cowley's Hist. Plants* IV. 177 The same Right-hand guides now the humble Stive, And Oxen Yoaks, that did fierce Nations drive.

† **stive**, *v.*[1] *Obs. rare.* [ME. *stīven*, OE. *stífian*, f. *stīf* STIFF *a.*] **a.** *intr.* To become stiff (OE. only). **b.** *trans.* To make stiff.

c **1000** ÆLFRIC *Gram.* xxvi. (Z.) 154 *Rigeo* ic stifige. **13..** *Will. Palerne* 3033 þe hote sunne hade so hard þe hides stiued, þat [etc.].

stive (staɪv), *v.*[2] Now chiefly *Sc.* [a. OF. *estiver*, otherwise adopted as STEEVE *v.*[2]] *trans.* To compress and stow (cargo) in a ship's hold. Also *transf.* to pack tightly; to crowd (with things or people). Also with *up*.

a **1320** *Sir Tristr.* 1169 In botes þai gun him stiue And drouȝ him to þe land. **1615** G. SANDYS *Trav.* I. 15 You would..admire if you saw them stiue it in their ships: enforcing a sacke as big as a wooll-packe into a roome at the first too narrow for your arme. *a* **1639** WOTTON *Parallel Essex & Buckhm.* (1641) 7 His chamber being commonly stived with friends or Suitors of one kinde or other. **1659** T. PHILIPOTT *Vill. Cant.* 2 Four Syllables..all confusedly shuffled and stiv'd into this one word Gavelkind. **1781** in *Hone's Every-day Bk.* II. 836 Corn [shall] be brought fairly to market, not stived up in granaries. **1844** 'JON. SLICK' *High Life N. York* II. 13 The cabin was so stived up with onion barrels..that I hadn't no room to fix up in. **1888** DOUGHTY *Arabia Deserta* I. 203 The locust meat is stived in leathern sacks.

stive (staɪv), *v.*[3] [app. a variant of STEW *v.*, a. OF. *estuver*. Cf. STIVE *sb.*[1] In mod. use often with mixture of the sense of STIVE *v.*[2], to pack tightly, and sometimes associated with STIFLE *v.*]

† **1.** *trans.* To boil slowly: = STEW *v. Obs. rare.*

? *c* **1390** *Forme of Cury* (1780) 37 Do the flessh therewith in a Possynet and styue [*printed* styne] it. [**1743** LYE in *Junius' Etymol.*, Stive or stew meat, *carnem lento igne coquere*. Su. *stufwa à stew*, Laconicum, q.v. Hinc to stive one, *Aliquem æstu ferè suffocare*.]

2. To shut up in a close hot place; to stifle, suffocate.

a **1722** LISLE *Husb.* (1757) 444 [The sparrow] chooses then, when the weather grows warm,..to build sub dio, and not to stive herself up in nests under the eaves of a house. [**1743**: see sense 1.] **1748** RICHARDSON *Clarissa* (1811) VII. 131, I have one half of the house to myself;..while..the two musty nieces are stived up in the other half. **1837** T. HOOK *Jack Brag* xvii, You did not suppose I was going to be stived up in this place. **1840** GEO. ELIOT in Cross *Life* (1885) I. 77 O how luxuriously joyous to have the wind of heaven blow on one after being stived in a human atmosphere. **1865** J. PAYN *Married beneath him* III. 181 What your husband needs is an immediate change of air and scene. He has been stived up here in town too long.

3. *intr.* To 'stew', suffocate.

1806 J. BERESFORD *Miseries Hum. Life* v. I. 83 The holes of happiness in which you have been stiving for the last two or three months. **1876** GEO. ELIOT *Dan. Der.* liv, One can get rid of a few hours every day in that way, instead of stiving in a damnable hotel.

b. Of a fighting-cock (cf. STOVE *v.* and STIVE *sb.*[3]).

1704 *Lond. Gaz.* No. 4063/4 The said Pens are now..built over the Pit, and very convenient to the Sparring and Stiving Rooms, much to the Advantage of the Feeders, and Cocks feeding, sparring and stiving.

Hence **stived** *ppl. a.* (chiefly in comb. ***stived-up***), deprived of fresh air; **'stiving** *vbl. sb., attrib.* in ***stiving-room*** (sense 3 b); **stiving** *ppl. a.*, suffocating.

1598 BRANDON *Octavia* II. B 7, What monstrous greefe, what horror, thus constrains My stiuing hart, his lodging to forsake. **1704** Stiving room [see 3 b]. **1847** L. HUNT *Men, Women & Bks.* (1876) 74 Sofa-bedsteads..in 'stived-up' little rooms. **1880** B. W. RICHARDSON in *Fraser's Mag.* Nov. 670 The stived-up children of the metropolis. **1894** N. BROOKS *Tales of Maine Coast* 59, I mounted to the fifth story of the rickety, stived building.

stive, obs. f. STEEVE *a.* and *v.*[1], STIFF *a.*

stiver ('staɪvə(r)), *sb.* Forms: 6 **stufer, stuver, styfer, stever,** 6–8 **styver,** 8 **stuyver,** 9 **stuiver,** 6– **stiver.** [a. Du. *stuiver*, (M)LG. *stüver*, whence mod.G. *stüber*, Da. *styver*, Sw. *styfver*. Of obscure origin: etymologists connect it with LG. *stūf* stumpy, cut short.]

1. *Hist.* A small coin (originally silver) of the Low Countries; applied to the nickel piece of 5 cents of the Netherlands (one-twentieth of a florin or gulden, or about a penny English).

1502 in *Lett. & Papers Rich. III & Hen. VII* (Rolls) II. 111 The crowne..is valued at xxxv[ti] stufers and an di. and xij. grotes sterlinge maketh only xxx[ti] stufers. **1527** E. LEE in *Ellis Orig. Lett.* Ser. III. II. 94 Doble ducats, single ducats, ..stufers, and black monaye. **1535** JOYE *Apol. Tindale* 22 The printer came to me agen and offred me ij stuuers and an halfe. **1543** RECORDE *Gr. Artes* K iij b, A single stiuer is 1 d, ob, q. The double stiuer is 3 d, q. **1547** BOORDE *Introd. Knowl.* xi. (1870) 153 A gelder areris is worth .xxiii. steuers: .xxiii. steuers is worth .iii. s. **1585** HIGINS *Junius' Nomencl.* 329/2 Fortie stiuers of Dutch coyne, which maketh a Noble of our monie: or a summe much thereabouts. **1697** DAMPIER *Voy.* (1729) II. I. 162 Some of them keep Tea-houses, where for a Stiver, a Man has near a Pint of Tea. **1756** MRS. CALDERWOOD in *Coltness Collect.* (Maitl. Club) 133 A stiver is rather more than our penny. **1838** *Murray's Handbk. N. Germ.* 4 The towing horse is ridden by a lad..who receives a few cents at each stage; and is well paid with a stiver. **1839** W. CHAMBERS *Tour Holland* etc. 27/1 The [school] fee is one cent. a-day, or the fifth part of a stiver, which is less than an English farthing.

2. Used (like *penny*) as a type of a coin of small value, or of a small amount of money; *occas.* a small quantity of anything, a 'bit'. ***not a stiver*** = nothing.

1622 FLETCHER *Beggars' Bush* I. ii, Set him free And you shall have your money to a Stiver. **1766** GOLDSM. *Vic. W.* xxxi, As for that lady's fortune, sir, you shall never touch a single stiver of it. **1822** BYRON *Werner* I. i. 409 He has not a stiver. **1842** BROWNING *Pied Piper* x, With him I proved no bargain-driver, With you, don't think I'll bate a stiver! **1872** CALVERLEY *Fly Leaves* 38, I come,..nor care a stiver; For trades are brisk and trades are slow, But mine goes on for ever. **1883** OLIVE SCHREINER *Afr. Farm* I. ix, That boy Waldo..has not done a stiver of work all day. **1909** *Blackw. Mag.* Nov. 672/7 They didn't care a stiver if my head was blown off.

3. *attrib.* and *Comb.*, as † ***stiver style***; † **stiver cramped** *a.*, short of money.

1649 J. JEPHSON in *Lovelace's Lucasta* To Author a 4 b, Though som thy prayse in rich stiles sing, I may In stiver stile write Love as well as they. **1785** GROSE *Dict. Vulgar T.*, *Stiver cramped*, needy, wanting money.

Hence **'stiverless** *a.*, without a stiver; penniless.

1839 J. P. KENNEDY *Rob of Bowl* xvii. (1860) 208 You go abroad unattended, stiverless.

stiver ('stɪvə(r)), *v. dial.* [f. ME. *stive* STIFF *a.* + -ER[5].] **1.** *intr.* To stand stiff. Chiefly of the hair, etc.: to bristle, become rough, stand on end.

1790 GROSE *Prov. Gloss.* (ed. 2), *Stivering* or *Stubvering up against*, standing stiff. West.

2. *trans.* To ruffle (the hair); to make it bristle or stand on end. Also with *up*.

1886, etc. in *Eng. Dial. Dict.* **1924** GALSWORTHY *White Monkey* I. viii. 61 Michael stivered his hair. **1926** —— *Silver Spoon* I. v. 34 Michael stivered up his hair.

Hence **'stivered** *ppl. a.*, **'stivering** *ppl. a.* Also **'stivery** *a.*, bristly, rough.

1832 *Blackw. Mag.* XXXI. 592 His tail he tuck'd into his pantaloons, With a Brutus, all stivering and hairy. *a* **1855** A. CROSSE *Memorials* (1857) 124, I saw that her hair was stivered; the cat was evidently ill. **1889** *Reports Provinc., Devon* (E.D.D.), The birds look big in winter with their feathers all stivered out. **1892** S. HEWETT *Peasant Speech* (E.D.D.), Didee iver zec sich a stivery head as 'er 'th agot? 'Er lüketh 's-of 'er'd been drawed drii a brimbly 'ädge back'ards. **1918** GALSWORTHY *Five Tales* 127 He looked like a stuffed man..sitting there, with..his stivered hair. **1928** —— *Swan Song* I. iii. 19 Dabbing at his hair, bright and stivery, he straightened his tie and ran down. **1939** N. MARSH *Overture to Death* v. 58 The stivered grass was washed with colour, and before him his own attenuated shadow appeared.

† **stivour.** *Obs.* [a. OF. **estiveor*, agent-n. f. *estiver* to play on the *estive*: see STIVE *sb.*[5]] A performer on a kind of bagpipe.

13.. *Guy Warw.* (1891) 396 Organisters & gode stiuours. **13..** *K. Alis.* 2566 (Laud MS.), Mery is þe blast of þe styuour. *c* **1330** *Arth. & Merl.* 6558 Þer were trumpes & fiþelers & stiuours & tabourers.

stivy ('staɪvɪ), *a.* [f. STIVE *v.*[3] + -Y.] Stuffy.

1849 ALB. SMITH *Pottleton Legacy* xxvi. 280 Kind spinsters are always found..to shut themselves up in stivy rooms on hot Sunday summer afternoons. **1899** M. HEWLETT in *Blackw. Mag.* Feb. 339/1 The sun of her smile was like a clean breath in the stivy den.

stiward, obs. form of STEWARD.

stiwe, obs. form of STEW *v.*

stiyng(e, var. forms of STYING.

‖ **stoa** ('stəʊə). *Gr. Antiq.* Pl. **stoas, stoai.** [Gr. στοά.] A portico, roofed colonnade; *spec.* the great hall at Athens (adorned with frescoes of the battle of Marathon), in which Zeno lectured, and from which his disciples were called Stoics; by Milton called 'the painted Stoa' (transl. of Gr. ἡ στοὰ ἡ ποικίλη: see PŒCILE).

1603 HOLLAND tr. *Plutarch's Mor.* 279 Call to minde..the ..famous Philosophers, either in Lycæum or the Academie: go to the gallerie Stoa [etc.]. **1671** MILTON *P.R.* IV. 253 His who bred Great Alexander to subdue the world, Lyceum there, and painted Stoa next. **1775** R. CHANDLER *Trav. Asia Minor* xviii. 59 Large quadrangular stoas or porticoes. **1842** W. C. TAYLOR *Anc. Hist.* ix. §3 (ed. 3) 230 At the east were erected two splendid stoai, or porticoes. **1898** *Edin. Rev.* Oct. 359 Temples and stoas were still standing.

stoach (stəʊtʃ), *v. dial.* Also 8 **stolch,** 9 **stooch, sto(t)ch.** [Of obscure origin: cf. STODGE *sb.*] *trans.* To trample (wet ground) into holes. Also *absol.* or *intr.* Comb. **stoach-way** (see quot. 1853).

1733 W. ELLIS *Chiltern & Vale Farm.* 20 Neither the Turnep, nor artificial Grass will answer, by reason of the Cattles stolching. **1836** W. D. COOPER *Sussex Gloss.* 31 *Stoach*, to make an impression on wet land, as oxen do in winter. E. **1853** *Ibid.* (ed. 2) 79 *Stoache-way*, the Channel at low water, which lies between the pier-head and the deep water, running through low sand. So used at Rye Harbour. **1910** KIPLING *Rewards & Fairies* 282 The ground about was poached and stoached with sliding hoof-marks.

Hence **'stoachy** *a.*, dirty.

1836 W. D. COOPER *Sussex Gloss.* 31 A stoachy road.

stoage, obs. form of STOWAGE.

stoak, *v. Naut.* ? *Obs.* (See quots. *a* 1625, 1644.)

a **1625** *Nomenclator Navalis* (Harl. MS. 2301), When the water cannot come to the well then we say that the Shipp is stoaked. **1644** MANWAYRING *Seamans Dict.* 102 When the limber-holes, have some ballast, or any thing else got into them, so that the water cannot passe, we say the limbers are Stoaked: also when any thing is gotten in, or about the bottom of the Pump, so that it cannot draw water, we say the Pump is Stoaked. (So **1658** in PHILLIPS; and in later Dicts.)

stoak, stoal(e, stoan(e, stoap(e, stoare: see STOKE, STOLE, STOOL, STONE, STOUP, STORE.

stoat (stəʊt), *sb.* Forms: 5 **s[t]ot,** 5–6 **stoote,** 5–9 **stote,** 9 **stoot,** 7– **stoat.** [Of obscure origin: there appears to be no ground for assuming connexion with STOT.] **a.** The European ermine, *Putorius ermineus* or *Mustela erminea*, esp. when in its brown summer coat.

c **1460** *Porkington MS.* 10 lf. 189 Þis byne þe bestes of þe stynkyng fute. The folmard..þe ottur þe stote and þe polcatte. **1486** *Bk. St. Albans* f iv b, The Squyrell, the Whitrat, the S[t] ot, and the Pulcatte. **1552** HULOET, Stoote, beast or vermyne whyche kylleth rabettes, *ferunculus*. **1570** LEVINS *Manip.* 178/7 A stote, vermine, *furunculus*. **1607** TOPSELL *Four-f. Beasts* 219 It is said..that if the head of a wolfe be hanged vp in a doue-cote, neither cat, Ferret, weasil, Stoate, or other noysome beast dare to enter therein. **1619** MIDDLETON *Tri. Love & Antiq.* D 1, The names of those Beasts, bearing Furr,..Ermine, Foyne, Sables,..Minck, Stote, Miniuer, [etc.]. *a* **1722** LISLE *Husb.* (1757) 417 When they are penned up they are more secure from the stote. **1768** PENNANT *Brit. Zool.* I. 84 The weesel being usually mistaken for a small stoat. **1823** E. MOOR *Suffolk Words*, *Stoot*, a species of pole-cat or weazle. **1872** TENNYSON *Gareth & Lynette* 871 Lion and stoat have isled together, knave, In time of flood. **1894** LYDEKKER *Roy. Nat. Hist.* II. 64 The stoat or, as it is generally called when in winter dress, the ermine (*Mustela erminea*), is closely allied to the weasel. **1897** 'OUIDA' *Massarenes* xxxix, You are as keen after gold as a stoat after poultry.

(*b*) *fig.*, esp. a treacherous fellow; a sexually aggressive man, a lecher.

1854 WISEMAN *Fabiola* II. vi. 173 You came here as a famous plot-hunter, a sort of stoat, to pull conspirators out of their nests. *a* **1960** E. M. FORSTER *Maurice* (1971) xxx. 138 His feeling for Dickie required a very primitive name... What a stoat he had been! **1978** C. EGLETON *Mills Bomb* xxii. 208 'Would it surprise you to learn that he was a fag?' 'You've got it wrong; everyone knew he was a stoat.'

b. *Comb.*, as ***stoat-hunting***; **stoat-weasel**, a stoat.

1836 MRS. SHERWOOD *Henry Milner* III. iii, To remember it was Sunday, and no day for stoat hunting. **1882** J. HARDY in *Proc. Berw. Nat. Club* IX. iii. 427 Stoat-weasels..still hold their ground.

stoat (stəʊt), *v. Tailoring.* [Of obscure origin.] *trans.* To sew with a particular kind of invisible stitch, which passes only half-way through the cloth. Hence **'stoated, 'stoating** *ppl. adjs.*; **'stoating** *vbl. sb.*

1888 *1st Rep. Sel. Comm. Sweating Syst.* 1029 Tailors' Log. Stoated and double pricked edges 3*s od.* **1888** *Daily News* 21 Sept. 4/7 Enduring fierce rebuke from 'the boss' for a shoulder awkwardly wadded, or a badly 'stoated' edge. **1901** HASLUCK *Tailoring* 21 There are three kinds of absolutely invisible stitches which are used to repair tears... These are stoating, fine-drawing, and rentering. *Ibid.*, The tear to be stoated must have firm edges; it is impossible to stoat ravelled edges such as most serges have.

stoat, dial. form of STOUT *sb.*, horse-fly.

stoater ('stəʊtə(r)). *Racing.* [Of obscure origin: ? identical with STOTER.] A heavy stake.

1860 *Sporting Mag.* Nov. 306 Owners back their horses for such 'stoaters,'..that [etc.]. **1861** *Ibid.* Dec. 448 We did not back her for 'a stoater,' or get 'on' for 'a monkey,' or 'a century,' or even wager that one 'pony' would win us another. **1862** *Baily's Mag.* Aug. 96 When it was known before starting the sum Lord Portsmouth stood on his filly, there was a perfect furore to back her, as a pony would be 'a perfect stoater' for him.

stoave, obs. form of STOVE.

stob (stɒb), *sb.*[1] Now only *Sc.* and *dial.* Also 7–9 **stobb.** [Partly a variant (sometimes merely graphic), partly a cognate, of STUB *sb.*[1], q.v. for the etymology. (It seems impossible accurately to separate the two words, as they appear always to have been to a great extent synonymous; the examples written with *o* are therefore placed here, even when it is not unlikely that they properly belong to STUB *sb.*[1]) Cf. STAB *sb.*[2]]

† **1.** A stump, portion remaining after mutilation.

c **1420** *Chron. Vilod.* 4326 Bot þe flesshe from þe stobbus of his lymus was clene a-way.

b. *fig.* (See quot.)

1825 BROCKETT *N.C. Gloss.*, *Stob*,..metaphorically,..an ignorant, stupid fellow.

2. A stick, a twig broken off.

1321 *Charter in Verse* (late copy) With grene ant wilde, stob ant stokke. **1513** DOUGLAS *Æneis* XI. ii. 18 Bund with the syonys or the twyistis sle Of small rammell or stobis of aikin tre [L. *virgis et vimine querno*]. **1827** TENNANT *Papistry Storm'd* 170 Sae stanes, stobs, sticks, come peltin' aff Dean Annan.

3. A stake; a post; also a gibbet. † ***rogue stob***, a whipping-post.

1530 LYNDESAY *Test. Papyngo* 169 Boreas blew one blast, ..Quhilk..blew hir.. Doun to the ground,..Vpon ane stob scho lychtit, on hir breist; The blude ruschit out. **1552** —— *Monarche* I. 1538 Quhalis and Monstouris of the seis Stickit on stobbis, amang the treis. **1550** *Abstr. Protocols Town Clerks Glasgow* (1894) I. 18 The twa biggit howssis nixt adjacent thairto upone the sammyn syide gangand to the lyne stobbis. **1626** in R. Welford *Hist. Newcastle* (1887) III. 276 For making clasps to the rogue stob, 1s. 2d. *a* **1670** SPALDING *Troub. Chas. I* (Bannatyne Club) I. 44 He was taken and headed, and his right hand sett upon ane stob. **1795** *Statist. Acc. Scot.* XV. 321 The different articles made from these woods are sold at the following prices on the spot: stobs at 4s. the hundred, four feet long; [etc.]. **1842** J. AITON *Dom. Econ.* (1857) 268 Almost every boy knows how to knock up a rabbit hutch... A few stobs, boards, and nails, is all that is required. **1860–62** *Trans. Tyneside Field Club* V. 90 (E.D.D.) In former times, a pilgrimage was sometimes made..to Winter's Stob, or gibbet, for a piece of the wood to rub the tooth with in toothache. **1882** *Trans. Glasgow Archaeol. Soc.* II. II. 129 Stobs had been inserted in the bank of the river. **1883** C. F. SMITH *Southernisms* in *Trans. Amer. Philol. Soc.* 53 *Stob*, 'a small post or stake or stump of a shrub,' commonly so used in many, if not all, parts of the South. **1893** T. N. PAGE *In ole Virginia* 140 A few hens loitering about..and a runty pig tied to a stob.

†**b.** (*to have* or *hold*) ***stob and stake***: to hold property (in a place). *Obs.*

1489 *Extracts Burgh Rec. Edin.* (1869) I. 57 Hafand nother stob nor stake within this towne. **1529** *Extracts Rec. Convent. Burghs Scot.* (1870) I. 510 That tha cum and duell within the burgh and hald the stob and stack within the same. **1596** *Extracts Aberd. Reg.* (1848) II. 133 All burgessis of gild..sall dwell,..hauld stob and stack, fyre and flett, within the burghs quhair thay are frie.

†**c.** ***every stob***: the whole of a building. *Obs.*

1716 *Wodrow's Corr.* (1843) II. 137 His mother..has the mill in farming, where every stob was burnt.

†**4.** A short thick nail. *Obs.*

1496 *Acc. Ld. High Treas. Scot.* I. 295 Item, for iij^c stobbis to the vyralis of the cartis, vs. iiijd. **1532–3** *Durham Househ. Bk.* (Surtees) 160 Pro 100 stobbys, pro molendino de Hessylden, 4d.

5. A thorn; a prickle; a splinter.

1637 RUTHERFORD *Let. to Meine* (1664) 167 Lest a stob strike up in your foot, and cause you to halt all your dayes. **1851** W. ANDERSON *Rhymes* (1867) 26 (E.D.D.) Pickin stobs frae laddies' feet.

6. A thatch-peg.

1837 *Finchale Priory Charters* etc. (Surtees) p. ccccl, The wooden pins or stobs used in fastening thatch to the roof of a building. **1844** H. STEPHENS *Bk. Farm* III. 1097 There are still other modes of thatching stacks, such as sticking in handfuls of straw..and keeping them down with stobs of willow.

7. A saddlers' awl. Cf. *stab-awl*, STAB *sb.*¹ 5.

1872 *N. & Q.* Ser. IV. IX. 476 The 'brog,' a small boring instrument, is in Scotland sometimes called 'a borin stob.' **1881** *Times* 4 Jan. 11/4 The man..said Cruickshank, a saddler, had deliberately stabbed him with a 'stob' or awl.

8. *Coal-mining.* (See quot.)

1883 GRESLEY *Gloss. Coal-mining* 241 *Stobb*, a long steel wedge used in bringing down coal after it has been holed.

9. *attrib.* and *Comb.*: **stob-feather** (see quot.); **stob-mill**, a windmill pivoted upon a central post; **stob-nail**, = sense 4; **stob-net**, a fishing net supported on stakes; **stob-pin**, = sense 4; **stob-thatch**, roofing consisting of broom or brushwood laid across the rafters; also *attrib.*; hence ***stob-thatched*** adj.

1825 BROCKETT *N.C. Gloss.*, *Stob-feathers, the short unfledged feathers that remain on a fowl after it has been plucked. **1882** *Archæol. Æliana* Ser. II. IX. 20 *Stob-mill of the antique mould. **1884** *Newcastle Daily Chron.* 28 Aug. 4 An old stob-mill..looks over the mural defences of Newcastle. **1728** *Extracts Burgh Rec. Glasgow* (1909) 308 A late method of fixing the iron bands to the trades of carts by square headed *stob naills. **1806** MORISON *Decis.* XXXIII. 14283 Salmon fishing in the river Leven, by means of *stob-nets. **1571** *Wills & Inv. N.C.* (Surtees 1835) 362, iiij^m *stob pynnes iiij^s. *c* **1748** *Ballad* in D. Mitchell *Hist. Montrose* (1866) 76 The roofs were made o' auld *stob thack, The wa's o' plastered fir. **1888** D. GRANT *Scotch Stories* 29 The dwellin' hoose..[was] a canty stob-thack but-an'-ben. **1792** *Statist. Acc. Scot.* II. 534 A very few of them have been *stob-thatched, or covered with a deep coat of straw. **1871** W. ALEXANDER *Johnny Gibb* (1873) 197 His cosy 'stob-thacket' house.

†**stob**, *sb.*² *Obs.* [f. STOB *v.*¹] = STAB *sb.*¹

1653 W. RAMESEY *Astrol. Restored* 258 Let the Roman emperor have a care of a stob.

†**stob**, *a. Obs.* [f. STOB *sb.*¹] Stumpy.

a **1500** *Anc. Scott. Proph.* i. 107 in *Bernard. de cura rei fam.* (E.E.T.S.), þar sall A batell be, Be-syde a stob crose of stane þat standis on A mure.

stob (stɒb), *v.*¹ *dial.* [Prob. f. STOB *sb.*¹ Cf. STAB *v.*] *trans.* To stab. Also *fig.*

1529 RASTELL *Pastyme* (1811) 132 Swanus..stobyd hym [Alphege] to deth at Grenewych. **1607** *Reg. Privy Council Scot.* XIV. 482 [They] with thair drawin suordis..stobbit the beddis within the said hous for my bodilie harme. **1632** LITHGOW *Trav.* III. 91 My designe is, to stob him with a knife this night. **1643** BAKER *Chron., Edw. VI*, 74 A Commissioner..was suddenly by a Priest stobbed into the body with a knife. **1678** SIR J. LAUDER (Fountainhall) *Hist. Notices* (Bannatyne Club 1848) I. 186 They say Major Johnston undertook to stob him, if he had attempted ane escape. **1683** TRYON *Way to Health* 456 No Swearing, nor stobbing Heaven with dreadful Execrations. **1700** in *Spalding Club Miscell.* (1846) III. 186 McPhersone came in to his house, and spilt his ale, and stobbed the bed, seeking the deponent.

stob (stɒb), *v.*² *Sc.* and *north. dial.* Also 6 *Sc.* stoib. [f. STOB *sb.*¹]

1. *trans.* (See quot. 1855.)

1550 *Abstr. Protocols Town Clerks Glasgow* (1894) I. 18 Twa howssis on the eist syide..as thai are now stobbit. **1605** *Ibid.* (1896) II. 116 Ane peice of waist grund..as the samin is alreddie stobbit and martchit. **1855** *Whitby Gloss.*, *Stob*, to stick stobs, or small posts or quasi-posts, into the ground for the purpose of defining the limits, or the shape of any thing, as a Railway, a house, an enclosure.

2. To roof with stob-thatch.

1535 STEWART *Cron. Scot.* (Rolls) III. 227 Trynchis [he] gart mak..And stoibbit thame with ryce quhen that wes done. **1900** C. MURRAY *Hamewith* 30 And the thatch ance sae neatly stobbit Has lang been scant and bare.

stob(b)all, stob-ball: see STOW-BALL.

†**'stobber.** *Sc. Obs.* In 7 stober. [f. STOB *v.*² + -ER¹.] ? One who roofs with 'stob-thatch'.

1650 in J. Davidson *Inverurie* (1878) 321 To Alex. Lassen, stober, 20 sh. [**1878** ibid. 322 The deals and wands, and the stobber's account, indicate repairs including some thatching work.]

stobe, obs. var. STUB *v.*

stoberlie, -nesse: see STUBBORNLY, -NESS.

†**'stobhert.** *Obs. rare*⁻¹. An alleged name for the hare.

a **1325** *Names of Hare* in *Rel. Ant.* I. 133.

stobill, stoble, stobul(l, obs. ff. STUBBLE.

stoburne, obs. form of STUBBORN.

†**'stobwort.** *Obs.* [? f. STOB *sb.*¹] Woodsorrel: = STAB-*wort*, STUBWORT.

1597 GERARDE *Herbal* Suppl., Stobwort is *Oxys.* **1665** LOVELL *Herbal* (ed. 2) 417 Stob-wort, see Wood sorrel.

stocade, variant of STOCKADE.

stocado: see STOCCADO, STOCKADO.

stocah, stocata: see STOKAGHE, STOCCADO.

stocbred: see STOCKBRIDGE.

stoccade, variant of STOCKADE and see next.

stoccado (stɒ'kɑːdəʊ), *sb. Obs.* exc. *arch.* Forms: 6–7 **stockado, stoccado, stoc(c)ata**, (7 **stookado**), 6 **stoccato**, 7 **stocado, stoc(c)ada**, 9 *arch.* **stoccata, stoccado, (stocado)**; 6–7 **stackado**, 7 **stacado**, 9 **staccato**; 8 **stoccade** (*anglicized, rare*). [Corruptly a. It. *stoccata*, f. *stocco* point of sword, dagger. Cf. the corresponding Sp., Pg. *estocada* (which may be the source of some forms), and Fr. *estocade* (from Sp.); and cf. -ADO 2.] A thrust or stab with a pointed weapon.

1582 HESTER *Secr. Phiorav.* II. xli. 123 [He] tooke hym by the coller and gaue him fiue stockadoes in the breast to haue slaine hym. **1595** SAVIOLO *Practise* I. 10 Let him [the scholar]..thrust his Rapier vnder his teachers, and giue him a thrust or stoccata in the belly. **1598** SHAKS. *Merry W.* II. i. 234. **1603** [see MANDRITTA]. **1657** LIGON *Barbadoes* 52, I have seen some of these Portugall Negres..play at Rapier and Dagger very skilfully, with their Stookados, their Imbrocados, and their Passes. **1698** FRYER *Acc. E. India & P.* 156 Whom when they meet they must give him the Way with a Cringe and Civil Salute, for fear of a *Stockado.* **1837** CARLYLE *Fr. Rev.* II. III. iii, We behold two men.. flourishing and thrusting, stoccado and passado. **1860** WHYTE MELVILLE *Holmby House* xv, [temp. *c* 1650] Your staccatos and passados, and cursed Italian tricks of fence.

fig. and *in fig. context.* **1596** HARINGTON *Metam. Ajax* Prol. B 5 b, I..entred the lists with him & fighting after the old English maner without the stockados, (for to voine or strike below the girdle, we counted it base and too cowardly) after halfe a score downeright blowes, we grew to be friends. **1656** EARL MONM. tr. *Boccalini's Advts. fr. Parnass.* (1674) A 2 b, My Author..gives sometimes very home and sharp Stockadoes. **1716** M. DAVIES *Athen. Brit.* II. 403 Those injur'd Fathers..are doubtless the more sensible of such Mortal Stoccades, as coming from pretended filial Hands.

Hence †**sto'ccado** *v. trans.*, to stab with a pointed weapon.

1676 D'URFEY *Madam Fickle* v. ii, 'Twas well my Lord your Valor interpos'd betwixt me and the danger, by Heaven I had been stockado'd else.

stoccado, -ata, var. ff. STOCKADO *Obs.*

stoce, var. *stows*, STOW *sb.*² (*Mining*).

stochastic (stəʊ'kæstɪk), *a.* [ad. Gr. στοχαστικός, f. στοχάζεσθαι to aim at a mark, guess, f. στόχος aim, guess.] **1.** Pertaining to conjecture. Now *rare* or *Obs.*

1662 J. OWEN *Animadv. on Fiat Lux* Pref. 4 But yet there wanted not some beams of light to guide men in the exercise of their Stocastick [*sic*] faculty. **17..** J. WHITEFOOT in *Sir T. Browne's Wks.* (1712) I. p. xxxvii, Tho' he [Browne] were no Prophet,..yet in that Faculty which comes nearest it, he excelled, *i.e.* the Stochastick, wherein he was seldom mistaken, as to future Events. **1720** SWIFT *Right of Preced. betw. Physicians & Civilians* 11, I am Master of the Stochastick Art, and by Virtue of that, I divine, that those Greek Words..have crept from the Margin into the Text.

2. a. Randomly determined; that follows some random probability distribution or pattern, so that its behaviour may be analysed statistically but not predicted precisely; ***stochastic process*** = ***random process*** s.v. RANDOM *a.* 1 b.

[**1917** L. VON BORTKIEWICZ *Die Iterationen* 3 Die an der Wahrscheinlichkeitstheorie orientierte, somit auf 'das Gesetz der Grossen Zahlen' sich gründende Betrachtung empirischer Vielheiten mö ge als Stochastik..bezeichnet werden. **1923** A. A. TSCHUPROW in *Metron* II. 461 Every stochastical (1) theory of statistics sees in the empirical statistical numbers images of certain really significant quantities—reflected confuse[d] images blurred..by the Chance. [*Note*] (1) I use the word 'stochastical' as synonymous to 'based on the theory of probability'—cf. J. Bernoulli, *Ars Conjectandi*, Basileae, 1713, p. 213 'Ars Conjectandi sive Stochastice nobis definitur ars metiendi quam fieri potest exactissimi probabilitates rerum' and L. v. Bortkiewicz, *Die Iterationen*.] **1934** *Proc. Nat. Acad. Sci.* XX. 376 A stochastic process is defined by Khintchine to be a one parameter set of chance variables: $x(t)$, $-\infty < t < \infty$. **1943** *Rev. Mod. Physics* XV. 32 That we should be able to idealize Brownian motion as a Markoff process appears very reasonable. But we should be careful not to conclude too hastily that every stochastic process is necessarily of the Markoff type. **1957** *New Scientist* 20 June 17/3 A new approach to population dynamics was needed, and quite recently this has been provided by J. G. Skellam in the form of a stochastic model which allows the experimentalist to regard his population as a random variable at each instant in time, and is much more flexible than the earlier deterministic equations. **1968** P. A. P. MORAN *Introd. Probability Theory* iii. 108 We have already dealt with some simple cases of successive trials in which the probabilities at each stage depend on what has happened before... As the successive stages can be regarded as successive instants of time the sequence of events may be regarded as a 'ramdom' or 'stochastic'..process. **1971** KIMURA & OHTA *Theoret. Aspects Population Genetics* iii. 33 In any finite population, gene frequencies are subject to stochastic change due to random sampling of gametes. **1979** *Sci. Amer.* Mar. 64/2 (Advt.), The key was recognizing that the star formation process was 'stochastic'. That is, new massive stars are not necessarily created adjacent to a supernova; rather, a probability exists for their formation.

b. *Mus.* Applied (orig. by Yannis Xenakis (b. 1922), Romanian-born Greek composer) to music in which the overall sound structure is determined, but internal details are left to chance or are established mathematically by composer or computer (by the laws of probability or otherwise).

1958 Y. XENAKIS in *Gravesaner Blätter* IV. 112 (*title*) In search of a Stochastic music. *Ibid.* 121 This *glissando* passage has been taken as an example, for it comprises every problem of this Stochastic music controlled by arithmetic. **1963** T. PYNCHON *V.* x. 292 He got around to talking stochastic music and digital computers with one technician. **1969** *Sat. Rev.* (U.S.) 28 June 56/2 Though much has been written, especially by Xenakis himself, on the technique of 'stochastic' music, most of it is utterly unintelligible to the layman. **1975** *New Yorker* 19 May 90/1, I heard a Balinese gamelan one night and the Strasbourg Battery in Yannis Xenakis's latest 'stochastic' composition the next. **1978** P. GRIFFITHS *Conc. Hist. Mod. Music* xi. 169 Iannis Xenakis.. has also used computers as calculating aids in the composition of his 'stochastic' music, where the musical form is made analogous to a stochastic process (i.e. one ruled by laws of probability, such as a sequence of dice throws).

Hence †**sto'chastical** *a.*; **sto'chastically** *adv.*; **stocha'sticity**, the property of being stochastic.

a **1688** CUDWORTH *Freewill* (1838) 39 We..may and often do proceed to making a judgment in the case one way or other, stochastically or conjecturally. *Ibid.* 40 There is need and use of this stochastical judging and opining concerning truth and falsehood in human life. **1947** *Biometrika* XXXIV. 228 The efficiency of any two tests would be identical, in the conditions stated, if the coefficient of correlation between them was ± 1 because then, of course, they would be functionally, and not stochastically, related. **1968** P. A. P. MORAN *Introd. Probability Theory* v. 247 X is said to be 'stochastically larger' than Y if $F(x) \leq G(x)$ for all x. **1971** *Jrnl. Statistical Computation & Simulation* I. 42 Refinement in modelling eventuates a requirement for stochasticity. **1979** *Nature* 9 Aug. 459/2 The explanation.. is to the contrary of the conventional explanation of these non-seasonal cycles in terms of demographic stochasticity.

stochiometry, obs. form of STOICHEIOMETRY.

stocious ('stəʊʃəs). *slang* (chiefly *Anglo-Ir.*). Also **stotious.** [Of uncertain origin.] Drunk, intoxicated.

1937 *News Chron.* 20 Feb. 8/6 Slang also appeals to our elementary sense of humour, as when we say of a man who is drunk that he is..stotious. **1949** C. GRAVES *Ireland Revisited* i. 20 Words to discriminate the various degrees of intoxication... You have..spifflu, langers, and stocious. The last word rhymes with atrocious and means thickly speaking drunk... We were unable to find anybody who had ever seen it in print. **1952** *Caribbean Quarterly* II. IV. 27 Since when you become so damn stocious? *a* **1966** 'M. NA GOPALEEN' *Best of Myles* (1968) 119 A young man charged with delivering them was found stotious in a doorway. **1970** M. KENYON *100,000 Welcomes* xx. 174 'She's stotious,' Rafferty said. **1980** J. O'FAOLAIN *No Country for Young Men* v. 115 'Coming home stocious five nights a week,' said Doris.

stock (stɒk), *sb.*¹ Forms: 1 **stocc**, 1–4, 6 **stoc**, 2–7 **stoke**, 3–7 **stocke**, **stok(ke**, (5 ? **stolke**), 5–6 **stokk**, 7 *Sc.* **stouk**, 4– **stock**. *Pl.* 3 **stocken**, 4 **stockus**, **stokez**, **stokken**, **stokkus**, **stoukz**, 4– 5 **stokkez**, 4–6 **stockys**, **stokkes**, 4–7 **stockis**, **stok(k)is**, 5–6 **stokkys**, 6 **stokys**, 7 **stox**. [OE. *stoc(c* masc., corresp. to OFris. *stok* tree-trunk, stump, OS. *stok* (Gallée) stick, pole (MLG. *stok* stump), (M)Du. *stok*, OHG., MHG. *stoc* stick, tree-trunk (mod.G. *stock* stick), ON. *stokk-r* tree-trunk, block, log (MSw. *stokk-er*, Sw. *stock*, Da. *stok* stick):—OTeut. **stukko-z*. Cf. Du. *stuk*, G. *stück* (:—OTeut. **stukkjo-m* neut., piece) and OFris. *stok* stiff. The connexions outside Teut. are doubtful: see Kluge, Franck, and Falk & Torp.

The Teut. word is the source of OF., Pr. *estoc* trunk, stump (mod.F. *étoc*, altered to *étau* vice), It. *stocco* rapier (whence OF. *estoc*).]

A. *sb.* **I.** Trunk or stem.

1. a. A tree-trunk deprived of its branches; the lower part of a tree-trunk left standing, a stump. *Obs.* or *arch.*

In this sense (also in b and c) often associated with *stone*.

862 *Charter* in *O.E. Texts* 438 Ðanne fram langan leaȝe to ðam won stocce. **971** *Blickling Hom.* 189 He ȝefeol on þone stocc be þære stænenan stræte þe is háten Sacra uia. **11..** *Fragm. Ælfric's Gram.* (1838) 3 Ligna, driȝe wude, truncus, stoc, stirps. *c* **1250** *Owl & Night.* 25 Þo stod on old stok þar byside. *c* **1325** *Sir Orpheo* 332 Over stok, and over stone. *c* **1374** Chaucer *Boeth.* v. met. i. (1868) 152 Þe stokkes araced wiþ þe flood [L. *vulsi flumine trunci*]. *c* **1480** Henryson *Orpheus* 179 For seke hir suth I sall, and nouthir stynt nor stand for stok no stone. **1509** Barclay *Ship of Fools* 269 b, Hange vp the scapler.. Vpon a tre clene dede, or rottyn stocke. **1590** Spenser *F.Q.* i. ix. 34 All about old stockes and stubs of trees, Whereon nor fruit nor leafe was euer seene. **1613** [Standish] *New Direct. Planting* 6 Seldome good Timber groweth of old stockes. **1704** N. Blundell *Diary* (1895) 22, I ploughed with a Culter.. to find Stocks. **1706** De Foe *Jure Div.* xi. 9 *note*, If the Parliament of England sets the Crown upon that Stock, (pointing to a Stump that stood by) I'll [etc.]. **1727** Swift *Poems Market-hill, Thorn* 33 The magpye, lighting on the stock, Stood chatt'ring. **1810** Scott *Lady of L.* i. vii, O'er stock and rock their race they take. **1837** Carlyle *Fr. Rev.* II. iv. vii, Over cliffs, over stock and stone. **1868** Cussans *Heraldry* (1893) 104 The Stump of a Tree is sometimes called a Stock. **1877** Stevenson *Will o' the Mill* i, Only he, it seemed, remained behind, like a stock upon the wayside.

†b. A log, block of wood; occas. wood as a material. *Obs.*

c **1000** Ælfric *Saints' Lives* xxxi. 856 Þær laȝon stoccas. *c* **1205** Lay. 626 Mid stocken & mid stanen stal fiht heo makeden. *c* **1386** Chaucer *Knt's. T.* 2076 Ne how the fyr was couched first with stree And thanne with drye stokkes clouen a thre. **1422** Yonge tr. *Secreta Secret.* 239 Suche a stomake is like a grete fyre that hath Powere to braunte grete shydis and stokkis. *c* **1450** *St. Cuthbert* (Surtees) 780 Made of stane and noȝt of stok. *c* **1485** *Digby Myst.* i. 154, I am right wele a-paid, if I do not wele, ley my hed vpon a stokke. **1501** Douglas *Pal. Hon.* ii. xxvii, Doun on ane stock I set me suddanelie. **1610** Holland *Camden's Brit.* (1637) 251 A stocke of wood hollowed [for a coffin]. **1792** G. Cartwright *Jrnl. Labrador* I. Gloss. p. xv, *Stock of Timber*, a piece of timber, intended to be sawed. **1806** Pike *Sources Mississ.* (1810) 61 My men sawed stocks for the sleds.

c. As the type of what is lifeless, motionless, or void of sensation. Hence, a senseless or stupid person.

1303 R. Brunne *Handl. Synne* 940 Dowun he smote hys mattok, And fyl hym self ded as a stok. *c* **1330** *Arth. & Merl.* 3855 Arthour on hors sat stef so stok. *c* **1407** Lydg. *Reson & Sens.* 6411 As deffe as stok or ston. *c* **1440** *Alphabet of Tales* 356 Evur sho talkid vnto hym wurdis to provoce hym to luste of his bodie, and yit be no wyse myght sho induce hym þerto,.. he was a stokk, sho sayd, & no man. **1569** Underdowne *Heliodorus* iv. 59 Yee vnhappy people, howe longe will ye sitte still, dombe like stockes? **1594** Spenser *Amoretti* xliii, That nether I may speake nor thinke at all, But like a stupid stock in silence die! **1640** Sir E. Dering *Carmelite* (1641) B ij, I am not so credulous to thinke every Stock a Stoicke. **1644** Milton *Educ.* 3, I doubt not but ye shall have more adoe to drive our dullest and laziest youth, our stocks and stubbs from the infinite desire of such a happy nurture then we have now [etc.]. **1714** Lady M. W. Montagu *Let. to Mrs. Hewet* Nov. (1887) I. 35, I am glad she is not such a stock as I took her to be. **1719** De Foe *Crusoe* ii. (Globe) 344 The Fellow stood mute as a Stock a good while. **1775** Sheridan *Rivals* iii. i, What a phlegmatic sot it is! Why, sirrah, you're an anchorite!—a vile, insensible stock. **1809** Malkin *Gil Blas* ix. vi. (Rtldg.) 320, I.. left him in the street like a stock, staring at my termagant loquacity. **1861** Dickens *Gt. Expect.* xxxviii, You stock and stone!.. You cold, cold heart! **1888** Barrie *When Man's Single* i, Joey Fargus was the stock's name. **1896** K. Snowden *Web of Weaver* xviii. 207 'Ye are not fain to see me, then?' I stood like a stock, letting her think so.

d. Applied contemptuously to an idol or a sacred image. Chiefly in the phrase ***stocks and stones*** = 'gods of wood and stone'.

c **1000** Ælfric *Deut.* xxviii. 36 Ðe þeouiað fremdum godum, stoccum and stanum. *a* **1225** *St. Marher.* 1 Heðene mawmez of stockes, ant of stanes, werkes iwrahte. *c* **1374** Chaucer *Troylus* iii. 589 He swor hir, yis, by stokkes and by stones, And by the goddes that in hevene dwelle. **1390** Gower *Conf.* II. 178 How myhte a mannes resoun sein That such a Stock mai helpe or grieve? *c* **1449** Pecock *Repr.* ii. ix. 198 Thei worschipiden ymagis of stoonys or of stockis. **1529** More *Dyaloge* i. Wks. 140/1 Of al our Ladies saith one, I loue best our Lady of Walsingam. And I saith yᵉ other our Lady of Ippiswitch. In whiche woordes what meneth she but her.. affeccion to the stocke yᵗ standeth in the chapel of Walsingam or Ippiswiche. *a* **1591** H. Smith *Sinful Mans Search* (1592) B 6, That ye be not seduced to offer your petitions to strange gods, as Saints, stockes or stones. **1611** Bible *Jer.* iii. 9, *Wisd.* xiv. 21. **1640** J. Taylor (Water P.) *Differing Worships* 4 Imploring aid.. From ragges and reliques, stones, and stocks of wood. **1655** Milton *Sonn.* xiii. 4. **1825** Scott *Talism.* xxviii, Those whom we regard as idolaters, and worshippers of stocks and stones. **1874** Sayce *Compar. Philol.* viii. 332 There was a worship of nature instead of stocks and stones.

†e. (*to lose*) ***stock and block***: everything, one's whole possessions. *Obs.*

1675 Brooks *Golden Key* Wks. 1867 V. 244 Adam, like the prodigal son,.. quickly lost stock and block, as some speak. **1725** N. Bailey *Fam. Colloq. Erasm.* (1733) 236 Before I came Home, I lost all, Stock and Block. **1775** J. Murray *Lett.* (1901) 194 Jack Clark.. offered to send Providence wagons to move us stock and block to a place of safety. **1809** Malkin *Gil Blas* xii. vi. (Rtldg.) 431, I had taken it for granted that.. the verb-grinders.. to whom I had given the plant of this Genoese bastard would lose stock and block.

†f. ***stock and stovel*** (Law): see quot. 1753. *Obs.*

?**15..** *Charter* in *Blount's Law Dict.* (1691) s.v. *Stoc*, Præterea si homines de Stanhal dicti Abbatis inventi fuerint in bosco prædicti W. cum forisfacto ad Stoc & ad Stovel,.. malefactor pro delicto, qui taliter inventus est, reddet tres solidos. **1753** *Chambers' Cycl.* Suppl., *Stoc and Stovel*, in our old writers, a forfeiture where any one is taken carrying *stipites* and *pabulum* out of the woods.

2. a. The trunk or stem of a (living) tree, as distinguished from the root and branches.

† (*to sell wood*) ***upon the stock***: standing.

1340 Hampole *Pr. Consc.* i. 676 What es man in shap bot a tre Turned up þat es doun,.. þe stok nest þe rot growand Es þe heved with nek folowand. **1382** Wyclif *Job* xiv. 9 His stoc at the smel of water shal burioune. *c* **1430** *Pilgr. Lyf Manhode* iii. xxi. (1869) 146 Sumtime the wodieres solden here wode up on the stok. *c* **1449** Pecock *Repr.* i. vi. 28 Tho bowis grewen out of stockis or tronchons, and the tronchons or schaftis grewen out of the roote. *a* **1500** in *Arnolde's Chron.* 168 Doo donge medlide with strawe aboute the stoke toward the roete of a good thiknes. ? *a* **1500** Bollarde in Turner *Dom. Archit.* (1851) I. 144 Take many rype walenottes, and water hem a while,.. and ther shalbe grawe therof a grett stoke, that we calle masere. **1526** *Pilgr. Perf.* (W. de W. 1531) 43 Of the whiche tree, fayth, hope, & charite, be compared to the stocke, to the barke, & to the sap. **1688** Holme *Armoury* ii. 84/2 The Stock [of a tree is] next to the root. **1697** Dryden *Virg. Georg.* ii. 264 Strong Stocks of Vines it will in time produce. **1705** tr. *Bosman's Guinea* 291 The Stock of these Trees, if they deserve that name, grow to once and a half or twice Man's height. **1846** Tennyson *Golden Year* 62 Like an oaken stock in winter woods. **1857** Henfrey *Elem. Bot.* §57 The Stock or caudex is an undivided woody trunk.

fig. **1340** *Ayenb.* 19 Þe oþer boȝ þet comþ out of þe stocke of prede zuo is onworþnesse. **1447** Bokenam *Seyntys, Anna* 110 Of this floure.. This gracyous Anne was stoke & rote. **1513** Bradshaw *St. Werburge* i. 3163 The tryed stock of truth and the grounde of grace Is pyteously decayed. **1531** Tindale *Expos. 1 John* (1537) 54 As ther is no synne in Christ yᵉ stock, so can ther be none in the quycke membres that lyue & grow in him. *a* **1536** *Songs, Carols* etc. (E.E.T.S.) 6 The blessid stoke þat yt on grew, Ytt was Mary, that bare Jhesu. **1647** Cowley *Mistress, Tree* iii, What a few words from thy rich stock did take The Leaves and Beauties all? **1812** Cary *Dante, Parad.* iv. 126 Thence doth doubt Spring, like a shoot, around the stock of truth. **1884** tr. *Lotze's Metaphysic* i. iv. 89 The impossibility.. of attaching the manifold of change by a merely outward tie to the unchangeable stock of the Thing.

b. The hardened stalk or stem of a plant. (Jam.) Chiefly *Sc.*

1629 *Orkney Witch Trial* in *N.B. Advertiser* Oct. 1894, [He] baid his wyff geve yow thrie or four stokis of kaill. **1783** Burns *Death Poor Mailie* 38 To slink thro' slaps, an' reave an' steal, At stacks o' pease, or stocks o' kail. **1913** J. G. Frazer *Golden Bough* (ed. 3) *Balder* II. xi. 193 One.. gave him several severe blows with the stock of a plant.

c. *Bot.* = rhizome.

1831 Macgillivray tr. *A. Richard's Elem. Bot.* ii. 47 The Stock or Rhizoma. This name has been given to the subterranean and horizontal stems of perennial plants, entirely or in part concealed under ground. **1863** Oliver *Bot.* (1873) 5 A portion of the stem, which is thickened and more or less buried underground,.. is called the stock.

3. Figurative uses developed from sense 2.

a. The source of a line of descent; the progenitor of a family or race. In *Law*, the first purchaser of an estate of inheritance.

c **1393** Chaucer *Gentilesse* 1 The firste stok, fader of gentilesse. *a* **1425** *Cursor M.* 9240 (Trin.) Þus was þe ton þe toþeres stok. *c* **1440** *Jacob's Well* 49 In ony of þise thre lynes afore-seyd, go to þe stok, þat is fadyr or modyr, & noumbre noȝt hem, but þe first persone, þat comyth of þat stok is þe first degre. **1526** *Pilgr. Perf.* (W. de W. 1531) 210 Go to yᵉ stocke of our progeny, & consyder it well. **1583** Melbancke *Philotimus* D iij, If a man should desire an herauld to sift out her pettigree,.. her stock would be found to be the maine sea, wereof she is nothing but the ouerture and ofscombe. **1594** T. B. *La Primaud. Fr. Acad.* ii. 15 Hee that was the stocke of all mankinde. **1620** T. Granger *Div. Logike* 292 The common stocke in a Kindred, or Tribe, is the Father, and Mother from whence the whole progeny, or issue is deriued. **1667** Milton *P.L.* xii. 7 Thus thou hast seen one World begin and end; And Man as from a second stock proceed. **1765** Blackstone *Comm.* I. iii. 210 The title to the crown is.. not quite so absolutely hereditary as formerly; and the common stock or ancestor, from whom the descent must be derived, is also different. Formerly the common stock was king Egbert; then William the conqueror. **1871** Freeman *Norm. Conq.* xviii. (1876) IV. 249 But one of Swegen's many sons might well become the stock of a new dynasty. **1886** F. W. Maitland in *Law Q. Rev.* Oct. 485 To constitute a new stock of descent a very real possession was necessary.

†b. The original from which something is derived. *Obs.*

a **1616** Beaum. & Fl. *Bonduca* v. iii, Brave soldier yeeld; thou stock of Arms and Honor, thou filler of the world with fame and glory. **1650** Fuller *Pisgah* iii. vii. 391 In some resemblance of the seven Planets, amongst which the Sun, the stock of light, stands in the midst. **1756** Burke *Subl. & B.* i. v. (1759) 57 The delight which arises from the modifications of pain confesses the stock from whence it sprung.

c. A line of descent; the descendants of a common ancestor, a family, kindred.

1382 Wyclif *1 Sam.* xvii. 55 Abner, of what stok descendide [Vulg. *de qua stirpe descendit*] this ȝong man? *c* **1386** Chaucer *Knt.'s T.* 693 Of his lynage am I, and his of spryng, By verray ligne, as of the stok roial. **1430–31** *Rolls of Parlt.* IV. 378/1 All the braunches of the Stok Riall. **1477** *Paston Lett.* III. 190, I.. ame better content nowe, that he sholde have hyr, than any other,.. consyderyd hyr persone, hyr yowthe, and the stok that she is comyn offe. **1547** *Bk. Marchauntes* e iiij b, A yong child comen of a good stocke and riche kinred. *c* **1586** C'tess Pembroke *Ps.* lxxii. ix, Eternall Lord, whom Jacobs stock adore. **1662** Stillingfl. *Orig. Sacræ* iii. iv. §1 They all were originally of the same stock. **1671** Milton *Samson* 1079 Men call me Harapha, of stock renown'd. **1693** G. Stepny in *Dryden's Juvenal* viii. (1697) 214 From a mean Stock the Pious Decii came. *a* **1704** T. Brown *On Beauties* Wks. 1730 I. 44 Unite two stocks to form the witty she, Dorinda's sense, and Flavia's repartee. **1827** Hallam *Const. Hist.* xvii. (1876) III. 341 The national prejudices ran in favour of their ancient stock of kings. **1840** Thackeray *Shabby-genteel Story* i, The Crabbs were of a very old English stock. **1857** G. A. Lawrence *Guy Liv.* xviii. 168 That girl comes of the wrong stock to give up anything she has fancied without a struggle. **1870** Bryant *Iliad* ii. I. 67 A warrior of the stock of Hercules was leader. **1879** Howells *Lady of Aroostook* iii, An ancestral consumption, his sole heritage from the good New England stock of which he came. **1899** *Allbutt's Syst. Med.* VIII. 296, I usually found the stock on both sides to be a highly 'nervous' one.

generalized use. **1873** Dixon *Two Queens* i. i. I. 5 Gonzales was of Hebrew stock. **1899** *Allbutt's Syst. Med.* VIII. 137 A lady of calm, well-balanced nervous system, well nourished and of healthy stock. **1900** J. Hutchinson in *Archives Surg.* XI. 210 Most local inflammations of the skin which are definitely blue, occur to those who are of gouty stock.

d. A race, ethnical kindred; also, a race or family (of animals or plants); a related group, 'family' (of languages). Also (cf. a, b), an ancestral type from which various races, species, etc. have diverged.

1549 Coverdale *Erasm. Par. Rom.* iv. 1 Of whom as father & beginner of theyr stocke, the whole nacion of Jewes are wont specially to crake & glory. **1610** Holland *Camden's Brit.* (1637) 121 One of Nemethus his progenie, that is, of the Scythian stocke. **1613** Purchas *Pilgrimage* (1614) 152 They haue Priests of the posteritie of Aaron which resteth in peace, who marrie not with any other but the men or women of their owne stocke. **1730** W. Wotton *Discourse Confusion Babel* 15 So that though this will invincibly prove the Gradation and Derivation of different Dialects from a common Stock, yet it will not prove the actual Formation of some essentially different Tongues which I here contend for. **1738** Wesley *Psalms* lxxx. x, Thou didst the Heathen Stock expel. **1774** Goldsm. *Nat. Hist.* III. 61 Were there but one of these wild animals, the enquiry would soon be ended; and we might readily allow it for the parent stock. **1813** Prichard *Phys. Hist. Man* vii. §6. 392 The interior of Malaya, where they have left remnants of their stock in the black savages of the mountains. **1815** Elphinstone *Acc. Caubul* (1842) I. 405 The languages of the inhabitants were probably all derived from the ancient Persian stock. **1822** *Malte-Brun's Univ. Geog.* I. 570 The stock or family of the languages of Eastern Asia, or of the Monosyllabic languages, differs entirely from that of the Indo-Germanic languages. **1849** Macaulay *Hist. Eng.* I. ii. 272 A population, sprung from the English stock, and animated by English feelings. **1859** Darwin *Orig. Spec.* i. (1872) 13 In the case of strongly marked races of some other domesticated species, there is presumptive or even strong evidence, that all are descended from a single wild stock. **1862** Huxley *Lect. Working Men* 140 We know that all varieties of pigeons of every kind have arisen by a process of selective breeding from a common stock, the Rock Pigeon. **1868** Gladstone *Juv. Mundi* ii. (1870) 41 Even this is considerably older than the date of any family which we can connect with.. the Hellenic stock. **1911** W. W. Fowler *Relig. Exper. Romans* iv. 69 When a stock or tribe (*populus*) after migration took possession of a district.

†e. Pedigree, genealogy; a genealogical tree. *Obs.*

c **1550** Cheke *Matt.* i. 1 (1843) 27 This is yᵉ book of Jesu Christes stock. **1552** Latimer *Serm., Christmas Day* (1584) 273 Shee boasted not of her stocke to be of the linage of noble king Dauid. **1615** Chapman *Odyss.* xi. 294 When, seuerally All told their stockes [Gr. ἑκάστη ὃν γόνον ἐξαγόρευεν]. **1657** Wood *Life* (O.H.S.) I. 225 In the north window opposite to the former is the stock of Jesse.

f. Kind, sort. Now *dial.* (see quot. 1787).

c **1450** Lydg. & Burgh *Secrees* 2001 Good breed of whete, ffesh that wel savours, Of tarrage and stok, good and holsom wyne. **1614** Jackson *Creed* iii. 101 It would argue either Antichristian blindness not to see, or impudency of no meaner stocke, not to acknowledge that [etc.]. **1787** W. H. Marshall *E. Norfolk* (1795) II. 389 *Stock*. Species of a crop. *Mod.* (*Norfolk*) Where did you get that stock o' wheat from? Oh, I ha' had that stock for years.

g. Feudalism. ***native*** (or ***villein***) ***of stock***, a mod. rendering of med.L. *nativus de stipite*, a serf by inheritance.

1828 tr. *Assession Roll* (Duchy of Cornwall) *11 Edw. III* in Manning & Ryland *Rep. Cases K.B.* (1830) III. 162 Robert Ceron, a villein of stock, holds the Lord Duke, in villenage, in Tyngaran, 1 messuage, 5 acres of land English. *Ibid.* 193 John, son of Ralph (Ranulf) of Tremaba, a villein of stock [foot-note *Nativus de stipite*], who at the last assession was admitted to one messuage.. is now granted.. To hold in form of stock [foot-note *in formâ stipitis*].

h. Used for: Inherited constitution, 'breed'. *rare.*

1866 Alger *Solit. Nat. & Man* iv. 243 His toughness of stock and copiousness of force enabled him to weather the storms of nearly a century.

4. A stem in which a graft is inserted.

c **1400** *Pylgr. Sowle* iv. ii. (Caxton 1483) 58 When that this graffe had taken kynde and moysture of this stock on whiche hit was ymped. *a* **1500** in *Arnolde's Chron.* (1811) 164 Take a graf of an apyll tree and graf it in a stoke of elme or aller and it shal bere redde aplys. **1577** Googe *Heresbach's Husb.* ii. 73 b, When you haue thus set in your graffe in the stocke. **1664** Evelyn *Kal. Hort., Jan.* (1679) 8 Gather Cyons for Graffs before the buds sprout; and about the latter end, Graff them in the Stock, Pears, Cherries and Plums. **1725**

Bradley's Family Dict. s.v. *Grafting*, The Stock for Slit-Grafting should be an Inch at least. **1858** CARPENTER *Veg. Phys.* §311 He chooses a stock, or stem deprived of its own buds, and cuts off its top in a sloping direction, so as [etc.]. **1903** W. H. HUTTON *Infl. Christianity* v. 225 He..grafted apples upon the wild stocks.

fig. *c* **1480** HENRYSON *Poems* (S.T.S.) III. 140 Fals titlaris now growis vp full rank, nocht ympit in the stok of cheretie. **1642** FULLER *Holy & Prof. St.* IV. iii. 250 He was contented to be the stock whereon Wolsey should be graffed. **1754** SHERLOCK *Discourses* I. vi. 197 When once they had grafted the Slips of Superstition upon the Stock of Nature. **1796** BURKE *Regic. Peace* i. 101 The wise Legislators..who aimed at..grafting the virtues on the stock of the natural affections.

†**5.** The 'trunk' of a human body. *Obs.*

Quot. 1590 is prob. a conscious transferred use of sense 1.

1387 TREVISA *Higden* (Rolls) III. 233 Þe stok of a man [L. *truncus homo*] fouȝt wiþ his teeþ as it were a wood beest. **1398** —— *Barth. De P.R.* v. l. (1495) 168 The stocke of the body begynnyth at the necke and stretchyth to the buttockes. *c* **1440** *Jacob's Well* 32 Þanne he bad, þat þe stok of his [body] schulde be leyde in a carte. *c* **1550** RAYNALDE *Birth Mankynde* I. (1565) 43 b, In this first figure is set forth the tronke or stocke of a womans body. **1590** SPENSER *F.Q.* I. viii. 10 He smote off his left arme..; Large streames of bloud out of the truncked stock Forth gushed.

†**6.** A post, stake. *Obs.*

c **1000** ÆLFRIC *Saints' Lives* xxvi. 260 Ða sæde se preost him Ic hæbbe of þam stocce þe his heafod on stod. *c* **1275** LAY. 16706 Samuel nam Agag þare king..and lette hime faste to one stocke [*c* 1205 stake] bynde. **1294** *Exch. Acc.* 5/2 Pro wyndase et wyndase stockez xv s. vi d. *c* **1375** *Sc. Leg. Saints* xix. (*Cristofore*) 568 Þane þe fellone tyrand king.. behynd his bak his handis bath til a gert stok gert bynd [hym] rath. **1382** WYCLIF *Josh.* x. 26 And Josue smoot, and slewȝ hem, and hongide vpon fyue stokkis [Vulg. *super quinque stipites*]. **1409–10** in Hudson & Tingey *Rec. Norwich* (1910) II. 56 [To William Morton, carpenter, for a] stok. **1548** LATIMER *Ploughers* (Arb.) 23 He shall lye sycke at theyr doore betwene stocke and stocke. **1599** PEELE *Sir Clyomon* xvi. 54 I'll beat thee like a stock. **1688** HOLME *Armoury* III. 311/2 Whipping Post (or Whipping Stock)..To this Post is [*sic*] Offenders and Petty Rogues and Vagabonds made fast while they are Whipt.

7. The main upright part of anything; the vertical beam, stem (of a cross).

1382 WYCLIF *Num.* viii. 4 The myddil stok [of the candlestick: Vulg. *medius stipes*]. *c* **1400** MAUNDEV. (Roxb.) ii. 5 Þe stock [of the Cross] þat stude in þe erthe..was of cedre. **1463** in *Fabric Rolls York Minster* (Surtees) 134 Thomæ Spence de Pontesfracto pro j stoke pro le tryndiles, 20 d. **1859** R. S. HAWKER in Baring-Gould *Vicar of Morwenstow* vii. (1876) 198 It was..a pentacle of stars, whereof two shone for the transome and three for the stock.

8. a. *pl.* An obsolete instrument of punishment, consisting of two planks set edgewise one over the other (usually framed between posts), the upper plank being capable of sliding up and down. The person to be punished was placed in a sitting posture with his ankles confined between the two planks, the edges of which were furnished with holes to receive them. Sometimes there were added similar contrivances for securing the wrists.

The synonymous med.L. *cippi*, F. *ceps*, suggest that this use of *stock* is an application of sense 6, the reference being to the two side-posts of the apparatus.

c **1325** *Gloss. W. de Bibbesw.* in Wright *Voc.* 163 E pur ço ke seygnur fet coingner Soun neif en ceps [*glossed* stockes] pur chastier. **13..** *E.E. Allit. P.* B. 46 On payne of enprysonment & puttyng in stokkez. **1362** LANGL. *P. Pl.* A. IV. 95 Bote Reson haue reuþe of him he resteþ in þe stokkes Also longe as I lyue. *c* **1380** *Sir Ferumb.* 1186 Bynd hem herde wyþ yre & steel, & pote hem in stokkes of trow. **1503** *Act 19 Hen. VII*, c. 6 §4 It shalbe lawefull..to put theym into the Stokkis and theym so to kepe till the next Market day. **1533** J. HEYWOOD *Pard. & Frere* 602 (Pollard) Wherfore by saynt John, thou shalt not escape me, Tyll thou hast scouryd a pare of stokys. **1598** SHAKS. *Merry W.* IV. v. 123 But that my admirable dexteritie of wit,..deliuer'd me, the knaue Constable had set me ith' Stocks, ith' common Stocks, for a Witch. **1620** *Reg. Mag. Sig. Scot.* 784/2 To hald and have stockis, joggis, prissounhousis, pit and gallous. **1620** ROWLANDS *Nt.-Raven* (1872) 3 Whores and Whoremongers trading for the Pox, And reeling Watch-men, carrying Rogues to Stox. **1632** in E. B. Jupp *Carpenters' Co.* (1887) 301 Theis workes..belong vnto the ..Carpenters..The makinge of..stocks cages and whipping postes. **1687** OTWAY *Soldier's Fortune* IV. i. 45 Constable, watch, stokes, stokes, stokes, murder—. **1769** BLACKSTONE *Comm.* IV. xxix. 370 [Other punishments] Such as whipping, hard labour in the house of correction, the pillory, the stocks, and the ducking-stool. **1841** HOOD *Tale of Trumpet* 701 Over the Green, and along by The George, Past the Stocks, and the Church, and the Forge. **1901** *Westm. Gaz.* 21 Dec. 10/1 Since my ordination (it was in 1870) I have seen a man in the stocks as a punishment for drunkenness. **1905** LD. COLERIDGE *Story Devonshire House* ii. (1906) 22 In the churchyard may be seen the time-worn stocks.

const. as sing. **1573** *New Custom* II. iii. C iij, Euery stockes should be full, euery prison, and iayle. **1612** [see c]. **1853** LYTTON *My Novel* III. ii, The stocks stood staring at him mournfully from its four great eyes. *Ibid.* III. xxiv, Now the stocks is rebuilt, the stocks must be supported.

†**b.** *sing. Obs. rare.*

1382 WYCLIF *Job* xiii. 27 Thou hast putte in the stoc [Vulg. *in nervo*] my foot. *c* **1460** *Oseney Reg.* 86 Noþer to put þere men in preson or in-to bondys or in-to stocke for oony trespase or forfet.

c. in figurative context.

1387–8 T. USK *Test. Love* I. iii. (Skeat) 144 Thus strayte, lady, hath sir Daunger laced me in stockes, I leve it be not your wil. *c* **1440** *Jacob's Well* 186 Whanne god settyth þe in stockys of sykenes, or in prisoun of deth-euyll. **1612** BEAUM. & FL. *Coxcomb* II. i, Was ever man but I in such a stockes? **1805** A. KNOX *Rem.* (1834) I. 27 Their feet are, as it were, made fast, in the stocks of appetite and passion. **1848** L. HUNT *Jar of Honey* Pref. 23 Put thine own pride and cruelty in the stocks. **1878** *Masque of Poets* 153 The world would end, were Dulness not, to tame Wit's feathered heels in the stern stocks of fact.

d. *loosely* in *pl.* †(*a*) Fetters. *Obs.* (*b*) The pillory.

c **1430** LYDG. *Bochas* VIII. vi. (1554) 180 b/1 This hardy princesse [Zenobia]..with stockes of gold [L. *aureis compedibus*] was brought to the cite. *c* **1825** CHOYCE *Log of Jack Tar* (1891) 26 They put his neck in the stocks and kept him there until he was sober. **1860** WHITTIER *Quaker Alumni* 102 The priestcraft that glutted the shears, And festooned the stocks with our grandfathers' ears.

e. *transf.* (*a*) *the shoemaker's stocks* (jocularly): Tight boots. (*b*) Applied to certain callisthenic contrivances formerly used in girls' schools.

1666 PEPYS *Diary* 22 Apr., Being in the shoemaker's stockes I was heartily weary. *a* **1700** B. E. *Dict. Cant. Crew*, *Shoe-makers-stocks*, pincht with strait Shoes. **1831** MRS. J. SANDFORD *Woman* xii. (1834) 182 The modern school-room ..might pass in succeeding centuries for a refined inquisition. There would be found stocks for the fingers, and pulleys for the neck, [etc.]. **1823** GRACE KENNEDY *Anna Ross* (ed. 6) 46 Her poor little feet were placed in stocks, because her Mamma said she turned her toes in when she walked. **1880** J. F. SOUTH *Househ. Surg.* (ed. 4) 331, I do not know whether that miserable invention, the stocks, is still in existence.

9. [? *transf.* from 8.] A frame in which a horse is confined for shoeing.

1875 KNIGHT *Dict. Mech.* 2391.

II. A supporting structure.

†**10. a.** The block or table on which a butcher or a fishmonger cuts his goods. *Sc. Obs.*

1488 *Extracts Burgh Rec. Edin.* (1869) I. 56 Baith in slaing and breking as a craftisman honestlie at his stok. **1508** *Ibid.* 114 It is ordanit that..the sellares and brekkaris of the greit fische haif thair stoks and grayth thairdone for that intent. *Ibid.*, At [= that] all thair [*sc.* the fleshers] stokis be of ane lenth. **1577** *Extracts Burgh Rec. Glasgow* (1876) I. 64 It sall nocht be lesum to na freman to hawe flesche stokis ma nor ane in the land marcat.

†**b.** *the Stocks, the Stocks Market*: the name of a market for meat, fish, etc. in the City of London, on or near the site of the Mansion House.

Stow *Survey* (1598) 178 alleges that the market was so called because it was built on the site where 'had stoode a payre of stockes, for punishment of offendors'; but this is probably a mere guess.

a **1350** *Chron. Edw. I & Edw. II, Ann. Lond.* (Rolls, 1882) I. 90 [In 1282 Henry le Waleis built] domos..apud Wolchirchehawe, quae vocantur Hales, Anglice Stockes. *c* **1483** *Chron. Lond.* (1827) 137 This yere [1450] the stokkes was divided bitwene fisshmongers and bochers. **1554** *Two London Chron.* (1910) 38 And at yͤ Stokes was a great pagaunte made at yͤ cities cost. **1587** FLEMING *Holinshed's Chron.* III. 1348/2 West towards the Stocks market. **1721** AMHERST *Terræ Fil.* No. 36. 192 A fruiterer's apprentice at Stocks-market. **1769** *De Foe's Tour Gt. Brit.* (ed. 7) II. 110 The Mansion-house, built in the Place where Stocks-market used to be kept.

†**c.** (See quot.) *Obs.*

Scott's explanation is perh. erroneous; his source may have used *black stock* in sense 14.

1831 SCOTT *Castle Dang.* i, When was it that I hungered or thirsted, and the black stock of Berkley did not relieve my wants? [*footnote*, The table dormant, which stood in a baron's hall, was often so designated.]

11. A gun-carriage. Cf. GUN-STOCK.

1496 *Acc. Ld. High Treas. Scot.* I. 289 Giffin for bering of a ryvin gunstok fra the Kingis Werk to Johne Lammys smythy to bynd it, xiiij d. **1497** *Naval Acc. Hen. VII* (1896) 246 Elmyn tres..for..makyng of Gonne stokkes for Gonnes belongyng to the seid Ship. **1578** *Invent. R. Wardr.* (1815) 248 Ane double cannon of fonte..montit upoun ane new stok. **1580** HOLLYBAND *Treas. Fr. Tong*, *Affuster*, as Affuster l'artillerie, to sette the artillerie in the stocke or frame. **1748** *Anson's Voy.* II. vii. 213 The Carpenters were ordered to fix eight stocks in the main and fore-tops, which were properly fitted for the mounting of swivel guns.

12. The outer rail of a bedstead; the side of a bed away from the wall; *pl.* a bedstead. *Obs.* exc. *Sc.* (local). Cf. BEDSTOCK. [So ON. *stokkr.*]

1525 tr. *Brunswyke's Handywork Surg.* lxxi. P ij b, And he must be bounde to .iii. or .iiii. places of yͤ bedstede and yͤ hole foote must be bounde to the stock that yͤ pacyent may not drawe it vp to hym. **1544** *Test. Ebor.* VI. 213 The bede and the stokes that I lie in. **1562** *Richmond Wills* (Surtees) 156 Stocks of a bedde and bleckfatts, iiij ˢ. **1629** Z. BOYD *Last Battell* 71 (Jam.) Hezekiah turned his backe to the stocke, and his face to the wall. **1775** GOLDSM. *Scarron's Com. Rom.* I. 35 It will be proper to observe that the bed was so placed as to be close to the wall; Rancour went into it first, and the merchant going after him lay at the stock which was considered as the place of honour. **1796** W. H. MARSHALL *Yorksh.* (ed. 2) II. 347 *Stock*; the outer rail of a bedstead; or the front side of a bed, which is placed against a wall.

13. a. *pl.* The framework on which a ship or boat is supported while in process of construction.

1422 *Foreign Acc.* 61, m. 43 (Publ. Rec. Office) Ad extrahend' et deducend' dictam navem extra idem wose supra stokkes in quâdam fossurâ vocatâ le dook..apud Deptford'. **1425** *Ibid.* 59, m. 22 d, Propter debilitatem et confracciones ejusdem posita fuit in quodam dok supra stokes ibidem de novo construend'. **1615** E. S. *Britains Buss* in Arber *Eng. Garner* III. 624 At length, I was informed.. that one Roger Godsdue, Esquire,..had on the stocks at Yarmouth, five Busses. **1627** CAPT. SMITH *Sea Gram.* i. 1 The stockes are certaine framed posts, much of the same nature upon the shore, to build a Pinnace, a Catch, a Frigot, or Boat, &c. **1638** HEYWOOD *Royal Ship* 13 Had not the famous Archimedes devised new Engines to rowle her [the vessel] out of the stocks into the water. **1670** *Lond. Gaz.* No. 4039/4 There is now upon the stocks an extraordinary large ship of 2500 Tuns. **1704** J. HARRIS *Lex. Techn.* I, *Stocks*; so the Ship-Carpenters call a Frame of Timber, and great Posts made a-shore to build Pinnaces, Ketches, Boats, [etc.] .. Hence we say, a Ship is on the Stocks, when she is a Building. **1755** *New-York Mercury* 14 July 3/1 One of the Gallies [is] planked and compleatly rigged on the Stocks. **1769** FALCONER *Dict. Marine* (1780). **1790** BEATSON *Nav. & Milit. Mem.* II. 34 Having..set upon the stocks two ships. **1810** WELLINGTON in Gurw. *Disp.* (1836) VI. 568 Having completed the boats which were on the stocks. **1875** *Comte de Paris' Hist. Civ. War Amer.* I. 448 They..only succeeded in destroying one of the stocks for ship-building.

b. *fig.*, esp. in phrase *on the stocks*, said e.g. of a literary work planned and commenced.

1669 C. F. *Pluto Furens* Ep. Ded., Until my other Play be finished, which is now on the Stocks. **1693** DRYDEN *Love Triumph.* IV. i, Farewel; you know I have other business upon the Stocks. **1765** FOOTE *Commissary* II. (1782) 45, I made these rhimes into a duet for a comic opera I have on the stocks. **1783** *Virginia Hist. Mag.* V. 390, I'm desirous to provide in the best manner I possibly can for my wife, a son, two daughters, and a child which I expect is in the stocks. **1828** P. CUNNINGHAM *N.S. Wales* (ed. 3) II. 281 A worthy elder, shocked at the scandal of such a numerous illegal progeny being all 'on the stocks' at once, waited on his pastor to condole upon the subject. **1836** J. H. NEWMAN *Lett.* (1891) II. 163, I have had a long letter on the stocks for you for the last fortnight. **1868** E. FITZGERALD *Lett.* I. 315 We shouldn't go off the stocks easy (pardon nautical metaphors). **1898** *Athenæum* 4 June 724/1 The 'Encyclopædia Britannica', the ninth edition of which was on the point of being put on the stocks.

14. *dial.* A ledge at the back or the side of a fireplace, on which a kettle or pot can be placed when removed from the fire: = HOB *sb.*[2] 1.

1592 WARNER *Alb. Eng.* IX. xlvii. (1612) 218 Cowring ore two sticks a crosse, burnt at a smoakie stocke. *a* **1613** OVERBURY *Wife*, *News* (1616) Q 6, That a Wise-rich-man is like the backe or stocke of the Chimney, and his wealth the fire, it receiues not for its owne need, but to reflect the heat to others good. **1823** E. MOOR *Suffolk Words*, *Stock*, the plate, or place, at the back of the fire, or immediately above it. **1854** MISS BAKER *Northampt. Gloss.*, *Stock*, the horizontal space at the side of a grate. *Mod.* (*Northants.*) I put the tea-kettle on one of the stocks and the saucepan on the other.

15. *Brick-making.* **a.** = *stock-board* (see 65).

1683 J. HOUGHTON *Collect. Lett. Improv. Husb.* II. vi. 188 In the middle we fasten with Nails a piece of board, which we call a Stock; this Stock is about half an Inch thick, and just big enough for the Mould to slip down upon. *Ibid.*, Then rubbing the Stock and inside of the Mould with Sand, with the Earth he forms a Brick. **1703** [see *stock-brick* in 65]. **1753** CHAMBERS *Cycl.* Suppl. s.v. *Brick*, Stock-bricks..are made on a stock, that is, the mould is put on a stock, after the manner of moulding or striking of tiles.

b. Short for *stock-brick* (see 65).

c **1738** in E. B. Jupp *Carpenters' Co.* (1887) 567 The Brickwork for £5. 10 per Rod and to do the same with Stocks. **1833** LOUDON *Encycl. Archit.* §79 To pave the back kitchen..with common stocks, bedded in sand. **1837** *Civil Engin. & Arch. Jrnl.* I. 34/1 Brickwork, consisting of sound, hard, and well-burned square stocks. **1858** SIMMONDS *Dict. Trade*, *Stocks*,..the red and grey bricks which are used for the exterior of walls and fronts of buildings. **1892** *Daily News* 16 Dec. 2/2 Decorated with red 'Newbiggin' stone and picked London stocks. **1905** *Pall Mall Gaz.* 29 May 8/2 Brick, of the kind known as dark purple stock.

16. The support of the block in which the anvil is fixed, or of the anvil itself.

1295 Stithistokke [see STITHY *sb.* 5]. **1790** COWPER *Odyss.* VIII. 336 To the stock he heaved His anvil huge. **1875** KNIGHT *Dict. Mech.* 2389 That to which others are attached, or in which they are inserted, as,..The anvil to its stock or pillar.

17. A stand or frame supporting a spinning-wheel or a churn.

1688 HOLME *Armoury* III. 286/2 The large Spinning Wheele..consists in these parts. The Stock standing on four Feet. The Standard [etc.]. **1858** ARNOT *Laws fr. Heaven* Ser. II. xlix. 400 She kept a Bible lying open on the 'stock' of the wheel.

†**18.** A roller for a map. *Obs.*

1737 in *10th Rep. Hist. MSS. Comm.* App. I. 479 The Maps are very large, there was no possible way of sending them by Post..than by rolling them upon a Stock.

†**19.** A perch for a bird. *Obs.* [So Du. *stok.*]

1575 TURBERV. *Bk. Falconrie* 79 When you haue showed hir the perche or stocke, and tyed hir vpon it, put with hir vpon the sayde pearche or stocke some Pullet.

III. A box, hollow receptacle. Cf. TRUNK *sb.* 2.

†**20.** An alms-box. [So G. (*almosen*)*stock*, Du. (*offer*) *stok*. Cf. F. *tronc.*] *Obs.*

c **1400** LOVE *Bonavent. Mirr.* (1907) 188 A coffre hauynge a hole abouen in manere of stokkes that ben now vsed in chirches. **1419** *Mem. Ripon* (Surtees) III. 146 Et in sal. unius hominis facientis j stok propter oblac. in le Crudys, 3*d.* ex convencione. **1504** *Acc. Ld. High Treas. Scot.* II. 266 Item, to the Kingis offerand in the stock at Sanct Duthois towm, xiiij s. **1527** *Churchw. Acc. St. Giles, Reading* 30 Of Willm A Dene for the stokk of the masse xlˢ.

†**21. a.** A trough; a basin; a stoup, esp. one used for holy water. (See *holy-water stock*, HOLY WATER 2.) *Obs.*

c **1450** *Maitl. Club Misc.* III. 203 Ane crem stok of siluer with ane closour of siluer. **1486** *Bk. St. Albans* b viij b, It behouyth that yowre hawke haue a fedyng stokke in hir mewe. **1500** *Will of Odingsellis* (Somerset Ho.), Holy Water stoke. **1554** in Fuller *Hist. Waltham Abbey* (1655) 17 A Stock of brass for the Holy-water. **1591** G. FLETCHER *Russe Commw.* (Hakl. Soc.) 135 They do not onely hallow their holie water stockes and tubbes ful of water, but all the rivers of the countrey once every yeere.

b. (See quot. 1877.)

1872 *Shipley's Gloss. Eccl. Terms* 334 Oil Box... Also called Oil Stock. **1877** F. G. LEE *Gloss. Liturg. & Eccl. Terms* 384 *Stock*... A vessel containing oils blessed for use in the Christian sacraments is so called in ordinary parlance.

22. (More fully *fulling-stock*, FULLING *vbl. sb.*) In a fulling-mill: Originally, the wooden trough or box in which the cloth is placed to be beaten by the 'faller' or the mallet; hence, this receptacle together with the 'faller'. In modern use, *stock* is often taken to denote the 'faller' or mallet itself.

1377 LANGL. *P. Pl.* B. xv. 445 Cloth.. is nouȝt comly to were, Tyl it is fulled vnder fote or in fullyng stokkes. **1506–7** *Durham Acc. Rolls* (Surtees) 252 Pro factura de lez stoke 13*s.* 4*d.* **1674** PETTY *Discourse Roy. Soc.* 64 The same is true of water gushing out upon the floats of under-shot Mills; as may be seen in the Stampers of Paper-Mills, the Stocks of Fulling-Mills [etc.]. **1677** YARRANTON *Eng. Improv.* 109 Our Fulling-Mills that we now have, our Fallers are taken up a great height, and so fall down into the Stock upon the Cloth. *Ibid.*, The Mills that go by Wind, the Fallers, or Feet, fall down perpendicular into the Stock, through a square hole, where the Cloth is, and so attracts no Wind, nor can any Air get into the Stock or Chest where the Cloth is. **1844** G. DODD *Textile Manuf.* iii. 103 The 'fulling-stocks',.. are hollow receptacles in which an enormous oaken hammer or stock vibrates up and down, each stock being kept in motion by machinery connected with a steam-engine. **1879** *Cassell's Techn. Educ.* IV. 342 By steeping the cloth in alkaline liquor, and beating it in the fulling stocks.

23. *Tanning.* (See quot. 1885.)

1882 PATON in *Encycl. Brit.* XIV. 383/2 The softening of these materials is helped and rendered thorough by working them for some time in the stocks after they have been well soaked. **1885** H. R. PROCTER *Tanning* 136 The 'stocks,'.. consist of a wooden or metallic box, of peculiar shape, wherein work 2 very heavy hammers, raised alternately by pins in a wheel, and let fall upon the hides, which they force up against the side of the box with a sort of kneading action.

IV. The more massive portion of an instrument or weapon; usually, the body or handle, to which the working part is attached.

24. a. The heavy cross-bar (originally wooden) of an anchor.

1346 *Exch. Acc.* 25/7 Pro ij hankerstokkes duorum ancor' ejusdem navis. **1407** *MS. Acc. Exch. K.R.* 44/11 (1) m. 3 In duobus ancrestokes inde faciendis. **1485** *Cely Papers* (Camden) 185 Item pd by me for iij hanker stolkes.. xv d. **1497** *Acc. Ld. High Treas. Scot.* I. 379 Item, for thre geestis to be stokkis to ankyrris, and other grath to the schippis, —s. **1615** E. S. *Britain's Buss* in Arber *Eng. Garner* III. 628 And so the four anchors, and their four stocks will come to £18 0 0. **1688** HOLME *Armoury* III. xv. (Roxb.) 29/1 The Anchor stock, is the peece of tymber fitly wrought and fastned at the nutts, below the eye, crossing the flookes. **1748** *Anson's Voy.* III. vi. 345 To fix two.. anchors into one stock. **1825** H. B. GASCOIGNE *Path Nav. Fame* 50 The circling Capstan merrily runs round, Until the Stock a proper height is found. **1839** URE *Dict. Arts* 45 The stock of the anchor is made of oak. **1867** SMYTH *Sailor's Word-bk.* 657.

b. Naut. phrase, *stock and fluke*.

1825 COBBETT *Rur. Rides* 9 Nov. (1885) II. 5 The new owner of the estate.. bought it 'stock and fluke' as the sailors call it; that is to say, that he bought movables and the whole. **1867** SMYTH *Sailor's Word-bk.*, *Stock and Fluke*, the whole of anything.

25. The block of wood from which a bell is hung.

1474–5 in Swayne *Churchw. Acc. Sarum* (1896) 20 It' in tymber for the stokke and uphongyng of the same [bell] xxij d. **1526–7** *Rec. St. Mary at Hill* (1905) 340 For mendyng of the Stokke of the Saunctus bell iiij d. **1706** in J. Watson *Jedburgh Abbey* (1894) 91 [To see if the bells] be sound in their hanging upon the stocks. **1871** WIGRAM *Change Ringing Disentangled* 1 He will see that it [the bell] is fastened to the under-side of a block of wood, called the 'stock'. **1906** RAVEN *Bells* 291 The bells are rung from the stock, without wheel or rope.

26. The 'hub' of a wheel.

1585 HIGINS *Junius' Nomencl.* 268/1 *Modiolus rotæ*,.. the stocke or naue wherein the spokes be fastened. **1876** VOYLE & STEVENSON *Milit. Dict.* 409/2 *Stock*, the nave of a wooden wheel. **1879** *Cassell's Techn. Educ.* IV. 206/1 The stock or hub.. should be in growth as near as possible the size required.

†**27.** = SADDLE-TREE. *Obs.*

1497 *Acc. Ld. High Treas. Scot.* I. 372 Item, agane ȝule, to turs our the Month, for ane stok of ane sadil. **1553** *Ibid.* X. 175 Item,.. for making of the stok and sadill heirto.

28. a. The wooden portion of a musket or fowling-piece; the handle of a pistol.

1541 *Act 33 Hen. VIII*, c. 6 §2 Any handgune.. shalbe in the stock and gonne of the lenghe of one hole Yarde. **1591** GARRARD *Art of Warre* 10 Raising up the crooked end of the stocke to his breast. **1641** J. LANGTON in *Lismore Papers* Ser. II. (1888) V. 8 Our men.. knocked some of them in the heade with the stocks of theire peeces. **1664** EVELYN *Sylva* viii. §4. (1679) 50 Walnut.. is of singular account.. with the Gunsmith for Stocks. **1719** DE FOE *Crusoe* I. (Globe) 261 The Captain.. knock'd him down with the Stock of his Musket. **1741** *Compl. Family-Piece* II. i. 320 As for Stocks, Walnut-Tree or Ash are very good for Use. **1830** *Hobart Town Almanack* 115 My trusty Manton, which falling under his right side,.. was broken in the handsome stock. **1860** *All Yr. Round* No. 71. 500 The stock is divided into the nose-cap, the upper, middle, and lower bands, the swell [etc.]. **1879** *Martini-Henry Rifle Exerc.* 42 Grasping the stock with the left hand.

b. Phrase, *stock, lock, and barrel* (also *lock, stock, and barrel*: see LOCK *sb.*² 5): the whole of a thing; also *advb.*, every whit, entirely.

1817 W. SCOTT *Let.* 29 Oct. (1933) V. 4 Like the Highlandman's gun, she wants stock, lock, and barrel, to put her into repair. **1830** GALT *Lawrie T.* II. viii. (1849) 66 Even the capital likewise—stock, lock, and barrel, all went. **1868** E. YATES *Rocks Ahead* III. iii, 'Cut the whole concern, stock, lock and barrel', said his lordship. **1905** *Times* 7 July 10/3 [Sir George White said:] He was not a Scotsman; he was.. lock, stock, and barrel an Irishman.

29. The handle (of a whip, fishing-rod, etc.).

1695 *Lond. Gaz.* No. 3044/4 All sorts of Whips, the Stocks of the best Greenland Whalebone. **1787** T. BEST *Angling* (ed. 2) 9 The best manner of making... Rods. The best time to provide stocks is in the winter solstice. **1882** STEVENSON *New Arab. Nts.* (1912) 321 The stock of a lance even rattled along the outer surface of the door.

30. The attachment of a seal.

1711 *Lond. Gaz.* No. 4815/4 Two Seals with Gold Stocks.

31. The part of a plough to which the share is attached.

1578 *Knaresb. Wills* (Surtees) I. 133 One new stocke and two plow cloutes, [etc.]. **1733** W. ELLIS *Chiltern & Vale Farm.* 318 Three Holes in the upper part of the Stock.

32. (More explicitly ***bit-stock***.) A carpenter's boring tool: = BRACE *sb.*² 6.

1794 *Rigging & Seamanship* I. 152 *Stock.* A wooden instrument to bore holes with, by fixing a bit in the lower end, and a pin with a round head in the other end. **1812** P. NICHOLSON *Mech. Exerc.* 126 Stock and Bits. **1858** SIMMONDS *Dict. Trade*, *Stock and bit*, an instrument for boring wood, used by carpenters; a centre-bit.

33. An adjustable wrench for holding screw-cutting dies.

1862 *Catal. Internat. Exhib., Brit.* II. No. 6139, Wrought-iron welded tubes; stocks, taps, and dies. **1902** P. MARSHALL *Metal Working Tools* 61 The die which cuts the thread is made in two halves, and is placed in a 'stock,' or holder, fitted with an adjusting screw... A set of stocks and dies consists of one stock with a series of interchangeable dies to cut threads of different sizes.

34. The shorter and thicker of the two pieces composing a **T**-square or an **L**-square.

1815 J. SMITH *Panorama Sci. & Art* II. 699 A thin flat ruler called the blade, let perpendicularly into the middle of another piece called the stock... The blade being laid on the paper, and the stock brought up close to the edge of the board, it is very readily used in ruling. **1857** W. BINNS *Elem. Orthogr. Projection* i. (1862) 6 Place the stock of the **T** square against the left hand side of the drawing-board. **1902** P. MARSHALL *Metal Working Tools* 15 This of course can only be the case when the blade and the stock have their respective inner and outer surfaces perfectly parallel.

35. In a plane, the block in which the plane-iron is fitted. †Also, the block carrying the axe of a 'maiden' or beheading instrument.

1639 in J. J. Cartwright *Chapters Hist. Yorks.* (1872) 339 They let runne the stock wth ye hatchet in. **1815** J. SMITH *Panorama Sci. & Art* I. 107 The block of wood in which the blade or Chisel of a plane is fixed, is called the stock.

36. The head of a brush (in which the bristles are inserted). Also, the wooden head of a wool-card.

1835 URE *Philos. Manuf.* 145 [The two rows of teeth] are fixed into a wooden stock or head *c*, which.. has a handle *d* fixed into it. **1837** WHITTOCK *Bk. Trades* (1842) 84 (Brush-maker), The wood, or 'stock', thus shaped has afterwards a number of small holes drilled through it at regular distances.

37. The wooden case of a lock.

1833 LOUDON *Encycl. Archit.* §84 And.. eight-inch fine plate stock locks (locks with a wooden back, or stock).

38. *Flax-dressing.* One of the beaters in a scutching-mill. (Cf. 22).

1776 YOUNG *Tour Irel.* (1780) I. 313 Two beetling cylinders,.. a pair of stocks, a washing wheel. **1860** *Ure's Dict. Arts* II. 234 Short arms, to which are nailed the stocks, which are parallelogram shaped blades of hard wood, with the edges partially sharpened.

V. Concrete senses of uncertain or mixed origin.

†**39.** A mouse-trap. [Cf. MOUSE-*stock* and Norw. *stok* trap (for birds).] *Obs.*

c **1175** *Lamb. Hom.* 53 þurh þe sweote smel of þe chese, he bicherreð monie mus to þe stoke.

40. A stocking. Now only *dial.* See NETHERSTOCK, UPPER STOCK.

The ***upper stock*** was the upper and wider part, and the ***nether stock*** the lower part, of the hose. Without the defining word, *stock* denoted the NETHERSTOCK or stocking.

1456–7 in *Fabric Rolls York Minster* (Surtees) 208 Meam subtuniculam de harden cloth, cum stokkes de correo. **1530** *Privy Purse Exp. Hen. VIII* (1827) 94 Euery one of them ij payer of hosen and ij payer of stockis. **1546** *Acc. Ld. High Treas. Scot.* IX. 27 Tua elnis fyne purpure welwote to be ane pair of stokes of hois to the said James.. viij li. **1564** *Reg. Privy Council Scot.* I. 308 Ane pair of almany stokkis of blak sating, drawin out with taffeteis. **1577–87** HOOKER *Chron. Irel.* 89/2 in *Holinshed*, He hit vpon the letter, bare it awaie in the heele of his stocke. *a* **1592** GREENE *Vision* Wks. (Grosart) XII. 209 His legs were small, Hosd within a stock of red. **1596** SHAKS. *Tam. Shr.* III. ii. 67 With a linnen stock on one leg, and a kersey boot-hose on the other. **1612** DRAYTON *Poly-olb.* XVI. 350 Before the costly Coach, and silken stock came in. **1876** *Mid-Yorksh. Gloss.* 137 Now then, I am ready for going—stock, shoes, and gaiter.

41. A swarm of bees.

[Cf. Du. *stok*, G. *stock*, a hive; but connexion is doubtful on account of the difference in sense. Cf. however quot. 1675, where the word appears to have the Du. sense.]

1568 *MS. Acc. St. John's Hosp., Canterb.*, There is a swarme found by Wylson and a seruante.. seruaunt to haue the fyrste swarme and Wilson the next and so the stocke remayne to the house. **1577** GOOGE *Heresbach's Husb.* IV. 177b, You may soone learne where theyr [*sc.* bees'] stockes [*L. examina*] be. **1649** OGILBY *Virg. Georg.* II. (1684) 89 In rugged Bark the Bees conceal their Stocks [L. *examina*]. **1675** GEDDE *New Discov. Bee-houses* 30 A stock full of Bees and Honey. **1679** M. RUSDEN *Further Discov. Bees* 68 A swarm in May, or June, is called a Stock at Michaelmas. **1793** *Trans. Soc. Arts* V. 287 The greatest number of Stocks of Bees, not fewer than thirty. **1877** A. I. ROOT *ABC Bee Culture* 158/1 Our pure Italian stocks could have been opened, and their queens removed, scarcely disturbing the cluster. **1930** W. HERROD-HEMPSALL *Bee-Keeping* I. vi. 315 A 'Swarm' is a cluster of bees and their queen only; a 'Colony' consists of the bees and queen living on combs containing brood.. and food; a 'Stock' includes the latter together with the home in which the bees are residing. **1980** R. J. & W. E. HOWE *Practical Beekeeping* vi. 49 When a stock of ten frames is broken up into a number of nuclei, the flying bees from these nuclei will return to their old stand.

42. The portion of a tally which was given to the person making a payment to the Exchequer.

The counterpart kept in the Exchequer was called the *foil* or *counterstock*. In Anglo-L. the terms were *stipes* and *folium*. Cf. F. *souche* (lit. tree-trunk), the longer of the two portions of a tally, hence also the counterfoils in a register or cheque-book.

a **1601** SIR T. FANSHAWE *Pract. Exch.* (1658) 98 The joyners of the tallies.. do see if the stock and the file do agree in hand, letter, and joyning. **1642** C. VERNON *Consid. Exch.* 44 The said stocke is delivered to the party that paid the money for his discharge, and the foile is cast into the Chamberlaines chest. **1671** E. CHAMBERLAYNE *Pres. St. Eng.* II. (ed. 5) 101 The Counterfoyles of the Talleys.. so exactly ranged.. that they may be found out, to be joyned with their respective Stock or Tally. **1714** [BP. ATTERBURY] *Eng. Advice to Freeholders* 4 Boroughs are rated on Royal Exchange, like Stocks and Tallies.

43. [Short for STOCK-GILLYFLOWER.] **a.** Any plant of the cruciferous genus *Matthiola*. **b.** ***Virginian stock***: the cruciferous plant *Malcolmia maritima*, having flowers somewhat resembling those of the stock-gillyflower.

1664 in *Verney Mem.* (1907) II. 208 To smell the sucklins and the stocks and to see the new trees grow. **1728–46** THOMSON *Spring* 533 The.. lavish stock that scents the garden round. **1760** J. LEE *Introd. Bot.* App. 328 Stock, Virginian, *Hesperis*. **1796** C. MARSHALL *Gardening* xix. (1813) 347 The French stock is very floriferous, and most apt to come double. **1844** LADY G. FULLERTON *Ellen Middleton* (1854) III. xx. 49 The delicate lilac flowers of the Virginian Stock. **1866** M. ARNOLD *Thyrsis* vii, And stocks in fragrant blow. **1894** BRIDGES *Garden Sept.* Poems (1912) 305 Stocks Of courtly purple, and aromatic phlox. **1908** R. BAGOT *A. Cuthbert* xix. 237 The sweet night-flowering stock.

44. a. A kind of stiff close-fitting neckcloth, formerly worn by men generally, now only in the army.

In the first quot. app. the collar-band of a shirt.

a **1700** EVELYN *Diary* June 1645, They [the Venetian nobility] also weare their collar open to shew the diamond button of the stock of their shirt. **1731** *Gentl. Mag.* I. 454 He lay in his Stock, which was so tight about his Neck, that it near strangled him. **1742** *Whyte's Poems* in Fairholt *Costume* (1860) 591 The stock with buckle made of plate Has put the cravat out of date. **1753** *Lond. Mag.* Oct. 480/2 Let the stock be well plaited, in fanciful forms. **1755** JOHNSON, *Stock*, something made of linen; a cravat; a close neckcloth. **1764** *Boston Even. Post* in Alice M. Earle *Costume Col. Times* (1894) 169 Newest fashion'd plaited Stocks. **1781** COWPER *Let. to Unwin* 23 May, My neckcloths being all worn out, I intend to wear stocks. In that case, I shall be obliged to you if you will buy me a handsome stock-buckle. **1802** C. JAMES *Milit. Dict.*, *Stock*, a part of an officer's dress which consists generally of black silk or velvet, and is worn round the neck... The soldier's stock is of black ribbed leather... Red stocks were formerly worn in the guards. **1806** SIR R. WILSON *Jrnl.* 11 Feb. *Life* (1862) I. 307 The issue of an order this morning for every officer in the garrison [of Cape Town] to wear black leather stocks! **1818** SCOTT *Rob Roy* i, He had the same.. suit of light brown clothes,.. the same stock, with its silver buckle. **1825** SIR H. COCKBURN *Memor.* ii. 131 The disclosure of the long neck by the narrow bit of muslin stock. **1837** DICKENS *Pickw.* ii, An old stock, without a vestige of shirt collar, ornamented his neck. **1840** J. P. KENNEDY *Quodlibet* x. (1860) 137 His shirt collar was turned down over a narrow horse-hair stock. **1868** *Queen's Regul. Army* §604*g*, The wearing of Stocks may be dispensed with on the line of March. **1892** KIPLING *Barrack-room Ballads, Cells* 16 But I fell away with the Corp'ral's stock, and the best of the Corp'ral's shirt.

b. An article of clerical attire, consisting of a piece of black silk or stuff (worn on the chest and secured by a band round the neck) over which the linen collar is fastened.

1883 *Offic. Yearbk. Ch. Eng.* p. iv. (Advt.), Clerical Collars and Stocks... Stuff Stocks 3/6; Silk do., 5/-; Stock Bands 5/6 per dozen.

45. The udder of a cow. Now *dial.*

1608 TOPSELL *Serpents* 218 Afterward that Cowes vdder or stocke dryeth vppe, and neuer more yeeldeth any milke. *Mod.* (Kent), This cow has a very large stock but I don't know that she'll give over-much milk.

46. A rabbit-burrow. Now *dial.* Cf. STOP *sb.*

1741 *Compl. Family-Piece* II. i. 303 The Bucks will kill their young ones, if they can come at them; and therefore Nature hath so decreed it, that the Does prevent them by stopping or covering their Stocks or Nests with Earth or Gravel. **1876** *Surrey Gloss.* **1883** *Hampsh. Gloss.*

VI. A fund, store.

The senses grouped under this head are not found in the other Teut. languages except by adoption from English. Their origin is obscure, and possibly several different lines of development may have blended. Thus the application of the word to a trader's capital may partly involve the notion of a trunk or stem (branch I) from which the gains are an outgrowth, and partly that of 'fixed basis' or 'foundation' (branch II): cf. FUND. Sense 47 may be derived immediately from that of 'money-box', and have given rise to uses coincident with senses of different origin. The application to cattle is primarily a specific use of the sense 'store', but the notion of 'race' or 'breed' (sense 3) has had some share in its development.

†**47.** A sum of money set apart to provide for certain expenses; a fund. *Obs.*

1463 *Bury Wills* (Camden) 17 A stoke to fynde yerly ij taperis lyght. **1547–8** in E. Green *Somerset Chantries* (1888) 10 Redy money gyven by Robte Holcombe to remayne in stocke to the saide use [*sc.* lights]. **1548** in Hudson & Tingey *Rec. Norwich* (1910) II. 126 All guylde stockis whatsoeuer their be withyn this citie shalbe employde towardes the fyndyng feyeng of the rever of the same citie. *c* **1550** *Yorksh. Chantry Surv.* (Surtees) II. 478 There is a stoke of xxij *s.* yeven to the finding of a light in the said chapell. **1553** *Inv.* in *Ann. Dioc. Lichf.* (1863) 7, xxj s. which remayned as a stoke to finde tapers in the churche. **1589** NASHE *Martin Marprelate* Wks. (Grosart) I. 80 That reuerend Elder of your Church, who being credited with the stocke of the poore,..was compelled to keepe it to himselfe, because [etc.]. **1638** R. BAKER tr. *Balzac's Lett.* (vol. III.) 156, I feare mee, the Stocke that was appoynted for paying of me, will goe some other way. **1645** in Arber *Transcr. Stationers' Reg.* (1875) I. 590 The Committee..resolued upon the Companies sudden setting upon the printing the Bible by a new Stock. **1663** GERBIER *Counsel* b 3, Venturing a stock to fetch *Aurum Horizontale* from the East Indies. **1676** EARL ESSEX in *Essex Papers* (Camden) 55 There will be a surplus of near 3000 l, [*MS.* 3000[d]] which may be kept in stock for any contingency. **1690** *Andros Tracts* II. 42 To make a Voluntary Subscription for a stock to bear the Charges of a Triall at Law. **1718** HICKES & NELSON *J. Kettlewell* II. xxv. 127 He set aside for a standing Stock..One Hundred Pound. [**1881** C. R. RIVINGTON *Rec. Stationers' Co.* 18 There were originally five different trading stocks, called respectively the Ballad Stock, the Bible Stock, the Irish Stock, the Latin Stock, and the English Stock.]

†**48. a.** A capital sum to trade with or to invest; capital as distinguished from revenue, or principal as distinguished from interest. *Obs.*

1526 *Pilgr. Perf.* (W. de W. 1531) 28 b, That rychesse he hath gyuen to vs as a stocke to occupy in our dayly exercyse, for the profyte of our owne soules. **1546** J. HEYWOOD *Prov.* II. ix. (1867) 77 How can ye now get thrift, the stocke beyng gone? Which is thonely thing to reise thrift vpon. **1561** AWDELAY *Frat. Vacab.* 8 Some yong Marchant man or other kynde of Occupier, whose friendes hath geuen them a stock of mony to occupy withall. **1573** *New Custom* II. iii. C iij b, The heyre Had substanciall reuenewes, his stocke also was faire. **1581** *Reg. Privy Council Scot.* III. 435 To..redeliver the same [*sc.* gold and silver] cunyeit to the said maister Thomas in prentit money, stok and proffite. **1613** J. WHITE *Two Serm.* (1615) 69 Prisoners, and distressed housholders, yong tradesmen that want stocks: must be thought on. **1614** RALEGH *Hist. World* v. ii. §2. 377 He thinkes that all this is too little for a stock, though it were indeede a good yearlie Income. **1677** YARRANTON *Eng. Improv.* 47 Let each County begin with two thousand Pounds Stock apiece. *Ibid.* 98 The Factors would joyn stock together, and set up our Trade in some other place. **1681–6** J. SCOTT *Chr. Life* (1747) III. 454 A Master coming to take account of his Servants, among whom he had entrusted a Stock of Ten Pounds. **1694** E. PHILLIPS tr. *Milton's Lett. State* 287 Lest he should lose his Ship and Lading, together with his whole principal Stock. *a* **1700** EVELYN *Diary* 13 Aug. 1641, The reson of this store of pictures and their cheapness proceedes from their want of land to employ their stock. **1760** *Cautions & Adv. Officers of Army* 8, I hope you will thoroughly weigh with yourself whether you are possessed of a sufficient Stock to enable you to discharge your Duty without repining.

fig. **1595** DANIEL *Civ. Wars* II. iv, And on the Hazard of a bad Exchange Have ventur'd all the Stock of Life beside. *a* **1652** J. SMITH *Sel. Disc.* v. iv. (1821) 155 To prepare our own souls more and more to receive of his liberality,..that the stock which he is pleased to impart to us may not lie dead within us. **1665** HOWARD *Ind. Queen* II. i, Why should you waste the Stock of those fair Eyes?

†**b.** ***to spend upon the stock***: to trench on one's capital. *Obs.*

1617 MORYSON *Itin.* I. 199 And lest by spending upon the stocke, my patrimony should be wasted I [etc.]. **1662** GURNALL *Chr. in Arm.* III. 253 That Minister must needs spend upon the stock, that hath no comings in from a constant Trade in his Study.

†**c.** An endowment for a son; a dowry for a daughter. Also *fig. Obs.*

1527 *Lanc. Wills* (Chetham Soc.) I. 17 Item to hyr son Justinean xx[li] to make hym a stokke w[t]. **1581** MULCASTER *Positions* v. (1887) 34 To write and read wel which may be iointly gotten is a prety stocke for a poore boye. **1605** *Lond. Prodigal* v. i. 400 Why this is well, and toward faire Luce's stocke, heres fortie shillings. *c* **1639** COWLEY *Misc., To Ld. Falkland* 32 Whilst we like younger Brothers, get at best But a small stock, and must work out the rest. **1685–6** STILLINGFL. *Serm.* (1698) III. i. 3 Therefore nothing would satisfie him [the young prodigal] unless he were intrusted with the Stock which was intended for him.

†**d.** ***in stock***: possessed of capital. ***out of stock***: without means. (Cf. *in, out of funds.*)

1648 in Willis & Clark *Cambridge* (1886) I. 256 In regard y[t] ye Colledge is wholey out of stocke,..y[e] chest-keepers wer requested to [etc.]. **1671** [S. COLLINS] *Pres. St. Russia* xii. 51 This put the man in stock, whereby he began to drive a Trade.

†**e.** fig. phrase. ***upon the stock of***: on the ground or basis of. *Obs.* Very frequent in Jer. Taylor.

1647 CLARENDON *Hist. Reb.* VI. §229 Which [help] they had no hope to procure but upon the stock of alteration of the government of the Church. **1649** JER. TAYLOR *Great Exemp.* II. vi. 11 He who beleeves upon the onely stock of education, made no election of his faith. *Ibid.* II. vii. 33 Upon the same stocke S. Chrysostome chides the people of his Diocese for walking, and laughing and prating in Churches. **1692** SOUTH *12 Serm.* (1697) I. 275 Few practical Errors in the world are embraced upon the Stock of Conviction, but Inclination. **1821** LAMB *Elia* Ser. I. *My First Play*, The theatre became to me, upon a new stock, the most delightful of recreations.

†**49. a.** An estate or property that produces income; a person's total property. *Obs.*

1552 LATIMER *Serm. St. John Evang.* (1584) 282 It shall not be a diminishing of theyr stockes, but it shall be rather an increase then a diminishing. **1579** SPENSER *Sheph. Cal.* July 192 They han great store and thriftye stockes. **1587** TURBERV. *Trag. Tales* (1837) 22 Whose land and fee descended orderly Unto the Sonne, with store of other stocks. **1646** CRASHAW *Steps* 97 The steward of our growing stocke. *c* **1665** MRS. HUTCHINSON *Mem. Col. Hutchinson* (1885) I. 185 But they, having stocks and families, were not willing to march as far as the army. *a* **1687** PETTY *Pol. Arith.* ii. (1691) 38 If the Stocks of laborious and ingenious Men.. should be diminished by a Tax, and transferred to such as do nothing at all, [etc.]. **1771** BEATTIE *Minstrel* I. xiv, An honest heart was almost all his stock.

†**b.** ***public stock***: the property held for public purposes by a nation, municipality, or community.

1663 PATRICK *Parab. Pilgrim* (1687) 115 A poor Widow, who had cast all her living into the publick stock. **1701** W. WOTTON *Hist. Rome* (*Marcus*) iv. 60 The Public Stock was well near exhausted by Verus's Prodigality. *c* **1710** CELIA FIENNES *Diary* (1888) 92 They have a great publick stock belonging to ye Corporation. **1770** LANGHORNE *Plutarch* (1879) I. 184/2 It appears..that the public stock of the Athenians amounted to 9700 talents.

c. Movable property.

1776 ADAM SMITH *W.N.* v. ii. II 412 The funds or sources, of revenue which may peculiarly belong to the sovereign or commonwealth must consist either in stock or in land.

†**d.** The aggregate wealth of a nation. *Obs.*

1640 PYM in Rushw. *Hist. Coll.* III. (1692) I. 22 By which means the Stock of the Kingdom is diminished. **1719** W. WOOD *Surv. Trade* 154 There is not anything more certain, than that our West-India Trade has greatly enlarged our Stock. **1729** SWIFT *Modest Proposal* 12 The Nation's stock will be thereby encreased fifty thousand pounds *per Annum.* **1796** BURKE *Regic. Peace* ii. (1892) 110 If we look to our stock in the Eastern world, our most valuable and systematick acquisitions are made in that quarter. **1825** M[c]CULLOCH *Pol. Econ.* II. ii. 92 The whole produce of industry belonging to a country is said to form its stock.

†**50. a.** The business capital of a trading firm or company. ***in stock*** (said of a person): in the position of a partner. *Obs.*

c **1600** HENSLOWE *Diary* (1845) 276 A Note of all suche bookes as belong to the Stocke. **1613** TAPP *Pathw. Knowl.* 233 Two Marchants are in Company, B putteth in 200 li more then A, B continueth in stocke 5 moneths, and A 7 moneths ½, they gaine one as much as the other; the question is [etc.]. **1669** W. A[GLIONBY] *Pres. St. United Provinces* 159 Many..put in different summes, which all together made up six hundred thousand pound, the first stock upon which this [Dutch East India] Company has built its prodigious Encrease. **1694** J. HOUGHTON *Collect. Improv. Husb.* No. 122 ⁋4 Lately a Company of Gentlemen have made a Stock for Improvement of Tanning with Birch-Bark... Their Tannery is at Holloway. **1697** *Lond. Gaz.* No. 3303/3 Each Member having Five hundred Pounds in the Stock of the Bank. **1798** HUTTON *Course Math.* (1806) I. 124 They admit K as a third partner, who brought into stock 2800*l.* **1844** H. H. WILSON *Brit. India* I. 494 As the state of the money market rendered it unadvisable to increase the Company's capital stock,..the Court applied to the House for such aid as [etc.].

b. In Bookkeeping by Double Entry, the heading (more fully ***stock account***: see 65.) of the ledger account which summarizes the assets and liabilities of the trader, firm, or company to whom the books belong.

1588 MELLIS *Briefe Instr.* D vij, Then for your Creditor goe to the letter S. and there enter stocke as followeth: Stocke is in folio 2. **1674** J. COLLINS *Introd. Merchants-Acc.* B 3 b, *John Speed* Debitor. January 2 To Stock owing by him..100 l. 00 s. 00 d. *Ibid.* B 4, *Per contra John Speed* Creditor. January 7 By Stock for Three Months rebate [etc.]. **1732** J. CLARK in *B. F. Foster's Double Entry eluc.* (1852) Pref. p. iii, Let it be supposed that the account of Stock is a real person employed to take care of my estate, and to render an account of the improvement he has made of it. **1771** *Encycl. Brit.* I. 589/2 Therefore this accompt is closed, by being debited or credited to or by Stock, for the difference of its sides. *Ibid.* 593/2 Accordingly in your new Journal, the several particulars on the Dr side must all of them be made Drs to Stock. *c* **1789** *Ibid.* (ed. 3) III. 368/2 Thirdly, Accounts of Stock, Profit, and Loss. **1828–32** WEBSTER, *Stock*, in *book-keeping*, the owner or owners of the books. **1852** B. F. FOSTER *Double Entry eluc.* (ed. 5) 4 When the assets exceed the debts, Stock or the proprietor is a creditor for the surplus, or, in the event of insolvency debtor for the deficiency.

†**51.** Money, or a sum of money, invested by a person in a partnership or commercial company. *Obs.*

c **1645** HOWELL *Lett.* (1650) II. 12 By reason of the generality of commerce,—the banks, adventures, the common shares and stocks which most have in the Indian and other companies,—the wealth doth diffuse it self here in a strange kind of equality. **1647** CLARENDON *Hist. Reb.* IV. §248 They [the Commons] were no way guilty of the troubles, the fears, and public dangers, which made men withdraw their stocks, and keep their money by them. **1685** *Caldwell Papers* (Maitl. Club) I. 146 The East India Companie..had very little advantage.. which he had reason to know, because he himselfe had a stock in it.

fig. **1686** GOAD *Celest. Bodies* III. ii. 434 When I consider that I do hereby advance a Stock towards the Discovery of the Cause, whether Celestial or no, I shall find some Mitigation of Censure. **1710** STEELE *Tatler* No. 225 ⁋2 All ..Deviations from the Design of pleasing each other when we meet, are derived from Interlopers in Society, who want Capacity to put in a Stock among regular Companions.

52. a. The subscribed capital of a trading company, or the public debt of a nation, municipal corporation, or the like, regarded as transferable property held by the subscribers or creditors, and subject to fluctuations in market value. Also, in particularized sense, a kind of stock, a particular fund in which money may be invested.

In expressions like *to buy or sell stocks*, the word may be partly an application of sense 42, 'tally'. Cf. quot. 1714 under that sense.

In modern British use the application of the word is narrowed; the subscribed capital of a public company is called *shares* when it is divided into portions of uniform amount, and *stock* when any desired amount may be bought or sold. In British use, also, when there is no specific indication, *stock* is usually taken to refer to those portions of the National Debt, the principal of which is not repayable, the government being pledged only to the payment of interest in perpetuity.

a **1692** POLLEXFEN *Disc. Trade* (1697) A 4 b, Whether any profit can arise to the Nation by the advance of Stocks. **1708** SWIFT *Abol. Chr.* Misc. (1711) 181 The Bank, and East-India Stock, may fall at least One *per Cent.* **1714** MACKY *Journ. Eng.* I. ix. 113 You will see Fellows, in shabby Cloaths, Selling Ten or Twelve Thousand Pounds in Stock, though perhaps he mayn't be worth at the same time Ten Shillings. *a* **1763** W. KING *Pol. & Lit. Anecd.* (1819) 105 Sir William..had a fair estate in land, a large sum of money in the stocks, and [etc.]. **1777** SHERIDAN *Sch. Scand.* III. i, He is forced to sell stock at a great loss. **1781** D. HARTLEY *Consid. Renewal Bank Charter* 18 One hundred pounds of Bank stock is now worth about 110 *l.* **1784** COWPER *Task* IV. 16 The fall of stocks. **1842** *Penny Cycl.* XXIII. 71/2 *Stocks*, a term applied to the various 'Funds' which constitute the national debt. **1845** M[c]CULLOCH *Taxation* III. ii. (1852) 450 Though it be true..that four and five per cent. stocks have always borne a lower relative value in the market than three per cent. stock, it is not true that [etc.]. **1889** *Act 52 & 53 Vict.* c. 32 §9 The expression 'stock' shall include fully paid-up shares. **1898** W. J. GREENWOOD *Business Pract.* 42 *Stock*, Capital in a lump sum divisible into unequal amounts, large or small, to suit investors, instead of in shares of fixed or equal instalments. English Government Consols are of this kind; also the stocks of some railway companies. **1913** *Times* 9 Aug. 17/6 Furness stock did not move on the announcement of an interim dividend at the rate of 2 per cent.

b. fig. phrase (colloq. or slang). ***to take*** (***large*** etc.) ***stock in*** (rarely ***of***): to be interested in, attach importance to, give credence to.

1870 'MARK TWAIN' in *Galaxy* Oct. 575/1 The 'chance' theory..is..calculated to inflict..pecuniary loss upon any community that takes stock in it. **1878** *Masque of Poets* 216 All which I do most potently believe, Taking large stock in Natural Selection. **1885** *Homiletic Rev.* Aug. 134 Educated, and I believe scientific men, took stock in it [Blue Glass theory of cure]. **1891** BRET HARTE *First Family Tasajara* v, I never took stock of that story. **1902** *Daily Chron.* 1 Apr. 6/3 There are many tales of the manifestation of natural gas in Sussex, which I do not take much stock in.

c. *fig.* Reputation, esteem, credit.

1930 *Times Lit. Suppl.* 17 Apr. 334/4 He found British stock very high in North Germany. **1942** *R.A.F. Jrnl.* 27 June (recto rear cover), The stock of the R.A.F. is high in the Soviet. **1955** *Times* 24 June 10/2 General Perón's stock still seemed to be rising to-day as the country gradually returned to normal conditions. **1979** A. BOYLE *Climate of Treason* viii. 237 This minor triumph sent up the personal stock of Philby.

53. a. A collective term for the implements (*dead stock*) and the animals (*live stock*) employed in the working of a farm, an industrial establishment, etc. See also ROLLING STOCK.

1519 *N.C. Wills* (Surtees 1908) I. 106 That my sonne.. have my ferme of Lenwyke..with the stocke theruppon. *a* **1676** HALE *Prim. Orig. Man.* (1677) 214 The Stock being exhausted one Year, left little for the supply of Tillage, Husbandry, or Increase for the next. **1788** PRIESTLEY *Lect. Hist.* v. xliv. 324 Cattle..bear a much lower price than corn, which requires more art, labour, and stock to raise it. **1826** *Art of Brewing* (ed. 2) 140 The costs of rents, of taxes, of agricultural stock, and of labourers' wages, are much less now than heretofore in our memory they have been. **1836** [MRS. TRAILL] *Backwoods of Canada* 26 Live and dead stock that go or are taken on board. **1841** W. SPALDING *Italy & Ital. Isl.* III. 246 The tenant was to find his own stock and tools. **1851** GREENWELL *Coal-Trade Terms, Northumb. & Durh.* 52 Colliery stock comprises the establishment of engines, waggons, horses, and materials of every description requisite to carry on a colliery. **1863** H. COX *Instit.* III. v. 658 Inspectors, who report on the sufficiency of the works and stocks of railways.

†**b.** Scots Law. ***stock and teind***: the gross produce of a farm, fishery, etc., without deduction of the tithe. *Obs.*

1574 in *Reg. Mag. Sig. Scot.* 1586, 367/2 Que salina esset libera a decimis, eo quod decime nunquam solite sunt separari, sed una *lie stok* et *teind* intromissa sunt. **1588** *Reg. Privy Council Scot.* IV. 280 Baith stok and teind thairof. [**1651** in Agnew *Hered. Sheriffs Galloway* (1893) II. 73 Salcharie pays in stock and teind thretty bolls victual, 300 marks money.]

c. = STOCK-CAR 2. *U.S.*

1951 *Sun* (Baltimore) 11 Oct. B24/1 The Philadelphia district will be well represented when the 100-mile National Championship, for sportsman stocks, gets the green flag at the Langhorne Speedway, Sunday. **1979** *Arizona Daily Star* 1 Apr. C12/5 Tucson Dragway will run its weekly racing program today, with the junior pro stocks..topping the racing.

54. *spec.* = LIVE STOCK; the animals on a farm; also, a collective term for horses, cattle, and sheep bred for use or profit.

1523–34 FITZHERB. *Husb.* 39 It is conuenient, that he rere two oxe calues, and two cowe calues at the least, to vpholde his stocke. **1608** ROWLANDS *Humors Looking Glasse* (1872) 15 This poore man had a Cow twas all his stocke. **1649** MILTON *Eikon.* 220 The people he accounts his Heard, his Cattell, the Stock upon his ground. **1660** F. BROOKE tr. *Le Blanc's Trav.* 348 They keep stocks of tame Deer. **1744** M. BISHOP *Life & Adv.* 4, I frequently rode out with him in a Morning to look at his Stock. **1796** W. H. MARSHALL *Yorksh.* (ed. 2) II. 347 *Stock*; livestock. **1801** *Farmer's Mag.*

Apr. 228 Drovers are now buying lean stock briskly at good prices. **1818** SCOTT *Hrt. Midl.* xliv, The proofs he had given of his skill in managing stock. **1851** H. STEPHENS *Bk. Farm* §4065 (1855) II. 240/1 Salted hay is much relished by all kinds of stock. **1890** 'R. BOLDREWOOD' *Col. Reformer* ix, But few stock were visible on the plain.

b. Applied to slaves.

1828–32 WEBSTER, *Stock*, in the West Indies, the slaves of a plantation. **1837** HT. MARTINEAU *Soc. Amer.* II. 41 Her [Virginia's] revenue is chiefly derived from the rearing of slaves as stock for the southern market.

55. a. A quantity (of something specified, whether material or immaterial) accumulated for future use; a store or provision to be drawn upon as occasion requires. Phrase, ***to lay in a stock.***

1638 ROUS *Heav. Acad.* i. 4 Let him gather a stock of them, and lay them up for his use. **1639** FULLER *Holy War* III. xi. (1640) 126 A Prince (as writers report) having a sufficient stock of valour in himself, but little happy in expressing it. *a* **1662** HEYLIN *Laud* (1668) 391 By making this agreement with them he put them into such a stock of Reputation, that [etc.]. **1693** C. DRYDEN *Juvenal's Sat.* VII. 200 But oh, what stock of Patience wants the Fool, Who wastes his Time and Breath in teaching School! **1711** in *10th Rep. Hist. MSS. Comm.* App. I. 142 When he has acquir'd to himself a good stock of reputation perhaps he will not envy ours. **1728** GAY *Let. to Swift* 16 May, I..am in hopes to lay in a stock of health. **1738** *Common Sense* (1739) II. 112 She dyes, alters, and turns her little Stock of Finery into all the Changes which Fancy and Affectation produce in every Brain of Quality. **1750** JOHNSON *Rambler* No. 109 ¶1 You have not yet exhausted the whole stock of human infelicity. **1771** FRANKLIN *Autobiog.* Wks. 1840 I. 18, I wanted a stock of words. **1774** GOLDSM. *Nat. Hist.* II. 133 When..a stock of provisions sufficient to support them the whole way, would be more than they could carry,..they [etc.]. **1790** BURKE *Fr. Rev.* Wks. 1808 V. 273 That stock of general truth, for the branches of which they contended with their blood. **1804** *Med. Jrnl.* XII. 305 It is frequently observed in the inoculated cow-pox. I have seen it..after I had been using matter from the same stock for upwards of three years. **1812** SHELLEY *Devil's Walk* xvi, For he is fat,.. How vast his stock of calf! **1843** [PYCROFT] *Hints to Freshmen* 16 Lay in a stock of Bryant's Regalias and Castle's Sylvas, to acquire condition in your absence. **1855** MACAULAY *Hist. Eng.* xii. III. 228 The stock of cannon balls was almost exhausted. **1907** J. A. HODGES *Elem. Photogr.* (ed. 6) 81 An ever-increasing stock of glass negatives.

†**b.** Complement of population; also, a large number (of persons). *Obs.*

1674 T. LOWER in *Jrnl. Friends Hist. Soc.* (1913) July 144 Seeinge such stockes of Quakers did resort to him. **1690** CHILD *Disc. Trade* (1698) 246 With us, after that with long civil wars the land was half unpeopled, so as till of late years, it came not to its full stock of people again.

c. *Mining.* (See quot.)

1709 T. ROBINSON *Nat. Hist. Westm. & Cumb.* xv. 85 To see that rich Vein, and the Stock of Ore upon the Bank, which was like a little Mountain. **1886** G. P. MERRILL in *Ann. Rep. Smithsonian Inst.* II. (1889) 525 *Stock*, the useful rock taken from a quarry. **1909** *Century Dict.* Suppl., *Stock*, the material removed from a quarry which is of suitable size to be worked into marketable articles.

56. a. The aggregate of goods, or of some specified kind of goods, which a trader has on hand as a provision for the possible future requirements of customers.

1696–7 *Act 8 & 9 Will. III*, c. 7 §10 The several Stockes of Paper Parchment Pastboard or Vellum. **1736** *Gentl. Mag.* VI. 591/2 They all brew great Quantities, which they keep by them as a Stock in Hand. **1814** SCOTT *Let.* in *Lockhart* (1837) III. x. 322 That having resolved, as they are aware, to relinquish publishing, you only wish to avail yourselves of this offer to the extent of helping off some of your stock. **1833** HT. MARTINEAU *Loom & Lugger* II. ii. 21 She might look through her father's stock many times. **1833** J. HOLLAND *Manuf. Metals* II. 112 A large depôt of arms had been established in the Tower; and it was known to some in the trade, that of this warlike stock the government were desirous to dispose. **1848** THACKERAY *Van. Fair* xxxv, The sculptors of those days had stocks of such funereal emblems in hand. **1851** HAWTHORNE *Ho. Sev. Gables* v. (1852) 59 'We must renew our stock, Cousin Hepzibah!' cried the little saleswoman. **1868** M. PATTISON *Academ. Org.* v. 167 We have not cared to keep on hand a larger stock than we could dispose of in the season. **1881** W. S. GILBERT *Foggerty's Fairy* I. (1895) 35 You are in trade?..So am I. Wholesale. What's your stock? *Tal.* Mine's cheese. **1885** *Manch. Exam.* 3 June 5/3 The market is reported to be glutted, and the production has of late been largely going into stock. **1899** *Daily News* 1 Nov. 3/1 The authorities at Enfield say that they are well supplied with these guns out at the Cape, and that they are working for stock.

b. take stock. In commercial use, to make an inventory of the merchandise, furniture, etc. in one's own (*rarely* in another's) possession, recording its quantity and present value. Hence *fig.*, to make a careful estimate of one's position with regard to resources, prospects, or the like. ***to take stock of***: to reckon up, evaluate; also *colloq.* to scrutinize (a person) with suspicion or interest.

1736 *Country Jrnl. or Craftsman* 14 Aug. 1/1 [Innkeeper to Exciseman.] Goodmorrow..Mr. Gage... I hope you have no Information against Me... Did you not take Stock but last Night? **1825** COLERIDGE *Aids Refl.* (1831) 184 How vague and general these [thoughts] are even on objects of Sense, the few who at a mature age have seriously set about the discipline of their faculties, and have honestly *taken stock*, best know by recollection of their own state. **1826** *New Monthly Mag.* XVI. 19 It may therefore be worth while at this commencement of a new year for us to balance accounts with our readers, and, in the trader's phrase, to 'take stock'. **1840** MACAULAY *Ess.*, *Clive* ¶7 The business of the servant of the Company was not, as now, to conduct the judicial, financial, and diplomatic business of a great country, but to take stock [etc.]. **1857** BORROW *Rom. Rye* xlvi, One day, being at a place called the Escurial, I took stock, as the tradesmen say, and found I possessed the sum of eighty dollars won by playing at cards. **1865** *Slang Dict.* 247 To take stock of one, to scrutinize narrowly one whom you have reason to suspect. **1867** W. JOHNSON in Farrar *Ess. Lib. Educ.* (1867) 333 You will find the historian taking stock of human knowledge for the end of the Middle Ages. **1877–81** VOYLE & STEVENSON *Milit. Dict.* Suppl. 36/2 A combatant officer appointed to 'take stock', either at home or abroad, is entitled to receive extra pay of 5*s.* a day. **1883** FROUDE *Short Stud.* IV. II. i. 166 It is, perhaps,..occasionally well to take stock of our mental experience. **1885** MISS BRADDON *Wyllard's Weird* ii, How is it that you who are so sharp could not contrive to spot him when you took stock of the passengers? **1893** *Times* 30 May 9/3 It is always the custom with practical politicians to take stock of what has been done ..and what can be done. **1896** *N. & Q.* Ser. VIII. IX. 158/2 A narrow squint window at the back of one of them enabled its occupant to take stock of any one who might knock at the door of his neighbour.

c. *in stock*: in the possession of the trader.

1618 in J. Charnock *Hist. Mar. Archit.* (1801) II. 237 There will remain in stock at Deptford 738 t. 14 c. 0 q. 9 lb. **1891** *Law Rep., Weekly Notes* 44/1 The defendant had about forty copies of the impression in stock which he desired to sell. **1898** W. J. GREENWOOD *Commerc. Corresp.* (ed. 2) 3, I intend to dispose of the whole of the goods in stock.

d. *Theatr.* A stock company; repertory. Chiefly *U.S.*

1916 *Variety* 27 Oct. 12/1 The Alcazar stock is enjoying satisfactory business. **1933** M. LINCOLN *Oh! Definitely* vii. 73 'He had been getting three pounds a week in stock' but would 'take two-ten for town'. **1937** *Daily Tel.* 14 Aug. 9/1 No money will induce them [*sc.* good actors] to bury themselves in Stratford..under 'stock' conditions. **1962** *Listener* 16 Aug. 242/2 Between her junior and senior years in college..she played summer stock.

57. a. The liquor made by boiling meat (with or without vegetables, etc.) and used as a foundation for soup.

1730 C. CARTER *Compl. Pract. Cook* 1 A good Stock of strong Broth Well made, and good Gravies well drawn off, are very principal Ingredients in the Composing of all Made-Dishes of boil'd Meats. **1747** H. GLASSE *Art of Cookery* ix. 78 An Oyster Soop. Your stock must be made of any Sort of Fish the Place affords. **1764** ELIZ. MOXON *Eng. Housew.* (ed. 9) 119 You must make your stock the day before you use it. **1844** H. STEPHENS *Bk. Farm* II. 169 Its decoction forms an excellent stock for various dishes. **1870** DICKENS *E. Drood* vi, Stock for soup became fragrant in the air of Minor Canon Corner. **1886** *Sat. Rev.* 6 Mar. 328/2 Vatel himself..would not have hesitated to make a stock for his master Condé, or his king Louis the Magnificent, out of cod's-heads.

b. *gen.* The raw material from which anything is made; material. Chiefly with prefixed word as in PAPER-stock, *soap-stock*.

1873 SPON *Workshop Rec.* Ser. I. 350 In its natural state, fat..is always associated with..foreign matters, which must be separated before it can be used as candle stock. **1875** Paper-stock [see PAPER *sb.* 12]. **1882** *Encycl. Brit.* XIV. 384/2 In these the stock is exposed to the strongest tanning liquors. **1924** S. LEICESTER *Pract. Stud. for Paper Manufacturers* v. 116 The mistakes in sizing are some of the most difficult to elucidate... The stock used may be the cause. **1963** R. R. A. HIGHAM *Handbk. Papermaking* ii. 45 Distinct variations occur between one batch of stock and another with regard to treatment, colour, temperature, consistency, retention of additives, etc.

c. Cinematographic film.

1897 C. F. JENKINS *Picture Ribbons* 27 The film is of transparent celluloid, one side of which is coated with a sensitive emulsion, that for the negative being much more rapid than the positive stock. **1909** *Moving Picture World* 3 July 11/2 The non-inflammable film stock is now being issued by so many manufacturers. **1938** *Times* 15 Mar. 12/3 A twelve-minute film on 16 mm. stock, shown privately in Liverpool. *Ibid.*, The technical quality of the film is excellent, super-panchromatic stock giving rich quality to shots which are themselves carefully composed. **1974** C. PRIEST *Your Bk. of Film-Making* i. 23 The film is twice as wide as 8 mm film stock.

58. *Card-playing.* **a.** In certain games, the portion of the pack of cards which is not dealt out, but left on the table to be drawn from according to the rules of the game.

[Cf. Du. *stok*, Norw. *stokk*, in the same sense.]

1584 R. SCOT *Discov. Witchcr.* XIII. xxvii. (1886) 273 Throw upon the Stocke the nether card. **1607** HEYWOOD *Wom. Killed w. Kindn.* (1617) E2b, This Queene I haue more then mine owne, you see. Giue me the stocke. **1674** COTTON *Compl. Gamester* vi. (1680) 65 [Gleek] The Dealer delivers the Cards by four till every one hath twelve, and the rest are laid on the Table, for the Stock, being in number eight. *Ibid.* vii. 69 [L'Ombre] There will remain thirteen Cards in the Stock. **1732** SWIFT *Poems, Beasts' Confess.* 193 He heard there was a club of cheats, Who..Could change the stock, or cog a dye. **1830** HARDIE *Hoyle* 44 (Piquet) *Talon*, or stock, is the eight remaining cards, after twelve are dealt to each person. **1878** H. GIBBS *Ombre* 19 After dealing he places the remaining thirteen cards before him, and they are called the Stock.

b. The set of cards used in a particular game (whether a pack, or one or more incomplete packs).

1584 R. W. *Three Ladies Lond.* II. Aiiij, Nowe all the Cardes in the stock are delte about. **1895** G. J. MANSON *Sporting Dict.*, [In Bezique.] *Stock*, the number of packs of cards corresponding with the number of players, shuffled together and ready to be dealt.

†**c.** = HAND *sb.* 23. *Obs.*

1637 RUTHERFORD *Lett.* (1836) I. 357 That Kirk and Commonwealth are in his hand, like a stock of cards, and that he dealeth the play to the mourners of Zion [etc.]. *c* **1641** CLEVELAND *Smectymnuus* Poems (1677) 39 So many Cards ith' Stock, and yet be bilk'd? **1659** *Shuffling, Cutting & Dealing* 6 Shall I not play? My Lord Protector hath given me a Stock, and I'le pack the Cards with all the Cavalier-Gamesters in the Town.

VII. 59. In imitation of compounds like LEANING-*stock*, WHIPPING-*stock*, where the sb. has the sense 1 b or 5, there have been formed many combinations of *stock* with a preceding vbl. sb., which designate a person as the habitual object of some kind of contemptuous or unpleasant treatment. (There is probably in these formations some notion of sense 1 c, the implication being that the person is treated as if incapable of feeling.) Examples, which appear in this Dictionary as main words or under their first element, are *floating-*, *gauring*, *gazing-*, *jesting-*, *laughing-*, *mocking-*, *pointing-*, *sporting-*, *talking-*, *torturing-stock*; the following quots. contain one or two nonce-words that have not been registered in their alphabetical place.

1545 HEN. VIII *Sp. Parlt.* (1642) A4, Not to dispute, and make Scripture a railing and taunting-stocke against Priests and Preachers. **1580** LYLY *Euphues & his England* (Arb.) 444 Then shall you be like stars to the wise, who are now but staring stockes to the foolish. **1630** B. JONSON *New Inn* I. vi. (1631) C2, Therefore [she] might indifferently be made The courting-stock, for all to practise on.

VIII. Combinations.

60. Similatively (with ref. to sense 1 c), as †*stock-log*; *stock-headed*, *-like* adjs. Also **stock-blind, -dead, -deaf** adjs., as blind (etc.) as a stock. Hence perh. **stock-full** *a. rare*$^{-1}$, chock-full, cramfull. Also STOCK STILL.

[Cf. Du. *stokblind*, G. *stockblind*; G. *stocktaub* stock-deaf; Du. *stokstijf*, G. *stocksteif* stiff as a poker; Du. *stokoud* very old; G. *stockdunkel*, *-finster* pitch-dark.]

1675 WYCHERLEY *Country Wife* II. i. 21 True Lovers are blind, *stockblind. **1802** BEDDOES *Hygeia* I. 32 He was stock-blind; so could not judge of me by my exterior. **1662** J. DAVIES tr. *Olearius' Voy. Ambass.* 136 A corpulent, fat Man..fell down *stock-dead, as soon as he came to the shrine. **1865** TYLOR *Early Hist. Man.* iv. 71 Though he is '*stock-deaf', he has a bodily feeling of music, and different instruments have different effects upon him. **1782** MISS BURNEY *Cecilia* v. xii, I'm sure the garden is so *stock full, that if there was to come many more, I don't know where they could cram 'em. **1904** M. HEWLETT *Queen's Quair* II. vii. 279 That *stock-headed starer out of painted eyes. **1878** BROWNING *Poets Croisic* lxi, Does he stand *stock-like henceforth? **1689** HICKERINGILL *Ceremony-Monger* iii. Wks. 1716 II. 408 [My Ceremony-Monger] is the great *Stock-logg of the Church, that has neither fire nor heat within.

61. In sense 4, as *stock-grower*, †*-head*; †**stock-grafted** *a.*, grafted by means of a slit or cleft in the stock; †**stock-grafting**, cleft-grafting.

1523–34 FITZHERB. *Husb.* §138 Take toughe cleye.. and ley it vppon the stocke-heed. **1707** MORTIMER *Husb.* (1721) II. 265 Medlars may be cleft, or Stock-grafted, on the White Thorn. **1731** MILLER *Gard. Dict.* s.v. *Grafting*, *Cleft Grafting*, which is also call'd *Stock* or *Slit-grafting*. **1842** LOUDON *Suburban Hort.* 562 As practised by the stock-growers in propagating plum and Paradise stocks.

62. In sense 52, as *stock* †*-bill*, *-board*, *-dealer*, *-list*, †*-office*, *-watering*; **stock certificate**, a document issued by the Treasury, entitling the holder to a certain amount of a particular government stock; **stock-indicator, -ticker**, a telegraphic instrument for recording variations in the price of stock; **stock receipt** (see quot.); **stock split** *U.S.*, the division of a stock into an increased number of shares; hence **stock splitting**; cf. *split-up* s.v. SPLIT-. Also STOCK-BROKER, etc.

1760–72 H. BROOKE *Fool of Quality* (1809) IV. 80 [He] produced bank and *stock bills to the amount of..five thousand pounds. **1872** CUYLER *Heart-Life* 123 The reckless gambling operations of *stock-boards or 'the street'. **1863** *Act 26 & 27 Vict.* c. 28 §6 A *Stock Certificate ..shall entitle the Bearer to the Stock therein described. **1902** *Westm. Gaz.* 30 Sept. 10/1 A firm of *stock-dealers. **1891** *Century Dict.*, *Stock-indicator. **1858** SIMMONDS *Dict. Trade*, **Stock-list*, a list published daily or periodically, enumerating the leading stocks dealt in; the prices current; the actual transactions, etc. **1737** J. CHAMBERLAYNE *St. Gt. Brit.* II. (ed. 33) 171 (South Sea office) Chief Clerk of the *Stock-office. **1901** CORDINGLEY *Dict. Stock Exch. Terms* 86 **Stock Receipt*. This is a Receipt, in printed form, filled in by the seller of Consols and other Registered Stocks and given by him to the buyer at the time the transfer is made. **1955** *Times* 6 July 9/3 According to the Associated Press, the directors of General Motors Corporation have to-day recommended a three-for-one *stock split to be voted on by stockholders at a special meeting on September 23. **1967** *N.Y. Times* (Internat. ed.) 11–12 Feb. 9/6 Your first bonus report will be our list of 30 stock split candidates. **1977** *Dædalus* Fall 85 Tests indicate that stock prices quickly adjust to changes in public information (announcements of stock splits, dividend increases, etc.). **1959** *Economist* 28 Feb. 788/1 *Stock splitting (the American equivalent of the British scrip or bonus issue). **1886** *Boston* (Mass.) *Jrnl.* 17 July 2/3 The *Stock Ticker. **1899** *Westm. Gaz.* 20 Apr. 10/2 A narrow strip of paper resembling a stock-ticker tape. **1883** *Nation* (N.Y.) 11 Oct. 307/2 '*Stock-watering' means simply an increase in the number of shares into which the property of a corporation is divided.

63. a. In sense 54, as *stock-agent*, *-auction*, *-breeder*, *-breeding*, *-carrying*, *-dealer*, *-driver*, *-driving*, *-farm*, *-farmer*, *-farming*, *-feed*, *-feeding*, *-food*, *-grower*, *-house*, †*-husbandry*,

-inspector, *-master*, *-minder*, *-owner* *-raiser*, *-raising*, *-ranch*, *-range*, *-rearing*, *-run*, *-sale*, *-station*, *-theft*, *-thief*, *-trader*, *-train*, *-yard*; *stock-proof* adj.; **stock and station** *Austral.* and *N.Z.*, used *attrib.* to designate firms or their employees dealing with farm products and supplies; **stock horse** *Austral.*, a horse trained to carry a stock-rider; **stock-hut** *Austral.*, the hut of a stockman; **stock-rider** *Austral.*, a man employed to ride after cattle on an unfenced station; **stock-riding**, the occupation of a stock-rider; **stock-route** *Austral.*, a right of way for travelling cattle through occupied land; **stock-whip** *Austral.*, a whip for driving cattle; also as *v. trans.*, to beat with a stock-whip. Also STOCK-CAR, STOCKHOLDER, -KEEPER (etc.), STOCKMAN.

1933 *Press* (Christchurch, N.Z.) 9 Sept. 15/7 Dealers and *stock-agents use various terms..to make failing mouthed sheep sound younger. **1977** *Weekly Times* (Melbourne) 19 Jan. 11/3 Barney, the stock agent, was looking him straight in the eye when he said: 'If I were you, Clarence, I'd sell the lot and run some sheep.' **1881** *Adelaide Observer* 22 Oct. 44/1 He was suspecious of all *stock and station salesmen. **1908** in D. J. Gordon *Handbk. S. Austral.* 327 (Advt.), Bagot, Shakes, & Lewis, Limited. Stock and station agents. **1930** L. G. D. ACLAND *Early Canterbury Runs* 1st Ser. ii. 13 Ford and Newton, who were the leading Christchurch Stock and Station Agents. **1965** G. MCINNES *Road to Gundagai* vii. 113 Here were the big mortgage and stock-and-station houses where wool was finally baled and cleaned for export. **1948** W. FAULKNER *Intruder in Dust* (1949) vi. 134 Monday was *stock-auction day at the sales barns behind the Square. **1815** *Sporting Mag.* XLV. 194 Mr. George Flower..Merino *stock-breeder. **1937** R. H. LOWIE *Hist. Ethnological Theory* viii. 114 This yields..the sequence of (a) hunting-gathering; hoe-culture; (c) hoe-culture with *stock-breeding; (d) 'agriculture'. **1957** *Times Lit. Suppl.* 8 Nov. 678/3 Professor Nichols makes a comprehensive review of the genetic basis of modern stockbreeding. **1866** J. MURRAY *Descr. Province Southland* 9 The *stock-carrying capacity of the natural herbage is of course variable. **1960** *Farmer & Stockbreeder* 12 Jan. 78/1 He brought back the idea of loose-housing..and introduced it at Langhill to cater for the additional stock-carrying capacity of the next-door, buildingless farm then being acquired. **1885** *Manch. Exam.* 17 Mar. 5/2 Duties on live meat in Germany fail in protecting *stockdealers. **1851** *Lyttelton* (N.Z.) *Times* 19 Apr., A settlement of whale-fishers and *stock-drivers. **1871** *Republican Rev.* (Albuquerque, New Mexico) 27 May 1/3 M. Maloney.. arrived here on Thursday, being sent ahead to employ stock drivers. **1867** H. PHILLIPS *Jrnl. Rockwood* 29 Sept. 88 (typescript), T.A.P. & I.I. *stock driving. **1874** J. C. McCOY *Hist. Sk. Cattle Trade* 92 [The farm] is allowed to lay awaste, whilst its owner has turned to stock-driving. **1806** *Sydney Gaz.* in O'Hara *Hist. N.S. Wales* (1817) 289 Well adapted either to an arable or *stock farm. **1848** *Senate Rep. 30th U.S. Congr. 1 Sess.* No. 75. 29 Some five hundred head of beef cattle were taken from the government stock farm. **1912** M. NICHOLSON *Hoosier Chron.* 27, I own a stock farm near Lexington. **1768** *Ann. Reg.* 149 The *stock farmers have greatly suffered, as the lambs were much hurt. **1894** *Harper's Mag.* Apr. 676/2 'Crit' Marston, the young blue-grass stock-farmer, is a favorite throughout all that section. **1865** TROLLOPE *Belton Est.* xvi. 183 In *stock-farming the chief thing is not to have too many beasts. **1915** *Edin. Rev.* Jan. 83 The Ana (or Aana) tree..is said to give the best *stock-feed in the whole world. **1960** *Farmer & Stockbreeder* 15 Mar. 113/1, I am growing ten acres each of stockfeed peas and beans. **1970** *Oxford Times* 30 Oct. 14 Demand for stockfeed potatoes would be far greater than usual. **1879** *Cassell's Techn. Educ.* III. 37 Crops used for *stock-feeding. **1894** *Jrnl. R. Agric. Soc.* Dec. 646 A proportion of the produce grown is retained on the farm, as *stock-food or litter. **1876** *Chamb. Jrnl.* 30 Dec. 845/1 The experience of *stock-growers from all sections for the last few years has proved [etc.]. **1846** H. WEEKES in Rutherford & Skinner *New Plymouth Settlement* (1940) I. vi. 124 'Peter' was an excellent *stock-horse, would follow cattle like a dog. **1865** H. KINGSLEY *Hillyars & Burtons* l, An aged stockhorse, which I had bought very cheap. **1808** *Sydney Gaz.* in O'Hara *Hist. N.S. Wales* (1817) 317 To be sold.. with a good dwelling-house, barn, stable, *stock-houses, and a capital stock-yard. **1801** *Farmer's Mag.* Aug. 285 The general run of the soil of this tract..renders it very eligible for what is called the *stock-husbandry. **1828** P. CUNNINGHAM *N.S. Wales* (ed. 3) II. 30 They..paid a visit to a *stock hut inhabited by three freemen, at Putty. **1888** *Century Mag.* Feb. 507/1 At every shipping point..*stock inspectors..jealously examine all the brands on the live animals or on the hides of the slaughtered ones. **1930** L. G. D. ACLAND *Early Canterbury Runs* 1st Ser. iii. 47 He then became Stock Inspector in the North Island, but quarrelled with his superiors. **1948** V. PALMER *Golconda* ii. 15 He might have been a country teacher or a stock-inspector. **1864** *Intell. Observer* Jan. 390 Veterinarians, sheep-breeders, *stock-masters, and others practically acquainted with the diseases of our domesticated animals. **1859** BARTLETT *Dict. Amer.* (ed. 2) 451 **Stock-minder*, one who takes care of cattle on the great prairies. **1865** *Daily Tel.* 18 Oct. 6/4 The Belgian Government has conferred a great boon..on its *stock-owners [by checking a cattle plague]. **1915** *N.Z. Jrnl. Agric.* 20 Feb. 190 If the long shoots of this plant [sc. *Eleagnus*] are interlaced while the hedge is growing it makes a close and excellent *stock-proof fence. **1960** *Farmer & Stockbreeder* 15 Mar. 123/2 The Monmouthshire style of hedging..gives a real stock-proof fence. **1874** RAYMOND *6th Rep. Mines* 314 A part..of the large grant.. on which numerous ranch-men and *stock-raisers are said to have settled. **1868** *Rep. U.S. Commissioner Agric.* (1869) 148 Study of plants, meadows, and *stock-raising. **1876** *Chamb. Jrnl.* 30 Dec. 845/1 Eventually the stock-raising interests will be driven to the northern buffalo grass region. **1871** in S. De Vere *Americanisms* (1872) 129 An *estancia* or *stock-ranch. **1859** BARTLETT *Dict. Amer.* (ed. 2) 451 **Stock-range*, the prairie or plain where cattle range or graze. **1882** *Century Mag.* Aug. 511/1 The hill country is all open as a stock-range. **1915** *Chambers's Jrnl.* Jan. 47/2 A son of his anticipated this kind of *stock-rearing many years ago in Manitoba. **1960** *Farmer & Stockbreeder* 29 Mar. 12/3 An 81-acre Northants stock-rearing and feeding farm has been sold for £9,800. **1862** *Cornhill Mag.* Jan. 31 Broke in by one of my *stock-riders up to fifteen stone. **1908** E. J. BANFIELD *Confessions of Beachcomber* II. iii. 314 A stockrider..in.. flash riding-boots. **1973** *Parade* (Melbourne) Sept. 30/2 The authorities were able to choose exactly the sort of men they wanted from the hundreds of adventurers, prospectors, settlers and stock-riders who offered their services. **1872** *Routledge's Ev. Boy's Ann.* 108/1 The Grant brothers had been doing some very tidy bits of *stock-riding too. **1890** 'R. BOLDREWOOD' *Col. Reformer* xviii, The stock-riding contingent. **1886** P. CLARKE *'New Chum' in Austral.* 197, I saw it on the *stock-route to Bathurst. **1901** M. FRANKLIN *My Brilliant Career* xxxiv. 286 An overgrown old orchard, skirting one of the great stock-routes. **1977** *Meanjin* (Austral.) XXXVI. I. 69 Cattle cross on the stockroutes. **1828** P. CUNNINGHAM *N.S. Wales* (ed. 3) II. 147 You oblige the settler to improve the grant, instead of keeping it as a mere *stock-run. **1948** W. FAULKNER *Intruder in Dust* (1949) vi. 134 *Stock-sale day unlike Sunday was a man's time. **1843** J. BACKHOUSE *Narr. Visit Austral. Colonies* xxiii. 264 Accompanied by the Agricultural Superintendent, we walked to a *stock-station..where three men are placed in charge of some cattle. **1847** A. HARRIS *Settlers & Convicts* xiii. 252 It was..not till noon..that we succeeded in finding the nearest stock-station. **1858** SIMMONDS *Dict. Trade*, *Stock-station*, a district for rearing and herding cattle. **1904** *Transvaal Agric. Jrnl.* July 573 *Stock theft has always been a great source of worry and trouble to the farming community of this country. **1955** L. G. GREEN *Karoo* xvii. 199 Crime in the karoo usually means stock-theft. *Ibid.* ix. 112 The hunt for a *stock-thief who fled into the poort. **1958** *Johannesburg Sunday Times* 28 Sept. 14/9 A quiet-spoken, slightly-built man has become the terror of stock-thieves in the Evaton and Losberg areas. **1942** W. FAULKNER *Go Down, Moses* 248 A back-street *stock-trader's boarding house. **1948** —— *Intruder in Dust* (1949) vi. 134 The men with their stock-trader walking-sticks not even stopping. **1859** BARTLETT *Dict. Amer.* (ed. 2) 451 **Stock-train*, a train of railroad cars loaded with cattle. ?**1906** in J. V. Allen *Cowboy Lore* (1971) I. 19 Another train run in to my stock train. **1961** R. P. HOBSON *Rancher takes Wife* xiv. 171 By the time the stock train pulled in..we had a count on the herd. **1852** *Harper's New Monthly Mag.* Dec. 25/1 The Australian 'stockman' is a sort of Europeanized Tartar... His food is beef and 'damper'... In his 'run' the stockman is king: his cattle are his subjects; his saddle is his throne; his sceptre is the *stock-whip. **1853** J. ROCHFORT *Adventures of Surveyor in N.Z.* iv. 42 If the natives had not lent her [*sc.* the mare] to me he would have gone over and stock-whipped them. **1857** W. HOWITT *Tallangetta* I. 100 The stock-whip, with a handle about half a yard long and a thong of three yards long, of plaited bullock-hide, is a terrible instrument in the hands of a practised stockman. **1901** M. FRANKLIN *My Brilliant Career* i. 4 Father came to my rescue, despatching the reptile with his stock-whip. **1936** I. L. IDRIESS *Cattle King* vi. 53 Wrap me in my stock whip and blanket, And bury me deep. **1955** J. CLEARY *Justin Bayard* viii. 111 He tried to hit me, and old Thaddeus stockwhipped him. **1958** R. STOW *To Islands* i. 17 What's the use of holding it against Mr. Heriot that he used to be a handy man with a stockwhip? **1802** *Barrington's Hist. N.S. Wales* x. 373 A young ox was missed from the *stock-yard at Toongabbe. **1858** R. S. SURTEES *Ask Mamma* lxvi. 300 The first result we see of a gentleman farming being the increase of the size of his stock-yard. **1869** *Bradshaw's Railway Man* XXI. 428 *Expended*... Union stock yards Chicago..§100,000. **1911** C. E. W. BEAN *'Dreadnought' of Darling* xv. 145 The wind..piled it uselessly, over every fence and stockyard. **1929** K. S. PRICHARD *Coonardoo* iv. 51 They wandered from the stock-yards to the shade-miah. **1958** L. DURRELL *Mountolive* viii. 162 The mauve-veiled evening voices of Alexandrians uttering stockyard quotations. **1963** *Times* 16 Jan. 6/6 Born in the stockyards district (where he still lives) and where as a 'stockyards cowboy' he once herded cattle from pen to pen. **1978** D. GREIG *Daisy* v. 54 In Chicago we stayed at the Hotel on Lake Michigan, near the famous Stockyards where, as they used to say, the unfortunate animals went in whole at one end and came out the other processed into fifty different products.

b. Indicating an animal that is chosen or kept for breeding purposes, as ***stock carp***, ***dog***, ***mare***, etc. Also ***stock-getter***.

1785 J. WOODFORDE *Diary* 20 Oct. (1926) II. 211 Mr. Townshend..sent me 20 brace and ½ of stock Carp. **1801** *Farmer's Mag.* Apr. 222 The season throughout has been remarkably favourable to stock sheep. **1851-61** MAYHEW *Lond. Labour* III. 15/2 A black tan terrier..which was the greatest stock dog in London of that day. **1854** *Poultry Chron.* II. 404 The purchase of fowls intended for stock-birds should not now be delayed. **1862** *Cornhill Mag.* Jan. 31 A handsome little stock-mare. **1862** H. H. DIXON *Scott & Sebright* iii. 165 Till within the last three years he [a stallion] was a very sure stock-getter. **1886** C. SCOTT *Sheep-Farming* 74 It..is only advisable with some very special stock-ram, whose progeny are valuable. **1891** *Century Dict.*, *Stock-fish*, ..fish adapted or used for stocking rivers, ponds, lakes, etc. **1909** *Westm. Gaz.* 13 Feb. 16/2 Another hundred good stock trout have been placed in the Henley waters. **1909** *Chamb. Jrnl.* Apr. 219/1 It is very difficult to get good stock-ducks of the pure Aylesbury strain.

64. In names of birds: **stock annet**, the common sheldrake, *Tadorna cornuta*; **stock drake** [cf. Da. *stok-*, Norw. *stokk-*, Sw. *stock-and*], **duck**, the mallard or wild duck, *Anas boscas*; **stock eagle**, **-eekle**, etc. [HICKWALL] *dial.*, the green woodpecker; **stock owl**, the eagle owl, *Bubo ignavus*; **stock pigeon** = STOCK-DOVE; **stock whaup**, the curlew, *Numenius arquata*.

1852 MACGILLIVRAY *Brit. Birds* V. 22 *Tadorna Vulpanser*. .. *Stockannet. **1772** FORSTER in *Phil. Trans.* LXII. 419 Mallard Drake... It is called *Stock Drake at Hudson's Bay. **1805** G. BARRY *Hist. Orkney Isl.* 301 The Mallard,.. our *stockduck. **1884** *Upton-on-Severn Gloss.*, **Stock-eekle*, a woodpecker. **1899** A. H. EVANS *Birds* (Camb. Nat. Hist.) 463 With which name [*sc.* 'Log-cocks'] may be compared that of 'Stock-eagle', i.e. 'Stump-eagle', given in the West of England to the Greater Spotted Woodpecker. *a* **1688** J. WALLACE *Descr. Isl. Orkney* (1693) ii. 16 Sometime the *Stock-oul and Bittern have been seen in this Country. **1805** G. BARRY *Hist. Orkney Isl.* 312 The Eagle Owl.., our *katogle* or stock-owl. **1783** LATHAM *Gen. Synopsis Birds* II. II. 604 *Stock Pigeon, *Columba ænas*. **1813** G. LOW *Fauna Orcad.* 80 The larger curlew, called here *Stock-Whap.

65. Miscellaneous special comb.: **stock account** *Book-keeping* (see 50 b); **stock beer**, beer that is stored for ripening before being drunk; **stock-board**, (*a*) the wooden board which forms the bottom of a brick-mould; (*b*) in an organ, the upper board of a soundboard, above the sliders, on which the pipes immediately rest; (*c*) see 62; **stock book**, a book in which an account is kept of goods in stock; also *spec.* a book in which a record is kept of the animals which make up the stock of a farm; †**stock-bow**, a crossbow; **stock-boy**, (*a*) *Austral.*, an Aboriginal employed to look after cattle or other stock; (*b*) *U.S.*, a boy employed by a business firm to look after stock; **stock-brick** [cf. sense 15], a hard solid brick, pressed in the mould; **stock-brush**, a brush with the bristles set in a flat stock or head; †**stock-buckle**, a buckle used to secure the stock or cravat; **stock-building** = STOCK PILING *vbl. sb.*; **stock-company**, (*a*) ? a joint-stock company; (*b*) a company the capital of which is represented by stock; **stock control** (see quot. 1943); **stock cube**, a cube of concentrated, dehydrated meat stock sold for use in making soups, stews, etc.; **stock culture**, an uncontaminated culture of a micro-organism maintained continuously and available as a source of experimental material; †**stockis-dynt** *Sc.* = *stingis-dint* (see STING *sb.*[1] 4); †**stock-drawers**, stockings; **stock-father**, the progenitor of a stock or race; †**stock-fowler**, a kind of cannon or mortar (cf. *stock-gun* and FOWLER 3); **stock-frost** *local*, ground-ice; **stock-gang**, a 'gang' or set of mill-saws arranged to cut a log into boards at one passage through the machine; †**stock-gold** *Theatr.*, 'property' gold; †**stock-gun** (cf. *stock-fowler*); †**stock-honey** (see quot.); †**stock-hose**, hose of stout material worn over thinner hose; †**stock-house**, a prison where offenders were set in the stocks; **stock-ice** *local* = *stock-frost*; **stock knife**, (*a*) a knife for cutting wood, *esp.* one used by a clogger for shaping the soles of clogs; (*b*) a cutting instrument pivoted on a block (cf. *stock-shave*); (*c*) a stockman's knife; **stock-maker**, a maker †(*a*) of gun-carriages; (*b*) of musket-stocks; (*c*) see quot. 1858; †**stock-nail** [cf. MDu. *stoknagel*], a thick nail; **stock-nut**, the hazel-nut; **stock-pot**, a pot in which stock for soups is boiled and kept; also *fig.*; †**stock-punished** *pa. pple.*, punished by being set in the stocks; **stock-purse**, a fund kept for the common purposes of a group of persons; **stock rail** *Railways*, each of the outer fixed rails at a set of points; **stock-room**, (*a*) a room in which reserve stock is stored; (*b*) a room in a hotel in which commercial travellers display their samples; **stock-saddle**, †(*a*) *Sc.* ? a saddle with a wooden tree; (*b*) in the Western U.S., a saddle with a heavy tree and steel horn to give resistance in using a lariat; **stock-saw**, a saw used in a stock-gang; **stock-shave** (see quot.); **stock-shears** (see quot.); †**stock-sleeve** (see quot.); †**stock-starve** *v. trans.*, to keep (a tradesman) short of stock; **stock-stone**, a flat stone fixed in a handle, used for scouring and stretching leather; **stock-tackle** *Naut.*, a tackle used for raising the stock of an anchor perpendicular; **stock-trail**, used *attrib.* to designate a gun-carriage in which the trail at the end of the stock rests upon the ground when the gun is unlimbered for firing; †**stock-tree** *Sc.*, ? a wooden saddle-tree; †**stock-wheel** *Sc.*, ? a wheel for a gun-carriage.

1771 *Encycl. Brit.* I. 589/2 *Stock-accompt..contains, upon the Dr side, the debts due by the merchant when the books were begun. The Cr side contains his ready money, effects and debts due to him at the same time. **1826** *Art of Brewing* (ed. 2) 64 Keep some *stock beer for flavouring your best ale. **1836** *Penny Cycl.* V. 404/2 The beer is by this means also rendered flat, which is necessary for stock or store beer that is to be kept some time before coming into use. **1850** E. DOBSON *Bricks & Tiles* I. 33 The brick mould is placed on a *stock board, which is made to fit the bottom of the mould. **1875** KNIGHT *Dict. Mech.*, *Stock-board* [in an organ]. **1835** J. F. COOPER *Monikins* I. ii. 32 Love was a sentiment much too pure and elevated for one whose imagination dwelt habitually on the beauties of the *stock-books. **1847** A. HARRIS *Settlers & Convicts* xiii. 260 Outside the yard..is..set a table with the stock book, pens, and ink, and in that the cattle are registered. **1882** W. D. HAY *Brighter Britain!* I. viii. 202 We keep a stock-book, in which every beast is entered. **1901** *Westm. Gaz.* 27 Aug. 2/1 The President..seats himself, pen in hand, at the [canteen] stock-book, while the subalterns run over the different articles. **1598** FLORIO, *Balista*, .. a crosse-bow, a *stock-bow or tillar. [**1887** *Kent. Gloss.*, *Stock-bow*, a cross-bow.] **1937** E. HILL *Great Austral. Loneliness* xli. 305 In Kimberley and the Territory lubras are even to-day recognised as the best '*stock-boys'. **1955** J. CLEARY *Justin Bayard* iv. 58 The stockboys had roped the piebald now and thrown a saddle on him. **1972** R. MILNER in W. King *Black Short Story Anthol.* 376 This receptionist thought I had come about a stock-boy job, you dig. **1979** D. ANTHONY *Long Hard Cure* x. 86 He owns a chain of department stores .. one of those self-made men, who went to work at fourteen as a stockboy. **1683** J. HOUGHTON *Collect. Lett. Improv. Husb.* II. vi. 186 We make two sorts of Bricks, Viz. *Stock-Bricks and Place-Bricks; the Stock-Bricks are made solid, strong, and .. hard. **1703** R. NEVE *City & C. Purchaser* 42 Stock-bricks .. are made upon a Stock, viz. The Mold is put on a Stock, after the manner of Molding, or Striking of Tiles. **1883** *Specif. Alnwick & Cornhill Rlwy.* 3 The whole of the bricks for the face of any work .. of the arches are to be stock bricks. **1693** MOXON *Mech. Exerc.* (1703) 249 Brishes, of three sorts, viz. A *Stock Brish, a Round Brish, and a Pencil. With these Brishes, they wet old Walls before they mend them. **1876** *Encycl. Brit.* IV. 403/2 Brushes with the tufts placed side by side on flat boards, as plasterers' brushes, are called stock-brushes. **1748** SMOLLETT *Rod. Random* xliv, A diamond *stock-buckle. **1815** SCOTT *Guy M.* xxxvii, A well-brushed black suit, with very clean shoes and gold buckles and stock-buckle. **1967** A. BATTERSBY *Network Analysis* (ed. 2) xiii. 221 They will be high during the first few months because of retail *stock-building. **1977** *Financial Results of Oil Majors 1976* (Shell Internat. Petroleum Co.) 8 The increase in demand, combined with some stock-building at the end of the year in anticipation of a significant rise in oil prices, raised oil production outside the USSR, Eastern Europe and China to 47 million barrels daily in 1976. **1827** —— *Surg. Dau.* Pref., Half-ashamed, .. yet half-proud of the literary *stock-company, in which he has got a share. **1905** *Outlook* 7 Oct. 471/1 Within the last two years there have been three exposures of gigantic stock-company frauds [in America]. **1943** *Princ. Production Control (B.S.I.)* 7 **Stock control*, the means by which the correct quantity and quality of material and components are made available according to the production plan, and excessive stocks avoided. **1962** A. BATTERSBY *Guide to Stock Control* v. 48 The calculations can conveniently be summarized on the Stock Control Form .. and a specimen set of figures is shown. **1976** J. LUND *Ultimate* iii. 29 They talked .. on the economics of warehousing and stock control. **1965** *Listener* 26 Aug. 317/2 Add enough water to almost cover the meat, and the *stock cubes. **1979** *Times* 29 Sept. 15/5 Do you keep a stockpot .. and boil it daily? .. Cookery books .. have a sneaky way of implying that stock cubes will never do. **1903** *Jrnl. Hygiene* III. 2 Gelatin plates were then made from the broth culture; if only a single species developed, agar tube-cultures were prepared and used as the *stock-cultures of the organism. **1979** *Jrnl. Appl. Bacteriol.* XLVII. 381 The maintenance of stock cultures of lactic acid bacteria in small microbiological laboratories may present a technical problem. **14..** *Burgh Lawis* xvii. in *Anc. Laws Scot.* (Burgh Rec. Soc.) 10 It is to wyt at in burgh sall nocht be herde bludewyt na yit *stockisdynt na merchet [etc.]. **1676** COLES *Dict.*, **Stock-drawers*, stockings. **1600** HOLLAND *Livy* v. xxiv. 196 Romulus .. the first *Stockefather and beginner of the cittie of Rome. *c* **1640** J. SMYTH *Lives Berkeleys* (1883) I. 207 Hee is the stock-father of that honored family of the Berkeleys of Wymondham. **1895** W. P. W. PHILLIMORE in *New Eng. Gen. Hist Register* Oct. 450 Edward Garfield, of Watertown, Mass., the stock-father of the American family. **1669** STURMY *Mariner's Mag.* I. ii. 19 See that our Murtherers and *Stockfowlers have their Chambers fill'd with good Powder. **1688** HOLME *Armoury* III. xviii. (Roxb.) 138/1 They are of some called Murthers and slings, or sling peeces, because they are slung in their holds to turne any way. Some call them Stock-fowlers; and Fowlers or Foulers. **1856** *N. & Q.* Ser. II. I. 151/2 *Stock-frost... The watermen of Norfolk unanimously believe in the possibility of the water freezing at the bottom of a river. **1908** *Nature* 30 Jan. 295/2 What is locally called 'stock frost' .. is known to the scientific world .. as 'ground ice'. **1875** KNIGHT *Dict. Mech.*, *Stock-gang. **1880** *Lumberman's Gaz.* Jan. 28 They [i.e. the rafts] are then cut into boards by 'stock gang' saws. **1713** *Guardian* No. 95 ¶1 Fourscore Pieces of *Stock-Gold, and thirty Pieces of Tin-Silver. **1465** *Paston Lett.* III. 436 Item, a *stokke gonne with iij. chambers. **1750** W. ELLIS *Mod. Husb.* V. i. 106 (E.D.S.) Those bees that swarmed the year before, we take up now, and then it is called 'stock-honey'. **1638** JUNIUS *Paint. Ancients* 155 They afterwards begun to use hose, drawing over them some thicker kind of *stock-hose. **1553** in W. H. Turner *Select. Rec. Oxford* (1880) 215 They .. had him .. to Bocardo, and did sette him in the *stocke howse. **1725** *Lond. Gaz.* No. 6403/4 Prisoner in the Stockhouse or Goal of Kingstone. **1879** *Hardwicke's Sci.-Gossip* XV. 142/2 What are the phenomena which go, in the Norfolk district at least, by the name .. of 'stock-frost', '*stock-ice?' **1583** *Rates Custom Ho.* C viij, Kniues called *stock kniues course vngilt the dosen, xvi.s. viii. d. **1799** J. WOOD *Princ. Mechanics* iv. (ed. 2) 93 Those [levers] in which the forces act on contrary sides of the center of motion, .. and those in which they act on the same side, as the stock knife. **1955** R. P. HOBSON *Nothing too Good for Cowboy* i. 16 He cut the moosehide wrapping with his stock knife. **1968** J. ARNOLD *Shell Bk. Country Crafts* 105 The shaping of clogs from these clefts is done with a stock knife... It consists of a stout blade with a long projecting handle. **1978** *Lancashire Life* Apr. 49/2 The tools a sole-cutter used were three in number—stock-knife, hollower and gripper. **1579** *Reg. Privy Council Scot.* III. 205 Wrichtis, *Stokmakaris and Quheill makaris. **1837** CARLYLE *Fr. Rev.* III. v. vi, Deft Stock-makers do gouge and rasp. **1858** SIMMONDS *Dict. Trade*, *Stock-maker*, a manufacturer of stiff neck-bands worn by men. **1596** *Shuttleworths' Acc.* (Chetham Soc.) 107 Stone nales, *stocke nailes, clagge nales. **1833** R. WALKER *Flora Oxfordsh.* 284 Corylus Avellana. Common Hazel-nut or *Stock-nut. **1845** E. ACTON *Mod. Cookery* i. 3 Never .. set the soup by in it, but strain it off .. and fill the *stock-pot immediately with water. **1853** SOYER *Pantroph.* 260 The Chief of the cooks, the Archimagirus, .. embraces at a single glance the series of stock-pots and brick stoves. **1891** AINGER in Edith Sichel *Life & Lett.* (1906) 253 The schoolboy verses .. will at once go into the Lamb 'Stock-pot' —my Commonplace Book. **1917** *Harrods Gen. Catal.* 964/1 Extra heavy bellied Stockpot, enamelled Pearl Grey outside and in. **1928** 'O. DOUGLAS' *Eliza for Common* x. 128 Some quite dull books read like that—as if the author had simply thrown everything in, a sort of stock-pot of a book. **1931** R. CAMPBELL *Georgiad* i. 18 His melancholy recipes for 'happiness' .. How to 'rechauffe' the stock-pot of desire. **1960** E. DAVID *French Provincial Cooking* 158 The pot .. is usually a tall straight-sided or slightly bulbous stock-pot made of earthenware, copper, enamelled iron, or heavy aluminium. **1982** *Daily Tel.* 14 Jan. 15/5 Put .. chine bone into stockpot, cover with water, .. and simmer. **1605** SHAKS. *Lear* III. iv. 140 (Qos.) Who is whipt from tithing to tithing, and *stock-punisht and imprisoned. *a* **1665** W. GUTHRIE *Serm.* in Tweedie *Sel. Biog.* (Wodrow Soc.) II. 75 We have all one common profession, interest, *stockpurse. **1802** C. JAMES *Milit. Dict.*, *Stock Purse*, a certain saving which is made in a corps, and which is applied to regimental purposes. **1832** G. DOWNES *Lett. Cont. Countries* I. 67 A small stock-purse is maintained, for the support of the enfeebled and superannuated. **1850** *Civil Engin. & Archit. Jrnl.* XIII. 270/1 The top of the switch not being mitred into the underside of the bearing surface of the *stock rail, it is not liable to be locked by the barbing over of the stock from the pressure of the wheels. **1890** W. H. COLE *Notes on Permanent-Way Material* i. 20 The points or switches are .. so adjusted to their respective stock-rails that when one switch is pressed against its stock-rail the other is drawn away, and thus one line of metals or the other is made continuous. **1935** E. BEAL *Railway Modelling in Miniature* ii. 36 Then solder the stock-rail for the other track. **1825** HANSARD *Typogr.* 243 Another large and convenient room, denominated the *Stock-room, in which the trading business of the [Stationers'] Company is transacted. **1877** '*The Road*': *Leaves Sk.-bk. Commerc. Trav.* 53 The Commercial-Room is ample; there are dining, coffee, bath and stock rooms. **1888** JACOBI *Printers' Vocab.* 133 *Stock room*, the department allotted to the storing of paper or printed stock. **1537–8** *Acc. Ld. High Treas. Scot.* VI. 380 For thre quarteris of fyne gray clath to cover ane *stok sadill to the Kingis grace. **1888** T. ROOSEVELT in *Century Mag.* Apr. 863/2 For a long spell of such work a stock-saddle is far less tiring than the ordinary Eastern or English one. **1875** KNIGHT *Dict. Mech.*, *Stock-saw. **1794** *Rigging & Seamanship* I. 152 **Stock-shave*, a large sharp-edged cutting knife, with a handle at one end and a hook at the other, by which it hooks in a .. staple .. driven in an elm block; it is used to pare off the rough wood from the shells of blocks, &c. **1688** HOLME *Armoury* III. 386/2 Two other working Tools of the Needle-makers. The first is their *Stock-Shears, with these they cut the Wyer to that length as the Needle is to bear. **1611** COTGR. s.v. *Lombard*, *Manche Lombarde*, a *stocke-sleeue; or fashion of halfe-sleeue, whose vpper part is raised, and full of plaits, or gathers. **1727** DE FOE *Eng. Tradesm.* (1732) I. vi. 67 Those adventures .. *stock-starve the Tradesman, and impoverish him in his ordinary business. **1875** KNIGHT *Dict. Mech.*, *Stock-stone. **1815** *Falconer's Dict. Marine* (ed. Burney), *Stock-Tackle. **1860** A. MORDECAI *Rep. Mil. Comm. Europe* (1861) 62 (Funk) These were no doubt designed for firing with larger charges .. than the *stocktrail carriage admits of. **1470** *York Memo. Bk.* (Surtees) I. 92 That .. no saddiller .. make any sadelles of trees that er calde *stokke trees or Scottes trees. **1547** *Acc. Ld. High Treas. Scot.* IX. 103 For tua botis .. hir *stoke quhelis and necessaris.

B. *adj.* (usu. in attributive use). That is kept in stock (see A 56 c).

1. a. Kept regularly in stock for sale, as ***stock book, lot, model; stock-type*** adj.; **stock shot** *Cinemat.* = *library shot* s.v. LIBRARY[1] 4; **stock size**, a size (of ready-made garments) regularly kept in stock; used *attrib.* or predicatively to designate a person whom such a size fits.

a **1625** FLETCHER *Nice Valour* v. iii, For they begin already to engross it, And make it a *Stock-book. **1858** COOPER *Ath. Cantabr.* I. 249 The Sick Man's Salve was long a stockbook with the Stationers' company. **1898** W. J. GREENWOOD *Commerc. Corresp.* (ed. 2) 31 We particularly wish to call your attention to the *stock lots as per particulars noted at foot. **1926** *Daily Colonist* (Victoria, B.C.) 4 July 3/1 (Advt.), The car was a *stock model in every respect except for a 48-gallon gasoline tank and changes in the top, back seat and tire carrier. **1941** B. SCHULBERG *What makes Sammy Run?* vi. 93 A shoe-string producer told him he had bought the *stock shots from *Hell's Angels*. **1974** *Radio Times* 14 Mar. 11/4 Processed chases up and down stock-shot ski slopes. **1897** *Daily News* 9 Jan. 6/3 The happy woman who possesses what we may call a *stock-size figure. **1900** *Ibid.* 28 July 6/7 Those who are fortunate enough to be a 'stock' size can save many shillings by buying these ready-made articles. **1952** M. LASKI *Village* xix. 262 Margaret was lucky, she was stock-size, not like Wendy herself who had always had to have everything made for her. **1980** *Country Life* 3 July 78/2 Our model girl was stock size and everything was too big for her. **1958** *Spectator* 1 Aug. 170/1 A *stock-type Vauxhall Velox.

b. Designating a medicinal or chemical preparation which is kept ready for use, or the vessel in which such a preparation is stored.

1863 J. HUGHES *Pract. Photogr.* (1866) 11 When you have done for the day, return what [collodion] remains back into the stock-bottle. **1882** *Encycl. Brit.* XIV. 390/1 These [chemicals] are mixed together in one large stock tank. **1898** *Allbutt's Syst. Med.* V. 424 If the specific gravity is to be lowered, this stock solution is diluted with water. **1907** J. A. HODGES *Elem. Photogr.* (ed. 6) 49 It is better to keep both the stock gold and the stock platinum solutions in the dark.

2. *Theatr.* ***stock author, burlesque, comedy, star***; **stock actor**, etc., a member of a stock company, or one who acts in stock pieces; also ***stock actress***; **stock character**, a dramatic character representing a type in a conventional manner and recurring in many works; (cf. sense 3 a below); **stock company**, a company who regularly act together at a particular theatre; **stock piece, play**, etc., one which forms part of a *répertoire*.

1839 MARRYAT *Diary Amer.* 2nd Ser. II. xiii. 121 The American **stock* actors, as they term those who are not considered as *stars*. **1865** W. DONALDSON *Recoll. Actor* 95 A large proportion of the stock actors were .. without talent or experience. **1921** E. O'NEILL *Diff'rent* II. 243 She resembles some passé *stock actress of fifty made up for a heroine of twenty. **1824** J. DECASTRO *Mem.* 154 T. Dibdin, esq., succeeded him .. as the *stock author of that theatre. **1864** 'P. PATERSON' *Glimpses of Real Life* xxv. 240 Jones keeps a stock author, and does not rely on outsiders. **1916** *Variety* 27 Oct. 12/1 *Stock burlesque at the Lyric is moderately successful. **1864** H. MORLEY *Jrnl.* 16 Jan. (1866) 325 The *gracioso* was a popular addition made by Lope de Vega to the *stock characters of a Spanish play. **1893** [see CLOAK *sb.* 6]. **1976** *Country Life* 12 Feb. 346/1 In *Albert Herring*, Britten took stock characters—pompous mayor, stolid policeman, .. overbearing lady of the manor. **1812** *Dramatic Censor 1811* 27/1 Among all the *stock comedies which the Theatres are in the habit of representing, this is, in our idea, one of the very best. **1830** G. COLMAN *Random Rec.* II. 6 Miss Lee's 'Chapter of Accidents', long and justly rated as a stock Comedy. **1864** P. PATERSON *Glimpses Real Life* 37, I .. being at the time one of the *stock company of the Beverley Theatre, New York. **1782** D. E. BAKER *Biogr. Dramatica* II. 84/2 The *Way to keep him* .. still stands on the *stock-list of the theatre. **1887** T. A. TROLLOPE *What I remember* II. xii. 209, I subsequently took Sir Anthony [in 'The Rivals'] which remained my *stock part for years. **1804** W. COOKE *Mem. C. Macklin* 408 It was always one of the *stock pieces which he engaged himself to perform. **1805** SOUTHEY in *Ann. Rev.* III. 76 Their classical stock pieces. **1843** *Ainsworth Mag.* IV. 135 His .. acting contributed greatly to the success of the drama, though it had not sufficient stamina to become 'a stock piece'. **1708** L. DOWNES *Roscius Anglicanus* 8 Note, That these being their Principal Old *Stock Plays. **1761** VICTOR *Theatres Lond. & Dublin* I. 65 Time .. wasted in rehearsing old Stock Plays, for the Sake of the new Performers to be introduced in them. **1807** *Director* I. 260 The Beggars Opera is what is termed a stock play with us. **1856** A. C. RITCHIE *Mimic Life* I. ii. 44 As the '*stock star' of a popular theatre, in Boston, she had shone several years in the dramatic firmament. **1847** *Theatr. Times* 11 Sept. 283/2 Mr. Gustavus V. Brooke is perhaps the greatest favourite in the provinces, as a *stock tragedian.

3. *fig.* in reference to intellectual or literary topics: Kept in stock for use; commonly used or brought forward, constantly appearing or recurring, in conversation, discussion, or composition; belonging to a staple or stock-in-trade of subjects, arguments, phrases, quotations, etc.; hence, commonplace, trite, conventional. Also with reference to fictional characters of a standardized or conventional type (cf. *stock character*, sense 2 above); also *transf.*

1738 SWIFT *Pol. Conversat.* Introd. 40 The old Stock-Oaths. **1803** MAR. EDGEWORTH *Pop. Tales*, *To-morrow* i, A line which has become a *stock* line among writing-masters' copies. **1835** DICKENS *Sk. Boz.*, *Mr. Watkins Tottle* ii. The master of the house, who was burning to tell one of his seven stock stories. **1853** KINGSLEY *Hypatia* ix. 109 The humble stock-phrases in which they talked of their labours of love. **1861** MILL *Utilit.* ii. 36 The stock arguments against utilitarianism. **1865** M. ARNOLD *Ess. Crit.* v. 172 Heine's .. utter rejection of stock classicism and stock romanticism. **1871** MORLEY *Crit. Misc.*, *Vauvenargues* 14 The stock moralist, like the commonplace orator of the pulpit, fails to touch the hearts of men. **1895** *Bookman* Oct. 26/2 The history has been sadly confused and distorted by stock quotations from the fathers. **1940** W. S. MAUGHAM *Books & You* p. xii, The characters .. are not very interesting, and most of them are the stock figures of Victorian fiction. **1951** M. MCLUHAN *Mech. Bride* (1967) 118/2 The 'good girl' is the nineteenth-century stock model which has long been merged with the mother image. **1960** [see EXURBANITE *a.*]. **1963** [see CLICHÉ 3]. *a* **1963** L. MACNEICE *Astrol.* (1964) vi. 200 Catering for stock-type 'individuals' (all humanity being divided into 12 groups). **1980** J. GARDNER *Garden of Weapons* II. vii. 185 A man full of bounce, like the stock uncle known to all large families.

b. Special collocations: **stock bowler** *Cricket*, a reliable but unspectacular bowler; hence **stock bowling**; **stock response**, an automatic and superficial reaction to a literary device (see quot. 1939); also *transf.* and *fig.*

1968 *Listener* 11 July 61/2 Connolly, in 1964 a strenuous but pedestrian fast bowler, has reduced his pace, developed swing and cut, and become an admirably steady *stock-bowler. **1976** J. SNOW *Cricket Rebel* 37, I could no more be regarded as a stock bowler relying on line and length to keep the scoring in check. *Ibid.* 77 Only occasionally did he call upon me to do a *stock bowling job with the intention of closing the game up. **1925** I. A. RICHARDS *Princ. Lit. Crit.* xxv. 203 Against these *stock responses the artist's internal and external conflicts are fought, and with them the popular writer's triumphs are made. **1939** BROOKS & WARREN *Understanding Poetry* 639 *Stock response*, the general uncritical response made on conventional or habitual grounds to a situation, subject, phrase, or word in literature. Advertisers frequently attempt to appeal to stock responses. **1957** A. THWAITE *Home Truths* 40 Or will it seem Merely the self-duped mind's harangue at Death, The stock-response still raging in the shroud? **1961** K. TYNAN *Curtains* I. 8 The stock response of terror in the face of matricide has vanished. **1966** 'K. A. SADDLER' *Gilt Edge* ix. 128 'Well,' he said continuing, and just in time as I was running out of stock responses. **1975** *Times* 20 Sept. 6/3 If Agatha Christie works almost entirely with what the critics call 'stock responses', she knows .. how to take advantage of our responding in a stock way to .. stock situations.

4. In non-*attrib.* use.

1966 *Listener* 25 Aug. 288/3 The authors gave us sharply observed characters—stock, but none the worse for it. **1977** *Hot Car* Oct. 88/2 The diesel stock with a servo. **1979** *Jrnl. R. Soc. Arts* Nov. 776/2 The stereotypes are used in a relatively straightforward way, as stock as the London brick.

†**stock**, *sb.*² *Sc. Obs.* [ONorthumbrian *stocc*, a. (O)Irish *stoc* (Gael. *stoc*), a trumpet. In Sc. the word seems to have been taken up afresh from Gaelic and associated with STOCK *sb.*¹

Initial *st* is very rare in native Irish words, and *stoc* is commonly believed to be a loan-word; but it occurs in early Middle Irish, so that adoption from English is improbable.]

a. *OE.* A trumpet. **b.** *Sc.* In the combs. **stock-horn, stock-in-horn, stock-and-horn,** a wind instrument formerly used in Scotland (see quots.).

a. *c* **950** *Lindisf. Gosp.* Matt. vi. 2 Bema *vel* stocc [gl. *tuba*]. **b. 1597** SKENE *De Verb. Sign.* s.v. *Menetum*, To blaw ane stock horne, quhilk commounlie is maid of Timmer & wood, or tree, with circles & girds of the same, quhilk is zet vsed in the Hie-lands and Iles of this realme. **1725** RAMSAY *Gentle Sheph.* I. i, When I begin to tune my stock and horn. **1815** *Notes to Pennecuik's Descr. Tweeddale* 96 (Jam.) The original genuine Scottish pastoral pipe, consisting of a cow's *horn*, a bower-tree *stock*, from *stoc*, in Gaelic, a pipe, called the *Stock-in-horn*, with stops in the middle, and an oaten reed at the smaller end for the mouth piece. **1827** *Hone's Every-day Bk.* II. 20 The *kythels*, or stock-and-horn, a musical instrument made of the thigh bone of a sheep and the horn of a bullock. **1844** *Ayrsh. Wreath* 170 The first instrument he played on was a stock and horn.

†**stock**, *sb.*³ *Obs.* [a. F. *estoc*, ad. It. *stocco*, prob. of Teut. origin: cf. STOCK *sb.*¹]

1. A thrusting sword. Also comb. *stock-sword*.

1513 DOUGLAS *Æneis* VII. xii. 59 Wyth round stok suerdis faucht thai in melle, Wyth poyntalis, or wyth stokkis Sabylyne. **1536** BELLENDEN *Cron. Scot.* x. xvi. (1821) II. 176 Thay..had..stok swerdis, quhom na armour micht resist. *a* **1572** KNOX *Hist. Ref.* Wks. 1846 I. 177 A stog sweard.

2. *Fencing.* A thrust with a pointed weapon.

1598 SHAKS. *Merry W.* II. iii. 36 To see thee passe thy puncto, thy stock, thy reuerse, thy distance, thy montant. **1602** *2nd Pt. Ret. fr. Parnass.* I. ii. (1606) B 3, Here is a fellow Iudicio that carried the deadly stocke [MS. *variant* stockado] in his pen. **1602** MARSTON *Antonio's Rev.* I. iii. B 2, And if a horned diuell should burst forth, I would passe on him with a mortall stocke. **1604** —— *Malcontent* II. ii. C 4, The close stock, o mortall wench.

stock (stɒk), *sb.*⁴ *Mining* and *Geol.* [a. G. *stock* (lit. 'stick').] **a.** (See quots.)

1882 GEIKIE *Text-bk. Geol.* IV. ix. §2. 597 The cavernous spaces dissolved out in some rocks..may be filled with..ores. Irregular metalliferous masses of this kind have long been known in Germany by the name of Stocks (*Stöcke*). **1901** RANSOME in *Ann. Rep. U.S. Geol. Surv.* II. 255 Stocks are those ore bodies commonly referred to as 'chimneys'.

b. A discordant intrusion of igneous rock which has a roughly oval cross-section and steep sides, and is smaller than a batholith.

1898 *Jrnl. Geol.* VI. 706 It will be found advantageous to discriminate between bysmalith and stock by limiting the term stock to such bodies as occupy nearly vertical tubes or funnels of indefinite depth in rocks of any and all kinds.. and which maintain such a relation to them as to appear to belong to the category of dikes. **1916** *Yukon Territory* (Canada Dept. Interior) iii. 35 Occasional pebbles derived from the various dikes and stocks outcropping along the valleys. **1944** [see LACCOLITH]. **1955, 1957** [see INTRUDE *v.* 5]. **1977** A. HALLAM *Planet Earth* 69/1 The upper surface [of a batholith] is generally irregular, with upwardly projecting stocks and dikes that may be the only surface clue to the much larger body at depth.

stock (stɒk), *v.*¹ Forms: 4–6 **stok(ke, 6 stoke, 5–7 stocke, 6– stock.** [f. STOCK *sb.*¹ (Independent formations relating to various senses of the sb.) Cf. Du. *stokken*, G. *stocken*, Sw. *stocka*, to provide (an anchor) with a stock, to hive (bees), to provide with sticks or props; *intr.* to stop flowing, come to a stop. Also G. *stöcken* to put in the stocks, to provide with sticks.]

I. Senses relating to material senses of the sb.

†**1.** *trans.* To set in the stocks; to punish by confining the feet (occas. the hands) in stocks; in early use, to subject to rigorous imprisonment. *Obs.*

c **1325** *Gloss. W. de Bibbesw.* in Wright *Voc.* 163 E pur co ke seygnur fet coingner [*glossed* stokken] Soun neif en ceps pur chastier. **1338** R. BRUNNE *Chron.* (1810) 121 Scho stokked [*ad fet mettre en ceppes*] Kyng Steuen. *c* **1374** CHAUCER *Troylus* III. 380 Rather deye I wolde,..stokked in presoun. **1430–40** LYDG. *Bochas* I. xv. (1554) 32 To liue in prison..And to be stocked under key and locke. *c* **1440** *Promp. Parv.* 476/2 Stokkyn, or settyn in stokkys, *cippo*. **1451** *Paston Lett.* I. 190 They stokked hym and hese sone at Swafham. **1534** MORE *Comf. agst. Trib.* III. Wks. 1245/2 He neither nedeth to coller vs nor to stocke vs for any feare of scaping away. **1571** *Life J. Story* in Morgan *Phoenix Brit.* (1732) I. 292 Some were stocked in both Feet and Arms; some also were stocked by both their Feet and by both their Thumbs, and so did hang in the Stocks. **1641** G. RALEIGH *Albania* 13 She came by a Constable stocking the Drunkard. *a* **1661** FULLER *Worthies, Yorks.* (1662) 191 The Hand steals, the Feet are stocked. **1694** PENN *Rise & Progr. Quakers* v. 85 Being often Stockt, Stoned, Beaten, Whipt and Imprisoned.

†**b.** *transf.* and *fig. Obs.*

1591 SYLVESTER *Du Bartas* I. vi. 77 The Dragon..doth fold About his fore-legs, fetter'd in such order, That stockéd there he now can stir no further. *a* **1618** —— *Job Triumph.* II. 333 In his Ruffe, and at his greatest height, Hee shall be stocked in full many a Strait.

¶ with allusion to STOCK *sb.*¹ 2.

a **1637** B. JONSON *Sad Sheph.* II. i, Whilst shee (poor Lasse) is stock'd up in a tree: Your brother Lorells prize!

†**c.** ? To fasten or confine (the tongue) as a punishment. *Obs.*

1568 V. SKINNER tr. *Gonsalvius' Sp. Inquisit.* 51 b, Streight way the felow should be sure to haue his mouth gagged, or his toung stocked, to teach him to be quiet.

2. To fasten to or fit with a stock: esp. **a.** To fix (a bell) to its stock.

1483–4 in Swayne *Churchw. Acc. Sarum* (1896) 34 The lytell Belle that was newe stokyt. **1600–1** in Garry *Churchw. Acc. St. Mary's, Reading* (1893) 86 Item to Richard hames for stoking the Belles & hanginge them, vijs. vjd. **1679** in *Trans. Shropsh. Arch. Soc.* Ser. III. (1908) VIII. 37 For stocking of yᵉ Treble Bell..6. 8. **1857** LUKIS *Church Bells* 28 The heavy expense..of taking the bell down to be stocked afresh.

b. To fit (a gun, crossbow) with a stock.

1539 in *Archæologia* XI. 436 A fowler of iron stokked and bounde with iron. **1541** *Acc. Ld. High Treas. Scot.* VIII. 119 Gevin to Johnne Drummond to stok ane grete culvering witht,..xviij s. **1634** W. WOOD *New Eng. Prosp.* (1865) 19 Our Gunnes that are stocked with English Wallnut. **1649** in W. M. Myddelton *Chirk Castle Acc.* (1908) 27 For stocking a crosse bow. **1747** *Gentl. Mag.* XVII. 101 A fine gun, which he forged, stocked, made, and completed himself. **1832** *Westm. Rev.* XVII. 327 Shungie the great warrior.. succeeded in stocking one of his musquets in a very elegant manner. **1904** *Field* 6 Feb. 209/3 There is..no other plan of efficiently stocking a ready-made gun.

c. *Naut.* To fix the stock upon (an anchor).

1769 COOK *Jrnl. 1st Voy.* (1893) 86 The Carpenter employ'd in stocking the Anchors. **1803** T. NETHERTON in *Naval Chron.* XV. 214 Those employed in..stocking anchors.

d. (See quot.)

1911 WEBSTER, *Stock*..3...to secure, by or to a stock; as, two plows *stocked* to one frame.

e. Naut. *to stock to*: to haul (an anchor) into a perpendicular position by means of a stock-tackle.

1815 *Falconer's Dict. Marine* (ed. Burney), To Stock-to the Anchor. *c* **1860** H. STUART *Seaman's Catech.* 57 It is then stocked to, and lashed, and the stock tackle is un-hooked. **1867** SMYTH *Sailor's Word-bk.*

†**3. a.** ? To cover (the leg) with a stock or stocking. *rare*⁻¹. **b.** To cover (hose) with some stronger material; to strengthen (stockings) with pieces of cloth sewn on. *Obs.*

1430–40 LYDG. *Bochas* IX. x. (1554) 201 b, Their breche enbroudred after yᵉ guise of old, Fret with pearle, legge stocked to the kne. **1520** in *Archæologia* XXV. 435 A yerd of black to stock my master's hose. **1545–6** *Acc. Ld. High Treas. Scot.* VIII. 443 Ane pair of hois of his gracis stokkit witht blew velvot. **1691** *Lond. Gaz.* No. 2633/4 Grey Breeches, and grey Stockings newly stock'd.

†**4.** ? To make a stock of, use as a stock for grafting. *Obs. rare*⁻¹.

1528 TINDALE *Wicked Mammon* G viij, God..planteth them in the garden of his mercye, and stocketh them & graffeth the spiryte of Chryst in them.

5. *Leather-manuf.* To beat (hides) in the stocks.

1883 R. HALDANE *Workshop Rec.* Ser. II. 367/1 When the skins are dry, they are 'stocked' with oil again.

II. 6. To root up, pull up by the roots (trees, stumps, weeds, etc.); to extirpate by digging or grubbing; to fell (a tree) by digging round and cutting its roots with a mattock or similar instrument.

a. simply.

c **1440** *Pallad. on Husb.* x. 92 This tyme is to be stocked euery tre. **1612** DRAYTON *Poly-olb.* XIV. 57 The painfull laborers hand shall stock the roots, to burne. **1686** PLOT *Staffordsh.* 210 Two able workmen were 5 days in stocking or felling it down. **1733** W. ELLIS *Chiltern & Vale Farm.* 300 Stocking them [*sc.* thistles] with an Iron Paddle. **1790** W. H. MARSHALL *Rur. Econ. Midl.* I. 102 Three methods of felling are here in use. Stocking, Axe-grubbing, and Axe-falling. **1839** SIR G. C. LEWIS *Gloss. Heref., To stock*,..To strike and wrench with an axe having a flat end. **1881** *Leicest. Gloss., Stock*, to cut off the branches from the trunk, or the long roots from the stump of a tree.

b. with *up* (very frequent); rarely *out*.

1458 *Anc. Deed* A. 7587 (P.R.O.), To stokke and hewe vppe to be þe Rotes alle maner of Busshes þornes and trees. **1523** FITZHERB. *Surv.* 4 b, Demeyne woode..whereof the lorde at his pleasure may assert, stocke vp by the rootes [etc.]. **1678** BP. H. CROFT *Second Call* 47 The Husbandman finding but a few Thistles and Briars in his Meadow, stocks them up. **1733** W. ELLIS *Chiltern & Vale Farm.* 134 The Root..should not be sawed or cut down at bottom, but stock'd and grub'd entirely up. **1798** J. MIDDLETON *Agric. Middlesex* 119 This tract of land..abounded with trees and bushes, which seemed to make it necessary for the cultivator to..stock out the roots. **1839** URE *Dict. Arts*, etc. 1194 Instead of stocking up his rattoons, holing, and planting the land anew, the planter suffers the stoles to continue in the ground. **1881** *Leicest. Gloss., Stock-up*, to stub up, grub up.

fig. **1579** TOMSON *Calvin's Serm. Tim.* 765/1 He saith wee must stocke vp all the thorns that are in vs. **1609** HOLLAND *Amm. Marcell.* XXX. iii. 381 That the occasion of discord might not possibly bee stocked up by the rootes, without [etc.]. **1643** TRAPP *Comm. Gen.* xxvi. 10 The Apostle Paul so strives to stock up by the roots that wretched opinion. **1674** J. B[RIAN] *Harv. Home* vii. 47 A root of bitter gall, And wormwood, never stockt up wholly.

c. *transf.* To pull up (stones, a fence); to break or loosen (the surface of the ground with a pick). Usually with *up*.

1802 W. HUTTON *Life* 78 At the foot of this artificial hill stood the castle. The people of the country have stocked up the stones to the very foundation for building and the roads. **1879** T. CODRINGTON *Macadamised Roads* 91 The practice of picking up or loosening the surface of a road with a pick, sometimes called 'stocking'. *Ibid.* 92 Picking or stocking up the surface before laying fresh materials. **1907** *Gentl. Mag.* July 38 This waste land would be only gradually stocked, or grubbed up.

III. To check in growth; to stiffen.

7. To stunt, check in growth (a plant or animal). Chiefly in pa. pple. *stocked* (mod. dial. also *stocken, stoken*). Also *intr.*, to be stunted in growth. *dial.*

1607 MARKHAM *Caval.* I. 88 If anye of them [*sc.* mares].. eyther through want of milke, or the doggednes of some vn-naturall quality, shall stocke and starue their foales. **1652** R. ROBINSON *Christ all & in all* xvii. (1656) 362 The husbandman useth to say of his corne in a time of long drought, that it is stocked, yet that corne when the raine comes, will shoot up. **1712** J. MORTON *Nat. Hist. Northamptonsh.* 385 The Corn that's thus discolour'd, is usually stock'd, as the Husbandmen call it, that is, does not come up to the Strength and Perfection of the rest that escapes this Injury. **1848** A. B. EVANS *Leicestersh. Words* 91 *Stocked*, stopped in growth. 'The lambs are almost stocked by the cold weather.' **1851** [see 9]. **1853** *Jrnl. R. Agric. Soc.* XIV. II. 452 The most profitable mode of bringing young or store stock to market is, never to allow them to 'stock', or be impeded in their growth. **1879** MISS JACKSON *Shropsh. Word-bk., Stoken*, stunted in growth; impoverished in condition; said of animals that have been badly fed and attended to.

†**8.** *refl.* ? To be stubborn, refuse obedience; to render oneself callous or incapable of feeling. *Obs.*

1610 J. ROBINSON *Justif. Separ.* i. 23 We must so enioy experienced good things, as we stock not our selves in respect of other things, as yet vntryed. **1634** CANNE *Necess. Separ.* 107 Sound comfort flowes from sincere obedience: and therefore whosoever stocks himselfe in any the least parts of the revealed will of God, he is as Iehu, rotten at the best, even when he manifesteth most shew of Religion.

9. *local.* To indurate (stone) by exposure to the weather. ? *Obs.*

1712 J. MORTON *Nat. Hist. Northamptonsh.* 489 Should the [Slate] Stones lie expos'd to Sun and Wind, before the Frosts appear, it would in such manner set or *stock* the Vein, as the Workmen speak, that they wou'd not cleave. **1851** STERNBERG *Northampt. Dial.* 106 Some kinds of stone are said to be *stocked*, when, by exposure to the weather, they become indurated. Wheat, also, is said to be *stocked* when its growth has been checked by an analogous cause.

10. *intr. Sc.* (See quot.)

1808 JAMIESON, *Stock*, to become stiff, to be benumbed... we say that one *stocks*, or that the limbs *stock*, from cold or want of exercise.

†**IV. 11.** *pass.* To have place in a stock or genealogy. *Obs. rare*⁻¹.

1611 B. JONSON *Catiline* III. F 4, A person both of Blood and Honor, stock't In a long race of vertuous Ancestors.

V. To supply with a 'stock', fund, or store.

12. *trans.* To supply or provide with stock or with a stock; e.g. to furnish (a farm, estate, etc.) with live or dead stock; to fill (a pond, river) with fish; to furnish (a shop) with a stock-in-trade; to store or supply with goods, commodities, appliances, etc.

1622 FLETCHER *Prophetess* v. iii, He has bought the great Farm..And stock'd it like an Emperour. **1648** *Hunting of Fox* 41 Your Cattell that should stocke your grounds. **1670** COVEL in *Early Voy. Levant* (Hakl. Soc.) 120 There were several sorts of fruit brought to us..with which we stock't ourselves. **1683** [R. NORTH] *Discourse Fish & Fish-ponds* xiii. (1713) 48 The Fish wherewith you stock the Waters. **1707** FREIND *Peterborow's Cond. Spain* 164 Your Lordship knows how well stock'd with Mony you left us. **1727** DE FOE *Eng. Tradesm.* (1732) I. vi. 61 Some Tradesmen are fond of seeing their shops well stock'd, and their warehouses full of goods. **1776** GIBBON *Decl. & F.* xiv. (1782) I. 504 The country was plentifully stocked with provisions. **1812** CRABBE *Tales* xxi. 180 Here, take my purse..('Tis fairly stock'd). **1832** HT. MARTINEAU *Hill & Valley* iv. 64 Some laid out their earnings in stocking a little shop. **1857** LIVINGSTONE *Trav.* iv. 85 Many of his cattle burst away from him... He stocked himself again among the Batleti. **1857** TROLLOPE *Barchester T.* xxxix, Instead of putting his money by to stock farms for his sons. **1899** LADY M. VERNEY *Verney Mem.* IV. 29 The cellar was stocked with Rhenish Wine.

b. in general, transferred, and figurative uses.

1623 MASSINGER *Bondman* III. iv, Shee from the magazine of her proper goodnesse, Stock'd me with vertuous purposes. **1655** FULLER *Ch. Hist.* III. 29 With many such memorable passages, the reader may stock himself from the pens of the civil Historians. **1695** J. EDWARDS *Perfect. Script.* 353 Here..occurs such a plenty..as is able to stock an antiquary of the first size. *a* **1701** MAUNDRELL *Journ. Jerus.* (1732) 45 Sidon is stockt well enough with Inhabitants. **1751** *Affecting Narr. of Wager* 9 The Island is thoroughly stock'd with Churches and Chapels. **1818** SCOTT *Br. Lamm.* xxx, Those legendary heroines, with whose adventures, for want of better reading, her memory had become stocked. **1829** CASSAN *Bps. Bath & Wells* 134 It looks not well, to see a Cathedral or diocese stocked with relatives and family connections. **1864** MᶜLAUCHLAN *Scott. Ch.* (1865) 416 David changed the priory into an abbey and stocked it with monks from Canterbury in 1124. **1885** *Truth* 28 May 841/1 The office is stocked with the scions of the families or the friends of Judges.

†**13.** To provide with capital or funds. *Obs.*

1615 E. S. *Britaines Busse* E 1 b, The First yeares cleare Gaine will stocke him or them so sufficiently for the use of this busse, as [etc.]. **1654** H. L'ESTRANGE *Chas. I* (1655) 123 Never King had a greater mind to the work, then King Charles, had he been stockt for it: but poverty..kept him short.

†**14.** To invest (money). Also with *in, out*. *Obs.*

1683 *Repr. Advantages Manuf. Woollen-cloath* 20 Each Member drawes a lot for every 100 Pound he Stocks in. **1710** in W. M. Morison *Dict. Decis.* (1817) 16187 Watson.. bequeathed..the sum of 5,400 marks Scots to be stocked in a responsible debtor's hand. **1794** *Cases Court Sess.* 70 Although this minister is to sell the marl, he does not apply the price to his own use; it is to be stocked out for the benefit of the incumbent.

15. To lay up in store; to form a stock or supply of (a commodity). Also with *up*.

1700 T. Brown *Amusem. Ser. & Com.* 114 Every day a Crop is gather'd, and every Night stockt up in Baskets. **1735** Dyche & Pardon *Dict.*, *Stock*,..also to lay in a large Quantity of any sort of Goods, &c. **1755–73** Johnson (ed. 4), *Stock*..to lay up in store; as, he stocks what he cannot use. **1823** Scott *Quentin D.* xviii, The wine was stocked in the deep vaults of Bracquemont, by my great-grandfather.

b. *esp.* To keep (goods) in stock for sale.

1884 *Bookseller* 1178/1 To refuse to stock the goods of the publishers who supply these cutters out. **1886** *Cyclist* 6 Oct. 1324/1 It will be perfectly safe to stock a well-considered variety of this style of machine. **1888** *Spectator* 21 July 1016 (Advt.), All the..Wholesale Houses regularly Stock it.

16. *absol.* To provide stock; to lay in a stock or supply. Also with *up*.

1850 *Jrnl. R. Agric. Soc.* XI. II. 613 Although my land is of very inferior quality, I stock heavily. **1876** Callis *Cutlery* (Brit. Manuf. Industr.) 173 His fellow, who works for a house that does not 'stock,' has to collect the material from half a dozen warehouses. **1890** 'R. Boldrewood' *Squatter's Dream* vii. 68, I shall decide to stock up as soon as the fences are finished. **1897** Howells *Landlord at Lion's Head* 416 She was over to Lovewell stockin' up for Thanksgivin'. **1908** *Nation* 22 Aug. 734/1 They 'stock' year by year: but they do so with fish reared from native spawn.

VI. Various technical and dial. senses.

17. *pass.* Of a female animal: To be impregnated.

1478, **1490** [see stocked 2]. **1894** *West Sussex. Gaz.* (advt.), Three-year-old Jersey Cow, stocked March 5th.

18. *trans.* To leave (a cow) unmilked in order that she may make a good show at market.

1683 Tryon *Way to Health* 485 Neither do our leathern Dublets stock their Cows, that is [etc.]. **1798** J. Lawrence *Treat. Horse* II. 156 There is also a cruel folly prevalent among cow-jobbers, namely that of stocking the cows, as it is called. **1847** [see stocking *vbl. sb.* 4].

19. *intr.* Of corn, grass, etc.: To send out shoots, sprout, tiller. ? Now only *Sc.*

1574 R. Scot *Hop Garden* (1578) 18 The Hoppe never stocketh kindelye vntyll it reache higher than the Poale. **1577** Googe tr. *Heresbach's Husb.* I. 37b, Yf you mingle Otes with the seede of Medica, and sowe them, they wyll cause them to stocke very well. **1799** J. Robertson *Agric. Perth* 164 Land in good order ought to be sown thin, because the grain will stock, the straw will be strong [etc.]. **1825** Jamieson. **1856** Morton *Cycl. Agric.*, *Provincialisms*, *Stocking* (Scot.), the tillering of grain crops in spring. *a* **1882** *Scotsman* (O.) About two months ago broad blanks were to be seen on many oatfields, and though they have stocked a little, the crop is yet far too thin.

20. *trans.* To sow (land) with grass or clover. Also with *down*: To lay down to grass, etc. *U.S.*

1828–32 Webster, *Stock*..to supply with seed; as, to *stock* land with clover or herdsgrass. *American farmers.* **1870** *Daily News* 16 Apr., In the following year it is sown to oats, and 'stocked down' with clover and grass seed. **1891** *Century Dict.*, *Stock*..to furnish with a permanent growth, especially with grass: as, to *stock* a pasture. **1911** Webster, *Stock down*, Agric., to sow, as plowed land, with seed of grass or other permanent forage crop.

b. Of weeds: ? To overrun, choke (land) with their growth.

1765 *Museum Rust.* IV. 187 If they are suffered to seed, they will soon stock the land.

21. To cause to be cropped or eaten by cattle; to use (land) as pasture.

1794 Vancouver *Agric. Cambridge* 188 The first year of the new grass it is stocked very hard with sheep. **1863** *Jrnl. R. Agric. Soc.* XXIV. 625 There is a limit to the extent to which we can stock and crop land. *Ibid.* 636 The best plan was to place them upon old grass-land, which had not been stocked with sheep through the previous part of the year. **1886** *W. Somerset Word-bk.* s.v., It is common to let pasture 'only to be stocked'—i.e. depastured, not to be mown for hay. **1909** *Nation* 18 Sept. 881/1 Fields of dry grey uneaten bennets that have been too sparsely stocked.

22. *intr.* Of live stock: To bear being crowded on pasture land.

1863 *Jrnl. R. Agric. Soc.* XXIV. 477 The Shropshires [i.e. sheep] upon the rich and heavy land of the Vales have this peculiar merit: they will stock thickly.

23. *trans.* **a.** To put (playing cards) together in a pack. **b.** To arrange or shuffle fraudulently.

1735 Dyche & Pardon *Dict.*, *Stock*,..in *Gaming*, to put the Cards together again without playing them. **1828–32** Webster, *Stock*..4. To pack; to put into a pack; as, to stock cards. **1865** *Slang Dict.* 247 To stock cards, is to arrange cards in a certain manner for cheating purposes. **1894** [see stocked *a.* 7].

stock (stɒk), *v.*[2] Now *dial.* [? ad. OF. *estoquier*, *estoquer*, to strike with the edge or point of a weapon. Cf. stock *sb.*[3] and stoke *v.*[1]]

†**1.** *trans.* To strike or hit with a thrust of a pointed weapon. *Obs. rare*$^{-1}$.

a **1625** Fletcher *Love's Cure* III. iv, In my young daies A Chevalier would stock a needles point, Three times together.

2. Of a bird: To peck, peck at; to make (a hole) by pecking. Also, to root *up* with the beak (cf. stock *v.*[1] 6). Also *intr.* To peck *away* (*at*).

1653 Baxter *Chr. Concord* 24 Some Birds first make their way into a hard tree by stocking a hole in it. **1674** Flavel *Husb. Spiritualized* xiii. 115 Corn..but slightly covered is stockt up as soon as it begins to sprout by Rooks and other devouring fowls. **1843** *Zoologist* I. 368 Rooks have at times seriously injured fields of young grass, by stocking up the red clover plants. **1844** E. Jesse *Sc. & T. Country Life* I. 213 He observed a young cock..stock with his beak the mice as fast as they fell to the ground. **1845** Darwin *Voy. Nat.* iii. (ed. 2) 57 The Polyborus Chimango..injures the potato-crops in Chiloe by stocking up the roots when first planted. **1890** *Glouc. Gloss.*, *Stock*, to peck; of a bird pulling up seed corn.. **1893** *Cornhill Mag.* Nov. 505 There were the old rooks stocking away at the grubs and chafers.

stockade (stɒˈkeɪd), *sb.* Also 8–9 stoccade, (9 stocade). [a. F. †*estocade*, corruption of *estacade*, a. Sp. *estacada*: see staccado, stockado.

In the 17th c. the Fr. word was occasionally miswritten *estocade*, by confusion with *estocade* sword-thrust, stoccado. This may be in part the source of the Eng. form.]

1. A defensive barrier of stakes or piles placed across a harbour or river, around a building, village, and the like; spec. in *Fortification*, a barricade for entrenchments and redoubts, usually made of timber, furnished with loopholes for gun-fire.

1614 Gorges *Lucan* II. 77 *marg.*, The like [*i.e.* a boom across the harbour's mouth] was vsed by the Spaniards before Antwerpe, which they termed a Stockade. **1777** Mason *Eng. Garden* II. 293 As, round some citadel, the engineer Directs his sharp stoccade. **1810** Wellington in Gurw. *Disp.* (1838) VI. 11 To secure effectually the breach on the left of the line..by a stockade. **1812** J. Henry *Camp. agst. Quebec* 19 The Fort..consisted of old Block-houses and a stocade. **1834–47** J. S. Macaulay *Field Fortif.* (1851) 92 Of Stoccades. If the work were a lunette, a stoccade, or strong palisade may be placed across the ditch. **1852** Doveton *Burmese War* i. 19 Rangoon..presented an assemblage of fragile bamboo tenements..encircled by a wooden fence,..known to us by the name of a 'stockade'. **1865** Livingstone *Zambesi* xxvii. 557 On the 11th October we arrived at the stockade of Chinsamba. **1879** *Cassell's Techn. Educ.* I. 162 Stoccades are formidable parapets constructed entirely of wood in situations not exposed to artillery fire... Ordinary stoccades consist of a row of upright timbers 12 or 14 inches in diameter, and from 10 to 15 feet in length. **1892** Col. G. Philips *Text Bk. Fortif.* (ed. 5) 74 A Stockade is a defensible rifle proof wall, made usually of timber or railway iron, and provided with loopholes to fire from.

2. *transf.* **a.** (See quot.)

1858 Simmonds *Dict. Trade*, *Stockade*, a fortification or fence of pointed stakes, in New Zealand called a pah; a cattle-pen.

b. *Hydraul. Engin.* A row of piles serving as a breakwater or as a protection to an embankment.

1891 *Century Dict.* **1895** *Daily News* 21 Mar. 5/3 One of the gales of February..destroyed 3,000 square yards of the stockade between Willop and Dymchurch.

c. A prison, esp. a military one.

1865 *Atlantic Monthly* Mar. 286/2 'Is it a pen?'.. 'Yes, yours,' retorted one of the guard, with a grin,—'the Stockade Prison.' **1882** W. D. Hay *Brighter Britain!* I. 23 A man..on a subsequent conviction, might be sent to the Stockade (prison) without the option of a fine. **1905** W. E. B. Du Bois *Souls of Black Folk* vii. 126 The high whitewashed fence of the 'stockade,' as the county prison [Dougherty, Georgia, U.S.] is called. **1906** *Daily Colonist* (Victoria, B.C.) 16 Jan. 2/5 [Two men] will be sent to the convict stockade on the islands in the tropics off the coast. **1945** *Richmond* (Va.) *News-Leader* 10 Oct. 8/1 'Stockade' in army language is synonymous with jail. **1979** P. Gosling *Zero Trap* xix. 191 'What's a glasshouse?'.. 'A prison,' Skinner explained... 'The stockade,' Laura amplified. 'That's what they call it in the [U.S.] Army.'

3. *attrib.* and *Comb.*, as ***stockade timber***, ***work***; ***stockade-like*** adj.; **stockade fort** [fort *sb.*[1] 1 c] *Brit. N. Amer.* and *U.S.*, a fortified trading station; **stockade tambour** (cf. tambour *sb.* 6).

1756 Washington *Lett.* Writ. 1889 I. 397, I am directed to evacuate all the *stockade forts. **1809** W. Irving *Knickerb.* (1861) 65 The land being thus fairly purchased of the Indians,..a stockade fort and trading house were forthwith erected. **1894** *Outing* (U.S.) XXIV. 337/1 A *stockade-like inclosure. **1892** Col. G. Philips *Text Bk. Fortif.* (ed. 5) 164 A *stockade tambour may be from 6 to 9 feet broad inside, and long enough for three or four men firing each way. **1879** *Cassell's Techn. Educ.* II. 129/2 This brings the loopholes close to the ground, and exposes as little as possible of the *stoccade timbers. *Ibid.*, As a rule the side and front walls are constructed of *stoccade work.

stockade (stɒˈkeɪd), *v.* [f. stockade *sb.*] *trans.* To protect or fortify with a stockade. Also with advs. *in*, *off*, *round*.

1755 T. Forbes in *C. Gist's Jrnls.* (1893) 150 This Fort was composed of four Houses built by way of Bastions and the intermediate Space stockaded. **1775** Adair *Amer. Ind.* 183 Having placed the dead on a high scaffold stockaded round. **1811** Wellington in Gurw. *Disp.* (1838) VII. 413 The breach at Badajoz can scarcely be more than stockaded. **1855** Kingsley *Westw. Ho!* xxi, We must..stockade a camp, and get our sick and provisions thither. **1864** Carlyle *Fredk. Gt.* XVI. xiv. IV. 474 Who landed, accordingly, on that rough shore; [and] stockaded themselves in. **1893** Selous *Trav. S.E. Africa* 297 João's town was well built and very strongly stockaded. **1897** Mary Kingsley *W. Africa* 148 A sweetly amicable style for factories, who as a rule firmly stockade themselves off from their next door neighbours.

Hence **stoˈckading** *vbl. sb.*, the action of the verb; also, *concr.* stockade-work.

1855 Kingsley *Westw. Ho!* xxi, I know nought about stockading; but Sir Francis would have given the same counsel. **1881** Mrs. C. Praed *Policy & P.* I. 59 Rough stockading..divided the settlers' paddocks from the road. **1897** Henty *On Irrawaddy* 175 Even the women had been compelled to labour in the work of stockading.

stockaded (stɒˈkeɪdɪd), *ppl. a.* [f. stockade *sb.* or *v.* + -ed.] Protected with a stockade.

1778 T. Hutchins *Topogr. Descr. Virginia* etc. 29 Ouiatanon is a small stockaded fort. **1834** M. Scott *Cruise Midge* ii, The fort..was a stockaded enclosure. **1908** Sir H. Johnston *G. Grenfell* I. xi. 197 They suddenly burst out of their own stockaded settlement on the rest of the town.

b. Of an island: Artificially formed by driving piles into the bed of the water.

1863 Lyell *Antiq. Man* 30 These 'stockaded islands,' as they [*i.e.* Irish lake-dwellings] have been sometimes called.

†**stoˈckado**, *sb.* *Obs.* Forms: 7 stocado, 7–8 stoccado, stoccata, 7, 9 stockado. [Altered form of staccado, as if f. stock *sb.*[1] Cf. stockade *sb.*] = stockade *sb.* 1.

[**1589** P. Ive *Fortif.* 38 Place in the riuer..a stackado of great piles to keepe an enemy out.] **1609** E. Grimestone *Gen. Hist. Netherl.* XII. 878 They of Antuerpe made new engines to breake and burne the bridge and Stocadoes [orig. F. *les estocades*] which the prince of Parma had made. **1615** Heywood *Foure Prentises* I. Wks. 1874 II. 242 Stockadoes, Palizadoes, stop their waters. **1638** R. Baker tr. *Balzac's Lett.* (vol. II) 204 A simple Captaine of Holland, who talkes nothing but Stoccadoes; and Circumvallation. **1783** W. F. Martyn *Geog. Mag.* II. 509 A small fort surrounded by Stoccadoes. **1809** *Ann. Reg.* 215 In order to protect them against fire ships, stockadoes, raised on piles, were placed 250 fathoms higher up the river.

b. *attrib.*, as ***stockado rail***; **stockado fort**, ? = *stockade fort* (see stockade *sb.* 3).

1760 *Brit. Chron.* 4 Apr. 326 It seems intended to surround the lawn in St. James's Park with a stoccado rail. **1766** Stork *Acc. E. Florida* 34 Forming a second communication between the stoccata fort..and fort Mosa.

†**stoˈckado**, *v.* *Obs.* [f. stockado *sb.*] = stockade *v.*, also with *about*, *round*.

1647 Sprigge *Anglia Rediv.* III. i. (1854) 133 Several works commanding one another,..being pallisadoed and stockadoed. **1699** Dampier *Voy.* II. I. 160 The back part is stockadoed round with great Trees, set up on end. **1701** C. Wolley *Jrnl. New York* (1860) 50 They fence and stockado their graves about. **1765** R. Rogers *Acc. N. Amer.* 246 The Indians..do not neglect to fortify themselves, many of their towns being well stockadoed.

Hence †**stockadoed** *ppl. a.*

1675 in *J. Easton's Narr.* (1858) 75 Where there is not a Block House or some stockadoed or palisadoed House.

stockado, variant of stoccado.

stockage (ˈstɒkɪdʒ). [f. stock *v.* after *pasturage*.] The action of putting cattle on land to feed on the crop. (Cf. stock *v.* 21.)

1884 *Advt.*, *Taunton*, *Somerset*, Sale of a small..Estate with excellent Homestead and right of Stockage on the Hill.

†**stockant**, *a.* *rare*$^{-1}$. [f. stock *sb.*[1] 8, after *couchant*, etc.] Frequently set in the stocks.

1652 Brome *Jovial Crew* II. E 1, *Mer.* Couchant and Passant, Guardant, Rampant Beggars. *Vin.* Current and vagrant— *Hil.* Stockant, whippant Beggars!

†**stockard**[1]. *Obs.* Alleged name of a bird.

1579 Hake *Newes out of Powles* iv. (1872) D ij b, Stent, Stockard, Stampine, Tantereuele, and Wigeon of the best. **1610** W. Folkingham *Art of Survey* IV. iii. 83 Fowling may be for the Bittour,..Pyntayl, Stockard, Duck, [etc.].

†**stockard**[2]. *Obs. rare.* ? = stocking *sb.*

1597 in Hore *Hist. Wexford* (1900) I. 280 One bed tik, 2 hatts, 3 prs. stockards, 24 lbs. pewter.

†**ˈstockbridge.** *Obs. rare.* Also stocbred. [a. MFlem. *stocbreet* (MLG. *stockbrêt*, MHG. *stockbreit*), lit. 'yard-wide' (*stok* yard measure, *breet* broad *a.*). The later form coincides with the name of a town in Hants.] Some kind of cloth.

1526 J. Hacket *To Wolsey* 4 July (*MS. Cott. Galba* B. IX. 22) The bourgessys of the sayd town [Bruges] cawssyd to bryng fro Andwerp and fro the Sclus manny kerseys and stocbreds. **1583** *Rates Custom Ho.* G ij, Rates for clothes... Streits Stockbridges Cardenals.

ˈstock-ˌbroker, stockbroker. [stock *sb.*[1]]

a. A broker who, for a commission, buys and sells stocks on behalf of clients.

1706 Phillips (ed. Kersey) s.v. *Broker*, *Stock-Brokers* are such as buy and sell Shares in the joynt Stocks of a Company, or Corporation, for any Person that shall desire them. **1746** W. Thompson *R.N. Adv.* (1757) 46 Usurers, Stock-Brokers, and Merchants. **1834** Marryat *P. Simple* i, My father had told me that Mr. Handycock was his stock-broker. **1867** Trollope *Chron. Barset* I. xxxvii. 320 A man may be a stockbroker though he never sells any stock.

b. **stockbroker belt**, any prosperous residential area in the Home Counties favoured by stockbrokers or other affluent businessmen; also *transf.* of similar areas elsewhere; usu. with *the*; similarly **Stockbroker('s Tudor**, a facetious term for a style of mock-Tudor architecture supposed to be favoured by such people.

1960 [see belt *sb.*[1] 5 a]. **1961** *Spectator* 14 Apr. 523 They live in the Sussex stockbroker-belt. **1968** *Listener* 22 Aug. 248/2 A moderately successful novelist..bored with his stockbroker-belt home. **1976** J. I. M. Stewart *Young Pattullo* ii. 24 She had been brought up in a stockbroker belt in the Home Counties. **1981** M. Jon *Wallington Case* iv. 24 It's a large house in..the stockbroker-belt, not far from Wilmslow. **1939** O. Lancaster *Homes Sweet Homes* 70 (*heading*) Stockbrokers Tudor. **1940** GRAVES & HODGE *Long Week-End* xi. 180 In 'Stockbroker's Tudor' houses.. ingenuity was displayed in olde-worlde disguise. **1958** J. CANNAN *And be a Villain* i. 6 Next best were these Stockbrokers' Tudor jobs built immediately before the first world war. **1959** *Good Food Guide* 98 Unlike Victorian Gothic, Stockbroker Tudor and such like varieties, this medieval mansion is perfect in every detail, except date. **1980** D. CLARK *Poacher's Bag* iv. 81 It had been an old inn. Now it had sprouted wings in stockbroker Tudor.

So **'stock-,brokerage, -,brokery**, the business of a stock-broker; **'stock-,broking** *vbl. sb.* and *ppl. a.*

1792 A. YOUNG *Trav. France* 513 The banking, money-changing, and stock-broking writers, with Necker at their head. **1837** CARLYLE *Fr. Rev.* I. III. viii, From the dens of Stock-brokerage. **1869** W. S. GILBERT *Bab Ball., Disillusioned* 29 With vulgar, coarse, stock-broking face. **1874** M. COLLINS *Transmigr.* III. viii. 127, I was specially anxious to transfer stockbrokery to Algy. **1885** *Law Rep., 15 Q.B. Div.* 116 An account in respect of stockbroking transactions carried on between them. **1896** *Daily News* 9 Nov. 3/4 He was now learning stockbroking in the city. **1952** S. KAUFFMANN *Philanderer* (1953) ii. 26 It reminded her of her father (a minor officer of a stockbrokerage firm). **1972** *Publishers Weekly* 6 Mar. 24/1 Her husband.. has his own stockbrokerage firm on Wall Street.

'stock-car. [f. STOCK *sb.*[1] + CAR *sb.*[1]] **1.** A truck or wagon for transporting cattle or other livestock by rail. *U.S.*

1858 *Pennsylvania Rail Road Ann. Rep.* 14 The rolling stock [included].. 188 Eight-wheeled Stock Cars. **1875** KNIGHT *Dict. Mech.* 2390 *Stock-car*, a railway-car for carrying cattle, horses, sheep, hogs, etc. **1898** KIPLING *Day's Work* 222 There were oil-cars, and hay-cars, and stock-cars full of lowing beasts. **1920** *Proc. 3rd Nat. Country Life Conf.* 12 They shot me across the country in a stock car. **1949** *Exciting Western* May 55/1 Another group was bringing the cattle up the Texas trail to ship east in the stock cars.

2. A racing car which has the basic chassis of an ordinary commercially produced vehicle but is extensively modified for use in racing. orig. *U.S.*

1914 *Automobile* 9 Apr. 792/2 It was a more strenuous test than ever staged in America in the days of stock cars. **1927** *Sat. Even. Post* 21 May 71 America's fastest stock car. **1935** EYSTON & LYNDON *Motor Racing & Record Breaking* viii. 73 They have been rivalled by reconstructed 'stock' cars. **1960** *Daily Tel.* 26 Sept. 1/8 (*heading*) Stock car ploughs into 10-deep crowd. **1982** *Times* 16 June 10/3 Andretti raced cars, stock cars, midgets, whatever presented itself.

3. *attrib.*, as ***stock-car driver, racer, racing***, etc.

1914 *Automobile* 9 Apr. 800/1 Chairman Richard Kennerdell and his Contest Board are at work on the stock car rules. **1955** *Times* 17 May 10/1 A woman stock car driver ..died in a Coventry hospital to-night from injuries received in an accident while she was competing in a stock car meeting. **1960** *News Chron.* 26 Sept. 1/5 He organises stock-car and jalopy racing. **1969** A. LURIE *Real People* 114 Nick Donato proposed that we should all go and watch what he called 'my kind of racing'—at the stock-car track over in Dryden. **1973** 'D. JORDAN' *Nile Green* vi. 29 Ramshackle, blaring taxis, weaving round the squares with the recklessness of stock-car drivers. **1976** B. BOVA *Multiple Man* (1977) viii. 87 Become a stock car racer. It's a helluva lot safer. **1976** A. DAVIS *Television* 67 The programmes close with classified results..including American and Gaelic football, stock car racing, canoe slalom and hurling.

stock-card. [f. STOCK *sb.*[1] + CARD *sb.*[1]] A large wool-card fastened to a stock or support. (See STOCK *sb.*[1] 2 a.)

1562 *Richmond Wills* (Surtees) 156 Stockcards and hande cards iij[s] iiij[d]. **1585** HIGINS *Junius' Nomencl.* 254/1 *Pecten*, .. a wooll card, or stocke card. **1688** HOLME *Armoury* III. 285/2 The Stock Card is of the same nature as the Wool Card only of a larger size, having a double handle fixt on the middle of the Board, by which the Workman holdeth with both Hands, and so Cards Wool (for it is only for Wool) upon another such like Card, but larger [etc.]. **1827** *Edin. Rev.* XLVI. 5 This..most ingenious..person adapted the stock-cards used in the woollen manufacture to the carding of cotton. **1835** URE *Philos. Manuf.* 170 The ancient plan of flat hand or stock cards.

Hence **†stock-card** *v. trans.*, to tease or scribble (wool) with a stock-card. **stock-carder**, one who uses a stock-card.

1728 CHAMBERS *Cycl.* s.v. *Woollen Manufactory*, A Pack.. of short Wool..employs..three Men to Sort, Dry, Mix, and make it ready for the Stock-Carder; five to Scribble, or Stock-Card it [etc.].

'stock-dove. Forms: see STOCK *sb.*[1] and DOVE. Also 4-6 -dowe, 5 -dowef. [Cf. Flem. †*stockduive* (Kilian), G. *stocktaube* (= *holztaube, hohltaube*). Prob. so named as living in hollow trees.

The conjecture that the name was given because this kind of pigeon was supposed to be the 'stock' or ancestral form of the domestic pigeon is unlikely.]

The wild pigeon, *Columba œnas*.

c **1340** *Nominale* (Skeat) 804 *Coloumbe ramer et vanele* Stokdowe and lapwynge. *c* **1425** *Voc.* in Wr.-Wülcker 640/3 *Hic palumbus*, stokedowef. *c* **1440** *Promp. Parv.* 476/2 Stokke Dowe, *palumba, palumbes*. *c* **1530** in *Archæologia* XXV. 498 To Osbert Reds sone, for bryngyng of stockdowes, ijd. **1584** LYLY *Sappho* IV. iii. 3 Me thought I saw a Stockdoue or woodquist, I knowe not how to tearme it. **1697** DRYDEN *Virg. Past.* I. 77 Stock-Doves and Turtles tell their am'rous pain. **1766** PENNANT *Brit. Zool.* I. 391 Rock-Pigeons have been often seen mixed with the flights of Stock Doves. **1867** TEGETMEIER *Pigeons* 13 The Stock Dove usually breeds in the hollows of decayed trees, sometimes in deserted rabbit burrows. **1895** LYDEKKER *Roy. Nat. Hist.* IV. 371 The stock-dove..often confused with the rock-dove, which it resembles in size and general colour, although distinguished by having the rump grey instead of white.

stocked (stɒkt), *a.* and *ppl. a.* [f. STOCK *sb.*[1] and *v.*[1] + -ED.]

†1. Set in the stocks, imprisoned. *Obs.*

c **1425** *Found. St. Bartholomew's* (E.E.T.S.) 27 Oure lord ihesu criste, the whiche losith stokkid men. *c* **1440** *Promp. Parv.* 476/2 Stokkyd, yn stokkys, *cip(p)atus*.

2. Of a female animal: Impregnated, breeding.

1478 *Acta Audit.* (1839) 74/2, xij stokit meris and a stag of a ȝere auld. **1490** *Acta Dom. Concil.* (1839) 146/2 A stokkit mere and hir foloware price iiij li.

3. Of a fire-arm, a tool: Furnished with a stock.

1497 *Naval Acc. Hen. VII* (1896) 290 Serpentynes.. stokked cxvj, vnstokked xxv. **1594** in *Highland Papers* (S.H.S. 1914) I. 183 He schot him with my reid stocket hagbit. **1635** *Relat. Maryland* vii. 45 Item, 2 Piercers stocked. **1648** *Bury Wills* (Camden) 217 My little black stocked peece inlayed with silver, and my case of redd stocked pistolls.

†4. Of hose. Cf. STOCK *v.*[1] 3 b.

1598 E. GUILPIN *Skial.* (1878) 48 The long stockt hose, or close Venetian.

5. Of a tree: ? Rooted up or felled.

a **1595** SOUTHWELL *St. Peter's Compl.* (1602) 72 Like stocked tree whose branches all doe fade.

6. Furnished with a stock or store. Also with adv., as ***well-stocked***.

a **1796** BURNS *'Thou's welcome, wean'* vi, Twill please me mair to hear an' see 't, Than stocket mailens. **1829** F. GLASSE *Belgic Past.* iii. 46 Had your sires toil'd a century, or more, With a stock'd farm, they had not heap'd the store Which Strephon claims. **1859** REEVE *Brittany* 228 We were led.. through a large and well-stocked garden. **1897** MEREDITH *Amazing Marriage* I. xv. 169 She could get up enthusiasm for a stocked hamper. **1909** *Edin. Rev.* Oct. 319 A barely stocked purse.

7. Of cards: Fraudulently arranged or dealt.

1894 J. N. MASKELYNE *Sharps & Flats* vi. 147 He is enabled to know when the stocked cards are being given off and who has them.

stocken-apple: see STOCKING-APPLE.

stocker ('stɒkə(r)). [f. STOCK *v.*[1] and *sb.*[1] + -ER[1].]

1. A workman who makes or fits stocks, esp. gun-stocks.

1641 *Sc. Acts Chas. I* (1870) V. 562/2 Stockeres of Gunes. **1881** GREENER *Gun* 249 The stocker upon receiving the stock first roughs it into shape. **1886** *Daily Tel.* 9 Feb. 7/5 Gun Maker. Wanted a stocker and screwer. **1892** SIMMONDS *Dict. Trade* Suppl., *Stocker*, a man engaged in making stock-locks.

2. A workman employed in felling or grubbing up trees. *local.*

1686 PLOT *Staffordsh.* 211 Under the hands of Francis Marshall, Thomas March, Stockers. **1890** *Gloucester Gloss.*, *Stockers*, men employed to clear out the butt of a tree ready for felling.

3. *local.* (See quot.)

1879 MISS JACKSON *Shropsh. Word-bk.*, *Stocker*, an implement used for 'stocking' up turnips; it has two prongs and a handle four feet long.

4. *U.S.* and *Canada*. An animal, esp. a young steer or heifer, sold to be finally butchered, but kept as stock until matured or fattened; distinguished from *killer*. (W. 1911.)

1881 *Chicago Times* 1 June, Stockers and feeders were dull and weaker. **1891** *Daily News* 2 July 6/4 Animals for fattening known as stockers. **1891** *Times* 1 Oct. 9/4 The bulk of the Canadians were only stockers.

5. *dial.* Fish of other kinds taken when fishing for herring or pilchards (E.D.D.); a sum of money accruing to a member of the crew as his share in this. Also *attrib.* as ***stocker-bait***.

1883 CLARK RUSSELL *Sailors' Lang.*, *Stocker-bait*, small fish given by smack-owners to their apprentices to sell for their own profit. **1904** in *Eng. Dial. Dict.* s.v., (Cornwall.) We get some mackerel and pollock in the pilchard nets or the herring nets. That goes for what we call 'stocker'. The crew divides that. **1914** *Times* 14 July, Stocker is explained as being money received from the sale of tails of a fish called the monk, roes, shell-fish, &c. *Ibid.*, They took the stocker, they sold it, and they handed the proceeds to some member of the crew for division between himself and the other members entitled to it.

6. A warehouseman or stock-keeper. Also (*U.S.*), an assistant engaged to look after stock held for sale by a business firm.

1921 *Dict. Occup. Terms* (1927) §940 *Stock keeper, stocker*, a warehouseman.. who keeps stock book showing amount of stock (as distinguished from stores). **1976** *Billings* (Montana) *Gaz.* 27 June 5-E/4 At age 14 or 15, cashiers, salesmen, stockers, baggers, gas pumpers, car washers,.. can work. **1979** *Arizona Daily Star* 5 Aug. (Advt. Section) 5/10 Full time person to work in our yard as salesperson and stocker.

7. *U.S. colloq.* A stock-car; a stock-car racer.

1976 *Harper's Mag.* Jan. 20 You simply can't believe the noise of these engines. Stockers, motorcycles, needlenosed dragsters,.. tear the night apart for hours. **1976** *Time* 27 Sept. 82/3 Stock cars... Richard Petty, king of the stockers, won $378,865 last year. **1978** *Time* 25 Sept. 88 Members of the National Association for Stock Car Auto Racing.. rolled up to the 'diplomatic entrance' in their Day-Glo colored 'stockers'.

stock exchange. a. A market for the buying and selling of public securities; the place or building where this is done; an association of brokers and jobbers who transact business in a particular place or market.

Often with capital initials as the name of a particular building, esp. that in the City of London.

1773 *Lond. Chron.* 13-15 July 50/3 Yesterday the Brokers and others at New Jonathan's, came to a resolution, that instead of its being called New Jonathan's, it should be named 'The Stock Exchange,' which is to be wrote over the door. **1809** *Morn. Herald* 18 May 3/3 Yesterday, being a Holiday, no Business was done at the Stock Exchange. **1887** *Encycl. Brit.* XXII. 557/1 In active times the business transacted daily on the London stock exchange amounts to an enormous total. **1905** MISS BROUGHTON *Waif's Progr.* ii. 17 He is on the Stock Exchange!

b. *attrib.*

1849 J. FRANCIS *Chronicles & Characters Stock Exchange* xv. 288 It was proved that one million had been wasted in commissions and military preparations; in Stock Exchange transactions and Stock Exchange jobbing. **1877** R. GIFFEN (*title*) Stock Exchange securities. **1922** JOYCE *Ulysses* 521, I shall..suck my thumping good Stock Exchange cigar. **1940** T. S. ELIOT *East Coker* III. 11 The Stock Exchange Gazette, the Directory of Directors. **1957** *Encycl. Brit.* XXI. 420/1 After 1954 all members of the council (from 30 to 36 in number) were to be elected by stock exchange members generally.

stockey, variant of STOCKY.

stock-fish, 'stockfish. For forms see STOCK *sb.*[1] and FISH *sb.*[1]; also 3 -fhis, 4 -fihs, -fys, 5 -fisch(e, -physhe, *pl.* -fyscheys. [Prob. a. (M)Du. *stokvisch* = MHG. *stocvisch* (G. *stockfisch*), MSw. *stokfisker* (Sw. *stockfisk*, Da. *stokfisk*); f. Du. *stok* STOCK *sb.*[1]; the reason for the designation is variously conjectured.] **1. a.** A name for cod and other gadoid fish cured by splitting open and drying hard in the air without salt.

1290 in J. Stevenson *Docum. illustr. Hist. Scot.* (1870) I. 139 Pro cc stokfhis, xviij*s*. **1350** in *Registr. Monast. de Winchelcumba* (1892) 264 Dimidium centum duri piscis de stocfish, videlicet coursfish. **1436** *Pol. Poems* (1859) II. 191 Of the comodius stokfysshe of Yselonde. **1450-4** in *Oxf. Stud. Soc. & Legal Hist.* (1914) IV. 199, ix[c] Stockfisshes and an c iiij[xx] Saltfisshes. **1555** EDEN *Decades* (Arb.) 303 From hense [Norway] is brought into all Europe a fysshe of the kindes of them whiche we caule haddockes or hakes indurate and dryed with coulde, and beaten with clubbes or stockes, by reason whereof the Germayns caule them stocke-fysshe. **1617** MORYSON *Itin.* III. 99 In Norway they catch great store of Stockfish, which they beate with cudgels, and dry with cold. **1796** MORSE *Amer. Geog.* II. 18 (Norway) Stock-fish in great numbers are caught and dried upon the rocks without salting. **1856** KANE *Arctic Expl.* I. ii. 22 The stockfish, dried in the open air, without salt.

b. In figurative, proverbial and jocular expressions. (Often with reference to the beating of the fish before cooking.)

1515 BARCLAY *Egloges* i. (1570) A ij, And as a stockfishe wrinkled is my skinne. **1552** HULOET, s.v. *Beate*, Beate often as a stockfyshe is beaten, *retundo*. **1560** BECON *Catech.* VI. Wks. I. 522 b, Those parents.. whiche furiously rage against their children, and without consideration beat them as stockfish. **1575** R. B. *Apius & Virginia* (facs.) Bj, As stout as a Stockefish. **1610** SHAKS. *Temp.* III. ii. 79 By this hand, Ile..make a Stockfish of thee. **1666** *Third Advice to Painter* 30 Beat him to Stock-fish, else he'l ne'r be good. **1680** OTWAY *Caius Marius* V. ii, As dead as a Herring, a Stock-fish or Door-Nail. **1841** DICKENS *Barn. Rudge* lvi, Old John sat, mute as a stock-fish. **1859** MEREDITH *R. Feverel* xxxvii, London is as dead as a stock-fish.

c. In contemptuous address to a person.

1596 SHAKS. *1 Hen. IV*, II. iv. 271 Away.. you stocke-fish.

d. *attrib.* and *Comb.*, as ***stockfish-bone, -monger, -sound***; **stockfish-hammer**, a hammer for beating the fish before cooking; **†stockfish-wood**, an American wood resembling logwood.

1299 In R. R. Sharpe *Cal. Lond. Lett.-Bk. C.* (1901) 55 Stocfismongers. **1350-1** in W. H. St. John Hope *Windsor Castle* (1913) I. 161 In Cvj stokfisshsondis emptis pro glu inde faciendo. *c* **1430** LYDG. *Min. Poems* 23 A stokefisshe boon in dirkeness ȝeveth a light. **1480-1** *Durham Acc. Rolls* (Surtees) 97, ij Stokfisshammers. **1699** DAMPIER *Voy.* II. II. 57 Of these sorts Bloodwood and Stock-fish-wood are of the natural growth of America. **1766** ENTICK *Lond.* IV. 6 Robert March, a stock-fish monger.

2. [ad. Afrikaans, f. Du. *stokvis* stockfish, hake.] Also **†stok-fish.** The South African hake, *Merluccius capensis*, of the family Gadidæ, a large marine food fish. *S. Afr.*

1823 W. W. BIRD *State of Cape of Good Hope in 1822* viii. 159 The hottentot, jacob evert, elft, hake or stockfish, the king klipfish, the steen brazen, and the stompneus are all of excellent quality. **1853** L. PAPPE *Edible Fishes Cape of Good Hope* 31 The cured or dried Cape Stok-fish is an excellent dish. **1913** W. W. THOMPSON *Sea Fisheries Cape Colony* ii. 48 The larger fish, such as..steenbras, stockfish,..are caught with fish bait. **1930** [see KINGKLIP]. **1947** K. H. BARNARD *Pict. Guide S. Afr. Fishes* iii. 83 The stockfish has become one of the mainstays of the South African fishing industry.

Hence **†'stockfished** *pa. pple.*, made hard as a stock-fish.

1654 GAYTON *Pleas. Notes* III. i. 68 So verily I believe, that our Knight's parts would be stockfisht, and solidated by continuall contusions, threshings, and quassations.

'stock-,gillyflower. Forms: see GILLYFLOWER; also 6 gyllofer, geleflour, gelle-flower, gille-, 7 jellyflower. [Cf. Flem. *stokvioliere* 'viola lignescens' (Kilian), now *stokviolier, -f(e)lier*, *stoffelier* (De Bo).] The plant *Matthiola incana*; so called as having a woody stem, in distinction from clove-gillyflower. (See also STOCK *sb.*[1] 43.)

1530 PALSGR. 276/2 Stocke gyllofer, *armorie bastarde.* **1548** TURNER *Names Herbes* 80 Purple and blew stockgelefloures. **1655** MOUFET & BENNET *Health's Improv.* iii. 19 Stock-gillyflowers. **1677** GREW *Anat. Plants*, etc. (1682) 271 The Purple Flower of Stock-July Flowers. **1894** BLACKMORE *Perlycross* xlii, With..stock-gilly flowers in their hands.

ˈstockˌholder.

1. One who is a proprietor of stock in the public funds or the funds of a joint-stock company, etc. Also (now *U.S.*) used more widely to include the meaning of 'shareholder'.

1753 *Scots Mag.* Mar. 116/1 The stockholders in the Silesia loan. **1776–83** JUSTAMOND tr. *Raynal's Hist. Indies* I. 359 The stock-holders will be mistrustful, the shares will be depreciated, and the Company will fall to ruin. **1844** H. H. WILSON *Brit. India* III. 498 The India stockholders would be left without any available means of realising their dividends. **1856** EMERSON *Eng. Traits, Wealth* Wks. (Bohn) II. 72 It draws the nobility into the competition as stockholders in the mine, the canal, the railway. **1883** *Harper's Mag.* Nov. 943/1 Its stockholders pocket comfortable dividends of seven per cent. **1904** *Athenæum* 2 July 8/1 The use of 'stockholders' in the sense of shareholders is admissible in a work designed for American readers only. **1912** *Times* 19 Oct. 18/5 The Three-and-a-Half per Cent. Debenture stockholders.

2. A member of the Stationers' Company. ? *Obs.*

1825 HANSARD *Typogr.* 276 The trading concerns [of the Stationers' Company] are managed by a regular committee of nine members; viz., the master, the two wardens, and six other stock-holders, who are annually chosen. *Ibid.*, The livery (stock-holders) are summoned to elect.

3. *Austral.* An owner of large herds of cattle or flocks of sheep.

1819 W. C. WENTWORTH *Descr. N.S. Wales* 97 The system which the great stockholders almost invariably pursue. **1824** E. CURR *Acc. Van Diemen's Land* 83 The most negligent stock-holders now carefully house their wool.

So **ˈstockholding** *vbl. sb.* or *ppl. a.*, (of or pertaining to) the action or business of a stockholder; also, (of or pertaining to) the practice of holding material in stock.

1830 *Debates in Congress* 10 May 927 The great stockholding interest, whose funds are in various stocks, which, altogether, constitute the national debt. **1961** *Wall St. Jrnl.* 26 Apr. 3 Ralph Gish, manager of the funds' investment departments, said common stock holdings have been increased in these industries. **1962** A. BATTERSBY *Guide to Stock Control* ii. 18 If the cost of the material goes up, the amount of capital invested in stock also increases, and so does the stockholding cost. **1965** *Mod. Law Rev.* XXVIII. v. 555 Loss to other outlets of fast-selling titles.. can have a devastating effect on stockholding booksellers. **1971** *Engineering* Apr. 123 (Advt.), This van is just one of many which provide a service from stock-holding depot to the customer... With 29 stock-holding depots strategically placed throughout the British Isles, you are assured personal service. **1981** *Times* 26 Jan. 15/2 A group of smaller stockholding concerns is said to have formed a consortium through which it can buy and distribute cheaper foreign produced steel. **1981** J. SUTHERLAND *Bestsellers* i. 18 The stockholding bookshop would be sacrificed to the bookstand in the supermarket.

Stockholm (ˈstɒkhəʊm). The name of the capital city of Sweden, used *attrib.* in **Stockholm syndrome** (see quots.); **Stockholm tar**, a kind of tar prepared from resinous pinewood and used in shipbuilding, skin ointments, etc.

1978 *Practitioner* Feb. 297/1 Mr Vaders had a mild case of 'Stockholm syndrome'... Named after the dramatic and unexpected realignment of affections in the Sveriges Kreditbank robbery, this syndrome consists of a positive bond between hostage and captor, and feelings of distrust or hostility on the part of the victim towards the authorities. **1980** C. MOOREHEAD *Fortune's Hostages* ix. 183 The phrase 'Stockholm syndrome' was coined, probably in America, to explain this strange affection the victims of kidnappings and sieges come to feel for the men who hold them prisoner. **1867** *Chambers's Encycl.* IX. 296/1 The Stockholm tar, which is so widely used in shipbuilding. **1929** R. HUGHES *High Wind in Jamaica* ii. 50 He did envy the chap whose job it was to dip his hand in a great pot of aromatic Stockholm tar, and work it into the dead-eyes. **1976** *Country Life* 5 Feb. 298/3 Sail-making..was very hard on the hand, and..open cracks in the skin, were a frequent source of trouble... For this 'Stockholm' tar was provided by the ship owners.

Stockholmer (ˈstɒkhəʊmə(r)). [f. prec. + -ER[1].] A native or inhabitant of Stockholm.

1938 *Daily Tel.* 22 Jan. 12/3 Modern Stockholmers..are accustomed to fairly substantial midday meals in restaurants. **1968** P. B. AUSTIN *On Being Swedish* iii. 21 To be *jäktad* (literally 'chased'), to be the victim of a mad whirl of engagements such as can only lead to stomach ulcers, is the contemporary Stockholmer's life-style. **1983** *Times* 30 June 13/4, I live in Stockholm and, like the vast majority of Stockholmers, buy a monthly card that gives me unlimited access to the underground and buses.

stockily *adv.*: see after STOCKY *a.*

stockinet (stɒkɪˈnɛt). Also **stockinett(e, stockinnet, stockingett(e, -nette.** [Prob. a perversion (as if f. STOCKING *sb.* + -ET[1], -ETTE) of the older *stocking-net*: see STOCKING *sb.* 6 b.]

1. A knitted textile fabric of considerable elasticity used chiefly in the making of undergarments. Also ***stockinet cloth, material.***

1824- [see 3]. **1862** *Catal. Internat. Exhib., Brit.* II. No. 4176, Woollen Manufacturers... [Exhibiting] Elastic stockingetts. **1880** *Cassell's Fam. Mag.* VI. 442 The stockingette material, or elastic cloth,..is being adapted to whole dresses, tunics [etc.]. **1881** *Ibid.* VII. 122 Stockingnette has proved this winter a bad investment. **1890** *Textile News* 20 June, Stockinettes and fancy woollens. **1905** *Daily News* 28 Mar. 12 An important clue was found in the discovery of three masks of black stockingette.

2. A garment made of stockinet. (Short for *stockinet pantaloons, shirt.*)

1837 T. HOOK in *New Monthly Mag.* L. 155 The dancing-master in his stockinets and pumps. **1838** POE *Narr. A. G. Pym* vii. Wks. 1895 V. 91 The shirt..was a blue stockinet, with large white stripes running across.

b. ? = STOCKING 1 b. (*nonce-use.*)

1864 TICKNOR *Life Prescott* 201 A full-length of Cortés,.. his nether extremities in a sort of stockinet, like the old cavaliers of the sixteenth century.

3. *attrib.* (or *adj.*) Made of stockinet.

1824 W. IRVING *T. Trav.* II. 28 He wore a pair of dingy-white stockinet pantaloons. **1884** *Girl's Own Paper* 29 Nov. 138/3 The lady working..wears a stockingette jacket.

stocking (ˈstɒkɪŋ), *sb.* Also 6–8 **stockin,** 7 **stocken,** (6 **stokyng**). [f. STOCK *v.*[1] (sense 3) + -ING[1].]

1. a. A close-fitting garment covering the foot, the leg, and often the knee, usually made of knitted or woven wool, silk, or cotton; now *spec.* as a woman's usu. diaphanous leg-covering (esp. of silk or nylon) reaching to the thigh. Chiefly *pl.*

1583 STUBBES *Anat. Abus.* II. 39 Othersome buy cloakes, ..caps, coates, stockings, and the like. **1586** *Acc. Bk. W. Wray* in *Antiquary* XXXII. 76 Mony for a p[r] of stokyngs. **1593** *Knaresb. Wills* (Surtees) I. 195 My best under stockinges. **1603** [see JERSEY[1] 1]. **1607** E. H. *Stow's Chron.* 477 This yeare 1589 was diuised and perfected the Art of knitting or weauing of silke stockings,..and diuerse other things by engines or steele Loomes by William Lee. **1613** SHAKS. *Hen. VIII*, I. iii. 30 Renouncing cleane The faith they haue in Tennis and tall Stockings, Short blistred Breeches. **1648** SIR J. TURNER *Mem.* (Bannatyne Club) 59 Riseing nixt morning, I misd one linnen stockine, one halfe silke one and one boothose, the accoustrement under a boote for one leg. **1697** *Lond. Gaz.* No. 3269/4 [Stolen] out of a Bag, half a dozen pair of Roll Stockins, and 18 pair of short Stockins. **1785** BURNS *1st Epist. J. Lapraik* ii, On Fasteneen we had a rockin, To ca' the crack and weave our stockin. **1812** *2nd Rep. Comm. Framework-Knitters* 93 Socks..are half-stockings, or rather what is called pantaloon stockings. **1902** ELIZ. L. BANKS *Newspaper Girl* 78, I hurriedly pulled on my stockings, buttoned my boots,..and started out.

Proverbial, etc. **1695** CONGREVE *Love for Love* II. i, *Nurse.* Pray Heav'n send your Worship good Luck..for you have put on one Stocking with the wrong side outward. **1739** BYROM *Jrnl. & Lit. Rem.* (1856) II. I. 223 The chief fault it had was that of King Stephen's stockings, the costing too little price.

†**b.** ? A kind of legging or long boot, a 'boot-hose' or 'boot-stocking'. *Obs.*

1676 WOOD *Life* 21 Apr. (O.H.S.) II. 344 To Mr. Prince for a pair of riding leather stockings, 5*s.*

2. A stocking used **a.** as a purse or receptacle for storing one's money; hence, a store of money; also with qualifying word, as *big, fat, long stocking.*

1873 A. G. MURDOCH *Lilts on Doric Lyre* 90 (E.D.D.) He wi' him had brocht A stocking weel padded wi' siller. **1876** S. R. WHITEHEAD *Daft Davie* iii. 57 She had a 'stocking' gathered to meet the wants of an evil day. **1899** G. FORD *Postle Farm* xxxvii. 192 Granfer's got money laid by in a stockin' up the chimney. **1903** FARMER *Slang* s.v., *Long-stocking* (common), means in plenty; resources.

b. as a receptacle for the presents supposed by children to be deposited in it by 'Father Christmas' (or, in *U.S.*, by Santa Claus) on Christmas eve.

1853 SUSAN & ANNA B. WARNER *Christmas Stocking* (1854) 3 Little Carl always hung up his stocking, and generally had it filled. **1883** *Harper's Mag.* Dec. 15/2 The saint who generously filled the Christmas stocking.

3. a. A surgical appliance resembling a stocking. ***elastic stocking***, a covering of elastic webbing worn as a remedial support for the leg, esp. when affected with varicose veins. **b.** A bandage for the leg of a horse.

[**1676** WISEMAN *Chirurg. Treat.* II. ii. 170 In stead of a Rowler I put on a laced Stocking.] **1875** KNIGHT *Dict. Mech.*, *Stocking*...(Farriery.) A device for remedying injuries to the tendons, varicose veins, etc., occurring in the lower part of a horse's leg. **1884** T. BRYANT *Surg.* I. 566 When exercise is allowed, steady pressure by a well-applied bandage..should be maintained, or an elastic stocking worn. **1894** [implied in STOCKINGED].

4. *transf.* Applied to the surface or coat of the leg (or the lower part of it) of a bird or beast, when of different colour from the body.

1821 SCOTT *Kenilw.* xl, 'And what didst thou learn there, forward imp?' 'To catch gulls, with their webbed feet and yellow stockings,' said the boy. **1856** H. H. DIXON *Post & Paddock* ii. 37 He was a very handsome rich bay, with a white stocking on his off hind leg. **1879** L. WRIGHT *Pigeon Keeper* 124 The Beard [kind of pigeon] is usually only white at the ends of the thighs, or the 'stockings'. **1893** R. LYDEKKER *Horns & Hoofs* 11 The absence of white 'stockings' as a distinctive feature of most of our domestic breeds [of cattle]. **1908** *Animal Management* (Vet. Departm., War Office) 33 When the white hair extends just above the fetlock it is sometimes called a sock, and when much higher a stocking or leg.

5. Phrases.

a. *to stand* (a specified height) ***in one's stockings***, i.e. without one's shoes. Cf. STOCKING-FOOT c.

1855 SMEDLEY *H. Coverdale* i, Harry Coverdale stood six feet one in or out of his stockings. **1883** *Harper's Mag.* Dec. 166/1 He stands over seven feet in his stockings.

b. ***to throw the stocking***: said with reference to an old custom according to which on the wedding night the bride's stocking was thrown among the guests; it was supposed that the person hit by it would be the first of the company to be married.

For other forms of this custom see *Eng. Dial. Dict.* s.v.

1694 N. H. *Ladies Dict.* 509/1 The Stockin being motioned, the Bride must sit up to have it thrown at her Nose, that the Batchellours may know by him that first hits it, who is to be marryed next. **1709** [W. KING] *Usef. Trans. Philos.* Mar. & Apr. 12 The Sack-Posset was eaten and the Stocking thrown. **1737** POPE *Hor. Epist.* I. i. 148 At am'rous Flavio is the stocking thrown? *a* **1833** ANDERSON *Cumbld. Ball.* (1904) 126 What! breyde forgat flingin the stokin. *a* **1845** BARHAM *Ingol. Leg.* III. *Wedding Day*, They all come ..To dance at her bridal, and help 'throw the stocking',—A practice that's now discontinued as shocking.

6. = *stocking web* (see 7 b).

1812 *Rep. Committee Framework Knitters Petit.* 18 There are goods made up into a large piece of stocking, and cut out, instead of being properly shaped on the stocking frame.

7. *attrib.* and *Comb.*: **a.** simple attrib., as ***stocking-heel, -manufactory, -manufacture, thread, -trade.***

1888 KIPLING *Story of Gadsbys* 1 (*stage direction*), Spreads *stocking-heel on open hand for inspection. **1891** HARDY *Tess* vii, I declare there's a hole in my stocking-heel! **1812** *1st Rep. Comm. Framework-Knitters* App. 48 Are you acquainted with the *stocking manufactory in general? **1765** *Par. Reg. Calverton* in Felton *Hist. Machine-wrought Hosiery* (1867) 30 The *Stocking manufacture very bad last year and this. **1833** J. RENNIE *Alph. Angling* 37 These water blood-worms..are not much thicker than a *stocking thread. **1819** *Rep. Sel. Comm. Framework-Knitters* 10 The number now employed in the *stocking trade in Leicester.

b. quasi-*adj.* with the meaning 'made with the stocking-stitch, knitted, made of stockinet', as ***stocking cloth, material, night-cap, -piece, stuff, -web***; **stocking-net** (rarely †*knit*; also *attrib.*), see quot. 1884 and cf. STOCKINET.

1880 *Cassell's Family Mag.* VI. 311/1 Bège tricot, woven as closely as possible to resemble *stocking-cloth. **1880** MRS. L. S. FLOYER *Hints Exam. Needlew.* 55 Pieces of *stocking material (coarse) for darning. **1804** in *Abridgm. Specif. Patents, Wearing Apparel* II. (1875) 19 A method of double seaming and uniting the inside of *stocking net work. *Ibid.*, *Stocking knit work. **1832** *Patent* in *Newton's Lond. Jrnl.* (1838) XII. 275 Machinery..for making or manufacturing stockings, stocking-net, or framework knitting. **1884** ROWLETT *Technol. Framework Knitting* I. 101 Stocking Net, *i.e.* plain framework made from woollen yarn on circular frames... Of late years this has largely come into use for ladies' jerseys. **1818** SCOTT *Rob Roy* xxviii, [He] wore the trews,..wove out of a sort of chequered *stocking stuff. **1843** *Penny Cycl.* XXVII. 180/2 One continuous thread forms both warp and weft, if we may apply these terms to the *stocking-web. **1884** *Cassell's Family Mag.* Feb. 185/2 The stocking-web jackets..fit the figure quite closely.

c. objective, as ***stocking-darning, -knitter, -knitting, -maker, -making, -manufacturer, -mender, -presser, -seller.***

1839 DICKENS *Nich. Nick.* ix, Mrs. Squeers being engaged in the matronly pursuit of *stocking-darning. **1728** CHAMBERS *Cycl.* s.v., The Company of *Stocking-knitters establish'd at Paris in 1527, took for their Patron St. Fiacre. **1921** *Dict. Occup. Terms* (1927) §374 *Stocking knitter*,..a frame hand..who attends a power-driven frame adjusted to knit elastic hosiery. **1830** SCOTT *Hrt. Midl.* Introd., She.. knit feet to country-people's stockings, which bears about the same relation to *stocking-knitting that cobbling does to shoe-making. **1619** *Canterb. Marriage Licences* (MS.), Starr of Cranbrook, *stocken-maker. **1779** in J. R. Anderson *Burgesses of Glasgow* (1935) 117 Wilson, Gabriel, stocking-maker. **1812** J. MELISH *Trav. in U.S.A.* II. 55 Professions exercised in Pittsburg:..stocking-makers, taylors, printers, book-binders. **1812** *1st Rep. Comm. Framework-Knitters* App. 44 There are four descriptions of persons concerned in the *stocking-making business. *a* **1876** M. COLLINS *Pen Sketches* (1879) I. 149 Avoiding the dreary stocking-making town of Shepton Mallet. **1793–4** *Matthews's Bristol Directory* 11 Bailey, Henry, *Stocking-manufacturer. **1594** NASHE *Terrors Nt.* Wks. (Grosart) III. 249 [They will] steale out a signe ouer a Coblers stall, lyke Aqua vitæ sellers and *stocking menders. **1686** *Lond. Gaz.* No. 2166/4 Mr. Edward Bonsaw, *Stocking-Presser. **1599** B. JONSON *Cynthia's Rev.* II. i, He beates a Tayler very well, but a *Stocking-seller admirably.

d. Special comb.; **stocking bar**, a counter or bar in a shop at which stockings are sold; **stocking board**, a board upon which stockings when wet are stretched and dried to shape; **stocking cap**, a knitted woollen hat with a long tapered end which hangs down from the crown; **stocking filler**, a small present suitable for putting in a Christmas stocking; also *fig.*; **stocking leg**, that part of a stocking which covers the leg; also as a receptacle for money (see 2 above); **stocking legger**, ? one whose occupation was the seaming of stocking-legs;

stocking loom, machine = STOCKING FRAME; †**stocking man**, a stocking-maker; **stocking mask**, a thin nylon stocking pulled over the face to disguise the features, used esp. by criminals; hence **stocking-masked** *a.*; **stocking needle**, a darning-needle; **stocking-sole**, the sole, or that part of a stocking which comes under the tread of the foot; ***in, on one's stocking-soles***, without one's shoes (cf. 5 a above and STOCKING-FOOT c); **stocking-stitch**, the stitch used in hosiery (see quot.); **stocking stuffer** *N. Amer.* = *stocking filler* above; **stocking-throwing** (see 5 b above); **stocking tights** = TIGHTS *sb. pl.* c; **stocking top**, the upper part or leg of a stocking; **stocking-trimmer** (see quot. 1858); **stocking-weaver**, one who weaves with a stocking-frame; **stocking-yarn**, the thread used in making hosiery. Also STOCKING-FOOT, STOCKING-FRAME.

1962 *Guardian* 23 Feb. 8/3 The idea of a *stocking bar came from America eight years ago. **1965** Stocking bar [see BAR *sb.*[1] 28 b]. **1862** *Catal. Internat. Exhib.* II. xxvii. 56 Glove and gauntlet trees and *stocking boards. **1902** *Daily Chron.* 14 Feb. 7/5 The captain offered him a *stocking-cap, and he objected to wear it. **1978** *Times* 4 Mar. 22/5 The fishermen still wear their shirts and trousers of Portuguese tartan and long black stocking caps. **1959** *Listener* 10 Dec. 1054/1 A useful *stocking-filler at 2s. is a gardener's measuring beaker, graduated for almost all fertilizers, insecticides, etc. **1973** *Radio Times* 20–27 Dec. 3 How's this for a stocking-filler? *Radio Times* has a complete Christmas package for you. **1979** M. BABSON *Twelve Deaths of Christmas* xx. 109 Just tiny bits and pieces. Stocking fillers, small tokens. **1861** R. QUINN *Heather Lintie* (1863) 225, I've.. A *stockin' leg weel crammed, I trow, Wi' glancin' gowd sae yelly. **1727** *Brice's Weekly Jrnl.* 10 Feb. 2 Thomas Herbert, jun. of London, *Stocking-legger. **1715** A. HILL *Acc. Beech-Oil Inv.* 12 And thus the ingenious *Stocking Loom.. was first invented. **1843** *Penny Cycl.* XXVII. 180/1 A singular confusion pervades the early history of the *stocking-machine. **1622** in *Crt. & Times Jas. I* (1848) II. 346 *Stocking-men, haberdashers, point-makers and other mean trades. **1966** *Times* 16 May 10 Three men in *stocking masks raided Martins Bank in South Audley Street. **1978** G. GREENE *Human Factor* I. ii. 25 He might object to a stocking mask all the same. **1971** *Daily Tel.* 24 Sept. 2/8 Six *stocking-masked bandits.. ambushed a lorry at Bethnal Green yesterday. **1977** N. ADAM *Triplehip Cracksman* xviii. 186 Corny stocking-masked villains. **1886** A. D. WILLOCK *Rosetty Ends* (1887) 148 So, takin' a bittie o' paper, he wrote on it, 'Dear Mary', an' wi' a *stockin' needle an' a bit worsit he steekit it on the inside o' the collar. **1607** TOPSELL *Four-f. Beasts* 575 Thereof [of the otter-skin] also in Germany they make.. *stocking-soles. **1827** SCOTT *Surg. Dau.* v, A gallant young fellow like you,.. six feet high on your stocking-soles. **1889** BARRIE *Window in Thrums* xxi, Tibbie went ben the house in her stocking-soles, but Jess heard her. **1805** *6th Rep. Deput Kpr. Publ. Rec.* App. II. 154 Specification of.. some new and improved kinds of *Stocking stitch, and warp work. **1839** URE *Dict. Arts* 648 The whole piece is composed of a single thread.. looped together in a peculiar manner, which is called stocking-stitch, and sometimes chain-work. **1976** *Globe & Mail* (Toronto) 7 Dec. 24/7 Rockefellers don't stress paperbacks this time of year—the market for *stocking stuffers is apparently limited. **1977** *Time* 17 Jan. 28/2 Around holiday season, stocking-stuffer items like *The Slipper and the Rose* usually show up, all covered in glitter and good will. **1885** *Scribner's Monthly Mag.* XXX. 393/1 *Stocking-throwing and other such customs long lingered among the backwoodsmen of the colonies. **1967** *Economist* 5 Aug. 517/1 Manufacturers report orders.. up by 23 per cent, mainly thanks to the invention of *stocking tights.. to go under mini skirts. **1977** J. WAINWRIGHT *Nest of Rats* I. i. 9 One leg of her stocking-tights badly torn. **1664** *Charter Framework-Knitters Co.* §26 And these [appointed members] to prove, try, and see whether all *stocking-tops,.. or any other thing.. be workmanlike wrought. **1859** GEO. ELIOT *Adam Bede* III. vi. liii. 305, I can count a stocking-top [in knitting] while a man's getting 's tongue ready. **1935** N. MITCHISON *We have been Warned* I. ii. 19 To wear the sgian dhu in his stocking top, as he was allowed to with the kilt. **1978** R. H. LEWIS *Antiquarian Bks.* ii. 47 Nina Hamnet.. remembered.. for her disconcerting habit of keeping her money in her stocking tops. **1723** *Lond. Gaz.* No. 6194/9 Henry Hunt, .. *Stocking-Trimmer. **1858** SIMMONDS *Dict. Trade*, *Stocking-trimmer*, a decorator or ornamenter of stockings; one who removes loose threads or imperfections. **1697** DE FOE *Ess. Projects* 24 For which I refer to the Engine it self, to be seen in every *Stocking-Weaver's Garret. **1866** CARLYLE *Remin.* I. 85 Joe Blacklock [was] a rickety stocking-weaver. **1835** URE *Philos. Manuf.* 343 So high is the character of their *stocking-yarns and threads. **1882** CAULFEILD & SAWARD *Dict. Needlework* 463 *Stocking Yarn*.. is Cotton thread, and is spun softer and looser than either Mule or Water Twist. Two threads are afterwards doubled together, and then slightly twisted round each other.

stocking ('stɒkɪŋ), *vbl. sb.* [f. STOCK *v.*[1] (occas. STOCK *sb.*[1]) + -ING[1].]

1. The action or process of fixing (a bell) to its stock, or furnishiing (a gun) with a stock.

1450 *Durham Acc. Rolls* (Surtees) 240 Et Joh'i Cales pro le stokkynge unius campane ad eccl. predictam, 4*d.* **1546** *Acts Privy Counc.* 23 May (1890) 423 Item; a warraunte.. for xx markes in preste to the saide Mr. Darcy for the stocking of gonnes and other thinges there. **1588–9** in Garry *Churchw. Acc. St. Mary's, Reading* (1893) 68 Item for the newe stokinge of the Bels, ij*s.* vj*d.* **1703** in *J. Watson's Jedburgh Abbey* (1894) 91 A collection at the kirk door for payment of the little bell's casting, stocking, and other expenses. **1844** *Queen's Regul. Army* 99 For the Stock and new stocking Muskets and Carbines.. 10*s.* 6*d.*

b. The parts forming the stock of a gun.

1532 *Acc. Ld. High Treas. Scot.* VI. 156 To tua pynouris that tursit the gunnis to the stokkin in the castell. **1858** GREENER *Gunnery* 395 From imperfections in the stocking of the gun. **1870** *Athenæum* 8 Oct. 471/1 Faults.. in.. the lever, the stocking, and the ammunition [of the Martini-Henry rifle].

2. a. The uprooting of trees or plants. Also with *up*. Also *pl.* (see quot. 1851). **b.** (See quot. 1611.)

c **1460** FORTESCUE *Abs. & Lim. Mon.* xiii. (1885) 141 As it now well apperith be the new husbondry þat is done þer.. in grobbyng and stokkyng off treis [etc.] **1534** [see sense 8, *stocking-iron*]. **1611** COTGR., *Tronquement*, a trunking, stocking, or cutting off. **1613** [STANDISH] *New Direct. Planting* 3 It were very conuenient, that the stocking vp of Woods were preuented,.. for.. within a very few years there wil be little or no wood left for any vse, the stocking & stubbing is so great. **1733** W. ELLIS *Chiltern & Vale Farm.* 363 The Felling and Stocking up of Trees. **1851** STERNBERG *Northampt. Dial.*, *Stockins*, land reclaimed from the woods.

3. The action of supplying with a stock or store; the furnishing (a farm) with cattle and implements or (a garden) with plants; also, keeping in stock.

1663 *Act 15 Chas. II*, c. 1 §15 All.. Implements of Husbandry, and all other things whatsoever, imployed in the Husbanding Stocking and Manureing of their.. Lands. **1766** BLACKSTONE *Comm.* II. 7 So long as it [migration] was confined to the stocking and cultivation of desart uninhabited countries, it kept strictly within the limits of the law of nature. **1813** SCOTT *Fam. Let.* 23 Mar. (1894) I. ix. 277, I have been here for some days directing.. the stocking of a garden. **1858** *National Rev.* Oct. 344 The natural pursuits of men make.. a complete stocking of the mind more.. necessarily a duty with them than with women. **1886** C. SCOTT *Sheep-Farming* 89 The only chance of rearing good lambs in such cases, lies in thin stocking, and giving a liberal supply of dry nourishing food. **1892** *Daily News* 5 Sept. 7/1 So far as the house coal trade is concerned,.. there is no reason for taking a despondent view... Winter stocking will soon set in in earnest.

b. *concr.* The cattle, farm implements, etc. as distinguished from the crops of a farm.

1730 T. BOSTON *View this & other World* 251 Abraham was rich in silver and gold, and Job in stocking. **1765** *Pet.* in *Walker v. Spence* 5 He had neither servants nor stocking proper for his farm. **1815** SCOTT *Guy M.* xii, And the furniture and stocking is to be roupit at the same time on the ground. **1818** MISS FERRIER *Marriage* xi, I shall advance you stocking and stedding. **1856** MORTON *Cycl. Agric.* II. 726/1 The stocking of a farm is the crop, cattle, and implements.

4. (See quot. and cf. STOCK *v.*[1] 18.)

1847 EVANSON & MAUNSELL *Managem. Childr.* (ed. 5) 50 *note*, Nurses who have not a good supply of milk will, occasionally, be found to adopt a practice commonly employed with milch cows when brought to market, and called by the cattle dealers, stocking; that is, they allow the milk to accumulate in their breasts.

5. Detention in the stocks.

1534 MORE *Comf. agst. Trib.* III. xx. (1553) S ij, That strayte kepynge, collerynge, boltynge, and stockynge,.. which.. is vsed in these speciall priesonmentes. **1563–83** FOXE *A. & M.* 1917/2 Then began they to threaten him with whippyng, stockyng, burnyng, and such like. **1679** PENN *Addr. Prot.* II. 220 Whence comes.. Beatings, Bruisings, Stockings, Whippings, and Spilling of Blood for Religion? **1822** SCOTT *Nigel* iii, Such idle suitors are to be.. punished for their audacity with stripes, stocking, or incarceration.

6. Treatment in the stocks of a fulling mill or tannery.

1883 R. HALDANE *Workshop Rec.* Ser. II. 367/1 After.. the drench, the skins are.. removed.. to the stocks, where they are beaten.. with heavy tilt-hammers. When soft, oil.. is sprinkled on them, and the 'stocking' is continued.

7. *slang.* (See STOCK *v.*[1] 23.)

1887 F. FRANCIS Jun. *Saddle & Mocassin* 228 A tender-foot got in amongst the gamblers on board.. and what with 'strippers', and 'stocking', and 'cold decks',.. he hadn't the ghost of a chance.

8. *attrib.* and *Comb.*, as (sense 1) ***stocking-room***, (sense 2) ***stocking-hoe***, †***-iron***, (sense 3) ***stocking plant***, ***-pot***.

1863 *Jrnl. Royal Agric. Soc.* XXXIV. 281 Some used *stocking-hoes and grubbed the ground 5 inches deep. **1534** MORE *Comf. agst. Trib.* III. xv. (1553) Q iiij b, He causeth like a good husband man his folke to come afield,.. and with their hookes & their *stocking yrons, grubbe vp these wicked wedes & busshes of our earthly substance. **1849** *Florist* 199 Those who are desirous of having *stocking plants [of pelargoniums] must cut their specimens down boldly. **1840** *Florist's Jrnl.* (1846) I. 153 The plants.. were raised from cuttings put into *stocking-pots. **1833** J. HOLLAND *Manuf. Metal* II. v. 106 The *stocking-room [for guns] is fitted with.. the tools usually found in a cabinet maker's shop.

stocking ('stɒkɪŋ), *v.* [f. STOCKING *sb.*]

1. *trans.* To furnish with stockings.

1755 JOHNSON, To *Stocking*, v.a., to dress in stockings. **1874** in W. Knight *J. C. Shairp* xiii. (1888) 315 The boys may be stockinged; will the mind be clothed and fed? **1892** *The Voice* (N.Y.) Apr. 28 Enough.. cotton to stocking every foot.

†**2.** To kill with a weapon consisting of a stone placed in the foot of a stocking. (Said of a soldier's wife or a camp-follower.) *Obs.*

1762 in *Grimston Papers* (MS.), As she had a regular education in Flanders, will be of great service when we come to action, in stripping, despatching, fleecing and stockinging the enemy.

stocking-apple. In 7 stocken-, -in, stoken-. [? f. STOCKING *vbl. sb.* in the sense 'keeping in stock'.] A kind of cider-apple. *local.*

1629 PARKINSON *Parad.* (1904) 588 The Stoken apple is a reasonable good apple. **1656** BEALE *Heref. Orchards* (1657) 45 The apples we commend for grafts, are the Stockin-apple [etc.]. **1676** WORLIDGE *Cyder* 163 The Stocken or Stoken-Apple is likewise in esteem there [in the cider countries], although not known by that name in many places. **1764** *Museum Rust.* II. x. 37 These [cider apples in Herefordshire] go under various names, as.. the stocking-apple,.. &c.

stockinged ('stɒkɪŋd), *ppl. a.* [f. STOCKING *sb.* or *v.* + -ED.]

1. Furnished with stockings or with a stocking.

1608 DEKKER *Work for Armourers* (1609) F 1 b, The kerzy stockingd Whoresons. **1693** DRYDEN *Juvenal* III. 397 Stockin'd with loads of fat Town-Dirt he goes. **1887** STEVENSON *Manse* in *Scribner's Mag.* I. 613/1 Nothing of this would cross the mind of the young student, as he posted up the Bridges with trim, stockinged legs.

transf. **1894** SALA *Lond. up to Date* 349 Those three slender quadrupeds, all stockinged and hooded.. which are being carefully conducted to a horse-box.

2. Of the foot: Covered with a stocking only.

1862 *Cornhill Mag.* May 570 She had taken her shoes off, and came in her stockinged feet up to my bedside. **1891** HARDY *Tess* xxxvii, He slid back the door-bar and passed out, slightly striking his stockinged toe against the edge of the door.

3. Of a bird: Feathered on the shank.

1855 *Poultry Chron.* III. 153 The Stomacher Pigeons.. are 'stockinged', or feathered to the toes with small feathers.

stockinger ('stɒkɪŋə(r)). [f. STOCKING *sb.* + -ER[1].] One who works at a stocking hand-loom, a framework knitter, stocking weaver.

1741 *Manch. School Reg.* (1866) I. 16 Thomas son of Thomas Steele of Manchester, Stockiner. **1812** *Rep. Committee Framework-Knitters Petit.* 30, I applied for work to what we call a bag-hosier, which is a master stockinger. **1843** *Penny Cycl.* XXVII. 181/1 [Stocking-frame]. There are three classes of operatives engaged: the 'winders',.. the 'stockingers', or 'framework knitters', who work the thread up into a knitted fabric; and the 'seamers'. **1873** *Echo* 22 Sept. 2/2 When.. all the collieries are opened out.. the 'stockinger' will disappear in favour of the miner.

stockingett(e: see STOCKINET.

stocking-foot. a. That part of a stocking which covers the foot.

1766 SHARP *Fracture* in *Phil. Trans.* LVII. 86, I do not always remove the shoe and stocking-foot. **1853** R. S. SURTEES *Sponge's Sp. Tour* lxviii, What a convenience to have one's wife's maid to sew on one's buttons, and keep one's toes in one's stocking-feet! **1884** ROWLETT *Technol. Framework Knitting* II. 342 Socks or half-hose. The feet are made in the same way as stocking feet.

b. As a purse or receptacle for money laid by. Chiefly *fig.*

1894 'H. HALIBURTON' *Furth in Field* II. 75 The cadger was just as eager to make the petty disbursement from his 'stocking-foot' or leather pouch. **1915** J. BUCHAN *Nelson's Hist. War* V. xl. 153 For them [*i.e.* the Treasury bonds] the peasant and the small tradesman brought out his store of gold from the stocking-foot.

c. (***in, on***) ***one's stocking feet***: with only one's stockings on one's feet, without one's shoes.

1802 R. ANDERSON *Cumbld. Ball.* (1808) 13 Wully.. in his clogs top teyme did beat; But Tamer, in her stockin feet, She bang'd him out and out. **1809** W. IRVING *Knickerb.* III. iii. (1820) 178 Leaving their shoes at the door, and entering devoutly on their stocking feet. **1854** THACKERAY *Newcomes* viii, Binnie found the Colonel.. arrayed in what are called in Scotland his stocking-feet. **1858** TROLLOPE *Doctor Thorne* xii, In his stocking-feet.. he was five feet five. **1901** THEODORA W. WILSON *T' Bacca Queen* xxvii. 247 Her husband was seated in stocking feet in the rocking-chair.

d. The loose or pendent part of a stocking-cap. *rare*[−1].

1921 D. H. LAWRENCE *Sea & Sardinia* v. 161 The old boy brings his stocking-foot over the left ear.

Hence **stocking-footed, (-feeted)** *a.*, having stocking-feet; in stocking feet.

1926 J. F. DOBIE *Rainbow in Morning* (1965) 99, I had a bay, white-faced, and stocking-footed horse called Buck. **1973** Stocking-feeted [see *leather-jacketed* s.v. LEATHER *sb.* 5 d].

stocking-frame. A machine for producing material composed of the looped stitch used in knitting; a knitting machine.

The invention of a machine for making plain stocking-net to supersede hand-knitting is believed to have been made in 1589 by William Lee M.A., St. John's Coll. Cambridge, a native of Woodborough, near Nottingham.

1710 *Lond. Gaz.* No. 4649/4 Wm. Brown,.. by Trade a Stocking-frame Smith. **1765** *Museum Rust.* IV. 392 Improvement of the Stocking-frame. **1881** *Encycl. Brit.* XII. 300/1 The inventor of the round stocking-frame was.. Sir Marc I. Brunel, who in 1816 patented his machine under the name of the *Tricoteur*.

stockingless ('stɒkɪŋlɪs), *a.* [f. STOCKING *sb.* + -LESS.] Without stockings.

1748 RICHARDSON *Clarissa* (1768) VIII. xix. 51 They were all slip-shoed; stockenless some; only under-petticoated all. **1775** S. J. PRATT *Liberal Opin.* cxiii. (1783) IV. 62 A little stockingless boy. **1825** [see SHOELESS]. **1869** ROSSETTI *Diary* 28 June, in *Athenæum* (1882) 15 July 79/1, I called on Trelawny... He retains his ancient habit of going stockingless. **1907** C. C. BROWN *China in Legend & Story* xvii. 246 His stockingless feet had been thrust into cheap shoes.

'stock-in-trade. Also †stock of trade (*obs.*).

a. The goods kept on sale by a dealer, shopkeeper, or pedlar. Also, a workman's tools, appliances, or apparatus.

[**1666** MARVELL *Let.* 13 Nov., Wks. 1776 I. 59 Catell, corn, and houshold furniture shall be excepted, and all such stock for trade, as is already tax'd by the land tax.] **1762–71** H. WALPOLE *Vertue's Anecd. Paint.* (1786) V. 214 He retired to Richmond, and.. sold part of his plates and stock in trade by auction. **1775** *Pennsylv. Even. Post* 20 June 258/1 To be sold, The Stock in Trade of the late Evan Morgan, deceased. **1851** Borrow *Lavengro* III. xix. 235-6 She..died, leaving me her cart and stock in trade.

b. *transf.* and *fig.* (esp. of mental equipment and resources). Also *attrib.*

1784 Barry *Lect. Painting* iv. Wks. 1809 I. 481 Men of mean intellects, who, incapable of meddling with the *ideal*, will operate solely with these mechanical principles, as their entire stock of trade. **1842** De Quincey *Cicero* Wks. VI. 185 Such charges were the standing material, the stock-in-trade of every orator. **1874** Sayce *Compar. Philol.* vii. 274 The conception of plurality was not part of the primary stock-in-trade of mankind. **1877** Black *Green Past.* i, A whole stock-in-trade of things that a good many girls seem to get on very well without. **1878** Lockyer *Stargazing* 233 The stock-in-trade of the modern astronomer. **1910** *Q. Rev.* Jan. 162 The manual labourer is himself his own stock-in-trade.

attrib. **1931** L. H. Myers *Prince Jali* ii. 26 The point was that his parents and the world each presented the other with something intelligible, they presented stock-in-trade figures between whom a stock-in-trade intercourse was possible. **1970** P. Oliver *Savannah Syncopators* 100 These repertoires of traditional songs, stock-in-trade lines and phrases and sudden original words and verses. **1977** *Word 1972* XXVIII. 190 Bloomfield discussed such stock-in-trade instances as *adder* (for *nadder*), *newt* (for *eft*), and *apron* (for *napron*), to illustrate one type.

stockish (ˈstɒkɪʃ), *a.* [f. stock *sb.* + -ish.]

1. Resembling a stock or block of wood; esp. of a person, excessively dull, stupid or 'wooden'.

1596 Shaks. *Merch. V.* v. i. 81 Naught so stockish, hard, and full of rage, But musicke for time doth change his nature. **1612** T. Taylor *Comm. Titus* i. 7 A stockish senselessnesse, or a sufferance of any evill, without any great sense of it. **1641** Ld. Brooke *Eng. Episc.* I. ix. 53 The issue will be slavish, grosse superstition, and stockish Idolatry. **1816** Colman *Br. Grins, Fire!* xvii, Touched by vivific flame, the stockish dirt Fermented, and became no more inert. **1842** Emerson *Lect., Transcendentalist* Wks. (Bohn) II. 285 These persons are not by nature melancholy,..they are not stockish or brute. **1842** J. Foster *Life & Corr.* (1846) II. 347 The stockish stupidity of those Chartists. **1881** Stevenson *Virg. Puerisque, Apol. Idlers* 124 Many..come out of the study with an..owl-like demeanour, and prove dry, stockish, and dyspeptic in all the better and brighter parts of life.

2. Short and thick-set, stocky. *rare*$^{-1}$.

1913 N. Munro *New Road* xviii, A stockish little man dressed in the Highland habit.

Hence **ˈstockishly** *adv.*, **ˈstockishness**.

1837 Browning *Strafford* III. iii, O stockishness! Wear such a ruff, and never call to mind St. John's head in a charger? **1846** —— *Soul's Trag.* II. Poems (1905) 358/1, I understand only the dull mule's way of standing stockishly. **1914** H. Newbolt *Aladore* xxvi, Then he stood before her stockishly, like a thing of wood.

stockist (ˈstɒkɪst). [f. stock *sb.*[1] + -ist.] One who stocks (certain) goods for sale.

1922 *Autocar* 10 Nov. 52 We are Stockists of High grade Cars. **1941** *Picture Post* 3 May 32/1 Write for style folder and name of nearest stockist to Swallow Raincoats Ltd. **1956** *People* 13 May 14/1 (Advt.), See the many other advantages at your local stockist. **1977** D. J. Elliott in D. Marcus *Best Irish Short Stories* II. 150 Our range of Sheer Elegance shampoos and lipsticks. Ask for samples at our nearest stockists.

†**stock-job**, *sb. Obs. rare*$^{-1}$. [Formed as next.] ? An act of stock-jobbing.

1719 D'Urfey *Pills* II. 101 Where Fools manage Bargains by way of Stock-jobb.

†**stock-job**, *v. Obs.* [Back-formation on stock-jobber, -jobbing.] **a.** *trans.* To apply the methods of stock-jobbing to, deal with according to the practices of a stock-jobber, employ in stock-jobbing; also *fig.* Also with complement, to bring *down*, throw *away*, bring *into* (a state), by these methods and practices.

1697 De Foe *Ess. Projects* 13 At last..it has been Stock-Jobb'd down to 10, 12, 9, 8 *l.* a Share. **1701** —— *Freeholder's Plea* Collect. Writ. 1703 I. 182 Let us be careful that we are not bought and sold, Stock-job'd into Ruin. **1703** T. Baker *Tunbridge-Walks* II. 23 Before I'de have a Wit inherit my Estate, I'de Stockjobb it away at Jonathan's. **1720** Ramsay *Rise & Fall of Stocks* 22 We madly, at our ain expenses, Stock-job'd away our cash and senses. **1721** —— *Answ. Burchet* 12 Let the greedy bike Stock-job the warld amang them as they like.

b. *intr.* To practise stock-jobbing.

1721 Amherst *Terræ Fil.* iv. 19 Only to enable one man.. to game, to wench, to stock-job, and indulge himself in all the vanities and vices of the world.

ˈstock-ˌjobber. **a.** A member of the Stock Exchange who deals in stocks on his own account; = jobber[2] 4.

a **1626** Sir J. Davies in Carte *Hist. Eng.* (1755) IV. 194/1 He had..played the stock-jobber in buying the debentures, tallies and ticquets,..at a great discompt. *a* **1692** Shadwell (*title*) The Volunteers, or the Stock-Jobbers. A Comedy. **1697** *Lond. Gaz.* No. 3280/2 An Act to Restrain the Number and Ill Practices of Brokers and Stock-Jobbers. **1723** *Ibid.* No. 6136/4 Thomas Shank,..Broker and Stockjobber. **1750** Johnson *Rambler* No. 20 ⁋5 The son of a wealthy stock-jobber, who spends his morning under his father's eye in Change Alley. **1755** —— *Dict.*, *Stockjobber*, a low wretch who gets money by buying and selling shares in the funds. **1838** Lytton *Alice* III. i, Lord Vargrave..was..suspected of selling his state information to stock-jobbers. **1858** Simmonds *Dict. Trade, Stock-jobber*, an outsider or intermediate agent between the buyer and seller of public securities, who makes a marginal price at which shares, etc. are to be bought or sold in the Stock-exchange.

b. *U.S.* 'A stockbroker; often used somewhat contemptuously or to suggest unscrupulousness' (W. 1911).

1833 *Niles' Reg.* XLIV. 570/1 The 'black-leg' in the gambling houses..more fairly takes the chances of the play, than the stock-jobber on 'change. **1895** in *Funk's Stand. Dict.* **1911** H. S. Harrison *Queed* 107 If a man became the greatest stock-jobber in the world, who would remember him after he was gone.

Hence **ˈstock-jobbery** *jocular*, stock-jobbing.

1882 Ogilvie, *Stock-jobbery*, the practice or business of dealing in stocks or shares: used in a disparaging sense. **1897** *Daily News* 22 May 5/1 Was the Jameson plan conceived or abetted in the interests of stock-jobbery?

ˈstock-ˌjobbing, *vbl. sb.* and *ppl. a.*

A. *vbl. sb.* The business of a stock-jobber; buying and selling of stock as practised by a jobber; *loosely*, speculative dealing in stocks and shares.

Often with unfavourable implication of rash or dishonest speculation; esp. with reference to the abuses of the early 18th c., which led to condemnation by Act of Parliament (see quot. 1734).

1692 Motteux *Gentl. Jrnl.* I. 12 The modern Trade, or rather Game, called Stock-Jobbing. **1694** J. Houghton *Collect. Improv. Husb.* No. 97 ⁋1 Joint Stocks, and of the various dealings therein, commonly called Stock-Jobbing. *a* **1700** B. E. *Dict. Cant. Crew, Stock-jobbing*, a sharp, cunning, cheating Trade of Buying and Selling Shares of Stock in East-India, Guinea and other Companies; also in the Bank, Exchequer, &c. **1711** Steele *Spect.* No. 114 ⁋5 Usury, Stock-jobbing, Extortion and Oppression, have their Seed in the Dread of Want. **1734** *Act 7 Geo. II*, c. 8 §1 The wicked, pernicious and destructive Practice of Stock-jobbing. **1874** L. Stephen *Hours in Libr.* (1892) II. iv. 117 The selfishness which degrades political warfare into a branch of stock-jobbing. **1888** E. J. Goodman *Too Curious* xii, All that has been said about stock-jobbing being morally as bad as betting on racehorses.

B. *ppl. a.* (and attrib. use of the vbl. sb.). That deals in stocks and shares; concerned with this business or traffic.

a **1692** Pollexfen *Disc. Trade* (1697) A 5 b, To advance Stocks, and Stock-Jobbing Trades. **1719** D'Urfey *Pills* II. 324 So may your wise Stock-jobbing Crimp go on. **1790** Burke *Fr. Rev.* 77 All you have got for the present is a paper circulation, and a stock-jobbing constitution. **1823** W. Cobbett *Rur. Rides* (1885) I. 321 Margate..is..thickly settled with stock-jobbing cuckolds at this time of the year. **1888** E. J. Goodman *Too Curious* xxii, This is really no stock-jobbing dodge, but a bonâ-fide thing.

ˈstock-ˌkeeper.

†**1.** ? An official in charge of a stock or fund of money (with jocular allusion to the punishment of the stocks). *Obs.*

1589 [Nashe] *Pasquil's Return* B iij b, The stocke-keeper of the Bridewel-house of Canterburie; he must carrie the purse, to defray their charges.

2. a. One who keeps cattle; a stock-farmer.

1912 *Times* 19 Oct. 7/4 Stock-keepers on both sides of the Channel had begun to hope that the necessary period of quarantine for Irish cattle might soon be at an end.

b. *Austral.*, etc. A herdsman or shepherd; = stockman 1.

1806 *Sydney Gaz.* in O'Hara *Hist. N.S. Wales* (1817) 264 Anthony Size, stock-keeper at Prospect. **1821** in E. Curr *Van Diemen's Land* (1824) 154 Prisoner servants employed ..as stock keepers. **1881** *Instr. Census Clerks* (1885) 37 Agricultural Labourer..Stock Keeper.

3. One who is in charge of the stock of a warehouse.

1902 *Daily Chron.* 9 Dec. 9/6 (Advt.), Situation in a London warehouse..as checker, stockkeeper, or clerk.

So **ˈstock-keep** *v.*, *nonce-wd.*, to tend cattle, etc. **ˈstock-ˌkeeping** *vbl. sb.*

1844 W. Wakefield in *N.Z. Company Rep.* (1845) XVII. 139 The sport of hunting them [*sc.* deer]..would afford a manly amusement to the young Colonists, fitting them for the more serious occupations of stock keeping and wool growing. **1886** C. Scott *Sheep-Farming* 30 Where..the farmer understands the business of stock-keeping and stock-feeding. **1890** 'R. Boldrewood' *Col. Reformer* x, [I can] drive bullocks, stock-keep, plough. **1907** M. C. F. Morris *Nunburnholme* 252 Stock-keeping was but little understood.

stockless (ˈstɒklɪs), *a.* [f. stock *sb.*[1] + -less.]

1. Without a stock; spec. of an anchor.

1886 *St. James's Gaz.* 14 Jan. 6/2 He fired off his stockless gun. **1901** *Westm. Gaz.* 5 July 1/2 Stockless anchors. **1909** *Light Keeper* June 3 The use of stockless anchors has now become universal in the mercantile marine.

2. Without agricultural stock.

1901 *Scotsman* 16 Apr. 8/3 The conclusion of the campaign will find the conquered colonies practically stockless.

ˈstock-lock. [f. stock *sb.*[1] + lock *sb.*] A lock enclosed in a wooden case, usually fitted on an outer door.

1365-6 in Brayley *Anc. Palace Westminster* (1836) 192, 18 stokloks. **1394** in *Archæologia* XXIV. 308, ij stoklokkes. **1416-17** *Durham Acc. Rolls* (Surtees) 614 In 10 stoklockys et aliis feturlockys. **1534-5** in W. H. St. John Hope *Windsor Castle* (1913) I. 264 For a doble hoopped stocke lock sett vppon the Colege garden dore to save the Kynges plaet locke oon to the begynnyng of somere, xvj d. **1601** *Shuttleworths' Acc.* (Chetham Soc.) 138 A stocke locke for the chamber dower at Symonston, viij^{d}. **1677** Moxon *Mech. Exerc.* ii. 21 Street-door Locks, called Stock-Locks. **1737** *Salmon's Country Builder's Estimator* (ed. 2) 111 Plate Stock-Locks. **1757** *Phil. Trans.* L. 106 Ripping off a small stock-lock from the door, [it] burst it open. **1771** Roland Le Virloys *Dict. Archit.* III. Vocab. 184 Stock-lock, *serrure à pêle* [= *pêne*] *dormant*. **1833** Loudon *Encycl. Archit.* §84 Stock locks (locks with a wooden back, or stock). **1842** *Penny Cycl.* XXII. 416/2, 191 men [employed] in the manufacture of stock-locks.

Hence †**ˈstock-lock** *v. trans.*, to double-lock. (? Some error.)

1771 Roland Le Virloys *Dict. Archit.* III. Vocab. 184 To Stock-lock, *fermer à double tour*.

ˈstockman.

1. A man employed to look after cattle or other live stock. Chiefly *Austral.*

1806 *Sydney Gaz.* in O'Hara *Hist. N.S. Wales* (1817) 295 The evidence of the stock-men, who did not attend [the inquest], being essential. **1830** *Hobart Town Almanack* 103 A group of Mr. E. Lord's stockmen. **1862** R. Henning *Let.* 2 Nov. (1966) 113 Mr Palmer was not at home, but we were received by an amiable stockman. **1881** *Instr. Census Clerks* (1885) 37 Agricultural Labourer...Stockman. **1891** T. E. Kebbel *Old & New* 167 Shepherds, waggoners and stockmen are paid at a higher rate. **1900** *Oxf. Times* 24 Nov. 1/4 Wanted,—Steady, Industrious Married Man for Breeding Flock, and as Stockman. **1911** C. E. W. Bean *'Dreadnought' of Darling* xi. 100 The subordinate hands on the station—..the groom, stockman, rouseabouts—live in the men's huts, close behind the homestead. **1929** K. S. Prichard *Coonardoo* 5 Nowadays..aboriginal stockmen usually receive a small wage as well as payment in kind by rations. **1944** *Living off Land* iv. 94 Before the sun rises..the stockman's 'boys' are back with the horses. **1962** A. Upfield *Will of Tribe* iii. 27 'You have two white stockmen.'..'Just the two,' replied the cattleman. **1978** O. White *Silent Reach* xviii. 191 'Where are the stockmen?'..'Out looking for the Dalziel girl.'

2. One who raises live stock; a stock-farmer.

1856 *Farmer's Mag.* Jan. 22 Such a division of labour between farmers and stockmen, and between farmers and dairymen, as has been found to work well in some parts of Scotland and England. **1886** C. Scott *Sheep Farming* 137 In those days the farmer who supplied the best food and the most whisky was accounted the best stockman.

Hence **ˈstockmanship**, the art of raising or looking after livestock.

1959 *Farmer & Stockbreeder* 22 Dec. (Suppl.) 7/2 As science develops...the art of good farming will remain—the art of knowing when and how to work the soil, the art of stockmanship. **1969** J. G. S. & F. Donaldson *Farming in Britain Today* II. xviii. 170 Efficient planning of the battery can almost eliminate the need for skilled stockmanship. **1979** *Daily Tel.* 1 May 11/2 Stockmanship, record-keeping, observation, simple disease control..will be the necessary tools of his [*sc.* the pigman's] trade.

ˈstock-ˌmarket.

1. a. A place where stocks or securities are bought and sold. **b.** The traffic in stocks and shares at such a place.

1809 R. Langford *Introd. Trade* 55 The dividend warrants..can be sold in the Stock Market. **1876** Bancroft *Hist. U.S.* III. vi. 370 He never grew giddy with the hazards of the stock-market. **1912** *Times* 19 Dec. 16/3 Stock markets on the whole were steady at the close, after opening dull.

c. *attrib.*

1930 W. C. Brooks *How Stock Market Really Works* viii. 121 There followed closely upon the Hatry crash the break of the stock market boom in New York. **1951** M. McLuhan *Mech. Bride* (1967) 7 Speed of communication and movement makes possible at the same time such diverse facts as stock-market operations, international armies, [etc.]. **1964** —— *Understanding Media* xxi. 207 The classified ads (and stock-market quotations) are the bedrock of the press. **1977** *Listener* 17 Apr. 204/1 The great stock market crash of 1929.

2. A cattle-market; trade in live stock.

1858 Simmonds *Dict. Trade, Stock-market*,..a place for the sale of cattle. **1890** 'R. Boldrewood' *Col. Reformer* xxiii, A favourable change would take place in the stock-market.

stock of trade: see stock-in-trade.

stock out. *Business.* [f. stock *sb.*[1] + out *adv.*] An occurrence of being out of stock of an item wanted by customers.

1957 Clark & Gottfried *Dict. Business & Finance* 339/1 Stock-out. **1967** E. Duckworth in Wills & Yearsley *Handbk. Management Technol.* 107 Because delivery from the wholesaler was so short the consequences of any 'stock out' would not be serious. **1969** J. Argenti *Managem. Techniques* v. 26 Symptoms: frequent stock-outs or frequent disposals of surpluses. **1979** *Washington Post* 22 June A 12/3 Its allocation rules 'do not prevent long lines, stockouts, and early closings at retail outlets'.

stockpile (ˈstɒkpaɪl), *sb.* orig. *U.S.* Also stock-pile, stock pile. [f. stock *sb.*[1] + pile *sb.*[3]]

1. A pile of coal or ore accumulated at the surface after having been mined.

1872 *Trans. Amer. Soc. Civil Engineers* II. 30 This covers the cost from miners' hands to cars or stock pile. **1912** C. E. van Barneveld *Iron Mining in Minnesota* 140 For lighter stripping work and stock-pile loading, the 70-C Bucyrus is quite largely used. **1958** *Engineering* 7 Feb. 188/1 Limestone is fed into a swing hammer-mill either direct from tipping lorries or by bulldozing from a stock pile.

2. a. A reserve or store of goods or commodities, esp. one accumulated in anticipation of shortage or market fluctuation.

1942 *Sun* (Baltimore) 15 Jan. 1/2 The facilities of new car dealers will be used to store for a year or more an estimated 130,000 new passenger automobiles under a 'stock pile' plan. **1943** *Times* 15 Dec. 5/6 The complete success achieved was due to..the statesmanship of all nations represented, especially those with resources outside their occupied lands and therefore able to make stockpiles of supplies at the expense of other nations less fortunate. **1957** *Economist* 30 Nov. 791/1 In the postwar years the cartel has not been restrictive. Helped by stockpile buying of industrial diamonds and by a demand for gems as a hedge against inflation, its policy has been to hold prices down rather than force them up. 1958 *Manch. Guardian* 25 Feb. 16/6 No wool from the British stockpile is included in this week's catalogue. 1962 *Economist* 20 Jan. 249/3 The United States will not now authorise sales of stockpile tin below £965 a ton. 1970 *Listener* 23 July 107/3 Most European countries keep a 2 months' stockpile of oil by government command. 1972 D. HASTON *In High Places* xii. 150 The supplies were flowing well through the icefall;..there was a great stockpile at Camp I.

b. *spec.* An accumulation of nuclear weapons.

1946 *Rep. Internat. Control Atomic Energy* (Dept. of State, Washington) III. i. 31 How can a strategic balance be maintained between nations so that stockpiles of fissionable materials will not become unduly large in one nation and small in another? 1947 *Nature* 11 Jan. 48/1 A.D.A. should take over..the right of ensuring that any dangerous products were consumed in [atomic] power plants and that no excessive stockpile be produced. 1955 [see ATOMIC *a.* 2 e]. 1957 *Times* 6 Nov. 9/6 Mr. Dulles said to-night that the United States was considering the problem of establishing stockpiles of nuclear weapons in Europe for N.A.T.O. forces' use in case of emergency. 1969 *Daily Tel.* 16 Sept. 22/7 The threat of nuclear war was increasing every day with the mounting nuclear stockpiles. 1976 *Survey* Summer–Autumn 193 The total explosive energy that could be released by the strategic stockpile is a measure frequently used to compare US and Soviet forces.

c. *fig.*

1945 J. STEINBECK *Cannery Row* xvii. 104 The sea rocks and the beaches were his stock pile. 1957 *Listener* 21 Nov. 826/1 Imperialist behaviour built stockpiles of national resentment. 1966 *Electronics* 31 Oct. 23 Stockpiles of good technical men in some of the aerospace companies. 1982 R. LUDLUM *Parsifal Mosaic* viii. 111 What he learned—what he *thinks* he learned—has turned him into a stockpile of nitro.

'stockpile, *v.* orig. *U.S.* [f. the sb.] **1.** *trans. Mining.* To heap up (ore, coal, etc.) in piles at the surface.

1921 E. W. DAVIS *Magnetic Concentration of Iron* 136 It may be necessary to mine, crush, and roast perhaps three tons of ore, cob, fine grind, and concentrate two tons of ore, dewater and agglomerate one ton of ore, stockpile one-half ton of ore, and dispose of two tons of tailings. 1937 —— *Magnetic Roasting of Iron Ore* 3 The ore being treated is a coarse tailing product rejected from existing concentration plants. It is in ideal physical condition for this process and is of no value at the present time, altho it has been mined, crushed, and stock-piled.

2. a. To accumulate a stock of (something); *spec.* to build up a stock of (nuclear weapons). Also *absol.*

1943 *Sun* (Baltimore) 28 Apr. 7/4 The Government at last began to 'stockpile' 100 octane gasoline. 1947 *Ibid.* 1 Jan. 6/3 It can be assumed that similar weapons..are now being perfected and stock-piled for future use. 1957 *Times* 18 Nov. p. xxxii/1 Decisions to buy and stockpile or to hold off and release stocks are, no doubt, dictated by consumer demand. 1959 *Listener* 16 July 88/2 President De Gaulle's refusal to allow American nuclear warheads to be stockpiled on French territory. 1974 G. MARKSTEIN *Cooler* lxxvii. 254 She..had stock-piled the pills the medical officer gave her until she had collected a fatal dose. 1976 *Country Life* 11 Mar. 638/2 It looked as if inflation would mean ever-advancing prices so wine merchants..started to stockpile.

b. *fig.*

1959 *News Chron.* 9 July 4/5 To stockpile acting talent of splendid calibre. 1959 *Daily Tel.* 2 Sept. 16/1 Employers urged to 'stockpile' labour. 1966 [see SACK *v.*[1] 8 a]. 1975 *Language for Life* (Dept. Educ. & Sci.) xxiv. 347 Pre-service education is not a phase in which the intending teacher must stockpile resources for a lifetime.

Hence **'stockpiled** *ppl. a.*; **'stockpiler.**

1951 *Business Week* 24 Nov. 26 (*heading*) Stockpilers are dipping in now and then to keep both civilian and military industry going. 1972 *Sci. Amer.* Jan. 22/1 There could be uncertainties about the performance of stockpiled weapons. 1979 *Guardian* 23 May 15/1 Agonised consumers deciding whether to take the stock-piled bread out of the freezer and fill it up with petrol.

'stockpiling, *vbl. sb.* orig. *U.S.* [f. STOCKPILE *v.* + -ING[1].] **1.** The action of making a stockpile of goods, raw materials, or nuclear weapons.

1943 *Sun* (Baltimore) 20 July 9/4 Suspension of purchases of Australian wool for stockpiling. 1946 *Rep. Internat. Control Atomic Energy* (Dept. of State, Washington) II. v. 25 It is, furthermore, clear that the stockpiling of appreciable quantities of fissionable material suitably denatured, must precede the development of these safe power reactors. 1953 E. HYAMS *Prophecy of Famine* 41 But to do so would upset our stock-piling and other contingency supplies. 1959 *Listener* 18 June 1066/2 France's refusal to allow stockpiling of American atomic weapons on French soil for the Nato fighter-bomber force.

2. *attrib.* and *Comb.*, as ***stockpiling act, policy, programme, purchase, purpose.***

1946 *Times* 26 July 7/1 This week President Truman has signed the Strategic and Critical Materials Stockpiling Act. 1945 *Sun* (Baltimore) 30 Mar. 7-0/5 The committee will review the food procurement and stockpiling policies of war agencies. 1943 *Ibid.* 20 July 9/4 Officials of agencies concerned with the stockpiling program. 1944 *Times* 14 Feb. 7/1 Certainly it would hardly be wise to start a 'stockpiling' programme. 1949 *Times* 10 Sept. 5/7 The article provides safeguards against..injuring British interests in their commercial export as a result of stockpiling purchases. 1947 *Sun* (Baltimore) 20 Dec. 2/4 To facilitate the procurement of such raw materials by the United States for stockpiling purposes.

stock still, 'stock-'still, *a.* [See STOCK *sb.*[1] 59 and cf. Du. *stokstil*, G. *stockstill.*] As still as a stock or log; quite motionless. Usually *to stand stock still*; rarely with other vbs. or *attrib.*

c 1470 *Gol. & Gaw.* 108 In stede quhare he lay, Stok still as ane stane. 1574 HELLOWES *Gueuara's Fam. Ep.* (1577) 81, I holde him not for a good beast, that when they lade him, will stand stock stil, and when they vnlade him will yerke out behinde. 1664 BUTLER *Hud.* II. ii. 230 Like Mules, who if th' have not their will To keep their own pace, stand stock still. 1712 ADDISON *Spect.* No. 407 ¶ 1 Our Preachers stand stock-still in the Pulpit. 1782 WOLCOT (P. Pindar) *Odes to R.A.'s* ix, A brother ensign spies the stock-still lad. 1841 DICKENS *Barn. Rudge* xxxiii, The clock—which was very near run down, and would have stood stock-still in half an hour. 1905 MISS BROUGHTON *Waif's Progr.* xviii. 200 A horrible suspicion..stopped the observer's feet stock still.

'stock-take, stocktake, *sb.* [f. the vb.] An instance of stock-taking.

1972 J. BROWN *Chancer* (1974) xii. 139 Three bad stock-takes and you're out. First stock-take I had it wasn't bad... The next big stock-take, the area manager, he came down. 1973 *Daily Tel.* 13 Apr. 18 The introductory work of stocktaking and separating VAT stock took two hours above that required by an efficient business for a normal necessary periodical stocktake. 1979 *Ibid.* 29 June 3/1 The committee decided to lock the door to ensure the 'privacy' of the club bars and stock after a stock-take before handing over to a new steward.

'stock-,taker. A person employed in stock-taking.

1794 in J. Lloyd *Old S. Wales Iron Works* (1906) 168 If any Slabs, Planks, etc., are delivered..an account of them must be taken by the Company's Agent or Stocktaker. 1892 *Labour Commission* Gloss., *Stock-takers*, the men who keep acount of the working of iron or of the iron..used in the process of working malleable iron. 1909 *Westm. Gaz.* 14 May 6/4 Abolishing the office of stocktaker, and entrusting the accountant..with the duty of verifying the stock.

'stock-,taking. [See STOCK *sb.*[1] 56 b.] A periodical examination, inventorying, and valuation of the stock or goods in a shop, warehouse, etc.

1858 SIMMONDS *Dict. Trade, Stock-taking.* 1861 *Draper & Clothier* III. 94/2 At Nottingham, the large houses have been engaged in stock taking. 1884 *Manch. Exam.* 14 Oct. 4/4 The stocktaking of this company..was made on Saturday.

b. *fig.*

1884 R. W. CHURCH *Bacon* 82 He sat down to make a minute stock-taking of his position and its circumstances. 1888 *Pall Mall Gaz.* 2 Apr. 11/1 The theological stocktaking with which this closing part of the century is busy.

Hence **'stock-take** *v.* (back-formation).

1892 MRS. H. WARD *David Grieve* II. 304 He would go over two or three times a year to stock-take and make up accounts.

'stock-work. *Mining.* Also **-werk.** [repr. G. *stockwerk.* See STOCK *sb.*[1] 55 c.] A deposit (esp. of tin) in which the ore is distributed through a large mass of rock.

1808 R. JAMESON *Syst. Mineral.* III. xi. 255 A Stock-werk, is a mountain-mass of greater or less extent, traversed in all directions by a very great number of small veins. 1839 URE *Dict. Arts* 1241 The Cornish ores occur..2. in stockwerks, or congeries of small veins. 1845 *Encycl. Metrop.* VI. 771/2 The stockwork of the German miners is to be considered as a mass of rock impregnated with metallic matters, in numerous small veins, which come together irregularly, so as to make particular parts extremely rich. 1881 RAYMOND *Mining Gloss., Stockwork* (Germ., *Stockwerk*). An ore-deposit of such a form that it is worked in floors or stories. It may be a solid mass of ore, or a rock-mass so interpenetrated by small veins of ore that the whole must be mined together. 1957 *Mineral. Mag.* XXXI. 588 In these the tin ores occur as stockworks of topaz-bearing greisen.

stocky ('stɒkɪ), *a.* [f. STOCK *sb.*[1] + -Y.]

†**1.** Made of a stock, made of wood. *Obs. rare*⁻¹.

Misprinted *stokly* in *Min. P. Vernon MS.* (E.E.T.S.).

a 1400 *Disp. Mary & Cross* 518 in *Leg. Rood*, On a stokky stede [i.e. the Cross] He Rod we Rede.

2. Of a plant: Of stout and sturdy growth; not 'drawn up', 'weedy', or spindling.

1622 DRAYTON *Poly-olb.* xxvii. 303 Those scattered trees ..send from their stocky bough, A soft and sappy Gum. 1846 J. BAXTER *Libr. Pract. Agric.* (ed. 4) II. 20 The plants so taken out must be planted on another compartment at the same distance, and they will come to full stocky hearts in April and May. 1883 W. ROBINSON *Eng. Flower Garden* II. 109 Vigorous stocky shoots from the buried joints of the plant. 1898 F. W. CARD *Bush Fruits* 360 It is generally believed that stockier and better plants are obtained from cuttings.

b. Of a root: Woody, as distinguished from fibrous.

1915 *Times* 25 Sept. 9/5 Take up some of the outer runners with good fibrous roots and replant them carefully at once. Old plants with stocky roots will not move well.

3. Of a person, animal, etc.: Of stout and sturdy build; short and thick-set.

1676 *Poor Robin's Intell.* 23–30 May 1/1 A well-set Fellow of very good natural parts, having a broad back, and a stocky leg, [etc.]. 1711 *Lond. Gaz.* No. 4917/4 Lost.., a stockey bright bay Gelding. 1712 ADDISON *Spect.* No. 433 ¶ 6 They had no Titles of Honour among them, but such as denoted some Bodily Strength or Perfection, as such an one the Tall, such an one the Stocky. 1725 *Brice's Weekly Jrnl.* 5 Nov. 4 He is a fair stocky Fellow. 1826 COBBETT *Rur. Rides* (1885) II. 174 A particular race of sheep, called the Cotswold breed... They are short and stocky. 1864 *Daily Tel.* 13 Aug., Well-built stocky horses, for artillery and other military work. 1888 *Harper's Mag.* Apr. 783 Sturdy and stocky as a Jersey bull. 1900 W. R. MOODY *Life D. L. Moody* vii. 69 A young man..short and stocky in figure.

Comb. 1905 GUNTER *Conscience of a King* vi. 90 A rather thickset stocky built woman.

b. *fig.* of a quality.

1882 H. E. SCUDDER *Noah Webster* i. 3 His square, upright tombstone..commemorates the stocky virtues of integrity and piety.

4. *dial.* ? Not amenable to control, intractable; full of spirits, boisterous.

1836 W. D. COOPER *Sussex Gloss., Stockey*, irritable, head-strong, and contrary, combined. 1856 GEO. ELIOT *Scenes* I. 86 Little Dickey, a boisterous boy of five..was squatting quiet as a mouse at her knee... He was a boy whom Mrs. Hackit, in a severe mood, had pronounced 'stocky'..; but seeing him thus subdued into goodness, she smiled at him. 1866 MRS. H. WOOD *Elster's Folly* II. xiii. 323 Afore that drownding of his Lordship last year, Davy was the boldest and stockiest rip going.

5. Of manner, etc.: Stiff, severe.

1876 JANE E. HOPKINS *Rose Turquand* ii, 'Good morning, Rose', said Mrs. Adair, in her stockiest tones, touching it with two frosty fingers.

Hence **'stockily** *adv.*, **'stockiness.**

1890 *Christian World Pulpit* XXXVIII. 359/1 The stockiness and sturdiness of coming generations. 1892 *Harper's Mag.* LXXXIV. 530/1 A pair of stockily built horses.

Stocyen, variant of STOICIAN. *Obs.*

stød (‖stœːd). *Linguistics.* [Da., lit. 'push, jolt'.] A glottal stop or catch (see quot. 1973).

1954 PEI & GAYNOR *Dict. Linguistics* 204 *Stød*, the Danish term for *glottal stop*.., often used by phoneticians for other languages, too. 1964 J. C. CATFORD in D. Abercrombie et al. *Daniel Jones* 36 *Voiced creak* may be one form of the 'stod' in Danish. 1973 J. D. O'CONNOR *Phonetics* vii. 237 Danish has the same stress system as English with the addition that each stressed syllable may or may not have the 'stød' or glottal stop added to it (in fact, it is rarely a complete stop but rather a short period of creaky voice). 1977 C. F. & F. M. VOEGELIN *Classification & Index World's Lang.* 140 Subdialectal division into Northern and Southern on the basis of the so-called 'stød' feature, usually a 'glottal creak' in Southern corresponding to pitch-stress phenomena in Northern Danish. 1980 *Amer. Speech* LV. 61 The Danish words that have the glottal catch or stød are generally those with accent 1 elsewhere in Scandinavia.

stoddy, rare variant of STITHY.

stode, obs. variant of STUD.

stodge (stɒdʒ), *sb.* [f. STODGE *v.*]

1. A thick liquid mixture.

a. Thick, tenacious mud or soil.

1825 J. JENNINGS *Observ. Dial. W. Eng., Stodge*, any very thick liquid mixture. 1881 WHITEHEAD *Hops* 44 In wet weather the horses feet make a great stodge in ploughing.

b. Food of a semi-solid consistency, esp. stiff farinaceous food; *spec.* heavy and usu. fattening food (often with little nutritional value). *colloq.*

1841 HARTSHORNE *Salop. Ant.* Gloss., *Stodge*, a thick mess of oatmeal and milk, or any food which is semi-solid. 1874 MRS. H. WOOD *Master of Greylands* xxiii, The soup I make is not a tasteless stodge that you may almost cut with the spoon. 1891 SARA J. DUNCAN *Amer. Girl in Lond.* xxiii. 247 Oh, we'd like to [eat] but we can't... We're still in training you know... Fellows have got to train pretty much on stodge. 1963 R. I. McDAVID *Mencken's Amer. Lang.* 296 *Pudding* implies what we normally call *stodge.* 1963 *Times* 13 Feb. 5/2 If the prisoner could not tolerate all the 'stodge' he became undernourished. 1976 *Milton Keynes Express* 25 June 4/5 Remember that no exercise programme will work if not backed by sensible eating patterns and cut out stodge from today. 1980 *Times* 28 Nov. 3/2 The writers complain of surviving on stodge like potatoes and rice.

2. a. 'Stodging', gorging with food. **b.** A heavy, solid meal. Chiefly *school slang.*

1894 N. GALE *Cricket Songs* 32 O Bowler, Bowler, when the Swells all frown And say your non-success is due to Stodge. 1903 FARMER & HENLEY *Slang* VI. 373/2 *Stodge*,.. a heavy meal. 1904 P. WHITE *Tri. Mrs. St. George* viii, Here was a real live soldier..eating mutton, potatoes, and greens —the usual Thursday stodge!—along with a lot of kids!

c. Food of any kind. *slang.*

1890 BARRÈRE & LELAND *Dict. Slang* II. 307/2 *Stodge*, ..(popular and thieves), food. 1917 'TAFFRAIL' *Sub* ii. 72 Cream, jam, mineral waters and all other sorts of 'stodge'. 1929 F. C. BOWEN *Sea Slang* 133 *Stodge*, food, generally used in the gunroom only. 1940 M. MARPLES *Public School Slang* 167 *Stodge* (Rugby),.. = food—e.g. 'I've got a box of stodge.'

3. 'Stodgy' notions.

1900 [see PLATITUDINAL *a.*]. 1902 ELINOR GLYN *Refl. Ambrosine* ix. 199 Avoid stodge..and..that sentimental mawkish dismal point of view, that dramatically wrote up over everything 'Duty' with a huge 'D.'

4. A hard effort; an unfulfilling occupation.

1846 J. C. PATTESON *Let.* in C. M. Yonge *Life J. C. Patteson* (1874) I. iii. 58 Reading books for the second or third time is light work compared to the first stodge at them. 1873 C. M. YONGE *Pillars of House* II. xxiv. 34 To let him go on here in the stodge is a bit of short-sightedness I can't understand.

5. = STODGER.

1922 E. V. LUCAS *Genevra's Money* xxiii. 152 How silly of us to think he was going to be a stodge.

stodge (stɒdʒ), *v.* [Of obscure origin; perh. phonetically symbolic after words like *stuff, podge*; cf. also STOG *v.*, STOACH *v.*]

1. a. *trans.* To fill quite full, to fill to distension. †Also, to stuff *in* as a filling material (*obs.*).

1674 DRYDEN in Johnson *L.P., Dryden* (1781) II. 21 It is a kind of gibblet porridge,..stodged full of *meteors, orbs, spheres* [etc.]. **1685** H. MORE *Paralip. Prophet.* xli. 357 To bring in the Ostrogoths here, is as if one stuffing a Pillow with feathers, should so forget himself, as to stodge in pieces of Brick or Clay. **1790** W. H. MARSHALL *Rur. Econ. Midl.* II. 443 *Stodged*; filled to the stretch; as a cow's udder with milk. **1854** MISS BAKER *Northampt. Gloss., Stodged*, filled to the stretch; crammed full... If things were crushed very closely into a sack, it would be stodged.

b. esp. To gorge with food.

1854 MISS BAKER *Northampt. Gloss.* s.v., Sometimes it is applied personally: 'If you eat all that, you will be stodged full'. **1860** *Hotten's Slang Dict.* 229. **1895** ALLBUTT in *Contemp. Rev.* Feb. 220 A 'City man'..stodges his stomach with rich food three times a day.

absol. **1911** BARRIE *Peter & Wendy* vii. 114 He could eat, really eat, if it was part of a game, but he could not stodge just to feel stodgy.

c. *fig.* Also *to stodge off*: to repulse by a surfeit.

1876 SIR J. PAGET *Mem. & Lett.* II. iv. (1901) 282 We had begun to feel 'stodged': the mediæval art at Florence, especially, had quite filled us. **1894** BLACKMORE *Perlycross* xxi, I thought I was a pretty plucky fellow,..but I'll show you where I was stodged off. **1909** *Westm. Gaz.* 11 Dec. 3/1 Alas! it is mostly fiction that gluts the market, 'stodges' the reader, and..kills the few living books.

2. *dial.* (See quots.)

a **1825** FORBY *Voc. E. Anglia, Stodge*, to stir up various ingredients into a thick mass. **1895** *Dial. Notes* (Amer. Dial. Soc.) I. VIII. 394 *Stodge*, to muss or mix up. Ind.

3. *pass.* To be stuck in the mud, to be bogged. (Cf. STOG *v.*[2])

1873 W. P. WILLIAMS & W. A. JONES *Gloss. Somerset* 36 Pendummer Where the Devil was stodged in the midst of zummer. **1902** C. G. HARPER *Cambridge, Ely*, etc. *Road* 54 Enfield Highway..was until quite recently stodged in sloughs.

4. *intr.* To work steadily *at* (something 'stodgy' or tedious). *colloq.*

1912 F. M. HUEFFER *Panel* I. iii. 93, I tell you, I'm tired! Used up! I must have comfort, quiet! I can't stodge away any more. *Ibid.* 98, I plodded and stodged for just that, and nothing else. **1928** —— *Last Post* II. iii. 259 They ought no longer to go stodging along in penury. **1939** D. JONES *Let.* 17 Jan. in R. Hague *Dai Greatcoat* (1980) ii. 89 Writing is odder than painting... One seems to stodge on and scratch out for hours and days and then sometimes..something breaks through. **1959** *Listener* 29 Oct. 748/2 Poor Dr. Bronowski seems fated to the *pas seul*... His fellows stodge around, looking severe and sagacious and sound and sensible.

5. To walk or trudge through mud or slush; to walk with short heavy steps. Occas. *trans.*, to trudge through (mud). *dial.* or *colloq.*

1854 A. E. BAKER *Northampt. Gloss.* II. 306 *Studging*, walking with short heavy steps; always used with the adjunct along. 'He goes *studging* along.' **1902** *Aberdeen Weekly Free Press* 7 June 3/6 A polissman wha was comin' stodgin' doon the street. **1920** W. DEEPING *Second Youth* xxiii. 195 The 'Old Man' and his orderly stodged back again up a waterlogged communication trench. **1929** —— *Roper's Row* viii. 83 She had seen the feet of cattle stodging the mire in Melfont. *Ibid.* xiii. 138 A very stout woman..stodged round the grave after the service was over.

Hence **stodged** *ppl. a.*, **'stodging** *vbl. sb.* and *ppl. a.*

1873 W. P. WILLIAMS & W. A. JONES *Gloss. Somerset.* 36 *Stodged* adj. stuffed with eating. **1898** ELLEN T. FOWLER *Conc. Isabel Carnaby* 124 Admiration is like porridge—awfully stodging, but you get hungry again almost as soon as you've eaten it. **1903** *Longm. Mag.* Oct. 527 The 'stodged' schoolboy again, for whom fielding out is a grievance. **1912** *Daily News* 31 Dec. 9 There must be no eating when not hungry and no 'stodging' between meals.

stodge-full, *a.* [f. vbl. phr. *to be stodged full*: cf. STODGE *v.* 1.] Full to distension or repletion.

1847 HALLIWELL, *Stodge-full*, quite full, or unable to contain more. **1883** *Chamb. Jrnl.* 725 Stodge-full of receipts for cattle drinks and sheep dressings.

stodger ('stɒdʒə(r)). *colloq.* [f. STODG(Y *a.* + -ER[1].] A stodgy person; one who is lacking in spirit or liveliness. Hence **'stodgery**, behaviour characteristic of such a person.

1905 *Punch* 25 Jan. 62/1 The other regular old stodgers who go to all the parties within a radius of six miles. **1907** *Punch* 9 Jan. 20/2 Well, father's quite right, they are the most awful stodgers. You know they are. **1920** W. DEEPING *Second Youth* iv. 31 If you were starving, Miles, I suppose you would walk down Oxford Street and say nothing. What stodgery! We middle-class people are hopeless!

stodgy ('stɒdʒɪ), *a.* [f. STODGE *v.* + -Y.]

1. a. Of a thick, semi-solid consistency.

1823 E. MOOR *Suffolk Words, Stodjy*, thick—clayey—clogsome. Such as a heavy road. **1887** *Kentish Gloss., Stodgy*, thick; glutinous; muddy. 'The church path's got middlin' stodgy.'

b. Of food, esp. of farinaceous food: Thick, glutinous.

1858 SPURDENS *Suppl. to Forby's Voc. E. Anglia, Stodgy*, thick, as porridge: *pulmentum crassum*. **1866** *Lond. Rev.* 2 June 608/2 A stodgy mass of paste in which potatoes and odds and ends of food have been mixed. *a* **1890** R. F. BURTON in Isabel Burton *Life* (1893) I. 74 This cannibal meal was succeeded by stodgy pudding. **1906** OLIVE C. MALVERY *Soul Market* ix. 156 The meat was almost raw, the potatoes stodgy.

c. Of food or a meal: Heavy, solid, hard to 'get through'.

1884 *Harper's Mag.* Oct. 709/2 The stodgy *table d'hôte*. **1889** C. KEENE in *Life* xiii. (1892) 409 It's a stodgy feed—soup, fish, flesh, and fowl, etc.

2. *fig.* Dull, heavy; wanting in gaiety or brightness. **a.** of literary composition, a subject of conversation, etc.

1874 L. TROUBRIDGE *Life amongst Troubridges* (1966) 89 We had meant to play Rats and Ferrets, but we had to begin a stodgy game of Old Maid. **1885** C. M. YONGE *Nuttie's Father* I. x. 111 One of the stodgey [*sic*] old clergymen in books. **1887** *Longman's Mag.* May 107 The most merciless and interminable romance that ever lowered the circulation of a magazine, and then appeared in three stodgy volumes. **1895** JOWETT in L. A. Tollemache *Benjamin Jowett* 8, I must make a bargain with you that, when we take a walk together, you don't put more than one of your stodgy questions! **1906** 'G. THORNE' *First it was ordained* 106 In England, art must be obvious and stodgy before people think it's respectable. **1907** *Academy* 28 Sept. 948 Stodgy sonnets to the moon. **1976** J. I. M. STEWART *Memorial Service* ii. 24 The stodgy lime-streaked effigy of Provost Harbage..is really more congruous with the spirit of the place. **1977** *National Observer* (U.S.) 1 Jan. 5/4 It was a stodgy old company when he came to it as president of the international division. **1977** *Time* 31 Jan. 13/2 Leidigkeit, 38, has brought scandal and notoriety to Bonn's Ermekeil Strasse, formerly a quiet, slightly stodgy row of shops, middle-class town houses and student flats.

b. of a person, ceremony, one's life. Also applied to other objects, activities, etc.

1895 *Brit. Weekly* 28 Mar. 370/1 There are experiences which grave the brow in spite of a man. But, on the other hand, to grow stodgy is no mark of grace. **1904** S. MACNAUGHTAN *Gift* II. ii. 127 The wedding was a stodgy affair. **1905** ELIN. GLYN *Viciss. Evangeline* 101, I have not felt like writing; these last days have been so stodgy,—sticky I was going to say! Endless infant talk!

c. *fig.* of a quality.

1894 DU MAURIER *Trilby* (1895) 74 It fosters..self-respect, and not a few stodgy practical virtues as well.

d. Applied *loosely* to music, its performance, interpretation, etc.

1934 C. LAMBERT *Music Ho!* v. 294 The stodgy and academic imagination of *Verklarte Nacht*. **1959** *Times* 12 Jan. 12/3 It was surprising that Miss Puppulo was so stodgy in some early miniatures at the start of the programme. **1974** *Early Music* Apr. 81 It is so easy..for four viols to be too stodgy. **1978** R. DONINGTON in J. M. Thomson *Future of Early Music in Britain* 14 The dodge..is to get that massive resonance without sounding in the least thick and opaque and stodgy and Straussian.

3. Of a person: Bulky in figure (usually connoting stiffness and clumsiness in movement).

1854 MISS BAKER *Northampt. Gloss.* s.v., He's a stodgy little man. **1879** J. PAYN *High Spirits* (ed. 2) I. 208 He was a stodgy, pursy, plethoric old fellow. **1895** *Century Mag.* Feb. 540 The stodgy plumpness of John Bull.

4. Of things: Bulky, 'fat', distended.

1860 GEO. ELIOT *Mill on Floss* I. v, 'You don't know what I've got in my pockets... 'No,' said Maggie. 'How stodgy they look.'

Hence **'stodgily** *adv.*, **'stodginess**.

1899 *Pall Mall Gaz.* 31 July 4/1 That portion of the reading public which likes its fiction solid even to stodginess. **1904** *Sat. Rev.* 2 Jan. 18/2 Subjects..when handled stodgily are not worth reproducing.

stodie, stodier, obs. ff. STUDY, STUDIER.

stodul, stodyll, obs. forms of STUDDLE.

stody, obs. form of STUDY *sb.* and *v.*

stœchados, variant of STECHADOS *Obs.*

‖**stœchas** ('sti:kæs). Also 6 **stechas, stichas**, 8 *erron.* **stæchas**. See also STECHADOS, STICKADOVE. [L., a. Gr. στοιχάς.

According to Pliny the plant was so called because imported from the *Stœchades* islands (Gr. Στοιχάδες, lit. 'standing in a row', f. στοῖχος row), now *Les Iles d'Hyères*.]

The plant French Lavender, *Lavandula stœchas*.

1548 TURNER *Names Herbes* 77 Stechas..may be called in english stichas or Lauender gentle. **1597** GERARDE *Herbal* II. clxx. 470 The later phisitions affirme, that Stœchas, and especially the flowers of it are most effectuall against paines of the head. **1725** *Bradley's Family Dict.* II. 6 K 4 b, The Stæchas is of a bitter taste and a little astringent. **1831** J. DAVIES *Manual Mat. Med.* 181 The Stœchas or French Lavender. *Lavandula stœchas*, Lin. A plant, native of the south of France... A syrup of stœchas, P., is prepared from this plant, and is added to antispasmodic mixtures.

stœchiogeny, -ology: see STOICH-.

stoel(e, obs. forms of STOLE *sb.*[1]

stoep (stu:p). *South Africa.* Also †**stoop** (cf. STOOP *sb.*[3]). [Du., related to STEP *sb.*[1] and *v.*

In the U.S. the Du. word has been adopted with the anglicized spelling STOOP.]

a. A raised platform or verandah running along the front and sometimes round the sides of a house of Dutch architecture.

1797 A. BARNARD *Let.* 10 July in *S. Afr. a Century Ago* (1901) 57 As for the young Dutchmen, I saw hardly any; the young ones prefer smoking their pipes on the *stoep*. **1798** —— *Jrnl.* 21 May in *Lives of Lindsays* (1849) III. 457 Their *stoop* was covered with a set of large idle boors in their blue jackets, sons of the family—men who do hardly anything beside eating and smoking. **1804** J. BARROW *Trav. Interior S. Afr.* II. ii. 104 He..parades the *stoop*, or raised platform before the door. **1805** *Gleanings in Afr.* ii. 17 A stone terrace, extending the whole length of the house, and elevated a few feet above the level of the street, is the grand promenade of the family; this is called the *Stoop*. **1822** BURCHELL *Trav. S. Africa* I. iii. 71 In front of each house, and of the same length, is a paved platform... This platform is called the *Stoep* (step). **1849** E. E. NAPIER *Excurs. S. Africa* I. 182 The 'stoep' is a narrow terrace raised outside most of the Dutch houses, where the owner may, towards evening, be generally seen smoking his pipe. **1883** OLIVE SCHREINER *Afr. Farm* II. vi. (1889) 201 On the 'stoep' a group of men and boys were smoking. **1890** *Pall Mall Gaz.* 20 Jan. 2/1 On the stoep—that terraced verandah which is the unfailing appendage of a Dutch house—the good wife stands to welcome us. **1939** tr. *E. N. Marais's My Friends the Baboons* ix. 101 We could follow the whole tragedy step by step from the stoep of Mr. van Heerden's house. **1966** E. PALMER *Plains of Camdeboo* ii. 26 A wide stoep running round three sides in the manner of Karoo houses. **1980** *Listener* 17 July 66/3 A farmer's wife in Natal..sitting..on the stoep.

b. *Comb.* ***stoep lantern, plant***; **stoep-room**, a small room having entrance and exit by the stoep only; **stoepsitter**, one who habitually sits idly on the stoep of his house.

1971 *Het Suid Western* 14 May 9 Wrought iron porch or *stoep lanterns, wired in new condition—R5 each. **1961** *Argosy* Mar. 20 She attended to her *stoep plants. **1880** HELEN M. PRICHARD *Friends & Foes in Transkei* xvii. 122 Two very miniature '*stoep-rooms', as they are called at the Cape. (Small rooms stolen out of each end of the verandah.) **1934** C. R. SWART *Africanderisms* (typescript), *Stoepsitters, ..a sluggard or lazy person; sometimes humorously applied by townsmen to farmers, who used to spend much of their time on the stoep, drinking their favourite beverage, coffee. **1948** O. WALKER *Kaffirs are Lively* 92 They don't work. They're stoep-sitters, coffee-tipplers and pipe-spitters. **1972** *Sunday Times* 24 Sept. 19 Topical remarks, especially by the three 'stoepsitters', are made through the play.

stof, obs. form of STUFF.

†**sto'ffado.** *Obs. rare*[−0]. [Prob. an error: cf. STUFFATA and It. *stoffa* STUFF *sb.*] (See quot.)

1688 HOLME *Armoury* III. 84/2 Stoffado, is a term for the Stuffing of any joint of Meat, or Belly of any Fowl, [etc.].

†**'stofne,** *v. Obs. rare*[−1]. [a. ON. *stofna*, to found, establish, f. *stofn* foundation, stem: see STOVEN.] *trans.* To found.

c **1200** ORMIN 14561 þatt erþliȝ shaffte mihhte ben þurrh hemm efftsone stoffnedd.

stog (stɒg), *sb.*[1] *Sc.* Also 6 **stogg.** [f. STOG *v.*[1] Cf. STUG *sb.*] A stab.

1587 W. FOWLER *Wks.* (S.T.S.) I. 69 So able war, and quik, for to awaird or to eshew the blow, the stogg, and prik. *c* **1590** J. STEWART *Poems* (S.T.S.) II. 93 Be dints and stogs of dochtie Durandal The craig and wreat he claiwe in stelpis small. **1863** J. NICHOLSON *Kilwuddie* I. xiv, In that famous muirlan' battle Trooper loons gat mony a stog.

stog (stɒg), *sb.*[2] *dial.* [f. STOG *v.*[2]] A sticking (in a bog).

1890 BARING-GOULD *Old Country Life* xiii, Though sure of a stogg to the girths in a bog.

stog (stɒg), *v.*[1] *Sc.* [Perh. f. *stog-* in *stog-sword*, var. *stock-sword* STOCK *sb.*[3] Cf. STOCK *v.*[2]]

†**a.** *trans.* To stab (a person); to prod or pierce (a thing) with a weapon. Also with *through*. Cf. STUG *v. Obs.*

a **1572** KNOX *Hist. Ref.* Wks. 1846 I. 361 One of the Bischopis sonis stogged throuch with a rapper one of Dundie. **1576** *Reg. Privy Council Scot.* II. 553 He come upoun him with a drawin swerd, and purposing to have slane him he stoggit him be chance throw the oxtare. **1607** *Ibid.* VII. 449 [They] with drawin swordis, durkis, and daigaris barbarouslie stoggit the daskis of the said scoole.

†**b.** *intr.* To make a stab with a weapon. *Obs.*

c **1590** J. STEWART *Poems* (S.T.S.) II. 31 Quhyls stiff thay stog, And quhyls they bend about To schaw tham maisters of the fensing art.

c. *trans.* To thrust the tool too deep in the wood in turning, chipping, or planing.

1825 JAMIESON.

d. To probe soil, a pool or marsh with a stick or pole.

1825 JAMIESON.

stog (stɒg), *v.*[2] [Perh. phonetically symbolic after *stick, bog* or the like. Cf. STODGE *v.*, STUG *v.*]

1. *pass.* To be stuck in mud, mire, bog or the like; to be bogged. Also *fig.*

1855 KINGSLEY *Westw. Ho!* v, If any of his party are mad, they'll try it, and be stogged till the day of judgment. There are bogs..twenty feet deep. **1863** —— *Water Babies* ii. 62 Stogged in a mire you never will be, I trust. **1883** M. G. WATKINS *In the Country* 7 Let them be in peace, unless you wish to be 'pixie-led', and left 'stogged' in a deep swamp. **1928** J. Y. T. GREIG *Breaking Priscian's Head* 60 Old pedantic grammarians stogged to the neck in Latin, have done their work too well.

2. *intr.* To walk clumsily or heavily; to plod *on.*

1818 HOGG *Brownie of Bodsbeck* iii, I slings aye on wi' a gay lang step;..Stogs aye on through cleuch and gill. **1824** MACTAGGART *Gallovid. Encycl.* 398 How angry did he [a corbie] hotch and stog, And croak about, Owreturning stanes. **1894** J. SHAW in R. Wallace *Country Schoolm.* (1899) 354 *Stog*, to walk heavily.

stoggie ('stɒgɪ), *sb. dial.* Also **stoggy.** [f. *stog-* in *stogdoo* Sc. var. of STOCKDOVE + -IE.] The stock-dove, *Columba œnas*.

1864 ATKINSON *Prov. Names Birds* s.v. **1890** J. NICHOLSON *Folk-Lore E. Yorksh.* 130 The stockdove..is locally known as a 'stoggie'.

stoggie ('stɒgɪ), *a. Sc.* and *dial.* Also **stoggy**. [Of obscure origin. Cf. STOCKY *a.*] Rough, rough and coarse, strongly made.

1825 JAMIESON, *Stoggie*, 1. Rough in a general sense, Upp. Clydes. 2. As applied to cloth, it denotes that it is both coarse and rough, ibid. **1895** *E. Angl. Gloss.*, *Stoggy*, thick, broad, and strongly made.

stogy ('stəʊgɪ), *a.* and *sb. U.S.* Now freq. **stogie**. Also **stoga**, **stoggie**. [Orig. *stoga*, short for *Conestoga*, the name of a town in Pennsylvania, used *attrib.* in *Conestoga wagon* (see Thornton *American Glossary*).

It is alleged that *stoga boots* and *stoga cigars* were so called because they were used by the 'stoga drivers', i.e. the drivers of the Conestoga wagons plying between Wheeling and Pittsburgh.]

A. *adj.* The distinctive epithet **a.** of a rough heavy kind of boots or shoes; **b.** of a long, slender, roughly made kind of cigar or cheroot.

a. a **1847** JOEL PALMER *Jrnl.* 117 (Thornton *Amer. Gloss.*) [I bought] a pair of stoga shoes, made in one of the eastern states. **1859** ALICE CARY *Pict. Country Life* 102, I want for you to make me a pair of tip-top stogy boots. **1876** DAVIS *Polaris Exp.* App. 669, 1 case men's stoga boots. **1892** GUNTER *Miss Dividends* (1893) 185 Stoggie boots aren't quite as nice as patent-leathers.

b. **1903** FARMER & HENLEY *Slang* VI. 373/2 *Stogy-cigar*, a rough coarse cigar. **1930** J. OMWAKE *Conestoga Six-Horse Bell Teams* 118 The Conestoga wagon gives its name to the Stogie cigar, a great thin coarse one, supposed to have been originally a foot long and made for the delectation of the wagoner.

B. *sb.* **a.** A 'stogy' boot. **b.** A 'stogy' cigar.

a. **1853** *Putnam's Mag.* July 31 Boot and shoe, pump and stoga, coming to that [*sc.* the gutter] at last. **1892** *Dialect Notes* (Amer. Dial. Soc.) I. 229 Kentucky Words... Conostogas:..brogans. (In Michigan 'stogies'.) **1908** GUNTER *Prince Karl* VII. 296 Rawdon cried: 'We've heard enough of you!' and with his own stogie kicked out the soap box from under the little desperado's feet.

b. **1873** J. O'CONNOR *Wanderings of Vagabond* 52 After the lunch liquors and cigars (red-eye and stogies), the best the place afforded, were introduced by the host. **1892** *Dialect Notes* (Amer. Dial. Soc.) I. 237 Notes from Missouri ...*Stogies*,..cheap cigars. **1897** KIPLING *Capt. Courageous* i. 6 'It would take more'n this to keel me over,' he said, ignorant that he was lighting that terrible article, a Wheeling 'stogie'. **1902** *Daily Record* 21 July 2 Stogies, Tobies and other cigars of a cheroot style. **1916** C. SANDBURG *Chicago Poems* 47 He lighted a three-for-a-nickel stogie. **1930** J. DOS PASSOS *42nd Parallel* 19 He was smoking a thin black stogy of a sort Fainy had never seen before. **1957** V. PACKARD *Hidden Persuaders* ix. 103 The man who puffs on his cigar is sucking his thumb while the man who chews vigorously on his stogie is a nail biter.

stoib, obs. Sc. f. STOB *v.*[2]

stoic ('stəʊɪk), *sb.* and *a.* Forms: 4 *pl.* **stoycis**, 6 **stoyck**, 6–7 **-icke**, **-ik(e**, **-yk(e**, **-ique**, 6–8 **stoick**, 7– **stoic**. [ad. L. *stōicus*, a. Gr. στωϊκός, f. στοά 'the Porch' in which Zeno lectured: see STOA. Cf. F. *stoïque*, It. *stoico*.

Wyclif's *stoycis* is L. *stoici* with an Eng. plural ending.]

A. *sb.*

1. (With capital initial.) One of a school of Greek philosophers (founded by Zeno, fl. *c* 300 B.C.), characterized by the austerity of its ethical doctrines for some of which the name has become proverbial (see 2).

1382 WYCLIF *Acts* xvii. 18 Forsothe summe Epicureis, and Stoycis [1388 Stoisens], and philosofris disputiden.. with him. **1575** GASCOIGNE *Glasse Govt.* Wks. 1910 II. 18 Aristo the Stoicke. **1589** NASHE *Anat. Absurd.* C 1 b. It is an old Question,..whether it were better to haue moderate affections, or no affections? The Stoicks said none. **1625** BACON *Ess.*, *Anger* (Arb.) 565 To seeke to extinguish Anger vtterly, is but a Brauery of the Stoickes. **1671** MILTON *P.R.* IV. 280 With those Sirnam'd Peripatetics, and the Sect Epicurean, and the Stoic severe. **1725** WATTS *Logic* (1822) 86 The Stoics..talk of fate, which is superior to the gods. **1837–9** HALLAM *Hist. Lit.* (1847) III. 11 Testi had taken.. Horace for his model; and perhaps like him he wished to appear sometimes a stoic, sometimes an epicurean.

attrib. **1725** YOUNG *Love Fame* I. 233 Fools grin on fools, and Stoic-like, support, Without one sigh, the pleasures of a court. **1891** FARRAR *Darkn. & Dawn* lx, And, therefore, Stoic-fashion, men must accustom themselves to regard all calamities as matters of indifference.

2. One who practises repression of emotion, indifference to pleasure or pain, and patient endurance.

1579 GOSSON *Sch. Abuse* (Arb.) 45, I make iuste reckoning to bee helde for a Stoike, in dealing so hardely with these people. **1596** SHAKS. *Tam. Shr.* I. i. 31 Onely (good master) while we do admire This vertue, and this morall discipline, Let's be no Stoickes, nor no stockes I pray. **1599** B. JONSON *Ev. Man out of Hum.* I. i, But Stoique; where (in the vast worlde) Doth that man breath, that can so much command His bloud and his affection? **1657** TRAPP *Comm. Job* i. 20 He stirreth not at the three first doleful tidings, but this fourth startleth him; for he was neither a Stoick, nor a stock. **1726** SWIFT *Stella's Birthday* 50 That patience under tort'ring pain, Where stubborn stoicks wou'd complain. **1771** BURKE *Let. Bp. Chester* Corr. (1844) I. 278 In some few things, I fancy I am grown almost a stoic; but your lordship's unkindness has attacked me on a side on which I was absolutely unguarded, and I bear it like a girl. **1809** CAMPBELL *Gertrude* I. xxiii, A stoic of the woods—a man without a tear. **1812** SCOTT in *Sotheran's Catal.* No. 12 (1899) 48, I am somewhat of a Stoic in family discipline, which was the old Scottish system. **1854** J. S. C. ABBOTT *Napoleon* (1855) I. i. 23 Stoic as he was, his stoicism then forsook him, and he wept like a child. **1855** TENNYSON *Maud* I. IV. iv, I..smile a hard-set smile, like a stoic, or like A wiser epicurean, and let the world have its way.

3. *Comb.*, as *Stoic-Christian*, *-Epicurean*, *-Megaric* adjs.

1933 A. N. WHITEHEAD *Adventures of Ideas* iii. 43 These doctrines have all weakened the Stoic-Christian ideal of democratic brotherhood. **1948** L. SPITZER *Linguistics & Lit Hist.* 15 *Pantagruélisme*, the name given by Rabelais to his stoic-epicurean philosophy. **1966** *Philos. Rev.* LXXV. 246 Rescher takes these..as evidence that Arabic logic was directly influenced by the Stoic-Megaric tradition.

B. *adj.*

1. Of or belonging to the school of the Stoics or to its system of philosophy.

1607 T. ROGERS *39 Art.* i. (1625) 5 The Stoike Philosophers. **1634** MILTON *Comus* 707 O foolishnes of men! that lend their ears To those budge doctors of the Stoick Furr. **1712** ADDISON *Spect.* No. 397 ¶1 As the Stoick Philosophers discard all Passions in general, they will not allow [etc.]. **1817** SCOTT *Rob Roy* xii, No Stoic philosopher, superior to his own passion and that of others, could have received an insult with a higher degree of scorn. **1848** LYTTON *Harold* x. ii, Harold's stern philosophy and stoic ethics were shaken to the dust.

2. = STOICAL *a.* 2.

1596 SPENSER *F.Q.* IV. Prol. iii, The which these Stoicke censours cannot well deny. **1807** CRABBE *Par. Reg.* III. 433 Yet far was he from stoic pride removed; He felt humanely, and he warmly loved. **1813** BYRON *Corsair* III. xxi, Full many a stoic eye and aspect stern Mask hearts where grief hath little left to learn. **1849** M. ARNOLD *To Gipsy Child* 29 Is the calm thine of stoic souls, who weigh Life well, and find it wanting..? **1913** MRS. F. H. BURNETT *T. Tembarom* x, The same factor may..have aided him to preserve a certain stoic, outward composure.

Hence †'**Stoicly** *adv.* (*rare*) = STOICALLY.

1612 W. MARTYN *Youth's Instruct.* 69 In your pleasures, not to be wanton, nor Stoickly to passe by them.

stoical ('stəʊɪkəl), *a.* Also 6–7 **-all**, and with capital initial. [f. L. *stōic-us* (see prec.) + -AL[1].]

1. Of or belonging to the Stoics; characteristic of the Stoic philosophy.

1432–50 tr. *Higden* (Rolls) IV. 205 This Cato was a philosophre of the stoicalle secte. **1586** T. B. *La Primaud. Fr. Acad.* I. 275 Standing much upon that stoicall opinion, that onely a wise and good man is free, and that all wicked men are bond men and slaves. **1662** STILLINGFL. *Orig. Sacræ* III. ii. §10 Which consequence is unavoidable on the Stoical Hypothesis of Gods being corporeal and confined to the World. **1778** REID *Ess. Active Powers Man* III. III. iii. 218 We cannot but admire the Stoical system of morals. **1869** LECKY *Europ. Mor.* I. ii. 237 The stoical system of ethics was in the highest sense a system of independent morals. **1887** MAHAFFY & GILMAN *Alexander's Empire* xxvii. 253 Such was already the result of Stoical teaching on the world!

2. a. Of temper or disposition, or its manifestations: Conformable to the precepts of the Stoic philosophy; characterized by indifference to pleasure and pain.

1571 GOLDING *Calvin on Ps.* lxi. 3 A hart that is benommed with Stoicall hardnes ageinst greefs and trubbles. **1596** LODGE *Marg. Amer.* 74 Now let each of you bethinke him of mirth not of majestie, I will have no stoicall humor in this arbour. **1622** PEACHAM *Compl. Gentl.* i. 2 For hardly they are to be admitted for Noble, who..consume their light..in contemplation, and a Stoicall retirednesse. **1739** CIBBER *Apol.* (1756) II. 31 My stoical way of thinking may be no rule for a wiser man's opinion. **1823** SCOTT *Quentin D.* vi, He looked around him in agony, and was surprised..to see the stoical indifference of his fellow-prisoners. **1856** FROUDE *Hist. Eng.* (1858) I. ii. 99 The English nation would have looked on with stoical resignation if pope and papacy had been wrecked together. **1874** GREEN *Short Hist.* viii. §10 We feel his [Milton's] inmost temper in the stoical self-repression which gives its dignity to his figures.

b. Of a person: Resembling a Stoic in austerity, indifference to pleasure and pain, repression of all feeling, and the like.

1577 NORTHBROOKE *Dicing* (1843) 83 If I should vtterly deny all kinde of such playes, then shoulde I bee thought too stoicall and precise. **1589** NASHE *Anat. Absurd.* B 1 b, Antient antiquitie was woont to bee such a stoycall obseruer of continencie, that women were not permitted so much as to kisse their Kinsmen. **1596** WARNER *Alb. Eng.* XI. lxi. (1602) 268 Nor was he stoicall in ought, but affable in all. **1612** SELDEN *Illustr. Drayton's Poly-olb.* VIII. 132 The Scythian was..so Stoicall, as not to care for the future, hauing prouision for the present. **1631** BRATHWAIT *Whimzies* 66 He is too stoicall that is wholly for his cell, and nothing for the world. *a* **1661** FULLER *Worthies, Essex* (1662) 332 One saith of him [Wm. Gilbert] that he was Stoicall, but not Cynicall, which I understand Reserv'd, but not Morose. **1849** MACAULAY *Hist. Eng.* vii. II. 170 He was a different man from the reserved and stoical William whom the multitude supposed to be destitute of human feelings. **1855** PRESCOTT *Philip II*, I. I. i. 7 Every one, even the most stoical, was touched by this..scene. **1891** HARDY *Tess* xxxiii, She had much questioned if they would appear at the parting moment; but there they were, stoical and staunch to the last.

Hence '**stoicalness**.

1727 BAILEY vol. II, *Stoicalness*, a holding the Principles of the Stoicks, that wise Men ought to be free from Passions, and that all Things were governed by Fate. **1818** in TODD.

stoically ('stəʊɪkəlɪ), *adv.* [f. prec. + -LY[2].]

1. In the manner of a Stoic; like the Stoics of old; in accordance with the principles of the Stoical philosophy.

1607 WALKINGTON *Opt. Glass* vii. 64 b, [A man] alwaies stoically visaged, like grout headed Archesilas. **1612** *Benvenuto's Passenger* II. i. 455 Though the Stoicks stoically haue held the contrarie. **1630** WADSWORTH *Pilgr.* iii. 25 The least fault he did they Stoically interpreted to bee equall to the greatest. **1682** SIR T. BROWNE *Chr. Mor.* III. §12 Be not Stoically mistaken in the equality of sins.

2. With the indifference or fortitude of a stoic.

1812 HENRY *Camp. agst. Quebec* 60 The laugh of the company was against me, but it was borne stoically. **1837** CARLYLE *Fr. Rev.* I. I. i, Paris is stoically calm. **1841** DICKENS *Barn. Rudge* ii, He tried to look stoically at the tavern. **1879** BEERBOHM *Patagonia* xi. 167, I sat down beside it waiting as stoically as I could for night-time.

stoicheiology (stɔɪkaɪ'ɒlədʒɪ), **stœchiology** (stiːkɪ'ɒlədʒɪ). *rare.* [f. Gr. στοιχεῖο-ν element + -LOGY. Orig. ad. the G. form *stöchiologie.*] The science of elements. **a.** In Oken's use: see quot.

1847 A. TULK tr. *Oken's Elem. Physiophilos.* 68 Stöchiology. Functions of the Elements. **1860** R. FOWLER *Med. Vocab.*, *Stœchiology*, a treatise on, or the theory of, elementary substances.

b. *Logic.* (See quot.)

1837–8 SIR W. HAMILTON *Logic* v. (1860) I. 72 We proceed to the doctrines which make up the science itself, and commence the First Great Division of Pure Logic—that which treats of its elementary or constituent processes,—Stoicheiology. *Ibid.* xxiv. II. 3 In its Stoicheiology or Doctrine of Elements, Logic considers the conditions of possible thought.

c. *Phys.* The study of the principles of animal tissues; a system of therapeutics based on this.

1875 J. F. CHURCHILL *Consumption* x. 385 My doctrine of stœchiology is diametrically opposed to this.

Hence **stoicheio'logical**, **stœchio'logical** *a.*

1875 J. F. CHURCHILL *Consumption* x. 384 Stœchiological medicine—Inhalants. *Ibid.* 391 This stœchiological doctrine ..gives us a fundamental classification of diseases.

†**stoicheio'matical**, *a. Obs. rare*[−1]. In 7 *erron.* **stocheio-**. [f. mod.L. *stoicheiōmatic-us* (ad. Gr. στοιχειωματικοί pl., persons who cast nativities, f. στοιχείωμα sign of the Zodiac) + -AL[1].] Pertaining to the casting of nativities.

1658 J. ROBINSON *Eudoxia* x. 55 The slow proreption of Every Sidus, out of his proper Sign almost unto the subsequent,..doth overturn the grand Pillar of Stocheiomatical Art [orig. *artis stoicheiomaticæ*].

So †**stoicheio'matic**, *sb. Obs.*, a caster of nativities.

1662 STANLEY *Hist. Chaldaick Philos.* I. III. iii. (1687) 1050/1 These the Greeks term also στοιχεῖα,..and the makers of them Stoicheiomaticks.

stoicheiometry (stɔɪkaɪ'ɒmɪtrɪ). *Chem.* Also †**stechi-**, †**stochi-**, **stœchi-** (stiːkɪ-), **stoichiometry**. [f. Gr. στοιχεῖο-ν element + -METRY.] The process or art of calculating or determining the equivalent and atomic weights of the elements participating in any chemical reaction; the science of estimating chemical elements; the branch of science concerned with the determination of atomic weights. (See also quot. 1880.) In mod. use, the quantitative relationship between the substances in a reaction or compound.

The term was introduced by J. B. Richter in his *Anfangsgründe der Stöchiometrie, oder Messkunst chemischer Elemente* (1792), to denote the determination of the relative amounts in which acids and bases neutralize each other.

1807 T. THOMSON *Chem.* II. 559, I have not been able to procure a sight of Richter's very curious..writings on Stechiometry, in which his observations on the fluates are to be found. **1825** W. HAMILTON *Hand-bk. Terms Arts & Sci.*, *Stochiometry*, the Geometry of chemical elements. **1880** TYNDALL *Heat* xviii. (ed. 6) 571 The doctrine of the conservation of force, or, as I should express it, Physical Stoichiometry. **1908** S. YOUNG (*title*) Stoichiometry. **1971** W. F. PICKERING *Mod. Analytical Chem.* iv. 153 It can also be used to determine the stoichiometry of reactions occurring in solution. **1975** R. F. BROWN *Organic Chem.* viii. 192 Stoichiometry, the weight relations in chemical reactions, must be kept in mind in the study of rates of reaction.

Hence **stoicheio-**, **stoichio-**, **stœchio'metric**, **-al** *adjs.*

1887 *Brit. Jrnl. Photogr.* 27 May 330/2 Much too small [a proportion of colouring matter] to represent a stoichiometrical composition. **1892** *Nature* 24 Mar. 497/2 The late Prof. Stas had left..a..memoir describing the results of several further stöchiometrical investigations. *Ibid.*, The stöchiometric relation of silver to potassium chloride. **1921** *Jrnl. Geol.* XXIX. 533 The stoechiometric relation between MgO and FeO in olivine and bronzite. **1962** J. H. WHITE *Inorganic Chem.* ix. 108 The formation of solid solution does not appear to be very different [from that of metallic compounds] except that..no stoichiometric relationship between the constituent metals exists. **1965** PHILLIPS & WILLIAMS *Inorganic Chem.* I. viii. 296 Metal fluorides but not hydrides are stoicheiometric.

†**stoichei'otical**, *a. Obs. rare*[−1]. In 7 **stoichioticall**. [f. late Gr. στοιχειωτικ-ός (f. στοιχειοῦν to enchant, f. στοιχεῖον element) + -AL[1].] Pertaining to magic.

1646 J. GREGORY *Notes & Observ.* (1650) 35 But the meaning of the Images [of the Emrods and Mice 1 Sam. vi. 5] is Stoichioticall.

†**Sto'ician**. *Obs.* In 4 **Stoi-**, **Stoycien**, **-yen**, **Stoisen**, 5 **Stocyen**. [a. F. *stoïcien* (14th c.), f. L. *stōic-us*: see STOIC and -IAN.] = STOIC *sb.* 1.

c **1374** CHAUCER *Boeth.* v. met. iv. (1868) 166 Philosophers þat hy3ten stoiciens. **1388** WYCLIF *Acts* xvii. 18 Epicureis, and Stoisens [1382 Stoycis]. **1426** LYDG. *De Guil. Pilgr.* 20182 And the Stocyens wolde Holden with me, (yiff they wer here). **1545** ASCHAM *Toxoph.* II. (Arb.) 165 Plato,

Aristotle, and the Stoicians. **1814** *Sporting Mag.* XLIII. 267 Have not Philosophers, Stoicians,..and Rhetoricians Left sense's cold, insipid shrine To bend 'fore Altars feminine?

stoicism ('stəʊɪsɪz(ə)m). [ad. mod.L. *stōicismus*, f. L. *stōicus*: see STOIC and -ISM. Cf. F. *stoïcisme* (17th c. in Hatz.-Darm.).]

1. (With capital initial.) The philosophy of the Stoics.

1626 [FEATLEY] *Pelagius rediv.* D 1 b, This Doctrine bringeth into the Church..Stoicisme. **1694** G. STANHOPE tr. *Epictetus' Mor.* Pref., The same Difficulty lies against Stoicism, with regard to Civil Society. **1712** ADDISON *Spect.* No. 243 ¶5 Stoicism, which was the Pedantry of Virtue, ascribes all good Qualifications, of what kind soever, to the virtuous Man. **1863** E. V. NEALE *Anal. Thought & Nature* 99 But when we meet stoicism in the works of Epictetus and Marcus Aurelius, we find a remarkable change. **1910** *Q. Rev.* Apr. 575 Stoicism, with a disposition to regard man as a self-sufficing unit, becomes aristocratic, whereas Christianity in its essential characteristics is democratic.

2. Conduct or practice conformable to the principles of the Stoics; austerity, repression of feeling, fortitude.

1630 BRATHWAIT *Eng. Gentlem.* (1641) 102, I admit of no such strict Stoicisme; but rather..to use wine or any such strong drinke to strengthen and comfort Nature. **1665** GLANVILL *Scepsis Sci.* xxvii. 168 This unmoved apathy in opinionative uncertainties, is a warrantable piece of Stoicism. *a* **1721** PRIOR *Vicar of Bray & Sir T. Moor* 577 Wks. 1907 II. 261, I am afraid your Lordship may grow Angry, which would be a little against Your Stoicism. **1820** W. IRVING *Sketch Bk.* II. 260 This last outrage overcame even the stoicism of the savage. **1855** MACAULAY *Hist. Eng.* xix. IV. 282 It was said that William so far forgot his wonted stoicism as to utter a passionate exclamation at the way in which the English regiments had been sacrificed. **1871** *Standard* 23 Jan., Paris received the news of General Chanzy's check..without losing its stoicism.

†**sto'icity.** *Obs. rare*⁻¹. [ad. F. *stoïcité*, f. L. *stōic-us* STOIC: see -ITY.] A stoical attitude.

1609 B. JONSON *Sil. Wom.* I. i, Leaue this Stoicitie alone, till thou maks't Sermons.

stoicize ('stəʊɪsaɪz), *v.* [f. L. *stōic-us* STOIC + -IZE.] *trans.* To render stoical, imbue with stoicism.

1718 C. HAYES tr. *Addison's Dissertation upon Roman Poets* 42 Pompey..ought to have been very much stoiciz'd indeed, who, despoil'd of all the Goods of Fortune, could place the Sum of his Felicity in meer naked Virtue. *a* **1864** T. ARCHER in *Mem.* (1867) 318 [This principle] may stoicize, may petrify your hearts.

stoicly *adv.*: see after STOIC.

Stoico- ('stəʊɪkəʊ), combining form of L. *stōicus* or Gr. *στωϊκός* STOIC, as in *Stoico-Platonic*, *-sybaritical* adjs.

1979 M. A. SCREECH *Rabelais* iii. 38 The inerrant Stoico-Platonic Christian sage. **1822** M. EDGEWORTH *Let.* 12 June (1971) 406 He and Harriet and Fanny too declare it is too much trouble to hold a parasol. I believe you too are of the same *Stoico-sybaritical* sect so I will waive the subject.

stoil-ball, obs. form of STOOL-BALL.

stoile, stoill: see STOLE *sb.*¹, STOOL.

stoir(e, obs. Sc. forms of STORE.

stoisen, variant of STOICIAN. *Obs.*

stoit (stɔɪt), *v. dial.* [? a. Du. *stuiten* to rebound, bounce (? adopted as a term of some ballgame). But cf. STOT *v.* in similar senses.]

1. *Sc.* **a.** *intr.* 'To rebound, bounce' (*Eng. Dial. Dict.*). **b.** To move unsteadily, stumble, lurch; to walk with unsteady movements. Also with *about*, *along*.

1719 W. HAMILTON *Ep. Ramsay* ii. 62 Wi' writing I'm sae bliert and doited, That when I raise, in troth I stoited. **1787** BURNS *To Miss Ferrier* iii, Last day my mind was in a bog, Down George's Street I stoited. **1794** —— *'Contented wi' little'* iv, Blind Chance, let her snapper and stoyte on her way. **1818** SCOTT *Hrt. Midl.* xxx, I wish ye had seen him stoiting about, aff ae leg on to the other, wi' a kind o' dot-and-go-one sort o' motion. **1864** LATTO *Tammas Bodkin* xii, We were stoitin' alang, deeply immersed in oor ain cracks.

2. Of pilchards: To leap above the surface of the water.

1825 *Encycl. Lond.* XX. 435/1 They call the jumping of the fish stoiting. **1836** YARRELL *Brit. Fishes* II. 101 The Herring..rarely springs from the water, or stoits, as it is called. **1899** BARING-GOULD *Bk. of West* II. xix. 315 The sean-boat is rowed in a circular course round where the fish are stoiting.

Hence **stoit** *sb.*, a lurch. Phr. *to play stoit*, to lurch or stagger.

1808 A. SCOTT *Poems* 164 But fegs, wi' mony a stoit an' stevel, She [*sc.* a filly] rais'd a trot. **1881** D. THOMSON *Musings among Heather* 118 Rab's road seem'd shorter than 'twas wide, For he play'd stoit frae side to side.

stoiter ('stɔɪtə(r)), *v.* *Sc.* and *north.* [Frequentative f. STOIT *v.* Cf. north. dial. *stotter*, *stauter*, *stowter* in similar senses (see *Eng. Dial. Dict.*).] *intr.* To swerve from side to side in walking; to walk with staggering or tottering steps; also with *up*.

c **1730** RAMSAY *Vision* xix, They stoyter hame to sleip. **1785** BURNS *Jolly Beggars* xvi, At length wi' drink and courting dizzy, He stoiter'd up and made a face. **1837** R. NICOLL *Poems* (1843) 91 Now wi' a staff about the dykes, He stoiters, auld, and beld and wan. **1893–4** STEVENSON *Heathercat* ii, Poor, blind, besotted creature—and I see you stoytering on the brink of dissolution.

Hence **'stoitering** *ppl. a.*, staggering, tottering. Also **stoiter** *sb.*, a stumble; phr. *to play stoiter*, to stagger.

1789 R. FERGUSSON *Poems* II. 86 Till he can lend the stoitering state a lift Wi' gowd in gowpins as a grassum gift. *a* **1838** RODGER *Poems, Colin Dulap* 59 While wauchlin' alang between sober and fou, Wi' a stoiter to this side, to that side a stap. **1890** J. SERVICE *Thir Notandums* vi. 31 Laird Speckie played stoiter to a corner and fell asleep.

stok, obs. form of STOCK.

‖**stokaghe.** *Obs.* In Johnson and later Dicts. **stocah.** [Irish *stócach*: cf. the later STALKO.] An attendant on a 'kerne' or Irish foot-soldier.

1596 SPENSER *State Irel.* Wks. (Globe) 672/1 He..thence-foorth becometh either an horseboy, or a stokaghe to some kearne. *Ibid.* 677/2 Kearne, Stokaghs, and Horseboyes.

Štokavian (ʃtɒ'kɑːvɪən), *sb.* (and *a.*). Also **Shtokavian, Stokavian, stokavian.** [f. Serbo-Croat *štokavščina* (*štokavski* adj.): see -IAN.] A widely spoken dialect of Serbo-Croat on which the literary language is based. Also *attrib.* or as *adj.*

[**1911** *Encycl. Brit.* XXIV. 695/2 Servian is sometimes called *shtokavski* because the Servian word for 'what' is *shto*, whereas the Croats say *cha* for *shto*, and therefore their language is called *chakavski*.] **1925** P. RADIN tr. *Vendryès's Lang.* 291 In Italy, in the province of Campobasso, there is a Serbo-Croatian colony..which..speaks a dialect of the Stokavian type. **1939** L. H. GRAY *Foundation of Lang.* 355 *Serbo-Croatian*, with three dialects conventionally named according to the way in which they form the word for 'what': *Štokavian* (the basis of the literary language), *Čakavian*, and *Kaykavian*. **1949** R. JAKOBSON *Slavic Languages* 4 Serbocroatian from East to West presents three basic groups: Štokavian, Čakavian and Kajkavian. **1964** M. PARTRIDGE *Serbo-Croatian* 13 Three distinct basic dialects exist in spoken Serbo-Croatian. They are referred to as *čakavian*, *kajkavian* and *štokavian* according to whether the word 'ča?', 'kaj?' or 'što?' is used respectively as the interrogative pronoun meaning *what?* **1974** *Encycl. Brit. Macropædia* XVI. 867/1 The literary Serbo-Croatian language was formed in the first half of the 19th century on the basis of the Shtokavian dialects that extend over the greater part of the Serbo-Croatian territory in Yugoslavia. **1976** *Language* LII. 375 The dat. sg. + *i* here..represents a morphological change rather than a phonological difference between kajkavian and štokavian. **1977** *Archivum Linguisticum* VIII. 91 In štokavian Serbo-Croat (on which the standard language is based), the rising accent is a disyllabic one.

†**stoke**, *sb.*¹ *Obs.* [OE. *stoc* neut. (gen. *stoces*); prob. f. the same root as *stoc(c* masc. (gen. *stocces*) STOCK *sb.*¹] = PLACE *sb.*, in various senses.

Common in place-names, as Bishopstoke, Winterstoke.

a **900** WÆRFERTH tr. *Gregory's Dial.* 12 þæt aborstene clif hreas þa of duneweard..oþ þæt hit com þær hit mynte feallan ofer þæt mynster, and þæt þonne wære hryre ealles þæs stoces. *Ibid.* 172 þa sona in Cassinum þæt stoc [*v.rr.* in C. þære stowe, on C. þam stocwic]. *c* **1200** ORMIN 1049 Uppo þatt oferrwerrc þeȝȝ haffdenn liccness metedd Off Cherubyn, & haffdenn itt O tweȝȝenn stokess metedd. *Ibid.* 15694 Inn oþre stokess nemmneþþ wel þa posstless hise breþre.

†**stoke**, *sb.*² *Obs.* [f. STOKE *v.*¹ Cf. STOCK *sb.*³ 3.] A thrust with a weapon, a stab.

13.. *K. Alis.* 7398 (Laud MS.), To don oþer vilanye Oiþer wiþ stoke oiþer wiþ dynte þat is al hir entente. *c* **1400** *Ywaine & Gaw.* 2481 Sethin with a stoke to him he stert, And smate the geant unto the hert.

†**stoke**, *sb.*³ *Obs.* [prob. a. Du. *stok*, lit. 'stick': see STOCK *sb.*¹] A yard in measurement.

1538 in *Lett. Suppress. Monasteries* (Camden) 180 Whych be compased in with the walles lxx. stokes of length, that is, fete ccx. **1547** *Ludlow Churchw. Acc.* (Camden) 30 Item,.. for mendynge the vestmentes, and for ij. stokes and a hallf of locram to lyne them withalle, iij s. vij d.

stoke(s (stəʊk(s)), *sb.*⁴ *Physics.* [f. STOKES¹. Proposed in Ger. by M. Jakob 1928, in *Zeitschr. f. techn. Physik* IX. 22/1.] The unit of kinematic viscosity in the C.G.S. system, equal to 1 cm.² sec.⁻¹

1931 G. BARR *Monogr. Viscometry* i. 4 Jacob [*sic*] has proposed that the C.G.S. unit be called the 'stokes', but the suggestion has not yet had time to bear fruit. **1934** [see CENTISTOKE(S)]. **1961** V. L. STREETER *Handbk. Fluid Dynamics* I. 14 The unit of one square centimeter per second is called a stoke. The centistoke (= 0·01 stoke) is often a more convenient unit. **1964** SABERSKY & ACOSTA *Fluid Flow* i. 10 In the c.g.s. system,..the unit of absolute viscosity..is called a poise, and the unit of kinematic viscosity, 1 cm.²/sec., is called a stoke.

†**stoke**, *v.*¹ *Obs.* [Perh. a. OF. *estoquier*: see STOCK *v.*²]

1. *trans.* To pierce, stab (a person).

a **1300** *Cursor M.* 24356 Wit spere þai stoked him wit wrang. *c* **1375** *Ibid.* 7667 (Fairf.) þe king þen hent a sper ful sharp to stoke him þorou-out þe wagh. *c* **1380** *Sir Ferumb.* 4615 And þan was Char[lis] wonder grym, And aȝeyn hym renneþ, & stokeþ hym By-twene ys browes rowe.

2. *intr.* To make a thrust (*at*).

c **1375** *Cursor M.* 7623 (Fairf.) þe king stoket at him wiþ a spere. *c* **1386** CHAUCER *Knt.'s T.* 1688 Ne short swerd for to stoke with poynt bitynge. ? *a* **1400** *Morte Arth.* 2554 Fulle stowttly they stryke, thire steryne knyghttes, Stokes at the stomake with stelyne poyntes.

3. *trans.* To thrust, drive home (a sword).

1513 DOUGLAS *Æneis* IX. vii. 140 The swerd, wyghtly stokit, or than was glaid Throu owt hys cost. *Ibid.* x. xiii. 135.

stoke (stəʊk), *v.*² Also 8 **stoak.** [Back-formation from STOKER.]

1. a. *trans.* To feed, stir up, and poke the fire in (a furnace), to tend the furnace of (a boiler). Also, to feed or build up (a fire), and with *up*.

1683, etc. [? Implied in STOKING *vbl. sb.*² c]. **1735** DYCHE & PARDON *Dict.*, *Stoak* or *Stoke* v. to stir up, rake, cook, feed and look after a great Fire, such as Brewers, Distillers, Glass-houses, &c. use. **1838** HOLLOWAY *Prov. Dict.*, To *stoke*, to stir the fire. **1864** *Reader* 2 July 9 Who shall stoke the furnace of the steamship? **1883** M. P. BALE *Saw-Mills* 224 In stoking Cornish or Lancashire boilers by hand three systems of firing are in vogue. **1909** G. M. TREVELYAN *Garibaldi* xi. 202 First the fires had to be lit and stoked. **1942** E. LANGLEY *Pea-Pickers* x. 148 The hut was warmed by a little red fire which the fair-haired comrade stoked. **1971** G. JONES in Jones & Elis *Twenty-Five Welsh Short Stories* 106 That night, when he went into the house, he saw that the big iron double bed had been moved down into the middle of the kitchen and a great furnace of a fire stoked up in the chimney.

absol. **1867–72** N. P. BURGH *Marine Engin.* (1881) 375 Stoke freely when under steam. **1892** *Black & White* 16 Jan. 76/1 The German ships had been stoking up.

b. *fig.*

1837 HOOD *Ode to R. Wilson* 391 Sufficiently by stern necessitarians Poor Nature, with her face begrim'd by dust, Is stok'd, cok'd, smok'd, and almost chok'd. **1882** BERESFORD-HOPE *Brandreths* III. xxxix. 95 It [a prize fight] was stoked by an Irish adventurer who [etc.]. **1915** *Blackw. Mag.* Aug. 265/1 Neither the British nor the German soldier has been able to stoke up that virulent hate.

c. To excite, thrill, elate. *slang* (chiefly *Surfing*).

1963 *Pix* 28 Sept. 63 A good stomping movement that 'stokes' the tourists is worth two extra points. **1965** *S. Afr. Surfer* I. 3/3 Your magazine stoked me out of my mind. *Ibid.* 7/1 We will let him stoke you on some of the modern variations of body riding.

2. *transf.* (*jocular*). To feed (oneself or another) as if stoking a furnace; to 'shovel' (food) into one's mouth steadily and continuously. Also *absol.* with *up*.

1882 *Pall Mall Gaz.* 12 July 2/2 Mr. Warton vigorously stoked himself with snuff in the exuberance of his delight. **1894** SALA *London up to Date* 34 He eats, or, rather, he 'stokes' his meal, till the veins in his forehead swell. **1897** MISS BROUGHTON *Dear Faustina* xv, The denizens of this A.B.C...are *stoking* themselves stolidly. **1900** KIPLING in *Daily Mail* 25 Apr. 4/4 So they stoked them—'the 'arf that 'adn't the use of their 'ands'—and they re-dressed their bandages. **1915** *Blackw. Mag.* May 686/1 There's folks as cant stoke hot tea upon sorsiges.

absol. **1882** BESANT *All Sorts* xvii, Dinner in the middle of the day, of course... At the East End everybody stokes at one. **1897** KIPLING *Capt. Courageous* ii. 41 Then they stoked in silence till Dan drew breath over his tin cup and demanded of Harvey how he felt. 'Most full.' **1901** 'R. ANDOM' *Troddles & Us & Others* iv. 47 Troddles stoked-up on bread-and-butter pudding to such an extent that I wondered how on earth he could..drag himself about. **1946** R. LEHMANN *Gipsy's Baby* 29, I have often noticed how much less greedy children of the proletariat are than others. One would imagine that they would be more absorbed in the problem of stoking up. **1975** J. SYMONS *Three Pipe Problem* xvi. 155 They sat in one of the high-backed compartments where the punters came to stoke up after their losses.

3. In combination, as *stoke-hearth*, *-house*. **stoke-up** *slang*, a large or sustaining meal.

1839 URE *Dict. Arts* 1248 The stoke-hearth [of a smelting furnace]. **1903** *Westm. Gaz.* 27 Jan. 7/1 It was heated by means of hot-water pipes, fed from a stoke-house. **1955** J. THOMAS *No Banners* xv. 133 Later..it would be possible to go to the black-market eating-houses for an occasional 'stoke-up'.

Hence **stoked** *ppl. a.*, (*a*) subjected to the action of the vb.; (*b*) (*slang*) excited; keen or 'hooked' *on*.

1902 *Daily Chron.* 2 May 6/1 Hand-stoked retorts were shut down, and now the whole of the gas is to be manufactured in inclined or mechanically stoked retorts. **1963** [see BOARD *sb.* 1 b]. **1968** *Surfer Mag.* Jan. 47/3, I realized they're really stoked. **1969** *Sunday Mail* (Brisbane) 2 Feb. 20/3 I'm stoked on Chinese food. **1970** *Studies in English* (Univ. Cape Town) I. 33 People bitten by the *surf bug*..are really *stoked* on surfing. **1976** *N.Y. Times Mag.* 12 Sept. 40/1 Something like 10 million Americans..are stoked on floating about three inches over the paved surfaces of planet earth. Their flotation device is the new, Nasworthy-improved skateboard. **1977** *Skateboard Special* Sept. 2/1 The guy was really stoked but he fell off a nose wheelie and ended up taking a trip to McDonalds.

stoke, obs. f. STOCK; obs. pa. t. and pa. pple. of STEEK *v.*

stokehold ('stəʊkhəʊld). [f. STOKE *v.*² + HOLD *sb.*²] An apartment containing the ship's boilers, where the stokers tend the furnaces.

1887 W. S. HUTTON *Pract. Engin. Hand-bk.* 112 Closed stokeholds working under air-pressure are better ventilated than open stokeholds. **1908** W. W. JACOBS *Salthaven* ii, In the stokeholds of Vyner & Son's steamships he talked learnedly on coal with the firemen.

b. *attrib.*

1893 *Westm. Gaz.* 28 Dec. 5/2 At one time the water in the ship was above the level of the stokehold plates. **1896** KIPLING *Seven Seas, M'Andrews' Hymn* 37 Three feet [of water] were on the stokehold-floor—just slappin' to an' fro.

stoke-hole. [Partly an adoption, partly a transl., of Du. *stookgat*, f. *stoken* to stoke + *gat* hole.]

1. The space in front of a furnace where the stokers stand to tend the fires; the aperture through which the fire is fed and tended; also *Naut.* a hole in the deck through which the fuel is passed for storage.

1660 *J. Okie's Lament.* xiv, I'le Cunningly retreat again into my warm Stoke Hole [of a brewery]. **1683** MOXON *Mech. Exerc., Printing* xviii. 163 The Stoke-Hole four Inches wide, and six Inches long. **1840** *Civil Engin. & Arch. Jrnl.* III. 349/2 The space between the engines and the boilers [of a steamship], usually called the stoke-hole. **1846** A. YOUNG *Naut. Dict.* 322 *Stoke-hole*, a scuttle in a steamer's deck, to admit fuel for the engine. **1892** E. REEVES *Homeward Bound* 147 Lascars are employed on the decks and Zanzibar men in the stoke-hole.

attrib. **1660** *J. Okie's Lament.* vii, They say I am indited, ..Would the Inditement was rak't in my Stoake hole Embers.

2. (See quot.)

1785 *Specif. of Phillips' Patent* No. 1477, That species of ..fireplaces commonly called copper holes or stoke holes.

†**3.** *fig.* *Obs.*

1768 [W. DONALDSON] *Life Sir B. Sapskull* I. iv. 32 They scower the inside of their flower-pots, at the same time they make a stoke-hole of their throats.

stoker ('stəʊkə(r)). Also 8 stoaker. [a. Du. *stoker*, agent-n. f. *stoken* to feed (a fire), to stoke.]

1. One who feeds and tends a furnace.

1660 *J. Okie's Lament.* i, Of a Famous Brewer my purpose is to tell,.. The Noble Stoker Okey that doth the rest Excel. **1706** PHILLIPS (ed. Kersey), *Stoaker*, one that looks after the Fire and some other Concerns in a Brew-house. **1707** [E. WARD] *Barbacue Feast* 9 The Stoaker..by the Help of Breath and Bellows, blew up as rare a Charcoal Fire as ever was kindl'd in Term-Time. **1798** M. NOBLE *Eng. Regicides* I. 104 John Okey..was first a dray-man, then a stoaker in a brewhouse at Islington. **1846** A. YOUNG *Naut. Dict.* 323 *Stoker* or *Fireman*, a person employed to feed and trim the fires for the boilers of marine steam-engines. **1853** LYTTON *My Novel* IX. i, Ten to one but he is saying—'Not sixteen miles and hour! What the deuce is the matter with the stoker?' **1879** *Cassell's Techn. Educ.* I. 284/2 The stoker should open the furnace-doors and push back a portion of the fuel, so as to make a space in front for the fresh supply.

b. *mechanical stoker*: an apparatus for automatically feeding fuel into a furnace.

1884 R. MARSDEN *Cotton Spinning* 349 Mechanical stokers.—The question of stoking by machinery is an open one. **1893** *Lightning* 9 Feb. 86/2 Lancashire boilers are used, fitted with Vicar's mechanical stokers.

c. *fig.*

1737 M. GREEN *Spleen* 320 A prince's cause, a church's claim, I've known to raise a mighty flame, And priest, as stoker, very free To throw in peace and charity. **1893** T. M. HEALY in *Westm. Gaz.* 2 Nov. 2/2 At its head was a moderate ..leader, averse, except when driven to it by the 'stokers' of the movement, to lend his approval to extreme demands.

2. *pl.* Small particles of black gritty matter which escape through the funnel of a steam-engine.

1899 F. T. BULLEN *Way in Navy* 67 These ships..provide us instead with a never-ceasing supply of 'stokers,' a sort of fine black hail of grit that covers everything. It is not soft like soot.

stokerage ('stəʊkərɪdʒ). *nonce-wd.* [f. STOKER *sb.* + -AGE.] The action or the services of a stoker.

1895 *Daily News* 25 Apr. 7/2 The absence of the necessity of stokerage,..and the simplicity of construction of the furnaces.

stokerless ('stəʊkəlɪs), *a.* [f. STOKER *sb.* + -LESS.] Without a stoker.

1862 *Illustr. Lond. News* 11 Jan. 51/3 You may as well try to stop a stokerless steam-engine as a savant.

stokery ('stəʊkərɪ). [f. STOKE *v.*[2] + -ERY.] A place where stoking is done.

1901 *Rep. Brit. Assoc.* 791 Very complete remains of baths were found, with two brick-built hypocausts and a stokery.

Stokes[1] (stəʊks). *Physics.* The name of Sir George *Stokes* (1819–1903), Irish-born physicist and mathematician, used in the possessive and *attrib.* to designate concepts and phenomena discovered by him or arising out of his work: **a.** *Stokes' theorem*: the theorem that the line integral of a vector function round a closed path is equal to the surface integral of the curl of the function over any surface bounded by the path.

1893 J. J. THOMSON *Notes Recent Res. Electr. & Magnetism* i. 10 Now by Stokes' theorem ∫ $(Xdx + Ydy + Zdz)$ taken round a closed circuit is equal to [etc.]. **1940** E. T. BELL *Development Math.* xviii. 364 Stokes' theorem, its proof, and its generalizations have developed into a thriving industry of modern analysis. **1975** R. L. FERRARI *Introd. Electromagnetic Fields* vi. 109 We have postulated Maxwell's equations in their integral form... Using the vector calculus rule, Stokes' theorem, these can be transformed into differential relationships required to hold everywhere in space.

b. *Stokes' law*: the statement (not always true) that in fluorescence the wavelength of the emitted radiation is longer than that of the radiation causing it. Also *Stokes' line, shift*, etc., with reference to spectral emission lines at a lower frequency than the stimulating or incident radiation.

[**1902** *Encycl. Brit.* XXXII. 124/1 According to the experimental law of Stokes, the wave-lengths of the fluorescent radiation are longer than those of the radiation which excites it.] **1926** R. W. LAWSON tr. *Hevsey & Paneth's Man. Radioactivity* v. 57 It is the same condition as that with which we meet in optics in connection with the occurrence of fluorescence according to Stokes' law. **1949** P. PRINGSHEIM *Fluorescence & Phosphorescence* ii. 163 The fourth row of the same table shows..the distances of the first Stokes line from the exciting line. *Ibid.* vii. 556 Even if the absorption and emission correspond to the same electronic transition,..relatively large Stokes shifts have a great probability [in crystal phosphors]. **1973** *McGraw-Hill Yearbk. Sci. & Technol.* 307/1 Other consequences of the transient nature of the scattering are that the Raman-shifted (Stokes) pulse is both narrowed in time and delayed with respect to the exciting pulse. **1975** D. H. BURRIN in Williams & Wilson *Biologist's Guide to Princ. & Techniques Pract. Biochem.* v. 146 The energy emitted from these molecules in regaining the ground state within a period of less than 10^{-8} s gives rise to a fluorescent peak, showing the Stokes' shift. **1978** P. W. ATKINS *Physical Chem.* xvii. 562 (*caption*) Stokes and anti-Stokes rotational Raman lines.

c. *Stokes' law* (or *formula*): the statement that the resisting force on a spherical particle moving through a fluid is $6\pi\eta Vr$ (where η is the viscosity of the fluid, V the speed of the particle, and r its radius), so that its limiting rate of fall is $2gr^2\rho/9\eta$ (where g is the acceleration due to gravity and ρ the difference in density between the particle and the fluid).

1910 *Rep. Brit. Assoc. Adv. Sci. 1909* 407 To test Stokes's formula for air, the size, density, and terminal velocity of fall of some spherical spores were determined. **1936** *Discovery* Nov. 349/2 This period [of settlement of dust particles] is dependent on the application of Stokes' law, and hangs on particle size, density, etc. **1968** P. A. P. MORAN *Introd. Probability Theory* ix. 431 Assume that the particle, besides being spherical, is large enough for Stokes law to give a good estimate of the resisting force. **1974** G. S. ORMSBY in P. L. Moore et al. *Drilling Practices Manual* vi. 158 Since Stokes Law applies in a sand trap, large quantities of barites..may be settled from weighted drilling fluids. **1983** *Sci. Amer.* Apr. 128/2 Many of the grains in Middle Eastern coffee are too large to fall according to Stokes's law.

Stokes[2] (stəʊks). The name of Sir Wilfrid *Stokes* (1860–1927), English engineer, used *attrib.* and *absol.* to designate a type of trench mortar invented by him.

1915 W. S. CHURCHILL *Let.* 7 Sept. in M. Gilbert *Winston S. Churchill* (1972) III. Compan. II. 1167 In the early part of June, Lloyd George and I were shown the Stokes gun in action. **1919** [see LEWIS[3]]. **1919** *Athenæum* 25 July 664/1 'Stokes', the name of the inventor of the T.M., has, by metonymy, come to mean the trench mortar gun itself (so 'Nissen' = hut; 'Armstrong' = o hut). **1923** KIPLING *Irish Guards in Great War* II. 146 Our own two-inch Stokes in the front line strove to cover the noise by separate rapid fire. **1930** G. B. SHAW *What I really wrote about War* (1931) 241 The thermit shower was produced by firing from Stokes guns a cloud of shells packed with it. **1974** A. PRICE *Other Paths to Glory* I. i. 16 Their dead hanging on the unbroken barbed wire among the dud shells and unexploded Stokes mortar bombs.

Stokes-Adams (stəʊks'ædəmz). *Med.* The names of William *Stokes* (1804–78) and Robert *Adams* (1791–1875), Irish physicians, who described the condition in 1846 (*Dublin Q. Jrnl. Med. Sci.* II. 73) and 1827 (*Dublin Hosp. Rep.* IV. 414) respectively, used *attrib.* to designate occasional transient cessation or extreme slowness of the pulse, esp. when caused by heart-block.

1903 R. H. BABCOCK *Dis. Heart* xxiv. 634 The diagnosis of Stokes-Adams disease presents difficulty when the paroxysms are characterized only by vertigo and increase of an already existing bradycardia. **1922** *Lancet* 13 May 933/2 In a woman of 49 with complete heart-block, who was under observation for seven days and nights, severe Stokes-Adams attacks were recurring almost every minute. **1947** SCHERF & BOYD *Cardiovascular Dis.* xxii. 318/1 In this book the term Stokes-Adams attacks will embrace all types [of circulatory standstill] resulting from a change of cardiac activity irrespective of whether they are due to cardiac standstill or tachycardia... We deal with a syndrome and not a disease entity. **1974** *Ciba Symposium* New Ser. XX. 133 AV blocks of all kinds, from first-degree block to complete block, including the Stokes-Adams syndrome.

stokesite ('stəʊksaɪt). *Min.* [f. STOKES[1] + -ITE[1].] A hydrated silicate of calcium and tin, $CaSnSi_3O_9.2H_2O$, found as colourless, transparent orthorhombic crystals.

1899 A. HUTCHINSON in *Phil. Mag.* XLVIII. 480 Among the specimens..recently acquired for the Cambridge Mineralogical Museum, has been found a crystal whose characters prove it to belong to a new mineral species. This mineral I propose to call Stokesite in honour of Sir George Gabriel Stokes, Bart., whose jubilee as Lucasian Professor was this year celebrated by the University. **1977** *Mineral. Mag.* XLI. 413 Stokesite in very small amounts has been reported at two localities in Czechoslovakia..while at Corrégo do Urucum, Brazil, it has been found..as spherical clusters of crystals up to 3 cm diameter.

†**'stoking,** *vbl. sb.*[1] *Obs.* [f. STOKE *v.*[1] + -ING[1].] The action of thrusting with a weapon.

1375 BARBOUR *Bruce* XVII. 785 With staffing, stoking, and striking Thar maid thai sturdy defending.

Comb. **1417** in *MS. For. Acc. 8 Hen., V*, G/1, xij debilibus stokyns sperres. **1420** in *MS. For. Acc. 3 Hen. VI*, H b, Cum .x. stoken' speres .viij. duodenis dartes.

stoking ('stəʊkɪŋ), *vbl. sb.*[2] [f. STOKE *v.*[2] + -ING[2].] The action of the verb; the operation of tending a furnace and feeding it with fuel.

1854 J. SCOFFERN in *Orr's Circ. Sci., Chem.* 193 Inequality of stoking, and inequality of water-supply are amongst the causes. **1884** *L'pool Mercury* 18 Feb. 5/4 The pumping of water in and for the prison is valued at £301..and stoking at £166.

b. *transf.* and *fig.*

1892 *Fabian News* Apr. 5/1 There is always a great waste of energy in canvassing, 'stoking up,' etc., by which no one is made any better or wiser. **1892** 'OUIDA' in *Fortn. Rev.* LII. 782 'Stoking'..is the one joy which never palls on the human machine, until he pays for it with dyspepsia and gout.

c. *attrib.*, as *stoking-hole, -iron, -place, -rod.*

1683 MOXON *Mech. Exerc., Printing* xi. ¶23 The *Stoking-hole lying far under the Caldron. **1794** *Trans. Soc. Arts* XII. 262 The stoking-hole of the furnace. **1876** E. M. SHAW *Fire Protection* 142 *Stoking irons..namely, 1 shovel, 1 rake, 1 pricker. **1741** SYMPSON *Hypocaust* in *Phil. Trans.* XLI. 856 The *Præfurnium*, (*Stoking-place). **1901** *Daily News* 5 Jan. 3/1 The caretaker brought a long *stoking rod.

stokked, obs. weak pa. pple. of STEEK *v.*[1]

1519 in *Fabric Rolls York Minster* (Surtees) 268 Nowe, often tymes, the dure is stokked.

Stokowskian (stə'kɒvskɪən), *a.* and *sb.* [f. the name of Leopold *Stokowski* (1882–1977), English-born American conductor + -AN.]

A. *adj.* Of, pertaining to, or characteristic of Stokowski.

1961 *Times* 19 June 9/2 Inappropriate infusions of Stokowskian sensuousness marred..his interpretation of Orff's *Carmina Burana*. **1977** *Gramophone* Apr. 1556/2 The Stokowskian concentration and persuasiveness will be hard for anyone to resist. **1978** *Ibid.* Jan. 1263/3 The Schubert is by Stokowskian standards given an unmagical performance.

B. *sb.* An admirer of Stokowski.

1975 *Gramophone* Aug. 322/2 It is very much a performance for Elgarians as well as for the Stokowskians. **1978** *Ibid.* Jan. 1308/2 Still, Stokowskians will want this, although I am sure they will lament with me that CBS scheduled this record before the *Pastoral* Symphony, which Stokowski was due to record when he died.

stokyn, obs. pa. pple. of STEEK *v.*[1] and *v.*[2]

stokyng, obs. form of STOCKING *sb.*

stol, rare obs. f. STALL *v.*[1]; obs. f. STOOL.

‖**stola** ('stəʊlə). *Ant.* [L. *stola*, ad. Gr. στολή: see STOLE *sb.*[1]] A long robe worn by Greek and Roman women; chiefly referred to as the distinctive dress of Roman matrons.

1728 CHAMBERS *Cycl.* s.v., The *Stola* of the ancient Romans, &c. was..a kind of Robe fitter for Women than Men. **1847** LEITCH tr. *C. O. Müller's Anc. Art* §341. 351 Among the higher ranks a dress similar to the Ionic came in fashion, to which belonged the Stola, consisting of a tunic with broad border. **1861** PALEY *Æschylus* (ed. 2) *Choeph.* 161 *note*, Βαθύζωνος..and βαθύκολπος..are epithets not very easily explained... Probably the loose and ample folds of the stola ..are meant. **1891** FARRAR *Darkn. & Dawn* i, The long *stola* worn by noble matrons.

stolated (stəʊ'leɪtɪd), *a. rare.* [f. L. *stolāt-us* (f. STOLA: see -ATE[2]) + -ED[1].] Wearing a stola or stole: **a.** *lit.* of a sculptured female figure; **b.** *transf.* in *Zool.* as rendering of mod.L. *stolatus*, the specific name of a snake.

1802 SHAW *Gen Zool.* III. 542 Stolated Snake..*Coluber Stolatus*. **1856** W. H. SMYTH *Roman Family Coins* 51 A stolated and helmed female.

stolch, obs. f. STOACH *v., dial.*

stolde, obs. pa. t. of STELL *v.*

†**'stoldred.** *Obs.* [App. f. ME. *stulþ* (a. ON. *stulð-r, stuld-r*, STOUTH) + -RED.] Stealth.

1654 E. JOHNSON *Wonder-working Provid.* 27 When the best choice our Orthodox Ministers can make is to take up a perpetuall banishment..their poore sheepe they may not feede, but by stoledred. **1657** BILLINGSLY *Brachy-Martyrol.* xxix. 107 Some little corn by stoldred brought to town, Each pound was valued at half a crown.

stole (stəʊl), *sb.*[1] Forms: 1 stol, 4, 6 stoele, 4–6 stoole, 4, 7 stool, 5 stoll, 5–6 stolle, 6 stoale, stoel, stoile, stoill, stoyle, stoyll, 7 stoal, 4– stole. [ad. L. *stola*, ad. Gr. στολή, orig. equipment, array, clothing, hence a robe, garment, f. root of στέλλειν to place, array. Cf. OF. *estole* (mod.F. *étole*), Sp., Pg. *estola*, It. *stola*. The use of L. *stola* = sense 2 has not been found earlier than the 9th century; its origin is obscure.]

1. A long robe. †**a.** In translations from or allusions to passages of the Vulgate or patristic texts. *Obs.*

first or *prime stole*, transl. of Vulg. *stolam primam* (Gr. στολὴν τὴν πρώτην), 'the best robe' in the parable of the Prodigal Son.

c **950** *Lindisf. Gosp.* Mark xii. 38 From uðuutum ðaðe wallas in stolum geonga. *a* **1000** *Durham Ritual* (Surtees) 45 Stol wvldres ʒiʒeride hine *stola glorie induit eum* [Ecclus. xlv. 7]. *a* **1340** HAMPOLE *Psalter* xxix. 15 He..vmgifs vs..with gladnes of þe first stole. **1380** *Lay Folks Catech.* (Lamb.

MS.) 1115 [Crist] wyle cloþe our sowlys..with þe stole of vndedlynesse. **1382** WYCLIF *Isa.* lxiii. 1 Who is this that cam fro Edom..? this shapli in his stole? *c* **1449** PECOCK *Repr.* IV. ix. 473 Pharisees..louen forto walke in stolis. *c* **1450** *Godstow Reg.* 17 Þat we ben cladde in a snow whyȝt stole Thorgh þe vertue of þe holy goost. *c* **1520** NISBET *N.T.*, *Apoc.* vi. 11 And quhite stolis, for ilk saule a stole, war gevin to thame. **1540** PALSGR. *Acolastus* v. v. Bb j b, Brynge forth ..at ones the fyrst stole. **1561** DAUS tr. *Bullinger on Apoc.* (1573) 92 The saintes (saith S. Gregory) enioy as yet but one stole or robe a peece. **1596** T. BELL *Surv. Popery* III. ix. 366 These (saith S. John) are they which came from great tribulation & washed their stoales, and made them white in the bloud of the Lambe. **1648** BP. HALL *Select Th.* xiii. 52 It must be the main care of our lives, how to put on Christ upon our souls: This is the prime stole wherewith the father of the Prodigal, graceth his returned son. **1649** JER. TAYLOR *Great Exemp.* III. Ad Sec xv. 95 They might be reinvested with a robe of his righteousnesse wearing that till it were changed into a Stole of glory [cf. Ecclus. xlv. 7]. *c* **1850** NEALE *Hymns East. Ch.* 94 In that same hour I lost the glorious stole Of innocence.

b. In poetic or rhetorical use. Often *fig.*

1590 SPENSER *F.Q.* I. i. 45 Her all in white he clad, and ouer it Cast a blacke stole. **1593** PEELE *Hon. Order Garter* B 4, Fame in a Stoale of purple, set with eyes, And eares, and tongues, carryed a golden Booke. **1597** SHAKS. *Lover's Compl.* 297 There my white stole of chastity I daft. *c* **1620** T. ROBINSON *Mary Magd.* I. 10 How night..Put on the glitteringe stole of brightest day. **1632** MILTON *Penseroso* 35 And sable stole of Cipres Lawn, Over thy decent shoulders drawn. **1742** SHENSTONE *Schcolmistr.* 64 A russet stole was o'er her shoulders thrown. **1753** T. WARTON *Ode Approach Summer* 255 When mild Morn in saffron stole First issues from her eastern goal. **1793** COLERIDGE *Songs of Pixies* 95 Graceful Ease in artless stole. **1845** L. HUNT *Poems, Fancy Concert* 37 With their singers in lily-white stoles. **1878** B. TAYLOR *Pr. Denkalion* II. ii. 61 The phantom purple underneath thy stole We see.

c. With reference to classical antiquity. (Cf. STOLA.) Also (in Scott) quasi-*arch.* with reference to mediæval costume.

1387 TREVISA *Higden* (Rolls) I. 223 In Albist[e]rio..were i-made white stolis for emperours [L. *ubi fiebant stolæ imperatorum*]. *c* **1510** *Virgilius* (Doesborcke) A iij b, And there he sawe his vnkell a fore hym stand in his emperly stole. **1725** POPE *Odyss.* VI. 88 The blooming virgin with dispatchful cares Tunics, and stoles, and robes imperial bears. **1790** COWPER *Odyss.* IV. 378 Beside him, Helen of the sweeping stole. **1811** SCOTT *Fam. Lett.* 4 Apr. (1894) I. 212 The lady..should I think have a sort of stole or loose upper garment. **1812** BYRON *Ch. Har.* II. ii, The warrior's weapon and the sophist's stole Are sought in vain. **1847** LEITCH tr. *C. O. Müller's Anc. Art* §246. 223 His courtiers in two different regularly alternating costumes,—the Median stole and the candys. **1850** BLACKIE *Æschylus* I. 110 See! my rent and ragged stole Speaks the conflict of my soul.

¶ **d.** Some writers have carelessly or ignorantly supposed the ecclesiastical 'stole' (sense 2) to be a gown or surplice.

1805 SCOTT *Last Minstrel* v. xxx, Behind, four priests, in sable stole, Sung requiem for the warrior's soul. **1831** CARLYLE *Sartor Res.* III. xi, The fair fabric of Society itself, with all its royal mantles and pontifical stoles. **1840** BARHAM *Ingol. Leg.*, *Jackdaw of Rheims* 35 Six little Singing-boys,—dear little souls! In nice clean faces, and nice white stoles. **1869** B. TAYLOR *By-Ways Europe* I. 219 Here the rustling of stoles and the muttering of prayers suggest incantation rather than worship.

2. *Eccl.* A vestment consisting of a narrow strip of silk or linen, worn over the shoulders (by deacons over the left shoulder only) and hanging down to the knee or lower.

c **1025** *MS. Laud* 482 f. 48 a, Scryde hine mid..alban & stolan & handline [etc.]. **13..** *K. Alis.* 4714 A withthe was heore stole, certes, With on othir they weoren y-gurte. *c* **1315** SHOREHAM *Poems* I. 1403 And nou þe stole a-fongeþ hy Ope here scholder lefte. *c* **1386** CHAUCER *Merch. T.* 459 Forth comth the preest with stole aboute his nekke. *a* **1400-50** *Wars Alex.* 1581 Þan fyndis he in þis o ire flote fanons and stolis Practisirs & prematis & prestis of þe lawe. **1481** CAXTON *Godfrey* cxli. 209 The men of the Chirche reuested with awbes and stooles. **1485** *Device for Coronation Hen. VII* in *Rutland Papers* (Camden) 18 The armyll is made in manner of a stole wovyn with gold & set with stones, to be putt by the Cardinall aboute the Kinges necke. *c* **1550** BALE *K. Johan* 1147 Put on yowr stolle then, and, I pray yow in Godes name, sytt. **1552** *Invent. Ch. Goods York*, etc. (Surtees) 42 Item, ij old whyt vestmentes with albe, and stoill, and fannells. **1561** T. NORTON *Calvin's Inst.* IV. xix. (1634) 329 Upon the Deacon that is ordered, the Bishop.. layeth a prayer booke and a Stoale upon his left shoulder. **1579** FULKE *Heskins Parl.* 84 M. Heskins mainteyneth reseruation by dipping of stoales, and linnen clothes in yͤ cup. **1764** in J. H. Harting *Hist. Sardinian Chapel* (1905) 23 Two copes with a large stole embroidered in gold thread, with gold fringe round the back. **1844** LINGARD *Anglo-Sax. Ch.* (1858) II. ix. 69 The usual episcopal vestments, the amise..stole [etc.]. **1865** WALCOTT *Cathedr.* 93 A canon was to wear in all places the insignia of his rank;..in England now a broad scarf instead of the narrow stole. **1877** J. D. CHAMBERS *Div. Worship* 48 The Stole, if worn by the Deacon, should be worn suspended over the left shoulder. **1885** *Notes on Angels* 38, 4. The Dominions, 5. The Virtues, and 6. The Powers wear albs down to the feet, golden girdles, and green stoles. **1904** MRS. CREIGHTON *Life Bp. Creighton* II. 35 Each man to be ordained priest was bidden to bring his stole in his hand.

†**b.** Often referred to as the vestment worn by a priest when engaged in exorcism or conjuration.

c **1450** LOVELICH *Graal* xlv. 312 Thanne the Goode Man took haliwater Anon, and his stole, and gan forth to gon. *c* **1590** GREENE *Fr. Bacon* IV. iii. 1835 Coniuring and adiuring diuels and fiends, With stole and albe and strange Pentagonon. **1598** BARCKLEY *Felic. Man* I. (1603) 55 Taking his stole and other instruments for his conjuration with him, to the sicke woman hee goeth. **1626** L. OWEN *Spec. Jesuit.* (1629) 42 When the Coniurer did but touch her with the stole or with some of his rotten Relikes.

c. *Hist.* In the names of certain knightly orders: see quots.

1728 CHAMBERS *Cycl.* s.v. *Stole*, *Order of the Stole*, an Order of Knights instituted by the Kings of Arragon... The first Time we hear of it is under Alphonsus V, who mounted the Throne in 1416... *Order of the Golden Stole*, a military Order at Venice; thus called from a golden Stole which the Knights wear over the Left Shoulder.

d. An embroidered strip of linen, hanging down in front of an altar.

1513 in *Archæologia* LXVI. 340 Itm a frontlett for an aulter wrought in the stole. **1845** *Ecclesiologist* IV. 103 We have not spoken of the stoles of the altar, because their use ..was never general... They occur in..Van Eyck's.. Adoration of the Lamb.

3. A woman's fur or feather garment, something in the shape of an ecclesiastical stole, worn over the shoulders and hanging down nearly to the feet.

1889 *Advt. Furs*, Victorias, Capes, Stoles, and Muffs, in every description of fur. **1892** *Lady* 29 Dec. 826/3 One sees a cloak lined with sable..accompanied by a stole and muff to match. **1904** *Daily Mail* 28 Mar. 1/4 Fashionable feather stoles, Good Feather,..10/6. **1906** *Ch. Times* 28 Dec. 848 Advt., Real Russian Sable Hair long throwover Stole with extra fine quality tails.

4. *attrib.* (senses 2, 3) as ***stole-end, -front, -tab***; ***stole-like***, adj. and adv.; **stole-fees** *pl.* [after G. *stolgebühren*] = SURPLICE-*fees*.

1896 *Daily News* 7 Mar. 6/3 Jackets..with Watteau pleats at the back and *stole ends in front. **1845** SARAH AUSTIN *Ranke's Hist. Ref.* v. iii. III. 83 The greater part of the *stole fees were abolished. **1897** TAUNTON *Engl. Black Monks* I. 56 Master Vicar..got his one-third clear, a house free of rent, and all his stole fees and dues. **1892** *Daily News* 16 June 6/1 The collar had *stole fronts, and the bodice was finished with black ribbons. **1876** ROCK *Textile Fabrics* 90 A *stole-like band of rich white tissue. **1865** *Direct Angl.* (ed. 2) 24 The Amyss..is a large fur cape..; its 'tippets', i.e. two strips of fur in front, fall, stole-like, below the knees. **1903** *Daily Chron.* 25 July 8/4 The collar..forms *stole-tabs upon the shoulders.

stole (stəʊl), *sb.*[2] Also 5–6 stoole, 6 stoolle, stowle. [Commonly identified with STOLE *sb.*[1], to which the unauthenticated sense of 'royal robe' is assigned. But there seems to be little doubt that the 'stole chamber', served by the Groom or Yeoman of the Stole, was originally the room containing the king's close-stool, and that the word is properly a variant of STOOL *sb.*[1] As, however, the word as thus used was for centuries entirely dissociated from *stool*, and latterly had a different spelling, it is necessary to treat it separately.

In accounts of coronation ceremonies the king is said to have worn an ornament resembling a stole (STOLE *sb.*[1] 2); but it does not appear that this was actually *called* a 'stole' until modern times. The view that the Groom of the Stole derived his designation from this ornament is quite improbable.

Sir H. Nicolas's supposition, that the 'stole' was a kind of packing-chest, is a mistaken inference from the *stole* and *male* being mentioned together in certain documents.]

1. ***groom of the stole***: the title of a high officer of the king's household (formerly sometimes also in the household of a prince of the blood), ranking next below the vice-chamberlain of the household. Also † ***yeoman of the stole***.

For the duties of the office as understood at various times, see the quots. In the household of a queen or a princess, the office and title were held by a lady. Under Queen Victoria no groom of the stole was appointed, and the office has not since been revived.

[? *a* **1480** in *Househ. Ord.* (1790) 41 The King's chamberlayn to assigne for the ii. garderobes and the King's chambre, for the male and stoole, and other stuffe nedeful, to the some of xii. or xvi. sompter horses. **1502** *Privy Purse Exp. Eliz. of York* (1830) 45 Item the vᵗʰ day of Septembre for cariage of the Quenes stole from London to Oxonford and from Oxonford to Langley, xiiij d. *Ibid.* 81 For bering shetes trussing sheetes and sheetes for the stoele.] **1455** in *Househ. Ord.* (1790) *18 Yomen of the Chambre [8 names]. Gromes of the Chambre [9 names]. Yoman of the Stoole, William Grymesby. **1526** *Ibid.* 156 It is the King's pleasure, that Mr. Norres shall be in the roome of Sir William Compton, not onely giveing his attendance as groome of the King's stoole, but also in his bed-chamber [etc.]. **1596** HARINGTON *Metam. Ajax* Answ. Let. A vj b, A seuenth (whome I woulde gesse by his writing to bee groome of the stoole to some Prince of the bloud of Fraunce) writes a beastly treatise onely to examine what is the fittest thing to wipe withall, alledging that white paper is too smooth [etc.]. **1647** CLARENDON *Hist. Reb.* v. §31 Groom of the Stole, which hath the reputation and benefit of being first Gentleman of the Bed-Chamber. **1669** E. CHAMBERLAYNE *Pres. St. Eng.* 262 Gentlemen of the Bed-Chamber, whereof the first is called Groom of the Stole, that is (according to the signification of the word in Greek, from whence first the Latines, and thence the Italian and French derive it) Groom or Servant of the Robe or Vestment. He having the Office and Honour to present and put on His Majesties first Garment or Shirt every morning, and to order the things of the Bed-Chamber. *Ibid.* 320 Officers and Servants belonging to Her Royal Highness the Dutchess [of York]. Groom of the Stole, Countess of Rochester. **1702** *Lond. Gaz.* No. 3820/3 His Excellency had Audience of His Royal Highness Prince George of Denmark, being received..by the Rt. Hon. the Lord Delawar, Groom of the Stool to His Royal Highness. **1710** J. CHAMBERLAYNE *Pres. St. Gt. Brit.* II. III. (ed. 23) 541 Sarah Dutchess of Marlborough, Groom of the Stole.

2. The office of Groom of the Stole.

1911 J. H. ROSE *Pitt & Gt. War* v. 125 Dundas requested that he should have the first claim for the Privy Seal for Scotland, provided that Lord Chatham did not take the Stole. **1911** RIKER *Henry Fox 1st Ld. Holland* II. x. 239 The man who..had once struggled, single-handed, to procure Bute the Stole.

3. *attrib.* in ***stole-chamber, -room.***

1532–3 in W. H. St. John Hope *Windsor Castle* (1913) I. 263 A Copple off Crosse Jamewis tynned ffor a new dore in the Kyngs stole chambre. **1676–7** *Ibid.* 315 The Kings Privy Backstairs & Closett and Stoole Roome. **1680–2** *Ibid.* 321 Isaac Thompson Engineer for making ijº new Close Stooles for his Maᵗⁱᵉ, One with two frames of Pullyes..and for Silvering the same to Keepe it from Rusting, & fitting & setting it up in his Mᵗⁱᵉˢ Stoole Roome. **1686–8** *Ibid.* 329 The lord Walgraves and Comptrollers Stoole Roomes.

stole (stəʊl), *sb.*[3] *Bot.* [Irregularly ad. L. *stolo*: see STOLON. (The anomalous form may have been due to confusion with *stole* var. STOOL *sb.*, tree-root.)] = STOLON.

1806 TURTON *Linné's Syst. Nat.* VII. Expl. Terms, *Stole*, a sucker or scion from the root of plants. **1832** *Planting* 91 in *Libr. Usef. Knowl.*, *Husb.* III, Stole.—The first stage of growth of a shoot emitted or sent out from the sides of a root or stub or coppice-stool. **1835** LINDLEY *Introd. Bot.* (1848) I. 182 The Stole (stolo), which may be considered the reverse of the sucker. **1866** *Treas. Bot.* 1101/2 Stole, stolon.

stole (stəʊl), *v.*[1] [f. STOLE *sb.*[1]]

1. *trans.* To provide (an altar, a church) with altar-stoles: see STOLE *sb.*[1] 2 d.

c **1475** *Crabhouse Reg.* (1889) 60 The Prioresse..pathed the chirche and the quere, and stolid it,..the veyl of the chirche with the auter-clothes in sute cost xl *s.* **1848** B. WEBB *Cont. Ecclesiol.* 165 A most singular altar is shewn in this window, stoled both in front and in the side. *Ibid.* 343 Several frontals are merely painted; but I remarked that they represented superfrontals properly fringed and stoled.

2. [See STOLED *ppl. a.*]

stole (stəʊl), *v.*[2] *rare.* [f. STOLE *sb.*[3]] *intr.* Of a plant: To develop stolons.

1824 LOUDON *Encycl. Gard.* (ed. 2) 1225/2 *Succisæ repullulant*, trees which stole, or which being cut over spring again. **1846** MRS. LOUDON *Gardening for Ladies* 80 The verb, to *stole*, which signifies the power most deciduous trees possess, of sending up new stems from the collar of their roots when cut down.

stole (stəʊl), *ppl. a.* Now *colloq.* [Strong pa. pple. of STEAL *v.*] = STOLEN *ppl. a.*

1393 LANGL. *P. Pl.* C. XVIII. 40 'Lord leyue' quaþ þe lede 'no stole þyng be here'. **1444** LYDG. in *Pol. Poems* (1859) II. 220 Tyl it be loost, stoole thyng is nat sought. **1884** *Encycl. Brit.* XVII. 359 Dead netting is a piece without either accrues or stole (stolen) meshes. **1923** [see HISN, HIS'N]. **1976** *Billings* (Montana) *Gaz.* 20 June 5-D/1 (Advt.), *Found* in Missoula: Male Great Dane Cross. Approx. 1½ yrs. old. Stole in Blgs. last Fall or Winter.

stole, pa. t. and pple. of STEAL *v.*; obs. f. STOOL.

stoled (stəʊld), *ppl. a.* [f. STOLE *sb.*[1] (? and *v.*[1]) + -ED.] Wearing a stole (in various senses of the sb.)

In the first quot. apparently misused for 'surpliced'.

1546–7 *Test. Ebor.* VI. 254 To every clerke iiij d. and every childe, being stolde, ij d. **1610** G. FLETCHER *Christ's Tri.* II. xvii, After them flewe the Prophets, brightly stol'd In shining lawne. **1629** MILTON *Hymn Nativ.* xxiv, In vain.. The sable-stoled Sorcerers bear his worshipt Ark. **1787** POLWHELE *Engl. Orator* II. 90 Where..amid the stoled Tribe Persuasion's swift-descending Genius swells The Oration's Period. **1808** SCOTT *Marmion* VI. Introd., That only night in all the year, Saw the stoled priest the chalice rear. **1839** MRS. BROWNING *Sabbath Morn.* xii, Though this sabbath comes to me Without the stolèd minister, Or chanting congregation. **1842** TENNYSON *Morte d' Arthur* 197 All the decks were dense with stately forms Black-stoled, black-hooded, like a dream. **1865** NEALE *Hymns Paradise* 43 The purple stoled Confessors. **1873** R. WILTON *Wood Notes* 33 At the Lord's Table, waiting, robed and stoled Till all had knelt around, I saw a sign.

stolen ('stəʊlən), *ppl. a.* Forms: see STEAL *v.* [Pa. pple. of STEAL *v.*] In senses of the verb.

1. Obtained by theft.

a **1300** *Cursor M.* 4875 Qua-so es tan wid stoln thing, He wil þat do him to hing. *c* **1380** WYCLIF *Wks.* (1880) 154 Þere comeþ a pardoner wiþ stollen bullis & false relekis. **14..** *Burgh Lawis* lxxxvii. in *Anc. Laws Scot.* (Burgh Rec. Soc.) 42 Of stollyn gudis fundyn in the fayre. *c* **1440** *Jacob's Well* 201 ȝif þou..kepyst treccherously in pryuite stolyn thynges or oþere thinges falsly get. **1583** *Leg. Bp. St. Androis* 325 in *Sat. Poems Reform.* xlv, Mercurius..Could not so weill of stowen geir tell, As could [etc.]. **1607** SHAKS. *Cor.* v. vi. 89 Do'st thou thinke Ile grace thee with that Robbery, thy stolne name Coriolanus in Corioles? **1611** BIBLE *Prov.* ix. 17 Stollen waters are sweet. *c* **1640** H. BELL *Luther's Colloq. Mens.* (1652) 309 The wealth of Popedom (saith Luther) is meerly robbed and stollen wealth. **1771** *Junius Lett.* lxv. 328 The stolen goods were found upon him. **1861** PALEY *Æschylus* (ed. 2) *Supplices* 897 *note*, [Hermes] the god of theft and abduction, and the recovery of stolen property. **1911** TREVELYAN *Garibaldi & Making of Italy* vii. 147 The men were disconsolately cooking some stolen lambs.

2. Accomplished or enjoyed by stealth, secret. Of a marriage: cf. STEAL *v.* 5 d.

13.. *Gaw. & Gr. Knt.* 1659 Such semblaunt to þat segge semly ho made, Wyth stille stollen countenaunce. *c* **1624** CHAPMAN *Hymn to Hermes* 158 To shun, of his stolne steps, the Tract. **1632** MASSINGER *City Madam* II. i, And pleasures stol'n being sweetest [etc.]. **1693** DRYDEN *Juvenal* x. 521 'Tis no stol'n Wedding, this; rejecting awe, She scorns to Marry, but in Form of Law. *a* **1797** BURNS '*Twas na her bonie blue e'e*', The bewitching, sweet, stown glance o' kindness. **1803** JANE PORTER *Thaddeus* i, I have already erred enough in consenting to this stolen marriage. **1832** S. WARREN *Diary Late Physic.* II. iv. 211 Few people, indeed, are so disposed to 'make the most' of their time at the opera as medical men, to whom it is a sort of stolen pleasure. **1837** DICKENS *Pickw.* liv, Arabella wrote..to say he had made a stolen match without her husband's father's consent. **1884** *J. Marshall's Tennis Cuts* 65 We remembered that no cricket had ever been half so delightful as those stolen single-wicket matches in our night-gowns. **1905** R. BAGOT *Passport* iii. 18 The girl at whom she had cast stolen glances of curiosity.

b. ***stolen march***: see STEAL *v.* 5 e.

1759 DILWORTH *Pope* 21 It appears by Mr. Pope's frequent stolen marches on the public [etc.]. **1766** GOLDSM. *Vicar* xvi, Our spirit took the alarm at this stolen march upon us.

c. Of a hen's nest: Made in a concealed place.

1854 *Poultry Chron.* I. 615 Eggs are to be sought after, and what a triumph is the discovery of a stolen nest!

3. Of time: Obtained by contrivance.

1585 HIGINS *Junius' Nomencl.* 367/1 Stolne time, or time gotten by snatches from other busines. **1611** B. JONSON *Catiline* I. i, These my retirements, and stolne times for thought.

4. In *Baseball*: see quots.

1897 *Encycl. Sport* I. 79/2 (Baseball) *Stolen Base*, a base obtained by a runner without help from a hit by a batsman. **1891** N. CRANE *Baseball* 61 The record is still hardly complete without showing the number of sacrifice hits and stolen bases by each player.

5. Of a crop: Interpolated in a rotation of crops.

1861 *Times* 10 Oct., Stolen crops of winter vetches..being also taken.

6. *Netting.* Of a mesh: Intentionally missed. (See STEAL *v.* 7.)

1884 [see STOLE *ppl. a.*].

7. *Comb.* **stolen-wise** *adv.*, stealthily.

1813 SCOTT *Bridal of Trierm.* II. xiii, And Lancelot, that evermore Look'd stol'n-wise on the Queen.

stolethery, obs. form of STOUTHERIE.

stolewise (ˈstəʊlwaɪz), *adv.* [f. STOLE *sb.*[1] + WISE *sb.*[1]] Draped like a stole.

1922 JOYCE *Ulysses* 19 Buck Mulligan slung his towel stolewise round his neck.

Stolichnaya (stɑːˈliːtʃnaɪə). [Russ., lit. 'of the capital, metropolitan'.] The proprietary name of a variety of Russian vodka.

1966 L. DEIGHTON *Billion-Dollar Brain* xi. 98 Stolichnaya ..the only vodka I will drink. **1969** *Official Gaz.* (U.S. Patent Office) 25 Feb. TM 145 Stolichnaya. V/O Sojuzplodoimport. **1973** *Radio Times* 20 Dec. 110/4, 1 bottle Russian vodka (Nureyev recommends Stolichnaya). **1975** *Trade Marks Jrnl.* 4 June 1163 Stolichnaya Vodka... 998,200. Vodka. Vsesojuznoje Objedinenie Sojuzplodoimport..32/34 Smolenskaja Square, Moscow, U.S.S.R.; Manufacturers and Merchants. —11th Sept. 1972. **1977** J. WAMBAUGH *Black Marble* (1978) i. 3 He.. stealthily withdrew the bottle of Stolichnaya from the pocket of his raincoat.

stolid (ˈstɒlɪd), *a.* [ad. L. *stolidus*, related to *stultus* foolish, f. root **stel-* to stand or cause to stand still: cf. STILL *a.* Cf. F. †*stolide* (16–17th c. in Godef.), Sp. *estólido*, It. *stolido.*

Not in Johnson 1755 (who has *stolidity*), and hardly occurring before the 19th c.]

Dull and impassive; having little or no sensibility; incapable of being excited or moved. Also of actions, demeanour, expression of countenance, etc.

c **1600** *Timon* II. iv. (1842) 31 That I..should bee caste into prison by stolidde, not by solidde, persons. **1623** COCKERAM I, *Stolide*, foolish. **1656** BLOUNT *Glossogr.*, *Stolid*, fooling, fond, leud of condition, unadvised, dull, doltish. **1816** SCOTT *Old Mort.* xiv, Morton recognised the stolid countenance of Cuddie Headrigg. **1831** CARLYLE *Sartor Res.* I. iv, With some half-visible wrinkle of a bitter sardonic humour, if indeed it be not mere stolid callousness. **1856** KANE *Arctic Expl.* II. xxix. 290 With a stolid expression of wonder, he stared for a moment. **1858** DORAN *Court Fools* 29 The philosophical envoy approached the stolid Roman. **1868** J. H. BLUNT *Ref. Ch. Eng.* I. 5 The stolid opposition with which their better aspirations were met by those in authority. **1902** MRS. LANE in *Fortn. Rev.* June 1009 How I wish I could clap a big, stolid, conservative, frost-bitten English matron into a snug American house.

Comb. **1862** WHYTE MELVILLE *Queen's Maries* II. 181 He was a stolid-looking fellow too. **1901** C. HOLLAND *Mousmé* 261 The dark consulting room with its stolid-looking oak-and-leather chairs.

Hence **ˈstolidly** *adv.*, **ˈstolidness**.

1727 BAILEY vol. II. *Stolidness*, Foolishness. **1857** DICKENS *Dorrit* I. xxx, As often as Mr. Blandois clinked glasses..Mr. Flintwinch stolidly did his part of the clinking. **1860** *All Year Round* No. 73. 552 There is a superb stolidness about her; a stolidness that could be wakened into savageness. **1867** PARKMAN *Jesuits N. Amer.* viii. (1875) 88 Often the patient was stolidly silent. **1877** E. R. CONDER *Basis Faith* ii. 81 These simple primary atoms, stolidly inert when none but its own kind are present. **1885** *Law Times* LXXIX. 37/2 Powers..of which vestries..have stolidly refused to avail themselves.

stolidify (stəˈlɪdɪfaɪ), *v. rare.* [f. L. *stolid-us* STOLID *a.* + -(I)FY.] *trans.* To render stolid.

1827 *Blackw. Mag.* XXI. 654 His brain was too stolidified, and too conversant with wine and good eating.

stolidity (stəˈlɪdɪtɪ). [ad. L. *stoliditāt-em*, f. *stolid-us* STOLID *a.* Cf. F. †*stolidité* (15–17th c. in Godef.), It. *stolidità.*] The attribute of being stolid; dull impassiveness; incapacity for feeling.

1563–83 FOXE *A. & M.* 1598/1 In which wordes note (good reader) not only the absurditie of doctrine, but also the solidity of the reason. **1607** TOPSELL *Four-f. Beasts* 629 Aristophanes reprouing the stolidity of the Athenians, calleth them sheepe. *a* **1661** FULLER *Worthies, Notts.* (1662) 316 Men in all Ages have made themselves merry with singling out some place, and fixing the staple of stupidity and stolidity therein. **1691** HARTCLIFFE *Virtues* 277 A principal defect of the Mind, which may be called Stolidity, or the Extremity of Dulness. **1826** DISRAELI *V. Grey* V. iii, The look of complacent and pompous stolidity. **1849** MISS MULOCK *Ogilvies* xix, Leigh's countenance relapsed into its customary stolidity. **1869** TOZER *Highl. Turkey* II. 221 We received the announcement with the stolidity of true Britons. **1910** *Q. Rev.* Apr. 567 His aim is to cultivate 'a good healthy stolidity'.

‖**stolkjærre** (ˈstulkjɛrə). Also **stolkjaerre.** [Norw. (Bokmål), f. *stol* seat, STOOL *sb.* + *kjærre* cart.] A two-wheeled cart with seats for two persons. Hence as *v. intr.*, to ride in such a cart.

1885 *One & a Half in Norway* 125 The court-yard of the station was quite busy with carrioles and stolkjærres. **1924** *Public Opinion* 9 May 454/2 The traveller in stolkjærre or automobile ascends to snow-mantled plateaux. **1932** *New Yorker* 9 Apr. 59/2 Yachting on the Trollfjord, stolkjærreing through the Naeroedal, automobiling in the Baltic Capitals.

stoll(e: see STEAL *v.*, STOLE *sb.*[1], STOOL.

stolled, -en, etc., obs. pa. pple. of STEAL *v.*

‖**Stollen** (ˈʃtɒlən). Also **stollen, Stolle.** [Ger.] A rich fruit loaf, often made with nuts added.

1906 E. OSWALD *German Cookery for English Kitchen* 200 Stolle... Prepare the yeast as in recipe 'Napfkuchen'. **1927** *Daily Express* 20 Dec. 5/3 Germany has a cake similar to the Polish Strutzel, called Stollen. The dough should be made in the same way with quarter pound each chopped mixed peel, melon, angelica, prunes, and raisins,..for a filling, and the icing made with lemon juice. **1959** H. SLESAR *Grey Flannel Shroud* (1960) i. 15 Fine European baked goods, the stollen and strudel and delicate little kuchen. **1975** *Woman* 17 May 15/3 There are more than 200 types of bread made in Germany, like..Stollen, a famous dryish bread filled with glacé fruit, almonds, raisins and currants. **1977** [see PFEFFERKUCHEN]. **1977** *Sunday Tel.* (Colour Suppl.) 5 June 13/2 Church remains an integral part of the day, the marzipan in the stollen bread.

stoln(e, obs. pa. pple. of STEAL *v.*

‖**stolo** (ˈstəʊləʊ). Pl. **stolones** (stəˈləʊniːz). [L.: see STOLON.]

1. *Bot.* = STOLON 1. *rare.*

1725 *Bradley's Family Dict.* s.v. *Elm*, Where the Suckers and Stolones are supernumerary. **1796** WITHERING *Brit. Plants* (ed. 3) I. 84 *Stolo*, a sucker. **1807** J. E. SMITH *Phys. Bot.* 120 When the *stolo* has taken root. **1849** BALFOUR *Man. Bot.* 638.

2. *Zool.* = STOLON 2. ***stolo prolifer***, the germ-stock of certain compound organisms.

1878 F. J. BELL tr. *Gegenbaur's Comp. Anat.* 391 The parent sending forth a runner (stolo) which is composed of form-elements belonging both to ectoderm and endoderm. *Ibid.*, What is performed in the Ascidiæ by means of off-shoots starting from the surface of the body, is carried out in the Cyclomyaria and Thaliadæ by a special organ—the germ stock or stolo prolifer. **1887** *Athenæum* 5 Feb. 194/2 The peculiar mode of budding in Pyrosoma..from a ventral stolo prolifer.

stolon (ˈstəʊlən). Also 9 † **stollen.** [ad. L. *stolōn-em*, *stolo*, sucker of a plant. Cf. F. *stolon.*]

1. *Bot.* (See quot. 1880.)

1601 HOLLAND *Pliny* XVII. i. I. 499 They of the noble Licinian familie had for their addition Stolons (that is to say, the unprofitable watershoots that put forth from the root or tree it selfe, and never prove or come to any good). **1802** R. HALL *Elem. Bot.* Dict., Stolon, *stolo*, a shoot or scion, from the root of a plant, by which it may be propagated. **1840** J. BUEL *Farmer's Comp.* 161 The habits of many plants, in sending abroad roots and stollens, to establish a progeny in fresh, unexhausted soil. **1861** BENTLEY *Man. Bot.* 112 The sucker can scarcely be said to differ in any essential particulars from the stolon. **1863** BERKELEY *Brit. Mosses* iii. 13 The tips of these creeping stolons rise above the surface. **1880** A. GRAY *Struct. Bot.* iii. 53 A Stolon is a prostrate or reclined branch which strikes root at the tip, and then develops an ascending growth, which becomes an independent plant. **1882** F. DARWIN in *Nature* 20 Apr. 580 The stolons of the strawberry.

2. *Zool.* Each of the connecting processes of the cœnosarc of a compound organism.

1846 DANA *Zooph.* iv. (1848) 58 These shoots are called stolons or creepers by Ehrenberg. **1856** W. CLARK *Van der Hoeven's Zool.* I. 78 The common body is made up of stolons, connecting tubes erect, ventricose, striated, each containing a Polyp. **1875** HUXLEY in *Encycl. Brit.* I. 130/2 The Zoanthidæ differ from the Actinidæ in little more than their multiplication by buds, which remain adherent, either by a common connecting mass or cœnosarc or by stolons. **1880** F. P. PASCOE *Zool. Classif.* (ed. 2) 294 *Stolons.* In zoology connecting processes of the cœnosarc, &c.

3. Comb. ***stolon-like*** adj.

1849–52 T. R. JONES in *Todd's Cycl. Anat.* IV. 1217/2 This stolon-like body is closed at the free extremity. **1882** *Garden* 28 Jan. 66/3 The corms produce long stolon-like shoots.

Hence **stoˈlonial** *a.*, of or pertaining to stolons.

1911 [see EPICARDIAC *a.*]. **1964** *Oceanogr. & Marine Biol.* II. 317 High salinities..caused..reduction of stolonial material and fusion of hydranths.

stoloniferous (stəʊ-, stɒləˈnɪfərəs), *a. Bot.* and *Zool.* [f. mod. L. *stolōnifer*, f. *stolōnem* STOLON: see -FEROUS.] Producing stolons.

1777 ROBSON *Brit. Flora* 6 *Stoloniferous*, having scions, suckers or barren shoots, as in Creeping Crowfoot and Meadow Bugle. **1786** ABERCROMBIE *Gard. Assist., Arrangem.* 65 Stoloniferous, or shoot-bearing Chinese saxifrage. **1840** J. BUEL *Farmer's Comp.* 161 Even the delicate stoloniferous rose is constantly changing its location in this way. **1865** *Intell. Observer* No. 40. 301 Traversed at D by a stoloniferous passage. **1872** BRADY in *Monthly Microsc. Jrnl.* July 33 [In the Foraminifera] It is not.. unusual to find..two segments connected by a stoloniferous tube. **1899** *Jrnl. R. Agric. Soc.* Mar. 113 So strong is the habit of stoloniferous growth.

Hence **stoloˈniferously** *adv.*

1864 COBBOLD *Entozoa* 264 The generally-received notion that the heads bud out stoloniferously, as it were, is altogether disproved.

‖**stolovaya** (staˈlɔvaɪə). [Russ.] A canteen, a cafeteria.

1943 E. M. ALMEDINGEN *Frossia* ix. 329 It is dinner time. Come on, let us eat at the station *stolovaya.* **1976** 'S. HARVESTER' *Siberian Road* vii. 75 The swingdoors of the *stolovaya* shut behind the Russian. **1982** *Spectator* 27 Mar. 21/3 The food in a Russian *stolovaya* (or 'diner').

stolp(e, obs. forms of STOOP *sb.*, post, STOUP.

STOLport (ˈstɒlpɔːt). orig. *U.S.* Also **STOL-port, stolport**, etc. [f. *STOL* (see S 4 a), after AIRPORT.] An airport for aircraft which need only a short runway for take-off and landing.

1968 *N.Y. Times* 14 Jan. 1/1 A stolport would serve planes that make a 'short take-off and landing'. They use runways much shorter than those required by commercial jets. **1968** *Science News* 7 Sept. 230 (*caption*) Frenetic ground travel to and from New York's main airports may be replaced by STOL-ports along the Hudson river. **1975** *Sunday Sun* (Toronto) 12 Oct. 17/1 As the plan suggests, the airport and the STOLport would take over all of Toronto's air travel eventually. **1976** *Globe & Mail* (Toronto) 16 Feb. 5/5 Nordair [is] getting permanent access to the Toronto island Airport and the Victoria STOLport in Montreal. **1980** *Times* 3 June 19/5 The company has drawn up plans for a 2,000ft 'stolport' (short takeoff and landing airport) in the east Shetlands basin. **1982** *Times* 24 June 3/4 A group of companies is proposing to build a small airport, to bring a different kind of transport interchange to the docklands known as a Stolport (Stol stands for short-take-off-and-landing).

stoltherie, -erye, obs. ff. STOUTHERIE.

stolyn, obs. pa. pple. of STEAL *v.*

Stolypin (staˈliːpɪn). [The name of Pyotr Arkadyevich *Stolypin* (1862–1911), Russian conservative statesman.] **1.** ***Stolypin's necktie***, the noose. *colloq.*

1909 J. R. WARE *Passing Eng.* 234/2 *Stolypin's necktie* (*Europ. Politics, 1897*), the final halter. This term was brought into fashion in 1907 (Nov.–Dec.), at a Duma then recently assembled in St Petersburg. One Rodicheff, an extreme Radical, brought in the term on 30th November 1907. **1974** *Encycl. Brit. Micropædia* IX. 583/1 Stolypin.. instituted a network of courts-martial... Within the few months of their existence they used 'Stolypin's necktie' (the noose) to execute more than 1,000 defendants.

2. Used *attrib.* and *absol.* to designate a type of railway carriage made for the transport of prisoners.

1970 HARARI & HAYWARD tr. *Amalrik's Involuntary Journey to Siberia* xi. 127 This was a so-called 'Stolypin' car, specially constructed for the transport of prisoners... They are named after the Tsarist Prime Minister and Minister of the Interior who introduced them after the first Russian Revolution of 1905. **1974** T. P. WHITNEY tr. *Solzhenitsyn's Gulag Archipelago* I. II. i. 491 The prisoners got used to calling this kind of railroad car a *Stolypin* car, or, more simply, just a *Stolypin.*

stolzite (ˈstɒltsaɪt). *Min.* [f. *Stolz* (see quot. 1868) + -ITE.] Tungstate of lead.

1868 DANA *Syst. Min.* (ed. 5) 606 Stolzite... Tungstate of Lead. *Ibid.* 607 This species was first made known, according to Breithaupt, by Dr. Stolz, of Teplitz. **1878** GURNEY *Crystallogr.* 78.

stom, var. of STAM *sb.*[3] *dial.*, STUM *sb.* and *v.*

‖**stoma** (ˈstəʊmə). Pl. **stomata** (ˈstɒmətə). [mod.L., a. Gr. στόμα mouth.]

1. *Anat.* and *Zool.* A small opening in an animal body; an aperture, orifice, pore (as of a lymphatic or other vessel, an air-tube, etc.).

1684 *Blancard's Phys. Dict.*, *Stoma*, the Mouth, as also the Mouths of any Vessels. **1875** W. TURNER *Introd. Hum. Anat.* I. 140 Scattered..over this surface are the minute orifices, or stomata, which open into lymphatic vessels. **1881** MIVART *Cat* 217 The lymphatic vessels communicate with the peritoneal cavity by definite apertures called stomata. **1888** ROLLESTON & JACKSON *Anim. Life* 240 The complete mesentery...will be seen to have two perforations. One of these, the inner septal stoma..is found universally among Sea-Anemones... The other perforation or outer septal stoma occurs in very few instances.

2. *Bot.* One of the minute orifices in the epidermis of plants, especially of the leaves, occurring as a slit between two (or in some cases more) cells of special structure (guard-cells), and opening into intercellular spaces in the interior tissue so as to afford communication with the outer air; a breathing-pore.

(Sometimes used for the whole structure, including the guard-cells.)

1837 P. KEITH *Bot. Lex.* 231 The leaves..inhale..gases through means of their stomata. **1851** CARPENTER *Man. Phys.* (ed. 2) 55 The stomata are bounded by two or more cells, in such a manner that they can be opened or closed by changes in the form of these. **1884** BOWER & SCOTT *De Bary's Phaner.* 34 The apparatus consisting of the pair of cells with the slit is called a pore or stoma. *Ibid.* 45 Stomata ..are completely absent in roots.

3. *Surg.* A permanent opening made into a hollow organ; *spec.* one made from outside the body. Freq. *attrib.*, as ***stoma patient, therapy***.

1937 R. SCHINDLER *Gastroscopy* xiv. 269 In cases of gastric resection the stoma of resection is generally easily seen if the 85° instrument is used. **1943** H. L. BOCKUS *Gastro-Enterol.* I. xxxi. 633 The stoma which is too large allows food to enter the jejunum immediately after eating. **1952** *Jrnl. Amer. Med. Assoc.* 25 Oct. 812/2 A special clinic devoted to intestinal stomas of all types has been established recently at the hospital. **1977** *Lancet* 15 Oct. 806/1 How often in a lifetime does a patient with an ileostomy have to return to hospital or seek advice from the Ileostomy Association or a stoma therapist? **1978** *Jrnl. R. Soc. Med.* LXXI. 519 All of these patients have become well rehabilitated, helped particularly by the excellent stoma-therapy services at these two hospitals. **1978** K. P. KRETSCHMER *Intestinal Stoma* 115 A stoma patient is well advised when entering an unfamiliar locality to inform himself first of bathroom facilities. **1980** *Recent Adv. Surg.* X. 281 Courses for the training of stomatherapists. **1981** *West Lancs. Evening Gaz.* 14 Jan. 14 (Advt.), Victoria Hospital Gastro Enterology Services Unit Stoma Therapy Nursing Service..are looking for a person who has the ability to communicate and assess the patient's psychological and social needs.

Hence **'stomal** *a.*

1952 W. M. CRAPPER in F. A. Jones *Mod. Trends Gastro-Enterol.* xviii. 464 A stomal ulcer may appear, as we have seen recently, where a woman aged 73 developed ulceration 9 months after gastro-jejunostomy for a duodenal ulcer. **1979** J. P. DELANEY et al. in Najarian & Delaney *Gastrointestinal Surg.* 191 The only way symptoms of stomal gastritis can be relieved is by diversion of the upper gastrointestinal juices away from the stomach.

‖**stomacace** (stəʊ'mækəsiː). *Path.* [L. *stomacacē* (Pliny), a. Gr. στομακάκη (Strabo), in the MSS. στομακάκκη, prob. f. στόμα mouth + κάκκη dung.

The second element is usually explained as κάκη vice; but this word occurs only in a moral sense.]

An ulcerous or scorbutic affection of the mouth; scurvy of the gums; ulcerative stomatitis.

1657 TOMLINSON *Renou's Disp.* 360 Britannica doth with a peculiar faculty respect stomacace [*mispr.* -cate] and scele-tyrbe. **1857** DUNGLISON *Med. Lex., Stomacace... Cancer Oris, Canker*..Fœtor of the mouth with a bloody discharge from the gums. **1897** *Allbutt's Syst. Med.* III. 334 Ulcerative Stomatitis (Phlegmonous stomatitis,.. Stomacace, Putrid sore mouth) is an affection of very varying severity.

stomacal: see STOMACHAL.

stomach ('stʌmək), *sb.* Forms: α. 4-6 **stomak**, 4-7 **-ake, -ac, -ack**, 5-7 **-acke**, (5 **-oke, -ocke**, 5-6 **-ok**, 6 **stommok, stummock, stomacque**, 7 **stamocke**, 8 *Sc.* **stamock**); β. 6 **stomache**, 6- **stomach** (9 *Sc.* **stammach**). [a. OF. *estomac, stomaque, stomeque* (mod.F. *estomac*) ad. L. *stomachus*, a. Gr. στόμαχος, orig. the throat, gullet, hence the mouth or orifice of any organ, esp. of the stomach, and later the stomach itself; f. στόμα mouth. Cf. Pr. *estomac*, Sp. *estómago*, Pg. *estomago*, It. *stomaco*.

The Gr. senses occur in Latin, where however the usual sense is 'stomach,' with various fig. applications, e.g. 'appetite,' 'indignation,' 'courage,' etc.]

1. a. In a human or animal body: The internal pouch or cavity in which food is digested.

In man, the stomach is a dilatation of the alimentary canal, occupying the upper part of the left side of the abdomen. In some animals there are several stomachs, through which the food passes in succession; thus in ruminants there are the first stomach (paunch, rumen), the second stomach (honeycomb, reticulum), the third stomach (omasum, psalterium), and the fourth or true stomach (abomasum).

13.. *E.E. Allit. P.* C. 274 & þer he [Jonah] festnes þe fete & fathmez aboute, & stod vp in his [the whale's] stomak, þat stank as þe deuel. *c* **1374** CHAUCER *Boeth.* III. met. xii. (1868) 107 þe fowel þat hyȝt voltor þat etiþ þe stomak or þe giser of ticius [erron. tr. L. *Tityi jecur*]. *c* **1374** —— *Troylus* I. 737. **1375** BARBOUR *Bruce* III. 542 That soucht nane othir salss thair-till Bot appetyt.. For weill scowryt war thar stomakys. **1398** TREVISA *Barth. De P.R.* v. xxxviii. (1495) 152 The stomak is beclipped in on place wyth the lyuer. *a* **1400-50** *Wars Alex.* 4436 Youre mawis ȝe fill,..Stuffis so ȝour stomake with stullis & of wynes, þat [etc.]. **1406** HOCCLEVE *La Male Regle* 150 A draght of wyn..To warme a stomak with. **1500-20** DUNBAR *Poems* xxvii. 52 In to his stommok wes sic ane steir, Off all his dennar quhilk he coft [*v.r.* cost] deir. **1526** *Pilgr. Perf.* (W. de W. 1531) 36 Somtyme of great replecyon or fyllyng of yᵉ stomacke, or surfet. *c* **1623** LODGE *Poor Mans Talent* E 2, The stomacke is the storehouse of the Bodie. **1650** BULWER *Anthropomet.* xi. 117 The Gullet moveth the meat into the Stomack by natural instruments. **1664** E. BROWNE *Jrnl.* in *Sir T. Browne's Wks.* (1836) I. 54, I being desirous to see the inside of a man's stomache, hee cut one up for me which hee had by him. **1686** tr. *Chardin's Trav. Persia* 168 It is not to be imagin'd what an empty stomach I had all the while that I was in Mingrelia. **1833** N. ARNOTT *Physics* I. III. v. 661 A full stomach produces tension and projection of the belly. **1834** McMURTRIE tr. *Cuvier's Anim. Kingd.* 482 In the middle of the inferior margin [of the rib in Medusæ] is the mouth, a wide aperture opening into a stomach placed transversely in the thickness of the rib. **1847** W. C. L. MARTIN *Ox* 144/2 The second stomach is the reticulum or honey-comb... The third stomach is termed manyplus, manyplies, manifold, and other names, in allusion to its internal foliations. **1873** MIVART *Elem. Anat.* 441 The stomach..is a simple, somewhat pear-shaped bag, curved so that its upper surface is concave. **1884** DAY *Fishes Gt. Brit.* I. p. lii, This gizzard-like stomach is evidently employed for grinding up hard food. **1901** *Daily Chron.* 26 July 3/4 The oyster and his fellow mollusca..like man himself,..possess that test of biological greatness, a true stomach.

transf. **1605** ROWLANDS *Hell's broke loose* 20 Our Purses may haue emptie stomackes all.

fig. *c* **1440** *Jacob's Well* 117 Takyth þe tryacle of my techyng in-to þe stomak of ȝoure soule.

†**b.** ***to defy*** or ***digest the stomach***: see DEFY *v.* 1 b, DIGEST *v.* 4 f.

c. ***on an empty stomach***: fasting. ***on a full stomach***: immediately after a copious meal.

1607 TOPSELL *Four-f. Beasts* 376 A Horsse may haue shortnesse of breath, by hasty running after drinking, or vpon a full stomach. **1663** BAYFIELD *Treat. De Morb. Capitis* 88 Barley masticated, or chewed, upon an empty stomach. **1744** BERKELEY *Siris* §3 About half a pint night and morning on an empty stomach. **1780** *Mirror* No. 98 When-ever he read on an empty stomach, he was apt to be disturbed with uneasy yawnings. **1865** ANNIE THOMAS *On Guard* xxvii. II. 178 Mrs. Green made some shadow of a protest against the brandy being taken on an empty stomach.

d. Viewed as the organ of digestion. Often with epithet, as *weak, strong, good*, etc.

c **1380** WYCLIF *Sel. Wks.* III. 133 þo stomak of a man schulde deffye his mete. *c* **1400** *Lanfranc's Cirurg.* 13 Forbede hem neiþir wiyn ne fleisch, for þe stomak þat is so feble ne myȝte nouȝt engendre nessessarie mater of blood þat longiþ to þe wounde. *c* **1430** LYDG. *Min. Poems* (Percy Soc.) 23 The wolf..Saide he [the lambe] maadde his water unholsom, His tender stomake to hinder and undispose. **1519** *Knaresb. Wills* (Surtees) I. 8 Hole in mynde and wake in stomak. **1599** BUTTES *Dyets drie Dinner* I 1, Signifying the holesomnesse thereof to a good stomacke. **1612** WOODALL *Surg. Mate* Wks. (1653) 70 Mace..strengtheneth the stomack. **1631** T. POWELL *Tom of All Trades* 31 A Citizens wife of a weake stomacke. **1669** DRYDEN *Tempest* II. (1670) 18 This [Brandy] works comfortably on a cold stomach. **1779** *Mirror* No. 9, I am a Scotsman of a good plain stomach. **1853** SOYER *Pantroph.* 73 The cucumber, although but little nutritious, does not agree with cold stomachs. **1856** *Athenæum* 26 Apr. 515/3 A brewage so composed can only be fitting for the stomachs of Belphegor and his brethren.

transf. **1612** STURTEVANT *Metall.* (1854) [115] The seuerall sorts of Raw matters, which are the things that the Stomack of the Furnace worketh upon.

fig. **1589** *Pappe w. Hatchet* in *Lyly's Wks.* (1902) III. 399 His conscience hath a colde Stomacke.

e. as the seat of hunger, nausea, discomfort from repletion, etc. ***to lie (heavy) on one's stomach***: (of food) to cause indigestion. (See also TURN *v.* 12, 12 b.)

c **1394** *P. Pl. Crede* 765 A great bolle-full of benen were betere in his wombe,..þan..comeren her stomakes wiþ curious drynkes. **1513** *Life Hen. V* (Kingsford 1911) 64 To ..indure the rage and boysterous of the sea, wᵗʰout accombrance and disease of his stomacke. *c* **1522** MORE *De quat. noviss.* Wks. 99/1 And than the head aketh, & the stomake knaweth, and the next meale is eaten wᵗ out appetite. **1567** *Gude & Godlie B.* (S.T.S.) 36 He wuld haif eitin with the swyne, His hungrie stomok to fulfill. **1610** SHAKS. *Temp.* II. ii. 118. **1649** JER. TAYLOR *Great Exemp.* Pref. ¶ 18 He knew that some appetites might be irregular, just as some stomackes would be sicke. **1709** T. ROBINSON *Vindic. Mosaick Syst.* 59 The Dog..when he finds himself sick at Stomach..presently runs to Grass, and having eaten it, it gives him a Vomit, and the Dog is well. **1711** SWIFT *Jrnl. to Stella* 5 Sept., I ate sturgeon, and it lies on my stomach. **1774** BURKE *Amer. Tax.* (C.P.S.) 95, I am sure our heads must turn, and our stomacks nauseate with them. **1786, 1807** [see SICK *a.* 1 c]. **1829** SOUTHEY *Pilgr. Compostella* IV. Poet. Wks. VII. 264 Not till he had confest,..did he feel His conscience and stomach at rest. **1842** MACAULAY *Ess., Freak. Gt.* ¶ 8 Sometimes he was forced to swallow food so nauseous that he could not keep it on his stomach. **1852** THACKERAY *Esmond* III. v, 'Twas the stomach that caused other patriots to grumble, and such men cried out because they were poor.

f. as the part of the body that requires food; hence, put for the body as needing to be fed.

1904 *Windsor Mag.* Jan. 268/2 'An army marches on its stomach.' '*C'est la soupe qui fait le soldat.*' These Napoleonic aphorisms..have been [etc.].

fig. *c* **1530** TINDALE *Jonas* Prol. A vij b, God oure father & scolemaster fedeth vs & teacheth [*printed* teached] vs according vn to the capacite of oure stomakes.

†**g.** Used to render L. *jecur* (liver) as the supposed seat of lust. *Obs.*

Cf. the original passage, *De Proeliis Alexandri*, 'Cupidinem deam iecoris existimas.'

1340-70 *Alex. & Dind.* 686 ȝe sain þat he [Cupidus] is a soþ god..þat haþ þe stomak in stat stifly to kepe, For þere þe hete that men han is holden wiþ-inne þat enforceþ þe flech folie to wirche. **1390** GOWER *Conf.* II. 177 Cupide..was the sire Of the stomak, which builleth evere, Wherof the Iustes ben the levere.

¶**2.** Some of the earlier anatomists (following, ultimately, Galen) attempted to restore to the word its original Gr. sense of œsophagus or gullet, and to give the name *ventricle* to what is 'improperly' called the stomach.

1541 COPLAND *Galyen's Terap.* 2 H j b, We must gyue medicaments to drynke to hym yᵗ hath his ventricle vlcerate, whiche vulgarily is called yᵉ stomacke, & yf the bulke yᵗ proprely is called yᵉ stomacke, yᵗ the grekes cal cesophagus [*sic*] be vlcerate, the sayd medycaments ought nat to be taken & swalowed at ones, but by lytel & lytell. **1578** BANISTER *Hist. Man* v. 68 The begynnyng of the stomache is at the roote of the toung, in the lower part of the iawes behynd Larinx. *Ibid.* 70 The Ventricle consisteth of two broad and thinne coates together ioyned, euen as the stomach or throte, but somewhat unlike. **1658** ROWLAND tr. *Moufet's Theat. Ins.* 1121, I mean by the stomach the mouth of the ventricle, taking the word stomach improperly, for properly it signifies the throat...the properly called stomach, that is, the throat is fenced with most strong bones.

3. The part of the body containing the stomach, the belly, abdomen; sometimes (formerly often) applied to the chest.

c **1375** *Sc. Leg. Saints* x. (*Matthew*) 488 He..his gret sorow for to slak, hyme-selfe into þe stomak strak, & ȝeld þe gaste. *c* **1400** *Laud Troy Bk.* 10929 He was al bare but his hauberke On his brest & his stomak. *c* **1440** *Gesta Rom.* xvi. 56 (Harl. MS.) þere came an arowe, & smote him at þe stomak, & he felle doun ded. **1530** PALSGR. 276/2 Stomake, *estomac, poictrine.* **1567** FENTON tr. *Bandello* xiii. (1898) II. 245 Her stomake also, some what raised by two rounde and precius dugges..was covered with a brave and softe vaile,.. whyche hyndred no waye the viewe of her travellynge brestes. **1585** T. WASHINGTON tr. *Nicholay's Voy.* II. vii. 37 b, About their neck and vpon their stomacke, they were many chaines, tablets, & other trynkets. *a* **1605** MONTGOMERIE *Misc. Poems* xxvii. 3, I wot ȝe neuer kneu A harte more treu with-in a stomok stik. **1748** SMOLLETT *R. Rand.* xxvii, Many cross-buttocks did I sustain, and pegs on the stomach without number. **1847** MARRYAT *Childr. N. Forest* iv, The dog..dragged himself on his stomach after Edward. **1863** KINGSLEY *Water-Bab.* vi. (1869) 271 So they lived miserably on roots and nuts, and all the weakly little children had great stomachs, and then died. **1888** RIDER HAGGARD *Maiwa's Revenge* i, Good crawled upon his stomach.

transf. **1848** THACKERAY *Van. Fair* lxii, With..his hand in the stomach of a voluminous white waistcoat. **1902** CORNISH *Naturalist Thames* 8 Barometers, if tapped violently in the centre of their mahogany stomachs.

†**4.** *Sc.* = STOMACHER. Also, a chest-covering for a horse. *Obs.*

1473-4 *Acc. Ld. High Treas. Scot.* I. 38 Deliuerit to Caldwele.. j elne of satyne for stomokis to the Quene. **1488-92** *Ibid.* 80 Item, in the same box, a stomok. **1500-20** DUNBAR *Poems* xxvii. 11 With mony lymmar loun,..Off stomok steillaris and clayth takkaris. **1506** [see SHAKER 6]. **1508** *Acc. Ld. High Treas. Scot.* IV. 22 Item for vj quartaris quhit dames to be foure stomo[k]is for hors housouris, xlij s. **1540-1** *Ibid.* VII. 423 The litill copburd of silver witht certane stomokkis, perle bedis, [etc.]. **1558** *Extracts Aberd. Reg.* (1844) I. 309 The wrangous reiffing and away taking fra hir of ane plyd,..ane bukrame approwne, ane stomak.

5. a. Appetite or relish for food. *Obs.* exc. (somewhat *arch.*) with const. *for*.

c **1386** CHAUCER *Sompn. T.* 139 The body is ay so redy and penyble To wake, that my stomak is destroyed. **1514** BARCLAY *Cyt. & Uplondyshm.* (Percy Soc.) 1 A lordes stomake & a beggers pouche Full yll accordeth. **1555** EDEN *Decades* (Arb.) 182 They haue no stomacke to their meate. **1560** T. WILSON *Rhet.* (1563) 72, I haue no liste to eate now, it is to earely for me, my stomacke is not yet come to me. **1590** SHAKS. *Com. Err.* I. i. 49 You haue no stomacke, hauing broke your fast. **1642** FULLER *Holy & Prof. St.* III. xiii. 185 A rich man told a poore man that he walked to get a stomach for his meat. *a* **1654** SELDEN *Table-T.* (Arb.) 88 'Tis a good rule, eat within your Stomach, act within your Commission. **1674-7** J. MOLINS *Anat. Observ.* (1896) 19 The Boy came to his Stomach, and would goe. *a* **1722** LISLE *Husb.* (1757) 271 Such working every other day..would get them a stomach to their meat. **1726** SWIFT *Gulliver* II. iii, I had quite lost my stomach, and was almost reduced to a skeleton. **1746** *Oxf. Sausage* (1764) 34, I..Rode for a Stomach. **1766** *Complete Farmer* s.v. *Purging*, Horses that fall off their stomach,.. should have a mild purge or two. **1841** JAMES *Brigand* v, Heaven send us all as good food as I have a good stomach. **1855** THACKERAY *Newcomes* II. xxxvii. 334 'You must go back to your dinner.' In vain I pleaded that I had no stomach for it. **1859** TENNYSON *Enid* 1062 And Enid took a little delicately, Less having stomach for it than desire To close with her lord's pleasure. **1867** HOWELLS *Ital. Journ.* 95 The lions had no stomach for Glaucus on the morning of the fatal eruption.

b. *fig.* Relish, inclination, desire (for something immaterial).

1513 DOUGLAS *Æneis* XIII. vi. 76 Agane his stomak..the contrak is ybrokken. **1596** SHAKS. *Merch. V.* III. v. 92 Nay, let me praise you while I haue a stomacke. **1610** —— *Tempest* II. i. 107 You cram these words into mine eares, against the stomacke of my sense. **1610** HOLLAND *Camden's Brit.* (1637) 313 These matters, I assure you, it goes against my stomacke to relate. **1622** BACON *Hen. VII*, 38 It was an Act against his stomacke, and put vpon him by necessitie and reason of State. *a* **1660** *Contemp. Hist. Irel.* (Ir. Archæol. Soc.) II. 27 The captain against his stamocke condescended. **1682** BUNYAN *Holy War* (1905) 369 The Captains..did do such execution with their stones, that they made him, though against stomach, to retreat. **1722** DE FOE *Plague* 65, I had no stomach to go back again to see the same dismal scene over again. **1793** DR. BURNEY in *Mme. D'Arblay's Diary & Lett.* (1891) III. 479, I have little stomach to write. **1870** EMERSON *Soc. & Solit., Books* Wks. (Bohn) III. 82 And if one lacks stomach for Mr. Grote's voluminous annals, the old slight and popular summary of Goldsmith.. will serve. **1902** BUCHAN *Watcher by Threshold* 186, I had no stomach for more mysteries.

6. a. Used (like 'heart', 'bosom', 'breast') to designate the inward seat of passion, emotion, secret thoughts, affections, or feelings. Now *rare*.

1482 *Cely Papers* (Camden) 131 The wyche y onderstond ye taked sor at yowre stomak. **1537** STARKEY in Strype *Eccl. Mem.* (1721) I. App. lxxxi. 197, I trust..your bounden duty to your Sovereign Lord & Master shal so prevail in your stomac, that you [etc.]. **1537** CRANMER *Let. to Crumwell* Misc. Writ. (Parker Soc.) II. 348 Your good mind to-wards me concerning my debts to the king's highness, which of all other things lieth most nigh unto my stomach. *a* **1548** HALL *Chron., Hen. VIII*, 164 b, They knew nothyng of all his doynges, whiche sore greved their stomackes. **1571** WALSINGHAM in Digges *Compl. Ambass.* (1655) 151 The common people ease their stomacks onely by uttering certain seditious words. **1599** Chapman *Hum. Day's Mirth* E 2b, Nay I do not cry, but my stomacke waters to thinke that you should take it so heauily. **1642** D. Rogers *Naaman* 346 Evill which causeth such a fulsomenesse and wearinesse in Gods stomacke. **1663** Butler *Hud.* I. iii. 222 This said, his grief to anger turn'd, Which in his manly stomach burn'd. **1707** Addison *Rosamond* II. ii. 16 My Stomach swells with secret Spight To see my fickle, faithless Knight .. So little his own Worth to know. **1721** Strype *Eccl. Mem.* I. I. xi. 98 Nor cared they to meddle openly against the Emperor, especially in this, which he took so much to Stomach. **1859** Earl Granville *Let.* in E. Fitzmaurice *Life Granville* (1905) I. xii. 344, I ought to.. tell you of.. the enormous weight off my stomach when I failed [to form a government]. **1965** E. B. White *Let.* July (1976) 533 The city is very strange this summer—alternately deserted and packed, and the nearness of Harlem always in everybody's stomach.

†**b.** ***to utter* (*the bottom of*) *one's stomach***: to disclose one's inmost thoughts. Similarly, ***to fish out the bottom of a person's stomach***. *Obs.*

1537 Cromwell in Merriman *Life & Lett.* (1902) II. 92 As you may therby fishe out the botom of his stomake, and aduertise his Maieste howe he standethe disposed towardes him. **1538** *Ibid.* 128, I cannot but.. be glad, that ye so frankely utter your stomache to me. **1604** Hieron *Preachers Plea* 28 But such as I am shall often heare them talke at libertie, and vtter the very bottome of their stomackes.

†**c.** In various phrases, ***to pierce one's stomach, sink* (*deep*) *into one's stomach, to stick in one's stomach***: said of something that makes a lasting (esp. painful) impression on the mind. *Obs.*

1387–8 T. Usk *Test. Love* II. viii. (Skeat) l. 15 It may not sinke in my stomake til I here more. **1509** Fisher *Funeral Serm. C'tess Richmond* Wks. (1876) 298 Dauyd sayth .. *zelaui super iniquos*.. it perceth my stomacke to se the rest & ease that synners often haue. *c* **1536** in *Priory of Hexham* (Surtees) I. App. p. clix, There is somewhat that stykkes in their stomakkes. *a* **1548** Hall *Chron., Edw. IV*, 207 These reasons.. sancke in the Dukes stomacke. **1565** Cooper *Thesaurus* s.v. *Mordeo*, Thy letters did much greue me, or pinche me at the stomake. **1579** Rice *Invect. agst. Vices* H j b, Now, therefore do I sore muse, how this question.. could sinke into any honest, & specially, into any Christian mans stomake, to demaunde, what [etc.]. **1643** Baker *Chron., Eliz.* (1653) 558 For this new Earl [of the Holy Empire] stuck in the stomachs of the English Barons, who inwardly grudged to give him place. **1691** Wood *Athenæ Oxon.* (1817) III. 369 Which usage sunk so deep into his stomach, that he [Selden] did never after affect the bishops and clergy. **1708** Mrs. Centlivre *Busy Body* v. iv, Does not your hundred pounds stick in your stomach? **1781** Cowper *Madan's Answ. Newton* 8 Which stuck in M.'s stomach as cross as a bone. **1809** Malkin *Gil Blas* x. vii. (Rtldg.) 356 This declaration stuck in his stomach. **1828** Carr *Craven Gloss.*, 'To stick in the stomach,' to remain in the memory with angry resentment.

†**7. a.** Temper, disposition; state of feeling with regard to a person; *occas.* friendly feeling, friendliness. *Obs.*

1476 Sir J. Paston in *Paston Lett.* III. 160 He also hathe tolde me moche off hys stomake and tendre faver that he owythe to yow. *c* **1489** Caxton *Sonnes of Aymon* xii. 288 And I behelde vpon my brederen, & knewe their stomackes. **1535** Coverdale *Prov.* xi. 17 He yͭ hath a gentle liberall stomacke, is mercifull. **1553** Brende *Q. Curtius* VI. 98 Antipater therefore which knew ful wel his stomake, durst not vse the victory according to his owne will. **1565** Cooper *Thesaurus* s.v. *Animus, Nec vnus in te ego hos animos gessi*, Not only I had that stomake towarde you. **1607** Topsell *Four-f. Beasts* 307 When he had gotten perfect intelligence and vnderstanding of the Horsses stomacke, he.. addressed himselfe to mount on his backe. **1610** Holland *Camden's Brit.* (1637) 51 The auxiliarie souldiers likewise were of the same stomach.

b. With various adjs. (e.g. *bold, high, proud, malicious*) or other qualifying words. (The combination of adj. and sb. is sometimes equivalent to the sb. in sense 8.)

c **1510** More *Picus* Wks. 5/1 He was verie quicke, wise, and subtile in dispicions, and had great felicitee therein, while he had that high stomak. **1535** Coverdale *Prov.* xvi. 18 After a proude stomake there foloweth a fall. **1536** in *Priory of Hexham* (Surtees) I. App. p. cxxxi, He did nothyng .. but of a willyng malicys stomak. **1548** Hall *Chron., Edw. IV*, 218 Erle of Warwicke, whose stoute stomacke, and invincible corage,.. caused death before.. old age. **1565** Cooper *Thesaurus, Sublimitas animi*, lofty stomake or courage. **1573** G. Harvey *Letter-bk.* (Camden) 14 A wurthi pattern of a noble stummock. **1576** Ralegh in Gascoigne *Steele Glas* (Arb.) 47 For spyteful tongs, in cankred stomackes plaste, Deeme worst of things, which best (percase) deserued. **1617** Hieron *Penance for Sin* xix. (1619) 283 It is scarcely to bee thought that that mans soule is truely taught of God, who is backward, especially out of height of stomake, to bee a Teacher vnto others. **1631** Quarles *Samson* iii, Great God! whose power hath so oft prevail'd Against the strength of Princes, and hast quail'd Their prouder stomackes. *a* **1661** Fuller *Worthies, Durh.* (1662) 294 This Ralph was a Prelate of High Birth, haughty Stomach, great Courtship, [etc.]. **1697** Dryden *Virg. Georg.* III. 322 Before his Training, keep him poor and low: For his stout Stomach with his Food will grow. **1709** Strype *Ann. Ref.* I. xxxv. 348 But Bourne, not-withstanding, had an angry Stomack against the Bishop. **1772** J. Fletcher *Logica Genev.* 29 The proud and haughty stomachs of the daughters of England are so maintained with divers disguised sorts of apparel, that [etc.]. **1835** Lytton *Rienzi* v. v, His stomach is too high for that now. **1881** Blackie *Lay Serm.* viii. 263 Middleton, soon after this hasty provocation of the stout old Scottish stomach, fell into discredit.

8. In various senses relating to disposition or state of feeling.

†**a.** Spirit, courage, valour, bravery. *Obs.*

Phrase, *to take stomach* (often with dat. of refl. pron.). *c* **1532** Du Wes *Introd. Fr.* in Palsgr. 904/2 The stomake, *le courage*. **1534** More *Comf. agst. Trib.* II. Wks. 1171/1 A merye tale wyth a frende, refresheth a manne.. and amendeth his courage and hys stomake. **1538** Starkey *England* (1878) 27 Yet the grete frute.. wych may.. yssue of the same may somewhat encourage vs and gyue vs stomake. **1540** Hyrde tr. *Vives' Instr. Chr. Wom.* (1592) I 3, Against these darts of the divell.. let her take the buckler of Stomacke. **1544** Bale *Exam. Oldcastle* 26 b, He toke stomake vnto him agayne. **1565** Cooper *Thesaurus, Afferre animum alicui*, to encourage; to geue stomake. **1569** Underdowne *Heliodorus* IV. 55 After shee knewe her selfe, and had taken stomake vnto her, shee.. saide [etc.]. **1571** *Homily agst. Disobedience* II. D j b, Lustie and couragious captaines, valiaunt men of stomacke. **1579** Fenton *Guicciard.* VII. (1599) 270 The king of Romains also taking stomack by the greatnesse of his son, solicited to passe into Italy. **1606** Shaks. *Tr. & Cr.* II. i. 137 Hector.. Will with a Trumpet,.. To morrow morning call some Knight to Armes, That hath a stomacke. **1611** Chapman *Iliad* IX. 335 Let him take stomacke to repell Troyes firie threatenings. **1645** Fuller *Good Th. in Bad T.* 172 John Courcy, Earl of Vlster, was chosen Champion for the English; A Man of great Stomack and Strength. **1663** Butler *Hud.* I. ii. 107 Instead of Trumpet and of Drum, That makes the Warrier's stomach come; A squeaking Engine he apply'd.

†**b.** Pride, haughtiness; obstinacy, stubbornness.

a **1513** Fabyan *Chron.* VII. 643 For yͤ great stomake of the father, yͭ he wolde not be condycioned with of yͤ sone. **1575–85** Abp. Sandys *Serm.* x. 169 Zeale without knowledge is not zeale but stomacke. **1590** Spenser *F.Q.* II. vii. 41 Sterne was his looke, and full of stomacke vaine. **1613** Shaks. *Hen. VIII*, IV. ii. 34 He was a man Of an vnbounded stomacke, euer ranking Himselfe with Princes. **1641** Milton *Animadv.* Wks. 1851 III. 239 They were.. for stomach much like to Pompey the great, that could indure no equall. **1674** J. Howard *Engl. Mounsieur* II. i. 26 Oh —is your stomack come down. **1692** R. L'Estrange *Fables* ccxv. 188 Now 'tis not Courage but Stomach, that makes many People Break, rather then they will Bend. **1765** Foote *Commissary* I. Wks. 1799 II. 9 Oh ho! what, I suppose his stomach's come down.

†**c.** Anger, irritation; malice, ill-will, spite; vexation, pique. *Obs.*

c **1540** *Life Bp. Fisher* (E.E.T.S.) p. xlix, Whereat the Cardinall tooke such hartie displeasure against the Emperour that ever after he bare him in stomacke. **1559** Abp. Parker in N. Johnston *King's Visit. Power* (1688) 216, I shall be bold in secretys to Wright it.. to avoid som Stomake that ellys might be taken. **1568** T. Howell *Newe Sonets* (1879) 139 Wordes be but winde, to purge his heate, His stomacke to abate. **1592** Wotton *Let.* 10 July *Reliq. W.* (1685) 675 Having left a stipend.. of 1200 Crowns, upon Stomach to see himself cross'd in the Court by the Archbishop of Pisa. **1603** Knolles *Hist. Turks* (1621) 440 Zemes more upon stomacke and desire of revenge, than [etc.]. **1611** Speed *Hist. Gt. Brit.* IX. xiii. §67 But the King vpon a stomacke doth it. **1633** Bp. Hall *Hard Texts* Eccl. x. 4 If the Prince be angry with thee, doe not in a stomach or froward pettishnesse give up thine office. **1641** Milton *Ch. Govt.* II. Wks. 1851 III. 140 Not suddenly to condemn all things that are sharply spoken, or vehemently written, as proceeding out of stomach, virulence and ill nature. **1643** Baker *Chron., Edw. I*, 131 Others of the nobility.. took stomach against him. *a* **1825** Forby *Voc. E. Anglia, Stomach*, anger.

9. *Brewing.* See quot. [Perhaps a corruption of some other word; perh. a fanciful use of 8 a.]

1835 W. Black *Brewing* 52 What is technically called the stomach or vinous vapour begins to be smelt, and continues to acquire strength until the process [of fermentation] is concluded. *Ibid.* 104 Stomach means the pungency, but more particularly the odour of the vapour evolved during fermentation; by which an experienced brewer should at all times be able to judge how the process is going on. **1882** E. G. Hooper *Man. Brewing* (ed. 2) 240 The proper cleansing point is fixed in different ways, and whilst one judges by the heat of the wort ceasing to rise, another goes by the diminution in pungency of the odour or 'stomach' exhaled.

10. *attrib.* and *Comb.* **a.** Simple attrib., pertaining to the stomach, as ***stomach-blood, -catarrh, -complaint, -digestion,* †*fit, muscle, ulcer, upset, -wall, -wound***; good for the stomach, as ***stomach-drink, -essence, -pill, powder, -wine***; **b.** objective and locative, as ***stomach-stretching; stomach-hating, -healing, -qualmed, -sick, -soothing, -turning, -twitched, -whetting, -worn***, adjs.; **c.** special comb., †**stomach-anger** *nonce-wd.*, concealed anger; **stomach-bag** = cheeselip[1] 2; **stomach cough**, a cough supposed to proceed from indigestion; †**stomach grief**, bitter anger; †**stomach-gut**, the duodenum; **stomach-piece** *Naut.* (see quot.); **stomach pocket**, *Zool.*, in Medusæ, a cavity serving as a stomach; **stomach-pouch**, (*a*) the protuberant abdominal pouch found in certain ducks and geese; (*b*) = prec.; **stomach-pump**, a kind of pump or syringe for emptying the stomach (esp. in cases of poisoning) or for introducing liquids into it; **stomach-staggers**, a variety of staggers (stagger *sb.*[1] 2) caused by distension of the stomach; **stomach sweetbread**, the pancreas, as distinguished from the 'throat sweetbread' or thymus; **stomach-syringe** = *stomach-pump*; †**stomach-tight** *a. Sc.*, hungry; *stomach-tooth* (see quot.); **stomach-tube**, (*a*) 'a siphon used in washing out the stomach'; (*b*) 'a feeding tube' (Dorland *Med. Lex.*); **stomach-warmer**, a flat vessel of tin-plate, to be filled with hot water and applied to the pit of the stomach; **stomach-wise** *adv.* (*nonce-wd.*), (crawling) on one's stomach; **stomach-worm**, (*a*) a common intestinal round worm, *Ascaris lumbricoides*, sometimes found in the human stomach (= maw-worm), (*b*) *slang* (see quot. 1788).

1640 Bp. Reynolds *Passions* xxxi. 317 Neither can I like that close and dissembled, that politick and *stomacke Anger, which cunningly shrowds it selfe under a calme and serene countenance. **1717** *Dict. Rust.* s.v. *Cheeslip-bag*, .. 'Tis the *Stomach-bag of a young Sucking Calf that never tastes any other food than Milk. **1847** W. C. L. Martin *Ox* 37 The first thing to be done is to clear the stomach-bag. **1666** G. Harvey *Morbus Angl.* xxx. (1672) 90 If the evacuated blood be florid, it's *Stomach-blood. **1910** *Daily Chron.* 5 Apr. 9/2 Niemeyer,.. speaking of the value of this fluid in *stomach-catarrh, is found saying [etc.]. **1824** Scott *St. Ronan's* iii, The gentlemen were as liable to *stomach complaints, as the ladies to nervous disorders. **1875** T. K. Chambers *Man. Diet* 287 '*Stomach cough' and 'Stomach sore throat'.. are best treated by [etc.]. **1899** *Allbutt's Syst. Med.* VIII. 369 The sensations accompanying *stomach and intestinal digestion are felt excessively. **1903** *Daily Chron.* 20 Feb. 3/5 Thus tea and coffee both retard stomach-digestion powerfully. **1766** *Complete Farmer* s.v. *Purging*, When horses lose their appetites after purging, it is necessary to give them a warm *stomach drink. **1672** G. Thomson *Let. to H. Stubbe* 25 A Vindication of the Author's *Stomach-Essence, and other effectual Remedies. *a* **1700** B. E. *Dict. Cant. Crew, Qualm*, a *Stomack-Fit. **1533** T. Wilson *Rhet.* 106 b, *Stomake grief [margin, *Iracundia*], is when we will take the matter as hote as a tost. **1585** Higins *Junius' Nomencl.* 31/2 *Intestinum primum*,.. the *stomach gutte, or maw gut. **1620** J. Taylor (Water P.) *Praise Hemp-seed* (1623) 21 Iniunctions for some *stomacke hating Fast. **1735** Somerville *Chace* I. 378 Each *Stomach-healing Plant Curious they crop. **1965** P. O'Donnell *Modesty Blaise* xviii. 199 Instinct tensed her *stomach-muscles an instant before the woman dropped on her with both knees. **1846** A. Young *Naut. Dict.* 14 *Apron*, or **Stomach-piece*, a piece of curved timber which is bolted on the inside of a vessel's main-stem, to strengthen it and to give shifts to its scarphs. **1875** Knight *Dict. Mech.*, *Stomach-piece*, a compass-timber fayed to the stem and keel. An apron. **1662** J. Degravere *Thesaurus Remed.* (ed. 2) 35 First clense downward with the *stomach pills. **1885** W. K. Brooks in *Mem. Boston Soc. Nat. Hist.* III. 361 The Narcomedusæ... Radial canals absent, or present as flat radial *stomach pockets. **1854** *Poultry Chron.* I. 498 The duck of this kind has at a very early age a great development of its '*stomach pouch.' **1871** Allman *Gymnobl. Hydroids* 84 The fact of their having twelve tentacles and twelve stomach-pouches instead of eight. **1911** E. Wharton *Ethan Frome* vii. 135 I've a good mind to go and hunt up those *stomach powders I got last year... Maybe they'll help the heart-burn. **1972** V. Canning *Rainbird Pattern* vi. 115 He was restless himself from a substantial dinner and lay awake for hours wishing he had brought some stomach powder. **1822–9** *Good's Study Med.* (ed. 3) I. 119 Until Dr. Physic proved the utility of the *stomach pump in the case of a child poisoned with laudanum, the invention gained little attention. **1899** Cagney tr. *von Jaksch's Clin. Diagn.* v. (ed. 4) 151 The handle is removed and the sound connected with a stomach-pump. **1611** Shaks. *Cymb.* III. iv. 193 If you are sicke at Sea, or *Stomacke-qualm'd at Land, a Dramme of this Will driue away distemper. **1613** Purchas *Pilgrimage* (1614) 289 He proued *stomack-sick to his expedition also. **1657** W. Rand tr. *Gassendi's Life Peiresc* I. 98 He withdrew himself [to sit by the Mainmast] that he might not be Stomach-sick. **1664** H. More *Exp. 7 Epist.* ix. 149 Christ here expresseth how nauseous and stomack-sick he is against his Church under this Intervall and Title of Laodicea. **1876** Bristowe *Th. & Pract. Med.* (1878) 201 Spirits of chloroform, bismuth, or other *stomach-soothing drugs. **1831** Youatt *Horse* vii. 103 In *Stomach-staggers the horse stands dull, sleepy, staggering. **1648** G. Daniel *Eclog* iii. 79 T'allay The *Stomacke-Stretchings of the former Day. **1822–9** *Good's Study Med.* (ed. 3) I. 119 A *stomach syringe, for diluting and washing away various poisons introduced into the stomach.. was first suggested by Renault. **1715** Ramsay *Christ's Kirk Gr.* II. xviii, But ithers that were *stomach-tight, Cry'd out, [etc.]. **1890** Billings *Nat. Med. Dict* II. 594 **Stomach tooth*, canine tooth of lower jaw of first dentition, so called because of gastric disturbance frequently accompanying its eruption. **1857** Dunglison *Med. Lex.* s.v. *Tube, Tube Œsophageal*, **Stomach Tube*, a long elastic gum tube, capable of being passed into the œsophagus or stomach. **1897** *Allbutt's Syst. Med.* III. 437 Emetics.. may be given when the use of the stomach-tube is inadvisable. **1875** Browning *Aristoph. Apol.* 197 The *stomach-turning stew. **1804** Coleridge *Lett.* (1895) 457, I am as asthmatic and *stomach-twitched as when with you. **1945** A. Huxley *Let.* 27 May (1969) 527 He interferes with the normal functioning of his own body and worries or strains himself into *stomach ulcers. **1961** L. Mumford *City in History* xv. 473 Definite ailments, like stomach ulcers and high blood pressure, seem to be aggravated by the strain of living, say, within sound of a busy motorway or airport. **1960** L. Cooper *Certain Compass* 23 Adrian said that he had a *stomach upset, and went back. **1976** D. Clark *Dread & Water* v. 102 Mugs.. if used communally.. can serve to pass germs among the party, causing stomach upsets. **1871** Allman *Gymnobl. Hydroids* 84 The internal surface of the *stomach walls. **1835** Dickens *Sk. Boz, River*, A flat bottle like a *stomach-warmer. **1858** Simmonds *Dict. Trade*, *Stomach-warmer* a metal vessel for holding hot water to place on the stomach. **1631** Quarles *Samson* x, Their *stomacke-whetting Sallats. **1677** J. Beale *Nurseries*, etc. ii. 24 Poitiers (where I always met with excellent *stomach-wine). **1750** J. Theobald *App. Medulla Med. Univ.* 67 Stomach Wine. Take Half an Ounce of Gentian-root, [etc.]. **1893** K. Grahame *Pagan Ess.* 131 Where a rabbit could go, a boy could follow, albeit *stomach-wise, and with one leg in the stream. **1647** Trapp *Comm. Mark* ix. 50. 27 *Stomach-worms are killed with salt. **1666** G. Harvey *Morbus Angl.* xvii. (1672) 35 Whence they are called Stomach or Maw-worms. **1788** Grose *Dict. Vulgar T.* (ed. 2) s.v., The stomach worm gnaws; I am hungry. **1812** [Southey] *Omniana* I. 229 The same man, sick, dyspeptic, and *stomach-worn. **1905** *Brit. Med. Jrnl.* 4 Mar. 471 The upper part of the *stomach wound was closed.

stomach ('stʌmək), *v.* Forms: see the sb. [f. STOMACH *sb.* Cf. L. *stomachārī* to be resentful, to be angry with, F. *s'estomaquer* to take offence.]

†**1.** *trans.* To be offended at, resent. *Obs.*

1523 CROMWELL in Merriman *Life & Lett.* (1902) I. 36, I stomak as a sory Subiect may doo, the high iniuries done by the saide Francoys. **1560** DAUS tr. *Sleidane's Comm.* 382 Than began he to stomack the matter, & was right sore offended. *a* **1591** H. SMITH *Restit. Nebuchadnezzar* 33 So God doth stomacke sinnes in those that beare his owne person. **1611** B. JONSON *Catiline* III. F 1 b, Publicke report, That giues you out, to stomacke your repulse. **1649** MILTON *Eikon.* 110 Parlament is call'd, not by the King, but by the Law, to be his Counselers & Dictators, though he stomac it. **1678** *Lively Oracles* II. ix. 246 We daily..receive those things with contentment..from an intimate..which if spoken by a stranger or enemy, would be despis'd or stomach'd. **1739** GRAY *Let.* Poems (1775) 47 Moreover I think I have reason to stomach your last piece of gravity. **1741** RICHARDSON *Pamela* (1824) I. 115 In such a manner as might show I would not disoblige on purpose, though I stomached this matter very heavily too. **1780** JOHNSON in *Boswell* (1904) II. 341 An Englishman would have stomached it, and been sulky. *a* **1825** FORBY *Voc. E. Anglia*, *Stomach*, to resent.

†**b.** with clause or infinitive as obj. *Obs.*

1587 NORTON tr. *Calvin's Inst.* IV. vii. (ed. 4) 377 *marg.*, The Bishop of Rome stomaking that the Bishop of Constantinople should come so neere as to bee made by a coun-cell next him in authoritie. **1594** *Mirr. Policy* (1599) K ij, When as Iulius Cæsar scorning a superior, and Pompey stomacking to haue any equall to himselfe, did both striue for the principality. *a* **1641** BP. MOUNTAGU *Acts & Mon.* (1642) 289 Alexander..stomacked that Antipater was all in all with his Father.

c. To be offended with (a person).

a **1548** HALL *Chron., Hen. IV*, 30 Jhon duke of Burgogn.. stomaked and envied the Duke of Orliance. **1583** STOCKER *Civ. Warres Lowe C.* IV. 52 b, The Magistrate and all the Citezeins did wonderfully stomacke the Catholickes, in so muche, that [etc.]. **1652–62** HEYLIN *Cosmogr.* III. (1676) 222/1 Both Nations hated by the Natives..but of the two the Spaniard looked on by the people as the more a Gentleman; the other stomached and despised for their sordid dealings. **1671** WOODHEAD *St. Teresa* II. ii. 6, I was very much stomacked by all my Monastery, because I would erect another, more recluse.

†**d.** *intr.* To take offence, feel resentment. *Obs.*

1567 PALFREYMAN *Baldwin's Mor. Philos.* To Rdr. (1600) A vj b, Not as though I..should swell or stomack against any man. **1591** SAVILE *Tacitus, Hist.* II. xxviii. 69 The Auxiliaries mourned the Legions stomacked. **1648** GAGE *West Ind.* 208 The good Archbishop..corrected some things in it..which we already hear they have stomached at. **1650** S. CLARKE *Eccl. Hist* (1654) I. 142 Herodias rageth afresh, stomacketh anew. *a* **1662** HEYLIN *Laud* (1668) 359 The Archbishop had long stomackt at the Insolencies of Matthews. **1706** PHILLIPS (ed. Kersey), To *Stomach* or *Stomach at*, to be angry at, to resent a thing. **1706** J. SERGEANT *Acc. Chapter Bp. Chalcedon* (1853) 85 The Cardinals..who..stomached at the authority of the chapter.

†**2.** *trans.* To excite the indignation of, to offend, vex. *Obs.*

1588 A. MUNDAY *Palmerin of Eng.* I. xi. (1639) E 1 b, Palmerin was chosen chiefe Defendant, which somewhat did stomack the sonnes of Primaleon. **1652–62** HEYLIN *Cosmogr.* III. (1676) 136/1 These insolent and unsufferable pranks committed so commonly by these masterful slaves so exceedingly stomached Bajazet the second, that [etc.]. **1675** ALSOP *Anti-Sozzo* 693 But the Apostle has said enough in this Chapter to stomack the Pride and Restifness of humane Wisdom.

3. To turn the stomach of, to nauseate. *rare.*

1796 ELIZA HAMILTON *Lett. Hindoo Rajah* (1811) II. 298 Some of us were so much stomached, that we did not much like to go. **1866** HOWELLS *Venet. Life* 76 It is not that the restaurants are very dirty—if you wipe your plate and glass carefully before using them, they need not stomach you.

†**4.** To inspire with resentment, fury or courage; to incite. *Obs.*

1541 PAYNEL *Catiline* xxxix. 56 b, Tell me I pray you, wherto serueth that oration? was it to stomake you ageynst the conspiracy [L. *an uti vos infestos conjurationi faceret*]? **1545** BALE *Image Both Ch.* I. vi. (1550) F j, When he had stomaked theim by the holy ghost, to shote forth his worde without feare. *a* **1548** HALL *Chron., Hen. VII*, 7 To encourage, stomacke and entyce many other to be aiders, assisters & partakers of the same conspiracy. *Ibid., Hen. VIII*, 163 b, Which fordele might perchance so stomacke him yͭ he would agre to no new condicions nor agrementes.

5. To brook, endure, put up with, tolerate.

1677 SIR H. CAPELL in *Essex Papers* (Camden) II. 128 Treas[urer] ill stomachs Ormond's carrying this businesse. **1814** LADY BURGHERSH *Lett.* (1893) 232, I confess I cannot stomach treating these people *de princes.* **1814** SCOTT *Wav.* lvii, So that Fergus was compelled to stomach this supposed affront. **1845** JAMES *Arrah Neil* vi, Dry stomached the affront till the time came for his revenge. **1861** HUGHES *Tom Brown Oxf.* xlii, In the end he could not stomach such a backsliding. **1862** *London Rev.* 30 Aug. 190 He cannot stomach 'a filthy compound of bones and alum'. **1874** *Slang Dict.* 311 *Stomach*, to bear with, to be partial to. Mostly used in a negative character,—as, 'I can't stomach that.' **1880** L. TENNYSON in *19th Cent.* Jan. 67 The first two evils he was obliged to stomach as best he might. **1887** BESANT *World went* iii, The study of the Latin language..he could not stomach. **1894** BARING-GOULD *Kitty Alone* III. 49 But that Pepperill's niece..should have the temerity to refuse his son was a fact he could not stomach.

6. To take into or retain on the stomach, to digest. *nonce-use.*

1822 PRAED *Poems* (1866) I. 66 Iron and steel, for an early meal, He stomached with ease. **1854** S. DOBELL *Balder* i. 3 Vales, mountains, trees, And stones of home,..anon Are stomached by mine hunger.

7. To climb by laying the stomach against.

1884 *Century Mag.* Dec. 195/1 Now creeping under an up-rooted tree..; then 'stomaching' a prostrate log three or four feet in height.

stomach-ache ('stʌmək,eɪk). Pain in the stomach or abdomen. Also *fig.*

1763 BICKERSTAFF *Love in Village* III. ix, Well, aunt, you have been complaining of the stomach-ach all day. **1839** J. H. NEWMAN *Lett.* (1891) II. 286, I must confess it has given me a stomach-ache. **1897** *Allbutt's Syst. Med.* IV. 241 In lead colic the more or less persistent 'stomach ache'..will usually assist in the diagnosis.

Hence **stomach-achey** *a.* (*nonce-wd.*) productive of stomach-ache.

1860 H. MAYHEW *Upper Rhine* ii. 65 A pickle that may be excellent..but which is sad stomach-achey wash. **1885** 'L. MALET' *Col. Enderby's Wife* III. ix, What a windy, stomach-achy sort of reward it promises to be!

stomachal ('stɒməkəl), *a.* [ad. mod.L. *stomachālis*, f. L. *stomach-us* STOMACH *sb.*: see -AL[1]. Cf. F. *stomacal* (in 16th c. *-chal*), Sp. *estomacal*, It. *stomacale.*]

1. Pertaining to the stomach, gastric; of the nature of or serving the purpose of a stomach.

1582 HESTER *Secr. Fiorav.* I. xxxviii. 45 Flebothomie euacuateth the stomochall humors that are cause of that corruption [in gout]. **1683** SNAPE *Anat. Horse* I. ix. (1686) 18 The Stomachal Arteries are twigs from the Coeliacal branch of the *Arteria magna.* **1841** *Penny Cycl.* XXI. 425/2 A curved longitudinal furrow, which circumscribes laterally the stomachal region. **1859** G. H. LEWES *Physiol.* I. iii. 201 Our knowledge of the stomachal process has been rendered more accurate. **1860** *Encycl. Brit.* XXI. 1000/1 Near the middle of the body the canal is dilated into a stomachal cavity. **1861** HULME tr. *Moquin-Tandon* II. VII. ii. 344 The alimentary canal [of the Oxyurus] has the appearance of three stomachal dilatations which succeed each other. **1871** W. A. HAMMOND *Dis. Nerv. Syst.* 49 In stomachal vertigo the attacks of dizziness are often severe. **1896** A. WILLEY in *Q. Jrnl. Microsc. Sci.* XXXIX. 336 The stomachal axis of Ctenoplana.

2. Of remedies: Good for the stomach.

1599 A. M. tr. *Gabelhouer's Bk. Physicke* 117/1 An excellent stomachalle pouldre. **1603** FLORIO *Montaigne* II. xxxvii. 436 Let her hardly remit this vocall lithernesse vnto evill, if it be neyther cordiall, nor stomacall. **1612** WOODALL *Surg. Mate* Wks. (1653) 63 They are very stomachal, for they refresh much the stomack. **1707** *Curios. Husb. & Gard.* 235 Balm..is..stomachal and diuretick.

†'**stomachate**, *a. Sc. Obs.* In 6 -chat, -chait, -kat. [ad. L. *stomachātus*, pa. pple. of *stomachārī*: see STOMACH *v.*] Indignant, angry.

c **1550** ROLLAND *Crt. Venus* II. 563 Richt stomakat in hart ay haiffand dreid. *Ibid.* III. 253 Than Venus said in mind half stomachat, Of the assyis nane salbe alterat. *Ibid.* IV. 227 For I lang eir was sa hie stomachait At Desperance for his greit rebellioun.

stomached ('stʌməkt), *a.* and *ppl. a.* Forms: see STOMACH *sb.* [f. STOMACH *sb.* and *v.* + -ED.]

1. Having a stomach. In quots. only as the second element of parasynthetic formations, having a stomach of the specified kind or condition.

1540 HYRDE tr. *Vives' Instr. Chr. Wom.* (1592) R 2, Likewise as of men, he who is most like stomacked unto a woman, nor lusty couraged, wil remember injurie longest. **1567** MAPLET *Gr. Forest* 83 b, There are some so eger and stout stomaked that they haue [etc.]. **1589** GREENE *Menaphon* (Arb.) 86 And with that Carmela was so full stomackt that she wept. **1615** S. WARD *Coal fr. Altar* 79 This want of reformation makes the queasie stomacked Brownists cast them selues out of our Church. **1710** FULLER *Pharm. Extemp.* a 3, When Patients are so weak Stomach'd..that they cannot..admit of the Bark. **1843** JAMES *Forest Days* (1847) 66 A jolly, large-stomached personage.

†**2.** In senses of STOMACH *v.*: Offended; incited, encouraged. *Obs.*

1599 JAS. I *Basil. Doron* To Rdr. (1603) A 4 b, I will the more narrowly rippe up the wordes, whereat they seeme to bee somewhat stomacked. **1623** COCKERAM I, *Stomaked*, angered, hartened. *c* **1712** G. GUTHRIE in *Monogr.* (1900) 10 Alexander suggested to his father that if he would allow him he could make money by his skill in musick, which the stomached father resented with no less than a pistoll.

stomacher[1] ('stʌmətʃə(r), 'stʌməkə(r)). Forms: 5 **stomakere, stomechere, stomachyr,** 5–6 **stomachere,** 5–6, 8 **stomager,** 6 **stomackger,** (8 **stomatcher**), 6– **stomacher.** [app. f. STOMACH *sb.* + -ER[1]: but see below.

The alleged F. *estomachier* appears to be recorded only by Palsgrave. If it be genuine, and the source of the Eng. word, it would account for the pronunciation ('stʌmətʃə(r)), which is given in the pronouncing dictionaries of Kenrick (1773), Sheridan (1780), Walker (1791), Smart (1836), Worcester (1860), in Cassell's *Encyclopædic Dict.* (1888), and in *Webster's Dict.* (1828–1886). The genuineness of this pronunciation is attested by the spellings *stomager* (1450, 1727), *stomackger* (1575), *stomatcher* (17..), and *stomacher* (*c* 1450 onwards): the spelling with *k* is evidenced only once (*c* 1466), though the word occurs frequently in writers who wrote the word *stomach* with *k*. The pronunciation ('stʌməkə(r)) was given by Ogilvie *Imperial Dict.* (1850) and appears in later editions of that work and in recent U.S. dicts. It is not impossible that *estomachier* was really formed in late Anglo-French, and is the source of the Eng. word. For the sense cf. the misuse of *stomach* for 'chest' (STOMACH *sb.* 3).]

†**1.** ? A waistcoat or pectoral of mail. *Obs. rare*[−1].

1450 in *Rep. MSS. Ld. Middleton* (1911) 114, I will..my felowe John Shipton for to have my dubbelet of mayell, my stomager of mayell, and a salet.

†**2.** A kind of waistcoat worn by men. *Obs.*

c **1450** *Coventry Myst.* (Shaks. Soc.) 241 A stomachere of clere reynes. **1466** *Mann. & Househ. Exp.* (Roxb.) 382 Item, the same day my mastyr paid fore a stomakere of velvet, ij.s. iiij.d. **1478** *Paston Lett.* III. 237, I beseche yow to sende me a hose clothe..and a stomechere and ij schyrtes. **1508–13** *Bk. Keruynge* in *Babees Bk* (1868) 282 Than warme his petycote, his doublet, and his stomachere. **1530** PALSGR. 276/2 Stomacher for one's brest, *estomachier.* **1575** TURBERV. *Falconrie* 16 The furryers doe vse their skynnes for stomackgers, to guard and defend the brest against the force of feruent colde. **1617** MORYSON *Itin.* III. 167 They use large stomachers of furre or lambe skinnes. *a* **1625** FLETCHER *Mad Lover* III. i, Talking to an old man is like a stomacher, It keeps his blood warm. **1693** CONGREVE *Double Dealer* III. i. (1694) 33 The first Favour he receiv'd from her was a piece of an old Scarlet Petticoat for a Stomacher. *a* **1700** EVELYN *Diary* May 1645 (Lucca), Embroidred stomachers generaly worn by gentlemen in these countries. **1702** BAYNARD *Cold Baths* II. (1709) 375 He wore a quilted Stomacher. **1715** tr. *Pancirollus' Rerum Mem.* I. IV. ii. 147 They wore also Stomachers, but in cold Weather most commonly woollen Shirts.

†**b.** A medicated cloth applied to the chest. *Obs.*

1577 FRAMPTON *Joyfull Newes* I. 7 In griefes of the Stomake, it [this plaister] doth a merueilous effect, applied after the maner of a Stomacher. **1584** COGAN *Haven Health* xlviii. 56 The herbe..put in a lynnen bagge and laide as a stomager next the skinne comforteth a colde stomacke well. **1682** *Digby's Chym. Secr.* II. 203 Take Wormwood..; of these make a Stomacher, and apply it.

3. An ornamental covering for the chest (often covered with jewels) worn by women under the lacing of the bodice.

1535 COVERDALE *Isa.* iii. 24 Instead of a stomacher [so **1560** (Geneva), **1611**, **1884** (Revised)], a sack cloth. **1566** *Engl. Ch. Furniture* (Peacock 1866) 56 Wherof his wief made of one a stomacher for her wench. **1580** LYLY *Euphues Eng.* To Ladies (Arb.) 222 If a Tailour make your gowne too little, you couer his fault with a broad stomacher. **1611** SHAKS. *Wint. T.* IV. iii. 226 Golden Quoifes, and Stomachers For my Lads, to giue their deers. **1653** H. COGAN *Diodorus Sic.* 161 The Goddesse Minerva..killed this cruell monster, and of her skinne made her selfe a stomacher. **1688** HOLME *Armoury* III. 94/2 The Stomacher is that peece as lieth under the lacing or binding on of the Body of the Gown. **1702** *Lond. Gaz.* No. 3806/8 Lost.., a Diamond Stomacher with a row of Rose Diamonds down the middle. *c* **1710** CELIA FIENNES *Diary* (1888) 252 Their stomatchers some were all Diamonds. **1727** DORRINGTON *Philip Quarll* 163 Which seem'd to adorn her Bosom far more than the richest Stomager made of Diamonds or Pearls could do. **1731** *Gentl. Mag.* I. 289 Sometimes the stomacher rises almost to the chin. **1737** *Ibid.* VII. 513/2 The Princess of Wales had on an exceeding rich Stomacher. **1761** *Brit. Mag.* II. 446 The rich diamond stomacher for our intended queen is quite finished. **1837** DICKENS *Pickw.* xlix, An old-fashioned green velvet dress, with a long waist and stomacher. **1868** *Morn. Star* 7 Mar., Ornaments: Diamond necklace and stomacher. **1880** *Cassell's Family Mag.* VI. 758/2 Several of the winter dresses are laced in front over a stomacher.

attrib. **1753** *Lond. Mag.* Sept. 396/2 Before, for your breast, pin a stomacher bib on.

†**b.** *transf.*

1611 SHAKS. *Cymb.* III. iv. 86 Away, away Corrupters of my Faith, you [*sc.* letters that she had carried in her bosom] shall no more Be Stomachers to my heart. **1613** DONNE *Epithalam.* 8 The houshold Bird with the red stomacher. **1717** J. DENNIS *Orig. Lett.* (1721) I. 33 You look full over Box Hill, and see the Country beyond it,..and, over the very Stomacher of it, see St. Paul's at five and twenty Miles Distance.

†'**stomacher**[2]. *Obs.* In 7 **stomaker.** [f. STOMACH *v.* + -ER[1].] One who 'stomachs' or resents.

1608 CHAPMAN *Byron's Trag.* v. R 3, By my loue.. command them To..proue no stomakers of my misfortunes.

stomacher[3] ('stʌməkə(r)). *Pugilism.* [f. STOMACH *sb.* + -ER[1].] A blow on the stomach.

1814 *Sporting Mag.* XLIII. 68 B. gave C. a stomacher. **1831** *Blackw. Mag.* XXX. 979 [He] seems to have given his adversary a facer and a stomacher, right and left. **1832** MARRYAT *N. Forster* xlvii, A stomacher, and both down!

stomachful ('stʌməkfʊl), *sb.* [f. STOMACH *sb.* + -FUL[2].] As much as will fill one's stomach.

1865 G. MACDONALD *Alec Forbes* II. xxv. 238 Ye'll be laid up yersel' gin ye dinna get a stammachfu' o' the caller air noo and than. **1891** HERMAN *His Angel* viii. 179, I guess you've had your stomachful of the law.

†'**stomachful**, *a. Obs.* [f. STOMACH *sb.* + -FUL[1].] Full of 'stomach' (STOMACH *sb.* 8).

1. Obstinate, self-willed. (Often said of horses; also of children.)

1600 SURFLET *Country Farm* I. xxiii. 130 If he [the ox] be stomackfull,..cause him to smell your hande oftentimes, that so hee may be acquainted with you. **1610** HOLLAND *Camden's Brit.* I. 623 A very shrewd, stout, and malapert stomackfull woman. **1633** T. ADAMS *Exp. 2 Peter* ii. 12. 835 A stomackfull horse, that will not be stopp'd in his carrier with the sharpest bit. **1643** T. GOODWIN *Trial Chr. Growth* 154 Like a stomachfull boy, that cryes he cannot have the victory, yet is weak, and easily laid on his back. **1676** MARVELL *Mr. Smirke* 61 (bis) But the few sincere or stomachful Bishops..expiated so in some measure, what they had committed in the Nicene Council. **1690** LOCKE *Educ.* §112 The obstinate or stomachful crying [of children] should by no means be permitted. **1710** M. HENRY *Expos. O. & N.T.* (1725) III. 522/2 A stomachful high-spirited Child must be subdued betimes. **1778** FOOTE *Trip to Calais* II. Wks. 1799 II. 361 You sullen, sulking, stomachful slut! **1797** MRS. A. M. BENNETT *Beggar Girl* (1813) V. 38, I suppose you was too stomachful to wait on her after the gentle-man died. **1828** CARR *Craven Gloss.*, *Stomach-full*, proud, obstinate.

2. Resentful, angry, malignant.
1610 Bp. Hall *Apol. agst. Brownists* Ep. Ded. 2 From the other, I receiued..a stomakfull Pamphlet. **1625** Purchas *Pilgrims* II. 1216 Thomas Becket was slaine in his Church at Canterburie..by..Courtiers..which had heard some stomackfull speeches of the King, touching the said Archbishop. **1765** J. Adams *Diary* 29 Dec., Wks. 1850 II. 169 Major Miller, forsooth, is very fearful that they will be stomachful at home, and angry and resentful.

3. Spirited, courageous.
1610 Guillim *Heraldry* III. xiv. (1660) 172 The Males are more stomachfull, and of greater courage than the Females. **1658** tr. *Porta's Nat. Magick* II. vi. 37 We see, how to generate a dog as stomackful as a Lion. **1676** Wycherley *Pl. Dealer* III. i. (1677) 39 Nay, but if I had but any Body to stand by me, I am as stomachful as another. **1809** W. Irving *Knickerb.* v. viii. (1861) 173 In the interim the stomachful heroes of Pyquag would have been choked with their own onions.

Hence †'**stomachfully** *adv.*; †'**stomachfulness**.
1611 Cotgr., *Ireusement*, irefully, wrathfully, stomackefully. **1614** Bp. Hall *Contempl.* v. *Golden Calf* 117 While so many thousand Israelites were slaine, that had stomachfully desired the Idoll. **1621** T. Granger *Eccles.* ix. 17. 248 Pride, stomachfulnesse, headinesse,..auaile little. **1664-5** Pepys *Diary* 28 Feb., I..did give her very provoking words, ..which she took very stomachfully, and reproached me justly with mine. **1682** Bunyan *Holy War* (1905) 302, I have often heard him say, and that with great stomachfulness, that he believed that there was neither God, Angel, nor Spirit. **1747** Richardson *Clarissa* (1749) II. 113 Only this Miss, That your stomachfulness had swallowed up your stomach. **1755** Johnson, *Chuffily*, surlily, stomachfully.

stomachic (stəʊˈmækɪk), *a.* and *sb.* [ad. L. *stomachicus*, a. Gr. στομαχικός, f. στόμαχ-ος stomach *sb.*: see -ic. Cf. F. *stomachique*, Sp. *estomáquico*, Pg. *estomachico*, It. *stomachico*.]

A. *adj.*

1. Of or pertaining to the stomach; gastric.
1656 Blount *Glossogr.* s.v. *Vein*, Stomachick vein (*vena stomachica*). **1677** tr. *Groeneveldt's Treat. Stone* 33 The stomachic branch of the sixt pair. **1690** J. Edwards *Demonstr. Exist. God* II. (1696) 60 Others hold that this stomachick ferment proceeds immediately from the blood. **1771** *Encycl. Brit.* I. 254/2 The stomachic plexus, formed by the eighth pair [of nerves]. **1799** *Med. Jrnl.* II. 398 The author..treats..of the great stomachic gland. **1808** Scott in *Lockhart* I. i. 49, I have..only had to complain of occasional headaches or stomachic affections. **1856** Emerson *Eng. Traits, Manners* Wks. (Bohn) II. 46 The Englishman speaks with all his body. His elocution is stomachic—as the American's is labial. **1875** H. C. Wood *Therap.* (1879) 51 The nitrate of silver is..useful in stomachic..diseases. **1881** *Encycl. Brit.* XII. 630/2 Whilst the mullet has a fleshy stomach like a bird, others have no stomachic dilatation.

b. Of an ailment: Caused by disorder of the stomach.
1878 A. M'L. Hamilton *Nerv. Dis.* 123 Stomachic Vertigo is common, and is produced, directly after a hearty meal, or else when the stomach is entirely empty.

†**2.** Having or subject to disorder of the stomach.
1656 Blount *Glossogr.* **1661** Lovell *Hist. Anim. & Min.* 238 Patridge,..it helps the cœliack and stomachick persons.

3. Good for the stomach.
1665 G. Harvey *Disc. Plague* (1673) 146 Likewise Pestilential stomachick Emplasters applied to the Stomach. **1732** J. Martyn tr. *Tournefort's Hist. Plants* I. 91 The root is stomachick, pectoral, diuretick, and provokes the menses. **1754-64** Smellie *Midwifery* II. 45 He ordered..three or four ounces every morning of the following Stomachick wine. **1833** L. Ritchie *Wand. by Loire* 110 A red wine celebrated for its rich colour and stomachic qualities. **1846** Soyer *Cookery* 58 This potage, though complicated, is very easily made with a little practice; it is entirely new, very stomachic and wholesome. **1876** Dunglison *Med. Lex. Tinctura Absinthii Composita*...Tonic, stomachic, vermifuge, and carminative. **1899** *Allbutt's Syst. Med.* VIII. 550 A stomachic or febrifuge mixture.

B. *sb.* A stomachic medicine.
1735 Bracken in *Burdon's Pocket Farrier* 41 *note*, It is a better Stomachick than most Compounds out of an Apothecary's Shop. **1850** Dickens *Dav. Copp.* vii, It was exactly the compound one would have chosen for a stomachic.

Hence **sto'machicness**. *rare*$^{-0}$.
1727 Bailey vol. II, *Stomachickness*, stomachick Quality, or Helpfulness to the Stomach.

stomachical (stəʊˈmækɪkəl), *a.* and *sb.* [f. stomachic + -al[1].] **A.** *adj.*

1. = stomachic *a.* 1.
1601 Holland *Pliny* xx. xvii. II. 66 Dieuches used..to give also the seed beaten to pouder with Mints in wine, for ..the defluxion Stomachicall. **1651** Biggs *New Disp.* §285 Whatsoever is taken in a surfet, above the native power of the stomachicall ferment. **1708** *Brit. Apollo* No. 38. 3/2 You must Chasten your Belly, And forbear the Stomachical Prizes. **1822** L. Sturgeon (*title*) Essays, Moral, Philosophical, and Stomachical, on the..Science of Good-living.

2. = stomachic *a.* 3.
1603 F. Hering *Cert. Rules* (1625) B2, Take three or foure cordiall and stomachicall pilles. **1725** *Bradley's Family Dict.* s.v. *Balm*, Balm-mint..is stomachical, cordial, and excites the Appetite and Wind.

†**B.** *sb.* = stomachic B *Obs.*
1657 *Physical Dict.*, *Stomachicals*, medicines peculiar to the stomach. **1689** J. Moyle *Abstr. Sea Chyrurg.*, These are inferiour to no stomachicals in the whole World.

Hence **sto'machically** *adv.*
1684 tr. *Bonet's Merc. Compit.* xvi. 565 As when they say, A Man swoons stomachically. **1898** *Daily News* 12 Jan. 6/6 He seemed to suddenly double up as if stomachically stricken.

stomaching (ˈstʌməkɪŋ), *vbl. sb.* [f. stomach *v.* + -ing[1].] The action of stomach *v.*; †feeling or cherishing indignation or bitterness.
1549 Cheeke *Hurt Sedit.* (1641) 14 Where disobedience is thought stoutnesse, and sullennesse is counted manhood, and stomaking is courage. **1582** N. T. (Rhem.) *2 Cor.* xii. 20 Contentions, emulations, stomakings. **1606** Shaks. *Ant. & Cl.* II. ii. 9 Tis not a time for priuate stomacking. **1671** Woodhead *St. Teresa* II. 99 When it is with Perturbation, and Passion, Stomacking, and repining at the Prioress, let them take it for a manifest Temptation.

†'**stomaching**, *ppl. a. Obs.* [f. stomach *v.* + -ing[2].] Full of malignity; given to cherish anger or resentment.
1577-87 Holinshed *Hist. Scot.* 260/2 The whole nation, against which the chiefest part of his booke seemeth to be a stomaching inuectiue. **1579** Tomson *Calvin's Serm. Tim.* 859/1 Wee are so stomaking of nature, that if a man displease vs we woulde that God shoulde straight wayes lighten against him.

†**sto'machious**, *a. Obs.* [f. stomach *sb.* + -ious.] = stomachous.
1611 Speed *Hist. Gt. Brit.* ix. vi. §69 A Lady no lesse proud, and stomachious then himselfe.

stomachless (ˈstʌməklɪs), *a.* [f. stomach *sb.* + -less.]

†**1. a.** Having no appetite. **b.** Unresentful. *Obs.*
1626 in *Cosin's Corr.* I. (Surtees) 87 You will say this is nothing. I feele it some thing yet, being weake and stomacklesse. **1697** R. Pierce *Bath Mem.* I. ii. 31 He was Stomachless, nautiated every thing they offer'd him to eat. **1722** *Phil. Trans.* XXXII. 30 This Application produced no considerable Alteration in the Dog; he neither appear'd sleepy nor stomachless. **1727** Bailey vol. II, *Stomachless*, wanting an Appetite; also, not apt to resent.

2. Destitute of a stomach.
1865 H. J. Slack in *Intell. Observer* VII. 96 A stomachless, organless thing, like the Gregarina.

Hence '**stomachlessness**.
1657 Trapp *Comm. Job* xxxiii. 21. 292 What marvel if.. extreme stomacklesness cause leaness and deformity.

†**stoma'chosity**. *Obs.*$^{-0}$ [ad. assumed L. **stomachōsitās*, f. *stomachōs-us*: see stomachous *a.* and -ity.] 'Anger, indignation, disdain.'
1656 Blount *Glossogr.*, *Stomachosity*.

†'**stomachous**, *a. Obs.* [ad. L. *stomachōsus*, f. *stomach-us* stomach *sb.*: see -ous.] **a.** Spirited, courageous. **b.** Resentful, bitter, irascible; stubborn, obstinate.
1547 Recorde *Judic. Uryne* A iii, Stomachouse horses, whiche contemptuously passe by the barkynge of curres. **1590** Spenser *F.Q.* II. viii. 23 Who..with sterne lookes, and stomachous disdaine, Gaue signes of grudge and discontentment vaine. *a* **1641** Finett *Philox.* 163 These and other the like Stommachous Speeches he let fall in my hearing. **1658** Phillips, *Stomachous*, angry, disdainfull.

Hence †'**stomachously** *adv.*
1593 G. Harvey *New Lett.* A3, I haue often bene compassionatly sory (or shall I say? stomachously angry) to read how [etc.].

stomachy (ˈstʌməkɪ), *a.* [f. stomach *sb.* + -y.]

1. Ready to take offence, irritable. *dial.*
1825 Jennings *Observ. Dial. W. Eng.* 73 *Stomachy*, obstinate, proud, haughty. **1829** Brockett *N.C. Gloss.* (ed. 2), *Stomachy*, easily offended, resentful—stomachful. **1876** Hardy *Ethelberta* xlvi, 'Now never be stomachy, my good soul,' cried Sol from the fireplace.

2. High-spirited. *dial.*
1896 Baring-Gould *Broom-Squire* i. 3 'He's a stomachy (sturdy) young chap,' she said, patting the babe with the now disengaged hand.

3. Big-bellied, paunchy. *dial.*
1889 Stevenson *Ballantrae* 21 A little, bald, solemn, stomachy man, a great professor of piety.

4. Of the voice or vocal sounds: deeply resonant, as if produced in the stomach. *colloq.*
1936 E. M. Forster *Abinger Harvest* II. 101 The soloist.. invites his 'friends' in a stomachy voice to rise in their shirt-fronts and shout. **1975** 'D. Rutherford' *Mystery Tour* iv. 71 His rich stomachy laugh.

stomager, obs. form of stomacher.

stomapod (ˈstɒməpɒd), *a.* and *sb. Zool.* [f. mod.L. *Stomapoda* neut. pl. (Latreille, 1817), irreg. f. Gr. στόμα mouth + ποδ-, πούς foot.] = stomatopod.
1833 Griffith tr. *Cuvier* XIII. 240 The Squillæ have received the denomination of Stomapods. *a* **1843** *Encycl. Metrop.* (1845) VII. 275/2 The two most highly developed Orders [of Crustaceans], viz. the Decapod and Stomapod. **1857** Agassiz *Contrib. Nat. Hist. U.S.* I. 110 In the classification of Dana, his first type embraces Decapods and Stomapods.

So **stoma'podiform** *a.*, having the form of, or resembling, a stomapod: applied to certain insect larvæ. **sto'mapodous** *a.* = *stomapod*; also applied to the mouth in certain arachnids, etc. when resembling or analogous to that of a stomapod crustacean.
1826 Kirby & Sp. *Entomol.* III. xxx. 165 [Primary Forms of Larvæ.] Stomapodiform... Ex. *Mantis. Ibid.* IV. xlvi. 309 Mouth... Stomapodous... When the Legs and Sternum act the part of Maxillæ, Labium, and Palpi. Ex. *Araneidæ*, *Scolopendra*, &c.

stomata, plural of stoma.

stomatal (ˈstɒmətəl, ˈstəʊ-), *a. Bot.* and *Zool.* [f. Gr. στοματ-, στόμα (see stoma) + -al[1].] Pertaining to or connected with a stoma or stomata; of the nature of a stoma; *loosely*, having stomata, stomatous.
1861 Bentley *Man. Bot.* 43 Generally..the stomatal cells are placed nearly or quite on a level with those of the epidermis. In other cases,..the stomatal cells are below the epidermal ones, while in some rare instances again they are above them. **1894** F. Darwin & Acton *Physiol. Plants* 93 Stomatal transpiration. **1897** *Nature* 17 June 167/1 The stomatal surface of a leaf.

stomate (ˈstəʊmət), *sb. Bot.* [app. formed as an Eng. sing. for the pl. *stomata*: see stoma. Cf. F. *stomate*, and stigmate.] = stoma 2.
1835 Lindley *Introd. Bot.* (1848) I. 137 In most plants the cuticle has..openings..called Stomates, Stomata, or Stomatia. *Ibid.* 141 Another singular kind of stomate. **1877** Huxley & Martin *Elem. Biol.* 73 Stomates are absent in the epidermis of the root.

stomate, *a. rare*$^{-0}$. [app. f. stoma + -ate[2]; but prob. a fiction of mod. Dicts. due to mistaking the sb. (see prec.) for an adj.] 'Having stomata' (Ogilvie *Suppl.* 1855: hence in later Dicts.).

stomatic (stəʊˈmætɪk), *a.* and *sb.* [ad. mod.L. *stomaticus*, a. Gr. στοματικός, f. στοματ-, στόμα mouth: see stoma and -ic. Cf. F. *stomatique*, It. *stomatico*, Sp. *estomático*. (The sb. is in L. *stomaticē*, a. Gr. στοματική, fem. of the adj.).]

1. a. *adj.* Of a medicine: Good for diseases of the mouth. **b.** *sb.* A 'stomatic' medicine. ? *Obs.*
The explanation in quot. 1656 is app. an error. In the bracketed quots. the word is misused for *stomachic*; the same blunder has been common in Fr., Sp., and It.
1656 Blount *Glossogr.*, *Stomatick*..that hath a sore or swelling in the mouth. **1657** Tomlinson *Renou's Disp.* I. vi. 10 *Stomatick* [medicaments] to the mouth. [**1678** Salmon *Lond. Disp.* 588/1 It is designed for a Stomatick to comfort and warm a cold and weak Stomach. **1683** —— *Doron Med.* II. 174 It is a good Cephalick, 'Stomatick' and hysterick. **1699** —— *Bate's Disp.* (1713) 242/1 Besides all this, it is an excellent Stomatick, strengthens the Ventricle, causes..a quick Digestion. **1741** *Compl. Family-Piece* I. i. 3 Take of the Stomatick-Pill with Gums.] **1857** Dunglison *Med. Lex.* s.v., Dentifrices, masticatories, &c., are stomatics.

2. *Bot.* and *Zool.* = stomatal.
1835 Lindley *Introd. Bot.* (1848) I. 141 The stomatic apparatus. **1890** *Hardwicke's Sci.-Gossip* XXVI. 172/2 The stomatic cells.

So †**sto'matical** *a. Obs.*
In the bracketed quots. the word is misused for *stomachical*; cf. the similar misuse of stomatic.
[**1547** Boorde *Brev. Health* ccclviii. 115 Let the pacient purge hym selfe..with pylles stomaticall.] **1601** Holland *Pliny* XXIII. vii. II. 170 This was the stomaticall medicine [L. *Hæc erat stomatice*] of the auncients. [**1662** Chandler *Van Helmont's Oriat.* 201 This is a sharp, hungry, stomatical [L. *stomachicum*], specifical, and humane ferment.]

stomatiferous (stɒməˈtɪfərəs), *a. Bot.* [f. mod.L. *stomat-* stoma + -(i)ferous.] Bearing stomata.
1866 *Treas. Bot.* 1101/2 *Stomatiferous*, bearing stomates.

‖**stomatitis** (stɒməˈtaɪtɪs, stəʊ-). *Path.* [mod.L. f. Gr. στοματ-, στόμα mouth + -itis.] Inflammation of the mucous membrane of the mouth.
1859 J. Tomes *Dental Surg.* 508 Follicular stomatitis is commonly associated with eruptions about the face and lips. **1899** *Allbutt's Syst. Med.* VIII. 527, I have traced the connection of impetigo with..ulcerative stomatitis [etc.].

Hence **stomatitic** (-ˈɪtɪk) *a.*, pertaining to or affected with stomatitis.
1901 *Lancet* 20 July 133/1 Those unhappy children who are born with teeth—blighted probably by stomatitic inflammation in utero—which are teeth but in name.

‖**stomatium** (stəʊˈmeɪʃ(ɪ)əm). Pl. **-ia**. [mod.L. dim. of stoma, on Gr. type *στομάτιον.] = stoma.
835 [see stomate]. **1866** *Treas. Bot.*, *Stomate*, *Stomatium*.

stomato- (ˈstɒmətəʊ, ˈstəʊ-), repr. Gr. στοματο-, combining form of στοματ-, στόμα mouth (see stoma): occurring in modern scientific terms, chiefly zoological. ‖ˌ**stomato'dendron** (pl. **-dendra**) [Gr. δένδρον tree], each of the dendritic branches bearing minute polyps in the family *Rhizostomidæ* of hydrozoans. ˌ**stomato'gastric** *a.* [gastric], pertaining to or connected with the mouth and stomach; applied to a system of visceral nerves in invertebrates. '**stomato**ˌ**gnath** [Gr. γνάθος jaw], a generic term for the hard structures or 'teeth' in the stomodæum of various classes of animals, as molluscs, crustaceans, annelids, rotifers, etc. **stoma'tology** [-logy], the scientific study of the mouth; hence ˌ**stomato'logical** *a.*, relating to stomatology; **stoma'tologist**, one versed in stomatology. '**stomato'morphous** (-ˈmɔːfəs), *a.*

Bot. [Gr. μορφή form], mouth-shaped. **'stomato,plasty** [-PLASTY], plastic surgery of the mouth (or of the *os uteri*); hence **,stomato'plastic** *a.*, pertaining to stomatoplasty. **stoma'toporoid** *a.* [f. mod.L. *Stomatopora* (f. Gr. πόρος pore) + -OID], resembling or characteristic of a coral of the fossil genus *Stomatopora*. **'stomato,scope** (-skəʊp) [-SCOPE], an instrument for examining the interior of the mouth. See also STOMATOPOD.

1859 HUXLEY *Oceanic Hydrozoa* 18 In the *Rhizostomidæ*, a complex tree-like mass, whose branches, the *stomatodendra, end in, and are covered with, minute polypites..is suspended from the middle of the umbrella. **1848** CARPENTER *Anim. Phys.* 342 Other small ganglia and nerves, connected with..mastication and digestion..are called *stomato-gastric. **1895** D. SHARP *Insects* I. 120 Stomato-gastric nerves of Cockroach. **1900** W. B. BENHAM in *Proc. Zool. Soc. 982 note*, I would suggest ..'*stomatognath' as a convenient term by which to refer to the various chitinous, or calcified, or siliceous 'teeth' or 'jaws' occurring as specialized thickenings of the lining of the stomodæum. **1913** *Times* 13 Aug. 3/3 At the final session of the *Stomatological Section the subject of dental disease as a cause of pain in remote parts of the body was discussed. **1913** *Publ. Opinion* 15 Aug. 166/2 The *stomatologists of the Medical Congress held a meeting in the Dental Hospital. **1895** *Westm. Gaz.* 22 June 8/1 The Science of *Stomatology. **1866** *Treas. Bot.* 1101/2 **Stomatomorphous*, mouth-shaped. **1857** DUNGLISON *Med. Lex.*, **Stomatoplastic*, **Stomatoplasty*. **1860** R. FOWLER *Med. Vocab.*, *Stomatoplasty*, the operation for remedying a contracted aperture of the mouth. **1880** *Brit. Med. Jrnl.* 27 Mar. 483/2 Stomatoplasty.—Dr. Mapother described a case of contracted mouth and nostrils from cicatrices after lupus. **1889** E. A. WALFORD in *Q. Jrnl. Geol. Soc.* XLV. III. 566 The interweaving of the *Stomatoporoid branches gives rise to another phase of growth, Tubuliporoid. **1855** DUNGLISON *Med. Lex.*, *Stomatoscope. **1866** *Sci. Rev.* July 62/3 The Stomatoscope..promises to be very useful in dental surgery,..It consists of a spiral wire of platinum..enclosed in a box-wood cup, and..brought to a red heat by the current..from a small galvanic battery; and a small mirror which reflects the light.

stomato'dæum. *Embryology.* [Intended as a correction (after *stomato-*) of the irregularly-formed STOMODÆUM.] = STOMODÆUM. Hence **stomatodæal** *a.* = STOMODÆAL.

1887 A. M. MARSHALL & HURST *Jun. Zool.* 141 The stomatodœum or anterior portion of the [alimentary] canal [of a crayfish]. **1888** HUXLEY & MARTIN *Elem. Biol.* (ed. 2) 171 The stomatodæum; a sac-like involution of the epidermis abutting against [the mesenteron]. **1893** A. M. MARSHALL *Vertebr. Embryol.* 148 The stomatodæal pit rapidly deepens.

stomatode ('stɒmətəʊd), *a.* and *sb.* *Zool.* [f. mod.L. *Stomatōda* neut. pl., irreg. f. Gr. στοματ-, στόμα mouth, on the supposed analogy of names like *Cestoda, Nematoda.*] **a.** *adj.* Pertaining to the *Stomatoda*, a group of *Protozoa* characterized by having a mouth. **b.** *sb.* A member of the *Stomatoda*.

1870 H. A. NICHOLSON *Man. Zool.* I. 59 The Infusoria, or Stomatode Protozoa.

stomatopod ('stɒmətəʊ,pɒd), *a.* and *sb.* *Zool.* [f. mod.L. *Stomatopoda* neut. pl., later and more correct form for Latreille's *Stomapoda*: see STOMAPOD.] **a.** *adj.* Belonging to the *Stomatopoda*, an order of malacostracous crustaceans, orig. (in form *Stomapoda*: see STOMAPOD) synonymous with *Gastrura*, now restricted to the family *Squillidæ*. **b.** *sb.* A stomatopod crustacean.

1877 HUXLEY *Anat. Inv. Anim.* vi. 361, I believe that the tergum of the seventh (or first thoracic) somite is obsolete, as in a Stomatopod.

So **stomatopodous** (-'ɒpədəs), *a.* = prec. **a.**

stomatous ('stɒmətəs), *a.* [f. mod.L. *stomat-* STOMA + -OUS.] Having or furnished with stomata. Also **'stomatose** *a.*

1880 WEBSTER Suppl., *Stomatous*. **1909** *Cent. Dict.* Suppl., *Stomatose*.

'stomber, *v. Obs.* exc. *dial.* [var. of *stamber*, STAMMER *v.*]

1. *intr.* To stumble.

1588 A. KING tr. *Canisius' Catech., Certane Prayers* 34 Thame that hes stombered thow liftes vp agane. **1879** MISS JACKSON *Shropsh. Word-bk.*, *Stombering*, walking in a heavy, stamping, stumbling way.

2. *trans.* To confuse. (Cf. STAMMER *v.* 4.)

1841 HARTSHORNE *Salop. Ant.* Gloss., *Stomber*, to confuse. **1879** MISS JACKSON *Shropsh. Word-bk.*, *Stombered*, confused. 'I got stombered o'er it.'

stomble, stomel(e, obs. forms of STUMBLE.

stomere, var. STUMMER *v. Obs.*, to stumble.

stomiatoid ('stəʊ-, 'stɒmɪətɔɪd), *sb.* and *a.* *Zool.* [f. mod.L. name of suborder *Stomiatoidei*, f. generic name *Stomias* (H. R. Schinz in G.L.C.F.D. Cuvier *Thierreich* (1822) II. 310), f. Gr. στόμ-α mouth + -IA[2]: see -OID.] **A.** *sb.* A deep-sea fish of the suborder Stomiatoidei, distinguished by a large mouth and rows of photophores on its sides. **B.** *adj.* Of or pertaining to a fish of this kind or the suborder as a whole.

1957 E. LE DANOIS *Fishes of World* vi. 178 The smaller stomiatoids with formidable teeth prey on other mid-water, deep-sea fishes. **1974** *Nature* 8 Nov. 98/1 They [*sc.* hatchetfishes] form one of the major groups of the stomiatoid fishes. **1976** *Jrnl. R. Soc. Arts* Apr. 251/2 Stomiatoid and lantern fishes..have large, highly sensitive eyes and marvellous arrays of light organs.

stomion ('stɒmiːɒn). *Gr. Archæol.* Pl. **stomia.** [a. Gr. στόμιον, dim. of στόμα mouth.] The entrance to an ancient tomb.

1934 E. GJERSTAD et al. *Swedish Cyprus Expedition* I. 35 Three chambers..roughly circular, or oval in shape with horizontal floors, and steeply sloping tunnel-shaped stomia. *Ibid.* 47 The proper dromos of Chamber B was never excavated. The stomion is very long and slightly curved eastwards. **1946** *Ann. Brit. School at Athens* XLI. 79 The tombs were entered by a narrow passage (*dromos*), sometimes wider below than above, with a rectangular doorway (*stomion* in *SEC* descriptions) closed by a limestone slab. **1969** V. KARAGEORGHIS *Cyprus* iii. 152 Towards the middle of the 7th century the same tomb was re-used by cutting a passage through the filling of the dromos of the first burial to provide access to the *stomion* of the chamber. **1970** *Mariner's Mirror* LVI. 390 Anchors.. were broken in antiquity before being used as fill in the stomion of a tomb last closed in the 11th century B.C.

stomium ('stəʊmiːəm). *Bot.* [mod.L., coined in Ger. (K. Goebel 1901, in *Organogr. d. Pflanzen* II. 753), f. Gr. στόμιον (see prec.).] In ferns, a part of the wall of the sporangium which ruptures to release the spores.

1905 I. B. BALFOUR tr. *Goebel's Organogr. of Plants* II. 575 A point of opening which we may designate the stomium occurs in all sporangia which discharge their spores into the air. **1936** A. J. EAMES *Morphol. Vascular Plants* xii. 263 The annulus [of the Cyatheaceæ] is complete and oblique (nearly vertical) with a poorly defined stomium. **1969** F. E. ROUND *Introd. Lower Plants* xiii. 156 The sporangial head has a cluster or ring of thickened cells (annulus) which acts as the dehiscence mechanism working on a weaker region of unthickened cells (stomium).

stomle, obs. form of STUMBLE *v.*

stommok, obs. form of STOMACH.

stomochord ('stɒməʊkɔːd). *Zool.* [f. Gr. στόμα mouth + χορδή CHORD *sb.*[1], after *notochord.*] Name proposed by Willey for the so-called 'notochord' of *Enteropneusta*: see quots. Hence **stomo'chordal** *a.*, pertaining to or having a stomochord.

1899 WILLEY in *Q. Jrnl. Microscop. Sci.* XLII. 234 MM. Delage and Hérouard retain the designation notochord applied by Bateson to the diverticulum from the throat which projects into the proboscis, where it acquires a rigid consistency and sustaining properties. I prefer to call this structure by a non-committal name, and propose the term stomochord. **1902** G. H. FOWLER in *Encycl. Brit.* XXIX. 251/1 The stomochord is a forward dorsal diverticulum of the gut in the collar region, which pushes before it the wall of the præ-oral body cavity or protocœle.

stomocke, -ok, -oke, obs. ff. STOMACH.

‖**stomodæum, -eum** (stɒməʊ'diːəm). *Embryology* and *Zool.* Pl. **-æa, -ea** (-'iːə). [mod.L. irreg. f. Gr. στόμα mouth + ὁδαῖος that is on or by the road.] The anterior portion of the digestive tract, beginning as an invagination of the epiblast.

1876 RAY LANKESTER in *Q. Jrnl. Microsc. Sci.* XVI. 64 A second invagination forms the true mouth and the stomodæum. [*Foot-note*] This term and its correlative 'proctodæum' I propose for the oral and anal invaginations. **1900** G. C. BOURNE in *Ray Lankester's Treat. Zool.* II. *Anthozoa* 7 The elongation of the mouth and stomodaeum confers a bilateral symmetry on the Anthozoan zooid.

Hence **stomodæal, -eal** (-'iːəl) *a.*, belonging to or constituting a stomodæum.

1883 RAY LANKESTER in *Encycl. Brit.* XVI. 637/1 (Mollusca) Both behind and before the stomodæal invagination. **1892** E. B. WILSON in *Jrnl. Morphol.* VI. 418 The stomodæal arc rapidly enlarges. *Ibid.*, The stomodæal glands.

stomok, obs. form of STOMACH.

stomp, *v.*[1] Used by Browning (to obtain a rime) for *stump* or *stamp*.

1845 BROWNING *Englishm. Italy* 272 And then will the flaxen-wigged Image Be carried in pomp Thro' the plain, while in gallant procession The priests mean to stomp.

stomp (stɒmp), *v.*[2] Chiefly *U.S.* (orig. *dial.*). [Var. STAMP *v.* in senses of branch II.] **1. a.** *intr.* = STAMP *v.* 2a. Also *fig.*

1803 J. DAVIS *Trav. U.S.A.* x. 382 He began to *stomp* upon me, and ax if I had yet got enough. **1936** C. CARMER *Listen for Lonesome Drum* 74, I stomped on his hand. **1961** C. MCCULLERS *Clock without Hands* vii. 148 He took down his records of German lieder.. and stomped on them, stomping with such despair and fury that not a groove of the records remained unshattered. **1971** B. MALAMUD *Tenants* 65 In the last piece Harry..is painted white by three brothers after they had considered stomping on him..for what he did. **1973** *Observer* 25 Nov. 28/4 They stomped all over Newport County.., winning 3–1.

b. = STAMP *v.* 2b.

1914 *Dialect Notes* IV. 156 *Stomp, v.i.*, var. of *stamp*, to strike the foot forcibly and noisily downward. **1917** *Ibid.* 400 *Stomp*.., tread heavily or noisily with one or more feet... 'He *stomped* on the floor as hard as he could.' **1928** J. PETERKIN *Scarlet Sister Mary* 147 Tell Doll not to stomp so hard. **1940** *Time* 29 July 40 They banged, rattled, beat, blew, stomped. **1969** *New Scientist* 17 July 119/2 The astronaut will be asked to stomp on the surface several times to produce observable seismic signals. **1982** B. CHATWIN *On Black Hill* xvi. 77 The bull bellowed; horses stomped in their stalls.

c. = STAMP *v.* 2e.

1919 E. POUND *Quia Pauper Amavi* 18 He stomped into my bedroom. **1941** *Time* 13 Oct. 15/3 Mr. Ford stomped out, grinding his teeth. **1953** W. BURROUGHS *Junkie* (1972) ii. 23 Whitey was stomping up and down the length of the bar trying to promote some free drinks. **1956** J. MASTERS *Bugles & Tiger* 87 Biniram unpacked my suitcase, threw my pyjamas on the bed, and stomped out. **1967** G. STEINER *Lang. & Silence* 138 He stomps like a boisterous giant through a literature often marked by slim volumes of whispered lyricism. **1971** B. W. ALDISS *Soldier Erect* 89 He came stomping along the edge—for a moment I thought he was going to dive in after me, boots and all! **1981** 'J. GASH' *Vatican Rip* vii. 61 I'd never seen people move so fast... Everybody simply stomped hurriedly past.

2. a. *trans.* = STAMP *v.* 3a. Also *fig.*

1916 in H. Wentworth *Amer. Dial. Dict.* (1944) 593/1 Before you stomp all that snow off. **1941** H. SKIDMORE *Hawk's Nest* 2 [She] stomped the red clay from her feet. **1954** *Ladies' Home Jrnl.* Oct. 116/3 Any passerby could look through the glass and see if the teacher inside were perhaps being pinned to the wall or stomped into the floor. **1971** B. PATTEN *Irrelevant Song* 40, I will make all that is possible step out of time To a land of giant hurrays! where the happy monsters dance And stomp darkness down. **1981** M. C. SMITH *Gorky Park* I. iii. 45 The host's carload entered, stomping snow off their boots.

b. *to stomp one's feet.* Cf. STAMP *v.* 3c.

c **1927–34** J. TOOMER in *Black Scholar* (1971) Jan. 8, I teased the girls. I sent notes. I stomped my feet and made strange noises. **1941** *Sat. Even. Post* 10 May 113/2 Fern stomped feet against the floor. **1955** *Birmingham* (Alabama) *News* 14 July 55/2 She stomped her feet in the manner in which she testified she saw Colin walking toward the car to take the battery. **1972** *Jazz & Blues* Nov. 5/1 They jitterbugged to 'One O'Clock Jump' and stomped their feet to 'Maple Leaf Rag'.

c. To stamp or trample on (a person, etc.). Also *transf.*

1934 C. CARMER *Stars fell on Alabama* 165, I fixes to stomp him to death... There I was stompin' jest like I'd stomped a thousand coons. **1942** *R.A.F. Jrnl.* 16 May 28 The Indians then began a victory dance. Before the dance was over..the..British fliers were stomping the ground in customary style. **1959** N. MAILER *Advts. for Myself* (1961) 201, I never could stomach the relish with which soldiers would describe how they had stomped some faggot in a bar. **1967** *Daily Progress* (Charlottesville, Va.) 1 May c2/6 Jerry got into an argument with his mother and his father shouted: 'I'm gonna stomp you!' **1975** D. LODGE *Changing Places* ii. 86 He saw Carol jumping up and down on the mountainous figure of the black wrestler, 'Stomp me baby, stomp me,' he moaned.

d. With *out.* = STAMP *v.* 3d. Chiefly *transf.*

1936 *Sun* (Baltimore) 4 Dec. 12/3 We are against crime. Crime should be 'stomped' out. **1940** W. FAULKNER *Hamlet* I. iii. 82 That first Snopes will turn around and stomp the fire out. **1941** *Time* 29 Dec. 22/1 Castillo would use his new powers..to stomp out Nazi propaganda agents. **1976** *Science* 10 Sept. 982/1 Despite government efforts to stomp it out..the banned anticancer drug Laetrile has a steady.. market..in the United States.

e. To beat *out* (a rhythm) with one's foot.

1973 *Black World* Mar. 61/2 Arms open wide, he stomped out a savage drum beat: 'Kill! kill! kill! kill!'

f. To tramp or trudge between (a series of places).

1977 'J. LE CARRÉ' *Hon. Schoolboy* xv. 331 He was reduced to stomping the air-freight agencies, asking about a firm called Indocharter.

3. Chiefly *Jazz.* **a.** *trans.* To perform (a dance) to a lively, stamping rhythm.

1926 B. KRENZ (*song-title*) Stomp your stuff. **1926** in R. S. Gold *Jazz Lexicon* (1964) 297 When they start dancin'—Stompin and prancin'—the dance called the sugar foot stomp. **1978** *Amer. Poetry Rev.* July/Aug. 45/2 'Stomping the blues' is also dancing with the get down style of dance-beat-oriented people.

b. With *off.* To beat (a tempo) with one's foot as a signal to a jazz band to start to play; also, to signal to (a band) in this way. Also *absol.* or *intr.*

1925 in R. S. Gold *Jazz Lexicon* (1964) 298 (*tune-title*) Stomp off, let's go. **1960** H. O. BRUNN *Story Orig. Dixieland Jazz Band* vi. 68 For this reason LaRocca was not allowed to 'stomp off' his band in the usual fashion. **1961** *Artesian* Winter 33 They stomped off the solid beat. **1970** W. APEL *Harvard Dict. Mus.* (ed. 2) 441/2 In the earliest forms of jazz the leader 'stomped off' the tempo (gave it by tapping his foot).

c. *intr.* To dance or play a stomp. Cf. STOMP *sb.* 1.

1925 (*tune-title*) Everybody stomp. **1929** (*tune-title*) I'm gonna stomp, Mr. Henry Lee. **1937** C. CONNOLLY in L. Russell *Press Gang!* 80 And then dancing, while..David stomps on the piano. **1957** D. HAGUE in S. Traill *Concerning Jazz* 112 A resurgence of swing in evidence..and Dixieland still stomping here and there. **1968** *Daily Mail* 16 Mar. 6/1 'Ullo, darlin', can you stomp?' my rocker friend Jonny asked gaily. I looked puzzled. 'It's the new Rocker dance,' he explained. **1974** *Ibid.* 16 Oct. 6/4 He does not stomp quite so energetically these days.

Hence **stomped** (stɒmpt) *ppl. a.*

1946 R. BLESH *Shining Trumpets* iv. 95 A stomped and hand-clapped rhythmic base. **1950** —— & JANIS *They all played Ragtime* ix. 176 Nor is erudite musical analysis needed to differentiate ragtime from jazz when one has heard him play the *Maple Leaf* in the authentic St. Louis manner and then follow with his own complex stomped version 'along the lines of jazz creation'.

stomp (stɒmp), *sb.* orig. and chiefly *U.S.* [f. STOMP *v.*[2]] **1. a.** Chiefly *Jazz.* A lively dance, usu. involving heavy stamping; also, a tune or song suitable for such a dance; stomping rhythm. Also *attrib.*

1912 (*tune-title*) Stomp dance. **1923** (*tune-title*) House rent stomp. **1926** *Amer. Mercury* Apr. 388/1 Hot jazz (which the Charleston and the Stomp—ye gods, what a name!—are bringing back, worse luck!). **1929** WODEHOUSE *Summer Lightning* iv. 108 Leopold's justly famous band, its cheeks puffed out and its eyeballs rolling, was playing a popular melody with lots of stomp in it. **1933** *Fortune* Aug. 90/3 Gene Gifford has composed and arranged some of the neatest exercises in *stomp* (very fast) time. **1940** *Swing* June 24/2 Fundamentally, there are two types of jazz—blues and stomps... Stomp tunes are gay; blues are mournful. **1952** *Mademoiselle* Dec. 120/3 The great era of the stomp was the twenties. **1956** H. KURNITZ *Invasion of Privacy* xiii. 85 She opened..with '*Vissi d'arte*' from Tosca..and to close, a hot and authentic stomp. **1968** *Daily Mail* 16 Mar. 6/5 Others did the stomp, an accelerated calypso, one of the most energetic and difficult dances I have ever tried to learn. **1977** J. WAINWRIGHT *Do Nothin' till you hear from Me* vii. 116 An outfit, straight from a 'viper session' could take a stomp, play it at..a nice, bouncy pace, and it came out faster than seemed mortally possible.

b. A heavy stamping step to the beat of such a dance.

1927 *Observer* 6 Feb. 15/7 Once you get the stomp—the peculiar beat of the foot—and you both hit the floor and not a neighbour's ankle, it is quite suitable as a ballroom dance. **1940** *Time* 25 Nov. 41/1 Dancer Massine [pieces out] simple footwork with deft body movements, well-timed claps and stomps. **1942** *Sat. Even. Post* 14 Feb. 20/2 A fast double shuffle that should have climaxed in a stomp. **1971** B. MALAMUD *Tenants* 217 Some of the youths try to imitate the newly married couples shaking their hips and shoulders but give it up and break into a stomp, shake, and whirl.

2. A party characterized by lively dancing to popular music; *spec.* a rent party.

1926 WHITEMAN & MCBRIDE *Jazz* viii. 177 The 'stomp' consisted of a barbecue with music afterwards, during and before. The guests raised a purse to save their host's home and also composed a new blues for the occasion. **1940** [see G.I. 2 a]. **1967** E. A. GOLLSCHEWSKY in *Coast to Coast 1965–66* 86 The stomp crowd breaking up down at the Junior Citizens' Hall. **1977** P. DICKINSON *Walking Dead* III. iii. 230 The villagers met..for dances—those noisy nights half-way between revivalist meetings and beer-hall stomp.

3. A heavy, tramping gait or walk; *on the stomp*: tramping or trudging from place to place.

1971 B. W. ALDISS *Soldier Erect* 205 The parade-ground stomp was out in Dimapur, where it raised too much dust; the fashion was for a sort of brisk stroll, a gun-fighter's walk. **1977** 'J. LE CARRÉ' *Hon. Schoolboy* xvi. 392 He went on the stomp for refugee and orphan stories. **1982** *Times* 6 Sept. 7/1 A stomp along the cliff path, talking all the way.

stompe, obs. form of STUMP.

†'**stomper**, *v. Obs. rare*[−1]. [f. STAMPER *sb.* (see sense 3 a).] *trans.* To pound with a pestle.

c **1420** *Liber Cocorum* (1862) 30 Take mustarde and let hit drye..Stomper hit in a morter fyne.

stomper ('stɒmpə(r)), *sb.* [f. STOMP *v.*[2] + -ER[1].]

1. *pl.* Shoes or boots; *spec.* large, heavy shoes. Cf. STAMPER *sb.* 4; *waffle stomper* s.v. WAFFLE *sb.*[1] *U.S. slang.*

1899 B. W. GREEN *Work-Bk. Virginia Folk-Speech* 366 *Stompers*, large heavy shoes. **1945** L. SHELLY *Jive Talk Dict.* 19/1 *Stompers*, pair of shoes. **1974** K. MILLETT *Flying* (1975) II. 233 The Left wears its jeans and stompers. **1979** B. MALAMUD *Dubin's Lives* vii. 257 Dubin wore two scarves.. waffle stompers, earmuffs.

2. *Jazz.* A person who performs a stomp.

1925 in B. Rust *Jazz Records 1897–1942* (1972) I. 758 (*recording artists*) The Dixie Stompers. **1927** *Music* 5 Jan. 50/2 (*heading*) Red and Miff's Stompers. **1944** *Amer. Speech* XIX. 268 In sharp contrast to the power-aggressiveness group [of names of boys' clubs] is a small but well defined group that might be called the rakish: Top Hats..Ramblers, Stompers, Hepcats. **1959** *Encounter* Sept. 51/1 Richard Waring..turns Oberon into a vocal, melodramatic, and *bravura* stomper. **1968** *Blues Unlimited* Nov. 17 A host of harpists, guitarists and stompers.

stompie ('stɒmpɪ). *S. Afr. slang.* [a. Afrikaans, dim. of *stomp* STUMP *sb.*[1]] A cigarette butt; also, a partially-smoked cigarette, esp. one stubbed out and kept for relighting later.

1947 L. ABRAHAMS in B. Sachs *H. C. Bosman: S. Afr. Opinion—Trek Anthol.* (1971) 235 He stubbed out the stompie on the kerb. Pushing it into his pocket, he came over. **1959** J. MEIRING *Candle in Wind* ii. 32 She pulled a stompie out of her pocket and lighted it. **1969** A. FUGARD *Boesman & Lena* 37 The whiteman stopped the bulldozer and smoked a cigarette... He threw me the stompie. **1981** A. PATON *Towards Mountain* v. 34 The smell [of tobacco smoke] was made worse by his habit of keeping stompies in his pockets, a stompie being a cigarette not fully smoked, then stubbed out, and stored away for future use.

stomping ('stɒmpɪŋ), *vbl. sb.* Chiefly *U.S.* [f. STOMP *v.*[2] + -ING[1].] **1.** The action of stamping or treading heavily.

1819 M. EDGEWORTH *Let.* 28 Jan. (1971) 164 Made such a stomping about the room that Mr. Sneyd could not think what was the matter. **1950** BLESH & JANIS *They all played Ragtime* ix. 166 The term 'stomp', used to designate a hot number of dynamic rhythm, was derived in New Orleans from the stomping of bare feet in the Bamboula and the Congo. **1976** *National Observer* (U.S.) 27 Mar. 2/5 The debate..was marked by howls, foot-stomping, angry exchanges.

2. *Jazz.* The action of dancing or playing a stomp.

1930 R. WRASKOFF (*song-title*) Stomping! Hot stomp. **1936** in R. S. Gold *Jazz Lexicon* (1964) 297 (*song-title*) Stomping at the Savoy. **1941** W. C. HANDY *Father of Blues* i. 6 That was real stomping. **1963** *Pix* 28 Sept. 62 Rubber soled sneakers are fine for stomping but you can get an extra two points for owning a pair of huaraches.

3. *transf.* An attack in which the victim is trampled upon. More generally, a beating. Cf. STOMP *v.*[2] 2 c. *U.S. colloq.*

1958 *Washington Post* 13 Sept. D3/5 A coroner's jury yesterday found Robert C. Gerald..responsible for the death by stomping of Hazel R. White. **1967** *Daily Progress* (Charlottesville, Va.) 1 May C2 (*heading*) Threatened with 'stomping' boy kills parents, granddad. **1971** J. MANDELKAU *Buttons* xiv. 155, I grabbed him by the hair when he didn't answer and started to swing him around and punch him in the face... You know what he cried? 'I know where it's at. I can take a stomping!' **1977** L. O'DONNELL *Aftershock* xv. 217 The beating and the stomping weren't necessary.

4. *Comb.*, as **stomping ground** = *stamping ground* s.v. STAMPING *vbl. sb.* 3.

1854 in *Amer. Speech* (1940) XV. 397/1 Crossing the top of said ridge to a white oak & 2 chesnut saplings by the edge of a stomping-ground. **1937** *Dialect Notes* VI. 617 This is the stomping ground of Pecos Bill. **1950** A. LOMAX *Mister Jelly Roll* 42 New Orleans was the stomping grounds for all the greatest pianists in the country. **1977** 'J. LE CARRÉ' *Hon. Schoolboy* xiii. 307 The East was his natural stomping ground.

stomping ('stɒmpɪŋ), *ppl. a.* Chiefly *U.S.* [f. STOMP *v.*[2] + -ING[2].] **1.** *Jazz.* That plays, or is played, in the manner of a stomp; exciting with a heavy, 'swinging' rhythm; also, that dances the stomp.

1927 H. FORD et al. (*song-title*) Stompin' fool. **1950** BLESH & JANIS *They all played Ragtime* viii. 160 New Orleans, not St. Louis, made the real impact on Chicago music,..as it developed into stomping jazz with much ragtime retained. **1956** M. STEARNS *Story of Jazz* (1957) xvi. 187 A series of stomping bands swung along this circuit. **1968** P. OLIVER *Screening Blues* v. 151 Joe Pullum, a Houston singer who was accompanied on *Joe Louis Is the Man* by Andy Boy's stomping piano. **1972** *Jazz & Blues* Sept. 12/2 The number seems to be based on 'Way Down Upon The Swanee River' but is played by Fats as a fast boogie-woogie piece with a stomping left hand.

2. = STAMPING *ppl. a. U.S.*

1942 *Time* 9 Feb. 28/2 Brazil's Aranha..announced to stomping, cheering crowds that Brazil..had..'broken her diplomatic and commercial relations with Germany'.

‖**stompneus** ('stɔmpnœs). *S. Africa.* [Du. = blunt nose.] Either of two edible fishes found off the coast of southern Africa, the red and silver *Chrysoblephus gibbiceps* or the silvery *Rhabdosargus globiceps*, both of the family Sparidæ. Also *stump-nose* (see STUMP *sb.*).

1705 tr. *Bosman's Guinea* 261 Several sorts of Bream, Stompneuses, or flat Noses. **1791** tr. *Le Vaillant's Trav. Africa* I. 22 There are plenty of fish at the Cape. Among those most valued..are..the stompneus [etc.]. **1945** *Cape Argus Mag.* 20 Oct. 1 Often we hooked two together—silverfish, panga, stompneus, elft. **1953** *Cape Times* 4 Mar. 2/4 Kabeljou, yellowtail, white stompneus and stockfish were all caught in Hermanus.

-stomy (stəmɪ), f. Gr. στόμ-α mouth, opening + -Y[3], used in *Surg.* to form the names of operations in which (*a*) an opening is made into the internal organ denoted by the preceding element, as in COLOSTOMY, GASTROSTOMY; or (*b*) a permanent connection is made between the internal organs indicated, as in *gastro-duodenostomy* and *gastro-gastrostomy* s.v. GASTRO-.

ston, obs. form of STONE, STUN.

stonage ('stəʊnɪdʒ). [f. STONE *sb.* + -AGE.]

†**1.** Stones collectively. *Obs.*

1618 CHAPMAN *Hesiod* II. 29 Draw ashore Thy Ship; and fence her round with stonage store, To shield her ribs against the humorous Gales.

2. Weight measured in stones. *nonce-use.*

1882 H. C. MERIVALE *Faucit of B.* II. II. i. 149 Six good feet of height, and a stonage coming nearer to fourteen than to thirteen on the average.

stonage, obs. form of STONEHENGE.

stonch, obs. form of STANCH *v.*

†**stond.** *Obs.* [App. a dial. variant of STAND *sb.*, adopted by certain writers in special uses.]

1. *Falconry.* Cf. STAND *sb.*[1] 7.

1580–3 GREENE *Mamillia* I. 4 b, The hawke that commeth at the first cal, wil neuer be stedfast on the stond. **1587** —— *Carde of Fancie* (1593) E 3 b, The Hawke that bates at euerie cast of the Lure will neuer be stedfast on the stonde.

2. Impediment, stoppage. (Only in Bacon.)

1605 BACON *Adv. Learn.* II. xxii. §10 That..you may work out the knots and stondes of the mind. **1612** —— *Ess., Studies* (Arb.) 11 Nay, thear is no stond or impediment in the wit, but may be wrought out by fit studies. *a* **1626** —— *Disc. touching Helps Intell. Powers* Resusc. (1657) 277 The Removing of the Stonds, and Impediments, of the Mind, doth often clear, the passage, and Current, to a Mans Fortune.

stond(e, obs. forms of STAND, STOUND.

stondard, -art(e, obs. forms of STANDARD.

stondenegosse, -gousse: see STANDENGUSS.

stonderde, -ert, obs. forms of STANDARD.

c **1550** *Battle of Otterburn* lvii, The stonderdes stode styll on eke a syde.

stone (stəʊn), *sb.* Forms: 1–3 (4–5 *Sc.* and *north.*) **stan**, 3 **stæn**, 3–5 **ston**, 4–5 **sten**, 4–6 **stoon** (5–6 **stoone**), 4–9 (*Sc.* and *north.*) **stane**, 5 *Sc.* **stayne**, (**stein**), 5–7 **stonne**, 6 **stoan(e**, **steane**, 6–7 *Sc.* **stain(e**, 7 *Sc.*, 8–9 *dial.* **stean**, 4– **stone**. [Common Teut.: OE. *stán* str. masc. corresponds to OFris. *stên*, (WFris. *stên*, *stien*, NFris. *stîn*, *stîæn*), OS. *stên* (LG., Du. *steen*), OHG. (MHG., mod.G.) *stein*, ON. *stein-n* (Sw., Da. *sten*), Goth. *stain-s*:—OTeut. **staino-z*, cogn. w. OSl. *stěna* (Russ. *stena*) wall, and Gr. στία, στῖον pebble.]

1. a. A piece of rock or hard mineral substance (other than metal) of a small or moderate size.

c **888** ÆLFRED *Boeth.* xxxiv. §xi, ʒif þu þonne ænne stan toclifst, ne wyrð he næfre ʒegadrod swa he ær wæs. *c* **1175** *Lamb. Hom.* 9 Me þe sculde nimen and..þe al to-toruion mid stane. *c* **1250** *Gen. & Ex.* 1604 He lay bi luzan ut on niʒt, A ston under hise heued riʒt. *a* **1310** *Cursor M.* 7581 He tok fiue stans rond. *c* **1412** HOCCLEVE *De Reg. Princ.* 1805 A stoon no thyng ne felith. **1573** TUSSER *Husb.* (1878) 80 The sticks and the stones go and gather vp cleene. **1686** W. HARRIS tr. *Lemery's Course Chem.* 214 There have been who gazing too earnestly upon the Stars above, have not perceived the stone at their feet, that caused them to stumble. **1798** COLERIDGE *Anc. Mariner* 17 The Wedding-Guest sat on a stone. **1812–16** PLAYFAIR *Nat. Phil.* (1819) I. 323 The Stones which have..been ascertained..to fall down from the air. **1833** *Penny Cycl.* I. 150/1 Aerolites, called also Meteoric Stones. **1875** JOWETT *Plato* (ed. 2) III. 64 A dog who..quarrels with the stones which are thrown at him.

†**b.** A rock, cliff, crag; a mass of rock; rocky ground. *Obs.*

c **825** *Vesp. Psalter* xxvi. 6 [xxvii. 5] In stane upahof mec. *c* **1000** *Rule St. Benet* (1888) 5 Hit ne feoll forþam þe hit wæs ʒestaðelod ofor þam stane. *c* **1200** *Trin. Coll. Hom.* 155 Sum of þe sed ful uppe þe ston and dride þere. *a* **1300** *Cursor M.* 16762 + 83 þe son wex merke, þe erth quoke, þe stons clef. *c* **1400** *Laud Troy Bk.* 4133 Lest thei..breke her schippus on cragges and stones. *c* **1430** *Prymer* (1895) 65 He ordeyned my feet on a stoon. **1513** DOUGLAS *Æneis* IX. vii. 174 Quhil the famyl and ofspring of Enee The stane immovable of the Capitolie Inhabitis. *a* **1700** EVELYN *Diary* Apr. 1646, Some of these vast mountaines were but one entire stone.

fig. *a* **1220** *Vices & Virtues* (1888) 27 And uppe þese stane ðe ðu hier hafst ʒenamd, Crist, godes sune, ich wille araren mine cherche. *c* **1400** *Rule St. Benet* 189 þis stone es crist, þat we on call. **1535** COVERDALE *Deut.* xxxii. 4 Perfecte are the workes of the Stone for all his wayes are righteous.

c. A meteorite; now *esp.* one containing a high proportion of silicates or other non-metals.

1628 J. HOSKINS *Let.* in N. Wallington *Hist. Notices* (1869) I. i. 14 As it is reported, there fell divers stones, but two is certain, in our knowledge. **1796** *Gentleman's Mag.* LXVI. 845/1 Various instances are alleged of such falling stones, or, as they may be denominated, extinguished meteors. **1802** *Phil. Trans. R. Soc.* XCII. 212 Have not all fallen stones, and what are called native irons, the same origin?.. Are all, or any, the produce or the bodies of meteors? **1809** *Jrnl. Nat. Philos.* XXIII. 233 Account of a meteoric stone..that fell in the circle of Ichnow. *Ibid.*, Several persons..got out the stone, which was above two feet beneath the surface of the snow... A professor of natural philosophy..considered it..as ferruginous. **1826**, etc. [see IRON *sb.*[1] 1 d]. **1977** A. HALLAM *Planet Earth* 24 Freshly fallen stones are usually quite cool to the touch.

d. A fashion shade of yellowish or brownish grey; stone-colour. Also *attrib.* or as *adj.* Cf. sense 19.

1848 E. RUSKIN *Let.* 10 May in W. James *Order of Release* (1947) v. 107 A stone silk dress with two broad flounces. **1865** M. EYRE *Lady's Walks in South of France* i. 10 The colours most in vogue are some shade of grey, stone, or buff. **1890** [see *box-cloth* s.v. BOX *sb.*[2] 24]. **1907** *Yesterday's Shopping* (1969) 157/2 Paints mixed ready for use... White, light stone, dark stone, middle stone, black. **1923** *Daily Mail* 2 June 1 In delightful shades of Fawn,..Dove Grey, Stone, Beaver. **1977** *Times* 18 Aug. 23/6 *Rover* 3·5 *litre*..blue with stone leather interior.

2. a. The hard compact material of which stones and rocks consist; hard mineral substance other than metal.

1154 *O.E. Chron.* (Canterb. MS.) an. 1020, Se cyng..let timbrian ðar an mynster of stane & lime. *c* **1200** ORMIN 4129 þatt cnif wass..Off stan, & nohht off irenn. *a* **1225** *Leg. Kath.* 266 Maumez of treo oðer of stan. **13..** *K. Horn* 905 (Harl.) A chirche of lym & ston. *c* **1384** CHAUCER *H. Fame* 70 The god of slepe..That dwelleth in a cave of stoon. *c* **1400** MAUNDEV. (Roxb.) i. 4 A brigg of stane þat es ouer þe ryuer. **1542** BOORDE *Dyetary* viii. (1870) 249 Stand nor syt long bareheed vnder a vawte of stone. **1590** in *Rep. Hist. MSS. Comm., Var. Coll.* IV. 284 Perceiving as well muche sand as stone..fetched from the sea-side. **1613** PURCHAS *Pilgrimage* (1614) 229 Mount Sinai..whose top..is hard stone of yron colour. **1774** GOLDSM. *Nat. Hist.* I. 27 We find layers of stone often over the lightest soils. **1826** *Art of Brewing* (ed. 2) 193 In Gloucestershire, and other parts of England, where stone is abundant. **1869** LOWELL *Cathedral* 283 Imagination's very self in stone!

b. as material for lithography.

c **1806** in *Archæol. Jrnl.* (1894) Ser. II. I. 111 The art of printing from stone called Polyautography. **1838** W. C. HARRIS *Narr. Exped. S. Africa* frontisp., Moselekatse, King of the Amazooloo. On Stone by W. C. Harris. **1864** *Scott. Metr. Psalter of 1635* title-p., Printed from stone, by Maclure and Macdonald, Lithographers to the Queen.

c. A particular kind of rock or hard mineral matter.

c **1400** tr. *Secreta Secret., Gov. Lordsh.* 87 Of propertez of stones, and of vertuz of herbes. **1480** CAXTON *Mirr. World* 92 In Archade is a stone whiche in no wyse may be quenchyd after it is sette a fire. **15..** in *Dunbar's Poems* (1893) II. 306 He knew the vertew of erb and stone. **1731** *Historia Lit.* III. 353 Semitransparent Stones, as Agat. **1796** KIRWAN *Elem. Min.* (ed. 2) I. 2 Stones differ from earths principally in cohesion and hardness. **1800** tr. *Lagrange's Chem.* I. 154 Many stones contain silex. **1841** *Penny Cycl.* XXI. 173/2 The material is a white calcareous stone, obtained in the neighbourhood.

d. *spec.* = PHILOSOPHERS' STONE.

1390 GOWER *Conf.* II. 88 This Ston..makth multiplicacioun Of gold. **1450** LYDG. *Secrees* 986 Al worldly tresour breeffly shet in Oon, Is declaryd in vertu of this stoon. **1610** B. JONSON *Alch.* Argt. 11. **1822** BYRON *Werner* III. i. 328 Thou more than stone of the philosopher!

e. = STONEWARE. Chiefly attrib.: see 17 b.

1642 *Rates of Merchandizes* 57 Whistles, cocks or Birds of stone. **1851** [see STONE-FRUIT 2].

†**f.** A mirror. *Obs. rare*⁻¹. Cf. *specular stone*, SPECULAR *a.* 1, 1 b.

1605 SHAKS. *Lear* V. iii. 262 Lend me a Looking-glasse, If that her breath will mist or staine the stone, Why then she liues.

g. ***artificial stone*** (see quot. 1967).

1722 *Brit. Pat.* 447 Thomas Ripley..and Richard Holt..have been at much labour..for the finding out and inventing 'A certain compound liquid metall never before known and used by the Antients or Moderns, by which artificiall stone and marble is made.' *c* **1778** [see LITHODIPYRA]. **1868** *Building News* 10 Apr. 248/2 *(heading)* Ransome's artificial stone. *Ibid.* 3 July 448/2 A method of manufacturing artificial granite..has just been patented by Mr. P. M. Parsons. **1935** *Economist* 9 Feb. 321/1 The two trades..which represent the largest consumers of cement are 'public works contracting, etc.', and 'artificial stone and concrete manufacturing'. **1935** [see RECONSTRUCTED *ppl. a.* a]. **1967** *Gloss. Highway Engin. Terms (B.S.I.)* 37 *Artificial stone*, a form of precast concrete in which the finished surface resembles that of natural stone.

3. a. As a type of motionlessness or fixity; esp. in phr. *(as) still as a stone.* ? *Obs.* (Cf. STONE-STILL.)

a **1225** *Leg. Kath.* 1253 Þᵗ nan ne seide na wiht, ah seten stille ase stan. **1390** GOWER *Conf.* I. 102 He lay stille as eny ston. **1535** COVERDALE *Exod.* xv. 16 Let feare and drede fall vpon them..that they maye be as styll as a stone. **1657** FULLER *Serm., Best Employm.* 12 Sit not there as a stone upon a stoole.

†**b.** As an emblem of stability or constancy; in phr. ***sad, stable, steadfast, true as stone.*** *Obs.*

c **1320** *Sir Tristr.* 115 Rohand, trewe so stan. *c* **1425** *Hampole's Psalter* Metr. Pref. 46 Euery word is sad as stone and sothly sayd, ful sykerly. *c* **1440** CAPGRAVE *Life St. Kath.* IV. 1251 He hath made hir hardy and stable as þe stoone. *c* **1450** *Godstow Reg.* 22, I wyl be as stedfast as any stone.

c. As a type of hardness, and hence as an emblem of insensibility, stupidity, deadness or the like; esp. in phrases of comparison with various adjs. as *blind, cold, dead, deaf, dumb, hard*, etc. (Cf. 19.)

a **1300** *Cursor M.* 12028 He fel dun ded as ston. **13..** *Seuyn Sages* (W.) 2359 He bicam blind so ston. *c* **1400** *Rom. Rose* 2409 Dom as a stoon. *c* **1400** *Pety Job* 318 in *26 Pol. Poems* 131 Me thynketh myn hert ys harder than a ston. **1500–20** DUNBAR *Poems* xv. 9 He that dronis ay as ane bee Sowld haif ane heirar dull as stane. **1599** SHAKS. *Hen. V*, II. iii. 26 All was cold as any stone. **1601** —— *All's Well* II. i. 76 A medicine..able to breath life into a stone. **1791** HAMPSON *Mem. Wesley* II. 133 The man continued as blind as a stone. **1837** P. KEITH *Bot. Lex.* 116 The albumen..in the seed of the coffee plant..is horny, and in that of the Date-palm it is said to be as hard as a stone. **1841** HOOD *Tale Trumpet* 42 She was deaf as a stone.

4. *transf.* and *fig.* Something resembling stone or a stone: **a.** in physical sense: A hard concretion.

1893 BARING-GOULD *Cheap Jack Zita* III. 119 The frost had set in..and..the Lark was turned to stone within its embankments.

b. in figurative sense, chiefly as the supposed substance of a 'hard' heart; also, a 'hard' or unfeeling person, or heart; †also, a stupid person, blockhead; a silent person.

1388 WYCLIF *Ezek.* xxxvi. 26 Y schal do awei an herte of stoon [1382 a stonen herte] fro ȝoure fleisch. *a* **1400** *Minor Poems fr. Vernon MS.* 618/266 Þe Iewes weoren harde stones. **1500–20** DUNBAR *Poems* lxxv. 40 Ȝour mvsing wald perss ane hairt of stane. **1591** SHAKS. *Two Gent.* II. iii. 11 He is a stone, a very pibble stone, and has no more pitty in him then a dogge. **1598** R. BERNARD tr. *Terence, Heautontim.* V. i, Signes..whereby I might haue perceiued it, had not I beene a very stone [*ni essem lapis*]. **1612** *Two Noble K.* I. i. 140 Your sorrow beates so ardently upon me, That it shall make a counter reflect gainst My Brothers heart, and warme it to some pitty, Though it were made of stone. *a* **1659** T. PESTEL *Psalm for Christmas Day Morning*, Joyn then all hearts that are not stone,..To celebrate this holy One. **1746** HERVEY *Medit.* (1818) 147 The heart of stone is taken away, and a heart of flesh..is introduced in its stead. *a* **1771** GRAY *Dante* 54 Nor wept, for all Within was Stone. **1837** DICKENS *Pickw.* xiv, Tom Smart said the widow's lamentations when she heard the disclosure would have pierced a heart of stone. **1852** MRS. STOWE *Uncle Tom's C.* xxxiv, He..said he should come back; but it didn't deceive me, I knew that the time had come. I was just like one turned into stone.

5. A piece of stone of a definite form and size (usually artificially shaped), used for some special purpose. (Often as the second element of a compound: cf. definitions below.)

a. for building, or as a part or element of a building. (See also COPING-STONE, CORNER-STONE, FOUNDATION-*stone*, etc.)

c **825** *Vesp. Psalter* ci. 15 [cii. 14] Forðon welȝelicad hefdun ðeowas ðine stanas his. *c* **1200** ORMIN 16285 Swa þeȝȝ stodenn..To wirkenn o þe temmple, þatt draȝhenn swerd wass inn an hannd, & lim & stan inn oþerr. *c* **1400** *Laud Troy Bk.* 3374 Noble Troye..A-doun is throwen, with ston an[d] wal. **1427** in Heath *Grocers' Comp.* (1869) 4 In here tyme..was the furste stoon leyd of the Groceres place in Conyhoope-lane. **1552** ABP. HAMILTON *Catech.* (1884) 28 A Mason can nocht hew ane evin aislair staine without directioun of his rewill. **1594** SHAKS. *Rich. III*, IV. i. 104 Looke backe with me vnto the Tower. Pitty, you ancient Stones, those tender Babes, Whom Enuie hath immur'd within your Walls. **1610** HOLLAND *Camden's Brit.* (1637) 696 With the stones hewed out of it..Sant Peters at Yorke was reedified. **1796** H. HUNTER tr. *St. Pierre's Study Nat.* (1799) II. 132 Water..diffused.. through the air..attaches itself, to the glass-windows and the polished stones of our houses. **1833** LOUDON *Encycl. Archit.* §79 To build all the foundations..with stones properly headed. **1867** H. MACMILLAN *Bible Teach.* xii. (1870) 232 It is built up, stone by stone, from the level of the earth.

b. for paving.

(See also HEARTHSTONE, PAVING-STONE, etc.)

1427–8 *Rec. St. Mary at Hill* (1905) 68 Also for a goter ston for þe same gate, xiiij d. **1612** *Two Noble K.* V. iv. 68 On this horse is Arcite Trotting the stones of Athens. **1682** *Lond. Gaz.* No. 1694/4 An Iron Grey Gelding,..a little tender-footed on the Stones. **1738** *Gentl. Mag.* VIII. 549/1 He was driven over the Stones in a Hackney Coach. **1840** DICKENS *Old C. Shop* xix, Horses clattered on the uneven stones. **1841** [see PAUPER 1 c]. **1851** MRS. BROWNING *Casa Guidi Wind.* I. 601 On the stone Called Dante's,—a plain flat stone, scarce discerned From others in the pavement.

c. A block, slab, or pillar of stone set up as a memorial, to impart information, or for some ceremonial purpose: *e.g.* as an altar, a monument, a boundary-mark, etc.

See also HOAR-STONE 2, MILESTONE, SHIRE-*stone*, STANDING STONE.

847 *Charter* in *O.E. Texts* 434 On ðone stan æt ðære flodan. *c* **1205** LAY. 9959 He lette a-ræren anan enne swuðe sælcuð stan: he lette þer on grauen sælcuðe run-stauen hu he Rodric of-sloh. **1297** R. GLOUC. (Rolls) 158 Evene vp riȝht & swiþe heiȝ, þat wonder hit is to se, þe stones stondeþ þere so grete. *a* **1300** *Cursor M.* 979 Ȝee sal do bren it on a stan. **1450–80** tr. *Secreta Secret.* lviii. 33 It was founde writen in a stone of þe tunge of Caldee. *c* **1470** HENRY *Wallace* I. 121 The croune he tuk apon that sammyne stane At Gadalos send with his sone fra Spane. **1581** *Cov. Leet Bk.* 822, & so Crosse ouer to the corner of Babethorp-wast vnto another stone there sett. **1598–1603** STOW *Surv.* (1908) I. 224 On the south side of this high streete..is pitched vpright a great stone called London stone. **1716** ADDISON *Freeholder* No. 18 ¶5 As ridiculously puzzled..as a man that counts the stones on Salisbury-plain, which can never be settled to any certain number. **1827** G. HIGGINS *Celtic Druids* 212 Some of these stones-erect have crosses cut upon them. **1831** SCOTT *Ct. Robt.* xx, The troth I had plighted to Hereward at the stone of Odin.

d. *spec.* = GRAVESTONE 2, TOMBSTONE.

13.. *Cursor M.* 193 (Gött.) Lazar þat ded lay vnder stan. **1303** R. BRUNNE *Handl. Synne* 8780 Lordes are besy aboute to haue Proude stones lyggyng an hye on here graue. **1436** *E.E. Wills* 105, I woll þat there be leyde vpon my body a stone of Marble. *a* **1585** MONTGOMERIE *Cherrie & Slae* 567 Than sall be graud vpon the stane Quhilk on thy graue beis laid [etc.]. **1687** A. LOVELL tr. *Thevenot's Trav.* I. 58 When the Grave is filled up, they erect a stone over the head of the deceased. **1750** GRAY *Elegy* 116 The lay, Grav'd on the stone beneath yon aged thorn. **1767** JAGO *Edge-hill* IV. 332 Alike the simple Stone And Mausoleum proud, his Pow'r attest, In wretched Doggrel, or elab'rate Verse. **1850** THACKERAY *Pendennis* lxxi, The stone closes over Harry the Fourth, and Harry the Fifth reigns in his stead. **1900** BP. W. How *Lighter Moments* 21 A stone-mason..brought a stone to put into the churchyard.

e. As an object of idolatrous worship; chiefly *pl.* in conjunction with ***stocks***: see STOCK *sb.* 1 d.

c **1400** *Apol. Loll.* 89 Wat honor of God is þis, to ren about bi tre, and stone, and formis, and honor as God veyn figeris?

†**f.** A gun-flint. *Obs.*

1611 BEAUM. & FL. *Knt. Burning Pestle* V. i, *Ralph.* Wheres the stone of this Peece? 2 *Sold.* The Drummer took it out to light Tobacco.

g. A rounded stone or pebble formerly used as a missile in war, being thrown with the hand, discharged from a sling, or shot from a fire-arm (cf. GUNSTONE); † *stone of iron*, a cannon-ball (*obs.*).

c **1205** LAY. 626 Mid stocken & mid stanen stal fiht heo makeden. *c* **1330** R. BRUNNE *Chron. Wace* (Rolls) 3030 Grete stones wyþ slynges [they] caste. *c* **1450** *Brut* 434 A traitour..shotte a Gonne, and the stone smot this good Erle of Salusbury. **1511** *Guylforde's Pilgr.* (Camden) 8 An other pece..shoteth a stone of irron of .ij. fote depe. *a* **1548** HALL *Chron., Hen. VIII*, 113 The Frenchemen shot out ordinaunce, quarelles and stones. **1573–5** GASCOIGNE *Flowers* Wks. 1907 I. 81 The harquebush doth spit his spight, with prety persing stones. **1581** A. HALL *Iliad* III. 47 The Greekes cease not to martch, their stones & darts at random flye. **1705** *Lond. Gaz.* No. 4097/1 They..ply the Enemy..with Bombs and Stones, from 6 Mortars. **1745** P. THOMAS *Jrnl. Anson's Voy.* 288 Each of those they had loaded with..Flint Stones and Shot. **1867** A. L. GORDON *Poems* (1912) 94 Like a bird on the wing, or a stone from a sling.

h. A shaped piece of stone for grinding or sharpening something, as a GRINDSTONE, MILLSTONE, WHETSTONE.

1578 *Invent. R. Wardr.* (1815) 260 Ane man mylne with hir stanys and hir haill tymmer werk. **1599** BRETON *Wil of Wit* (Grosart) 11/1 The stone, that Wit must whet himselfe uppon. **1751** *N. Jersey Archives* XIX. 1 A Large..grist-mill, with two pairs of stones. **1886** STEVENSON *Kidnapped* xxvi, Shearers worked all day in a field..and we could hear the stones going on the hooks.

i. A flat slab or tablet for grinding something upon, or for smoothing or flattening something (see also FLATTENING-*stone*, SLEEKSTONE, etc.); in *Printing* = IMPOSING-*stone*; also a slab of stone for lithography (see 2 b).

14.. *Crafte of Lymnynge* in *E.E. Misc.* (Warton Club) 72 Grynde vermelone one a stone with newe glayre. *a* **1550** [see *mustard-stone*, MUSTARD *sb.* 4 c]. **1573** *Art Limming* 5 b, Grind Synapour lake & Synapour topes ech by him selfe on a Painters stone. **1683** MOXON *Mech. Exerc., Printing* xvii. ¶2 The Stone is commonly about eighteen Inches diameter, having both its Sides truly Rub'd flat and smooth. *Ibid.* xxiv. ¶17 They are to be Ground with a Mullar on a smooth Marble Stone. *c* **1806** in *Archæol. Jrnl.* (1894) Ser. II. I. 112 A drawing..intended to be printed is made on a stone with a pen and a particular ink or with a kind of chalk. **1827** FARADAY *Chem. Manip.* xix. (1842) 535 Glass may be ground on almost any flat stone with a coarse grain, by means of a little sharp sand and water. **1886** FURNIVALL in *Shaks. Ven. & Ad.* (1st Qo. facs.) p. xix, *Troilus and Cressida* is partly on the stone.

j. A heavy stone used in athletic sports. Phrases, ***to cast, put,*** or ***throw the stone***: see also PUT *v.*¹ 2, *v.*² 2.

c **1300–1816** [see PUT *v.*¹ 2, *v.*² 2]. **1518** H. WATSON *Hist. Oliver of Castile* (Roxb.) C i b, Dysportes..vsed by noble men..as..tennys, lepe, sprynge, wrastle, cast the stone, cast the barre, or ony other games. **1561** HOBY tr. *Castiglione's Courtier* I. (1577) D vj, It is meet for hym also to haue the Arte of swymming, to leape, to runne, to caste the stone. **1620** [see CURLING-STONE]. **1638** NABBES *Totenham-Court* II. ii. (Bullen) I. 120 He pitcheth the barr and throws the stone. **1824** [see HOG *sb.*¹ 10]. **1849** *Chambers's Inform.* II. 649/2 Each person..causing his stone to slide towards the opposite end of the rink. **1891** [see CURLING-STONE].

†**6.** A vessel of stone, or of stoneware; a stone jar, cistern, etc. *Obs.* (Cf. STEAN.)

c **1450** LOVELICH *Grail* lv. 165 Thanne let he fyllen a ston [Fr. *vne cuue*]..Ful of water. *c* **1450** *Mirk's Festial* 52/8 Þen bade Ihesus seruandus full syxe stones þat stoden þer wyth watyr. **1470–85** MALORY *Arthur* IV. viii. 128 Oute of that pype ranne water..in a stone of marbel. *a* **1722** LISLE *Husb.* (1757) 206 The maltsters used to fling the barley out of the cistern or stone into the floor.

7. a. A precious stone: see PRECIOUS *a.* 6 a. *spec.* in *S. Afr.*: a diamond.

c **825** *Vesp. Psalter* xviii. 11 [xix. 10] Wilsum ofer gold & stan. *c* **1200** ORMIN 8170 Eȝȝwhær bisett Wiþþ deorewurrþe staness. *c* **1300** *Havelok* 1633 A gold ring drow he forth anon, An hundred pund was worth þe ston. **1340** *Ayenb.* 140 He louede betere þe bestes þet god him made þanne he dede gold oþer stones of pris. *c* **1386** CHAUCER *Clerk's T.* 1062 With a coroune of many a riche stoon Vp on hire heed. *c* **1475** *Rauf Coilȝear* 468 His Basnet was bordourit and burneist bricht With stanes of Beriall cleir, Dyamountis and Sapheir, Riche Rubeis in feir. **1503** DUNBAR *Thistle & Rose* 102 This lady..crownit him with dyademe Off radyous stonis. **1568** GRAFTON *Chron.* II. 383 A riche crowne of gold garnished with stone and pearle. **1594** SHAKS. *Rich. III*, I. iv. 27 Inestimable stones, vnvalewed Iewels. **1611** —— *Cymb.* II. iv. 40 Sparkles this Stone as it was wont? **1753** *Lond. Mag.* Oct. 480/2 His buckles of stones, of five guineas price. **1884** MRS. CAREY-HOBSON *At Home in Transvaal* 184 He had placed no stones in the bank since Graham had been on the Fields. **1891** E. GLANVILLE *Fossicker* xxix. 292 The cooling mud has closed around the 'stones', taking the impress of every angle and facet. **1910** H. A. MIERS in *Encycl. Brit.* VIII. 161/2 The River Diggings on the Vaal river are still worked upon a small scale... The stones, however, are good. **1946** S. CLOETE *Afr. Portraits* 109 His favourite stone was his blink klippie—his shining stone—the first diamond to be found in Africa. **1972** *Panorama* Dec. 27 'Stones' are usually over one carat (a carat being 200 milligrams). Anything smaller falls in the 'melee' category.

b. *Criminals' slang.* A diamond (see also quot. 1955).

1904 'No. 1500' *Life in Sing Sing* 252/2 *Stone*, diamond. **1936** J. CURTIS *Gilt Kid* xxiv. 240 Ten nicker for a little stone like that. **1955** D. W. MAURER in *Publ. Amer. Dial. Soc.* xxiv. 122 A man's tie-pin, seldom worn nowadays, was a prop. If it had a diamond setting, it was referred to as a stone.

c. *Austral.* Opal or opal-bearing material; an opal; *to be on stone*, to have struck opal stone. Also *N.Z.* (see quot. 1965).

1895 *Rep. N.S.W. Dept. Mines* 68 A patch of stone was taken about the end of the year which brought £1,200. **1921** K. S. PRICHARD *Black Opal* iv. 33 You don't suppose Jun'd try to take the stones off of him, do you? **1924** T. C. WOLLASTON *Opal* iv. 61 The men were not 'on stone', it seemed, but perhaps I could change the luck? **1965** G. J. WILLIAMS *Econ. Geol. N.Z.* iii. 20/2 *Stone*, a miner's term for payable [*sc.* auriferous] quartz. **1967** A. KALOKERINOS *In Search of Opal* 18 Stones that are worth $2,000 or more on the field are found at a rate that would not exceed one per week.

8. a. A lump of metallic ore. *Obs.* exc. in ***stone of tin***, a lump of tin ore.

c **888** ÆLFRED *Boeth.* xxxiv. §8 Þa gyldenan stanas, & þa seolfrenan, & ælces cynnes ȝimmas. **1778** W. PRYCE *Min. Cornub.* 81 A few Stones of Tin are found. **1895** *Times* 7 Jan. 3/4 The agents report good stones of tin coming from Trevannance engine shaft.

†**b.** = LOADSTONE. *Obs.*

1390 GOWER *Conf.* III. 293 He hath his rihte cours forth holde Be Ston and nedle, til he cam To Tharse. **1436** *Libel Eng. Policy* in *Pol. Poems* (Rolls) II. 191 Of Yseland to wryte is lytille nede,..Men have practised by nedle and by stone Thider-wardes wythine a lytel whylle. **1631** W. FOSTER *Sponge Weapon-salve* 25, I deny that the Loadstone doth worke upon the North-pole. The pole rather workes upon the stone.

9. = HAILSTONE.

1422 YONGE tr. *Secreta Secret.* 198 God keste ham dovne wyth grete Stonys of hawle. 1606 SHAKS. *Ant. & Cl.* III. xiii. 160 If I be so, From my cold heart let Heauen ingender haile, And poyson it in the sourse, and the first stone Drop in my necke. 1753 *Scots Mag.* June 307/1 Some of the stones measured three inches about.

10. a. A hard morbid concretion in the body, esp. in the kidney or urinary bladder, or in the gallbladder (GALL-STONE); also an intestinal concretion in some animals (***bezoar stone***: see BEZOAR 2 a): = CALCULUS 1. Also, the disease caused or characterized by the formation of such a concretion; lithiasis. (In hawks = CRAY[1] 2.)

c1000 *Sax. Leechd.* II. 238 On þære blædran stanas weaxað. 1398 TREVISA *Barth. De P.R.* VII. lv. (1495) 268 Of gleymy humours in the reynes and in the bledder comyth the stone. 1483 CAXTON *Cato* e viij b, [Mustard] purgeth.. the brayne and heyleth and breketh the stone. 1486 *Bk. St. Albans* C vij b, When yowre hawke may not metese then she hathe thatt sekenes calde the stoon. 1533 ELYOT *Cast. Helthe* (1541) 23 Chese ingendreth yll humours, and bredeth the stone. 1597 GERARDE *Herbal* II. cccciii. 888 The seede and roote of Saxifrage drunken with wine..breaketh the stone in the kidneies and bladder. 1620 VENNER *Via Recta* viii. 177 To liue fettered with gouts,..& tormented with stones. 1621 BURTON *Anat. Mel.* II. v. I. v. 474 Bezoar stone... I haue seene [some] that haue beene much displeased with faintnesse,..& taking the weight of three grains of this stone..haue beene cured. 1628 in Foster *Eng. Factories India* (1909) III. 206 Very sick, being newly cutt for the stone. 1709 STEELE *Tatler* No. 27 ¶2 In the Pangs of the Stone, Gout, or any acute Distemper. 1797 M. BAILLIE *Morbid Anat.* (1807) 373 Stones have some-times been found in the cavity of the uterus. 1846 G. E. DAY tr. *Simon's Anim. Chem.* II. 442 Of 59 small stones taken from a man aged 45 years, 24 consisted of urate of ammonia and 35 of uric acid. 1859 JEPHSON *Brittany* vii. 89 Mineral waters, said to be beneficial in cases of stone and dropsy. 1897 *Allbutt's Syst. Med.* IV. 233 The stones may have passed into the bowel.

b. A hard natural formation in an animal.

See also *crab-stone* (CRAB *sb.*[1] 13), *ear-stone* (EAR *sb.*[1] 10).

1605 [see CRAB'S-EYE]. 1661 LOVELL *Hist. Anim. & Min.* Isagoge d 6, All kinds of stones found in the heads of fishes, powdred and drunk in wine, help the collick. *Ibid.* 190 Crab. .. The eyes or stones..breake the stone.

11. a. A testicle: chiefly in *pl.* *Obs.* exc. in vulgar use. (See also BALLOCK-*stone*.)

1154 *O.E. Chron.* an. 1124 ad fin., Six men spilde of here ægon & of here stanes. 1387 TREVISA *Higden* (Rolls) IV. 289 þe rotynge of his priue stones. a1450 *Knt. de la Tour* 71 They toke a knyff, and cutte awey the monkes stones. 1542 BOORDE *Dyetary* xviii. (1870) 277 The stones of a cockrell, & the stones of other beestes that hath not done thyr kynde, be nutrytyue. 1617 MORYSON *Itin.* I. 163 The Toscanes hold Rammes stones fried for a great daintie. 1668 CULPEPPER & COLE *Barthol. Anat.* Introd., The action of the Liver is blood-making, of the Stones, Seed-making. 1713 J. WARDER *True Amazons* 10 In the very shape of the Stones of a Lamb.

†**b.** In old names of various species of orchis, as DOGSTONES, *fool's stones* (FOOL *sb.*[1] 7 c), *fox-stones* (FOX *sb.* 16); hence used in *plural* as a generic term for 'orchis'. *Obs.*

1562 TURNER *Herbal* II. 152 Ye other kindes [of orchis] ar in other countrees called fox stones or hear stones, & they may after ye Greke be called dogstones. 1597 GERARDE *Herbal* I. xcvii. 155, I haue placed it..next vnto the Lillies, before the kinds of *Orchis* or stones. *Ibid.* xcviii. 156 *Tragorchis*, or Gotes stones:..*Testiculus odoratus*, or sweete smelling stones:..*Testiculus Pumilio*, or Dwarffe stones.

12. The hard wood-like endocarp of a *stone-fruit* or drupe, inclosed by the pulpy pericarp, and inclosing the seed or kernel. Also applied to the hard seeds of some pulpy fruits, as the grape.

1523–34 FITZHERB. *Husb.* §140 Cheryes..maye be sette of stones. 1591 A. W. *Bk. Cookrye* 10 b, Great Raisins, the stones taken out. 1603 SHAKS. *Meas. for M.* II. i. 110 Cracking the stones of the foresaid prewyns. 1620 VENNER *Via Recta* vii. 120 In the eating of Grapes..that neither the skinnes, nor the kernels or stones in them be swallowed downe. 1796 WITHERING *Brit. Plants* (ed. 3) I. 252 Prunus. .. S[eed] Vessel nearly globular, pulpy, including a nut or stone. 1870 HOOKER *Stud. Flora* 108 Bird Cherry..Stone globose. 1882 VINES tr. *Sachs' Bot.* 122 The stone is the inner layer of the fundamental tissue of the same foliar structure of which the outer layers form the succulent flesh of the fruit.

13. A name for a domino.

1865 *Compl. Domino-player* 19 [At vingt-et-un] the dealer then slides the players one domino or stone each. 1870 *Routledge's Ev. Boy's Ann.* 274 Stones... The name by which the domino is called at vingt-et-un.

14. a. A measure of weight, usually equal to 14 pounds avoirdupois (⅛ of a hundredweight, or half a 'quarter'), but varying with different commodities from 8 to 24 pounds. The stone of 14 lb. is the common unit used in stating the weight of a man or large animal. (Collective pl. usually *stone*.) See also STONE-WEIGHT.

139. *Earl Derby's Exp.* (Camden) 76/16 Pro x stone lini. a1400 *Sir Perc.* 2024 The clobe wheyhed reghte wele,..The hede was of harde stele, Twelve stone weghte! There was iryne in the wande, Ten stone of the lande. 1465 *Manners & Househ. Exp.* (Roxb.) 200 Item, in aparayll of the said shippe; ropes for hyr srowde, the wyche weyid xv. stone .ij. li., prise the stone, xxj.d. 1474 *Stat. Winch.* in *Cov. Leet Bk.* 396 The wich kepes weyght & mesure l li. the halfe C, xxvti li. the quartern, xij li. & halfe the halfe quartern, þe wich was called of olde tyme beyng Stone of London, & vj li. & a quartern ys the halfe Stone, as it appereth in Magna Carta. 1483 in *Acta Dom. Concil.* (1839) 83*/2, ix stane of chese,.. ten stane of butter. 1495 *Act 11 Hen. VII*, c. 4 §2 Be it also enacted that ther be but only..xiiij lb. to the stone of Wolle. 1520 *Cov. Leet Bk.* 668 That no taloe be solde by-twene this & the next lete a-bove ij s. the Stonne. 1542 RECORDE *Gr. Artes* (1575) 203 In woolle..the 14 pounde is not named halfe quarterne, but a Stone. 1609 SKENE *Reg. Maj., Stat. Robt. III*, 56 b, The stane to wey woll and other things, sould haue fiuetene punds. Ane stane of walx, aucht. Twelue London punds makes ane stane. 1674 JOSSELYN *Two Voy.* 15 Of Sugar and Spice 8 pound make the stone. 1730 CHENY *List Horse-Matches* 68 Fourteen Hands to carry Nine Stone. 1825 R. P. WARD *Tremaine* I. xviii. 123 He rose up, as well as sixteen stone would permit. 1845 G. DODD *Brit. Manuf.* IV. 96 The wool comes in bags containing about ten stones each—a 'stone' in this commodity being twenty-four pounds. 1846 *Baxter's Libr. Pract. Agric.* I. 213 A calf..eighteen weeks old, weighing..33 stone. 1887 'M. RUTHERFORD' *Revol. Tanner's Lane* i. (ed. 8) 7 A drayman weighing about eighteen stone. 1913 *Times* 19 Aug. 14/5 Quotations per stone of 8 lb...Beef..Mutton.

b. A piece of metal of this weight, used in weighing, or (as in quot.) as a standard.

1556 *Peebles Burgh Rec.* (1872) 235 The commoun stane to be put in sure keping in the commoun Kist.

c. In phr. ***to give a stone and a beating to*** (Racing slang): to outrun easily, despite carrying a heavier weight. Also *transf.*, to surpass. Now *rare*.

1885 *Daily News* 4 Feb. 5/2 *Canis vulpis* is, as a rule, able to give, intellectually speaking, and in language germane to the matter, 'a stone and a beating' to the majority of his pursuers. 1906 *Punch* 18 Apr. 286/3 Their Smokeroom is deliciously comfy, and can give a stone and a beating to ours at the Camellia.

15. In collectors' names of certain moths: see also MOCHA[1] 2.

1775 M. HARRIS *Engl. Lepidoptera* 45 Phalæna... Stone, mocha... Stone, pale mocha. 1832 J. RENNIE *Consp. Butterfl. & Moths* 64 Xylina... The Stone (*X. petrificata*..) Wings..pale grey brown. *Ibid.* 114 *Ephyra*... The Mocha Stone (*E. porata*..).

16. Proverbial phrases. †**a.** ***to boil, roast,*** or ***wash a stone***: to labour in vain, expend effort with no result. *Obs.*

1522 SKELTON *Why not to Court* 109 They may..elles go rost a stone. 1546 J. HEYWOOD *Prov.* II. ii. (1867) 46, I doo but roste a stone. In warmyng hir. c1548 in Strype *Eccl. Mem.* (1822) II. II. 316 Or els he washeth a stone, that is to say, he laboureth in vayne. 1895 *Westm. Gaz.* 22 May 6/1 Like the old saying:—'Boil stones in butter and you shall sup the broth.'

b. ***to kill two birds with one stone***: to accomplish two different purposes by the same act or proceeding.

1656 [see BIRD *sb.* 6]. 1696 *Growth of Deism in Eng.* 11 Thereby they kill two or three Birds with one stone. 1847 MRS. SHERWOOD *Fairchild Fam.* III. xxi. 273 So..she will be killing two birds with one stone.

c. ***to leave no stone unturned*** (also formerly ***to move, roll,*** or ***turn every stone*** or ***all stones***): to try every possible expedient in order to bring about a desired result.

c1550 *Dice-Play* B vj, He wil refuse no labor nor leaue no stone vnturned, to pick vp a penny. 1569 UNDERDOWNE *Heliodorus* VIII. 108 b, Now turne euery stoane, deuise al maner of meanes. 1600 HOLLAND *Livy* XXV. xxiii. 565 Hee would leave no stone unrolled, but trie all waies that could be devised. 1637 GILLESPIE *Eng. Pop. Cerem.* Epist. B 1 b, They make so much adoe, and move every stone against us. 1648 J. BEAUMONT *Psyche* x. lxx, Still he persever'd all stones to roll, Which might that one in Judas' Bosom move. 1670 G. H. tr. *Hist. Cardinals* II. III. 190 [He] has left no stone unturn'd to arrive at his designs. 1791 BURKE *Corr.* (1844) III. 349 We shall not be negligent; no stone will be left unturned. 1873 STANLEY *Serm. East* 108 He left no stone unturned to do the work which was set before him.

d. (*a*) †***to roll the stone***: to discuss a matter (*obs.*). (*b*) ***to set*** (†***put***) ***a stone rolling***: to start a course of action which may lead to unforeseen, esp. disastrous, consequences. (*c*) Prov. ***a rolling stone gathers no moss***: see MOSS *sb.* 3 b, ROLLING STONE 1. (*d*) †***to stand on a rolling stone*** (etc.): to be in a precarious position where one is likely to fall or suffer disaster (*obs.*).

1581 R. GOADE in *Confer.* III. (1584) Q iiij, This stone hath bene rowled enough. 1592 KYD *Spanish Trag.* I. iii. 317 Whose foote is standing on a rowling stone. 1602 FULBECKE *Pandectes* 78 How murther hath beene punished..I haue shewed I hope sufficientlie..so that I shall not need here to rowle the same stone. 1613 SHAKS. *Hen. VIII* v. iii. 104, I told ye all When we first put this dangerous stone a rowling, 'Twold fall vpon our selues.

†**e.** ***to spring*** or ***be sprung of*** (***a, the***) ***stone***: used in similative expressions indicating the absence of any known ancestry or kinsfolk. *Obs.*

1297 R. GLOUC. (Rolls) 6720 Seint Edward in normandie was þo bileued al one As bar, as wo seiþ, of þe kunde as he sprong of þe stone. a1300 *K. Horn* (Camb.) 1026 Horn him ȝede alone, Also he sprunge of stone. a1400 *Sir Perc.* 1043 Als he ware sprongene of a stane, Thare na mane hym kende.

†**f.** ***to take a stone*** (***up***) ***in the ear***: (of a woman) to lapse from virtue. *slang.* *Obs.*

1691 SHADWELL *Scowrers* II. 19 Did you see who went off with your Aunt! is she given to stumble? will she take a Stone in her Ear? 1702 T. BROWN *Lett. fr. Dead* Wks. 1730 II. 92 Madam, I much rejoice to hear, You'll take a stone up in your ear; For I'm a frail transgressor too.

g. ***to throw*** (***cast***) ***a stone*** or ***stones*** (***at***): to make an attack (upon), or bring an accusation (against). So ***to cast the first stone*** (in allusion to John viii. 7).

1568 *Sat. Poems Reform.* xlvii. 83 Quhat cummer castis the formest stane,..At tha peure winschis ȝe wranguslie suspect. 1579 FULKE *Heskins' Parl.* 325 Will not all the Grammarians, Logicians, and Rhetoricians..throwe stones at him? a1633 [see GLASS *sb.*[1] 1]. 1670 [see GLASS WINDOW]. 1674 HICKMAN *Hist. Quinquart.* (ed. 2) 109 The Doctor, as if he were perfectly free from this crime, thus throweth his stones at others. 1754 SHEBBEARE *Matrimony* (1766) II. 102 Thee shouldst not throw stones, who hast a Head of Glass thyself. 1827 SCOTT *Chron. Canongate* v, It is not, however, prudent to commence with throwing stones, just when I am striking out windows of my own. 1869 [see GLASS-HOUSE 2].

h. ***stone of stumbling*** (†***scandal,*** †***slander,*** etc.): an occasion of scandal or stumbling, a stumbling-block (Vulgate *petra scandali*). †***stone of touch*** = TOUCHSTONE (*obs.*).

1382 WYCLIF *Isa.* viii. 14 The Lord..shal be..in to a ston ..of offencion [1388 a stoon of hirtyng], and in to a ston of sclaunder [COVERD. stone to stomble at, ye rock to fall vpon; 1611 for a stone of stumbling and for a rocke of offence] to the two houses of Irael. 1604 A. CRAIG *Poet. Ess.* (1873) 13 Be thou the stone (precellent Prince) of tuch, For to secerne the honest mindes from such. 1639 S. DU VERGER *Camus' Admir. Events* 111 She was accounted as a stone of scandall which ought to bee cast forth of the City. 1695 tr. *Misson's Voy. Italy* II. 107 His Authority has been always a Stone of Stumbling to those who are wont to make Prejudice their Rule of Faith. 1911 B. NIGHTINGALE *Ejected of 1662 in Cumbld. & Westmld.* I. 701 Hutchinson's error has..been quite a stone of stumbling to subsequent writers.

i. Phrases of comparison, with adjs. (***cold, dead, hard,*** etc. ***as*** (***a***) ***stone***): see 3 c.

17. *attrib.* passing into *adj.* **a.** Consisting of stone; made or built of stone.

a1000 *Cædmon's Gen.* 1700 (Gr.) Him on laste bu stiðlie stantorr. a1000 *Ruin* 39 (Gr.) Stanhofu stodan. 1402–3 *Durham Acc. Rolls* (Surtees) 217, 1 stanetrogh et 1 tretrogh. 1420 *Engl. Misc.* (Surtees) 17 The stane house toward the kynges strete. c1483 in Nicolas *Chron. Lond.* (1827) 7 In this yere the stone brigge of Londone was first begoune to make. 1552 HULOET, Stone crosse, *pyramis*. a1578 LINDESAY (Pitscottie) *Chron. Scot.* (S.T.S.) I. 176 [He] bigit money stain house. 1610 HOLLAND *Camden's Brit.* (1637) 333 A very goodly stone bridge of arch-work. 1663 GERBIER *Counsel* 18 The Stone or wooden Figure. a1672 WOOD *Life* (O.H.S.) I. 43 M. Anthony Wood..was borne in an antient stone-house opposite.. Merton Coll. a1728 WOODWARD *Fossils Method* II. 39 The Stone-Weapons,..were all cut out, and made, before the Discovery of Iron. 1766 SMOLLETT *Trav.* I. 351 The olives..are..ground into a paste by a mill-stone, set edge-ways into a circular stone-trough. *Ibid.* II. 46 A range of antient Roman stone-coffins. 1776 G. SEMPLE *Building in Water* 89 The Water that had fallen on the Urn from the Lime-stone..had petrified and made a Stone-crust on the outside thereof. 1805 R. W. DICKSON *Pract. Agric.* I. Plate XIII, A common stone roller..for rolling arable lands. 1829 SCOTT *Anne of G.* xiv, The sword, escaping from his hold, rolled on the stone floor with a heavy clash. 1833 TENNYSON *Lady Clara* 23 The lion on your old stone gates. 1837 DICKENS *Pickw.* xxii, At last he reached a stone hall. 1841 BREES *Gloss. Civil Engin.* 24 Stone blocks were introduced in place of wooden sleepers. 1908 [MISS E. FOWLER] *Betw. Trent & Ancholme* 29 A stone quern.

b. Made of stoneware; also *transf.* of ginger-beer contained in stoneware bottles.

c950 *Lindisf. Gosp.* Mark xiv. 3 & mið-ðy ȝebrocen wæs þæt stan fæt to-dælde..ofer heafud his. 1479–81 *Rec. St. Mary at Hill* (1905) 101 Item, for a stone potte to put in oyle, j d ob. 1547 *Test. Ebor.* (Surtees) VI. 256 My stone cup withe the silver cover. c1600 *Acc. Bk. W. Wray* in *Antiquary* XXXII. 80 Beate them well in a stone morter. 1626 in Jewitt *Life Wedgwood* (1865) 37 To grant vnto them our royall priveledge for 'The sole making of the Stone Potte, Stone Jugge, and Stone Bottle', within our Dominions. 1642 *Rates of Merchandizes* 54 Stonebirds or Whistles. [Cf. *Ibid.* 57 Whistles, cocks or Birds of stone.] 1676 WORLIDGE *Vinet. Brit.* 103 Glass-bottles are preferr'd to Stone-bottles, because that Stone-bottles are apt to leak. a1756 ELIZA HAYWOOD *New Present* (1771) 215 Always keep your pickles in stone jars. 1782 COWPER *Gilpin* 66 Mistress Gilpin..Had two stone bottles found, To hold the liquor that she lov'd. 1851–4 TOMLINSON *Cycl. Arts* (1867) II. 196/2 The contents of the basket are turned into a stone or iron vessel. 1884 *B'ham Daily Post* 28 July 3/4 Mineral-water Trade..stone beer. 1904 H. BESWICK *Last Karkawber* etc. 37 While I sipped my stone-ginger.

c. Applied to substances in a solid or massive (as distinct from liquid or powdered) form, as ***stone alum***, STONE-BLUE, ***stone ochre***, STONE-PITCH.

1608 TOPSELL *Serpents* 42 Mustard-seede three scruples, ..Stone-Allom and Opopanax, of either halfe an ounce. 1815 J. SMITH *Panorama Sci. & Art* II. 802 A thin coat of gold size..composed of stone ochre ground in fat oil.

d. Of, pertaining or relating to stone or stones (in various senses).

1826 A. C. HUTCHINSON *Pract. Observ. Surg.* 313 The paucity of stone cases occurring in tropical climates. 1833 LOUDON *Encycl. Archit.* §1244 Constructing them..either on the wooden model or the stone model. 1879 RUSKIN *Hortus Incl.* (1887) 67 It is delightful of you to be interested in that stone book. 1911 W. W. SKEAT in *Folk-lore* (1912) XXIII. 60 The best-known stone superstition is that the celt was a thunderbolt.

e. *ellipt.* Belonging to the STONE AGE.

1864 J. HUNT tr. *Vogt's Lect. Man* xii. 340 The stone skull ..is still narrower than the Lapp skull. *Ibid.* 368 The stone people of Europe knew of no metal. 1880 DAWSON *Fossil Man* i. (1883) 7 The earlier Stone folk are known to us only by their graves.

f. (from 11.) Of male domestic animals: Not castrated, entire, as ***stone-ass, -colt, -ram,*** STONE-HORSE; †thence allusively of men = lascivious, lustful, as ***stone-priest, -puritan***.

1602 CHETTLE *Hoffman* II. (1631) C 3, I could helpe you now to a stone mule, a *stone-asse. a1722 LISLE *Husb.* (1757) 355 A mare takes a stone-ass. 1691 *Lond. Gaz.* No. 2710/4 A Cream-coloured young *Stone-Colt. 1778 *Eng. Gazetteer* (ed. 2), Benager..near Mendip-hills; has a fair for stone colts at Whitsuntide. **1608** *Merry Devil Edmonton* IV. i. (facs.) E 1, The *stone Priest steales more venison then halfe the country. **1663** DRYDEN *Wild Gallant* v. ii, Who have I got, a Stone-Priest by this good Light. **1614** B. JONSON *Barth. F.* III. ii, Fine ambling hypocrites! and a *stone-puritane. **1764** *Ann. Reg.* II. 10/1 Their winter garment is made of deer or *stone-ram skins with the hair on.

g. With preceding numeral, forming an attrib. or adj. phrase, in sense (*a*) set with a (specified) number of (precious) stones; (*b*) weighing (so many) stone; hence *transf.* applied to the prize in a race in which the horses carry the specified weight.

1683 *Lond. Gaz.* No. 1865/8 A Seven Stone Diamond Ring. **1705** *Ibid.* No. 4149/4 A 12 Stone Plate..will be run for..by Hunters.

18. Obvious Combinations (unlimited in number): **a.** attrib. as ***stone-cliff, -heap, -marl*** (MARL *sb.*[1] 1 b), ***-merchant, -quarry, -ship, -volley, -worship***, etc. **b.** objective, etc., as ***stone-caster, -digger, -gatherer, †-graver, -hewer, -setter, -shooter, -worshipper; stone-casting, -cleaving, -darting, -eating, -haunting, -moving, -rolling, -throwing, -worshipping*** sbs. and adjs.; ***stone-like*** adj. **c.** instrumental, locative, and parasynthetic, as ***stone-builder; stone-arched, -bearded, -bladed, -built, -coated, -edged, -faced, -flagged, -floored, -headed, -horned, †-living*** (living in stone), ***-paved, -pillared, -ribbed, -roofed, -strewn***, etc., adjs.; ***stone-face*** vb.

1822 SCOTT *Nigel* x, The old *stone-arched hall. **1922** JOYCE *Ulysses* 141 A man supple in combat: stonehorned, *stonebearded, heart of stone. **1893** H. BALFOUR in *6th Ann. Rep. Univ. Mus. Oxford* 24 *Stone-bladed axe. **1837** CARLYLE *Fr. Rev.* II. I. x. Spade-men, barrow-men, *stone-builders. **1913** SIR H. JOHNSTON *Pioneers Australasia* viii. 266 This vanished race of stone-builders whose works stretch across the Pacific. **1798** *Times* 28 June 4/1 A large *stone-built Farm House. **1598** GRENEWEY *Tacitus, Ann.* II. v. (1622) 39 The Captaine..commaunded the sling-casters and *stone-casters to let freely at them. *a* **1400** *Octovian* 895 At wrestelyng, and at *ston castynge, He wan the prys. **1644** DIGBY *Nat. Soul* Concl. 457 In halfe yeare nights;..in perpetuall *stonecleauing coldes. **1884** KNIGHT *Dict. Mech.* Suppl. 866/2 Stone cleaving Machine..for dividing granite. **1912** E. POUND *Ripostes* 26 Storms, on the *stone-cliffs beaten. **1767** *Phil. Trans.* LVII. 411 A clean *stone-coated retort. **1769** PENNANT *Brit. Zool.* III. 145 The stone-coated worms which the fishermen call hadock meat. **1599** NASHE *Lenten Stuffe* 12 Their *stondarting engines. **1562** in *Archæologia* XXXVI. 301 To Dorye the *stone dyggere.. for xxxiij. dayes dyggynge of stone and chalke. **1864** in *Life W. Pennefather* (1879) 389 Including stone-diggers, there were representatives from more than thirty..villages. **1815** KIRBY & SP. *Entomol.* xii. (1818) I. 391 The *stone-eating caterpillars recorded in the Memoirs of the French Academy..are now known to erode the walls..solely for the purpose of forming their cocoons. **1895** K. GRAHAME *Golden Age* 45 Terrace of shaven sward, *stone-edged. **1852** WIGGINS *Embanking* 125 The cost of *stone-facing a sea-bank. **1632** LITHGOW *Trav.* VIII. 375 Where huge and hilly lands Haue *stone-fac'd scurrile bounds. **1874** *Contemp. Rev.* Oct. 762 The churches are proud of their stone-faced interiors. **1932** W. FAULKNER *Light in August* xvi. 355 This time he indicates the stonefaced woman; she may or may not be listening to what he is saying. **1973** M. WOODHOUSE *Blue Bone* ix. 82 The Eisenwald Volksklinik was..a huge stonefaced structure. **1904** E. WHARTON *Italian Villas* i. 53 The house is built about three sides of a raised *stone-flagged terrace. **1978** J. WAINWRIGHT *Jury People* v. 16 The room had a stone-flagged floor. **1841** DICKENS *Barn. Rudge* lviii, A *stone-floored room. **1875** KNIGHT *Dict. Mech.* 2396/2 **Stone-gatherer*, a machine for picking up loose surface stones in fields. **1894** LADY M. VERNEY *Verney Mem.* III. 132 Stone-gatherers should be set to work on some of the fields. **1530** TINDALE *Exod.* xxviii. 11 After the worke of a *stonegrauer..shalt thou graue the .ii. stones with the names of the childern of Israel. **1933** AUDEN *Poems* (ed. 2) 43 By pot-holed becks A bird *stone-haunting, an unquiet bird. **1829** G. GRIFFIN *Collegians* I. viii. 170 The difference which existed between..an English halberd and a *stone-headed gai-bulg. **1904** SPENCER & GILLEN *North. Tribes Central Australia* xxiii. 671 A stone-headed spear. **1382** WYCLIF *2 Kings* x. 8 Puttith hem at the two *stone hepis [Vulg. *ad duos acervos*]. **1868** *N. & Q.* 15 Aug. 165/2 The game Set-a-Foot is still played by the rising generation who frequent Park Square, Regent's Park, under the name of Stone Heaps. **1941** F. THOMPSON *Over to Candleford* 356 They ran..and wrestled the whole way, or pushed each other over stone-heaps or into ditches. **1977** *New Yorker* 17 Oct. 37/3 Her stone heap... My mother spreads out soapy white laundry on these stones, so that the hot sun will bleach them even whiter. **1579–80** NORTH *Plutarch, Alcib.* (1595) 217 Many carpenters, masons, *stone hewers, and other workmen. **1837** CARLYLE *Fr. Rev.* II. vi. viii, Heavy Monge the Mathematician, once a stone-hewer. **1922** *Stone-horned [see *stone-bearded* above]. **1776** DA COSTA *Elem. Conchol.* 2 A Shell..a kind of *stone-like calcareous covering..in which the whole animal..lives included as in a house. **1855** LYNCH *Rivulet* XXVI. i, While the law on stone is written, Stone-like is the mighty word. **1631** W. FOSTER *Sponge Weapon-salve* 25 But of *Saxanimalia* *stone-living creatures never did I heare. **1760** R. BROWN *Compl. Farmer* II. 44 Cow-shut or *stone-marle is commonly found under clay. **1805** R. W. DICKSON *Pract. Agric.* I. 238 It is distinguished..into shell, clay, and stone *marle*..the stone marle has different proportions of sand united with the calcareous matter and the clay. **1610** HEALEY *St. Aug. Citie of God* XVIII. xiii. 678 The fiction..of Amphion and his *stone-mooving musicke. *a* **1593** MARLOWE *Ovid's Elegies* III. i. 3 A *stone-pau'd sacred spring. **1819** SCOTT *Leg. Montrose* xiii, On the floor of a damp and stone-paved dungeon. **1601** HOLLAND *Pliny* VII. lvi. I. 188 Cadmus.. found out *stone quarries first. **1837** CARLYLE *Fr. Rev.* III. VI. iii, He has to fly again, to skulk, round Paris, in thickets and stone-quarries. **1817** SCOTT *Harold* IV. i. 2 The long Gothic aisle and *stone-ribb'd roof. **1936** L. B. LYON *Bright Feather Fading* 19 The bone-Bare garden steep, the stone-ribbed land. **1606** SYLVESTER *Du Bartas* II. iv. I. *Tropheis* 1045 *Stone-rowling Tay. **1903** *Daily Chron.* 31 Mar. 9/1 Wheelbarrow races and stone-rolling competitions. **1825** R. WILSON *Hist. Hawick* 56 The building..being *stone-roofed, was preserved. **1725** *Lond. Gaz.* No. 6432/5 Simon Dyer,..*Stone-setter. **1849** W. R. O'BYRNE *Naval Biog. Dict.* 850/2 An attempt to sink two *stone-ships at the entrance of the harbour. **1875** JOWETT *Plato* (ed. 2) III. 700 Two archers, two slingers, three *stone-shooters. **1853** M. ARNOLD *Poems* 179 The climbing gourd-plant's leaves Muffled its walls, and on the *stone-strewn roof Lay the warm golden gourds. **1974** R. ADAMS *Shardik* x. 71 The bear's trail led on through the bushes to emerge in open, stone-strewn woodland. **1598** GRENEWEY *Tacitus, Ann.* XIII. ix. (1622) 191 The sling-casters and *stone-throwers had a place appointed them. **1880** GOLDW. SMITH *Cowper* ii. 32 He..became the mark for a little *stone-throwing. **1881** W. E. FORSTER in T. W. Reid *Life* (1888) II. 321 An obstructing, stone-throwing mob. **1861** M. PATTISON *Ess.* (1889) I. 45 A *stone-vaulted kitchen. **1837** CARLYLE *Fr. Rev.* I. III. viii, It has passed from..duelling..to street-fighting; to *stone-volleys and musket-shot. **1838** AKERMAN in *Numism. Jrnl.* II. 216 The *stone-worship of the ancients illustrated by their coins. **1844** LINGARD *Anglo-Sax. Ch.* (1858) I. iv. 152 *note*, We forbid *stone-worshippings.

19. a. In adverbial comb. with adjs. or pples., in similative sense (cf. phrases in 3), and hence occas. as a mere intensive (= very, completely): as in ***stone-asleep, †-astonied, -bright, -cold*** (also in quasi-advb. attrib. use, esp. in phr. ***stone cold sober*** = utterly sober), ***-comfortless, -dead, -deaf, -dumb, -hard, †-naked, †-old*** (Sc. *staneauld*), ***-silent***; STONE-BLIND, also STONE-STILL *adv.* and *adj.* Also with adjs. of colour (which may also be used as sbs.), as ***stone-brown, -buff, -grey***.

1826 HOOD *Last Man* 64 The folks were all *stone-asleep. **1596** R. L[INCHE] *Diella* (1877) 60 *Stone-astonied, like a Deare at gaze. **1916** E. POUND *Lustra* 26, I have known the *stone-bright place, The hall of clear colours. **1894** R. B. SHARPE *Birds Gt. Brit.* I. 65 Eggs.—Four to six in number. Ground-colour, *stone-brown..scribbled and blotched all over with black. **1882–4** *Yarrell's Brit. Birds* (ed. 4) III. 561 The nestling is of a *stone-buff on the upper parts. **1592** BRETON *Pilgr. Paradise* (Grosart) 12/1 Thou *stone-colde hart. **1836** T. HOOK *G. Gurney* I. 139 The lamb was stone cold, and the fish boiled to pieces. **1855** MILMAN *Lat. Chr.* XIV. iii. (1864) IX. 123 His text-book was the rigid, stone-cold Sentences of Peter the Lombard. **1913** F. H. BURNETT *T. Tembarom* xxxiv. 435 It'd be stone-cold safe to rush things. **1937** T. RATTIGAN *French without Tears* III. i. 65 Are you stone-cold sober? **1958** A. SILLITOE *Saturday Night & Sunday Morning* vii. 111 We've been stone-cold sober since Canning Circus. **1969** C. ARMSTRONG *Seven Seats to Moon* v. 59, I could have been stone-cold-dead in Chicago! **1979** O. SELA *Petrograd Consignment* 144 Unlike the other revolutionaries, the Bolsheviks..were resolutely stone-cold sober. **1924** D. H. LAWRENCE in M. Magnus *Mem. Foreign Legion* 13 There I had a big and lonely, *stone-comfortless room. *c* **1290** *St. Agnes* 76 in *S. Eng. Leg.* 183 He fel a-doun *stan-ded. **1531** TINDALE *Expos. 1 John* (1537) 55 We were stone dead and wythout lyfe or power to do or consent to good. **1590** SPENSER *F.Q.* II. xi. 43 As when Ioues harnesse-bearing Bird from hie Stoupes at a flying heron..The stone-dead quarrey fals. **1719** DE FOE *Crusoe* II. (Globe) 331 He dropt down stone-dead. **1888** BRYCE *Amer. Commw.* lxxxix. III. 217 Keep up the fight until it [the power of corruption] is stone dead. **1837** LOCKHART *Life Scott* (1839) IX. 197 A man almost literally *stone-deaf could not discharge..the highest duties of a parish-priest in a satisfactory manner. **1872** A. J. C. HARE *Story My Life* (1900) IV. xvi. 50 She is quite stone-deaf, so we..correspond on a slate. **1888** F. R. STOCKTON in *Century Mag.* Feb. 622, I did say to myself.. Now Elizabeth is so *stone dumb that she'll jus' stay here an' do the little I tell her to do. **1878** TRIMEN *Regiments Brit. Army* 21 Its uniform when raised was *stone-grey. **13..** *E.E. Allit. P.* B. 884, & steken þe ȝates *ston-harde wyth stalworth barrez. *a* **1400** *Minor Poems fr. Vernon MS.* 618/222 Iewes ston-hard in sinnes merk. **1594** SHAKS. *Rich. III*, IV. iv. 227 The murd'rous Knife was dull and blunt, Till it was whetted on thy stone-hard heart. **1875** TENNYSON *Q. Mary* I. v, He is..Stone-hard, ice-cold—no dash of daring in him. *c* **1450** *Mirour Saluacioun* (Roxb.) 77 ȝe tirvid hym *stone naked aȝeinward scornfully. *c* **1800** *Johnnie o Cocklesmuir* xi. in Child *Ballads* III. 9 By there came a *stane-auld man. **1862** CARLYLE *Fredk. Gt.* XII. x. (1865) IV. 235 Friedrich..was *stone-silent on this matter. **1769** J. WEDGWOOD *Let.* 1 Dec. (1965) 85 We have nobody making white ware here, only *stone white ware. **1949** E. POUND *Pisan Cantos* lxxxiv. 129 Carrara Snow on the marble Snow-white against stone-white.

b. Intensively with adjs. in non-similative use (after *stone-broke* adj., sense 20 a below): completely, utterly, 'plumb', as ***stone crazy, drunk, mad***, etc. Also in adj. relation to sb., complete, utter, 'dead'; excellent. Cf. *stone ginger* (b), sense 20 a below. *slang.*

1928 *Lawn Tennis & Badminton* 23 June 255/2 Few could have foreseen that the two doubles would have been the 'stone certainties' for Britain that they proved to be. **1933** PARTRIDGE *Words, Words, Words!* 214 India gives us ..*piache*, mad... On the analogy of *stone mad, stone piache* was employed for a change. **1935** Z. N. HURSTON *Mules & Men* (1970) I. iii. 66 You must be stone crazy! Why, dis hide is worth five thousand dollars. **1947** K. TENNANT *Lost Haven* ix. 126 Oh, don't let him think of the punt again—that was the stone finish! **1959** *Esquire* Nov. 70 *Stone*, adjective meaning complete. Example: He's a stone musician. **1960** *Observer* 25 Dec. 7/7 If..he were stone rich and lived in a big drum in the country. **1968** *Blues Unlimited* Dec. 12 First things developed was the set of four reissue albums labelled 'Legendary Masters'; three being stone blues albums. **1970** D. M. DAVIN *Not here, not Now* III. vi. 202 This was the finish, the stone end of it. **1978** *N.Y. Times* 30 Mar. A21/1 A little later another patrol..declared him stone drunk, and confiscated his documents and his car keys.

c. As *adj.*, excited; intoxicated with drink or drugs, 'stoned'. *U.S. slang. rare.*

1945 L. SHELLY *Jive Talk Dict.* 19/1 *Stone* (adj), excited or intoxicated. **1960** R. G. REISNER *Jazz Titans* 165 *Stone*, drunk or high.

20. a. Special comb.: **†stone-bag**, ? a bag carried on board ship, containing stones to be used as shot; **stone-bark** *Bot.*, bark consisting chiefly of hardened and thickened cells (cf. *stone-cell*); **stone-barrow** [BARROW *sb.*[3]], a barrow for carrying stones; **†stone-binder** = OSTEOCOLLA; **stone-boiler**, one who practises *stone-boiling*; **stone-boiling**, the process of boiling water by putting hot stones in it, as practised by certain primitive peoples; **stone-brash** [BRASH *sb.*[2]], a subsoil consisting of loose broken stone; also *attrib.*; **stone-breaker**, a person employed in, or a machine used for, breaking stones; so **stone-breaking**; **stone-broke** *a. slang*, 'hard up', ruined (cf. *stony-broke*, STONY *a.* 6 c); **stone bruise** chiefly *N. Amer.*, an injury to the feet caused by walking on stony ground; hence **stone-bruised** *a.*; **stone-buckle**, a buckle set with precious stones; **stone-butter** [after G. *steinbutter*; cf. *rock-butter* BUTTER *sb.*[1] 3], a name for alum occurring in soft masses greasy to the touch; **stone-canal** *Zool.*, a canal forming part of the water-vascular system in Echinoderms, usually with calcareous walls, leading from the madreporic plate to the circumoral water-vessel; **†stone-case**, (*a*) ? an enclosed millstone for grinding apples for cider; (*b*) a case to contain a stone; **stone cell** *Bot.*, one of a number of greatly hardened and thickened cells occurring in certain plants; **stone-china**, a kind of stoneware (see quot. 1825); **stone circle** *Archæol.*, = CIRCLE *sb.* 12; **stone cist** *Archæol.*: see CIST 1 a; **†stone-colic**, colic attributed to the presence of a stone in the kidneys (see 10); **stone-colour**, the (usual) colour of stone, a yellowish or brownish grey, also *attrib.*; so **stone-coloured** *a.*; **stone-craft**, the art or skill of working in stone; sculpture; **stone cream**, a traditional blancmange-like sweet served cold on a base of jam; **stone-crusher**, a machine for crushing or grinding stone, a stone-breaker; **stone-delf** (now *dial.*) a stone-quarry; **†stone-doublet** *slang*, a prison; **†stone-drawer**, (*a*) a surgical instrument for extracting a stone from the bladder; (*b*) a man who digs stone from a quarry, a quarryman; **stone-dresser**, one who dresses or shapes stone for building; also, a machine for this purpose; so **stone-dressing** (also *attrib.*); **stone-drop** (*nonce-wd.*), poetic name for a stalactite; **stone-dust**, dust or powder made of particles of broken stone; hence **stone-dusting**, the introduction of stone-dust to the air in a mine to render the coal-dust less combustible; **stone-dust** *v. trans.*, with place as obj.; **stone-eared** *a.*, 'hard of hearing', deaf (in quot. in *fig.* sense); **stone-eater**, a conjuror who pretends to swallow stones (see also 20 b); **stone-element** *Bot.*, a hard element of tissue (cf. *stone-cell*); **stone-engraving**, the art or process of engraving on stone, lithography; **stone era** = *stone period*; **stone-etching**, the art or process of etching on stone; **stone-eyed** *a.*, (*a*) ? having the eyes fixed or motionless; (*b*) dull-sighted, 'blind' (*fig.*); **stone face** *U.S. colloq.*, a person whose features reveal no emotions; a poker-faced person; esp. in phr. ***great stone face*** in playful allusion to Hawthorne's tale (see bracketed quot. 1850); **stone-fall**, a fall of meteoric stones, or of loose stones on a mountain slope; **stone fence**, (*a*) a fence made of stones, a stone wall; (*b*) *U.S. slang*, name for various intoxicating drinks (see quots.); **stone-field**, an expanse of ground covered with large stones; *spec.* = FELSENMEER; **stone frigate** *Naut. slang*, a Naval shore establishment or barracks (see quot. 1948); formerly *spec.* a naval prison; also *transf.*; **stone-gall** [GALL *sb.*[2] 4]: see quot.; **stone garland** *Geomorphol.*, a low bank or terrace of large stones occurring on a steep slope and curved downwards so as to resemble a garland or necklace; **stone-getter**, a workman who gets stone from a quarry, a quarryman; **stone ginger**, (*a*) (see sense 17 b); (*b*) *slang*, a certainty, a 'sure thing' (cf. sense 19 b above); also as *adj.*, certain; **†stone-glass** = *glass-stone* (see GLASS *sb.*[1] 16); **stone-grave**, †(*a*) = *stone-pit*; (*b*) a prehistoric grave containing stone implements (also *attrib.*); **†stone-grist**, ? the privilege of using a grindstone; **stone-ground**

a., ground by means of millstones: cf. *stone-mill* (*c*); **stone guard**, an attachment serving to prevent stones entering the air-intake system of a motor vehicle or aeroplane; a similar device protecting another part of a vehicle; † **stone-gun**, a gun for firing stone shot; **stone-hammer**, a hammer for breaking or rough-dressing stones; **stone-hand** (*Printing*) = STONEMAN[1] 1; **stone harmonicon**: see quot., and cf. *rock harmonicon* (ROCK *sb.*[1] 9); **stone-head**, the top of the stratum of solid stone or bed-rock beneath the loose or soft superficial deposit; also = next; **stone-heading** *Coal Mining*, a heading driven through stone or rock; **stone-hearted** (now *rare*) = STONY-HEARTED; **stone-heled (-healed, -hilled)** *a.* [HELE *v.*[2] 2], covered or roofed with stone (*obs.* or *dial.*); **stone-honey** (see quot.); † **stone-hook**, ? one of a pair of hooks for lifting blocks of stone; **stone kist**, var. *stone cist* above; **stone-knife** *House-painting*, a larger form of palette-knife used for mixing colours on the slab; **stone-layer** (? *obs.*), a workman who lays stones in building (cf. *bricklayer*); **stone-laying**, the laying of stones in building; *spec.* the ceremonial laying of the foundation-stone of a public building, esp. a church; **stone-lifter**, (*a*) a machine for hoisting stones; (*b*) a name for the Australian fish *Kathetostoma læve*, of the family *Uranoscopidæ*; **stone-lime**, lime made from limestone (as distinguished from *chalk-lime*); **stone line** *Geomorphol.*, a layer of isolated stones between subsoil and underlying rock; also, the line of stones that this appears as in a section through the soil; **stone-marble** *Bookbinding*, one of the many ways of marbling books; † **stone marl** = next; **stone marrow** [after G. *steinmark*, latinized by Agricola as *stenomarga*], name for a kind of spongy limestone (= LITHOMARGE); **stone-mill**, (*a*) a mill for grinding stone, a stone-crusher; (*b*) a machine for dressing stones; (*c*) a mill in which millstones (not rollers) are used for grinding the flour; so **stone-milled** *a.* = *stone-ground*; † **stone-mushroom**, ? = *mushroom coral* (MUSHROOM 6 c); † **stone-nail**, ? a nail for fixing stone slates (cf. STONE-BROD); **stone net** *Geomorphol.*, a network of stone rings or polygons; **stone-oil**, a name for a kind of bitumen (see quot. 1838), or for petroleum or rock-oil; also erron. applied to a mixture of petrosilex and water used as a glaze for pottery; **stone pavement** *Geomorphol.*, an area of ground covered with large flattish stones; **stone period** *Archæol.*, = STONE AGE; also, a portion of the stone age; also *attrib.*; **stone-pit**, a pit from which stones are dug, a quarry; **stone-plant**, † (*a*) a fossil or petrified plant (= ROCK-PLANT 1); (*b*) a plant growing in stony or rocky places (= ROCK-PLANT 2); **stone-pock** *Path.*, a hard suppurating pimple; a disease characterized by such pimples, as acne; **stone-polisher**, one engaged in polishing stones for building or other purposes; also, a machine for this purpose; so **stone-polishing** (also *attrib.*); **stone polygon** *Geomorphol.*, a naturally occurring arrangement of stones in the approximate form of a polygon; **stone-printer**, a lithographic printer; **stone-put** *Sc.* [PUT *sb.*[1] 2] = STONE'S THROW; **stone ring**, (*a*) *Geomorphol.*, a natural circle of stones on the ground, similar to a stone polygon; (*b*) *Archæol.* = *stone circle*; **stone river**, a dense, stream-like accumulation of rocks and large stones occurring along a valley bottom or down a slope; *esp.* one of those in the Falkland Islands; † **stone-roche** = ROCK *sb.*[1] 2 a; **stone run** = *stone river* above; **stone-saw**, a saw, usually without teeth, for cutting stone into blocks or other shapes for building or other purposes; **stone-sawyer**, a man who works a stone-saw; **stone-sclerenchyma** *Bot.*, sclerenchyma or hard tissue formed of *stone-cells*; **stone-shower**, a shower or fall of meteoric stones; † **stone-shrub**, name for a kind of coral; **stone-slate**, a roofing slate made of thin stone; **stone-square** *Brewing*, a square fermenting-tank made of stone; **stone-squarer**, one who squares or shapes stone for building, a stone-cutter, stone-dresser; **stone stripe** *Geomorphol.*, one of the evenly spaced bands of coarse rock debris separated by finer material that occur on slopes in cold environments; **stone tint** = *stone-colour*; **stone-turf**, ? a hard or compact kind of turf; **stone-user**, one who uses stone for weapons, etc., a man of the STONE AGE; so **stone-using** *a.*; † **stone-wring** (*Sc.* **stane-**), ? = *stone-colic*; **stone-yard**, a yard in which stone-breaking or stone-cutting is done; *fig.* a part of the sea full of rocks. See also STONE AGE, STONE-AXE, STONE-BLIND, STONE-BOAT, STONE-BOW, etc.

1346 *MS. Acc. Exch. K.R.* 25/7 no. 2 In emendacione.. iiij. anulorum ferri pro iiij. *stonbagges et ij. ligulis ferreis pro le top castel. **1388** in Nicolas *Hist. Royal Navy* (1847) II. 476, iii. stonebagges febles. **1884** BOWER & SCOTT *De Bary's Phaner.* 540 In other cases [these cells] form larger groups, ..inserted in the soft tissue, the number and size of which may increase in the older parts of the cortex.. so that the old cortex has been appropriately termed '*stone-bark' by Hartig. *c* **1470** HENRYSON *Mor. Fab.* XIII. (*Frog & Mouse*) xx, To the war better beir the *stane barrow, Than to be matchit with ane wickit marrow. **1480–1** *Durham Acc. Rolls* (Surtees) 96 Pro factura unius hollbarowe et 2 stanebarowes, 6d. **1791** G. WALLIS *Motherby's Med. Dict.* (ed. 3) 563/2 *Osteites, Osteocolla*, called also..*stone-binder. **1865** TYLOR *Early Hist. Man.* ix. 262 A North American tribe,.. the Assinaboins or '*Stone-Boilers'. *Ibid.*, This intermediate process, which I propose to call *Stone-Boiling. **1883** tr. *Joly's Man before Metal* II. i. 204 *note*, The process known as 'stone-boiling', which consists in obtaining boiling water by means of stones heated directly in the fire and then dropped in the water. **1677** PLOT *Oxfordsh.* 242 Another sort of Land they call *Stone-brash, consisting of a light lean Earth and a small Rubble-stone. **1794** T. DAVIS *Agric. Wilts* 149 The stone-brash land in the north-west part of the district. **1860** *Times* 4 Jan. 10/5 A flinty soil sucks its surface dry, a thin Stonebrash soil lets the rain run through it. **1827** S. RODMAN in B. Swan *New Bedford in 1827* (1935) 8 Occupied most of the day at my house lot. Made a further trial of my *stone breaker, the weight raised by a horse. **1843** BETHUNE *Scott. Peasant's Fireside* 127 My attention was arrested by one of the stonebreakers. **1868** *Rep. U.S. Commissioner Agric.* (1869) 355 The cost..has.. been..reduced by the introduction of the 'Blake Stone-Breaker'. **1851** MAYHEW *Lond. Labour* I. 357 We found that we could obtain employment at *stone-breaking. **1873** *Spons' Dict. Engin.* VII. 2544 Blake's Stone-breaking Machine. **1888** RUTLEY *Rock-Forming Min.* 12 Not every kind of hammer..is suitable for stone-breaking. **1886** H. BAUMANN *Londinismen* 196/2 *Stone-broke. **1888** F. HUME *Mme. Midas* I. ii, I'm nearly stone broke. **1889** BESANT *Bell St. Paul's* I. 7 The stone-broke sporting man. **1933** *Bulletin* (Sydney) 20 Dec. 10/3 There was a hardy war-time story of a stonebroke Digger. **1981** O. BERNIER *Pleasure & Privilege* xii. 197 Naples wasn't exactly short of nobility... Some were stone broke. **1805** LEWIS & CLARK *Orig. Jrnls. Lewis & Clark Expedition* (1904) II. 290 We have a lame crew just now,..one with a bad *stone bruise. **1885** *Cent. Mag.* Nov. 29/1 Angy, who was complaining of a stone-bruise, got up. **1976** T. WALKER *Spatsizi* xi. 122 The continuous descent over rough ground lamed one saddle horse with a stone bruise. **1909** 'O. HENRY' *Roads of Destiny* xxi. 354 Five of my best staff-officers fell, suffering extremely with *stone-bruised heels. **1748** SMOLLETT *Rod. Random* xliv, A set of *stone buckles for the knees and shoes. **1756** A. MURPHY *Apprentice* I. i, Wearing stone-buckles, and cocking his hat. **1796** KIRWAN *Elem. Min.* (ed. 2) II. 14 [Alum] is found in soft brittle masses, that feel somewhat greasy, and thence called by the Germans *Stone Butter. **1887** H. BURY in *Phil. Trans.* CLXXIX. II. 277 The tube thus formed..is the equivalent of the '*stone-canal' of other Echinoderms. **1664** DR. SMITH in *Evelyn's Pomona* 46 The Cider that is ground in a *Stone-case is generally accused to taste unpleasantly of the Rinds, Stems and Kernels of the Apples. **1664** PEPYS *Diary* 27 Aug., Thence to my case-maker for my stone case. [Cf. 19 Aug. *ante*..a case, for to keep my stone, that I was cut of, in.] **1875** BENNETT & DYER tr. *Sachs's Textbk. Bot.* ii. 106 The polyhedral *stone-cells (sclerenchyma) in the flesh of pears are arranged in groups. **1884** BOWER & SCOTT *De Bary's Phaner.* 540 'Stone-cells' in the external cortex. **1825** J. NICHOLSON *Oper. Mech* 479 *Stone-china is formed of a compound of Cornish-stone and clay, blue clay, and flint. **1847** DICKENS *Haunted Man* i, It's surprising how stone-chaney catches the heat, this frosty weather. **1827** HIGGINS *Celtic Druids* 234 From these stones, the place became called the place of the *stone circle. **1831** SCOTT *Ct. Robt.* xx, The practice of youths and maidens plighting their troth at the stone circles dedicated, as it was supposed, to Odin. **1901** *Scotsman* 12 Mar. 4/8 Six distinct varieties of stone circles. **1888, 1934** *Stone cist [see *passage grave* s.v. PASSAGE *sb.* 16 b]. **1603** FLORIO *Montaigne* III. xiii. 651 Since I have had the *stone-chollike. **1695** *Phil. Trans.* XIX. 77 Nephritick Pains, commonly called, the Stone-Colick. **1663** GERBIER *Counsel* 83 A fair *Stone-colour in oyl. **1762–71** H. WALPOLE *Vertue's Anecd. Paint.* (1786) II. 193 In a corner in stone colour is a statue of peace. **1808** *Fashionable Biogr.* 75 Light stone-colour musquito pantaloons. **1894** R. B. SHARPE *Birds Gt. Brit.* I. 34 In some specimens the ground-colour of the egg is yellowish or creamy stone-colour. **1770** *Phil. Trans.* LXI. 254 A kind of light *stone-coloured varnish. *c* **1850** LYTTON in *Life & Lett.* (1883) I. 117 A comely plump matron in a stone-coloured silk gown. **1903** J. R. HARRIS *Dioscuri in Christian Legends* 37 We recognized *stonecraft amongst the arts of the Dioscuri. **1931** *Catholic Bull.* (Dublin) June 578 Metal-work, stone-craft, and architecture. **1861** MRS. BEETON *Bk. Househ. Managem.* 747 *Stone cream of tous les mois...½ lb. of preserve, 1 pint of milk, 2 oz. of lump sugar, 1 heaped tablespoonful of tous les mois, 3 drops of essence of cloves, 3 drops of almond-flavouring... When rather cool, but before turning solid, pour the cream over the jam. **1973** E. SPRIGGE *Life of Ivy Compton-Burnett* v. 78 They liked fish, too, and junket, and that old favourite among puddings, stone cream. **1875** KNIGHT *Dict. Mech.* 2391/1 **Stone-crusher*, a mill for grinding stone or ore. **1912** *Blackw. Mag.* Aug. 265 These wagons are emptied direct into a stone-crusher. ?**972** *Charter of Eadgar* in Birch *Cartul. Sax.* III. 586 Andlang sices to þan *stan ȝedelfe. **1356** in Owen & Blakeway *Hist. Shrewsbury* (1825) II. 462 Versus le Whyte standelf. **1894** *Yorks. Weekly Post, Xmas No.* 1, Boggart Hole is a forsaken stone-delf. **1694** MOTTEUX *Rabelais* IV. xii, In danger of miserably rotting within a *stone Doublet. **1767** THORNTON tr. *Plautus* II. 322 *note*, He talks of the prison as of a garment; like as the cant-word is with us,..a Stone-doublet. **1775** JEKYLL *Corr.* (1894) 19 A stone doublet, which fathers have a legal right to clap upon their sons for extravagance. **1597** A. M. tr. *Guillemeau's Fr. Chirurg.* 16 b/2 A little *stone-drawer, may be vsed to drawe out a bullet. **1703** T. N. *City & C. Purchaser* 19 An ancient experienced Stone drawer. **1858** SIMMONDS *Dict. Trade*, *Stone-dresser, one who tools, smooths, and shapes stone for building purposes. **1875** [see STONE-CUTTER 1 b]. **1845** *Builder* 15 Feb. 83/2 *Stone Dressing Machinery. **1897** *Allbutt's Syst. Med.* IV. 728 Constant exposure to dust..as in..stone-dressing. **1810** SOUTHEY *Kehama* XIII. v, Hung Like *stone-drops from the cavern's fretted height. **1896** M. E. WILKINS *Madelon* xxix. 330 Damned foolishness, that does more harm to the world than the shattering of all the commandments into *stone-dust. **1920** *Chambers's Jrnl.* Mar. 266/2 This fact is taken advantage of to localise explosions in some American mines by mixing the first rush of air with stone-dust. **1930** *Engineering* 28 Feb. 295/3 *Stone-dusting in coal mines was not considered to be injurious in Poland. **1975** *Telegraph* (Brisbane) 13 Nov. 16/2 No agreement was reached between union and management on stone dusting Kianga No. 1. **1895** *Dublin Rev.* Apr. 356 Had Mr. Swinburne been less stone-eyed and less *stone-eared. **1820** SCOTT *Monast.* Answ. Introd. Ep., The guisards, the *stone-eater, and other amusements of the season. **1884** BOWER & SCOTT *De Bary's Phaner.* 127 The *stone-elements ('stone-cells' of the Pharmacologists), so called after the stony bodies in the flesh and stalk of many pears, which are composed of them. **1891** *Century Dict.*, *Stone-engraving. **1911** MCEWEN *Hist. Ch. Scot.* I. vii. 144 The Scottish type of Stone-engraving. **1873** MATH. BLIND tr. *Strauss' Old Faith & New* 231 This *stone-era already bears a certain stamp of civilization. **1807** J. LANDSEER *Lect. Engraving* 143 The *Stone-etching is calculated..to render a faithful fac-simile of a painter's sketch. **1890** HALL CAINE *Bondman* I. v, Stephen Orry grew woebegone and *stone-eyed. **1895** [see *stone-eared* above]. [**1850** HAWTHORNE *Great Stone Face* in *Nat. Era* 16 Jan. 16/1 The Great Stone Face, then, was a work of Nature..formed on the perpendicular side of a mountain by some immense rocks, which had been thrown together in such a position, as, when viewed at a proper distance, precisely to resemble the features of a human countenance.] **1949** *Life* 5 Sept. 82/2 (*heading*) The great *stone face [of Buster Keaton]. **1960** *Newsweek* 25 Jan. 90/2 Here is the Great Stone Face on the most famous element of this vanishing art, his dead pan. **1972** J. MOSEDALE *Football* iv. 47 Even in high school his classmates called him the 'Great Stone Face'. **1977** *Rolling Stone* 21 Apr. 88/3 Only a stoneface could resist smiling. **1868** LOCKYER *Elem. Astron.* §310 A third *stonefall occurred at Orgueil, in the south of France, on the..14th of May, 1864. **1901** *Westm. Gaz.* 26 July 5/3 The mountain this year is more difficult than usual... Stone-falls have been frequent. **1809** *Stone-fence [see COBBLER 3]. **1844** 'JON. SLICK' *High Life New York* I. 37, I might as well a been talking to a stun fence. **1856** KINGSLEY in *Life & Lett.* xiv. (1879) II. 29 Climbing cliffs, and shoving down stone fences. **1859** FOWLER *Southern Lights* 52 *A Stone-fence*. Ginger-beer and brandy. **1872** SCHELE DE VERE *Americanisms* 217 Now he is asked to take a Stone Fence, and now a Railroad, but both are simple whiskey. **1889** *Pall Mall Gaz.* 20 June 3/2 'Stone fence' is the euphonious cognomen given to whisky which is drunk with cider instead of water. **1906** *Jrnl. Geol.* XIV. 103, I feel sure that these immense block-fields of Bear Island are formed in quite the same manner as the Falkland stone-runs... The only differences between the two occurrences are differences of topography and age: in Bear Island a great plain forming a *stone-field, in the Falkland Islands valleys filled at the bottom by stone-rivers. **1959** A. H. MCLINTOCK *Descr. Atlas N.Z.* p. xv, At the timber line there is a locally heavy scrub belt..passing into snow-tussock grasslands, stone-fields, and herb moor. **1978** O. WHITE *Silent Reach* viii. 87 It gets harder when you hit the ..stonefields. **1917** M. T. HAINSSELIN *Grand Fleet Days* iv. 15 Where I met her was in a *Stone Frigate—that is to say, a Naval Shore Establishment. **1929** F. C. BOWEN *Sea Slang* 134 *Stone frigate*, a naval gaol or, more recently, any shore establishment. **1948** PARTRIDGE *Dict. Forces' Slang.* 182 *Stone frigates*, Royal Naval Barracks or Shore Establishments; they are usually named after the old frigates. **1955** 'N. SHUTE' *Requiem for Wren* iii. 81 She found that *H.M.S. Mastodon* was a stone frigate. It was Exbury Hall, about three miles up the Beaulieu River from the Solent. **1979** *Mariner's Mirror* LXV. 51 H.M.S. *Thunderer* (our title as a 'stone frigate') has since prospered... It is planned amongst other things to produce a book on the history of the college. **1850** OGILVIE, **Stone-gall*, the name given by workmen to a roundish mass of clay, often occurring in variegated sandstone. Stone-galls lessen the value of stones for building. **1932** E. ANTEVS *Alpine Zone Mt. Washington Range* iv. 62 A balsam fir forest..grows normally up to the *stone garland. **1977** R. J. SMALL *Study of Landforms* x. 326 If the slope becomes a little steeper, the ploygons give way to 'stone garlands'. **1688** HOLME *Armoury* III. 394/1 The Mattock..is much used with *stone Getters in Quarries. **1870** *Inquiry Yorksh. Deaf & Dumb* 4 He has been employed as a stone-getter, and stone-dresser. **1936** J. CURTIS *Gilt Kid* iv. 41 It was *stone-ginger, you thought, that you'd get a smashing job up here. **1943** J. A. W. BENNETT in *Amer. Speech* XVIII. 90 'That's a stone ginger' (a dead certainty) conceals the name of a famous and unbeatable horse, Stone Ginger [in New Zealand]. **1972** G. F. NEWMAN *You Nice Bastard* 348 *Stone ginger*, a million; certainty. **1585** HIGINS *Junius' Nomencl.* 413/2 Glasse stone, or *stone glasse, which may be cut into very small and thin panes, which in old time they vsed in stead of glasse windowes. *c* **1205** LAY. 31881 þat folc flah in to wuden.. leien in þa *stan-graffen. **1878** J. C. SOUTHALL *Epoch of Mammoth* xv. 264 Another find of this sort..occurring in a large stone-grave near Stubnitz. **1883** *Science* II. 25/1 Mound-builders and stonegrave people. **1235–52** *Rentalia Glastonb.* (Somerset Rec. Soc.) 224 Henricus Faber pro j *stanegrist xijd. per annum. **1905** *Macm. Mag.* Nov. 50 It is hoped the public are beginning to insist upon having *stone-ground flour. **1936** *Times* 19 Oct. 8/4 The chromium-plated radiator has an integral *stoneguard. **1947** *Jrnl. R. Aeronaut. Soc.* LI. 287/2 The best solution of the problem of the stone guard would be to abolish the guard, and eliminate stones and other refuse by momentum-separation. **1958** *Times* 22 Sept. 12/6 Superficially it [*sc.* a motor car] had many attractive qualities..a detachable silver stone-guard before the radiator. **1981** *Buses* Dec. 535/1 This ex-Liverpool Atlantean..has acquired a stone guard in front of the windscreens. **1495** *Naval Acc. Hen. VII* (1896) 194 *Stone gonnes of yron in the Wast of the seid Shipp. **1411** in *Finchale Priory Charters* etc. (Surtees) p. clviii, Item ij *stanehammers. Item ij hamers pro sclattis. **1533–4** in W.

H. St. John Hope *Windsor Castle* (1913) I. 264 For iij stone hamors ffor the bryklayers to work wyth...xviij^{d}. **1875** KNIGHT *Dict. Mech.* 2398/1 *Stone-hammer*, a chipping hammer used by stone-masons in rough-dressing stone. **1896** *Daily News* 7 Dec. 12/5 Overseer wanted for Evening and Weekly. Must be a..smart *stone hand. **1921** Stone hand [see IMPOSER b]. **1978** L. DAVIDSON *Chelsea Murders* xxv. 156 He..was rapidly rewriting lines for the stone-hand. **1875** KNIGHT *Dict. Mech.*, **Stone Harmonicon*, a musical instrument consisting of a number of bars or slabs of stone,..played like the dulcimer. **1708** J. C. *Compl. Collier* (1845) 15 To dig till we sink down to the *Stone-head. **1883** GRESLEY *Gloss. Coal-mining* 242 *Stone-head*. 1. A heading driven in stone. 2. (N.) The first hard stratum met with underlying quicksand. **1892** *Labour Commission* Gloss., **Stone Headings*, Drivages other than coal formed in stone. **1569** T. NORTON *Warn. agst. Papists* A ij, He is obstinately *stone harted. **1640** J. TAYLOR (Water P.) *Differing Worships* 9 St. Steven..prayd..For his stone-hearted stony enemies. **1899** *Daily News* 11 Oct. 8/4, I would not be stone-hearted. **1578** LYTE *Dodoens* I. xxxii. 46 Tyled, or *stone healed houses. *Ibid.* II. iii. 151 Olde walles & stonehilled houses. **1623** G. MARKHAM *Eng. Housew.* 47 Take the iuice of red Fennell, and the iuyce of Sen greene and *stone hony, and mixe them very well together. **1623** C. BUTLER *Fem. Mon.* vi. (1634) 108 While it continueth liquid, ..it is called Live-hony, when it is turned white and hard (euen like unto sugar) it is called Corn-hony, or Stone-hony. **1814** tr. *Klaproth's Trav. Cauc.* 263 The stone-honey..is dissolved in water, and drunk. **1909** *Westm. Gaz.* 14 Apr. 4/1 The Chinese histories of 1,800 years ago,..frequently speak of 'stone honey' as coming from Tonquin and the various States of India. **1396-7** *Durham Acc. Rolls* (Surtees) 214, 1 par de *stanhokes. **1426-7** *Rec. St. Mary at Hill* (1905) 66 A peire stone hokis. **1926** *Stone kist [see *round barrow* s.v. ROUND *a.* 15a]. **1980** D. K. CAMERON *Willie Gavin* vi. 54 There was hardly a year when the winter ploughs did not turn up an old hunter..crouched still in his cold stone-kist. **1875** E. A. DAVIDSON *House-painting*, etc. 1 A *Stone Knife. **1562** in *Archæologia* XXXVI. 301 To one other *stone leyere for .x. dayes,..iiij s. ij d. **1669** *Canterb. Marriage Licences* (MS.), John Mathewes,..stonelayer. **1562** in *Archæologia* XXXVI. 302 In Masonrye worke and *stone leynge. **1898** J. T. FOWLER *Durham Cathedral* 22 On the occasion of the stone-laying. **1884** KNIGHT *Dict. Mech.* Suppl. 867/1 **Stone lifter*. Shepherd's lifter..has a pair of eccentric lever griping jaws, pivoted in a frame. **1898** MORRIS *Austral Eng.* 441 *Stone-lifter*, a Melbourne name for the fish *Kathetostoma læve*. **1707** MORTIMER *Husb.* (1721) I. 86 The *Stone-Lime is much the best for Land. **1847** A. SMEATON *Builder's Man.* 27 Builders are accustomed..to use more sand with stone-lime than with chalk-lime. **1938** C. F. S. SHARPE *Landslides & Related Phenomena* iii. 24 This layer [of rock fragments] outcrops in natural and artificial cuts and marks the approximate boundary between the base of..the 'B' horizon of the soil and the 'C' horizon or parent rock material. Where well developed it appears as a broken line of stones suggesting the name **stone-line* here used. **1969** C. OLLIER *Weathering* iv. 46 The profiles in many tropical countries have rock..overlain by a stone line, overlain in turn by fairly uniform, fine grained 'soil'. **1975** R. V. RUHE *Geomorphology* vii. 127/3 A stone-line surface usually differs topographically from the present land surface. **1818** *Art Bookbinding* 82 *Stone marble. **1681** GREW *Musæum* III. §iii. iii. 347 *Stone Marrow. *Stenomarga Agricolæ*, i.e. *Saxi Medulla*: because found between the Commissures of great Stones. **1839** URE *Dict. Arts* 771 Spongy limestone, usually called Agaric mineral, stone marrow, etc. **1875** KNIGHT *Dict. Mech.* 2398/2 *Stone-mill. **1901** *Daily Chron.* 7 Aug. 7/6 Bread composed of *stone-milled flour. **1687** *Stone-Mushromes [see *stone-shrub*]. **1469-70** in Swayne *Churchw. Acc. Sarum* (1896) 13 Et in iiij m'l clauis voc' *stone nayle occupatis supra Capellam be' Marie. **1586** *Shuttleworths' Acc.* (Chetham Soc.) 31 For a quarterone of a thousand of stone nalles, vj^{d}. **1612** *Ibid.* 201 Twoe hundreth of stone naile for the leades, vij^{d}. **1688** HOLME *Armoury* III. 300/1 Stone Nails, or Lath Nails. **1949** *Jrnl. Geol.* LVII. 143 *Stone nets, stone stripes, and soil stripes have formed on high, flat erosion surfaces..in the Wind River Mountains, Wyoming. **1977** D. & V. WEYMAN *Landscape Processes* iv. 69/2 Stripes are found on slopes above 4° and seem to be stone nets elongated by downslope movements of slope debris. **1838** T. THOMSON *Chem. Org. Bodies* 721 This bitumen [found at Bechelbronn (Bas Rhin)] ..is known in the neighbourhood under the name of *stone oil. **1880** JANVIER *Practical Keramics* 154 The proportions.. for the best glaze are about ten of petrosilex and water (stone-oil) to one of lime and water (fern oil, lime oil). **1969** E. WATSON tr. *Tricart's Geomorphol. of Cold Environments* II. ii. 109 Moist Climates with Severe Winters: Mountain Type... Stone polygons and stone stripes (as well as *stone pavements, which are typical), are fairly frequent. **1977** D. & V. WEYMAN *Landscape Processes* iii. 52/1 In general, desert surfaces show only a shallow weathering layer. Bare rock outcrops are common and many other areas have a stone pavement of coarse material. **1849** W. J. THOMS tr. *Worsaae's Primeval Antiq. Denmark* II. iii. 106 The cromlechs of the *stone-period. **1864** J. HUNT tr. *Vogt's Lect. Man* xii. 342 The Lapps present..in their cranial structure a greater affinity with the stone-period people than with the Romanic-type. **1880** DAWSON *Fossil Man* i. (1883) 11 A still earlier Stone period, that more properly named the Palæolithic, appears to be indicated by [etc.]. *c* **1325** in *Kennett's Par. Antiq.* (1818) I. 570 Quatuor rodæ terræ jacent super le *Staneputtes. **1525** in *Archæologia* XXV. 478 For dyggyng of xliiij lode of stone & for makyng of the stone pytte. *a* **1728** WOODWARD *Nat. Hist. Fossils* I. (1729) 107 Found frequently in the Stone-pits about Oxford. **1859** *Sporting Mag.* Jan. 4 [The fox] went to ground in a stone-pit. **1676** *Phil. Trans.* XI. 736 In a Mine where the *Stone-plants grow. **1883** STEVENSON *Silverado Squatters* 236 About the spurs of the tall pine, a red flowering stone-plant hung in clusters. **1818-20** E. THOMPSON *Cullen's Nosol. Meth.* (ed. 3) 332 Acne; *Stone Pock. **1822-9** *Good's Study Med.* (ed. 3) V. 584 When this species becomes inflamed, it lays a foundation for a varus or stone-pock. **1704** *Collect. Voyages & Trav.* III. 656/1 The *Stone-Polishers make them thinner. **1875** KNIGHT *Dict. Mech.*, **Stone-polishing Machine*, a machine for giving the final dressing and gloss to the surface of stone. **1924** HUXLEY & ODELL in *Geogr. Jrnl.* LXIII. 208 We propose here to style the two forms '*stone-polygons' and 'fissure-polygons' respectively. The stone-polygons are represented at one extreme by isolated stone-circles, while at the other they may become drawn out into a series of elongated mud-strips, separated by strips of stone. **1950** [see PATTERNED *ppl. a.* b]. **1970** R. J. SMALL *Study of Landforms* x. 327 The reason why stone polygons as a whole vary so much in size (their diameters range from 0·5 to 15 metres) is not understood. **1819** J. HODGSON in J. Raine *Mem.* (1857) I. 260, I called..at a *stoneprinter's in Lincoln's Inn Fields. **1896** N. MUNRO *Lost Pibroch* (1902) 70 A *stone-put further. **1924** *Geol. Mag.* LXI. 509 *(heading)* Formation of '*stone rings' in rocks which are being shattered by frost action. **1954** J. R. R. TOLKIEN *Fellowship of Ring* I. vii. 141 The stone-rings upon the hills. **1957** J. K. CHARLESWORTH *Quaternary Era* I. xxvii. 572 The severer frost in the lower, sodden layers produces the finer material and brings it to the surface, pushing the coarser to the sides. The stone-rings so produced grow outwards from their centres to build a polygonal network. **1980** *Sci. Amer.* July 67/1 As a result the term now coming into favour as a description of these megalithic enclosures is stone ring. **1877** C. W. THOMSON *Atlantic* II. iv. 246 At the mouth of the valley the section of the '*stone river' exposed by the sea is like that of a stone drain on a huge scale. **1894** J. GEIKIE *Gt. Ice Age* (ed. 3) xl. 723, I do not think there can be much doubt that the 'stone-rivers' of the Falkland Islands are of the same nature and origin as the rubble-drifts already described in connection with the glacial phenomena of Europe. **1956** W. EDWARDS in D. L. Linton *Sheffield* 20 Newer Drift... This is well developed on the hillsides in the Millstone Grit country—for example, on Burbage Moor.. —its content of large gritstone blocks betraying its presence, especially where these are concentrated in 'stone-rivers'. **1969** C. OLLIER *Weathering* xii. 214 Block-streams (stone rivers) also have sharp edged and angular blocks, and occur in the same areas as blockfields. *c* **1200** *Vices & Virtues* 45 For us eft to warnin wið ðo *stan-roches of ðe harde hierte. **1906** *Jrnl. Geol.* XIV. 101 The large old *stone-runs of the Falkland Islands evidently were formed in a period of the past with a climate more severe than the present. **1950** *Geol. Mag.* LXXXVII. 106 The stone runs of the Falklands extend over a greater area than is at present exposed, since they are masked by vegetation. **1843** HOLTZAPFFEL *Turning* I. 169 The *stone-saw, a smooth iron blade fed with sand and water. **1890** 'M. RUTHERFORD' *Miriam's Schooling* etc. 155 He sat at one end of the heavy stone-saw, with David Trevenna, at the other. **1845** G. DODD *Brit. Manuf.* IV. 17 If we watch..a *stone-sawyer, we shall.. see that the saw frequently 'jars'. **1884** BOWER & SCOTT *De Bary's Phaner.* 540 The formation of *stone-sclerenchyma. **1687** A. LOVELL tr. *Thevenot's Trav.* I. 166 We bought of these poor Greeks several stone-Mushromes, which in that place are got out of the Red-sea; as also small *Stone-shrubs, or branches of Rock, which they call white Coral. **1530** PALSGR. 706/1, I sclate a house with *stone slates, *je couuers de pierre*. **1880** SIR E. BECKETT *Bk. Building* (ed. 2) 183 In some places a thin kind of stone slates are used,..they make picturesque roofs but rather heavy. **1882** E. G. HOOPER *Man. Brewing* (ed. 2) 237 There is another system of fermentation..known as the *stone-square system. The fermenting tank here is a large square, constructed of stone. **1888** F. FAULKNER *Mod. Brewing* (ed. 2) 187 The original closed box, denominated a Yorkshire stone square. **1611** BIBLE *1 Kings* v. 18 And Solomons builders, and Hirams builders, did hewe them, and the *stone-squarers. **1934** *Proc. Geologists' Assoc.* XLV. 174 Fig. 24.. shows the *stone-stripes in cross section one to two inches thick lying in shallow depressions in the clay-loam. **1978** A. L. BLOOM *Geomorphology* xv. 363 Like sorted polygons, stone stripes require active freeze-thaw processes but are not restricted to regions of permafrost. **1833** LOUDON *Encycl. Archit.* §235 The cement chimney shafts to be coloured..of a good warm *stone tint. **1797** *Encycl. Brit.* (ed. 3) XII. 105/2 That called in England by the name of *stone-turf contains a considerable proportion of peat. **1915** H. R. HALL *Anc. Hist. Near East* ii. 32 The earlier Greeks ..were still *stone-users. **1870** GREENWELL in *Jrnl. Ethnol. Soc.* (N.S.) II. 420 The supply of flint [at Grime's Graves], in itself a mine of wealth to a *stone-using people. *c* **1500** *Rowlis Cursing* 61 in Laing *Anc. Poet. Scot.*, The *stane-wring, stane and stane blind. **1858** SIMMONDS *Dict. Trade*, **Stone-yard*, a contractor's or other yard where paupers are set to break stones. **1886** STEVENSON *Kidnapped* xiii. 115 If I had kent of these reefs..it's not sixty guineas..would have made me risk my brig in sic a stoneyard! **1899** A. C. BENSON *Life Abp. Benson* I. v. 161 A small walled garden..with a rockery of broken carvings from the stone-yards.

b. In names of animals, as **stone-bass**, †*(a)* a fish of the genus *Pagrus*, found in the West Indies; *(b)* a fish of the genus *Polyprion* (family *Serranidæ*), characterized by a bony ridge on the operculum, and serrated spines on the anal and ventral fins; **stone-bird**, *(a)* the vinous grosbeak = MORO^{3}; *(b)* = *stone-snipe (a)*; **stone-biter**, *(a)* the hawfinch; *(b) Orkney & Shetl.* the common cat-fish or wolf-fish [= Icel. *steinbítr*, Da. *stenbider*, Norw. *steinbit*, Du. *steenbijter* (Kilian)]; **stone-borer**, a bivalve mollusc that bores into stones or rocks; **stone-cat**, a N. American freshwater cat-fish of the genus *Noturus*; **stone-centipede**, a centipede of the family *Lithobiidæ*, found in stony places; **stone-coral**, hard or sclerodermatous (as distinguished from sclerobasic), or massive (as distinguished from branching) coral; **stone-crab**, *(a)* name for various species of crab (see quots.); *(b)* applied locally in *U.S.* to the dobson or hellgrammite, the larva of a neuropterous insect, used as a bait in angling; **stone-crawfish**, a European species of crawfish or crayfish, *Astacus torrentium*; **stone-cricket**, a wingless insect of the genus *Ceuthophilus* or other genera of *Locustidæ*, found under or among stones; **stone curlew**, see CURLEW 3; **stone-eater**, = *stone-borer*; **stone falcon** [G. *steinfalke* (Gesner)], a name for the merlin; **stone-fish**, a name for various fishes harbouring under stones (see quots.); esp. the highly venomous *Synanceja verrucosa*, of the family Scorpænidæ, a bottom-dwelling fish resembling a small rock, found in tropical seas and bearing venom glands at the base of the dorsal fin spines; **stone-flower** = STONE-LILY; **stone-fox** [= Du. *steenvos*], the Arctic fox, *Canis lagopus*; † **stone-grig** [GRIG *sb.*^{1} 3], local name for a species of eel or lamprey; **stone hawk** = *stone falcon*; **stone-lifter** (see 20a); **stone-loach**, a species of loach, *Cobitis barbatula*; **stone-lugger** = *stone roller*; **stone-marten**, the beech-marten (*Mustela foina*), or its fur; **stone-owl**, *U.S.* the saw-whet owl, *Nyctala acadica*, which frequents quarries or rocks; **stone-pecker** (*Sc.* stane-), local name for the TURNSTONE, and for the purple sandpiper, *Tringa striata* or *maritima*; **stone-perch**, a small fish allied to the perch (= POPE *sb.*^{1} 6, RUFF *sb.*^{1} 2); **stone-piercer** = *stone-borer*; **stone-plover**, see PLOVER 2; **stone roller**, name for two N. American fresh-water fishes (see quots., and cf. *stone-lugger* and *stone-toter*); **stone-runner**, a name for the ringed plover, or the dotterel; also applied to some species of sandpiper; **stone-snipe**, *(a)* the stone-curlew, *Œdicnemus scolopax*; *(b)* a large N. American bird of the snipe family, *Totanus melanoleucus*; also applied to other species of *Totanus*; **stone-sponge**, a lithistid sponge; **stone-sucker**, a fish belonging or allied to the genus PETROMYZON, a LAMPREY (see the etymologies of these words); **stone-thrush**, a local name of the missel-thrush; †**stone-tivet** [? TEWHIT], ? the lapwing; **stone-toter** [TOTE *v.*], a N. American fresh-water fish, *Catostomus* or *Hypentelium nigricans*, also called *stone-lugger* or *stone-roller* (see quot. 1817); also applied to the genus *Exoglossum*. See also STONEBUCK, STONECHAT, STONE-FLY, STONE-HATCH, STONE-SMATCH.

1698 FRYER *Acc. E. India & P.* 12 There is another Fish they call a *Stone-Bass,..of a Colour sandy, but has a Relish equal to our Soles. **1725** SLOANE *Jamaica* II. 286 *Pagrus totus argenteus*..A Stone-Basse. This is taken in all the Rivers of this Island,..they are altogether of a white Colour, and are..one of the best sort of Fish they have in Jamaica. **1822** COUCH in *Trans. Linn. Soc.* XIV. 81 Sciæna... Stone Basse—This species, which is common in more southern latitudes..approaches the Cornish coast under peculiar circumstances. When a piece of timber covered with Barnacles is brought by the currents from the regions which these fishes inhabit, considerable numbers of them sometimes accompany it. **1883** *Fisheries Exhib. Catal.* 270 Special Line,..used in fishing for Stone Bass or Wreck-fish. **1731** MEDLEY *Kolben's Cape G. Hope* II. 157 There are in the Cape countries great numbers of Haw-Finches... They are call'd likewise *Stone-Biters. **1743** *Phil. Trans.* XLII. 612 Other Fish, as Sharks, Holly-butts,..Stone-biters. **1854** A. ADAMS etc. *Man. Nat. Hist.* 153 *Stone-borers (Saxicavidæ). **1882** JORDAN & GILBERT *Syn. Fishes N. Amer.* 97 *Noturus*, *Stone Cats. **1854** A. ADAMS etc. *Man. Nat. Hist.* 266 *Stone-Centipedes (Lithobiidæ). **1880** F. P. PASCOE *Zool. Classif.* 32 Sclerodermata. (*Stone-corals.) **1713** PETIVER *Aquat. Anim. Amboinæ* Tab. i, *Cancer saxatilis* ..*Stone Crab. **1853** T. BELL *Stalk-eyed Crustacea* 165 Northern Stone-crab. *Lithodes Maia*. **1884** GOODE *Nat. Hist. Aquat. Anim.* 772 The Stone Crab, *Menippe mercenarius*,..is one of the two edible species of Crabs occurring upon the Southern Atlantic coast of the United States. **1815** S. BROOKES *Conchol.* 157 *Stone Eater. *Mytilus lithophagus*. **1854** WOODWARD *Mollusca* II. 243 The boring shell-fish have been called 'stone-eaters' (lithophagi). **1656** BLOUNT *Glossogr.*, **Stonefaulcon* (*Lithofalcus*..) so called from the stones and rocks where she *eyries*, or builds her nest. **1678** RAY *Willughby's Ornith.* II. ix. 80 The Stone-Falcon,..*Falco Lapidarius*. **1862** WOOD *Illustr. Nat. Hist.* II. 77 The Merlin..from this habit of perching on pieces of stone..has derived the name of Stone Falcon. **1668** CHARLETON *Onomast.* 135 *Alphestes*..Belgis Stein-Fish, i.e. *Stone-fish. **1710** SIBBALD *Hist. Fife* 51 *Gunnellus Cornubiensium*, the Butter Fish of the English, our Fishers call it the Stone-fish. **1881** DAY *Fishes Gt. Brit.* I. 204 Shanny or shan:..Stone-fish, Parnell. **1896** *Strand Mag.* XII 354/2 Another fish that is unpleasant to meet is that known as the stone-fish. It is small,..but its bite is poisonous. Apparently, it makes its home under the pearl shell, for it is only when picking up a shell that a diver is bitten. **1908** E. J. BANFIELD *Confessions of Beachcomber* I. iv. 143 Beware of the stone fish.., the death adder of the sea. **1947** I. L. IDRIESS *Isles of Despair* xxxv. 234 The lancet of the hideous little stone fish in his salamander coat. **1971** *Islander* (Victoria, B.C.) 20 June 5/2 The ugliest fish in the sea (and one of the most dangerous) is the stonefish. **1847** ANSTED *Anc. World* iii. 49 The simple forms of the crinoids or *stone-flowers. **1832** J. BREE *St. Herbert's Isle* 48 Through the night the hungry *stone-fox howls. **1884** *Chamb. Jrnl.* 5 Jan. 10/1 The stone-foxes and wolverines having destroyed the povision depôts. **1666** MERRETT *Pinax* 188 *Lampetra parva fluviatilis*..*Herefordiensibus*, a *Stone Grig. **1736** AINSWORTH, The *stone hawk, *lithofalco*. **1863** H. G. ADAMS *Birds of Prey* 46 The Merlin..makes its..nest..in the holes generally amid pieces of rock, hence one of its common names, Stone or Rock Hawk. **1825** HONE *Every-day Bk.* I. 697 When he essay'd to war on dace, bleak, bream, *stone-loach or pike. **1883** DAY *Fishes Gt. Brit.* II. 204 Stone-loach, due to its fondness for secreting itself beneath a stone. **1882** JORDAN & GILBERT *Syn. Fishes N. Amer.* 130 *Catostomus nigricans*, Stone Roller, Hammer-head; *Stone lugger. *Ibid.* 149 *Campostoma anomalum*, Stone-roller; Stone-lugger. **1841** J. H. FENNELL *Nat. Hist. Quadrupeds* 106 *note*, Besides beech marten, it is called *stone marten, martern, marteron, martlett, and mousehunt. **1882** CAULFEILD & SAWARD *Dict. Needlework* 463/1 Stone Marten..This fur is much esteemed throughout Europe. **1869–73** T. R. JONES *Cassell's Bk. Birds* II. 87 The *Stone Owls (*Athene*). *Ibid.* The Stone Owl Proper (*Athene noctua*). **1904** *Brit. Med. Jrnl.* 17 Sept. 644 Transformations undergone by a blood parasite of the stone-owl when taken into the stomach of a mosquito. **1731** MEDLEY *Kolben's Cape G. Hope* II. 157 The *Stone-pecker. The Dutch call this Bird *Strand Loper*, i.e. Shore-Courser. **1885** SWAINSON *Prov. Names Birds* 187 Turnstone..Stanepecker (Shetland Isles). *Ibid.* 194 Purple Sandpiper (*Tringa striata*).. Stanepecker (Shetland Isles). **1888** GOODE *Amer. Fishes* 2 The *Stone-perch, Pope, Ruffe,..which somewhat resembles the Perch,..is..not found in America. **1713** PETIVER *Aquat. Anim. Amboinæ* Tab. 19/13 *Pholas*..*Stone Peircer. **1768** PENNANT *Brit. Zool.* (1776) I. 293 This [red-headed Linnet] seems to be the species known about London under the name of *stone redpoll. **1802** MONTAGU *Ornith. Dict.*, s.v. *Redpole*, Lesser, Numbers [are] frequently taken about London..: it is there called Stone Redpole. **1878** C. HALLOCK *Sportsman's Gaz.* 386 The 'stone toter', or '*stone roller', is a far better variety. **1882** Stone Roller [see *stone-lugger*]. **1681** GREW *Musæum* I. §4 iv. 77 The Egg of a *Stonerunner. **1802** MONTAGU *Ornith.* s.v., *Stone-runner*, many of the Sandpipers so called. **1849** *Zoologist* VII. 2392 The ringed plovers are 'stone-runners'. **1785** PENNANT *Arct. Zool.* II. 468 *Stone Snipe. With a black bill: head, neck, and breast spotted with black and white... Double the size of a Snipe. **1864** WEBSTER, *Stone-snipe*,..a large snipe (*Gambella melanoleuca*), common in the United States. **1887** *Cassell's Encycl. Dict.*, *Stone-snipe*, stone-curlew,..*Œdicnemus scolopax*. **1753** *Chambers' Cycl.* Suppl., *Petromyzon*, the *stone sucker,..a genus.. comprehending the lamprey, etc. **1851** GOSSE *Nat. Hist., Fishes* 319 *Petromyzonidæ*. (Stone-suckers.) **1885** SWAINSON *Prov. Names Birds* 2 Missel Thrush... *Stone thrush (Dorset). **1579** HAKE *Newes out of Powles* iv. (1872) Dij b, *Stonetiuets, Teale, and Pecteales good, with Busterds fat and plum. **1817** PAULDING *Lett. fr. South* (Bartlett), The most singular fish in this part..is..the *Stone-toter, whose brow is surmounted with several little sharp horns, by the aid of which he totes small flat stones.. in order to make a snug little inclosure for his lady. **1868** SIR J. RICHARDSON etc. *Mus. Nat. Hist.* II. 123 The species of *Exoglossum* are named 'Stone-toters,' because they pile up little heaps of small stones, among which they deposit their spawn.

c. In names of plants (either growing in stony places, or having some part hard like stone), or their fruits, etc.: as † **stone apple** = *stone pippin*; **stone basil**, the wild basil, *Calamintha Clinopodium*, or basil-thyme, *C. Acinos*; **stone-beech**, a variety of the common beech (see quot.); **stone-berry**, the dwarf cornel of N. America, *Cornus canadensis*; **stone-brake**, the rock-brake or parsley-fern, *Allosorus crispus*; **stone bramble**, a species of bramble, *Rubus saxatilis*, growing in stony places, with bright red fruit; **stone-clover** = HARE'S-FOOT 1; **stone-fern**, *Asplenium Ceterach*; also applied to other ferns growing in stony places (see quots.); † **stone-grape**, ? a grape with stones or hard seeds; **stone-leek**, the rock or Welsh onion, *Allium fistulosum*; in quot. 1904 app. misused for HOUSELEEK; **stone-lichen**, any lichen growing on stones or rocks; spec. *Parmelia saxatilis* (= STANERAW); **stone liverwort** = LIVERWORT 1; **stone-mint**, the American dittany, *Cunila Mariana*; † **stone-moss**, ? the orchil lichen, *Roccella tinctoria*; **stone orpine**, *Sedum reflexum*; † **stone-pepper**, an old name for STONECROP; † **stone pippin**, a variety of apple (? with hard fruit); **stone-root**, a N. American aromatic labiate herb, *Collinsonia canadensis*, also called *horse-balm* or *rich-weed*; † **stone-rue**, an old name for the fern WALL-RUE, *Asplenium Ruta-muraria*; **stone-seed**, English rendering of *Lithospermum*, a genus of *Boraginaceæ*, so called from their hard 'seeds' or capsules; **stone-turnip**, a variety of turnip; **stone-weed**, (*a*) = *stone-seed*; (*b*) local name for knotgrass, *Polygonum aviculare*; (*c*) ? a weed growing on stone or rock; **stonewood**, name for various trees with very hard wood (see quots.), or the wood itself. See also STONEBREAK, STONECROP, etc.

1741 *Compl. Family-Piece* II. iii. 383 Apples. [July.] Deux Ans or John Apple, *Stone Apple, Oaken Pin. **1597** GERARDE *Herbal* II. ccxiii. 548 *Acynos*. *Stone Basill. **1886** BRITTEN & HOLLAND *Plant-n.*, Basil, Field, Stone, or Wild. Book-names for *Calamintha Clinopodium* and *C. Acinos*. **1884** BOWER & SCOTT *De Bary's Phaner.* 532 An.. individual variation in those stems of Fagus silvatica occasionally occurring which are called *Stone-beeches, and are conspicuous from their thick, furrowed bark. **1837** P. H. GOSSE in *Life* (1890) 107 Here the scarlet *stoneberry (*Cornus Canadensis*) was abundant. **1796** WITHERING *Brit. Plants* (ed. 3) III. 304 Stone Fern. Crisped Fern. Parsley Fern. *Stone Brakes. **1744** J. WILSON *Synopsis Brit. Plants* 117 *Chamærubus saxatilis*... The *Stone-bramble, or Raspis. **1552** HULOET, *Stoneferne herbe, *Asplenium, Citrac, Scolopendra*. **1777** JACOB *Catal. Plants* 38 *Pteris aquilina*, Small-branched Stone-Fern. **1796** [see *stone-brake*]. **1820** T. GREEN *Univ. Herbal* II. 218 *Osmunda Crispa*; Curled Osmunda, or Stone Fern. **1863** PRIOR *Plant-n.*, Stone-fern, from its growth on stone-walls, *Ceterach officinarum*. *c* **1475** *Pict. Voc.* in Wr.-Wülcker 810/17 *Hic acinus*, a *stongrape. **1866** *Treas. Bot.* 40/2 The Welsh Onion..is a native of Siberia and certain parts of Russia, where it is known as the Rock Onion, or *Stone Leek. **1904** A. C. BENSON *House of Quiet* (1910) 164 The stone-leek on the roof of mellowed barns. **1861** *Stone lichen [see STANERAW]. **1854–67** *Stone-mint [see *dittany* 5]. **1681** GREW *Musæum* III. §ii. i. 326 The several Styriæ or Capillary parts..growing together almost like those of the little *Stone-Moss. **1763** in *6th Rep. Dep. Kpr. Publ. Rec.* App. II. 132 Making Orchell from Rock or Stone Moss. **1777** ROBSON *Brit. Flora* 318 *Byssus aurea*... Saffron Byssus. Silken Stone-moss. **1866** *Stone Orpine [see STONEHORE]. **1597** GERARDE *Herbal* Tables Eng. Names, Stone hore, that is *Stonepepper, or Stone crop. **1767** ABERCROMBIE *Ev. Man his own Gardener* (1803) 671/2 Apples..Kirtin pippin, *Stone pippin. **1848** BARTLETT *Dict. Amer.* 335 *Stone-root*, a plant used in medicine. Its properties are diuretic and stomachic. **1872** SCHELE DE VERE *Americanisms* 399 The Stone-Root (Collinsonia canadensis), the flowers of which have an odor like lemons, is also known as Rich Weed from this fragrance. **1548** TURNER *Names Herbes* 86 Saluia vita or Ruta muralis..maye be called in english *Stone Rue, or wal Rue. **1578** LYTE *Dodoeus* III. lxviii. 408 *Ruta Muraria*, Stone Rue, or Wall Rue. **1833** *Wauldby Farm Rep.* 105 in *Libr. Usef. Knowl., Husb.* III, The variety called the white *stone turnip. **1847** DARLINGTON *Amer. Weeds* 243 Field Lithospermum. *Stone weed. Gromwell... Formerly a reputed cure for the stone in the bladder, from the stony-like appearance of its seeds. **1847** HALLIWELL, *Stoneweed*, knot-grass. *Suffolk*. **1913** M. HEWLETT in *Engl. Rev.* Mar. 534 Her garment..seemed to grow upon her as a creeping stone-weed grows. **1863** BATES *Nat. Amazon* ix. 238 A suitable canoe..of about six tons' burthen, strongly built of Itaüba or *stone-wood, a timber of which all the best vessels in the Amazons country are constructed. **1889** MAIDEN *Usef. Plants Australia* 390 *Callistemon salignus*..'Stonewood'. *Ibid.* 604 *Tarrietia argyrodendron*..'Stonewood'.

stone (stəʊn), *v.* Forms: see prec.; also (*Sc.* and *north.*) 4 **stain**, 6 **staan, staen**. [Early ME. *stānen*, f. *stān* STONE *sb.* Cf. STEEN *v.*]

1. a. *trans.* To throw stones at, pelt with stones; *esp.* to put to death by pelting with stones.

c **1200** *Ormin* 1968 3ho munnde affterr þe laȝheboc To dæþe ben istanedd. *a* **1300** *Cursor M.* 19456 Þar-for on steuen all þai stert, þai draf him vte o tun allan, And þai demed him to stain. **1382** WYCLIF *Exod.* xvii. 4 What shal Y do to this puple? ȝit a litil while, and it shal stonen me. *c* **1400** MAUNDEV. (Roxb.) x. 40 Þe kirke of saynt Steuen, whare he was staned to deed. *c* **1450** *Mirour Saluacioun* (Roxb.) 142 Ysay prophete was sawen and stonyd was Jeremye. **1535** COVERDALE *Matt.* xxi. 35 The huszbandmen caught his seruauntes: one they bett,..the thirde they stoned. **1596** DALRYMPLE tr. *Leslie's Hist. Scot.* I. 123 Gif a Sou eit his ȝoung, stane him [L. *lapidibus obruito*], and eit nocht his flesche. **1611** SHAKS. *Wint. T.* IV. iv. 807 Some say hee shall be ston'd: but that death is too soft for him (say I). **1781** GIBBON *Decl. & F.* xxx. II. 149 Cowards were stoned to death. **1843** LYTTON *Last Bar.* I. vi, Were he to walk the streets, they would stone him. **1909** *Blackw. Mag.* Sept. 367/2 Henry splashed about in the shallows, stoning the little fishes.

b. In colloq. phr. ***stone the crows***: see CROW *sb.*[1] 3 d. Similarly ***stone me***: an exclamation of astonishment.

1961 SIMPSON & GALTON *Hancock* 38 *Tony*: Any room for a littl'un? (*Laugh*). *They stare at him frostily. Tony (laugh dries)*: Cor, stone me. **1967** *Listener* 21 Dec. 815/2 Mrs. Dale speaks. 'Why hello, Jim—Cor, stone me, what a booze up we had last night up the BMA.' **1979** J. WAINWRIGHT *Tension* 183 Stone me!—next thing I know I have a..hand-grenade here in my pocket.

†**2.** To turn into stone, or make hard like stone; to petrify. (Chiefly *fig.*) *Obs.*

1604 SHAKS. *Oth.* v. ii. 63 O periur'd woman, thou do'st stone my heart. **1634** HABINGTON *Castara* (Arb.) 38 Till I shall see That heart so ston'd and frozen, thaw'd in thee. **1853** MISS SHEPPARD *C. Auchester* II. 64 When André looked up, he..seemed almost stoned with surprise.

3. a. To furnish or fit with stones; to pave, or build up, with stone or stones. (See also quot. 1877.) Also, to cover or shut *up* with stones (also *fig.*).

1600 *Weakest goeth to Wall* C 3, Were your streets through ston'd with Dyamonds. **1703** S. SEWALL *Diary* 16 Apr. (1879) II. 77 He is stoning the Cellar. **1877** E. LEIGH *Cheshire Gloss.* 201 To stone a road, is to put large stones or boulders on the road, to force carriages, carts and horses to go over the fresh laid metal, instead of the beaten part of the road. A dangerous but general custom in Cheshire. **1889** V. McNABB *Let.* 24 Apr. in F. Valentine *Father Vincent McNabb* (1955) I. ii. 62 Every little fountain of grief seems stoned up. **1890** *Church Bells* 3 Jan. 80/1 The vacant space above and at the sides being stoned in. **1893** BARING-GOULD *Cheap Jack Zita* II. xvii. 72 When a highway has been new stoned. **1953** A. BRYANT *Story of England* iii. 68 His [*sc.* Jesus'] body had vanished from the tomb in which it had been stoned up.

†**b.** To administer stones to (a falcon) as a purgative. *Obs.*

1618 LATHAM *New Bk. Falconry* (1633) 147 They be as hard Hawkes as any be, and must bee stoned and set to a sound stomacke when they should flie.

c. (with *out*) ? To displace by stone. *nonce-use*.

1858 HAWTHORNE *Fr. & Ital. Note-bks.* (1871) II. 58 The earth, I think, is too much stoned out of the streets of an Italian city—paved..quite across, with broad flagstones.

4. To rub or polish with a stone; to sharpen on a whetstone; in *Leather Manuf.* to scour and smooth with a stock-stone.

1688 [see STONING *vbl. sb.* 3]. **1878** MRS. H. WOOD *Pomeroy Abb.* II. xvii, I was on my hands and knees, stoning the passage flags. **1884** F. J. BRITTEN *Watch & Clockm.* 201 Brass services are generally 'stoned' preparatory to polishing, that is, rubbed square with a blue stone or water of Ayr stone and water or oil. **1885** H. R. PROCTER *Tanning* 183 In the Lancashire district, butts are generally ..'stoned', so as to remove the whole of the bloom. **1885** STEVENSON *Child's Gard. Verses* (1895) 83 When the scythe is stoned again.

5. To take the stones out of (ground); to clear or free from stones. ? *Obs.*

c **1475** *Cath. Angl.* 359/2 (Addit. MS.), To Stane, *depetrare, petras remouere*. **1563** HYLL *Art Garden.* (1593) 46 It needeth not after to be weeded or stoned. **1628** [see STONING *vbl. sb.* 4].

†**6.** To deprive of the testicles, castrate, geld. *Obs.*

1584 *Shuttleworths' Acc.* (Chetham Soc.) 20 The smith of Ecclestone for stoninge work horsies, xvj[d].

7. To take the stones out of (fruit): see prec. 12.

1639 O. WOOD *Alph. Bk. Secrets* 19 With..a few Raysins of the Sun stoned. **1665** W. HUGHES *Compl. Vineyard* 17 This way you may also make Gooseberry Wine,..Wine of Plumbs, &c., but these last must be stoned. **1675** HANNAH WOOLLEY *Gentlew. Comp.* 187 Goosberries.., cut off their heads and stone them. **1709** W. KING *Art of Love* v. 703 Stoning currants in whole bunches. **1769** MRS. RAFFALD *Eng. Housekpr.* (1778) 241 Stone a pound and a half of cherries. **1845** ELIZA ACTON *Mod. Cookery* (ed. 2) 416 The peaches and apricots should be merely skinned, halved, and stoned. **1874** MRS. H. WOOD *Master of Greylands* xix. 225 With not a raisin in the house stoned for plum-pudding!

8. *intr.* Of a fruit (drupe): To form a stone in the process of growth.

1842 LOUDON *Suburban Hort.* 479 A few days before, and a few days after, the crops begin to stone, is the most critical period in forcing. *Ibid.* 592 The peach border will require occasional watering,..but water ought to be withheld when it is stoning and when it is ripening. **1852** *Beck's Florist* 176 The fruit sets well and stones freely.

9. a. To become intoxicated with drink or drugs (with *out*, to the point of unconsciousness). **b.** *trans.* To render intoxicated or (*fig.*) ecstatic. Also *refl.* Chiefly as (*ppl.*) *a.*: see STONED *ppl. a.* and *a.* 7. *slang* (orig. *U.S.*).

1952 G. MANDEL *Flee Angry Strangers* 139 I'd rather stay with the tea. It's great pod. I don't want to stone out. **1959** *Jazz* Fall 290, I heard Phineas Newborn play 'I'll Remember April' two Mondays ago at The Five Spot and he completely stoned me. *a* **1961** T. CAPOTE in WEBSTER (1961) s.v., Planned to stone himself with vodka. **1972** J. BROWN *Chancer* iii. 38 You smoke Egyptian Black, that will stone you out of your head.

stone, obs. form of STUN *v.*

stone, obs. Sc. pa. pple. of STEAL *v.*

stone age. a. *Archæol.* The period or stage in the development of human culture which is marked by the exclusive or greatly predominant use of stone as material for weapons and implements, in contradistinction to the later 'ages' in which bronze or iron was used.

The *stone age* is divided into the PALÆOLITHIC and NEOLITHIC periods.

[**1863** LYELL *Antiq. Man* ii. (ed. 2) 10 The age of stone in Denmark coincides with the period of the first vegetation, or that of the Scotch fir.] **1864** J. HUNT tr. *Vogt's Lect. Man* xii. 343 Long heavy skulls, which differ entirely from those of the stone-age. **1874** PITT-RIVERS *Evol. Culture, Princ. Classif.* (1906) 14 The Fijians..at the time of their discovery were still in the stone age.

attrib. **1878** J. C. SOUTHALL *Epoch of Mammoth* iv. 45 In the Stone-Age lake-stations, pottery (hand-made) is found in abundance. **1910** HADDON *Races of Man* 20 The Tasmanians..never advanced beyond an early stage of stone-age culture.

b. *fig.*, esp. as the type of an outmoded or unsophisticated era. Also *attrib.* and as *adj.*

1927 KIPLING in *Maclean's Mag.* 15 Sept. 52/4 The old lady..was primitive Stone-Age—bless her! She looked on us as a couple of magicians. **1937** F. SCOTT FITZGERALD *Let.* 5 July (1964) 15 The girls who were what we called 'speeds' (in our stone-age slang) at sixteen were reduced to anything they could get at the marrying time. **1959** M. LASKI *Offshore Island* III. 84 I've enjoyed civilization too much to be happy in a new stone age. **1973** R. THOMAS *If you can't be Good* (1974) xvi. 147 Back in the mid-fifties was back in the stone age. It was way before the Pill. **1981** *Quarto* May 4/2 In the age of computerised type-setting, the technology of the book trade seems more and more stone age.

stone-axe.

1. A two-edged axe used for hewing stone.

c **1000** ÆLFRIC *Gloss.* in Wr.-Wülcker 141 *Bipennis*, twibille *uel* stanæx. ? *c* **1357** *Durham Acc. Rolls* (Surtees) 560 Pro Stanaxes, Hakkes, [etc.]. **1483** *Cath. Angl.* 359/2 A Sstane axe, *vbi* A mason Axe. **1533** *MS. Rawl.* D. 776 lf. 147 b, For a stone axe ffor lyk vse. **1875** KNIGHT *Dict. Mech.*, *Stone-axe*, an axe with two somewhat obtuse edges, used in spawling and hewing stone.

2. An axe made of stone.

1864 H. WOODWARD in *Intell. Observ.* V. 180 Stone axe of Serpentine. **1865** LUBBOCK *Preh. Times* iv. (1878) 98 The North American stone axe or tomahawk.

stone-blind (ˌstəʊn'blaɪnd), *a.* (*sb.*) (Also as two words.) [STONE *sb.* 19.] Blind as a stone; completely blind. **a.** *lit.*

c **1375** *Sc. Leg. Saints* xii. (*Matthias*) 420 Sic a drynk þat quha-euire of it cane taste, he worde stane-blynde. **1591** GREENE *Conny Catching* II. Wks. (Grosart) X. 85, I haue seen men ston-blind offer to lay bets. **1742** *Phil. Trans.* XLII. 264 The famous Statuary Ganibasius,..though stone-blind, could by Feeling make a Statue in Clay. **1891** KIPLING *Light that Failed* xiii, Dick Heldar..has gone blind... He has been stone-blind for nearly two months.

b. *fig.* (In quot. 1849 a humorous strengthening of BLIND *a.* in sense 10.)

1596 DALRYMPLE tr. *Leslie's Hist. Scot.* I. 128 Quha now, nocht stane blind,..wil nocht sinceirlie grant, the forme of Scotland..to be elegant? **1648** *Petit. Eastern Assoc.* 17 So stoneblinde, as not to see..worse in themselves. **1849–50**

DICKENS *Dav. Copp.* xxiii, A little half-blind entry where you could see hardly anything, a little stone-blind pantry where you could see nothing at all. **1864** LOWELL *Rebellion* Writ. 1890 V. 119 In disputable matters, every man sees according to his prejudices, and is stone-blind to whatever he did not expect or did not mean to see.

Hence **stone-blindness.**

1868 MILMAN *St. Paul's* xiii. 345 Laud's stone-blindness to the signs of the times. **1869** SPURGEON *Treas. Dav.* xxiv. 4 Stone-blindness in the eyes arises from stone in the heart.

†**c.** as *sb.* = *stone-blindness. Obs. nonce-use.*

c **1500** *Rowlis Cursing* 61 in Laing *Anc. Poet. Scot.*, The stane-wring, stane and stane blind.

stone-blue. [See STONE *sb.* 17 c and BLUE *sb.* 2 b; cf. POWDER-BLUE.]

1. A compound of indigo with starch or whiting, used by laundresses. Also *attrib.*

1675 in *Abridgem. Specif. Patents, Bleaching* etc. (1859) 7 [The art] of making out of the vseless dust or powder of indigo, stone blewe, flatt indigo, and powder blewe. **1786** *Act 26 Geo. III* c. 51 §21 Great Quantities of Starch are used in the making of Stone Blue. **1836** E. HOWARD *R. Reefer* xxxvii, A washerwoman's stone-blue bag. **1836–41** BRANDE *Chem.* (ed. 5) 1091 Stone-blue is a compound of indigo or prussian blue and the inferior kinds of starch.

2. The blue colour of this, or a dress of this colour. (Cf. POWDER-BLUE 2.)

1860 C. BRONTË *Emma* in *Cornh. Mag.* Apr. 494 Bright stone-blue is a colour they like in dress. **1906** *Daily Chron.* 5 Oct. 4/5 Mrs. Cyril Ward, in stone-blue. **1962** *L. L. Bean Catal.* Spring 11 Ladies Knee Sox..Colors: Stone Blue, Stone Green.

'stone-boat.

1. A boat for transporting stones.

c **1336** *Durham Acc. Rolls* (Surtees) 533 Qui..reduxerunt Batellum vidz. le Stanbate. **1471** *Extracts Burgh Rec. Edin.* (1869) I. 25 Of ilk stane bot lossand in the havin j d. **1505** *Acc. Ld. High Treas. Scot.* II. 280 Ane stane bote at the New Havin. **1875** KNIGHT *Dict. Mech.* s.v. *Stone-vessel*, De Cessart's machine for throwing large stones into the sea consisted of a pontoon carrying an inclined plane [etc.]. [*title of figure*] De Cessart's Stone-Boat.

2. *U.S.* (chiefly *North.*) and *Canad.* A flat-bottomed sled used for transporting or removing stones, and for other purposes.

1859 N. P. WILLIS *Convalescent* 75 A *stone-boat* would run glibly over such a shallow snow! **1875** KNIGHT *Dict. Mech.* s.v., The rise in front enables the stone-boat to ride over small obstacles. **1901** 'R. CONNOR' *Man from Glengarry* 189 In the afternoon the colt was put through her morning experience, with the variation that the stone-boat was piled up with a fairly heavy load of earth and stone. **1906** *Daily Chron.* 21 Sept. 4/4 They fetch the water every day in a barrel fixed in a kind of sled called a stone boat. **1962** J. ONSLOW *Bowler-hatted Cowboy* viii. 79 A stone-boat is best described as a heavy wooden sled, on which can be hauled rocks and stones..dead cows, sick cows, or other heavy objects.

stone-bow ('stəʊnbəʊ). [Cf. MHG. *steinboge* = sense 2, ON. *steinboge* = sense 1.]

1. [BOW *sb.*[1] 3.] An arch of stone. *Obs.* exc. as the name of one of the gates of Lincoln.

Beowulf 2545 Ʒeseah ða be wealle Stondan stanboȝan.

†**2.** [BOW *sb.*[1] 4.] A kind of cross-bow or catapult used for shooting stones. *Obs.*

1419 *Liber Albus* (Rolls) I. 278 Quod nullus portet arcum vocatum 'Stonebowe'. **1543** *Acts Privy Council* (1890) I. 104 Breaking wyth stonebowes off certeyne wyndowes. **1601** SHAKS. *Twel. N.* II. v. 51. **1611** BEAUM. & FL. *King & No K.* v. i, Children will shortly take him for a Wall And set their Stone-bows in his forehead. **1660** *Act 12 Chas. II* c. 4 Sched. s.v., Bowes, vocat. stone-bowes of steel, the piece, x. s.

stonebreak ('stəʊnbreɪk). ? *Obs.* [f. STONE *sb.* + BREAK *sb.*[1] (or *v.*), after Du. *steenbreek* (†*-breke* Kilian) = G. *steinbrech.*] = SAXIFRAGE 1. (See also quot. 1739 and cf. BREAKSTONE.)

1548 TURNER *Names Herbes* 87 The other duche saxifrage hath leaues lyke Tyme & it may be called in english Time-stonebreake. **1597** GERARDE *Herbal* II. ccxcv. 693 The first is called..white Saxifrage, or white Stonebreake: The second is called golden Saxifrage, or golden Stonebreake. **1739** P. MILLER *Gard. Dict.* II. Index, Stone-break, see *Alchymilla* and *Saxifraga.* **1863** PRIOR *Plant-n.*, Stone-break,..so named from its supposed power of rending rocks, and thence employed to break stone in the bladder, *Saxifraga.*

†**stone-brod.** *north. Obs.* Also stan-, stane-. [f. STONE *sb.* + BROD *sb.*[1]] A nail or peg for fixing stone slates; a slate-pin.

1363–4 in *Finchale Priory Charters* etc. (Surtees) p. lxiv, Et vᵐ de stanbrods et lednaill' emptis. **1419** in *Fabric Rolls York Minster* (Surtees) 38 In v. m stanebrod, 6s. 8d. **1457** *Ibid.* 69, xxj. m stonebrodes. **1543** *Mem. Fountains Abb.* (Surtees) 404 For one thousande stonebrode xiij d.

stonebuck ('stəʊnbʌk). Also 7–8 -bock. [f. STONE *sb.* + BUCK *sb.*[1]; found in OE., but formed afresh in the 16th c. after the Ger. form.]

1. The ibex: = STEINBOCK.

c **1000** ÆLFRIC *Gram.* ix. (Z.) 68 *Hic cynyps* þes stanbucca. **1585** HIGINS *Junius' Nomencl.* 51/2 *Tragelaphus*,..a stone-buck or goathart. **1668** CHARLETON *Onomast.* 7 *Capra Ibex* ..The Stone-bock. **1749** WEST *Odes Pindar*, etc. (1753) I. 253 The..branching Stone-buck bearded like a Goat. **1910** A. HILLIERS *Master Girl* ii. 59 She could see that chamois and stone-buck had come down.

2. = STEENBOK. *rare*⁻⁰. (Perh. an error.)

1855 OGILVIE Suppl., *Stone-buck*, the steinbok [1833 steenbok], an animal of the antelope kind.

stone-cart. A cart for carrying stones.

? *c* **1357** *Durham Acc. Rolls* (Surtees) 559 In flekes empt. pro le Stankart pro calce et sabulo cariand. 2s. **1557** in *Lancs. & Cheshire Wills* (1884) 61 Implements of husbandrye..a stone carte. **1867** J. K. HUNTER *Retrosp. Artist's Life* iii. (1912) 28 It was what was known as a stone cart—one without sides.

stone-cast, stone's cast. Now *rare.* [CAST *sb.* 1 c.] = STONE'S THROW.

a. *a* **1300** *Cursor M.* 15605 A stancast þan fra þaim he yode. *a* **1400–50** *Wars Alex.* 3614 Mare þan a stanecast..be-fore his kniȝtis all He standis vp. *c* **1520** SKELTON *Magnyf.* 2174, I warant the, it is but a stone caste. **1634** SIR T. HERBERT *Trav.* 106 It has a River a stone cast over. **1730** T. BOSTON *Mem.* x. 280, I was told that one was a-dying little more than a stone-cast from the church. **1862** MRS. CARLYLE *Lett.* III. 127 This house is within a stone-cast of the sea.

β. **1387** TREVISA *Higden* (Rolls) I. 215 Pilers as hiȝ as a stones cast. **1485** *Yorks. Archæol. Soc., Record Ser.* XLI. 3 The house of one William Slatter..is..a stonys cast fro the house of John Johnson. **1562** *Child Marriages* 206 They mett William Plumpton a stones cast from the old house. **1634** SIR T. HERBERT *Trav.* 29 His body..buried..where not a stones cast further, sleepes Tom Coriats bones. **1793** SMEATON *Edystone L.* §87 We got within a stone's cast of the rock. **1886** T. FROST *Remin. Country Journalist* viii. (1888) 96 Within a stone's cast of the parish church.

stonechat ('stəʊntʃæt). [f. STONE *sb.* + CHAT *sb.*[2], 'from the similarity between its alarm note and the striking together of two pebbles' (Swainson).] A small bird, *Pratincola* (or *Saxicola*) *rubicola*, inhabiting heaths, commons, etc. in Britain and various parts of Europe. (Also called ***stonechat warbler***.) Also improperly applied to several allied species, as the whinchat, *P. rubetra*, and the wheatear, *S. œnanthe*. Also, with defining word, applied to other species.

1783 LATHAM *Gen. Synopsis Birds* II. I. 448 Stone-Chat ..*Motacilla rubicola.* **1797** BEWICK *Brit. Birds* I. 233 The Stonechat, Stone-smit[c]h, Moor Titling. **1817** STEPHENS in *Shaw's Gen. Zool.* X. 709 Stone-chat Warbler. (Sylvia Rubicola.) **1839** MACGILLIVRAY *Brit. Birds* II. 279 *Fruticicola Rubicola.* The Black-headed Bushchat. Stonechat. Stonesmich. Stonechatter. **1865** A. L. ADAMS in *Pop. Science Rev.* IV. 326 A good many stone-chats spend the winter in Britain. **1872** J. H. GURNEY *Andersson's Birds Damara Land* 102 *Pratincola torquata* (Linn.) South-African Stone-chat. **1873** E. BALFOUR *Cycl. India* (ed. 2) V. 573/2 The pied stone-chat (Saxicola picata) may be seen hopping about in the Dekhan.

Also called **stone-chacker, -chatter, -chatterer, †-check** (STEINCHEK). Also **stone-clink**; STONE-SMATCH, -SMITCH, etc.

1853 F. O. MORRIS *Brit. Birds* III. 170 Wheatear. Fallow-chat. White-tail. *Stone-chacker. **1544** TURNER *Avium Præcip.* I 1 b, Qualis est auicula Anglis *stonchattera, aut mortettera dicta. **1783** LATHAM *Gen. Synopsis Birds* II. I. 450, I have ever thought it exactly imitating the clicking of two stones together, one being held in each hand. If others have thought the same, it will easily account for the reason of its being called the Stone-Chatter. **1837** M. DONOVAN *Dom. Econ.* II. 145 The Stonechatter, although an insignificant little bird, is prized by lovers of curious eating. **1823** A. SMALL *Rom. Antiq. Fife* 235 The little light blue bird called the *Stone-chatterer, from its delighting to be amongst, and building its nest under stones. **1668** CHARLETON *Onomast.* 88 *Cæruleo*, the Clot-bird, Smatch, or *Stone-Check. **1885** SWAINSON *Prov. Names Birds* 11 Stonechat..*Stone clink; Chickstone.

stone-coal ('stəʊn,kəʊl). (Also as two words.) [Cf. Ger. *steinkohle*, Du. *steenkool.*]

†**1.** Mineral coal, as distinguished from charcoal: = COAL *sb.* 5. *Obs.*

1585 HIGINS *Junius' Nomencl.* 377/2 Seacole: Smithes cole: stone cole. **1602** R. CAREW *Cornwall* I. 21 Stone cole, fetched out of Wales. **1673** H. STUBBE *Further Vind. Dutch War* App. 126 To digg for any Quarry of Stone, or Mine for Oare, or Stone-coles. **1741** *Phil. Trans.* XLI. 672 This Bishoprick (Liege) has rich Mines of *Houille* or Stone-coal.

2. Any hard variety of coal, esp. anthracite.

1708 J. C. *Compl. Collier* (1845) 19 The Stone-Coal is so called because it has a sort of Stone, which is in the Bed or Vein of Coal. **1712** *Phil. Trans.* XXVII. 541 A Coal like Cannal-Coal, by the Miners called Stone-Coal. **1823** W. PHILLIPS *Min.* (ed. 3) 366 Slaty Anthracite..is found in the coal-formation near Walsal in Staffordshire (Stone Coal). **1877** RAYMOND *Statist. Mines* 237 Lignite, shale, stone-coal, and fire-clay. **1883** GRESLEY *Gloss. Coal-mining* 242 *Stone coal*, anthracite,..Also certain other very hard varieties of coal.

stonecrop ('stəʊnkrɒp). Forms: 1 stáncrop, 4–5 stancroppe, 5 stoon-, stoncroppe, 5–6 stoncrop, 5–8 stone crop, 6 stone croppe, 7 stone cropp, 8–9 stone-crop, 7– stonecrop. [OE. *stáncrop*: see STONE *sb.* and CROP *sb.* (? sense 3).] The common name of *Sedum acre* (N.O. *Crassulaceæ*), a herb with bright yellow flowers and small cylindrical fleshy sessile leaves, growing in masses on rocks, old walls, etc.; also applied (with or without defining word) to other species of *Sedum*, esp. those of similar growth, and of allied genera, as the N. American *Penthorum.*

c **1000** *Sax. Leechd.* II. 354 Cassuc þefan þorn, stan crop. *a* **1387** *Sinon. Barthol.* (Anecd. Oxon.) 17 *Crassula minor*, vermicularis, an. stancroppe. *c* **1400** *Lanfranc's Cirurg.* (1894) 185 Leie þerevpon a lynnen cloop wet in þe iuys of stooncroppe. *c* **1450** *M.E. Med. Bk.* (Heinrich) 113 Item drynke stancroppe wyþ wermot & hit wol slee hem. **1548** TURNER *Names Herbes* 72 Sedum... The seconde kynde is called in English thryft or stoncroppe. The thyrd kinde is called in Englishe Mouse tayle or litle stoncroppe. **1678** PHILLIPS (ed. 4), *Stonecrop*,..an Herb of a very hot temperature, sharp and biting. **1777** JACOB *Catal. Plants* 103 *Sedum annuum*, Mountain Stone-crop. *Ibid.* 104 *Sedum reflexum*, Yellow Stone-crop, or Prick-madam... *Sedum acre*, Stonecrop, or Wall-pepper. **1782** J. SCOTT *Poet. Wks.* 100 Along my wall the yellow stonecrop grows. **1862** MISS BRADDON *Lady Audley* i, An ancient wall..overgrown with trailing ivy, yellow stonecrop, and dark moss. **1866** *Treas. Bot.* 861/1 *Penthorum sedoides* commonly goes by the name of Virginian Stonecrop in the United States.

b. ***stonecrop tree, shrub*** or ***tree stonecrop***: names for *Suæda* (*Salsola*) *fruticosa.*

c **1710** PETIVER *Catal. Ray's Eng. Herbal* Tab. viii, Tree Stonecrop. **1721** MORTIMER *Husb.* II. 189 The greater Stone-crop Tree is a beautiful green. **1796** WITHERING *Brit. Plants* (ed. 3) II. 278 *Salsola..fruticosa*..Shrub Stone-Crop, or Glasswort.

stone-cutter ('stəʊn,kʌtə(r)).

1. One who cuts or carves stone; a workman engaged in shaping stone for building, ornamental, or other purposes; one who carves figures or inscriptions on stone.

stone-cutter's disease or ***phthisis***, an affection of the lungs, incident to stone-cutters, caused by inhaling the fine dust of the stones.

1540 in *Lett. & Papers Hen. VIII* (1898) XVI. 195 Dirrike Johnson, stone cutter. **1585** HIGINS *Junius' Nomencl.* 505/1 *Lapicida*,..a quarrier: a hewer of stone: a stone cutter. **1605** SHAKS. *Lear* II. ii. 63. **1684** BOYLE *Porousn. Solid Bodies* vi. 101 The invention of staining or colouring white Marble,.. casually lighted upon by an ingenious Stone-cutter in Oxford. **1724** DE FOE *Tour Gt. Brit.* I. III. 69 This Island [Portland]..the Inhabitants being almost all Stone-Cutters, we found there was no very poor People among them. **1829** S. SHAW *Staffordsh. Potteries* 131 The old Inscription was almost effaced, when two of the parish servants..paid a stone cutter to sink the letters. **1866** A. FLINT *Princ. Med.* (1880) 186 *Chalicosis pulmonum* is the name given to the pulmonary changes induced by the inhalation of stone-dust. It is also called stone-cutter's phthisis. **1877** RUSKIN *St. Mark's Rest* iv. (1894) 47 Desiring to show, not a mere symbol of a living man, but the man himself, as truly as the poor stone-cutter can carve him. **1896** LEASK *Hugh Miller* ii. 44 He was feeling the first effects of the stone-cutters' disease. **1908** W. M. RAMSAY *Luke the Physician* xii. 362 Then I conjecture that..the stone-cutter accidentally omitted the fourth hexameter.

b. A machine for cutting or shaping stone.

1875 KNIGHT *Dict. Mech.*, *Stone-cutter*, a machine for working a face on a stone or ashlar... It differs from the stone-dresser, which may be said to begin its duty after the surface is fairly flattened. **1884** *Ibid.* Suppl. s.v. *Stone Cutting Machine*, Atchison's stone cutter.

†**2.** A surgeon who 'cuts for the stone' (CUT *v.* 26 b); a lithotomist. *Obs.*

1655 MOUFET & BENNET *Health's Improv.* (1746) 218 No People in the World are more subject [than the Netherlanders] to that Disease [*sc.* stone], as the Number and Excellency of Stone-cutters in that Country may plainly prove. **1787** *Phil. Trans.* LXXVIII. 32 The Egyptians..had ..not only regular physicians..but likewise stone-cutters, oculists, aurists, &c.

So **'stone-,cutting**, the process or art of cutting or shaping stone; also *attrib.*

1611 COTGR., *Statuaire*, (the art of) Stone-cutting, or Statue-making. **1828** P. NICHOLSON (*title*) A popular.. treatise on Masonry and Stone-cutting. **1838** HT. MARTINEAU *Western Trav.* I. 225 The stone-cutting department.

stoned (stəʊnd), *ppl. a.* and *a.* [f. STONE *v.* and *sb.* + -ED.]

1. Pelted with stones.

1483 *Cath. Angl.* 359/2 Stanyd, *lapidatus.*

2. †**a.** Built of stone; fortified with stone. *Obs.*

a **1400–50** *Wars Alex.* 4352 Make we na vessall of virre.. Ne store staned strenthis.

b. Paved with stones.

1868 *Rep. U.S. Commissioner Agric.* (1869) 356 Depressions in the stoned surface cannot be well repaired without 'picking up' the metal to the depth of several inches.

†**3.** Made of stoneware: = STONE *sb. attrib.* (17 b). *Obs. rare*⁻¹.

1593 *N. Country Wills* (Surtees) II. 157 Twoe stoned pottes garnished with silver.

4. a. Of a male animal (esp. a horse): Having testicles, not castrated, entire: = STONE *sb. attrib.* (17 f). ? *Obs.*

1513 DOUGLAS *Æneis* IV. Prol. 59 Quhow thine vndantit mycht Constrenis so sum tyme the stonit hors. **1535** COVERDALE *Jer.* v. 8 In the desyre of vnclenely lust they are become like the stoned horse. **1559** in Kempe *Losely MSS.* (1836) 177, I do geve unto William More, esquire, thre stoned coltes and thre geldinges. **1617** MORYSON *Itin.* III. 133 They have no Gueldings or ambling Nagges,..but commonly use trotting and stoned Nagges. **1688** *Phil. Trans.* XVIII. 121 There is a Law, that no Horse shall be kept stoned under a certain size.

†**b.** *transf.* Lascivious: cf. STONE *sb.* 17 f. *Obs.*

1607 R. C[AREW] tr. *Estienne's World of Wonders* 184 These stoned Priests haue manifested by their practises [etc.].

†**5.** Of fruit: Having a stone or stones. *Obs.*

1513 DOUGLAS *Æneis* III. ix. 111 Stanit heppis, quhilk I on buskis fand. **1681** GREW *Musæum* II. §i. ii. 188 A Stoned-Fruit in shape..like a Quince. **1705** BEVERLEY *Hist. Virginia* II. iv. (1722) 112 Of stoned Fruits, I have met with three good Sorts: viz., Cherries, Plums, and Persimmons.

6. Of fruit: Deprived of the stone or stones.

1728 E. S[MITH] *Compl. Housew.* (ed. 2) 256 Put in 2 handfuls of ston'd Raisins. **1743** *Lady's Companion* (ed. 4) I. 438 Put in some Capers, ston'd Olives, and a Drop of Vinegar. **1764** ELIZA MOXON *Eng. Housew.* (ed. 9) 159 A pound of ston'd gooseberries. **1846** SOYER *Gastron. Regen.* 533 Line a charlotte mould..with various kinds of fruits (such as stoned cherries, strawberries, [etc.]). **1902** *Daily Chron.* 15 Feb. 8/4 Butter a pudding mould, and cover the inside with stoned raisins.

7. *slang.* **a.** Drunk, extremely intoxicated (see also quot. 1952). Freq. const. *on.* Chiefly *predic.*, esp. in phr. ***to get stoned.*** Cf. STONE *sb.* 19c. orig. *U.S.*

1952 *Life* 29 Sept. 67/2 Like boiled snails, bop jokes certainly are not everybody's dish, but those who acquire the taste for them feel cool, gone, crazy and stoned. *Ibid.* 67/3 *Stoned*, drunk, captivated, ecstatic, sent out of this world. **1955** *Amer. Speech* XXX. 305 *Stoned out of his skull*, intoxicated to an intense degree. **1957** J. KEROUAC *On Road* (1958) I. xiii. 90, I had finished the wine..and I was proper stoned. **1968** *Listener* 28 Nov. 735/2 He would only be taken in charge if he was drunk: were he to spend his ten shillings on getting stoned out of his mind the police would happily accommodate him. **1972** R. REID *Canadian Style* (1973) iv. 144 Then they all laugh and get stoned. **1976** P. CAVE *High Flying Birds* ii. 18 We drive off the ferry at Roscoff late in the afternoon, both well and truly stoned on cut-price booze.

b. In a state of drug-induced euphoria, 'high'; also, incapacitated or stimulated by drugs, drugged. orig. *U.S.*

1953 ANSLINGER & TOMPKINS *Traffic in Narcotics* 315 *Stoned*, under the influence of drugs. **1956** 'E. MCBAIN' *Cop Hater* (1958) ix. 85 You're an H-man..and we know you copped three decks a little while back. Are you stoned now, or can you read me? **1967** M. M. GLATT et al. *Drug Scene* viii. 97 Addicts know these dangers, one for example describing graphically how in a 'stoned' state he had stepped out in front of a car. **1971** 'D. HALLIDAY' *Dolly & Doctor Bird* x. 129 They're all lying around in there wearing beads and stoned out of their skulls on French Blues. **1981** M. LEITCH *Silver's City* viii. 65 If he'd been pissed, he reflected, instead of stoned, he might still be in khaki, but, as it was, the old man had a down on drugs, and so it was a dishonourable discharge or nothing.

c. *fig.*

1952 [see sense 7 a above]. **1963** R. I. MCDAVID *Mencken's Amer. Lang.* 742 A cool cat..is..much of the time stoned on wine, pot.., heroin or an overdose of Zen Buddhism. **1969** *Listener* 17 July 88/3 We are, by any definition, stoned on liberty, smashed by self-fulfilment; the real need now is for silence and what used to be called classical restraint—and irony. **1980** *Times Lit. Suppl.* 31 Oct. 1220/5 He [*sc.* Tom Robbins] is also a moralist, and although superficially he belongs to the 'stoned' school of American fiction, along with Brautigan, Kotzwinkle et al, there is a more interesting comparison to be made with the work of Aldous Huxley.

d. With *out.*

1968 A. DIMENT *Great Spy Race* iii. 39 He..[was] chortling in his stoned out way. Tim was really blocked. **1972** R. K. SMITH *Ransom* I. 23 Joyboy had been a stoned-out junkie. **1977** *Rolling Stone* 13 Jan. 51/1 We even have a comedy collection—the Firesign Theatre's *Forward into the Past*, a double album's worth of puns, alliterations, slapstick and stoned-out mayhem.

stonedemel, variant of STOUNDMEAL.

stone-dike, -dyke. (Also as two words.) [Cf. G. *steindeich.*] A dike constructed of stone; a stone fence or embankment. Also *attrib.* (in quot. = enclosed with a stone-dike).

1553-4 *Extracts Burgh Rec. Edin.* (1871) II. 289 The making of the stane dike on the north side of the South Loch, to hauld in the watter thairof. **1731** *Mem. Capt. Creichton* in *Swift's Wks.* (1762) X. 225 Sir John Cogheran lay with a Party, in a Stone-Dike-Park, about ten Miles off. **1842** J. AITON *Dom. Econ.* (1857) 159 Stone-dikes are of all fences the readiest and most complete... Stone-dike inclosures are generally of dry stone.

Hence **stone-dike** *v.*, *intr.* to build stone-dikes; **stone-diked** (-daɪkt) *a.*, enclosed with stone-dikes; **stone-diker**, one who builds stone-dikes.

1870 J. BROWN *Lett.* (1907) 201 They had been stonedyking since October. **1897** *Daily News* 30 Sept. 6/2 Some village sanctuary on a Yorkshire or Lancashire upland among the stone-dyked fields. **1901** R. M. F. WATSON *Closeburn* iii. 37 David was a stone-dyker by trade.

stone-fly. An insect of the family *Perlidæ*, whose larvæ are found under stones in streams; esp. *Perla bicaudata*, much used (in the larval or the perfect state) as a bait in angling; also, an artificial fly made in imitation of this. Also *attrib.*

a **1450** *Fysshynge w. Angle* (1883) 23 In May take a ston flye and þe bub vndur þe cow torde and the dor worme [etc.]. **1653** WALTON *Angler* iv. 97 There are as many sorts of flies as there be of fruits:..as the dun flie, the stone flie, the red flie, [etc.]. **1741** *Compl. Family-Piece* II. ii. 334 The Stone or May Fly, the Body make of Black Wool.., and the Wings make of a Drake's Down. **1841** E. NEWMAN *Hist. Insects* 107 The May-flies or caddews, stone-flies, &c., frequent watery places. **1872** J. G. WOOD *Insects at Home* 265 Larvæ of May-flies..I take in plenty, but not one single Stone-fly larva have I found. **1896** LYDEKKER *Roy. Nat. Hist.* VI. 171 The stone-flies (*Perlidæ*).

stone-fruit.

1. [STONE *sb.* 12.] A fruit having the seed or kernel surrounded by a 'stone' or hard endocarp within the pulp; a drupe. (Also collectively: cf. FRUIT *sb.* 2a.)

1523-34 FITZHERB. *Husb.* §140 All maner of stone fruite, and nuttes. **1600** SURFLET *Country Farm* III. xliv. 511 Plum trees, and other trees bearing stone fruit. **1675** COTTON *Planters Man.* title-p., All sorts of Fruit-Trees, whether Stone-fruits, or Pepin-fruits. **1842** LOUDON *Suburban Hort.* 441 It ought not to be gathered till it is quite ripe, which in stone fruits and berries is known by its softness and fragrance. **1883** *Evang. Mag.* Oct. 460 The kind of fruit called a 'Drupe,'..generally known as a 'stone-fruit'.

attrib. **1721** MORTIMER *Husb.* (ed. 5) II. 305 Stone-Fruit Trees generally bear on the Branches of the foregoing Year. **1855** DELAMER *Kitch. Gard.* (1861) 145 Stone-fruit-trees are almost always budded instead of being grafted.

2. (As two words.) [STONE *sb.* 2e, 17b.] Imitation fruit made of stoneware, used as chimney ornaments.

1851 MAYHEW *Lond. Labour* I. 371/1 Of stone fruit there are now usually six street sellers... The fruit is principally made at Chesterfield in Derbyshire... The most saleable fruits are apples, pears, peaches, apricots, oranges, lemons, and cucumbers. The cucumbers, which are sometimes of pot as well as of stone..are sometimes made to serve for gin-bottles.

stonegall, corrupt form of STANIEL, the kestrel.

1602 FULBECKE *2nd Pt. Parallel* Ep. Ded. 2 A pray to be pursued, not of the Stonegalle, the Muskette, and the Merlin, but of..birdes of an higher wing. **1863** H. G. ADAMS *Birds of Prey* 47 The Kestrel, variously called Kastrel, Windhover, Stonegall, Steingall or Stannel.

stonege, obs. form of STONEHENGE.

stonehatch ('stəʊnhætʃ). [f. STONE *sb.* + ? stem of HATCH *v.*[1] (see quot. 1882-4).] The ring-plover or stone-plover, *Ægialitis hiaticula.*

1852 MACGILLIVRAY *Brit. Birds* IV. 116 *Charadrius Hiaticula.* The Common Ring-plover... Stonehatch. Stone Plover. **1882-4** *Yarrell's Brit. Birds* (ed. 4) III. 258 The nest is only a slight hollow in the sand..; but sometimes ..lined or covered with a number of small stones about the size of peas, upon which the eggs are laid, and this habit has gained for the Ringed Plover..the provincial name of Stone-hatch.

Stonehenge (stəʊn'hɛndʒ). Forms: α. 2 Stanenges, Stanenheng, Stanheng, 3-4 Stonheng(e, 5 Stone hengles, Stonehenges, 5- Stonehenge. β. 6 stonege, 7 stonage. [f. STONE *sb.*; the second element may have meant something 'hanging' or supported in the air: cf. OE. *hęngeclif* 'præruptum' (*Suppl. to Ælfric's Glossary*); in the compound the word was prob. originally plural.

A spurious form *Stanhengest* occurs in some Latin chronicles (*a* 1500) in connexion with a story of a massacre of British nobles by Hengist at Stonehenge.]

Name of a celebrated stone circle on Salisbury Plain; hence applied allusively to similar structures elsewhere.

α. **11..** HENRY OF HUNTINGDON *Hist. Angl.* I. (Rolls) 12 Quatuor autem sunt, quæ mira videntur in Anglia... Secundum est, apud Stanenges. **11..** GEOFFREY OF MONM. *Hist. Brit.* XI. iv. (1844) 204 Intra lapidum structuram sepultus fuit, quæ haud longe a Salesberia mira arte composita, Anglorum lingua Stanheng nuncupatur. **1297** R. GLOUC. (Rolls) 3222 Ac arst was þe king ybured..Wiþinne þe place of stonheng [*v. rr.* þe stonheng; stonhenge]. **1470** HARDYNG *Chron.* lxx. (1812) 117 The Giauntes carole,.. The stone hengles [*v.r.* Stonehenges], that nowe so named been. *Ibid.* lxxxvi. 150 Whiche called is the stone Hengles [*v.r.* Stonehenge]. **1610** HOLLAND *Camden's Brit.* I. 251 (Wilshire) Certaine mighty and unwrought stones,..upon the heads of which, others like ouerthwart peeces do beare and rest crossewise,..so as the whole frame seemeth to hang: whereof we call it Stonehenge. *a* **1722** TOLAND *Hist. Druids* Coll. Pieces (1726) I. 23 Hard by is her Temple; being a sort of diminutive Stonehenge. **1801** J. BARROW *Trav. S. Africa* I. 373 The..fragments..rolling from the upper ridges, had tumbled on each other, forming natural.. colonnades, and Stonehenges. **1821** SCOTT *Pirate* xl, A rising ground, whence they commanded a full view of the Orcadian Stonehenge. **1840** DICKENS *Old C. Shop* xxxvi, A dreary waste of cold potatoes, looking as eatable as Stonehenge.

β. **1547** BOORDE *Introd. Knowl.* i. (1870) 120 Vpon the playn of Salysbury is the stonege, whyche is certayne great stones, some standyng, and some lyenge ouerthawart. **1647** G. TOOKE *Belides* 39 As who with skill,..his journey manage will, Does often from the beaten road withdraw, Or to behold a Stonage, taste a Spaw, Or [etc.]. *a* **1670** [GIBBONS] *Fools Bolt soon shot at Stonage* in Hearne *P. Langtoft's Chron.* II. 505 The Israelites..did by God's command erect a stonage of twelve Stones in the midst of Jordan. **1701** C. LESLIE *Short Method with Deists* I. (ed. 3) 17 Ther is the Stonage in Salisbury-Plain. Everybody knows it. *Ibid.* 18 Now let us Compare this with the Stonage, as I may call it, or Twelve Great Stones set up at Gilgal.

†**stonehore.** *Obs.* Also 5 stonore, 6 stonnord, 7 stonnard, (ston-chore). [f. STONE *sb.*; the second element is obscure.] = STONECROP (*Sedum acre* or *S. reflexum*).

a **1400-50** *Stockh. Med. MS.* 173 Stonore or stoncrop: *crassula minor.* **1541** *Bk. Properties Herbs* B vj, Crassula minor. Thys herb is called Stonehore or Stonecroppe. **1579** LANGHAM *Gard. Health* 623 Stonhore or wall-pepper, causeth vomite, taken with vineger,..and is good against feuers. **1597** GERARDE *Herbal* II. cxxxvii. 415 The Englishmen [call this] Stonecrop and Stonehore, little Stonecrop, Pricket, [etc.]. *Ibid.* Suppl., Stonnord is Stonecrop. **1640** PARKINSON *Theat. Bot.* 735 Wee [call it] in English Prickmadam, Stonecrop or Great Stonecrop,.. Stonehore and Mousetaile. **1665** LOVELL *Herbal* (ed. 2) 417 Stone hore, see Stone pepper, or Stone crop. Stonnard and Ston-chore, see Stonecrop.

stone-horse. [STONE *sb.* 17f.] An uncastrated or entire horse; a stallion. Now only *dial.*

1600 J. PORY tr. *Leo's Africa* III. 156 They carrie stone-horses about with them, which for a certaine fee, they will let others haue to couer their mares. **1679** SHADWELL *True Widow* III. 43 I'll hold you six to four of the Gelding against the Mare; gold to silver on the bay Stone-horse against the Flea-bitten. **1781** W. BLANE *Ess. Hunting* (1788) 69 The Doctor galloped his grey stone-horse forty miles on end. **1847** NICOLAS *Sir C. Hatton* 340 In the 33rd Hen. VIII. an Act was passed that..every other person whose wife wore any French hood..should maintain one stone trotting horse. [The Act itself has *stoned.*]

b. Applied allusively to a man.

1580 FULKE *Dangerous Rock* 167 But what if your popish geldings, by neying at euery mans wife,..proue them selues to be stone horses. **1640** SHIRLEY *St. Patrick* v. i. H 2, Cannot a Mare come into the ground, but you must be leaping you stone horses.

c. *attrib.*

1546 in Phillipps *Wills* (*c* 1830) 487 A stone horsse colte. **1728** E. S[MITH] *Compl. Housew.* (ed. 2) 243 Strain the Posset on 7 or 9 globules of Stone-Horse dung tied up in a cloth. **1836** R. FURNESS *Astrologer* II. Wks. (1858) 152 Bear's grease,..fox-lungs, stone-horse warts.

stone jug. (Also with hyphen.)

1. A jug made of stoneware.

1596 SHAKS. *Tam. Shr.* Ind. ii. 90 Yet would you..raile vpon the Hostesse of the house,..Because she brought stone-Iugs, and no seal'd quarts. **1906** *Westm. Gaz.* 22 June 8/2 The Apollinaris Co...now bottles the water in stone jugs.

2. *slang.* A nickname for Newgate prison, or for a prison in general.

1796 *Grose's Dict. Vulgar T.* (ed. 3), *Stone jug*, Newgate, or any other prison. **1838** DICKENS *O. Twist* xliii, He shall be kept in the Stone Jug, Charley, like a gentleman.

3. *Rhyming slang.* = MUG *sb.*[5] Cf. STEAMER 11.

1923 J. MANCHON *Le Slang* 296. **1974** P. WRIGHT *Lang. Brit. Industry* xiv. 128 When the Duke of Edinburgh visited one of the Astley collieries in the 1950s, he so satisfied the miners..that one of them was moved to say to the local press, 'He's no stone jug, you mon.' This was the highest possible praise from a South Lancashire miner.

†**stone-lath.** *north. Obs.* In 4 stanlat, 5 stanelatte. A lath on which stone slates were fastened with 'stone-brods' (see STONE-BROD).

1370-1 *Durham Acc. Rolls* (Surtees) 209 Et in mill. stanlat empt. cum cariagio ad dictam ecclesiam, 12s. 1d. **1421** *Fabric Rolls York Minster* (Surtees) 44 In m. m. stanelattes emptis, cum cariagio de Byrnand de Cattall, 14s. 8d.

stoneless ('stəʊnlɪs), *a.* [f. STONE *sb.* + -LESS.] Destitute of stone or stones; having or containing no stone.

1823 COBBETT *Rur. Rides* (1885) I. 264 A fine, buttery, stoneless loam. **1898** F. DAVIS *Silchester* 62 In a stoneless country, the fabric of the deserted city would rapidly be appropriated as building material.

b. Having no tombstone.

1834 *Fraser's Mag.* X. 654 The nameless, stoneless, lime-filled grave-hole. **1882** J. WALKER *Jaunt to Auld Reekie* 162 A digging sexton..points to a stoneless grave.

c. Of fruit: see STONE *sb.* 12.

1815 J. SMITH *Panorama Sci. & Art* II. 673 Barberry,.. stoneless. **1860** *Times* 14 Nov. 9/6 A favorite fruit with the Chinaman is the classic lotos..; it is full of stoneless kernels. **1879** *Cassell's Techn. Educ.* I. 243/2 Stoneless sultana raisins from Smyrna.

Hence **'stonelessness.**

1891 *Athenæum* 30 May 708/1 Is it quite certain that the vallum..is not..marked by the same virtual stonelessness?

stonelet ('stəʊnlɪt). *nonce-wd.* [f. STONE *sb.* + -LET.] A little stone.

1899 *Edin. Rev.* Apr. 326 Black and white stonelets.

stone-lily.

Name for a fossil crinoid or encrinite, from its resemblance to a lily on its stalk.

1808 PARKINSON *Organic Rem.* II. 174 The Encrinus, *Lilium lapidium*, or Stone Lily. **1828** G. YOUNG *Geol. Surv. Yorks. Coast* 207 Zoophytes distinguished by the names Encrinites and Pentacrinites, or the more familiar term Stone lilies. **1881** *Cassell's Nat. Hist.* V. 154 Other Groups, such as the Stone Lilies and Sea Anemones.

stoneman ('stəʊnmən). Pl. **-men.**

1. *Printing.* A compositor who imposes pages of type on the imposing-stone.

1875 SOUTHWARD *Dict. Typogr.* **1904** DE VINNE *Mod. Book Composition* 301 (Cent. Suppl.) Front and tail margins can be most accurately made by the stoneman, for they cannot be predetermined with precision by guesswork.

2. *Coal Mining.* A man employed in driving stone-headings, and in making and repairing 'roads'.

1883 GRESLEY *Gloss. Coal-mining.* **1891** *Star* 8 July 3/4 All the enginemen were doing eight hours shifts, while the stonemen and others did still more.

3. A man who works in stone; a stone-cutter, stonemason.

1912 E. RHYS in *Engl. Rev.* Nov. 517 He saw the bob-tailed rabbits above the stoneman's pit.

stonemason ('stəʊn,meɪs(ə)n), *sb.* [f. STONE *sb.* + MASON *sb.*[1]] A workman who shapes and lays stones in building: = MASON *sb.*[1] 1.

stonemason's lung (Path.): cf. *stone-cutter's disease* (STONE-CUTTER 1).

1758 C. SMITH *Let.* 23 Feb. in *Lett. to Washington* (1899) II. 269 Our Stone Masons has been Sick, Ever Since you have been Away, and our Stone Work is much Behind hand. **1809** *Lond. Chron.* 22 Aug. 181/2 Seven stone-masons were landing a stone in Cumberland-street. **1824** SCOTT *St. Ronan's* ii, Jock Ashler the stane-mason, that ca's himsell an arkiteck. **1905** ROLLESTON *Dis. Liver* 185 An analogous form [of hepatic cirrhosis] associated with stonemason's lung-silicosis.

Hence **stonemason** *v.*, *trans.* to carve or work as a stonemason; **stone-masonry**, the art of, or work executed by, a stonemason: = MASONRY 1, 2.

1859 DICKENS *Lett.* (1880) II. 95 One of the balustrades of the destroyed old Rochester bridge has been.. presented to me by the contractor.. and has been duly *stonemasoned and set up on the lawn. **1818** SCOTT *Hrt. Midl.* xxxii, Despite the superior advantage of *stone-masonry. **1897** A. DRUCKER tr. *Ihering's Evol. Aryan* 110 The difference between timber-work and stone-masonry.

stonen (ˈstəʊnən), *a.* Now only *dial.* or *rare arch.* Forms: α. 1 **stǣnen**, 3 **stænen**, 2–3 **stenen**. β. 2–3 **stanen**, 4 **stoonen**, 5 **stonun**, 5–6 **-yn**, (7 **stoneing**), 3–5, 9 **stonen**. [OE. *stǣnen* = OFris. *steinen*, OHG., MHG. *steinîn*, Goth. *stainein-s*:—OTeut. **stainīno-* f. **staino-z* STONE *sb.* The β forms are refashioned after the sb.]

1. Made or consisting of stone: = STONE *sb. attrib.* (17 a).

a **900** *O.E. Martyrol.* 15 May 82 God sealde.. his bebodu.. on twam stænenum bredum. *c* **1205** LAY. 9241, & al abuten ouer al he makede stænene wal. *Ibid.* 12424 Ænne strongne stanene wal. *Ibid.* 14227 þer uppe stenene [**1275** stonene] wal. *a* **1225** *Ancr. R.* 378 Ineiled o rode, and ine stonene þruh biclused. **1388** WYCLIF *2 Cor.* iii. 3 Writun.. not in stony [*v.r.* stonen] tablis, but in fleischli tablis of herte. *c* **1400** *Apol. Loll.* 90 þe heþun men had sex kyndis of similacris, cleyen, treen, brasun, stonun, silueren, & golden. *c* **1450** *Brut* 404 Grete houngir brekithe herd stonen wall yn hir grete nede. **1528** in Phillipps *Wills* (*c* 1830) 106 My great stonyn trough. **1643** in *N. & Q.* 5th Ser. VIII. 497/1 He pulled down a stoneing cross. **1879** FARRAR *St. Paul* II. 103 Ye are our Epistle, says St. Paul,.. written.. not on stonen tablets, but on fleshen tablets. *Mod. dial.* (*Berks.*) Have you come over the stonen bridge? [i.e. a stone thrown across a ditch or narrow stream.]

†**b.** *fig. Obs.*

971 *Blickl. Hom.* 105 Hie wæron stænenre heortan & blindre. **1430–40** LYDG. *Bochas* IV. ix. (1554) 105 b, No man had so hard a stonen hert That might.. his iyen kepe drye.

2. Made of stoneware: = STONE *sb. attrib.* (17 b).

c **1000** *Ags. Gosp.* John ii. 6 þær wæron soðlice aset six stænene [*c* **1160** *Hatton* stenene] wæter-fatu. *c* **1200** ORMIN 14029 Sexe stanene fetless. *c* **1440** *Promp. Parv.* 477/1 Stonyn pott or oþer wessel.

stone-parsley. The umbelliferous herb *Sison Amomum*; also applied to *Seseli Libanotis* and other species (Mountain Stone-parsley), *Sison* being then sometimes distinguished as Bastard Stone-parsley.

1548 TURNER *Names of Herbes* 61 Petroselinum named in latine Apium saxatile is not our commune persely.. but.. an other herbe, as I do thynke,.. Whiche may be called in englishe stone persely or Lumberdy parsely. **1635** SWAN *Spec. Mundi* (1670) 218 There is Apium Hortense, garden-parsley; and apium palustre, water parsley (which is Smallage) and Apium montanum, mountain Parsley; and Petrapium, or Petroselinum Macedonicum, which we in England call Stone Parsley. **1744** J. WILSON *Synopsis Brit. Plants* 68 *Sium aromaticum Sison Off*... Bastard Stone-parsley. *Ibid.* 72 *Apium petræum seu montanum album*... Mountain Stone Parsley. **1857** ANNE PRATT *Flower. Pl.* III. 5 Sison (Stone Parsley). **1858** A. IRVINE *Handbk. Brit. Plants* 592 *Libanotis*... Mountain Stone-Parsley.

stone-pine. [= F. *pin de pierre*; cf. also G. *steinpinie* (in some Dicts.). The reason for the name is obscure; it has been supposed to refer to the hardness of the seeds.] A species of pine-tree, *Pinus Pinea*, a native of Southern Europe and the Levant, with edible seeds. Also applied to other species, as *P. Cembra* (Swiss Stone-pine).

1759 P. MILLER *Gard. Dict.* (ed. 7) s.v. *Pinus*, The cultivated Pine Tree, commonly called the Stone Pine. **1785** MARTYN *Lett. Bot.* xxviii. 444 The Stone-Pine has also double leaves. **1846** LINDLEY *Veg. Kingd.* 229 [The seeds] of the Stone Pine of Europe, Pinus Pinea,.. [and of] Pinus Cembra, Pinus Lambertiana.. are all eatable when fresh. **1887** G. NICHOLSON *Dict. Gard.* s.v. *Pinus*, *P. Cembra.* Swiss Stone Pine.

attrib. **1822** *Hortus Angl.* II. 498 P[inus] Pinea. Stone Pine Tree. **1874** STEWART & BRANDIS *Flora N. West India* 516 The celebrated Stone Pine forest.. near Ravenna. **1875** KINGSTON tr. *Jules Verne's Abandoned* vii. (1880) 90 [The monkey] ate with relish some stone pine almonds.

stone-pitch. ? *Obs.* [f. STONE *sb.* (see 17 c) + PITCH *sb.*[1] Cf. G. *steinpech*, bitumen.]

1. Pitch in the solid form; hard or dry pitch.

c **1450** *M.E. Med. Bk.* (Heinrich) 174 Spaynysche code & stanpicche. [*Harl. MS.* 1600 half a pond of stanpiche.] **1579** LANGHAM *Gard. Health* 493 Stone or drie Pitch, hath the vertues of Tarre or liquid Pitch, but not so strong. **1610** HOLLAND *Camden's Brit.* I. 411 Plankes of oke with nailes driven into them, cemented with stone-pitch. **1668** CHARLETON *Onomast.* 236 *Bitumen*.. Stone-Pitch.

2. (Meaning obscure.)

1589 in H. Hall *Soc. Eliz. Age* (1886) 225 Supper eodem. A shoulder of mutton,.. Bred & beare,.. Stone pytche.

stoner[1] (ˈstəʊnə(r)). Also 4 **staner.** [f. STONE *v.* + -ER[1].] One who stones or pelts with stones (esp. so as to kill).

a **1350** *Stephen* 217 in Horstm. *Altengl. Leg.* (1881) 30 Saul, þat þe staners clothes held. *c* **1440** *Promp. Parv.* 477/1 Stonare, or he þat stonythe.. *lapidator.* **1623** BINGHAM *Xenophon* 99 The stoners of the Ambassadors. **1680** C. NESSE *Church Hist.* 359 With this word, as with a stone, he knockt those stoners, for such they would have been to the woman, on the head. **1867** LIDDON in J. O. Johnston *Life & Lett.* v. (1904) 110 The stoners of St. Stephen.

stoner[2] (ˈstəʊnə(r)). [f. STONE *sb.* + -ER[1].]

†**1.** One skilled in precious stones: = LAPIDARY *sb.* 1 b. *Obs.*

c **1440** *Gesta Rom.* lxv. 286 (Harl. MS.) Gwido.. went to a stoner, and saide to hym, 'good man, I pray þe tell me þe vertu of þis ston.'

2. In comb. with prefixed numeral: A person weighing, or a horse carrying, (so many) stone (STONE *sb.* 14).

1862 WHYTE MELVILLE *Inside Bar* iii. 264 Your nags is hardly thirteen-stoners, sir—not in a country like this. **1896** CONAN DOYLE *Rodney Stone* xvii. 293 'Your man brought the scale down at thirteen-three and Harrison at thirteen-eight.' 'He's a fifteen-stoner from the loins upwards', cried Dutch Sam.

stone-raw. Southernized form of STANE-RAW.

1802 SCOTT *Minstrelsy* II. 215 The usual dress of the fairies is green; though on the moors, they have been sometimes observed in heath-brown, or in weeds dyed with the stoneraw, or lichen. **1853** G. JOHNSTON *Bot. E. Bord.* 265 *Parmelia saxatilis*... Stoneraw: Staney-rag. It is employed.. in dyeing stockings and nightcaps of a dirty orange-brown colour.

†**ˈstonern,** *a. Obs.* [Corrupt form of STONEN: cf. EARTHERN, and G. *steinern*.] = STONEN 1.

1753 W. MAITLAND *Hist. Edin.* I. i. 11 The Buildings which before had Stonern Fronts, were now converted into Wood. **1822** SCOTT *Nigel* ii, The West-Port is of stonern work.

stonery (ˈstəʊnərɪ). *rare.* [f. STONE *sb.* + -ERY.] An artificial collection or pile of stones; a rockery.

1833 LOUDON *Encycl. Archit.* §1979 Stoneries, as they are sometimes called, might be made little geological museums. **1889** *Advt.*, Seeds for Stonery or Grotto.

Stonesfield (ˈstəʊnzfiːld). Name of a village in Oxfordshire: used *attrib.* in **Stonesfield slate** (*Geol.*), a stratum of thin-bedded limestone and calcareous sandstone forming part of the Great Oolite series in Oxfordshire and Gloucestershire.

Stonesfield slates, i.e. slabs of limestone from this formation, are used for roofing.

1839 G. ROBERTS *Dict. Geol.*, *Stonesfield*, near Oxford; slate containing pterodactyles, &c., a lower portion of the great oolite. **1855** *Orr's Circ. Sci.*, *Inorg. Nat.* 71 Great oolite, Stonesfield slate, Fuller's earth. **1865** PAGE *Handbk. Geol. Terms*, *Stonesfield Slate*,.. celebrated for its being the rock in which English geologists first detected mammalian remains.. of Secondary epoch. **1885** GEIKIE *Text-bk. Geol.* VI. iii. (ed. 4) 795 The fossils of the Stonesfield Slate are varied and of high geological interest.

stone-shot.

1. [SHOT *sb.*[1] 14.] Stones used as missiles, esp. as shot for cannon: cf. STONE *sb.* 5 g. Also a single stone used as a cannon-ball.

1667 PEPYS *Diary* 28 Apr., A ship of near 500 tons was there found.. supposed of Queene Elizabeth's time,.. with a great deal of stone-shot in her,.. which was shot then in use. **1712** MOTTEUX *Quix.* III. viii. (1749) I. 184 The other slaves.. pouring vollies of stone-shot at the guards. **1876** VOYLE & STEVENSON *Milit. Dict.* 410/1. **1910** *Encycl. Brit.* II. 685/2 [In 1807] a stone-shot weighing some 700 lb. cut the mainmast of Admiral J. T. Duckworth's flagship in two.

†**b.** [SHOT *sb.*[1] 7 b.] The act of discharging stones from a gun. *Obs.*

1692 in *Capt. Smith's Seaman's Gram.* II. xvi. 125 In loading your Gun for a Stone-shot you are not to give her the same Charge of Powder as for one of Lead or Iron.

2. [SHOT *sb.*[1] 8.] = STONE'S THROW.

1847 TENNYSON *Princess* v. 51 He show'd a tent A stone-shot off.

stone-smatch, -smitch (stəʊnsmætʃ, -smɪtʃ). Also **-smach, -smich**, corruptly **-smick, -smickle.** [f. STONE *sb.* + SMATCH *sb.*[2] Cf. G. *steinschmätzer*.] A name for the STONECHAT (also applied to the wheat-ear).

1668 WILKINS *Real Char.* 151 Living.. upon stony places or open Heaths.. Stone Smich. *a* **1672** WILLUGHBY *Ornith.* II. xv. §3 (1676) 169 *Oenanthe nostra tertia*: *Muscicapa tertia* Aldrov... The Moor-Titling: The Stone-smich or Stone-chatter. **1709** J. LAWSON *Hist. Carolina* 146 The Snow-Birds are most numerous in the North Parts of America... They are like the Stones Smach, or Wheat-Ears. **1736** AINSWORTH, Stonesmickle (bird), *Muscinapa.* **1790** GROSE *Prov. Gloss.* (ed. 2) Suppl., *Stone-chat* or *Stone-smatch*, the bird called in the south a wheat-ear. **1797** [see STONECHAT].

stone's throw (ˈstəʊnz,θrəʊ). Also (*rarely*) **stone-throw.** [THROW *sb.*[2] 6.] The distance that a stone can be thrown by the hand; vaguely used for a short or moderate distance.

α. **1581** A. HALL *Iliad* III. 45 For who can see a stones throw of ought thing in land or plaine? **1712** [see THROW *sb.*[2] 6]. **1832** R. & J. LANDER *Exped. Niger* II. viii. 3 The Niger here is not more than a stone's-throw across at present. **1889** JESSOPP *Coming of Friars* v. 218 Three mighty churches, all within a stone's throw of one another.

β. **1875** MCILWRAITH *Guide Wigtownsh.* 19 The ruins of the little chapel are within a stone-throw of the road. **1895** W. M. MACPHERSON *Ch. & Priory Monymusk* i. 41 The little Romanesque church and tower.. were built.. within a stone throw of their altar.

stone-still, *adv.* and *predicative adj.* [See STONE *sb.* 19 and STILL *adv.* and *a.*; cf. STOCK-STILL.] As still as a stone; perfectly still or motionless. Usually after *sit, stand, lie*, etc.

a **1225** *Ancr. R.* 414 Sitte ȝe mid Marie ston-stille ed Godes fet, and hercneð him one. *c* **1375** *Sc. Leg. Saints* i. (*Peter*) 491 þe body lay stan still. *c* **1475** *Hunt. Hare* 42 Jac Wade hase a dogge.. wyll take a bull, And hold hym ston-styll. **1595** SHAKS. *John* IV. i. 77, I will not struggle, I will stand stone still. **1608** L'ESTRANGE *Vis. Quev.* vii. 212 At the very name of Priest,.. Lucifer stood stone-still, as mute as a fish. ? **1718** POPE *Let. to Duke Buckhm.* Wks. 1886 X. 149, I imagined it had been a village in Amphion's time, where all the cottages having taken a country dance together, had.. stood stone-still with amazement ever since. **1859** MEREDITH *R. Feverel* i, She lay stone-still in a trance of terror.

†**b.** Perfectly quiet or silent. *Obs.*

1338 R. BRUNNE *Chron.* (1725) 266 Nouþer suld werri bi lond, no in water bi schip, Bot hold þam stone stille in pes at þer cuntre. *c* **1425** *Seven Sag.* (P.) 1735 Scho sewyd hyr modyr wylle, And went hom al ston stille.

†**ˈstonesuck.** *Obs.* In 3 **stoansuke.** [f. STONE *sb.* + SUCK *v.*] Parsley.

c **1265** *Voc. Plants* in Wr.-Wülcker 556/11 *Petrosillum*, peresil, stoansuke.

stonewall, *sb.* Also **stone-wall** and as two words.

1. A wall built of stones; now esp. of rough stones without mortar, as a fence between fields, etc.

c **825** *Vesp. Psalter* lxi[i]. 4 Stanwalle [*dative*: gl. *macheriæ*]. *c* **1205** LAY. 15846 Nulle hit nauere god.. þæt þi castel stonde.. ne nauere þi stan wal stille ne ligge. *c* **1385** CHAUCER *L.G.W.* 713 There was but a ston wal hem betweene. **1463** *Bury Wills* (Camden) 20 The stoon wal be the strete syde. **1546** J. HEYWOOD *Prov.* (1867) 39 Hunger perseth stone wall. **1621** in *Trans. Cumb. & Westm. Archæol. Soc.* (1903) III. 155 That all the Tennants.. make their dike.. with Stonewall Five foote high with Cape and Coble. ? *c* **1640** LOVELACE *Poems*, *To Althea* iv, Stone Walls doe not a Prison make. **1768** PENNANT *Brit. Zool.* II. 269 Hills, especially those that are fenced with stone walls. **1856** EMERSON *Engl. Traits* v, Wks. (Bohn) II. 43 The last Reform-bill took away political power from a mound, a ruin, and a stone-wall, whilst Birmingham and Manchester.. had no representative. **1908** [MISS E. FOWLER] *Betw. Trent & Ancholme* 21 A low stone wall and coping.

2. a. Used as an epithet for one who seeks to confound by dogged resistance. Chiefly applied to Thomas Jonathan ('*Stonewall*') Jackson (1824–63), Confederate general during the American Civil War.

1862 *Texas Almanac Extra* 18 Sept. 1/1 Stonewall Jackson was marching on Baltimore with 40,000 men. **1863** G. MEREDITH *Let.* 7 Jan. (1970) I. 185 Busy my good sir, so as to drive the pen as fast as Stonewall Jackson is driving the federals. **1867** *John Lillywhite's Cricketers' Compan.* 46 'Young Stonewall'—as he [*sc.* H. Jupp] has been called—was in immense form. **1902** E. B. V. CHRISTIAN in Alverstone & Alcock *Surrey Cricket* iii. 82 The eleven.. received very valuable additions in Tom Humphrey and Jupp, or 'young Stonewall', the 'old Stonewall' being Mortlock, who still played. **1970** R. LOWELL *Notebook* 120 Above your fire the blood-crossed flag of the States, A Stonewall Jackson, a Twenty-two at half-cock.

b. *Australian Polit. slang.* Parliamentary obstruction, or a body of obstructives: cf. *stonewall* vb., etc. below.

1876 *Victorian Hansard* Jan. XXII. 1387 (Morris) Mr. G. Paton Smith wished to ask.. whether the six members.. constituted the 'stone wall'.. which was to oppose all progress? **1898** *Daily News* 22 Oct. 2/1 The New Zealand Legislation.. indulging in what is known in colonial parlance as a 'stone wall'.

3. *attrib.* and *Comb.*

1880 'BROOKSBY' *Hunting Countries* II. 201 Stonewall jumping. *Ibid.* 205 Here you get on to the stone wall country, and may not see a hedge all day. **1885** F. GALE *Hon. Robert Grimston* iii. 25 The well-known stone-wall cricketer, Mr. A. Haygarth. **1890** *Catholic News* 20 Sept. 7/3 It displayed.. the usual stone-wall stupidity. **1895** LD. SALISBURY in *Standard* 6 July 5 When a Standing Committee by a stonewall majority passed every word of a Bill in spite of every attempt to amend it. **1895** J. N. PENTELOW *England v. Australia* 37 Lucas played the stonewall game. **1901** *Daily-Chron.* 29 Aug. 6/3 What excellent stone-wall jumpers almost all the horses were. **1932** E. BOWEN *To North* vi. 57 He played.. a stonewall game and beat Emmeline.

Hence **stonewall** *v.* (*a*) *intr.*, *Cricket slang*, to block balls persistently, to play solely on the defensive; also *transf.*; (*b*) *Polit. slang*, (orig. *Australian*, now chiefly *N. Amer.*), to obstruct business by lengthy speeches or otherwise, to practise obstruction; also *trans.* to obstruct (business); also, to block (an enquiry, request, etc.); to obstruct (a person or organization). **stone-walled** (-wɔːld) *a.*, having or enclosed by a stone wall or walls. **stonewaller**, one who 'stone-walls' (in either sense). **stone-walling** *vbl. sb.*, (*a*) the process of walling with stone; *concr.* (usually as two words) stone walls collectively, or a length of stone wall; (*b*) *Cricket* and *Polit. slang*, persistent blocking or obstruction (see *stonewall* vb. above); also *attrib.* **stone-walling** *ppl. a.*, that 'stonewalls', obstructive.

1889 *Played On* 34 A brother professional.. began to *stone-wall in a distracting manner. 'Take care of your wicket and let the runs take care of themselves,' was his motto. **1914** *Daily News* 15 Apr. 9 Complaint that the Church has been too long stone-walling was made at the annual conference of the Wesley Guild. **1916** *Contemp. Rev.* Nov. 576 Obstruction did not merely consist in stonewalling Government business. **1964** M. Gowing *Britain & Atomic Energy 1939–1945* xiii. 344 The Combined Policy Committee discussed the matter but the Americans stonewalled. **1972** *Accountant* 23 Mar. 373/2 Often in the past, the Budget speech has been preceded by the unreality of questions to the Chancellor which his junior Ministers have had to stonewall with the traditional: 'I cannot anticipate my right hon. Friend's Budget statement.' **1974** *Newsweek* 11 May 23/2 The President himself.. served notice that he would stonewall any further demands for tapes in the Watergate scandal. **1974** *Globe & Mail* (Toronto) 10 Dec. 6/2 What the Government does not seem to realize is that in the process of stonewalling the Opposition, it has, itself, compromised the independence of Mr. Munro. **1976** D. Hiro *Inside India Today* 260 The Congress administration stonewalled again, when Mishra died.. and the opposition demanded a 'high power' inquiry. **1982** *Daily Tel.* 25 Jan. 12/7 The Nixon administration.. also gave the world 'stonewall' as a verb and then got out in the attempted practice thereof. **1786** G. Frazer *Dove's Flight* 41 She takes her flight to her *stone-walled refuge. **1891** *Field* 7 Mar. 345/3 Barchard in goal..showed marvellous stopping powers... In him the North possess a regular '*stonewaller'. **1895** J. N. Pentelow *England v. Australia* 20 Boyle gave the young stonewaller still better assistance. **1958** *Economist* 2 Aug. 361 He indicated to the Austrians that he thought Mr Dulles the chief western noman and habitual stonewaller. **1971** *Jamaican Weekly Gleaner* 17 Nov. 27/1 Mrs. A. D. Scott, regarded as one of the toughest stonewallers ever to play locally, was not very happy on the very fast surface. **1799** A. Young *View Agric. Lincoln.* 32, 518 yards of chopped *stone walling. **1875** *Encycl. Brit.* II. 388/2 Over this structure there was clearly another..as extensive remains of fine stone-walling still exist. **1880** *Gentl. Mag.* Jan. 64 If '*stone-walling' tactics are adopted by the oppositionists. **1892** *Pall Mall Gaz.* 5 Sept. 1/2 It is for cricket such as this..that the opponents of stone-walling sigh. **1902** *Daily Chron.* 23 Apr. 3/2 Of 'stone-walling' cricketers, Lord Granville [Gordon] entertains a very poor opinion.

stoneware ('stəʊnwɛə(r)). (Also with hyphen, or as two words.) A hard dense kind of pottery ware, made from very siliceous clay, or a mixture of clay with a considerable amount of flint or sand.

1683 *Digby's Chym. Secr.* II. 207 Take an Earthen Pan of Stone-ware. **1747** Berkeley *Tar-water in Plague* Wks. III. 487, I use tar-water made in stone ware or earthen very well glazed. **1827** Faraday *Chem. Manip.* xv. (1842) 373 Bottles ..on sand, placed in a bowl or cup of common stone ware. **1880** Janvier *Pract. Keramics* 136 Very fine stonewares, mostly iron-body, are made in Japan and China.

b. *attrib.*

1783 *J. Tait's Directory Glasgow* (1872) 54 Oliphant Francis, stone ware dealer, King's street. **1807** T. Thomson *Chem.* (ed. 3) II. 302 The paper, while still moist, is applied to the stoneware biscuit and pressed upon it. **1829** S. Shaw *Staffordsh. Potteries* 173 His beautiful and excellent Stone Ware Pottery. **1833** N. Arnott *Physics* (ed. 5) II. 39 A black stone-ware teapot..will radiate away 100 degrees of its heat in the same time that a pot of polished metal will radiate only 12 degrees. **1854** Ronalds & Richardson *Chem. Technol.* (ed. 2) I. 229 The smoke and hot gases are caused to circulate in an extensive series of metallic or stoneware flues. **1884** C. T. Davis *Bricks, Tiles*, etc. (1889) 308 The interval between the South Amboy fire-clay bed and the stoneware clay bed.

stone-weight. (Now usually as two words.) A measure of weight: = stone *sb.* 14. Also, a piece of metal of this weight, used in weighing, or as a standard.

a **1400** [see stone *sb.* 14 a]. **1552** *Extracts Rec. Convent. Burghs Scot.* (1870) I. 2 The stane wecht of Lanark. **1628** in *Maitl. Club Misc.* III. 369 For bringing from Edinburgh to Stirling xiij stane wecht of Calk oyle and Culloures. **1658** Gurnall *Chr. in Arm.* II. 33 If a pound weighs down the scale, there is no doubt then but a stone weight will do it. **1835** *Act 5 & 6 Will. IV*, c. 63 §11 By local Customs..the Denomination of the Stone Weight varies.

stonework ('stəʊnwɜːk). (Also with hyphen, or occas. as two words.) [Cf. OS. *stênwerk*, MHG., mod.G. *steinwerk*.]

1. Work built of stone; masonry.

c **1000** Ælfric *Saints' Lives* xxvii. 29 He..worhte þa of seolfre ænne heahne stypel on stanweorces gelicnysse. **1387** Trevisa *Higden* (Rolls) II. 81 Vawtes of stoonwerk wonderliche i-wrouȝt. **1412–20** Lydg. *Troy Bk.* II. 698 With spoutis þoruȝ & pipes..From þe ston-werke to þe canel rauȝt. **1556** *Chron. Grey Friars* (Camden) 75 The goodly stoneworke that stode behynde the hye alter. **1609** Holland *Amm. Marcell.* xxiv. i. 241 The scluces or floudgates made of stone worke. **1776** G. Semple *Building in Water* 73 All that soft Slutch would be thrown out, and a firm Stone-work put in the Place of it. **1837** *Penny Cycl.* IX. 165/2 A course of stone work imbedded in cement. *a* **1894** Layard *Autobiog.* (1903) I. iii. 146 The Lion of St. Mark carved in the stone-work.

b. Artistic work of any kind executed in stone.

1910 D. G. Hogarth in *Encycl. Brit.* I. 248/1 The magnificent gold work of the later period..should be compared with stone work in Crete, especially the steatite vases with reliefs found at Hagia Triada.

2. The process of working in stone, as in building; the labour or task of a mason.

1793 Smeaton *Edystone L.* §93 Whether there was any kind of mortar or cement used in the stone-work. **1870** J. L. Aikman *Centenary Anderston Ch., Glasgow*, Hist. Sk. 60 The stone-work was let to Mr. Broom, builder.

b. *Coal Mining.* The work of driving headings through stone or rock: cf. *stone-heading* (stone *sb.* 20).

1883 Gresley *Gloss. Coal-mining* 242 *Stone work*, driving of drifts or galleries in measures.

So **stone-worker**, a worker in stone; one who shapes or carves stone, as in building or sculpture. **stone-working**, the process of working in stone (also *attrib.*). **stone-works**, (*a*) an establishment for preparing stone for building, decorative, or other purposes; (*b*) an establishment for making artificial stone.

1898 *Allbutt's Syst. Med.* V. 253 The pulmonary fibrosis of metal-grinders, of *stone-workers..and some other trades, is popularly known as consumption. **1875** Knight *Dict. Mech.*, *Stone-working Tools. **1905** Miss A. S. Griffith tr. *Capart's Prim. Art Egypt* ii. 50 As a question of stone-working it is astonishing to find primitive man making rings in flint. **1731** W. Halfpenny *Perspective* 34 Mr. Allen's *Stone-Works, near the City of Bath. **1878** Jewitt *Ceramic Art* I. 163 At the commencement Mr. Ransome had ..his stone-works at Ipswich.

stonewort ('stəʊnwɜːt). [f. stone *sb.* + wort. Cf. G. *steinwurz*.] Name for several different plants.

†**1.** The fern *Asplenium Ceterach*, also called *stone fern* (stone *sb.* 20 c). *Obs.*

1585 Higins *Junius' Nomencl.* 135/1 *Scolopendrium, calcifraga*,..fingerferne: ceterach or stonewoort. **1647** Hexham I. (Herbs), Fingerferne, or stone-wort, *Steen-varen.*

2. With defining words, applied to species of *Sison* and other umbelliferous plants. (Cf. stone-parsley.)

1796 Withering *Brit. Plants* (ed. 3) II. 300 *Sison Amomum*... Bastard Stone Parlsey. Hedge Stonewort. *Ibid.*, [*S.*] *segetum*... Corn Parsley, or Stonewort. **1799** J. Hull *Brit. Flora* I. 62 *Sison inundatum*... Water Stonewort. *Ibid.*, *Sison verticillatum*,..Verticillate Stonewort. **1865** *Sowerby's Eng. Bot.* (ed. 3) IV. 107 *Sison Amomum*... Hedge Stonewort. *Ibid.* 108 *Trinia vulgaris*... Glabrous Stonewort.

3. A book-name for the genus *Chara*, from the calcareous deposits on the stem; also extended to the N.O. *Characeæ*.

1816 T. Green *Univ. Herbal* I. 285 *Chara Tomentosa*; Brittle Chara, or Stonewort. *Ibid.*, *Chara Vulgaris*; Common or Stinking Chara, or Stonewort. *Ibid.*, *Chara Flexilis*; Smooth Chara, or Stonewort. **1854** A. Adams etc. *Man. Nat. Hist.* 535 Stone-worts (Characeæ). **1875** Huxley & Martin *Elem. Biol.* 42 Stoneworts (Chara and Nitella).

stoney ('stəʊnɪ). *dial.* Also *Sc.* **staney, stanie; stonie.** [Var. stony *a.*] A child's coloured marble made of stone or a stone-like material.

1856 *N. & Q.* 2nd Ser. I. 283/2 Stone marbles are called *stoneys*, and clay ones *commoneys*, though *Dutch alleys* are only *stoneys* enamelled. **1868** *Little Corporal* May 67/3 Chinies, Stonies, and Agates, some large and some small. **1885** 'J. Strathesk' *More Bits from Blinkbonny* (ed. 2) ii. 33 Those played with were called 'taas', and consisted of 'marbles, stanies, frenchies, moral-leggers', etc. **1919** W. Wingate *Poems* 74 Reddies and stanies for 'moshie' or 'ring'. **1956** G. E. Evans *Ask Fellows who cut Hay* xxiv. 215 Single marbles were placed in a long line, as many marbles as there were players... The player stood at the end of the line, an agreed distance from the first marble, or *stoney* as it was called. **1965** *Press & Jrnl.* (Aberdeen) 13 Apr. 6/4 A good 'staney', a hard stone boolie which could be hurled against the school wall without breaking.

stoney, var. of stony *a.* and *v.*

stong, obs. pa. t. and pa. pple. of sting *v.*[1]

stong(e, obs. or north. ff. stang *sb.*[1] and *sb.*[2]

stongke, obs. pa. t. of stink *v.*

† **'stonied**, *ppl. a.*[1] *Obs.* [f. stony *v.* + -ed[1].] Stupefied, benumbed, etc. Cf. astonied.

a **1340** Hampole *Psalter, Prayer Habakkuk* 510 In manaunce of endles fyre, þou sall make þaim as stunayd men for wa þat is cumand till þaim. **1382** Wyclif *Prov.* xvi. 30 [He] that with stoneȝid eȝen [1388 iȝen astonyed; Vulg. *attonitis oculis*] thenketh shreude thingis. **1602** tr. *Guarini's Pastor Fido* IV. v. M 1, Fresh water may restore her stonied sprights. **1682** D'Urfey *Butler's Ghost* 134 That tumbling backwards o're a Stool, The stunnied Statesman with the blow Was left at the mercy of his Foe.

† **'stonied**, *ppl. a.*[2] *Obs. rare.* [f. as if **stony* vb., f. stony *a.* + -ed[1].] That has become hard as a stone, stony.

1590 Fenne *Frutes, Hecubaes Mishaps* Cc 4 b, What stonied heart..would this not make to melt?

stonify ('stəʊnɪfaɪ), *v. rare.* [f. stone *sb.* or stony *a.* + -fy.] *trans.* To make stony, or turn into stone; to petrify. Also *absol.*

1610 Holland *Camden's Brit.* I. 363 Wilkes of stone or Shell-fish stonified. **1633** J. Fisher *Fuimus Troes* II. v. D 1 b, Whose most vgly shapes..[they] May kill, and stonifie without all weapons. **1763** *Ann. Reg., Char.* 28/2 Flints..are .., if the expression may be allowed, more *stonified* than other stones. **1887** W. C. Russell *Frozen Pirate* I. xi. 160 The temperature below had not the severity to stonify me to the granite of the men at the table.

Hence **'stonified** *ppl. a.* Also **'stonifiable** *a.*, capable of being stonified.

1662 J. Chandler *Van Helmont's Oriat.* 247 Every stonyfiable juyce hath its own determined..hardness. **1882** R. C. Maclagan *Scott. Myths* 144 This stonified head. **1890** W. C. Russell *Ocean Trag.* III. xxxiii. 218 The stonified ship [a ship encrusted with shells, etc.] shook to the mighty discharge.

stonily ('stəʊnɪlɪ), *adv.* [f. stony *a.* + -ly[2].] In a stony manner. Chiefly *fig.*: cf. stony *a.* 5 a.

a **1845** Barham *Ingol. Leg.*, *Blasph. Warn.* 722 And very few saw..A small stony Saint... Beckon stonily downward to some one below. **1859** W. H. Gregory *Egypt in 1855–6* II. 35 The huge columns of the central hall, the colossal figures gazing stonily upon me..fell like a waking nightmare upon my imagination. **1899** Conan Doyle *Duet* 248 Harrison began to laugh, and then turned stonily solemn.

stoniness ('stəʊnɪnɪs). [f. as prec. + -ness.] The quality or condition of being stony.

1. *lit.* The fact of having the character of stone, or being full of stones (or of hard substance like stone).

1600 Surflet *Country Farm* II. liv. 369 Figges... Their stonines or being without stones. **1665** Sir T. Herbert *Trav.* (1677) 38 Arabia Petrea (named so either from the Stoniness thereof or from Petra..the Capital City). **1789** W. H. Marshall *Glouc.* II. 40 Notwithstanding the stoniness of the soil.

b. *concr.* Stony matter or deposit. *rare.*

1653 Blithe *Eng. Improv. Impr.* (ed. 3) 33 Oft-times thou commest immediately unto a little Gravill, or Stoniness. **1760** R. Brown *Compl. Farmer* II. 5 Where anything of small gravel or stonyness is to be found.

2. *fig.* Hardness, insensibility, unfeelingness.

1571 Golding *Calvin on Ps.* xviii. 26. 62 God hardeneth himself..and becometh steely against their stonnynesse. **1626** J. Cotton in *Ussher's Lett.* (1686) 339 Before the Heart be changed from Stoniness to Brokenness. **1854** T. T. Lynch *Lett. to Scattered* etc. (1872) 383 The stoniness of his own heart may remain.

stoning ('stəʊnɪŋ), *vbl. sb.* [f. stone *v.* + -ing[1].] The action of the verb, in various senses.

1. Pelting with stones; esp. (in ancient times) as a form of capital punishment.

a **1300** *Cursor M.* 19467 Quils þai him wit staning queld. *c* **1400** *Sc. Trojan War* II. 1595 With mony bitter panes Of stanyng of hir moder schene. *c* **1440** *Promp. Parv.* 477/1 Stonynge, *lapidacio.* **1548** *Elyot's Dict.*, *Lapidatio*, a stonyng, a hurlynge of stones. **1657** Billingsly *Brachy-Martyrol.* viii. 27 The Christians underwent all wrongs, As Scourgings, stonings. **1849** M. Arnold *Sick King in Bokhara* 112 They..sentenc'd him..To die by stoning. **1886** C. Bigg *Chr. Platonists Alexandria* iv. 117 He narrowly escaped stoning in the streets.

2. Paving, building up, or repairing with stones. Also *concr.*

1797 J. Curr *Coal Viewer* 13 These roads..are laid.. upon wood, (after..stoneing about ten or twelve inches thick for a foundation). **1819** [see garland *sb.* 7]. **1867** *Jrnl. R. Agric. Soc.* Ser. II. III. II. 664 At the entrances to large rivers it was sometimes necessary..to have careful stoning, because the work was frequently tested by heavy seas.

3. Rubbing or scouring with a stone. Also *attrib.*

1688 Holme *Armoury* III. 92/2 (Wool carding) Stoning of it [*sc.* the Card] is burnishing of it. **1882** *Encycl. Brit.* XIV. 387/1 In machine currying the tanned hides..are struck out in a 'stoning' machine. **1884** Knight *Dict. Mech.* Suppl., *Stoning Jack*, a machine in which the jack is furnished with a stock stone to work the leather.

4. Clearing (ground) of stones; taking the stones out (of fruit).

1628 Bp. Hall *Fast Serm.* 27 To what purpose is the fruitfulnesse, fencing, stoning, if the ground yeeld a plentiful Crop of..Weedes? **1747** Mrs. Glasse *Cookery* 154 To preserve Gooseberries whole without stoning.

5. Formation of the stone in fruit. Also *attrib.*

1842 Loudon *Suburban Hort.* 475 The setting and stoning of fruit... The fruit is thinned before and after the stoning season. *Ibid.* 484 When the stoning is completed and the fruit begins to swell.

'stoning, *ppl. a.* [f. as prec. + -ing[2].] That stones, in senses of the vb.; †petrifying.

1623 W. Lisle *Ælfric's O. & N. Test.* To Rdrs. ¶4 To mould the dow of artificiall marble, and bake it in Killes for building..or tempered with clammy and stoning waters, to plaster and polish it with tooles appliable vnto all formes. **1891** Meredith *One of our Conq.* xxxii, A man whose appearance breathed of offering her common ground, whereon to meet and speak together, unburdened by the hunting world, and by the stoneing world.

† **'stonish**, *a. Obs.* [f. stone *sb.* + -ish[1].] Resembling, or having the character of, stone; stony. (Chiefly *fig.*)

c **1450** *Mirour Saluacioun* (Roxb.) 158 Harde and stonysshe ware yͭ hert. **1530** Palsgr. 302 *Pierreux*, stony or stonysshe. **1551** Robinson tr. *More's Utopia* II. (1895) 206 Is there annye man so possessed wyth stonyshe insensibilitie..?

† **'stonish**, *v. Obs.* Forms: 5 *Sc.* **stunys, stonisch,** 5–6 *Sc.* **stonis, -ys, -eis,** 6 *Sc.* **stwnys, stunnys;** 6 **ston(n)ysh(e,** 6–7 **stonish.** [aphetic f. astonish *v.*] *trans.* To stun mentally, shock, surprise. = astonish *v.* 2–4.

c **1470** Henry *Wallace* VI. 549 The fyrst cownter so gret abaysing maid, That all the ost was stunyst of that sicht. *c* **1470** *Rauf Coilȝear* 175 For I am stonischit at this straik, that hes me thus steird. **1513** Douglas *Æneis* XI. i. 44 So that ..na delay May stoppin ȝou, nor stunnys ane other day Be ȝour awin sleuth. **1530** Palsgr. 736/2, I stonyshe, *jestonne.* He stonyshyd me. **1592** Shaks. *Ven. & Ad.* 825 Whereat amas'd..Or stonisht, as night wandrers often are, Their light blowne out..Euen so confounded in the darke she lay. **1612** T. Taylor *Comm. Titus* i. 15 Labour in hearing the word, to finde it..to shake and stonish thy soule.

Hence †**'stonished** *ppl. a.*, †**'stonishing** *vbl. sb.* Also †**'stonishment.**

c **1520** M. Nisbet *N.T. in Scots* Acts iii. 10 And thai war fillit with wonndring, and stonysing of mynde [1388 Wyclif stoniynge]. **1530** Palsgr. 276/2 Stonnyshyng abashing, *estonnissement*. **1594** R. C[arew] *Tasso* II. xxi, T'was stonishment [It. orig. *stupor*]..If t'were not loue that stir'd his villaine hart. **1595** Spenser *Amoretti* xvi, The whiles my stonisht hart stood in amaze.

stonk (stɒŋk). [? Echoic.] **1.** *dial.* Also **stunk.** (See quot. 1841). Also, a game of marbles; a coloured marble.

1841 Jamieson *Dict. Sc. Lang.* II. 503/1 *Stunk*, the stake put in by boys in a game, especially in that of marbles. **1896** *Manch. City News* 10 Oct., The game is called 'stonks' oftener than marbles. *Ibid.*, A brown or other coloured marble is a 'stonk' and counts one.

2. *Mil. slang.* A concentrated artillery bombardment. Also *fig.*

1944 W. Robson *Let.* 8 May (1960) 94 Our gunners were in readiness for the great stonk we requested at nightfall. **1947** D. M. Davin *Gorse blooms Pale* 197, I wasn't so crackers I wasn't still listening for that bloody stonk to come screaming down on us. **1961** *Times* 27 Nov. 6/5 The 'stonks' that Mr. Brown and his regional organizers are now going to bring down. **1975** D. Clark *Premedicated Murder* iv. 65 'We were AGRA.' 'Army Group Royal Artillery.. thickening up on other people's stonks and barrages.' **1981** Ld. Harewood *Tongs & Bones* ii. 45 You could never tell.. if your arrival would bring down an artillery 'stonk' on your head.

Hence as *v. trans. Mil. slang*, to bombard with concentrated artillery fire.

1944 *Daily Tel.* 15 May 6 Here was one more message before we left—that British troops on a captured ridge were being 'stonked' heavily. **1946** R. Allen *Home made Banners* xi. 136 Moaning Minnie..was the name they gave to the German multiple mortars that stonked their positions, wherever they were, a minimum of twice and a maximum of several dozen times in each twenty-four hours.

stonk(e, -en, obs. pa. t. and pple. of STINK *v.*

stonker ('stɒŋkə(r)), *v. slang* (chiefly *Austral.* and *N.Z.*). [f. STONK + -ER[5].] *trans.* To render useless; to put out of action, thwart. Also, to kill, destroy; to defeat or outwit. Now chiefly as *pa. pple.*

1919 W. H. Downing *Digger Dial.* 48 *Stonker*, exterminate; kill; strike out. **1928** *Bulletin* (Sydney) 15 Feb. 26/4 Then one [shell from a gun] comes in and stonkers 'Iggins and the Company Sergeant-Major. **1941** Baker *Dict. Austral. Slang* 72 *Stonker*, to defeat, outwit, put out of action. **1945** R. L. Seddon *Whims of W.A.A.F.* 4 Benzine restrictions have stonkered my car. **1959** G. Slatter *Gun in my Hand* xiv. 201 He went and stepped on a bloody mine. Stonkered the poor bastard properly.

Hence **'stonkered** *ppl. a.* (also *spec.* drunk; excessively intoxicated; extremely tired).

1924 *Truth* (Sydney) 27 Apr. 6 *Stonkered*, to be very drunk. **1925** Fraser & Gibbons *Soldier & Sailor Words* 271 *Stonkered*, put out of action. **1932** A. W. Upfield *Royal Abduction* 250 'Why don't they shut off the confounded thing?' 'Too stonkered with surprise, I'll bet.' **1940** F. Sargeson *Man & Wife* (1944) 76 Once they were a bit stonkered the boys would want to have a bo-peep at the bird while he was asleep. **1948** V. Palmer *Golconda* xix. 161 There were one or two old chaps on the executive who were glad enough to see me stonkered. **1963** A. Lubbock *Austral. Roundabout* 44 Two on 'em there was, lyin' stonkered in the road. **1967** K. Giles *Death & Mr. Prettyman* ii. 59 It won't help. I know when I'm stonkered. **1970** *Private Eye* 22 May 16 I'm pretty stonkered. Where can we get a snooze round here?

stonkerd, obs. form of STUNKARD *a.*

stonnard, stonnord: see STONEHORE.

stonne, obs. form of STONE.

stonore, variant of STONEHORE.

stont, variant of STOUND *sb.*, STUNT *a.*

stont(e: see STAND *v.*, STINT *v.*

stony ('stəʊnɪ), *a.* Forms: 1 **stániȝ,** 3 **stoni,** 3–4 **stani,** 4–5 **stany,** 5–6 **stonye,** 6 **stoany,** *Sc.* **staany,** 6–7 **stonie,** 7 *Sc.* **stanie,** 7– **stoney,** 4– **stony.** [OE. *stániȝ* = OHG. *steinag*, Goth. *stainah-s* :—OTeut. **stainaȝo-*, *-aχo-*, f. **staino-* STONE *sb.*: see -Y. (OE. had also *stǽniȝ*:—OTeut. type **stainīȝo-*.)]

1. a. Abounding in, or having the character of, stone or rock; full of rocks; rocky. Now *rare* or *Obs.*

†*Stony sea*: the Adriatic.

c **975** *Rushw. Gosp.* Matt. xiii. 5 þæt oþere þonne ȝefeollon on staniȝ lond. *c* **1325** *Metr. Hom.* 52 That gat that ledes Til hel..es stany and thornye Wit couaitys, and glotounye, [etc.]. *c* **1382** Wyclif *Acts* xxvii. 27 In the stoony see [Vulg. *in Adria*]. *c* **1440** *Gesta Rom.* viii. 19 (Harl. MS.) The wey toward the cite was stony, þorny, and scroggy. *a* **1500** *Medulla Gram.*, *Adriaticus*, stonye. **1526** Tindale *Mark* iv. 5 Some [seed] fell on a stony [**1611** on stony; R.V. 1881 on the rocky] grounde, where it had not moche erth. **1638** Junius *Paint. Ancients* 92 Hee betooke himselfe to a stony place of a reasonable height. **1709** T. Robinson *Nat. Hist. Westmld. & Cumbld.* xv. 87 Those high, steep, and stony Mountains, which are called the Skrees. **1832** Tennyson *Mariana in the South* iv, Day increased from heat to heat, On stony drought and steaming salt.

b. Full of or abounding in stones; containing many stones.

c **1400** *Promp. Parv.* 477/1 Stony, or full of stonys, *lapidosus, petrosus*. *c* **1440** *Pallad. on Husb.* XIII. 38 In stony grounde ek loueth he to stonde. **1538** Elyot *Dict.*, *Calculosus locus*, a stonye place. **1669** Worlidge *Syst. Agric.* (1681) 260 Eels commonly abscond themselves under stones in stony Waters. **1765** *Museum Rust.* IV. 219 He excludes both stoney and clayey soils from the use of his plough. **1815** J. Smith *Panorama Sci. & Art* II. 587 A gravelly soil consists chiefly of small stones from the size of a pea to that of a walnut, but when a large proportion of the stones are of the latter size or larger, the land is said to be stony. **1855** Tennyson *Brook* 39, I chatter over stony ways.

†**c.** Of fruits: Having a stone; also, abounding in stone-like seeds. *Obs.*

1585 Higins *Junius' Nomencl.* 97/1 *Pomum calculosum, lapidosum*,..stonie fruite, or such fruit as hath a grauellie core. **1681** Langford *Plain Instr. Fruit-trees* 135 The English [Quince] is the most stony. **1683** Poyntz *Pres. Prosp. Tobago* 8 Guavers are a Fruit that's very stony. **1784** Cowper *Task* I. 120, I fed on scarlet hips and stony haws.

2. †**a.** Made of stone. *Obs.*

1382 Wyclif *2 Cor.* iii. 3 Writun..not in stoony [**1388** stony, stonen] tablis but in fleischly tablis of herte. *c* **1447–8** *Shillingford Lett.* (Camden) 85 Wher was never no stale but a stony walle. **1551** T. Wilson *Logic* E iij, Euen as Moses receyued the same [law] of God in stony tables. **1611** Coryat *Crudities* 58 A faire stonie Bridge. **1612** *Two Noble K.* v. i. 62 The stony girthes of Citties. **1776** Goldsm. *Nat. Hist.* I. 382 Another noise..like the rattling of a great cart, upon a stony pavement.

b. Of the nature of stone.

1695 Woodward *Nat. Hist. Earth* II. (1723) 78 The Stoney Matter of the Strata. **1827** Faraday *Chem. Manip.* xiii. (1842) 302 Ordinary earthy or stony matter. **1871** G. Macdonald *Sonn. conc. Jesus* xiv, When the soaring skylark sings How shall the stony statue strain to hear?

c. Consisting of stones; *occas.* inflicted by stones. Chiefly *poet.* ? *Obs.*

c **1586** C'tess Pembroke *Ps.* lxxix. i, Jerusalem..hath suffred..utter wrack, To stony heapes her buildings turned. **1611** Coryat *Crudities* 103 A certaine stony circle that appeareth a little aboue the ground. **1657** Billingsly *Brachy-Martyrol.* iv. 19 Holy Steven Did through a Stony-volley go to heaven. **1697** Dryden *Æneid* ix. 1092 His golden helm gives way with stony blows Battered. **1736** Gray *Statius* I. 18 Batter Cadmus walls with stony showers.

d. Of a meteorite or meteoritic material consisting mostly of silicates and other non-metals.

1802 *Phil. Mag.* XIII. 23 (*heading*) Experiments and observations on certain stony and metalline substances which at different times are said to have fallen upon the earth. **1866** *Catal. of Meteorites* (Geol. Survey of India) 8 Two classes of meteorites or solid bodies which have been known to fall to the earth's surface, namely, 1st, stony masses, or aërolites, (often with particles of iron)—and 2nd, masses chiefly iron, or aërosiderites. **1898** *Amer. Jrnl. Sci.* CLV. 63 It seems probable that certain of the stony meteorites that have been found are really the masses in which some of the iron nodules, formed perhaps many miles distant, were embedded at the moment they entered our atmosphere. **1926** E. A. Fath *Elem. Astron.* xiv. 196 The three classes have the following general composition:..Iron Meteorites... Stony-iron Meteorites... Stony Meteorites. —These consist essentially of silicate minerals with minor amounts of metallic alloys and sulphides. **1981** *Times* 23 Jan. 14/5 The fossil falls into the class known as 'H-chondrite', stony meteorites containing a large amount of iron.

3. Pertaining or relating to stone or stones. *rare.*

1847 Tennyson *Princess* iii. 343 Chattering stony names Of shale and hornblende, rag and trap and tuff, Amygdaloid and trachyte. **1849** H. Miller *Footpr. Creator* xv. (1874) 290 The stony science. **1864** Ruskin in *Reader* IV. 678/1, I ..have been at stony work ever since, as I could find time.

4. a. Resembling stone in consistence; hard like stone; very hard.

1523–34 Fitzherb. *Husb.* §137 A peare or a warden wolde be graffed in a pyrre-stocke,..and some men graffe theym in a whyte-thorne, and than it wyll be the more harder and stonye. *c* **1586** C'tess Pembroke *Ps.* cv. ix, Noe rayny cloude but breakes in stony haile. **1664** Evelyn *Kal. Hort.*, *Feb.* (1679) 10 Set all sorts of Kernels and stony-Seeds. **1834** McMurtrie *Cuvier's Anim. Kingd.* 470 A layer of stony granules, which form an extremely indurated crust. **1857** Dickens *Dorrit* II. i, The thin, hard, stony wine. **1897** *Allbutt's Syst. Med.* III. 884 Formation of a stony concretion..in the nose..a rhinolith.

b. Of a quality (as hardness, colour): Like that of stone.

1565 Cooper *Thesaurus*, *Lapidea duritia*, a stonie hardenesse. **1796** Withering *Brit. Plants* (ed. 3) IV. 64 Root single, central, of a stony consistence. **1897** *Allbutt's Syst. Med.* IV. 747 There is very marked induration..often stony hardness. **1910** W. Parker in *Encycl. Brit.* XI. 352/2 In colour they range from a pale stony or yellowish shade to a rich dark brown.

5. *fig.* **a.** 'Hard', insensible, or unfeeling, as if consisting of stone; hardened, obdurate.

? *c* **1230** *Hali Meid.* 22 Stani were his heorte ȝef ha ne mealt i teares. *a* **1250** *Prov. Ælfred* B. 694 He hauit stoni herte, no-þing him ne smerteþ. **1526** *Pilgr. Perf.* (W. de W. 1531) 288 b, The herte begynneth to..melte..whiche before was all harde and stony as a flynte. **1595** Markham *Sir R. Grinuile* To Earl Sussex 4 Sauing the Muse by stonie times vndoone. **1596** Shaks. *Merch. V.* iv. i. 4 A stonie adversary, an inhumane wretch, Vncapable of pitty. *a* **1640** J. Ball *Treat. Covt. Grace* (1645) 340 A fleshie heart cannot be received by a stony, but the stony is removed by the fleshie. **1648** J. Beaumont *Psyche* xiv. cxlii, From the staring People's stony eye He of compassion not one drop had wrung. **1847** C. Bronte *Jane Eyre* iv, She introduced me to the stony stranger. *a* **1854** H. Reed *Lect. Eng. Hist.* x. (1856) 187 The tyrant's indurated and stony conscience.

absol. **1667** Milton *P.L.* xi. 4 Prevenient Grace descending had remov'd The stonie from thir hearts.

b. Rigid, fixed, motionless; destitute of movement or expression: esp. of the eyes or look.

1642 H. More *Song of Soul* III. iii. 44 Some Giant..With stony staring eyes. **1813** Scott *Trierm.* II. xxvi, Long shall close in stony sleep Eyes for ruth that would not weep. **1855** Tennyson *Maud* I. xiii. 22 He..Gorgonised me from head to foot With a stony British stare.

c. Of fear, grief, silence, etc.: 'Petrifying', stupefying: having no relief.

1590 Spenser *F.Q.* I. vi. 37 Suddein cold did ronne through every vaine, And stony horrour all her scences fild. *Ibid.* II. viii. 46 The stony feare Ran to his hart. **1794** W. Blake *Songs Exper.*, *Earth's Answ.* 4 Stony dread! **1882** 'Edna Lyall' *Donovan* iv, A stony speechless sorrow. **1911** M. Beerbohm *Zuleika Dobson* vii. 90 The Duke did not try to break the stony silence in which Zuleika walked. **1979** A. Brink *Dry White Season* iv. iv. 301 They were still staring at me in stony silence, their young dark faces expressionless.

d. *slang.* Short for *stony-broke* (see 6).

1886 [see BROKE *ppl. a.* 3]. **1890** [R. C. Lehmann] *Harry Fludyer* 122 Pat said he was stoney or broke or something but he gave me a sov. **1894** W. H. Wilkins & H. Vivian *Green Bay Tree* I. 25, I shall be quite stony if this goes on. **1905** Vachell *Hill* ix. 193 You'll have to wait till I have the money. I'm stoney now.

6. Combinations, etc. **a.** In advb. comb. with adjs., as †*stony-blind* (= STONE-BLIND), *-pitiless*. **b.** Parasynthetic formations, as *stony-eyed*, *-faced*, *-jointed*, *-toed*, *-winged* adjs. **c.** Special comb. and collocations: † **stony bone** (tr. med.L. *os petrosum*: see PETROSAL; cf. ROCKY *a.*[1] 3 a), the petrous portion of the temporal bone, containing the internal ear; **stony-broke** *a.* (*slang*) = *stone-broke* (STONE *sb.* 20 a); † **stony coal** = STONE-COAL; **stony cobbler** (see quot.); **stony colic,** colic due to an intestinal concretion (cf. *stone-colic*, STONE *sb.* 20 a); **stony coral** = *stone-coral* (STONE *sb.* 20 b); **stony-iron** *sb.* and *a.*, used to designate meteorites which contain appreciable quantities of both stony material and iron; † **Stony Mountains,** the Rocky Mountains (see ROCKY *a.*[1] 1 b); † **stony sage** (see quot.).

1587 W. Fowler *Wks.* (S.T.S.) I. 39/73 The man is *stony blinde that can not see the Sun. **1615** Crooke *Body of Man* 487 The *stony-bone. **1677** tr. *Groeneveldt's Treat. Stone* 9 The *Os petrosum*, or Stony-bone in the Organ of our Hearing. **1890** *Stony-broke [see *pebble-beached* adj. s.v. PEBBLE *sb.* 5 b]. **1894** Astley *50 Yrs My Life* II. 84 Though stony broke, it still reposes on my sideboard. **1895** Marie Corelli *Sorrows of Satan* x, I'm cleaned out—'stony-broke', as the slang goes. **1617** Moryson *Itin.* III. 93 The County of Namures..hath Mines of Iron and plenty of *stony Coale. **1880** Day *Fishes Gt. Brit.* I. 82 Little- or lesser-weever:..*Stony-cobbler. **1822–9** *Good's Study Med.* (ed. 3) I. 252 Enterolithica. *Stony colic. From bezoards and other intestinal concretions. **1882** *Cassell's Nat. Hist.* VI. 277 The *Stony Corals are well-known forms of animal life. **1859** 'O. Meredith' *Wanderer* (ed. 2) 177 Each *stony-eyed corpse there. **1933** M. Arlen *Man's Mortality* xv. 315 Manteuffel, staring *stony-faced towards the darkness..appeared not to have heard his question. **1975** F. Bresler *You & Law* 81 Even in this stony-faced sector of the law, fairness prevails. **1918, 1962** *Stony-iron [see MESOSIDERITE]. **1969** *Times* 9 Apr. 7/3 Stony-iron meteorites have been found in several Hopewell burial mounds. **1978** D. W. Sears *Nature & Origin of Meteorites* iii. 73 Stony-iron meteorites are traditionally defined as having approximately equal proportions of stony material and iron. At various times, four groups of stony-iron meteorites have been defined, but since two of these contain only one meteorite each we need here consider only two in any detail: the pallasites and the mesosiderites. **1767** Ellis *Corallines* in *Phil. Trans.* LVII. 408 The *stony-jointed Corallines. **1811** Pinkerton *Mod. Geog.* 542 The ridge called the *Stoney Mountains. **1818–22** *Encycl. Metrop.* XIV. 305/2. **1604** *Meeting of Gallants at Ordinary* (Percy Soc.) 7 Are not my Acts More *stony-pittilesse? **1548** Turner *Names Herbes* 73 Sideritis prima..may be called in englishe walsage or *stonisage. **1845** Dickens *Chimes* i. 6 A breezy,..blue-nosed, red-eyed, *stony-toed, tooth-chattering place it was, to wait in, in the winter-time. **1855** Bailey *Mystic* 45 Dragon *stony-winged.

†**'stony,** *v. Obs.* Forms: 4–5 **stoney, stonay, stunay,** 4 **stonye, (stoneȝe),** 5 **stuny, stonyyn** (*Promp. Parv.*), 7 **stunny,** 4–7 **stony.** *Pa. t.* 4 **stoneyd, stoneȝed,** *Sc.* **stonait, -ayit,** 5 **stonayd(e, stonaid,** 4–7 **stonyed.** *Pa. pple.* 4 **stoneyd, -eyed,** *Sc.* **stonayit,** 4–5 **stonayd,** 5 **-ayde, -ayed,** *Sc.* **stonayt,** 5–6 **stonyed,** (6 **stonied),** 7 **stunnied.** See also STOYNE *v.* [Aphetic f. ASTONY *v.* (Prob. sometimes confused with STUN *v.*)]

1. *trans.* To stupefy with noise or with a shock to the mind or feelings, benumb the faculties of (a person); to confound, amaze. Also *pass.*

c **1330** R. Brunne *Chron. Wace* (Rolls) 16629 Cadwaladres, when he þys herde,..Stoneyed he was a wel god prowe. *a* **1340** Hampole *Psalter, Prayer Habakkuk* 510 *In furore obstupefacies gentes*..in breth þou sall stunay genge. *c* **1340** —— *Pr. Treat.* 43 þise wordes when I here thaym or redis þam stonyes me and makis me gretly ferd. **1375** Barbour *Bruce* I. 299 Thair wes nane auentur that mocht Stunay hys hart. **1399** Langl. *Rich. Redeles* II. 125 þus ȝe derid hem vnduly.., And stonyed hem with stormes þat stynted neuere. *c* **1450** in Aungier *Syon* (1840) 354 Yf the hyghe mas be bygon they schalle synge Ab inimicis..withe oute the chirche, for stonyeng of the preste at auter. **1470–85** Malory *Arthur* III. vii. 107 Syr gauayne was so stonyed of the deth of this fair lady that he wiste not what he dyd. **1596** Spenser *F.Q.* v. xi. 30 Then gan she cry much louder then afore,..And Belge selfe was therewith stonied sore. **1612** Dekker *Lond. Tri.* C 4 b, *Envy*... Come You clouen-footed-brood of Barathrum Stop, stony her, fright her with your shreekes. **1660** Boyle *New Exp. Phys. Mech.* v. 52 So loud and vehement a noise, as stony'd those that were by. **1688** S. JOHNSON *Purgatory Prob'd* Pref. 1 This Miracle stunnied the Dominicans for some time.

2. To amaze or stupefy with a blow, stun.

c **1330** R. BRUNNE *Chron. Wace* (Rolls) 12377 Arthur was stoneyd, stakered, & stynt, But ȝut fel he nought for þat dynt [of the giant]. **1370** *Lay-Folks Mass-Bk.*, App. IV. 354 Lord greue ȝe not for þat dunt He stoneyed me and made me stunt Stille out of my steuene. *c* **1400** *Sege Jerusalem* (E.E.T.S.) 50 þe worst wrecche in þe wone; may on walle lygge, Strike doun with a ston; & stuny many knyȝtes. *c* **1450** *Merlin* xvi. 265 But he was stonyed of the stroke that he myght not stonde on his feet. **1470–85** MALORY *Arthur* I. xvi. 58 He.. smote hym on hyhe vpon the helme a grete stroke and stonyed hym sore. **1642** R. CARPENTER *Experience* II. vii. 163 [They] cut off their fingers, when many of them were alive, and onely stunnied. **1645** FEATLY *Dippers Dipt* (1646) 2 *margin*, The venturous Scotchman was so stunnied with this blow that he gave in.

3. To induce insensibility or loss of function in (a body or limb); to benumb, deaden.

1382 WYCLIF *Gen.* xxxii. 32 Therthurȝ that he towchide the synwe of his hipe, and it was stoneyd [Vulg. *obstupuerit*, 1388 dried]. **1398** TREVISA *Barth. De P.R.* XVII. cxii. (Tollem. MS.), Oyle may be so colde, þat he schall stony þe membre þat is bawmid þerwith. *c* **1403** LYDG. *Temple of Glas* 683 Bicause he seith, þat stoneiþ al my bloode, I am so symple & she is so goode. *c* **1530** *Judic. Urines* III. ii. 48 Yf that parte of the hede be agreued & stuffed or stonyed, through euyll humours and fumosites. **1684** tr. *Bonet's Merc. Compit.* IX. 335 The things that kill or stony them [i.e. worms] are all bitter, sharp, inciding, astringent things.

4. *intr.* To be stupefied with wonder or with fear.

1382 WYCLIF *Isa.* xiii. 8 Eche to his neȝhebore shall stoneȝe [1388 schal wondre. Vulg. *stupebit*]. *Ibid.* xix. 16 In that dai Egipt shal be as wymmen, and thei shul stoneȝen and dreden. **1436** *Libel Eng. Policy* in *Pol. Poems* (Rolls) II. 200 By lande and see so welle he hym acquite, To speke of hym I stony in my witte. *c* **1440** *York Myst.* xxx. 223 Loo! he stonyes for vs, he stares where he standis.

5. To break, crush.

c **1440** *Promp. Parv.* 476/2 Stonyyn, or brese werkys, *briso*.

Hence † **'stonying** *vbl. sb. Obs.*

c **1315** SHOREHAM *Poems* I. 954 þer-fore þy schryfte, man, schel be Wyþ-oute stoneynge. **1382** WYCLIF *Jer.* xix. 8 And Y shal sette this cite in to stoneyng [1388 wondring. Vulg. *in stuporem*]. **1398** TREVISA *Barth. De P.R.* XVII. ix. (1495) N vj b, Anetum sodde wyth oyle releasyth shrynkynge & stonyenge of synewes [L. *rigorem nervorum*]. *c* **1430** *Life of St. Kath.* (Gibbs MS.) 76 Whiche hath turned us alle in suche stonyynge and merueylyng. *c* **1530** *Judic. Urines* II. xii. 40 b, Litargia the lytargye is a stonyng of the brayne, wᵗ forgetfulnes. *Ibid.* 42 [This] sheweth brestyng bresyng or stonyng of sum veyne in yᵉ body. **1665–6** *Phil. Trans.* I. 223 The other [person struck by thunder or lightning].. besides a present stonying or numness, had no other hurt.

stony-hearted (ˌstəʊnɪˈhɑːtɪd), *a.* Having a stony heart; cruel, unfeeling, merciless.

1569 UNDERDOWNE *Heliodorus* VII. 93 There is no man so stoany harted, but he shal be made to yeelde with our flatteringe allurmentes. **1596** SHAKS. *1 Hen. IV* II. ii. 28 The stony-hearted Villaines. **1603** KNOLLES *Hist. Turks* (1638) 44 For who was so stony hearted; whom his sweet words and abundant teares.. might not haue moued. **1822** DE QUINCEY *Opium Eater* I. (1903) 183 So then, Oxford Street, stony-hearted stepmother,.. at length I was dismissed from thee! *a* **1851** D. JERROLD *St. Giles* xv. 150 His coarse and stony-hearted brethren at the bar.

Hence **stony-'heartedness.**

1673 HICKERINGILL *Greg. F. Greybeard* 258 They are so rooted in pride, stony heartedness and opinion of themselves. **1888** *Voice* (N.Y.) 19 Jan. 5 Mayor Chapin.. refuses to perform the marriage ceremony... His stony-heartedness will blight the joy of many an intending Brooklyn couple.

†**stoo**, *int. Obs. rare.* An exclamation used to urge on hounds. Cf. STABOY, STEEBOY.

1673 (*title*) S'too him Bayes: Or some Observations upon the Humour of Writing Rehearsal's Transpros'd. **1692** *Christ Exalted* §cv. 85 In bringing out his Molossi and whaffling Whelps, and crying, Stoo Dogs, stoo.

stoo, variant of STOW *v.*², *dial.*, to crop.

stoobber, stood, obs. ff. STUBBER, STUD.

stooge (stuːdʒ), *sb. slang* (orig. *U.S.*). [Origin unknown; the possibility that it represents an altered form of *student* has been suggested (students having frequently been employed as stage assistants).] **1. a.** A stage hand. **b.** A stage assistant, esp. one who acts as the butt or foil for a leading character; a feed, straight man. **c.** The assistant of a conjuror or similar performer. **d.** *transf.*

1913 *Sat. Even. Post* 1 Nov. 64/4 Ben, I want you to plant one of your stooges in that coop with a couple of smoke-pots, so that we'll get the effect of Jack coming through the thickest of it. **1929** *Variety* 24 July 1/1 Stuges perform on the floor with dead-pan faces and unconscious feet beating out the time-step. **1936** R. E. SHERWOOD *Idiot's Delight* II. iii. 129, I was a stooge for Zuleika, the Mind Reader. **1936** WODEHOUSE *Laughing Gas* xxii. 238 You expect me, do you, not only to act as a stooge for you in front of the camera, but to sit smiling in the background while you horn in and swipe my interview? **1940** —— *Eggs, Beans & Crumpets* 166 She's a conjuror's stooge.. A conjuror's assistant, don't you know. **1941** *Punch* 14 May 468/1 A lament for the absence of that long-suffering, superbly resilient feminine stooge, *Margaret Dumont* [as partner of the Marx brothers]. **1955** W. R. MATTHEWS *Brit. Philosopher as Writer* 12 In it [*sc.* one kind of philosophical dialogue] the author sets up one or more 'stooges', who.. can be made to ask just the questions which he, in the person of another character, can answer. **1967** M. ARGYLE *Psychol. Interpersonal Behaviour* vi. 112 Subjects took part in three three-minute discussions with stooges trained to stare, at distances of two, six and ten feet. **1977** *Spare Rib* June 28/2 Our humour is inter-reactive, there's no stooge. **1979** *Sci. Amer.* May 22/1 A common method of cheating is to rely on what magicians call a 'stooge': someone who is watching behind a screen and sending secret signals to the psychic by any one of scores of little-known techniques. **1982** *Jewish Chron.* 9 July 10/3 Their roles—ventriloquist and dummy, reciter and interrupter, smart alec and stooge.

2. A newcomer, a novice (in certain *spec.* contexts: see quots.).

1930 J. LAIT *Big House* i. 6 A first-timer [in prison] is a 'stooge'. **1935** J. HARGAN *Gloss. Prison Lang.* 8 *Stooge*, first offender. **1942** FORBES & ALLEN *Ten Fighter Boys* 55 As the squadron was on readiness most of the day, training was difficult to do, but we did some. However, within a fortnight the squadron moved south to 'K': we stooges were left behind with one pilot to finish off training.

3. A person whose function is merely to carry out another's directions; an unquestioningly loyal or obsequious subordinate, a lackey; a person used as an instrument by someone behind the scenes, a cat's paw. Also *fig.*

1937 H. G. WELLS *Brynhild* vi. 85, I have to.. proclaim you. Be your Aaron. Your John the Baptist. Your—Stooge! **1937** —— *Star Begotten* vii. 128 He assembled by wire and telephone all his most trusted henchmen, tools, stooges, subordinates, intimates. **1944** *Times* 6 Jan. 8/3 'If the Beveridge plan is adopted, does it mean that we shall all become State stooges?'.. 'No... I have been a Civil servant myself, and I rather resent the suggestion that a Civil servant is a stooge.' **1948** *Observer* 7 Mar. 4/2 Communists have no use for democratic Socialists except as stooges, and the end they are working for is not Socialism but the totalitarian police-State. **1951** *Negro Hist. Bull.* (U.S.) Feb. 111/1 Black stooges mouthing the sentiments of the white politicians. **1952** R. A. KNOX *Hidden Stream* xvii. 157 If I see a rather nice picture in a shop and.. buy it, is that because.. I can't resist buying it? But if so, surely my will is not really free: it is just a sort of stooge. **1957** M. SPARK *Comforters* iii. 69 At first I thought she was running a gang, but now, all things considered, I think she may be their stooge. **1960** *Washington Post* 28 Apr. A 22/1 But.. his habit of surrounding himself with stooges and sycophants, inevitably led to the debacle after an egregiously fraudulent election. **1978** *Detroit Free Press* 5 Mar. A 11/1 Joshua Nkomo and Robert Mugabe.. branded the moderate African leaders as 'sworn stooges of Premier (Ian) Smith'.

4. *R.A.F.* In war-time: a flight during which one does not expect to encounter the enemy. Also *attrib.* and in *stooge-around*.

1942 T. RATTIGAN *Flare Path* I. 37 It's a raid, I suppose. *Teddy.* It's not exactly a practice stooge-around. **1945** C. H. WARD-JACKSON *It's a Piece of Cake* 57 *Stooge patrol*, a patrol on which the pilot does not see, or expect to see, the enemy. **1952** M. TRIPP *Faith is Windsock* v. 86 At one stage we saw a Fortress orbiting slowly, presumably on a stooge with a team of W/Ops jamming enemy frequencies.

5. *attrib.* and *Comb.*

1940 *Punch* 1 May 482/3 His Lordship.. was taken on as a stooge fiance in order to camouflage Felicity's unprincipled intentions. **1948** PARTRIDGE *Dict. Forces' Slang* 183 *Stooge pilot*, a pilot employed in flying-training aircraft carrying untrained navigators or gunners. **1957** R. N. CAREW HUNT *Guide to Communist Jargon* xxxiii. 115 The Communists.. introduced one-party government, and the various stooge-parties the existence of which they permitted had no influence in determining policy. **1958** *Observer* 16 Mar. 17/6 The sententious, almost stooge-like, quality associated with the chorus in Greek tragedy.

stooge (stuːdʒ), *v.* [f. the sb.] **1.** *intr.* To act as a stooge (senses 1 and 3) (*for* someone). *slang.*

1939 R. CHANDLER *Big Sleep* xviii. 135 We're glad to stooge for a shamus of his standing. **1955** J. THOMAS *No Banners* xxii. 214 One of the *Milice* degenerates who stooged for the Gestapo. **1973** 'G. BLACK' *Bitter Tea* viii. 122 For a time Jeremy stooged in espionage, but that must have hurt his feet. **1979** *Sci. Amer.* May 22/3 That Strang often stooged for Geller is well established.

2. *slang* (orig. *R.A.F.*). Of an aircraft: to cruise (*about*, *around*, etc.). Hence *gen.*, to drift, wander, move randomly.

1941 *Illustr. London News* 9 Aug. 165/2 (*caption*) We just stooged about watching the bombers drop their loads. **1942** T. RATTIGAN *Flare Path* I. 19 We were stooging along over the Dutch coast. **1942** [see BEAT *v.*¹ 40 i]. **1953** G. HEYER *Detection Unlimited* xiii. 208 Stooging round with me, and thinking how much better you could do the job yourself. **1956** 'J. WYNDHAM' *Seeds of Time* 136 The streets became.. full of crowds stooging around. **1958** M. K. JOSEPH *I'll soldier no More* xiii. 238 Been in 691 Squadron, stooging around the Channel ports all winter. **1973** 'N. GRAHAM' *Murder in Dark Room* xviii. 128, I noticed the Austin in the mirror... That made me think I'd seen another black Austin stooging around fairly recently.

Hence **'stooging** *vbl. sb.*

1944 *Times* 26 Jan. 4/2 Anti-submarine patrols form another vitally important part of the Coastal Air Force's work; it is often dull, monotonous 'stooging', but is also often well rewarded. **1960** D. STOREY *This Sporting Life* I. ii. 62, I don't want the thought of your stooging always lying over me. **1978** J. GARDNER *Dancing Dodo* xviii. 134, I did some stooging—keeping cave, you know.

stook (stʊk), *sb.*¹ Forms: 5–6 **stowk, stouke,** 5–7 **stowke,** 5–6, 8–9 *dial.* **stouk,** 6 **stuk,** 9 *dial.* **stuck,** 6– **stook.** [ME. *stouk*, a. or cogn. w. MLG. *stûke* (WFlem. *stuik*) = HG. dial. *stauche* fem.; formally coincident (though etymological identity is doubtful on account of the difference of meaning) with a widespread Teut. word meaning sleeve: MLG. *stûke*, OHG. *stûhha* (MHG. *stûche*, mod.G. *stauche*), (O)Icel. *stúka* (? from Ger.).

The form *stook* is orig. n. dial.: cf. *hoose* (huːs) = house. It has, however, become current in other dialects, though the regular forms *stowk* and *stuck* are also used.]

1. = SHOCK *sb.*¹ 1.

14.. *Nom.* in Wr.-Wülcker 725/31 *Hec congelima*, a scowk [*read* stowk]. *c* **1460** *Towneley Plays* xxx. 315 His hede is like a stowke hurlyd as hoggys. **1494** in W. Ross *Busby & Neighb.* i. (1883) 22 Ilk person haffand ane pleugh—sall pay ane thraif of aits.. and ilk half-pleugh a stouk. **1530** TINDALE *Exod.* xxii. 6 Yf fyre breake out and catch in the thornes, so that the stoukes of corne.. be consumed therwith. **1586** *Durham Wills* (Surtees) II. 132 Otes, reaped anno 1586, ccxl threves, at v stookes a boll. 28l. 16s. **1620** MARKHAM *Farew. Husb.* xiii. 103 [They] lay them in stoucks of twenty or of foure and twenty sheaues a piece. *c* **1730** RAMSAY *Fable* XIX. 68 They'll start at winlestraes, yet never crook, When Interest bids, to lowp out o'er a stowk. **1785** BURNS *To J. M'Math* i, While at the stook the shearers cow'r To shun the bitter blaudin' show'r. **1812** SIR J. SINCLAIR *Syst. Husb. Scot* I. 333 Carts in this way will easily carry at once from ten to twenty stooks. **1827** HOOD *Ruth* iv, Thus she stood amid the stooks, Praising God with sweetest looks. **1865** W. WHITE *Eastern Eng.* II. 64 The great undulating upland stretches away to the southwards field after field; here waving grain, there rows of 'stooks'. **1894** *Times* 23 July 13/1 The prospect which a fortnight ago seemed certain of seeing wheat in stook by the end of the month is rapidly vanishing. **1898** J. A. GIBBS *Cotswold Village* 36 The vicar's man went into the cornfields and placed a bough in every tenth 'stook'. **1916** *Times* 4 Aug. 3 The cutting of winter oats is now common in the home counties, and the crops are bulking well in stook.

attrib. **1743** R. MAXWELL *Sel. Trans. Soc. Improv. Agric. Scot.* 328 The Lint is tied and set up Stook-ways. **1876** *Whitby Gloss.*, *Stookbands*, twisted straw ropes for sheaf-binding.

¶ **b.** Used for: A pile, mass.

1865 E. BURRITT *Walk to Land's End* 327 No furzy hill in the two counties wearing a stook of rocks on its head for hair-pins, could be better fitted [etc.]. **1892** HENLEY *Song of Sword, Lond. Voluntaries* i. 41 [The trees] stand Beggared and common, plain to all the land For stooks of leaves.

c. *stook of duds*: see quot. 1901.

1831 CARLYLE *Sartor Res.* III. x, In Scotland, again, I find them entitled *Hallanshakers*, or the *Stook-of-Duds* Sect; any individual communicant is named *Stook-of-Duds* (that is, Shock of Rags), in allusion, doubtless, to their professional Costume. **1901** *Eng. Dial. Dict.* s.v. *Stook sb.*¹ 2. *Stook-of-duds*, a person so wrapped up as to suggest a shock of corn.

2. A bundle of straw. *dial.*

1571 in *Reg. Mag. Sig. Scot.* 1576, 709/1, 3 den. for thre stoukis (*sarcinis*) of custome stray. **1876** *Whitby Gloss.* s.v., 'A stook of straw', a bound bundle for thatching with. **1901** JANE BARLOW *Ghost-bereft* 86 The furze 'ill be thick as a stook of good thatch ivery day of the year.

†**3.** A cock (of hay). *Obs. rare.*

1600 SURFLET *Country Farm* IV. vi. 638 You must make it [your hay] into a high cocke with a narrow top..; and although there come no raine, yet it will be good to make these great stoukes [orig. F. *meulons*].

4. *Coal-mining.* [Perh. a different word: cf. STOOP *sb.*¹] **a.** The portion of a pillar of coal left to support the roof.

1826–30 T. WILSON *Pitman's Play* (1843) 59 They jenkin a' the pillars doon, And efter tyek the stooks away. **1840** *Civil Engin. & Arch. Jrnl.* III. 68/2 In the Newcastle pits.. blocks or 'stooks' of considerable strength are suffered to remain, for the purpose of protecting the colliers from the exfoliation of the roof. **1883** GRESLEY *Gloss. Coal-mining* 242 *Stook* [Northumb. & Durham], a pillar of coal about four yards square, being the last portion of a full-sized pillar to be worked away in board and pillar workings. **1891** KIPLING *City Dreadf. Nt.* 82 The chipped-away legs of the pillars [of coal] are called 'stooks'.

b. *stook and coil, stook and feathers*: see quots.

1808 BALD *Gen. View Coal Trade Scot.* 12 (Jam.) The mode then practised in sinking through hard strata, was by a set of tools termed stook and coil, or stook and feathers... Two long slips of iron, named the feathers, were placed down each side of the hole, and betwixt these a long tapering wedge, termed the stook was.. driven down. **1883** GRESLEY *Gloss. Coal-mining* 242 *Stook and feather*, a wedge for breaking down coal, worked by hydraulic power, the pressure being applied at the extreme inner end of the drilled hole. **1886** J. BARROWMAN *Sc. Mining Terms* 64 *Stook and Coil*, or *Stook and Feathers*, a mode of wedging rocks.

†**stook** (stʊk), *sb.*² *Obs. slang.* Also stoock. [Possibly ad. G. *stück* piece.] A pocket-handkerchief. Also *Comb.*, as **stook-buzzer, -hauler**, one who steals pocket-handkerchiefs.

1859 HOTTEN *Dict. Slang* 103 *Stook*, a pocket-handkerchief. *Stook hauler*, or *buzzer*, a thief who takes pocket-handkerchiefs. **1862** H. MAYHEW *London Labour* Extra vol. 25 *Stook-buzzers*, those who steal handkerchiefs. **1889** E. SAMPSON *Tales of Fancy* 18 A dirty face, and a still more dirty 'stook'. **1893** P. H. EMERSON *Signor Lippo* xiv. 48 All I get is my kip and a clean mill tog, a pair of pollies and a stoock.

stook (stʊk), *v.* [f. STOOK *sb.*¹: cf. MLG. *stûken*, WFlem. *stuiken*, G. *stauchen*.] *trans.* To set up (sheaves) in stooks. Also with *up*.

c **1575** SIR J. BALFOUR *Practicks* (1754) 220 The fruitis of the samin benefice beand separate fra the ground, be scheiring, stouking or stakking thairof. **1592** *Sc. Acts Jas. VI* (1814) III. 583/2 Quhen as the cornis ar standand vpon the grounde stoukit. **1611** COTGR., *Endizeler les gerbes*, to stonke [*read* stouke], or shocke vp sheaues of corne; to set, or make them vp in (tenne-sheaued) half-thraues. **1652** LAMONT *Diary* (Maitl. Club) 43 About Dundie in Angus ther was beare stowked. **1765** *Museum Rust.* IV. 457 If the flax be so short and branchy as to appear most valuable for seed, it ought, after pulling, to be stooked. **1794** A. PRINGLE *Agric. Westmorland* 31 Four men may cut, tie, and stook, a customary acre in a day. **1823** A. SMALL *Rom. Antiq. Fife*

135 Corn,..taken out of a place where it has not much air to dry it, and stooked up thick on the ground. **1851** H. STEPHENS *Book of Farm* (ed. 2) II. 336/1 The corn is stooked upon the ridge where it grew. **1887** HALL CAINE *Deemster* viii, They were stooking the barley in the glebe.

b. *absol.*

1641 BEST *Farm. Books* (Surtees) 54 Oftentimes a painfull fellowe will not refuse to stooke after 7 or 8 Sythes, if the binders will but..throwe him in the sheaves. **1799** J. ROBERTSON *Agric. Perth* 159 Seven reapers generally have a man to bind and stook after them. **1868** G. MACDONALD *R. Falconer* I. 262 Lasses to cut, and lasses to gether, and lasses to bin', and lasses to stook.

Hence **stooked** *ppl. a.*, **'stooking** *vbl. sb.*

1575 Stouking [see the vb.]. **1787** BURNS *Answ. Gudwife Wauchope-House* i, Still shearing, and clearing The tither stooked raw. **1844** H. STEPHENS *Bk. Farm* III. 1066 In stooking, bean-sheaves are set up in pairs against one another. **1884** *Pall Mall Gaz.* 21 June 6/1 The cutting, the 'stooking', and the gathering into the stackyard of their corn. **1884** *St. James's Gaz.* 22 Aug. 14/2 Fields of shocked or stooked corn. **1900** CROCKETT *Fitting of Peats* iv. *Love Idylls* (1901) 27 After the manner of stooked sheaves in a harvest-field.

stook, dial. variant of STOUK *sb.* handle.

stookado, rare obs. form of STOCCADO.

stooke, obs. pa. t. and pa. pple. of STICK *v.*

stooker ('stʊkə(r)). [f. STOOK *v.* + -ER[1]] One who arranges sheaves in stooks.

1641 BEST *Farm. Bks.* (Surtees) 54 Wee allowe one stooker usually to 3 binders or 6 Sythes. **1822** J. WILSON *Lights & Shadows Sc. Life* 214, I was a stooker and a bandster on the Corn-rigs. **1904** *Dundee Advertiser* 20 July 5 Where the stookers have been able to keep up, what was..a waving mass of golden grain is now a regular succession of rows of stooks.

stookie ('stukɪ), *Sc.* and *north. dial.* Also **steuke, stoukie.** [dial. var. STUCCO *sb.*] **1.** Plaster of Paris; any plaster-like substance.

1796 *Edin. Mag.* May 385 The carved wood an' polish'd stoukie. **1948** *Proc. Sc. Anthrop. & Folklore Soc.* III. iii. 83 When the doorstep had been washed, the careful housewife could draw designs and patterns with white 'stookie'. **1968** in *Sc. Nat. Dict.* (1974) IX. 60/3 My stooky halfed in two and I had to go back into hospital.

2. A plaster statue, a wax figure or dummy. Also *transf.*, a slow-witted person, a blockhead.

a **1828** T. BEWICK *Howdy & Upgetting* (1850) 13 Dinna sit there leyke steuke, and sit and say nowse. **1895** W. C. FRASER *Whaups of Durley* xv. 219 Jamie sat like a stookey wi' a face as red as a partan's tae. **1903** J. LUMSDEN *Toorle* 193 Because, ye stupid stookie, I step aside for none. **1931** A. J. CRONIN *Hatter's Castle* II. iii. 256 Did ye notice the stookies in the window? **1934** J. BUCHAN *Free Fishers* xix. 314 Give her your arm..and don't stand glowering like a stookie. **1948** *Aberdeen Press & Jrnl.* 27 May 4/1 The civic representatives all standing like 'stookies' as they had not got the words of the Psalm they were singing.

'stookless, *a.* [f. STOOK *sb.*[1] + -LESS.] Without a stook or stooks.

1883 A. WILSON *Nether Lochaber* lviii. 371 The field from head-rig to head-rig is but bare and stookless stubble.

stool (stu:l), *sb.* Forms: 1 stool, 1-2 stól, 3-4 stol, 4 stule, 4-7 stole (also 9 in sense 13), stoole, 5 stoll, 5-6 stolle, 6, 8 stoul, (6 stoule, -lle, stoale, stowle, stoel, *north.* stoile), 6-7 stowell, (stowll), 5- stool; *Sc.* 4-6 stule, 6 stuill, -yll, stwyll, stul(l, stwle, 7 stuile. [Com. Teut.; OE. *stól* masc. = OS. *stôl* (Du. *stoel*), OHG., MHG. *stuol* (mod.G. *stuhl*), ON. *stóll* (Sw., Da. *stol*), Goth. *stōl-s* throne:—OTeut. **stōlo-z*, prob. f. root **stō-*: *sta-* to STAND. Cf. OSl. *stolŭ* throne, seat.]

†**1. a.** Any kind of seat for one person; often, a chair of authority, state, or office; esp. a royal or episcopal throne. (Hence occas. = SEE *sb.*[1] 2 b.) *Obs.*

porphyry stool: cf. *porphyry chair*, PORPHYRY 5 b.

c **897** ÆLFRED *Gregory's Past. C.* lvi. 435 Swa micle swa se bið beforan ðe on ðæm stole [L. *cathedra*] sitt ðæm oðrum ðe ðær ymb stondað. *a* **1000** *Cædmon's Gen.* 260 (Gr.) Wið þone hehstan heofnes wealdend, þe siteð on þam halȝan stole. *a* **1100** *Gerefa* in *Anglia* (1886) IX. 264 Man sceal habban.. sceamelas, stolas, læflas. *c* **1205** LAY. 12657 A þan daȝen at seint Pauwel wes þe ærchebiscop stol [*c* **1275** stolle]. *Ibid.* 24287 þe biscop stole [*c* **1275** stol] wes at sein Aaron. ? *a* **1300** *Shires England* 13 in *O.E. Misc.*, þis bispryche wes hwylen two bispriche, þeo oþer stol wes at remmesbury. *c* **1320** *Seuyn Sag.* 1889 [The barber] set her on a stol,..And gan to smiten hire on the veyn, And sche bledde. **1375** BARBOUR *Bruce* II. 151 The Bruce..raid to Scone, for to be set In kingis stole, and to be king. *c* **1375** *Sc. Leg. Saints* xxxiii. (*George*) 541 On þe morne gert he grathit be a stule in place of Iugment. **1387-8** T. USK *Test. Love* I. v, Suche persons as loven the first sittinges at feestes, the highest stoles in churches and in hal. *a* **1450** *Knt. de la Tour* xxiii. 33 Sethe y am come and must sitte, late me haue sum quyshon or a stole. **1535** COVERDALE *Ps.* xciii. [xciv.] 20 Wilt thou haue eny thinge to do with the stole of wickednesse [1611 Bible, throne of iniquitie; Luther *dem schädlichen Stuhl*]. **1549** ALLEN *Jude's Par. Rev.* iv. 1 Gods stoole or seate in heauen sygnified the euerlastynge state and continuaunce of the power..of god. **1558-9** in J. W. Burgon *Life Gresham* (1839) I. iv. 248 Before the stoole of estate satt an other mayde. **1648** MILTON *Observ. Art. Peace* Wks. 1851 IV. 568 In vain were the Bishops..forbid to sit..in the House, if these men ..be permitted more license on their Presbyterial Stools. **1677** W. HUGHES *Man of Sin* II. xii. 227 How? Bring Paul to the Porph'ry Stool?

fig. phrases. **1565** T. STAPLETON *Fortr. Faith* 27 If Scripture telleth vs it [*i.e.* the church] is at Wittenberg,.. then the Ciuill Lutherans haue the church only: Caluin, Illyricus, Osiander, and all their adherents are put beside the stoole. **1579** W. WILKINSON *Confut. Familye of Loue* B i b, Right discerning..commeth..by them that are set in the right place of iudgement by the Lord himselfe, and not by those that sitt on their owne stoole. **1818** SCOTT *Br. Lamm.* xxviii, He is an old man, and a minister of state... You had more need to think of making up to Miss Lucy Ashton the disgrace..than of interfering with a man too old to fight, and on too high a stool for your hand to reach him.

†**b.** A church pew *Obs.*

1570 *Minute-bk. Archdeaconry of Essex* 5 b (MS.), He refusyth to syt in the stole where the church wardens do place him. **1616** *Min. Archdeaconry of Colchester* fol. 27 (MS.), A couple that came to be married, which, by.. custome, should have sitten in the stoole aforesayd.

†**c.** ? A seat by a grave or tomb. *Obs.*

1463 *Bury Wills* (Camden) 15 No stoon to be steryd of my graue, but a pet to be maad vnder the ground sille ther my lady Schardeloue was wont to sitte, the stoolys removyd, and the body put in. **1526** *Cartular. S. Nicholai Aberd.* (New Spalding Club) I. 155 Our collectour..shall ȝeirlie sett ane honest stuill apoun ye said Jhonis sepultur decorit with bakin and arress as wss is. **1537** *Reg. Aberd.* (Maitl. Club) I. 414 Tway schillingis to þe sacristene for þe settyng of þe stwyll at his graif. **1539** in *Abstr. Protocols Town Clerks Glasgow* (1897) IV. 119 That the said vicar..warne the sacrista minor of revestry to cuyr ane stuyll honestlie and fynd twa wax preckattis byrneand..aboue the lair of Jhonn Painter.

†**d.** A seat for an offender. See CUCKING-STOOL, CUTTY-STOOL, PINING-*stool*, *stool of* REPENTANCE.

c **1308** [see CUCKING-STOOL]. **1562** *Maitland Club Misc.* III. 327 In ye essemble of ye congregacion to syt vpon ye penitent stul tym of ye seruice. **1714** GAY *Sheph. Week* III. 105 Where the high stool On the long plank hangs o'er the muddy pool, That stool, the dread of every scolding quean. **17..** W. FORBES *Dominie Depos'd* I. xxiv, Sae shall they never mount the stool, Whereon the lassies greet an' howl. *Ibid.* II. xxvii, Ye've play'd the fool, Anither now your post maun bruik, An' you the stool.

e. *West Africa.* (See quots.)

1819 BOWDICH *Mission to Ashantee* 231 Saï Tootoo..was presented with the stool, or made king. *Ibid.* 236 This monarch..raised his favourite captains to the vacant stools, uniting three or four in one. *Ibid.*, *footnote*, 'To succeed to the stool,'..is the common expression for succeeding to a property even in private life. The same stool, or seat, descends through many generations. **1909** D. MOORE *We Two in West Africa* 146 On the 'Coast'..the chief of a tribe is said to be on the stool of that tribe... The word stool is nearly always used instead of tribe.

2. a. A wooden seat (for one person) without arms or a back; a piece of furniture consisting in its simplest form of a piece of wood for a seat set upon legs, usually three or four in number, to raise it from the ground.

The OE. instances belong properly to the general sense 1. Often with qualifying word indicating its form or use, as *round, three-legged, camp-, music-stool* and the like.

[*c* **725** *Corpus Gloss.* (Hessels) T 309 *Tripes*, stool. *c* **1000** *Sax. Leechd.* II. 76 ðewyrc þonne stol of þrim treowum ni an ðyrele site on bydene.] **1390** GOWER *Conf.* III. 224 The kinges fol Sat be the fyr upon a stol. *c* **1425** *Cast. Persev.* 2599 in *Macro Plays* 154 Worldis wele is lyke a iij-foted stole, it faylyt a man at hys most nede. **1434-** [see JOINT-STOOL]. *c* **1520** SKELTON *Colin Clout* 30 Let hym go to scole, On a thre foted stole That he may downe syt. **1592** *Arden of Feversham* V. i. 131 Place Mosbie, being a stranger, in a chaire, And let your husband sit vpon a stoole. **1610** HOLLAND *Camden's Brit.* (1637) 441 Young lads..with stooles fastened to their buttockes to milke [ewes]. **1631** GOUGE *God's Arrows* IV. §15 In the garret were set some stooles, and chaires for the better sort. **1709** STEELE *Tatler* No. 80 ¶3 A servant brought a round Stool, on which I sat down. **1784** COWPER *Task* I. 86 Thus first necessity invented stools, Convenience next suggested elbow-chairs. **1886** W. J. TUCKER *E. Europe* 310 The legs and seats of the stools, —for chairs there were none,—were coloured in harmony with the rest.

b. A high seat of this kind for convenience of writing at a high desk; more fully *office stool*. Hence, a situation as clerk in an office.

1836 DICKENS *Let.* ? 27 July (1965) I. 157 If you write me word that you will give him a stool, he shall sit himself upon it forthwith. **1837** [see OFFICE *sb.* 12]. **1842** TENNYSON *Audley Court* 44 Oh! who would cast and balance at a desk, Perch'd like a crow upon a three-legg'd stool? **1852** DICKENS *Bleak Ho.* xx, Mr. Guppy suspects everybody who enters on the occupation of a stool in Kenge and Carboy's office, of entertaining..sinister designs upon him.

c. A low short bench or form upon which to rest the foot, to step or kneel. Chiefly = FOOTSTOOL. Sometimes used as a child's seat.

a **1225** *Ancr. R.* 166 Vor þi alle þe halewen makeden of al þe world ase ane stol [*v.rr.* scheomel, schamel] to hore uet, uorto arechen þe heouene. **1377** LANGL. *P. Pl.* B. v. 394, I may nouȝte stonde ne stoupe ne with-oute a stole knele. **1382** WYCLIF *Matt.* xxii. 44 Til that I put thin enmyes a stole of thi feet. **1398** TREVISA *Barth. De. P.R.* XIV. ii. (1495) 465 The erthe is callyd the stole of goddys owne fete. **1468** in *Archæologia* X. 197 Item, payd Will. Pylche for makyng of the stole to the funte and keverynge of the same, xx d. *c* **1440** *Promp. Parv.* 476/2 Stool, *scabellum*. **1567** *Gude & Godlie Ball.* 50 And war the warld ten tymes sa wyde,..Unworthie it war, ȝit to the, Under thy feit ane stule to be. **1827** LYTTON *Pelham* xii, You must not lounge on your chair—nor put your feet upon a stool. **1858** —— *What will He do* I. vi, Sophy left her seat, and placed herself on a stool at her grandfather's knee.

†**d.** *stool and ball*, the implements used in the game of STOOL-BALL. *Obs.*

1619 *Pasquil's Palm* (1877) 152 When country wenches play with stool & ball.

3. *fig.* **a.** Proverb, *to fall, come to the ground, sit between two stools*: to incur failure through vacillation between two different courses of action.

1390 GOWER *Conf.* I. 15 Bot it is seid..Betwen tuo Stoles lyth the fal, Whan that men wenen best to sitte. *Ibid.* II. 22 O fol of alle foles, Thou farst as he betwen tuo stoles That wolde sitte and goth to grounde. *a* **1536** *Prov.* in *Songs, Carols* etc. (E.E.T.S.) 129 Betwen two stolis, the ars goth to grwnd. **1613** PURCHAS *Pilgrimage* (1614) 610 Guageda betwixt two stooles had vnquiet sitting, paying tribute both to the Kings of Telensin, and the Arabians. **1717** PRIOR *Alma* I. 231 Poor Alma sits between two stools. **1765** LD. HOLLAND in Jesse *Selwyn & Contemp.* (1843) I. 380, I only hope Sir Charles Bunbury has not lost his Paris place, and dropped, as I fear he has, between two stools. **1857** TROLLOPE *Barchester T.* xx, Truly he had fallen between two stools. **1867** —— *Chron. Barset* xxxv, She was like to fall to the ground between two stools,—having two lovers, neither of whom could serve her turn.

b. Phrases.

1605 SHAKS. *Macb.* III. iv. 82 But now they rise againe With twenty mortall murthers on their crownes, And push vs from our stooles. **1730** T. BOSTON *Mem.* x. (1899) 276 The work was begun on Thursday with a sermon on Amos vi. 1, which I believe drew the stool from under most of us. **1749** FIELDING *Tom Jones* I. xiii, One of the Maxims..is, when once you are got up, to kick the Stool from under you. In plain English, when you have made your Fortune by the good Offices of a Friend, you are advised to discard him as soon as you can.

†**4.** The lair of a hare; = FORM *sb.* 21, SEAT *sb.* 10.

1607 TOPSELL *Four-f. Beasts* 271 In such places doth the Hare seek her lodging... Then let him [the hunter] draw his nets round about them..and then raise her from her stoole.

5. a. A seat enclosing a chamber utensil; a commode; more explicitly *stool of ease*. Also, a privy.

For *groom of the stool* (*stole*), see STOLE *sb.*[2]

1410-1869 [see CLOSE-STOOL]. **1501** *Acc. Ld. High Treas. Scot.* II. 25 Item,..giffin for ane stule of es bocht to the King viij d. **1516-17** *Rec. St. Mary at Hill* (1905) 292 Paid for makyng clene of the Rectors stolys ij d. **1528** A prevey stole [see PRIVY *a.* 8 c]. **1561** *Invent. R. Wardr.* (1815) 139 Item ane stuill of ease coverit with crammosie broun velvot. **1573** L. LLOID *Pilgr. Princes* (1586) 145 The Emperour Heliogabalus was killed vpon his stole at his easement. **1645** MILTON *Colast.* 13, I send them by his advice to sit upon the stool and strain. **1768-74** TUCKER *Lt. Nat.* (1834) II. 147 If Alexander and Cæsar could never be easy off the stool, I would not deny them that needful utensil.

b. In phrases originally meaning 'the place of evacuation', now (without *the*) the action of evacuating the bowels.

1542 BOORDE *Dyetary* viii. (1870) 248 Than go to your stole to make your egestyon. **1558** WARDE tr. *Alexis' Secr.* 32 b, The sayde pylles..prouoke not to the stoole. **1602** *2nd Pt. Return fr. Parnass.* I. ii, They..write as men go to stoole, for needes. **1676** MARVELL *Mr. Smirke* 33 Though they be, reading Papers of State, or at the Stool more seasonably [he] obtrudes his Pamphlet. **1705** *Phil. Trans.* XXV. 2110 He did not go to Stole for a fortnight or three weeks together. *Ibid.* 2111 When he dy'd it was nine weeks after he had any Stole. **1726** SWIFT *Gulliver* III. vi, Men are never so serious, thoughtful, and intent, as when they are at stool. **1871** NAPHEYS *Prev. & Cure of Dis.* III. ix. 980 To go to stool twice a day. **1899** *Allbutt's Syst. Med.* VII. 263 When the veins are congested by straining at stool.

c. The action of evacuating the bowels; an act of discharging fæces. *by stool*: by fæcal as distinguished from other means of evacuation.

1533 ELYOT *Cast Helthe* (1541) 38 b, By experience and diligent serch by their stoole, their nourices shal perceyve what digesteth wel. **1596** HARINGTON *Metam. Ajax* C 5, Hee heard him say, hee thanked God, hee had had a good stoole. **1623** HART *Arraignm. Urines* i. 2 Having his vacuations by stoole as orderly as other healthfull men. *a* **1625** FLETCHER *Noble Gent.* v. i, I fear this loss of honor will give him some few stools. **1663** PEPYS *Diary* 24 May, Having taken one of Mr. Holliard's pills last night it brought a stool or two this morning. **1682** *Digby's Chym. Secrets* II. 228 A second Dose ..will work either by Stool or Vomit, or Sweat. **1783** WESLEY *Jrnl.* 16 Mar., It gave me four or five and twenty stools, and a moderate vomit. **1843** R. J. GRAVES *Syst. Clin. Med.* X. 110, I do not feel the least anxiety if the patient remains without having a stool for two or three days. **1875** H. C. WOOD *Therap.* (1879) 106 The stools are at times normal in character and frequency.

fig. **1592** NASHE *Four Lett. Confut.* 11 A Letter whereof his inuention had a hard stoole, and yet it was for his ease.

d. A discharge of fæcal matter of a specified colour, consistency, etc.; the matter discharged (chiefly *pl.*).

1597 A. M. tr. *Guillemeau's Fr. Chirurg.* 3 b/2 The patient can nether retayne his vrine, *Sperma*, or Stole. *Ibid.* 4/1 His vrine bloodye; his stoels like matter. **1607** TOPSELL *Four-f. Beasts* 104 Her nature is to hide her own dung..the little Mouse being able by that stoole, to smell the presence of her mortall foe. **1698** SLOANE in *Phil. Trans.* XX. 69 Stools resembling the Dregs of Wine. **1789** W. BUCHAN *Dom. Med.* (1790) 497 He must..drink freely of water-gruel to prevent bloody stools. **1845-6** G. E. DAY *Simon's Anim. Chem.* II. 386 Calomel is frequently given..: its administration is succeeded by numerous, very green, bilious stools. **1871** GARROD *Mat. Med.* (ed. 3) 97 It often produces in children the so-named calomel stools, or green-coloured fæces.

†**6.** A frame upon which to work embroidery or tapestry. *Obs.*

c **1385** CHAUCER *L.G.W.* 2352 So that she werkyn & enbroude couthe And weuyn in hire stol the radyuore. ?*c* **1475** *Promp. Parv.* 305/2 (Camb. MS.) Lyncet, a werkynge stole, *liniarium*. **1502** *Privy Purse Exp. Eliz. of York* (1830) 7 Item..for the stuff and making of iiij working stoles for the Quene..vs. iiij d. **1513** *Papers 5 Hen. VIII* No. 4101 (P.R.O.), A frontlett for an aulter wrought in the stole. **1523** SKELTON *Garl. Laurel* 790 To weue in the stoule sume were full preste, With slaiis, with tauellis, with hedellis well drest. **1538** ELYOT *Dict., Licia*, be thredes, whiche sylke women do weaue in lyncelles or stooles. *a* **1548** HALL *Chron., Hen. VIII*, 7 On their heades bonets of Damaske, syluer flatte wouen in the stole.

7. *Naut.* **a.** (See quot. 1867. Cf. CHANNEL *sb.*[2]) **b.** (See quot. *c* 1850.) **c.** (See quot. 1846.)

a. 1711 W. SUTHERLAND *Shipbuild. Assist.* 37 Backstays or Topmast Shrouds are to be fasten'd down to the Channels, or Stools fixed for that purpose. **1867** SMYTH *Sailor's Word-bk., Stool*, a minor channel abaft the main channels, for the dead-eyes of the backstays.

b. 1750 BLANCKLEY *Nav. Expositor. c* **1850** *Rudim. Navig.* (Weale) 153 *Stools*,..ornamental blocks for the poop lanterns to stand on abaft.

c. 1797 *Encycl. Brit.* (ed. 3) XVII. 395/2 This line will represent the lower edge of the rail that comes to the middle stool. **1830** HEDDERWICK *Mar. Archit.* 120 *Stools*, pieces of plank which are bolted edgeways to the quarters of small vessels, to form the mock quarter-galleries. **1846** A. YOUNG *Naut. Dict.* 323 *Stool*, the lowest transom of a vessel's stern-frame; or, more correctly, a chock introduced beneath the lowest transom: to it the lower ends of the fashion-pieces are secured.

8. *Brickmaking.* A brick-moulder's shed or workshop; also, the gang of workmen employed in one shed; also, a moulder's bench.

1693 J. HOUGHTON *Collect. Improv. Husb.* No. 70 ¶1 There are usually employed about a Stooles Work four Men, and two Boyes: The first, an Earth-maker that prepares the Earth. The second a Carter..to bring the Earth to the Stool. *Ibid.* ¶3 A Stool does ordinarily make.. eight Thousand in a Day. **1850** E. DOBSON *Bricks & Tiles* I. 34 In slop moulding, the mould is simply laid on the moulding stool. *Ibid.* 37 The area occupied by each stool is greater than in making slop-moulded bricks. **1886** *Standard* 10 May 8/5 To be let, a brickfield with four stools. **1891** *Ibid.* 24 Jan. 2/8 To distribute the funds to the different fields according to the number of stools or moulders' sheds worked.

9. *Arch.* The sill of a window. *Obs.* exc. *U.S.*

1663 GERBIER *Counsel* 88 For the Capitol, to the stooles of those windowes. **1682** SIR C. WREN in W. H. St. John Hope *Windsor Castle* (1913) II. 387 By cleansinge from moss & weeds all the coapings of the Buttresses,..the stooles of the Windowes,..[etc.]. **1891** *Century Dict.* s.v., *Stool of a window*, or *window-stool*, in arch., the flat piece on which the sash shuts down, corresponding to the sill of a door. **1911** WEBSTER s.v. [adds] In the United States, the narrow shelf fitted on the inside against the actual sill.

10. a. A base or stand upon which a thing is set to raise it above the ground or general surface.

1481-3 in W. H. St. John Hope *Windsor Castle* (1913) II. 404 Cxx et xxxviij pedibus Chaptrelles et Braces. xvij Stolys. xlii. Botraces. cix panelles. **1535** COVERDALE *2 Chron.* iv. 14 He made the stoles also and ye kettels vpon the stoles [Luther *Gestühle*]. **1554-5** *Extracts Burgh Rec. Edin.* (1871) II. 309 For twa greit bakis to be stullis to the malt myln [etc.]. **1566** *Reg. Mag. Sig. Scot.* 763/2 Dicti commendatarius [etc.] sustentarent dimidietatem scabelli lie mylne stuill. **1641** *Invent. Goods C'tess Arundel* in *Burlington Mag.* (1911) Nov. 98/1 In the Seller..is noething, but two stowelles to sett beare on & two Shelues. **1683** MOXON *Mech. Exerc., Printing* xv. ¶2 So much of this Bottom-Plate..is called the Stool,..because on it the lower end of the Matrice rests. **1827** FARADAY *Chem. Manip.* iv. (1842) 97 This furnace..being raised upon a stool so as to bring the aperture of the air-chamber to a level with the nozzle of the bellows. **1888** JACOBI *Printers' Vocab.* 133 *Stool*, a platform or stage on which paper or printed work is stacked.

b. The stand of a beehive. ? *Obs.*

1523-34 FITZHERB. *Husb.* §122 Set a stole or a forme nyghe vnto the swarme,..shake the bees in-to the hyue, and shortely sette it vppon the stole. **1609** C. BUTLER *Fem. Mon.* (1634) 14 As many as fall beside the stool, when it waxeth dark, ten to one they lie abroad all night. **1774** *Phil. Trans.* LXV. 274 We have seen fleas..swarming at the mouths of these holes like bees on the stools of their hives.

11. A bench, counter, table, trestle. *Sc.* and *north.*

1519 *Reg. Aberd.* (Maitl. Club) II. 177 The baikhouss witht..ij bakin stulis. **1559** *Richmond Wills* (Surtees) 135 The mylke house..a fleke, a stole. **1559** *Peebles Burgh Rec.* (1872) 257 The inqueist findis Thomas Dikesone in the wrang for..castin of his [John Edmond's] flesche stule in the gutter. **1870** J. K. HUNTER *Life Studies of Char.* xlvi. 282 There was nae word o' John comin' wi' the spokes and stools [trestle for a coffin].

12. *Mining.* (See quot. 1851.)

1653 MANLOVE *Lead-mines* 62 Then must the Miners chase the stole to th' stake; From meer to meer. **1670** PETTUS *Fodinæ Reg.* 86 And the Miners shall work their Meers duly, and shall chuse their Stool on that one part there as he may find Mine between two Walls. **1747** HOOSON *Miner's Dict.* N iv b, When the old-man is cleared out from a Shaft-foot, Forfield, Stool, or Stope, we say we have bared it. **1778** W. PRYCE *Min. Cornub.* 63 The end or stool of the vein will run of itself, like sand. **1851** TAPPING *Gloss. to Manlove, Stool*, is where the miners leave digging deeper and work in the ends forward; the end before you is called the stool... The term stool has also another signification, which is so far as the miner cuts before him, which is about two yards high.

13. [Cf. Du. *stoel* in similar uses. (In technical language sometimes spelt *stole.*)] **a.** The stump of a tree which has been felled; also the head of the stump, from which new shoots are produced.

1577-87 HOLINSHED *Chron.* I. 195/2 When a grene tree is cut in sunder in the middle, and the part cut off is caried three acres bredth from the stocke, and returning againe to the stoale, shall ioine therewith. **1686** PLOT *Staffordsh.* 209 The stooles or stumps of many trees. **1769** D. BARRINGTON *Indig. Trees* in *Phil. Trans.* LIX. 33 No pine or fir ever shoots from the stool. **1842** LOUDON *Suburban Hort.* 286 If a graft is inserted either in the collar or stool, or in the amputated head, it will give an immediate direction to the sap. **1844** H. STEPHENS *Bk. Farm* I. 116 The stools of hard-wood trees,..set on end.., form a very durable flooring. **1874** LYELL *Elem. Geol.* xxiv. 421 All the stools of the fossil trees dug out by us divided into four parts. **1886** *Cheshire Gloss.* s.v. *Stoo*, Clap yon owd stoo a' top o' th' foire. **1899** R. MUNRO *Prehist. Scotland* ii. 29 As evidence..we can still point to the stools of huge trees, at the bottom of extensive tracts of moorland peat.

b. *Forestry.* A stock or stump of a tree felled or headed for the production of coppice-wood, underwood, saplings, or young timber. Also a set or group of stumps.

a **1722** LISLE *Husb.* (1757) 365, I proposed to cut coppice-wood for the fire: my woodward said, it would not hurt the stools to cut it so late, but it would never..burn well. **1827** STEUART *Planter's G.* (1828) 298 The making up into one set or stool separate plants of the same species. **1832** *Planting* 41 in *Libr. Usef. Knowl., Husb.* III, The parent wood of coppice stools is most frequently suffered to rise too high from the roots. **1880** JEFFERIES *Gt. Estate* (1881) 82 Between the stoles [of the copse]..the ground was quite covered in spring with dark-green vegetation. **1894** *Jrnl. R. Agric. Soc.* June 243 The [willow] rods being cut off close to the stools.

c. *Forestry* and *Horticulture.* The base of a plant cut down to produce shoots or branches for layering. Also, a plant laid down for layering (*rare*).

1789 *Trans. Soc. Arts* VII. 126, I have likewise procured several small stools of the black mulberry [for propagating]. **1813** C. MARSHALL *Gardening* xix. (ed. 5) 317 In order to obtain suckers and shoots for layers [of elm], stools are to be formed, by cutting down some young trees, almost close to the ground. **1825** *Greenhouse Comp.* I. 221 Where entire plants are layed down to produce layers, they are called stools; and the main root remains there as a stool for several years. **1842** LOUDON *Suburban Hort.* 711 Having been much troubled with caterpillars on our gooseberry stools in the nursery. **1880** C. R. MARKHAM *Peruv. Bark* 223 He afterwards went round to all the old stools and put in as many layers from them as possible.

d. *Horticulture.* The base containing the latent buds in plants which annually throw up new stems or foliage to replace the old.

1790 *Phil. Trans.* LXXX. 350 Stool of [sugar] canes (which is the assemblage of its numerous roots where the stems begin to shoot out) is almost impenetrable to rain. **1824** LOUDON *Encycl. Garden.* §3339 Stools [of the strawberry] of two years standing, which have borne one crop, may be put into pots in August. **1839** URE *Dict. Arts* 1194 Rattoons (a word corrupted from *rejettons*) are the sprouts or suckers that spring from the roots or stoles of the canes that have been previously cut for sugar. **1842** *Florist's Jrnl.* (1846) III. 95 Chrysanthemums may be struck and the old stools turned out. **1846** *J. Baxter's Libr. Pract. Agric.* (ed. 4) II. 231 As the finest..of these fruits [raspberries] are ..the produce of strong and well-ripened canes, it becomes necessary that the stools should have every advantage afforded them. **1877** S. HIBBERD *Amateur's Kitchen Gard.* 158 Manure should be spread around the stool to insure some benefit to the roots of the [rhubarb] plant. **1882** *Garden* 14 Jan. 17/3 Each stool consisting of about eight canes.

e. A cluster of stems or foliage springing from a stool or from the same root; the complement of stalks produced by one grain of corn.

1712 J. MORTON *Nat. Hist. Northamptonsh.* 154 They much resembled the Bottom of a Cluster, or Stool, as it is here called, of large Rushes. **1807** *Prize Ess. & Trans. Highl. Soc.* III. 476 A single stole of corn growing in a dung hill, has plenty of air, light, and heat. **1880** F. W. BURBIDGE *Gardens of Sun* v. 94 Each tuft or stool [of rice] being about eight inches from its neighbours. **1882** *Contemp. Rev.* Aug. 233 From one wheat grain there were eighty-five stalks to the stool. **1887** BLACKMORE *Springhaven* III. vii, His shelter was a stool of hazel, thrown up to repair the loss of stem. **1894** —— *Perlycross* vii, A great stool of fern.

f. *a fine, good stool* (of clover, of timber): clover or timber well stooled (see STOOL *v.* 3).

1801 *Farmer's Mag.* Nov. 461 This year, the field was in barley, and yielded seven bolls per acre, leaving as fine a stool of young clover and rye-grass as ever I saw. **1814** *4th Rep. Comm. Irish Bogs* II. 188 The country possesses a good stool of timber.

transf. **1831** J. WILSON *Noct. Ambr.* Wks. 1856 III. 327 Hecate a beauty! I aye thocht she had been a furious fricht —black-a-viced, pockey-ort, wi' a great stool o' a beard.

g. A shoot or layer from the stump or base of a plant. [Confused with L. *stolo*: see STOLE *sb.*[3], STOLON.]

1818 TODD, *Stool*, 4. [*stolo* Latin], a shoot from the trunk of a tree. **1821** S. F. GRAY *Brit. Plants* I. 52 Stool, *Stolo.* A branch from the head of the root, bending down, taking root, and emitting leaves. **1824** MACTAGGART *Gallovid. Encycl.*, *Stowl* or *Stole*, a scion from a root.

†**14. a.** The scar left by a wound, a cicatrix. *Obs. rare*$^{-1}$. (Cf. STADDLE *sb.* 6.)

1601 HOLLAND *Pliny* xx. i. II. 36 The root [of wild cucumber]..reduceth the stooles or skars left after any sore ..to their fresh and native colour againe.

†**b.** The 'eye' of an apple, pear or quince.

1671 GREW *Anat. Plants* I. vi. §2 Most of them [i.e. the branches of the endocarp of an apple] enarching themselves towards the Cork or Stool of the Flower. *Ibid.* II. §9 [of a pear]. *Ibid.* §10 [of a quince].

†**15.** The head or top of a mushroom. (Cf. *stool* in TOADSTOOL *sb.*) *Obs. rare*$^{-1}$.

1743 PICKERING *Seeds of Mushrooms* in *Phil. Trans.* XLII. 595, I began with one of the Gills carefully separated from the Head, or Stool, without bruising.

16. *U.S.* (See quot.)

1881 INGERSOLL *Oyster-Industr.* (Hist. Fish. Industr. U.S.) 249 *Stools.*—Material spread on the bottom for oyster spawn to cling to.

17. †**a.** ? Some part of a plough. *Obs. rare*$^{-1}$. (Possibly an error.) **b.** The shank of a rake or hay-fork (*Northumbld. Gloss.* 1893-4).

1523-34 FITZHERB. *Husb.* §5 It is necessarye for hym to lerne to make his yokes, oxe-bowes, stooles, and all maner of plough-geare.

18. *U.S.* **a.** A decoy-bird (perh. short for *stool-pigeon*), esp. one used in shooting wildfowl; also a perch upon which a decoy-bird is set. (Cf. STALE *sb.*[3], STALL *sb.*[2]) Also *transf.*, a person employed as a decoy by criminals.

1825 *Huntington* (N.Y.) *Town Rec.* (1889) III. 322 No person [shall] be permitted to gun with macheanes or stools in sd. Town. **1847** J. ROACH *Let.* 20 May in T. Coleman *Passage to America* (1972) xi. 183 There is three hundred emigrants in the Rochester tonight... The head man is a 'Stool'—make him jump. **1859** BARTLETT *Dict. Amer.* (ed. 2) 452 *Stool*, an artificial duck or other water-fowl used as a decoy. **1872** SCHELE DE VERE *Americanisms* 211 Stool-Pigeon... In the former [literal signification] it means the pigeon, with its eyes stitched up, fastened on a stool, which can be moved up and down by the hidden fowler. **1874** J. W. LONG *Amer. Wildfowl* xvii. 205 Wood-ducks..are not easily decoyed, either by stools or calls. **1895** G. J. MANSON *Sporting Dict., Stool*, a decoy for snipe, plover, and peach-birds. **1902** GREENOUGH & KITTREDGE *Words* 363 A stool pigeon..is a 'decoy pigeon', so called from its being tied to a stool.

b. A police informer. Cf. *stool-pigeon*, sense 19 b.

1906 G. E. STEVENS *Wicked City* 233 Under others were inscribed: 'He is a "stool".'.. 'He was croaked by the cops.' **1915** J. LONDON *Jacket* ii. 10 They laughed at him and turned him away..for the stool that he was. **1932** E. WALLACE *When Gangs came to London* xv. 129 I'm not so sure that I want to tell you anything—I never was a stool. **1939** J. STEINBECK *Grapes of Wrath* xx. 338 I'll come for ya tonight. Maybe I'm wrong. There's stools aroun' all a time. **1962** B. COBB *Murder: Men Only* i. 12 He said he wasn't a stool, he wasn't giving anybody away.

19. a. *attrib.* and *Comb.*, (sense 2) as *stool cover*; (sense 5), as †*stool door*, †*house*, †*pan*; (sense 13), as *stool-growth*, *shoot*; (sense 7 c), as *stool rail*; appositive (sense 1), as *stool stone*; objective, as *stool-bearer*, *-bearing*, *-casting*; similative, as *stool-like* adj.

1518 *Perth Hammermen Bk.* (1889) 2 The *stule berer. **1821** S. F. GRAY *Brit. Plants* I. 42 *Stool-bearing. *Stoloniferæ.* Throwing out stools, *stolones*, which take root. **1637** LD. WARISTON *Diary* 23 July (S.H.S.) 265 Thair rayse ..sik ane outcrying quhat be the people's murmuring, mourning, rayling, *stoolcasting, as the lyk was never seien. **1837** A. HAYWARD *Lett.* (1886) I. 60, I am quite charmed with the *stool-cover. **1564** in *Archæol. Cant.* (1874) IX. 234 Itm payd..for makyng and setting on of ij payer of Charnayles [hinges] uppon a *stoole doore, vjd. **1909** *Nation* 1 May 156/2 We push through the rods of the *stool-growth with difficulty. **1541-2** *MS. Rawl. D.* 781 lf. 160 Item in y^e *Stolle howse ij quarelles mendyd—jd. **16..** in *Archæologia* LXIV. 390 The Stowll hous. **1868** *Rep. U.S. Commissioner Agric.* (1869) 251 A hedge becomes thin at the base..the sap ascending and forming a spreading, *stool-like form of growth. **1620** in *Unton Inventories* (1841) 26, xj *stoole panns. **1688** HOLME *Armoury* III. xiv. (Roxb.) 9/2 He beareth Gules, a stoole pan, or close stoole pan, Argent. **1797** *Encycl. Brit.* (ed. 3) XVII. 395/2 Set off the depth of the middle *stool rail above the line already drawn. **1907** *Blackw. Mag.* Apr. 488/2 Self-sown seedlings and *stool-shoots being then left to come up naturally. **1664** J. WEBB *Stone-Heng* (1725) 198 One only simple Circle of about twelve Slabbs of Stone, with a *Stool-stone for the King.

b. Special comb.: **stool-bed** (see quot. 1879); **stool-bent** (see quot. 1789); **stool-crab** (see quot.); **stool land** *West Africa* (see quot., cf. 1 e); **stool-mail** *Sc.*, a fine imposed upon a person condemned to the stool of repentance; **stool-pigeon**, (*a*) *U.S.*, a pigeon fastened to a stool as a decoy; chiefly *fig.* of a person employed, especially by gamblers, as a decoy; (*b*) a police informer; **stool-pipe** (see quot.); †**stool table**, ? a table on trestles; †**stool-wagon** [G. *stuhlwagen*], a German chaise.

For *stool-chamber*, *-room*, see STOLE *sb.*[2]

1859 F. A. GRIFFITHS *Artil. Man.* (1862) 126 Place *stool-bed and quoin. **1879** *Cassell's Techn. Educ.* II. 391/2 A third point of support..for the gun..is supplied..by a 'quoin'.. placed immediately under the breech, and resting on a block called a 'stool-bed'. **1789** J. LIGHTFOOT *Flora Scot.* 1131 *Juncus squarrosus.* *Stool-Bent. *Scotis australibus.* **1835** S. OLIVER [W. A. Chatto] *Rambles Northumbld.* 165 Spreats and stool-bent, which, in moist places, always indicate the spot where the pedestrian may be sure of firm footing. **1880** *E. Cornw. Gloss.*, *Stool-crab, the male of the edible crab, *Platycarcinus pagurus.* **1909** D. MOORE *We Two in West Africa* 146, I..mean the lands belonging to the tribe governed by the chief in question. On the 'Coast' these are called *stool lands. **1837** *Voluntary Ch. Mag.* Nov. 493 It was poinded by the session because its owner would not pay the *stool-mail for having had a bastard child. **1830** *Workingman's Gaz.* (Woodstock, Vermont) 1 Dec. 79/2 A wag who keeps an oyster cellar in Newark advertises, among other things, 'wildbirds domesticated and *stool pigeons trained to catch voters for the next Presidency—warranted to suit either party.' **1836** W. IRVING *Astoria* I. 137 One man ..was used like a 'stool pigeon', to decoy the others. **1844** [see ROPER 5]. **1845** *Yankee* (Boston) 9 Aug. 2/6 If this business is so profitable to thieves, how much do those [*sc.* police officers] make out of it who encourage the stool pigeon business? **1849** *Bankers' Mag.* Aug. 89 The senior high constable of Philadelphia..recollected that Harry White.. who he had been lately using as a 'stool pigeon', or secret informer, had informed him..that 'a big thing' was coming off shortly. **1850** *Congress. Globe* 18 July 1403/1 Sheltering this aggression, on the part of the United States, behind 'poor New Mexico', who is only a stool-pigeon. **1859**

Bartlett *Dict. Amer.* (ed. 2) 452 *Stool-pigeon*, a decoy robber, in the pay of the police, who brings his associates into a trap laid for them. **1865** *Pall Mall Gaz.* 13 Nov. 2 The harrowing narrative of 'Antilles' may be after all only an ingenious 'stool-pigeon,' concocted for the purpose of terrifying the Republican party. **1906** L. H. Vincent *Amer. Literary Masters* 46, I am not going to be made a stool-pigeon to attract birds of passage that may be flying about. **1910** E. A. Walcott *Open Door* 134 Rafferty..assured the chief that he would pass word to certain stool-pigeons to keep their eyes and ears open for trace of the missing canvas. **1930** *Times Lit. Suppl.* 4 Dec. 1047/3 Occasionally a masterful rogue arose who shot a few people as 'stool-pigeons', even though they had never imparted any information to the police. **1974** J. Thomson *Long Revenge* ii. 23 A stool pigeon planted in a local Gestapo prison to eavesdrop on the detainees. **1886** J. Barrowman *Sc. Mining Terms* 64 *_Stool-pipe, Stool-piece_, the pipe on which a column of pipes rests. **1630** *Maldon* (Essex) *Documents* Bundle 217 No. 22 In the hall..1 *stoole table. **1829** *Sporting Mag.* XXIV. 201 Four horses were next put to the *stool-wagon, and we drove to Faulenrost.

stool (stu:l), *v.* Also 6, 9 **stole**. [f. stool *sb.*]

1. *trans.* To put or set (a person) on a stool.

a. To condemn (a person) to the stool (of repentance). *nonce-use.* In quot. *absol.*

1682 Hickeringill *Hist. Whiggism* ii. 38 Horning, Cursing, Damning, Imprisoning, Stooling or Fooling upon the Stool of Repentance.

b. *West Africa.* (Cf. stool *sb.* 1 e.)

1898 R. A. Freeman *Trav. Ashanti* i. 3 Until the king [of Ashanti] had been enthroned on the gold stool his title was not officially recognised... But the ceremony of 'stooling' a new king was one that involved considerable expense.

2. *intr.* To evacuate the bowels; also *trans.*, to evacuate as excrement.

1545 Raynalde *Byrth Mankynde* Pj, The greate labour and payne the whiche the partie hath in..enforsynge her selfe other to stole or to make water. **1843** R. J. Graves *Syst. Clin. Med.* v. 57 They are..almost constantly confined to bed except when rising to stool.

3. Of a plant: To throw up young shoots or stems; of corn, grass, herbage, to throw out lateral shoots producing a thick head of stems or foliage. Also with *out, forth.*

1789 *Trans. Soc. Arts* I. 260 Some sorts of Cotton did not rattoon or stool so well as others. **1790** W. H. Marshall *Midl.* II. 443 To *Stool*; to ramify as corn. **1795** Vancouver *Agric. Essex* 152 Strong and luxuriant shoots stool forth. **1830** M. T. Sadler *Law Popul.* I. 93 Wheat is one of those plants which, according to the phraseology of agriculturists, stools; that is, throws out lateral roots capable of producing separate stems. **1844** H. Stephens *Bk. Farm* III. 857 New grass, if moderately eaten down in spring, stools out, and affords a thicker cutting at hay time. **1853** G. Johnston *Nat. Hist. E. Bord.* I. 121 The herbage..does not spread nor stool upon the ground. **1869** Blackmore *Lorna Doone* xxxviii, I worked very hard in the copse of young ash,.. cutting out the saplings where they stooled too close together.

fig. **1835** *Tait's Mag.* II. 491 From the original hardy stem of the Surrey yeomen, this vigorous branch 'stooled out', and put forth arms.

4. a. *trans.* To entice (wild-fowl) by means of a decoy-bird; also *intr.* (of a bird) to come (well) to a decoy. *U.S.*

1842 W. P. Hawes *Sporting Scenes* i. 55 I'll tell you all about that..the next time we're stooling snipe together. **1859** Bartlett *Dict. Amer.* (ed. 2) 452 *Stooling*, decoying ducks or other fowls by the means of 'stools'. **1874** J. W. Long *Amer. Wild-fowl* xviii. 209 Widgeon..stool well to almost any decoys.

b. *intr.* To act as a stool or stool-pigeon; to inform *on* (someone). Chiefly *U.S. slang.*

1911 [see boob *sb.* 1]. **1938** *Amer. Speech* XIII. 191/2 *To stool*, to act as a stool-pigeon. **1950** Patterson & Conrad *Scottsboro Boy* iii. v. 224 There were little mice in Kilby. They ran in the cells. They weren't the trouble that the big rats were, though, them that stooled on you. **1960** 'E. McBain' *See them Die* v. 48 You'd stool on Pepe for that rotten cop?.. A stoolie is a stoolie. **1973** 'B. Mather' *Snowline* xi. 133 'I stand in a sort of special relationship with these bums. If they thought I was stooling on them—well, you see what I mean?' 'No,..I don't see that putting me in touch..could possibly be construed as stooling. I'm not a policeman.'

5. *Mining.* To work (a vein). Cf. stool *sb.* 12.

1824 Mander *Derbysh. Miner's Gloss.* 69 Then it is common to say, the vein is Stoled, or Stooled, ten or twelve fathoms.

stool, obs. form of stole *sb.*[1] and *sb.*[2]

'stool-ball. [f. stool *sb.* + ball *sb.*

The 'stool' was the wicket (see stool *sb.* 2 d); perh. it was originally an ordinary stool.]

1. An old country game somewhat resembling cricket, played chiefly by young women or, as an Easter game, between young men and women for a 'tansy' (tansy 3) as the stake. Still played (in modified forms) by women and children in some districts, esp. in Sussex. (Quite distinct from stow-ball.)

a **1475** *Myrc's Par. Pr.* 11 *note*, Hand ball, fott ball, stoil ball & all manner other games out cherchyard. **1564** in *Shirburn Ball.* (1907) 48 [At Midsummer sessions at Maldon, 1564, complaint was made against the constables that they had suffered] stole-ball [to be played on Sundays]. **1567** Drant *Horace's A.P.* Biiij, The stoole ball, top, or camping ball if suche one should assaye As hath no mannour skill therin,..Theye all would..laughe at hym aloude. *a* **1586** Sidney *Arcadia, Sonn.* (1622) 493 A time there is for all, my mother often sayes, When she with skirts tuckt very hie, with gyrles at stoolball playes. **1612** *Two Noble K.* v. ii. 101 *Wooer.* What shall we doe there, wench? *Daugh.* Why, play at stoole ball. **1615** Chapman *Odyss.* vi. 139 Till which time (hauing din'd) Nausicae With other virgins, did at stool-ball play. **1648** Herrick *Hesper.*, *Stool-ball* (1915) 238 At Stool-ball, Lucia, let us play, For Sugar-cakes and Wine; Or for a Tansie let us pay, The loss or thine, or mine. **1677** *Poor Robin's Almanack* 19 Apr., Observ., Young men and maids Now very brisk, At Barley-break and Stool ball frisk. **1711** Steele *Spect.* No 71 ¶2 Betty [was] a publick Dancer at May-poles, a Romp at Stool-Ball. **1715** N. Blundell *Diary* (1895) 134 The Young Weomen treated ye Men with a Tandsey as they had lost to them at a Game at Stoole Balle. **1801** Strutt *Sports & Past.* ii. iii. §11. 76, I have been informed, that a pastime called stool-ball, is practised to this day in the northern parts of England. **1898** *Encycl. Sport* II. 412 Stool-ball... The game..has of late years changed considerably... Thus, while formerly the hand was used to strike the ball, a bat is now used... The stools have been superseded by 'targets', which are round boards..fastened to posts.

attrib. **1614** Breton *I would & I would not* lxxix, Paryaway, And for a Tanzey, goe to Stoole-Ball-play. **1615** Chapman *Odyss.* vi. 165 Her meane was this (though thought a stool-ball chance).

2. A ball used in the game described above.

1690 *Pagan Prince* xiv. 42 And when they see a Cannon Bullet coming toward ye..[they] will catch it like a Stool Ball, and throw it to the Devil. **1819** Scott *Ivanhoe* xxvi, Kind service cannot be chucked from hand to hand like a shuttlecock or stool-ball.

stoole, obs. form of stole *sb.*[1] and *sb.*[2]

stoole(n, obs. pa. pple. of steal *v.*

stoolie ('stu:lɪ). *U.S. slang.* [f. stool *sb.* 18 b or *stool(-pigeon)* (s.v. stool *sb.* 19 b) + -ie.] A police informer, a stool-pigeon.

1924 G. C. Henderson *Keys to Crookdom* 419 *Stool pigeon*, a spy, stoolie, squealer. One who betrays his fellow crooks. **1930** 'E. Queen' *French Powder Mystery* p. xiv, Without the stool-pigeon a huge percentage of felonies would remain unsolved... Our problem is to find a 'stoolie' who will part with the tip. **1947** *Sun* (Baltimore) 13 Sept. 8/1 Victor Mature..succeeds in winning sympathy for Nick against odds, overcoming even the stigma which attaches to the stoolie. **1958** 'E. McBain' *Killer's Payoff* (1960) viii. 79 The policeman trusted the stoolie's information... The stoolie trusted the policeman... Cops were averse to working with pigeons they did not know and trust. **1960** [see stool *v.* 4 b]. **1974** T. P. Whitney tr. *Solzhenitsyn's Gulag Archipelago* i. iii. 128 'There is no way out! You have to confess to everything!' whisper the stoolies who have been planted in the cell. **1978** LaRosa & Tanenbaum *Random Factor* (1979) 60 When Parker put the pressure on, some stoolie somewhere would turn the man he was looking for.

stooling ('stu:lɪŋ), *vbl. sb.* [f. stool *v.* and *sb.* + -ing[1].]

1. The action or process of evacuating the bowels; also, *concr.* the matter evacuated.

1599 Minsheu *Span. Gram.* 81 *Rézias camaras.* Strong stoolings. *a* **1610** Healey *Epictetus* (1636) 82 To bee alway conversant in corporall matters:..in much eating, drinking, stooling. **1695** *New Light Chirurg. put out* 38 The Stooling of bloody Excrement. **1895** Elworthy *Evil Eye* 74 'Tis a very bad thing to throw a child's stooling in the fire.

2. The action of throwing up young shoots or stems; of corn, etc., the forming of a thick head from lateral shoots.

1854 Miss Baker *Northampt. Gloss.*, *Stooling*, the second germination of corn. **1868** *Rep. U.S. Commissioner Agric.* (1869) 254 Trimming does thicken the surface of the hedge by causing a stubbed, stooling form of growth. **1901** *Dundee Advertiser* 15 Jan. 4 The 'stooling' or tillering habits of these varieties [of oat] being weak.

3. *concr.* The framework supporting a mill (cf. stool *sb.* 10).

1558 in *Reg. Mag. Sig. Scot.* 1565, 411/1 Sustentarent dicta molendina in omnibus necessariis, nisi tantum in *ly stuling* quod [etc.]. **1606** *Ibid.* 616/1 *Lie stuilling* cum *mylnedame* et *mylneleid* sustentando.

stoolle, obs. form of stole *sb.*[2]

†'stool-work. *Obs.* [? f. stool *sb.* 6 + work *sb.*] Embroidery or tapestry work of the kind made on a 'stool'.

1526 in Gutch *Collect. Cur.* (1781) II. 315 Item deliverid oone corse of Stole Wurke for the same Buckill and Pendent, xiij s. iiij d. *c* **1534** in J. Lewis *Life Bp. Fisher* (1855) II. 297 A vestment..wyth a crose of golde of stole warke wroght wyth daysys. **1547** in Feuillerat *Revels Edw. VI* (1914) 14, viij partlettes of Blewe Sarcenet with colers of golde stoleworke. **1547** *Inv. of Guarderobes, etc.* (Harl. MS. 1419) 408 b, A Horne of Brasse garnisshed with nedle worke with a Bawdricke of Stole worke. *a* **1548** Hall *Chron., Hen. VIII*, 83 Bonnettes of stoole worke of golde of damaske. *c* **1555** in Feuillerat *Revels Q. Mary* (1914) 192, iiijor Quoyffes sylver & gylte stoleworke.

stooly ('stu:lɪ), *a.* [f. stool *sb.* + -y.] Of the nature of a stool (see stool *sb.* 13).

1868 *Rep. U.S. Commissioner Agric.* (1869) 258 There will be layers enough when the hedge is again laid to admit of these stakes being cut out if they become stooly where previously cut off.

stoom, stoomp: see stum, stump.

stoon(e, obs. forms of stone.

stoop (stu:p), *sb.*[1] Now only *dial.* Forms: α. 5 **stolpe**, 5–9 **stulp(e**, 6 **stoulpe**. β. 5–7 **stowpe**, 6 **stuipe, stouppe, stowppe**, 6–8 **stoope**, 6–9 **stoup(e**, 7–9 **stope, stowp**, (7 **stoppe**), 7– **stoop**. [Late ME. *stulpe, stolpe*, a. ON. *stolpe* (Icel. *stólpi*, Sw., Da. *stolpe*); prob. cogn. w. Russian *stolb* post, pillar.

It is doubtful whether the word has any connexion with MLG. and early mod.Du. *stolpe, stulpe* lid (according to Kilian also beam, rafter), mod.Du. *stolp, stulp*, mod.G. *stulpe* (from LG.).

The β forms may possibly partly represent a distinct but synonymous word, a. or cogn. w. OFris. *stûpa*, MLG., MDu. *stûpe* whipping-post, stake, punishment of flogging, MHG. *stûpe* (from MLG.; mod.G. *staupe*) flogging.]

1. A post, pillar.

α. **1439** *Rec. Carpenters' Co.* (1914) II. 4 Paide for ij Stulpes and ye settinge up. *c* **1440** *Promp. Parv.* 481/1 Stulpe, or stake, *paxillus*. *c* **1450** *Brut* 462 Whan the Kyng had riden thurgh Suthwerk, and come to the stulpes without London Brigge. **1490–1** *Rec. St. Mary at Hill* (1905) 167 Item, to Byrd, carpenter, for stolpes & Reylles, viij s. iij d. *Ibid.* 168 Paide to paris ffor settyng of stulpis and ledgis & nayllis..v d. **1494** in *Househ. Ord.* (1790) 127 The cradle to have five stolpes, three at the head, and twoe at the feet, and the King's armes on the middle stolpe. **1530** Palsgr. 277/1 Stoulpe before a doore, *souche*. **1555** Phaer *Æneid* ii. (1558) Ej b, The walles with skalyng ladders layde, & stulps of scaffolds hie, And vp by stayres thei clyme. **1579** *Abstr. Dewsbury Court Roll* in *Yorks. Archæol. Jrnl.* XXI. 410 Roger Hirste shall make a newe gate and new stulpes. **1736** Ainsworth *Lat.-Eng. Dict.* Art. T, Save that the transverse plank lay not quite on the top of the erect stulp, but across it a little lower.

β. **1463** in *Fabric Rolls York Minster* (Surtees) 134 For a newe stowpe to ye grate yates, 10 d. **1552** *Acc. Ld. High Treas. Scot.* X. 112 Item, to ane turnour turnand stoupis of beddis and charis in the said castell..iij li. iiij s. **1600** in Hore *Hist. Newmarket* (1885) I. 95 Whereas Hugh Wyrrall, gentleman, had caused a stoope to be sett on Doncaster More at the west end of the horse race. **1682** W. Blundell *Cavalier's Notebk* (1880) 267 The stoop, commonly called the chair, where the horse course on Crosby Marsh doth usually begin and end. **1685** Cotton tr. *Montaigne* (1711) I. xxxviii. 335 Stoops dive deeper and deeper into the earth by being moved up and down. **1709** in *Slingsby's Diary* (1836) 193 Upon her Lady-ships promise that the said Gate, & Stoups, & all things belonging to it should be hung. **1756** Mrs. Calderwood in *Coltness Collect.* (Maitl. Club) 226 A chair, with one carved bar close to the bottom behind, eight other turned bars, the stoops and four cross bars in the back, a rush bottom. **1770** *E. Heslerton Inclos. Act* 6 Guarded with substantial stoops and rails. **1823** Willson *Gloss. Gothic Archit.* (ed. 2) 21 *Stoup*, a post. A pedestal, or small pillar, for a statue to stand upon. **1829** Glover *Hist. Derby* I. 190 Substantial stone stoops or posts for gates are in general use.

in fig. context. **1637** Rutherford *Lett.* (1664) 254 Our Salvation is fastened with God's own hand and with Christ's own strength to the strong stoup of God's unchangeable nature. Mal. 3. 6.

2. *fig.* A person or thing that supports or sustains; a 'prop', 'pillar'. *Sc.*

a **1572** Knox *Hist. Ref.* iv. Wks. 1848 II. 411 Ledingtoune and the Maister of Maxwell were that nycht the two stoupeis of his chair. **1640** R. Baillie *Lett. & Jrnls.* (Bannatyne Club) I. 282 Since he heard of Ratcliffe prisoned, and Wentford's death, his two stoups, his heart is a little fallen. **1721** Ramsay *To Earl Dalhousie* 2 Dalhousie of an auld descent, My chief, my stoup, and ornament. **1821** Galt *Ann. Parish* xxvi. (1895) 167 All [invited] in addition to our old stoops from the neighbouring parishes. **1863** R. Paul in B. Bell *Mem.* (1872) 266 He..is..a great stoop to the Free Church. **1896** Barrie *Marg. Ogilvy* ii, He was a great 'stoup' of the Auld Licht kirk.

†3. *Cant.* The pillory. *Obs.*

1795 Potter *Dict. Cant* (ed. 2). **1812** J. H. Vaux *Flash Dict.*

4. *Mining.* (See quot. 1881.) **stoop-and-room** = *pillar-and-stall*: see pillar *sb.* 7.

1881 J. Sands *Sk. Tranent* 30 'Stoops', or massive pillars of coal, were left to support the roof. **1881** Raymond *Mining Gloss.*, Stoop-and-Rooms. **1888** B. H. Brough *Mine-Surv.* 7 The 'post and stall' system,..known..in Scotland as 'stoup and room', and the 'long-wall' system. **1890** Wallace *Alston Moor* 141 (E.D.D.) From these levels short cross-cuts were made..into the vein, and its contents mined by stoups. **1899** *N.B. Daily Mail* 21 June 5 The adjoining 'stoop' was finished last Wednesday. That was about half a mile from the pit bottom.

5. *attrib.* as †**stoop bedstead**; (sense 4) **stoop-road, -side**; **stoop-net**, a fishing-net supported on a pole.

1593 *Wills & Inv. N.C.* (Surtees 1860) 228 In the south turrett. One *stoupe bedstead, teaster, valens and curtaines. **1806** Morison *Decis.* XXXIII. 14271 The *stoop-net is quite a different kind of net from the pock-net, being a much larger net, with the mouth of it fastened to three pieces of wood, fixed in the form of a triangle. To this triangle is fixed a large pole, by which a person in a boat holds it while he is fishing. **1883** Gresley *Gloss. Coal-mining* 243 *_Stoop roads_, roads driven in the solid or whole coal on the stoop and room system. **1887** P. McNeill *Blawearie* 33 Hanging his lighted lamp on the *stoopside.

stoop (stu:p), *sb.*[2] Also 6–7 **stoupe, stoope**, 7 (? *erron.*) **stop(pe**. [f. stoop *v.*[1]]

1. An act of stooping; a bending of the body forwards; a bow.

1571 Campion *Hist. Irel.* (1633) 69 The Generall also himselfe, digging with a pykeaxe, a desperate villaine.. watched his stoope, and clove his head with an axe. **1603** B. Jonson *Sejanus* i. (1605) B 3, *Cor.* Here comes Seianus. *Sil.* Now obserue the stoupes, The bendings, and the falls. *Arr.* Most creeping base! **1668** Dryden *Even. Love* Epil. 14 Up starts a Mounsieur, new come o'er, and warm In the French stoop, and the pull-back o' th' Arm. **1760** C. Johnston *Chrysal* (1822) I. 263 Some unlucky stoop burst the string that tied his breeches. **1833** Chalmers in Hanna *Mem.* (1851) III. 370 A passage often narrow and requiring a very low stoop. **1885** *Spectator* 25 July 977/2 His trick was done by a peculiar method of stooping, and of concealing the stoop behind a skirt.

transf. **1684** R. Waller *Nat. Exper.* 130 The Amber being hung at liberty by a thread in the Air,..when it was rubb'd and heated, made a stoop to those little Bodies, which likewise proportionally presented themselves thereto, and readily obey'd its call.

b. *fig.* A condescension, a voluntary descent from superiority or dignity.

1636 SHIRLEY *Duke's Mistr.* III. i. (1638) E 2 b, Have you obteyn'd so much As one stoope to your wanton avarice, One bend to please your inflam'd appetite? **1681** DRYDEN *Span. Friar* IV. ii, Can I, can any Loyal Subject see With Patience, such a Stoop from Sovereignty? **1842** J. SHERMAN in Allon *Mem.* (1863) 294 To give us a claim to all His perfections..is such a stoop of the Divine Majesty as exceeds the utmost stretch of human imagination. **1856** SPURGEON *Serm. N. Park St. Pulpit* 720 It would have been a stoop more immense than if a seraph should have changed himself into an emmet. **1890** *Spectator* 22 Nov., She certainly 'stoops to deceit' often enough for the stoop to leave a very vivid impression on the reader's mind.

†**c.** *to give the stoop*: to bow; *fig.* to yield, give way. *Obs.*

1623 B. JONSON *Time Vind.* (1640) 94 T' have giv'n the stoop, and to salute the skirts Of her, to whom all Ladies else are flirts! *a* **1670** HACKET *Abp. Williams* II. (1693) 186 O that a King should give the stoop to such as these?

2. A stooping attitude; a temporary or permanent bent position of the back or shoulders.

1716 LADY M. W. MONTAGU *Let. to Lady Rich* 20 Sept., I can assure you that..a small stoop in the shoulders, nay, even gray hairs, are no objection. **1825** *Lond. Med. & Phys. Jrnl.* LIV. 210 On the Means generally used with the intention of curing a Stoop. **1862** MISS BRADDON *Lady Audley* x, The lazy horses..dropping their heads with a weary stoop under the afternoon sunshine. **1863** GEO. ELIOT *Romola* v, His tall spare frame had the student's stoop of the shoulders. **1899** *Allbutt's Syst. Med.* VIII. 77 Associated with the forward stoop is a tendency to take quick steps. **1904** A. C. BENSON *House of Quiet* xix. (1907) 115 He was a tall thin man, with a slight stoop.

†**3.** Descent, declivity (of a mountain); a downward slope or incline. *Obs.*

1611 SPEED *Hist. Gt. Brit.* IX. x. §7 As he was entring into Savoy, at the stoope, or descent of the Alpes, very many of the..Peeres of England met him. **1711** *Milit. & Sea Dict.* (ed. 4) s.v. *Chemise*, When the Soil was sandy and loose; and therefore could not support it self, without allowing it too great a *Talus*, or Stoop.

b. *dial.* (See quot.)

1854 MISS BAKER *Northampt. Gloss.*, *Stoop*, a fall of water in a river.

4. The action of descending from a height; *spec.* the swoop of a bird of prey on its quarry, or the descent of a falcon to the lure. Also *fig.*

c **1586** C'TESS PEMBROKE *Ps.* CXIX. Q. i, Lett not these that soare to high By my low stoope, yet higher fly. *a* **1586** SIDNEY *Arcadia* III. (1598) 261 (Amphialus' Dream 56) More swift then falcons stoope to feeding Falconers call. *c* **1611** CHAPMAN *Iliad* XXIII. 91 Like matter vaporous The spirit vanisht vnder earth, and murmur'd in his stoope. *a* **1616** BEAUM. & FL. *Wit without M.* IV. i. (1639) G 4 How daintily she [the lady] flies upon the lure, and cunningly she makes her stoopes. **1645** WALLER *To Mutable Fair* 16 Poems 120 Now will I wander through the ayre, Mount, make a stoope at every Fayre. **1774** GOLDSM. *Nat. Hist.* VI. 48 Some water-fowls subsist by making sudden stoops from above, to seize whatever fish come near the surface. **1823** BYRON *Age of Bronze* vii, Vulture-plumed guerrillas, on the stoop For their incessant prey. **1845** DARWIN *Voy. Nat.* iii. (1879) 54 Its stoop..is very inferior in force and rapidity to that of a hawk. **1885–94** BRIDGES *Eros & Psyche* Nov. 12 As an eagle..checks his headlong stoop With wide-flung wing. **1891** HARTING *Bibl. Accipitr.* 230 *Stoop*, the swift descent of a falcon on the quarry from a height.

5. Comb.: **stoop-necked** *a.*, having the neck bent downwards; **stoop-shouldered** *a.*, having a stoop in the shoulders.

1773 *Pennsylv. Gaz.* 7 July 3/3 Run away from the subscriber, an English servant girl,..about 20 years of age, a little stoop shouldered. **1887** C. G. D. ROBERTS *Poems* (1903) 56 Black on the ridge, against that lovely flush, A cart, and stoop-necked oxen. **1899** *Royal Mag.* Feb. 384/1 An old woman of seventy, thin, stoop-shouldered—from long years of bending over her cobbler's bench.

stoop (stuːp), *sb.*³ *U.S.* and *Canada.* Also 9 stoop. [a. Du. *stoep*: see STOEP.] **a.** 'An uncovered platform before the entrance of a house, raised, and approached by means of steps. Sometimes incorrectly used for *porch* or *veranda.*' (*Cent. Dict.*)

1789 *Massachusetts Spy* 20 Aug. 3/2 Several persons were in a stoop and at windows within fifteen or twenty feet from the tree. **1833** [MRS. TRAILL] *Backwoods of Canada* ix. (1836) 142 The Canadians call these verandahs 'stoups'. **1837** HAWTHORNE *Amer. Note-bks.* 13 July (1883) 58 Councillors seated about, sitting on benches near the bar, or on the stoop along the front of the house. **1856** MISS WARNER *Hills Shatemuc* ii, He was cleaning the harness of the wagon, and he took it out into the broad stoop outside of the kitchen door. **1883** STEVENSON *Across the Plains* (1896) 16 The clear, bright, gardened townships spoke of country fare and pleasant summer evenings on the stoop.

b. stoop ball *N. Amer.*, a ball game resembling baseball, but in which the ball is thrown against a stoop or building rather than to a batter.

1941 B. SCHULBERG *What makes Sammy Run?* ix. 166 Kids yelling at each other in a stoop-ball game. **1947** *Commentary* May 463/2 As one of a large family of games such as stoopball..it demands an ability to maneuver freely. **1959** J. D. SALINGER in *New Yorker* 6 June 102/2 Stoopball, for the information of rural readers, is a ball game played with the support of a flight of brownstone steps or the front of a apartment building. **1978** G. A. SHEEHAN *Running & Being* vii. 90 We knew our block... Knew which steps to get pointers in stoop ball.

stoop (stuːp), *v.*¹ Pa. t. and pa. pple. **stooped** (stuːpt). Forms: 1 stúpian, 2–4 stupen, 4–7 stoupe (4 stope), 5 stowpe, 7 stoup, 6 stoope, 6– stoop. [OE. *stúpian* wk. vb. corresp. to MDu. *stûpen* (WFlem. *stuipen*, now conjugated strong), ON. *stúpa* (once, in inf.; MSw., Sw. *stupa* wk. vb., Norw. *stupa* str. vb.); related by ablaut to OTeut. *staup- STEEP *adj.* For the phonology of the mod.Eng. form cf. *coop*, *droop*, where ME. *ū* before *p* has similarly remained unchanged instead of becoming (aʊ).]

I. To bow down, to descend.

1. a. *intr.* Of a person: To lower the body by inclining the trunk or the head and shoulders forward, sometimes bending the knee at the same time. Often with *down.*

c **893** ÆLFRED *Oros.* VI. xxiii, þæt he swa oft sceolde stupian swa he to his horse wolde, & he þonne se cyning hæfde his hrycg him to hliepan. *a* **1225** *Juliana* 72 As ha schulde stupen ant strecchen forð þe swire [*sc.* to be beheaded]. *c* **1275** *Passion our Lord* 559 in *O.E. Misc.*, He adun stupede and lokede myd eye. *a* **1300** *Cursor M.* 13728 He stuped dun, and wit his hand He wrat a quil in to þe sand. **1303** R. BRUNNE *Handl. Synne* 5613 He stouped down to seke a stone. **13..** *K. Alis.* 1103 Alisaundre anvied was; Over the table he gon stoupe, And smot Lifias with the coupe. **1377** LANGL. *P. Pl.* B. v. 394, I moste sitte..I may nouȝte stonde ne stoupe ne with-oute a stole knele. *c* **1380** *Sir Ferumb.* 4065 As lef me were her stope adoun, & lete gurd of myn heued. **1388** WYCLIF *John* xx. 5 And whanne he stoupide, he sai the schetis liynge, netheles he entride not. *a* **1400** *Octouian* 1141 In haste the geaunt stupte adoun, With the left hond to take vp the fachoun. *c* **1400** *Rom. Rose* 2662 Than shalt thou stoupe, and lay to ere, If they within a-slepe be. *c* **1450** *Merlin* vii. 119 He..smote the kynge loth vpon the helme that he made hym stoupe on the arson of his sadell. **1470–85** MALORY *Arthur* IX. xxxiii. 391 Thenne sir Tristram was ware of hym & there he stouped a syde. *a* **1500** *Abraham* 378 in *Brome Bk.* 66 But, fader, wyll I stowppe downe lowe, ȝe wyll not kyll me with ȝowre sword, I trowe? **1530** PALSGR. 737/2, I stowpe downe to take upe a thyng, *je me penche.* **1553** EDEN *Treat. New Ind.* (Arb.) 25 All suche as wayte on hym, stoup downe & make lowe curtesie. **1565** COOPER *Thesaurus* s.v. *Pronus*, Thou stoupest downe & drinkest water. **1584** COGAN *Haven Health* i. (1612) 3 Stouping and rising oftentimes,..these doe excercise the backe and loines. **1590** SPENSER *F.Q.* I. v. 12 He..with so exceeding furie at him strake, That forced him to stoupe upon his knee. **1603** G. OWEN *Pembrokeshire* (1891) 253 A man on horsbacke, may well ride vnder it, without stowpinge. **1603** B. JONSON *Panegyre K. Jas.* 23 Beside her stoup't on either hand, a maid. **1649** E. REYNOLDS *Hosea* vii. 124 Angels..stoope down with their faces towards the mercy Seat. **1697** DRYDEN *Virg. Georg.* III. 169 The Youthful Charioteers with heaving Heart..Stoop to the Reins, and lash with all their Force. **1794** MRS. RADCLIFFE *Myst. Udolpho* xxxviii, Dorothée, now stooping to pick up something that had dropped from among the papers, suddenly exclaimed [etc.]. **1847** C. BRONTË *Jane Eyre* xxxiv, He raised his head suddenly from the desk over which he was stooping. **1863** GEO. ELIOT *Romola* xii, He had just stooped to reach his manuscript, which had rolled down. **1900** L. HUXLEY *Life Prof. Huxley* II. vi. 65 To stoop over the microscope was a physical discomfort.

¶**b.** In ME. poetry occas. used for: To fall headlong. *Obs.*

13.. *Sir Beues* 3817 Taile ouer top he made him stoupe. *c* **1400** *Destr. Troy* 7256 He hit on his helme with a heuy sword, þat greuit hym full gretly, gert hym to stoupe. *c* **1430** *Syr Gener.* (Roxb.) 3821 With his launce grete and square To Sir Abel grymlie he bare That he made him low stoupe Bakward ouer his hors croupe.

c. Said of the head or shoulders.

1375 BARBOUR *Bruce* VIII. 297 With hedis stowpand and speris straucht Richt to the kyng thar vay thai raucht. **1576** GASCOIGNE *Grief of Joye* II. li, Owre showlders stowpe, wᶜʰ erst stood bolt upright. *a* **1616** ? BEAUM. & FL. *Faithful Friends* I. i. MS. Dyce Collect. No. 10. 4 The Sabines are in Armes, whose Stuborn neckes These many yeares stoopt to the yoake of Roome. **1663** BUTLER *Hud.* I. i. 286 His Back, or rather Burthen show'd As if it stoop'd with its own load.

†**d.** Of a quadruped: To crouch. *Obs.*

1590 SPENSER *F.Q.* I. vi. 25 He would learne The Lyon stoup to him in lowly wise. *a* **1625** FLETCHER *Nice Valour* IV. i, This fellow..Stoops like a Cammell, that Heroick beast, At a great load of Nutmegs.

e. Of a dog: To put its nose to the ground to find a scent.

1523–34 FITZHERB. *Husb.* §41 It is harde to make an olde dogge to stoupe. **1781** P. BECKFORD *Th. Hunting* (1802) 91 When your young hounds stoop to a scent,..you may then begin to put them into the pack. **1897** [see STOOPING *vbl. sb.*].

2. *fig.* **a.** To 'bow' to superior power or authority; to humble oneself, yield obedience. Const. *to*, *under.* Now somewhat *rare.*

1530 PALSGR. 737/2 Thought you be never so prowde a varlet, I wyll make you stowpe or you go. **1535** COVERDALE *Job* ix. 13 He is God..the proudest of all must stoope vnder him [Luther: *unter ihn müssen sich beugen*]. **1555** EDEN *Decades* (Arb.) 52 Stoope Englande stoope, and learne to knowe thy lorde and master. **1570** LEVINS *Manip.* 221/30 To stoupe, *humiliare se.* **1610** HOLLAND *Camden's Brit.* (1637) 118 By the Scots that infested them out of Ireland, they were made to stoop. *c* **1640** SHIRLEY *Cont. Ajax & Ulysses* (1659) 128 Early or late, They stoop to fate, And must give up their murmuring breath, When they pale Captives creep to death. **1642** FULLER *Holy St.* II. xxi. 134 Here Drake received a dangerous wound, though he valiantly conceal'd it for a long time, knowing if his heart stooped, his mens would fall. **1646** H. P. *Medit. Seige* 98 He hath..made his desires stoope unto his reason. **1666** DK. NEWCASTLE in *11th Rep. Hist. MSS. Comm.* App. v. 14 His..victory over his enemies, which will make all his neyghbor kinges stoope to him. **1710** O. SANSOM *Acc. Life* 43 Because I would not stoop under them,..to promise to go to no more Meetings..they Fined me Five Pounds. *a* **1715** BURNET *Own Time* III. (1724) I. 523 The Duke now seemed to triumph in Scotland. All stooped to him. **1752** YOUNG *Brothers* IV. i, Tho' Thrace by conquest stoops to Macedon, I know my rank. **1837** THIRLWALL *Greece* xxix. IV. 104 A Spartan generally found it the hardest of all things to stoop.

†**b.** To submit *to* something burdensome. *Obs.*

1611 B. JONSON *Catiline* IV. i, Good and great men: that know how To stoupe to wants, and meete necessities. **1621** T. WILLIAMSON tr. *Goulart's Wise Vieillard* 105 Why should hee which knowes, and takes himselfe to be a man,..refuse to put vnder his shoulder and stoope to those ieopardies, burthens, and crosses. **1621** in Foster *Eng. Factories Ind.* (1906) 265 More losse then wee have reason to stoope unto. **1647** N. BACON *Disc. Govt. Eng.* I. iv. 13 It had been better for them to have stooped to hard conditions with the Picts.

c. To condescend *to* one's inferiors or *to* some position or action below one's rightful dignity.

1579 W. WILKINSON *Confut. Fam. Love* 18 God.. stoupeth and lispeth with us that we may understand him. **1661** BOYLE *Style Script.* (1675) 241 The Divine inspirer of the Scripture, ev'n when his style seems most to stoop to our capacities, doth yet retain a prerogative above meerly humane writings. *a* **1669** STILLINGFL. *Six Serm.* v. 195 Is Religion a beggarly and contemptible thing, that it doth not become the greatness of your mindes to stoop to take any notice of it? **1671** TRENCHFIELD *Cap Gray Hairs* (1688) 4 And tho some Fathers..have undertook to give advice unto their Sons;..yet there's not any (that I know of) hath stoopt so low, to give advice to an Apprentice. **1687** T. BROWN *Saints in Uproar* Wks. 1730 I. 78, I can hardly believe that such nice, well-bred ladies, as those are, would stoop to so vile a drudgery. **1703** DE FOE in *15th Rep. Hist. MSS. Comm.* App. IV. 61 Nor is there anything so mean (which I can honestly stoop to do) that I would not submit to, to obtain her Majesty's favour. **1766** GOLDSM. *Vicar* xxx, If you can stoop to an alliance with a family so poor as mine, take her. **1773** —— (*title*) She stoops to conquer. **1820** W. IRVING *Sketch Bk.* I. 195 Stooping from his high estate to sow the sweet flowers of poetry and song. **1868** BROWNING *Ring & Bk.* I. 139 A Latin cramp enough..But interfilleted with Italian streaks When testimony stooped to mother-tongue. **1867** FREEMAN *Norm. Conq.* (1876) I. iv. 193 The Aquitanian princes now and then stooped to pay a nominal homage.

d. To lower or degrade oneself morally; to descend *to* something unworthy.

1743 BULKELEY & CUMMINS *Voy. S. Seas* Ded. p. iv, A British Seaman hath a Spirit too brave to stoop to so degenerate a Practice. **1751** JOHNSON *Rambler* No. 96 ¶5 Many whom their conscience can scarcely charge with stooping to a lie, have [etc.]. **1855** MACAULAY *Hist. Eng.* xxi. IV. 555 He..was incapable of stooping to an act of baseness. **1891** FARRAR *Darkn. & Dawn* xxxiv, Her son stooped to the most ignoble methods for rendering her life miserable.

3. a. Of a thing: To incline from the perpendicular; to bend down; to slope; to hang over.

c **1000** *Sax. Leechd.* III. 266 Ȝyf seo sunne hine [the new moon] onælð ufan þonne stupað he [*i.e.* has the concave side inclined downward]. **1340** *Ayenb.* 151 U or he nimþ hede þet his tour ne hongi ne stoupi. *c* **1374** CHAUCER *Troylus* II. 968 As flouris, thurgh cold of nyghte Yclosid, stoupyn in her stalkys lowe. **1422** YONGE tr. *Secreta Secret.* 233 He that hath a longe noose and Sum-whate stowpynge and strachynge toward the mouthe, he is worthy and hardy. *Ibid.* 234 Who-so hath a leiand Plate noose amyd, stoupynge to-warde the butte, he is a iogoloure. **1592** SHAKS. *Ven. & Ad.* 1028 The grasse stoops not, she treads on it so light. **1615** J. TAYLOR (Water P.) *Fair & Foul Weather* B 1 b, With a troope Of full mouth'd windes, that made great oakes to stoope. **1702** *Milit. Dict.* s.v. *Bomb*, Rowling down Bombs upon them along a Plank set stooping towards their Works. **1683** TEMPLE *Mem.* Wks. 1731 I. 419 Nimeguen is seated upon the Side of a Hill, which..stoops upon the River Waal. **1827** SCOTT *Highl. Widow* i, The rocks and precipices which stooped down perpendicularly on our path. **1829** —— *Anne of G.* ii, He felt the huge cliff on which he stood, tremble, stoop slowly forward, and gradually sink from its position. **1885** *Athenæum* 23 May 669/1 The crests of the rushes..are not stirred sufficiently to make them stoop.

†**b.** Of a heavenly body: To bend its course downward; to begin to descend. *Obs.*

1615 CHAPMAN *Odyss.* XII. 444 In Nights third part; when stars began to stoope; The Cloud-assembler, put a Tempst vp. **1631** KNEVET *Rhodon & Iris* IV. iii. G 2 b, I saw the blazing meteor stoupe, And bend his course toward the humble Center.

†**c.** *Naut.* To heel over. *Obs.*

1663 SIR W. PETTY in Rigaud *Corr. Sci. Men* (1841) I. 103 Our vessel..hath sailed by and large, to the admiration of some hundred seamen..for..keeping a wind,..not stooping, staying and steering. **1691** T. H[ALE] *Acc. New Invent.* 121 The line unto which she stoops upon a Wind of either side. *Ibid.* 124 The Ship upon a Wind, is to stoop upon a certain Angle.

4. To stand or walk with the shoulders bent or the upper part of the body inclined forwards; esp. to have habitually or permanently this kind of attitude.

1340 HAMPOLE *Pr. Consc.* 777 His sight wax dym..His bak waxes croked, stoupand he gas. **1387** TREVISA *Higden* (Rolls) II. 185 In his elde þe stature boweþ and crokeþ and stoupeþ adoun. **1474** CAXTON *Chesse* II. ii. (1883) 29 So olde that he stowped & quaqued for age. **1530** PALSGR. 737/2 Sche is but a yong wenche and yet sche stowpyth and sche were an owlde woman. **1605** *Proclam. Search T. Percy* 5 Nov., He stoupeth somewhat in the shoulders. **1611** BIBLE *2 Chron.* xxxvi. 17 The king of the Caldees..had no compassion vpon..olde man, or him that stouped for age. **1776** *Pennsylv. Even. Post* 30 Apr. 220/1 Two..servant women. One..tall and lusty, stoops in her shoulders. **1838** LYTTON *Alice* II. iii, Cissy, my love, don't stoop so. **1856** COMPAING & DEVERE *Tailor's Guide Cutting* 9 A man stoops, when, instead of standing upright, he usually carries his body forward, and becomes shorter in front and longer behind. **1905** ELIN. GLYN *Viciss. Evangeline* 89 She was very tall and thin, and stooped dreadfully.

†**5. a.** To descend from a height. *Obs.*

1608 B. JONSON *Masque at Ld. Hadington's Marr.* Wks. (1616) 939 Venus, is this a time to quit your carre? To stoope to earth? to leaue alone, your starre, Without your influence? **1633** P. FLETCHER *Purple Isl.* XI. xxxv, Soon stoops the speedie Herauld through the aire. **1697** DRYDEN *Virg. Georg.* IV. 75 The winged Nation wanders thro' the Skies,.. Then stooping on the Meads and leafy Bow'rs, They skim the Floods, and sip the purple Flow'rs. **1847** TENNYSON *Princess* vii, The cloud may stoop from heaven and take the shape With fold to fold, of mountain or of cape.

†**b.** To be lowered in amount or degree. *Obs.*

1572 MALIM tr. *Martinengo's Famagusta* 9b, All our prouision within the Citie stooping very lowe. **1608** CHAPMAN *Byron's Consp.* I. ii. 182 Your highnesse makes the light of this Court stoope, With your so neere departure.

6. a. Of a hawk or other bird of prey: To descend swiftly on its prey, to swoop (const. *at*, *on*); also, to descend to the lure. Also *fig.*

1575 TURBERV. *Falconrie* 123 The Almaines doe flee at the Pye with a lease or twoo caste of Falcons at once, and they make them to mownte and to stowpe. **1577** GRANGE *Golden Aphrod.* G ij b, With lure I play the Faukner kinde,.. I shake my fiste, I whistle shrill, but nought will make hir stoupe. **1590** SPENSER *F.Q.* II. xi. 43 As when Joves harnesse-bearing Bird from hye Stoupes at a flying heron with proud disdayne. **1621** BURTON *Anat. Mel.* II. ii. III. (1624) 208 A Hawke.. when the game is sprung, comes down amaine, & stoupes vpon a sudden. **1675** TRAHERNE *Chr. Ethics* 457 An eagle cannot stoop at flies. **1717** BOLINGBROKE *Let. to Sir W. Windham* (1753) 147 Whether the priest had stooped at the lure of a cardinal's hat,.. I know not. **1779** SHERIDAN *Critic* I. i, The follies and foibles of society are subjects unworthy the notice of the comic muse, who should be taught to stoop only at the.. blacker crimes of humanity. **1825** SCOTT *Betrothed* xxiii, At length one of the falcons had reached a pitch from which she ventured to stoop at the heron. **1828** SIR J. S. SEBRIGHT *Hawking* 27 The magpie is to be driven from his retreat, and the hawk, if at a good pitch, will stoop at him as he passes to another bush. **1847** C. BRONTE *Jane Eyre* (ed. 2) Pref., Fielding could stoop on carrion, but Thackeray never does. **1895** J. G. MILLAIS *Breath fr. Veldt* (1899) 121 Tawny eagle stooping at wounded steinbuck.

b. *trans.* = To stoop at or on. ? *Obs.*

1575 TURBERV. *Falconrie* 154 Then shall you first cast off a well quarried or make Hawke, and let hir stoupe a fowle vpon a brooke or a plashe. **1583** T. WATSON *Poems* (Arb.) 83 In time all haggred Haukes will stoope the Lures. **1607** DEKKER & WEBSTER *Northw. Hoe* V. i. G 4b, See the hawke that first stoopt my phesant is kild by [etc.]. **1618** FLETCHER *Loyal Subj.* I. ii, He flies to stoop our favours.

II. Causative uses.

7. a. *trans.* To cause to bow down, bring to the ground; *fig.* to humiliate, subdue. Now *rare.*

c **1205** LAY. 25950 Mon ne mæi mid strenðe stupen hine to grunde. **1594** KYD *Cornelia* II. 153 [Caesar] that toyld To stoope the world and Rome to his desires. **1594** CHAPMAN *Shadow of Nt.* B iij, Shoote, shoote, and stoope his pride. *c* **1600** *Distr. Emperor* IV. iii. in Bullen *O. Pl.* (1884) III. 236, I cannot stoope the harte of Ganelon. *c* **1611** CHAPMAN *Iliad* VI. 407 The Gods may stoupe me by the Greekes. **1615** —— *Odyss.* V. 321 He fell to felling downe; And twentie trees he stoopt, in litle space. **1616** NICCOLS *Overburies Vis.* (1873) 13 Hee, whose conquering stroke Did stoope our neckes to Norman rule. *a* **1630** S. PAGE *Ps.* xi. 6 in Spurgeon *Treas. Dav.* I. 155 [The snares] of our own sins.. Keep down our heads, and stoop us that we cannot look up. **1742** YOUNG *Nt. Th.* IX. 855 Turn we, nor will hear.. what they [the stars] would impart For man's emolument, sole cause that stoops Their grandeur to man's eye? **1839** *Blackw. Mag.* XLVI. 279 The worst symptom is at home, in the wretched impolicy which stoops Government to the rabble. **1856** LEVER *Martins of Cro' Martin* xli, A very large, powerfully-built man, somewhat stooped by age. **1901** JANE BARLOW *Ghost-bereft* 65 The wind in the trees stooped the straightest that stood All its own way.

†**b.** *passive.* To be curved downwards. *Obs.*

1681 GREW *Musæum* I. §5 i. 100 The Brasilian Frog-fish.. hath a black Horn on his Forehead, stooped forwards.

8. a. To bow (the head, †face, neck, knee); to incline (one's ear). Also *to stoop an eye on* (? nonce-use), to deign to glance at.

1634 MILTON *Comus* 333 Thou fair Moon.. Stoop thy pale visage through an amber cloud. **1655** W. HAMMOND *On death of Brother* Poems 67 But stoop thine eare ill-councelld youth, and hark. **1771** *Muse in Miniature* 146 To him I stoop the penitential knee. **1777** POTTER *Æschylus, Prometh. Chain'd* 56 *Chorus.* What, shall high Jove bend to a greater lord? *Prometheus.* And to a yoke more galling stoop his neck. **1818** SCOTT *Hrt. Midl.* xxii, With his face stooped against his hands. **1825** —— *Talism.* vii, He then stooped his lofty crest, and entered a lowly hut. **1831** JAMES *Phil. Augustus* I. xv, He pushed his way through the foliage, stooping his head to prevent the branches striking him in the face. **1860** TYNDALL *Glac.* I. xxii. 155 In getting through the rocks.. I once had occasion to stoop my head. **1885–94** BRIDGES *Eros & Psyche* May xix, Here Zeus, in likeness of a tawny bull, Stoop'd on the Cretan shore his mighty knee. **1904** WEYMAN *Abbess of Vlaye* xi, This puling girl on whom the Captain of Vlaye had stooped an eye.

b. *refl.* or quasi-*refl.* = sense 1.

1808 SCOTT *Marm.* VI. xxx, She stoop'd her by the runnel's side. **1814** —— *Lord of Isles* III. xii, Where Coolin stoops him to the west, They saw upon his shiver'd crest The sun's arising gleam. **1849** ROCK *Ch. of Fathers* I. viii. (1903) III. 65 While he.. stoops him down to read the legend.

c. *fig.* To condescend to apply (one's thoughts, etc.) to something unworthy.

1598 SYLVESTER *Du Bartas* I. i. 143 Let other-some (whose fainting Spirits do droop) Down to the ground their meditations stoop. **1698** COLLIER *Short View* i. 3 I'm sorry the Author should stoop his Wit thus Low. **1718** POPE *Iliad* XI. 95 None stoop'd a Thought to base inglorious Flight. **1866** LYTTON *Lost Tales Miletus* Pref. p. vii, In this selection I have avoided.. the more licentious themes, to which.. the Boccacios of Miletus sometimes stooped their genius.

†**9. a.** To let down, lower, 'vail'. Often *Naut.* and *Mil.* to lower (a sail, an ensign). *Obs.*

1530 TINDALE *Gen.* xxiv. 14 The damsell to whom I saye, stoupe doune thy pytcher and let me drynke. **1593** DRAYTON *Sheph. Garland* IX. xv, With that fayre Cynthya stoups her glittering vayle, And diues adowne into the Ocean flood. **1597** —— *Heroic. Ep., Q. Isab. to Rich. II*, 104 Nor durst his slugging Hulks approch the strand, Nor stoop'd a top as signall to the Land. **1612** —— *Poly-olb.* VIII. 212 Nor with that Consull ioyn'd, Vespasian could.. make them stoope their saile. **1639** S. DU VERGER tr. *Camus' Admir. Events* 180 Fortune is constrained to stoope her ensign before her. **1672** T. VENN *Milit. Observ.* 175 You shall see some Ensigns let fly their Colours, when they should sink them; and some to stoop them to Pesants or Comrades, when Superiors have gone unsaluted. **1687** A. LOVELL tr. *Thevenot's Trav.* II. 24 They made many bows to the East lifting up the right hand to their head, and then stooping it down to the ground. **1697** COLLIER *Ess. Mor. Subj.* II. 56 A Man must stoop his hand for his Friend, and raise him up towards his own Ground. *fig.* *a* **1619** FOTHERBY *Atheom.* (1622) Pref. p. xviii, The highest points, which I have carefully indeauoured to stoop and demitte, euen to the capacitie of the very lowest.

b. Of a bird, etc.: To direct (its flight) downwards.

1810 SCOTT *Lady of L.* II. xxxiii, Like the ill Demon of the night, Stooping his pinions' shadowy sway Upon the nighted pilgrim's way. **1824** —— *St. Ronan's* vi, This is not the way of the world, my good sir, to which even Genius must stoop its flight.

†**10.** To put down, stake (money) on a game.

c **1550** *Dice-Play* (Percy Soc.) 27 He that will not stoop a dodkin at the dice, per chaunce at cardes will spend God's cope. **1591** GREENE *2nd Pt. Conny Catching* (1592) B 4b, The Conny-catchers.. began to lay the plot how they might make him stoope all the money in his purse. **1592** —— *Def. Conny Catching* To Rdr., Some that would not stoope a farthing at cardes, would venter all the byte in their boung at dice.

†**11.** To plunge (a knife) *in* a person's body. *Obs.*

1662 LAMONT *Diary* (Maitl. Club) 145 [He] was strangled in his bed priuately, and, fearing he sould recouered, a knife was stooped in his throat.

12. To tilt (a cask). Now *dial.* Cf. STEEP *v.*[2] 1.

a **1670** HACKET *Abp. Williams* I. (1692) 59 To stoop this Vinacre to the very Lees. **1788** G. KEATE *Pelew Isl.* xxv. 312 The only conveniency they had of keeping water.. was in thick bamboos, that had a bore of five or six inches diameter; these they placed upright, and stooped them when they wanted to pour any out. **1823** J. BADCOCK *Dom. Amusem.* 161 Stoop the vessel sideways. **1838** HOLLOWAY *Prov. Dict.*, To *stoop*, to put a piece of wood behind a cask that is nearly empty, so as to raise the hinder part, in order to let the contents run out.

13. To train (a dog) to 'stoop' for a scent. Cf. 1 e.

1781 P. BECKFORD *Th. Hunting* (1802) 85 It is now time to stoop them to a scent. **1826** J. COOK *Fox-hunting* 23 You will soon find they [the young hounds] will 'down with their noses' without being unnaturally stooped to Hare.

III. 14. *Comb.*: **stoop crop** *N. Amer.*, a crop whose cultivation demands stoop labour; †**stoop-frog** (? *nonce-wd.*), an oppressor of frogs (the King Stork of the fable); **stoop labour** *N. Amer.*, agricultural labour performed in a stooping (or squatting) position; **stoop tag** *N. Amer.* = SQUAT TAG.

1928 *Sat. Even. Post.* 10 Mar. 170/2 He does heavy field work—particularly in the so-called '*stoop crops' and 'knee crops' of vegetable and cantaloupe production. **1939** J. STEINBECK *Grapes of Wrath* xix. 316 Lettuce, cauliflower, artichokes, potatoes—stoop crops. **1967** *PTA Mag.* (U.S.) June 5 He was one of the migrant workers who follow the course of stoop crops through California fields and valleys. **1602** WARNER *Alb. Eng.* VI. xxxii. 160 This *stoope-Frog Æsops Storke. **1943** *Sun* (Baltimore) 3 Aug. 11/1 Asparagus cutting ordinarily is a specialized *stoop-labor job. **1959** *Economist* 7 Mar. 876/1 Some harvesting can be done mechanically, but most crops still require back-breaking 'stoop' labour. **1972** *Islander* (Victoria, B.C.) 23 Apr. 13/2 Most moved down to southern Ontario to do back-breaking stoop labor in its sugar-beet fields. **1979** G. SWARTHOUT *Skeletons* 89 There are eight million illegals in the country... It would be one thing if they were all agricultural—stoop labor, fruit- and produce-pickers, so on. **1898** F. P. DUNNE *Mr. Dooley in Peace & War* (1899) 179 Little Flora an' little Fauna playin' *stoop-tag aroun' a whale.. or engagin' in some other spoort iv childhood! **1955** W. GADDIS *Recognitions* I. iii. 146 The critics!.. They're like a bunch of old maids playing stoop-tag in an asparagus patch.

†**stoop**, *v.*[2] *Obs. rare.* [f. STOOP *sb.*[1]] *trans.* To mark *out* with 'stoops' or posts.

1663 W. BLUNDELL *Crosby Rec.* (1880) 222 This course, as it is now used upon the marshes.. was stooped out by me ..A.D. 1654. **1756** in Picton *L'pool Munic. Rec.* (1886) II. 154 Ordered,.. that the horse causeway.. be repaired at the expence of the Corporation so for as it extends within our liberties; and to be stoop'd out.

stoop, var. STOUP; obs. form of STUPE.

stoop and roop, roop and stoop, *advb. phr. Sc.* and *north. dial.* [Of obscure origin; the 18th c. forms point to ME. *ū* as in STOOP *v.*[1] Probably this and *stout and rout* in quot. *c* 1375 are corruptions of some rhyming phrase, of which perh. only the first word was significant. Cf. Da. *rub og stub* (Norw. *rubb og stubb*, Sw. *rubb och stubb*) and the Sc. and north. dial. *stump and rump* in the same sense.] Completely, entirely.

[*c* **1375** *Sc. Leg. Saints* xxxvii. (*Vincencius*) 353 þane gert he his body bere al bare to bestis.. til ete hyme bath stout & rout.] **1728** RAMSAY *Monk & Miller's Wife* 184 They snapt her up baith stoup and roup. *c* **1746** J. COLLIER (Tim Bobbin) *View Lancs. Dial.* (1770) 21 Tum took Care oth' tother, steawp on reawp. **1816** SCOTT *Bl. Dwarf* x, We are ruined stoop and roop. **1826** J. WILSON *Noct. Ambr.* Wks. 1855 I. 161 You set yoursel to listen to a no verra bricht discoorse, as if you had taken an oath to devour't frae stoop to roop. **1834** M. SCOTT *Cruise Midge* i, And tipping the wink, we hove him bodily stoop and roop overboard.

stooped (stuːpt), *ppl. a.* [f. STOOP *v.*[1] + -ED[1].]

1. a. On which a bird of prey is stooping. **b.** Of a bird of prey: That has swooped down.

1606 CHAPMAN *Gentl. Usher* I. i. A 2b, A cast of Faulcons on their merry wings, Daring the stooped prey that shifting flies. **1819** KEATS *Lamia* I. 67 While Hermes on his pinions lay, Like a stoop'd falcon ere he takes his prey.

2. Of the head or shoulders: Bent downwards. Of a person: Bowed, having a stoop, stooping.

1865 SWINBURNE *Chastelard* I. i. 8 Which one is that, stooped somewhat in the neck, That walks so with his chin against the wind? **1873** MISS BROUGHTON *Nancy* xxii. II. 61 Barbara's stooped head is hidden by her hands. **1876** *World* No. 115. V. 13 He is paler, and stooped, and supports his tottering steps with a stout walking stick. **1881** MAY LAFFAN in *Macm. Mag.* XLIV. 380 A little stooped old woman. **1897** HOWELLS *Landlord at Lion's Head* 238 Over their stooped shoulders.. Westover saw Alan.

3. Of a vessel: Tilted, inclined.

1865 SWINBURNE *Poems & Ball.*, *Ilicet* 49 The stooped urn-filling, dips and flashes.

stooper ('stuːpə(r)). [f. STOOP *v.*[1] + -ER[1].]

1. (See quot. 1854.)

1784 *Cries of London* 101 Any Work for the Cooper?.. Whene'er a vessel gets a bruize By slipping off the stooper, Old Farrell I would have you chuse, As soon as any Cooper. **1854** MISS BAKER *Northampt. Gloss.*, *Stooper*, a wedge for stooping or tilting a barrel.

2. One who stoops or bends down; one who has a stoop.

1892 *Daily News* 3 Mar. 5/3 At one lace-making village.. it was observed that there were no 'stoopers' except the invalids and weakly ones. **1912** D. CRAWFORD *Thinking Black* iv. 59 Good gleaners must be good stoopers.

†**stoop-gallant**, *sb.* [f. STOOP *v.*[1] + GALLANT *sb.* = F. *trousse-galant*, recorded *a* 1590 in Paré *Œuvres* XXII. v. (1641) 530.

The Fr. equivalent is an objective compound of the vb.-stem; it is uncertain whether the Eng. word is a compound of the same type, or a phrase with the verb in the imperative and the sb. used vocatively. Cf. the following quot.

1551 *Loughborough Register* in J. Nichols *Hist. Leicester* (1804) III. II. 891/2 The Swat, called New Acquaintance, alias Stoupe, Knave, and know thy Master.]

Something that humbles 'gallants'; originally, a name for the 'sweating sickness'; later used *gen.* Also *attrib.* or *adj.*

1551 in *Gentl. Mag.* (1808) LXXVIII. II. 1057 The hote Sickness, called Stup-gallant. *a* **1560** T. HANCOCK in *Narr. Reform.* (Camden) 82 The posting swet, that posted from towne to towne, throwghe England, and was named stope gallant, for hytt spared none, for ther were dawncyng in the cowrte at 9 a'clocke thatt were deadd or aleven a'clocke. *a* **1571** BP. J. LESLIE *Hist. Scot.* (Bannatyne Club) 81 Thair wes ane seknes universallie in the moneth of September [1510] in Scotland,.. it wes callit be the peple stoup galland. **1579** SPENSER *Sheph. Cal.* Feb. 90 Youngth is a bubble.. Whose way is wildernesse, whose ynne Penaunce, And stoopegallaunt Age the hoste of Greeuaunce. **1583** MELBANCKE *Philotimus* K ij, Old cramped sires in their stoupe gallant age. **1596** NASHE *Saffron Walden* Wks. 1910 III. 114 Comedie vpon Comedie he shall haue... One shal bee called.. *Stoope Gallant*, or *The Fall of pride.* **1862** WRAXELL tr. *Hugo's Les Misérables* III. lxvii. 332 Your stoop-gallant is called cholera.

¶ Used allusively as verbal phrase.

a **1661** FULLER *Worthies, Surrey* (1662) 84 His Lordship.. enforced them to stoop gallant, and to vail their Bonnets for the Queen of England.

stoopid ('stuːpɪd), *a.* and *sb.* Non-standard (often joc. or playful) repr. of STUPID *a.* and *sb.*

1848 THACKERAY *Vanity Fair* xl. 362 Hold your tongue, you stoopid old fool. *Ibid.* lv. 499 Shut your mouth, you old stoopid. **1854** MRS. GASKELL *Let.* 2 Sept. (1966) 303 Many happy returns of your birthday.. I hope it won't be a 'stoopid' day. **1902** F. G. ELLERTON *Let.* 11 Aug. in S. Bailey *John Bailey* (1935) 83 Glad you had a little slap at that stoopid old Swinburne. **1913** R. BROOKE *Let.* 24 ? Nov. (1968) 537 I'm going to spend 5 days a week there, and three in London (that's 8, stoopid). **1956** N. MARSH *Off with his Head* (1957) x. 211 Lor', Dulcie, what a stoopid gel you are. **1978** C. STORR *Winter's End* xi. 131 'I didn't like your being angry with me.' He began with a denial.. then checked himself. 'I was stoopid.'

stooping ('stuːpɪŋ), *vbl. sb.* [f. STOOP *v.*[1] + -ING[1].] The action of the verb, in its various senses; an instance of this.

1398 TREVISA *Barth. De P.R.* VIII. xiii. (1495) 320 In aege ..the planete mars disposyth to stowpynge and crokydnesse. *c* **1412** HOCCLEVE *De Reg. Princ.* 1019 Stomak is on whom stowpyng.. Annoyeth soore. **1592** *Soliman & Pers.* 1481 Nay, then, I see, my stooping makes her proud. **1653** H. COGAN tr. *Pinto's Trav.* xix. 65 Looking towards the point of the Island from whence the Kite came, we perceived divers others, that in their flying made many stoopings. **1754** CHATHAM *Lett. to Nephew* v. 34 As to the carriage of your person, be particularly careful.. not to get a habit of stooping. **1799** UNDERWOOD *Dis. Childhood* (ed. 4) II. 87 The height which he may have lost in consequence of that stooping which the disorder had induced. **1897** *Encycl. Sport* I. 583/1 (Hunting, fox) *Stooping* (of hounds), putting their noses to the ground. A hound is said to stoop to a scent when he has once taken to speaking to it.

b. *Comb.*: †**stooping-horse** = STALKING-HORSE.

1659 D. PELL *Impr. Sea* 22 *note*, Counterfeit Religion is made a mere stooping horse of.

stooping ('stu:pɪŋ), *ppl. a.* [f. STOOP *v.*^{1} + -ING^2.] That stoops.

1. Of the body, head, shoulders, etc., also of the posture: Bowing down, inclining or leaning forward; chiefly, having a habitual stoop, as from age or infirmity.

c **1290** *Clement* 238 in *S. Eng. Leg.* 330 Pouere and stoupinde and miseise, he bi-gan to siken sore. *c* **1386** CHAUCER *Merch. T.* 494 Whan tendre youthe hath wedded stoupyng age. **1422** YONGE tr. *Secreta Secret.* 223 Hey vprerid shuldris; the body Sumwhate Stowpynge. **1538** ELYOT *Dict.*, *Cernuus*, stowpynge or lookynge downewarde. **1558** PHAER *Æneid* VIII. (1562) Bbj, Y^e king him self of stoupyng age Eneas next him toke for mate. **1593** SHAKS. *Rich. II*, III. iii. 48 How farre off from the mind of Bullingbrooke It is, such Crimson Tempest should bedrench..King Richards Land, My stooping dutie tenderly shall shew. **1609** HEYWOOD *Brit. Troy* VIII. xv. 172 They can make..the Foole wise, The stooping Straight. **1771** SMOLLETT *Humphry Cl.* 6 May (1815) 71 Mrs. Tabitha Bramble is..flat-chested, and stooping. **1807** J. BARLOW *Columb.* III. 497 Forbear to tell my stooping sire His darling hopes have fed a coward fire. **1816** SCOTT *Bl. Dwarf* iv, Getting up from his stooping posture. **1875** JOWETT *Plato* (ed. 2) III. 103 The usurer with stooping walk pretends not to see them. **1908** W. CHURCHILL *Mr. Crewe's Career* vii. 95 Mr. Crewe was ushered out by the stooping Secretary.

Comb. **1594** LYLY *Mother Bombie* I. 111 He doats, he is stooping old, and shortly must die.

b. Of things: Inclined from the perpendicular.

1621 G. SANDYS *Ovid's Met.* V. (1632) 183 Wandring in the Ort-yard, simply shee [Ceres] Pluckt a Pomegrannet from the stooping Tree. **1915** *Glasgow Herald* 28 May 8 On the farther side (seen by me past the shoulder of a dark alder and stooping scrub of hazels..upon the nearer bank).

†**2.** Of a person's fortunes: Declining. *Obs.*

1608 *Yorks. Trag.* I. iii. 15 A good and sure reliefe To al his stooping fortunes. **1611** SPEED *Hist. Gt. Brit.* IX. xvi. (1623) 841 King Henries fortunes in France were desperately stooping.

3. Of a bird of prey: That is making its stoop.

1754 BOYER *Gt. Theat. Honour* (ed. 2) 116 Stooping (is said of a Bird of Prey that makes a stoop at the Game), *Fondant.* **1895** CROCKETT *Men of Mosshags* viii. 59 The wide pleasant moors where..the stooping wild birds cried all the livelong day.

Hence '**stoopingly** *adv.*, with the body bent or bowed down.

1530 PALSGR. 842/2 Stowpyngly, *en cambrant.* **1547** BOORDE *Brev. Health* (1552) 59 *Gibbositas*... In Englyshe it is named crokydnes of the backe or shoulders, makyng a man to go stoupyngly. **1561** T. NORTON *Calvin's Inst.* III. 240 We may safely folow the Scripture, whiche as with a motherly pace goeth stoupyngly [L. *submissius graditur*], least it shoulde forsake our weakenesse. **1825** *New Monthly Mag.* XIV. 130 He walks stoopingly. **1871** *Daily News* 21 June, The well-known figure, somewhat stoopingly, progressed to the seat apportioned. **1906** E. V. LUCAS *Listener's Lure* 63 The giant stoopingly emerged from the back compartment.

'**stoopy**, *a. rare.* [f. STOOP *sb.*^{2} or *v.*^{1} + -Y.] Having a stoop.

1905 MRS. BARNES-GRUNDY *Vacill. Hazel* vi. 82 A young, stoopy man walked into the room.

stoor(e: see STIR, STORE, STOUR.

stoot(e: see STOAT, STUT.

‖'**stooter.** *Obs.* In 6-7 stoter. [Du. *stooter.*] A Dutch coin worth two stuivers and a half.

1598 W. PHILLIP tr. *Linschoten* I. xxx. 58 There are many Indians that are daily hired..and haue 12. *Basarucos* the day, which is as much as two stiuers or a stoter. **1609** ROWLANDS *Dr. Merrie-man* (1877) 14 Now for a Stoter you a Box may haue, That will the liues of halfe a dozen saue. **1616** B. JONSON *Devil an Ass* III. iii. 32 Where could you ha' ..Beene satisfied with a leape o' your Host's daughter, In garrison, a wench of a stoter! or, Your Sutlers wife, i' the leaguer, of two blanks! **1811** P. KELLY *Univ. Cambist* I. 14 Amsterdam... [Silver Coins] Stooters, [reckoned] at $2\frac{1}{2}$ Stivers.

stooth (stu:θ). *dial.* Forms: 3-9 stothe, 5 stuthe, stoth, 6 stoothe, stoith, (pl. stoithez, stoys), 9 stooth. [Either repr. OE. *stuðu* var. of *studu* STUD *sb.*, or a. the equivalent ON. *stoð.*]

1. A post, an upright lath; now only one of the upright battens in a lath-and-plaster wall. **b.** Comb. ***stooth-and-plaster***; †**stooth-stone**, a stone post.

1295 *Acc. Exch. K.R.* m. 13 Et xxij s. in Trussurs, Girdelinges et Stothes emptis de eodem. **1352-3** *Ely Sacr. Rolls* (1907) II. 152 Pro cariagio de ix^{xx} sparris et cc stothys quercinis, 18 s. 6 d. **1410-11** in Hudson & Tingey *Rec. Norwich* (1910) II. 58 [For two spars, 3] stothis [and other timber]. **1453** *Mem. Ripon* (Surtees) III. 160 Et de 3*d.* sol. pro stuthes de ligno eidem operi. *c* **1460** *Promp. Parv.* (Winch. MS.) 440 S[t]oth of an hows, *posticulus.* **1497-8** in *Fabric Rolls York Minster* (Surtees) 90 Emendacione unius les stothe in zona pro cornu Sancti Willelmi. *c* **1530** *Ibid.* 355 Operantibus super reparacionem murorum stabuli circa soletrees et stoothes,..etc. 13 s. 2 d. **1532-3** *Durham Househ. Bk.* (Surtees) 173 Pro sarracione $1\frac{1}{2}$ rod in wyndbalks, stoys, pouynchys, 4 s. 8 d. **1533-4** *Ibid.* 270 Pro sarracione 1 rod in bords et stoythez, 2 s. 8 d. **1552** in *Fabric Rolls York Minster* (Surtees) 355 For setting in ij stothes. **1566** *Leverton Churchw. Acc.* in *Archæologia* XLI. 364, ii altar stones for stothe stones. **1893** H. D. RAWNSLEY in *Westm. Gaz.* 14 Nov. 2/1 He..showed me the stooth and plaister partition that had at one time formed his [Wordsworth's] bedroom outer wall.

†**2.** A stud or knob. *Obs.*

1397 *Durham Acc. Rolls* (Surtees) 445 Et vj stothes deaurat. ex donacione domini Ricardi de Castro Bernardi. **1428** in *Engl. Misc.* (Surtees) 1 For stuthes of xxxiij gyrdels of menged metaill..tin and lede. ? *c* **1475** *Reg. Guild Corpus Chr. York* (Surtees) 295 A blak gyrdill, ye pennaunt and ye buccle golde, with vij stuthes,..a blew girdill, pennaunt and ye bocle silver and gilt, with xxxij stothez.

†**3.** The list of a web of cloth. *Obs.*

c **1440** *Promp. Parv.* 476/2 Stothe, of a clothe [*Winch.* stoth], *forago.*

Hence †'**stoothed** *a.*, having studs.

1467 *York Memo. Bk.* (Surtees) I. 165 Ther shall no man ..make or garre make any double stothed girdilles to sell.. uppayn of iijs. iiij*d.*

stoothe (stu:ð), *v. dial.* Also 6 stothe, 9 stooth. [f. STOOTH.]

†**1.** *trans.* To garnish with studs or knobs. = STUD *v. Obs.*

1530 *Knaresb. Wills* (Surtees) I. 26 A gyrdell stothed with sylver.

2. To furnish (a wall) with the framework on which the lath-and-plaster is fixed; to build with lath and plaster.

1825 JAMIESON *Stooth.* **1833** LOUDON *Encycl. Archit.* §925 The whole of the insides of the external walls are to be properly stoothed (battened). *a* **1860** J. YOUNGER *Autob.* (1881) 365, I could only bring him to an agreement to stooth the bed-length of the damp back wall,..for which stoothing I engaged to pay him full five per cent. in advance of rent.

Hence **stoothed** *ppl. a.*; '**stoothing** *vbl. sb.*, the action of the vb.; *concr.* a wall or partition of lath and plaster; also *attrib.*

1770 HUTTON *Mensuration* 591 Ceiling joists to both storys. Stoothed partitions. Deal flooring. **1788** W. H. MARSHALL *Yorksh.* II. 356 *Steathing*; a lath and plaister partition. **1833** LOUDON *Encycl. Archit.* §980 Roofing, lintels,..stoothings (stud-work, or quartering; that is, wooden framework for lath and plaster partitions). *Ibid.* §982 The ceilings of all the rooms, passages, and of the staircase with stoothing partitions, to have two-coated lath-plaster. **1833** RAINE *Brief Acc. Durham Cath.* 108 Portions of the stoothing were removed. **1884** *Congregational Year Bk.* 401 The clerestory arches are constructed of rough framing and stoothing. **1893** S. O. ADDY *Hall of Waltheof* 173 This wooden framework which fills up the interstices is locally known as 'studding' or 'stoothing'.

stoove, stoover: see STOVE, STOVER.

stoowre, obs. form of STOWER^1.

†**stop**, *sb.*^{1} *Obs.* Forms: 1 stoppa, 4-6 stoppe, 5-6 stopp, 4-9 stop. [OE. *stoppa* wk. masc. = OS. *stoppo*:—WGer. **stoppon-* f. OTeut. **stup-* ablaut-var. of **staup-*: see STOUP.]

1. A pail or bucket.

c **725** *Corpus Gloss.* B. 147 *Blohonicula*, stoppa. *c* **890** WÆRFERTH tr. *Gregory's Dial.* 11 þa becom an fisc in þone wæterstoppan. *c* **1000** ÆLFRIC *Gloss.* in Wr.-Wülcker 123/24 *Situla*, stoppa. *c* **1340** *Nominale* (Skeat) 497 Paile.. Stoppe. **1397-8** *Durham Acc. Rolls* (Surtees) 601 Pro stoppes correi empt. pro camera d'ni Prioris. *c* **1440** *Promp. Parv.* 477/1 Stoppe, vessel for mylkynge, *multra.* **1491** *Acta Dom. Concil.* (1839) 195/2 Five barellis,..thre treyn stoppis. **1548** in Hudson & Tingey *Rec. Norwich* (1910) II. 174 To serche for stoppes, roopes, ladders and bokettes of lether. **1787** W. H. MARSHALL *E. Norfolk* (1795) II. 389 *Stops*, small well-buckets. **1895** *E. Angl. Gloss.*, *Stop*, the bucket of a well; formerly any bucket.

2. A holy-water stoup.

1419 Holiwaterstop [see HOLY WATER 2]. **1426-7** *Rec. St. Mary at Hill* (1905) 67 Also for primyng of þe haly water stop, viij d. **1483** *Act 1 Rich. III*, c. 12 That no merchaunt Straungier..brynge into this Realme of Englond.. halywater stoppes. **1552** in *Archæol. Cant.* (1874) IX. 273 Item a holy water stopp of latten.

3. *Sc.* A pitcher, flagon, tankard. Also *attrib.*

1489 *Acta Dom. Concil.* (1839) 131/1 A stop compto^r, a gret pot, & a half galloun stop. **1490** *Acc. Ld. High Treas. Scot.* I. 175 A water stop of siluer. **1491** *Acta Dom. Concil.* (1839) 176/2 A quarte stop price ij s. **1496** *Acc. Ld. High Treas. Scot.* I. 321 For five vnce of siluir of maid werk in a stop lid of the Kingis. **1540** *Ibid.* VII. 312 Ane silver stop weyand xij pund wecht twa unces. **1697** *Invent.* in *Scott. N. & Q.* (1900) Dec. 90/2 A tinn quart stop, a pynt.

stop (stɒp), *sb.*^{2} Forms: 5-7 stopp, 6-7 stoppe, (stope), 5- stop. [f. STOP *v.* Cf. MDu. *stoppe* (mod.Du. *stop* fem., bung, darn).]

I. Action of stopping.

1. a. The action or an act of impeding, obstructing, or arresting; the fact of being impeded or arrested; a check, arrest, or obstruction (of motion or activity).

1544 BETHAM *Precepts War* I. clxxxviii. I iij b, That thy souldiours maye haue plentye, withoute any stop or entercourse of theyr enemyes. **1592** *Soliman & Pers.* I. v. 15 Through which our passage cannot finde a stop Till it haue prickt the hart of Christendome. *c* **1610** SIR J. MELVIL *Mem.* (Bannatyne Club) 350 They..entrit into the toun without stop. **1690** T. BURNET *Theory Earth* III. ix. 76 Therefore we must not suppose such an Universal stop of waters. **1722** DE FOE *Col. Jack* ii, He..had the money paid him without any stop or question asked. **1738** [G. SMITH] *Cur. Relat.* II. 314 There was a general Stop of Trade. **1837** CARLYLE *Fr. Rev.* II. I. xi, Our Federate Volunteers will file through the inner gateways... Nay there, should some stop occur, [etc.]. **1848** THACKERAY *Van. Fair* xvi, If people only made prudent marriages, what a stop to population there would be!

b. An act of stopping the ball in a ball-game.

1773 J. DUNCOMBE *Surrey Triumphant* xlix, Davis, for stops and catches fam'd.

c. The order given to a fire-brigade station not to continue sending out in force. Also ***stop-message.***

1872 *Routledge's Ev. Boy's Ann.* 114/2 Roused me four times..for stops for chimbleys [*note*, a fireman's warning]. **1890** *Times* 25 Apr. 10/2 The fire was so well under control that a stop message was despatched.

†**d.** ***to give a stop to*** (an agent or activity): to check or arrest the progress of. *Obs.*

a **1586** SIDNEY *Arcadia* II. (Sommer) 175 b, But Basilius (swearing he would put out her eyes, if she stird a foote to trouble his daughter) gaue her a stoppe for that while. **1611** G. H. tr. *Anti-Coton* 63 Words that had given vs the stop, had they been put in the entrance (of his discourse). **1678** BUTLER *Hud.* III. i. 286 In hast I snatch'd my weapon up, And gave their Hellish Rage a stop. **1693** LOCKE *Educ.* §107 'Tis a great Step towards the mastery of our Desires, to give this stop to them, and shut them up in Silence.

†**e.** ***to make (a) stop of*** = f. *Obs.*

1633 BROME *Antipodes* I. vii. (1640) D 1 b, What's he? One sent, I feare, from my dead mother, to make stop Of our intended voyage. **1638** R. BAKER tr. *Balzac's Lett.* (vol. II.) 56 This is..not to make a stoppe of contentments but to husband them. **1673** TEMPLE *Ireland* Wks. 1731 I. 110 This made a sudden and mighty Stop of that Issue of Money.

f. ***to put a stop to*** (an activity, something active): to check, restrain; to arrest the progress of; to bring to an end, abolish.

1678 DRYDEN *Tr. & Cr.* I. i. (1679) 3 But you grave pair, ..Must put a stop to these incroaching ills. **1687** A. LOVELL tr. *Thevenot's Trav.* I. 26 For putting a stop to these fires, there are men called *Baltadgis.* **1702** *Reasons for addressing his Maj. to invite the Electress*, etc. 2 Putting all imaginable Stops to what they cannot barefac'dly hinder. **1735** JOHNSON *Lobo's Abyssinia, Descr.* xi. 111 That a stop might be put to the inroads of the Galles. **1789** BRAND *Hist. Newcastle* II. 304 The coal-trade at Newcastle was for some time put a stop to by a mutiny of the keelmen. **1879** M. J. GUEST *Lect. Hist. Eng.* xvii. 166 Henry..put a stop to this. **1885** 'MRS. ALEXANDER' *Valerie's Fate* ii, This is very curious,..and must be put a stop to.

g. An act of stopping and questioning a suspected person.

1968 J. LOCK *Lady Policeman* iii. 21 These stops winkled out the juveniles who had absconded. **1970** P. LAURIE *Scotland Yard* ii. 47 He appreciates encouragement, and has been advised..about stops on the street.

2. In certain specific uses: A veto or prohibition (*against*); an embargo (*upon* goods, trade); a refusal to pass tokens; an order stopping payment of a bank note, cheque, or bill.

stop of the exchequer, the suspension of payment of the Government debt to the London goldsmiths in 1672.

1634 in J. Simon *Ess. Irish Coins* (1749) 115 Complaints.. concerning the stop and refusall of farthing tokens. **1675** *Essex Papers* (Camden) I. 293 To take off the stopp in the Court of Excheq^r against the Convicting of Papists. **1723** *Lond. Gaz.* No. 6133/4 A Stop is put against any Claim at the South-Sea-Office. *a* **1734** R. NORTH *Life Ld. Keeper Guilford* (1826) I. 178 Hence proceeded the stop of the Exchequer. **1855** F. PLAYFORD *Pract. Hints Investing Money* 44 A 'Writ of Distringas' is a process, by which persons beneficially interested in any Stock standing in the name of other parties may..place a *Distringas* or stop on the transfer thereof. **1863** H. COX *Instit* III. vii. 683 *note*, An Order in Council..directed a stop to be made of payment of Exchequer moneys. **1892** CORDINGLEY *Commerc. Guide* 160 A 'stop' is usually put on bank notes, cheques, bills of exchange, bonds and similar documents when they have been lost or stolen. The 'stop' consists in writing a letter to the banker from whom the documents are payable, giving him instructions not to pay them, or not to do so without inquiry. **1907** —— *Lond. Commerc. Dict.* 162 In such cases ..it is usual to land the goods on arrival and put a 'Stop' upon them—that is, instruct the wharfinger..not to part with them until the freight has been paid.

3. The act of filling or closing up an aperture.

1593 SHAKS. *2 Hen. VI*, III. i. 288 A Breach that craues a quick expedient stoppe.

4. a. The act of coming to a stand; a halt in a journey or walk; a cessation of progress or onward movement. Often coupled with *stay.* Phr. ***to make a stop.***

? **1575** BLUNDEVIL *Art of Riding* II. iv. E v b, I tolde you before, that you shuld trot your horse right out in the midle forowe betwixte the ringes vntill you come to the place of stop. *c* **1586** C'TESS PEMBROKE *Ps.* CIV. ix, Thou makst the sunne..Well knowe the start and stop of dayly race. *a* **1625** FLETCHER *Hum. Lieut.* III. i, When he took leave now, he made a hundred stops. **1648** J. BEAUMONT *Psyche* II. xlix, How Kingdoms sprung, and how they made their stop, I well observ'd. **1697** DRYDEN *Virg. Georg.* III. 173 No Stop, no Stay, but Clouds of Sand arise. **1776** ENTICK *London* I. 489 The next stop was at a pageant at Leadenhall. **1805** WORDSW. *Waggoner* I. 36 Many a stop and stay he makes. **1839** DICKENS *Nich. Nick.* xxv, Mrs. Crummles advancing with that stage walk which consists of a stride and a stop alternately. **1887** F. FRANCIS Jun. *Saddle & Mocassin* 168 He [the pony] would check and counter-check in mid-career each break of the truant's with stops and turns so sudden, that once [etc.].

b. A halt or stay occupying some considerable space of time; a stay or sojourn made at a place, esp. in the course of a journey.

1650 R. STAPYLTON *Strada's Low C. Wars* III. 50 Her husband Octavio Duke of Parma (who never liked the stop of the Spanish army in the Netherlands). **1659** RUSHW. *Hist. Coll.* I. 76 From thence [they] rode Post to Paris, where they made some stop. **1719** DE FOE *Crusoe* II. (Globe) 581 Nor did we make any long Stop here, but hastned on towards Jarawena. **1793** L. WILLIAMS *Children's Friend* I. 221 So I staid, upon thorns. And father, uneasy at my stop, came soon afterwards. **1881** J. HATTON *New Ceylon* v. 137 From six in the morning till about eight in the evening they held their way, with but three stops of about half an hour each. **1895** *Cornh. Mag.* Oct. 407 The train was a good deal behind time, and therefore the stop was curtailed as much as possible.

c. A place at which a halt is made; a stopping-place (for coaches, etc.).

1889 *Pall Mall Gaz.* 2 Jan. 4/2 The next stage was to Cuckfield, to which stop the team consisted of four geldings. **1913** *Daily Graphic* 26 Mar. 7/4 There should be separate and fixed stops for 'buses and trams.

5. A block or obstruction of traffic caused by the overcrowding of vehicles.

a **1626** BACON *Apoph.* §86 Wks. 1778 I. 539 A citizen of London passing the streets very hastily, came at last where some stop was made by carts;..where being in some passion that he could not suddenly pass [etc.]. **1683** LUTTRELL *Brief Rel.* I. 249 The justices of peace..have..made an order for the clearing the narrow streets of hackny coaches, to prevent any stops that may happen thereby. **1690** CROWNE *Eng. Frier* III. 27 As soon as ever the stop of coaches is over, my Lady will drive like mad. **1712** STEELE *Spect.* No. 515 ¶1 To St. Paul's Church-yard, where there was a Stop of Coaches attending Company coming out of the Cathedral. **1739** *Joe Miller's Jests* No. 205 A Fellow once standing in the Pillory at Temple-Bar, it occasioned a Stop, so that a Carman with a load of Cheeses had much ado to pass.

6. a. A cessation, coming to a pause or end (of any activity, process, etc.).

1483-4 *Cely Papers* (Camden) 146 Yff they schuld be stoppyd ther wold come noo moo merchauntes heder the whych schuld cause a grett stopp. **1596** SHAKS. *1 Hen. IV*, v. iv. 83 And Time, that takes suruey of all the world, Must haue a stop. **1634** MILTON *Comus* 552 At which I ceas't, and listen'd them a while, Till an unusuall stop of sudden silence Gave respit [etc.]. **1690** LOCKE *Hum. Und.* III. vii. §5 Here it intimates a stop of the Mind, in the course it was going, before it came to the end of it. **1752** tr. *Rameau's Treat. Musick* 69 These Cadences introduce a Sort of a Stop or Rest, during a Piece. **1889** *Eng. Illustr. Mag.* Dec. 256 The band came to a stop. **1897** *Allbutt's Syst. Med.* II. 916 In tobacco intermittence the patient is always conscious of the stop and roll forward [of the heart].

b. A pause or breaking-off made by one speaking.

1561 HOBY tr. *Castiglione's Courtier* II. (1900) 199 Here M. Bernarde makinge a little stopp. **1593** SHAKS. *Rich. II*, v. ii. 4 *Yorke.* Where did I leaue? *Duch.* At that sad stoppe, my Lord, Where [etc.]. **1604** —— *Oth.* III. iii. 120 And for I know thou'rt full of Loue, and Honestie, And weigh'st thy words before thou giu'st them breath, Therefore these stops of thine, fright me the more. **1663** PATRICK *Parab. Pilgr.* xvi. (1687) 137 The first words..which he uttered when the other made a little stop, was this vehement exclamation. **1848** DICKENS *Dombey* xli, The smiling and unconscious look of Florence brings him to a dead stop. **1859** MEREDITH *R. Feverel* xxxviii, Her voice sounded to him like that of a broken-throated lamb, so painful and weak it was, with the plaintive stop in the utterance.

†**c.** Hesitation, holding back; a pause for consideration before acting. *Obs.*

1535 COVERDALE *Isa.* xliv. 7 Let him tell you forth planely thinges, that are past and for to come: yee and that without eny feare or stoppe. **1560** PILKINGTON *Aggeus* E v, And almost as many yeres haue we..buylded our owne houses goodly without any stoppe or feare. **1561** HOBY tr. *Castiglione's Courtier* II. (1900) 138 Nor to geve himselfe so for a prey to friend..that without stoppe a manne shoulde make him partaker of all his thoughtes.

†**d.** *at a stop*: at a standstill; at a nonplus.

a **1626** BACON *Holy War* Misc. Wks. (1629) 98 At which sudden Question, Martius was a little at a stop. **1685** LADY RUSSELL in *Buccleuch MSS.* (Hist. MSS. Comm.) I. 342 Lord Dorset's match seems to be at a stop. **1722** DE FOE *Plague* (1884) 127 As Navigation was at a Stop.

†**e.** The 'end' or purpose of an action. *Obs.*

1551 RECORDE *Pathw. Knowl.* Epist. to King, All do agre, that felicitie is and ought to be the stop and end of all their doynges.

II. Something that stops, arrests, or blocks.

7. a. Something that arrests or hinders motion or activity; an impediment, obstacle. ? *Obs.*

c **1508** WOLSEY in *Lett. Rich. III & Hen. VII* (Rolls) I. 446 That ther shuld be in hym no stop [nor] let but perfygt indever that suche a amyte and confederacon s[hould be made] suerly betwyx them. **1513** DOUGLAS *Æneis* IX. iii. 160 Quhat meyn thai be this myddill mantill wall? This litill stop of dykis and fouseys all? **1526** TINDALE *Eph.* ii. 14 He ..whych..hath broken doune the Wall in the myddes, that was a stoppe bitwene vs. **1548** HALL *Chron., Hen. IV*, 25 For the which cause he conceiued so great an hatred.. against the Duke of Orleaunce (as the onely stop and let of his..renoume). **1588** SHAKS. *L.L.L.* I. i. 70 These be the stops that hinder studie quite. **1635-56** COWLEY *Davideis* III. 948 He curst the Stops of Form and State, which lay In this last Stage like Scandals in his Way. **1665** HOOKE *Microgr.* 131 A stiff, hard, and hollow Cane, or Reed, without any kind of knot, or stop, from its bottom. **1725** N. ROBINSON *Th. Physick* 31 The Dregs or Fæces [will] descend, and surmount all those Stops, Letts, and Impediments, that arise from the Plicæ or Wrinkles of the Intestines.

†**b.** Something that finishes or brings to an end.

a **1586** SIDNEY *Arcadia* IV. (1598) 326 Blessed be thou, o night,..thou art the stop of strife, and the necessarie truce of approching battels. **1628** [see 18 b].

8. a. A weir or dam across a river; a sluice or floodgate. ? *Obs.*

1585 HIGINS *Junius' Nomencl.* 391/2 *Septum*,..a sluce: a floudgate, or water stop. **1641** J. TAYLOR (Water P.) *Last Voy.* A 4 b, Every Stoppe and Weare. **1681** DELAUNE *Pres. St. Lond.* 199 They took care to clear..the River Westward of about 79 Stops or Hatches, consisting of divers great Stakes and Piles, erected by Fishermen for their private lucre. **1793** *Rep. Comm. Ho. Comm.* (1803) XIV. 233 Between Day's and Sutton Locks there requires a stop or pound lock at or near Clifton Ferry. **1800** *Trans. Soc. Arts* XVIII. 283 Two stops or cloughs, one to each lock, which serve as lock-gates to the south end.

b. A blind alley in a maze.

1666 G. HARVEY *Morbus Angl.* xxvi. (1672) 58 Like a Labyrinth divided into several stops, turnings or windings, where at each division we must halt, [etc.]. **1718** SWITZER *Ichnogr. Rust.* II. 219 Six different entrances, whereof there is but one that leads to the centre, and that is attended with some difficulties and a great many stops. **1882** *Encycl. Brit.* XIV. 181/1 The key to reach this resting place is to keep the right hand continuously in contact with the hedge from first to last, going round all the stops.

9. a. A piece of mechanism (e.g. a pin, bolt, shoulder, a strip or block of wood) which checks the motion or thrust of anything, keeps a part fixed in its place, determines the position to which a part shall be brought, etc.

1523-34 FITZHERB. *Husb.* §139 Thou muste haue made redy a ponch of harde wood, with a stop and a tenaunte on the one syde. **1552** HULOET, Stoppe whych reteygneth a wheale of hys course, *sufflamen.* **1770** LUCKOMBE *Hist. Printing* 314 On the hither end of this square pin is made a sholder or stop. **1784** BRAMAH in *Repert. Arts & Manuf.* (1796) V. 222 The said key, by having a stop, or some mark whereby to limit or determine the length of its push against the said levers, sliders, &c. puts a period to each of their motions. **1845** G. DODD *Brit. Manuf.* IV. 203 The plank or piece of wood, while being planed, is kept firmly down upon the bench by means of a stop or fastening at the end. **1857** W. COLLINS *Dead Secret* IV. i, [He] touched the stop of the musical box so that it might cease playing when it came to the end of the air. **1870** TYNDALL *Heat* i. §6. 5 The current generated would dash the needle violently against its stops and probably derange its magnetism. **1897** *Encycl. Sport* I. 342/1 (Driving), *Stops*, hooks upon the shafts which prevent the harness from slipping forward. **1897** *Allbutt's Syst. Med.* II. 229 Stops should be fixed in the sash-grooves, so that neither sash can be opened more than six inches. **1901** *J. Black's Carp. & Build., Home Handicr.* 24 A bench iron or 'stop' should be screwed down on forward end of bench for holding work during planing.

b. *Joinery.* Each of the pieces of wood nailed on the frame of a door to form a rebate against which the door shuts.

1833 LOUDON *Encycl. Archit.* §239 Stops (a term variously applied, but chiefly to slips nailed on for doors or shutters to shut against). **1881** YOUNG *Every Man his own Mechanic* §836 The door must then be removed, and stops..nailed to the sides of the jambs and the under surface of the lintel.

†**c.** *Watchmaking.* ? A mark on the dial of a stop-watch indicating a fraction of a second. *Obs.*

1701 *Lond. Gaz.* No. 3692/4 Lost.., a Watch with a double Case.., with Minutes, Seconds, and Stops.

d. *Clockwork.* A contrivance to prevent overwinding.

1675 J. S[MITH] *Horolog. Dial.* 38 You must first wind it [a watch] up right..not too hastily, least you force the stop, and break the string. **1873** NELTHROPP *Watch-work* 145 Foreign watches are usually made without the fusee..; when such is the case, a Geneva stop is used, which consists of a small wheel placed on the barrel-arbor, having but one tooth. **1875** KNIGHT *Dict. Mech.* s.v. *Stop-work*, It is better to so organize the stop that the strongest and weakest powers of the spring be rejected.

e. *Bookbinding.* (See quot.)

1880 ZAEHNSDORF *Art of Bookbinding* 177 *Stops*, small circular tools, adapted to 'stop' a fillet when it intersects at right angles; used to save the time 'mitreing' would occupy.

f. *Lace-making.* A junction of the different sets of warp-threads, taken as a basis for measurement in Jacquard weaving.

1891 *Century Dict.*

10. *Naut.* **a.** A piece of small line used to fasten or secure anything.

1846 A. YOUNG *Naut. Dict.* 323 *Stop*, a temporary fastening for a rope; generally of rope-yarn... A Stop, also means a projection for anything to rest or bear upon. **1875** BEDFORD *Sailor's Pocket Bk.* vii. 216 When the boat is beached, the stops which hang the gangboards alongside are to be let go. **1887** *Daily Tel.* 10 Sept. 2/5 The jib..had been sent up in stops.

b. A projection at the upper part of a mast.

1846 [see a]. **1867** SMYTH *Sailor's Word-bk.*, *Stop*, a small projection on the outside of the cheeks of a lower mast, at the upper parts of the hounds.

c. *Shipbuilding.* (See quot.)

1891 *Century Dict.* s.v., *Single stop*, the scoring down of the carlines between the beams, by which means a carline is prevented from sinking any lower than its intended position. The double stop is generally used for deeper carlines than the single stop.

11. *Arch.* An ornamental termination to a chamfer.

1825 J. NICHOLSON *Operat. Mech.* 604 In grooving, the stops are paid over and above. **1845** *Builder* 15 Nov. 551/1 Figures 1, 2, 3, and 4,..shew Norman stops to chamfers, in Sherburn church, Yorkshire.

12. *Optics.* A perforated plate or diaphragm used to cut off marginal rays of light round a lens. Cf. DIAPHRAGM *sb.* 4 a. Also in *Photogr.*, a diaphragm or (orig.) a perforated plate for reducing the effective diameter of the lens of a camera or enlarger (now usu. built into the apparatus); hence used as a unit of change of relative aperture (or exposure or film speed), a reduction of one stop being equivalent to a halving of any of these.

1831 BREWSTER *Optics* xliii. 361 The stop or diaphragm must be placed half way between the two lenses. **1858** SUTTON & WORDEN *Dict. Photogr.* 255 The principle of this form of lens will be best understood by discussing, in the first place, the case of a single plano-convex lens, with a stop in front. **1883** *Photogr. Simplified* 23 Always focus with the largest stop, so as to get as much light as possible, and afterwards insert a stop which gives the necessary sharpness. **1888** RUTLEY *Rock-Forming Min.* 28 The eye-piece must of course be provided with a stop. **1902** G. B. SHAW *Let.* 11 Aug. (1972) II. 282 A slow plate and a suitably small stop will prolong the exposure sufficiently to make it manageable by hand with a cap. **1955** MORGAN & LESTER *Leica Man.* (ed. 13) ii. 75 With lenses of short focal length, the addition of 62·5mm extension results in the true aperture being nearly 2 stops smaller than the marked f-numbers. **1961** G. MILLERSON *Telev. Production* iii. 36 Lens diaphragms are graduated in units called stops or f-numbers. **1977** H. INNES *Big Footprints* II. iii. 179 The light's going to be tricky... It'll soon be dusk. If I were you I'd open up a stop. **1979** *Amat. Photographer* 10 Jan. 90/1 The extra two stops of film speed obtained by raising 400ASA to 1600 are invaluable under such conditions.

13. Something that stops an aperture; a plug.

1770 *Phil. Trans.* LX. 317 The stop of cotton must now be taken out of the throat. **1862** *Catal. Internat. Exhib.* II. x. 18 Patent india-rubber stops to make air-tight joints.

III. *Music.*

14. a. In an organ, a graduated set of pipes producing tones of the same quality. ? Orig. applied to the slider which controls such a set.

c **1500** in Grose *Antiq. Repert.* (1809) IV. 407 The swete Organe Pipis comfortith a stedfast mynde, Wronge handlynge of the stoppis may cause yem sipher fro ye kynde. **1513** in Kerry *Hist. St. Lawrence's, Reading* (1883) 60 It. payd for ij lokks to the same organs, one for the stopps and the other for the keyes, xj d. **1541** *Ludlow Churchw. Acc.* (Camden) 8 For mendynge one of the stoppes of the great organs..viij d. **1542** in *Archæol. Jrnl.* XVIII. 139 Item oone peir of doble Regalles with two stoppes of pipes coverid with purple vellat. **1667** MILTON *P.L.* VII. 596 All Organs of sweet stop. **1782** W. HOOPER *Rational Recr.* (ed. 2) II. 237 The stops of an organ have various denominations, according to the sounds they are to produce; some of which are diapason, principal, fifteen, twelfth, [etc.]. **1804** GRAHAME *Sabbath* 71 The organ breathes its distant thunder-notes,..And now the tubes a soften'd stop controls. **1887** RUSKIN *Præterita* II. 9 Accompanying flourishes by Mr. Marshall on the trumpet stop.

b. The handle or knob by which a set of organ pipes is turned on or off; a stop-knob, draw-stop.

1585 HIGINS *Junius' Nomencl.* 354/2 *Epistomium*,..the stop in a paire of organs, whereby the sound is made hie or lowe. **1852** SEIDEL *Organ* 35 On both sides of the manual.. there is a number of handles or buttons..called stops. **1883** *Grove's Dict. Mus.* III. 718/2 *Stops.* This word is used in two senses—for the handles or draw-stops which are placed near the organ-player, and by which he can shut off or draw on the various registers; and for the registers themselves.

c. In the harpsichord, a handle controlling a lever by which the position of a jack could be varied so as to modify the tone produced.

1730 in *Abridgm. Specif. Patents, Music* (1871) 1 It will keep much longer in tune than any harpsichords that have octave stops. **1879** *Grove's Dict. Mus.* I. 689/2 He [Hans Ruckers] contrived, after the example of the organ, a second keyboard, and stops to be moved by the hand, for the control of the registers or slides of jacks acting upon the strings.

15. a. The closing of a finger-hole or ventage in the tube of a wind instrument so as to alter the pitch; a metal key used for this purpose. Also, the hole or aperture thus closed.

c **1500** in Grose *Antiq. Repert.* (1809) IV. 407 The Recorder of his kynde the meane doth desyre, Manyfolde fyngerynge and stoppes bringith hy from his tunes clere, Who so lyst to handill an instrument so goode, Must se in his many fyngerynge yt he kepe tyme, stop and moode. **1579** GOSSON *Apol. Sch. Abuse* (Arb.) 68 God forbidde, quoth the piper, that your misestie should be so miserable, as to knowe these fantastical toyes any better, their effeminate stops are not worth a straw. **1597** SHAKS. *2 Hen. IV* Ind. 17 Rumour is a Pipe..of so easie, and so plaine a stop, That..The still discordant, wauering Multitude, Can play vpon it. **1630** DRAYTON *Muses Eliz., Nimph.* iii. 413 Teaching euery stop and kaye, To those vpon the Pipe that playe. **1637** MILTON *Lycidas* 188 He touch'd the tender stops of various Quills. **1705** ADDISON *Italy, Rome* 322 The same Variety of Strings may be observ'd on their Harps, and of Stops on their Tibiæ. **1846** LANDOR *Hellenics, Theron & Zoe* 61 The sobs that choakt my flute, the humidity..that gargled on the stops. **1913** SIR H. JOHNSTON *Pioneers Australasia* vi. 205 The flutes upon which the people [of Tahiti] played had only two stops.

b. The act of pressing with the finger on a string of the violin, lute, etc., so as to raise the pitch of its tone. Also, the part of the string where pressure is made in order to produce a required note; sometimes mechanically marked, as by the frets of a lute or guitar. ***full stop***, a chord in producing which all the strings are stopped.

1530 PALSGR. 276/2 Stoppe of a lute. **1574** F. KE tr. *A. Le Roy's Instruct. Lute* 6 There bee ordinarily eight stops in nomber: whereof euery one containeth but halfe a tune or note. **1599** SHAKS. *Much Ado* III. ii. 62 His iesting spirit, which is now crept into a lute-string, and now gouern'd by stops. **1610** DOWLAND *Var. Lute-lessons* C 1 b *marg.*, To know how to strike single strings, being found amongst full stops. **1626** BACON *Sylva* §105 If a Man would endeuour to raise or fall his Voice, still by Halfe-Notes, like the Stops of a Lute. **1659** C. SIMPSON *Division-Violist* I. 6 Where the Stopps are Wide (as amongst the Fretts,) the Fourth or Little Finger, is of more use, then Lower down, where the Stopps are more Contract. **1678** DURFEY *Trick for Trick* IV. ii. 40 Hee'l Fiddle and make a noise, but the Devil a stop he knowes, or when he fiddles in Tune. **1876** STAINER & BARRETT *Dict. Mus. Terms, Stop* (1) the pressure by the nngers of the strings upon the fingerboard of a stringed instrument. (2) A fret upon a guitar or similar instrument.

†**c.** ***to keep stop***, ? to keep in tune or correct pitch. *Obs.*

c **1500**: see a. **1585** HIGINS *Junius' Nomencl.* 354/1 *Modos concidere & frangere*,..to breake time: not to keepe stop, or to fall from the higher tunes to the lower.

16. *fig.* or *transf.* Now chiefly with reference to the organ; in the earlier quots. app. sometimes vaguely used for 'note', 'key', 'tune'. In modern use freq. in phrase ***to pull out all the stops***, to make every possible effort.

1576 GASCOIGNE *Steele Gl.* (Arb.) 59 But sweeter soundes, of concorde, peace, and loue, Are out of tune, and iarre in euery stoppe. **1605** *1st Pt. Jeronimo* II. iv. 35 Haue euery sillable a musick stop, That, when I pause, the mellody may moue [etc.]. **1684** ROSCOMMON *Ess. Transl. Verse* 349 A skilful Ear in Numbers shou'd preside, And all Disputes without Appeal decide. This ancient Rome and Elder Athens found, Before mistaken stops debauch'd the sound. **1821** SHELLEY *Epipsych.* 85 Sweet as stops Of planetary music heard in trance. **1850** S. DOBELL *Roman* vii. Poet. Wks. (1875) 138 Fortune..Play'd a flourish ere she changed her awful stop for evermore. **1865** M. ARNOLD *Ess. Crit.* Pref. p. xiv, Knowing how unpopular a task one is undertaking when one tries to pull out a few more stops in that..somewhat narrow-toned organ, the modern Englishman. **1927** *Oxford Mag.* 20 Oct. 3/2 He may be said to have 'pulled out all his stops'. He gave the University a speech which for ease, eloquence and felicity could not readily be surpassed or indeed equalled. **1955** A. L. ROWSE *Expansion of Elizabethan England* 123 As his rebellion progressed Tyrone had to pull out the Catholic stop. **1957** *Economist* 5 Oct. 20/2 A Russian admiral on a good will naval visit to the Syrian port of Lattakia was serenading nationalism with all the right stops out. **1965** MRS. L. B. JOHNSON *White House Diary* 20 Dec. (1970) 341 This evening we gave a State Dinner... We opened up all the stops and the Christmas carols rang forth. **1974** A. PRICE *Other Paths to Glory* I. vi. 77 'But they have no idea who did it?' 'Not from what I heard... I know they're pulling out all the stops, though.' **1978** P. MCCUTCHAN *Blackmail North* ii. 20 We'll be doing our best, all stops out.

IV. *Grammar.*

17. a. A mark or point of punctuation.

[**1590**: see 21.] **1616** T. SCOT *Philomythie* G 3 b, Thy folly was in fault rashly to draw, Thy articles without aduise at law. There wanted stops, pricks, letters, here and there. **1623** MIDDLETON *More Dissemblers* III. ii. 77, I can write fast and fair, Most true orthography, and observe my stops. **1740** CHESTERF. *Lett.* I. lxi. 173, I hope too that he makes you read aloud, distinctly, and observe the stops. **1802** MAR. EDGEWORTH *Moral T., Forester* xv, The corrector of the press scarcely had occasion to alter a word, a letter, or a stop. **1862** CALVERLEY *Verses & Transl.* (ed. 2) 38 Who..talked in such a hurry And with such wild contempt for stops and Lindley Murray. **1906** H. W. & F. G. FOWLER *King's Engl.* iv. 225 It is a sound principle that as few stops should be used as will do the work.

b. ***mind your stops***: *lit.* said to a child reading aloud; in quot. *transf.* (colloq.).

1830 MARRYAT *King's Own* xx, Mind your stops, my Jack of the Bone-house, or I shall shy a biscuit at your head.

c. *Versification.* In Guest's nomenclature, a break (in verse as spoken or read aloud) which is required by the sense: distinguished from *pause*, which denotes a break required by the metre.

1838 GUEST *Engl. Rhythms* I. I. vii. 148, 154, 158. **1852** R. W. EVANS *Versif.* 59 Whenever he [*sc.* Virgil] adds a stop to the pause, he is wont to break its force by putting a monosyllable after it.

d. *Cryptography.* A character representing a punctuation mark.

1915 [see NULL *sb.*[1] b]. **1939** F. PRATT *Secret & Urgent* 18 *Stops* are punctuation marks, usually sentence endings, for which special characters are provided, sometimes placed after each word.

e. Short for *full stop*: (*a*) as used, spelt out, in a telegram; (*b*) = PERIOD *sb.* 11 b.

1936 [see LITERARY *a.* 3 b]. **1964** F. CHICHESTER *Lonely Sea & Sky* xxxii. 333 Another exciting telegram..which read, 'Delighted to see that you have achieved your ambition to beat your own record Stop.' **1977** *Times* 7 Oct. 15/5 Sir, Almost all who write you on this subject assume that high productivity is desirable, stop.

18. full stop. a. The end of a sentence; the single point or dot used to mark this; a period, full point.

1596 SHAKS. *Merch. V.* III. i. 17 *Sal.* Come, the full stop. **1665** HOOKE *Microgr.* 3 A point commonly so call'd, that is, the mark of a full stop, or period. **1729** S. PALMER *Gen. Hist. Printing* I. 93 Their periods are distinguished by no other points than the double and single one, i.e., the colon and full stop. **1748** J. MASON *Ess. Elocution* 24 You are not to fetch your Breath (if it can be avoided) till you come to the Period or Full stop. **1886** *Athenæum* 30 Oct. 559/3 In spite of much use and abuse of full stops, the writer's meaning is often far from clear.

b. *transf.* and *fig.* in various senses, e.g. a complete halt, check, stoppage, or termination; an entire nonplus. Also = PERIOD *sb.* 11 b.

1628 EARLE *Microcosm., Sergeant* (Arb.) 57 He is the Period of young Gentlemen, or their full stop, for when hee meets with them they can go no farther. **1655** FULLER *Ornithol.* (1867) 258 She therefore that hath not the modesty to die the Relict of one man, will charge through the whole Army of Husbands, if occasion were offered, before her love will meet with a full stop thereof. **1711** BUDGELL *Spect.* No. 77 ¶1 After we had walked some time, I made a full stop with my Face towards the West. **1719** W. WOOD *Surv. Trade* 233 All Persons depending on the Turkey Trade, were at a full Stop for many Months. ? **1727** SWIFT *Gulliver, Introd. Let. fr. Capt. Gulliver*, Seeing a full stop put to all abuses and corruptions, at least in this little island. **1798** FERRIAR *Engl. Historians* 237 The story thus comes unexpectedly to a full stop. **1815** SCOTT *Guy M.* xlvii, He drew up his reins.., and made a full stop. **1861** GEO. ELIOT *Let.* 6 Oct. (1954) III. 456 There is a point of disgust.. which one feels must make a full stop, and call for a *Finis* in friendship. **1923** P. SELVER tr. *Capek's R.U.R.* I. 10 It was in the year 1920 that old Rossum the great physiologist, who was then quite a young scientist, betook himself to this distant island for the purpose of studying the ocean fauna, full stop. **1962** *Observer* 1 July 8/5 The controversy has been between those who say yes, full stop, and those who say yes, but... **1971** R. AMBERLEY *Ordinary Accident* x. 92 Once he sends for a lawyer then that will be full stop.

19. *Phonetics.* **a.** The complete closure of the orinasal passages in articulating a mute consonant. **b.** A consonantal sound in the formation of which the passage of the breath is completely obstructed; a stopped consonant, a mute.

1669 HOLDER *Elem. Speech* 11 The Letters, as they have their natural Production by the several checks or stops, or (as they are usually called) Articulations of the Breath or Voice in their passage from the Larynx through the Mouth or Nose, made by the instruments of Speech. **1873–4** H. SWEET in *Trans. Philol. Soc.* 106 A peculiar feature of Danish is its aspiration of the voiceless stops at the beginning of a syllable.

V. Miscellaneous specific and technical senses (some of mixed or uncertain affinity).

20. *Fencing.* (See quot.) Cf. *stop-thrust* in 30, and F. *coup d'arrêt.*

c **1450** *Fencing with Two-handed Sword* in *Reliq. Antiq.* I. 308 An in stop, and an owte stop, and an hawke quartere. *Ibid.*, Two quarters and a rownde a stop thou hym bede. *Ibid.* 309 Thy stoppis, thy foynys, lete hem fast rowte. **1771** LONNERGAN *Fencer's Guide* 82 On Guard in Quarte-over-the-arm. Make a full thrust at me in Quarte [etc.]..; thus you stop me. Note, that you must conserve a little of your whole longe, that your stop may be planted with more force. **1891** *Century Dict., Stop*..17. In *fencing*, the action whereby a fencer, instead of parrying a blow and then thrusting, allows a careless opponent to run on his sword-point. He may hasten the stop by extending the sword-arm.

21. †**a.** In the manège: A sudden check in a horse's career. *Obs.* **b.** In driving: (see quot. 1897).

? **1575** BLUNDEVIL *Art of Riding* II. i. D vj, Secondly, you must teach him to be light at stoppe. **1590** SHAKS. *Mids. N.* v. i. 120 He hath rid his Prologue, like a rough Colt: he knowes not the stop. **1597** —— *Lover's Compl.* 109 What rounds, what bounds, what course, what stop he makes! **1598** FLORIO, *Parare*,..the stop in the action of horsemanship. **1897** *Outing* XXX. 255 Whenever a sharp turn is being made always be prepared to put on the 'stop'. *Ibid.*, Lift your left hand, drop your right over all reins and give the 'stop' firmly.

†**22.** *Hunting.* ? A check given to the hounds. ***to hunt upon the stop***, ? to hunt with frequent pauses, as in hunting with stop-hounds; in quot. *fig.*

1590 COCKAINE *Treat. Hunting* B iv b, At euery ouer putting off the hounds, or small stop, euery huntsman that hath a horne ought to begin his rechate. **1615** S. WARD *Coal fr. Altar* 78 If any step a little forward, do not the rest hunt vpon the stop?

23. a. *Pugilism.* A guard or attack that prevents a blow from getting home.

1812 *Sporting Mag.* XL. 66 Maltby, however, has some slight notion of the stop. **1828** EGAN *Boxiana* IV. 154 Abbot showed that he was not destitute of science, and made some good stops. **1861** LEVER *One of them* ix, The stranger not only 'stopped' every blow of the other, but followed each 'stop' by a well-sent-in one of his own.

b. *Wrestling.* A counter to any particular fall or hold.

1840 D. WALKER *Defensive Exerc.* 12 Particular falls and their stops.

24. A hole in the ground in which the doe-rabbit secures her litter. Cf. STAB *sb.*[3] and STOCK *sb.*[1] 45.

1669 WORLIDGE *Syst. Agric.* (1681) 174 On the other side ..let the places be left for the Does to make their stops in. **1823** COBBETT *Rur. Rides* (1885) I. 357 As pleased as..when I had just found a rabbit's stop, or a black-bird's nest. **1908** *Nation* 6 June 340/2 An occasional rabbit stop opened from above and emptied of its young.

25. *Fox-hunting.* A particular area in which a man is deputed to stop the earths.

1826 J. COOK *Fox-hunting* 65 If, after this notice, you run to ground in any particular man's stop, you had better discharge him [the earth-stopper] immediately.

26. *Shooting.* A person posted in a particular place in order to keep the game within range after it has been started.

1897 *Encycl. Sport* I. 442/2 (Gamekeepers), The stops must be in their places long before the actual beating begins. **1905** GLASFURD *Rifle in Ind. Jungle* 332 The tiger has not been in any way located by any 'stops' which the *shikári* may have posted.

27. a. The indentation in the face of a dog between the forehead and the nose.

1867 *Dogs Brit. Isl.* (ed. 'Stonehenge') 70 The 'stop' (which is an indentation between the eyes) should extend up the face [of the bulldog] a considerable length. **1884** *Live Stock Jrnl.* 5 Sept. 227/2 Bull-dogs:..a nice brindle, hardly enough chop, but good stop and wrinkle.

b. In a cavy (see quot. 1913).

1902 *Fur & Feather* 19 Sept. 233/1 Capital stops, nice cheeks, good top collar. *Ibid.*, Only 1 stop, this about its only fault. **1913** G. GARDNER *Cumberland's Cavies* (ed. 2) 75 [In Dutch-marked cavies] The 'stops', or white markings, to the hind feet, should be about an inch long.

28. *Card-playing.* In Pope Joan and similar games, a card which stops the run of a sequence. Hence *pl.*, the game of Newmarket.

1808 C. JONES *Hoyle's Games Impr.* 161 (Pope Joan) One [card is] turned up for trump, and about six or eight left in the stock to form stops:..the four kings and the seven of diamonds are always fixed stops. **1830** 'E. TREBOR' (R. Hardie) *Hoyle Made Familiar* 81 (Commit.) A spare hand is dealt in the middle of the table, for the purpose of making stops in the playing, which is by sequences. **1886** W. B. DICK *Mod. Pocket Hoyle* (ed. 11) 343 Newmarket, or Stops. This game is played in a similar manner to the game of 'Boodle'. **1895** G. J. MANSON *Sporting Dict., Stop*, a card in Newmarket which balks or stops the further play in a sequence. **1897** R. F. FOSTER *Compl. Hoyle* 466 Newmarket, or Stops.

†**29.** *Cricket.* A fielder standing three or four yards behind the wicket, a little on the off side. *Obs.* Cf. BACK-STOP b, *long-stop* s.v. LONG *a.*[1] 18 d.

1773 in H. T. Waghorn *Cricket Scores, Notes, &c.* (1899) 90 All England. May, Lumpey, bowlers; Minshul, Miller, Parmore (stop). Hampshire. Bret, Nyren, bowlers; Small, Sutton, Lear (stop). **1851** W. CLARKE in W. Bolland *Cricket Notes* 129 In laying out your field, you should be careful in selecting good men for your principal places, such as wicket keeper, point, stop, short slip.

VI. 30. Comb.: **stop band** *Electronics*, a band of frequencies which are highly attenuated by a filter; **stop bath** *Photogr.*, a bath for arresting the process of the preceding bath, esp. development, by neutralizing any of its chemical that may still be present; **stop bead** [BEAD *sb.* 6 b] (see quot. 1964); **stop-block**, †(*a*) a block of wood indicating the position of a fire-cock; (*b*) a buffer at the termination of a railway-line; **stop-boy**, a boy employed to keep the game within range (see 26); **stop-buffer** = *stop-block* (*b*); **stop-butt**, a slope or bank constructed behind the targets at a rifle range to stop bullets; **stop button**, a button or switch which is pressed or pulled to stop the action of a machine; †**stop cater trey**, some kind of false dice (cf. *stop-dice*); **stop chords** *Jazz*, chords played on the first beat of every bar or every other bar, as the only accompaniment to a solo; **stop chorus** *Jazz*, a solo accompanied by stop chords; **stop-cleat** *Naut.* (see CLEAT *sb.* 2); **stop-clock** (cf. STOP-WATCH *sb.*); **stop-cloth**, a cloth used in cleaning a chimney to prevent the soot from spreading into the room; **stop-coin** = *stop-quoin*; **stop consonant** = sense 19 b; **stop-cylinder**, a printing press in which the cylinder is stopped to permit the return of the reciprocating carriage; **stop-day**, a day on which colliers stop work; †**stop-dice**, some kind of false or loaded dice; cf. *stopped dice*, STOPPED *ppl. a.* 4; **stop-dog** = *stop-hound*; **stop-drill**, a drill with a shoulder or collar to limit the depth of penetration; **stop-finger**, a device for arresting motion in machinery; †**stop-galliard**, ? a galliard in which the music and dancing were abruptly broken off; **stop-gate**, (*a*) a gate placed across a railway; (*b*) a gate by which the water in one section of a canal can be shut off from the next in case of damage to the bank; (*c*) a stop-valve; **stop-ground** = GROUND *sb.* 6 d; **stop-handle** = *stop-knob*; **stop-hound**, a hound trained to hunt slowly and to stop at a signal from the huntsman; **stop-knob**, the handle which is pulled out to open a particular stop in an organ; **stop lamp**, a light on the rear of a motor vehicle, which is automatically illuminated when the brakes are applied; **stop light**, (*a*) = *stop lamp* above; (*b*) *N. Amer.* = *stop sign* below, also *fig.*; **stop list**, (*a*) a list of persons, etc., deprived of particular rights, privileges, or services; *spec.* a list of persons with whom members of an association are forbidden to do business; (*b*) a list of prohibited books; (*c*) a list of words to be omitted from a concordance or index; hence **stop-list** *v. trans.*, to include in a stop list; **stop log**, a log or plank, or a beam or plate of concrete or steel, fitting between vertical grooves in walls or piers to close a water channel; **stop-mount** = sense 12; **stop-net**, (*a*) a net thrown across a river or tidal channel to intercept fish; (*b*) a net to stop the ball, in various games; **stop-netting** = *stop-net* (*b*); **stop-order**, (*a*) an order issued by the Court of Chancery to stay payment of funds in the custody of the Court; (*b*) an order directing a broker to buy or sell stock at a specified price, in order to limit loss; **stop-piece, -pin**, a piece or pin serving to arrest some moving part; **stop-plank** (see quot.); **stop-plate**, (*a*) in a lock (see quot. 1837); (*b*) in a journal-box (see quot. 1884); **stop-quoin, -coin**, a quoin used for keeping a gun steady; †**stop-rice** *Mining* [perh. to STOPE *sb.*[2]], ? wood for making stop-rods; **stop-ridge** *Archæol.*, a ridge on a celt, pipe, etc. which prevents one part from slipping too far over another; **stop-rod,** (*a*) *Mining* [? to STOPE *sb.*[2]], in *pl.*, the wattling of the shafts of a mine; (*b*) *Weaving*, a rod which forms part of the mechanism for stopping the motion of the loom; †**stop-screw,** a screw which clamps a movable part when it is required to be fixed; **stop-seine** *Fisheries* (see quot. 1884); **stop sign,** a sign indicating that traffic should stop; *N. Amer.* spec., a red traffic-light; **stop signal,** a signal indicating whether a train should stop; **stop-stroke** *Croquet*, a stroke which drives a croqueted ball to a distance, while leaving the striker's ball more or less stationary; **stop-tap** = STOPCOCK; **stop-thrust** *Fencing*, a thrust delivered at the opponent at the moment when he advances for attack (cf. 20); **stop time** *Jazz*, a stop chorus or a series of stop chords; **stop-valve,** a valve which closes a pipe against the passage of fluid; **stop volley** *Lawn Tennis* (see quot. 1928); **stopway,** an area at the end of an airfield runway in which an aircraft can be stopped after an interrupted take-off; **stop-wither** *Whaling* (see quot.); **stop-wool** *Hatmaking* (see quot.); **stop word,** a word (usu. one of a set of the words most frequently occurring in a language or text) that is automatically omitted from or treated less fully in a computer-generated concordance or index; **stop-work,** a mechanism to prevent the overwinding of the spring of a watch, etc.

1922 *Stop band [see *passband* s.v. PASS *sb.*[2] 18b]. **1959** KUH & PEDERSON *Princ. Circuit Synthesis* xiii. 200 The frequency where the pass- and stopbands coalesce is called the cutoff frequency. **1978** *Internat. Jrnl. Electronics* XLV. 247 Filters are designed with various frequency characteristics for the pass band and the stop band and also with predefined zeros in the stop band. **1898** H. MACLEAN *Pop. Photographic Printing Processes* iv. 42 To counteract some more or less over-toning..what is termed a '*stop' bath is used. **1967** E. CHAMBERS *Photolitho-Offset* v. 58 The required number of contacts are made on lith type plates, developed, passed into the stop-bath and etch-bleached in the usual manner. **1980** D. FRANCIS *Reflex* xiii. 151, I set out the trays of developer and stop bath and fixer. **1876** *Encycl. Brit.* IV. 496/1 An inner or *stop bead is mitred round on the inside to complete the groove or channel for the lower sash. **1964** J. S. SCOTT *Dict. Building* 155 *Stop bead*, a bead mitred round the inner edge of a sash window to prevent the inner sash from swinging into the room. **1976** R. DAY *All about House Repair & Maintenance* 62 Broken sash cords are easily removed... First remove the stop bead on the inside. **1707** *Act 6 Anne* c. 31 §1 The Top of such *Stop-blocks to lie even with the Pavement of each Street or Place. **1853** *Repts. Principal Accid. Railways* 233 A short siding with strong stop blocks at the end. **1902** *Land & Water* 25 Oct. 616/3 *Stop boys should not make such a noise or be placed in such a position as to frighten the birds into breaking at the wrong place. **1881** M. REYNOLDS *Engine-driving Life* 69, I was once in a train which the driver could not stop, and we went right into the *stop-buffers. **1864** A. WALKER *Rifle* (ed. 2) 114 If at a smaller angle it would, instead of acting as a *stop-butt [etc.]. **1923** KIPLING *Land & Sea Tales* 177 The long shed of the Village Rifle Club reeked with the oniony smell of smokeless powder, machine-oil, and creosote from the stop-butt. **1963** W. H. FULLER *Small-Bore Target Shooting* i. 25 Stop butt or bullet catchers. **1940** N. MARSH *Surfeit of Lampreys* (1941) xiv. 209 When we'd got about half-way d-down she started screaming... I shoved down the *stop button. So we stopped... Just below the first floor. **1977** J. WAINWRIGHT *Day of Peppercorn Kill* 120 He glanced at the tape-recorder, pressed the 'stop' button and said, 'We need a new reel.' **1605** *Lond. Prodigal* I. i, Fullomes, *stop cater traies, and other bones of function. **1606** CHAPMAN *M. D'Olive* IV. i. F 3, I haue learned but three sorts [of pronounds]; the Goade, the Fulham, and the Stop-kater-tre; which are all demonstratiues. **1941** *Musical Q.* Jan. 52 The second chorus is played with great feeling by the clarinet to a background of '*stop chords', a very effective device of the New Orleans style. **1958** R. HARRIS in P. Gammond *Decca Bk. of Jazz* iii. 45 *Dipper Mouth* with a hot theme stated by the ensemble; a superb Dodds solo against stop chords; [etc.]. **1942** BERREY & VAN DEN BARK *Amer. Thes. Slang* §578/10 *Stop chorus, a chorus in which the orchestra plays only one note in every one or two measures as a background for a tap dancer or other soloist. **1968** P. OLIVER *Screening Blues* ii. 67 The singer 'reading on down' to each new chapter [in sermon-like recitations] against the stop chorus of the pianist or a full jazz band. **1794** *Stop-cleats: see CLEAT *sb.* 2. **1869** SIR E. REED *Shipbuild.* xiii. 250 Upon the upper and lower stays Stop-cleats are riveted and serve to prevent the rudder from being put over past a certain angle. **1881** *Times* 15 Jan. 5/6 The time being taken by a *stop-clock. *c* **1742** in *Hone's Everyday Bk.* II. 526 [The coffin] is covered with a Chimney-sweeper's *Stop-cloth. **1975** *Stop consonant [see PRESSURIZATION]. **1978** *Maledicta* II. 111 Rising tones in Thai do not co-occur in syllables ending in a stop consonant. *a* **1877** KNIGHT *Dict. Mech.* I. 671/2 The *stop-cylinder press, designed for woodcut printing. **1980** B. CRUTCHLEY *To be Printer* ii. 21 'And what do you know about printing?' I was about to reply..: 'Well, I can tell the difference between a two-rev and stop-cylinder,' (those were basic types of printing machine). **1879** CROSBY *Chr. Preacher* vii. 191 The Sabbath is a *stop-day. **1900** *Westm. Gaz.* 4 Dec. 5/2 It is believed that another stop day will shortly be observed by the colliers of South Wales with a view to restricting the output of coal. **1540** PALSGR. *Acolastus* IV. ii. S iv, Dyce of aduantage, or false dyce, or *stoppe dyce. **1592** GREENE *Def. Conny Catching* To Rdr., Gourds, stoppe-dice, high-men, low-men. *c* **1767** G. WHITE *Selborne, To Pennant* vi, They gave him [the deer], by their watches, law, as they called it, for twenty minutes; when, sounding their horns, the *stop-dogs were permitted to pursue. **1843** HOLTZAPFFEL *Turning* I. 342 This is frequently regulated by boring holes..with a *stop-drill. **1875** KNIGHT *Dict. Mech.*, *Stop-finger, a device in a silk-doubling machine for stopping the motion of the bobbin if the thread break. **1884** F. J. BRITTEN *Watch & Clockm.* 248 The chain would raise the end of the stop finger. **1594** PLAT *Jewell-ho.* II. 39 Mee-thinks I am now in the midst of a *stop galiard, &..coulde finde in my hearte to commaunde the Violands to cease, and so to breake off. **1790** *Act 30 Geo. III*, c. 82 §58 The Person or Persons making every such Cut shall ..make, erect, and maintain a *Stop Gate or Stop Gates on every such Cut, in order to prevent the Water being drained ..out of the said Canal. **1793** *Act 33 Geo. III*, c. 95 §40 Every Horse..which shall..travel upon any such Rail or Waggon Way,..and shall pass through or by any Stop Gate ..erected upon or across the same. **1872** D. STEVENSON *Canal & River Engin.* (ed. 2) 16 It is necessary to introduce stop-gates at short intervals of a few miles,..so that in the event of a breach occurring, the gates may be shut, [etc.]. **1898** *Daily News* 14 Dec. 6/3 An engine,..over-running the stopgate, ran down an incline at a great rate. **1902** *Science* 10 Jan. 66 (Cent.) The closing of the stop-gate [= valve] is instantaneous. *a* **1819** REES *Cycl.* s.v. *Etching*, This varnish or composition (which is called **stop-ground*) being sufficiently dry, the aquafortis may be poured on the plate. **1858** J. BARON *Scudamore Organs* 19 They had no notion how the sound was..modified, beyond knowing that.. certain *stop handles [must be] pulled out or pushed in during the playing of the instrument. **1711** BUDGELL *Spect.* No. 116 ¶3 Sir Roger, being at present too old for Fox-hunting,..has disposed of his Beagles and got a Pack of *Stop-Hounds. **1781** P. BECKFORD *Th. Hunting* (1802) 261 Were fox-hounds to stop, like stop-hounds, at the smack of a whip, they would not do their business the worse for it. **1887** W. S. PRATT in W. Gladden *Parish Problems* 435 The notion that his organ consists merely of a set of keys and *stop-knobs. **1959** *Motor Man.* (ed. 36) viii. 217 Sidelamps, headlamps, rear lamps and *stop lamps should also be examined for bulb failure. **1979** *Southern Star* (Eire) 29 Sept. 2/6 Defendant was fined £3 for having no stop lamp, £3 for having no rear lamp and £3 for having no number plate lighting. **1930** D. MACKAIL *How Amusing!* 190 His *stop-light flickered almost ceaselessly as he crawled round the square. **1931** O. NASH *Hard Lines* 45 But there is no stoplight For a talkative cosmoplite. **1950** *How to drive Car* (ed. 18) xi. 88 Most cars are now fitted with direction indicators and 'stop' lights. The latter are automatic if properly maintained and come on when the brakes are applied. **1978** *Verbatim* Sept. 7/2 The tremendous role that traffic signals play in our national consciousness (it can be argued that the entire Interstate system was built in order to get around—and under and over—stoplights). **1920** *Daily Tel.* 18 May 16/5 The association published his name on their *stop list, the object of which was to prevent all members of the association having any trade relations with the offending agent. **1949** *Rep. Committee on Resale Price Maintenance* 54 in *Parl. Papers 1948–49* (Cmd. 7696) XX. 383 Only the 'open price-cutter' who advertised that he was committing a breach of the conditions of sale was immediately stop-listed. **1958** *Times* 13 Mar. 11/3 A nation with what is reported to be over 1,000 books on the stop-list had got enough censorship. **1963** *Times* 28 Jan. 9/2 Merseyside was on the original list but within a few months, because of the motor industry's plans and other new projects, was put on the stop-list. Last week it was restored to the active list. **1963** [see *re-list* vb. s.v. RE- 5a]. **1970** *Computers & Humanities* IV. 167 This program segment provides for two stoplists. **1974** *Times* 5 Feb. (Europa Suppl.) p. xiv/5 With credit cards the vendor has to check against the stop list (to check on people who have had their accounts stopped, or cards that have been reported missing). **1975** O. SELA *Bengali Inheritance* xxi. 185, I intend to hold your passport... I'm also putting you on a stop list at Kai Tak [airport]... I don't want you disappearing. **1979** J. E. ROWLEY *Mechanised In-House Information Syst.* I. 74 Words in a title are compared with a stop-list, to suppress the generation of useless index entries. **1930** *Engineering* 6 June 725/3 Each weir is divided into six bays by piers, between which *stop logs can be placed, while for emergency regulation..low level Stoney sluices are provided. **1973** *Detroit Legal News* 30 Aug. 13/2 Two feet of the south stop-log chamber wall at the Fairview Pumping Station was removed and had to be replaced with new reinforced concrete. **1879** *Cassell's Techn. Educ.* IV. 312/2 The paper *stop-mount should be printed in black. **1634–5** *Ir. Act 10 Chas. I*, c. 14 (1678) 426 Setting of *stop-Nets, Still-Nets or standing-Nets fixed upon posts..in the Rivers where the Salmon should passe up from the Sea. **1808** COL. HAWKER *Diary* (1893) I. 8 Went fishing with a casting net and a stop net. **1881** *Cassell's Nat. Hist.* V. 138 The stop-net is then shot out towards the land across the direction in which the fish are moving, so as to intercept them. **1891** GRACE *Cricket* 223 A piece of ground..thirty to forty yards long,..with stop-nets, will serve your purpose [for practice]. **1927** *Stop-netting [see RUN-BACK 2]. **1981** *Sunday Tel.* 4 Oct. 16/3 A badly-flighted lob cleared the stop-netting. **1875** W. ROYLE *Laws Funds* etc. 75 A *Stop Order is a proceeding merely applicable to funds in the Court of Chancery. **1840** in *Newton's Lond. Jrnl.* Conj. Ser. XVI. 326 One of the ends of the locking lever..is brought by the force of the main spring against or into coincidence with a ruby pallat or *stop-piece. **1869** RANKINE *Machine & Hand-tools* Pl. N 1, Two adjustable *stop pins, *i*, are fixed at points corresponding to the period for reversing the motion of the machine. **1840** H. S. TANNER *Canals & Rail Roads U.S.* 260 **Stop planks*, dams on the line of a canal to prevent the loss of water in case of accident. **1837** HEBERT *Engin. & Mech. Encycl.* II. 108 A circular *stop-plate, to prevent the withdrawal of the bolt [of a lock] till the circular plate, which is put in rotation by clock-work, shall have revolved so as to bring a notch opposite the end of the bolt. **1884** KNIGHT *Dict. Mech.* Suppl., *Stop Plate*, a metallic plate in the inside of a journal-box which forms an end-bearing for the axle and checks its end-motion. **1859** F. A. GRIFFITHS *Artil. Man.* (1862) 112 *Stop quoins. *c* **1860** H. STUART *Seaman's Catech.* 12 When do you use stop Coins? When fighting lee guns, or with distant charges. **1653** MANLOVE *Customs Lead-Mines* 258 *Stoprice, Yokings, Soletrees, Roach and Ryder. **1747** HOOSON *Miner's Dict.* K 1, Ordinary Timber or Stoprice. **1877, 1894** *Stop-ridge [see PALSTAVE]. **1902** A. J. EVANS in *Ann. Brit. Sch. Athens* 1901–2, 14 The mouthpiece of each tube is provided with a stop-ridge. **1747** HOOSON *Miner's Dict.* s.v. *Brouse*, Brouse [is] a course sort of Stoping,..put into the Pannes, at the Back of the *Stoprods, or Bangrets, in Sinking,..to hold the Geer from falling down. **1680** MOXON *Mech. Exerc.* xiv. 237 The *Stop-screw, to take out when the Hollow Axis moves in the Moving Coller. **1825** *Encycl. Lond.* XX. 435/1 This *stop-sean is left in the water, till, by successive tuckings, night after night, all the fish are taken therefrom. **1884** DAY *Fishes Gt. Brit.* I. p. c, Common seines or stop-seines are such as are lifted at once with the enclosed fishes into the boat. **1899** BARING-GOULD *Bk. West* II. *Cornw.* xix. 315 The boat.. then shoots this tuck-sean within the stop-sean. **1934** *Amer. Speech* IX. 114/2 Those who drive have to make allowances for *stop streets* and **stop signs*. **1951, 1972** [see RUN *v.* 40d]. **1976** *S. Wales Echo* 27 Nov. 9/3 Pleaded guilty by letter to failing to conform to a stop sign while on his motor-cycle. **1923, 1963** *Stop signal [see HOME B. 2d]. **1868** WHITMORE *Croquet Tactics* 15 The *stop stroke is made as follows. Place the balls in line and touching;..bring the mallet head sharply down on the ball you strike. **1895** *Jrnl. R. Inst. Brit. Architects* 14 Mar. 350 Pipes should be run on inside walls and fitted with several *stop-taps. **1861** G. CHAPMAN *Foil Practice* 20 The Time Thrust is a sudden attack..; it is designated..a *Stop Thrust when it arrests the adversary on his advance. **1889** W. H. POLLOCK etc. *Fencing* (Badm. Libr.) 91 The Stop-thrust (i.e. *Coup d'Arrêt*). **1929** *Musical Q.* XV. 611 As to what possibilities such free-will tricks as the jazz 'break', *stop-time, the harmony chorus, an exaggerated syncopation, etc., hold for the development of musical form beyond jazz itself, he would be bold who would predict. **1966** *New Yorker* 11 June 135 The Onward was playing 'Victory Walk', an engaging stop-time number. **1978** *N.Y. Times* 30 Mar. C16/2 Even in strongly swinging situations, jumping brightly through crisply muted breaks and stop time, the singing flow of Mr. Vaché's playing is never lost. **1829** *Nat. Philos., Hydraulics* ii. 13 (U.K.S.) *K* is the *stop-valve, covering the top of the feed-pipe. **1915** M. E. MCLOUGHLIN *Tennis as I play It* 56 That is when a '*stop-volley' is employed to drop a ball just over the net. **1928** B. NUTHALL *Learning Lawn Tennis* 106 One of the most useful strokes in the game..is what is called the 'stop volley'... It is necessary to be quite close to the net to play it. The racket is just put in the way of the ball, which drops dead on the other side of the net. **1978** *Times* 4 July 19/2 Ground strokes were spiced with many a delicate angled cross-court chip, the stop volley, the lob and smash. **1960** in *Guide to Civil Land Aerodrome Lighting* (*B.S.I.*) 7 **Stopway*, a defined rectangular area at the end of a runway which has been selected or prepared as a suitable area in which aircraft can be stopped after an interrupted take off but which is not suitable for use as part of the runway. **1980** *Observer* 2 Nov. 6/8 A..DC-10 from Delhi ran from the runway on to the stopway, the hard section on either side, which is meant to be firm enough to take the weight of aircraft. **1820** SCORESBY *Acc. Arctic Reg.* II. 224 The little reverse barb, or '*stop wither' as it is called,..prevents the harpoon from being shaken out by the ordinary motions of the whale. **1839** URE *Dict. Arts* 637 Round the edge of the tip or crown [of a silk hat], a quantity of what is called *stop wool is to be attached..which will render the edge soft and elastic. **1969** *Computers & Humanities* III. 135 If *stop words are desired, the user can either specify his own or request a standard list which is encoded within BIBCON. **1979** J. E. ROWLEY *Mechanised In-House Information Syst.* I. 74 The stop-list or stopword list contains words under which entries are not required, such as the, he, is, a and in some circumstances, machine, processing, plant, etc. **1982** *N. & Q.* Oct. 385/1, I understand that a microfiche concordance of the stop words will soon be available. **1869** *Horolog. Jrnl.* 1 Apr. 91/1 Dispensing with *stop works, which..are objectionable when economy is an object.

stop (stɒp), *v.* Pa. t. and pa. pple. **stopped** (stɒpt), †**stopt.** Also 4–6 **stoppe,** 4–7 **stopp,** 4 **stope;** *Sc.* 4, 7 **stope,** (6 **stoip**), 6, 8–9 **stap.** [OE. **stoppian* (only in *forstoppian*, occurring once: see sense 8a and cf. FORSTOP *v.*) corresponding to OLow Frankish (*be*)*stuppôn* to stop (the ears), (M)Du., (M)LG. *stoppen* (whence Icel., Sw. *stoppa*, Da. *stoppe*), WFris. *stopje*, MHG., mod.G. *stopfen*, to plug, stop up; a Com. WGer. adoption of popular L. or Rom. **stuppāre* to stop or stuff with tow or oakum (evidenced by It. *stoppare*, Pr., Sp. *estopar*, OF. *estouper*, mod.F. *étouper*), f. L. *stuppa* tow (It. *stoppa*, Sp. *estopa*, OF. *estoupe*). The sense 'bring or come to a stand' is a specially English development, but in marine and railway use the Eng. word has been widely adopted in other langs., as F. *stopper*, G., Du. *stoppen*, Sw. *stoppa*, Da. *stoppe*.

The AF. *estopper* (latinized *estoppare*), whence ESTOP *v.*, is to be regarded as adopted from the Eng. verb rather than as a variant of OF. *estouper*.]

I. To fill up, plug, close up.

1. *trans.* To close up (an aperture) by stuffing something into it, by building it up, or by placing something before it. **a.** To block up (a way of entrance or exit, an aperture for the passage of light, air, sound, and the like). Also with *up*.

c **1375** *Sc. Leg. Saints* xxiii. (*Seven Sleepers*) 164 þai..of þe cawe þe mouth of stane stopyt wele. *c* **1400** MAUNDEV. (Roxb.) xxix. 132 þe 3ates þat Alysaundre gert stoppe with grete stanes and syment. **1480** *Coventry Leet Bk.* 460 The seid dore owe to be stopped vp. **1600** SHAKS. *A.Y.L.* IV. i. 165 Shut that, and 'twill out at the key-hole: stop that, 'twill flie with the smoake out at the chimney. **1632** LITHGOW *Trav.* x. 457 Stop the holes of the doore with double Matts. **1744** M. BISHOP *Life & Adv.* 22 My Business was to stop the Touchhole, whilst the other spunged it. **1867** SMYTH *Sailor's Word-bk.*, *Stop the Vent*, to close it hermetically by pressing the thumb to it. **1891** RIDER HAGGARD *Nada* xv, The gates [of the kraal] were stopped with thorns.

fig. **1596** SHAKS. *1 Hen. IV*, IV. i. 71 Wee..Must..stop all sight-holes, euery loope, from whence The eye of reason may prie in vpon vs. **1605** —— *Macb.* I. v. 45 Stop vp th' accesse and passage to Remorse, That no compunctious visitings of Nature Shake my fell purpose.

†**b.** To close the mouth of (a pit or hole). *Obs.*

1382 WYCLIF *2 Kings* iii. 19 And alle the wellis of watiris ȝe schuln stoppen. *c* **1425** *Cursor M.* 6726 (Trin.) If any mon makeþ a pit And siþen wol not stoppe hit If ox or asse or oþere beest Falle þerinne [etc.]. *c* **1440** *Promp. Parv.* 477/2 Stoppyn a pytte or an hole, *opilo, obstruo, obturo.*

c. To block the mouth of (an animal's hole or earth); *spec.* in *Foxhunting* (see quots. 1686, 1897). †Also with *up*. Also, to block up the earths in (a particular district).

1530 PALSGR. 736/2, I stoppe a hoole or an yerth of any beest in the ground, *je bouche*... I have stoppyd all the foxys hooles and therefore he can nat scape us. **1576** TURBERV. *Venerie* 192 The Huntsman which would haue good pastime at this vermine, shall do well to stop vp his earthes. **1686** BLOME *Gentl. Recr.* II. 88 Having found a Foxes Earth, about Midnight.. cause all his Holes to be stopt.. except the main Hole or Eye,.. which stop not until about Day-break, for fear of stopping him in. **1781** P. BECKFORD *Th. Hunting* xxiii. 306 [Digging of foxes.] Stop all the holes, lest the fox should bolt out unseen. *Ibid.* 308 [Oxford toast.] Hounds stout, and horses healthy, Earths well stopp'd, and foxes plenty. **1880** 'BROOKSBY' *Hunting Countries* II. 198 For the border meets of either [Hunt] the neighbouring territory is always 'stopped' by the other. **1897** *Encycl. Sport* I. 547/2 (Hunting), It was his [*sc.* the earth-stopper's] duty to proceed to the earths situated in the country which was to be drawn the next day, and carefully to stop them with earth or faggots about the hour of midnight.

d. To close with the finger or with a mechanical substitute (a ventage or finger-hole of a wind-instrument) in order to produce a particular note.

1832 BREWSTER *Nat. Magic* viii. 204 Seven of these regulated the motions of the seven fingers for stopping the holes of the flute.

e. Said of the obstruction: To block, choke up. Also in *passive*, to be choked up *with* (dirt, etc.). Now chiefly with *up*.

1508 DUNBAR *Tua Mariit Wemen* 99 And gory is his tua grym ene.. And gorgeit lyk twa gutaris that wer with glar stoppit. **1576** TURBERV. *Venerie* 193 When your Terriers are out of breath, or that the Belles [on their collars] are stopped and glutted vp with earth. **1606** SHAKS. *Tr. & Cr.* II. i. 87 This Aiax.. Has not so much wit.. As will stop the eye of Helens Needle. **1648** J. BEAUMONT *Psyche* VIII. clxxvi, His mouth the coal-black foam here stoping. **1864** PUSEY *Daniel* 416 Of a well the whole [entrance] was.. covered.. by a stone,.. to keep it.. from being stopped by sand. **1885** *Law Times' Rep.* LII. 723/1 One of the stack pipes was stopped up with leaves and dirt.

†**f.** *intr.* in passive sense: To become choked up. *Obs.*

1576 TURBERV. *Venerie* 194 The Colerake to clense the hole and to keepe it from stopping vp. **1712** J. JAMES tr. *Le Blond's Gardening* 197 Quills which.. have but one Hole for the Water to issue at.. not being so subject to stop, as the flat ones. **1792** *Trans. Soc. Arts* X. 52 Injured.. by a leading land-ditch stopping, which overflowed that part of the field.

†**2.** *absol.* To make a closure or obstruction. *Obs.*

a **1225** *Ancr. R.* 72 Ase ȝe muwen iseon þe water, hwon me punt hit, & stoppeð biuoren wel, so þet hit ne muwe aduneward, þeonne is hit ined aȝein uor to climben upward.

3. *trans.* To make (a way) impassable by blocking up its passage or outlet.

a. To block, choke up (a road, channel, harbour, and the like). Also with *up*.

13.. *K. Alis.* 1224 He stopped [*Laud MS.* forstopped] heore way, y-wis, That ther no myghte, to heore fode, Come to heom no gode. **1375** BARBOUR *Bruce* XVII. 306 The schippis com in sic plente,.. That all the havyn wes stoppit then. **1544** BETHAM *Precepts War* I. lii. D j b, Yf thou wylt stoppe an hauen (my consayle is) to fyll a shyppe full of greate stones, and then to drowne the same shyp, ouerthwarte in the hauen. **1588** T. HUGHES *Misfort. Arthur* III. iii. 10 The mustering traines Stop vp the streetes. **1667** MILTON *P.L.* x. 291 Mountains of Ice, that stop th' imagin'd way Beyond Petsora Eastward. **1790** BEATSON *Nav. & Mil. Mem.* I. 159 The enemy sunk the ship at the mouth of the harbour, which stopped up the channel. **1831** *Society* I. 276 The Countess of Avon's carriage stopping the way. **1848** DICKENS *Dombey* lvii, Warehouses, with waggons at the doors, and busy carmen stopping up the way. **1911** CROCKETT *Smugglers* xix, On the other [side of the hall] was a stand for the bicycle.. which partially stopped the fairway.

fig. **1596** DALRYMPLE tr. *Leslie's Hist. Scot.* I. 344 The Balie had stopet the way of freindschip betueine him and ffrance. **1644** MILTON *Areop.* (Arb.) 48 Evill manners are as perfectly learnt without books a thousand other ways which cannot be stopt. **1882** A. BAIN *James Mill* iii. 88 He had induced Sir Francis Burdett to offer to transfer the interest of £1000,.. but legal difficulties stopped the way.

b. To close (a road) to the public. Also with *up*.

In this sense *to stop up* implies a physical barrier; the simple verb may refer to a mere prohibition of passage.

1423 *Coventry Leet Bk.* 56 The said hyȝe way þat leedyth from Allysley way to Coundull is stoppyd, wher hit owȝte to be open. **1598** STOW *Surv. Lond.* 187 The other end [of the lane] is builded on and stopped vp by the Chamberlaine of London. **1684** BUNYAN *Pilgr.* ii. 65 These ways are since stopt up with Chains, Posts, and a Ditch. **1821** CLARE *Vill. Minstr.* I. 50 Inclosure came, and every path was stopt. **1885** *Law Rep.* 14 *Q.B. Div.* 747 The railway company had.. altered and stopped up a certain road.

c. *to stop one's way*: to stand in one's way, bar one's passage, oppose one. *lit.* and *fig.*

1338 R. BRUNNE *Chron.* (1725) 179 Slayn alle may þou se, þat þi way stopped [AFr. *tes vayes estopaynt*]. **1596** SHAKS. *Tam. Shr.* III. ii. 237 Touch her who euer dare, Ile bring mine action on the proudest he That stops my way in Padua. **1697** DRYDEN *Æneid* II. 918, I went; but sad Creusa stopp'd my way, And cross the Threshold in my Passage lay.

4. a. To fill up, repair, make good (a breach, hole, crevice, or defective place of any kind). Also with *up*. So ***to stop a leak*** (lit. and fig.).

to stop a gap: see GAP *sb.*[1] 1, 2.

1388 WYCLIF *2 Esdras* iv. 7 Whanne Sanaballat hadde herd.. that the brekyng of the wal of Jerusalem was stoppid [Vulg. *quod obducta esset cicatrix muri*]. *c* **1450** *St. Cuthbert* (Surtees) 4088 Hay or clay to him he toke, And stoppid creuys in ilk a noke. **1523-34** FITZHERB. *Husb.* §127 And to pleche downe the bowes of the same tree, to stoppe the holowe places [in a hedge].. yf all the holowe and voyde places wyll not be fylled and stopped, than scoure the old dyche, and cast it vp newe. **1582** N. LICHEFIELD tr. *Castanheda's Conq. E. Ind.* I. lxxv. 153 b, Willyng them not to bee a fearde, but to goe forwarde in stopping the leake. **1665** *Phil. Trans.* I. 80 The Chinks are stopt with Parchment pasted or glewed upon them. **1724** RAMSAY *Health* 295 He causes stop each cranny in his room. **1771** *Encycl. Brit.* II. 515/2 (*Etching*) The operator must be attentive to the ground, that it does not fail in any part, and where it does to stop up the place with the above composition. **1901** W. R. H. TROWBRIDGE *Lett. her Mother to Eliz.* vi. 27 It would cost such a lot to stop the leaks in a seven-acre roof.

fig. **1593** SHAKS. *2 Hen. VI*, v. ii. 83 We shall to London get,.. where this breach now in our Fortunes made May readily be stopt. **1597** HOOKER *Eccl. Pol.* v. ix. §2 There.. will be alwaies.. breaches and leakes moe then mans wit hath hands to stop. *c* **1616** BACON *Advice to Villiers* in *Cabala* (1663) 43 His Majesty in his time hath religiously stopped a leak that did much harm.

b. To plug (the seams of a boat) with oakum, tow, or other caulking material; †to caulk (a ship). Also ***to stop up***.

1535 COVERDALE *Ezek.* xxvii. 9 The eldest and wysest at Gebal were they, that mended & stopped thy shippes. **1585** HIGINS *Junius' Nomencl.* 223/2 To stoppe the ioynts of ships with mosse, okam, or tow: properly called to calke. **1865** VISCT. MILTON & W. E. CHEADLE *N.-W. Passage by Land* ii. 24 The continual leaking of our rickety canoes obliged us to .. spend hours in attempting to stop the seams.

c. *Plastering, House-painting*, etc. To fill up or make good the holes in (a surface to be covered with a wash, paint, or other material); †to close (the joints of brick-work), to 'point' (POINT *v.*[1] 8 a).

1557-8 in W. H. St. John Hope *Windsor Castle* (1913) I. 258 To the same for painting prymering stoping gilding and varnishing of a greate Lyon. **1680-2** *Ibid.* 321 John Grove Plaisterer for washing stopping and Whiting the Kings and Queens Backstaires, [etc.]. **1693** MOXON *Mech. Exerc.* (1703) 245 A Brick Trowel to.. stop the joints. **1842** *Civil Engin. & Arch. Jrnl.* V. 337/2 The walls.. of a light buff colour, rubbed down and stopped. **1903** HASLUCK *House Decoration* viii. 117 Priming must be done before stopping the work... When dry, the work is rubbed down.. and all nail-holes are stopped with putty.

d. *Dentistry.* To fill the cavity of (a decayed tooth) with a stopping.

1592 LYLY *Midas* III. ii, If your tooth be hollow it must be stopt, or puld out. **1657** J. COOKE tr. *J. Hall's Sel. Observ. Engl. Bodies* 87 To stop the tooth with a little Camphire. **1896** BADEN-POWELL *Matabele Campaign* xii, One had his teeth peculiarly stopped with gold. **1907** H. WALES *Yoke* xi, He [a dentist] stopped a tooth for me two years ago.

e. *Glazing.* To fasten (a quarrel or pane of glass) in a window; to putty (glass) in a sash.

1533 in W. H. St. John Hope *Windsor Castle* (1913) I. 262 For stopyng off vij quarelles in the same window. **1858** *Skyring's Builders' Prices* 93 Crown Glass, Stopped in Old Sashes.

†**5.** To mend (a garment); to make good or mend (cloth, metal-work) with an inferior material.

c **1481** CAXTON *Dialogues* viii. 34 Euerard the vpholster Can well stoppe [Fr. *estoupper*] A mantel hooled. **1541** *Act 33 Hen. VIII*, c. 18 §3 Nor shall falsefye or untrulie make or stoppe any manner Kerseyes withe flockes [etc.]. **1645** in W. M. Williams *Ann. Founders' Co.* (1867) 98 No Founder.. shall fill or stop with Lead and Brass Works made up by them.

†**6.** To stanch the bleeding of, bind up (a wound). *Obs.* (Cf. 14 d.)

13.. *Sir Beues* 1936 A keuerchef to him a drouȝ.. To stope mide is wonde. *c* **1400** *Siege Jerus.* (E.E.T.S.) 48 Leches.. Waschen woundes with wyn & with wolle stoppen. **1470-85** MALORY *Arthur* XIV. x. 654 Thenne he stopped his bledyng wounde with a pyece of his sherte. **1599** *Warn. Faire Wom.* II. 579 O stoppe my woundes if ye can. *Old Iohn.* Ioane, take my napkin and thy apron, and bind vp his wounds.

fig. **1594** SHAKS. *Rich. III*, v. v. 40 Now ciuill wounds are stopp'd, Peace liues agen. **1602** CHETTLE *Hoffman* I. (1631) B 2, My hart still bleeds Nor can my wounds be stopt, till an incision I'ue made to bury my dead father in.

7. a. To close (a vessel or receptacle) by blocking its mouth with a cover, plug, or other stopper; similarly, to close (the mouth of a vessel); also, to shut up (something) *in* a stoppered vessel. Also with *down, up*.

c **1420** *Liber Cocorum* (1862) 34 And do hit [venison] in a barel þenne;.. Stop wele þo hede for wynde and sone. *a* **1425** tr. *Arderne's Treat. Fistula*, etc. 92 Putte þat liquour.. into a vessel aȝeyn and stoppe þe vessel þat þer come none aier out. *c* **1460** *Play of Sacrament* 629 in *Non-Cycle Myst. Plays* 77, I stoppe thys ovyn, wythowtyn dowte, With clay.. That non heat shall cum owte. **1558** WARDE tr. *Alexis' Secr.* 31 b, Hauinge putte and left all these thinges in a violle well stopped, the space of two dayes. **1588** *Marprel. Epist.* (Arb.) 11 For men wil giue no mony for your book, vnles it be to stop mustard pots. **1607** TOPSELL *Four-f. Beasts* 552 Afterwards they put them vp in glasses, and stop the mouth close. **1634** PEACHAM *Compl. Gentl.* viii. (1906) 71 Having as it were given you a taste, and stopped up the vessell againe. **1712-14** POPE *Rape Lock* II. 126 Whatever spirit.. His post neglects.. Shall.. Be stopp'd in vials, or transfix'd with pins. **1737** BRACKEN *Farriery Impr.* (1757) II. 176 Keep it close stopped in a Bottle for Use. **1766** *Complete Farmer* s.v. *Vinegar*, Which being drawn off.. and preserved in another cask, well stopped down, will continue perfect, and fit for use. **1826** *Art of Brewing* (ed. 2) 5 The beer in the cellar carefully stopped up. **1869** TYNDALL *Notes Lect. Light* §148. 22 A tube of any kind stopped watertight will answer for this experiment.

b. *Organ-building.* To close (an organ pipe at its upper end) with a plug or cap.

1782 W. HOOPER *Rational Recr.* (ed. 2) II. 231 The wooden pipes [of the organ] are square, and their extremity is stopped with a valve or tampion of leather. **1879** *Organ Voicing* 25 This in either case will be a 4-ft. pipe, stopped.

8. To obstruct the external orifice of (a bodily organ) by putting something in or on it or by pressing the parts together.

a. *to stop* (one's own or another's) *ear* or *ears*. Also *fig.*, to render oneself deaf *to* something, refuse to listen, to close one's mind against arguments, etc.

[*c* **1000** *Sax. Leechd.* II. 42 Ðenim þonne þæt seaw.. do on þa ilcan wulle wring on eare & mid þære ilcan wulle forstoppa þæt eare.] **1340** *Ayenb.* 257 Stoppe þine earen mid þornes, and ne hyer naȝt þe queade tongen. **1382** WYCLIF *Prov.* xxi. 13 Who stoppeth his ere at the cri of the pore. *c* **1440** *Jacob's Well* 217 þerfore stoppe þis gate of þin erys fro þe feend. **1565** COOPER *Thesaurus*, *Obdere ceram auribus*, to stoppe the eares with waxe. **1578** H. WOTTON *Courtlie Controv.* 58 Hee perceyued hir eares stopped, and hearte hardened agaynste all perswasions of consolation. **1594** in *Cath. Rec. Soc. Publ.* (1908) V. 289 It is thought he had stopped his ears with wull at his deathe, for he never answered word to any thinge they said. **1607** HIERON *Discov. Hypocr.* 11 When Steuen preached, there was shouting and stopping the eares. **1747** WESLEY *Prim. Physic* (1759) 56 Drop three or four Drops into the Ear,.. and stop it with black Wool. **1815** J. CORMACK *Abol. Fem. Infanticide Guzerat* viii. 127 The avarice of the Jahrejahs, which was so powerful as to stop the ear against the most tender pleadings of nature. **1830** *Forrester* II. xi. 201 'Oh! horrid, horrid!' exclaimed Peggy, stopping her ears. **1896** HOUSMAN *Shropshire Lad* xix, And silence sounds no worse than cheers After earth has stopped the ears.

b. *to stop* (one's own or another's) ***mouth***: *lit.*, as with a gag or muzzle; *fig.* to compel or induce to be silent; occas. †to satisfy (a person's) appetite. Also, ***to stop the mouth of*** (a lion), to prevent him from devouring his prey.

a **1300** *Cursor M.* 17438 Thise knyghtes anon we yeftes bede That we may stoppe her mowthe with mede. **1382** WYCLIF *Heb.* xi. 33 Thei stoppiden the mouthis of lyouns. *c* **1450** *Mirk's Festial* 58 The þrid skylle was forto stoppe mowthes, lest þay had sayde þat þay dyd not þe lawe. *a* **1548** HALL *Chron., Rich. III*, 40 Some saie yt he had a smal office or a ferme to stoppe his mouthe with al. **1599** SHAKS. *Much Ado* II. i. 321 Speake cosin, or (if you cannot) stop his mouth with a kisse, and let not him speake neither. **1632** J. HAYWARD tr. *Biondi's Eromena* 28 The Baron of Ianque ..(lest the Lady Admirall should cry out) held close her mouth stopt up with the sheetes. **1648** BP. HALL *Breath. Devout Soul* 35 Under heaven there can be no bounds set to this intellectuall appetite: O do thou stop the mouth of my soul with thy self, who art infinite. **1714** BUDGELL tr. *Theophrastus* ii. 9 He.. stops his Mouth with his Handkerchief that he may not laugh out. **1722** WOLLASTON *Relig. Nat.* vii. 148 The controversy may be fairly decided, and all mouths eternally stopped. **1781** COWPER *Conv.* 480 Give it the breast, or stop its mouth with pap! **1859** FITZGERALD *Omar* xxv, Their Words to Scorn Are scatter'd, and their Mouths are stopt with Dust. **1888** 'J. S. WINTER' *Bootle's Childr.* xiv, They wanted to know.. who it was, and—and I just said it was my sister by way of stopping their mouths.

c. *to stop one's nose, nostrils.* ? *Obs.*

c **1420** *Sir Amadace* (Camden) vii, Butte suche a stinke in the chapelle he hade, That.. He stopput his nace with his hude. **1565** LARKE *Bk. Wisdom* H iv, They passed by a place where there was a deade Horse, which dyd stynke verie sore, wherfore the Heremite did stoppe his nose. **1604** SHAKS. *Oth.* IV. ii. 77 Heauen stoppes the Nose at it, and the Moone winks. **1681** DRYDEN *Abs. & Achit.* II. 457 Now stop your noses, Readers, all and some, For here's a tun of Midnight work to come. **1697** —— *Virg. Georg.* IV. 423 They stop his Nostrils, while he strives in vain To breath free Air.

†**d.** *to stop* (a person's) ***eyes*** or ***sight***: to cover the eyes with a bandage, the hand, or other obstruction to the sight; also = to shut one's eyes. *Obs.*

c **1380** *Sir Ferumb.* 1162 þe bond þat is fysage was bounde wyþ to stoppen is louely siȝt, þay ounbounde. **1530** PALSGR. 737/1, I stoppe ones eyes, I cover them with my hande, or with a clothe, that he shall nat se. *a* **1677** BARROW *Creed* (1697) 28 We cannot without stopping our eyes exclude that light.

9. a. To close up, choke, obstruct (a canal, duct, passage or pipe in the animal body); to block the passage or passages of (a bodily organ). Also with *up*.

1398 TREVISA *Barth. De P.R.* III. xviii. (1495) d vj, And yf yt sinew [*sc.* the auditory nerve] be stopped or greued wt some euyll, yt lettyth thoffyce therof. *c* **1530** *Judic. Urines* II. iv. 22 As somtyme the bladder and sometyme the necke of the bladder is stopped.. and stuffed and dystempred throgh excesse of vnkynde hete. **1573-5** GASCOIGNE *Flowers* Wks. 1907 I. 81 The smoulder stops our nose with stench. **1577** B. GOOGE *Heresbach's Husb.* III. 141 The frostye grasse at this time of yeere, doo stoppe their heades with rhume. **1837** P. KEITH *Bot. Lex.* 394 If the passage through the nostrils should happen to be stopped up, as by a cold, or by any internal swelling.

In fig. context. **1597** SHAKS. *2 Hen. IV*, IV. i. 65 To.. purge th' obstructions, which begin to stop Our very Veines of Life.

†**b.** *pass.* Of a person: To be afflicted with an obstruction of the bodily passages or organs. *Obs.*

c **1400** *Lanfranc's Cirurg.* 300 þe blood..wole boile vpward to þe brest,..þat þe pacient schal be ful ny3 stoppid [L. *quod patiens suffocatur*]. **1541** W. C. *Bk. Prop. Herbes* A v b, It is medicinable and curable for those men that be stopped in the breste. **1579** TOMSON *Calvin's Serm. Tim.* 252/1 As these men whiche haue bene a great while in a stincking place, become, as it were stopped.

†**c.** ***stop my vitals*** (see STAP).

a **1700** B. E. *Dict. Cant. Crew, Stop my Vitals*, a silly Curse in use among the Beaux. [Cf. STAP 1696–1839.]

†**d.** To make costive, to bind. Also *absol. Obs.*

1545 ELYOT *Dict.*, *Aluum sistere*, to stoppe or bynde. **1548** *Elyot's Dict.* s.v. *Sisto*, *Aluum sistere*, to stoppe or bynde the bealy. **1584** COGAN *Haven of Health* N j, Bread that cometh hotte from the ouen is vnholsome. The reason is, bycause it stoppethe moche. **1631** WIDDOWES *Nat. Philos.* 45 It stoppeth the belly, and nourisheth but little. **1733** W. ELLIS *Chiltern & Vale Farm.* 281 The one [fodder] to scour them, the other to stop and fat them.

†**10. a.** To shut up, block up (a person or thing *in* a place). Also with adv. *in*, *up*. *Obs.*

c **1315** SHOREHAM *Poems* VII. 578 Wy nedde hy [devils] be ine helle y-stopped For euere mo. **1340** HAMPOLE *Pr. Consc.* 7368 Þai salle be pressed togyder swa harde, Als þai war stopped togyder in ane oven. *a* **1400** *Minor Poems fr. Vernon MS.* xxix. iv. 122 Thi hosebonde haþ my child ibrent, I-stopped him in a glouwyng houen. *a* **1400–50** *Wars Alex.* 5496 And raryfey, a rich ray, he in þe roche stoppis. *c* **1440** *Alphabet of Tales* 227 As þis mason was brekand ane old wall, he fand a grete som of golde stoppyd in a hole. *c* **1440** *Pallad. on Husb.* IV. 959 For thy yf combes ronke of hony wepe, Thre dayes stopped vp at home hem kepe. **1576** TURBERV. *Venerie* 196 When you haue stopped them in thus. **1590** SHAKS. *Com. Err.* I. ii. 53 Stop in your winde sir, tell me this I pray? **1594** —— *Rich. III*, I. iv. 38 But still the enuious Flood Stop'd in my soule, and would not let it forth. **1634** W. WOOD *New Eng. Prosp.* (1865) 38 The English..do crosse the Creekes with long seanes or Basse Netts, which stop in the fish. **1693** J. WARDER *True Amazons* (1713) 96 Prevented by a timely stopping up of the Bees, I do not mean by stopping them up quite.

†**b.** ***to stop out***: to shut out, exclude. ***to stop off***: to keep back (a crowd). *Obs.*

c **1530** TINDALE *Jonas* (title), With what keyes it is so opened that the reader can be stopped out with no sotilte or false doctrine of man. **1685** STILLINGFL. *Orig. Brit.* iv. 174 Nothing would ever be able to stop out the Arian Heresie but the Nicene Faith. **1722** in *Rutland Mag.* (1905) July II. 68 Pd. to ye men yt stop't off the crowd.

†**c.** To exclude *from*. *Obs.*

1567 *Gude & Godlie Ball.* 81 The decreit, and scharp hand wryte, That stoppit vs fra the Father quyte, Furth of the myndis he withdrew.

11. a. To thrust, push (a thing, more rarely a person) *in*, *into* a receptacle or place; also, †to thrust (a boat under water). Chiefly *Sc.*

c **1375** *Sc. Leg. Saints* xxxiii. (*George*) 458 And tak he gert salt smal & stope in til his wondis al. *a* **1572** KNOX *Hist. Ref.* Wks. 1846 I. 204 A galay..was so doung with the cannoun and other ordinance, that she was stopped under watter, and so almost drowned. **1607** MARKHAM *Caval.* VII. 26 Take two little round balles of flaxe or soft towe, and dipping them therein, stop them into the horses eares. **1686** tr. *Chardin's Trav. Persia* 134 He caus'd this Vizier to be stopp'd into the mouth of a cannon. **1704** N. N. tr. *Boccalini's Adv. Parnass.* I. 108 She stopt these *Billet-deux* into her Master's Hand. **1871** W. ALEXANDER *Johnny Gibb* xvii. 125, I..throws on my waistcoat an staps my feet in'o my sheen. **1915** G. SINCLAIR *Poems* 122 A wee black box was stappit Amang the frozen clay.

b. *Sc.* and *north.* To thrust in the point or end of (a thing), to insert; to put in (a plant), hence ***to stop in***, to plant.

1731 J. MONCRIEF *Poor Man's Physician* in H. G. Graham *Social Life Scot.* (1901) I. vii. 52 Stop the finger into a cat's ear and it will be whole in half an hour. **1826** GALT *Last of Lairds* xxxviii, I planted that [tree]..; I dibbled the yearth, and stappit it in there. **1828** CARR *Craven Gloss.*, '*To stop in*,' to plant. **1829** BROCKETT *N.C. Gloss.* (ed. 2), *Stop*, to thrust; e.g. to stop the poker into the fire. **1896** A. J. ARMSTRONG *Cobblers o' Kirkiebrae* 167 (E.D.D.) He..staps pushioned preens through bonnie wee butterflies.

†**c.** To press (a thing) *to the nose*. *Obs.*

1607 TOPSELL *Four-f. Beasts* 553 Some Marchants when they are to buy muske stop it to their noses, and holding their breath run halfe a stones cast, afterwards they pul it from their Nose.

12. a. To cram (a receptacle with something); also ***to stop full***. *Obs.* exc. *Sc.*

c **1400** *Melayne* 1289 Þay..with grete stones Graythe gounnes stoppede those gones, With peletes vs to payne. *c* **1420** *Liber Cocorum* (1862) 34 Take tenderons of sauge with owte lesyng, And stop one fulle up to þo ryng. **1719** DE FOE *Crusoe* (Globe) 579 We stopped his [the idol's] Eyes, Ears, and Mouth, full of Gun-Powder. **1768** ROSS *Helenore* 137 Then I'll bang out my beggar dish, An' stap it fou o' meal. **1814** A. WILSON *Loss o' the Pack* 19 Dear I lo'ed her, and..Stapped her pouches fu' o' preens and laces.

†**b.** To stuff, pad (a dummy, garment, cushion, etc. *with* straw, flock or other material). *Obs.*

c **1400** *Pilgr. Sowle* (Caxton) IV. xxix. (1859) 61 Ymages made of clothe, stopped with strawe. **1525** BERNERS *Froissart* II. xliv. 59 b/2 The heed [of the dart] perced all the plates of his cote of mayle and a iacke stopped with sylke. **1620** in W. O. Blunt *Ch. Chester-le-Street* (1884) 85 For flockes to stopp the quishions, 2 s. **1621** MARKHAM *Hungers Prevention* 50 Stoping it with dry Strawe [etc.]..let it [the Stalking-horse] be painted as neere the colour of a Horse as you can deuise. **1626** B. JONSON *Staple of N.* II. iv, Hee has offer'd To..preserue Each haire falls from him to stop balls with all.

†**c.** *Cookery.* To fill (the inside of a bird, a fruit, and the like) with herbs, spices, etc. preparatory to cooking. Also, ***to stop full***. Cf. STUFF *v.*

1342–3 [see STOPPED *ppl. a.* 1]. *c* **1390** *Forme of Cury* xxxiv. (1780) 25 Take persel and sawge.., take garlec and grapes and stoppe the Chikennes ful. *c* **1420** *Liber Cocorum* 48 Fyrst stop þy capone with saveray, With persyl, a lytil ysope. *c* **1450** *Douce MS. 55* (Bodl.) xxvii, Take quinces and stopp hem whith ynne with hole pepyr. **1541** W. C. *Bk. Prop. Herbes* G j b, Thys is called Persly..and it is good in potage and to stoppe chyckens. **1599** H. BUTTES *Dyets drie Dinner* M ij, Lamprey..stop the mouth with a Nut-meg, and the other holes with Cloves: then fry it.

†**d.** *Dicing.* To load (dice). *Obs.*

1596 LODGE *Wits Miserie* 41 As for Dice, he hath all kind of sortes,..some stopt with quick siluer, some with gold, some ground. *Ibid.*, He stabs if you touch his stake, and stop me his dice, you are a villaine.

†**e.** To plug (the feet of a horse) with something as a dressing; also, to pad (a horse) round the body with straw. *Obs.*

1577 B. GOOGE *Heresbach's Husb.* III. 122 b, You must stop his hoofes with Cowe doung. *Ibid.* 123 For al halting [of horses]... Mingle Hemp with the white of an egge, and stop the foote with all. **1614** MARKHAM *Cheap & Good Husb.* I. i. 8 Walke not nor wash not [your horse] at all,..but set him vp warme, well stopt, and soundly rubbed with cleane litter. *Ibid.*, Stop not your horses fore-feete with Cowes dung, till hee be sufficiently cold. **1623** *Ibid.* I. v. (ed. 3) 51 Cloath him, and stop him round with wispes. *Ibid.* 52. **1852** BURN *Naval & Mil. Techn. Dict.* II. *s.v.*, To stop a horse's feet, *remplir les pieds d'un cheval*.

13. To press down (the tobacco in a pipe) with or as with a tobacco-stopper.

1848 ALB. SMITH *Chr. Tadpole* xix. 167 He stopped the tobacco in his pipe with his little finger.

II. To bring to a stand.

14. *trans.* To prevent the passage of by blocking the channel or outlet. **a.** To dam, keep back, block the channel of (water, a stream, and the like). Also with advs. *back*, *up*.

1398 TREVISA *Barth. De P.R.* IV. iv. (1495) e vij b, Clyffes & strondes stoppen and hold in the flood of the see. **1421** *Coventry Leet Bk.* 31 With filthe, dong and stonys the watur [is] stoppyd of his cours. **1590** SPENSER *F.Q.* II. iv. 11 The bankes are ouerflowen, when stopped is the flood. **1697** DRYDEN *Virg. Past.* VIII. 4 The Rivers stood on heaps, and stopp'd the running Flood. **1776** GIBBON *Decl. & F.* (1787) II. xviii. 108 By the labour of the Persians, the course of the river was stopped below the town, and the waters were confined. *c* **1790** *Encycl. Brit.* (ed. 3) V. 100/1 A frame-work ..closely calked, will stop back the whole or the greatest part of it [water in a mine]. **1821** CLARE *Vill. Minstr.* I. 136 Boys came..Stopping up the mimic rills, Till they forc'd their frothy bound.

transf. and *fig.* **1592** SHAKS. *Rom. & Jul.* IV. i. 12 Her Father..hasts our marriage, To stop the inundation of her teares. **1622** FLETCHER & MASS. *Prophetess* III. iii, It is not in thy power to turn this destiny, Nor stop the torrent of those miseries. **1835** T. MITCHELL *Acharn. of Aristoph.* 651 *note*, A princess, high-minded, yet gentle, with the current of her feelings stopped, when their tide ran purest.

b. To intercept (light, air, heat, etc.). ***to stop out***, to exclude. Also, †to exclude the light from (a thing).

1393 LANGL. *P. Pl.* C. XXI. 285 Ac rys vp ragamoffyn, And reche me alle þe barres..And ich shal lette þis lorde, and hus light stoppe; Ar we þorw bryghtnesse be blent. **1508** STANBRIDGE *Vulgaria* (W. de W.) B iv, Thou stoppest my light, *Interpellas lumen.* **1530** PALSGR. 700/1, I shadowe a thyng, I stoppe it that it can nat apere clerely, *je fais vmbre*. **1538** ELYOT *Dict.*, *Obstruere luminibus*, to lette that a manne canne not loke out of hys wyndowes, or to stoppe his lyghtes. **1594** *1st Pt. Contention* (1843) 39 *York*...Duke Humphrey ..well made away, None then can stop the light to Englands Crowne. **1619** W. WHATELY *Gods Husb.* I. (1622) 39 To turne day into night, by shutting the windowes..to stop out the Sun-shine. **1856** W. B. CARPENTER *Microscope* 129 The object (provided it be of a nature to stop enough light) is seen bright upon a dark field. **1892** *Photogr. Ann.* II. 194 These will form rabets and stop out the wind and weather.

c. ***to stop the breath*** (more rarely ***the wind***) ***of***: to prevent the respiration of, to suffocate, stifle, choke; hence, to cause to die. †Also with *up*.

c **1400** MAUNDEV. (Roxb.) xxii. 99 Þe preste..castez a clath on his mouth and stoppez his wynde. **1534** MORE *Comf. agst. Trib.* III. xx. S vj, If the doore shoulde be stoppe vpon me, I would weene it would stoppe vp my breath. **1581** PETTIE *Guazzo's Civ. Conv.* I. (1586) 42 Those which blow forth such blasts [of slander], deserue to haue their winde stopt with a halter. **1652** C. B. STAPYLTON *Herodian* XVIII. xxxiv, They rusht into his Tent and stopt the breath Of all save few. **1780** R. TOMLINSON *Slang Pastoral* 11 Will no blood-hunting foot-pad..Stop the wind of that nabbing-cull, constable Payne? **1785** BURNS *Death & Dr. Hornbook* ix, Ye're maybe come to stap my breath.

d. To stanch (bleeding, blood).

1573–5 GASCOIGNE *Adv. Mr. F. J.* Wks. 1907 I. 390 When they..had all in vayne sought many waies to stoppe hir bleeding. **1685** in P. Wright *New Bk. Martyrs* (1784) 795/2 Lord, if it be thy holy will, stop this issue of christian blood, and let my guiltless blood be the last spilt on this account. **1748** RICHARDSON *Clarissa* VII. 414 The motion set both his wounds bleeding afresh; and it was with difficulty they again stopped the blood. **1825** SCOTT *Talism.* xiv, He..stopped with styptics and bandages the effusion of blood which followed. *Ibid.* xxviii, Its [the stone's] virtues are still applied to for stopping blood.

15. a. To arrest the onward movement of (a person or thing); to bring to a stand or state of rest; to cause to halt on a journey; also, to prevent the departure or starting of. †Const. *of* (one's passage) and with double obj. by omission of *of*.

c **1440** *Promp. Parv.* 477/2 Stoppyn, or wythe stondynge a beest of goynge or rennynge, *sisto, obsto.* **1523** BERNERS *Froissart* I. cccxxxiii. 308/2 But they were nat men ynowe to stoppe theym their way. **1530** PALSGR. 736/2, I stoppe a thefe that is ronnyng a waye, *je arreste*. Stoppe the thefe for Godes sake. **1590** NASHE *1st Pt. Pasquil's Apol.* A 4, If I muster and traine my men a newe, that the enemies of God ..may be stopt of theyr passage and driuen backe. **1614** BACON *Charge touching Duels* 33 In case I be aduertised of a purpose in any to goe beyond the sea to fight, I may haue granted his Maiesties writ of *Ne exeat regnum* to stoppe him. **1665** MANLEY *Grotius' Low-C. Warres* 315 The Prince.. sending before some Horse, which should hinder and stop the Enemy, at the Passage over the Maes. **1670** G. H. *Hist. Cardinals* I. III. 82 A Cardinal stops his Coach to another that is his Senior. *a* **1700** EVELYN *Diary* 29 Oct. 1660, Going to London, my Lord Maior's shew stopp'd me in Cheapside. **1714** SWIFT *Hor. Sat.* II. vi. 111 I'm stopp'd by all the Fools I meet, And catechis'd in ev'ry street. **1726** —— *Gulliver* I. ii, We found our fingers stopt with that lucid substance. **1761** *Lond. Chron.* 24–26 Dec. 622/2 Thursday night three highwaymen stopped several waggons on Northall Common. **1809** *Med. Jrnl.* XXI. 218 The catheter ..appeared to be stopt by the neck of the bladder. **1821** SCOTT *Kenilw.* xiv, Tressilian and his attendants were stopped and questioned repeatedly by sentinels. **1860** TYNDALL *Glac.* I. xxiii. 164, I was at length stopped by the dislocated ice. **1867** S. W. BAKER *Nile Trib.* v. 97 The common belief that the scales of a crocodile will stop a bullet is very erroneous. **1876** J. W. BARRY *Rlwy. Appliances* 293 The responsibility of stopping a train in all other emergencies is given without question to the engine-driver. **1901** T. R. GLOVER *Life & Lett. Fourth Cent.* vii. 157 To declare war on him, means to stop the corn-ships at once.

b. ***stop thief!*** a cry for help to arrest a running thief. Also *slang* (see quot. 1857).

1714 A. SMITH *Lives Highwaymen* (ed. 2) I. 67 He espy'd Cox,..and crying out *Stop Thief*, he was apprehended in St. Clement's Church-Yard. **1758–65** GOLDSM. *Ess.* vi. [xxi.] (Globe) 303/2, I had not gone far from the house when I heard behind me the cry of 'Stop thief!' **1857** 'DUCANGE ANGLICUS' *Vulgar Tongue* 20 *Stop Thief*, meat stolen. 'I have got this piece of *stop thief*.' I stole this piece of raw meat. Th[ieves]. **1887** *Times* 26 Aug. 10/2 Prosecutor having called out 'stop thief' he was apprehended.

c. To bring down (a bird) with the gun. Also, to arrest the rush of (a charging enemy or wild beast) with rifle-fire. (Said also of the bullet and of the wound produced.) Also, to hit (game).

1845 *Punch* 25 Jan. 46/2 Out they [*sc.* the hares] rushed from every quarter—so many—that it was often impossible to 'stop' more than one out of half-a-dozen. **1862** LD. W. LENNOX *Recreat. Sportsm.* I. 151 At the first [pigeon-shooting] handicap Moncrieff stopped a bird at seventy-five yards. **1892** GREENER *Gun* (ed. 5) 208 An 8-bore [rifle] will frequently fail to stop the charge. **1896** *Times* 16 Dec. 5/2 The task of making a Lee-Metford bullet which, without losing its ranging powers, should still inflict a wound sufficiently severe to stop even the most determined fanatics. **1898** G. W. STEEVENS *With Kitchener to Khartum* xxxiii. 285 The officer assailed put a man-stopping revolver bullet into him, but it did not stop him.

d. *Fencing*, *Pugilism*, etc. To check (an adversary, his stroke, weapon, etc.) with a counter movement or stroke; to counter (a blow, a manœuvre in wrestling, etc.) Also ***to stop short***.

1714 PARKYNS *Inn-Play* (ed. 2) 47 [*Wrestling.*] Then go to the Flying Mare, and if he stops that, give him your Elbow under his Chin. **1765** ANGELO *Sch. Fencing* 26 You may stop his blade short, by keeping your wrist [etc.]. **1771** LONNERGAN *Fencer's Guide* 82 Make a stamp with your foot, and thrust forward at me; thus you stop me. *Ibid.* 83 Then finish in a Quarte-over-the-arm in like manner with a Stop. Thus you stop in Low Quarte. **1823** 'JON BEE' *Dict. Turf* 214 *Stop a blow*, (ring), to prevent its alighting on the part intended by means of the guard, or position of defence, i.e. the fore-arm or elbow. **1840** D. WALKER *Defensive Exerc.* 14 [Wrestling.] It is sometimes possible to stop the hipe by clapping the knees instantly together. *Ibid.* 67 [Single-stick.] The usual blow at the head... To stop this, raise the hand a little. **1889** A. HUTTON *Cold Steel* 34 The vertical cut 7, if given at the head, should be stopped by the Head parry.

absol. **1857** G. A. LAWRENCE *Guy Liv.* iv. 32 His adversary ..stopped and countered as coolly as if he had only the gloves on. **1865** A. L. GORDON *Poems, Ye Wearie Wayfarer* IV. iv, Don't stop with your head too frequently (This advice ain't meant for a nigger).

e. *colloq.* (orig. *Mil.*). To be hit by (a bullet). Phrases ***to stop one***: to be hit or killed; ***to stop a packet***: see PACKET *sb.* 1 f.

1901 *Boy's Own Paper* 5 Oct. 14/2 After the battle of Spion Kop, one man, who was hit in seven places, said that he had stopped a whole volley himself. **1915** *Sphere* 6 Nov. 144/1 A man's troubles begin rather than end when he 'stops' a German or Turkish bullet. **1916** E. V. LUCAS *Vermilion Box* clxxxiv. 213 Poor boy, I do so hope he manages not to 'stop one'—which is what being hit is called here. **1929** J. BUCHAN *Courts of Morning* I. xiii. 152 If I hadn't thought of that head-crashing dodge, I think I might have stopped a bullet. **1933** H. S. WALPOLE *Vanessa* IV. i. 682 Maurice stood there wishing that he might 'stop one' before he had to go over the top. *a* **1976** A. CHRISTIE *Autobiogr.* (1977) v. ii. 234 You stop one, you've had it, and you've left behind a young widow.

f. To drink; usu. in phr. ***to stop one***, to take a drink. *Austral. slang.*

1924 *Truth* (Sydney) 27 Apr. 6 *Stop one*, to take a drink. **1929** K. S. PRICHARD *Coonardoo* xxix. 279 Geary poured himself a drink. 'Hi, Dick,' he called, 'could you stop one?' **1936** A. RUSSELL *Gone Nomad* x. 78 Then, jerking his finger knowingly, 'I s'pose yer could stop one?' I could. I needed that rum. **1937** PARTRIDGE *Dict. Slang* 835/2 *Stop a pot*, 'to quaff ale,' C. J. Dennis.

16. In certain games. **a.** *Tennis.* (*a*) To keep off (the ball) from the dedans, winning-gallery, or grille. †(*b*) *absol.* ? To mark or record the stops or chases.

(*a*) **1822** [R. LUKIN] *Treat. Tennis* in J. Marshall *Tennis* (1878) 196 To stop the ball, that is, merely to prevent it entering the dedans, &c., is not sufficient. **1895** G. J. MANSON *Sporting Dict., Stop,* to prevent (by a volley) a ball from entering an opening.

(*b*) **1530** PALSGR. 737/1, I stoppe on ones syde, as one that is a stoppar in a tenes play or at the foote ball, *je garde.* I wyll stoppe on your syde. *a* **1548** HALL *Chron., Hen. VIII,* 98 b, On saterday the kyng & the Emperor playd at tennice.. agaynst the princes of Orenge and the Marques of Brandenborow, & on the Princes syde stopped the Erle of Deuonshyre and the lorde Edmond on the other syde.

†**b.** *Cricket.* (*a*) Of a batsman: To play (a ball) defensively, without attempting to hit it away. Also *absol.* (*b*) *absol.* Of a fieldsman: To field the ball, to act as fieldsman. ***to stop behind,*** to act as longstop. *Obs.*

(*a*) **1833** NYREN *Yng. Cricketer's Tutor* (1902) 34 How to stop a shooting-ball dropped short of a length... This backward movement will give you a better sight of the ball, and more time for stopping it. *Ibid.* 150 Every loose, hard hitter would learn to stop, and play as safe a game as possible. **1856** *Househ. Words* 2 Feb. 59/2 They cut a good deal oftener and stop much less, perhaps, than they used to do.

(*b*) **1744** LOVE *Cricket* (1754) I. 11 Expert to bowl, to run, to stop, to throw. **1833** NYREN *Yng. Cricketer's Tutor* (1902) 22 No substitute in the field shall be allowed to..stop behind to a fast bowler.

17. To intercept and detain in transit.

1604 E. G[RIMSTONE] *D'Acosta's Hist. Indies* VII. xxvi. 576 Where they continued many daies, stopping their victuals, nor suffering any to enter or issue forth. **1661** MARVELL *Corr.* Wks. 1875 II. 51, I have yours of 22, I wish you had had mine of 19th, but all were stopped. **1667** STURMY *Mariner's Mag., Penalties & Forfeit.* To Merchants (1669) n 2 b, Your Goods have been seised..and Ships stopp'd and hindred in their Voyages.

18. a. To withhold (a sum of money) in paying wages or other debt, on the ground of some counter-claim.

1427 *Coventry Leet Bk.* 113 And þat hit be rered be þe comen seriant, or els þat hit be stopped vppon the hire of þe seid comen seriant. **1495–6** *Rec. St. Mary at Hill* (1905) 220 Item, payd to thomas Mundys,..wyche he stoppyth in his hondes in party payment that is owyng hym for nayll, the quitrent that belongyth to owre chyrch. **1538** ELYOT *Dict., Resignatum æs,* wages stopped for negligent seruice in warres. **1597** SHAKS. *2 Hen. IV,* v. i. 24 And Sir, doe you meane to stoppe any of Williams Wages, about the Sacke he lost..at Hinckley Fayre? **1612–13** FLETCHER *Coxcomb* IV. (1647) 111/2 [Viola has broken a glass] *Moth.* Did you so? be sure I'le stop it, 'twill make a good gap in your quarters wages. **1668** in *10th Rep. Hist. MSS. Comm.* App. v. 61 Your Grace was pleased to order the said fees to be stopt in the hands of the King of Armes. **1734** POPE *Sat. Hor.* II. ii. 63 Nor stops, for one bad cork, his butler's pay. **1741** *Col. Rec. Pennsylv.* IV. 510 Since £1,500 out of the £2,500 said to be Expended has been stopt out of my support. **1832** *Min. Evid. Comm. Factories Bill* 203 They stop 1*s.* a week of every hand upon the premises. **1887** *Spectator* 9 July 932/1 A new kit was now supplied to him, and sixpence a day stopped out of his money to pay for it.

indirect passive. **1802** C. JAMES *Milit. Dict.* s.v. *Stoppages,* Soldiers are directed to be stopped one shilling and sixpence per week.

†**b.** To deprive (a person) *of* his pay. *Obs.*

1594 *1st Pt. Contention* ix. 44 Tis thought my lord, your grace..stopt the soldiers of their paie.

c. ***to stop it out:*** to save the cost of a thing by economizing *in* (something else). *colloq.*

1863 MRS. CRAIK *Mistress & Maid* xii, 'It will do no harm to enquire the price. I might stop it out in omnibuses.' For this was the way every new article of dress had to be procured—'stopping it out' of something else.

d. To withhold (goods) as security or in lieu of payment.

1761 *Ann. Reg.* IV. *Chron.* 123 An action brought against a carrier for stopping a goose..because the gentleman did not pay the porter a shilling for..carrying it to the gentleman's house. **1864–5** TROLLOPE *Can you forgive her?* iii, What do you think of Mrs. Green wanting to charge me for an extra week, because she says I did not give her notice till Tuesday morning? I won't pay her, and she may stop my things if she dares.

19. To give instructions to a banker not to cash (a bank note, bill, or the like). Similarly ***to stop payment*** (of a note).

1713 *Lond. Gaz.* No. 4619/11 It being stop'd at the Bank. **1722** *Post Man* 16–19 June 2/1 With several Notes in it, being of no Value to any but the Owner, Payment being stopt. **1722** DE FOE *Col. Jack* (1840) 21 They [the bills] would be stopped. **1884** E. YATES *Recoll.* II. 194 The numbers of the notes were known, payment of them was stopped. **1892** CORDINGLEY *Commerc. Guide* 63 To 'stop' a cheque, in cases where it has been lost or stolen, is to give written instructions to the banker it is drawn upon not to pay the cheque when presented.

20. a. To cause (a person) to desist from or pause in a course of action or conduct. Const. *from, in,* †*of;* also with gerund as second obj. Also ***to stop short,*** to check abruptly.

Orig. a fig. use of sense 15, often with reference to a metaphorical way or course.

1393 LANGL. *P. Pl.* C. v. 150 Mede..on men of lawe gan wynke, in sygne þat þei sholde, with som sotel speche Reherce þo a-non ryght, þat myghte reson stoppe. **1561** HOBY tr. *Castiglione's Courtier* I. (1900) 76 It is a stray out of the way in which he would have profited, had he not bene stopped in it. **1592** KYD *Span. Trag.* III. xiv. 74 My L., it lyes not in Lorenzos power To stop the vulgar, liberall of their tongues. **1611** BIBLE *2 Cor.* xi. 10 No man shall stop mee [*marg.,* Gr. this boasting shal not be stopped in me.] of this boasting in the regions of Achaia. **1816** SCOTT *Old Mort.* xliv, What can be done to stop him from running headlong on ruin? **1837** CARLYLE *Fr. Rev.* I. v. iii, Your National Assembly, stopped short in its Constitutional labours, may, [etc.]. *Mod.* I wish you would stop him circulating those rumours.

b. To cause (a person) to break off in narrative or speech. Const. *from, in.* Also ***to stop short.***

1545 ELYOT *Dict.* s.v. *Opprimo, Opprimere orationem alicuius,* to stoppe one in his tale. **1604** SHAKS. *Oth.* II. i. 199, I cannot speake enough of this content, It stoppes me heere. **1697** J. LEWIS *Mem. Dk. Glocester* (1789) 23 But when my Lady Governess..began to tell the Duke the sad news, he stopped her. **1784** P. WRIGHT *New Bk. Martyrs* 795/2 He then was stopped from saying any more. **1825** SCOTT *Betrothed* xviii, The chaplain had arrived at some convenient pause in the lecture, where the Archbishop stopped him with, '*Satis est, mi fili.*' **1889** F. E. GRETTON *Memory's Harkback* 121 'Yes, my lord; but—–' Garrow stopped him short. 'Not one word more, sir, if you please.'

c. To cause (a thing) to cease action. Now *rare.*

1377 LANGL. *P. Pl.* B. XVIII. 415 Was neuere werre in þis worlde..so kene þat ne..pees þorw pacience, alle perilles stopped. **138.** WYCLIF *Sel. Wks.* III. 360 And þus þe puple myȝte wiþdrawe þer almes fro wickide preestis, and þe pride of preestis shulde be stoppid, bi which þei envenemyn þe puple. **1593** SHAKS. *3 Hen. VI,* III. iii. 14 From such a cause, as fills mine eyes with teares, And stops my tongue. **1672** VILLIERS (Dk. Buckhm.) *Rehearsal* IV. i. (Arb.) 101 Hold, stop your murd'ring hands. **1777** W. DALRYMPLE *Trav. Sp. & Port.* iv, I fortunately came in and stopped her hand.

21. a. To restrain or prevent (a person) from a contemplated action. Const. as in 20.

c **1470** HENRY *Wallace* IX. 30 He leit no word than walk off his menge, Or Inglismen had stoppit him his wiage. **1530** PALSGR. 737/1, I stoppe, I hynder or let one of any purpose that he is about, *je empesche.* **1611** SHAKS. *Wint. T.* II. i. 187 Now, from the Oracle They will bring all, whose spirituall counsaile had Shall stop, or spurre me. **1697** J. LEWIS *Mem. Dk. Glocester* (1789) 22, I was ordered..to go..for Dr. Radcliffe,..but Mr. Pierce..told them he was in no danger, and we were stopt. **1801** J. THOMSON *Poems Sc. Dial.* 15 So whan ye find yoursells incline To steal a rag,..O! stop yoursells o' that design. **1874** RUSKIN *Fors Clav.* IV. xxxix. 69 If any one likes to go, nobody will stop them. **1908** R. BAGOT *A. Cuthbert* vii. 66 He was about to place the chair near to that of the lady,..but Jim stopped him. *a* **1917** *Mod.* Why didn't you stop him sending that letter? **1951** M. KENNEDY *Lucy Carmichael* II. iii. 94 You..make an entrance if you like. I'm not stopping you. **1970** *Globe & Mail* (Toronto) 28 Sept. 23/2 (Advt.), Make the break with Tradition. What's to stop you? Certainly not the price. **1973** R. THOMAS *If you can't be Good* (1974) xx. 180 'I wanta see Connie Mizelle,' he said. 'What's stopping you?' 'Not a damn thing,' he said. 'Let's go.'

†**b.** *Law.* To bar, hinder, preclude. Const. *from, to* with *inf.* = ESTOP 2. *Obs.*

1534 tr. *Lyndewode's Const. Provinc.* 39 b, The free testament makynge is let and the chyrche, & other aboue named, be malyciously stopped from theyr ryght. **1595** SHAKS. *John* II. i. 562 Iohn to stop Arthurs Title in the whole, Hath willingly departed with a part. **1711** in *Nairne Peerage Evid.* (1874) 141 And all others perills burdens dangers and inconveniences..which may anywayes stop trouble or pre-judge them in the peaceable possession thereof.

c. To stay, suspend (proceedings); to prevent (a decree, etc.) from taking effect.

1690 *Acts of Sederunt* (1790) 185 Where any act, decreet or protestation being pronounced, without debate in the cause, is thereafter stopped upon application of one of the parties. **1774** BP. HALLIFAX *Anal. Rom. Civil Law* (1795) 126 An Inhibition is issued from the Superior Court to the Inferior, to stop Proceedings.

(*b*) ***to stop the show*** (orig. *U.S.*); to cause an interruption of a performance by provoking prolonged applause or laughter, or requests for encores. Cf. ***show-stopper, -stopping*** adj. s.v. SHOW *sb.*[1] 22.

1926 *Amer. Speech* I. 437/1 When an act proves to be such a wow that it is forced to respond to encore after encore and the remainder of the acts on the program must wait until the audience will allow them to go on, it is said to 'stop the show cold'. **1933** *Fortune* Aug. 92/1 Jim Europe had stopped the show with *St. Louis Blues.* **1957** R. HART-DAVIS *Let.* 19 May in *Lyttelton-Hart-Davis Lett.* (1979) II. 103 The Gibbon quotation stopped the show long enough for me to consult my scrappy notes. **1966** 'M. RENAULT' *Mask of Apollo* vi. 107 This line, as I had feared it might, stopped the show. **1977** *Times* 13 June 15/4 *The Merchant of Venice* [was] performed by the Ibadan Boys' Grammar School... A British widower['s]..son..was cast as the Prince of Morocco. His opening line stopped the show: 'Mislike me not for my complexion—.'

d. To give a still picture of (a moving object).

1937 *Star* (Kansas City) 8 Aug. 3 The camera 'stops' the action of a chorus in training. **1937** *Discovery* Nov. 353/1 Anyone can find a gannet, and any shutter working to 1/500 sec. will 'stop' it. **1950** A. HUXLEY *Themes & Variations* 161 On Alexander's [tomb] the monster has been 'stopped', as the photographers say, in the act of shooting up from the doorway leading into the vault.

†**22.** To hamper, hinder, impede the course or progress of (affairs, a project, etc.); to hinder (a person) in action or in some proceeding. Sometimes with clause as object. *Obs.*

c **1380** WYCLIF *Wks.* (1880) 159 Where worldly prestis schullen for here..ydelnesse & pride stoppe cristene men to knowe god. **1436** *Libel Eng. Policy* in *Pol. Poems* (Rolls) II. 178 For this wee see welle every day at eye, Geftes and festes stopene oure pollicye. **1538** STARKEY *England* 36 Puttyng in exercyse many honest and vertuse affectys of mannys mynd, wych els schold be..stoppyd and let by penury and pouerty. **1594** SHAKS. *Rich. III,* I. ii. 35 What blacke Magitian coniures vp this Fiend, To stop deuoted charitable deeds? **1721** RAMSAY *Prospect of Plenty* 105 The Dutch, say they, will strive your plot to stap.

23. a. To cause to cease, put an end to (a movement, activity, course of events).

c **1400** *Destr. Troy* 10105 But Pollexena..Abated the bremmes in his bale yre, And stoppet the strif of his strong hert. **1426** W. PASTON in *P. Lett.* I. 26, I wot not whether it were best in any sermon or other audience..to declare aught of this matier in stoppyng of the noyse that renneth in this case. **1526** *Pilgr. Perf.* (W. de W. 1531) 64 But stoppe it [suspicyon] betyme, and suffre it neuer to growe to iudgement. *a* **1670** SPALDING *Troub. Chas. I* (1850) II. 337 Quhilk wold give the Southland men aneuche ado, and stop thair cuming heir. **1820** SHELLEY *Oedipus Tyr.* II. ii. 40 For God's sake stop the grunting of those Pigs! **1827** SCOTT *Chron. Canongate* v, But I stopped her doubts, by assuring her it had been part and pendicle thereof in my forefathers' time. **1831** GREVILLE *Mem.* (1874) II. 158 Gurney overheard one juryman say to another, 'Don't you think we had better stop the case? It is useless to go on.' **1848** MILL *Pol. Econ.* III. ix. §2 (1876) 306 Even if this small annual supply were stopt entirely. **1898** 'MERRIMAN' *Roden's Corner* xviii. 193 In plain English, it is murder, and it must be stopped at any cost. You understand?

b. To prevent the coming-on of.

1538 STARKEY *England* 180 Of thys we must have regard, and stoppe al occasyon therof as much as we may. **1608** SHAKS. *Per.* I. ii. 98 With thousand doubts How I might stop this tempest ere it came. **1840** THACKERAY *Barber Cox* Jan., I..popped my shaving brush into Mr. Bar's mouth—a capital way to stop angry answers. **1891** FARRAR *Darkn. & Dawn* viii, It was only with difficulty that Seneca and Burrus had been able to stop more tragedies.

24. a. To cease from, discontinue (an action, employment, etc.).

1525 BERNERS *Froiss.* II. ccxxxvii. 306 b/2 Whan they had this warnynge they stopped their commyng to the kyng. **1592** SHAKS. *Rom. & Jul.* V. iii. 54 Stop thy vnhallowed toyle, vile Montague. **1599** —— *Hen. V,* II. iv. 69 Turne head, and stop pursuit. **1795** *Gentl. Mag.* LXV. II. 539/1 Barley was so dear that brewers had stopped brewing. **1818** SCOTT *Br. Lamm.* xxi, Prithee, stop thy gambling cant for one instant. **1848** THACKERAY *Van. Fair* lxvi, I say I will not have it: and Dobbin, I beg, sir, you'll stop it. **1853** M. ARNOLD *Scholar Gypsy* xii, The blackbird picking food Sees thee, nor stops his meal, nor fears at all. **1860** DENISON *Clocks & Watches* (ed. 4) 343 The clock stopped striking. **1878** JEVONS *Primer Pol. Econ.* 66 Nobody should be allowed suddenly to stop work in a way endangering other people.

b. ***to stop payment:*** to declare oneself unable to meet one's financial obligations. Also in shortened form ***to stop.***

1766 BLACKSTONE *Comm.* II. xxxi. 479 It has been determined expressly, that a banker's stopping or refusing payment is no act of bankruptcy. **1818** SCOTT *Rob Roy* xxii, But what will that be to the news that Osbaldistone and Tresham have stopped! **1864** MRS. RIDDELL *Geo. Geith* xxxv. III. 29 The bank has stopped payment. **1879** RUSKIN *Let.* 31 Oct., Wks. 1908 XXXIV. 238 Written contracts are all very well, but if the contractor stops payment—where are you? **1898** W. J. GREENWOOD *Commerc. Corresp.* (ed. 2) 40 The house mentioned in yours of the 3rd inst. is daily expected to stop payment.

c. To put an end to the issue of (an allowance).

1839 DICKENS *Nich. Nick.* viii, She has..stopped his..pocket-money. **1865** H. KINGSLEY *Hillyars & Burtons* xxvi, Suppose, sir, that I was..to stop your allowance?

25. To cause (a machine or piece of mechanism) to cease working or going. ***to stop the press:*** to suspend the operation of printing (esp. in order to give opportunity to make some insertion).

1538 ELYOT *Dict., Sufflamen,* that wherwith a wheele is retained or stopped of his course. **1703** DE FOE in *15th Rep. Hist. MSS. Comm.* App. IV. 76, I shall continue to stop the press in this case till I hear your opinion. **1765** BICKERSTAFF *Maid of Mill* I. i, Stop the mill there; and..hoist yon sacks of flour upon this cart lad. **1815** *Morn. Chron.* 22 June 3/2 We stop the press to announce the most brilliant and complete Victory ever obtained by the Duke of Wellington. **1825** J. NICHOLSON *Oper. Mech.* 237 To stop the engine, the cocks at K and Y should be shut. **1860** in *Abridgm. Specif. Patents, Watches* etc. (1871) 51 Mechanism..for stopping and starting watches. **1883** M. P. BALE *Saw-Mills* 32 A new method of stopping engines by electricity.

26. To arrest the oscillation, vibration, or unsteady motion of; to keep immovable or steady.

1669 STURMY *Mariner's Mag.* VII. xxix. 42 Let a stander by stop one end of a Thred on the Glass at D. *Ibid.* v. xii. 78 The Piece to be Mounted higher or lower, until you bring the Bead..and the Mark all in one Line, stop the Piece in that position with a Coyn.

27. *Mus.* To press down (a string of a violin, lute, and the like) with the finger (*rarely* with a key) in order to shorten its vibrating length and thereby produce certain intermediate sounds; hence, to produce (a note, sound) by this means; to use (a finger) for this purpose. Also with *down.*

c **1500** in Grose *Antiq. Repert.* (1809) IV. 406 In myddest of the body [of the Lute] the stryngis sowndith best, For stoppide in the freytes they abydeth the pynnes wrest. **1574** F. KE tr. *A. Le Roy's Instruct. Lute* 64 b, Thou muste also vnderstande, how, and with whiche fingers the strynges of the Lute must be stopped. *Ibid.* 68 b, The first .C. of the first stoppe..must be stopped with the seconde finger. **1626** BACON *Sylva* §156 In Lutes, and Instruments of Strings, if you stop a String high..the Sound is more Treble. **1676** MACE *Musick's Mon.* 84 Then be ready to stop down (*β,*) with the Fore-finger. *Ibid.* 85 After your Stopt Note..you are not to take up that Finger, which you last Stopt, until necessity require. **1784** in *Abridgm. Specif. Patents, Music* (1871) 15 The manner of stopping the British lyre is..peculiar to the instrument, which instead of being stopped by the fingers..is stopped and the tone given by small keys.

1867 MACFARREN *Harmony* i. 8 An instrument such as the violin whose notes are stopped by the fingers.

absol. **1762** STERNE *Tr. Shandy* V. xv, I will this moment stop three hundred and fifty leagues out of tune upon my fiddle, without punishing one single nerve that belongs to him.

28. *Naut.* **a.** To bring (a ship) to anchor by gradually checking the cable. Phr. ***to stop the cable***: to prevent it running out too fast. ***stop her!*** see quot. 1867; also, on small steamers and motor-boats, the command to stop the engine.

1627 CAPT. SMITH *Sea Gram.* vii. 31. **1644** MANWAYRING *Seamans Dict.* 101 When they come to an Anchor, and have let run-out as much..of Cabell..as will make the ship ride, or that the ship be in a current, where it is best to stop her a little by degrees, then they say, Stopp the ship; and so hold-fast the Cabell, and then veere-out a little more, and so stopp her fully, to let her ride. *Ibid.* 103 The use of them [*sc.* stoppers] is chiefly..to stopp the cabels, when they come to an Anchor, that it may goe-out by little and little. **1775** DALRYMPLE *Voy.* in *Phil. Trans.* LXVIII. 404 At noon, close reefed top-sails, stopt the cable, and came to sail. **1834** SIR F. HEAD *Bubbles Brunnen Nassau* 6 The word of command, 'Stop her!' was loudly vociferated by a bluff, short, Dirk Hatteraick-looking pilot. **1841** [see EASE *v.* 9]. **1867** SMYTH *Sailor's Word-bk.*, *Stop Her!*, an order to check the cable in being payed out.

b. ***to stop the tide***: to prevent the ship being carried with the tide.

1627 CAPT. SMITH *Sea Gram.* x. 47 To Tide ouer to a place, is to goe ouer with the Tide of ebbe or flood, and stop the contrary by anchoring till the next Tide. **1708** *Lond. Gaz.* No. 4422/7 We came to an Anchor to stop the Flood. *Ibid.* No. 4431/15 They have anchor'd and stop'd the Tide. **1835** SIR J. ROSS *N.-W. Passage* ii. 25 We were obliged to stop the tide off Port Kale.

c. To tie up with thin rope. Also ***to stop up***.

1770 *Phil. Trans.* LX. 191 The maintop-mast back stay, to which the chain is stopped, to prevent its swinging about. **1875** BEDFORD *Sailor's Pocket Bk.* v. (ed. 2) 155 It is advisable to bend the cable..to the crown of the anchor, stopping it with spun-yarn to the ring. **1882** NARES *Seamanship* (ed. 6) 50 How are the footropes fitted? With a cut splice, being stopped out on each side to the guys.

29. *Horticulture.* To pinch out the head of (a plant); to remove (a shoot or a portion of it) by pinching. Also ***to stop back***.

1699 L. MEAGER *Art of Gardening* 66 August... Release and unbind the Buds you have Inoculated, if they have taken; prune and stop them. **1794** MCPHAIL *Treat. Cucumber* 67 When the seedling plants have one or two joints, I stop them, after which they generally put forth two shoots. **1796** C. MARSHALL *Garden.* xiv. (1813) 193 Stopping the plants is to be performed about a week before they leave the seed bed. **1842** LOUDON *Suburban Hort.* 495 To concentrate the vigour of the plant, the shoots are stopped repeatedly as they advance in growth. **1849** *Florist* 256 Stop back young plants that have been struck this season.

fig. **1875** DOWDEN *Shakespere* 282 When Shakspere finds himself shooting up too rapidly he 'stops' himself, as gardeners do a plant.

30. *Arch.* To cause (a rib, shaft, chamfer, etc.) to terminate (in a specified form or position).

1835 R. WILLIS *Archit. Mid. Ages* vii. 97 Sometimes, however, the diagonal ribs are stopped by corbels near their imposts. *Ibid.* 98 The vaulting shafts are all stopped before they reach the ground. **1848** RICKMAN *Archit.* 36 The flutes are stopt square, and not as usual rounded at the ends.

31. *Bird-catching.* To subject (a call-bird) to a process which causes it to moult prematurely. ? *Obs.*

1768 PENNANT *Brit. Zool.* II. 332 We have been lately informed by an experienced bird-catcher, that he pursues a cooler regimen in stopping his birds.

32. *Phonetics.* To check the flow of (breath or voice) in articulation. Cf. STOPPED *ppl. a.* 7.

1867 A. M. BELL *Visible Sp.* 12 In forming Consonants, the breath or voice is stopped or squeezed, with an effect of percussion, sibilation, buzzing, or vibration, in some part of the guttural or oral passage.

33. Technical uses with advs.

a. stop down. *trans.* To reduce the aperture of (a lens) by means of the stops. Also *absol.* and *intr.* for *pass.*

1892 *Photogr. Ann.* II. p. cxxiii, The Lenses..will work full aperture for portraits and groups, and when stopped down a little, will produce landscape and architectural photos. **1907** J. A. HODGES *Elem. Photogr.* (ed. 6) 21 The sharpness of the picture can..be greatly improved by the simple expedient of 'stopping down'. **1971** P. PURSER *Holy Father's Navy* xiv. 75 Can you stop down to make it look like dusk? **1978** *SLR Camera* Aug. 46/1 As the lens is focused through these various degrees of magnification the lens automatically stops down.

b. stop off. *trans.* (*a*) In *Moulding*, to adapt (a mould) to a new design by shortening or obliterating some part of it; also *refl.* of a mould. (*b*) In *Etching*, *Electroplating*, etc.: = *stop out.*

(*a*) **1843** HOLTZAPFFEL *Turning* I. 354 If the pattern be too long, or that it be temporarily desired to obliterate some few parts, the mould is made of the full size and stopped-off. **1885** [HORNER] *Pattern Making* 53 We make a special box to fill up the print as well as to core the hole out, or, in brief, to 'stop itself off.'

(*b*) **1856** G. GORE *Pract. Chem.* 77 Many articles which are to receive deposits require to have portions of their surface 'stopped off', to prevent the deposit spreading over those parts. **1907** *Edin. Rev.* July 233 The lines of an etching may be darkened or again 'stopped off'.

c. stop off = senses 21 a, 23 b, and 24 a. Now *rare* or *obs.*

1891 W. B. YEATS *Let.* 21 Jan. (1954) I. 162 Ellis..may do some of my chapters himself... Providence has stopped off his terrible activity for the present with twelve lectures for the University Extension. **1892** —— *Lett.* (1954) II. 201, I helped to stop off another man of learning the other day who came trying to get a book from Unwin to do. **1902** H. JAMES *Wings of Dove* VII. xxv. 382 Having suffered him to insist almost convicted her of indelicacy. Why hadn't she stopped him off? **1904** G. B. LANCASTER *Sons o' Men* 47 Stop that row, Tommy... Stop it off. **1929** T. E. LAWRENCE *Let.* 22 July (1938) 666 Dirty Dogs, they *have* stopped off poor Trotsky.

d. stop out. *trans.* (*a*) In *Etching*, to obliterate or cover with a varnish (the marks, lines, or other parts of a plate which are to be kept from the acid in the process of biting in). Also *absol.* (*b*) In *Electrotyping*, *Calico-printing*, etc.: see quots.

1811 *Self Instructor* 548 If any scratches..or mistakes be committed in the etchings, they are to be stopped out. **1815** J. SMITH *Panorama Sci. & Art* II. 775 If any parts require to be stopt out, use turpentine-varnish and lamp-black, and with a camel's hair brush pass over those parts you consider of sufficient depth. **1871** HAMERTON *Etcher's Handbk.* 78 Bracquemond..stopped-out sixty times, in order to get sixty degrees of depth in his lines. **1892** *Temple Bar* Sept. 56 The lettering of plates may be stopped-out or burnished away or covered up for the striking off of misleading impressions.

(*b*) **1838** in *Newton's Lond. Jrnl.* Conj. Ser. XVI. 63 Certain apparatus, by which I stop out or protect any desired portions of the cloth or fabric, whilst it is under the operation of dyeing. **1885** LOCK *Workshop Rec.* Ser. IV. 214/2 [Electrotyping.] The mould is next 'stopped out', by brushing liquid wax on those portions of the frame and wax upon which no deposition is intended to take place.

e. stop over. *trans.* In *Moulding*: see quot.

1885 [HORNER] *Pattern Making* 53 'Stopping-over' means filling up the upper portion of the print level with the face of the mould, after the core has been placed in position.

III. To come to a stand, cease to move or act.

34. a. *intr.* To cease from onward movement, to come to a stand or position of rest. More emphatically ***to stop dead, stop short*** (see DEAD, SHORT *advs.*). Said of a person or other living creature, also of an inanimate thing driven or propelled.

1530 PALSGR. 736/2, I stoppe, as a horse or cart doth, whan they be goyng on the way, *je jocque.* **1597** SHAKS. *2 Hen. IV*, I. i. 38 (Qo.) After him came spurring hard A gentleman.. That stopt by me, to breathe his bloudied horse. **1670** DRYDEN *Tyr. Love* IV. ii, As some faint pilgrim..Sometimes resolved to fetch his leap, and then Runs to the bank, but there stops short again. **1709** *Tatler* No. 114 ¶1, I saw a Coach stop at my Door. **1770** CUMBERLAND *West Indian* I. vi, Stop, stay a little, Charles, whither are you going in such haste? **1736** GRAY *Statius* I. 40 Sure flew the disc from his unerring hand, Nor stopp'd till it had cut the further strand. **1821** SCOTT *Kenilw.* v, He again paced the room in silence, stopped, filled and drank a cup of wine. *Ibid.* xxiv, Pulling the reins with all his might, and ejaculating, 'Stop! stop!' **1852** F. S. WILLIAMS *Our Iron Roads* x. 227 On a train stopping, or travelling slowly through an intermediate station. **1855** KINGSLEY *Westw. Ho!* xii, Sebastian Cabota, ..being in want of provisions, stopped short at the mouth of that mighty South American river. **1907** J. H. PATTERSON *Man-Eaters of Tsavo* xv. 169 All of a sudden, however, the jackal stopped dead for a second, and then made off out of sight.

fig. **1595** SHAKS. *John* v. vii. 67 [The king dies.] *Hen.* Euen so must I run on, and euen so stop.

b. *spec.* of a horse: See quot. 1679.

? **1575** BLUNDEVIL *Art of Riding* II. ii. D viij b, The horse by this meanes learneth .iii. lessons at once,..firste to tread the ringe, secondly to stop, and thirdly to turne. **1601** SHAKS. *Jul. C.* IV. i. 32 It is a Creature that I teach to fight, To winde, to stop, to run directly on. **1679** A. LOVELL *Indic. Univ.* 215/2 To stop a Horse is, to make him stay short on his buttocks... That Horse stops well. **1697** DRYDEN *Virg. Georg.* III. 183 The Lapithæ..taught the Steed to bound;.. To stop, to fly, the Rules of War to know.

c. To pause, stay on the or one's way (*to* do something). Also ***to stop short***.

1711 ADDISON *Spect.* No. 129 ¶9 He stopt short at the Coach, to ask us how far the Judges were behind us. **1825** SCOTT *Talism.* ix, The baron, however, was a little later of entering the tent.., stopping, perchance, to issue some orders. **1837** DICKENS *Pickw.* xxxviii, You've been stopping to over all the posts in Bristol, you idle young scamp! **1873** RUSKIN *Fors Clav.* III. xxx. 10 It seemed to him that everybody stopped as they passed, to look at his cart.

35. a. To make a halt on a journey, esp. to halt and remain for rest and refreshment. Of a coach, train, boat, or other public conveyance: To halt at a specified place to pick up and set down passengers, etc.

1743 BULKELEY & CUMMINS *Voy. S. Seas* 107 The greatest Part of the People must be oblig'd, at every Place we stop, to go on Shore in Search of Provisions. **1794** MRS. RADCLIFFE *Udolpho* xxxv, The postilions stopped at the convent..to take up Blanche. **1832** J. H. NEWMAN *Lett. & Corr.* (1891) I. 295 The vessel not being allowed to stop over tomorrow. **1837** DICKENS *Pickw.* xxii, It was at the door of this overgrown tavern, that the London coach stopped, at the same hour every evening. **1849** MACAULAY *Hist. Eng.* xvi. III. 677 Thence he travelled to London, stopping by the road at the mansions of some great lords. **1856** MISS ISAB. BIRD *Englishw. in Amer.* 160 While stopping at a station another lady entered. **1901** ALLDRIDGE *Sherbro* xxiii. 235 We..marched on..until we reached the old shed, where we had stopped three days before.

b. ***to stop over***: to make a halt (*at* a place) and proceed by a later conveyance. Similarly ***to stop off***. orig. *U.S.*

1855 *Knickerbocker* XLVI. 604 He had 'stopped off', he said, to see a friend. **1857** M. J. HOLMES *Meadow-Brook* xvi. 182 Wishing to see a friend of his who lives here, we have stopped over one train. **1873** 'MARK TWAIN' & WARNER *Gilded Age* xxiv. 218 Once when you renewed your ticket after stopping over in Baltimore. **1884** SIR J. W. DAWSON in *Handbk. Canada* 86 By stopping over at Dalhousie..the following localities may be visited. **1892** *Harper's Mag.* Feb. 437/2, I stopped off overnight to see about something for a friend. **1897** *Outing* (U.S.) XXIX. 563/2 Yet would I counsel the traveler whose way lies by Avignon to stop off, if only for an hour, in order to ascend the Rocher des Doms. **1913** *Blackw. Mag.* Jan. 98/2 It was arranged that the party should 'stop off' at a small place..on the main line, and should thence by motor 'side track'..to another small town. **1925** D. H. LAWRENCE *Let.* ?7 Nov. (1962) 864 It is great fun stopping off in Switzerland to see you. **1952** M. LASKI *Village* xii. 173 'Shall we stop off soon and eat our lunch?' asked Roy and at the next field-gate they dismounted. **1970** G. F. NEWMAN *Sir, You Bastard* viii. 244 Stopping off after court for an early liquid lunch. **1971** *Daily Tel.* 29 Dec. 10 Many people suffer from jet fatigue and on long-distance routes often go to the additional expense of stopping over somewhere on the way to recuperate.

c. ***to stop in***: to pay a brief visit, 'drop in'. *U.S.*

1904 *Dialect Notes* II. 421 *Stop in*, *vb. i.*, to call. 'I *stopped in* at his house one day.' **1925** T. DREISER *Amer. Tragedy* (1926) I. II. xxxvi. 402 He stopped in, not at all sure that on this first occasion he would be able to broach the dangerous subject. **1953** J. CHEEVER in *New Yorker* 22 Aug. 23/2 He was rude to his friends when they stopped in for a drink. **1963** *Jrnl. Amer. Med. Assoc.* 26 Oct. 459/1 He was found dead in his crib by a family friend who had stopped in at the home. **1979** *Yale Alumni Mag.* Apr. (Suppl.) cn17/3 Classmates are eagerly invited to stop in!

d. With *by*: (*a*) as *adv.*, = sense 35 c above; (*b*) as *prep.*, to call at, visit (a place). orig. *U.S.*

1905 *Dialect Notes* III. 96 *Stop by*, *v. phr.*, to call, to visit. 'I believe I'll *stop by* and see Bud.' **1923** *Ibid.* V. 244 *Stop by*, v. phr., to visit. '*Stop by* my house.' **1928** F. N. HART *Bellamy Trail* v. 172 They were going to stop by for her. **1943** T. PRATT *Barefoot Mailman* i. 11, I picked him up when I stopped by at St. Augustine. **1953** N. GORDIMER *Lying Days* II. v. 48 It was Ludi, he would stop by at the old Plaskett's on the way to say hullo—. **1957** *New Yorker* 2 Nov. 89/3 Don't wait..stop by your favorite shop and try one today. **1964** MRS. L. B. JOHNSON *White House Diary* 8 Apr. (1970) 103, I had asked Mrs. MacArthur and her son ..to stop by the White House to warm up and have a cup of tea. **1973** M. AMIS *Rachel Papers* 20, I mentioned that Gloria would probably be stopping by later on.

36. a. (Cf. STAY *v.*[1] 8, which is often preferred as more correct.) To remain, prolong one's stay in a place; to stay (*to* dinner, *at* home, *with* a person). Also *to* with *inf.* Also quasi-*trans.*, to remain for (a ceremony, a meal, etc.).

1801 tr. *Gabrielli's Myst. Husb.* III. 123 If your Honour and you, Madam, will stop to dinner with us. **1805** MOORE *Mem.* (1853) I. 181 Now, by stopping in town to-morrow, I shall..get off the necessity of returning to town so soon as I otherwise should do. **1832** J. H. NEWMAN *Lett. & Corr.* (1891) I. 254 Let him [come up alone and] go into your rooms, and do stop in Devonshire a good while. *Ibid.* 275 Did I consult my wishes I should stop at home. **1857** HUGHES *Tom Brown* II. vii, I never stop the Sacrament... I've never been confirmed. **1858** TROLLOPE *Dr. Thorne* xxix, But you'll stop and take a bit of dinner with us? **1864** MRS. RIDDELL *Geo. Geith* xxi. II. 88 The butler..went straight off to Granny, and gave her notice; and she actually raised his wages, and prayed him to stop. **1898** RIDER HAGGARD *Doctor Therne* 10, I could stop in Mexico for three months. **1901** W. R. H. TROWBRIDGE *Lett. her Mother to Eliz.* xix. 94, I am sure the society at Lucerne would have bored me if I had stopped much longer.

b. With advs., as *away*, *out.* ***to stop on***, to continue in one place or employment. ***to stop up***, to remain 'up' at one's college or university; *colloq.* to sit up instead of going to bed. ***to stop out***: *spec. N. Amer.*, to interrupt one's higher education for a time in order to pursue some other activity.

1815 *Zeluca* II. 86 You stopped away from Spire on Tuesday. **1819** J. H. NEWMAN *Lett. & Corr.* (1891) I. 42 [At the end of the term he writes] The Fellows have been very kind, have said we might stop up as long as we like. **1848** THACKERAY *Van. Fair* lxi, Georgy stopped away from school. **1857** MRS. GASKELL *Charlotte Brontë* II. 148 Mr. Brontë and old Tabby went to bed... But Charlotte.. stopped up,—it was very tempting,—late and later. **1889** *Spectator* 14 Sept., This..is their notion of a career, and.. to 'stop on' in the village is to accept a great disappointment. **1926** I. S. COBB *Some United States* xi. 257 I'm a Virginian —at present stopping out in Kentucky. **1942** BERREY & VAN DEN BARK *Amer. Thes. Slang* §214/7 *Stop out*, to stay away from home all night. **1971** *Less Time, More Options* (Rep. Carnegie Commission on Higher Educ.) vii. 28 Colleges and universities can assist by..encouraging students to have work or service experience before entering college, to stop out while in college to obtain it, or both. **1977** *N.Y. Times* 16 Jan. IV. 9/1 Paul Marantz is stopping out. He's one of the estimated two million college undergraduates..who last year left school to spend some time in the outside world, or to try out some other form of education, but who do plan to return eventually and earn their degrees.

c. To sojourn as a visitor, resident, or guest.

1797 MRS. A. M. BENNETT *Beggar Girl* (1813) V. 37 They wanted her to let Miss stop with them. **1839** LEVER *Harry Lorrequer* ii, You will dine with us to-day at seven..: but make your arrangements to stop all night and to-morrow. **1859** G. TICKNOR *Life* II. xxii. 439 Sir Henry Holland..has been stopping with the President. **1859** DASENT *Pop. Tales Norse* 344 She gave the man leave to stop the night. **1901** W. R. H. TROWBRIDGE *Lett. her Mother to Eliz.* vi. 26 Clandevil is stopping at Astley Court.

37. a. To leave off doing what one is actually engaged in for the moment. Const. *from.* Also ***to stop short***, to leave off abruptly.

1594 SHAKS. *Rich. III*, IV. ii. 45 Hath he so long held out with me, vntyr'd, And stops he now for breath? **1727** POPE *Macer* 9 There he stopped short, nor since has writ a tittle.

1826 SCOTT *Jrnl.* 12 Mar., I was interrupted by a slumberous feeling which made me obliged to stop once or twice. **1861** PALEY *Æschylus* (ed. 2) *Choeph.* 904 *note*, The transcriber having begun to copy the next verse, and stopping short on discovering his error. **1885** W. W. STORY *Fiammetta* ii. 32 The groups of reapers that stopped from their work to gaze at the passing train. **1894** J. T. FOWLER *Adamnan* Introd. 74 And here, he said, I must stop, let Baithene write the rest.

b. To pause in speech or narrative; to break off in the middle of a sentence. Also *to stop short*, to pause abruptly. †Also *refl.*

1579 W. WILKINSON *Confut. Fam. Love* Brief Descr. ☛ iiij b, Yea quoth Vitels..the same mynde must be in you which was in Christ, and there he stopped him [*i.e.* did not complete the quotation]. **1592** SHAKS. *Rom. & Jul.* II. iv. 98 *Ben.* Stop there, stop there. *Mer.* Thou desir'st me to stop in my tale against the haire. **17..** POPE *Imit. Hor.* I. vii. 84 'Harley, the Nation's great Support,'—But you may read it; I stop short. **1816** SCOTT *Old Mort.* xxxviii, He had just recollection sufficient to stop short in the midst of the dangerous sentence. **1862** MISS BRADDON *Lady Audley* xxxiii, 'There's Luke, too tipsy to help himself,..there's Mr. Audley asleep—.' Phœbe Marks stopped suddenly at the mention of Robert's name. **1862** MRS. BROWNING *Last Poems, King's Gift* i, Now what has the messenger brought her,..To make her stop short in her singing?

c. To pause in a course of conduct (*to* think, question oneself).

1865 FLOR. MARRYAT *Love's Confl.* I. xix. 328 She herself never stopped—she dared not stop—to ask herself why or wherefore she felt thus.

d. *imper.*, used as an injunction to pause in or desist from any procedure, as speech, argument, criticism, and the like. Also in the phrase *stop a moment!*

1570 FOXE *A. & M.* (ed. 2) III. 2164/2 At last his chaplaynes cryed, stoppe, stoppe my Lord, for now he wyll recant. **1738** POPE *Epil. Sat.* II. 52 *P.* To tax Directors,.. Still better, Ministers, or, if the thing May pinch ev'n there —why lay it on a King. *F.* Stop! stop! *P.* Must Satire, then, nor rise nor fall? **1759** JOHNSON *Rasselas* ix, 'Stop a moment', said the Prince; 'is there such depravity in man as that he should' [etc.]. **1839** LEVER *Harry Lorrequer* xxx, 'Well, are you satisfied that this is his handwriting?'.. 'Why, of course—but stop—you are right; it is not his hand.' **1848** ALB. SMITH *Chr. Tadpole* xlvii. 408 'We will knock the neck [of the bottle] off with a stone.' 'Stop, Sir,' said the stranger. 'Excuse me—this is the way to do it.' **1865** FLOR. MARRYAT *Love's Confl.* I. xix. 336 He..drew out the packet of letters. 'Confound it!' where was the one in his mother's handwriting? The rest were all there—stop! were they? **1887** O. WILDE *Canterville Ghost* v, 'Stop!' cried Virginia, stamping her foot, 'it is you who are rude, and horrid, and vulgar'.

e. *Bridge.* To refrain from increasing one's bid beyond a specified level. Const. *in*.

1959 *Listener* 5 Feb. 265/1 The British pair stopped in Five Hearts. **1964** FREY & TRUSCOTT *Official Encycl. Bridge* 533/1 *Stopping below game*, the decision to 'stop on a dime' in two no trump or three of a major may be influenced by a variety of factors.

38. a. To leave off, stay, desist (in a course of action or a pursuit, or from one's customary action or employment). Const. *from*, *to* with *inf.* Also *to stop short*.

1689 *Sc. Acts* (1875) XII. 61/2 Letters..ordering the Judges to stoppe and desist sine die to determine causes depending before them. **1850** MCCOSH *Div. Govt.* II. i. (1874) 146 Every event has a cause, and in tracing up causes we must stop at length at a great first cause. **1901** W. R. H. TROWBRIDGE *Lett. her Mother to Eliz.* xxi. 99 Lady Beatrice, who really at her age ought to stop, got a blow on her forehead [at hockey].

b. To limit one's activity *at* a certain point; to refrain from exceeding a certain degree or extent.

1737 *Gentl. Mag.* VII. 539, I..attended the innocent but unfortunate Men to the Scaffold... I did not stop here, for I carried the Head of Captain Green to the Grave. **1744** KAMES *Decis. Crt. Sess. 1730–54* (1799) 81 If the rule be ones established that a man has power over his neighbour's property..there is no possibility to stop short. **1770** CUMBERLAND *West Indian* IV. iii, *Louisa.* Hold, are you mad? I see you are a bold, assuming man, and know not where to stop. **1771** *Junius Lett.* xlii, The woman, who admits of one familiarity, seldom knows where to stop, or what to refuse. **1819** SCOTT *Ivanhoe* xxviii, His charity would willingly have stopped short at Ashby. **1860** ROUS in *Baily's Mag.* I. 75, I know the point to stop at, and how far the public will support me in my policy.

c. To stay in action, to hesitate, 'stick'. Const. *at*. *to stop at nothing*, to be prevented by no obstacle.

1676 DRYDEN *Aureng-zebe* II. 29 The World is made for the bold impious man; Who stops at nothing, seizes all he can. **1704** CIBBER *Careless Husb.* v. 63 'Tis Possible you'll stop at Nothing to preserve it. *c* **1738** POPE *On Receiving Standish* 24 You'd write..on ivory, so glib, As not to stick at fool or ass, Nor stop at Flattery or Fib. **1907** J. H. PATTERSON *Man-Eaters of Tsavo* ii. 20 They stopped at nothing..in order to obtain their favourite food.

39. a. Of a thing: To cease its motion or action. Of a process: To cease activity; to come to pause or end.

a **1529** SKELTON *E. Rummyng* 29 Her nose..Neuer stoppynge, But euer droppynge. **1594** KYD *Cornelia* II. 186 Whereat my blood stopt in my stragling vaines; Mine haire grew bristled. **1605** SHAKS. *Macb.* II. iii. 104 The Spring, the Head, the Fountaine of your Blood Is stopt, the very Source of it is stopt. *Macd.* Your Royall Father's murther'd. **1663** BAYFIELD *Treat. De Morb. Capitis* 181 The more he bled, the more his Fever abated, and when it was gone, the blood stopped. **1707** MORTIMER *Husb.* 574 It flushes violently out of the Cock for about a Quart, and then stops on a sudden. **1765** *Museum Rust.* IV. 181 The purging stopped the fourth day. **1771** *Junius Lett.* xliv. (1788) 254 Their whole proceeding stops; and there they stand, ashamed to retreat, and unable to advance. **1816** J. SMITH *Panorama Sci. & Art* II. 482 Crystallization goes on but very slowly in closed vessels; and in most instances wholly stops. **1830** R. KNOX *Béclard's Anat.* 247 The ulceration stops and heals. **1839** D. MILNE in *Trans. R. Soc. Edin.* XIV. 458 The Kirtle, a river which runs from Dumfriesshire into the Solway Frith, stopped, on the 17th February 1748, for five hours. **1901** W. R. H. TROWBRIDGE *Lett. her Mother to Eliz.* xxix. 141 Yesterday it rained..and when it stopped for a few minutes there was such a nasty fog.

b. Of a machine, etc.: To cease working or going. Also *to stop dead*.

1789 COWPER *Let. Mrs. Throckmorton* 18 July, Your clock in the hall has stopped. **1839** DICKENS *Nich. Nick.* ii, My watch has stopped. **1903** A. MACLAREN *Last Sheaves* 182 You have weaving machines..that whenever a thread breaks stop dead.

40. a. Of an immaterial thing: To have its limit of operation at a specified point. Of a series: To come to an end.

1733 POPE *Ess. Man* III. 128 There stops the Instinct, and there ends the care. **1741–2** CHALLONER *Missionary Priests* (1803) II. 19 But the severities exercised against catholics did not stop here. **1806** *Med. Jrnl.* XV. 533 That any particular mode of treatment should stop at such supposed line, and that then an opposite mode of cure should be thought necessary. **1874** GROSS *Algebra* II. 23 If a series stops at some one term, it is called a finite series. **1911** H. BINDLOSS *Hawtrey's Deputy* xi, His comprehension stopped at such details as these.

b. Of a material thing: To come to an end (in space). *to stop short*, to end abruptly.

1887 S. O. RIDLEY in *Challenger Rep.* XX. 204 Every alternate fascicle of the main skeleton stops short a little way below the surface. **1915** *Blackw. Mag.* Mar. 338/1 Alleys, each of which stopped with a dead end.

IV. 41. [From STOP *sb.*[2]] *trans.* To furnish with stops or punctuation-marks, to punctuate.

1776 *Critical Observ. Books* I. 25 Thus Bergler rightly stops these lines; for if a comma be made after στυφελιξη [etc.]. **1802** DIBDIN *Edit. Classics* 39 *note*, These verses are stopp'd according to the Harleian Catalogue. **1826** LANDOR *Imag. Conv.*, *Alfieri & Salomon* Wks. 1846 I. 191/1 Guicciardini, if his sentences were properly stopped, would be found in general both full and concise. **1885** G. ALLEN *Babylon* x, That letter wasn't all spelt right, or stopped right.

42. *Versification.* To conclude or divide (a line of verse) with a 'stop'. Cf. STOP *sb.*[2] 17 c, STOPPED *ppl. a.* 8. Also *intr.* (cf. 37 b).

1857 C. B[ATHURST] *Rem. Differ. Shaks. Versif.* 148, I think Shakspeare had a preference, where the line is completely stopped in the middle, for a break upon the short syllable. *Ibid.* 202 Blank verse, unbroken, is still totally separate from complete rhyme, as having no tendency to stop at every other line.

V. 43. Combinations of the verb with a sb. in objective relation: †**stop-gamble**, †**stop-game**, a situation that ends or interrupts the game; †**stop-hole**, a plug; **stop-loss** *a.*, (of an order to sell stock, etc.) intended to save further loss than has been already incurred by falling prices; **stop-motion**, a device for automatically stopping a machine or engine when something has gone wrong; **stop-mouth** *a. nonce-wd.*, intended to keep people silent; **stop-press** *sb.* (see quot. 1888); also *attrib.* or *adj.* (of an issue of a newspaper or a particular column), containing late news inserted after printing has begun; †**stop-ship** [tr. Gr. ἐχενηΐς], the remora; **stop-tap**, the time at which drinks cease to be served in a public house; †**stop-throat** *a. nonce-wd.*, that tightly enwraps the throat; **stop-water** *Naut.*, (*a*) something fixed or towed overboard to retard the motion of a ship; (*b*) a plug or other contrivance for making a joint water-tight; (*c*) *gen.* (? *nonce-use*) an obstacle to the flow of water. Also STOP-GAP.

1579 J. STUBBES *Gaping Gulf* E v, A most strange dreame it is of theirs who will haue thys match a bridle to the french king, a snaffle to Spayn, and a *stopgamble to all practises of competition for popery. **1659** GAUDEN *Tears Ch.* IV. xx. 566 No violence and injustice can be proper to usher in true Christian Religion and Reformation: these methods have made them so stunted and ricketly, that they are come to a *stop-game. **1562** TURNER *Baths* 2 My counsell is yt euery bath haue an hole in the bottome, by the whych the *stophole taken out ye bath should be clenged. *c* **1711** PETIVER *Gazophyl.* VII. lxv, The Cover or Stop-hole of the *Cochlea cœlata.* **1901** *Scotsman* 8 Apr. 9/7 Many fresh *stop-loss orders were put on the market. **1851** *Mechanics' Mag.* Jan. 54/2 An Improvement in *Stop-motion of Looms. **1902** THORNLEY *Cotton Combing Machines* 210 There are two or three descriptions of stop motions which are applied to combers when required. **1823** in *Spirit Publ. Jrnls.* 261 The accumulated expences of renewals, interest, stamps, *stop-mouth and forbearance money. **1881** *Manch. Even. News* 17 Mar. 3 The *stop-press edition of the Daily Chronicle says [etc.]. **1888** *Encycl. Brit.* XXIII. 703/1 In machines which printed from the type, late telegrams could only be inserted by a 'stop-press'; that is, the printing was interrupted while the alteration was being made. **1910** *Spectator* 16 July 103/1 The 'stop press' column of an evening newspaper. **1591** SYLVESTER *Du Bartas* I. v. 444 O *Stop-ship say, say how thou canst oppose Thy selfe alone against so many foes? **1672** JOSSELYN *New Eng. Rarities* 29 Remora, or Suck Stone, or Stop Ship. **1938** F. D. SHARPE *Sharpe of Flying Squad* xxiii. 240 Bob said that they hadn't *passed by* any public houses and that it was after '*stop tap' that they were passing the shop. **1940** DYLAN THOMAS *Portr. Artist as Young Dog* 228 If you go for a constitutional after stop-tap along the sands you might as well be in Sodom and Gomorrah. **1960** V. JENKINS *Lions down Under* 103 The 'five o'clock, to six o'clock swill' in the bars of New Zealand cities—for 'stop-tap' is at six—is also a phenomenon to be avoided. **1975** R. LEWIS *Part of Virtue* vi. 147 Next evening, after stop tap, he was putting some crates out behind the pub. **1600** ROWLANDS *Lett. Humours Blood* xxvii. 33 Why in the *Stop-throate fashion doth he go, With Scarfe about his necke? **1794** *Rigging & Seamanship* II. 337 *Stopwaters.. on the lee quarter.., may cause the ship to veer. **1820** SCORESBY *Acc. Arctic Reg.* II. 450 Making a stop-water between two of the frames of timber on the fore part of the leak. **1832** GEN. P. THOMPSON *Exerc.* (1842) II. 324 If London Bridge could have kept out the first stroke of the pick-axe, the old stop-water would have been there still. **1844** *Civil Engin. & Arch. Jrnl.* VII. 95/2 It offers little or no resistance to the speed of the vessel as a stopwater. **1869** SIR E. REED *Shipbuild.* xi. 228 A stop-water formed of Canvas steeped in paint,..must be fitted between the continuous plates and angle-irons.

b. *Cinematogr.* Combinations of the verb with a sb., with reference to the technique of stopping the camera between frames in order to produce special effects, esp. animation; as *stop-action*, *-frame*, *-motion*, *-shot*, etc.

1912 F. A. TALBOT *Moving Pictures* 201 When the 'stop' call was given the witch disappeared from the stage... The strange effects produced in the witch's cave were obtained both by double printing and the 'stop-motion'. **1915** J. B. RATHBUN *Motion Picture Making* 73 Trick street scenes, commonly known as 'stop' pictures. **1933** G. H. SEWELL *Commercial Cinematography* x. 155 Stop-motion is..the method of cine-photography in which one, two, or three frames..are taken at one time, the camera being stopped and the subject re-arranged after each shot or group of shots. **1959** HALAS & MANVELL *Technique Film Animation* xxii. 274 The technique for stop-action puppet work must be worked out in terms of single motion-picture frames. **1966** *Listener* 14 July 67/1 The stop-shots neatly made each point. **1968** *Guardian* 22 Mar. 10/4 The stop-frame technique in which the puppets are photographed separately for each movement. **1976** R. B. PARKER *Promised Land* (1977) xx. 122 Powers was quiet. We all were. It was like a stop frame in instant replay. **1980** *Sci. Amer.* Apr. 84/1 A glass is a solid that can be regarded as a stop-action photograph of a liquid.

44. Substantival or attributive uses of verbal phrases: **stop and frisk** *a.*, of or pertaining to the stopping and searching of suspects by the police; so **stop-and-search**, **stop-search-question**; **stop-and-start** *a.*, alternately stopping and starting; **stop-back**, a contrivance for temporarily arresting the flow of water in a pipe or watercourse (now *spec.* a lump of clay inserted for this purpose); **stop-me-and-buy-one**, a travelling vendor of refreshments, usu. ice-creams [from the slogan on the refrigerated box at the front of Wall's Ice-Cream tricycles]; also *attrib.*; **stop-off**, (*a*) something which stops the working of a machine; in quot. *attrib.*; (*b*) the act of stopping off (see 35 b); a place where one stops off; also *attrib.*; **stop-out**, (*a*) *colloq.*, one who stays out late; (*b*) *N. Amer.*, a student who interrupts his or her studies for a time in order to pursue some other activity; an interruption of studies for this purpose; also *attrib.*; **stop-over** (also **stopover**), (*U.S.*), (*a*) the act of 'stopping over' (see 35 b) or breaking one's journey to go on by a later conveyance; also *attrib.*; (*b*) permission given to a passenger to break his journey (now *rare* or *obs.*); (*c*) a place where a journey is broken; also *fig.*; **stop-short** *a.* (*nonce-wd.*), that stops short of its proper object.

1967 *Economist* 21 Oct. 286/1 The cases to be heard this year are a mixed bag. Those involving the criminal law and the police—particularly '*stop and frisk' laws—may be the most controversial. **1975** *New Yorker* 2 June 101/1 A Terry stop is what civil libertarians sometimes refer to as stop-and-frisk. **1974** *Spartanburg* (S. Carolina) *Herald* 25 Apr. A 10/1 A federal court judge began hearing arguments Wednesday on whether to halt the hotly debated police 'Operation Zebra' *stop-and-search dragnet for the black killer or killers of 12 whites. **1950** J. G. DAVIS *Dict. Dairying* 62 The feed to the dies is done with a variable *stop-and-start motion, allowing the strip time to stop while the die punches out the shape. **1961** *Times* 4 May 13/6 The stop-and-start tendencies of our economy. **1976** *Woman's Day* (U.S.) Nov. 50/2 If you do a lot of stop-and-start driving,..change every three months or 3,000 miles. **1790** *Act 30 Geo. III.* c. 21 §1 Stand Pipes, Service Pipes,..*Stopbacks, Valves, Fire Plugs. [**1935** *Automobile & Carriage Builders' Jrnl.* LXXV. 4/1 'Stop me and buy one.' The latest type of cycle carrier for ice-cream vending.] **1935** *Food* Oct. 3/1 A holiday spent in a number of South Coast towns suggests that England is ..becoming as ice-cream-minded as North America. The last three hot summers have provided a golden harvest for the familiar tricycle. But even more recent..has been the appearance..of the 'ice-cream parlour'... 'Come in and have one' is evidently proving as alluring a slogan as the more familiar '*Stop me and buy one'. **1936** N. COWARD *To-Night at 8.30* 49 Asked if I'd got an ice-cream wafer... What did she think I was, a 'Stop me and buy one'? **1939** N. MONSARRAT *This is Schoolroom* xi. 228 To..buy an ice from the stop-me-and-buy-one man. **1947** DYLAN THOMAS *Let.* 11 Apr. (1966) 300 There were stop-me-&-buy-one bicycle boys selling, not ice-cream, but bottles of Chianti. **1979** D. ROBINSON *Eldorado Network* III. xliii. 288 Ice cream. Stop-me-and-buy-one, the Eldorado man on a tricycle. **1869** RANKINE *Machine & Hand-tools* Pl. K 9, The *stop-off motion..is very simple. **1912** J. SANDILANDS *Western Canad. Dict. & Phrase-bk.*, *Stop-off* or *stop-over privileges*, an arrangement made with the ticket agent to break a railway journey at some place where the passenger wishes to make a short halt. **1931** C. BEATON *Jrnl.* Feb. in *Wandering Years*

(1961) x. 226 En route for home there was a three-week stop-off in Paris. **1947** *Sun* (Baltimore) 18 Jan. 4/2 Is the police court merely a stop-off between one back room and the next? **1958** *Times Lit. Suppl.* 7 Mar. 125/3 London, New York, Paris, Rome come to life not as tourist centres, holiday stop-offs, but as places of work. **1977** *Horse & Hound* 14 Jan. 25/2 Cost of the trip is £530 return (excursion, 21 days–6 months, no stop-offs). **1906** E. Dyson *Fact'ry 'Ands* ii. 24 'See,' cried Annie—'See, you dirty *stop-out!' She placed the hat on the floor and danced wildly amongst the feathers. **1941** Baker *Dict. Austral. Slang* 72 *Stop-out*, an inveterate gadabout, esp. a woman. **1966** F. Shaw et al. *Lern Yerself Scouse* 27 *Yer a derty stopout*, you are a nocturnal reveller. **1971** *Less Time, More Options* (Rep. Carnegie Commission on Higher Educ.) vi. 13 That service and other employment opportunities be created for students between high school and at stop-out points in college. *Ibid.* 21 Those who plan to continue with academic study either directly or after a stop out. **1971** *Time* 27 Sept. 79/3 Still, many stop-outs do better academically than their less-seasoned classmates, if only because they are a year older. **1974** *Globe & Mail* (Toronto) 31 Oct. 1/5 The so-called stopout students, those who postponed entering university immediately after high school graduation, now are starting to go back to school. **1881** *Harper's Mag.* Apr. 767/2 They are allowed *stop-over tickets which give them the privilege of turning their stock out at any place for the winter, and then sending them on in the spring to market. **1884** *Advt. Illinois Central Railroad*, Tourist-tickets from Chicago to Texas,..via New Orleans, with stop-over privileges to visit the Exposition there. **1885** *Outing* (U.S.) Nov. 150/2 There I took advantage of what, in railroad parlance, is called a 'stop-over'. **1893** Samborn *S. California* 97 The schedule of trains allows of convenient stop-overs. **1895** *Outing* (U.S.) XXVII. App. 27 By stop-over privileges at every point of interest, the Northern Pacific Railroad enables tourists to visit this wonderful region. **1905** *Chambers's Jrnl.* Jan. 87/1 At Vancouver I stepped on board a Canadian Pacific Railway steamer bound for Hong-kong, with a stop-over on my second-class ticket. **1909** *Public Ledger* (Philad.) 24 June 11/4 Philadelphia is named as a stop-over point in excursions. **1928** *Blue Peter* July p. iv (Advt.), A Convenient Stopover. Honolulu is a regular port of call for passenger steamers crossing to or from the Orient. **1953** I. Levin *Kiss before Dying* I. ii. 11 College would only be an unnecessary stopover on the road to..success. **1959** *Economist* 20 June 1106/1 Mr Khrushchev will round off his Scandinavian tour in August by a two or three day stop-over in Helsinki. **1976** *National Observer* (U.S.) 22 May 18/6 From New York the round-trip economy fare is about $1,600, with stopover privileges in London and Nairobi. Because it's a very long flight, you can use the stopovers. **1973** *Time Out* 2–8 Mar. 10/3 More recently they have been performing *stop-search-question late night patrols in Hornsey which have resulted in such serious crime detection as arresting people with a quid's worth of dope. **1747** Richardson *Clarissa* (1811) I. xxx. 213 Proud of *exterior* advantages!—must not one be led by such a *stop short pride, as I may call it, in him or her who has it, to mistrust the *interior*?

stop: see stoop *sb.*^{2}

stop-and-go (stɒp ənd gəʊ), *a.* Also **stop and go.** [f. stop *v.* + and *conj.* + go *v.*] **1.** = stop-go *adj.* 1.

1926 G. Frankau *My Unsentimental Journey* xi. 145 St. Louis; where the men..have the most elaborate 'stop and go' signs for their traffic. **1935** D. L. Sayers *Gaudy Night* viii. 177 Its modern bustle of cars and complication of stop-and-go lights. **1942** *Policy on Rotary Intersections* (Amer. Assoc. State Highway Officials) 1 There is discussion of design speeds, interweaving lengths, curves, geometric shapes, sight distance, roadway widths, cross slope, curbs, islands, lighting, stop-and-go control and special adaptations of rotary intersections. **1962** N. Freeling *Love in Amsterdam* I. 61 Don't use your brain. Be a farmer holding a stop-and-go sign.

2. = stop-go *adj.* 2.

1943 F. L. Wright *Autobiogr.* (rev. ed.) iv. 329 No need to get tangled up in spasmodic stop-and-go traffic. **1972** *Jazz & Blues* Nov. 32/1 He also evinces real invention over the stop-and-go rhythms of *Departure*. **1977** 'E. McBain' *Long Time no See* vii. 94 His stop-and-go typing irritated Carella.

3. = stop-go *adj.* 3.

1961 *Times* 5 Jan. 11/5 The short-term 'stop-and-go' remedies of recent years..deal with the symptoms rather than the disease. **1961** *Hansard Commons* 7 Nov. 850 Before the right hon. Member for Monmouth we had the present Prime Minister as Chancellor. He was a 'stop and go' man. **1962** *Listener* 10 May 817/2 The new-found interest in planning in Tothill Street was a direct reaction to the stop-and-go policies of 1959 and 1960.

stopbank (ˈstɒpbæŋk). *Austral.* and *N.Z.* Also **stop-bank.** [f. stop *sb.*^{2} + bank *sb.*^{1}] A levee, an embankment.

1950 G. Wilson *Brave Company* xiii. 196 The clean lines of the river and the stopbank. **1958** S. Ashton-Warner *Spinster* 54 All them kids on the stopbank. **1965** S. T. Ollivier *Petticoat Farm* xv. 198 Stop-banks were raised against rivers. **1977** *N.Z. Herald* 5 Jan. 1–6/4 The Auckland Harbour Board controls to the tidal boundary at Bonds Rd, Matatoki, a vast acreage that has built up outside the stopbanks.

stopcock (ˈstɒpkɒk). [f. stop *sb.*^{2} or *v.* + cock *sb.*^{1} 12.] A tap or short pipe furnished with a valve operated from the outside by turning a key or handle, for the purpose of stopping or permitting as required the passage of liquid, air, steam, gas or the like. (Sometimes improperly applied to the key or handle by which the valve is turned.)

1584 in Hudson & Tingey *Rec. Norwich* (1910) II. 393 The sayd maynepype and pypes, systerne, cockes and stopcockes. **1653** H. More *Antid. Ath.* II. ii. §8 (1712) 44 Apply a tapering Valve of Brass to the lower branch of the Stopcock of the Receiver well emptied of Air, as before, and turn the Key of the Stopcock. **1664** Pepys *Diary* 25 Dec., Some family offences, such as my having of a stopcock to keepe the water from them. **1755** *Gentl. Mag.* XXV. 494 At one end of this cylinder there is screwed a pneumatic gun.. furnished with a stop-cock, to be used occasionally. **1790** *Act 30 Geo. III* c. 21 §1 Such Pipes, Stop Cocks, Plugs [etc.]. **1844** H. Stephens *Bk. Farm* II. 209 The common stop-cock, with a lengthened tail passing downward. **1894** *Times* 12 July 14/1 The stopcock..was placed in the service pipe leading from the water main into the adjoining house.

b. *attrib.*

1797 J. Curr *Coal Viewer* 63, 2 Feeding cocks made in the stop cock way, with a hole in the key to turn by hand occasionally. **1857** Miller *Elem. Chem., Org.* 21 The stop-cock tube, *c*, is connected with an exhausting syringe. **1901** *Westm. Gaz.* 21 Feb. 2/3 The consumers..are to be compelled to put 'stop-cock' boxes in the pavements outside their houses.

†**stope**, *sb.*^{1} *Obs.* Also 6 **stoppe.** [a. OF. *estoup(p)e, estoppe*:—L. *stuppa* tow, oakum. Cf. stupe.] **a.** Tow for burning. **b.** Oakum.

1552–3 in Feuillerat *Revels Edw. VI* (1914) 108 A dragons mowthe of plate with stoppes to burne like fier. **1569** R. Androse tr. *Alexis' Secr.* IV. I. 36 Take of the stope, or caulking which they take out of olde shippes.

stope (stəʊp), *sb.*^{2} *Mining.* [App. cogn. w. step *sb.*^{1}, but the phonological relation is obscure.]

†**1.** A step or notch in the side of a pit, or in an upright beam, to receive the end of a stemple or cross-piece. Also *attrib. Obs.*

1747 Hooson *Miner's Dict.* S 4, Instead thereof in either end is made a Step or Stope with a Gouge, and the ends of the Forks sharpned like the Edge-end of a Stemple for to stand in those Stopes. **1824** J. Mander *Derbysh. Miners' Gloss.* 69 *Stope*, a Hole or Step cut into the side or any other firm place, where there is occasion to set Stemples. **1836** R. Furness *Astrologer* Gloss. *Poet. Wks.* (1858) 175 *Stope and Coil*, or *Stope and Quoin.* In ancient times, the stope was a hole bored in the rock, in order to introduce the quoin or wedge to burst it open.

2. A step-like working in the side of a pit.

1747 Hooson *Miner's Dict.* U 2 b, Thus many men may work at once, taking each a Stope before him, one after another, and consequently raise more Ore. **1747** *Gentl. Mag.* XVII. 327 On the 6th of April..there happened a very great explosion, which beat down a good deal of the partitions, and some of the stops [*sic*] under ground, and a part of the coal took fire by the damp. **1758** Borlase *Nat. Hist. Cornw.* 169 The men work in stopes, that is, in several degrees or steps one above another. **1860** *Ure's Dict. Arts* (ed. 5) III. 469 The overburden being removed, the clay is dug up in stopes: that is, in successive layers or courses, and each one being excavated to a greater extent than the one immediately below it, the stopes resemble a flight of irregular stairs.

b. *attrib.*, as in *stope-working*; **stope drill**, a portable rock-drill, used in stoping.

1908 *Daily Report* 27 Aug., Rand stope drills..enter the competition early next year. **1910** *Chamb. Jrnl.* 7 May 358/2 By the time 'stope' working is commenced in the Cobalt silver-mines Canada will have first place among the silver-producing countries of the world.

stope (stəʊp), *v.* [f. stope *sb.*^{2}] **1.** *trans.* To cut (mineral ground) in stopes; to excavate horizontally, layer after layer; to extract (ore) by this process. Also with *out*. Also *absol.*

1778 W. Pryce *Min. Cornub.* 142 They found it most adviseable to sink Shafts down upon the Lode, to cut it at some depth, and then to Drive and Stope east and west upon the course of the Lode. **1886** *Encycl. Brit.* XXI. 230/2 The salt is stoped out in longitudinal and transverse galleries, and large vaulted chambers, supported by massive pillars. **1887** *Times* (weekly ed.) 9 Dec. 1/7 Many thousands of tons of stone, richly laden with gold, are ready to be stoped. **1896** Mériot *Eng.-Fr. Dict. Terms Finance*, etc. 226 *Stope*,..to break and extract the ore. *Ibid.*, *Stoping*,..breaking out the payable ore.

2. *Geol.* Of magma or a magmatic body: to make *its way* by stoping; also, to subject to stoping.

1908 *Amer. Jrnl. Sci.* CLXXVI. 19 The latter are regarded as then stoping their way up into the overlying shell. **1932** F. F. Grout *Petrogr. & Petrol.* III. 202 No batholith is known to have stoped its way to the actual surface. *Ibid.* 203 Some rocks are stoped and assimilated more readily than others. **1962** W. T. Huang *Petrology* iv. 104 If the specific gravity is lower than the corresponding solid rock, a magma could stope its way into rocks of similar chemical composition.

Hence **stoped** *ppl. a.*

1932 F. F. Grout *Petrogr. & Petrol.* III. 203 The stoped blocks may dissolve before moving far. **1970** K. C. Jackson *Textbk. Lithol.* ii. 38 The margin of the magma body becomes cluttered with scattered stoped blocks of wall rock.

stope: see step *v.*, stoop *sb.*^{1}, *v.*^{1}, stop *sb.*^{2}, *v.*, stoup.

†ˈ**stopel.** *Obs. rare.* [f. OTeut. **stōp-* ablaut-variant of **stap-*: see step *v.* and -el^1.] **a.** A footprint. **b.** A step of a flight of stairs.

971 *Blickl. Hom.* 127 þæt mon æfre þurh þæt mæȝe a þy maran dæl on þæm stoplum ȝewercean. *c* **1200** *Trin. Coll. Hom.* 165 On þe steire of fiftene stoples fro neþewarde to uuewarde.

stopell(e, obs. forms of stopple *sb.*^{1}

stopen, obs. pa. pple. of step *v.*

ˈ**stoper.** [f. stope *v.* + -er^1.] One who stopes.

1875 J. H. Collins *Metal Mining* 46 Stopers paid at per ton.

ˈ**stop-gap.** [f. stop *v.* + gap *sb.*^{1} (From the phrase *to stop a gap*: see gap *sb.*^{1} 2 b and 6 b.)]

†**1.** An argument in defence of some point attacked. *Obs.*

1533 More *Debell. Salem* Wks. 986/2 But yet hath this good man one stoppe gappe for me stil, to proue alwai that mi sample is not lyke.

2. Something that temporarily supplies a need; a makeshift. Also, of a person: One who temporarily occupies an office, etc. until a permanent appointment can be made.

1691 Shadwell *Scowrers* IV. i. 35 Reads. *Yet I have sent you a bill for 25ol. to receive...* This won't do, but thou art a good Dad, 'tis a pretty Stop Gap. **1731** *Fall of Mortimer* I. i. 9, I hate your Stop-gaps; they were never good for England. **1774** Foote *Cozeners* I. Wks. 1799 II. 147, I must desire you to find out some other agent: I declare off! you sha'n't make a stop-gap of me! **1804** Collins *Scripscrap.* p. vi, A Bit or a Scrap often serves, as a Stop-gap, to fill up the Void of an idle Hour. **1827** Hare *Guesses* Ser. I. 1 Moral prejudices are the stopgaps of virtue. **1883** *Athenæum* 8 Sept. 299/1 Altogether his volume is merely a stopgap pending the appearance of the book which is to supersede Mill. **1911** J. H. Rose *Pitt & Gt. War* xx. 447 Addington soon made it apparent that he was no stop gap.

3. An utterance intended to fill up a gap or an awkward pause in conversation or discourse.

[**1684**: see 5.] **1707** J. Stevens tr. *Quevedo's Com. Wks.* (1709) 416 A Compliment..is the common Stop gap. [*a* **1764**, **1885**: see 5.] **1886** H. W. Lucy *Diary Gladstone Parlt.* 211 Besides, if he is ever at a loss for a word, he can always throw in 'I am not one of those who', or 'I venture to say'. These stop-gaps..have been found very convincing.

4. In physical sense: Something to stop up a hole. *rare.*

1872 Geo. Eliot *Middlem.* xli, A bit of ink and paper, which has long been an innocent wrapping or stop-gap, may at last be laid open under the one pair of eyes which [etc.].

5. *attrib.* passing into *adj.*, with sense 'filling a gap, pause, etc.'

1684 J. Lacy *Sir H. Buffoon* I. 5 There's my Ladies little Dog..; then a Horse stolen or stray'd... Then there's the old stop-gap *Ditto*; and these are for ever and ever the news of the Gazette. *a* **1764** Lloyd *Ode to Genius* 20 Vain every phrase in curious order set, On each side leaning on the (stop-gap) epithet. **1885** *Proc. Amer. Soc. Psych. Research* I. 312 (Cent.) The 'well's' and 'ah's', 'don't-you-know's', and other stop-gap interjections. **1885** J. Chamberlain *Sp.* 13 June 146 What will be known in history as the 'Stop-gap' Government.

stop-go (stɒp gəʊ), *a.* and *sb.* [f. stop *v.* + go *v.*] **A.** *adj.* **1.** Of signs or lights: indicating alternately to traffic that it should stop or that it should go.

1918 *Wells Fargo Messenger* Feb. 94/3 The copper flashed us a smile as he gave his stop-go apparatus another twist. **1952** M. Steen *Phoenix Rising* ii. 50 They were..held up.. by 'Stop'-'Go' signs. **1965** *Motor* 17 July 1/2 The long queues of cars waiting at the wrongly timed stop-go lights.

2. Alternately stopping and going, or acting and not acting.

1960 *Times* 10 Oct. 16/1 In their new 'stop-go' style they were infinitely the more dangerous. **1973** 'M. Innes' *Appleby's Answer* iii. 32 Their taxi made only a tedious stop-go progress. **1980** *Times Lit. Suppl.* 2 May 503/4 Would that English historical journals discussed, for example, the implications for future research of the stop-go policy of recruitment of graduates to history departments.

3. *Econ.* Of, pertaining to, or designating a policy of alternately restricting demand, in order to contain inflation, and expanding credit, in order to reduce unemployment.

The earlier designation of the policy was *stop-and-go* (see stop-and-go *a.* 3).

1962 *Daily Tel.* 21 Feb. 10 It is precisely these 'stop-go' policies of successive Chancellors which have been a major cause of our export troubles. **1965** *Listener* 3 June 817/2 The British Government then in office found its negotiating position undermined by gossip and arguments at home about the imminence of devaluation of the pound sterling as the only way out of the old stop-go circle. **1971** *Business Week* 13 Nov. 146/3 Yet Ulman and Flanagan conclude that governments have a strong tendency to choose stop-go policies. **1975** J. De Bres tr. *Mandel's Late Capitalism* xiv. 455 The 'Stop-Go' pattern of the British economy in the first post-war Tory era is the classical example of such a relatively autonomous credit cycle. **1979** *Dædalus* Spring 47 In Sweden, special factors reduced the country's vulnerability to uncontrollable money wage increases, hence to disruptive policies of the stop-go variety.

B. *sb. Econ.* A stop-go policy; the economic cycle resulting from this.

1964 S. Brittan *Treasury under Tories* vii. 208 This was the event which turned the business community violently against 'stop-go' and made it look with a less jaundiced eye on national planning. **1966** *Listener* 2 June 808/2 Does more inflation mean more difficulties with the balance of payments and more 'stop-go'? **1972** *Accountant* 23 Mar. 365 What evidence is there to convince management and industry that the new phase of expansion which the Chancellor's proposals should generate will not, as on so many previous occasions, culminate within some 18–24 months in a revival of 'stop-go' and balance of payments difficulties? **1976** K. Joseph *Monetarism is not Enough* 10 We refused to believe that it was the drug which had caused the need for a stop, hence we still say 'stop-go', but it is the go which causes the stop, not vice-versa.

†ˈ**stopine.** *Obs. rare.* [? ad. It. *stoppino* (used in the sense of 'wick'), f. *stoppa* tow. (The It. original has *stoppata*.)] = stupe.

1582 Hester *Secr. Fioravanti* II. vii. 88 Laie on [the impostume] a stopine wet with..white of an Egge. *Ibid.* III.

lxxxiv. 111 The sinewes of an Oxe beyng dried and made linte to make tentes or stopines, is most excellent.

stoping ('stəʊpɪŋ), *vbl. sb.* [f. STOPE *v.* + -ING[1].]
a. The action of the verb STOPE.
1778 W. PRYCE *Min. Cornub.* 97 When met with in stopeing, or driving as aforesaid, they commonly say, 'It is a stope of dead ground.' **1903** *Westm. Gaz.* 16 Sept. 9/1 We have good reason to believe that actual stopings.. will expose a much larger amount than can now be seen.
attrib. **1877** RAYMOND *Statist. Mines & Mining* 320 Besides this, stoping ground for 10 men is opened. **1884** KNIGHT *Dict. Mech.* Suppl. 868/1 *Stoping Drill* (Mining.) One for excavating drifts or horizontally lying beds or steps [etc.].
b. *Geol.* The process by which intruding magma detaches blocks of the surrounding rock.
1903 R. A. DALY in *Amer. Jrnl. Sci.* CLXV. 272 (*heading*) The hypothesis of overhead stoping† by deep-seated magmas. [*Note*] †A technical mining term meaning to excavate upwards or sideways to remove ore. **1903** —— in *Bull. U.S. Geol. Surv.* No. 209. 102 Magmatic stoping would tend to weaken the earth's crust immediately above the intruding body. **1939** BAILEY & WEIR *Introd. Geol.* xlii. 237 On the whole, stoping is probably the most important method of emplacement. **1977** A. HALLAM *Planet Earth* 69/1 Intrusions are emplaced in various ways: for example, ..by stoping, a process of gradual movement involving the dislodging of the blocks of country rock and their incorporation—perhaps even assimilation—into the magma.

stople, obs. form of STOPPLE *sb.*[1], *sb.*[2]

stopless ('stɒplɪs), *a.* [f. STOP *sb.*[2] + -LESS.] Without a stop or stops. **a.** Unceasing. **b.** Of a pipe: Having no stops. **c.** Without punctuation.
1660 DAVENANT *Poem K. Chas. II's Return* 14 Making a civill and staid Senate rude, And stoplesse as a running multitude. **1899** *Academy* 11 Nov. 543/2 A slouching figure playing imaginary tunes on a stopless pipe. **1903** W. JERROLD in *Great Thoughts* 10 Jan. 248/1 The voice gives out before the end of the first stopless stanza of over 60 lines.
Hence **'stoplessness.**
1859 *Sat. Rev.* 19 Feb. 220/1 Sometimes she works herself up into a state of utter stoplessness—at others, she gives half a page in which the pause of a comma is all the time allowed for refreshment anywhere.

stoppability (stɒpə'bɪlɪtɪ). *rare.* [f. next (though recorded earlier): see -ITY.] Lack of resistance to stoppage.
1897 *Allbutt's Syst. Med.* IV. 389 To judge of the force or 'stopability' of the pulse it is best to use two fingers and both hands in feeling it.

stoppable ('stɒpəb(ə)l), *a.* [f. STOP *v.* + -ABLE; cf. STOPPABILITY.] That can be stopped.
1934 in WEBSTER. **1977** *Time* 3 Jan. 20/1 Stop most anyone you see—they're generally stoppable—and he or she will soon be spinning you a web of recollection to entertain you both. **1982** *Economist* 16 Oct. 18/1 The dangers threatening Lebanon's Palestinians are not academic; they are both foreseeable and stoppable.

stoppage ('stɒpɪdʒ). [f. STOP *v.* + -AGE.] The action of stopping, the condition of being stopped.
1. Deduction from payments; a sum 'stopped' or deducted from the pay of a soldier, workman, or servant.
1465 *Paston Lett.* II. 221, I told hym that.. I wold pay hym his dewte without any stoppage. **1747** in *Col. Rec. Pennsylv.* V. 140 The Private Men at the rate of 6d. Sterling per Day, out of which a Stoppage must be made of 4d. for their Provisions. **1802** C. JAMES *Milit. Dict.*, *Stoppages*, in a military sense, deductions from a soldiers pay, the better to provide him with necessaries, &c. **1831** *Act 1 & 2 Will. IV* c. 37 §23 Such Stoppage or Deduction.. shall not be in any Case made from the Wages of such Artificer, unless [etc.]. **1855** MACAULAY *Hist. Eng.* xx. IV. 525 His anxiety that she should receive her income regularly and without stoppages was honourable to him. **1883** GRESLEY *Gloss. Coal-mining* 243 *Stoppages*, deductions from miners' wages, such as rent, candles, blacksmith's work, field club, etc. **1912** *Daily News* 8 Mar. 2 A miner works nearly a whole day for stoppages, lamp oil (permanent), tools, doctor, etc.
†**2.** An obstacle, hindrance. *Obs.*
c **1450** *Cov. Myst.* (Shaks. Soc.) 196 To blynde the devyl of his knowlache, And my byrthe from hym to hyde, That holy wedlok was grett stoppage.
3. a. Obstruction of a road, passage, stream, or current; †*concr.* something that obstructs.
1540 PALSGR. *Acolastus* II. iii. Lij, I haue ouer passed all stoppages of wayes .i. all suche lettes of passage [etc.].. as myght lette me on my waye. **1621** BP. HALL *Heaven upon Earth* §6, I haue seene a little streame of no noise, which vpon his stoppage hath swelled vp. **1643** BAKER *Chron.*, *Edw. III*, 174 An Act was made in this Kings time, that all Weares, Mils and other stoppages of Rivers.. should be removed. **1773** J. FLETCHER *Dreadful Phenom.* title-p., A particular Account of the sudden Stoppage of the River Severn. **1787** JEFFERSON *Writ.* (1859) II. 104 Those States have suffered by the stoppage of the channels of their commerce.
b. A 'block' of the traffic in a street.
1727 *Daily Post* 4 Feb. 1/3 The High Bailiff of Westminster.. was ordered to take Care to prevent the Stoppages in the Streets leading to the Parliament House. **1835** DICKENS *Sk. Boz, Mr. Watkins Tottle* ii, When he got into Fleet-street, there was 'a stoppage,' in which people in vehicles have the satisfaction of remaining stationary for half an hour, [etc.]. **1870** DISRAELI *Lothair* xxi, Broughams whirled and bright barouches glanced, [etc.].. There were stoppages in Bond Street.
c. Closing up of a vessel.
1725 *Bradley's Family Dict.* s.v. *Restoring of Cider*, The.. Flatness of this Liquor is often occasion'd by the too free Admission of the Air into the Vessel, for want of right Stoppage.
4. *Path.* Obstructed condition of a bodily organ.
1575 TURBERV. *Faulconrie* 233 You shall finde it ease your hawke greatly and ridde a greate parte of the filthie matter that breadeth the stoppage in his head. **1666** W. BOGHURST *Loimogr.* (1894) 32 A very great stoppage at the brest.. by degrees all her stopping and lisping left her. **1686** S. MEADE in *Jrnl. Friends' Hist. Soc.* (1914) Oct. 168 Nathanaell had a loosenesse for aboue 2 weekes, which.. carried of his flegme & stoppage at his stomacke. **1704** *Lond. Gaz.* No. 3986/4 A Stoppage in his Nose. **1758** *Phil. Trans.* L. 522 But about that age [he] was afflicted with stoppages, which often threw him into convulsive fits. **1799** UNDERWOOD *Dis. Childhood* (ed. 4) III. 107 The slightest sympton of which, is that called the Snuffles, or stoppage of the nose. **1818–20** E. THOMPSON *Cullen's Nosol. Method.* (ed. 3) 319 Order I. Paraphymata. Local Changes.. 41 *Emphragma.*—Stoppage. **1899** *Allbutt's Syst. Med.* VIII. 889 The stoppage of the nose.. constitutes a serious impediment to respiration.
5. Arrest or detention of a traveller, or of goods being conveyed from place to place. ***stoppage in transitu, in transit*** (Law): see quot. 1862.
1621 in Foster *Eng. Factories Ind.* (1906) 354 In our last wee advised you the stoppage off the Dutches goods likewise by Saffy Caun. **1649** in *Verney Mem.* (1907) I. 446 There being a generall stoppage of all letters. **1777** COOK *Third Voy.* III. i. (1784) II. 13 This stoppage of a favourite article, without assigning some reason, might have occasioned a general murmur. **1817** W. SELWYN *Law Nisi Prius* (ed. 4) II. 1169 Chap. xxxvii. (heading of chapter) Stoppage in Transitu. **1862** J. W. SMITH *Man. Common Law* 267 Stoppage in transitu is the resumption by a vendor of the possession of goods which have been transmitted to, but have not yet come into the actual or constructive possession of, a purchaser who has become insolvent. **1911** J. H. ROSE *Pitt & Gt. War* iv. 103 Grenville refused to discuss or explain the stoppage of certain cargoes of grain destined for French ports.
6. a. The action of stopping or causing to cease.
1657 J. COOKE tr. *J. Hall's Sel. Observ. Engl. Bodies* xcv. 302 The stoppage of Vrine and Strangury.. may be joyned together, the one being a totall the other a partiall suppression of Urine. **1696** FLOYER *Humours* (J.) The stoppage of a cough, or spitting, increases phlegm in the stomach. **1727** A. HAMILTON *New Acc. E. Ind.* II. xli. 106 This Stoppage of Trade and Fishing.. made a great Noise among the poorer Sort. **1813** J. THOMSON *Lect. Inflam.* 253 The distance in the canal to which this stoppage of the pulsation extends, varies in different cases. **1863** H. COX *Instit.* I. vii. 85 The House of Lords complained of this stoppage of the issue of writs by the Commons. **1908** *Animal Managem.* (War Office) 326 Stoppage of bleeding is the first point to be attended to if it is serious.
b. Discontinuance of supply.
1865 DICKENS *Dr. Marigold* viii, Thereby leading to.. the total stoppage of the unfortunate young man's beer.
7. a. Cessation of movement or activity; a stop or halt in a journey.
1794 MRS. RADCLIFFE *Myst. Udolpho* viii, She raised her eyes on the sudden stoppage of the carriage. **1840** HOOD *Up Rhine* 49 Our first stoppage was at Dortrecht on Dort. **1856** MISS ISAB. BIRD *Englishw. in Amer.* 159 We ran three hundred miles through central Michigan in ten hours, including stoppages. **1865** TYNDALL *Fragm. Sci.* (1871) 426 An abrupt stoppage of sensation. **1897** MEREDITH *Amazing Marr.* I. xv. 169 They had a hamper and were independent of stoppages for provision. **1913** *Times* 13 Sept. 18/5 Unless there is an improved demand we shall soon be hearing of the stoppage of looms through lack of work.
b. A cessation of work owing to disagreement between employer and employees; a strike or a lock-out.
1902 *Encycl. Brit.* XXV. 554/1 The adjustment of differences that might otherwise lead to stoppage. *Ibid.* XXXIII. 14/1 To distinguish stoppages as strikes or lock-outs according to the source of the original demand for a change of conditions would lead to a very arbitrary and misleading classification. **1926** *Publishers' Circular* 29 Dec. 895/3, 1926... The year of the General Stoppage. **1966** *Listener* 1 Sept. 302/2 An American-owned engineering works in north-west London is to close down because of stoppages and the economic squeeze. **1976** *West Lancs. Evening Gaz.* 8 Dec. 1/2 More than 350 Blackpool Corporation busmen agreed unanimously to give authority to the TGWU's North Lancashire District Committee to call them out on a one-day stoppage in support of their Fylde colleagues.
8. *Comm.* The action of stopping payment.
1817 W. BELOE *Sexagenarian* II. 189 It is no less singular, that this failure did not occasion the bankruptcy, or cause stoppage of payment, in any other house. **1828** P. CUNNINGHAM *N.S. Wales* (ed. 3) II. 95 It was indeed a stoppage of payment without a concomitant bankruptcy, two things hitherto synonymous in England. **1846** MCCULLOCH *Brit. Empire* (1854) II. 33 There was.. a pretty severe run upon the Bank of England, and it was at length apprehended that she might be obliged to make a temporary stoppage. **1864** MRS. RIDDELL *Geo. Geith* xxxvi, Norton's stoppage has ruined me. **1891** *Law Times* XC. 377/1 He had been concerned in floating several companies, the stoppage of one of which, it is stated, has ruined a number of persons.

stoppall, obs. form of STOPPLE *sb.*[1]

†**'stoppance.** *Obs.* [f. STOP *v.* + -ANCE.] Something used in stopping or forming a stoppage.
1493 *Ir. Act 8 Hen. VII* (1621) 51 Now of late the said Riuers and Podells be filled and stopped, as well by the inhabitants.. in estopping or casting of stoppance out of their houses, as doung of beasts as by Tanners [etc.].

stoppe: see STOP *sb.*[1], *sb.*[2], *v.*, STOPE *sb.*[1]

stopped (stɒpt), *ppl. a.* [f. STOP *v.* + -ED[1].] In senses of the verb.
†**1.** (Sense uncertain: ? Stuffed.) *Obs.*
1342–3 *Durham Acc. Rolls* (Surtees) 38 In ij stopped salmon emp. iiij s.
2. a. Obstructed, blocked. Of a hole or crevice: Filled up.
c **1440** *Promp. Parv.* 477/2 Stoppyd, *obstructus.* **1578** H. WOTTON *Courtlie Controv.* 237 My stopped eares thou haste compeld to heare. **1582** BENTLEY *Mon. Matrones* ii. 145 Open thou the stopped eares of mine hart. **1796** COLERIDGE *To a Friend* [Lamb] 35 With stopped nostril and glove-guarded hand. **1881** TRIPPLIN & RIGG *Saunier's Watchmakers' Handbk.* 279 To clear a stopped hole in a screw-plate. **1899** *Westm. Gaz.* 15 Feb. 5/1 Stopped gas-pipes or burst water-pipes.
†**b.** Having the voice obstructed; hoarse. *Obs.*
1456 SIR G. HAY *Gov. Princes* Wks. (S.T.S.) II. 157 Sum man [is] stoppit as a crok, and sum clere syngand as a nychtingale.
c. ***stopped-up***: obstructed, suffering from obstruction.
c **1611** CHAPMAN *Iliad* xv. 222 [He] found great Hector, sitting vp, not stretcht vpon his bed, Nor wheasing with a stopt-vp spirit. **1667** *Phil. Trans.* II. 547 Upon taking a slight cold, she was so stop't up, that she could only whisper. **1855** BROWNING *Andrea del Sarto* 80 In their vexed, beating, stuffed and stopped-up brain.
d. *Bridge.* (See quots.) Cf. STOPPER *sb.* 7 e.
1901 R. F. FOSTER *Foster's Bridge* 35 A Suit is Stopped when you can make one trick in it, or can compel the adversary to quit it and lead something else. **1929** M. C. WORK *Compl. Contract Bridge* iv. 20 A suit is stopped when the bidder holds such cards in it that he can be sure of taking at least one trick in that suit.
3. Of a vessel, tube, etc.: Closed with a plug or stopper. Of an organ-pipe: Closed at the top. ***stopped diapason***: see DIAPASON *sb.* 7.
1601 DANIEL *Civ. Wars* VI. xlix, They Mineralls combustible do finde, Which in stopt concaues placed cunningly They fire. **1694** WALLER in *Phil. Trans.* XVIII. 155 A stopt Organ-Pipe is an Eighth to the same one. **1720** MRS. BRADSHAW in *C'tess Suffolk's Lett.* (1824) I. 69 You are as close as a stopped bottle, and do not give one the least account how things go on your side of the water. **1827** FARADAY *Chem. Manip.* xv. (1842) 390 Broken up and put into stopped bottles. **1841** J. BISHOP *Hamilton's Dict. Mus. Terms* App. 117 *Stopt Diapason*, the name of an organ-stop; so called from having its pipes stopped at the top with a wooden plug, by which it is tuned. **1867** TYNDALL *Sound* 187 There is no theoretic limit to the subdivision of an organ-pipe either stopped or open. In stopped pipes we begin with a semi-ventral segment, and pass on to 3, 5, 7, &c. semi-ventral segments. **1880** *Grove's Dict. Music* II. 490 A hollow, rather sweet tone, similar to that of a stopped organ pipe. **1891** HARDY *Tess* xiv, The stopt-diapason note which her voice acquired when her heart was in her speech.
†**4.** Of dice: Loaded. (Cf. STOP *v.* 12 d). *Obs.*
1600 ROWLANDS *Lett. Humours Blood* (1874) 59 His stopt Dice with Quick-siluer neuer misse.
5. *Mus.* (See quots.)
1676 MACE *Musick's Mon.* 68 An Open String is more sweet, and Freer of Sound, than a stopt String. *Ibid.* 85 Never take up any Stopt Finger.. till you have some necessary Vse of It. *Ibid.* 103 The Stopt-Shake, is (only) differing from the Open-Shake, in that you [etc.]. **1801** BUSBY *Dict. Mus.*, *Stopt*, an epithet applied to the strings of a violin, violoncello, &c. when brought into contact with the finger-board by the pressure of the fingers.
6. a. Caused to cease; brought to a standstill; barred from further progress or action.
a **1586** SIDNEY *Arcadia* III. xix. (1912) 468 Gynecia.. besought him to make no delay; using such gestures of compassion insteed of stopped words, that [etc.]. **1599** PORTER *Angry Wom. Abington* (Percy Soc.) 14 *Mis. Bar.*.. Shall I be chid For such a ——. *Mis. Gou.* What a? nay mistresse speake it out; I scorne your stopt compares. **1850** HANNAY *Singleton Fontenoy* I. viii, Things are very bad.. Nothing but turnings out, stopped mills, and riots. **1891** MEREDITH *One of our Conq.* xxviii, The face of a stopped watch. **1898** *Westm. Gaz.* 27 Apr. 8/2 A passenger on board a stopped steamer said that.. the soldiers.. are enthusiastic for war.
b. Of a bank-note, cheque, etc.: see STOP *v.* 19.
1865 MRS. RIDDELL *Maxw. Drewitt* xxix, Robbery of two thousand pounds.. assaulting a constable.. passing the stopped notes. **1891** *Daily News* 18 July 4/7 A vendor could sell a legally stopped bond, which he knew to be so stopped, to a purchaser who did not know it was stopped.
7. *Phonetics.* Of a consonant-sound: Formed by complete closure of the orinasal passages; explosive.
1874 SWEET in *Trans. Philol. Soc.* 539 The conversion of an open into a stopped consonant is, of course, anomalous. **1885** *Encycl. Brit.* XVIII. 787/1 *margin*, Stopped sounds.
8. *Versification.* Of a line: Ending with the conclusion of a sentence or clause.
1874 FLEAY in *Trans. New Shaks. Soc.* I. 2, I cannot speak definitely as to the stopped-line test, not having worked it out. **1875** A. W. WARD *Eng. Dram. Lit.* I. iv. 361 A 'stopped' line is one in which the sentence, or clause of the sentence, concludes with the line.
9. *Carpentry.* Of a chamfer, housing, etc.: closed, not running the whole length of a member. Cf. STOP *v.* 30.
1918 *Woodwork Joints* 167 The sketch to the right shows 'stopped housing', the groove coming to within ½in. of the front edge of the shelf. **1934** P. A. WELLS *Design in Woodwork* ii. 15 The number of joints can be trebled by variations such as 'through', 'stopped' or 'secret' dovetails. **1949** W. J. WEST *Woodwork* ix. 78 To cut stopped housings start by using a mallet and chisel to chop out a slot of the required depth. **1979** A. B. EMARY *Woodworking* iii. 18 At

(a) is seen the stopped housing joint where the recess has been terminated a short distance from one edge and the piece which fits into the recess has been cut to fit round the stopped end.

stoppel, -ell(e, obs. forms of STOPPLE *sb.*[1]

stopper (ˈstɒpə(r)), *sb.* [f. STOP *v.* + -ER[1].]
1. A person who stops (see the senses of the verb).

†**a.** One who obstructs the course of (a river); one who stops or fills up holes or chinks.

1480 *Coventry Leet Bk.* 455 They maken dayly als gret diligens as they can to knowe the stoppers of the seid Comien Ryuer,..and when eny be perceyued they ben punysshed. **1611** BIBLE *Ezek.* xxvii. 9 Thy calkers [*marg.* or, stoppers of chinks, Heb. strengthners].

b. *Hunting.* = *earth-stopper* (EARTH *sb.*[1] II).

1848 *Rural Amusem.* 125 The stopper belonging to the pack rarely neglected stopping these earths in the night before the meet.

c. One who brings to a stand or causes to cease.

1533 BELLENDEN *Livy* IV. (S.T.S.) II. 124 þe remanent tribunis, quhilkis war stopparis of þe law Agrarie. **1597** MIDDLETON *Wisd. Solomon* iv. 17 When wail is weales, & stelth is welths chiefe stopper. **1611** COTGR., *Estancheur*, a stopper (of an issue of blood, &c.). **1617** MORYSON *Itin.* II. 22 If any be stopped from following of his track the stopper shall answere the goods so tracked. **1913** H. S. WILKINSON in *Rep. 7th Ann. Mtg. Hist. Assoc.* 3 How..could a leader.. find a multitude of his fellow creatures willing to make themselves stoppers of bullets and to part with life itself in obedience to a word..?

d. *Pugilism.* (See STOP *v.* 15 d.)

1840 BLAINE *Encycl. Rural Sports* §4038 He was..an excellent 'stopper', hitting with his right and stopping with his left.

†**e.** *Tennis.* (See quot. 1585.)

a **1548** HALL *Chron., Rich. III* 35 b, The best stopper that he hath at tenyce shall not wel stoppe without a faulte. *c* **1550** *Dice-Play* (Percy Soc.) 43 Another was rid of his six hundred pounds, at tennis, in a week by the fraud of his stopper. **1585** HIGINS *Junius' Nomencl.* 296/2 *Factor*,..the stopper, or he that marketh the chase in playeng, at tennise specially.

f. A player whose office it is to stop balls; in *Cricket*, a wicket-keeper.

1744 in *Lillywhite's Scores* (1862) I. Pref. 10 When ye Ball has been in Hand by one of ye Keepers or Stopers..He may go where he pleases till ye next Ball is bowled. **1847** HALLIWELL, *Stopper*, a person at tennis, football, and other games, who stops the balls. **1904** *Daily Chron.* 21 May 9/4 This Sussex stumper..is the best 'stopper' in England.

g. *Assoc. Football.* A player whose function is to block attacks on goal from the middle of the field. Also *attrib.* as ***stopper centre-half.***

1934 D. JACK *Soccer* 124 The defensive pivot..is essentially a 'stopper', a destructive player if you like. **1941** *Daily Mail* 10 Feb. 4/2 Though occasionally outwitted by Lawton, Dykes made himself a nuisance as a stopper. **1951** *Sport* 16–22 Mar. 9/1 He was an admirable foil for two clever attacking halves, for he was a stopper pure and simple. **1961** *Times* 10 Feb. 19/6 A fundamental change in tactics with the arrival of the 'stopper' centre-half. **1978** *Time* 3 July 53/2 He spent the first half, at his own behest, in the unlikely role of a stopper on Paolo Rossi—and very nearly gave away a goal.

2. a. Something that stops up a hole or passage.

1591 PERCIVALL *Sp. Dict.*, *Rombon*, a stopper, *Obturatorium.* **1701** C. WOLLEY *Jrnl. New York* (1860) 29 The surest..stopper of the Pores of their Bodies against the Winter's cold. **1721** MORTIMER *Husb.* II. 333 To tun it up into a Cask,..which stop up only with a loose stopper for two or three Days;..put a Peg into the vent hole loose. **1768** TUCKER *Lt. Nat.* II. I. v. 98 Imagining..that the orifices of these nerves are provided with stoppers which the mind draws up at pleasure to give the animal spirits admittance. **1799** SIR T. MUNRO in Gleig *Life* vii. (1849) 117, I pulled two stoppers of lint out of my ears. **1844** DUFTON *Deafness* 85 Sometimes the stopper of wax is removed by a single syringing. **1875** E. WHITE *Life in Christ* v. xxviii. (1878) 471 Thus the opponent's mouth is shut with a stopper of his own invention. **1888** RUTLEY *Rock-Forming Min.* 7 The stop-cock being closed and the stopper removed from the upper orifice.

fig. **1824** MISS MITFORD *Village* I. 64 Lucy never intended to marry this commodious stopper of love-gaps.

b. *spec.* A plug for closing the neck of a bottle, the end of a tube, or the hole for the egress of fluid from any vessel.

Not usually applied to a cork or bung; most commonly it denotes a solid piece of glass, the lower part of which is shaped to fit the neck of a bottle, while the upper part is fashioned to serve as a handle.

1667 *Phil. Trans.* II. 522 A Silver Tube, with a Silver Stopper. **1719** D'URFEY *Pills* (1872) VI. 296 The Hole that let the Liquor run, Was wanting of a Stopper. **1807** T. THOMSON *Chem.* (ed. 3) II. 228 A phial closed with a ground stopper. **1843** *Penny Cycl.* XXVII. 464/1 The patent caoutchouc stoppers, which, besides being..cheaper than corks, can [etc.]. **1881** TYNDALL *Ess. Floating Matter Air* 32 In a third series [of experiments] the cork stoppers used in the first and second series were abandoned, and glass stoppers employed. **1883** H. J. POWELL *Glass-making* 74 Finally the stopper is ground into the mouth of the decanter. **1913** P. D. SCOTT-MONCRIEFF *Paganism & Chr. Egypt* ii. 25 *note*, The old 'Canopic' vases..had stoppers in the form of genii supposed to protect the dead.

fig. **1852** THACKERAY *Esmond* III. ix, There is no such word as enough as a stopper for good wine.

c. A cork or plug for the mouth of a muzzle-loading musket, to keep out moisture and dust.

1802 C. JAMES *Milit. Dict.* **1859** F. A. GRIFFITHS *Artill. Man.* (1862) 38 The men will be directed to replace their stoppers.

d. = *pipe stopper, tobacco stopper* (see PIPE *sb.*[1] 11 b; TOBACCO 3).

1622 J. TAYLOR (Water P.) *Water-Cormorant* C 2, A pyde coat Page, Who..his Tobacco fils, With stopper, tongs, and other vtensils. **1693** *Humours Town* 63 As the destruction of Pipes is the multiplication of Stoppers, so [etc.]. **1731–8** SWIFT *Pol. Conversat.* ii. Wks. VI. 328 They say, that the Corruption of Pipes, is the Generation of Stoppers. **1736** [I. H. BROWNE] *Pipe of Tobacco* ii. 8 Lip of Wax, and Eye of Fire:..And thy swelling ashey Crest, With my little Stopper prest. **1885** J. PAYN *Talk of Town* II. 201 Flattening the tobacco in his pipe with its stopper.

e. The plug of a 'stopped' organ-pipe.

1852 SEIDEL *Organ* 80 The stopping is effected by a sort of capsule, similar to the lid of a round brass box, called the stopper. **1879** *Organ Voicing* 25 If..the stopper and joints of the pipe are sound.

f. = STOPPING *vbl. sb.* 4 d.

1879 *Cassell's Techn. Educ.* IV. 207/2 The nail holes, &c., are stopped with hard-stopper made of dry lead mixed with Japan gold size. **1912** H. J. BUTLER *Motor Bodies* 115 Some add turps and tub lead to help the stopper to harden. This hard stopper is forced in carefully with the putty knife.

†**3.** Anything that produces constipation. *Obs.*

1528 PAYNELL *Salerne's Regim.* M ij, Breadde made with littel leuen nourishethe the moche, but the norishement therof is a stopper. **1584** COGAN *Haven Health* iv. 23 Bread ouer-sweete is a stopper.

†**4.** *Anat.* (See quot. and OBTURATOR 1.) *Obs.*

1686 SNAPE *Anat. Horse* IV. cxx. 187 Two Muscles called *Obturatores*, or Stoppers, because they fill up the wide hole between the *Os pubis* and Hip-bone.

†**5.** A shoemaker's tool: = *stopping-stick* (STOPPING *vbl. sb.* 7). *Obs.*

1599 DEKKER *Shoemaker's Holiday* II. iii. (1610) C 3 b, Heark you skomaker, haue you al your tooles, a good rubbing pin, a good stopper, a good dresser [etc.].

6. The upper pad of the sole of a greyhound's foot.

1853 'STONEHENGE' *Greyhound* vii. 158 When the cut is severe, as for instance, at the root of 'the stopper'. **1856** —— *Brit. Rural Sports* I. III. vii. 201 If a Stopper is detached from the leg.., it is far better to remove the hanging portion with the knife.

7. Something that causes to cease or brings to a stand. **a.** *gen.*, esp. in the phrase ***to put a stopper on*** (? with mixture of sense 2), to put a stop to. *colloq.* or *slang.*

1828 EGAN *Boxiana* IV. 188 The Lively Kid met with a stopper to his rush on the nob. **1830** MARRYAT *King's Own* xl, If you don't clap a stopper on that jaw of yours, by George, we'll cobb you. **1841** DICKENS *Barn. Rudge* lviii, If it rested with him to decide, he would put a final stopper on the bird, and his master too. **1859** GEN. P. THOMPSON *Audi Alt.* II. xcix. 88 The stopper has been put upon the utterance of ideas on both sides the Channel. **1898** B. BURLEIGH *Sirdar & Khalifa* vii. 107 A bullet so treated expands mushroom fashion upon striking any object and becomes a veritable 'stopper'. **1901** *Wide World Mag.* VI. 501/1 A hit, evidently, for the animal's progress became immediately slower. Then Armstrong put in the stopper, his bullet piercing the neck. **1911** MAX BEERBOHM *Zuleika Dobson* v. 56 But that rejection..is no stopper to my suit.

b. *Mech.* An appliance for stopping machinery.

1871 *Abridgm. Specif. Patents, Watches* etc. 111 Whenever a stopper is pressed against the collar, the arbor, and therefore the seconds hand, ceases to rotate. **1875** KNIGHT *Dict. Mech.*, *Stopper* (Railway Engineering), A trailing-brake formerly used on inclined planes. It..was thrown into action by the pressure of the cars, if the rope broke. **1903** *Westm. Gaz.* 15 Jan. 2/1 Ramsbottom.. invented.. the weft-fork-stopper for looms. This stopper, as its name implies, stops the loom when the weft breaks.

c. *Hunting.* An obstacle that is impassable or causes delay.

1832 *Q. Rev.* XLVII. 237 The fence at the top is impracticable—Meltonicé, 'a stopper;' nothing for it but a gate, leading into a broad lane. **1859** EARDLEY-WILMOT *Reminisc. T. Assheton Smith* (1860) 44 The famous story of Lord Kintore coming once to a 'stopper' in the Vale of White Horse, which defied the whole field. **1859** *Sporting Mag.* Mar. 159 They..crossed the old canal, which was another stopper, and allowed the fox to get a long way ahead.

d. *Rowing.* The after part of a rowlock.

1897 J. JEFFERY *Rowing* 8 That part against which the oar is pressed in rowing is called the 'thowl', and the opposite, or after-thowl, is called the 'stop', or 'stopper'. **1904** G. RIXON *Rowing & Sculling* 2 In some stock gigs it will be found that there is not sufficient room between the thowl and stopper, causing the oar to stick or 'lock' on a full reach forward.

e. *Bridge.* A card of such value that it can reasonably be counted on, in conjunction with other cards in the same suit, to take a trick in that suit. Cf. STOPPED *ppl. a.* 2 d.

1901 R. F. FOSTER *Foster's Bridge* 112 When the make is original, a guarded king is very likely a stopper in the dealer's suit. **1913** F. IRWIN *Auction High-Lights* 101 To bid 'a no-trump' declares nothing actually, except general help. The bid is often made on three stoppers. *Ibid.* 105 Four diamonds to the jack might not prove a stopper if the card next to the jack did not happen to be the ten-spot, but it is, and a sequence-stopper is always safe. **1933** *Times* 24 Jan. 13/4 This is a conventional and artificial response. It does not guarantee a 'stopper' in Spades. **1959** T. REESE *Bridge Player's Dict.* 222 Some players bid 1 NT on a fair balanced hand even when they have no stopper. **1978** *Detroit Free Press* 2 Apr. 19c/2 If North has a diamond stopper, he bids no trump.

f. Something which attracts and holds attention; something striking or impressive. *colloq.* Cf. *show-stopper* s.v. SHOW *sb.*[1] 22.

1968 *Punch* 21 Feb. 269/1 'What's your snap reaction, Jack?' broke in Gringeworth. 'It's um, well, certainly a stopper,' said Tubstraw. 'My God! It's the stopper of the century!' exclaimed Gringeworth. **1973** *Times* 21 Feb. 13/8 'A memorable image.' 'It's a stopper.'

8. *West Indian.* A tree of the genus *Eugenia.*

1884 SARGENT *Rep. Forests N. Amer.* 88 *Eugenia buxifolia*. .. Gurgeon Stopper. Spanish Stopper. *Ibid.* 89 *Eugenia monticola*... Stopper. White Stopper. *Ibid.*, *Eugenia procera*... Red Stopper.

9. a. *Naut.* (See quots. 1769.)

For *cat-, cathead-, dog-, ring-, wherrit-, wing-stopper*, see the prefixed words.

1626 CAPT. SMITH *Accid. Yng. Seamen* 30 Nealed too, looke to your stoppers, your Anchor comes home, the ships a drift. **1644** MANWAYRING *Seamans Dict.* 102. **1711** W. SUTHERLAND *Shipbuild. Assist.* 153 Stoppers of Anchors... Stoppers of the Bit. **1769** FALCONER *Dict. Marine* (1780) s.v. *Anchor*, The anchor is suspended at the cat-head by its stopper. *Ibid.*, *Stoppers*,..certain short pieces of rope, which are usually knotted at one, or both ends... They are either used to suspend any weighty body, or to retain a cable, shroud, &c. in fixed position [etc.]. **1829** MARRYAT *F. Mildmay* xx, The stoppers were cut, and the anchors dropped.

b. *Fisheries.* (See quot.)

1883 R. F. WALSH *Ir. Fisheries* (Fish. Exhib. Publ.) 11 At the bottom of the nets another rope runs from end to end, and this is called the 'foot line'... Suspended from this foot line..are other ropes, each 27 feet long, and called 'stoppers'.

10. *Comb.* **stopper-berry tree**, the Barbados cherry, *Malpighia glabra*; **stopper-bolt** *Naut.* (see quots.); **stopper-hitch** *Naut.* (see quot.); **stopper-hole** (see quot.); **stopper-knot** *Naut.*, a kind of knot used for the ends of stoppers; **stopper-net** (see quot.).

1750 G. HUGHES *Barbados* 176 The *Stopper-Berry Tree; Lat. Malpighia. **1711** W. SUTHERLAND *Shipbuild. Assist.* 37 To have *Stopper-bolts for the Cables. **1875** KNIGHT *Dict. Mech.*, *Stopper-bolt*, a large ring-bolt driven in the deck of a ship before the main-hatch, for securing the stoppers to. **1876** VOYLE & STEVENSON *Milit. Dict.* 410/2 **Stopper-hitch*, a knot for stoppering the fall of a tackle, &c. **1869** S. J. V. DAY *Puddling* in Rankine *Machine & Hand-tools*, In the lower side of the charging door an opening is formed called the **stopper-hole*, through which the puddler introduces his *rabble* for working up the mass of iron. *c* **1860** H. STUART *Seaman's Catech.* 56 A thimble is spliced in one end and a 'double wall' or deck *stopper-knot, is made on the other. **1792** G. CARTWRIGHT *Jrnl. Labrador* I. Gloss. p. xv, **Stopper-net*, a large net for catching seals, which is made to fit the place in which it is fixed.

Hence ˈ**stopperless** *a.*, without stoppers.

1863 DICKENS *Uncomm. Trav.* xxii, The stopperless cruets on the spindle-shanked sideboard were in a miserably dejected state.

stopper (ˈstɒpə(r)), *v.* [f. STOPPER *sb.*]
1. *trans. Naut.* To secure with a stopper.

1769 FALCONER *Dict. Marine* II. (1780), *Bosser le Cable*, to stopper the Cable. **1834** MARRYAT *P. Simple* xv, Jump down, then, and see it [the cable] double-bitted and stoppered at thirty fathoms. **1883** *Man. Seamanship for Boys* 234 The first reef-pendant is stoppered and hitched round the boom.

2. To close or secure (a bottle, etc.) with a stopper. Also with *down.*

1868 *Rep. U.S. Commissioner Agric.* (1869) 441 The milk-can is filled full of milk, and so stoppered down that there is no room for the least motion to churn the milk. **1915** *Morning Post* 21 June 8/1 A quart bottle very carefully stoppered.

b. *Metallurgy.* (See quot.) Also with *down.*

1884 W. H. GREENWOOD *Steel & Iron* xx. §770 The metal is run into the several moulds, which are each 'stoppered'.. either with an iron plate, or simply by throwing on a shovelful of sand, which is then covered with an iron plate, wedged down [etc.]. *Ibid.* xx. §809 The ingots are properly stoppered down, by throwing a shovelful of sand into the mould on the top of the still fluid metal, and then covering it with an iron plate fastened down by a cross bar [etc.].

3. To fit with a stopper.

1827 FARADAY *Chem. Manip.* xv. (1842) 361 The bottles should be wide-mouthed and accurately stoppered. **1860** *Repert. Patent Invent.* Dec. 443 Improvements in Closing or Stoppering Bottles, Jars, and other Receptacles. **1883** H. J. POWELL *Glass-making* 73 The mouth of the vessel to be stoppered.

4. *slang.* To stop; to 'put the stopper on'.

1821 SCOTT *Pirate* xxxix, Stopper your jaw, Dick, will you? **1905** *Daily Chron.* 24 Apr. 3/4 This elegant Cyril Wentworth, who gaily 'stoppers' men and women by the dozen if they happen to thwart him in the slightest degree.

stoppered (ˈstɒpəd), *ppl. a.* [f. STOPPER *v.* + -ED[1].] Fitted with a stopper.

1803 *Phil. Trans.* XCIII. 38 A curved and stoppered tube. **1827** FARADAY *Chem. Manip.* xxiv. 622 Receive the gas when good into stoppered bottles. **1869** S. J. V. DAY *Puddling* 4 in Rankine *Machine & Hand-tools*, A row of stoppered holes.

stoppering (ˈstɒpərɪŋ), *vbl. sb.* [f. STOPPER *v.* + -ING[1].] The action of STOPPER *v.*

1805 in *Polwhele's Trad. & Recoll.* (1826) II. 577 In ten minutes our rigging was past all stoppering. **1859** F. A. GRIFFITHS *Artill. Man.* (1862) 107, (4) The proper stoppering of the fall, when necessary.

attrib. **1877** *Encycl. Brit.* VI. 402/2 Many substitutes have been proposed for cork as a stoppering agent.

stopping (ˈstɒpɪŋ), *vbl. sb.* [f. STOP *v.* + -ING[1].]
I. 1. a. The action of the vb. STOP in various senses.

1375 BARBOUR *Bruce* VI. 169 The vpcom wes then Dittit with slayn hors and men; Swa that his fayis, for that stopping, Micht not cum to the vp-cummyng. *c* **1470** HENRY *Wallace* v. 114 Fyrst, to the hunde it mycht gret stoppyn be.

1487-8 *Rec. St. Mary at Hill* (1905) 132 Paide to a dawber for stoppyng of an hole in Sir Iohn lovyers chamber,.. iij d. 1552 HULOET, Stoppynge of wynde, *asthma, obstructio.* 1592 BACON *Observ. Libel* Resusc. (1657) 125 For the Stopping of Traffique.. I refer my Self to the Custome-Books. 1677 F. NORTH *Philos. Ess. Mus.* 28 Pipes may be helped by the strength of the blast, and fretted Instruments by a favourable stopping. 1697 DE FOE *Ess. Projects* 321 All discounting of Wages,.. stopping of Pay, and the like, to be adjusted by stated and Publick Rules. 1764 *Museum Rust.* IV. 18, I pinch off with my nail such branches as accompany the fruit, to the thickness of about two crown-pieces, which I call stopping. 1842 LOUDON *Suburban Hort.* 613 Pruning may be rendered almost unnecessary by disbudding, disleafing, and stopping. 1873-4 H. SWEET in *Trans. Philol. Soc.* 107 The voice stops (g), (d) and often (b) are weakened after vowels by imperfect stopping. 1875 E. A. DAVIDSON *House-painting*, etc. 12 Stopping consists in filling in and making good all nail-holes, bad joints, cracks, &c. with putty, or with a paste made of putty and white lead, called hard stopping. 1881 GROVE *Dict. Mus.* III. 717 *Stopping*, the technical term for the operation of pressing the fingers on the strings of a violin, viola, etc., necessary to produce the notes. *Double Stopping* is the producing of two notes at once. 1902 *Land & Water* 35 Oct. 616/3 Very naturally they [the boys] prefer a day's stopping [in the coverts] to a day school.

b. Combined with advs., ***stopping down, off*** (also *attrib.*), ***out, -over, up.*** (See the related verbal phrases under STOP *v.*)

1904 KILBEY *Hand-camera Photogr.* 39 This is the chief use of 'stopping down'. 1856 G. GORE *Pract. Chem.* 77 'Stopping off' to Prevent Deposition. 1875 KNIGHT *Dict. Mech.* 2407 *Stopping off* (*Founding*), a term applied to the filling up with sand of a portion of a mold, when the casting is desired to be smaller than the pattern from which the mold is formed. 1942 BERREY & VAN DEN BARK *Amer. Thes. Slang* §45/2 Small town,.. *stopping-off place.* 1966 'A. HALL' *9th Directive* iv. 41 I'll need up-to-the minute information.. final itinerary.. stopping-off points, so forth. 1807 LANDSEER *Lect. Engraving* 232 Either by partial stoppings out, or the increased pressure of his Etching-needle. 1838 in *Newton's Lond. Jrnl.* Conj. Ser. XVI. 64 These stopping-out apparatus are not limited as to their forms or dimensions. 1880 HAMERTON *Etching & Etchers* (ed. 3) App. 338 Stopping-out varnish. 1971 *Time* 27 Sept. 79/1 The trend of stopping out is growing.. partly because the draft law now gives young men with high lottery numbers a new freedom. 1977 *N.Y. Times* 16 Jan. IV. 9/1 Stopping out .. has become so popular on some campuses that the notion of graduating in four years seems almost quaint. 1932 *New Yorker* 4 June 38 You leave Seattle July 9, and do a bit of stopping-over at Yokohama, Tokio, and other Japanese ports. 1671 PHILLIPS (ed. 3), *Suffocation*, a choaking, stifling, or stopping up of the breath. 1721 MORTIMER *Husb.* II. 330 The principal Cause that there hath been so much bad Cyder made in most parts of England, was the too early stopping of it up. 1805 *Shipwright's Vade-M.* 136 *Stoppings-up*, the poppets, timbers, &c. used to fill up the vacancy between the upper-side of the bilgeways and the ship's bottom, for supporting her when launching. 1886 *Encycl. Brit.* XXI. 821/1 s.v. *Shipbuilding*, There should be at least two chains on each side secured to the fore-poppets, .. and two on each side to the stopping-up. 1912 H. J. BUTLER *Motor Bodies* 114 Opinion is divided as to when the stopping up should take place. Some painters do it now, while others leave it till the filling up.. is done.

2. The placing of stops, punctuation.

1728 CHAMBERS *Cycl.*, *Stops, Stopping*, in Grammar. 1837 J. H. NEWMAN *Proph. Office Ch.* 180 They use some anomalous criticism, or alter the stopping, or amend the text, &c. 1880 N. T. (*Rev. Vers.*), Pref. iii. 4 d, Great care has been bestowed on the punctuation. Our practice has been to maintain what is sometimes called the heavier system of stopping. 1902 T. S. OMOND in *N. & Q.* Ser. IX. IX. 276/2 His [Browning's] punctuation.. seems an attempt to supply that rhetorical arrangement of clauses which modern stopping altogether ignores.

†**3.** *Path.* Obstructed conditions of an organ: = STOPPAGE 4. *Obs.*

1398 TREVISA *Barth. De P.R.* XIX. xlix. (1495) 891 Soure thynges openyth stoppynges of the splene and of the lyuour. 1528 PAYNELL *Salerne's Regim.* F 4 b, They open the opilations & stoppynges that are wonte to be engendred in suche persons. 1657 COLES *Adam in Eden* cxlv, The Extraction thereof is a Singular remedy against the yellow Jaundice, and Stoppings of the Liver, Spleen, and Womb. 1741 A. MONRO *Anat.* (ed. 3) 86 A *Coryza*, or stopping of the Nose from any other Cause.

fig. 1646 JENKYN *Remora* 33 What coolings were there in our love, what stoppings in our bowels.

II. Concrete uses.

4. a. Something inserted to stop a hole, crevice, or passage.

1585 HIGINS *Junius' Nomencl.* 264/1 *Endiæum*,.. the stopping of the glister pipe, which is of cloth, and hangeth by a thred. 1823 J. BADCOCK *Dom. Amusem.* 162 The access of air being prevented by a stopping of paste or mortar so made. 1842 LOUDON *Suburban Hort.* 259 The water in the inner pot.. is prevented from escaping through its bottom by the clay stopping at *a*. 1876 PREECE & SIVEWRIGHT *Telegraphy* 230 A stopping of yarn should be rammed into the socket of the pipe before the joint is made.

†**b.** Decayed honey filling the cells of a comb.

1609 C. BUTLER *Fem. Mon.* i. (1623) D ij, So they might live in secula, if.. the abundance of noisome stopping would suffer them to abide the Hiues. *Ibid.* vi. (1623) O ij [see COOM *sb.*[1] 3].

c. *Farriery.* A pad charged with grease inserted within the shoe for the purpose of keeping the horse's foot moist.

1580 BLUNDEVIL *Curing Horses Dis.* cxliv. 62 b, Stop him with Turpentine and Hogs grease molten togither, and laid on with a little towe or flaxe, and then clap on the shooe to keepe in the stopping. 1828 S. F. GRAY *Suppl. Pharmacopœias* (ed. 4) 464 Stoppings for the feet. Tallow 2 lb. [etc.].

d. A composition used to stop holes or crevices.

1823 P. NICHOLSON *Pract. Builder* 417 Filling up cracks and defects with putty, called stopping. 1883 R. HALDANE *Workshop Rec.* Ser. II. 127/1 The 'stopping', as this mixture [of size and whiting] is called, is pressed into the cracks [of the picture] by means of a palette-knife. 1901 J. BLACK *Carp. & Build., Home Handicr.* 43 [Before painting] any knots or resinous places in the woodwork should be coated with 'stopping,' or red lead in varnish.

e. *Dentistry.* The material used for stopping a hollow tooth.

1863 TREVELYAN *Compet. Wallah* (1866) 151 As a dentist once said to me, 'All is not stopping that glitters.' 1896 *Punch* 11 Jan. 24/2 You mustn't bite anything for two hours at least, or you'll spoil the stopping.

5. †**a.** A dam, embankment. *Obs.*

1575 in W. H. Turner *Select. Rec. Oxford* (1880) 375 The banks and stoppings of the waters aboute Sowthe bridge.

b. *Mining.* (See quots.)

1708 J. C. *Compleat Collier* (1845) 46 Care of the Air must be taken in general, That it be not too much Dispersed, or too much liberty given for want of Stoppings. *c* 1790 *Encycl. Brit.* (ed. 3) V. 103/2 The passage.. must be closed up.. by a partition of deals, or by a wall built with bricks or stones, to prevent the air passing that way. This building is called a stopping. 1839 URE *Dict. Arts* 986 By means of such stoppings placed in the boards next the dip-head level, the air can be transported to the right hand or to the left for many miles. 1911 *Act 1 & 2 Geo. V*, c. 50 §42 (3) All stoppings between main intake airways and main return airways.

6. *Archery.* (See quot.)

1801 T. ROBERTS *Engl. Bowman* 294 *Stopping*, the extreme part or head of the pile, which is solid.

III. 7. *attrib.* and *Comb.*, in sense 'bringing to a stand', as in ***stopping effect, power, quality***; 'coming to a stand, halting', as in ***stopping distance, -point***; 'filling holes or crevices', as in ***stopping-instrument, -knife, -material, -tool***; **stopping-ground** *Etching* (see quot.); **stopping house** *Canad.*, a house offering accommodation to travellers; a boarding-house or rooming-house; **stopping mixture** *Etching*, a composition to be used as a stopping-ground; †**stopping pan**, a pan for melting materials for making 'stoppings' (sense 4 c); **stopping-place**, (*a*) a place at which a person or thing stops; (*b*) *Canad. Hist.*, a stopping house, or a settlement where groups of travellers customarily stop for food and lodging; **stopping rule** *Statistics*, any rule in sequential testing or sampling for deciding when an investigation should be terminated, dependent on the cumulative trends in the results obtained; **stopping station**, one of the stations at which an express train stops; †**stopping stick**, a shoemaker's tool (? for filling crevices).

1947 *Highway Code* 10 The good driver knows how *stopping distances increase with speed, and drives accordingly. 1907 J. H. PATTERSON *Man-Eaters of Tsavo* xxiv. 279 As a matter of fact, however, it [the bullet] went clean through him [the charging lion] without having the slightest *stopping effect. 1837 *Penny Cycl.* IX. 442/1 The parts which are bitten-in enough, are now to be covered with what is called *stopping-ground, which is a mixture of lamp-black and Venice turpentine. 1883 *Prince Albert* (Saskatchewan) *Times* 18 Apr. 1/5 The road from Carrot River crosses the South Saskatchewan at this point where there is now a first class ferry and *stopping house. 1912 H. FOOTNER *New Rivers of North* 235 None of the stopping-houses along this trail have progressed beyond the most primitive stage. They provide a floor for you to sleep on and a fire-place, in some cases a stove for you to cook your food on; that is all. 1970 R. & J. PATERSON *Cranberry Portage* i. 4, I got a stoppinghouse here... My rooms is all full up. 1862 *Chamb. Encycl.* III. 497/2 To be firmly pressed with a blunt-pointed *stopping-instrument or 'plugger' into all the interstices of the hollow of the tooth. 1823 P. NICHOLSON *Pract. Builder* 422 Glaziers are likewise furnished with *stopping knives. 1815 J. SMITH *Panorama Sci. & Art.* II. 767 If the ground be any where broken up, a composition called the *stopping mixture, must be immediately applied to it. 1580 BLUNDEVIL *Curing Horses Dis.* cxv. 53 b, Then fill both his feete with Hogges grease, and bran fried togither in a *stopping Pan. 1827 A. SHERWOOD *Gazetteer Georgia* 37 *Camp c.* in the N.W. part of the Warren.. and well known as a *stopping place. 1836 C. FOX *Jrnl.* 31 Aug. in *Memories of Old Friends* (1882) ii. 5 Dr. Buckland was an outside *compagnon de voyage*, but often came at stopping places for a little chat. 1848 W. TEMPLETON *Locomot. Eng.* (ed. 2) 73 In nearing any station or stopping place, the steam must be shut off. 1878 J. M. LEMOINE *Chronicles of St. Lawrence* 21 When being jolted in a two-wheeled post stage, without springs, over these villainous roads, the traveller will do well to fix beforehand the stopping places (for meals), as hostelries are few and far between. 1909 A. D. CAMERON *New North* 28 We 'make tea' at Sturgeon Creek (the Namao Sepee of the Indians), the first of the 'stopping-places' or Waldorf-Astorias of the wilderness. 1950 Stopping place [see LAY-BY *sb.* 1 c]. 1854 *Poultry Chron.* I. 504 The improvement in these birds is so continuous, that it is hard to say where their *stopping-point will be found. 1896 *Times* 16 Dec. 5/2 In the Chitral campaign the *stopping powers of the Lee-Metford rifle bullet were shown to be so small that [etc.]. 1898 B. BURLEIGH *Sirdar & Khalifa* vii. 106 The soldiers have no faith in the *stopping quality of the Lee-Metford bullet. 1953 *Jrnl. R. Statistical Soc.* B. XV. 9 Thus if a history of the population is available over some period of time, $\lambda + \mu$ can be estimated from the observed number of incidents and the U_i, and $\lambda/(\lambda + \mu)$ from the proportion of the incidents that are births; the details will depend on the *stopping rule. 1960 P. ARMITAGE *Sequential Med. Trials* ii. 17 The design of the trial is determined entirely by the stopping-rule. 1978 *Brit. Jrnl. Cancer* XXXVIII. 760/1 Investigators were also asked whether they used any formal or informal stopping rules for the early termination of trial if treatment differences should develop. 1840 *Civil Engin. & Arch. Jrnl.* III. 32/2 One of the '*stopping stations' of all the second class trains being opposite. 1891 *Daily News* 3 Apr. 5/5 Only Bletchley,.. Stirling, and Perth are stopping stations by these specially fast trains. 1597 DELONEY *Gentle Craft* I. Wks. (1912) 89 The whetstone, the *stopping-stick, and the paring knife. 1823 P. NICHOLSON *Pract. Builder* 371 The plasterer likewise employs several small tools, called *stopping and picking-out tools.

stopping ('stɒpɪŋ), *ppl. a.* [f. STOP *v.* + -ING[2].]

†**1.** *Med.* Tending to cause stoppage; astringent, constipating. *Obs.*

1398 TREVISA *Barth. De P.R.* XVII. cxiv. (1495) Sj, The substaunce [of cole] without the Juys is stoppynge & byndynge. 1562 TURNER *Herbal* II. 66 The sede & roote of it [nymphea] with the yelow floure dronken with rede stopping and tart wyne ar good agaynst.. isshues. 1608 ARABELLA STUART *Let.* 8 Dec. in Lefuse *Life* (1913) 206, I have sent your lordship some of the stoppingest meat that is [*sc.* cheese]. 1666 G. HARVEY *Morbus Angl.* xxxiii. (1672) 103 Then you must resolve to live without Victuals, there being no meat in the world, but what may be excepted against, in saying this is windy, and that is stopping, &c.

2. That stops, in senses of the verb. ***stopping oyster***: see OYSTER *sb.* 1 c. ***stopping train***: a train which stops at some or all intermediate stations on a particular line.

a 1529, 1542 [see OYSTER *sb.* 1 c]. 1676 MACE *Musicks Mon.* 104, I must, with the Stopping Finger (only) cause the *a*, to sound, by taking it off, in a kind of a Twitch. 1854 *Repts. Accid. Railways* 23 The train book kept at Weedon station.. shows the time of arrival and departure of every stopping train. 1888 *Pall Mall Gaz.* 31 Aug. 4/2 If a stopping omnibus is an obstruction, so is a stopping cab.

stopple ('stɒp(ə)l), *sb.*[1] Forms: 4-6 **stopell**, 5 **stopelle, -ylle**, 5-7 **stoppell, stople**, 6 **stoppall, -elle, -ull**, 6-9 **stoppel**, 9 *dial.* **stapple**, 6- **stopple**. Cf. STOUPAILLE, ESTOPPEL. [Partly f. STOP *v.* + -EL[1], -LE: partly aphetic f. ESTOPPEL.]

I. 1. a. An appliance for closing the orifice of a vessel, tube, etc.; a stopper, cork, bung, or plug. Now somewhat *rare*; usually replaced by STOPPER.

139. *Earl Derby's Exped.* (Camden) 72 Et per manus eiusdem pro j stopell pro j botell. *c* 1440 *Promp. Parv.* 477/2 Stoppell, of a bottel or oþer like, *ducillus.* 1471 RIPLEY *Comp. Alch.* III. vi. in Ashm. (1652) 140 Make thy Stopell of glas. *c* 1480 HENRYSON *Mor. Fab.*, *Wolf & Fox* xix, The fraudfull foxe.. with his teith the stoppell, or he stint, Pullit out. 1526 in Gutch *Collect. Cur.* (1781) II. 325 Item deliveryd the.. burnysshing of twoo Flagons and mending the Cheynis and Stoppells. 1600 SURFLET *Country Farm* III. lxii. 574 Euerie one of the [furnace] mouthes shall haue his stopple. *Ibid.* v. xxiii. 725 They draw forth the thinnest of the licour.. by a stopple which they haue for the purpose in the bottome of the fat. 1601 HOLLAND *Pliny* XXXIII. iv. II. 468 No sooner are the stopples driven and shaken out, but the water gusheth foorth amaine. 1613 PURCHAS *Pilgrimage* (1614) 184 The stopple of a Vessell, if it be of Hempe or Flax, may not be thrust in. 1626 MIDDLETON *Wom. beware Wom.* III. iii. 103 Like a cloth-stopple in a cream-pot. 1718 J. CHAMBERLAYNE *Relig. Philos.* (1730) II. xviii. §6 All the Stopples that are used to the Phials.. are corroded by the Particles that ascend. 1823 J. BADCOCK *Dom. Amusem.* 75 Let a phial be provided, which has a cork-stoppel. 1849 EASTWICK *Dry Leaves* 44 Among the ornaments.. suspended over the tomb were some stopples of decanters. 1865 E. C. CLAYTON *Cruel Fortune* II. 289 Mademoiselle Marie took up the phial,.. extracted the stopple, sniffed at the contents, then replaced the stopple.

†**b.** *transf.* and *fig. Obs.*

1508 DUNBAR *Tua Maritt Wemen* 339 Than with a stew stert out the stoppell of my hals. 1565 JEWEL *Repl. Harding* (1611) 361 The Councell of Salesgunstadium hath straitly charged, that no Priest presume, to say more than three Masses vpon one day,.. which also is a great stopple to M. Hardings *Totquot.* 1628 in Rushw. *Hist. Coll.* (1659) I. 586 Which might serve for a sufficient stopple for the Doctors mouth, to keep in his Doctrine of Necessity. 1691 RAY *Creation* II. (1704) 304 Therefore were there no Shuts or Stopples made for the Ears.

†**c.** *Mus.* The plug of a stopped organ-pipe. Also (see quot. 1801). *Obs.*

1771 ROLAND LE VIRLOYS *Dict. Archit.* III. Vocab. 184 Stopple of an organ, *biseau d'orgue.* 1801 BUSBY *Dict. Mus.* (1811), *Stopples*, certain plugs with which the ancients stopt or opened the holes of a flute.. in order to accommodate its scale.. to some particular mode. 1876 STAINER & BARRETT *Dict. Mus. Terms.*

d. = *ear-plug* (*b*) s.v. EAR *sb.*[1] 17. *U.S.*

a 1961 in WEBSTER, s.v., A stopple must be fitted into the ear canal so that noise does not leak around the edges. 1965 J. M. CAIN *Magician's Wife* (1966) xvi. 121 He must put stopples in his ears to account for his failure to answer, in case his phone had rung. 1977 *New Yorker* 12 Sept. 161/3 (Advt.), Noise? No problem. Flents Ear Stopples seal it out.

†**2.** A stopping or pad (of wet cotton). *Obs.*

1560 WHITEHORNE *Ord. Souldiours* (1588) 39 b, Put in the trumbe a handfull of serpentine pouder vnmixt, next a handfull of the foresaid mixture, after a little pouder, then a stoppell of cotten wet in oyle of gineper.

†**3.** A name for some marine animals. *Obs.*

1713 PETIVER *Aquat. Anim. Amboinæ* Tab. 5/6 *Blatta oblonga maxima*.. Great Oval Horn-stopple. *Ibid.* 10/3 *Umbilicus marinus niger*.. Black Bone stopple.

4. *Comb.*, as ***stopple-cork, -maker***; †**stopple-pear**, some variety of pear (? shaped like a stopper).

a 1849 J. C. MANGAN *Poems* (1859) 38 Wrench the *stopple-cork! 1481 CAXTON *Reynard* (Arb.) 16 His fader was Macob the *stoppelmaker. 1664 EVELYN *Kal. Hort.*,

Dec. (1679) 30 Pears,.. Gascogne-Bergomot, Scarlet-pear, *Stopple-pear.

†**II. 5.** The action of stopping; a stoppage, prohibition. (Cf. ESTOPPEL 2, 2 b.) *Obs.*

1578 SIR F. KNOLLYS in *MS. Rawl. D. 23* lf. 19 b, To stoppe hir Maiesties owne marchantes from theyre free vente at Hanborroe, hoping that by the stoppall thereof, they shall [etc.]. **1598** MARSTON *Sco. Villanie* II. vii. 205 Their only skill rests in Collusions, Abatements, stoppels, inhibitions. **1600** W. WATSON *Decacordon* (1602) 314 Neither Matchiuel, nor any that euer yet was in Europe [come] neere vnto the Iesuits for Atheall deuises to preuent the stoppels of their stratagems. **1651** J. S. *Prince of Priggs Revels* III. 10 He'l soon recover all by his collusions, Abatements, stoppels, inhibitions.

'stopple, *sb.*^{2} *Sc.* and *north.* Also 7 **stople,** 9 **stapple.** The stem of a tobacco-pipe. (See PIPE-STAPPLE.)

1681 COLVIL *Whigs Supplic.* (1751) 55 Some have their faces and their throples All scratched with tobacco stoples. *a* **1730** T. BOSTON in Morrison *Mem.* (1899) 6 He.. broke in pieces a part of a tobacco-pipe..; bidding the devil beat him as small as that pipe-stopple, if [etc.]. **1898** *Shetland News* 5 Feb. (E.D.D.), He.. ramm'd da strae twartree times introw da stapple o' his pipe.

stopple ('stɒp(ə)l), *v.* [f. STOPPLE *sb.*^{1}] *trans.* To put a stopple on; to close with a stopple.

? **1795** COWPER *Moralizer Corrected* 7 [He] Stoppled his cruse, replac'd his book Within its customary nook. **1834** H. MILLER *Scenes & Leg.* xix. (1857) 283 Macglashan.. received the stoup, stoppled with a bunch of straw. **1857** THOREAU *Maine W.* ii. (1912) 183 A little vial, containing matches, stoppled water-tight.

stopple, obs. var. STOUPLE, STUBBLE.

stoppo ('stɒpəʊ). [f. STOP *sb.*^{2} or *v.* + -O^2.]

1. *slang.* A rest from work.

1938 J. PHELAN *Lifer* xii. 120 What's the chances for a 'stoppo', Reg?

2. *Criminals' slang.* An escape, a get-away, esp. in phrase ***to take stoppo***, to make a rapid escape in order to avoid detection. Freq. *attrib.*, with reference to rapid escape by car, in ***stoppo car, driver, man.***

1935 G. INGRAM *Cockney Cavalcade* v. 78 'I took stop-o.' In other words, ran away from the police. **1949** PARTRIDGE *Dict. Underworld* 712/1 *Take stoppo*, to be obliged to run away... To take heed when the look-out cries 'Stop!' **1974** *Listener* 7 Nov. 595/3 Boys who are going to be stoppo drivers—driving stolen escape cars. **1975** M. KENYON *Mr Big* xx. 192 Walk, then, to the stoppo car... And wait... Till Slicker comes. **1978** J. GARDNER *Dancing Dodo* xxxv. 279 Dobson.. held the clutch down, took off the hand brake and let his toe press gently on the accelerator... 'It's a stoppo man's take-off,' the instructor said.

stoppull, obs. form of STOPPLE *sb.*^{1}

†**'stopsel.** *Obs. rare*$^{-1}$. [a. Du. *stopsel*, in Kilian glossed *stuppa* (tow), f. *stoppen* to stuff, stop: see STOP *v.*] An incendiary missile, consisting of tow, brimstone, etc.

1489 CAXTON *Faytes of A.* II. xxxv. K iiij b, They muste haue appareylled redy pitche, oyle brymstone and towe to make with all grete stopselles that shal be shoten thykke to the engyns of theyre enemyes tyl that they be sette a fyre.

†**stopull.** *Obs. rare*$^{-1}$. [Of obscure origin and meaning; perh. an error for **scopull* ad. L. *scopulus* rock.]

1506 *Guylforde's Pilgr.* (Camden) 13 Ouer ayenst the forsayd yle of Cirigo to y^e see wardes is y^e Stopull or Cragge called in Greke Ouago. **1517** *Torkington's Pilgr.* (1884) 19 The Stopull of Craggs called in Greke Obaga.

'stop-watch, *sb.* A watch which indicates fractions of a second by a hand that may be instantly stopped by pressure on a spring or catch, so as to record an exact moment or period of time; chiefly used for timing races.

1737 BRACKEN *Farriery Impr.* (1757) II. 166 Provided he is truly try'd by a stop Watch. **1867** in C. A. Wheeler *Sportascrapiana* 214 Place a practical man with one of M'Cabe's stop-watches at the finishing point. **1888** MRS. CUSTER *Tenting on Plains* xii, The General, with his stop-watch in hand.

b. *fig.* Also *attrib.*

1806 J. BERESFORD *Miseries Hum. Life* VII. lxi, Automata —people who regulate all their thoughts, words, and actions, by the stop-watch. **1817** *Examiner* No. 505. 554 The uncle .. being a stop-watch person always in a hurry. **1821** LAMB *Elia* Ser. I. *Old Benchers*, He was at once.. his guide, stop-watch, auditor, treasurer. **1896** SAINTSBURY *Hist. 19th Cent. Lit.* v. 228 The critic looks only at the weak parts, and he judges the weak parts only by the stop-watch. [Cf. Sterne *Tr. Shandy* III. xii.]

stop-watch ('stɒpwɒtʃ), *v.* [f. the sb.] *trans.* To time with a stop-watch.

1973 J. WAINWRIGHT *Devil you Don't* 19 We being timed? .. Stop-watched? **1977** B. FREEMANTLE *Charlie Muffin* xvii. 166 Cuthbertson.. had insisted on final rehearsals.. stop-watching the journey and testing the surveillance.

stop-work ('stɒpwɜːk), *a.* Also as one word. [f. STOP *v.* + WORK *sb.*] **1.** *Austral.* and *N.Z.* Designating a meeting that requires employees to stop working in order to attend. Also *ellipt.* as *sb.*

c **1926** 'MIXER' *Transport Workers' Song Bk.* 25 With their silly bluff and twaddle, And their stop-work meetings, too, By which I'm not allowed to work Till their business is through. **1941** *Argus* (Melbourne) 15 Nov. 3/6 A stopwork meeting of builders' workers. *Ibid.*, Mr. Howitt said congress regretted the stopwork meeting. **1946** K. TENNANT *Lost Haven* (1947) x. 138 Jack Starbrace called a little stop-work meeting and addressed it. **1957** *Landfall* 11 Apr. 278 But it was a good day for a stop-work. **1977** *N.Z. Listener* 15 Jan. 6/4 A great many immigrants, probably the majority, were never involved in any kind of trade unionism in Britain and would not have recognised a 'stop-work' meeting if they had actually fallen over one!

2. *N. Amer.* Designating an order requiring work to stop.

1972 *Even. Telegram* (St. John's, Newfoundland) 28 June 1/1 The federal cabinet has authorized a stop-work order. **1973** *N.Y. Law Jrnl.* 26 July 2/1 This is an article 78 proceeding to rescind a 'stop work' order issued by the New York City Department of Buildings.

stopylle, obs. form of STOPPLE *sb.*^{1}

†**stor.** *Obs.* [OE. *stór* masc., rendering L. *storax* and *tus*; perh. a. L. *storax* (see STORAX).] Incense.

c **1000** ÆLFRIC *Hom.* I. 116 Hi.. him ȝeoffrodon.. gold and recels and myrran... Se stor [ȝetacnode] ðæt he is soð God. *c* **1250** *Kent. Serm.* in *O.E. Misc.* 26 Hi wolden offri him gold, and stor, and Mirre. *c* **1265** *Voc. Plants* in Wr.-Wülcker 556/44 *Olibanus*, encens, stor. *c* **1315** SHOREHAM *Poems* v. 160 Gold, myrre, stor, were here offrynges. **1340** *Ayenb.* 211 Þet stor huanne hit is ope þe uere smelþ zuete. **1387** TREVISA *Higden* (Rolls) I. 99 In Arabia is store, mir, and canel.

b. *Comb.*: **stor-fat**, a censer.

c **1000** *Sign Language* in *Techmer's Zeitschr.* (1885) II. 120 Ðonne þu storfæt habban wille, þonne wend þu þine hand ofdune and weȝe hi, swilce þu styre. *c* **1200** *Vices & Virtues* 143 Swa go upp mine ȝebede to-foren ðe, swa ðat stor dieth ut of storfate!

stor, obs. form of STAR *sb.*^{1}, STOUR.

storable ('stɔərəb(ə)l), *a.* Also **storeable.** [f. STORE *v.* + -ABLE.] Capable of being stored.

1868 *Daily News* 26 Aug., Live meat is not a portable or storeable article. **1871** R. S. BALL *Exper. Mechanics* §544. 262 Gunpowder is.. energy in a compact and storable form. **1907** *Nation* 9 Mar. 69/2 In some districts storable fruits are hard to find.

storacke, obs. form of STORAX.

storage ('stɔərɪdʒ). Also 9 **storeage.** [f. STORE *v.* + -AGE.]

1. Capacity or space for storing.

1612–13 FLETCHER *Coxcomb* I. i. (1647) 99/1 They are made like Carrecks, only strength and storage. **1706** PHILLIPS (ed. Kersey), *Storage*, Warehouse room for Goods. **1848** S. C. HOMERSHAM *Rep. to Directors M.S. & L. Rlwy.* 55 The storage that can be made available to receive the flood water from this area of drainage ground now stands as follows. **1946** GOLDSTINE & VON NEUMANN in J. von Neumann *Coll. Wks.* (1961) V. 24 It may be seen from the fact that each binary digit requires essentially one relay or one pair of vacuum tubes.. that this form of storage rapidly becomes quite expensive. **1964** T. W. MCRAE *Impact of Computers on Accounting* ii. 38 These early machines.. were fitted with magnetic tape storage. **1973** C. W. GEAR *Introd. Computer Sci.* vii. 309 We must develop a scheme for allocating storage as it is needed and 'recovering' it when structures using it are deleted.

2. a. The action of storing or laying up in reserve; the condition or fact of being stored.

1828 WEBSTER, *Storage*, the act of depositing in a store or warehouse for safe keeping; or the safe keeping of goods in a warehouse. **1868** *Daily News* 15 July, The Belgian government have determined.. to prohibit the manufacture, storage, or transport of that dangerous compound [nitroglycerine] in Belgium. **1869** E. A. PARKES *Pract. Hygiene* (ed. 3) 13 The chances of contamination of the water during storage are very great. **1879** M. PATTISON *Milton* xiii. 207 Milton's diction is the elaborated outcome of all the best words of all antecedent poetry, not by a process of recollected reading and storage, but [etc.]. **1907** J. A. HODGES *Elem. Photogr.* (ed. 6) 159 Precautions should be taken for dry storage.

b. ***cold storage***: the storing of provisions in refrigerating chambers as a means of preserving them from decay. Also *attrib.* Similarly *cool storage* (see quot. 1906).

1877 *Illustr. London News* 3 Mar. 203/1 A.. company called Cold Storage Wharf.. undertakes to provide cold storage accommodation for fresh meat.. and all produce of a perishable nature, from all parts of the world. **1895** *Daily News* 23 Nov. 3/2 We have now a very large capital.. invested in cold storage premises in various parts of London. **1906** *Westm. Gaz.* 27 July 7/3 To ensure that the cheese is delivered in uniform good condition the temperature of the four chambers.. will be maintained at 45deg. to 48deg. This is known as 'cool storage,' which is distinct from cold storage. **1926** *Daily Express* 11 May 1/3 No difficulty was experienced at any of the cold storage centres. **1933** *Discovery* Apr. 126/1 Canning and freezing both eliminate the risk of spoilage by moulds and bacteria which are a constant danger in cold storage. **1946** *Nature* 21 Dec. 920/2 Fruit cold-storage research has continued.

fig. **1897** *Outing* XXX. 367/1 Still that stony stare and his reiterated, impertinent queries... A cold-storage air arose between us. **1907** W. JAMES *Pragmatism* vi. 231 When may a truth go into cold-storage in the encyclopedia? and when shall it come out for battle? **1920** W. PERRETT *Peetickay* 3 It seemed.. that the thing to do would be to apply the stenographic principle to the consonants... That plan is now in cold storage. **1951** A. HUXLEY *Let.* 22 July (1969) 637 It seems to be rather a shame that this anthology-with-comments, which cost me a lot of work.. should remain indefinitely in cold storage. **1979** A. BOYLE *Climate of Treason* xi. 420 If he did idly question why the Soviet Union had kept their guests in cold storage for so long, Philby soon found a ready answer.

c. *Electr.* (See quot. 1893.)

1881 S. P. THOMPSON in *Jrnl. Soc. Arts* XXX. 30/1 The Storage of Electricity. **1893** SLOANE *Electrical Dict.*, *Storage of electricity*. Properly speaking electricity can only be stored statically or in static condensers, such as Leyden jars. The term has been popularly applied to the charging of secondary or storage batteries, in which there is really no such thing as a storage of electricity, but only a decomposition and opposite combination brought about, which leave the battery in a condition to give a current.

d. *Computers.* The placing or keeping of data and instructions in a device from which they can be retrieved as needed.

1909 *Sci. Proc. R. Dublin Soc.* XII. 80 The present design of the machine provides for the storage of 192 Variables of twenty figures each. **1945** J. VON NEUMANN in B. Randell *Origins Digital Computers* (1973) 358 R has also the properties of a memory. Indeed, it is the natural medium for long time storage of all the information obtained by the automatic device on various problems. **1958** *Listener* 11 Dec. 983/2 For high-speed storage, the magnetic cores of the present machines will give way to films of special iron alloys deposited *in vacuo* upon ceramic plates. **1978** J. P. HAYES *Computer Archit. & Organization* v. 325 The physical processes involved in storage are sometimes inherently unstable, so that stored information may be lost over a period of time.

3. A place where something is stored.

1775 in ASH. **1865** E. BURRITT *Walk Land's End* vii. 241 The whole of Dartmoor seems to be a storage of this valuable stone [*sc.* granite].

4. Rent paid for warehousing.

1775 in ASH. **1809** R. LANGFORD *Introd. Trade* 134 Storage, warehouse rent. **1817–8** COBBETT *Resid. U.S.* (1822) 232 This very salt; when brought here from England, has all the charges of freight, insurance, wharfage, storage, to pay. **1862** WATERSTON *Man. Commerce* 303 Storeage, a charge for warehouse rent.

5. *attrib.*, as ***storage bin, capacity, charge, company, device, dump, house, hut, medium, pile, power, register, rent, reservoir, -room, space, warehouse.***

1900 *Engineering Mag.* XIX. 753/1 The *storage bins for ore, limestone, and coke. **1868** in *Encycl. Brit.* (ed. 9) XVI. 458/1 Sixty-seven reservoirs.. having a *storage capacity of 336,000,000 feet. **1884** *Law Times Rep.* XLIX. 742/2 The charges in question were warehouse and *storage charges. **1884** *Pall Mall Gaz.* 19 July 5/2 The prospects of electric light companies in general, and *storage companies in particular, have of late been so much overcast that [etc.]. **1946** *Electr. Engin.* LXV. 389 Each is a complete adding and subtracting machine, and functions as a *storage or memory device. **1955** *IRE Trans. Electronic Computers* IV. 16/1 This report deals with a storage device utilizing magnetic cores to achieve fairly large amounts of information storage with a relatively moderate amount of circuitry. **1972** D. LEWIN *Theory & Design Digital Computers* vi. 185 Storage devices may have either destructive or non-destructive read-out of the stored data. **1882** *Rep. Prec. Met. U.S.* 98 *Storage dumps have been built. **1856** MISS WARNER *Hills Shatemuc* viii, The mill and *storeage house kept and owned by Mr. Cowslip. **1894** *Westm. Gaz.* 8 May 5/1 On making inquiries as to who were in the *storage hut at the time. **1947** A. W. BURKS et al. in J. von Neumann *Coll. Wks.* (1963) V. 40 There still remains the problem of automatic integration of this *storage medium with the machine. **1966** *Sci. Amer.* Sept. 80/1 Magnetic materials.. supply the principal storage medium in computers. **1913** *Times* 9 Aug. 19/3 At the present time there are 13,114 tons of coal in the *storage pile. **1881** S. P. THOMPSON in *Jrnl. Soc. Arts* XXX. 34/2 *Storage power lessened by heat. **1946** *Ann. Computation Lab. Harvard Univ.* I. 14 Each *storage register consists of twenty-four electro-magnetic counter wheels. **1965** HOLLINGDALE & TOOTILL *Electronic Computers* 114 In most computers an individual storage register is not a separate entity, either physically or conceptually, and the term *storage location* is more appropriate. **1868** *Routledge's Ev. Boy's Ann.* 341, I paid a month's *storage rent in advance. **1877** RAYMOND *Statist. Mines & Mining* 91 For a supply of water during the dry season we rely almost exclusively upon our *storage-reservoirs. **1848** S. C. HOMERSHAM *Rep. to Directors M.S. & L. Rlwy.* 37 This amount of *storage room is by no means large. **1891** *Daily News* 24 Oct. 7/4 On going into the storage-room he saw a number of pieces of meat. **1936** *Discovery* May 158/1 It may well revolutionise library methods and solve the eternal question of *storage-space. **1979** D. MALLETT *Greatest Collector* ix. 84 Richard Wallace .. bought no furniture, not wishing, perhaps, to add to the already acute problems of storage space. **1904** *Westm. Gaz.* 15 Dec. 11/3 The paper also recommended a system of *storage warehouses as a remedy for low prices arising from exceptionally large crops.

6. Special comb.: **storage battery**, a secondary battery in which a supply of electricity is accumulated; **storage-bellows** (see quot.); **storage cell**, an electrical accumulator; **storage heater**, (*a*) a heating apparatus for railway carriages, operating by means of stored heat; (*b*) = *night storage heater* s.v. NIGHT *sb.* 14; hence **storage heating**, heating by means of storage heaters; **storage life** (see quot. 1971^1); **storage location** *Computers*, a place in a store capable of storing one unit of data and usu. specifiable by an address; **storage protection** *Computers*, the protection of storage locations against unauthorized or accidental reading or writing; **storage ring** *Physics*, an approximately circular accelerator in which particles can be effectively stored by being made to circulate continuously at a high energy; **storage station**, a place at which electric current is stored for distribution for lighting purposes; **storage tank**, a tank for storage (e.g. of petrol); **storage tube** *Electronics*, any of various kinds of electron tube which store the information or image applied to them so that it can be retrieved at a later time; **storage tuber**, a tuber forming a reservoir of nourishment for the plant; **storage unit**, (*a*) one of a set of domestic cupboards; (*b*) a unit that serves as storage for a computer; **storage wall**, a partition wall consisting of cupboards, often designed to be opened from either side.

1881 S. P. THOMPSON in *Jrnl. Soc. Arts* XXX. 35/2 This is one of the rocks on which amateur constructors of *storage batteries have come to grief. **1898** A. TREADWELL *Storage Battery* 206 Probably the largest installation for the operation of storage-battery cars is in Paris. **1891** *Century Dict.* s.v. *Organ*, **Storage-bellows*, horizontal bellows into which the feeders open, and in which the air is kept at a uniform pressure by means of weights. **1881** S. P. THOMPSON in *Jrnl. Soc. Arts* XXX. 30/2 It is doubly difficult to find, in the electric accumulator or *storage cell, anything which can be called stored electricity. **1894** *Westm. Gaz.* 10 Dec. 8/1 The *storage heater is partially filled with a solution of salt water or acetate of soda. **1961** *Listener* 19 Oct. 629/1 For an existing house the storage-heater system works out very favourably. A good-looking storage-heater with thermostatic control..costs £22 10s. 6d. **1977** B. PYM *Quartet in Autumn* x. 88 Mrs Pope's sister apparently being too mean to switch on the storage heaters before January. **1961** *Listener* 19 Oct. 629/1 A *storage-heating installation. *Ibid.* 629/2 The chief disadvantage of storage-heating is the comparatively slow reaction to sudden big outside-temperature changes. **1971** *Gloss. Terms Quality Assurance* (*B.S.I.*) 8 **Storage life*, the specified length of time prior to use for which items which are inherently subject to deterioration are deemed to remain fit for use under prescribed conditions. **1971** *Country Life* 9 Sept. 643/1 How can the storage life of vacuum-packed bacon be extended? **1949** D. R. HARTREE *Calculating Instruments & Machines* 96 Different means have to be used for identification of a *storage location on a wire. **1964** T. W. MCRAE *Impact of Computers on Accounting* i. 10 If we have 100 storage locations, each one of which can store one character, we will divide this up into ten words, each word containing ten storage locations. **1965** G. B. DAVIS *Introd. Electronic Computers* 223 A *storage protection feature is an optional feature not usually found on small computers. **1970** O. DOPPING *Computers & Data Processing* ix. 128 In a computer with storage protection, a program can modify the contents of storage only within a prescribed area assigned to the program. **1956** G. K. O'NEILL in *Physical Rev.* CII. 1418/2 (*heading*) *Storage-ring synchrotron: device for high-energy physics research. *Ibid.*, Two 'storage rings', focusing magnets containing straight sections one of which is common to both rings, are built near the accelerator. **1965** *New Scientist* 18 Mar. 692/2 They accelerated two comparatively low energy beams of electrons to 300 MeV in a linear accelerator; they steered these beams into two 'storage rings' built adjacent to one another in the form of a figure of eight, and finally made them collide head-on at the point where the two rings touch. **1978** *Nature* 20 July 202/1 PETRA, Europe's 19 GeV on 19 GeV electron-positron storage ring under construction..near Hamburg, has circulated its first beam around the ring and stored it 'for several minutes'. **1889** *Daily News* 28 Nov. 6/1 The electric current will in the first place be transmitted..from Draycott-place to the three '*storage' stations. **1897** P. DAWSON *Electric Rlwys.* etc. 366 The required compressed air is carried in a *storage tank provided under each car. **1946** *Radar: Summary Rep. & Harp Project* (U.S. Nat. Defense Res. Comm., Div. 14) 144/1 *Storage tube. **1947** *Electronics* Sept. 80/1 Specific applications of this storage tube include use in simultaneous multicolor and three-dimensional presentation of radar or sonar data. **1975** D. G. FINK *Electronics Engineers' Handbk.* VII. 30 The correlation is a storage tube that receives a visual input to a photoemissive film..and later compares the original image with a similar image. **1914** BOWER *Address Brit. Assoc.* in *Nature* 24 Sept. 103/1 The plant is well known to botanists as regards its external features, its annual *storage tuber, [etc.]. **1951** *Catal. of Exhibits, South Bank Exhib., Festival of Britain* 125/2 *Storage unit. **1964** T. W. MCRAE *Impact of Computers on Accounting* vii. 199 A magnetic tape reel is a remarkably compact storage unit. **1978** J. MCNEIL *Consultant* xi. 117 Two lines of storage units ran at right angles to the wall. **1978** J. KELLOCK *Elements of Accounting* xii. 215 Hardware includes the storage unit, arithmetic unit, control unit, and all the input and output devices used with the computer. **1945** NELSON & WRIGHT *Tomorrow's House* xi. 132 (*caption*) It is only a step to the use of such equipment [*sc.* storage cabinets] to form the walls themselves—a device which we have named the '*storagewall'. **1959** *House & Garden* July 43/2 The dining-room, linked to the kitchen by a storage wall. **1970** *Observer* 18 Oct. 35/1 Ideally, every room in every house needs a storage wall.

storap, obs. form of STIRRUP.

storax (ˈstɔəræks). Also (4 torax), 6 stora(c)ke, 7 storaxe. Cf. STYRAX. [a. L. *storax*, an early adoption of Gr. στύραξ: see STYRAX. Cf. F. *storax*, It. *storace*, Sp., Pg. *estoraque*.]

1. A fragrant gum-resin described by ancient writers. In early mod. use applied (perh. correctly) to the resin of the tree *Styrax officinalis*; in later commercial and pharmaceutical use to the balsam of the tree *Liquidambar orientale* (more explicitly ***liquid storax***).

1382 WYCLIF *Ecclus.* xxiv. 21 As torax [*c* **1388** as storax], and galban,..and as Liban not kut, I smekede my dwelling. **1483** CAXTON *Golden Leg.* 51 b/2 Presente to that man yeftes a lytyl Reysens & hony Storax stacten therebinthe & dates. **1542** BOORDE *Dyetary* xxvii. (1870) 290 Take of storax calamyte half an vnce. **1543** TRAHERON *Vigo's Chirurg.* v. 267 b/1 Then put therunto..of liquide storax .3. vi. **1577** FRAMPTON *Joyful News* I. 7 Mingled with a little Storake, Amber & Muske. **1648** HERRICK *Hesper., Another on Julia* 210 How can I chuse but kisse her, whence do's come The Storax, Spiknard, Myrrhe, and Ladanum. **1694** PECHEY *Compl. Herbal* 333 The resin of Storax, which is sold in the Shops is two-fold, dry and liquid. The dry is called Storax-Calamite..because it is put up in Reeds. **1712** E. COOKE *Voy. S. Sea* 363, 3 Bales Storax. **1820** T. GREEN *Univ. Herbal* II. 637 But the only kinds now to be found in the shops are the Pure and the Common Storax; the former is..of a yellowish or reddish-brown appearance, and interspersed with whitish tears... This has been called Storax-in-the-lump, or Red Storax; and the separate tears, Storax-in-the-tear. The Common Storax is in large masses, [etc.]. **1838** EMERSON *Addr. Cambridge, Mass.* Wks. (Bohn) II. 192 The religious sentiment..is the embalmer of the world. It is myrrh and storax, and chlorine. **1859** HOOKER in *Man. Sci. Enquiry* (ed. 3) 423 None of the storax found in commerce in modern times is derived from *Styrax officinale* L.

2. The tree *Styrax officinalis*.

1694 PECHEY *Compl. Herbal* 333 A Storax, with the Leaves of Maple, grows in the Lord Bishop of London's curious Garden. **1842** *Penny Cycl.* XXIII. 181/1 *Styrax officinalis*, officinal Storax.

3. *attrib.*, as ***storax-ointment, -pill, -plant, -tree***; **storax-worts** *pl.*, Lindley's name for the N.O. *Styracaceæ*.

1753 *Chambers' Cycl.* Suppl. App., *Storax-tree*, in botany, the English name of the styrax. **1783** S. CHAPMAN in *Med. Commun.* I. 267 The storax pill was desired to be repeated. **1846** LINDLEY *Veg. Kingd.* 593 Storax worts are sparingly distributed, for the most part through the tropical or sub-tropical regions of both hemispheres. **1876** HARLEY *Royle's Mat. Med.* 414 The Storax Tree. A tree resembling the plane.., 20 to 60 feet high. **1891** *Century Dict.* s.v. *Ointment*, *Storax ointment*, liquid storax and olive-oil.

storb, variant of STURB *v. Obs.*

†**storbilon.** *Obs. rare*⁻¹. [a. OF. *estorbillon*, extended form of *torbillon* (mod.F. *tourbillon*), f. L. *turbo* spinning-top, whirlwind.]

A whirlwind.

c **1315** SHOREHAM IV. 7 Senne makeþ storbylon, þar scholde be godes peys.

stordy, obs. form of STURDY.

store (stɔə(r)), *sb.* Forms: 3-7 stor, 4 stoer, 4-5 stoor, 5 stour, stoher, 5-6 stoore, 6 stoare, stowre, *Sc.* stoire, stoyr, 9 *dial.* stoar, 6-7 stoir, 3- store. [ME. *stor*, aphetic f. ASTORE *sb.*, a. OF. *estor* (= Pr. *estor*, Anglo-L. *staurum, instaurum*) vbl. noun f. *estorer*: see STORE *v.* (The W. *ystôr*, Irish *stór*, Gael. *stòr*, are from English.)]

1. a. *sing.* (without indef. art.) That with which a household, camp, etc., is stored; food, clothing, and other necessaries, collected for future use. Now *rare*. †Also furniture (of a house or building).

1297 R. GLOUC. (Rolls) 8138 So þat þe cristinemen adde þer þe maistrie & tresour founde & stor inou. **13..** *Sir Beues* 1295 Þe palmer nas nouȝt wiþouten store, Inouȝ a leide him be-fore Bred and flesc out of his male. **13..** *Coer de L.* 1656 They schyppys armes, man and stede, And stoor, her folk al with to fede. *c* **1330** *Poem Evil Times Edw. II* 387 in *Pol. Songs* (Camden) 341 For beof ne for bakoun, ne for swich stor of house. *c* **1400** *Gamelyn* 354 Who made the so bolde For to stroien my store of my housholde. *c* **1440** *Jacob's Well* 128 Whan þou seruaunt stelyst in house mete & drynke, henne or chekyn, or oþer stoor. *c* **1470** HENRY *Wallace* v. 1036 Bath breid and aylle, gud wyne and othir stor. **1542-3** *Act 34 & 35 Hen. VIII*, c. 10 §4 It shalbe lawfull to everye persone..to make coverlettes..for theyre owne use or store of theyre householdes. **1570** LEVINS *Manip.* 174/16 Store of house, *supellex, res familiariæ*. **1581-2** *Wills & Inv. Durham* (Surtees) III. 91 To my wife..my farmehold in Buckton, the tower with all things belonging, and all the store upon it. **1582** in Feuillerat *Revels Q. Eliz.* (1908) 356 For the hire of three cartes to remove the store of the office to Wyndesor. **1667** MILTON *P.L.* v. 322 Small store will serve, where store, All seasons, ripe for use hangs on the stalk. **1821** SHELLEY *Hellas* 556 The garrison of Patras Has store but for ten days. *fig.* **1835** T. MITCHELL *Acharn. of Aristoph.* Introd. p. viii, In the Iliad and Odyssey..the Spartans found..ample store for cultivating that love of genealogies and antiquities, which characterised them.

†**b.** *to keep, take to* or *for one's own store*: to appropriate, take possession of. *Obs.*

c **1385** CHAUCER *L.G.W.* 2337 He..kepte her to his usage and his store. **1387** TREVISA *Higden* (Rolls) VII. 25 Þe earle..took þe mayde to his owne store [L. *suis usibus puellam applicuit*]. **1390** GOWER *Conf.* I. 239 It is other mannes riht, Which he hath taken..To kepe for his oghne Stor. **1426** LYDG. *De Guil. Pilgr.* 8563 Thys, the blyssyd saphyr trewe, ..Kep hyt for thyn owne stoor, ffor yt saueth euery soor.

c. *collective pl.* Articles (such as food, clothing, arms, etc.) serving for the equipment and maintenance of an army, a ship; occas. of a household, etc. Cf. MARINE STORES.

1636 in Rymer *Fœdera* (1735) XX. 126 The King..granteth to John Wells, the Office of Clerk and Keeper of all his Majesty's Stores and Storehouses at Deptford Strond, Chatham, [etc.]. **1664** *Act 16 Chas. II*, c. 5 §4 Whereas diverse of his Majestyes Stores and Ammunition pertaining to his Navy and Shipping or Service thereof are imbezilled and filched away. **1736** *Gentl. Mag.* VI. 443 Ordnance and Stores sent by his Majesty's Order in Council, dated April 3, 1735. **1802** C. JAMES *Milit. Dict.*, *Stores, Military*, are provisions, forage, arms, clothing, ammunition, &c. **1845** DISRAELI *Sybil* v. vi, Now dark streets of frippery and old stores, now market-places of entrails and carrion. **1846** A. YOUNG *Naut. Dict.* 324 *Stores of a vessel*, the ropes, sails, provisions and other outfit with which she is supplied. **1875** JOWETT *Plato* (ed. 2) III. 683 The docks were full of triremes and naval stores. **1889** MRS. HAWEIS *Art of Housekeeping* 92 Hints for the Storeroom. It is better to give out stores daily than weekly, and weekly than monthly.

†**2.** Live stock. In later use chiefly in phrases ***young, old store***. *Obs.*

a **1300** *Cursor M.* 2447 Bot fra þair store [*v.rr.* stor, stoor] bigan to sprede þe pastur þam bigan to knede. *c* **1375** *Ibid.* 1517 (Fairf.) Iobal was his eldest sone stoer of fee he dalt wip. *c* **1386** CHAUCER *Prol.* 598 His lordes..swyn, his hors, his stoor, and his pultrye, Was hoolly in this Reues gouernyng. *a* **1440** *Sir Degrev.* 72 Grett herdus in the playnus Wyth muchelle tame store. **1530** PALSGR. 276/2 Store of horses, *monture*. **1536** BELLENDEN *Cron. Scot.*, *Cosmogr. Albion* viii. (1821) I. p. xxxiii, Merchand with Cathnes lyis Sutherland, ane proffitable cuntre baith for store and cornis. **1538** ELYOT *Dict.*, *Armentum*, store of horse or nete. *Ibid.*, *Pecuaria*, store of catell. **1551** ROBINSON tr. *More's Utopia* I. (1895) 55 After farmes pluckyd downe, and husbandry decayed, ther is no man that passyth for the breadyng of yonge stoore [L. *non sunt qui fœturam curent*]. **1590** R. PAYNE *Brief Descr. Ireland* (1841) 13 Swine will not be full growen before they be two yeeres old: so the first yeere you can kill but your old store. **1596** DALRYMPLE tr. *Leslie's Hist. Scot.* I. 49 Marr..rache in store and pastural. *a* **1688** J. WALLACE *Descr. Orkney* ii. (1693) 16 Eagle[s] or Earns, and Gleds are here in plenty, and very harmfull to the young store. **1697** DRYDEN *Virg. Georg.* IV. 795 Four Heifars from his Female Store he took.

†**3.** A body of persons. *Obs.*

13.. *E.E. Allit. P.* A. 847 And þaȝ vch day a store he feche, Among vus commez non oþer strot ne stryf. *c* **1460** *Towneley Myst.* XII. 457 Ye ar of the old store, It semys you, Iwys. **1563** A. NEVILLE in *B. Googe's Eglogs* (Arb.) 23 By this alone The olde renowmed Stoore Of Auncient Poets lyue.

4. a. Sufficient or abundant supply (*of* something needful). †Hence (more fully, ***great, good store***), abundance, large number or quantity (of something whether desirable or not).

Proverb, *store is no sore*, i.e. abundance does no harm. **1471** RIPLEY *Comp. Alch.* XII. viii. in Ashm. (1652) 186 For wyse men done sey *store ys no sore*. **1500-20** DUNBAR *Poems* xiv. 59 Sic stoir of vyce, sa mony wittis vnwyce Within this land was nevir hard nor sene. **1568** GRAFTON *Chron.* II. 202 He helped forwarde that good store of forfeites and fines were gathered into the kingis treasury. **1570-6** LAMBARDE *Peramb. Kent* (1826) 121 They [the Danes] armed more store of chosen souldiers and entred the River of Thamise with five & thirtie Saile. *c* **1572** GASCOIGNE *Flowers* Wks. 1907 I. 63 Store makes no sore. **1594** PLAT *Jewell-ho.* II. 8 Ships..are pestred..with exceeding store of mice. **1598** HAKLUYT *Voy.* I. 54 In certaine places thereof are some small store of trees growing, but otherwise it is altogether destitute of woods. **1612** *Two Noble K.* I. iii. 6 Store never hurtes good Gouernours. **1615** G. SANDYS *Trav.* 249 Hereabout are great store of Tarantulas: a serpent peculiar to this countrey. **1653** H. COGAN tr. *Pinto's Trav.* xxii. 79 Having first given orders to his Junks to shoot continually at the town..wheresoever they perceived any store of people assembled. **1659** HAMMOND *Ps.* xxxviii. Annot. 206 Applying the words to his streights in general, store of which it is certain he had. **1677** WOOD *Life* (O.H.S.) II. 371 Great store of snow fell that day. **1705** tr. *Bosman's Guinea* 180 Plunder is their chief aim, instead of which they often get good store of blows. **1712** MOTTEUX *2nd Pt. Quix.* xliii. (1749) IV. 62 You can't eat your cake and have your cake; and store's no sore. **1759** R. BROWN *Compl. Farmer* 44 This kind must have great store of food. **1844** THACKERAY *Box of Novels* Wks. 1899 XIII. 415 Think of all we owe Mr. Dickens,..the store of happy hours that he has made us pass. **1853** M. ARNOLD *Scholar Gypsy* ix, Oft thou hast given them store Of flowers.

†**b.** Plenty; abundance (of food or necessaries).

1560 DAUS tr. *Sleidane's Comm.* 55 b, Yᵉ common people leaving theyr daily labor, toke such things as they neded of others yᵗ had store. **1590** LODGE *Euphues Gold. Leg.* B 4 b, Riches (Saladyne) is a great royalty, & there is no sweeter phisick than store. *a* **1642** FULLER etc. *Abel Rediv.*, *Grynaeus* (1651) 536 Christ, as in life, so He in death is store. [= L. *Christus ut in vita, sic quoque morte lucrum est.*] **1711** POPE *Temple Fame* 450 Of loss and gain, of famine and of store. **1712** SWIFT *Fable Midas* 49 By starving in the Midst of Store, As t'other Midas did before.

†**c.** *in* (*great, good*) *store*: in abundance. *Obs.*

1600 FAIRFAX *Tasso* VII. xxv, It was a fountaine from the liuing stone, That powred downe cleere streames, in noble store. **1607** TOPSELL *Four-f. Beasts* 137 There is no region or countrey in the world, where these are not bred in some store, as shall be declared afterwarde in the particular discourse of euery kind of Dogges. **1621** tr. *Ir. Act 28 Hen. VI*, c. 3 Whereas the theeues and euil doers encrease in great store. **1700** S. L. tr. *Fryke's Voy. E. Ind.* 288 Goats are in good store here.

d. Used *adv.* or as postpositive or predicative adj. = 'in store', in plenty, abundant(ly). Also ***good, great store***. Now *arch.* and *dial.*

1569 PRESTON *Cambises* 858 (Manly) The poets wel, in places store, of my might doo expresse. **1577** HANMER *Anc. Eccl. Hist., Evagr.* v. xix. 500 Then there were captiues great store, and cheape inough. **1578** T. N. *In Commend. Lyte's Dodoens*, Till Rembert he, did sende additions store. *a* **1586** SIDNEY *Ps.* XXV. xi, Behold my foes, what stoare they be. **1604** E. G[RIMSTONE] tr. *Acosta's Hist. Indies* III. xxii. 187 Peru doth surpasse it in one thing, which is wine, for that there growes store, and good. *c* **1610** *Women Saints* 24 And whereas no Saints want enuious enemies, as our Sauiour had store, and [etc.]. **1619** J. TAYLOR (Water P.) *Kicksey Winsey* B 5 b, Your stockes are poore, your Creditors are store, Which God increase, and decrease, I implore. **1624** CAPT. SMITH *Virginia* v. 170 Numbers of Mulberies, wild Oliue-trees store. **1648** MILTON *Ps.* lxxxviii. 9 For cloy'd with woes and trouble store Surcharg'd my Soul doth lie. **1650** B. *Discolliminium* 13 We shall have as many changes as my Mare hath paces, and she hath pretty store. **1673** RAY *Journ. Low C.* 5 In..Bruges..are no more than seven Parish Churches but of Monasteries or Religious Houses..good store, 60 according to Golnitz. **1694** J. CLAYTON *Acc. Virginia* in *Phil. Trans.* XVIII. 125 Wolves there are great store. **1718** POPE *Iliad* IX. 62 Ships thou hast store. **1810** SCOTT *Lady of L.* III. i, The race of yore..Told our marvelling boyhood legends store, Of their strange ventures. **1830** JAMES *Darnley* iv. I. 60 There might be seen the inimitable ham of York, with manifold sides of bacon,.. and cheeses store. **1855** *Whitby Gloss.* s.v., 'He likes the situation good store,' that is, very much.

5. a. A person's collective possessions; accumulated goods or money. † *to gather to store*: to hoard up money.

1303 R. BRUNNE *Handl. Synne* 6117 He gadred vn-to store fast, þat hys purs he fylled at þe last. **1596** SHAKS. *Merch. V.* I. iii. 54 *Shy.* I am debating of my present store, And by the neere gesse of my memorie I cannot instantly raise vp the grosse Of full three thousand ducats. **1615** CHAPMAN *Odyss.* XI. 226 Or if my store My wife had kept together. **1693** DRYDEN *Persius* VI. 183 Increase thy Wealth, and double all thy Store. **1700** —— *Ovid's Met.* VIII. *Baucis & Phil.* 34 Though little was their Store, Inur'd to Want, their Poverty they bore. **1753** MISS COLLIER *Art Torment.* II. ii. 111 If you bring no fortune to your husband, you should be as insolent as if you had increased his store by thousands. **1779** J. NEWTON *Olney Hymns* II. lviii. 252, I envy not the worldling's store, If Christ and heav'n are mine.

b. *transf.* and *fig.*

1684 DRYDEN *To Mem. Mr. Oldham* 11 O early ripe! to thy abundant Store What could advancing Age have added more? **1697** —— *Virg. Georg.* III. 482 The salacious Goat encreases more; And twice as largely yields her milky Store. **1770** GOLDSM. *Des. Vill.* 59 For him light labour spread her wholesome store.

†**6. a.** Something precious; a treasure. *Obs.* (see b).

1410 in *26 Pol. Poems* ix. 181 And arraye ȝow wel þerfore To resceyue god, ȝoure soules store. **1412–20** LYDG. *Chron. Troy* I. 2114 It sitteth nat a womman lyue alone; It is no stor but þei haue more þan oon. *c* **1426** *Abraham's Sacrif.* 216 in *Non-Cycle Myst. Plays* (1909) 32 She was wont to calle me hir tresoure and hir store.

b. In various phrases with the sense 'to value, esteem, prize; make account of': † *to tell, make, hold, set* (*great, little, no*) *store of* (obs.); † *to set at* (*much, little*) *store* (obs.); *to set* (*great,* etc.) *store by*; *to* †*put, set* (*great,* etc.) *store upon*.

c **1386** CHAUCER *Wife's Prol.* 203 And by my fey I tolde of it no stoor They had me yeuen hir gold and hir tresoor. *c* **1400** *Beryn* 4 For hem þat hold no store Of wisdom. **1413** in *26 Pol. Poems* xii. 28, I wolde set hit at lytel store. *c* **1440** LYDG. *Horse, Goose & Sheep* 440 But here this sheepe..Set litill stoor of swerd or Arwis keene. *c* **1460** *Towneley Myst.* III. 92 Bi me he settis no store. **1525** BERNERS *Froiss.* II. c. [xcvi.] 293 They wolde make no stoore of hym. **1540** PALSGR. *Acolastus* I. i. D iv, If thou..set any store by thy helth. **1553** BRENDE *Q. Curtius* Q iii, If I shoulde make a little store of them, for whome I had done so muche [L. *si, in quos tam magna contuleram, viliores mihi facerem*]. **1561** T. HOBY tr. *Castiglione's Courtyer* IV. (1577) Y iv, Hee deserued not to haue anye more store made of him. **1569** UNDERDOWNE *Heliodorus* IV. 59 And therefore I should lose that I sette moste stoare by. **1600** W. WATSON *Decacordon* (1602) 159 They [the Jesuits] make no more store of a man or woman's life,..then they do of the death of a dogge or a mouse. **1737** BRACKEN *Farriery Impr.* (1757) II. 108 Those Medicines which will do the greatest Feats are least Store set by. **1768** STERNE *Sent. Journ.*, *Starling* (1778) II. 36 The bird had little or no store set by him. **1797** MRS. A. M. BENNETT *Beggar Girl* (1813) III. 241 The precious metal, on which they set so high a store. **1860** RUSKIN *Unto this last* iv. §61 Much store has been set for centuries upon the use of our English classical education. **1862** LATHAM *Channel Isl.* III. xiv. (ed. 2) 331 Upon the Icelandic sagas many have put great store. **1876** FREEMAN *Norm. Conq.* (ed. 2) I. App. 674 The reader will not be inclined to set much store by the authority of Osbern. **1895** *Law Times* XCIX. 546/2 Students..though they may attend classes..do not rely on or..set much store by them. **1908** J. B. MAYOR in *Expositor* July 19 She sets more store by her own vow than by the promise of the Messiah.

†**c.** *to stand* (a person) *in store*: to be valuable to. *Obs.*

? **1463** *Paston Lett.* (1904) IV. 65 It shuld stand me in gret stoher if it mygth be do closly and suerly.

7. a. A stock (of anything material or immaterial) laid up for future use. Phrase, *to lay in a store*.

1487–8 *Rec. St. Mary at Hill* (1905) 137 Beside this Ther is spente of your stoor, in lathes, xxiij c. **1573–80** TUSSER *Husb.* (1878) 53 Thresh barlie thou shalt, for chapman to malt. Else thresh no more but for thy store. *c* **1600** SHAKS. *Sonn.* xxxvii. 8 For whether beauty, birth, or wealth or wit, ..Entitled in thy parts do crowned sit, I make my love engrafted to this store. **1725** WATTS *Logic* (1736) 71 You.. will obtain a rich Store of proper Thoughts and Arguments upon all Occasions. **1774** GOLDSM. *Nat. Hist.* VIII. 54 Their leaves must be gathered..and kept in a dry place, if it be necessary to lay in a store. **1808** SCOTT in *Lockhart* I. i. 45 My desk usually contained a store of most miscellaneous volumes. **1841** THACKERAY *Gt. Hoggarty Diam.* xii, All day she sat working at a little store of caps and dresses for the expected stranger. **1842** LOUDON *Suburban Hort.* 407 The greater part of the nourishment to the seeds being furnished by the store laid up in the plant. **1845** JAMES *Arrah Neil* ii, Whenever I have an opportunity I lay in a store in my own stomach for the journey. **1875** MANNING *Mission Holy Ghost* Pref. p. ix, These united would make a precious store for students and for preachers. **1881** S. P. THOMPSON in *Jrnl. Soc. Arts* XXX. 31/2 A piece of coal represents a store of energy. So does a bag of hydrogen gas. So does a piece of zinc.

†**b.** The stock of a tradesman; the tools, etc. of a workman. *Obs.*

1605 BACON *Adv. Learn.* I. vi. §16 As if wee should iudge or construe of the store of some excellent Ieweller, by that only which is set out toward the streete in his Shoppe. **1615** E. S. *Britain's Buss* A 3, Thirdly, the particulars of her Carpenters store; and of her Stewards store.

c. *collect. plural.* Stocks, reserves; often in immaterial sense, treasures, accumulated resources.

1520 *Coventry Leet Bk.* 674 A veu was takon by the said Maier and his brethern what stores of all Maner of Corne, and what nombre of people was then within the said Cite. **1697** DRYDEN *Virg. Past.* VII. 76 Lavish Nature laughs, and strows her Stores around. **1697** POTTER *Antiq. Greece* IV. i. (1715) 162 To fasten to some Part of their Body the most precious of all their Stores. **1699** T. BAKER *Refl. Learn.* Pref. A 2 b, And then it must be done by reasons borrow'd from the Stores of Learning. **1748** GRAY *Alliance* 14 Instruction on the growing Powers Of Nature idly lavishes her Stores. **1780** *Mirror* No. 80 An author, who..has added to the stores of natural history the following very curious facts. **1807** CRABBE *Par. Reg.* III. 388 Then we beheld her turn an anxious look From trunks and chests, and fix it on her book ..; And then once more, on all her stores, look round. **1854** *Poultry Chron.* II. 65 If they can climb these glorious hills, ..lay in stores of health and fresh air [etc.].

8. a. Storage, reserve, keeping. Now somewhat *rare*. Phr. *to keep* (young animals) *for store*: cf. 13 c and 9.

1487–8 *Rec. St. Mary at Hill* (1905) 135 Item, for mendyng of ij olde lockes with the keyes for stor. **1555** EDEN *Decades* (Arb.) 110 Certeine fruites..whiche they reserue for store as wee doo chestnuttes. *c* **1600** SHAKS. *Sonn.* xi. 9 Let those whom Nature hath not made for store, Harsh featureless and rude, barrenly perish. **1625** B. JONSON *Staple of N.* V. vi, The vse of things is all, and not the Store. **1638** R. BAKER tr. *Balzac's Lett.* (vol. III.) 3 Base wares get no value by Store. **1667** MILTON *P.L.* VI. 515 Sulphurous and Nitrous Foame..they reduc'd To blackest grain, and into store conveyd. **1707** MORTIMER *Husb.* 185 Some esteem them the best Pigs to keep for Store that suck the foremost Teats. **1811** *Regul. & Orders Army* 26 It is their duty to control..the Issue, and Delivery into Store, of all Articles of Camp Equipage. **1859** REEVE *Brittany* 6 Two boxes of chemicals, one for use and the other for store.

b. *in store*: in reserve, laid up for future use. Hence (of events or conditions in the future) *in store for*: awaiting (a person).

c **1386** CHAUCER *Clerk's Prol.* 17 Youre termes, youre colours, and youre figures, Keepe hem in stoor, til so be that ye endite Heigh style. *c* **1421** in *26 Pol. Poems* xix. 13 Man! is þe laft no loue in store? **1497** *Naval Acc. Hen. VII* (1896) 124 Wheles in store Shodd iiij pair Bare xiiij pair. **1535** COVERDALE *Isa.* xxxvii. 30 This yeare shalt thou eate that is kepte in stoare, & the next yeare soch as groweth of himself. **1550** CROWLEY *Epigr.* 712 For unlesse ye repent, God hath vengeaunce in store. **1590** SPENSER *F.Q.* II. x. 20 Then for her sonne..was young,..In her owne hand the crowne she kept in store, Till ryper yeares he raught. **1651** HOBBES *Leviath.* III. xl. 255 They alwaies kept in store a pretext, either of Justice, or Religion, [etc.]. **1657** in *Verney Mem.* (1907) II. 61, I shall be confident that Heaven hath a perticuler blessing in store for mee and for my family. **1732** BERKELEY *Alciphr.* vi. §5, I have so many objections in store you are not to count much upon getting over one. **1849** MACAULAY *Hist. Eng.* iii. I. 306 *note*, It was determined.. that a hundred and seventy thousand barrels of gunpowder should constantly be kept in store. **1857** DICKENS *Dorrit* I. xxxv, What such surprise can be in store for me? **1874** *Punch* 25 Apr. 180/1 Better days are in store for men and husbands. **1913** WILLCOCK *Sir H. Vane* iv. 56 Nothing but humiliation was in store for Vane.

9. A sheep, steer, cow or pig acquired or kept for fattening. (From the attributive use 13 c, to which quot. 1620 may belong.)

1620 *Inv. Wm. Toller* in *Essex Rev.* (1907) XVI. 206, 1 stor and a cowbullocke iijli xs. **1776** A. YOUNG *Tour Irel.* (1780) I. 45 Pigs. Bought in stores in September, at 7s. to 20s. each. **1812** *Examiner* 7 Sept. 564/1 Fat stock rather cheaper, but stores, with the exception of pigs, still dearer. **1815** *Hist. John Decastro* IV. 15 Take my brother his rent..and you may set out in the morning to fetch the stores..it is my positive order that no goads be used. **1844** *Jrnl. R. Agric. Soc.* V. I. 74 The practice with regard to feeding pigs..is to put up early in the spring some strong stores of twelve-months old. **1874** RANKEN *Domin. Australia* xiii. 233 They then, if 'stores', pass to the rich salt-bush country of Riverina. **1890** 'R. BOLDREWOOD' *Col. Reformer* xx, I have to meet a man about a largish lot of stores that we're dealing over. **1898** MORRIS *Austral Eng.*, *Store*, a bullock, cow, or sheep bought to be fattened for the market. **1901** *Scotsman* 3 Apr. 7/3 Stores met a fair trade, and fat cattle brought satisfactory returns. **1911** *Daily News* 1 May 6 May is the month..when the paddock is alive with frolicsome little pigs, fast growing into 'stores'

†**10.** Means for storing, receptacles for storage.

1497 *Naval Acc. Hen. VII* (1896) 123 Store for cranes & gynnes..ij chestes.

11. a. A place where stores are kept, a warehouse; a storehouse. Also *fig.*

1667 MILTON *P.L.* VII. 226 The golden Compasses, prepar'd In Gods Eternal store, to circumscribe This Universe. **1707** J. LOGAN in *Penn & Logan Corr.* (1872) II. 231 We are to have a good store there to put thy goods in. **1755** JOHNSON. **1828–32** WEBSTER, *Store*, a storehouse; a magazine, a warehouse. Nothing can be more convenient than the stores on Central wharf in Boston. **1899** *Westm. Gaz.* 24 Aug. 5/1 The structure was used as a military hay and fodder store. **1911** SIR H. CRAIK *Earl Clarendon* xx. II. 159 Her naval stores and arsenals were equipped with careful industry.

b. *Computers.* = MEMORY *sb.* 2 d.

1837 C. BABBAGE in B. Randell *Origins of Digital Computers* (1973) 21 The Store may be considered as the place of deposit in which the numbers and quantities given by the conditions of the problem are originally placed, in which all the intermediate results are provisionally preserved, and in which at the termination all the required results are found. **1919** A. MACFARLANE *Lect. on Ten Brit. Physicists* 80 Directive cards to transfer numbers from the store to the mill and from the mill to the store. **1948** *Nature* 8 May 712/1 The general ideas for a large automatic calculating machine are to be found in the designs of Charles Babbage for an 'analytical engine'... It was to work by means of plungers passing through punched cards, and was to contain a 'store' for numbers... The main components of any digital computing machine were then described... There must be a store to hold numbers and instructions. **1948** *Proc. R. Soc.* A. CXCV. 283 Stores have been operated with thirty-two lines and with sixty-four lines, each line containing thirty-two digits; 12 in. diameter cathode-ray tubes were used. **1964** F. L. WESTWATER *Electronic Computers* iv. 59 To read a word out of the store we have to open a gate at the end, and this permits pulses to escape. **1968** *Brit. Med. Bull.* XXIV. 191/1 The basic configuration of any computer consists of a store, a suitable input and output device, and a control mechanism. **1977** *Sci. Amer.* Sept. 130/1 In the context of electronics 'memory' (or, in British usage, 'store') usually refers to a device for storing digital information.

12. A place where merchandise is kept for sale. **a.** Chiefly *N. Amer.* and elsewhere outside the U.K. In early use, a shop on a large scale, and dealing in a great variety of articles (see quot. 1808). Now, equivalent to the British use of SHOP *sb.* 2. Also in phr. *to keep, tend store*.

The use of the word in this sense has not become common in the U.K. except in *Comb.*, as *chain store, department store* (see under the first elements), *store detective* (see sense 13 d below), in which it still refers to a large shop.

1740 *Pennsylv. Gaz.* 24 Apr. 4/2 At his store opposite the George in Arch Street. **1752** *Ibid.* 25 June 4/3 Where Mr. Samuel Burge kept store. **1757** WASHINGTON *Lett.* Writ. 1889 I. 490, I..beg the favor of you to choose me..as much thread as is necessary in Mr. Lewis' Store, if he has them. If not, in Mr. Jackson's. **1772** *Boston Gaz.* 23 Nov. (Thornton s.v. *Tend*) A person that can tend Store or wait on a private Gentleman. **1808** ASHE *Trav.* I. 40 It [Pittsburg] possesses upward of forty retail stores. *Ibid. foot-n.*, The common name for the places of sale in America and the colonies; differing from shops in being generally larger, and always dealing in a vast variety of articles. **1836** [MRS. TRAILL] *Backw. Canada* 124 A store is..nothing better than what we should call..at home a 'general shop'. **1839** W. WAKEFIELD in *N.Z. Jrnl.* (1840) No. 9. 112 It partly belongs to Captain Mayhew, an American, who has a store on it. **1844** 'JON SLICK' *High Life N. York* I. 2 They told me that he kept store away down Pearl street. **1861** MRS. MEREDITH *Over the Straits* II. 41 Some tolerably good 'stores' (as we designate those colonial Shops-of-all-work). **1862** *Times* 1 Sept. 5/1 At one corner of the street was a little provision and drapery store kept by an old woman. *a* **1872** in Schele De Vere *Americanisms* 641 He wanted to write up books, to tend store, or do anything to make an honest living. **1875** W. MCILWRAITH *Guide to Wigtownsh.* 43 Here are two or three little grocery stores. **1880** *Austral. Town & Country Jrnl.* 14 Feb. 314/4 This great city (of the future) is yet unbuilt, except one public-house and a store, blacksmith's shop, and very small telegraph and post office. **1907** J. H. PATTERSON *Man-Eaters of Tsavo* i. 11 [Mombasa] has several excellent stores where almost anything, from a needle to an anchor, may readily be obtained. **1956** H. G. DE LISSER *Cup & Lip* ii. 22 The shops—or stores, as they are invariably called in the West Indies—were open. **1975** *Encounter* Jan. 41/2 But for chrissake—that's 'Christ's sake' in American, chaps—has anybody ever gone away from a shop—meaning 'store', youse guys—empty-handed through ignorance of some one of these local variants?

b. In Great Britain after about 1850, the word became current in the designation *co-operative store*, denoting the shop in which a co-operative trading society exposes goods for sale (originally to its own members only, but later usually also to the outside public). Commonly in *plural* ('The Stores'), applied esp. to the establishment of any of the larger London co-operative societies, consisting of a number of departments, each dealing in a separate class of goods. In imitation of this use, the plural ('——'s Stores', '—— & Co.'s Stores') was often adopted as the designation of a trading establishment resembling 'The Stores' in extent and in multifariousness of business.

1852 [see CO-OPERATIVE *a.*]. **1865** *Sat. Rev.* 21 Jan. 79/2 The first development of the principle which obtained considerable results was the Co-operative Store. **1881** *St. James's Mag.* XL. 389 Ladies of highest rank and fashion struggling through crowds of ill-clad people at the Stores. **1889** MRS. HAWEIS *Art of Housekeeping* 97 These materials are bought infinitely cheaper at the Stores, than at the chemists. *Mod.* I know nothing about local prices; I deal at the Stores.

pl. const. as *sing.* **1914** *Times* 28 Aug., The head of a great stores has explained to a representative of *The Times* some of the difficulties with which [etc.].

13. *attrib.* † **a.** with the sense 'of the nature of store', 'hoarded up'. *Obs. rare.*

a **1626** BACON *Advt. Holy War* Misc. Wks. (1629) 100 Of this Treasure, it is true, the Gold was Accumulate, and Store Treasure, for the most part. **1633** T. JAMES *Voy.* 57 Wee made bags of our store shirts.

b. Designating a receptacle, repository, depot or transport for stores or supplies, as *store-back, -bag, -barn, -box, -cage, -cask, -cellar, -chamber, -city, -closet, -cupboard, -drawer, -loft, -place, -pond, -shed, -shop, -tent, -tub, -vat*; *store-boat, -craft, -sloop, -vessel*, etc. Also STOREHOUSE, STORE-ROOM.

1839 URE *Dict. Arts* 406 Discharging the purified spirit into the *store-back. **1730** J. SOUTHALL *Treat. Buggs* 10, I open'd my *Store-Bags, took out one Piece of Beef, some Biscuits and a Bottle of Beer. **1926** D. H. LAWRENCE *David* xii. 87 And she shall have her handmaidens about her, and her *store-barns of wool. **1797** *State Papers & Publick Documents U.S.* (1815) II. 436 On the 21st of January, the ice began to give way, and their *store-boat arriving on the 28th, they proceeded on the 31st for the Natchez. **1822** J.

Woods *Two Yrs.' Resid. Illinois* 87 The master of the store-boat..had freighted his boat with store-goods and fruit. 1898 *Daily News* 26 Aug. 5/2 These store-boats will be towed by the British gunboats to every camp which we form near the Nile. 1944 T. D. Clark *Pills, Petticoats, & Plows* 25 In the Louisiana sugar belt, barge store boats eased along the back ways of sugar plantations receiving stolen goods. 1826 Samouelle *Direct. Collect. Insects & Crust.* 68 *Store Boxes. 1677 N. Cox *Gentl. Recr.* iii. 60 If you would know whether your Canary-bird be in health before you purchase him, take him out of the *Store-cage, and put him in a clean Cage alone. 1773 *Gentl. Mag.* XLIII. 515 Two men.. attempting to go down a ladder into a large *store-cask, in order to clean it, were immediately suffocated. 1656 *Act Commw.* c. 19 (1658) 453 The..Store-houses, Ware-houses, *Store-cellars..of every Vintner or Retailer. 1624 in *Archæologia* XLVIII. 148 In the *Storechamber. 1611 Bible *2 Chron.* viii. 6 All the *store-cities [*1 Kings* ix. 19 cities of store] that Solomon had, and all the charet-cities. 1825 T. Hook *Passion & Princ.* v, The..key of the *store-closet. 1796 W. Vaughan *Exam.* 7 Coal-barges..converted into floating *store-craft, in order to save the expense of wharfage. 1841 C. Fox *Jrnl.* 5 May in *Mem. Old Friends* (1882) vii. 123 We went all over his comfortable house.. choosing papers, positions of *store cupboards, and other important arrangements. 1903 Kath. Tynan *Hon. Molly* xxix. 308 The store-cupboard, the linen-closet, the china-closet. 1865 Ruskin *Sesame* i. §36 One of the newspaper paragraphs which I am in the habit of cutting out and throwing into my *store-drawer. 1612 in *Antiquary* (1906) XLII. 29/1 Imprimis in the *Store lofte foure iron wedgs.. and other olde iron and lumber. 1852 Hanna *Mem. Dr. Chalmers* IV. 401 An old deserted tannery whose upper storeloft, approached from without by a flight of projecting wooden stairs, was selected. 1507 *Reg. Privy Seal Scot.* I. 223/1 Al and sindri his and tharis landis,..stedynnis, *store placis, grangis, [etc.]. 1879 Ld. Coleridge in E. H. Coleridge *Life & Corr.* (1904) II. 238 To treat it [a chapel] as a store-place for tools and ladders. 1708 *Lond. Gaz.* No. 4453/3 Large *Store-ponds, and Sun-ponds for making of Brine. 1879 Castle *Law of Rating* 76 They were rateable for a *store-shed. 1888 C. M. Yonge *Our New Mistress* xii. 109, I went into one of those great *store shops where they sell all sorts of things. 1972 E. White in W. King *Black Short Story Anthol.* 366 Jill..passes the store-shops of the Jews. 1776 Mickle tr. *Camoens' Lusiad* Introd. p. xl, Here the *store-sloop, now of no farther service, was burnt by order of the admiral. 1870 *Routledge's Ev. Boy's Ann.* 592 A *store-tent where most of the Iron Barkers bought their groceries. 1845 G. Dodd *Brit. Manuf.* IV. 127 The paint.. is conveyed into *store-tubs. 1826 *Vintner's, Brewer's* etc. *Guide* 122 *Store vats..for keeping beer till wanted for sale. 1791 Smeaton *Edystone L.* §85 To moor a *store-vessel in the neighbourhood of the rocks.

c. Designating animals kept for breeding or as part of the ordinary stock of a farm, also animals bought lean to be fattened; as ***store beast, bullock, cattle, cow, pig, sheep, sow, stock, swine***; **store-farm**, a farm on which cattle are reared, a stock farm; also *store-farmer, -farming, -master*.

1602 *Inv.* in *Collect. Archæol.* (1863) II. 111 One sow and ij store pigges. 1681 Flavel *Meth. Grace* xi. 245 'Tis better like store-cattle to be kept lean and hungry, than with the fatted ox to tumble in flowery meadows. 1683 *Lond. Gaz.* No. 1872/4 Ten Scotch Store-Bullocks. 1733 W. Ellis *Chiltern & Vale Farm.* 353 If they are eat off with Store-sheep. 1764 in *Morison's Dict. Decis.* (1806) XXXIII. 14512 The said William Porteous, and others, store-masters and tenants in the parishes of Lesmahago, [etc.]. 1772 *Ann. Reg.* 110/1 The mortality has been as great in most of the other store-farms. 1787 Winter *Syst. Husb.* 227 Stale meat.. should be cleared out, and given to store swine. 1801 *Farmer's Mag.* Apr. 220 The sheep-graziers or store masters, who occupy much of the higher parts of the country. 1808 Forsyth *Beauties Scot.* V. 271 The store-farmer, who rears the sheep. 1815 *Hist. John Decastro* IV. 15 A journey of forty miles to bring home a lot of store beasts to take place of the fat lot which had been just sold. 1822 W. J. Napier (*title*), A Treatise on Practical Store-Farming. 1823 E. Moor *Suffolk Words*, *Store*, applied to a domestic animal, especially to a sow, means one kept for breeding. 'A store sow.' 1844 Stephens *Bk. Farm* II. 71 The store-sheep in Scotland—that is, the ewe-hoggs—are always fed as fully as the wether-hoggs which are intended to be fattened. 1858 Simmonds *Dict. Trade*, *Store-master*, the tenant of a store farm, that is, a sheep walk in Scotland. 1885 Mrs. C. Praed *Head Stat.* xvii. I. 283 Oh, we are not fit for anything but store-cattle: we are all blady grass and brigalow scrub. 1901 *Scotsman* 3 Apr. 7/3, 191 fat cattle, 486 store cattle, 76 fat sheep, 120 store sheep.

d. Chiefly *N. Amer.* and elsewhere outside the U.K. In sense 'of or belonging to a store or shop', as ***store-book, -boy, buyer, detective, -girl, porch, -rent***; 'purchased or purchasable at a store', as ***store boots, cheese, clothes, goods, pants, shirts, sugar, tea, teeth***; **store church**: see quot. 1948; = *storefront church*; **store pay** (see quot. 1848). Also storekeeper.

1741 Tailfer etc. *Narr. Georgia* 29 And we may safely affirm (and appeal to the Store-Books for the Truth of it) that [etc.]. 1876 Besant & Rice *Golden Butterfly* xxxi, A stove-pipe hat, store boots, and go-to-meetin' coat. 1840 Maury in Mrs. Corbin *Life* (1888) 33 A shop-boy, or as we say in the West, a store-boy. 1965 *Harper's Bazaar* Feb. 21/3 The entirely new role of the store buyer. 1980 *Times* 12 Aug. 8/4 Store buyers..still come to Paris, but..to see the ready-to-wear. 1982 *Times* 3 Aug. 6/1 This week, there weren't any store buyers. 1863 P. S. Davis *Young Parson* 61 One plate of 'store cheese', and a half a bread-basket of ginger crackers. 1894 *Rep. Vermont Board Agric.* XIV. 25 A full cream store cheese is run through a grinder. 1948 H. L. Mencken *Amer. Lang.* Suppl. II. x. 591 A *store-church* is one set up in a vacant store or in the front room of a dwelling house. 1961 C. Himes *Black on Black* (1973) 60 She hid in Rev'end Sinner's store church when she run away. 1840 *Knickerbocker* XVI. 262, I felt an awe of young ladies in 'store clothes'. 1859 Bartlett *Dict. Amer.* (ed. 2) 453 *Store clothes, store goods*, clothing or other articles purchased at a store, as opposed to those which are home made. 1872 [see *boiled shirt* s.v. boiled *ppl. a.* 2]. 1944 B. Johnson *As much as I Dare* 294 These young men did not want to give up their store clothes. 1907 *St. Nicholas* Oct. 1106/2 He wondered how the store detectives worked to find a man who might be picking pockets in a great crowd. 1968 J. Lock *Lady Policeman* xix. 157 They had been detained by the store detective. 1979 R. Rendell *Make Death love Me* vi. 59 A woman had grabbed him and he'd only just escaped the store detective. 1822 J. Woods *Two Yrs'. Resid. Illinois* 75 There were twelve tons of store-goods [on board]. 1891 'O. Thanet' *Otto the Knight* 4 Thar, store pants an' gallowses! Make haste an' putt 'em on! 1932 *Atlantic Monthly* Apr. 475/1 Steve-john..was..a bronze perfection—Celini's 'Perseus' in store pants. 1942 W. Stegner *Mormon Country* 126 Smart alecs had money to jingle in their store pants. 1842 R. H. Bonnycastle *Canada & Canadians* II. 180 A quintal of fish..is worth 12*s*. 6*d*. in hard cash, or 14*s*. 6*d*. store pay. 1848 Bartlett *Dict. Amer.* App. 411 *Store pay*, payment made for produce or other articles purchased, by goods from a store, instead of cash. 1891 S. M. Welch *Recoll. Buffalo 1830–40* 353 The workmen were to receive.. only half cash, the remainder in trade—store pay, *i.e.*: in orders on the employers or other stores for such goods as they needed. 1905 J. S. Carter *Story of Dundas* 51 The store-keeper bought the settlers' produce but would give them only trade in return, or what was known as 'store pay'. 1934 C. M. Wilson *Backwoods Amer.* ii. 16 Hired boys are among the most cherished perpetrators of store-porch mirth. 1949 B. A. Botkin *Treas. S. Folklore* p. xix, The rural south is a land of the out-of-doors come up to the door and even indoors, where the 'gallery', the store-porch, the kitchen..are made for story-telling. 1800 *Publ. Acts U.S.* 6th Congr. 1. c. 57 §1 The expense of the navy store at Philadelphia, comprising storekeeper's salary, clerk hire, store rent [etc.]. 1872 Schele de Vere *Americanisms* 206 Store-sugar, or sugar made from the cane. 1843 'R. Carlton' *New Purchase* I. ix. 64 'Tisn't nun of your spice-wood or yarb stuff, but the rale, gineine *store* tea. 1872 Schele de Vere *Americanisms* 395 It was soon discovered that store-tea was all over the interior of the country the name for genuine tea. 1878 *Brooklyn Monthly* June 185/1 It occurred to me that a brief description of the sensations experienced might be of interest to any of my readers who are contemplating a new set of 'store teeth'. 1891 *Century Dict.* s.v., *Store* teeth (humorously used for *false teeth*). 1951 C. Lynch-Robinson *Last of Irish R.M.s* vi. 113 When I first got my new 'store teeth' in, they worried me. 1975 *Budget* (Sugarcreek, Ohio) 20 Mar. 8/6 Mrs. Gintz is a sister to O. K. Brown, the dentist that pulled my last teeth, and made me some store teeth.

e. Pertaining to 'the Stores' (see 12 b), as *store price*.

1889 Mrs. Haweis *Art Housekeeping* 115 The calculation is based on the prices of the best London tradesmen [etc.]. .. West-end dairyman, fruiterer, greengrocer, and fishmonger; baker and grocer (Store prices).

14. In *Comb.* with adjs. or ppl. adjs., as **store-bought**, bought (often ready-made) from a store; also *fig.*; also **store-boughten** *U.S.*; **store-wide**, operating or applying throughout the whole of a store.

1952 J. Steinbeck *East of Eden* xvi. 181 Would you say they were made clothes or store bought? 1953 *Manch. Guardian Weekly* 1 Oct. 2 She swayed like a riven oak over her failure to compete with 'powder and store-bought hair'. 1962 *Times* 4 May 9/6 It has become 'common sense' to substitute a store-bought, ready-made universe for the disquieting uniqueness of actuality. 1970 *Islander* (Victoria, B.C.) 22 Nov. 5/1 Those home-garden farmers aimed for near total independence from store-bought produce. 1981 *Farmstead Mag.* Winter 63/2 Pickled mushrooms..bring an outrageous price, in delicatessen shops, if you can find them and the storebought ones don't taste nearly as good as those pickled at home. 1883 Zeigler & Grosscup *Alleghanies* 91 Two good-natured-looking young men dressed in..'store-boughten' coats, and homespun pantaloons. 1933 L. I. Wilder *Farmer Boy* viii. 54 Clothes..made of store-boughten cloth, woven by machines. 1974 M. Laurence *Diviners* ii. 29 Storeboughten cookies are looked down on. 1938 *Sun* (Baltimore) 8 Sept. 3/1 A union demand for..a store-wide seniority plan. 1979 *Tucson* (Arizona) *Citizen* 3 Oct. 10/A (Advt.), Tremendous storewide savings.

store (stɔə(r)), *v.* Forms: 4 stoore, 6 stoare, 7 *Sc.* stoir, stor, 3– store; *pa. pple.* 3–4 istored, 4–5 ystored, -id. [Aphetic var. of astore *v.*, a. OF. *estore-r* to build, establish, furnish, stock, fortify, restore:—L. *instaurāre*, whence instauration. Cf. enstore, instore *vbs.* Sense 4 is prob. a new formation on store *sb.*]

1. a. *trans.* To furnish, supply, stock (a person, place, etc.) *with* something.

1264 *Pol. Songs* (Camden) 70 The Kyng of Alemaigne.. Brohte from Alemayne mony sori gost to store Wyndesore. *c*1275 Lay. 13412 Alle þine castles ich habbe wel istored. 1338 R. Brunne *Chron.* (1810) 160 Isaac did it store, to hold for tuo ȝere. *c*1386 Chaucer *Shipm. T.* 273 Certein beestes þat I moste beye To stoore with a place þat is oures. *c*1450 *St. Cuthbert* (Surtees) 1788 He tellit before þat an egle suld him store. 1530 Palsgr. 737/2 I have storyd my parkes and my pondes. 1586 Ferne *Blaz. Gentrie* 226 That noble familie..stored the crowne of England, well nigh the space of foure hundreth yeares. *a*1595 Southwell *St. Peter's Compl.* (1602) 15 Sweet volumes stoard with learning fit for Saints. 1595 Shaks. *John* v. iv. 1, I did not thinke the King so stor'd with friends. *a*1661 Fuller *Worthies, Wilts* 155 After he had stored himself with home-bred Learning. 1720 De Foe *Capt. Singleton* vi. (1840) 99 We stored ourselves.. with flesh and roots. 1722 N. Blundell *Diary* (1895) 187, I sent two Doz. yong Pigeons to Mr. Plumbe to Store his Dove-Coat. 1837–40 W. Irving *Wolfert's R., Mountjoy* (1855) 69 These studies..store a man's mind with valuable facts. 1857 Livingstone *Trav.* Introd. 2 His memory was stored with a never-ending stock of stories. *a*1883 J. Russell *Remin. Yarrow* iv. (1894) 84 Most of the lakes are stored with pike, perch, eels, and trout.

absol. (for *refl.*) 1803 *Naval Chron.* IX. 494 The *Prevoyante*..is storing at this port.

†**b.** const. *of*. *Obs.*

*c*1400 Maundev. (1839) xix. 207 No Cytee of the World is so wel stored of Schippes, as is that. 1422 Yonge tr. *Secreta Secret.* xiii. 142 Bethynke the that thow be well y-storid of whete and of corne. 1511 *Guylforde's Pilgr.* (Camden) 59 Where some of vs went a londe..to store vs of newe vytaylles. 1633 C. Farewell *East-Ind. Colation* 41 Theyr Wives and Concubines (whereof they are stored according to theyr states). 1657 R. Ligon *Barbadoes* 19 The Leeward Ilands,..of which the Bay of Merixo [*read* Mexico] is well stor'd.

†**c.** To dose *with* (drugs or medicines). *Obs.*

1722 De Foe *Hist. Plague* (1754) 36 Storeing themselves with such Multitudes of Pills, Potions, and Preservatives,.. that they..even poison'd themselves before-hand.

2. a. To reinforce, provide for the continuance or improvement of (a stock, race, breed). *Obs.* exc. *Sc. dial.* in *to store the kin*: see quot. 1866.

*a*1300 *Cursor M.* 2940 [Lot's daughter speaks], I think man-kind sal perist be, Bot it be stord wit me and þe. 1607 Topsell *Four-f. Beasts* 626 The sheepe of Spaine were of no reckoning til they were stored with the breed of England. 1866 Gregor *Banffsh. Gloss.*, *Store the kin*, to live; very often used, with a negative, of a person to appearance dying; as, 'He's unco ill; a doot he winna store the kin lang'. 1909 C. Murray *Hamewith* 90 Content gin mony towmonds still we're left to store the kin.

†**b.** To produce as offspring; also, to breed, rear (young animals). *Obs.*

1611 Heywood *Golden Age* iv. i. H 2, Or shall a stranger beare you to your tombe, When from your owne blood you may store a Prince To do those sacred rights. 1629 *Orkney Witch Trial* in *County Folk-Lore* (1903) III. 80 He..storit never ane calff of fyftene ky be the space of thrie yeirs.

†**3.** To restore (what is ruined or weakened). *Obs.*

1387 Trevisa *Higden* (Rolls) VII. 189 Harald..stored Herford, and closid it with kesting up of a diche [*Herefordiam instaurans vallo cingit*]. *c*1400 *Destr. Troy* 727 [She] Storet thee to strenght & þi stythe londes. 14.. *Guy Warw.* (Cambr. MS.) 3842 And thorowowt my londe fare And store ageyne, þat lorne was are.

4. a. To keep in store for future use; to collect and keep in reserve; to form a store, stock or supply of; to accumulate, hoard.

1600 Shaks. *A.Y.L.* ii. iii. 40, I haue fiue hundred Crownes..Which I did store to be my foster Nurse. 1620 T. Granger *Div. Logike* 120 How many seedes the sleepy poppy stores. 1671 Milton *Samson* 395 My capital secret, in what part my strength Lay stor'd. 1791 Cowper *Iliad* iv. 165 Safe stored it lies, By many a Chief desired. 1820 Keats *Eve St. Agnes* xx, All cates and dainties shall be stored there. 1842 Tennyson *Dora* 50 But Dora stored what little she could save, And sent it them by stealth. 1874 L. Stephen *Hours in Libr.* (1892) I. viii. 270 The vast accumulation of incoherent facts..stored in a capacious memory. 1881 S. P. Thompson in *Jrnl. Soc. Arts* XXX. 30/2 In the electric accumulator, by which we want to store electric currents, we use a chemical storage. *Ibid.* 32/1 In an ounce of gunpowder is stored about 10,000 foot-pounds of energy. 1893 D. J. Rankin *Zambesi Basin* xiv. 241 The drink [thus made] is consumed immediately after its manufacture, and is never stored.

fig. 1842 Tennyson *Ulysses* 29 And vile it were For some three suns to store and hoard myself.

absol. 1906 M. Sellers *Eastland Co.* (Camden) Introd. 58 When there was a glut they stored; when there was a scarcity they threw goods into the market.

b. With *up, away*, †*in*.

1552 Huloet, Store vp, *repono*. 1561 T. Hoby tr. *Castiglione's Courtier* i. (1577) F iij b, The true glory, that is stored vppe in the holy treasure of letters. 1601 Shaks. *All's Well* ii. i. 111 Many receits he gaue me, chieflie one, Which ..He bad me store vp, as a triple eye, Safer then mine owne two. 1718 *Free-thinker* No. 89. 237 Their Memory increases by daily storing up a Variety of Knowledge. 1770 G. White *Selborne, To Pennant* 22 Feb., I never could find that they stored in any winter provision, as some quadrupeds certainly do. 1866 *Sci. Rev.* Sept. 96/2 This curious property of acetate of soda enables us, by means of it, to store up and recover solar heat at pleasure. 1879 Lubbock *Sci. Lect.* i. 10 She [a bee]..goes back to the hive, stores away her honey, and returns..for another supply. 1881 S. P. Thompson in *Nature* 2 June 106/1 The currents stored up in the secondary battery are however not stored up as accumulations of electricity. 1912 J. S. M. Ward *Brasses* xv. 103 He stored them away and forgot all about them.

c. *spec.* To deposit (goods, furniture, etc.) in a store or warehouse for temporary preservation or safe-keeping.

1899 *Grocery* 15 May 125/3 [He] exhibited some California Newtown pippins, which had been stored since last December, as an instance of what cold storage could do. *Mod.* I shall store my furniture and spend a year in travelling.

d. *Computers.* To retain a physical representation of (data or instructions) that enables them to be subsequently retrieved.

1909 *Sci. Proc. R. Dublin Soc.* XII. 78 An Analytical Machine must have some means of storing the numerical data of the problem to be solved. 1937 H. H. Aiken in *IEEE Spectrum* (1964) Aug. 69 It is necessary that numbers may be removed from the calculating units and temporarily stored in storage positions. 1945 J. von Neumann in B. Randell *Origins Digital Computers* (1973) 356 A distinction must be made between the specific instructions given for and defining a particular problem, and the general control organs which see to it that these instructions..are carried out. The former must be stored in some way. 1948 *Nature* 8 May 712/2 In all these machines there is provision for storing numbers, say in the scale of 2, in certain places. 1964 F. L. Westwater *Electronic Computers* ix. 144 Inside a computer, alphabetical characters and numerals are both stored as numbers. 1972 D. Lewin *Theory & Design Digital*

Computers vi. 184 The speed of computers is limited by the time required to store and retrieve information.

e. *Computers.* To transfer *into* a store or storage location.

1964 *Ann. N.Y. Acad. Sci.* CXV. 654 The speed of the computer is fixed by the length of time required to read information from or store information into one of the 1,024 .. 12-bit memory locations. **1973** C. W. Gear *Introd. Computer Sci.* ii. 37 The CPU can be told to load a number into its accumulator from a specific cell in the memory .. or to store a number from the accumulator into memory.

5. Of a receptacle: To hold, keep, contain, have storage-accommodation for.

1911 *Concise Oxf. Dict.* s.v., A single cell can store 2000000 foot-pounds of energy.

6. *Comb.*: **store-and-forward** *Telecommunications*, used *attrib.* with reference to a data network in which messages are routed to one or more intermediate stations where they may be stored before being forwarded to their destinations.

1963 *On Line Data Processing* (Inst. Electr. & Electronics Engineers) 63 The store and forward switching system must interconnect with line switching facilities. **1980** R. L. Freeman *Telecommunication Syst. Engin.* ix. 429 The ARPANet connects dispersed computers of various manufacture and varying design. The subnet providing that connection is a form of store and forward system and must deal with such problems as routing, buffering, synchronization, [etc.].

Hence **'storing** *vbl. sb.* (also *attrib.*) and *ppl. a.*

1494–5 *Rec. St. Mary at Hill* (1905) 214 Item, for storyng of the bemelight & canstikes .. ij s j d. **1573–80** Tusser *Husb.* (1878) 35 No storing of pasture with baggedglie tit. *a* **1586** Sidney *Ps.* iv. vi, Whose store .. Of grain and wine fills stoaring place. **1667** Milton *P.L.* v. 324 Save what by frugal storing firmness gains To nourish. **1726** Leoni *Alberti's Archit.* I. 98*a* The gathering together and storing up the fruits of the harvest. **1884** *Pall Mall Gaz.* 13 Sept. 9/1 The lofts over the stable were used as a storing place for hay and straw. **1901** *Scotsman* 3 Apr. 7/4 There was a moderate show of storing cattle. **1907** A. C. Benson *Altar Fire* 150 What would be idleness in another is for him a storing of forces.

store: see stir *v.*, story, stour, stower *sb.*[1]

stored (stɔəd), *ppl. a.* [f. store *v.* + -ed[1].]

1. a. Laid up in store; kept in reserve as a store or stock; accumulated, hoarded.

1581 A. Hall *Iliad* v. 80 Sith fate no children did him leaue He forced was his stored wealth to strangers to bequeaue. **1605** Shaks. *Lear* ii. iv. 164 All the stor'd Vengeances of Heauen fall On her ingratefull top. **1879** W. Cory *Lett. & Jrnls.* (1897) 449 The stored water on which one's gardening depends. **1881** S. P. Thompson in *Nature* 2 June 106/2 A dozen times as much stored energy. **1885** *Athenæum* 28 Nov. 698/1 His three volumes are the stored harvest of a long .. life. **1897** *Allbutt's Syst. Med.* IV. 609 Only a small portion of the stored fat in the body comes directly from that consumed with the food.

b. with *up*, *away*.

1859 Lever *Dav. Dunn* lxxv. 658 You .. know little of the stored-up happiness your very name has afforded me for many a day. **1890** L. C. Miall *Obj. Lessons fr. Nature* ii. xv. 196 You have only to dry .. the plant to get back a good deal of its stored-up energy. **1900** *Everybody's Mag.* III. 581/1 Others came to offer certain stored-away preserves.

c. ***stored program***, a program that is stored in a computer in the same way as data, *esp.* one that can be automatically manipulated like data; freq. *attrib.*

1957 D. D. McCracken *Digital Computer Programming* i. 4 We speak of modern computers as being stored program machines. **1964** *Ann. N.Y. Acad. Sci.* CXV. 654 The LINC is a small stored-program digital computer which uses transistor circuitry and a random-access ferrite-core memory. **1970** O. Dopping *Computers & Data Processing* vi. 93 The use of a stored program, which can be modified by the machine itself, is one of the basic ideas in the design of a computer. **1983** *Sci. Amer.* Jan. 92/3 The stops and combination pistons [of the organ] .. are under the control of microprocessors having stored-program capabilities.

2. Stocked, furnished or supplied with a store. Also with qualifying adv.

1612 Bacon *Ess., Greatness Kingd.* (Arb.) 472 Walled Towns, stored Arcenals and Armories. **1835** J. Duncan *Beetles* (Nat. Libr.) 81 A well-stored cabinet of Coleoptera. **1865** Lea in Mrs. Lecky *Mem. Lecky* (1909) 45 Your richly stored pages show how much there is to be learned. **1882** Bain *James Mill* vi. 277 Men of stored and cultivated minds.

storefront, *sb.* (and *a.*). orig. and chiefly *U.S.* Also store-front, store front. [f. store *sb.* + front *sb.*] **1. a.** The side of a shop facing the street; (a building with) a shop window.

1880 G. W. Cable *Grandissimes* 376 A large porte-cochère .. [opened] upon the banquette immediately beside and abreast of the store-front. **1922** F. Farrington *Meeting Chain Store Competition* iii. 37 You can make your store front as conspicuous as a red front Atlantic and Pacific Tea Co. store front and still make it infinitely more attractive. **1945** *Planning Store of Tomorrow* (National Retail Merchants Assoc.) 6/1 Some are specialists on store fronts, but can do or supervise an intelligent job on interior layout. **1962** E. Snow *Red China Today* (1963) lxx. 538 Some of the old foreign store fronts (such as Whiteaways) now exhibited shining lathes and other machines. **1974** R. L. Simon *Wild Turkey* iii. 19 [A] shocking pink storefront temporarily labeled 'The Institute of Oral Love'. **1977** *Guardian Weekly* 4 Dec. 12/5 This indifference .. turns storefronts not into show-cases for the articles sold by the shops but into museums of all the goods that were once sold there or will be sold at some future date. **1979** *United States 1980/81* (Penguin Travel Guides) 73 This little deli is just a storefront on a shopping-center strip, so look carefully.

b. A room or rooms at the front of shop premises, esp. as used for some other purpose.

1972 *N.Y. Times* 3 Nov. 22/2 The two fully staffed and fully equipped Nixon storefronts in the area contain busy volunteers. **1973** *Houston Chron.* (Texas Mag.) 14 Oct. 2/1 The Hare Krishna sect .. is big business. It began in an East Village store front in New York. **1976** *National Observer* (U.S.) 7 Feb. 20/3 Performances first held in storefronts and lofts and later in streets, parks, and other public places. **1982** S. Paretsky *Indemnity Only* vii. 83 She ran a clinic in a shabby storefront down the street.

2. *attrib.* and *Comb.*, as ***storefront cinema, headquarters, industry, location, restaurant, theatre, window***; **storefront church**, a shop building used as a church or meeting place, esp. by small evangelical groups; also ***storefront mission, synagogue, temple***.

1938 C. Himes *Black on Black* (1973) 167 For one hundred and fifty dollars he leased a storefront church in the heart of the slums and poverty. **1957** *Economist* 28 Sept. 1031/2 The Negro newcomer from the South .. may attend a 'storefront church', of uncertain denomination, in a rented shop with the display window painted over. **1968** P. Oliver *Screening Blues* ii. 62 Infinitely smaller, but important because of their numbers and their devout followings of tiny congregations, are the multitude of store-front churches which line the streets in the Negro areas of the main urban centres. **1973** A. Dundes *Mother Wit* 175 Professor Dillard .. examines the names of store-front churches... The individual words in store-front church names may be SE (Standard English). **1967** *Daily Tel.* 16 Feb. 19/6 The Storefront Cinema .. is a rented shop that has been converted into a miniature cinema. **1976** *National Observer* (U.S.) 3 Apr. 5/1 He has more than 25 store-front headquarters in every one of the state's nine congressional districts. **1967** *Economist* 6 May 563/2 Everywhere in Bangkok there are store-front industries where people are beating metal, mending things by hand, getting used to machines. **1970** *Globe & Mail* (Toronto) 25 Sept. 11/4 Government information centres in 'store-front locations'. **1978** *Sunday Mail TV Suppl.* (Brisbane) 23 July 2/2 The pair operate a store-front mission in a lower class area. **1978** *Chicago* June 208/1 We've always liked to brag about Chicago's Mom-and-Pop storefront restaurants. **1975** A. Bergman *Hollywood & Le Vine* (1976) vii. 80 A store-front synagogue in Brooklyn. **1965** D. Henderson in S. Henderson *Understanding New Black Poetry* (1973) iii. 269 The ritual is black The ritual is in the storefront temple On the corner. **1973** E. Bullins *Theme is Blackness* 7 Sweating out long, hot summers in store-front theaters. **1976** *National Observer* (U.S.) 2 Oct. 15/1 A Teletype machine, set in the store-front window of the bureau.

3. *attrib.* passing into *adj.* **a.** Of, pertaining to, or designating legal aid or citizen's advice organizations which operate from shop premises in order to be easily accessible.

1971 *Sunday Sun* (Brisbane) 31 Oct. 20/2 Why .. can't we have legal offices in poor areas offering cheap legal aid along the lines of America's 'store-front' lawyers. **1973** *Courier-Mail* (Brisbane) 9 June 1/3 A 'store front' legal and general advice system will be available cheaply to Brisbane people in a few weeks. **1973** *Globe & Mail* (Toronto) 2 Aug. 8/7 (Advt.), Store-front Citizenship Office now open .. to answer your questions about how you can become a Canadian citizen. **1974** *Index-Jrnl.* (Greenwood, S. Carolina) 18 Apr. 6/1 A group called Resource One operates a storefront 'people's computer', a cross between a hip encyclopedia and a community bulletin board. **1974** *Courier-Mail* (Brisbane) 25 Apr. 2/4 Australia's first 'store front' legal aid office will open in Ipswich tomorrow. **1975** *Weekend Mag.* (Montreal) 1 Nov. 8/2 Robert Cooper .. is a lawyer with an extraordinary string of .. achievements in his chosen field, including the opening of Canada's first storefront law office. **1979** N. Hartley *Quicksilver* i. 19 Storefront law offices, giving free legal advice to minority groups.

b. Of, pertaining to, or characteristic of a storefront church.

1972 J. L. Dillard *Black English* v. 217 We see evidence of formal styles of Negro Non-Standard in the speech of the storefront preachers. **1973** *Black World* Sept. 31 'Tambourines' has the impelling, fervent, and nervous rhythms of the 'store-front' spiritual or gospel hymn. **1976** *National Observer* (U.S.) 1 May B 2/3 Store-front religion offered solace and precious respectability to mothers whose families were collapsing around them. **1978** J. Updike *Coup* (1979) v. 173, I hope that stuff hasn't taken you in; it's just our usual native storefront I'm-comin'-home-Jesus routine.

†**'storeful**, *a. Obs. rare*[−1]. [f. store *sb.* + -ful.] Copiously supplied, opulent.

1598 Florio, *Vberifero*, plentifull .. rich, store-full, fat.

'storeholder.

1. = storekeeper 1.

1869 *Daily News* 8 Sept., The charge of conspiracy against a storeholder and a foreman in the Woolwich Arsenal.

b. The possessor of a store of something. ? *nonce-use.*

1907 Saintsbury in *Q. Rev.* Jan. 144 That marvellous storeholder of Balzacian treasures, the Vicomte de Spoelberch de Lovenjoul.

2. A receptacle for a store of a commodity.

1886 *Pall Mall Gaz.* 9 Dec. 4/1 Upon compression, the gas is turned into wrought iron storeholders.

'storehouse. [f. store *sb.* + house *sb.*]

1. A building in which goods are stored.

1348 *MS. Acc. Exch. K.R.* 470/18 m. 9 Pro vna serura noua empta pro hostio del storhus vj. d. **1463** *Bury Wills* (Camden) 22 She to haue the storehous therto to leye in hire stuffe. **1526** Tindale *Luke* xii. 24 Which nether have stoore housse ner barne. **1605** Shaks. *Macb.* ii. iv. 34 Where is Duncans body? *Macd.* Carried to Colmekill, The Sacred Store-house of his Predecessors, And Guardian of their Bones. **1664** Pepys *Diary* 12 July, And fine storehouses there are and good docks. **1748** *Anson's Voy.* iii. ii. 307 One of these huts .. the Indians made use of for a store-house. **1857** Ruskin *Pol. Econ. Art* i. §9 Laying up your wheat wisely in store-houses for the time of famine. **1890** *Rlwys. Amer.* 300 The supplies are .. delivered at the General Storehouse.

b. *attrib.* and *Comb.*

1497 *Naval Acc. Hen. VII* (1896) 240 The vtter Storhouse Dore in the seid Ship. **1540** Palsgr. *Acolastus* ii. iv. M iv b, Now that I am become the storer or storehouse keper of this puissant lorde. **1548** in Feuillerat *Revels Edw. VI* (1914) 40, ij° croked boltes ffor the store howse dore. **1809** in *Orders in Council Nav. Service* (1866) I. 257 Clerk and Storehouse Keeper. **1816** *Ibid.* 260 One Storehouse Labourer. **1833** *Ibid.* 190 The first and second classes of storehouse labourers, who are men charged with an important trust of great responsibility. **1886** *Ibid.* (1888) V. 125 We would recommend that Your Majesty may be graciously pleased to sanction the appointment of a Storehouseman (Civil rating) to that Ship .. and to be assisted by a Yeoman of Storerooms.

2. *transf.* and *fig.* Often, a store or treasury from which something may be obtained in plenty; an abundant source (*of*).

1578 Banister *Hist. Man* v. 72 The liuer, the shoppe or storehouse of bloud. **1589** Greene *Menaphon* (Arb.) 68 Arcadie, storehouse of Nimphs, and nurserie of beautie. **1590** Spenser *F.Q.* ii. vi. 6 She .. greatly ioyed merry tales to faine, Of which a store-house did with her remaine. **1671** Milton *P.R.* ii. 103 My heart hath been a store-house long of things And sayings laid up, portending strange events. **1690** Locke *Hum. Und.* ii. x. §2 Memory, which is as it were the Store-house of our Ideas. **1846** Wright *Ess. Mid. Ages* I. v. 203 The history .. published by Geoffrey of Monmouth opened a rich storehouse of fiction for the poets who followed. **1856** Sir B. Brodie *Psychol. Inq.* I. ii. 59 The brain .. is the store-house of past sensations. **1881** Westcott & Hort *Grk. Test.* Introd. §5 Books that are professedly storehouses of information.

storekeeper (ˈstɔəkiːpə(r)).

1. One who has charge of a store or stores; one who superintends the receipt and issue of stores; *spec.* an officer or official in charge of naval or military stores.

1618 in J. Charnock *Hist. Mar. Archit.* (1801) II. 238 Under storekeepers, Chatham. **1663** Pepys *Diary* 5 Mar., Troubling me and other friends for getting him a place (that is, storekeeper of the Navy at Tangier). **1704** Chamberlayne *Pres. St. Eng.* iii. (ed. 21) 532 Yeoman-Sadler and Store-keeper. *Ibid.* 575 Officers of Her Majesty's Yards. At Chatham... Store-keeper. **1751** Johnson *Rambler* No. 113 ¶8 That the best storekeeper was the mistress's eye. **1798** Hinderwell *Hist. Scarborough* 81 Besides whom, the military establishment consists of R. V. Drury, Esq. Store-keeper; a Barrack-Master, [etc.]. **1809** *Lond. Chron.* 1 July 2/3 Mr. John Trotter, jun. the Storekeeper-General, and some of the other heads of departments, have gone to Portsmouth. **1838** Lytton *Alice* iv. v, The post of Storekeeper to the Ordnance. **1876** *N. Amer. Rev.* CXXIII. 300 A dishonest store-keeper at a distillery. **1890** *Rlwys. Amer.* 307 Everything in the nature of material .. passes through the Store-keeper's books.

2. *N. Amer.*, *Austral.* etc. A shopkeeper.

1741 P. Tailfer etc. *Narr. Georgia* 107 Augusta .. is principally if not altogether, inhabited by Indian Traders and Store-keepers. **1775** A. Burnaby *Trav.* 38 The chief of the inhabitants are storekeepers or public officers. **1817** M. Birkbeck *Notes Journ. Amer.* (1818) 97 The store-keepers (country shopkeepers we should call them) of these western towns. **1857** D. P[useley] *Rise Australia* etc. 421 Geelong .. Richardson, S., storekeeper. **1858** Simmonds *Dict. Trade*, *Store-keeper*, .. the name for a retail dealer or shop-keeper in the Colonies, who keeps a miscellaneous assortment of all kinds of commodities. **1887** F. Francis Jun. *Saddle & Mocassin* 61 To and fro flitted a few busy store-clothed store-keepers and clerks.

b. *U.S. slang.* An article that remains so long on hand as to be unsaleable.

1891 *Century Dict.*

storeman (ˈstɔəmən).

1. A man placed in charge of stores or supplies; a storekeeper, esp. in the army.

1859 F. A. Griffiths *Artil. Man.* (1862) 113 No. 10 .. performs the general duties of storeman. **1910** *Blackw. Mag.* Feb. 256/2 The accused [soldier], a man of long service and excellent character, was 'storeman' of his company.

2. A workman employed in the storage of goods.

1885 *Weekly Echo* 5 Sept. (Cass.) The question of wages of shifters and store-men has been referred to arbitration.

3. *N. Amer.*, *Austral.* etc. One who keeps, or serves in, a 'store' or 'stores'; a shopkeeper, shopman. Also **storesman**.

1858 Simmonds *Dict. Trade*, *Storeman*, the keeper of a general store; a shopman, one who serves in a store. **1862** F. Sinnett *Acc. S. Australia* 34 Rates of wages obtainable .. Storemen, 7s. to 8s. [per day]. **1885** *Macm. Mag.* Feb. 281/2 If the storesman is .. engrossed in .. excited talk it is generally about a bond which wants renewing, or an ostrich, or some oranges or mealies, or the next clip of wool.

storer (ˈstɔərə(r)). Also 6 stoarer, storyar, *Sc.* storour(e, -are, storrour, stourour. [f. store *v.* and *sb.* + -er[1].]

1. One who, or a thing which, stores or keeps in store.

1513 Douglas *Æneis* vii. ix. 23 Tirrheus thair fader was fee maister, and gyde Of studis, flokis, bowis; and heyrdis wyde, As storoure to the king, did kep and ȝime. *Ibid.* xii. Prol. 263 Welcum stourour of alkynd bestiall. **1540** Palsgr. *Acolastus* ii. i. I iij, The storer of some well moneyed mayster .i. the keper or ouerseer of the prouision for householde. **1571** Golding *Calvin on Ps.* lxix. 10 Y[e] trew rule of Godlynesse .. whereof y[e] church is y[e] faithful storer.

1640 T. Brugis *Marrow of Physicke* I. 55 Memory is the sure storer of all things, as in a magazine. **1864** E. A. Parkes *Pract. Hygiene* 89 Sulphurous Acid Gas.—The bleachers in cotton and worsted manufactories, and storers of woollen articles, are most exposed to this gas.

b. One who hoards, lays by, or makes provision, *for* (a need).

1599 Hayward *1st Pt. Life Hen. IV*, 59 The King in peace no stoarer for war. **1622** Mabbe tr. *Aleman's Guzman d'Alf.* I. 26 My Mother was a storer, a thrifty Wench. **1907** *Athenæum* 14 Sept. 307/1 The coal-tit is undoubtedly a storer for the future.

†**c.** ? A partner or shareholder in a joint-stock undertaking. *Obs.*

1623 in *Trans. New Shaks. Soc.* (1885) 499 The said Thomas Greene..was a fellow Actor or player of and in the Companie..of the late queenes Matie Queene Anne,..and a full adventurer, storer and sharer of in and amongst them.

d. One who stocks or peoples.

1690 C. Nesse *Hist. & Myst. O. & N. Test.* I. 125 To him who was the first storer of the world [*sc.* Adam].

2. Something kept to produce a store or stock. **a.** = standel 1. ? *Obs.*

1543 [see standel 1]. **1572** *B.N.C. Munim.* 24. 27, Storyars. **1670** J. Smith *Eng. Improv. Reviv'd* 100 About 2 years after the planting one of the best plants is to be reserved as a Standil or Storer. **1721** Mortimer *Husb.* II. 109, I divided my Trees into three sorts, *viz.* first Storers, which I reckoned all to be that were under 12 Inches Circumference; secondly, Saplings, which I called all under 24 Inches Circumference; and what was two Foot Circumference..I reckoned Timber-trees. **1792** *Jrnls. Ho. Comm.* 13 Feb. 234/1 Storers, or Saplings.

†**b.** A number of animals kept for breeding. *Obs.*

1569 in W. H. Turner *Select. Rec. Oxford* (1880) 330 They have put fyve swannes upon the water to be storer for the Cytye.

'store-room.

1. A room set apart for the storing of goods or supplies, esp. those of a ship or household.

1746 P. Yorke in G. Harris *Ld. Chanc. Hardwicke* (1847) II. 293 He..saw powder, shot, & bonnets distributed to them out of a store-room, whereof his Lord kept the key himself. **1748** *Anson's Voy.* III. i. 301 The Gunner's fore store-room. **1780** *Mirror* No. 93 When he gives out the wine from the cellar, and the groceries from the store-room. **1846** A. Young *Naut. Dict.* 77 In frigates,..the gunner's, boatswain's, and carpenter's store rooms are in the fore cockpit. **1857** Ruskin *Pol. Econ. Art* i. §10 You will see the good housewife taking pride..in her well-dressed dish, and her full store-room. **1886** [see storehouse 1 b].

attrib. **1750** Blanckley *Naval Expos.* 90 *Storeroom lanterns*, a triangular Light placed at the Bulk-head of the Boatswain and Carpenter's Store-Rooms. **1897** 'Sarah Grand' *Beth Bk.* xii. (1898) 95 He led the way..to the store-room door.

2. Room or space for storage.

1783 Justamond tr. *Raynal's Hist. Ind.* IV. 457 Tobacco ..pays two sols six deniers per quintal to the government for store-room. **1887** *Spons' Househ. Man.* 100 If the cupboards are taken up to the ceiling line,..increased storeroom would be provided for clothing not immediately required.

'store-ship, 'storeship. A government ship employed to carry military or naval stores.

1693 *Lond. Gaz.* No. 2888/3 *Susanna* Bomb Storeship. **1705** *Ibid.* No. 4187/3 This day sailed hence Her Majesty's Ship the Lizard with three Store-ships. **1788** Gibbon *Decl. & F.* xlvi. IV. 511 A fleet of gallies, transports, and store-ships, was assembled in the harbour. **1790** Beatson *Nav. & Mil. Mem.* II. 66 This being the first expedition of importance that had neither store-ship, hospital-ship, fire-ship, or tender, to accompany it. **1834** J. D. Lang *Hist. Acc. N.S. Wales* (1837) I. 48 His Majesty's store-ship Guardian had been despatched from England..with a large supply of provisions and other stores for the settlement. **1915** *Daily Tel.* 24 Aug. 8/7 The movement of men-of-war, transports, and storeships across Baltic waters.

storesman: see storeman 3.

storey, storeyed: see story *sb.*², storied.

‖**storge** ('stɔːgiː). Also storgé, -è, -ē, -ee, -èe, -ée. [Gr. στοργή, related to στέργειν to have natural affection to, to love.] Natural affection; usually, that of parents for their offspring.

1637 Bastwick *Litany* I. 11/1 We must be louing progenitors & although they doe *ex officio* abandon and renounce, both honesty and storge at once, yet we may not. **1764** T. Hutchinson *Hist. Mass.* vi. (1765) 463 The Storgée in the parent might be observed towards their young. **1809** R. Cumberland *John de Lancaster* I. 23 The storgee, or natural affection of my daughter-in-law towards her infant. **1835** Kirby *Habits & Inst. Anim.* II. xviii. 258 But first, I must say something of that *Storge*, or instinctive affection, which is almost universally exhibited by females for their progeny. **1850** Thackeray *Pendennis* I. ii, I could have.. adored in her the Divine beneficence in endowing us with the maternal *storgē*, which..sanctifies the history of mankind. **1880** S. Cox *Comm. Job* 524 The Ostrich resembles the stork..; but lacks its pious, maternal *storgé*.

storgeon, obs. form of sturgeon.

†**'storial,** *a. Obs.* Also storyal. [Aphetic var. of historial. Cf. It. *storiale*.] Of, pertaining to or of the nature of history.

c **1385** Chaucer *L.G.W.* 702 And this is storyal soth, it is no fable. *c* **1449** Pecock *Repr.* III. vii. 320 And here y make an eende of Scripture storial ensaumpling. *c* **1450** *J. Shirley's Cron. Chaucier* heading, Þe nyene worshipfullest Ladyes þat in alle cronycles and storyal bokes haue beo founden of trouþe of constaunce and vertuous or reproched womanhode. **1575** Laneham *Let.* (1871) 26 Certain good harted men of Couentrée..made petition that they moought renu noow their olld storiall sheaw.

storiation (stɔərɪ'eɪʃən). [f. story *v.* + -ation.] Decoration with artistic designs representing historical, legendary, or emblematic subjects.

1884 *Times* 20 Nov. 4/5 The artistic decoration of the dome of St. Paul's..should..provide places for proper storiation. **1893** Stannus in *Jrnl. Soc. Arts* 10 Feb. 262/1 Storiation is that section of the rules of Applied Art which governs (*a*) the Selection and (*b*) the Representation of Meaning in the decoration of objects.

Hence (by back-formation) **'storiate** *v.*, **'storiated** *ppl. a.*

1889 *Art Jrnl.* Mar. 91/2 The mania for the acquisition of storiated title-pages has led to the cruel spoliation of thousands of rare old books. **1893** Stannus in *Jrnl. Soc. Arts* 10 Feb. 262/2 There are 3 mental Stages in the process of storiating an object.

storie, obs. form of stir *v.*

storied ('stɔərɪd), *a.*¹ and *ppl. a.* [f. story *sb.*¹ and *v.*¹ + -ed. Cf. med.L. *historiātus*, OF. (*h*)*istorié*.]

1. Ornamented with scenes from history or legend by means of sculpture, painting, needlework or other art; also, inscribed with a legend or memorial record.

1481 Caxton *Myrr.* I. v. 25 Clerkis..that haue the precyous bookes richely lymned storyed and wel adoubed. **1624** Wotton *Archit.* II. 98 As for other Storied Workes vpon Walles, I doubt our Clime bee too yeelding and moist, for such Garnishment. *Ibid.* 101 Marking in certaine Storied Sculptures, of oulde time, how precisely the parts and Lines of the Figures..doe meete. **1632** Milton *Penseroso* 159 And storied Windows richly dight, Casting a dimm religious light. **1750** Gray *Elegy* 41 Can storied urn or animated bust Back to its mansion call the fleeting breath? **1792** S. Rogers *Pleas. of Mem.* I. 53 The storied arras.. With old achievement charms the wildered sight. **1808** Scott *Marmion* v. Introd. 185 As the ancient art could stain Achievements on the storied pane. **1862** Thrupp *Anglo-Saxon Home* 227 They occasionally wrought the storied mantles worn by kings at their coronation, on which mythological and historical subjects were delineated. **1876** Swinburne *Erectheus* 1727 One fair chaplet..To hang for ever from thy storied shrine.

2. Celebrated or recorded in history or story.

1725 Pope *Odyss.* IV. 440 Each known disaster of the man disclose,..Recite them! nor in erring pity fear To wound with storied grief the filial ear. **1746** Francis tr. *Horace, Art of Poetry* 387 They scorn'd to take from Greece the storied Theme, And dar'd to sing their own domestic Fame. **1832** Tennyson '*Love thou thy Land*' i, Love thou thy land, with love far-brought From out the storied Past, and used Within the Present. **1877** Mrs. Oliphant *Makers of Flor.* vii. 183 The many historical places..which attract the spectator in the storied city of Florence. **1903** *Athenæum* 1 Aug. 151/1 To set out upon as adventurous and entertaining a career as that of any of his storied forbears in Baghdad.

storied ('stɔərɪd), *a.*² Also storeyed. [f. story *sb.*² + -ed.] Having stories, divided into stories.

Frequently in parasynthetic formations, as *one-*, *two-*, *three-storied*, for which see the first element.

1624 Wotton *Archit.* I. 40 We meane in a Dorique, Ionicall, Corinthian Porch, or Cloister, or the like of one Contignation, and not in Storied buildings. **1820** Shelley *Prometh. Unb.* IV. 344 Each crag-like tower, and storied column. **1855** Hawthorne *Eng. Note-Bks.* (1883) I. 582 It seemed possible to shake hands from one jutting storied old house to another. **1858** Merivale *Rom. Emp.* (1865) VI. liii. 356 A vast extent of gardens, with their baths, their fish-ponds, and their storied terraces. **1903** *Architect* 24 Apr. 269/1 A porch may often be carried up to form a storeyed tower with happy effect.

storier ('stɔərɪə(r)). Also 5–7 storyer. [In sense 1, aphetic variant of historier; in senses 2, 3 f. story *sb.*¹ or *v.*¹ + -er¹.]

†**1.** A chronicler, historian. *Obs.*

1387–8 T. Usk *Test. Love* III. iv. (Skeat) 257 In goodnes of gentil manliche speche, without any maner of nyceté of storiers imaginacion,..he passeth al other makers. *c* **1400** tr. *Secreta Secret., Gov. Lordsh.* 100 Swylk er customyd to be wel spekyng, wel taght, curteys, and good storyers. *c* **1449** Pecock *Repr.* III. xii. 351 Forwhi noon fundamental cronicler or storier writith therof, saue Girald. *c* **1555** Harpsfield *Divorce Hen. VIII* (1878) 232 We now add Bede himself, whom the said storyers do follow. **1570–6** Lambarde *Peramb. Kent* 22 For proofe whereof, I will call to witnesse Thomas Spot..bycause he only (of all the Storiers that I haue seene) reporteth it. *a* **1640** Jackson *Creed* XI. xli. Wks. 1673 III. 718 Had the spirit of God been storyer of their lives, we should have had notice of their often trippings.

2. The teller of a story; a story-teller. *nonce-uses.*

1826 Disraeli *Viv. Grey* v. xiii. 237 'But it is a very curious story.'..'Oh! so is every story, according to the storier.' **1830** —— *Let.* 25 Aug., *Home Lett.* vii. (1885) 54 Some smoking in sedate silence, some telling their beads, some squatting round a storier.

3. *dial.* One who tells 'stories' or fibs.

1877 *N.W. Linc. Gloss.* **1908** [Miss E. Fowler] *Trent & Ancholme* 52 She's a storier. Why she was sayin' there was a ghost.

storiette, storyette (stɔərɪ'ɛt). [f. story *sb.*¹ + -ette. Cf. novelette.] A very short story.

1889 Farmer *Americanisms.* **1892** *Star* 30 Dec. 1/7 The new year will see the *Penny Illustrated Paper* well to the fore with an exceptionally attractive series of new storiettes. **1897** *Athenæum* 20 Nov. 689/3 A well-established Syndicate requires storiettes of 1,200 to 1,500 words each. **1899** Roberton *Novel-reader's Handbk.* 74 Mr. Kipling has also a number of storyettes scattered through the magazines. **1907** F. T. Bullen *Advance Australia* xxiv. 261 There are.. four serial stories..twelve short stories, and about fifty storyettes.

storify ('stɔərɪfaɪ), *v.*¹ *rare.* [f. story *sb.*¹ + -fy.] *trans.* To picture, delineate or record (a historical event or fact); to celebrate in history or story. Also *absol.* Hence **'storifying** *vbl. sb.*¹ (*attrib.*)

1616 J. Lane *Contn. Sqr.'s T.* III. 320 And looke what natures selfe hathe not supplyed, shall by queint painters hand bee storifyed [in Cambuscan's theatre]. **1675** J. Smith *Chr. Relig. Appeal* I. 70 His third [year] was so barren of Action, had so little wind stirring: as Tacitus complains his storifying Vein is becalm'd, his Pen can find no Pasturage in that Years Occurrences. **1830** *Fraser's Mag.* I. 44 So 'tis plain that a sure means of gaining fame malice is; And many's the name which through it has been storified.

storify ('stɔərɪfaɪ), *v.*² [f. story *sb.*² + -fy.] *trans.* To arrange (beehives) in stories. Hence **'storifying** *vbl. sb.*² (also *attrib.*).

1827 E. Bevan *Honey-bee* 99 This shed..is adapted either to storifying or single hiving. *Ibid.* 111 Side boxes occupy a great deal more room than storifying boxes. **1888** R. C. Day *Mod. Bee-keeping* in *Good Words* May 355/1 He finds himself in doubt between the 'combination' system, the 'storifying' system, [etc.].

storiologist (stɔərɪ'ɒlədʒɪst). Also **storyologist.** [f. next + -ist.] A student of storiology.

1862 J. F. Campbell *Tales W. Highl.* IV. 309 And then with a fossil incident picked out of the stratum in which it was first found, the 'storyologist' may proceed to pick out other notions in the same way. **1877** W. R. S. Ralston in *Academy* 17 Feb. 130 These literary legends are the bug-bears of scientific 'storiologists'. **1902** *Folk-Lore* June 221, I warmly commend M. Dottin's volume to all storyologists.

storiology (stɔərɪ'ɒlədʒɪ). Also **storyology.** [f. story *sb.*¹ + -(o)logy.] The systematic study of popular tales and legends, with regard to their origin and development.

1860 J. F. Campbell *Pop. Tales W. Highl.* I. Introd. 11 The following collection is intended to be a contribution to this new science of 'Storyology'. **1862** *Ibid.* IV. 308 Now if 'storyology' be a science, it is worthy of a system and systematic study. **1877** W. R. S. Ralston in *Academy* 17 Feb. 129 A fair sample of the Basque contribution to comparative 'storiology'. **1900** B. Taylor (*title*), Storyology: Essays in Folklore, Sea-lore, and Plant-lore.

Hence ˌ**storio'logical** *a.*, of or pertaining to storiology.

1891 *Daily Graphic* 19 Oct. 9, I have a dozen storyological friends. **1904** *Folk-Lore* Mar. 60 Examples of storyological research.

†**'storize,** *v. Obs. rare*⁻¹. [aphetic f. historize.] *trans.* To represent in imagery.

1594 *Zepheria* xxxiv. F 1 b, The pompous gallerie, Wherein were storiz'd to mine eye sweet obiects, Embroydred all with rare immagerie.

storjon, obs. form of sturgeon.

stork (stɔːk), *sb.* Forms: 1 storc, (3 steorc), 3–7 storke, 4– stork. [OE. *storc* masc. = OS., (M)LG., (M)Du. *stork*, NFris. *stork, stourk, störk*, OHG. *storah, stork* (MHG. *storch, storc*, mod.G. *storch*, dial. *stork*), ON. *stork-r* (Sw., Da. *stork*):—OTeut. **sturko-z*.

Usually referred to the Teut. root **sterk-* (see stark *a.*), the name being supposed to refer to the apparent stiffness or rigidity in the bird's manner of standing. Some regard the word as cogn. w. Gr. τόργος vulture. The names of the stork in various eastern European langs. are commonly believed to be from Teut.: OSl. *strŭkŭ*, Russ. *sterkh*, Lith. *starkus*, Lett. *starks*, Magyar *eszterag*, Albanian *sterkjok*.]

1. A large wading bird of the genus *Ciconia*, allied to the ibis and heron; characterized by having long legs and a long stout bill.

Usually, the name denotes the White Stork (*Ciconia alba*), which stands over three feet high, and has brilliant white plumage with black wing-coverts and quills, and red legs. In summer it is an inhabitant of most parts of the Continent of Europe. A less common European species is the Black Stork (*C. nigra*). The American Stork (*C. maguari*) belongs to South America.

a **800** *Erfurt Gloss.* 259 in *O.E. Texts* 52 *Ciconia*: storc. *c* **1000** Ælfric *Hom.* I. 404 Storc and swalewe heoldon ðone timan heora to-cymes. *a* **1225** *Ancr. R.* 132 Þe steorc [*v.rr.* strucion, ostrice] uor his muchele flesche makeð a semblaunt uorte vleon,..auh þet fette drauhð euer to þer eorðe. *c* **1330** R. Brunne *Chron.* (Rolls) 14574 He liuede in kerres, as doþ þe stork. *c* **1381** Chaucer *Parl. Foules* 361 The stork the wrekere of a-vouterye. **1398** Trevisa *Barth. De P.R.* XII. ix. (1495) 419 A storke is messager of spryngynge tyme. *c* **1425** *Eng. Conq. Irel.* 28 Storkes & swalewes & oþer somer foules we haue aftyre I-loked. *a* **1529** Skelton *P. Sparowe* 469 The storke also, That maketh his nest In chymneyes to rest. **1584** Greene *Mirr. Modesty* Wks. (Grosart) III. 39 The Storke neuer medleth but with his mate. **1648** Bp. Hall *Sel. Th.* li. 149 The Stork is said to have taught man the use of the glyster. **1667** Milton *P.L.* VII. 423 There the Eagle and the Stork On Cliffs and Cedar tops their Eyries build. **1678** Ray *Willughby's Ornith.* III. ii. 287 The American Stork, called by the Brasilians Maguari of Marggrave. **1738** Albin *Nat. Hist. Birds* III. 77 The Black Stork. **1774** Goldsm. *Nat. Hist.* (1824) II. v. iii. 350 The Dutch are very solicitous for the preservation of the stork in every part of the republic. **1838** *Murray's Handbk. N. Germ.* 30 A number of tame storks may be seen stalking about in the fish-market of the Hague.

b. Applied to birds of allied genera: (see quots.).

1869–73 T. R. JONES *Cassell's Bk. Birds* IV. 59 The Whale-headed Stork, or Shoe-beak (*Balæniceps rex*)..is extremely numerous on the marshy grounds and rain-beds near the White Nile. *Ibid.* 71 The Giant Storks (*Mycteria*). *Ibid.* 75 The Clapper-billed Storks, or Shell-eaters (*Anastomas*), inhabit Africa and Southern Asia. *Ibid.* 91 The Field Storks (*Arvicolæ*)..are natives of South America. **1872** J. H. GURNEY *Andersson's Birds Damara Land* 281 *Ephippiorhynchus senegalensis*, Bon. Saddle-billed Stork. *Ibid.* 282 *Leptoptilus crumeniferus*, Cuv. African Marabou Stork.

c. *fig.* and *allusive.*

With reference to supposed habits of the stork (see quots. 1580, 1642; cf. quots. *c* 1381 and 1584 in 1); to the fable of the frogs who chose a stork for their king; to the German and Dutch nursery fiction that babies are brought by the stork; etc.

1555 *Instit. Gentl.* G iij b, And well worthye are all such to loose yᵉ name of gentry, because like Storcks deuourers of their owne kinde, in running out of their profession, they distroy themselues. **1580** LYLY *Euphues & his England* (Arb.) 363 Ladyes vse their Louers as the Storke doth hir young ones, who pecketh them till they bleed with hir bill, and then healeth them with hir tongue. *Ibid.* 416 Constancy is like vnto the Storke, who wheresoeuer she flye commeth into no neast but hir owne. **1597** J. PAYNE *Royal Exch.* 48 You..maliciously accuse vs.., reiectinge you and your vilde opinions sythens the fyrst hatchinge therof by your grandsire Storck. **1597** DONNE *Poems, Calm* 4 The fable is inverted, and farre more A blocke afflicts, now, then a storke before. **1631** MASSINGER *Emperor East* II. i, Like Æsops folish Frogges..if hee proue a Storke, they croke and rayle Against him as a tyranne. **1642** FULLER *Holy & Prof. St.* I. vi. 15 He is a stork to his parent, and feeds him in his old age. **1784** COWPER *Task* v. 282 Thus kings..became..Storks among frogs, that have but croak'd and died. **1823** SCOTT *Quentin D.* xxi, I wish we have not got King Stork, instead of King Log.

2. The bird or its flesh an article of food.

c **1460** J. RUSSELL *Bk. Nurture* 433 in *Babees Bk.* (1868) 144 Pecok, Stork, Bustarde & Shovellewre, ye must vnlace þem in þe plite of þe crane. ? *c* **1475** *Sqr. lowe Degre* 323 Both storkes and snytes ther were also, And venyson freshe. **1513** *Bk. Keruynge* in *Babees Bk.* (1868) 271 For standarde, venyson roste,..bustarde, storke, crane. **1620** VENNER *Via Recta* iii. 64 The Storke is of hard substance, of a wilde sauour, and of very naughty iuyce.

†**3.** Some kind of fish. ? A shark. *Obs. rare*⁻¹.

1600 DALLAM in *Early Voy. Levant* (Hakl. Soc.) 95 A great fishe called a storke, of a marvalus length, did follow our ship,..waytinge for a praye.

4. A variety of the domestic pigeon. More fully ***stork pigeon.***

1855 *Poultry Chron.* III. 140/1 Storks. *Ibid.* 320 The Stork Pigeon. The Stork... They derive their name from their plumage bearing considerable resemblance to that of a stork. **1881** LYELL *Pigeons* 88 When well marked, the stork is considered one of the finest feather varieties in Germany. *Ibid.*, The..stork or wing pigeon of Germany.

5. (See quot.)

1750 T. WRIGHT *Orig. Theory Universe* 25 Her [*sc.* the moon's] whole Globe appeared to us very conspicuously within a manifest circle. You..told me that that kind of phænomenon the country people called a Stork, or the old moon in the new one's arms.

6. *attrib.*, as ***stork-assembly, -flight, -kind, -migration, -tribe***; parasynthetic and similative, as ***stork-billed*** adj., ***stork-fashion*** adv., ***stork-like*** adj. and adv.

1730–46 THOMSON *Autumn* 853 The *stork-assembly meets,..Consulting..ere they take Their arduous voyage through the liquid sky. *c* **1875** *Cassell's Nat. Hist.* III. 349 The *Stork-billed Kingfishers (*Pelargopsis*). **1888** *Myra's Jrnl.* 1 Apr. 210/2 The skater must poise on one leg only, *stork-fashion. **1837** CARLYLE *Fr. Rev.* I. VII. v, In this manner..they, a wild unwinged *stork-flight,..wend their way. **1774** GOLDSM. *Nat. Hist.* (1824) II. v. iii. 360 A bird of the *stork kind. **1652** BP. HALL *Balm of Gilead* 213 Sometimes indeed..some *Storke-like disposition repaies the loving offices done by the Parents. **1872** COUES *N. Amer. Birds* 262 The pterylosis is more or less completely stork-like. **1913** J. R. HARRIS *Boanerges* xxxii. 312 It seems to be more likely that the swan migration is independent of the *stork migration. **1895** LYDEKKER *Roy. Nat. Hist.* IV. 306 The *Stork tribe.

stork (stɔːk), *v. U.S. slang.* [f. the sb., with reference to the nursery fiction that babies are brought by the stork: see sense 1 c.] *trans.* To make pregnant.

1936 A. HUXLEY *Eyeless in Gaza* xxv. 353 What would you do if the fever frau had the misfortune to be storked? **1968** R. STOUT *Father Hunt* (1969) xiii. 157 'Didn't she stop because she was pregnant?'.. 'Yes,' he said. 'She was storked.' **1977** *Amer. Speech 1975* L. 67 *Stork vt*, make pregnant. 'Jim storked her; that's why she's not back up here this year.'

'storkbird. *nonce-wd.* [f. STORK *sb.* + BIRD *sb.*] = STORK *sb.*

1922 JOYCE *Ulysses* 416 Madam, when comes the storkbird for thee?

storken ('stɔːk(ə)n), *v. Sc.* and *north.* Also 5–6 storkyn, 7– sturken. [a. ON. *storkna* to coagulate, corresp. to OHG. *kistorchanên* to become rigid, Goth. *gastaurknan* to dry up, f. Teut. root **sturk-* ablaut-var. of **stark-*: see STARK *a.*]

1. *intr.* To become stout, sturdy, strong; to grow, thrive, gain strength.

c **1425** WYNTOUN *Cron.* I. xvi. 1528 This Iubiter..Scho gert be fosterit tenderly, Till he wes passit all ȝouthheid And storkynnit [MS. Cott. starkynnyt] in stout manheid. **1500–20** DUNBAR *Poems* lxxv. 48 My stang dois storkyn with ȝour towdie. **1691** RAY *N.C. Words* (ed. 2) 71 To *Sturken*; to grow, thrive. **1851** *Cumbld. Gloss.*, *Storken*, to gain strength. **1894** *Northumbld. Gloss.* s.v., Newly-hatched chickens are often kept under cover for a day or two until they are 'weel storkened'.

2. To be stiffened with cold, to congeal. (Said esp. of blood or melted fat.)

1570 LEVINS *Manip.* 61/36 To storken, *congelari.* **1684** G. M[ERITON] *Praise Yorksh. Ale* (1685) 47 The Fatt's all storken'd here, a sham to see. *Ibid.* Clavis 108 To Storken, is to cool, or wax stiff or hard. **1691** RAY *N.C. Words* (ed. 2) 149 To Storken. Gelu adstringi. **1781** J. HUTTON *Tour to Caves* (ed. 2) Gloss. 97 *Storken*, to congeal, or coagulate like melted wax or tallow. **1785** —— *Bran New Wark* (E.D.S.) 339 Your minister was freetned, the hairs of his head stood on end, his blead storkened.

storkish ('stɔːkɪʃ), *a.* [f. STORK *sb.* + -ISH.] Of, pertaining to, or resembling a stork; like that of a stork.

1592 R. D. *Hypnerotomachia* 91 b, Antigone the daughter of Laomedon solaciously delighting hir selfe in hir storkish plumes. **1600** W. WATSON *Decacordon* (1602) 336 Like storkish kings they came vpon vs poore frogs with minaces of death to him that first should leape out of the puddle from vnder their tyranny. **1842** THACKERAY *Sultan Stork* I, They ..greeted it in the true storkish language. 'Good morning,' ..said the stork.

storkling ('stɔːklɪŋ). [-LING.] A young stork.

1802 W. GIFFORD tr. *Juvenal* xiv. 110 And the fledg'd storklings..Seek the same reptiles through the devious brake. **1898** E. P. EVANS *Evol. Ethics* vii. 232 A goose's egg, which..produced a gosling instead of the expected storkling.

stork's bill. [Cf. G. *storchschnabel* (*schnabel* beak, bill), OS. *storkesnevel* (in sense 1).]

1. A book-name for a plant of the genus *Erodium* (N.O. *Geraniaceæ*), esp. *E. cicutarium* or *E. moschatum*. †Also in corrupt forms *stocks-bill* (Ray *N.C. Words*, 1691), *stockbill* (Withering *Brit. Pl.*, ed. 3, 1796, III. 608).

1562 TURNER *Herbal* II. 9 This kynde [of Geranium] is called in Englishe Pinke nedle or starkis [*sic*] byll. **1597** GERARDE *Herbal* II. cccxliii. 795 Of knobbed Cranes bill..it is also called..in English Storks bill. *Ibid.* cccxliv. 796 Musked Storkes bill. **1657** S. PURCHAS *Pol. Flying-Ins.* I. xv. 94 Bees gather of these flowers following..In May:.. Storks-bill, Mous-ear, [etc.]. **1825** SIR J. E. SMITH *Eng. Flora* III. 229 *Erodium.* Stork's-bill. *Ibid.*, *E. cicutarium.* Hemlock Stork's-bill. *Ibid.* 230 *E. moschatum.* Musky Storks'-bill. *Ibid.* 231 *E. maritimum.* Sea Stork's-bill. **1898** MISS YONGE *John Keble's Parishes* xiv. 162 On the road-side have sprung up..the Stork's bill, *Erodium moschatum.*

attrib. **1845–50** MRS. LINCOLN *Lect. Bot.* App. 101/2 *Erodium ciconium* (stork-bill geranium).

2. A plant of the genus *Pelargonium* (N.O. *Geraniaceæ*).

1825 *Greenhouse Comp.* I. 65 *Pelargonium Barringtonii*, a splendid flower..considered the first of storksbills. **1829** T. CASTLE *Introd. Bot.* 146 One extensive genus, called pelargonium or stork's-bill, upwards of one hundred and fifty species of which are natives of the Cape of Good Hope. **1848** SCHOMBURGK *Hist. Barbados* 602 Pelargonium humifusum. Trailing Stork's Bill. **1866** *Treas. Bot.* 1102/1.

†**3.** *Surg.* = CROW-BILL 2. *Obs. rare.*

1671 PHILLIPS (ed. 3), *Storks bill*, a Chirurgions Instrument, the same as Crows bill which see.

†**4.** A derisive gesture: = L. *ciconia*. *Obs.*

1616 B. JONSON *Cynthia's Rev.* v. ii, You giue him the Reuerse stroke, with this Sanna, or Storkes-bill.

storm (stɔːm), *sb.* Also (1 stearm *north.*), 3–7 storme (3 steorm, storem, 5 stourme, starme). [Com. Teut. (not recorded in Gothic): OE. *storm* masc. corresp. to Fris., OS. (MLG., Du.) *storm*, OHG. (MHG., mod.G.) *sturm*, ON. *storm-r* (Sw., Da. *storm*):—OTeut. **sturmo-z* (whence Rom. **stormo*: see STOUR *sb.*¹), f. root **stur-* (? **stwer-*) of STIR *v.*]

I. 1. a. A violent disturbance of the atmosphere, manifested by high winds, often accompanied by heavy falls of rain, hail, or snow, by thunder and lightning, and at sea by turbulence of the waves. Hence sometimes applied to a heavy fall of rain, hail, or snow, or to a violent outbreak of thunder and lightning, unaccompanied by strong wind.

More explicitly *storm of hail*, †*lightning*, *rain*, †*thunder*; also with the sb. prefixed, as HAILSTORM, RAIN-*storm*, SNOW-STORM, THUNDER-STORM.

c **825** *Vesp. Ps.* xlix. 3 Fyr in ȝesihðe his beorneð & in ymbhwyrfte his storm strong. *Ibid.* liv. 9 Ic bad hine se mec halne dyde from lytelmodum & storme. *c* **950** *Lindisf. Gosp.* Matt. xvi. 3 To dæȝ [bið] stearm, faȝas forðon unrotlic heofon. *c* **1000** *Sax. Leechd.* III. 274 Seo lyft ðe we ymbe sprecað astihð up fornean oð þone monan & abyrð ealle wolcna stormas. *a* **1122** *O.E. Chron.* (Laud MS.) an. 1070 þa com an mycel storm & to dræfede ealle þa scipe þær þa gersumes wæron inne. *c* **1175** *Lamb. Hom.* 143 Ech eorþe scal hwakien on his ecsene alse deoð þe see in storme. *c* **1200** *Trin. Coll. Hom.* 161 Storemes falleð in þe sæ, and to-worpeð hit. *a* **1225** *Juliana* 76 As ha weren in wettre com a steorm [*v.r.* strom] & draf ham to londe. *a* **1225** [see STILL B 2]. *c* **1386** CHAUCER *Knt.'s T.* 1122 Ther ran a rumbel and a swough As though a storm sholde bresten euery bough. *c* **1400** *Destr. Troy* 7631 The stourme wex still. *c* **1440** *Promp. Parv.* 477/2 Storm, wedyr, *nimbus, procella, altanus.* Storm, yn the see, *turbo.* *c* **1475** *Rauf Coilȝear* 23 His steid aganis the storme staluartlie straid. **1594** KYD *Cornelia* I. 82 The windie storme Doth topside-turuey tosse thee as thou flotest. *Ibid.* II. 93 Enemies..Beat backe like flyes before a storme of hayle. **1597** DONNE *Poems, Storm* 32 And what at first was call'd a gust, the same Hath now a stormes, anon a tempests name. **1610** SHAKS. *Temp.* II. ii. 19 Heres.. another Storme brewing, I heare it sing ith' winde. **1621** in Foster *Eng. Factories Ind.* (1906) 280 A storme of thunder and rayne came. **1627** CAPT. SMITH *Sea Gram.* x. 47 A Storm is knowne..not to bee much lesse than a tempest, that will blow downe houses, and trees vp by the roots. **1665** SIR T. HERBERT *Trav.* (1677) 126 That night we..were entertained by..a sudden storm of rain, thunder, and lightning. **1725** DE FOE *Voy. round World* (1840) 18 The wind setting in at South-west, blew a storm. **1735** JOHNSON *Lobo's Abyssinia, Voy.* i. 2 We had our Rigging somewhat damag'd by a Storm of Lightning. **1788** WESLEY *Jrnl.* 6 Oct., When I came into the town, it blew a storm... But it fell as suddenly as it rose. *Ibid.* 25 Nov., Though it blew a storm, and was piercing cold, we were sufficiently crowded at Dover. **1805** SCOTT *Let.* 18 Aug. in *Lockhart* (1837) II. ii. 60 The most dreadful storm of thunder and lightning I ever witnessed. **1847** TENNYSON *Princess* IV. 256 Like the mystic fire on a mast-head, Prophet of storm. **1861** DICKENS *Lett.* (1880) II. 156 The storm was most magnificent at Dover. **1895** *Law Times Rep.* LXXIII. 156/2 Two vessels..drifted through the violence of a storm on to the toe of a breakwater.

in figurative context. *c* **897** ÆLFRED *Gregory's Past. C.* ix. 58 Hwæt is ðonne ðæt rice & se ealdordom buton ðæs modes storm, se symle bið cnyssende ðæt scip ðære heortan? **1599** SHAKS. *Much Ado* v. iv. 42 Why what's the matter? That you haue such a Februarie face, So full of frost, of storme, and clowdinesse. **1740** C. WESLEY *Hymn, Jesu, lover of my soul* i, Hide me, o my Saviour, hide, Till the storm of life is past. **1850** TENNYSON *In Mem.* xxxiii. 1 O thou that after toil and storm Mayst seem to have reach'd a purer air.

b. Used *spec.* as the distinctive appellation of a particular degree of violence in wind. In mod. *Meteorology*: An atmospheric disturbance which in the Beaufort scale is classed as intermediate between a whole gale and a hurricane, having a wind-force estimated at 10–11 and a limit of velocity at from 56–75 miles per hour.

1801 CAPPER *Observ. Winds & Monsoons* Pref. p. xxiii, The tempest..is..the same as a hurricane, or whirlwind: I shall therefore use these words synonimously, and place them in the first order, or degree of violent winds. The storm, or what the English seamen call a hard gale, is likewise, I believe, nearly the same; I shall, therefore, make use of the former for the land, and the latter for the sea term, and reckon these in the second class. **1858** FITZROY *Meteorol. Papers* III. 94/1 [Beaufort Scale.] 11 Storm. **1867** SMYTH *Sailor's Word-bk.* s.v. *Storms*, That is a storm which reduces a ship to her storm stay-sails, or to her bare poles.

c. *spec.* A snowstorm. Also, a quantity of fallen snow. *Sc.*

1681 FOUNTAINHALL *Chronol. Notes* (1822) 8 A great storm of snow had fallen. *c* **1730** BURT *Lett. N. Scot.* (1754) II. xviii. 67 There fell a very great Storm (as they call it) for by the Word Storm they only mean Snow. **1787** [J. BEATTIE] *Scoticisms* 119 They turned him out,..though there was a storm of snow lying on the ground.

d. A period of hard weather with frost and snow. *Sc.* and *N. Amer.*.

1880 J. COLQUHOUN *Moor & Loch* I. 239 Even the sea-worm having failed at the end of that long continued storm. **1887** I. R. *Ranche Life Montana* 24 This 'storm', as they call the spell of cold weather, lasted about 10 days.

e. ***magnetic storm***: a magnetic disturbance observed simultaneously over a considerable portion of the globe.

1860 SABINE in *Proc. Roy. Soc.* X. 634 The casual magnetic disturbances, or magnetic storms. **1871** *Nature* 5 Oct. 441/1 Observations upon magnetic storms in higher latitudes.

f. In pl. *ellipt.* for storm windows. *N. Amer.*

1952 *Home Building in Canada* Oct.–Nov. 22/2 If you are wondering which windows and when to protect with storms, the answer is simple—all of them, from October to April. **1968** *Globe & Mail* (Toronto) 17 Feb. 45 (Advt.), Complete with drapes, aluminum, storms and screens. **1973** *N.Y. Law Jrnl.* 1 Aug. 3/2 Alwin J. Dovale, installer of storms and screens. **1977** *Chicago Tribune* 2 Oct. II. 7/1 Maybe next year I can afford real storms with the money I'll save on utility bills.

g. *Proverbial phrases.*

a storm in a teacup (and earlier phrases: see quots.): a great commotion in a small community or about a trifling matter. [Prob. after L. *fluctus excitare in simpulo* (Cic.).] ***any port in a storm***: see PORT *sb.*¹ 1 c.

1590 GREENE *Neuer too late* II. (1600) L 3 b, No storme so sharpe to rent the little Reede. **1603** DRAYTON *Bar. Wars* III. lv, Let's feare no Storme, before we feele a Showre. **1642** FULLER *Holy & Prof. St.* v. xiv. 415 At last he is as welcome as a storm. **1678** DK. ORMOND *Let. Earl Arlington* 28 Dec., in *Hist. MSS. Comm., Ormonde MSS.* IV. 292 Our skirmish seems to be come to a period, and compared with the great things now on foot, is but a storm in a cream bowl. **1770** *Gentl. Mag.* XL. 560 He [has]..Been in a storm; this is a sea-phrase for being less than dead-drunk. **1830** *Ibid.* C. I. 49/2 Each campaign, compared with those of Europe, has been only, in Lord Thurlow's phrase, a storm in a wash-hand basin. **1872–** [see TEA-CUP c]. **1878** [see SLOP-BASIN].

2. *transf.* A heavy discharge or downfall (of missiles, blows).

Beowulf 3117 þonne stræla storm strengum ȝebæded scoc ofer scildweall. **1600** FAIRFAX *Tasso* XI. xxxiv, Adrastus first ..through the falling storme did vpward clime Of stones, dartes, arrowes, fire, pitch and lime. **1615** KYD *Span. Trag.* I. ii. 53 Thicke stormes of bullets ran like winters haile. **1667** MILTON *P.L.* I. 172 The Sulphurous Hail Shot after us in storm. *Ibid.* VI. 546 This day will pour down..no drizling show'r, But ratling storm of Arrows barbd with fire. **1777** POTTER *Æschylus, Persians* 486 Whilst broken rocks..And storms of arrows crush'd them. **1817** SCOTT *Harold* VI. xv, Then rose His mace, and with a storm of blows The mortal and the Demon close. **1849** W. S. MAYO *Kaloolah* ii. (1850) 24 She [the frigate] sent forth a storm of shot.

fig. **1842** TENNYSON *St. Sim. Styl.* 7 Battering the gates of heaven with storms of prayer.

3. *fig.* and in figurative context. **a.** A violent disturbance of affairs whether civil, political, social or domestic; commotion, sedition, tumult. More definitely ***storm of rebellion, state, strife, war***, etc. Freq. in phr. ***to weather the storm***.

a **1000** *Andreas* 1236 (Gr.) Storm upp aras æfter ceaster-hofum, cirm unlytel hæðnes heriȝes. *c* **1315** SHOREHAM *Poems* vii. 716 For þou [*sc.* the serpent] areredst þerne storm And alle þys hete, Acorsed be þou bestes by-syde. *c* **1420** *Chron. Vilod.* 940 Ryȝt so holy chyrche after þat starme Shalle haue þe maystre atte lest. **1477** EARL RIVERS (Caxton) *Dictes* 1 Subgette and thral vnto the stormes of fortune. **1593** SHAKS. *2 Hen. VI*, III. i. 349, I will stirre vp in England some black Storme, Shall blowe ten thousand soules to Heauen, or Hell. **1614** BACON *Charge touching Duels* 9 It may cause suddaine stormes in Court, to the disturbance of his Maiestie. **1671** [see WEATHER *v.* 4 b]. **1713** POPE *Prol. to Addison's Cato* 21 A brave man struggling in the storms of fate. **1741** KAMES *Decis. Crt. Sess. 1730–52* (1799) 33 Newlands dreading the storm, had retired out of the country. **1802** CANNING *Song*, Here's to the pilot that weather'd the storm! [*i.e.* Pitt.] **1849, 1853** [see WEATHER *v.* 4 b]. **1855** MACAULAY *Hist. Eng.* xii. III. 207 A violent storm broke forth. Daly was ordered to attend at the bar. **1868** FREEMAN *Norm. Conq.* II. ix. 361 A monk of the house, who ..contrived to weather all storms, and died in possession of his Abbey. **1924** *Nation & Athenæum* 26 Jan. 603/1 His plight was serious; but he weathered the storm. **1934** F. W. CROFTS *12.30 from Croydon* viii. 95 He had come to an arrangement with his uncle whereby he hoped to weather the storm.

b. A tumultuous rush (of sound, tears, etc.); a vehement utterance (of words); a violent outburst (of censure, ridicule, etc.); a passionate manifestation of feeling.

1602 tr. *Guarini's Pastor Fido* IV. viii. M 2 b, That.. afterward dost mooue A thousand stormes of sighes, of teares, of plaintes. **1611** BIBLE *Transl. Pref.* ¶ 1, For, was there euer any thing proiected, that sauoured any way of newnesse..but the same endured many a storme of gaine-saying, or opposition? **1615** CHAPMAN *Odyss.* IX. 435 With stormes of whistlings [Gr. πολλῇ ῥοίζῳ] then, his flocks he draue Vp to the mountaines. **1693** DRYDEN *Persius* I. 36 The Prose is Fustian, and the Numbers lame. All Noise, and empty Pomp, a storm of Words. **1712** ADDISON *Spect.* No. 407 ¶ 4 How much more they would have been alarmed, had they heard him actually throwing out such a Storm of Eloquence. **1781** COWPER *Table-T.* 491 The strings are swept with such a pow'r, so loud, The storm of music shakes th' astonish'd crowd. **1832** WARREN *Diary Physic.* II. iii. 124 He concluded amid a storm of applause. **1847** TENNYSON *Princess* v. 477 At which the storm Of galloping hoofs bare on the ridge of spears And riders front to front. **1849** MACAULAY *Hist. Eng.* iv. I. 484 He..faced the storm of invective which burst upon him from bar, bench, and witness box, with the insolence of despair. **1891** FARRAR *Darkn. & Dawn* xxviii, Octavia disburdened the long-pent agony of repression in..a storm of weeping.

c. Commotion or unrest (of mind or soul); a tumultuous assemblage (of thoughts, feelings).

1569 UNDERDOWNE *Heliodorus* VII. 89 A whole storme of thoughtes in a manner ouerwhelmed her. **1728–46** THOMSON *Spring* 299 These, and a thousand mixed emotions more,..vex the mind With endless storm. **1729** G. ADAMS tr. *Sophocl., Antig.* III. v. II. 51 Still the same Violence of the Storms of her Soul torments her. **1864** TENNYSON *Aylmer's F.* 322 Sir Aylmer reddening from the storm within, Then broke all bonds of courtesy, and crying 'Boy' [etc.]. **1894** HALL CAINE *Manxman* III. xii. 170 She.. covered up her head in the clothes as before, but with a storm of other feelings.

d. ***storm and stress*** [G. *Sturm und Drang*]: used to designate the movement in German literature about 1770–82, due to a school of young writers characterized by extravagance in the representation of violent passion, and by energetic repudiation of the 'rules' of the French critics. See also STURM UND DRANG.

Sturm und Drang, the title of a play by F. M. Klinger (1776), was seized upon by the historians of literature as aptly expressing the spirit of the school to which the author belonged.

1855 G. H. LEWES *Goethe* I. III. i. 140 [1771] The period known as the Storm and Stress period was then about to astonish Germany, and to startle all conventions, by works such as Gerstenberg's *Ugolino*, Goethe's *Götz von Berlichingen*, Klinger's *Sturm und Drang* (from whence the name), and Schiller's *Robbers*. **1900** F. H. STODDARD *Evol. Eng. Novel* iv. 144 That group of men whom collectively we take to illustrate the early Storm and Stress.

transf. **1839** LONGF. *Hyperion* II. viii, Did you never have the misfortune..to know one of the benefactors of the human race, in the very 'storm and pressure period' of his indiscreet enthusiasm? **1879** FARRAR *St. Paul* II. 411 Written during the years A.D. 57 and 58, a period pre-eminently of storm and stress in the Apostle's life. **1900** G. C. BRODRICK *Memories* 227, I never knew John Bright personally until his time of storm and stress was over.

e. ***up a storm*** adv. phr., vehemently, violently, with enthusiasm or energy. *U.S. colloq.*

1953 J. STREET *Civil War* iv. 55 The editors just r'ared back in the omnipotence of Jove and pontificated up a storm. **1956** B. HOLIDAY *Lady sings Blues* (1973) xviii. 149 After Marietta taught me, I knitted up a storm and got real fancy. I made cable-knit sweaters for Bobby Tucker and his little boy. **1965** *Charlottesville* (Va.) *Daily Progress* 29 Apr. 6/1 When I ask him to go to the store for me he starts to wheeze up a storm and tells me he is a sick man. **1967** *Boston Sunday Herald Mag.* 30 Apr. 19/3 Right now she's cooking up a storm in preparation for the rash of friends who will be stopping by on their way to Expo. **1972** *TV Guide* (U.S.) 15 Jan. A54/1 Aretha Franklin sings up a storm and impersonates top female vocalists. **1974** K. MILLETT *Flying* (1975) v. 518, I will console myself with material goods. I will shop up a storm. **1983** *Oxford Times* 29 Apr. 3/7 Youngsters from the First Yarnton Brownies have been knitting up a storm to make a blanket for Mother Theresa in India.

4. *Path.* **a.** A paroxysm, violent access (of pain or disease). Now chiefly with qualifying word, as ***asthmatic, rheumatic storm***.

1545 RAYNALDE *Byrth Mankynde* 58 Another dyette there is, the whiche she ought to obserue in yᵉ tyme of labour: when the stormes and thronges begyn to come on. **1612** SHELTON *Quixote* I. III. iii. (1620) 134 He swet, and swet againe, with..excessiue swoonings. This storme and mishap endured about some two houres. **1897** *Allbutt's Syst. Med.* III. 39 All these together as phenomena of the same rheumatic storm. **1898** *Ibid.* V. 288 The asthmatic storm flits about the lung, now here, now there. **1899** *Ibid.* VII. 819 We should expect the final storm of grave symptoms [in an attack of convulsions] to be preceded by indications of gradual failure.

b. ***brain storm, nerve storm***: see quots.

1890 BILLINGS *Med. Dict.*, *Nerve-storms*, sudden attacks or paroxysms of neuroses or functional nervous disease. **1894** G. M. GOULD *Illustr. Dict. Med.*, *Brain-storm*, a succession of sudden and severe phenomena, due to some cerebral disturbance.

II. [f. STORM *v.*]

5. *Mil.* **a.** A violent assault on a fortified place.

1645 CROMWELL in Carlyle *Lett. & Sp.* (1845) I. 225 The day and hour of our storm was appointed. *Ibid.* 226 The General's signal unto a storm, was to be, The..discharging four pieces of cannon. **1665** BOYLE *Occas. Refl.* II. iii. (1848) 107 A Fortress, whose Defendants are not Treacherous, can scarce be taken otherwise than either by Famine, or Storm. **1748** *Anson's Voy.* II. xi. 255 We should have carried the fort by storm. **1813** WELLINGTON in Gurw. *Desp.* (1838) X. 548, I believe the Storm ought to take place by daylight. **1840** W. C. BURNS in I. Burns *Life* ix. (1870) 204 He served at eight storms, and twelve general engagements. **1869** FREEMAN *Norm. Conq.* (1875) III. xii. 168 An attempt at a storm was beaten back by the defenders.

b. ***to take by storm***: to take possession of by a sudden attack; to carry by assault.

1687 A. LOVELL tr. *Thevenot's Trav.* I. 72 At length they took the Town by storm. **1734** tr. *Rollin's Anc. Hist.* (1827) I. 149 The town was taken by storm. **1870** ROGERS *Hist. Glean.* Ser. II. 49 The rioters took Norwich by storm.

fig. **1847** C. BRONTË *Jane Eyre* xxxiii, How I looked while these ideas were taking my spirit by storm, I cannot tell. **1889** JESSOPP *Coming of Friars* i. 27 The Franciscans..were taking the world by storm.

III. 6. *attrib.* and *Comb.*: **a.** simple attrib., as ***storm-blast, -burst, -drop, -flake, -gust, -lift, -month, -rack, -shock, -song, -spirit, -sprite***; also ***storm-like*** adj. and adv.

1817 COLERIDGE *Anc. Mar.* I. 41 And now the *Storm-blast came. *a* **1849** MANGAN *Poems* (1859) 69 The *storm-burst is over. **1836** KEBLE in *Lyra Apost.* (1849) 167 Now the big *storm-drops fall. **1876** *Storm flake [see *scroll-leaved* adj. s.v. SCROLL *sb.* 6 a]. **1860** TYNDALL *Glac.* I. xxvii. 198 Wild *storm-gusts, sent down against us from Mont Blanc himself. **1870** MORRIS *Earthly Par.* III. IV. 372 The storm began To rumble, and the *storm-lift moving slow, Over a full third of the sky to grow. *a* **1586** SIDNEY *Arcadia* III. *Amphialus' Dream* (1605) 261 Whereout with sudden fall ..There came a chariot faire..Whose *stormelike course staid not till hard by me it bided. **1607** CHAPMAN *Bussy d'Ambois* II. i. 101 Storme-like he fell, and hid the feare-cold Earth. **1705** MRS. CENTLIVRE *Basset-Table* IV, I am rough and storm-like in my temper. **1894** *Stonyhurst Mag.* Feb. 233 And like the *storm-months smote the earth. **1878** O. WILDE *Ravenna* 14 As from the *storm-rack comes a perfect star! **1926** J. N. CAMERON in *Oxford Poetry* 14 The haggard storm-rack of disastrous days. **1849** CHRISTINA ROSSETTI *Poems* (1904) 118/1 See the ancient pine that stands the firmer For the *storm-shock that it bore. **1925** BLUNDEN *English Poems* 40 While on her soul the *stormsong bursts, and groanings Knell through roof and flue. **1929** —— *Near & Far* 41 *Storm-spirit, coil your lightnings round mad towers. **1817** SCOTT *Harold* III. ix, When the *storm-sprite shrieks in air.

b. instrumental, as ***storm-armed, -beat, -beaten, -bitten, -bound, -damaged, -driven, -encompassed, -laden, -rent, -swept, -threatened, -tormented, -torn, -tossed, -troubled, -washed, -worn*** adjs.

1591 SYLVESTER *Ivry* 174 *Storm-arm'd Auster cruell. **1590** SPENSER *F.Q.* II. xii. 32 Here may thy *storme-bet vessel safely ride. **1814** SCOTT *To Dk. Buccleuch* 64 On every storm-beat cape. **1582** STANYHURST *Æneis* I. (Arb.) 37 Lyke plodding *stormebeaten haglers. **1600** SHAKS. *Sonn.* xxxiv. 6 To dry the raine on my storme-beaten face. *a* **1639** T. CAREW *Poems* (1651) 28, I float Far from the shore, in a storm-beaten boat. **1855** MACAULAY *Hist. Eng.* xviii. IV. 191 Some stormbeaten pinnacle of rock. **1939** W. B. YEATS *Last Poems* 6 A small forgotten house that's set On a *storm-bitten green. **1830** CARLYLE in Froude *Life* (1882) II. 66 After so many weeks of *storm-bound inactivity. **1980** *New Age* (U.S.) Oct. 26/1 Eight acres of *storm-damaged apricots. **1841** J. G. WHITTIER *Poet. Wks.* (1898) 190/2 Loose rock and frozen slide, Hung on the mountain-side, Waiting their hour to glide Downward, *storm-driven! **1900** W. S. CHURCHILL in *Morning Post* 1 Jan. 6/2 These tall figures, full of animated movement, clad in dark flapping clothes, with slouch, storm-driven hats. **1817** SHELLEY *Revolt Islam* VII. xxxvii, Like the fires that flare In *storm-encompassed isles. **1899** MACKAIL *Morris* II. 27 The *storm-laden air that he began to feel around him. **1794** COLERIDGE *To Yng. Lady* 21 Amid the yelling of the *storm-rent skies! **1850** E. B. BROWNING *Poet. Wks.* (1904) 141/1, I lack your daring, up this storm-rent chasm To fix with violent hands a kindred god. **1805** SCOTT *Last Minstrel* VI. xxi, Where restless seas Howl round the *storm-swept Orcades. **1977** *Storm-threatened [see QUANTUM 5 d]. **1844** POE in *Columbian Mag.* Dec. 275/2 *Storm-tormented ocean of his thoughts. **1876** J. G. WHITTIER *Poet. Wks.* (1898) 247/2 The *storm-torn plumes Of old pine-forest kings. *c* **1958** E. M. FORSTER *Life to Come* (1975) 199 They flew round and round the basilica.., they shot through its roof into the storm-torn night. **1610–11** J. DAVIES (Heref.) *Paper's Compl.* (Grosart) 78/1 Looke downe..Vpon Thy Church *storme-tossed euery houre. **1842** CARLYLE *Past & Pr.* I. vi. 48 Through all these stormtost seas,..the Supreme Powers are driving us. **1850** E. BRONTË *Wuthering Heights* 489 No coward soul is mine, No trembler in the world's *storm-troubled sphere. **1840** THACKERAY *Shabby-genteel Story* ii, The *storm-washed shores of Margate in winter. **1885** TENNYSON *Dead Prophet* v, A *storm-worn signpost not to be read.

c. objective, as ***storm-bringer; storm-boding, -breathing, -portending, -presaging*** adjs.

1672 DAVENANT *Masque* (1673) 365 The *storm-boading Whale. **1594** CHAPMAN *Shadow of Nt.* D ij, *Storme-breathing Lelaps. **1552** HULOET, *Storme brynger, ..*nimbifer*. **1582** STANYHURST *Æneis* I. (Arb.) 35 But with a flaw suddeyn chauffing stormbringer Orion, Spurnt vs too the waters. **1845** BAILEY *Festus* (ed. 2) 198 A *storm-portending cloud. **1809** SCOTT *Poacher* 143 The waning moon, with *storm-presaging gleam.

d. Special comb.: **storm apron** *U.S.*, a waterproof sheet used to cover the front of an open carriage in wet weather; **storm-area**, the area of the earth's surface over which a storm spreads itself; also *fig.*; **storm-beach** (see quot.); **storm-bell**, (*a*) [cf. G. *sturmglocke*] an alarm bell; (*b*) (see quot. 1910); **storm-belt**, a belt or zone in which storms occur periodically; **storm boat** *Mil.*, a light but powerful boat used for conveying attacking troops across rivers; **storm-breeder** (see quot.); **storm card**, a transparent disc marked with lines representing the wind-directions of a cyclonic storm, to be placed over the ship's position on the chart in order to ascertain the course of the storm-centre; **storm cellar** orig. and chiefly *U.S.*, a cellar or dugout made to be a place of refuge from a storm; also *transf.* and *fig.*; **storm centre**, the central area of a cyclonic storm, characterized by comparative calmness; *fig.* the central point around which a storm of controversy, trouble, etc. rages; the seat of disease, sedition, and the like; **storm choke**, a safety valve installed in an oil-well pipe below the ocean surface, designed to stop the oil flow should it exceed a predetermined rate as a result of damage at the wellhead; **storm-circle** = *storm-card*; **storm-clock**, (*a*) [G. *sturmglocke*], *nonce-use* an alarm bell; (*b*) a meteorograph, spec. one devised by Sir F. Ronalds (*Cent. Dict.* Suppl. 1909); **storm-cloud**, a heavy cloud which threatens or comes with rain; also *fig.*; **storm coat** orig. and chiefly *U.S.*, a waterproof coat or heavy overcoat for use in stormy weather; **storm collar**, a coat-collar which may be turned up and fastened close round the neck; **storm-compass** = *storm-card* (Cent. Dict.); **storm-cone** = CONE *sb.*[1] 9; **storm-current** (see quot.); **storm door** orig. *U.S.*, an outer or supplementary door for use in stormy weather; **storm drain**, a drain built to carry away excess water in times of heavy rain; **storm-drum**, a canvas cylinder hoisted in conjunction with the storm cone as a weather-signal; = DRUM *sb.*[1] 8 b; **storm-fire** = CORPOSANT; **storm flag**, (*a*) *U.S.*, each of the flags used in the U.S. system of storm-signalling (*Cent. Dict.*); (*b*) the smallest national flag used at posts and flown only in stormy weather (W. 1911); **storm-flap**, a piece of material designed to protect an opening or fastening from the effects of rain, as on a tent, coat, etc.; **storm-glass**, a hermetically sealed tube containing a solution which becomes flocculent on the approach of a storm; **storm-god**, a deity supposed to rule the storms; so also **storm-goddess; storm-head window**, a kind of dormer window; †**storm-hole**, ? an opening made in a wall for letting out water resulting from a storm; **storm-house** *U.S.*, a temporary shelter against storm for workmen (*Cent. Dict.*); also, a shelter from the weather on a boat; **storm-jacket**, a weather-proof jacket; **storm-jib** *Naut.* (see quot. 1867); **storm-kite** (see quot.); **storm lantern** orig. *U.S.* = *hurricane-lamp* s.v. HURRICANE 3 a; **storm-light**, the lurid light seen in a stormy sky; also = CORPOSANT; **storm mizen, -pane** (see quots.); **storm-path** = *storm-track*; **storm-pavement** (see quot.); †**storm-pole** *Mil.*, each of a series of stakes driven into a defensive work as a protection against assault; **storm-porch**, a porch for the protection of an outer door from storms; **storm power** = *storm-god*; **storm-proof** *a.*, (*a*) impervious to storm; also, protected from or affording protection from stormy weather; (*b*) proof against storming or assault; also *fig.*; **storm rubber** *N. Amer.*, a rubber overshoe; **storm-sail** (see quot. 1867);

storm sewer *U.S.* = *storm drain* above; **storm shutter**, an outside window-shutter for use in stormy weather; **storm-signal**, a signal exhibited at coastguard stations, etc., to give warning of the approach and direction of dangerous winds; also *fig.*; hence **storm-signalling** *vbl. sb.*, the signalling of storms; also *attrib.*; **storm-spencer** = *storm-trysail*; **storm-stayed, (-staid)**, chiefly *Sc.*, prevented by stress of weather from making or continuing a journey; **storm-staysail**, a staysail of reduced dimensions for use in a storm; **storm-stead** *a. Sc.* = *storm-stayed*; **storm surge** *Oceanogr.*, an abnormal raising of the sea level in a region as a result of the wind and atmospheric pressure changes associated with a storm; **storm-system**, the group of low-pressure areas (revolving round a centre of lowest pressure) constituting a cyclonic storm; **storm track**, the path traversed by the centre of a cyclonic storm; **storm-trysail** (see quot. 1867); **storm-warning**, warning of the approach of a storm obtained by meteorological observation; **storm-water**, (*a*) an abnormal amount of surface water resulting from a heavy fall of rain or snow; also *attrib.*; (*b*) *poet.*, water agitated by a storm; **storm-wave**, an abnormally heavy wave due to cyclonic disturbance which rolls across the ocean and frequently causes the inundation of low-lying coast lands; also *fig.*; **storm wind**, the wind which accompanies a storm; also *fig.*; *spec.* a wind having a speed within certain limits (see quots. and cf. STORM *sb.* 1 b); **storm window**, (*a*) = *storm-head window*; (*b*) an outer window to protect the inner from the effects of storms (Cassell 1888); (*c*) *N. Amer.*, a detachable window put up in winter to form an insulating double window; †**storm-winnock (-windoik)** *Sc.* = prec. (*a*); **storm-zone** = *storm-belt*.

1895 *Montgomery Ward Catal.* Spring & Summer 591/2 **Storm Aprons.* These aprons are held firmly in position on the dash..forming an unbroken water-shed over front of dash. No mud, snow, or rain can settle inside of carriage. **1943** L. I. WILDER *These Happy Golden Years* xxix. 260 Back in his [buggy] seat, he unrolled the rubber storm apron. **1853** W. R. BIRT *Handbk. Law of Storms* 29 The above considerations lead to a most important division of the *storm area. **1898** *Daily News* 8 Nov. 4/7 As the day for the meeting of the Czar's Conference on Peace draws near, the storm-area seems to be steadily extending. **1882** GEIKIE *Text-bk. Geol.* III. I. iii. 277 Accumulations of gravel or '*storm-beaches' are often thrown up by storms, even above the level of ordinary high-tide mark. **1837** CARLYLE *Fr. Rev.* III. I. iv, At two o'clock the *stormbell shall be sounded,.. all Paris shall rush..and have itself enrolled. **1910** *Encycl. Brit.* III. 688/2 A storm-bell warns travellers in the plain of storms approaching from the mountains. **1891** *Century Dict.*, *Storm-belt. **1945** *Sun* (Baltimore) 27 Feb. 3/1 The sergeant..took them back to the road to carry the *stormboat down to the river and launch it. **1945** *Finito! Po Valley Campaign* (15th Army Group) 12 Each 20-foot, powered, plywood storm boat. **1867** SMYTH *Sailor's Word-bk.*, **Storm-breeders*, heavy cumulo-stratus clouds. **1844** *Storm card [see *storm circle*]. **1920** G. ADE *Hand-Made Fables* 30 The Money-lender beat it to a *Storm-Cellar. **1929** J. F. DOBIE *Vaquero of Brush Country* 151 Storm cellars in north Texas, Oklahoma, and Kansas still preserve its architecture. **1962** F. I. ORDWAY et al. *Basic Astronautics* xii. 503 One.. suggestion is that a special 'storm cellar' be constructed within the spacecraft, a well-shielded area into which the crew could retreat. **1971** J. H. GRAY *Red Lights on Prairies* ii. 36 When the first oratorical thunder clapped, the chief, the mayor..took to the storm cellars to wait for the storm to blow over. **1977** J. CLEARY *Vortex* i. 8 People build storm cellars to retreat to. **1894** *Harper's Weekly* 7 Apr. 315 It establishes a sort of Weather Bureau of disease, and..is to show..where the *storm centres of communicable disease are. **1900** A. CHURCH & PETERSON *Nervous & Mental Dis.* (ed. 2) 181 The initial or signal symptom..becomes highly significant as pointing to the storm-center, the point of greatest instability and usually the seat of organic disease. **1900** *Jrnl. Sch. Geog.* (U.S.) June 228 To fix the direction of the storm centre from the vessel, it is thus only necessary to face the wind. **1965** *Listener* 30 Sept. 481/2 Europe is no longer the storm centre in world affairs. The clouds have shifted to Asia. **1978** M. PUZO *Fools Die* xxix. 335 She was having a good time standing outside the party storm center. **1966** P. HINDE *Fortune in North Sea* viii. 154 The first safety valve is installed and left at the bottom of each production well at sea, and is known as the *Storm Choke. **1975** *North Sea Background Notes* (Brit. Petroleum Co.) 40 Precautions are taken to shut down production automatically on any failure of the wellhead or flow-line by installing suitable safety valves. These are the 'storm choke' in the well bore, ..and the surface safety valve. **1844** H. PIDDINGTON *Horn-bk. of Storms* 5 The horn plates in the pockets of this book are what is called Col. Reid's Hurricane, or *Storm, circles, or cards. **1819** SCOTT *Leg. Montrose* xiv, 'That,' said he, 'must be the alarm—the *storm-clock, as the Germans call it.' **1822** —— *Maid of Isla* ii, Her white wing gleams through mist and spray, Against the *storm-cloud. **1830** J. F. WATSON *Annals of Philadelphia* 179 In the year 1749, I met with the incidental mention of a singular over-coat, worn by captain James as a *storm coat, made entirely of beaver fur. **1849** THOREAU *Week Concord Riv.* 250 He ran along over the wet stones like a wrecker in his storm coat. **1897** *Outing* (U.S.) XXX. 162/2 Stormcoat. **1953** 'S. RANSOME' *Drag Dark* (1954) i. 16 The corpse..wore..a tan gabardine storm-coat, and big galoshes. **1974** 'J. ROSS' *Burning of Billy Toober* i. 7 His stiff-fabric stormcoat. **1981** *Daily Tel.* 30 Mar. 18/5 Snug, high-collared storm coats are ready to roam Tibetan mountains. **1898** *T. Eaton & Co. Catal.* Spring & Summer 124/1 Men's Klondike mining coats,..with 6-inch *storm collar and capot to pull over the head. **1899** [see EMPIECEMENT]. **1931** *Daily Mail* 26 May 1/4 (Advt.), West Riding suiting coats... Smart Storm Collar and pull-in Belt. **1863** in Fitzroy *Rep. Meteorologic Office* (1864) p. xi. *note*, This morning the *storm cone was hoisted. **1843** H. PIDDINGTON in *Jrnl. Asiatic Soc. Bengal* XII. I. 398 The '*storm current' may be briefly described as circular streams on the circumferences of rotatory storms. **1878** E. B. TUTTLE *Border Tales* 29 The horses..broke loose from the stable, and begun gnawing the *storm doors in front of the officers' quarters. **1939** H. M. MINER *St. Denis* ii. 25 Storm doors or built-on entries are put on the houses in winter. **1977** *Grimsby Even. Tel.* 27 May 17/7 (Advt.), Freehold semi-detached house... Porch with storm door. Entrance Hall. **1960** C. ACHEBE *No Longer at Ease* ii. 16 His car was parked close to a wide-open *storm drain from which came a very strong smell of rotting flesh. **1974** N. GORDIMER *Conservationist* 218 The English-language evening paper published a picture of a pet dog being rescued from a flooded storm-drain by the fire brigade. **1866** *Daily Tel.* 18 Jan. 4/5 It is not because occasional perturbations..baffle the reckonings of science, that meteorology should be ignored —four times out of five the *storm-drum is right. **1881** *Times* 19 Jan. 10/3 This evening the south storm-drum is hoisted at the semaphore at the Dockyard. *a* **1847** ELIZA COOK *Birds* v. 21 The *storm-fire burns, but what care they? **1883** A. I. MENKEN *Infelicia* 38 Heed not the storm-fires that so terribly burn in the black sky. **1896** *Weather Bureau Bull.* (U.S.) No. 80. 7 Two *storm flags (red with black centers), displayed one above the other,..announce the expected approach of tropical hurricanes. **1929** *T. Eaton & Co. Catal.* Spring & Summer 373/1 Palmetto Tent... Insect-proof mosquito door and rear window with *storm flap operated from inside. **1968** J. IRONSIDE *Fashion Alphabet* 41 *Trench-coat*... This short-cape effect is often called a 'storm cape' or 'storm flaps'. **1972** *Village Voice* (N.Y.) 1 June 13/2 (Advt.), Nylon Mountain Tent... Rear screen window with storm flap. **1973** *Shooting Times & Country Mag.* 7 July 37/2 (Advt.), Zip full length from neck to hem, covered by storm flap. **1823** *Mech. Mag.* I. 174 Those glasses..which are sold in the shops of opticians, under the name of '*Storm Glasses'. **1864** SPENCER *Biol.* 78 The relation between the phenomena occurring in the storm-glass and in the atmosphere respectively, is really not a correspondence at all. **1877** C. P. TIELE *Outl. Hist. Relig.* 113 In this conflict he [*Indra vritrahan*] is surrounded by the Maruts or *storm-gods, led by Rudra. **1869** TOZER *Highl. Turkey* II. 320 The character of a *storm-goddess, in which she [the Lamia] thus appears. **1833** LOUDON *Encycl. Archit.* §455 The next characteristic is the *storm-head window. **1419** *Mem. Ripon* (Surtees) III. 146 Et in salar. Will. de Cloke, carpentarii, emendantis diversos defectus in le Ales, et facientis *Storm-holes. **1836** T. POWER *Impressions Amer.* I. 31 She..had stump-royal masts, and a *storm-house abaft. **1839** *Southern Lit. Messenger* V. 8/2 The James Cropper..was fitted with..a storm house over the wheel. **1887** *Harper's Mag.* Dec. 119/1 Two men..were bending down at the storm-house in front of her parlor-door. **1844** H. MILLER in W. K. Leask *Life* iv. (1896) 109 Encased in his ample-skirted *storm-jacket of oiled canvas. *c* **1810** W. HICKEY *Mem.* (1960) xiii. 207 It blew so hard we could scarcely carry a close-reefed mainsail and *storm-jib. **1833** MARRYAT *P. Simple* xlvii, Another try-sail and a storm-jib were expanded to the wind. **1867** SMYTH *Sailor's Word-bk.*, *Storm-jib*, in cutters, the fifth or sixth size: the inner jib of square-rigged ships. *Ibid.*, **Storm-kite*, a contrivance for sending a hawser from a stranded vessel to the shore. **1895** *Montgomery Ward Catal.* Spring & Summer 553/2 Cold Blast or *Storm Lantern: is made on the same principle as street lamps, with wind break. **1923** W. DEEPING *Secret Sanctuary* xx. 207 He ..lit the storm-lantern he used at night, and extinguished the lamp. **1964** D. VARADAY *Gara-Yaka* vi. 51, I hurried to the hut with a storm lantern. **1976** *Norwich Mercury* 17 Dec. 6/7 If the light fails, you use a storm lantern. **1843** EMERSON *Misc. Papers, Carlyle* Wks. (Bohn) III. 315 It is not serene sunshine, but everything is seen in lurid *storm-lights. **1906** *Month* June 629 That the poets..should many of them allude to the mysterious storm-lights in their poems, is not surprising. **1794** *Rigging & Seamanship* I. 135 **Storm Mizen.* This sail is triangular, and..bends on the fore part to a horse, abaft and parallel to the mizen-mast. **1875** KNIGHT *Dict. Mech.*, **Storm-pane*, a supplementary, framed sheet of glass, to substitute, in an emergency, for a broken pane in a lighthouse. **1888** STEVENSON *Across the Plains* (1892) 176 The reflectors scratched, the spare lamp unready, the storm-panes in the storehouse. **1850** W. R. BIRT *Hurricane Guide* 55 The lower and upper branches of the *storm paths of the Northern Atlantic. **1875** KNIGHT *Dict. Mech.*, **Storm-pavement*, the sloping stone paving which lines the sea-face of piers and breakwaters. **1647** J. SPRIGGE *Anglia Rediv.* (1854) 257 The line, both upon the bulwarks and the curtain was strongly set with *storm-poles. **1879** *Lumberman's Gaz.* 15 Oct., Houses..should be protected at every much-used entrance, by *storm-porches. **1869** RUSKIN *Q. of Air* i. §20 Another beneficent *storm power, Boreas, occupies an important place in early legend. **1594** NASHE *Unfort. Trav.* C 4, Sailers doo pitch their apparell to make it *storme proofe. **1886** N. L. WALFORD *Parl. Generals of Civil War* 258 There had not been sufficient time..to make them [*sc.* the fortifications] storm-proof. **1901** Storm-proof [see COVER-ALL, COVERALL *sb.*]. **1909** *Chambers's Jrnl.* May 335/2 The lamp is stormproof, and is unaffected by cold weather, while it constitutes the safest form of street-lighting that has yet been devised. **1911** J. H. ROSE *Pitt. & Gt. War* vii. 192 The constitution had suffered dilapidation, but it was storm-proof. **1968** R. M. PATTERSON *Finlay's River* 224 So I set up a good storm-proof camp on a level point between two streams. **1895** *Montgomery Ward Catal.* Spring & Summer 522/3 Woman's *Storm Rubber: nothing better for wet weather. **1924–25** *T. Eaton & Co. Catal.* Fall & Winter 146/2 Women's first quality Black Storm Rubbers with round toes and low heels. **1840** R. H. DANA *Bef. Mast* xi, We came down to double-reefed topsails and the *storm-sails. **1867** SMYTH *Sailor's Word-bk.*, *Storm-sail*, a sail made of stout No. 1 canvas, of reduced dimensions, for use in a gale. **1887** W. E. S. FALES *Brooklyn's Guardians* iii. 43 The improvements contemplated the repairing of the great thoroughfares..; the construction of *storm sewers. **1941** *Sun* (Baltimore) 16 Sept. 9/3 Silting-up of the channel, due, it is said, to discharge from storm sewers. **1978** J. IRVING *World according to Garp* iv. 77 The storm sewers bogged. **1834** E. W. BRAYLEY *Graphic & Historical Illustrator* 395/1 All the windows..are protected by *storm-shutters. **1908** *Westm. Gaz.* 18 Mar. 10/1 All the windows, too, have storm-shutters. **1863** in Fitzroy *Rep. Meteorologic Office* (1864) p. xi. *note*, Drum *storm signal hoisted at noon. **1867** SMYTH *Sailor's Word-bk.*, *Storm-signal*, the hoisting of a danger-flag. Also, Fitzroy's drum and cone, which show the direction of the expected gale. **1905** W. O'BRIEN *Recoll.* vii. 136 We who knew Egan's storm-signals, saw the tips of his ears redden and a bright scarlet point appear in the centre of his cheeks. **1875** *Chamb. Journal* 2 Jan. 8/1 *Storm-signalling apparatus is supplied by the Board of Trade. **1857** M. F. MAURY in D. F. M. Corbin *Life* (1888) 135 The *storm-spencer had been blown away. **1491** *Acta Dom. Conc.* (1839) 203/1 In the accioun..tueching þe takin of a schip & gudes..*stormestaid & drevin to þe Erlis fery. **1787** BURNS *Let. W. Cruikshank* June, I was storm-staid two days at the foot of the Ochill Hills. **1856** KANE *Arct. Expl.* II. xxii. 216 An abrupt change of the weather gave us a howling gale outside, and we were all of us storm-stayed. **1880** MISS BIRD *Japan* I. 344 The *yadoyas* are crowded with storm-staid travellers. **1850** L. HUNT *Autob.* II. 255 We set the fore *storm-staysail anew. **1513** DOUGLAS *Æneis* III. iii. (*heading*), How Troiane goddis apperis to Enee, And how that he was *stormested on the see. **1632** LITHGOW *Trav.* III. 94, I stayed sixteene dayes, storme-sted with Northernely winds. **1888** BARRIE *Auld Licht Idylls* ii. 41 Storm-stead shows used to emphasize the severity of a Thrums winter. **1929** A. T. DOODSON *Rep. Thames Floods* 5 If there are no tidal predictions available the problem of separating the *storm surge from the tidal oscillation is by no means easy. **1956** *Proc. R. Soc.* A. CCXXXVII. 325 The problem [of the mathematical solution of tides in a closed channel] is increased in difficulty when a storm surge of a non-periodic character is superposed upon the periodic tide. **1970** D. A. ROSS *Introd. Oceanogr.* vii. 229 In the Gulf Coast area of the United States, storm surges have been known to raise the water level as much as 7m. **1897** *Daily News* 26 Jan. 7/1 Later in the day the *storm-system continued to increase in depth. **1838** W. REID *Law of Storms* 430 The *storm tracks here traced. **1851** H. MELVILLE *Moby Dick* III. xxxvii. 213 A *storm-trysail was set further aft. **1867** SMYTH *Sailor's Word-bk.*, *Storm-trysail*, a fore-and-aft sail, hoisted by a gaff, but having no boom at its foot, and only used in foul weather. **1967** L. S. TAWES *Coasting Captain* 259, I slacked off my storm trysail sheet. **1867** A. BUCHAN *Meteorol.* 9 *Storm-warnings. **1883** *Encycl. Brit.* XVI. 158/1 Weather Forecasts and Storm Warnings. **1879** *Cassell's Techn. Educ.* III. 394 *Storm-waters, as they may be called,..fall in such quantities within..an hour or two as entirely to overcharge all ordinary systems of drainage. **1887** MEREDITH *Ball. Tragic Life* 92 Howled and pressed the ghastly crew, Like storm-waters over rocks. **1905** *Daily Chron.* 3 July 6/7 Heavy rain began to come down—so heavy that the storm-water sewers were not able to take it off. **1839** D. MILNE in *Trans. R. Soc. Edin.* XIV. 486 This *storm-wave (for such it may not improperly be termed) moved..through the Atlantic in a N.NE. direction. **1874** LISLE CARR *Judith Gwynne* I. iv. 120 Her bosom would heave with a great storm-wave of passionate emotion. **1839** LONGF. *Hyperion* I. vii, The *storm-wind came from the Alsatian hills. **1873** HAMERTON *Intell. Life* II. iv. (1876) 72 Like..a steamer with a storm-wind directly against her and an iron-bound coast behind. **1892** G. F. X. GRIFFITH tr. *Fouard's St. Peter* 78 The storm-winds of trial swept over them. **1923** Storm wind [see GALE *sb.*[3] 1 a]. **1959** *Gloss. Meteorol.* (Amer. Meteorol. Soc.) 545 *Storm wind*, in the Beaufort wind scale, a wind whose speed is from 56 to 63 knots (64 to 72 mph). **1824** SCOTT *Redgauntlet* Let. iv, There were what are called *storm-windows in the roof. **1933** L. I. WILDER *Farmer Boy* xxii. 174 They fitted storm doors and storm windows on the house. **1956** W. R. BIRD *Off-Trail in Nova Scotia* ii. 51 She's always nagging Sam to take off the storm windows, whitewash the fence. **1978** *Detroit Free Press* 5 Mar. C21/1 (Advt.), 3 Track Storm Window $20.95 each. **15..** *Aberd. Reg.* (MS.) (Jam.) The bigging of the *storme-windoik. **1889** R. HINMAN *Eclectic Physical Geogr.* vi. 94 The regions between 40° and 70° latitude are the great *storm zones of the world.

e. In names of certain birds, the movements or cries of which are supposed to presage a storm: **storm-bird**, (*a*) = *storm-petrel*; (*b*) = *thunder-bird* b (see THUNDER *sb.* 6); (*c*) a local name (Norfolk) for the fieldfare (Swainson); **storm cock**, the missel-thrush; also locally applied to the fieldfare and the green woodpecker (Miss Jackson *Shropsh. Word-bk.*); **storm-finch** (†*-finck*, †*-fink*) = *storm-petrel*; **storm-petrel**, *Procellaria pelagica* (cf. STORMY *a.* 3); **storm thrush**, the missel-thrush.

These words are sometimes used *fig.* to designate a person whose activity is a sign of impending discord.

1752 J. HILL *Hist. Anim.* 514 [The Petrel] was first mentioned in the Stockholm Transactions, under the name of Procellaria, or the *Storm-bird. **1867** GOLDW. SMITH *3 Eng. Statesmen* (1882) 34 Lady Carlyle—a storm-bird of this parliamentary storm. **1913** R. HARRIS *Boanerges* xxv. 267 The Arabian Storm-bird or thunder-bird. **1769** G. WHITE *Selborne, To Barrington* 2 Nov., Missel-bird, *Turdus viscivorus*... Is called in Hampshire and Sussex the *storm-cock. **1819** M. EDGEWORTH *Let.* 26 Jan. (1971) 160 When a dark black cloud threatens a heavy shower..then the storm-cock cries or screams. **1896** A. E. HOUSMAN *Shropshire Lad* 17 So braver notes the storm-cock sings To start the rusted wheel of things. **1902** G. BRENAN *House of Percy* II. ii. 32 Charles Paget—storm-cock of Catholic agitation. **1978** *Country Life* 7 Sept. 630/1 The mistle thrush..will sing in the wildest weather and fully justify its vernacular name of storm-cock. **1661** LOVELL *Hist. Anim. & Min.* Isagoge a 6 [Aquatic birds] as the..*stormfinck. **1804** BEWICK *Brit. Birds* II. 249 Stormy Petrel. Storm Finch, or Little Petrel. **1867** SMYTH *Sailor's Word-bk.*, *Storm-finch*, the petrel, or Mother Cary's chicken. **1833** P. J. SELBY *Illustr. Brit. Ornith.* II. 533 Common *Storm-Petrel. *Ibid.* 537 Fork-tailed Storm-Petrel. **1885** NEWTON in *Encycl. Brit.* XVIII. 712/1 The common Storm Petrel, *Procellaria pelagica*,..is the 'Mother Carey's chicken' of sailors, and is widely believed to be the harbinger of bad weather. **1854** Miss Baker *Northampt. Gloss.*, *Storm-cock* or **Storm-thrush.* The missel-thrush. **1913** *Engl. Rev.* Apr. 157 Like a storm-thrush piping its warning.

storm (stɔːm), *v.* [f. storm *sb.* (OE. had *styrman*, early ME. sturme *v.*)]

1. *intr.* Of the elements or weather: To be tempestuous or stormy, to rage.

14.. *Chaucer's Boeth.* i. met. vii. (1868) 29 þe trouble wynde þat hyȝt auster stormyng [*Camb. MS.* turnyng: L. *mare volvens*] and walwyng þe see medleþ þe heete. **1564** T. Stapleton tr. *Staphylus' Apol.* Pref. 3 As the quiet passanger when the sea stormeth. **1579** Spenser *Sheph. Cal.* Dec. 131 So now he [winter] stormes with many a sturdy stoure. **1612** Drayton *Poly-olb.* x. 74 From Shetland straddling wide, his foote on Thuly sets: Whence storming, all the vast Deucalidon hee [Boreas] threts.

fig. c **1611** Chapman *Iliad* i. 148 That..he, whose bow thus stormd For our offences, may be calmd.

b. *impers.* To blow violently; also to rain, snow, etc. heavily. Now only *U.S.*

1530 Palsgr. 130 *Il tempeste*, it stormeth. **1598** W. Phillip tr. *Linschoten* 5/2 The nearer wee are vnto the land, the more it stormeth, raineth, thundreth and calmeth.

1840 R. H. Dana *Bef. Mast* v, Throughout the night it stormed violently—rain, hail, snow and sleet beating upon the vessel. **1848** Bartlett *Dict. Amer.* 336 *To storm*, to blow with violence; impersonally, as, *it storms.* We use it improperly in the sense of to rain or to snow. **1856** Miss Warner *Hills Shatemuc* xix, Come in..it is going to storm hard... It's going to be a bad storm;—you'll be better under here. **1858** M. F. Maury in D. F. M. Corbin *Life* (1888) 168 It is now snowing and storming furiously. **1872** 'Mark Twain' *Innoc. Abr.* ii. 20 It was still raining. And not only raining, but storming. 'Outside'..there was a tremendous sea on. **1894** *Chamb. Jrnl.* 16 June 376/1 Oh, but the nuts fall much more quickly when it storms.

c. *transf.* To rush with the violence of a storm.

1842 Tennyson *Vis. Sin* 25 The music..Rose again from where it seem'd to fail, Storm'd in orbs of song, a growing gale. **1854** —— *Charge of Light Brigade* iii, Storm'd at with shot and shell, Boldly they rode and well, Into the jaws of Death.

2. *trans.* To make stormy. In quots. *fig.* to trouble, vex, disturb. Also *pass.*

1597 Shaks. *Lover's Compl.* i, I..Ere long espied a fickle maid..Storming her world with sorrowes, wind and raine. **1878** Browning *Poets of Croisic* lxiv, Our simulated thunder-claps Which tell us counterfeited truths—these same Are—sound, when music storms the soul, perhaps? —Sight, [etc.]. **1883** H. W. Beecher in *Chr. World Pulpit* XXIV. 122/3, I honour men who are stormed like the ocean, whose sky is dark, on whom the waves of trouble roll.

3. *intr.* To complain with rough and violent language; to rage. Const. *at*, *against* (a grievance or person).

1553 *Respublica* i. iii. 211 *Avar.* Feyth, manne, I spake but even to prove your pacyence, that yf thowe haddest grunted or stormed thereat, *Adul.* Naie, fewe times doe I vse suche lowde manier as that. *Ibid.* iii. vi. 935 Ye muste storme & sharpelye take hym vp for stumbling. **1570** Foxe *A. & M.* (ed. 2) 1225/1 The Priestes..began to grudge & storme against Tyndall. **1586** A. Day *Eng. Secretorie* ii. (1625) 26 Such odde kinde of reports..the least whereof would make you storme to the gall. **1596** Shaks. *Merch. V.* i. iii. 138 Why looke you how you storme, I would be friends with you. **1603** Knolles *Hist. Turkes* (1621) 1254 Storming against their Generall for not being a coward, as they themselves were. c **1611** Chapman *Iliad* v. 868 O Father stormst thou not To see vs take these wrongs from men? **1642** D. Rogers *Naaman* 15 Oh they storme and rage as a Beare robbed of her Whelpes. **1741** Richardson *Pamela* (1824) I. 90 She curses and storms at me like a trooper. **1797** Mrs. Berkeley *Poems of G. M. Berkeley* Pref. p. ccxxviii, Mrs. Berkeley used to storm nobly on these occasions. **1813** Byron *Br. Abydos* i. xiii, And he so often storms at nought. **1867** Trollope *Chron. Barset* I. xiv. 120 He'll storm and threaten and stop the supplies for a month or so. **1885** *L'pool Daily Post* 30 June 4/7 They storm like very demons when anyone ventures to hint that the Highland crofter is not the paragon of the human race. **1889** Barrie *Window in Thrums* xii. 108, I do not want to storm at the man.

b. quasi-*trans.* with complement.

1839 Bailey *Festus* 286 Although..they may have put God from them—Disowned His prophets..and stormed His curses back to Him; yet..He can pity still. **1891** Kipling *Light that Failed* xv. 335 Dick roused, struck him over the head with the butt, and stormed himself wide awake.

4. *pass.* To be exposed to the severity of the weather; to suffer severely from cold. Now *dial.*

c **1440** *York Myst.* xiv. 16 And yf we here all nyght abide, We shall be stormed in þis steede. c **1636** Strafford in Browning *Life* (1892) 187 He was found dead..and in a cold night and lodging, stormed to death. **1828** Carr *Craven Gloss.*, *Storm'd*, starved, pinched with cold.

5. *trans.* To make (seed-hay) storm-proof by piling the sheaves in small stacks. *local.*

1862 *Jrnl. R. Agric. Soc.* XXIII. 63 Ere it [the rain] arrives ..several acres of his hay-seed are already in the field stack. Thus it is saved, by being stormed, as the local [Warwickshire] phrase well expresses it.

6. *Mil.* To make a vigorous assault on (a fortified position); to take or attempt to take by storm or assault.

1645 Cromwell in Carlyle *Lett. & Sp.* (1845) I. 227 By means of this entrance of Colonel Hammond they did storm the Fort on that part which was inward. **1646** in *10th Rep. Hist. MSS. Comm.* App. i. 54 The General Major of the horses wold haue the wallis of the citie stormit vpoun all quarteris. **1651** Lamont *Diary* (Maitl. Club) 32 They stormed Dundie, and caried the towne. **1692** Prior *Ode imit. Hor.* 31 All Day to Mount the Trench, to Storm the Breach. **1820** W. Irving *Sketch Bk.* II. 260 Several of their bravest officers were shot down in the act of storming the fortress. **1874** Green *Short Hist.* i. §6. 49 Æthelred stormed the Danish camp at Benfleet.

b. *transf.* and *fig.*

1652 R. Loveday *Hymen's Præludia* 301 He basely resolves to storm her chastity. **1697** Collier *Ess. Mor. Subj.* ii. (ed. 2) 99 Thus People are stormed out of their Reason and Inclinations; plagued into a Compliance; and forced to yield in their own Defence. **1703** S. Sewall *Diary* 16 Mar. (1879) II. 75 So should we patiently..sing the Praises of God,..though Storm'd by the last efforts of Antichrist. **1730** T. Boston *Mem.* xii. (1899) 395 The toothache has stormed my lower teeth so that I think they are beginning to give way too. **1812** Byron *Ch. Har.* i. xlix, Here the bold peasant storm'd the dragon's nest. **1820** Keats *Eve of S. Agnes* x, A hundred swords Will storm his heart, Love's feverous citadel. **1841** Thackeray *Gt. Hoggarty Diam.* x, She would have stormed Lady Jane Preston's door, and forced her way up-stairs. **1855** Macaulay *Hist. Eng.* xvi. III. 697 At last it seemed that heaven had been stormed by the violence of supplication: the truth came out, and many lies with it. **1910** Ld. Rosebery *Chatham* x. 220 Pitt had apparently determined, in the jargon of that day, to storm the Closet.

7. *intr.* **a.** *Mil.* To rush to an assault or attack.

1632 *Swed. Intelligencer* ii. 47 The Scots..forced the garrison into the inner port; they Storming in together with them. **1645** Cromwell in Carlyle *Lett. & Sp.* (1845) I. 226 Colonel Montague and Colonel Pickering, who stormed at Lawford's Gate..presently entered. *Ibid.*, The Major-General's regiment being to storm towards Froom River. **1859** Hawthorne *Fr. & It. Note-bks.* (1872) II. 267 A great gap in the ramparts—it may have been a breach which was once stormed through. **1860** Froude *Hist. Eng.* V. 207 Again the next day they stormed up to the walls. **1877** Tennyson *Harold* v. i, Our javelins Answer their arrows. All the Norman foot Are storming up the hill.

b. *transf.* To rush with violence.

1837 Carlyle *Fr. Rev.* I. ii. vii, How, in this wild Universe, which storms in on him..shall poor man find.. footing to stand on. **1863** Longf. *Wayside Inn*, i. *Falcon* 98 The boy, rejoicing in his strength, Stormed down the terraces from length to length. **1870** Tyndall *Fragm. Sci.* (1879) I. v. 133 On placing the flame at some distance below the beam, the same dark masses stormed upwards.

Hence **stormed** *ppl. a.*, taken by storm.

1841 James *Brigand* ii, The cold wind rushed in fiercely like a besieging army into a stormed city. **1888** E. A. Freeman *Four Oxf. Lect.* 95 It is our one recorded example of the fate of a stormed town.

stormable (ˈstɔːməb(ə)l), *a.* [f. storm *v.* + -able.] That can be taken by storm.

1645 Cromwell *Let.* 6 Oct. in *Carlyle* (1845) I. 233 We.. made a breach in the wall near the Black Tower, which after about 200 shot, we thought stormable, and purposed on Monday morning to attempt it. **1829** Shipp *Mem.* II. 185 The breaches began to wear a stormable appearance. **1885** *Where Chineses Drive* 162 It was surrounded by a moat, and not easily stormable.

† **stor'matical, 'stormical**, *adjs. Obs. nonce-words.* [See -atic and -ical.] Stormy. (Invented to render F. *bourrasqueux.*)

1634 W. Tirwhyt tr. *Balzac's Lett.* (vol. I.) 91 Should I ..sayle vpon the Ocean in the stormaticall seasons of the yeare [Fr. *ès bourrasqueuses saisons de l'année*]. **1654** Baker tr. *Balzac's Lett.* i. 31 In the stormical seasons of the year.

stormer (ˈstɔːmə(r)). [f. storm *v.* + -er¹.]

1. One who storms or rages; one who makes a wild agitation.

1617 Collins *Def. Bp. Ely* ii. ix. 358 The Iesuites, those stormers against the authoritie of heathen Magistrates ouer beleeuers. **1886** *Pall Mall Gaz.* 10 Feb. 8/1, I wish we could make people see that we are not merely wild stormers, but that we have definite, sober economic theories.

2. One who takes by storm; a member of a storming party.

1655 Earl Orrery *Parthen.* ii. ii. III. 148 The Assaliants admir'd to finde the Breach so well defended,..but the Day no sooner appear'd than the Stormers wonder ceas'd by another. **1828–40** Napier *Penins. War* xvi. v. (Rtldg.) II. 362 On the breach, at the head of the stormers. **1889** J. G. Alger *Englishmen in Fr. Rev.* 52 The widows and orphans of the stormers of the Tuileries.

stormful (ˈstɔːmfʊl), *a.* [f. storm *sb.* + -ful.] Abounding in or subject to storms; tempestuous, stormy. *lit.* and *fig.* (A favourite word with Carlyle.)

1558 Phaer *Æneid* viii. (1562) Bbiij, Store of strugling wynds & stormful clouds of cloddid raine. **1591** Sylvester *Du Bartas* i. v. 576 From jeopardy Of stormfull Seas. a **1756** Collins *Superstit. Highlands* 67 They know what spirit brews the stormful day. **1837** Carlyle *Fr. Rev.* II. v. xi, This Camp of Twenty-thousand, could it be other than of stormfullest Sansculottes? **1883** J. Payn *Kit* xxxii, To shape his thoughts in less vehement and stormful fashion.

Hence **'stormfully** *adv.*, **'stormfulness.**

1831 Carlyle *Sartor Res.* ii. iii, With a stormfulness.. under which the boldest quailed. *Ibid.* iii. viii, We..haste stormfully across the astonished Earth. **1904** M. Maclean *Lit. Celts* xviii. 350 A hundred and sixty years pass stormfully by.

stormical: see s.v. stormatical.

stormily (ˈstɔːmɪlɪ), *adv.* In 5 **stormely**. [f. stormy + -ly².] In a stormy manner.

c **1450** *Mirk's Festial* 205 þe wynde [began] stormely forto blow. **1830** De Quincey *Bentley* Wks. 1862 VI. 39 My own belief sets in stormily towards the same conclusion. **1847** C. Brontë *Jane Eyre* ii, Her cap flying wide, her gown rustling stormily. **1860** Froude *Hist. Eng.* V. 344 The interview ended stormily. **1889** Mary E. Carter *Mrs. Severn* iii. ix, The sky was stormily beautiful.

storminess (ˈstɔːmɪnɪs). [f. stormy + -ness.] Stormy quality.

1587 Golding *De Mornay* xi. 180 The storminesse thereof [*sc.* of the wind]. **1631** T. Powell *Tom of All Trades* 3 The stormynesse of the sea of state. **1796** *Ann. Reg.* (Otridge), *Hist. Europe* 198/2 The storminess of the weather increased to such a degree, that..the French admiral determined to quit his position. **1894** Jeaffreson *Bk. Recoll.* I. ii. 27 School-boys..never feared the capricious storminess of his freakish..irritability. **1913** Gretton *Mod. Hist.* I. xii. 284 The shock had added to the storminess of events.

storming (ˈstɔːmɪŋ), *vbl. sb.* [-ing¹.] The action of the vb. storm.

1461 *Bale's Chron.* in *Six Town Chron.* (1911) 137 The last day of novembr was a marvelous and dredful sturmyng and noys of the comones and of lordes men at Westminster. **1622** J. Taylor (Water P.) *Shilling* C5b, Such storming, fretting, fuming. **1661** *Reg. Privy Counc. Scot.* Ser. iii. I. 26 Gunnis taken..at the stormeing of Dundy. **1667** J. Caryl *Eng. Princess* ii. v. 20 Slow Treaties will to stormings him oblige, Who leisure wants to take the Fort by Siege. a **1774** W. Whitehead *Epist. form Grove* 11 For here, for all my master's storming, I'm sure we strangely want reforming. **1913** G. Edmundson *Church in Rome in 1st Cent.* vi. 169 The storming and burning of the Capitol by the foreign mercenaries of Vitellius.

storming (ˈstɔːmɪŋ), *ppl. a.* [-ing².]

1. That storms or rages.

1557 *Tottel's Misc.* (Arb.) 242 And all my storming dayes be past, and weather waxeth faire. **1591** Spenser *Ruins of Time* 404 Wise words..Recorded by the Muses, liue for ay; Ne may with storming showers be washt away. **1619** A. Newman *Pleasures Vision* 10 Blowne and tost, like ships in storming wind. **1622** J. Taylor (Water P.) *Farew. Tower Bottles* A4b, Showring hayleshot, from the storming heau'n. **1837** Carlyle *Fr. Rev.* III. v. v, A dumb inarticulately storming Whirlwind of things. **1852** Tennyson *Ode Death Wellington* 155 Thank Him who isled us here, and roughly set His Briton in blown seas and storming showers. **1905** *Daily Chron.* 14 July 3/1 The learned doctor is in a storming fury.

absol. **1712** Steele *Spect.* No. 438 ¶4 The Hectoring, the Storming, the Sullen, and all the different Species and Subordinations of the Angry.

2. That attacks in order to take by storm; chiefly in ***storming party***.

1802 C. James *Milit. Dict.*, *Storming Party*, a select body of men, consisting generally of the grenadiers, who first enter the breach, &c. **1829** Shipp *Mem.* II. 185 The storming parties were ordered to be in readiness about two o'clock. **1864** Skeat *Uhland's Poems* 69 The storming hosts rush on. **1894** Wolseley *Life Marlborough* II. lxv. 195 The ecstasy of reckless daring which takes possession of the soldier in a storming party. **1894** Blackmore *Perlycross* xi, Three old Officers..brave men as ever led a storming column.

Hence **'stormingly** *adv.*

a **1600** Hooker *Wks.* (1888) II. 593 But there are, whose stubborn spirits will..hereupon stormingly reply.

† **'stormish**, *a. Obs. rare.* [f. storm *sb.* + -ish¹.] Stormy.

c **1430** Lydg. *Min. Poems* (Percy Soc.) 245 Stormysshe as Marche, with chaungis ful sodeyne. **1530** Palsgr. 326/1 Stormysshe, stormy as the wether is, *tempesteux*.

stormless (ˈstɔːmlɪs), *a.* [f. storm *sb.* + -less.] Free from storms.

c **1500** Q. Shaw in Pinkerton *Anc. Sc. Poems* (1786) I. 133 Tho the air be fair, and stormles. **1591** Sylvester *Du Bartas* i. v. 918 Whatsoever other Monster haunts In Storm-less Seas. **1765** J. Brown *Chr. Jrnl.* 73 That I might enter into endless calms of peace, and stormless mansions of felicity. **1819** R. Sheil *Evadne* iii. i. 42 May your days, Like a long stormless summer, glide away. **1867** Swinburne in *Fortn. Rev.* Oct. 422 That unfooted grove of the God, sunless and stormless in all seasons of wind or sun.

Stormont (ˈstɔːmɒnt). The name of a suburb of Belfast, used to denote: (*a*) the administration presided over by the Secretary of State for Northern Ireland (the Northern Ireland Office), housed at Stormont Castle; (*b*) the Northern Ireland parliament which met at the Parliament House in the grounds of Stormont Castle from 1920 until its suspension in 1972.

1934 H. Maxwell *Ulster was Right* 9 The Act which created Stormont provided also for a similar Parliament in Dublin. **1935** *Frontier Sentinel* 22 June 4/4 The strongest supporter of Stormont rule. **1938** *Irish News* 3 Feb. 2/3 Stormont is not a de jure Government. **1949** St. J. Ervine *Craigavon Ulsterman* iii. x. 418 Some very queer fish have been elected to Stormont,..but Stormont, at its worst, has never declined to the depths of Leinster House. **1957** *Times* 9 Dec. p. ii/3 The Government of Northern Ireland Act by which Stormont was established in 1920 was not a response to local demands. **1971** H. Wilson *Labour Govt.* xxxv. 719 Our own back-benchers expressing their criticisms of Stormont and the Unionists in speeches designed to strengthen the arm of the Home Secretary. **1972** *Guardian* 25 Mar. 1/2 Mr Brian Faulkner, who has been Northern Ireland's sixth Prime Minister..will tender his resignation on Tuesday... He will end the existence of that..provincial assembly which has become known..by the name of the building where the Parliament sits—Stormont. **1975** *Times* 10 Sept. 1/3 Stormont officials attempted to put a brave face on the situation.

'storm-trooper. Also **storm trooper, stormtrooper.** [f. as next + -er¹.] **1.** A member of the storm-troops, esp. the Nazi S.A.

1933 *Palestine Post* 2 Apr. 4/1 The Nazi storm-troopers at noon on Friday, cleared the Berlin law courts of Jewish judges. **1941** B. Schulberg *What makes Sammy Run?* vi.

101 'Jews,' he said bitterly..like a storm-trooper. **1958** *Listener* 14 Aug. 238/2 The Nazi storm-trooper. **1973** R. LACEY *Sir Walter Raleigh* xvii. 129 The ordinary English levies..were no match for the Spanish stormtroopers. **1976** J. MCCLURE *Rogue Eagle* iii. 57 Formidable fellow like Vorster, ex-stormtrooper general. **1977** A. ECCLESTONE *Staircase for Silence* v. 89 He did not foresee a time when.. stormtroopers and commandos would appear.

2. *transf.* and *fig.*

1943 C. HIMES *Black on Black* (1973) 220, I suppose you have been reading about the birth of the storm troopers in Los Angeles, the reincarnation, or rather I should say, the *continuation* of the vigilantes, the uniformed Klansmen. **1956** R. MACAULAY *Towers of Trebizond* ii. 23 Some of the leaflets had 'Catholic Commandos' printed on them, and others 'Protestant Storm Troopers', and Father Chantry-Pigg did not know which of these two bands of warriors he disliked most. **1958** *Spectator* 1 Aug. 163/2 The toughest Nationalists, Plaid Cymru's Storm Troopers. **1976** *Birmingham Post* 16 Dec. 4/1 The Gay movement in the city is concerned about a kind of creeping apathy coming over some of its former storm-troopers. **1978** M. PAGE *Pilate Plot* (1979) x. 160 A place within..easy reach in which Von Hassen's storm-troopers would find their activities heavily restricted.

'storm-troops, *sb. pl.* Also storm troops. [tr. G. *sturmtruppen.*] **1. a.** = *shock troops* s.v. SHOCK *sb.*[3] 8 b. Also *fig.*

1917 *Punch* 27 June 409/3 Special 'storm troops'—men picked for their youth, vigour and daring, to carry out counter-attacks—are now a feature of the German Armies. **1922** C. E. MONTAGUE *Disenchantment* ix. 125 Canadians and Australians..were the 'storm troops', the men who had to be sent for to do the tough jobs. **1924** J. ROSS *Years of My Pilgrimage* xxx. 283, I had heard from my friend, Sir Henry Wilson, F.M., that the use of storm troops was an extravagant way of utilizing men. **1933** J. BUCHAN *Prince of Captivity* III. i. 274 They were violent German nationalists ..true storm-troops, ready for any forlorn hope and prepared to use any means however devilish. **1943** C. DAY LEWIS *Word over All* 42 Spent as storm-troops after defeat or triumph, Deeply indifferent. **1973** *Black Panther* 11 Aug. 8/3 Tommassi said he was offered $5,000 to use his storm troops as registrars.

b. *spec.* The troops of the Nazi STURMABTEILUNG.

1923 *Times* 15 Jan. 10/4 Bands of 'storm troops' paraded the streets, singing the Fascist war songs. **1933** *Granta* 26 Apr. 370/1 We believe that only now has come the time to see these issues in themselves, out of the context of cruelty and outrage which Herr Hitler's storm-troops created for them. **1954** B. & R. NORTH tr. *M. Duverger's Pol. Parties* I. i. 36 In the case of the National Socialist Storm Troops the initial element was the squad (*schar*). **1982** T. KENEALLY *Schindler's Ark* xxxiii. 344 An influential officer in the S.A. (the Sturmabteilung, or Storm Troops).

2. *sing.* **a.** A branch or detachment of storm troops.

1935 [see NAZI *a.*]. **1938** J. CARY *Castle Corner* 483 A soldier picked by lot for the storm troop.

b. *attrib.*

1939 S. SPENDER tr. *E. Toller's Pastor Hall* I. 14 Go and ask the Stormtroop Leader to come in. **1958** *Times* 3 Sept. 11/3 The outbreaks will have served a useful purpose if they oblige the public to understand that the Storm Troop mentality exists in England, too. **1981** *Listener* 2 July 7/1 Röhm..was jailed on 29 June [1934] by a worried Heines, and other storm-troop leaders..were due to arrive the next day.

Hence **'storm-troop** *v. intr.*, to behave in an aggressive manner like storm-troops; so **'storm-trooping** *ppl. a.*

1960 *News Chron.* 5 Jan. 4/5 The storm-trooping bird-brains of Notting Hill. **1974** *Times* 10 May 22/6 The National Union of Students goes storm-trooping about the country's universities suppressing..freedom of speech. **1977** *Sounds* 9 July 31/3 This is the nucleus of the band, who charge in with a stormtroopin' instrumental romp through the Byrds 'Eight Miles High'.

stormy ('stɔːmɪ), *a.* [f. STORM *sb.* + -Y.]

1. Of the weather, season, air, sky, sea, etc.: Characterized by storm or tempest; tempestuous. Of a place or region: Subject to storms.

a **1200** in *Anglia* XI. 369 Hit byð..windiȝ sumer and storemiȝ and ȝeswyncfull hærfest. *a* **1300** *Cursor M.* 22691 A stormi dai, a stret of au. ? *a* **1366** CHAUCER *Rom. Rose* 455 And if the wedir stormy were For colde she shulde haue deyd there. **1390** GOWER *Conf.* I. 35 Now be the stormy wynter shoures. **1535** COVERDALE *Ps.* liv. 8, I wolde make haist to escape, from the stormy wynde and tempest. **1590** SPENSER *F.Q.* III. viii. 21 And all his windes Dan Aeolus did keepe, From stirring vp their stormy enmitie. **1637** MILTON *Lycidas* 156 Beyond the stormy Hebrides. **1764** GOLDSM. *Trav.* 167 Where the bleak Swiss their stormy mansions tread. **1799** J. ROBERTSON *Agric. Perth* 356 The wildest and most stormy mountains in Scotland. **1860** TYNDALL *Glaciers* I. xxiii. 164 A wild stormy morning. **1885** *Manch. Exam.* 15 May 5/6 An Atlantic steamer..ploughing its course across stormy oceans.

2. *fig.* Of persons, their temper or looks; of times, events, circumstances, etc.

a **1340** HAMPOLE *Psalter* Prol. 3 Now with halesome lare drouyd & stormy saules it bryngis in til clere & pesful lyf. *c* **1374** CHAUCER *Troylus* II. 778 For loue is yet þe meste stormy lyf. *c* **1386** —— *Clerk's T.* 939 O Stormy peple, vnsad, and euere vntrewe. **1412-20** LYDG. *Chron. Troy* I. 2245 His stormy cruel aventure. *Ibid.* III. 4079 Allas! Fortune,..Whan folk most triste in þi stormy face..þanne is þi Ioye aweye to turne & wryþe. **1592** *Arden of Feversham* III. v. 113 Nothing shall hide me from thy stormy looke. **1597** SHAKS. *2 Hen. IV*, I. i. 164 Your health, the which if you giue-o're To stormy Passion, must perforce decay. **1641** J. JACKSON *True Evang. T.* iii. 193 That Religion which is more turbulent, seditious, and stormy, let it be throwne over-board to lighten the ship of the Church. **1700** DRYDEN *Cymon & Iph.* 257 While stormy Cymon thus in secret said [etc.]. **1831** GREVILLE *Mem.* (1874) II. 153 There was.. every promise of a stormy session. **1849** MACAULAY *Hist. Eng.* ii. I. 223 Shaftesbury and Buckingham..appeared at the head of the stormy democracy of the city. **1891** SMILES *Mem. J. Murray* I. xvii. 443 The discussion was long and stormy before the meeting broke up. **1915** J. KELMAN *Salted with Fire* iv. 40 In the stormy times in which his lot was cast emergencies were constantly arising.

b. *Path.* of inflammation.

1899 *Allbutt's Syst. Med.* VI. 903 Meningitis is usually so stormy in its manifestation that [etc.].

3. Associated or connected with storms; indicative, predictive, or symbolical of storms. *poet.*

1560 ROLLAND *Seven Sages* 24 Anone thay spy into the Firmament Ane stormie sterne that troublit thair Intent. **1697** DRYDEN *Virg. Georg.* I. 419 Now sing we stormy Stars. **1761** GLOVER *Medea* v. v. 94 Grim Neptune yonder shakes his stormy trident. **1842** TENNYSON *Sir Galahad* 25 When down the stormy crescent goes.

b. *stormy petrel*: the bird *Procellaria pelagica.* Also *fig.*, a person who delights in strife, or whose appearance on the scene is a harbinger of coming trouble.

1776 PENNANT *Zool.* II. 553 Stormy Petrel. **1847** LD. CAMPBELL *Chancellors* ccviii. VII. 479 Eldon..came to London..on account of rumours of a dissolution of the Ministry. He went, with some, by the name of the 'Stormy Petrel', being supposed to delight in such convulsions. **1892** *World* 6 Apr. 15 (Brewer), Dr. von Esmarch [a physician] is regarded at court as a stormy petrel, and every effort was made to conceal his visit to the German emperor.

4. Relating to or concerned with storms. *poet.*

1725 POPE *Odyss.* I. 232 A duteous people, and industrious Isle, To naval arts inur'd, and stormy toil.

storne, obs. form of STERN *sb.*[1]

‖**stornello** (stɔːˈnɛləʊ). Pl. stornelli (-liː). [It.] A short popular Italian lyric, usually improvised.

1873 'OUIDA' *Pascarel* I. iv. 57 Many and many a time.. I have..repeated the stornelli to an enthusiastic circle of blacksmiths [etc.]. **1885** *Encycl. Brit.* XIX. 272/2 Most of the Italian rispetti and stornelli seem to be improvisations.

storoppe, obs. form of STIRRUP.

storre, obs. form of STAR *sb.*[1], STIR *v.*, STOUR *a.*

storrie, obs. form of STORY *sb.*[2]

storrope, obs. form of STIRRUP.

stort, error for SCART *sb.*[1] (cormorant).

1635 BRERETON *Jrnl.* (Surtees 1914) 26 (Bass Rock) Abundance of fowle breed here: solem geese: storts: [etc.].

storte, obs. form of START *sb.*[1]

Storting ('stɔəˌtɪŋ). Also **Storthing.** [Norw. *storting*, formerly *-thing*, f. *stor* great + *ting, thing* assembly (see THING *sb.*[2]); cf. ON. *stórþing* œcumenical council.] The Norwegian parliament.

1834 S. LAING *Jrnl. Resid. Norway* (1836) 115 The Parliament, or Storthing, is elected and assembled once in three years, and sits for three months, or until the business is dispatched. **1840** R. G. LATHAM *Norway & Norwegians* II. 86 The thus elected Representatives shall constitute the Storting of the Kingdom of Norway. **1893** *Nation* (N.Y.) 21 Aug. 153/3 If a bill is passed unchanged by three successive Storthings, it becomes law without the royal sanction. **1955** *Times* 23 June 11/6 King Haakon VII..was formally elected by the Storting, the Norwegian Parliament, on November 18, 1905. **1964** *Ann. Reg. 1963* 267 The Storting on 28 March passed a Bill concerning Norway's participation in a common defence system for the European section of NATO. **1977** *Time* 26 Sept. 17/3 From the beginning, the race for control of the Storting (Parliament) had been regarded by most Norwegians as a 'destiny election' for the Labor Party's brand of socialism.

†**'stortkyn, 'stotterkyn.** *Obs.* [Form uncertain; perh. a corruption of some Du. word; see -KIN.] Some measure of quantity.

1501 *Acc. Ld. High Treas. Scot.* II. 28 Giffin for ij stortkynnys of girthis, ilk ane contenand xxxiiij skeynȝeis; ilk stotterkin xvij s.; summa xxxiiij s.

†**'storven,** *ppl. a. Obs.* [regular str. pa. pple. of STARVE *v.* Cf. STARVEN *ppl. a.*] Dead; also *absol.* Also of an animal: That has died of disease.

a **1225** *Leg. Kath.* 1043 He wið his steuene þe storuene astearde. **1390** GOWER *Conf.* I. 194 Riht as of an hungri Pie The storve bestes ben awaited. **1482** [see GALL-BITTEN *a.*].

story ('stɔərɪ), *sb.*[1] Pl. stories ('stɔərɪz). Forms: 3-7 storie, 4 *Sc.* stoury, 4-5 store, 4-6 stori, 5-7 storye, 5 stoory, 4- story. *Pl.* 4 storis, storijs, -yss(e, 4-5 storys, -yies, stor(r)ius, 4-7 storyes, 6 storeis, storyis, 4- stories. [a. AF. *estorie* (OF. *estoire*, later in semi-learned form *histoire*):—L. *historia*: see HISTORY. Cf. It. and med.L. *storia.*]

I. † **1. a.** A narrative, true or presumed to be true, relating to important events and celebrated persons of a more or less remote past; a historical relation or anecdote. *Obs.*

In early use the most frequent application was to passages of Bible history and legends of saints. In quot. 1303, although the possessive denotes authorship, the sb. prob. retains the general sense.

a **1225** *Ancr. R.* 154 Me schal, leoue sustren, tellen ou þeos storie [*v.r.* storien] uor hit were to long to writen ham here. *a* **1300** *Havelok* 1641 þat sholen ye forthward ful wel leren [*MS.* heren], Yif þat ye wile þe storie heren. *a* **1300** *Cursor M.* 3410 Now es god at vnder tak þe store tell of ysaac. **1303** R. BRUNNE *Handl. Synne* 11452 She chese þat vertu, oure lady, So seyþ magnificat, here owne storye [Fr. *En Magnificat qe ele feseit*]. **1320-30** *Horn Ch.* 4 Stories ye may lere Of our elders that were Whilom in this land. *c* **1380** WYCLIF *Sel. Wks.* I. 71 A storye of Joon Baptiste. *c* **1386** CHAUCER *Prol.* 709 He was in chirche a noble ecclesiaste, Wel koude he rede a lesson or a storie But alderbest he song an Offertorie. *c* **1400** MAUNDEV. (Roxb.) ii. 6 As þe story of Noe beres witness. **1526** *Pilgr. Perf.* (W. de W. 1531) 5 Whan they here the precher..reherse ony fygures or storyes of the lawe of Moyses. **1559** *Mirr. Mag.*, *Richard Earl of Camb.* Introd., By that this was ended, I had found out the storie of Richard earle of Cambridge. **1621** BURTON *Anat. Mel.* III. iii. III. (1624) 480 Paulus Æmilius..hath a Tragicall story of Chilpericus the first his death. *a* **1628** PRESTON *Breastpl. Love* (1631) 152 David had many great infirmities, as we see in the whole story, the whole relation of his life. **1642** JER. TAYLOR *Episc.* (1647) 25 So they being sent forth by the holy Ghost, departed into Seleucia. This is the story, now let us make our best on't.

†**b.** ***Clerk of the Stories***: Petrus Comestor, the author of the *Historia Scholastica.* Also ***Master in*** or ***of the Stories***: see MASTER *sb.* 12 b.

1362 LANGL. *P. Pl.* B. VII. 73 Catoun kenneth men þus and þe clerke of þe stories. **1387** TREVISA *Higden* (Rolls) I. 65 þe Maister of the stories sayth. [**1450** *Harl. transl.*, *ibid.*, After the Maister in storyes.]

†**c.** A historical incident. *Obs.*

c **1449** PECOCK *Repr.* II. xiii. 225 Euereither of these stories were doon eer eny lawe was ȝouun to the Iewis.

†**2.** A historical work, a book of history. *Obs.*

13.. *Coer de L.* 4852 And as I fynde in hys story, He seygh come St. George, the knyght, Upon a stede good and lyght. **1338** R. BRUNNE *Chron.* (1810) 51 A thousand was þe date & sex & pritty, Whan Knoute kyng died, so sais þe story. **1340-70** *Alex. & Dind.* 467 We raiken to oure romancus & reden þe storrius þat oure eldrene on erþe or þis time wroute. **1387** TREVISA *Higden* (Rolls) I. 297 Herodotus þe writer of stories. *Ibid.* II. 7 This Britayne is acounted an holy lond bothe in oure stories and also in stories of Grees. *c* **1440** *Generydes* 3481 Generides his swarde toke in his hande, Claryet it hight, the store tellith me so. *c* **1449** PECOCK *Repr.* III. xii. 351 Ech fundamental storie speking of this said voice seith and storieth, that [etc.]. **1574** WHITGIFT *Def. Aunsw.* II. 98 And yet in lawfull matters, not expressed in the Scriptures, I know not to whome we should resorte to know the vse and antiquitie of them, but to the Councels, stories, and doctors. **1634** PEACHAM *Compl. Gentl.* xv. (1906) 186 Ordericus Vitalis the Monke, in his Normane Story saith. **1684-5** SOUTH *Serm.* (1715) I. 304 Examples of this, we have both in Holy Writ, and also in other Stories. **1708** CHAMBERLAYNE *St. Gt. Brit.* I. III. x. (1743) 220 Records of this Nation, without which no Story of the Nation can be written or proved. **1756** AMORY *Buncle* (1825) I. i. 17 When I had done with antient history, I sat down to the best modern stories I could get, and read of distant nations.

†**3.** In generalized sense: Historical writing or records; history as a branch of knowledge, or as opposed to fiction. Also, the events recorded or proper to be recorded by historians: = HISTORY *sb.* 4 c. *Obs.*

a **1300** *Cursor M.* 7038 In grece þan regned Preamus As ald stori telles vs. **13..** *K. Alis.* 670 (Laud MS.) þis is nouȝth romaunce of skof, Ac storye ymade of maistres wyse. **1387** TREVISA *Higden* (Rolls) II. 345 Verrey storie [L. *vera historia*] seiþ þat Saturnus þe fader and Iupiter þe sone hadde twie kingdomes [etc.]. *c* **1430** LYDG. *Min. Poems* (Percy Soc.) 85 The chieldren of Seth in story ye may se, Flowryng in vertu by longe successiouns. **1568** ABP. PARKER *Let.* 4 July *Corr.* (1853) 328 In story it is reported that the prince of the realm by right is not *Dominus Hiberniæ*, but *Rex Hiberniæ.* **1570-6** LAMBARDE *Peramb. Kent* (1826) 89, I will shewe you out of Beda and others the content and storie of this Ile. **1611** BIBLE *Transl. Pref.* ¶ 1 As many as know story, or haue any experience. **1612** SELDEN *Illustr. Drayton's Poly-olb.* XI. 379 As Robert of Glocester, according to truth of Story hath it. *a* **1626** BACON *Sp. Speaker's Excuse* Wks. 1778 II. 242 This is no part of a panegyric, but merely story. **1644** MILTON *Areop.* (Arb.) 54 Who is so unread or so uncatechis'd in story, that hath not heard of many sects refusing books as a hindrance. **1647** WARD *Simple Cobler* (1843) 2 Those that are acquainted with Story know. **1666** DRYDEN *Ann. Mirab.* Pref. ¶ 1 The destruction being so swift..as nothing can parallel in Story. **1692** PRIOR *Ode Imit. Hor.* xii, 'Tis no Poet's Thought, no flight of Youth, But solid Story, and severest Truth. **1728** MORGAN *Algiers* I. iv. 93 Have we not any Instances in Story of some such-like Deportment practised by politer and more refined Nations? **1768** H. WALPOLE *Hist. Doubts* 20 With every intention of vindicating Richard, he does but authenticate his crimes, by searching in other story for parallel instances of what he calls policy.

4. a. A recital of events that have or are alleged to have happened; a series of events that are or might be narrated.

1375 BARBOUR *Bruce* I. 1 Storys to rede ar delitabill, Suppos that thai be nocht bot fabill: Than suld storyss that suthfast wer,..Hawe doubill plesance in heryng. *c* **1400** *Destr. Troy* 419 Ouyd, þat feynit in his fablis & other fele stories. **1594** SHAKS. *Rich. III*, IV. iii. 8 Dighton and Forrest, whom I did suborne To do this peece of ruthfull Butchery, ..Wept like to Children, in their deaths sad Story. **1602** tr. *Guarini's Pastor Fido* v. I. N 3 b, But twilbe too Too troublesome to tell the storie of my life. **1653** LD. VAUX tr. *Godeau's St. Paul* 44 But to understand this better, tis necessary we take the course of this Story a little higher. **1667** MILTON *P.L.* VII. 51 He with his consorted Eve The storie heard attentive. **1725** POPE *Odyss.* XXIII. 324 Intent he hears Penelope disclose A mournful story of domestic woes. **1796** H. HUNTER tr. *St. Pierre's Study Nat.* (1799) II. 247, I shall give this story in the simplicity of style of the old Translator of Pliny. **1843** PRESCOTT *Mexico* VI. viii. (1864) 407 The whole story has the air of a fable, rather than of history! **1862** MISS BRADDON *Lady Audley* xxxvii, He told the story of George's disappearance, and of his own doubts and fears. **1883** TYLOR in *Encycl. Brit.* XV. 199/1 Among the magi the interpretation of dreams was practised, as appears from the story of the birth of Cyrus.

b. *transf.*

1611 Beaum. & Fl. *Philaster* III. i, How that foolish man, That reads the story of a womans face, And dies believing it, is lost for ever. **1828** Duppa *Trav. Italy*, etc. 3 His [Raffaello's] great and commanding excellence is in..the art of telling a story with such appropriate feeling and expression, as no other artist ever yet approached. **1849** Ruskin *Seven Lamps* vi. §7. 169 Better the rudest work that tells a story or records a fact, than the richest without meaning.

†**c.** Purport, meaning conveyed. *Obs.*

1340–70 *Alex. & Dind.* 609 ȝe ne vndurstonde nouht þat stounde þe storie of þis wordus, þat god hereþ no gome but for his goode dedus, & for no bestene blod. **1399** Langl. *Rich. Redeles* Prol. 82 Þe story is of non estate þat stryuen with her lustus, But þo þat ffolwyn her fflessh.

d. With possessive: A person's account of the events of his life or some portion of it.

1604 Shaks. *Oth.* I. iii. 165 She..bad me, if I had a Friend that lou'd her, I should but teach him how to tell my Story, And that would wooe her. **1663** Tuke *Adv. Five Hours* I. 4 Let's tell our Stories, that we soon shall see, Which of us two excells in Misery. **1667** Milton *P.L.* VIII. 522 Thus have I told thee all my State, and brought My Storie to the sum of earthly bliss Which I enjoy. **1797** [Frere & Canning] *Knife-grinder* in *Anti-Jacobin* No. 2. 15/2 As soon as you have told your Pitiful story. **1818** Scott *Hrt. Midl.* xlvi, 'Ye maun gang up wi' me to the Lodge, Effie,' said Jeanie, 'and tell me a' your story'. **1894** B. Thomson *South Sea Yarns* 81 And then she told him her whole story.

e. With possessive or followed by *of*: The series of events in the life of a person or the past existence of a thing, country, institution, etc., considered as narrated or as a subject for narration. Also in catch-phrase ***that's the story of my life***, etc., used of something that supposedly epitomizes one's life or experience.

Originally = history 4b; but in modern use (from association with sense 5) implying that the course of events referred to has the kind of interest which it is the aim of fiction to create. (So often in titles of books.)

a **1700** Evelyn *Diary* 6 Sept. 1676, The famous beauty and errant lady the Dutchesse of Mazarine (all the world knows her story). **1711** Swift *Cond. Allies* 65 The Prudence, Courage and Firmness of Her Majesty..would, if the Particulars were truly related, make a very shining Part in Her Story. **1712** Addison *Hymn* in *Spect.* No. 465 The Moon..nightly..Repeats the Story of her Birth. **1734** tr. *Rollin's Anc. Hist.* (1827) II. III. 161 Several other Kings of Babylon with whose story we are entirely unacquainted. **1878** Herford (*title*) The Story of Religion in England. **1885** L. Oliphant *Sympneumata* 135 The story of woman upon earth has been different from the beginning to that of man. **1888** E. Clodd (*title*), The Story of Creation. **1898** 'Merriman' *Roden's Corner* i. 10 Many objects in the room had a story, had been in the daily use of hands long since vanished. **1910** J. McCabe *Prehist. Man.* i. 14 If we take the entire story of the stratified rocks to extend to over 55 million years. **1964** *Punch* 11 Mar. 385/3 It's the story of my life—looking for small watch-straps. **1969** *Time* 30 May 22/3 In 13 years, he's been a hard-liner in criminal cases. That's the story of his life.

5. a. A narrative of real or, more usually, fictitious events, designed for the entertainment of the hearer or reader; a series of traditional or imaginary incidents forming the matter of such a narrative; a tale.

Often applied more or less *spec.* to a tale told to children, a nursery tale, and to a tale handed down by popular oral tradition, a folk-tale (the two classes partly coincide). When denoting a literary composition, the word is sometimes applied to a long work of fiction, a romance or novel, esp. when considered with reference to its series of incidents (cf. c), but more commonly to a short tale or novelette.

1500–20 Dunbar *Poems* lvii. 7 Sum singis, sum dancis, sum tellis storeis. **1597** J. King *Jonas* (1618) 355 Now wee haue Arcadia, and the Faery Queene, and Orlando Furioso, with such like friuolous stories. ?**1605** Drayton *Poems Lyr. & Past.* Eglog vi. F 1, Summers longst day shall sheepheards not suffice to sit and tell full storyes of thy prayse. **1632** Milton *L'Allegro* 101 With stories told of many a feat, How Faery Mab the junkets eat. **1692** S. Shaw *Diff. Humours Men* 30, I doubt you would be laught at as bad as the Crow in the Story. **1866** Freeman *Hist. Ess.* Ser. I. (1871) 9 A romance without a shadow of truth may be exquisitely beautiful as a story. **1867** Max Müller *Chips* (1880) II. xxii. 213 Stories become extinct like dodos and megatheria. **1886** *Morning Post* 8 Sept. Bk.-review, It is a brilliant story..which will be avidly read.

b. In generalized sense: Traditional, poetic, or romantic legend or history.

1794 Mrs. Radcliffe *Myst. Udolpho* xxxv, She almost fancied herself approaching a castle, such as is often celebrated in early story, where the knights look out from the battlements on some champion below. **1796** Watson *Apol. Bible* 40 They are sensible that the gospel miracles are so different, in all their circumstances, from those related in pagan story. **1802** Wordsw. *To the Small Celandine* 6 Long as there are violets, They will have a place in story. **1816** Scott *Bl. Dwarf* ii, Old Martin Elliot of the Preakin-tower, noted in Border story and song. *a* **1839** Praed *Poems* (1864) II. 11 Or die in fight, to live in story. **1855** Lynch *Rivulet* LXXXII. i, Breathe on us for the passing day The powers of ancient story.

c. Succession of incidents, 'plot' (of a novel, poem, or drama).

1715 Parnell *Pope's Iliad* I. *Ess. Homer* 38 While his Works were suffer'd to lie in an unconnected manner, the Chain of Story was not always perceiv'd, so that they lost much of their Force and Beauty by being read disorderly. **1772** Johnson in *Boswell* (1904) I. 455 Why, Sir, if you were to read Richardson for the story, your impatience would be so much fretted that you would hang yourself. **1779** *Mirror* No. 31 The great error..into which novel-writers commonly fall, is, that they attend more to the story and to the circumstances they relate, than to giving new and just views of the character of the person they present. **1868** D. Cook *Nts. at the Play* (1883) I. 88 Sundry bursts of patriotic oratory..close the second act effectively, but otherwise help the story in no way. **1877** *Ibid.* II. 159 The story set forth by the play. **1897** *Strand Mag.* Dec. 634/2 As the life of the body is the blood, so the life of the novel is the 'story'. **1902** A. Dobson *S. Richardson* iv. 94 In *Grandison*..the movement of the story for the most part advances no more than a rocking-horse.

d. An incident, real or fictitious, related in conversation or in written discourse in order to amuse or interest, or to illustrate some remark made; an anecdote. ***good story***: often, an amusing anecdote.

a **1679** J. Ward *Diary* (1839) 129, I have heard a merrie storie of a certain scholar, that [etc.]. **1771** *Junius Lett.* lxvii. 331 The following story will serve to illustrate the character of this respectable family. **1779** *Mirror* No. 5 He is as much a pedant as his quondam tutor, who..tells stories out of Herodotus. **1781** Cowper *Conversat.* 203 A story, in which native humour reigns, Is often useful, always entertains. **1858** Hawthorne *Fr. & Ital. Note-bks.* (1871) I. 126, I capped his story by telling him how [etc.]. **1888** Bryce *Amer. Commw.* cxi. III. 597 A deliberate and slow delivery ..has the advantage of making a story or jest tell with more effect.

¶ **e.** Used for: A subject of story. Also, a theme for mirth, a dupe.

1603 Shaks. *Meas. for M.* I. iv. 30 Sir, make me not your storie. **1703** Rowe *Ulysses* IV. i, 'Till I had been a Story to Posterity. **1756** C. Smart tr. *Horace, Epist.* I. xiii. (1826) II. 229 Rather than..turn your paternal name of Asina into a jest; and make yourself a common story [L. *et fabula fias*].

6. a. An allegation, statement; an account or representation of a matter; a particular person's representation of the facts in a case. Phrase, ***the story goes that...***: it is reported. ***to be all in one story, to be in the same story***: (of a number of persons) to agree in their account of a matter (usually implying collusion).

1601 Shaks. *All's Well* v. iii. 229 The story then goes false, you threw it him Out of a Casement. **1653** Ramesey *Astrol. Restored* 28 Inventing and affirming detracting and most abusive speeches and stories. **1661** Pr. Rupert in *11th Rep. Hist. MSS. Comm.* App. v. 7 The stori is this, the Elector Pallatin hath ben pleased to write to a Prive Consellor of this court [Vienna] in these terms [etc.]. *a* **1670** [S. Collins] *Pres. St. Russia* (1671) 41 But as the story goes, she fail'd of her promise. **1686** tr. *Chardin's Trav. Persia* 159, I kept constant to this story, not knowing any better way to conceal my self. **1700** N. Rous in *Jrnl. Friends' Hist. Soc.* (1912) IX. 184, I find Brother Dykes continues in his old story. **1760–72** H. Brooke *Fool of Qual.* (1809) I. 24, I find all the world in the same story. **1770** Goldsm. *Des. Vill.* 210 And e'en the story ran that he could gauge. **1775** Sheridan *Duenna* II. iii, I find they are all in a story. **1823** Lockhart *Sp. Ball., Escape of Gayferos* x, And of Gayferos' slaughter a cunning story [they] made. **1833** Greville *Mem.* (1874) II. 340 He [Lyndhurst] told me his story, which differs very little from that which Arbuthnot had told me at Downham. **1838** Dickens *O. Twist* xvii, They're all in one story, Mrs. Mann. That out-dacious Oliver has demogalized them all! **1855** Macaulay *Hist. Eng.* xviii. IV. 234 The Queen..had been informed that stories deeply affecting the character of the navy were in circulation. **1865** Livingstone *Zambesi* v. 126 A Chief..remarked that parties had come before, with as plausible a story as ours. **1898** J. K. Fowler *Rec. Old Times* 114 The story goes that the following colloquy took place. **1905** *Times Lit. Suppl.* 14 July 223/3 Dr. Murray has a slightly different story [of the origin of pasquinade].

†**b.** A mere tale, a baseless report. *Obs.*

1662 J. Davies tr. *Olearius' Voy. Ambass.* 93 Were it granted that this is but a story, as it seems to be no other. **1665** Granvill *Scepsis Sci.* x. 53 And it may be more than a Story, that Nero derived much of his cruelty from the Nurse that suckled him. **1685** Jas. II in *Lond. Gaz.* No. 2006/3 But that is not the onely Story has been made of Me. **1692** Luttrell *Brief Rel.* (1857) II. 376 Merchant letters are silent herein, so hoped to be a story. **1705** E. Ward *Hud. Rediv.* III. iv. 27 Tell 'em, the Church declines in Glory, They cry, they hope 'tis all a Story. **1796** Watson *Apol. Bible* 74 Is it a story, that our first parents fell from a paradisiacal state?

†**c.** ***to make a story***: to cause a scandal. *Obs.*

1652 Dorothy Osborne *Lett. to Sir W. Temple* (1888) 29 He has made a story with a new mistress that is worth your knowing.

d. Phrases. ***the whole story***: the full account of the matter, all that there is to be said. †***to be out of the story***: to misunderstand the state of things. ***(that is) another story***: a matter requiring different treatment. ***(to be) the same story***: a repetition of some occurrence; similarly ***a different story***. ***the old story***: see old *a.* 7e.

1668 Temple *Let. to Ld. Halifax* Wks. 1731 II. 89 There is the whole Story; that you may see how much you are either biass'd, or mistaken in all the rest you say of it. **1778** *Arminian Mag.* I. 194 Alas, Sir, you are as much out of the Story now as ever. **1818** Scott *Heart Midl.* II. xiii. 308 But if she's gaun to look after the kye at St. Leonard's, that's another story. **1865** Ruskin *Sesame* i. §33 If the scientific man comes for a bone or a crust to *us*, that is another story. **1905** *American Mag.* May 107/1 It has been the same story in every strike the man has undertaken, though it has been a longer job in most cases. **1940** A. Christie *Sad Cypress* II. iii. 128 As a matter of fact, it was Nurse O'Brien who set me on the track; but that's another story. **1958** 'Castle' & 'Hailey' *Flight into Danger* i. 20 The met report was reasonable... In a month or so's time it'll be a very different story. **1966** 'H. Calvin' *Italian Gadget* v. 64 'Brains?.. I haven't shown much evidence of them here... But that's another story,' he added hastily. **1979** J. Crosby *Party of Year* xxiii. 146 Let's look at the back stairs.—Same story there... The door was of steel.

e. orig. *U.S.* A narrative or descriptive article in a newspaper; the subject or material for this. Now chiefly = *news story* s.v. news *sb.* (*pl.*) 6b.

1892 *Harper's Weekly* 9 Jan. 42/3 When one reporter is given the whole of a 'story', his instructions always leave him more or less discretion, but when several men are assigned to different parts of one 'story', each one has instructions which must be followed to the letter. **1898** *Scribner's Mag.* May 572 'Where's your story?' asked the city editor. 'There wasn't any story to write,' replied the new reporter, ..'finally the [peace] meeting broke up in a free fight; so I came back, sir.' **1902** Eliz. Banks *Newspaper Girl* 95 A girl artist and I were told by our editor to go out and get up a true story on 'The Hottest Day among the New York Poor'. **1905** E. Wallace *Four Just Men* v. 86 'A very good story,' said the chief complacently, reading the proofs. **1942** *Sphere* 27 June 409/1 Each regional editor acquires stories from his own Embassy or exiled Government as well as sending out his own reporters for stories of special interest to his country. **1961** C. Willock *Death in Covert* xii. 203 One headline said: *Regency Bucks Ride Again*, and the sub-head to the same story complained: *Last time a man was blown up.* **1976** *Task of Broadcasting News* (B.B.C.) II. 17/1 'Story' is only a journalist's professional jargon for an item of news. The proper place for it is a news bulletin.

7. *colloq.* Euphemism for: A lie. Hence (in vulgar use, esp. among children) ***you story!*** = 'you story-teller', 'liar'.

a **1697** Aubrey *Lives, Sir H. Blount* (1898) I. 110 Two young gentlemen that heard Sir H. tell this *sham* so gravely ..told him they wonderd he was not ashamed to tell..storys as, &c. **1740** Richardson *Pamela* II. 272, I believe, Woman, said she, thou tellest me a Story. **1763** Bickerstaff *Love in Village* III. ix, You strike me, because you have been telling his worship stories. **1770** Wesley *Jrnl.* 21 Mar., You were always good Children, and never told stories. **1834** Dickens *Sk. Boz, Steam Excurs.*, The unfortunate little victim was accordingly led below, after receiving sundry thumps on the head from both his parents, for having the wickedness to tell a story. **1854** Miss Baker *Northampt. Gloss.*, *Story*, a softened term for a lie. **1869** *Routledge's Ev. Boy's Ann.* 561 Saying, as the little girls in the streets do, 'Oh, you story!' **1880** Mrs. Lynn Linton *Rebel of Family* II. ix. 201 Now, Eva,..I know all about you, so do not begin to deny and tell stories. **1884** *Life & Lett. Bayard Taylor* I. 11 The boy.. went home, telling his mother that there was no school,—the first and only 'story,' she says, that he ever told her. **1893** W. S. Gilbert *Utopia* II, Oh, you shocking story! **1901** W. Pett Ridge *Lond. Only* ii. 38 'Least bit bandy, surely?' remarked her sister. 'Oh, you story!' exclaimed Rhoda, with indignation. 'His legs are as straight as straight.'

†**II. 8. a.** A painting or sculpture representing a historical subject. Hence, any work of pictorial or sculptural art containing figures. *Obs.* [So med.L. ***historia, storia*** (Du Cange), OF. ***histoire*** (Godef.).]

1388 Wyclif *1 Kings* vii. 24 Tweyne ordris of grauyngis conteynynge summe stories [1382 Two ordris of storye grauyngis: Vulg. *duo ordines sculpturarum striatarum* (? misread *storiatarum*)]. *c* **1400** Maundev. (Roxb.) xxi. 94 In þase platez er storys of kynges and knyghtes and batales. *c* **1449** Pecock *Repr.* II. ii. 139 In the sidis of the same ymage he made stories in ymagerie..as it is open iijᵉ. Reg. vijᵉ. c. *c* **1470** Harding *Chron.* XLI. iv, He died so, and in his temple fayre Entoumbed was, with stories all about. **1533** *Coron. Q. Anne* in *Bibl. Curiosa* (1884) 29 The standarde whiche was costly and sumptuously garnisshed with gold and asure with armes and stories. **1563** B. Googe *Eglogs* etc. (Arb.) 114 The walles were raysed hye And all engraued with Storyes fayre of costlye Imagrye. **1577** Harrison *England* II. v. [II. i.] 76b in *Holinshed*, As for our Churches themselues..all Images,..and monumentes of Idolatry, are remooued,..onely the storyes in glasse windowes excepted. **1610** Holland *Camden's Brit.* (1637) 548 In the walles whereof are engraven the stories of Christs Passion and other things. *a* **1700** Evelyn *Diary* 8 May 1654, I also call'd at Mr. Ducie's, who has indeede a rare collection of the best masters, and one of the largest stories of H. Holbein. *Ibid.* 20 July, The dining-roome..richly gilded and painted with story by De Creete.

†**b.** Subject (of a painting or sculpture). *Obs.*

a **1700** Evelyn *Diary* 3 Jan. 1666, There are some mezzo-relievos as big as the life, the storie is of the Heathen Gods.

III. 9. *attrib.* and *Comb.*, as in ***story-ballet, -film, -group, -maker, -monger, -plot, -reader, -weaving, -wright, -writing***. Also **storyboard**, a large surface on which is displayed a series of rough drawings representing a shot-by-shot breakdown of a planned film (*spec.* used of advertising commercials); **story-book**, a book containing stories, esp. children's stories; also *occas.* a novel or romance; also *attrib.*; freq. *fig.* with allusion to the conventionally happy ending of children's stories or popular romances (cf. fairy-tale); **story conference**, a meeting of editorial and production staff to discuss a film script; †**story-dresser**, one who gives a novel form to history; **story editor**, one who advises on the content and form of film or television scripts; †**story-faith**, historical faith (see historical *a.* 2); **story-line**, an outline of the principal stages by which a story (esp. a film script) unfolds; also *transf.*; †**story's man** (***stories man***), the authority for a story; †**story-painter**, a historical painter; **story-paper**, a journal that contains works of fiction; †**(in) story wise** *adv.* (*a*) historically; (*b*) in the manner of 'story' or historical painting or sculpture; †**story-work**, historical painting or sculpture (see sense 8); **story-writer**, †(*a*) an official chronicler, historiographer; (*b*) a historian; (*c*) a writer of stories or tales; †**story-wrought** *a.*, adorned with 'story-work'. Also STORY-TELLER, -TELLING.

1951 *Ann. Reg. 1950* 396 '*Story ballets' with music that had been specially composed to fit a ballet scenario. **1964** *Listener* 23 Apr. 668/2 Story-ballets on special scenarios. **1942** *Amer. Cinematographer* Apr. 188/3 A *story board is a large 4 x 8 foot piece of wallboard or celotex, on which the story sketches are pinned in rows with aluminum push-pins. **1952** *Jrnl. Soc. Mot. Pict. & Television Engineers* LIX. 298/1 The storyboard will then show how much time is to be consumed between these majors. **1962** *Rep. Comm. Broadcasting 1960* in *Parl. Papers* 1961–2 (Cmnd. 1753) IX. 259 70 The story-boards or scripts of all advertisements are scrutinised by the Advertising Copy Committee. **1975** R. Hill *April Shroud* xii. 154 A huge sheet of card pinned to the wall. On it were pasted a series of drawings... 'Yeah, that's my story board.' **1711** Swift *Harrison's Tatler* No. 5 ¶2 My Maid left on the Table..one of her *Story-Books (as she calls them) which I..found full of strange Impertinences,..Of poor Servants that came to be Ladies [etc.]. **1790** Cowper *Let.* 23 Mar., The Odyssey, which is one of the most amusing story-books in the world. **1818** Scott *Hrt. Midl.* xxxix, The Duke in person with laced coat, gold-headed cane, star and garter, all, as the story-book says, very grand. **1844** C. M. Yonge *Abbeychurch* xiv. 298 It is only a failure in story-book justice. Lucy is too noble a creature to be rewarded in story-book fashion. **1848** Thackeray *Van. Fair* xlv, Her simple little fancies shrank away tremulously, as fairies in the story-books before a superior bad angel. **1883** Miss M. Betham-Edwards *Disarmed* xi, Can things come right for us, as they do in story-books? **1908** A. Kinross *Joan of Garioch* xlv. 298 The silent horsemen all about me were figures from a story-book of old romance. **1913** E. C. Bentley *Trent's Last Case* xv. 309 The national fondness for doing things in a story-book style. *a* **1944** K. Douglas *Alamein to Zem Zem* (1946) xix. 124 She looked like a story-book nurse, clean, slim, pretty, and smiling. **1973** P. Moyes *Curious Affair of Third Dog* iii. 32, I call that a real story-book happy ending. **1926** G. Frankau *My Unsentimental Journey* xvi. 217 Casey Williams explained a *story-conference, which appears to be something like a board meeting. **1975** R. L. Simon *Wild Turkey* (1976) xi. 71, I found the producer's office... Graskow was in the middle of a story conference. **1592** Nashe *Pierce Penilesse* 20 Any *Storie dresser..that sets a new English nap on an olde Latine Apothegs. **1621** Burton *Anat. Mel.* Democr. to Rdr. (1624) 7 Our Poets steale from Homer,..Divines vse Austins wordes verbatim still, and our story dressers doe as much. **1940** I. Crump *Our Movie Makers* ii. 21 In every studio there is a *story editor, with numerous assistants who are always on the watch for stories. **1950** C. Beranger *Writing for Screen* xx. 165 The story then goes to the head of the department, the story editor. If the story editor approves of it, he in turn gives it to an associate producer or to the studio head who can order its purchase. **1966** *Writing for BBC* v. 24 A post peculiar to [television] Drama Group is that of the Story Editor... He is concerned with the content of the script, rather than its technical requirements... His role..is that of adviser, not 'rewrite man'. **1981** N. Tucker *Child & Book* v. 142 Story editors may be pushed fairly hard to think of new material for plots. **1531** Tindale *Expos. 1 John* iv. (1538) 65 We beleue not only wyth *story fayth, as men beleue old cronicles, but we beleue [etc.]. **1937** A. Calder-Marshall in C. Day Lewis *Mind in Chains* 64 Proceeding from the lot of the film-worker to the nature of capitalist *story-films, we find that they have a uniform basis. **1961** K. Reisz *Technique Film Editing* i. 36 This contempt for the simplest requirement of a story-film—the ability to create the illusion of events unfolding in logical sequence. **1904** Jessie Weston in *Romania* XXXIII. 342 Remnants of a once popular and widely-spread *story-group connected with the deeds of Gawain and his kin. **1941** B. Schulberg *What makes Sammy Run?* vi. 103 I've been after them to make a Jefferson picture..if I can only hammer out the goddam *story line. **1956** *B.B.C. Handbk. 1957* 82 The most noticeable trend in variety production has been recent efforts to develop the situation comedy-type show with the continuing story-line. **1967** M. McLuhan *Medium is Massage* 92 Older societies.. demanded story lines. Today's humor, on the contrary, has no story line—no sequence. **1972** G. Jones *Kings, Beasts, & Heroes* I. i. 8 'The Three Stolen Princesses' is an elaborate and complicated type of folktale..tolerating a considerable choice of alternatives by the story-teller without losing its story line. **1422** Yonge tr. *Secreta Secret.* 162 Dares..that was att the Segee of the nobill Cite of Troy, and therof the *stori-makere. **1913** R. C. Maclagan *Our Ancestors* xxiv. 285 It is no wonder that the story-makers should ascribe its use in royal ceremonial as taking place in Ireland. *a* **1661** Fuller *Worthies, Huntingdon.* (1662) 49 Mr. Parker (I tell you my story and my *stories-man) an industrious Antiquary, collecteth out of the Records of the Church of Ely, that [etc.]. **1668** R. L'Estrange *Vis. Quev.* vii. 315 Where are the *Story-Mongers? The Masters of the Faculty of Lying? That Report more than they Hear [etc.]. **1634** Peacham *Compl. Gentl.* xii. (1906) 110, I call Reubens to witnesse, (the best *story-painter of these times). **1886** F. H. Burnett *Little Lord Fauntleroy* xi. 218 Then he looked at the *story papers. **1888** R. L. Stevenson *Beggars* ii, He had a vulgar taste in letters; scarce flying higher than the story papers. **1890** Hartland *Science of Fairy Tales* i. (1891) 2 The outlines of a *story-plot among savage races are wilder and more unconfined. **1903** A. Lang in *Folk-Lore* June 155 Now I have already insisted that captured slaves..and commerce in all ages must have diffused story-plots. **1844** Dickens *Chimes* i, It is desirable that a story-teller and a *story-reader should establish a mutual understanding as soon as possible. **1889** *Spectator* 9 Nov. 640/2 Never raising him above his true level, which was that of an artist in *story-weaving. **1565** Calfhill *Answ. Treat. Crosse* Pref. 6 b, At the firste, Images among Christen men, were only kept in priuate houses: paynted or grauen in *story wise. **1571** Golding *Calvin on Ps.* xviii. 8. 58 Yit dooth not David report theis things in story-wyse; but [etc.]. **1572** Roscarrocke in Bossewell *Armorie* Pref. Verses, All the walls with imagery, were grauen storie wise. **1608** Hieron *Defence* I. 46, I might put him in mind, that some learned men observe Mathew not to alleadge that testimony; but to report storie wise, how the Scribes did alleadge it to Herod. **1601** Holland *Pliny* xvi. xxxiii. I. 479 Thereof [of Cypress] are drawne many vinets and borders about *storie-workes in colours. **1611** Cotgr., *Historier*,..to flourish, or beautifie Wainscot or Tapistrie with Histories, or Storie-worke. **1659** Torriano, s.v. *Storie*, To beautifie with storie-work, *historiare*. **1903** Christabel Coleridge *C. M. Yonge* vi. 163 Miss Dyson had generous insight enough to know that her friend was a far better *story-wright than herself. **1483** *Cath. Angl.* 366/2 A *Story wryter (writter A.), *historiagraphus*. **1535** Coverdale *1 Esdras* ii. 25 Then wrote the kynge to Rathimus the story wryter [LXX. τῷ γράφοντι τὰ προσπίπτοντα]. **1552** Huloet, Story writer, *historiographus*. **1621** Bp. Mountagu *Diatribæ* 407 The particular remembrances of such use..either neuer were in being, for want of Story-writers in barbarous times..or [etc.]. **1905** A. R. Wallace *My Life* II. 135 Frank Stockton, perhaps the most thoroughly original of modern story-writers. **1552** Huloet, Story wrytyng, *historiographia*. **1606** Sylvester *Du Bartas* II. iv. II. *Magnif.* 267 Her wide-side Robes of Tissue passing price, All *story-wrought with bloudy Victories.

story, *sb.*², **storey** ('stɔːrɪ). Pl. stories, storeys. Forms: 5 storye, 6 storie, (storrie, store), 7– storey, ? 4, 5– story. [First in AL. form *historia*; hence prob. the same word as STORY *sb.*¹, though the development of sense is obscure.

Possibly *historia* as an architectural term may originally have denoted a tier of painted windows or of sculptures on the front of a building: see STORY *sb.*¹ 8, and cf. the Latin quot. 1398 below and sense 2.

The current view that the word is a. OF. *estoree (f. *estorer* to build, furnish: see STORE *v.*) is untenable on account of the AL. form *historia* (from 12th c.).

The following are examples of the Anglo-Latin use of *historia* in the architectural sense:—

a **1200** Hugo Candidus *Cœnob. Burgensis Hist.* 93 in Sparke *Hist. Angl. Scriptt.* (1723) In suo etiam tempore [*sc.* W. de Waterville, 1155–75] tres historiæ magistræ turris erectæ sunt. *a* **1300** *Gesta Sacristarum* in Arnold *Mem. St. Edmund's Abbey* (Rolls) II. 291 Qui [Abbot Sampson 1135–1211] tempore officii sui pro majori parte chorum consummavit unam istoriam in majori turre ad ostium occidentali. **1339–40** *Ely Sacrist Rolls* (1907) II. 96 Pro fenestris superioris istoriæ novi operis. **1398** in *Hist. Dunelm. Script. tres* (Surtees) p. clxxxi, Supra quodlibet studium erit unum modicum et securum archewote, supra quod, spacio competenti interposito, erit una historia octo fenestrarum..et desuper istam historiam fenestrarum erunt honesta alours et bretesmontz batellata et kirnellata.]

1. Each of the stages or portions one above the other of which a building consists; a room or set of rooms on one floor or level.

In this use synonymous with FLOOR *sb.* 5; but while in England the term FIRST-FLOOR is applied to the floor above the ground-floor, the numbering of 'stories' (so named) usually begins with the ground floor, so that the 'first-floor' is identical with the 'second story,' and 'a house of one story' has a ground-floor only. A different usage is shown in quot. 1850, and appears to be not wholly obsolete.

Quot. *a* 1400, though the reading is app. the scribe's conjectural emendation of an obscure passage, may perh. be taken as attesting the existence of the sb. at the date of the MS.; the passage was prob. supposed to refer to the addition of 'stories' or upper stages to towers.

a **1400** *R. Gloucester's Chron.* 3756 (Harl. MS.) Hii bygonne her heye tounes strengþy [*Cotton MS.* & strengþede] vaste aboute, Her castles & storys [*Cotton MS.* & astori], þat hii mygte be ynne in doute. *a* **1490** Botoner *Itin.* (Nasmith, 1778) 282 Turris Sci Stephani Bristoll.. habet 4 storyes, et ibi in quarta storia sunt campanæ. In superiori historia tres orbæ in qualibet panella. **1569** Stocker tr. *Diod. Sic.* III. viii. 113 b, He caused an engine to be made called *Helepolis*,..in which were .ix. stories or sellers deuided one from another with planchers of wood. **1585** Higins *Junius' Nomencl.* 181 *Tristega*,..a house of three sollers, floores, stories or lofts one ouer another. **1590** Lucar *Lucarsolace* I. xxi. 34 By the art..you may tell..what space is betwene storie and storie in any house or other building. **1600** J. Pory tr. *Leo's Africa* VIII. 307 It is built very stately..and is of three stories high. **1625** Bacon *Ess., Of Building* (Arb.) 552–3 This vpon the Second Story. Vpon the Ground Story, a Faire Gallery..: And vpon the Third Story likewise, an Open Gallery. **1672** Marvell *Reh. Transp.* I. 39 Annoyances incident to such as dwell in the middle story. **1693** Dryden *Juvenal* iii. 326 Thy own third Story smoaks. **1723** *Present State of Russia* I. 43 All the Inhabitants of Petersbourg who had Houses but one Story high. **1741** P. Tailfer etc. *Narr. Georgia* 107 The Orphan-house..has two Stories besides Cellars and Garrets. **1763** *Museum Rust.* (ed. 2) I. 76 The granary..consists of seven stories of floors. **1766** Entick *Lond.* IV. 360 The basement story is very massy. **1773** G. A. Stevens *Trip to Portsmouth* ii. 20 Three story is na height at all—my town hoose at bonny Edingburgh is up the aught story. **1815** Scott *Guy M.* iii, The..narrative..was interrupted by the voice of some one ascending the stairs from the kitchen story. **1819** Shelley *Let. to T. L. Peacock* 26 Jan., Sel. Lett. (1882) 95 The houses [in Pompeii] have only one story, and the apartments..are very lofty. **1837** Carlyle *Fr. Rev.* II. v. iii, A Brigand Court-Martial establishes itself in the subterranean stories of the Castle of Avignon. **1840** Dickens *Barn. Rudge* i, With its overhanging storeys, drowsy little panes of glass, and front bulging out and projecting over the pathway. **1850** Parker *Gloss. Archit.* (ed. 5) I. 447 In domestic and palatial architecture the stories are thus enumerated from the lowest upwards. Basement or underground story... Ground story or ground-floor... First-story... Then follow second, third, and so on. **1852** Mrs. Stowe *Uncle Tom's C.* xxxii, A wide verandah of two storeys running round every part of the house. **1864** C. Geikie *Life in Woods* vii. 132 A wooden schoolhouse..a single story high. **1874** Ruskin *Fors Clav.* IV. xlvi. 222 The little house..having..two windows over the shop, in the second story. **1899** *Daily Chron.* 24 Jan., The inhabitants have taken refuge in the upper storeys of the houses.

b. *transf.* and *fig.* Anything compared to a story of a building; one of a series of stages or divisions lying horizontally one over the other.

1625 Massinger *New Way* IV. i, Not the..feare of what can fall on me hereafter, Shall make me studie ought but your aduancement, One story higher. An Earle! if gold can do it. *a* **1631** Donne *80 Serm.* ii. (1640) 14 God shall raise thee one peece by peece, into a spirituall building; And after one Story of Creation, and another of Vocation, [etc.]. **1648** J. Beaumont *Psyche* XXIV. clxxx, If Lucifer had never walk'd upon Complete Felicitie's transcendent Stories,..His Loss had finite been. **1687** A. Lovell tr. *Thevenot's Trav.* II. 40 Here you may see a very lovely Cascade of nine or ten Stories. **1693** Evelyn *De La Quint. Compl. Gard., Refl. Agric.* 67 The Leaves..grow upon the Boughs Chequerwise, in little Stories or Steps at a small distance from each other. **1727** A. Hamilton *New Acc. E. Indies* I. xxxi. 384 His Effigie is..carried..in Procession mounted on a Coach four Stories high. **1727** Pope, etc. *Art of Sinking* xiii. 74 A Rhetorical Chest of Drawers, consisting of three Stories. **1762–71** H. Walpole *Vertue's Anecd. Paint.* (1786) III. 199 He painted in an age when the women erected edifices of three stories on their heads. **1763** Mills *Pract. Husb.* IV. 354 Three branches should be left..in the circumference of the tree, to from what is called the first story. At three feet above them, three other branches are left... The tree is to be formed into stories, in this manner, up to the top. **1768** Tucker *Lt. Nat.* (1834) II. 545 To try how all the principles and precepts of religion, morality, and common prudence, in several stories supported by one another, may be rationally erected. **1826** J. T. Smith *Bk. for Rainy Day* (1845) 238 Among the old dandies of this description of wig we may class Mr. Saunders Welch,..he had nine stories. **1842** Tennyson *Will Waterproof* 70 High over roaring Temple-bar, And set in Heaven's third story, I look at all things..thro' a kind of glory. **1874** Aldrich *Prud. Palfrey* xi. (1885) 172 It is so easy to add another story to the high opinion which other people have of you.

c. *the* or *one's upper story*: jocularly used for the head as the seat of the mind or intellect.

1699 Bentley *Phalaris* 304 He..must have Brains..as well as Eyes in his Head. A man that has that Furniture in his upper Story, will discover [etc.]. **1771** Smollett *Humphry Cl.* 10 June iii, What you imagine to be the..light of grace, I take to be a deceitful vapour, glimmering through a crack in your upper story. **1817** Keats *Lett.* Wks. 1889 III. 57 By this means, in a week or so, I became not over capable in my upper stories. *a* **1837** John Scott in Lockhart *Scott* (1837) III. xi. 351 His neighbour..cast many a curious sidelong glance at him, evidently suspecting that all was not right with the upper story. **1884** *Harper's Mag.* Dec. 88/1, I wuz born weak in th' upper story.

2. Each of a number of tiers or rows (of orders, columns, window mullions or lights, etc.) disposed horizontally one above another.

1412 [see CLERESTORY]. **1449** in *Cal. Proc. Chanc. Q. Eliz.* (1830) II. Pref. 54 Uppon þe furste flore in þe second story ..shullen be xviij wyndowes haunsed. **1518–19** *Rec. St. Mary at Hill* (1904) 302 Paid for makyng of a fote of glas in the upper store in the Middyll Ile, iiij d. **1564** in Willis & Clark *Cambridge* (1886) II. 569 Item for scoweryng and newe trimmyng fower stories of olde yron at ij^s. vj^d. the storie, xj^s. **1624** Wotton *Archit.* I. 39 Where more of these Orders then one, shalbe set in seuerall Stories or Contignations, there must bee an exquisite care, to place the Columnes precisely, one ouer another. **1663** Gerbier *Counsel* 36 It stands so much higher, as..the third story of Columns. **1811** Milner *Eccles. Archit. Eng.* Pref. p. xv, The mullions of these windows, being continued down to the bottom of their story. **1849** Ruskin *Seven Lamps* v. §13. 148 The side of that church has three stories of arcade. *a* **1878** Sir G. Scott *Lect. Archit.* (1879) I. 88 The capitals which prevail in the upper storeys of the choir..I cannot think so early.

3. Comb.: **story box**, one of a series of boxes (for keeping bees) arranged one over the other (cf. STORIFY *v.*); **story post, rod** (see quots. 1842); †**story wig**, one with several rows of curls.

1780 J. Keys *Pract. Bee-Master* §170. 70 By keeping Bees both in *story and collateral boxes at the same time, I have ..found [etc.]. **1663** Gerbier *Counsel* 67 Oaken Carcasse, ground plates nine inches one way, seven inches the other; *Story Posts backwards nine inches one way and six inches the other. **1842** Gwilt *Archit.* Gloss., *Story Posts*, upright timbers disposed in the story of a building for supporting the superincumbent part of the exterior wall through the medium of a beam over them; they are chiefly used in sheds and work-shops. **1823** P. Nicholson *Pract. Builder* 199 The *Story-rod is a rod of wood, equal in length to the height of the stairs. **1842** Gwilt *Archit.* Gloss., *Story Rod*, one used in setting up a staircase, equal in length to the height of the story, and divided into as many parts as there are intended to be steps in the staircase, so that they may be measured and distributed with accuracy. **1826** J. T. Smith *Bk. for Rainy Day* (1845) 238 The earliest engraved portraits of Dr. Johnson exhibit a wig with five rows of curls, ..commonly called 'a *story wig'.

story ('stɔːrɪ), *v.*¹ [f. STORY *sb.*¹]

1. *trans.* In early use, to record historically; to relate the history of (*obs.*); in later use, to tell as a story, to tell the story of. Often with clause as obj. Now *rare*; very common in the 16–17th c., esp. quasi-impers. in passive, *it is storied that*...

The original sense appears occasionally down to the end of the 17th c., but from the middle of the century, or even earlier, it is often difficult to determine whether the older or the newer use is intended. Cf. the sb.

a **1450** *Knt. de la Tour* cxv. 156 She owithe well forto be ..storied in scripture with other good ladyes. *c* **1449** Pecock *Repr.* III. xii. 351 Ech fundamental storie speking of this seid voice seith and storieth that it was mad in the eir. *Ibid.* 353 And this Eusebi..took up on him for to write and storie the hool lijf and the deeth of the same Constantyn. **1563** Foxe *A. & M.* 1353/1 It were a large and long proces to story al the doinges, trauailes, and wrytynges of this Christian Bishop [Latimer]. **1610** Guillim *Heraldry* III. xvii. (1611) 159 It is storied, that the old Eagles make proofe of their yong by exposing them [etc.]. **1621** Bp. Mountagu *Diatribæ* 209 Their Tithes are not onely storied to haue been payed, but are strictly commanded to be payed. **1634** Milton

Comus 516 What the sage Poets..Storied of old in high immortal vers Of dire Chimera's and inchanted Iles. **1649** PRYNNE *Demurrer to Jews' Remitter* 41 Nicholas Trivet.. thus stories the Jews banishment. **1652** SPARKE *Prim. Devot.* (1663) 583 On our British isles too (story some) This Canaanite bestowd first Christendom. **1657** G. THORNLEY *Daphnis & Chloe* 90 Daphnis then storied to her what he had seen. **1672** GALE *Crt. Gentiles* I. III. ii. 33 Truth wrapt under these fables..as tis evident, by what is storied of the Floud. **1701** HOWE *Some Consid. Pref. Enquiry* 7 That..which is storied of Plato, that having one in his Academy that [etc.]. **1796** COLERIDGE *Ode to Departing Yr.* 67 With many an unimaginable groan Thou storied'st thy sad hours! **1813** W. TAYLOR in Robberds *Mem.* II. 414 Are you not afraid of seeing the Peninsula evacuated before you have storied the ancient explosions of independence? **1864** *Spectator* 538 A people who would lay all laws e'er sung Or storied at thy feet.

†**b.** With adv. *to story forth*: to proclaim the story of. *to story out*: to invent stories of; also, ? to unravel the true story of. *Obs.*

1591 *1st Pt. Troub. Raigne K. John* E 4, My tongue is tunde to storie forth mishap. *Ibid.* G 4 b, I goe my selfe, the ioyfulst man aliue To storie out this new supposed crime. *a* **1661** HOLYDAY *Juvenal* x. (1673) 188 Men once beleiv'd, Athos was sail'd about, And all that lying Greece dares story-out [L. *et quicquid Graecia mendax Audet in historia*.]

2. To decorate with paintings or sculpture; to represent in painting or sculpture. Cf. STORY *sb.*[1] 8.

1387–8 T. USK *Test. Love* II. xiii. (Skeat) 76 Purtreytures storied with colours medled. **1812** CARY *Dante, Purg.* x. 66 There, was storied on the rock [It. *Quivi era storiata*] The exalted glory of the Roman prince..Trajan the Emperor. **1844** HOOD *Haunted Ho.* III. 285 Rich hangings, storied by the needle's art, With Scripture history, or classic fable. **1853** MRS. GASKELL *Ruth* i, A window of stained glass, storied all over with armorial bearings. **1854** TALFOURD *Castilian* III. iv, The walls Of alabaster, storied with the deeds Of saints and martyrs.

Hence **'storying** *vbl. sb.*, the action of the vb.; †a historical narrative; also **'storying** *ppl. a.*

c **1449** PECOCK *Repr.* II. i. 133 Þi his writing in storiyng or cronycleing. *Ibid.* III. xii. 354 The seid Damesis storiyng writun by Damasus long sithen Constantyn died. **1793** COLERIDGE *Kisses* 1 Cupid, if storying Legends tell aright, Once fram'd a rich Elixir of Delight. **1820** J. H. WIFFEN *Aonian Hours* (ed. 2) 153 Thou hast thy records which surpass Or storying stone, or sculptured brass!

'story, *v.*[2] *Obs.* [f. STORY *sb.*[2]] *trans.* To arrange in 'stories' or strata one over the other.

1692 BENTLEY *Boyle Lect.* iv. 12 All the parts of an undisturbed Fluid are either of equal Gravity, or gradually placed and storied according to the differences of it.

storyette: see STORIETTE.

'storyful, *a. nonce-wd.* [-FUL.] Rich in story.

1846 J. C. MANGAN *Poems, The Lovely Land* 24 This is.. Some lone land of genii days, Storyful and golden!

storyless ('stɔərılıs), *a.* [f. STORY *sb.*[1] + -LESS.] Having no story or stories.

c **1836** DARLEY in *Friendsh. Miss Mitford* (1882) II. 4 You have..a substantive..taste for poetry itself, when you can thus like storyless abstraction better than a tale of some.. human interest. **1849** *Fraser's Mag.* XL. 42 Even storyless and songless Java is for us embalmed in one line verse of Heber's Missionary Hymn. **1867** *Athenæum* 9 Nov. 607/3 The author is as story-less as the knife-grinder.

'story-,teller. [f. STORY *sb.*[1] + TELLER.] One who tells stories.

1. One who is accustomed to tell stories or anecdotes in conversation.

1709 STEELE *Tatler* No. 132 ⁋10 There is nothing more ridiculous than an old trifling Story-Teller. **1711** ADDISON *Spect.* No. 247 ⁋8 As for newsmongers, politicians, mimics, story-tellers,..they are as commonly found among the men as the women. *a* **1763** W. KING *Lit. & Polit. Anecd.* (1819) 72 A story teller is the most agreeable or the most disagreeable character we can meet with. **1862** *Fraser's Mag.* July 46 He was also a *bon-vivant*, a diner-out, and a story-teller.

2. Euphemistically: A liar. *colloq.*

1748 RICHARDSON *Clarissa* (1811) III. 20 Wicked story-teller! **1770** WESLEY *Jrnl.* 21 Mar., 'But,' says he [a boy of nine], 'you quarrel with God's word;..So you make God a Story-teller.' **1796** MME. D'ARBLAY *Camilla* II. 63 He is a very learned gentleman, and no more a story-teller than I am myself. **1814** *Sporting Mag.* XLIII. 371, I always believed you to be one of the greatest story tellers in England, but I find you have spoke the truth to day. **1825** T. HOOK *Sayings* Ser. II. *Man of Many Fr.* I. 196 Oh, you story-teller, Tom! **1862** MRS. H. WOOD *Mrs. Hallib.* II. ii, What an old story-teller she must be.

3. One whose business it is to recite legendary or romantic stories.

1777 J. RICHARDSON *Dissert. Language* 57 Professed story-tellers..are of early date in the East. **1813** BYRON *Giaour* 1334 *note*, The coffee-house story-tellers who abound in the Levant, and sing or recite their narratives. **1841** SPALDING *Italy & Ital. Isl.* III. 266 A profession peculiar to Italy and the East,—that of the Story-tellers. **1846** MILL *Diss. & Disc.* (1859) II. 310 The Greek religion appears in them too much as a sort of accident, the arbitrary creation of poets and storytellers. **1908** *Hibbert Jrnl.* Oct. 27, I have paid special attention to public story-tellers.

4. Applied to a writer of stories.

1814 SCOTT *Wav.* lxv, These circumstances will serve to explain such points of our narrative as, according to the custom of story-tellers, we deemed it fit to leave unexplained, for the purpose of exciting the reader's curiosity. **1861** HUGHES *Tom Brown at Oxf.* xvii, The exigencies of a story-teller must lead him away from home now and then. **1885** MISS GATTY *Jul. H. Ewing* i. 3, I have promised the children to write something for them about their favourite story-teller, Juliana Horatia Ewing.

transf. **1879** *Social Notes* IV. 114 Hogarth was a story-teller in the strictest sense of the term; his series of chapters correspond closely to the novelist's chapters.

5. The teller of a particular story.

1851 D. JERROLD *St. Giles* xiv. 138 Again was he pressed to rehearse the tale, whilst mugs of ale rewarded the story-teller. **1883** MISS M. BETHAM-EDWARDS *Disarmed* iii, The story-teller suddenly broke down, as if thrilled and set a-tremble with the potency of his own words. **1911** SWANTON *Ind. Tribes Lower Misciss.* (Bureau Amer. Ethnol.) 323 *note*, The storyteller added that there were other parts of the myth, which he had forgotten.

'story-'telling, *sb.* The action of telling stories.

1709 STEELE *Tatler* No. 2 ⁋1, I am not in Humour for telling a Tale, and nothing in Nature is so ungrateful as Story-Telling against the Grain. **1713** *Guardian* No. 42 (1756) I. 182 Story-telling is therefore not an art, but what we call a 'knack'. **1837** LOCKHART *Scott* I. vii. 202 He soon became as famous for his powers of story-telling among the lawyers of the Outer-House, as he had been among the companions of his High School days. **1882** R. L. STEVENSON in *Longman's Mag.* I. 75 The early part of 'Monte Christo', ..is a piece of perfect story-telling. **1894** B. THOMSON *South Sea Yarns* Introd. p. vii, In the great bure of Raiyawa there was a story-telling. **1903** *Sat. Rev.* 26 Dec. 806/1 He has not the gift of storytelling. **1911** W. P. KER *Engl. Lit. Medieval* vi. 177 There is a large section of medieval story-telling which is in a different condition.

attrib. **1897** G. ALLEN *Type-writer Girl* iv. 44 The clear-cut outlines, the translucent hues,..the story-telling faculty, each charmed and beguiled me. **1904** *Daily Chron.* 26 Sept. 4/5 Mr. Morrison has rare constructive skill, as all his story-telling work has shown.

'story-,telling, *a.* That tells stories, in various senses of the sb.; addicted to anecdote; exercising the art of the story-teller in literature or otherwise; *colloq.* lying, mendacious.

1766 FORDYCE *Serm. Young Women* (1767) I. iv. 145 The vulgar story-telling tribe [*i.e.* novelists]. **1839** SIR W. HAMILTON in R. P. Graves *Life* (1885) II. 301, I resemble only too much the inveterate story-telling button-holder. **1840** THACKERAY *Catherine* i, What a naughty story-telling woman! **1848** —— *Van. Fair* viii, I have heard a brother of the story-telling trade, at Naples,..work himself up into such a rage [etc.]. **1863** LONGF. *Wayside Inn* Prel. 168 The story-telling bard of prose, Who wrote the joyous Tuscan tales Of the Decameron.

stose, obs. form of STOWCE.

stoss (stoːs, ‖ʃtoːs), *a. Geol.* [G. *stoss-*, f. *stossen* to push, thrust.] Designating the side of any object that faces a flow of ice or water; also *transf.* Freq. in *stoss-side* [partial tr. G. *stoßseite*, †also used]; *stoss-and-lee* attrib. phr. (see quot. 1947).

[**1848** J. G. CUMMING *Isle of Man* xv. 249 The general appearance of its eastern, as compared with its western side, described by Swedish naturalists under the term *stoss seite* or weathered side, indicates in some measure that fact.] **1878** C. H. HITCHCOCK *Geol. New Hampshire* III. III. ii. 180 The sides most worn are those which have been struck. We often speak of the struck or *stoss* and the lee sides of these rounded edges. **1891** R. D. SALISBURY *Geol. Surv. New Jersey* 47 There was also more rapid erosion upon the north or stoss side of hills than upon the southern or lee side. **1905** J. GEIKIE *Structural & Field Geol.* xx. 310 The smoothed face is termed the Stoss-seite, and the non-glaciated face, the Lee-seite. **1920** [see LEE SIDE b]. **1928** T. C. CHAMBERLIN *Two Solar Families* 180 Let us picture the accretions..as running in convergently at one end of the axis of the core (the stoss end) and as running out divergently at the other (the lee end). **1947** R. F. FLINT *Glacial Geol. & Pleistocene Epoch* v. 72 The persistently asymmetric arrangement of bosses and small hills in a strongly glaciated district, each hill having a comparatively gentle abraded slope on the stoss side and rougher quarried slope on the lee side, is termed stoss-and-lee topography. **1968** R. W. FAIRBRIDGE *Encycl. Geomorphol.* 435/1 These small glaciated knobs generally display a gently sloping, striated and polished upstream (stoss) slope and an oversteepened lee slope. **1971** I. G. GASS et al. *Understanding Earth* xiii. 171/1 The abundant ripples of beaches are..about 1 cm high... They move forward under the current by stoss-side erosion and lee-side avalanching.

stot (stɒt), *sb.*[1] Also 1, 3–9 **stott**, 5–7 **stotte**, 6–7 **stoote**, 5–7, 9 **stote**. [OE. *stot(t* masc.; perh. cogn. w. ON. *stút-r* bull (MSw. *stut-er*, Sw., Norw. *stut*, Da. *stud* young ox); the root may be OTeut. **stut-* ablaut-var. of **staut-* to thrust, push: see STOT *v.* The identity of the word in sense 1 and senses 2–3 is, however, not quite certain.]

†**1.** A horse. In OE. ? one of an inferior kind.

a **1100** *Bury St. Edm. Rec.* in Napier *Contrib. OE. Lexicogr.* 56 Ðæt is vii oxen..& ii stottas [glossed *equi uiles*]. [**1222** in *Domesday of St. Paul's* (Camden) 93 Ad .xii. boves & quatuor stottos.] *c* **1250** *Owl & Night.* 495 Þe sulue stottes yne þe stode Beþ boþe wilde and marewode. **1377** LANGL. *P. Pl.* B. xix. 262 And grace gaue pieres, of his goodnesse, foure stottis, Al þat his oxen eryed, þey to harwe after. *c* **1386** CHAUCER *Prol.* 615 This Reue sat vp on a ful good stot, That was al pomely grey, and highte Scot. *c* **1440** *Promp. Parv.* 477/2 Stot, hors, *caballus*.

2. A young castrated ox, a steer. *north.*

1251 *Cal. Charter Rolls* (1903) I. 373 [For twenty oxen or] stottes [or as many cows without young]. *a* **1300** *Cursor M.* 10386 To godd þe lambes he gaf to lottes, And to þe pouer þe bul scottes [*sic*; *Gött.* stostis]. *a* **1400–50** *Wars Alex.* 4267 Hald we no hors for na harow ne na horned stottis. *c* **1460** *Towneley Myst.* xiii. 518 If I any shepe fott, Aythor cow or stott. **1558** in J. Croft *Excerpta Ant.* (1797) 26 Item, x Stotts of iij Yeres old. **1597** MONTGOMERIE *Cherrie & Slae* 1099 The man may ablens tyne a stot That cannot count his kinsch. **1641** BEST *Farm. Bks.* (Surtees) 144 Two fatte kyne, two fatte stottes, two leane stottes, eight calves. **1791** NEWTE *Tour Eng. & Scot.* 192 There is nothing more common than to see small horses, jack-asses, stotts, or two years old bullocks, and even boar swine, all yoked together. **1814** SCOTT *Wav.* xi, Killancureit talked..of..gimmers, and dinmonts, and stots, and runts. **1844** H. STEPHENS *Bk. Farm* II. 129 Stot in some places means a bull of any age. **1883** M. PATTISON *Mem.* i. (1885) 45 Transported from a desert moor where were no inhabitants but Highland 'stots'.

3. A heifer. *north.* (Cf. 4 a.)

[**1371** in *Fabric Rolls York Minster* (Surtees) 123 De 6s. pro stota wayf apud Herswyk.] **1677** W. NICOLSON *Gloss. Brigant.* in *Trans. R. Soc. Lit.* (1870) IX. 320 Stot, a heifer. **1904** *Eng. Dial. Dict.* (Yorks.).

4. †**a.** As a term of contempt for a woman. *Obs.*

c **1386** CHAUCER *Friar's T.* 332 'Nay, olde Stot, that is nat myn entente' Quod this Somonour. *c* **1450** *Cov. Myst.* (Shaks. Soc.) 217 Come forthe, thou stotte, com forthe, thou scowte. **1481** BOTONER *Tulle on Old Age* (Caxton), He [Flamininus] syttyng at borde was exhorted by a rebawde stotte of his, that [etc.]. *a* **1500** *Medulla Gram.*, *Prostibulum*, a hous of stottys.

b. A stupid, clumsy person. *Sc.* and *dial.*

1877 *Holderness Gloss.*, *Stot*, a foolish or awkward person. **1894** CROCKETT *Raiders* v, The great stot of a farm lad.

5. *Comb.*, as *stot-beef*, *-hide*, *-ox*, †*-stable*; **stot-calf**, a castrated bull-calf; † **stot-plough** = *fool-plough* (FOOL *sb.*[1] 6).

1820 *Blackw. Mag.* VIII. 85 We have made shift to swallow a pound of *stot-beef, which in the West Country, beats our stot-beef here all to sticks. **1800** TUKE *Agric. N. Riding* 253 The time for rearing calves is December and January for '*stot-calves'. **1532–3** *Durham Househ. Bk.* (Surtees) 205, 2 kye hyds et 1 *stothyde. **1586–7** *Shuttleworths' Acc.* (Chetham Soc.) 35 A *stotte oxe. **1778** W. HUTCHINSON *View Northumbld.* II. Anc. Customs 18 Others, in the same kind of gay attire [at Christmas], draw about a Plough, called the *Stot Plough. **1377** in *Cal. Close Rolls* (1913) 509 [(Mendlesham, Suffolk). A house called] *stotty-stable.

stot (stɒt), *sb.*[2] *Sc.* [related to STOT *v.*]

1. The act of rebounding; a rebound; a rebounding blow. *at* or *on the stot*, (to catch or take) on the rebound; in quots. *fig.* *to play stot*, to rebound, bounce (Eng. Dial. Dict.).

1513 DOUGLAS *Æneis* IX. xi. 10 On bos helmys and scheildis the weyrly schot Maid rap for rap, reboundand wyth ilk stot. *c* **1590** MONTGOMERIE *Misc. P.* xxiv. 23 Lurking Love, vha lang had lyne in wait, Persaving tym, he took me at a stot. **1637** R. MONRO *Exped.* II. 118 They are possessed instantly with a Panicke feare, especially being taken at the Stot or rebound, before they have time to disgest their feare. **1821** *Blackw. Mag.* X. 4 She set it down with a stot. **1914** *The Scot at Hame & Abroad* 1 Oct. 5/1 Had I gaun back I wad a been stravaigin' the toon lookin' for you, instead o' catchin' ye, on the stot, as it were.

2. A leap or spring, esp. in dancing. Hence, the swing or rhythm of a tune. *to keep stot*, to keep step or time (*with*); also *fig.*

c **1590** J. STEWART *Poems* (S.T.S.) II. 9 To sport ȝour hienes vith my ruid reherse, In hoip of pardon thocht sum stots I tyn. *c* **1620** Z. BOYD *Zion's Flowers* (1855) 49 Wee have great neede the stots of time to keepe. **1637** RUTHERFORD *Lett.* (1664) 38 A wrong step or a wrong stot in going out of this life. *Ibid.* 154, I finde it a difficult matter to keep all stots with Christ. *c* **1700** *Country Wedding* xvi. in *Watson's Collect.* III. (1711) 51 Well danc'd Eppie and Jennie! He that tynes a Stot o' the Spring, Shall pay the Piper a Pennie. **1822** GALT *Provost* xxxix, Those behind the curtain, who thought to bounce out with a grand stot and strut before the world. **1859** *Sporting Mag.* Oct. 237 The little bay..cantered down the course..at every third or fourth stride giving a proud little stot.

stot (stɒt), *v. Sc.* and *north.* [Of obscure origin; perh. in some way belonging to the Teut. root **stut-*: **staut-* to thrust, push, knock; in Goth. *stautan*, ON. *stauta* (Sw. *stöda*, Da. *støde*), OS. *stôtan* (Du. *stooten*), OHG. *stôzan* (G. *stossen*). Cf. STOIT *v.*]

1. *intr.* To rebound, bounce (*from*, *off*); to fall or impinge with a bounce (*on*, *against*); to jump, start, spring.

1513 DOUGLAS *Æneis* x. vi. 96 Dartis sevin Alsammyn thai kest.. Of quham sum dyd, but harm or other deyr, Stot from hys scheild, his hewmet, or hed geyr. *c* **1620** Z. BOYD *Zion's Flowers* (1855) 93 It leapes, it stots, and stayes not. **1821** GALT *Ann. Parish* xxvi, He attempted to fling it at Sambo, the black lad's head, but it stottit against the wall, and the lid flying open, the whole mustard flew in his own face. **1822** —— *Provost* xxxi, The bailie..stotted out of his chair with the spunk of a birslet pea. **1895** CROCKETT *Men of Mosshags* xxiii, The elshin that had stottit on to the floor.

b. *fig.*

c **1590** MONTGOMERIE *Misc. P.* iii. 36 Sho [Fortune] stottis at strais, syn stumbillis not at stanis. **1616** W. HAIG in J. Russell *Haigs* (1881) 158 If God had not made him stot upon some circumstances in that writ given to your Majesty.

2. To move with a jumping or springing step, to bound along; also *trans.* (causative). Also, to stagger, lurch, move unsteadily.

1801 W. BEATTIE *Parings* (1873) 43 (E.D.D.) Hame we stot through thick and thin. **1824** MISS FERRIER *Inher.* lxviii, They stotted along, side by side, but a full yard asunder. **1858** SURTEES *Ask Mamma* xxxviii. 158 Out sprung puss and went stotting and dotting away with one ear back and the other forward. **1901** G. DOUGLAS *House with Green Shutters* 267 See how the stot stots about the ring. **1903** *Union Mag.* July 312/2 McEwan..unable to carry the heavy coffin 'stotted' it from step to step down a steep tortuous High Street stair.

Hence **'stotting** *ppl. a.* Also **'stotter**, a ball that bounces or rebounds.

1853 SURTEES *Sponge's Sp. Tour* (1893) 311 Bang! went the other barrel, which the hare acknowledged by two or three stotting bounds and an increase of pace. **1896** W. PARK Jr. *Game of Golf* 52 They should be good 'stotters'—that is to say, when dropped on a flagstone or pavement they should rebound with a clear, hard click.

stot, obs. form of STOAT.

†**stotay(e**, *v. Obs.* Also 4 **stotey(e**. [? ad. OF. *estoutoier, estoteier* to fall into disorder.] *intr.* To falter, totter; to come to a stand.

? *a* **1400** *Morte Arth.* 1435 Bot ȝitt oure stale one a strenghe stotais a lyttille, Alle to-stonayede with þe strokes of þa steryne knyghtez. *Ibid.* 3467 Furth he stalkis a stye by tha stille euys, Stotays at a hey strette, studyande hyme one. *Ibid.* 4271 Than he stotays for made, and alle his strenghe faylez. *a* **1400** *Pistill of Susan* 285 Alle þei stoteyd and stoode, þis ferlys to frayne.

†**stote**, *v. Obs.* [Cf. STOTAYE *v.*, STUT *v.*]

1. *intr.* To stand still, halt, stop.

13.. *E.E. Allit. P.* A. 149 Abowte me con I stote & stare To fynde a forþe. *c* **1400** *Anturs of Arth.* ix, It stottyde, it stounnede, it stode als a stane. *a* **1440** *Sir Degrev.* 226 Anone to the forest they found, There they stoted a stound. *c* **1470** *Gol. & Gaw.* 678 Right styth, stuffit in steill, thai stotit na stynt, Bot buskit to battaille.

2. To stammer, stutter.

c **1325** *Gloss. W. de Bibbesw.* in Wright *Voc.* 173 Jo vy cy vener mester Hughe, Ke reyn ne parle s'yl ne bue [*glossed* bote he stote]. *c* **1340** *Nominale* (Skeat) 174 *Femme iupe et ledement hue* Woman houtith and foule stotith. *c* **1400** *Destr. Troy* 3881 A litle he stotid. **14..** *R. Gloucester's Chron.* 8573 (Digby MS. 205 lf. 112) Stotynge & most when he was in wraþe or in strif. *c* **1440** *Promp. Parv.* 477/2 Stotyn, *titubo, blatero.*

3. *trans.* To cause to halt, stop.

1375 BARBOUR *Bruce* III. 66 For wondyr that he suld swa Stot [*ed.* 1616 Stoney] thaim, him allane but ma.

Hence †**'stoting** *vbl. sb.*; †**'stoting** (*stotting*) *ppl. a.*, stammering.

c **1440** *Promp. Parv.* 478/1 Stotynge, *titubatus, titubacio.* **1567** FENTON *Trag. Disc.* v. (1898) I. 230 [He was so tongue-tied in presence of his lady] that he colde neither pleade for hymself at lardge, nor yet playe the parte of a stotting solicitor.

stote, obs. form of STOAT, var. STOT *sb.*[1]

†**'stoter**, *sb.*[1] *Obs. rare*[−1]. [f. STOTE *v.* + -ER[1].] One who stutters.

c **1440** *Promp. Parv.* 477/2 Stotare, *tituballus, blesus.*

†**'stoter**, *sb.*[2] *Obs. slang.* Also 8 **stoater, stouter.** [a. Du. *stooter*, f. *stooten* to knock, push.] A violent blow.

1694 MOTTEUX *Rabelais* IV. lxvii, Vinet lent him such a swinging stoater with the Pitch-fork.., that down fell Signore on the ground. *a* **1700** B. E. *Dict. Cant. Crew*, *Stoter*, a great Blow. *Stoter him*, or *tip him a Stoter*, settle him, give him a swinging Blow. **1769** *Stratford Jubilee* II. i. 28 Giving him a stouter on the noggin, I laid him as flat as a flaunder. **1785** GROSE *Dict. Vulgar T.*

†**'stoter**, *v. Obs. slang.* [f. STOTER *sb.*[2]] *trans.* To hit hard; to fell with a heavy blow.

1690 D'URFEY *Collin's Walk* I. 17 He..knew, by wisdom outward, What Ox must fall, or Sheep be stoter'd. *a* **1700** [see STOTER *sb.*[2]]. **1705** VANBRUGH *Mistake* v. 48 Why, Madam, have you no Pity, no Bowels? [To Leonora.] Stand and see one of your Husbands stoter'd before your Face?

stoter, variant of STOOTER *Obs.*

†**stoteye.** *Obs. rare.* [a. OF. *estotie, estoutie* hardihood, audacity, bold attack.] Impetuous valour, hardihood in attack.

c **1350** *Will. Palerne* 4985 Hade he had his ost he wold asaide þere to haue with stoteye & strengþe stoutli hire wonne. *c* **1400** *Pride of Life* 36 Not I neuir non suc Of stotey ne off strynt.

stoth(e: see STOOTH and STOOTHE *v.*

stothele, obs. form of STUDDLE.

‖**stotinka** ('stotinka). Usu. in *pl.* **-ki**. [Bulg.] A Bulgarian unit of currency, one-hundredth of a *lev*; a coin of this value.

1892 F. C. HIGGINS *Introd. Copper Coins Mod. Europe* 91 *Bulgaria*, 1881.—2, 5, and 10 'Stotinki'. **1902** *Encycl. Brit.* XXVI. 451 The monetary unit is the *lev*, or 'lion'.. nominally equal to the franc, with its submultiple the *stotinka* (pl. *-ki*), or centime. **1933** *Whitaker's Almanack* 546/1 Bulgaria—*Lev* of 100 *Stotinki*. **1976** A. GREY *Bulgarian Exclusive* vii. 48 I'll bet you fifty *stotinki* that he'll start telling us anti-communist jokes.

stotious, var. STOCIOUS.

stotter ('stɒtə(r)), *v. Sc.* and *north.* Also **stoter, stotre, stutter.** [f. STOT *v.* + -ER[1]. Cf. STOITER, STUTTER, TOTTER *vbs.*] *intr.* To stumble, stagger.

1781 J. HUTTON *Tour to Caves* (ed. 2) Gloss. 97 *Stoter*, or *stotre*, to stumble. **1785** *Bran New Wark* l. 365 She stottered, she fell. **1893** STEVENSON *Catriona* xi, I never could abye the reek of them since I could stotter on two feet.

stotterel ('stɒtərəl). *north.* Also 6 **stotrell, stottrele**, 9 **stotteril.** [dim. of STOT *sb.*[1]: see -REL.] A small stot or bullock.

1532-3 *Durham Househ. Bk.* (Surtees) 205 Et in 3 stotterels emptis de Willielmo Hall..25s. **1542** in *Richmond Wills* (Surtees) 37 One why strik, or one stotrell. **1574** *Ibid.* 248, xxij stotes and stottreles and iiij bules. **1876** *Whitby Gloss.*, *Stotteril*, or *Stot*, a young ox.

stotty ('stɒtɪ). *north. dial.* [Origin unknown.] In full, ***stotty cake.*** A soft roll split and filled with meat or cheese.

1971 *Guardian* 5 July 4/6 The traditional local [Tyneside] foods such as leek and suet puddings, stotty cake. **1975** *Times* 20 Sept. 11/5 The bar snacks..include..stotties, which are a local version of a bap, split and filled with meat or cheese. **1982** *Times* 12 Aug. 3/4 Most of the gunners come from north-east England, and Councillor Joseph Hall, Mayor of Sunderland, welcomed them as they left their aircraft. They were given..large portions of locally made pease pudding and stotty cake.

stou, obs. form of STOW *sb.*[1], *v.*[1]

stouf(fe, obs. forms of STOVE *sb.*[1]

stoufe, obs. form of STUFF.

stough, stought, obs. ff. STOW *sb.*[3], STOUT *a.*

stouith, variant of STOUTH *Obs.*

stouk (staʊk, stʊk), *sb. dial.* Also **stowk, stook.** [Of obscure origin.] The handle of a pail or other vessel.

1674 RAY *N.C. Words* 46 A Stowk..the handle of a Pail. **1688** HOLME *Armoury* III. xiv. (Roxb.) 5/1 [A pottinger] is an half round vessell in the belly without a brime, some haueing two eares, but most onely one eare or handle or stouke as the countrey terme is. **1817** WILBRAHAM *Cheshire Gloss.* in *Archæologia* XIX. 38 *Stowk*, a stalk or handle of a pail. **1879** MISS JACKSON *Shropsh. Word-bk.*, *Stouk*, a handle, as of any wooden or earthenware vessel. **1882** *W. Worcestersh. Gloss.* Add. *s.v.*, Please, 'm, I took 'old o' the jug, an' the stook come off in my 'and.

stouk, *v. dial.* [f. STOUK *sb.*] *trans.* To fit with a handle or handles. Also *absol.*

1686 PLOT *Staffordsh.* iii. §27. 123 When they are dry they stouk them, i.e. put Ears and Handles to such Vessels as require them. **1820** WILBRAHAM *Cheshire Gloss.* 63 To *Stouk* or *Stowk*, to put ears or handles to such vessels as require them. **1829** S. SHAW *Staffordsh. Potteries* 104 Vessels..with loop handles *stouked* to the sides. *Ibid.* 166 A good workman could *throw, turn*, and *stouk*.

Hence **'stouker**, one who fits vessels with handles; **'stouking** *vbl. sb.*

1809 in Jewitt *Life Wedgwood* (1865) 105 Fletcher was a 'Stouker' by trade. I gave him a pint of ale to show my handlers the old way of 'Stouking'. **1829** S. SHAW *Staffordsh. Potteries* 104 The Stouker..was the workman who affixed handles, spouts, and other appendages. *Ibid.* 123 Some of the black tea pots are glazed, but not all; and the *stouking* branch seems improved in all the specimens.

stouk(e, obs. forms of STOCK *sb.*[1], STOOK.

stoul(e, stoulle, obs. forms of STOOL.

stoulpe, obs. form of STOOP *sb.*[1]

stoun (stuːn), *v.* Now *Sc.* and *north.* Forms: 4 **stoune, stowne,** (*pa. pple.* **stouned, stund**), 5 **stounne**, 7 **stown**, 6- **stoun.** [Aphetic a. OF. *estoner*: see ASTONE *v.* Cf. STUN *v.* and STOUND *v.*[2]]

†**1.** *trans.* **a.** To stun, stupefy, as with a blow; to benumb. **b.** To stupefy with amazement, astound. *Obs.*

a **1300** *Cursor M.* 12963 Hu bot lepe dun to þe grund, þat þi bodi be noght stund. **13..** *Gaw. & Gr. Knt.* 242 Þer-fore to answare was arȝe mony aþel freke, & al stouned at his steuen, & ston-stil seten. **13..** *E.E. Allit. P.* C. 73 When þat steuen was stynt, þat stowned his mynde. **1591** HARINGTON *Orl. Fur.* xxxvi. liv. (1634) 302 But though the shield brake not, gramercy charme, Yet vnderneath the shield it stound his arme. **1596** SPENSER *F.Q.* v. xi. 29 So was he stound with stroke of her huge taile. **1613** T. HEYWOOD *Brazen Age* II. ii. C 3, My beauty, that charms Gods, makes men amaz'd, And stownd with wonder. **1631** HENSHAW *Horæ Succ.* 389 The wicked..thinkes not of it till it come; and when it is come can think of nothing but that and is stown'd with the thought of it.

2. *intr.* To be stupefied or benumbed.

c **1400** *Anturs of Arth.* ix. 109 It stottyde, it stounnede, it stode als a stane.

stound (staʊnd, stuːnd), *sb.*[1] Forms: 1-3 **stund**, 3 **stunde**, 3-5 **stonde**, 4-6 **stond**, (4 **stunt**, 4-5 **stont**), 3-6 **stounde** (4 **stounte**), 4-6 **stownd(e**, (5 **stowndde, stouunde, stowunde**), 4- **stound**; 6 **stowne**, 8-9 *Sc.* **stoun.** [Com. Teut. (wanting in Gothic): OE. *stund* fem. = OFris. *stunde*, OS. *stunda* (Du. *stond*), OHG. *stunta* space of time (MHG., mod.G. *stunde* hour), ON. *stund* (Sw., Da. *stund*):—OTeut. **stundō*.]

1. A time, while; a short time, moment. *Obs.* exc. *dial.*

a **1000** *Andreas* 1210 Nis seo stund latu þæt þe wælreowe witum belecgað. *a* **1225** *Ancr. R.* 190 A sicnesse of ane stunde. *a* **1275** *Prov. Ælfred* 312 So his mani wimman.. Scene under scete, and þoh hie is scondes ful in an stondes wile. *a* **1300** *Cursor M.* 24496 Quen i him had in armes fald, ..þan bigan mi gle to gru,..And neud me mi stondes [*Gött.* stundis]. *a* **1300** *Fragm. Pop. Sci.* (Wright) 13 That is evene above thin heved, aboute the nones stounde. **14..** *Erthe upon Erthe* 34/75 God lytyd in erth, blyssed be that stounde! *c* **1440** *Alphabet of Tales* 412 Evur he contynewid in syngyng, prayers-saying, and wurshippyng our Lady vnto þe stounde of dead. **1579** SPENSER *Sheph. Cal.* Sept. 56 Hobbin, ah hobbin, I curse the stounde, That euer I cast to haue lorne this grounde. **1602** DAVISON *Rhapsody* (1611) 39 Wo worth the stund wherein I tooke delight To frame the shifting of my nimble feete. **1603** B. JONSON *Entert. Althrope* 2 Now they Print it on the Ground With their feete in figures round, Markes that will be euer found, To remember this glad stound. **1616** R. C. *Times' Whistle*, etc. (1871) 129 Soe death is heer and yonder in one stound. **1819** W. TENNANT *Papistry Storm'd* (1827) 25 Scrimply there pass't a stound o' time. **1838** HOLLOWAY *Prov. Dict.*, *Stound*, a short period of time.

b. As advb. accus.

a **1000** *Boeth. Metr.* xxv. 68 Ðæt is wyrse ȝet, þæt he winnan nyle Wið ðæm anwalde ænige stunde. *a* **1123** *O.E. Chron.* an. 1106, On þære forman længten wucan..ætywyde an unȝewunelic steorra, & lange stunde þeræfter wæs ælce æfen ȝesewen. *c* **1200** ORMIN 6576 Þatt sume off ure little flocc..Hemm wendenn oþerr stund fra Crist. *c* **1200** *Moral Ode* 149 (Trin. Coll. MS.) Hadde he finded sume stunde he wolde seggen oðer. *c* **1205** LAY. 3117, & þus ane stonde [*c* **1275** stunde] hit stod æ ðon ilka. *a* **1300** *X Commandm.* 22 in *E.E.P.* (1862) 16 Alas wrecchis whi do we so hit mai noȝt hold vre lif a stunde. *a* **1300** *Cursor M.* 14557 In ephraim dueld he a stunde And þeþen-ward son can he funde. **13..** *Bonaventura's Medit.* 878 Fro wepyng she ne myȝt stynte no stounde. *a* **1340** HAMPOLE *Psalter* li. 5 Þof he lat þe lif a stunt in welth. *c* **1400** *Assump. Virg.* 727 (Add. MS.) And euer þei cryede many a stounde, 'Alas'! [etc.]. *c* **1450** *St. Cuthbert* (Surtees) 7012 Þidir he went, and bade a stont. **1519** HORMAN *Vulg.* 56 He was so abasshed, that he was almoste mad, and stoode styffe a stownde. **1557** *Tottel's Misc.* (Arb.) 257 Elde..Will turne eche blysse into a blast, Which lasteth but a stounde. **1567** TURBERV. *Epit.* etc. 91 Vlysses wiues renowne Unsitting is for hir whose loue endureth but a stowne. **1591** SYLVESTER *Du Bartas* I. ii. 609 So that this vapour, never resting stound, Stands never still, but makes his motion round. **1594** R. C[AREW] *Godfrey of Bulloigne* (1881) 85 Like him that lookes ech stond with bared necke, When cruell axe shall his liues warrant checke. **1600** FAIRFAX *Tasso* XIX. xxviii, His legges could beare him but a little stound. **1895** *E. Angl. Gloss.* s.v., He stayed a long stound.

†**c.** In advb. phrases with preps., e.g. ***for, in, on a (little) stound, in many stounds, in that stound. by stounds***: at intervals, from time to time, by turns. ***umbe stound***: see UMSTOUND. *Obs.*

c **1205** LAY. 8815 Hærde bi-ðrungen i wel feole stunden. *a* **1225** *Ancr. R.* 310 A mon þet hefde al þene world awold, & hefde, uor his cweadschipe, uorloren al on one stunde. *a* **1225** *Juliana* 7 Ant efter lutle stounde wið ute long steuene. *a* **1250** *Prov. Ælfred* 395 Ac al he schal for-leten on a litel stunde. **13..** *Gaw. & Gr. Knt.* 1567 Bot ȝet þe styffest to start bi stoundez he made. *c* **1350** *St. Christina* 179 in Horstm. *Altengl. Leg.* (1881) 95 He was so stonayd in þat stunt He strake him self fast in þe frunt. *c* **1374** CHAUCER *Boeth.* IV. met. vi. (1886) 111 The moyste thinges stryuynge with the drye thinges yeuen place by stowndes. *a* **1400** *Pistill of Susan* 167 Alle hire seruauns þei shont And stelen a-wey in a stont. **1513** DOUGLAS *Æneis* II. x. 80, I within ane litle stound, The clud of dirknes from thi sicht sall cleir. *a* **1529** SKELTON *P. Sparowe* 34 Within that stounde,..in a sounde I fell downe to the grounde. **1575** *Gammer Gurton* Prol. 7 He quyetly perswaded with her in that stound Dame Chat, her deare gossyp, this needle had found. **1591** SYLVESTER *Du Bartas* I. vi. 364 Abiding, for a stown, Pale, cold, and sense less, in a deadly swown.

†**d.** ***often-, oft-stounds***: often. [Cf. OFTEN-*sithes*, *-whiles*, OFTENTIMES.] ***that stounds*** [? advb. genitive]: at that moment. *Obs.*

1303 R. BRUNNE *Handl. Synne* 3083 Ʒyf þou delyte þe oftyn stoundes, yn horsys, haukys, or yn houndes. *a* **1400** *Octouian* 893 Men blamede the bochere oft stoundys For hys sone. *a* **1400** *King & Hermit* 56 He blew thrys, vncoupuld hundes; They reysed þe dere vp þat stondes.

†**e.** ? An hour. *Obs.*

c **1325** *Lai le Freine* 207 To-day, right in the morning, Sone after the first stounde, A litel maiden-childe ich founde.

†**f.** The time for doing something; one's 'hour' or opportunity. *Obs.*

a **1225** *Leg. Kath.* 1263 Nu is ower stunde! **1297** R. GLOUC. (Rolls) 10873 In þe kinges chaumbre..was A clerc ifounde..He made him as bi wit, so þat it was ifounde, þat it was bi speke to sle þe king, wan he sei stounde. *c* **1330** R. BRUNNE *Chron. Wace* (Rolls) 11332 Al þe nobleye couthe y nought telle, Ne y naue no stounde þer-on to dwelle.

2. †**a.** Contextually: A hard time, a time of trial or pain. *Obs.*

a **1000** *Riddles* (Tupper) xiii. 19 No ic þa stunde bemearn ne for wunde weop. *c* **1250** *Owl & Night.* 706 Þe Nihtegale ..hedde onswere god ifunde Among alle hire harde stunde. *c* **1300** *Cursor M.* 17152, I..sufferd her þis herd stondes, and ded on þis rode tre. *c* **1374** CHAUCER *Anel. & Arc.* 238 Alas! the harde stounde. **1590** SPENSER *F.Q.* I. viii. 25 Such percing griefe her stubborne hart did wound, That she could not endure that doleful stound.

b. Hence, a sharp pain, a pang; a fierce attack, a shock. Chiefly *northern.* Also (*Sc.*), a thrill (of delight).

c **1300** *Cursor M.* 24541 In sterin stanging was i stadd, Sa war mi stundes store. **13..** *E.E. Allit. P.* B. 1540 Þe stronge strok of þe stonde strayned his ioyntes. **1375** BARBOUR *Bruce* III. 140 He rouschit doun off blud all rede, As he that stound feld off dede. *c* **1400** *Rom. Rose* 4472 What avayleth hir good wille, Whan she ne may staunche my stounde ille? **1500-20** DUNBAR *Poems* lxxii. 98 Than straik at me with mony ane stound. *c* **1550** ROLLAND *Crt. Venus* I. 641 As he that said, to his hart straik ane stound. **1567** *Gude & Godlie Ball.* 99 Lyke deidly dartis thow geuis stang & stound. **1579** SPENSER *Sheph. Cal.* May 257 Iesus..keepe your corpse from the carefull stounds, That in my carrion carcas abounds. **1596**

—— *F.Q.* VI. vi. 5 Their wounds..had festred privily; And ranckling inward with unruly stounds, The inner parts now gan to putrify. 1659 H. MORE *Immort. Soul* III. xiv. 477 The stounds and agonies of Death. 1788 BURNS *To the Weavers gin ye go* 16 But every shot and every knock, My heart it gae a stoun. 1789 —— *Blue-eyed Lassie* 11 And aye the stound, the deadly wound, Cam frae her een sae bonnie blue. 1825 BROCKETT *N.C. Gloss.*, *Stound*, the sensation or first impression of sudden pain, arising from a knock or blow. 1827 J. WILSON *Noctes Ambr.* Wks. 1855 I. 355 My heart has gien a sudden-stoun o' uncommunicable delicht. 1834 PRINGLE *Afr. Sk.* 17 Oft as he feels gaunt hunger's stound. 1878 SIR T. MARTIN tr. *Heine* 18 Then I felt a stound through all my frame.

c. Roar, violent noise.

1627 DRAYTON *Nymphidia* liv, By the Thunders dreadfull stound. 1658 BURTON *Comment. Itin. Antoninus* 150 After this storm and stound..it flourished again. 1837 CARLYLE *Fr. Rev.* I. v. iv, One can fancy with what dolorous stound the noon-tide cannon..went off there.

†**3.** Station, position. *Obs.*

1557 GRIMALDE in *Tottel's Misc.* (Arb.) 104 What power haue you so great..To pluck, to draw, to rauish hartes, and stirre out of ther stownd? 1566 DRANT *Horace, Sat.* II. iii. F viij, Stande still in stounde, kepe whishte (I say) whilste I doe proue you mad. 1567 —— *Ep.* xvi. *To Quintius* E vij, Well might thou saye that freshe Tarent were brought into this stounde. *Ibid.* F j, He hath forsoke of manlines the stounde [L. *locum virtutis deseruit*]. 1570 LEVINS *Manip.* 220/40 A stound, *statio, terminus*. 15.. *Pater Sapientiæ* lxxx. in Ashm. (1652) 204 For when the Larke ys weary above in hys stound, Anon he falleth right downe to the ground.

†**4.** Used for: STADIUM. *Obs. rare*$^{-1}$.

[Perh. some error: cf. G. *stunde* (hour) as an itinerary measure.]

1656 W. DU GARD tr. *Comenius' Gate Lat. Unl.* §524. 155 A hundred twenty-five Geometrical paces, make a stound or furlong.

stound (staʊnd, stuːnd), *sb.*^{2} Now *dial.* Also 8 **stownd.** [App. f. STOUND *v.*^{2}; but perh. a use of STOUND *sb.*^{1} 2 b, modified by association with the vb.] A state of stupefaction or amazement.

1567 GOLDING *Ovid's Met.* XIII. (1593) 298 [He] raised soberly his eye-lids from the ground (On which he had a little while them pitched in a stound). 1596 SPENSER *F.Q.* IV. vi. 12 Lightly he started up out of that stound. 1610 FLETCHER *Faithf. Sheph.* II. ii. (1634) D 1, Whilst the sound Breakes against heaven, and drives into a stound The amazed Shepherd. 1667 PEPYS *Diary* 3 Apr., This put us all into a stound. 1674 N. FAIRFAX *Bulk & Selv.* 120 We having warily held, the stirr'd body not to be at rest, or in a stound or pause at all, but alwayes to be either stirring or bearing. 1677 GILPIN *Dæmonol.* (1867) 440 Though at first some good men were overawed to..recant,..yet..after the stound and dazzle of the temptation was over, they recoiled so resolutely upon them, that [etc.]. 1714 GAY *Sheph. Week.* Prol. 23 Thus we stood as in a stound. 1767 MICKLE *Concub.* II. Introd., In musefull Stownd Syr Martyn rews His Youthhedes thoughtlesse Stage. 1819 W. TENNANT *Papistry Storm'd* (1827) 194 Flew frae ae pillar to the tither, Syn in a stound did drap. 1859 MISS MULOCK *Life for Life* II. 184, I laugh now..to recollect what a stound it gave us both, this utterly improbable..tale.

†**stound,** *sb.*^{3} *dial. Obs.* [Unexplained var. of STAND *sb.*^{2}] (See quots.)

1674 RAY *N.C. Words* 46 A *Stound* q. Stand; a wooden Vessel to put small Beer in. [So in many later Glossaries.] 1706 PHILLIPS (ed. Kersey), *Stound*, a Vessel of Earth or Wood that stands on end. 1721 MORTIMER *Husb.* II. 332 If the quantity of your choicest Cyder be too great for your Bottles, you may..make use of..Stounds of Flanders Earth.

stound, *v.*^{1} Also 3 **stunde.** [f. STOUND *sb.*^{1}]

†**1.** [STOUND *sb.*^{1} 1.] *intr.* To remain, stay. *Obs.*

Cf. obs. dial. '*Stound*, to stop, stand still, esp. in order to listen' (Suffolk and Essex): see *Eng. Dial. Dict.*

c 1250 *Gen. & Ex.* 1987 Ðor was in helle a sundri stede, wor ðe seli folc reste dede; ðor he stunden til helpe cam. *Ibid.* 3211 Ðor he stunden for to sen quilc pharaon wið hem sal ben. *c* 1330 R. BRUNNE *Chron. Wace* (Rolls) 10902 When Arthur felde þat he was wounded, Noþyng he ne stinte ne stounded. 14.. *Sir Beues* (S.) 1283 On knee he him set, he nolde stound, And ȝaue vp his deth with his hold.

2. [STOUND *sb.*^{1} 2 b.] †**a.** *trans.* To affect with a 'stound' or pang; to cause great pain to. *Obs.* **b.** *intr.* To be acutely painful; to smart, throb. Only *Sc.* and *north.*

c 1500 KENNEDY *Passion of Christ* 450 Thai hurt his [back] and all his body þai fret, Saris his senonis and stoundis all his wanis. *Ibid.* 552 On him to luk þair stomok sair it stoundis. 1513 DOUGLAS *Æneis* X. x. 135 So tyll hys hart stoundis the prik of deith. *a* 1585 MONTGOMERIE *Cherrie & Slae* 741 His wounds ȝit, quhilk stounds ȝit, He gat them than throw thee. 1678 J. BROWN *Life of Faith* I. vii. (1824) 137 Every ingredient that affecteth thee stounds his heart. 1724 RAMSAY *Health* 294 For the least noise stounds thro' his ears like death. *a* 1792 BURNS *Bonie Wee Thing* 3 And my heart it stounds wi' anguish, Lest my wee thing be na mine. 1825 BROCKETT *N.C. Gloss.*, *Stound*, to ache, to smart, to be in pain. 1848, 1910 [see STOUNDING *ppl. a.*^{1}].

stound (staʊnd, stuːnd), *v.*^{2} Now *dial.* Also 4, 7 **stund,** 5 **stond.** [Aphetic var. of ASTOUND *v.*, or extended form of STOUN *v.*]

1. *trans.* To stun as with a blow; to stupefy, benumb; to stupefy with astonishment, bewilder.

a 1300 *Cursor M.* 7558 Quat! wyns þou i am a hund, Wit þi stans me for to stund? *a* 1420 *Aunters of Arthur* xlvii. 602 (Douce MS.) The knighte of corage was cruel and kene, And withe a stele bronde þat sturne oft stonded. 1587 HARRISON *England* III. vii. 231/1 in *Holinshed*, Mastiffes..take also their name of the word mase and theefe..bicause they often stound and put such persons to their shifts. 1600 HOLLAND *Livy* I. xli. 24 That the king was stounded with a sudden blow [L. *sopitum fuisse regem subito ictu*] but the weapon did not go very deep into his body. 1609 T. HEYWOOD *Brit. Troy* XII. xci. 262 But him the Woorthy stounded with a blow. *a* 1617 BAYNE *Lect.* (1634) 302 The Chirurgion bindeth and stoundeth before cutting, that the patient may be lesse grieved. 1629 in *Bibl. Regia* II. 236 The fatal blow given your most loyal servant..hath so stounded our University as (like a body without a soul) she stirs not. 1672 MARVELL *Reh. Transp.* I. 218 They are slain every mother's son of them. Yet perhaps they are but stounded and may revive again. 1678 BUNYAN *Pilgr.* I. 221 At the sight..of this River, the Pilgrims were much stounded. 1689 *Dialogue Timothy & Titus* 4 I'le protest you've stunded me. *a* 1825 FORBY *Voc. E. Anglia*, *Stound.* 1. To stun. 2. To overcome with astonishment.

†**2.** *intr.* To be bewildered or at a loss.

1531 in W. H. Turner *Select. Rec. Oxford* (1880) 98 The seid Mayer and Burgeys many tymes stound and be in grett ambuyguyte to execute such old graunts.

'stounded, *ppl. a.* [f. STOUND *v.*^{2} + -ED^{1}.] Stunned; astonished.

1757 E. PERRONET *Mitre* II. lxxxvii, The news makes all their Sur-loins crack: Down drops each stounded head. 1819 W. TENNANT *Papistry Storm'd* (1827) 76 Whan to his stoundit ear there comes The blair o' trumpets and o' drums.

†**'stounding,** *vbl. sb.*^{1} *Obs.* [f. STOUND *v.*^{1} + -ING^{1}.] **a.** Lingering, delay. **b.** *pl.* Remains.

? *a* 1400 *Morte Arth.* 491 Wythowttyne more stownntynge they schippide theire horsez. 1650 *Presbyt. Rec. Inverurie* in J. Davidson *Inverurie* (1878) 306 The mistress was delyvered and thereafter the pains left her, except some stoundings of the grinding.

'stounding, *vbl. sb.*^{2} [f. STOUND *v.*^{2} + -ING^{1}.] Benumbing.

1637 RUTHERFORD *Lett.* (1836) I. 296 Christ's 'Not yet,' is a stounding of all the limbs and liths of the soul.

'stounding, *ppl. a.*^{1} *north.* [f. STOUND *v.*^{1} + -ING^{1}.] Smarting, acutely painful.

1848 J. HAMILTON *Happy Home* vi. (1871) 132 Writhing nerves and stounding bones. 1910 D. CUTHBERTSON in *Poets of Ayrshire* 280 Our hearts a stounin' pain aft feel.

'stounding, *ppl. a.*^{2} [f. STOUND *v.*^{2} + -ING^{1}.] Stunning; astounding.

1608 DEKKER *Dead Term* A 3, Many a stounding blow hath he taken on his head. 1674 N. FAIRFAX *Bulk & Selv.* 87 That stounding and surprizing Essex Writer. 1819 KEATS *Otho* IV. ii. 95 Unless Retraction follow close upon the heels Of that late stounding insult.

†**'stoundmeal,** *adv. Obs.* Forms: 1 **stund-, stuntmælum,** 2 **stundmele,** 4–5 **stound(e)mele,** 4 **stowndmeel,** 5 **stonedemel.** [OE. *stundmǽlum*: see STOUND *sb.* and -MEAL.]

1. At intervals, from time to time.

c 1000 ÆLFRIC *Gram.* xxxviii. (Z.) 238 *Vicissim* stundmælum. *c* 1000 *Ags. Gloss.* in *Haupt's Zeitschr.* (1853) IX. 438/2 *Alternatim* (gl. *singulatim*, marg. *separatim*) tvæmendlice *vel* stundmælum. *c* 1200 *Trin. Coll. Hom.* 113 And wunede mid his disciples noht alegate ac stundmele. *c* 1350 *Will. Palerne* 736 A-wai wold it neuer but gan to studie stoundemele so stifly þer-onne þat lelly be a litel while his langure gan wex. 1382 WYCLIF *Num.* x. 7 Whanne forsothe the puple is to gederynge togidre, shal be symple criynge of trompes, and not stowndmeel thei shulen ȝolle. *c* 1400 *Rom. Rose* 2304 The lyf of loue is ful contrarie, Which stounde mele can ofte varie. 1426 LYDG. *De Guil. Pilgr.* 19179 Thus stoundemel ȝe may hym se Some tyme swymme, som tyme fflee. *c* 1430 —— *Min. Poems* (Percy Soc.) 159 Som folk pesible, som contrarious, Stonedemel now hevy and now lihte. 1481 CAXTON *Reynard* xvii. (Arb.) 40 The foxe loked on the kyng stoundmele, and was glad in his herte.

¶**b.** quasi-*adj.* That exists at times.

c 1400 *Rom. Rose* 3784 Who serueth loue can telle of woo; The stoundemele ioie mote overgoo.

2. Gradually.

c 1000 ÆLFRIC *Gram.* xxxviii. (Z.) 228 *Sensim*, stundmælum. *c* 1374 CHAUCER *Troylus* v. 674 Þis wynde þat moore and moore þus stoundemele encresseth in my face. *c* 1400 *Ragman Roll* 62 in Hazl. *E.P.P.* I. 72 And now cometh age, foo to your beaute, And stelyngly it wastyth stownde-mele.

stoune, obs. Sc. pa. pple. of STEAL *v.*

stoung(e(n, obs. pa. t. and pple. of STING *v.*^{1}

stoup (stuːp). Forms: α. (chiefly *Sc.* and *north.*) 4–6 **stowpe,** 6–9 **stowp,** 6 **stolp,** 6–7, 9 **stoupe,** 6– **stoup;** β. 6–7 **stoope,** 7–9 **stoop;** γ. (4 *Latin* **stopa**), 5–8 **stope,** 6–7 **stoap(e;** δ. *Sc.* 6 **stoip,** 7 **stoype.** [a. ON. *staup* neut. (Norw. *staup*, Sw. *stop*) = OE. *stéap* masc., MDu. *stoop* masc. (Du. *stoop* masc. and fem.), MLG. *stôp* masc., OHG., MHG. *stouf* (mod.G. dial. *stauf* masc.):—OTeut. **staupo-*. Cf. STOP *sb.*^{1}

Prob. some of the forms are due to the influence of the MDu. or MLG. equivalent: see note to sense 2.]

1. A pail or bucket; also ***water-stoup***. Now only *Sc.* †Formerly also, a large jar or small cask for holding liquids. (Cf. STOP *sb.*^{1} 1.)

α. 1397 in *Finchale Priory Charters* etc. (Surtees) p. cxvii, Item iiij stowpes de coreo. 1574 in *Richmond Wills* (Surtees) 247 In the brewe house..vij. seaes, ij skiles, ij. stoupes. *a* 1670 SPALDING *Troub. Chas. I* (Bannatyne Club) I. 44 It is said that their sister, with ane trein stoup, slew ane called Mercer..Dumbar. 1708 *Invent.* in E. D. Dunbar *Soc. Life Former Days* (1865) 212 A laddle, a watter stoup, three cies. 1822 GALT *Provost* xxxiii, Even lasses were fleeing to and fro, like water nymphs with urns, having stoups and pails in their hands. 1912 R. M. FERGUSON *Ochil Fairy Tales* 13 Two wooden stoups or pitchers full of water.

β. 1634 BRERETON *Trav.* (Chetham Soc.) 53 Here along this passage are thirty-six stoopes placed at equal distances.

γ. [1390 *Earl Derby's Exped.* (Camden) 9 Pro j stopa et di. mellis. *Ibid.* 14 Pro vij^{xx} viij stopis vini Rochell.] 1411 in *Finchale Priory Charters* etc. (Surtees) p. clvi, Item vj tankards et j stope de corio. 1427–8 *Durham Acc. Rolls* (Surtees) 142 In iij. ollis nuncupatis Stopez. 14.. *Nom.* in Wr.-Wülcker 728/28 *Hec cupa*, a stope. 1554 *Acc. Ld. High Treas. Scot.* X. 234 Item, for platis, dischis, bukatis, and stopis, xv s. 1595 DUNCAN *App. Etym.* (E.D.S.), *Amphora*, a stope.

2. A drinking-vessel, of varying dimensions; a cup, flagon, tankard. Also as a measure of definite quantity; often with defining word, as ***gill, pint, quart stoup***. Now *Sc.* and *north.*, and as a literary archaism. (Cf. STOP *sb.*^{1} 3.)

In some of the quots. used to represent a foreign form, e.g. Du. *stoop*, Sw. *stop*.

α. 1500–20 DUNBAR *Poems* xl. 26 Off wyne owt of ane choppyne stowp, They drank twa quartis, sowp and sowp. 1533 *Acc. Ld. High Treas. Scot.* VI. 179 For mending of ane of the Kingis silver stolpis..viij s. 1543–4 *Extracts Burgh Rec. Edin.* (1871) II. 115 Stowppis of mesour. 1573 *Sc. Acts Jas. VI*, c. 57 (1597) 27 Everie Barrell of herring and quhit-fisch, [sall] conteine nine gallones of the samin stope. 1586 *Extracts Burgh Rec. Edin.* (1882) IV. 475 All persouns quha hes any fals stowpes clowrit in the sydes. 1610 BEAUM. & FL. *Scornf. Lady* II. ii, Lets haue a bridling cast before you goe. Fils a new stoupe. 1617 MORYSON *Itin.* III. 286 Each Student in the Vniversitie hath eighty measures of wine (vulgarly called *Stoup*) allowed him free from imposition. 1638 *Reg. Mag. Sig. Scot.* 315/1 To mark and stamp all firlottis..quart-stoupis, pynt, chopein and mutchekin stoupis. 1721, 1786 [see MUTCHKIN b]. 1754 E. BURT *Lett. N. Scot.* (1818) I. 157 Their capacious pint pot which they call a stoup. 1785 GROSE *Dict. Vulgar T.*, *Stoup*,..a vessel containing a size or half a pint, is so called at Cambridge. 1814 SCOTT *Wav.* xvi, The Baron ordered a stoup of usquebaugh. 1879 'OUIDA' *Cecil Castlemaine* 7 Scarce stopping for a stoup of wine. 1895 SNAITH *Mistr. Dorothy Marvin* xxvii, A big stoup o' cider.

β. 1589 HAKLUYT *Voy.* 824 Also they shal sell wines by the pype, and by the gallon, quart, or Stoope they shall not sell [in Russia]. 1601 SHAKS. *Twel. N.* II. iii. 14 Marian I say, a stoope of wine. 1617 MORYSON *Itin.* I. 62 For each measure of wine..I paid ten grosh, which measure is called a stoope, and is somewhat bigger then the English quart. 1708 W. KING *Art of Cookery* 85 A cauldron of fat beef, and stoop of ale. 1753 HANWAY *Trav.* (1762) I. II. xi. 51 Liquors are sold by the stoop, of which three are equal to an English gallon. 1771 SMOLLETT *Humphry Cl.* 3 Sept., This is brought in a pewter stoop, shaped like a skittle. 1864 D. G. MITCHELL *Wet Days* 131 The monks might send him now and then a stoop of their wine. 1869 BLACKMORE *Lorna D.* xxix, Parson took a stoop of cider.

γ. 1452 *Paston Lett.* Suppl. (1901) 44 Ye shul have a stope of bere to comforte yow. *c* 1483 CAXTON *Dialogues* 7 *Cannes de deux lots*, Cannes of two stope,..*Lotz et demy lotz*, Stopes and half stopes. 1502 *Acc. Ld. High Treas. Scot.* II. 295 Ane tyn quart and ane poynt stopes. 1533 *Ibid.* VI. 165 For iij quart stopis, xviij d. 1591 [? NASHE] *Prognostication* B 3, Englishe Beere shall there [in Denmark] be woorth fiue pence a stoape. 1592 GREENE *Black Bks. Messenger* Ep. Rdr., He would steale ouer in to the Lowe Countries, there to tast three or foure Stoapes of Rhenish wine. 1602 SHAKS. *Ham.* V. ii. 278 Set me the Stopes of wine vpon that Table. 1609 DEKKER *Gull's Horn-bk.* Proem. 4 The Switzers stoap of Rhenish. 1657 in *10th Rep. Hist. MSS. Comm.* App. I. 38 Tow silver stoapes. 1673 DRYDEN *Amboyna* v. i, [Dutchman loq.] Boy, give me some Tobacco, and a stope of Wine. 1713 *Phil. Trans.* XXIX. 57, 30 Rotterdam Stopes (making each about 3 English Quarts).

δ. 1530 in A. Laing *Abbey of Lindores* (1876) 490 It. iiij half gallonis stoippis, xj q^{r}t stoippis iiij poynt stoppis. ? *a* 1550 *Freiris of Berwick* 66 in *Maitland Poems* (1786) 67 Dame, fill ane stoip of aile. 1663 *Invent. Ld. J. Gordon's Furniture*, Twa quart stoypes.

3. A vessel to contain holy-water, usu. a stone basin set in or against the wall of the church-porch, or within the church close to the entrance-door.

The form *stoup* is modern. It represents the earlier *stop*, *stope*: see γ below and STOP *sb.*^{1} 2; cf. STOCK *sb.*^{1} 21.

α. 1793 DENNE in *Archæologia* XI. 131 The holy-water stoup, fixed near the doors of churches, is sometimes called *labrum*. *Ibid.* 150, 365 *note*. 1829 BLOXAM *Princ. Gothic Archit.* xi. 65. 1848 LYTTON *Harold* IV. vi, Near the doorway ..was the stoupe or aspersorium for holy-water. 1899 *Q. Rev.* Apr. 470 The famous alliance between the stoup and the sabre, which has reorganised the politics of France.

β. 1784 DENNE in J. Thorpe *Custumale Roffense* (1788) 99 These basins or stoops were sometimes made of metal, but generally of stone.

γ. 1500 *Invent. Ch. Goods Canterb.* in *Gentl. Mag.* (1837) Dec. 569/2 A stope, off lede, for the holy wat^{r} atte the churche dore.

†**4.** *attrib.*, as ***stoop-can, -glass***. *Obs.*

1608 H. CLAPHAM *Errour Right Hand* 53 See you that cherry-cheeked Damsell that tooke vp there the Stoop-kan. 1626 BACON *Sylva* §796 Take a Stock-Gilly-Flower, and tye it gently vpon a Sticke, and put them both into a Stoope Glasse.

stoup, obs. form of STOOP, STUPE.

†**stoupaille.** *Obs. rare*$^{-1}$. [ad. OF. *estoupail* or *estoupaille* plug: see ESTOPPEL and STOPPLE.] ***to make a stoupaille of***, to stop up, close with a plug.

1426 LYDG. *De Guil. Pilgr.* 24110 Of grace thou shalt not faille So that thou make a stoupaille Of the hooles that open be In thyn handes.

†**stoupe.** *Obs. rare*$^{-1}$. [Of obscure origin and meaning; but cf. OF. *estoupe* cheat, deception.]
1297 R. GLOUC. (Rolls) 5432 So þat heo mid childe was & þoȝte hire so sor Ar þat child were ybore, þat he ne willed it nammor Come nammor to þulke stoupe, vor me ne miȝte hire bringe þat ȝo wolde euere eft in monnes bedde come vor eny þinge.

stoupful ('stu:pfʊl). [f. STOUP + -FUL.] As much as a stoup will hold.
1590 in *Law's Memor.* (1818) Pref. p. xxviii, A stoupfull of poisoned aill. **1824** CARLYLE *Let.* 18 Sept. in Froude *Life* (1882) I. 235, I have swallowed, say about two stoupfuls of castor oil since I came hither. **1892** J. S. FLETCHER *When Chas. I was King* (1896) 295, I see you have drunk all the ale—shall I fetch you another stoupful?

stouph(e, obs. forms of STOVE.

†**stouple.** *Obs.* Also 7 **stoupell, stopple.** [ad. F. †*estoupille, étoupille*, f. *étoupe*:—L. *stuppa, stūpa* tow.] = QUICK-MATCH.
1634 J. B[ATE] *Myst. Nature* 65 How to make stouple, or prepare cotten-week to prime your fire-works with. **1688** HOLME *Armoury* III. xvi. (Roxb.) 91/2 The stouple or primeing [of the rocket]. *Ibid.* 92/1 When the fire is come to the stoupell, that will fire the cloth. **1696** R. H. *Sch. Recreat.* 33 A Quill of Wild Fire..or Stopple.

stouple, obs. form of STUBBLE.

stouppe, obs. form of STOOP *sb.*[1]

stour (stur), *sb.*[1] Forms: 3–4 **stur(e, 4–9 stoure, stowre, 5 store, (6 stourre), 5–8 stowr, 6–9 stower, 8–9 stoor, 4– stour.** [a. AF. *estur*, OF. *estour* (N.E. dial. *stour*), *estor, estorn* = Pr. *estorn-s*, It. *stormo* tumult, conflict, a. Teut. **sturmo-z* STORM *sb.* The etymological identity of senses 4 and 5 with the other senses is doubtful.]

I. 1. An armed combat or conflict; esp. a contest in battle; a fight. *Obs.* exc. *arch.*
a **1300** *Cursor M.* 7466 A man o þair gains an of vr, If vrs mai him win in stur [*other texts* stoure, stour(e)s]. *Ibid.* 7752–3 Gain saul þai gaf batail strang... In hard strur [*read* stur] þai samen mett. Ful snaip it was þair stur and snell. *c* **1325** *Metr. Hom.* 23 Bot werdes haht and hey tures Getes thir cite men fra stures. *c* **1330** R. BRUNNE *Chron. Wace* (Rolls) 730 Lordynges..þat fledde fro þe grete stour. *c* **1386** CHAUCER *Monk's T.* 380 She that helmed was in starke stoures [*Ellesm.* shoures] And wan by force townes stronge and toures. *c* **1400** *Destr. Troy* Prol. 28 Now of Troy forto selle..Of the stoure & þe stryffe when it distroyet was. *c* **1430** *Pilgr. Lyf Manhode* II. civ. (1869) 113, I am ladi and ..constablesse of alle stoures in cheuachyes, ther as baners ben desplayed. *c* **1489** CAXTON *Sonnes of Aymon* i. 42 Moche grete and merueyllouse was the stoure, and the bataill soo fyers. **1500–20** DUNBAR *Poems* lxxxvi. 26 The quhilk, with mony bludy woundis, in stour, Victoriusly discomfeit the dragoun. **1592** WYRLEY *Armorie, Ld. Chandos* i, Prooued knights In martial feats and battelous stoure. **1612** DRAYTON *Poly-olb.* XVI. 69 Those braue spirits in all those balefull stowres, That with Duke Robert went against the Pagan powers. **1667** J. M'KENZIE in *Highland Papers* (S.H.S. 1916) II. 22 Both parties met wt a terrible stour fighting handsomlie on both sides. **1803** W. S. ROSE *Amadis* 96 Man to man, and horse to horse oppos'd, the stower began. **1808** SCOTT *Marmion* IV. xxxii, When joins yon host in deadly stowre. **1816** —— *Old Mort.* xxxvii, 'Then ye saw a bonny stour,' said Cuddie, 'that sall serve me for fighting a' the days o' my life'. **1846** PROWETT *Prometheus Bound* 21 Whose pointed lances on their foes Bear down the battle's stour. **1904** J. PARKINSON *Lays of Love & War* 81 War unto him is his birthright, The stour of the battle his breath.

†**b.** Phrases. ***stiff, stith, strong in stour***; also rarely ***good, fast, bold in stour.*** *Obs.*
a **1300**, *?a* **1366** [see STIFF *a.* 13]. *a* **1300–1400** [see STITH *a.* 6]. **1338** R. BRUNNE *Chron.* (1725) 6 A stiffe knyght in stoure. *Ibid.* 213 Edward & Edmunde, knyght gode in stoure. *a* **1400** *Minor Poems fr. Vernon MS.* lv. 37 þer nis non so strong in stour,..From þat day forþ,..Of his strengþe he lest a quantite. *c* **1435** *Torr. Portugal* 1655 Welcom, sir knyght, That fast art in stoure. *c* **1460** *Towneley Myst.* xxv. 131 He is..of so mekill myght, And styf in euery stoure. **1500–20** DUNBAR *Poems* lxxvii. 33 The Bruce, that euir was bold in sto[u]r. **1508** *Ibid.* vii. 9 Welcum in stour most strong, incomparable knight. [**1857** SIR F. PALGRAVE *Norm. & Eng.* II. 352 The Danes were very stiff in the stour.]

†**2.** *fig.* **a.** Conflict with death, death-struggle, esp. in ***hard, death-stour, bale-stour*** (see BALE *sb.*[1] 8). *Obs.*
a **1300** *Cursor M.* 15647 Quen suete o blod vt of him brast, þat sua on erth fell. Quen he was risen vt o þis sture til his felaus come he. **1340** HAMPOLE *Pr. Consc.* 1838 þe payn of þe dede..þat es þe hard stour at þe last ende, When þe saule sal fra þe body wende. *Ibid.* 5812, I yhelde my saul in þis dede stour Til þe Loverd. *c* **1450** *St. Cuthbert* (Surtees) 5374 þai prayed þe confessour To bring þat man oute of þat stour. **1552** LYNDESAY *Monarche* 5161 Deith..Quham wysedome may nocht contramand, Nor strenth that stoure may nocht ganestand!

†**b.** A conflict waged with immaterial weapons; a struggle with pain or adversity. *Obs.*
c **1450** *St. Cuthbert* (Surtees) 111 Whan þai þole mekill' in stoures, Tene and tray of tormentoures, To sere men þaire sufferynge Is ensample of gude lyuynge. *c* **1460** *Towneley Myst.* xiv. 497 In strong stowre now ar we sted; what may we say? **1535** STEWART *Cron. Scot.* II. 47 Honorious of Rome the empioure, That tyme with seiknes staid wes in ane stour. *a* **1536** *Songs, Carols* etc. (E.E.T.S.) 68 Styfly to stond in euery stowr Agaynst the fende & all his methe. **1585** FETHERSTONE tr. *Calvin on Acts* xiii. 8. 296 The same stoure haue we at this day with a number of brablers. **1686** J. RENWICK *Let.* 18 Feb. in *Life* Biog. Presbyt. (1827) II. 276 The Lord..hath helped you to stand with a poor despised Party in many Stours for his Interest. **1807–10** TANNAHILL *Poems* (1846) 48 Thus youth and vigour fends itsel'; While dowless eild, in poortith cauld Is lanely left to stand the stoure.

†**3.** Used by Spenser and his imitators for: Time of turmoil and stress. *Obs.*
1579 SPENSER *Sheph. Cal.* Jan. 51 And eke tenne thousand sithes I blesse the stoure [*Glossed by E. K.* a fitt], Wherein I sawe so fayre a sight, as shee. *Ibid.* May 156 When approchen the stormie stowres. **1590** —— *F.Q.* I. ii. 7 Then gan she waile and weepe, to see that woefull stowre. *Ibid.* III. ii. 6, I haue beene trained vp in warlike stowre. *Ibid.* IV. ix. 39 But thus turmoild from one to other stowre, I wast my life. **1597** BP. HALL *Sat.* II. iii. 35 So haue I seene in a tempestuous stowre, Some breer-bush shewing shelter from the showre. **1620** QUARLES *Feast for Worms* Med. ii. D 2 b, God..shield all good men from such stormy stowre. **1642** H. MORE *Song of Soul* I. i. 53 Wks. (Grosart) 18/53 And shall not he..rise, and in his wrathfull stour..quell the haughty enemy. **1742** SHENSTONE *Schoolmistr.* xix, All, all but He, the Author of it's Shame,..regret it's ruthful Stour. **1767** MICKLE *Concub.* I. xxxi, Now to the Goal they fly—in franticke Stowre. **1811** H. MACNEILL *Bygane Times* 49 When wives and dochters, without thrift..can mak nae shift To screen themsels frae tempest's stour.

†**b.** Used by Greene, Lodge, and others, probably by misapprehension of Spenser, for: Occasion, place. *Obs.*
1583 MELBANCKE *Philotimus* A a iij b, When ye Græcians were in suspence, whether to march on to giue onset of battaile, at the same stoure, drad flakes of lightning fire were darted down from heauen. **1589** LODGE *Scillaes Metam.* A 4 b, Clore she gathered Amaranthus flower, And Nais Aiax blossom in that stowre. **1589** GREENE *Menaphon, Melicertus Ecl.* 39 He chose her chinne; and from that happie stowre He neuer stints in glorie to appeare. **1590** —— *Never too Late, Palmer's Verses* 41 The birds at euerie stowre Do tempt the heauens with harmonie diuine. **1595** *Locrine* II. v. 111 For Strumbo the cobler At this same stoure, at this very houre, Lies dead on the ground. **1600** LODGE in *England's Helicon* E 1 b, Oft from her lap at sundry stoures, He leapt, and gathered Sommer flowres.

4. Tumult, uproar; commotion, fuss. Now *Sc.* and *dial.*
[Perhaps partly a variant of STIR *sb.*[3]; cf. the *y* forms of STIR *v.*]
c **1440** *Bone Flor.* 1659 Sche glyste up wyth the hedeows store, A sorowfull wakenyng had sche thore. **1570** LEVINS *Manip.* 175/9 A stoore, *commotio, turbatio.* **1724** WODROW *Corr.* (1843) III. 116, I see he is to take Bishop Burnet in task;..and I am content I have so masterly a writer..some way to stand betwixt me and the stour, so to say. *c* **1730** RAMSAY *Masque* 197 Minerva mim, for a' your mortal stoor, Ye shall with billy Bacchus fit the floor. **1833** G. N. BROWN *York Minster Screen* 150 (E.D.S. No. 76) An t' bairns all roo'red to see their moother roore, Ah nivver i my life seed sike a stoore. **1879** HARDY *Wessex Tales* (1889) 262 Oh, there's such a stoor, Mrs. Newberry..! The king's excise-men can't get the carts ready nohow at all! **1915** SIR J. WILSON *Lowland Scotch in Lower Strathearn* 206 Sic a stoor uboot naything.

b. A storm; esp. a driving storm. *Sc.* and *north.*
1827 J. WILSON *Noct. Ambr.* I. 278 The other horse grows obstinate wi' the sharp stour in his face. *a* **1878** H. AINSLIE *Pilgr. Land Burns* etc. (1892) 218 Then look, ere midnight's past For a stour frae the nor-wast. **1891** ATKINSON *Moorland Parish* 362 It would have been alike impossible to see or read [the burial service] in such a fierce, savage stour; and the sharp, hard sleet and roughened snow were driven against..my neck and face.

II. 5. Flying dust raised by the rapid movement of a person or things, or by the wind; hence a deposit of dust; also dust from material undergoing mechanical treatment. *Sc.* and *north.*
1456 SIR G. HAYE *Law Arms* (S.T.S.) 61 Sa began the grete bataill sa vigorous, that the stour strake in the hevin of the crueltee of that mortall bataill. *c* **1470** HENRY *Wallace* VII. 579 The strang stour rais, as reik, vpon thaim fast. *Ibid.* x. 29 The tothir ost mycht nocht no dedis se, For stour at rais. **1513** DOUGLAS *Æneis* VII. xi. 57 The dusty pouder vp dryvand wyth a stour. *Ibid.* IX. ii. 3 The Troianis..A dusty sop vprysand gan do se, Full thik of stour vp thringand in the ayr. *a* **1578** LINDESAY (Pitscottie) *Chron. Scot.* (S.T.S.) II. 39 The battellis ioynit so cruellie that they might nocht be sene for the stour and reik of poullder. **1786** BURNS *To Mountain Daisy* i, For I maun crush amang the stoure Thy slender stem. **1808** J. MAYNE *Siller Gun* II. 121 Alang the roads it left out-ower ye Sic clouds o' stour, Ye coudna see yer thumb before ye. **1836** CARLYLE in *Academy Suppl.* 17 Sept. (1898) 272/1 The huge smoke and stour of that tumultuous Manchester. **1894** CROCKETT *Lilac Sunbonnet* 46 Ye couldna see his legs or coat-tails for stour as he gaed roon'. **1905** *Blackw. Mag.* Jan. 120/2 She went down on her knees to blow aside a pile of white peat 'stour'.

†**b.** A cloud of spray. *Sc. Obs. rare.*
1513 DOUGLAS *Æneis* III. vi. 130 The large fludis suppis thrise in ane swelth, And wther quhilis spowtis in the air agane, Drivand the stour to the sternis, as it war rane. **1822** H. AINSLIE *Pilgr. Land of Burns* 179 The siller stour That bowses frae the linn.

c. Phrases. (Sc.) ***like stour***: very swiftly or vigorously. ***to blow, cast, throw stour in one's eyes***: fig. (cf. DUST *sb.*[1] 4). ***to kick up, make, raise a stour***: to raise a dust; *fig.*, to make a disturbance or fuss.
a **1788** BURNS *'O Tibbie, I hae seen the day'* ii, Yestreen I met ye on the moor, Ye spak na, but gaed by like stoure. **1870** J. K. HUNTER *Life Studies Char.* 135 Thoo sees I am preachin' awa' here like storr. **1894** CROCKETT *Raiders* (ed. 3) 322, I saw our men..drive like stour across the yard and in at the open gate.
1823 GALT *R. Gilhaize* xv, My grandfather being eager to throw stour in his eyes. **1883** R. CLELAND *Inchbracken* xviii. 136 Do you tak me for a fule, to think ye're to blaw the stour i' my e'en that gate?
1786 BURNS *Ordination* iii, This day the Kirk kicks up a stoure. **1837** R. NICOLL *Poems* (1843) 179 Wha raised at Marston such a stour And made the tyrants fear folk? **1896** A. LILBURN *Borderer* xxii. 169 Tschuh, tschuh, tscha, oh confound you and yer brush together..! Kicking up such a stour. **1897** BEATTY *Secretar* xviii. 154 What gars ye mak sic a stour at sic a time?

†**6.** *to stour*: ? to the ground. *Obs.*$^{-1}$.
c **1557** ABP. PARKER *Ps.* lxxx. 13 Why hast thou beat his closure downe..?..The tushy bore..doth route it vp to stoure.

stour, stoor (stur), *a.* and *sb.*[2] *Obs.* exc. *Sc.* Forms: 1 **stór, 3–5 stor, (3** *Lay.* **steor), 3–5 store, 4–6 stoore, 5 storre; 3–6 stur, 4–6 sture, 5–9 stoor, 6 stur; 4–6, 9 stoure, 4–9 stour, 4, 6, 7** *north.* **stowre, 6–7 stower;** *Sc.* **6, 8 stuir.** [Apparently two words have been confused: (1) Late OE. *stór*, a. ON. *stór-r* (Sw., Da. *stor*) great. Cf. OFris. *stór* great, OS. *stôri* (gl. *inclitus*); the root is prob. **stō-* ablaut-var. of **sta-* to STAND. (2) ME. *stūr*, cogn. w. MLG. *stûr*, MDu. *stuur, stûre* (med. Flem. *stuur*; Du. has the derivative *stuursch*) rough, wild, furious, harsh; it is uncertain whether the affinities are with STEER *a.* or with STIR *v.*
Owing to the uncertainty of the phonetic import of some of the forms, the two words cannot be distinctly separated.]

A. *adj.*

†**1.** Of natural agencies: Violent, fierce. *Obs.*
a **1122** *O.E. Chron.* (Laud MS.) an. 1085, Swa stor þunring & lægt wes swa þat hit acwealde maniȝe men. *c* **1205** LAY. 25740 þer uuen on heo iseȝen a fur þat wes muchel and swiðe stor. *c* **1400** *Ywaine & Gaw.* 373 The store windes blew ful lowd. **1460** *Lybeaus Disc.* 1766 A fere stark and store Was lyght. **14..** *Pol. Rel. & L. Poems* (1903) 131/256 On a grene hill he sawe a tre, The Savoure of hit was stronge & store.

†**b.** Of a fight, battle: Fiercely contested. *Obs.*
c **1205** LAY. 1709 þær wes feiht swiðe strong on alche haue hit wes stor þer wes..moni cniht feie. **1338** R. BRUNNE *Chron.* (1725) 72 þer þe bataile was stoure an abbay wild he haf wrouht.

†**c.** Of conditions: Causing great pain or hardship, hard, severe, grievous. *Obs.*
c **1205** LAY. 7333 þu [Cæsar] ært icumen of Rome þine word beoð swiðe store of ure londe þu axest ȝeld. *a* **1300** *Cursor M.* 24541 Sa war mi stundes store. *c* **1350** *Med. MS.* in *Archæologia* XXX. 384 Ye playster..is good..To leyn on place yer styngyng is, It drawyth awey ye smert so stoure.

†**d.** Of sound: Great in volume, loud. (Cf. 6 b.)
c **1440** *York Myst.* xxxi. 242 My lorde it astonys hym, youre steuen is so store. *a* **1489** CAXTON *Blanchardyn* 162 As of the stour dynnyng and noyse that their horses made treddyng and wallopyng..vpon the grounde. **1500–20** DUNBAR *Poems* xxi. 63 Quhen the angell blawis his bugill sture.

e. quasi-*adv.* Violently, fiercely.
a **1300** *Floriz & Bl.* 228 (Camb. MS.) Fram flore in to flore þe strimes vrneþ store. *c* **1470** *Rauf Coilȝear* 16 The wind blew out of the Eist stiflie and sture. **1885** 'S. MUCKLEBACKIT' (J. Lumsden) *Rural Rhymes* 91 Thou wearie, eastlin' blast Frae 'Lumsden's Hole' that stormest stoure!

†**2.** Great in number, numerous. *Obs.*
c **1205** LAY. 3821 He gadere ferde þe wes feondliche stor. *c* **1250** *Gen. & Ex.* 842 On-kumen was cadalamor, king of elam, wið ferding stor. *a* **1300** *Havelok* 2383 þer he yet on hunting for, With mikel genge, and swiþe stor. **1338** R. BRUNNE *Chron.* (1725) 313 þe poyntes were so store. *a* **1400–50** *Wars Alex.* 1534 Store starand stanes strekilland all ouire [the garment]. *Ibid.* 1741 þou may reȝt lycken þe store strenthe of oure stoure to sternes of þe heuen.

†**3.** Great in degree. *Obs.*
c **1205** LAY. 349 He was mete-custi þat is monscipe steor. *Ibid.* 9126 Muchele is & stor þe eiȝe. *c* **1250** *Owl & Night.* 1473 (MS. Cott.) Wundre me þungþ wel starc & stor Hu eni mon [etc.].

†**4.** Of material things: Great in size, stout, massive, bulky; also *rarely* great in extent of surface. (In some of the quots. approximating to sense 7.) *Obs.*
?a **1300** *Shires England* 28 in *O.E. Misc.* 146 Ac þis wes hwile þreo bisscop-riche, for-þi her to hereþ .viii store schire, and on half schire. *c* **1375** *Sc. Leg. Saints* xix. (*Christopher*) 339 Quhen þat christofore þis prayere had mad,..His staf, þat was sture & stark, was cled with lewis, & with bark. ?**13..** *Adultery* 158 in *Archiv Stud. neu. Spr.* LXXIX. 421 An huge tre, stark & stoure. *c* **1400** *Sc. Trojan War* (Horstm.) 198 Of Pallas a tempile full stoure. *c* **1450** *Bk. Curtasye* 822 in *Babees Book* (1868) 326 He..Awoydes þo borde in-to þo flore, Tase away þo trestis þat ben so store. *c* **1470** HENRY *Wallace* x. 956 Thai..Brak byggyngs doun quhilk had bene stark and stur. **1513** DOUGLAS *Æneis* XI. xi. 45 For in his hand..had he A bustuus speir, percace, baith styth and stuir. **1549** LATIMER *7th Serm. bef. Edw. VI.* A a vj, It was..a greater payne..then when the stower nayles were knocked and driuen throughe hys handes and fete. **1674** N. FAIRFAX *Bulk & Selv.* 138 For body being a stour unweildsom thing,..it cannot stir without asking another bodies leave to crowd by.

†**b.** Of length: Great, immoderate, inordinate.
c **1400** *Destr. Troy* 3042 Hir nose..Stondyng full streght & not of stor lenght.

5. Of persons or animals: Strong, sturdy, stalwart.
a **1310** in Wright *Lyric P.* xxx. 87 Ne is no quene so stark ne stour,..that ded ne shal by-glyde. **1375** BARBOUR *Bruce* x. 158 He wes a stout carle and a sture. *a* **1400–50** *Wars Alex.* 3937 þan floȝe þar..of þa foule Backes, Als store & als stalword as þire sedill dowis. *c* **1400** *Laud Troy Bk.* 16413 The quene..rydyng..Opon a stede strong & store. *c* **1450**

HOLLAND *Howlat* 500 Was nane so stur in the steid micht stand him a start. **1513** DOUGLAS *Æneis* v. viii. 20 The tother of lymmis biggar and cors mair stur is. **1535** STEWART *Cron. Scot.* (Rolls) I. 20 His buirlie bodie, that wes bayth strang and stuir. **1633** G. HERBERT *Temple, Ch. Porch* xx, Constancie knits the bones, and makes us stowre. **1793** *Carlop Green* (1817) 116 Stiff, still, stuir, hard-grown Baillie Brock. **1814** SCOTT *Wav.* xlii, That grey auld stoor carle, the Baron o' Bradwardine.

Comb. *a* **1400–50** *Wars Alex.* 1702 (Ashm. MS.), Askis þam.. Bathe of his statoure & his strenth if he ware store ben [*Dublin MS.* sture-baned].

†**b.** of bearing, countenance, speech. *Obs.*

c **1375** *Sc. Leg. Saints* xx. (*Blase*) 149 þane sad hym blase [= Blasius] with stur chere: certis, þu art a foule. *c* **1386** CHAUCER *Merch. T.* 1123 O stronge lady stoore, what dostow? *c* **1400** *Destr. Troy* 3763 Achilles was.. a stythe man in stoure, storest of wille. *c* **1470** *Gol. & Gaw.* 87 With stout contenance and sture he stude thame beforne. *a* **1510** DOUGLAS *K. Hart* II. 395 Go to the King, with sture voce can he say, Speir gif ony office he hes for me. *a* **1529** SKELTON *Agst. Scottes* 12 They are so stowre, So frantyke mad. **1530** PALSGR. 326/1 Stowre of conversacyon, *estourdy*. **1560** ROLLAND *Seven Sages* 68 He was sa stout and sture, Of his lyfe tuk na cure. **1567** GOLDING *Ovid's Met.* Epist. 11 Such as were most wyld, stowre, feerce.. and bent Ageinst good order, were by him perswaded to relent.

†**c.** of a stroke, pace. *Obs.*

c **1400** *Destr. Troy* 1193 Bothe batels on bent brusshet togedur; With stithe strokes and store. *c* **1470** HENRY *Wallace* IV. 780 Quhen that he was with out, Rycht fast he ȝeide, a stour pais and a stout. *c* **1590** J. STEWART *Poems* (S.T.S.) II. 27/452 Thow happelie did find Thy fortoune now that from his stricking stuir [*sc.* the kicking of a horse] So hes eschewit saif vntuitchit suir.

6. Of a person: Stiff, unbending, stubborn; stern, surly. Also of looks, etc.

1303 R. BRUNNE *Handl. Synne* 11471 ȝyf þou meke þe to þy prest, þou mekes þe to Goddes brest; ȝyf þou be to hym ful stour, þou doust to God grete dysonour. *c* **1400** *Laud Troy Bk.* 3845 But non of hem thei ones gret, But sette hem doun with semblaunt store. *c* **1447** in *Invent. Jarrow & Wearmouth* (Surtees) 241 Will'm of Hilton.. wt hy and stoor countenance entreed yr qweer.. wt outyn ony.. reuerence ..to ye blessid sacrament. *a* **1500** *Ratis Raving* III. 367 Na falow the nocht with our gredy, Na with our still men, na our sture. **1555** WATREMAN *Fardle Facions* II. i. 110 The Occean, whiche where he cometh by Easte Asie, is called Eous,.. and aftre the name of the stoure Scithiane, vpon the Northe Scythicus. **1642** J. ROUS *Diary* (Camden) 121 For that he shewed himselfe crosse and stower, he was committed to the Fleet. **1789–90** BURNS *Five Carlins* xvii, Says Black Joan frae Crichton Peel, A carline stoor and grim. **1815** SCOTT *Guy M.* xxxix, A muckle sture fearsome-looking wife. **1846** CHALMERS in Hanna *Mem.* (1852) IV. xxiv. 456 There's some of your stour orthodox folk just over ready to stretch the Bible to square with their catechism.

Comb. **1816** SCOTT *Old Mort.* iv, That dour stour-looking carle.

b. Of a voice: Harsh, rough. (Cf. 1 d.)

1785 BURNS *Addr. to Deil* viii, When wi' an eldritch, stoor quaick, quaick, Amang the springs, Away ye squatter'd like a drake. **1828** CARR *Craven Gloss.*, *Stoar, stour*, harsh, deep-toned. *Ibid.* II. 294, I tell's him i' a stoar voice, as lang as I'se maister o' this house [etc.]. **1894** 'H. HALIBURTON' (J. L. Robertson) *Furth in Field* 9 The farmer.. demanded in a stoor voice..'whether' [etc.]. **1894** R. REID *Poems* 46 Nae merle at e'enin' his melody starts.. But a corbie's maybe, or some ither as stoor.

7. Coarse in texture, harsh, rough, stiff.

c **1400** MAUNDEV. (Roxb.) xxxi. 140 In thase iles..er schepe als mykill as oxen, bot þe woll of þam es grete and sture. *c* **1440** *Alphabet of Tales* 184 And he sett befor þaim sture brede & salte. **1530** PALSGR. 326/1 Stoure, rude as course clothe is, *gros*. *Ibid.* 630 This rubbynge of your gowne agaynst the wolle wyll make it sture to the syght: *ce frotter de vostre robbe contre la layne laruyda quant a la veue.* **1545** RAYNALDE *Byrth Mankynde* I. 2 The Skin.. in sume one person [is] moore stowre & styffe then in sume other agayne. **1545** ASCHAM *Toxoph.* II. (Arb.) 131 A fenny goose, euen as her flesh is blacker, stoorer, vnholsomer, so is her fether for the sa ne cause courser stoorer and rougher. **1567** GOLDING *Ovid's Met.* VIII. (1593) 195 And eke the skin with bristles stur right griesly he hir gaue. **1691** RAY *S. & E. Country Words, Sturry*, inflexible, sturdy, and stiffe. *Stowre* is used in the same sense, and spoken of cloth, in opposition to limber. *a* **1825** FORBY *Voc. E. Anglia, Stour*, stiff, stout. .. In our use, it seems rarely, if ever, applied to any thing but strong vegetable growth.. In Suffolk.. it is applied to land which works stiff.

†**B.** *sb.*[2] [Cf. A. 7.] A thick place (in cloth).

1472 *5th Rep. Hist. MSS. Comm.* 436/2 [The cloth is to be clear of] rowe, stour, cokell, vagite, grete hole or any other defaute.

Hence †'**storlic** *a.*, strong, fierce.

c **1205** LAY. 10647 þat feht wes swiðe storlic [*c* **1275** storlich].

stour (stur), *v.* *Sc.* and *north.* Also stoor. [f. STOUR *sb.*[1] II.]

1. *intr.* Of a substance: To rise up in a cloud of dust or powder; to fly. Of snow: To drive.

1788 W. H. MARSHALL *Yorksh.* II. 356 To *Stoor*; to rise up in clouds, as smoke, dust, fallen lime, &c. **1860** RAMSAY *Remin.* v. (1867) 87 In speaking of the dryness of the soil on a road in Lanarkshire, a farmer said, 'It stoors in an oor'. **1891** ATKINSON *Moorland Parish* 360 It was a wild day indeed, the snow stouring in blinding clouds.

2. (See quot.)

1811 WILLAN in *Archæologia* XVII. 160 *Stour*, to raise dust, to make a bustle.

Hence '**stouring** *ppl. a.*

1891 ATKINSON *Moorland Par.* (ed. 2) 361 The stouring snow which blew directly into one's face and eyes.

stour, obs. form of STORE; var. STOWER *sb.*[1]

stourb, variant of STURB *v.* *Obs.*

stourdi, obs. form of STURDY *a.*

stoure: see STIR *v.*, STOUR, STOWER *sb.*[1]

stourly ('sturlɪ), *adv.* Forms: 3 storliche; *Sc.* 4–5 sturly, 5 stwrly, 5–6 sturely, 8–9 stourly. [f. STOUR *a.* + -LY[2].]

†**1.** Greatly. *Obs.*

a **1225** *Leg. Kath.* 1268 Is nu se storliche unstrenget ower strengðe.

2. *Sc.* Fiercely, violently; stoutly, vigorously.

c **1375** *Sc. Leg. Saints* l. (*Catherine*) 1028 þane þat tyrand ..rathly ruschit to and fra,..& sturly stampit als, & steryt. *c* **1470** *Rauf Coilȝear* 860 The kene Knicht in that steid stakkerit sturely. **1572** *Sat. Poems Reform.* xxxviii. 74 Giue ..we..hald vs togidder, Baith surely, and sturely, and stoutly gainstand thame. **1793** T. SCOTT *Poems* 375 (E.D.D.), I heard a horn fu' stourly blawn. **1888** DOUGHTY *Trav. Arabia Deserta* I. 127 He looked stourly about him, who should speak next. **1898** J. PATON *Castlebraes* ii. 49 Swuftly an' stourly, I laid ma Heezel Rung, a second swash, athwart the safter pairs.

stourm, stourne: see STORM *sb.*, STERN *a.*

stourness ('sturnɪs). *Obs.* exc. *Sc.* [f. STOUR *a.* + -NESS.] The condition of being 'stour'; †sturdiness; †roughness; largeness.

c **1400** *Destr. Troy* 9015 Kyng Seppidon.. Bounet vnto batell.. And to Neptilon anon,.. As by stowrnes of strenght, streght on hym met. *Ibid.* 10345 And troiell.. trayturly he slogh, Noght þurgh stowrenes of strokes, ne with strenght one; But [etc.]. **1530** PALSGR. 277/1 Stournesse, *estourdisseure*. **1866** T. EDMONDSTON *Shetl. & Orkney Gloss.*, *Stourness*, largeness, bigness, Shetland.

stourre, obs. form of STOUR *sb.*, STOWER *sb.*[1]

stoury ('sturɪ), *a.* *Sc.* and *north.* Also 9 stoory. [f. STOUR *sb.*[1] 5 + -Y.] Characterized by flying dust or driving snow; also, covered with dust.

a **1792** BURNS *Weary Pund o' Tow* iii, And ay she took the tither souk To drouk the stourie tow. **1803** R. ANDERSON *Ball. Cumbld.* (1808) 62 The Bible ligs stoury abuin the duir head. **1823** GALT *R. Gilhaize* xlvii, The stoury rafters of an auld bigging. **1898** *Blackw. Mag.* Jan. 21 The dry and stoury alleys of the fir-wood.

stoury, obs. form of STORY *sb.*[1]

stoush (staʊʃ), *v.* *Austral.* and *N.Z. slang.* Also †stouch. [Orig. uncertain: perh. rel. to *stashie* uproar, quarrel (*E.D.D.*, *S.N.D.*).] To thrash or beat (a person); to punch or strike; to fight.

1893 J. A. BARRY *Steve Brown's Bunyip* 66 I'll get stoushed over this job yet. Brombee's got it in for me. **1894** *Bulletin* (Sydney) 5 May 13/3 'Then 'e biffed me.' 'And did yer stouch him back?' **1900** H. LAWSON *On Track* 148 'If you don't,' said Steelman, 'I'll stoush you.' **1924** KIPLING *Debits & Credits* (1926) 309 'What *your* crowd down under are suffering from is growing pains. You'll get over em in three hundred years or so— if you're allowed to last so long.' 'Who's going to stoush us?' Orton asked fiercely. **1941** K. TENNANT *Battlers* xxvi. 281 What with not being allowed to stoush any of the coves in charge of this turnout. **1945** [see QUILT *v.*[2] a]. **1965** E. LAMBERT *Long White Night* 79 Get out of that bloody car while I stoush yer!

stoush (staʊʃ), *sb.* *Austral.* and *N.Z. slang.* Also †stouch. [f. the vb.] Fighting; also, *to take stoush*, to receive a beating. A brawl or fight; a scrap, 'punch-up'.

1908 H. FLETCHER *Dads & Dan between Smokes* 32 He looked as though he liked bein' hit an' took stoush fer breakfast every mornin'. **1914** C. J. DENNIS in *Bulletin* (Sydney) 16 July 47/1 Wot's jist plain stoush wif us.. is 'valler' [*sc.* valour] if yer far enough away. **1924** *Truth* (Sydney) 27 Apr. 6 *Stouch*, a fight; to assault. **1945** R. S. CLOSE *Love me Sailor* 149 It was like the old days when I got Ernie into some stoush ashore just for the hell of fighting him out of it. **1952** J. CLEARY *Sundowners* (1960) iii. 129 The warmonger. You start any more stoushes.. and.. it'll be the finish of you. **1966** *Weekly News* (N.Z.) 22 June 59/4 The final folly was that it was the Lions and not Otago who were principally responsible for the 'stoush' of the first half of Saturday's game. **1970** D. M. DAVIN *Not here, not Now* IV. i. 229 I've played football against him. He's a good man in the stoush, no doubt about that.

stout (staʊt), *sb.*[1] Now *dial.* Forms: 1–2 stút, 4 stoute, 7 stowt(e, 7–9 stut, 9 stoat, 6– stout. [OE. *stút*, of obscure etymology.] A gadfly, horse-fly; also applied to a gnat.

Higins (quot. 1585), prob. by mistake, uses it for the candle-fly or moth; Florio follows this, using *fire-fly* for 'a fly living in the fire' (Cooper s.v. *Pyrausta*).

c **1000** ÆLFRIC *Voc.* in Wr.-Wülcker 121/24 *Culex*, stut. **1387** TREVISA *Higden* (Rolls) V. 159 þe snowtes of olyfauntes and his hors eren were so ful of gnattes and stoutes and of greet flyes [L. *culicibus et ciniphibus*] þat þey [etc.]. **1585** HIGINS *Junius' Nomencl.* 72/2 *Pyrallis*,.. a candle flie: a stout, or millers soule [*printed* foule]. **1598** FLORIO, *Pirausta*, a fire-flye or worme bred and liuing in the fire, and going from it dieth, and flieth into the leame of a candle: some call it a candle-flie, a stout, a miller-fowle, or bishop. **1616** J. LANE *Contn. Sqr.'s T.* XI. 383 And blusshinge welkin fell with stowtes to playe at novum. **1657** R. LIGON *Barbadoes* 62 Musketos, who bite and sting worse then the Gnats and Stouts, that sting Cattle in England. **1666** MERRETT *Pinax* 199 *Tabanides*, a Burrel-fly, stout, Brees, Clog or Cling. **1674–91** RAY *S. & E.C. Words*, A Stut: a Gnat: Somerset. **1852** *Berks. Gloss.*, *Stout*, a sharp stinging fly. **1879** JEFFERIES *Wild Life in S.C.* 199 A boy armed with a spray of ash, with which he flicks off the stoats that would otherwise drive the animals frantic. **1898** MISS YONGE *John Keble's Parishes* xvi. 193 The large fly, popularly called a stout, as big as a hornet, lays eggs under the skin of cows.

attrib. *a* **1887** JEFFERIES *Field & Hedgerow* (1889) 229 The peculiar low whir of the stoat-fly.

b. *Newfoundland.* (See quot.)

1903 A. C. P. HAGGARD *Sporting Yarns* 205 The huge 'stouts', a gadfly of great biting power, used to attack my head and neck terribly. **1905** —— *Bond of Sympathy* 60 A.. ferocious insect, thicker than, and about the size of a hornet, which it resembles in being barred with black and yellow. This formidable insect, the Newfoundlanders call the Stout.

stout (staʊt), *sb.*[2] Also 7 stoutt. [Prob. elliptical for *stout ale* or *stout beer* (STOUT *a.* 11), though in our quots. these are not found till much later.] †**a.** 'A cant name for strong beer' (J.) *Obs.* **b.** In present use, a strong variety of porter.

1677 R. HAWTREY *Let., Egerton MS.* 2716 We will drink your healths both in stoutt and best wine. *a* **1700** B. E. *Dict. Cant. Crew, Stout*, very strong, Malt-Drink. **1719** D'URFEY *Pills* V. 83 We will frolick in Stout, And banish all Care in a Mug. **1720** SWIFT *Poems, To Stella* 32 Or kindly, when his credit's out, Surprise him with a pint of stout. **1762** W. BURTON *Let.* in *Add. MS.* 32933, lf. 273 The Porter brewers likewise make a beer of an extraordinary strength called Stout, that will bear being make weaker by mixing it with small. **1816** *Times* 25 Jan. in *Hone's Every-day Bk.* I. 462 Each house was supplied with Brown Stout. **1848** ALB. SMITH *Chr. Tadpole* xxvi. 237 A bottle of stout and a biscuit. **1882** BESANT *All Sorts* Prol. I. I. 12 Messenger, Marsden, and Company's Stout, their XXX, [etc.].

stout (staʊt), *a.* and *adv.* Forms: 3–4 stute, 3–7 stoute, 4 stut, 4–7 stowt(e, 5 *Sc.* stult, 5–6 stought, 7 stoutt, 4– stout. [a. OF. *estout* (NE. dial. *stout*), earlier *estolt*, *estult*, brave, fierce, proud; of Teut. origin: cf. OFris. *stult* proud, MLG. *stolt* stately, proud, (M)Du. *stout* proud, OHG., MHG., mod.G. *stolz* proud (in MHG. also foolish):—WGer. **stulta-*. The ON. *stollz* is from HG., and the later ON. *stolt-r* (= MSw. *stolt-er*, Sw., Da. *stolt*) from LG.

According to some scholars the WGer. word is an adoption (with remarkable development of meaning) of L. *stultus* foolish. Others regard it as native Teut., from **stult* ablaut-var. of **stelt-* (? to walk stiffly): see STILT *sb.*]

A. *adj.* **I.** Proud, fierce, brave, resolute.

†**1. a.** Proud, haughty, arrogant. Often coupled with *proud*. *to make it stout*: to swagger. *Obs.*

c **1315** SHOREHAM *Poems* vii. 410 Alle hy weren ydryuen out, Wyþ lucyfer þat was so stout. *c* **1330** *Spec. Gy de Warw.* 623 Ac þu, fersse man, þat art so stout, And heih of mod, and herte proud. *c* **1400** *Rom. Rose* 6158, I mene of fals Religious, That stoute ben, and malicious [Fr. *des felons, des malicieus*]. *c* **1400** *Brut* 2 Albyne bycome so stoute & so sterne, þat sche told litel prys of her lord. *c* **1400** *Sowdone Bab.* 1825 Thai made it both stoute and gay. *c* **1421** *26 Pol. Poems* xxi. 73 How of hem han hertis stoute þat reweþ non pore þat han penaunce. *c* **1440** *Jacob's Well* 74 Whan þou art in þat estate,.. þanne wexist þou stowt & fell, and puttyst out þi venym of pride. **1535** COVERDALE *Isa.* x. 12 The noble and stoute Kynge of Assiria. **1552** HULOET, Stowt, *superbus, superciliosus*. *a* **1586** SIDNEY *Arcadia* I. v. (1912) 32 A man mightie in riches & power, and proude thereof, stubbornly stout. **1593** SHAKS. *2 Hen. VI*, I. i. 187 As stout and proud as he were Lord of all. **1635** PAGITT *Christianogr.* III. (1636) 22 If he be stout and proud, he is not of God. **1656** BAXTER *Reformed Pastor* 177 Can we once conceive of him as purposely washing.. his servants feet, and yet be stout and Lordly still? **1669** R. MONTAGU in *Buccleuch MSS.* (Hist. MSS. Comm.) I. 452 If we are as high and as stout as they, I am confident we shall bring them a pin lower. *a* **1803** [see PROUD-HEARTED]. **1851** STERNBERG *Northampt. Gloss.*, *Stout*, proud.

†**b.** Stately, magnificent, splendid. *Obs.*

a **1310** in Wright *Lyric P.* xvi. 52 Heo is dereworthe in day, Graciouse, stout, ant gay. **13..** *E.E. Allit. P.* A. 935 If þou has oþer lygynges stoute, Now tech me to þat myry mote. **1362** LANGL. *P. Pl.* A. II. 12 *note*, Of reed gold so ryche redilyche I-dyȝte Wiþ precioue stoones so stoute stondynge þer-ynne. *a* **1400** *Launfal* 985 Up stod the quene and ladyes stoute. *c* **1400** *26 Pol. Poems* xxv. 537, I that was full stoute and gay, froll horyble am now opon to se. **1430–50** *Erthe upon Erthe* IV. 25 Why scholde erthe a-pon erthe goo stowte and gay?

†**2. a.** Fierce, furious. *Obs.*

c **1300** *Beket* 512 Sire Hughe Eorl of Chestre, and Eorl Williem of Ferers, Were at this parlement, stout ynou and fers. **1303** R. BRUNNE *Handl. Synne* 4036 He.. sagh a bere wylde and stoute. **1338** —— *Chron.* (1725) 48 þe burgeis of London were wroþe & stoute. *c* **1421** *26 Pol. Poems* xxi. 139 Drede no tyrauntes sterne and stoute May sle þy body. *c* **1450** LOVELICH *Merlin* 2687 Vndyr wheche water ben there set Tweyne wondirful Stowte dragowns. **1590** SPENSER *F.Q.* III. XII. 25 Emongst them was sterne Strife, and Anger stout. **1600** HOLLAND *Livy* I. xlvi. 32 The younger Tullia, a stout dame and a proud.

†**b.** Formidable, menacing; terrible in appearance. *Obs.*

1338 R. BRUNNE *Chron.* (1725) 74 Tiþynges com him fulle stoute, þat a grete oste & stark,.. Were aryued in Humbere. *Ibid.* 115 þise men lift per standard, that stoute was & grim. *c* **1375** *Sc. Leg. Saints* xix. (*Christopher*) 469 þat [þa] wemane speryt has with stut vysage & auchtful spek. *c* **1420** ? LYDG. *Assembly of Gods* 313 Hys colour was.. Foule,.. hys eyen gret & stoute. *c* **1470** HENRY *Wallace* x. 78 Quha couth behald thair awfull lordly wult, So weill beseyn, so forthwart, stern, and stult. *a* **1550** *Freiris Berwik* 196 in *Dunbar's Poems* (1893) 291 The gudwyfe spak than, with a visage stowt. **1601** CHESTER *Love's Mart.* (1878) 27 A huge Tower of brasse,.. Able to bide the raging Foes stout frowne.

†**c.** Of pain: Severe. *Obs.*

c **1425** AUDELAY *XI Pains of Hell* 144 in *O.E. Misc.* 227 Faste þei wente þis pepul a-boute, Wiþ moni turmentes grete and stoute.

3. a. Valiant, brave; undaunted and vigorous in conflict or resistance. Also, *stout fellow*: see FELLOW *sb.* 9a. Now somewhat *arch.* (chiefly *attrib.* of soldiers).

13.. *K. Alis.* 869 (Laud MS.), Nicholas of cartage Hardy man stout & sauage. *c* **1325** *Lai le Freine* 249 He was stout, of gret renoun And was y-cleped Sir Guroun. **13..** *E.E. Allit. P.* B. 1184 Stoffed wyth-inne with stout men to stalle hem þer-oute. **1375** BARBOUR *Bruce* II. 390 Thocht he wes stout and hardy,.. Thar mycht na worschip thar awailȝe. **1572** HULOET (ed. Higins), Stoute or aduenturous, *audaculus.* **1586** A. DAY *Eng. Secretorie* I. (1595) 74 Grieue, replied the stout couragious Citizen, yea, euen I. **1590** SPENSER *F.Q.* II. x. 54 Stout Bunduca. **1591** SHAKS. *1 Hen. VI*, III. iv. 19 A stouter Champion neuer handled Sword. **1595** *Phrases Lat. Aldi Manutii* 106 Fortis pro salute patriæ. Stout in the quarrell, or valiant for the safe-guard of his country. **1625** BACON *Ess., Suspic.* (Arb.) 528 They [*sc.* these defects] take Place in the Stoutest Natures: As in the Example of Henry the Seuenth..: There was not a more Suspicious Man, nor a more Stout. **1656** T. STANLEY *Hist. Philos.* v. xxix. (1687) 194 In this Sence we call all Souldiers stout, and sometimes call imprudent and rash persons stout, when we speak not of the perfect Vertues. *a* **1661** FULLER *Worthies, Westmorld.* (1662) 136 That Stout Prelate who when the Scots invaded England,.. utterly routed and ruined them. **1690** LOCKE *Educ.* §96 (1693) 114 Some Men by the unalterable Frame of their Constitutions are Stout, others Timorous. **1727** A. HAMILTON *New Acc. E. Indies* I. xviii. 216 Cowards are generally stout when Dangers are at a Distance, and so was our General, who had never seen a Sword drawn in Anger. **1842** BORROW *Bible in Spain* xxvi. (Pelh. Libr.) 186 Legends the most wild are related of the manner in which the stout soldier fell. **1849** MACAULAY *Hist. Eng.* v. I. 647 His arm had been.. shattered in the battle; and, as no surgeon was at hand, the stout old soldier amputated it himself. **1890** CONAN DOYLE *White Company* xxvii, I have heard that he is a very stout and skilful soldier.

absol. *c* **1470** *Gol. & Gaw.* 831 So sal ye stonay yone stowt, suppose he be strang.

†b. Hardy, strong in endurance. *Obs.*

1576 WOOLTON *Chr. Man.* Lvjb, We receaue fashions and condicions of our companions... Effeminate men and softlings, cause the stoute man to waxe tender. **1708** J. CHAMBERLAYNE *Pres. St. Gt. Brit.* I. III. viii. 274 Which grievous kind of Death [*Peine forte et dure*] some stout Fellows have sometimes chosen.

c. Of courage, the 'heart', etc.: Undismayed.

1508 DUNBAR *Tua Mariit Wemen* 485 Sum stalwardly steppis ben, with a stout curage. *a* **1548** HALL *Chron., Edw. IV*, 238b, Thys ende had the valiant hart and stoute courage of duke Charles of Burgoyn. **1663** BUTLER *Hud.* I. ii. 299 Yet Talgol was of Courage stout, And vanquish'd oftner than he fought. **1781** COWPER *Expost.* 358 To quell the valour of the stoutest heart. **1831** SCOTT *Jrnl.* 9 Apr., Their courage is much stouter than I apprehended. **1837** CARLYLE *Fr. Rev.* II. I. ii, A man stout of heart. **1841** HELPS *Ess.* II. *Educ. Man Business* 79 He should be courageous... Besides a stout heart, he should have a patient temperament.

d. Of a conflict, assault, or resistance: Vigorous.

1582 N. LICHEFIELD tr. *Castanheda's Conq. E. Ind.* I. lxxiv. 152 Our men.. made with the enimies a valyant and stout skirmish. **1587** FLEMING *Contn. Holinshed* III. 1406/1 In a letter written.. out of Spaine, in the yeare 1577, it is set downe.. that the state of Christendome stood vpon the stout assailing of England. **1595** SHAKS. *John* IV. ii. 173 When aduerse Forreyners affright my Townes With dreadfull pompe of stout inuasion. **1812** CARY *Dante, Parad.* XII. 95 He.. Smote fiercest, where resistance was most stout. **1858** CARLYLE *Fredk. Gt.* II. x. (1865) I. 109 To the last they always made stout fight for themselves. **1890** P. H. HUNTER *Story of Daniel* i. 12 The Assyrian monarch offered a stout resistance.

†e. Strenuous, energetic. *Obs.*

1600 HOLLAND *Livy* VI. xxxiv. 241 L. Sextius, a stout young man [L. *strenuo adolescente*]. *c* **1610** *Women Saints* 175 The lawes which Salomon prescribeth to such a stoute and paynefull woman. **1635** R. N. tr. *Camden's Hist. Eliz.* I. 59 He performed stout service. **1661** LOWTHER in *Extr. S.P. rel. Friends* II. (1911) 118 For the incourragiinge all to be active and stowte in a tyme soe necessary. **1664** H. MORE *Myst. Iniq.* 302 They may be receiving (though not in such a passive way as it does not involve with it some stout effort of their own). **1711** SWIFT *Jrnl. to Stella* 10 Nov., Stella is naturally a stout walker, and carries herself firm.

†4. a. Of persons: Firm in resolve, unyielding, determined. *Obs.* exc. as in d.

1568 GRAFTON *Chron.* II. 58 He.. with wordes of great consolation did courage him to be stoute in the quarrell he toke in hand. **1591** HARINGTON *Orl. Fur.* Apol. Poetrie ¶iiijb, Bishop Fisher, a stout Prelat.. was assaid by King Henrie the eight for his good will and assent for the suppression of Abbeys. **1594** SHAKS. *Rich. III*, I. iii. 340 Heere come my Executioners, How now my hardy stout resolued Mates, Are you now going to dispatch this thing? *c* **1610** *Women Saints* 100 She being but a girle receyued the faith of Christ, wherein she grew so feruent and stoute, that [etc.]. **1631** *Proverb* in J. Done *Polydoron* 43, I stout and thou stout, who shall carry the Dirt out? **1639** FULLER *Holy War* II. xlv. (1640) 106 Askelon was stout, and would not surrender. **1711** SWIFT *Jrnl. to Stella* 6 Dec., We reckon we have a majority of ten on our side in the House of Lords; yet I observed Mrs. Masham a little uneasy: she assures me the Queen is stout. **1720-1** *Lett. fr. Mist's Jrnl.* (1722) II. 235 All the several Parties among us exact that of us, which they will by no Means practise themselves. They are all stiff and stout, and maintain their several Posts resolutely. **1729** SWIFT *Poems, Grand Question* 55 Madam, I always believ'd you so stout, That for twenty Denials you would not give out. **1815** J. W. CROKER in *C. Papers* 27 July (1884) I. 75 He was very stout about travelling all night and every night when we left Paris, and seemed only to fear my laziness or reluctance. **1815** WELLINGTON in Gurw. *Desp.* (1838) X. 169 But if we are stout we shall save the King whose government affords the only chance for peace.

†b. In bad sense: Obstinate, intractable, stubborn, rebellious. *Obs.*

c **1410** HOCCLEVE *Mother of God* 82 Thogh that oure hertis steerne been & stoute. *c* **1412** —— *De Reg. Princ.* 2639 Is non so good, as lat vs mollifie Our hertes stoute to his genterie. *a* **1620** J. DYKE *Right Receiving* (1640) 55 The stoutest, sturdiest, and most rebellious spirit that ever was. **1620** QUARLES *Feast for Wormes* Med. xi. I2b, Lord.. Subdue our Passions, Curb our stout Affections. *a* **1639** W. WHATELEY *Prototypes* I. xix. (1640) 194 If any of you have beene stoute against God Pharaoh-like, let him [etc.]. **1646** SLINGSBY *Diary* (1836) 181 Yᵉ one being mild and tractable, yᵉ other stout, covetous, and impatient of a companion. **1788** WESLEY *Wks.* (1872) VI. 301 The stout, the hard-hearted, will melt before you. *a* **1834** J. H. NEWMAN *Par. Serm.* I. xvii. 260 He has to overcome that resistance from his old stout will and hardened heart.

c. Of utterances or demeanour: Resolute, defiant. *arch.*

1390 GOWER *Conf.* II. 378 Bot where he spak in Grece aboute, He herde noght bot wordes stoute. *c* **1420** ? LYDG. *Assembly of Gods* 439 On a rewde maner he salutyd all the rout, With a bold voyse, carpyng wordys stout. **1470-85** MALORY *Arthur* I. vii, There was but little meekenesse, for there was stout and hard words on both sides. **1553** BRENDE *Q. Curtius* Bv, Hereupon Alexander with many stowte and dispiteful wordes, departed from his father. **1565** T. STAPLETON *Fortr. Faith* 102 This stoute assertion of that impudent frier. **1611** BIBLE *Mal.* iii. 13 Your words haue bin stout against me, saith the Lord. **1634** PEACHAM *Compl. Gentl.* i. (1906) 17 To these and such, I oppose Marius, and that stout reply of his in *Salust.* *a* **1653** BINNING *Common Princ. Chr. Relig.* Wks. (1735) 37/2 It is not big and stout Words that will prove it. *a* **1656** USSHER *Power Princes* II. (1683) 229 In the like manner Hosius, that old Confessor, beginneth his stout, but dutiful Letter which he wrote unto him. *a* **1700** EVELYN *Diary* 11 July 1691, This stout demeanor of the few Bishops who refus'd to take the oathes. **1729** TINDAL tr. *Rapin's Hist. Eng.* XVII. IX. 30 James returned a stout Answer, and vindicated himself for not having performed his Promise. **1810** WELLINGTON in Gurw. *Desp.* (1836) VI. 207, I have a letter from the Governor of the 13th in which he holds stout language. **1868** J. H. BLUNT *Ref. Ch. Eng.* I. 54 A month after this stout despatch.. Wolsey was nominated principal legate.

d. Of a partisan, an advocate, an enemy: Uncompromising.

1586 A. DAY *Eng. Secretorie* I. (1595) 37 That which.. there is none (were it the stoutest enemie that euer liued) but wil most highlie commend. *a* **1661** FULLER *Worthies, Suffolk* (1662) 57 Robert Grosthead.. was a stout Opposer of Popish Oppression in the Land. **1835** J. W. CROKER in *C. Papers* 10 Mar. (1884) II. 267 His enemies are not very stout, and are united only on the one point of opposing him. **1850** W. IRVING *Goldsm.* xxxi. 302 Johnson, who was a stout unbeliever in Rowley. **1861** BROUGHAM *Brit. Const.* xi. 155 A claim admitted by even the stoutest advocates of the Romish Church. **1913** *Times* 14 May 7/6 When Philip the Bold.. married Margaret, the heir of France's stout enemy, Flanders.

5. a. Of a fox: Capable of long runs; enduring.

1714 TYLDESLEY *Diary* (1873) 147 Went a hunting to Sullum, and ffound ditto ffox... Had a noble chace, but he proved too stout and bette us quit outt. **1880** 'BROOKSBY' *Hunting Countries* II. 195 The woodland foxes of course are stout; and they travel long distances before they die. **1894** *Pall Mall Gaz.* 20 Dec. 10/3 A stout fox found in Owston Wood broke away on the Melton side.

b. Of a horse: Characterized by endurance or staying power: contrasted with *speedy.* Hence ***stout blood.***

1773 GOLDSM. *Stoops to Conq.* v. ii, *Tony.* Stout horses and willing minds make short journeys, as they say. **1796** J. LAWRENCE *Treat. Horses* I. 196 The term stout, in equestrian language, applies invariably to the courage, not the substance of the horse. **1818** 'W. H. SCOTT' *Brit. Field Sports* 511 We have upon the Turf, two old and customary divisions of Race Horses, which according to their peculiar constitutional temperament, we classify as *speedy* or *stout.* **1833** *Q. Rev.* XLIX. 387 It is worthy of remark, that in his stud, a regard is paid to what is termed stout blood. *Ibid.* 388 A stout horse ends his race to advantage up hill; a speedy jade down hill. **1860** ROUS in *Baily's Mag.* I. 19 For the encouragement of the breed of strong stout horses. **1861** J. H. WALSH & LUPTON *Horse* 75 About twenty horses have been in training, and among these he has had the luck to have one extraordinarily stout mare.

II. Physical senses.

6. a. Strong in body; of powerful build. Now only *U.S. dial.*

c **1386** CHAUCER *Prol.* 545 The Millere was a stout carl for the nones Ful byg he was of brawn, and eek of bones. **1390** GOWER *Conf.* II. 244 Mars, which god of Armes was, Hath set two Oxen sterne and stoute. *c* **1440** *Promp. Parv.* 478/1 Stowt, or stronge, *robustus.* **1765** *Museum Rust.* IV. 208 Our reaps are put by gatherers, women or stout boys, into sheets. .. Two stout men carry these. **1784** COWPER *Task* I. 481 Till the stout bearers lift the corpse again. **1791** SMEATON *Edystone L.* §297 The high wages we were obliged to give, to induce stout labourers to face the perils of the service. **1796** JANE AUSTEN *Sense & Sens.* xxxviii, They must get a stout girl of all works. **1800** *Med. Jrnl.* IV. 222 He is tall, well proportioned, thin, but pretty stout for his years. **1804** *Ibid.* XII. 114, I forgot to mention that this woman was suckling a stout boy, twelve months old. **1822** SHELLEY *Goethe's Faust* ii. 2 Would you not like a broomstick? As for me I wish I had a good stout ram to ride. **1842** LOUDON *Suburban Hort.* 315 This bank.. will by its weight furnish such resistance to the action of the top of the tree, that a stout man, on applying himself to a rope tied to the upper part of the stem, will generally be unable to displace the root. **1882** 'MARK TWAIN' *Stolen White Elephant* 269 Your word 'stout' means 'fleshy'; our word 'stout' usually means 'strong'. **1913** *Dialect Notes* IV. 54 That calf's terrible stout; he pretty near pulled me all over the field. **1962** W. FAULKNER *Reivers* iv. 82 Let Lucius get out... He's younger than me and stouter too for his size.

b. In robust health, 'strong', esp. with reference to recovery from illness. *Obs.* exc. *Sc.*

1697 J. LEWIS *Mem. Dk. Glocester* (1789) 50 The Duke was not the stoutest child, and had been subject to a watry mouth, which now grew better. **1780** S. J. PRATT *Emma Corbett* (ed. 4) III. 51, I cannot be more explicit till I know what present health you are in... Tell me that you are very stout and you shall hear more. **1797** HAN. MORE in Visctess. Knutsford *Life & Lett. Z. Macaulay* (1900) 177 He as usual overworks himself, and is not, I think, very stout, though certainly very happy. **1811** SARAH LADY LYTTELTON in Mrs. H. Wyndham *Corr.* (1912) 119 All this fine weather will help poor, dear old Granny Lucan to get stout again. **1813** *Ibid.* 145 It being Sunday, and I feeling very stout, ventured out at noon. **1817** MARIA EDGEWORTH *Ormond* vii, Then if you are quite stout again, I shall want you to row me across the lake. *c* **1825** MRS. CAMERON *Houlston Tracts* II. xxxiv. 4 The week after-wards, Ellen said to her husband, on Sunday morning, 'Now, William, I am got so stout, that I think we may return to our old habits, and go to church twice a-day.' **1838** WHATELY in *Life* (1866) I. 417 We have been two months in England for J.'s health, who is better, though far from stout. **1844** H. HEUGH in Macgill *Life* xxiv. (1852) 431, I have not felt so stout for a great while, wind and weather notwithstanding. **1848** DICKENS *Dombey* viii, 'The child is hardly,' said Mr. Dombey, 'as stout as I could wish.' **1884** ANNIE SWAN *Carlowrie* x. 162 Ye're no' lookin' very stoot, Mrs. Dalrymple,.. I doot ye're workin' ower sair.

7. With reference to intensity or force. **†a.** Of a wind: Strong. *Obs.*

c **1400** *Destr. Troy* 1981 A stithe man to the stere hade, & a stoute wynde, Were blouen to þe brode se in a bir swithe. **1533** J. HEYWOOD *Play Wether* (1903) 1089 A water-myller .. sayde the wynde was so stout The rayne could not fale. **1670** NARBOROUGH *Jrnl.* in *Acc. Sev. Late Voy.* I. (1694) 21 A stout gale and a great Sea.

†b. Of sound: Strong, harsh. *Obs.*

c **1440** *York Myst.* xix. 3 Stent of youre steuenes stoute. *c* **1482** J. KAY tr. *Caoursin's Siege of Rhodes* (1870) ¶ 1 f [The Turks] made thenne a stoute and horryble crye, as they haue in theyr guyse afore that they begynne to fyghte. **1545** BALE *Image Both Ch.* I. i. Ciiij, A loud shyrle voyce.. whiche was so vehement, and stought to my iudgement, as it had bene yᵉ noise of a great trompe. **1545** ASCHAM *Toxoph.* I. (Arb.) 39 Musicke inuented by the Dorians [having] a manlye, rough and stoute sounde in it.

c. *Path.* Of a heart-beat: Strong.

1898 *Allbutt's Syst. Med.* V. 927 The deliberate rhythm, some forty in the minute, in which each reluctant beat, stout as it was, seemed as if it might be the last effort.

8. a. Of buildings, rocks, trees, etc.: Capable of defying attack; strong.

c **1400** *Destr. Troy* 8388 The walles vp wroght on a wise faire With stones full stoute, stithest of vertue. *c* **1600** SHAKS. *Sonn.* lxv. 7 When rocks impregnable are not so stout,.. but Time decays? **1610** —— *Temp.* v. 45 To the dread ratling Thunder Haue I giuen fire, and rifted Ioues stowt Oke With his owne Bolt. **1909** *Q. Rev.* Oct. 455 The stout dam with its marble bridge stood longer.

b. Of a ship: Strongly built; capable of bearing rough weather.

1622 in Foster *Eng. Factories Ind.* (1908) II. 114 Hath made us promyse to furnishe three stoutt shippes. **1685** *Act 1 Jas. II*, c. 18 Preamble, Where many stout Shipps were yearely built for the Coale and other Trade. *a* **1700** EVELYN *Diary* 6 Feb. 1652, I embark'd early in the packet-boat, but put my goods in a stouter vessell. **1779** HERVEY *Nav. Hist.* II. 165 A stout ship commanded by Cornelius Van Velsen blew up. **1788** GIBBON *Decl. & F.* lxviii. VI. 488 Five stout and lofty ships were guided by skilful pilots. **1868** *Rep. Munitions War* 266 We must be content with.. a stout fighting ship, to the exclusion of a fast-sailing one.

c. Of a machine: Durably constructed, strong.

1702 *Lond. Gaz.* No. 3819/8 Stout, able, Water Corn-Mills to be Sold, well customed, also fit for London-work. **1833** J. HOLLAND *Manuf. Metal* II. 247 The following cut.. represents a stout and useful crushing mill for ordinary purposes.

9. Of plants and their parts: Strong in growth; thick, not slender.

1573-80 TUSSER *Husb.* (1878) 120 Now downe with the grasse vpon hedlonds about, that groweth in shadow, so ranke and so stout. **1791** COWPER *Yardley Oak* 117 Yet is thy root.. A quarry of stout spurs, and knotted fangs. **1841** *Florist's Jrnl.* II. 2 The pistil is yellowish, with a shade of green and brown, and it is stout and fleshy. **1845** *Ibid.* VI. 156 The plant is altogether of a much stouter habit, and is remarkable for the large size of the foliage. **1870** *Daily News* 16 Apr., The oats are harvested, and in the next year the clover and grass are 'stout'. **1882** VINES tr. *Sachs' Bot.* 16 The stouter species of the genus *Spirogyra.* **1882** *Garden* 7 Jan. 8/1 The plants.. should be kept well up to the light, as this.. keeps them stouter.

†10. Of soil: ? Firm, not boggy. *Obs.*

1764 *Museum Rust.* II. 80 If the land be stout and good, there is a chance for the seed to stand for a crop.

†11. Of liquor: Having 'body' or density. Chiefly of ale or beer: cf. STOUT *sb.*² *Obs.*

1698 FRYER *Acc. E. India & P.* 242 The Wine.. being of so stout a Body that it is not subject to decay presently. **1733** W. ELLIS *Chiltern & Vale Farm.* 131, I have known a considerable Quantity of Stout-bear spoiled, by brewing with Pond-water wherein its [*sc.* the Ash's] Leaves fell. **1742** *London & Country Brew.* I. (ed. 4) 22 For Stout Butt-beer. This is the strongest Butt-beer that is brewed from brown Malt. **1771** *Encycl. Brit.* I. 669/2 For stout-beer is commonly drawn one barrel off a quarter of malt. **1818** MAGINN in *Blackw. Mag.* IV. 324 While we sung and we laugh'd, and the stout ale quaff'd. **1826** *Art of Brewing* (ed. 2) 69 Stout ales.. labour under one material want—that of spiritual vigour.

12. a. Of persons: Thick in the body, not lean or slender; usually in unfavourable sense, inclined to corpulence; often *euphemistically* = corpulent, fat.

1804 ABERNETHY *Surg. Observ.* 94 A gentleman of a stout make, and about 40 years of age. **1807** *Med. Jrnl.* XVII. 430 A short stout man. **1833** LYTTON *Godolphin* v, An old gentleman, of the age of sixty-three, in a bob-wig, and inclined to be stout. **1840** THACKERAY *Barber Cox* Dec., We tried a gallopard, which I found anything but easy; for since

I am come back to a life of peace and comfort, it's astonishing how stout I'm getting. **1845** BUDD *Dis. Liver* 166 Madame Mazet, æt. 34, of very strong constitution, and very stout. **1848** THACKERAY *Van. Fair* xli, 'She is stouter too, and altogether improved,' continued Miss Rosalind, who was disposed to be very fat. **1856** COMPAING & DEVERE *Tailor's Guide Cutting* 6 We term a man slender in the waist, if this part of the body is small compared with the size of the breast measure. He is stout when, on the contrary, the waist is large in comparison with the breast. *Ibid.*, Figures 3, 4, and 5 shew stout waists... A man is not stout because he measures so many inches, but because he is larger in the waist than the usual proportion. **1864** TENNYSON *Enoch Arden* 747 Stout, rosy, with his babe across his knees. **1866** P'CESS ALICE *Mem.* (1884) 121 Uncle looks very well, but he grows very stout, I think. **1888** MISS BRADDON *Fatal Three* I. i, The gentleman was middle-aged and stout. **1892** ASHBY-STERRY *Lazy Minstr.* 231 That young maidens, slim and shy, May grow old and stout and sly. **1899** LADY M. VERNEY *Verney Mem.* IV. 167 His military bearing is giving way to a slouching gait as he grows older and stouter.

b. Of animals, their limbs or parts: Thick, massive. Of certain moths: Thick in the body. ***stout dart***: the moth *Agrotis ravida*.

1832 J. RENNIE *Consp. Butterfl. & Moths* 54. **1840** MACGILLIVRAY *Man. Ornith.* I. 114 Bill.. moderately stout or rather slender. *Ibid.* 115 Feet rather stout. **1869** E. NEWMAN *Brit. Moths* 335.

c. ***stout party***, a fat person (*humorously*). Esp. in catch-phrase ***collapse of stout party*** (see quot. 1975).

1855 *Punch* 25 Aug. 80/1 (*caption*) *Stout Party*: Well, I'm sure! What can possess those skinny creatures to wear round hats, I can't think,—making themselves so conspicuous! **1949** M. ALLINGHAM *More Work for Undertaker* vii. 102 'Do you will the stout party to give you the sixpences?' he ventured. **1957** R. G. C. PRICE *Hist. Punch* iii. 96 The florescence of the 'collapse of stout party' type of caption comes later [than the 1860s]. **1959** [see PEARLY *sb.* b]. **1975** R. PEARSALL *Collapse of Stout Party* 4 To many people Victorian wit and humour is summed up by *Punch*, when every joke is supposed to end with 'Collapse of Stout Party', though this phrase tends to be as elusive as 'Elementary, my dear Watson' in the Sherlock Holmes sagas.

13. a. Of a material object or substance: So thick as to be strong or rigid.

1765 *Museum Rust.* IV. 107 It was admitted by all, that no hemp.. had a sufficient strength of harle for making stout cordage, but the hemp of Riga and Petersburge. **1801** J. THOMSON *Poems Sc. Dial.* 25 I'd hang them in a gude stout tow, Wha are the wyte o't. **1815** J. SMITH *Panorama Sci. & Art* II. 209 On a stout board GH, are firmly jointed two uprights LM. **1825** SCOTT *Talism.* i, A stout poniard. **1833** J. HOLLAND *Manuf. Metal* II. 103 The barrel intended to be bored is fastened at the breach or stouter end by means of a strong screw. **1834** MCMURTRIE *Cuvier's Anim. Kingd.* 313 The web of some exotic species is formed of such stout materials that it will arrest small Birds. **1847** DE QUINCEY *Sp. Mil. Nun.* v. 10 One stout needle. **1857** MILLER *Elem. Chem., Org.* 12 It is made of stout sheet-iron. **1859** JEPHSON *Brittany* vi. 67 Those stout woollen petticoats. **1875** HUXLEY & MARTIN *Elem. Biol.* xiii. 196 Cut away the front of the pelvis with a stout pair of scissors. **1891** *Law Times* XCII. 79/1 This almanack.. is pasted on very stout cardboard. **1907** J. A. HODGES *Elem. Photogr.* (ed. 6) 121 Strips of stout paper.

b. Of bacon: see quot. 1905.

1905 W. H. SIMMONDS *Pract. Grocer* III. 108 Regarding weight and sizes, the wholesale dealers classify the best branded Irish bacon as lean sizable, prime sizable, lean stout, prime stout, and lean sixes... English smoked bacon is cut in sides,.. each classified into lean sizable, sizable, medium, stout medium, and heavy. **1913** *Times* 9 Aug. 19/6, 84s. to 90s. for lean sizeable [bacon], 83s. to 87s. for lean stout, and 83s. to 88s. for stout sizeable.

III. 14. *Comb.*, as ***stout-looking*** adj.; also in many parasynthetic derivatives, as ***stout-armed, -bodied, -limbed, -minded, -sided, -soled, -winged, -worded*** adjs.; † **stout-stomached** *a.*, high-spirited, obstinate. Also STOUT-HEARTED *a.*

1878 E. C. G. MURRAY *Russians of To-day* 87 A smart flagellation or two at the hands of a *stout-armed wardress. **1859** *Stout-bodied moths [see SLENDER *a.* 11]. **1913** SIR H. JOHNSTON *Pioneers Australasia* v. 173 The people being very black, strong and *stout-limbed. **1830** SCOTT *Hrt. Midl.* Introd., A little, rather *stout-looking woman. **1908** W. R. NICOLL *'Ian Maclaren'* ix. 169 The then Bishop of Liverpool, the *stout-minded English Evangelical, better known as J. C. Ryle. *a* **1612** RALEGH *Let. to Pr. Henry* Sceptick etc. (1651) 128 In a well conditioned Ship, these things are chiefly required. 1. That she be strong built. 2. Swift in sail. 3. *Stout-sided. **1891** C. T. C. JAMES *Rom. Rigmarole* 6 The Squire's were broad-welted, *stout-soled ones. **1549** LATIMER *2nd Serm. bef. Edw. VI* (Arb.) 57 He was a *stoute stomaked chyld. **1560** BECON *Catech.* IV. Wks. I. 386 Howe earnestly that stout stomacked and couragious Matrone Iudith rebuked them for this theyr impaciency. **1626** *Maldon* (Essex) *Docum.* Bundle 208. No. 9, A good stout-stomacked gelding, full of mettle. **1648** J. BEAUMONT *Psyche* XXI. xvi, *Stout-winged Eagles ne'r were made to be Consorts to flitting Dunghil flies. **1863** *Athenæum* 22 Aug. 234/2 The Judges were strong-minded and *stout-worded men.

B. *adv.* **a.** = STOUTLY *adv.* Now *rare.* † ***to bear oneself stout***: to behave haughtily or defiantly.

1338 R. BRUNNE *Chron.* (1725) 296 A man þat beris him stoute, whan þat he suld bowe, In chance if þat he loute, he [etc.]. **1436** *Pol. Poems* (Rolls) II. 196 [England's] sonne wente aboute in alle the worlde stoute. *c* **1470** *Gol. & Gaw.* 78 Ane bright fyre couth he se Birnand full stout. **1581** A. HALL *Iliad* IX. 152 In bloudie warre right stout thou playst. **1622** BACON *Hen. VII*, 55 [The French King's] Subiects.. beare themselues stout vpon the strength of the Duke of Britaine. **1726** DYER *Country Walk* 11 A beautiful variety Of strutting cocks, advancing stout. **1863** W. C. BALDWIN *Afr. Hunting* ii. 32 The pony.. proved himself a good one, running very stout and fast.

b. *Comb.* with pa. pples.

1842 LOVER *Handy Andy* xii, A *stout-built peasant. **1890** D. DAVIDSON *Mem. Long Life* iv. 75 He was a short, stout-built man. **1595** DANIEL *Civ. Wars* I. lii. Wks. (Grosart) II. 31 Which publique death.. made his *stout-defended cause appeare With such a face of Right, as that [etc.]. **1823** SCOTT *Quentin D.* ii, His comrade was a *stout-formed, middle-sized man. **1820** —— *Abbot* xiv, The mock dignitary was a *stout-made, under-sized fellow.

stout (staʊt), *v.* [f. STOUT *a.*]

† **1.** *intr.* To be defiant; to act in a defiant or stubborn manner. *Obs.*

1303 R. BRUNNE *Handl. Synne* 3403 And ȝyf he yn folye begynne to stoute, þan bereþ he þe deuylys baner aboute. *Ibid.* 10923 Lewed man, þou shalt cursyng doute, And to þy prest þou shalt nat stoute. *c* **1330** —— *Chron. Wace* (Rolls) 6361 *note*, For Conan gan þat oper rebuk, & reuiled [*v.r.* Conan stouted] hym wyþ wordes þore. **1583** GOLDING *Calvin on Deut.* lxi. 366 They fall to stouting against him. **1616** J. LANE *Contn. Sqr.'s T.* VII. 193 His silken standard.. which blazd a lion, pard, and prowlinge beare, in a feild gules. These on thigh bullwarcke stowted.

2. quasi-*trans.* † **a.** ***to stout it*** = sense 1. *Obs.*

1570 *Marr. Wit & Sci.* IV. i. C iij b, Nay you must stoute it, and face it out with the best. *a* **1624** BP. M. SMITH *Serm.* i. (1632) 5 For all our vilenesse.. we will not be acknowne of it, but contrariwise stout it with him and beard him. *Ibid.* vii. 130 Others made it their care to strowt it, and to stout it, and to braue it in costly apparell. **1644** PRYNNE *Check to Britannicus* 5 If they by his own sentence (though penitent) endured the halter, I am certaine he still stouting it, much more deserues the Axe. **1670** T. BROOKS *Wks.* (1867) VI. 372 None stout it against Jesus Christ as hypocrites do.

b. ***to stout it out***: to persist in a defiant attitude, e.g. when detected in a falsehood, or when hard pressed; to 'brave it out'. Now *rare.*

a **1639** W. WHATELEY *Prototypes* I. xi. (1640) 105 O that we could be so desirous of unity, not stouting it out as many do. **1644** PRYNNE & WALKER *Fiennes' Trial* 93 The Defendant was so far from this fault of stouting it out over-long; that he deserves to lose his head for yeelding Bristol up too soone. **1650** TRAPP *Comm. Lev.* xxvi. 23 The wicked refuse to receiv corrections:.. they stout it out, and will not stoop. **1658** GURNALL *Chr. in Arm.* II. verse 15. vi. §3. 366 He will not debase his Sovereignty to treat with a wretch that stands to his armes, and stouts it out with him. **1690** C. NESSE *Hist. & Myst. O. & N. Test.* I. 145 They had stubbornly stouted it out with God. **1848** ELIZA GURNEY in A. J. C. Hare *Gurneys of Earlham* (1895) II. 255 When.. I saw William Forster standing at the hall-door, looking unutterably sad, I felt I could stout it out no longer, and completely broke down. **1897** *Advance* (Chicago) 25 Mar. 372/1 Robins have either been belated or some of them determined upon stouting it out all the season through.

† **c.** ***to stout out***: to 'brazen out' (a matter); to persist obstinately in the defence of (a besieged place). *Obs.*

1568 HARDING *Detect. Errours Jewel's Def.* 67 b, First he auoucheth his shamelesse lye boldly, as though where truth faileth, for shew of proufe, the matter might be stowted out. **1644** PRYNNE & WALKER *Fiennes' Trial* 93 That a French Author.. affirmed; it was a capitall offence to stout out a place overlong.

d. To get (something) *away from* a person by importunity. *rare*⁻¹.

1812 HT. SHELLEY *Lett.* (1889) 27 You can say you wish to look at them [Shelley's MS. Poems], and then you may be able to stout them away from him.

† **3.** *trans.* To defy. *Obs.*

1303 R. BRUNNE *Handl. Synne* 2948 But þere þe wyfe ys aboute þe gode man for to stoute.

Hence † **'stouting**, *vbl. sb.*, boastfulness, pride, defiance.

1630 I. C. *Handkercher for Parents Wet Eyes* 42 'Tis not stouting, and stomacke, and pettishnesse, but meekenesse, and patience, and humility, makes God propitious.

† **stout and rout.** *Sc.* See STOOP AND ROOP.

stouten ('staʊt(ə)n), *v.* [f. STOUT *a.* + -EN[5].]

1. *trans.* To make stout.

1834 L. HUNT *Lond. Jrnl.* I. Suppl. p. iv/2 Men may surely learn how to stouten their legs, as well as to improve their stockings. **1887** D. C. MURRAY & HERMAN *Traveller Returns* xiv. 213 But however she stoutened her heart. **1910** *Q. Rev.* Jan. 217 Sympathy should be stoutened by a certain detachment.

2. *intr.* To grow stout.

1863 'HOLME LEE' *A. Warleigh* I. 113 John stoutening fast into rectorial dignity. **1865** MRS. WHITNEY *Gayworthys* xv, He did not stouten much as summer came on. **1890** *Pictorial World* 7 Aug. 186/3 He felt her perceptibly stiffening, and stoutening, and bonyfying in his clasp.

Hence **'stoutening** *vbl. sb.*

1853 RUSKIN *Stones Venice* I. App. xv. 385 Much hardening of hands and gross stoutening of bodies in all this.

'stouter. (See quot. 1792) ? *Obs.* Cf. STROUTER.

1792 G. CARTWRIGHT *Jrnl. Labrador* I. Gloss. p. xv, *Stouter*, very strong shores, which are placed round the head of a stage or wharf, to prevent them from being damaged by ships or boats. **1819** L. A. ANSPACH *Hist. Island Newfoundland* 430 The place where the operation of curing the cod-fish is performed, is a *stage* or covered platform erected on the shore, with one end projecting over the water, which is called the *stage-head*, and which is fortified with stouters.

stouter, var. STOTER *sb.*[2] *Obs.*

† **'stoutess.** *Obs.* In 5 stowtesse. [f. STOUT *a.* + -ESS[2].] Stoutness; courage; bravery.

1422 YONGE tr. *Secreta Secret*, 180 To Speke wyth good Spirite and breth appartenyth to the hardy, for that tokenyth hardynesse of herte, grete takynge on, and Stowtesse.

† **'stoutfully**, *adv. Obs. rare*⁻¹. [f. STOUT *a.* + -FUL + -LY[2].] = STOUTLY.

a **1578** LINDESAY (Pitscottie) *Chron. Scot.* (S.T.S.) II. 261 [They] maid stoutfullie and manfullie to the feildis to meit and resist thame as they mycht.

† **stouth.** *Sc.* and *north. Obs.* Forms: 4 **stulth, stulþ**, 5 **stouth, stoutht, stuth**, 6 **stouith**, 6, 9 **stowth.** [Northern ME. *stulþ*, a. ON. *stulþ-r* (Icel. *stulð-r, stuld-r*), f. OTeut. **stul-* ablaut-var. of **stel-*: see STEAL *v.*]

1. Theft. Often coupled with *reif*: cf. STOUTHREIF.

a **1300** *Cursor M.* 28461 Stulth o mete and drink did i. **1429** in *Cal. Doc. rel. Scot.* (1888) 405 Gif.. he knew never of the stoutht of the hale gude no[r] of that pert that is fundin with him. **1456** SIR G. HAY *Gov. Princes* Wks. (S.T.S.) II. 88 Unlautee engenderis outhir ref, stouth, pillery or rubbery. **1497** *Reg. Privy Seal Scot.* I. 12/1 For the reif and stuth of the gudis and insicht being in the sammyn. **1530** LYNDESAY *Test. Papyngo* 529 Quhat stouith, quhat raif, quhat murther, & myschance! **1535** STEWART *Cron. Scot.* (Rolls) III. 101 With reif and stouth, spulȝe and oppressioun. **1589–90** *Reg. Privy Council Scot.* IV. 453 Manifest reiffis and stouthis committit upoun his Hienes peceable and gude subjectis. **1610** *Extracts Aberd. Reg.* (1848) II. 304 The frequent pykrie and stouthis in the cuntrie. **1652** in *Cromwellian Union* (S.H.S. 1902) 61 The vnsufferable robberies and stouthis daylie committit on both sydes of the border. **1701** in W. R. Mackintosh *Cur. Incid. Rec. Kirkwall* (1892) 110 The crymes of thift, reiff, stouth, and ressate of thift are punishable by death. **1791** LEARMONT *Poems* 46 (E.D.D.) Great geer by stouth and rief, He's filcht frae mony Indian chief.

2. Stealth, clandestine transaction. (Jam.)

1513 DOUGLAS *Æneis* XII. Prol. 212 Sum rownys to hys fallow, thame betwene, Hys mery stouth and pastans lait ȝistrene.

stouth and routh. [Prob. some error: cf. STOUT AND ROUT.] A quasi-archaic phrase used by Scott in the sense of: Plenty, abundance.

1816 SCOTT *Antiq.* xi, It's easy for your honour and the like o' you gentlefolks, to say sae, that hae stouth and routh, and fire and fending.

† **'stoutheart.** *Obs. rare*⁻¹. [f. STOUT *a.* + HEART *sb.*] A stout-hearted person.

1553 GRIMALDE *Cicero's Offices* I. (1558) 29 A true, and wise stouthearte iudgeth that honesty, which nature chiefly foloweth, to stande in deedes, and not in glory.

stout-hearted, *a.* Having a stout heart; courageous, undaunted; †stubborn, intractable.

1552 HULOET, Stowt harted or stomaked, *graucicors.* **1568** GRAFTON *Chron.* II. 334 When the king and his Lords sawe the demeanour of the people, the stowtest hearted of them that were with the king were afrayed. **1611** BIBLE *Isa.* xlvi. 12 Hearken vnto me, ye stout hearted, that are farre from righteousnesse. **1613** HIERON *Minor Saints* Wks. 1614 I. 31 Wee are generally stout-hearted, and will not yeelde to the terrour of the Lord. **1788** WESLEY *Jrnl.* 29 Mar., It was given me to speak strong words, such as made the stout-hearted tremble. **1841** DICKENS *Barn. Rudge* lxi, A few of the stoutest-hearted were armed and gathered in a body on the green. **1847** HELPS *Friends in C.* I. i. 18, I think, however, that the view is a stouthearted one. **1855** MACAULAY *Hist. Eng.* xiii. III. 273 There were indeed many stouthearted nonconformists in the South; but scarcely any who in obstinacy.. could bear a comparison with the men of the school of Cameron. **1905** LYALL *Life Marq. Dufferin* I. i. 12 His descendants were stout-hearted country gentlemen after his kind. **1906** W. A. CRAIGIE *Anc. Scand. Relig.* ii. 30 Snorri describes him as 'the bravest and stoutest-hearted of the gods'.

Hence **stout'heartedly** *adv.*; **stout'heartedness.**

a **1683** OWEN *Holy Spirit* (1693) 39 The Reliefs which.. carnal Security and Stoutheartedness in Adversity do offer. **1826** E. IRVING *Babylon* I. Introd. 17 Leaving them long to welter in the wo from which their stout-heartedness would not be warned. **1873** SYMONDS *Grk. Poets* vii. 212 For his cardinal virtue Euripides chose what the Greeks called εὐψυχία, stout-heartedness. **1884** *Brit. Q. Rev.* Apr. 418 Mr. Mackintosh proceeds stout-heartedly in his great work.

stoutherie. *Obs.* exc. *Sc.* Also 5 **stolethery, stoltherie, -ye.** [f. *stulþ*, STOUTH + -ERY.] Theft, stealing; also stolen goods.

c **1440** *Alphabet of Tales* 8 The money at þou hase taken of þi bruther, it is stoltherye. *Ibid.* 9 Euer sen I forsuke to take swilk stolethery I hafe abundid & waxin ryche of gudi[s]. *Ibid.* 222 þe fadur þeroff, garte call it Latro, because it was getten be stoltherie. **1864** LATTO *Tam. Bodkin* x. 92 To find oot the loons that had received the unleisum stoutherie.

'stouthreif. *Sc. Obs.* exc. *arch.* Also 5 **stowthrefe**, 5–7 **stouthreif**, 6 **stouthe reif, stowth reif**, *pl.* **stouthisreiffis**, 7, 9 **stouth-rife**, 9 **stouthreef, -rief.** [f. STOUTH + REIF; perh. altered from *stouth and reif.*] Theft with violence; robbery.

1493 in Pitcairn *Crim. Trials* I. *15 For Stouthreif of a bonnet & quhyngare from the s[d] Robert. **1493** *Reg. Privy Seal Scot.* I. 5/1 For the stowthrefe of thre oxin and kye fra the larde of Howmend. **1566** *Reg. Privy Council Scot.* I. 489 Crymes of slauchtir, stowth reif, thift, resset of thift. *a* **1578** LINDESAY (Pitscottie) *Chron. Scot.* (S.T.S.) I. 177 Everie lord.. was suorne.. to cause stouthe reif and slaughter to be punished. **1578** *Extracts Burgh Rec. Edin.* (1882) IV. 91 Heivylie oppressit be the stouthisreiffis and vtheris enormiteis of the thevis. **1587** *Sc. Acts Jas. VI* (1814) III. 451/1 Only landit men.. convict of þe crymes of commoun thift resett of thift or stouth reiff.. sall incur the cryme and pane of tressoun. **1678** SIR G. MACKENZIE *Crim. Laws Scot.* I. xix. §v. (1699) 99 Theft may be divided into common

Theft, which is Theft so properly called, or Stouth-rife, which is violent Theft, and is a complex of Theft and Robbery. **1828** Scott *F.M. Perth* ii, Thou canst frame locks and bars to defend the property of the weak against the stouthrief and oppression of the strong. [Frequently in Scott.] **1881** *Blackw. Mag.* Apr. 518 We love the old ballads of stouthrief and blood-feuds.

stoutish (ˈstaʊtɪʃ), *a.* [f. STOUT *a.* + -ISH[1].] Somewhat stout, in senses of the adj.

1835 Dickens *Sk. Boz, Parlour Orator*, A stoutish man of about forty. **1883** Stevenson *Treas. Isl.* xviii, The captain.. turned out..a coil of stoutish rope. **1912** *Nation* 24 Aug. 758/2 Messrs. Constable publish his proposed washing-list in a stoutish volume.

†**ˈstoutly**, *a. Obs.* [f. STOUT *a.* + -LY[1].] Stout, valiant.

1338 R. Brunne *Chron.* (1725) 221 Stoutly was þat stoure, long lastand þat fight. *c* **1614** Sir W. Mure *Dido & Æneas* I. 349 'Stay, stowtly ȝowthes!' (she sayes), 'who heir resorte.'

stoutly (ˈstaʊtlɪ), *adv.* [f. STOUT *a.* + -LY[2].]

1. Valiantly, bravely, with courage and energy; manfully.

13.. *Sir Beues* 683 Beues stoutliche in þat stounde Haf vp is heued fro þe grounde. **1375** Barbour *Bruce* XI. 158 In ilkane war weill ten thousand, That thoucht thai stalwardly suld stand In the battale and stoutly ficht. **1422** Yonge tr. *Secreta Secret.* 134 Thay hath longe afor wel deseruyd in battaille and dyuers Stowres stowtly demenet ham-Selfe in grete yonge-man-hode. **1540** Palsgr. *Acolastus* III. i. N iv b, He..playeth his parte stoutely or lyke a man. **1549** Coverdale etc. *Erasm. Par. 1 Tim.* iii. 8–13 Lyke as in a seculer commen wealthe he is called to be a Mayor, that before vsed himselfe stowtely in the wardenshyp. **1593** Shaks. *Lucr.* 1209 Faint not faint heart, but stoutlie say so be it. **1610** Healey *St. Aug. Citie of God* I. xi. 21 Whole armies..went stoutly to these slaughters. **1833** Ht. Martineau *Brooke Farm* vi. 78, I..walked as stoutly as any of them to where the surgeons were. **1904** *Verney Mem.* II. 342 When a traveller of unwonted courage stoutly defeated the gentlemen who meant to rob him.

†**b.** By means of valour. *Obs.*

1649 J. H. *Motion to Parl.* 13 You have done great things for us, and equall to what hath been done in any Nation, either stoutly or fortunately.

†**2.** Haughtily, proudly, arrogantly. *Obs.*

a **1547** J. Croke *Thirteen Ps.* (Percy Soc.) 13 And when I slyde, both hele and toes, Then stowtly they of me do speake. **1572** Huloet (ed. Higins), Stoutly, proudly, or arrogantly, *superbè, elatè, arroganter* [etc.]. **1632** Milton *L'Allegro* 52 While the Cock..Stoutly struts his Dames before.

3. Resolutely, firmly, uncompromisingly.

1303 R. Brunne *Handl. Synne* 3521 And ȝyf he wyl nat with feyre lere, þan mayst þou speke stoutly to hym withoute wraþþe, wurdys ful grym. *a* **1533** Frith *Disput. Purgat.* Wks. (1573) 19/1 Rastell..would stoutely affirme that the body suffereth neither well nor woe, ioy nor payne, good nor euill. **1568** Grafton *Chron.* II. 777 Sithence he had once begonne, he would stoutly go thorowe. **1579** E. K. in *Spenser's Sheph. Cal.*, Gen. Argt., It is..stoutely mainteyned with stronge reasons of the learned, that the yeare beginneth in March. **1682** Norris *Hierocles* Pref. 3 To rail stoutly against Popery. *a* **1703** Burkitt *On N.T.* John ix. 38 Behold this blind man..stoutly defending the gracious author of his cure. **1779** *Mirror* No. 34 Miss Betsy denied stoutly that she ever sung at all. **1840** Thackeray *Catherine* vii, She stoutly swore that no parents could ever desert their children. **1858** Trollope *Dr. Thorne* xxxiv, The doctor..at once resolved stoutly that he would not go. **1880** 'Ouida' *Moths* I. i. 21 'What for should they not listen?' said Fräulein Schroder stoutly. **1891** *Speaker* 2 May 564/1 The admiration even of those who were most stoutly opposed to his political opinions.

†**4.** Stubbornly, contumaciously. *Obs.*

15.. *Wyf of Auchtirmwchty* 100 in *Bannatyne MS.* (Hunter. Club) 345 Scho hard him, and scho hard him not, Bot stowtly steird the stottis abowt. **1631** Gouge *God's Arrows* I. §22. 30 Others would be emboldened..to carrie themselves stoutly against God.

5. Vigorously, with might and main, lustily. ? *Obs.*

1399 Langl. *R. Redeles* I. 114 ȝe cleued to knavis..þat..stirid ȝou stouttely till ȝe stombled all. *c* **1482** J. Kay tr. *Caoursin's Siege of Rhodes* ¶ 10 (1870), They casted agaynes the tour thre hondred grete stones of bombardes and brake the toure stoutely and put it in a grete danger to be ouerthrawn. **1684** Otway *Atheist* IV. i. 42 I'll swinge her the stoutlier, for alienating his Affections from his natural Father. **1709** T. Robinson *Vind. Mosaick Syst.* 90 [Wood-Ants] with Burthens of green Leaves upon their Backs, so big that one can scarce see the Insect for the Burthen, and yet they march stoutly. **1773** Goldsm. *Stoops to Conq.* I. ii, Drive up the yard, and call stoutly about you. **1810** Scott *Lady of L.* I. vi, The gallant stag swam stoutly o'er. **1815** —— *Guy M.* xlv, Dinmont, I say, fell stoutly upon the good cheer.

†**b.** with reference to drinking. *Obs.* (Common in 17–18th c.)

1617 Moryson *Itin.* III. 51 The Novocomians [are said] to eate without end and drinke stoutly. **1687** A. Lovell tr. *Thevenot's Trav.* III. 24 To let the World see that he could drink stoutly, on the Top of his Pyramid there is a large Stone-cup. **1749** Fielding *Tom Jones* XVIII. xiii, These two therefore sat stoutly to it, during the whole evening.

6. Strongly, massively, solidly; so as to be stout or thick, or with the addition of something stout.

c **1350** *Will. Palerne* 1950 Alle on stalworþ stedes stoutliche i-horsed. **1604** Shaks. *Oth.* II. i. 48 His Barke is stoutly Timber'd. *a* **1825** Forby *Voc. E. Anglia*, *Spile*, a wedge of wood stoutly pointed with iron. **1891** *Hardwicke's Sci-Gossip* XXVII. 55 The species are rather more stoutly built than the *Tipulinæ*. **1892** Lady F. Verney *Verney Mem.* II. 193 They..manufactured a wooden cannon from an elm tree, stoutly hooped with iron.

7. *Comb.*

1648 J. Beaumont *Psyche* VII. ccx, Dark Bats,..Surprised by a stoutly-flashing Flame. *Ibid.* XVI. i, Whose stoutly-paradoxick Essence founds Its dearest Health upon its deepest wounds. **1833** Nyren *Yng. Cricketer's Tutor* (1902) 94 He was a short and rather stoutly-made man. **1872** Coues *N. Amer. Birds* 216 A large stoutly-built hawk. **1881** *Cassell's Nat. Hist.* V. 359 Bees..are generally rather stoutly-built insects.

stoutness (ˈstaʊtnɪs). [f. STOUT *a.* + -NESS.] The quality or condition of being stout.

†**1.** Pride, haughtiness, arrogance. *Obs.*

1375 Barbour *Bruce* VII. 356 For quhar a hert is rycht vorthy, Agane stoutnes [it] is ay stout. **1398** Trevisa *Barth. De P.R.* VI. xviii. (1495) 204 And god commaundeth that the lordes be not besye to wynne and gete theyr owne joye and stowtnes. *c* **1400** *Brut* 124 He..bicome a gode man and an holy, and lefte al maner pride & stoutenesse. **1535** Coverdale *Jer.* xlviii. 29, I knowe hir stoutnesse [1611 pride]. **1548** Udall *Erasm. Par. Matt.* v. 5 Stowtnes and styfnes is hated of al men. **1552** Latimer *Serm. 3rd Sund. Epiph.* (1584) 309 b, Beware of pride and stoutnes. **1570** Jewel *Def. Apol.* II. iii. (1571) 119 Doubtlesse..the Councel of Aphrica meante the stoutenesse of the Cleregie, and not of the Nobles: the pride of Rome, and not of Aphrica. **1572** Huloet (ed. Higins), Stoutnes, proudeness, or arrogancie, *fastus, arrogantia, ferocitas*, [etc.]. **1600** Holland *Livy* XLII. xiv. 1123 Besides, the stoutnes used by Harpalus (the principall person of the embassie)..exasperated their stomackes. **1607** Shaks. *Cor.* v. vi. 27 His stoutnesse When he did stand for Consull, which he lost By lacke of stooping.

2. Bravery, valour, courageousness. Now *rare*, exc. in ***stoutness of heart***.

c **1470** *Gol. & Gaw.* 799 Is nane sa stalwart in stour, with stoutnes to stand. **1553** Brende *Q. Curtius* A iij, In an excellent capitaine nature must geve the chiefest partes, that is to say: hardines, stowtenes of stomacke, wyth a natural wisdome and understanding. **1561** Hoby tr. *Castiglione's Courtier* I. (1577) C ij b, Dyuerse calamities, which hee alwayes bore out with such stoutnesse of courage, that [etc.]. *a* **1575** tr. *Pol. Verg. Eng. Hist.* I. (Camden, No. 36) 39 At the lengthe, having conflicte with wilde beastes, [he] made a beastlie ende, and thus..to miche stoutenes beecamme his owne confusion. *a* **1586** Sidney *Arcadia* III. xvii. (1912) 452 [She] was an Amazon, and therefore had gotton a habite of stoutnes above the nature of a woman. **1631** Gouge *God's Arrows* v. §6. 416 Stoutnesse and courage of mind. **1666** Pepys *Diary* 17 Sept., Sir Thomas Clifford, who appears..much set by at Court for his activity in going to sea, and stoutness every where. **1691** Hartcliffe *Virtues* 119 As Stoutness of mind very well agrees with Meekness, and therefore Moses, who was indeed a Person of the most undaunted Courage, is said in Scripture to be the meekest Man upon Earth. **1727** Bailey vol. II, *Stoutness*, Courageousness, Boldness. **1822** Lamb *Elia* Ser. I. *Decay of Beggars*, The common cripple would despise his own pusillanimity, viewing the hale stoutness, and hearty heart, of this half-limbed giant. **1827** Pollok *Course T.* II. 770 He..Amidst vindictive thunders lets them try The stoutness of their heart.

3. Firmness, resoluteness.

1561 Eden *Art Navig.* Pref. ℂℂ i, Accoumpting..rashnesse for hardinesse, impudencie for stoutnesse. **1577** Vautrollier *Luther on Ep. Gal.* 48 Our stoutnes therfore in this matter is godly and holy. **1642–4** Vicars *God in Mount* 132 These with the rest discovered aboundance of stoutnes and resolution. **1799** Han. More *Fem. Educ.* (ed. 4) I. 8 Let her..not make herself amends by the stoutness of her orthodoxy for the badness of her temper.

†**4.** Stubbornness, intractability, rebelliousness. *Obs.*

c **1400** *Rom. Rose* 1936 He is a fool in sikernesse, That with daunger or stoutnesse Rebellith ther that he shulde plese. *c* **1440** *Promp. Parv.* 478/2 Stowtnesse, or vnbuxumnesse, *rebellio*. **1560** *Bps. Addr.* in Strype *Ann. Ref.* (1709) I. xviii. 214 Not in any respect of Self-Will, Stoutness, or striving against her Majesty. **1570** Jewel *Def. Apol.* II. xviii. (1571) 350 But perceiuing that the King was much moued and misliked his stoutnesse, the next night folowing, he fled ouer into France, and afterwarde sought aide of the Pope. **1599** Sandys *Europæ Spec.* (1632) 174 Hee opposeth a proud stoutnesse and intractable obstinacie. *a* **1654** Gataker *Antid. Errour* (1670) 51 Either out of a stoutnes of stomack, and a stifnes of self-wil, or out of an extream malice and inveterate hatred against the person. **1768–74** Tucker *Lt. Nat.* (1834) II. 534 There is a stoutness, and an aversion to inferiority rooted in all men, which must be managed with great delicacy.

5. *Sporting.* In animals, esp. horses and foxes: Staying power, endurance.

1818 'W. H. Scott' *Brit. Field Sports* 511 Horses..able to carry weight,..and more distinguished for stoutness, in the Turf phrase, namely stoutness of heart, or ability to last, than for speed. **1826** J. Cook *Fox-hunting* 61, I could enumerate many other capital runs to prove the stoutness of the Essex foxes. **1856** 'Stonehenge' *Brit. Rural Sports* I. III. ii. 156 Stoutness [in the greyhound] depends partly upon general muscular development. **1883** *Times* 22 Oct. 10/2 He [a racehorse] appears to be bred rather for speed than for stoutness. **1901** *Daily Chron.* 20 Nov. 4/2 A capital day's sport was witnessed at this club gathering,..hares running with great stoutness.

6. In physical senses:

a. Strength of body or limbs (now *rare*).

c **1440** *Promp. Parv.* 478/2 Stowtnesse, or strenghe, *robur*. **1866** Seeley *Ecce Homo* iii. (ed. 8) 23 No one doubted the stoutness of Samson's sinews.

b. Corpulence.

1838 Lytton *Alice* II. ii, Mr. Merton was..fair, and inclined to stoutness. **1899** 'A. Hope' *King's Mirror* XIV. 139 He grew indolent; his stoutness increased. **1902** Mrs. Barnes-Grundy *Thames Camp* 49 Long hours of idleness..tend to encourage a dreadful infirmity called 'stoutness'.

c. Massiveness; strength due to thickness.

1845 *Florist's Jrnl.* (1846) VI. 156 Our plant however is by no means possessed of the huge size and stoutness for which *D. speciosum* is remarkable. **1870** Hooker *Stud. Flora* 409 *Carex vulpina*..Perigynia compressed, ribs variable in stoutness. **1915** *Blackw. Mag.* Aug. 198/2 In spite of the stoutness of our tackle, they broke us.

†**ˈstouty**, *a. Obs. rare.* In 6 stoutty, stowty. [f. STOUT *a.* + -Y.] Stout, valiant, strong.

a **1529** Skelton *Duke of Albany* 78 Ye duke so doutty, So sterne, so stoutty. —— *Agst. Garnesche* i. 10 Ye stronge sturdy stalyon, so sterne and stowty.

stouve, stouver, stouwe: see STOVE, STOVER, STOW.

stovaine (ˈstəʊveɪaɪn). *Pharmacy.* [a. F. *stovaïne*, formed after *cocaïne* (see COCAINE); the first element is obscure.] A local anæsthetic, discovered by Fourneau in 1903 (*Comptes Rendus* Feb. and May 1904).

1904 *Jrnl. Chem. Soc.* LXXXVI. II. 501 Toxicity of Amyl Chlorohydrin (Stovaine). **1910** *Chamb. Jrnl.* Feb. 142/1 This new weapon of the surgeon called Stovaine, created considerable interest in the medical world.

stove (stəʊv), *sb.*[1] Forms: 6 stofe, stouf(fe, stowf(f)e, 6–7 stoave, stoove, 7 stouph(e, stouve, 5– stove. See also STOW *sb.*[3] [OE. had *stofa* wk. masc., hot air bath (once, as gloss on *balneum*), and the related *stuf-bæð* (*Leechdoms* III. 92, 132) in the same sense. The word, however, seems not to have survived, but to have been taken up afresh in the 15–16th c. from MLG. or MDu. *stove* fem. (Du. *stoof*) = OHG. *stuba* fem. (MHG. *stube* heated room, mod.G. *stube* sitting-room), ON. *stofa*, *stufa* fem. (Sw. *stufva*, *stuga* cottage, Da. *stue* room); the Scandinavian words are prob. adopted from LG. The relation between the WGer. **stub-* and the late L. or Rom. *stūfa*, *stūfāre* (see STEW *sb.*[2] and *v.*[2], STUFE) is uncertain.]

†**1. a.** A hot air bath; a sweating-room; = STEW *sb.*[2] 3, STUFE. *Obs.*

In the second quot. the pl. is used with sing. construction.

1456 Sir G. Haye *Gov. Princes* Wks. (S.T.S.) II. 142 Here declaris the noble the maneris of baithis and of stovis. *Ibid.* 143 Thare mon be grete consideracioun to make wele a bathis or a stovis. **1562** Bullein *Bulwark, Bk. Sick Men* (1579) 24 b, Idle bodies..are made warme, by..Oyle, bathing in warme water, or going into yᵉ Stoue. **1579** J. Louthe in *Narr. Reform.* (Camden) 58 This was to hym in stede of a stowffe called Laconicum. **1579–80** North *Plutarch, Cimon* (1595) 525 As they were rubbing of him with oile in his stoue or hotte house. **1587** Harrison *England* II. x. 187/2 in *Holinshed*, As for stooues we haue not hitherto vsed them greatlie, yet doo they now begin to be made in diuerse houses of the gentrie..., who build them not to worke and feed in as in Germanie and else where, but now and then to sweat in. **1595** Duncan *App. Etym.* (E.D.S.), *Vaporarium*, a hot stofe. **1599** B. Jonson *Ev. Man out of Hum.* IV. viii, You shall sweat there with..losing your monie at primero, as well as in all the stoves in Sweden. **1603** Holland *Plutarch's Mor.* 864 Neither used they the stouph or bath together. **1607** Topsell *Four-f. Beasts* 517 The dung..of mice..rubbed vpon the head of any one who is troubled with the scurfe or skaules thereon in a bath or stoue, will presently expell and driue them quite away. **1612** Drayton *Poly-olb.* IV. 304 The Pentecosts prepar'd at Carleon in his Court,..her Temples and her Groues, Her Palaces, her Walks, Baths, Theaters, and Stoues. **1629** H. Burton *Truths Tri.* 293 That riuer in hell..is now become a hot dry stoue, called Purgatory. **1658** W. Burton *Comment. Itin. Antoninus* 213 This I guess to be a Stouphe or hot-house to bath in. **1683** *Digby's Chym. Secr.* II. 200 When the Patient is Sweating in the dry Stove. *a* **1700** Evelyn *Diary* 8 Feb. 1645, Neere to this cave are the natural stoves of St. Germain. **1715** Leoni *Palladio's Archit.* (1742) I. 101 A lukewarm Room..from which they enter'd into the hot stove. **1756** C. Lucas *Ess. Waters* I. 230 You may have ..more or less vapor..which can not be done in the common suffocating stoves at the Hummums.

†**b.** A closed basket for 'stoving' or sweating a gamecock. *Obs.*

1631 Markham *Country Contentm.* I. xix. (ed. 4) 111 You must haue deepe straw baskets made for the purpose,..and there let your Cocke stoue and sweate till the Euening. But before you put him into the stoue, you shall [etc.].

†**2.** A sitting-room or bedroom heated with a furnace. Chiefly with reference to Germany, the Low Countries, Scandinavia, or Russia. (Cf. STEW *sb.*[2] 2.) *Obs.*

? **1545** Brinklow *Complaynt* 36 b, Euen the porest man..may boldly come into their hall or stoue, thei being at dynar. **1559** Morwyng *Evonym.* 70 Certaine of the Germaines that lyve in stouffes, that is hot houses, the winter time, make in them lowe fornaices. **1600** Hakluyt *Voy.* III. 392 Here they found houses of foure stories high,..and in most of them were Stooues for the Winter season. *a* **1608** Dee *Relat. Spir.* I. (1659) 212 In the excellent little Stove, or Study of D. Hageck his house lent me, by Bethlem in old Prage. **1617** Moryson *Itin.* III. 77 (*bis*) In stead of fier they vse hot stoues.., which are certaine chambers or roomes, hauing an earthen ouen cast into them. *Ibid.* 103 All the passengers lie together in the warme stoaue, with those of the Family, both Men and Weomen. **1621** Burton *Anat. Mel.* I. ii. IV. v. (1624) 136 How tedious is it to them that liue in Stoues & Caues halfe a yeare together; as in Island, Muscovy, or vnder the Pole it selfe. **1634** W. Wood *New Eng. Prosp.* (1898) 68 Hee busles better through a world of cold in a frost-paved wildernesse, than the furred Citizen in his warmer Stoave. **1642** Fuller *Holy & Prof. St.* II. ix. 86 When a certain Frenchman came to visit Melanchthon, he found him in his stove with one hand dandling his child.., and in the other hand holding a book. *a* **1700** Evelyn *Diary* 23 Sept. 1680, All the inhabitants retiring to their stoves. **1706** Farquhar *Recruiting Officer* III. ii, I might have marry'd a German Princess, worth fifty thousand Crowns a Year, but her Stove disgusted me.

3. A hothouse for plants.

1695 *Phil. Trans.* XIX. 395 A new black Maiden Hair.. now growing in his Majesty's Stoves at Hampton Court. **1739** P. MILLER *Gard. Dict.* II. 5 B 2 b, A Catalogue of such Plants as should be placed in a Stove. **1793** R. STEELE *Ess. Gardening* 115 A General Stove, 160 feet in length, and of proper width and height, is capable of containing a prodigious collection of plants. **1804** CHARLOTTE SMITH *Conversations*, etc. I. 65 In the stove the natives of the torrid zone; in the conservatory the inhabitants of milder regions. **1869** A. R. WALLACE *Malay Archipelago* (1890) 85 In our stoves these varied conditions can be supplied to each individual plant. **1895** AMHERST *Gardening* 282 The climbing plants which adorned the stove.

4. A heated chamber or box for some special purpose.

1640 T. BRUGIS *Marrow of Physicke* II. 142 So set your Plate in a warme Stove, or Oven. **1706** PHILLIPS (ed. Kersey), *Stove*... Among Confectioners, it is a little Closet well stopt up on all Sides; where there are several stories or rows of Shelves, one above another, made of Wires, to hold the Sweet-meats that are to be dried. **1769** MRS. RAFFALD *Engl. Housekpr.* (1778) 245 When they are cold take them out and lay them on glasses, put them into a stove, and turn them every half hour. **1774** GOLDSM. *Nat. Hist.* V. 168 The artifical method of hatching chickens in stoves, as is practised at Grand Cairo. **1811** A. T. THOMSON *Lond. Disp.* (1818) 241 They are.. killed by the steams of boiling vinegar, and dried either by the sun or in a stove. **1835** URE *Phil. Manuf.* 146 When all the wool is gathered on the teeth, the comb is placed with its points in the stove. **1867** SMYTH *Sailor's Word-bk.* 660 A stove, is a kind of kiln for warping timber in. **1881** RAYMOND *Mining Gloss.*, *Stove*, the oven in which the blast of a furnace is heated. **1885** HUMMEL *Dyeing Textile Fabrics* 112 The sulphur stove—a spacious brick chamber which can be charged with sulphur dioxide. **1897** *Allbutt's Syst. Med.* II. 969 The drawing or emptying of 'stoves' is regarded as the most dangerous part of white-lead making.

5. An apparatus for heating (orig., for heating a 'stove' in sense 1 or 2). Cf. STEW *sb.*[2] 1 b.

a. A closed box or vessel of earthenware, porcelain, or (now more usually) of metal, portable or fixed, in which heat is produced either by combustion of fuel or electrically, for use in warming rooms, cooking, etc.

Often with defining word, indicating the purpose for which the stove is used, as in *cooking stove*, or the kind of fuel employed, as *anthracite, coal, gas, oil stove*.

Quots. 1562 and 1591 perh. do not belong to this sense.

[**1562** BULLEIN *Bulwark, Bk. Sick Men* (1579) 6 Make a fyer of Charcoales, or a stoue, which is a fyer secret felt, but not seene. **1591** G. FLETCHER *Russe Commw.* ii. 4 In the extremitie of winter, if you holde a pewter dishe.. in your hand.. (except in some chamber where their warme stoaues bee) your fingers will friese faste vnto it.] *a* **1618** *Rates of Merchandizes* H 4, Iron Stoues the peece, xl.s. **1623** T. ADAMS *Barren Tree* 4 A Candle is made to light vs, not to heate vs: a Stoue is made to heate vs, not to light vs. **1624** in *Archæologia* XLVIII. 138 In your closet a litle chare, the marble morter, the stove, your owne cabinet and bookes, a target, [etc.]. **1642** FULLER *Holy & Prof. St.* I. xii. 39 Though there be no fire seen outwardly, as in the English chymnies, it may be hotter within, as in the Dutch stoves. **1691** J. GIBSON in *Archæologia* XII. 181 In one of the lesser gardens is a large green house divided into several rooms, and all of them with stoves under them, and fire to keep a continual heat. **1693** EVELYN *De La Quint. Compl. Gard.*, *Cult. Orange-trees* 21 The Heat of Char-coal.. in some hidden Stove, or Earthen Pan. **1702** S. SEWALL *Diary* 16 Jan., A good fire in the stove warm'd the room. **1715** *Lond. Gaz.* No. 5325/4 Stoves fix'd to the Chimneys. **1735** DYCHE & PARDON *Dict.*, *Stove*, a small close Fire, sometimes used for drying Sugars, Sweet-meats, &c. **1747** MRS. GLASSE *Cookery* ii. 26 Do it over a Stove or slow Fire till the Rice begins to be thick. **1816** T. L. PEACOCK *Headlong Hall* viii, With pick-axes and gunpowder, a hanging stove and a poker. **1833** J. HOLLAND *Manuf. Metal* II. 173 The close fire-places, or stoves properly so called, the principle of which is the emission of hot air. **1853** SOYER *Pantroph.* 248 Place them on the stove or gridiron, and you will, by these means, obtain a delicate and tempting dish. **1853** MRS. MOODIE *Life in Clearings* 373, I have seen the grandmother in a wealthy family ironing the fine linen, or broiling over the cook-stove. **1854** RONALDS & RICHARDSON *Chem. Technol.* (ed. 2) I. 216 Chamber stoves are constructed to disseminate heat by the direct contact of air with the heated surface, which is obtained by burning fuel on a grate, closely surrounded on all sides except below the bars, by a good conducting or absorbing material. **1879** *Cassell's Techn. Educ.* II. 395/1 On the Continent.. the.. scarcity of fuel.. early led to the introduction of the hot-air stove. **1909** *Mission Field* June 60 There is at present no heating system of any kind in the school beyond the old-fashioned stoves in each room.

b. Applied to the metal structure of a more or less open fireplace; a 'grate'.

This use, common in England, appears to be unknown in the U.S.

a **1756** ELIZA HAYWOOD *New Present* (1771) 252 To rub the stove and fire-irons. **1794** MRS. RADCLIFFE *Myst. Udolpho* x, On the next morning Emily ordered a fire to be lighted in the stove of the chamber where St. Aubert used to sleep. **1817** W. BELOE *Sexagenarian* II. 143 He would.. offend the delicacy of his hostess by contaminating.. the brightness of her stoves.. with the distillations of tobacco. **1848** DICKENS *Dombey* viii, An empty room.. made ghastly by a ragged fireplace without any stove in it. **1861** T. L. PEACOCK *Gryll Gr.* xxii, It would not suit the stoves of our modern saloons.

†**c.** *Naut.* (See quot.) *Obs.*

1750 BLANCKLEY *Nav. Expositor*, *Stoves* are square Boxes made of Plank filled with Bricks, and when fitted with an Iron Ring and small Bars, are for burning Charcoal, in order for the Cook to dress the Admiral's or Captain's Victuals on.

d. A foot-warmer containing burning charcoal, such as is used in the Low Countries [Du. *stoof*].

1716 GAY *Trivia* II. 338 The Belgian stove beneath her Footstool glows. **1883** OLIVE SCHREINER *Afr. Farm* I. v, Under her feet was a wooden stove.

6. *attrib.* and *Comb.*: in sense 2, as †***stove-window***; in sense 3, as ***stove-flower, -heat, -plant, -shrub, -thermometer***; in sense 4, as ***stove-dry*** vb., whence ***stove-dried*** adj.; in sense 5, as ***stove-brush, -chimney, -coal, -door, -fitter, -fitting, -grating, -lid*** (U.S.), ***-maker, -manufacturer, -oven, -piping, -setter, -setting, -tile, -wood*** (U.S.); ***stove-heated, -warmed*** adjs.; **stove enamel**, a vitreous enamel that is sufficiently heat-resistant to be used on stoves; hence **stove-enamelled** *a.*, **stove-enamelling**; †**stove-fire** (see quot. 1769); **stove-glass** (see quot.); **stove-grate**, (*a*) = sense 5 b; (*b*) see quot. 1875; **stove-house** = sense 3; **stove lifter** *N. Amer.*: see LIFTER 2 a; **stove-polish**, black lead or other substance used for polishing stoves; †**stove-pot** (see quot. for *stove-fire*); **stove-room**, †(*a*) = sense 2; (*b*) = sense 4; **stove-truck** (see quot.); **stove-tub** = sense 4.

1858 SIMMONDS *Dict. Trade*, **Stove-brush*, a housemaid's polishing-brush, for blackening or shining a grate. **1730** *Inventory R. Woolley's Goods* (1732) 8 A *Stove Chimney. **1736** AINSWORTH *Eng.-Lat. Dict.*, A blower (in a stove chimney) *ferreum ignis suscitabulum*. **1881** RAYMOND *Mining Gloss.*, *Stove-coal. **1895** *Daily News* 15 Oct. 3/5 Stove coal 15s. **1868** *Rep. Munitions of War* 188 Having a door resembling an ordinary *stove-door. **1766** *Complete Farmer* s.v. *Moth*, As this corn (which had not been *stove-dried) was old and dry enough, it was but seldom ventilated. **1752** *Gentl. Mag.* XXII. 348 (Porcelain) Rooms for throwing, turning, and *stove drying the ware. **1907** *Yesterday's Shopping* (1969) 11/1 *Stove enamel polishing paste.. tin, 0/2. **1949** KIRK & OTHMER *Encycl. Chem. Technol.* IV. 165 White baking finishes may be classified in four general types: (1) kitchen-cabinet enamels, (2) refrigerator finishes, (3) washing-machine finishes, and (4) stove enamels... Stove enamels are intended for use on the trimmings for stoves... A maximum temperature of 200°F is encountered. **1958** *Observer* 13 Apr. 10/2 A durable finish chromium rather than aluminium, and vitreous enamel.. rather than stove enamel. **1912** C. H. B. QUENNELL in L. Weaver *House & its Equipment* 103 A few years ago, and in the case of the cheaper ones to-day, baths were '*stove-enamelled'. **1977** *Custom Car* Nov. 85/1 (Advt.), 100E Jaguar IRS complete with crossmember, stove enamelled, all new parts. **1939** *Jrnl. R. Aeronaut. Soc.* XLIII. 607 It is desirable therefore, that in cases where *stove-enamelling treatments or other processes involving re-heating at elevated temperature have to be applied to duralium, [etc.]. **1769** MRS. RAFFALD *Eng. Housekpr.* (1805) Descr. Plate, The Plate is the design of three *stove-fires for the kitchen, that will burn coals or embers instead of charcoal..; the coals are burnt in cast iron pots,.. CC Stove pots in which the fire is made. **1903** *Daily Record & Mail* 22 Aug. 2 George Morrow.. a *stovefitter. **1870** DISRAELI *Lothair* xxxi, She held.. a vast bouquet entirely of white *stove flowers. **1891** *Century Dict.* s.v. *Glass*, **Stove-glass*, sheets of mica used in the fronts of stoves, etc. **1730** *Inventory R. Woolley's Goods* (1732) 8 In the Dining-Room... A *Stove Grate. **1753** HOGARTH *Anal. Beauty* viii. 43 Those branches fixt to the sides of common old-fashion'd stove-grates by way of ornament. **1841** in *Inquiry, Yorks. Deaf & Dumb* (1870) 26 Jos. Fellows, stove-grate fitter, Rotherham. **1862** *Catal. Internat. Exhib.* II. No. 5971 Wholesale ironmonger and stove-grate manufacturer. **1875** KNIGHT *Dict. Mech.* 2412 *Stove-grate*, the grid or series of bars on which the fuel rests in a stove. **1890** W. W. MERRY in *More Echoes Oxf. Mag.* (1896) 96 By the *stove-grating I can see the stoker. **1852** GLADSTONE *Glean.* IV. 184 The growth of those democratic principles which the present system is forcing with *stove-heat to maturity. **1894** C. L. JOHNSTONE *Canada* 67 The heat of the stove-heated kitchen prevented me from sleeping. **1860** GOSSE *Rom. Nat. Hist.* (1866) 178 Choice plants that I have been used to see fostered and tended in pots in our *stove-houses at home. **1876** 'MARK TWAIN' *Tom Sawyer* i. 17 She could have seen through a pair of *stove lids just as well. **1929** W. FAULKNER *Sound & Fury* 318 'I came in here to burn them up'.. I says, looking at him and opening the stove lid. **1886** *Harper's Mag.* Nov. 835/1 We'll have a real egg and cinder flip with the hot *stove-lifter in it when we get back. **1927** M. DE LA ROCHE *Jalna* xxv. 306 She up and shied the stove lifter at my 'ead. **1843** *Civil Engin. & Arch. Jrnl.* VI. 422/2 This is a stigma on the *stove-makers of London. **1858** SIMMONDS *Dict. Trade*, *Stove-maker*, a founder and caster of stoves and ranges, for grates and fire-places. **1843** *Civil Engin. & Arch. Jrnl.* VI. 422/1 As a *stove manufacturer, I have [etc.]. **1855** E. ACTON *Mod. Cookery* (rev. ed.) ii. 70 Set the dish into a gentle oven... A *stove-oven, if the heat be properly moderated, will answer for the baking. **1968** *Globe & Mail* (Toronto) 13 Feb. 30/4 (Advt.), 4 Bedrooms, large family room. Fireplace! Walkout! Stove Oven! **1838** *Penny Cycl.* XI. 219/2 A communication.. made of one or more ranges of iron *stove-piping. **1901** *J. Black's Carp. & Build., Home Handicr.* 64 An old piece of stove-piping. **1778** W. COWPER *Let.* 3 Dec. (1904) I. 151, I made Mr. Wrighte's gardener a present of fifty sorts of *stove plant seeds. **1812** *New Botanic Gard.* I. 10 A pleasing variety among other stove plants. **1842** LOUDON *Suburban Hort.* 19 Hothouse plants, which may be either dry stove plants.. or damp stove plants. **1858** SIMMONDS *Dict. Trade*, **Stove-polish*, black-lead. **1905** *Daily Chron.* 13 Apr. 5/3 The blacklead and stove-polish business. **1769** *Stove-pots [see *stove-fire*]. **1706** S. SEWALL *Diary* 27 Feb. (1879) II. 155 Passing out of the *Stove-Room into the Kitchen. **1756–7** tr. *Keysler's Trav.* (1760) IV. 239 Fowls here live in the same apartment or stove-room with the owners. **1825** *Gentl. Mag.* XCV. I. 163 He went into a stove-room, in which sulphur, hay, &c. were burning at the same time. **1840** *Penny Cycl.* XVIII. 473/1 Immediately behind him is the stove-room, in which the moulds are ranged on shelves. **1846** DODD *Brit. Manuf.* VI. 181 Sail-making. Besides the bleach-field there is.. a 'stove-room', in which the flax can be exposed to any required degree of temperature. **1898** *Daily News* 18 June 9/4 Bricklaying, jobbing, drains, *stove setting, &c. **1850** *Florist* 202 A handsome *stove-shrub. **1786** ABERCROMBIE *Gard. Assist.* 354 The proper degree of heat.. may be determinable by a *stove thermometer. **1860** *Inventory Objects Mus. Ornamental Art, S. Kensington* 51/1 German enamelled *stove tile; allegorical figure under an arcade.—Dated 1567. **1936** *Burlington Mag.* Sept. 111/1 The occurrence.. on the jug of a relief corresponding to one on a green-glazed stove-tile. **1960** R. G. HAGGAR *Conc. Encycl. Cont. Pott. & Porc.* 269/2 Stoves and stove-tiles were made from the sixteenth until the eighteenth centuries, the earlier stove-tiles having flat surfaces with relief decorations and concave cylindrical backs. **1875** KNIGHT *Dict. Mech.*, **Stove-truck*, a truck employed in cannon-foundries for moving pieces of ordnance. **1797** *Encycl. Brit.* (ed. 3) XVII. 433/2 They should be stoved in a stove by the heat of a flue, and not in a baker's oven or a *stove tub. **1911** *Chamb. Jrnl.* Sept. 566/2 Their wives have their duties in the close and *stove-warmed houses. **1560** DAUS tr. *Sleidane's Comm.* 164 Lookynge downe out of the *stowffe wyndowe into the courte vnderneth. **1680** R. L'ESTRANGE *Twenty Sel. Colloq. Erasm.* 60 The Master of the Inn puts his head out of the Stove window. **1867** D. R. LOCKE *Swingin' round Cirkle* 159, I held a stick of *stove wood suspended over his head. **1929** W. FAULKNER *Sound & Fury* 332 Then she.. stacked stovewood into her crooked arm. **1972** *News & Observer* (Raleigh, N.C.) 30 Dec. 4/2 We don't hear much about stove wood [nowadays].

stove, *sb.*[2] *Sc.* and *north.* [Cf. STEW *sb.*[3]] A steam; a mist rising from the ground.

1513 DOUGLAS *Æneis* VII. Prol. 89 The callour air.. Maid seik warm stovis. *Ibid.* XII. Prol. 46 Moich hailsum stovis ourheildand the slak.

stove (stəʊv), *v.*[1] Also 7 stoove. [f. STOVE *sb.*[1] Cf. Du. *stoven*, which may be partly the source.]

†**1. a.** *trans.* To subject to a hot-air bath. *Obs.*

1456 SIR G. HAY *Gov. Princes* Wks. (S.T.S.) II. 143 Quhen the man suld stove him, he suld first entre the first chaumer, that is calde.

†**b.** To sweat (a gamecock). Also *intr.* of the cock: To undergo sweating. Cf. STOVE *sb.*[1] 1 b. *Obs.*

1631 MARKHAM *Country Contentm.* I. xix. (ed. 4) 111 Then putting in your Cocke, couer him with sweete strawe vp to the top, and then lay on the lidde close, and there let your Cocke stoue and sweate till the Euening. **1686** BLOME *Gentl. Recr.* II. 279/2 Each time Stove and Scour him [the Cock] according to the nature of his Heats, long Heats requiring longer Stoving, as also greater Scouring.

†**2.** To keep up the heat of (fire). *Obs. rare*$^{-1}$.

1590 GREENE *Never too late* I. (1600) E 2 b, As the minerals of Ætna stoue fire,.. so young yeeres are incident to the heate of loue.

3. To put (plants) in a hothouse.

1625 BACON *Ess., Gardens* ¶ 1 For December, and Ianuary, and the Latter Part of Nouember, you must take.. Orenge-Trees; Lemon-Trees; and Mirtles, if they be stooued [*v.r.* stirred]. **1691** J. GIBSON in *Archæologia* XII. 188 These more nice and curious plants, that need closer keeping are in warmer rooms, and some of them stoved when he thinks fit. **1851** *B'ham & Midl. Gardeners' Mag.* Aug. 140 Tulips,—These will, of course, be all dryed, cleaned, stoved, and in their places.

†**4.** To keep (persons) in heated rooms. *Obs.*

1627 FELTHAM *Resolves* I. xviii. (1628) 55 While the rich lye stoued in secure reposes. **1801** A. YOUNG *Autob.* 6 June (1898) 364 Charming weather for the country,.. and I am stoved up in this horrid place. **1802** BEDDOES *Hygeia* v. 15 Mistaken medical opinions.. induced physicians to stove their patients.. in hot, close rooms.

5. a. To dry in a stove or heated chamber: *Naut.* to dry (ropes) in this manner to prepare them for tarring.

a **1625** *Nomenclator Navalis* (Harl. MS. 2301). **1664–5** [see STOVING *vbl. sb.*]. **1736** J. LEWIS *I of Tenet* (ed. 2) 39 *Stow* or *Stove Ropes*, to dry them in an Oven. **1794** *Rigging & Seamanship* I. 57 *Stoving* is placing of white rope in an iron stove or oven,.. which makes the rope more limber.. to receive the tar. **1851** KIPPING *Sailmaking* (ed. 2) 45 Bolt ropes formerly were stoved in a stove, by the heat of a flue, and tarred afterwards. **1914** A. DEANE *Belfast Art Gall. & Museum* (Quarterly Notes No. 26) 8 The [clay] pipes are then laid in the sun, if the weather permits, for partial drying, or stoved previous to heating in the kiln.

b. To heat so as to fuse a coating to the object being coated. Also *absol.*, and *intr.* (of the coating) for *pass.*

1951 *Industrial Finishing* IV. 184/1 Unless the article is suspended approximately equidistant from the emitting surfaces there will be a risk of it being unevenly stoved. **1954** *Archit. Rev.* CXVI. 132 The undersides of most metal deckings are ribbed, and the steel ones are usually finished with red oxide, 'stoved' on. **1962** D. W. HISLOP in H. W. Chatfield *Sci. Surface Coatings* xviii. 531 A finish which stoves in half an hour at 150°C on sheet metal may require three times as long.. at the same temperature when applied to a heavy casting. *Ibid.* 532 To be sure that a finish has been stoved adequately, a recording instrument is used with a thermocouple in contact with the painted metal. *Ibid.* 537 These lamps may be arranged in banks to give a high heating intensity. They enable paint films on suitable objects.. to be stoved in times of a few seconds. **1977** *Hot Car* Oct. 73/1 It first etches and then stoves so that the finished coating (they say) is a really corrosion resistant lacquer around five times the thickness of factory wheel lacquer. **1979** J. D. SANDARS et al. *Man. Colour Matching* 129 Apply 25–30 micron dry films to burnished degreased mild steel. Stove for appropriate times.

6. To stew (meat or vegetables). Now *Sc.* and *north.*

1738 *Ochtertyre House Bk.* (S.H.S.) 150 Dinner lambs head stoved. **1741** *Compl. Family-Piece* I. ii. 115 Stove it well in good Gravy one Hour, and send it whole to Table.

1747 Mrs. Glasse *Cookery* ii. 44 Pigeons stoved. **1867** J. K. Hunter *Retrosp. Artist's Life* xvii. (1912) 178 Plenty of potatoes stoved with the broo made an excellent dinner.

7. To fumigate with sulphur; to disinfect with sulphur or other fumes.

1805 Luccock *Nat. Wool* 171 The well-known mode of stoving cloth by the fumes of sulphur. **1844** G. Dodd *Textile Manuf.* ii. 73 The cloth was first bleached; the squares were printed by cylinder with a mordant of acetate of iron; then stoved; then passed through a caustic emulsion. **1915** *Blackw. Mag.* No. 589/2 All clothing, even if issued brand-new on the eve of departure from a hospital in France, has to be stoved when it reaches English soil.

8. To heat (a building) with stoves; to provide with stoves. *rare.*

1808 Sarah Lady Lyttelton *Corr.* (1912) 53 The house is so well stoved and fired it is quite a delightful temperature.

†**stove**, *v.*² *Sc. Obs.* [f. stove *sb.*²] *intr.* Of smoke: To pass in clouds.

1756 Mrs. Calderwood in *Coltness Collect.* (Maitl. Club) 164 A long table where the carles smoak, so that, when a scoot passes, you see the smoak stoving out at the windows.

stove (stəʊv), *v.*³ [f. *stove*, pa. pple. of stave *v.*] *trans.* = stave *v.* 2.

1820 Oxley *Jrnls. Exped. N.S. Wales* 17 The large boat had got stoved against a tree under water. **1883** Stevenson *Treas. Isl.* xx, I'll stove in your old blockhouse like a rum puncheon. *Ibid.*, Drop shooting poor seamen, and stoving of their heads in while asleep. **1894** *Westm. Gaz.* 7 Dec. 5/1 And her bulwarks were stoved and washed away.

stove (stəʊv), *ppl. a.* [irreg. pa. pple. of stave *v.*] **1.** Chiefly *Naut.* That has been 'stove in'. Also **stove-in**.

1850 H. Melville *White Jacket* I. iv. 20 Eternally talking of line-tubs, Nantucket, spermoil, stove boats, and Japan. **1897** Kipling *Captains Courageous* iv. 98 They found..a gin-bottle, and a stove-in dory, but nothing more. **1899** F. T. Bullen *Idylls of Sea* xvi. 124 One of the most frequent experiences in this perilous trade [whale-fishing] is that of a 'stove' boat. **1979** 'A. Hall' *Scorpion Signal* xix. 223 A stove-in radiator with rusty water blowing out of it.

2. stove-up. Run-down, exhausted; worn out. Chiefly *predic.* of persons. *N. Amer. slang.*

1901 A. C. Hegan *Mrs Wiggs of Cabbage Patch* ix. 127 If I was n't so stove up, an' nobody was n't lookin', I'd jes' skitter 'round this here yard like a colt! **1942** Berrey & Van den Bark *Amer. Thes. Slang* §129/12 *Physically run-down*, ..stove-up. **1955** R. Hobson *Nothing too Good for Cowboy* xvi. 175 You look stove-up, boy, what's the trouble with that hind leg of yours? **1960** H. Lee *To kill Mockingbird* viii. 81 Mr. Avery'll be in bed for a week—he's right stove up. He's too old to do things like that. **1974** D. Sears *Lark in Clear Air* i. 18 An elderly man in levis and stove-up range-boots was..in the lower bunk.

stove, irreg. pa. t. and pa. pple. of stave *v.*

stoved (stəʊvd), *ppl. a.*¹ [f. stove *v.*¹ + -ed¹.] †**1.** Of a fire: Kept burning in a stove. *Obs.*

1693 Evelyn *De La Quint. Compl. Gard., Direct. Melons* Advt. 4 It is certain, that a Naked or Stov'd Fire, pent up within the House,..must needs be extreamly Noxious and Pernicious to these Delicate and Tender Plants.

2. *Sc.* Of meat or vegetables: Stewed.

1728 Ramsay *Fables, Monk & Miller's Wife* 133 The stov'd or roasted we afford Are aft great strangers on our board. **1756** Mrs. Calderwood in *Coltness Collect.* (Maitl. Club) 149 All sorts of stewes or stoved things. **1867** J. K. Hunter *Retrosp. Artist's Life* i. (1912) 10 She gave me my dinner of stoved potatoes.

3. Heated by a stove. Also, kept in a heated room.

1802 Beddoes *Hygeia* v. 60 The carpeted, stuccoed, and stoved sitting room. *a* **1835** McCulloch *Attributes* (1837) III. xliii. 147 It is no trial to bring a caged and stoved animal from a hot climate and then to decide that it cannot live out of a stove.

4. Dried in a stove or oven. ***stoved salt***: see quot. 1892.

1800 Henry *Epit. Chem.* (1808) 182 The various forms under which it [common salt] appears, of stoved salt, fishery salt, bay salt, &c. arise rather from differences in the size and compactness of the grain than [etc.]. **1808** H. Holland *Agric. Cheshire* in W. H. Marshall *Rev. Rep. Agric.* (1810) II. 93 In making the stoved, or lump salt, as it is called, the brine is brought to a boiling heat. **1852** Fincham *Shipbuilding* III. (ed. 3) 32 It was found that the stoved planks were fresher and tougher. **1880** *Daily News* 28 Oct. 3/8 Sugar... Stoved goods and Paris loaves continue firm. **1892** *Labour Commission* Gloss., *Stoved Salt*, boiled salt drawn out of the pans, put into wooden moulds, and afterwards taken into the stoves or hot-houses for the purpose of being thoroughly dried. All table salt is stoved salt.

5. ***stoved enamel*** = *stove enamel* s.v. stove *sb.*¹ 6.

1926–7 *Army & Navy Stores Catal.* 311 The patent 'Peveril' grate..in best bright black stoved enamel, which does not require blackleading. **1967** *Times Rev. Industry* May 53/3 A good deal of paint is exported as the cellulose finish of a car, the stoved enamel surface of a washing machine or the paintwork of a jet airliner.

stoved, *ppl. a.*² = stove, stoven *ppl. adjs.*

1798 O'Keeffe *Wild Oats* I. i, I'm as empty as a stoved keg.

stoveful ('stəʊvfʊl). [f. stove *sb.*¹ + -ful.] A quantity that fills a stove; as much as a stove can contain.

1838 *Civil Engin. & Arch. Jrnl.* I. 380/2 Your apparatus, with rather less fuel, has thoroughly dried each stove-full in ten days.

stovel, corrupt form of stoven.

15.., **1753**; see stock *sb.* 1 f.

stoveless ('stəʊvlɪs), *a.* [f. stove *sb.*¹ + -less.] Having no stove.

1889 *Advance* (Chicago) Nov. 7 Their shivering women, in stoveless hovels. **1906** *Macm. Mag.* No. 8 Ah, those stoveless rooms in Milan and Brescia!

'stoven, *sb. Obs.* exc. *dial.* Also 4 **stovyn**, 7 **stovene**. [OE. *stofn* masc. and fem. = ON. *stofn* masc.] **a.** A stem or trunk of a tree. **b.** A sapling, shoot from the stump of a tree. Also *fig.*

c **1000** Ælfric *Gloss.* in Wr.-Wülcker 137/29 *Stipes*, stofn. *c* **1000** in Napier *Gloss.* i. 117 *Surculos*, stofnas. *Ibid.* 1665 *Progenie propaganda*, mid ȝestrenendlicere stofne. **1295** *Acc. Exch. K.R.* 5/8 m. 5 Et xix. d. in Stouenes emptis..ad Galeam. *a* **1300** *Cursor M.* 8243 Quen all was cled a-boute þat tre, A siluer cercle son naild he, þat was þe stouen for to strength. **1334–5** in *Blount's Law Dict.* (1691) s.v. *Zuche*, Concedimus dilecto valecto nostro Ric. de Stelley omnes Zucheos aridos, qui Anglice vocantur Stovenes infra Hayam nostram de Beskewood. [**1524** *Yorks. Deeds* (Yorks. Archæol. Soc.) II. 39 To sufficiently fence all trees, stoven, and under-growth]. *a* **1640** Jackson *Creed* xi. iv. (1657) 3347 The diffusion of life..from the roots into the stemmes, stovens or branches. **1788** W. H. Marshall *Yorks.* II. 356 *Stoven*, a shoot of a tree. **1821** Clare *Vill. Minstr.* II. 176 How sweet to be thus nestling deep in boughs, Upon an ashen stoven pillowing me. **1854** Miss Baker *Northampt. Gloss.*, *Stoven*, a stump, either growing or put into the ground as a post. **1896** J. K. Snowden *Web of Weaver* v, It was strangely ordered that my happiness and my shame should grow on one stoven (stock, or stem).

stoven ('stəʊv(ə)n), *ppl. a.* [irreg. pa. pple. of stave *v.*] = stove *ppl. a.*

1851 H. Melville *Moby Dick* II. xiv. 122 The terrific wreck of the stoven planks. **1892–3** Froude *Lect. Counc. Trent* vi. (1896) 140 The sands were littered with drowned bodies, stoven casks, and shattered boxes. **1900** W. S. Davis *Friend of Caesar* xiii. 258 It was madness to embark on the stoven craft.

'stove-pipe.

1. Each of the pipes by which hot air is conveyed in a 'stove' or hothouse.

1699 Evelyn *Kal. Hort.* (ed. 9) 165 [The plants] as they are placed nearer, or farther from the Noses of the Stove-pipes, enjoy the several Climats and Degrees of Warmth which shall be found most..agreeable to them.

2. A metal pipe attached to a stove to carry off the smoke.

1858 Lardner *Hand-bk. Nat. Phil.* 273 If a stove pipe be observed ascending through a room, it will be easy to show that [etc.]. **1861** C. Benson in *Macm. Mag.* Feb. 276 He.. finally clutched at the stove-pipe to save himself [falling]. **1896** Kipling *Seven Seas, Three Sealers* 18 It was the sealer *Northern Light*..With a stovepipe stuck from a starboard port. *Ibid.* 26 A stovepipe seen through the closing mist, it shows like a four-inch gun. **1898** 'Merriman' *Roden's Corner* i. 3 A shop..where ancient pieces of stove-pipe and a few fire-irons are exposed for sale.

attrib. **1882** *U.S. Rep. Prec. Met.* 627 The pipes are.. jointed together in stove-pipe fashion.

3. *colloq.* or *slang.* **a.** (Originally *U.S.*) A tall hat of cylindrical shape, a 'top hat', 'chimney-pot'. Also ***stove-pipe hat.***

1851 *Illustr. Lond. News* 27 Sept. 395/2 Every male who wears the present stove-pipe section head-gear. **1857** J. D. Borthwick *Three Yrs. California* xxii. 333 Here and there some forlorn individual exhibited himself in a black coat and stove-pipe hat. **1883** F. M. Crawford *Dr. Claudius* x, His servant arrayed him in the purple and stove-pipe of the higher civilization. **1886** W. J. Tucker *E. Europe* 429 The brimless black velvet 'stove-pipe' hats worn by the girls on Sundays. **1902** J. F. Rusling *European Days & Ways* 319 Derby and slouch hats, and sack coats, instead of 'stove-pipes' and Prince Alberts.

b. *pl.* Trousers. More recently, *spec.* = *drain-pipe* (fig.) s.v. drain *sb.* 5. Also *attrib.*, as ***stove-pipe trousers.***

1863 B. Brierley *Chron. Waverlow* 147 Their calves were ..hidden betwixt the seams of the more modern 'stove pipes' (trousers). **1955** T. H. Pear *Eng. Social Differences* vii. 176 Narrow stove-pipe trousers. **1970** *Globe Mag.* (Toronto) 26 Sept. 5/2 The greasers..wear stove pipes, grey with pin stripes. **1978** *Sunday Times Mag.* 18 June 43/2 The names are Mazurca and Maier, cheap pink shirts against blond hair, stovepipe trousers above bare ankles and feet.

c. A portable trench mortar. *U.S. Mil.*

1920 H. H. Bissell *Hist. Sixty-Third U.S. Infantry* 37 It didn't prevent their finding ranges, or getting the maximum of performance out of the old 'Stove-pipes'. **1957** R. Leckie *Helmet for my Pillow* vi. 236, I remained..spared the ordeal of carrying mortar shells to the 'stove-pipe' crews.

stover ('stəʊvə(r)), *sb.*¹ Now *dial.* Also 6–7 **stoover**, **stouver**, **stower**. [Aphetic variant of estover.]

†**1.** The provision of food (for persons or animals) necessary for a journey or a sojourn. *Obs.*

13.. *Seuyn Sag.* (W.) 2606 Thai..fond hire that night stouer, And left here alone. **13..** *K. Alis.* 1866, Anon was.. Y-charged mony a selcouth beste, Olifauns, and eke camailes, With armure, and eke vitailes;..Assen and muylyn, with heore stoveris. *c* **1330** *Arth. & Merl.* 7611 For wonderliche þai weren bliþe Of þe eiȝtte & stouers, þat þai brouȝt, þo pauteners. *a* **1320** *Sir Tristr.* 1149 A schip þou bring me tille, Mine harp to play me þare, Stouer ynouȝ to wille To kepe me, son ȝou ȝare.

2. †**a.** *gen.* Winter food for cattle. *Obs.*

1557 Tusser *100 Points Husb.* xxxvii, If barne rome will serue, lay thy stoouer vp drye, and eche kinde of strawe, by hitselfe let it lie. **1563–83** Foxe *A. & M.* 271/1 He plowed vp the fieldes, that there should no stouer be found to serue their horses. **1567** Golding *Ovid's Met.* v. (1593) 116 Dame Ceres..made corne and stover soft to grow upon the ground. **1577** Harrison *England* I. xiii. 38/1 in *Holinshed*, The haye of our lowe meddowes is..not so profitable, for stouer and forrage as yᵉ higher meades be. **1578** Timme *Calvin on Gen.* vi. 22. 189 Noah..had much more businesse and trouble in prouiding stouer and prouinder for beastes themselues. **1600** Holland *Livy* xxiii. xlviii. 506 The corn was..so well grown, that the blade therof yeelded good forage & stouver for the horses. **1610** Shaks. *Temp.* iv. i. 63 Ceres..Thy Turphie-Mountaines, where liue nibling Sheepe, And flat Medes thetchd with Stouer, them to keepe. **1622** Drayton *Poly-olb.* xxv. 145 And others from their Carres, are busily about, To draw out Sedge and Reed, for Thatch and Stouer fit. **1634–5** *Ir. Act 10 & 11 Chas. I*, c. xvii. (1678) 474 The..improvident care of the owners, that neither provide fodder, nor stover for them [*sc.* cattle] in winter, nor [etc.]. **1657** S. Purchas *Pol. Flying-Ins.* 118 Whereas gloomy cold and close weather, shuts them in and saves stover. **1674** Ray *S. & E.C. Words*, *Stover*: Fodder for cattel, as hay, straw or the like, *Ess.*

fig. **1609** Holland *Amm. Marcell.* xvi. v. 56 Gathering together certaine forage and stoover (as it were) for to feed his mind [L. *quasi pabulum animo..conquirens*].

b. *spec.* In various applications according to locality: Hay made from clover; broken straw, etc. from the threshing-floor; stubble. (See quots.)

1669 Worlidge *Syst. Agric.* 276 *Stover*, Straw. **1733** W. Ellis *Chiltern & Vale Farm.* 84 A good Crop of Peas, or other Stover in great Quantities has been taken off. *Ibid.* 381 These Creatures are of prodigious Service in converting Stover to one of the best of Dungs. **1763** *Museum Rust.* (ed. 2) I. 191 Neither is the haulm so good, as it will not serve for stover for our cattle in the winter. **1787** W. H. Marshall *E. Norfolk* II. 389 *Stover*, a general term for the different species of fodder arising from thrashed corn, whether it be straw, chaff, or 'colder'. **1788** —— *Yorks.* II. 45 The stover (that is, the pulls and points of the [rape-] straw broken off in thrashing) is as acceptable to them [*sc.* cattle] as hay. **1823** E. Moor *Suffolk Words*, *Stuva* or *Stover*, clover made into hay. **1840** *Jrnl. R. Agric. Soc.* I. iii. 255 The land not producing then stover sufficient to keep any stock worth mentioning. **1854** Miss Baker *Northampt. Gloss.*, *Stover*, or *Sturver*, haulm, stubble; the second mowing or growth of clover. **1883** C. Wilson in *Harper's Mag.* Jan. 271/2 The.. annual yield of corn stover in its various forms is not less than 120,000,000 tons. **1889** Hissey *Tour in Phaeton* 140 At Woodbridge we observed..the notice 'Stover sold here'.

†**3.** Used for: ? Reeds. (Cf. quot. 1622 in 2 a.)

1621 Markham *Fowling* 9 They loue also..Fennes,.. ouer-growne with tall and long rushes, reads, seges, stouer, or any other kinde of Couert. **1638** W. Lisle *Heliodorus* i. 7 Where th' ouer-floods of Nile Fall int' a Dale vnmeatly midward deepe, Though nigh the banks to muddy fen it creepe. This Stouer breeds, which some for pasture take. **1895** *E. Angl. Gloss.*, *Stiver* or *Stover* marsh litter or marsh stuff.

stover ('stəʊvə(r)), *sb.*² [f. stove *v.*¹ + -er¹.] One who stoves.

c **1600** in *Rep. MSS. Ld. Middleton* (1911) 169 [Rules to be observed by miners in the coalpits.] This is our master's comandment that all you stovers of the feild shalle make your just account unto your undermen everye nowne and every nyght what you have gett and sould. **1832** Thackrah *Effects Arts etc. on Health* 58 The Stovers of Woollen Articles are also exposed to the evolution of sulphurous vapour. **1835** Ure *Philos. Manuf.* 400 The stovers, in bleach-works and print-works, hang their cloth in temperatures much above 100° Fahr. **1861** *Internat. Exhib. 1862, Alph. Lists Trades* 39 Stovers. **1902** *Brit. Med. Jrnl.* 15 Feb. 380/1 Hatting Operatives... Proofers including 'stovers'..and 'steamers'.

†**'stover**, *v. Obs.* [? f. stover *sb.*¹] *intr.* ? To stand *up* like stubble, to bristle *up*.

1633 Ford *Love's Sacrif.* ii. i, Beard be confin'd to neatnesse, that no haire May stouer vp to pricke my mistris lip.

stovies ('stovɪz), *sb. pl. Sc.* and *north. dial.* [f. stove *v.*¹ 6.] A dish of potatoes stewed in a pot; a potato stew. Also *attrib.*

1893–4 R. O. Heslop *Northumb. Words* II. 687 Hey! lass, is the stavies [*sic*] no ready yit? **1894** J. Inglis *Oor Ain Folk* iv. 40 One day there was a fine dish of 'stoved taties' for dinner... The lads would..have 'the stovies' finished before he had a chance to start. **1907** in *Ochtertyre Ho. Bk. Accomps* 258 *Stovies*, potatoes stewed fine with dripping or fat bacon, onions and spice, and served hot. **1939** M. Spring Rice *Working-Class Wives* vi. 144 Her main dish is 'stovies' made with onions, potatoes and water; she never puts either dripping or meat into them. **1971** S. Walker *Highland Cookbk.* 77 Plain stovies are excellent with beef stew or mince..Put as many peeled and sliced potatoes as you need in a pot [etc.]. **1973** *Courier & Advertiser* (Dundee) 26 Feb. 7/1 A liquid gas portable stove..would have barely supported our stovie pot!

stoving ('stəʊvɪŋ), *vbl. sb.* [f. stove *v.*¹ + -ing¹.] **a.** The action of stove *v.*¹ in various senses.

1456 Sir G. Hay *Gov. Princes* Wks. (S.T.S.) II. 143 Efter the stoving and bathing, men suld sytt on faire bynkis on thai herberis. **1664–5** Pepys *Diary* 13 Feb., We had good discourse touching stoveing and making of cables. **1676** (*title*) Practical and Short Discourse of Stoving and Bathing. **1845** G. Dodd *Brit. Manuf.* Ser. v. 73 Conversion of gyle into vinegar... This process of acetification is technically called 'stoving'. *Ibid.* 165 Hat-making... After another 'stoving' by which the spirit is evaporated [etc.]. **1862** C. O'Neill *Dict. Calico Printing* 7/2 *Ageing*; known also as Stoving or Hanging. The operation of exposing printed or mordanted goods to the action of the air. Formerly the ageing or hanging rooms were kept hot by flues or steam pipes, whence called stoves, a name which they still retain in some places, though heat may not be used. **1882** Crookes *Dyeing & Tissue-Printing* 4 Wool is bleached by the action of the fumes of burning sulphur... This process is generally known as 'stoving'.

b. *attrib.*

1456 SIR G. HAY *Gov. Princes* Wks. (S.T.S.) II. 143 Efter the sesone of ilke bathing and stoving time. **1686** BLOME *Gentl. Recr.* II. 279/1 Take them [Cocks] out of the Stoving-Baskets, and.. put them into the Pens. **1879** *Cassell's Techn. Educ.* IV. 338/2 The gases having done their work here, are carried off by the flues into the stoving-room, where they are made to do duty a second time in drying the salt. **1952** *Industrial Finishing* V. 201/2 How efficiency of drying.. can be increased with existing stoving equipment. **1962** D. W. HISLOP in H. W. Chatfield *Sci. Surface Coatings* xviii. 531 All paint stoving ovens can be a hazard as the solvent vapour/air mixture is a potential fire risk. **1972** *Materials & Technol.* V. viii. 215 The use of these oils in water-thinnable stoving paints has been more successful. *Ibid.* xi. 363 Anti-corrosive stoving primers for cars. **1982** W. M. MORGANS *Outl. Paint Technol.* (ed. 2) I. xiii. 221 The combination of urea resin with non-drying alkyd is used very widely for stoving finishes of almost all types.

stow, *sb.*[1] *Obs.* exc. *dial.* (sense 3). Forms: 1 stów, 3 -stouwe, stowe, 4 steowe, stou, 9 *dial.* stow. [OE. *stów* fem. = OFris. *stô*, ON. **stó* in *eldstó* fireplace:—OTeut. **stōwō* f. **stō-* (*sta-*): see STAND *v.*]

1. = PLACE *sb.* in various senses; a place on the surface of the earth or in space; occas. a place in a book or writing. Cf. ERDINGSTOW.

The word survives in the names of many towns and villages, sometimes separately, as Stow in Cambridgeshire, Stowe in Buckinghamshire, Stow-on-the-Wold; more frequently as the terminal element, as in Chepstow.

Beowulf 1372 Nis þæt heoru stow. *c* **888** ÆLFRED *Boeth.* xxxiii. §5 Þu eart æʒðer ʒe weʒ, ʒe ladþeow, ʒe sio stow ðe se weʒ to ligð. *a* **1175** *Cott. Hom.* 219 For wan hi beoð þuss icweðe me scel sigge, an oðre stowe. *c* **1200** *Trin. Coll. Hom.* 207 He haueð.. gon.. seldere þenne he sholde to his chirche, and to oðre holie stowen. *c* **1205** LAY. 1209 Makian ich wlle on þine nome mæren ane stowe. ? *a* **1300** *Shires England* 5 in *O.E. Misc.*, þe breade of Engle londe is þreo hundred myle brod from Dewyes steowe to Doueran. *a* **1310** in Wright *Lyric P.* xxxv. 98 On stou ase thou stode,.. Thou restest the under rode.

2. (See quot.) *rare*$^{-1}$.

c **1440** *Promp. Parv.* 478/1 Stowe, streythe passage betwyx ij. wallys or hedgys, *intercapedo.*

3. *dial.* (See quot.)

1856 MORTON *Cycl. Agric.* II. 726/1 *Stow* or *Tray.* (Lincolns.), a sheep-hurdle.

stow (stəʊ), *sb.*[2] *Mining.* Also 7-9 stowe, 9 stoe. [App. a sing. form evolved from STOWCE (to which the first quot. may belong).]

†**1.** = STOWCE. *Obs.*

? **1550** in Pettus *Fodinæ Reg.* (1670) 93 And if any Gentleman or other man have any Ground lying in the Mine called The Kings Field of the Mine, they shall keep them lawfully with Stows and Timber. **1653** MANLOVE *Lead-Mines* 5 (E.D.S.) They may make crosses, holes, and set their Stowes, Sink Shafts, build Lodges, Cottages, or Coes. *a* **1661** FULLER *Worthies, Derby.* (1662) 229 He that stealeth Oar twice, is fined, and the third time struck through his hand with a Knife unto the haft into the Stow, and is there to stand until death, or loose himself by cutting off his hand. **1681** T. HOUGHTON *Rara Avis in Terra* Gloss. (E.D.S.) *Stows*, seven pieces of wood.. fastened with pins of wood together; two are called soul-trees; two, stow-blades; two, hang-benches; and a spindle: these stows give a miner, or any person that owns them, as good right to a meer or meers of ground (so that every meer have a pair of stows set on them) as a deed of conveyance doth to any purchaser. **1836** R. FURNESS *Astrol.* I. Poet. Wks. (1858) 133 Then would he dress a helm,.. Make stows, and keep the heavy hours alive.

†**2.** A nick in the 'stow-blade'. *Obs.*

1851 TOPPING *Manlove's Customs Lead Mines* Gloss. 33/1 They have a nick in the top like an arrow's head, called a stow.

3. Comb. ***stow-fork*** = STOW-BLADE.

1824 MANDER *Derbysh. Miner's Gloss.* 68 In the Wapentake of Wirksworth they [the Stoces] contain seven pieces of wood, viz. two Sole-trees, two Hang Benches, two Stoe-forks, and one Spindle.

stow (stəʊ), *sb.*[3] *Obs.* exc. *techn.* Forms: 6-8 stowe, 7 stough, 7- stow. [Variant of STOVE *sb.*[1]]

†**1.** In various senses of STOVE *sb.*[1]: A hot-air bath; a heated room or chamber; a hothouse for plants; a closed fireplace. *Obs.*

In quot. 1599 the spelling *stowis* is prob. merely an example of the writing of *w* for *v* in Sc., and has no phonetic significance.

[**1599** *Sc. Acts Jas. VI* (1816) IV. 187/2 Fewall.. is alreddie brocht to ane grit decay within the boundis of þis realme by the excessiue spending.. þairof for laik of the formes of killis, stowis, and furnessis eftermentionate.] **1614** MARKHAM *Cheap & Good Husb.* II. i. 114 To set Hens in the winter time in stowes or ouens is of no vse with vs in england. **1627** HAKEWILL *Apol.* (1630) 399 They could neither eate nor drinke vnlesse they had first bathed or had sweat in a stough. **1652–62** HEYLIN *Cosmogr.* I. (1682) 145 To keep the heat of their Stows from going out, or any cold from coming in. **1655** HARTLIB *Ref. Silk-worm* 30 Iohn Tradeskin.., by the advantage of putting his Trees, and other Plants into a warm house in winter or a stow, nurses up those things faire and fragrant, which would without that help either dye or be dwarft. **1713** PETIVER in *Phil. Trans.* XXVIII. 218 The Dutchess of Beaufort shewed me this [plant] in her Stows at Badmington. **1721** MORTIMER *Husb.* II. 267 Commit them early to their shelter, where they may intirely be preserv'd from the Frost; you may give them a gentle Stow, and attemper the Air with a Fire of Charcoal during the extream rigour of the Winter. **1730** *Inventory D. Bond's Goods* (1732) 18 A small Stow and Fender. **1731** *Inventory T. Warren's Good* (1732) 32 One Cupboard, 2 Stowes.

2. *Tin-plate making.* (See quot. 1875.)

1839 URE *Dict. Arts* 1253 A range of rectangular cast-iron pots is set over a fire-flue in an apartment called the stow. **1875** KNIGHT *Dict. Mech.* 2413 *Stow*, a raised structure containing the furnace and set of pots used in the manufacture of tin-plate.

stow, *sb.*[4] *Sc.* and *dial.* Also stove; for other forms see *Eng. Dial. Dict.* s.v. *Stove.* [f. STOW *v.*[2]]

1. The stump of a tree or shrub.

1774 HUTCHINSON *Hist. Cumb.* (1794) I. 102 The bottoms, or stoves, of some of the trees,.. which appeared to be then lately cut down.

2. A thick slice (of cheese).

1715 RAMSAY *Christ's Kirk Gr.* II. xx, A kebbuck syn.. pat on the sheaf, In stous that day.

stow (stəʊ), *v.*[1] Pa. t. and pa. pple. **stowed** (stəʊd). Forms: 4 **stau, staw, stew, stouwe, stue, stywe,** 4-7 **stowe,** 5 **stou, stowyn,** 6 **stoe,** 7 **stoaw, stooe,** 4- **stow.** *Pa. pple.* 4 **i-stewid,** 7 **stoad.** [f. STOW *sb.*[1] Cf. BESTOW *v.*

OE. appears to have one example, *stouuiʒan* (= **stówian*) 'retentare' (*Corpus Gl.* c 725); but the meaning of the lemma is obscure, and the vb. recorded from the 14th c. onwards is prob. an independent formation.]

†**1. a.** *trans.* To place; to put in a certain place, position, or situation. *Obs.*

13.. *E.E. Allit. P.* B. 113 Wheþer þay wern worþy, oþer wers, wel wern þay stowed. *Ibid.* 352, & when ʒe arn staued, styfly stekez yow þerinne. *Ibid.* 360 Al wer stawed & stoken, as þe steuen wolde. **1362** LANGL. *P. Pl.* A. v. 39 Leste þe kyng and his counseil ʒor comunes apeire, And beo stiward in oure stude til ʒe be stouwet [*v.rr.* stewed, stuede, stuyd, stywed, stowed] betere. *c* **1374** CHAUCER *Troylus* III. 1271 (MS. Gg.) And for þou.. Hast holpin þere I likly was to steruyn And me ben I-stewid [*other MSS.* bistowed] in so hi a plase. **1387** TREVISA *Higden* (Rolls) III. 277 Tullius.. seiþ þat Socrates.. cleped philosofie from hevene into erþe, and stowed [L. *collocavit*] philosofie in citees. *c* **1440** *Promp. Parv.* 478/1 Stowyn, or cowche to-gedyr, *loco, colloco.* **1555** PHAER *Æneid* II. (1558) F ij, And captiue children stode, and tremblyng wifes in long aray Were stowed about and wept. **1592** WARNER *Alb. Eng.* VIII. xli. (1612) 198 His eie had stoed her in his heart. **1593** SHAKS. *Lucr.* 119 Till sable Night.. in her vaultie prison, stowes the daie.

refl. **1594** R. CAREW *Tasso* (1881) 10 Part campt abroad, part them in circuit stowe, Another part within Tortosa lay.

b. To lodge, quarter, find room for (persons). Now only in derogatory sense (after 3).

1604 SHAKS. *Oth.* I. ii. 62 Oh thou foule Theefe, Where hast thou stow'd my Daughter? **1607** ROWLANDS *Diogines Lanth.* C 1 b, If thou hast roome to stooe him in thy Tunne, He will be ready both to goe and runne. **1687** A. LOVELL tr. *Thevenot's Trav.* I. 277 There they lodge as well as they can, some having little Rooms made of wood, to which they go up by Ladders, and are stowed three or four together in one. **1707** PRIOR *Satire upon the Poets* 76 You've no Friend left, but trusting Landlady, Who stows you on hard Truckle, Garret high. **1739** 'C. DODD' *Ch. Hist. Eng.* II. 170/2 She stowed her children in a pair of panniers, and so proceeded on her journey. **1759** ROBERTSON *Hist. Scot.* II. VIII. 47 Mrs. Beatrix Ruthven was brought.. as one of their gentlewomen, into the court in the evening, and stowed in a chamber prepared for her by the queen's direction. **1760–72** H. BROOKE *Fool of Qual.* (1809) IV. 130 The coaches came, and Harry assisted.. in carrying.. and gently stowing the maimed and wounded into some of them. **1788** WESLEY *Jrnl.* 8 July, We were much distrest at Rotheram for want of room, the rain driving us into the house. However we stowed in it as many as we possibly could. **1821** SCOTT *Kenilw.* xxxi, I will but see him stowed, and be back with you presently.

†**2.** To invest (money); to apply (money or goods) to a particular purpose; to spend. (Cf. BESTOW *v.* 5, 5 b.) *Obs.*

Sometimes written *'stow*, as if short for *bestow*.

c **1440** *Promp. Parv.* 478/1 Stowyn, or waryn, or besettyn, as men don moneye or chaffer, *commuto.* **1616** R. C. *Times Whistle* 2544 If thou dost flow In thy frank guiftes, and thy golde freely stow, The principall will make thy pennance ebbe. **1617** FLETCHER *Mad Lover* Prol., Remember, ye'ar all venturers; and in this Play How many twelve-pences ye have 'stow'd this day. **1742** YOUNG *Nt. Th.* VIII. 7 And yet Lorenzo still affects the world; There, stows his treasure. **1762** *Gentl. Mag.* XXXII. 287/1 When you stows eighteen pence in cakes & beer, To treat that dirty trollup, Mall Rosevear.

3. a. To place in a receptacle to be stored or kept in reserve. †Rarely with *up*.

1456 SIR G. HAYE *Law Arms* (S.T.S.) 111 To stou up his suerd in his furrell. *c* **1586** C'TESS PEMBROKE *Ps.* XLIX. v, Death in the pitt his carrion foode doth stow. **1596** SPENSER *F.Q.* IV. vii. 6 His neather lip was.. like a wide deepe poke .. In which he wont the relickes of his feast And cruell spoyle, which he had spard, to stow. **1601** R. JOHNSON *Kingd. & Commw.* (1603) 224 It was fiercelie assaulted, and as valiantly defended, vntil the fire began to take hold vpon the bulwarke wherein their prouision of gunpowder was stowed. **1683** [R. NORTH] *Discourse Fish & Fish-ponds* xvi. (1713) 62 Some use to put up Fish in Baskets or Hampers for Carriage, stowing them with Grass between. **1706** E. WARD *Wooden World Diss.* (1708) 53 He's soon equipped for his Journey, for he stows all his Baggage in his Pockets. **1720** OZELL *Vertot's Rom. Rep.* II. IX. 51 [That they] had brought home not only their Purses fill'd with Gold and Silver, but had likewise stow'd it in to Pots and Vessells. **1862** CALVERLEY *Verses & Transl.* (ed. 2) 64, I.. Place 'neath my head the *havre-sac* Which I have stowed my little all in. **1874** SYMONDS *Sk. Italy & Greece* (1898) I. ii. 33 Raftered lofts to stow the hay. **1877** *Five Yrs. Penal Serv.* iii. 246 She'd smug a whole piece of silk and stow it under her petticoats.

absol. **1824** SCOTT *Redgauntlet* ch. xv, The Miller, or old Peel-the-Causeway, will tell you where to stow.

b. *jocularly.* To find room for (a quantity of food).

1833 L. RITCHIE *Wand. by Loire* 54 We are still filled with curiosity.. to know how they contrive to stow all they eat.

4. *Naut.* **a.** To place (cargo) in proper order in the hold or other receptacles in a ship; also, to store (provisions, etc.) between decks.

Possibly influenced by the (etymologically unconnected) Du. *stouwen* in the same sense.

1555 *Instit. Gentl.* E vj, Ptolomye.. caused all thys golde and siluer.. to bee put into certayne shippes.., and ordeyned that holes shoulde be made in the bottoms of the sayde vessels wherin he had stowed him selfe and the mony. **1598** FLORIO, *Stipare*,.. Also to presse downe hard, to stowe as merchandise is in a ship. **1627** CAPT. SMITH *Sea Gram.* vii. 33 Stowage or to stow, is to put the goods in Howle in order. **1633** T. JAMES *Voy.* 74 There stowd we a But of Wine also. **1644** MANWAYRING *Seamans Dict.* 103 To *Stowe*, is to put any goods in Howld (in order, for else we say it is not stowed, but lyes in howld) also we call it stowing betweene the Decks of [*read* if] any goods or victuals be placed in order upon the Decks: but it is not used in this kind to small things, as to a Chest or the like. **1661** GODOLPHIN *View Admir. Jurisd.* Introd. [a 5 b], He may not over-charge or over-lade his Ship, nor stowe Goods above her birth-mark. **1725** POPE *Odyss.* II. 439 The Goddess shov'd the vessel from the shores, And stow'd within its womb the naval stores. **1743** BULKELEY & CUMMINS *Voy. S. Seas* 3 Here we employ'd most of our Time in getting aboard Water, and stowing our dry Provisions between Decks. **1748** *Anson's Voy.* II. x. 241 They take on board a much greater quantity of water than can be stowed between decks,.. yet.. even a three months store of water could never be stowed in a ship so loaded. **1800** COLERIDGE *Wallenstein* I. vii, I am but the ship in which his hopes were stow'd. **1821** SHELLEY *Boat on Serchio* 74 Stow the eatables in the aft locker. **1845** STEPHEN *Comm. Laws Eng.* (1874) II. 134 Goods stowed upon the deck. **1849** MACAULAY *Hist. Eng.* I. v. 651 The human cargoes were stowed close in the holds of small vessels. **1883** BRETT in *Law Times Rep.* (1884) XLIX. 768/2 Part of the timber which was stowed on the deck was jettisoned by the captain of the vessel.

b. To fasten down (persons) under the hatches for confinement or safety.

1602 MARSTON *Antonio's Rev.* II. iv. E 1 b, Antonio's bride, pure heart, defam'd, and stoad Vnder the hatches of obscuring earth. **1610** SHAKS. *Temp.* I. ii. 230 The Marriners all vnder hatches stowed. **1622** FLETCHER *Sea-Voy.* I. i, *Mast.* Clap this woman under hatches.. For heaven's sake stoaw this woman. **1644** WINTHROP *Hist. New Eng.* (1826) II. 192 They.. had stowed the lady and her people under hatches.

c. To put (guns, oars, furniture, etc.) in the proper receptacles on board.

c **1595** CAPT. WYATT *Dudley's Voy.* (Hakl. Soc.) 58 [He] caused his leiftenant.. to commaunde the gunners to make readie all such great peeces of ordinance as weare not allreadie dismounted and stowed. **1596** SAVILE *Libell Sp. Lies* 24 As for the Oares.. they had stoed them aboarde their Shippes. **1700** DRYDEN *Fables, Ceyx & Alcyone* 107 Some stow their Oars or stop the leaky Sides. **1726** SWIFT *Gulliver* I. viii, I took out my other cables, which were stowed in one of the ships. **1857** C. GRIBBLE in *Merc. Marine Mag.* (1858) V. 8 [They] stowed the anchors. **1867** SMYTH *Sailor's Word-bk.*, *Stowing Hammocks*, placing them in a neat and symmetrical order in the hammock-netting.

d. To furl (a sail).

1644 MANWAYRING *Seamans Dict.* 103 Also the placing and laying of the top-sailes in the top, is called Stowing the top-sailes. **1769** FALCONER *Dict. Marine* II. (1780), *Dedans*, when expressed of the sails, imports furled or stowed. **1823** W. SCORESBY *Jrnl.* 302 We close-reefed the top-sails, and stowed the courses. **1836** MARRYAT *Pirate* i, The men were .. stowing away the foretopmast-staysail. **1885** LADY BRASSEY *The Trades* 465, 8 A.M.—Stowed foresail... 10 P.M. —Stowed topgallant sail.

e. ***to stow down***: to put down into a vessel's hold; in quot., to yield (a certain quantity) to be stowed down.

1850 SCORESBY *Cheever's Whalem. Adv.* xii. (1858) 178 That whale stowed us down eighty-five barrels of oil.

f. Of a ship: To have stowage-room for; to hold. ? *Obs.*

1615 E. S. *Britaines Buss* in Arber *Eng. Garner* III. 635 The Buss can conveniently stow at once but 34 Last of Caske. **1617** FLETCHER *Mad Lover* IV. i, Shall thy black Bark those guilty spirits stow That kill themselves for love? **1645** WINTHROP *Hist. New Eng.* (1826) II. 240 He entertained as many as his ship could stow.

5. a. *Naut.* To fill (the hold of a ship, etc.) with cargo; to load (a ship). Also, to fit up (a ship), supply with necessaries.

1692 *Capt. Smith's Seaman's Gram.* I. xvi. 78 *Stowing the Hold*, is when they take goods into the Hold. **1703** *La Hontan's Voy. N. Amer.* I. 127 Upon that occasion I repeated my Presents; in compensation of which my Pirogues were stow'd with Beef as full as they could hold. **1755** MAGENS *Insurances* II. 16 If.. a Master overloads his Ship or stows it unskilful. **1845** *Encycl. Metrop.* VI. 383/1 This officer is directed.. to obtain the most correct information he can of the manner in which the hold was stowed when she was last in commission. **1856** KANE *Arct. Expl.* I. xix. 234, I find upon my return the brig so stowed and refitted that four days would prepare us for sea.

b. *transf.* To fill (a receptacle), to pack (*full*, *close*) with things or persons; to crowd with contents.

1710 C. SHADWELL *Fair Quaker Deal* I. i. 15 [A sailor speaks.] Pshaw, who would not stand all this, to have their upper and lower Teer well Stow'd with Flip? **1758** WESLEY *Jrnl.* 11 Oct., The House was stowed as full as possible, but still many were constrained to stand without. **1785** BURNS *To W. Simpson* 24 Ye Enbrugh Gentry! The tythe o' what ye waste at cartes Wad stow'd his [Fergusson's] pantry! **1815** SCOTT *Guy M.* xxxix, The lawyer afterwards compared his mind to the magazine of a pawnbroker, stowed with goods of every description, but [etc.]. **1817** COLERIDGE *Biogr. Lit.* II. 207 The passage boat.. was stowed close with all people of all nations. **1849** CUPPLES *Green Hand* iii.

(1856) 33 The window [of the shop] was stowed full of cakes of cavendish, twists of negrohead, and coils of pigtail. **1850** R. G. CUMMING *Hunter's Life S. Afr.* (1902) 52/1 The morning was spent in stowing the waggons, greasing the wheels, [etc.].

6. stow away. a. *trans.* To remove and store until required; to put (a thing) away in a secret or not readily accessible place, or where it will be out of the way; occas. to put or lodge (a person) in out-of-the-way quarters, or in a place of concealment; *jocularly*, to 'put out of sight', 'dispose of', eat up (quantities of food).

1795 VANCOUVER *Agric. Essex* 23 Successive hoeings [of the carrots] will cost about four pounds per acre: and gathering, lopping, tailing, and stowing away, will be about four pounds per acre more. **1825** T. HOOK *Sayings* Ser. II. *Passion & Princ.* vi, He was 'stowed away' in a manner perfectly suitable, as the chambermaid thought, to the condition of an outside passenger..who..carried his own portmanteau up stairs. **1833** HT. MARTINEAU *Vanderput* i. 1 The bales of merchandize which could not be stowed away before dark. **1847** C. BRONTË *Jane Eyre* v, At last the guard returned; once more I was stowed away in the coach. **1857** DUFFERIN *Lett. High Lat.* vii. (ed. 3) 133 We had some difficulty about stowing away the legs of a tall philosopher. **1858** M. TUCKETT *Diary* 24 Nov. (*c* 1975) 21 We stowed away a good breakfast. **1865** LIVINGSTONE *Zambesi* vii. 169 They..eat till it becomes physically impossible for them to stow away any more. *a* **1881** A. BARRATT *Phys. Metempiric* (1883) 253 On the spiritual theory, past ideas..must be imagined to be stowed away in some fashion, to exist all the time till they happen to be wanted. **1885** CHITTY in *Law Times' Rep.* LIII. 83/2 The plate..is now stowed away in the strong room of a bank.

refl. **1849** CUPPLES *Green Hand* xi. (1856) 114 Then I shins aloft up a tree, where I stowed myself away till noon.

b. *intr.* for *refl.* To conceal oneself on board a ship, train, or aeroplane; to be a STOWAWAY.

1879 STEVENSON *Ess. Trav., Amateur Emigrant* (1905) 62 He had now made up his mind to stow away. **1916** *Daily Chron.* 3 Feb., They escaped and reached Gibraltar on a steamer on which they had stowed away. **1929** R. HUGHES *High Wind in Jamaica* vii. 168 Otto was a Viennese by birth, but had stowed away in a Danube barge when he was ten years old, had taken to the sea, and thereafter generally served in English ships. **1973** *Times* 8 Aug. 7/3 A Brazilian youth was sent home..after stowing away on board a South African Airways aircraft by mistake.

†**7.** *slang.* **a.** *intr.* To cease speaking, 'shut up'. *Obs.* **b.** *trans.* To desist from.

1567 HARMAN *Caveat* (1869) 84 Stow you, holde your peace. **1676** COLES, *Stow your whids*, c[anting], speak warily. *a* **1700** B. E. *Dict. Cant. Crew*, *Stow*, you have said enough. **1796** *Grose's Dict. Vulgar T.* (ed. 3), *Stow you*, be silent, or hold your peace. **1806** *Naval Chron.* XV. 18 A sailor.. bawled..for those aloft to stow their jabber. **1812** J. H. VAUX *Flash Dict.* s.v., To *stow* any business, employment, or mode of life, is the same as to *stash it*, &c. *Ibid.*, *Stow*, *stow it*, or *stow-faking*, an intimation from a thief to his pall, to desist from what he is about. **1838** DICKENS *O. Twist* xv, 'Stow that gammon,' interposed the robber, impatiently. **1857** 'DUCANGE ANGLICUS' *Vulgar Tongue* 20 *Stow your mag*, hold your tongue. *L[ow] Life.* **1865** H. KINGSLEY *Hillyars & Burtons* xxxiii, 'Stow larks, Jimmy,' said the constable. **1882** 'OUIDA' *Under Two Flags* xxv. (1890) 391 'Stow that, sir,' cried Rake, vehemently. **1884** HENLEY & STEVENSON *Adm. Guinea* III. ii. (1892) 232 *Pew.* Stow your gab (seizing his wrist).

†**8.** Obscure or uncertain senses: **a.** ? To bring to a stand; **b.** ? To arrest, imprison. *Obs.*

a. *c* **1440** *Promp. Parv.* 478/1 Stowyn, or charyn ageyne[,] cowpyn, idem quod Stoppyn.

b. *c* **1450** *Cov. Myst., Wom. Adultery* (1841) 217 *Accusator.* Stow that harlot sum erthely wyght... *Juvenis.* ȝiff any man stow me this nyth, I xal hym ȝeve a dedly wownde. **1546** GARDINER *Declar. Joye* 15 Ye crye stowe the thefe, to hyde your selfe with the noyse. **1614** R. TAILOR *Hog hath lost Pearl* II. C 3 b, My lord and father hath put them all to the bastinado twice this morning already; not a wayting woman but has been stowed ifaith.

9. *Comb.* **stow-board** *Mining* (see quots.); **stow-down**, the action of stowing down (cargo); that which is stowed down (see 4 e); **stow-master**, a man in charge of the stowing of a boat; **stow-road**, **stow-wood** (see quots.).

1851 GREENWELL *Coal-trade Terms, Northumb. & Durh.* 53 **Stow-board*, a board driven for convenience of stowage. **1860** *Mining Gloss., Newcastle Terms* 64 *Stowbord*, a place into which rubbish is put. **1883** GRESLEY *Gloss. Coal-mining* 243 *Stow-board*, a board or heading in which débris is stowed. **1857** P. COLQUHOUN *Oarsman's Guide* 22 One [man] should do the cooking;..another act as *stow-master. **1886** J. BARROWMAN *Sc. Mining Terms* 65 **Stow road*, an abandoned road in which debris is stowed. **1846** A. YOUNG *Naut. Dict.* 324 **Stow-wood*, billets of wood used as chocks for steadying casks in a vessel's hold.

stow, *v.*[2] Now only *Sc.* and *dial.* Also 7 **stowe**, 7–9 **stoo**; for other forms see *Eng. Dial. Dict.* s.v. *Stove*. [The various dialectal pronunciations —(staʊ) in Suffolk, (stuːv) in Cumberland, (stu) in Sc.—seem to point to a ME. **stūven*, f. **stūf* a. ON. *stúf-r*, stump. (The mod. dial. STOW *sb.*[4], however, is f. the verb.) Cf. ON. *stýfa* to cut off.] *trans.* To crop, cut close; *esp.* to cut off (ears), crop the ears of (a sheep); to lop off the branches of (a tree), or the leaves of (a plant); to trim (a hedge); to cut (a cheese) down to the rind.

1513 DOUGLAS *Æneis* VI. viii. 41 Half hedis spulȝeit, of stowit his eris tuay. **15..** LYNDESAY [*Satyre* 1939] in *Bannatyne MS.* (Hunter. Club) 503 Quhae devill maid yow a gentillmann wald nocht stow [1602 cut] your luggis? **1600** PORY tr. *Leo's Africa* VI. 271 They will stow the palme-trees also to the very stocks. **1618** W. LAWSON *Orch. & Gard.* (1623) 15 If you use to stowe or top your tree too much.. such a kinde of stowing is a kinde of smothering, or choaking the sap. **1641** BEST *Farm. Bks.* (Surtees) 80 Yow are neaver to carry a lambe but by the foreleggеs,..and in stowinge of them yow are..to double the eare eaven and to cutte of the toppes as rownde as yow can without forkinge. **1691** RAY *N.C. Words* 70 *Stood*; Cropt: Sheep are said to be stoo'd whose Ears are cropt, and Men who wear their Hair very short. **1712** J. JAMES tr. *Le Blond's Gardening* 173 By cutting the Palisade down to four or five Foot high, or by stowing it close with the Hedging-Bill. *a* **1774** FERGUSSON *Rising of Session* Poems (1845) 28 After their yokin, I wat weel, They'll stoo the kebbuck to the heel. **1818** SCOTT *Hrt. Midl.* xlix, A drunken Jacobite laird wished for a Bothwell-Brigg whig, that 'he might stow the lugs out of his head.' **1818** —— *Rob Roy* xxxiv, I wad stow the tongue out o' the head o' ony o' them that suld presume to say ower again ony speech held wi' me in their presence. **1823** E. MOOR *Suffolk Words*, *Stow*, rhyming to *now*. To cut the boughs of a pollard tree close to the head. *a* **1846** RODGER *Poems* (1897) 100 They pu'd their ain fruit, and they stoo'd their ain kail. **1903** *Westmorld. Gaz.* 27 June 5/2 Came astray, in March, rough ewe..stowed near ear, no other marks.

†**stow**, *v.*[3] *Mining. Obs.* [f. STOW *sb.*[2]] *trans.* To supply with stows. Also *absol.*

? **1550** in Pettus *Fodinæ Reg.* (1670) 92 Also by the old Custom Miners ought to have Wood of the Kings Wood to stow and timber their Groves under the Earth and above. *Ibid.* 93 A man may go home and fetch his Tools to work with, and Timber to stow with.

†**stow**, *int.* Also **stowe**. A call addressed to a hawk by a falconer to make it come to his fist.

c **1520** SKELTON *Magnyf.* 968 Stowe, byrde, stowe, stowe! It is best I fede my hawke now. —— *Ware the Hauke* 73 The fauconer..cryed, Stow, stow, stow! **1575** TURBERV. *Faulconrie* 182 Make them come from it [the perch] to your fist eyther much or little, with calling and chirping to them, saying: Towe, Towe, or Stowe, Stowe, as Falconers vse, and when they come feed them. **1621** BRATHWAIT *Nat. Embassie* etc. 250 But stow bird stow, See now the game's a foote. **1847** HALLIWELL (citing *Gent. Rec.* ii. 58).

stowable ('stəʊəb(ə)l), *a.* [f. STOW *v.*[1] + -ABLE.] Capable of being stowed.

1610 FOLKINGHAM *Feudigr.* I. viii. 19 A blackish moulde which is light,..mellow, of moderate warmth, not stowable in the primer continent. **1845** STOCQUELER *Handbk. Brit. India* (1854) 84 Besides being more easily stowable in a cabin .., they [*sc.* portmanteaus] can bear a good deal of tumbling about in holds and baggage-rooms.

stowadore, obs. form of STEVEDORE.

stowage ('stəʊɪdʒ). Also 4 **stouuage, stouwage**, 6–7 **stoage**, 8 **stowidge**. [f. STOW *v.*[1] + -AGE. First in Anglo-Latin form *stowagium*. Cf. Du. *stouwage, stuwage*.]

1. The action or operation of stowing cargo on board ship, or goods in a warehouse, etc.

[**1352** *Exch. Acc.* Q.R. 20 no. 27 (Publ. Rec. Office) De xd. pro portagio xxvj. dicr' pellium boum..de navi usque in domum Southantonie, et de xij d. pro stouuag' eorundem [*sic*] ibidem in eadem domo.] **1390** *Earl Derby's Exped.* (Camden) 22 Et per manus eiusdem pro strycage et stouwage xij doliorum vini et floure, x s. vj d. *a* **1513** FABYAN *Chron.* VII. (1811) 391 By meanes of the sayd marchauntes straungers, it was at this day brought to passe that they myght hyre to them houses for to dwell in, and for stowage of theyr wares. **1586** *Acts Privy Council* (1897) XIV. 217 Certaine cellers and stoarehouses built of late on the cliftes and sea coast for the stoage of pilchardes. **1594** J. DAVYS *Seaman's Secr.* II. (1607) 16 Being an instrument portable, of easie stowage. **1626** CAPT. SMITH *Accid. Yng. Seamen* 5 The quarter Maisters hath the charge of the hold for stowage, rommageing, and trimming the shippe. **1733** W. ELLIS *Chiltern & Vale Farm.* 252 Even here they can't enjoy a Cellar for the Stowage of their Liquors. **1784** J. KING *Cook's 3rd Voy.* VI. v. III. 294 On Wednesday we had finished the stowage of the holds. **1840** R. H. DANA *Bef. Mast* iii, The mate..has the charge of the stowage, safe-keeping, and delivery of the cargo. **1865** DICKENS *Mut. Fr.* II. i, From his early childhood up, his mind had been a place of mechanical stowage. **1883** *Manch. Exam.* 6 Nov. 5/4 Board of Trade officers..will supervise the loading, stowage and general equipment of the vessels. **1891** *Law Rep., Weekly Notes* 61/1 The goods were stolen during the stowage after they were on board by one of the stevedores' men. **1907** 'Q.' (Quiller-Couch) *Poison Isl.* xi, The coachman..anon breaking off to direct the stowage of a parcel.

transf. (*jocular.*) **1833** M. SCOTT *Tom Cringle* xvi, A large dish of scalding..hasty pudding..with which Wagtail was in the habit of commencing his stowage at breakfast.

b. Manner in which the contents of a ship are stowed.

1769 FALCONER *Dict. Marine* (1780), *Stowage*, the general disposition of the several materials contained in a ship's hold, with regard to their figure, magnitude, or solidity. **1866** ARNOULD *Marine Insur.* III. i. (ed. 3) II. 667 The casks however had not shifted their places, in other words, 'the stowage was not damaged'. **1867** SMYTH *Sailor's Word-bk.* s.v. *Stowage*, Owners and masters are legally liable to the losses by bad stowage or deficient dunnage.

†**2.** A duty levied on goods stowed. *Obs.*

[**1434** in H. Swinden *Gt. Yarmouth* (1772) 56 *note*, Seisiti fuerunt de..alia custuma vocata stowagio, videlicet, duobus denariis de quolibet pondere dolii cujuscunque mercandise ..in portu predicto posite seu stowate capiendis.]

3. The condition or process of being stowed or placed in a receptacle.

1611 SHAKS. *Cymb.* I. vi. 192 'Tis Plate of rare deuice, and Iewels Of rich and exquisite forme..And I am something curious, being strange To haue them in safe stowage. **1856** KANE *Arctic Expl.* I. xv. 181 By one in the morning we had our discarded excess of pemmican and the boat once more in stowage.

b. The condition of being closely filled or packed.

1825 HONE *Every-day Bk.* I. 438 Clouds of tobacco-smoke..declare the full stowage of each apartment.

4. Room or accommodation for stowing anything; internal capacity of a warehouse or a receptacle of any kind.

1547 *Acts Privy Council* (1890) II. 466 Though he had not convenient stowage for the same [vytayls]. **1579** FENTON *Guicciard.* II. (1599) 544 They approched it vnder the benefite of a caske or vessell of wood..within which was stowage for 300 men. **1612** BODLEY *Will* in Macray *Ann. Bodl. Libr.* (1890) 406 There must..be very great want of conueyance & stowage for Bookes. **1622** FLETCHER *Beggar's Bush* IV. i, When by your leave..We could have stoage for a little cloth, Or a few wines. **1634** W. WOOD *New Eng. Prosp.* (1865) 58 Yet being a heavy commodity, and taking but a little stoage, it is cheaper to carry such commodities out of England. **1655** FULLER *Hist. Camb.* 166 His industrious minde had vast stoäge for words. **1703** *La Hontan's Voy. N. Amer.* I. 26 But those [canoes] of a larger size will easily afford stowage for fourteen Persons. **1748** *Anson's Voy.* II. x. 247 The small stowage necessary for the silver. **1817–8** COBBETT *Resid. U.S.* (1822) 164 He must lay in his store [of potatoes] at the beginning of winter... And, where is he to find stowage? He has no caves. **1869** *Daily News* 13 July, The ordinary amount of 700 tons, which is the stowage of both the Northumberland and Agincourt. **1889** WELCH *Text Bk. Naval Archit.* ii. 28 This is more important in ships of moderate dimensions having relatively large stowage in the the upper bunkers.

b. *jocularly.* Capacity for food.

1651 BIGGS *New Disp.* ¶ 282 To wish that he had not.. crammed the stowage of his body so much. *a* **1716** SOUTH *Serm.* (1744) VIII. 8 What were all the fasts..of the late Reformers, but the forbearing of dinners? that is, the enlarging the stowage, and the redoubling the appetite, for a larger supper? **1819** SCOTT *Leg. Montrose* vi, 'I have still some stowage left for beef and bannocks,' said the Captain.

5. A place in which something is stowed.

a **1641** BP. MOUNTAGU *Acts & Mon.* (1642) 409 There must be a supply of soules for men to be borne, either by new creating of new soules, or by assuming them already created, as out of a Promptuary, Repository, or some Stowage of soules. **1641** MILTON *Animadv.* 53 They may as well sue for Nunneries, that they may have some convenient stowage for their wither'd daughters. **1710** C. SHADWELL *Fair Quaker Deal* v. 60 Faith I'll treat my Jenny [*pulls out a large rich Purse*] with this Purse of Gold; the weighty Stowage of a fair hundred Guineas. **1805** W. TAYLOR in *Ann. Rev.* III. 314 Malta and Gibralter would be convenient stowages for such recruits. **1848** *Jrnl. R. Agric. Soc.* IX. II. 571 A room under the stowage or cooling-room. *Ibid.* 572 The floor of the stowage.

b. A receptacle for stowing cargo.

1815 *Falconer's Dict. Marine* (ed. Burney) s.v. *Stranded*, A cargo packed in Mr. Dickenson's patent iron stowages.

6. That with which a vessel is or is to be stowed.

1622 FLETCHER *Sea-Voy.* I. i, Let the Ship sinck or swimme; we ha nere better luck, When we ha such stoage as these trinkets with us, These sweet sin-breeders. **1778** FOOTE *Trip Calais* I. Wks. 1799 II. 329, I must take t' other trip to the port, for your stowage. **1823** LAMB *Elia, Old Margate Hoy*, Not many rich, not many wise, or learned, composed at that time the common stowage of a Margate packet.

7. *Mining.* (See quot.)

1886 J. BARROWMAN *Sc. Mining Terms* 65 *Stowage*, or *stowing*, in longwall, the space from which the mineral has been extracted and which has been filled with debris.

8. *attrib.*, as **stowage capacity, house, space**; **stowage goods** (see quot.); **stowage room**, (*a*) space for stowing goods; (*b*) a room in which hops are placed after drying.

1871 *Routledge's Ev. Boy's Ann.* Apr. 248 Her *stowage capacity was not over 100 tons. **1863** A. YOUNG *Naut. Dict.* 395 **Stowage goods*, those which usually pay freight according to their bulk. **1547** *Acts Privy Council* (1890) II. 466 The furnisshing and coveryng of the *stowage houses. **1763** W. ROBERTS *Nat. Hist. Florida* 64 To make *stowage-room for the corn of the new year. **1805** R. W. DICKSON *Pract. Agric.* II. 754 An adjoining room constructed for the purpose, which is called the stowage room. **1844** DICKENS *Mart. Chuz.* xvi, The more ample stowage-room he had for dollars. **1890** W. J. GORDON *Foundry* 74 It is almost impossible to realize the *stowage space of one of these huge liners.

stowaway ('stəʊəweɪ). [f. vbl. phrase *stow away*: see STOW *v.*[1] 6.] **1.** A person who hides in a ship in order to escape payment of passage-money, to get to sea unobserved, or to escape by stealth from a country. Hence also, one who steals a passage by aeroplane.

1850 *Morning Chron.* 22 July 6/1 All the passengers were summoned on deck that their names might be read over, their tickets produced, and a search made in the steerage, and in every hole and corner of the ship, for 'stow-aways'. **1854** *Ann. Reg.* 191 He had been seized as a 'stow-away'. **1885** *American* XI. 78 Forty-seven stowaways were found in the hold of one vessel. **1922** [see SCRATCH *sb.*[1] 5 b]. **1973** *Times* 8 Aug. 7/3 (*heading*) Stowaway takes wrong flight.

2. *gen.* Something stowed away. Also, a place where things may be stowed.

1913 E. F. BENSON *Thorley Weir* iii, For all these weeks Charles had never touched the cupboard except to insert some further stowaway. **1915** W. J. LOCKE *Jaffery* xx, Of all the stowaway places under my control..only one is locked. **1928** *Daily Express* 21 Mar. 5/3 The window-seat top lifts up, and this makes another good stowaway for toys.

†**stow-ball.** *Obs.* Also 7 **stopball, stoball, stob-ball, stobball.** [Of obscure origin.

Commonly identified with STOOL-BALL; but the games appear to have been very dissimilar, and the corruption of *stool-ball* into *stoball, stobball* seems hardly probable. Possibly the first element may be STOB *sb.*, denoting the club or 'staff'.]

An outdoor ball-game commonly played in the 16–17th c. (see quots.). Also *attrib.*

1634 *Abp. Laud's Visit.* in *4th Rep. Hist. MSS. Comm.* App. 144/1 This whole churchyard is made a receptacle for all ydle persons to spend their time in stopball, and such lyke recreacions. *c* **1640** J. SMYTH *Hund. Berkeley* (1885) 10 The large and levell playnes..in the vale of this hundred..doe witnes the inbred delight, that both gentry, yeomanry, rascallity, boyes and children, doe take in a game called Stoball... And not a sonne of mine, but at 7. was furnished with his double stoball staves, and a gamster therafter. **1679** LOCKE in Ld. King *Life* (1830) I. 248 The sports of England, which, perhaps, a curious stranger would be glad to see, are ..shooting in the long-bow and stob-ball, in Tothill Fields. *a* **1686** AUBREY *Nat. Hist. Wilts* (1847) 117 Stobball-play is peculiar to North Wilts, North Gloucestershire, and a little part of Somerset near Bath. They smite a ball, stuffed very hard with quills and covered with soale leather, with a staffe, commonly made of withy, about 3 [feet] and a halfe long... A stobball-ball is of about four inches diameter, and as hard as a stone. **1694** E. CHAMBERLAYNE *Pres. St. Eng.* III. vii. 463 The Citizens and Peasants have..Skittles or Nine-pins, Shovel-board, Stow-ball, Goffe, [etc.]. **1801** STRUTT *Sports & Past.* II. iii. 82 A pastime called Stow-ball is frequently mentioned by the writers of the sixteenth and seventeenth centuries, which, I presume, was a species of goff, at least it appears to have been played with the same kind of ball. **1907** F. W. HACKWOOD *Old Eng. Sports* 144 In the English modification of Goff, the club employed was not unlike the bandy-stick... In the sixteenth and seventeenth centuries this game was also known as Stow-ball.

b. A ball used in this game.

1678 LITTLETON *Lat.-Eng. Dict., Paganica*,..a goff-ball, a stow-ball, stuffed with feathers.

stow-blade. *Mining.* Also stoblade. [f. STOW *sb.*[2]] Each of two upright pieces of wood, a foot in length, connected at the top with the sole-trees of a stow or stowce.

1681 [see STOW *sb.*[2] 1]. **1747** HOOSON *Miner's Dict.* K 1, Two Irons..are put into each end of the Turntree, and run in the Slots of the Stoblades. **1851** TAPPING *Manlove's Customs Lead Mines* Gloss. 33/1 Two upright pieces of wood called stow-blades, about one foot long, [etc.].

'stow-boat. *local.* [Of obscure origin; perh. an alteration of STALL-BOAT, from association with STOW *v.*[1] Cf. STOW-NET.

This view gains some support from the forms *storbanting, storbatin*, given in the *Eng. Dial. Dict.* as the Suffolk pronunciation of '*Stow-boating*, (1) dredging up stone at sea for making Roman cement (Kent); (2) fishing for sprats (Suff.).' But the final *l* in *stall* is normally dropped only in northern and north midland dialects.]

A kind of boat used in fishing for sprats. Also *attrib.* Hence **'stowboating** *vbl. sb.*

1833 *Rep. Sel. Comm. Brit. Channel Fisheries* 11 The Stow-boat Fishery, or Catching of Sprats for Manure. *Ibid.*, There are at present from 400 to 500 Boats engaged in Stow-boating on the Kentish Coast only. *Ibid.* 58 How many men are there on board the stow-boats? **1883** *St. James's Gaz.* 21 Dec. 6/1 It is to the stow-boats..that the London poor owe their chief supply of these valuable little fish.

stowbornes, obs. form of STUBBORNNESS.

stowce (stəʊs). *Mining.* Also 7 stose, 8–9 stoce, 9 stowse. See also STOW *sb.*[2] [Of obscure origin; possibly a contraction of *stothes*, pl. of *stothe*, STOOTH.] *sing.* and *pl.* A kind of windlass for drawing up ore; in Derbyshire, a special form of this apparatus; also, a model of this, intended not for working, but to comply with the old law which provides that the presence of an owner's 'stowce' on a mining tract secures his right of possession. Hence **stowce** *v., trans.*, to mark (a 'meer' of ground) with 'a pair of stowces'.

1664 in Tapping *Manlove's Customs Lead Mines* (1851) Gloss. 33 If there be any miner..that has any grove or meer of ground in the mines, he or they shall keep the same in lawful possession both stosed and yoked,..we mean one pair of stoses and one yoking of timber in all men's sight. **1747** HOOSON *Miner's Dict.* F 2, In the High Peak the Cross and Stake holds Possession, but while a Man may go home to fetch his small Stoce's to set on it. **1802** MAWE *Min. Derbysh.* Gloss. (E.D.S.), *Stowces*, [a] drawing-stowce, a small windlass. *Ibid.*, *Stowces*, pieces of wood of particular forms and constructions placed together, by which the possession of mines is marked; a pair of stowces possess a mear of ground. **1824** MANDER *Derbysh. Miner's Gloss.* 68 *Stoce.* First. Under this head is described the Miners drawing Stoce, also the Stoce of Pretence or Possession. *Ibid.* 69 The Stocing is placing the Stoce on the surface of the land under which the Mine lies, by the Miners, to denote how far their title extends. **1829** *Glover's Hist. Derby* I. 75 Small models of stowses..came in use, as the means of keeping possession. **1851** TAPPING *Manlove's Customs Lead Mines* Gloss. 33/1 *Stowe* or *Stowse*, or, as sometimes called, a *Possession* or *Stowse of Pretence*, is a machine which formerly was the only apparatus for drawing up the ore in tubs from the mine. It is constructed of seven pieces of timber, [etc.]. **1876** *Mid-Yorksh. Gloss.*, *Stoarces*, a frame to support a wooden roller, in the process of heaving or hoisting by hand; Nidd[erdale]. **1883** GRESLEY *Gloss. Coal-mining* 243 *Stowses*, a windlass or wallow.

stowe, pa. t. (pl.) of STY *v.*

stowed (stəʊd), *ppl. a.* [f. STOW *v.*[1] + -ED[1].] In senses of the vb.; also *stowed-away* (STOW *v.*[1] 6).

¶ By Fairfax used for: Having a position in space.

1674 N. FAIRFAX *Bulk & Selv.* 81 That unto a stowsomness or local respect between two stowed beings, 'tis not only needful they should be both bulky;..but [etc.]. **1753** *Chambers' Cycl.* Suppl. s.v. *Roussin*, A strong well knit, well stowed horse. **1856** J. W. PALMER *Up & Down Irrawaddi* 219 (Cent.) We pointed to the white rolls of stowed hammocks in the nettings.

stowell, obs. form of STOOL.

stower ('staʊə(r)), *sb.*[1] *Obs.* exc. *dial.* Forms: 4 sture, 4–5 store, 4–5, 9 stoure, 5 staure, stourre, 5–9 stowre, 6 stoowre, stowir, 6–9 stour, 8 stowr, 7– stower. [a. ON. *staur-r*, stake.]

1. A stake, hedge-stake; a pale; a pole, post. ***stower-and-daub***: = *wattle and daub* (see DAUB *sb.*[1]) † ***stick and stower*** (***stour***): see STICK *sb.*[1] 3 c.

1371 in *Fabric Rolls York Minster* (Surtees) 355 Uni homini amputanti stoures..pro parietibus domorum..per diem, 4 d. **1374** in Willis & Clark *Cambridge* (1886) I. 238 Dormannes giystes et etiam stures cum pertinenciis pro mediis parietibus in dictis cameris sub et supra. *c* **1375** *Sc. Leg. Saints* xix. (*Christopher*) 224 þane in his hand he hynt his store. **1417–18** *Durham Acc. Rolls* (Surtees) 302 Pro staures emptis pro shepehekkys apud le Holme, 16 d. *c* **1420** *Avow. Arth.* vii, Butte sette my head opon a store, Butte giffe he flaey 30 alle fawre. *c* **1440** *Alphabet of Tales* 158 He gatt hym a stowre, & gnew vppon þe tone end & made it sharpe with his tethe, & þrustid hym selfe evyn thrugh þerwith. **1481–2** in *Finchale Priory Charters* etc. (Surtees) p. ccclv, Et in stowrys et virgis emptis pro eodem, xvj[d]. **1513** DOUGLAS *Æneis* IX. viii. 149 Apon a speyr, Or heich sting or stour of the fyr tre. **1674** RAY *N.C. Words* 45 A *Stowre*,..a hedge-stake. **1792** *Statist. Acc. Scot.* II. 16 Pock-net fishing..is performed by fixing stakes or stours (as they are called) in the sand. **1798** *Sporting Mag.* XII. 166 Cut from thence a certain number of stakes and stowers.

2. Each of the upright staves in the side of a wagon.

1641 BEST *Farm. Bks.* (Surtees) 35 Wee sende worde to the wright to come and see that the axle-trees and felfes of the waines bee sownde..and likewise to putte in stowers wheare any are wantinge. **1691** RAY *N.C. Words* (ed. 2) 70.

3. A rung of a ladder.

1674 RAY *N.C. Words* 45 *Stowre*, a round of a ladder.

4. A punt-pole.

1777 in C. W. Hatfield *Hist. Notices Doncaster* (1866) I. 194 Five men, with long 'stowers' and boat hooks were placed at St. Mary's. **1822** BEWICK *Mem.* ii. (1862) 18 We then set to work with a 'boat-stower' to push it [a piece of ice] off shore. **1889** *Linc. Chron.* 16 Nov. (E.D.D.), Deceased had hold of the stower, and pushed the boat off.

5. *Naut.* (See quot.)

1863 A. YOUNG *Naut. Dict.* 449 *Wrain-staff*, Wrung-staff, or 'Dwang-staff', also called a Stower, or Twisting-staff, a sort of stout billet of tough wood tapered at the ends so as to go into the ring of the wrain-bolt for the purpose of setting-to the planks.

stower ('stəʊə(r)), *sb.*[2] Also *dial.* stowyer. [f. STOW *v.*[1] + -ER[1].] One who stows; one who stows a ship, a stevedore; one of a fishing crew whose work is to stow the net; a miner whose work is to pack up stone.

1769 FALCONER *Dict. Marine* II. (1780), *Arrimeur*, a stower. **1867** SMYTH *Sailor's Word-bk.* s.v. *Stowage*, The stower seldom consults the specialities of the vessel's construction. **1886** *Newcastle Daily Chron.* 23 Nov. (E.D.D.), The packing is done by a class of men called stowers. **1892** P. H. EMERSON *Son of Fens* vii. 64 Go down into the net-room where the stowyer get it and stow it up. **1906** *Dundee Advertiser* 28 May, A Lochee woman,..wife of a stower residing in South Road.

†**stower**, *v.* [f. STOWER *sb.*[1]] *trans.* To fence with stakes; ? *intr.* to fix stakes. Hence **stowering** *vbl. sb.* (in quots. *attrib.*).

c **1555** R. TROUGHTON in *Archæologia* XXIII. 23 A Comon wateryng place ther called Hedgedyke, late stowered for Catall to drynke at. *Ibid.*, I..asked of hyme howe he liked the newe stowered wateryng place. **1557–8** in R. W. Goulding *Louth Old Corpor. Rec.* (1891) 109 It. for dī hundreth of tray nailles & dī c of stowring nailles, ij[d]. **1611–12** *Knaresb. Wills* (Surtees) II. 34 One stowering womble.

stower: see STOUR, STOVER *sb.*

stowf(f)e, stowidge, obs. ff. STOVE, STOWAGE.

stowin(e, obs. Sc. pa. pple. of STEAL *v.*

stowing ('stəʊɪŋ), *vbl. sb.*[1] Also 5 *Sc.* stollin. [f. STOW *v.*[1] + -ING[1].]

1. The action of the verb in various senses.

c **1440** *Promp. Parv.* 478/1 Stowynge, or yn dede puttynge [*v.r.* in stede puttinge] *locacio, collocacio. Ibid.*, S(t)owwynge, or a-geyne cowpynge or chargynge [*v.rr.* charynge, stowynge or ageyne chasinge], *obsistencia, resistencia.* **1467** *Sc. Acts Jas. III* (1814) II. 87 That na merchandis gudis be revin nor spilt with vnresonabel stollin. **1619** in Foster *Eng. Factories India* (1906) 137 They beg ..'that good regard also be had unto the qualitie, packinge, and stowinge of all the comodities you send'. **1835** DICKENS *Sk. Boz, Astley's*, Then pa drilled the boys, and directed the stowing away of their pocket-handkerchiefs. **1900** F. T. BULLEN *With Christ at Sea* xiii. 260 My first duty was to superintend the stowing of the cargo.

2. *concr.* (See quot.)

1860 *Mining Gloss., Newcastle Terms* 64 *Stowing*, rubbish put into old workings to fill them up.

3. *Comb.*

1883 *Pall Mall Gaz.* 30 Aug. 11/1 There will be a stowing room for 20 tons of provisions. **1896** *Daily News* 19 Mar. 3/6 The coal bunkers will have a stowing capacity of nine hundred tons.

†**'stowing**, *vbl. sb.*[2] *Obs.* [f. STOW *v.*[2] + -ING[1].]

1. The action of the verb; lopping of trees.

1618 W. LAWSON *New Orch. & Gard.* (1623) 15 Such a kinde of stowing is a kinde of smothering, or choaking the sap.

2. *concr.* in *pl.* (See quot.) *Sc.*

1788 PICKEN *Poems* 63 O' meals ait-parritch was the best, Or stowins, e'en right poorly drest. *Ibid.* Gloss., *Stowins*, small cuttings taken from young greens.

stowk(e, stowle, obs. ff. STOOK, STOLE *sb.*[2], STOOL.

stowll, obs. form of STOOL.

stowmpe, obs. Sc. form of STUMP.

stown(e: see STEAL *v.*, STOUN *v.*, STOUND *sb.*[1]

stownd(e, obs. forms of STOUND *sb.*[1]

'stow-net. [See STOW-BOAT, and cf. STALL NET.] A kind of net used in fishing for sprats.

1871 *Echo* 15 Dec., The vessels engaged in the fishing are called stow-boats, and the nets used stow-nets. **1883** *Fisheries Exhib. Catal.* 3 The gigantic funnel-shaped stow-net, by which thousands of tons of sprats are caught.

'stownlins, *adv. Sc.* Also stowlins, stowenlins (see *Eng. Dial. Dict.*). [f. *stown* = STOLEN *ppl. a.* + -LING[2], -LIN(G)S.] By stealth; secretly.

1786 BURNS *Halloween* x, Rob, stownlins, prie'd her bonie mou.

stowp(e, obs. forms of STOOP, STOUP.

stowr(e: see STORE, STOUR, STOWER *sb.*[1]

stowse, variant of STOWCE.

†**'stowsome**, *a. nonce-wd.* [f. STOW *v.*[1] + -SOME.] Having position in space. Hence †**'stowsomeness**.

1674 N. FAIRFAX *Bulk & Selv.* 77 It loses its stowsomness or location. *Ibid.* 81 We have taken away all stowsom medlings. *Ibid.* 82 There is room between, but no roomthy or stowsom respect.

stowt(e, stowth: see STOUT, STOUTH.

stowyn, obs. Sc. pa. pple. of STEAL *v.*

stox, obs. pl. of STOCK *sb.*[1]

stoydel, obs. form of STUDDLE.

stoyle, stoyll, obs. forms of STOLE *sb.*[1]

†**stoyne**, *v. Obs.* [var. of STONY *v.*; the form has not been satisfactorily accounted for. Cf. *astoyned* var. of ASTONIED *ppl. a.*] **a.** *trans.* To stun with a blow or with a shock of amazement, fear, and the like. Chiefly *pass.* **b.** *intr.* To be stunned.

c **1400** *Destr. Troy* 7431 Ector, for þe stithe stroke stoynyt no thyng. *c* **1450** CAPGRAVE *S. Kath.* Prol. 109 þe preest is stoyned as thow he turned wer. New ioye, new thowte had he than þere! *Ibid.* 1837 Thei sey hir resons and hir grete euydens Whiche stoyned the clerkis alle tho ben there. **1460** —— *Chron.* (Rolls) 124 There cam a wind, and brast the dores ope with swech a violens that thei stoyned on the walle. **1555** PHAER *Æneid* II. (1558) F ij, I stoynyd, and my heare vpstood, my mouth for feare was fast. **1563** SACKVILLE *Induct. Mirr. Mag.* xxxiv, Next sawe we Dread al tremblyng how he shooke,..Stoynde and amazde at his owne shade for dreed.

Hence †**'stoyning** *vbl. sb.*

1594 CAREW *Tasso* (1881) 44 So by your fame to fright, and stoyning brought Are Realmes about.

stoype, stoyr, obs. Sc. ff. STOUP, STORE.

stoytene, obs. Sc. var. STUDDING (*sail*).

stoythe, obs. variant of STOOTH.

14.. *Nom.* in Wr.-Wülcker 735/9 *Hec stipa*, a stoythe.

STP (ɛs tiː piː). orig. *U.S.* Also S.T.P. [Prob. f. the initial letters of *S*cientifically *T*reated *P*etroleum, the commercial name of a motor-oil additive which was being extensively advertised when the drug first appeared.] A synthetic hallucinogenic drug chemically related to amphetamine but having effects similar to those of LSD; 2,5-dimethoxy-4-methylamphetamine.

1967 *Village Voice* (N.Y.) 13 Apr. 7/2 STP is a new psychedelic drug which..has become the most sought-after high on the psychedelic scene. **1967** *Guardian* 4 July 7/1 A new drug being used by the 'hippies' who inhabit San Francisco... For want of a name the hippies call it STP—a trade mark for an oil additive. **1969** *Oz* May 21/2 Alexander 'Sashe' Shulgin, the brilliant chemist who is best known to the public for his synthesis of STP (which was later illegally distributed in a dose form twice that 'recommended'). **1971** *It* 2–16 June 8/5 Those 80,000 doses of S.T.P. in the peanut butter jar that we were saving for an emergency. **1974** M. C. GERALD *Pharmacol.* xvii. 328 DOM is 2,5-dimethoxy-4-methylamphetamine to the chemist and STP (serenity, tranquillity, and peace) to the drug user.

stra, Sc. and north. form of STRAW.

strabery, variant of STRAWBERRY.

strabism (ˈstreɪbɪz(ə)m). Also 7 **strabisme**. [Anglicized form of STRABISMUS. Cf. F. *strabisme*.] = STRABISMUS.
1656 BLOUNT *Glossogr.*, *Strabism*..the squintness in the eyes. **1658** PHILLIPS, *Strabisme*, a looking a squint. **1661** LOVELL *Hist. Anim. & Min.* 417 The strabisme, or squintnesse, caused, by evil conformation, custome, or disease. **1755** JOHNSON, *Strabism*, a squinting; act of looking asquint. **1774** GOLDSM. *Nat. Hist.* (1824) I. xxix. 238 Hence proceeds that awkward look which is known by the name of strabism. **1807** *Med. Jrnl.* XVII. 526 Perfectly formed eyes have little inducement to wander into habits of strabism. **1914** *Contemp. Rev.* Apr. 507 Some Spanish critics have lately attributed the defects in his [El Greco's] drawing to strabism and astigmatism.

strabismal (strəˈbɪzməl), *a. Path.* [f. STRABISMUS + -AL[1].] = STRABISMIC *a.*
1891 *Century Dict.* **1898** *Syd. Soc. Lex.*
Hence **straˈbismally** *adv.*, squintingly.
1893 E. SALTUS *Madam Sapphira* 120 Mrs. Snaith..eyed him strabismally, then..addressed the floor.

strabismic (strəˈbɪzmɪk), *a. Path.* [f. STRABISM-US + -IC.] Of, pertaining to, or affected by strabismus. Also *fig.*
1855 *Lancet* 12 May 479/1 If the strabismic eye be brought into play, it assumes a normal condition, and moves in obedience to the will. **1875** H. H. WALTON *Dis. Eye* 385 Strabismic vision. **1915** H. DE SÉLINCOURT *Realms of Day* ii. 8 The weak and dim-eyed, who blame life for their own strabismic will-lessness. **1955** W. GADDIS *Recognitions* II. viii. 695 A small figure clutching a filthy dollar bill fixed him with a strabismic stare. **1975** *Nature* 20 Nov. 199/1 If a kitten is made strabismic by sectioning an eye muscle..their neurones are found to receive input from one eye or the other, but very few receive input from both.
Hence **straˈbismical** *a.*, suffering from strabismus.
1866 *Athenæum* 20 Jan. 92/3 When strabismical statisticians number the peeresses who find daily solace in gin-palaces. **1889** *Science* 10 May 364/2 Should a child be born with..a strabismical eye, or distorted limbs, he is accepted as a healer of coming generations.

strabismometer (ˌstreɪbɪzˈmɒmɪtə(r)). [f. STRABISM-US + -(O)METER.] An instrument for measuring the degree of strabismus.
1869 *Lancet* 27 Nov. 733/1 Mr. Zachariah Laurence's strabismometer..consists of an ivory plate moulded to the conformation of the lower lid. **1876** DUNGLISON *Med. Lex.*
Hence **ˌstrabisˈmometry**, the act or practice of measuring the degree of strabismus.
1889 *Syd. Soc. Lex.*

‖**strabismus** (strəˈbɪzməs). *Path.* [mod.L., ad. Gr. στραβισμός, f. στραβίζειν to squint, f. στραβός squinting (whence L. *strabus* in the same sense).] An affection of the eyes in which the axes of vision cannot be coincidently directed to the same object; squinting, a squint.
convergent or ***internal strabismus***, a turning inward of the eyes, CROSS-EYE; ***divergent*** or ***external strabismus***, a turning outwards of one or both eyes.
1684 *Blancard's Phys. Dict.*, *Strabismus*, Squinting, is occasioned by the Relaxation, Contraction, Distorsion, too great Length, or too great Shortness of the Muscles which move the Eye. **1771** *Encycl. Brit.* III. 155/1 A Strabismus, commonly called squinting. **1846** F. BRITTAN tr. *Malgaigne's Man. Oper. Surg.* 294 For external strabismus, a flap of the internal portion of the conjunctiva is removed. **1884** T. BRYANT *Pract. Surg.* (ed. 4) I. 409 Convergent strabismus is the most common of all. *Ibid.* 412 Divergent strabismus..is often the result of myopia.
b. *fig.* Perversity of intellectual perception.
1844 H. ROGERS *Ess.* (1860) III. 111 His prejudices have wholly clouded his common sense, or produced an incurable *strabismus* of intellect. **1846** *Ibid.* (1874) I. iv. 198 Any one ..not afflicted with polemical *strabismus*, would as soon affirm that [etc.]. **1881** E. CAIRD *Ess. Lit. & Philos.* (1892) I. 193 A review which supposes man to be afflicted with a kind of intellectual *strabismus*, so that he can never see with one of his mental eyes without shutting the other.
c. *attrib.*
1864 *Lancet* 17 Dec. 689/2 The Strabismus operation made easy. **1875** KNIGHT *Dict. Mech.*, *Strabismus-forceps*, a straight or curved pinchers..for holding the muscles to be divided in correcting strabismus. **1876** T. BRYANT *Pract. Surg.* (1884) I. 411 Strabismus hook. Strabismus scissors.

strabometer (strəˈbɒmɪtə(r)). [f. *strabo-* (see next) + -METER.] = STRABISMOMETER.
1875 KNIGHT *Dict. Mech.* **1876** DUNGLISON *Med. Lex.*
Hence **straˈbometry** = STRABISMOMETRY.
1900 *Lancet* 13 Jan. 104/1 Professor Edmund Landolt of Paris..considers that there are three methods of measuring the amount of deviation or strabometry.

strabotomy (strəˈbɒtəmɪ). *Path.* [ad. F. *strabotomie* (mod.L. *strabotomia*), f. *strabo-* taken as comb. form of STRABISMUS: see -TOMY.] The operation of dividing one or more of the muscles of the eye as a remedy for strabismus.
1857 DUNGLISON *Med. Lex.* **1898** *Syd. Soc. Lex.*
Hence **strabotome** (ˈstreɪbətəʊm), a knife used in the operation of strabotomy.
1875 KNIGHT *Dict. Mech.* **1888** *Cassell's Encycl. Dict.*

†**ˈstrabrod.** *north.* [f. *stra*, north. f. STRAW + BROD *sb.*[1]] A wooden pin used in fastening thatch.
1335-6 *Durham Acc. Rolls* (Surtees) 529 In xxv^m de Strabrod. **1372-3** *Finchale Priory Charters* etc. (Surtees) p. lxxxvii, Schotnaile, stanbrodd, strabrodd, [etc.]. **1847** HALLIWELL, *Strabrods*, the wooden pins or stobs used in fastening thatch to the roof of a building.

strac, obs. pa. t. of STRIKE *v.*

‖**stracchino** (strakˈkino). Also **strachino**. [It. *stracchino* adj. and sb., designating 'an excellent and very soft kind of cheese'.] ***stracchino cheese***, a variety of cheese made in the north of Italy.
1832 G. DOWNES *Lett. Cont. Countries* I. 503 The atmosphere of this place is saturated with the odour of *stracchino* cheese, the village being crowded with manufactories of it. It is softer than cream cheese, and the taste is better than the smell, which is rank and oppressive. **1857** DICKENS *Dorrit* I. i, He gets..white bread, strachino cheese, and good wine by it. **1880** *Encycl. Brit.* XIII. 452/1.

‖**stracciatella** (strattʃaˈtella). [It.] A soup made with stock, eggs, and cheese.
1954 E. DAVID *Italian Food* 66 *Stracciatelle*, a Roman soup but common all over Italy, and extremely good. **1963** R. CARRIER *Great Dishes of World* 54 Stracciatella alla Romana... Bring chicken stock to a fast boil and add egg mixture. **1978** *Chicago* June 221/1 A sumptuous selection of delectables: stracciatella fiorentina, soup made with whipped egg and spinach and topped with cheese. **1981** M. NABB *Death of Englishman* I. iii. 95 *Stracciatella!* Good fresh broth, eggs laid ten minutes ago.

strache, strachle: see STRETCH, STRAUCHLE.

Stracheyan (ˈstreɪtʃiːən), *a.* [f. the name of the English biographer and critic Giles Lytton *Strachey* (1880–1932) + -AN.] Of, pertaining to, or characteristic of Strachey or his style of writing.
1927 *Observer* 9 Oct. 6/2 Mr. Burdett's 'Gladstone'.. owes to Mr. Strachey nothing but its size; it is a Victorian revaluation on a Stracheian scale. **1958** *Sunday Times* 22 June 6/4 A profusion of fancy adjectives and Stracheyan present participles. **1967** *Punch* 25 Oct. 639/2 The tone of it, if not derisive and iconoclastic in quite the Stracheyan manner, is none the less far from hushed and reverential. **1974** K. CLARK *Another Part of Wood* v. 174, I had escaped from the infection of Stracheyan irony that influenced my chapter on the Ecclesiologists.

stracht: see STRAIGHT and STRETCH *v.*

strack, obs. form of STRAKE *sb.*

stract, *a. Obs.* exc. *dial.* Also 8 **strackt**, 9 **strack**. [Aphetic f. DISTRACT *a.*] = DISTRACT *ppl. a.* 4, DISTRACTED *ppl. a.* 5.
1598 R. BERNARD tr. *Terence, Adelphos* IV. ii, He came afterwards as one stract and besides himselfe. *c***1746** J. COLLIER *View Lanc. Dial.* (1770) 28 On neaw I'r so strackt woode, I'r arronly moydert. **1818** R. WILBRAHAM *Chesh. Gloss.*, *Stract*, adj., abbreviation of distracted. **1877** E. LEIGH *Chesh. Gloss.*, s.v. *Strack*, 'Lave the poor wench alone —oo's strack, oi tell ye.'

Strad (stræd). *colloq.* Short for STRADIVARIUS.
1884 HAWEIS *Musical Life* III. i. 218 The exquisite sweetness and freshness of the Dolphin 'Strad.' excited most admiration. **1908** *Daily News* 29 Feb. 7 The trade in Strads is confined to a very few dealers.

strad, obs. pa. t. of STRIDE *v.*

ˌstradaˈmetrical, *a. rare.* [f. It. *strada* STREET *sb.*: see -METRY.] Of or pertaining to the measurement of streets or roads.
1852 N. S. SHRAPNEL (*title*), The Stradametrical Survey of London,..Containing the mean distances, with their relative cab fares, from all the principal streets..in London, to the Great Exhibition. **1853** *Househ. Words* VII. 246/1 We commenced our stradametrical survey of Rotterdam..and at about five o'clock..I was left with my little portmanteau at the proper house. **1855** OGILVIE Suppl., *Stradometrical.*

†**stradarolle.** *Obs. rare*[−1]. [ad. It. *stradaruolo*, f. *strada* street.] A highwayman.
1562 J. SHUTE tr. *Cambini's Two Comm.* ii. 25 This subtill olde Ruter sent to Scanderbeg a messager, requiring him to fyght with him like a prince..and not..lyke a stradarolle and thefe [*cosi da stradarolo*].

straddle (ˈstræd(ə)l), *sb.* [f. next.]
I. The action of the verb.
1. a. The action of walking, standing, or sitting with the legs wide apart. Also *transf.* and *fig.*
1611 MIDDLETON & DEKKER *Roaring Girl* III. i. F 2, I knew you by your wide straddle. ? **1771** WALPOLE *Let. Lady Coke* ? Oct.–Nov., Lett. 1904 VIII. 99 You are, I know, Madam, an excellent walker, yet methinks seven leagues at once are a prodigious straddle for a fair lady. **1784** H. MACNEILL *Whip* Poet. Wks. 1801 I. 100 No female Phaetonians then Surpass'd the boldest of our men In gesture, look, and straddle. **1815** *Hist. John Decastro & Bat* II. 272 However he made a straddle of it, and took the crown thereof very well between his knees.
transf. and *fig.* **1780** COWPER *Rep. Adjudged Case* 14 Your lordship observes they [the spectacles] are made with a straddle, As wide as the bridge of the Nose is; in short, Designed to sit close to it, just like a saddle. **1914** LLOYD GEORGE in *Times* 20 Sept. 4/4, I do not believe he [*sc.* the German Emperor] meant all these speeches; it was simply the martial straddle he had acquired.

b. The distance between the feet or legs of one who straddles.
*c***1842** G. D. PRENTICE *Prenticeana* (1860) 110 A writer in the 'True Whig' justly represents Mr. Tyler as standing with 'a foot on one boat and a foot on the other'... Although his Accidency's legs are not of the shortest, his straddle is becoming inconveniently wide. He will soon be as badly split as his party. **1864** in WEBSTER. **1934** H. VINES *This Green Thicket World* 21 The two springs that were little more than a man's straddle apart boiled up.
2. a. *U.S. Exchange slang.* A 'privilege' or speculative contract in any one market or class of commodities, covering both a 'put' and a 'call' —that is, giving the holder the right at his option (1) of calling, within a specified number of days, for delivery of an ascertained quantity of the commodity at a stated price, or (2) of delivering to the person to whom the consideration had been paid an ascertained quantity of another (or, less usually, of the same) commodity at a stated price. Hence, applied to an analogous contract on the Stock-exchange. Also called *spread-eagle* (*Cent. Dict.* 1891).
1883 *Harper's Mag.* Mar. 598/2 They [*sc.* N.Y. brokers] always talked of 'margins' and 'puts' and 'calls,' and 'straddles.' **1892** STEVENSON & L. OSBOURNE *Wrecker* i. 25 My father..was trying at this time a 'straddle' in wheat between Chicago and New York. **1893** CORDINGLEY *Guide Stock Exch.* 123 *Straddle*..is also an American term for a 'Put and Call,' but used when the price is the same whether the Stock is 'put' or 'called'. **1902** *Longman's Mag.* Apr. 485 The lady's wealth is based on a successful Straddle, operated..in—Bristles—Hog's Bristles and Lard.
b. In British use: see quot.
1902 *L'pool Corn Trade Assoc. Ltd.*, *Section J*, Bye-laws relating to Brokerages on grain futures. *Straddles.* When a broker executes an order to buy grain deliverable in a certain specified month, executing at the same time an order to sell the same quantity and description deliverable in another specified month, he shall be at liberty to carry out both transactions for one brokerage.
3. *U.S. Politics* (*colloq.*). An attempt to take an equivocal or non-committal position in a party platform (*Cent. Dict.* 1891).
[*c***1842**: see sense 1 b above.] **1843** *Knickerbocker* XXII. 233 These are..subjects for the straddle. The fence..is our only..safety on these p'ints. **1883** *American* VI. 100 That his demand for an endorsement of free trade could not be yielded to, and that expediency demanded a 'straddle' that could be explained either way. **1890** C. L. NORTON *Polit. Americanisms* 109 *Straddle*, a stock-broker's term which acquired a political meaning during the campaign of 1884.
4. *Poker.* A doubling of the 'blind' or stake by one of the players.
1864 W. B. DICK *Amer. Hoyle* 177 If the dealer choose, he may, in turn, double the *straddle*. **1882** *Poker; how to play it* 49 The straddle is nothing more than a double blind. **1897** [see STAY *v.*[1] 13].
5. A positioning of discharged shots, bombs, etc., such that some fall short of and some beyond the target (see also quot. 1973), esp. used as a deliberate form of attack or for range-finding. Freq. with reference to naval warfare. Cf. STRADDLE *v.* 5 c; STRADDLING *vbl. sb.*
1915 in M. Gilbert *Winston S. Churchill* (1972) III. Compan. I. 486 Four rounds will be wasted for every hit made in addition to the rounds used before the straddle is obtained. **1918** [see STRADDLE *v.* 5 c]. **1926** *Sci. Amer.* Aug. 104/1 They were liable to be wrecked by the first 'straddle' of an enemy's salvo. **1944** *Times* 27 Apr. 4/7 Depth charges were dropped from a low height in a perfect straddle. **1973** J. QUICK *Dict. Weapons & Military Terms* 423/1 In range, or in deflection, when projectiles from a salvo fall both over and short of, or to both the left and right of, the target, a straddle is obtained.
II. Something which straddles or is straddled.
6. †**a.** (Meaning obscure.) *Obs.*
1684 *Phil. Trans.* XIV. 666 Land Carriage by draught, is by Wheele-barrows, Straddles, Carts of 2 wheels, Sleds, Wagons [etc.].
b. = SADDLE *sb.* 3.
1825 JAMIESON. **1837** LOVER *Rory O'More* I. xi. 253 From the rudely constructed straddle of the sorry animal,..a budget containing the implements of the tinker's trade, depended. **1882** E. O'DONOVAN *Merv Oasis* II. xlviii. 308 A beam..was in turn attached to a straddle fastened to the back of a camel.
7. *Mining.* (? *U.S.*) Each of the vertical timbers by which the different sets are supported in a shaft (*Cent. Dict.* 1891).
III. 8. Comb.: **straddleback** *adv.*, with the legs astraddle; **straddle-band**, the band which secures the 'straddle' on a horse's back; **straddle-bob** *dial.*, a black beetle (cf. STRADDLE-BUG); **straddle-breech** *a.*, a contemptuous epithet applied to one who straddles; **straddle carrier**, a vehicle for manœuvring large containers, bulk loads of timber, etc., by straddling and lifting them beneath its chassis; **straddle-fashion** *adv.*, in a straddling position, astride; **straddle harvester, machine**, an agricultural device which straddles rows of bushes or plants, etc., to facilitate the picking of the fruit; **straddle-leg(s** *adv.*, with the legs astride; also *attrib.*; **straddle-legged** *a.*, having the legs set wide apart; *adv.*, with the legs astride; **straddle mill** (see quot. 1911); also as *v. trans.*; so **straddle milling** *vbl. sb.*, the milling of

two parallel faces of a workpiece simultaneously by means of a pair of cutters on a single shaft; **straddle-pipe, -plough** (see quots.); **straddle truck** = *straddle carrier* above; **straddleways** *adv.* = *straddle-wise* adv.; **straddle-wise** *adv.* = *straddle-fashion.*

1839 Thackeray *Leg. St. Sophia of Kioff*, She gets on the Prior's shoulder *straddleback. **1901** Jane Barlow *From Land of Shamrock* 288, I noticed the *straddle-band lookin' uncommon quare and wake. **1847** Halliwell, **Straddlebob*, a blackbeetle. *I. Wight.* **1682** T. Flatman *Heraclitus Ridens* No. 60 (1713) II. 126 Then there was our old *Straddle-breech Friend. **1950** *Dock & Harbour Authority* XXXI. 157/2 Another method of conveying baulks of timber, iron pipes and other similar goods is by petrol or diesel driven '*straddle' carrier. **1969** *Jane's Freight Containers 1968–69* 9/1 Provisions for straddle carrier handling. **1977** D. Grossman *Samsom Management Lexicon* vi. 36 At the extreme, straddle carriers may have a span wide enough to straddle several railway tracks or roadways and are used for the *intermodal* transfer of containers between road and rail. **1873** *Routledge's Young Gentl. Mag.* Nov. 32/2 Seating himself *straddle-fashion across a chair. [**1967** *Amer. Fruit Grower* May 20/1 (*caption*) Also a straddle-type, the Krebs harvester..has hand shakers on both sides.] **1976** 'D. Halliday' *Dolly & Nanny Bird* vii. 85, I lurched creaking up the stairs like a blackcurrant *straddle harvester. **1836** Haliburton *Clockm.* Ser. i. xxxii, That Captain has nothin to do all day, but sit *straddle legs across his tiller. **1868** *Routledge's Young Gentl. Mag.* 597 Over the shaft were fastened three poles, straddle-legs fashion. **1892** P. H. Emerson *Son of Fens* vii. 60, I went and sat straddle-leg across the horse of the bowsplit. **1817** Hazlitt *Pol. Ess.* (1819) 213 The monstrous *straddle-legged figure of that legitimate monarch, Henry VIII. **1858–9** Russell *Diary India* (1860) I. xiv. 229 The wives of the binneahs who sit straddle-legged on the tiniest of donkeys. **1975** *N.Z. Jrnl. Agric.* Sept. 39/2 The larger British '*straddle' machines..are used to harvest some berry fruits. **1898** *Straddle mill [see *side mill* s.v. side *sb.*[1] 27]. **1905** W. S. Leonard *Machine-Shop Tools* (ed. 3) xxvi. 436 The straddle-mill..is of course the quickest for shapes having an even number of sides. **1911** Webster, *Straddle mill*, a milling cutter..commonly used in pairs a fixed distance apart so as to straddle the work, for sizing nuts, boltheads, etc. **1919** H. D. Burghardt *Machine Tool Operation* ii. xii. 255 When any considerable number of pieces are to be milled it will be advisable to straddle-mill them. **1922** P. Gates *Jigs, Tools & Fixtures* v. 53 In the case of the component at b calling for '*straddle' milling, the fixture can be made adaptable, so that in the case of horizontal machines..the fixture could be arranged on angle plate..and vertically 'straddle' milled. **1954** Straddle milling [see *side milling* vbl. sb. s.v. side *sb.*[1] 27]. **1875** Knight *Dict. Mech.*, **Straddle-pipe*, (Gas), a bridge-pipe connecting the retort with the hydraulic main. *Ibid.*, **Straddle-plow*, a plow with two triangular, parallel shares, a little distance apart, and used for running on each side of a row of dropped corn, to cover the seed. **1958** *Listener* 25 Sept. 458/1 The [timber] yards, where the fork-lift and *straddle trucks scurry about loading and stacking. **1968** *N.Z. News* 25 Dec. 5/5 Straddle trucks are by no means new to the timber industry, but this vehicle..offers features never before incorporated in these utility vehicles. **1919** H. S. Walpole *Secret City* i. iii. 10, I can imagine Lawrence standing *straddleways on the deck of the *Jupiter*, his short thick legs wide apart. **1865** Le Fanu *Guy Deverill* II. xiv, Little Linnett, mounted *straddlewise on his chair.

straddle ('stræd(ə)l), *v.* Also 6–8 **stradle.** [Frequentative f. *strād-* ablaut-var. of *strīd-* stride *v.*: see -le. Cf. striddle, stroddle *vbs.*]

1. a. *intr.* To spread the legs wide apart in walking, standing, or sitting; to stride *about*.

1565 Cooper *Thesaurus* s.v. *Varix, Varico,*..vel *Varicor* .., to goe wide with the knees and legges: to straddle:.. to goe stradlynge. **1567** Golding *Ovid's Met.* xiii. (1587) 172 See how their vdders ful do make them straddle. **1605** *1st Pt. Jeronimo* ii. iii. 83 Thou hast made his legs straddle too much like a Frenchman: for shame, put his legs closer. **1612** Drayton *Poly-olb.* x. 73 [Boreas] From Shetland stradling wide, his foote on Thuly sets. **1619** Middleton *Tri. Love & Antiq.* C 2 b, She being the first that taught women to ride sideling on horsebacke, but who it was that taught 'em to ride stradling, there is no Records so immodest that can shew me. **1685** *Lond. Gaz.* No. 2074/4 An able white Gelding,..has all his paces, Straddles very much with his hinder Legs. **1735** Dyche & Pardon *Dict.*, *Straddle*, to stretch or extend the Legs wider than common. **1784** Cowper *Task* vi. 676 Some noble lord Shall..wrap himself in Hamlet's inky cloak, And strut, and storm, and straddle, stamp, and stare, To show the world how Garrick did not act. **1906** Charlotte Mansfield *Girl & Gods* xi, 'How do you do?' she said, entering the tiny sitting-room where Colonel Vibrant straddled in front of the fire.

b. To stand or stride *across*, *over* (a wide space, etc.), *from* one stepping place *to* another at a distance; to sit astride *on*, *across*.

1678 Bunyan *Pilgr. Progr.* i. (ed. 2) 93 Then Apollyon stradled [*ed. 1* strodled] quite over the whole breadth of the way, and said,..prepare thy self to die. **1760** H. Walpole *Let. to H. S. Conway* 19 Sept., Can't he make..Johnson straddle cross a river and come back with six heads of hussars in his fob? **1818** Scott *Roy Roy* xxx, His foot slipping, as he straddled from one huge fragment of rock to another. **1826** Hood *Recipe for Civiliz.* 45 Tartar grooms, that merely straddle Across a steak and warm their saddle. **1853** Kane *Grinnell Exp.* ii. (1856) 18, I felt as if I could straddle from the main hatch to the bulwarks. **1859** Tennyson *Guinev.* 266 Down in the cellars merry bloated things..straddling on the butts While the wine ran. **1885** *Manch. Exam.* 7 Aug. 5/6 Ministers who passed in and out had to straddle or leap over his long legs. **1898** J. M. Cobban *Angel of Covenant* i. 6, I straddled across the slab-step of the door, and dared him with the ashen cudgel I carried.

c. Of the legs: To stand wide apart.

1634 Sir T. Herbert *Trav.* 38 [An idol] resembling a man ..his legs stradling, very wide. **1687** A. Lovell tr. *Thevenot's Trav.* i. 163 Their Pack-saddles are so broad that they are very uneasie to ones Legs, which must straddle very wide. **1889** 'Q.' (Quiller-Couch) *Splendid Spur* x, Under a trunk extraordinary broad and strong, straddled a pair of legs that a baby would have disown'd. **1897** J. Gordon *Village & Doctor* 3 On he went..with head well back and legs straddling wider apart at every step, floundering in the heavy snow.

d. *transf.* of a thing, esp. of a thing having legs; also, to divaricate, sprawl. Also with complement and *fig.*

1596 Nashe *Saffron Walden* V 2, He would..splinter our pens til they stradled again, as wide as a paire of Compasses. **1662** Shirley *Honoria & Mammon* Wks. 1833 VI. 48 Her teeth straddle. **1670** Eachard *Cont. Clergy* 66 There is one [passage] in Genesis, as I well remember, that is like a pair of compasses stradling! **1680** Moxon *Mech. Exerc.* xii. 204 The Chopping-Block..hath three Legs in it, that stand stradling out from the underside. **1875** Browning *Inn Album* i Lubber prose o'ersprawls, And straddling stops the path from left to right. **1909** *Durham Archæol. Trans.* p. xxxi, A modern screw-pile bridge now straddles its ungainly length across the Tyne. **1916** C. N. & A. M. Williamson *Car of Destiny* xiv, [We] crossed the Pisuergo by a long-legged bridge straddling across the river bed. **1969** B. Rubens *Elected Member* ii. 18 Now, it was Norman, on the same bed, with a different illusion, but an illusion all the same, while between his father and Dr Levy in the kitchen, straddled the same uneasy truth.

e. *spec.* Of the spokes of a wheel: To stand with the ends staggered (Webster 1911).

1875 [see straddling *ppl. a.*].

2. To walk with the legs wide apart; *dial.* 'to swagger, strut' (*Eng. Dial. Dict.*).

1802 D. Wordsworth *Jrnl.* 8 Feb. (1941) I. iii. 108 We met our patient bow-bent Friend... He straddled and pushed us with all his might; but we soon outstripped him. **1825** J. Neal *Bro. Jonathan* III. 10 Bless my heart—how you do straddle about! **1848** Dickens *Dombey* xxvi, Major Bagstock..straddled along the shady side of the way. **1851** D. Jerrold *St. Giles* xii. 121 You straddle on to the tradesman who stands behind a little mountain of eggs. **1895** Sir H. Maxwell *Duke of Britain* i. 9 Petilius tossed off his bumper..and straddled off to the parade ground.

†3. *slang.* (See quot.) *Obs.*

1735 Dyche & Pardon *Dict.*, *Straddle*,..also in Sports and Gaming to play who shall pay the Reckoning.

4. *trans.* To set (the legs) wide apart (in standing or walking). In quots. with *out*, †*asunder*.

1565 Cooper *Thesaurus* s.v. *Diduco, Diductum stare*, to stande stradlyng the legges a sunder. **1831** Carlyle *Sartor Res.* i. v, Man..stands..insecurely enough; has to straddle out his legs, lest the very wind supplant him. **1840** Dickens *Old C. Shop* iv, Mr. Quilp..straddling his legs out very wide apart, stooped slowly down. **1893** Selous *Trav. S.E. Africa* 151, I watched them [giraffes] drinking, straddling out their forelegs by little jerks, until their feet were yards apart.

5. a. To sit, stand, or walk with one leg on either side of; to stride over; to bestride. Also *fig.*

1823 D'Israeli *Cur. Lit.* 2nd Ser. I. 51 Arion, with a grotesque motion, is straddling a great trout. **1841** Catlin *N. Amer. Ind.* (1844) II. xlvi. 95 Charley [the horse] was caught and dressed and straddled. **1859** *Habits of Gd. Society* vii. 251 Straddling a chair, and tilting it up may be pardonable in a bachelor's rooms. **1863** Bates *Nat. Amazons* xii. (1864) 397 In climbing between the box and the wall, it [*sc.* a monkey] straddled the space. **1908** E. Œ. Somerville *Further Exper. Irish R.M.* 26, I straddled the window-sash, and arrived in the room with a three-cornered tear in the shoulder of my coat. **1970** A. Toffler *Future Shock* xx. 424 Advanced telecommunications mean that participants in a social future assembly need not literally meet in a single room, but might simply be hooked into a communications net that straddles the globe. **1981** *Economist* 24 Jan. 28/2 Bank holding companies can straddle state lines (including foreign banks that were lucky enough to establish branches before the 1980 deadline).

b. *transf.* To stand or lie across or on both sides of (something).

1890 *Century Mag.* May 130/1 'Let him take a seat with me in the buggy.' 'That is best perhaps, as he would know better how to avoid the stumps and straddle the ruts.' **1907** J. A. R. Marriott *Life Ld. Falkland* 314 A cavalry skirmish ..enabled the King to win the race to Newbury and so straddle the London road. **1911** [see *straddle-mill*, straddle *sb.* 8].

c. *Gunnery* To fire at (a target) with shots, bombs, etc., so that they fall in a straddle (sense 5). (See also quot. 1941.)

1916 Sir J. Jellicoe *Disp.* 24 June, in *Battle of Jutland* 54 *Colossus*..was hit,..and other ships were straddled with fair frequency. [*Ed. note* i.e. shots were falling on both sides of the ship, but not hitting her.] **1918** 'B. Copplestone' *Silent Watchers* viii. 165 When, say, the shots of one salvo fall beyond the mark and the shots of the next come down on the near side, the mark is said to be 'bracketed'. When the individual shots of a salvo fall some too far and others too short, the mark has been 'straddled'. A *straddle* is a closed-in bracket. **1941** *Christian Sci. Monitor* 6 Mar. 4/7 'To straddle a target'..no longer means..range-finding shots placed each side of the target. To the bombardier, the phrase describes the split-second triggering of a stick of bombs upon an objective. **1943** *Sun* (Baltimore) 28 Aug. 2/4 The crew of a plane..sprayed the deck of one submarine with machine-gun bullets, straddled it with depth charges and caused the U-boat to explode internally.

6. *U.S. colloq.* 'To occupy or take up an equivocal position in regard to; to appear to favour both sides of'. Also *intr.* and *absol.* (*Cent. Dict.* 1891.)

1838 J. C. Neal *Charcoal Sk.* 133 Sometimes I was a-one side, sometimes a-t'other, and sometimes I straddled till the election was over, and came up jist in time to jine the hurrah. **1878** *N.Y. Tribune* 29 Mar. 4/5 Whenever Mr. Randall doesn't straddle a question, he gets on the wrong side of it. **1880** *Daily Union* (San Diego, Calif.) 5 Sept. 1/3 For once in his life, therefore, Hendricks didn't straddle. He put both feet down on the wrong side, and tipped the whole party up. **1884** *Nation* (N.Y.) 3 July 4/1 The platform..contains the well-known plank 'straddling' the tariff question. **1884** *Boston* (Mass.) *Traveller* Aug., It should be remembered that he never straddled the negro question. **1906** *N.Y. Even. Post* 6 Dec. 8 Eleven Senators answered yes, four no, and four straddled.

7. *Poker.* To double (a stake, bet). Also *absol.*

1864 W. B. Dick *Amer. Hoyle* 177 The 'blind' may be doubled by the player to the left of the eldest hand, and the next player to the left may at his option *straddle* this bet. **1872** [see blind *sb.* 8]. **1882** *Poker; how to play it* 49 C can straddle B's ante by putting in the pool two chips. *Ibid.* 50 A good player very rarely straddles. **1885** B. L. Farjeon *Sacred Nugget* xvii, He put in [the pool] a bank-note, and said, 'Five pound blind'. Antonio..put in an I.O.U. for ten pounds, saying 'I straddle you'. *Ibid.*, Mike Patchett went ten pounds blind; he [Antonio] straddled it with twenty. **1897** R. F. Foster *Compl. Hoyle* 179 (Poker) The player to the left of the age may straddle the blind by putting up double the amount put up by the age.

8. ***to straddle the market*** (see quots.). *U.S. Exchange slang.*

1870 W. W. Fowler *Ten Years in Wall St.* 128 Going long and short of stocks, at the same time, is what is technically called 'Straddling' the market. **1900** S. A. Nelson *ABC Wall St.* 161 A speculator who has bought and is long of one stock, and sold and is short of another, has straddled the market. **1907** M. Rollins *Money & Investments* 383 *Straddle the market*, an understanding of 'Selling Short' is first necessary. One has 'straddled the market' when he is 'short' of one stock and 'long' of another.

Hence '**straddling** *vbl. sb.*

1673 Bunyan *Diff. Judgm. Water-Baptism* 44 Your putting in that way of his receiving which is invisible to us, is but an unhandsome straddling over my Argument, which treateth only of a visible receiving. **1761** Victor *Theatres Lond. & Dublin* II. 74 By walking the Decks of the Ship from a Boy, he had contracted a Stradling in his Gait. **1919** *Athenæum* 23 May 360/1 For a well-known method of range-finding..the Navy [has] the term 'straddling'. **1949** *San Francisco News* 14 Mar. 14/2 Despite the local board's straddling, the Legislature, fortunately, voted to continue the centers for another year. **1957** O. Parkes *British Battleships* lxxviii. 458 He proposed that the armoured cruiser..should be placed at his disposal for..'straddling' tests.

straddle ('stræd(ə)l), *adv.* [advb. use of straddle *sb.*] = astraddle, astride. Also const. *of*.

1857 *Quinland* I. 24 He found a crazy fellow sitting straddle of a grave, holding on to the tombstone. **1866** Brogden *Prov. Lincs.*, *Straddle*, astride. **1898** J. C. Harris *Tales of Home Folks* 244, I boun' ef I had a hoss an' could ride straddle I'd ketch 'im. **1919** J. Masefield *Reynard the Fox* 12 Molly Wolvesey riding straddle. **1930** W. Faulkner *As I lay Dying* 79 They had already dragged the backboard back from where Quick found it upside down straddle of the ditch about a mile from the spring. **1935** Z. N. Hurston *Mules & Men* i. vii. 163 It's a story 'bout a man sittin' straddle of a cow.

'**straddle-bug.** *U.S.* Also **straddlebug.** [cf. *straddle-bob*, straddle *sb.* 8.] **1.** A long-legged beetle, esp. *Canthon lævis.* Also *attrib.* (similative).

1839 Longf. *Hyperion* i. vi. (1852) 37 There is one [sketch] on the wall there, which is beautiful, save and except that straddle-bug figure among the bushes. **1862** R. H. Newell *Orpheus C. Kerr Papers* xx. (1866) 124 Now that I look at him, he reminds me of an old-fashioned straddle-bug.

2. *colloq.* A politician who is non-committal or who equivocates; one who 'straddles' (sense 6).

1872 *Kansan* (Newton, Kansas) 5 Sept. 2/1 We think it well that the people..not see quite so much of the straddle-bug business carried on by a few. **1896** *N.Y. Sun* 13 May 1/3 McKinley isn't a gold-bug, McKinley isn't a silver bug, McKinley's a straddle-bug. **1939** *Newsweek* 21 Aug. 14/2 If we nominate conservative candidates, or lip-service candidates, on a straddlebug platform, I personally..will find it impossible to have any active part in such an unfortunate suicide of the old Democratic party. **1948** *Sat. Even. Post* 10 July 33/3, I will not support either a conservative or a straddlebug.

straddler ('strædlə(r)). [f. straddle *v.* + -er[1].] One who or something which straddles.

1863 Bates *Nat. Amazons* ix. (1864) 265 A suitable tree was found for the shell of the boat... The expanding of the log thus hollowed out is a critical operation... Wooden straddlers..are inserted into the opening. **1882** *Poker; how to play it* 49 The player to the left of the last straddler..must be the first to declare whether he will make good the straddle, and so on. **1889** *Voice* (N.Y.) Jan. 10 Contemptible straddlers of great and solemn issues. **1911** Webster, *Straddler*,..a. *Railroads.* A tool that straddles the rail to bear upon the projecting ends of a tie plate, used in driving tie plates into the track. b. A weeding hoe that straddles a row.

straddling ('strædlɪŋ), *ppl. a.* [f. straddle *v.* + -ing[2].]

1. That straddles, in the senses of the verb.

1592 Nashe *P. Penilesse* A 3, At length..I lighted vpon an old straddling Usurer. **1615** Crooke *Body of Man* 102 *Epiplois postica*..diuided into two stradling branches. *a***1652** Brome *Mad Couple* (1653) To Stationer, No stradling Tetrasyllables are brought To fill up room, and little spell, or nought. **1679** *Lond. Gaz.* No. 1403/4 A Strawberry py'd Gelding,.. all his paces, and a stradling gate behind. **1765** H. Walpole *Let. to Miss Anne Pitt* 25 Dec., May the chimney be widened, without which it can never be a French chimney, which is always very low and straddling? **1831** Youatt *Horse* x. 165 [In anchylosis] the horse..has a curious straddling action. **1848** Dickens *Haunted Man* i. 9 The shadows..making..the very tongs upon the hearth, a straddling giant with his arms a-kimbo. **1875** Knight *Dict. Mech.*, *Straddling* (Vehicle), applied to spokes when they are arranged alternately in two circles in the hub. Also said to be *staggered*.

2. *Bot.* Divaricate.

1796 Withering *Brit. Plants* (ed. 3) I. 84 *Straddling* (divaricatus) branches standing wide from each other. *Ibid.* II. 26 Bulbs straight, not much straddling. **1825** *Greenhouse Comp.* II. 25 Malva *divaricata*, straddling Mallow.

Comb. **1822** *Hortus Angl.* II. 399 Straddling-branched Star Wort.

straddly ('strædlı), *a. rare*$^{-1}$. [f. straddl(e *v.* + -y^1.] That straddles; long-legged.

1921 E. M. Forster *Let.* 21 July in *Hill of Devi* (1953) 98 Returned on foot, buying some toys—straddly black horses, but they will be difficult to pack.

†**strade.** *Obs. rare*$^{-1}$. [? a. OF. *estrade* 'escarmouche' (Godefr.)] ? Skirmish, scuffle.

c **1400** *Rowland & Otuel* 476 The Nasell of his helme of-glade Dowun bi-fore hym in the strade.

strade, obs. pa. t. of stride *v.*

stradiot ('strædıɒt). *Hist.* Also 6 **stradiott, stradiote, stradyate.** [ad. It. *stradiotto*: see estradiot. Cf. F. *stradiot.*] = estradiot.

a **1533** Berners *Huon* clxxxix. 761 This great stradiot is come well at a poynte for or he departe he shall pay for our scot & expence. *a* **1548** Hall *Chron.*, *Hen. VIII*, 28 Among the Frenchmen were certaine light horsmen called Stradiotes with..smal speres and swerdes like semiteries of Turkay. **1567** Fenton *Trag. Disc.* v. 95 Leauyng the miserable stradyates..to the guide and gouernemente of their fortune. **1643** Baker *Chron.*, *Edw. IV*, 108 The Duke of Burgoigne..had promised..to bring..foure thousand Stradiots or light horse. **1825** Scott *Talism.* xxiv, A gallant band of twelve hundred Stradiots, a kind of light cavalry raised by the Venetians in their Dalmatian possessions. **1878** Villari *Machiavelli* (1892) I. i. xii. 498 This general was captured on the road by the Stradiotes of Venice.

Stradivarius (strædı'vɛərıəs). Also **Straduarius** (strædju:'ɛərıəs). [a. L. *Stradivarius*, *Straduarius*, latinized forms of the name of Antonio *Stradivari*, a noted Italian maker of stringed instruments in the 17th c.] A violin or other stringed instrument made by Stradivari or his pupils. Also *attrib.*

1833 Fardely tr. *Otto's Treat. Violin* 33 One of his [Amati's] Violins, in good condition, is almost preferable to a Stradiuarius. **1865** Dickens *Mut. Fr.* iii. xiii, He had a Straduarius violin to dispose of. **1874** Boddam-Whetham *Western Wand.* 185 One of the orchestra lost a Straduarius violin worth 1,400 dollars. **1887** Conan Doyle *Study in Scarlet* (1892) 38 My companion prattled away about..the difference between a Stradivarius and an Amati.

stradlings ('strædlıŋz), *adv. dial.* [f. straddle *v.* + -lings.] Astride.

1823 E. Moor *Suffolk Words.* *a* **1825** [see sidelings 5].

stradometrical, variant of stradametrical.

strae, straemash: see straw, stramash.

strafe (strɑ:f, streıf), *v. slang.* Also **straff.** [From the Ger. phrase *Gott strafe England*, 'God punish England', a common salutation in Germany in 1914 and the following years.] *trans.* Used (originally by British soldiers in the war against Germany) in various senses suggested by its origin: To punish; to do damage to; to attack fiercely; to heap imprecations on; also *absol.* In later Mil. usage, to attack from low-flying aircraft with bombs or machine-gun fire, etc.; also *transf.* and *fig.*

1915 A. D. Gillespie *Lett. from Flanders* (1916) 240, I never saw a billet like this for flies... We are trying poison too, but however we may 'strafe' there are just as many left. *Ibid.* 251 They only sent a few shells, and the first seemed to burst in their own trench..and I expect someone will be 'strafed' for it. **1916** *Times Lit. Suppl.* 10 Feb. 62/1 The Germans are called the Gott-strafers, and strafe is becoming a comic English word. **1916** *MS. Let. fr. Front* (Feb. or Mar.) There is not much Hun artillery fire, but as our guns strafe them well every day, I expect they will wake up and return the compliment. **1916** *Daily Mail* 1 Nov. 4/4 The word *strafe* is now almost universally used. Not only is an effective bombardment of the enemy's lines or a successful trench raid described by Tommy as 'strafing the Fritzes,' but there are occasions when certain 'brass hats'..are strafed by imprecation. And quite recently the present writer heard a working-class woman..shout to one of her offspring 'Wait till I git 'old of yer, I'll strarfe yer, I will!' **1916** 'Boyd Cable' *Action Front* 45 Straff the Germans and all their works, particularly their mine works! **1917** J. M. Grider *War Birds* (1927) 33 A regular army West Point major came over from Paris to look us over Sunday and straffed hell out of us in front of the British colonel and his staff. **1918** Galsworthy *Five Tales* 273 If I did my duty as a special, I should 'strafe' her for that. **1925** *Atlantic Monthly* Nov. 657 They're going to strafe us when we start out. **1942** *R.A.F. Jrnl.* 3 Oct. 36 Within ten minutes, enemy aircraft were straffing the ship. **1944** *Sun* (Baltimore) 12 Dec. 20/1 Most of the fighter escort of the 1,600 bombers..dropped to telephone-pole level to strafe trucks and trains heading from Frankfurt to the Saarbrucken battle zone. **1959** N. Mailer *Advts. for Myself* (1961) 42 They started to strafe the beach and the trenches. **1965** *Listener* 16 Dec. 1012/1 At least the latter straffed right and left with an energetic disregard for anything but her own sense of superiority. **1979** B. Parvin *Deadly Dyke* xv. 81 The Stone Cottages were..in need of repair, their paintwork peeling and strafed by the Fenland winds. **1982** *Daily Tel.* 18 Jan. 4/8 Filipino officials have denied a claim by Tokyo that their air force strafed the Japanese oil tanker.

Hence '**strafer**; '**strafing** *ppl. a.*

1916 O. Seaman *Made in England* 31 Is it the absent strafer's kiss On whose account this plaint they utter? **1930** C. R. Samson *Fights & Flights* 98 We left a car to attend to the Zeppelin strafers and take their mechanics away. **1979** M. Page *Pilate Plot* iv. 50 Some illusory protection from any Turkish Air Force strafer that appeared overhead. **1979** R. Cox *Auction* ii. 41 Strafing fighters passed so low that they were often below the level of the hill.

strafe (strɑ:f, streıf), *sb. slang.* Also **straff.** [f. the vb.] A fierce assault; an attack from low-flying aircraft. Also *fig.*, a reprimand.

1915 in *Naval Rev.* (1916) IV. 267 The usual daily straff. **1916** *Blackw. Mag.* Feb. 284/1 Intermittent strafes we are used to. **1918** J. M. Grider *War Birds* (1927) 73 The C.O. and Capt. Horn, our new flight commander, were all set for a big straff because we were supposed to be back at nine. **1935** D. L. Sayers *Gaudy Night* xvii. 372 We was expectin' a bit of a strafe. **1939** *War Illustr.* 11 Nov. 288/1 (*heading*) German officer called Polish campaign a 'strafe' expedition, not a war. **1944** *R.A.F. Jrnl.* Aug. 262 Jerry is up to his nightly strafe. **1979** *Guardian* 24 July 19/1 The people who organize dinners..for foreign panjandrums have..received a rocket... The subject of the strafe was the standard of food. **1980** J. L. Carr *Month in Country* 69 I'd prayed eloquently enough in my signal-pit during big strafes.

strafe, obs. Sc. pa. t. of strive *v.*; var. straif.

Stra'ffordians, *sb. pl. Hist.* [-ian.] A name applied to the fifty-nine members of the House of Commons who voted against the bill for the attainder of Thomas Wentworth, earl of Strafford.

1641 Whitelocke *Mem.* 2 May, This multitude..posted up at Westminster the names of all those members of the house of commons who had voted for the earl, and called them Straffordians. **1647** Clarendon *Hist. Reb.* iii. §141. **1906** *Cambr. Mod. Hist.* IV. ix. 289.

strafing ('strɑ:fıŋ, 'streıfıŋ), *vbl. sb. slang.* Also **straffing.** [f. straf(e *v.* + -ing^1.] Fierce attacking; bombarding; bombing or machine-gunning from low-flying aircraft. Also *fig.*, a dressing-down.

1915 in *Naval Rev.* (1919) IV. 267 Not much straffing on either side. **1919** E. H. Jones *Road to En-Dor* vii. 70 The escape..was followed by a very severe 'strafing' of the whole camp. **1923** *Contemp. Rev.* Jan. 16 Mr. Bonar Law endured this moral strafing with dogged heroism. **1927** E. W. Springs *Nocturne Militaire* 75 I'm going to get a strafing when I get in. **1945** *Finito! Po Valley Campaign* (15th Army Group) 27 Spitfires and Mustangs weaved in strafing sorties over the enemy's positions. **1969** I. Kemp *Brit. G.I. in Vietnam* iii. 60 Diving aircraft..swept close past us on their strafing runs. **1971** S. Hill *Strange Meeting* iii. 169 But when the strafing finally stopped, everything just went quiet. **1979** T. Barling *Olympic Sleeper* iv. 51 Let us hope the Zionists don't make a strafing run on the ship.

†**strag,** *v. Obs.*$^{-0}$ *intr.* ? To walk with a crutch; ? to straddle. Hence **stragging** *vbl. sb.*

c **1440** *Promp. Parv.* 478/2 Stragyn, *patento, strigio.* St(r)agyng, *patentacio.*

†**strage.** *Obs.* [ad. L. *strāges.*] Slaughter.

a **1632** T. Taylor *God's Judgem.* ii. iii. (1642) 39 Not sating himselfe with the strage of men, his tyrrany usurped upon women. **1635** Heywood *Hierarchy Angels* 549 He did as much dammage and made as great slaughter on his Enemies, as he had receiued strage or execution from them. **1689** T. Plunket *Char. Gd. Commander* Ded. 5 Some haue the Laurel won by blood and strage.

straggle ('stræg(ə)l), *sb.* In 5–6 **stragill, -yll.** [f. straggle *v.*^{1}]

†**1.** Phr. *at, to* (*the*) *straggle*, in straggling order. *Sc. Obs.*

c **1470** Henry *Wallace* x. 683 At stragyll raid quhat Scot mycht formest pas. *Ibid.* 699 The frayit folk, at stragill that was fleand. **1513** Douglas *Æneis* xii. xi. 4 A few menȝe persewand our the plane, Quhilk at the stragill fled in all thar mane. **1549** *Diurn. Occurr.* (Bannatyne Club) 49 Thaj tarijt nocht, bot past away with all spulȝie thaj mycht get. The Scottis followit thame to the stragill.

2. A body or group of scattered objects; an irregular or fitful emergence (*of* something); a thin, lank, or untidy growth (of hair). Also *Comb.*

1865 Carlyle *Fredk. Gt.* xix. vi. V. 539 Here are some private utterances of his, throwing a straggle of light on those points. **1869** —— in Mrs. Carlyle *Lett.* I. 266 With a considerable straggle of audience, I found this artist industriously fiddling. **1906** F. S. Oliver *Alex. Hamilton* iii. vi. 238 Where now there is but a thin straggle of stunted trees. **1978** H. Wouk *War & Remembrance* i. 7 His once-thick brown hair was a gray straggle. **1979** C. MacLeod *Family Vault* xviii. 117 Edith, puffy-faced and straggle-haired, stumped upstairs.

straggle ('stræg(ə)l), *v.*^{1} Forms: 5 **stragyll,** 5–6 **stragel,** 5–8 **stragle,** 6– **straggle.** [Of somewhat uncertain etymology; perh. an alteration of *strackle frequentative f. strake *v.*: see -le. Cf. dial. *strackle-brain*, *strackling*, a giddy, thoughtless person (which, however, may be connected rather with *stract* distract *a.*) The dial. *strag* a vagabond, a stray pigeon, may perh. be a back-formation from the verb.]

1. a. *intr.* To wander or stray *from* the proper road, one's companions, etc.; to rove without fixed direction; to go up and down dispersedly. Often conjugated with *be*. Often with adv., as *about*, *abroad*, *away*, *behind*.

c **1400** *Master of Game* (MS. Digby 182) xxxv, þe forster shulde haue men redely þere too meete with hym, þat þei go no ferther nor stragle aboute. *c* **1450** *Brut* 576 Both horse-men and footemen, with huntyng of hem, were stragelt abrode ouer all þe feldys, and were al out of array. **1461** *Paston Lett.* II. 3 Thei haue no capteyn ner rewler..and so thei stragyll abowte be them self. **1583** Stubbes *Anat. Abus.* ii. (1882) 89 [They] runne stragling and rouing..from towne to towne. **1589** Greene *Menaphon* (Arb.) 23 To see if any of his ewes and lambes were straggled downe to the strond. **1642** Fuller *Holy & Prof. St.* iii. xi. 178 There is no danger that weak folks if they walk abroad will straggle farre. **1669** Dryden *Tempest* iii. (1670) 34 He..looks about him like a Callow-bird Just straggl'd from the nest. **1707** Mortimer *Husb.* 195 Turkeys being very apt to straggle will often be laying their Eggs in secret places. **1711** Addison *Spect.* No. 130 ⁋1 They [the gipsies] generally straggle into these Parts about this Time of the Year. **1768** G. White *Selborne, To Pennant* 28 Nov., It is very extra-ordinary..that a bird so common with us should never straggle to you. **1776** Pennant *Brit. Zool.* (ed. 4) I. 142 When the first crowd [of seals] is past, they kill as many as straggle behind. **1788** G. Keate *Pelew Isl.* x. 111 Captain Wilson's servant, who was straggling about with his gun to kill some fowl for dinner. **1877** H. Saunders in *Proc. Zool. Soc.* (1878) 171 An individual of this species [*Larus affinis*] which had straggled to Greenland.

b. *spec.* of a soldier: To wander from the line of march, stray from one's company. Also of a ship: To stray from the line of battle. Of a sailor: To be absent from his ship without leave or overstay his leave.

1529 Rastell *Pastyme* (1811) 227, .xx. archers whiche straggled from theyr companye. **1598** Barret *Theor. Warres* iv. i. 102 To be carefull that the souldiers straggle not. **1648** Gage *West Ind.* 201 She was somewhat far stragled from the rest of the ships. **1760** *Cautions & Advices to Officers of Army* 171 Keep then at the head of your Pelotoon..and suffer not the Men of it to straggle or break their Rank. **1790** Beatson *Nav. & Mil. Mem.* I. 188 The Rear-Admiral's division had straggled, and was a great way astern of the centre. **1831** Scott *Ct. Robt.* vii, If any straggle from their standards, or insult the country by marauding. **1863** A. Young *Naut. Dict.* 395 People who have overstaid their leave of absence, or straggled. **1913** *Q. Rev.* Oct. 555 They sickened or straggled or frankly deserted.

†**c.** Of a merchant: To intrude into a market where he has no licence to trade; to 'interlope'. *Obs.* Cf. straggler c, straggling *ppl. a.* b.

1588 *Acts Privy Council* XVI. 83 The Merchauntes..goe straggling about all the countrey adjoyninge, forstallinge, inhansinge, and raysinge the pryce of all kynd of commodytyes there. **1601, 1622** [see straggling *vbl. sb.*].

d. *transf.* and *fig.* (of persons and things).

1588 Greene *Metamorph.* (1617) G 4b, Be thou stedfast and no doubt thou shalt not finde him stragling. **1632** tr. *Bruel's Praxis Med.* 329 The collicke..doth straggle ouer the whole region of the belly. **1641** Milton *Prel. Episc.* Wks. 1851 III. 77 That sovran Book which we had fondly straggl'd from. *a* **1661** Fuller *Triana* (1867) 188 Vices straggle not alone, but go in companies. *c* **1698** Locke *Cond. Underst.* §29 Wks. 1714 III. 414 He that will observe Children, will find, that even when they endeavour their utmost, they cannot keep their Minds from straggling. **1711** Addison *Spect.* No. 129 ⁋6 One of the last Year's little Muffs had by some means or other straggled into those Parts. **1758** L. Temple *Sketches* (ed. 2) 35 To compress within three Lines, what must otherwise straggle into four. **1848** Dickens *Haunted Man* (1887) 5 Its sun-dial in a little bricked-up corner, where no sun had straggled for a hundred years. **1885** *Athenæum* 7 Feb. 193 Goldsmith..straggled into literature as the humble hack of Griffiths the bookseller. **1891** C. E. Norton *Dante's Hell* xxv. 138 Here let the novelty be my excuse if my pen straggle a little.

e. Of a plant, branch, etc.: To grow irregularly or loosely; to spread or shoot too far. Also, of hair: to spread in lank or untidy strands. Cf. straggling *ppl. a.* c.

1693 Evelyn *De La Quint. Compl. Gard.*, *Culture Orange-trees* 25 To Cut away..all that part which grows out of due Rank, and stragles beyond its bound. **1762** R. Lloyd *Author's Apol.* 179 Though prudence, and our nature's pride May wish our weaknesses to hide, And set their hedges up before 'em, Some sprouts will branch, and straggle o'er 'em. **1841** Browning *Pippa Passes* i. Poems (1905) 167 How these tall Naked geraniums straggle! **1940** R. Chandler *Farewell, my Lovely* xvii. 106 Her dirty hair straggled on the pillow. **1958** A. Sillitoe *Saturday Night & Sunday Morning* i. 17 Her hair straggled untidily over the pillow.

f. Of inanimate objects: To be arranged dispersedly or irregularly; to be situated apart from any main body or from one another. Of a town, building, etc.: To be built irregularly and without compactness. Of a road, river, fence, etc.: To wind in an irregular course.

1611 Speed *Theat. Gr. Brit.* xx. (1614) 39/1 The forme thereof is somewhat circular, with many indents to fetch in those Townes that are dispersedly stragled into her next Shire. **1613** Purchas *Pilgrimage* viii. i. 607 Sometimes they finde it [silver] straggling, in peeces, not holding any continuing Veine. *a* **1661** Fuller *Worthies*, *Norf.* (1662) 250 This said William Paston.., lies buryed in Norwich; so that his corps..do straggle from the Sepulture of their Ancestors, who..were all interred at Paston. **1662** J. Davies tr. *Olearius' Voy. Ambass.* 31 The River Oder,..staggles so, as that to come to the City from Dam side, a man must pass over six bridges. **1818** Scott *Br. Lamm.* xii, A little hamlet which straggled along the side of a creek. **1850** Hawthorne *Scarlet L.* xvi, The road,..straggled onward into the mystery of the primeval forest. **1866** G. Macdonald *Ann. Q. Neighb.* iii. (1878) 26 In another direction the houses went straggling away into a wood. **1890** 'R. Boldrewood' *Col. Reformer* xvi, The..township..straggled around the edge of a sombre watercourse.

¶**2.** Misused for straddle *v.* *rare*$^{-1}$.

Cf. dial. *straggle-bug* = straddle-bug, *strag-legs* (Ireland) = straddle-legs.

1609 Holland *Amm. Marcell.* xxii. xi. 206 The whole multitude..came upon Georgius, whome they haled and tugged with his legs and feet wide stragling.

3. †**a.** *trans.* To scatter, disperse. *Obs. rare.*

1589 Bigges *Summarie Drake's W. Ind. Voy.* 19 The dead body of one of our boyes, found by them stragling all alone, from whom they had taken his head and his heart, and had stragled the other bowels about the place.

b. *passive.* To be placed stragglingly. *U.S.*

1898 Secretan *To Klondyke & Back* 110 At this time the 'City' consisted of several hundred tents, straggled along in the mud for about a mile and a half. **1902** *Munsey's Mag.* XXVI. 479/2 Few have seen the little, old town straggled along the backwater.

Hence **'straggled** *ppl. a.*

1641 Shirley *Cardinal* v. iii. (1652) 62 Ha? if the Dutchess in her stragled wits, Let fall words to betray me to the Cardinal. **1682** Dryden & Tate *Abs. & Achit.* ii. 1124 Thronging and busie as Hyblæan Swarms, Or stragled Souldiers Summon'd to their Arms. **1787** P. Oliver 18 Mar. in *T. Hutchinson's Diary* II. 424 Having nothing but a rusty straggled nail to write with. **1805** Collingwood 24 Oct. in Nicolas *Disp. Nelson* (1846) VII. 217 The remnant of the Combined Fleet..stood up to leeward of my shattered and straggled charge as if meaning to attack them. **1884** 'V. Lee' *C'tess Albany* iii. 27 Its straggled, black and filthy streets. **1887** *Pall Mall Gaz.* 15 July 5/1 A rocky, splashing streamlet..fringed with patches of gorse and straggled belts of natural wood.

straggle ('stræg(ə)l), *v.*^{2} [Of obscure origin.] *trans.* To rough-dress (a grindstone). Cf. straggling *vbl. sb.*^{2}

In recent Dicts.

straggle-brained, *a.* [f. straggle *v.*^{1} + brain *sb.* + -ed.] Having wandering wits.

1725 P. Walkden *Diary* (1866) 11 A wandering straggle-brained clergyman. **1887** Hall Caine *Son of Hagar* ii. xiii, The straggle-brained guest had been lit to his bed.

straggler ('stræglə(r)). Also 6–8 **stragler,** 6 **strag(g)eler, strageller,** 7 *Sc.* **straggillar.** [f. straggle *v.*^{1} + -er^{1}.] One who, or a thing which, straggles.

1. One who wanders or roves without fixed direction; one who strays from his companions or from the regular route; †a gadabout; †a camp-follower, a tramp, vagabond.

1530 Palsgr. 277/1 Straglers after an army, *bidaulx, truandaille.* **1585** Higins *Junius' Nomencl.* 486/2 *Desertor,*.. a straggeler, or forsaker of his fellowes. **1592** Greene *Disput. Conny-catchers* D 3, A Maid shoulde not be a stragler, but like the Snayle, carry her house on her heade. **1594** Shaks. *Rich. III*, v. iii. 327 Let's whip these straglers o're the Seas againe. **1610** Beaum. & Fl. *Scornf. Lady* i. (1616) B 4 b, *Wel.* .. Is your Ladie at home? *Abi.* She is no stragler Sir. **1617** Boys *Expos. Proper Ps.* ii. 33 Euen so the Church of God wandereth as a straggler and as a stranger in the wildernesse of this world. **1729** Swift *Direct. Serv., Butler* (1745) 35 Note, That Bottles missing are supposed to be half stolen by Stragglers and other Servants. **1773** J. Berridge *Wks.* (1864) 131 Satan may as well bar up his gates; he will not catch a single straggler. **1828** Lytton *Pelham* lxiv, I rode over the ground, in the hope of finding some solitary straggler of our party. **1883** Miss M. Betham-Edwards *Disarmed* xli, In an incredibly short space of time the vast pleasure-grounds were cleared of the last straggler.

transf. and *fig.* **1583** Greene *Mamillia* ii. (1593) H 3, Æneas a verie stragler, yet Dido neuer founde halting. **1612** Drayton *Poly-olb.* xvii. 56 But Homesdale raised Hills, to keep the straggler [a river] in. **1748** *Anson's Voy.* Introd. (c) 4 b, The Manila ships are the only ones which have ever traversed this vast ocean, except a French straggler or two.

2. a. *Mil.* A soldier who leaves the line of march or falls out of the ranks. †Also, a scout or skirmisher.

1589 Warner *Alb. Eng.* v. xxv. (1612) 118 Vntill a desperate Stragler with an arrow pierst his head. **1601** R. Johnson *Kingd. & Commw.* (1603) 160 He had lost his carriages with some fewe straglers that had marched disorderly. **1617** Moryson *Itin.* ii. 81 Our straglers that went out retired to the firm ground. **1644** in *10th Rep. Hist. MSS. Comm.* App. i. 53 He..tuik fourtie men and many horses and slew many of thair straggillars. **1707** *Lond. Gaz.* No. 4337/2 Col. Hill..assembled the Stragglers of the English Regiments into a Body. **1813** Wellington 19 July in Gurw. *Desp.* (1838) X. 545 There are many stragglers still out. **1878** Bosw. Smith *Carthage* x. 205 He now rested for a time to recruit his troops, and to allow stragglers to rejoin him.

fig. **1589** Puttenham *Eng. Poesie* iii. xix. (Arb.) 240 This maner of speech is termed the figure of digression by the Latines,..we also call him the *straggler* by allusion to the souldier that marches out of his array. **1625** Gill *Sacr. Philos.* Pref., Although it be not lawfull for mee to handle either sword or speare; yet because I wish well to these holy wars, I have as a stragler brought my baskets of stones. **1850** Blackie *Æschylus* II. Notes 308 These Australians and Africans may be mere imbecile stragglers who have been dropt from the great army of humanity in its march. **1879** Proctor *Pleas. Ways Sci.* v. 119 The two meteors..may have been stragglers from the main body.

b. *Naut.* A sailor who is absent from his ship without leave or who overstays his leave.

1670 Covel in *Early Voy. Levant* (Hakluyt Soc.) 134 We saw some of the Straglers posting down in wonderful haste. **1699** Dampier *Voy.* II. ii. 15 The Captain was not among them; and they were afraid to tell the Spaniards so, for fear of being all hanged for Straglers. **1815** *Falconer's Dict. Marine* (ed. Burney), *Stragglers* are seamen who desert and abscond from his Majesty's ships. **1887** *Queen's Regul. Nav. Service* §728. 289 The Constable, or other person bringing Deserters or Stragglers on board. **1891** *Daily News* 22 Jan. 7/3 Sidney Stevens,..dressed in the uniform of a sailor, was charged before Mr. John Dickinson with being a 'straggler.'

†**3.** A merchant who intrudes into a market without licence to trade there; an interloper. *Obs.*

1591 Q. Eliz. *Let. to Emp. Russia* 14 Jan. in Hakluyt *Voy.* (1599) I. 500 To purge your Countrey of such straglers of our subiects, as..are not of the Company of our merchants. **1601** J. Wheeler *Treat. Comm.* 55 *marg.*, The pedlarlike dealing of the English straglers at the Narue.

4. An animal that strays from its habitat or companions; esp. a migratory bird found at a place outside its usual range; *spec.* in Austral. and N.Z., a stray unbranded animal or one that falls behind or is overlooked in a round-up. Also *fig.*

a **1552** Leland *Itin.* (1768) I. 74 There resorte many redde Dere strageglers to the Mountaines of Weredale. **1594** Barnfield *Affect. Sheph.* (Arb.) 30 If any [sheep] prove a Straggeler From his owne fellowes in a forraine field. **1647** Fuller *Good Th. in Worse T.* 118 Those Straglers [*sc.* deer]..being out of the Protection, because out of the Pale of the Parke. **1760** *Ann. Reg.* 127/1 The magistrates..have ordered all dogs to be muzzled..and all stragglers to be destroyed. **1830** Lyell *Princ. Geol.* (1835) III. 72 These animals of more southern seas can be considered only as stragglers attracted to our shores..by an abundant supply of food. **1848** H. W. Haygarth *Recoll. Bush Life Austral.* vi. 56 Innumerable animals of every kind of brand, and others with no brand at all, and known as 'stragglers', are mixed with the herds in the interior. **1852** Macgillivray *Brit. Birds* IV. 398 Very few [species] are permanently resident in Britain; but, with stragglers, we make up a pretty considerable list. **1860** G. Duppa in S. S. Crawford *Sheep & Sheepmen Canterbury* (1949) v. 46 Complete dipping flock..deliver stragglers. **1890** 'R. Boldrewood' *Col. Reformer* xviii, The stragglers or strayed cattle. **1899** W. T. Greene *Cage Birds* 40 The Blue-headed Wagtail..is rather an accidental straggler to our shores than a resident species. **1928** 'Brent of Bin Bin' *Up Country* xvii. 296 Then I'm going to have a good fling and settle down with a straggler if I can't get the bell ewe. **1933** L. G. D. Acland in *Press* (Christchurch, N.Z.) 16 Dec. 21/8 *Straggler*, sheep that has been left on the country at a muster. It is usual to go over the country again to pick them up. **1953** O. E. Middleton in C. K. Stead *N.Z. Short Stories* (1966) 186 Shepherding the stragglers would be Charlie's strong-eyes, Beau and Belle. **1972** P. Newton *Sheep Thief* 188 Sheep that have been missed in a main muster are 'stragglers'. To get them in may necessitate a special muster.

5. A plant, branch, etc., that grows irregularly or shoots too far; also, a plant, fruit, etc., found growing singly or apart from others of its kind. Similarly, a stray lock of hair. Also *fig.*

1553 Ascham in *Lett. Lit. Men* (Camden) 14 And I in a manner alone of that tyme left a standing straggler, peradventur, though my frute be very smaul, yet,..I may yet be thought somwhat fitt for seede. **1630** Bp. Hall *Occas. Medit.* liii. (1633) 125 There you see a cluster, whose grapes touch one another, well ripened; heere you see some straglers, which grow almost solitarily, greene and hard. **1703** Pope *Vertumnus* 38 Sometimes his pruning-hook corrects the vines, And the loose stragglers to their ranks confines. **1825** Lamb *Elia* ii. *Wedding*, My friend the Admiral..did not at once shove up his borrowed locks..to betray the few grey stragglers of his own beneath them. **1840** *Mental Culture* 27 Field and hedgerow stragglers, exposed to all weathers, will never reach their full stature. **1863** Lyell *Antiq. Man* 16 In the antecedent bronze period there were no beech trees, or at most but a few stragglers.

straggling ('stræglɪŋ), *vbl. sb.*^{1} [-ing^{1}.] **a.** The action of straggle *v.*^{1}

1601 J. Wheeler *Treat. Comm.* 53 Such stragling by free, and vnfree English vsed in Germanie, and the townes of the Lowe Countries out of the Marte townes, is so vnseemely, vnmerchantlike [etc.]. **1622** [E. Misselden] *Free Trade* 80 Having lost their Priuiledges, partly by their owne Stragling. **1847** *Infantry Man.* (1854) 99 The prevention of straggling is..part of the duties of a rear guard. **1862** *Queen's Regul. Nav. Service* 213 In cases of Desertion, a reward not exceeding 3*l.*, and in cases of Straggling not exceeding 1*l.*, is to be paid. **1893** *Nation* (N.Y.) 2 Feb. 86/2 Straggling cuts a considerable figure in Col. Allan's as well as in other Southern estimates of Lee's forces.

b. *spec.* in *Nucl. Physics*, a spread of the energies, ranges, etc., of charged particles about a mean value as a result of collisions undergone in their passage through matter.

1912 *Phil. Mag.* XXIII. 902 After going a given time the α particles will have straggled out, and some will be moving faster than others. I have not succeeded in finding the amount of this straggling. **1930** E. Rutherford et al. *Radiations from Radioactive Substances* iv. 112 The first experiments to estimate the straggling of the α particles were made by the scintillation method. **1950** D. Halliday *Introd. Nucl. Physics* iv. 121 We can have straggling effects caused by varying energy losses in the source (source straggling), by departure of the beam from parallelism (angular straggling), and by characteristics of the detecting and recording equipment (instrument straggling). **1971** *Canad. Jrnl. Physics* XLIX. 1015 (*caption*) Comparison of experimental and theoretical range and range straggling values of ^{224}Ra ions in gases. **1979** *Physical Rev.* A. XIX. 111/1 Measurements of the energy straggling of ^{16}O ions with energies from 5 to 50 MeV passing through Al foils of thickness 100–500μg/cm^{2} were described.

c. *attrib.* **straggling-money** *Naut.* (see quots.).

1815 *Falconer's Dict. Marine* (ed. Burney), *Straggling-Money*, a compensation allowed to persons on their apprehending and bringing on board any stragglers, or deserters, from his Majesty's ships or vessels. **1867** Smyth *Sailor's Word-bk.*, *Straggling-money.* If a man be absent from his duty without leave, but not absent long enough to be logged as *run*, and is brought on board, a deduction is to be made from his wages at the discretion of the captain; not, however, to exceed the sum of £1.

'straggling, *vbl. sb.*^{2} [f. straggle *v.*^{2} + -ing^{1}.] A method of rough-dressing a grindstone (see quots.).

1850 Holtzapffel *Turning* III. 1109 In straggling, or ragging, the stone is kept running as usual whilst a piece of soft iron about a quarter or half an inch square..is wriggled against the edge of the stone by a motion of the wrist. **1875** Knight *Dict. Mech.*, *Straggling*, the process of working down the face of a grindstone to a regular shape, or of removing metallic particles which have become imbedded therein.

'straggling, *ppl. a.* [-ing^{2}.] That straggles.

a. Of persons, animals, ships, etc.: Straying apart from companions or the main body; roving or wandering at random; †vagabond, vagrant.

†*straggling mate*: a stray member of a company.

1589 Bigges *Summarie Drake's W. Ind. Voy.* 36 Lest by some stragling Spaniards from the land, they might be warned by signes from comming in. **1590** Greene *Orl. Fur.* i. i. 170 What is Orlando but a stragling mate, Banisht for some offence by Charlemaine. **1592** Bacon *Observ. Libel Resusc.* (1657) 121 A wrangling Neighbour, that may Trespass, now and then, upon some Stragling ships of ours. *c* **1611** Chapman *Iliad* x. 178 To approue, if any stragling mate He can surprise neare th' vtmost tents. **1632** *Swed. Intelligencer* i. 116 In passing thorow which [forest] many of his stragling Souldiers were knockt downe by the Boores of the Countrey. **1634** Milton *Comus* 499 Hath any ram.. Slip't from the fold..Or straggling weather the pen't flock forsook? **1643** *Docq. Lett. Lat. at Oxf.* (1837) 20 For restrayning of straggling and idle people from following the Army. **1748** *Anson's Voy.* ii. iii. 151 They had now and then a straggling canoe or two of Indians. **1776** Adam Smith *W.N.* i. xi. (1869) I. 232 Some miserable pasture, just sufficient to keep alive a few straggling, half-starved cattle. **1841** Elphinstone *Hist. Ind.* II. 143 The straggling survivors of his party assembled at the same place. **1842** Lover *Handy Andy* xix, There were some straggling spectators besides, to witness the affair. **1866** Miss Braddon *Lady's Mile* i. 1 Some half-dozen nurse-maids with their straggling charges. **1883** Coues in *Encycl. Amer.* I. 528/2 Aside from the straggling *Haliaëtus albicilla* and the South American harpy.., only two eagles are known to occur in North America.

†**b.** Of a merchant: That trades in a market of which he is not free; interloping. Said also of trade thus practised. *Obs.*

c **1592** Horsey *Trav.* etc. (Hakl. Soc.) 290 All interloperes and straglyng Englishemene lyving in that contrey [Russia]. **1601** J. Wheeler *Treat. Comm.* 54 The gouerned and well-ordered trade of the M.M. Aduenturers Companie, is farre to be preferred before a dispersed, stragling, and promiscuous trade. *Ibid.* 55 A number of stragling Marchants resorting thither out of this Realme, the trade was vtterly spoiled. **1622** [E. Misselden] *Free Trade* 81 Which is an effect of a stragling vngouerned Trade. [**1851** Mayhew *Lond. Labour* II. 21/1 This traffic [in second-hand weapons], which is known as a 'straggling' trade, pursued by men who are at the same time pursuing other street-callings.]

c. Of hair, plants, a hedge, etc.: Growing irregularly or dispersedly; shooting or spreading too far.

1674 tr. *Scheffer's Lapland* 12 Their hair is thin, short and flaggy, their beard stragling and scarce covers their chins. **1697** Dryden *Virg. Georg.* i. 358 Twine The Sallow Twigs to tye the stragling Vine. **1707** *Curios. in Husb.* 254 Take off the Roots that are too long, and stragling. **1770** Goldsm. *Des. Vill.* 193 Beside yon straggling fence that skirts the way. **1784** Cowper *Task* ii. 446 First we stroke An eye-brow; next, compose a straggling lock. **1851** Helps *Comp. Solit.* vi. 85 She..held up a straggling but pretty weed. **1860** Thackeray *Lovel* ii. (1861) 48 This gentleman with..the straggling beard. **1862** Miss Braddon *Lady Audley* i. 5 They must have fallen but for the straggling ivy.

d. of inanimate moving objects, of the direction or course of a moving body, of handwriting, etc.

1560 Phaer *Æneid* ix. (1562) Cc iij b, I se ye stragling starrs yt from the poale their course declynes. **1581** Pettie *Guazzo's Civ. Conv.* i. (1586) A 5, I doubt not nowe but to escape a few stragling shot in a light skirmish. **1627** May *Lucan* x. T 3 b, Hence nature did His stragling waues within high mountaines hide. **1822** Byron *Juan* vii. lxxxvi, With straggling light The stars peep through the vapours. **1847** Lever *Knt. Gwynne* xxiii, The writing was straggling and irregular. **1871** L. Stephen *Playgr. Eur.* (1894) v. 134 We marched steadily forwards in a long straggling line.

e. *fig.* of immaterial things (e.g. thoughts, looks, words).

1589 Greene *Menaphon* (Arb.) 63 When your straggling eye..would bee gadding throughout euerie corner of our companie. **1608** Downame in *Eng. Hist. Rev.* (1909) Apr. 245 A few stragling sentences quoted out of the Fathers. *a* **1614** D. Dyke *Myst. Self-Deceiv.* xxii. 276 The spirit of prayer..chaseth away all stragling thoughts. **1615** Brathwait *Strappado* 10 May I speake more, for I am in a vaine, To cull strange things out of a stragling braine. **1676** Wycherley *Pl. Dealer* ii. i, *Oliv.* He a Wit!..he's only an Adopter of straggling Jests and fatherless Lampoons. **1678** Shadwell *Timon* 50 O stragling Senses, whither are you going? **1747** *Frauds & Abuses Coal Trade* (ed. 3) 13 To be Runner to a Coal-Owner to distribute Bills, and collect straggling Debts. **1854** Carlyle in Froude *Life Lond.* (1884) II. 156 It must have been fourteen years later before I..began to have some distant straggling acquaintance of a personal kind with him.

f. Of stationary objects: Scattered or arranged irregularly. Of a road, tract of country: Winding irregularly, having an irregular outline. Of a house, town, etc.: Built irregularly and uncompactly.

1604 E. G[RIMSTONE] *D'Acosta's Hist. Indies* IV. v. 217 There are two different kindes [of silver], the one they call stragling, the other fixed and setled. **1615** G. SANDYS *Trav.* III. 150 In the vally on the East side of the Citie, are many stragling buildings. **1700** DRYDEN *Fables, Char. Good Parson* 61 Wide was his Parish; not contracted close In Streets, but here and there a straggling House. **1778** *Eng. Gazetteer* (ed. 2) s.v. *Bicister*, 'Tis a long, straggling town. **1835** DICKENS *Sk. Boz, Parl. Sketch*, That..ungainly-looking man,..with the straggling black trousers, which reach about half-way down the leg of his boots. **1838** LYTTON *Alice* V. i, A straggling, irregular, but picturesque building. **1860** TROLLOPE *Castle Richmond* vi, The straggling mahogany table in the centre of the room, whose rickety legs gave way and came off whenever an attempt was made to move it. **1870** E. PEACOCK *Ralf Skirl.* II. 187 An inn with a straggling collection of houses near it. **1894** WEYMAN *Under Red Robe* ii, The cottages..ran in a straggling double line with many gaps.

g. Occurring casually or occasionally, 'stray'.

1618 in J. Charnock *Hist. Mar. Archit.* (1801) II. 231 Wherein is sett downe how of the 182 sailes wanting, 104 may be supplyed with stragling sailes of other shipps.

Hence **'stragglingly** *adv.*

1579-80 NORTH *Plutarch, Dion* (1595) 1047 The other that could not get in in time, fledde straglingly vp and downe. **1650** A. B. *Mutat. Polemo* 24 So they stragglingly departed like fools. **1668** *Lond. Gaz.* No. 230/2 About 160 German Souldiers being straglingly arrived at Milan, were by the Governours Order disposed of. **1693** EVELYN *De La Quint. Compl. Gard.* II. 190 If we be not careful to thin it, ..it..grows weak, and shoots its Leaves straglingly outward. **1774** GOLDSM. *Nat. Hist.* II. 220 [The Tartars] have but little beard, which grows straglingly on the chin. **1818** *Ann. Reg., Chron.*, etc. 479/1 The town stands stragglingly on an abrupt slope. **1884** HOWELLS in *Harper's Mag.* Dec. 125/1 Roberts, Lawton, and Bemis follow stragglingly.

straggly ('strægli), *a.* [f. STRAGGLE *v.*[1] and *sb.* + -Y.] Characterized by straggling.

1862 J. A. SYMONDS *Let.* 2 Feb. (1967) I. 327 The evergreens..are growing very straggly in parts. **1866** CARLYLE *Remin.* (1881) I. 152 At the riding-house..was a kind of straggly group, or small crowd, with redcoats interspersed. **1880** MISS BROUGHTON *Second Thoughts* I. iii, A shaky, straggly old man's hand. **1882** *Garden* 2 Sept. 204/3 The spike has numerous long straggly branches. **1890** J. HATTON *By Order of Czar* IV. i, His hair long and straggly.

straght, obs. Sc. form of STRAIGHT.

straghte, obs. pa. t. of STRETCH *v.*

†**'stragler.** *Obs. rare*[−1]. [? jocularly f. L. *astragal-us*, Gr. ἀστράγαλ-ος (see ASTRAGAL) + -ER, after *straggler*.] *pl.* The game of hucklebones.

c **1650** *MS. Ashmole* 788 lf. 162 The game of Astragalls alias straglers.

stragular ('strægjʊlə(r)), *a.* [f. STRAGUL-UM + -AR.] Of or pertaining to the stragulum.

1891 *Century Dict.*

'stragule. *Bot. rare.* [a. F. *stragule* or ad. L. *strāgulum* covering.] The inner involucrum of the flowers of grasses.

1821 S. F. GRAY *Brit. Plants* I. 122 Glumelle. Stragule, Corolla, Interior glume [etc.].. The internal particular involucrum of the flowers of the grasses.

‖**stragulum** ('strægjʊləm). *Ornith.* [L. *strāgulum* spread, covering, carpet.] = MANTLE *sb.* 9.

1891 *Century Dict.*

†**'strahlite.** *Min. Obs.* [f. G. *strahl-stein* (its earlier name; f. *strahl* sunbeam = ἀκτίς) + -ITE.] Actinolite.

1823 BROOKE *Introd. Crystallogr.* 453 Amphibole.. Actynolite; Actinote; Strahlite.

strai, obs. form of STRAW, STRAY.

straibere, obs. form of STRAWBERRY.

straic(h)t(e, obs. forms of STRAIGHT, STRAIT.

straid, obs. Sc. pa. t. of STRIDE *v.*

straif. *Obs.* exc. *dial.* Also 4 *pl.* **streyves, strayves**, 6 **straiff, strayff**, 9 **strafe.** [Alteration of STRAY *sb.*, to match *waif.*] A stray animal or thing. Chiefly in ***waif and straif***: see WAIF *sb.*

1377 LANGL. *P. Pl.* B. Prol. 94 Of wardes and wardmotes, weyues and streyues [1393 C. I. 92 strayues]. **1447** *Shillingford Lett.* etc. (Camden) 99 He and his predecessours..have had view of Frank Plegge weif and straif and all other profits longing to a viewe. **1509-10** *Durham Acc. Rolls* (Surtees) 195 *Redd. Ass.* De ancaragia nil hoc anno, nec de wryk, nec de strayff, nec de wayff, nec de infanketheyff hoc anno. **1535-6** *Act 27 Hen. VIII*, c. 26 §23 Lordes Marchers..shall haue..Wayff, Straiff, Infanthef, Outfanthef, Treasoure Troves. **1876** *Whitby Gloss., Waif and Straif*, articles, by chance, washed up on the beach by the sea, as wreck materials; here they are the property of the manor owner. **1879** MISS JACKSON *Shropshire Word-bk., Strafe*, a stray animal.

straif, obs. Sc. pa. t. of STRIVE *v.*

straight (streɪt), *a.*, *sb.* and *adv.* Forms: α. 4 (**straȝfte**), **strayth, streiȝet, streighte, streiht**, 4-5 **streiȝt**, 4-7 **streght**, 4-8 **streight**, 5 (**strath**), **streȝt, streith, streught, streygth, streyȝte, streyȝthte**, 5-6 **streghte**, 5-8 **streyght(e**, 6 **strayght(e**, (*Sc.* **strecht**), 8 *Sc.* **straicht**, 4- **straight**. β. *Sc.* 4 **stracht, strauȝt, strauht, strawt**, 4-5 **straȝte**, 4-7 **straght**, 4-9 **straucht, straught**, 6 **strauch.** γ. *Sc.* 5 **stright, stryȝte**, 6 **stricht.** δ. 4 **straitt**, 4-5 **streit(e, streyt(e**, 4-6 **strayt(e**, 5 **straict**, 5-8 **straite**, 5-9 **strait.** [ME. *streȝt, straȝt*, orig. an adjectival use of the pa. pple. of *strecchen* to STRETCH.]

A. *adj.*

†**1. a.** As ppl. adj.: Extended at full length. *Obs.*

c **1400** *Destr. Troy* 7677 With a streught arme he keppit the caupe on his clene sheld. **14..** *Fifty-first Ps.* 45 in *Pol. Rel. & L. Poems* (1903) 281 Sithe þi flesche, lord, was furst perceyued And for oure sake laide streiȝt in stalle. *a* **1420** *Aunters of Arthur* 534 Hit was no ferly, in faye, His stedes startun on straye, With steroppus fulle stryȝte. **1596** DALRYMPLE tr. *Leslie's Hist. Scot.* I. II. 133 Quhairfor Ferithar receiuet the kingis Waipone, to wit, a naikit sworde, a bent and straucht out wande, in thir dayes called a sceptre.

†**b.** Spread out, broad. *Obs.*

? *a* **1366** CHAUCER *Rom. Rose* 119 And somdel lasse it was than Seine, But it was straighter [Fr. *plus espandue*] wel away.

2. a. Not crooked; free from curvature, bending, or angularity.

c **1350** *Libeaus Desc.* (Kaluza) 942 Hir nose was streiȝt [*Cotton MS.* strath] and riȝt. *c* **1369** CHAUCER *Dethe Blaunche* 942 Hyt [*sc.* her neck] was white, smothe, streght and pure flatte Wyth-outen hole. *c* **1400** *Destr. Troy* 1574 The Stretis were streght & of a stronge brede. *c* **1420** *Liber Cocorum* (1862) 35 On alle these fowles tho legges schune bene, Summe cralled, sum streȝt, as I haue sene. **1523-34** FITZHERB. *Husb.* §4 The plowes that goo with wheles, haue a streyghte beame. **1563** *Mirr. Mag., Jane Shore* xx, And bent the wand that might haue growen ful streight. *a* **1577** SIR T. SMITH *Commw. Eng.* I. (1589) 2 A rule is alway to be vnderstoode to be straight. **1611** SHAKS *Cymb.* III. i. 38 There is no mo such Cæsars, other of them may haue crook'd Noses, but to owe such straite Armes, none. **1661** J. CHILDREY *Brit. Baconica* 129 This River is a very streight and broad river. **1667** PRIMATT *City & C. Builder* 52 Let him in the buying his timber, buy the streightest he can light on. **1678** R. L'ESTRANGE *Seneca's Mor.* (1702) 213 A streight Stick in the Water appears to be crooked. **1697** DRYDEN *Virg. Georg.* III. 121 Upright he walks, on Pasterns firm and straight; His Motions easy; prancing in his Gate. **1728** CHAMBERS *Cycl.* s.v. *Stairs*, Straight Stairs..are such as always fly, that is, proceed in a Right Line, and never wind. **1737** *Gentl. Mag.* VII. 190 The Bill was hardly discernable, so I cannot say whether it was Streight or Crooked. **1767** GOOCH *Treat. Wounds* I. 234 We are to consider the..shape of the weapon; whether it has a strait, or a rising edge. **1786** BURNS *Vision* I. xi, And such a leg!.. Sae straught, sae taper, tight and clean. **1796** WITHERING *Brit. Plants* (ed. 3) II. 123 Panicle stiff and straight. **1796** KIRWAN *Elem. Min.* (ed. 2) I. 162 Fracture presents..mostly streight and parallel, rarely curved fibres. **1808** PARSONS *Trav. Asia* xi. 230 The streets are all strait. **1839** LINDLEY *Introd. Bot.* 485 Straight (*rectus*); not wavy or curved, or deviating from a straight direction in any way. **1842** LOUDON *Suburban Hort.* 138 This requires a blade with a straight edge like those of the pruning-knives now in general use. **1896** *Law Times Rep.* LXXIII. 615/1 The railway line..was perfectly straight for a distance of over 700 yards.

absol. **1718** PRIOR *Solomon* I. 190 Water and Air the varied Form confound; The Strait looks crooked, and the Square grows round.

b. ***straight line***: a line uniform in direction throughout its length; *Geom.* = *right line*, which is now rare.

1398 TREVISA *Barth. De P.R.* III. xvii. (1495) 61 One manere of the syghte is by strayte lynes vpon the whyche the lyknesse of the thyng that is seen cometh to the syghte. *c* **1537** DE BENESE *Measurynge Lande* A iiij, Of lynes one is a straygth lyne hangyng, y[e] seconde is a straygth lyne ouerthwarte [i.e. perpendicular and horizontal]. **1551** [see RIGHT *a.* 2]. **1610** BOLTON *Elem. Armories* 87 Armorial Lines are in their first diuision Straight, or Crooked. Againe the Straight are either Direct, or Oblique. **1649** JER. TAYLOR *Gt. Exemp.* I. Ad Sec. viii. 118 Of all lines the straight is the shortest. **1697** POTTER *Antiq. Greece* II. xiv. I. 287 Instead of ascending in a streight Line, it [the flame] whirled round. **1726** LEONI *Alberti's Archit.* I. 9 *a*, The strait Line is a Line drawn from one Point to another, the shortest Way. **1799** HAN. MORE *Fem. Educ.* (ed. 4) I. 240 Why in teaching to draw do you begin with strait lines and curves? **1840** LARDNER *Geom.* ii. 25 If from any proposed point P, several straight lines be drawn to a given straight line AB. **1870** B. STEWART *Elem. Physics* §25. 28 The method of representing forces by straight lines. **1884** tr. *Lotze's Metaph.* 182 If we proceed onwards in a straight line, we shall, admittedly, never come to the end of the line. **1885** LEUDESDORF *Cremona's Proj. Geom.* 75 Through *M*..draw two straight lines to cut *u* in *A* and *B*.

c. Of a human form, a back: Erect, not crooked or stooping.

1599 SHAKS. *Hen. V*, v. ii. 168 A good Legge will fall, a strait Back will stoope, a blacke Beard will turne white. **1826** F. REYNOLDS *Life & Times* I. 232 He was young, tall, strait, and good-looking. **1855** TENNYSON *Brook* 70 A daughter of our meadows,..Straight, but as lissome as a hazel wand. **1868** GEO. ELIOT *F. Holt* i. I. 31 You are as straight as an arrow still.

d. Of a limb, etc.: Held with the joint not flexed.

1765 ANGELO *Sch. Fencing* 18 Keep a strait arm, in order to throw off his point. *a* **1774** GOLDSM. *Surv. Exp. Philos.* (1776) II. 169 As painful as it would be to stretch out a finger streight that was contracted by an inflammation. **1940** W. FAULKNER *Hamlet* III. ii. 200 Lying flat on his back in the darkness with his eyes open and his arms straight beside him, thinking of nothing. **1955** *Simple Gymnastics* ('Know the Game' Ser.) 6/1 When your knees are as high as this, squeeze your legs together and lay back with straight arms.

e. Of hair: Not curly or waved.

1748 SMOLLETT *Rod. Random* xiii. (1768) I. 83 My hair.. hung down upon my shoulders, as lank and streight as a pound of candles. **1774** *Pennsylv. Gaz.* 23 Feb. 5/3 A native Irish servant man,..fair complexion, straight fair hair. **1886** H. W. LUCY *Diary Gladstone Parlt.* 239 His pale face, his straight black hair.

f. *Printing.* ***straight accent***: a macron.

1888 JACOBI *Printer's Vocab.* 134 *Straight accents*, another term for long accents, thus—ā ē ī ō ū.

g. *Arch.* (See quots.)

[**1666** *Act 18 & 19 Chas. II*, c. 8 §5 Archworke of Bricke or Stone either straight or circular.] **1812** P. NICHOLSON *Mech. Exerc.* 237 All vaults which have a horizontal straight axis, are called straight vaults. **1828** —— *Masonry* 110 *Straight walls*, those which have plane surfaces.

h. *Anat.* The distinctive epithet of certain structures (= mod.L. *rectus*).

1585 HIGINS *Junius' Nomencl.* 31/2 *Intestinum rectum*,.. the straight gut, or the arse gut. **1749** HARTLEY *Observ. Man* I. i. §3. 99 The Four strait Muscles of the Eye. **1840** W. J. E. WILSON *Anat. Vade M.* (1842) 339 The Straight or fourth sinus is the sinus of the tentorium. **1879** HARLAN *Eyesight* ii. 30 The straight muscles, acting together, tend to draw it [the eyeball] backwards, while the oblique muscles are so placed as to oppose this tendency.

i. *Zool.* and *Bot.* (See quots.)

1822 J. PARKINSON *Outl. Oryctol.* 171 The additions which this author has made to the genera of straight multilocular shells. **1841** *Penny Cycl.* XXI. 183/2 Mirbel has proposed a classification of ovules. When the ovule has grown regularly with the hilum and chalaza at the base and the foramen at the apex, it is called a *straight* ovule, or *orthotropous*. **1854** A. ADAMS, etc. *Man. Nat. Hist.* 373 Straight-Foraminifers (Vaginulidæ).

j. Of the front of a coat or dress: Not fitting closely to the chest.

1893 *Daily News* 5 Apr. 7/1 This shape is fitted in towards the waist at the back, but the fronts are 'straight,' a tailor's technicality for 'not fitting'. **1906** *Daily Chron.* 19 Sept. 4/4 The dress-improver and even the 'straight-front' were in the panoply of the society dame of nineteen centuries ago.

3. Direct, undeviating. **a.** Of a way or course: Leading directly to its destination; not deviating or circuitous. Also in fig. context.

13.. *E.E. Allit. P.* A. 691 By wayez ful streȝt he con hym strayn [Vulg. *Sap.* x. 10 *Deduxit per vias rectas*]. *c* **1386** CHAUCER *Knt.'s T.* 832 Duc Theseus the streighte wey hath holde And to the launde he rideth hym ful right. *c* **1425** *Hampole's Psalter* Metr. Pref. 32 This is þe way to mannys syȝt; euen streygth wiþ out deseyt. **1488** *Cal. Anc. Rec. Dublin* (1889) I. 493 And so forth the streyght wey till they came to Kylmagergan. **1500-20** DUNBAR *Poems* lxxvi. 1 Quhat is this lyfe bot ane straucht way to deid. **1526** *Pilgr. Perf.* (W. de W. 1531) 22 This waye of religyon, whiche is the streyght waye to the perfeccyon of grace. **1533** BELLENDEN *Livy* II. 6 Þan was It found expedient to send Icelius brother and numitorius son..þe strauchest way þai mycht to þe portis. **1535** COVERDALE *Luke* iii. 4 Prepare the waye of the Lorde, and make his pathes streight. **1568** GRAFTON *Chron.* II. 28 He without long tariyng or aduisement, tooke the streight way to the sea syde. **1627** ABP. ABBOT in Rushw. *Collect.* (1659) I. 456 To keep things in a streight course, sometimes in fits of the Gout, I was forced by my Servants to be carried into the Court. **1736** BUTLER *Anal.* I. v. 93 If we were to suppose a strait Path marked out for a Person. **1820** SCOTT *Monast.* xxiii, While, in pursuit of his interest, he made all the doubles which he thought necessary to attain his object, he often..missed that which he might have gained by observing a straighter course. **1859** GEO. ELIOT *Adam Bede* xxxvii, Hetty..asked the straightest road northward towards Stonyshire.

(*b*) *fig.*, in collocation with *narrow*, esp. in phr. ***straight and narrow path***, a course of conventionally moral and law-abiding behaviour; freq. *ellipt.* in colloq. usage as ***straight and narrow***. Cf. *strait and narrow* s.v. STRAIT a. 3 b.

The latter use is a misinterpretation of Matt. vii. 14 'Because strait is the gate, and narrow is the way which leadeth vnto life, and few there be that findе it.'

1842 J. E. LEESON *Hymns & Scenes of Childhood* 25 Loving Shepherd, ever near, Teach Thy lamb Thy voice to hear; Suffer not my steps to stray From the straight and narrow way. **1912** T. DREISER *Financier* xxiii. 253 In his younger gallivantings about places of ill repute, and his subsequent occasional variations from the straight and narrow path, he had learned much of the curious resources of immorality. **1930** J. DOS PASSOS *42nd Parallel* IV. 275 Robbins..said that he..would have to follow the straight and narrow. **1959** D. BUCKINGHAM *Wind Tunnel* xx. 161 He had unwittingly caused Madelaine to take a far more serious step off the straight and narrow. **1970** *Times* 13 Feb. 10/4 It may be counted for consistency..that the White Paper should not have flinched..once again to sign-post the straight and narrow path. **1978** F. WELDON *Praxis* x. 73 It's only the fear of pregnancy which keeps girls on the straight and narrow.

b. Of a look: Bold, steady.

c **1400** *Destr. Troy* 3758 Stokyn ene out stepe with a streught loke. **1898** G. B. SHAW *You never can Tell* II. 241 She takes his hand and presses it, with a frank, straight look into his eyes. **1922** T. S. ELIOT *Waste Land* (1923) ii. 12 He wants a good time. And if you don't give it him, there's others will, I said... Then I'll know who to thank, she said, and give me a straight look.

c. Of an aim, a stroke, a throw, etc.: Directed precisely to the mark.

1833 NYREN *Yng. Cricketer's Tutor* 33 All straight balls should be played straight back. **1837** DICKENS *Pickw.* vii, The ball flew from his hand straight and swift towards the centre stump of the wicket. **1859** RUSKIN *Two Paths* i. §32 The workman's whole aim is straight at the facts, as well as he can get them. **1884** *Sat. Rev.* 26 Jan. 108/1 The clumsy round-armed hit [in boxing]..is not esteemed so highly as a

d. Of gunpowder: = *straight-shooting*: see C.

1899 F. V. KIRBY *Sport E.C. Africa* xxvii. 302, I had made up my mind to use my rifle, with the straightest powder I had. **1900** POLLOK & THOM *Sports Burma* 262 One need not necessarily burn straight powder.

e. *colloq.* Of an utterance: Outspoken, unreserved. Also, straightforward, not evasive. ***straight talk***: a piece of plain speaking.

1894 ASTLEY *50 Yrs. Life* I. 326, I made a vow..that I would never open that infernal Euclid book again, and, what is more, I never will! so that is straight. **1895** *Westm. Gaz.* 11 Sept. 2/2 The jury..attributed the accident solely to the neglect of the Conservators... That is pretty straight. **1900** *Ibid.* 1 Sept. 1/2 One candidate..is already consoling himself in advance with the thought of the Straight Talks he will give the..deputations that are certain to descend upon him. **1903** *Ibid.* 9 Jan. 2/2 It was a night of Straight Talks. **1959** A. SILLITOE *Loneliness of Long-Distance Runner* ii. 178 'You'll get five years in Borstal if you don't give me a straight answer,' he said. **1973** J. PORTER *It's Murder with Dover* vii. 70 Dover generously gave him a straight answer to a straight question. 'No,' he said. **1979** 'A. HAILEY' *Overload* IV. viii. 333 Nim, give me the straight dope behind this Yale thing. What went wrong?

f. ***the straight tip*** (*colloq.*): see TIP *sb.*[4] b.

g. *Lawn Tennis.* Applied to the sets in a match where the winner has not conceded a set. Also *fig.*

1895 *Official Lawn Tennis Bull.* 4 July 103 Stevens's persistent and accurate ground-strokes from the base-line, and his ability to reach and return everything safely proved too much for Fischer, who was beaten rather badly in straight sets. **1911** *Wright & Ditson's Official Lawn Tennis Guide* 12 Except in the second set of this match, the two Doyles..were completely outclassed and Waidner and Gardner made rather easy work, winning in straight sets. **1936** E. C. POTTER *Kings of Court* vi. 99 If Brookes had been able to hold his service..it might have gone for a straight-set win. **1949** D. C. COOMBE *Hist. Davis Cup* 222 Petra won both his singles in straight sets. **1961** *Times* 4 Jan. 11/3 Miss McAlpine should have won in straight sets. **1971** LAVER & COLLINS *Educ. Tennis Player* xxiii. 273, I picked up a little Spanish in that stretch of straight-set victories. **1980** *Guardian* 20 Sept. 10/3 (*heading*) Straight set winners.

h. Consecutive, in unbroken sequence. *colloq.* (orig. *U.S.*).

1899 J. LONDON *Let.* 30 Apr. (1966) 35 He spent 48 straight hours with me a couple of days before he went. **1963** *Wall St. Jrnl.* 25 Jan. 31/3 American Photocopy Equipment stock was the most active stock for the second straight day. **1971** LAVER & COLLINS *Educ. Tennis Player* xxv. 291 I had won 30 straight matches since losing to Newcombe in June, the week before Wimbledon. **1976** *Morecambe Guardian* 7 Dec. 8/9 Vale got off to a good start through their No. 1 Mike Ashby who won in fine style in three straight games. **1977** *Listener* 10 Mar. 295/1 Company earnings..had reflected their 16th straight annual gain.

i. *Racing.* Designating a bet which backs (a horse, etc.) to win. Cf. PARI MUTUEL.

1928 *Daily Sketch* 10 Aug. 20/4 It..can be used either for straight or place betting. **1974** P. ARNOLD *Bk. Gambling* viii. 88/1 If there are three to six runners, a straight forecast pool is also run. Bettors are required to name the first two horses to finish, in the correct order. **1976** *Webster's Sports Dict.* 427/2 *Straight*,..[in] parimutuel betting. First place at the finish. When a straight wager is made, the bettor collects only if the competitor wins.

j. Straightforward, simple, uncomplicated. *colloq.*

1936 *Discovery* Aug. 254/1 It is possible to perceive a sharp demarcation between what may be called 'straight dowsing' and 'divination proper'. **1957** *Times Lit. Suppl.* 18 Oct. 625/3 Any editor worth his salt is grateful to have slips, oversights, straight mistakes and insensitivities pointed out. **1962** *Times* 5 July 15/5 The tapes all emerged as inferior in straight comparisons. **1972** WODEHOUSE *Pearls, Girls, & Monty Bodkin* x. 143 Would he be cut in on the gross receipts, do you think, or is he on a straight salary?

†4. Of a mountain: Steep. *Obs.* (chiefly *Sc.*)

1475 *Bk. Noblesse* (Roxb.) 15 The streit high monteyns of Pirone. **1533** BELLENDEN *Livy* II. xxi. (S.T.S.) I. 218 þai fled vp throw ane strate montane. **1549** *Compl. Scot.* Ep. Ded. (1873) 2 The quhilkz volffis ar nocht the rauand sauuage volffis of strait montanis ande vyild fforrestis. *a* **1800** *Bonny Lizie Lindsay* xxiii. in Child *Ballads* IV. 262/2 The mountains were baith strait and stay.

5. ***straight angle.*** **†a.** A right angle (*obs.*); **b.** in mod. use, an angle of 180°.

1601 HOLLAND *Pliny* II. xviii. I. 13 Those raies that come sidelong..give but a darke and dim light..in comparison of them that fall directly with straight angles. **1707** MORTIMER *Husb.* 431 The best Figure for a Kitchin-Garden..is a Square of straight Angles. **1889** DUPUIS *Elem. Synth. Geom.* §36. 17 One-half of a circumangle is a straight angle, and one-fourth of a circumangle is a right angle.

6. a. Of conduct: Free from crookedness; frank, honest. Hence of persons and their attributes. Also in mod. colloq. use, law-abiding as opp. criminal. Cf. *to go straight* (*b*), sense 5 of the adv. below.

The present use (chiefly *colloq.*) is unconnected with that of the 16–17th c.

1530 PALSGR. 326/1 Strayght, ryght in condycions, *juste.* **1541–2** *Act 33 Hen. VIII*, c. 15 §1 The..good order strayte and true dealing of the inhabitauntes of the said towne [Manchester]. *a* **1628** PRESTON *New Covt.* (1634) 233 To describe to you a right and straight man, when his end is right, and his rule is right. **1642** EARL LEVEN *Let.* 28 Nov. in *Scott. Jrnl. Topog.* (1847) I. 73/2, I am aboundantly persuaded of your integrity and straught desyres for the peace..of or poor distressed kingdome.

1864 KIMBALL *Was he Successful?* 43 (Hoppe) You are honest too—straight as a shingle. **1890** *Spectator* 22 Nov., There exists..a sort of instinctive appreciation of honesty which..gives enormous influence to any big squatter who is really upright and 'straight'. **1893** *Jrnl. R. Agric. Soc.* Mar. 1 Having the reputation of being a fearless and independent divine, a straight man, true to his cloth and calling. **1901** BP. W. STUBBS in *Ch. Q. Rev.* Apr. 9, I think there never was such a life, so long, so brave, so devoted, so straight. **1904** SHUDDICK *How to arrange with Creditors* 32 If the debtor..has been what is called a straight man, the creditors..accept his proposal of a composition. **1908** W. W. FOWLER *Soc. Life Rome* vi. 200 It is on the whole a pleasing letter... The reader shall be left to decide for himself whether it is perfectly straight and genuine. **1977** J. WAINWRIGHT *Day of Peppercorn Kill* 37 Inky was straight. .. Ten years ago, Inky had walked away from prison..and, since that day, he hadn't put a foot wrong.

†b. Right, proper, fitting. *Obs.*

1538 STARKEY *England* 38 Vertue..schowyth vs the ryght vse and streght, both of helth, strenghth, and beuty.

c. Of a person: Well-conducted, steady. Chiefly in ***to keep straight.*** Also, of a woman: Virtuous, chaste.

1853 C. M. YONGE *Heir of Redclyffe* II. v. 70 If the right motives did not suffice to keep one straight..why then I should be..utterly good for nothing. **1868** A. L. GORDON *Let.* Poems (1912) 370 She tried hard to cheer me up and keep me straight. **1876** 'OUIDA' *Winter City* vi. 125 If only people 'keep straight' for the sake only of what other people say of them. **1886** —— *House Party* vii. (1887) 163 Do you really think that to have any influence on English public life it is necessary..to keep so very straight, as regards women, I mean, you know? **1890** *Pall Mall Gaz.* 21 May 5/1 Mr. Dolling amused his audience..by his description of a 'straight girl,' *i.e.*, one a young fellow not merely walked out with, but intended to marry. **1893** SALTUS *Madam Sapphira* 133 As God is my witness that girl is as straight as your sister. **1894** WILKINS & VIVIAN *Green Bay Tree* I. 185 She ..meant to marry him in two or three years, if he proved he could keep straight in the meanwhile. **1908** R. BAGOT *A. Cuthbert* viii. 83 And, now Jim came to think of it, she had shown that she was 'straight'. A woman who wasn't would have behaved—well, differently.

d. *slang* (orig. *U.S.*). Conventional, respectable, socially acceptable. Also *spec.* (*a*) heterosexual; not practising sexual perversions; (*b*) not using or under influence of drugs; sober, abstinent.

1941 G. W. HENRY *Sex Variants* II. 1176 *Straight*... Also employed as meaning not homosexual. *To go straight* is to cease homosexual practices and to indulge—usually to re-indulge—in heterosexuality. **1959** M. ZANE *Easy Living* vii. 90 'You don't want a slug [of brandy], huh?' 'No thanks. I'm straight.' **1960** WENTWORTH & FLEXNER *Dict. Amer. Slang* 524/1 *Straight*,..honest; normal. Depending on the context, denotes that the person referred to is not dishonest, not a drug addict, not a homosexual, and so forth. **1965** *San Francisco Examiner* 5 Sept. 5/1 A lot of us have 'straight' friends. **1966** A. YOUNG in A. Chapman *New Black Voices* (1972) 147 Why dont you buy this joint off me so I can be straight for lunch. **1967**, etc. [see FREAK *sb.*[1] 4c]. **1968** *Globe & Mail Mag.* (Toronto) 13 Jan. 6/1 Some straight (heterosexual) people also go there to watch the drag show (a floor show put on by men dressed and acting like women). **1971** *Psychol. Today* May 43/1, I can see patterns, form, figures, meaningful designs in visual material that does not have any particular form when I'm straight. **1971** 'M. UNDERWOOD' *Trout in Milk* xx. 167 'Every perversion catered for.'.. 'And what's yours, Mr Slatter?'.. 'I'm straight.' **1975** *N.Y. Times Bk. Rev.* 30 Nov. 42/3 A fastidiously distant man without the hint of a sex life, straight or otherwise. **1976** J. CROSBY *Snake* (1977) ix. 43 Few of the revolutionary youth..threw it all up and came back to the straight world. **1978** V. MARTIN *Set in Motion* v. 96, I wish I had some dope. I haven't been straight this long in years. **1981** Q. CRISP *How to become a Virgin* vi. 88 All his spare attention was given to pointing out which bars were gay or had been gay, which restaurants were straight though run by homosexuals and so on.

7. a. Not oblique; either vertical or horizontal. Hence, ***a straight eye***: ability to see whether an object is placed straight.

c **1600** SHAKS. *Sonn.* cxxi. 11, I may be straight though they them selues be beuel. **1865** DICKENS *Mut. Fr.* I. vi, In its whole constitution it had not a straight floor. **1901** *Daily News* 21 Sept. 6/4 As to the machine stitching, there is very little difficulty about that to anyone who has a straight eye. *Mod.* I don't think that picture is quite straight.

b. *Cricket.* Of the bat: Held so as not to incline to either side. Freq. in phr. ***to play a straight bat*** and varr. Also *fig.* Hence, ***straight play***, play with the bat held straight.

1843 'A WYKHAMIST' *Pract. Hints on Cricket* 7 The secret of all good Batting..is the playing with a straight or upright Bat. **1851** W. CLARKE *Pract. Hints on Cricket* in E. V. Lucas *Hambledon Men* (1907) 167 By the handle of the bat being nearer the bowler than the blade (always bearing in mind to keep it straight), the ball will be prevented from rising. **1851** PYCROFT *Cricket Field* iii. (1854) 45 [He] always insisted on keeping the left elbow well up; in other words, on straight play. **1897** *Encycl. Sport* I. 219/2 (Cricket), 'How beautifully straight his bat is!' is a remark often made about a good batsman. As a matter of fact 'upright' would be a more correct term than 'straight', but 'straight' is the almost invariable epithet. **1944** BLUNDEN *Cricket Country* vii. 79 He simply played the straight-bat game. **1973** *Times* 11 June 13/7 The British too..owed much of their greatness to their own self-esteem, and to the legend of straight bat, stiff upper lip, probity and detachment. **1975** *Times* 1 Dec. 5/1 Mr Wilson and Mr Callaghan intend to play a straight bat at the EEC conference. **1979** 'J. LE CARRÉ' *Smiley's People* (1980) xiv. 164 When it came to the big stuff he always played a straight bat.

8. a. Predicatively: In proper order, not ruffled or disarranged. Esp. in colloq. phr. ***to keep a straight face*** (**†*one's face straight***): to refrain from laughing.

1831 *Society* I. 64 The pleasure of seeing her kept his temper straighter than usual. **1837** CARLYLE *Fr. Rev.* II. I. ii, It would make all so straight again. **1847** HELPS *Friends in C.* I. vi. 92, I prefer real life..where there is no third volume [as in a novel] to make things straight. **1860** THACKERAY *Lovel* iii, Lay them books straight. Put the volumes together, stupid! **1885** 'MRS. ALEXANDER' *Valerie's Fate* iii, Come and put your hair straight. **1887** P. FENDALL *Sex to Last* III. x. III. 220 Five minutes' conversation..will set everything straight. **1888** HONNOR MORTEN *Hospital Life* 73 The small patients lay quiet in their cribs; everything was straight for the night. **1897** *Spectator* 25 Sept. 408/1 The story..is one which few people, to use an expressive vulgarism, will be able to read 'with a straight face'. **1953** H. MILLER *Plexus* (1963) iv. 137 All I felt called upon to do was to keep a straight face and pretend that everything was kosher. **1972** J. PORTER *Meddler & her Murder* x. 128 Miss Jones..managed to keep a straight face... The margarine represented a small secret triumph. **1974** *Scotsman* 22 Apr. p. ix, Only in oil can you break off kelly and set down on rams while keeping a straight face.

b. *colloq.* Of accounts: Settled up, leaving nothing owing.

1613 *Nottingham Rec.* IV. 316 Southwell pence beinge in arrerage..Maister Hill..shall pay the same..and so to sett ytt straight for this tyme. **1798** T. MORTON *Speed the Plough* IV. i. (1800) 52 Zur Philip did send vor I, about the money I do owe 'un; and said as how he'd make all strait between us. **1900** *Westm. Gaz.* 12 Apr. 7/1 He goes away with a straight book.

c. Of a person: Having settled one's differences (*with* another); also, having balanced one's account, 'even'; free from debt.

1730 P. WALKDEN *Diary* (1866) 108 This morning Thomas Harrison had my horse a gate with a load of oats to the Lum..in return for his horse that I had once thither with a load of oats, so that we are now straight in the case. **1894** MRS. DYAN *Man's Keeping* (1899) 262 She..urged him to strive to get straight once more with his conscience and his God. **1914** F. M. FORD *Let.* 22 Dec. (1965) 60 Of course if Conrad is not yet straight I don't want to exact this. **1960** *Jazz Rev.* Sept.–Oct. 14 He was straight at this time —saved his money and everything. **1966** *Listener* 8 Sept. 335/2 In the ten years after the war we made a huge effort to get straight by austerity and stringent controls.

d. In colloq. phrases, as ***to get*** (***something***) ***straight***, to make (something) clear, to reach an understanding; ***to keep*** (***someone***) ***straight***, to keep (someone) informed.

1862 J. BLACKWOOD *Let.* 17 Mar. in *Geo. Eliot Lett.* (1956) IV. 22, I suppose there is nothing in your remarks about language to clash with my paper last month. Keep me straight about this. **1920** S. LEWIS *Main St.* xiv. 167 Will,.. I must get this straight. Some one said..all the doctors hate each other. **1946** MEZZROW & WOLFE *Really Blues* viii. 124 Get this straight, we pure-and-simple jazzmen didn't scoff the 'serious' composers. *Ibid.* xi. 194 When he got straight on my version of *My Blue Heaven* I played the second harmony sax part along with him. **1946** J. B. PRIESTLEY *Bright Day* x. 320 I'm going to risk telling you something... It's all ancient history, but..we might as well get it straight.

e. *U.S. slang.* Of a drug-user: drugged, 'high' (HIGH *a.* 16 c). Cf. sense 6 d above.

1946 MEZZROW & WOLFE *Really Blues* xii. 217, I know I'm gonna get straight now, I know you gonna put me on. **1951** *Life* 11 June 120/1 While the cops were in the apartment they seized five teen-agers who came up to be put straight. **1965** *Life* 26 Feb. 86/4 Once the addict has had his shot and is 'straight' he may become amiably, though briefly, industrious. **1971** E. E. LANDY *Underground Dict.* 178 *Straight*,..1...off drugs; clean. 2. A drug addict will use the word 'straight' to mean to use a drug—eg. *I've got to get straight.*

9. orig. *U.S.* **a.** Unmixed, undiluted; of spirits, 'neat'. Also qualifying a designation of a political party: Strict, rigid, extreme. ***to vote the straight ticket***: to vote for all the official candidates of one's party; also *fig.*

1856 *N.Y. Courier & Enquirer* Sept. (Bartlett), The present candidate of the straight Whigs for the Vice-Presidency. **1857** *N.Y. Times* 14 Oct. (ibid.), The straight Republican Convention is to meet to-morrow. **1862** J. R. MORRIS in *Congr. Globe* 7 July 3158/3, I supported the straight Democratic ticket. **1865** VISCT. MILTON & W. B. CHEADLE *N.-W. Passage by Land* ii. (1867) 33 As a Yankee would express it, they were geese and ducks 'straight'—*i.e.*, without anything else whatever. **1873** LELAND *Egypt. Sketch-Bk.* 146 Pains have been taken to add ornament, though every other structure near it be of mud 'straight' —or unmingled and plain. **1874** *Slang Dict.* 312 *Straight*, an American phrase peculiar to dram-drinkers; similar to our word neat. **1879** TOURGEE *Fool's Err.* vii. 28, I allers did like my liquor clar,—clar an' straight. **1892** W. PIKE *Barren Ground N. Canada* 128 We had bread at every meal, which is in itself a luxury after four months of straight meat. **1901** W. CHURCHILL *Crisis* viii. 432 Stephen had never learned to like straight whiskey. **1934** J. O'HARA *Appointment in Samarra* (1935) vi. 171 You want ginger ale with yours, or straight? **1940** H. G. WELLS *Babes in Darkling Wood* II. iii. 194 She'll give up the ice, I expect, and settle down to straight Martini and gin. **1950** 'D. DIVINE' *King of Fassarai* xv. 119 'I'd like a coke.'.. 'Little rum in it?'.. 'Straight coke.' **1977** M. HINXMAN *One-Way Cemetery* xx. 146 She handed him his glass. 'Soda?' 'Straight.' **1979** *Guardian* 30 Oct. 10/4 People who vote the straight green ticket—rucksacks, sperm whales, recycling, and free-range hens.

b. ***straight poker, whist***, etc.: the game in its unmodified form. ***straight four, five, six, straight flush***: see quots.

1864 W. B. DICK *Amer. Hoyle* 167 It [*sc.* Twenty-Deck Poker] is controlled by the same rules as Common or Straight Poker. **1882** *Poker; how to play it* 56 A Straight Flush (that is, a sequence of five cards, all of the same suit). *Ibid.* 72 Straight Poker or Bluff, as it is sometimes called, is played with a pack of fifty-two cards. **1895** G. J. MANSON *Sporting Dict.*, *Straight Five*, a sequence or rotation of fives. *Ibid.*, *Straight Four.* **1901** R. F. FOSTER *Bridge* Introd. p. xii, Bridge..has completely taken the place of straight whist.

c. Of a grade of flour (see quots.).

1859 BARTLETT *Dict. Amer.* (ed. 2) 454 *Straight*, even or uniform in quality. A term used in Commerce, and particularly among flour-dealers. **1883** E. INGERSOLL in *Harper's Mag.* June 78/1 Bakers..use what is known as 'wheat' or 'straight' flour, which is the product of the five reductions, all the subsequent processes through which the middlings pass in making fine flour being omitted.

d. *Mus.* Applied to a kind of jazz characterized by adherence to a score or set orchestration and a lack of improvisation, or to a player of this kind of jazz. Also, of music or a musician: 'serious' or dance-band as opposed to jazz; = LEGITIMATE *a.* 2 e.

1926 *Melody Maker* Feb. 15/2 His father was.. one of the finest 'straight' saxophonists in the world. **1927** *Ibid.* Apr. 329/3 The band is well drilled.. but relies on stereotyped orchestration and 'straight' rendering. Moreover, there is nothing like enough solo work. **1928** [see HOT *a.* 8 g]. **1934** S. R. NELSON *All about Jazz* ii. 40 This training is very useful where an orchestra has played for the cabaret, or any diversion where 'straight' music is employed. **1936** *Swing Music* Apr. 37/1 Red Nichols was.. a great 'straight' jazz trumpet. **1938** *Oxf. Compan. Music* 777/2 It appears that the terms *Straight Jazz* (or *Sweet Jazz*) and *Hot Jazz* apply respectively to jazz played as written and jazz in which the extempore element is prominent. **1947** *Penguin Music Mag.* May 28 Antony Hopkins has been much more affected by the jazz element in other 'straight' composers' works than by the original thing. **1961** *Guardian* 16 Mar. 11/1 [He] is a 'straight' musician with some experience of jazz. **1971** *Daily Tel.* 20 Jan. 10/6 A programme which covered fields as diverse as Renaissance polyphony, newly-commissioned music, both straight and jazzy, and swinging close-harmony arrangements.

e. Of animals: pure-bred. Cf. *straight-bred*, sense 9 a of the adv. below.

1972 P. NEWTON *Sheep Thief* x. 80 They were straight merinos and pretty touchy to handle.

10. a. *Theatr.* 'Serious' as opposed to popular or comic. Cf. LEGITIMATE *a.* 2 b.

1895 *N.Y. Dramatic News* 6 July 2/1 Trilby is the only 'straight' theatrical entertainment now left in New York. **1908** *Variety* 16 May 15/1 A steady succession of comedy numbers.. gave the two 'straight' acts closing the bill an almost impossible task to accomplish. **1928** *Observer* 1 Jan. 11/4 Miss Gertrude Lawrence will then make her first appearance in 'straight' drama. **1928** *Punch* 23 May 582/3 The character-actors have no doubt an easier task than the 'straight' actors. **1932** *Daily Express* 27 June 3/3 Being determined to go into straight plays, she learned some poetry. **1937** *Sunday Express* 21 Feb. 21/5 Luckily he has Naunton Wayne handling his best lines, revealing in his first straight part an easy sense of situation and character to back up his known comedy brilliance. **1959** H. PINTER *Birthday Party* I. 4 This is a straight show... No dancing or singing. .. They just talk. **1970** *Guardian* 19 Aug. 6/4 Feldman.. has since appeared as a straight man.. in a couple of Johnny Speight TV plays. **1981** V. GLENDINNING *Edith Sitwell* xi. 151 Edith.. loved music halls, which she preferred to the straight theatre.

b. *Vaudeville.* Applied to a performer who assumes a passive role as a feeder (FEEDER 11) or butt for a comedian; also *transf.*

1923 *N.Y. Times* 15 July VI. 1/6 The method of the comedy team remains more or less unvaried. The team is composed, in the first place, of a comedian and a 'straight' man. **1933** P. GODFREY *Back-Stage* iii. 37 The music-hall cross-talk act, where one of the characters is 'straight' and the other the comedian. **1957** [see FEEDER 11]. **1961** *Sunday Express* 18 June 19/1 For eight years he had been 'straight man' to Sid Field, one of the great comics. **1973** R. HILL *Ruling Passion* II. ii. 101 Pascoe looked doubtful. He was used to playing Dalziel's straight man. **1979** J. BARNETT *Backfire is Hostile!* i. 26 Smith knew he was being used as a straight man but played along with it.

c. Applied to a 'serious' novel, film, etc. which employs the conventional techniques of its art form.

1936 'J. TEY' *Shilling for Candles* vi. 59 She was at that time shooting her her first straight film. **1942** H. HAYCRAFT *Murder for Pleasure* ix. 203 Mr. Carr-Dickson.. has been an incomparable boon to the English 'straight' detective story. **1953** A. UPFIELD *Murder must Wait* x. 90, I write.. straight novels, not these beastly thrillers. **1977** *Listener* 30 June 866/4 Most crime reviewers have.. been arraigned by novelists who think they would have got better treatment in straight novel columns. **1981** F. MCSHANE *Sel. Lett. R. Chandler* p. xv, He.. rendered the actualities of American life as vividly and independently as any 'straight' novelist.

11. *Comb.* **a.** Parasynthetic formations, unlimited in number, as ***straight-barred, -barrelled, -billed, -bitted, -bodied, -edged, -fibred, -grained, -hammed, -horned, -jointed, -leaved, -legged, -limbed, -minded, -necked, -nosed, -ribbed, -shaped, -sided, -stocked, -tusked, -veined, -winged*** adjs.

1832 J. RENNIE *Consp. Butterfl. & Moths* 171 The *Straight-barred Elm (*Cnephasia rectifasciana*). **1709** *Lond. Gaz.* No. 4540/8 Stray'd or Stoln,.. a black Gelding,.. full chested, *streight barrel'd. **1811** SHAW *Gen. Zool.* VIII. 329 One of the most beautiful of the *strait-billed Humming-Birds. *c* **1875** *Cassell's Nat Hist.* III. 309 The Parrots are divided into two large sections,.. the Parrots proper.. and.. the straight-billed Parrots (*Psittaci orthognathi*). **1665** REA *Flora* I. 4 With a *straight-bitted Spade, or Turving-Iron.. they will easily be flaied and taken up. **1603–26** BRETON *Mad World* (Grosart) 8/1 A.. faire-handed, small-footed, *straight-bodied.. gentlewoman. **1689** *Lond. Gaz.* No. 2493/4 A Bay Mare,.. streight Body'd,.. strayed.. on the 30th past. **1833** LOUDON *Encycl. Archit.* §690 Wooden hooping, or *straight-edged laths, may be substituted for iron. **1886** *Encycl. Brit.* XXI. 819/2 s.v. *Shipbuilding*, Plank is either worked in parallel strakes, when it is called 'straight-edged', or [etc.]. **1785** ROY in *Phil. Trans.* LXXV. 434 Very *straight-fibred deal was not.. affected.. by the humidity of the air. **1753** F. PRICE *Brit. Carpenter* (ed. 3) 6 With some good, dry, and *strait-grain'd English oak. **1843** HOLTZAPFFEL *Turning* I. 52 Straight-grained pines and mahogany. **1903** *Westm. Gaz.* 31 Oct. 7/1 The purse is made of straight-grained, dark green morocco leather. **1714** TICKELL in Steele *Poet. Misc.* 181 Truss-thigh'd, *straight-ham'd, and Fox-like form'd his Paw. **1854** A. ADAMS etc. *Man. Nat. Hist.* 200 *Straight-horned Snout-Beetles (Orthocerata). **1887** MORRIS *Odyss.* XII. 348 His straight-horned oxen. **1711** *Lond. Gaz.* No. 4849/4 [Of a horse.] *Strait jointed behind. **1833** LOUDON *Encycl. Archit.* § 239 To lay good.. straight-jointed floors in the sitting-rooms and passage. **1553** PAYNELL tr. *Dares Phryg. Destr. Troy* C v b, Polixena... her members well made and well proporcioned, long fingerde, *streight legged. **1898** CONAN DOYLE *Trag. Korosko* v. 137 He walked slowly away, with his straight-legged military stride. **1909** MRS. H. WARD *Daphne* iii. 49 The chairs and sofas were a trifle stiff and straight-legged. **1622** BACON *Hen. VII*, 246 Hee was a Comely Personage, a little aboue Iust Stature, well and *straight limmed, but slender. **1860** FORSTER *Gr. Remonstr.* 102 Robert Car was a poor but handsome young Scot,.. straight-limbed, well-favoured,.. and smooth-faced. **1841** THACKERAY *Gt. Hoggarty Diam.* vii, 'Mr. Titmarsh,' says he,.. 'you seem to be an honest, *straight-minded young fellow'. **1839** YARRELL *Suppl. Brit. Fishes* 47 The *Straight-nosed Pipe-Fish, *syngnathus ophidion*. **1821** S. F. GRAY *Brit. Plants* I. 75 Nervature... *Straight-ribbed, *rectinervia, penninervia*. Ribs running in a straight line. **1825** SCOTT *Talism.* i, A long, broad, *straight-shaped, double-edged falchion. **1816** J. SMITH *Panorama Sci. & Art* I. 144 A *straight-sided canopy is sometimes used. **1871** W. MORRIS in Mackail *Life* (1899) I. 268 A terrible chasm, deep, straight-sided, and with water at the bottom. **1598** BARRET *Theor. Warres* 33 A straight-stocked peece, I hold for the better. **1882** W. B. DAWKINS in *Contemp. Rev.* Aug. 307 The *straight-tusked elephant. **1839** LINDLEY *Introd. Bot.* 132 *Straight-veined [leaves]. **1854** A. ADAMS etc. *Man. Nat. Hist.* 209 *Straight-winged Insects (Orthoptera).

b. In concord with sb., forming combs. used *attrib.* or as adjs., as in ***straight-line, -needle, -tube.***

1843 *Penny Cycl.* XXV. 425/2 The square or *straight-line chuck.. is peculiar to the rose-engine. **1884** F. J. BRITTEN *Watch & Clockm.* 249 [A] Straight Line Lever.. a form of Lever Escapement chiefly used in foreign watches, in which the escape wheel arbor, the pallet staff, and the balance staff are planted in a straight line. **1900** *Engineering Mag.* XIX. 728 A straight-line motion of a moveable piston. **1875** KNIGHT *Dict. Mech.* 2120/2 The sewing-machine for leather is similar to the ordinary *straight-needle machine, but is stronger. **1901** *Scotsman* 13 Mar. 10/7 Four types of large *straight tube boilers.

c. Special combinations and collocations: **straight A('s)** *U.S.*, uniform top grades; **straight arch**, an arch having radiating joints but a straight intrados and extrados line; **straight-armed** *a. Cricket*, with the arm unflexed; *spec.* designating a style of round-arm bowling with a straight arm, or an exponent of this style (now *Hist.*); **straight arrow** *N. Amer. slang*, an honest or genuine person; also as *adj.* and *adv.*; **straight-backed** *a.*, (*a*) *lit.* of a person, an animal, a chair, etc.; (*b*) not bending the back for work, idle; (*c*) not given to lounging, energetic; **straight bit** (see quot.); **straight block**, a kind of joiner's plane; **straight chain** *Chem.*, a chain of atoms that is neither branched nor closed in on itself to form a ring; usu. *attrib.* (with hyphen); **straight-claw** *Zool.*, a bird of the genus *Orthonyx*; **straight coal** *Mining* (see quot.); **straight cut** *Cinemat.*, a complete cut between sequences (as opposed to a fade or a dissolve); **straight drive** *Cricket*, a drive in which the ball is struck back down the pitch towards or past the bowler; also as *v. trans.*; hence **straight driver, straight driving** *vbl. sb.*; **straight-edge(d) razor** = *straight razor* below; also *ellipt.*; **straight eight** *Mech.*, (a motor vehicle having) an internal combustion engine with eight cylinders arranged in a straight line; freq. *attrib.*; similarly ***straight four, straight six***; (cf. IN-LINE *a.* 1 a); **straight-faced** *a.*, solemn, serious (cf. sense 8 a); hence **straightfacedly** *adv.*, **straightfacedness**; **straight fight**, an election in which there are only two candidates; **straight goods** *U.S. slang*, the truth; an honest person; **straight-grain(ed)** *a.* (see quot. 1929); **straight-haired** *a.*, (*a*) having straight hair, leiotrichous; (*b*) puritanical, prim; hence **straight-hairedness**; **straight-horn** *Zool.*, an animal of the family *Orthoceratidæ*; **straight hosiery** (see quot.); **straight job** *U.S. slang*, a single-unit truck, one with its body built directly on to its chassis; **straight-joint floor** *Arch.* (see quot.); **straight leg** *U.S. Mil. slang*, a member of the ground staff as opposed to one of the flying personnel (see also quot. 1967); **straight mute**, a simple cone-shaped mute for a trumpet or trombone; **straight-necked** *a.*, having a straight neck; (of a fox) running with a straight neck or without deviation; **straight pein** *a.*, designating a type of hammer which has the pein in line with the handle; freq. *absol.* as *sb.*; **straight razor**, a razor with a long blade that folds into its handle for storage, a cut-throat razor (see CUT-THROAT 1 d); **straight-run** *a. Chem.*, (of a petroleum fraction) produced by distillation without cracking or other chemical alteration of the original hydrocarbons; **straight stall** *Mining* = *straight coal*; **straight stitch**, in *Embroidery*, a single, short, detached stitch; also as *adj.*, designating a simple type of sewing-machine; hence **straight-stitching** *a.*; **straight-tail** *Ornith.* (see quot.); **straight-time** *a.* orig. and chiefly *U.S.*, of or relating to remuneration received for work performed within normal or regular hours; also *absol.* (cf. OVERTIME *sb.* a); **straight-wing**, an insect of the family *Orthoptera*. Also STRAIGHT-EDGE.

1926 *Amer. Oxonian* July 98 It isn't merely four years of football, four years of *straight A, and ten thousand activities that make a winner [of a Rhodes Scholarship]. **1948** *Chicago Daily News* 20 Sept. 18/2 In pre-medical college Jim. S. was a brilliant student—straight A's. **1960** *Encounter* Nov. 29/1 The straight-A students.. sometimes slipped away without anyone's noticing. **1980** *TWA Ambassador* Oct. 77/2, I have a daughter who is the movie-star type, brighter than hell and has straight A's in college. **1663** GERBIER *Counsel* 63 *Staight Arches. **1842** *Civil Engin. & Arch. Jrnl.* V. 251/2 Straight Arch, or Plat Band, with joints converging to a common centre. **1827** *Sporting Mag.* Nov. 11/1 If necessary, admit the *straight-armed bowling, allowing it to go as high as the shoulder, so that the back of the hand be kept under when the ball is delivered. **1828** *Ibid.* Feb. 244/2 Straight-armed bowlers are invariably slow bowlers. **1934** W. J. LEWIS *Lang. Cricket* 31 Various obsolete names applied to round-arm bowling when it was first introduced: .. *straight-arm* (or *-armed*) *bowling*, i.e. with the arm extended horizontally. **1961** *Times* 12 July 4/5 Suttle gathering runs with that curiously rigid, straight-armed hook of his. **1969** *Time* 22 Aug. 43 The new eco-activists include groups as *straight-arrow as the Girl Scouts. **1969** *New Yorker* 11 Oct. 194 Smith, a wonderfully old-fashioned straight arrow. **1977** C. MCFADDEN *Serial* (1978) xliv. 95/1, I keep trying to tell you, I'm really a straight arrow. **1978** *Daily Colonist* (Victoria, B.C.) 6 Sept. 31/3 Tell the truth no matter what. And be straight-arrow about it. **1978** J. L. HENSLEY *Killing in Gold* iv. 52, I hated not playing it straight-arrow with Ed. **14..** in *Harrow. Hell* Introd. 25 The horss hath xxv propertes... After the asse, well-mouthid, well-wyndid, *stregth-bakked. **1819** M. EDGEWORTH *Let.* ? 10 Mar. (1971) 181 Lady Elizabeth's mother a fine straight-backed thin dried benevolent smiling eyed looking woman whom I like much. **1830** COBBETT *Rur. Rides* (1885) II. 356 No straight-backed, bloated fellow,.. called a publican. **1847** W. C. L. MARTIN *Ox* 48/1 Excellent cattle,.. large, staight-backed, deep, and broad-breasted. **1859** GEO. ELIOT *Adam Bede* xl, The mother's a whimpering thing..; however, she's a straight-backed, clean woman, none of your slatterns. **1915** BEGBIE *Cage* ii. 41 The grandmother in a straight-backed chair, the child on a stool at her feet. **1883** GRESLEY *Gloss. Coal-mining* 244 **Straight bit*, a flat or ordinary chisel for boring. **1812** P. NICHOLSON *Mech. Exerc.* 105 The *Straight Block is used for shooting short joints and mitres, instead of the jointer. **1890** J. B. TINGLE tr. *E. Hjelt's Princ Gen. Org. Chem.* I. ii. 18 If the carbon atoms of a nucleus are joined together in a single *straight chain, they are said to form a simple or normal chain. **1934** *Jrnl. Franklin Inst.* CCXVIII. 145 Among organic chemical compounds the straight-chain hydrocarbons are of particular interest because of the simplicity of their properties. **1965** PHILLIPS & WILLIAMS *Inorg. Chem.* I. iv. 138 A relatively simple example is provided by the difference between the branched and straight-chain hydrocarbons. **1971** Straight chain [see *ladder polymer* s.v. LADDER *sb.* 6]. **1894–5** LYDEKKER *Roy. Nat. Hist.* III. 438 The.. yellow-headed *straight-claw (*Orthonyx ochrocephalus*), is characterised by the short and straight beak. **1883** GRESLEY *Gloss. Coal-mining* 244 **Straight coal*, an excavation made in the Thick coal, having the solid coal left on three sides of it. **1953** K. REISZ *Technique Film Editing* iii. 245 While the spectator is still laughing, he is already plunged—through a *straight cut—into the next sequence. **1959** Straight cut [see CUT *sb.*[2] 15]. [**1877** C. BOX *Eng. Game Cricket* xxvi. 449 *Drive*, a hard forward hit; it is designated on, off, or straight according to the course taken by the ball.] **1898** K. S. RANJITSINHJI *With Stoddart's Team* (ed. 4) iv. 72 McKenzie plays with a very straight bat,.. most of his runs being obtained by *straight drives on either side of the bowler. **1927** G. A. TERRILL *Out in Glare* v. 95 Clement played his first ball defensively; .. off-drove the next for three. Fosbery straight-drove the next for two. **1959** J. FINGLETON *Four Chukkas to Australia* xvi. 135 He straight-drove Davidson. **1971** *Times* 15 Feb. 8/2 Jenner .. made some punishing straight drives off Lever. **1925** *Country Life* 8 Aug. 214/1 Of all the glorious *straight drivers I have ever seen, commend me to J. N. Crawford. **1904** P. F. WARNER *How we recovered the Ashes* vii. 119 There was a Lyons-like power about his *straight driving. **1972** *Sat. Rev.* (U.S.) 27 May 4/2 When I was a small boy, my father used a *straight-edged razor... I tried using a straightedge, but I was a generation too late... I went over to the safety razor. **1973** J. ROSSITER *Manipulators* i. 8 He shaved his flat cheeks.. with a straight-edge razor. **1926** A. HUXLEY *Jesting Pilate* II. 197 Heroes invariably have the time to drive in *Straight-Eights from Salt Lake City to New York. **1928** *Punch* 17 Oct. 439/3 Several new 'straight eight' cars have recently been announced. The advantages of the eight-in-line unit are obvious. **1954** *Motor Man.* (ed. 35) ii. 25 (*caption*) Daimler Straight-eight 36 h.p. petrol engine. **1963** BIRD & HUTTON-STOTT *Veteran Motor Car* 53 This formed the basis for the small, fast revving straight-eights so particularly associated with the name of Bugatti. **1982** *Times Lit. Suppl.* 5 Mar. 249/5 The engine of the Type-41 Bugatti illustrated.. is a straight-eight with all its cylinders in line. **1975** *Business Week* 30 June 14/2 Pierce was, Crichton tells us with the *straight-faced assurance that makes his readers wonder what is fiction and what is fact, 'a man destined to be so notorious that Queen Victoria herself expressed a desire to meet him'. **1983** *Washington Post* 6 Mar. H 6/3 O'Down just turned 21. With the innocence of the newly famous, he's straight-faced when he says, 'I want to grow old gracefully.' **1977** *Guardian Weekly* 17 July 11/3 They were told *straight-facedly [that] the new Israeli premier was going all out to convince the Arabs that in their own interests Israel should keep the West Bank. **1982** *N. & Q.* Apr. 142/1 One cannot help feeling that the straight-facedness of the glossing.. detracts from the complete understanding of the passage. [**1900** *Times* 3 Oct.

8/2 Dundee, where there will this time be a straight party fight, without the interposition of a labour candidate.] **1910** *Times* 12 Jan. 9/1 Another very noticeable feature of the London elections is that there will be a *straight fight between the Government candidate and the Opposition nominee in all but three constituencies. **1957** *Ann. Reg. 1956* 26 Comparisons had been complicated by the appearance or disappearance of Liberal candidates. Here..the comparison was between two straight fights. **1959** *Motor Man.* (ed. 36) ii. 38 The crankshaft is arranged so that the pistons operate in exactly the same manner as they do in a *straight-four engine. **1892** *Harper's Mag.* Dec. 138 I'm givin' yu' *straight goods, yu' see. **1903** B. KENNEDY *Sailor Tramp* I. xix. 156 What do I know..about him? Why that he's all right. That he's straight goods. **1922** E. O'NEILL *Anna Christie* III. 181 You'd die laughing sure if I said that meeting you that funny way that night in the fog, and afterwards seeing that you was straight goods stuck on me, had got me to thinking for the first time. **1922** —— *Hairy Ape* IV. 40 Is all dat straight goods? **1880** J. W. ZAEHNSDORF *Art Bookbinding* xx. 88 Should the leather be '*straight grain', it must only be creased in the one direction of the grain. **1929** C. J. H. DAVENPORT *Roger Payne* ii. 44 He [*sc.* Roger Payne] found that if a piece of morocco was slightly damped, and then vigorously rolled on itself by hand, that all its original markings became much more apparent. This leather when dry was found to have acquired a permanent surface configuration like a series of small, more or less parallel, wavy lines, which is now known as 'straight grain', largely found, for the first time, on many of Payne's finest bindings. **1963** Straight-grain [see *paste grain* s.v. PASTE *sb.* 8]. **1892** W. L. ANDREWS *Roger Payne* 16 The materials used by Roger Payne as coverings for his bindings were almost without exception either *straight-grained morocco or russian leather. **1956** H. M. NIXON *Broxbourne Library Styles & Designs Bookbindings* 193/1 Material: Red straight-grained morocco, over pasteboards. **1841** MIALL in *Nonconformist* I. 242 One may hear timid, down-looking, *straighthaired dissenters who speak as small as a halfpenny whistle. **1910** J. MCCABE *Prehist. Man* vii. 102 One of the great divisions of humanity, the 'straight-haired' men, or Leiotrichi. **1850** HUXLEY in L. Huxley *Life & Lett.* (1900) I. 52, I had expected a good deal of *straight-hairedness (if you understand the phrase) and methodistical puritanism, but I find it quite otherwise. **1861** P. P. CARPENTER in *Rep. Smithsonian Instit. 1860*, 167 They belonged to the Family *Orthoceratidæ*, or *Straight-horns. **1892** *Labour Commission* Gloss., **Straight Hosiery*, articles made by cutting up into lengths a long seamless piece..and stitching upon them a stocking foot or sheet sleeve. **1955** *Amer. Speech* XXX. 92 **Straight job*, a single-unit truck, usually equipped with dual wheels. **1978** S. BRILL *Teamsters* v. 170 About thirty trucks, all 'straight jobs' (that is, one-unit vehicles rather than tractors pulling trailers) were backed against a ramshackle warehouse. **1842** GWILT *Archit.* §2168 The chief sorts of floors may be divided into those which are *folded*,..and those which are **straight joint*, in which the side joints of the boards are continuous throughout their direction. **1951** *Sun* (Baltimore) 24 July 17/3 Witnessing the maneuver from the sidelines were a number of anxious ground officers or '*straight legs'. **1967** *Everybody's Mag.* (Austral.) 18 Jan. 36/2 Today, in Vietnam, Australians are again catching up on American Army slang... An airborne soldier is called a Trooper, and he knows his counter-part on the ground as a Straight-leg. **1926** *Melody Maker* Feb. 23/1 The modern player must be prepared to use every kind of mute, and novelties are constantly being produced. Most of the latter provide 'stunt'..effects as against the '*straight' mute, which merely softens the tone of the instrument. **1961** A. BERKMAN *Singers' Gloss. Show Business Jargon* 61 The most popular mutes for trumpet and trombone are the Straight Mute, which softens the volume about fifty per cent, retaining a certain amount of 'attack' quality; the Cup Mute, [etc.] **1577** B. GOOGE *Heresbach's Husb.* III. 127 He is coloured lyke a fallowe Deare, *straight necked, and hye, like an Ostryge, his head something higher then a Cammels. **1887** *Field* 19 Feb. 232/3 They missed the good straight-necked fox from this covert which was brought to hand not long since at Terringham. **1900** *Westm. Gaz.* 12 Jan. 3/1 Scent was not of that reliable description which conduces to straight-necked foxes. **1904** J. L. BACON *Forge-Practice* i. 11 Several other types..are illustrated... *A* is a *straight-pene, ..and *C*, a riveting-hammer. **1957** R. LISTER *Decorative Wrought Ironwork* ii. 11 Hammers..used by blacksmiths vary considerably in size and shape. One type is called a *straight pane*; its head has a slightly convex face at one end and a wedge-shaped termination or pane (sometimes formerly called a *pen*) at the other. **1964** [see PEIN *sb.*]. **1975** R. A. SALAMAN *Dict. Tools* 223/1 The Scotch pattern [of hammers used in coopering] has a round face with chamfered neck... The straight pane is used for flaring hoops..to follow the bulge of the cask. **1959** E. FENWICK *Long Way Down* v. 41 If you can use plain soap and don't mind a *straight razor. **1976** 'TREVANIAN' *Main* (1977) iv. 73, I use a straight razor. **1921** *Nat. Petroleum News* (U.S.) 15 July 76/2 Such a product as 68–70 *straight-run gasoline is made principally from fresh crude. **1934** *Industr. & Engin. Chem.* May 501/1 Similar studies were made of a 'reformed' gasoline produced by cracking a West Texas straight-run gasoline. **1973** HADLEY & TURNER in G. D. Hobson *Mod. Petroleum Technol.* (ed. 4) xii. 441 The petroleum chemicals industry can call upon a variety of feedstocks, including natural gas and straight-run oil fractions. **1973** *Guardian* 11 June 7/4 The Datsun 240K GT Skyline..[has] an ordinary *straight-six cylinder engine. **1860** *Mining Gloss., S. Staffs. Terms* 80 **Straight Stall*, an excavation made into the thick coal, having the solid coal left on three sides of it. **1918** E. A. ARCHER *Needlecraft* ix. 99, I will start with chain-stitching... Start by taking a *straight stitch on the line. **1934** M. THOMAS *Dict. Embroidery Stitches* 194 Straight or Stroke Stitch consists of single isolated satin stitches of any desired length and worked in any required direction over short traced lines which have to be covered. **1961** *Observer* 28 May 33/1 The cost of a sewing-machine can vary... Simple straight-stitch machines can be had for £25 to £30 hand operated. **1967** E. SHORT *Embroidery & Fabric Collage* ii. 51 Even on a simple *straight-stitching domestic machine a wide variety of effects may be obtained. **1843** *Penny Cycl.* XXV. 272/2, 21st Race [of Humming-birds]. The *Straight-tails... Bill very short; tail composed of long, delicate, pointed, graduated feathers. **1944** *Sun* (Baltimore) 13 Oct. 7/7 *Straight-time earnings (which include incentive payments and merit increases). **1958** *Listener* 10 July 43/2 The widely recognised problem of maintaining reasonable balance of earnings between semi-skilled workpeople paid by results and others—possibly highly skilled—who are traditionally paid on a straight-time basis. **1971** *Daily Colonist* (Victoria, B.C.) 7 Oct. 1/3 The construction workers..were working 60-hour weeks at straight time for an hourly rate of $2.27. **1842** LOUDON *Suburban Hort.* 100 *Orthoptera* (*Straight-wings).

B. quasi-*sb.* and *sb.*

1. The adj. used *absol.* (quasi-*sb.*) in certain phrases.

†**a.** ***upon straight***: upright, erect. *Obs.*

c **1400** *Destr. Troy* 3841 Burthen hade ynoghe The fete of þat freke to ferke hym aboute, Or stond vppo streght for his strong charge.

b. ***on the straight***: (*a*) along a straight line, not following irregularities of contour; (*b*) parallel with the side, as opposed to 'on the cross' = diagonally; (*c*) *slang*, behaving reputably.

1663 GERBIER *Counsel* 48 Work rated on running measure, and on the straight. **1894** *Paris Mode* I. 31/2 It is usually cut on the cross... The material is folded over to form a triangle, and in anything cut out of it in this position the threads run differently to what is cut on the straight. **1900** E. WALLACE *Writ in Barracks* 103 O the garden it is lovely—That's when Jerry's on the straight!

c. ***out of straight***: deviating from the required straight form or position; not duly rectilinear, level, or perpendicular; awry.

1678 MOXON *Mech. Exerc.* iv. 66 You have the less danger that the Joynt is wrought out of straight. **1683** *Ibid., Printing* xvi. 144 He may find out whether either or both of the Carriages are out of straight. **1851–61** MAYHEW *Lond. Labour* III. 24/1 The bone broke..and in growing together again it got out of straight.

†**d.** ***to take the straight*** (in measurement): to measure in a straight line. *Obs.*

1805 *State, Fraser of Fraserfield* 186 (Jam.) That the distance..taking the straight, and leaving the small angles and turns of the banks unnoticed, is about 2060 feet.

e. ***the straight***: the truth. Esp. in phr. ***to get (at)*** or ***hear the straight***. *U.S.*

1866 C. H. SMITH *Bill Arp* 35 You should git the straight of it from one who seen it with his eyes. **1900** E. A. DIX *Deacon Bradbury* 266 You've heared th' straight of it, Mr. Leavitt. **1902** G. H. LORIMER *Lett. Self-Made Merchant* xviii. 271 No one except the widow ever really got at the straight of Bud's conduct. **1951** H. GILES *Harbin's Ridge* xviii. 161, I wanted to get the straight about this piece of land Faleecy John wanted. **1977** 'L. EGAN' *Blind Search* iii. 38 Tell you something, I never heard the straight of that anyway. **1982** 'W. R. DUNCAN' *Queen's Messenger* xxv. 372 It will be recorded properly in the archives... The straight of it will exist.

2. A straight form or position; a level.

1645 QUARLES *Sol. Recant.* i. 2 Not all this knowledge can reduce the state Of crooked nature to a perfect Straight. **1688** HOLME *Armoury* III. xviii. (Roxb.) 142/1 Mounture the Morter, elevate the mouth of it from a streight to such a degree of height as is necessary for the slinging or casting out of the granado to the distance or place required. **1812** P. NICHOLSON *Mech. Exerc.* 142 Winding Sticks are..for the purpose of ascertaining whether a surface be straight or not, if not, the surface must be brought to a straight by trial. **1904** GALLICHAN *Fishing Spain* 162 The rod flew back to the straight, and the line came mournfully limp to the bank. A grand fish lost!

3. a. A straight portion, e.g. of a race-course (see quot. 1897), railway, or road; also *fig.* ***straight of breadth*** (*Naut.*): see quot. 1846; ***back straight***: see BACK- B.; ***home straight*** = HOME-STRETCH (cf. STRETCH *sb.* 8).

1846 A. YOUNG *Naut. Dict.* 325 *Straight of breadth*, in shipbuilding, the space before, at, and abaft the dead-flat, in which the ship is of the same uniform breadth. **1864** *Field* 16 July 41/2 Three-quarters of a mile from home Fisherman's Daughter began to draw up to the leaders; on entering the straight she went up to Spitfire Kitty, and heading her ..went on with the lead. **1894** CROCKETT *Raiders* xlii. 355 The beast that hunted me gaining ever on the straight, and I at the turnings. **1897** *Daily News* 13 Sept. 7/2 Then there are frequent and long stretches of 'straight,' that delight of the railway engineer. **1897** *Encycl. Sport* I. 62/2 (Athletics) *Straight*, the section of the track between the last bend and the winning post. **1903** *T.P.'s Weekly* 2 Jan. 248/1 Good, I'm in the straight now!.. Thank Heaven that's done. **1913** *Times* 1 Sept. 12/1 Seremond..retained his place, and when presently the field turned into the straight he was still in front. **1953** K. AMIS *Lucky Jim* i. 15 The car darted forward on to the straight. **1958** *Times* 20 Aug. 2/7 Miss Itkina, of Russia, used the inside lane intelligently and was well ahead of the opposition entering the long home straight. **1968** P. DICKINSON *Weathermonger* iv. 59 You'll have to do the map-reading... I'll teach you as soon as we come to a safe bit of straight where we can't get surprised. **1976** *West Lancs. Even. Gaz.* 13 Dec. 9/1 (Advt.), Scalextric, including pits, chicane, straights, 90 degree. **1977** *Arab Times* 14 Dec. 10/2 In the longer sprint, the 400 m, Ayad Mooshari and Ali Sulaiman were easily the strongest runners in the home straight.

b. *Aeronaut.* A run or flight in a straight line (without turning).

1911 *Aeroplane* 19 Oct. 471/2 In evening Sabelli rolling and Richey doing straights on brevet machine, the latter damaging chassis slightly in landing. **1914** H. ROSHER *In Royal Naval Air Service* (1916) i. 20 Yesterday I did five straights (straight flights) alone.

4. *Geom.* A straight line. *rare.*

1892 G. B. HALSTED *Elem. Synth. Geom.* 4 The intersection of two planes is called a straight line, or simply a straight. **1904** —— *Rational Geom.* 3 Two distinct straights cannot have two points in common.

5. a. In Poker and other games: A series of five cards in sequence but not of the same suit. ***inside straight***, four cards which will form a straight if a fifth card of a particular value is added.

1841 *Spirit of Times* 1 May 102/1 This last name [*sc.* Falseful] is taken from the players of *twenty-deck poker*, and is used by them to represent a '*straight*', or ace, king, queen, jack, and ten. **1866** C. H. SMITH *Bill Arp* 39 The Yankees had a strait, which would have taken Forrest and raked down the pile. **1882** *Poker; how to play it* 16 A Sequence (sometimes called a 'straight'). *Ibid.* 55 If more than one player holds a straight, the straight headed by the highest card wins. **1894** MASKELYNE *Sharps & Flats* 84 A 'four'; which can only be beaten when 'straights' are played by a 'straight flush'—in other words, a sequence of five cards, all of the same suit. **1897** R. F. FOSTER *Compl. Hoyle* 182 (Poker), In straights, the highest card of the sequence wins. **1903** 'O. HENRY' *Roads of Destiny* 210 He always would play jack, queen, king, ace, deuce for a straight. **1934** M. ELLINGER *Poker* 163 The odds against filling an inside straight flush are 3 to 1. **1951** *Amer. Speech* XXVI. 99/2 *Inside straight*, a possible straight which is open in the middle, for example: 4-5-7-8. It takes a gun shot to hit it. **1968** V. NABOKOV *King, Queen, Knave* p. ix, I can only hope that my good old partners, replete with full houses and straights, will think I am bluffing. **1977** G. V. HIGGINS *Dreamland* i. 11 Never draw to an inside straight.

b. *Shooting.* A perfect score, with every shot fired making a hit.

1903 *Forest & Stream* 21 Feb. 160/1 In the 10-bird event Wade..and Curran each made a straight. **1931** L. B. SMITH *Better Trapsmanship* vii. 101 In the Atlantic Indian shoot in September, 1927, there were two 100 straights turned in for the championship. **1976** *Shooting Mag.* Dec. 36/2 Three more straights [in skeet shooting] were shot by Minards, P. Spear and J. Cording.

6. *slang.* **a.** orig. *U.S.* Unadulterated or very strong whisky. Cf. sense 9 a of the adj.

1862 *Harper's Mag.* Aug. 312/1 [The] primer was simply a gill of Bourbon straight. **1905** 'O. HENRY' in *N.Y. World Mag.* 12 Nov. 8/1, I managed to soak in a little straight. **1928** *Collier's* 29 Dec. 42/2 There is Juarez whisky, for instance. It is sometimes called 'American Straight'.

b. A cigarette, esp. one containing ordinary tobacco as opposed to marijuana.

[**1923** J. MANCHON *Le Slang* 296 *A straight = a straighter = a straight cut*, une cigarette en tabac de Virginie.] **1959** *Esquire* Nov. 70 J *Straight*,..an ordinary cigarette. **1973** W. TUTE *Resident* iii. 53 'I..never will be a dope head. I don't drop and I don't smoke—except straights.' 'You mean ordinary cigarettes?' 'Yes.' **1977** *Radio Times* 1–7 Apr. 41/4 *Straights*, cigarettes.

7. a. *Vaudeville.* A stooge; a 'straight' performer (see sense 10 b of the adj. above).

1933 P. GODFREY *Back-Stage* xviii. 228 They had teamed up together, with Dora doing the 'straight' and Fred the red-nosed comedy stuff. **1941** J. P. MARQUAND *H. M. Pulham, Esquire* xxix. 312 'A straight,' Bill said. 'Don't you know what a straight is? A straight's someone in a skit who has all the jokes thrown at him.'

b. In absol. use of the adj. (sense 6 d): one who conforms to the conventions of society; one who does not take drugs; a heterosexual. *slang* (orig. *U.S.*).

1967 *Observer* (Colour Suppl.) 4 Dec. 28 *Straight*, conventional person, one who does not use cannabis. **1967** W. & J. BREEDLOVE *Swinging Set* xii. 146 The easy atmosphere..the abundant evidence of abundant wealth attract not only 'straights', but a variety of sexual thrill-seekers. **1968** J. D. MACDONALD *Pale Grey for Guilt* (1969) xii. 152 We don't bug the straights and why shouldn't they leave us alone? **1969** *Gandalf's Garden* IV. 25/2 George King ..has spent his life in a service that causes Straights to back away muttering 'crack-pot'. *c* **1971** *Come Together* III. 7/1, I have danced with a boy at a straight party where we were the only two gay people and the straights were looking at us. **1974** 'K. ROYCE' *Trap Spider* vii. 111 'I'm not having the stink of pot in this place.'.. 'You straights are all the same.' **1974** K. MILLETT *Flying* (1975) III. 279 Unctuous homosexual eager to prove its human worth to these archetypical straights. **1977** *Gay News* 24 Mar. 10/4 It was a campaign shared and supported by a number of gays—even straights. **1980** *Daily Mirror* 10 Apr. 13/4 Straights prefer 'mums and dads' type pop music made by bands like Boomtown Rats, Blondie and, more recently, Police.

8. A shoe designed to be worn on either foot.

1934 *Times* 5 Feb. 13/5 In the seventeenth century men's and women's shoes and slippers seem without exception to be straights. **1968** J. IRONSIDE *Fashion Alphabet* 125 During the Dark Ages, shoes were cut as 'straights', both shoes having the identical shape. **1976** *Sunday Post* (Glasgow) 26 Dec. 6/5 My late father used to tell of bootmaking in his young day. People ordering footwear had to say they wanted a right and left. Otherwise they were supplied with 'straights', which fitted either foot.

C. *adv.*

Certain similative phrases, as ***straight as a dart, as a stick***, etc., which primarily belong to the adj., are sometimes used colloq. in various senses of the adv. to which they have no pertinence.

1. In a straight course or line. **a.** In a straight course; directly to or from a place; without deviation or circuit; by the shortest way. Also in modified sense (often indistinguishable from sense 2): Without any intermediate destination or interruption of journey.

13.. *Bonaventura's Medit.* 1122 Se cryst aftyr hys deþ: For þy synne streyght to helle he geþ. *c* **1350** *Will. Palerne* 3592 þe Kinges sone..gart his [stede] goo, and streiȝet to him rides. *c* **1374** CHAUCER *Troylus* II. 1461 But to his neces hous, as streyt as lyne, He com. **1375** BARBOUR *Bruce* XIV. 22 Till Irland held he straucht his way. *c* **1400** *Destr. Troy* 959 Jason..stird ouer the streame streght to þe lond. **14..** *Hymns Virg. & Christ* 13 For myȝtili þou roos, & ran Streiȝt vnto þi fadir in trone. *c* **1440** *Ps. Penit.* (1894) 58 Delyvere me lord from my fon felle, For straught to the yfled am y. *c* **1450** in Aungier *Syon* (1840) 284 He schal not come at the seyd grate, but he schal go streghte into the monastery.

c **1500** *Melusine* xix. 69 Hold strayte this way and ye shal not mys of it. **1528** MORE *Dyalogue* IV. Wks. 271/2 They make a vysage as though they came streight from heauen to teache them a newe better waye. *a* **1533** BERNERS *Huon* lxiv. 220 There shall ye fynde your brother Huon, who is come strayte fro beyond yᵉ see. *c* **1643** LD. HERBERT *Autobiog.* (1824) 139 This piece of eloquence moved me so much that I went straight to his Excellency. **1687** A. LOVELL tr. *Thevenot's Trav.* I. 204 When we had seen all these things, we took our way streight to Jerusalem. **1704** SWIFT *Batt. Bks.* 253 Fame..fled up strait to Jupiter. *c* **1730** RAMSAY *Vision* xxvii, He mountit upwarts..Straicht to the milkie way. **1845** DISRAELI *Sybil* IV. vi, The nearest way to it is straight along this street. **1858** MRS. CARLYLE *Lett.* II. 380 Are you going straight to London? **1876** TREVELYAN *Life Macaulay* I. i. 16 The captain..brought a party of sailors straight to the Governor's house.

b. with advs., †*forth* (obs.), *forward, on.*

a **1400** *Minor Poems fr. Vernon MS.* xxiii. 200 þat vr fot mowe þen go Streiht forþ wiþ-outen lettyng. *c* **1450** CAPGRAVE *St. Aug.* xxv. 34 With þe next wynd he and his felauchip sailed streit on-to Cartage. **1535** STEWART *Cron. Scot.* (Rolls) II. 441 Fra Striuiling straucht on to the Eist se. **1782** MISS BURNEY *Cecilia* IX. iii, When felicity is before us ..we proceed strait forward. **1876** J. SAUNDERS *Lion in Path* iii, He went straight on to the noble palace that had been placed at the service of James II some few years before. **1887** J. ASHBY-STERRY *Cucumber Chron.* 7 She tells me, I am to keep round to the right and go straight on. I follow her directions and pass by the Priory.

c. In a straight line, not crookedly.

1530 PALSGR. 842/2 Strayt, nat crokedly, *droyt*. **1538** ELYOT *Dict.*, *Adamussim*, by rule, streight as a lyne. **1576** GASCOIGNE *Steele Gl.* 718 O that al kings, would..Hold euermore, one finger streight stretcht out, To thrust in eyes, of all their master theeues. **1655** MARQ. WORCESTER *Cent. Inv.* §76 To write in the dark as streight as by day or candle-light. **1710** SWIFT *Jrnl. to Stella* 3 Nov., I cannot write straighter in bed, so you must be content. **1875** JOWETT *Plato* (ed. 2) V. 346 The drunken man..cannot be expected to walk straight either in body or mind. **1912** WAKELING *Forged Egypt. Antiq.* ix. 102 It is not correctly shaped and should not be cut straight off across the bottom.

†**d.** With reference to position. Directly (opposite), due (east, etc.). *Obs.*

1512 *Act 4 Hen. VIII*, c. 1 §1 The haven of Brest lyeth streight ayenst the South see costes of..Cornwall. **1530** PALSGR. 823/1 Strayght over agaynste,..*vis a vis*. **1820** BELZONI *Egypt & Nubia* II. 237 The tomb faces the north-east, and the direction of the whole runs straight south-west.

e. In a straight direction; not obliquely; directly to a mark or object, or following a moving object without deviation.

1535 COVERDALE *Prov.* iv. 25 Let thine eye lyddes loke straight before the. **1552** ABP. HAMILTON *Catech.* (1884) 28 A man..can nocht..gyd his lyif evin and strecht to the plesour of God without direction of the commandis. **1601** *Reg. Mag. Sig. Scot.* 449/1 Discending eist the said gait lineallie throche the lie, straucht throw the Brounfauld. **1638** JUNIUS *Paint. Ancients* 27 The statues..standing in a lifelesse posture with..their hands hanging straight downe. **1669** STURMY *Mariner's Mag.* I. ii. 4 When you espy any Island,..by looking straight upon the Compass, you shall know upon what Point of the Compass the Object beareth from you. **1678** MOXON *Mech. Exerc.* v. 95 And straight through the Stuff, as Work-men call it; that is, in a Geometrical term. perpendicularly through the upper and under-side. **1812** *Sporting Mag.* XXXIX. 187 The combatants hit strait with one hand at the head. **1821** SCOTT *Kenilw.* xiv, Each..looked straight upon the wall which was opposite to them, without speaking to his companion. **1833** NYREN *Yng. Cricketer's Tutor* (1902) 13 If such an accident should happen, and the ball have been delivered straight to the wicket. **1857** G. A. LAWRENCE *Guy Liv.* iii. 17 He not only went straight as a die, but rode *to* hounds instead of *over* them. **1865** A. TROLLOPE *Hunting Sk.* 8 And he will ride this year!.. He will ride straight. **1886** STEVENSON *Kidnapped* iv, He..looked this time straight into my eyes. **1890** CONAN DOYLE *White Company* viii, I am a man who shoots straight at his mark. **1897** HENTY *At Agincourt* i. 13 There is not one of his age who can send an arrow so straight to the mark. **1907** J. H. PATTERSON *Man-Eaters of Tsavo* xxvii. 299 Our party of five, including one lady who rode and shot equally straight.

f. With additional notion, which sometimes becomes the substantive sense: All the way, continuously to the end; 'right' *across, through,* etc. †Also with reference to time.

1446 LYDG. *Nightingale Poems* i. 198 Fro morow to nyght be-tokenes All the tyme, Syth thou wast born streyght tyll þat thou dye. **1756** NUGENT *Montesquieu's Spir. Laws* VIII. xxi. (1758) I. 181 [They] march strait up to the capital. **1840** PARKER *Gloss. Archit.* (ed. 5), *Reveal, Revel*... The term is principally used in reference to apertures which are cut straight through a wall, like modern doors and windows.

g. *to think straight*: to think clearly or logically. *colloq.*

a **1916** H. JAMES *Sense of Past* (1917) II. 60 He had already ..asked himself when he should be able so to detach himself as to think at all straight about his book. **1973** 'C. AIRD' *His Burial Too* xiii. 115, I can't begin to think straight as it is. **1980** P. G. WINSLOW *Counsellor Heart* x. 137 He rubbed his forehead. 'I haven't been thinking straight. Excuse me.'

2. a. Immediately, without delay: = STRAIGHTWAY. Now *poet.* or *arch.*

a **1300** *Cursor M.* 9484 Nu has him sathanas in wald,..To wais seruis straitt he him eild. *c* **1375** *Sc. Leg. Saints* xli. (*Agnes*) 312 He gert thonnir & fire-slacht Stirk done þe payanis þar stracht. **1478** *Maldon* (Essex) *Court Rolls* Bundle 50, No. 10b, They ii. spake no word, butt streyte they smete at him wyth her wepynes. *c* **1520** SKELTON *Magnyf.* 1592 Let se what ye say; shewe it strayte. **1530** PALSGR. 813/2 Straycht, *a coup*. **1580** G. HARVEY *Three Proper Lett.* 38 If so be goods decrease, then straite decreaseth a goods friend. *a* **1608** RALEGH *Poems, Lie* 48 And when they do reply, straight giue them both the lie. **1632** LITHGOW *Trav.* I. 32 [She] fell straight in a sound. **1642** H. MORE *Song of Soul* II. App. 69 His Fiat spoke and streight the thing is done. **1674** J. HOWARD *Engl. Mounsieur* III. v. 34 *Wel.* Is your Lady within? *Porter.* I am not sure sir, but i'le inform you strait, your patience a little sir. **1705** STANHOPE *Paraphr.* II. 134 Whereupon the whole herd streight ran down a precipice, and were choaked in the Water. **1722** A. PHILIPS *Briton* III. v. 32 My Chariot straight; another, for the Prince. **1755** RIDLEY in *World* No. 155 V. 130 Strait a voice more dreadful than thunder burst out. **1760–72** H. BROOKE *Fool of Qual.* (1809) II. 59 She burst into tears, and straight quitted the room. **1798** COLERIDGE *Anc. Mar.* VII. vii, The boat came close beneath the ship, And straight a sound was heard. **1843** MACAULAY *Horatius* xix, The bridge must straight go down. **1849** LONGF. *Build. Ship* 1 Build me straight..a goodly vessel. **1871** R. ELLIS *Catullus* li. 9 When as I look'd on thee..Straight my tongue froze, Lesbia.

†**b.** followed by prep. Immediately *after, upon,* at the same time *with* something. Also with adv., ***straight after, forth, forthwith, upon, with.*** *Obs.*

1570–6 LAMBARDE *Peramb. Kent* 3 For straight vpon the death of Edward the Confessor, William of Normandy.. demaunded the Crowne. **1576** GASCOIGNE *Philomene* Wks. 1910 II. 184 Whom he no sooner sawe..But streight therwith his fancies fume All reason did convince. **1578** TIMME *Calvin on Gen.* i. 25 For this is the simple purpose of Moses, to shewe that the worlde..was not finished streight after the beginning, but [etc.]. *a* **1591** H. SMITH *Serm.* (1594) 358 Straight vpon this, he [*sc.* David] sayth: It is not so with the wicked. **1654** T. WHALLEY in *Ussher's Lett.* (1686) 604 Read, if you please, his Epistle, *ad Albertum Marchionem*, Dedicatory, straight after the midst.

1536 *Stories & Proph. Scripture* H iv b, And when the people creyed thus & the trompets sounded, then fell the walles of the toune [of Jericho] streyght forthwith all. **1543** GRAFTON *Contn. Harding* (1812) 568 The quene..straight vpon shewed theim the same Peter. *Ibid.* 579 When he saw that thei [*sc.* the gates] could not easely be betten downe with any thyng, streight with he set fyre on theim. **1610** HOLLAND *Camden's Brit.* (1637) 273 Dying straight after without issue.

c. ***straight off***, † ***straight an end***: immediately, at once, without deliberation or preparation. See also STRAIGHTAWAY *adv.*

1778 *Learning at a Loss* II. 147 'Twas at his House they [two lovers] broke cover. And then took off strait an End to Edinburgh. **1873** *Punch* 18 Jan. 29/1 If ever I meet a woman with lots of tin, who's faultlessly beautiful, I shall marry her straight off. **1879** MISS BRADDON *Clov. Foot* xxxvi, One of those tip-top firms in the City would have gone straight off to take counsel's opinion.

3. In an erect posture, upright. Also ***straight up. straight set up***: having an erect figure.

1535 COVERDALE *1 Esdras* ix. 46 And whan he had red out the lawe, they stode all straight vp vpon their fete. **1718** RAMSAY *Christ's Kirk Gr.* III. xviii, They..sat straught Upon 't. **1852** MRS. STOWE *Uncle Tom's C.* vii, 'Mas'r,' said Tom—and he stood very straight—'I was jist [etc.].' **1899** G. B. SHAW *You Never Can Tell* II. (1907) 261 *Waiter*... Very high-spirited young gentleman, sir: very manly and straight set up.

†**4.** As an intensive (= STARK *adv.*) in ***straight blind, dead.*** *Obs.*

1387 TREVISA *Higden* (Rolls) III. 97 He put out his eiȝen in Reblata, and lad hym so in Babilon streiȝt blynde. *c* **1400** *Song of Roland* 691 Bothe streght ded the horse and his selue.

5. Honestly, honourably. Esp. in phr. ***to go straight***: (*a*) *colloq.*, to behave honourably; (*b*) *colloq.*, to reform, to desist from criminal activities (cf. sense 6 a of the adj.); (*c*) *slang*, to conform to social conventions, *spec.* by renouncing drugs or homosexuality (cf. sense 6 d of the adj.).

1845 DISRAELI *Sybil* II. xiii, 'Don't you think, Warner,' said his wife, 'that you could sell that piece to some other person?'.. 'No!' said her husband, fiercely. 'I'll go straight.' **1864** *Field* 2 July 4/1 Mr. Merry who runs his horses so straight, and who is backed with the same confidence as Lord Glasgow. **1888** [see GO v. B. 4 a]. **1888** *Times* 26 June 4/5 As a rule I believe they [*sc.* jockeys] run very straight. It is ridiculous to suppose that they are generally dishonest. **1893** F. ADAMS *New Egypt* 27 There's always room in a place like this for anyone who'll..act straight, and be content with a reasonable profit. **1940** BLUNDEN *Poems 1930–40* 76 Fixing his pinchers on the snake, Thus spake The crab: 'It's Time for you, mate, To go straight; No more crooked habits.' **1968** [see DO v. B. 11 l]. **1973** *To our Returned Prisoners of War* (U.S. Secretary of Defense, Public Affairs) 5 *Go straight*, (1) Give up the use of drugs. (2) Return to an approved life style. **1977** D. E. WESTLAKE *Enough!* ii. 59 'He's a fag.'.. 'Well, maybe he's trying to go straight.'

6. Frankly, outspokenly. Also ***straight out*** and used *colloq.* as *int.* or intensively: really, certainly, definitely.

1874 A. J. MUNBY *Diary* 22 Apr. in D. Hudson *Munby* (1972) 366 'Mrs Skeats,' I said to her, quite straight, 'Do you really think I could wish to be a lady?' **1877** SPURGEON *Serm.* XXIII. 56 Speak right straight out and do not be afraid. **1880** G. R. SIMS *Dagonet Ballads, Told to Missionary* ii, Give it us straight now, guv'nor,—what would you have me do? **1894** A. CHEVALIER *in Humorous Songs*, 'Straight,' says I, 'I'm on the job, for better or for wuss.' **1898** J. ARCH *Story Life* xii. 285 As my custom has ever been I spoke straight. **1898** J. D. BRAYSHAW *Slum Silhouettes* 3, I could kill yer wiv my little finger. I could, straight. *a* **1900** S. CRANE *Gt. Battles* (1901) 201 He knew how to speak straight as a stick to the common man. **1900** G. SWIFT *Somerley* 124 You're a good 'un to tell me straight out like this. **1907** H. RASHDALL *Theory of Good & Evil* II. 89 *n.*, Nietzsche..often says straight out what some of our English self-realizers only hint. **1914** D. H. LAWRENCE *Prussian Officer & Other Stories* 211 I'm awfully sorry, I am, straight, Lois. **1949** J. R. COLE *It was so Late* 61 She was a smasher—straight she was! **1969** D. FRANCIS *Enquiry* xi. 141 'You've never seen nothing like it,' he said. 'You wouldn't know it was a car, you wouldn't straight.'

7. orig. *U.S.* **a.** *slang.* Without adornment, admixture, or dilution. Cf. sense 9 a of the adj.

1869 S. BOWLES *Our New West* 135 We had to take our victual and drink 'straight',—plain ham and bread and butter and black coffee,—or go without. **1873** J. H. BEADLE *Undeveloped West* 528 We lived on Navajo bread, coffee, and 'commissary butter', straight. **1902** L. MCKEE *Land of Nome* 234 It was a rude shock..when I saw 'Little Casino' standing by the bar and drinking her whisky straight. **1947** *This Week Mag.* 10 May 13/2 She was a bold..camp in days gone by and still drinks her liquor straight.

b. *Jazz.* ***to play (it) straight***: to play without improvisation, but according to a score or set orchestration. Cf. sense 9 d of the adj. above.

1933 *Fortune* Aug. 90/3 It seems to be congenitally impossible for Negro dance musicians to play *straight*. **1934** S. R. NELSON *All about Jazz* iii. 66 Listen to the tune played 'straight', or as written. **1948** MANONE & VANDERVOORT *Trumpet on Wing* 26 Then we would play it straight. **1960** M. T. WILLIAMS *Art of Jazz* iii. 18 The average listener is disappointed in anything played 'straight'.

c. *colloq.* In a straightforward or simple manner; without embellishment or affectation; seriously, without 'hamming'. Cf. senses 10 a, c of the adj. above.

1961 A. BERKMAN *Singers' Gloss. Show Business Jargon* 84 *Straight*, (Mus.) As written, with no variations. (Thea[tr.]) without comedy (e.g. 'play it straight'). **1975** *Country Life* 25 Dec. 1799/1 He was able to render these [folk] songs 'straight', not in the cultured, genteel manner usually affected on the concert platform. **1976** *S. Wales Echo* 23 Nov. 1/4 Eric and Ernie played it straight but still had their 'audience' laughing. **1978** *N.Y. Times* 30 Mar. c16/1 One can strike for authenticity: collect old scripts and have them read, straight, by good actors.

8. *U.S. colloq.* Consecutively, in a row. Cf. sense 3 g of the adj. above.

1949 H. ROBBINS *Dream Merchants* (1950) 45 Haven't you got any other films? People are getting tired of the same show for three weeks straight. **1951** R. BRADBURY *Silver Locusts* 106 He had been working in one of the new colonies for ten days straight, and now he had two days off and was on his way to a party. **1973** [see SERIES 17 a]. **1976** *National Observer* (U.S.) 7 Feb. 9/4 It [*sc.* a stove] has an automatic thermostat that adjusts the damper, and can be loaded to burn for 12 hours straight.

9. *Comb.* **a.** With pples., forming adjs., as ***straight-cut, -falling, -flung, -flying, -going, -growing, -grown, -hanging, -made, -shooting, -sliding, -spoken, -standing***; also with agent-noun, as ***straight-goer***; † **straight-bounded**, bounded by straight lines; **straight-bred** *a.*, pure-bred, descended from one breed only (cf. sense 9 e of the adj.); **straight-cut** *a.*, (*a*) cut on straight lines; (*b*) *slang*, honest, respectable; (*c*) applied to cigarettes made from tobacco with the leaves cut lengthwise into long strands; freq. *absol.* as *sb.*; † **straight-pight**, having a tall and erect figure; **straight shooter** *slang* (chiefly U.S.), an honest person (cf. *square shooter* s.v. SQUARE *a.* 15 a).

1614 T. BEDWELL tr. *Schoner's De Num. Geom.* 43 Each of them is a right-angled and *straight-bounded figure. **1898** *Breeder's Gaz.* XXXIV. 199/3 The Gazette is asked for information in reference to certain so-called 'pure' or '*straight-bred' strains of pedigreed cattle. **1840** THACKERAY *Shabby-genteel Story* viii, He wore..a black *straight-cut coat, and light drab breeches. **1868** G. M. HOPKINS *Jrnl.* 14 Aug. (1959) 185 Fine. There were the travelling stack clouds with straight-cut under-sides. **1884** *Illustr. London News* 18 Oct. 383/1 Cigarette smokers..will find the Richmond Straight Cut No. 1 superior to all others. **1895** *Irish Times* 16 July 3 (Advt.), Kinney's straight-cut cigarettes. **1927** G. W. DEEPING *Kitty* ii. 21, I want some cigarettes,—straight-cuts—. **1936** J. CURTIS *Gilt Kid* xiv. 139 He could..pick up a girl, even a straight-cut, and have her walk arm-in-arm with him. **1939** JOYCE *Finnegans Wake* 156 As British as bondstrict and as straightcut as when that broken-arched traveller from Nuzuland. **1887** *Daily News* 24 June 2/1 The *straight-falling folds of pale grey silk that fall round the slim shape of a fair-haired, dreamy-eyed woman. **1896** KIPLING *Song of the English, England's Answ.* 26 Now ye must speak to your kinsmen,..After the use of the English, in *straight-flung words and few. **1925** J. GREGORY *Bab of Backwoods* ii. 17 Whatever Dick Gale had done pointed the *straight-flying arrow for Bab's following. **1857** G. A. LAWRENCE *Guy Liv.* xxvi. 248 Foxes were strong and plentiful..and during two months of open weather, many a *straight-goer had died gallantly in the midst of the wide pasture-grounds. **1865** A. TROLLOPE *Hunting Sk.* 2 Though the nature of their delight is a mystery to *straight-going men, it is manifest enough, that they do like it [*sc.* hunting]. **1884** TENNYSON *Cup* I. i. 86 [You] may be foil'd like Tarquin, if you follow Not the dry light of Rome's straight-going policy. **1765** *Museum Rust.* III. 242 Some small poles of ash, willow, or any *strait-growing wood,.. must be procured. **1888** EMILY GERARD *Land beyond Forest* li. 305 What more glorious than those *straight-grown stems. **1935** *Amer. Speech* X. 192/1 [In writing on fashion] adjectives [*sic*] in combination with present participles are common, as in *much-looking* and **straight-hanging*. **1960** *Times* 18 Jan. 15/2 Straight-hanging coats with flat backs are a speciality. **1581** C. T. in Farr *Sel. Poetry Eliz.* (1845) 395 My *straight-made lims I will not crooke, To think of death, of deuill, or God. **1611** SHAKS. *Cymb.* v. iv. 164 Beauty..for Feature, laming The Shrine of Venus or *straight-pight Minerva. **1928** S. LEWIS *Man who knew Coolidge* II. 155 'I'll make the law and you furnish my fee,' he used to say—but laughingly, of course, because he was a real square *straight-shooter. **1969** G. M. BROWN *Time to Keep* 176 'He's the decentest skipper ever I sailed with... Strict, but fair in his dealings.' 'A straight shooter.' **1978** M. PUZO *Fools Die* xxxiii. 376 She came from a place where the people were straight shooters. **1901** CONAN DOYLE in *Wide World Mag.* VIII. 113/1 The hard-riding, *straight-shooting sons of

Australia and New Zealand. **1902** *Westm. Gaz.* 30 Aug. 3/1 He..only hopes that, in the matter of 'straight-shooting powder,' his master's guests will prove equal to the occasion. **1869** RANKINE *Machinery & Millwork* 314 A *straight-sliding slide-valve. **1848** LOWELL *Biglow P.* Ser. I. vii. 5 I'm a *straight-spoken kind o' creetur 'Thet blurts right out wut's in his head. **1859** BARTLETT *Dict. Amer.* (ed. 2) 454 *Straight-spoken*, plain-spoken; downright; candid. **1913** D. H. LAWRENCE *Sons & Lovers* xii. 334 The big, *straight-standing woman was trying to estimate the situation.

b. Certain phrases in which *straight* qualifies another adv. are sometimes used *attrib.* or *predicatively*, becoming adjs. (when *attrib.* they are usually hyphened), as ***straight-through***, etc.; **straight-ahead**, simple, straightforward; *spec.* (orig. *U.S.*) with reference to popular music, pure, unadorned; **straight-up**, (*a*) perpendicular; (*b*) *colloq.*, exact, complete; true, trustworthy; also as quasi-*adv.* (i) truthfully, honestly; = STRAIGHT *adv.* 6; (ii) *U.S.*, unmixed, undiluted (cf. sense 9 a of the adj.); **straight-up-and-down**, simple, presenting no difficulties; also candid, straightforward. Also STRAIGHTAWAY, STRAIGHTFORTH, STRAIGHTFORWARD, STRAIGHT-OUT *adjs.*

1836 HALIBURTON *Clockm.* Ser. I. xxxvi, No strong-minded, *straight-a-head, right up and down man does that. **1895** *Outing* XXVII. 200/1 A plain, straight-ahead skater. **1911** MARETT *Anthropol.* iv. 95 On the other hand, to improve the physical environment is fairly straight-ahead work, once we can [etc.]. **1964** *Down Beat* 17 Dec. 30 'McSplivens' is a straight-ahead blues. **1977** *It* May 27/2 Just high energy, straight ahead rock 'n roll of the seventies. **1904** *Punch* 30 Mar. 234/2 After one *straight-through reading of this strange story, an entire class had to pass an examination in it. *c* **1590** MONTGOMERIE *Sonn.* xxxii. 2 The lillie..Vhose staitly stalk so *streight vp is and stay. **1662** J. DAVIES tr. *Olearius' Voy. Ambass.* 205 Having on the very top of it a great Rock streight up. **1910** A. BENNETT *Clayhanger* I. ix. 71 This new Licensing Act will close every public-house..at eleven o'clock, and a straight-up eleven at that! **1936** J. CURTIS *Gilt Kid* v. 52 But Maisie was the only girl he had ever loved! That was straight-up. **1963** L. DEIGHTON *Horse under Water* xlix. 211 'What's the trouble?' I asked. 'I'm being followed,' he said. 'Really,' I said. 'Straight up,' he said. 'I wasn't sure until today.' **1973** W. J. BURLEY *Death in Salubrious Place* vii. 150, I don't know where he is, Mr Gill, straight up, I don't. **1975** B. GARFIELD *Death Sentence* (1976) v. 30 He..beckoned the barmaid. 'Dewar's straight up, darlin'.' **1976** *Listener* 8 Jan. 23/1 It proved to be a completely wasted sacrifice, for the programme it gave space to..was a straight-up disaster. **1979** D. SANDERS *Queen sends for Mrs Chadwick* 137 You might have something going there. That's if this is straight up. **1982** R. HILL *Who guards a Prince* II. vii. 149 You looked honest to me..and you sounded like a straight-up guy. **1859** BARTLETT *Dict. Amer.* (ed. 2) 455 **Straight up and down*, plain; candid; honest. **1903** *Daily Chron.* 15 Apr. 3/6 A straight-up-and-down business of the kind..should be a more attractive investment for British capitalists than the average run of gold and diamond mining schemes.

straight (streɪt), *v.* Forms: α. 5 **streȝt**, 5–9 **streight**, 6 **strayght**, 6– **straight**; β. *Sc.* 4 **stracht**, 4–5 **straucht**, 9 **straught**. [f. STRAIGHT *a.*]

†**1.** *trans.* To stretch (e.g. a body on the rack); to stretch *out* (one's limbs); to extend, stretch forth (a spear); *refl.* to lie *down* flat. *Obs.*

to straight a rope, to be hanged.

1375 BARBOUR *Bruce* II. 348 Thai straucht thar speris, on athir syd. *c* **1375** *Sc. Leg. Saints* iii. (*Andrew*) 645 And bad his tormentoris but bad þane one þe croice þai suld hym stracht. *Ibid.* xxii. (*Laurence*) 337, & þar-eftyre gert hyme straucht In til framis with al þare macht. *c* **1400** tr. *Secreta Secret., Gov. Lordsh.* 69 Whenne þou risys fro slepe þou salt goo a lytyl, & euenly streight out þy membres. *c* **1480** HENRYSON *Fox, Wolf & Cadger* 185 ȝe mon..straucht ȝow doun in middis of the way. **1500–20** DUNBAR *Poems* lxxii. 67 Unto the crose of breid and lenth, To gar his lymmis langar wax, Thai straitit him with all thair strenth. *a* **1800** *Lang Johnny More* vii. in Child *Ballads* IV. 398/1 Whan the king got word o that, A solemn oath sware he, This weighty Scot sall strait a rope, And hanged he shall be.

†**2.** *refl.* and *intr.* To direct one's course, go. *Obs.*

a **1400–50** *Wars Alex.* 2032 Fra þe streme of struma he streȝtis & still mournes. *Ibid.* 3206 He streȝt him to struma & ouire þe streme ridis.

3. *trans.* To make straight, straighten. In later use chiefly *Sc.*, to straighten (a stream, a boundary), to lay out (a corpse).

1530 PALSGR. 738/1, I strayght a thyng that is crokyd or bendyd, *je redresse*. Strayght my wande, I praye you. **1583** MELBANCKE *Philotimus* A iv, The smith cooleth his yron to straight it & strenghthen it. **1612** T. TAYLOR *Titus* ii. 6 (1619) 404 Experience wisheth vs to..straight a tree while it is a twigge. **1725** P. WALKER *Life Peden* Biog. Presbyt. (1827) I. 74 She..straighted his Body, and covered him with her Plaid. **1765** A. DICKSON *Treat. Agric.* (ed. 2) 295 If a view to inclosing makes it necessary to straight the ridges, the levelling them should be the work of several years. **1776** ADAM SMITH *W.N.* I. i. 6 One man draws out the wire, another straights it, a third cuts it. **1799** J. ROBERTSON *Agric. Perth* 365 Some brooks, which ran slowly with a winding course..have been streighted. **1818** SCOTT *Br. Lamm.* xxiii, If the dead corpse binna straughted, it will girn and thraw, and that will fear the best o' us. **1833** LOUDON *Encycl. Archit.* §936 All the ceilings..are..to be properly straighted (made even or smooth with the edge of a board or float). **1838** W. BELL *Dict. Law Scot.* s.v. *Marches*, By the act 1699, c. 17, landholders may apply for a streighting of marches, and the judge ordinary may streight them. **1861** MRS. STOWE *Pearl Orr's Isl.* 18 Zephaniah Pennel straighted his tall form,—before bowed on his hands.

†**b.** To compose, clear up (care). *Obs.*

1604 BRETON *Pass. Sheph.* (Grosart) 9/1 Thus let all your Cares be straited.

Hence '**straighted** *ppl. a.*

1835 *Fraser's Mag.* XII. 13 The widow herself was a dead and straighted corpse.

straight, obs. form of STRAIT.

straight-arm, *a.* and *sb.* [STRAIGHT *a.* 1 d.]

A. *adj.* Performed with the arm stiff or unflexed; *spec.* in *Cricket* = *straight-armed* adj. s.v. STRAIGHT *a.* 11 c (now *Hist.*).

1807 *Sporting Mag.* July 192/1 The straight-arm bowling, introduced by John Willes, Esq. **1946** E. O'NEILL *Iceman Cometh* III. 177 [Rocky] Leans over the bar and stops Lewis with a straight-arm swipe on the chest. **1977** *Time* 21 Nov. 28/2 New Jersey's Democratic Governor Brendan Byrne, whose self-effacing campaign style consists of a strained smile and straight-arm salute.

B. *sb. N. Amer. Football.* An act of warding off an opponent or making room for oneself with the arm held straight. Also *fig.* Cf. *stiff-arm* s.v. STIFF *a.* 21 c.

1903 W. T. REID in W. Camp *How to play Football* (ed. 2) 85 Under no circumstances can a back use his 'straight-arm' more effectually than in the broken field running that forms such a big part of back-field work. **1927** G. S. LOWMAN *Pract. Football* xii. 225 He must have good use of the straight-arm and must be able to hit and pivot. **1951** M. MCLUHAN *Mech. Bride* (1967) 141/2 The numerous variants on straight-arm tactics, from lynch law to the third degree, all reduce to inner panic as their origin. **1969** *Maclean's Mag.* Aug. 3/1 He had to get his kicks, like many of us, by watching the Good Guys belt the Bad Guys and imagining that it was him down there, handing out straight-arms.

Hence as *v. trans.* and *intr.* (also *transf.*); **straight-arming** *vbl. sb.*

1934 WEBSTER, Straight-arm *v. trans.* **1934** CRISLER & WIEMAN *Pract. Football* vii. 81 (*heading*) Straight-arming. **1966** R. H. RIMMER *Harrad Experiment* (1967) 95 They stamped on feet, straight-armed, jammed people in the middle, and cursed them. **1980** 'R. B. DOMINIC' *Attending Physician* xix. 174 Ben..did not pause, but straight-armed his way through the human barrier.

'**straighta,way**, *a.*, *sb.*, and *adv.* [The phrase *straight away* (see C below) used *attrib.*]

A. *adj.* Of a shot: Aimed at a bird flying 'straight away'. Also said of the bird. Of a ride, a course in rowing or sailing: Continuous in direction and time; similarly of other courses or paths: direct, without bending or turning.

1874 J. W. LONG *Amer. Wild-fowl* i. 41 Straight-away shots they usually kill better than any others, because little or no calculation is required. **1883** *Standard* 18 Jan. 3/7 Another straightaway row to Iffley was indulged in. **1889** C. LANCASTER *Art of Shooting* 72 Longer shots may be made at crossing than at straight-away birds. *Ibid.* 75 The Straightforward Shot. This class of shot may be considered under three headings—straight-away, high straight-away, and low straight-away shots. **1894** *Outing* XXIV. 175/1 It was a straight-away gallop, our horses straining every nerve and muscle to the utmost. **1898** KIPLING in *Morn. Post* 5 Nov. 5/3 Once again we headed W.N.W...at an average speed of between thirteen and fourteen knots on a straightaway run of three hundred and fifty miles. **1903** G. V. HOBART *Out for Coin* 89 Out of the chute in to the straightaway course they foamed, that heaving, seething mass of horseflesh. **1913** *Captain* Sept. 1072/2 In straight-away flights even higher speeds have been established. **1977** *New Yorker* 16 May 115/1 The fifteenth, a straightaway 490-yard par 5, can be reached with two big blows.

B. *sb.* A straight course in rowing or sailing. Also, a straight section of a road or racecourse, etc. Cf. STRAIGHT *sb.* 3. Chiefly *U.S.*

1878 C. HALLOCK *Hallock's Amer. Club List & Sportsman's Gloss.* p. xi, *Straight-away*, a straight course without a turn, for racing boats. **1895** G. J. MANSON *Sporting Dict.*, *Straightaway*, a straight course without a turn for racing boats. **1909** *Century Dict.* Suppl., *Straightaway*, a race-course which is without turn or curve; also a race which is run without turning or curving. **1926** E. HEMINGWAY *In our Time* xiii. 188 Finally they made the last turn and came into the straightaway. **1935** *Sun* (Baltimore) 31 Jan. 11/6 On straightaways, Lieutenant Klein said, these pursuit planes made still higher speeds with the '100-octane'. **1954** [see PROP *v.*[1] 4]. **1957** J. KEROUAC *On Road* (1958) III. ix. 234 A long Nebraskan straightaway. **1966** J. PEARL *Crucifixion of Pete McCabe* (1967) iii. 30 Once they were on the wide main highway, McCabe relaxed... Donovan could not get in too much trouble on the straightaway. **1978** L. PRYOR *Viper* ii. 31, I backed off the throttle for the U-turn at the end of the straightaway.

C. *adv.* Also (esp. in earlier use) written as two words. Immediately, at once, without deliberation or preparation.

1662 TUKE *Adv. Five Hours* I. (1663) 7 We Prisoners made, were hurri'd streight away To their Quarters. **1885** P. M. THORNTON *Harrow Sch.* 80 We read of a Mr. Thomas Page,..to whom was paid £306. 16s. 6. straight away. **1910** *Sphere* 20 Aug. p. vi/1 Radley flies a mile straight-away at a speed of 75 miles an hour. **1911** SIR W. RAMSAY in *Expositor* Apr. 360 He assumes straight away that the end of man and the aim of man's life is to be righteous. **1923** *Daily Mail* 26 May 9 It was so evident that Evander had been badly hurt that he was straightaway withdrawn. **1948** M. LASKI *Tory Heaven* v. 65, I said straightaway..that I'd like to be a land-agent. **1978** *Church Times* 23 June 14/1, I would confess straightaway that I have often envied my Anglican brethren when I was in the pastoral ministry.

'**straight-edge.** A narrow strip of hard wood, steel, or brass, with one edge cut perfectly straight, used to test the accuracy of a plane surface, or as a guide for a cutting instrument.

1812 P. NICHOLSON *Mech. Exerc.* 142 The Straight Edge is a piece of stuff or board made perfectly straight on the edge, in order to make other edges straight. **1816** J. SMITH *Panorama Sci. & Art* I. 24 A perfectly straight steel ruler, for which we shall adopt the technical term, by calling it a *straight edge*. **1879** R. ROUSE *Sci. & Pract. Geom.* 17 A straight-edge or ruler. **1907** J. A. HODGES *Elem. Photogr.* (ed. 6) 106 An ebonite straight-edge.

b. *Printing.* (See quot. 1888.)

1888 JACOBI *Printers' Vocab.* 134 *Straight-edge*, a long wooden or metal stick used for squaring up the pages in a forme in order to obtain correct register in printing. **1890** W. J. GORDON *Foundry* 188 The machine had now the impression cylinder, the inking rollers, the straight-edge, and the travelling table of 1790.

straighten ('streɪt(ə)n), *v.* Also 6–9 **streighten**, 8–9 **straiten.** [f. STRAIGHT *a.* + -EN[5].]

1. a. *trans.* To make straight (what is bent or crooked); also with *out*. With *up*, to bring on to a straight or level course.

1542 UDALL tr. *Erasm. Apoph.* 235 A thing is said in latin *corrigi*, & in englyshe to be emended or streightened, yt is reproued or disallowed, and also that of crooked is made straight. **1594** HOOKER *Eccl. Pol.* IV. viii. §3 A crooked stick is not streightned vnlesse it be [etc.]. **1641** QUARLES *Enchir.* IV. xcix, While he [a child] is a tender Twigge, streighten him. **1697** DRYDEN *Virg. Georg.* I. 684 The crooked Scythes are streightned into Swords. **1727** H. BLAND *Milit. Discipl.* 41 The Soldiers are immediately to straiten their Ranks and Files. **1742** YOUNG *Nt. Th.* III. 371 Virtue..straitens nature's circle to a line. **1751** BANKTON *Instit. Laws Scot.* I. 282 The incloser may apply to the judge ordinary..to visit the ground, straiten and regulate the marches with the best conveniency. **1765** ANGELO *Sch. Fencing* 7 In these motions the arm should be straitned. **1775** ADAIR *Amer. Ind.* 425 They can fresh stock their guns..and streighten the barrels, so as to shoot with proper direction. **1841–71** T. R. JONES *Anim. Kingd.* 38 The delicate..stems of the *Vorticellæ*, which on the slightest touch shrink into spiral folds, and again straighten themselves to their full extent. **1844** KINGLAKE *Eothen* xix, I straightened myself in my stirrups. **1856** KANE *Arctic Expl.* II. vii. 76 He is sitting up congratulating himself that he can nearly straighten his worst leg. **1904** E. H. COLERIDGE *Life Ld. Coleridge* II. 287 He did not like hard work, but he straightened himself and bowed to the yoke. **1911** GRAHAME-WHITE & HARPER *Aeroplane* 136 Instead of performing the evolution which is known as 'straightening up' a machine, just before coming into contact with the ground, M. Chavez continued on his downward course, at a steep angle, and struck the ground with great violence.

b. In hand wool-combing: To comb wool for the second time.

1886 W. CUDWORTH *Rambles round Horton* vii. 75 She 'jigged' and he 'straightened'.

2. To unravel, disentangle, clear up (what is confused or intricate). Also *transf.* of persons: to put (someone) right, esp. by explanation. Now chiefly with *out*.

1577 tr. *Bullinger's Decades* II. viii. 193 So that to judge, is to streighten and to make plaine. **1894** D. L. MOODY in W. R. Moody *Life* (1900) Pref. 5 What I want is that you should correct inaccuracies and misstatements that it would be difficult to straighten out during my life. **1898** 'MERRIMAN' *Roden's Corner* xxxii. 341 Marguerite took occasion to congratulate herself,..in the fact that..'things' were beginning to straighten themselves out. **1900** H. C. BEECHING in *Monthly Rev.* Nov. 88 There are not a few moral questions that I should like to hear straightened out. **1956** B. HOLIDAY *Lady sings Blues* (1973) iv. 42 Excuse me, Mom, I'm sorry, but I got to straighten this whore out. **1979** W. STYRON *Sophie's Choice* xii. 355 Look, Sophie, you're confusing me. Straighten me out. Please.

3. To put in order, tidy up. Also in slang use (see quot. 1970).

1867 in J. Lucas *Stud. Nidderdale* (1882) 281 Cum don on thi' bonnet an' shawl, An' streighten thi' cap an' thi' hair. **1884** *Manch. Exam.* 28 Nov. 5/2 An English mob..eager to straighten up their difficulties and begone before the Riot Act was read. **1890** 'R. BOLDREWOOD' *Col. Reformer* xiii, We straightened the horses after a bit—there was two dead and one with a broken leg. **1901** ANTROBUS *Wildersmoor* 297, I'll send Granny up here to straighten things a bit. **1944** C. HINES *Black on Black* (1973) 198, I had to get them people straight and get 'em straightened fast. **1946** MEZZROW & WOLFE *Really Blues* xii. 216 I'm short a deuce of blips but I'll straighten you later. **1970** C. MAJOR *Dict. Afro-Amer. Slang* 110 *Straighten*, to straighten someone is to tell her or him the truth or to pay back money borrowed.

4. a. *intr.* To become straight. *to straighten up* (orig. U.S.): to rise to an erect posture; *slang*, to adopt an honest course of life; also in *gen.* use, to adopt a straight or level course. Similarly *to straighten out* (also *fig.*).

1891 KIPLING *Light that Failed* xiii. 256 Dick's shoulders straightened again, for the words lashed like a whip. **1897** *Trans. Amer. Pediatric Soc.* IX. 168 After a series of such oscillations..he straightens up, regains his breath, and the paroxysm ends with a long, sighing inspiration. **1907** JEAN WEBSTER *Four-Pools Myst.* xix. (1916) 198 He has been dishonest, but unintentionally so. He wishes to straighten up and lead a respectable life. **1914** [see FLATTEN *v.* 2 b]. **1917** *Times* 5 July 6/5 Two machines..swerved and one started to fall for some hundreds of feet before it straightened out and regained flying speed. **1921** *Rev. of Reviews* Aug. 99/2 The..expectations..that the Silesian tangle was straightening out have proved quite illusory. **1939** G. B. SHAW *In Good King Charles's Golden Days* I. 31 Newton straightens up and stares. **1940** W. FAULKNER *Hamlet* I. ii. 36 All of a sudden they [*sc.* mules] straightened out and I mind how I was thinking what a good thing it was they was pointed away from the wagon when they straightened out.

b. *colloq.* To settle *up* an account or debt (with someone).

1915 D. H. LAWRENCE *Let.* Dec. (1948) 66 But I haven't had the bill yet: I will straighten up with you when it comes. **1966** *Amer. Speech* XLI. 297 *Straighten up*, pay a bill.

5. *trans.* To bribe or corrupt. Also with *out*. *slang* (orig. *U.S.*).

1923 E. WALLACE *Missing Million* xxiii. 182 They said they'd tried to straighten you. **1960** [see KNOCK *v.* 12 i]. **1976** J. O'CONNOR *Eleventh Commandment* v. 67, I didn't fancy being in the hands of the Wiltshire police. I couldn't straighten them, but I had one in London straightened. **1982** *Observer* 15 Aug. 22/4 Somebody who has been successfully bribed to do something has been 'straightened out'.

Hence **'straightened** *ppl. a.*

1665 DRYDEN *Ind. Emp.* v. ii, Fasten the Engines; stretch 'em at their length, And pull the straightned Cords with all your strength. [*They fasten them to the rack, and then pull them.*] **1897** MARY KINGSLEY *W. Africa* 125 In which case offer him a straightened-out hairpin.

straighten, var. STRAITEN *v.*

straightener ('streɪt(ə)nə(r)). [f. STRAIGHTEN *v.* + -ER[1].] One who or something which straightens.

1611 COTGR., *Dresseur*, a straightener, directer, leueller. **1832** HT. MARTINEAU *Hill & Valley* iv. (1833) 61 They saw ..the straighteners who straighten the bars when they are hot, and mark them with the stamp of the works where they are made. **1875** KNIGHT *Dict. Mech.* 2414/2 Fig. 5940 is a railway-rail straightener.

straightening ('streɪt(ə)nɪŋ), *vbl. sb.* [f. STRAIGHTEN *v.* + -ING[1].] **a.** The action of the verb, in various senses. Also with *out*.

1730 A. GORDON *Maffei's Amphith.* 274 The Space is taken up by the straightning of the Roof. **1839** URE *Dict. Arts*, etc. 881 Whereby he effects..the straightening of the wires [for needles]. **1860** J. G. HOLLAND *Miss Gilbert* i, Bearing the doctor in his gig, and stopping here and there at the houses of his patients without the straightening of a rein. **1884** *Manch. Exam.* 29 Sept. 5/3 Their project contemplates the deepening, widening, and straightening of the rivers Mersey and Irwell. **1892** *Labour Commission* Gloss., *Straightening*, putting rails under the press to straighten them when they have become bent in cooling. **1900** 'MARK TWAIN' in *McClure's Mag.* XIV. 287/1 With this straightening-out and classification of the dreamer's position to help us, perhaps we can put ourselves in his place. **1916** *Med. Press & Circular* 10 May 421/2 Nothing can be more reprehensible than the repeated straightening of the uterus by means of the uterine sound. **1978** S. BRILL *Teamsters* vi. 226 She went to a friend of Arnie's who she thought was straight..and asked him to talk to Arnie for her about straightening out.

b. *attrib.*

1688 HOLME *Armoury* III. 387/1 Instruments of the Needle-makers:..a Streightning file. *Ibid.* 388/2 Tools in much use with the Horn-maker;..the Streightning-Tongs. **1869** RANKINE *Machine & Hand-tools* Pl. P 6. 4 The action of the straightening mandrel. **1884** KNIGHT *Dict. Mech.* Suppl., *Straightening Block*, the anvil on which buckled saws are straightened.

straightening ('streɪt(ə)nɪŋ), *ppl. a.* [-ING[2].]

1850 W. C. BENNETT *Poems, Baby May* 15 Clutching fingers; straightening jerks. **1894** *Outing* XXIV. 440/1 An ear that is jarred by the twang of a straightening blade of grass.

straight forth, 'straightforth, *adv.* and *a.* Now *rare*. [STRAIGHT *adv.* 9 b.]

A. *adv.* **1.** Directly in front or onwards.

1530 PALSGR. 827/1 Strayght forthe afore, *tout droyt deuant*. **1570** BILLINGSLEY *Euclid* I. Post. ii. 5 b, To produce a right line finite, straight forth continually. *c* **1590** MARLOWE *Faustus* 813 (1604) D i b, The streetes straight forth, and pau'd with finest bricke. **1601** HOLLAND *Pliny* VI. xvii. I. 124 And this part of the Orientall Indians, which lieth directly streight forth,..containeth 1875 miles. **1830** J. WRIGHT *Retrospect* i. 27 Straightforth before us rolls the pleasing past. **1850** HAWTHORNE *Scarlet L.* x, He seldom, nowadays, looked straightforth at any object.

2. Immediately, at once.

1577 GRANGE *Golden Aphrod.* C iv, Who (obeying hir heste) straightfoorth ascended to the Mount Pernassus. **1590** SPENSER *Muiop.* 325 She smote the ground, the which streight foorth did yield A fruitfull Olyue tree. **1854** H. MILLER *Sch. & Schm.* iii. (1858) 41, I quitted the dame's school..; and was transferred straightforth to the grammar school of the parish.

†**B.** *adj.* Straight-shaped. *Obs.*

1567 MAPLET *Gr. Forest* 30 The Almonde tree in Greeke is called *Amygdalê*, in Latine Nux longa, a long and straight forth kinde of Nutte.

straight forward, straight'forward, *adv.* and *a.* [STRAIGHT *adv.* 9 b.]

A. *adv.* Directly in front or onwards; in direct order.

1809 MALKIN *Gil Blas* VIII. xii. (Rtldg.) 306 Tell him all the circumstances straightforward as they happened. **1830** HERSCHEL *Study Nat. Phil.* I. ii. (1851) 22 To walk uprightly and straight-forward on firm ground. **1832** HT. MARTINEAU *Demerara* iii. 39 Old Robert could not be got to answer a question straight-forward or to tell anything without contradicting himself twenty times. *c* **1850** *Arab. Nts.* (Rtldg.) 727 He proceeded straight forward on his journey without deviating either to the right or left.

B. *adj.*

1. Of movement, vision, etc.: Proceeding or directed straight forward.

1807 ROLAND *Fencing* 24 Those kind of straight-forward thrusts. **1815** MME. D'ARBLAY *Diary* 20 Mar., The desire of obtaining intelligence made Madame d'Henin most unwilling to continue a straightforward journey. **1859** HAWTHORNE *Fr. & It. Note-bks.* (1871) II. 291 Its peculiar expression eludes a straightforward glance, and can only be caught by side glimpses. **1867** LONGF. *Dante. Inf.* i. 3 Midway upon the journey of our life I found myself within a forest dark, For the straightforward pathway had been lost.

2. Of language, narrative, or exposition: Direct, without circumlocution or digression.

1806 J. BERESFORD *Miseries Hum. Life* vii. Introd. (ed. 3) 132 You put my poor stock of straight-forward phraseology quite upon the stretch to reach after you! **1875** JOWETT *Plato* (ed. 2) IV. 40 Of many..benevolent actions we can give a straightforward account by their tendency to promote happiness. **1895** J. H. ROUND in *Bookman* Oct. 25/2 The book..[is] a straightforward, readable narrative in a very reasonable compass. **1913** *Times* 13 Sept. 15/6 They had had a straightforward statement of affairs from Mr. Barry.

3. Of an action or process: Continuous in one direction, undeviating.

1817 MALTHUS *Popul.* III. 170 It has proceeded in a very straight-forward manner to spend great sums in war, and to raise them by very heavy taxes. **1824** DIBDIN *Libr. Comp.* p. iv, A sedulous and straight-forward cultivation of the pursuit in question. **1850** DENISON *Clock & Watch-m.* 161 We must have some more violent method than the straight forward expansion of one metal over that of another.

4. Presenting a clear course; free from difficulties.

1833 HT. MARTINEAU *Brooke Farm* xi. 131 It all seems straightforward enough now, if I can but get this appointment.

5. Of persons, their dispositions or conduct: Consistent, undeviating in purpose, single-minded. Also (now usually), free from duplicity or concealment; frank, honest, outspoken.

1829 P. EGAN *Boxiana* 2nd Ser. II. 601 The *Streatham Youth* is a *straight-forward* fellow—*honest* upon all occasions. **1834** MARRYAT *P. Simple* vii, 'He may be a fool, sir,' observed he to the captain, aside; 'but I can assure you he is a very straight-forward one.' **1845** DISRAELI *Sybil* IV. v, He is a man; with clear, straightforward ideas, a frank, noble presence. **1845–6** TRENCH *Huls. Lect.* Ser. II. i. 160 Serving with a straightforward and downright obedience..God. **1850** W. IRVING *Mahomet* II. 18 His next movement was indicative of his straight-forward cut-and-thrust policy. **1874** SPURGEON *Treas. Dav.* ci. *title*, It is David all over, straightforward, resolute, devout; there is no trace of policy or vacillation. **1874** GREEN *Short Hist.* ix. §10. 702 He was thoroughly straightforward and true to his own convictions. **1911** RIKER *Henry Fox 1st Ld. Holland* I. ii. 86 Lacking a straightforward and practicable policy, they were helpless to combat a party which [etc.].

Comb. **1875** G. JOHN in R. W. Thompson *Life* (1908) 352 Wei is a plain, honest, straightforward-looking man.

straight'forwardly, *adv.* [-LY[2].] In a straightforward manner.

1. Honestly, frankly, without reserve.

1839 JAMES *Louis XIV*, I. 279 The question was even put to it straightforwardly, whether it pretended, or not, to circumscribe the royal authority. **1864** J. H. NEWMAN *Apol.* 429 He avoided..having any thing to do with two-faced persons, who did not go simply and straightforwardly to work in their transactions. **1903** DE BLOWITZ *Mem.* 234 The friend who unfortunately, and quite straightforwardly, led us into this frightful speculation.

2. In consecutive order, without digression or intricacy.

1874 RUSKIN *Fors Clav.* xxxvii. 12, I do not pretend to tell you straightforwardly all the laws of nature respecting the conduct of men; but some of those laws I know [etc.]. **1906** *Daily Chron.* 16 July 3/2 'Bess of the Woods' is a quite straightforwardly told tale of the life of well-to-do country folk in the eighteenth century.

straight'forwardness. [-NESS.] The quality of being straightforward.

1805 W. TAYLOR in *Ann. Rev.* III. 46 He..wins his easy way to the reader's sympathy..by the straight-forwardness of his course. **1853** LANDOR *Last Fruit, Louis Philippe & Guizot* 14 The lover of straitforwardness and truth. **1871** SWINBURNE *Ess. & Stud.* (1875) 293 In both plays there is a perfect unity of action, a perfect straightforwardness of design. **1911** A. C. DIXON in *The Fundamentals* V. 86 The Gospel writers..simply tell right out what they saw in all simplicity and straightforwardness.

straight'forwards, *adv.* = STRAIGHTFORWARD *adv.* 1.

1555 J. BRADFORD in Coverdale *Lett. Martyrs* (1564) 296 Looke not on this side or that side, or behynd you as Lothes wyfe dyd; but strayght forwardes on the ende.

straightish ('streɪtɪʃ), *a.* and *adv.* [f. STRAIGHT *a.* and *adv.* + -ISH.] Somewhat straight.

1683 MOXON *Mech. Exerc., Printing* xxii. ¶8 If he should stick the Point of the Bodkin straight or straightish down upon any part of the Letter. **1793** MARTYN *Lang. Bot.* Straightish, *rectiusculus*. **1802** R. HALL *Elem. Bot.* 88 Sisymbrium. Silique opening, valves straightish. **1830** LINDLEY *Nat. Syst. Bot.* 152 Embryo included, either straightish or curved. **1886** RUSKIN *Præterita* I. xii. 429, I like oval faces,..with straightish, at the utmost wavy,..hair.

straight-lined, *a.* Composed of or containing straight lines; having the form of a straight line; rectilinear.

1571 DIGGES *Pantom.* I. *Elem.* B j b, Of straight lined angles there are three kindes. **1656** tr. *Hobbes' Elem. Philos.* (1839) 120 A strait-lined triangle. **1673** FLAMSTEED in Rigaud *Corr. Sci. Men* (1841) II. 171 He was pleased to shew me a straight-lined projection for finding the hour by inspection. **1764** DODSLEY *Leasowes* in *Shenstone's Wks.* (1777) II. 300 Now we turn upon a sudden into a long strait-lined walk in the wood. **1801** *Farmer's Mag.* Apr. 129 Measuring off from a straight lined hedge,..he takes one length of the poles for the half or crown of the first ridge. **1808** J. WEBSTER *Nat. Philos.* 115 They conducted water across hills and vallies by straight-lined ducts. **1898** A. BROWNE in *Daily News* 10 Mar. 6/3 Across this opaque covering a straight-lined scratch is made with a needle or knife.

†**'straightly,** *a. Obs.* [f. STRAIGHT *a.* + -LY[1].] Tense, stretched.

1422 YONGE tr. *Secreta Secret.* 230 Tho that have the braons of the shuldres ryght strayghtly whan thay mewyth ham, tokenyth that thay bene stronge and hardy.

straightly ('streɪtlɪ), *adv.* [f. STRAIGHT *a.* + -LY[2].]

1. In a straight manner; in a straight line; directly.

1395 PURVEY *Remonstr.* (1851) 46 Siche lawis ben directli, other straightli, or openli, contrarie to the truthe. **1398** TREVISA *Barth. De P.R.* XIII. vi. (Bodl. MS.) He renneþ scharpelich & swiftelich and straiȝteliche as it were. **1426** LYDG. *De Guil. Pilgr.* 11640 My glovys streythly on to sette. **1586** MARLOWE *1st Pt. Tamburl.* II. i, But tell me..What stature wields he, and what personage? *Mena.* Of stature tall, and straightly fashioned. *a* **1677** BARROW *Serm.* iii. Wks. 1687 I. 27 God's word..is a lamp unto our feet,..teaching us to walk streightly and surely, without erring or stumbling. **1804–6** SYD. SMITH *Mor. Philos.* (1850) 231 Firmness and constancy of purpose, that withstands all solicitation, and, in spite of all danger, goes on straightly to its object, is very often sublime. **1867** F. FRANCIS *Angling* v. (1880) 150 Let him deliver the fly straightly and well. **1867** C. J. SMITH *Syn. & Antonyms* 24 To allude is to make such a reference to a subject as does not straightly refer to, but, as it were, plays about it.

2. Straightway, immediately. *poet. rare.*

1830 TENNYSON *Sonn.* '*Could I outwear*', Could I thus hope my lost delights renewing, I straightly would commend the tears to creep From my charged lids. **1868** MORRIS *Earthly Par.* I. (1870) 252 Make no tarrying, But straightly set thyself to do this thing.

straightness ('streɪtnɪs). [-NESS.] The quality of being straight, in various senses of the adj.

1530 PALSGR. 277/1 Streightnesse rightnesse, *droicteur*. **1534** WHITINTON *Tullyes Offic.* I. (1540) 36 This is the offyce of a man of armes:..in all chaunces to kepe streyghtnesse and honesty. *a* **1577** SIR T. SMITH *Commw. Eng.* I. (1589) 2 Ye right rule whereby the Artificer and the Architect doe iudge the straightnes of euery mans worke. *a* **1732** T. BOSTON *Crook in Lot* (1805) 7 We do not reckon it a crooked thing, which though forcibly bended..presently recovers its former straightness. **1882** MISS BRADDON *Mt. Royal* ix, The straightness and purity of the girl's purpose upheld her. **1915** W. K. HOLMES *Ballads of Field & Billet* 49 He likes to boast to youngsters of his age, The straightness of his back, his sight, his health.

'straight-out, *a.* and *sb.* Chiefly *U.S.* [attrib. use of the phrase *straight-out*: see STRAIGHT *adv.*]

A. *adj.* Unrestrained; going all lengths. Also straightforward, unqualified, genuine. In party politics = STRAIGHT *a.* 9.

1848 W. ARMSTRONG *Stocks* 9 The Stock is to be delivered and paid for upon a certain day—these are sometimes termed straight out contracts. **1856** *N.Y. Commercial Adv.* May (Bartlett), We feel what a blessed thing it is just now to be a straight out Whig. **1856** MRS. STOWE *Dred* II. xxxi. 337 Anne was indignant—with that straight out and generous indignation which belongs to women. **1859** BARTLETT *Dict. Amer.* (ed. 2) 454 *Straight out*, pure; genuine; unsophisticated. **1860** KEITT in *Congr. Globe* 1 Feb. 651/2 A straight-out nominee of your party. **1873** 'MARK TWAIN' *Gilded Age* xxv. 228 Buying committees for straight-out cash on delivery. **1888** BRYCE *Amer. Commw.* II. I. II. 269 The electors..give little thought to the personal qualifications of the candidates, and vote the 'straight out ticket.' *Ibid.* VI. ciii. III. 481 The congregation of Plymouth Church were mostly 'straight out' Republicans. **1912** T. DREISER *Financier* 57, I don't like it as well as I do the straight-out brokerage business. **1915** *Morn. Post* 9 Apr. 8/5 That, says the Post, was a straightout policy of lawlessness and terrorism. **1947** A. P. GASKELL *Big Game* 118 It's not just a straight-out romance? **1973** E. S. GARDNER *Case Postponed Murder* (1977) viii. 106 It isn't any trap. It's a straight-out business proposition.

B. *sb.* One who votes a 'straight' party ticket, an uncompromising partisan.

1840 *Nashville Whig* 17 Aug. (Thornton *Amer. Gloss.*), The company of Straight-Outs..are the representatives of a hardy race of honest log cabin pioneers. **1872** *Nation* (N.Y.) 22 Aug. 113 (Cent.), Other Straight-outs, as they call themselves,..cannot take Grant and the Republicans.

†**'straightwards,** *adv. Obs. rare.* [f. STRAIGHT *a.* + -WARDS.] In a straight direction.

1644 DIGBY *Nat. Bodies* xxxv. §1. 296 This transparent body, hangeth as it were straightwardes, from the forehead towards the hinder part of the head.

straightway ('streɪtweɪ), *adv.* [f. STRAIGHT *a.* + WAY *sb.*]

†**1.** By a direct course, straight from or to a place. *Obs.*

1461 *Paston Lett.* II. 38 Item, sir, thys day cam on John Waynflet from the Kyng streyt weye. *c* **1485** *Digby Myst.* III. 427 Serys, I abey your covnsell in eche degre; strytt waye þethyr woll I passe. **1486** *Bk. St. Albans* d j b, Crepe softely towarde the fowle: from yowre hawke streght way. **1587** HARRISON *England* II. vi. 167/2 in *Holinshed*, The merchant would haue thought that his soule should haue gone streightwaie to the diuell, if he should haue serued them with other than the best.

2. Immediately; without interval or delay; at once. Now only *literary*.

1526 TINDALE *Matt.* iv. 20 They strayght waye lefte there nettes. *Ibid.*, *John* xxi. 3 They..entred into a shippe strayght waye. *Ibid.*, *Rom.* ix. 7 Nether are they all children strayght way be cause they are the seede of Abraham. **1576** FLEMING *Panopl. Epist.* 248 Whiche if he sought not to recompence by reuengement, then was he thought straightway a cowardly beast. **1666** G. HARVEY *Morbus Angl.* ix. (1672) 25 Grief protracted to some space of time, doth inevitably absorb the fleshy parts of the body, and strait-way hasten to a perfect Consumption. **1714** PRIOR *Viceroy* 66 That he, O! Ciel, without trial, Straitway shou'd hanged be. **1786** *Har'st Rig* xvi, This being done, they straughtway gang Into the barn. **1816** COLERIDGE *Statesm. Man.* 18 But let the winds of passion swell, and straitway men begin to generalize. **1838** DICKENS *Nickleby* xxviii, She straightway sat down and indited a long letter. **1852** THACKERAY *Esmond* II. vii, They dazzle him, so that the past becomes straightway dim to him. **1867** MORLEY *Burke* 240 It is too commonly asserted, and straightway accepted, that the Revolution destroyed, but contributed nothing to the yet greater task of reconstruction.

straightways ('streɪtweɪz), *adv.* Now *rare* or *Obs.* [See -WAYS.]

1. Immediately, without delay: = STRAIGHTWAY 2.

c **1530** BERNERS *Arthur Lyt. Bryt.* (1814) 434 Than the king said,..let them come hyder: and so they were incontinent sente for, and they came thyder streyght wayes. **1567** MAPLET *Gr. Forest* 80 He holdeth fast in his clawes little stones, which in their falling from him straight wayes awaketh him. **1573–80** TUSSER *Author's Life* viii. *Husb.* (1878) 207 From Paules I went, to Eaton sent, To learn streight waies, the latin phraies. **1575** R. B. *Apius & Virginia* (facs.) E j b, To master reward I straight waies will go. **1603** STOW *Surv.* (1908) II. 132 Richard Talbot Bishop of London, streghtwayes after his consecration deceased, saith Euersden. **1611** BIBLE *2 Macc.* xiv. 16 So at the commandement of the captaine, they remooued straightwayes from thence. **1625** BACON *Ess.*, *Cunning* (Arb.) 443 Like to him, that hauing changed his Name, and walking in Pauls, Another suddenly came behind him, and called him by his true Name, whereat straightwaies he looked backe. **1695** LD. PRESTON *Boeth.* I. 14, I the Leader do straightways retreat with my Party into a Fortress. **1812** SOUTHEY *Omniana* I. 324 And he went straightways to the house of the woman.

†**2.** In a straight line. *Obs.*

1771 *Phil. Trans.* LXI. 235 They are first extended streightways, and appear like two bristles.

'straightwise, *adv. rare.* [-WISE.] = STRAIGHTWAY 2.

1588 A. KING tr. *Canisius' Catech.* 223 Whairfor straght wyse thay heare the word of Christ. **1839–52** BAILEY *Festus* (1854) 73 Surely thou camest straightwise from the stars.

straigne, obs. form of STRAIN *v.*[1]

straik (streɪk), *sb.*[1] *Sc.* and *north.* Also 9 **strake, straike, straick.** [f. STRAIK *v.*]

†**1.** *by straik*: by 'straiked' or levelled (as distinguished from heaped) measure. Also *attrib.* in *straik measure. Sc. Obs.*

1549 *Extracts Aberd. Reg.* (1844) I. 264 That frathinfurth na maner of malt nor beir that cumis to the guid tovnn to sell be mett in tymes cumyng bot with ane straik mesour. **1567** *Sc. Acts Jas. VI* (1814) III. 39/2 It is desyrit ane straik mett be maid vniuersalie through all þe realme. **1587** *Ibid.* 521/2 For eschewing of fraud hes thocht expedient that all wictuall in tyme cuming salbe mesorit be straik.

2. The normal proportion of malt for a brewing.

App. only in Scott; the quots. do not seem to justify the usual rendering 'bushel' (cf. STRIKE, STROKE *sbs.*).

1820 SCOTT *Abbot* xix, With a single straike of malt to counterbalance a double allowance of water. **1821** —— *Pirate* iv, The 'bern'..never quitted hold of the tankard with so much reluctance as when there had been..a double straik of malt allowed to the brewing. **1823** —— *Quentin D.* Introd., A double straick of John Barleycorn.

†**3.** A measure of timber. *Obs. rare*[-1].

1542 *Acc. Ld. High Treas. Scot.* VIII. 95 Ane straik of buirdis, as the bill of compt thairupoune beris.

4. A piece of wood coated with sand or emery, used for sharpening scythes; = STRICKLE, STRIKE *sb.*

1844 H. STEPHENS *Bk. Farm* III. 1063 The sharpening should always be finished with the straik or strickle. **1894** CROCKETT *Lilac Sunbonnet* vii. 59 The clear metallic sound of the 'strake' or sharpening strop.

straik (streɪk), *sb.*[2] *Sc. rare.* ? A narrow channel in a stream.

1847 STODDART *Angler's Comp.* 42 The rocky straiks and clippers that afford facilities for fish to cut or wear through the line. *Ibid.* 259 In rapid water, such as the necks of streams, straiks, and eddies, the plying and working of the hook is not always requisite.

straik (streɪk), *v. Sc.* Also **strake.** [Normal Sc. form of STROKE *v.* (q.v. for other senses).] *trans.* To level (corn, etc.) in a measure. Hence **straiked** *ppl. a.*

1579 *Extracts Rec. Convent. Burghs Scot.* (1870) I. 81 Sua that all fourletis, pekis, and vther mesouris war maid of the lairgnes of the heipit mett, to be straikit and nocht heipit. **1582** *Extracts Burgh Rec. Edin.* (1882) IV. 236 Conform to the awld just mesour of the realme in straiket mett. **1684** A. SYMSON in W. Macfarlane *Geogr. Collect.* (S.H.S.) II. 101 One boll of good and sufficient meal straked measure. **1685** PEDEN in P. Walker *Life* Biog. Presbyt. (1827) I. 95 Christ knows well, whether Heaping or Straiking agrees best with our narrow Vessels, for both are alike to him. **1894** CROCKETT *Raiders* xvii. 158 The bushel-stoup of their iniquity was nearly full measure, heaped and running over, and it would soon be straked with the Lord's own level and plumb line.

straik, obs. f. STRAKE; obs. Sc. f. STROKE; obs. Sc. pres. stem and pa. t. of STRIKE *v.*

† **'straiken, 'straiking.** *Sc.* and *north. Obs.* Also 6 **straikin, straken, straykyng, streakings,** 6, 8 **strakins,** 8 **straikens.** [Of obscure origin.] A kind of coarse linen. Also *attrib.*

1531–2 *Durham Househ. Bk.* (Surtees) 67, 1 peayce curse straykyngs. **1557** *Wills & Inv. N.C.* (Surtees) I. 159, ix pare of lyne shetts & iij pare of streakings iiij[l] xvj[s] viij[d]. **1569** *Ibid.* 303 Item one fether bedtyke xij[d]—sex yerds of strakins v[s]. **1577** *Ibid.* 415 Tenn payer of harden and straken sheats. **1593–4** *Extracts Munic. Acc. Newcastle* (1848) 32 Paide for a strakin short to him and for sewing ytt, 16*d.* **1643** *Melrose Regality Rec.* (S.H.S.) I. 100 Ane straiking serk. **1703** LADY G. BAILLIE *Househ. Bk.* (S.H.S.) 172 For 20 ells strakins at 6s. 6d. **1793** *Statist. Acc. Scot.* VI. 169 Some coarse tweels, some harns and straikens. **1884** *Good Words* May 326/2 His shirt is made of the strong old-fashioned coarse linen called 'straiken'.

† **strail.** *Obs.* Forms: 1 **strǣl, stréaȝl, strél,** 4–5 **strale, strayl,** 4–6 **straile, strayle,** 5–6 **strayll(e.** [OE. **strǣȝl* (recorded forms *stréaȝl, strǣl, strél*) fem., repr. an early adoption of L. *strāgula*, f. *strā-* root of *sternĕre* to lay down, spread.] A woollen bed-covering, a blanket.

c **725** *Corpus Gloss.* (Hessels) A 932 *Aulea*, streaȝl. *Ibid.* S 514 *Stragu[l]a*, strel. *c* **1000** in Napier *OE. Glosses* i. 1035 *Stragularum*, stræla, hwitla, wæstlinga. *a* **1300** *E.E. Psalter* vi. 7 (Harl. MS.) With my teres witerli Mi straile sal I wete for-þi. **1310–11** *Durham Acc. Rolls* (Surtees) 506 In 2 paribus de strayles emp. 12*s.* **1397** in *Finchale Priory Charters* etc. (Surtees), p. cxvii, Item j par de strales antiquum. *c* **1440** *Promp. Parv.* 478/2 Strayle, bed clothe, *stamina, stragula.* *a* **1500** *Medulla Gram.*, *Stragula*, burell, Rayclothe, motteley. *Stragulum, idem* or a strayle. **1532** *Visit. Dioc. Norwich* (Camden) 263 Fiat injunctio quod utantur strailes more antiquo et non linthiaminibus uti jam faciunt omnes. **1532** *Durham Househ. Bk.* (Surtees) 132, 1 payr straylls.

Comb. **1438** *Will of Refhan* (Somerset Ho.), John Studley Straylweber.

strain (streɪn), *sb.*[1] Forms: 1 **stréon, stríon,** 2–3 **streon,** 3–4 **stren,** 3–7 **strene,** 4 **streone,** 4–6 **streen,** 5–7 **straine,** 6–7 **streine, streyne,** 7 **streene,** 9 *dial.* **strene,** 7– **strain.** [OE. *stréon, stríon* neut., a shortened form (recorded only in North.) of *ȝestréon, ȝestríon* (see I-STREON) = OS., OHG. *gistriuni*, related to *(ȝe)stréonan, (ȝe)strienan, (ȝe)strýnan* to acquire, gain (also to beget, procreate) = OHG. *(ga)striunen*, f. OTeut. (pre-Teut.) root **streu-* to pile up; cf. L. *struēs* pile, *struĕre* to build.

The normal form in mod.Eng. would be *streen*; the actual form, which is found in the 15th c., but did not finally prevail until the 17th c., is due to association with STRAIN *sb.*[2] or *sb.*[3] The related STRENE *v.* did not survive beyond the 14th c., and therefore did not undergo the perversion of form.]

†**I. 1.** Gain, acquisition; treasure: = I-STREON 1. *Obs.*

c **950** *Lindisf. Gosp.* Matt. vi. 21 Ðer is strion ðin [Vulg. *ubi est thesaurus tuus*]. *c* **1250** *Prov. Ælfred* 184 in *O.E. Misc.* 113 Acte nis non eldere stren [*Jesus MS.* istreon], ac it is Godis lone. *c* **1275** LAY. 18609 þe castles gode were of his hilderne streone.

II. †**2.** Begetting, generation: = I-STREON 2.

Not recorded in OE., the supposed instance in *Bæda's Hist.* I. xxvii. being due to an erroneous reading.

c **1200** ORMIN 127 þatt naffdenn þeȝȝ þurrh þeȝȝre streon Ne sune child, ne dohhterr. *Ibid.* 18889 Off moderr & off faderr stren. *c* **1200** *Trin. Coll. Hom.* 19 Ure helende crist is his onlepi sune, noht after chesunge ac after strene.

†**3.** The germinal vesicle in the yolk of an egg.

c **1305** *Pop. Treat. Sci.* (1841) 132 Urthe is a-midde the hevene as the streon a-midde theye. *c* **1420** *Liber Cocorum* (1862) 51 Breke ten egges in cup fulle fayre,..þo strene also þou put away. **1585** HIGINS *Junius' Nomencl.* 54/2 *Oui vmbilicus*,..the streine or kenning of the egge. **1596** BARROUGH *Meth. Phisick* I. xxxviii. (1639) 61 Then put into the eye the streines of egs, ordered as I declared before. **1600** SURFLET *Country Farm* I. xii. 64 Take..sixe springs or straines of egges that are verie new. **1681** W. ROBERTSON *Phraseol. Gen.* (1693) 523 The strain of an egg, *umbilicus ovi.* **1764** ELIZA MOXON *Eng. Housew.* (ed. 9) 116 Take the yolks of two eggs and beat them very well, leaving out the strain.

4. Offspring, progeny: = I-STREON 3. Also *fig. Obs.* exc. *arch.*

c **1175** *Lamb. Hom.* 133 Vre drihten cleopede monnes streon sed. *c* **1200** ORMIN 16396 Forr þatt hiss stren all shollde ben Todrifenn & toskeȝȝredd. *a* **1225** *Ancr. R.* 208 Ne not ich none sunne þet ne mei beon iled to one of ham seouene, oðer to hore streones. *a* **1225** *Juliana* (Bodl. MS.) 55, & wel bi semeð þe to beon & bikimeð to beo streon of a swuch strunde. **13..** *King Alis.* 511 A god..That hath y-laye by the quene, And bygete on hire a steorne streone. **1315** SHOREHAM *Poems* i. 1777 For te destruwen oure stren. **1621** QUARLES *Esther* xviii, That remainder of proud Haman's straine, Their hands haue rooted out. **1839–52** BAILEY *Festus* 175 Child of the royal blood of man redeemed, The starry strain of spirit, thence we are.

5. Pedigree, lineage, ancestry, descent.

c **1205** LAY. 29725 Of Bruttisce streonen. *c* **1386** CHAUCER *Clerk's T.* 101 Bountee comth al of god, nat of the streen Of which they [children] been engendred and ybore. *c* **1450** LOVELICH *Grail* xxxviii. 345 A veleynes sone was he tho, and I-comen of a schrewed streen. **1470–85** MALORY *Arthur* II. i. 77 He must be a clene knyght withoute vylony and of a gentil strene of fader syde and moder syde. *c* **1530** *Crt. of Love* 370 For though thy-self be noble in thy strene, A thowsand-fold more nobill is thy quene. **1596** SPENSER *F.Q.* v. ix. 32 Sacred Reuerence, yborne of heauenly strene. **1599** SHAKS. *Much Ado* II. i. 394 Hee is of a noble straine, of approued valour, and confirm'd honesty. **1600** FAIRFAX *Tasso* v. xlii, Let them in fetters plead their cause (quoth hee) That are base peasants, borne of seruile straine. **1615** CHAPMAN *Odyss.* XIV. 286 From ample Crete I fetch my Natiue straine; My Father wealthy: whose house [etc.]. **1624** HEYWOOD *Gunaik.* I. 49 Young Epaphus..To Phaeton objects, that he was bred Of mortall straine. **1813** SCOTT *Trierm.* I. i, Where is the maiden of mortal strain, That may match with the Baron of Triermain?

6. a. The descendants of a common ancestor; a race, stock, line.

c **1330** *Arth. & Merl.* 1021 For þe misbeȝeten stren Quic y schal now doluen ben! *c* **1400** *Rom. Rose* 4859 Bicause al is corumpable, And faile shulde successioun, Ne were ther generacioun Our sectis strene for to save. *c* **1440** *Sir Gowther* 202 Thow comest never of Crists strene, Thou art sum fendes sone y wene. **1470–85** MALORY *Arthur* XIII. viii. 622 He is..of the best men of the world comen and of the strene of alle partyes of kynges. **1569** *Irish Act 11 Eliz.* c. I. (1621) 315 Least that any man..might be ledde..to thinke that the strene or lyne of the Oneyles should..hold or possesse anie part of the dominion..of Ulster. **1589** WARNER *Albion's Eng.* VI. xxxi. (1592) 140 Of that Streene shall Fiue at length re-raigne. **1597** BEARD *Theatre God's Judgem.* (1612) 465 His carkasse..was hanged vpon a gallowes, and all his kindred and children put to death, that there might not one remaine of his straine. **1624** QUARLES *Job Milit.* x. Med. xxviii, And left his Empire to another Straine. **1676** SHADWELL *Virtuoso* I. i, It must needs be so; for Gentlemen care not upon what Strain they get their sons, nor how they breed 'em, when they have got 'em. **1688** DRYDEN *Brit. Rediv.* 216 And for his Estian race and Saxon strain Might reproduce some second Richard's reign. **1700** PRIOR *Carmen Sec.* 73 Charlemain, And the long Heroes of the Gallic Strain. **1876** GEO. ELIOT *Deronda* lxiii. IV. 247, I come of a strain that has ardently maintained the fellowship of our race.

b. Any one of the various lines of ancestry united in an individual or a family; an admixture of some racial or family element in a genealogy.

1863 WHYTE MELVILLE *Gladiators* I. ii. 26 It might have been the strain of Greek blood which filtered through his veins, that tempered his Roman courage..with the pliancy, essential to conspiracy and intrigue. **1865** *Pall Mall Gaz.* 8 June 11 These animals are usually a cross between the bulldog and the mastiff, and are all the better if dashed with a strain of the bloodhound. **1884** W. C. SMITH *Kildrostan* 93 She's just a Highland lady Touched with an Eastern strain. **1897** *Times* 11 Mar. 12/2 Lord Coventry..said..He had not bought horses in Ireland as hunters which had any strain of hackney or cart-horse blood. **1902** R. BAGOT *Donna Diana* ix. 103 The features were regular..with something about..the moulding of the nose and chin that suggested a strain of Jewish blood.

7. A race, breed; a variety developed by breeding. **a.** of animals.

1607 MARKHAM *Caval.* I. (1617) 26, I..know, that if a man will continue his breede altogether in one straine, without any alteration or strangenesse [he] shall in the ende finde his studd to decay. **1615** CHAPMAN *Odyss.* XIV. 31 By them, Mastiues as au tere As sauage beasts, lay euer. Their fierce straine Bred by the Herdsman. **1634** BRERETON *Trav.* (Chetham Soc.) 32 Coach-mares, bred but of his own strain. *c* **1650** in Thoms *Anecd.* (Camden) 47 The cocke was match't, and bearing Sir Thomas Jermin's name... Everyone wond'red to see Sir Thomas his streine cry Craven. **1697** DRYDEN *Virg. Past.* ii. 55 Two Kids..Both fleck'd with white, the true Arcadian Strain. **1708** J. CHAMBERLAYNE *St. Gt. Brit.* I. I. iii. (1743) 12 The Sheep of Cotswold have so fine a Wool, that the Spanish strain ('tis said) came from a Present of Edward I. made of these Sheep to Alphonso King of Spain. **1759** R. BROWN *Compl. Farmer* 46 The former hogs of the cross strain. **1847** W. C. L. MARTIN *Ox* 70/1 Crosses with the Hereford were tried,..but soon, after one or two generations, the defects of the Glamorganshire strain reappeared. **1854** *Poultry Chron.* I. 246/2 To keep up a stock of first-rate fowls it is necessary every other year to cross the strain. **1859** DARWIN *Orig. Spec.* i. 34 Eminent breeders try by methodical selection, with a distinct object in view, to make a new strain or sub-breed, superior to anything existing in the country. **1868** *Field* 4 July 22/2 Two Pups of his strain of the above breed [of St. Bernard's]. **1872** L. WRIGHT *Illustr. Bk. Poultry* 207 *Strain*, a race of fowls which, having been carefully bred by one breeder or his successors for years, has acquired an individual character of its own which can be more or less relied upon. **1884** *Expositor* Jan. 35 The animals which man has bred into new and specialized strains.

b. of plants.

1845 *Florist's Jrnl.* (1846) VI. 42 It has..taken a number of years to obtain what florists term a 'strain' of flowers likely to lead to great results. **1849** J. F. WOOD *Midland Florist* iii. 121 Every tulip grower is aware of the importance of getting a good strain of any given variety. **1908** *Ch. Times* 20 Mar. 392/4 Begonias, gold medal strain, equal to any in the kingdom.

c. of microbes, etc.

1897 *Allbutt's Syst. Med.* II. 636 Numerous strains of vaccine lymph have, from time to time been raised from the equine source. **1904** *Brit. Med. Jrnl.* 3 Dec. 1508 Another point leading to a similar interpretation is observed in some strains of B. anthracis.

(*b*) *spec.* as ***strain 19, Strain 19***: a strain of the bacterium *Brucella abortus* which is used as a live vaccine against brucellosis in cattle and as a killed vaccine in horses.

1930 *Jrnl. Agric. Res.* XLI. 669 Strain 19 that had been isolated one and one-half years previously was used in the preparation of the vaccine administered to calves. **1959** *Vet. Ann.* I. 88 There have been several reports of infection of human beings with strain 19 vaccine. **1970** T. G. HUNGERFORD *Dis. Livestock* (ed. 7) 718/2 Injection of Strain 19 into the horse is followed by severe systemic reaction... As a result, killed Brucella abortus vaccine was originally used, but it is thought that the living Strain 19 giving a violent reaction offers a better hope of success.

8. a. Inherited character or constitution.

1603 B. JONSON *Sejanus* I. i, 'Tis wee are..degenerate from th' exalted streine Of our great Fathers. **1605** SHAKS. *Lear* v. iii. 40 Sir, you have shew'd to day your valiant straine And Fortune led you well. *a* **1671** TILLOTSON *Serm.* iii. 135 Intemperance and Lust breed infirmities and diseases, which being propagated, spoil the Strain of a Nation. **1681** W. ROBERTSON *Phraseol. Gen.* (1693) 1176 A strain, *indoles.* **1853** C. BRONTE *Villette* ii, Neither in mien nor in features was this creature like her sire, and yet she was of his strain; her mind had been filled from his, as the cup from the flagon.

b. An inherited tendency or quality; a feature of character or constitution derived from some ancestor; hence, in wider sense, an admixture in a character of some quality somewhat contrasting with the rest.

1598 SHAKS. *Merry W.* II. i. 91 For sure vnlesse he know some straine in mee, that I know not my selfe, he would neuer haue boorded me in this furie. **1605** *Lond. Prodigal* III. ii. 172 Such mad straines as hee's possesst withall. *a* **1627** HAYWARD *Edw. VI* (1630) 7 Because Heretickes for the most part haue a straine of madnesse, he thought it best to apply her with some corporall chastisements. **1633** HEYWOOD *Eng. Trav.* I, The French is of one humor, Spaine another, The hot Italian hee's a straine from both. **1704** SWIFT *Mech. Operat. Spir.* in *Tale Tub*, etc. 289 A Fanatick Strain, or Tincture of Enthusiasm. **1885** 'MRS. ALEXANDER' *Valerie's Fate* i, She really has a strain of nobility under all her flightiness. **1899** P. H. BROWN *Hist. Scot.* II. ii. I. 95 There was in him a strain of superstition which distorted his vision in all matters concerned with the church. **1906** *Lit. World* 15 Nov. 489/2 There was..a strain of insanity in the family.

†**c.** A characteristic instance (of a person's qualities). *Obs.*

1685 TEMPLE *Gardening* Wks. 1770 III. 204 It was no mean strain of his philosophy to refuse being secretary to Augustus. **1695** —— *Hist. Eng.* (1699) 146 It looks like a Strain of his usual Boldness and fearless Temper.

9. a. A kind, class, or sort (of persons), as determined by community of character, conduct, or degree of ability. Now *rare.*

1598 SHAKS. *Merry W.* III. iii. 97 *Mist. Page.* Hang him dishonest rascall: I would all of the same straine, were in the same distresse. **1600–9** ROWLANDS *Knaue of Clubbes* 32 A Cittie wanton full of pride and lust, Of Venus straine and disposition iust. **1642** D. ROGERS *Naaman* 57 And that by the confession even of some of his owne straine. **1645** FEATLY *Dippers Dipt* (1646) 21 So we haue had but too just cause to complain of the like outrages committed by some of the Zelots of that Straine. **1647** N. BACON *Disc. Govt. Eng.* ii. 4 Their [*sc.* the Druids'] high conceipt of their excellency above the ordinary straine of men. *a* **1660** *Contemp. Hist. Irel.* (Ir. Archæol. Soc.) I. 172 The Councell that grannted such power to a partie of that straine, were malitiously intended. **1693** DRYDEN *Persius* v. 164 Thou, who lately of the common strain, Wert one of us. **1746** FRANCIS tr. *Hor., Sat.* I. i. 131 A bold Wench, of right Virago Strain. **1847** EMERSON *Poems, Threnody* 141 The world..was not ripe yet, to sustain A genius of so fine a strain.

b. A kind, class, or grade (of things). ? *Obs.*

1612 T. TAYLOR *Titus* i. 1. (1619) 24 The contemplation of things of an higher strain. **1646** J. MAXWELL *Burd. Issachar* 4 All crimes and scandals of highest strain, namely, such as are civilly punishable by death. **1695** WOODWARD *Nat. Hist. Earth* v. (1723) 249 But these Alterations are of a quite different Strain. **1702** S. PARKER tr. *Cicero's De Fin.* IV. 231 Hitherto your Objections have been Vulgar and of Course; and therefore I promise myself you have a higher Strein in Reserve.

10. *Comb.* ***strain-specific*** adj.; ***strain-specificity.***

1964 M. HYNES *Med. Bacteriol.* (ed. 8) xxiv. 350 Many examples are now known of viruses which cause malignant tumours in animals. Most are species-specific or even strain-specific. **1947** *Ann. Rev. Microbiol.* I. 362 There was a sharp strain specificity with sedimented antigen and less with the residual.

strain (streɪn), *sb.*² Forms: 5 stren, 5–7 straine, 6 *Sc.* streinȝe, strenȝae, 6–7 strayn(e, streine, streyne, 7 streyn, *Sc.* strienȝie, 7–8 strein, 7– strain. [f. STRAIN *v.*¹]

†**I. 1.** A strainer. *Obs.*

1432 in Gross *Gild Merch.* (1890) II. 233 For a straine 2 d. *c* **1467** *Noble Bk. Cookry* (1882) 26 Streyn the broth through a stren. **1655** R. YOUNGE *Charge agst. Drunkards* (1863) 3 Custom hath made it to passe through them, as through a tunnel, or streine [1658, strainer].

II. Action or result of straining.

†**2.** Constraint, bondage. *Obs.*

a **1510** DOUGLAS *K. Hart* I. 274 Thair saw he Lust by law [ly] vnder lok, In streinȝe strong fast fetterit fute and hand.

†**3.** Compulsion. *Obs.*

1532 *Abstr. Protocols Town Clerks Glasgow* (1897) IV. 46 The forsaydis Thomas and Jonet..sull pas frele, withowt ony impediment and strenȝae ane mark of anwell. **1602** MARSTON *Antonio's Rev.* IV. iii, What I here speake is forced from my lips By the pulsive straine of conscience. **1632** LITHGOW *Trav.* x. 487 What by dread or straine, you can not worke nor do. **1648** J. BEAUMONT *Psyche* XII. ix, Moderation's Discipline may prove No Task of Duty, but a Strein of Love.

4. A result of straining. **a.** An injury done to a limb or part of the body, esp. to a muscle or tendon, through being forcibly stretched beyond its proper length. Often coincident with SPRAIN.

1558 in Feuillerat *Revels Q. Mary* (1914) 251, I ame not able to ryde nor shalbe I fear this iij or iiij dais by reason of a strayn. **1580** LYLY *Euphues & Eng.* Wks. 1902 II. 204 Saying that in thinges aboue reach, it was easie to catch a straine; but impossible to touch a Star. **1614** LATHAM *Falconry* (1633) 135 This is a very speciall thing to comfort the sinewes ouer strained, and to cure and asswage the anguish of the straine. **1670** E. BORLASE *Latham Spaw* 51 His Servant..got a strain in his back, lifting more than he could well master. *a* **1673** P. D. *Mare of Collingtoun* in *Watson's Collect.* I. (1706) 60 It will be good against the Pine Of any Wriest or Strienzie. **1735** DYCHE & PARDON *Dict., Strain*,..also an Extorsion of the Sinews beyond their natural Tone, sometimes called a Sprain. **1789** W. BUCHAN *Dom. Med.* (1790) 597 Strains are often attended with worse consequences than broken bones. **1842** *Penny Cycl.* XXII. 383/1 Sprain, or Strain, is an injury of muscular or tendinous tissues, resulting from their being forcibly stretched beyond their natural length.

†**b.** A failure under trial. *Obs.*

1596 BARLOW *Three Serm.* ii. 81 For thogh the godly haue their slips and straines, yet it greeueth them.

5. a. A stretch, extreme degree, height, pitch (of a quality, activity, etc.). Now *rare.*

Some of the examples below might perhaps be referred to STRAIN *sb.*¹ 9 or 8 c.

1576 GASCOIGNE *Steele Gl.* (Arb.) 59 But had he seene, the streine of straunge deuise, Which Epicures, do now adayes inuent, To yeld good smacke, vnto their daintie tongues:.. Then would he say, that [etc.]. **1609** HOLLAND *Amm. Marcell.* XXVI. vii. 292 More odious than Cleander; who governing as Præfect..in a high straine (as it were) of outrage and madnesse, made havocke..of divers mens estates. **1627** HAKEWILL *Apol.* (1630) 411 Yet Heliogabalus went a straine farther, and put it to a baser use. **1631** R. BOLTON *Comf. Affl. Consc.* vii. (1635) 43 Crowne Him with the concurrence of all created earthy exellencies, to the utmost and highest straine. **1648** J. BEAUMONT *Psyche* XII. clxvii, No Epicurean ambition e'r Its liquorish self screw'd to so high a strein As to affect a Draught so rich as this. **1664** WOOD *Life* (O.H.S.) II. 2 The undergraduates..arrived to strang degree and streyn of impudence. **1667** [SIR J. STUART & STIRLING] *Napthali* 91 This is a strain of wickedness above all that former times could imagine. **1685** STILLINGFL. *Orig. Brit.* v. 275 This is a Strain beyond Geffrey, who never thought of bringing the British Language from the Plain of Sennaar. **1708** SWIFT *Abol. Chr.* (1717) 13 To Break an English Free-born Officer only for Blasphemy, was..a very high strain of absolute Power. *a* **1715** BURNET *Own Time* (1766) I. 228 It was thought..an odd strain of clemency if it was intended he [Milton] should be forgiven. **1717** POPE *Let. to Earl Halifax* 1 Dec., It is, indeed, a high Strain of Generosity in you, to think of making me easy all my Life. **1817** JAS. MILL *Brit. India* v. vi. II. 574 Justice was administered..without any peculiar strain of abuse. **1822** LAMB *Elia* Ser. II. *Bks. & Reading*, I knew a Unitarian minister, who was generally to be seen upon Snowhill.., between the hours of ten and eleven in the morning, studying a volume of Lardner. I own this to have been a strain of abstraction beyond my reach. **1875** JOWETT *Plato* (ed. 2) IV. 161 Saying the same thing in different ways..is a strain of art beyond the reach of most of us.

†**b.** Utmost capacity, reach. *Obs.*

1593 DRAYTON *Sheph. Garland* Eglog iii. v, Faire Betas praise beyond our straine doth stretch, Her notes too hie for my poore pipe to reach. **1599** B. JONSON *Ev. Man out of Hum.* Induct., May our Minerua Answere your hopes, vnto their largest straine! **1599** —— *Cynthia's Rev.* I. v. (1601) C 4 b, O how..base a thing is Man, If he not striue t'erect his groueling thoughts Aboue the straine of flesh?

†**c.** Standard of requirement. *Obs.*

1605 BACON *Adv. Learn.* II. xxii. §9 That wee beware wee take not at the first either to High a strayne or to weake: for if, too Highe in a diffident nature you discourage, in a confident nature, you breede an opinion of facility.

†**d.** ? A 'stretch' of country. *Obs. rare*⁻¹.

1614 GORGES *Lucan* VI. 215 That long stretching Malean straine That shelues so farre into the maine.

†**6.** A strained construction or interpretation.

1579 W. WILKINSON *Confut. Fam. Love* 26 b, The first straine wheron this further hereticall accord was to be stretched, was this. **1609** [W. BARLOW] *Answ. Nameless Cath.* 38 What a trifling Sophister this is, to picke quarels at words, by wrests and streines, neither to purpose nor to sense. **1616** JAS. I *Sp. Starre-Chamber* 20 June 20 It must not bee Sophistrie or straines of wit that must interprete, but either cleare Law, or solide reason. **1629** CHAS. I *Decl. 3rd Parlt.* Wks. 1662 II. 16 Finding..such sinister strains made upon Our Answer to that Petition..We resolved [etc.]. **1707** *Col. Rec. Pennsylv.* II. 334 We declare [this] to be a meer straine and a most unjust Imputation. **1720** LD. CHANC. PARKER in W. P. Williams *Chancery Cases* (1740) I. 517 It was a strange Construction to take Pains by a Strain in Law, to place a Remainder in Fee *in Nubibus.* **1726** SWIFT *Gulliver* I. iv, This, however, is thought to be a mere strain upon the text: For the words are these: 'That all true' [etc.]. **1731** —— *Verses Death Dr. Swift* 327 Not strains of law,..nor jury picked, Prevail to bring him in Convict.

†**7.** Something strained or squeezed out. *Obs.*

c **1616** CHAPMAN *Batrachom.* 3 Lyurings (white-skin'd as Ladies:) nor the straines Of prest milke, renneted.

8. a. A strong muscular effort; †*spec.* an effort to vomit, a retching; a straining at stool.

In quots. 1590, 1607 app. used for: A step, pace (? with notion of stately or ponderous movement.)

1590 GREENE *Never too Late, Canzone* 37 Her pace was like to Iunoes pompous straines When as she sweeps through heuens brasse-paued way. **1592** KYD *John Brewen* Wks. (1901) 290 He began to vomet exceedingly, with such straines as if his lungs would burst in pieces. **1601** HOLLAND *Pliny* XXII. xxi. II. 126 As many as live thereof, are infested ..neither with the dysenterie..ne yet with the troublesome offers and streins to the seege without doing any thing. **1607** TOPSELL *Four-f. Beasts* 101 This beast..doth not moue his right and left foote one after another, but both together,.. whereby his whole body is remoued at euery step or straine. *c* **1630** DONNE *Serm.* xxxiii. (1640) 322 The holy Ghost.. deales not with him, as a Painter, which..passes his pencill an hundred times over every muscle,..but..as a Printer, that in one straine delivers a whole story. **1726** LEONI *Alberti's Archit.* I. 74*a*, The Rise..was only for so little a way, that a beast heavy loaden cou'd get over it at one strain. **1771** R. JAMES *Diss. Fevers* (ed. 8) 40 He had several strains for two hours, but never vomited. **1884** W. F. BUTLER *Nile Boat Song* in *Pall Mall Gaz.* 16 Oct. 4/2 Row, my boys, row away... Bend to the strain, men!

b. ***at (full, utmost) strain, on the strain***: straining, using strong effort. Cf. ASTRAIN *adv.*

1851 MRS. BROWNING *Casa Guidi Wind.* II. 290 With her wide eyes at full strain. **1868–70** MORRIS *Earthly Par.* III. 432 A dismal wedding! every ear at strain Some sign of things that were to be to gain. **1884** *Graphic* 16 Aug. 166/1 Till..even nine at night they are perpetually on the strain. **1885–94** BRIDGES *Eros & Psyche* May 20 Adonis..spear in hand, with leashed dogs at strain. **1900** F. T. BULLEN *With Christ at Sea* xi. 227 They were all labouring at utmost strain to try and save the ship.

c. Extreme or excessive effort; a straining *at* or *after* some object of attainment; †laboured or affected diction or thought.

1683–6 *Dryden's Plutarch, Jul. Cæsar* (1693) IV. 416 Yet with the utmost streins of their valour, they were not able to beat the enemy out of the field. **1713** JOHNSON *Guardian* No. 4 ¶2 'Tis observable of the Female Poets and Ladies Dedicatory, that..they far exceed us in any Strain or Rant. **1839** HALLAM *Lit. Europe* IV. vii. §5. IV. 501 The Dialogues of the Dead..are condemned by some critics for their false taste and perpetual strain at something unexpected and paradoxical. **1870** MORLEY *Crit. Misc., Vauvenargues* (1871) I. 21 Men think and work on the highest level when they move without conscious and deliberate strain after virtue. **1905** J. H. JOWETT *Passion for Souls* 84 There shall be strenuousness without strain!

9. a. A forcible stretching of a material thing; force tending to pull asunder or to drag from a position. In later use with wider sense: Force or pressure tending to cause fracture, change of position, or alteration of shape; also, the condition of a body or a particle subjected to such force or pressure.

1602 MARSTON *Ant. & Mel.* I, Heele snap in two at every little straine. **1818** P. BARLOW in *Encycl. Metrop.* III. 61/1 Our object is to investigate the conditions of equilibrium between the resistance of solids, and the strains to which they may be exposed. **1827** FARADAY *Chem. Manip.* xx. (1842) 548 That by directing the pull on the bottle a little on one side or the other, the strain upon the stopper may be equal or nearly so on the two sides. **1827–8** HERSCHEL in *Encycl. Metrop.* IV. 565 The general problem, then, to investigate the actual state of strain of any molecule at any moment is one of some complexity. **1842** GWILT *Archit.* Gloss., *Strain*, the force exerted on any material tending to disarrange or destroy the cohesion of its component parts. **1867** SMYTH *Sailor's Word-bk., Set up rigging*, to take in the slack of the shrouds, stays, and backstays, to bring the same strain as before, and thus secure the masts. **1884** SARGENT *Rep. Forests N. Amer.* 355 Table III. Behavior of the principal woods of the United States under transverse strain. **1888** BURT *Stand. Timber Meas.* 312 Table of Breaking Strains.

b. *Physics.* In mod. use, after Rankine and Thomson: see quots.

1850 RANKINE *Misc. Sci. Papers* (1881) 68 Although the word *strain* is used in ordinary language indiscriminately to denote relative molecular displacement, and the force by which it is produced,..I shall..use it, throughout this paper, in the restricted sense of relative displacement of particles, whether consisting in dilatation, condensation, or distortion; while under the term *pressure* I shall include [etc.]. **1879** THOMSON & TAIT *Nat. Phil.* I. I. §154 We have now to consider the very important kinematical conditions presented by the changes of volume or figure experienced by a solid or liquid mass... Any such definite alteration of form or dimensions is called a Strain.

c. ***to take the strain***, in a tug of war: see quots.; *fig.*, to assume a burden, take a responsibility.

1912 *Games & Nav. Milit. Tournament* 3 The pulls will be started by the Referee by word of mouth:—'Take the strain', on which both teams will put a strain on the rope without pulling. **1927** W. E. COLLINSON *Contemporary English* 38 Among the other field sports I might single out..the tug of war with its expressions to take the strain (i.e. when each side pulls the rope taut before the signal for the tug is given by the dropping of a handkerchief), and to pull one's weight .., both of which lend themselves to figurative use.

10. In immaterial applications of sense 9 a.

†**a.** *pl.* Trials, hardships. *Obs.*

a **1628** F. GREVIL *Sidney* (1652) 18 Any man..forced, in the straines of this life, to pass through any straights or latitudes of good or ill fortune.

b. Pressure or exigency that severely taxes the strength, endurance, or resources of a person or thing, or that imperils the permanence of a feeling, relation, or condition.

1853 MRS. GASKELL *Ruth* xxxi, I should not have been surprised last night if he had dropped down dead, so terrible was his strain upon himself. **1858** LYTTON *What will He do?* XII. ix, The reaction that follows all strain upon purpose. **1860** TYNDALL *Glac.* I. xxvii. 196 The strain upon the horses [was] very great. **1876** GEO. ELIOT *Deronda* xv. I. 295 A difference of taste in jokes is a great strain on the affections. **1897** MARY KINGSLEY *W. Africa* 217 He was..a bright, intelligent young Frenchman; but..the strain of his responsibility had been too much for him. **1894** LADY M. VERNEY *Verney Mem.* III. 5 He had been often driven to borrow money of Sir Ralph..but their friendship had stood the strain. **1898** CONAN DOYLE *Trag. Korosko* v. 123 My Arabic won't bear much strain. I don't know what he is saying. **1908** R. BAGOT *A. Cuthbert* xxiii. 309 His voice broke suddenly, and Sonia realised the strain he had been putting upon himself to meet his trouble quietly and courageously.

c. Strained relations, tension.

1884 *Chr. World* 30 Oct. 821/1 The strain between the two Houses could, he thought, only be relaxed by mutual concessions.

d. *Life Insurance.* An expense or financial liability incurred by an insurance office which is not covered by reserves accumulated from the relevant policies.

1910 *Encycl. Brit.* XIV. 670/2 It is obvious that office B, which has a margin of income 50% greater than that of office A, is so much better able to bear any unusual strain in addition to the ordinary expenditure. **1929** F. L. COLLINS in R. C. Simmonds *Life Assurance Text-bk.* 128 The true risk which the office runs consists not in the whole sum assured, but in the difference required in the case of death to supplement the reserve value which it already has in hand ... technically termed the 'strain'. **1941** *Economist* 15 Mar. 344/1 When a premature death occurs, the loss to the office, known technically as the 'strain', is the difference between the policy moneys payable and the reserve carried, and it follows that this 'strain' will be much greater in the case of a young life than an old one. **1965** Fisher & Young *Actuarial Practice of Life Assurance* I. ii. 29 The net premium method of valuation failed to take account of this uneven incidence of expenses and caused what is termed a new business strain. It required the setting up of initial reserves which could not have been derived from the first premium since that had been largely or even entirely expended in the cost of the first year's risk and expenses.

11. Phr. ***strain and stress*** (with reference to senses 9 and 10; cf. ***stress(es) and strains*** s.v. stress *sb.* 6).

[**1842** *Penny Cycl.* XXIII. 101/2 *Strain and Stress.* ([See] *Materials, Strength of.*)] **1856** *Phil. Trans. R. Soc.* CXLVI. 488 (*heading*) On the measurement of strains and stresses. **1857** E. B. Browning *Aurora Leigh* v. 385 We, staggering 'neath our burden as mere men, Being called to stand up straight as demi-gods, Support the intolerable strain and stress Of the universal. **1872** J. G. Whittier in *Pennsylvania Pilgrim* 94 Take from our souls the strain and stress, And let our ordered lives confess The beauty of thy peace. **1935** *Discovery* Sept. 270/1 Many [stelae] have successfully resisted the strains and stresses of the passing centuries. **1941** H. G. Wells *You can't be too Careful* v. i. 240 After a tremendous constructive effort after the war, and after a phase of experimental strain and stress. **1962** J. Dill in *Into Orbit* p. xix, Space flight..would expose the Astronauts to greater strains and stresses, both physically and mentally, than most pilots had ever had to face.

III. (Cf. strain *v.*[1] V.)

12. *Mus.* A definite section of a piece of music: see quots. 1841–75.

1575 Gascoigne *Posies, Gr. Knt.'s Farew. Fansie* Wks. 1907 I. 381 In Hyerarchies and straynes, in restes, in rule and space, In monacordes and mouing moodes, in Burdens vnder base. **1589** *Pappe w. Hatchet* in *Lyly's Wks.* (1902) III. 413 Martin, this is my last straine for this fleech of mirth... I must tune my fiddle, and fetch some more rozen. **1597** Morley *Introd. Mus.* 180 Canzonets..(wherein little arte can be shewed being made in straines, the beginning of which is some point lightlie touched, and euerie straine repeated except the middle). **1598** Bastard *Chrestol.* II. xxi. 40 He hath rimes and rimes, and double straynes: And golden verses, and all kindes of veynes. **1599** B. Jonson *Cynthia's Rev.* v. v. (1601) L 2, Stage-dir., They daunce the 1. Straine. **1662** Playford *Skill Mus.* I. xi. 35 The double Bars are set to divide the several Strains or Stanzaes of the Songs and Lessons. **1676** Mace *Musick's Mon.* 127 If at any time you chance to meet with a Strain, consisting of Odd Barrs, peruse That Strain well. **1841** J. A. Hamilton *Dict. Mus. Terms* (ed. 13) 66 *Strain*, a portion of a movement divided off by a double bar. **1873** H. C. Banister *Mus.* 171 A musical idea or passage, more or less complete in itself, and terminating, most frequently, with a Perfect Cadence.. constitutes a Rhythmical Period, or Strain. **1875** Stainer & Barrett *Dict. Mus. Terms, Strain*, a musical subject forming part of, and having relation to, a general whole.

13. a. In wider sense, a musical sequence of sounds; a melody, tune. Often *collect. pl.*

1579 Gosson *Apol. Sch. Abuse* (Arb.) 68 Pypers are sore displeased bicause I allow not their new streines. ? **1617** Sir W. Mure *To Prince Charles* 4 Montgomery..often ravischt his harmonious ear W[t] straynes fitt only for a prince to heir. **1637** Milton *Lycidas* 87 That strain I heard was of a higher mood. **1687** Norris *Misc.* 89 Soft melting strains of Music. **1697** Dryden *Virg. Georg.* iv. 746 She supplies the Night with mournful Strains, And melancholy Musick fills the Plains. **1735** Fielding *Universal Gallant* Epil., By the vast sums we pay them for their strains, They'll think, perhaps, we don't abound in brains. **1775** Sheridan *Duenna* I. i, Tell me, my lute, can thy soft strain So gently speak thy master's pain? **1794** Mrs. Radcliffe *Myst. Udolpho* xxvii, Emily recollected the mysterious strains of music that she had lately heard. **1820** W. Irving *Sketch Bk.* I. 347 When a soft strain of music stole up from the garden. **1827** Keble *Chr. Yr., Morning* 37 As for some dear familiar strain Untir'd we ask, and ask again. **1851** Longf. *Golden Leg.* iv. *Road to Hirschau*, This life of ours is a wild æolian harp of many a joyous strain. **1859** Sala *Tw. round Clock* 108 The enlivening strains of the brass band. **1875** Jowett *Plato* (ed. 2) V. 14 Notes are struck which are repeated from time to time, as in a strain of music.

b. *transf.* A passage of song or poetry. †Also, ? a passage, verse (of the Bible).

1563 Golding *Calvin on Job* 135 b, This is not the naturall meening: and such as take it so, neuer knewe the intent of the holy Ghost as touching this streyne [Fr. *quant à ce passage*]. **1583** —— *Calvin on Deut.* ii. 18 b, That then is the thing that wee haue to marke vppon this streyne [Fr. *en ce passage*]. **1632** Milton *Penseroso* 174 Till old experience do attain To something like Prophetic strain. **1643** Sir T. Browne *Relig. Med.* I. §44 There be many excellent straines in that Poet [Lucan]. **1697** Dryden *Virg. Past.* iv. 1 Sicilian Muse, begin a loftier strain! **1751** Johnson *Rambler* No. 93 ⁋3 Interest and passion..will for ever bid defiance to the most powerful strains of Virgil or Homer. **1766** [Anstey] *Bath Guide* i. 14 Here teach fond Swains their hapless Loves In gentle Strains to weep. **1770** Goldsm. *Des. Vill.* 423 Aid slighted truth with thy persuasive strain. **1833** Tennyson *Miller's Dau.* 66 A love-song I had somewhere read, An echo from a measured strain. **1847** Emerson *Repr. Men, Goethe* Wks. (Bohn) I. 392 There are nobler strains in poetry than any he has sounded. **1858** J. Martineau *Stud. Christ* 41 Who, having the strains of David, would pore over Leviticus? **1879** Geo. Eliot *Theo. Such* ii. 32, I might have poured forth poetic strains which would have anticipated theory.

c. A stream or flow of impassioned or ungoverned language. (Either in favourable or unfavourable sense.) ? *Obs.*; common in 17–18th c.

1649 Milton *Eikon.* vi. 50 The Simily..I was about to have found fault with, as in a garb somwhat more Poeticall then for a Statist: but meeting with many straines of like dress in other of his Essaies,..I begun to think that [etc.]. *a* **1677** Barrow *Serm.* (1716) I. 159 When a man is..fiercely angry..he blustereth and dischargeth his choler in most tragical strains. **1699** T. Baker *Refl. Learn.* xv. 178 Macrobius speaks of his [*sc.* Hippocrates'] knowledge in such lofty strains, as are only agreeable to God Almighty. **1713** Steele *Englishman* No. 55. 355 Addresses came..with foolish Strains of Obedience without Reserve. **1741** Hume *Ess. Mor. & Polit.* xvi. (1748) 144 Shall we assert, that the Strains of ancient Eloquence are unsuitable to our Age? **1742** C. Yorke in G. Harris *Life Ld. Hardwicke* (1847) II. 21 Dean Swift has had a statute of lunacy taken out against him. His madness appears chiefly in most incessant strains of obscenity and swearing.

14. Tone, style, or turn of expression; tone or character of feeling expressed; tenor, drift, or general tendency or character (of a composition or discourse).

1622 J. Taylor (Water P.) *Water-Cormorant* Pref., I haue thought good to sympathize a subiect fit for the time, and I haue done my best to handle it in a sutable straine. **1665** Boyle *Occas. Refl.* Introd. Pref. (1848) p. xxi, When he writes of Ants and Flies, he does it in a Strain worthy of the same Pen, that so loftily describes the Destruction of Troy. **1678** R. Barclay *Apol. Quakers* v. §xxi. 161 It is contrary to the very strain of the Context. **1681** W. Robertson *Phraseol. Gen.* (1693) 1176 A strain in speech, *stylus, sermo.* **1684** Bunyan *Pilgr.* II. Introd., To study what those Sayings should contain That speak to us in such a Cloudy strain. **1708** Swift *Baucis & Phil.* 11 Where, in the Strolers canting Strain, They begg'd from Door to Door in vain. **1761** Hume *Hist. Eng. to Hen. VII*, I. i. 23 Their writings, which as appears from the strain of his own wit,..he [Gregory] had not taste nor genius sufficient to comprehend. **1777** Priestley *Matter & Spir.* Pref. p. xix, It is, I presume, sufficiently evident from the strain of my publications, that general applause has not been my object. **1786** Cowper *Let.* 19 Feb., My friend Bagot writes to me in a most friendly strain. **1808** W. Wilson *Hist. Dissenting Ch.* II. 56 For a serious, evangelical strain of preaching,..he was equalled by few ministers in his day. **1817** Jas. Mill *Brit. India* iv. v. II. 164 Clive wrote with much sharpness to the Nabob; and Meeran apologized in the most submissive strain. **1826** W. Irving *Babylon* I. II. 69 And among the heathen also, if we may judge from the strain of many of their writings. **1849** Macaulay *Hist. Eng.* vi. II. 141 But his letters to England were in a very different strain. **1870** J. Bruce *Life of Gideon* iv. 74 Observe the strain and character of that wonderful reply. **1902** R. Bagot *Donna Diana* x. 113 At times Frau von Raben would talk in a mysteriously sympathizing strain, as though inviting her confidence.

†**IV. 15.** The track of a deer. (Cf. strain *v.*[1] 18 b.) *Obs.*

1612 Capt. Smith *Virginia* Wks. (Arb.) I. 71 So watching his best aduantage.., hauing shot him [a deer] hee chaseth him by his blood and straine till he get him. **1652** J. Wright tr. *Camus' Nat. Paradox* iv. 82 The Hunts-men, who were more in pain for the straying of their Master, than their missing of the Stag, whose Strain they could not finde, all their Hounds being at a loss. **1659** Howell *Lex. Tetragl., Partic. Voc.* iii, The strain, view, slott, or footing of a deer.

V. 16. *attrib.* and *Comb.*, as ***strain-bearing***, ***case***, ***-sensation***; ***strain-free***, ***-veined*** adjs.; **strain ageing** *vbl. sb. Metallurgy*, the cold working of iron and steel followed by ageing, either at room temperature or at temperatures up to the recrystallization temperature; also, the resultant increase in hardness and decrease in ductility; so **strain-aged** *ppl. a.*; **strain-band** *Naut.* (see quot. 1867); **strain energy**, (*a*) *Mech.*, energy stored in a body as a result of work performed on it; (*b*) *Chem.*, the excess heat of formation of a cyclic molecule over the value calculated from similar bonds in unstrained molecules; **strain gauge** *Engin.*, a device for indicating the strain of a material or structure at the point of attachment; **strain hardening** *vbl. sb. Metallurgy*, increase in strength and hardness and decrease in ductility of a metal as a result of strain ageing; so **strain-harden** *v. intr.*, to undergo strain hardening; **strain-hardened** *ppl. a.*; **strainmeter** *Engin.* = *strain gauge* above; **strain rosette** *Engin.* = rosette *sb.* 5 f; **strain-slip cleavage** *Geol.*, a rock structure in which there are parallel, closely-spaced shear planes with transverse microscopic folds between adjacent ones.

1966 *Trans. Metall. Soc. A.I.M.E.* CCXXXVI. 1198/1 (*heading*) The yield-point phenomenon in *strain-aged martensite. **1979** *Jrnl. Materials Sci.* XIV. 386 A strain-aged low carbon (~ 0·1% C) temper-rolled 16-gauge sheet steel which has been subjected to..ageing temperatures of 80 and 100°C. **1934** *Proc. Amer. Soc. Testing Materials* XXXIV. II. 48 The authors have applied the principle that *strain ageing and blue brittleness of ferrous materials are but different manifestations of the same phenomenon. **1967** A. H. Cottrell *Introd. Metall.* xxi. 394 In mild steel strain ageing usually takes a few days at room temperature, or about 30 minutes at 100°C, the rate being controlled by the diffusion of nitrogen and carbon atoms. **1867** Smyth *Sailor's Word-bk.*, *Strain-bands, bands of canvas sustaining the strain on the belly of the sails, and reinforced by the linings, &c. **1899** Whiteing *5 John St.* xix. 194 She [a mare] is a tower of strength, as carefully constructed for *strain-bearing as an Arctic ship. **1898** *Allbutt's Syst. Med.* V. 954 The disease in the cardio-arterial cases is 'progressive' and in the rheumatic or *strain cases not necessarily so. **1926** Pippard & Barrow *Building Res. Board Techn. Paper* No. 1. 2 The total *strain energy of the beam is made up of three components due to bending, torque and shear. **1939** *Jrnl. Amer. Chem. Soc.* LXI. 1871/2 The relative heats of hydration may be employed to evaluate the strain energy in cyclopentene only after correction has been made for these steric effects. **1976** A. L. Ternay *Contemp. Org. Chem.* vii. 197 The cyclopentane ring is puckered and..the cyclohexane ring exists largely in the chair form. If these compounds did not adopt these geometries, their strain energy would increase. **1977** Willems & Lucas *Struct. Analysis for Engineers* (1978) iii. 34 For the purposes of this text..all work done by external actions A_i acting through corresponding displacements D_i will be converted into kinetic and strain energy, and no energy losses will occur. **1946** *Nature* 26 Oct. 583/1 Well-annealed glass is *strain-free when uniformly heated. **1978** *Solid State Communications* XXVII. 713 (*heading*) Ferromagnetic resonance in strained and strain-free single crystal nickel films. **1910** *Engin. Rec.* LXI. 767/2 (*caption*) *Strain gauge or extensometer for deformation of webs or beams. **1948** 'N. Shute' *No Highway* i. 9 He had a few strain gauges mounted on various parts of the structure. **1972** L. M. Harris *Introd. Deep-water Floating Drilling Operations* xv. 160 Strain gauges on marine-riser joints have been used to evaluate fatigue damage and to locate stress concentrations. **1977** *Proc. R. Soc. Med.* LXX. 172/2 Mouth pressure and œsophageal pressure are monitored using strain-gauge transducers. **1959** C. E. Birchenall *Physical Metall.* vi. 124 Alloys always *strain-harden more effectively than pure metals. **1968** B. Avitzur *Metal Forming* viii. 201 When a material is deformed at a temperature above its crystallization temperature, it does not strain-harden. **1914** W. Rosenhain *Introd. Stud. Physical Metall.* xiii. 300 All ordinary wrought metals show signs of 'cold work' and are more or less *strain-hardened. **1960** *Jrnl. Appl. Physics* XXXI. 687/1 It is usually difficult to study the behavior of individual dislocations in strain-hardened crystals because so many dislocations are present. **1914** W. Rosenhain *Introd. Stud. Physical Metall.* xiii. 300 It is generally desirable to continue the working operations until a moderately low temperature is reached. This will result in slight *strain-hardening of the metal. **1973** J. G. Tweeddale *Materials Technol.* II. iv. 75 In metallic materials particularly, and in some other crystalline materials, mechanical deformation in certain circumstances gives rise to strain hardening. **1916** *Metallurgical & Chem. Engin.* XIV. 551/1 The *strainmeter is not affected by vibration, and it can be used under difficult conditions. **1939** *Jrnl. R. Aeronaut. Soc.* XLIII. 544 The strain meter..first made it possible to investigate the behaviour of the fast-moving and more inaccessible parts, such as crankshaft, airscrew, etc., during flight. **1979** *Bull. Seismol. Soc. Amer.* LXIX. 1983 Four invar-wire strainmeters have been operated in shallow trench sites..beside the San Andreas fault. **1938** *Engin. News-Record* 10 Mar. 370/3 The strains and stresses computed on the above form are pictured, in relation to the *strain rosette on the plating, in Fig. 6. **1950** J. H. Meier in M. Hetényi *Handbk. Exper. Stress Analysis* 400 The equi-angular strain rosette..is best suited in cases where the direction of the principal strains cannot be established approximately before test. **1894** J. E. Creighton & Titchener tr. *Wundt's Hum. & Anim. Psychol.* 247 When we are trying to remember a name or are pondering a difficult problem we notice the presence of *strain-sensations. **1886** T. G. Bonney in *Q. Jrnl. Geol. Soc.* XLII. I. 95 Subsequent work..has thrown additional light upon the..kind of cleavage..in which the cleavage-planes cut across the undulating bands of the constituent minerals. Of this structure I possess one or two excellent examples.. which makes it clear that the structure is an example of the *strain-slip cleavage (Ausweichungs-Clivage) of Dr. Heim. **1954** J. F. Kirkaldy *Gen. Princ. Geol.* x. 127 Less perfectly graded rocks..may develop not the true slaty cleavage, due to re-orientation of the minerals, but a strain-slip cleavage, produced by closely spaced planes of movement. **1969** Bennison & Wright *Geol. Hist. Brit. Isles* vii. 137 The first thrusts have been folded by N-S fairly open folds and associated asymmetric small folds have a strain-slip cleavage. **1922** Joyce *Ulysses* 714 The cause of a brief sharp unforeseen heard loud lone crack emitted by the insentient material of a *strainveined timber table.

†**strain**, *sb.*[3] *Obs.* Also 6 **streyne, streen**, 6–7 **straine.** [Of obscure origin; cf. MDu., MLG. *strene* (Du. *streen*), OHG. *streno* (MHG. *strene*, mod.G. *strähne*), skein, hank.]

1. A thread, line, streak.

c **1520** Skelton *Magnyf.* 1571 The streynes of her veynes as asure inde blewe. **1545** Raynalde *Byrth Mankynde* 22 When the water hath to passe throw so narow passage, it makith the longer iourney and yeldith the smaller thred or streen. **1590** Greene *Never too late* (1600) G 4, Her face like siluer Luna in her shine, All tainted through with bright vermillion straines. **1613** Purchas *Pilgrimage* VII. xi. (1614) 706 Barrius..is of opinion, That the violent currents of the Tides..raise vp from the bottom that redde floore..and cause, by the motion of the same vnder the water, that rednesse in the vpper face thereof:..and the threeds or straines of this rednesse are lesse in the greater and more spacious Sea-roome.

2. = strand *sb.*[4] 1.

c **1586** J. Davys in Hakluyt *Voy.* (1589) 786 The straines of one of our cables were broken.

3. A barb or filament of a (peacock's) feather. (Cf. strand *sb.*[4] 3 b.)

1651 T. Barker *Art of Angling* (1653) 6 Another flie, the Body made of the strain of a Pea Cocks feather. **1662** R. Venables *Exper. Angler* iii. 28 Take one strain of a Peacocks feather (or if that be not sufficient, then another).

†**strain**, *sb.*[4] *Obs. rare*[−1]. In 6 **strayne.** [Aphetic f. distrain *sb.* Cf. strain *v.*[2]] A distraint.

1526 *Croscombe Churchw. Acc.* (Somerset Rec. Soc.) 38 Ther was payde owtte of the chyrch box for all the parysch whane ther was a strayne taken for the lorde [*i.e.* of the manor for chief rent], xx[s].

strain (streɪn), *v.*[1] Forms: 4 **strayn, strayny**, 4–5 **streny, streyn**, 4–6 *Sc.* **strenȝe**, 5–6 **stren(e**, 4–7 **strane, strayne, streine**, (7 **strein**), 4–8 **streyne**, 6 **straigne, -ygne, streigne, -ygne**, *Sc.* **strengȝe**, strenye, 6–7 straine, 6– strain. [ME. *streyne*, etc., a. OF. *estrein-*, *estreign-*, *estren-*, stem of *estreindre*, *estraindre* (mod.F. *étreindre*) to bind tightly, clasp, squeeze, corresp. to Pr. *estrenher*, Cat. *estrenyer*, Sp. *estreñir*, It. *strignere*, *stringere*:—L. *stringĕre* to bind tightly, to draw tight, tighten: see STRINGENT *a.*

The sense 'to draw tight' (whence branch II below) is app. not recorded for OF. *estraindre*, though it was prob. not wholly wanting, as it is the earliest sense to appear in Eng.; the L. *stringere* was common in this sense. Branches III, IV, and V seem to be purely Eng. developments.]

I. To bind tightly; to clasp, squeeze.

1. †**a.** *trans.* To bind fast; to confine in bonds. *Obs.*

1340 HAMPOLE *Pr. Consc.* 7181 Þai salle be.. In helle hard bonden,.. And straytely streyned ilka lym. **1426** LYDG. *De Guil. Pilgr.* 7207 With a gyrdel off ryhtwysnesse, Thy reynys strongly for to streyne [*pour bien estraindre fort les reins*]. **1483** CAXTON *Golden Leg.* 177/1 Saynt peter was empryosoned in a strayte place wherin he was strayned. **1513** DOUGLAS *Æneis* II. vii. 78 Baith hir tendir handis War strengȝeit sair, ybound in hard with bandis.

fig. **1382** WYCLIF *Num.* xxx. 14 If she auowe, and bi ooth streyne hir self [1388 byndith hir silf; Vulg. *se constrinxerit*]. *c* **1435** in Kingsford *Chron. London* (1905) 21 Bondes of Liegeaunce.. in which they weren or ben bounden to me, or in eny other wyse Streynyd. **1532** MORE *Confut. Tindale* Wks. 394/1 And with these woordes of hys own, will I strayne him fast and sure.

b. To fasten, attach firmly. Const. *to*, or with *together*. *lit.* and *fig. Obs.* exc. (*rarely*, influenced by sense 2) with the sense: To attach by compulsion.

1387 TREVISA *Higden* (Rolls) VII. 109 Kyng Kanute,.. þat he myȝte streyne [L. *astringeret*] þe reme of Engelond more faste unto hym, wedded to his wyf Emme the queene. **1391** CHAUCER *Astrol.* I. §14 Thorw wich pyn ther goth a litel wegge.. þat streyneth alle thise parties to hepe. *c* **1450** *Maitl. Club Misc.* III. 201 Item ane salter befor the Licentiatis stal strenyeit. **1508** DUNBAR *Tua Mariit Wemen* 59 It is agane the law of luif, of kynd, and of nature, Togidder hairtis to streine, that stryveis with vther. **1530** TINDALE *Exod.* xxxix. 21 And they strayned the brestlappe by his ringes vnto the ringes of the Ephod, with laces of Iacincte. **1856** MERIVALE *Rom. Emp.* IV. xxxiv. 105 It was requisite to strengthen and draw closer the bonds which strained them to the conquerors.

†**c.** To stanch (blood). *Obs. rare*$^{-1}$.

c **1425** tr. *Arderne's Treat. Fistula* etc. 79 Also puluer of vitriol combuste streyneþ blode in euery place if it be putte by itself or with iuyse of any herbe streynyng blode.

†**d.** To constrict (the organic tissues). *Obs. rare.*

1533 ELYOT *Cast. Helthe* I. 8 b, Flewme stiptik or binding,.. hath the tast lyke to grene redde wyne, or other lyke, straynyng the tunge. **1548** *Elyot's Dict.*, *Astrictus gustus*, a rough or sharpe tast, that streigneth the tongue.

2. a. To clasp tightly in one's arms. *Obs.* exc. as in b.

c **1374** CHAUCER *Troylus* III. 1205 This Troilus in armes gan hir streyne. **1590** SPENSER *F.Q.* III. ii. 34 So hauing said, her twixt her armes twaine She straightly straynd. **1597** DRAYTON *Heroic Ep.*, *Owen Tudor to Q. Kath.* 39 Euen as a mother comming to her child... With tender armes his gentle necke doth straine. **1613** SHAKS. *Hen. VIII*, IV. i. 46 Our King has all the Indies in his Armes, And more and richer, when he straines that Lady. **1697** DRYDEN *Virg. Georg.* IV. 726 In vain, with folding Arms, the Youth assay'd To stop her flight, and strain the flying Shade.

b. esp. ***to strain*** (a person) ***to one's bosom, heart***, and the like.

1789 CHARLOTTE SMITH *Ethelinde* (1814) V. 297 'She is mine!' continued he; straining her to his bosom. **1809** CAMPBELL *Gertrude* I. xxiii, He said—and strain'd unto his heart the boy. **1883** FRANCES M. PEARD *Contrad.* xxii, He strained her to him again. **1891** FARRAR *Darkn. & Dawn* xxxv, He strained her again and again to his heart.

3. To clasp tightly in the hand.

a. †To press, squeeze (another's hand or fingers, a person by the hand) in love or farewell (*obs.*). Also (*rarely*), to clasp (one's own hands) forcibly.

1518 H. WATSON *Hist. Oliver of Castile* (Roxb.) C 4, He toke his leue of the quene, the whiche dydde strayne his fyngres togyder at the departynge. **1523** BERNERS *Froiss.* I. x. 9 [He said] I gyue you leue, and kyste hym, streynynge hym by the hande, in sygne of great loue. **1652** GAULE *Magastrom.* 330 She strained her husbands hand, and concluded both her speech and life with these complaining words. **1888** 'J. S. WINTER' *Bootle's Childr.* viii, 'Mrs. Ferrers,' cried Lassie, straining her thin hands together, 'don't *break* it to me, please. Tell me the whole truth at once.'

b. To grip, grasp tightly (a weapon, etc.). *Obs.* or *arch.*

1590 SPENSER *F.Q.* II. vii. 21 The one in hand an yron whip did strayne, The other brandished a bloudy knife. *Ibid.* III. v. 21 The third brother.. droue at him with all his might and maine A forrest bill, which both his hands did straine. **1825** SCOTT *Talism.* xv, 'Name her not..' said the King, again straining the curtal-axe in his gripe, until the muscles started above his brawny arm.

†**c.** Of a bird (esp. a hawk) or beast: To seize (its prey) in its claws. Chiefly *absol. Obs.*

1426 LYDG. *De Guil. Pilgr.* 17528, I Gryppe and streyne lyk a Gryffoun, And faste I holde ther-with-al Coper, yren, and ech metal. **1486** *Bk. St. Albans*, *Hawking* a vj b, The .ix. [term belonging to hawking] she streynith and not Clithith nor Cratchith. **1530** PALSGR. 738/1, I strayne, as a hauke doth, or any other syche lyke fowle or beest in theyr clawes, *je estraings.* Were a good glove I reede you, for your hauke strayneth harde. **1575** TURBERV. *Faulconrie* 214 When they are unable.. to performe their parts.. as not to be able to flee or strayn yᵉ pray wᵗ their pownces. **1596** SPENSER *F.Q.* VI. iv. 22 [The bear] Gnashing his cruell teeth at him in vaine, And threatning his sharpe clawes, now wanting powre to straine.

4. To constrict painfully, as with an encircling cord. Also in wider sense: †To hurt by physical pressure; to pinch.

1375 *Sc. Leg. Saints* xxii. 646 Sancte laurens.. be þe areme can hyme strenȝe [*brachium ejus strinxit*] rycht sayre and Increly. **1426** LYDG. *De Guil. Pilgr.* 8257 Thys glouys bynde me so sore,.. And al the remnaunt.. off armure, Me streyneth so on euery syde, That [etc.]. *c* **1500** KENNEDY *Passion of Christ* 379 Thai strenȝeit þai fair handis with a string. **1586** *Withals' Dict.* (1599) 65, I wot wel where my shooe pincheth or straineth me. **1618** W. LAWSON *New Orch. & Gard.* (1626) 27 Take well tempered morter, soundly wrought with chaffe or horsedung (for the dung of cattell will grow hard, and straine your graffes). **1712–14** POPE *Rape Lock* IV. 101 Was it.. For this with fillets [you] strain'd your tender head? **1830** TENNYSON *To —— i*, The wounding cords that bind and strain The heart until it bleeds.

†**5. a.** To compress, contract, diminish (in bulk or volume); to draw *together* (the brows). *Obs.*

1398 TREVISA *Barth. De P.R.* XIV. xlix (Tollemache MS.), [The field is] streynid in winter with froste and with colde, and swellid in somer with brennynge and with hete [L. *hyeme gelu et frigore constringitur*]. **1432–50** tr. *Higden* (Rolls) I. 57 The see callede Pontus, diffusede from þens towarde the northe makethe the see callede Propontides. And from thens hit is streynede also into vjᶜ passes [L. *stringitur in secentos passus*]. **1445** tr. *Claudian* in *Anglia* XXVIII. 271 Thi yiftes be not streyned In noon smal boke thei may be writen. *c* **1530** *Judic. Urines* II. iii. 17 b, This feuer.. is knowen by straynyng togyder of the browis.

†**b.** *refl.* To squeeze oneself *through* (a narrow passage). Also with *out*. *Obs.*

1603 KNOLLES *Hist. Turkes* (1621) 1211 By straining himselfe out at a little window.. he in safetie got downe to the ground. **1606** S. GARDINER *Bk. Angling* 37 Some like slimy and slipperie eeles, no sooner find themselues entangled in the nette, but they seeke to wind and straine out themselues. *a* **1678** MARVELL *Appleton Ho.* 31 As practising, in doors so strait, To strain themselves through Heavens Gate.

†**c.** To derive (a word) by contraction. *Obs. rare*$^{-1}$.

1614 CAMDEN *Rem.*, *Names* 101 Pernel, from Petronilla, Pretty-stone, as Piere and Perkin strained out of Petre.

†**6.** To press hard upon, afflict, distress. *Obs.*

13.. *E.E. Allit. P.* C. 234 Styffe stremes & streȝt hem strayned a whyle. **1382** WYCLIF *Gen.* xxxi. 40 Day and nyȝt with hoot and coolde Y was streynyd [1388 angwischid; Vulg. *æstu urebar* (? misread *urgebar*) *et gelu*]. *c* **1385** CHAUCER *L.G.W.* 2684 And cold as eny frost now waxeth she, For Pite by the herte hire streynyth so. *c* **1477** CAXTON *Jason* 116 He might not speke.. his herte was so closed and strained with anguissh. **1513** DOUGLAS *Æneis* VI. ix. 58 In quhat pvnition, panis, and distres, Bene saulis ȝondir strenȝeit [L. *quibusve urgentur poenis*]? **1580** G. HARVEY *Three Proper Lett.* 40 Such pleasaunce makes the Grashopper so poore, And ligge so layde, when winter doth her strayne. **1730** T. BOSTON *Mem.* vi. (1899) 77 Being strained with this message I laid it before the Lord.

†**7. a.** To bridle, control, restrain. *Obs.*

Often with allusion to Ps. xxxi[i]. 9 (Vulg. *constringe*).

a **1340** HAMPOLE *Ps.* xxxi[i]. §12 In keuel and bridel streyn þaire chekis. **1340** *Ayenb.* 263 Þet is to zigge huych mayne to moche slac and wylles uol ssel by: bote yef þe ilke uaderes stefhede hise strayny and ordayny. *c* **1346** HAMPOLE *Prose Tr.* 6, I.. said þat I wald ryse and blesse vs in þe name of þe Haly Trynytee, and scho strenyde me so stallworthely þat I had no mouthe to speke, ne no hande to styrre. **13..** *Gaw. & Gr. Knt.* 176 A stede ful stif to strayne. *c* **1400** *Apol. Loll.* 74 Þe loue of Goddis lawe.. schuld streyn men fro þis Office. **1414** BRAMPTON *Penit. Ps.* (Percy Soc.) 11 And streyne here chekys fro woordys y-dell, That kan noȝt holdyn here tungys stylle. **1434** MISYN *Mending Life* 112 Besy kepyng of þi vtward wittis, þat tastyn[g] sauerynge, herynge & seynge vndyr þe bridyll of gouernans wysely be strenyd. **1529** MORE *Dyaloge* I. Wks. 168/2 So hath God euer kepte man in humilite, straynyng him with yᵉ knowledge of confession of his ygnoraunce. **1533** —— *Answ. Poysoned Bk.* Ibid. 1054/2 Pray him.. to draw you, and as the Prophet sayth to pray him strayn your iawes with a bitte and a brydle. **1558** PHAER *Æneid* I. A ij, You gave me might these stormy winds to strain or make to blow. **1591** SPENSER *M. Hubberd* 1190 Of men of armes he had but small regard, But kept them lowe, and streigned verie hard. **1595** HUNNIS *Joseph* 42 He did refraine and straine himselfe, as it had not been he.

†**b.** To restrict, confine. *Obs.*

1566 PAINTER *Palace Pleas.* I. 260 When they happened to be strayned to straight lodging, the maried gentleman would not sticke to suffer his frend to lye with him and his wife.

†**8. a.** To force, press, constrain (*to* a condition or an action). Also const. *to* with inf. *Obs.*

c **1374** CHAUCER *Compl. Mars* 220 To what fyn made the god that sit so hye, Benethen him, love other company, And streyneth folk to love, malgre hir hede? *a* **1400** *Pauline Epist.*, *2 Cor.* v. 14 (1916) 112 *Caritas enim christi urget nos.* .. Forwhy þe charite of crist streynes vs. *a* **1400–50** *Wars Alex.* 3549, I hope þou wenes at we be like to þire lethire Persyns, þat þou þi lordschip to loute has now on late strayned. **1456** SIR G. HAYE *Law Arms* (S.T.S.) 94 Folk may nocht be strenȝeit to mak weris. **1528** MORE *Dyaloge* II. Wks. 200/1 The profe.. semeth me not very stronge nor able & sufficient to strayne a man to consent thereto. **1531** *Reg. Privy Seal Scot.* 98/1 He is oblist and strenȝeit to mak continuale residence and service at the said chaplanriis. **1551** T. WILSON *Logic* II. L ij, Some of these causes worke by the force and violence of nature, some by an outward powre, beyng strained thervnto. **1559** *Mirr. Mag.*, *Dk. Glouc.* xix, How stoutly we dyd the king strayne The Rule of his realme wholy to resygne. **1595** SHAKS. *John* III. iii. 46 Making that idiot laughter keepe mens eyes, And straine their cheekes to idle merriment. **1603** KNOLLES *Hist. Turks* (1621) 590 Who doubts but the enemie,.. strained by necessitie,.. will prey vpon your countries, houses, and goods?

†**b.** To incite (a person) to exertion, to urge.

1581 A. HALL *Iliad* I. 8 Agamemnon, whome anger forward straines.

†**c.** To urge, insist upon (a thing). Also *absol.*

1380 WYCLIF *Sel. Wks.* III. 240 Þei schulde teche þat whosoevere approves þis, confermes hit, or streynes hit, he synnes ageyns God. **1576** FLEMING *Panopl. Epist.* 260 Hee sheweth howe readie hee is, not onely in taking paines himselfe, but in strayning his friendes ayde also, that such meanes may be wrought. **1604** SHAKS. *Oth.* III. iii. 250 Note if your Lady straine his Entertainment With any strong, or vehement importunitie, Much will be seene in that.

†**d.** To compel to go. *Obs.*

13.. *E.E. Allit. P.* A. 691 By wayez ful streȝt he con hym strayn [after *deduxit per vias rectas*, Vulg. *Sap.* x. 10].

†**9. a.** To extract (liquor or juice) by pressure: to squeeze out. Also *intr.* Of a juice: To exude.

1483 *Cath. Angl.* 368/1 To Stren iuse of herbis (or herbys), *exsuccare.* **1583** H. HOWARD *Defensative* I j b, That we may beware of those that strayne Oyle out of a Flint. **1621** H. ELSING *Lords' Debates* (Camden) 56 That a favourable construccion be made, &c., and not to the squiesing of blood out of wordes... Yt was a greate mistakeing to say 'to streyne blood out of wordes'. **1707** *Curios. Husb. & Gard.* 94 These Juices strain out of their own accord.

fig. **1709** POPE *Ess. Crit.* 608 [They] Still run on Poets, in a raging vein, Ev'n to the dregs and squeezings of the brain, Strain out the last dull droppings of their sense. **1735** —— *Prol. Sat.* 182 The Bard.. Just writes to make his barrenness appear, And strains, from hard-bound brains, eight lines a year. **1781** COWPER *Table-t.* 533 From him who rears a poem lank and long, To him who strains his all into a song.

†**b.** To extort (money, confessions, etc.). *Obs.*

1596 SHAKS. *Merch. V.* IV. i. 184 *Por.* Then must the Iew be mercifull. *Iew.* On what compulsion must I? Tell me that. *Por.* The quality of mercy is not strain'd. **1678** SIR G. MACKENZIE *Crim. Laws Scot.* II. xx. §ii. (1699) 230 His Majesties Advocat is still a party interested, and so should not be allowed to deal with the Witnesses; for thereby he may strain from them what otherwise they would not depone. *a* **1699** J. KIRKTON *Secr. Hist. Ch. Scot.* (1817) 314 Yet when he or his friends talked in the English parliament, and had a mind to strain money from it, they spoke of a warre with France.

II. To tighten, draw tight, stretch.

10. To extend with some effort; to subject to tension, to stretch.

a. To draw tight (a band, bandage, bonds). Also *absol.*

c **1300** *Beket* (Percy Soc.) 1475 The straples were istreynd hard ynouȝ. *c* **1400** *Lanfranc's Cirurg.* 297 Binde it [the wart] wiþ a strong þreed, & streine wel þe þred & drawe him awei wiþ þe þreed. **1541** COPLAND *Guydon's Quest. Chirurg.* L ij, Hede must be taken to strayne to harde or to loose [upon the hurt place]... And some put to double clothes, and strayne them and sewe them on the place. **1697** DRYDEN *Virg. Georg.* IV. 596 But thou, the more he varies Forms, beware To strain his Fetters with a stricter Care.

in fig. context. **1707** NORRIS *Treat. Humility* vi. 237 This strains the hard knot of poverty yet harder, and makes it pinch more sensibly. **1757** BURKE *Abridgm. Eng. Hist.* Wks. 1842 II. 544 There may be a danger in straining too strongly the bonds of government.

†**b.** To stretch and hold extended (a body or its limbs on a cross, on the rack, etc.). *Obs.*

a **13..** *Cursor M.* 16762 + 126 His armes wore so streyned oute [on the Cross]. *a* **1400** *Minor Poems fr. Vernon MS.* 643 And strayte I-streynet on þe Rode, Streyned to druye on Rode-tre, As parchemyn oweþ for to be. **1483** CAXTON *Golden Leg.* 289/2 He dyde doo strayne and payne them in the torment of Eculee. *a* **1500** *St. Patrick's Purgatory* 355 in *Brome Bk.* 93 Whyll þat þey streynyd forth hys fete [etc.]. **1526** *Pilgr. Perf.* (W. de W. 1531) 254 b, Some affirmeth that he was first streyned on lyeng wyde open on the grounde.

c. To extend and make taut (a line, wire, etc.), to stretch (material *on* a frame, *over* a surface, etc.). Also with *out*.

a **1400–50** *Wars Alex.* (Dubl. MS.) 792* Than strenys he hys streropes & streȝt vp sittes. *Ibid.* 840* [He] Stranes owt hys sterops & sternly lokez. **1523** BERNERS *Froiss.* I. xviii. 25 Ther they founde CCC. caudrons made of bestis skynnes,.. strayned on stakes ouer the fyre, full of water. **1539** in *Vicary's Anat.* (1888) App. III. 4. 173 [Five Banners, which] waving & Strayned with the wynde.. made a goodly Showe. *a* **1548** HALL *Chron.*, *Hen. VIII*, 66 b, This house was couered with coardes strayned by craft... Ouer their coardes was streyned wollen clothes of light blew. **1573** in Feuillerat *Revels Q. Eliz.* (1908) 201 Nayles to strayne the Canvas. **1605** B. JONSON *Volpone* IV. i, On the one [wall] I straine me a fayre tarre-paulin; and, in that, I stick my onions, cut in halfes. **1627** CAPT. SMITH *Sea Gram.* v. 21 The Ties.. doe carry up the Yards when wee straine the Halyards. **1761** GRAY *Fatal Sisters* 6 Glittering lances are the loom, Where the dusky warp we strain. **1818** SCOTT *Br. Lamm.* xvi, The hook is fixed; we will not strain the line too soon. **1820** C. HAYTER *Introd. Perspective* 255 The vellum.. must be strained tight, by tacking on a straining frame. **1827** FARADAY *Chem. Manip.* x. (1842) 257 The temporary cover thus formed fits the mouth of the vessel tightly, is strained level over its surface. **1893** *Law Times* XCV. 104/2 The barbed wire fence.. was strained to posts.. 6 ft. high.

†*quasi-intr.* for *pass.*

1683 MOXON *Mech. Exerc.*, *Printing* xxii. ¶6 He pulls the Cord as hard.. as he can; and keeping the Cord straining, whips it again about the Head and other sides of the Page.

transf. and *fig.* **1590** GREENE *Orl. Fur.* I. ii, Although the mystic vayle straind ouer Cynthia Hinders my sight from noting all thy crue. **1634** J. ROBINSON *Lawfulness of Hearing Ministers* Wks. 1851 III. 360 To strain the strings of this imagined proportion to make them meet, and to suppose the church to be as the altar, yet [etc.].

d. To tighten up (the strings of a musical instrument) so as to raise the pitch. Also with *up*.

1387 TREVISA *Higden* (Rolls) II. 377 Mercurius.. putte seuene strenges to þe harpe.. and þey putte to þe strenges and streyned [L. *strinxit*] hem in þis manere. **1587** GOLDING *De Mornay* i. 4 Not so much as two strings beeing of one selfesame nature, can agree in one tune, without the wit of a man that can skil to streine them and to slacke them as he seeth it good. **1626** BACON *Sylva* §184 Wherby you shall discouer..the Proportion likewise of the Sound towards the String, as it is more or lesse strained. **1888** *Encycl. Brit.* XXIV. 244/1 The sympathetic strings were..strained to pitch..by means of additional pegs.

fig. **1602** MARSTON *Antonio's Rev.* IV. iii, Castilio, Forobosco, all Straine up your wits, winde up invention Unto his highest bent. *a* **1626** BRETON *Daffodils & P.* (Grosart) 20/2 A harte (not harpe) is all her instrument, Whose weakned stringes all out of tune she stranes. **1781** COWPER *Truth* 385 Man..in ev'ry sense a wretch, An instrument, whose cords, upon the stretch, And strain'd to the last screw that he can bear, Yield only discord in his Maker's ear.

†e. To stretch (cloth) fraudulently. *Obs.*

1514–15 *Act 6 Hen. VIII* c. 9 The byer..shall not..streyne nor do to be streyned in bred the same Clothes..by teyntour or wynche. *c* **1560** *Maldon* (Essex) *Docum.* Liber B. fol. 55b, Whether they shalbe stretched or streyned or pressed with the hott presse.

†f. To extend (a thing), to stretch to the full length. Also with *forth*, *out*. Also *intr.* for *refl.*

1398 TREVISA *Barth. De P.R.* v. vi. (1495) 111 The eye shall not be straynyd to ferre oute nother areyd to hyghe. *c* **1450** CAPGRAVE *St. Gilbert* xl. 120 In hir creping þe senewes whech were contract be-fore in hir lendes [loins], þei brak and streyned oute to swech largenesse þat [etc.]. **1485** CAXTON *Chas. Gt.* 47 Olyuer..aroos oute of hys bedde and began for to scratche [? *read* stratche] and strayne hys armes and to fele yf it were possyble to hym to bere armes.

†g. To elongate by hammering. *Obs.*

1674 RAY *Collect. Words, Wire Work* 132 They take little square bars, made like bars of steel and strain i.e. draw them at a Furnace with a hammer..into square rods.

11. *fig.* **a.** To force the meaning or sense of (words, an ordinance, decree, etc.); †to distort the form of (a word). Also *absol.*

1449 PECOCK *Repr.* I. xi. 58 The vndirstonding, bī which summen streynen forto speke of the writing which we han now of the Newe Testament. **1596** SHAKS. *1 Hen. IV*, IV. i. 75 *Wor.* This absence of your Father drawes a Curtaine [etc.]... *Hotsp.* You strayne too farre. I rather of his absence make this vse: [etc.]. **1604** —— *Oth.* III. iii. 218, I am to pray you, not to straine my speech To grosser issues. **1605** VERSTEGAN *Dec. Intell.* i. 14 The ancient German names beeing by latin or other authors strayned and drawn vnto their ortography, according to their fancies. **1614** RALEGH *Hist. World* III. i. §8. 15 Neuerthelesse wee finde many and good Authors, who..are well contented to straine these prophecies with vnreasonable diligence vnto such a sense. **1665** BOYLE *Occas. Refl.* (1675) Pref. 16 If..I may have at any time a little Strain'd the Similitude, the better to accommodate it to my present Theme, and Design. **1753** CHALLONER *Cath. Chr. Instr.* 170 The Protestant Translation has strained the Text to make it say more than the Original. **1785** BURKE *Sp. Nabob of Arcot's Debts* Wks. 1842 I. 341 And, lastly, and above all, not to be fond of straining constructions, to force a jurisdiction. **1849** MACAULAY *Hist. Eng.* iv. I. 488 Defective laws should be altered by the legislature, and not strained by the tribunals. **1884** *Law Rep. 27 Chanc. Div.* 638, I think that..I am not straining the effect of the order in saying so.

b. To transgress the strict requirements of (one's conscience), to violate the spirit of (one's oath).

1592 KYD *Sp. Trag.* III. iv. 8 And he that would not straine his conscience For him that thus his liberall purse hath stretcht, Vnworthy such a fauour may he faile. **1596** SPENSER *State Irel.* Wks. (Globe) 618/2 They make noe more scruple to pass [judgement] agaynst an Englishman, and the Queene, though it be to strayne theyr othes, then to drinke milke unstrayned. **1877** OWEN *Wellesley's Desp.* Introd. 16 The exigencies of the war..had induced Lord Cornwallis to strain his conscience so far as to write a letter, which was to have the binding force of a Treaty.

c. To force (prerogative, power, etc.) beyond its legitimate extent or scope.

1605 BACON *Adv. Learn.* I. vii. §9 The temperate use of the Prerogative [of Q. Elizabeth], not slackened, nor much strayned. **1733** POPE *Ess. Man* III. 290 'Twas then, the studious head..Taught Pow'r's due use to People and to Kings, Taught not to slack, nor strain its tender strings. **1883** FROUDE *Short Stud.* IV. I. x. 108 The Crown retains prerogatives at present which would be fatal to it if strained.

†d. To apply or use (a thing) beyond its province. *Obs.*

1592 SHAKS. *Rom. & Jul.* II. iii. 19 Nor ought so good, but strain'd from that faire vse, Reuolts from true birth, stumbling on abuse. **1599** —— *Much Ado* IV. i. 254 For to strange sores strangely they straine the cure. **1621** in Foster *Eng. Factories Ind.* (1906) 269 He denyeth that hee hath any way taxt the Councell or strained his pen..beyond due bounds or reason. **1638** JUNIUS *Paint. Ancients* 229 Nothing marreth the life and spirit of the invented things so much, as to force and strain them to a fore-determined purpose. **1647** *Hamilton Papers* (Camden) 146 Because you had assured me you were to goe out of town I strained not the time that prest me exceedingly.

e. *to strain a metaphor* (see quot.).

1783 BLAIR *Lect.* I. xv. 313 If the resemblance..be long dwelt upon, and carried into all its minute circumstances we make an allegory instead of a metaphor... This is called straining a Metaphor.

f. *to strain a point*: to exceed one's usual limits of procedure, to do more than one is bound to do or go further than one is entitled to go in a matter. Cf. STRETCH *v.*

1596 LAMBARDE *Peramb. Kent* (ed. 2) 401 He would not sticke to straine a point, so that he might glorifie Saint Thomas thereby. **1661** GODOLPHIN *View Adm. Jurisd.* Introd. [a 5], In time of war they strain a point to drive a Colourable Trade. **1757** SIR B. KEENE *Desp.* 26 Sept. in *10th Rep. Hist. MSS. Comm.* App. I. 219 Tho' we should have strain'd a Point to serve Him. **1857** G. A. LAWRENCE *Guy Liv.* xxxiv. 343 We've not quite so much proof as I could wish. It would be straining a point to arrest him, as it stands. **1873** BROWNING *Red Cott. Nt.-Cap C.* 393 You must be generous, strain point, and call Victory, any the least flush of pink Made prize of.

†g. To insist upon unduly, to be over-punctilious about. *Obs.*

1665 DRYDEN *Ind. Emperor* III. ii, I'le not strain Honour to a point too high; I sav'd your Life, now keep it if you can. **1711** ADDISON *Spect.* No. 99 ¶5 In Books of Chivalry, where the Point of Honour is strained to Madness.

h. *to strain courtesy*: see COURTESY *sb.* 1 c.

†i. To raise to an extreme degree. *Obs.*

1609 HOLLAND *Amm. Marcell.* xxviii. ii. 327 To the end that a duple authority, and the same strained to the height [L. *erectaque sublatius*], might patch matters together. **1612** CAPT. SMITH *Virginia* 28 All their actions, voices and gestures, both in charging and retiring, were so strained to the hight of their quallitie and nature, that [etc.]. **1697** DRYDEN *Æneis* VII. 536 Nor yet content, she strains her Malice more, And adds new Ills to those contriv'd before.

j. *to strain up*: to force up to a higher scale of estimation; to 'screw up' (rents, usury) to an oppressive rate.

1599 SANDYS *Europæ Spec.* (1632) 218 In all places they are permitted to streine up their Vsury to eighteene in the hundred upon the Christian. **1769** BLACKSTONE *Comm.* IV. xi. 142 Both of these species are also either felonious, or not felonious. The felonious breaches of the peace are strained up to that degree of malignity by virtue of several modern statutes. **1905** *Westm. Gaz.* 23 Aug. 8/2 'What is to be understood by "straining rents"?'..'I have known houses, built to let at 11s. a week, gradually strained up to 14s.'

k. To raise to a high state of emotional tension.

1667 MILTON *P.L.* VIII. 454 My earthly by his Heav'nly overpowerd, Which it had long stood under, streind to the highth In that celestial Colloquie sublime,..sunk down, and sought repair Of sleep. **1820** LAMB *Elia* Ser. I. *South-sea House*, While he held you in converse, you felt strained to the height in the colloquy. **1867** H. MACMILLAN *Bible Teach.* ii. (1870) 31 Each sense was strained, by the sublimity around, to its utmost tension.

l. To make excessive demands upon, tax severely (resources, credit, friendship, etc.). Also, †to tax severely the resources of (a person).

1609 DEKKER *Ravens Alm.* F 1, The Farmer carefull of his day, because he knew the hard conscience of the Usurer, straind himselfe and his friends, and prouided the money. **1642** FULLER *Holy & Prof. St.* II. xxi. 140 Great spirits, having mounted to the highest pitch of performance, afterwards strain and break their credits in striving to go beyond it. **1673** *Essex Papers* (Camden) I. 57, I am much deceiv'd if they are not willing to straine themselves very far on any such publick acc^t. **1798** in Owen *Wellesley's Desp.* (1877) 754 The Company have, from such considerations, strained their own means to put their servants on the most liberal footing. **1855** MACAULAY *Hist. Eng.* xxii. IV. 701 The King had strained his private credit in Holland to procure bread for his army. **1888** BURGON *12 Gd. Men* II. xi. 308 There were occasions..when Eden strained those friendships severely. **1912** *Eng. Hist. Rev.* Oct. 712 His [Burke's] succour to the distressed French exiles had strained his scanty resources to the breaking-point.

m. To raise (matters, relations between parties) to a dangerous state of tension. Cf. STRAINED *ppl. a.*

1671 MILTON *Samson* 1348 Consider, Samson; matters now are strain'd Up to the highth, whether to hold or break.

12. a. To stretch (sinews, nerves, muscles) beyond the normal degree (as the supposed condition of intense exertion); hence, to force to extreme effort, exert to the utmost (one's limbs, organs, powers). *to strain every nerve* (*fig.*): to use one's utmost endeavours.

1446 LYDG. *Nightingale Poems* ii. 73 This bridde.. Syngeth as that she wold hir-self dismembre, Streyneth hir throte, peyneth hir brest at al. **1548** *Elyot's Dict.* s.v. *Intendo*, I must streigne a sinewe or stretche a veyne, to begyle this olde man. **1576** FLEMING *Panopl. Epist.* 261 To make them al amends therfore in the behoofe of one, I must straine mine abilitie. **1584** COGAN *Haven Health* i. 3 They streine more one part of the body than an other, as shooting the armes, running the legges, &c. **1611** SHAKS. *Cymb.* III. iii. 94 He sweats, Straines his yong Nerues, and puts himselfe in posture That acts my words. **1671** MILTON *Samson* 1646 This utter'd, straining all his nerves he bow'd. **1777** JOHNSON *Let. Mrs. Thrale* 27 Oct., Some strain their powers for efforts of gaiety. **1821** SCOTT *Kenilw.* xxx, That memorable discharge of fireworks..which Master Laneham ..has strained all his eloquence to describe. **1837** CARLYLE *Fr. Rev.* II. v. i, All Constitutional Deputies did strain every nerve. **1841** ELPHINSTONE *Hist. Ind.* I. 345 This last exercise only operates on the arms and chest, but the others strain every muscle in the frame. **1855** KINGSLEY *Heroes* IV. iii. (1868) 251 His father sat..and strained his old eyes across the sea, to see the ship afar. **1856** *N. Brit. Rev.* XXVI. 158 When we view them with two eyes..the muscles of the eyeball are not strained. **1894** MISS L. ALMA-TADEMA *Wings of Icarus* 159, I strained my ears in vain for a sound.

b. *intr.* for *refl.* of the eyes or ears.

1855 BROWNING *Ch. Roland* xviii, No sound, no sight as far as eye could strain. **1943** J. WEDGE in K. Rhys *More Poems from Forces* 313 Ears are straining for a distant 'boom'.

c. To force (the voice) above its natural compass.

1913 *Times* 14 May 8/5 He seemed to be straining it [*sc.* his voice] upon the high notes.

d. *Photogr.* (See quot.)

1890 WOODBURY *Encycl. Dict. Photogr.* 385 But if brought nearer than a certain point, the lens will be what is termed 'strained,' and the image will become dreadfully distorted.

13. To injure or alter by excessive tension.

a. To injure (a limb, muscle, tendon, etc.) by stretching or over-exertion; to sprain. Also *refl.* of a person or animal.

1612 *Benvenuto's Passenger* I. iv. 313, I haue strayned one of my feete. **1711** SWIFT *Jrnl. to Stella* 3 Oct., I have strained the thumb of my left hand with pulling him. **1726** —— *To Janus* 22 Prudes decay'd about may tack, Strain their necks with looking back. **1788** MRS. ANNE HUGHES *Henry & Isab.* IV. xxxiii. 240 Mrs. Maitland, having..strained one of her ancles. **1890** CONAN DOYLE *White Company* xxviii, I strained a sinew on the day that I slew the three men at Castelnau. **1891** M. ROBERTS *Land-travel & Sea-faring* 131 Devilskin strained himself..by treading on a loose stone. **1899** *Allbutt's Syst. Med.* VIII. 18 Nerves and muscles may be acutely 'strained'. The word is placed between inverted commas to shew that it is used in its popular sense... Whether this is due to the stretching of fine nerve-twigs it is scarcely possible to decide.

b. To impair or imperil the strength of (a material thing) by excessive tension or disruptive force.

1730–46 THOMSON *Seasons, Autumn* 320 Strained to the root, the stooping forest pours A rustling shower of yet untimely leaves. **1771** SMOLLETT *Humph. Cl.* 10 July (1815) 222 Crossing a deep gutter, made by a torrent, the coach was so hard strained, that one of the irons which connect the frame snapped. **1859** TENNYSON *Enid* 1007 But Geraint's [lance], A little in the late encounter strain'd, Struck.. home, And then brake short. **1868** *Chamb. Jrnl.* 13 June 381/2 The ship had strained herself a good deal, owing to the heavy cargo of railway-iron she had stowed in her hold. **1884** *Law Times* LXXVII. 26/2 A tug towed at her for an hour and a half before she was got off, during which time her decks and waterways were much strained.

c. *Physics.* (See quot. 1856.) Also *intr.* for *refl.*

1850 RANKINE *Misc. Sci. Papers* (1881) 82 When the body is strained, therefore, the pressure is the resultant of the variations of all those forces, arising from the displacements of the atomic centres from their natural relative positions. **1856** SIR W. THOMSON in *Phil. Trans.* CXLVI. 481 If a stone, a beam, or a mass of metal, in a building, or in a piece of framework, becomes condensed or dilated, in any direction, or bent, or twisted, or distorted in any way, it is said to experience a strain, to become strained, or often in common language, simply 'to strain'. **1879** THOMSON & TAIT *Nat. Phil.* I. I. §154 Thus a rod which becomes longer or shorter is strained.

III. To press through a filtering medium, to filter. (Cf. 9.)

14. a. To press (a liquid) through a porous or perforated medium which keeps back the denser portions or the solid matter held in suspension; to free (solid matter) from the contained or accompanying liquid by this process; to purify or refine by filtration. Also *absol.*

In mod. use *to strain* is to pass through a medium having visible pores, as hair-cloth or muslin, while *to filter* refers to the use of a medium such as paper, a layer of charcoal, a bed of sand, etc.

c **1386** CHAUCER *Pard. T.* 210 Thise Cookes, how they stampe, and streyne [L. *alius contundit et colat*], and grynde And turnen substaunce in-to Accident. **1398** TREVISA *Barth. De P.R.* XIX. lx. (1495) 897 Fyrste vyneygre is sodde wyth necessary herbes..thenne the vyneygre is streynyd and clensyd. *c* **1420** *Liber Cocorum* 9 Take ryse..And þorowgh a strynour þou hom strene. *Ibid.* 40 Breke eyren and streyne hom thorowghe a clothe. **1523–34** FITZHERB. *Husb.* §44 Styrre it aboute, and than streyne it thorowe an olde clothe. **1591** A. W. *Bk. Cookrye* 5b, Then..strain the yolkes of Egges with Vinager, and put them into your broth. *Ibid.* 9b, Then straine a little bread and put it in. **1697** DRYDEN *Virg. Georg.* II. 330 First an Osier Colender provide Of Twigs..(such toiling Peasants twine, When thro' streight Passages they strein their Wine). **1731** in *10th Rep. Hist. MSS. Comm.* App. I. 269 Some people have such an aversion to them [snails] that they can't get down any liquid into wch they are but strain'd. **1811** A. T. THOMSON *Lond. Disp.* (1818) 668 Macerate for fourteen days in a stopped glass bottle, and strain. **1826** *Art Brewing* (ed. 2) 153 The juice must then be strained through a coarse hair-sieve, to keep back its grosser particles. **1901** J. BLACK *Carp. & Build., Home Handicr.* 50 Boil a little common size.., strain through muslin into a clean pan.

b. said of natural agencies.

1610 HOLLAND *Camden's Brit.* (1637) 562 Three fountaines walme out of the ground streined, as it should seeme, through a veine of Alum. **1774** GOLDSM. *Nat. Hist.* (1776) I. 194 [He] contends that rivers must be supplied from the sea, strained through the pores of the earth.

c. *transf.* and *fig.*

1387 TREVISA *Higden* (Rolls) I. 5 Of þe whiche þinges our litel konnynge myȝte nouȝt take knowleche,..but besines of writers to oure vnkunnynge hadde i-holde and i-streyned mynde of olde dedes [L. *transfunderet.. memoriam transactorum*]. **1589** *Pappe w. Hatchet* in *Lyly's Wks.* (1902) III. 402, I will boyle thee, straine thee, and then drie thee, so that of a lubber,..I will at last make a dram of knaues powder. **1606** SHAKS. *Tr. & Cr.* IV. v. 169 Faith and troth, Strain'd purely from all hollow bias drawing: Bids thee.. welcome. **1662** E. HOPKINS *Funeral Serm.* (1685) 21 So a Christian, when he is strained through the grave, loseth all his brackishness, all his dreggs and scumme, and becomes pure and holy. **1785** COWPER *Task* II. 438 The nasal twang Heard at conventicle, where worthy men, Misled by custom, strain celestial themes Through the prest nostril, spectacle-bestrid. **1819** SHELLEY *Cenci* V. ii. 169 *Judge.* Let tortures strain the truth till it be white.

d. To remove (liquid) by filtration, drain off. Const. *from*. Also with *out*, *off*.

15.. in *Oxf. Archd. Will Reg.* (*N. & Q.* 11th Ser. 1914, IX. 268/1) Then streyne the licour from the barley. **1558** WARDE tr. *Alexis' Secr.* 40 Let it boyle..vntil it be diminished of the third part, than straine it out softly. **1640** T. BRUGIS *Marrow of Physicke* II. 142 Straine all the thin water from them through a faire Cloth. **1747** MRS. GLASSE *Cookery* 12 Let it [the gravy] stew till it is quite rich and good; then season it to your Taste with Salt, and then strain it off. *Ibid.* 15 Then take out your Tripe and strain the Liquor out.

fig. **1848** H. ROGERS *Ess.* (1860) I. 275 It is a translation of a translation, in which the beauties of Plato are strained off by a double process.

¶ **e.** To take out (something) from a liquid by straining.

This use seems hardly to occur exc. in ***strain out a gnat*** (after L. *excolare*), † ***strain a gnat***, in Matt. xxiii. 24. (For the better known rendering of this text see 21.)

1526 TINDALE *Matt.* xxiii. 24 Ye blinde gydes which strayne out a gnat and swalowe a cammyll. [So also **1535** Coverdale, **1539** Cranmer, **1560** Geneva.] **1564** *Brief Exam.* *******b, None of them..did strayne a Gnat, and swallowe a Camell. **1582** N.T. (Rheims) *Matt.* xxiii. 24 That straine a gnat. **1589** WARNER *Alb. Eng.* VI. xxxi. (1602) 153 Precisians..In Loue doe swallow Cammels, whilest they nicely straine a Gnat. **1616** B. PARSONS *Magistr. Charter* 23 Straine not out gnats, then, neither swallow downe camels. **1881** BIBLE (R.V.) *Matt.* xxiii. 24 Which strain out the gnat.

15. a. *intr.* for *refl.* To filter; to trickle. Also *fig.*

1588 MARLOWE *2nd Pt. Tamburl.* III. iv, I feele..all my entrals bath'd In blood that straineth from their orifex. **1594** KYD *Cornelia* III. iii. 118 My griefe is lyke a Rock, whence (ceaseles) strayne Fresh springs of water at my weeping eyes. **1626** BACON *Sylva* §1 The Sea water passing or Strayning through the Sandes, leaueth the Saltnesse. **1725** *Bradley's Family Dict.* s.v. *Honey* ¶6 To the end that the Honey may strain gently through the Bag. **1897** F. T. JANE *Lordship, Passen, & We* v. 57 The speech that he made was a tidy long one... It all strained out to telling us how that we should make up to the Radicals.

b. Of a stream: To flow. *rare.*

1612 DRAYTON *Poly-olb.* I. 226 So Touuy straineth in. *Ibid.* VI. 343 But, backe, industrious Muse; obsequiously to bring Cleere Seuerne from her sourse; and tell how she doth straine Downe her delicious Dales. **1915** J. BUCHAN *Nelson's Hist. War* III. xxi. 98 The river [Oder] in many places strains in mazy channels and backwaters among isles matted with dwarf willows and alders.

16. *trans.* To sow or let fall (seed) in a furrow (i.e. not broadcast). Also with *in. local.*

1733 W. ELLIS *Chiltern & Vale Farm.* 28 By this one Ploughing may be sown Beans, either strained in the Thoroughs,..or else by sowing the Beans all over the Field. *Ibid.* 80 Strain in the Acorns by a Man's Hand in two Thoroughs. *Ibid.* 333 Peas are sowed by straining them in Thorough by Thorough.

IV. To exert oneself. (Cf. sense 12.)

17. *refl.* To exert oneself physically. In later use, to exert oneself so as to be in danger of injury. Now *rare* or *Obs.*

13.. *E.E. Allit. P.* A. 551, & þenne þe fyrst by-gonne to pleny & sayden þat þay hade trauayled sore, þese bot an oure hem con streny. **1377** LANGL. *P. Pl.* B. XIV. 233 Whan he streyneth hym to streche þe strawe is his schetes. *a* **1400–50** *Wars Alex.* 2809 Slike a seknes for-sothe is on my-selfe halden, þat I ne may streyne me ne stere for stondis so hard. **1470–85** MALORY *Arthur* XVIII. xvii. 755 Syre Launcelot strayned hym self soo straytly with soo grete force to gete the hors forward that the buttom of his wound brast. **1538** *St. Papers Hen. VIII*, I. 586 They do yet best, consideryng His Grace is yet tendir, that he shuld not streyn hym self..till he come above a yere of age. **1580** HESTER tr. *Fioravanti's Disc. Chirurg.* 27 b, [For those ruptured.] Keepe thy house with as much ease as thou mayest, and strayne not thy selfe in any wise. **1640** BROME *Sparagus Garden* IV. vii, Hold, sir, hold, pray use this whistle for me, I dare not straine my selfe to winde it I.

fig. **1574** tr. *Marlorat's Apocalips* 11 Sathan hath streyned himselfe too the vttermost too bring in such things.

18. *intr.* **a.** To make violent and continuous physical effort; to exert oneself to the utmost. Also with *forward, together.*

1340–70 *Alisaunder* 349 Steedes stirred of þe stede strane men under. **1556** *Aurelio & Isab.* (1608) B iij, After that these two knightes had longe ynough strained together. **1592** *Arden of Feversham* IV. iv. 72 Come, Francklin, let vs strain to mend our pace. **1654** VILVAIN *Enchir. Epigr.* III. lxxix. 75 b, The six first Princes for the kingdom strained, But it by a slight horstrick Darius gained. **1704–13** POPE *Windsor Forest* 155 See the bold youth strain up the threat'ning steep. **1849** MACAULAY *Hist. Eng.* vii. II. 194 The patience with which he had seen a boatman on a canal strain against an adverse eddy. **1853** G. JOHNSTON *Nat. Hist. E. Bord.* I. 18 A man would strain to leap its current. **1862** [PYCROFT] *Cricket Tutor* 33, I am far from sanctioning the fashion of straining forward at balls which there is plenty of time to play back. **1893** BRIDGES *Founder's Day, Eton* v, Or whether..dashing The oars of cedar skiffs, ye strain Round the rushes and home again.

b. *spec.* of a deer. (See quot. 1575.)

1575 TURBERV. *Venerie* 242 Termes of the Hart... When he bounceth by vpon all foure, then he tryppeth, and when he runneth verie fast, then he streyneth. **1735** SOMERVILLE *Chase* III. 543 As o'er the Turf he [the stag] strains. **1810** SCOTT *Lady of Lake* I. vii, Nor nearer might the dogs attain, Nor farther might the quarry [stag] strain.

c. *transf.* of a thing viewed as endowed with power to make effort. Also with *along.*

1819 BYRON *Juan* II. xiii, The wind sung, cordage strain'd, and sailors swore. **1858** in *Merc. Marine Mag.* V. 200 The ship straining along under a heavy press of sail. **1863** MRS. GASKELL *Sylvia's L.* iii, [A] courtyard in which there grew two or three poplars, straining upwards to the light.

d. To pull forcibly (*at* a rope, leash, rein).

1791 COWPER *Odyss.* XV. 353 Then, straining at the halyards, hoised the sail. **1825** SCOTT *Talism.* xxiv, King Richard looked..at the Nubian and his dog; but the former moved not, nor did the latter strain at the leash. **1871** TYNDALL *Fragm. Sci.* (1879) I. vi. 197 The blue-jackets strained in concert. **1881** *Daily Tel.* 28 Jan., The brig.. mounted the seas as though she were straining at a chain cable.

fig. **1808** SCOTT *Marmion* I. Introd. 92 When the frantic crowd amain Strain'd at subjection's bursting rein.

†**e.** *trans.* To direct (one's steps) hastily; to make (one's passage) with effort. *Obs.*

1579 H. C. *Forest of Fancy* F j b, Straight wayes my steppes I straind To bewties bower and there ariude. **1760** *Ann. Reg.* 24/2 In straining their passage thro' morassy ground several soldiers dropped down on their march.

19. *intr.* To use one's utmost endeavours; to strive vigorously. Const. *to* with inf., *after, for, to* (the attainment of some object).

1593 DRAYTON *Ecl.* v. 152 Stay there good Rowland, whether art thou rapt, beyond the moone that striuest thus to strayne. **1607** SHAKS. *Timon* I. i. 143 This Gentleman of mine Hath seru'd me long: To build his Fortune, I will straine a little, For 'tis a Bond in men. **1683** W. LLOYD in *Lett. Lit. Men* (Camden) 188, I will strein hard to allow him 20 li a year. **1721** SWIFT *Wonder of Wonders* 6 When in Office, no one..does his Business better. He hath sometimes strained hard for an Honest Livelyhood. **1750** JOHNSON *Rambler* No. 58 ¶3 They are unable..to strain in the race of competition, or to stand the shock of contest. **1797** *Monthly Mag.* III. 226 They exhibit the author as straining after novelty by eccentric distances, and by movements out of cathedral time. **1828** D'ISRAELI *Chas. I*, I. vi. 175 Both sides were straining to reconcile the most repulsive difficulties. **1841** MYERS *Cath. Th.* III. §41. 149 A mind open to all theories but straining after none. **1890** GOSCHEN *Sp. Ho. Comm.* 18 Apr., in *Hansard* 908 In case of war every one strains for gold.

20. † **a.** To retch, heave, make efforts to vomit.

1679 V. ALSOP *Melius Inquir.* I. i. 41 They swallowed them [the articles] with some Reluctancy, and are now reaching and straining with many a sowre face, to disgorge..the Hook of the Article. **1727** SWIFT *Poison. E. Curll* Misc. 1732 III. 19 He..fell a vomiting and straining in an uncommon and unnatural Manner.

b. To make efforts to evacuate the bowels; more fully ***to strain at stool.*** Also with *down.*

1645 MILTON *Colast.* 13, I send them by his advice to sit upon the stool and strain. **1797** UNDERWOOD *Dis. Childhood* (1799) III. 192 They [*sc.* young children] should be set on the chair, and not suffered to play until they have had an opening, for which they should strain. **1897** *Allbutt's Syst. Med.* III. 981 The patient should be directed to strain down, as this action will give a view of the interior of the anus. **1899** *Ibid.* VI. 839 Straining at stool may be the immediate cause of the rupture of a retinal vessel. *Ibid.* VII. 244 When the patient was made to strain, as at stool, the rate of flow of the fluid was doubled.

21. ***to strain at***: to make a difficulty of 'swallowing' or accepting (something); to scruple at. Also (rarely), †***to strain to do*** something.

This use is due to misunderstanding of the phrase 'strain at a gnat' in Matt. xxiii. 24. It has been asserted that 'straine *at*' in the Bible of 1611 is a misprint for 'straine *out*', the rendering of earlier versions (see 14 e). But quots. 1583 and 1594 show that the translators of 1611 simply adopted a rendering that had already obtained currency. It was not a mistranslation, the meaning intended being 'which strain the liquor if they find a gnat in it'. The phrase, however, was early misapprehended (perh. already by Shaks. in quot. 1609), the verb being supposed to mean 'to make violent effort' (see sense 18).

[**1583** GREENE *Mamillia* II. B 3 b, Most vniustly straining at a gnat, and letting passe an elephant. **1594** J. KING *On Jonas* (1599) 284 They have verified the olde proverbe in strayning at gnats and swallowing downe camells. **1611** BIBLE *Matt.* xxiii. 24 Ye blind guides, which straine at a gnat, and swallow a camel.]

1609 SHAKS. *Tr. & Cr.* III. iii. 112 (Qo. 1) *Vliss.* I do not straine [*Fol.* (*hypermetrically*) straine it] at the position, It is familiar, but at the authors drift. **1670** SOUTH *Serm.* (1727) III. 110 He who hates his Enemy with a Cunning equal to his Malice, will not strain to do this or that good Turn for him, as long as it does not thwart..the main Design of his utter Subversion. **1677** R. WITTY *Gout Raptures* To Rdr. A 5 b, If any man strain at the Verse which is not in the usual mode, let him read the Lyrick Poets in Greek, who I think have taken more liberty then I. **1737** *Gentl. Mag.* VII. 546 The old Proverb, Strain at a Gnat, and swallow a Camel.

† **V. 22. a.** *trans.* To use (the voice) in song; to play upon (an instrument). **b.** To utter in song. **c.** *intr.* To sing. *Obs.*

Of uncertain origin; possibly developed from 10 d and 12. The related senses of STRAIN *sb.*² (11–12) seem to be derived from this use of the verb, but have prob. reacted upon it.

a. 1580 LYLY *Euphues* Wks. 1902 II. 58 Vnder a sweete Arbour of Eglentine, the byrdes recording theyr sweete notes, hee also strayned his old pype, and thus beganne. Gentle-menne, [etc.]. **1583** MELBANCKE *Philotimus* C ij b, Hark how the strumpet can straine her voice, to delighte with her deceite. **1600** FAIRFAX *Tasso* XI. ii, First let the priests..With sacred hymnes their holy voices straine. **1601** W. PERCY *Cuckqueanes & Cuckolds Errants* III. v. (Roxb.) 40 Then let the Goldsmith now for to streyne him, while I my self beare, to him, a Burden. **1602** MARSTON *Antonio's Rev.* I. v, Intreat the musick straine their instruments With a slight touch. **1648** J. BEAUMONT *Psyche* XV. ccxc, As to the Confines of the spheres they drew, His Harp and Voice their Chanter strein'd as high.

b. 1589 GREENE *Menaphon* (Arb.) 66 With this the Shepheard was mute..: but at length..to..make his olde Mistris some new musicke, he strained foorth this dittie. **1592** SHAKS. *Rom. & Jul.* III. v. 28 It is the Larke that sings so out of tune, Straining harsh Discords, and vnpleasing Sharpes. **1648** J. BEAUMONT *Psyche* XI. ccIxiii, He..strein'd his Ejulation To Horror's tune.

c. 1602 MARSTON *Ant. & Mel.* v, First let their voyces strain for musicks price. **1612** DRAYTON *Poly-olb.* II. 7 But as my subiect serues, so hie or lowe to straine. *Ibid.* XII. Argt., The Muse..Relating many glorious deeds, Of Guy of Warwick's fight doth straine.

†**strain,** *v.*² *Law. Obs.* [Aphetic form of DISTRAIN *v.* Cf. STRAIN *sb.*⁴] **a.** *trans.* To distrain (a person). Const. *for.* = DISTRAIN *v.* 7.

c **1450** *Godstow Reg.* 506 That they may streyne hym in all his tenementis, and hold the distreynynges, tille hit were fully I-satisfied of the arrerages of the forsaid rente. **1489** *Acc. Ld. High Treas. Scot.* I. 102 To Sperdour to pass to strenȝe Alexander Cambell for siluer he wes awande. *a* **1500** *Paston Lett.* Suppl. 167 Or ellys a wolle dystrayne me..as a hath strayne [*sic*] my tenenttes byfore for thys mater and costys. **1607** *Melrose Regality Rec.* (S.H.S.) I. 36 The judge ..ordanis the officer to poynd and strenze the defendar for thrette thre schilingis four pennyis.

b. *absol.* or *intr.* To levy a distress. Const. *for, on, upon* (a thing), *of, on* (a person or thing). = DISTRAIN *v.* 8.

1503 *Plumpton Corr.* (Camden) 178 They should either have the rent, or be suffered to streyne on such guds as they fond on the ground. *Ibid.* 180, I wold have streaned, but ther could no man shew me which was your ground. **1511** in *Exch. Rolls Scot.* XIII. 445 *note*, Unlawis, amerciamentis, and eschutis..[to] raise and uplift and for the samyn to strenye gif neid beis. **1586** *Acts Privy Counc.* (1897) XIV. 88 Then shall he [the Sheriff] straine uppon his landes and goodes for the payment thereof. **1633** ROWLEY *Match at Midn.* I. i, *Smith.* [This is] A vice sir, that I would faine bee furnisht with a little money upon 't... [I bought it] of a fat Cooke, that strain'd of a Smith for's rent. **1636** in *Parish Bks. St. Julian's, Shrewsbury* (MS.) I. 16 It: paid for 5 warants to Strayne on those who refuse to pay. **1675** in J. P. Earwaker *E. Cheshire* (1877) I. 116 Spent when we went to straine of the Quakers, Iˢ 8ᵈ. **1697** in *Col. Rec. Pennsylv.* I. 523 He wold demand, collect, or strain for yᵉ sd assessment. *a* **1718** W. PENN *Wks.* (1726) I. 673 Fining and Straining for Preaching and being at a Meeting.

fig. **1647** TRAPP *Comm. 1 Cor.* ix. 17 God will strain upon no man. All his servants are a free people.

c. *trans.* To seize (goods) by way of distress = DISTRAIN *v.* 9.

1455 in W. Fraser *The Lennox* (1874) II. 72 All our gudis mouable and vnmouable.., for to be tane, strenzet, poundyt, and..to be away hade. **1467** *Maldon* (Essex) *Court Rolls* Bundle 43. no. 3ᵛ, In his voydyng the said Gate streynyd the goodis & cattells that he fownde within the said place. **1529** *Acc. Ld. High Treas. Scot.* V. 380 Item,..to the currouris that past to strenȝe the bischop of Sanctandrois gudis for the temporalitie of Dunfermling iiij li. **1565** COOPER *Thesaurus* s.v. *Pignus*, A man may not..seise or strayne ones ploughe in way of distresse. **1576** GASCOIGNE *Steele Glas* 1102 When baylifes strain, none other thing but strays. **1681** W. ROBERTSON *Phraseol. Gen.* 1176/1 To strain a mans goods, *pignora cædere.*

strain (streɪn), *v.*³ [f. STRAIN *sb.*¹] *intr.* **a.** ***to strain back***: to go back in pedigree (*to* an ancestor).

1856 H. H. DIXON *Post & Paddock* ii. (1860) 35 Tomboy strains back to Sorcerer, through Jerry and Smolensko. **1871** *Daily News* 7 Dec., One of his exhibits strains back to the Gledmere flock.

b. ***to strain after***: to inherit the characteristics of.

1888 MRS. RIDDELL *Nun's Curse* I. vi. 97 You do not 'strain after' most of your family, for there has not been a Conway of Calgarry..that could bear to hear the truth.

†'**strainable,** *a.*¹ *Obs.* Forms: 5 strenabylle, strayne-, 6 strayn-, streyn(e-, strein-, stren-, 6–7 strain(e)able. [f. STRAIN *v.*¹ + -ABLE.]

1. Coercive, compulsive, compulsory.

1483 *Cath. Angl.* 368/1 Strenabylle, *artabilis, co-, coarcibilis.* **1577–87** HOLINSHED *Chron.* III. 828/1 Being hastned forward through the strenable force of destinie. **1592** BACON *Observ. Libel* Resuscit. (1657) 117 The Entring, and Sifting, into Mens Consciences,..which is Rigorous, and Straineable, Inquisition.

2. In physical sense: Violent, exerting great force. Chiefly of wind and weather.

1497 *Naval Acc. Hen. VII* (1896) 249 The wynde contraryed & the wether was so Strayneable that scace they gate into Lymyngton haven. *a* **1548** HALL *Chron., Rich. III*, 41 A prosperous and strenable wynde. **1566** PAINTER *Pal. Pleas.* I. 69 The night being darke and the billowes going high and streinable. **1581** MULCASTER *Positions* xxix. (1887) 109 Some [exercises] be verie vehement, strong, and strainable.

3. Of the voice: ? Full, powerful, sonorous.

1569 NEWTON *Cicero's Olde Age* 17 b, The office and function of an Oratoure consisteth not only in wytte and eloquence, but also in a loude durablenesse, and strainable voice. **1576** —— *Lemnie's Complex.* I. vi. 37 He..vseth a liuelye & straynable voyce [L. *viua intentaque voce*].

Hence †'**strainableness;** †'**strainably** *adv.*

1511 *Guylforde's Pilgr.* (Camden) 60 The wynde blew not so straynably as byfore. *a* **1542** WYATT *Poems*, '*Go burning Sighs*', With pitefull plaint & scalding fyer that oute of my brest doeth straynably stert. **1581** LD. BURLEIGH in Nicolas *Mem. Sir. C. Hatton* (1847) 177, I do..pray you..not to have the Earl deale withal strainably, but only by way of advice. **1587** FLEMING *Contn. Holinshed* III. 1549/1 By building of which bridge ouer so swift & great a streame, the passage was set open..which before (by reason of the strenablenesse of the water) was not passable.

†'**strainable,** *a.*² *Scots Law. Obs.* Forms: 6 stren(e)ȝeable, strengyabill, strenyeabill, 6–7 strenȝeabill, -ell, streinȝeable. [aphetic f. DISTRAINABLE. Cf. STRAIN *v.*²] Subject to distraint, liable to be distrained.

1508 *Cartular. S. Nich. Aberd.* (New Spalding Club) I. 205 Ay and quhile We prouid to thame ane plaice als strenȝeabill for ye pament of ye saide sex markis in ye ȝeir. **1540** *Rec. Elgin* (New Spalding Club) I. 51 The prouest and bailȝeis commandat the officiaris to pund termlye ony strengyabill bigging of the forsaid landis. **1609** SKENE *Reg. Maj., Stat. Alex. II* 18 b, Gif they haue na strenzeabell gudes. *Ibid., Quon. Attach.* xxxvii. 84 Ilke frie man may be borgh for himselfe..swa he be responsall, and strenzeabill to the judge.

strained (streɪnd), *ppl. a.* [f. STRAIN *v.*[1] + -ED[1].]

1. Subjected to physical tension. Of a rope, etc.: Stretched tight.

1640 J. GOWER *Ovid's Festiv.* IV. 82 The strained ropes mens toilsome hands do wring. **1769** J. GRANGER *Biogr. Hist. Eng.* II. 563 One represents her dancing on a strained, the other vaulting on a slack rope. **1854** *Pereira's Polarized Light* (ed. 2) 143 The immediate effect of heat on one part of a piece of glass is to put all the surrounding parts into a strained state. **1859** JEPHSON *Brittany* iv. 39 Their well-formed ankles [shown to advantage] by their tightly strained black stockings. **1869** RANKINE *Machine & Hand-tools* Summary Princ. 1 If a previously strained body, upon the removal of the stress, recovers its free shape, it is said to be perfectly elastic. **1888** T. WATTS *Burd. Armada* in *Athenæum* 18 Aug. 224/2 And now, amid the tempest's din Each Spaniard in the strained Vasana pales.

2. Of a part of the body: Injured by over-exertion of the muscles, etc. Said also of an animal suffering from such an injury.

1611 COTGR., *Seton*,..the rowelling, or roping of a bruised, or strained horse. **1753** RICHARDSON *Grandison* (1754) II. x. 64 A wry face, and a strained neck, denoting her difficulty to get down but a lark's morsel. **1829** J. LAWRENCE *Horse* 185, I have, now and then, heard of a strained ankle as the consequence [of a lady's jumping from her saddle]. **1899** *Allbutt's Syst. Med.* VIII. 175 These cases..which are often called 'strained back,' etc.

3. Of the voice, gaze, attention, 'nerves', etc.: Exerted by an abnormal effort or to an abnormal degree. Of look or expression: Showing signs of nerve-tension.

a **1542** WYATT *Penit. Ps.* xxxii. Proem. 32 Wt strained voyce againe thus cryth he. **1577** KENDALL *Flowers of Epigr.* 80 With strained throates God saue the kyng they crie, and crie alowde. **1606** WOTTON *Life & Lett.* (1907) I. 343 Whom welcoming with a very high and strained voice. **1697** CONGREVE *Mourn. Bride* II i. 19 O my strain'd Heart. **1806** SURR *Winter in Lond.* I. 75 Fixing his strained eyes upon a portrait of Dr. Enfield which hung over the chimney. **1818** SCOTT *Hrt. Midl.* xv, The person who sung kept a strained and powerful voice at its highest pitch. **1841** DICKENS *Barn. Rudge* lxi, With eager eyes and strained attention. **1863** MRS. OLIPHANT *Salem Chapel* xxi, Afraid to relax her strained nerves even by leaning back or forward. **1908** R. BAGOT *A. Cuthbert* xxviii. 368 The strained, drawn expression, telling of mental suffering.

4. Of conduct, demeanour, gestures, etc.: Produced under compulsion or by deliberate effort; artificial, forced, not spontaneous or natural.

c **1400** *Rom. Rose* 7325 My lemman, Streyned-Abstinence [*m'amie Contrainte-Astenance*]. **1588** W. R. *Engl. Ape* 23 Theyr strayned modesty, and theyr counterfayte coynesse. **1597** SHAKS. *2 Hen. IV* I. i. 161 (Qo.) This strained passion doth you wrong my lord. **1612** *Two Noble K.* III. iii. 56 Foole, Away with this straind mirth. **1628** FELTHAM *Resolves* I. vi. 13 If you search for high and strained Carriages; you shall for the most part, meete with them, in low men. **1865** DICKENS *Mut. Fr.* I. xiii, Thoroughly used to him as he was, he found something new and strained in him [*sc.* his friend] that was for the moment perplexing. **1898** KIPLING *Day's Work* 210 The strained, eye-shirking talk at dinner till the servants had withdrawn.

5. Of language, construction put upon words or actions, etc.: Employed or interpreted in a laboured, far-fetched, or non-natural sense; wrested or distorted from the natural meaning or intention; pressed, forced. Of a conception, supposition, etc.: Pushed beyond what is natural or reasonable.

c **1600** SHAKS. *Sonn.* lxxxii. 10 When they haue deuisde What strained touches Rhethorick can lend. **1651** HOBBES *Leviath.* III. xlii. 304 Which is a strange, and very much strained interpretation. **1747** LD. CHANC. HARDWICKE in G. Harris *Life* (1847) I. 374, I own I thought this a strained construction, and did not scruple to say so. **1768** H. WALPOLE *Hist. Doubts* 64 There is nothing strained in the supposition of Richard's sparing his nephew. **1857** C. B[ATHURST] *Rem. Differ. Shaks. Versif.* 42 There is nothing pompous, strained, ranting. **1885** *Law Times* LXXVIII. 386/2 Surely this is rather a strained construction to put upon the 26th section?

6. Of a regulation, enactment, prerogative, etc.: Pushed or urged beyond what is equitable. Of personal relations, a situation, etc.: Subjected to a dangerous degree of tension, forced to a point where a rupture becomes imminent.

1735 tr. *Rollin's Anc. Hist.* x. i. §2 IV. 273 Was it not a wise amendment of what was too strained and excessive in that law of Lycurgus? **1880** *Daily News* 2 Nov., The situation was thought 'strained' even in a disturbed Oriental country. **1899** P. H. BROWN *Hist. Scot.* II. ii. I. 77 The peace between the two kings was of short duration. On the Easter following their treaty a trifling incident again placed them in strained relations. **1911** CRAIK *Edward Earl of Clarendon* I. iii. 69 Charles..resolved to summon a Parliament. The first step in the surrender of a strained prerogative was taken.

7. Passed through a strainer or colander.

1591 A. W. *Bk. Cookrye* 12 So boyle them in the broth and thicke it with strained bread. **1596** BARROUGH *Meth. Phisick* (ed. 3) 436 To the strained decoction, put the iuice of quince peares and pomegranates. **1611** COTGR., *Pressis*, cullisses, or strained meats. **1675** HANNAH WOOLLEY *Gentlew. Comp.* 131 A Gallandine-sauce made with strained Bread, Vinegar [etc.]. **1731** ARBUTHNOT *Aliments* iii. (1735) 68 If the Plant be boil'd in the same Water, the strain'd Liquor is call'd the Decoction of the Plant. **1871** GARROD *Mat. Med.* (ed. 3) 170 Reduce the strained liquor to three pints.

fig. **1606** SHAKS. *Tr. & Cr.* IV. iv. 26 (Qo.), Cressid I loue thee in so strain'd a purity.

†**8.** Having a strain or melody; formed into melody. *Obs.*

1589 PUTTENHAM *Eng. Poesie* II. i. (Arb.) 79 The harmonicall concents of the artificial Musicke, consisting in strained tunes. **1601** WEEVER *Mirr. Mart.* lxxix. B 8 Whose strayned ditties most melodicall.

Hence **'strainedly** *adv.*, **'strainedness.**

1571 GOLDING *Calvin on Ps.* ix. 7. 27 Others more streynedly interpret it. **1639** N. N. tr. *Du Boscq's Compl. Woman* II. 59 Hence it is they live with so much strainednesse, and that there is nothing even or natively done in their behaviours. **1697** G. KEITH *2nd Narr. Proc. Turner's Hall* 26 He unfairly and strainedly defends G. Fox's words. **1891** H. C. HALLIDAY *Someone must suffer* I. viii. 184 She entered, smiling rather strainedly. **1901** Strainedness [see *over-elaboration* s.v. OVER- 29 d].

strainer ('streɪnə(r)). Forms: 4 **streignour, streyngoure, -your,** ? **streinor, stryn(n)or,** 4–5 **streynour(e, straynour(e, strenour,** 5 **straynowr(e, -woure, streynȝour, strener, strenyor, -yowre, streneyour, strynour,** 5–6 **streyner, strenȝoure,** 6 **streynyowr, straygner, strenear, -ere, -yer,** 7 **streiner,** 5–7 **strayner,** 6– **strainer.** [f. STRAIN *v.*[1] + -ER[1]; but the early forms suggest that there may have been an AF. ****estreignour***, f. *estreign-* STRAIN *v.*[1]]

1. a. A utensil or device for straining, filtering, or sifting; a filter, sieve, screen, or the like.

1326–7 *Durham Acc. Rolls* (Surtees) 15 In 20 ulnis linee tele pro naprouns et streyngoures. **1348–9** *Ibid.* 43 In Streynyours. **139.** *Earl Derby's Exped.* (Camden) 22/3 Pro xl virges de streynours ad iij d., x s. *c* **1420** *Liber Cocorum* (1862) 9 þorowgh a strynour þou hom strene. *c* **1481** CAXTON *Dialogues* 8 For to make..sauses thorugh the strayner. **1527** *Luton Trin. Guild* (1906) 188 Payd for A gelebag and a strenere v d. **1533** in *Kal. & Inv. Exch.* (1836) II. 294 Item a strᵉyner of golde for orrenges. **1599** A. M. tr. *Gabelhouer's Bk. Physicke* 41/2 Then straygne them through a clothe or straygner. **1640** T. BRUGIS *Marrow of Physicke* II. 155 Let it run through a woollen strainer. **1707** MORTIMER *Husb.* 216 Pour it..into a Strainer of fine thin Linen, or of twisted Hair. **1824** SCOTT *St. Ronan's* x, The silver strainer, on which..the lady of the house placed the tea-leaves. **1846** A. YOUNG *Naut. Dict.* 254 *Rose*, or *Strainer*, a plate of copper or lead perforated with small holes, sometimes placed upon the heel of a pump to prevent any thing being sucked in which might choke the pump. **1889** WELCH *Text Bk. Naval Archit.* xi. 123 The ejector is surrounded by a strainer and placed in an ejector tank. **1894** *Outing* XXIV. 435/1 A basket of gravel and dirt is thrown into a bamboo strainer.

b. Applied to natural structures or processes which perform the function of filtering.

1626 BACON *Sylva* §93 The Cause of Orient Colours in Birds..is by the Finenesse of the Strainer. **1666** G. HARVEY *Morbus Angl.* xxii. (1672) 51 The office of the Lungs is only to serve the heart in the capacity of Aereal strainers, to strain the Air. **1737** BRACKEN *Farriery Impr.* (1756) I. 12 All the little Glands and Strainers of the Body. **1772** PENNANT *Tours in Scot.* (1774) 169 The apertures to the gills very long, and furnished with Strainers. **1841–71** T. R. JONES *Anim. Kingd.* 826 Seeing that in some whales there are about three hundred plates composing the outer row on each side of the mouth, the reader may form some idea of the extent of this enormous strainer. **1880** HUXLEY *Crayfish* ii. 53 So is the cuticle of the stomach calcified..to give rise..to a filter or strainer, whereby the nutritive juices are separated from the innutritious hard parts of the food.

c. *transf.* and *fig.*

1621–31 LAUD *Serm.* (1847) 44 The blessings..come not immediately from God to the people,..but they are strained ..through the man, and therefore must relish a little of the strainer, him and his mortality. **1648** WINYARD *Midsummer-Moon* 4 Hee is a strainer, retaines all the dreggs, and clarifies the University as milke and whites of eggs doth Ippocras. **1666** T. WATSON *Godly Man's Pict.* 255 He put his body to no other use, but to be a strainer for meat and drink to run thorow. **1732** POPE *Ess. Man* II. 189 Lust, thro' some certain Strainers well refin'd, Is gentle love. **1813** *Examiner* 26 Apr. 266/1 To them may be traced, through different strainers, almost all the fictions of European romance.

2. a. A device for stretching or tightening.

1527 in *Archæologia* XXXVI. 222 Item syx banner clothys and foure streyners and eyght pools too the same. **1688** HOLME *Armory* III. 396/2 A [Sadlers'] Strainer..is made of Wood [etc.]..with this the Girth web is fastned and drawn streat upon the Sadle trees; or in such places where the Girth requires straining. **1883** J. SCOTT *Farm Roads* etc. 83 The wires are strained by a portable strainer.

b. *N.Z. ellipt.* for *strainer post* below.

1933 E. JONES *Autobiogr. Early Settler* xviii. 77, I know of a wire fence which was erected with wire strainers 70 years ago. **1950** *N.Z. Jrnl. Agric.* Apr. 347/3 Reinforced concrete strainers and intermediate posts are preferable to wood. **1961** B. CRUMP *Hang on a Minute, Mate* 43 They'd been splitting the short ends of logs into posts and strainers.

3. (See quot.)

1891 *Century Dict.*, *Strainer*... In carriage-building: (*a*) A reinforcing strip or button at the back of a panel. (*b*) Canvas glued to the back of a panel to prevent warping or cracking.

4. *Comb.*: †**strainer-cloth**, a cloth used for filtering; **strainer post** chiefly *N.Z.* = *straining post* s.v. STRAINING *vbl. sb.* 6 a; **strainer-vine**, *Luffa acutangula* (Grisebach *Flora W. Ind. Islands* 788).

1444 *Compota Domest.* (Abbotsf. Club) 21 Pro bultyngclothes strenourclothes [etc.]. **1483** CAXTON *Golden Leg.* 432 b/2 He..ware for a Shyrte a Stamyn or Streyner clothe. **1537** in *Myrr. Our Ladye* Introd. 31 Strayner cloth j pece. **1921** H. GUTHRIE-SMITH *Tutira* xviii. 148 A kerosene case nailed to the top of a strainer-post. **1950** *N.Z. Jrnl. Agric.* Apr. 347/3 At the ends of each fence should be a good strainer post stayed in position in the normal way. **1965** S. T. OLLIVIER *Petticoat Farm* ix. 132 If she walked round the drain she could climb on the corner strainer post and get a view of the house. **1968** J. ARNOLD *Shell Bk. Country Crafts* 101 End or corner strainer posts are supported by diagonal struts.

strainful ('streɪnfʊl), *a.* [f. STRAIN *sb.*[2] + -FUL.] Causing or filled with strain; stressful.

1935 G. FRANKAU *Three Englishmen* lxix. 607 It came to Andrew—not for the first time in these strainful days—how great, whatever the outcome of this ordeal, would be the relief of its end. **1957** *Psychol. Rev.* LXIV. 142/2 There is no built-in incentive for the foreigner to maintain a cognitively strainful regimen of attending further to speech sounds.

strainge, -er, obs. ff. STRANGE, STRANGER.

straining ('streɪnɪŋ), *vbl. sb.* [f. STRAIN *v.*[1] + -ING[1].]

1. The action of stretching, extending, drawing tight, wrenching, etc.; the fact of being stretched, wrenched, etc.

c **1400** *Lanfranc's Cirurg.* 199 A Mannes lyme bicomeþ smal wiþ greet streynyng of ligaturis þat takiþ awei þe norisching of þe lyme. **1463–4** *Rolls of Parlt.* V. 501/1 Brode Cloth..after almanere rakkyng, streynyng or teyntyng therof. **1562** TURNER *Herbal* II. 83 The ach that commeth by the wrinchyng or strenyng [*printed* streuyng] of any ioynte. *a* **1647** in *Archæologia* XII. 263 The ship went away without any straining of screws or tackles. **1748** *Anson's Voy.* II. iv. 157 The water the *Pink* had made by her working and straining in bad weather. **1805** SCOTT *Last Minstr.* IV. xx, So near they were, that they might know The straining harsh of each cross-bow. **1860** W. COLLINS *Woman in White* vii, The drawings..require careful straining and mounting. **1865** SWINBURNE *Poems & Ball.*, *Lamentation* 69 With straining of oars.

2. a. Excessive exertion of the voice, lungs, eyes, etc.

1585 HIGINS *Junius' Nomencl.* 347/2 *Bombyces*,..long pipes which are very hardly filled with breath, and not without great straining of the breath. **1591** SHAKS. *1 Hen. VI*, I. v. 10 My brest Ile burst with straining of my courage. **1639** N. N. tr. *Du Bosq's Compl. Woman* I. 28 The strayning of their countenance discovers, they have not modestie enough for silence, no more then sufficiency for discourse. **1680** OTWAY *Caius Marius* IV. i, It is the Lark, and out of Tune she sings With grating Discords and unpleasing Strainings. **1712** ADDISON *Spect.* No. 407 ¶1 Those Strainings of the Voice, Motions of the Body, and Majesty of the Hand, which are so much celebrated in the Orators of Greece and Rome. **1832** S. WARREN *Diary Physic.* II. iii. 122 There was..no knitting of the brows, or painful straining of the eyes. **1876** GEO. ELIOT *Deronda* xv. I. 292 An uncommonly fine girl... Really worth a little straining to look at her.

b. A violent muscular effort to evacuate the bowels, etc.

1613 PURCHAS *Pilgrimage* (1614) 721 In the ascent he and all the rest were surprised with so sudden panges of straining and casting, and some also of scouring, that the Sea-sicknesse is not comparable hereunto. **1677** GILPIN *Dæmonol.* (1867) 307 That vomit..cannot be done without sickness, straining, and torture. **1899** *Allbutt's Syst. Med.* VII. 241 The percentage of total solids in the fluid passed during straining, was less than half that passed when the patient remained passive.

c. The making a violent effort or strong endeavour (*to* do something, *after* an end or object).

1580 LYLY *Euphues Eng.* (Arb.) 422 The Nightingale, which is saide with continual strayning to singe, to perishe in hir sweete layes. **1665** BOYLE *Occas. Refl.* IV. xiii. (1848) 248 The Shore being fixt, and immoveable, instead of making that come to him, his very strainings drew him and his Boat to that. **1800** COLERIDGE in J. D. Campbell *Life* (1894) 107, I find that I can without any straining gain 500 guineas a year. **1890** *Spectator* 1 Nov., Grand projects of street-improvement, many of which are mere strainings after a needless grandeur. **1898** M. HEWLETT *Earthwork out of Tuscany* (1899) Pref. p. xii, The straining of Botticelli to express the ineffable.

3. An urging or pressing too far, laying undue stress upon; wresting or distortion of meaning, forced construction or interpretion.

1528 MORE *Dyaloge* Wks. 107/2, I haue in these matters bidden him be bolde, without any strayning of curtesie. **1654** JER. TAYLOR *Real Pres.* 116 By some straining, the Lamb slain might signifie the slaying the Egyptians. **1855** MACAULAY *Hist. Eng.* xv. III. 527 The words of the Act.. may, without any straining, be construed as the Court construed them. **1908** *Athenæum* 31 Oct. 535/2 They were forced into resisting such strainings of the prerogative as the Declaration of Indulgence.

4. a. Filtering, sifting, expressing.

1548 *Elyot's Dict.*, *Expressio*, a streynyng. **1583** MELBANCKE *Philotimus* C c/ij b, The streyning of a gnat is not swallowing of a cammell. **1640** BP. HALL *Chr. Moder.* I. xiii. 141 The presse is prepared for the grapes and Olives, and..neither of them will yeeld their comfortable and wholsome juyce without an hard strayning. **1718** QUINCY *Compl. Disp.* (1719) 66 Gums and inspissated Juices..are seldom fit for use before straining. **1883** *Encycl. Brit.* XVI. 691/2 Probably a straining of water from solid particles is effected by the lattice-work of the ctenidia or gill-plates.

b. *concr.* Something strained or extracted by straining; usually a strained liquor.

1580 BLUNDEVIL *Curing Horses Dis.* lxix. 29 Cast not awaie the sodden Barlie with the rest of the strainings. **1669** ROWLAND *Schroder's Chym. Disp.* I. iii. 6 *Succus*, in Shops are Expressions or Strainings, such as will mix with Water. **1887** A. M. BROWN *Anim. Alkaloids* 82 The residue is filtered by pressure, and the united strainings are subjected to boiling or evaporation.

5. *Saddlery.* (See quot. 1875.)

1871 *Saddlers' Gaz.* 1 May 12/1 The webs used for the manufacture of a saddle are termed straining web, cross straining and diaper web. **1875** KNIGHT *Dict. Mech.*, *Straining*, a piece of canvas or leather, which, being drawn tightly over the tree, forms the foundation for the seat of the saddle... It is called the straining, because the stretch is taken out of it by repeated wettings and stretchings.

6. *attrib.* and *Comb.* **a.** in sense 1: **straining-arch**, an arch designed to resist end-thrust; **straining-beam** (see quot. 1825); **straining-frame**, a frame on which paper, canvas, etc. is stretched; **straining-leather** (see quot. and sense 5); **straining-piece** = *straining-beam*; **straining-pillar, -post**, a post from which wire fencing is stretched tight; **straining-sill** or **-cill** (see quot. 1825); **straining-web** (see 5).

1848 RICKMAN *Archit.* (ed. 5) Descr. Engrav. p. xli, The angel corbel carries another arch, known as a *straining arch. *a* **1805** ROBISON *Syst. Mech. Philos.* (1822) I. 545 The *straining beam and the trussbeam above it. **1825** J. NICHOLSON *Oper. Mech.* 572 *Straining-beam*; a piece of timber placed between two others, called *queen-posts*, at their upper ends, in order to withstand the thrust of the principal rafters. **1762–71** H. WALPOLE *Vertue's Anecd. Paint.* (1786) III. 80 On the *straining frame was written Gerard Soest pinxit. **1815** J. SMITH *Panorama Sci. & Art* II. 747 The paper designed for a transparency must be fixed on a straining frame, such as that of a drawing board without its pannel. **1875** KNIGHT *Dict. Mech.*, **Straining-leather*, a kind of web forming the seat of a hussar-saddle. *a* **1805** ROBISON *Syst. Mech. Philos.* (1822) I. 669 The great use of the *straining piece is to give a firm abutment to the inner struts, without allowing any lateral strain on the stretcher. **1842** *Civil Engin. & Arch. Jrnl.* V. 361/2 Long straining-pieces reaching from one post to another. **1883** J. SCOTT *Farm Roads* etc. 85 *Straining-pillars and posts fitted with ..winding brackets. **1882** *Worc. Exhib. Catal.* III. 20 Strained wire fencing..with two kinds of *straining posts. *a* **1805** ROBISON *Syst. Mech. Philos.* (1822) I. 547 The *straining sill Q gives a firm abutment to the principal braces. **1825** J. NICHOLSON *Oper. Mech.* 572 *Straining-cill*; a piece of timber placed upon the tie-beam at the bottom of two queen-posts, in order to withstand the force of the braces.

b. in sense 4, as *straining-bag, -cloth, -spoon, -tower*.

1725 *Bradley's Family Dict.* s.v. *Sugar* ¶ 1 Passing it thro a *Straining-Bag. **1742** *Lond. & Country Brew.* IV. (ed. 2) 311 A Bag made of *Straining-cloth, such as Dairy Women use to pass their Milk through. **1915** J. LONDON *Let.* 26 Jan. (1966) 445 Note his..pasteurization of utensils and of straining-cloths over the milk-pails. **1912** C. MACKENZIE *Carnival* xxxvi. 342 Here were also brass ladles and *straining spoons and a pair of bellows. **1960** H. HAYWARD *Antique Coll.* 269/2 *Straining spoon*, spoon with pierced bowl, found either in large sizes for gravy or similar use or in teaspoon size with thin, tapering stem and pricket top, used for skimming leaves from teacups. **1887** *Pall Mall Gaz.* 21 Oct. 5/2 There will be a *straining tower at Vyrniew [*i.e.* Vyrnwy], a profusion of filter-beds at Oswestry.

ˈ**straining**, *ppl. a.* [-ING².] That strains, in various senses of the vb.

1530 PALSGR. 326/1 Straynyng, *constraintif.* **1534** MORE *Comf. agst. Trib.* III. xxvii. (1553) V vij b, Yᵉ crewel stretching and straining payne, farre passing any crampe. **1584** B. R. tr. *Herodotus* I. 26 b, Fetching from the bottom of his hart a deepe and streyning sigh. **1794** MRS. RADCLIFFE *Myst. Udolpho* xxxiv, The straining cordage bursts, the mast is riven. **1838** W. C. HARRIS *Narr. Exped. S. Africa* xxx. 289 But neither fount, nor pool, nor running stream, greeted my straining gaze. **1888** F. HUME *Mme. Midas* Prol., Holding the straining sail by a stout rope twisted round his arm. **1898** *Allbutt's Syst. Med.* V. 281 Much harm may be done by straining efforts in defœcation.

†**b.** Astringent, styptic. *Obs.*

1398 TREVISA *Barth. De P.R.* XVII. liii. (1495) 634 Iuy is medicinable thouh it be bytter and is streynynge. **1552** HULOET, Streygninge or bitinge as ginger..[etc.], *stipticus*.

Hence ˈ**strainingly** *adv.*

1828 *Blackw. Mag.* XXIII. 773 Stood he strainingly upright. **1831** TRELAWNY *Adv. Younger Son* cxxiii, The tense cords strainingly drawn from heart to brain. **1883** MISS BROUGHTON *Belinda* I. xiii, Belinda has opened the envelope, and is staring strainingly at the paper.

strainless (ˈstreɪnlɪs), *a.* [f. STRAIN *sb.*² + -LESS.] Produced without strain; free from strain. Hence ˈ**strainlessly** *adv.*

1907 G. B. SHAW *John Bull's Other Island* II. 39 Aunt Judy comes down the hill,..a contented product of a narrow, strainless life. **1927** *Daily Tel.* 10 Feb. 16/4 Eluding the volleying vigilance of the Australian by drives as supremely accurate as they were strainlessly produced. **1927** N. V. SIDGWICK *Electronic Theory of Valency* xiv. 237 We are.. not justified in assuming..that the resulting angles are 'strainless'. **1975** R. F. BROWN *Org. Chem.* xii. 322 It was not until 1890 that Sachse proposed strainless ring puckering for cyclohexane and larger rings.

strainometer (streɪˈnɒmɪtə(r)). [f. STRAIN *sb.*² + -OMETER.] = *strain gauge, strainmeter* s.v. STRAIN *sb.*² 16.

1915 *Jrnl. Iron & Steel Inst.* XCI. 605 The strainometer, besides measuring the axial deformation, enables the amount of bending to be accurately calculated. **1978** *Invest. Urology* XVI. 208/2 The strainometer constantly monitored changes in vas deferens diameter which occurred with spontaneous contractions.

straint (streɪnt). *rare.* [Partly a. OF. *estrainte, estreinte* (mod.F. *étreinte*), n. of action f. *étreindre* to STRAIN; partly a nonce-formation, after *restraint, constraint*, to serve as a sb. to STRAIN *v.*] Application of force or pressure.

1534 *Prymer in Engl.* O v, When we are driuen to suche an harde straynte [**1538** straynt] that we can not tel what to do. **1596** SPENSER *F.Q.* V. ii. 14 Sir Artegall..Vppon his iron coller griped fast, That with the straint his wesand nigh he brast. *a* **1876** G. DAWSON *Shaks. & other Lect.* (1888) 304 Friendship..is above the straints and restraints of destiny.

strainth, obs. Sc. form of STRENGTH.

strais, obs. Sc. pl. of STRAW.

strait (streɪt), *a.*, *sb.*, and *adv.* Forms: 3 strect, 3–7 streit(e, 4–6 streyt(e, strayt, strayth, 4–6, 9 *dial.* stret, (5 strete, 6 streayte, strayet), 4–7 strayte, straite, 4 (strecte, streȝt), streyghte, straiȝt, *Sc.* strat, 4–6 *Sc.* strate, 5 streiȝt, (streihte, straeict), strayȝt(e, streith, streythe, (straytt), 5–7 streyght, 5–9 straight, 6–7 streighte, 6–9 straight, (6–7 -e), 6 strayght(e, straicte, 6–7 streict(e, 7 streigt, 5–6 stryte, 3– strait. [ME. *streit*, a. OF. *estreit* tight, close, narrow, also as sb., narrow or tight place, strait of the sea, distress (mod.F. *étroit* narrow) = Pr. *estreit*, Sp. *estrecho*, Pg. *estreito*, It. *stretto*:—L. *strictus* (see STRICT *a.*) pa. pple. of *stringĕre* to tighten, bind tightly: see STRAIN *v.*, STRINGENT *a.*] **A.** *adj.*

I. In physical senses: Tight, narrow.

1. a. Of a garment, etc.: Tight-fitting, narrow. *Obs.* exc. *dial.*

1387 TREVISA *Higden* (Rolls) I. 353 þey..haueþ..straiȝt hodes [L. *capuciis strictis*]. **1398** —— *Barth. De P.R.* V. xxix. (1495) 140 A rynge that is streyghte on a fyngre and may not be take of afore mete, maye easely be take of after mete. *c* **1400** *Rom. Rose* 2271 Streite gloves. **1459** *Paston Lett.* I. 475, j. nothir gowne of clothe of golde, with streyht slevys. **1551** in Feuillerat *Revels Edw. VI* (1914) 58 A Iyrkyn for the Tumbler strayte to his bodye. **1599** SHAKS. *Hen. V*, III. vii. 57 You rode like a Kerne of Ireland, your French Hose off, and in your strait Strossers. **1605** BACON *Adv. Learn.* II. xxii. §8 For he mought see that a streight gloue wil come more easily on with vse. **1612–26** BRETON *Wits Priv. Wealth* (Grosart) 8/1 And strait Shooes fill the feet full of cornes. **1658** A. Fox tr. *Wurtz' Surg.* III. x. 246 Bind the wound slackly, and let the party not put on too straight clothes. **1693** LOCKE *Educ.* §11 That your Sons Cloths be never made strait. **1713** *Guardian* No. 32 ¶7 The Third..appeared in Cloaths that were so strait and uneasie to him, that he seemed to move with Pain. **1767** STERNE *Tr. Shandy* IX. ii, His blue and gold had become so miserably too strait for him. **1779** FORREST *Voy. N. Guinea* II. xiv. 330 The men go generally in white waistcoats,..with white breeches, sometimes strait, sometimes wide. **1888** *Sheffield Gloss.*, *Stret*, tight, too small. 'Her dress were that stret at shoo couldn't stride o'er t' brook.'

†**b.** Of bonds, a knot: Tightly drawn. *Obs.*

1561 HOBY tr. *Castiglione's Courtier* II. (1900) 138, I allowe well, that this knott, which is so streicte, knitt or binde no mo than two. **1569** *Reg. Privy Council Scot.* II. 62 [He] sall incontinent..be put in strait irnis. **1600** HOLLAND *Livy* XXIV. vii. 513 [He] lift up his foot, making as though he would loose and slacke a streight knot of his sho latchet. **1656** RIDGLEY *Pract. Physick* 163 If the parts swell hard, it [the bandage] is too straight; if it swell not, it is too loose. **1725** *Bradley's Family Dict.* s.v. *Snakes*, By a streight Ligature below the Wound.

fig. **1583** GOLDING *Calvin on Deut.* i. 3 He is..our Father and hath adopted us to be his Children, and moreouer tied us to him by a much streiter Band: in that he hath redeemed us. **1595** SPENSER *Amoretti* lxxi, Right so your selfe were caught in cunning snare of a deare foe,..in whose streight bands ye now captiued are. **1628** FELTHAM *Resolves* I. lxxxv. 245 So they [hearts] cloze againe after discussion, many times in a straighter Tye.

†**c.** Of an embrace: close. *Obs.*

1596 SPENSER *F.Q.* IV. viii. 63 She to him ran, and him with streight embras Enfolding said, And liues yet Amyas?

†**d.** Tense, not lax. *Obs.*

1578 BANISTER *Hist. Man* I. 19 And yet the Articulation [of the vertebræ] not left to strayte, but slacke inough..for the turnyng of the head on eche side. **1732** ARBUTHNOT *Rules of Diet* i. §21 in *Aliments* etc. II. (1736) 283 All those who have lax Fibres and Vessels are naturally cooler than those that have strait.

†**e.** Of the chest: Constricted, 'tight'. Of the breath: Difficult, 'short'. *Obs.*

1561 HOLLYBUSH *Hom. Apoth.* 6 Then becommeth a man strayght about the cheste or stomake, & his heat is dry. **1695** *Phil. Trans.* XIX. 80 Her Breath was streight, as is usual to fat People, especially when she went up a pair of Stairs.

2. a. Scanty or inadequate in spatial capacity; affording little room; narrow. Of bounds, limits: Narrow. Now *rare* exc. in *too strait*.

c **1290** *St. Brendan* 255 in *S. Eng. Leg.* 226 A luytel hauene and swyþe streit huy founden atþe laste. Þat vnneþes heore schip miȝte þerinne come, Aunker for to caste. *c* **1374** CHAUCER *Boeth.* III. met. ii. (1868) 68 Brid þat syngiþ..in þe wode and after is inclosed in a streit cage. *c* **1375** *Sc. Leg. Saints* vii. (*Jacobus mi.*) 762 He sa sted wes..þat he mycht nothire syt no ly; sa strate to hyme wes þat herbry. *c* **1386** CHAUCER *Miller's T.* 202 Myn hous is streit. **1426** LYDG. *De Guil. Pilgr.* 18076 By large mesure I can byen, and streight mesure I sell ageyn. **1509** FISHER *7 Penit. Ps.* cii. Wks. (1876) 171 Where as somtyme we were spredde almoost thrugh the worlde, now we be thraste downe into a very streyght angyll or corner. **1513** MORE in Hall *Chron., Edw. V* (1548) 6 b, The kynge was goyng to horsebacke, because he would leaue the lodgyng for them, for it was to straight for bothe the compaignies. **1600** E. BLOUNT tr. *Conestaggio* 4 Portugall was then obscure, vntilled, poore, and reduced into streight limits. *a* **1659** BP. BROWNRIG *Serm.* (1674) I. vii. 101 The Sun is made for the World, not for any streighter Region. **1707** *Curios. in Husb. & Gard.* 332 Within the streight Bounds of that small Vessel. **1724** BP. WILSON in Keble *Life* (1863) II. 625 Because of a very numerous family..for which the vicarage-house was too strait. **1797** *Encycl. Brit.* (ed. 3) II. 490/2 Where the space is straitest, the earth moves more slowly than where it is widest. **1839** MRS. BROWNING *Sabbath Morn.* ix, Too strait ye are, capacious seas, To satisfy the loving! **1879** FROUDE *Cæsar* v. 41 The hunting and pasture grounds were too strait for the numbers crowded into them.

fig. **1340** *Ayenb.* 54 Þo þet libbeþ be fisike: hy healdeþ þe mesure of ypocras þet is lite an strait. **1634** W. WOOD *New Eng. Prosp.* (1865) Addr. Rdr., Any thing stranger than ordinary, is too large for the straite hoopes of his apprehension. **1668** DRYDEN *Dram. Poesy* 19 But in how straight a compass soever they have bounded their Plots and Characters, we will pass it by, if they have regularly pursued them. **1787** *Printer's Gram.* 21 It is therefore to be wished that the intermixing Roman and Italic may be brought to straighter limits. **1875** WHITNEY *Life Lang.* iii. 35 One may ..have reached in some single department..the furthest limits of his predecessors' knowledge, and found them too strait for him.

b. Of a place of confinement. *lit.* and *fig.* *Obs.*

c **1460** SIR R. ROS *La Belle Dame* 563 in *Pol. Rel. & L. Poems* (1903) 101 It is grete dures and discomfort To kepe an hert in so streyt a presoun, þat hathe but on body for his disport. **1483** CAXTON *Golden Leg.* 177/1 Saynt Peter was enprysoned in a strayte place wherin he was strayned. **1594** NASHE *Unfort. Trav.* (ed. 2) L 2 b, To the straightest prison in Rome he was dragged. **1614** RALEGH *Hist. World* II. v. iii. §5. 436 All such Prisoners as he had of the Romans, he held in streight places, loden with yrons.

3. a. Of a way, passage, or channel: So narrow as to make transit difficult. Now *rare* in lit. sense.

13.. *K. Alis.* 6114 Theo wayes weore so strayte, and fyle, That mon no hors, by twenty myle, No myghte come the toun nigh. **1375** BARBOUR *Bruce* VI. 362 His vit hym schawit the strat entre Of the furde, and the ysche alsua. **138.** WYCLIF *Serm.* Sel. Wks. I. 14 Þe nett is brood in þe bigynnyng, and after streit in ende. *c* **1425** tr. *Arderne's Treat. Fistula* etc. 33 Þe mouþe of þe vlcere was ouer streit. **1481** CAXTON *Godfrey* xviii. 47 Certayne..strayt entrees that ben as yates of the londe. **1560** DAUS tr. *Sleidane's Comm.* 265 To open the strayte passages in the Alpes. **1611** SHAKS. *Cymb.* v. iii. 11 The strait passe was damm'd With dead men. **1619** DRAYTON *Bar. Wars* v. xli, Where, through strait Windowes, the dull Light came farre. **1697** DRYDEN *Virg. Georg.* II. 330 When thro' streight Passages they strein their Wine. **1768** G. WHITE *Selborne, To Pennant* 12 Mar., The owners slit up the nostrils of such asses as were hard worked; for they, being naturally strait or small, did not admit air sufficient. **1819** SCOTT *Ivanhoe* xlii, If the stairs be too strait to admit his fat carcass, I will have him craned up from without. **1855** MACAULAY *Hist. Eng.* xiii. III. 354 That road was so steep and so strait that a handful of resolute men might have defended it against an army.

b. *fig.* and in figurative context. Now *arch.* after Bible use, esp. as ***strait and narrow*** (*ellipt.*), a conventional, limited procedure or way of life; cf. *straight and narrow* s.v. STRAIGHT 3 a.

a **1340** HAMPOLE *Psalter* xvi. 6 Gif grace þat þe charite of my lufers be perfit in þe strayt stretis of þi counsails. **1382** WYCLIF *Matt.* vii. 13 Entre ȝe bi the streyt ȝate. **1555** J. BRADFORD in Coverdale *Lett. Martyrs* (1564) 296 The way of Christe is the strayte waye. **1600** J. BODENHAM *Belvedére* 228 No wise man likes in such a life to dwell, Whose wayes are strait to heauen, but wide to hell. **1681** DRYDEN *Sp. Fryar* Epil., There is no Dives in the Roman Hell. Gold opens the strait gate, and lets him in. **1720** SEWEL *Hist. Quakers* (1795) I. Pref. 14 Such who finding the strait way too narrow for them, left it. **1836** J. GILBERT *Chr. Atonem.* ii. (1852) 39 The way to life is strait. **1952** S. KAUFFMANN *Philanderer* (1953) xv. 247 Not that I wandered from the respectable bourgeois strait-and-narrow. **1979** *Listener* 1 Mar. 322/2 She seems to feel it is rather daring of her to be the great defender of Arnold Bennett's reputation—and I felt she might have risked one or two dashes off the strait and narrow.

†**4. a.** Having little breadth or width; narrow. *Obs.*

c **1391** CHAUCER *Astrol.* 14 A label..schapen lik a rewle, save that it is streit & hath no plates on either ende. *c* **1400** MAUNDEV. (1839) v. 45 Egypt is a long Contree; but it is streyt, that is to seye narow. **1486** *Bk. St. Albans, Her.* c ii b, Ther is an oder cros aquall straythyr in the myddis then in thenddys. **1527** R. THORNE in Hakluyt *Voy.* (1589) 253 A certain straight Sea called *Estrecho de todos Sanctos*.

†**b.** Of cloth, ribbon, etc.: Narrow. *Obs.*

1439 *Rolls of Parlt.* V. 30/1 Unreasonable mesure, both of brode clothe and streite. **1480** *Wardr. Acc. Edw. IV* (1830) 136 Riban off silk: streyte xj unces di'; brode ix yerdes. **1503** *Privy Purse Exp. Eliz. of York* (1830) 104 Item payed to Cristofore Ascue for v yerdes of Streyt white by him delivered.

5. Special collocations: **strait gulf**, †**horehound** (see quots.); **strait jacket** *sb.* and *v.* = STRAIT WAISTCOAT *sb.* and *v.*; **strait-jacketed** *ppl. a.*, confined in a strait jacket (chiefly *fig.*); **strait-jacketing** *vbl. sb.* and *ppl. a.*; **strait work** (see quot.). Also STRAIT WAISTCOAT.

1867 SMYTH *Sailor's Word-bk.*, **Strait Gulf*, an arm of the sea running into the land through a narrow entrance channel, as the Gulf of Venice. **1548** TURNER *Names Herbes* 77 Stachys..maye be named in englishe litle Horehounde or *strayte Horehound. **1814** SCOTT *Let.* in *Lockhart* (1837) III. iii. 119 A madman, whom..he has..by the wholesome discipline of a bull's pizzle and *strait-jacket, brought to.. his senses. **1901** *N. Amer. Rev.* Feb. 198 They intended.. to put the national government and the national life into a strait-jacket. **1863** READE *Hard Cash* II. xix. 313 The keepers, the very moment the justices left the house, would ..*strait-jacket them, and starve them. **1891** *Harper's Mag.* July 220/1 Distrusting all efforts of school-masters to strait-jacket our speech into formulas borrowed from the Latin. **1894** G. B. SHAW *Let.* 2 Dec. (1965) I. 462 The dramatist is so *strait-jacketed in theories of conduct that he cannot even state his conventional solution clearly. **1937** *Times Lit. Suppl.* 16 Oct. 743/3 It is a great story, a little strait-jacketed by the official style of the *communiqués*. **1955** Straitjacketed [see *lock-step* s.v. LOCK *sb.*² 20]. **1950** *Times* 20 Mar. 3/3 Tendencies towards reducing Socialist democracy to a minimum, including the *strait-jacketing of opinion and the suppression of the initiative of the people. **1965** K. H. CONNELL in Glass & Eversley *Population in Hist.* xvii. 433 The Malthusian theory, freed of its mathematical strait-jacketing, had a precise relevance to Irish conditions. **1977** *N.Y. Rev. Bks.* 26 May 17/1 Paradoxically, he finds liberation in a succession of instrumental works, the Trio, Symphony, Concerto, and two Quartets, all written according to certain principles of Schoenberg's new, reputedly strait-jacketing twelve-tone system. **1979** *Time Out* 5–11 Oct. 20/3 The possible straitjacketing effect of producing another revue. **1883** Gresley *Gloss. Coal-mining* 244 **Straight work* or *Strait work*, the system of getting coal by headings or narrow work. **1904** *Daily Chron.* 19 Mar. 9/5 Coal was got from mines either by the wide-work system or by straight-work.

II. Strict, rigorous.

†**6. a.** Of conditions, sufferings, punishment, etc.: Pressing hardly, severe, rigorous. *Obs.*

c **1205** Lay. 22270 He wolde westen his lond and..mid fure mid stele streit gomen wurchen. **1340** Hampole *Pr. Consc.* 4736 [The day of dome] es þe mast day þat ever was yhitte, And þe straytest and þe mast harde. *c* **1400** tr. *Secreta Secret., Gov. Lordsh.* 90 But here ys no stede to shewe of so hard and streyt science. *c* **1421** Lydg. *Horse, Goose & Sheep* 392 in *Pol. Rel. & L. Poems* (1903) 31 At a streight neede thei can weel staunche blood. **1512** *Act 4 Hen. VIII*, c. 20 Preamble, The said John Tailer..and many other felons, [etc.]..dwellyd in a strayte and parlous Countrey for your sayd Besecher or any other your true subgettes without great jopertie of theire lyves to take and arrest theym. **1538** Starkey *England* i. iv. 120 Yf we coud deuyse a punnyschment more strayttur then deth, hyt were necessary to be ordenyd. *a* **1540** Barnes *Wks.* (1573) 202 If there were a generall Councell,..there must needes folow, both ouer him & you a streight reformation. **1550** Crowley *Last Trumpet* 1451 For God wyll punyshe in straite wyse Such as wyth him wyl be so bolde. **1550** in Strype *Eccl. Mem.* (1721) II. 239 We delight more in Clemency than the streit administration of Justice. **1596** Spenser *F.Q.* v. v. 33 Bound vnto me, but not with such hard bands Of strong compulsion, and streight violence, As now in miserable state he stands. **1642** D. Rogers *Naaman* 30 When he [God] hath them upon the hip by any deepe and straight sore and extremity.

†**b.** Of modes of living, diet, etc.: Involving hardship or privation; severely regulated. *Obs.*

c **1300** *St. Brandan* (Percy Soc.) 35 There he was abbot of an hous.., and there he ladde a full strayte and holy lyfe. *c* **1380** Wyclif *Sel. Wks.* III. 473 What ever þou haldes to þe of þo auter, over a streyte lyvelode ande symple cloþing, hit is not þine. *c* **1450** tr. *De Imitatione* iii. xi. 79 Þei shull gete liberte of mynde [þat] entriþ into streiȝt lif. **1579** Lyly *Euphues* Wks. 1902 I. 252 If this seeme too straight a dyet for thy straininge disease, or to holy a profession, for so hollow a person. **1582** Hester *Secr. Fioravanti* i. xxiii. 26 Neither let them keepe any straight Diette. **1594** Nashe *Unfort. Trav.* (ed. 2) M 4, To such straight life did it thence forward incite me, that..I married my curtizan,..and hasted..out of the Sodom of Italy. **1613** Purchas *Pilgrimage* (1614) 379 [He] led a streight life in continencie and austerity. *Ibid.* 426 They..in their Monasteries, are very abstinent in eating and drinking, containe their bodies in strait chastitie, [etc.].

†**c.** Of a religious order, its rules, etc., also of a sect: Rigorous, strict. *Obs.*

c **1386** Chaucer *Prol.* 174 The reule of seint Maure or of seint Beneit, By cause that it was old and som del streit. *c* **1440** *Jacob's Well* xxvi. 178 Þe chanoun, after, schroof hym to þe bysschop of þat synne, & entryd in-to a streytere relygyoun. *c* **1490** Caxton *Rule St. Benet* 119 Þat they maye ..execute the hole rewll and the better kepe it than it is accordyng to the abyte & their streyte professyon. **1577** tr. *Luther's Comm. Galat.* v. 19 (1580) 270 b, The Carthusians or Charterhouse monkes, whose order..is of all other the straitest & sharpest. **1579** W. Wilkinson *Confut. Fam. Love* 50 There is a confession in the Family of H. N. more streight than euer was in the tyme of Popery.

7. †**a.** Of a person, an agent: Severe, stern, strict, exacting in actions or dealings. *Obs.*

1297 R. Glouc. (Rolls) 5406 So streit he was þat þei me leyde amidde weyes heye, Seluer þat nomon ne dorste hit nyme vor beye hor eye. *c* **1400** *Apol. Loll.* 45 If þei haue streit conscience to faile in þis þat hemself haþ bound him to, þei schuld haue mikil more to faile in þis þat Crist haþ bound hem to. *c* **1440** *Alphabet of Tales* 11 Hur susters þe nonnys purseyvid, & was passand fayn þerof, becauce sho wa[s] so strayte vnto þaim, at þai myght have a cauce to accuse hur in. **1526** Tindale *Luke* xix. 21, I feared the, because thou arte a strayte man: thou takest vp that thou laydest nott doune. **1549** Coverdale etc. *Erasm. Par. Jude* 22 b, That whiche Pharao that straight and intolerable lorde was vnto them, the deuil was the same vnto vs. **1600** Holland *Livy* ix. xvi. 324 He was a man besides for seueritie streight, and of right great command..ouer his allies and confederates. **1607** Shaks. *Timon* i. i. 96 Fiue Talents is his debt, His meanes most short, his Creditors most straite. **1612** T. Taylor *Comm. Titus* i. 7 Such infirmities the Lord will not be so straite in.

b. Rigorous in principles; strict or scrupulous in morality or religious observance. *arch.*

1526 Tindale *Acts* xxvi. 5 For after the most straytest [Gr. ἀκριβεστάτην] secte of oure laye lived I a pharisaye. **1577** Northbrooke *Dicing* (1843) 51 *Age.* Although they do, yet, for my parte, I will not bee so straite or scrupulous. **1603** Shaks. *Meas. for M.* ii. i. 9 Let but your honour know (Whom I beleeue to be most strait in vertue) That [etc.]. **1777** Priestley *Matt. & Spir.* Ded., Educated, as you know I was, in the very straitest principles of reputed orthodoxy. **1875** Lowell *Spenser* Writ. 1890 IV. 314 There is a verse, ..'Like that ungracious crew which feigns demurest grace,' which is supposed to glance at the straiter religionists. **1890** *Spectator* 12 July, He never lost the confidence even of the most strait of his fellow-Churchmen, while the more advanced felt that they had his fullest sympathy.

8. a. Of a commandment, law, penalty, vow: Stringent, strict, allowing no evasion. *Obs.* exc. *arch.*

c **1375** *Sc. Leg. Saints* xix. (*Cristofore*) 621 He.. commawndment gef strat þar-to. **1390** Gower *Conf.* II. 211 For that a man scholde al unthryve Ther oghte no wisman coveite, The lawe was noght set so streite. *a* **1400** *Minor Poems fr. Vernon MS.* liv. 193 A strayt couenaunt I-mad þer was Bi-twene me and Sathanos. **1485–6** *Coventry Leet Bk.* 527 The oth & charge of the Recorder, which in diuers thynges me thinketh full streyte. **1535** Coverdale *Ps.* cxviii. 4 Thou hast geuen strayte charge to kepe thy commaundementes. **1560** Daus tr. *Sleidane's Comm.* 278 b, The Duke of Wirtemburg hath accorded vpon moste straite conditions. **1596** Shaks. *1 Hen. IV*, iv. iii. 79 And now (forsooth) takes on him to reforme..some strait Decrees, That lay too heauie on the Common-wealth. **1612** T. Taylor *Comm. Titus* i. 6 His..strait charge to all posteritie, that one man should cleaue to one wife. **1630** R. N. tr. *Camden's Eliz.* i. 16 The Queene set forth a straight Proclamation, that they should not handle any such questions. **1870** Tennyson *Coming of Arthur* 261 Then the King..Bound them by so strait vows to his own self, That [etc.].

†**b.** Of a legal instrument: Stringently worded, peremptory. *Obs.*

1503 in *Acc. Fam. of Innes* (1864) 91 Sesing and letters of assedatioun in the stratest forme can be devisit be the said Robert. **1565–6** *Reg. Privy Council Scot.* I. 417 Quhairunto we obleis us as said is in the stratest forme and sickir style of obligatioun that can be divisit. **1632** Lithgow *Trav.* x. 481 Hee..obtained a strait warrant to command the Gouernour ..to deliuer mee ouer in the English hands.

9. †**a.** Of actions, proceedings: Conducted with strictness. *Obs.*

c **1430** Lydg. *Min. Poems* (Percy Soc.) 240 But Jhesu be my staff and my potent, Ovir streyt audit is lik t'encoumbre me. *c* **1440** *Alphabet of Tales* 355 Hafe compassion on hym, at ye make hym no lettyng when he commys afor þe strayte iugement of almyghtie God. *c* **1450** Capgrave *Life St. Gilbert* xxxii. 108 There þei dede rede þe myracles and discussed hem with grete diligens and streyt examination. **1530** Palsgr. 277/1 Strayte dealyng, *rigeur*. **1541** Elyot *Image Gov.* 17 He was exhorted to advaunce his astate..in princely porte,..leauyng his affabilitee and straight obseruacion of his lawes. **1586** *Privy Council Let.* in *Maldon* (Essex) *Borough Deeds*, Bundle 149 No. 12 Your owne example in the straite kepinge of these orders..will greatlie further the observinge of the same amonge the meaner sort. **1599** *Warn. Faire Wom.* ii. 895 Strait inquisition and search is made.

b. Of guard, watch, imprisonment: Rigorous, strict. Cf. 2 b. Now *rare.*

1423 Jas. I *Kingis Q.* 25 In strayte ward and in strong prisoun. **1432–50** tr. *Higden* (Rolls) IV. 341 Seynte Iohn Baptiste was heded after that he hade bene in streyte kepynge or in prison in this yere. **1554** Ridley in Coverdale *Godly Lett. Martyrs* (1564) 61 We are..separated..and much straite watching of the baylifes is about vs that there be no priuy conference amongest vs. **1639** Fuller *Holy War* v. vi. 238 He had a strait watch set upon them. **1641** Milton *Ch. Govt.* i. i. 6 Yea though she be well instructed, yet is she still under a more strait tuition. **1716** Lady M. W. Montagu *Let. To C'tess Mar* 21 Nov., She endures all the terrors of a strait imprisonment. **1837** Carlyle *Fr. Rev.* III. iv. iii, Back to thy Arrestment, poor Brissot; or indeed to strait confinement.

†**c.** Of a siege: Close. *Obs.*

1603 Drayton *Heroic Ep.* vi. (Bl. Prince to C'tess Salisb.) 80 Thy brest..That may be batter'd, or be vndermin'd, Or by straite siege for want of succour pin'd. **1647** May *Hist. Parlt.* iii. vi. 101 Gloucester was thus beseiged, and the seige so straight, that no intelligence could possibly arrive at it. **1657** Trapp *Comm. Job* v. 20 [God delivered] the Rochellers by a miraculous shoale of shel-fish, cast up into their town in a strait seige.

III. Limited in scope, degree, or amount.

†**10.** Scanty, poor in degree. *Obs.*

a **1300** *Cursor M.* 24745 Þof mans wijt be neuer sa strait, Sco mai well bring it vnto nait.

11. †**a.** Of fortune, means, circumstances: Limited so as to cause hardship or inconvenience; inadequate. *Obs.* Cf. straitened *ppl. a.*

c **1386** Chaucer *Friar's T.* 128 My wages been ful streite and ful smale. *c* **1400** *Sowdone Bab.* 2533 Therefore sende we to Charles,..And certyfye him of oure strayȝte beinge. *a* **1617** Bayne *On Eph.* (1658) 25 A great Heir is often held to strait allowance. **1647** Clarendon *Hist. Reb.* i. §131 If he had not..been too much grieved and wrung by an uneasy and strait fortune, he would have been an excellent man of business. **1706–7** J. Logan in *Pennsylv. Hist. Soc. Mem.* X. 197 Money is hard to be got out of the Treasury these strait times. **1722** Wollaston *Relig. Nat.* ix. 181, I am not of opinion..that virtue and prudence can always..mend a strait fortune. **1741** 'T. Betterton' *Mem. Mrs. Anne Oldfield* 1 Mrs. Oldfield being left in strait Circumstances, She and Daughter lived for some time with her Sister. **1780** A. Nash in Sparks *Corr. Amer. Rev.* (1853) III. 108 They were very soon reduced to strait allowance.

b. Of a person: In want *of*, straitened *for*. *Obs.* exc. *dial.*

1662 J. Strype in *Lett. Lit. Men* (Camden) 178 If you are not too straight of money, send me some. **1866** W. Gregor *Banff Gloss., Stret*... (3) In want of; as 'He's gey stret o' siller.' **1881** *Leicestersh. Gloss.* s.v. *Stret*, 'As we're so stret for speakers to-dee,' was the commencement of an oration at an agricultural dinner.

12. Of words: Limited in application or signification. *Obs.* exc. *dial.*

c **1380** Wyclif *Sel. Wks.* III. 415 And, for hit were to streyte to lordship of Crist to be a special lord of Jude or Jerusalem, þerfore he bad þat þei schulde calle him Lorde. **1480** *Coventry Leet Bk.* 456 The seid Maire & his Brethern seyn that the wordes in the seid Tripartite be not so speciall & streyt as the seid prior taketh hem. **1558** Traheron *Expos. John* G iij, The worlde in this place signifieth al men. For it can not be taken in a straighter sense. **1654** Z. Coke *Logick* 78 When a word is larger or straighter then the thing meant thereby, let another word, if it may be had, be put in the room. **1901** J. Prior *Forest Folk* iii. 36, 'I never—that is hardly ever—quarrel about anything.' 'That "hardly ever's" a bit stret for what's in't.'

†**13.** Strictly specified, exact, precise, definite; esp. of an account, exactly rendered. *Obs.*

1340 Hampole *Pr. Consc.* v. 5644 For men sal þan strayte acount yhelde Of alle þair tyme. **1580** Lyly *Euphues* Wks. 1902 I. 308 Wee shall all bee cyted before the Tribunall seate of God to render a straight accompt of our stewardshyp. **1619** Hieron *Penance for Sin* xiv. Wks. 1620 II. 217 Touching the word Create: in strait speaking, it betokeneth the making of a thing of nought. **1638** T. Whitaker *Tree Hum. Life* 4 To prescribe a pondus or streight weight and measure of nutriment to all tempers.

14. Of friendship, alliance, etc.: Close, intimate. Now *rare.*

c **1530** Berners *Arth. Lyt. Bryt.* (1814) 1 He was sworne of the kynges preuye and streayte counsayle. **1561** Hoby tr. *Castiglione's Courtier* ii. (1900) 137 Suche as are coopled in streicte amitie and unseparable companye. **1568** J. Fen tr. *Osorius' Confut. Haddon* i. 1 Both for the streight friendshippe, as also for the long acqueintaunce betwene vs. **1587** Golding *De Mornay* ii. 18 There ye see yet a streighter vnitie. *a* **1617** Bayne *On Eph.* (1658) 162 There is a most neer and strait union among the faithful. **1626** Bacon *New Atl.* 25 By that time..I was fallen into straight Acquaintance, with a Merchant of that Citty, whose Name was Ioabin. **1647** Clarendon *Hist. Reb.* iv. §259 As a compliment to this kingdom, with which it [Spain] was then in strait alliance and confederacy. **1650** Earl Monm. tr. *Senault's Man become Guilty* 19 The difficulty is to know how the Soul..contracts Sin... To this I answer, that her streight union with the body is one cause of her sin. **1873** H. Rogers *Orig. Bible* i. (1875) 24 Or any similar strait alliance ..of religion and morality.

†**15. a.** Reluctant and chary in giving; close, stingy, illiberal. *Obs.*

c **1290** *Beket* 335 in *S. Eng. Leg.* 116 Of is ordres he was ful streit..and he was in grete fere For-to ordeinen ani Man: bote he þe betere were. **1390** Gower *Conf.* II. 390 Avarice, ..Thurgh streit holdinge and thurgh skarsnesse Stant in contraire to Largesse. *c* **1412** Hoccleve *De Reg. Princ.* 1784 Of þin annuitee, þe paiement,..Þou dredest, whan þou art from court absent, Schal be restreyned, syn þou now present Vnneþes mayst it gete, it is so streit. *Ibid.* 4522 But if so be, ..Thow [a miser] correcte thy greedy appetyt, And of streit kepynge empte þy delyt. *c* **1440** Lydg. *Secrees* 763 Twen moche and lyte A mene to devise Of to mekyl And streight Coveitise. *a* **1475** Ashby *Active Policy* 253 [To be] Ne to liberal for no frendlynesse. Ne ouer streit for noo necessite. **1483** *Vulgaria abs Terentio* 17 To be more sparynge and streytere [L. *vt frugalior sim*]. **1595** Shaks. *John* v. vii. 42, I begge cold comfort, and you are so straight And so ingratefull, you deny me that. *a* **1628** Preston *Breastpl. Love* (1631) 62 Not to use them [our opportunities] because wee have straight hands and narrow hearts, is a signe we want love to Christ.

b. Of a person's 'heart': Contracted in sympathies, narrow. (Cf. *strait-hearted, -ness*, in 17.)

1760 Sterne *Serm. Luke* x. 36–7 How often do you behold a sordid wretch, whose strait heart is open to no man's affliction, taking shelter behind an appearance of piety.

IV. Combinations.

16. In parasynthetic adjs., as ***strait-bodied, -breasted, -breeched, -chested, -clothed, -coated, -necked, -sleeved, -toothed, -waisted***.

1601 B. Jonson *Poetaster* iv. i, This *straight-bodied Citty attire..will stirre a Courtiers blood. *a* **1668** Lassels *Italy* (1698) I. 61 Genoa look'd..like a proud young lady in a strait-bodied flower'd gown. **1585** Higins *Junius' Nomencl.* 453/2 That is narrow or *streite breasted. **1666** *Char. Mary-Land* (1869) 68 The *straight-breecht Commonalty of the Spaniard. **1620** Venner *Via Recta* vi. 95 They are..hurtfull to the phlegmaticke..and them that are *straight chested. *c* **1450** *Brut* 297 Þe wemmen..were so *strete cloþed þat þey lete hange fox tailes..with-inforþ hire cloþis, forto hele and heyde hire ars. **1858** Mrs. Gore *Hecklington* I. xiv. 301 The *strait-coated young Reverence who replaced at the parsonage his defunct wide-skirted father-in-law. **1808** Jamieson Addit. s.v. *Buck*, To make a guggling noise, as liquids when poured from a *strait-necked bottle. **1561** Daus tr. *Bullinger on Apoc.* (1573) 16 b, This cleaueth iust to the body, and is so narrow and *strayte sleeued, that there is no wrincle at all in the garment. **1700** *Transactioneer* 18 One wide-toothed Comb, One *strait-toothed Comb. **1725** *Bradley's Family Dict.* s.v. *Drying Hemp*, There must be..an open or wide-tooth'd, or nick'd Brake, and a close and strait-tooth'd Brake [for hemp or flax]. *c* **1450** *Brut* 297 Long large and wyde cloþis..; & anoþer tyme schorte cloþis & *stret-wasted.

17. Special comb.: †**strait-handed** *a.*, close-fisted, grasping, stingy; hence †**strait-handedness**; †**strait-hearted** *a.*, ungenerous, exacting, mean; hence †**strait-heartedness**; †**strait-mouthed** *a.*, reticent, uncommunicative; †**strait-winded** *a.*, short of breath.

1600 G. Abbot *Jonah* 38 They who are otherwise *straight-handed enough in promoting that which is good, will spare no cost at all to further that which is evil. **1679** J. Goodman *Penitent Pardoned* iii. vi. (1713) 378 God is neither narrow hearted, nor strait-handed. **1649** Bp. Hall *Cases Consc.* iv. iii. 410 The Romish doctrine makes their *strait-handednesse so much more injurious, as the cause of separation is more just. **1759** Sterne *Tr. Shandy* II. xvii, A *strait-hearted, selfish wretch. **1646** P. Bulkeley *Gospel Covt.* iii. 269 There is a *straightheartedness..towards the Lord, in not ministering to the things which concern his worship; the least portion is enough. **1664** R. Atkyns *Orig. & Growth Printing* 13 Some of them..are so *streight-mouth'd, that they do not declare the whole Truth of what they know on our Part. **1601** Holland *Pliny* xxii. xxii. II. 131 The white [Sowthistle]..is thought to bee as good as Lectuces, for those that be *streight winded, and cannot take their breath but vpright.

B. *sb.*

1. a. A narrow confined place or space or way generally. Now *rare* or *Obs.*

1352 Minot *Poems* vi. 56 A bare now has him soght Till Turnay þe right gate, Þat es ful wele bithoght To stop Philip þe strate. *c* **1450** *Merlin* x. 160 Thei rode forth..to the straite be-twene the wode and the river. **1544** BETHAM *Precepts War* II. xlvii. L ij, What is to be done when we do fyght in straites. Yf bothe the hostes mete and ioyne in strayte places, and neyther wyll recule,..then myne aduise is, [etc.]. **1590** SPENSER *F.Q.* II. vii. 40 He brought him through a darksome narrow strait To a a broad gate. **1606** SHAKS. *Tr. & Cr.* III. iii. 154 Honour trauels in a straight so narrow Where one but goes abreast. **1672** J. LACY tr. *Tacquett's Milit. Archit.* 28 It cannot entertain a good quantity of Souldiers to defend it by reason of its straits. **1719** DE FOE *Crusoe* II. (Globe) 582 It was in a narrow Strait, between two..Woods, that we pitch'd our little Camp for that Night. **1850** MRS. BROWNING *Poems, Finite & Inf.* I The wind sounds only in opposing straits.

in fig. context. **1611** BIBLE *Lam.* i. 3 All her persecutors ouertook her betweene [1885 (*Revised*) within] the straits.

†**b.** *pl.* with sing. sense. *Obs.*

1545 RAYNALDE *Byrth Mankynde* 135 Cheiflye fomente them on the strayghts betwene the fundament and the coddes. **1609** BIBLE (Douay) *Num.* xxii. 24 The Angel stoode in the streictes of two walles [Vulg. *in angustiis duarum maceriarum*]. **1741** MIDDLETON *Cicero* II. x. 467 We got through the straits of the morass and the woods.

2. *fig.* **a.** A narrow or tight place, a time of sore need or of awkward or straitened circumstances, a difficulty or fix. Now *rare* in *sing.*; still common in *plural.*

sing. **1544** BETHAM *Precepts War* I. cxxxvii. G vij, Whych thing is not to be done, but in a great strayte, & vrgent necessitie. **1642** EARL OF CORK in *Lismore Papers* Ser. II. (1888) V. 117 By..deceiuing the trust imposed vpon you, you put two gentlemen to a greate streighte. **1692** R. L'ESTRANGE *Fables* ccccxxx. 407 The Lion finding what a Streight he was in, gave one Hearty Twitch, and got his Feet out of the Trap. **1748** RICHARDSON *Clarissa* (1811) III. 241 The streight, which the discovery of my brother's foolish project had brought me into. **1821** SCOTT *Kenilw.* xxx, I would advise you to tell your strait to the Earl's chamberlain —you will have instant redress. **1847** TENNYSON *Princess* I. 84 Take me: I'll serve you better in a strait. **1879** CHRISTINA ROSSETTI *Seek & Find* 34 The sun..at the voice of one man ..stood still; in the strait of another it retrograded.

pl. **1565** JEWEL *Repl. Harding* XII. xv. 474 But here marke thou, gentle Reader, into what straites these men be driuen. **1600** SHAKS. *A.Y.L.* v. ii. 71, I know into what straights of Fortune she is driuen. *a* **1628** F. GREVIL *Sidney* (1652) 18 That any man being forced, in the straines of this life, to pass through any straights, or latitudes of good, or ill fortune, might [etc.]. **1671** MILTON *P.R.* II. 415 Thy self Bred up in poverty and streights at home. *a* **1687** PETTY *Pol. Arith.* (1690) 48 Upon these occasions,..Merchants are put to great straights and inconveniences. **1756** MRS. CALDERWOOD in *Coltness Collect.* (Maitl. Club) 200 He keept them in great straits for money. **1849** HT. MARTINEAU *Hist. Peace* v. ix. (1877) III. 379 Never were the Whig rulers reduced to more desperate straits. **1894** *Solicitors' Jrnl.* XXXIX. 3/1 The defendant..is known to be in straits financially.

b. A dilemma; a difficulty of choice. ? *Obs.* Cf. STRAIT *v.*

In quot. 1611 only a contextual use of sense 2.

1611 BIBLE *Phil.* i. 23 For I am in a strait betwixt two [Gr. συνέχομαι δὲ ἐκ τῶν δύο]. *a* **1643** CARTWRIGHT *Siege* II. vi, The Straight is this, Either you must ruine th' Effect, or lose Your beauty by consenting.

†**c.** *straits of time*: pressure or insufficiency of time. *Obs.*

1612 BRINSLEY *Lud. Lit.* vii. 84 In hearing parts in straights of time, thus we may examine only in those places where we most suspect the negligence. *a* **1703** BURKITT *On N.T.* Matt. xxvii. 61 It was done in haste, by reason of the straits of time.

d. In generalized sense: Privation, hardship.

1837 CARLYLE *Fr. Rev.* II. II. ii, They..did often deliver the Aristocrat brother officer out of peril and strait. **1872** *Daily News* 27 Sept., There will be almost an unprecedented amount of suffering and strait in our large towns.

3. a. A comparatively narrow water-way or passage connecting two large bodies of water.

When used as a geographical proper name, the word is usually *pl.* with sing. sense, e.g. ***the Straits of Dover, of Gilbraltar*** (formerly †***of Morocco***), ***of Magellan, of Malacca***, and ***the Straits*** as short for any of these; with regard to ***Bass('s) Strait(s, Torres Strait(s***, usage is divided, while ***Davis Strait*** rarely appears in the plural form. The use of the pl. for the sing. began in the 15th c. A few writers, chiefly of gazetteers, use the sing. consistently throughout.

the Straits: in 17–18th c. usually = the Straits of Gibraltar; later, where there is no contextual indication, chiefly = the Straits of Malacca.

sing. **1375** BARBOUR *Bruce* III. 688 As is the raiss of Bretangȝe, Or strait off Marrok in-to Spanȝe. *c* **1386** CHAUCER *Man of Law's T.* 366 The Strayte Of Marrok. **1527** R. THORNE in Hakluyt *Voy.* (1589) 251 They may return through the streight of Magellan. **1585** T. WASHINGTON tr. *Nicholay's Voy.* II. x. 43 b, We entred the streit of Hellespont. **1610** HOLLAND *Camden's Brit.* (1637) 671 The small narrow streight of Menai. **1703** *La Hontan's Voy. N. Amer.* I. 83 We entered the Streight of the Lake of Huron, where we met with a slack Current of half a League in breadth, that continued till we arriv'd in the Lake of St. Claire. **1774** J. BRYANT *Mythol.* I. 262 The narrow streight into the Euxine sea was a passage of difficult navigation. **1807** G. CHALMERS *Caledonia* I. II. vii. 319 *note*, Passengers used to speak across the streight from Mull to Hy. **1833** MRS. BROWNING *Prometh. Bound* Poet. Wks. (1904) 153 That strait, called Bosphorus. **1887** W. D. GAINSFORD *Winter's Cruise Mediterr.* 294 At 1 p.m. we rounded Tarifa, and at 4.30 were off Trafalgar, and through the Strait. **1896** KIPLING *Seven Seas, M'Andrews' Hymn*, Fra' Deli clear to Torres Strait.

pl. **1439** *Rolls of Parlt.* V. 31/2 Contres beyonde the Streytes of Marrok. **1547** BOORDE *Introd. Knowl.* xxxvi. (1870) 213 They [Moors] wyl come ouer the straytes. **1582** STANYHURST *Æneis* III. (Arb.) 83 The sea..Italye disioyncting with short streicts from Sicil Island. **1614** RALEGH *Hist. World* II. xxviii. §2. 632 They returned home by the pillars and streights of Hercules (as the name was then) called now the straights of Gybraltar. **1669** STURMY *Mariner's Mag., Penalties & Forf.* I Commodities of the Levant Seas may be brought from any Port within the Straights. **1775** *Cont. Sterne's Sent. Journ.* III. 177 You may drop the bloody dagger in the streights of Dover and Calais, to cleanse its sanguinary blade. **1812** BYRON *Ch. Har.* II. xxii, Through Calpe's straits survey the steepy shore. **1884** CAVENAGH *Remin. Ind. Official* vii. 259 A succession of men-of-war and transports belonging to both nations passed through the Straits. The hospitality of Government House [Singapore] was tendered to all. **1887** C. D. BELL *Glean. Tour Palestine* etc. 313 Passing through the straits of Abydos, the vessel made her quiet way..into the Sea of Marmora.

b. *transf.* and *fig.*

? *c* **1600** COWLEY *Ess.* ix. *Shortn. Life*, It is, alas, so narrow a Streight betwixt the Womb and the Grave, that it might be called the *Pas de Vie*. **1666** G. HARVEY *Morbus Angl.* iii. (1672) 9 The Infant..makes its sally out of the Womb, that's now grown too little to give it any longer harbour; and having thus passed the Streights, it's tossed into the wide world. **1805** WORDSW. *Waggoner* I. 10 Where the scattered stars are seen In hazy straits the clouds between. **1850** TENNYSON *In Mem.* lxxxiv. 39 Mine own [spirit]..hovering o'er the dolorous strait To the other shore.

c. *pl.* Short for *Straits Settlements*, the name formerly given to the British possessions in the Malay peninsula collectively (near the Straits of Malacca).

1884 CAVENAGH *Remin. Ind. Official* vii. 372, I left the Straits a most flourishing colony. *Ibid.*, I must always look back with pleasure to my connection with the Straits.

d. *pl.* ***up the Straits*** (see quot. 1962); in the Mediterranean. *Naut. slang.*

1916 'TAFFRAIL' *Pincher Martin* i. 2 'Er commander's a werry nice gentleman; 'e was shipmates along o' me in th' *Duncan* up the Straits six year ago. **1962** W. GRANVILLE *Dict. Sailors' Slang* 115/1 *Straits, up the*, serving on the Mediterranean Station in the Straits of Gibraltar.

†**4.** A narrow pass or gorge between mountains; a defile, ravine. *Obs.*

1375 BARBOUR *Bruce* IV. 458 Syne till a strate thai held thair way. *c* **1400** MAUNDEV. (Roxb.) xiv. 64 Fra Tortouse passez men..by land thurgh þe straytes of mountaynes and felles. *c* **1450** *Merlin* xv. 256 The kynge..sente hym worde to mete with hym at the streite of the roche magot. **1525** BERNERS *Froiss.* II. xv. 12, I wolde not counsayle you to passe the mountayns of Northumberlande, for there be mo than .xxx. streightes and passages. **1560** DAUS tr. *Sleidane's Comm.* 391 Having won the straites of thalpes. **1585** T. WASHINGTON tr. *Nicholay's Voy.* IV. xv. 129 Through which narrow streights, Alexander..made his armie to pass. **1627** MAY *Lucan* IV. F 5 b, Below safe passages are found Through windings darke; which straights if once the foe Had in possession. Cæsar well did know [etc.]. **1753** HANWAY *Trav.* (1762) II. III. i. 86 Leonidas..defended the streight of Thermopilæ with four thousand men. **1778** PENNANT *Tour Wales* (1883) I. 111 They suffered the enemy to march along the streights of the country, till their forces were entangled in the depths of the woods.

5. A narrow strip of land with water on each side, an isthmus. Now *rare.* (*poet.*)

1562 J. SHUTE tr. *Cambini's Two Comm.* 20 b, The walle of Esmilia, that was buylded vpon the straite called Isthmos. **1568** HACKET tr. *Thevet's New found World* lxx. 113 Daryen, a straight of lande [Fr. *detroit de terre*], so named of the Riuer of Daryen. *a* **1586** SIDNEY *Arcadia* I. xii. (1912) 74 Afterward he passed..to the Corinthians, prowde of their two Seas, to learne whether by the streight of that Isthmus, it was possible to know of his [Diaphantus'] passage. **1601** HOLLAND *Pliny* IV. vii. I. 75 At the streights of Isthmus [*ab Isthmi angustiis*] beginneth Hellas. **1632** LITHGOW *Trav.* VI. 297 Diuers have attempted to digge through this strait to make both Seas meete for a nearer passage to India. **1777** ROBERTSON *Hist. Amer.* II. (1851) I. 156 He supposed this strait or isthmus to be situated near the gulf of Darien. **1842** TENNYSON *Morte d' Arthur* 10 A chapel..That stood on a dark strait of barren land. On one side lay the Ocean, and on one Lay a great water.

6. A narrow part (of a river); *pl.* 'narrows'. Now *rare* or *Obs.*

? **1427–9** *Rolls of Parlt.* IV. 364/2 Many diverses straites and daungers been in the entryng into the river of Humbre out of the See. **1568** HACKET tr. *Thevet's New found World* xxv. 40 b, The straight of our riuer being about a gunne shotte brode. **1610** HOLLAND *Camden's Brit.* (1637) 199 That little river Lid, here at the bridge, gathered into a streight, and pent in between rocks, runneth down amaine. **1665** MANLEY *Grotius' Low-C. Wars* 481 Coming to the River..whose long and narrow Streights & Fords were very troublesome to passe. **1836** W. IRVING *Astoria* II. 189 The long and terrific strait of the river set all further progress at defiance.

†**7.** A narrow lane, alley, or passage. *Obs.*

1614 B. JONSON *Barth. F.* II. vi, Looke into any Angle o' the towne (the Streights or the Bermuda's) where the quarrelling lesson is read. *a* **1637** —— *Underwoods, Ep. to Sackville* 82 These men..turne Pyrats here at Land, Ha' their Bermudas and their streights i' th' Strand. **1622** J. TAYLOR (Water P.) *Water-Cormorant* D 2 b, And passing through a narrow obscure strait, The thieving knaue the purse he nimbly nims. **1712** [see PASS *sb.*[1] 3 f.]

8. The narrow part (of anything tubular); a narrow passage in the body.

1558 WARDE tr. *Alexis' Secr.* (1568) 105 By that meanes it maye stoppe the strayte of the funnell. **1567** MAPLET *Gr. Forest* 40 Dictamus is an Herbe..very wonderfull in losening & vnbinding the straights of the bodie. **1831** R. KNOX *Cloquet's Anat.* 119 This strait..is circumscribed anteriorly by the symphysis of the pubes, on the sides by the rami. **1881** *Trans. Obstetr. Soc. Lond.* XXII. 41 The vaginal stricture necessitating the performance of the operation through a narrow unyielding strait. **1890** G. M. GOULD *New Med. Dict.* s.v. *Pelvis, Straits of Pelvis*, superior and inferior, the planes of the inlet and outlet.

†**9.** *pl.* Cloth of single width, as opposed to BROADCLOTH. (Cf. A. 4 b.) *Obs.*

1429 *Rolls of Parlt.* IV. 361/1 Fyn Streites of Essex for xxiiii s. a pece, commen Strettes xvi s. **1483** *Act 1 Rich. III*, c. 8 All maner Clothes called Straytes to..conteigne..in brede a yerde wᵗ yn the listes. **1545** *Rates Custom Ho.* d iij, vi Strayghtes for a clothe. **1553** *Act 7 Edw. VI*, c. 9 An Acte for the true makinge of white playne streightes and pynned white streightes in Devon and Cornwall. **15..** *Christ's Kirk* 13 in *Bannatyne MS.* (Hunter. Club) 283 Thair schone wes of the straitis. **1706** PHILLIPS (ed. Kersey), *Straights* or *Streights*, a sort of narrow Kersey, or woollen Cloth.

10. A tile about half the usual breadth used at the gable ends of a tiled roof.

1703 T. N. *City & C. Purchaser* 257 *Strait*, A Term us'd by Bricklayers, it is half, (or more, or less than half) a Tile in breadth, and the whole length. They are commonly us'd at the Gable-ends..to cause the Tiles to break Joint. **1887** *Dict. Archit.* (Archit. Publ. Soc.) s.v. *Straight.*

11. *attrib.* and *Comb.* as in sense 'of or pertaining to the Straits (of Gibraltar, Malacca, etc.)', also 'suitable for ships bound thither'; **Straits-born** *a.*, born in the Straits Settlements; **Straits Chinese**, a Chinese born in one of the former Straits Settlements; also *attrib.* or as *adj.*; **Straitsman**, (*a*) a ship suitable for the Straits; (*b*) *Australian* (see quot. 1846); **straits oil**, a type of fish-oil (see quot. 1902), formerly made from fish caught in the straits between Newfoundland and Labrador; also *ellipt.*

1907 *Q. Rev.* July 180 The Straits-born Chinaman. **1897** *Straits Chinese Mag.* Mar. 1/2 A Straits Chinese Magazine has been started; and although its name indicates that it will mainly be controlled and carried on by Straits Chinese, nevertheless within its columns will be discussed all matters of interest to Straits people generally. **1968** *Radio Times* 28 Nov. 20/2 Straits Chinese: Joyce Galbraith recalls..the Chinese she knew in Singapore. **1969** J. M. GULLICK *Malaysia* i. 28 The modern descendants of the earliest wave of Chinese immigration several centuries ago are the 'Straits Chinese' whose forebears intermarried with local women. **1970** M. PEREIRA *Pigeon's Blood* xiv. 156 The manager..was a Straits Chinese by the name of Yee-Shen, originally a native of Malacca. **1693** LUTTRELL *Brief Rel.* III. 7 The Streights fleet and their convoy. *Ibid.* 10 The Dutch Streights and West India fleets are arrived. **1799** *Hull Advertiser* 13 July 2/1 The good brigantine Lady Bruce.. would make an excellent coaster or streightsman. **1846** J. L. STOKES *Discov. in Australia* II. xiii. 449 Straitsmen is the name by which those who inhabit the eastern and western entrance of Bass Strait are known. **1850** *Rep. U.S. Comm. Patents 1849* 165, I..claim..the combination of the straits oil with the magnesia. **1897** C. T. DAVIS *Manuf. Leather* (ed. 2) 229 The oil is clarified and bleached by boiling and filtering. Thus refined it is called 'straits'. **1902** *Rep. U.S. Comm. Fish & Fisheries* 226 'Straits oil' and 'bank oil' were formerly well-known grades of cod oil, but these are now made entirely from menhaden. **1686** in T. H[ale] *Acc. New Invent.* (1691) 69 Which upon due enquiry will appear to be very little more than a good Streights sheathing, and not above half so much as an East-India sheathing.

C. *adv.*

1. a. Tightly. *Obs.* exc. *dial.*

c **1200** *Trin. Coll. Hom.* 197 *Nos sumus quasi serpentes terre corpore adherentes*... We bed alse þe neddre, hie smuȝð strect bi þe eorðe. *c* **1374** CHAUCER *Troylus* IV. 1689 After that þei longe compleined hadde And ofte I-kiste & streite in Armes folde That þe day gan rise. *c* **1375** *Sc. Leg. Saints* xxxiii. (*George*) 288 þai þat schupe þaim to duel stil, strat stekine set þe ȝettis til. *c* **1386** CHAUCER *Prol.* 457 Hir hosen weren of fyn scarlet reed Ful streite yteyd. *c* **1400** *Destr. Troy* 2815 By the Regions of Rene rode þai ferre, Streit by the stremys of the stithe londys. *c* **1420** ? LYDG. *Assembly of Gods* 539 Sodeynly..constreynyd..Was the ground to close hys superfyciall face So strayte that to scape Eolus had no space. *c* **1450** *Mirk's Festial* 9 þay bonden hym to þe crosse ..so hard and strayte, þat þe blod wrast apon yche a knot. **1523–34** FITZHERB. *Husb.* §56 To be lose-skinned, that it stycke not harde nor streyte to his rybbes. **1534** MORE *Dial. Comf. agst. Trib.* III. xxvii. (1553) V vij b, The scorneful crowne of sharpe thornes beaten doune vpon hys holye head so strayte and so depe, that on euerye parte hys blessed bloude issued out. **1561** HOBY tr. *Castiglione's Courtier* II. (1900) 197 The two..layed hande upon Cesar with me and helde him streict. **1596** DALRYMPLE tr. *Leslie's Hist. Scot.* II. 7 So strate vses the knot of vertue to be knutt betueine gud men. **1601** B. JONSON *Poetaster* III. iv, Sirrah, boy, brace your drumme a little straighter. **1684** R. WALLER *Nat. Exper.* 38 Close then the folds of the Bladder, and bind it very strait round the Neck. **1884–6** *Chester Gloss.*, *Stret*, tightly. 'Tee it stret,' tie it tightly.

†**b.** With close bonds of fealty, friendship, servitude, etc. *Obs.*

1375 *Sc. Leg. Saints* xxxvii. (*Vincencius*) 401 For þo he brynt wes in þe fyre,..stratar to god wes he bundine. *c* **1400** *Beryn* 3643 Geffrey with his wisdom held hem hard & streyte. **1590** SPENSER *F.Q.* I. xii. 18 For by the faith, which I to armes haue plight, I bounden am streight after this emprize. **1592** NASHE *P. Penilesse* 37 God, who raineth him [*sc.* the devil] so straight, that except he let him loose he can doo nothing. **1672** A. MARVELL *Reh. Transp.* I. 28 Some that meddle in it do it chiefly in order to fetter men straiter under the formal bondage of fictitious Discipline.

†**2.** Close; with narrow opening. *Obs.*

c **1440** *Pallad. on Husb.* I. 134 And kitte hem streit [L. *strictius*] aftir thi good vyndage, And, grapis fewe yhad, let kitte hem large [L. *latius*]. **1641** MILTON *Ch. Govt.* I. vii. 30 And still the ofter we loose [the offers], the straiter the doore opens, and the lesse is offer'd.

†**3.** In a crowded condition; with insufficient room. *Obs.*

c **1450** LOVELICH *Grail* xlviii. 21 For so streite here, sire, we Sitte,..In distresse And In Mal Ese. **1551** ROBINSON tr. *More's Utopia* II. v. (1895) 159 To thintent the sycke..shuld not lye to thronge or strayte.

†**4.** In strait or careful keeping, securely; in close confinement or strict custody. *Obs.*

c **1330** R. BRUNNE *Chron. Wace* (Rolls) 16311 Haue þys y þen herte ful streit, How þey haue don vs many deseit. *c* **1385** CHAUCER *L.G.W.* 723 For in that cuntre Maydenys been I-kept for gelosye Ful streyte lyst they dedyn sum folye. *c* **1386** —— *Merch. T.* 885 Thogh they [Piramus and Tesbee] were kept ful longe streite oueral They been accorded rownynge thurgh a wal. *c* **1400** *Destr. Troy* 615, I hete you.. The flese for to fecche, and ferke it away; And withstond all the stoure þat it strait yemys. **1461** *Paston Lett.* II. 52 The Duc of Somerset, [and others]..are comen into Normandy out of Scotland, and as yette they stand strete under arest. **1470–85** MALORY *Arthur* VIII. xxxv. 327 He took la beale Isoud home with hym and kepte her strayte that by no meane neuer she myght wete nor sende vnto Trystram nor he vnto her. **1568** GRAFTON *Chron.* II. 376 He did emprison them..commaundyng the Jaylours to kepe them streyt in Irons. **1611** BIBLE *1 Macc.* xiii. 49 They also of the towre in Ierusalem were kept so strait, that they could neither come foorth, nor goe into the countrey.

5. Severely, oppressively; so as to cause hardship. Now *rare.*

a **1300** *Cursor M.* 24849 Strangli strait þan war þai stadd. **1303** R. BRUNNE *Handl. Synne* 3814 He durst come oute on no party Of alle þe twelue monþe..So was he beseged streyte. **13..** *E.E. Allit. P.* B. 880 þus þay þrobled & þrong & þrwe vmbe his erez, & distresed him wonder strayt. **1390** GOWER *Conf.* I. 214 His fader grete werres hadde With Rome, whiche he streite ladde. *c* **1440** *Generydes* 1462 Generydes..hym [a prisoner] delyueryd onto Anasore, A gentill knyght keping the prison ther, To kepe hym hard and strayte in his office. **1460** W. PASTON in *P. Lett.* I. 516 He saythe it schuld go streythe with zow wytheowt zowr witnesse were rythe sofycyent. **1568** GRAFTON *Chron.* II. 10 They were..compelled to eate all kinde of Vermine,..so harde and streit they were kept by the warre. **1837** CARLYLE *Fr. Rev.* III. IV. viii, Danger drawing ever nigher, difficulty pressing ever straiter.

†**6. a.** With strictness of conduct or rule. *Obs.*

1390 GOWER *Conf.* I. 167 Of these lovers that loven streyte. *c* **1400** *Apol. Loll.* 36 þei kepe more specialy þe þingis, & þe biddingis enioynid of men, & streytar þan biddingis & þingis enioynid of God. *c* **1400** *Rule St. Benet* (Prose) ii. 6 þa þat ere froward and recles, Lede þaim þe straiter. *c* **1450** CAPGRAVE *Life St. Gilbert* xxii. 95 þei desired þat he schuld sumwhat tempir þe gret hardnesse of religion and suffir hem not to be kept so streith as þei wer be-for. **1535** COVERDALE *Ps.* cxviii. 128 Therfore holde I straight all thy commaundementes, and all false wayes I vtterly abhorre.

†**b.** With rigorous exactness; with strict correctness; exactly, precisely. *Obs.*

1338 R. BRUNNE *Chron.* (1725) 84 Tuenty ȝere had he þe land & nien moneth streite. *Ibid.* 139 Henry dred disceite, He wild, that his conant were holden stable & streite. *c* **1375** *Sc. Leg. Saints* xxxv. (*Thaddæus*) 80 Fore quhais [saulis] þu mon reknynge ȝeld, [as] strate as for þine. *a* **1450** MYRC *Par. Pr.* 1424 Whether hyt [the sin] be gret or smal, Open or hud, wyte þow al... Byd hym telle euen straȝt. **1590** H. SMITH *Magistr. Script.* 2 And though they iudge here, yet they shall be iudged hereafter, and giue account of their stewardship how they haue gouerned, as straite as their subiectes how they haue obeyed.

7. Graspingly, stingily. *Obs.* exc. *dial.*

1390 GOWER *Conf.* II. 136 The more he hath of worldis good, The more he wolde it kepe streyte. **1853** W. WATSON *Poems* 16 (E.D.D.) They grip their gear sae stret They live an' die in their ain debt.

8. Comb. with pa. pples., as *strait-besieged, -braced, -embraced, -tied.* Also STRAIT-LACED *a.*

1648 J. BEAUMONT *Psyche* IX. xviii, When sly Danger near Our *strait-besieged Soul or Body draws. **1847** TENNYSON *Princess* Prol. 36 O miracle of women,..O noble heart who, being strait-besieged By this wild king to force her to his wish, Nor bent, nor broke. **1627** DRAYTON *Agincourt* cxc. 39 The dreadfull bellowing of whose *strait-brac'd Drumes, To the French sounded like the dreadfull doome. **1648** J. BEAUMONT *Psyche* I. clxxiv, Those arms that courteous Vine About her *strait-embraced Elm doth throw. *c* **1520** SKELTON *Magnyf.* 852 Beyonde Measure My sleue is wyde, Al of Pleasure My hose *strayte tyde.

†**strait,** *v. Obs.* Forms: see the adj. [f. STRAIT *a.*]

1. *trans.* ? To brace up to effort.

[Perh. a different word: cf. ON. *streita-sk* to struggle.]

1340–70 *Alex. & Dind.* 756 Summe [of your idols] ȝou strenkþen to striue & straiten ȝour minde, & somme eggen in ese to eten and to drinke.

2. As rendering of Vulg. *coartare, artare,* lit. to press together, contract.

a **1340** HAMPOLE *Psalter* xxxiv. 6 And aungel of lord straitand [Vulg. *coartans*] þaim. **1382** WYCLIF *Job* xviii. 7 The goingis of his vertue shul be streitid [Vulg. *artabuntur*]. —— *Joel* ii. 8 Eche shal not streyte [Vulg. *non coartabit*] his brother, eche shuln go in his path.

3. To narrow (e.g. the course of a river, a street).

1421 *Coventry Leet Bk.* 31 That þe Ryuer and the brokes ..& allso the Red-dyche be enlargid..þe wiche, be encrochment of dwellers of both sydes, be strayted and narrowid, & with filthe, dong and stonys the watur stoppyd of his cours. **1510** *Sel. Cases Star Chamber* (Selden Soc.) II. 69 [He] made..many wharffes stathes & keyes..Wherby the seide porte is greatly streyted and hurted..and shippes ..applyeng the same for straytnes therof oftymes in greate Jeopardie. **1530** PALSGR. 738/1 It is to wyde, you muste strayght it. **1606** *Court Rolls* 174/16 *Wickham* [Essex] *View* 23 Sept. (P.R.O.), Henry Finch hath straited the way in Mosepett Lane to the great annoyance of the King's people. **1610** HOLLAND *Camden's Brit.* I. 1 The sea is so streited, that some thinke the land there was pierced thorow, and received the seas into it. **1615** *Manwood's Lawes Forest* xxiii. §7. 228 If any man haue stopped or strayted any Church-way, Mill-way, or other wayes..you shall do us to weet thereof.

b. *intr.* To become narrowed, to narrow.

a **1552** LELAND *Itin.* (1910) V. 52 Dargwent..casteth owt an arme of his abundant water that maketh a poole,..and afterward strayteth, and at the last cummeth ynto Dargwent, and so maketh an isle.

4. To shut up in or force into a narrow space.

c **1420** ? LYDG. *Assembly of Gods* 1633 Lyke as Eolus, beyng at hys large, Streytyd hym sylf thorow his owne lewdenesse. **1534** MORE *Treat. Passion* Wks. 1347/2 The tyme shall come whan..the churche by persecucion [shal be] so straughted into so narow a corner, that..it shall seeme that there shall bee than no chrysten countreyes left at all. **1571** CAMPION *Hist. Irel.* vii. (1633) 23 All sorts brake truce and amity with the Gyants, and straited them up so, that from all corners of the land, they must needes assemble into one field. **1579** FENTON *Guicciard* VIII. 442 At the beginning our towne was strayted. **1579–80** NORTH *Plutarch, Crassus* (1595) 610 He..straighted the battell of his footemen [Amyot *estroissit la bataille de ses gens de pied*]. *c* **1611** CHAPMAN *Iliad* XIV. 28 Which..yet suffisd, to hide them, though their men Were something streighted [Gr. στείνοντο δὲ λαοί]. **1612** J. DAVIES (Heref.) *Muse's Sacrif.* (Grosart) 83/2 My Body's but the Prison of my Soule; which straits her more, the more that Prison's free. **1641** BEST *Farm. Bks.* (Surtees) 21 Your best way will bee to howse them all night, viz.:—to lye them in some howse or barne wheare they may not bee straited for roome.

5. a. ? To do violence to, to mar.

1390 GOWER *Conf.* II. 341 Bot for he wolde be nomore Among the wommen so coveited, The beaute of his face streited He hath.

b. To press hardly upon.

1460 CAPGRAVE *Chron.* (Rolls) 309 Ther took he a preest of the secte, and othir servauntis of his, whom the lord Bergeveni streyted so, that thei told wher Oldcastelle was hid. **1594** in *Highl. Papers* (S.H.S.) I. 186 My Lord Argyll had straitit him verie sore about a band quhilk he had with Huntly. **1614** GORGES *Lucan* x. Argt., Cæsar..By ship to Pharos takes his flight. Where being straighted by his foes, From thence by swimming safely goes.

c. To bring into straits, subject to hardship.

1579–80 NORTH *Plutarch, Sertorius* (1595) 633 Hauing straighted his enemies with scarcitie of victuals. **1633** *Orkney Witch Trial* in *Abbotsford Club Misc.* 152 Scho and hir haill fammillie was straitit with drouth for the space off xx dayis ore ane mounth. *c* **1640** MURE *Ps.* cvii. 28 While straited thus in these extreams Wnto the Lord they cry. **1654** VILVAIN *Enchir. Epigr.* v. xii. 95 Exter..Hath with ten sieges grievously bin streited.

d. In *passive,* To be hard put to it, to be at a loss, to be nonplussed.

1611 SHAKS. *Wint. T.* IV. iv. 365 If your Lasse Interpretation should abuse, and call this Your lacke of loue, or bounty, you were straited For a reply. **1624** T. WHITE *Repl. Fisher* 357 We are not so straighted for words. **1646** R. BAILLIE *Anabaptism* (1647) 37 When in their debates against the baptism of infants they are straited with consequences from the circumcision of infants. **1647** TRAPP *Comm. Rev.* xvii. 18 The Rhemists are so straited that they know not which way to turn them.

6. To tighten (a knot).

a **1542** WYATT in *Tottel's Misc.* (Arb.) 66 And if I did, the lot, That first did me enchayne: May neuer slake the knot, But strayght it to my payne.

7. To confine, restrict *to* a person, time, etc.; to confine *within* limits.

1581 J. BELL *Haddon's Answ. Osor.* 102 b, His doctrine being not straighted within the boundes of Nature. *Ibid.* 399 Yet ought not this power be so narrowly streighted either to one Byshop onely..as though there were none other Remission of Sinnes.

b. To restrict in choice. Const. *between, betwixt* (alternatives, options).

1633 WARISTON *Diary* (S.H.S.) 110 Being straited by God (as I thought) betuixt three unsupportable burdens. **1637** GILLESPIE *Engl. Pop. Cerem.* II. ix. 51 He is greatly mistaken, whiles he thinkes that a man can be so straited betwixt two scandalls, that he cannot choose but give the one of them. **1642** D. ROGERS *Naaman* 30 Straighted betweene the choice of either famine, warre, or pestilence.

c. To restrict in freedom of action.

1533 MORE *Apol.* 249 Yet are they streyghted by the playne law that they may not so do at the seconde, whan the man is relapsed. **1613** HEYWOOD *Silver Age* III. i, *Juno.* Nor powers of heaven shall straight me till the deaths Of yon adultress and her mechal brats. *a* **1617** BAYNE *Lect.* (1634) 272 God in none of these [things] is straited. **1642** D. ROGERS *Naaman* 149 Selfe hath hidebound thee and straited thee in thine owne bowells.

8. To keep ill supplied, to stint.

1513 SIR E. HOWARD in Ellis *Orig. Lett.* Ser. III. I. 149, I have geven such ordre in dispendyng of our vitaill that ther was never Army so straited, nat by one drynkyng in a day, wich I know well hath byn a grete sparyng. **1564** HARDING *Answ. Jewel* xvii. 165 Herein I am more encombred with store, then straighted with lacke. **1601** HOLLAND *Pliny* XVIII. xxi. I. 581 And surely, I doe find this rule of his most true, ..in case a man have land ynough for to let his grounds.. rest every second yeare. But how if a man is streighted that way, and hath no such reach and circuit lying to his living? **1607** BP. HALL *Art Div. Medit.* iv. Wks. (1625) 107 God hath not straited vs for matter, hauing giuen vs the scope of the whole world. **1669** W. MONTAGU in *Buccleuch MSS.* (Hist. MSS. Comm.) I. 446 We are so straighted here in our charities, as we can furnish as yet but two hundred pistoles towards all the Church charities.

9. To reduce the duration or period of.

1571 T. BANNESTER *Let. to Cecil* 29 Mar. (P.R.O.) They went from yt, and streyghted owr yerelye Pencyon or Allowance to iij yeres. **1581** J. BELL *Haddon's Answ. Osor.* 403 b, Whereas Gregory the 11. reduced the Jubilee to the 33. yeare..Paule 2. and Sixtus the 4...streighted the Jubilee to the 25. yeare, in the yeare 1475.

10. To limit in amount or degree; also, to impute limitation to.

1533 MORE *Answ. Poysoned Bk.* Wks. 1121/2, I..sayed.. that Frith was but a foole so to straite and to limite the power of almightye god. **1596** BABINGTON *Profit. Exp.* 185 Now in the time of his Gospell his goodnes is not streyted or diminished. **1647** H. MORE *Song of Soul* II. iii. IV. xli, So that the durance of the Deity We must contract, or strait his full Benignity.

Hence †**'straited** *ppl. a.*

1581 A. HALL *Iliad* VII. 125 Lycurgus..slue him downe in strayted lane [στεινωπῷ ἐν ὁδῷ], where club he could not weeld. **1642** H. MORE *Song of Soul* I. ii. 42 But that full right ..did so unbind His straited sprights, that [etc.].

strait, obs. form of STRAIGHT.

straiten ('streɪt(ə)n), *v.* Forms: 6 **streyghten, streyten,** 6–7 **streiten,** 6–8 **streighten,** 6–9 **straighten,** 7 **straicten, strayten,** 7– **straiten.** [f. STRAIT *a.* + -EN[5].]

1. *trans.* To render strait or narrow; to narrow, contract (an opening, a passage, road, stream, etc.). Now somewhat *rare.*

1552 HULOET, Streyghten or make narrow, *angusto.* **1603** STOW *Surv.* 84 The number of..carts and coatches, more then hath beene accustomed, the streetes and lanes being streightned, must needes be daungerous. **1604** E. G[RIMSTONE] tr. *Acosta's Hist. Indies* III. xviii. 176 The river being there straightened, and forced betwixt two high steepe rockes: the water falles directly downe. **1628** COKE *On Litt.* 3 An ancient grant..that a way leading to their common should not be streightened. **1660** BOYLE *New Exper. Phys. Mech.* xxiii. (1682) 92 Into the latter [the Philosophical egg] we put a..rod of solid glass to straiten the Cavity of the neck by almost filling it up. **1683** SALMON *Doron Med.* I. 322 [This] straitens the Pores and Passages of the Body. **1695** in *Hertford Sessions Rolls* (1905) I. 420 [Enclosing part of a highway] by which means the said highway is much straightened. **1712** J. JAMES tr. *Le Blond's Gardening* 43 Trees on the Sides, coming to..grow thicker, will in Time ..streighten a Walk very considerably. **1715** DESAGULIERS *Fires Impr.* 51 The Funnel..shou'd have several divisions to cut the Wind. Some have indeed streighten'd this Passage. *c* **1804** JANE AUSTEN *Watsons* in Leigh *Mem.* (1871) 321 In passing through the latter, where the passage was straitened by tables, Mrs. Edwards and her party were for a few moments hemmed in. **1822–7** GOOD *Study Med.* (1829) III. 14 The throat is rough and straightened from the second day of the eruption. **1895** PETRIE *Egypt. Tales* Ser. I. 62 The tow-path..was straitened..: on the one side of it was the water, and on the other side of it grew his corn.

transf. **1638** FORD *Fancies* IV. i. 49 We shall flourish. Feed high henceforth, man, and no more be streightend Within the limits of an emptie patience.

†**b.** To close the ranks of (an army). *Obs.*

1590 SIR J. SMYTHE *Disc. Weapons* 3 b, That a squadron of armed men..being readie to encounter with another squadron,.. ought to streighten and close themselues by frunt and flanckes. *a* **1609** SIR F. VERE *Comm.* (1657) 95 The water now grew very high, so as both we and they were forced to streighten our front.

†**c.** *to straiten one's hand*: to become niggardly. *Obs.*

1622 MABBE tr. *Aleman's Guzman d' Alf.* I. 251 My friends ..had already cast mee off, streightning more and more their hand towards mee.

†**d.** Phrase, *to straiten* (a person's) *quarters.* (Cf. sense 4 b.) *Obs.*

1647 CLARENDON *Hist. Reb.* VI. §237 The winning of Ciceter..which, being upon the edge of Wiltshire, Barkshire, and Oxfordshire, shrewdly straitened the King's quarters. **1741** MIDDLETON *Cicero* II. x. 395 Distressing him by straitening his quarters. **1781** GIBBON *Decl. & F.* xxx. (1787) III. 150 The Barbarian was gradually invested, on every side, by the troops of the West..; his quarters were straightened; his convoys were intercepted.

2. *intr.* To become narrow, to narrow.

1601 HOLLAND *Pliny* V. xxxii. I. 114 Being past this gulfe, the sea beginneth to streighten againe, and the land to meet neere together. **1615** G. SANDYS *Trav.* II. 117 This arme of the Nile is as broad at Rosetta as Thames about Tilbury, streightning by little and little. **1731** T. GORDON *Tacitus, Agricola* II. 360 But a tract of territory huge and unmeasurable stretches forward to the uttermost shore, and straightning by degrees, terminates like a wedge. **1823** J. THACHER *Milit. Jrnl. Amer. Rev.* 96 We behold Lake Champlain widening and straitening as banks and clifts project into its channel. **1853** G. J. CAYLEY *Las Alforjas* II. 28 The valley..shortly after this began to straiten, till it came at last to so narrow a gorge..that [etc.].

†**3.** *trans.* To tighten (a knot, cord, bonds). *Obs.*

c **1645** HOWELL *Lett.* (1650) II. xvi. 28 You have much streightned that knot of love which hath bin long tied between us. **1659** MILTON *Treat. Civ. Power* 58 As well may he loos'n that which God hath strait'nd, or strait'n that which God hath loos'nd, as [etc.]. **1741** 'T. BETTERTON' *Hist. Engl. Stage* v. 66 Shewing the Teeth, and straitening the Lips on them, shews Indignation and Anger. **1742** POPE *Dunc.* IV. 29 Morality..Gasps, as they straiten at each end the cord.

†**b.** To render more strict or rigorous. *Obs.*

1751 H. WALPOLE *Let. to Mann* 1 May, On this his confinement was straitened. **1753** RICHARDSON *Grandison* (1781) III. 46 Her Mother's wickedness giving occasion the more to streighten her education.

4. To confine in or force into a narrow space; to hem in closely. Also with *in.* Now *rare.*

1570–6 LAMBARDE *Peramb. Kent* 79 Vortimer..so streightned the Saxons in this Ile.., that for a colour they sent Vortiger to treate with him of peace. ? **1605** DRAYTON *Poems Lyr. & Past., Man in Moone* H 3, Wherin you might view A sea that somwhat straytned by the land, Two furious tydes raise their ambitious hand One gainst the other. **1622** MABBE tr. *Aleman's Guzman d' Alf.* II. 216 They seemed.. to be like vnto straw, which..if you restraine and straiten it, ..it will shoot it selfe out. **1626** BACON *Sylva* §115 Waters, when they beat vpon the Shore, or are straitned (as in the falls of Bridges;)..giue a Roaring Noise. **1637–38** in Willis & Clark *Cambridge* (1886) I. 119 Y[e] wind could not there be straightned by Clare Hall, w[ch] scarce reacheth to y[e] fourth part of y[t] height. **1648** GAGE *West Ind.* 123 The chiefest mountains which straighten in this City and valley are two.

1652 Nedham *Selden's Mare Cl.* 172 An In-land Sea, which in som places beeing streightned with Land on every side, exceed's not the breadth even of a River. **1667** Milton *P.L.* i. 776 So thick the aerie crowd Swarm'd and were straitn'd. **1684** *Contempl. St. Man* ii. vi. (1699) 196 The Bodies of the Damned..shall be so straitned and crowded together in that Infernal Dungeon. **1698** Norris *Pract. Disc.* IV. 33 The Heavenly Plant is too much streightned and bound up to thrive, and cannot shoot forth its Branches very far. **1862** Stanley *Jew. Ch.* (1877) I. xvi. 311 The small tribe of Dan, already straitened between the mountains and the sea.

b. said of a hostile army.

1603 Knolles *Hist. Turkes* (1621) 944 Who..with all speed compassed in his enemies, and straightning them on both sides, tooke some of them alive,..and [etc.]. **1667** Milton *P.L.* ix. 323 If this be our condition, thus to dwell In narrow circuit strait'nd by a Foe. **1849–50** Alison *Hist. Europe* liv. §47. VIII. 509 Finding himself daily more closely straitened by the insurgents [he] was obliged to retire.

5. To narrow or restrict the freedom, power, or privileges of (a person). *arch.*

a **1586** Sidney *Arcadia* i. iv. (1912) 25 Their [*sc.* your daughters'] education by your fatherly care, hath beene hetherto such, as hath beene most fit to restraine all euill:..not greeuing them for want of wel-ruled libertie. Now to fall to a sodain straightning them, what can it doo but argue suspition? **1611** Bible *Micah* ii. 7 Is the Spirit of the Lord straitned [*marg.* or, shortened]? **1619** Sanderson *Serm. Ad Clerum* i. (1632) 24 The liberty of a Christian..is then infringed, when the Conscience is bound and streitned, by imposing vpon it an opinion of doctrinall Necessity. *a* **1653** Binning *Sinner's Sanct.* xiv. Wks. (1735) 233 Was it the Satisfaction of his Justice that straitned him, and put a Necessity of this upon him? **1701** Sir D. Hume *Diary Parl. Scot.* (Bannatyne Club) 52 What was moved seemed to him to straiten the King... So this was let fall. **1858** J. Martineau *Stud. Christ.* 108 Our spirit..is so straitened by the bands of sin..that there is no freedom.

†**b.** To deprive partially, abridge *of* (a possession or privilege). *Obs.*

1523 Fitzherb. *Surv.* 8 b, And also the lordes haue enclosed a great parte of their waste groundes and streytened their tenauntes of their commyns therin. **1621** Elsing *Debates Ho. Lords* (Camden) 114 The peticioner to be called in and herde. Yf he fynde himselfe streightened of his proofes for not beinge herde, then to gyve him longer daye. **1647** Howell *Lett.* (1650) III. xv. 27 The King is streightned of that liberty he formerly had in the Isle of Wight.

†**c.** To restrict *from* doing something. *Obs.*

1622 *Relat. Engl. Plant. Plymouth, New Eng.* 65 Some who out of doubt in tendernesse of conscience,..are straitned and doe straiten others, from going to forraine plantations.

†**d.** To bind stringently. *Obs.*

1652 Howell *Giraffi's Rev. Naples* ii. 129 While thus in the Countrey there was a course taken to straiten the people to the Obedience of his Majesty, there was no time lost in Naples.

6. To narrow or restrict in range, scope, or amount.

1645 Pagitt *Heresiogr.* (ed. 2) 46 Because else the grace of God to his people is now..lessened and straitned more then before. **1650** Jer. Taylor *Holy Living* iv. §7 (1676) 237 Let not young beginners in Religion..straiten their liberty by vows of long continuance. **1653** H. More *Antid. Ath.* ii. ix. (1712) 67 The reason why Birds are Oviparous..but do not bring forth their young alive, is..that neither the Birds of prey, the Serpent nor the Fowler, should streighten their generations too much. **1708** Addison *Pres. St. War* 8 We may only add, that the same Causes which streighten the British Commerce, will naturally enlarge the French. **1709** T. Robinson *Vindic. Mosaick Syst.* 79 The Divine Providence..so streightens their Increase, that they [Tigers] may not be too offensive and destructive, either of Man or Beast. **1778** Hartley *Swedenborg's Heaven & Hell* (1851) Pref. p. xlviii, God forbid that we should go about to straiten that mercy towards others (though even devils), to which the very best of us stand indebted. **1781** Cowper *Retirem.* 234 As woodbine weds the plant within her reach, ..But does a mischief while she lends a grace, Strait'ning its growth by such a strict embrace. **1801** S. Turner *Hist. Anglo-Sax.* iv. v. (1807) I. 276 A vigilant armed peasantry.. secured the property of the country, and straitened the supplies of the invader. **1855** Milman *Lat. Christ.* ix. ii. (1864) V. 212 They declared that they had no design to straiten the rights of the Holy See. **1863** Kinglake *Crimea* I. 34 The conquest of the shores of the Bosphorus..would straiten the range of England's authority in the world. **1868** Rogers *Pol. Econ.* xv. (1876) 211 It is supposed, and generally with reason,..that profits must fall, and so business must be straitened. **1871** Morley *Carlyle* in *Crit. Misc.* Ser. i. (1878) 163 It is a question of temperament how violently either of them straitens and distorts the normal faculties of vision.

7. To reduce to straits; to subject to privation, hardship, or distress. Often said of besiegers, sometimes with mixture of sense 4 b.

1611 Bible *Jer.* xix. 9 The siege and straitnesse, wherewith their enemies..shall straiten them. **1645** in *Verney Mem.* (1904) I. 400 Chester is certainly very much straitened, and if not suddenly relieved doubtless will be lost. **1665** Manley *Grotius' Low-C. Wars* 127 After he had encamped in all the Parts adjacent to Bruxels, endeavouring to straiten the City, by wasting and consuming all the Fruits of the Ground. **1759** Hume *Hist. Eng. Ho. Tudor, Edw. VI*, ii. I. 323 De Thermes..took the fortress of Broughty, and.. straitened the English at Haddington. **1778** *Phil. Surv. S. Irel.* 324 With a threat to streighten them if they refused to comply. **1838** Prescott *Ferd. & Is.* ii. xi. III. 101 The viceroy..endeavoured to straiten the garrison there by desolating the surrounding country. **1867** Trollope *Chron. Barset* I. xxxii. 267, I am sore straitened, and brought down into the very dust by misfortune.

†**b.** In *passive*, To be at a loss, to be 'hard put to it'. *Obs.*

1647 May *Hist. Parlt.* iii. vi. 101 The Parliament..were much straightned how to proceed in the businesse, with the expedition which was required.

c. To inconvenience by insufficiency of something specified (as time, space, supplies of any kind). Const. *for*, †*in*, †*of*, †*with*. Now only in *passive* (somewhat *arch.*).

1620 Sanderson *Serm. Ad Pop.* ii. (1632) 291, I will not ..straiten my selfe of time for the delivery of what I am now purposed to speake. **1634** Sydenham *Serm.* (1637) 75 They are not..so straightned with time,..but they might sequester one solemne houre for the service of the Lord. **1655** Stanley *Hist. Philos.* i. xi. (1687) 29/1 These young Men, streightned in time, underwent the Yoke, and drew the Chariot of their Mother forty five Stadia. **1661** Marvell *Corr.* Wks. (Grosart) II. 60 We are as much straitned in paper and time at present as we shall be always large in affection and service to you. **1663** Gerbier *Counsel* 12 Staires ought to be so long, that the Attendants on each side..may not be streightned for roome. **1665** Manley *Grotius' Low-C. Wars* 219 That by shutting up their Haven, he might straighten the Townsmen of Provision. **1697** Dryden *Virg. Georg.* iv. 218 But streighten'd in my Space, I must forsake This Task; for others afterwards to take. **1706** *Col. Rec. Pennsylv.* II. 260 Finding themselves straitned in time,..requested [etc.]. **1761** Hume *Hist. Eng. to Hen. VII* (1762) I. ix. 310 The garrison [of Verneuil], being straitened for provisions, were obliged to capitulate. **1817** W. H. Havergal in Jane M. Crane *Rec. Life* (1882) 19 The arranging and planning it [his Sunday School] has straitened me much for time. **1853** J. H. Newman *Hist. Sk.* Ser. ii. i. i. (1873) 6 If straitened for provisions, they [the Tartars] ate the chargers which carried them to battle.

d. To render short of money.

1699 Bentley *Phal.* 457 The Romans being straitned in the First Punic War, lower'd their Brass Money Five parts in Six. **1712** Addison *Spect.* No. 295 ¶1 The Education of these my Children..streightens me so much, that [etc.]. **1719** De Foe *Crusoe* ii. (Globe) 508 My Nephew furnishing me with..a Letter of Credit..that I might not be straiten'd whatever might happen. **1796** Mme. D'Arblay *Camilla* IV. 320 It shall value him fifty pound a-year more to his income, if I straighten myself never so much. **1818** Hallam *Mid. Ages* viii. iii. (1819) III. 91 The king, in short, was more straightened than ever. His distresses gave no small advantage to the commons. **1857** Kingsley *Two Y. Ago* xxv, The old man thanked God for his good son, and only hoped that he was not straitening himself to buy luxuries for a useless old fellow. **1860** Froude *Hist. Eng.* VI. 488 The works had fallen again into ruin; and Mary, straitened by debt,..and a supposed obligation to make good the losses of the clergy, had found neither means nor leisure to attend to them.

†**8.** To hamper, impede in action. *Obs.*

1607 T. Ridley (*title*), A view of the civile and ecclesiasticall law, and wherein the practise of them is streitned, and may be relieued within this land. **1662** H. Newcome *Diary* (Chetham Soc.) 87, I preached but was a little streitned by a cold. **1664** Power *Exp. Philos.* i. 53 So Inartificial is Art when she is pinched and streitned in her Workmanship. *a* **1683** Owen *Holy Spirit* (1693) 264 This a Man hath when he is not from any Internal Defect, or from any outward Consideration streightened in the Declaration of those things. **1726** Wodrow *Corr.* (1843) III. 234 But pray do not straiten yourself with any thing I cast in, and please dash down any thing that is proper for me to help.

Hence **'straitening** *vbl. sb.* and *ppl. a.*

† *straitening circumstances* (obs.) = straitened circumstances.

1598 Stow *Surv.* 231 After that is Grubstreete, more then halfe thereof to the straightning of the streete. **1646** H. P. *Medit. Seige* 130 When a fort or Garrison cannot be gotten neither by treatie, nor by streightning, the last attempt is commonly by storming. *a* **1652** J. Smith *Sel. Disc.* ix. 465 Separating them from those circumstantiating and straitening conditions of time and place. **1667** Milton *P.L.* vi. 70 Nor obvious Hill, Nor streit'ning Vale,..nor Stream divides Thir perfet ranks. **1692** Locke *Consid. Lower. Interest* 115 The Landed Man finds himself aggrieved, by the falling of his Rents, and the streightning of his Fortune. *a* **1732** T. Boston *Crook in Lot* (1805) 17 Providence..keeps them still in straitening circumstances. **1751** in J. J. Vernon *Parish of Hawick* (1900) 189 In case..his Widow should be reduced to straitning circumstances. *a* **1788** Gilson *Serm.* xvii. 498 They ardently long to be removed to that state themselves, where the straitening ties of sense, or corporeal relation, shall cease to hamper or keep down the soul. **1849** Ruskin *Seven Lamps* i. §11. 21 The nice balance between the straitening of effort or enthusiasm on the one hand, and vainly casting it away upon the other.

straitened ('streɪt(ə)nd), *ppl. a.* [f. straiten *v.* + -ed[1].] In various senses of the verb.

1. Contracted, narrowed; insufficiently spacious.

1602 [J. Willis] *Art Stenogr.* A 5, Stenographie, signifieth a straightned or compendious Writing. **1694** Addison *Poems, Virg. Georg.* iv. 375 First then a close contracted space of ground, With streighten'd walls and low-built roof they found. **1760–72** H. Brooke *Fool of Qual.* (1809) III. 154 The king's lion..traversed the limits of his straightened dominions. **1800** Ht. Lee *Canterb. T.* (ed. 2) III. 153 He was..in lodgings rather straitened and inconvenient. **1822–7** Good *Study Med.* (1829) V. 80 About half an inch within the orifice of the urethra, at which part the passage feels peculiarly straitened. **1842** Tennyson *Locksley H.* 62 Cursed be the gold that gilds the straiten'd forehead of the fool! **1866** Rogers *Agric. & Prices* I. xxiii. 601 Anticipations of excessive demand or of exceedingly straitened supply. **1890** Bridges *Shorter Poems* iii. vii, We steered Along a straitened channel flecked with foam.

†**b.** Limited in power or range of action.

a **1665** J. Goodwin *Being filled with the Spirit* (1867) 328 They that bring up such a report as this upon the Spirit, as that he is but a finite spirit, a created spirit, a straitened spirit, what do they do else but [etc.].

c. Contracted in intelligence or sympathy.

1712 Waterland *Serm.* Wks. 1823 VIII. 374 That we may not..grow straitened and narrow in our affections. **1860** Warter *Sea-board & Down* II. 400 He has but a limited and a straitened mind who [etc.].

d. *straitened circumstances*: inadequate means of living, poverty. Also *straitened income, means.*

a **1766** Mrs. F. Sheridan *Sidney Bidulph* (1796) IV. 4 They believed she was in straitened circumstances. **1813** *Sketches of Character* (ed. 2) I. 21 There remained but a straightened income for the widow. **1838** Dickens *Nich. Nick.* x, To remind her of her straitened and altered circumstances. **1877** Mrs. Oliphant *Yng. Musgrave* I. 7 So far as his straitened means and limited stables permitted.

2. Confined in narrow space; having too little room; closely besieged.

1757 W. Wilkie *Epigoniad* vi. 175 Now, when hostile pow'rs With strictest siege invest our strait'ned tow'rs. **1854** S. Dobell *Balder* i. Poet. Works 1875 II. 11 You floors, in whose black oak The straitened hamadryad lives and groans.

3. Drawn tight; tightened.

1665 Dryden *Ind. Emp.* v. ii, Fasten the Engines; stretch 'em at their length, And pull the streightened Cords with all your strength. **1716** Pope *Iliad* v. 325 My Horses here detain, Fix'd to the Chariot by the straiten'd Rein. **1742** Young *Nt. Th.* iv. 397 Or holds he furious storms in streighten'd reins, And bids fierce whirlwinds wheel his rapid car?

4. Reduced to hardship or privation; having straitened means (see 1 d).

1716 Pope *Iliad* v. 255, I..thought the Steeds (your large Supplies unknown) Might fail of Forage in the straiten'd Town. **1888** Bryce *Amer. Commw.* cii. III. 438 But even in the East a good many may come from straitened homes. **1911** G. M. Trevelyan *Garibaldi & Making of Italy* ii. 36 Sums..which represented the widow's mite in many straitened Italian households.

straith, obs. form of strath.

†**'straithead.** *Obs.* [f. strait *a.* + -head.]

a. Tightness, constriction. **b.** Closefistedness.

a **1400** *Stockh. Med. MS.* ii. 304 in *Anglia* XVIII. 315 ȝif eyther lewyd or prest Hawe gret streythed at hys brest, Modirworte late hym takyn. *c* **1440** *Jacob's Well* 119 Anoþer sqware of þis wose in coueytise, is straythed in kepyng ryches.

†**'straiting,** *vbl. sb. Obs.* [f. strait *v.* + -ing[1].] = straitening *vbl. sb.*

1421 *Coventry Leet Bk.* 31 Dyuers perels had afortyme by floodys thurgh stoppyng and strayting of the same Ryvers. **1472–5** *Rolls of Parlt.* VI. 159/1 The outrageous enhaunsyng and streytyng of Weeres. **1591** Jas. VI *Let.* 12 June in *New Discov. Pontif. Pract. Persec. J. Udall* (1643) 43 Requesting you..that..it may please you to let them be relieved of their present straite,..respecting both their former merit,..and the great slander which could not faile to fall out upon their further straiting for any such occasion.

strait-lace, *v.* [Back-formation from strait-laced *a.*] *trans.* and *intr.* (for refl.) To lace tightly, confine. Hence **strait-lacing** *vbl. sb.* and *ppl. a.* Also **strait-lacer** (in quot. *fig.*).

1636 W. Durham in *Ann. Dubrensia* (1877) 10 Then they repine at their streight-lacing shore, Prohibiting their passage to his dore. **1662** Glanvil *Lux Orient.* vi. 69 Is not this to slurr his goodnesse! and to straight-lace the divine beneficence? **1675** Hannah Woolley *Gentlew. Comp.* 80 Endeavouring by strait-lacing to be as slender in the middle as the Strand-May-pole is tall in its height. **1693** Locke *Educ.* §11, I have seen so many Instances of Children receiving great harm from strait-lacing. **1700** Congreve *Way of World* iv. v, I denounce against all strait-Laceing, Squeezing for a Shape, 'till you mold my boy's head like a Sugar-loaf. **1776** Sir J. Reynolds *Seven Disc. R. Acad.* (1778) 313 The strait lacing of the English ladies. **1811** Lamb *On Trag. Shaks.* Wks. (1876) 563 How cruelly this operates upon the mind, to have its free conceptions thus cramped and pressed down to the measure of a strait-lacing actuality, may be judged from [etc.]. **1820** T. Mitchell *Aristoph.* I. p. xxx, A course of straight-lacing and cool diet was bringing her a little more into compass. **1913** J. L. Paton *J. B. Paton* xvii. 309 A well-meaning straitlacer.

strait-laced (ˌstreɪt'leɪst), *a.* [f. strait *adv.* + laced *ppl. a.*]

†**1.** Wearing stays or bodice tightly laced. *Obs.*

1626 Moryson *Shaks. Europe* (1903) 485 The [Irish] wemen generally are not straight laced..and the greatest part are not laced at all. **1650** Bulwer *Anthropomet.* Pref., No Maid here's handsome thought, unless she can With her short Palms her streight-lac't body span. **1693** Locke *Educ.* §11 We should as certainly have no perfect children born, as we have few well-shaped that are strait-laced. **1698** Fryer *Acc. E. India & P.* 394 A Plump Lass being in more esteem than our Slender and Strait-laced Maidens.

transf. **1648** J. Beaumont *Psyche* ix. lii, The strait-lac'd Insect's slender Brood could ne'r Shrink up themselves into a scanter dress.

b. Of a bodice, etc.: Tightly laced. *rare.*

Cf. quot. *c* 1430, where *strait laced* is not a compound, but two words.

[*c* **1430** Lydg. *Min. Poems* (Percy Soc.) 201 Hire crowpe doth the semys shrede, Whan they so streyght lasyd been.] **1855** Macaulay *Hist. Eng.* xviii. IV. 148 It was never, he [Child] declared with much spirit, found politic to put trade into straitlaced bodices.

2. *fig.* †**a.** Of things: Narrow in range or scope.

1549 Coverdale etc. *Erasm. Par. 1 Tim.* ii. 1–7 Lest Christian loue shoulde appeare to be but a straite laced loue. **1579** G. Harvey *Two Other Lett.* (1580) 64 He might haue spared..that same restrictiue, & streightlaced terme, Precisely. **1583** Golding *Calvin on Deut.* vi. 4–9. 272 But this exposition is too straite laced, and attaineth not to the verie meaning of Moses. **1686** Goad *Celest. Bodies* i. xi. 41 Natural Causes are not so straight-lac'd.

†**b.** Of persons: Shut up within oneself, uncommunicative, morose, unsympathetic. *Obs.*

1546 J. Heywood *Prov.* I. xi. (1867) 31 He is so hy in thinstep, and so streight laste, That pryde and couetyse withdrawth all repaste. **1549** Coverdale etc. *Erasm. Par. Ephes.* Prol. ¶ iiij, Whan were maisters more vnlouyng or strayterlaced to their seruauntes? **1571** Golding *Calvin on Ps.* xxvii. 10. 102 All mortal men who are of nature nigardly & streitlaced [L. *qui natura maligni sunt ac restricti*]. **1579** Lyly *Euphues* (Arb.) 54 Commonly if they be adorned with beautie, they be straight laced, and made so high in the insteppe, that they disdaine them most that most desire them. **1691** Norris *Pract. Disc.* 297 Is it then possible for a Man seriously..to contemplate the..Goodness of God, and ..to be selfish and strait-laced, niggardly and covetous?

†**c.** Obstinate, indisposed to yield; grudging in gifts or concessions. *Obs.*

1560 Daus tr. *Sleidane's Comm.* XII. 162 b, He requested them, that they woulde not be ouer streight lased, but to graunt to so muche as they myght with a saufe conscience. **1579–80** North *Plutarch, Galba* (1595) 1113 Titus Iunius.. onely made the Emperour straight laced to all others, whilest he himselfe tooke vnreasonably of all men. **1588** J. Udall *Diotrephes* (Arb.) 23 If it be not vnreasonable, you may assure your selfe of it, for you know, that I haue neuer bin strait laced againste you, or anye of your friends. **1600** Holland *Livy* XXII. lix. 468 Our fathers also, notwithstanding they were most streightlaced, and hardly brought to capitulat and compound for peace, yet sent Embassadours..to redeeme their Captives. **1601** F. Godwin *Bps. of Eng.* 523 The Pope was somewhat strait laced in admitting him.

d. Of persons, their habits, opinions, etc.: Excessively rigid or scrupulous in matters of conduct; narrow or over-precise in one's rules of practice or moral judgement; prudish.

1554 T. Martin *Marr. Priestes* vi. K iiij, He had to doe with certaine holy and straite lased heretikes, whiche denied it to be lawful for a Christian man after his baptisme to retourne to his wife. **1598** Dallington *Meth. Trav.* V 2, They of the Reformed Religion may not Dance, being an exercise against which their strait-laced Ministers much inueigh. **1639** Saltmarshe *Pract. Policie* 175 Doe not alwaies stand upon the nice puntilioes..of state and place..; these that doe not observe this, are a little too strait laced for businesse either civill or religious. **1659** in *Trans. Roy. Hist. Soc.* (N.S.) XVII. 114 If hee or any man else in this place were soe straite laced that they could nott endure such thinges [as a market on Sunday], they might depart the towne. **1688** Shadwell *Sqr. Alsatia* III. iv, I am not streight-lac'd; but when I was young, I ne'er knew any thing gotten by wenching, but duels, claps, and bastards. **1705** Hickeringill *Priest-Cr.* II. ii. 16 This strait-lac't Doctrine seems contrary to the Justice, Mercy and Holiness of God. **1707** Filmer *Def. Plays* A 6 b, Had these strait-lac'd Gentlemen once gain'd their Point against Plays. **1857** Gladstone *Glean.* VI. lii. 81 Gibbon, no straightlaced judge,..records his judgment [etc.]. **1870** R. Brough *Marston Lynch* xxix. 311 They have such ridiculously strait-laced notions. **1884** Sala *Journ. due South* I. i. (1887) 22 At no time during the period..have the print-sellers of the gay capital been very straight-laced. **1904** L. Stephen *Eng. Lit. & Soc. 18th C.* iv. 162 Richardson seemed to be a narrow, straitlaced preacher.

†**e.** Hampered by narrow rules of procedure.

1766 [? G. Grenville] *Sp. agst. Susp. Prerogative* (ed. 3) 14 But if that strange thing should fall out, our constitution is not so strait laced as to let a nation die or be stifled, rather than it should be helped by any but the proper officers. **1791** Jefferson *Writ.* (1830) IV. 527 Will Congress be too strait-laced to carry the constitution into honest effect?

Hence **'strait,lacedness.**

1876 M. & Fr. Collins *Vill. Comedy* II. xii. 150 This division of the people led in time to a general appearance of priggishness and straitlacedness in the village. **1903** A. McNeill *Egregious English* 38 Their assumption of morality and puritanical straitlacedness is admirable.

straitly ('streɪtlɪ), *adv.* [f. strait *a.* + -ly[2].]

1. Tightly. *Obs.* or *arch.*

1338 R. Brunne *Chron.* (1725) 337 He did þam fettre wele, streitly & right hard. *a* **1425** tr. *Arderne's Treat. Fistula*, etc. 29 þof al it be bounden riȝt streitly at þe first tyme ȝitte vnneþe schal þe fretyng be complete in som men by a moneþ. **1483** Caxton *Golden Leg.* 407/3 Thenne eche kyssed other and embraced straytely. **1579** Tomson *Calvin's Serm. Tim.* 255 Let ye Ministers of Gods word learne to be straitlier laced then other men. **1598** Grenewey *Tacitus, Ann.* XIV. ii. (1612) 200 Nero..embraced hir more streightly then hee was accustomed. **1653** H. More *Conject. Cabbal.* 228 The soul may deem her self too straitly girt up. **1752** 'Sir H. Beaumont' *Crito* 19 If it be a Child of the tenderer Sex, she must be bound yet more streightly about the Waist and Stomach. **1820** Scott *Monast.* xxxi, Even that ruffian hesitated to draw the cord straitly. **1850** Neale *Med. Hymns* 12 Let thy loins be straitly girded.

†**2.** Urgently. *Obs.*

1340 Hampole *Pr. Consc.* 5597 Þe croyce on whilk he dieghed for man Sal stratly pray ogayne þe þan. *c* **1440** *Alphabet of Tales* 15 A monke þat hight Hubertus..when he sulde dy,..askid straytlie þat þe abbott myght com vnto hym & assoyle hym.

3. Narrowly; within narrow limits.

c **1400** *Ywaine & Gaw.* 674 At aither entre was, i wys, Straytly wroght, a port-culis. *a* **1504** *Erthe upon Erthe* (1911) 28/39 Erth hath closed them ful streytly in his bowre. *a* **1619** Fotherby *Atheom.* II. i. §8 (1622) 185 Yet is our capacity so much straitlier limited, that it cannot reach to any of their limits. **1851** Carlyle *Sterling* II. v, I remember finding him lodged straitly but cheerfully,..in a little cottage on Blackheath. **1877** Conder *Basis of Faith* v. 230 Nature.. straitly restrains that latent capacity for variation, so freely evolved under the hand of man.

b. With reference to a siege or the like: Closely, narrowly, strictly.

1303 R. Brunne *Handl. Synne* 3811 Þo was he beseged so streytly, þat he durst come oute on no party. **1474** Caxton *Chesse* III. ii. (1883) 90 His gardes whiche wacchid and kept straytly thys forteresse. **1610** Holland *Camden's Brit.* (1637) 205 William the Conquerour, most straightly beleaguered it. **1728** Morgan *Algiers* I. 170 His..Wizir.. revolted, and straitly besieged him. **1889** Rider Haggard *Cleopatra* I. iv, And for answer Achillas marched on Cæsar, and besieged him straitly in the Bruchium at Alexandria.

†**c.** *straitly stead*: placed in straits, sore beset.

1375 Barbour *Bruce* VII. 216 The kyng so stratly stad wes thair, That he wes neuer ȝeit swa stad. *c* **1400** *Melayne* 42 He was full straytly stede. *c* **1440** *York Myst.* xxii. 187 Me thynke þat ȝe ware straytely stedde, Lorde, with þis fende þat nowe is fledde.

†**d.** *to look straitly to*: to watch narrowly. *Obs.*

c **1450** *St. Cuthbert* (Surtees) 5022 He was so straytely loked to. **1568** Hacket tr. *Thevet's New found World* xlii. 66 They dare doe no faulte: for their husbandes doe looke straightly to them [Fr. *car les maris les regardent de prés*]. *a* **1569** Kingesmill *Man's Est.* viii. (1580) 42 If I have sinned, then thou wilt streightly looke unto mee. **1588** D. Rogers in Ellis *Orig. Lett.* Ser. II. III. 151 Who of late did his best to escape away, which is the occasion that he is now the streightlier looked unto.

†**4.** In a niggardly manner. *Obs.*

1340 *Ayenb.* 34 Auarice..zuo disordene him ssewep in pri maneres..ine wynnynge boldeliche ine ofhealdinge streytliche ine spendinge scarsliche. **1614** in *Liber Deposit. Archd. Colcestren.* 1612–16 lf. 70 The Testator was kept so barely and so straightly from victualls by his wife, that he was driven vpon necessitie often tymes to begg.

5. Strictly, rigorously, stringently; with strictness of observance. Now only *arch.* with respect to commands, questions, or obligation.

c **1290** *Beket* 163 in *S.E. Leg.* 111 So streitliche heo fraynede him. *a* **1300** *Cursor M.* 6105 Moyses..straitlike forbed þat þai Suld [etc.]. *c* **1380** Wyclif *Wks.* (1880) 322 Siþ þe contrarie is soþ, to whiche þise ordris ben streytliche sworen. **1461** in *Jarrow & Wearmouth* (Surtees) 245, I John Lawyson, be ye Auctoryte of our holy fadre ye pope,.. inhibite straeictly and command..ye priour of yis cathederall church..that [etc.]. **1495** *Act 11 Hen. VII*, c. 3. Preamble, Dyvers enquestes..streitly sworne and charged before the seid Justices to enquyre of the premysses. **1586** T. Bowes tr. *La Primaud. Fr. Acad.* I. xxxix. 390 Amongst the famous..personages of olde time, no vertue was.. straightlier kept and observed than Faith and Fidelitie. **1594** Shaks. *Rich. III*, IV. i. 17 (Qo.), I may not suffer you to visite him, The King hath straightlie [Fol. strictly] charged the contrarie. **1611** Bible *1 Sam.* xiv. 28 Thy father straitly charged the people with an oath. **1676** Owen *Worship of God* 31 Jesus Christ streightly enjoyns His disciples. **1837** Carlyle *Fr. Rev.* II. VI. vi, They question him straitly on that Mayor's Order to resist force by force. **1872** Tennyson *Gareth & Lynette* 785 Bound am I to right the wrong'd, But straitlier bound am I to bide with thee. **1878** Bosw. Smith *Carthage* xii. 244 He straitly charged Minucius to follow his policy, and on no account to risk a battle in his absence. **1879** Butcher & Lang *Odyss.* IV. 63 Son of Atreus, why dost thou straitly question me hereof?

†**b.** With regard to diet or mode of living. *Obs.*

c **1375** *Sc. Leg. Saints* xviii. (*Mary Egypt*) 103 [þai] straytly þe lyfe cane leyde anerly in vatyre & brede. *c* **1470** *Paston Lett.* II. 419 He purposith to lesse his howshold, and to leve the streytlyer. **1480** Caxton *Chron. Eng.* III. (1520) 25 b, They lyved straytlyer than other men dyd.

†**c.** In close confinement; under strict control.

1375 Barbour *Bruce* XVIII. 512 And bad haf him avay in hy, And luk he kepit war stratly. **1535** Coverdale *1 Macc.* xiii. 49 They in the castell at Ierusalem were kepte so strately, that they coude not come forth. **1579** Northbrooke *Dicing* (1843) 96 If thy daughter be not shamefast, holde hir straitly, least she abuse hir selfe thorow ouermuch libertie. **1633** T. Stafford *Pac. Hib.* I. vii. 51 They were presently caried to Castle Lyshin,..and there straightly kept in Irons. **1687** *Pennsylv. Arch.* I. 98 And the said Pirats,..to cause to be streightly imprisoned and kept in safe Custody.

†**d.** With reference to punishment, judgement, etc.: Rigorously, unsparingly, severely. *Obs.*

a **1340** Hampole *Psalter* cxlii. 2 Do noght straytly wiþ me in þi dome. *Ibid.*, *Song of Hannah* 5 Straytly demand ȝoure ald errours. **1467** *Coventry Leet Bk.* 336 Vppon peyn streitly to be punysshed be þe Meir for the tyme beyng. **1560** *MS. Cott. Cal.* B. 10. lf. 290 The bishops have of late..dealt streightly with some persons of good religion. **1590** Spenser *F.Q.* II. viii. 29 So streightly God doth judge. **1668** R. Steele *Husbandm. Calling* v. (1672) 121 Taking occasion from his straits, to deal straitly with him.

†**e.** Precisely, exactly. *Obs.*

a **1395** Hylton *Scala Perf.* (W. de W. 1494) 93 Also thise wordes that I write take hem not to streytly but there that the thynkith by gode auysement that I speke to shortly..I praye the amende it. **1398** Trevisa *Barth. De P.R.* XIV. xlviii. (1495) 484 Moost streyghtly to speke Ager is a felde that is not conteynyd in certayne mesure of lynes. *c* **1400** *Beryn* 95 For had ye countid streytly, & no thing lefft be-hynde, I myȝte have [etc.].

6. With reference to alliance or union: Closely, intimately. *arch.* (Very common in 16–17th c.)

c **1480** Henryson *Fables, Sheep & Dog* 33 Quhilk wer confidderit straitlie in ane band. **1485** Caxton *St. Wenefryde* 19, I shal the straitlyer be confedered to yow. **1596** Dalrymple tr. *Leslie's Hist. Scot.* I. 327 The hartes of the tua kingis straitlie knutt agane throuch beneuolent and true luue. **1614** Ralegh *Hist. World* V. i. §4. 333 The Selinuntines were streightly allied to the Syracusians. **1684** *Contempl. St. Man* II. iv. (1699) 160 By how much a delectable Object is more..straightly united to the Faculty; by so much greater is the Joy and Delight which it produces. **1690** Locke *Hum. Und.* III. ix. §17 Weight..a Quality as straitly join'd with that Colour [yellow] as its Fusibility. **1871** R. Ellis *Catullus* xci. 7 Yea tho' mutual use did bind us straitly together.

straitness ('streɪtnɪs). [f. strait *a.* + -ness.]

1. The quality of being strait, in various senses. **a.** Tightness; insufficiency or scantiness of breadth, area, or spatial extent, narrowness.

1382 Wyclif *2 Macc.* xii. 21 It was vnable to be ouercummen, and hard in goynge to, for streytnesse of places. *c* **1391** Chaucer *Astrol.* I. §21. 33 For the streitnesse of thin astrelabie. *c* **1430** Lydg. *Min. Poems* (Percy Soc.) 50 No maryner durst take on hond To cast an anker, for straytnes of passage. *c* **1520** Barclay tr. *Sallust's Jugurth* liv. 76 b, Thus cowde nat the soudyours..contynue togyder at their worke..for strayetnes and dyfficultie of the place. *c* **1530** *Judic. Urines* II. vii. 27 Another may be by strettenes of ye waies of ye vryne fro ye raines to ye bladder. **1691** T. H[ale] *Acc. New Invent.* p. lxxxii, The great straitnes of the River. **1715** Leoni *Palladio's Archit.* (1742) I. 13 In leaving too little space between..Columns, the streightness of the vacancy will make them appear too thick. **1849–50** Alison *Hist. Europe* lxxxviii. §51. XIII. 155 The streets in the old part of the town are narrow,..but their straitness only renders them the more imposing. **1902** Buchan *Watcher by Threshold* 269 He felt the torture of his collar and the straitness of his clothes.

fig. **1622** Bacon *Adv. Holy War* Misc. Tracts (1629) 132 It is a great Errour, and a Narrownesse, or Straightnesse of Minde, if any Man thinke, that Nations [etc.]. **1648** *Eikon Bas.* xi. 95 If the straitnesse of my Conscience will not give me leave to swallow down such Camels. **1662** Gurnall *Chr. in Arm.* III. xxv. §2. 215 Because of the penury and streightness of these appellations. **1868** J. J. S. Perowne tr. *Ps.* cxxx. 7 Notes, Such is the straitness of our heart,..that it [redemption] far exceeds all our capacity.

†**b.** Tightness of the chest; difficulty or 'shortness' (of breathing). *Obs.*

1398 Trevisa *Barth. De P.R.* v. xxiv. (Bodl. MS.) In alle þese is..streitenes of breeþ. *c* **1530** *Judic. Urines* III. iv. 49 b, If that mater..come to the throte goll, it causeth straethnys and horsenes & grete dysese. *Ibid.*, It causeth cough & streythnes of breth. **1576** Baker *Gesner's Jewell of Health* 72 The water..helpeth the straitnesse of the breast. **1578** Lyte *Dodoens* III. lxxi. 415 The disease called Asthma, whiche is a straightnesse in drawing of breath. **1580** T. Newton *Approved Medicines* 32 b, The fume of the leaues..healpeth the coughe, & straightnes of winde. **1637** Wotton *Let. to Sir E. Bacon* Reliq. (1672) 467 Since the late cold weather, there is complicated with it a more Asthmatical straitness of respiration then heretofore. **1683** Salmon *Doron Med.* II. 377 Heart-burning, Sowr Belchings, straightness of Breathing. **1710** Fuller *Pharmacop.* 272 [The Lohoch] is of excellent service against..straitness of Breath. **1725** *Bradley's Family Dict.* s.v. *Nightingale*, There is another Disease incident to these Birds, which is called the Streightness or Strangling in the Breast.

c. Strictness, rigour, severity.

c **1375** *Sc. Leg. Saints* xxvii. (*Machor*) 406 In honest conuersacione & stratnes of relygione. *c* **1460** *Play Sacram.* 737, I shew yow the streytnesse of my greuance. **1551** T. Wilson *Logic* I. G iij b, Christ..byndeth vs to a more straightnesse, that not only we should do none euill, but that also we shoulde consent to none euyll. **1603** Shaks. *Meas. for M.* III. ii. 269 If his owne life, Answere the straitnesse of his proceeding, It shall become him well. **1772** Fletcher *Appeal* Wks. 1795 I. 183 The straitness of the heavenly rule will soon shew thee how very far gone thy..nature is from original righteousness. *a* **1842** Arnold *Hist. Rome* xliv. (1843) III. 249 The straitness of the blockade could no longer be endured.

†**d.** Parsimony, stinginess. *Obs.*

c **1460** Metham *Wks.* (1916) 94 Yff this cornere be iuste off bothe lynys metyng to-gydyr scharp..yt sygnyfyith couetyse and streytnes in kepyng off money. **1461** *Paston Lett.* II. 38 Ther shal no thyng hurte hym but youre streytnesse of mony to hym. **1653** Whitelocke *Swed. Amb.* (1772) I. 47 This straightnes of the councell raysed many serious thoughts in Whitelocke.

†**e.** Scantiness, limited amount. *Obs.*

c **1698** Locke *Cond. Underst.* §3 Wks. 1714 III. 391 The Straitness of the Conveniences of Life amongst them. **1725** N. Bailey *Fam. Colloq. Erasm.* (1733) 120 You see, not the Affluence, but the Straitness of my Fortune. **1772** [Shrubsole & Denne] *Hist. Rochester* 105 By the straitness of its income..is this diocese unluckily distinguished from almost every other see in the kingdom.

†**f.** *straitness of time*: = 'straits of time', strait *sb.* 2 c. *Obs.* (Very common in the 16–17th c.)

1545 Ascham *Toxoph.* I. (Arb.) 48 These two thinges, straytenesse of tyme, and euery man his trade of liuing, are the causes that so fewe men shotes. **1570** Dee *Math. Pref.* A iiij b, Though I haue ben pinched with straightnes of tyme. **1621** Elsing *Debates Ho. Lords* (Camden) 5 The collecions are made soe well as the streightnes of the tyme woulde permitte. **1657** in *Burton's Diary* (1828) II. 229 In regard of the straitness of time, you have always let loose that rule by a proviso.

g. Straitened condition (of circumstances). *rare.*

1740 Ld. Harrington *Let.* in *10th Rep. Hist. MSS. Comm.* App. I. 275 The extreme Streightness of my Family Circumstances. **1829** Everett *Orat.* (1850) II. 13 He was never employed in [public affairs],..the straitness of his circumstances keeping him close to his trade.

†**2.** *concr.* A strait place. *Obs.*

1625 Purchas *Pilgrims* II. 1124 Where..is the narrowest and streightest passage of the Streight. This streightnesse [Bab-el-Mandeb], of the neighbouring people..is called *Albabo.*

†**3.** Want of room. *Obs.*

1586 in J. Morris *Troubles Cath. Forefathers* (1875) 76 And as many [are] pestered into every chamber as it will receive, by reason of which throng and straitness oftentimes infectious sicknesses do reign amongst vs. **1611** Bible *Job* xxxvi. 16 Euen so would he haue remooued thee out of the strait into a broad place, where there is no straitnesse. **1633** T. Stafford *Pac. Hib.* II. x. 192 The rest of the Armie.. lodged there..although with great straightnesse, the place contayning not aboue two hundred houses. **1775** *Ann. Reg.* 137* Having been before much incommoded by the streightness in which they were confined in Boston.

4. Hardship, distress; privation, straitened circumstances. (Cf. 1 g.) *arch.*

a 1340 HAMPOLE *Psalter* xvii. 22 When we suffire fleysly straytnes, he ledis vs in gastly breed. 1436 *Rolls of Parlt.* IV. 498/2 They have suffred right grete streitenesse, as well in their Persones as in their Godes. 1535 COVERDALE *Job* xxxvi. 15 The poore delyuereth he out of his straytnesse, and comforteth soch as be in necessite and trouble. 1737 WHISTON *Josephus, Wars* VI. ix. §3 An army which.. occasioned so great a straitness among them that there came ..a famine. 1742 T. BARNARD *Char. Lady E. Hastings* 41 Add..free and frequent Remission of Debts, in Cases of Straitness or Insolvency. 1845 J. H. NEWMAN *Development* 302 The need and straitness of the Church had been great. 1879 CHRISTINA ROSSETTI *Seek & Find* 211 In these two passages [of the Bible] summer wears an aspect of..hope..; winter, one which forebodes aggravated affliction, straitness, trial.

plural. a 1676 HALE *Hist. Common Law* xi. (1713) 212 The Laws of the Twelve Tables..had many other Streightnesses and Hardships which were successively remedied. 1868 BROWNING *Ring & Bk.* IV. 643 They needs must..publish all abroad The straitnesses of Guido's household life.

strait waistcoat, *sb.* A garment for the upper part of the body, made of strong material and admitting of being tightly laced, used for the restraint of violent lunatics or prisoners, and sometimes as a means of punishment.

There are various forms of this appliance; in some there are long sleeves with no opening, which can be tied together at the back; in others the arms are covered by the body of the garment.

1753 RICHARDSON *Grandison* (1754) III. xxi. 271 She threatened her then with the Strait Waistcoat, a punishment at which the unhappy Lady was always greatly terrified. 1773 CRISP *Let.* in *Mme. D'Arblay's Early Diary* (1889) I. 261, I shall..have a strait waistcoat immediately put on him, debar him the use of pen, ink, and paper [etc.]. 1837 CARLYLE *Fr. Rev.* III. III. viii, Within year and day we hear of her in madhouse and strait-waistcoat. 1881 BESANT & RICE *Chapl. Fleet* II. xviii, They had put the strait-waistcoat over him, which pinned his arms to his sides.

fig. 1824 LADY GRANVILLE *Lett.* 23 June (1894) I. 304, I put a strait-waistcoat upon my thoughts as the only way of keeping them within bounds. 1851 RUSKIN *Stones Venice* I. i. 22 The English Gothic was confined, in its insanity, by a strait-waistcoat of perpendicular lines.

b. *attrib.*

1837 CARLYLE *Fr. Rev.* II. I. ii, Neither indeed is there madness, of the strait-waistcoat sort. 1891 C. T. C. JAMES *Rom. Rigmarole* 159 Assuming as jaunty..a step as the strait-waistcoat tightness of my riding costume permitted.

Hence **strait-'waistcoat** *v. trans.*, to confine in a strait waistcoat; **strait-'waistcoating** *vbl. sb.*

1837 DICKENS *Pickw.* xxxix, Ve thought ve should ha' been obliged to strait-veskit him last night. 1859 W. ANDERSON *Disc.* Ser. II. (1860) 89 The maniac-like strait-waistcoating of worldliness. 1859 SALA *Tw. round Clock* (1861) 213 Till their own troublesome bodies..are securely shackled and strait-waistcoated up, and carted away in police-vans to deep-holded ships. 1874 HARDY *Far fr. Mad. Crowd* xli, Such strait-waistcoating as you treat me to is not becoming in you at so early a date.

strak, obs. f. STROKE; obs. pa. t. of STRIKE *v.*

strake (streɪk), *sb.*[1] Also α. 6 **strack, strak, straake,** 7 **straak,** 6–8 **straik;** β. 6 **streake,** 6–9 **streak.** [ME. *strake*, app. belonging to the OTeut. root **strak-* whence **strakjan*, OE. *stręccan* STRETCH *v.* Cf. NFris. (Sylt) *straak* a stretch, *straake* v. to stretch oneself.

It is perh. impossible to distinguish accurately between this word and STREAK *sb.*[1] (:—OE. *strica*). From the 16th c., in some dialects, *streak* has been a possible phonetic spelling of *strake* sb.[1], and *strake* of STREAK *sb.*[1] The two words, etymologically unconnected, have developed senses nearly coincident, and have to some extent coalesced.

There is also some confusion between this word and *strake* northern form of STROKE *sb.*]

1. a. A section of the iron rim of a cart-wheel. **b.** A strip of iron attached to the left side of a plough (= PLOUGHSTRAKE).

α. 1330–1 *Exchequer Acc.* K. R. Bundle 18 no. 34 (Publ. Rec. Off.), xii. strak' ferri pro rotis carectarum. 1334–5 *Durham Acc. Rolls* (Surtees) 526 In reparacione I strakis, 35 straknaill' et 4 wyndbandes, 23*d.* 1407–8 in Hudson & Tingey *Rec. Norwich* (1910) II. 55 [To the same for] carte strakes, cloutes [and nails]. 1519 tr. *Rentale Dunkeld.* (S.H.S.) 299 Making 4 lie straikis of iron for lie extreis, 4*d.* 1538 ELYOT *Dict.*, *Canthus*, the yron wherwith the extremytie of wheeles be bounden, the straake of a carte. 1539 *Archæologia* XI. 439, 23 stracks of iron for saker and fawcon whelys. 1587 *Wills & Inv. N.C.* (Surtees 1860) 308, xj straikes of iron, for byndyng a paire of wheles. c 1611 CHAPMAN *Iliad* xx. 347 His body..Which Grecian horse broke with the strakes, naild to their chariot wheeles. 1710 J. HARRIS *Lex. Techn.* II, *Straiks*, in Gunnery, are Plates of Iron of the length and breadth of one of the 6 Felloes, which serve for the Round of the Wheel of a Gun-carriage. 1794 W. FELTON *Carriages* (1801) I. 112 The strake is the short iron with which the common wheel is rung. 1832 *Scoreby Farm Rep.* 3 in *Libr. Usef. Knowl., Husb.* III, The plough.. is..made of ash-wood, with a mould-board and slips, or strakes of cast iron. 1888 HARDY *Wessex Tales* II. 187 The waggon-wheels be without strakes. 1894 A. JESSOPP *Random Roaming*, etc. 138 The next best substitute for tyres, to wit, thick iron plates, called strakes, attached to the fellies by long spikes.

β. 1565 COOPER *Thesaurus*, *Vietus*, an hoope, or a streake of a carte. 1683 *Pat. Office* 229. 1 A new Invencion of makeing severall things of Iron..as Streaks or Tire for Wheeles, &c. 1797 J. CURR *Coal Viewer* 15 The corf.. contains neat measure clear of the boxes which cover the wheels, to the streak, 20491 solid inches. 1858 *Straith's Fortif. & Artillery* (ed. 7) II. 121 The English tire is on in six pieces, called streaks. 1876 VOYLE & STEVENSON *Milit. Dict.* 411/2 *Streak*, iron plate fastened in pieces to form the tire round the circumference of gun-carriage or other wheels [etc.].

2. A stripe of different colour from the rest of the surface of which it forms part: = STREAK *sb.*[1]

1398 TREVISA *Barth. De P.R.* XVI. iii. (Tollemache MS.) Alabaster is a white stone with strakes of diuerse coloure. 1496–7 *Rec. St. Mary at Hill* (1905) 33 A diaper towell.. with vj strakis at euerye ende. 1537 BIBLE ('Matthew') *Gen.* xxx. 37 Iacob toke roddes of..hasell & of chestnot-trees, & pylled whyte strakes [so 1611; COVERDALE, strekes] in them. 1555 EDEN *Decades* (Arb.) 381 Summe lowe places..looke like redde cliffes with white strakes like wayes a cable length a piece. 1577 B. GOOGE *Heresbach's Husb.* III. 116 b, Others commend the blacke, specially if he haue either white starre in his forhed, or strake downe his face. 1589 GREENE *Tullies Love* Wks. (Grosart) VII. 123 The purest Chrisolite hath his strakes. 1590 SPENSER *F.Q.* II. iv. 15 His burning eyen, whom bloody strakes did staine. 1610 GUILLIM *Heraldry* III. xiv. (1611) 131 His colour most commonly sandie with a blacke strake along his backe. 1662 J. DAVIES tr. *Olearius' Voy. Ambass.* 70 As soon as their Maids become marriageable, they make several blew strakes in their faces. a 1700 EVELYN *Diary* June 1645, They weare very long crisped haire, of severall strakes and colours. 1735 DYCHE & PARDON *Dict.*, *Strake*,..also any Stroke or Mark of a different Colour upon Cattle, Fruit, &c. 1750 W. ELLIS *Mod. Husb.* III. i. 131 (E.D.S.) Mix beaten salt regularly with [the butter],..else the buttermilk, whey, and salt will shew themselves in strakes. 1879 G. MACDONALD *Sir Gibbie* li, There's ae unco black ane [cloud] yon'er..wi' a straik o' white, aboot the thrapple o' 't.

3. *Naut.* Each of the several continuous lines of planking or plates, of uniform breadth, in the side of a vessel, extending from stem to stern. Hence, the breadth of a plank used as a unit of vertical measurement in a ship's side.

binding-strake, see quot. 1867. *garboard strake*, see GARBOARD.

α. 1419 ALCETRE in Ellis *Orig. Lett.* Ser. II. I. 69 At the making of this Letter yt [*sc.* the ship] was in this estate, that ys to wetyng xxxvj strakys in hyth ybordyd, on the weche strakys byth ylayde xi bemys. 1537 *St. Papers Hen. VIII*, I. 569 The greate tymber of the ship is alredy framed, and thre strakes therof planked. 1627 CAPT. SMITH *Sea Gram.* xi. 53 By ripping off the plankes two or three strakes vnder water. 1727 BAILEY vol. II. s.v. *Strake*, *To heel a Strake* [Sea Term], a Ship is said so to do, when she inclines or hangs more to one Side than another, the Quantity of a whole Plank's Breadth. 1769 FALCONER *Dict. Marine* (1780), *Black-strakes*, a range of planks immediately above the wales in a ship's side. 1840 *Civil Engin. & Arch. Jrnl.* III. 349/2 The lower 6 strakes which form the bottom, and extend from the keel-plate to the turn of the bilge, are clinker-built. 1867 SMYTH *Sailor's Word-bk.* 102 *Binding-strakes*, thick planks on the decks, in midships, between the hatchways. Also the principal strakes of plank in a vessel. 1892 KIPLING *Barrack-r. Ballads, The 'Bolivar'* 143 We..Heard the seas like drunken men pounding at her strake. 1894 *Act 57 & 58 Vict.* c. 60, Sch. 2 (1) Deducting the average thickness of the ceiling which is between the bilge planks and limber strake. 1896 KIPLING *Seven Seas, Derelict* 75 The footless, floating weed Folds me and fouls me, strake on strake upcrawling. 1914 *Blackw. Mag.* Apr. 501/2 The yawl was now being raised a strake that she might follow the long boat.

β. a 1612 RALEGH *Let. to Pr. Henry* Sceptick etc. (1651) 130 Which with a deep keel and standing streak she would perform. 1748 *Anson's Voy.* I. x. 104 The ship heeled afterwards two streaks to port. 1773 *Cook's 1st Voy.* III. iv. in Hawkesw. *Voy.* III. 567 He reported that three streaks of the sheathing, about eight feet long, were wanting. 1797 S. JAMES *Narr. Voy.* 192 Hove the ship six streaks out of water. 1840 R. H. DANA *Bef. Mast* xxxv. 134 We painted her on the outside, giving her open ports in her streak. 1856 'STONEHENGE' *Brit. Rural Sports* II. VIII. iii. 475/1 When first these boats were introduced, they were almost always built of four or five streaks, or planks, on each side. 1863 READE *Hard Cash* xiv, The Agra rose a streak; and the next wave carried her a little farther in shore.

b. ? Erroneous definition.

1688 HOLME *Armoury* III. 166/2 *Strake*, is a seam between two Planks. 1704 J. HARRIS *Lex. Techn.* I.

†**4.** A reef in a sail. *Obs.*

1399 LANGL. *Rich. Redeles* IV. 80 For ne had þei striked a strake..And abated a bonet or þe blast come, þey had be þrowe ouere þe borde backewarde ichonne.

†**5.** A strip, narrow tract (of land or water). *Obs.*

1503 in *Trans. Roy. Hist. Soc.* (1902) 152 Beyng yn a strake of a meadowe lyeng yn the bak syde of Crambroke. 1511 *Guylforde's Pilgr.* (Camden) 12 This Morrea is.. almoste inuyrounde with the see, excepte one strake of a .vj. myle brode, whiche yeueth entre into Grecia. 1577–87 HARRISON *England* II. iv. 155 in *Holinshed*, Lach lade, which is parted from the main countie of Barkeshire by a little strake of Oxfordshire. a 1578 LINDSAY (Pitscottie) *Chron. Scot.* (S.T.S.) I. 336 Ane great fowsie and strak of watter.

b. A stretch of ground travelled over. Also, length of stride; speed in travelling, pace.

1558 PHAER *Æneid* VIII. (1562) Cc I, Thei through ye thornie downs..in armour iointly ryde, hie shoutes vprise, & clustring strakes thei gallup. 1804 in *Daily Chron.* (1904) 25 Aug. 4/7 [Her horse had] much the shorter strake of the two. 1823 W. TENNANT *Card. Beaton* V. vii. 171 Aweel, we've haen a fine straik, an' are now safe hame agen. 1865 MRS. WHITNEY *Gayworthys* xvi, 'Well, I'm restless,' replied Gershom,..'she's [the ship's] going a good streak, ain't she? We'll be in by to-morrow night, they say.'

†**6.** A ray, beam of light. *Obs.*

c 1400 *Three Kings Cologne* (1886) 34 Þe sterre..is nothyng liche to sterres þat be peynted here in diuers places: ffor hit had iiij many longe strakys and beemys. 1594 NASHE *Terrors Nt.* Wks. 1904 I. 354 Bloody streamers, blasing Comets, fire strakes. a 1633 AUSTEN *Medit.* (1635) 28 So.. Followes him a heavenly strake, Darting Light through all his path. 1825 R. CARRUTHERS in F. Miller *Poets Dumfriesh.* (1910) 224 In quiet lang straiks the holie licht lay On the swaird.

7. A swath (of mown grass); a wisp (of straw).

1585 HIGINS *Junius' Nomencl.* 124/2 *Fœni striga*,..the swathe or strake of grasse, as it lyeth mowne downe with the sithe. 1909 JANE BARLOW *Irish Ways* I To darn his thatched roof with strakes of straw.

†**8.** A wheel-rut. *Obs.*

1617 MINSHEU *Ductor* s.v., The Strake of a wheele [is so called]..because it makes a strake in the ground as it goeth. 1655 tr. *Sorel's Com. Hist. Francion* III. 53 At last, lighting into the Concave of a strake [F. *horniere*] made by the Wheel of the Sun's Chariot, there my Course was stopp'd.

9. *Comb.*: **strake-nail**, a kind of nail used for fastening the strakes to the wheel; †**strake-shide**, a piece of wood forming one of the timbers of a saw-pit; **strake-tire**, a tire composed of strakes.

1334–5 *Strake-nail [see 1]. 1570 *Wills & Inv. N.C.* (Surtees 1835) 329, I do gyue..vnto my Godsonn Mychiell tompson..a great naill tull & a straicke naill tull. 1802 C. JAMES *Milit. Dict.*, *Streak-Nails* are those which fasten the streaks to the fellies of the wheels. 1536 *Churchw. Acc. Yatton* (Somerset Rec. Soc.) 150 Payd for drawyng of *strake schyd to ye sayd pytte, v^d. 1837 W. B. ADAMS *Carriages* 95 The application of what is called a 'hoop tire' instead of a '*strake tire'.

†**strake,** *sb.*[2] *Hunting. Obs.* [Belongs to STRAKE *v.*[2]] Some particular signal with the horn.

c 1400 *Master of Game* (MS. Digby 182) xxxv, þan shulde he blowe a moot and strake withoute þe moote in þe mydle forto drawe men togedre. 1470–85 MALORY *Arthur* x. lii. 500 And alle the blastes that longen to all maner of gamen. Fyrste to the vncoupelynge, to the sekynge,..and to strake, and many other blastes and termes. 1576 TURBERV. *Venerie, Meas. Blowing* (1908) 251 The Strake to the Fielde. To be blowen with twoo windes. *Ibid.* 254 A Strake of nyne, to drawe home the companie. With twoo windes.

strake (streɪk), *sb.*[3] *Mining.* Also **strek, streke.** [Of obscure origin.

Possibly the same word as STRAKE *sb.*[1]; cf. *strake-shide* (STRAKE *sb.*[1] 9) and *side-strakes*, used dial. for the two longitudinal timbers of a sawpit (*W. Som. Wd.-bk.*); it seems likely that the word was applied in the plural to the boards lining the washing pit, and then to the whole apparatus.]

a. A shallow pit for the purpose of washing ore. **b.** A wooden box without ends, used for the same purpose.

1758 BORLASE *Nat. Hist. Cornwall* 203 In several pits made for that purpose called the strakes, it [the poorer sort of ore] is washed clean. 1778 PRYCE *Min. Cornub.* 226 At the higher end is a circular pit called the Strêk or Strep, large enough to contain four hand barrows full of slime. *Ibid.* 227 The rough grains lie at the bottom of the strêk. *Ibid.* 233 The strêke or strakes is made of two deal boards laid flat for a bottom fourteen inches in the ground. 1860 *Mining Gloss., Cornw.* 24 *Strake*, a launder, or box of wood without ends, in which the process of washing or tying is performed.

c. *Gold-mining.* An apparatus for concentrating the stamped ore.

1887 J. A. PHILLIPS & BAUERMAN *Elem. Metall.* (ed. 2) 789 The discharge from the screens..is..conducted over inclined strakes each 20 inches in width and 22 feet in length, which have a fall of 1 in 10. These strakes are made of well-seasoned $1\frac{1}{2}$ inch planks nailed to triangular frames.

d. *attrib.*

1839 DE LA BECHE *Rep. Geol. Cornwall*, etc. xv. 593 The stony part, from its great volume, accumulated at the lower end or tail of the strake-boards. 1887 J. A. PHILLIPS & BAUERMAN *Elem. Metall.* (ed. 2) 789 Each end of the strake-frame is supported [etc.].

†**strake,** *sb.*[4] *Obs. rare*[−1]. [Either the northern form of STROKE *sb.* (misused, as the scene is Shrewsbury), or an error for STRIKE *sb.*] A bushel: = STRIKE, STROKE *sbs.*

1706 FARQUHAR *Recruiting Officer* III. i, *Bull.* Come Ruose, Ruose, I sold fifty Strake of Barley to day in half this time.

strake (streɪk), *v.*[1] *Obs.* exc. *dial.* [app. f. OTeut. root **strak-* whence **strakjan* to STRETCH. Cf. NFris. *straake*, to stretch oneself.]

1. *intr.* To move, go, proceed.

13.. *Bonaventura's Medit.* 661 To hys fete anon þan þey straked. c 1369 CHAUCER *Dethe Blaunche* 1312 And with that worde, ryght anoon They gan to strake forth [*Skeat conjectures* They gon forth straken (*or* striken)], al was doon For that tyme the herte huntynge. 1394 *P. Pl. Crede* 82 Wiþ sterne staues and stronge þey ouer lond strakeþ. 1860 MISS YONGE *Hopes & Fears* I. 290 Some villanous slander, of course, there is, but it is no business of yours to be straking off to make it worse.

†**2.** To extend, stretch. *Obs.*

1594 R. C[AREW] *Tasso* (1881) 74 A beard bigge, bushy, knotted gristelly: From wrapped muzzle down his rough bosom strakes.

†**strake,** *v.*[2] *Hunting. Obs.* [Of obscure origin: cf. STRAKE *sb.*[2]] *trans.* To sound (a particular call) on the horn. Also *absol.* or *intr.* Hence †'**straking** *vbl. sb.*

13.. *Gaw. & Gr. Knt.* 1364 Strakande ful stoutly mony stif motez. *Ibid.* 1923. a 1400–50 *Wars Alex.* 1386 Steryn steuyn vp strake strakid þar trumpis. c 1400 *Master of Game* (MS. Digby 182) xxxiii, And whan þer is nought ylefte, þan shulnde þe lorde gyfe hym luste, and elles þe maistre of þe game..shulde strake in þis wyse: þat is to say blowe .IIII. moot a litell lenger þan þe first IIII. *Ibid.* xxxv, þei shulde strake þe assise þat longeth to þe herte slayne with strength. *Ibid.*, And alle oþere hunters shall strake þe common strakynge as is aboue deuysed and seyde. 14.. in *Rel. Ant.* I. 152, I shall blowe a mote, and aftirward I shall strake after myn houndes. **1470-85** MALORY *Arthur* IX. xxi. 370 Thenne kyng Mark blewe and straked and there with his knyghtes came to hym. **1576** TURBERV. *Venerie, Meas. Blowing* (1908) 252 The Straking from Couert to Couert. With twoo windes.

†**strake**, *v.*[3] *Obs.* Also 6-7 *Sc.* straik. [perh. a northern form of STROKE *v.* But cf. STREAK *v.*[2]]

1. *trans.* ? To sharpen, whet.

1483 *Cath. Angl.* 367/1 To Strake, *affilare.*

2. To rub lightly, esp. with an unguent or the like; to smear, grease. Also with *over.* Also to smear (an unguent, etc.) *upon* something.

1506 *Acc. Ld. High Treas. Scot.* III. 203 Item, for mending of thre irn boltis and straking of ane axtree, xviij s. **1535** COVERDALE *Ezek.* iv. 12 Barly cakes shalt thou eate, yet shalt thou first strake them ouer with mans donge, y[t] they maye se it. **1561** HOLLYBUSH *Hom. Apoth.* 7 Let hys lamed lymmes be straked wyth water of Lauender. *Ibid.* 21 Strake thys [*sc.* a lotion] oft about hys heade. **1578** LYTE *Dodoens* I. ii. 6 With the same [preparation]..they vse to rubbe and strake painefull bleered eyes. **1579** LANGHAM *Gard. Health* 68 Bengewin..Being straked on the eyes with Hony, it quickeneth the sight. **1588** A. KING tr. *Canisius' Catech.* 72 It [*sc.* the chrism] is in this sacrament straiked be solemn cæremonie vpon the forhead. **1600** SURFLET *Country Farm* I. xxv. 159 Afterward you shall strake the shorne sheepe all ouer their skins with your drie hande, moistened in oile and wine mingled togither, to comfort them withall. **1676** ROW *Contn. Blair's Autobiogr.* xii. (1848) 427 Others thought he was but straking cream in their mouths first.

3. To draw (something) along a surface.

c **1530** *Interl. Beauty & Gd. Prop. Women* C ij, A foule rough bych..strakyng her body along on the gras.

Hence †**straking** *vbl. sb. concr.*

1409 *Acc. Exch. K.R.* 44/11 (3) m. 3 In .j. lagena incasti [*sic*] empta..et expendita in reparacione del strakynge pro pictura eiusdem [bargie].

strake (streɪk), *v.*[4] [f. STRAKE *sb.*[1]]

†**1.** *trans.* To mark with lines, to streak. *Obs.*

1537 [cf. STRAKED *ppl. a.*]. **1552** in *Archæologia* XLIII. 236, j red hangynge of silke straked withe golde. **1577** B. GOOGE *Heresbach's Husb.* I. 31 The stalke is..straked [L. *strigato*] like to the greater Fearne. **1591** PERCIVALL *Sp. Dict., Rayar,*..to strake out. **1600** HAKLUYT *Voy.* III. 392 They..brought..many mantles of cotton straked with blew and white. **1613** PURCHAS *Pilgrimage* (1614) 699 Faire Iacinthes, that are good Iewels, straked like as it were with Naturall veines. **1718** J. FOX *Publ. Spirit* 13 Just when the Morning Goddess..strak'd with infant Light the Eastern Skies.

2. *intr.* To become streaky.

1911 MASEFIELD *Everlasting Mercy* (1912) 56 The peacock screamed, the clouds were straking, My cut cheek felt the weather breaking.

strake (streɪk), *v.*[5] *Mining.* Also 8 streke. [f. STRAKE *sb.*[3]] *trans.* To wash (ore) in a strake. Also *Gold-mining*, to concentrate (ore) by means of strakes.

1778 PRYCE *Min. Cornub.* 233 Throwing aside the poorer part, which is afterwards to be streked and washed. **1839** DE LA BECHE *Rep. Geol. Cornwall*, etc. xv. 592 The poorer ores were put aside to be straked. **1882** *Rep. Ho. Repr. Prec. Met. U.S.* 608 Their plan of concentration being principally what is called 'straking', consisting of a number of fixed inclined trays 30 feet in length.

strake: see STRAIK, STRIKE *v.*, STROKE.

straked (streɪkt), *a.* [f. STRAKE *sb.*[1] + -ED[2].] Of a wheel: Furnished with strakes.

a **1571** JEWEL *Serm.* (*Josh.* vi. 1-3) (1583) A vij b, The Ægyptians had mightie chariots, straked and barred with yron. **1801** W. FELTON *Carriages* I. 111 There are three descriptions of wheels, viz:—the straked, the hooped, and the patent rim.

straked, *ppl. a.* Now *rare.* Also 7 stracked. [f. STRAKE *v.*[4] Cf. STREAKED.] Streaked, striped.

1537 BIBLE ('Matthew') *Gen.* xxx. 40 And the shepe conceaued before the staues & brought forth straked, spotted and partie. **1585** HIGINS *Junius' Nomenclator* 273/2 A straked target. **1597** GERARDE *Herbal* I. xix. 25 The White Chameleon grasse, or straked grasse. **1664** BEALE in *Evelyn's Pomona* 26 A Red-strak'd Must. *Ibid.*, These and other differences, Straked, Must [1683 Straked-Must], right Red-strake, Red-red-strake, &c. **1688** HOLME *Armory* II. 183/1 Roed and Stracked like a Leopard. **1727** BAILEY vol. II, *Straked*, having Strakes or Lines. **1939** A. RANSOME *Secret Water* xxix. 343 He could not help smiling..at the memory of the savages ringed, straked and spotted in the war-paint of mud.

straken, -ins, var. ff. STRAIKEN.

strakur, obs. var. STREAKER, hound.

straky ('streɪkɪ), *a.* Now *dial.* [f. STRAKE *sb.*[1] + -Y.] Streaky.

1650 VENNER *Via Recta* (ed. 3) 197 Bloudwort..is well known by the red strakie colour of the leaves. **1886** *W. Som. Wordbk.* s.v., I likes bacon straky, nit all fat. **1887** BLACKMORE *Springhaven* ix, The weariless tide..gurgled with a quiet wash along the straky bends.

†**strale**. *Obs.*[−0] ? Also starle. [Cf. Flem. *straal* (De Bo; Kilian 16th c. *straele*), a use of *straal* beam, ray, orig. arrow; also Flem. *ster* (lit. 'star') in the same sense.] The pupil of the eye.

1574 WITHALS *Dict.* 62/2 The strale [1562, 1566 starle] of the eye, *pupilla.*

strale: see STRAIL, STREALE.

†**strall**. *Obs.*[−1]. [a. Du. *straal.*] A beam, ray.

a **1618** SYLVESTER *Sonnets* xii, The fiery Strall of Jove.

stram (stræm), *v. U.S. colloq.* and *dial.* (now *Obs.* or *rare*). [Perh. suggested by words like STROLL, TRAMP.] *intr.* To stretch out the limbs; to walk in a flourishing manner.

1792 F. BURNEY *Jrnl.* 27 June in *Jrnls. & Lett.* (1972) I. 209 He bowed without looking at her, & she strammed away, still, however, keeping in sight. *a* **1852** F. M. WHITCHER *Widow Bedott Papers* (1856) xxv. 306 She..strammed right across the room and sot down. **1866** W. GREGOR *Dial. Banffshire* 184 *Stram, v.n.* to walk with a rude, noisy step. **1869** MRS. STOWE *Oldtown Folks* xliii. (1870) 489 Well, Sam, ..take an old woman's advice, and don't go stramming off another afternoon. **1890** *Dialect Notes* I. 19 *Stram*, flourish the limbs. It is used in two ways: (1) 'to go stramming along the street', 'to stram about the room', that is, stride with ado and bustle; and (2) 'to stram about in bed' = flounder, kick about. **1927** *Amer. Speech* III. 138 A young child crying and displaying temper was said to 'kick and stram'. This word *stram* means in older English 'to recoil with violence and noise', which gives a vivid picture of a child in a tantrum.

Hence as *sb.*, a long, hard walk; also '**stramming** *ppl. a.*

1869 MRS. STOWE *Oldtown Folks* xliii. (1870) 483 Do you think she ever could have made me a great stramming, threshing, scrubbing, floor-cleaning machine, like herself? *Ibid.* xlv. 511, I hed sech a stram this mornin', 'n hain't hed nothin' but a two-cent roll.

†**stramage**. *Obs.*[−1] [a. OF. **estramage*, f. *estramer* to spread with straw or rushes :—pop.L. **strāmināre* from L. *strāmen* straw.] Rushes with which a floor is strewed.

14.. *Promp. Parv.* 480/2 (MS. H.) Strowynge or stramage, *stramentum* [Pynson *stramagium*].

stramash (strə'mæʃ), *sb.* Chiefly *Sc.* Also *Sc.* straemash. [Belongs to STRAMASH *v.*]

1. An uproar, state of noise and confusion; a 'row'.

1821 GALT *Ann. Parish* xii. 124 This stramash was the first time that I had interposed in the family concerns of my people. **1823** —— *R. Gilhaize* xiv, There's like to be a straemash amang the Reformers. *a* **1840** J. RAMSAY *Poems, Sports Fasten's-een* v, Mark ye yon fish..He's laughin' at the grand stramash, And thinks he's safe frae harm. **1840** BARHAM *Ingol. Leg., House-Warm.* xxi, Oh! what a fearful 'stramash' they are all in! **1861** H. KINGSLEY *Ravenshoe* xxxvi, Last year at Oxford, I and three other University men ..had a noble stramash on Folly Bridge. That is the last fighting I have seen. **1896** *Spectator* 28 Mar. 444 The Muscular Christians rebelled at these ideas with a stir and stramash audible to all men.

2. A state of ruin, a smash. *to go (to) stramash*: to be ruined.

1819 W. TENNANT *Papistry Storm'd* (1827) 2 And fearfu' the stramash and stour, Whan pinnacle cam doun and tow'r. **1829** BROCKETT *N.C. Gloss.* (ed. 2), *Stramash*, a complete overthrow, with great breakage and confusion. **1896** 'IAN MACLAREN' *Kate Carnegie* 364 It's been rotten,..for a while, an' noo it's fair stramash. **1910** N. MUNRO in *Blackw. Mag.* Jan. 32/1 My business would go to stramash.

stramash (strə'mæʃ), *v. dial.* [app. onomatopoetic: cf. SMASH.

Notwithstanding the curiously close resemblance in sense, the commonly alleged derivation from It. *stramazzare* (see STRAMAZON) is out of the question.]

(See quot. 1788.)

1788 W. H. MARSHALL *Yorksh.* II. 356 To *Stramash*; to crush, or break irreparably; to destroy. **1880** J. F. S. GORDON *Chron. Keith* 70 Choking the lums with a divot (which occasionally stramashed the Tea Pots).

†**stramazo**. *Obs. rare*[−1]. [a. It. *stramazzo.*] = next.

1605 SYLVESTER *Du Bartas* II. iii. I. *Vocation* 769 Such thrusts, such foyns, stramazos, and stoccados.

†**stramazon**. *Fencing. Obs.* Also 6-7 stramazone, 6, 9 -zoun, 7 -son, -zoon, stramison, 9 stramaçon. [ad. It. *stramazzone* (also *stramazzo*) a knock-down blow, f. *stramazzare* to knock (a person) down, f. *stramazzo* straw mattress, straw strewn on the floor, f. *strame*:—L. *strāmen* straw. Some of the forms are influenced by F. *estramaçon*: see ESTRAMAZONE.] 'A vertical downward cut in rapier fence, which is delivered at the head with the part of the weapon close to the point' (Hutton, *Fixed Bayonets* 1890, Gloss. s.v. *Stramazzone* It.).

1595 *Saviolo's Practise* I. F 2, He may giue him a slicing or cutting blow, which we call *Stramazone.* **1599** B. JONSON *Ev. Man out of Hum.* IV. iv, But I..made a kind of stramazoun, ran him vp to the hilts, through the doublet. **1603** DEKKER *Wonderf. Yeare* D 4, He [Sickness] has his.. Stramazones and Stoccataes at his fingers ends. **1637** NABBES *Microcosm.* II. i. C 2 b, Then have wee..our stramisons, passatas, carricadas, amazzas and incartatas. **1651** J. S. *Prince of Priggs Revels* I. 2 Drink deep my brave boyes of the Bastinado Of Stramazons, Tinctures [etc.]. *a* **1668** DAVENANT *Man's the Master* v. i. (1669) 67 *D. Lewis.* I have lost blood... *D. Ferd.* I'st by Stoccado, or Stramason? **1826** SCOTT *Woodstock* xix, But where is the rascal I killed?—I never made a fairer *stramaçon* in my life.

‖**strambotto** (stram'bɔtto). Pl. strambotti. [It.] An Italian verse form of eight lines, common esp. in the 15th and 16th centuries and freq. set to music.

1914 G. WARRACK *Folk Songs of Tuscan Hills* p.v., Of the verse-form which belongs to the Sicilian equivalent of the *Rispetto*, the *Canzona* or *Strambotto*, an octave of lines alternately rhyming, there is said to be only one example amongst the Tuscan poems. *Ibid.*, Tigri notes that the octave poems amongst the *Rispetti* are sometimes also in the Pistoian mountains called *Strambotti* (a word derived.. from *strani motti* = 'strange words, quaint conceits'); some writers give this name to the Sententious Rispetti. **1931** J. TORBARINA *Italian Influence on Poets of Ragusan Republic* II. iii. 143 Their origin..is the ottava of the Italian *strambotto.* Though it had its prime towards the end of the preceding century, the *strambotto* continued to flourish far into the Italian Cinquecento. **1960** *New Oxf. Hist. Music* III. xi. 395 The collection [*sc.* the fourth book of Petrucci's frottole] contains 47 *strambotti*, 19 *frottole*, 14 *ode*, and 9 *sonetti.* The appearance of *strambotti* in such great number is noteworthy, for although their artistic value is low indeed, from this form developed the later *ottava rima.* **1980** *Early Music* Jan. 104/2 Among the other compositions there is a *barzelletta* setting and a *strambotto* both by Cara, a number of *ballate mezzane*, and a sonnet.

stramel, variant of STRUMMEL, straw.

stramin ('stræmɪn). [ad. Da. *stramin*, maker's name for the material.] A kind of coarse sacking formerly used for making nets for sea fishing.

1914 *Jrnl. Marine Biol. Assoc. U.K.* X. 328 The nets used were constructed on the system of the Petersen young-fish trawl, and three qualities of material were used. These were coarse sacking ('Stramin'), with mesh $\frac{1}{16}$" square; cheesecloth,..and mosquito netting. **1925** *Ibid.* XIII. 769 The material known as 'stramin',..on account of its cheapness and durability compared with silk makes large nets for everyday use a possibility. **1936** *Nature* 30 May 915/1 The larger tunicates were abundant in the stramin net. **1959** H. BARNES *Oceanogr. and Marine Biol.* ii. 25 (*caption*) Large stramin net coming to the surface. This is made from fairly coarse material and is used to catch the larger zooplankton organisms. **1970** *Jrnl. Marine Biol. Assoc. U.K.* L. 709 The previous stramin mesh has been replaced with a knitted Terylene material, which has a higher porosity than stramin, and is less expensive than either stramin or nylon.

stramineous (strə'mɪnɪːəs), *a.* [f. L. *strāmine-us* (f. *strāmen* straw) + -OUS.]

1. Consisting of or relating to straw; *fig.* valueless.

1621 BURTON *Anat. Mel.* I. ii. IV. vii. (1624) 148 His sole study is for words, that..not a syllable [be] misplaced, to set out a stramineous subiect. **1641** C. BURGES *Serm.* 5 Nov. 33 Much ado made about a supposed stramineous Miracle of Garnets face found in a straw. **1658** J. ROBINSON *Endoxa, Calm Ventil.* II. 123 Upon a suddain approach of the warmed Electrick, the stramineous bodies will, at first, a little recede. **1900** SAINTSBURY *Hist. Criticism* I. 66 He not only seems to be dealing with men of straw, but answers them with, as Luther would say, a most 'stramineous' argument.

2. *Bot.* Straw-coloured; dull pale yellow.

1845-50 MRS. LINCOLN *Lect. Bot.* 204/1 *Stramineous*, straw-like, straw-coloured. **1871** W. A. LEIGHTON *Lichen-flora* 99 Ochroleucous or stramineous.

stramison: see STRAMAZON.

'**strammel**. *Obs.* exc. *dial.* Also stramel. [Of obscure origin: cf. dial. *scrammel* in the same sense, also STRUMMEL.] 'A lean, gaunt, ill-favoured person or animal' (Miss Jackson *Shropsh. Word-bk.*).

1706 E. WARD *Hud. Rediv.* I. xii. 19 Strutting about on hide-bound Strammel, Mounted like Turk upon a Camel. **1711** —— *Quix.* I. 28 When thus he had prepar'd his Stramel, Tall as an Elephant or Camel. **1879** in Miss Jackson *Shropsh. Word-bk.* art. *Scrammel, Shammel*, A great strammel of a pig.

stramonium (strə'məʊnɪəm). Also 7 strammonium, 8 stramonia. [a. mod.L. *stramonium* (Parkinson 1629), *strammonium* (F. Columna 1592), *stramonia* (Fuchs 1542, given as Italian), of uncertain origin. Cf. F. *stramoine* (more usually *stramonium*), Sp., Pg. *estramónio*, It. *stramonio.*

The Russian synonym *dur'man* is said by Miklosich to be adopted from the Kazan Tartar *turman*, 'a medicine for horses'. It seems possible that *stramonia* may be altered from an earlier form or a dialectal variant of the Tartar word.]

1. The solanaceous plant *Datura Stramonium*, the THORN-APPLE. ***purple stramonium***: the purple thorn-apple, *Datura Tatula.*

1677 GREW *Anat. Plants* IV. III. v. (1682) 188 The Seed-Case of Stramonium or Thorn Apple, is divided into Four Closets. **1694** Strammonium [see THORN-APPLE]. **1706** PHILLIPS (ed. Kersey), *Stramonia*,..the Apple of Peru, or Thorn-Apple. **1741** *Compl. Fam.-Piece* II. iii. 357 Tender annual Flowers,..such as..double-flowering Stramonium. **1881** *Harper's Mag.* Oct. 648 See this long bouquet of Bouncing-Bet, stramonium and pansy. **1906** TUCKWELL *Remin. Radical Parson* x. 140, I had seen a heavy profit reaped by a shrewd farmer who took it at a low rate on poppies, henbane, and stramonium.

2. A narcotic drug prepared from this plant.

1802 *Med. Jrnl.* VIII. 427, I have found the stramonium especially beneficial in cases of mania attended with little or no fever. **1887** MOLONEY *Forestry W. Afr.* 395 The properties of stramonium are regarded as anodyne and anti-spasmodic.

3. *attrib.*

1840 PEREIRA *Elem. Mat. Med.* II. 865 Stramonium seeds, bruised. **1856** G. B. WOOD *Therap. & Pharmacol.* I. 809 Stramonium Leaves. *Ibid.* 810 Stramonium Root. **1868** GARROD *Mat. Med.* (ed. 3) 291 In extracting the alkaloids from corresponding parts of belladonna and stramonium plants. **1888** *Pall Mall Gaz.* 22 May 6/1 Stramonium cigarettes.

stramony ('stræmənɪ). Also **strammony**. Anglicized form of STRAMONIUM.

1842 BRANDE *Dict. Sci.* etc., *Stramony* or Thorn Apple.

stramp, *sb. Sc.* [f. STRAMP *v.*] A stamp of the foot.

a **1578** LINDESAY (Pitscottie) *Chron. Scot.* (S.T.S.) I. 222 The strampe of Mr Patrickis was so sade upoun his brotheris footte. **1828** MOIR *Mansie Wauch* ix. 80 This was a stramp on his corny toe.

stramp (stræmp), *v. Sc.* [Perh. suggested by *stamp*, *tramp*, *stride*. Cf. G. *strampfen* in the same sense.]

1. *intr.* To set down the foot firmly; to tread heavily *on* something.

c **1423** JAS. I *Good Counsel* 19 (Camb. MS.), Stramp [*Bannatyne MS.* Graip] or thou slyd, and crep furth one the way. *c* **1480** HENRYSON *Orpheus & Euryd.* 105 (Bannatyne MS.) Scho strampit [*Asloan* trampit] on a serpent vennemus. *a* **1508** DUNBAR *Tua Mariit Wemen* 493 And him befor, with my fut fast on his I stramp. **1529** LYNDESAY *Compl.* 288 Now in the court seindell he gois, In dreid men stramp vpon his tois. **1536** BELLENDEN *Cron. Scot.* (1821) II. 86 All wemen that strampis on this sepulture sall be ay barrant. *a* **1578** LINDESAY (Pitscottie) *Chron. Scot.* (S.T.S.) I. 222 To that effect [he] strampit sadlie on his brotheris foott. **1616** *Orkney Witch Trial* in C. Rogers *Soc. Life Scot.* (1886) III. 300 His hors strampit vpon the leg of the said lamb and brak it. **1828** MOIR *Mansie Wauch* ii. 23 A fat and dumpy man..stramped on a favourite Newfoundland dog's tail.

2. *trans.* To tread upon; to trample *down. lit.* and *fig.* †*to stramp away, forth*: to stamp out.

1535 STEWART *Cron. Scot.* (Rolls) II. 266 Forbad also..in streit, To mak ane cors quhair men ȝeid on thair feit, That it sould not dishonorit be so far, Vnder thair feit to stramp into the glar. **1552** LYNDESAY *Monarche* 5795 Papis, for thare traditionis..Quhilk Christis Lawis strampit down. **1556** *Rec. Elgin* (New Spalding Club 1903) I. 31 That nane ..tak vpone hand to eitt distroy or stramp donne ony growand cornes with thair horssis. **1563** WINȜET tr. *Vincent. Lirin.* Wks. (S.T.S.) II. 76 The noueltie being strampit doun. *a* **1578** LINDESAY (Pitscottie) *Chron. Scot.* (S.T.S.) I. 85 It had bene goode..that the Earle..had bene rootted out of memorie, cleane strampit away. *Ibid.* 94 Deservand..his memorie to be abussit and strampit fourtht for ewer. **1589** R. BRUCE *Serm.* (1843) 52 The wicked are sayd to stramp the blood of Christ under their feet. **1866** J. SMITH *Merry Bridal* 7 His minnie..Had met his faither's ardent gaze, When at the burnie strampin' claes, Wi' coaties toshly kiltit.

strample ('stræmp(ə)l), *v. Sc.* [f. STRAMP *v.* + -LE.] *trans.* = STRAMP *v.* 2.

a **1610** SIR J. SEMPLE in *Sempill Ballatis* (1872) 253 Still strampl'd doune with sturte. **1896** P. A. GRAHAM *Red Scaur* xxii. 339 He rode the horse at you, as if he'd liked to strample you to death.

stran, variant of STRAND *sb.*[4]

strand (strænd), *sb.*[1] Forms: 1 **strand**, 2–6 **strande**, 3–6 **stronde**, 3–8 **strond**, (3 **straunde**, 6 **strounde**), 3– **strand**. [OE. *strand* (? neut.) = OFris. *strônd* (WFris. *strân*, *straun*, NFris. *strön*, *strunn*), MLG. *strant* (*strand-*) masc. (whence Du. *strand* neut., mod.G. *strand* masc.), ON. *strǫnd* (*strand-*) fem., border, edge, coast (Sw., Da. *strand*).]

1. a. The land bordering a sea, lake, or †river; in a more restricted sense, that part of a shore which lies between the tide-marks; sometimes used vaguely for coast, shore. Cf. SEA-STRAND. Now *poet.*, *arch.* or *dial.*

c **1000** *Ags. Gosp.* Matt. xiii. 48 þa hi þa þat nett uppatuȝon & sæton be þam strande. *Ibid.* John xxi. 4 Witodlice on ærne merȝen se hælend stod on þam strande. *a* **1066** *Charter of Eadweard* in Kemble *Cod. Dipl.* IV. 221 Ic ciðe eow ðæt Urk min huskarl habbe his strand eall, forneȝen hys aȝen land.. and eall ðæt to his strande ȝedryuen hys, be minum fullan bebode. *c* **1200** ORMIN 11155 Forr Crist, son summ he fullhtnedd wass & stiȝhenn upp o strande. *c* **1205** LAY. 17586 Þer heo nomen hauene..scipen eoden a þat strond, cnihtes eoden a þat lond. *c* **1250** *Gen. & Ex.* 2717 And moyses druȝ him to ðe strond, And stalle he dalf him ðe sond. *c* **1290** *Mary Magd.* 471 in *S. Eng. Leg.* 475 Þe prince stap out of þe schipe:..Opon þe stronde he ȝaf a lupe. *c* **1330** R. BRUNNE *Chron. Wace* (Rolls) 14049 Seuen hundred schipe lyn by þe stronde. *c* **1384** CHAUCER *H. Fame* 148 The Armes and also the man That first came..Vnto the strondes of Lauyne. **1390** GOWER *Conf.* II. 232 Thei ben comen sauf to londe, Wher thei gon out upon the stronde Into the Burgh. *c* **1430** LYDG. *Min. Poems* (Percy Soc.) 50 A lowe ground ebbe was fast by the strond, That no maryner durst take on hond To cast an anker. **1544** BETHAM *Precepts War* I. lii. Djb, Wherby other shyppes can not well arryue at anye strounde, ne yet go out of the hauen. **1593** PEELE *Honour of Garter* 15 The channel that divides The Frenchmen's strond fro Britain's fishy towns. *c* **1595** DONNE *Sat.* II. 78 Shortly (as the sea) hee will compasse all our land; From Scots, to Wight; from Mount, to Dover strand. **1632** J. HAYWARD tr. *Biondi's Eromena* 26 They walked along the strond, till they came to his Barke. **1681** DRYDEN *Abs. & Achit.* I. 272 The Joyful People throng'd to see him Land, Cov'ring the Beach and blackning all the Strand. **1718** PRIOR *Alma* II. 535 The Strand, Which compasses fair Albion's Land. **1759** *Ann. Reg.* 36/1 Quebec..consists of an upper and lower town, the lower..is built upon a strand, at the foot of a lofty rock. **1796** H. HUNTER *St.-Pierre's Stud. Nat.* (1799) II. 155 James Cartier and Champlain represent the strands of the lakes of North-America as shaded by stately walnut-trees. **1817** SHELLEY *Rev. Islam* I. xvi, On the bare strand Upon the sea-mark a small boat did wait. **1871** COUCH *Polperro* ii. 32 The next object of notice..is the beach, or 'strand', inside the old quay. **1911** E. BEVERIDGE *North Uist* vi. 132 Six [of the island-forts] are easily accessible over the strand at ebb-tide.

fig. **1649** JER. TAYLOR *Gt. Exemp.* Pref. ⁋25 God brought Moses law into the world to be as a strand to the inundation of impiety.

†**b.** in certain rhyming and alliterative phrases used in charters. *Obs.*

? **11..** *Charter of Eadweard* (A.D. 1066) in Kemble *Cod. Dipl.* IV. 192 Ic nelle..ðat ðær any man any onsting habbe on any þ[i]ngen oðe on any timen be strande ne bi lande buton [etc.]. **1155** *Charter Hen. II* in *Anglia* VII. 220 Saca & Socne, on strande & on Streame, on wudan & on feldan, tolles & theames, grithbriches & hamsocne & forstalles & infangenes thiafes & fleamene frimtha ofer heore aȝene men. **1208** *Rot. Chart.* (1837) 184/1 Habeant..omnia predicta.. cum soka et saca..et cum aliis consuetudinibus..warwagio suo bilaunde & bistraunde [etc.]. [**1706** PHILLIPS (ed. Kersey), *Strand and Stream*, an Expression formerly us'd for an immunity or freedom from Custom, and all Impositions upon Goods or Vessels by Land or by Water.]

†**c.** A quay, wharf, or landing-place by the side of navigable water. *Obs.*

den and strand: see DENE *sb.*[2] 2.

1205 *Rot. Chart.* (1837) 153/1 Habeant [barones de Hastinges] strand [*printed* strand] & dene apud Gernemue. **1577–87** HOLINSHED *Chron.* III. 1097/1 Sir Thomas Wiat hauing with him foureteene ensignes,..marched to Detford strand, eight miles from Detford. **1600** J. PORY tr. *Leo's Africa* VIII. 301 A most impregnable castle, which standeth vpon the strand or wharfe of the port. *c* **1600** in T. Brown *Misc. Aulica* (1702) 254 If any that hath a House or Land adjoining do make a Strand, Stairs, or such like, they pay forthwith Rent to the City of London. **1637** MILTON *Comus* 876 By Leucothea's lovely hands, And her son [*sc.* Portunus] that rules the strands. **1707** *Lond. Gaz.* No. 4397/3 He was ..one of the Elder Brothers of Trinity-House of Deptford-Strond. **1859** BARTLETT *Dict. Amer.* (ed. 2) 455 The Dutch on the Hudson River apply the term to a landing-place; as, the strand at Kingston.

d. ***the Strand***: the name of a street in London; originally so called as occupying, with the gardens belonging to the houses, the 'strand' or shore of the Thames between the cities of London and Westminster.

1246 *Misc. Rolls, Chancery* Bd. 3 No. 2 m. 1 Domos.. extra muros Ciuitatis nostre London, in vico qui vocatur le Straunde. **1601** F. GODWIN *Bps. Eng.* 262 Walter de Langton..built also..the pallace by the Strond at London. **1613** SHAKS. *Hen. VIII*, v. iv. 55 [She] cryed out Clubbes, when I might see from farre, some forty Truncheoners draw to her succour, which were the hope o' th' Strond where she was quartered. **1691** WOOD *Ath. Oxon.* II. 226 James Heath [was] Son of Rob. Heath the Kings Cutler, living in the Strand leading from London to Westminster. **1729** POPE *Dunc.* II. 28 Where the tall may-pole once o'er-look'd the Strand. **1790** PENNANT *London* 126–7, I shall resume my account at the opening of the Strand into Charing-Cross, by observing, that in the year 1353, that fine street the Strand was an open highway, with here and there a great man's house, with gardens to the water-side. **1823** BYRON *Island* II. xix, But less grand, Though not less loved, in Wapping or the Strand.

e. Used vaguely (like SHORE *sb.*[1] 1 c) for country, region, esp. a foreign country. Chiefly *poet.*

c **1386** CHAUCER *Prol.* 13 Thanne longen folk to goon on pilgrimages And Palmeres for to seken straunge strondes. *c* **1400** *Roland & Otuel* 1215 An hundrethe knyghtes of Turkeye Bare his Mawmettes hym by And paste ouer that strande. *c* **1590** GREENE *Fr. Bacon* (1594 facs.) F 3, Drugges ..Found in the wealthy strond of Affrica. **1704** COBB *Poems* (1709) 57 Sail, Happy Prince, to that expecting Strand Where wealthy Tagus rowls his golden Sand. **1821** SHELLEY *Hellas* 1028 Let Freedom and Peace flee far To a sunnier strand.

¶**2.** Used for SHORE *sb.*[4] *Obs.* (? *nonce-use.*)

1635 B. JONSON *Epigr. To a Friend* 13 Seek out some hungry painter, that..Will well design thee to be view'd by all, That sit upon the common draught or strand [*rhyme* brand].

3. a. *attrib.* and *Comb.*, as ***strand bank, bird, bush, -plant***; † **strand boat**, a shore boat; **strand fishery**, a coast fishery pursued from the shore (Webster *Suppl.* 1902); **strandflat** [partial tr. Da. *strandflade*, lit. 'beach expanse' (H. Reusch 1894, in *Norges Geol. Undersøgelse* No. 14. 1)], a very wide rocky platform, close to sea level, that extends along much of the Norwegian coastline between cliffs and the sea; (with *a* and *pl.*) any particular part of this; † **strand hedge** *Isle of Man*, a fence on the sea shore; **strand ice** (see quot.); **strand knife** *Whaling*, a knife for cutting blubber; **strand-line** *Geol.* (see quot.); **strand-nut** (see quot.); † **strand plat**, the beach or seashore; † **strandward** in advb. phr. *to* (*the*) ***strandward***, in the direction of the beach or sea-shore.

1881 tr. *Nordenskiold's Voy. 'Vega'* II. xiv. 225 At Nunamo the *strand-bank was gay with an exceedingly rich magnificence of colour. **1755** *Gentl. Mag.* XXV. 319 Among other birds in this country [Norway] are some that haunt the coast..called *strand birds. **1860** WRAXALL *Life in Sea* iii. 49 The Strand Birds, which live on the verge of the ocean, and on the beach deserted by the tide. **1670** CAPT. J. SMITH *Eng. Improv. Reviv'd* 268 To carry on this great Trade, they [the Hollanders] have 700 *Strand-boates. **1863** W. C. BALDWIN *Afr. Hunting* vii. 282 The inyala is only to be met with in the *strand bush along the coast. [**1906** *Q. Jrnl. Geol. Soc.* LXII. 87 Raised rock-platforms of marine origin.. were found along the Norwegian coast, and had been termed strandflade or 'coast-plane [*read* -plain]' by Dr. Reusch.] **1922** *Skrifter utgit av Videnskabsselskabet i Kristiania 1921: Mat.-Nat. Kl.* No. 11. 60 At Tangen, on the south side of Sogne Fjord,..there is a well-marked *strandflat..on which the houses are situated. **1934** R. A. DALY *Changing World Ice Age* v. 166 Along the coast of southern Norway the strandflat is a composite of three benches, with inner edges respectively 30 to 40 meters and 15 to 18 meters above sea and a few metres..below sea-level. **1940** *Geogr. Jrnl.* XCVI. 96 The origin of strandflats has interested many writers. **1954** W. D. THORNBURY *Princ. Geomorphol.* xvii. 436 The Strandflat along the west coast of Norway, which is thought by some to be of marine origin, has a maximum width of 40 miles. **1972** J. L. DAVIES *Geogr. Variation Coastal Devel.* vi. 87 The enormous width of strandflats in some places makes it difficult to conceive of them as extraordinarily extensive shore platforms and their origin remains obscure. **1723** in H. STOWELL *Life Wilson* App. I. (1819) 337 [Isle of Man] By the governor's granting licence to inclose the lands of several persons under their *strand hedges. **1897** tr. *Nansen's Farthest North* II. vii. 346 Close to our den there was an opening in the *strand-ice. *Note*, Ice which is frozen fast to the bottom, and is therefore left lying like an icy base along the shore. **1820** SCORESBY *Acc. Arctic Reg.* II. 299 Process of Flensing... The blubber..is received upon deck by the boat-steerers and line-managers: the former with *strand-knives divide it into portable cubical, or oblong pieces. **1910** *Encycl. Brit.* XI. 658/2 Proof of recent emergence of land is supplied by what are called 'raised beaches' or '*strand-lines', that is, lines of former shores marked by sheets of littoral deposits, or platforms cut by shore-waves in rock. **1860** J. F. CAMPBELL *Tales W. Highl.* I. Introd. 9 On the stormy coasts of the Hebrides,..fishermen..find..objects, somewhat like flat chestnuts.. which they call..*strand-nuts. **1906** *Daily Chron.* 13 Aug. 3/2 Most of the Hawaiian *strand-plants that are dispersed by the currents are found in America. **1582** STANYHURST *Æneis* II. (Arb.) 78 Father Anchises his palms from *strond plat inhauncing On gods heunlye cryeth. *c* **1400** *Beryn* 3138 So, walkyng to the *Strondward, wee bargeynyd by the wey. **1582** STANYHURST *Æneis* II. (Arb.) 56 Soom run to vessels too strondward swiftlye retyring.

b. In the names of birds, beasts, etc. that frequent the shores of seas, lakes, or estuaries, as **strand-plover**, **strand-runner** (see quots.; cf. STRANDLOOPER 2); **strand-wolf** [Du.], the name given in S. Africa to the striped hyena (*Hyæna brunnea*).

1772 RUTTY *Nat. Hist. Dublin* I. 324 The *Strand Plover, by some called, the Stone Plover. **1885** SWAINSON *Prov. Names Birds* 181 Grey plover (*Squatarola helvetica*)... Strand plover (Cork). **1706** PHILLIPS (ed. Kersey), **Strand-Runner*, a Bird of the bigness of a Lark, with a four-square Bill resembling a Rasp, which runs on the Rocks of Spitsberg and feeds on Worms. **1786** G. FORSTER tr. *Sparrman's Voy. Cape of Good Hope* I. 165 Two other voracious animals of this kind are found in Africa, which are distinguished by the names of mountain-wolf and *strand-wolf. **1826** A. SMITH *Catal. S. Afr. Mus.* I. 14 Striped Hyæna of the English. Strand Wolf of the Dutch. **1881** *Encycl. Brit.* XII. 420/2 If the strand wolf (*Hyæna villosa*) of the Cape colonists is only a variety of this species [*Hyæna striata*].

strand (strænd), *sb.*[2] Chiefly *Sc.* and *north.* Forms: 3, 6 **strond**, **strund**, 4 **stronde**, 3– **strand**. [App. connected with STRIND[2], though the phonological relation is obscure.

The first quot. is from a work belonging to a group of writings (the 'Katharine group'), which show a curious mixture of midland and even northern forms with their markedly southern dialect. (The regular Southern form *strund* occurs in the same text.) Otherwise the word is purely northern, exc. for its occurrence in the Wyclif Bible and in Wyclif's sermons, and once in Spenser (who may have imitated Douglas).]

†**1.** A stream, brook, rivulet; *transf.* a stream (of blood, etc.). *Obs.*

a **1240** *Ureisun* in *Lamb. Hom.* 189 Þe ilke fif wallen þet of þi blisfulle bodi sprungen and strike dun strondes [*Cotton MS.* Ibid. p. 202 strundes] of blode. *a* **1300** *Cursor M.* 1033 In middes þat land a welle springes, Þat rennes out wit four strandes. *a* **1340** HAMPOLE *Psalter* cix. 8 *De torrente in via bibit*..Of þe strand in way he drank. **1340–70** *Alex. & Dind.* 140 He dide him forþ to flod þat phison is called,..From perlese paradis passeþ þe stronde. **1357** *Lay Folks Catech.* (Lamb. MS.) 192 Our lady was ful of grace as a stronde ful of watyr. **1388** WYCLIF *Num.* xiii. 24 Thei ȝeden til to the stronde of clustre [1382 the rennynge watir of the clustre]. *Ibid.*, *Deut.* ix. 21 Y..castide [it] forth in to the stronde [1382 streem], that cam doun fro the hil. *a* **1400–50** *Wars Alex.* 5280 Was neuir na cristall so clere as was þa clere strandis. *Ibid.* 4202, 5507. *c* **1470** HENRY *Wallace* IX. 975 A litill strand he fand, that ran hym by. **1552** LYNDESAY *Monarche* 4038 The strandis of blude ran throuch the stretis. **1595** *Reg. Mag. Sig. Scot.* 92/1 Ane strand and rynner of watter that flowis furthe of the said wall. **1632** LITHGOW *Trav.* VI. 255 In all the bounds of Arabia Deserta ..there is no such matter, as Brooke, or strand, much lesse a Riuer. **1650** *Sc. Psalms* lxxxiii. 9 Do to them as to Midian, Jabin at Kison strand. **1722** W. HAMILTON *Wallace* 247 A Strand of Water running by. **1805** SCOTT *Last Minstr.* I. xxv, He pass'd the Peel of Goldiland, And cross'd old Borthwick's roaring strand. **1809** DONALDSON *Poems* 39 Ye wives lament..Let tears rin like the Keppin stran'. **1901** *Gallovidian* III. 74/1 [The sweat] wus rinnin' frae their neb-en's in strauns.

fig. *a* **1340** HAMPOLE *Psalter* xvii. 5 Þe strandis of wickidnes [Vulg. *torrentes iniquitatis*] has drouyd me. *c* **1375** WYCLIF *Sel. Wks.* II. 255 And al þis is a stronde of love, þat stronger may no love be. For where is welle of more love, than [etc.].

attrib. **1587** *Reg. Mag. Sig. Scot.* 469/1 Rex..concessit ..$\frac{2}{16}$ partes terrarum..haben. ex australi antiquos muros petarum Jo. Purdie ad *lie Strandheid*.

¶ **2.** Used by Douglas and Spenser for: The sea, a sheet of water.

1513 DOUGLAS *Æneis* I. iv. 5 Eneas and his feris, on the strand Wery and forwrocht, sped tham to the nerrast land. **1590** SPENSER *F.Q.* II. vi. 19 By this time was the worthy Guyon brought Vnto the other side of that wide strond, Where she was rowing.

3. *Sc.* A channel, gutter.

1565 *Reg. Mag. Sig. Scot.* 387 Canalem, vulgariter ane strand vel a syk. **1721** RAMSAY *Rise & Fall of Stocks* 90 Children.. In summer dam up little strands, Collect the drizzle to a pool. **1810** SIR A. BOSWELL *Edin.* Poet. Wks. (1871) 53 There in the dirty current of the strand, Boys drop the rival corks. **1903** J. LUMSDEN *Toorle* I. iii. 14 Ye scaur the vera deuks That plouter i the strand alang the street.

Comb. **1822** SCOTT *Nigel* xv, He has three bairns, they say; they will help him bravely to grope in the gutters. Your good lordship may have the ruining of him again, my Lord, if they have any luck in strand-scouring.

† **strand**, *sb.*[3] *north. Obs.* [? Altered form of STRIND[1].] Line of descent, pedigree; offspring, descendants: = STRAIN *sb.*[1]

a **1300** *Cursor M.* 9497 He wat born of frely strand [*rhyme* errand]. *Ibid.* 10157 Bot o þe toþer sister strand, þat ioachim had til husband, þan sal we first vr stori drau.

strand (strænd), *sb.*[4] Also 5–8 strond, 8 strang, 8–9 *dial.* stran, 9 *Sc.* strawn. [Of obscure origin; connexion with STRAIN *sb.*[3], or with OF. *estran, estren* rope, is not proved.]

1. Each of the strings or yarns which when twisted together or 'laid' form a rope, cord, line, or cable. Also, a ply (of worsted). *dial.* Also *attrib.*, as ***three strand rope***.

1497 *Naval Acc. Hen. VII* (1896) 244, ij cabulles.. of iiij strondes.., iiij hawsers.. wherof oon of iij Strondes. **1627** CAPT. SMITH *Sea Gram.* v. 26 The Wall knot.. is a round knob, so made with the strouds [*sic*] or layes of a rope, it cannot slip. *Ibid.* ix. 43. **1644** MANWAYRING *Seamans Dict.* 18 A Cabell is a three-strand Roape. **1674** RAY *S. & E.C. Words*, *Strand*, one of the twists of a line; be it of horse-hair or ought else. *Suss.* **1755** MAGENS *Insurances* I. 182 They were obliged to cut a Cable of four Strangs to Pieces. **1794** MORSE *Amer. Geog.* 425 Machinery, to.. spin flax and hemp into threads or yarns, fit for.. sail cloth, oznabrigs, twine, and the strans or yarns for cordage. **1800** *Naval Chron.* III. 474 Three strond shroud-laid rope. **1821** J. SMYTH *Pract. of Customs* (1821) 74 Every Cable.. is composed of three strands, every strand of three ropes, and every rope of three twists. **1898** MRS. C. P. PENBERTHY *Warp & Woof of Cornish Life* ii. 13, I darned the hole with worsterd, and twas blue, dark blue worsterd, and twas five strans thick.

transf. **1863** BATES *Nat. Amazons* I. ii. 47 Some [tree-stems] were twisted in strands like cables.

fig. **1816** SCOTT *Antiq.* xix, The three strands of the conversation, to speak the language of a rope work, were again twined together into one undistinguishable string of confusion. **1855** TENNYSON *Maud* I. XVIII. vii, The dusky strand of Death inwoven here With dear Love's tie, makes Love himself more dear.

b. Each of the lengths of twisted wire used to form a wire-rope, cable, or electric conductor.

1860 *Chamb. Encycl.* I. 522/1 The [Atlantic] cable.. was composed of a strand of seven wires of pure copper, coated with.. gutta percha,.. and finally bound round with iron wires. **1875** BEDFORD *Sailor's Pocket Bk.* x. 313 Wire rope usually consists of 6 strands round a hempen core; each strand consists of 6 wires round a smaller hempen core. **1891** *Pall Mall Gaz.* 16 Mar. 2/1 A special form of cable has been laid, consisting of four conductors each composed of a strand of seven copper wires.

2. Each of the threads or strips of a woven or plaited material; hence a thread or strip drawn from such material.

1802–12 BENTHAM *Ration. Judic. Evid.* (1827) II. 691 When, instead of the G.R., comes the broad arrow on timber, or the strand in sail cloth, then comes the doubt.. as between written and real evidence. **1878** HUXLEY *Physiogr.* 71 Connected by means of a strand of cotton with a small reservoir of water. **1914** *Daily News* 30 Sept. 3, [I] had to pull a strand of good Irish homespun from my coat before I could lash it to the mast-head.

fig. **1868** NETTLESHIP *Ess. Browning's Poetry* v. 130 A garment in which fear made many strands. **1904** S. H. BUTCHER *Harvard Lect.* 195 The Platonic dialogues are another case in point. Several strands of thought are here subtly interwoven.

3. Transferred senses.

a. A string of beads, pearls, and the like; also the material on which they are strung.

1825 JAMIESON *s.v.*, A strawn of beads. **1860** WHITTIER *Truce of Piscataqua* 46 In his wigwam.. Sits a woman all alone, Wampum beads and birchen strands Dropping from her careless hands. **1876** *Surrey Gloss.*, *Strand*, a stalk of grass. The children make what they call a strand of straw-berries, *i.e.* they take a long stalk and thread it full of them. **1886** SHELDON tr. *Flaubert's Salammbô* 14 Strands of pearls attached to her temples.

b. A barb or fibre of a feather. (Cf. STRAIN *sb.*[3] 3.)

1847 STODDART *Angler's Comp.* 93 Hoffland's Fancy [fly]... Body: reddish, dark brown silk, red hackle, two or three strands of ditto for tail.

c. A tress or a filament of hair.

1870 *Echo* 19 Oct., His long hair, not unconscious of a grey strand, hangs over a forehead lofty and massive. **1904** H. G. WELLS *Food of Gods* III. ii. 233 The breeze had stolen a strand or so of her hair too. **1915** *Q. Rev.* Oct. 359 Four hundred years after her death.. they [Junot's soldiers] found among her bones the thick strands of the marvellous yellow hair which the old books tell of.

d. A thread or filament in animal or vegetable structure.

1877 FOSTER *Phys.* III. i. (1878) 394 A sensory nerve in its simplest form may be regarded as a strand of eminently irritable protoplasm. **1879** CALDERWOOD *Mind & Brain* 50 Molecular changes in the brain are consequent upon impulses propagated along the strands of nerve fibres. **1887** GARNSEY & BALFOUR *De Bary's Fungi* 18 The hyphae form by their union elongated branching strands (fibrous or fibrillose mycelia). **1904** *Brit. Med. Jrnl.* 10 Sept. 583 The strands and nodes of the cytoplasmic reticulum which traverse this ground substance vary a great deal in thickness.

e. Each of the pieces into which a strip of metal is divided by slitting (see quot.).

1876 *Encycl. Brit.* IV. 218/1 The metal for wire drawing is rolled into long strips.. and cut into 'strands' by means of slitting rolls.

4. *Comb.*: **strand ground** (see quot.); **strand-hook**, a hook to which strands of cordage are fastened in the process of tempering; also *attrib.*

1882 CAULFEILD & SAWARD *Dict. Needlework* 463/1 **Strand ground*. This ground is used to connect sprays of Honiton Lace, and is formed of irregular Bars made on the Pillow and with two Bobbins. **1825** J. NICHOLSON *Oper. Mech.* 431 Thus bringing all the strands to an equal tension, without one *strand-hook making more revolutions than another. *Ibid.*, The strand hook spindles.. are so contrived, for the tempering of the strands, that any one or more of them may.. be made to slide.

strand (strænd), *v.*[1] [f. STRAND *sb.*[1] Cf. Du., G. *stranden*, Da. *strande*, Sw., Icel. *stranda*, intr. to run aground.]

1. *trans.* To drive or force aground on a shore, esp. on the sea-shore; also *rarely* of a river, to leave aground (by the ebbing of the tide).

1621 in Foster *Eng. Factories Ind.* (1906) 264 The last yeare.. all taken or stranded by the Portugall. **1666** DRYDEN *Ann. Mirab.* ccli, As those who live by Shores with joy behold Some wealthy Vessel split or stranded nigh. **1680** *Lond. Gaz.* No. 1508/1 The *Adventure*, and *Bristol*.. are come up so close with him, that we doubt not but they will either take or strand him. **1697** DRYDEN *Virg. Georg.* III. 809 Mighty Phocæ, never seen before In shallow Streams, are stranded on the Shore. **1723** DE FOE *Col. Jack* (1840) 297 To run the ship on shore to save our lives and so, stranding our vessel, spoil both sloop and cargo. **1777** COOK *Voy. S. Pole* III. xi. 158 They likewise asserted that neither she, nor any other ship, had been stranded on the coast. **1837** CARLYLE *Fr. Rev.* III. v. iii, The corpses of the first were flung into the Rhone, but the Rhone stranded some. **1843** BETHUNE *Scott. Peasant's Fire-side* 117 The vessel was stranded in a gale during the night, on the west coast of England.

2. *transf.* and *fig.* Chiefly in *passive*.

1837 CARLYLE *Fr. Rev.* II. VI. v, Your National Assembly, like a ship waterlogged, helmless, lies tumbling;.. and waits where the waves of chance may please to strand it. **1850** BLACKIE *Æschylus* II. 64 Thy pride will strand thee on a worser woe. **1860** TYNDALL *Glac.* II. viii. 264 When a glacier diminishes in size it leaves its lateral moraines stranded on the flanks of the valleys. **1874** RUSKIN *Fors Clav.* IV. xxxvii. 3, I am left utterly stranded and alone in life and thought. **1876** MISS BRADDON *J. Haggard's Dau.* I. 5 A man of superior mind, stranded for life in such a place as Combhaven, might naturally think himself a king. **1880** GOLDW. SMITH *Cowper* ii. 22 At thirty-five he was stranded and desolate. **1885** A. SETH *Scott. Philos.* ii. 68 When he [Hume] had given free scope to his logical acuteness, he stranded himself equally with his masters on the consequences he arrived at.

3. *intr.* To run aground.

1687 A. LOVELL tr. *Thevenot's Trav.* I. 17 It blowing so fresh, and we having all our Sails abroad, the Ship in all probability should have stranded. **1705** tr. *Bosman's Guinea* 418 They belong'd to a small French Pyrate, which stranded there about ten Days before. **1796** MORSE *Amer. Geog.* II. 68 Lost 6 or 7 ships of the line, two by catching fire.. and the others by stranding on the sandbanks. **1864** TENNYSON *Enoch Arden* 548 Half the night, Buoy'd upon floating tackle and broken spars, These drifted, stranding on an isle at morn. **1887** *Pall Mall Gaz.* 17 Feb. 7/2 The Guion Line steamer *Wisconsin* stranded yesterday during a fog on the outer bar,.. and remained fast.

fig. **1901** *Munsey's Mag.* (U.S.) XXV. 668/1 An old fellow in Mariposa County, California, who stranded there when the current of the forty niners ebbed out of the hills. **1908** H. WALES *Old Allegiance* ix. 148 So I stranded in a remarkable quandary.

Hence **'stranding** *vbl. sb.* and *ppl. a.*

1817 W. SELWYN *Nisi Prius* (ed. 4) II. 882 To constitute a stranding it is essential that the vessel should be stationary; the striking on a rock where the vessel remains for a minute and a half only, is not a stranding, though she thereby receives an injury, which eventually proves fatal. **1884** SIR T. BRASSEY in *19th Cent.* Mar. 445 Careless shipmasters and mates are responsible for many collisions and strandings. **1904** H. G. WELLS *Food of Gods* II. ii. 190 Big frogs, bigger trout and stranding carp.

strand (strænd), *v.*[2] [f. STRAND *sb.*[4]]

1. *intr.* Of a rope: To break one or more of its strands. Also *trans.*, to break one or more of the strands of (a rope).

a **1780** G. GILBERT in Besant *Capt. Cook* (1890) 169 The hawser we had reeved for that purpose being so rotten, that it stranded in five or six places as we were heaving. **1841** R. H. DANA *Seaman's Man.* 128 A rope is stranded when one of its strands is parted or broken by chafing or by a strain. **1853** KANE *Grinnell Exp.* xii. (1856) 88 In another attempt a four-inch hawser will be stranded without producing the slightest effect.

2. *trans.* To form (a rope) by the twisting of strands.

1886 *Encycl. Brit.* XX. 846/1 Wire ropes are stranded.. in machines which do not differ in essential features from the ordinary rope-making machinery.

3. To insert a strand or filament in (a texture). Also *fig.*

1894 J. E. DAVIS *Elem. Mod. Dressmaking* 116 Very careful workers strand their button-holes—*i.e.* carry a thread of silk across each edge over which to work the stitch. **1911** WEBSTER, *Strand*,.. 3. To weave a strand in, as with a needle in mending a garment; as, to strand a stocking; to strand a hole or rent. **1914** *Blackw. Mag.* Nov. 581/2 Time.. has.. prettily stranded her black hair with grey.

† **'strandage.** *Obs.* [f. STRAND *sb.*[4] + -AGE.] A charge or toll levied upon fish or other commodities landed on a 'strand'.

1419 *Liber Albus* (Rolls) I. 234 La nief.. dorra ii deniers pur straundage. **1598** STOW *Surv.* 161 In the raigne of Edwarde the thirde, euery great ship landing there [*sc.* at Billingsgate], paide for strandage two pence. **1711** MADOX *Hist. Exchequer* xviii. 534 The issue of divers Tronages with several small strandages.

‖ **Strandbad** ('ʃtræntbɑːd, ‖'ʃtrantbaːt). Also **Strand-Bad**. [Ger.] In Germany and in German-speaking countries: a bathing-place by natural waters, an open-air swimming-pool.

1939 N. MONSARRAT *This is Schoolroom* III. xvii. 391 We had.. our first bathe in a little Strand-Bad sheltered by trees. **1959** P. TOWNEND *Died o' Wednesday* ix. 149 From a multi-coloured knot of bathers at the river *Strandbad* occasional faint cries drifted up to the terrace.

stranded ('strændɪd), *ppl. a.*[1] [f. STRAND *v.*[1] + -ED.] That has been driven ashore; that has run aground.

1703 PRIOR *Ode to Mem. Col. George Villiers* 43 Some from the stranded Vessel force their Way. **1729** POPE *Dunc.* II. 287 He.. climb'd a stranded lighter's height, Shot to the black abyss, and plung'd downright. **1810** SCOTT *Lady of L.* III. i, [They] Wait on the verge of dark eternity, Like stranded wrecks. **1872** EARL OF PEMBROKE & G. H. KINGSLEY *S. Sea Bubbles* i. 9 The only thing then to be done is to lie quietly where you are, like a stranded whale. **1914** A. PLUMMER *Churches in Brit.* I. iv. 122 The stranded vessel was got off the beach.

b. *transf.* and *fig.* (Cf. STRAND *v.*[1] 2.)

1851 RUSKIN *Stones Ven.* (1874) I. i. 24 [The works of Claude and the Poussins] may be left without grave indignation to their poor mission of furnishing drawing-rooms and assisting stranded conversation. **1869** LECKY *Europ. Mor.* I. i. 89 Some stranded nation apart from all the flow of enterprise and knowledge. **1885** *Pall Mall Gaz.* 19 Feb. 5/1 The author.. is already favourably known.. for his finished pictures of this strange, stranded old-French life. **1901** *Scotsman* 5 Nov. 6/8 The fog lifted a little and the immense array of stranded omnibuses and vans would be able to find their way home.

stranded ('strændɪd), *ppl. a.*[2] [f. STRAND *v.*[2] and *sb.*[4] + -ED.]

1. Of a rope: Having one or more strands broken.

1815 *Falconer's Dict. Marine* (ed. Burney), *Stranded*,.. speaking of a cable or rope, signifies that one of its strands is broken. **1823** W. SCORESBY *Jrnl.* 311 Our movements.. were effected by means of a stranded (or partly broken) rope. **1888** W. E. NICHOLSON *Gloss. Coal Trade Northumb. & Durh.* (E.D.D.).

2. Composed of (a specified number of) strands.

1875 BEDFORD *Sailor's Pocket Bk.* x. 313 A four-stranded rope is about one-fifth weaker than a three-stranded one.

3. Composed of strands of wire (STRAND *sb.*[4] 1 b).

1888 *Encycl. Brit.* XXIII. 114 The stranded form [of submarine cable] was suggested by Prof. W. Thomson at a meeting of the Philosophical Society of Glasgow in 1854. **1899** J. PENNELL in *Fortn. Rev.* LXV. 120 In the Bowden brake the power is applied by a coiled wire, with a stranded wire inside it. **1903** KELSEY *Contin. Current Dynamos* 199 A stranded conductor is used on account of the immunity thereby obtained from eddy currents.

4. Of a fur garment: made of skins which have been cut into diagonal strips and resewn.

1935 O. HACKING *Home Furriery* iii. 16 Work the next cut in the same way, breaking through the little joins in the centre and sides piece by piece... This way of dealing with the skin gives lovely stranded effects. **1977** *Lancashire Life* Dec. 109/2 (Advt.), A gorgeously rich coat in warm-coloured pastel mink has big revers, beautifully stranded sleeves and a full skirt for perfect winter warmth and elegance. **1978** *Times* 26 Aug. 22/7 Fully stranded new mink coats from £950.

'strander. [f. STRAND *v.*[2] + -ER[1].] *spec.* An operative employed in electric cable manufacture.

1881 *Instr. Census Clerks* (1885) 47 Electrical apparatus maker.. Land Cable:.. Wire Winder. Strander.

'stranding *vbl. sb.*[2] [f. STRAND *v.*[2] + -ING[1].]

a. The action of the vb., esp. in rope-making (in quots. *attrib.*).

1825 J. NICHOLSON *Oper. Mech.* 436 The backward movement of the stranding-sledge.. towards the bottom of the rope-walk by which strands are drawn out. **1884** *Pall Mall Gaz.* 17 Apr. 11/1 This work of binding the copper wires together is performed by a small 'stranding machine'.

b. In the working of furs: (see quots. 1950, 1968).

1935 O. HACKING *Home Furriery* iii. 15 (*caption*) Dropping and stranding. **1950** *N.Z. Jrnl. Agric.* June 597/1 Some technical terms in [fur] workmanship.. should be understood... Stranding or letting out means cutting and sewing a pelt in such a way that it becomes longer and narrower than it was originally; it is done with mink and fitch. **1968** J. IRONSIDE *Fashion Alphabet* 153 *Stranding.* This is the process of lengthening and narrowing a skin by cutting and resewing in a series of diagonal strips.

strandless ('strændlɪs), *a.* [f. STRAND *sb.*[1] + -LESS.] Without a strand or beach.

1894 A. AUSTIN in *Blackw. Mag.* Sept. 315/1, I could.. still see the sweeping, swirling coils of strandless water running in and out of the black honeycombed abysses.

†**'strandling.** *Obs.* Forms: 3 stranlyne, -ling, 4 -lyng, strenlyng, strandling(e, -lyng(e. [Of obscure origin.] Some kind of fur; ? the fur of the squirrel taken at Michaelmas.

c **1299** *Durham Acc. Rolls* (Surtees) 495 In 5 fururis de Stranlyne, 52*s.* 6*d.*.. In 6 furur. de Stranling ad capusc., 22*s.* **1303–4** *Acc. Exors. R. de Gravesend* (Camden) 55 De duabus capis de persico furratis de Strenlyng. **1305** in *Munim. Magd. Coll. Oxf.* (1882) 145 Cum perrula de stra[n]dlings. *c* **1314** *Liber Horn* fol. 249 b (Guildhall MS.) in *N. & Q.* 11th Ser. (1912) V. 170/2 Strandling est Squirel contre le feste Seint Michel. **1327** in Riley *Memorials* (1868) 153 A fur of stra[n]dlynge of 6 tiers. **1327** in *Compotus Rolls Obedientiaries St. Swithun's, Winch.* (1892) 256 In j furura de grosso Strandling et alia de minuto Strandling. *c* **1330** R. BRUNNE *Chron. Wace* (Rolls) 11194 Manteles... Of meneuer, stranlyng, veyr, & gris. **1334–5** in *Compotus Rolls Obedientiaries St. Swithun's, Winch.* (1892) 236 In xij furruris de grossa Strandlinge... In iiij furruris de Meyn Strandlynge.

Strandlooper, Strandloper ('strɑːntlʊpə(r)). Also with lower-case initial. Rarely as two words or with hyphen. [a. Afrikaans *strandloper*, f. Du. *strand* STRAND *sb.*[1] + *looper* walker: cf. LAND-LOPER.]

1. *S. Afr.* Any of several sand-plovers of the genus *Charadrius*, found in coastal regions.

1731 G. MEDLEY tr. *Kolb's Descr. Cape of Good Hope* II. 157 The Dutch call this Bird *Strand Loper*, i.e. Shore-Courser. **1875–84** R. B. SHARPE *Layard's Birds S. Afr.* 662 *Ægialitis tricollaris* (Vieill.)... This pretty little Plover, the Strandlooper of the colonists, is common throughout the colony. [**1972** *Evening Post* (Port Elizabeth) 9 Sept. 2 They [*sc.* ostriches] find the little sandplovers (strandlopertjies) on the farm a nuisance. These little birds dart at them frequently.]

2. *S. Afr.* **a.** A member of a people, related to the Bushmen and Hottentots, living on the southern shores of S. Africa from prehistoric times until the present millennium. **b.** A member of a people, perh. to be identified with the above, found on the Namibian coast.

1838 [see SALDANIER]. **1846** J. SUTHERLAND *Mem. Kaffirs*, etc. *S. Afr.* II. 29 For a little tobacco the strandloopers will always fetch firewood for the cooks. **1900** *Jrnl. Anthropol. Inst.* XXX. 47, I have not much to say about the remains of the 'strand loopers' or 'shore walkers', as they have been called, from their habit of life. **1913** *Daily News* 16 Dec. 9 The Strandlopers lived on the coast before the Dutch went into South Africa. **1919** H. H. JOHNSTON *Compar. Study Bantu & Semi-Bantu Lang.* I. ii. 23 This Strandlooper either co-existed alongside the Bushman or preceded and was followed by this specialized desert negro. **1928** C. DAWSON *Age of Gods* i. 11 There is reason to think that this race [*sc.* Boskop Man] was the ancestor of the modern South African Hottentot and Bushman, for the remains of an intermediate type—the vanished race of Strandloopers—has been discovered and all three types agree in certain cranial characteristics. In size of brain, however, there is a steady diminution from the 1,700 c.c. or more of Boskop through the Strandlooper skulls. **1948** L. G. GREEN *So Few are Free* xvi. 216 Some authorities believe that the 'Strandlopers', extinct in South Africa, may survive on the Kaokoveld coast. **1951** [see *river-debris* s.v. RIVER *sb.*[1] 5 d]. **1956** *Cape Times* 27 July 3/5 Three Hottentots of the *strandloper* race, said to be the last of their kind, attended a gathering of Kaokaoveld Natives addressed by.. Dr. Verwoerd.. in the north-west of South West Africa. **1975** *Eastern Province Herald* (Port Elizabeth) 4 Aug. 4 A skeleton believed to be that of a Strandloper Hottentot, who was buried in the traditional position with legs drawn up and hands placed across the knees, has been unearthed near Sedgefield, the coastal resort. **1981** *Sci. Amer.* Aug. 92/1 They appeared to fill a niche at the edge of western Europe similar to that of the aboriginal Tasmanians in the Pacific, the Patagonians in sub-polar South America and the Hottentot 'strandloopers' of South Africa.

3. *Archæol.* Usu. *pl.* Any prehistoric people who were nomadic about coastal areas or inland shores.

1935 *Proc. Prehistoric Soc.* I. 12 The strandloopers who have left the kitchen-middens in Denmark. **1939** V. G. CHILDE *Dawn Europ. Civilization* (ed. 3) i. 8 *Asturian* is the term applied to the culture of strandloopers who succeeded the Azilians on the coasts of North Spain. **1956** *Antiquity* XXX. 48 A peripheral culture, which has lost its vitality, a 'strand-loper' type of existence. **1974** G. JENKINS *Bridge of Magpies* ii. 37 The investigation of sea-shore middens belonging to *Strandlopers*—'Seashore Walkers'—who were a vanished Stone Age race of Sperrgebeit nomads. **1975** J. G. EVANS *Environment Early Man Brit. Isles* v. 103 In the north of Britain, and especially along the coasts of the North Channel, groups of people known as 'Strandloopers', who subsisted to a considerable extent on shellfish, are represented by the Larnian and Obanian industries.

4. A beachcomber or vagrant.

1939 JOYCE *Finnegans Wake* 110 What child of a strandlooper but keepy little Kevin.. would ever have trouved up on a strate that was called strete a motive for future saintity by euchring the finding of the Ardagh chalice by another heily innocent and beachwalker. **1952** *Chambers's Jrnl.* Feb. 87/2 The man turned out to be a strandlooper—a coloured beachcomber, one who shared the food of the gulls.

Hence **'strandlooping** *ppl. a. Archæol.*, nomadic about coastal areas or lake shores; also as *vbl. sb.*

1959 *New Scientist* 12 Mar. 562/1 The Kennet of about 7,000 years ago was a series of connected lakes surrounded by forest, a site which must have been ideal for a strand-looping people. **1975** J. G. EVANS *Environment Early Man Brit. Isles* v. 105 For part of the year, the inhabitants probably forsook their industrial and strandlooping activities and moved inland to obtain their living by other means. **1976** J. HAWKES *Atlas of Early Man* 44/2 Strand looping as well as fresh water and sea fishing intensified. **1978** R. BRADLEY *Prehist. Settlement of Britain* 94/1 Early fishing, fowling and strandlooping are all compatible with one another.

‖**Strandveld** ('strændvɛlt, ‖'strantfɛlt). *S. Afr.* Also †strand veld, Strandveldt, etc.; strandveld. [Afrikaans, f. Du. *strand* STRAND *sb.*[1] + *veld* VELD.] The southernmost coastal strip of Africa, in the district of Bredasdorp.

1875–84 R. B. SHARPE *Layard's Birds S. Afr.* (rev. ed.) 47 Mr. John Van Byl's farm, Nacht-wacht in the Strand-Veldt. **1880** *Trans. S. Afr. Philos. Soc.* I. III. 196 The variety is usually termed the 'Strandveldt' (sea-coast) locust. **1912** *S. Afr. Agric. Jrnl.* July 35 In the Bredasdorp district it [*sc.* lamziekte] occurs on the flats of the strand veld and is prevalent along the mountain ranges in the strand veld. **1953** *Cape Times* 3 Apr. 2/6 *Bredasdorp*... Mr. Hennie Geldenhuys has.. killed two lynx which marauded farms in the strandveld area of the district in the summer. **1974** *Standard Encycl. S. Afr.* X. 319/2 The Strandveld is.. a marine terrace, some 30 to 45 metres above sea-level... The main portion is the Western Strandveld, round Elim, which is level or undulating and where agriculture is practised... To the south of the town of Bredasdorp lies the Eastern Strandveld, a drier terrain of chalky dune-sand.

strane, obs. form of STRAIN *v.*[1]

strang: see STRAND *sb.*[4], STRANGE *a.*, STRONG *a.*

strange (streɪn(d)ʒ), *a.* Also 3–7 **straunge**, 4–6 **straung**, 4–7 **strang**, 5 **strawnge**, **straunce**, **straunche**, 6 **straenge**, **straynge**, **straing**, *Sc.* **strenge**, 6–7 **strainge**. [a. OF. *estrange* (mod.F. *étrange*) = Pr. *estranh*, *estrang*, Sp. *estraño*, Pg. *estranho*, Rum. *străin*, It. *strano* adj., *stranio*, *strangio* sb.:—L. *extrāneus* external, foreign (see EXTRANEOUS), f. *extrā* adv. outside, without.]

I. †**1.** **a.** Of persons, language, customs, etc.: Of or belonging to another country; foreign, alien. *Obs.*

1297 R. GLOUC. (Rolls) 379 Þe king made him vroþ inou, .. þat strange men in is owe lond dude a such trespas. **1338** R. BRUNNE *Chron.* (1810) 36 In Ingland neuer before was kynge lufed so wele, Ne of the folk strange non honourd so mykelle. **1387** TREVISA *Higden* II. 159 Þe Flemmynges þat woneþ in þe weste side of Wales haueþ i-left her straunge speche and spekeþ Saxonliche i-now. **1471** CAXTON *Recuyell* (Sommer) 303 They wold not haue the luste and true blood of egypte, but the strange blood whiche they shold take & make sacrefice therof. **1483** *Cath. Angl.* 367/2 Strawnge, *alienus, barbarus*. **1572** ABP. PARKER *Let.* 13 Dec. *Corr.* (Parker Soc.) 411 To be first sent out to the reader, both English and strange. **1588** SHAKS. *L.L.L.* IV. ii. 134 One mounsier Berowne, one of the strange Queenes Lords. **1621** J. TAYLOR (Water P.) *Superbiæ Flagellum* A 6, Ancient Bards, and Poets in strange toungs. **1642** *Rates of Merchandizes* 66 That if any English transport Coales in strange Bottoms to pay Strangers Custome. **1755** MAGENS *Insurances* II. 236 If a strange Master, that never was on the River Elbe before, takes a Pilot on board in foreign Parts.

†**b.** Of a country or other geographical feature: Situated outside one's own land. *Obs.*

1297 R. GLOUC. (Rolls) 5838 Þat hii & al þat lond bineþe ssolde be ydo þoru folc of strange londe. *c* **1386** CHAUCER *Prol.* 13 And Palmeres for to seken straunge strondes. *Ibid.* 464 She hadde passed many a straunge strem. **1389** in *Eng. Gilds* (1870) 35 Also ȝef ony broþer or sister deye in straunge cuntre, in cristendom or in hethenesse. **15..** *Jerusalem reioss* 11 in *Dunbar's Poems* 322 Thre Kingis of strenge regionis To the ar cumin. **1614** RALEGH *Hist. World* III. vii. § 5. 84 Long abode in a strange ayre, and want of supplie, had much enfeebled the Athenians. **1722** A. PHILIPS *Briton* I. ii. 6 In a strange Land His *Manes* shall not wander, unappeas'd.

2. Belonging to some other place or neighbourhood; unknown to the particular locality specified or implied. Of a place or locality: Other than one's own.

c **1290** *St. Brendan* 292 in *S. Eng. Leg.* 227 An straunge man eche daye it bringuth In-to ovre celere, i-wis. **1390** GOWER *Conf.* III. 233 For whan a man mai redy finde His oghne wif, what scholde he seche In strange places to beseche To borwe an other mannes plouh. **1421** *Coventry Leet Bk.* 27 That no man throw ne cast at noo straunge man, ne skorn hym. **1487–8** *Rec. St. Mary at Hill* (1905) 129 Item, Resseyued of Margarete Bull for þe buriall of a straunge childe, ij s. **1555** *Ludlow Churchw. Acc.* (Camden) 65 Received of m[r] Whytlege for the beryalle of a straunge man in the churche, vj s. viij d. **1662** W. KILBURNE in *Extr. S.P. rel. Friends* II. (1911) 148 Within these three weeks last past I have taken notice of many strange faces which frequent this meeting. **1732** SWIFT *Exam. Abuses Dubl.* Misc. 1735 V. 363 A strange Dog happens to pass through a Flesh-Market. **1859** GEO. ELIOT *Adam Bede* xlix, There's all the sewing to be done, an' I must have a strange gell out o' Treddles'on to do it. **1892** *Photogr. Ann.* II. 760 The address should be given in full, as tourists in strange towns have otherwise difficulty in finding the place. **1894** J. PAYN *Gleams of Memory* 9 Strange clergymen were much put out by it [*sc.* the old squire's snoring], and would make significant pauses in their discourse.

†**3.** Belonging to others; not of one's own kin or family. *Obs.*

1338 R. BRUNNE *Chron.* (1810) 87 Purchaced þing men gyues,.. tille a man is strange for his seruise. *c* **1386** CHAUCER *Merch. T.* 196 Yet were me leuere þat houndes had me eten Than þat myn heritage sholde falle In straunge hand. *c* **1510** *Robt. Deuyll* (1827) 15 Ye to do justice upon hym [*sc.* your son] as on a straunge man. *a* **1533** BERNERS *Golden Bk. M. Aurel.* vi. (1535) 10 For perfyte knowlege of thynges,.. it behoueth to haue strange aduyse, clere vnderstandynge, and propre experience.

4. ***strange woman***: a harlot. (With *the*, as denoting the class.)

After many passages in the Book of Proverbs. The adj. renders two different Heb. words, *nokrīyāh* and *zārāh*, both which have the sense 'not one's own (wife)' (see 3).

1535 COVERDALE *Prov.* ii. 16 That thou mayest be delyuered also from the straunge woman [so later versions], and from her that is not thine owne. **1614** B. JONSON *Barth. Fair* II. iv. (1631) 23 *Ins.* If I can.. but rescue this youth, here out of the hands of the lewd man and the strange woman. **1886** RUSKIN *Præterita* I. xi. 346 No fear of my being tempted by the strange woman, for was I not in love?

†**5.** Added or introduced from outside, not belonging to the place or person where it is found, adventitious, external. In *Surg.* = FOREIGN *a.* 5.

c **1386** CHAUCER *Wife's T.* 305 For gentillesse nys but renomee Of thyne auncestres for hire heigh bountee, Which is a strange thyng to thy persone. *a* **1425** tr. *Arderne's Treat. Fistula*, etc. 83 It haþe in it a vertue putrefactyue by which he putrefieþ straunge humours comyng to a wounde. **1557** EDGEWORTH *Serm.* Repert. A j. Adulteringe womens heare with strange colours, &c. is controlinge of Gods handy worke. **1578** LYTE *Dodoens* III. lxxxvi. 440 This is a strange plante, and not found in this Countrie, except in the gardens of some Herboristes. **1590** SPENSER *F.Q.* III. xii. 11 Yet his owne face was dreadfull, ne did need Straunge horrour, to deforme his greisly shade. **1597** A. M. tr. *Guillemeau's Fr. Chirurg.* 5/3 The strange thinges are ether externall,.. or anye substance of our bodyes, as splinters or parcells of bones, which we esteme straunge, because they are noe more partakers of our lyfe. **1672** WISEMAN *Treat. Wounds* II. v. 30 Cleanse the Wound first from all strange Bodies.

†**6.** With *from*: Alien, far removed; diverse, different. *Obs.*

c **1380** WYCLIF *Sel. Wks.* III. 431 Alle þes bodiliche signes ben straunge fro charite. *Ibid.* 511 Þerfore no newe secte of religioun, straunge fro Cristis secte, shulde have begunne. *c* **1440** *Pallad. on Husb.* III. 91 A witty man tacth preued thyng, & change He macth, that lond from lond be not to strange. **1456** *Coventry Leet Bk.* 294 To be estraunged from his Crafte.. and to be reputed & holden as straunge from eny benyvolence of this Cite. **1577** HANMER *Anc. Eccl. Hist., Euseb.* VI. xxxii. 112 Beryllus.. went about to establyshe forrayne and straunge doctrine from the fayth.

7. Unknown, unfamiliar; not known, met with, or experienced before. Const. *to*.

13.. *K. Alis.* 4817 Hy ledden hym.. In the straungest peryl of Inde. **1390** GOWER *Conf.* III. 252 In strange place and doun thei lihte And take a chambre. *c* **1391** CHAUCER *Astrol.* ii. § 17 Rubric, To knowe the verrey degree of any maner sterre straunge or vnstraunge after his longitude. **1500–20** DUNBAR *Poems* xiv. 9 So nyce array, so strange to thair abbay. **1513** DOUGLAS *Æneis* VII. iii. 45 As ȝow art careyt tyll ane strange cost [L. *ignota ad litora vectum*]. **1551** RECORDE *Pathw. Knowl.* To Rdr., Straung paths ar not troden al truly at the first. **1603** SHAKS. *Meas. for M.* IV. ii. 209 You know the Charracter I doubt not, and the Signet is not strange to you? **1611** BIBLE *Transl. Pref.* ¶5 Euen S. Hierome himselfe calleth the Hebrew tongue barbarous, belike because it was strange to so many. **1655** MOUFET & BENNET *Health's Improv.* (1746) 261 Strange things are ever best liked. **1768–74** TUCKER *Lt. Nat.* (1834) II. 567 Until they become familiar with nurse and mamma, and then they take violent distaste at strange faces. **1830** GREVILLE *Mem.* (1874) II. 29 The next Parliament.. is besides very ill composed—full of boys and all sorts of strange men. **1842** TENNYSON *Morte D'Arthur* 238 Among new men, strange faces, other minds. **1867** SMYTH *Sailor's Word-bk.*, *Strange Sail*, a vessel heaving in sight, of which the particulars are unknown. **1889** *Universal Rev.* 15 Feb. 251 One good jump on a strange horse shows standard horsemanship.

†**8.** Of a kind that is unfamiliar or rare; unusual, uncommon, exceptional, singular, out of the way. *Obs.* (Merged in 10.)

13.. *Coer de L.* 268 Kyng Rychard gan hym dysguyse In a ful strange queyntyse. *c* **1330** R. BRUNNE *Chron. Wace* (Rolls) 116 And forsoth I couth noght So strange Inglis as þai wroght. **1340** HAMPOLE *Psalter* Pref. 4 In this werke .i. seke na straunge ynglis, bot lyghtest and commonest. *c* **1374** CHAUCER *Anel. & Arc.* 202 The kynde of mannes herte is to delyte In thing that straunge is. **1390** GOWER *Conf.* I. 89 Strange aventures forto seche, He rod the Marches al aboute. **1412–20** LYDG. *Chron. Troy* II. 4187 The straunge metis, þe manere of þe seruyse, I haue noon englische al for to deuyse. **1553** T. WILSON *Rhet.* III. 86 This should first be learned, y[t] we neuer affect any straunge ynkehorne termes, but so speake as is commonly receiued. **1554–5** in Feuillerat *Revels Q. Mary* (1914) 173 Verey fayer quaint and strange attier. **1585** T. WASHINGTON tr. *Nicholay's Voy.* IV. xxv. 141 Skins of al sorts, of liuely colours, straunge and diuers aboue al.. in the world. **1663** HEATH *Flagellum* (1672) 24 And all by such uncouth and strang passes, such unexpected.. contingency of things.

9. **a.** Exceptionally great (in degree, intensity, amount, etc.), extreme. (Now tending to merge in 10.)

c **1380** WYCLIF *Wks.* (1880) 454 But þis abusioun were to straunge. **1573–80** TUSSER *Husb.* (1878) 62 Sea rages in winter be sodainly strange. **1585** T. WASHINGTON tr. *Nicholay's Voy.* II. xv. 50 The last [earthquake].. was so straunge and fearful for the space of xviii. dayes continually. **1606** SHAKS. *Ant. & Cl.* II. ii. 157, I did not think to draw my Sword 'gainst Pompey, For he hath laid strange courtesies, and great Of late vpon me. **1663** PATRICK *Pilgrim* xxvi, The ensuing part of the road was very dangerous,.. and of a strange length. **1719** DE FOE *Crusoe* I. (Globe) 227 His Eyes sparkled, and his Countenance discover'd a strange Eagerness. *Ibid.* 300 Taking Devilish long Strides, and shuffling along at a strange Rate. **1752** FOOTE *Taste* I. i, I have a strange Mind to leave you to yourselves. **1818** SCOTT *Hrt. Midl.* xxxiii, Strange was the courage and address which he displayed in his pursuits. **1828** CARR *Craven Gloss.*, *Strange*, great. 'A strange deal.' **1849** MACAULAY *Hist. Eng.* vii. II. 195 The fall of the Hydes had excited throughout England strange [1858 ed., extreme] alarm and indignation. **1875** JOWETT *Plato* (ed. 2) IV. 33 The aspiration after good has often lent a strange power to evil.

b. quasi-*adv.*, qualifying an adj.: Very, extremely. Also ***strange and —***. Now *dial.*

1667 WOOD *Life* (O.H.S.) II. 102 March 6,..began the strange cold weather with great winds. **1669** STURMY *Mariner's Mag.* I. ii. 17 The Sea breaks strange and dangerous. **1888** G. M. FENN *Dick o' the Fens* 133, I've got a straänge nice lot o' bait. *Ibid.* 160, I'm straänge and glad you've caught him.

10. a. Unfamiliar, abnormal, or exceptional to a degree that excites wonder or astonishent; difficult to take in or account for; queer, surprising, unaccountable.

c **1374** CHAUCER *Troylus* v. 120, I wot yow þenketh straunge, No wonder is, for it is to yow newe, Thaqueyntaunce of þese Troians to chaunge For folk of Grece þat ye neuere knewe. **1390** GOWER *Conf.* I. 24 Me thoghte I syh upon a Stage Wher stod a wonder strange ymage. **1461** *Paston Lett.* II. 39 The gydyng of youre adversary hath been in many causez ryght straunce. **1549** LATIMER *Ploughers* (Arb.) 29 And nowe I would aske a straung question. **1568** GRAFTON *Chron.* II. 27 Many straunge and wonderfull sightes were seene this present yere in the skie. **1610** SHAKS. *Temp.* v. i. 242 This is as strange a Maze, as ere men trod. **1620** I. C. *Two Merry Milk-maids* IV. i. L 3, But this is very strange. *Fre.* But not so strange as true, I am a witnesse of it. **1779** *Mirror* No. 57 They complained that I was a strange fellow, who hated company. **1782** MISS BURNEY *Cecilia* IV. ii, Will you not think me very strange if I should take the liberty to consult you upon some business? **1823** BYRON *Juan* XIV. ci, 'Tis strange—but true; for truth is always strange; Stranger than fiction. **1842** BROWNING *Pied Piper* v, 'Come in!'—the Mayor cried, looking bigger: And in did come the strangest figure! **1860** TYNDALL *Glac.* I. xv. 103 It seemed strange that a man should be there alone. **1875** JOWETT *Plato* (ed. 2) I. 188 The professors of education are strange beings.

absol. **1815** SHELLEY *Alastor* 112 Whatsoe'er of strange Sculptured on alabaster obelisk,..Dark Ethiopia in her desert hills Conceals. **1839** T. MITCHELL *Frogs of Aristoph.* Introd. p. cvi. *note*, Æschylus..loved exceedingly the strange and the exciting.

†**b.** ***to think (it) strange of*** (or ***concerning***): to be surprised at. *Obs.*

1585 T. WASHINGTON tr. *Nicholay's Voy.* I. xvii. 19 b, He had vnderstanding, that the Frigate..was of Malta, whereof he thought very straunge [Fr. *ce qu'il trouuoit estrange & mauuais*]. **1611** BIBLE *1 Pet.* iv. 12 Beloued, thinke it not strange [Gr. μὴ ξενίζεσθε] concerning the fiery triall, which is to try you.

c. ***strange to say, tell,*** etc., used parenthetically: cf. SAY *v.*[1] 11. Similarly ***strange enough.***

[**1576** GASCOIGNE *Steele Gl.* (Arb.) 68 Strange tale to tel: all officers be blynde.] **1697** DRYDEN *Æneis* II. 930 While I held my Son,..Strange to relate, from young Iulus Head A lambent Flame arose. **1853** KANE *Grinnell Exp.* xxii. (1856) 170 Strange enough, during the night, Captain Austin.. entered the same indentation. **1859** FITZGERALD *Omar* lx, And, strange to tell, among that Earthen Lot Some could articulate, while others not. **1862** MISS BRADDON *Lady Audley* viii, Strange to say, George Talboys, who very seldom observed anything, took particular notice of this place.

d. quasi-*int.* 'An expression of wonder' (J.); 'an elliptical expression for *it is strange* (W. 1828).

c **1670** WALLER *St. James's Park* Poems (1722) 163 Strange! what Extremes shou'd thus preserve the Snow, High on the Alps, or in deep Caves below. **1694** LOCKE *Treat. Govt.* (ed. 2) I. xi. §147 Strange! that Fatherly Authority should be the only Original of government, and yet all Mankind not know it; and Stranger yet, that [etc.]. **1725** [see TWEEDLE-].

e. *Particle Physics.* Epithet of those subatomic particles that have a non-zero value of the strangeness quantum number.

So called orig. because they had lifetimes much longer than was expected from their being produced by the strong interaction.

1956 M. GELL-MANN in *Nuovo Cimento* IV. Suppl. 850 We shall refer to the nucleon.., the antinucleon.., and the pion..as 'ordinary particles' to distinguish them from the 'strange particles', K-particles and hyperons. **1965** H. MUIRHEAD *Physics Elem. Particles* i. 20 The discoveries of new particles have occurred sometimes as a result of a theoretical impetus and sometimes by accident. The strange particles fall into the latter category. **1973** L. J. TASSIE *Physics Elem. Particles* vi. 51 A typical strange particle is the Λ°, an uncharged particle which decays with a mean lifetime of $2{\cdot}5 \times 10^{-10}$ s. **1974** FRAUENFELDER & HENLEY *Subatomic Physics* xiii. 358 To construct strange mesons and strange baryons, at least one strange quark is needed. **1975** *Physics Bull.* Apr. 177/1 There are two nonstrange quarks, u and d, a doublet under SU(2), and a strange quark which is a singlet under SU(2). **1977** *Sci. Amer.* Oct. 58/3 There must be a set of lightest strange particles, which have no states of lower mass to which they can give the *s* quark. These are the *K* mesons and the lambda baryon (Λ).

†**11.** Of persons: **a.** Unfriendly; having the feelings alienated. **b.** Distant or cold in demeanour; reserved; not affable, familiar, or encouraging; uncomplying, unwilling to accede to a request or desire. *Obs.*

1338 R. BRUNNE *Chron.* (1810) 50 Olaf in Norweie..bare him ouer strange to þe kyng Knoute. ? *a* **1366** CHAUCER *Rom. Rose* 1065 These losengers thorough flaterye Haue maad folk ful straunge be There hem ought be pryue. **1423** JAS. I *Kingis Q.* cii, And though I was vnto ȝour lawis strange, By ignorance, and noght by felonye. **1509** HAWES *Past. Pleas.* xxxiv. (Percy Soc.) 173 Be straunge unto hym, as ye knowe nothyng The perfite cause of his true commyng. **1538** ELYOT *Dict.* Addit., *Auersus*, straunge, vnacquaynted. *a* **1568** A. SCOTT *Poems* (S.T.S.) xxi. 18, I fand hir of ane staffage kynd, Bath staitly, strange, and he. **1592** SHAKS. *Rom. & Jul.* II. ii. 102, I should haue beene more strange, I must confesse. *a* **1593** MARLOWE *Edw. II*, II. iv. 1162 If he be straunge and not regarde my wordes. **1633** ROWLEY *Match at Midn.* III. i. F 4 b, I was strange, in the nice timerous temper of a Maid. **1700** CONGREVE *Way of World* IV. v, *Mil...* Let us never Visit together, nor go to a Play together, But let us be very strange and well bred. **1763** CHURCHILL *Night* 87 The strange reserve, the proud affected state Of upstart knaves grown rich, and fools grown great.

†**c.** Sparing *of* (one's favour). *Obs.*

1548 HALL *Chron., Edw. V* 3 b, Some were reconsiled and growen into his fauoure, of the whiche he was neuer straunge, when it was with true herte demaunded.

†**d.** ***to make oneself strange***: to be distant or unfriendly. *Obs.*

1390 GOWER *Conf.* I. 144 He [*sc.* Nebuchadnezzar] kneleth in his wise and braieth, To seche merci and assaieth His god, which made him nothing strange, Whan that he sih his pride change. *Ibid.* III. 195 And for he wolde his herte glade, He lihte and made him nothing strange. **1566** PAINTER *Palace Pleas.* (1569) I. 232 b, Myne aduise is, that by litle and litle, you do make your selfe straunge, and vse no more your wonted grace vnto him.

†**e.** ***to look strange***: to look at a person as if one did not know him. *Obs.*

1590 SHAKS. *Com. Err.* v. i. 295 Why looke you strange on me? you know me well. *c* **1600** —— *Sonn.* lxxxix. 8, I will acquaintance strangle and looke strange.

12. Of a person: Unfamiliar or unacquainted with something (specified or implied); †inexperienced or unversed *in*; fresh or unaccustomed *to*; unpractised or unskilled *at*.

1561 HOBY tr. *Castiglione's Courtier* II. (1577) H vi b, And whan he hath it [promotion], let him not shewe himselfe new or straunge in it. **1590** SHAKS. *Com. Err.* II. ii. 151 In Ephesus I am but two houres old, As strange vnto your towne, as to your talke. **1607** —— *Timon* IV. iii. 56, I know thee well: But in thy Fortunes am vnlearn'd, and strange. **1770** LUCKOMBE *Hist. Printing* 323 An understanding Pressman knows..how to give a strange joyner and smith instructions to make a Press. **1868** BROWNING *Ring & Bk.* II. VI. 86 Though as strange at the work As fribble must be. **1911** *Concise Oxf. Dict.* s.v., [I] am strange to the work.

13. ***to make (it) strange***: to make difficulties, refuse to assent or comply, be reluctant or unwilling; to hold back, keep a stand-off attitude; to be distant or unfriendly; to affect coyness; to pretend not to understand; to affect or feel surprise, dislike, indignation, etc. Const. *of* (= about) a matter, etc.; *to* (do something); also to ***make strange at.*** †**a.** ***to make it strange.*** *Obs.*

c **1386** CHAUCER *Reeve's T.* 60 And straunge he made it of hir mariage. *c* **1386** —— *Frankl. T.* 495 He made it straunge, and swoor, so god hym saue, Lasse than a thousand pound he wolde nat haue. *c* **1440** *Gesta Rom.* xlix. 220 What! deer love, whi makest þow hit nowe so straunge to me? *c* **1530** BERNERS *Arth. Lyt. Brit.* (1814) 351 Though she make it straunge & deny you at the fyrst, yet be not ashamed therwith, & she shall loue you the better. **1566** PAINTER *Palace Pleas.* (1575) I. 249 b, The husbande hearinge him saye so, commaunded his wyfe to kisse him, which she did although she made it straunge, either for the Lordes desire or for husbands request to do the same. **1591** SHAKS. *Two Gent.* I. ii. 102 She makes it strange, but she would be best pleas'd To be so angred with another Letter.

b. ***to make strange.*** Also (esp. in earlier use) const. *at, of.* Now *dial.* and *N. Amer.*

1456–7 *Paston Lett.* I. 406 Whan he maket straunge to ley dowun the condempnacion. **1549** SOMERSET etc. in Strype *Eccl. Mem.* (1721) II. II. 102 If they shal make strange to have the same [treaty] so confirmed. *a* **1553** UDALL *Royster D.* v. vi. (Arb.) 84 *R.* Thei wer not angry then. *M.* Yes at first, and made strange. **1565** COOPER *Thesaurus* s.v. *Delicium, Delicias facere*, to make strange and dally, because he would be intreated. **1598** CHAPMAN *Blinde Beg. Alexandria* D 2 b, Therefore beautious Ladie make not strange, To take a freind and adde vnto thy Ioyes. **1602** ROWLANDS *Greenes Ghost* 46 Maister Doctor at the first made strange of the matter, and seemed verie loth to deale in it. **1633** FORD *'Tis Pity* II. i, Sir, now you know my house, pray make not strange. **1655** tr. *Sorel's Com. Hist. Francion* IX. 18 This brown lasse did make a request to the Shepherd for her, but at the first he seemed to stand off, and to make strange thereat. **1727** DE FOE *Hist. Appar.* viii (1840) 134 However, she made still strange of it. **1773** C. DIBDIN *Deserter* I. vii, How strange you make of this matter! **1904** *Eng. Dial. Dict.* V. 804/2 *Strange...* 1. *adj...* *W*[*est*]*m*[*oreland*]. Also said of one who professes to be in ignorance of some matters it is well known he understands. 'Thoo's neea casion to makt seea strange, thoo knows o' t'time.' **1937** P. K. DEVINE *Devine's Folk Lore of Newfoundland* 33 *To make strange*, to be afraid or timid. 'Don't make strange,' said to a guest sitting down to eat. **1966** *Amer. Speech* XLI. 295 [Newfoundland] *Don't make strange.* Said to make a guest feel at home. **1974** P. GZOWSKI *Bk. about this Country* 173/1 The luxury of a babysitter is rare—besides, the baby makes strange, and no babysitter with knowledge aforehand would come near!

II. *absol.*, passing into *sb.*

†**14.** A strange person, stranger; in pl. sense, strangers. Also *rarely* in pl. form. *Obs.*

Trevisa has *straungene* as genit. pl.

a **1325** *MS. Rawl. B. 520* lf. 31 b, Felonies i don to straunge. *c* **1325** *Prose Ps.* xciii. 6 Hij slowen wydowes and strange. *c* **1374** CHAUCER *Troylus* II. 411 (Campsall MS.) Allas what shulde straunge to me don When he þat for my best frend y wende [etc.]. **1387** TREVISA *Higden* V. 321 In holy place I now reste in straungene londe. *c* **1400** *Destr. Troy* 2975 þou couet to se þat straunge, þat was stoute. *c* **1400** *Laud Troy Bk.* 7182 ȝe may ȝit kyng Thoas chaunge For on of oure or for som strange. **1477** in *Engl. Miscell.* (Surtees 1890) 27 Item William Panter..maid afray of ij stranghis.

†**15.** *pl.* News. *Obs. rare*$^{-1}$.

a **1500** *Coventry Corpus Chr. Plays* II. 4 Where nevis and strangis be cum of lately, Affermyng the seyng of old profecie.

III. 16. Comb., forming adjs.

a. parasynthetic, as ***strange-plumaged, -tongued***; **b.** prefixed as compl. to pres. pples., as ***strange-looking, -sounding***; **c.** adverbially (now *rare*), as ***strange-achieved, -composed, -digested, -moulded***, etc.

1534 MORE *Comf. agst. Trib.* III. xx. Wks. 1246/1 He may be a minstrell & make melodye you wotte wel with some other instrument, some straunge fashioned peradeunture, that neuer was seene before. **1549** COVERDALE etc. *Erasm. Par. Eph.* Prol. ¶ij, So diligent to continue & aduaunce their popyshe pryuate masses & other straunge tounged seruice. **1597** SHAKS. *2 Hen. IV*, IV. v. 72 For this, they haue ingrossed and pyl'd vp The canker'd heapes of strange-atchieved Gold. **1601** —— *Jul. C.* I. iii. 33 Indeed, it is a strange disposed time. **1607** TOURNEUR *Rev. Trag.* I. i. A 3, Some strange digested fellow..Of ill-contented nature. *Ibid.*, Ile be that strange composed fellow. **1627** MAY *Lucan* I. B 1, Strange formed Meteors the thicke ayre had bred. **1756** HOME *Douglas* II. (1757) 28 The red moon..Cross'd and divided by strange-colour'd clouds. **1814** SCOTT *Diary* 10 Aug. in *Lockhart* (1837) III. iv. 171 One of their boats comes off, a strange-looking thing without an entire plank in it. **1820** W. IRVING *Sketch Bk.* (1859) 53 Some strange-favored being. **1842** BORROW *Bible in Spain* xxv, They were conversing with each other in a strange sounding dialect. **1859** TENNYSON *Elaine* 796 Under the strange-statued gate. **1868–70** MORRIS *Earthly Par.* III. 75 Among strange-plumaged bird, Strange-fruited tree, and strange-clad maid. **1917** D. H. LAWRENCE *Look! We have come Through!* 135 Also she who is the other has strange-moulded breasts.

†**strange**, *v. Obs.* Also 5–6 **straunge**, 5 **straunche.** [ad. OF. *estranger*: see ESTRANGE *v.*]

1. *trans.* To remove, banish, keep apart *from* an accustomed place, condition, relations, etc.

c **1430** *Pilgr. Lyf Manhode* III. li. (1869) 162 Ye shulden now be me ful sweete and deere, ne were j so aloyned and straunged from yow. **1450** *Rolls of Parlt.* V. 216/2 He shuld be straunged from his high Presence, and from his Court. *c* **1450** *Knt. de la Tour* 58 And for that dede we were.. straunged from gret ioye and blisse. **1547** *Bk. of Marchantes* b j b, The pore people ae so vndertrod, grawen, devoured, and so straunged for [= from] y^e knowledge of God. **1559** *Mirr. Mag., Mowbray banished* xxi, I that was exylde for aye, My enmy straunged but for a ten yeares daye.

2. To make strange or different, alter.

1390 GOWER *Conf.* II. 329 For anon after he was changed And from his oghne kinde stranged, A lappewincke mad he was. *Ibid.* III. 77 The See his propre kinde changeth, And al the world his forme strangeth. **1567** DRANT *Hor. De Arte Poet.* A ij, By wittie composition its excellente to heare A knowne worde straunged hansumlye. **1638** BRATHWAIT *Barnabees Jrnl.* IV. (1818) 167 Musing I should be so stranged, I resolv'd them, I was changed.

3. To alienate in feeling or affection, estrange *from* (rarely *of*).

1460 *Paston Lett.* I. 507 That I schulde..sodenly have departed in to these parties,..and that I straunched me from sertein persones to moche. **1483** CAXTON *Golden Leg.* 266/2 She lad the lyf of an heremyte and al Straunged fro the world. *c* **1500** *Melusine* xiii. 48 Are ye as now so straunged of vs that ye marye you without that we know therof tyl the day of weddyng? **1580** HOLLYBAND *Treas. Fr. Tong, Estrangé*, stranged, alienated. **1623** WODROEPHE *Spared Hours Soldier* 364 Vice and Laizinesse, which offuscate & diffame the Children of good Houses, stranging them from their God. **1641** TOMBES *Leaven Phar. Wil-worship* (1643) 9 It strangeth the mindes of people and Ministers from learning, and studying Gods word. *a* **1656** BP. HALL *Rem. Wks.* (1660) 146 Did we love our Father in Heaven as Children could we strange ourselves from his interest? **1691** *D'Emiliane's Frauds Rom. Monks* 47, I might have had good reason to infer from their behaviour, that their Hearts were much stranged from the words of their Lips. **1715** tr. *C'tess D'Anois' Wks.* 93, I thought him quite strang'd from me.

b. To make (a person) a stranger *to* (a sentiment).

1390 GOWER *Conf.* II. 190 Whan ther is lacke in hem above, The poeple is stranged to the love Of trouthe, in cause of ignorance. *Ibid.* III. 210 He which that wolde himselve strange To Pite, fond mercy so strange, That he withoute grace is lore.

4. ? To grudge (something valuable) *to* (a person); *refl.* to refuse (*to* grant something).

1439 *Rolls of Parlt.* V. 24/1 By cause of which Statuyt thus made, the Chaunceller of England for the tyme beyng, hath straunged hem oft tymes to graunt Licences. *c* **1489** CAXTON *Blanchardyn* 71 That sore lytyll that god hath lent me of goodes sholde not be straunged vnto hym by me, for he is worthy to haue mykel more.

5. *intr.* To depart, estrange oneself *from*; to be removed or become alienated *from.*

c **1380** WYCLIF *Sel. Wks.* I. 12 Crist shulde be our maister, and we shulden not strange from him. *Ibid.* 79 Men shulden speke her wordis as Goddis lawe spekiþ, and strange not in speche from undirstondinge of þe puple. **1390** GOWER *Conf.* III. 6 Mi wittes changen And alle lustes fro me strangen.

6. To become strange or changed. *Obs.*

1390 GOWER *Conf.* II. 264 And riht so as hir jargoun strangeth, In sondri wise hir forme chaungeth.

7. To be surprised, wonder. Const. *at*, dependent clause, or *to* and inf.

1639 FULLER *Holy War* IV. ii. 169 Whereat I should strange more, but that [etc.]. **1648** GEREE *Red Horse* 7 Strange not then at changes. **1654** GAYTON *Pleas. Notes* III. i. 69 Thou wouldst not much strange that I doe before-hand conforme my selfe to the Ceremony. **1664** BUTLER *Hud.* II.

i. 9 Is't not enough to make one strange, That some mens fancies should ne'er change? **1671** *True Non-Conformist* 472, I strange you should accuse Henry the Eight of a civil Papacy, and so inconsequently acquit al his Successors. *a* **1691** G. FOX *Jrnl.* (1827) I. 80, I stranged at it. **1696** ELIZ. WEST *Mem.* (1865) 53, I stranged mightily what might be the reason that the mills were going. **1757** MRS. GRIFFITH *Lett. Henry & Frances* (1767) II. 158 J. M. is in this house, offered me his company, and stranges much, as the waiter phrases it, why I should thus chuse to be alone. **1788** SHIRREFS *Poems* (1790) 164, I strange to hear ye speak in sic a stile. **1880** *Antrim & Down Gloss.* s.v., I strange very much that you didn't come.

b. *trans.* To wonder at.

1641 R. HARRIS *Abners Funerall* Ep. Ded., Madam, Strange not my slownesse.

c. To surprise.

1657 GAULE *Sap. Justif.* 74 It stranges me still, that [etc.].

Hence †**stranged** *ppl. a.*, made strange; †'**stranging** *vbl. sb.*, wondering.

1581 T. HOWELL *Deuises* K iij b, What straunged sight hath me dismaide. **1658** GURNALL *Chr. in Arm.* II. verse 15. xvi. 456 This very thing made one of the Disciples ask Christ with no little stranging at it, Lord [etc.].

†'**strangeful,** *a. Obs. rare*$^{-1}$. [f. STRANGE *a.* + -FUL.] Full of strangeness. Hence †'**strangefully** *adv.*

1591 SYLVESTER *Du Bartas* I. ii. 878 O Frantick France! why dost not Thou make use Of strangefull Signes, whereby the Heav'ns induce Thee to repentance? **1664** *Depos. Cast. York* (Surtees) 124 His daughter Alice, of the age of 17, hath beene for six weeks lastly past most strangfully and wonderfully handled.

'**Strangelove.** Also strangelove. The name of the character Dr. *Strangelove* from the film of that title (1963) directed by Stanley Kubrick, used *transf.* to designate one who ruthlessly considers or plans nuclear warfare. Freq. *attrib.* and with *Dr.*

1968 *Listener* 16 May 638/1 Dr Strangelove is still at it... He has realised that the hydrogen bomb may yet prove to be a limited..means of annihilating the human race. His current concern is with finding ways of doing it more cheaply..and with greater gusto. **1972** *Village Voice* (N.Y.) 1 June 10/4 In the strangelove language of the AEC, the accident exceeded the 'maximum credible accident' established as a possibility for the installation in the AEC's Hazards Summary. **1973** *Guardian* 22 Feb. 11/3 The Strangelove school, of which Dr Kissinger is a charter member, sees the world as a series of problems that can be manipulated by US money, technology, and bombs. *Ibid.* 28 Feb. 10/6 Professor William Shockley the exponent of sterilisation for low IQ subjects..went into a Dr Strangelove act. **1975** *University* (Princeton Univ.) Winter 5/1 *The Physicists* makes a Strangelove even out of Einstein. **1976** 'R. B. DOMINIC' *Murder out of Commission* xv. 137 Dean Kennison was no Dr Strangelove, yearning to set off bigger and better bangs. **1980** *Times* 12 Aug. 10/7 Nervousness about a latterday Dr Strangelove getting his itchy finger on the button.

Hence (**Dr.**) '**Strangelovean, -ian** *a.*; '**Strangelovism,** a word or expression characteristic of one who toys with the concept of nuclear war.

1967 *Newsweek* 27 Mar. 47 Words like deterrent, credibility, overkill and doomsday machine became familiar, and were even kidded in such movies as 'Dr. Strangelove'. Now development of anti-ballistic missiles has produced a second generation of Strangelovisms. **1969** *Washington Post* 23 Apr. A16/4 Mendel Rivers..suggested that nuclear weapons be used if necessary to 'bring this crowd to its knees'... Such 'strangelovisms' from that source are of course not new. **1971** P. DICKSON *Think Tanks* 4 Outside Washington, D.C.,..a group of analysts is fighting the wars of the 1990's in a $50,000 Strangelovean game room to see who wins, why, and with what weapons. **1977** *Time* 11 Apr. 13/1 The concepts are often Strangelovean. **1978** *Chatelaine* (Canada) Dec. 41/3 There was something Dr. Strangelovian about these top-level intellectuals who discussed top-secret scenarios.

strangely ('streɪn(d)ʒlɪ), *adv.* [f. STRANGE *a.* + -LY^{2}.]

†**1.** In a foreign or outlandish manner. *rare*$^{-0}$.

1483 *Cath. Angl.* 367/2 Strawngely, *extranee, barbare, peregrine.*

†**2.** In an unfriendly or unfavourable manner; with cold or distant bearing. *Obs.*

c **1374** CHAUCER *Troylus* v. 955 And straungely she spak and seyde þus. **1461** *Paston Lett.* II. 59, I have spoken with hem of that matre..and I have found the[m] too straunchely disposed. **1548** HALL *Chron., Edw. V* 23 b, When the protector had harde the proposicion, he loked very strangely therat. **1560** DAUS tr. *Sleidane's Comm.* 278 b, He answered somwhat straungly [L. *paulo respondet alienius*]. *c* **1600** SHAKS. *Sonn.* xlix. 5 When thou shalt strangely passe, And scarcely greete me with that sunne thine eye. *Ibid.* cx. 6, I haue lookt on truth Asconce and strangely. *a* **1707** PATRICK *Autobiogr.* (1839) 25 Look not strangely upon him because he differs from thee in some opinions.

†**3.** In a way that is unusual or exceptional; in an unusual sense. *Obs.* (Merged in 5.)

1533 MORE *Confut. Barnes* Wks. 807/1 Heretikes, whiche bee straungers from the housholde of Christes catholike church, and whiche doe strangely rehearse and strangely declare Christes catholyke scrypture, agaynste the knowen catholike doctrine. **1581** PETTIE *Guazzo's Civ. Conv.* III. (1586) 122 b, If you take it not so, me thinkes..you take it too strangelie, and too obscurelie.

†**4.** In an uncommon or exceptional degree; very greatly, extremely. *Obs.* (Merged in 5.)

1387-8 T. USK *Test. Love* I. iii. (Skeat) l. 59 The storm so straungely..gan..us assayle. **1610** SHAKS. *Temp.* IV. i. 7 Thou Hast strangely stood the test. **1618** in Foster *Eng. Factories Ind.* (1906) 32 Hee was straungely importunate with me to give him leave to goe. **1665** in *Verney Mem.* (1907) II. 243 The Sicknesse is strangely increased. **1671** SALMON *Syn. Med.* III. xxii. 395 Camomil,..it strangely cureth Agues. **1705** HEARNE *Duct. Hist.* (ed. 2) I. 155 Civil Prudence..sparkles strangely in his Institution of Cyrus. **1707** PRIOR *Sat. Poets* 109 How fine your Plot, how exquisite each Scene! And play'd at Court, would strangely please the Queen. **1719** DE FOE *Crusoe* I. (Globe) 122 The Heat of the Sun bak'd them strangely hard.

5. In a manner so unusual or exceptional as to excite wonder or astonishment; surprisingly, unaccountably, oddly.

a **1450** *Knt. de la Tour* 64 A gentill woman..come to a fest so straungely atyred and queintly arraied..that all that sawe her come ranne towardes her to wonder. **1590** SPENSER *F.Q.* III. ii. 18 By strange occasion she did him behold, And much more strangely gan to loue his sight. **1599** DALLAM in *Early Voy. Levant* (Hakluyt Soc.) 85 The which myls be verrie straingly made. **1610** SHAKS. *Temp.* III. iii. 40 They vanish'd strangely. *a* **1652** BROME *Queenes Exch.* v. i, *Osr.* Is Offa mad? *Keep.* O quite besides himself, and talks the strangeliest Of his fathers murder. **1712** STEELE *Spect.* No. 306 ⁋8 The Vagaries of Fancy which so strangely misled you. **1775** SHERIDAN *Rivals* v. i, This fellow runs strangely in my head. **1849** MACAULAY *Hist. Eng.* vi. II. 13 Men who had never before had a scruple had on a sudden become strangely scrupulous. **1874** GREEN *Short Hist.* iii. §6. 144 Strangely as the two men differed from each other, their aim was the same. **1888** BURGON *Lives 12 Gd. Men* I. ii. 116 Mankind show themselves strangely forgetful of their chiefest benefactors.

6. quasi-*Comb.* (The adv. qualifying a ppl. adj. or adj.; often hyphened when the use is attributive.)

1598 CHAPMAN *Hero & Leander* III. 183 Most strangely-intellectuall fire. **1605** SHAKS. *Macb.* IV. iii. 150 Strangely visited people All swolne and Vlcerous. **1633** FORD *Love's Sacrif.* IV. H 2 b, Some strangely-shap'd man-beast. **1648** J. BEAUMONT *Psyche* II. clxxv, His strangely-potent Wand's petard. **1777** BURKE *Corr.* (1844) II. 172 So strangely-timed a piece of adulation. **1851** HELPS *Comp. Solit.* xiii. 273 This mass of strangely-mingled materials.

strangeness ('streɪn(d)ʒnɪs). [-NESS.]

1. a. The quality of being strange, foreign, unfamiliar, uncommon, unusual, extraordinary, etc. (see the adj.).

c **1386** CHAUCER *Pars. T.* ⁋340 That precious clothyng is cowpable..for his strangenesse and degisynesse. *c* **1440** *Promp. Parv.* 479/1 Strawngenesse, *extraneitas.* **1531** ELYOT *Gov.* III. xviii, For the straungenesse of it, I will reherce a notable historie. **1577** B. GOOGE *Heresbach's Husb.* I. 37 b, You must geue them but little at once, lest the strangenesse of the foode [L. *novitas pabuli*] hurt them. **1612** BACON *Ess., Beauty* (Arb.) 210 There is no excellent beauty, that hath not some strangenesse in the proportions. **1638** WILKINS *Discov. World in Moon* I. i. 1 The strangenesse of this opinion is no sufficient reason why it should be rejected. **1768–74** TUCKER *Lt. Nat.* (1834) II. 567 Novelty is different from strangeness; one is engaging, the other unpleasant. **1847** JAMES *Convict* iii, The first strangeness of new arrival wore off with the two guests. **1860** TYNDALL *Glac.* II. xvii. 316 There is a strangeness about the place which repels you. **1861** DICKENS *Lett.* (1880) II. 152 This did not tend to cheer the strangeness I felt. **1885** *Manch. Exam.* 20 Mar. 4/7 Witnesses..declared that her strangeness of manner was subsequent to the marriage.

b. quasi-*concr.* With *pl.*: Something strange; a strange circumstance, object, event, or the like. †Without *pl.*: Strange matter, strange stuff.

a **1566** R. EDWARDS *Damon & Pithias* (facs.) B iv, Some strangenesse there is, that breedeth this musinge. **1568** HACKET tr. *Thevet's New found World* xxii. 36 Certaine others being ignorant doe write yet more strangenesse. **1604** E. G[RIMSTONE] tr. *Acosta's Hist. Indies* III. xxi. 186 For that it is rare and extraordinarie to see a Countrie where it never raines nor thunders; men desire naturally to know the cause of this strangenes. **1651** JER. TAYLOR *Serm.* I. vii. 83 New accidents and strangenesses of Providence. **1804** COLERIDGE *Lit. Rem.* (1836) II. 414 Fond of the curious, and a hunter of oddities and strangenesses. **1883** ABP. BENSON in *Standard* 28 June 2/3 All their teaching would have a substantial basis and staple, instead of excitement and strangenesses, which ended where they began.

†**2. a.** Absence of friendly feeling or relations; discouraging or uncomplying attitude towards others; coldness, aloofness. *Obs.*

c **1386** CHAUCER *Shipm. T.* 386 Ye han maad a manere straungenesse Bitwixen me and my cosyn daun Iohn. *c* **1400** *Rom. Rose* 3611 Nor straungenesse was in him sene, No more than he ne had wrathed bene. **1470–85** MALORY *Arthur* VII. xix. 242 Allas faire lady..I haue not deserued that ye shold shewe me this straungenes. **1540–1** ELYOT *Image Gov.* (1556) 25 b, Changyng affabilitee into straungenesse and stately countenance. **1575** TURBERV. *Falconrie* 129 Vntill..shee be familiar with the man without any straungenesse or coynesse. **1607** CHAPMAN *Bussy d'Ambois* II. ii. 192 Alas, I fear my strangeness will retire him. **1669** R. MONTAGU in *Buccleuch MSS.* (Hist. MSS. Comm.) I. 452 The King here lives at so much distance and strangeness with me. **1718** HICKES & NELSON *J. Kettlewell* I. viii. 30 Some strangeness had..intervened betwixt him and his Old Friends. **1752** JOHNSON *Rambler* No. 194 ⁋2 He practises the stare of strangeness, and the smile of condescension. **1766** C. BEATTY *Tour* (1768) 47 All anger and strangeness of mind might be for ever done away.

†**b.** *to make strangeness*: to show oneself unfriendly or uncomplying. *Obs.*

c **1407** LYDG. *Reson & Sens.* 4829 Ther was no wight that sayde nay Nor made thoo no straungenesse, For the porter ydelnesse Lete hym in and that in hast. *a* **1513** FABYAN *Chron.* v. cxxxiv. (1811) 118 Where straungenesse was made by the ruler of yᵉ hous for the receyte of those relykes, tyll a myracle or dyuyne token there was shewyd.

3. *Particle Physics.* A quantized property of hadrons, now attributed to the *s* quark, that is conserved in strong and electromagnetic interactions but not in weak ones and is represented by a quantum number S equal to the hypercharge of a particle minus its baryon numbers.

1956 M. GELL-MANN in *Nuovo Cimento* IV. Suppl. 852 Since we have $S = 0$ for ordinary particles and $S \neq 0$ for 'strange' ones we refer to S as 'strangeness'. **1960** *New Scientist* 5 May 1126/2 Like electric charge, the total magnitude of strangeness remains constant in a nuclear process. Not so, however, for the decay phenomena... Decay forces violate strangeness-conservation. **1963** S. TOLANSKY *Introd. Atomic Physics* (ed. 5) xxiii. 397 Whilst the strangeness number seems to play a basic part in the baryon reactions it does *not* operate in the base of the leptons... The concept of isospin is hardly appropriate to the leptons and with this falls away the significance of strangeness too. **1965** H. MUIRHEAD *Physics of Elementary Particles* ix. 396 The classification of particles using the hypercharge quantum number is more economical in numbers than one involving strangeness. **1972** [see HYPERCHARGE]. **1981** *Sci. Amer.* June 57/1 Strangeness conservation is now understood to be not a fundamental principle like energy conservation..but a consequence of the detailed theory of the strong interactions.

stranger ('streɪndʒə(r)), *sb.* (and *a.*) Forms: 4 **strangere,** 4–5 **straungere,** 4–6 **straunger,** 5 **strangier, -yer, straungeour, -ior, -yer, strawnger(e, strayngour, strongere, strounger,** (6 **strenger**), 5–6 *Sc.* **strainger, strangear,** 6 **straungier,** 4– **stranger.** See also ESTRANGER. [Aphetic a. OF. *estrangier* (mod.F. *étranger*) = Pr. *estrangier*, Sp. *extrangero*, Pg. *estrangeiro*, It. *straniere, straniero*:—popular L. **extrāneārius*, f. L. *extrāne-us*: see EXTRANEOUS and STRANGE *adjs.*

The OF. word (like its equivalents in the other Rom. langs.) is primarily and chiefly an adj.; in Eng. the subst. use is primary, such adjectival uses as exist (see 13 below) being almost wholly developed from the attributive use of the sb.]

1. a. One who belongs to another country, a foreigner; chiefly (now exclusively), one who resides in or comes to a country to which he is a foreigner; an alien.

Now somewhat *rare*; the recent examples show mixture of sense 2 or 4.

1375 BARBOUR *Bruce* XX. 402 And to the lord Dowglass gaf he The waward, for to leid and steir All haill the strangeris with him weir. *c* **1375** *Sc. Leg. Saints* xxvii. (*Machor*) 26 God mad hym to rest syn in france, in toron, til honouryt be, set þare a strangere was he. *c* **1460** J. RUSSELL *Bk. Nurture* 1109 More ouer take hede he must to aliene commers straungeres, and to straungers of þis land, resient dwelleres. **1487** WRIOTHESLEY *Chron.* (1875) I. 2 One Martin Swarte, a straunger, slayne all in a feild that they made againste the Kinge. **1493** *Sc. Acts Jas. IV* (1814) II. 234/1 Quhene ony schip of alienaris or strangearis of vþer realmes cummys in þe havin of Leith. *c* **1511** *1st Eng. Bk. Amer.* (Arb.) Introd. p. xxxii, We kepe also the poure people with our almes alle that cometh be it strenger or of oure owne people. **1569** in *Southampton Court Leet Rec.* (1905) I. 58 That none wᵗʰin the towne of Southampton englishe or stranger by enne butter other then for theire owne stowere. **1597** MORLEY *Introd. Mus.* Pref., Then was I forced to runne to the workes of manie, both strangers and Englishmen..for a solution..of my doubt. **1611** BIBLE *Transl. Pref.* ⁋11 As St. Augustine saith; A man had rather be with his dog than with a stranger (whose tongue is strange vnto him). **1650** A. COWLEY in T. Brown *Misc. Aulica* (1702) 134 His Forces compos'd of about six hundred Strangers, and the rest drawn out of the Islands, are about two thousand. **1651** HOBBES *Leviath.* II. xix. 101 Strangers (that is, men not used to live under the same government, nor speaking the same language). **1667** MILTON *P.L.* XII. 358 At last they seise The Scepter, and regard not Davids Sons, Then loose it to a stranger. *a* **1700** EVELYN *Diary* (1879) I. 3 In the judgement of Strangers as well as Englishmen it [*sc.* Wotton] may be compared to [etc.]. **1729** T. COOKE *Tales* etc. 213 If stated Rules are observed..the Facility of learning the Language will be no small Inducement to the Study of it in Strangers. **1870** DK. OF ARGYLL *Iona* i. 14 The story..that a British chief invited the Saxon stranger from across the German Sea. **1871** FREEMAN *Norm. Conq.* IV. xvii. 55 In a generation or two the stranger ceased to be a stranger. The foreign spoiler.. insensibly changed into the son of the soil. **1906** W. A. CRAIGIE *Relig. Anc. Scandinavia* iv. 57 In Sweden, indeed, strangers appear to have run some risk of being selected as victims.

†**b.** Something that comes from abroad; *esp.* an exotic plant. *Obs.*

1578 LYTE *Dodoens* I. lxxxvii. 440 The apple of Perow is a stranger also [*Ibid., supra*: a strange plant]. **1597** GERARDE *Herbal* I. lxxxiii. 133 The last [flower] is a stranger in England, yet we haue it and the rest in our gardens. **1657** COLES *Adam in Eden* cxi, There are divers Sorts of Wood-binds, some..known throughout the Land;..others are strangers, or not so well known. **1669** STURMY *Mariner's Mag.* VII. xi. 17 This Declining Dial being a Stranger with us, followeth the fashion of his own Country. **1732** LYTTELTON *Progr. Love* ii. 69 A Bird..Whose yellow Plumage shines like polish'd Gold; From distant Isles the lovely Stranger came, And bears the fortunate Canaries Name.

2. a. One who is not a native of, or who has not long resided in, a country, town, or place. Chiefly, a new comer, one who has not yet become well acquainted with the place, or (cf. 4) one who is not yet well known.

1447 BOKENAM *Saints* i. (*Marg.*) 881 Allas, quod he, euene as a straunger And as vnknowyn also in this cuntre Ineuytabylly I must deyin her. **1592** GREENE *Upst. Courtier* C 2, Because I am a stranger in this land, & but here lately arriued, they wil hold me as an vpstart. **1596** SHAKS. *Tam.*

Shr. II. i. 90 Pardon me sir, the boldnesse is mine owne, That being a stranger in this Cittie heere, Do make my selfe a sutor to your daughter. *a* **1626** BACON *New Atlantis* 5 He came to conduct vs to the Strangers House... The Strangers House is a faire and spacious House, built of Brick, [etc.]. **1794** MRS. RADCLIFFE *Myst. Udolpho* vi, I cannot show you the way, for I am almost a stranger here. **1845** GOSSE *Ocean* iv. (1849) 178 But of all the constellations that stud the sky of the southern hemisphere, there is none that more strikes a stranger than the Southern Cross. **1860** *Merc. Marine Mag.* VII. 311 Some allowance is to be made for him from the fact of his being a stranger in these seas.

transf. *a* **1767** M. BRUCE *Ode to Cuckoo* 1 Hail, beauteous Stranger of the wood! Attendant on the Spring! **1811** HOGG *Verses to Comet of 1811*, 9 Stranger of heaven! I bid thee hail! **1864** SEMMES *Cruise Alabama & Sumter* I. 64 The Governor at once proceeded to take legal opinion as to the propriety of permitting the suspicious stranger [the Sumter] to coal. **1892** EMILY LAWLESS *Grania* I. 179 Leaning against a big boulder, a 'stranger' like the one that blocked the mouth of their own gully.

†**b.** In parochial registers: A person not belonging to the parish. *Obs.*

The Latin equivalent *extraneus* (*extranea*) was also commonly used.

1507–8 *Rec. St. Mary at Hill* (1905) 262 R' of stevyn sawnderson for the beryell of a stranger, xij d. **1517–18** *Ibid.* 299 Ress' for the buryall of a straunger in þe greate chirche-yard.. viij d. **1585** in *Trans. Essex Archæol. Soc.* (1863) II. 128 A poore child beinge a stranger bapt[d] the 13th of Julye.

†**c.** *strangers' silver* (Sc.).

1591 *Exch. Rolls Scot.* XXII. 156 Borrowit fra the said clerk of register be his majestie of the straingeris siluer consignit in his handis.

3. a. A guest or visitor, in contradistinction to the members of the household. Now chiefly with mixture of sense 4.

to make a stranger of: to treat with ceremony, not as one of the family. Chiefly with negative.

c **1400** MAUNDEV. (1839) iv. 29 At grete Festes and for Straungeres, thei setten Formes and Tables. **1420–2** LYDG. *Thebes* II. 1468 The fresshnesse of Her heuenly cheres So agreable was to the straungeres,.. that.. hem thoght it lik a thyng Celestial. **1430–40** *Bk. Curtasye* 801 in *Babees Bk.* 326 But he sende hit to ony strongere, A pese þat is hym leue and dere. *c* **1450–60** *Bp. Grosseteste's Househ. Stat.* Ibid. 330 Commaunde ye the officers that they admitte your knowlechyd men, familiers frendys, and strangers, with mery chere. *c* **1470** *Gol. & Gaw.* 1155 He gart at ane sete burd the strangearis begin, The maist seymly in sale ordanit thame sete. *c* **1470** *Rauf Coilȝear* 214 Gyll, lat the cop raik for my bennysoun; And gar our Gaist begin, and syne drink thow to me; Sen he is ane stranger, me think it ressoun. **1509** FISHER *Funeral Serm. C'tess Richmond* Wks. (1876) 296 The housholde seruauntes muste be put in some good ordre. The straungers of honeste.. must be consydered. **1519** in *Archæologia* XXV. 425 Straungers in ye same week Imprimis Mr Roger Woodows & his wyff, & his iiij servants from Sondaye till Wedynsdaye. **1577** H. RHODES *Bk. Nurture* in *Babees Bk.* 102 If that a straunger syt thee neare, See thou make him good cheare. **1667** MILTON *P.L.* v. 316 And what thy stores contain, bring forth and poure Abundance, fit to honour and receive Our Heav'nly stranger. **1699** DAMPIER *Voy.* II. i. v. 93 That part that fronts the Gate, has a pretty neat room, which seems to be designed for the reception of Strangers. **1766** GOLDSM. *Vic. W.* xxxii, He now resides.. at a relation's house,.. seldom sitting at the side-table, except when there is no room at the other; for they make no stranger of him.

transf. **1577** B. GOOGE *Heresbach's Husb.* II. 76 A ground drye, fatte, and well laboured with the Mattocke, wherein the stranger may be well cherished [L. *aduenis hospitale*].

b. Any of the things which are popularly imagined to forebode the coming of an unexpected visitor, e.g. a floating tea-leaf in the cup; an excrescence on the wick of a candle, causing guttering; a piece of soot flapping on the bar of the grate; a moth flying towards one.

1798 COLERIDGE *Frost at Midnight* 20 Only that film, which flutter'd on the grate, Still flutters there... Ah me!.. How often in my early school-boy days, With most believing superstitious wish Presageful have I gaz'd upon the bars, To watch the *stranger* there! **1838** G. WILSON *Let.* in Jessie A. Wilson *Mem.* iii. (1860) 136 Have you seen any strangers floating in your tea? **1862** C. C. ROBINSON *Dial. Leeds* 423 *Stranger*, a name given to the soot-flakes which peel off, and flutter on the bars of fire-grates [etc.]. **1870** *Brand's Pop. Antiq.* (ed. Hazl.) III. 181 A kind of fungus in the candle, he [*sc.* Grose] observes, predicts the visit of a stranger from that part of the country nearest the object. [Addit. note] This is called a stranger. **1894** R. LEIGHTON *Wreck Golden Fleece* 84 Pausing only to take up the silver snuffers and clip a 'stranger' from the wick of the guttering candle. **1896** PROUDLOCK *Borderland Muse* 7 Oh see, Granny, see! A stranger sae bonnilie flaps on the bars.

4. a. An unknown person; a person whom one has not seen before; also in wider sense, a person with whom one is not yet well acquainted. Phrases, *a perfect, a total, an utter stranger*. Const. *to*.

c **1385** CHAUCER *L.G.W.* 1075 And, for he was a straunger, somwhat she Lyked him the bet, as.. To som folk ofte newe thing is swote. *c* **1489** CAXTON *Blanchardyn* xii. 43 Incontynente that she felte her self to be thus sodaynly kyst of a man straunger out of her knowlege, she [etc.]. **1522** MORE *De quat. Noviss.* Wks. 81/1 So that if thou consider this well, thou maist loke vpon deth, not as a stranger, but as a nigh neibour. **1601** SHAKS. *Twel. N.* I. iv. 4 The Duke.. hath known you but three dayes, and already you are no stranger. *a* **1700** EVELYN *Diary* 30 Jan. 1653, At our own parish Church a stranger preach'd. **1719** DE FOE *Crusoe* I. (Globe) 283 When I came to England, I was as perfect a Stranger to all the World, as if I had never been known there. **1798** SOPHIA LEE *Canterb. T., Young Lady's T.* II. 488 Sir Edward, perceiving.. a person quite a stranger to him. **1825** LYTTON *Zicci* i, But the stranger had an air and tone with him it was impossible to resist. **1876** J. PARKER *Paracl.* I. viii. 114 He [Christ] has always been a stranger, viewed with suspicion. **1893** D. DAVIDSON *Mem. Long Life* viii. (ed. 2) 198 Mr. Bell was sitting at breakfast, when a stranger entered his bungalow. **1908** R. BAGOT *A. Cuthbert* v. 41 After all, you must remember that up to a few days ago you were a comparative stranger to your aunt Jane.

transf. **1878** H. S. LEIGH *Town Garland* 77 Helvellyn I have never seen, While Snowdon is a stranger quite. **1889** GRETTON *Memory's Harkback* 168 Would I not drive myself? No; I could drive a horse of my own, but would have nothing to do with a stranger.

b. Said playfully of a newborn child. Usu. *little stranger*.

'Welcome, little stranger!' was a quotation common in the early part of the 19th century, and sometimes printed or embroidered on articles for nursery use.

a **1674** T. TRAHERNE *Centuries of Meditations* (1927) III. ii. 151, I was a little stranger, which at my entrance into the world was saluted and surrounded with innumerable joys. **1787** J. WOODFORDE *Diary* 6 May (1926) II. 320 Mrs. Custance was brought to bed of a Boy about 11 o'clock this Morn'. She with the little stranger as well as can be expected. **1829** SCOTT *Guy M.* Introd., 'I fear from your looks,' said the father, 'that you have bad tidings to tell me of my young stranger'. **1856** H. MAYHEW *Rhine* 41 A medical bulletin, informing you of that day's state of health of some 'little stranger' and its mother within. **1896** KIPLING *Seven Seas, Three-decker* 14 We never talked obstetrics when the Little Stranger came.

c. *Vocatively*. Orig. in rustic use in the U.S., a customary mode of address to one whose name is unknown. Now in gen. colloq. use, to address one who has not been seen for some time.

1817 M. BIRKBECK *Notes Journ. Amer.* (1818) 81 On my way.. a man.. hailed me with the common, but to us quaint appellation of 'stranger'. **1827** J. F. COOPER *Prairie* ix, I should be better pleased, stranger,.. to be sure the creature was a beast at all. **1884** PHILLIPPS-WOLLEY *Trottings of Tenderfoot* 33 Mighty big feet of yourn, ain't they, stranger? **1934** E. O'NEILL *Days without End* II. 59 Hello, Stranger. **1969** *New Yorker* 3 May 34/3 'Well, stranger, where've you been?' she greeted me. 'Why didn't you come back like you said?' **1973** *Weekly News* (Glasgow) 11 Aug. 5/1 (*caption*) Hello, there, stranger! **1977** F. PARRISH *Fire in Barley* iii. 31 'Mornin', stranger,' said.. the landlord. 'How's the old lady keepin'?' 'Fairish,' said Dan.

d. Predicatively, said of one whose visits have long ceased. Similarly in phr. *to be* (*quite*) *a stranger* and varr., said of an infrequent visitor. †Also, one who never visits (a place), an absentee *from*.

1530 PALSGR. 625/2, I make my selfe a straunger for leavyng to resorte to a place, *je me aliene*. **1540** —— *Acolastus* I. i. Dj, *Pel.* Hast thou not herde tell.. of my sonne? *Ev.* What studyeth he..? *Pel.* To make hym selfe a straunger from his fathers howse [etc.]. **1580** G. HARVEY *Three Proper Lett.* 37, I am lately become a maruellous great straunger at myne olde Mistresse Poetries. **1620** [G. BRYDGES] *Horæ Subs.* 174 To make themselues altogether strangers from the Court and Towne is too strict. **1706** DE FOE *Appar. Mrs. Veal* (1732) 3, I am surprized to see you, you have been so long a Stranger. *c* **1807** JANE AUSTEN *Watsons* in J. Leigh *Mem. Jane Austen* (1871) 349 'So Emma,' said he, 'you are quite a stranger at home.' **1860** C. M. YONGE *Friarswood Post-Office* vii. 115 Ha! Harold King! Well, to be sure, you are a stranger! **1884** ANNIE SWAN *Carlowrie* x. 161 'Eh, Miss Ritchie, what a stranger!' exclaimed Mrs. Dalrymple's pleasant voice. **1910** A. BENNETT *Clayhanger* III. vii. 378 'Well, Mr. Clayhanger,' said the steward... 'You're quite a stranger.' **1916** JOYCE *Portrait of Artist* (1969) 219 You are a great stranger now. **1937** A. UPFIELD *Mr. Jelly's Business* xx. 211 Hello, Mr. Muir! You're quite a stranger. **1962** G. AVERY *Greatest Gresham* ix. 162 Well, if it isn't the kiddies from next door. Why, you are strangers these days.

e. *Austral.* and *N.Z.* An animal which has strayed from a neighbouring flock or herd.

1852 J. R. CLOUGH *Jrnl.* 11 Feb. in *Deans Lett. 1840–54* (1937) 290 Branded 57 calves.. counted all the other cattle; 201 of them strangers. **1933** L. G. D. ACLAND in *Press* (Christchurch, N.Z.) 16 Dec. 21/8 *Stranger*, a sheep of a neighbour's on your own run. **1965** J. S. GUNN *Terminol. Shearing Industry* II. 28 *Stranger*, a strange sheep, probably from an adjoining property, which has joined the flock being shorn. **1972** P. NEWTON *Sheep Thief* xvi. 137 There was nothing unusual in.. having a few 'strangers' (neighbour's sheep) on the place.

5. a. A non-member of a society. Now *rare*.

? *c* **1376** in *Eng. Gilds* (1870) 76 Also þat no brother no sister ne shalle discuse þe counseil of þis fraternite to no straungere. **1556** *Rec. Inverness* (New Spald. Club) I. 3 For withhalding of.. strangeris nocht to be excepit amangis thame as burges or gild broder. **1576** in W. M. Williams *Ann. Founders' Co.* (1867) 65 To comyte to prison those two Strangers which do refuse to be sworne to observe.. Ordynances of theyre sayde Companye. **1879** H. C. POWELL *Amateur Athletic Ann.* 22 Portal, of Balliol, had little difficulty in taking the first prize in the 300 yds. strangers' handicap [at Corpus sports]. **1892** *Photogr. Ann.* II. 607 Brechin Photographic Association... The use of the dark room.. is granted to strangers at the nominal charge of 1s. per month.

b. *Parliament.* One who is not a member or official of the House, and is present at its debates only on sufferance. So occas. with reference to a court of justice.

I spy strangers: the formula used by a member in demanding the expulsion of strangers from the House.

1705 *House of Commons Jrnl.* 31 Oct. 6/2 *Ordered*, That the Serjeant at Arms, attending this House, do, from time to time, take into his Custody any Stranger or Strangers, that he shall see, or be informed of to be, in the House, or Gallery, while the House, or any Committee of the Whole House, is sitting. **1795** tr. *C. P. Moritz's Trav.* 58 The members call aloud to the gallery, *withdraw! withdraw!* On this the strangers withdraw. **1809** *Hansard's Parl. Deb.* XIV. 255 The gallery was not re-opened to strangers, and the house shortly afterwards divided on Mr. Canning's Amendment. **1835** DICKENS *Sk. Boz, Parl. Sk.*, We will try our fortune at the Strangers' gallery, though the nature of the debate encourages very little hope of success. **1861** BROUGHAM *Brit. Const.* xix. 322 Each court should have the power of excluding strangers in certain cases. **1886** H. W. LUCY *Diary Gladstone Parlt.* 120 The galleries over the clock were all full, strangers displaying an undying interest in the proceedings.

6. A person not of one's kin; more fully, *stranger in blood*. Also, a person unconnected by ties of friendship or the like. †*to put on the stranger*: to affect a distant manner.

1535 COVERDALE *Ps.* lxviii. 8, I am become a straunger vnto my brethren, and an aleaunt vnto my mothers children. **1809** MALKIN *Gil Blas* XII. i. (Rtldg.) 423, I came up to pay my devotions; but whim.. determined her to put on the stranger, and receive my compliments with so discouraging a coldness, as to throw me into some little confusion. **1860** HAWTHORNE *Transform.* xxiii, That Miriam—until yesterday her oldest friend—had a right to be told.. that henceforth they must be for ever strangers.

7. a. One who has no share in (some privilege or business). Const. *of, from*. ? *Obs.*

1483 CAXTON *G. de la Tour* d vj, We and alle the world were delyuered to the perille of the deth of helle and made straungers of the greete ioye of paradys. *c* **1535** NISBET *Prol. Rom.* Wks. (S.T.S.) III. 323 Heythen quhilkis ar strangers from the lyf of Gode. **1611** SIR J. DIGBYE *Let.* 2 Feb. in *10th Rep. Hist. MSS. Comm.* App. I. 559 The French Ambass[r] here is much dejected that he has been made a mere stranger in this business.

b. *Law.* One not privy or party to an act. Const. *to*. Also, one not standing towards another in some relation implied in the context.

1543 tr. *Act 1 Rich. III*, c. 7 The sayde fyne to be a fynall ende, and to conclude aswell pryueys as straungers to the same. **1642** tr. *Perkins' Profit. Bk.* x. §691. 298 The feoffees.. are strangers unto the lease [AF. *ils sont estranges a le lease*]. **1765** BLACKSTONE *Comm.* I. xiv. 418 If a servant.. by his negligence does any damage to a stranger, the master shall answer for his neglect. **1766** *Ibid.* II. xxi. 356 Strangers to a fine are all other persons in the world, except only parties and privies. **1818** CRUISE *Digest* (ed. 2) V. 367 If a feoffment from the *cestui que use* to a stranger, after he had conveyed the use, would have made the fine undoubtedly good, the like feoffment would [etc.]. **1842** GREENLEAF *Evid.* I. §522. 672 (Funk) It is also a most obvious principle of justice, that no man ought to be bound by proceedings to which he was a stranger.

†**8.** Something alien; something that has no place in (a class, the nature of a thing, a person's character, thoughts, or discourse). Const. *to*. *Obs.*

1602 MARSTON *Ant. & Mel.* I. B 4 b, Pish, tis our nature to desire things That are thought strangers to the common cut. **1605** SHAKS. *Macb.* IV. iii. 125, I.. Heere abiure The taints, and blames, I laide vpon my selfe, For strangers to my Nature. *a* **1625** FLETCHER *Nice Valour* v. ii, The name of envy is a stranger here. *a* **1653** BINNING *Sinner's Sanct.* v. Wks. (1735) 183 It is no Wonder that we cannot speak any Thing to Purpose of this Subject,.. because it is indeed a Mystery to our Judgments, and a great Stranger to our Practice. **1703** ROWE *Fair Penit.* Ded., Those violent Passions which have been always Strangers to so happy a Temper as your Grace is Mistress of. **1715** J. HUGHES *Spenser's Wks.* I. Remarks p. xciv, Before his [Spenser's] time, Musick seems to have been so much a Stranger to our Poetry, that.. we have very few Examples of Verses that had any tolerable Cadence. **1722** A. PHILIPS *Briton* I. v. 10 A Friend accounted long, I felt her Charms, When Yvor was a Stranger to her Thoughts. **1838** T. MITCHELL *Clouds of Aristoph.* 461–2 *note*, Language derived from the art of war appears to have been no stranger to the mouth of Socrates.

9. Predicatively, *a stranger to* ——: Unacquainted with, ignorant of. (Distinct from sense 4.)

†**a.** Unacquainted with (a person, place, book, etc.). *Obs.*

1697 DRYDEN *Æneis* Ded. (e) 3 b, Long before I undertook this Work, I was no stranger to the Original. **1710** FELTON *Diss. Classics* (1718) 123 There is so much.. Beauty in the Classics, that 'tis impossible to translate them so ill, as utterly to deface them, and quite spoil the Entertainment they afford those who are Strangers to them in their Native Tongue. **1721** [T. THOMAS] *Urry's Chaucer* Pref. i 2, As for my self, I was equally a stranger to Mr. Urry and his Undertaking, till some time after his Death. **1776** COOK *2nd Voy.* I. iii. I. 67 Fearing to run, in thick weather, into a place to which we were all strangers,.. I tacked in twenty-five fathom water.

†**b.** Ignorant of (an art, a language, etc.). *Obs.*

1665 BOYLE *Occas. Refl.* iii. 61 Though one that were a Stranger to the Art of Gardening, would think, that [etc.]. **1688** —— *Final Causes* i. 28 A great Book, written in some Indian Language, which he is utterly a Stranger to. **1741–2** CHALLONER *Mem. Missionary Priests* Pref., We must be utterly strangers to the history of that reign.. if we deny that they [tortures] were in use in those times.

†**c.** Unaware of (a fact, state of things, something that has happened). Also with clause, *to be no stranger*, not to be unaware *that*. *Obs.*

1693–4 *Phil. Trans.* XVIII. 43 Had any Person, a stranger to what had been done, seen the Stumps, he would have supposed nothing less than an actual Cautery had been applyed. **1731–8** SWIFT *Pol. Conversat.* iii. 190 *Lady Answ.* They say, she's quite a Stranger to all his [*sc.* her husband's] Gallantries. **1748** *Anson's Voy.* II. iv. 166 The enemy was still a stranger to our having got round Cape Horn. **1763** *Museum Rust.* I. 327 They are no strangers that new beans will.. give a horse the gripes. **1831** SCOTT *Ct. Robt.* xiii, 'I am no stranger,' said the Varangian, 'to the pride of your heart, or the precedence which you assume over those who have been less fortunate in war than yourselves.'

d. Having no experience of; unaccustomed to. Said of persons and things.

1633 FORD *Broken H.* III. iv, I am no stranger to such easie calmes As sit in tender bosomes. **1684** BUNYAN *Pilgr.* II. (1693) 138 There are many that go upon the Road, that rather declare themselves Strangers to Pilgrimage, than Strangers and Pilgrims in the Earth. **1713** STEELE *Guardian* No. 17 ¶8 The Mother assured him that..[her daughter] was a Stranger to Man. **1728** LAW *Serious C.* iii. (1732) 32 A stranger to watchings, fastings, prayers, and mortifications. **1785** J. PHILLIPS *Treat. Inland Navig.* 28 Seamen are..preferred, for conducting the barges and boats, to people entirely strangers to the water. **1796** MORSE *Amer. Geog.* II. 262 They [*sc.* Polish cavalry] are strangers to all discipline. **1826** LAMB *Pop. Fallacies* xii, It grew up without the lullaby of nurses, it was a stranger to the patient fondle. **1831** SCOTT *Ct. Robt.* xxvi, This singular dialogue, in which he had assumed a tone to which his daughter was a stranger, and before which she trembled. **1833** T. HOOK *Parson's Dau.* II. ii, A report..that his lordship was shortly to return to Dale Cottage, set the heart of the Parson's Daughter into a sort of palpitation, to which..it had been a perfect stranger. **1835** DICKENS *Sk. Boz, Mr. Watkins Tottle* ii, The dirty floor had evidently been as long a stranger to the scrubbing-brush as to carpet or floor-cloth. **1843** *Fraser's Mag.* XXVIII. 654 He was described as a stranger to dissipation. **1863** FAWCETT *Pol. Econ.* II. v. 185 No man.. would willingly change a business to which he has been accustomed..for one to which he would be a stranger.

10. In popular names of animals.

a. *Labrador.* (See quot.)

1792 G. CARTWRIGHT *Jrnl. Labrador* I. Gloss. p. xv, *Stranger*, a water-fowl of the duck kind.

b. Certain species of moths.

1832 J. RENNIE *Consp. Butterfl. & Moths* 70 The Stranger (*Mamestra Aliena*,..) appears in June. *Ibid.* 214 The Stranger Knot-horn (*Phycita advenella*). **1869** E. NEWMAN *Brit. Moths* 415 The Stranger (*Hadena peregrina*).

c. The Australasian fish, *Odax richardsonii.*

1875 *Spectator* (Melbourne) 19 June 81/1 Common fish, such as..garfish, Strangers, Silvers, and others. **1891** *Australasian* (Melbourne) 15 Aug. 320 Melbourne markets. Salmon 5s. to 6s.; stranger 2s. to 4s. **1898** MORRIS *Austral Eng.* 422.

†**11.** A name for some form of stanza. *Obs.*

13.. R. BRUNNE *Chron. Wace* (Rolls) 86 If it were made in ryme couwee, Or in strangere or enterlacé.

12. *slang.* A guinea.

1785 GROSE *Dict. Vulgar T.*

13. *attrib.*, passing into *adj.*

a. That is a stranger (in senses 1–5). Often hyphened.

stranger-guest (cf. *guest-friend*, GUEST *sb.* 6): invented by Pope as a rendering of Gr. ξένος; used occas. by other writers for a stranger (sense 1 or 4) who is received as a guest.

1421 *Coventry Leet Bk.* 29 Allso we command that no maner of Straunger vitaler þat bryngithe See fische..to this cite for to sell, that he sell no maner of suche fische..till hit be ix of the cloke. *c* **1485** *Digby Myst.* I. 80 + 17 My lord,.. ther were iij straunger kynges but late in your presence, that went to bedlem. **1543** *Star Chamber Cases* (Selden Soc.) II. 267 The Straunger seller and the Straunger byer do appoynt to mete at the said faire. **1596** SHAKS. *Merch. V.* I. iii. 119 You that did..foote me as you spurne a stranger curre Ouer your threshold, moneyes is your suite. **1607** —— *Per.* II. iii. 67 Alas my Father, it befits not mee, Vnto a stranger Knight to be so bold. *c* **1619** DRUMM. OF HAWTH. *Conv. w. B. Jonson* (1842) 4 His [Ben Jonson's] judgement of stranger poets was: That he thought not Bartas a Poet, but a Verser... That Guarini [etc.]. **1622** MALYNES *Anc. Law-Merch.* 326 That no Corporation..shall let any house or dwelling place to any stranger Vsuror. *a* **1653** BINNING *Common Princ. Chr. Relig.* Wks. (1735) 31/2 Thus poor Stranger-Gentiles.. come to share with Abraham, Isaac, and Jacob. **1687** A. LOVELL tr. *Thevenot's Trav.* I. 248 Besides these are the Stranger Christians, Turks and Jews; the stranger Christians are either Franks or Greeks. **1697** DRYDEN *Æneis* VIII. 165 He said; and downward hasting to the Strand, Embrac'd the Stranger Prince, and join'd his Hand. **1725** POPE *Odyss.* I. 156 The stranger Guest the royal Youth beheld. *Ibid.* I. 515, VII. 223, XV. 548. **1767** JAGO *Edge-hill* I. 237 To chear The Stranger-Guest. **1810** SCOTT *Lady of L.* II. xiv, What think'st thou of our stranger guest? **1812** BYRON *Ch. Har.* I. xc, How many a doubtful day shall sink in night, Ere..Freedom's stranger-tree grow native of the soil! **1813** SHELLEY *Q. Mab* IV. 121 Ah! to the stranger-soul, when first it peeps From its new tenement..how stern..a tract is this wide world! **1825** WATERTON *Wand. S. Amer.* IV. i. 287, I saluted him as one stranger gentleman ought to salute another when he wants a little information. **1859** TENNYSON *Marr. Geraint* 286 Pardon me, O stranger knight. **1869** TOZER *Highl. Turkey* II. 287 Her enchantment is removed..by means of a stranger prince.

b. Pertaining to a stranger or to strangers; also, situated abroad; foreign.

1593 NORDEN *Spec. Brit., Cornw.* (1728) 98 Salt-ashe.. hath anchorage and soylage of all straunger ships. **1593** SHAKS. *Lucr.* 99 But she that neuer cop't with straunger eies, Could picke no meaning from their parling lookes. **1593** —— *Rich. II*, I. iii. 143 You cousin Herford..Shall..tread the stranger pathes of banishment. **1598** BARRET *Theor. Warres* IV. i. 119 The Spaniards will not permit any souldier of a straunger nation to beare office among them. **1598** MARSTON *Met. Pigmalion's Image* Reactio 60 Raile..At all Translators that do striue to bring That stranger language to our vulgar tongue. **1671** R. MONTAGU in *Buccleuch MSS.* (Hist. MSS. Comm.) I. 501 Commissions will..be given out for all the stranger troops that are to be raised. **1685** in *Verney Mem.* (1907) II. 402 [She begged him to burn her letters, that] no stranger eye may censure them hereafter. **1697** DRYDEN *Virg. Georg.* IV. 502 O Sister! not with causeless Fear possest, No Stranger Voice disturbs thy tender Breast. **1810** MONTGOMERY *West Indies* II. 215 Condemn'd..in stranger-isles to bear,..Through life's slow journey, to its dolorous close, Unseen, unwept, unutterable woes. **1812** BYRON *Ch. Har.* I. xiii. 9 Perchance my dog will whine in vain, Till fed by stranger hands. **1837** HALLAM *Lit. Europe* I. I. iv. §25 The north of Italy still endured the warfare of stranger armies. **1880** RUSKIN *Bible of Amiens* I. i. 2 And of these, the fruits of her hands,..she sent also portions to stranger nations.

c. Not one's own (or its own); alien. *rare.*

1577 B. GOOGE *Heresbach's Husb.* II. 75 b, Some delight to be set in trees, and not in the grounde: and when they haue no soyle of their owne, they liue in a stranger [L. *cum suam sedem non habeant, in aliena viuunt*]. **1642** H. MORE *Song of Soul* II. II. ii. 39 Long 'tis till water boild doth stranger heat controul. *a* **1763** SHENSTONE *Elegies* xiii. 13 Life is that stranger land, that alien clime. **1850** TENNYSON *In Mem.* cii, The roofs, that heard our earliest cry, Will shelter one of stranger race.

14. *Comb.*, as ***stranger-like***, ***-tongued***, adjs.; **stranger-born** *a.*, of foreign birth (the first example is doubtful); **stranger-wise** *adv.*, as a stranger.

1473 *Rolls of Parlt.* VI. 78/2 The which Michell Potter.., *straunger born, not made nor beyng Denizein, late purchased. **1870** BRYANT *Iliad* XVI. 687 The slain, though stranger-born, Had been a pillar of the realm of Troy. **1868** BROWNING *Ring & Bk.* VII. 19 A pretty church,..Yet *stranger-like,—while this Lorenzo seems My own particular place, I always say. **1824** SYMMONS *Æschylus' Agamem.* 112 Bred in strange land, in city *stranger-tongued. **1616** SURFLET & MARKHAM *Country Farm* I. i. 2 Either little, or very *stranger-wise, acquainted with them. *a* **1894** AUGUSTA WEBSTER *Mother & Dau.* (1895) 16 Child, I'd needs love thy beauty strangerwise.

Hence **'strangerdom**, **'strangerhood**, **'strangership**, the condition or fact of being a stranger.

1867 MISS MULOCK *Fair France* i. (1871) 6 The glorious independence of total *strangerdom. **1857** J. HAMILTON *Less. Gt. Biog.* 218 No stiffness, no mien of *strangerhood, to the redeemed of other countries. **1890** H. M. STANLEY *Darkest Africa* I. xi. 293 This began the exchange of friendly intercourse. Strangerhood was broken. **1824** LÆTITIA M. HAWKINS *Mem.* I. 290 It was her care to put every body at ease; it was her delight to break the barrier of *strangership. **1829** BENTHAM *Justice & Cod. Petit.* 188 In a case where.. the party..is by strangership, relative indigence, or bad character, disabled from finding any security. **1834** DE QUINCEY *Autob. Sk.* Wks. 1853 I. 221 His next care was.. to withdraw me the stranger from any oppressive feeling of strangership. **1881** MACFARREN *Counterpoint* iii. 8 And the 7th note has an effect of strangership in any key.

stranger ('streɪndʒə(r)), *v.* [f. STRANGER *sb.*]

†**1.** *trans.* To make a stranger of; to alienate.

1605 SHAKS. *Lear* I. i. 207 Will you with those infirmities she owes,..Dow'rd with our curse, and stranger'd with our oath, Take her or leaue her.

2. To make strange.

1863 W. LANCASTER *Praeterita* 70 Homeless home is strangered with a shade, That moves us weeping from familiar doors.

strangle ('stræŋg(ə)l), *sb.* [f. STRANGLE *v.*]

†**1.** The action of strangling; strangulation. *Obs.*

c **1386** CHAUCER *Knt.'s T.* 1600 Myn is þe strangle [*So Lansd.; other MSS.* stranglyng] and hangyng by þe þrote. *a* **1603** T. CARTWRIGHT *Confut. Rhem. N.T.* (1618) 373 Divers lewd traditions..as of Iudas breaking the rope where-with he hung himselfe, directly contrary to Luke, who writeth that he dyed of that strangle.

fig. **1641** MILTON *Animadv.* 8 An injurious strangle of silence.

†**2.** = STRANGLES. *Obs.*

1607 MARKHAM *Caval.* VII. 70 For betwixt the Strangle and the Glanders is but this difference, that [etc.].

3. = *strangle-hold* (in 4).

1890 E. HITCHCOCK in *Outing* Nov. 117/1 The man unfortunate enough to be under the neck-stretching hold of a 'Nelson', or in the grip of a 'strangle', both of which holds are now usually barred in competition. **1906** in F. R. Toombs *How to Wrestle* 65 Now we consider a strangle from the rear.

4. *Comb.* †**strangle-halt**, ? = STRINGHALT; **strangle-hold** *Wrestling*, a hold which stops the adversary's breath; also *fig.*

1624 L. W. C. *Perf. Disc. Horse* D 2 b, For the Strangle-halt. **1893** *Lippincott's Mag.* Feb. 210 In the 'strangle' hold, an opponent's head is caught under the arm, and the unfortunate man is compelled to acknowledge defeat or be choked into insensibility. **1901** H. McHUGH *John Henry* 83 Day after to-morrow he'll flash the intelligence on me that he has invented a strangle-hold line of business that will put Looey Harrison on the blink. **1930** G. B. SHAW *Apple Cart* p. x, This purely inhibitive check on tyranny has become a stranglehold on genuine democracy. **1939** *Daily Tel.* 18 Dec. 6/4 Hitler knows and fears the stranglehold of the British and Allied blockade. **1980** I. COLEGATE *Shooting Party* (1982) 7 The strangle-hold of the rich on the life-blood of the working man.

strangle ('stræŋg(ə)l), *v.* Forms: 4 **strangel(le, strangul**, 4, 6 **strangil**, 5 **strangli**, **strang(e)lyn**, 6 **strangyll**, **straungle**, **strongle**, 7 **strengle**, 4– **strangle**. See also ASTRANGLE, ESTRANGLE *vbs.* [a. OF. *estrangler* (mod.F. *étrangler*) = Pr. *estranglar*, *estrangolar*, Sp., Pg. *estrangular*, It. *strangolare*, *strangulare*:—L. *strangulāre*, a. Gr. στραγγαλᾶν, f. στραγγάλη halter, cogn. w. στραγγός twisted.]

1. a. *trans.* To kill by external compression of the throat, esp. by means of a rope or the like passed round the neck.

1303 R. BRUNNE *Handl. Synne* 972 Ne here helpe hadde be, þat was so nere, þe hand me hadde strangled here. **1338** —— *Chron.* (1725) 33 þe kyng tok þis pantelere, & strangled him right þore. **13..** *K. Alis.* 5305 The other lep on an olyfaunt,..And strangled hym in litel stounde. **1340** HAMPOLE *Pr. Consc.* 8408 þai [*sc.* the damned] salle be fulle ..Of hatred..Swa þat ilk ane wald with other fyght, And strangelle other, if þai myght. *c* **1380** WYCLIF *Wks.* (1880) 476 Knytte þis coorde to mannus þrote & it myȝte soone strangle þis man. **1426** LYDG. *De Guil. Pilgr.* 8245 Thys gorger..strangleth me almost vp ryht, That I may nat speke a-ryht. *c* **1430** —— *Min. Poems* (Percy Soc.) 238 This name Jhesus..Is for to seyne..Our strong Sampson that stranglyd the lioun. *c* **1450** *Merlin* i. 4 She henge herself and was strangelid to death. *c* **1500** *Three Kings' Sons* (1895) 132 He..drewe the rope so fast, that was aboute his nek, that he had strangild him, had not his folkes cried on him, and seide that it was the hangmans office,..to do so foul a dede. **1530** PALSGR. 738/2 He held me so harde by the throote that he hade allmost stranglyd me. *a* **1533** BERNERS *Huon* lxxxi. 249 Your brother Gerarde [ought] to be hanged and strangled. **1555** *Instit. Gentl.* L v b, This Narcissus then accordyngly entered into the chaumbre of Comodus, and by force strangled him to deathe. **1563–83** FOXE *A. & M.* 1079/2 Tindall..was..then strangled first by the hangman, and afterward with fire consumed. **1577–87** HARRISON *England* II. xi. 184/2 in *Holinshed*, He is either hanged aliue in chaines ..(or else vpon compassion taken first strangled with a rope). **1588** SHAKS. *L.L.L.* V. i. 142 He shall present Hercules in minoritie: his enter and exit shall bee strangling a Snake. **1602** CHETTLE *Hoffman* IV. (1631) H 2, Weapons draw blood..Then strangle her, here is a towell sir. **1613** BEAUM. & FL. *Philaster* V. iii. (1620) 57 Vnlesse it be some snake, or something like your selfe, That in his birth shall strengle you. **1663** *Unfort. Usurper* IV. iv. 50 He strangles Alexius with the Bowstring. *a* **1700** EVELYN *Diary* 21 Oct. 1678, The murder of Sir Edmondbury Godfrey, found strangl'd about this time. **1726** AYLIFFE *Parergon* 52 Our Saxon Ancestors compelled the Adulteress to strangle herself. **1774** GOLDSM. *Nat. Hist.* V. 134 As for small birds, they are its usual food. It seizes them by the throat, and strangles them in an instant. **1800** *Med. Jrnl.* IV. 327 The os uteri encircled round the neck of the fœtus like a collar, insomuch that the fœtus was strangled. **1892** R. BUCHANAN *Come live with Me* iii. 30 Geoffrey's fingers itched to strangle him out of life.

b. *fig.*

a **1591** H. SMITH *Trump. Soule* A 5 b, Strangle sinne in thy cradle, for all the wisedome in the world wil not help thee else. **1678** STILLINGFL. *Serm.* xvi. (1707) 249 If this be the way to reconcile us to their Communion, have we not great reason to be fond of returning into the Bosom of such a Church which may strangle us as soon as it gets us within her Arms? **1870** J. BRUCE *Gideon* x. 179 They would be eager to strangle this insurrection in the birth.

c. To constrict painfully (the neck or throat).

c **1450** *Mirk's Festial* 79 þat þrote þat spake þe wordes of traytery..was ystrangled with þe grynne of a rope. **1540** PALSGR. *Acolastus* II. i. H ij, I haue a throte bolle almoste strangled .i. snarled or quarkennyd with extreme hunger. **1886** C. E. PASCOE *Lond. To-day* xli. (ed. 3) 355 The cravat has passed out of memory..and the 'stock' is only to be seen occasionally strangling the neck of a stout City magnate.

†**d.** *intr.* To be at close grips, to struggle *with.*

1595 *Locrine* I. i. 29 In vaine, therefore, I strangle [ed. 1664 struggle] with this foe.

2. a. *trans.* In wider sense: To kill by stoppage of breath; to smother, suffocate, choke. Now *rare.*

to strangle down (nonce-use): of a whirlpool, to choke as it engulfs.

a **1300** *Havelok* 640 Y was þe[r]-with [*i.e.* with a gag] so harde prangled, þat i was þe[r]-with ney strangled. *c* **1450** *Brut* II. 352 þei token þe fetherbed..and cast hit aboue hym; ..and sum lay vpon þe fethir bed apon hym, vnto þe tyme þat he were ded... And þus þei strangled þis worthi Duk vn[to] the deth. **1483** CAXTON *Cato* 5 An ensample how the auaricious man ete iiii pyeces of golde and how the fourthe strangled hym. **1504** ATKYNSON tr. *De Imit.* I. xxiii. 173 Some etynge haue be strangled. **1574** T. NEWTON *Health Mag.* L ij, If a liuinge Mullet be put into wine and choked or strangled therin, whatsoeuer man drinketh of the same wyne, shall [etc.]. **1592** SHAKS. *Rom. & Jul.* IV. iii. 35 Shall I not then be stifled in the Vault?.. And there die strangled ere my Romeo comes. **1599** HAYWARD *1st Pt. Hen. IV*, 40 He was strangled under a feather bedde. **1728** CHAMBERS *Cycl.* s.v. *Damps*, A Labourer, who was sent down [the well] to recover it [a hammer], ere he reach'd the Water, was strangled. **1833** MRS. BROWNING *Prometh. Bound* Wks. 1850 I. 189 With Necessity's vortices strangling me down! **1888** *Spectator* 14 Jan. 49 Over a territory of ten thousand square miles..the soft water passed, silently strangling every living thing.

†**b.** To kill by poison or the like; *rarely*, by the sword. *Obs.*

c **1374** CHAUCER *Boeth.* I. pr. iv. (1868) 19 Al þouȝ I hadde ben accused þat I wolde..strangle [L. *ingulare*] prestys wiþ wicked swerde [etc.]. *c* **1443** LYDG. in *Pol. Poems* (Rolls) II. 214 Hanybal,..At the laste, stranglyd with poisoun, Of marcial ire koude lyve nevir in pees. **1535** COVERDALE *Jer.* XV. 3 The swearde shal strangle them [Luther *Mit dem Schwerdt, dass sie erwürget werden*]. *a* **1578** LINDESAY (Pitscottie) *Chron. Scot.* (S.T.S.) I. 407 Or they come he was nearhand strangled to death be the extreme melancollie. **1602** MARSTON *Antonio's Rev.* I. i, That I should drop strong poyson in the boawle,..That it should worke..And strangle him on sodaine. **1607** TOPSELL *Four-f. Beasts* 237 Galen saith, if it be eaten without Hony, water, and salt, it curdleth in the belly of a man like a cheese and strangleth him.

†**c.** said of a wild beast, a devil. *Obs.*

1303 R. BRUNNE *Handl. Synne* 3189 For me ys come þe fende of helle... Ryȝt now shal he me strangle and cheke, Ne shal y neuer aftyr speke. *c* **1330** *Arth. & Merl.* 688 þat ich niȝt þe deuel com & strangled hir owhen grom. *c* **1386** CHAUCER *Knt.'s T.* 1160 Yet saugh I..The hunte strangled with the wilde beres. **1386** —— *Pars. T.* 768 They been the deueles wolues that strangle the sheepe of Ihesu crist. **1390** GOWER *Conf.* III. 197 The Jew..strangled was of a leoun. *c* **1400** *Solomon's Bk. Wisdom* 243 þere seuen hungri lyouns weren pereinne all ydytte, ffor þai hym strangle scholden. **1447** BOKENAM *Seyntys, Agnes* 394 þe deuyl hym stranglyd in þat place. **1481** CAXTON *Myrr.* II. xvi. 102 Hym sholde seme anon in his slepe dremyng that all the deuyllis of helle shold come to hym and strangle hym. **1484** —— *Fables of Auian* xiv, The lyon wold haue strangled hym. *a* **1700** EVELYN *Diary* 18 Mar. 1644 This country so abounds with wolves, that a shepherd whom we met told us one of his companions was strangled by one of them the day before. **1751** *Gentl. Mag.* XXI. 555 A sort of wolves, which attack.. children, of whom they have already strangled and devoured about thirty.

absol. **1611** BIBLE *Nahum* ii. 12 The Lion did teare in pieces enough for his whelpes, and strangled for his Lionesses.

3. a. *transf.* To choke, hinder the growth of (a plant) by crowding; †to stifle, quench (a fire, heat) (*obs.*); to impede the action of (an internal bodily organ) by compression; to suppress (a laugh, a yawn).

1382 WYCLIF *Matt.* xiii. 7 Forsothe other seedis felden amonge thornis; and the thornis wexen vp and strangliden hem [Vulg. *suffocaverunt ea*]. *c* **1530** *Judic. Urines* I. iii. 6 b, Therfore kynde hete is theked and straungled. *Ibid.* II. iv. 21 And moche water quencheth & cheketh & strangleth feble fyre. **1605** SHAKS. *Macb.* II. iv. 7 Byth' Clock 'tis Day, And yet darke Night strangles the trauailing Lampe. **1614** JACKSON *Creed* III. To Indifferent Rdr. a 6 Like the Iuy alwaies greene, because not set to bring forth fruit vnto saluation, but rather to choake and strangle the plants of life. **1621** BURTON *Anat. Mel.* I. ii. II. ii. (1624) 63 As a Lampe is choaked with a multitude of oyle,.. so is the naturall heat with immoderate eating strangled in the body. **1707** MORTIMER *Husb.* 387 Young Trees will be strangled with.. any rank growing Corn or Weeds, if [etc.]. **1829** SCOTT *Anne of G.* xxxii, The poor King.. saw.. the fatal cabinet.. and dolefully calculated how many yawns he must strangle ere he sustained the consideration of its contents. **1897** *Allbutt's Syst. Med.* IV. 476 The presence of large quantities of this intrusive substance strangling the secreting structures. **1898** *Ibid.* V. 788 [The symptoms] occur.. also where the heart is strangled and compressed by dense fibrous thickening.

b. *fig.* with various notions. To prevent the growth or rise of; to hamper or destroy by excessive restrictions; to suppress. Also with *off*.

1611 SHAKS. *Wint. T.* IV. iv. 47 Be merry (Gentle) Strangle such thoughts as these, with any thing That you behold the while. **1642** H. MORE *Song of Soul* III. iii. 41 Consuming anguish, styptick bitternesse, Doth now so strangle their imperious will. **1658–9** in *Burton's Diary* (1828) III. 321 It is not fit to debate whether it shall be in the power of any person or persons to strangle the debates and pains of this House. **1661** COTTERELL tr. *Calprenède's Cassandra* II. II. (1676) 145 Too inconsiderable to strangle your interests. **1710** PRIDEAUX *Orig. Tithes* App. *Reasons for Bill* 1 As often as a Bill was brought into Parliament for this purpose, it was always encountered with another.. and the latter constantly strangled the former. **1898** MEREDITH *Odes, Napoleon* vi, Her surest way to strangle thought. **1911** J. H. ROSE *Pitt & Gt. War* iii. 72 The exclusive privileges retained by the Dutch had almost strangled the trade of Antwerp. **1918** D. H. LAWRENCE *New Poems* 38 The frost has.. ruthlessly strangled off the fantasies Of leaves.

4. *intr.* To be choked or suffocated.

1338 R. BRUNNE *Chron.* (1725) 55, I praye God if it wer so I strangle of þis brede. **1662** R. MATHEW *Unl. Alch.* 8 He could not.. lie down in his bed; and if he had assayed to do it, then he should strangle. **1848** THACKERAY *Bk. Snobs* xxii, He came down.. with a surly scowl on his.. face, strangling in a tight, cross-barred cravat. **1889** STEVENSON *Master of Ballantrae* ix. 228 Some foul and ominous nightmare, from the which I would awake strangling. **1897** *Bookman* Jan. 116/1 Strangling in our starch we can rally him [Byron] familiarly on his limp collars.

5. Comb.: †**strangle-goose** *slang*, a poulterer (Grose *Dict. Vulgar T.* 1785); †**strangle-tare** [transl. of Gr. ὀροβάγχη, f. ὄροβος tare, vetch + ἄγχ-ειν to choke, strangle], Turner's name for the Broomrape (*Orobanche*); by later writers sometimes applied to some other parasitic plants; **strangle-vetch, -weed** = *strangle-tare*.

In some modern books *strangle-tare, -vetch, -weed* are given as popular names, but it does not appear that they have had any real currency.

1562 TURNER *Herbal* II. 71 It hath the name of Orobanche, that is chokefitche or strangletare. **1597** GERARDE *Herbal* Table Eng. Names, Strangle weede, and Strangle tare, that is Orobanch. **1693** *Urquhart's Rabelais* III. li, Unto whom it is more contrarious and hurtful than the Strangle-weed, Choak fitch is to the Flax. **1796** WITHERING *Brit. Plants* (ed. 3) III. 638 Strangle Vetch, or Tare. **1861** ANNE PRATT *Flower. Pl.* IV. 77 The Broomrapes.. have in country places the old name of Strangleweed. **1863** PRIOR *Plant-n.*, *Strangle-tare*, a tare that strangles, *Vicia lathyroides*, and also a plant that strangles a tare, *Cuscuta Europæa*.

strangleable ('stræŋg(ə)ləb(ə)l), *a. nonce-wd.* [f. STRANGLE *v.* + -ABLE.] Capable of being strangled.

1753 CHESTERF. *Let. to Son* 19 Oct., I own, I am glad that the capital strangler should, in its turn, be *strangle-able*.

strangled ('stræŋg(ə)ld), *ppl. a.* [f. STRANGLE *v.* + -ED[1].] In senses of the verb.

1. *lit.* †Also *absol.* (= what is strangled) literal rendering of Acts xv. 20.

1382 WYCLIF *Acts* xv. 20 That thei absteyne hem fro.. stranglid thingis [Vulg. *a suffocatis*; Gr. ἀπὸ τοῦ πνικτοῦ; Tindale 1534 from strangleyd]. **1593** SHAKS. *2 Hen. VI*, III. ii. 170 Staring full gastly, like a strangled man. **1618** J. SPRINT *Cassander Angl.* 17 When the Apostles decreed the abstaining from blood and strangled. **1795** SOUTHEY *Joan of Arc* III. 65 Richemont.. drove the Loire Sends the black carcass of his strangled foe. **1828** *Ann. Reg.* 375/1 The blood in a strangled or suffocated person rises to the head, and gives the face a livid appearance.

b. *Path.* = STRANGULATED.

1846 BRITTAN tr. *Malgaigne's Man. Oper. Surg.* 423 When the strangled portion [of a hernial tumour], which formed a sort of plug, is returned, the rest follows easily. **1899** *Allbutt's Syst. Med.* VIII. 897 The skin of the strangled portion [of the little toe] is not materially altered in appearance.

2. *transf.* and *fig.* Suppressed, prevented from growing or developing.

1812 COLERIDGE *Remorse* v. i. 41 How the half sounds Blend with this strangled light! **1847** TENNYSON *Princess* v. 15 A strangled titter, out of which there brake On all sides.. Unmeasured mirth. **1854** LD. LYTTON in Lady B. Balfour *Lett.* (1906) I. 58 Each step forward.. would have to be trodden over some relinquished dream, or some strangled instinct. **1898** MEREDITH *Odes, Napoleon* vi, Her strangled thought got breath.

b. Of a voice [after F. *voix étranglée*]: Choked with emotion, uttered with difficulty. *rare.*

1900 LUCY B. WALFORD *One of Ourselves* xiv, 'Come home this minute,' she said, in a cold, strangled voice.

stranglement ('stræŋg(ə)lmənt). [f. STRANGLE *v.* + -MENT.] Strangling, choking of voice.

1837 C. LOFFT *Self-form.* I. 250 The third [speech was] a mere struggle of elocution against stranglement.

strangler ('stræŋglə(r)). [f. STRANGLE *v.* + -ER[1].] **1. a.** One who or something which strangles. *lit.* and *fig.* ***strangler's grip*** = strangle-hold (STRANGLE *sb.* 4).

1552 HULOET, Strangler, *suffocator.* **1602** MARSTON *Antonio's Rev.* IV. iii, My selfe will be thy strangler, unmatcht slave. **1606** SHAKS. *Ant. & Cl.* II. vi. 130 The band that seemes to tye their friendship together, will bee the very strangler of their Amity. **1753** [see STRANGLEABLE]. **1844** *P. Parley's Ann.* V. 355 Though.. the cords of the strangler and the sword of the headsman be ready for me. **1895** *Westm. Gaz.* 9 Oct. 2/1 The strangler's grip is another trick which some men practise, though not very often with success, as the police know it and watch for it.

b. *spec.* in *Bot.*, an epiphytic plant which eventually sends its roots to the ground and smothers its host.

1895 J. RODWAY *In Guiana Forest* 91 The strangler is now ready for its deadly work. The forest giant.. is bound by cords which are stronger than iron bands. **1952** P. W. RICHARDS *Tropical Rain Forest* ii. 21 The third section of dependent plants, here termed stranglers.. begin life as epiphytes and later send roots to the ground. **1960** N. POLUNIN *Introd. Plant Geogr.* xiv. 435 Stranglers.. begin life as epiphytes but later send down roots to the soil. **1976** *Hortus Third* (L. H. Bailey Hortorium) 288/1 *Clusia*.. dioecious trees and shrubs, occasionally more or less epiphytic or stranglers.

c. *attrib.* and *Comb.* as ***strangler fig, vine***; **strangler tree** *U.S.*, a tree of the genus *Clusia*, growing usually as a parasite on some other tree.

1909 *Century Dict.* Suppl., Strangler tree. **1955** *Sci. Amer.* Apr. 74/2 The strangler fig in the tropical jungle, which kills other trees to reach the light, is a rare type. **1962** *Times* 6 Apr. 7/2 Strangler figs.. envelope and kill other trees. **1976** *Publishers Weekly* 12 Jan. 50/3 'Nanny' grows upon the family like a strangler vine upon a tree.

2. = CHOKE *sb.*[1] 7.

1925 E. W. KNOTT *Carburettor Handbk.* i. 29 Easy starting devices... First, stranglers or air chokes which reduce the main air supply by means of a suitable shutter or similar device, the use of which increases the suction on the main fuel orifice or jet far beyond the normal state of affairs. **1976** J. WATSON *Understanding your Car* v. 27 A second butterfly valve, mounted above the spray tube.. is known as a strangler, and by cutting off most of the air it greatly increases the suction on the jet to give a very rich mixture for starting.

strangles ('stræŋg(ə)lz). Also 7 stranga's, strangies. [Orig. pl. of STRANGLE *sb.*]

†**1.** A disease in horses and other animals, characterized by inflamed swellings in the throat: = STRANGULLION 1. *Obs.*

1600 SURFLET *Country Farm* I. xxiii. 137 For the strangles or glandules which happen vnder the oxe his throat,.. plucke away their glandules, and [etc.]. **1601** HOLLAND *Pliny* XXVI. xv. II. 268 Sideritis hath a peculiar vertue for to cure swine of their squinsies or strangles. **1624** L. W. C. *Perf. Disc. Horse* C 3, For the Strangles. Cut him betweene the lawes, and take out the Kirnels. **1686** *Lond. Gaz.* No. 2154/4 Stolen.., a dark brown Gelding 14 hands high,.. hath had the Stranga's in two places under the Jaw.

2. An infectious febrile disease of equine animals, caused by the bacterium *Streptococcus equi*.

1706 PHILLIPS (ed. Kersey), *Strangles*, the thick Humour, which young Horses void at their Nostrils. **1753** J. BARTLET *Gentl. Farriery* x. (1754) 104 The methods above recommended in the strangles. **1831** YOUATT *Horse* viii. 123 Glanders have often been confounded with strangles, and by those who ought to have known better. Strangles are peculiar to young horses. **1891** H. S. CONSTABLE *Horses, Sport & War* 66 Every horse.. during the time its throat is choked up, and nerves paralysed by strangles is a roarer. **1908** *Animal Managem.* (War Office) 313 Strangles is a fever of young horses, the prominent feature of which is an abscess which develops between the branches of the lower jaw.

attrib. **1897** *Allbutt's Syst. Med.* II. 515 The matter from a newly-opened farcy.. is usually distinguishable from staphylococcus pus, and strangles pus.

strangling ('stræŋglɪŋ), *vbl. sb.* [f. STRANGLE *v.* + -ING[1].]

1. The action of the vb. STRANGLE.

c **1386** CHAUCER *Knt.'s T.* 1600 Myn is the stranglyng and hangyng by the throte. **1398** TREVISA *Barth. De P.R.* VII. xxviii. (Bodl. MS.), Sqynancy is strangeling of þe þrote. **1538** ELYOT *Dict.*, *Suffocatio*, a stranglynge. **1585** HIGINS *Junius' Nomencl.* 427/1 *Incubus*,.. a kinde of disease called the night mare or witch, being a certeine pressing downe and strangling of the bodie. **1611** BIBLE *Job* vii. 15 My soule chooseth strangling: and death rather then my life. **1649** LAMONT *Diary* (Maitl. Club) 12 It was thought.. that she wronged her selfe, ether by strangling, or by poyson. **1719** DE FOE *Crusoe* I. (Globe) 29 But between the Wound.. and the strangling of the Water, he dyed just before he reach'd the Shore. **1820** SCOTT *Monast.* x, They say the Primate recommends a little strangling and burning in aid both of censure and of sword. **1914** *Eng. Hist. Rev.* Oct. 768 It seems to us improbable that they would have killed him by strangling.

†**2.** *Path.* Strangulation, stricture. *Obs.*

1563 T. HYLL *Art Garden.* (1593) 76 The hearb brused with oyle.. dooth help the strangling of the priuitie. **1590** BARROUGH *Meth. Phisick* 191 Svffocation or strangling of the wombe is nothing else but a drawing backe of it to the vpper partes. **1725** *Bradley's Family Dict.* s.v. *Nightingale*, Another disease incident to these Birds.. is called Streightness or Strangling in the breast.

†**3.** *pl.* ? = STRANGLES *Obs.*

1624 L. W. C. *Perf. Disc. Horse* A 4 b, *Stranglings*, is a swelling in the Throat.

4. *attrib.*

1592 *Soliman & Pers.* v. ii. 7 See that your strangling cords be ready. **1911** J. G. FRAZER in *Manch. Oriental Soc. Jrnl.* 108 The strangling-net is then undone.

strangling ('stræŋglɪŋ), *ppl. a.* [f. STRANGLE *v.* + -ING[2].] That strangles, in senses of the vb.

1606 BRYSKETT *Civ. Life* 108 Their praises and soothings are but strangling morsels smeared ouer with hony. *a* **1618** SYLVESTER *Tobacco Battered* 143 In them Both, a strangling vertue note, And both of them doe worke upon the Throte. *a* **1682** SIR T. BROWNE *Misc. Tracts* (1684) 88 Cockle, wild strangling Fitches, Bindweed. **1692** SOUTH *Serm.* (1697) I. 16 Weeping.. is the Discharge of a big and a swelling grief, of a full and strangling discontent. **1822–27** GOOD *Study Med.* (1829) I. 631 The suffocative convulsion.. must produce that strangling constriction or straitness which is a pathognomic sign of asthma. **1844** MRS. BROWNING *Drama of Exile* 1789 Tree by tree, with strangling roots. **1897** *Allbutt's Syst. Med.* III. 45 The tight strangling grip of the inelastic fibrous sac.

stranglon, -guelyon, etc.: see STRANGULLION.

stranguary, -ery, obs. ff. STRANGURY.

†'**strangulate,** *sb. Obs. rare*[−1]. [ad. L. *strangulātum*, neut. pa. pple. of *strangulāre* to STRANGLE.] A strangled animal.

1702 C. MATHER *Magn. Chr.* v. ii. (1852) 262 The principal entanglements of their idolatry lay in these four things: of idolathytes, fornication, blood, and strangulates.

strangulate ('stræŋgjʊlət), *a. Bot.* [ad. L. *strangulātus* pa. pple. of *strangulāre* to STRANGLE.] = STRANGULATED *ppl. a.* 3.

1866 *Treas. Bot.* 1102/1 *Strangulate*, contracted and expanded in an irregular manner.

strangulate ('stræŋgjʊleɪt), *v.* [f. L. *strangulāt-* ppl. stem of *strangulāre*: see STRANGLE *v.*]

†**1.** *trans.* To choke, stifle, suffocate. *Obs.*

1665 M. N[EDHAM] *Med. Medicinæ* 327 This.. strangulates all thoughts of devising more potent Medicins, or of introducing other Methods.

2. *Path.* and *Surg.* To constrict or compress (an organ, duct, etc.) so as to prevent circulation or the passage of fluid; to remove (a growth) by constricting it with a ligature.

1771– [implied in STRANGULATED *ppl. a.*]. **1875** BUCKLAND *Log-Book* 222 When the horn [of the deer] has attained its full development the 'burr' appears at the base of the horn, and strangulates the blood-vessels. **1876** GROSS *Dis. Bladder* 151 On removing the obturator the growth is fairly exposed, and can be strangulated, cut, scraped, or torn away. **1876** BRISTOWE *Th. & Pract. Med.* (1878) 33 If, after injecting them, the operation of twisting, and thus strangulating, one testicle was performed.. violent inflammation with sloughing.. took place. **1897** *Allbutt's Syst. Med.* III. 794 A loop of bowel is snared and acutely strangulated. *Ibid.* IV. 355 The new fibroid tissue gradually contracts,.. and narrows and strangulates the tubes which it involves.

b. *transf.* To choke (a plant); to prevent the flow of sap in (a tree). Also *fig.*

1835 SOUTHEY *Doctor* interch. vii. (1848) 165 The creepers of literature, who suck their food, like the ivy, from what they strangulate and kill. **1841** *Florist's Jrnl.* (1846) II. 129 In order to arrest this same elaborated sap in the branches, every plan of reversing, or ringing, or strangulating them, is advised to prevent it sinking to the roots.

3. To prevent respiration in (a person) by constriction of the trachea; = STRANGLE *v. rare.*

1829 LANDOR *Imag. Conv.*, *Penn & Ld. Peterborough* Wks. 1853 I. 548/1 If we cry out, there is always a hand in readiness to stop our mouths, and to stifle and strangulate such as would resist.

Hence '**strangulating** *ppl. a.*

1822–27 GOOD *Study Med.* (1829) V. 81 We often meet with a troublesome phimosis, either of the strangulating or incarcerating kind. **1828** *Blackw. Mag.* XXIII. 412 Struggling in the many-fingered grasp of the strangulating heather. **1871** NAPHEYS *Prev. & Cure Dis.* III. xii. 1056 The cough becomes more difficult and strangulating.

strangulated ('stræŋgjʊleɪtɪd), *ppl. a.* [f. STRANGULATE *v.* + -ED[1].]

1. *Path.* and *Surg.* Of a vessel, an intestine: Congested by constriction and the arrest of circulation. ***strangulated hernia***: a hernia so constricted that the circulation in the protruded part is arrested.

1771 J. S. tr. *Le Dran's Observ. Surg.* (ed. 4) 184 The strangulated Portion of the Intestine was no larger than a

Cherry. **1788** H. HELSHAM in *Med. Commun.* XIII. 280 (*title*), Sudden fatal termination of a Case of Strangulated Hernia. **1836-9** *Todd's Cycl. Anat.* II. 745/1 The volume of a strangulated intestine is always increased. **1899** *Allbutt's Syst. Med.* VI. 342 The retinal vessels seem strangulated or constricted.

fig. **1857** *Fraser's Mag.* LVI. 535 The..most pressing City improvement is the widening of this strangulated metropolitan gullet.

2. *Ent.* Of the head, abdomen, or thorax of an insect: Constricted or greatly narrowed.

1819 SAMOUELLE *Entomol. Compend.* 196 Head cordiform, abruptly strangulated at its junction with the thorax.

3. *Bot.* Of a plant-stem: Contracted by or as if by a ligature.

1849 BALFOUR *Man. Bot.* 639. **1856** HENSLOW *Bot. Terms.* In recent Dicts.

strangulation (stræŋgjʊˈleɪʃən). Also 6 **strangulacion.** [ad. L. *strangulātiōn-em*, n. of action f. *strangulāre*: see STRANGLE *v.* Cf. F. *strangulation* (Cotgr.).]

1. The action or process of stopping respiration by compression of the air-passage, esp. by a sudden and violent compression of the windpipe; the condition of being strangled by such compression.

1542 BOORDE *Dyetary* ix. (1870) 251 Surfeting causeth strangulacion and soden death. **1646** SIR T. BROWNE *Pseud. Ep.* II. v. 84 So a sponge is mischievous,..because being received into the stomack it swelleth, and..induceth at last a strangulation. **1661** J. CHILDREY *Brit. Baconica* 40 Its tast is manifestly acide without astriction, but..causing an extream hot strangulation in the mouth. **1793** BEDDOES *Scurvy* 81 Had he been carefully observed, his countenance would have shewn signs of strangulation. **1869** DICKENS *Mut. Fr.* I. iv, She stopped to pull him down from his chair in an attitude highly favourable to strangulation. **1874** FARRAR *Christ* I. iv. 43 He had ordered the strangulation of his favourite wife. **1883** *Encycl. Brit.* XV. 781/1 [Medical Jurisprudence.] Strangulation may be accomplished by drawing a cord tightly round the neck, or by forcibly compressing the windpipe (throttling).

fig. **1831** CARLYLE *Sartor Res.* III. iv, To make air for himself in which strangulation, choking enough to a benevolent heart, the Hofrath founds..this Institute [for the Repression of Population].

†**b.** In full, ***strangulation of the matrix*** or ***womb***: hysteria. (Cf. SUFFOCATION c.) *Obs.*

1601 HOLLAND *Pliny* XXXII. x. II. 448 Castoreum.. helpeth them when by rising of the mother they are in daunger of strangulation. **1615** CROOKE *Body of Man* 218 The strangulation or suffocation of the matrix, which we call fits of the mother. **1634** T. JOHNSON *Parey's Wks.* XXIV. xliv. 939 The strangulation of the wombe.

2. *Path.* and *Surg.* Constriction (of a bodily organ, duct, etc.) so as to stop circulation or the passage of fluids.

1749 GATAKER tr. *Le Dran's Oper. Surg.* 55 If the wound penetrates one of the *musculi recti*, the skin causes a strangulation in the first place. **1807** M. BAILLIE *Morbid Anat.* 200 A rupture without any strangulation of the intestine. **1890** F. TAYLOR *Pract. Med.* (1891) 765 There may be severe attacks of so-called strangulation of the [movable] kidney.

3. *transf.* Excessive constriction of a channel or passage.

1882 A. GEIKIE *Geol. Sketches* vi. 141 At a point about half a mile or less from the foot of the glacier the valley suddenly contracts... At a point where the strangulation takes place the glacier lies in a kind of basin.

4. *concr.* A strangulated part; a constriction. *spec.* in *Nat. Hist.*

1828 STARK *Elem. Nat. Hist.* II. 185 Head separated from the body by a strangulation.

†**ˈstrangulative,** *a. Obs. rare.* [f. L. type **strangulātīvus*, f. *strangulāre*: see STRANGLE *v.* and -ATIVE.] That strangles or stops respiration.

1647 A. ROSS *Myst. Poet.* xi. (1648) 266 Medea is the name of a poysonable herb..called..in English dogs-bane; but our dogs-bane hath no such strangulative quality. **1657** TOMLINSON *Renou's Disp.* I. II. xiii. 262 One sort of Ephemerum is lethal and strangulative.

strangullion (strænˈgʌljən). Forms: 5-6 **stranguyllyon,** (6 **-guillyon, -guil(l)ion, -guelyon, stranglon**), 6 **strangulyon,** 6-7 **strangulion,** 6- **strangullion.** [a. OF. *stranguillon, estranguillon* (mod.F. *étranguillon*), ad. It. *stranguglione* :—popular L. **strangulionem*, f. L. *strangulāre* to STRANGLE: see -ION[1].]

1. A disease of horses, characterized by inflammation and swelling of the glands of the throat. †Also *rarely*, a similar disease in human beings, a quinsy.

1481 CAXTON *Reynard* xxxii. (Arb.) 82 Yf ony man be seke ..of colyk, stranguyllyon, stone, fystel or kanker. **1523-34** FITZHERB. *Husb.* §88 Stranguelyon is a lyght dysease to cure, and a horse wyl be very sore sycke therof. **1555** *Extracts Burgh Rec. Stirling* (1887) 64 It is fund that Thomas Bwyhes twa hors that hes stranglon that ar infeccatife. **1580** BLUNDEVILL *Curing Horses Dis.* lxv. 25 Of the glanders, and strangulion, so called according to the Italian name, Stranguijlione. Most Ferrers doe take the glanders and strangulion, to be all one disease, but it is not so, for the glanders is that which the Physicians call Tonsillæ, and the strangulion is that which they call in Latin, Angina,..and we commonlie call it in English, the Squinancie, or Quinzie. **1727** *Bradley's Family Dict.* s.v. *Glanders*, Those Humours ..frequently produce the Strangullions, Diseases in the Throat [etc.]. **1847** W. C. L. MARTIN *Ox* 139/1 The submaxillary and parotid glands are, from various causes, subject to acute inflammation and swelling called strangullion.

†**b.** (See quot.) *Obs.*

1756 OSMER *Treat. Horse* III. iii. (ed. 5) 121 A case..of.. tumefied gland on the ileum, and consequent strangulation of the guts beneath it, vulgarly termed strangullion. *Ibid.* III. iv. 125 This last kind of colic..is what the writers and farriers indiscriminately call 'the strangullion', or 'twisting of the guts', for such they always suppose it to be.

¶**2.** Used incorrectly for STRANGURY. *Obs.*

1530 PALSGR. 277/1 Stranguyllyon a sicknesse, *chauldepisse.* **1538** *St. Papers Hen. VIII*, III. III. 30, I besech you, because of my stranguillyon, gett me lycence to ryd apon a pyllyon. **1593** NASHE *Christ's T.* 51 b, When on your death-beddes you shall lye, and cry out of the Stone, the Strangullion and the Goute, you shall not be heard. **1614** MARKHAM *Cheap & Good Husb.* I. xxiv. 21 Of the Strangullion. This is a sorenesse in the horses yard..: the signes are, hee will pisse oft, yet but a drop or two at once. **1655** MOUFET & BENET *Health's Improv.* 105 Their flesh being salted cureth Strangullions and the stone not confirmed. **1678** PHILLIPS (ed. 4), *Strangury*..is vulgarly called the *Strangullion.*

†**stranˈgurion.** *Obs.* Also 6 **-yon,** 6-7 **-ian.** [A confusion of STRANGURY and STRANGULLION.] = STRANGURY.

1547 RECORDE *Judic. Ur.* 64 b, A disease named y[e] strangury, (whiche sum corruptely call the Stranguryon) in whiche dysease, the uryne doth contynually drop furth as fast as it commyth into the bladder. **1562** TURNER *Herbal* II. 97 Knotgrasse..is good for the strangurian for it doth manifestly bryng furth water. **1616** BULLOKAR *Eng. Expos.*, *Strangurion*, a disease when one cannot make water, but by drops, and that with great paine. **1622** S. WARD *Life of Faith* (1627) 85 Here thou shrinkest to thinke of the gout, collicke, stone, or strangurian.

strangurious (strænˈgjuːrɪəs), *a. rare*[−1]. [ad. late L. *strangūriōsus*, f. *strangūria* STRANGURY: see -OUS.] Of, pertaining to, or characteristic of strangury; affected with strangury.

1733 CHEYNE *Eng. Malady* III. iv. 321, I was often fretted with strangurious Symptoms. **1898** *Syd. Soc. Lex.*

strangury (ˈstræŋgjʊərɪ). *Path.* Forms: 6-7 **strangurie,** 6 **-ye,** 7 **stranguery,** 7-9 **stranguary,** 4- **strangury.** [ad. L. *strangūria*, a. Gr. στραγγουρία, f. στραγγ-, στράγξ drop squeezed out + οὖρον urine. Cf. F. *strangurie* (14th c. in Hatz.-Darm.).]

1. A disease of the urinary organs characterized by slow and painful emission of urine; also the condition of slow and painful urination.

[**1398** TREVISA *Barth. De P.R.* VI. xxi. (1495) 211 He that hath that dysease..that hyghte Stranguria, pyssyth ofte and lytyll.] *a* **1400-50** *Stockh. Med. MS.* 133 For þe strangury. **1522** MORE *De quat. Noviss.* Wks. 77/2 Parcase ye stone or the strangurye, haue put thee..to no lesse torment. **1651** JER. TAYLOR *Holy Dying* iv. §5. (1727) 144 The Axe is much a less affliction than a strangury. **1687** LUTTRELL *Brief Rel.* (1857) I. 425 The lord chancellor is lately taken very ill with the stone and strangury. **1691** WOOD *Ath. Oxon.* II. 584 He ..had never either Gout, Stone, Stranguery, or Head-ach. *c* **1720** GIBSON *Farrier's Dispens.* x. (1734) 238 This is adapted to Horses that are subject to the Stone and Strangury. **1765** STERNE *Tr. Shandy* VIII. iii, I hope they have got better of their colds,..fevers, stranguries, [etc.]. **1794** G. ADAMS *Nat. & Exp. Philos.* I. xi. 488 In calculous complaints of the urinary passages and in habitual stranguaries. **1847** W. C. L. MARTIN *Ox* 153/1 Sometimes there is great stranguary, but this is not an invariable symptom. **1875** H. C. WOOD *Therap.* (1879) 502 Complete strangury was not produced, but there was some difficulty in passing the urine. **1883** *American* V. 205 M. Louis Blanc had been suffering terribly for the past two years from a strangury.

fig. **1692** CROWNE *Regulus* II, Wine they will have, and have no stoppage of Wine here, give my Trade the Strangury?

¶**2.** By erroneous etymological association with STRANGLE, the word has sometimes been supposed to mean a disease due to strangling or choking.

a. *fig.*

1698 FARQUHAR *Love & Bottle* III. i, But why a Scribler, Madam?.. Is my Countenance strain'd, as if my head were distorted by a Stranguary of thought? **1847** THACKERAY *Contrib. to Punch* Wks. 1899 VI. 98 Everybody stopped. There was a perfect strangury in the street.

b. *Bot.* (See quot.; the sense appears in dictionaries, but evidence of its actual use is wanting.)

1840 PAXTON *Bot. Dict.*, *Strangury*, a disease produced on plants by tight ligatures.

†**ˈstrangy,** *a. Obs. rare.* In 6 **straungy, -gie, straunge** (*disyllabic*), **strangie, -gy.** [app. f. STRANGE *a.* + -Y.] Strange.

1555 PHAER *Æneid* II. C iij b, Some gasyd at the straungy gift that there to pallas stood. *Ibid.* III. H iij, That night in wodes w[t] straunge [disyllabic; so also in 1562: eds. 1584-1600 *read* straungy, strangie] sightes & monsters far from kind We troublyd were... Whan sodenly, from out the woodes,..A straungy man to sight apperes. *Ibid.* v. P j, All nakyd on some strangy sand onburyed lye thou must. **1594** R. C[AREW] *Godfrey of Bulloigne* II. li, To Mahound rather I impute aboue This straungy myracle. **1597** TOFTE *Laura* I. xxxix. in Arber *Garner* VIII. 294 Her heart, by th' other's made, in strangy wise, Hard as a rock.

stranskiite (ˈstrænskɪaɪt). *Min.* [ad. G. *stranskiit* (H. Strunz 1960, in *Naturwissenschaften* XLVII. 376/1), f. the name of I. N. *Stranski* (b. 1897), Bulgarian-born physical chemist: see -ITE[1].] An arsenate of zinc and copper, $Zn_2Cu(AsO_4)_2$, found as blue triclinic crystals.

1960 *Amer. Mineralogist* XLV. 1315 (*heading*) Stranskiite. **1978** *Ibid.* LXIII. 213 Inclusions of intergrown stranskiite, $Zn_2Cu(AsO_4)_2$, and schultenite, $PbHAsO_4$, in massive tennantite from Tsumeb, Southwest Africa, have been investigated by X-ray diffraction and X-ray fluorescence.

strany (ˈstrænɪ). A local name of the Common Guillemot.

1804 BEWICK *Brit. Birds* II. 175 Guillemot... Strany. **1831** G. MONTAGU *Ornith. Dict.* (ed. 2), Willock (*Uria Troile*, Latham)... Provincial. Guillem. Sea Hen... Strany. **1896** NEWTON *Dict. Birds.*

†**stranyelour.** *Sc. Obs. rare*[−1]. ? Corrupted form of STRANGULLION.

c **1500** *Rowlis Cursing* 63 in *Bannatyne MS.* (Hunter. Club) I. 300 The stranyelour and grit glengoir,..Mott fall vpoun thair kankart corss.

strap (stræp), *sb.* Also 6-7, (9 *Sc.*) **strapp,** 6-7 **strappe,** (7 *Sc.* **strape**). [dial. form of STROP *sb.* The early examples are either Sc. or nautical; in Sc. the form is normal: cf. *tap, drap* = TOP, DROP.]

1. a. A leather band, thong; in recent use, a flat band or strip of leather of uniform breadth. (Cf. STROP *sb.* 1.)

1685 *Rec. Scott. Cloth Manuf. New Mills* (S.H.S.) 105 Anent allowing of the stocken weavers oyle, strape and cords ordered that they be allowed oyle but noe strape nor cord. **1687** LOVELL tr. *Thevenot's Trav.* II. 87 They have a stick, with a strap of leather, like a bow, but very slack. **1706** PHILLIPS (ed. Kersey), *Strap*, a Thong of Leather. **1796** J. LAUDERDALE *Poems* 68 (E.D.D.) Providence did bless the seed, Sae brought it forth unto the strap. **1824** MACTAGGART *Gallovid. Encycl.* 439 *Strapps*, bands for binding grain with. **1827** SCOTT *Highl. Widow* v, I, who have gone for years with only a strap of deer's hide to tie back my hair.

b. as used for flogging. Hence, the application of the strap as an instrument of punishment.

c **1710** CELIA FIENNES *Diary* (1888) 217 My horse was quite down in one of these holes full of water but by y[e] good hand of God's providence.., for giving him a good strap he fflounc'd up againe. **1712** ADDISON *Spect.* No. 499 ¶5 A lively Cobler, that..had scarce passed a Day in his Life without giving her the Discipline of the Strap. **1874** H. CALDERWOOD *On Teaching* ii. 19 'A thrashing-mill', as an ingenious school-fellow named a teacher given to the rough and ready use of the strap. **1905** *Westm. Gaz.* 20 May 6/2 I got strap for that.

c. *transf.* Something resembling a leather strap in form.

a **1680** BUTLER *Rem.* (1759) I. 195 On both Sides of his Noddle Are Straps o' th' very same Leather; Ears are imply'd, But th' are mere Hide. **1837** P. KEITH *Bot. Lex.* 167 The stem of an ash-tree thus flattened terminated in a strap of about two inches in breadth. **1845** GOSSE *Ocean* i. (1849) 43 From a shallow cup..spring two or three long, olive-coloured straps [of the sea-thong], each of which becomes divided into two.

†**d.** A snare for birds. Also *fig.* [Cf. Du. *strop* in the same sense.] *Obs.*

1584-7 GREENE *Carde of Fancie* (1593) K I, Is the bird inticed to the strap by the shewe of the nets? **1602** ROWLANDS *Greenes Ghost* (1626) B I, As for Conicatching, they cleape it Batfowling, the wine the Strap, and the cards the Limetwigs.

e. A rope (of onions); a cluster, bunch (of fruit). *Sc.* and *north.*

1816 SCOTT *Old Mort.* x, They winna string the like o' him up as they do the puir Whig bodies..like straps o' onions. **1894** *Northumbld. Gloss.*, *Strap*, a cluster, a bunch; especially applied to red or white currants.

2. *Naut.* = STROP *sb.* 2.

a **1625** *Nomenclator Navalis* (Harl. MS. 2301). **1644** MANWAYRING *Seaman's Dict.* 103 A *Strap* a roape which is spliced about any block, that the block thereby may be made fast, to any place where they have occasion to use it: by the eye which is made in the Strap. **1745** P. THOMAS *Jrnl. Anson's Voy.* 27 We broke the Straps of the Main-Sheet and Clugarnet Blocks. **1794** *Rigging & Seamanship* I. 57 *Strap*, a number of yarns platted together with an eye at one end, to put a stick through [in ropemaking]. **1837** HEBERT *Engin. & Mech. Encycl.* I. 180 Blocks are suspended by straps, either of rope or iron. **1860** LD. W. LENNOX *Pict. Sporting Life* II. 137 Away went the strap of the mainsheet. **1862** F. A. GRIFFITHS *Artil. Man.* (ed. 9) 107 Wooden blocks are generally bound on the outside..with a grummet, which is called 'the strap' of the block.

Phrase. **1852** *Bentley's Misc.* XXXI. 59 We can't keep strap and block together, no how at all.

3. A narrow strip of leather, cloth, or other material fitted with a buckle as a fastening and for adjustment.

1688 HOLME *Armoury* III. 93/1 Strapps, are Leathers fastned to the sides of the Tree [of a saddle], to draw the Girths streight under the Horse Belly. *Ibid.* 93/2 End straps for tying, or buckling the ends to the Belly Girths. **1827** J. F. COOPER *Prairie* I. i. 22 To release his own rifle from the strap. **1833** J. HOLLAND *Manuf. Metal* II. 317 The leather part of bridles and other straps usually pass through metal rings, after which they are fastened with buckles. **1885** FAIRHOLT *Costume* (ed. 3) II. 386 Straps as well as leathern points were used in great numbers for the adjustment of armour. **1898** *Encycl. Sport* II. 298/1 (Rowling) *Straps*, the leather bands looped through holes in the stretcher, between which and the stretcher itself the oarsman's feet are placed. **1901** P. N. HASLUCK *Tailoring* iii. 44 The right strap [at the back of a waistcoat] should be shaped at the narrow end.., and a buckle put on the left one. **1915** *Blackw. Mag.* Apr.

493/2 'We'll have to step out' concluded M'Cabe, shortening the strap of his game-bag and settling it on his back.

4. a. A short band formerly attached to the bottom of each leg of a pair of pantaloons or trousers passing from side to side under the shank or waist of the boot. Chiefly *pl.*

1837 DICKENS *Pickw.* xiv, 'Damn my straps and whiskers', says Tom, 'if this [the weather] ain't pleasant, blow me!' **1848** THACKERAY *Van. Fair* lvi, Master George wore straps, and the most beautiful little boots like a man. **1878** HARE *Story of Life* (1896) I. 291 For many years afterwards, all young gentlemen wore straps to their trousers.

b. = SHOULDER-STRAP 2.

1802 C. JAMES *Milit. Dict.* s.v.

c. A band, usually elastic, inside the skirt of a lady's riding-habit, forming a loop in which the toe or the heel is inserted, so as to keep the skirt in its place.

1884 MRS. KENNARD *Right Sort* x, Stirrup proceeded to adjust her skirt satisfactorily and place her feet in the elastic straps.

5. A looped band. **a.** A looped band of leather or cloth attached to the top of a boot to draw it on.

1601 SHAKS. *Twel. N.* I. iii. 13 And so bee these boots too: and they be not, let them hang themselues in their owne straps. *a* **1625** FLETCHER *Captain* II. ii, And by all likelihoods he was begotten Between a stubborn pair of Winter-boots; His body goes with straps, he is so churlish. **1688** HOLME *Armoury* III. 13/2 The Straps are those Leathers sowed within the Boot on each side to draw them on. **1860** LD. W. LENNOX *Pict. Sporting Life* I. 209 The boots being short, and finished with very broad straps, which hung over the tops and down to the ankles.

b. A band or loop of leather to be grasped by the hand or arm, esp. as a means of steadying oneself in a moving vehicle.

1842 LOUDON *Suburban Hort.* 375 A deal plank to tread upon, with a strap at each end to drag it along either way. **1861** MRS. RIDDELL *City & Suburb* i, 'Now then', yelled out another conductor, balancing himself with a strap, while he stooped to open the door of his omnibus. **1897** C. T. DAVIS *Manuf. Leather* xxvii. (ed. 2) 415 The straps which are used in street cars to hold to when the cars are crowded.

6. *Mech.* A band or belt by means of which motion is communicated from one wheel, shaft, or pulley to another. = BAND *sb.*[2] 7.

1790 W. NICHOLSON in *Repert. Arts* (1796) V. 157 These three cylinders are connected, either by cogs or straps at the edges of each. **1835** URE *Philos. Manuf.* 47 The endless strap or belt which descends from the driving shaft to the steam pulley. **1860** *All Year Round* 26 May 163 The straps glide smoothly enough about the wheels [of the machine].

7. *Surg.* **a.** (See quot. 1706. Cf. STROP *sb.* 5.)

1706 PHILLIPS (ed. Kersey), *Strap*,.. In Surgery, a sort of Band usually made of Silk, Wooll, or Leather, to stretch out Members, in the setting of broken or disjoynted Bones.

b. A strip of adhesive plaster used to hold together the edges of a wound, fasten on a dressing, etc.

1749 GATAKER tr. *Le Dran's Oper. Surg.* 430 In order to keep the skin even with the flesh,.. we apply two straps of plaister over the lint. **1813** J. THOMSON *Lect. Inflam.* 285 The utility of stiches, in some of the wounds.. has been denied.. and the uniting bandage and adhesive strap.. may .. be advantageously substituted.

8. a. A razor-strop: = STROP *sb.* 3. *Obs.* exc. *dial.*

1758 JOHNSON *Idler* No. 40 ¶9 The dispute about straps for razors, now happily subsided. **1797** *Encycl. Brit.* (ed. 3) IX. 743/2 The powder of black-lead serves also to cover the straps for razors. **1809** MALKIN *Gil Blas* II. vii. ¶2 Two razors.. with a strap to set them. **1859** BARTLETT *Dict. Amer.* (ed. 2) 455 *Strap*, a razor-strop is, with us, generally called a razor-strap.

b. *slang.* A barber.

Hugh Strap, a barber, is one of the characters in Smollett's Roderick Random, 1748.

1865 *Hotten's Slang Dict.* (ed. 3) 248 *Strap*, a barber.

9. A narrow band of iron or other metal used in the form of a plate, loop, or ring for fastening a thing in position, holding together timbers, parts of machinery, etc.

[**1573-4, 1603-4**: see STROP *sb.* 4.] **1620** in Swayne *Sarum Church-w. Acc.* (1896) 172 Twoe new strapps for bell wheles, waying vij li. 2s. 4d. **1753** F. PRICE *Brit. Carpenter* (ed. 3) 17 The prick'd posts.. being tyed to the back of the rafter.. with iron straps. **1833** LOUDON *Encycl. Archit.* §1584 Straps to tie together the wall-plates at the external angles of the building. **1848** RONALDS & RICHARDSON *Knapp's Chem. Technol.* I. 234 The iron straps for strengthening the furnace. **1874** *Spon's Dict. Engin.* VIII. 2938 A strap is a band or strip of metal, usually curved to clasp or hold other parts; as a beam-strap, a spring-strap; especially the U-shaped part of a strap-head which clasps and holds the brasses.

10. A projection on a metal article, narrowed and flattened for screwing down to a wooden surface or for slipping under a metal plate; esp. each or one of the leaves of a strap-hinge.

1831 J. HOLLAND *Manuf. Metal* I. 140 The cheeks or straps of the shovel. *Ibid.*, The middle inside, where the handle is to be inserted, being kept open by the driving of an iron chisel down between the straps. **1833** LOUDON *Encycl. Archit.* §630, *q* is the part [of a strap-hinge] screwed to the under side of the flap; and *r* the strap or part which is inserted under the top of the table, into an iron plate, *s*. **1847** BRANDON *Anal. Goth. Archit.* 100 That [hinge] in Plate I has the strap continued quite through, and is finished with an ornamental termination.

11. †**a.** ? A piece of timber serving to fasten two objects together. *Obs.*

1588 *Shipping Lists of Dundee* in D. Wedderburne *Compt. Bk.* (S.H.S.) 217 Ye said schip now come from norrovay contenand.. thrie hundreth & fyve dousone daillis viij dousone of tymmer twentie strappis ane hundreth vnder-girths of aik fyve dousone of crockit tymmer ane thousand steyngis thrie small maistis. **1739** C. LABELYE *Westm. Bridge* 24 These Sides [of the Caisson] were fastened to the Bottom, or Grating, by 28 Pieces of Timber.. call'd Straps, about 8 Inches broad, and about 3 Inches thick, reaching and lapping over the Top of the Sides.

b. *Mining.* (See quots.)

1883 GRESLEY *Gloss. Coal-mining* 244 *Straps*, old iron way rails put up between the coal face and the front rank of props, in long-wall stalls, for supporting a tender roof. **1886** J. BARROWMAN *Sc. Mining Terms* 65 *Strap*, a plank supported at each end to uphold the roof strata. **1892** *Labour Commission Gloss.*, *Straps*, lengths of wood, either round or flat and from four to eight feet long, placed up to the roof and across the working places of a mine. At either end they are supported by props called legs.

12. *Bot.* **a.** (See quot. 1796.) **b.** = LIGULE 1.

1796 MARTYN *Lang. Bot.* s.v., Strap. *Ligula.* An appendage to the leaf in some Grasses. **1862** DARWIN *Fertil. Orchids* v. 171 The labellum.. is remarkable by being joined to the base of the column by a very narrow, thin, white strap. **1900** B. D. JACKSON *Gloss. Bot. Terms*, *Strap*, the ligule of a ray floret in Compositæ.

13. *Anglo-Irish.* A term of abuse applied to a woman or girl.

1842 LOVER *Handy Andy* ii, 'You infernal old strap!' shouted he, as he clutched up a handful of bottles.. and flung them at the nurse. *c* **1848** J. KEEGAN *Leg. & Poems* (1907) 454 You lie, you Orange strap.. you were insulting every one you met.

14. *slang.* Credit, trust. Phr. *on (the) strap.*

1828 CARR *Craven Gloss.*, *Strap*, credit, trust. **1876** W. CUDWORTH *Round abt. Bradford* 146 Meal and milk.. were had from the neighbouring farmhouses, and in reckoning for the latter a system of 'strap' then existed which was easily checked by both buyer and seller. This was done by what was called a 'milk stick'. *a* **1890** J. BROWN *Literæ laureatæ* (1890) 106 With willing hand I drain the brazen tap, Or draw the cork, or estimate the strap. **1894** HALL CAINE *Manxman* IV. ix, It was a trick of the devil to deal with you, and forget to pay strap (the price). *Ibid.* V. xxi, Himself going round to pay the grocer what had been put on 'strap' while he was at Kinsale. **1896** *Daily News* 21 Feb. 6/7 There was plenty to be had without paying for it. No one else paid that he saw. Whether they had 'strap' he did not know.

15. An energetic spell of work. (Cf. STRAP *v.* 4.)

1840 COL. HAWKER *Diary* (1893) II. 173 Had a stiff pianoforte lesson from Bertini, who by mere chance dropped in, and invited me to a good 'strap'.

16. *Typogr.* Short for *strap-line*, sense 18 below.

1960 A. HUTT *Newspaper Design* vii. 128 Essentially the strap is a single-line affair. **1981** A. GRAHAM-YOOLL *Forgotten Colony* xviii. 238 A photograph of the man.. was splashed over the front page of the Buenos Aires evening newspaper.. with a strap that read: 'This is how our English friends see us.'

17. *attrib.* and *Comb.* **a.** simple attrib., as ***strap-end***, ***-tab***; with the meaning 'made or consisting of a strap', as (sense 3) ***strap-muzzle***; also 'that has a strap', as ***strap watch***; (sense 5 b) ***strap-handle***; **b.** objective, as ***strap-maker***, ***strap-wielding***; **c.** similative, as ***strap-like*** adj.

1909 T. SHEPPARD in *Trans. Hull Sci. Club* IV. II. 62 The part with a swivel is attached to the brass at the *strap-end. **1892** *Photogr. Ann.* II. 533 A polished mahogany stained case with leather *strap handle for carrying. **1835-6** *Todd's Cycl. Anat.* I. 785/2 At the same epoch there are formed anteriorly.. two pairs of small *strap-like bodies. **1770** *Ann. Reg.* 73/2 He was a clog *strap-maker. **1889** *Daily News* 7 Nov. 7/2 When the ordinary *strap muzzle was used, if drawn too tightly, a dog could not drink. **1913** E. T. LEEDS *Archæol. Anglo-Sax. Settlements* iii. 56 Other objects include the bronze *strap-tab. **1926** *Daily Colonist* (Victoria, B.C.) 11 July 9/4 (Advt.), *Strap Watch. Guaranteed accurate and dependable. Handsome case. Leather strap. **1962** K. ORVIS *Damned & Destroyed* xxiv. 181, I dropped my eyes to my strap-watch. **1910** I. MACINTOSH in *Poets of Ayrshire* 331 His reputation for *strap-wielding made roots respected.

18. Special comb.: **strap-bar**, (*a*) (see quot.); (*b*) a bar which carries the strap-fork *q.v.* (*Cent. Dict.* Suppl. 1909); **strap-block** (see quot.); **strap-bolt** *sb.*, a bolt with a flattened end for screwing down to a surface; **strap-bolt** *v. trans.*, to fasten *down* with a strap-bolt; **strap-bound** *a.* in ***strap-bound-block*** (see quot.); **strap brake**, a brake consisting of a friction strap applied to a cylindrical bearing surface; esp. a dynamometer brake on this plan; **strap-butt** [BUTT *sb.*[11]], leather for the making of bands, belts, straps, etc. (see quot. 1904); **strap-cap**, a cap with bands to fasten under the chin; **strap-end** *Archæol.*, the metal fastening on a strap (sense 3); **strap-fork**, an apparatus with prongs for guiding the driving-belt of a machine from one pulley to another; **strap-form** *a. Bot.*, ligulate (cf. STRAP-SHAPED *a.*); **strap-game**, a swindling game = FAST AND LOOSE (*Cent. Dict.* 1891); **strap handle** *Ceramics*, a handle on a vessel such as a jug or ewer which is in the form of a loop and flattened like a narrow strap; hence **strap-handled** *a.*; **strap-head** (see quot. 1875); **strap hide**, a hide suitable for or used for the making of straps (cf. *strap-butt*); **strap hinge**, a hinge with long leaves or flaps for screwing down to a surface; also a hinge with one leaf lengthened for insertion into an iron plate; **strap iron**, (*a*) (see quot. 1833); (*b*) *U.S.*, iron in the form of long narrow strips (cf. *strap-rail*); **strap-laid** *a.*, (of a rope) made in a flat form by binding together two or more hawser-laid ropes; **strap leather**, leather for making straps; **strap-line** *Typogr.*, a subsidiary heading printed above a headline; **strap-oil**, *slang*, flogging with a strap; **strap-ornament**, ornamentation in *strap-work*; **strap-oyster** *U.S.* (*local*) (see quot.); **strap-rail** *U.S.*, a flat railroad rail laid upon a continuous longitudinal sleeper (*Cent. Dict.* 1891); hence **strap railroad, railway, road** *U.S.*, a railroad constructed with strap-rails; **strap shoe**, a shoe fastened by means of a strap across the instep; **strap skein** *U.S.*, a strengthening iron band or a series of such bands placed upon a wooden spindle of an axle bar (see SKEIN *sb.*[2] 2); **strap solder** (see quot. 1896); †**strap-spear-shaped** *a. Bot.*, (of a leaf) flattened or strap-shaped at the base with a spear-shaped head; **strapwork** (see quot. 1854); also *attrib.*; **strap-worm**, a cestoid worm of the family *Ligulidæ*; **strapwort**, a small annual plant belonging to the genus *Corrigiola* found in the extreme south-west of England. Also STRAP-SHAPED *a.*

1887 J. A. PHILLIPS & BAUERMAN *Elem. Metall.* (ed. 2) 647 There are also two bars, called '*strap-bars,' connecting the first transverse bar at the wider end with the ring. **1875** KNIGHT *Dict. Mech.*, *Strap-block* (Nautical), a block with a strap around it, and an eye worked at the lower end for attachment to a hook upon deck for a purchase. **1795** HERSCHEL in *Phil. Trans.* LXXXV. 359 They were all screwed down by *strap-bolts. *Ibid.* 360 The lower end is *strap-bolted down upon the beams. **1794** *Rigging & Seamanship* I. 157 **Strap-bound-blocks* are single blocks, with a shoulder left on each side, at the upper part, to admit the strap through, a little above the pin. **1902** S. SHELDON & H. MASON *Altern.-Current Machines* 240 The power output of the motor is absorbed in a *strap brake. **1885** H. R. PROCTOR *Tanning* 200 In the case of *strap-butts, the currying is.. far less elaborate. **1904** P. N. HASLUCK *Harness Making* ii. 38 Black strap butts are the best part of the hide from which the belly and shoulder have been cut. **1820** in Alice M. Earle *Two Cent. Costume Amer.* (1903) II. 501 The women.. had two kinds... One was called a *strap-cap; it came under the chin; the other was called round-cord cap, and did not come over the ears. **1973** *Oxf. Univ. Gaz.* CIII. Suppl. v. 18 *Mr A. R. Lake*: Presented a 12th-century bronze *strap-end from near Bicester, Oxon. **1977** *Antiquaries Jrnl.* LXII. 420 Belt-buckles and strap-ends of the later Roman Empire. **1902** THORNLEY *Cotton Combing Machines* 7 *Strap Fork. **1845-50** MRS. LINCOLN *Lect. Bot.* Vocab., **Strap-form*, ligulate. **1847** *Knickerbocker* XXIX. 281 He was accused of having 'come the *strap-game' over a native. **1873** J. H. BEADLE *Undevel. West* vii. 140 A score of 'smart Alecks' relieved of their surplus cash by betting on the 'strap game'. **1939** J. D. S. PENDLEBURY *Archaeol. Crete* iii. 134 The small size of the *strap handles is also an indication of date. **1972** *Trans. Oriental Ceramics Soc.* XXXVIII. 65 A stoneware ewer, ovoid with a short spreading neck and double strap-handle. **1957** V. G. CHILDE *Dawn Europ. Civilization* (ed. 6) vii. 131 *Strap-handled Jugs. **1864-86** WEBSTER, **Strap-head*. **1875** KNIGHT *Dict. Mech.*, *Strap-head*, a journal-box secured by a strap to a connecting-rod. **1862** *Catal. Internat. Exhib.*, *Brit.* II. No. 4671, Brown *Strap Hides. **1737** HOPPUS *Salmon's Country Build. Estim.* (ed. 2) 107 *Strap Hinges, are sold by the Dozen. **1833** LOUDON *Encycl. Archit.* §630 The end flaps.. are made to put on or to take off as required, by means of what are called strap-hinges. *Ibid.* §1584 Fix on each side of the principals two long double wrought-iron *strap irons (binding plates of iron).. secured by thirteen screw-bolts. **1883** INGERSOLL in *Harper's Mag.* Jan. 199 The track is rudely built.., the rails being heavy strap-iron bolted upon string pieces. **1839** URE *Dict. Arts* 1072 A three-inch *strap-laid rope. **1897** C. T. DAVIS *Manuf. Leather* xxvi. (ed. 2) 414 Large sides are used for bag leather and for *strap leather. **1960** A. HUTT *Newspaper Design* vii. 128 The use of subsidiary lines—**strap-lines* over headings, *tag-lines* following them—has become a feature of headline practice. *Ibid.*, *Strap-lines* are most suitable over double-column headlines. **1979** *Guardian* 9 Oct. 10/7 Lord Beaverbrook.. sometimes put a strap-line over the story saying that the piece didn't represent editorial policy. **1847** HALLIWELL, **Strap-oil*, a severe beating. It is a common joke on April 1st to send a lad for a pennyworth of strap-oil, which is generally ministered on his own person. **1895** *Daily News* 27 May 6/6 A vase-shaped sugar castor,.. chased with cherubs and *strap ornament in relief. **1881** INGERSOLL *Oyster-Industr.* (Hist. Fish. Industr. U.S.) 249 **Strap-oyster*, the long, slender form which grows in mud. **1874** B. F. TAYLOR *World on Wheels* I. xiii. 105 Years ago, he rode on a train of the old Toledo & Adrian Railway—*strap-rail at that. **1948** *Exhibit Finder* (Museum of Sci. & Industry, Chicago) 3 The story of the early days of railroading is further traced by samples showing the progress of rail manufacture from strap rail, flat as a pancake, to the heavy crowned rail of today. **1911** WEBSTER, **Strap railroad* or *railway*. **1861** N. A. WOODS *Prince of Wales in Canada* xviii. 357 The first part of the journey was over what is termed a '*strap road,' one of the most unsafe varieties of railway ever used. **1903** *Daily Chron.* 10 Jan. 8/4 Patent leather *strap shoes. **1891** *Century Dict.* *Strap-skein. **1885** P. J. DAVIES *Pract. Plumbing* I. 44 *Strap Solder. **1896** *Ibid.* II. 801 *Strap solder*, solder run into strips. **1796** WITHERING *Brit. Plants* (ed. 3) I. 85 **Strap-spear-shaped* (lineari-lanceolatum). *Ibid.* II. 30 Blossom of 3 petals, the 2 upper strap-spearshaped. **1854** FAIRHOLT *Dict. Terms Art*, **Strap-work*, a peculiar kind of ornament, adopted extensively in the fifteenth and sixteenth centuries (particularly in Flanders and Germany) .. which consists of a narrow fillet or band, folded and crossed, and occasionally interlaced with another. **1901** *Illustr. Lond. News* CXVIII. 912 Above the monogram is a strapwork panel. **1854** A. ADAMS etc. *Man. Nat. Hist.* 361 *Strap-Worms (Ligulidæ). **1896** tr. *Boas' Text-bk. Zool.* 151 The Strap-worm, *Ligula simplicissima*, parasitic in the digestive tract of different Water-birds. **1799** J. HULL *Brit. Flora* I. 66 *Corrigiola littoralis*, Sand *Strapwort.

strap (stræp), *v.*[1] [f. STRAP *sb.* (Cf. STROP *v.*)]

1. a. *trans.* To furnish with a strap; to fasten, bind, or secure with a strap or with straps. Also with *on*, *up*, *together*.

1711 W. SUTHERLAND *Shipbuild. Assist.* 141 A general Proportion for strapping every Block in a Ship. **1735** DYCHE & PARDON *Dict.*, *Strap*, to fasten down with a Strap. **1776** G. SEMPLE *Building in Water* 35 Let your Mauls be well hooped and strapped with Iron. **1837** DICKENS *Pickw.* ii, His scanty black trousers..were strapped very tightly over a pair of patched and mended shoes. **1843** LEFEVRE *Life Trav. Phys.* III. III. iv. 120 A tin case strapped over his shoulders. **1860** TYNDALL *Glac.* I. ii. 15, I strapped on my knapsack. **1861** SALA *Dutch Pict.* xviii. 282 The barouche..had a hamper strapped behind it. **1873** BLACK *Pr. Thule* xxiv, [She] asked ..if all her portmanteaus were strapped up. **1874** THEARLE *Naval Arch.* §280. 292 They are also carefully strapped with two rivets on each side of the butt. **1885** MISS BRADDON *Wyllard's Weird* i, He began to collect all this literature and to strap it neatly together. **1909** *Daily News* 20 Oct. 7/1 'It is blowing a bit hard', was the intrepid aviator's remark as he strapped himself to his seat on the machine.

b. *Surg.* To apply straps of adhesive plaster to (a wound, etc.); to fasten (dressing) *on* with plaster; ***to strap up***, to dress and bandage (a wound or a person, *i.e.* his wound).

1843 R. J. GRAVES *Lect. Clin. Med.* xxx. 385 But [he] expected some improvement from strapping the ulcer with real adhesive plaster. **1872** O. W. HOLMES *Poet Breakf.-t.* v. (1885) 110 He..strapped up my cut. **1902** *Munsey's Mag.* XXVI. 583/2, I awoke and found Low..ready to take off my bandages and dress my wound... And after he had strapped me up again the baroness came in with my breakfast. **1905** H. D. ROLLESTON *Dis. Liver* 118 The local pain and tenderness [should be] relieved..by strapping the hepatic region with narrow strips of plaster as if for fractured ribs.

c. To bind and hang (a person). Also with *up*. Also *intr.*, to be hanged. *Sc.*

1815 SCOTT *Guy M.* xxxiii, I am done up already, and if I must strap for it, all shall out. **1815** —— *Let.* in *Lockhart* III. xi. 381 A full account of the affair of 1745, with the trials.. of the poor plaids who were strapped up at Carlisle.

d. To fasten, bind, or secure (a strap) tightly.

1818 SCOTT *Rob Roy* xxxiv When they strapped the horse-girth ower my arms, I might hae judged what was biding me.

e. ***to strap*** (oneself) ***in***: in an aircraft, to fasten one's safety belt. Also *absol.* (occas. with *up* or without *adv.*).

1913 *Flight* 20 Sept. 1040/2 Neither the pilot nor passenger was strapped in. **1919** J. BUCHAN *Mr. Standfast* I. ix. 173 He signalled to me to strap myself in..and he proceeded to practise 'stunts'—the loop, the spinning nose-dive, and others. **1958** 'CASTLE' & 'HAILEY' *Flight into Danger* v. 72 Better strap yourself in... You must have watched the pilot quite a lot. **1962** L. DEIGHTON *Ipcress File* v. 31 The steward helped him strap in. **1970** 'R. LLEWELLYN' *But we didn't get Fox* vii. 69 She waited for me to strap, started a jet..and taxied down the loop. **1977** *R. Air Force Yearbk.* 29 The excellent leverage of the straps is a noteworthy point and enables the pilots to strap in tightly and securely. **1977** 'O. JACKS' *Autumn Heroes* v. 69 Gerry Steinberg was strapping up beside his pilot.

f. *intr.* for *pass.* To admit of being fastened by means of a strap.

1924 A. D. SEDGWICK *Little French Girl* I. v. 37 Grey shoes strapping across the instep with a buckle.

2. To beat with a strap or leather thong.

1735 DYCHE & PARDON *Dict.* **1832** *Min. Evid. Comm. Factories Bill* 193 When I got home I saw her shoulders, and I said, 'Ann, what is the matter?' she said, 'The over-looker has strapped me.' **1854** THACKERAY *Newcomes* I. ii. 20 Many and many a time had his own father..strapped and beaten him. **1887** *Pall Mall Gaz.* 21 Dec. 7/1 The two little girls were strapped again. With faces marked by the strap they fled.

3. To sharpen (a razor, knife) by applying it to a strap or strop: = STROP *v.* Now *rare* or *Obs.*

1785 J. COLLIER *Musical Trav.* 119 Still strapped he his inexorable razor. **1823** *Blackw. Mag.* XIV. 592/1 He had not 'strapped' the razor enough—or he had strapped it too much. **1845** S. JUDD *Margaret* I. xvii. (1881) 149 Strapping his knife on the edge of the kit. **1850** THACKERAY *Pendennis* lxviii, Mr. James Morgan laid out the silver dressing-case, and strapped the shining razor. **1856** [see HONE *v.*[3]].

4. *intr.* To work closely and energetically (*at* a task); to buckle *to* one's work. Also with adv., as *to*, *away*. *slang.*

1823 EGAN *Grose's Dict. Vulgar T.*, *Strap*, to work. The kiddy would not strap, so he went on the scamp. **1836** COL. HAWKER *Diary* (1893) II. 103 Writing, reading, and strapping hard at my long-lost music. **1849** ALB. SMITH *Pottleton Leg.* xxxi. 347 Pedestrians..strapping away at the rate of four miles and a half per hour. **1851** MAYHEW *Lond. Labour* II. 233/1 The strapping masters, or those who make the men (by extra supervision) 'strap' to their work, so as to do a greater quantity of labour in the usual time. **1891** *Cornhill Mag.* July 65 Maisie strapped to, and got a berth as a nursery governess.

5. *trans.* To groom (a horse).

1854 MISS BAKER *Northampt. Gloss.*, *Strap*, to groom a horse. **1875** *My First 'Wine'* 20 When the groom took off his [a horse's] clothes to strap him,..my hopes of winning.. vanished altogether. **1881** A. C. GRANT *Bush Life Queensld.* xxv. (1882) 254 Tommy..leads the Bey [a racehorse] off to be thoroughly strapped and clothed [after the race].

6. To give credit for (goods). *dial.* or *slang.*

1862 C. C. ROBINSON *Dial. Leeds* 423 'Yuh mun strap muh this missis wal Seterder neet.'..'D' yuh strap here māaster?' **1896** *Evesham Jrnl.* 26 Sept. (E.D.D.), Witness said she had not got a sixpence, and prisoner offered to 'strap' it with her.

7. Comb.: **strap-down** *a.* *Astronautics*, applied to an inertial guidance system in which the gyroscopes are fixed to the vehicle rather than mounted in gimbals; **strap-on** *a.*, that can be attached by a strap or straps; in *Astronautics*, applied to a booster rocket mounted on the outside of the main rocket so as to be jettisonable; also as *sb.*, such a booster.

[**1962** FERNANDEZ & MACOMBER *Inertial Guidance Engin.* viii. 308 The strapped-down gyro reference package..has become widely used as a guidance aid in ballistic missiles where high accuracy is not required.] **1963** SLATER & AUSMAN in C. T. Leondes *Guidance & Control Aerospace Vehicles* iii. 82 A system of this sort..is sometimes inelegantly called 'strapdown'. **1983** *Times* 8 June 2/8 The IMU system uses specially designed and positioned gyros attached to the body of the missile, called strapdown gyros. **1966** *Sci. News* 13 Aug. 107 Solid propellant strap-ons could be used to raise the Saturn V's orbital payload..to as much as 427,000 pounds. **1968** *New Scientist* 31 Oct. 231 The vehicle..appeared to have a two-stage core with four strap-on boosters. **1975** *Aviation Week* 12 May 21/1 Viewed from below a climbing booster, the procedure would appear like the petals of a flower opening if all four strap-ons separated at the same moment. **1981** J. SUTHERLAND *Bestsellers* x. 111 Such 'novelties' as strap-on shark fins. **1982** *Aviation Week* 14 June 18 The U.S. vehicle..uses strap-on solid boosters and integral liquid propulsion to launch itself.

strap (stræp), *v.*[2] *dial.* [Alteration of STRIP *v.*] (See quots.)

1854 MISS BAKER *Northampt. Gloss.*, *Strap* or *Strip*, to draw the last milk from a cow. **1881** *Leicester Gloss.*, *Strap*, to drain the last milk from the udder by a peculiar motion of the thumb and finger. Often metaphorically used for draining anything dry.

S-trap: see S I. 2c.

strapade, strapado(e, obs. ff. STRAPPADO.

'strap-hang, *v. colloq.* Also **straphang.** [Back-formation from prec.] *intr.* To be a straphanger in a railway carriage, etc. Also *fig.*

1908 O. JESPERSEN in *Englische Studien* LXX. 119 You strap-hang on the Subterranean. **1917** *Daily Mail* 28 Aug. 2/5, I think those weary girls look like tired little flowers as they strap-hang for half an hour or more. **1931** GALSWORTHY *Maid in Waiting* vii. 55 The only..difference ..between Parties is that one Party sits in the National 'Bus, and the other Party strap-hangs. **1937** W. H. AUDEN in Auden & MacNeice *Lett. from Iceland* v. 55 The bowler hat who straphangs in the tube. **1959** *Times Lit. Suppl.* 24 Apr. 237/4 Miss Charles straphangs from fashion on a journey whose destination does not interest her. **1974** K. ROYCE *Trap Spider* viii. 141, I still wonder what happened to her; it's not usually a happy ending with girls who strap-hang with rats like Laurie Yates. **1982** BARR & YORK *Official Sloane Ranger Handbk.* 100/1 In the Europe Supermarket in Old Brompton Road, or strap-hanging in the tube from Gloucester Road, astonishingly you meet *more* people you know.

Hence **'strap-hanging** *vbl. sb.* and *ppl. a.*

1919 *Electrician* LXXXII. 497/2 The somewhat elaborate provision made for 'strap hanging'. **1920** *Cycling* 5 Feb. p. i (Advt.), The strap-hanging problem is easily solved by the satisfied owner of a Rudge-Whitworth. **1928** *Daily Express* 22 Dec. 7/2 (*heading*) Straphanging rule dispute. **1945** [see KEYNOTE *v.*]. **1957** L. DURRELL *Justine* I. 53 Here, where the general impression of British culture suggested parsimony, indigence, intellectual strap-hanging—here I would pass the evening alone. **1972** C. FREMLIN *Appointment with Yesterday* i. 8 Every strap-hanging commuter in London.

straphanger ('stræphæŋə(r)). *slang.* [f. STRAP *sb.* + HANG *v.* + -ER.] A passenger who is compelled to stand and hold on by the strap in a full omnibus, compartment of a railway carriage, etc.; also *fig.*, one who commutes to work by public transport.

1905 *Daily News* 30 Jan. 3 Mr. W. Lestocq..has espoused the cause of the long-suffering 'straphanger'. **1905** *Punch* 8 Nov. 341/2, I am a Straphanger. I am one of a million swaying souls who travel underground to the vast city. **1915** W. CATHER *Song of Lark* II. v. 195 In the street-car..she sat staring at the waistcoat buttons of a fat strap-hanger. **1950** A. J. DEUTSCH in D. Knight *100 Yrs. Sci. Fiction* (1969) 169 The other seats were filled, and there were a dozen or so strap-hangers. **1981** *Times* 5 Aug. 10/4 Washington.. commuters.. are not strap-hangers like New Yorkers, Londoners and Parisians.

strapless ('stræplɪs), *a.* [f. STRAP *sb.* + -LESS.] Without a strap; not fitted with straps. *spec.* of women's dress: without shoulder straps; also *absol.*

1846 LYTTON *Lucretia* II. Prol., A sturdy wanderer, with thick shoes and strapless trousers. **1935** *Mademoiselle* Feb. 91/3 Strapless and backless brassiere. **1946** *Vogue* Aug. 90/2 In another seventy-five years he'll probably be all for Picasso and your strapless frock. **1955** N. FITZGERALD *House is Falling* i. 13 Her strapless, white swim-suit. **1969** A. LURIE *Real People* 92 Anna May came out, in a cerise strapless satin evening gown. **1973** *Country Life* 8 Mar. 633/2 Slinky dresses that have the finest straps or are completely strapless. **1980** *Daily Tel.* 13 Oct. 19/3 Strongest revival of all—the straight-across strapless.

‖**strapontin** (strapɔ̃tɛ̃). [Fr.] A tip-up seat, usu. additional to the ordinary seating in a theatre, taxi, etc., esp. in France.

1926 W. J. LOCKE *Old Bridge* v. xviii. 270 Perella insisted on sitting on the little seat, so that Silvester should be at the back with Beatrice. 'He loves it—hates *strapontins*.' **1927** *Observer* 29 May 12/3 As for the strapontins, which, at every performance of a successful play, block up all the gangways, actors and managers agree that they are dangerous. **1934** H. MILLER *Tropic of Cancer* 179 Carl was sitting opposite us, on the *strapontin*. **1965** P. H. NEWBY *One of Founders* iv. 113 Hedges..climbed in behind Prudence, seated himself on a well-upholstered strapontin, and allowed himself to be driven off.

strappado (stræ'peɪdəʊ, -'ɑːdəʊ), *sb. Obs.* exc. *Hist.* Forms: (6 **stappado, strippado, stroppado**), 7 **strappada, strappadoe,** 6– **strappado**; *pl.* 6–7 **strappadoes,** (6 **-das**); 6–8 **strapado,** (7 **strapadoe,** 8 **strapade**). [ad. F. *strapade*, *estrapade*, ad. It. *strappata*, f. *strappare* to drag, pull, snatch; for the quasi-Sp. ending see *-ado*.]

1. A form of punishment or of torture to extort confession in which the victim's hands were tied across his back and secured to a pulley; he was then hoisted from the ground and let down half way with a jerk; also an application of this punishment or torture; also the instrument used.

1560 J. FRAMPTON in Strype *Ann. Ref.* xx. (1709) I. 232 And forthwith I was plucked up again; and after a while let down again. And being put down well near dead..of this Torment of the Stappado [*sic*], they asked me [etc.]. **1568** V. SKINNER *Gonsalvius' Discov. Pract. Spanish Inquis.* 24b, They..bid the hangman to slip the ropes suddenly, that he may fall downe with a sway, and in the halfe way to stop and geue him the Strippado: which being done with a trice, al his whole body is out of frame. **1583** GREENE *Mamillia* I. 22b, Or the superstitious Essenians..had had Licurgus for their iudge, they had in mine opinion purchased y[e] strapado for their paines. **1585** T. WASHINGTON tr. *Nicholay's Voy.* II. x. 44b, The one..hadde presently three stroppados at the yardes arme of the gally. **1596** SHAKS. *1 Hen. IV*, II. iv. 262. **1598** FLORIO *Worlde of Wordes* Ep. Ded. a4, One saies of Petrarche for all: A thousand strappadas coulde not compell him to confesse, what some interpreters will make him saie he ment. **1670** R. LASSELS *Voy. Italy* II. 254 And a pocket pistol found about you..is enough to make you be sent to the Gallies with *tre tratti di corda*, that is, the strappada thrice. **1725** *Lond. Gaz.* No. 6343/1 *Turin*... A few Days ago an Advocate underwent the Punishment of the Strapade. **1855** KINGSLEY *Westw. Ho!* vii, I have had too much of the rack already, and the strappado too, to care much what man can do unto me. **1888** H. C. LEA *Hist. Inquisition* I. 400 *note*, In some witch trials of 1474 in Piedmont the oath to tell the truth was enforced with excommunication and '*tratti di corde*,' or infliction of the torture known as the strappado.

†**b.** as a punishment used in military discipline.

1622 F. MARKHAM *Epist. Warre* III. vii. 106 [The Provost Marshal] is..to see all places of Execution..furnished with ..Gallowes, Gybbets, Scaffolds, Pillories, Stocks or Strappadoes. **1671** SIR J. TURNER *Pallas Armata* xxvii. 348 Military Punishments, which reach not to Death, are the Strappado, hanging up by the Thumbs, [etc.]. **1688** HOLME *Armoury* III. 310/2 There are several other Punishments used by Military Officers for the Chastising of Offending Soldiers, as..the half Strappado, the whole Strappado... The Half Strappado, is to have the Mans hands tyed cross behind his Back, and so by them be drawn up to a considerable height, and so let down again... The Whole Strappado, is when the person is drawn up to his height, and then suddenly to let him fall half way with a jerk.

†**c.** *transf.* and *fig. Obs.*

1594 *Selimus* H4 Marrie that had bene the way to preferment, downe Holburne vp Tiburne: well ile keepe my best ioynt from the strappado. **1598** E. GUILPIN *Skial.* (1878) 32 He's a Strappado, rack, and some such paine To base lewd vice. **1615** BRATHWAIT (*title*) A Strappado for the Diuell. *Ibid.* To Rdr., Be honest still and thou art out of the swing of this strappado. **1626** J. YATES *Ibis ad Cæs.* II. 14 Truth hath alwaies given her enemies such Strappadoes, that it wresteth some words of confession from them against their will. **1650** FULLER *Pisgah* II. iv. 109 O sad strapado of the soul, to be hoised up so high, and then cast down suddenly so low. **1691** ABP. SANCROFT *Fam. Lett. to North* (1757) 23 My old pain in my right shoulder, which gives me the strappada sometimes, when I put on my doublet.

¶**2.** Erroneously taken to mean 'chastisement by blows' (J.). [Cf. STRAP *sb.* 1b, STRAP *v.* 2.]

1668 R. L'ESTRANGE *Vis. Quev.* vii. 311 If I dye, let my Boy Robin have the Strappado, three hours a day, to be duly paid him during Life. **1704** T. BAKER *Act at Oxf.* II. ii. 24 [*The Beadles give him a Blow on the Back with a Stick.*] *Dri.* Sir! *Blo.* That Strappado, Sir, is to inform your Body, you are..putting on the more decent Habit of a Doctor. **1712** STEELE *Spect.* No. 509 ¶3 The Benches around are so filthy, that no one can sit down, yet the Beadles and Officers have the Impudence at Christmas to ask for their Box, though they deserve the Strapado. **1716** M. DAVIES *Athen. Brit.* II. To Rdr. 8 Having a Pope-Sinon to undergo the voluntary Operations of his own Party's Satyrical Lashes and Mootly Strapades. **1769** BICKERSTAFFE *Padlock* I. viii, He gave me the strappado on my shoulders, and the bastinado on the soles of my feet.

†**stra'ppado,** *v. Obs.* [f. STRAPPADO *sb.*]

1. *trans.* To torture or punish with the strappado. Also *fig.*

1596 NASHE *Saffron Walden* O3, A Gentleman..that was no straunger to such bandyings as had past betwixt vs, was desirous to see how he lookt since my strappadoing and torturing him. **1607** HEYWOOD *Woman Kild* (1617) G3b, Oh to redeeme mine honor, I would..Be rack'd, strappado'd, put to any torment. **1641** MILTON *Animadv.* 12 They had neither bin hal'd into your Gehenna at Lambeth, nor strappado'd with an Oath *Ex Officio* by your bow men of the Arches.

¶**2.** To beat with a strap. (Cf. STRAPPADO *sb.* 2.)

1655 tr. *Sorel's Com. Hist. Francion* VI. 14, I will beat her soundly for it with the Brims of my Hat, although she better doth deserve to be strappadoed [orig. F. *qui meriteroit plustost les estriuieres*].

strapped (stræpt), *ppl. a.* [f. STRAP *v.*^{1} + -ED^1.]
1. a. Furnished with a strap, bound or fastened with a strap or with straps.
1784 COWPER *Task* IV. 6 He [the post] comes,.. With spatter'd boots, strapp'd waist, and frozen locks. **1809** *Catal. Bks.*, Hymns,.. morocco, gilt edges, 7*s*... strapped, 7*s*. 6*d*. **1864** E. BURRITT *Walk fr. Lond. to John O'Groats* 316 Strapped pantaloons. **1909** H. BEGBIE *Cage* i. 2 He hurrried to school with.. a strapped bundle of books under his arm.
b. *Dressmaking* and *Tailoring*. Trimmed with straps; *spec.* of a seam, etc.: Strengthened by overlaying with piece of stronger material.
1892 *Stratford-on-Avon Herald* 18 Nov. 6/1 The strapped corsage, cuffs and turn-down collar being of velvet. **1894** *Daily News* 20 June 6/4 Another lady affects.. a covert coat with manly pockets and strapped seams. **1909** *Daily Mail* 6 Aug. 1/6 Gentlemen's Riding Breeches; in tough wearing whipcord,.. strapped buckskin.
2. *slang* (orig. *U.S.*). Short of money. Now freq. const. *for*. Also in extended use and ***cash-strapped*** adj.
1857 *Nat. Intelligencer* Oct., (Bartlett) No go. Lowndes is strapped. **1876** *Daily News* 5 Oct. 6/1 The tramp.. does not awaken sympathy like the 'strapped' journeyman in search of a job. **1913** EDITH WHARTON *Custom of Country* I. iv. 44 'Fact is,..' he said,..'I'm a little mite strapped just this month.' **1935** *Sun* (Baltimore) 13 Mar. 2/6 PWA is not yet 'strapped' for funds. **1936** L. C. DOUGLAS *White Banners* ix. 193 If he had been strapped, the chances were he would have bought a hat to-day. **1936** M. FRANKLIN *All that Swagger* xlviii. 437 Also she was strapped for ready money. **1952** WODEHOUSE *Pigs Have Wings* i. 23 A bit strapped for the ready, eh? **1958** L. WOLFF *Low Level Mission* iii. 76 The Axis powers had always been strapped for oil; the specter of a shortage.. haunted the two dictators. **1960** J. LODWICK *Asparagus Trench* 7 Fortunately, neither was strapped for children. **1968** *Sunday Mail Mag.* (Brisbane) 8 Dec. 13/3 Strapped for cash he and the dancers tossed their luggage by night from fire escape. **1973** *Times* 7 Dec. 18/7 (*caption*) If only we could be sure the Stringalongs are as strapped for petrol as we are, we could risk asking them to dinner. **1976** *Time* 5 Apr. 37/1 Cash-strapped Chrysler is stepping up preparations to bring out its first domestic subcompact late next year. **1977** *Time* 25 July 48/3 By the spring of 1974, the whipsaw effect of recession and rising costs—particularly for oil which fuels 80% of Con Ed's generating capacity—left the company strapped. **1979** *Church Times* 2 Nov. 10 The Roman Church is almost everywhere strapped for ready cash. **1982** *Times* 18 Dec. 9/1 Cash-strapped countries like Iran and Libya are producing flat out.

strapper^1 ('stræpə(r)). [f. STRAP *v.*^{1} + -ER^1.]
1. a. A 'strapping' or tall and robust person; one above the average stature and strength of build. (Chiefly applied to women. Cf. STRAPPING *ppl. a.*)
1675 WYCHERLEY *Country Wife* III. ii, Come let us go too: Madam, your Servant. (*To* Alithea.) Good night Strapper. —(*To* Lucy [Alithea's maid].) **1690** *Pagan Prince* xxviii. 77 This Goddess.. took him up in her Arms (for your Pagan Goddesses are all Strappers). **1706** ESTCOURT *Fair Example* I. i, She's a Strapper, and I'm a Pigmy. **1751** SMOLLETT *Per. Pickle* xcv, Ah! you strapper, what a jolly bitch you are! **1802** G. COLMAN *Br. Grins, Elder Bro.* (1804) 118 Isaac ey'd Toby,.. And saw he was a strapper,—stout and tall. **1842** J. WILSON *Chr. North* (1857) I. 157 She is what is delicately called a strapper, rosy-armed as the morning. **1847** C. BRONTË *Jane Eyre* xx, A strapper—a real strapper, Jane: big, brown, and buxom.
†**b.** *transf.* A monstrous lie, 'whopper'. *Obs.*
1677 W. HUGHES *Man of Sin* I. x. 46 Did not the Pope deliver Trajan's, the Heathenish Persecuting Emperor's Soul from Hell, as they assure us; and whereof, with other strappers of the same breed, you will hear more fully hereafter? *Ibid.* III. iii. 58 Such another Strapper is their talk about Christs Shrowd, or Winding-sheet.
2. One who straps or grooms horses. Esp. *Austral.* in later use.
1828 *Sporting Mag.* XXIII. 19, I found him in the yard, looking pretty slippery after the strappers. **1891** *Field* 7 Mar. p. xxix/1 Will any Gentleman recommend a strong, active man as Groom, under coachman;.. must be thorough stableman, good strapper, and experienced with hunters. **1963** M. L. WEST *Gallows on Sand* i. 3 The strappers who stood round the tracks in the misty mornings trying to pick Saturday's winners. **1970** *Sunday Truth* (Brisbane) 19 July 30/6 He checked to see if he was registered as a strapper with any turf club in the country.
3. *slang*. An unremitting worker.
1851 MAYHEW *Lond. Labour* II. 305/1 They are all picked men in the shop—regular 'strappers', and no mistake.
4. A labourer employed temporarily at busy seasons; an extra hand. Also see quot. 1892. *dial.* or *local*.
1888 *Berksh. Gloss.*, *Strapper*, a journeyman labourer coming for work at harvest time or hay making. **1892** *Labour Commission Gloss.*, *Strappers*, There is a system in vogue at the docks by which the conveyance of goods from the dock-quays to the piling grounds is done by contractors... Sometimes they require more men, and these are called strappers.
5. A worker who furnishes or secures a thing with straps.
1881 *Instructions to Census Clerks* (1885) 79 Leather Goods.. Maker. Strapper. **1921** *Dict. Occup. Terms* (1927) §047 *Strapper*, puts up straps of wood or steel in support of roof in machine cut coal face. *Ibid.* §345 *Strapper*, attaches straps to bags, trunks, etc.

strapper^2 ('stræpə(r)). *dial.* [? f. STRAP *v.*^{2} + -ER^1. Cf. STROPPER.] (See quots.)
1777 *Terrier* in J. P. Briscoe *Old Nottinghamsh.* (1881) 37 Item: For every Milch Cow a composition of twopence, and for every Strapper (a cow that yields but little milk [Ed.]) one penny halfpenny. **1854** MISS BAKER *Northampt. Gloss.*, *Strappers*, cows that are nearly dry, that yield little milk.

†**'strappet.** *Obs. rare*$^{-1}$. [? f. STRAP *sb.* + -ET^1.] A small strip.
1665 in *Hist. Springfield, Mass.* (1899) II. 214 There is grannted to Lawrence Bliss Some Small nookes & Strappetts of Meddow & Swamp lying in the corners of his meddow.

strapping ('stræpɪŋ), *vbl. sb.*^{1} [See -ING^1.]
1. The action of STRAP *v.*^{1}; also an instance of this.
1806 SHERIDAN in *Sheridaniana* (1826) 200 Oh! I'll give them—a strapping! **1832** MARRYAT *N. Forster* xlv, He.. was better pleased when superintending the mousing of a stay or the strapping of a block. **1876** DUNGLISON *Med. Lex.*, *Strapping*, the dressing of ulcers by means of straps or strips of adhesive plaster, linen, &c. **1914** *Blackw. Mag.* Feb. 161/1 Slappings, strappings, and curses were the portion of Maria Assunta.
2. *concr.* **a.** *Surg.* Adhesive plaster for binding up wounds.
1818 S. F. GRAY *Suppl. Pharmacopœias* 243 Adhesive Plaisters, Strapping,.. much used by surgeons to close the lips of wounds, and retain dressings. **1898** EVA C. E. LÜCKES *Gen. Nursing* vii. 86 The strapping for fractured ribs should be cut three inches wide.
b. Iron straps or bands for stengthening woodwork, etc.
1862 F. A. GRIFFITHS *Artil. Man.* (ed. 9) 107 The iron strapping is retained in its place by means of the pin.
c. Leather straps for harness, machinery, etc.
1882 J. PHILIPSON *Harness* 17 Such parts of the hide.. as are most suitable.. for traces, backbands, and other heavy strapping. **1885** *Harper's Mag.* Jan. 280/1 [Leather.] Strapping, staying, and all kinds of binding are sold by the gross.
d. *Dressmaking.* Trimming composed of narrow bands.
1898 *Westm. Gaz.* 31 Mar. 3/1 Velvet strappings.. are quite *de rigueur* this spring. **1901** *Daily News* 16 Feb. 6/7 The black-cloth gown.. trimmed with black silk strappings. **1904** *Ibid.* 13 June 5 The waistband and strappings on the bodice were of yellow velvet.
3. *attrib.* and *Comb.*, as ***strapping plate***; **strapping-master, -shop** (see quots.); **strapping-tin**, a tin containing hot water, on the outside of which surgical plaster is warmed.
1851 MAYHEW *Lond. Labour* II. 233/1 The *strapping masters, or those who make the men (by extra supervision) 'strap' to their work, so as to do a greater quantity of labour in the usual time. **1860** *Eng. & For. Mining Gloss.* (ed. 2) 24 (Cornw. Terms) **Strapping plates*, the iron plates by which the connection rods are fastened to each other. **1851** MAYHEW *Lond. Labour* II. 304/1 The shops where this system is enforced are termed '*strapping-shops', as indicative of establishments where an undue quantity of work is expected from a journeyman in the course of the day. **1898** EVA C. E. LÜCKES *Gen. Nursing* vii. 86 The nurse.. handing the surgeon the strips.. duly warmed by placing the non-adhesive side of the plaster across the hot-water *strapping tins.

'strapping, *vbl. sb.*^{2} *dial.* [f. STRAP *v.*^{2} + -ING^1.] (See quots.)
1854 MISS BAKER *Northampt. Gloss.*, *Strappings*, *Strippings*, *Stroakings*, the last milk drawn or drained from a cow in milking. **1881** *Leicestersh. Gloss.*, *Strappings*, the last milk forced from the udder, particularly rich in quality.

strapping ('stræpɪŋ), *ppl. a.* Also 8 *Sc.* **strapan,** 8–9 *Sc.* **strappan.** [f. STRAP *v.*^{1} + -ING^2. Cf. STRAPPER^1.] Originally of a young woman: †Full of activity, vigorous, lusty (*obs.*). Now of a person of either sex: Strongly and stoutly built, robust, sturdy.
1657 G. THORNLEY *Daphnis & Chloe* (1893) 24 And, now and then, one of the bolder strapping girles would catch him in her arms, and kisse him. **1698** FRYER *Acc. E. India & P.* 234 They are Strapping Sunburnt Lasses. **1707** J. STEVENS tr. *Quevedo's Com. Wks.* (1709) 55 One of these three young Men was taller than I by the Head, so that you may guess what a strapping Fellow he was, for I am none of the least. **1725** RAMSAY *Gentle Sheph.* III. ii. (1769) 48 Patie's grown a strapan lad. **1749** H. WALPOLE *Let. to Mann* 12 Sept., The Richcourts are arrived, and have brought with them a strapping lad of your Count. **1785** BURNS *Cotter's Sat. Nt.* viii, A strappan youth; he takes the Mother's eye. **1793** —— *Meg o' the Mill* ii, The Miller was strappin, the Miller was ruddy. **1824** MISS MITFORD *Village* I. 42 The under damsel, was a stout strapping country wench. **1859** GEO. ELIOT *Adam Bede* ii, Well, it's a pretty spot,.. and one meets some fine strapping fellows about too. **1869** BLACKMORE *Lorna D.* xiii, This Nicholas Snowe was to come in the evening, with his three tall comely daughters, strapping girls. **1902** *Times* 24 July 5/1 They.. are the finest-looking men you want to see; all well-built, strapping fellows.
b. *transf.* Big, 'whopping'. *rare.*
1819 W. TENNANT *Papistry Storm'd* (1827) 134 Sanct Salvador's lang strappan steeple Had peltit five hours to the people. **1863** TREVELYAN *Compet. Wallah* (1866) 62 It is.. a new.. doctrine.. that protection is afforded to a traffic by loading it with a strapping duty. **1893** *Outing* Oct. 3/2 The team was a span of strapping mules.

†**'strapple,** *sb. Obs.* Forms: 1 **strapul,** 3 **strapel,** 4–5 **straple,** 5 **strapul, strapylle, strapil.** [OE. *strapul* masc., of obscure origin.] A covering for the lower part of the leg, forming the complementary part of the 'breech', consisting of a fillet or band laced or bound round the limb.
c **1000** ÆLFRIC *Gloss.* in Wr.-Wülcker 125 *Tubroces*, *uel brace*, strapulas. *a* **1225** *Ancr. R.* 420 Sum wummon inou-hreaðe wereð þe brech of heare ful wel i-knotted, and þe strapeles adun to hire uet, i-laced ful ueste. *c* **1290** *Beket* 1443 in *S. Eng. Leg.* 147 He hadde of harde here Schuyrte and brech streit i-novȝ:.. þe strapeles weren swiþe streite. **1387** TREVISA *Higden* (Rolls) V. 355 [He said] þat þey were liche to mares wiþ white legges up to þe þiȝes, for þat tyme þe Longobardes usede strapeles [*v.r.* straples; 1432–50 usede.. whyte listes; L. *usque ad suras candidis fasceolis uterentur*] wiþ brode laces doun to þe sparlyver. **14..** in *Rel. Ant.* (1843) I. 82 Ther stode wonus a coke on Seynt Pale stepull toppe, and drewe up the strapuls of his brech. **14..** *Lat.-Eng. Voc.* in Wr.-Wülcker 582 *Femorale*, a strapul. **14..** *Nominale* Ibid. 734 *Hec tribrica*, the strapuls of a pare brek. *c* **1440** *Promp. Parv.* 478/2 Straple, of a breche (MS. *K.* strappyl), *femorale*, *feminale*. *c* **1475** *Pict. Voc.* in Wr.-Wülcker 775 *Hoc tibiale*, a strapylle. **1483** *Cath. Angl.* 367/2 þe Strapils of breke, *tribraca*.

'strapple, *v. Obs.* exc. *dial.* [f. STRAPPLE *sb.*]
†**1.** *trans.* To furnish with 'strapples' or coverings for the legs. *Obs.*
1607 CHAPMAN *Bussy d' Ambois* III. ii. 14 Slaue flatterie (like a Rippiers legs rowl'd vp In bootes of haie-ropes) with Kings soothed guts Swadled and strappl'd, now liues only free.
2. To bind or make fast with bands. Also *fig.*
c **1611** CHAPMAN *Iliad* XVI. 438 His ruine startl'd th' other steeds: the geres crackt, and the raines Strappl'd his fellowes. *c* **1624** —— *Hymn to Hermes* 720 Hermes.. did forth-with cut and bow Strong Osiers in soft folds, and strappl'd strait One of his hugest Oxen. **1659** C. NOBLE *Mod. Answ. to Immod. Queries* 8 'Tis also a stumbling stone, and a gin, and a snare, to entangle and strapple some feeble judgements. **1888** *Sheffield Gloss.*, *Strapple*, to bind, make fast with a cord, strap, &c.

strappy ('stræpɪ), *a.* [f. STRAP *sb.* + -Y^1.] Of footwear or clothes: having straps.
1977 *Observer* (Colour Suppl.) 31 July 18/3 Bags, handluggage, strappy evening sandals. **1978** *Detroit Free Press* 16 Apr. (Detroit Suppl.) 20 (Advt.), Strippy, strappy stripes of canvas, wedged high, to put spring snap in your steps. **1980** *Daily Tel.* 21 July 13/1 There are strappy Fifties-style sundresses.

'strap-shaped, *a.* Long, narrow and flat in shape. **a.** *spec.* in *Bot.* = LIGULATE *a.* 1.
1796 WITHERING *Brit. Plants* (ed. 3) I. 229 Anthers strap-shaped. *Ibid.* II. 30 Lower lip [of blossom] oblong-strap-shaped. **1806** TURTON *Linné's Syst. Nat.* VII. Expl. Terms, *Strap-shaped*, nearly of the same width all along. **1890** *Hardwicke's Sci.-Gossip* XXVI. 206 Our sketch of the ox-eye daisy, showing the outer and usually strap-shaped florets converted into barren tubular florets.
b. *gen.*
1826 KIRBY & SP. *Entomol.* xxx. III. 231 This cocoon is.. composed of small rectangular strap-shaped pieces of the fine upper skin, or epidermis of the twig upon which it rests. **1893** TUCKEY *Amphioxus* 136 The fibrilla [*sic*] grow.. to such an extent that from being thread-like in form they become strap-shaped.

Strasbourg ('stræzbɜːg, ‖'ʃtraːsburg). Also 7 **Stras-, Strawsborough, Strasbrow,** 7– **Strasburgh,** 9– **Strasburg.** [G. *Strassburg*, Fr. *Strasbourg*.] The name of the principal town of Alsace, used *attrib.* in the names of various articles.
Strasbourg embroidery (see quot.). ***Strasbourg finch*** (see quot.). ***Strasbourg goose***, a goose fattened in such a way as to enlarge the liver for use in pâté de foie gras (see PÂTÉ^3 1 a). ***Strasbourg linen***, a kind of linen imported from Strasbourg. ***Strasbourg match***, an aromatic match for fumigating wines. ***Strasbourg onion*** (see quot.). ***Strasbourg pâté***, formerly = *Strasbourg pie*, but now usu. a goose pâté not enclosed in pastry. ***Strasbourg pie***, a pie made of fatted goose liver: see PÂTÉ^3 1. ***Strasbourg turpentine***, turpentine obtained from the Silver Fir *Abies Picea*.
1882 CAULFEILD & SAWARD *Dict. Needlework* 426 *Roman Work*. Also known as..*Strasbourg Embroidery,.. and differing but slightly from Richelieu Guipure. **1815** STEPHENS in *Shaw's Gen. Zool.* IX. 538 *Strasburgh Finch. *Fringilla argentoratensis*... Found in the neighbourhood of Strasburgh, where it goes by the name of the Gyntel. **1857** C. M. YONGE *Dynevor Terrace* I. xv. 240 A *Strasburg goose nailed down and crammed before a fire becomes a Strasburg pie. **1877** E. S. DALLAS *Kettner's Bk. of Table* 277 The liver of the Toulouse duck.. is by most good judges preferred even to that of the Strasbourg goose. **1969** J. FRASER *Clap Hands* v. 76 Byron's passion for Liquorice Allsorts was rapidly diminishing... Every week.. he was fed a large box of them, like a Strasbourg goose. **1642** *Rates of Merchandizes* 40 *Strasborough or Hamborow linnen. **1657** *Acts of Interregn.* (1911) II. 1215 Linnen Cloth called.. Strasborough or Hamborough Linnen. **1682** *Privil. Cit. Lond.*, *Scavage Tables* 52 Strasbrow Linnen. **1851** *Butler, Wine-dealer* etc. 27 The *Strasbourg, or aromatic matches, are to be preferred for wines. **1731** MILLER *Gard. Dict.* s.v. *Cepa Cepa oblonga*. The *Strasburgh Onion. *Ibid.* The best Onions for keeping are the Strasburgh kind, which is an oval-shap'd Bulb. **1860** DICKENS *Uncommercial Traveller* (1861) xiv. 204 An unopened *Strasbourg pâté fresh from Fortnum and Mason's. **1980** D. BLOODWORTH *Trapdoor* x. 56 They sat perched on high stools.. with a pot of taramasalata,.. an opened tin of Strasbourg pâté, a loaf of brown bread. **1838** THACKERAY *Yellowplush* (1865) 27 He sent me out.. for wot's called a *Strasbug-pie—in French, a '*patty defau graw*.' **1869** H. S. LEIGH *Carols of Cockayne* 169 Turtle and salmon and Strasbourg pie. **1687** J. SMITH *Art Painting* xix. (ed. 2) 91 Take good *Strasburg Turpentine, and warm it. **1861** BENTLEY *Man. Bot.* 659.
b. Used to designate the European Parliament, established in 1958, which has its seat in the

premises of the Council of Europe at Strasbourg.

1972 *Guardian* 14 July 10/2 There is now some recognition at Strasbourg that with the coming of new members it must change its ways. *Ibid.* 23 Oct. 12/2 No doubt progress towards an effective European Parliament must take time. There are nevertheless measures which can be taken at once to lift Strasbourg out of its futile and legalistic rut. **1976** *Times* 8 Mar. 13/1 (*heading*) Who governs, Strasbourg or Westminster?

strase, obs. pl. of STRAW.

strass[1] (stræs). [a. G. *strass*, F. *stras* (*Dict. Acad.* 1762); said to be from the name of the inventor, Josef Strasser.] A vitreous composition used as a basis in the manufacture of artificial stones: = PASTE *sb.*[1] 5.

1820 *Ann. Reg.* *453/1 What is technically called 'Strass', and which forms the basis and body of all artificial stones. **1844** *E. A. Parnell's Appl. Chem.* II. 44 The variety of glass known by the name of *Strass* [*foot-n.* So called from the name of its German inventor], which is used as a general colourless basis for factitious gems, on account of its remarkable lustre. **1876** 'OUIDA' *In Winter City* vi, She threw them all into the shade as a rose diamond throws stars of strass.

attrib. **1908** *Ladies' Field* 4 Apr. 197/1 Strass ornaments imitating peacock's feathers.

strass[2] (stræs). [a. F. *strasse*, in Cotgr. *estrace*, *estrasse*, 'raw silk thats so ruffled, or tangled, as it cannot be wound', ad. It. *straccio*.]

1. (See quot.) *rare.*

[**1858** SIMMONDS *Dict. Trade*, *Strasse* (French), the waste or refuse of silk in working it up into skeins.] **1875** KNIGHT *Dict. Mech.*, *Strass*..2 (Silk.) The refuse of silk in the process of working into skeins.

2. A kind of waxed straw with a silky appearance, used for dress trimmings, etc.

1926 *Westm. Gaz.* 10 Mar. 7/3 Raspberry red strasse (a sort of waxed straw) was made into rosettes for a trimming on one black frock. **1927** *Daily News* 8 Apr. 2/2 Beneath the large strass-trimmed finish to the belt in front fell a full panel of white georgette trimmed with strass.

strata, pl. of STRATUM.

stratagem (ˈstrætədʒəm). Forms: 5–7 **stratageme, 6 -geeme, 7 stratigem, 6– stratagem.** [a. F. *stratagème* (= Sp., Pg. *estratagema*, It. *stratagemma*), ad. (with alteration of vowel in the second syllable) L. *stratēgēma*, a. Gr. στρατήγημα a piece of generalship, stratagem, f. στρατηγεῖν to be a general, f. στρατηγός STRATEGUS.]

1. An operation or act of generalship; usually, an artifice or trick designed to outwit or surprise the enemy.

1489 CAXTON *Faytes of A.* II. i. 91 Whiche subtilites and wylis are called stratagemes of armes. **a 1548** HALL *Chron.*, *Hen. VI*, 173 b, Therle of Salisbury..knewe the slaightes, stratagemes and pollecies of warlike affaires. **1555** EDEN *Decades* (Arb.) 93 By this stratageme or policie, they came sodenly vppon Maiobanexius, and tooke hym prisoner. **1639** R. WARD *Animadv. Warre* I. 329 Breda..was once by the Hollander surprized, by a Stratagem of a Boate laden with Turffe, in whose Keele was imbarqued very closely divers valiant Gentlemen. **1653** H. COGAN tr. *Pinto's Trav.* v. 12 He was advertised by spies what stratagems the enemy would use against us. **1719** DE FOE *Crusoe* I. (Globe) 269, I presently thought of a Stratagem to fetch them back again. **1840** THIRLWALL *Greece* lvii. VII. 261 Antigonus..surprised the victors by a stratagem something like Lysander's at Ægos-potami. **1865** LIVINGSTONE *Zambesi* ix. 190 Attempting to carry out the skilful plans and stratagems of some eminent leader.

fig. **1665** BOYLE *Occas. Refl.* Introd. (1848) p. xxxi, In the spiritual Warfare, where our Adversary is the old Serpent, Stratagems are as Lawful as Expedient. **1859** GEO. ELIOT *Adam Bede* xii, It is the favourite stratagem of our passions to sham a retreat, and to turn sharp round upon us at the moment we have made up our minds that the day is our own.

b. In generalized sense: Military artifice.

1599 SHAKS. *Hen. V*, IV. viii. 113 Without stratagem, But in plaine shock, and euen play of Battaile. **1717** LADY M. W. MONTAGU *Let. to C'tess Mar* 30 Jan., The Turks once more attempted to gain it [Raab] by stratagem. **1853** SIR H. DOUGLAS *Milit. Bridges* 200 In the following campaign, by having recourse to stratagem, he succeeded better. **1874** BANCROFT *Footpr. Time* i. 77 He then turned his arms against Babylon which he took by stratagem after a long siege.

2. Any artifice or trick; a device or scheme for obtaining an advantage.

1588 *Marprel. Epist.* (Arb.) 38, I doubt not in my visitation, but to get a hundreth of these stratagemes. **1592** KYD *Sp. Trag.* II. i. 35, I haue already found a stratageme, To sound the bottome of this doubtfull theame. **1662** J. DAVIES tr. *Olearius' Voy. Ambass.* 12 It was a Stratageme of the Inhabitants, who had incens'd the Bees, purposely to prevent our lodging in the Village. **1728** YOUNG *Love Fame* VI. 187 For her own breakfast she'll project a scheme, Nor take her tea without a stratagem. **1750** JOHNSON *Rambler* No. 35 ¶10, I shall not trouble you with a history of the stratagems practised on my judgement. **1830** HERSCHEL *Stud. Nat. Phil.* 2 His existence would be one continued subterfuge or stratagem. **1879** FARRAR *St. Paul* (1883) 680 The stratagem was for the time..successful.

b. In generalized sense: Skill in devising expedients; artifice, cunning.

1588 SHAKS. *Tit. A.* II. i. 104 'Tis pollicie and stratageme must doe That you affect. **1737** BRACKEN *Farriery Impr.* (1757) II. 81 A Horse is a noble Creature, naturally strong and courageous, and, for this Reason, he is not endowed with so much Stratagem as others of less account. **1837** THIRLWALL *Greece* xxxv. IV. 361 Notorious for his mastery in the arts of stratagem and intrigue. **1872** GEO. ELIOT *Middlem.* vi, Obliged to get my coals by stratagem.

†**3.** Used loosely for: A deed of blood or violence. *Obs.*

1588 GREENE *Pandosto* (1607) G 4 To close up the Comedie with a Tragicall stratageme, he slew himselfe. **1589** —— *Tullies Love* (1616) K 3, The Senators seeing what bloudy stratagems would insue of this strife, if it were not pacified, sent for the Consuls. **1592** in J. Morris *Troubles Cath. Forefathers* (1877) 50 Of these late executions, you shall have shortly a more particular and true advertisement, by a priest who was present at the stratagem. **1593** SHAKS. *3 Hen. VI*, II. v. 89 What Stra[ta]gems? how fell? how Butcherly? Erreoneous, mutinous, and vnnaturall, This deadly quarrell daily doth beget? **1601** YARINGTON *Two Trag.* II. ii. in Bullen *O. Pl.* IV, Blood-sucking Avarice, and all the Sinnes, That hale men on to bloodie stratagems. **1606** G. W[OODCOCKE] *Hist. Justine* XXXVII. ii. 116 Fearing his enemies would compasse the treason by stratigem, which they could not by poyson [L. *ne inimici, quod veneno non potuerant, ferro peragerent*].

†**stratage'matic**, *a.* *Obs.* Also 7 **strategematick.** [a. obs. F. *strategematique* (16th c. in Godefroy), *stratag-* (Cotgr.), or ad. L. *stratēgēmatic-us*, f. *stratēgēmat-*, *stratēgēma* STRATAGEM.] Relating to, versed in, stratagem or strategy.

1589 PUTTENHAM *Eng. Poesie* I. viii. (Arb.) 35 Of this sorte of phantasie are all good Poets, notable Captaines stratagematique, all cunning artificers and enginers. **1629** MAXWELL tr. *Herodian* VI. 3 *marg.*, In which words the excellent Author hath couched both the parts of Warre: viz. Tactick and Strategematick. **1646** J. HALL *Horæ Vac.* 163 Greece and Rome did most excell in the art of War, whether the Tactick or the Stratagematick part. **1650** —— *Paradoxes* 93 Many great stratagematick wits, have no better ways either of startleing their enemies, or retaining their friends, then by increasing the shew of their dangers.

†**stratage'matical**, *a.* *Obs.* = prec.

1611 CORYAT *Crudities* 375 In these wals are many strong and auncient Towers..being built with a pretty kinde of stratagematicall invention. **1612** [see STATIZE *v.*].

Hence †**stratage'matically** *adv.* *Obs.*

1592 G. HARVEY *Four Lett.* F 2 The fine Discouerer, and curious Intelligencer, goe inuisible, & stratagematically discry many hidden priuities of publique, and priuate misgouernment.

†**strata'gematist.** *Obs.* [f. (with alteration of the second vowel) Gr. στρατηγηματ-, στρατήγημα STRATAGEM + -IST.] One versed in stratagem.

1609 TOURNEUR *Funeral Poem on Sir F. Vere* 556 Where he shew'd all wherein wit can assist The workings of a stratagematist. **1684** tr. *Agrippa's Van. Arts* viii. 45 Sophisters..like Stratagematists fly for Refuge to the strength of Memory.

stratagemical (strætəˈdʒɛmɪkəl), *a.* ? *Obs.* [irreg. f. STRATAGEM + -IC + -AL[1].] Belonging to, concerned with, of the nature of, stratagem.

1585 DANIEL *P. Jovius' Disc. Imprese* etc. H iij, A Calthrope, a Stratagemical instrument vsed in warre. **1599** R. LINCHE *Anc. Fiction* V iiij, The house of Mars..is built in an obscure corner of Thracia, where the people wholly giue and addict themselues to warres and stratagemicall policies. **1600** W. WATSON *Decacordon* (1602) 331 Their [the Jesuits'] paradoxall, pragmaticall, and stratagemicall doctrine. **1688** ? SWIFT *Tripos* in J. Barrett *Ess. Life Swift* (1808) 76 His wife, who, to gain entirely his affections, sent him this stratagemical epistle. **1838** B. CORNEY *Controv.* 12 In every species of controversy, there is scope for the exercise of stratagemical ingenuity.

Hence **strata'gemically** *adv.*

1600 W. WATSON *Decacordon* (1602) 104 Which to performe stratagemically, they commended his said Vncle exceedingly. **1838** B. CORNEY *Controv.* 12 A fact or argument of an inconveniently formidable nature, may be met stratagemically.

†**stratagemitor.** *Obs. rare.* [irreg. f. STRATAGEM + L. agent-suffix -(I)TOR.] ? A deviser of stratagems.

1600 W. WATSON *Decacordon* (1602) 102 As politicall a stratagemitor as I thinke hath bene in any age. *Ibid.* 160 That Atheall stratagemitor. **1612** T. JAMES *Jesuites Downefall* 49 A dangerous Polypragmon,..Atheall Stratagemitor.

†**strata'gemous**, *a.* *Obs. rare*⁻¹. [f. STRATAGEM + -OUS.] Of, or consisting of, stratagems.

1606 WARNER *Alb. Eng.* XV. xcv. 379 [Guy Faux] Hels stratagemous Quintessence, Romes selfe-created Foe.

stratal (ˈstreɪtəl, ˈstrɑː-), *a.* [f. STRAT-UM + -AL[1].] Of or belonging to a stratum (or strata).

1875 A. SMITH *New Hist. Aberdeensh.* II. 1232 The stratal direction of the vein. **1966** S. M. LAMB *Outl. Stratif. Gram.* 1 These several systems may be called stratal systems, and each may be said to be associated with a stratum of linguistic structure. **1967** D. G. HAYS *Introd. Computational Linguistics* viii. 162 A stratal conversion is a mapping or transduction of the representation of an utterance on one stratum into the representation of the same utterance on an adjacent stratum.

stratarchy (ˈstrætɑːkɪ). *rare*⁻¹. [ad. Gr. στραταρχία, the office of a general, f. στρατάρχης, also στράταρχος, a general, f. στρατ-ός army + ἄρχ-ειν to rule.] The system of rule in an army.

1877 GLADSTONE in *19th Cent.* Mar. 18 A hierarchy..is broadly distinguished from a *stratarchy*, from the corps of officers of an army, where an absolute obedience is due from the private soldier, and from every successive grade, to a superior.

†**strata'rithmetry.** *Obs. rare*⁻¹. [irreg. f. Gr. στρατ-ός army + ἀριθμ-ός number + -μετρία -METRY.] The art of drawing up an army or body of men in a given geometrical figure, and of estimating the number of men contained in such a figure.

1570 J. DEE *Math. Pref.* a iij, Moreouer, of the former knowledge Geometricall, are growen the Skills of Geographie, Chorographie, Hydrographie, and Stratarithmetrie. *Ibid.* a iiij b. [**1802** C. JAMES *Milit. Dict.* has the correct form *Stratarithmometry*.]

stratche, strate, obs. ff. STRETCH *v.*, STREET.

†**stratege.** *Obs. rare*⁻¹. [ad. Gr. στρατηγ-ός. Cf. F. *stratège* (also *stratègue*).] = STRATEGUS.

1808 MITFORD *Hist. Greece* v. §4. I. 287 The Athenian Stratege..was the general officer.

strategetic (strætɪˈdʒɛtɪk), *a.* [ad. Gr. στρατηγητικ-ός, f. στρατηγεῖν: see STRATAGEM.] = STRATEGIC.

1848 W. H. KELLY tr. *L. Blanc's Hist. Ten Y.* II. 393 Fieschi had invented the fatal machine with views entirely strategetic. **1862** TROLLOPE *N. Amer.* II. 151 He..entertained an idea that Cairo was the nucleus or pivot of all really strategetic movements in this terrible national struggle. **1870** ANDERSON *Missions Amer. Board* IV. xxxii. 210 Acquainted with the field, with its wants, and its strategetic points.

strategetical (strætɪˈdʒɛtɪkəl), *a.* [f. prec. + -AL[1].] = prec.

1828 NAPIER *Penins. War* I. iv. I. 54 Hence Zaragoza..was a strategetical point of importance [*ed.* 1851 I. 33 was of strategic importance]. **1849–50** ALISON *Hist. Europe* lxxxiv. §67. XII. 445 A city of the highest importance in a strategetical point of view, as being the place where several roads..intersect each other.

strategian (strəˈtiːdʒɪən). *rare.* [Formed as STRATEGY + -AN.]

†**1.** Used by Holland to render Pliny's *strategia* (στρατηγία), a government or province. Cf. STRATEGY 1. *Obs.*

1601 HOLLAND *Pliny* VI. ix. I. 119 This is well knowne, that divided it [Armenia] is into certaine regiments, which they call Strategians.

2. A strategist.

1901 HORNUNG *Black Mask* vi. 107 Raffles..was both strategian and tactician, and we all now know the difference between the two. **1912** A. F. WHYTE in *Everyman* 15 Nov. 135 The strategians of the corrupt party.

strategic (strəˈtiːdʒɪk, -ˈtɛdʒɪk), *a.* and *sb.* [a. F. *stratégique* or ad. Gr. στρατηγικ-ός of or pertaining to a general, f. στρατηγ-ός STRATEGUS.]

A. *adj.* **1.** Of or belonging to strategy; useful or important in regard to strategy.

strategic point [= F. *point stratégique*], a position determined as important in a plan of campaign.

1825 J. A. GILBERT *Expos. Princ. Milit. Comb.* 3 Strategic movements and manœuvres. *Ibid.* 67 Choosing a field of battle which has all the advantage of a good strategic position. **1855** TWEMLOW *Consid. Tactics & Strategy* (ed. 2) 172 The importance of strategic reserves. **1861** JEFF. DAVIS *Message to Confederate Congr.* 18 Nov., Our armies were marched into that State to repel the enemy and prevent their occupation of certain strategic points which would have given them great advantages in the contest. **1894** *Engineer* 9 Mar. 199/1 The strategic railway connecting Tientsin with Shan-hai-Kwan.

transf. **1886** H. W. LUCY *Diary Gladstone Parlt.* 133 The Sergeant-at-Arms..more than once has had occasion to sally forth from his chair, and by strategic movements interrupt that gentleman's unauthorised advance towards the table.

2. Of, pertaining to, or designating nuclear weapons intended to destroy an enemy's capacity to make war. Cf. TACTICAL *a.* 1 c.

1957 *Listener* 26 Dec. 1056/1 Nobody has managed..to draw an effective distinction between 'strategic' and 'tactical' atomic weapons. **1957** *Times* 18 Nov. p. x/2 Between 1946..and 1950, strategic stockpiling had hardly begun. **1958** *Spectator* 21 Feb. 219/1 If Russia were to launch a major attack on the West, even with conventional forces only, the West would have to hit back with strategic nuclear weapons. **1961** *Listener* 14 Dec. 1012/1 The idea was not to create a complete system of strategic deterrence under Nato, but one large enough to meet certain specific problems. **1965** H. KAHN *On Escalation* v. 92 A high degree of escalation could easily be involved..if it were a strategic-weapons submarine. **1969** *Times* 27 Oct. 9/1 The discussions which will open between the United States and Russia in Helsinki next month are...the long awaited Salt discussions—the strategic arms limitation talks. **1978** *Orbis* XXII. 319 A desire to strengthen the linkage between theater- and strategic-nuclear forces. **1979** *Financial Rev.* 28 Sept. 10/5 It is not that the doctrine of strategic deterrence is being discarded, but that it is being constantly adapted to new technologies as each side seeks to prevent the other from gaining a decisive advantage.

3. Of, pertaining to, or designating materials essential to a country for fighting a war.

1958 *Economist* 26 July 283 A relaxation of the embargo on strategic exports to communist countries has been in the wind for some time. **1959** *Listener* 10 Dec. 1023/1 On the British side there is the question of the so-called strategic controls. This is the agreement between Great Britain and certain other Western countries not to export to the U.S.S.R. certain goods which might be used for military purposes. **1969** PLANO & OLTON *Internat. Relations Dict.* iii. 76 Some of the most critical strategic materials include foodstuffs, aluminum, cadmium, cooper, magnesium, [etc.]. **1981** *Financial Rev.* (Sydney) 24 Apr. 54/2 Germanium is one of about two dozen metals called 'strategic' because they are vital to defence and industry, but available in large supplies only from foreign sources.

4. Special collocations: ***strategic bombing***, the bombing of an enemy's territory with the aim of disrupting its economy and destroying morale; hence ***strategic bomber***, an aircraft used for this purpose; cf. TACTICAL *a.* 1 b; ***strategic hamlet***, a settlement or reservation for accommodating potential terrorists or their supporters under surveillance (esp. with reference to the Vietnam war); ***strategic studies***, the analysis of conflict in international relations in all its aspects.

1961 *Listener* 14 Dec. 1012/1 If it becomes unwise..to consider basing MRBMs or strategic bombers in Europe. **1977** *Sci. Amer.* Aug. 26/3 The Backfire's capability as a strategic bomber—defined as a bomber that can reach the other country's territory—is certainly less significant than that of U.S. bombers based in Europe or on aircraft carriers. **1941** *Nineteenth Cent.* Sept. 163 Bombing of cities..is a true example of strategic bombing. **1966** *Listener* 27 Oct. 616/2 The very foundation stone of the independent service—strategic bombing—becomes a stumbling block. **1963** *Times* 21 Jan. 9/7 A vast campaign to build 'strategic hamlets' has been launched in every province... President Ngo Dinh Diem has described 1962 as the 'year of the strategic hamlets'. **1973** *Black Panther* 30 June 11/3 Smith's program involves the concepts of the 'strategic hamlet' and 'pacification'; to round up peasants from areas where guerilla forces show signs of gathering support (they will then be relocated to centers where they are surrounded by police barricades). **1975** *New Yorker* 5 May 131/1 What were *we* doing to the South Vietnamese, with our 'strategic hamlets' and 'free-fire zones'? **1959** *Times* Feb. 12/1 The chairman and council of the Institute for Strategic Studies held a reception yesterday evening. **1981** *Listener* 5 Nov. 530/1, I..started a postgraduate seminar in strategic studies.

B. *sb.* The strategic art, strategy. **a.** *sing.* [= Gr. ἡ στρατηγική (sc. τέχνη).] *rare.*

1860 GEN. P. THOMPSON *Audi Alt.* III. cxxii. 68 Frederic was the great improver in this which may be called the 'Strategic of Battle'.

b. *pl.* [= Gr. τὰ στρατηγικά.]

1852 *Fraser's Mag.* XLVI. 88 All the details of submarine tactics and strategics. **1853** STOCQUELER *Mil. Encycl.* s.v. *Tactics*, Tactics, as distinct from strategics [*printed* strategies], imply the disposition and formation of troops in presence of an enemy. **1863** DICEY *Federal St.* II. 2 At Washington, during the war, every militia officer.. considered himself justified in talking about Jomini and Vauban and the science of strategics.

strategical (strəˈtiːdʒɪkəl, -ˈtɛdʒɪkəl), *a.* [f. prec. + -AL[1].] = prec. adj.

1838 R. N. MAGRATH *Hist. Sk. Art of War* 152 His well combined strategical operations, his system of presenting concentrated masses to isolated corps [etc.]. **1852** E. YATES *Elem. Strategy* 10 Strategical Reserves are detachments from the main body left to guard the communications. **1856** MACDOUGALL *Theory of War* i. 63 Every point on the theatre of war..which conduces in any manner to strengthen your line of operations (or of communication), is a strategical point. **1883** *Manch. Exam.* 6 Nov. 4/7 The rebels..have taken up a strategical position on a height commanding a ravine below.

strategically (strəˈtiːdʒɪkəlɪ, -ˈtɛdʒɪkəlɪ), *adv.* [f. prec.: see -ICALLY.] In a strategic manner; as regards strategy, according to the principles of strategy.

1810 C. JAMES *Milit. Dict.* (ed. 3), *Strategically*, according to the principles of strategy; done out of sight of an enemy. **1855** TWEMLOW *Consid. Tactics & Strategy* (ed. 2) 205 Frederic the Great was strategically and tactically surprised at Hochkirk by Laudon and Daun. **1861** G. M. MUSGRAVE *By-Roads in Picardy* 298 The English position..was strategically a warranty of their preservation; for they could not be attacked in flank or in rear. **1912** W. B. WOOD in *Eng. Hist. Rev.* Oct. 797 Tactically a drawn battle, Resonville was strategically a Prussian victory.

strategician (strætɪˈdʒɪʃ(ɪ)ən). *rare*⁻¹. [f. STRATEGIC + -IAN.] A strategist.

1862 WRAXALL tr. *Hugo's Les Misérables* I. cvi. 395 Great strategicians [F. *stratégistes*] have their eclipses.

strategist (ˈstrætɪdʒɪst). [a. F. *stratégiste*, f. *stratégie* STRATEGY.] One versed in strategy.

1838 J. MITCHELL *Thoughts on Tactics* 30 Strategy.. presupposes in the strategist a perfect knowledge of tactics. **1877** GREEN *Hist. Engl. People* I. 426 Edward..had shewn himself as consummate a strategist in the campaign as a tactician in the field. **1912** G. O. TREVELYAN *Geo. III & Fox* I. i. 18 The elder Pitt..was a maritime strategist of the highest order.

transf. **1872** LOWELL *Milton* Writ. 1890 IV. 99 He was a strategist rather than a drill-sergeant in verse. **1911** SIR H. CRAIK *Life Ld. Clarendon* I. iii. 74 Pym's wonderful astuteness as a parliamentary strategist.

strategize (ˈstrætɪdʒaɪz), *v. U.S.* [f. STRATEGY + -IZE.] *intr.* To formulate a strategy or strategies; to plan a course of action. Hence **ˈstrategizing** *vbl. sb.*

1943 *Sun* (Baltimore) 8 Nov. 6/3 The delay in bringing the bill to the House floor for action developed because both sides were 'strategizing'. **1977** *Dædalus* Fall 134 Four competing hypotheses can be posed for the explanation of kinship rules: detailed genetic control, rational strategizing, complete cultural determinism, and coupled cultural and genetic control. **1978** *New Scientist* 21 Sept. 873 Men in dark suits and homburg hats will be commissioning think tanks to strategize. **1983** *Washington Post* 3 June A 3 Back in those days [*sc.* the 1960s]..you didn't have to strategize and study and do the kind of homework on your cases that you have to do now.

‖**strategus** (strəˈtiːgəs). *Gr. Hist.* Pl. -gi (-dʒaɪ). Also with Gr. ending **strategos** (strəˈtiːgɒs), pl. -oi. [L. *stratēgus*, a. Gr. στρατηγός (Doric στρατᾱγός), f. στρατ-ός army + -ᾱγ-, ἄγειν to lead. Cf. STRATEGE.] A commander-in-chief or chief magistrate at Athens and in the Achæan league (also in Harrington's imaginary commonwealth).

1656 HARRINGTON *Oceana* (1700) 123 The Strategus is first President of the Senat, and General of the Army. **1728** CHAMBERS *Cycl.* **1808** MITFORD *Hist. Greece* xli. §1. IV. 528 It was found convenient that the strategus, the first general, should have a discretionary power to call extraordinary assemblies of the people. **1847** GROTE *Greece* II. xxxi. IV. 192 The stratêgi or generals, who were always elected by show of hands of the assembled citizens. **1909** GWATKIN *Early Ch. Hist.* I. vi. 92 Even Constantine was a strategos of Athens in the direct succession of Themistocles and Phocion.

strategy (ˈstrætɪdʒɪ). Also 9 **strategie**. [a. F. *stratégie* (Du Pinet's tr. Pliny, 1562), ad. Gr. στρατηγία office or command of a general, generalship, f. στρατηγ-ός STRATEGUS.]

†**1.** A government or province under a strategus: cf. STRATEGIAN 1. *Obs. rare*⁻¹.

1688 MORDEN *Geog. Rect., Armenia* 343 Pliny accounted 120 Strategies Governments or particular Jurisdictions of every Province.

2. a. The art of a commander-in-chief; the art of projecting and directing the larger military movements and operations of a campaign.

Usually distinguished from *tactics*, which is the art of handling forces in battle or in the immediate presence of the enemy.

1810 C. JAMES *Milit. Dict.* (ed. 3) s.v., Strategy differs materially from *tactic*; the latter belonging only to the mechanical movement of bodies, set in motion by the former. **1825** J. A. GILBERT *Expos. Princ. Milit. Comb.* 11 The second combination is the art of bringing the mass of one's forces as rapidly as possible on the decisive point of the primitive line of operation, or of the accidental line. It is what is vulgarly called strategy, but strategy relates only to the mode of executing this second combination. **1827** SCOTT *Napoleon, View Fr. Rev.* xi. II. 73 A brave and excellent soldier, but with no idea of strategie [*sic*] or tactics, save those current during the Seven Years War. **1889** A. T. MAHAN *Sea Power* Introd. 8 Before hostile armies or fleets are brought into contact (a word which perhaps better than any other indicates the dividing line between tactics and strategy).

b. An instance or species of this.

1833 MACAULAY *Ess., War of Succession* ¶7 Where something different from ordinary strategy was required in the general. **1868** FARRAR *Seekers* Concl. (1875) 320 By copying the strategy of the battle of Beth Horon. **1913** R. LUCAS *Ld. North* I. vii. 277 His strategy was to hold the Hudson River and isolate the New England States.

c. *transf.*

1837 W. IRVING *Capt. Bonneville* I. 103 The captain had here the first taste of the boasted strategy of the fur trade. **1849** C. KNIGHT *Ht. Martineau's Hist. Peace* I. ii. 19 The battle against this tax was one of the most remarkable examples of Parliamentary strategy that was ever displayed. **1878** A. P. STANLEY *Addr. & Serm. in Amer.* Pref. to Serm. (1883) 83 It has been too often the conventional strategy of theological argument, in dealing with books or persons with whom we differ, to give no quarter.

d. In (theoretical) circumstances of competition or conflict, as in the theory of games, decision theory, business administration, etc., a plan for successful action based on the rationality and interdependence of the moves of the opposing participants; also *transf.* (see quot. 1979).

1944 VON NEUMANN & MORGENSTERN *Theory of Games* i. 44 The same arguments which forced us to consider sets of imputations instead of single imputations necessitate the abandonment of that narrow concept of 'standard of behavior'. Actually we shall call these sets of rules the 'strategies' of the game. **1954** *Psychol. Bull.* LI. 406/2 A *strategy* is a set of personal rules for playing the game. For each possible first move.., your opponent will have a possible set of responses. **1965** H. I. ANSOFF *Corporate Strategy* vi. 118 A *grand* or *mixed* strategy is a statistical decision rule for deciding which particular pure strategy the firm should select in a particular situation. **1969** R. FARQUHARSON *Theory of Voting* iv. 20 Any procedure can be represented as a game by assuming that each voter makes a plan in advance regarding the course of action he will take in every division which can arise. Any such plan may be called a 'strategy'—the voter's set of strategies constitutes the complete range of such possible plans. **1979** *Science* 25 May 795/2 Gideon Louw..laments the widespread biological use of the word 'strategy' because of the implication of rational choice..but..there is no simpler way to label possible evolutionary designs.

3. *Gr. Hist.* The office of a STRATEGUS. *rare*⁻¹.

1869 A. W. WARD tr. *Curtius' Hist. Greece* III. iii. II. 456 Among the offices requiring a certain capacity..there was none more important than the generalship or *Strategy* [G. *Strategie*]. *Ibid.* 458 Pericles, besides the authority of a Strategy prolonged to him in an extraordinary measure, also filled the office of superintendent of the finances.

Hence **ˈstrategy** *v. trans.*, to force (a person) *into* (a position) by strategy. **ˈstrategying** *vbl. sb.*, exercise of strategy. (Both *nonce-wds.*)

1858 CARLYLE *Fredk. Gt.* IX. x. (1872) III. 157 We hear there is marching, strategying in the Parma Country. **1894** CLARK RUSSELL *Good Ship Mohock* I. i. 21 Not the gods themselves could have strategied me into wedlock.

Stratfordian (strætˈfɔːdɪən), *sb.* (*a.*). [f. the name of the town *Stratford*-upon-Avon, War., birthplace of William Shakespeare + -IAN.]

1. One who lives in or was born in Stratford-upon-Avon.

1821 J. SAUNDERS *Let.* 8 June in A. Mathews *Mem. Charles Mathews* (1839) III. ix. 204 Intreating a line when you have anything desirable to impart to the Stratfordians. **1909** 'MARK TWAIN' *Is Shakespeare Dead?* 58 Stratfordians who were not Stratfordians of Shakespeare's day, but later comers. **1963** *Times* 12 Feb. 11/4 It is likely that the Stratfordians thus deprived of some edification from the pulpit were less put out than those who now find the harmonies of a concert-platform sadly broken.

2. A supporter of the view that Shakespeare was the author of the plays generally attributed to him. Also as *adj.* Cf. SHAKESPEARIAN *a.* (and *sb.*) b.

1908 G. GREENWOOD *Shakesp. Probl. Restated* 172 Really, really, there must be some limits even to Stratfordian demands on our credulity! *Ibid.* 226 The futilities which are gravely trotted out by enthusiastic Stratfordians as valuable evidence to illustrate the life of Shakespere. **1912** [see *overprove* s.v. OVER- 27 a]. **1930** P. ALLEN *Case for E. de Vere as Shakespeare* 6, I remained an orthodox Stratfordian until 1923. *Ibid.* 26 All these discoveries and inferences..were fast and firmly establishing the case for Oxford, at the same time that they were destroying utterly the Stratfordian arguments. **1962** *Economist* 28 July 364/2 His work..made him a 'convinced Stratfordian'.

strath (stræθ). *Sc.* Also 7 **strathe, straith.** [a. Gael. *srath* = Ir. *srath, sratha*, W. *ystrad*.] A wide valley; a tract of level or low-lying land traversed by a river and bounded by hills or high ground.

1540 *Reg. Mag. Sig. Scot.* (1883) 464 Terras de Auchnahay Auchalane, Dugerre, Kinloch, Auchranich, cum lie Strath, cum le Clasche et le Claschebrek. **1639** SIR R. GORDON *Geneal. Hist. Earld. Sutherld.* (1813) 4 The valies which doe ly upon the banks of these rivers and inlets of water, as they doe ascend from the sea to the mountanes, ar called Strathes. **1721** RAMSAY *Poet's Wish* i, Those fair straths that water'd are With Tay and Tweed's smooth streams. **1750** COLLINS *Ode Superstit. Highlands* iv, When, o'er the wat'ry strath, or quaggy moss, They see the gliding ghosts unbodied troop. **1753** *Stewart's Trial* 203 The deponent answered, that he had seen no person from the strath (or vale) of Appin. **1814** SCOTT *Wav.* xiii, A ridge of distant and blue hills, which formed the southern boundary of the strath, or valley. **1873** GEIKIE *Gt. Ice Age* xii. 154 The river Clyde..flows towards the north-west in a valley that gradually expands to a broad open strath.

†**b.** *loosely.* A stretch of flat land by the waterside. *Obs.*

1699 G. TURNBULL *Diary* in *Scot. Hist. Soc. Misc.* (1893) I. 383 The place is pretty pleasant, close by Forth watarside, att the foot of Craigmor, betwixt which and the watar there is a strath very proper for walking. *c* **1730** BURT *Lett. N. Scot.* (1818) I. 290 A strath is a flat space of arable land lying along the side or sides of some capital river between the water and the feet of the hills.

strath, obs. form of STRAIGHT.

strathspey (stræθˈspeɪ). ? Also 7 **stravetspy.** [f. the Sc. place-name *Strathspey* (= the strath of the river Spey).

If the form *stravetspy* (quot. *a* 1653) be genuine and belong to this word, the mod. form would seem to be due to popular etymology.]

a. A lively dance or reel for two dancers. **b.** The music or tune (usually in common time) used to accompany this dance. Also †***strathspey minuet.***

a **1653** Z. BOYD *John Baptist* in G. Neil *Z. Boyd's Flowers of Zion* (1832) p. xxx, To please the King, the Morrice dance I will; Stravetspy, and after, last of all, The Drunken Dance I'le dance within that hall. **1756** MRS. CALDERWOOD in *Coltness Collect.* (Maitl. Club) 195 Lady Hellen and Lord Garless danced a strathspey minuet. **1791** BURNS *Tam o' Shanter* 117 Nae cotillion brent-new frae France, But hornpipes, jigs, strathspeys, and reels, Put life and mettle in their heels. **1810** SCOTT *Lady of L.* II. xi, Nor would my footsteps spring more gay In courtly dance than blithe strathspey. **1818** —— *Rob Roy* xxii, He..sate himself down on the oak table, and whistled a strathspey. **1882** J. F. S. GORDON *Shaw's Hist. Moray* I. 239 He was one of the best violinists in the north and excelled in Strathspeys.

straticulate (strəˈtɪkjʊlət), *a. Geol.* and *Min.* [f. mod.L. **strāticul-um* (dim. of L. *strātum* STRATUM) + -ATE[2]] Arranged in thin layers. So **straticuˈlation**, arrangement in thin layers.

1880 DANA *Man. Geol.* (ed. 3) 82 Beds consisting of thin and even subordinate layers, separable or not so, are said to be straticulate. *Ibid.* 685 Agate, and much stalagmite, are straticulate, but not properly stratified. **1895** *Ibid.* (ed. 4) 244 Planes of bedding or straticulation in the ice.

stratification (strætɪfɪˈkeɪʃən). [ad. med.L. *strātificātiōnem*, n. of action f. *strātificāre*: see STRATIFY *v.* and -FICATION. Cf. F. *stratification* (1656 in Hatz.-Darm.).]

1. †**a.** The action of depositing something in layers; *spec.* (see quots.). *Obs.*

1617 WOODALL *Surg. Mate* (1639) 274 *Stratification*, or *stratum superstratum* well knowne to Chymists, and used in cementation, is strewing of corroding powder, or the like, upon plates of metall by course. *Ibid.* 266 Stratifications [*sic*]. **1669** tr. *Benguinus' Tyroc. Chym.* 25 Stratification is a corrosion by corrosive powders. It is thus made, [etc.]. **1669** ROWLAND *Schroder's Chym. Disp.* I. xiv. 21 Stratification in Beguin comprehends the whole Art of Calcination, by which the Plates are made brittle, this they say is Cæmenting. **1704** J. HARRIS *Lex. Techn.* I, *Stratification*, or *stratum super stratum*, as the Chymists call it, is putting different Matters *Bed upon Bed*, or one layer upon another, in a Crucible in order to Calcine a Metal or Mineral. **1787** R. WATSON *Chem. Ess.* V. 251 Copper combined with sulphur by stratification and cementation... *Æs ustum.* **1815** J. SMITH *Panorama Sci. & Art* II. 301 *Stratification*, an operation in which bodies are placed alternately in layers, in order that they may act upon each other when heat is applied to them. **1882** *Encycl. Brit.* XIV. 385/1 It was formerly the practice in England..to tan by the process of stratification, for which purpose a bed of bark is made..; upon this is laid the hide, then bark, then a hide, and so on.

b. The placing of seeds close together in layers between layers of moist sand, peat, or the like in order to preserve them or promote germination; also extended to the placing of seeds in such a medium other than in layers.

1914 MOON & BROWN *Elem. of Forestry* vi. 103 Commercial houses rarely practice stratification, because they have storehouses where moisture conditions are kept uniform. **1928** *Jrnl. Forestry* XXVI. 775/2 Stratification of these seeds for one to four months previous to planting has been found to hasten greatly their germination. **1976** H. L. EDLIN *Nat. Hist. Trees* xiv. 181 The seeds of ash trees..and many other common genera..require stratification for sixteen months.

2. The formation, by natural process, of strata or layers one above the other; the fact or state of existing in the form of strata, stratified condition; also, the manner in which something is stratified.

a. *Geol.* The formation of strata in portions of the crust of the earth by successive deposits of sedimentary matter; the manner in which a portion of the crust of the earth is stratified.

1795 J. HUTTON *Theory Earth* II. ix. II. 307 This summit is of solid granite, a mass in which there is no stratification. **1796** KIRWAN *Elem. Min.* (ed. 2) I. 420 A total absence of stratification near the crater. **1802** PLAYFAIR *Illustr. Huttonian Theory* 500 Thus by the waste and subsequent stratification of the land the direction of gravity is continually altered. **1830** LYELL *Princ. Geol.* I. 203 The planes of stratification are perfectly parallel. **1838** POE *A. Gordon Pym* xviii. Wks. 1865 IV. 146 The very rocks were novel in their mass, their color, and their stratification. **1851** RICHARDSON *Geol.* (1855) 135 There are three distinct forms of structure frequently present in rocks of this nature: stratification, joints, and slaty cleavage. **1878** A. C. RAMSAY *Phys. Geog.* iv. 38, I have shown how aqueous rocks may generally be known by their stratification.

b. *concr.* A stratum produced by this process. **1808** W. RICHARDSON in *Phil. Trans.* XCVIII. 220 Regular stratifications on the summits of hills and mountains, have been long a stumbling block to theorists. **1822** J. PARKINSON *Outl. Oryctol.* 267 The matrix of these fossils is evidently a portion of the same stratification which occurs at Pappenheim.

c. *Biol.* and *Path.* The thickening of a tissue by the deposition or growth of successive thin layers.

1875 tr. *De Bary* in *Jrnl. Bot.* Oct. 301 In *Chara fragilis*, ..this membrane shows a copious tender stratification after the carbonate of lime has been dissolved. **1876** tr. *Wagner's Gen. Pathol.* 200 The form, color, and stratification of the impacted piece. **1880** BESSEY *Bot.* 32 During the increase of the cell-wall in thickness, an appearance of stratification arises in it. **1887** T. W. SHORE *Elem. Biol. Vegetable* 10 Observe..Stratification of the cuticle, i.e. the appearance of lines in it, parallel to the surface of the section. **1899** CAGNEY tr. *von Jaksch's Clin. Diagn.* iv. (ed. 4) 115 In some diseases, as in abscess and gangrene of the lung there is marked stratification of its [i.e. the sputum's] parts.

d. *Electr.* The striated appearance assumed by an electric discharge passing through a highly rarefied gas.

1856 T. R. ROBINSON in *Proc. R. Irish Acad.* VI. 429 When a Leyden jar (each coating about a foot) was connected with the terminals, the stratification was well seen in each direction of the current. **1858** J. P. GASSIOT in *Phil. Trans.* I The phenomenon of stratifications in the discharge *in vacuo* were subsequently observed in Paris by M. Ruhmkorff. **1866** R. M. FERGUSON *Electr.* (1870) 193 The cause of this stratification is as yet a matter of speculation.

e. *transf.* and *fig.* Chiefly with reference to the geological use, and *spec.* in *Sociology*, the formation and establishment of social or cultural levels resulting from differences in occupation and political, ethnic, or economic influence.

1860 MAURY *Phys. Geog.* (Low) xxii. §885 Let us, in imagination, divide these depths..into any number of stratifications or layers of equal thickness. **1862** BURTON *Bk. Hunter* (1863) 113 The library is the great intellectual stratification in which the literary investigator works. **1879** BARING-GOULD *Germany* I. 2 The stratification of the German classes, and of the aristocracy, is most peculiar. **1889** A. SIDGWICK in *Jrnl. Educ.* Feb. 117 That there is not a chance of saving much time by improved methods and proper stratification. **1910** D. G. HOGARTH in *Encycl. Brit.* I. 248/2 (*Aegean Civiliz.*), By exact observation of stratification, eight more periods have been distinguished by the explorer of Cnossus. **1927** P. SOROKIN *Soc. Mobility* ii. 13 Unstratified society..is a myth which has never been realized in the history of mankind... The forms and proportions of stratification vary, but its essence is permanent. **1944** S. PUTNAM tr. *da Cunha's Rebellion in Backlands* ii. 117 It was natural that the deep-lying layers of our ethnic stratification should have cast up so extraordinary an anticlinal as Antonio Conselheiro. **1962** *Guardian* 22 June 20/2 The so-called gulf between science and literature ..led to no social stratification. **1981** R. FLETCHER *Sociol.* vii. 200 Specific interest groups and a changing ethnic composition are the elements most likely to be troublesome in..problems of social stratification.

f. The existence in a lake or other body of water of two or more distinct layers differing in temperature, density, or the like.

1898 *Amer. Naturalist* XXXII. 26 It is in a condition of 'inverse stratification', as Forel calls it, when the colder water is above the warmer. **1935** P. S. WELCH *Limnology* iv. 51 Exceptional meteorological conditions may..prevent stratification completely. **1952** *Phil. Trans. R. Soc.* B. CCXXXVI. 355 (*heading*) Water movements in lakes during summer stratification. **1972** M. G. GROSS *Oceanography* vii. 191 Well-developed density stratification of the open ocean inhibits strong vertical currents. **1973** P. A. COLINVAUX *Introd. Ecol.* xviii. 249 If a lake is highly productive, thermal stratification has some interesting consequences for the bottom water.

g. Variation in the richness of the fuel-air mixture during the period of its introduction into the cylinder of an internal-combustion engine.

1922 H. R. RICARDO *Internal-Combustion Engine* I. v. 75 In order to increase the range of power as far as possible, every effort is made to encourage stratification. **1981** *Sci. Amer.* May 45/1 The stratification also makes it possible to burn fuel-air mixtures so lean in fuel that they would not burn if the fuel were uniformly mixed with the air.

3. *Statistics.* The (usu. notional) division of a population into distinct groups from each of which a proportion of an overall sample may be taken.

1920 A. L. BOWLEY *Elements of Statistics* (ed. 4) II. iv. 336 The stratification of a universe of measurable objects is also treated by Mr. Yule. **1934** *Jrnl. R. Statistical Soc.* XCVII. 608 This method of stratification..gives an improvement in precision. **1957** KENDALL & BUCKLAND *Dict. Statistical Terms* 282 The process of stratification may be undertaken on a geographical basis, *e.g.* by dividing up the sampled area into sub-areas on a map. **1966** *Rep. Comm. Inquiry Univ. Oxf.* II. 420 In drawing the sample stratification by college and subject was used to the greatest possible extent. **1967** G. WILLS in Wills & Yearsley *Handbk. Management Technol.* 187 This process of stratification..can only be carried out if you have details of the relevant population of shops by region, type, etc. **1977** *Lancet* 28 May 1142/2 With stratification for hospital, age, and year of admission, the maximum-likelihood estimate of uniform risk ratio was 3·3.

4. *attrib.*

1884 A. GEIKIE in *Nature* 13 Nov. 30/1 These thrust-planes..could not be distinguished from ordinary stratification-planes.

stratificational (strætɪfɪ'keɪʃənəl), *a.* [f. STRATIFICATION + -AL[1].] **1.** *Linguistics.* Of or pertaining to the concept of language as a series of strata or structural layers, esp. ***stratificational grammar, linguistics***, whereby language is envisaged and analysed in terms of a number of different strata, each with its own rules of formation and related to each other.

1962 S. M. LAMB (*title*) Outline of stratificational grammar. *Ibid.* 3 The code relating each pair of neighboring strata is a set of *stratificational rules*. *Ibid.* 6 Stratificational analysis may be described as a process of *emicization* followed by the description of the results. **1966** *Georgetown Univ. Monogr. Ser. Lang. & Linguistics* XVII. 87 The picture of the organization of language in terms of four strata can conveniently be called stratificational. **1968** P. M. POSTAL *Aspects Phonol. Theory* iv. 89 By abandoning any vestige of a natural relation between phonetic and phonemic representations, stratificational phonemics has completely lost contact with these early motivations. **1970** *Canad. Jrnl. Linguistics* XV. 97 Since this hypothesis is independent of the concept of strata, it seems sensible to call the grammar to be developed here a *relational network grammar*, rather than a stratificational grammar. **1972** D. G. LOCKWOOD *Introd. Stratificational Linguistics* i. 5 Stratificational theory may eventually be able to provide evidence on the relation of the neural networks to the storage of knowledge. **1977** P. STREVENS *New Orientations Teaching of English* vi. 79 Very little..stratificational theory..could be thoroughly taught and learned during, say, a two-year training college course.

2. Of or pertaining to social or cultural strata.

1963 *New Society* 3 Oct. 30/3 The evolution of American jazz has been correctly recognised..as a musically expressed protest movement against the existing stratificational order. **1968** *Canad. Jrnl. Linguistics* XIII. 126 The variables studied..showed stratificational patterns clearly identifiable with different social levels of the community.

Hence **stratifi'cationalism**, adherence to the theory that language comprises several structural layers; **stratifi'cationalist**, one who holds this theory.

1968 *South Atlantic Bull.* Mar. 1/3 Dashing across the empty plains from a distant Danish horizon comes a new band, the troop of Stratificationalism. **1969** R. I. MCDAVID in *2nd & 3rd Lincolnland Conf. on Dialectology* (1972) 1 There seems to be diffidence on the part of Lamb's stratificationalists. **1973** *Amer. Speech 1969* XLIV. 287 Pike or Lamb might charge that James D. McCawley's 'Prelexical Syntax' is arcane from the point of view of a tagmemicist or stratificationalist. **1978** *Language* LIV. 170 If it can be said to have a dominant philosophy, it would be stratificationalism.

stratified ('strætɪfaɪd), *ppl. a.* [f. STRATIFY *v.* + -ED[1].] **1.** Disposed in strata or layers.

a. *Geol.* Of rocks, a portion of the earth's crust.

1799 [see POLYGENOUS *a.* 1]. **1802** PLAYFAIR *Illustr. Huttonian Theory* 65 In the view now given of metallic veins they have been considered as traversing only the stratified parts of the globe. **1813** BAKEWELL *Introd. Geol.* (1815) 29 Stratified mountains or rocks are those which are composed of layers of stone, laid over each other. **1832** DE LA BECHE *Geol. Man.* (ed. 2) 35 In the accompanying Table, rocks are first divided into Stratified and Unstratified. **1854** H. MILLER *Sch. & Schm.* xxi. (1860) 228 The deposit.. consists..of alternate beds of limestone, sandstone and stratified clay. **1889** *Hardwicke's Sci.-Gossip* XXV. 69 The absence of large erratic blocks in the stratified beds may indicate a period of extreme glaciation. **1897** G. P. MERRILL *Rocks* etc. 34 The term massive is applied to such igneous rocks as show no sign of bedding or stratification, while limestones, sandstones, and such other rocks as are arranged in more or less parallel layers are described as stratified.

b. in various applications; said, e.g., of incrustations, animal or vegetable tissues, a solid or fluid substance.

1809 J. KIDD *Min.* I. 38 The calcareous incrustation..is of a stratified appearance. **1859** PARKINSON *Optics* (1866) 106 In this way the law of variation of density of a stratified medium may be expressed. **1887** T. W. SHORE *Elem. Biol. Vegetable* 13, 1. The thin common cell wall, or middle lamella. 2. The much thicker stratified thickening of the cell wall. **1897** *Allbutt's Syst. Med.* III. 360 The internal surface [of the œsophagus] is covered with stratified squamous epithelium.

c. *Electr.* (Cf. STRATIFICATION 2 d.)

1856 *Rep. Brit. Assoc.* II. 10 On the Stratified Appearance of the Electrical Discharge. By W. R. Grove. **1865** *Ibid.* II. 15 On the Change of Form and Colour which the Stratified Discharge assumes when a Varied Resistance is introduced in the Circuit of an Extended Series of the Voltaic Battery. **1873** J. C. MAXWELL *Electr. & Magnetism* I. 369 On Stratified Conductors. Let a conductor be composed of alternate strata of thickness c and c' of two substances whose coefficients of conductivity are different.

d. Placed in alternate layers with something else.

1855 J. SCOFFERN in *Orr's Circ. Sci., Elem. Chem.* 490 The stratified copper leaves..are taken out.

e. Of a lake or other body of water: exhibiting stratification. [tr. F. *stratifié* (F. A. Forel 1880, in *Bibliothèque Univ.: Arch. des Sci. physiques et nat.* IV. 94).]

1881 *Proc. Boston Soc. Nat. Hist.* XXI. 66 In summer the return current takes place at no great depth, because then the water is stratified according to its temperature. **1910** E. M. WEDDERBURN in Murray & Pullar *Bathymetrical Surv. Sc. Fresh-Water Lochs* I. 104 As winter draws on the lake becomes thermally stratified. **1957** G. E. HUTCHINSON *Treat. Limnol.* I. v. 334 Not only can a lake oscillate as a whole, but if it is stratified, the various layers of different density can oscillate relative to one another. **1972** M. G. GROSS *Oceanography* xi. 301 Tidal currents [in an estuary] cause mixing between layers, so that the waters become only moderately stratified. **1980** G. E. FOGG in Barnes & Mann *Fund. Aquatic Ecosystem* ii. 37 Sometimes lakes are permanently stratified, as for example in tropical regions.

f. *Sociol.* (Cf. STRATIFICATION 2 e.)

1927 P. SOROKIN *Social Mobility* ii. 11 If the economic status of the members of a society is unequal, if among them there are both wealthy and poor, the society is *economically stratified*. **1960** V. PACKARD *Status Seekers* xxii. 325 Life is said to be more stable and serene in clearly stratified societies. **1969** C. D. DARLINGTON *Evol. of Man & Soc.* xviii. 422 The urban society was still stratified and even more highly stratified, but the strata and their boundaries had changed.

g. ***stratified charge***: in an internal-combustion engine, a rich mixture for ignition in each cycle followed by a lean one for combustion, usu. achieved by having a side chamber in each cylinder into which the mixture for ignition is introduced; freq. *attrib.*

1931 D. R. PYE *Internal Combustion Engine* vi. 148 (*caption*) Thermal efficiencies obtainable at weak petrol-air mixtures with 'stratified charge' operation. **1953** H. R. RICARDO *High-Speed Internal Combustion Engine* (ed. 4) xviii. 366 Two alternative schemes were tried:..(2) The use of a stratified charge in which the mixture immediately in the zone of the sparking-plug is very much richer than that in the main body of the combustion space. **1976** *National Observer* (U.S.) 22 May 9/4 The Japanese car is..powered with a larger version of the stratified-charge engine. **1981** *Sci. Amer.* May 45/1 Direct-injection stratified-charge engines have efficiency advantages comparable to those of the diesel.

2. *Statistics.* Employing, or obtained by means of, the technique of stratification.

1920 A. L. BOWLEY *Elements of Statistics* (ed. 4) II. iv. 333 In a non-stratified selection we should have had $\sigma = \cdot 0141$. **1934** *Jrnl. R. Statistical Soc.* XCVII. 567 This method has been called by Professor Bowley the method of stratified sampling. **1956** *B.B.C. Handbk.* 1957 104 This Survey employs part-time interviewers..who each day question some four thousand people—a sample or cross-section of the adult public... (Technically speaking, the sample used is a stratified quota sample.) **1980** *Nature* 1 May 5/3 One [technique] is stratified sampling, in which the site was first divided into 20 metre by 20 metre squares, and then four randomly selected one metre by one metre trenches excavated within each of the larger squares.

stratiform ('strætɪfɔːm), *a.*[1] [ad. F. *stratiforme*, as if ad. L. type **strātiformis*, f. *strātum*: see STRATUM and -FORM.]

1. *Geol.* Disposed in the form of strata; showing apparent stratification.

1805 [S. WESTON] *Werneria* 8 Concrete carbonate of lime ..is fistular, or in pipes or cylinders, or strati-form in layers. **1811** PINKERTON *Petral.* I. 91 The other formation belongs to his [Werner's] Floetz, horizontal, or stratiform rocks. **1839** DE LA BECHE *Rep. Geol. Cornwall*, etc. vi. 163 This tendency to be divided or cleave in a stratiform manner is highly deceptive. **1856** PAGE *Adv. Text-bk. Geol.* xx. (1876) 416 But as we descend..we find stratiform layers of shells. **1883** R. D. IRVING in *3rd Ann. Rep. U.S. Geol. Surv.* 118

Seven layers of stratiform amygdaloid running from 3 to 20 feet in thickness.

2. Forming or formed into strata or layers; *spec.* in ***stratiform cartilage***, 'cartilage covering the bone in an osteo-aponeurotic canal for a tendon' (*Syd. Soc. Lex.*, 1898).

1834 *Good's Study Med.* (ed. 4) II. 555 A very thin layer spread over serous membranes, the stratiform, or membraniform, melanosis. **1847** *Todd's Cycl. Anat.* IV. 104/2 Stratiform deposition is that occurring on serous surfaces in layers. **1871** T. H. GREEN *Introd. Pathol.* ii. 12 The punctiform and stratiform redness of hyperæmia.

So †**'stratiformed** *a. Geol.* (see quot.).

1811 PINKERTON *Petral.* I. Introd. p. xxix, A stratified rock [in Werner's nomenclature] implying that the strata are of one and the same substance; while the Floetz..often present beds of different substances. But this distinction is not of such utility or importance as to necessitate the introduction of a barbarous word; and if stratified be not precise, we may use stratiformed with Daubuisson.

'stratiform, *a.*[2] [f. STRAT-US: see -FORM.] Resembling stratus clouds.

1853 KANE *Grinnell Exp.* xxxv. (1856) 321 Long, stratiform illuminated clouds. **1885** [see CUMULIFORM *a.*]. **1944** H. C. WILLETT *Descriptive Meteorol.* iv. 92 These high stratiform clouds are spread over large areas where convection is extensive in the lower atmosphere. **1978** *Bull. Amer. Meteorol. Soc.* LIX. 518 (*heading*) An analytical model of snowflake growth in stratiform clouds.

stratify ('strætɪfaɪ), *v.*[1] [ad. F. *stratifier*, ad. mod.L. *strātificāre*, f. *strātum*: see STRATUM and -FY.]

1. a. *trans.* 'To range in beds or layers' (J.); *spec.* in *Metallurgy*, to range in alternate layers (metals and reagent substances) in a crucible.

1661 LOVELL *Hist. Anim. & Min.* 193 Crowfish..may be put into barrels, having myrtle leaves stratified. **1669** ROWLAND *Schroder's Chym. Disp.* I. xiv. 21 To *Stratify*,..is when Minerals are laid with Powders, Layer upon Layer, first Powder, then Plates of Metals; then Powder, to the end. **1670** W. SIMPSON *Hydrol. Ess.* 6 Artificial vitriol..made by a cementation of plates of copper stratified with common salt and sulphur. **1706** PHILLIPS (ed. Kersey) s.v., To Stratify Gold and Cement..is to lay a Bed of Paste call'd Cement, then a Plate of Gold, then another Layer of Cement, then another Plate of Gold; and so on, till the Crucible be full. **1799** G. SMITH *Laboratory* I. 185 Stratify thin plates of brass in an earthen pipkin with powdered sulphur and antimony. **1825** J. NICHOLSON *Oper. Mech.* 340 The iron..must be put into..a cementing pot, and stratified with powdered charcoal. **1826** W. C. OTTLEY *Dict. Chem. & Min.* Introd. Vocab., *Stratify*, to cause two or more bodies to act upon each other by placing them in any vessel in alternate layers. **1845** DODD *Brit. Manuf.* Ser. v. 184 The hide is then transferred to a pit containing stronger ooze, or else is stratified with crushed bark. **1853** SOYER *Pantroph.* 240 They..wash them [*sc.* anchovies] in soft or salt water, and stratify them in barrels with salt. **1855** J. SCOFFERN in *Orr's Circ. Sci., Elem. Chem.* 438 Bars of wrought iron are stratified with charcoal.

†**b.** In *passive*: To be placed in alternate layers *with* something else. *Obs.*

1789 MILLS in *Phil. Trans.* LXXX. 83 The gneiss..is in ribs from two to twelve inches thick, and is stratified by intermediate ribs of red granite of about an inch thick. **1789** E. DARWIN *Bot. Gard.* I. (1791) 38 *notes*, Iron is found.. stratified with clay coals or argillaceous grits. **1829** *Good's Study Med.* (ed. 3) I. 616 We find the hydatids..sometimes stratified with layers of albuminous and friable matter.

c. To preserve or promote the germination of (seeds) by stratification.

1905 *Terms Forestry & Logging* (U.S. Dept. Agric., Bureau of Forestry) 23 *Stratify*, to preserve tree seeds by spreading them in layers alternating with layers of earth or sand. **1916** J. W. TOUMEY *Seeding & Planting* vii. 104 Some of the pines and junipers germinate so slowly that the seed is usually stratified for a year before sowing. **1949** *Q. Jrnl. Forestry* XLIII. 169 The seed is stratified in wet sand for six weeks before sowing at a temperture of 34° F. **1960** *New Scientist* 12 May 1210/3 When seeds of certain shrubs or trees are stratified—stored in moist sand at 41° F. to break their dormancy—the amount of moisture in the sand may markedly influence the percentage germination subsequently achieved.

2. a. *Geol.* Of natural agencies: To deposit (rocks) in strata or beds; to produce (a portion of the earth's crust) in the form of strata; to form strata in. Chiefly in *passive*.

1794 R. J. SULIVAN *View Nat.* I. 49 They contain..other vestiges of organic substances; and are always stratified. **1805** JAMESON *Min. Descr. Dumfries* 94 An extensive quarry, where a great rock mass of limestone is exposed: it is distinctly stratified. **1821** T. DWIGHT *Trav.* II. 480 A vast mass of blue limestone, horizontally stratified. **1862** DANA *Man. Geol.* 554 While the glaciers were disappearing, many a stream or lake would have existed to stratify the drift. **1863** LYELL *Antiq. Man* 37 If the mud pierced through had been thrown down by the river in ancient channels, it would have been stratified. **1867** —— *Princ. Geol.* II. xxiv. (1875) I. 617 Composed chiefly of indurated Tufa like Monte Nuovo, stratified conformably to its conical surface. **1878** A. H. GREEN, etc. *Coal* i. 6 Both sandstones and shales are divided into layers or beds, and are said to be stratified.

b. *transf.* and *fig.*

1851 MRS. BROWNING *Casa Guidi Wind.* I. 631 Good lovers of our age to track and plough Their way to, through time's ordures stratified. **1872** O. W. HOLMES *Poet Breakf.-t.* ii. 67 Society stratifies itself everywhere. **1897** BP. CREIGHTON in *Daily News* 22 Jan. 6/5 Its methods had been found effective in a younger country less stratified than our own. **1900** *Pilot* 28 Apr. 256/2 The mound from its great height must represent a series of stratified ruins. **1912** J. L. MYRES *Dawn of Hist.* viii. 168 This style [of pottery] was found in the important because well-stratified site at Phylakopi.

c. *Statistics.* To subdivide (a population) into groups in order to take a stratified sample. Also *absol.*

1949 F. YATES *Sampling Methods for Censuses & Surveys* iii. 25 A population may be stratified for two or more different characteristics... Thus we may stratify farms according to size and according to geographical regions. **1966** *Rep. Comm. Inquiry Univ. Oxf.* II. 420 It was possible to stratify by college and proposed subject. *Ibid.* 424 The names under Social Studies were further stratified according to college thus: Nuffield, St. Antony's, and others. **1967** G. WILLS in Wills & Yearsley *Handbk. Management Technol.* 187 In most cases..the statistician can..stratify the list of 27,000 names [of shops] in terms of the region of the country they are in, [etc.]. **1970** J. E. FREUND *Statistics* xi. 285 Stratified sampling..can be very effective provided one stratifies with respect to truly relevant characteristics of the population.

3. *intr.* To assume the form of strata. Also, to become stratified.

1856 T. B. BUTLER *Philos. Weather* i. 13 (Funk) Currents of air do not mingle but stratify. **1935** P. S. WELCH *Limnology* iii. 15 Criteria which would make a lake include only those bodies of standing water which are of considerable expanse and which are deep enough to stratify thermally. **1980** R. S. K. BARNES in Barnes & Mann *Fund. Aquatic Ecosystems* i. 14 Water bodies stratify when stable density differences are generated, often as a result of surface heating.

Hence **'stratifying** *vbl. sb.*

1706 PHILLIPS (ed. Kersey), *Stratification*, (in Chymistry) a stratifying or putting different Matters Bed upon Bed [etc.].

'stratify, *v.*[2] ? *nonce-wd.* [f. L. *strāta* road (see STREET *sb.*) + -(I)FY.] *trans.* To furnish with a system of roads.

1881 C. WORDSWORTH *Ch. Hist.* I. ii. 15 The Greek Empire..had facilitated national intercourse by sea. The Roman Empire, by its great military roads, accelerated that intercourse by land. Greece and Rome navigated and stratified the world.

stratigrapher (strəˈtɪɡrəfə(r)). [f. STRATIGRAPHY: see -GRAPHER.] One versed in stratigraphy; one who describes or delineates strata.

1883 A. GEIKIE in *Nature* 15 Feb. 357/1 He is an excellent stratigrapher. **1897** *Natural Sci.* Dec. 418 The stratigrapher is expected to map solid rock through its drift covering.

stratigraphic (strætɪˈɡræfɪk), *a.* [f. STRATIGRAPHY: see -GRAPHIC. Cf. F. *stratigraphique.*] = next. Also *transf.* and *fig.*

1877 LE CONTE *Elem. Geol.* (1879) 401 The lower portion is very barren of fossils, and this means of correcting the stratigraphic conclusion was at first nearly wanting. **1880** *Nature* 22 Jan. 290/1 Stratigraphic observations on the pre-carboniferous formation of Valtellina and Calabria. **1884** *American* VIII. 300 Geography and Stratigraphic Geology. **1896** J. P. SMITH in *Proc. Amer. Philos. Soc.* Nov. 222 The absence of a paleontologic or stratigraphic break was a sufficient reason for calling the beds in question Upper Coal Measures rather than Permian.

transf. **1912** *Man* XII. 134 Throughout the Old World the careful study of quaternary implements, and stratigraphic analysis of the conditions accompanying the different types, almost always make it possible to date a quaternary industry by the typical forms contained in it. **1972** *Computers & Humanities* VII. 39 One of the most characteristically archaeological of these uses is the generation and printing of stratigraphic backplots of artifacts and other items in a site.

fig. **1976** *Jrnl. Asian Studies* XXXV. 636 Another stratigraphic approach to Indian society.

stratigraphical (strætɪˈɡræfɪkəl), *a.* Sometimes *erron.* **strata-**. [Formed as prec.: see -ICAL.] Pertaining to stratigraphy.

1817 W. SMITH (*title*) Stratigraphical System of Organized Fossils. **1849** MURCHISON *Siluria* iii. (1859) 43 The rock unquestionably occupies the same stratigraphical position as the Lingula Flags of Wales. **1857** PORTLOCK in *Q. Jrnl. Geol. Soc.* XIII. p. xci, The stratigraphical distribution of the fossils enumerated. **1869** HUXLEY in *Sci. Opin.* 28 Apr. 486/1 What is termed stratigraphical geology is neither more nor less than the anatomy of the earth. **1883** HULKE in *Q. Jrnl. Geol. Soc.* XXXIX. Proc. 64 The advantages likely to accrue from such international uniformity of stratigraphical terms. **1892** LAPWORTH in *Nature* 18 Aug. 372/2 What is known as stratigraphical geology, or the study of the geological formations.

Hence **stratiˈgraphically** *adv.*, in stratigraphical respects; with reference to stratigraphy.

1831 A. SEDGWICK in *Proc. Geol. Soc.* I. 274 He [*sc.* W. Smith] made large collections of fossils; and the moment an opportunity presented itself he arranged them all stratigraphically. **1857** H. MILLER *Test. Rocks* x. 418 Both stratigraphically and palaeontologically the place in the scale of the Niagara graveyard can be definitely determined.

stratigraphist (strəˈtɪɡrəfɪst). [f. STRATIGRAPHY + -IST.] = STRATIGRAPHER.

1879 W. KEEPING *Fossils Upware & Brickhill* (1883) 27 The value of the species is thereby..considerably increased both to the Naturalist and Stratigraphist. **1892** LAPWORTH in *Nature* 18 Aug. 373/1 The brilliant stratigraphists of the end of the last century.

stratigraphy (strəˈtɪɡrəfɪ). [f. L. *strāti-* combining form of *strātum*: see STRATUM and -GRAPHY. Cf. F. *stratigraphie.*]

1. The branch of geology that is concerned with the order and relative position of the strata of the earth's crust.

1865 *Reader* 4 Mar. 248/2 While accepting as a basis in theoretical geology the principles of Hutton, and in stratigraphy the work of William Smith, he [etc.]. **1891** BLAKE in *Q. Jrnl. Geol. Soc.* XLVII. 341 Nor did he see any reason to doubt the correctness of his stratigraphy there.

2. The stratigraphical features (of a country, etc.); the order and relative position of the strata.

1882 A. GEIKIE in *Nature* 7 Dec. 121/2 His monograph embraces the stratigraphy, palæontology, structure, eruptive rocks, and contact-metamorphism of the district. **1892** LAPWORTH in *Nature* 18 Aug. 373/2 A formation, which is the unit of geological stratigraphy, is a rock sheet composed of many strata possessing common lithological characters.

transf. **1912** *Man* XII. 135 Dr. Peabody said that the perfect stratigraphy in Europe is contrasted with a vague stratigraphy in America. There the paleolithic form persists in later periods and Chellean types are found on the surface.

stratiote ('strætɪəʊt). *rare.* In 7 -ot. [ad. Gr. στρατιώτης, f. στρατιά army.] A soldier (in ancient Greece; also used by Harrington with reference to his imaginary commonwealth).

1656 HARRINGTON *Oceana* Wks. (1700) 174 The Constable who is to officiat at the Urn, shall, after the manner of the Elders, elect every fifth Man of their whole number..to be a Stratiot or Deputy of the Youth. **1873** BURTON *Hist. Scot.* I. iii. 115 The lighter equipped stratiote of Greece.

†**stratiˈotic,** *a. Obs.*[−0] [ad. Gr. στρατιωτικός military, στρατιωτική the military arts, f. στρατιώτης soldier, f. στρατιά army.] (See quot.)

1656 BLOUNT *Glossogr.*, *Stratiotick* (*stratioticus*) warlike, pertaining to War.

strato- ('strɑːtəʊ, 'streɪtəʊ). **1.** Combining form of STRATUS, used to form names for mixed types of cloud-structure in which the 'stratus' form is present as an element modifying one of the other forms: **strato-'cirrus**, a cloud resembling cirro-stratus, but more compact in structure; hence **strato-cirrous** *a.*; **strato-'cumulus** = *cumulo-stratus*; hence **strato-'cumulous** *a.* Also used in forming other terms, as **'stratotype** *Geol.*, a particular group of strata chosen as defining a named stratigraphic unit or boundary; freq. *attrib.*; **'stratovol,cano** *Geol.* [ad. G. *strato-vulkan* (K. von Seebach 1866, in *Zeitschr. d. deutsch. geol. Ges.* XVIII. 644)], a volcano built up of alternate layers of lava and ash.

1816 W. TAYLOR in *Monthly Mag.* XLII. 35 Such clouds should be called strato-cirrous. **1898** *Jrnl. Sch. Geog.* (U.S.) Oct. 310 The sky..was overcast with strato-cumulus and cumulus clouds. **1965** *Bull. Amer. Assoc. Petroleum Geologists* XLIX. 1701/1 The most effective means of providing a chronostratigraphic unit with fixed and uniform limits..appears to be by the designation of a specifically bounded section of rock strata as the stratotype of this unit. **1969** *Proc. Geol. Soc. Lond.* Aug. 142 A standard stratigraphical scale expresses the relative ages of rock in agreed terms defined by boundary points in stratotype sections. **1972** J. A. COUVERING in Bishop & Miller *Calibration of Hominoid Evolution* 247 State-age names..are put in quotation marks when used in a sense which differs from the strict definition of the stratotype. **1978** *Nature* 16 Nov. 258/2 The rich foraminiferal and molluscan faunas at these localities establish the correlation of the beds..with the Jemmys Point Formation in Gippsland, the stratotype of the Kalimnan Stage (early Pliocene). [**1885** A. GEIKIE *Text-bk. Geol.* (ed. 2) 227 Von Seebach..distinguished two volcanic types. 1st, Bedded Volcanoes (Strato-Vulkane), composed of successive sheets of lava and tuffs, and embracing the great majority of volcanoes.] **1957** G. E. HUTCHINSON *Treat. Limnol.* I. i. 25 The typical large volcano with a well-developed crater is an intermediate or composite structure, usually built of alternating layers of lava and cinders, and therefore called a stratovolcano. **1973** *Sci. Amer.* Aug. 67/1 These later lavas form the great stratovolcanoes, some still active, that dominate the Andean chain. **1977** *Whitaker's Almanack 1978* 1037/2 Merapi, a strato-volcano on the island of Java, has been active for several centuries.

2. [f. STRATO(SPHERE.] **a.** Used to form the names of various kinds of high-altitude aircraft, as ***stratocruiser***, ***-fortress***, ***-freighter***, ***-jet***, ***-liner***, ***-plane***, ***-tanker***.

All but *stratoplane* are the names of aircraft built by the Boeing Airplane Company, but only *Stratoliner* (formerly also *Stratocruiser*) is a proprietary name (in the U.S.).

1944 *Sun* (Baltimore) 15 Nov. 8/2 An announcement by the Boeing Aircraft Company of a 'Stratocruiser' for postwar production... A military prototype of the Stratocruiser..is undergoing tests. **1966** D. FRANCIS *Flying Finish* iv. 48 The pressurized stratocruiser which took us [to New York]. **1953** *Britannica Bk. of Year* 28/1 The Boeing YB-52, an eight-engine jet swept-wing Stratofortress designed gradually to replace the intercontinental B-36, made its first flight. **1981** *Nature* 17 Dec. 606/2 The massive wide-area saturation bombing from B-52 stratofortresses alone ultimately added up to 800,000 tonnes of bombs. **1947** *Sun* (Baltimore) 10 July 2 (*caption*) The Boeing Aircraft Company's 'Stratocruiser', passenger-carrying counterpart of the 'Stratofreighter', is shown as it takes off on its initial test flight at Seattle. **1947** *Daily Progress* (Charlottesville, Va.) 18 Dec. 10/1 The XB4 Stratojet, described as potentially the world's most powerful plane, made its initial test hop yesterday. **1955** *Times* 20 June 3/5 One 'Stratojet' bomber succeeds another as the latest weapon of defence. **1938** *Sun* (Baltimore) 8 June 3/2 Two other new transports, the Boeing 'Stratoliner' and the Douglas DC-4. **1939** *Official Gaz.* (U.S. Patent Office) 26 Dec. 805/1 Boeing Aircraft Company... Stratoliner. For airplanes and structural parts thereof. **1955** M. MCCARTHY *Sights &*

Spectacles (1959) 162 Stratoliners from Kansas City ferry-in patrons for *Guys and Dolls*. **1933** *Daily Progress* (Charlottesville, Va.) 16 Nov. 6/4 Clues to the tail-winds that may push future strato-planes on high-speed flights through the stratosphere were sought..here today by astronomers watching the Leonid meteor shower. **1936** *Discovery* Apr. 125/2 The efficiency of the reaction-motor beginning where that of the propeller leaves off, at approximately the 10-mile level,..raises the question as to whether certain makers of hush-hush 'stratoplanes' are not working along the wrong lines. **1955** *Ann. Rep. 1954* (Boeing Airplane Co.) 15/2 The new military airplane, to be known as the KC-135 Jet Stratotanker, will be an advanced version of the prototype. **1980** *Times* 1 Feb. 3/3 (*caption*) A woman stratotanker pilot in the United States Air Force at RAF Fairford, Gloucestershire, yesterday, after a refuelling mission.

b. Used in the sense 'travelling in, suitable for travel in, the stratosphere', in **stratonaut** [f. *-naut* after AERONAUT, ASTRONAUT], **stratosuit**.

1934 *Amer. Speech* IX. 236/2 According to C. E. Mason, the New York *Times* coined the word *stratonaut* to describe venturers in the stratosphere. **1936** *Nature* 27 June 1053/1 A general introduction which is packed with references to Magellan and Copernicus on one hand, and the stratosphere explorers (*stratonauts*) and theoretical investigators of the expanding universe on the other. **1937** C. G. PHILP *Conquest of Stratosphere* 6 Seventy-four years ago..those gallant pioneers, Glaisher and Coxwell,..claimed to have reached a height of 7 miles, into the lower stratosphere..without a single essential of the modern stratonaut, for they had no oxygen apparatus. **1945** *Sun* (Baltimore) 23 June 3/2 (*caption*) An airman wears a new flexible pressurized 'Strato-suit' of rubberized fabric..for use in high-altitude flying. **1949** *Jrnl. Brit. Interplanetary Soc.* VIII. 40 Doubtless considerable improvements have been effected in stratosuits since the Haldane-Davis original.

stratocracy (strəˈtɒkrəsɪ). Also 7 stratocratie. [f. Gr. στρατό-ς army + -κρατία: see -CRACY. Cf. F. *stratocratie*.] Government by the army; military rule; a polity in which the army is the controlling power.

1652 *Observ. Forms of Govt.* 8 Their Monarchy was changed into a Stratocratie. **1656** BLOUNT *Glossogr.*, *Stratocracy* (Gr.) military Government; where a Commonwealth is governed by an Army or by Soldiers. **1659** GAUDEN *Slight Healers* (1660) 61 A game of Government wholly new to England, called Stratocracy. **1758** *Monthly Rev.* 27 They [the English *c* 1650] felt in their turns all the inconveniences of an Oligarchy, a Democracy, and a Stratocracy. **1815** GRATTAN *Sp.* 25 May (1822) III. 374 Sir, the French Government is war; it is a stratocracy. **1832-4** DE QUINCEY *Cæsars* Wks. 1859 X. 102 The government of an imperator was.. permanent stratocracy having a moveable head. **1899** *Spectator* 7 Oct. 485/2 The greatest danger to the permanent progress of Europe..is the possibility of a period of stratocracy.

So **ˈstratocrat**, one who embodies military rule; **stratoˈcratic** *a.*, pertaining to stratocracy.

1840 G. RAYMOND in *New Monthly Mag.* LVIII. 463 Having, with a stratocratic 'privilege', forcibly appropriated the person of a young Polish female. **1892** *Spectator* 11 June 809/1 The triumphant stratocrat whom their [the Roman oligarchy's] system tended to produce.

stratography (strəˈtɒgrəfɪ). *rare*$^{-1}$. [f. Gr. στρατός army + -γραφία -GRAPHY.] Military science.

1841 D'ISRAELI *Amen. Lit.* (1867) 607 A great commander by land and by sea, he was critical in all the arts of stratography.

stratopause (ˈstrætəʊpɔːz). *Meteorol.* [f. STRATO(SPHERE + PAUSE *sb.*] The upper limit of the stratosphere, separating it from the mesosphere. (In current use at a greater height than formerly: cf. STRATOSPHERE 2.)

1950 S. CHAPMAN in *Jrnl. Atmospheric & Terrestrial Physics* I. 121 Taking stratosphere to denote the nearly isothermal region above the troposphere, its upper boundary, where the temperature first begins to increase upwards more rapidly than is common in the lower stratosphere, would be the stratopause. **1963** *Q. Jrnl. R. Meteorol. Soc.* LXXXIX. 156 At its meeting in June 1962, the executive committee of the World Meteorological Organization passed a resolution on the terminology..for the high atmosphere. It is as follows:..(a) Stratosphere: Region (situated between the tropopause and stratopause) in which the temperature generally increases with height. (b) Stratopause: The top of the inversion layer in the upper stratosphere (usually around 50 to 55 km). **1979** *Jrnl. Atmospheric Sci.* XXXVI. 1616/1 Large [meridional wind] oscillations are seen near the stratopause (~ 50 km) with a period of about 2 days and an amplitude as large as 30 m s^{-1}.

straˈtopedarch. *Hist. rare.* [ad. Gr. στρατοπεδάρχης, f. στρατόπεδο-ν camp + -άρχης ruler.]

1855 MILMAN *Lat. Chr.* VI. 266 *note*, Demetrius the great Stratopedarch. **1895** W. M. RAMSAY *St. Paul the Traveller* xv. 347 When the party reached Rome, the centurion delivered his charge to his superior officer, who bears the title Chief of the Camp (Stratopedarch) in the Greek text.

stratose (ˈstreɪtəʊs), *a. Bot.* [f. STRAT-UM + -OSE.] Stratified; arranged in layers.

1881 FARLOW *Mar. Algæ* 51 Subgenus Eucladophora. Plants tufted, or, at times, stratose, not united into spongy masses by rhizoidal branches. **1900** B. D. JACKSON *Gloss. Bot. Terms*, *Stratose*, in distinct layers.

stratosphere (ˈstrætəsfɪə(r)). [f. STRATUM + -O + SPHERE *sb.*]

†**1.** *Geol.* [ad. G. *stratosphäre* (E. Suess *Das Antlitz der Erde* (1901) III. I. i. 4).] (See quots.) *Obs.*

1908 H. B. C. SOLLAS tr. *Suess's Face of Earth* III. i. 2 So great is the part played by stratified deposits in the structure of the earth's crust that we might be tempted to speak of the *stratosphere* of the earth in contradistinction to the *scoriosphere* of the moon. **1909** *Ibid.* IV. xv. 546 The stratosphere, or younger sedimentary envelope has been formed almost entirely at the expense of the Sal envelope.

2. *Meteorol.* The region of the atmosphere extending from the top of the troposphere up to a height of about 50 km. (the stratopause), in the lower part of which there is little temperature variation with height in temperate latitudes and in the higher part the temperature increases with height; formerly, the lower part of this region only (up to a height of about 20 km.).

1909 *Sci. Abstr.* A. XII. 208 (*heading*) Variation in height of the stratosphere (isothermal layer). **1909** W. N. SHAW *Free Atmosphere in Region of Brit. Isles* 47 M. Teisserenc de Bort has introduced the words 'troposphere' and 'stratosphere' to denote these two layers. *Ibid.* 48 Such evidence as we have goes to show that the stratosphere is a region of comparative calm. **1923** *Daily Mail* 26 Feb. 5/4 In this stratosphere it has been ascertained from balloon soundings that the temperature ceases to fall with an increase in height,..up to a level of 13½ miles, the highest attained so far by any instrument of man. **1934** *Discovery* Mar. 57/2 Professor Piccard, the Belgian physicist, was the first to make a successful flight [by balloon] into the stratosphere. **1937** *Jrnl. R. Aeronaut. Soc.* XLI. 414 It is likely to be many years before stratosphere flight, flights at heights of 40,000 feet and over, will become the commercially paying proposition which its enthusiasts believe it ultimately will be. **1951** 'J. WYNDHAM' *Day of Triffids* ii. 39 Somewhere high up in the stratosphere, he and Comrade Baltinoff found themselves attacked by the planes. **1951** [see *exosphere* s.v. EXO-]. **1960** M. NICOLET in J. A. Ratcliffe *Physics of Upper Atmosphere* ii. 19 The stratosphere is essentially that region where the temperature increases, or at least does not decrease, with altitude. **1963** [see STRATOPAUSE]. **1980** *Nature* 27 Nov. 347/1 Air samples, collected cryogenically at different heights of the stratosphere, were analysed for carbon dioxide.

3. *Oceanogr.* The bottom layer of the ocean, in which (by analogy with the original meaning of sense 2) there is little temperature variation with depth.

1937 *Nature* 26 June 1085/1 The oceanic troposphere, like the corresponding section of the atmosphere, is a relatively shallow layer marked by steep temperature gradients which contrast strongly with the more even conditions of the stratosphere. **1942** H. U. SVERDRUP et al. *Oceans* iv. 141 From analogy with the atmosphere, Defant (1928) has applied the terms troposphere and stratosphere to two different parts of the ocean. Troposphere is applied to the upper layer of relatively high temperature that is found in middle and lower latitudes and within which strong currents are present, and stratosphere to the nearly uniform masses of cold deep and bottom water. *Ibid.*, Within the oceanic stratosphere the salinity is very uniform. **1966** R. W. FAIRBRIDGE *Encycl. Oceanogr.* 940/2 The oceanic stratosphere refers to the nearly uniform masses of cold deep water and bottom water.

4. *transf.* and *fig.* An upper region, esp. in a hierarchy; a high, or the highest, plane, level, or rank.

1951 M. MCLUHAN *Mech. Bride* (1967) 62/1 The bathroom has been elevated to the very stratosphere of industrial folklore. **1952** *Observer* 3 Feb. 5/8 Their father was a big Paris dealer who moved in the stratosphere with Anatole France and de Goncourt. **1958** *Listener* 9 Oct. 578/2 To come down from the stratosphere of critical intentions to the rough terrain of poetry itself. **1965** B. SWEET-ESCOTT *Baker Street Irregular* vii. 188 Since August 1943 the stratosphere had begun to take our work in the Balkans seriously. *a* **1974** R. CROSSMAN *Diaries* (1975) I. 609 They were astonished that Harold had upped me into the stratosphere. **1975** *Country Life* 16 Jan. 138 With the fall-front secretaire..we are well-up in the stratosphere in terms of furniture... It was sold for 45,000 gn. **1980** *Daily Tel.* 3 Nov. 16 At various times she has advanced three different reasons for keeping the [minimum lending] rate in the stratosphere.

stratospheric (strætəˈsfɛrɪk), *a.* [f. prec. + -IC.] **1.** Of or pertaining to the stratosphere; occurring or performed in the stratosphere.

1920 W. J. HUMPHREYS *Physics of Air* x. 191 Let a stratospheric column be dropped bodily a distance *dh*, and let the surrounding air come in until equilibrium is again established. **1935** *Jrnl. R. Aeronaut. Soc.* XXXIX. 194 This plea is often put forward by the protagonists of so-called stratospheric aviation. **1945** *Washington Post* 10 Oct. 1/3 Development of even greater bombers capable of operating at stratospheric altitudes..is a certainty. **1959** *Daily Tel.* 30 Nov. 1/6 A balloon descending from a stratospheric study of the planet Venus landed safely in a meadow 20 miles north of Manhattan, Kansas, to-day. **1980** *Nature* 27 Nov. 347/2 The stratospheric CO_2 mixing ratio is not constant with height but rather decreases with increasing height.

2. *fig.* On a scale, from a point of view, or of a pitch, so high as to be suggestive of the stratosphere; *esp.* of a cost: = ASTRONOMICAL *a.* 1 b.

1935 *Sun* (Baltimore) 16 Feb. 2/1 This bill..requires Congress to abdicate. It requires the country to lean on a dubious dream... Changes made by the Senate committee ..in no sense change the stratospheric realities of the bill itself. **1958** K. GOODWIN in P. Gammond *Decca Bk. of Jazz* xiii. 149 His ability to produce stratospheric screamers with apparent ease was utilized to add bite and drive to the brass sections. **1966** *Economist* 19 Nov. 778/1 It might at least consider supporting stratospheric French suggestions for so-called 'solving of the key currency problem' by the admitted archaism of raising the world price of gold. **1973** *Daily Tel.* 17 Nov. 29/3 To prevent gilt-edged prices from falling even further and yields from escalating to even more stratospheric heights. **1980** *Jewish Chron.* 29 Feb. 17/3 Stratospheric admission prices for a suburban commercial venture.

stratoˈspherically, *adv. colloq.* [f. prec. + -AL[1] + -LY[2].] To a stratospheric degree, 'astronomically'.

1946 J. W. DAY *Harvest Adventure* xx. 331 This type of oratory was something very rich and rare, obviously from an intellect stratospherically above the plain, blunt, and fairly honest opinions held by the rank and file of Newark Labour. **1961** B. FERGUSSON *Watery Maze* x. 237 The stratospherically high priority afforded him for the journey did not really do him much good.

stratous (ˈstreɪtəs), *a.* [f. STRAT-US + -OUS.] Of clouds: = STRATUS *attrib.*

1816 W. TAYLOR in *Monthly Mag.* XLII. 35 These are called stratous clouds, from their sinking quashed appearance.

Stratovision (ˈstrætəʊvɪʒən). *U.S. Television.* Also **stratovision**. [f. STRATO(SPHERE + TELE)VISION.] A proprietary name for a system whereby television programmes are broadcast to a wide area by retransmission from a circling aircraft.

1945 *Cleveland* (Ohio) *Plain Dealer* 10 Aug. 1/5 The stratovision system simply puts the antenna and transmitter in an airplane flying in lazy circles 30,000 feet above the earth. **1946** *Official Gaz.* (U.S. Patent Office) 14 May 197/1 *Stratovision* for radio receiving and/or transmitting sets, television receiving and sending apparatus, [etc.]. **1948** *Sun* (Baltimore) 6 Oct. 19/4 If the World Series goes beyond five games, the East Coast and mid-West can see the remaining contests. A linking of the two networks by stratovision plane would provide the largest audience in television broadcast history. **1959** *Washington Post* 24 Dec. A1/7 Four transmitters on the Purdue campus will send two simultaneous programs to the plane, which will travel in a 10-mile circle 23,000 feet above Montpelier... The system, known as 'stratovision', is designed to explore the value of the plane in reaching hundreds of thousands of students at one time. **1964** B. GROB *Basic Television* (ed. 3) v. 85 The UHF channels 66 to 83 are available for experimentation with this airborne television system called stratovision.

strattli, obs. form of STRAITLY.

stratula (ˈstreɪtjuːlə), *sb. pl.* [a. mod.L. type **strătula*, pl. of **strătulum*, dim. of STRATUM.] (See quots.)

1853 DE LA CONDAMINE in *Q. Jrnl. Geol. Soc.* IX. 273 *note*, May not the word *stratula* be coined to describe those smaller subdivisions of strata which are frequently oblique? I should then say that the stratula here dip to the east. **1876** A. H. GREEN *Phys. Geol.* ii. §7. 83 The thicker layers of bedded rocks are usually spoken of as Beds or Strata, and the thinner as Laminæ or Stratula.

stratum (ˈstrɑːtəm, ˈstreɪtəm). Pl. **strata** (ˈstrɑːtə, ˈstreɪtə); 9- *rarely* stratums. [a. mod.L. use of L. *strātum*, lit. something spread or laid down (in classical use with the senses 'bed-cover', 'horse-cloth', 'pavement'), neut. pa. pple. of *sternĕre* to throw down, lay prostrate, spread out. Cf. F. *strate* fem. (1865 in Littré).]

1. *gen.* A quantity of a substance or material spread over a nearly horizontal surface to a more or less uniform thickness; a layer or coat; esp. one of two or more parallel layers or coats successively superposed one upon another.

The mod.L. phrase *stratum super stratum* (cf. quot. 1699) was often used in Eng. context by writers of the 17th c.: see e.g. quot. 1617 s.v. STRATIFICATION 1.

a. *sing.*

1599 A. M. tr. *Gabelhouer's Bk. Physicke* 54/1 Take a Copper basen,..insparge on the bottome therof a stratum of sault, and on that sault a row of mature Strawberryes. **1677** PLOT *Oxfordsh.* 249 [He] first laid at the bottom green Black-thorn bushes, and on them a stratum of large round stones. **1699** EVELYN *Acetaria* App. P 4, Cover the Bottom of the Jar with some Dill, an Handful of Bay-Salt, &c. and then a Bed of Nuts; and so stratum upon stratum as above. **1799** *Phil. Trans.* LXXXIX. 154 The stratum of soil, sixteen feet thick, placed above the decayed trees, seems to remove the epoch of their sinking and destruction, far beyond the reach of any historical knowledge. **1800** tr. *Lagrange's Chem.* II. 338 Scrape off..the stratum of verdigrise which covers each side of the plate. **1816** T. L. PEACOCK *Headlong Hall* viii, Covering the whole with a stratum of turf. **1834** J. DALTON *Meteorol. Observ.* (ed. 2) App. 197 The thickness of a stratum of clouds..is also variable from a few yards to three or four hundred or more. **1846** *J. Baxter's Libr. Pract. Agric.* (ed. 4) I. 313 To prevent the attacks of slugs and worms, some cultivators recommend a stratum of lime..to be placed at the bottom of the bed. **1851** NICHOL *Archit. Heav.* 22 In the midst of a *stratum* or bed of stars. **1860** TYNDALL *Glac.* I. xviii. 132 The blue gleams which issued from the broken or perforated stratum of new snow. **1867** BAKER *Nile Trib.* vi. (1872) 79 It had been entirely denuded of the loam that had formed the upper stratum.

b. pl. *strata.*

a **1700** KEN *Hymnotheo* Poet. Wks. 1721 III. 46 Thus of each Age..The Strata there of Graves distinct remain. **1777** ROBERTSON *Hist. Amer.* x. Notes, Wks. 1851 VI. 301 According to M. de Condamine, there were regular strata of building in some parts of Atun-Cannar, which he remarks as singular. **1807** T. THOMSON *Chem.* (ed. 3) II. 418 Thus there were three strata of liquids in the vessel: the acid lowermost, and the alcohol uppermost, separated from each other by the water. **1837** BARHAM *Ingol. Leg., Spectre of Tappington,* Rescued from the grave in which they [his breeches] had been buried, like the strata of a Christmas pie.

¶**c.** The form *strata* used as sing., with pl. *stratas. Obs.*

1735 DYCHE & PARDON *Dict., Strata,* a Layer or Bed of different Soil or Matter. **1766** J. BARTRAM *Jrnl.* 9 Jan. 29 A high bluff of sand.. under which was a strata four foot thick, of a brownish soft sand stone. **1768** HAMILTON *Vesuvius* in *Phil. Trans.* LIX. 20 The soil consists of stratas of lavas, ashes, pumice, and now-and-then a thin stratum of good earth.

2. A bed of sedimentary rock, usually consisting of a series of 'layers' or 'laminæ' of the same kind, representing continuous periods of deposition.

The precise application of the term has varied, some geologists having used it as equivalent to 'layer' or 'lamina'. In the collective plural *strata,* which is much the most frequent use, the distinction between the different uses commonly dissappears.

a. *sing.*

1699 J. BREWER in *Phil. Trans.* XXII. 485 This Stratum of green Sand and Oyster-shells is.. nigh 2 foot deep. **1709** T. ROBINSON *Nat. Hist. Westmorld. & Cumb.* v. 27 Flints.. make up no particular Stratum of this Earth, but are a sort of Mundick. **1772** PENNANT *Tours Scot.* (1774) 267 This whole stratum lies in an inclined position. **1804** J. BARROW *Trav. S. Africa* II. 82 In the same stratum.. I discovered several large masses of pyramidal crystals of quartz. **1830** LYELL *Princ. Geol.* I. 203 One stratum, composed of many layers, is of a compact nature and fifteen feet thick; it serves as an excellent building stone. **1863** DANA *Man Geol.* 91 A *stratum,* the collection of layers of one kind which form a rock as it lies between beds of other kinds... A stratum may consist of many layers. **1872** JENKINSON *Engl. Lake Distr.* (1879) 36 When ascending from Long Sleddale the stratum of limestone is observed in the gill on the left.

b. pl. *strata.*

1671 H. O. tr. *Steno's Prodr. Diss. Solids* 37 To the Sediments of Fluids do belong the Strata or Beds of the Earth. **1695** WOODWARD *Nat. Hist. Earth* (1702) 29 Shells.. fell to the bottom at the same time that the Chalky Particles did, and so were entombed in the Strata of Chalk. **1706** PHILLIPS (ed. Kersey), *Strata*.. the Layers or Beds of different kind of Earthy Matter, that lie one over another without any regular Order, in the most part of the whole Globe of Earth. **1730–46** THOMSON *Autumn* 1359 The mineral strata there, Thrust blooming thence the vegetable world. **1738** T. STORY in *Mem. J. Logan* (1851) 155 Scarborough.. at whose high cliffs and the great varieties of strata therein and their present positions, I further learned and was confirmed in some things. **1784** COWPER *Task* III. 151 Some drill and bore The solid earth, and from the strata there Extract a register by which [etc.]. **1842** *Penny Cycl.* XXIII. 105/2 In Geology, both the separately deposited layers of rock, and the rocks formed of these similar layers, accumulated together, have received the name of strata. **1847** TENNYSON *Princess* iii. 154 That afternoon the Princess rode to take The dip of certain strata to the North. **1875** DAWSON *Dawn of Life* ii. 9 The.. Laurentian strata.. are seen to underlie.. the Silurian beds. **1877** HUXLEY *Physiogr.* ii. 24 The successive layers of rock, or as they are technically called *strata.*

c. pl. *stratums.* (Not in scientific use.)

1843 MR. & MRS. S. C. HALL *Ireland* III. 170 The black irregular rocks, the stratums of many colours and the *débris* of a sloping bank.

3. A region of the atmosphere, of the sea, or of a quantity of fluid, assumed for purposes of calculation as bounded by horizontal planes.

a. *sing.*

1796 H. HUNTER tr. *St. Pierre's Study Nat.* (1799) I. 38 That vast stratum of frozen air which surrounds our Globe, about a league above the surface. **1834** MRS. SOMERVILLE *Connex. Phys. Sci.* §xiii. (1849) 113 Sir James Ross, who found a stratum of constant temperature in the ocean at a depth depending on the latitude. **1842** GROVE *Lect. Progr. Phys. Sci.* 18 No action is perceptible in the intervening stratum of liquid. **1850** RANKINE *Misc. Sci. Papers* (1881) 22 A portion of a spherical stratum of atmosphere surrounding an atomic centre. **1877** HUXLEY *Physiogr.* vi. 84 The carbonic acid.. would tend to settle down in a stratum near the ground.

b. pl. *strata.*

1787 *Crit. Rev.* LXIV. 302 It was found that the change really arose from the drier air above, mixing with the inferior strata. **1812–16** PLAYFAIR *Nat. Phil.* (1819) I. 245 If, therefore, the heights from the surface be taken increasing in arithmetical progression, the densities of the strata of air will decrease in geometrical progression. **1854** TOMLINSON tr. *Arago's Astron.* 163 But gases being extremely compressible, the lower strata.. are necessarily more compressed. **1858** JENYNS *Observ. Meteorol.* 204 The temperature of the lower strata of the air.

4. *Biol.* etc. One of a number of layers composing an animal or vegetable tissue.

a. *sing.*

1846 G. E. DAY tr. *Simon's Anim. Chem.* II. 99 If a normal stratum of epithelium is no longer formed,.. the changes impressed on the fluid must be different from those which it would undergo during the ordinary secretion of healthy mucus. **1866** *Treas. Bot.* 1102/2 *Stratum,* a layer of tissue. **1884** BOWER & SCOTT *De Bary's Phaner.* 554 The cells of the endodermis.. often form the outermost stratum of the cork-layer. **1899** *Allbutt's Syst. Med.* VIII. 600 The collagenous tissue of the uppermost stratum of the cutis may now undergo a distinct sclerotic change.

b. pl. *strata.*

1741 A. MONRO *Anat.* (ed. 3) 3 The.. *Strata* or Layers, of which the *Periosteum* is composed. **1860** LAYCOCK *Mind & Brain* II. 359 Under certain circumstances the [ganglionic] cells are arranged in layers or strata. **1884** BOWER & SCOTT *De Bary's Phaner.* 83 The strata or crusts are superposed on the cuticle in the form of a continuous membrane.

5. *Electr.* (Cf. STRATIFICATION 2 d.)

1856 T. R. ROBINSON in *Proc. R. Irish Acad.* VI. 428 The meniscoid strata were at first very distinct, but faded away in a few seconds.

6. *fig.* in various applications (chiefly after sense 2): A portion of a body of institutions, beliefs, etc., proceeding from one historical period or representing one stage of development; a level or grade in social position or culture; the part of a population belonging to a particular level in station or education, as *social stratum*; and the like. **a.** *sing.*

1807 G. CHALMERS *Caledonia* I. 229 *note,* The first stratum of names on the map of North-Britain is Cambro-British;.. the second stratum.. superinduced on the former, was the Gaelic. **1850** CARLYLE *Latter-day Pamph.* iii. 39 From the lowest and broadest stratum of Society.. there was born,.. a Robert Burns. **1862** STANLEY *Jew. Ch.* (1877) I. xix. 369 In modern times they have practically been drawn from one stratum of society. **1870** MAX MÜLLER *Sci. Relig.* (1873) 318 Odin belongs to the same stratum of mythological thought as Dyaus in India. **1877** MISS YONGE *Cameos* I. ii. 17 The Caroline race were Franks,.. a mixture of Roman and Gallic, with only an upper stratum of the true Frank. **1886** T. H. S. ESCOTT in P. Bailey *Leisure & Class in Victorian England* (1978) iii. 58 A social movement.. is now steadily progressing on a lower social stratum. **1902** L. STEPHEN *Stud. Biogr.* IV. vii. 261 The habit of reading spread to a lower social stratum. **1914** *Blackw. Mag.* Oct. 505/2 He sprang from that stratum of the middle class.. which owes its immediate fortunes to commercial enterprise. **1927** P. SOROKIN *Social Mobility* 141 There has never existed a society in which vertical social mobility has been absolutely free and the transition from one social stratum to another has had no resistance. **1973** E. BERCKMAN *Victorian Album* 50 This murder.. must have been in too drab a social stratum.. to attract even contemporary attention.

b. pl. *strata.*

1850 CARLYLE *Latter-day Pamph.* iii. 38 In the lowest broad strata of the population.. are produced men of every kind of genius. **1867** A. BARRY *Sir C. Barry* ii. 43 The superimposed strata of Greek, Roman, Saracenic and Gothic architecture. **1876** BIRCH *Monum. Hist. Egypt* 15 Leaving as open questions the contemporaneity or sequence of the dynasties, but recognising them as representing strata of time. **1890** BLACKIE *Ess. Mor. & Soc. Int.* 298 In fact a large proportion of the upper strata of English is merely Latin and Greek in a very thin disguise. **1890** W. JAMES *Princ. Psychol.* I. iv. 121 Habit.. keeps different social strata from mixing. **1913** SIR T. BARLOW in *Times* 7 Aug. 8/2 The.. study of small variations in the ordinary diets of adults and children.. in different social strata and in different countries. **1937** R. H. LOWIE *Hist. Ethnological Theory* vi. 57 It is hard to understand how Morgan could have missed the social strata of the caste-ridden Oceanians. **1968** G. P. MITCHELL *Dict. Sociol.* 182 In theory social strata are made up of individuals and families.

c. *Statistics.* Each of the groups into which a population is divided in the technique of stratified sampling.

1920 A. L. BOWLEY *Elements of Statistics* (ed. 4) II. iv. 332 It may happen.. that the universe consists of different regions or strata in which the chances are different, and the question arises whether we should proceed at random.., or.. partially arrange the choice so as to take the same proportion out of each region or stratum. **1952** A. HALD *Statistical Theory with Engin. Applications* xvii. 495 In sampling investigations of industrial products stratified sampling is often useful. For example, when a lot is being loaded a random sample of items may be taken from every truckload, the truckloads being the strata. **1960** *Jrnl. Amer. Statistical Assoc.* LV. 105 If the sample is allocated to the strata in proportion to the number of elements in the strata, it is virtually certain that the stratified sample estimate will have a smaller variance than a random sample of the same size. **1980** HAWKINS & WEBER *Statistical Analysis* xi. 295 Stratified sampling is appropriate only if the variable of interest is relatively homogeneous within strata and heterogeneous among strata.

¶**d.** The form *strata* used as sing., with pl. *stratas.*

1937 *Times Lit. Suppl.* 27 Nov. 910/2 He marries a penniless girl of a lower social strata than himself. **1946** M. PEAKE *Titus Groan* 159 The mixture of cunning and honesty which he did not yet perceive to be a still deeper strata of Steerpike's cleverness. *Ibid.* 177 The abstract language with which they communicated their dizzy stratas of conjecture. **1971** *Timber Trades Jrnl.* 14 Aug. 20/2 The era of the family business is now a complex structure of top, middle and lower stratas. **1980** *Good Housekeeping* Nov. 181/4 After this comes a strata of accessories.

7. a. *attrib.* (in pl. form.)

1814 JAMESON in *Mem. Wernerian Soc.* II. 223 Two contiguous portions of rock, whether separated by strata-streams or not. **1839** URE *Dict. Arts* 748 The flat veins, or strata veins, seem to be nothing else than expansions of the matter of the vein between the planes of the strata. **1842** SELBY *Brit. Forest Trees* 351 The strata-like form the branches naturally assume. **1955** T. H. PEAR *Eng. Social Differences* i. 23 Within the wholesale trade there are interesting strata-differences. **1962** *Conveyancing (Strata Titles) Act* in *Statutes of New S. Wales 1961* 129 'Strata plan' means a plan which.. shows the whole or any part of the land comprised therein as being divided into two or more strata, whether or not any such stratum is divided into two or more lots. **1977** [see b below]. **1982** *Polit. Sci. Q.* XCVII. 482 The manipulation of ethnicity or of strata-local forces.

b. (in sing. form.)

1955 T. H. PEAR *Eng. Social Differences* vi. 144 Neighbouring families for whom class-consciousness.. was usually submerged below stratum-consciousness. **1977** *Dædalus* Fall 73 Country-wide strata consciousness and a less pronounced stratum formation of ethnic, religious, or regional elements.

c. Special Combs.: **strata-bound** *a.*, confined to a single stratum or group of strata; **strata title** *Austral.* and *N.Z.*, the freehold or leasehold of or title to a stratum or storey (or more than one) of a building.

1962 *Econ. Geol.* LVII. 272 It is.. reasonable to expect that a majority of strata-bound ore fields will be readily explainable on explicit grounds of tectonic history. **1979** *Nature* 15 Nov. 247/1 Uranium mineralisation, for the most part, is strata-bound and occurs in breccia matrix and vugs. **1962** *Statutes of New S. Wales 1961* 128 (*title*) Conveyancing (strata titles) act. **1977** *Courier-Mail* (Brisbane) 7 Apr. 17/2 Many strata title (home units) property owners risk serious financial loss because of inadequate legal insurance on their units. **1977** *N.Z. Herald* 5 Jan. 2-16/2 (Advt.), Home unit, Avondale, as new, strata title, 2 brms, internal garage.

stratus ('strɑːtəs, 'streɪtəs). *Meteorol.* [a. L. *strātus* (*u* stem), f. *strā-*, *sternĕre* to spread, lay down. (See quot. 1803, and cf. STRATUM.)] One of the simple forms of cloud, having the appearance of a broad sheet of nearly uniform thickness, usually existing at low elevations.

1803 L. HOWARD *Modif. Clouds* (1865) 4 *Stratus,* a widely extended, continuous, horizontal sheet, increasing from below upward. *footn.* This application of the Latin word *stratus* is a little forced. But the substantive *stratum,* did not agree in its termination with the other two [*cirrus, cumulus*], and is besides already used in a different sense even on this subject, e.g. a stratum of clouds; yet it was desirable to keep the derivation from the verb *sterno,* as its significations agree so well with the circumstances of this Cloud. **1831** BREWSTER *Nat. Magic* vi. (1833) 141 A thin stratus or 'fog bank' appeared in the same quarter. **1858** JENYNS *Observ. Meteorol.* 199 Hence a mist will often appear in damp places, while in others, where dews are of constant occurrence, a mist, *i.e. stratus,* may be a rare thing. **1882** PIDGEON *Engineer's Holiday* II. 216 Extending.. a considerable distance towards the zenith, lay a thick horizontal layer of stratus, above which was blue.

attrib. **1860** TYNDALL *Glac.* I. xviii. 122 A gray stratus cloud had drawn itself across the neck of the Matterhorn. **1883** *Harper's Mag.* May 888/2 In that low mass of stratus clouds which overhung the sunset there was now a wild convulsion.

strauch(t: see STRAIGHT, STRETCH *v.*

†**straught,** *a. Obs.* [Aphetic f. DISTRAUGHT *a.*] Distraught, out of one's mind. Also, bereft *of* (one's wits, mind).

a **1529** SKELTON *Agst. Ven. Tongues* Wks. 1843 I. 133 My scoles are not for vnthriftes vntaught, For frantick faitours half mad and half straught. **1530** PALSGR. 429/2, I am straught, *je suis enragé.* He is straught, *il est enragé.* **1566** PAINTER *Pal. Pleas.* (1569) I. 147 He seemed rather to bee a man straught.. than lyke one that had hys wittes. **1566** DRANT *Horace, Sat.* I. vi. Dvb, The moste of men, wil thincke me straughte of witte. **1567** GOLDING *Ovid's Met.* VI. (1593) 150 Betweene his duskie wings he caught Orithya straught for feare. **1579–80** NORTH *Plutarch, Agesilaus* (1595) 668 Seely women also.. ranne vp and downe, as straught of their wits. **1584** R. SCOT *Discov. Witchcr.* VII. xi. 144 Being now straught of mind, desperate, and a verie foole. *c* **1600** DAY *Begg. Bednall Gr.* IV. i. (1881) 72 Stumbling? what! stumbling? I think the fellow be straught.

Hence †'**straughtness,** '**straughtedness.**

1530 PALSGR. 277/1 Straugh[t]nesse madnesse, *amence.* **1552** HULOET, Strawghtnes of the mynd by reason of fear, *panicus.* **1583** GOLDING *Calvin on Deut.* xxviii. 979/2 For vntill God haue brought vs to this straughtednesse, we be altogether blockish. [Fr. *Car iusques à tant que Dieu nous ait amenez à ceste furie, nous sommes stupides du tout.*]

straught: see STRAIGHT *a.* and *v.*, STRETCH *v.*

strauhe, strauht, obs. ff. STRAW, STRAIGHT.

strauht(e, obs. pa. t. and pa. pple. of STRETCH *v.*

straunc(h)e, straung(e, obs. ff. STRANGE.

straunde, obs. form of STRAND *sb.*[1]

straungeour, -er(e, etc., obs. ff. STRANGER.

straungle, obs. form of STRANGLE *v.*

Straussian ('straʊsɪən), *a.* and *sb.* [f. the name of (1) the German composer Richard *Strauss* (1864–1949), or (2) the Viennese family of composers of whom Johann *Strauss* II (1825–99) was the foremost member + -IAN.]

A. *adj.* **1.** Of, pertaining to, or characteristic of the music of Richard Strauss.

1910 G. B. SHAW in *Nation* 19 Mar. 969/2 To those of us who are neither deaf nor blind nor anti-Straussian critics (which is the same thing), she was a superb Elektra. **1949** A. HUXLEY *Ape & Essence* ii. 24 Flawlessly pure of all Wagnerian lubricity and bumptiousness, all Straussian vulgarity! **1954** *Grove's Dict. Mus.* (ed. 5) VIII. 129/1 He wrote.. some fine songs for voice and orchestra,.. of which 'Hymnus' and 'Gesang der Apollopriesterin' (Op. 33) are the most characteristic of Straussian rapture. **1963** *Times* 8 Mar. 15/3 Earlier in the work he had not shown the same ability to sustain a true Straussian intensity of feeling. **1979** *Guardian* 26 Mar. 14/5 It was no disappointment to find Italian verismo rather than Straussian opulence.

2. Of, pertaining to, or characteristic of the music of the Strauss family.

1935 *Punch* 8 May 561/2 The scheme and time of the play.. has prevented him from suggesting or—except in a brief snatch of the *Blue Danube*—borrowing from the glories of the Straussian epoch. **1958** *Listener* 21 Aug. 285/1 The commonplace of a Straussian waltz.

B. *sb.* An admirer of Richard Strauss; an exponent of his music.

1959 *Times* 17 Nov. 16/4 With that renowned Straussian, Mr. Rudolf Kempe, now.. available to take charge, the London Symphony Orchestra assembled all its forces on

Sunday..so that the second half of the programme could be devoted to *Also sprach Zarathustra*. **1967** *Guardian* 13 June 7/3 Straussians all think it [sc. *Die Frau ohne Schatten*] *the* masterpiece. **1977** *Gramophone* June 64/1 A lack of sensuousness and ardour in the first half of the work is something which many Straussians won't readily forgive.

strauth, obs. pa. pple. of STRETCH *v.*

†'**stravagant**, *a.* and *sb.* *Obs.* [ad. It. *stravagante*, or aphetic ad. med.L. *extrāvagantem*: see EXTRAVAGANT.]

A. *adj.* Irrelevant, unsuitable, extraordinary: = EXTRAVAGANT *a.* 4, 5, 6.

1565 HARDING *Let.* in Strype *Ann. Ref.* (1709) I. App. xxx. 57, I made no foretalk to your strauagant Chalenge, till [etc.]. **1579** FENTON *Guicciard.* 823 Of which stravagant manner of dealing not being hable to excuse themselves by any reason, they attributed all to the working of the holy Ghost. **1613** CHAPMAN *Mask Inns of Court* (1614) A 3 The Torch-bearers habits were likewise of the Indian garb, but more strauagant then those of the Maskers.

B. *sb.* **a.** Something irrelevant. **b.** A vagrant.

1565 T. STAPLETON *Fortr. Faith* 8 To go to the matter alleaged directly without idle twanges, and rouing strauagants from the purpose. **1592** *Nobody & Somebody* C i, I was carried afore the Constable but yesterday, and they tooke mee vp for a strauagant. **1608** DAY *Hum. out of Breath* III. i. (1860) 31 *Flo.* Away you sharking companion. *Asp.* How? *Flo.* Wandring strauagant, that like a droane flies humming from one land to another.

stravaig (strə'veɪg), *v.* Chiefly *Sc.*, *north*, and *Ir.* Also **stravague**, **stravag(e**. [? Aphetic form of EXTRAVAGE *v.* (? for **extravague*).] *intr.* To wander about aimlessly. Also in general literary use, and occas. *trans.* with *road* as obj. Hence **stra'vaiging** (-gɪŋ) *vbl. sb.* and *ppl. a.* Also **stra'vaiger** (-gə(r)).

1802 [see VAGUE *v.*[1] 1 *β*]. **1821** GALT *Ann. Parish* xiii, Lady Macadam's hens and fowls..being great stravaggers for their meat. **1825** J. WILSON *Noctes Ambr.* Wks. 1855 I. 25 The belts o' plantations are no very wide nor the sherubberies stravagin awa' into wild mountainous regions o'..breckans. **1825** BROCKETT *N.C. Gloss.*, *Stravaiging*, strolling about. **1831** S. LOVER *Legends & Stories of Ireland* p. xxiv, *Stravaig*, to ramble. **1842** J. WILSON *Chr. North* III. 293 Those heartless clouds that keep stravaigging over mountain-tops. **1871** BLACK *Dau. Heth* xxiv, 'Nonsense!' said Lady Drum. 'Would you have an old woman like me stravaiging about the shore by myself?' **1876** C. M. YONGE *Three Brides* I. xvi. 279 Her own children, which it is a shame to see stravaging about the place! **1884** ANNIE SWAN *Carlowrie* x. 152 Miss Ritchie's peacock had taken what she called a stravagin' turn. **1887** HENLEY *Villon's Straight Tip* 23 At any graft, no matter what, Your merry goblins soon stravag. **1901** G. DOUGLAS *Ho. with Green Shutters* 26 Where have you been stravaiging to? **1905** A. I. SHAND *Days of Past* xiv. 275 Those stravaiging cottage cats. **1929** E. BOWEN *Last September* I. viii. 93 They do be stravaging about always and not contented at all. **1934** T. E. LAWRENCE *Let.* 23 Nov. (1938) 830 Visit it, sometime, if you still stravage the roads of England in a great car. **1958** S. BECKETT *From Abandoned Work* 14, I might be sprawling in the sun now sucking my pipe..wondering what there was for dinner, instead of stravaging the same old road in all weathers.

strave, obs. pa. t. of STRIVE *v.*

Stravinskian (strə'vɪnskɪən), *a.* (and *sb.*). Also **Stravinskyan**. [f. the name of *Stravinsky* (see below) + -AN.] Of, pertaining to, or characteristic of the Russian-born composer Igor Fyodorovich Stravinsky (1882–1971) or his music. Also as *sb.* = STRAVINSKYITE.

1925 F. TOYE *Well-Tempered Musician* iii. 74 Stravinsky himself was put up to defend Tchaikowsky, at whom all the Stravinskians..had been constantly sneering for years. **1947** D. MILHAUD in *Stravinsky's Poetics of Music* p. xi, The *Poetics of Music* brings to light the indissoluble relationship between the two aspects of the Stravinskyan temperament: that is, his music and his philosophy. **1958** *Times* 22 Feb. 3/7 Wishart had absorbed his Stravinskian predilection. **1962** *Times* 29 Mar. 8/5 Sir William, whose attitude to critics is Stravinskyan..is ready to forecast critical reactions to his work. **1968** *Listener* 1 Aug. 153/2 Britten's exuberant cantata..is informed by a Stravinskian economy of gesture and dramatic style. **1978** *Gramophone* July 174/1 The second [movement is] a sonata—very Stravinskian yet it could not be by Stravinsky but only by Malcolm Williamson.

So **Stra'vinskyite**, a devotee of Stravinsky's music.

1924 C. GRAY *Survey Contemp. Music* 132 The devotees of the Russian ballet, the Stravinskyites, seek the satisfaction of normal human activities in art. **1949** G. F. KNIGHT in *Penguin Music Mag.* IX. 82 The majority of the musical world divided into two irreconcilable camps: the Stravinskyites and the Anti-Stravinskyites. **1961** *Times* 12 Apr. 6/5 Elsewhere all praise—and a rap on the knuckles for all those Stravinskyites who stayed at home.

straw (strɔː), *sb.*[1] Forms: *α.* 1 **stréaw**, **strau**, 3 **strauȝ**, **strauue**, 3–7 **strawe**, 5 **strauhe**, **strawh**, 4– **straw**; *β.* 1 **stréow**, **streu(w**, **strew** (*pl.* **strewu**); *γ.* 1 **stré**, 1–5, 9 *dial.* **stree**, 4–6 **stre** (*pl.* **stren**), 5–6, 8–9 *dial.* **strey**, 7–9 *dial.* **strea**, **streea**, **streay** (7 *pl.* **strease**); *δ.* 3–9 *north.* **stra** (5 *pl.* **strase**), 6–7 *Sc.* **strai**, **stray** (*pl.* **strais**), 6–9 *Sc.* **strae**; *ε.* 5 **strowh**, 5–6 *Sc.* and *north.* **stro**, **stroye**, 7 **stroe**, 5–7 **strowe**. [Com. Teut. (not found in Gothic): OE. *stréaw* neut. = OFris. *strê* (NFris. *strâi*, *stre*, WFris. *strie*), OS., MLG., MDu. *strô* (Du. *stroo*) neut., OHG., MHG. *strô* neut., gen. *strawes*, *strôwes* (mod.G. *stroh* masc.), ON. *strá* neut. (Sw. *strå*, Da. *straa*):—OTeut. **strawo-*, f. root **strau-*: *streu-*: see STREW *v.*

The ON. form *strá* is prob. in part the source of the Sc. and Northern *stra*, *strae*, etc. and of the North Midland and Northern *stro*, though in some dialectal areas the normal phonetic development from OE. would issue in forms coincident with these. The Scottish *stro* of the 15–16th c. is a literary alteration of *stra*.]

I. *Collective sing.*

1. a. The stems or stalks (*esp.* dry and separated by threshing) of certain cereals, chiefly wheat, barley, oats, and rye. Used for many purposes, e.g. as litter and as fodder for cattle, as filling for bedding, as thatch, also plaited or woven as material for hats, beehives, etc.

c **1000** ÆLFRIC *Gram.* iv. (Z.) 8 *Foenum*, gærs oððe streow [*v.rr.* streaw, strau]. *Ibid.* xiii. (Z.) 83 *Foenum* strew [*v.rr.* streow, streaw, strau]. *c* **1000** *Sax. Leechd.* III. 114 Bærne þanne streuw. *c* **1000** ÆLFRIC *Hom.* I. 404 Sume hi cuwon heora ȝescy,..sume streaw. *a* **1300** *Cursor M.* 7204 His bandes al he brac in tua, Als þai had ben made bot on stra. *c* **1374** CHAUCER *Troylus* III. 859 How is this candele in the strawe y-falle? **1377** LANGL. *P. Pl.* B. XIV. 233 Whan he streyneth hym to streche þe strawe is his schetes. *c* **1380** WYCLIF *Sel. Wks.* I. 119 Swepte as þe pament from hilyyng of stree. **1388** —— *Isa.* lxv. 25 A lioun and an oxe schulen ete stree. **1422** YONGE tr. *Secreta Secret.* 239 Suche a stomake is likenyd to the litill fire, that may brande but flex or stree. *c* **1440** LYDG. *Horse, Goose & Sheep* 196 As pilwes been to chaumbris agreable, So is hard strauhe litteer for the stable. *c* **1450** CAPGRAVE *St. Gilbert* vi. 71 On his bed had our maystir Gilbert..no bolstering but strawe. *c* **1460** *Oseney Reg.* (1913) 144 þe chaffe schall Abide togedur with þe strow to me and to my heyres. *c* **1480** HENRYSON *Test. Cresseid* 439 And for thy Bed tak now ane bunche of stro [*rime-words* tho, ago]. **1491** in *Acta Dom. Concil.* (1839) 222/1 For hay & stra price xxiiij s. **1501** *Acc. Ld. High Treas. Scot.* II. 124 Item, ..to James Dog to by stray to the Kingis chamir in Invernes, xvj d. **1523–34** FITZHERB. *Husb.* §6 Horses..must haue.. strawe for lytter. **1549** in Feuillerat *Revels Edw. VI* (1914) 43 For Strawe to Stuff the baggs, iiij[d]. *a* **1568** A. SCOTT *Poems* (S.T.S.) xxxv. 19 Lyk dust and stro [*rime-word* no] Bene vaneist w[t] the wind. **1579** in *3rd Rep. Hist. MSS. Comm.* 402/2 Yeirlie ane wedder, ane creill full of peittis and ane sled full of stray. **1593** *Extracts Munic. Acc. Newcastle* (1848) 31 Paide for stro, candle, drinke, and stringe, which bounde the semynaries armes before he was executed, 9*d.* **1637** MILTON *Lycidas* 124 Their lean and flashy songs Grate on their scrannel Pipes of wretched straw. **1657** LAMONT *Diary* (Maitl. Club) 100 None should be obleidged to bring any oatts to the English troupe horses any longer, but only stra hireafter. **1688** HOLME *Armoury* II. 173/2 Blend Fodder, is Hay and Straw mixed. *c* **1730** BURT *Lett. N. Scot.* (1754) II. xxiii. 233 He dy'd at Hame, lik an auld Dug, on a Puckle o' Strae. **1765** *Museum Rust.* IV. 221 The straw of rye is much more valuable, both for thatching, bedding and fodder than the straw of wheat. **1797** MRS. RADCLIFFE *Italian* x, Paolo soon after turned into his bed of straw. **1832** *Veg. Subst. Food Man* 45 The straw of summer wheat is more agreeable to cattle than that produced from winter sowing. **1848** THACKERAY *Van. Fair* xix, She had the street laid knee-deep with straw; and the knocker put by. **1868** *Rep. U.S. Commissioner Agric.* (1869) 417 It [*sc.* wheat] stooled out much more than either, and was uniform in ripeness and length of straw. **1875** W. PATERSON *Notes Milit. Surv.* (ed. 3) 80 Load of straw = 36 trusses each of 36 lbs.

b. *fig.* with reference to the small value of straw in comparison with the grain, or to its ready inflammability.

c **1386** CHAUCER *Man of Law's T.* 603 Me list nat of the chaf or of the stree Maken so long a tale as of the corn. *c* **1400** *Rom. Rose* 6354, I..go thurgh alle regiouns, Seking alle religiouns. But to what ordre that I am sworn, I take the strawe, and lete the corn. **1610** SHAKS. *Temp.* IV. 52 Strongest oathes, are straw To th' fire ith' blood.

†**c.** Thatch, thatched houses. *Obs.*

1665 SIR T. HERBERT *Trav.* (1677) 27 A small Village of Straw unworthy the notice.

d. The colour of straw, a pale brownish-yellow.

1799 in M. Edgeworth *Parent's Assistant* (1800) (ed. 3) VI. 119 Mr. Davis, slate-color and straw. **1897** *Sears, Roebuck Catal.* 231/2 Silk Mitts..in the following colors:.. sky blue, lemon, straw, cardinal. **1923** *Daily Mail* 19 Feb. 5 A full range of new colourings, including Peach, Lemon, Straw, Rose. **1942** *R.A.F. Jrnl.* 3 Oct. 15 A heavy, oily liquid, from straw to black in colour. **1978** A. S. BYATT *Virgin in Garden* xi. 111 Red was defiance, gold avarice, straw plenty. Green was hope, but sea-green was inconstancy.

2. Phrases. **a.** ***to make bricks without straw***: said with allusion to *Exodus* v.

The current form and application of the saying are hardly justified by the narrative. The Israelites were not required to make bricks without straw (which was an indispensable binding material for sun-dried bricks), but to gather the straw for themselves instead of having it furnished to them. The phrase, however, now commonly means '(to be required) to produce results without the means usually considered necessary'. Cf. the accurate use in quot. 1661.

1658 in *Verney Mem.* (1907) II. 79 It is an hard task to make bricks without straw. **1661** DK. ORMONDE in *11th Rep. Hist. MSS. Comm.* App. v. 10 If they will not let that [act] passe..and yet will have us keepe armys, is it not requireing a tale of bricks, without allowing the straw. **1874** L. STEPHEN *Hours in Library* I. vi. 271 It is often good for us to have to make bricks without straw. **1883** MISS M. BETHAM-EDWARDS *Disarmed* i. I. 5 The fact is, you are fast being spoiled. But your task from to-day will be to make bricks without straw. No appeal shall induce me to have pity on you.

b. ***in the straw***: in childbed, lying-in. So ***out of the straw***, recovered after childbearing.

In quot. 1786 the phrase is taken to refer to the practice of laying down straw (to deaden noise) before a house where there is a confinement. It is doubtful whether this was the original meaning, though the practice was common.

a **1661** FULLER *Worthies, Lincs.* (1662) 149 Our English plain Proverb, *De Puerperis*, they are in the Straw; shows Feather-Beds to be of no ancient use amongst the Common sort of our Nation. **1705** [E. WARD] *Hudibras Rediv.* IV. 18 We sipp'd our Fuddle, As Women in the Straw do Caudle. **1772** *Grimston Papers* (MS.), I hope your neighbour, Mrs. G., is safe out of the straw, and the child well. **1786** BURGOYNE *Heiress* I. i, You take care to send [*sc.* cards] to all the lying-in ladies? *Prompt.* At their doors, Madam, before the first load of straw... *Prompt.* (Reading his memorandum as he goes out). Ladies in the straw—Ministers, &c...never a better list [etc.]. **1822** DE QUINCEY *Confess.* (1823) 120 In the phrase of ladies in the straw, 'as well as can be expected'. **1832** MARRYAT *N. Forster* xv, They found the lady *in the straw*.

c. ***in the straw***: (of corn) not yet threshed.

1701 C. WOLLEY *Jrnl. New York* (1860) 59, I paid for two load of Oats in the straw 18 shillings. **1702** *Act 1 Anne* Stat. II. c. 10 §14 All Carts with..Corn in the Straw.

d. ***to run to straw***: see RUN *v.* 69 e.

1659 GAUDEN *Slight Healers* (1660) 89 Physitians that are not by much study..run out to Atheism (as some corn in lusty ground doth to straw and halm). *a* **1722** LISLE *Husb.* (1757) 13 You will find, that in such a case the corn will run out to a straw. **1765** [see RUN *v.* 69 e]. **1857** LIVINGSTONE *Trav.* xii. 215 It..would make corn run entirely to straw.

e. ***man of straw***: (*a*) a person or thing compared to a straw image; a counterfeit, sham, 'dummy'; similarly, ***a face of straw***, etc.; (*b*) an imaginary adversary, or an invented adverse argument, adduced in order to be triumphantly confuted; (*c*) a person of no substance, esp. one who undertakes a pecuniary responsibility without having the means of discharging it; (*d*) a fictitious or irresponsible person fraudulently put forward as a surety or as a party in an action.

1599 *Return fr. Parnass.* I. i. 231 [He] braggs..of his liberalitie to schollers..: but indeed he is a meere man of strawe, a great lumpe of drousie earth. **1615** DANIEL *Hymen's Tri.* II. i. Wks. (1623) 283 Idolatrize not so that Sexe, but hold A man of strawe more then a wife of gold [= Fr. proverb: 'Un homme de paille vaut une femme d'or']. **1624** GATAKER *Transubst.* 92 To skirmish with a man of straw of his owne making. **1652** R. SAUNDERS *Balm to heal Relig. Wounds* 82 He..strikes at randome at a man of straw. **1675** WYCHERLEY *Country Wife* IV. iii. 67, I will not be your drudge by day, to squire your wife about, and be your man of straw, or scare-crow only to Pyes and Jays; that would be nibling at your forbidden fruit. **1677** *2nd Packet Adv. to Men of Shaftesbury* 52, I rather suppose the Some that say so never were men of God's making, but mere men of straw set up by Master Bencher, for a Tryal of his own Skill in Confutation. *a* **1734** NORTH *Exam.* III. vii. (1740) 508 The Verity of all such Suppositions denied, off drops the Vizor, and a Face of Straw appears. **1768–74** TUCKER *Lt. Nat.* (1834) I. 253 What is this but placing the essence of virtue in her outside, making her a man of straw, an empty covering containing nothing within? **1823** 'JON BEE' *Dict. Turf* 167 'Man of straw', a bill-acceptor, without property —'no assets'. **1837** DICKENS *Pickw.* xxi, If the defendant be a man of straw, who is to pay the costs, Sir? **1840** DE QUINCEY *Style* Wks. 1859 XI. 218 It is always Socrates and Crito, or Socrates and Phædrus,..in fact, Socrates and some man of straw or good-humoured nine-pin set up to be bowled down as a matter of course. **1876** L. STEPHEN *Hours in Library* II. ii. 67 But no man can dispense with the aid of a living antagonist, free from all suspicion of being a man of straw. **1885** *Law Times' Rep.* LIII. 484/1 The real plaintiff may assign his interest to a man of straw, and in such a case the court will require security to be given.

†**f.** ***a pad in the straw***: see PAD *sb.*[1] 3. *Obs.*

†**g.** *Mil.* ***for straw***: (see quots.). *Obs.*$^{-0}$

[A rendering of Fr. *à la paille*, from the phrase *aller à la paille*, 'to go in search of straw for the horses', hence 'to be allowed a short interval of rest from carrying arms'.]

1702 *Milit. Dict.* (1704) s.v., For Straw, is a word of command to dismiss the Soldiers when they have grounded their Arms, so that they be ready to return to them upon the first firing of a Musket, or beat of Drum. [Hence **1706** PHILLIPS (ed. Kersey); and many later Dicts.]

†**h.** ***to condemn to straw***: to declare worthy of a madhouse. *Obs.*

1779 JOHNSON *L.P.*, *Dryden* (1868) 163 Virgil would have been too hasty if he had condemned him [Statius] to straw for one sounding line.

3. a. Extended to denote the stalks of certain other plants, chiefly pease and buckwheat. ***poppy straw***: see POPPY *sb.* 8.

c **1325** *Gloss. W. de Bibbesw.* in Wright *Voc.* 156 Pernet dount de pessas [*gloss*] pese stree. **1579** E. K. *Gloss. to Spenser's Sheph. Cal.* 256 Vetchie, of Pease strawe. **1687** A. LOVELL tr. *Thevenot's Trav.* II. 126 These Bottles are covered with the Straw of Canes. **1760** R. BROWN *Compl. Farmer* II. 83 The straw [of buckwheat] is good fodder for cattle. **1795** VANCOUVER *Agric. Essex* 178 To discontinue the practice of burning the straw of coleseed, mustard, coriander, carraway. **1805** R. W. DICKSON *Pract. Agric.* II. 628 The haulm or straw of the potatoe. **1892** *Gardeners' Chron.* 27 Aug. 237/2 Messrs. Carter should have preferred it if the straw [of a pea] had not been so long.

b. *U.S.* Pine needles.

1856 OLMSTED *Slave States* 321 The leaves, or straw, as its foliage [*i.e.* that of the yellow pine] is called here. **1860** WHITMAN *Amer. Feuillage* 36 The ground in all directions is cover'd with pine straw.

c. In plant-names, as ***camel's straw***, ***sea straw***.

1516 *Gt. Herbal* ccclxxxvi. (1529) X iij b, Squinante is an herbe that is called camelles strawe, bycause camelles do eate it. *c* **1711** PETIVER *Gazophyl.* x. 91 Sussex Sea-straw.

4. The straw of wheat or other cereal plants plaited or woven to form a material for hats and bonnets; a kind or variety of this material, or an imitation of it (made, e.g., from paper).

1730 MRS. ELIZ. THOMAS *Metam. Town* (1731) 20 Straw, lin'd with Green, their May-day Hats. **1783** O'KEEFFE *Birth-day* 17 With her stockings green, and her hat of straw. **1859** *Ladies' Cabinet* Nov. 278/1 Plain Dunstable straws continue to be worn. **1895** *Daily News* 20 Mar. 7/1 Paper straws are among the new things... Hats and bonnets made of these straws are inexpensive. **1902** *Daily Chron.* 1 Feb. 8/3 The newest straw resembles the petals of a flower, and is called chrysanthemum straw; also there is more lace straw going to be worn than last year.

II. A single stem of a cereal, etc.

5. a. A stem of any cereal plant, esp. when dry and separated from the grain; also, a piece of such a stem.

c **1200** *Vices & Virtues* 135 Ne lat hie [*Honestas*] nawht ðe hande pleiȝende mid stikke, ne mid strawe. *a* **1225** *Ancr. R.* 296 Þe cwene seide ful soð þet mid one strea brouhte o brune alle hire huses, þet muchel kumeð of lutel. *c* **1374** CHAUCER *Troylus* II. 1745 In titering, and pursuite, and delayes, The folk devyne at wagginge of a stree. **1426** LYDG. *De Guil. Pilgr.* 1837 Lych hornys of a lytell snayl, Wych..for a lytel strawh wyl shrynke. *c* **1450** *Bk. Curtasye* 94 in *Babees Bk.*, Clense not thi tethe..With knyfe ne stre, styk ne wande. **1601** SHAKS. *Jul. C.* I. iii. 108 Those that with haste will make a mightie fire, Begin it with weake Strawes. **1675** OWEN *Indwelling Sin* xvii. (1732) 233 No more Impression ..than Blows with a Straw would give to an Adamant. **1732** POPE *Ess. Man* ii. 276 Behold the child, by Nature's kindly law, Pleas'd with a rattle, tickled with a straw. **1815** J. SMITH *Panorama Sci. & Art* II. 817 The communication may be maintained by any slight tube, as a straw, or a reed. **1897** E. HOWLETT in *W. Andrews' Legal Lore* 92 In some manors the surrender [of lands] is effected by the delivery of a rod, in others of a straw.

transf. **1587** T. NEWTON *Herbal for Bible* xxvii. 150 Another kinde of Reede..hath a long, round and hollowe stalke or strawe, full of knottie ioints.

†**b.** *Collective plural* = sense 1. *Obs.*

1390 GOWER *Conf.* I. 143 In stede of mete gras and stres, ..He syh. *c* **1440** *Pallad. on Husb.* III. 362 With rysshes or with stren me most hem bynde [L. *tunc iunco aut ulmo aut uimine stringimus*]. **1583** *Leg. Bp. St. Androis* 299 Reasing the devill..With..Palme croces, and knottis of strease.

c. *Poet.* = OAT *sb.* 5. *rare.* (Cf. quot. 1637 in 1.)

1588 SHAKS. *L.L.L.* v. ii. 913 When Shepheards pipe on Oaten strawes. **1697** DRYDEN *Virg. Past.* III. 37 Dunce at the best; in Streets but scarce allow'd To tickle, on thy Straw, the stupid Crowd.

d. A straw in the shoe is said to have been the sign by which loafers about the courts of law advertised their readiness to perjure themselves for money. Cf. *straw-shoe* in 14.

1743 FIELDING *Jon. Wild* I. ii, An eminent gentleman, .. who was famous for so friendly a disposition, that he was bail for above a hundred persons in one year. He had likewise the remarkable humour of walking in Westminster-hall with a straw in his shoe.

e. *Bot.*

1776 J. LEE *Introd. Bot.* Explan. Terms 378 Culmus, a Straw, properly the Trunk of Grasses. **1796** WITHERING *Brit. Plants* II. 80 Straws round, and somewhat flattened. **1821** SIR J. E. SMITH *Gram. Bot.* 6 *Culmus*, a Culm or Straw, the peculiar stem of Grasses, is leafy, cylindrical [etc.]. **1839** LINDLEY *Introd. Bot.* I. ii. 84 From the caulis, Linnæus, following the older botanists, distinguished the culmus or straw, which is the stem of Grasses.

f. *Mining.* (See quot.)

1860 *Engl. & For. Mining Gloss., Staffs. Terms* 80 *Straw*, a fine straw filled with powder and used as a fuse. **1886** J. BARROWMAN *Sc. Mining Terms* 65 *Straw*, or *strae*, a fuse composed of a straw filled with gunpowder.

g. A hollow tube (orig. of straw or glass, now usu. paper or plastic) through which a drink is sucked.

1851 *London at Table* III. 52 *Mississippi Punch.* Let them use a glass tube or straw to sip the nectar through. **1860** BARTLETT *Dict. Americanisms* (ed. 3) 90 *Cobbler*,..a drink made of wine, sugar, lemon, and pounded ice, and imbibed through a straw or other tube. **1872** 'A. MERION' *Odd Echoes Oxf.* 21 Come let the mackerel soused be brought,..The cider-cup and straws. **1883** SCHELE DE VERE in *Encycl. Amer.* I. 201/1 With the various drinks invented by Americans came into use the straws—slender tubes of wheat, or even of glass—through which beverages are sucked up, or, as it is called, imbibed. **1888** RUSKIN *Præterita* III. ii. 57, I..saw the Bishop of Oxford taught by Sir Robert Inglis to drink sherry-cobbler through a straw. **1926** 'O. DOUGLAS' *Proper Place* xxxi. 286 She..soon had Alistair supremely happy drinking lemonade through a straw. **1926** [see *soda straw* s.v. SODA[1] 9]. **1953** DYLAN THOMAS in *Listener* 17 Sept. 459/2 They gave him a bottle with a straw. **1967** R. A. WALDRON *Sense & Sense Devel.* vi. 116 A drinking-*straw* is nowadays usually made of plastic. **1982** H. ENGEL *Ransom Game* viii. 45, I settled for a vanilla shake... The straw stood up unaided in..the froth.

h. Used as a means of deciding something by chance (lit. by choosing the shortest (or longest) from among several straws held so as to conceal one end); phr. *to draw a straw* or *straws*, to draw a lot or lots.

1832 [see DRAW *v.* 34]. **1939** WODEHOUSE *Uncle Fred in Springtime* i. 13 It was the person on whom life had thrust the..task who must be considered to have drawn the short straw. **1959** R. BRADBURY *Day it rained Forever* 47 Sundays we draw straws for who wears the suit the extra night.

6. A small particle of straw or chaff, a 'mote'.

c **950** *Lindisf. Gosp.* Matt., Introd. 17 Lytles strees *vel* micles beames. *Ibid.* Matt. vii. 3 Huæt ðonne ȝesiistu stre *vel* mot in eȝo broðres ðines. *c* **1050** *Voc.* in Wr.-Wülcker 405/33 *Fistucam*, strewu, eglan. *c* **1400** *Rule St. Benet* ii. 5 In þi broþir ehe þu ses a stra, And noht a balke in þin aȝen. *c* **1407** LYDG. *Reas. & Sens.* 6084 Awmber..ryght myghty in werkyng..For to drawe to him strawys. **1523-34** FITZHERB. *Husb.* §27 Take good hede, that the sherers of all maner of whyte corne cast not vppe theyr handes hastely, for thanne all the..strawes..flieth ouer his heed. **1639** DU VERGER tr. *Camus' Admir. Events* 99 Amber will draw unto it any manner of strawes except of the hearb Basill. **1750** tr. *Leonardus' Mirr. Stones* 108 Being heated with rubbing, gagates attracts straws and chaff.

7. a. Often used as a type of what is of trifling value or importance, as in ***not to care a straw*** (***two, three straws***), and similar phrases.

c **1290** *St. Michael* 151 in *S. Eng. Leg.* 304 Nis nouþe no man aliue þat hire couþe habbe i-wust so wel, Ne so hire i-fed and hire child þat ne costnede nouȝt a straw3. *a* **1300** *Havelok* 315 He let his oth al ouer-ga, þerof ne yaf he nouth a stra. *c* **1369** CHAUCER *Dethe Blaunche* 718 Socrates..ne counted nat thre strees Of noght that fortune koude doo. *c* **1400** *Ywaine & Gaw.* 2655 By his sar set he noght a stra. *c* **1412** HOCCLEVE *De Reg. Princ.* 1670 Swiche vsage is Not worþ a strawe. *c* **1430** *Pilgr. Lyf Manhode* IV. liii. (1869) 201 Deth, j drede þee nouht a straw. **1513** DOUGLAS *Æneis* XII. xiv. 22 Thou fers fo, Thy fervent words compt I nocht a stro. **1593** SHAKS. *Lucr.* 1021, I force not argument a straw, Since that my case is past the help of law. **1692** R. L'ESTRANGE *Fables* xxix. 29 'Tis not a Straw matter whether the Main Cause be Right or Wrong. **1780** *Mirror* No. 103 An explanation, besides exposing me to their resentment (but that I did not value a straw), would have [etc.]. **1861** HUGHES *Tom Brown at Oxf.* iii, Drysdale, who didn't care three straws about knowing St. Cloud. **1887** *Spectator* 1 Oct. 1304 The British Government..does not care one straw what religion its subjects profess.

†**b.** ***a straw for —***: an expression of contempt.

c **1374** CHAUCER *Troylus* v. 362 A strawe for alle swevenes signifiaunce! *c* **1412** HOCCLEVE *De Reg. Princ.* 622 But straw vnto hir reed! wolde I [etc.]. *c* **1460** *Play Sacram.* 205 Yea yea master a strawe for talis that manot sale. **1513** DOUGLAS *Æneis* I. Prol. 33 Stra for thys ignorant blabring imperfyte Beside thi polyte termis redemyte. *a* **1529** SKELTON *Bouge of Court* 341 Naye, strawe for tales, thou shalte not rule vs. **1549** CHALONER *Erasm. Praise Folly* A j b, In whiche poinct, a strawe for all these cankerd philosophers, and sages, who saie [etc.]. **1562** J. HEYWOOD *Prov. & Epigr.* (1867) 119 Back (quoth the woodcocke): Straw for the (quoth the dawe). **1598** R. BERNARD tr. *Terence* (1607) *Andria* IV. ii, A straw for such as would haue vs two at debate.

†**c.** Used as an exclamation, = rubbish! nonsense! *Obs.*

c **1412** HOCCLEVE *De Reg. Princ.* 1874 Ye straw! let be! *Ibid.* 5191 Straw! be he neuer so harrageous, If he & she shul dwellen in on house, Goode is he suffre. *c* **1520** SKELTON *Magnyf.* 564 Tushe, a strawe! *a* **1529** —— *E. Rummyng* 535 A strawe, sayde Bele, stande vtter, For we haue egges and butter. —— *Manerly Margery* 5 Tully valy, strawe, let be, I say!

d. A trifle; a frivolous ground of quarrel, a trifling difficulty.

1692 [J. WILSON] *Vindic. Carol.* i. 17 Here also he quarrels at Straws. **1782** MISS BURNEY *Cecilia* VI. vii, My passions will not, just now, be irritated by straws. **1828** CARLYLE *Misc.*, *Burns* (1840) I. 367 Mighty events turn on a straw. **1858** TROLLOPE *Dr. Thorne* xxxiii, When he spoke of the difficulties in his way, she twitted him by being overcome by straws.

8. a. In certain proverbs, and allusive senses derived from them. (See quots.)

a. 1748 RICHARDSON *Clarissa* VII. 12 A drowning man will catch at a straw, the Proverb well says. **1823** SCOTT *Quentin D.* xxxv, Love, like despair, catches at straws. **1853** MRS. GASKELL *Ruth* xxx, That hope was the one straw that Mr. Bradshaw clung to. **1908** R. BAGOT *A. Cuthbert* xxv. 331 He had been compelled, however, to suppress both his shame and his pride, and grasp at the straw held out to him.

b. 1848 DICKENS *Dombey* ii, As the last straw breaks the laden camel's back, this piece of underground information crushed the sinking spirits of Mr. Dombey. **1874** S. WALPOLE *Life Perceval* II. vii. 260 The difference about the grant to the Prince was of course only the last straw. The load on Lord Wellesley had been long intolerable. **1897** *Allbutt's Syst. Med.* II. 865 In ordinary cases of the disease there is often some minor exciting cause which acts as a 'last straw'. *Ibid.* VII. 693 Sunstroke may act as the 'last straw'.

c. *a* **1654** J. SELDEN *Table-Talk* (1689) 31 Take a straw and throw it up into the Air, you shall see by that which way the wind is. **1799** W. COBBETT *Porcupine's Works* (1801) X. 161 'Straws' (to make use of Callender's old hackneyed proverb) 'Straws serve to show which way the wind blows.' **1823** BYRON *Don Juan* XIV. viii, You know or don't know that great Bacon saith 'Fling up a straw, 'twill show the way the wind blows.' **1835** LYTTON *Rienzi* II. iii, The Provençal, who well knew how to construe the wind by the direction of straws. **1846** *Fraser's Mag.* XXXIII. 131 This straw shews the peculiar superstitiousness of Johnson's mind. **1852** BRISTED *Five Yrs. Eng. Univ.* (ed. 2) 365 One of the smallest possible straws may be taken as an indication of the direction in which the *aura popularis* now set. **1861** READE *Cloister & H.* lvi, And such straws of speech show how blows the wind. **1915** *Daily News* 28 Dec. 4 Occasional tavern brawls between German and Bulgarian officers are no doubt only straws, but the lesson they point is reinforced by [etc.]. **1927** A. ADAMS *Ranch on Beaver* vii. 99 'As straws tell which way the wind blows,' remarked Sargent, 'this day's work gives us a clean line on these company cattle.' **1939** MADGE & HARRISSON *Britain, by Mass-Observation* ii. 107 Yet through agents in the constituencies, and straws in the wind like West Leicester, came a slightly better indication of popular sentiment. **1960** C. P. SNOW *Affair* xxv. 334 There have been other things, straws in the wind, maybe, which give reason to think that contemporary standards among a new scientific generation are in a process of decline. **1975** *Language for Life* (Dept. Educ. & Sci.) xii. 189 These are straws in the wind. What they indicate is the degree to which learning and the acquisition of language are interlocked. **1983** *Listener* 27 Jan. 3/1 As MPs have already pointed out in the debate, Captain Nick Barker of HMS *Endurance* had detected straws in the wind.

9. In various phrases.

†**a.** ***to turn every straw, leave no straw unturned***: to search everywhere for something lost.

a **1225** *Ancr. R.* 324 He secheð hine anonriht, & to-went euerich strea uort he beo ifunden. **1575** *Gammer Gurton's Needle* I. iv. 12 So see in all the heaps of dust thou leave no straw vnturned.

†**b.** ***to lay a straw***: to stop, desist. ***there a straw!*** = here I will stop. *Obs.*

c **1480** HENRYSON *Orph. & Euryd.* 241 Off sik musik to wryte I do bot dote, Tharfor at this mater a stra I lay. *c* **1550** [G. WALKER] *Manif. Detect. Diceplay* B ij, Well, as to that, there lay a strawe tyll anone, that the matter lede vs to speake more of it. **1568** V. SKINNER tr. *Gonsalvius' Sp. Inquis.* 63 There they were enforced to lay a straw. **1580** G. HARVEY *Three Proper Lett.* iii. 49 You may communicate as much.. as you list,..with the two Gentlemen: but there a strawe, and you loue me: not with any one else, friend or foe. *a* **1600** DELONEY *Gentle Craft* II. iii. Wks. (1912) 157 Nay soft, there lay a straw for feare of stumbling (quoth Robin). **1601** HOLLAND *Pliny* IX. xxxvi. I. 258 If I should lay a straw here, and proceed no further in this discourse of Purples.

†**c.** ***to break a straw*** [= Fr. *rompre la paille*]: to quarrel. *Obs.*

1542 UDALL tr. *Erasm. Apoph.* 61 b, I prophecie..that Plato and Dionysius wil ere many dayes to an ende breake a straw betwene theim.

d. ***to draw, gather, pick straws***: (of the eyes) to be sleepy.

1691 MRS. D'ANVERS *Academia* 36 Their Eyes, by this time all drew Straws. **1694** MOTTEUX etc. *Gentl. Jrnl.* Apr. 84 It growing then towards eleven a clock, the City Ladies Eyes began to draw Straws. **1731-8** SWIFT *Pol. Conversat.* iii. Wks. 1738 VI. 344 *Miss.* Indeed, my Eyes draw Straws (she's almost asleep). **1796** J. WOLCOT (P. Pindar) *Orson & Ellen* v. 125 Their eyelids did not once pick straws. **1825** J. WILSON *Noctes Ambr.* Wks. 1855 I. 29 But would you believe it, my beloved Shepherd, my eyes are gathering straws. **1892** *Illustr. Sporting & Dram. News* 5 Nov. 270/2 'That period—probably two o'clock a.m.—when the eyes of chaperons begin to draw straws'.

e. ***to have straws in one's hair*** (and varr.): to be insane, eccentric, or distracted.

1890 'L. CARROLL' *Nursery 'Alice'* x. 39 That's the March Hare, with the long ears, and straws mixed up with his hair. The straws showed he was mad—I don't know why. Never twist up straws among *your* hair, for fear people should think you're mad!] **1923** WODEHOUSE *Inimitable Jeeves* vii. 72 When your uncle the Duke begins to feel the strain a bit and you find him in the blue drawing-room sticking straws in his hair, old Glossop is the first person you send for. **1925** —— *Carry On, Jeeves!* vi. 142 His [*sc.* a psychiatrist's] outlook on life has become so jaundiced through constant association with coves who are picking straws out of their hair. **1937** D. L. SAYERS *Busman's Honeymoon* xviii. 346 (*heading*) Straws in the hair. **1962** 'S. WOODS' *Bloody Instructions* ix. 100 Dennis Dowling..brought with him an atmosphere of mingled drama and insanity. Antony thought: 'definitely straws in the hair' as soon as he opened the door.

10. Applied to various things shaped like a straw.

†**a.** *pl.* = *jack-straws*, JACK-STRAW 2. *Obs.*

1765 H. WALPOLE *Let. to C'tess Suffolk* 9 July, They (I mean my bones) lie in a heap over one another like the bits of ivory at the game of straws.

b. *Austral.* A walking-stick insect, a phasmid.

1827 HELLYER in *Bischoff's Van Diemen's Land* (1832) 177, I caught one of those curious insects the native straw; it is, I apprehend, a nondescript.

c. A long slender needle.

1862 MORRALL *Hist. Needle-making* 39 The Straws are suited for millinery and light work, and they are often made double length, for sewing fents in Manchester. **1882** CAULFEILD & SAWARD *Dict. Needlework* 464 Straws..are needles of a particular description, used in hat and bonnet making.

d. A slender kind of clay pipe.

1882 *Worc. Exhib. Catal.* III. 28 Tobacco pipes. 10-inch Straws.

e. ***cheese straw***: a thin stick of pastry, containing cheese. ***potato straw***: see POTATO *sb.* 7.

1877 *Cassell's Dict. Cookery* 119. **1892** T. F. GARRETT *Encycl. Cookery* I. 350.

f. A plastic phial in which bull semen is stored for artificial insemination.

1966 *Canad. Jrnl. Compar. Med. & Vet. Sci.* XXX. 109 The use of plastic straws would..encourage volume storage of high quality semen from young sires. *Ibid.* 111/1 Better fertility results can be anticipated with straw packaged semen as compared with that packaged in glass ampoules. **1982** *Sunday Times* 12 Sept. 45/2 The firm..specialises in artificial insemination..in cattle, and expects Pickles [*sc.* a bull] eventually to produce 40,000 'straws', or phials, of semen a year. These straws will be frozen, and sold to cattle breeders all over the world at about £50 a time.

III. 11. A straw hat.

1829 P. EGAN *Boxiana* 2nd Ser. II. 681 *Hall*..went briskly into the ring, and tossed up his Dunstable straw. **1849** *Theatr. Programme* No. 5. 45/2 (Advt.), Charles Vyse, manufacturer of Leghorns and Straws to the British and Foreign Courts.—30 Ludgate-street. **1863** *Baily's Mag.* Jan. 357, I hung my saturated 'straw' upon a bush. **1902** HICHENS *Londoners* 159 I've only brought a straw.

IV. In Combination.

12. ***attrib.*** (passing into *adj.*), with sense 'made of straw'. See also STRAW HAT.

1442 *Will of R. Cottingham* in Fairholt *Costume* II. 387 A blak stra cappe. **1599** HAKLUYT *Voy.* II. II. 83 Their houses are..layde all ouer with strawe-pallets, whereupon they doe both sit in stead of stooles, and lie in their clothes with billets vnder their heads. **1624** in *Archæologia* XLVIII. 148 A strowbasket. **1679** M. RUSDEN *Further Discov. Bees* 2 The keeping of Bees in Box-hives, I call by the name of Colonies, to distinguish them from those kept only in Straw-hives.

1699 EVELYN *Kal. Hort., Nov.* (ed. 9) 134 Cover also your most delicate Stone-fruit and Murals, skreening them with Straw-hurdles. **1707** *Curios. Husb. & Gard.* 257 Cover the Earth with good Straw-Mats. **1848** THACKERAY *Van. Fair* xxii, A straw bonnet with pink ribbons. **1871** MACDUFF *Mem. Patmos* vii. 87 Hovering around the straw-pallet of some Lazarus-beggar.

13. Obvious combinations: **a.** Simple attrib., with the sense 'of or pertaining to straw or straws', as in ***straw-end, -fire, -market, -mow, -pad, pulp, -rick, -stack***; designating a receptacle for straw, as ***straw-barn, -barton, -house, -loft, rack.***

1557 TUSSER *100 Points Husb.* xl, But serue them with haye, while thy straw stoouer last, they loue no more strawe, they had rather to fast. **1591** SYLVESTER *Ivry* 289 When his fury glowes, 'Tis but as Straw-fire. **1657** BILLINGSLY *Brachy-Martyrol.* II. vii. 196 How like you (John) your lodging and your fare? Willis said, Well, had I a straw-pad here. **1662** A. COOPER *Stratologia* VI. 52 A timerous Footman.. In a Straw-mough had hid himself for fear. **1677** MIEGE *Dict. Eng.-Fr.*, A Straw-house, *paillier, le lieu où l'on tient la paille.* **1721** MORTIMER *Husb.* (ed. 5) I. 143 What Corn you stack must be bound up in Sheaves, that so the Ears of the Corn may be turned inward, and the Straw-ends out. *a* **1722** LISLE *Husb.* (1757) 213 Nor did he think it more dangerous than other grass, unless cattle came hungry to it out of the straw-barton. *Ibid.* 215 They.. were foddered in the straw-house. *a* **1747** HOLDSWORTH *Remarks on Virgil* (1768) 323 A street.. formerly called La Rue de Fourrage: where the straw-market was kept. **1812** SIR J. SINCLAIR *Syst. Husb. Scot.* I. 15 The straw-barn.. should be so large as to pile up the straw of two stacks when threshed. **1833** LOUDON *Encycl. Archit.* §1142 Straw-racks are placed in the sheds. **1837** CARLYLE *Fr. Rev.* III. IV. iii, They lie in straw-lofts, in woody brakes. **1886** W. J. TUCKER *E. Europe* 187 Strawstacks, and haystacks, and maizestacks. **1888** CROSS & BEVAN *Text-bk. Paper-Making* vi. 101 The presse-päte system is largely adopted for straw pulp. **1891** HARDY *Tess* xxxii, To inquire how the advanced cows were getting on in the straw-barton. *Ibid.* xlvii, The old men on the rising straw-rick. **1937** E. J. LABARRE *Dict. Paper & Paper-Making Terms* 238/2 Straw pulp is prepared by cooking straw with soda.

b. objective, as ***straw-carrier, -clutching, -cutter, -cutting,*** etc.

1656 COLLOP *Poesis Rediv.* 64 Th' straw-gatherers of Egypt. **1790** W. H. MARSHALL *Midland Counties* II. 443 *Straw-cutter*, a cutter of straw, &c. into chaf. **1805** *Trans. Soc. Arts* XXIII. 51 He purchased a straw-chopper, that the horses corn might be mixed with straw. **1837** CARLYLE *Fr. Rev.* I. v. ix, After all that straw-burning, fire-pumping, and deluge of musketry. **1844** H. STEPHENS *Bk. Farm* II. 196 Straw-cutters are of very various construction. *Ibid.*, Straw-cutting machines. **1869** *Spons' Dict. Engin.* I. 229 The straw-shaker [in a threshing-machine] should pass the straw at the rate of 75 to 80 ft. a-minute. **1884** J. SCOTT *Barn Implem.* (1885) 145 The 'Straw-Elevator,' driven in connection with the threshing-machine. **1891** C. ROBERTS *Adrift Amer.* 23 The straw carrier of the thrashing machine. **1962** L. DAVIDSON *Rose of Tibet* iii. 65 Every bit of straw-clutching, every bit of hope.. was followed instantly by a reaction of dismay.

c. instrumental and parasynthetic, as ***straw-bottomed, -built, -crowned, -roofed, -stuffed, -thatched*** ppl. adjs.

1577 HARRISON *England* III. i. 96/1 in *Holinshed*, In some places it [malt] is dryed with woode alone, or strawe alone.. but of all the strawe dryed is the most excellent. **1598** BP. HALL *Sat.* IV. ii. 14 So rides he mounted on the market-day Vpon a straw-stu'ft pannell, all the way. **1613** [STANDISH] *New Direct. Planting* 21 Cottages and such like Straw-thatched houses. **1667** MILTON *P.L.* I. 773 Thir [*sc.* the bees'] Straw-built Cittadel. **1738** P. WHITEHEAD *Manners* 4 'Midst the mad Mansions of Moor-fields, I'd be A straw-crown'd Monarch, in mock majesty. **1746** J. WARTON *Ode to Fancy* 30 Where never human art appear'd, Nor ev'n one straw-rooft cott was rear'd. **1749** SMOLLETT tr. *Le Sage's Gil Blas* (1750) II. IV. xi. 137 We quitted the hermitage, leaving .. two old straw-bottomed chairs. **1750** GRAY *Elegy* 18 The swallow twitt'ring from the straw-built shed. **1820** KEATS *Cap & Bells* xxix, Many as bees about a straw-capp'd hive. **1824** CAMPBELL *Theodric* 501 Till reaching home, terrific omen! there The straw-laid street preluded his dispair. **1837** DICKENS *Pickw.* xlii, Had he been inspecting a wooden statue or a straw-embowelled Guy Fawkes. **1899** HOWELLS *Ragged Lady* 286 The tubes of straw-barreled Virginia cigars.

14. a. Special comb.: **straw bail** (see quots.); †**straw-bait** = *straw-worm*; **straw ballot** = *straw vote*; **straw basher** *slang*, a straw hat or boater; **straw-bed**, (*a*) a bed or mattress filled with straw, a paillasse; (*b*) = *straw-ride* a; **straw bid, bidder** *U.S.* (see quot.); **straw-blond(e** *a.*, applied to hair of a pale, yellowish blond colour; also *absol.*, this colour; **straw-board**, coarse yellow millboard made from straw pulp, used for making boxes, book-covers, etc.; also, a piece of this material; **straw bond** *U.S.* (see quot. and cf. *straw bail*); **straw boots** *dial.*, wisps of straw tied round the feet and legs; hence as a nickname for the 7th Dragoon Guards; **straw boss** orig. *U.S.*, a subordinate or assistant foreman; **strawboy** *Ir.* (see quots.); **straw braid** = *straw-plait*; **straw-bug** *slang*, a strawberry; †**straw-burn** *v. trans.*, to fertilize (land) by burning straw upon it; hence †**straw-burning** *vbl. sb.*; **straw cat**, the pampas cat (*Cent. Dict.* 1891); †**straw coat**, a coat trimmed with straw; **straw cotton** (see quot.); **strae-dead** *a. Sc.* [cf. ON. *strádauða*], quite dead; **straw-death**, *Sc.* strae- [cf. Norw. *straadaude*, Da. *straadød*], a natural death in one's bed; †**straw deer**, an alleged name for the hare; †**straw-device**, a worthless or harmless device; **straw-drain**, a drain filled with straw (Webster 1828–32); **straw-driver**, ? one who practises horses on a straw-ride; **straw-dry** *a.*, as dry as straw, very dry; **straw-dynamite** (see quot.); **straw embroidery** (see quot. 1882); **straw-fiddle**, a xylophone in which the wooden bars are supported on rolls of twisted straw; **straw-foot**: see HAY-FOOT; **straw-fork**, a pitchfork; **straw-gold**, the colour of straw; = sense 1 d above; **straw-knife**, a knife used for cutting and splitting straw; **straw-laths**, *pl.* the laths on which straw is fastened in thatching; **straw-like** *a.*, resembling straw; *fig.* light or worthless as straw; **strawline**, a light rope used to pull a heavier one into position, esp. in *Logging*; **straw-man**, (*a*) a figure of a man made of straw; (*b*) a 'man of straw' (Webster 1911); **straw-mote** *dial.*, a single stalk of straw; **straw-necked** *a.*, having straw-like feathers on the neck; designating an Australian ibis (see quot.); **straw-needle**, a long thin needle used for sewing together straw braids (*Cent. Dict.*); cf. 10 c; **straw-pale** *a. rare*$^{-1}$, as pale as straw; **straw paper**, paper made from straw bleached and pulped; **straw plait, plat**, a plait or braid made of straw, used for making straw hats, etc.; hence **straw-plaiter**; **straw-plaiting** *vbl. sb.* and *gerund*; also *concr.*, an article made of straw plait; **straw poll** orig. *U.S.* = *straw vote*; **straw potatoes**, very thinly cut potato chips; **straw ride**, (*a*) a track laid with straw on which horses are exercised in winter; (*b*) *U.S.* 'a pleasure-ride in the country, taken in a long wagon or sleigh filled with straw, upon which the party sit' (*Cent. Dict.*); **straw ring**, a ring of plaited straw used to support a round-bottomed vessel in an upright position; **straw rope**, a rope made of twisted straw, used e.g. to secure thatching; also *attrib.*; †**straw-shoe**, a name given to a hanger-on of the law-courts (to be known from his having a straw sticking out of his shoe) who was prepared to swear to anything wanted; **straw-splitter**, one who makes over-nice distinctions, a quibbler; similarly **straw-splitting** *vbl. sb.* and *ppl. a.* (see SPLIT *v.* 5 b and cf. HAIR-SPLITTER, -SPLITTING); **straw-stem**, a wine-glass stem pulled out of the substance of the bowl; hence, a wine-glass having such a stem (*Cent. Dict.*); **straw tick** *U.S.* [TICK *sb.*^{2}], a straw-filled mattress; **straw vote** orig. *U.S.*, an unofficial vote taken in order to indicate the relative strength of opposing candidates or issues; **straw wine**, a luscious wine made from grapes dried or partly dried in the sun on straw; **straw wisp**, a small bundle or twist of straw; also *fig.*; hence **straw-wisped** *a.*, enwreathed with a straw wisp; †**straw woad**, some variety of woad; **straw-work**, work done in plaited straw; **straw-worm**, the caddis-worm; **straw-yellow** *sb.* and *a.* = STRAW-COLOUR, -COLOURED. Also STRAW YARD.

1853 *N. & Q.* Ser. I. VII. 86/1 *Straw bail is, I believe, a term still used by attorneys to distinguish insufficient bail from 'justifiable' or sufficient bail. **1859** BARTLETT *Dict. Amer.* (ed. 2) 455 *Straw bail*, worthless bail; bail given by 'men of straw', i.e. persons who pretend to the possession of property, but have none. **1932** *Straw ballot [see *straw poll* below]. **1967** *Canad. Ann. Rev. 1966* 63 RIN.. polled 27·7 per cent of the vote in a Université de Montréal straw ballot. **1901** *Straw basher [see BASHER^2]. **1931** A. J. CRONIN *Hatter's Castle* II. xii. 421 A stiff, board-like straw-basher. **1632** G. SANDYS *Ovid's Met.* xv. Notes 520 So Cod-bates, and *Straw-bates which ly vnder water [turn] into May-flies. **1585** HIGINS *Junius' Nomencl.* 247/1 *Culcita stramentitia*,.. a *straw bed, or pad of straw. **1671** WOODHEAD *St. Teresa* II. 263 The Straw-bed, the ordinary Bed of the Discalced. **1856** 'STONEHENGE' *Brit. Sports* II. I. ix. 352/1 Some [colts] being at once physicked, and exercised afterwards upon straw-beds, &c. **1889** FARMER *Americanisms*, **Straw bid*, a worthless bid; one not intended to be taken up. **1928** E. O'NEILL *Strange Interlude* I. 25 Her *straw-blond hair, framing her sunburned face, is bobbed. **1973** A. HUNTER *Gently French* v. 47 Her hair was a warm straw blonde. **1850** *Rep. Commissioner Patents 1849* (U.S. Patent Office) 305 [The] said process is peculiar to the use of *strawboard. **1862** *Harper's Mag.* June 135/1 He was making a personal examination of straw-board shoes provided for those who have gone to be soldiers. **1875** KNIGHT *Dict. Mech.*, Straw-board. **1881** GREENER *Gun* 409 In the said slots were placed sheets of straw-board of uniform texture and thickness. **1885** G. F. GREEN in Rattray & Mill *Forestry & Forest Products* xviii. 474 Wood-pulp boards, straw-boards, and mill-boards are sometimes referred to as 'paste-boards'. **1956** H. WILLIAMSON *Methods Bk. Design* xix. 321 Millboards are harder and more solid than strawboards. **1889** *Century Dict.* s.v. *Bond*, **Straw bond*, a bond upon which either fictitious names or the names of persons unable to pay the sum guaranteed are written as names of sureties. **1715** tr. *C'tess D'Anois' Wks.* 493 Admiral Sharp-Cap dispatcht away John Prattle-Box, Courier in Ordinary of the Closet, with his *Straw-Boots [*botté de paille*] to inform the King. **1832** D. VEDDER *Orcadian Sk.* Poems, etc. (1878) 298 His legs were completely enveloped in twisted straw, generally known by the name of 'strae boots'. **1879** *All the Year Round* 5 Apr. 370/1 The Seventh [Dragoon Guards] has been known indifferently as the Black Horse,.. and as the Virgin Mary's Guard; but its more popular pseudonym is the Straw Boots. **1894** W. H. CARWARDINE *Pullman Strike* ix. 117 These employees.. had been so ground between the upper millstone of 'low wages' and the nether millstone of 'high rents', the continued oppression of the '*straw bosses', [etc.]. **1915** S. LEWIS *Trail of Hawk* II. xiii. 132 He had laughed away the straw boss who tried to make him go ask for a left-handed monkey-wrench. **1945** 'N. SHUTE' *Most Secret* viii. 172 Them Frenchies won't work right without they have a straw-boss. **1976** L. ST. CLAIR *Fortune in Death* x. 98 Dimestores, cafeterias, moving to a new job.. every time some greasy straw boss ran his hand up my skirt. **1894** C. R. BROWNE in *Proc. R. Irish Acad.* 3rd Ser. III. 352 Mr. Michael Lavelle.. informs me that he has heard that sometimes, on the occasion of a wedding, '*straw-boys' go round with long straw masks on, and if they do not get either money or liquor will threaten to break the windows and furniture of the house. **1937** C. M. ARENSBERG *Irish Countryman* iii. 106 The 'strawboys'—privileged masqueraded figures whose mock-dangerous invasion of the wedding feast has been dignified to represent a last remnant of a primeval bride-capture. **1968** A. GAILEY in *Folk Life* VI. 90 In parts of Fermanagh there survive even to the present day traces of an old ceremony performed by groups of.. young men, disguised latterly in.. straw masks.., but in former times.. wearing complete suits of straw. They interrupted the festivities following the solemnisation of marriages in the country districts, and were known simply as the Strawboys. **1864** *Harper's Mag.* Oct. 578/2 He laid all kinds of evil results at the door of *straw braid. **1875** KNIGHT *Dict. Mech.* 2417/1 The Leghorn, or Italian straw-braid. **1882** CAULFEILD & SAWARD *Dict. Needlework* 463/2 Straw Braids are made in very long lengths, and are sewn together by means of long thin Needles, called Straws. **1908** A. HUXLEY *Let.* 29 June (1969) 28 Latest News Stop Press *Strawbugs for tea. **1959** I. & P. OPIE *Lore & Lang. Schoolch.* ix. 155 These syllables [sc. *-bug, -gog*, etc.] are used.. to replace the second half of a word, as: newbug, rasbug, strawbug, goosegog, and wellygogs. **1799** A. YOUNG *Agric. Lincoln.* 267 He *straw-burnt a piece in the middle of a field preparing for turnips. *Ibid.* 268 This *straw-burning husbandry I found again at Belesby. **1783** *European Mag.* Mar. 190/1 Paillasses, or *straw-coats, are very much in use. **1882** CAULFEILD & SAWARD *Dict. Needlework* 464 **Straw Cotton*.. is a wiry kind of thread, starched and stiff,.. exclusively made for use in the manufacture of straw goods. **1820** *Glenfergus* xviii. II. 218 Gin ye dinna haste ye, doakter, .. it may be *strae dead afore ye come on till 't. **1785** BURNS *Dr. Hornbook* xxv, Whare I kill'd ane, a fair *strae-death, By loss o' blood, or want o' breath. **1865** KINGSLEY *Herew.* iv, Dead is he, a bed-death,.. A straw-death, a cow's-death. **1868** G. MACDONALD *R. Falconer* I. xxiii. 305 She's gane, an' no by a fair strae-deith (death on one's own straw) either. *a* **1325** *Names of Hare in Rel. Ant.* I. 133 The *strauder, the lekere. **1599** B. JONSON *Cynthia's Rev.* III. ii. (1601) F 1 b, As if I knew not how to entertaine These *Straw-deu ses. **1828** *Sporting Mag.* XXII. 183 Mr. Darvill.. commenced life as a *straw-driver in a country racing stable. **1951** W. DE LA MARE *Winged Chariot* 47 Unlike the plant called 'everlasting', this [*sc.* poetry] Never *straw-dry, sapless, or sterile is. **1963** *Glamour* Nov. 23 Even hair that's straw-dry turns silky. **1889** CUNDILL *Dict. Explosives* 61 **Straw Dynamite* is a mixture of nitro-glycerine with nitro-cellulose made from straw. **1862** *Catal. Internat. Exhib., Brit.* II. No. 4432 *Straw embroidery. **1882** CAULFEILD & SAWARD *Dict. Needlework* 464 *Straw Embroidery*.. consists in tacking upon black Brussels silk net or yellow coloured net, leaves, flowers, corn, butterflies, &c. that are stamped out of straw, and connecting these with thick lines made of yellow filoselle. **1867** TYNDALL *Sound* iv. 137 Instead of using the cord, the bars may rest at their nodes on cylinders of twisted straw; hence the name *straw-fiddle sometimes applied to this instrument. **1573–80** TUSSER *Husb.* (1878) 35 Flaile, *strawforke and rake. **1858** SLIGHT & BURN *Farm Implem.* 479 The straw-fork.. has rather longer prongs. **1963** A. LUBBOCK *Austral. Roundabout* 3 Here are fine expenses of pasture, turning to *straw-gold in summer. **1977** J. AIKEN *Last Movement* i. 20 Her hair had been.. a pale Scottish straw-gold. **1862** *Catal. Internat. Exhib., Brit.* II. No. 6527 Chaff machine knives, and *straw knives. **1391** *Mem. Ripon* (Surtees) III. 107 Et in cc *stralates [*printed* stralanes] emp. pro domo in tenura Joh. Knygth, 16*d.* **1433–4** in *Fabric Rolls York Minster* (Surtees) 54 In m.ccc strelattes emptis pro grangia decimali ibidem reparanda, 6s. 6d. **1485** *Nottingham Rec.* III. 231, vij. bonches of stree lattes. **1742** YOUNG *Nt. Th.* II. 78 He loudly pleads The *straw-like trifles, on life's common stream. **1848** GOULD *Birds Australia* VI. Pl. 45 The shafts of the feathers are produced into long lanceolate straw-like and straw-coloured processes. **1956** *Amer. Speech* XXXI. 152 **Strawline*,.. a small-size wire rope which hauls the heavy logging cables into position. **1975** *Islander* (Victoria, B.C.) 22 June 7/4 A strawline was taken across the river by boat, then each cable was pulled to the other side by the horses. **1594** T. B. *La Primaud. Fr. Acad.* II. 567 A scarre-crowe to make them afraide, as wee vse to deale with little children and with birdes by puppets and *strawe-men. **1890** FRAZER *Golden Bough* II. 247 Sometimes a straw man was burned in the 'hut'. **1896** L. T. HOBHOUSE *Theory of Knowl.* 59 The straw man was easily enough knocked over by the critic who set him up. **1934** A. WOOLLCOTT *While Rome Burns* 76, I have often challenged one of these straw-man authorities. **1946** KOESTLER *Thieves in Night* 328 The authorities.. only got the Rumanian captain and his crew, who couldn't give away much as all their dealings had been with straw men under assumed names. **1981** 'M. HEBDEN' *Pel is Puzzled* xviii. 180 He seemed active enough, but there seemed an awful lot lacking in him... Was he really just a straw man? **1747** *Straw-Motes [see MOTE *sb.*^{1} 4]. **1874** HARDY *Far fr. Mad. Crowd* lii, Then Gabe brought her some of the new cider, and she must needs go drinking it through a straw-mote. **1848** GOULD *Birds Australia* VI. Pl. 45 *Geronticus* [or *Carphibis*] *spinicollis*. *Straw-necked Ibis. **1922** W. B. YEATS *Seven Poems* 13 Under the shadow of stupid *straw-pale locks. **1854** *Househ. Words* IX. 86/2 A secret mode of making *straw-paper. **1862** MISS YONGE *C'tess Kate* i, Forgetting everything in the interest of her drawing on a large sheet of straw paper. **1800** *Repert. Arts* etc. (1801) XV. 19 A new and improved Manufacture of

*Straw-Plat, made of split Straw. 1842 S. C. HALL *Ireland* II. 164 The manufacture of straw-plait is to be found in every house. 1846 MRS. GORE *Eng. Char.* (1852) 68 The hereditary race of *straw-plaiters. 1834 MCCULLOCH *Dict. Comm.* (1844) s.v. *Hats*, The wives and daughters of the farmers used to plait straw for making their own bonnets, before *straw-plaiting became established as a manufacture. 1849 LYTTON *Caxtons* II. ii, He would stand an hour at a cottage door, admiring the little girls who were straw-platting. 1862 *Catal. Internat. Exhib., Brit.* II. No. 4849 Straw plaitings, straw hats and bonnets. 1932 C. E. ROBINSON *Straw Votes* iv. 52 The newspaper or magazine conducting a *straw poll by the ballot-in-the-paper method prints a straw ballot in the publication for a certain period of time before an election. 1944 *Chicago Tribune* 26 Oct. 12/2 (*heading*). New deal area lifts F.D.R. in N.Y. straw poll. 1958 *Spectator* 6 June 722/1 In my own straw poll I found two electors who were going to vote Liberal for the first time. 1978 *Nature* 6 Apr. 484/3 A straw poll taken three weeks ago at a meeting of faculty professors..voted 23 to 3 against approving the proposal. 1904 C. H. SENN *New Cent. Cookery Bk.* (rev. ed.) 596 Pommes Pailles (*Straw Potatoes). 1959 *Times* 6 Apr. 13/5 Serve with sweet corn and straw potatoes. 1856 'STONEHENGE' *Brit. Sports* II. I. x. 357/1 The *straw-ride is generally made by using the long litter of the stable laid down round a large paddock. 1881 DU CHAILLU *Land Midn. Sun* II. 434 A custom which reminded me of the 'straw ride' parties common in the rural districts of the United States. 1895 *Outing* XXVI. 408/1 Invitations to sailing parties, straw rides or picnics. 1641 FRENCH *Distill.* i. (1651) 41 The lower gourd or recipient set upon *straw-rings. 1763 'THEOPH. INSULANUS' *Second Sight* 9 As he was going out of his house on a morning, he put on *straw-rope garters instead of those he formerly used. 1837 CARLYLE *Fr. Rev.* III. VII. iii, See Pichegru's soldiers, this hard winter,..in their 'straw-rope shoes and cloaks of bast-mat'. 1844 H. STEPHENS *Bk. Farm* II. 11 Assorted straw.. is put..thick above the turnips for thatch, and kept down by means of straw-ropes. 1826 *Q. Rev.* XXXIII. 344 We have all heard of a race of men, who used in former days to ply about our own courts of law, and who, from their manner of making known their occupation, were recognized by the name of *Straw-shoes. An advocate or lawyer, who wanted a convenient witness, knew by these signs where to meet with one,..'Then come into court and swear it?' And Straw-shoe went into the court and swore it. 1844 SMYTH *Cycle Celestial Obj.* I. 384 *note*, A certain straight-laced *straw-splitter objects to the terms *rising* and *setting*, as being highly improper when applied to fixed points. 1828 PUSEY *Hist. Enq.* I. 16 The endless *straw-splittings of the schoolmen. *Ibid.* 35 Abounding..in straw-splitting distinctions. 1881 MORLEY *Cobden* xxxi. II. 323 They were wasting time in mere strawsplitting. 1854 G. W. CURTIS *Potiphar Papers* ii. (1866) 55 A dozen of the delicately-engraved *straw-stems that stood upon the waiter. 1931 *Amer. Speech* VII. 169 Most of these [mattresses and ticks] were filled with corn husks, straw or hay, and were called 'husk ticks', 'hay mattresses', and '*straw ticks'. 1949 L. I. WILDER *Long Winter* viii. 68 They must fill the straw ticks with hay, because there was no straw in this new country. 1954 W. FAULKNER *Fable* 195 He was sleeping on a straw tick in the lodge room over the store. 1866 *Cleveland* (Ohio) *Leader* 6 Oct. 4/2 A *straw vote taken on a Toledo train yesterday resulted as follows; A. Johnson 12; Congress, 47. 1887 *San Francisco Thunderbolt* 4 Nov. 1. The straw vote taken at the 'Report' office is unreliable. 1906 *Daily Chron.* 24 Oct. 4/5 'Straw' votes, which have recently been taken in the New York State campaign, indicate that Mr. Hearst will be badly beaten. 1977 R. HOLLAND *Self & Social Context* v. 175 A special session on legal registration produced a straw vote which revealed an even balance of viewpoint. 1824 A. HENDERSON *Hist. Anc. & Mod. Wines* 172 The liquor.. receives the name of *straw wine (*vin de paille*). 1833 REDDING *Mod. Wines* vii. 208 Straw wines are made in Franconia. 1508 DUNBAR *Flyting* 213 *Stra wispis hingis owt. a 1678 in *Evelyn's Pomona* 407 Instead of the straw-wisp, a Basket may be fitted, which with a little straw within will keep the Fruit in better order. a 1761 [S. HALIBURTON & HEPBURN] *Mem. Magopico* v. (ed. 2) 18 The man is..a plain undesigning nose o' wax, a cat's paw, a straw wisp. 1861 MRS. H. WOOD *East Lynne* I. iv, In spite of his smock frock, his *straw-wisped hat, and his false whiskers,..she knew him for her brother. 1612 *Sc. Bk. Customs* in *Halyburton's Ledger* (1867) 332 Woad called Iland grene woad or stra woad the tun i^c^xx li. a 1700 EVELYN *Diary* 1646 (Milan), They have curious *straw worke among the nunns, even to admiration. 1798 *Monthly Mag.* June 429 The principal manufacture is straw-work..which is confined to about six or eight miles round Dunstable. 1882 CAULFEILD & SAWARD *Dict. Needlework* 463 Cabinets, boxes, and cardcases..decorated with a covering of coloured Straw-work, much resembling Mosaic work. 1653 WALTON *Angler* xii. 232 There is also another Cadis called by some a *Straw-worm. 1796 KIRWAN *Elem. Min.* (ed. 2) I. 29 *Straw yellow. 1831 BREWSTER *Nat. Magic* xxxiv. (1833) 285 The finest varieties..transmit a straw-yellow tint. 1843 PORTLOCK *Geol.* 214 From yellowish-brown to rich straw yellow.

b. In book-names of certain moths, with reference to their colour (see quots.).

1775 M. HARRIS *Engl. Lepidoptera* 45 Phalæna..310 Straw, clouded. 1819 SAMOUELLE *Entomol. Compend.* 427 Botys cespitalis. The Straw-barred. 1832 RENNIE *Butterfl. & Moths* 49 The Straw Underwing..appears about June. *Ibid.* 116 The Straw Belle. *Ibid.* 188 The Dingy Straw (*Depressaria costosa*). *Ibid.* 193 The Dingy Straw (*Recurvaria Silacella*). 1869 E. NEWMAN *Brit. Moths* 98 The Straw Belle (*Aspilates gilvaria*). *Ibid.* 295 The Straw Underwing (*Cerigo Cytherea*).

†**straw**, *sb.*[2] *Obs.* Apparently some foreign denomination of weight.

1540 *Act. 32 Hen. VIII*, c. 14 §2 [Freight from Denmark] Item for everie strawe of wax of xvj C. weight xiiij s.

straw (strɔː), *a.* Short for STRAW-COLOURED.

1842 *Penny Cycl.* XXIII. 3/2 The annexed are the tempering heats, colours, and uses of steel of different degrees of hardness:—430° Fah., very faint yellow; for lancets. 450° pale straw; razors and surgeons' instruments. 1862 M. BROWN *Catal. Postage Stamps* (ed. 2) 21 Letters in each corner of stamp. 3 d. pink, 4 d. vermilion, 9 d. straw.

straw (strɔː), *v.*[1] Pa. t. and pa. pple. **strawed** (*rarely* pa. pple. **strawn**). *Obs.* exc. *arch.* Also 4 **strauwe**. [App. repr. a dial. pronunciation (with rising diphthong) of OE. *streawian* var. of *streowian* STREW *v.*] = STREW *v.*

1. *trans.* To scatter, spread loosely; to scatter (rushes, straw, flowers, etc.) on the ground or floor, or over the surface of something; to scatter or sprinkle (something in powder) over a surface.

c 1200 ORMIN 8193 To strawwenn gode gresess þær, þatt stunnkenn swiþe swete. a 1300 *Floriz & Bl.* (Camb. MS) 436 Cupen he let fulle of flures, To strawen in þe maidenes bures. c 1375 *Sc. Leg. Saints* xlii. (*Agatha*) 254 þane bad he Schellis & brynnand cole straw in þe floure. c 1385 CHAUCER *L.G.W.* 207 (Fairf.), I bad hem strawen [*v.rr.* strawe, strowe(n)] floures on my bed. c 1400 *Destr. Troy* 12145 Hire blod all aboute aboue hit was sched, And strawet in þe strete, strenklit full þik. c 1430 *Two Cookery-bks.* I. 23 Take pouder Pepir, & Canelle, & straw þer-on. c 1440 *Sir Eglam.* 376 Bryght helmes he fonde strawed wyde, As men of armys had loste ther pryde. c 1449 PECOCK *Repr.* II. xiv. 230 Now sche berith aischis out, now sche strawith rischis in the halle. 1483 CAXTON *Golden Leg.* 417/3 Thenne Julyan..dyd doo Strawe Salte on the body. 1526 TINDALE *Matt.* xxi. 8 Other cut doune braunches from the trees, and strawed [so 1611; 1881 *Revised* spread; Gr. ἐστρώννυον] them in the waye. 1578 LYTE *Dodoens* III. xxvii. 354 Aloë, made into powder & strawen vpon newe blooddy woundes, stoppeth the blood, and healeth the wounde. 1594 *Gd. Huswifes Handmaid Kitchin* 22 b, Take great Raisons and minse them small, and plucke out the kernels, and strawe them in the bottome of your pie. 1657 W. COLES *Adam in Eden* cxlix, The affected place being bathed with the decoction thereof, and the powder strawed on afterwards. 1725 BOURNE *Antiq. Vulg.* iv. 26 That other Custom of strawing Flowers upon the Graves of their departed Friends, is also derived from a Custom of the ancient Church. 1765 A. DICKSON *Treat. Agric.* III. (ed. 2) 379 The strawing small chaff..on the bottom of the pigeon-house, is very proper. 1828 CARR *Craven Gloss.*, *Straw*, to spread grass, when mown to strew. 1896 KIPLING *Seven Seas* 8 We have strawed our best..To the shark and the sheering gull.

†**b.** With *abroad*. *Obs.*

1549 COVERDALE etc. *Erasm. Par. 1 Tim.* i. 1–7 In stedde of the sure doctrine of Christ, they strawe abrode vayne smokes & mystes of Jewishe questions. 1576 FOXE *A. & M.* (ed. 3) 990/2 After that..the Cardinall, vnderstode these bookes of the Beggars supplication..to be strawne abroade in the streetes of London,..the sayd Cardinall [etc.]. 1579–80 NORTH *Plutarch, Solon* (1595) 106 Some say, the ashes of his body were after his death strawed abroade through the Ile of Salamina.

c. *absol.* (The chief modern use, in allusion to Matt. xxv. 24.)

1526 TINDALE *Matt.* xxv. 24 Which..gadderest where thou strawedst not [1611 where thou hast not strawed (1880 *Revised* where thou didst not scatter); Gr. διεσκόρπισας]. c 1586 C'TESS PEMBROKE *Ps.* CXII. viii, He gives where needs, nay rather straweth, His justice never ending. 1861 LOWELL *Washers of Shroud* 26 Still men and nations reap as they have strawn. 1914 J. K. GRAHAM *Anno Dom.* 76 The soul.. anticipates an epoch of halcyon splendour when it shall gather where it has strawed.

2. To cover (the ground, a floor, etc.) with something loosely scattered, e.g. rushes, straw, flowers. Now *rare* or *Obs.*

13.. *K. Alis.* 1026 With rose, and swete flores, Was strawed [*Laud MS.* ystrewed] halles, and bouris. c 1350 *Will. Palerne* 1617 Eche a strete was striked & strawed wiþ floures. c 1380 *Sir Ferumb.* 2690 Al þe feldes þoȝte y-strawed of dede men al aboute. c 1386 CHAUCER *Squire's T.* 606 Though thou..strawe hir cage faire and softe as silk. c 1450 *Mirk's Festial* 39 Hys hall was yche day of þe ȝere new strawed, yn somer wyth grene rosches, and yn wyntyr wyth clen hay. 1544 PHAER *Pestilence* (1553) L vi, It is good in hote time, to straw ye chamber ful of willow leues and other fresh boughes. 1572 MASCALL *Plant. & Graff.* (1592) 64 The blacke Figges..being dried in the Sunne, and then laied in a vessell in beddes one by an other, & then sprinkled or strawed all ouer, euerie laie with fine Meale. 1587 T. NEWTON *Herbal for Bible* xvi. 94 With the which [sedge] many in this Countrie do vse in Sommer time to strawe their Parlours, and Churches. 1591 SAVILE *Tacitus, Hist.* IV. i. 169 The streetes were strawed with dead carcases. 1596 DANETT tr. *Comines* (1614) 304 And gather vp the launces wherewith the place lay strawed. 1631 WEEVER *Anc. Funeral Mon.* 41 Which..hath beene sprinkled with the bloud..and strawne with the ashes, of those blessed Saints. 1650 T. B[AYLY] *Worcester's Apoph.* 23 We had..laid some loose boards, and strawed the new made floar with rushes.

fig. 1606 DEKKER *Seven Sins Lond.* Wks. (Grosart) II. 30 Their seruants, wiues and children strawing the way before him with curses. 1676 BAKER in Rigaud *Corr. Sci. Men* (1841) II. 2 You have most ingeniously strawed the way for its invention.

†**3.** To make or lay (a bed). Also *absol.* *Obs.*

13.. *St. Gregory* (Vernon MS.) 574 þe wyf strauwede [*Cotton MS.* (older text) strowiþ] him ful soft þer he in Chaumbre schulde leyn. 1540 PALSGR. *Acolastus* III. v. R j b, Commaunde the seruantes to make or strawe a bedde. *Ibid.*, Cause..a bryde bed to be strawen for vs.

4. To be strewn or spread upon.

1593 *Extracts Munic. Acc. Newcastle* (1848) 29 Paide for earbes and rushes which strawde the chapple, 2s. 1896 HOUSMAN *Shropshire Lad* iv, And the tent of night in tatters Straws the sky-pavilioned land. 1898 WOLLOCOMBE *From Morn till Eve* i. 8 The green rushes that strawed the hall.

straw (strɔː), *v.*[2] Also 5 **strowe**. [f. STRAW *sb.*[1]]

1. *trans.* To supply with straw.

c 1440 *Promp. Parv.* 480/2 Strowyn, or lyteryn, *stramino*. c 1481 CAXTON *Dialogues* ix. 49 Gyue heye to the hors, And strawe them well. [Fr. *et les estraines bien.*] 1483 —— *Gold. Leg.* 44/1 And brought hym in and strowed his cameles and gaf them chaff and heye.

2. *intr.* (*slang.*) See quot.

1851 MAYHEW *Lond. Labour* I. 215 The practice of what is called 'strawing', or selling straws in the street, and giving away with them something..forbidden to be sold,—as indecent papers [etc.].

Hence **strawed** *ppl. a.*; '**strawing** *vbl. sb.*

1851 MAYHEW *Lond. Labour* I. 239, I have already alluded to 'strawing'. 1887 HISSEY *Holiday on Road* 103 Farmsteads ..with..their deeply strawed yards.

strawberry ('strɔːbərɪ). Forms: see STRAW *sb.* and BERRY *sb.*[1]: also 4–6 **straubery**, 5–6 **strebere**, 6 **strai-**, **strawbere**, 7 **-berre**, **strewbery**, **stra-**, **strawbury**. [OE. *stréaw-*, *stréow*, *stréa-*, *stréuberiȝe*, f. *stréaw* STRAW *sb.*[1] + *beriȝe* BERRY *sb.*

No corresponding word is found in any other Teut. lang. The reason for the name has been variously conjectured. One explanation refers the first element to STRAW *sb.*[1] 2, a particle of straw or chaff, a mote, describing the appearance of the achenes scattered over the surface of the strawberry; another view is that it designates the runners (cf. STRAW *sb.*[1] 3).

The view of Kluge, that OE. *stréaw-* in *streawberiȝe* is cogn. w. L. *frāgum* strawberry, is not phonologically satisfactory, and is also open to objection on other grounds.]

I. 1. a. The 'fruit' (popularly so called) of any species of the genus *Fragaria*, a soft bag-shaped receptacle, of a characteristic colour (scarlet to yellowish), full of juicy acid pulp, and dotted over with small yellow seed-like achenes. It is eaten alone or crushed with sugar and cream (or wine). The wild or wood strawberry is smaller than the cultivated kinds.

c 1000 ÆLFRIC *Gloss.* in Wr.-Wülcker 136/14 *Fraga*, streaberige. 1328–9 *Exch. K.R. Mem. Rolls*, 2 Edw. III, m. 166, 1 furcam de argento pro strauberiis. c 1340 *Nominale* (Skeat) 693 *Frese rouge*, streberie. c 1450 *Two Cookery-bks.* II. 75 And streberies, if hit be in time of yere. ? a 1500 *London Lickpenny* ix. (MS. Harl. 542) Hot pescods, one gan cry, strabery rype, and chery in the ryse. 1541 in *MSS. Dk. Rutland* (Hist. MSS. Comm.) IV. 314 To a servaunte..that brought streberes to my Lorde Roose, iiijd. 1542 BOORDE *Dyetary* xiii. (1870) 267 Rawe crayme vndecocted, eaten with strawberyes or hurtis, is a rurall mannes banket. 1620 VENNER *Via Recta* vii. 126 The wilde or voluntary Strawberies..are not so good as those that are manured in gardens. 1655 WALTON *Angler* I. v. (1661) 118 We may say of Angling as Dr. Boteler said of Strawberries; Doubtless God could have made a better berry, but doubtless God never did. 1788 J. HURDIS *Village Curate* (1797) 75 To Godstow bound..For strawberries and cream. 1862 CALVERLEY *Verses & Transl.* (ed. 2) 17 At my side she mashed the fragrant Strawberry.

b. A sea anemone, probably a variety of *Actinia equina*, the body of which resembles a strawberry.

1856 G. TUGWELL *Man. Sea-Anemones* ii. 33 Here is 'the strawberry', whose body is mottled with red and green, after the fashion of that pleasant fruit. 1856 GEO. ELIOT *Jrnl.* 8 May–26 June in *Lett.* (1954) II. 243 It was a crescendo of delight when we found a 'Strawberry'..in a low tide pool. 1971 *Oxf. Bk. Invertebrates* 14/1 Particularly common is the 'strawberry' variant [of the beadlet anemone] in which the body is crimson with green spots.

c. The fruit of certain seaweeds resembling a strawberry. (Perhaps a misunderstanding by Kipling.)

1897 KIPLING *Capt. Cour.* iii. 53 The hook had fouled among a bunch of strawberries, red on one side and white on the other.

2. The plant of the genus *Fragaria* which bears this fruit: a stemless herb with trifoliate leaves, white flowers, and slender runners which trail on the ground.

c 1000 *Sax. Leechd.* I. 138 Ðeos wyrt ðe man fraga & oðrum naman streawberȝean nemneð. a 1387 *Sinon. Barthol.* (Anecd. Oxon.) 22 *Fragaria, Fraser*, straubery. 1530 PALSGR. 277/1 Straubery an herbe, *fraysier*. 1563 HYLL *Art Garden.* (1593) 107 The Strawberrie is accounted among those hearbs that grow in the fieldes of their owne accorde. 1578 LYTE *Dodoens* I. lviii. 84 The Strawberrie with his small and slender hearie branches, creepeth alongst the ground. 1866 *Treas. Bot.* 504 The Pine Strawberries have generally large flowers and fruit, with foliage of a darker green..than that of the scarlets. 1870 H. MACMILLAN *True Vine* v. (1872) 224 The fragrance that is absent from the leaf and the blossom of the strawberry is apparent in the delicious fruit.

3. A representation of the fruit as an ornament.

1523 in *Archæologia* XXXVIII. 360 A leyer of sylver, doble gylte, with a straibere on þe topp. 1533 in *Kal. & Inv. Exch.* (1836) II. 291 Item a salte of golde wrought w^t^ braunches of strawburyes w^t^ a tufte of strawburyes or hawes opon the cover. 1604 SHAKS. *Oth.* III. iii. 435 A Handkerchiefe Spotted with Strawberries.

4. Short for *strawberry colour*, *red*, etc.

1688 *Lond. Gaz.* No. 2364/4 A light Sorrel Nag, inclining to a Strawberry. 1897 *Sears, Roebuck Catal.* 222/1 They [*sc.* scarves] consist mostly of combination colors, just a few of which are blue, lavender, light green, cherry, strawberry, [etc.]. 1922 JOYCE *Ulysses* 492 A blond feeble goosefat whore in a tatterdemalion gown of mildewed strawberry lolls spreadeagle in the sofacorner. 1954 [see ALIZARIN]. 1974 *Harrod's Xmas Catal.* 19 Luggage..in colourful Vinyl: light tan, orange, blue, or strawberry.

5. Short for *strawberry jam*.

1890 R. C. LEHMANN *Harry Fludyer* 6 Cook says she is pleased you liked the jam, but there are only three of the strawberry left, and would you like some of the gooseberry?

6. Applied to things resembling a strawberry in shape or colour. **a.** An emery bag in the shape of a strawberry.

1903 K. D. WIGGIN *Rebecca of Sunnybrook Farm* vi. 66 She polished her needles to nothing, pushing them in and out of the emery strawberry. **1937** [see *emery cushion* s.v. EMERY *sb.* 3]. **1976** P. CLABBURN *Needleworker's Dict.* 99/1 *Emery cushion* (emery bag, emery ball, strawberry), small pincushion, often in the shape of a strawberry, which is filled with emery powder... If needles become damp and rusty they are run through the cushion to make them shiny and smooth again.

b. A sore or bruise, esp. one caused by friction with the ground. *N. Amer. colloq.*

1921 *Daily Colonist* (Victoria, B.C.) 13 Oct. 11/4 'Strawberry', or open sore, on his hip, caused by sliding bases and constantly reopened. **1937** *Pittsburgh Press* 11 Jan. 27/5 Here are some expressions commonly used..; *Strawberry*, a bruise from sliding [etc.]. **1981** *Washington Star* 19 Mar. D 1 'Look at that,' he said, hitching up his knickerbockers to reveal matching strawberries just above both knees, red and angry-looking. At least, they used to call them 'strawberries'. He still does.

c. A nose having the colour of a strawberry, esp. as the result of heavy drinking.

1949 PARTRIDGE *Dict. Slang.* (ed. 3) Addenda 1188/1 *Strawberry*,..a red nose: Cockney's. **1980** C. SMITH *Cut-out* ix. 62 His nose..had turned..to the characteristic boozer's strawberry.

II. *attrib.* and *Comb.*

7. *attrib.*, passing into *adj.* Resembling a strawberry in colour. Also ***strawberry pink, red, roan, crushed strawberry***, etc.

1675 *Lond. Gaz.* No. 1038/4 Stolen..A strawberry Mare. **1690** *Pagan Prince* xxx. 83 A grave Gentleman with a Strawberry Countenance. **1854** *Poultry Chron.* I. 263/1 In colour they are mealy or strawberry, the wings barred with a redder tint. **1864** BOUTELL *Her. Hist. & Pop.* xxviii. 435 A strawberry-roan horse salient. **1897** G. ALLEN *Type-writer Girl* i, Our modern novelists dress her up afresh in the princess robe of the day (sage green or crushed strawberry). **1899** *Westm. Gaz.* 13 Apr. 3/1 A strawberry and white cow. **1939** JOYCE *Finnegans Wake* 207 The lellipos cream to her lippeleens and the pick of the paintbox for her pommettes, from strawbirry reds to extra violates. **1952** A. G. L. HELLYER *Sanders' Encycl. Gardening* (ed. 22) 113 [*Cirrhopetalum*] *Amesianum*, old gold, single haired, lower sepals strawberry-red. **1956** G. DURRELL *My Family & Other Animals* ii. 28 (*heading*) The strawberry-pink villa.

8. a. Simple attrib., as ***strawberry bed, blossom, border, box*** (also *fig.*), ***garden***, **†*-prick*** (= *seed*), ***root, runner, seed, time***.

1535 in E. Law *Hampton Crt. Pal.* (1885) 372 For gathering of 34 bushells of strawberry rot. **1573–80** TUSSER *Husb.* (1878) 41 Wife, into thy garden, and set me a plot, with strawbery rootes. **1619** *Depositions Bk., Archd. Essex & Colchester* 117b, Deponit that, in Strabury tyme was twelve moneth, [etc.]. **1681** GREW *Musæum* I. §7. i. 160 In colour, shape, and bigness like a Strawberry-seed. **1682** WHELER *Journ. Greece* I. 45 The curious Plants I here took particular notice of, are these:..9. Lychnis, with Flowers, speckled, like the Strawberry-pricks. **1699** EVELYN *Kal. Hort., Mar.* (ed. 9) 34 You can hardly over-water your Strawberry-Beds in a dry Season. *Ibid.* Aug. 99 Pluck up Strawberry Runners. *a***1700** EVELYN *Diary* 8 May 1654, A vineyard, planted in strawberry borders. **1787** J. WOODFORDE *Diary* 15 Oct. (1926) II. 352, I was very busy this morning in my Garden making some new Strawberry Beds. **1802** WORDSW. *Foresight* 3 Strawberry blossoms, one and all, We must spare them. **1892** W. B. YEATS *Countless Kathleen* ii. 34 My asparagus and strawberry beds Are trampled into clauber. **1936** 'R. HYDE' *Passport to Hell* vi. 93 Life just one strawberry-box after another. **1951** *Dict. Gardening* (R. Hort. Soc.) IV. 2042/1 An infected Strawberry bed should be cleared by burning all the plants. **1965** G. MCINNES *Road to Gundagai* iii. 35 All about us they [*sc.* passengers] were vomiting into 'strawberry boxes'.

b. Designating a confection or drink in which strawberries are an ingredient or flavouring, as **†*strawberry ale, water, wine***; ***strawberry cream, ice (-cream), jam, jelly, shortcake***.

1523 in W. H. Turner *Select. Rec. Oxford* (1880) 49 For strawbery ale and a posset iiij[d]. **1621** BURTON *Anat. Mel.* II. v. I. vi. (1624) 327 Strawbury water. **1669** *Sir K. Digby's Closet opened* 127 Strawberry Wine. **1792** J. WOODFORDE *Diary* 26 June (1927) III. 359 Dinner..a very fine Leveret rosted, Strawberry Cream, Jelly. **1818** S. F. GRAY *Suppl. Pharmacopœias* 291 Strawberry jelly. **1841** L. B. SWAN *Jrnl.* 20 June (1904) 28 We had a new dish, 'Strawberry Short Cake' very fine indeed. **1846** SOYER *Cookery* 552 Fill it with strawberry ice. **1861** [TREVELYAN] *Horace at Univ. Athens* (1862) 12 Pitching into strawberry-jam Like wranglers at their tea. **1862** MRS. I. WILLIAMSON *Pract. Cookery* (ed. 5) 151 Strawberry Cream. **1890** R. C. LEHMANN *Harry Fludyer* 8 Afterwards a strawberry ice cream landed on his shirt-front. **1953** G. W. BRACE *Spire* xi. 93, I had strawberry shortcake... Hot biscuits, yellow cream, and quite often wild berries.

c. Parasynthetic and similative, as ***strawberry-breasted, -coloured, -like***.

1688 *Lond. Gaz.* No. 2310/4 A Strawberry colour'd Gelding above 13 hands. **1756** W. TOLDERVY *Hist. 2 Orphans* IV. 196 An open chaise, drawn by a pair of strawberry coloured horses. **1862** ANSTED *Channel Isl.* IV. xxi. (ed. 2) 496 Its bright red strawberry-like berries. **1875** B. MEADOWS *Clin. Observ.* 15 The child is peevish,..with relaxed bowels, and a strawberry-like tongue. **1878** G. M. HOPKINS *Poems* (1967) 77 Star-eyed strawberry-breasted Throstle.

9. a. Special comb.: **strawberry bass** *U.S.*, the fish *Pomoxys sparoides*; **strawberry blite**, a herb, *Chenopodium capitatum*, with triangular leaves and heads of small flowers followed by fruit resembling a strawberry; **strawberry blond(e)** *a.*, applied to hair of a light reddish blond colour; as *sb.*, the colour itself; a person with hair of this colour; **strawberry bush**, (*a*) = *strawberry shrub*; (*b*) the shrub *Euonymus americanus*, with crimson and scarlet pods; †**strawberry cinquefoil**, the genus *Potentilla*; **strawberry clover** = *strawberry trefoil* (Prior *Plant.-n.* 1863); †**strawberry cockle**, some kind of shell-fish; **strawberry comb**, a cock's-comb resembling a strawberry; **strawberry crab** (see quot.); **strawberry dish** *Silver-work* (see quot. 1977); **Strawberry Fields** *slang* [prob. f. *Strawberry Fields Forever*, title of a song (1967) by John Lennon and Paul McCartney] = LSD[2]; **strawberry finch**, the amadavat; **strawberry geranium** (see quot.); **strawberry guava**, a shrub or small tree, *Psidium cattleianum*, of the family Myrtaceæ, native to tropical America and bearing white flowers and large edible berries; also, the red or yellow fruit of this tree; **strawberry-headed trefoil** = *strawberry trefoil*; **Strawberry Hill** *Archit.*, the name of the house in Twickenham bought in 1747 and rebuilt by Horace Walpole after the Gothic style, used *attrib.* to designate the style of early Gothic Revivalist architecture inspired and epitomized by this house; **strawberry-mark**, a birth-mark or nævus resembling a strawberry; **strawberry pear**, the fruit of the W. Indian cactus *Cereus triangularis*, or the plant itself (*Treas. Bot.* 1866); **strawberry perch** *U.S.* = *strawberry bass*; **strawberry pot**, a large garden pot with pockets in its sides, designed to contain growing strawberry plants; **strawberry shrub** *U.S.* = CALYCANTHUS; **strawberry spinach** = *strawberry blite*; **strawberry tomato** *U.S.*, a ground-cherry of the genus *Physalis* or its edible fruit; **strawberry tongue** (see quot.); **strawberry tree**, † (*a*) = sense 2; (*b*) = ARBUTUS 1; also = MADROÑO; (*c*) *U.S.* = *strawberry bush* b; **strawberry trefoil**, *Trifolium fragiferum*; **strawberry vine** = sense 2; **strawberry weevil**, a small black and white beetle, *Anthonomus signatus*, found in eastern North America, where it lays its eggs in strawberry buds, so that no fruit is formed; **strawberry wire**, the runner of the strawberry plant; †**strawberry wise**, †**with** = sense 2.

Also, in recent U.S. dictionaries, in names of insects injurious to the fruit or plant, as ***strawberry borer, moth, sawfly, worm***, etc.

1867 T. F. DE VOE *Market Assistant* 294 Calico bass, speckled bass, or partridge-tailed bass.—This fish is also known among our fishermen as the '*strawberry bass'. **1882** JORDAN & GILBERT *Syn. Fishes N. Amer.* 465 *Pomoxys sparoides*,..Strawberry Bass. **1947** B. W. DALRYMPLE *Panfish* 81 You'd think there be Strawberry Bass..in there. **1753** *Chambers' Cycl.* Suppl. App., **Strawberry-blite.* **1900** L. H. BAILEY *Cycl. Amer. Hort.* I. 290/2 The common Strawberry Blite..has been introduced to the trade as a pot-herb. **1943** FERNALD & KINSEY *Edible Wild Plants* iii. 180 The Strawberry-Blite, one of the most striking plants of Canadian clearings, on account of its masses of brilliant red pulpy fruits, may be used as a potherb like spinach. **1970** *Beaver* Winter 23 Strawberry spinach, also known as.. strawberry blite, is similar to its close cousin, lamb's quarters. **1884** E. W. NYE *Baled Hay* 98 That is what is.. sprinkling my *strawberry blonde hair with gray. **1887** *Courier-Jrnl.* (Louisville, Kentucky) 6 Feb. 12/2 Seventeen young women, with hair ranging from strawberry blonde to deep crimson, are seated..on a long platform. **1895** PALMER & WARD *Band played On* (song) 4 Casey would waltz with a strawberry blond, And the Band played on. **1958** *Daily Express* 17 Mar. 1/4 An unassuming strawberry blonde. **1977** B. BAINBRIDGE *Injury Time* ii. 19 Alma's hair, rinsed to an unusual shade of strawberry blonde. **1847** DARLINGTON *Amer. Weeds* (1860) 135 *Calycanthus*..*Strawberry-bush. **1856** A. GRAY *Man. Bot.* (1860) 81 *Euonymus Americanus*, Strawberry Bush. **1753** *Chambers' Cycl.* Suppl. s.v. *Pentaphylloides*, The erect *pentaphylloides*, called by authors the *strawberry-cinque-foil. **1713** PETIVER *Aquat. Anim. Amboinæ* 4/2 Red *Strawberry Cockle. **1815** BURROW *Elem. Conchol.* 195 Cardium Fragum. White Strawberry Cockle. C. Unedo. Strawberry Cockle. **1746** in *Poultry Chron.* (1855) III. 439 Yellow Dun, low *strawberry comb. **1850** [A. WHITE] *Spec. Anim. Brit. Mus.* IV. *Crustacea* 8 *Eurynome aspera*, *Strawberry Crab. **1941** *Burlington Mag.* Aug. 68/1 A set of four *strawberry dishes—also silver-gilt, by Paul Crispin, 1734. **1977** FLEMING & HONOUR *Penguin Dict. Decorative Arts* 766/1 *Strawberry dish*, a type of late C17–C18 English silver dish, deeper but no larger than a plate, rather thin with punched decorations in the C17, more substantial and usually with a scalloped rim in the C18. It is improbable that such dishes were used originally only for strawberries. **1971** *Tel.* (Brisbane) 27 Oct. 3/1 A youth had seven tablets of LSD, known as '*Strawberry Fields', when picked up in a city hotel by detectives. **1976** H. FERGUSON *Confessions Long Distance Acid Head* 22 Then came the fatal trip which led..to my fleeing to India to forget. I was on Blue Cheer, I think, though it could have been Strawberry Fields. **1880** BESSEY *Bot.* 526 *Saxifraga sarmentosa*, the so-called *Strawberry Geranium, a fine basket plant from China. **1901** L. H. BAILEY *Cycl. Amer. Hort.* III. 1460/2 *Strawberry Guava. Shrub or small tree, 10–20 ft. high... Pulp fleshy, soft and juicy, purplish red next the skin,..sweet and acid, with a strawberry-like fragrance and flavor. **1976** *Monitor* (McAllen, Texas) 7 Nov. 1C/1 (*caption*) The strawberry guava, a shrublike tree, produces a fig-like fruit almost cherry-sized that can be eaten raw and can also be made into jellies. **1822** *Hortus Anglicus* II. 271 *Strawberry headed Trefoil. **1836** R. GRIFFIN *Hist. Audley End* v. 127 The chapel..was newly fitted up..according to the fashion of the day, with.. clustered pilasters, and a groined ceiling, in the style called after its patron, **Strawberry Hill Gothic.* **1891** T. G. BONNEY in *Hist. Houses of United Kingdom* 90 A room..now serves as a chapel... It is..a specimen of Strawberry Hill Gothic. **1928** A. HUXLEY *Point Counter Point* xix. 344 The fantastic towers and pinnacles of Gattenden Castle, built.. in the most extravagant style of Strawberry Hill Gothic. **1977** *Times* 6 Aug. 3/3 The eleventh duke [of Norfolk] rebuilt it [*sc.* Arundel Castle] in the Strawberry Hill baronial fantasy style. **1847** J. M. MORTON *Box & Cox* (at end), Have you such a thing as a *strawberry mark on your left arm? **1877** C. HALLOCK *Sportsman's Gazetteer* 378 *Strawberry Perch... *Pomoxys hexacanthus.* **1888** GOODE *Amer. Fishes* 69 In Lake Erie, and in Ohio generally, it is the 'Strawberry Bass', 'Strawberry Perch' or 'Grass Bass'. **1946** M. FREE *All about House Plants* ix. 67 '*Strawberry pots' made of earthenware..are much used, suitably planted, for patio decoration in California. **1977** JELLICOE & ALLEN *Town Gardens to live In* xi. 125/2 (*heading*) A handmade strawberry pot. It will take twenty-eight plants. **1731** MILLER *Gard. Dict., Chenopodio-morus; major*..commonly call'd *Strawberry Spinage. **1862** M. D. COLT *Went to Kansas* ix. 133 The *strawberry tomatoes..are indigenous to the soil. **1867** A. GRAY *Man. Bot.* (1874) 382 *Physalis Alkekengi.* Strawberry Tomato. **1919** E. L. STURTEVANT *Notes on Edible Plants* 432 *P. lanceolata*..was among the strawberry tomatoes grown at the New York Agricultural Experiment Station in 1886. **1969** *Oxf. Bk. Food Plants* 126/2 The ground cherry, which is also called 'Strawberry Tomato'.., is an annual, native in parts of eastern and central North America. **1876** DUNGLISON *Med. Lex.*, **Strawberry Tongue*, a characteristic appearance of the tongue in scarlatina, in which, after the clearing away of a thick white fur, the organ becomes preternaturally red and clean. **14..** *Lat.-Eng. Voc.* in Wr.-Wülcker 584/29 *Fragus*, a *streberytre. **1548** TURNER *Names Herbes* 16 Arbutus.. may be called in english strawberry tree, or an arbute tree. *a***1687** PETTY *Polit. Surv. Irel.* (1719) 109 That part of Kerry called Desmond, where the Arbutus or Strawberry Tree groweth in great Quantity. **1792** A. MENZIES *Jrnl.* 2 May in *Menzies' Jrnl. of Vancouver's Voy.* (1923) 20 The Oriental Strawberry Tree..at this time a peculiar ornament to the Forest by its large clusters of whitish flowers & ever green leaves, but its peculiar smooth bark of a reddish brown colour will at all times attract the Notice of the most superficial observer. **1813** H. MUHLENBERG *Catalogus Plantarum Americæ Septentrionalis* 25 *Euonymus Americanus*, (burning bush, strawberry tree). **1838** J. C. LOUDON *Arboretum & Fruticetum Britannicum* II. 1117 The Arbutus, or Strawberry Tree... Robust evergreen shrubs, or low trees. **1845** A. GRAY *Bot. Text-bk.* (ed. 2) 376 Euonymus Americanus (sometimes called Strawberry-tree). **1866** *Trans. Illinois Agric. Soc.* VI. 391 The Strawberry Tree, with its delicate foliage, green wood and beautiful berries. **1975** D. MCCLINTOCK *Wild Flowers of Guernsey* 155 The Strawberry Tree..has established itself in Jersey. **1731** MILLER *Gard. Dict., Trifolium; fragiferum*... *Strawberry-Trefoil. **1867** AUGUSTA WILSON *Vashti* iii, I.. pull out grass and weeds from the *strawberry vines. **1884** *Ann. Rep. Michigan State Hort. Soc. 1883* 155 This *strawberry weevil..was described by Thomas Say. **1929** AUCHTER & KNAPP *Orchard & Small Fruit Culture* xiv. 486 Strawberry Weevil..lays its eggs in the flower buds and then girdles the stem so as to prevent further development. **1976** *Islander* (Victoria, B.C.) 30 May 10/2 Another expense was combating the strawberry weevil. **1601** HOLLAND *Pliny* xxv. ix. II. 228 *marg.*, The leaves of Cinquefoile are much like to the Strawberrie leafe: But as the one hath no fruit or berrie at all, so the other (to wit, the *Strawberrie-wire) puts forth but three leaves. **1879** MISS JACKSON *Shropsh. Word-bk.*, *Straberry-wires*, strawberry-runners. *c* **1000** ÆLFRIC *Gloss.* in Wr.-Wülcker 136/15 *Framen*, *streaberiewisan. *c* **1440** *Promp. Parv.* 478/2 Strawbery wyse [*Winch. MS.* strawbyry vyse], *fragus.* *c* **1450** *M.E. Med. Bk.* (Heinrich) 177 Tak bugle, streberywyse, mene consond [etc.] **1483** *Cath. Angl.* 367/1 A *Straberi wythe, *fragus.*

†**b.** In allusion to Latimer's condemnation of preachers who preach only once a year (see quots. below), as ***strawberry preacher, preaching, sermon***; ***strawberry-wise*** adv.

1549 LATIMER *Ploughers* (Arb.) 20 The preachynge of the worde of God vnto the people is called meate... Not strauberies, that come but once a yeare and tary not longe. .. The people muste haue meate that muste be familier and continuall, and dayly geuen vnto them to fede vpon. Many make a strauberie of it, ministringe it but once a yeare, but such do not thoffice of good prelates. **1566** in *Latimer's Serm.* (Parker Soc. 1844) 62 *note*, A pitious case it is, that now in all Oxford there is not past five or six preachers, I except strawberry preachers. **1605** F. MASON *Author. Ch.* (1607) 24 Wherefore that in stead of strawberie Sermons there might bee a more plentifull prouision in the house of God, our Church hath decreed, that [etc.]. **1606** S. GARDINER *Bk. Angling* 107 Then would not Sermons bee so daintie as they are, which come from some strawberre-wise, that is, once a yeere. **1615** HIERON *Dignitie of Preaching* 14 That, which old Latimer..once blamed vnder the witty terme of strawbery-preaching. **1648** E. SPARKE *Shute's Sarah & Hagar* Pref. b j b, These are no Strawberry-Sermons, pick'd and cull'd out with long vagaries.

Hence †**'strawberried** *ppl. a.*, marked with a strawberry-mark. **'strawberrying** *vbl. sb.*, gathering strawberries (in phr. ***to go strawberrying***).

1634 SHIRLEY *Example* IV. i, I can gather Warme Snowe from her faire brow, her chin, her neck,..Sated with these, I'le finde new appetite, And come a wanton strawberying to her cheekes. **1675** *Lond. Gaz.* No. 1035/4 Strayed away.., a gray Gelding,..Strawberried in the near Cheak. **1856** SUSAN WARNER *Hills of Shatemuc* viii, I wonder who'll go strawberrying with them?

strawberry leaf. The leaf of the strawberry plant. Also, †the plant itself (*obs.*). Also *attrib.*

[*c* **1000** *Sax. Leechd.* II. 350 Streawbergean leaf.] *c* **1265** *Voc. Plants* in Wr.-Wülcker 558/28 *Fraga*, fraser, streberilef. **1548** TURNER *Names Herbes* 38 Fragraria is called in english a strawbery leafe, whose fruite is called in englishe a strawbery. **1893** *Morning Post* 8 Mar. 8/2 Another rosaceous pest is the little strawberry-leaf beetle.

b. In allusion to the row of conventional figures of the leaf on the coronet of a duke, marquis, or earl.

1827 MOORE *New Creation of Peers* 32 If coronets glistened with pills 'stead of pearls, And the strawberry-leaves were by rhubarb supplanted! **1844** DISRAELI *Coningsby* v. iii, Who, if he carried the county and the manufacturing borough also, merited the strawberry-leaf. **1875** J. GRANT *One of Six Hundred* iv. 32 It was among the strawberry leaves she chiefly expected to find a husband for her daughter—a marquis at least.

Hence **strawberry-leaved** *a.*

1894 K. GRAHAME *Pagan Papers* 107 Duchesses..rapt.. from their strawberry-leaved surroundings. **1883** LD. R. GOWER *Remin.* I. v. 71 The ducal strawberry-leaved land.

straw-breadth, straw's breadth. Now *rare.* The breadth of a straw. Formerly often referred to as a typically small distance.

α. **1577** GRANGE *Golden Aphrod.* etc. S iv, Yet I truste yee will accepte of me for my well meanyng, who am not therein a strawe bredth incomparable to Cleanthes. **1596** HARINGTON *Anat. Metam. Aiax* L iiij, This skrew must.. appeare through the planke not aboue a straw-breadth on the right hand. **1676** MACE *Musick's Mon.* 60 Leaving about a Straw-bredth or two betwixt Paper and Paper. **1722** TICKELL *Kensington Gard.* 310 More tall he seems to rise, And struts a straw-breadth nearer to the skies. **1730** T. BOSTON *Mem.* vii. (1899) 153 There was a spit..sticking in the wall of the house, with the small end of it outmost. I rushed inadvertently my face on it, and the wound I got was about a straw-breadth beneath the eye. **1816** SCOTT *Old Mort.* xxxiii, Awaiting till the sword destined to slay him crept out of the scabbard gradually, and as it were by straw-breadths.

β. **1577** tr. *Bullinger's Decades* IV. vii. (1592) 713 Christians ..do not..go a strawes bredth from the diuine scriptures.

†**straw brede.** *Obs.* Also 6 *Sc.* straybrede. [f. STRAW *sb.*[1] + BREDE *sb.*[2]] = prec.

14.. *Guy Warw.* 8149 Nother flewe a strawe brede. **1508** DUNBAR *Tua Mariit Wemen* 234 Scho suld not stert for his straik a stray breid of erd.

strawcht, obs. pa. t. and pple. of STRETCH *v.*

straw colour. The colour of straw, a pale yellow. Also *attrib.* or *adj.* = STRAW-COLOURED.

1589 *Acc. Bk. W. Wray* in *Antiquary* XXXII. 78, vij q[trs] stroye coler canvesse, vj s. viij d. **1590** SHAKS. *Mids. N.* I. ii. 95, I will discharge it, in either your straw-colour beard, your orange tawnie beard [etc.]. **1737** W. SALMON *Country Builder's Estimator* (ed. 2) 101 Orange-Colour, Lemon-Colour, Straw-Colour, Pink-Colour, and Blossom-Colour, ground in Oil, from 10d. to 1s. per lb. **1815** STEPHENS in *Shaw's Gen. Zool.* IX. I. 184 This bird is sometimes found entirely of a pale straw-colour. **1882** *Cassell's Nat. Hist.* VI. 289 It is of a bright straw colour when living.

straw-coloured, *a.* Of the colour of straw; pale light yellow.

1585 in *Cath. Rec. Soc. Publ.* V. 111 A strawe couloured fustion dublet laide on with red Lace. **1625** HART *Anat. Ur.* I. v. 47 The next vrine was of a pale straw coloured yellow. **1756** C. LUCAS *Ess. Waters* I. 145 St. Paul's Church-yard-pump. upon evaporation, gives a straw-colored matter. **1826** KIRBY & SP. *Entomol.* IV. xlvi. 279 Straw-coloured (*Stramineus*). Pale yellow with a very faint tint of blue. **1871** *Cassell's Nat. Hist.* I. 311 The Straw-coloured Bat, ..*Natalus stramineus.* **1898** CONAN DOYLE *Tragedy of Korosko* ix. 296 A straw-coloured moustache.

strawen ('strɔːən), *a.* *Obs.* exc. *arch.* Also 5 **strowen,** 6–7 **strawne.** [f. STRAW *sb.*[1] + -EN[4].] Made of straw.

1459 in *Paston Lett.* I. 477 Item, ij. strawen hattis. *c* **1550** *Vertuous Scholehous* K iij b, The Celibate lyfe is a strawen Loue, whiche euery houre is broken and rent asunder of one worde onely. **1577** GOOGE *Heresbach's Husb.* III. 122 b, The legges must be often rubbed with a strawen wispe. **1580** FULKE *Dang. Rock* xviii. 307 Luther calleth it [the Epistle of James] a strawen Epistle. **1590** SPENSER *F.Q.* v. v. 50 Let him lodge hard, and lie in strawen bed. **1597** BP. HALL *Sat.* III. vii. 66 Lik'st a strawne scar-crow in the new-sowne field, Reard on some sticke, the tender corne to shield. **1609** C. BUTLER *Fem. Mon.* (1634) 34 In some countries they use strawn Hives. **1636** *Coach & Sedan* B j, Cudgell'd thick on the backe..with broad shining lace (not much unlike that which Mummeres make of strawen hatts). **1861** READE *Cloister & H.* xxxi, Like wee icicles a-melting down from strawen eaves. **1864** ALLINGHAM *Lawrence Bloomfield* vii. 95 Oona..in her accustom'd strawen chair.

†'**strawer**[1]. *Obs.* [f. STRAW *v.*[1] + -ER[1].] One who 'straws' or squanders.

1460 *Extracts Aberd. Reg.* (1844) I. 405 Wat Cutlaris wife ..is knawin a strawer of her husbands gudis.

'**strawer**[2]. [f. STRAW *v.*[2] + -ER[1].] (See quot.)

1851 MAYHEW *Lond. Labour* I. 239 The strawer offers to sell any passer by in the streets a straw and to give the purchaser a paper which he dares not sell..political, libellous, irreligious, or indecent.

strawflower ('strɔːflaʊə(r)). *N. Amer.* [f. STRAW *sb.*[1] + FLOWER *sb.*] = EVERLASTING *sb.* 4; esp. *Helichrysum bracteatum*, a perennial herb of the family Compositæ, native to Australia, whose variously coloured flowers are often dried and preserved.

1924 L. H. BAILEY *Man. Cultivated Plants* 786 Strawflower..frequently grown as an 'everlasting'. **1933** L. BLOOMFIELD *Language* x. 160 The *straw-* in *strawberry* is phonetically the same as the *straw-* in *strawflower.* **1972** F. MASON *Roads to Liberty* 10 She had tucked a pair of blue-dyed strawflowers into the dark hair above her ear.

strawght(e, strawhte, obs. pa. t. of STRETCH *v.*

strawh, obs. form of STRAW.

straw hat. Also **strawhat** and with hyphen.

1. a. (Formerly often hyphened.) A hat made of plaited or woven straw.

1453 in Sharp *Cov. Myst.* (1825) 190, iiij surplis & iiij stre hatts. *a* **1500** *Bale's Chron.* in *Six Town Chron.* (1911) 133 In a blewe gown of velvet..and a strawe hat upon his heed. **1603** FOWLDES *Homer's Battle Frogs & Mice* (1634) C 3, Next with a corslet they defend the heart, Not made of steele, but of an old straw-hat. **1697** *Lond. Gaz.* No. 3325/4 A Straw Hat lined with Painted Callicoe. **1712** STEELE *Spect.* No. 304 ¶9 An Handmaid in a Straw-Hat. **1837** DICKENS *Pickw.* vii, Several other gentlemen dressed..in straw hats, flannel jackets, and white trowsers. **1890** ELIZ. CARMICHAEL tr. *Björnson's In God's Way* II. i. 57 Their light summer clothes,..felt hats, straw hats, tulle hats.

b. *attrib.* (Now usually hyphened.)

1795 VANCOUVER *Agric. Essex* 27 A straw-hat manufactory has lately been established. **1835** URE *Philos. Manuf.* 255 An obscure straw-hat manufacturer.

2. *U.S. Theatr.* A summer theatre; a theatre operating during the summer only and presenting various productions or companies. Freq. *attrib.*

1935 *Variety* 12 June 62/4 (*heading*) Nearly 100 straw hat troupes will dot eastern landscape. **1936** A. GREEN in *Esquire* Sept. 160/3 A summer stock (legit) is a 'straw hat'. **1946** *Life* 5 Aug. 81/1 More than 125 straw-hat theaters now adorn the eastern sea-coast. **1948** *Sun* (Baltimore) 24 June 16/1 They appeared in the same roles last year on the strawhat circuit. **1952** *Ibid.* 10 June (B* ed.) 10/1 The play is not the thing this week at the Maryland strawhat. **1968** *N.Y. Times Bk. Rev.* 23 June VII. 5/4 They finagle their way into the strawhat dramatic workshop of a famous theater guru.

Hence **straw-hatted** *a.*, wearing a straw hat; **straw-hatter**, a straw-hat theatre, or play presented in one; **straw-hatting** *vbl. sb.*, work in straw-hat theatres.

c **1730** RAMSAY *Betty & Kate* ii, The strae-hatted maid. **1884** HOWELLS *Silas Lapham* (1891) I. 141 A straw-hatted population, such as ours is in summer. **1949** *N.Y. Times Mag.* 21 Aug. 24/4 The trick of operating a successful straw-hatter is to build up a steady clientele—a sizable number of people who get the habit of regular attendance because they have learned that the general average of production is good. **1950** *Richmond* (Va.) *Times-Dispatch* 9 Dec. 5/1 Strawhatting is arduous. **1954** *Wall St. Jrnl.* 4 Aug. 9 The Howard Lindsay-Russell Crouse straw hatter ('Life with Father') subsequently made Broadway.

'**strawish,** *a.* *rare.* [f. STRAW *sb.*[1] + -ISH.] Resembling straw.

1562 TURNER *Herbal* II. (1568) 110 Herbe fyvelefe..hath small strawish braunches a span longe. **1598** J. FLORIO *Worlde of Wordes* 253/1 *Pagliaresco*, made of strawe, strawish. **1978** B. FREEMANTLE *Clap Hands* viii. 50 Thinning strawish hair... A very ordinary sort of man.

strawless ('strɔːlɪs), *a.* [f. STRAW *sb.*[1] + -LESS.] Made without straw, containing no straw (in allusion to *Exodus* v; see STRAW *sb.*[1] 2 a). Also in fig. context.

1691 SIR T. P. BLOUNT *Ess.* v. 96 After this, among the Ægyptians was that of the Strawless Tax. **1859** W. H. RUSSELL in *Times* 24 Mar. 9/3 Perhaps something like it.. might have been seen..when the children of Israel were making strawless bricks. **1870** *Daily News* 17 May, To create a character out of the strawless clay which is so frequently provided by the dramatic author, requires a most trying effort of the imagination. **1896** J. F. MCCURDY in Hilprecht *Recent Res. in Bible Lands* 11 The great discovery of the 'treasure city' of Pithom with its straw-less bricks.

strawnge, -er(e, obs. ff. STRANGE, STRANGER.

strawt(e, obs. Sc. form of STRAIGHT; obs. pa. t. and pa. pple. of STRETCH *v.*

strawy ('strɔːɪ), *a.* Also 8–9 **strawey.** [f. STRAW *sb.*[1] + -Y.]

1. Consisting of, of the nature of, full of straw.

1552 HULOET, Strawye, or of strawe, *stramineus.* **1557** *Tottel's Misc.* (Arb.) 268 Some birdes can eate the strawie corne, And flee the lime the fowlers set. **1597** GERARDE *Herbal* I. vii. 8 A strawie stalke. **1664** BOYLE *Exper. Colours* iii. 34 The Lateral and Strawy parts [of ripe corn]. **1786** ABERCROMBIE *Gard. Assist.* 19 Having some strawey mulchy dung lay it on the ground over the roots. **1805** R. W. DICKSON *Pract. Agric.* II. 604 The strawy litter from the fold-yard. **1854** *Jrnl. R. Agric. Soc.* XV. I. 15 The hay is coarse and strawy. **1881** ELEANOR A. ORMEROD *Man. Injur. Insects* 148 Any long strawy lumps left on the surface will shelter the fly.

2. Made with straw; filled, thatched, or strewed with straw.

1568 T. HOWELL *Arb. Amitie* (1879) 65 The yoked Oxe doth smell his strawie stall. *a* **1593** MARLOWE *Ovid's Elegies* II. ix. 18 Rome if her strength the huge world had not fild, With strawie cabins now her courts should build. **1610** G. FLETCHER *Christ's Vict.* I. lxxxii, The strawy tent, Where gold, to make their Prince a crowne, they all present. **1736** W. THOMPSON *Nativity* 28 The strawy Shed, Where Mary, Queen of Heaven, in humbless Lay. **1859** CAPERN *Ballads & Songs* 110 Swaddled in a strawy bed, Lies the babe of Bethlehem. **1860** DICKENS *Uncomm. Trav.* xii, I departed from Dullborough in the strawy arms of Timpson's Blue-Eyed Maid [a coach].

3. Resembling straw in texture, colour, etc.

1668 WILKINS *Real Char.* 84 A yellowish flower, of a dry strawy consistence. **1839** URE *Dict. Arts* 93 The water.. acquires a yellowish tinge, and a strawy smell. **1879** 'ALIPH CHEEM' (Yeldham) *Lays of Ind* (ed. 6) 105 You'll see him turn a strawy hue.

4. *fig.* Light, empty, or worthless as straw.

1583 FULKE *Def.* Answ. Pref. 13 Luther..sayth, the epistle of Iames in comparison of these, is strawye, or like straw. **1606** SHAKS. *Tr. & Cr.* v. v. 24 (Qo.) And there the strawy Greekes ripe for his edge Fall downe before him, like a mowers swath. **1641** MILTON *Animadv.* 32 The iron, the brasse, and the clay of those muddy and strawy ages that follow. **1662** J. CHANDLER *Van Helmont's Oriat.* 76 Therefore by a strawie argument, the Maxim of the Schooles falls to the ground. **1957** T. HUGHES *Hawk in Rain* 20 With love so like fire they dared not Let it out into strawy small talk.

straw yard. 1. A yard littered with straw, in which horses and cattle are wintered. Also *attrib.*

1787 W. H. MARSHALL *E. Norfolk* (1795) II. 378 *Cow-par*, straw-yard; fold-yard. **1789** —— *Glouc.* II. 76 His practice is to buy in large Welch bullocks at Gloucester... He gives them the run of the straw yard the first winter. **1801** *Farmer's Mag.* Aug. 251 Winterers, or straw-yard cattle, intended for next summer's grass. **1844** *Queen's Regul. Army* 371 Horses bought in the Winter, are, generally, subject to diseases in coming from straw-yards, or from the open fields, into Stables. **1904** *Blackw. Mag.* Aug. 185/2 Spacious straw-yards for artillery bullocks.

2. *slang.* (See quot.)

1851 MAYHEW *Lond. Labour* II. 138/2 The night asylums or refuges for the destitute (usually called 'straw-yards' by the poor).

3. *colloq.* A (man's) straw hat.

1900 *Westm. Gaz.* 23 Apr. 9/2 The same hatter had sold two score 'strawyards' by noon to-day.

Hence **straw-yarder** *slang.* (See quot.)

1853 *N. & Q.* Ser. I. VII. 342/2 A seaman..said that the captain..had manned his ship with a 'lot of straw-yarders.' .. I was told that a 'straw-yarder' was a man about the docks who had never been to sea.

stray (streɪ), *sb.* Also 6 **strey,** 6 *pl.* **stras.** See also STRAIF. [Two formations: (1) a. AF. *stray, estrai*, verbal noun f. AF., OF. *estraier* STRAY *v.*[2]; (2) f. STRAY *v.*[2]]

I. 1. *Law.* A domestic animal found wandering away from the custody of its owner, and liable to be impounded and (if not redeemed) forfeited: = ESTRAY *sb.* (For *waifs and strays* see WAIF.)

[**1228** in *Mem. Ripon* (Surtees) I. 57 Et habent catalla felonum,..et wrek et weyf, stray, curiam suam et cognicionem de falso judicio.] **1498–9** *Durham Acc. Rolls* (Surtees) 194 Rec. 12 d. pro una ove vocata a hog capta pro 1 le stray in de (*sic*) Hemyngburgh. **1523** FITZHERB. *Surv.* 29 And if no man come within the yere and the day and to make suffycient proue that the catell is his than it is forfayte to the lorde as a strey. **15..** *Order for Swans* §20 *Archæologia* XXXII. 427 If the Maister of the Swannes, or his Deputy, do seaze or take vp any Swannes, as strayes for the Kings Maiestie. **1598** MANWOOD *Laws Forest* xv. 86 [The unclaimed beasts] were taken and seised by the Officers of the Forrest, to the vse of the king, as Strayes of the Forrest. **1599** B. JONSON *Ev. Man out of Hum.* I. ii. (1600) C iij b, The Lord of the soile ha's all wefts and straies here, ha's he not? *a* **1634** COKE *Inst.* IV. (1648) 280 No Fowle can be a stray but a Swan. **1711** *Lond. Gaz.* No. 4893/4 A..Horse, and a very little Bay-Nag, were taken up as Strays. **1805** WORDSW. *Prelude* v. 335 Some intermeddler still is on the watch To drive him back, and pound him, like a stray Within the pinfold of his own conceit. **1808** *Sporting Mag.* XXXI. 25 Cattle or horses, which, under the denomination..of strays or damage-feasant, are impounded by the Lord of the Manor.

b. *transf.*

1593 SHAKS. *2 Hen. VI*, IV. x. 27 Heere's the Lord of the soile come to seize me for a stray, for entering his Fee-simple without leaue. **1597** DELONEY *Gentle Craft* I. xv. Wks. (1912) 134 If that your heart be fled away, And it be taken for a Stray. **1639** FULLER *Holy War* III. xiii. 130 Leopoldus Duke of Austria..as being Lord of the soil, seised on this Royall stray ['this loose lion' i.e. Richard I]. **1713** C'TESS WINCHELSEA *Misc. Poems* 259 Shou'd I as a Stray be found, And seiz'd upon forbidden Ground.

2. An animal that has strayed or wandered away from its flock, home, or owner.

c **1440** *Promp. Parv.* 478/2 Stray beest þat goethe a-stray, *vagula.* **1543** in *Lett. & Papers Hen. VIII*, XVIII. II. 118 For drywyn the mor for stras iiij men ij days..to met and wagys iijs. ijd. *c* **1550** SIR J. CHEKE *Matt.* xviii. 13 Wold not he leave nijnti and nijn [sheep] on ye hilles, and go to seek ye strai. **1616** W. BROWNE *Brit. Past.* II. iv. 98 A youthfull Shepheard..Missing that morne a sheepe out of his Fold, Carefully seeking round to finde his stray. **1792** HORSLEY *Serm.* (1816) III. xl. 224 Just as the owner of a large flock is solicitous for the recovery of a single stray. **1797** HT. LEE *Canterb. T., Trav. T.* (1799) I. 203 Anxiously had she sought the brood, and most carefully had she replaced the little stray. **1887** F. FRANCIS Jun. *Saddle & Mocassin* 161 One of our steers..that got driven off with a bunch of strays which the San Simon boys was taking back. **1899** *Speaker* 23 Dec. 309/2 The sheep are folded—all but three ewes a-missing—Davie..speaks in a disconsolate voice of the three strays in the mountain.

†**b.** A person who wanders abroad; one who runs from home or employment. *Obs.*

1557 *Tottel's Misc.* (Arb.) 163 At Bacchus' feast none shall her mete..nor gasyng in an open strete, nor gaddyng as a stray. **1735** DYCHE & PARDON *Dict.*, *Stray*, a..Person that is run away from his Discipline, &c.

c. *fig.* One who has gone astray in conduct, opinion, etc.

1605 SYLVESTER *Urania* xliii, Anon from error's mazes Keeping th' unsteady, calling back the straies. **1614** —— *Little Bartas* 987 The Spirit..Which brings the straies home to Thy holy Fold. **1691** SHADWELL *Scowrers* v. 53 No pow'r but Love could thus call back a stray, From all the crooked Paths, to the right way. **1711** in *10th Rep. Hist. MSS. Comm.* App. v. 187 Nor is Heaven such a toy, as to be gained for a song, whatever the strayes of religion think.

1788 D. Gilson *Serm.* ix. 254 Is it [the Church] only to be an open Common—for the reception of every Stray?

d. A homeless, friendless person; an ownerless dog or cat. Also in the phrase ***waifs and strays***: see WAIF.

1649 *Valentine & Orson* ix. 43 They uttered forth many reproachful words against him, saying, that..he was but a found stray, poore, base, without any knowne Parents or Friends. **1864** [F. W. Robinson] *Mattie* II. 78 A stray whom no one would claim as child, sister, friend. **1889** *Harper's Mag.* Mar. 545/2 There is also a school for strays and truants..which re-enforces the public schools. **1892** *Daily News* 2 Apr. 6/6 Greater facilities are now offered than formerly in conveying the strays to the Home [for Lost Dogs].

e. Something that has wandered from its usual or proper place; something separated from the main body; a detached fragment, an isolated specimen.

1798 Sophia Lee *Canterb. T., Young Lady's T.* II. 208 It is a stray of my own; composed when I was a little rustic, wandering in the woods. **1824** Miss Mitford *Village* I. 252 The keys, will sometimes be found, with other strays, in that goodly receptacle. **1866** Swinburne *Poems & Ball.* 220 Such dead things..As the sea feeds on, wreck and stray And castaway. **1888** Goode *Amer. Fishes* 111 It is certainly not found in the Gulf of Mexico, unless as a stray. **1891** Stevenson *Let. W. C. Angus* Apr., Wks. 1912 XXV. 70 If you will collect the strays of Robin Fergusson, fish for material, collect any last re-echoing gossip, command me to do what you prefer.

†**f.** *collect.* A number of stray beasts; a body of stragglers from an army; *fig.* those who are astray from the faith. *Obs.*

1597 Shaks. *2 Hen. IV*, IV. ii. 120 Strike vp our Drummes, pursue the scatter'd stray. **1611** Speed *Hist. Gt. Brit.* IX. vi. 53 Restore with me Religion and Discipline to the ancient splendor therof..; reduce the stray, enlighten our ignorance, polish our rudenesse. **1717** Addison *Ovid's Metam., Transf. Battus,* [He] cried out, 'Neighbour, hast thou seen a stray Of bullocks and of heifers pass this way?'

3. *Electr.* (See quot. 1912.)

1901 *Westm. Gaz.* 16 Dec. 6/3 The general impression in America is..that Marconi has been premature in announcing his success... Thomas Edison..says, 'Marvellous! marvellous! but let us not forget that there are such things as electric strays.' **1912** *Nature* 21 Nov. 345/2 Due to atmospheric causes, there is [*sic*] generally audible in the telephone receiver clicks and noises commonly spoken of as atmospherics or strays.

II. †**4.** The action of straying or wandering.

For *o strai, on (the) stray, out of stray* see ASTRAY *adv.*

a **1300-** [see ASTRAY *adv.*]. *c* **1400** *Destr. Troy* 6258 Lokis well to þe listis, þat no lede passe! If any stert vpon stray, strike hym to dethe. *c* **1400** *26 Pol. Poems* iv. 14 Stoken in presoun as best fro stray. *c* **1440** *Promp. Parv.* 478/2 Stray, or a-stray, *vagacio, palacio.* **1530** Palsgr. 277/1 [In 'Table of Substantives'] Stray wandring, *au large.* **1535** *Act 27 Hen. VIII*, c. 7 §2 If..any maner of beaste or quycke cattell..come into any of the said forestes by strayes theffe stolen or otherwise. **1605** Shaks. *Lear* I. i. 212, I would not from your loue make such a stray, To match you where I hate. **1614** W. B. *Philos. Banq.* (ed. 2) 121 Yet in his youth was he accessary to the errour of his yeeres, following the whole sway and stray of youth. **1615** Brathwait *Strappado* 10 Lasse it is nothing for maides now adaies For which of them (though modest) hath not straies. **1623** Lisle *Ælfric on O. & N. Test.* To the Prince xxxv, As long as these, and Riuers all elsewhere, Their moulten Crystall poure by crooked strayes Into the Maine. **1793** *Gentl. Mag.* Oct. 913/2 [Art.] A Naturalist's Stray.

5. The right of allowing cattle to stray and feed on common land. *north.* Also ***stray of rabbits*** (see quot. 1877).

1736 F. Drake *Eboracum* I. vii. 240 Land..over which the poor freemen of each ward have a particular stray for their cattle from Michaelmas to Lady-day. **1776** *Foston Incl. Act* 4 Right of stray, or other right. **1828** Carr *Craven Gloss., Stray,* a right of depasturing on commons. **1880** *Spectator* 21 Aug. 1065 The mountain land over which the tenants have had for generations a right of stray for their cattle.

b. A piece of unenclosed land on which there is a common right of pasture: = COMMON *sb.* 5.

At Harrogate, 'The Stray' is the name of a large piece of grass land round which the principal houses are built.

1889 *Harper's Mag.* Nov. 843/2 The eight hundred acres, more or less, in six different 'strays' without the walls [of York], belonging to the four ancient wards, and on which freemen have exclusive right to depasture their cattle.

6. *Naut.* Deviation (of a sounding-line) from the perpendicular: = STRAY-LINE 2. Also = STRAY-LINE 1; in Comb. **stray-mark**, 'the mark at the junction of the stray and log lines' (Adm. Smyth).

1628 Digby *Voy. Mediterr.* (Camden) 91 Sounding from a shippe in a forcible gale is very vncertaine, because of the much stray of the line.

stray (streɪ), *a.* [Partly an aphetic variant of ASTRAY (cf. LONE *a.* from ALONE); partly attrib. use of STRAY *sb.*]

1. Of an animal: That has wandered from confinement or control and goes free; that has straggled from a flock; of a domestic animal, etc., that has become homeless or ownerless. †Also rarely of a person.

1607 Topsell *Four-f. Beasts* 663 His seruants seeing a stray Sow come among them, the owner whereof they did not know, presently they slew her. **1634** Milton *Comus* 315 If your stray attendance [= attendants] be yet lodg'd, Or shroud within these limits. **1671** —— *P.R.* I. 315 An aged man..Following..the quest of some stray Ewe. **1832** Ht. Martineau *Life in Wilds* v. 58 He saw a herd of buffaloes. ..Arnall determined that if a stray one came within shot, he would take aim at it. **1875** Maine *Hist. Inst.* ix. 261 The right of the lawful possessor of land to..impound stray beasts which are damaging his crops. **1908** [Miss E. Fowler] *Betw. Trent & Ancholme* 143 A little stray lamb who left the fold.

b. *fig.*

1749 Fielding *Tom Jones* XVIII. viii, Whether the good-natured world will suffer such a stray-sheep to return to the road of virtue. **1862** Goulburn *Personal Relig.* IV. v. (1873) 287 To seek the stray sheep in the wilderness of the world.

2. Of a cable: Loose, slack. Cf. STRAY *sb.* 7 and STRAY-LINE.

1791 Smeaton *Edystone L.* §128 Hill's company were employed on board the buss, heaving the stray cable [etc.].

3. Of a person or thing: Separated from the main body; occurring away from the regular course or habitat; isolated.

1796–1842 Wordsw. *Borderers* II. 766, I was going To waken our stray Baron. *a* **1834** Newman *Par. Serm.* (1836) III. xxii. 360 In the cavern, or the desert, or the mountain, where God's stray servants lived. **1837** Carlyle *Fr. Rev.* I. v. vi, Their infinite hum waxing ever louder, into imprecations, perhaps into crackle of stray musketry. **1849** W. S. Mayo *Kaloolah* vii. (1850) 65 The little medical knowledge that I had picked up by stray reading. **1867** H. Latham *Black & White* 22 In one of the corridors we fell in with a stray Professor, who..showed us over the whole building. **1872** Jenkinson *Guide Eng. Lakes* (1879) 318 The desolate grandeur of the scenery which there meets the eye of the stray visitor. **1873** Tristram *Moab* iii. 39 Not even a stray salsola or salicornia to relieve the flat sand beds. **1907** J. A. Hodges *Elem. Photogr.* (ed. 6) 33 The detection of stray beams of light coming from chinks and cracks in the door.

†**4.** Strolling, vagrant. *Obs. rare.*

1620 in *Southampton Court Leet Rec.* (1907) I. 578 The spoyle therof is Cheifelie occasioned by the sufferinge of Straye players to acte their enterludes ther.

5. *Electr.* (See quots.)

1893 Sloane *Electr. Dict., Stray Field.* In a dynamo or motor the portion of the field whose lines of force are not cut by the armature windings. *Ibid., Stray Power.* The proportion of the energy wasted in driving a dynamo, lost through friction and other hurtful resistances.

stray (streɪ), *v.*[1] *Obs.* exc. *dial.* Also 5 **strie.** [OE. *strēgan* (**strīegan*, **strīgan*) = Goth. *straujan*, f. Teut. root **strau-*: **streu-*: see STREW *v.*] *trans.* To strew.

c **1000** *Seafarer* 97 (Gr.) þeah þe græf wille golde stregan. *c* **1440** *Pallad. on Husb.* IV. 670 For rayn, in sonne yf thou ne mayst hem drie, Hote askis may this fleykis vnder strie In house in stede of sonne. *Ibid.* XII. 381, 507. **1560** *Ludlow Churchw. Acc.* (Camden) 95 For russes to straye the seate before the pilpett. **1658** A. Fox tr. *Würtz Surg.* I. iv. 13 They cause thereby infinite wrongs,..as if they had strayed the wounds full of venom. *Ibid.* I. iv. 13 When you stray that pouder into [it.] *Ibid.*, Must not the wound being straid full, be bound up. *Ibid.* I. iv. 14 The in-strayed pouder. **1886** *Cheshire Gloss., Stray,* to strew, to scatter.

stray (streɪ), *v.*[2] Also 4–6 **straye**, 6 **straie**, (**straigh**). [Aphetic var. of ASTRAY, ESTRAY *vbs.*, a. OF. *estraier*:—Rom. **estragare* (Pr. *estragar*), contraction of **estravagare*, repr. L. *extrā vagārī* to wander outside: see EXTRAVAGANT *a.*

The view that the OF. verb is a derivative of L. *strāta* STREET *sb.* is on phonological grounds untenable.]

1. *intr.* To escape from confinement or control, to wander away from a place, one's companions, etc. Const. *from, into,* also with *abroad, away, off.*

13.. *E.E. Allit. P.* B. 1199 And þay stoken so strayt, þat þay ne stray myȝt A fote fro þat forselet to forray no goudes. *c* **1330** R. Brunne *Chron. Wace* (Rolls) 12878 God tent til al his men he tok, When þey astraied, whideward [*v.r.* where þei straied whidire] þey schok. **1338** —— *Chron.* (1725) 219 [*Edwardus evasit de carcere Herfordiæ.*] In to þe watere he straied, & passed wele þat flode. *c* **1450** *Cov. Myst.* (1841) 74 Go do what ȝe lyst; se ȝour bestys not stray. *a* **1513** Fabyan *Chron.* (1811) 484 Sir Iohn de Vyenne, encountred l. sperys and xx. archers that were strayed frome theyr hoste. **1573–80** Tusser *Husb.* (1878) 40 Go stie vp thy Bore, least straying abrode, ye doo see him no more. **1590** Sir J. Smyth *Disc. Weapons* 11 b, That no man vpon paine of death being landed, shall straggle or stray abroad. **1653** W. Ramesey *Astrol. Restored* 173 If thou wouldst buy..Swans..to remain or keep from straying, let *Scorpio* be preferred. **1667** Milton *P.L.* III. 476 Here Pilgrims roam, that stray'd so farr to seek In Golgotha him dead, who lives in Heav'n. **1704–13** Pope *Windsor Forest* 165 Here too, 'tis sung, of old Diana stray'd, And Cynthus' top forsook for Windsor shade. **1722** Diaper tr. *Oppian's Halieut.* I. 658 Sea-Calves by Night far from the Waters stray. **1831** James *Philip Augustus* I. ii, Has thy falcon strayed? Say, 'twas a vile bird ..and call it a good loss. **1879** Froude *Cæsar* xvii. 287 To keep the legion within the lines, and not to allow any of the men to stray. **1888** 'J. S. Winter' *Bootle's Childr.* ix, The four elder children had strayed off to the hall to see what was going on there.

b. of an inanimate thing.

13.. *E.E. Allit. P.* A. 1173 My hede vpon þat hylle was layde, þer as my perle to grounde strayd. **1557** Phaer *Æneid* VII. (1558) Tiij b, Poison..Whiche from that serpent shed, & al her lymmes infecting straied. **1697** Dryden *Virg. Georg.* II. 507 Be bold To lop the disobedient Boughs, that stray'd Beyond their Ranks. **1738** Gray *Propertius* II. i. 8 If the loose Curls around her Forehead play, Or lawless, o'er their Ivory Margin stray. **1855** *Orr's Circ. Sci., Inorg. Nat.* 43 It has been assumed..that the earth was originally in a state of igneous fusion, from which it has cooled down by radiation... No one, however, has explained where this lost heat has strayed. **1873** Burton *Hist. Scot.* V. lvi. 121 The town had strayed beyond the wall built round it after the defeat at Flodden. **1908** [Miss E. Fowler] *Betw. Trent & Ancholme* 13 The Vines strayed down the west side of the old paddock wall.

2. To wander up and down free from control, to roam about. Const. *about, along, in, through* (a place); also with *about* adv.

1398 Trevisa *Barth. De P.R.* XV. lxix. (1495) 514 Galon people in Affrica stretche fro the south to the Hesperi Ocean, whiche men go aboute and stray in desert [L. *pervagans in desertis & discurrens*]. *c* **1425** *Castle Persev.* 2052 in *Macro Plays* 138 Hys enmys strayen in þe strete, to spylle man with spetows spot. *c* **1440** *Promp. Parv.* 478/2 Strayyn, or gon a-stray, *palo, vagor.* **1530** Palsgr. 738/1, I straye, I wander about and wot nat whyther I go, *je erre...* Yet the boye strayeth alone some where, God gyve grace that a beggar mete nat with hym. *Ibid.*, I stray about, as a masterlesse parson doth, *je vagabonde...* He doth nought but stray abowt and wyll do no labour in the worlde. **1556** Hoby tr. *Castiglione's Courtier* Ep. Transl. (1577) A ij, This Courtyer hath long strayed about this realme. **1590** Spenser *F.Q.* I. iii. 3 Yet she..Farre from all peoples prease, as in exile, In wildernesse and wastfull deserts strayd, To seeke her knight. **1610** Shaks. *Temp.* I. ii. 417 He hath lost his fellowes, And strayes about to finde 'em. **1632** Milton *L'Allegro* 72 Russet Lawns, and Fallows Gray, Where the nibling flocks do stray. **1697** Dryden *Virg. Georg.* IV. 158 When the Swarms are eager of their Play, And loath their empty Hives, and idly Stray. **1742** Gray *Eton* 13 Ah fields belov'd in vain, Where once my careless childhood stray'd. **1789** W. L. Bowles *Sonn. Cherwell*, Cherwell, how pleas'd along thy willow'd edge Erewhile I stray'd. **1850** Tennyson *In Mem.* cii. 14 Yea, but here Thy feet have stray'd in after hours With thy lost friend among the bowers. **1866** Augusta Wilson *St. Elmo* iii, But you are too young to be straying about in a strange place.

b. of an inanimate thing, the fingers, etc. Also *fig.* of a person, his thoughts, wishes, etc.

1647 Cowley *Mistr., Change* i, Love walks the pleasant Mazes of her Hair; Love does on both her Lips for ever stray. **1750** Gray *Elegy* 74 Their sober wishes never learn'd to stray. **1789** Cowper *Ann. Memorab.* 22 As the bee..So I from theme to theme display'd In many a page historic stray'd. **18..** Shelley *Queen of my Heart* iii, How I love to gaze As the cold ray strays O'er thy face. **1831** James *Philip Augustus* I. iv, Through the mazes of whose hair his other hand was straying. **1842** Browning *Pied Piper* vi, And his fingers, they noticed, were ever straying As if impatient to be playing Upon this pipe. **1873** Helps *Anim. & Mast.* i. (1875) 27 It strays from one topic to another, in the most eccentric fashion. **1885** 'Mrs. Alexander' *At Bay* i, Again her deft fingers strayed over the notes. **1909** Stacpoole *Pools of Silence* xxx, These thoughts..just came and strayed across his mind.

c. Of a stream: To meander.

1591 Shaks. *Two Gent.* II. vii. 31 And so by many winding nookes he [*sc.* the current] straies..to the wilde Ocean. **1643** Denham *Cooper's H.* 160 Where Thames amongst the wanton Vallies strays. **1700** Dryden *Acis, Polyph., & Galatea* 78 More clear than Ice, or running Streams, that stray Through Garden Plots. **1754** Gray *Progr. Poesy* 85 What time, where lucid Avon stray'd, To Him the mighty Mother did unveil Her aweful face.

†**d.** *trans.* To wander in, over, or through (a place). Also, to cause (the eye) to wander (over something). *Obs.* or *nonce-uses.*

1613 Heywood *Silver Age* III. i. G 1 His maw vnstaunch't He still the thicke Nemean groues doth stray. **1729** Savage *Wanderer* II. 106 To his my Sighs, to his my Tears reply! I stray o'er all the Tomb a watry Eye! **1844** A. Maclagan *Scotch Blue-bell* 29 How oft wi' rapture ha'e I strayed The mountain's heather crest.

3. *intr.* To wander from the direct way, deviate.

1561 Hoby tr. *Castiglione's Courtier* I. (1577) E iij, As he that walketh in the darke..and therefore many tymes strayeth from the right way. **1590** Spenser *F.Q.* I. i. 10 When weening to returne, whence they did stray, They cannot finde that path. **1593** Shaks. *Rich. II*, I. iii. 206 Farewell (my Liege) now no way can I stray, Saue back to England, all the worlds my way. **1604** E. G[rimstone] *D'Acosta's Hist. Indies* IV. xxx. 291 Being straied in the mountaines, not knowing which way he shoulde passe. **1912** J. L. Myres *Dawn of Hist.* ix. 191 A strong inducement to the nomad to stray into the richer pasture.

4. *fig.* **a.** To wander from the path of rectitude, to err.

c **1325** *Metr. Hom.* (1862) 52 Bot in our gat lis Satenas.. And spies ful gern ef we straye, And haldes noht the riht way. **1457** Harding *Chron.* in *Eng. Hist. Rev.* (1912) Oct. 740 Scotland hool, which shulde your Reule obaye As Souereyn lorde, for whiche thay prowdly stray. **1548** Udall, etc. *Erasm. Par. Luke* xxii. 54–62 Neither was he lyke to haue made any ende of straying out of the righte waye. **1552** [see ERR *v.*[1] 2]. **1690** Prior *Consid. 88th Ps.* iii, Nor refuge could I find, nor friend abroad, Straying in vice, and destitute of God. **1712–14** Pope *Rape Lock* I. 91 Oft, when the world imagine women stray, The Sylphs thro' mystic mazes guide their way. **1780** Cowper *Doves* i, Reas'ning..Man yet mistakes his way, While meaner things, whom instinct leads, Are rarely known to stray. **1831** N. P. Willis *Brown University* 32 A heavenward spirit, straying oftentimes, But never widely. **1902** Violet Jacob *Sheep-Stealers* xii, It was the direst necessity which had induced George Williams to stray so far across the line of honesty.

b. To wander or deviate in mind, purpose, etc. Said also of the mind or thoughts.

1390 Gower *Conf.* III. 371, I was out of mi sounee affraied, Wherof I sih my wittes straied, And gan to wclepe hem hom ayein. **1577** Grange *Golden Aphrod.* L j, But why seeme I thus to stray from my texte? **1581** Pettie *Guazzo's Civ. Conv.* II. (1586) 56 b, It is a thing unseemely..in talke to straye to farre from fit and usuall matters. **1709** Pope *Ess. Crit.* 104 Then Criticism the Muses hand-maid prov'd, To dress her charms, and make her more belov'd: But following wits from that intention stray'd. **1766** Goldsm. *Vic. W.* xiv, But, sir, I ask pardon, I am straying from the question. **1813** Scott *Rokeby* I. xii, Still from the purpose wilt thou stray! Good gentle friend, how went the day?

†**c.** *trans.* (causative.) To cause to err or deviate; to distract. *Obs.*

1561 T. HOBY tr. *Castiglione's Courtyer* III. (1577) Q v, We shal know.. as touching the vnderstanding of great matters, that they doe not straye oure wittes, but rather quicken them. *Ibid.* Q vj, The loue of the Damsell Laura sometime strayed him from it. **1590** SHAKS. *Com. Err.* v. i. 51 Hath not else his eye Stray'd his affection in vnlawfull loue?

stray, obs. Sc. form of STRAW.

'strayaway. [f. STRAY *v.*[2] + AWAY *adv.*] An animal that strays away; a straggler.

1820 KEATS *Isabella* xvii, Quick cat's-paws on the generous stray-away. **1868** BROWNING *Ring & Bk.* v. 1198 What did he else but.. Leave, like a provident shepherd, his safe flock To follow the single lamb and strayaway?

strayed (streɪd), *ppl. a.* [f. STRAY *v.*[2] + -ED[1].] That has gone astray, *lit.* and *fig.*

1529 *Supplic. to King* (E.E.T.S.) 28 To call agayne the strayed shepe in-to the ryght waye. **1590** H. R. *Defiance to Fortune* B 3 b, Searching for the straied beastes of his saide maister Miller. **1615** BRATHWAIT *Strappado* 10 Yea I know som which may lament with thee For their straide daughters. **1634** MILTON *Comus* 503, I came not here on such a trivial toy As a stray'd Ewe. **1653** H. COGAN tr. *Pinto's Trav.* xv. 51 He had slain at times in strayed Vessels above an hundred Portugals. **1707** KEN in W. L. Bowles *Life* (1831) II. 296, I rejoice that my strayed sheep are reduced under his government. **1895** ZANGWILL *Master* II. ix. 233 A strayed sparrow hopped dolefully.. on the floating platform. **1897** *Allbutt's Syst. Med.* II. 1033 Kidney, spleen, pleura, and the urinary passages have sheltered strayed specimens of these parasites at times.

strayer ('streɪə(r)). [f. STRAY *v.*[2] + -ER[1].] One who strays, in the senses of the verb.

1519 HORMAN *Vulg.* 263 b, He called ageyne the strayers out of ordre. **1570** FOXE *A. & M.* (ed. 2) 1912/1 A great straier abroad in all quarters of the realme to deface and impeach the springing of Gods holy Gospel. **1575–85** ABP. SANDYS *Serm.* vii. §15. 113 All sinners are straiers: for sinne maketh a diuision betweene God and man. **1638** RUTHERFORD *Lett.* (1881) 50 Ye faithful pastors yet amongst the flocks..; Or any weak, tired strayers who cast but half an eye after the Bridegroom. **1868** BROWNING *Ring & Bk.* IV. 1245 For the priest, spritely strayer out of bounds,.. Let him be relegate to Civita. **1908** *Academy* 4 Jan. 308/2 We suspect that, like 'the old prophet,' he is a confirmed strayer from his beat.

straygne, -er: see STRAIN *v.*[1], STRAINER.

straying ('streɪɪŋ), *vbl. sb.* [f. STRAY *v.*[2] + -ING[1].] **a.** The action of the verb, in various senses; also, an instance of this.

1548 *Elyot's Dict., Erratio*, a goyng out of the waie, a wandryng, a straiyng abrode, a rouyng. **1583** GOLDING *Calvin on Deut.* viii. 47 What els are the wais of the world but straiings, so as euery man gaddes in and out when they once turne their backes vpon God. **1632** SANDERSON *Serm. Ad Aulam* ii. (1681) 22 Those strayings also and outsteppings, whereof Gods faithfullest servants are now and then guilty. **1643** ROUS *Ps.* xlv. 18 (1646) 76 Our heart's not turn'd back, from thy way, our steps no straying made. **1786** G. FRAZER *Dove's Flight* 39 Observe the pidgeon in her straying from the flock. **1820** KEATS *Isabella* xviii, How could they find out in Lorenzo's eye A straying from his toil? *a* **1857** H. BONAR *Hymns of Faith & Hope* 33 Cease, my soul, thy strayings! **1876** M. ARNOLD *Lit. & Dogma* 244 Those learned inquirers ..who were so busy about the strayings of Ulysses, so inattentive to their own. **1889** H. E. HANDERSON tr. *Baas' Hist. Med.* 495 *note*, Patin was the first who observed a case of tubal pregnancy, ascribing it to a straying of the ovum.

b. Gerundially in *to go a-straying*. Now only *arch.*

a **1586** SIDNEY *Ps.* xiv. 3 And loe, he findes that all a straying went. **1884** *Eng. Illustr. Mag.* Dec. 152/2 Thoughts that had gone astraying half across the globe. **1936** AUDEN *Look, Stranger!* 56 And Garbo's and Cleopatra's wits to go astraying.

straying (streɪɪŋ), *ppl. a.* [f. STRAY *v.*[2] + -ING[2].] That strays, in the senses of the verb. **a.** Of a person, animal, etc.

1585 T. WASHINGTON tr. *Nicholay's Voy.* III. xv. 99 Duryng these blind and straying peregrinations, they carry none other apparrell then a little cassock. **1593** A. CHUTE *Beautie Dishonoured* (Budig 1908) 95 Neuer did flocke to old Vlisses Queene, In wearie absence of her straying knight, Neuer more woers [etc.]. **1681** FLAVEL *Meth. Grace* xxviii. 475 The straying bullock needs a heavy clog. **1831** MARY W. SHELLEY *Swiss Peasant* Tales x. (1891) 189 Or a straying cow would lead him far into the depths of the stormy hills.

b. Of a thing. †*straying star*: a planet; cf. ERRANT *a.* 9 b.

1585 T. WASHINGTON tr. *Nicholay's Voy.* II. ix. 42 b, The seuen straying starres. **1601** HOLLAND *Pliny* II. xlv. I. 22 The straying starres or planets. **1612** *Two Noble K.* I. v. 15 This world's a Citty full of straying Streetes, And Death's the market place, where each one meetes.

c. *fig.*

1553 *Short Catechism* 7 b, Hearin is debarred al kind of filthy & strayeng lust. *a* **1586** SIDNEY *Ps.* i. 1 He blessed is who neither loosely treads The straying steps as wicked councel leads,.. Nor yet [etc.]. *c* **1600** SHAKS. *Sonn.* xli. 10 And chide thy beauty, and thy straying youth. **1690** NORRIS *Beatitudes* (1692) 9 To reduce straying man to his true Good and Happiness. **1867** M. E. GRANT DUFF *Notes fr. Diary 1851–1872* (1897) II. 78 He writes of these straying sheep without bigotry.

straykyngs: see STRAIKEN.

'stray-line. *Naut.* [f. STRAY *a.* (or STRAY *sb.* 7) + LINE *sb.*]

1. (See quot. 1867.)

1703 DAMPIER *Voy.* III. I. 99 An extraordinary Care ought to be used in heaving the Log, for fear of giving too much Stray-Line in a moderate Gale. **1867** SMYTH *Sailor's Word-bk., Stray line of the log*, about 10 or 12 fathoms of line left unmarked next the log-ship, in order that it may get out of the eddy of the ship's wake before the measuring begins, or the glass is turned.

2. = STRAY *sb.* 6.

1769 FALCONER *Dict. Marine* II. (1780), *Derive*.. the stray-line, or allowance made for stray-line, occasioned by a ship's falling to leeward, when sounding, in deep water.

3. *Whaling.* That part of the tow-line which is in the water when fast to a whale.

1820 SCORESBY *Acc. Arctic Reg.* II. 232 A portion of five or six fathoms of the line first put into the boat called the 'stray-line', is left uncovered, by that which follows.

4. A submerged or floating line fastened at one end only.

1888 HARDY *Wessex Tales* II. v. 143 They'll string the tubs to a stray-line, and sink 'em a little-ways from shore.

strayling ('streɪlɪŋ). [f. STRAY *a.* or *v.* + -LING[1].

Cf. *changeling, wildling*. The word coincides formally with a possible dim. of STRAY *sb.*, but in the quots. it has not the dim. sense.]

A stray thing or person.

1838 LYTTON *Leila* III. i. 31 It may win a new strayling to the Immortal Fold. **1881** G. ALLEN in *Cornhill Mag.* June 705 Sometimes garden kinds, escaped from cultivation.. sometimes American straylings. **1904** *Blackw. Mag.* Jan. 156/1 We owe a greater debt to our own countrymen than to the straylings from Russia.

straymer, obs. form of STREAMER.

strayinge, -our: see STRANGE, STRANGER.

strayngth, obs. form of STRENGTH.

stray-running, *ppl. a. rare*[−1]. [f. STRAY *a.* or *v.*[2] + RUNNING *ppl. a.*] That runs astray.

1914 D. H. LAWRENCE *Prussian Officer & Other Stories* 251 What am I frightened of him for? Why, for you, you stray-running little bitch.

stre, strea, streach(e: see STRAW, STRETCH.

†**stread**, *sb. Obs. rare*[−1]. App. a constable's 'beat' or district.

1518 *Star Chamber Cases* (Selden Soc.) II. 136 Euery Constable warnyd wythin hys stread euery man to be in the Fen in the mornyng.

streak (striːk), *sb.*[1] Forms: *α.* 1 strica, 4 stric, stryk, 5 strick(e, 5–6 stryke, 5–7 strike; *β.* 5 strek, 5–6 streke, 6 streeke, 6–7 streek, streake, 6– streak. [OE. *strica* wk. masc., f. weak-grade of the Teut.-root **strīk-*: see STRIKE *v.* The *α* and *β* forms represent a difference of dialectal phonetic development: in the *α* forms the *ĭ* remained (cf. *prick* sb.:—OE. *prica*); in the *β* forms the OE. *ĭ* in open syllable became ME. *ē* (with *strēke* cf. *week*, ME. *wēke*:—OE. *wicu*). It is probable that the spelling *strike, stryke* in the late 16th and early 17th c. sometimes represents a pronunciation (striːk), so that these forms would really belong to the *α* class. Cf. Goth. *strik-s*, OHG., mod.G. *strich* masc., MDu. *strēke* (Du. *streek* fem.), which agree in sense and root-grade with the Eng. sb.]

†**1. a.** A line, mark, stroke; esp. one used as a sign or character in writing or as a unit or degree in measurement. *Obs.*

α. *c* **1000** ÆLFRIC *Hom.* II. 200 An strica oððe an stæf [L. *iota unum aut unus apex*] ðære ealdan æ ne bið forȝæᵹed oðþæt hi ealle ᵹefyllede beon. **1387** TREVISA *Higden* (Rolls) III. 249 Esdras.. fonde up newe manere titles and strikes [L. *apices litterarum*] to write among þe lettres. *c* **1391** CHAUCER *Astrol.* II. §12. 24, & endith in the nexte strik of the plate. *Ibid.*, Techyng by swych strikes the howres of planetes by ordre as thei sitten in the heuene. *c* **1400** *Destr. Troy* 3024 The shede þurghe þe shyre here shone as þe lilly, Streght as a strike, straght þurgh the myddes. *c* **1460** [see *β*.]. **1530** PALSGR. 58 There is a stryke above the hed of *au*, by cause the accent of the worde is there. **1598** W. PHILLIP tr. *Langenes' Voy. Ships Holland E. Ind.* 11 We found that our Compasses helde two Strikes to farre Northwarde. **1610** HOLLAND *Camden's Brit.* I. 178 Upon this Exchequer board is laid a cloth.. rewed with strikes distant one from another a foote. **1611** tr. *Serlio's Archit.* IV. vii. 34 b, The strickes of the Columnes, which were call Chanels or hollowings, shall be 24. in number.

β. *c* **1440** *Promp. Parv.* 479/1 Strek, or poynt be-twyx ij. clausys yn a boke (*S.W.* poyntinge of ij. clauses), *liminiscus*. *c* **1460** J. METHAM *Wks.* 89 Yef in the same lyne be suche strykys descende and in the myddys be cutte or deuyded with other lynes or strekes. **1545** in *Archæologia* XLIII. 237, iiij copys of ymagerye worke with strekes of golds. **1594** BLUNDEVIL *Exerc.* I. xxvii. (ed. 7) 65 Minutes are marked with one streek over the head, seconds with two streekes, thirds with three streekes. **1633** B. JONSON *Tale Tub* IV. i. Scene interloping 41 *Cle.* Zure, you can gage 'hun. *Med.* To a streake, or lesse: I know his diameters, and circumference. **1650** BULWER *Anthropomet.* xxii. 238 Men and women use to cut three streaks on their body. **1664** POWER *Exp. Philos.* I. 7 View them [the wings of the butterfly] in the Microscope, and you may see the very streaks of the Coelestial pencil that drew them. **1735** DYCHE & PARDON *Dict.*, *Streak*, a Line or Mark make to put Things in order by, &c.

†**b.** A cutting stroke. *Obs. rare*[−1].

1725 *Bradley's Family Dict.* s.v. *Pears*, Give them [*sc.* the pears] a streak upon the Head with the point of a Knife.

2. a. A thin irregular line of a different colour or substance from that of the material or surface of which it forms a part.

α. **1585** HIGINS *Junius' Nomencl.* 414/2 Marble hauing white specks or stricks in it.

β. **1577** GRANGE *Golden Aphrod.* H iv b, And teares with streakes doth paynte Their lether cheekes. **1646** SUCKLING *Poems* (1648) 39 For streaks of red were mingled there, Such as are on a Katherne Pear. **1666** G. HARVEY *Morbus Angl.* xxi. (1672) 50 A high coloured Urin with a number of small streeks of fat, swimming a top in the form of a Cobweb. **1667** MILTON *P.L.* XI. 879 But say, what mean those colour'd streaks in Heavn [*sc.* a rainbow]. **1718** PRIOR *Solomon* I. 77 While the fantastic Tulip strives to break In two-fold Beauty, and a parted Streak. **1784** COWPER *Task* VI. 241 Not a flow'r But shows some touch, in freckle, streak, or stain, Of his unrivall'd pencil. **1796** WITHERING *Brit. Plants* (ed. 3) III. 613 Petals.. purple, with 3 or 4 darker streaks. **1845** BUDD *Dis. Liver* 220 Streaks of a black substance were observed in the matter which was vomited. **1845–7** LONGF. *Evang.* II. iv. 172 Then there appeared and spread faint streaks of gray o'er her forehead. **1860** TYNDALL *Glac.* II. xxvii. 381 We observe blue streaks, from a few inches to several feet in length, upon the walls of the same crevasse. **1876** O. C. STONE in *Jrnl. R. Geogr. Soc.* XLVI. 57 They paint the face with streaks by means of a rose-coloured lime. **1890** *Hardwicke's Sci.-Gossip* XXVI. 265/2 The appearance of Jupiter is very different from that of Mars. On his surface we see grey.. streaks or belts. **1899** *Allbutt's Syst. Med.* VIII. 595 Papules rarely arise, but there are often red scaly streaks on the face. **1911** WEBSTER s.v., Bacon with a streak of lean and a streak of fat.

b. A line of colour, less firm and regular than a stripe, occurring as a distinctive mark on the coat of an animal, the plumage of a bird, the body or wings of an insect. Also *fig.*

α. **1567** MAPLET *Gr. Forest* 70 [This aspis] is of white colour,.. beset with black spots or strikes. **1626** *Maldon* (Essex) *Docum.* Bundle 208 No. 9 A tall darkeish graye gelding,.. haveing a white stricke on one side.

β. **1641** J. JACKSON *True Evang. T.* I. 74 Too much of the Leopard.. in our spots, and streaks, with sinfull customes, and habits. **1687** LOVELL tr. *Thevenot's Trav.* I. 237 This Ass had a black List down the back, and the rest of its Body was all begirt with white and Tawny streaks. **1697** DRYDEN *Virg. Georg.* IV. 150 The better Brood [of bees].. Are mark'd with Royal streaks of shining hue. **1815** STEVENS in *Shaw's Gen. Zool.* IX. I. 29 There is a short streak at the angles of the mouth, beneath the eye, sometimes whitish, sometimes yellow. **1882–4** *Yarrell's Brit. Birds* (ed. 4) III. 561 The black loral streak.. is assumed the second year.

c. In the names of moths, etc.

1704 PETIVER *Gazophyl.* II. Tab. xi, *Papilio minor fuscus, duplici linea inferne prædítus*, The brown double Streak. **1775** M. HARRIS *Engl. Lepidoptera* 45 Phalæna... Streak. **1815** BURROW *Elem. Conchol.* 206 Patella Mammillaris. Black Hair Streak Limpet. **1832** J. RENNIE *Butterfl. & Moths.* **1872** J. G. WOOD *Insects at Home* 461 The Moth which is appropriately termed the Streak (*Chesias spartiata*).

d. *Min.* The line of coloured powder produced by scratching a mineral or fossil, or the mark made by rubbing it on a harder surface.

1794 KIRWAN *Elem. Min.* I. 26 External characters. These are colour, shape, lustre,.. colour of streak &c. **1796** *Ibid.* (ed. 2) I. 183 Its streak somewhat glossy. **1805** WEAVER tr. *Werner's Ext. Char. Fossils* 190 Solid fossils.. when scraped .. yield a powder, presenting the same, or a different, colour from that of the fossil; and also the same or a more or less different lustre. This is called the streak. **1849** J. NICOL *Man. Min.* 487 Kobellite... Colour blackish lead-grey to steel-grey; streak black. **1888** CROOKES *Mitchell's Pract. Assaying* (ed. 6) 239 Cinnabar has both a red colour and a red streak.

e. *Biol.* etc. A linear mark, stria. Also, a narrow tract in a tissue.

primitive streak: see PRIMITIVE *a.* 8.

1837 P. KEITH *Bot. Lex.* 34 If the streak of the parenchyma is to be regarded as a good evidence. But this streak is not discernible in all stems. **1856** HENSLOW *Bot. Terms, Streak*, a straight line formed by a vein, by colour, by indentation, &c. *Ibid.*, *Stria* (a groove or furrow), a streak. **1859** SEMPLE *Diphtheria* 20 We often see a long, narrow streak, of a dark red colour, which extends into the pharynx. **1899** *Allbutt's Syst. Med.* VII. 716 The degeneration may be more intense in certain streaks; as in the posterior root-zones, or in Goll's tracts.

f. *Glass-making.* (See quot. 1807.)

1807 T. THOMSON *Chem.* (ed. 3) II. 512 *Streaks*. These are waved lines, often visible in glass, which interrupt distinct vision. **1832** G. R. PORTER *Porcelain & Gl.* 197 Large plates,.. to be perfect, require to be without streak or bubble.

g. *Bacteriology.* A light scratch made with the bacteria-covered point of a needle on the surface of the mass to be infected. Cf. *streak-culture* in 8.

1892 G. M. STERNBERG *Man. Bacteriol.* I. viii. 75 We commonly make a streak upon the surface of cooked potato or solidified blood serum in studying the development of various bacteria on these culture media. **1893** W. R. DAWSON tr. *Schenk's Man. Bacteriol.* 57. **1939** A. J. SALLE *Fund. Princ. Bacteriol.* ix. 133 The last streaks should thin out the culture sufficiently to give isolated colonies. **1969** SIROCKIN & CULLIMORE *Practical Microbiol.* ii. 17 It will be observed that away from the initial streak, the growth is less dense and discrete colonies are present.

h. *Hairdressing.* A strand or strands of hair fashionably tinted, esp. in a light colour. Cf. HIGH LIGHT 1 b.

1949 *Queen* 21 Dec. 39 Light streaks are again fashionable. These can be tinted to match an evening dress—the colour can be washed out next day. **1956** ASHLEY & STEVENSON *Hair Design & Control* xi. 127 When introducing blonde streaks, or tipping, it assists to segregate the streak or section of hair concerned by means of a piece of cloth or Cellophane. **1966** J. S. COX *Illustr. Dict. Hairdressing* 144/1 *Streaks*, light strands of hair deliberately contrived to enhance the appearance. **1979** R. RENDELL *Make Death love Me* v. 40 She and Pam argued as to whether it was possible to put blonde streaks in one's hair at home.

3. a. A faint line of light (esp. of the dawn) diversifying the darkness. Also *fig.*

1592 SHAKS. *Rom. & Jul.* II. iii. 2 The gray ey'd morne smiles on the frowning night, Checkring the Easterne Cloudes with streaks of light. **1605** —— *Macb.* III. iii. 5 The West yet glimmers with some streakes of Day. **1697** DRYDEN *Æneis* IX. 477 And see the scatter'd Streaks of dawning day. **1812–16** J. SMITH *Panorama Sci. & Art* I. 450 When we look at a candle..with our eyes almost closed, streaks of light appear to dart upwards and downwards. **1837** CARLYLE *Fr. Rev.* II. III. vi, Darkness..with here and there some streak of faint lurid light. **1881** S. R. MACPHAIL *Relig. House Pluscardyn* xii. 114 The grey streaks of Reformation dawn speedily forced themselves upon public attention. **1885** 'MRS. ALEXANDER' *At Bay* v, The first faint streaks of daylight were stealing across the eastern sky.

b. A flash of lightning, etc.

1781 COWPER *Heroism* 18 While through the stygian veil that blots the day, In dazzling streaks, the vivid lightnings play. **1828** CARLYLE *Misc., Burns* (1840) I. 352 Streaks of hell-fire quivering madly. **1847** *Illustr. Lond. News* 10 July 19/3 She saw a streak of lightning shoot in an oblique direction. **1863** AYTOUN *Lays Scott. Cavaliers, Exec. Montrose* xiii, And the jagged streak of the levin-bolt Lit up the gloomy town.

c. *slang.* ***streak of lightning***, ? a glass of gin (cf. LIGHTNING *sb.* 2). ***like a streak, like streaks***: with the swiftness of lightning; also ***quick as a streak*** and *transf.*

1839 *Knickerbocker* XIII. 298, I see him yesterday afternoon..starting off like a streak, to go to Norridgewock. **1849** C. LANMAN *Lett. from Alleghany Mts.* xi. 89 The water wheeled my head round to the hole, and in I went quick as a streak. **1859** C. MACKAY *Life & Liberty Amer.* I. 169 'Ginsling,' 'brandy-smash', 'a streak of lightning', [etc.]. **1887** M. E. WILKINS *Humble Romance* 376 He went past me like a streak when I was coming up the road. **1901** *Daily Chron.* 26 Sept. 6/2 Workman was running like a 'streak,' to use the local phrase. **1901** *Scribner's Mag.* XXIX. 501/1 We worked like streaks. **1920** C. SANDBURG *Smoke & Steel* 138 Maybe I will light out like a streak of wind.

d. *slang* (orig. *U.S.*). A rapid move; (a journey undertaken at) a fast rate. Also *fig.*

a **1861** T. WINTHROP *John Brent* (1862) xxii. 243 She's got the old man to take care of and follow off on his next streak. **1865** A. D. WHITNEY *Gayworthys* 141 She's going a good streak, ain't she? **1875** J. G. HOLLAND *Sevenoaks* iv. 60 We'll wopse 'im up in some blankits, an' make a clean streak for the woods. **1909** R. A. WASON *Happy Hawkins* 280 She was in the habit of estimatin' just how little nourishment it would take to run her to the next feed, gettin' it into her in the shortest possible time, an' then makin' a streak for it. **1960** *Twentieth Cent.* Dec. 556 His streak to stardom.

e. ***to talk a streak***, to talk fast or constantly; ***to talk a blue streak***: see *blue streak* (*b*) s.v. BLUE *a.* 13.

1915 J. LONDON *Jacket* v. 37 He sleeps most of the watch, and we can talk a streak. **1968** T. WOLFE *Electric Kool-Aid Acid Test* xxvii. 373 Robertson's talking a streak. It's a grand speech.

4. a. A long irregular narrow strip of land, water, etc.; a line of colour representing a distant object in a landscape.

the silver streak: the English Channel; see SILVER *sb.* 21 and cf. quot. 1870 below.

1727 DYER *Grongar Hill* 118 See on the mountain's southern side..How close and small the hedges lie! What streaks of meadows cross the eye! **1818** KEATS *Lett.* 20 July (1895) 173 The first glance was a streak of waters deep in the Bases of large black Mountains. **1841** BROWNING *Pippa Passes* I. Poems (1905) 167/2 Ah, the clear morning! I can see St. Mark's: That black streak is the belfry. **1842** TENNYSON *Œnone* 55 Far-up the solitary morning smote The streaks of virgin snow. **1865** W. G. PALGRAVE *Journ. Central & E. Arabia* II. 128 Though separated from it by a streak of desert. **1870** GLADSTONE in *Edin. Rev.* Oct. 588 Happy England!..happy..in this, that the wise dispensation of Providence has cut her off, by that streak of silver sea,..partly from the dangers, absolutely from the temptations which attend upon the local neighbourhood of the Continental nations. **1872** JENKINSON *Guide Eng. Lakes* (1879) 274 The white streak of water running down the face of the mountain is Sour Milk Gill. **1883** MORFILL *Slavonic Lit.* i. 6 There is also a thin streak of Little Russian population in the kingdom of Hungary, north of the Carpathians. **1907** J. LONDON *Before Adam* viii, When we reached the edge of the forest he was no more than a streak in the distance.

b. *colloq.* (orig. *Austral.*). A tall, thin person.

1941 BAKER *Dict. Austral. Slang* 73 *Streak*, a tall, lean person. **1947** K. TENNANT *Lost Haven* iii. 57 Thank goodness he hadn't told that long, gabbling streak about Cherry. **1959** I. & P. OPIE *Lore & Lang. Schoolch.* ix. 169 There is a fusion of terms between those for the thin and lanky lad and those for the overgrown... Epithets include: ..streak or streaker, Tower of London, walking barge pole, [etc.]. **1966** *Listener* 3 Mar. 317/1 That long streak of misery in a blue shirt.

5. a. The horizontal course of a stratum of coal (cf. STRETCH, STRIKE *sbs.*). **b.** A stratum or vein (of metal ore).

1672 G. SINCLAIR *Hydrostaticks* (1683) 273 The Coal..hath its three principal dimensions,..Longitude, Latitude, and Profundity... The Longitude is nothing else but what is termed by the Coal-hewers, the Streek. **1686** PLOT *Staffordsh.* iii. 129 According to the course of the row or streek of the coal. **1789** J. WILLIAMS *Min. Kingd.* I. 334 The streeks or flat veins. *Ibid.* 339 By the word streek they mean stretch, or a vein between the strata which stretches or spreads in a horizontal position. **1872** SCHELE DE VERE *Americanisms* 171 He hopes..to strike it very rich, as soon as he comes to the pay-streak, that is, the lode or vein which is to repay him for all his labors. **1904** S. E. WHITE *Blazed Trail Stories* xii, Here a pocket, there a streak, yon a clear ten feet of low-grade ore.

6. a. An intermixture (of some contrasting or unexpected quality, esp. in a person or his character); an inherited strain. ***a streak of red***: a strain of American ('Red') Indian blood.

1647 COWLEY *Mistr., Wisdom* Poems (1905) 86 With your grave Rules from musty Morals brought: Through which some streaks too of Divinity ran. **1762** *Ann. Reg., Charac.* 32/2 Broad streaks of folly now and then appear through all the grave wisdom..of those mighty statesmen. **1856** MRS. STOWE *Dred* I. ix. 121 Just act, now, as if you'd got a streak of something in you. **1865** GROTE *Plato* II. xxiii. 158 There is..a streak of eccentricity in his character. **1885** W. D. HOWELLS *Silas Lapham* (1891) II. 175 He always did have that close streak in him. **1889** *Spectator* 28 Dec., The deep and unscrupulous craft which lay in streaks through all Cavour's great character. **1890** J. AITCHISON *Signa Christi* i. 23 The streak of immorality would have run through the whole history. **1908** W. CHURCHILL *Mr. Crewe's Career* vii. 84, I can't understand Victoria. She really has influence with these country people... Sometimes I think Victoria has a common streak in her. **1913** *Play Pictorial* No. 134. 82 A woman even suspected of a 'streak of red' is scarcely within the pale.

b. A temporary run (of luck). In phr. ***(on) a losing*** (or ***winning***) ***streak***, (experiencing) a series of losses (or wins). Hence, a series (of games, etc.) of a specified kind.

1843 *Knickerbocker* XXI. 303, I had 'struck a streak of bad luck'. **1865** 'MARK TWAIN' in Harte & 'Twain' *Sk. Sixties* (1926) 205 There never was a bad James in the Sunday-school books that had such a streak of luck as this sinful Jim. **1871** B. HARTE *Luck of Roaring Camp* 34 We've had a streak of bad luck since we left Poker Flat. **1882** *Poker; how to play it* 94 The player in this seat should not come in..under a pair of court cards, unless he happens to be in a streak of good luck. **1900** UPWARD *Ebenezer Lobb* 114 He said he found luck did come in these queer streaks. **1912** C. MATHEWSON *Pitching in a Pinch* xi. 233 But what's a new hat against a losing streak or a batting slump? **1950** *Daily Ardmoreite* (Ardmore, Okla.) 30 Apr. D. 6/2 Last year's edition of the Indians set one of the hottest paces in the league before folding with a long losing streak. **1963** A. BARON *Lowlife* xi. 107 The old song inside my head, *don't be mad, don't walk out of a winning streak.* **1967** *Boston Globe* 5 Apr. 51/5 It is also fair enough to figure the 76ers will end the Celtics' streak of eight straight National Basketball Assn. titles. **1968** *Globe & Mail* (Toronto) 3 Feb. 35/6 Toronto Marlboros snapped Montreal Junior Canadiens' unbeaten streak at 10 games. **1968** Winning streak [see *goal-tending* vbl. sb. s.v. GOAL *sb.* 6]. **1972** 'H. CARMICHAEL' *Naked to Grave* xvi. 183 Mrs Davey won quite a lot of money... She said something to him about Mrs Davey's winning streak. **1973** G. MOFFAT *Deviant Death* ix. 125 The police were on a losing streak and they knew it. The questions were just form. **1976** *New Yorker* 15 Nov. 162/1 'We're on a winning streak. We're on a hot roll,' one city official said happily last summer, during the triumphal series of events that began with Operation Sail and extended through other local Bicentennial celebrations. **1980** *Times* 19 Feb. 11/5 Their winning streak includes the Boat Race record. **1976** *Cumberland News* 3 Dec., Gilsland's Station Hotel team, playing in the Irthing Valley Sunday League, are still in a winning streak.

7. Any of various virus diseases of plants which cause discoloured stripes to appear on their leaves; = *streak disease*, sense 8 below.

1930 *Discovery* June 196/1 Other important virus diseases of plants include..streak of maize,..and many others. **1936** J. JOHNSON in *Phytopathology* XXVI. 285 The writer has repeatedly observed a disease of tobacco in the field that is characterized by a necrosis of, or along, the veins of the leaf. .. The term 'tobacco streak' is..proposed as perhaps the simplest and most suggestive for this malady. **1939** *N.Z. Jrnl. Sci. & Technol.* A. XX. 365 In New Zealand, pea-streak has not been observed other than at Palmerston North. **1952** GRAM & WEBER *Plant Dis.* iii. 387/2 Heavy dressings of stable manure make the symptoms of tomato streak worse. **1963** L. BOS *Symptoms Virus Dis. in Plants* 39 The term 'streak', such as in 'cocksfoot streak' or 'pea streak', is confusive and insufficient. The name does not indicate whether the streak is chlorotic or yellow, such as in 'cocksfoot streak', or is necrotic, such as in 'pea streak'. **1977** J. KRANZ et al. *Diseases, Pests & Weeds in Tropical Crops* 21 Maize streak has not been reported from Europe or the Americas.

8. *attrib.* and *Comb.*, as ***streak-like*** adj.; **streak camera**, a camera which uses the principles of streak photography; also, an electron-optical analogue of this allowing the resolution of events of the order of a picosecond duration and used esp. in high-speed spectroscopy (see quots. 1973, 1977); **streak culture**, a bacterial culture made by drawing the point of an infected needle or the like over the surface of a solid culture medium; **streak disease** = sense 7 above; **streak fallowing** (see quot.); **streak-flowered** *a. Bot.*, striate; **streak lightning**, forked lightning; **streak photography**, a form of photography in which film is automatically and rapidly moved past the open shutter of a camera, allowing a one-dimensional record of high-speed events to be made which can be reconstituted optically; so **streak photograph**; **streak plate**, (*a*) *Bacteriology*, (a vessel containing) a streak culture; (*b*) *Min.*, a small tablet of unglazed porcelain on which minerals may be rubbed to ascertain the colour of the streak (sense 2 d); **streak powder** (see quot., cf. 2 d); **streak stitch** (see quot.); **streak vein**, ? = sense 5 b; **streak virus**, a virus causing a streak disease in plants.

1962 *Sci. Amer.* May 102/2 For this purpose we use a *streak camera. **1973** *Ibid.* June 60/2 In the streak camera, which has an electronic circuit fast enough to measure picosecond events, light from a slit is focused onto a cathode where electrons are released and accelerated towards a phosphorus substance, which emits light. A voltage increasing with time..streaks the electrons across the phosphor so that electrons released at earlier times appear at a different position on the phosphor than electrons released later. **1977** *Jrnl. R. Soc. Arts* CXXV. 772/2 Direct linear measurement of pulse durations by electronoptical streak-cameras, in which the time-into-space transformation is brought about by deflecting an electronoptical slit image across the output phosphor of an image-tube. **1892** G. M. STERNBERG *Man. Bacteriol.* I. viii. 75 Koch made '*streak cultures' by drawing the point of a platinum needle, charged with bacteria, over the surface of a gelatin or agar plate. **1893** W. R. DAWSON tr. *Schenk's Man. Bacteriol.* 60 Blood serum ..is principally adapted for surface or *streak* cultures (*Strichculturen*). **1926** A. BULLEID *Text-bk. Bacteriol.* vii. 62 An examination of the culture tube with the naked eye will reveal the presence of 'colonies' on or in the medium, according to whether the culture was made on the surface (streak culture) or into the medium (stab or shake culture). **1923** W. F. BEWLEY *Dis. Glasshouse Plants* vi. 132 The organism from the tomato can cause a number of 'stripe' or '*streak' diseases of other plants. **1925** *Rep. Proc. Imperial Bot. Conf.* 132 (*heading*) Streak disease, an infectious chlorosis of sugar-cane. *Ibid.* 133 Streak disease in maize has been known in Natal for many years. **1938** *Jrnl. Agric. Res.* LVI. 747 A virus disease of peas.., manifested by a streaking of the stems and leaves and a spotting of the pods, was observed under greenhouse conditions..in the fall and winter of 1934. The disease..resembles the streak disease described by Linford, in 1929, as occurring in pea fields throughout the United States. **1970** LIEBSCHER & KOEHLER tr. *Fröhlich & Rodewald's Pests & Dis. Tropical Crops* 240 Leaves [of sugar cane] infected with streak disease exhibit light-coloured, short and long streaks along the veins. **1677** PLOT *Oxfordsh.* 243 There is a sort of tillage..which they call *streak-fallowing; the manner is, to plough one furrow and leave one. **1822** *Hortus Anglicus* II. 186 Sisyrinchium Striatum. **Streak flowered Sisyrinchium.* **1916** *Chamb. Jrnl.* Aug. 560/1 It was *streak lightning that was observed. **1876** *Clin. Soc. Trans.* IX. 87 Small white *streak-like spots. **1950** *Jrnl. Appl. Physics* XXI. 448/2 (*caption*) *Streak photograph illustrating the motion of the platform of the instrument shock testing machine. *Ibid.* 445/1 Methods of *streak photography are easy to perform and can often be done with ordinary laboratory equipment. **1952** G. A. JONES *High Speed Photogr.* ix. 181 Streak photography is mainly of value in the case of luminous objects. **1980** *Sci. Amer.* May 102/2 The course of growth over time also appears to be continuous, as can be seen in time-lapse motion pictures, multiple-exposure photographs and streak photographs. (A streak photograph is made with a camera in which the lens is left open and the film moves at a constant speed.) **1895** *Buck's Handbk. Med. Sci.* Suppl. 83/1 '*Streak-plates' are made on gelatine and agar, after the medium has been poured in the plates and become solidified, by drawing an infected needle across them in four or five parallel courses. **1898** BRUSH & PENFIELD *Man. Determ. Mineral.* (ed. 15) v. 228 The streak of a mineral.. may be quickly determined by rubbing it on a piece of white, unglazed porcelain... Pieces of unglazed porcelain, called streak plates, are made especially for this purpose. **1964** J. SINKANKAS *Mineral. for Amateurs* viii. 202 Hematite crystals appear quite black, but when rubbed across a porcelain streak plate, the characteristic deep red trace shows the true color. **1966** *McGraw-Hill Encycl. Sci. & Technol.* III. 616/2 Streak plates are incubated in a closed vessel in which the air is replaced by an inert oxygen-free gas. **1857** DANA *Man. Min.* (1862) 56 The color of a surface that has been rubbed or scratched..is called the streak, and the powder abraded, the *streak-powder. **1882** CAULFEILD & SAWARD *Dict. Needlework* 464 In hand-made laces the veins of leaves or flowers are made with an open line, that is sometimes designated *Streak Stitch. **1789** J. WILLIAMS *Min. Kingd.* I. 404 In Derbyshire..great attention is paid to all the *streak veins. **1930** *Ann. Appl. Biol.* XVII. 623 Our maize *streak virus was taken from a naturally streaked maize plant. **1948** *Phytopathology* XXXVIII. 421 To determine the incidence of the streak virus in wild and crop plants, collections were made in areas near infected tobacco fields.

streak (stri:k), *sb.*[2] *slang* (orig. *U.S.*). [f. STREAK *v.*[2] 6 d.] An act of running naked in a public place; = STREAKING *vbl. sb.* [2] 4. Also *attrib.* Cf. STREEK *v.* 5.

1974 *Newsweek* 4 Feb. 63/3 A student who participated with 125 others in a co-educational streak has been suspended from school. **1974** *Daily Tel.* 11 Mar. 16 High spirits may account for some streaks, and sheer frustration or a desire to insult society for others. **1974** *Newsweek* 18 Mar. 42/3 Any number of other streak-watchers didn't react at all. **1980** *Times* 5 Jan. 3/5 [He] ran down Dean Street, Soho, on New Year's Eve, wearing only shoes while taking part in a 'streak' for charity.

streak (stri:k), *v.*[1] *Obs.* exc. *dial.* Forms: 5–6, 9 streke, 6 streyk(e, 6–7 streak(e, 7, 9 streek. [? a. ON. *strjúka* to stroke, rub, wipe; but cf. STRAIK *v.* (*Sc.*), STRAKE *v.*[3], STRIKE *v.*, STROKE *v.*]

1. *trans.* To stroke.

c **1440** *Promp. Parv.* 479/2 Strekyn, as menn do cattys, or hors or howndys, *palmito.* **1851** W. ANDERSON *Rhymes* (1867) 60 (E.D.D.) Streek my hair.

2. To make level, flat, or even; *spec.* to level (corn, etc.) to the rim of a measure by passing a piece of straight wood over it. Cf. STRAIK *v.*, STRIKE *v.*

c **1440** *Promp. Parv.* 479/2 Strekyn or make pleyne, *complano. Ibid.*, St(r)ekyn, or streke mesure, as buschellys and oþer lyke, *hostio.* **1829** BROCKETT *N.C. Words, Streek*, to measure corn exactly. *Ibid.*, *Streeked-measure*, exact measure—in opposition to heaped measure. **1841** HARTSHORNE *Salopia Ant.* Gloss., *Streke*, to strike with a streckle.

†**3.** To polish or make smooth by rubbing; to iron (clothes). *Obs.*

1567 DRANT *Horace, Ep.* Ded. *ij, The verie Crounes and Scepters of best Monarks and princes had bene rustie, wembde, and warpde with obliuion, hadd not they with the goodly eloquence of greate clarkes, and Poettes, ben streked and filed. **1823** E. MOOR *Suffolk Words, Streek*, to iron clothes.

†**4.** ? To sweep; to clean by sweeping, rubbing, or the like. *Obs.*

1492 *Churchw. Acc. St. Mary, Oxon* (Wood MS. D. 3 lf. 261) Item for streking of the church 4 times, xvi d... Item for streyking the roffe of the church, xii d. **1498** *Churchw. Acc. Croscombe* etc. (Somerset Rec. Soc.) 66 Item for strekyng the wyndows and wallys, iiii[d]. **1516** *Ibid.* 73 Item ffor strekyng off y[e] chercheerd, iiii[d].

†**5.** To rub or smear (a surface) *with* (some soft or liquid substance). *Obs.*

1545 RAYNALDE *Byrth Mankynde* II. vi. (1552) 87 In the water of this decoction beyng warme, dyp a spunge,.. fomenting, soking, & streking the back with the same. **1561** HOLLYBUSH *Hom. Apoth.* 6 Wyth thys wyne streke the lymmes greued. **1590** SHAKS. *Mids. N.* II. i. 257 And with the iuyce of this Ile streake her eyes.

†**6.** ? To spread, lay evenly. *Obs.*

?*c* **1440** *Anc. Cookery* in *Househ. Ord.* (1790) 471 Then take the same stuff, and streke above the trenchours al hote. **1517** in *Archæologia* XLVI. 205 Paid to Alson hog for strekyng of the straw mete & wages, iij d.

†**7.** To pass (one's hand) over a surface. *Obs.*

1607 DEKKER & WILKINS *Jests* 38 Two of them meete him at a corner, and only with streaking of their hands on his hose, gesse whether this bayte be worth the nibling at.

†**8.** *intr.* To rub softly or make strokes *with* an implement *upon* (a surface). *Obs.*

1607 TOPSELL *Four-f. Beasts* 410 Lay vnto the place a peece of shoomakers waxe made like a flat cake,.. and with your iron not made ouer hot, streek softly vpon it too and fro, vntill the said wax be throughly melted into the sore.

Hence '**streaking** *vbl. sb.*[1]; *pl.* the last milk that comes before the cow's udder is empty.

1658 GURNALL *Chr. in Armour* II. verse 15 xiii. §1. 424 This was Christs fare-well Sermon, the very streakings of that milk, which he had fed them withall. **1866** BROGDEN *Prov. Lincs, Strappings, Streakings, Strokings*, the last milk given by a cow.

streak (striːk), *v.*[2] Forms: 5–6 streke, 6 streeke, 6–7 streake, 6– **streak**. [f. STREAK *sb.*[1] Cf. STRAKE *v.*[4]]

†**1.** *trans.* ? To cancel by drawing a line or lines across. *Obs.* (Cf. STRIKE *v.*)

c **1440** *Promp. Parv.* 479/2 Strekyn, or cancellyn a thynge wrytyn, *cancello, obelo.* **1594** BLUNDEVIL *Exerc.* I. v. (1597) 7 b, Streeke out the 48. and also the first figure of your Diuisor which is 5. **1595** T. EDWARDS *Cephalus & Procris* (Roxb.) 28 Affection is the whole Parenthesis, That here I streake, which from our taske doth misse.

2. a. To mark with lines or stripes of a different colour, substance, or texture; to form streaks on or in.

1595 T. EDWARDS *Narcissus* (Roxb.) 55 Now Phœbus gins ..To streake the welkin with his darting beames. **1612** DRAYTON *Poly-olb.* xiv. 254 No browne, nor sullyed black the face or legs [of the Cotswold sheep] doth streak. **1660** F. BROOKE tr. *Le Blanc's Trav.* 354 Some pieces of Rock streaked with gold and silver. **1667** MILTON *P.L.* IV. 623 To morrow ere fresh Morning streak the East With first approach of light. **1784** tr. *Beckford's Vathek* (1868) 22 The clear blue sky appeared streaked over with streams of blood. **1847** TENNYSON *Princess* v. 188 Pure as lines of green that streak the white Of the first snowdrop's inner leaves. **1888** F. HUME *Mme. Midas* I. Prol., The sudden line of white foam every now and then streaking the dark green waves. **1913** *Illustr. Lond. News* 22 Feb. 238/3 Large mines of rock-salt streaked here and there by riband-like veins of sylvine. *fig.* **1711** STEELE *Spect.* No. 118 ⁋3 This Affliction in my Life has streaked all my Conduct with a Softness, of which I should otherwise have been incapable.

b. *Bacteriology.* To draw an infected needle or the like lightly over the surface of a solid culture medium in order to initiate a culture in which there is a varied density of growth: used with either the needle or the medium as obj. Also, to transfer (a bacterial specimen) in this way.

1910 [implied at STREAKING *vbl. sb.* 1]. **1927** R. A. KELSER *Man. Veter. Bacteriol.* vi. 70 By going to the end of the streak with a sterile needle and streaking that portion down, the end of such down streak will contain but very few bacteria. **1934** A. T. HENRICI *Biol. of Bacteria* xii. 203 It is often advisable to streak a second or even a third plate without recharging the wire loop. **1949** KELLY & HITE *Microbiology* xi. 147 The specimen is streaked out with a sterile inoculating needle. **1969** SIROCKIN & CULLIMORE *Practical Microbiol.* ii. 17 Streak out a loopful of the broth culture using the aseptic techniques described. **1976** WILLIAMS & SHAW *Micro-Organisms* x. 124 (*caption*) Streaking a plate with pure cultures. **1977** *Lancet* 29 Oct. 906/1 A bacteriological loop is used to sweep across the surface of a young culture of the isolate and is then streaked across one end of the strip. **1980** *Nature* 21 Feb. 793/1 Faecal specimens were collected on sterile 'Culturettes'..and streaked onto MacConkey plates.

c. *Hairdressing.* To tint (the hair) with streaks (STREAK *sb.*[2] 2 h). Cf. STREAKING *vbl. sb.*[2] 3.

1965 R. CORSON *Fashions in Hair* xiv. 625 Women developed an experimental urge and began streaking their hair.

3. To form or prolong in streaks.

1895 P. HEMINGWAY *Out of Egypt* II. 181 He looked at the great oaks standing motionless, at the answering shadows streaked along the meadows.

4. *intr.* †**a.** Of a comet: To emit rays or streamers of light. *Obs.*

1606 HEYWOOD *2nd Pt. Q. Eliz. Troub.* (1609) E 2, Looke how it streakes, what doe you thinke of it? *Shir.* Tis a strang Comet M. Hobson.

b. Of lightning: To break forth in a streak.

1849 CUPPLES *Green Hand* xiv. (1856) 139, I saw a blue flare of lightning streak out betwixt the bank of grey haze and the cloud that hung over it. **1902** *Westm. Gaz.* 2 July 2/3 Perhaps, however, lightning can streak into many places at once.

5. To become streaked or streaky.

1870 *Pall Mall Gaz.* 25 Nov. 12/2 His locks are thinning and his whiskers streaking with silver. **1879** *Cassell's Techn. Educ.* III. 231 Paper at all liable to streak should be toned slowly.

6. a. To go or advance quickly; to go at full speed, to rush. Also with *off, out, up,* etc. [Originally a respelling of STREEK *v.* 5, probably through assoc. with STREAK *sb.* 3 c.]

1768 A. ROSS *Fortunate Shepherdess* 51 O'er hill an' dale she forcefully did dreel; A' road to her was bad an' gueed alike, Nane o't she wyl'd, but forret still did streak. **1834** *New Monthly Mag.* XLI. 465 Away we 'streaked' at the rate of twelve miles an hour against the current. **1844** 'JON. SLICK' *High Life N. York* I. 159 The door-bell rung, and in streaked five or six fellers. **1888** P. GILLMORE *Days & Nights by Desert* xx. 170 True, it was wounded; but as it 'streaked' across the plain, from the pace it was going, no one would have thought so. **1893** *Field* 22 Apr. 581/3 A flock of teal come 'streaking' down towards me. **1897** *Outing* XXIX. 439/1 A strong, young, spiked buck came streaking through the Chêniere. **1914** *Times* 26 Nov. 6 Discretion seems the better part of valour when one streaks through in one's car. **1915** H. ROSHER *In Royal Naval Air Service* (1916) 50, I climbed to 2,000 feet and streaked off over the Channel. **1931** *Punch* 28 Oct. 456/1 The village kids..used to spend most of their leisure in pushing the door ajar in order to set it [*sc.* an electric bell] going and then streak for home. **1955** 'A. GILBERT' *Is she Dead Too?* vii. 128 'So you opened the door—' 'And Tom [*sc.* a cat] streaked out.' **1973** E. LEMARCHAND *Let or Hindrance* viii. 94, I got out at last, and streaked up to the bungalow.

b. with *it.*

1833 [SEBA SMITH] *Lett. J. Downing* ii. (1835) 32, I streaked it round the corner of the stone-fence to head him off. **1844** 'JON. SLICK' *High Life N. York* I. 132, I put on my hat, and streaked it down tu Peck slip. **1894** CROCKETT *Raiders* (ed. 3) 156 Streekin' it for the Ferrytoon o' Cree as fast as the horses can birl.

c. *trans.* To cause to move fast or like lightning.

1912 W. DEEPING *Sincerity* xviii. 137 She shot well, very few of her arrows streaking their way through the sunlight to stand slantingly in the grass. **1928** *Daily Express* 19 June 17/2 He hit only three 4's, and..streaked one from Staples dangerously through the slips when 28. *Ibid.* 25 June 17 Chapman..'streaked' several shots through the slips. **1970** J. HOWARD *Please Touch* 2 When supersonic transports streak 330 passengers to their destinations.

d. *intr.* To run naked in a public place as a stunt. Cf. STREAK *sb.*[2] *slang* (orig. *U.S.*).

1973 [implied at STREAKING *vbl. sb.*[1] 4]. **1974** *Runner's World Mag.* Feb. 9/1 During the winter of 1958–9 a group of us 'streaked' all over Berkeley. **1974** *Daily Tel.* 5 Mar. 3/6 At Memphis State University, the dean issued a warning that students caught 'streaking' would be suspended. **1974** *Globe & Mail* (Toronto) 18 Mar. S1/1 Phil Esposito, stripped as though to streak, held court in the cluttered quarters, tall, dark, unquiet. **1979** *Daily Tel.* 12 Jan. 9/3 The girls..had danced on the lawns in the nightdresses, 'streaked' to chapel and enjoyed midnight parties.

Hence '**streaker**[2], one who runs naked in a public place; also *attrib.*; **streak-in** [-IN[3]], a communal act of running naked in a public place.

1973 *Time* 10 Dec. 14/2 Streakers generally race nude between two unpredictable points. **1974** *Newsweek* 4 Feb. 63/3 One Los Angeles radio station broadcast 'streaker alerts' to warn the populace that naked youths were on the loose. **1978** D. BLOODWORTH *Crosstalk* xiii. 104 The streaker had invaded the Brasserie Lipp in Paris at lunchtime. **1978** J. IRVING *World according to Garp* xi. 210 A young woman had reported that she was approached by an exhibitionist —at least, by a streaker. **1974** *Kingston* (Ontario) *Whig-Standard* 8 Mar. 3/2 The mass streak-in started near Victoria and Leonard Halls. **1974** *Times* 9 Mar. 4/8 Some of the students were arrested when a 'streak-in' turned into a riot.

streak: see STRAKE *sb.*[1] and STREEK *v.*

streaked (striːkt), *ppl. a.* [f. STREAK *v.*[2] + -ED[1]. Cf. STRAKED *ppl. a.*]

1. Marked with streaks; striped, striate. Often in specific names of animals and plants.

1596 SHAKS. *Merch. V.* I. iii. 80 That all the eanelings which were streakt and pied Should fall as Iacobs hier. **1611** —— *Wint. T.* IV. iv. 82 Streak'd Gilly-vors (Which some call Natures bastards). **1656** BEALE *Heref. Orchards* (1657) 46 For cider, the streak't must is most commended. **1665** LOVELL *Herbal* (ed. 2) 419 Streaked grasse, see Lady lace grasse. **1681** GREW *Musæum* I. §v. iii. 114 The Streaked File-Fish. *Capriscus striatus.* **1758** BORLASE *Nat. Hist. Cornw.* 203 The poorer sort, which is the streaked or dredged ore. **1774** GOLDSM. *Nat. Hist.* (1776) III. 242 The true streaked tiger. **1796** WITHERING *Brit. Plants* (ed. 3) I. 85 *Streaked*, marked with depressed, but not always parallel lines. **1801** [C. STEWART] *Elem. Nat. Hist.* I. 352 *Trigla lineata.* Streaked Gurnard. **1855** *Orr's Circ. Sci., Inorg. Nat.* 207 Bath stone..is..usually of a warm cream tint, often streaked. **1868** SIR J. RICHARDSON etc. *Mus. Nat. Hist.* I. 260 The Streaked Sparrow-hawk (*Accipiter virgatus*).

b. Of flesh-meat, esp. bacon: = STREAKY 2 b.

1687 MIEGE *Gt. Fr. Dict.* II. s.v., A fine streaked Bacon, *du petit Lard.* **1725** *Bradley's Family Dict.* s.v. *Potage*, A Border of young streak'd Bacon. **1845** D. JERROLD *Time Works Wonders* I. 2 I've some beautiful bacon, sir, Such pink and white! Streaked, sir, like a carnation. **1846** J. BAXTER *Libr. Pract. Agric.* (ed. 4) II. 92 The fat is inter-mixed among the fibres of the muscles, giving the meat a streaked or marbled appearance.

2. *U.S. dial.* Confused, ashamed, agitated; uneasy, scared, alarmed. Usually *to feel* or *look streaked.*

1833 [SEBA SMITH] *Lett. J. Downing* ii. (1835) 29, I begun to feel pretty streaked for our folks when I see what was done on Boston Common. **1837** HALIBURTON *Clockm.* Ser. I. iv. 26 If he was in your House of Commons, I reckon he'd make some of your great folks look pretty streaked. **1848** LOWELL *Biglow P.* Ser. I. ii. 19, I tell ye I felt streaked The fust time 't ever I found out wy baggonets wuz peaked.

Hence '**streakedness.** *rare*$^{-0}$.

1727 BAILEY vol. II, *Variegatedness*, Speckledness, Streakedness.

streaker[1] ('striːkə(r)). Forms: 4 strecour, 6 strekour, 9 **streaker.** [ME. (Sc.) *strecour*, prob. a. AF. **stracour* (*stracur, strakur*, quot. 1287): cf. OF. *estrac* track.]

1. A kind of swift hound for the chase. *north.*

[**1287** in G. J. Turner *Sel. Pleas Forest* (1901) 149 Cum uno stracur nigro. *Ibid.*, Cum duobus leporariis..et cum uno strakur griseo.] **1375** BARBOUR *Bruce* VI. 487 A sleuthhund had he thar alsua..; And sum men sais ȝeit that the kyng As a strecour hym nwrist had. **1840** COLQUHOUN *Moor & Loch* 44 If the foxes escape the guns, as they commonly do, 'the streakers' are slipped upon them. *Footnote.* A breed between the largest size of greyhound and foxhound.

†**2.** *Sc.* A term of abuse for a person. *Obs.*

1500–20 DUNBAR *Poems* lx. 17 Stuffettis, strekouris, and stafische strummellis.

†**3.** ? A beaker, goblet. *Obs. rare*$^{-1}$.

Prob. a different word, or misprint for *beaker*.

1694 MOTTEUX *Rabelais* IV. xv. 63 A swindging Streaker of Briton Wine.

streaker[2]: see STREAK *v.*[2]

streaking *vbl. sb.*[1]: see STREAK *v.*[1]

streaking, *vbl. sb.*[2] [STREAK *v.*[2]]

1. The action of STREAK *v.*[2]; *concr.* a series or arrangement of streaks.

1677 COLES *Eng.-Lat. Dict.*, A Streaking, *distinctio.* *a* **1820** J. R. DRAKE *Amer. Flag* 8 She..striped its pure celestial white With streakings of the morning light. **1845** LINDLEY *School Bot.* (1866) 133 The sepals have a deep brown streaking at the back. **1898** G. W. CABLE *Grandissimes* viii. 43 Hair *en queue*, the handsomer for its premature streakings of grey.

b. *Bacteriology.* See STREAK *v.*[2] 2 b.

1910 HISS & ZINSSER *Text-bk. Bacteriol.* viii. 148 (*heading*) Separation of bacteria by surface streaking. **1949** KELLY & HITE *Microbiology* xi. 147 Though the streaking must be done carefully and according to some plan, it must be performed speedily. **1973** R. G. KRUEGER et al. *Introd. Microbiol.* iv. 169/1 Aerobic organisms..are inoculated onto the surface of the solidified medium by a procedure called streaking.

2. *Television.* A picture condition in which the trailing edges of areas of a particular colour are extended by streaks of the complementary colour.

1956 AMOS & BIRKINSHAW *Television Engin.* II. (*caption facing* p. 27) An image of test card C as reproduced by a video-frequency amplifier giving short-term streaking. **1975** B. GROB *Basic Television* (ed. 4) xix. 411 The streaking is especially evident trailing to the right after the edges of numbers or letters in the picture... The cause is phase distortion with time delay for low video frequencies up to about 200 kHz.

3. *Hairdressing.* (See quot. 1966.)

1966 J. S. COX *Illustr. Dict. Hairdressing & Wigmaking* 144/1 *Streaking*, the bleaching of a few strands of hair in the coiffure. **1975** *Time Out* 30 May 63/4 (Advt.), Streaking including cut & blow £5.50. **1976** *Southern Even. Echo* (Southampton) 3 Nov. 2/3 (Advt.), Fashion cutting, blow drying, shampoo and set and streaking.

4. The act of running naked in a public place. Cf. STREAK *v.*[2] 6 d, STREAK *sb.*[2]

1973 *Time* 10 Dec. 14/2 Another statistic in a growing Los Angeles-area fad: streaking. **1974** *Washington Post* 6 Mar. B 3 Lady Godiva established the political importance of streaking. **1977** D. MORRIS *Manwatching* 210 The phenomenon of 'streaking'..is a strange example of an act that *only* has value as a deliberate Overexposed Signal.

streakings: see STRAIKEN.

streaky ('striːkɪ), *a.* Also 7 **streeky.** [f. STREAK *sb.*[1] + -Y. Cf. STRAKY.]

1. Of the nature of a streak or streaks; occurring in, consisting of, streaks.

1670 G. HARVEY *Little Venus Unmask'd* 46 Virulent Whites, being thick streeky, and sometimes thin, sharp, and gnawing. **1687** DRYDEN *Hind & P.* III. 1293 For now the streaky light began to peep. **1700** —— *Fables, Flower & Leaf* 586 The Life is in the Leaf, and still between The Fits of falling Snows appears the streaky Green. **1748** RICHARDSON *Clarissa* (1811) VIII. 156 The paint lying in streaky seams. **1821** JOANNA BAILLIE *Metr. Leg., Wallace* x, As lightning.. At first but like a streaky line In the hush'd sky. **1849** CUPPLES *Green Hand* xiii. (1856) 123 The line of the horizon ..with a streaky white haze overlying it. **1916** *Connoisseur* Aug. 239/1 The latter [picture] was somewhat reminiscent of Gainsborough in the streaky handling of the sky and foliage.

2. a. Marked with streaks; streaked.

1745 T. WARTON *Pleas. Melancholy* 72 The blushes of the streaky west. **1811** *Self Instructor* 519 Ivory..coarse grained or fine, streaky or the contrary. **1862** CALVERLEY *Verses & Transl.* (ed. 2) 2 When I..sent those streaky lollipops home for your fairy suction. **1872** J. H. GURNEY *Andersson's Birds*

Damara Land 183 *Poliospiza gularis* (Smith). Streaky-headed Grosbeak. **1883** *Hardwich's Photogr. Chem.* (ed. 9) 331 The Print Marbled and Streaky.—These defects are often seen before the print is toned.

b. Of flesh-meat, esp. bacon: Having lean and fat in alternate streaks. Also *absol.* as *sb.*

1838 DICKENS *O. Twist* xvii, The layers of red and white in a side of streaky bacon. **1848** THACKERAY *Van. Fair* xxviii, Good streaky beef, really mingled with fat and lean. **1969** *Listener* 17 Apr. 535/3 An angst-ridden fly on the ceiling: 'What is my life? Hanging about dustbins, crawling up drains, promiscuous sex on a rasher of *streaky*. There must be more to life than just pleasure.' **1973** *Tel.* (Brisbane) 5 Apr. 29/3 If she [*sc.* a housewife] wants half-a-pound of streaky she is likely to be called 'dear' by Britain's grocers. **1979** A. PARKER *Country Recipe Notebk.* vi. 82 Pot-roasted pork streaky (belly of pork) is better cold than hot.

3. *fig.* Variable, uneven (in character or quality); changeable, uncertain (in operation or activity). *colloq.*

1898 BARTRAM *Whiteheaded Boy* x. 216, I believe Finoucane to have been, as regards courage, what I should call 'streaky'. **1899** A. C. BENSON *Life E. W. Benson* I. iv. 117 The incongruous and streaky additions [to the school-buildings]. **1899** *Daily News* 4 Oct. 3/2 The wind, however, was streaky, and did not hit the boats at the same time. **1903** *Westm. Gaz.* 7 July 3/1 Raphael did not begin well, his first thirty or forty runs being very streaky.

4. *slang.* **a.** Irritable, ill-tempered. **b.** *U.S.* = STREAKED 2.

1848 in Bartlett *Dict. Amer.* s.v. *Streaked*, I never did feel so streaky and mean before. **1860** *Hotten's Slang Dict.* 229 *Streaky*, irritated, ill-tempered. *a* **1872** in Schele de Vere *Americanisms* 637 A man needn't be afraid to feel streaky, when his mule's about giving out and the Ingins begin to yell like a pack of coyotes.

Hence **'streakily** *adv.*; **'streakiness.**

a **1750** A. HILL *Wks.* (1753) II. 185, I..walked homeward, in the brownness of the night, which had shadowed over the fields, with a melancholy streakiness, from the paleness of the moonshine. **1873** BESANT & RICE *My Little Girl* II. ix. 109 He has no perception of the beauties of nature, save in the streakiness of beef. **1874** J. FERGUSSON *St. Paul's* in *Contemp. Rev.* Oct. 759 It shows that what was meant to suggest strength is a mere sham, only a little bit of inlay, which, besides its streakiness, violates every principle of..construction. **1885** LOCK *Workshop Rec.* Ser. IV. 390/2 It would be next to impossible to obtain a coating perfectly free from streakiness. **1896** *Brit. Birds, Their Nests & Eggs* I. 111 They [the eggs] are dull greenish-white, mottled, or streakily spotted with olive.

streal, variant of STREEL.

streale. *Obs.* exc. *dial.* Also 3 stral. [OE. *strǽl* (Anglian *strēl*) masc. and fem., corresp. to OS. *strâla* fem. (MLG. *strâl*, *strâle* masc. and fem.), MDu. *strael* masc., *strâle* fem. (Du. *straal* masc.), OHG. *strâla* fem. (MHG. *strâl*, *strâle* masc. and fem., mod.G. *strahl* masc.):—OTeut. **strǣlo-z*, *-ō*, cogn. w. OSl., Russian *strela* arrow.] An arrow.

?**680** *Ruthwell Cross Inscr.* in *O.E. Texts* 126 Miþ strelum ȝiwundad. **971** *Blickl. Hom.* 199 He..mid ȝeættredum stræle ongan sceotan. *c* **1205** LAY. 5695 Ofte heo letten grund-hat læd gliden heom an heore hæfd, stockes & stanes & strales hate. **1853** W. D. COOPER *Provinc. Sussex* 79 *Streale*, an arrow. E[astern Sussex].

stream (striːm), *sb.* Forms: 1 stréam, stréaum, stréom, 2–6 strem(e, 3 strime, striem, stræm, (stram), 3 streume, (4 stremme), 4–7 streem(e, 5–6 streym(e, 5–7 streame, 3– stream. [Com. Teut. (not recorded in Gothic): OE. *stréam* masc. = OFris. *strâm* (WFris. *stream*, NFris. *strôm*, *strûm*), OS. *strôm* (Du. *stroom*), OHG., MHG. *stroum* (mod.G. *strom*), ON. *straum-r* (Sw. *ström*, Da. *strøm*):—OTeut. **straumo-z*:—pre-Teut. **stroumo-s*, f. Indogermanic root **srou-* (: **sreu-*: **srŭ-*) to flow.

Among the many cognates outside Teut. are Skr. *sru* (3rd sing. pres. *sravati*) to flow, *sruta* fluid; Gr. ῥέ(ϝ)ειν to flow, ῥεῦμα a flow, ῥό(ϝ)ος current; OSl., Russ. *struya* stream; OIrish *sruaim* stream, *sruth* (= MWelsh *frut*, mod.Welsh *ffrwd* stream).]

1. a. A course of water flowing continuously along a bed on the earth, forming a river, rivulet, or brook.

c **875** *Erfurt Gloss.* 2036 in *O.E. Texts* 102 *Torrentibus*, streaumum. *a* **1000** *Boeth. Metr.* xx. 172 Swa stent eall weoruld.., streamas ymbutan. *c* **1205** LAY. 21323 Nu he stant on hulle & Auene bi-haldeð hu ligeð i þan stræme stelene fisces. *c* **1250** *Gen. & Ex.* 2096 Ðo drempte pharaon king a drem, ðat he stod bi ðe flodes strem. *a* **1300** *Cursor M.* 1316 He saw a spring Of a well..Þat oute of ran four gret stremmes; Gyson, fison, tigre, eufrate. *c* **1386** CHAUCER *Prol.* 464 She hadde passed many a straunge strem. **1470–85** MALORY *Arthur* IV. xix. 144 Aboue ther by was the hede of the streme a fayr fontayne. *a* **1552** LELAND *Itin.* (1910) V. 72 For there the streme of Isis breaketh into many armelets. The fery [Hinkesey] selfe is over the principal arme or streame of Isis. **1668** DRYDEN *Ess. Dram. Poesie* 62 'Tis like the murmuring of a stream, which not varying in the fall, causes at first attention, at last drowsiness. **1709** T. ROBINSON *Nat. Hist. Westmorld. & Cumb.* viii. 48 The River Eden..takes into its Stream the Rivers Eamont and Lowther, which make a considerable Increase to it. **1745** *Sc. Transl. & Paraphr.* xxiv. 1 Say, grows the Rush without the Mire? the Flag without the Stream? **1782** COWPER *Comparison* 9 Streams never flow in vain; where streams abound, How laughs the land with various plenty crown'd! **1833** TENNYSON *Lady of Shalott* IV. ii, The broad stream bore her far away, The Lady of Shalott. **1837** W. IRVING *Capt. Bonneville* III. 9 The Lower Nez Percés range upon the Way-lee-way, Immahah, Yenghies, and other of the streams west of the mountains. **1871** RUSKIN *Arrows of Chace* (1880) II. 160 The first thing the King of any country has to do is to manage the streams of it.

b. Appended to a river-name. Now only *poet.*

c **950** *Lindisf. Gosp.* John i. 28 Ofer iordanen ðone stream [L. *trans. Jordanem*]. *c* **1205** LAY. 21275 Þa al wes Auene stram mid stele ibrugged. *c* **1275** *Moral Ode* 244 in *O.E. Misc.*, Ne may hit quenche no salt water ne auene strem ne sture. **1627** MAY *Lucan* III. E 6 Now downe the streame of Rodanus the fleet From Stæchas comes to sea. **1808** BYRON *'Well! thou art happy'* 35 Oh! where is Lethe's fabled stream? **1896** HOUSMAN *Shropshire Lad* xxviii, High the vanes of Shrewsbury gleam Islanded in Severn stream.

c. *poet.* as a type of pure water for drinking.

c **1205** LAY. 19757 For þe King ne mai on duȝeðe bruken nanes drenches buten cald welles stræm. **1671** MILTON *Samson* 546 Nor did the dancing Rubie Sparkling, out-powr'd,..Allure thee from the cool Crystalline stream. **1738** GRAY *Propertius* III. v. 47 Famine at feasts, and thirst amid the stream.

d. In *plural*, the waters (of a river). *poet.*

1500–20 DUNBAR *Poems* lxxxviii. 26 Thy Ryuer..Whose beryall stremys, pleasaunt and preclare, Under thy lusty wallys renneth down. **1594** KYD *Cornelia* IV. ii. 13 O beautious Tyber, with thine easie streames That glide as smothly as a Parthian shaft. **1627** MAY *Lucan* III. E 1, And where vnder sea Alphæus sends his streames to Sicily. **1824** SCOTT *St. Ronan's* i, A river of considerable magnitude pours its streams through a narrow vale.

e. A rivulet or brook, as contrasted with a river.

1806 *Gazetteer Scot.* (ed. 2) 610 Whithern..a royal borough..seated on the bay of Wigton, where a small stream of water falling into it forms a harbour. **1834** LYTTON *Pompeii* III. iii, The Sarnus;—that river, which now has shrunk into a petty stream. **1876** VOYLE & STEVENSON *Milit. Dict.* 412/1 *Stream*, a small land current of water.

2. a. Flow or current of a river; force, volume, or direction of flow.

14.. in Parker *Dom. Archit.* (1859) III. 42 Then the strenghe of the streme astoned hem stronge. **1508** DUNBAR *Golden Targe* 28 Doun throu the ryce a ryuir ran wyth stremys, So lustily agayn thai lykand lemys, That [etc.]. **1530** PALSGR. 693/2, I ronne, as the streame of any ryver or water dothe, *je cours.* **1590** SHAKS. *Com. Err.* I. i. 87 My wife and I..Fastned our selues at eyther end the mast, And floating straight, obedient to the streame, Was carried towards Corinth. **1609** HOLLAND *Amm. Marcell.* XXIII. ii. 221 He departed from thence by the very edge of the river bankes, where the streame was big by occasion of other brookes conflowing thither on every side. **1653** HOLCROFT *Procopius, Gothic Wars* II. xxiii. 66 Soon after, the River had the wonted stream and was Navigable again. **1662** R. VENABLES *Exper. Angler* iii. 37, I could never..discern perfectly where my flie was, the wind and stream carrying it so to and again, that [etc.]. **1768–74** TUCKER *Lt. Nat.* (1834) II. 460 As in rivers,..whose very essence is incompatible with a real identity: for the essence of a river consists in having a stream, that is, a perpetual change of waters. **1889** MRS. PENNELL in *Century Mag.* Aug. 484 For two persons who knew nothing about boats and could not swim, the Thames journey with such a stream running was not promising.

†**b.** A flood, unrestrained outbreak of waters.

c **950** *Lindisf. Gosp.* Matt. vii. 27 Cuomon streamas [L. *venerunt flumina*] & ȝebleuun windas. *a* **1300** *Cursor M.* 1852 Til seuensith tuenti dais war gan þe streme it stud ai still in-an.

c. A current in the sea. Cf. GULF STREAM.

1375 BARBOUR *Bruce* III. 684 Quhar als gret stremys ar rynnand,..As Is the raiss of bretangʒe. *c* **1386** CHAUCER *Prol.* 402 To rekene wel his tydes, His stremes, and his daungers hym bisides. **1546** in *Sel. Pleas Crt. Admiralty* (1894) I. 148 Fyndynge the sayde shyppe..dryvynge with the streamys as a wayff and forsaken of all creatures. **1596** DALRYMPLE tr. *Leslie's Hist. Scot.* I. 59 It swallyis vp hail schipis, and throuch the violence, and vehement force of contrare workeng of the wais of the sey, quhen ilk streme stryues with vthir, drounes thame in the deip. **1687** *Relat. De Chaumont's Embassy Siam* 17 The Streams were so great, and running sometimes against us, that we were forced oft to cast Anchor; for when the Calm took us, the Streams forcibly carried us a great distance. *a* **1830** J. RENNELL *Currents Atlantic Ocean* (1832) 22 The Equatorial Current ..is, doubtless, the most powerful and the longest extended stream of all those in the Atlantics. **1849** CUPPLES *Green Hand* ii. (1856) 17, I have seldom seen the Stream [i.e. the Gulf Stream] so distinct hereabouts.

d. The middle part of a current or tide, as having the greatest force of flow.

1398 TREVISA *Barth. De P.R.* XIII. xviii. (1495) 448 Comynly the streme hath most fresshe water and most clene grounde, and rennyth moost swyftly than any other parte of the ryuer. **1867** SMYTH *Sailor's Word-bk.*, *Stream*, Anglo-Saxon for flowing water, meaning especially the middle or most rapid part of a tide or current.

†**e.** *to break the stream*: to pass through water belonging to the jurisdiction of one port in order to load or unload at another port. *Obs.*

1496 *Maldon* (Essex) *Court-rolls* Bundle 56 No. 4b, Misericordia xii d. de Willelmo Heyward quod fregit le streyme usque heybregge cum navicula sua.

f. Phrases. (*a*) ***against, with the stream.*** Often in fig. context (cf. 6), e.g. ***to strive against the stream***, to resist the influences of one's environment, to oppose prevailing tendencies; ***to go, sail, swim with the stream***, to yield to pressure of circumstances or example. (*b*) ***down, up (the) stream***, † ***downward the stream.***

(*a*) *c* **1000** *Sax. Leechd.* III. 70 Sing þis..horse on þæt wynstre eare on yrnendum wætre & wend þæt heafod onȝean stream. *c* **1175** *Lamb. Hom.* 51 [Heo] bi-gon to swimmen forðward mid þe streme. *c* **1205** LAY. 4531 Scipen þer heo funden makede muchul sæ-flot and ferden mid streme. **1390** GOWER *Conf.* II. 93 Riht as a Schip ayein the strem, He routeth with a slepi noise. *c* **1489** CAXTON *Sonnes of Aymon* xxviii. 582 By the grete strenghte of the fysshes it [*sc.* the corpse] was taried, and went noo ferder with the streme by the wille of our lorde. **1546** J. HEYWOOD *Prov.* II. v. (1867) 55 Foly it is to spourne against a pricke, To stryue against the streme, to winche or kicke Against the hard wall. **1555** EDEN *Decades* (Arb.) 195 Turnynge the stemmes or forpartes of their shyppes ageynst the streame. **1579** TOMSON *Calvin's Serm. Tim.* 54/2 Yet suffer we all these things to passe, and goe with the streame. **1592** NASHE *Strange Newes* Wks. 1904 I. 321 This..is nothing else but to swim with the streame. **1593** —— *Christ's T.* 59 b, Because the multitude fauours Religion, he runnes with the streame, and fauours Religion. **1638** R. BAKER tr. *Balzac's Lett.* (vol. II.) 43, I have done it against the streame of my resolution quite. **1668** DRYDEN *Ess. Dram. Poesie* 57 To tell you, how much in vain it is for you to strive against the stream of the peoples inclination. **1708** *Constit. Watermen's Co.* xxix, If any Waterman Rowing with the Tide or Stream, shall neglect to give Notice or Warning..to all Persons Rowing cross or against the Stream or Tide. **1711** *Let. to Sacheverel* 30 There is hardly a Man, who does not swim with the Stream, that has not been..insulted. **1714** POPE *Let.* 25 July, Wks. 1737 II. 115 No man ever rose to any degree of perfection in writing, but thro' obstinacy and an inveterate resolution against the stream of mankind. **1736** GRAY *Tasso* 15 Against the stream the waves secure he trod. **1937** W. R. INGE *Rustic Moralist* IV. i. 234 What ought the helpless *intelligentsia* to do? Not to float with the stream, a feat which any dead dog can accomplish.

(*b*) *a* **1300** *Cursor M.* 4780 He sagh a-pon þe water reme Caf flettand dunward þe strem. **1560** DAUS tr. *Sleidane's Comm.* 360 b, They brought in vitayle both vp the streame and down [L. *aduerso & secundo flumine*]. *c* **1643** LD. HERBERT *Autobiog.* (1824) 133 But the river being deep and strong in that place where he entered it, he was carried down the stream.

g. Naut. *in*, †*upon the stream*: see quot. 1863.

1473–4 *Acc. Ld. High Treas. Scot.* I. 67 His schip and gudis that wes fundin vpon the streme and na man with hir, and was eschetit as the Kingis eschete. **1564** *Reg. Privy Council Scot.* I. 280 Thair schippis hes lang tyme lyne on the Streme, and the maist part of thame becum lek. **1577** *Ibid.* II. 626 For bying and resset of unlauchful gudis upoun the streame. **1860** *All Year Round* 28 July 379/2 She's in the stream, sir. Yonder she [a yacht] lays. **1863** A. YOUNG *Naut. Dict.* 396 A vessel in a river is said to be in the stream, when she is lying off from the shore so that they have to communicate with her by means of boats.

†**3.** Used vaguely (*sing.* and *pl.*) for: Water, sea. *Obs.*

c **950** *Lindisf. Gosp.* Matt. viii. 18 Fara *vel* gaa ofer luh *vel* stream [L. *trans fretum*]. ? **11..** *Charter of Eadweard* (A.D. 1066) in Kemble *Cod. Dipl.* IV. 193 Tolles and teames, on strande and on streame. *c* **1205** LAY. 3227 Þa olde King.. lette heo fo[r]ðe liðen ofer þa stremes. *Ibid.* 6116 Ofer þane saltne strem. *a* **1300** *Cursor M.* 1843 On þe streme þe arche can ride. **13..** *K. Horn* 105 (Harl. MS.) Þare fore þou shalt to streme go. *c* **1385** CHAUCER *L.G.W.* 2508 (Skeat) Yit hath the streem of Sitho [Ovid *Sithonis unda*] nat y-broght From Athenes the ship. *c* **1470** *Gol. & Gaw.* 460 Schipmen our the streme thai stithil full straught. **1513** DOUGLAS *Æneis* XII. Prol. 187 On salt stremis wolx Dorynda and Thetis, By rynnand strandis Nymphis and Naedes. **1551** EDW. VI *Lit. Rem.* (Roxb.) II. 327 Also the French embassadour was advertised [of the Flemish ships]; who answered that he thought him sure inough when he came into our streames, —terming it so. **1577–87** HOLINSHED *Chron.* III. 811/1 Whereas peace was yet betweene England and Scotland, that they contrarie to that, as theeues & pirats, had robbed the kings subiects within his streames. *a* **1593** MARLOWE *Ovid's Elegies* III. v[i]. 81 Tis said the slippery streame held vp her brest. **1614** GORGES *Lucan* x. 419 With fleetes he cuts the Ocean streames.

4. a. A flow or current of water or other liquid issuing from a source, orifice, or vessel. Often *hyperbolically* in sing. or pl. for a great effusion of blood or tears.

971 *Blickl. Hom.* 59 Ealle þa ȝewitaþ swa swa wolcn, & swa swa wæteres stream, & ofer þæt nahwær eft ne æteowaþ. *c* **1205** LAY. 30991 Blod orn in þe weiȝe stremes swiðe brade. *a* **1225** *Ancr. R.* 112 So largeliche..vleau þet ilke blodi swot ..þet te stremes vrnen adun to þer eorðe. *a* **1225** *Leg. Kath.* 2479 Þet ter rinneð aa mare eoile iliche riue, & strikeð a stream ut of þat stanene þruh. *a* **1225** *St. Marher.* 5 Þæt tet blod barst ut ant strac adun of hire bodi as stream deð of welle. *a* **1300** *Floriz & Bl.* (Camb. MS.) 228 In þe tur þer is a welle... He vrneþ in o pipe of bras..Fram flore in to flore þe strimes vrneþ store. *a* **1300** *Havelok* 2687 On þe feld was neuere a polk þat it ne stod of blod so ful þat þe strem ran intil þe heel. **1398** TREVISA *Barth. De P.R.* v. lxi. (1495) 177 The veynes haue that name, for they ben the wayes..of the stremes of the fletynge of the blood. *c* **1400** *Destr. Troy* 10661 Myche watur he weppit..Ouer-flowet his face, fell on his brest With streamys out straght þurgh his stithe helme. **1591** SPENSER *Teares of Muses* 230 She lowdly did lament and shrike, Pouring forth streames of teares abundantly. **1594** SHAKS. *Rich. III*, v. v. 37 Traitors..That would reduce these bloudy dayes againe, And make poore England weepe in Streames of Blood. **1625** N. CARPENTER *Geog. Delin.* II. ix. (1635) 144 Certaine pits being digged into the grounde 2 hundred or three hundred feet deep, will discouer many great Streams of Water. **1697** DRYDEN *Æneis* IX. 470 The Wound pours out a Stream of Wine and Blood. *a* **1700** EVELYN *Diary* 23 May 1645, Last of all we came to the labyrinth in which a huge colosse of Jupiter throws out a streame over the garden. **1798** ROSCOE tr. *Tansillo's Nurse* I. (1800) 33 Say can ye choose a nurse from broad St. Giles? Heedless what venom taints the stream she gives. **1812** BYRON *Ch. Har.* I. lxxx, To meditate 'gainst friends the secret blow,..whence life's warm stream must flow. **1815** J. SMITH *Panorama Sci. & Art* II. 121 The water thus collected, runs in a continued stream out of the box. **1831** JAMES *Phil. Augustus* I. iii, From the strong muscular arm of the knight, a stream of blood was just beginning to flow into a small wooden bowl held by a page. **1855** *Poultry Chron.* III. 299 Glasses may be prepared..by pouring a thin stream of melted wax down the side of the glass. **1881** MRS. R. T. COOKE *Somebody's Neighbors* 84 The sharp streams of milk spun and foamed into the pail below. **1899** LADY M. VERNEY

Verney Mem. IV. 79 Wine and ale..flowed in streams. **1913** *Times* 13 Aug. 3/4 Drugs..which will kill the parasite in the blood and lymph streams of the body, have no effect upon the parasites in the brain.

†**b.** Strength or volume of flow. *Obs.*

c **1290** *S. Eng. Leg.* 17 þat blod sprong out with gret strem. **1707** Floyer *Physic. Pulse-Watch* 282 We must observe the Colour, Stream and Pulse in Bleeding, and stop as the Colour changes, or the Stream falls.

c. A current or flow of air, gas, electricity.

a **1722** Lisle *Husb.* (1757) 211 They find great relief by the stream of air which runs along the rutts. **1753** Henry in *Phil. Trans.* XLVIII. 1 A stream of wind instantly ensued, the violence of which nothing could resist. **1777** Cavallo *Electricity* 208 And if the excitation of the cylinder is very powerful, dense streams of fire will proceed from the rubber. **1795** *Ibid.* (ed. 4) II. 117 With such machines, the power of Electricity should be so regulated, as to apply every degree of it with facility and readiness; beginning with a stream issuing out of a metal point. **1836–41** Brande *Chem.* (ed. 5) 491 When a stream of sulphuretted hydrogen gas is passed through it. *a* **1866** B. Taylor *Poems, Voy. Dream* 66 Sweep downward streams of air.

†**d.** An effluvium. *Obs.*

1677 Gilpin *Dæmonol.* (1867) 83 Those conceits that men have of God, whereby they mould and frame Him in their fancies,..are streams and vapours from this pit. *Ibid.* 454 These temptations..are like the opening of a sepulchre, which sends forth a poisonous stream which may infect those that loathe and resist it. *a* **1680** Glanvill *Sadducismus* I. v. (1681) 23 Nature for the most part acts by subtile streams and aporrhœa's of minute particles.

†**e.** An emanation. *Obs.*

a **1300** *Cursor M.* 18986 Yur eldrin men sal dremes dreme, And o mi gast þai sal ha streme. *c* **1374** Chaucer *Troylus* I. 305 He..was full unwar that love had his dwellinge Withinne the subtile stremes of hir yen. *c* **1420** ? Lydg. *Assembly of Gods* 1855 With fantasyes, tryfyls, illusions & dremes, Wyche poetys call Morpheus stremes.

f. See on stream *adv. phr.* and *a.*

5. *transf.* **a.** An uninterrrupted succession of persons, animals, or things, moving constantly in the same direction.

1600 E. Blount tr. *Conestaggio* 289 The which inuested her rounde with a great streame of fire and shotte. *c* **1611** Chapman *Iliad* xvi. 359 And then lay ouerthrowne Numbers beneath their axle-trees; who, (lying in flight's streame) Made th' after chariots iot and iumpe in driuing ouer them. **1639** Fuller *Holy War* II. xxvii. (1647) 79 Emmanuel the Emperour..fortified his cities in the way, as knowing there needed strong banks where such a stream of people was to passe. **1759** Johnson *Rasselas* xviii, He followed the stream of people. **1827** Faraday *Chem. Manip.* xvii. (1842) 453 A stream of bubbles should be disengaged. **1838** Dickens *Nich. Nick.* xxxii, Streams of people apparently without end poured on and on. **1849** Macaulay *Hist. Eng.* vii. II. 238 At present a constant stream of emigration runs from Ireland to our great towns. **1857** Livingstone *Trav.* vi. 124 Very large flocks of swifts were observed flying over the plains... I counted a stream of them.

†**b.** A line, streak. *Obs.*

1597 Skene *De Verb. Sign.* s.v. *Actilia*, Partial gilt, with spranges or streames of Gold fuilȝie. *a* **1722** Lisle *Husb.* (1757) 133, I perceived..a stream or streak of a brown stain, the breadth of a pin, in the first joint above the root.

c. *Tin-mining.* (See quot. 1855.)

1778 W. Pryce *Min. Cornub.* 133 The principal part of the Stream..is intermixed with stones, gravel, and clay. **1855** J. R. L[eifchild] *Cornwall Mines* 200 This stream-tin is either met with in a pulverized sandy state, in separate stones called shodes, or in a continued course of stones... This course is called a stream.

d. In a polar ice-field: see quot.

1817 Scoresby in *Ann. Reg., Chron.* 531 It [*sc.* a collection of pieces of drift-ice] is called a stream when its shape is more of an oblong. **1835** Sir J. Ross *Narr. 2nd Voy.* Explan. Terms p. xv, *A stream*, a number of pieces of ice joining each other in a ridge or in any particular direction. **1853** Kane *Grinnell Exp.* xiv. (1856) 101 Broken floes running out into 'streams' were on all sides of us.

6. *fig.* **a.** In various applications, e.g.: A continuous flow of discourse, words, or of time; a continuous series of testimonies, events, or influences tending in one direction; an outflow (of beneficence, etc.), an influx (of wealth, revenue).

Wordsworth's expression ***stream of tendency*** (quot. 1814) is often mentioned with ridicule by writers of the first half of the 19th c. It was subsequently in common use.

c **900** Wærferth tr. *Gregory's Dial.* 94 Her yrneð up se æftra stream þære godcundan spræce, se cymð of þære rynelan þæs gastlican æsprynges. **1523** Cromwell in Merriman *Life & Lett.* (1902) I. 30 Whereoff there were no dowte but that ryght haboundant stremys shuld from his most liberall magnyfysence be dereuyed into euery parte of this his Realme to the grete Inryching..of..all suche as hereafter showld lyue under hys obeysaunce. **1585** T. Washington tr. *Nicholay's Voy.* Ep. Ded., This flowing streame of wordes. **1597** Shakes. *2 Hen. IV* iv. i. 70 Wee see which way the streame of Time doth runne. **1630** Prynne *Anti-Armin.* 177 The constant streame of ancient, of moderne Interpreters haue giuen this orthodox receiued Exposition. **1681** in *Nairne Peerage Evid.* (1874) 14 Charles R. Our soveraigne lord knowing that it belongs to his majesty's crowne and prerogative royall to confer dignities and titles of honour on his well deserving subjects from whence as from the fountaine all the streames of honour doe flow. **1692** Ray *Disc.* iii. xi. (1693) 355, I have already given many Testimonies of the ancient Fathers and Doctors of the Church, and could, if need were, produce many more, the whole stream of them running this way. **1710** Felton *Diss. Classics* (1718) 71 For this is to speak or write English in Purity and Perfection, to let the Streams run clear and unmix'd, without taking in other Languages in the Course. **1719** Waterland *Vind. Christ's Div.* Contents, Query xxviii, Whether it be at all probable..that the whole Stream of Christian Writers should mistake in telling us what the Sense of the Church was. **1739** Hume *Treat. Hum. Nature* II. iii. 276 When we turn our thought to a future object, our fancy flows along the stream of time. **1769** Burke *Corr.* (1844) I. 189 It must be of infinite importance, that the whole stream of the petitions should, as much as possible, run one way. **1775** Johnson *Tax. no Tyr.* 65 The quit-rents ..will pour large streams of wealth into the royal coffers. **1814** Wordsw. *Excurs.* ix. 87 To commune with the invisible world, And hear the mighty stream of tendency Uttering, for elevation or our thought, A clear sonorous voice. **1846** J. S. Mill in *Edin. Rev.* Oct. 356 Authentic history, as we ascend the stream of time, grows thinner and scantier. **1858** Carlyle *Fredk. Gt.* x. viii. II. 678 Friends are encouraged..to keep up a stream of talk. **1874** Stubbs *Const. Hist.* I. i. 3 The original stream of influence has been turned aside in its course. **1875** E. White *Life in Christ* iii. xxiii. (1876) 355 For there is a broad and deep stream of evidence to show [etc.]. **1896** L. T. Hobhouse *Theory of Knowl.* ii. xix. 465 Think of the whole page as the stream of time advancing from the top downwards. **1900** J. E. Ellis in *Corr. relat. Polit. Situation S. Africa* 12 We want a stream of facts concerning suppression of telegrams, opening of letters, arbitrary arrests, [etc.]. **1914** B. Russell *Our Knowl. External World* vi. 167 A truer image of the world..is obtained by picturing things as entering into the stream of time from an eternal world outside.

b. The prevailing direction of opinion or fashion. †Also, the majority, main body (of a class of persons).

1614 Bacon *Charge touching Duels* 12 Yet the streame of vulgar opinion is such, as it imposeth a necessity vpon men of value to conforme them-selues; or else there is no liuing or looking vpon mens faces. **1651** N. Bacon *Disc. Govt. Eng.* ii. i. 6 He reflected upon God in common events, more ordinarily then the general streame of the Clergy did in those dayes. **1669** R. Montagu in *Buccleuch MSS.* (Hist. MSS. Comm.) I. 427, I find the stream of this Court to run mightily against him.

†**c.** *to give stream to*: to set in motion (one's power). *Obs.*

c **1611** Chapman *Iliad* I. 272 Atrides! giue not streame To all thy powre, nor force his prise; but yeeld her still his owne, As all men else do.

d. ***stream of thought*** = stream of consciousness.

1890 W. James *Princ. Psychol.* II. xix. 79 This consciousness must have the unity which every 'section' of our stream of thought retains so long as its objective content does not sensibly change. **1921** J. Varendonck *Psychol. of Day-Dreams* iv. 293 Only such terminations of fore-conscious streams of thought as are in relation with acknowledged desires..of our conscious life can come to the surface. **1938** W. S. Maugham *Summing Up* 223 Of the other experiments that have been made [by the novelist] the most important is the use of the stream of thought... It was tempting to explore greater depths of character by an imaginative picture of the subconscious of the persons of his invention. **1961** *John o' London's* 2 Feb. 109/3 The author includes many..remarks..on the Ulysses characters, providing fascinating insights into what Joyce was getting at with his stream-of-thought vignettes.

e. *Educ.* A division in a school according to ability or to subjects studied; a group of pupils selected in this way.

1938 [see multilateral *a.* 4]. **1946** M. L. Jacks *Total Education* iv. 59 The Headmaster of a Senior School tells me that his main difficulty lies not with the A stream nor with the C stream,..but with that solid mass in the middle. **1953** *Manch. Guardian* 11 May 6/10 On entry at eleven, each child is given intelligence tests and group tests in arithmetic and English, and on the result is placed in the appropriate stream (both the Douglas schools have a six-stream, Ramsey a four, and Castle Rushen a three-stream entry). **1959** *Observer* 20 Dec. 22/2 Perhaps we can totter along somehow, and for a time, by prolonging the 'stream' system into university education. **1966** J. Partridge *Middle School* iii. 41 It is clearly recognized that the 'A' stream contains the most intelligent boys and the 'D' stream the least. **1977** J. Aiken *Last Movement* i. 31, I never actually taught her.. because she was in the science stream and I was tutoring in business methods.

†**7.** A ray or beam of light; the tail of a comet.

c **1368** Chaucer *Compl. Pity* 94 Let som streem of your light on me be sene. *c* **1391** —— *Astrol.* i. §13. 7 A Square plate perced with a certein holes..to resseyuen the stremes of the sonne by day. *c* **1402** Lydg. *Compl. Bl. Knt.* 592 His brighte bemes and his stremes al Were in the wawes of the water fal. **1473** Warkw. *Chron.* 16 The Erle of Oxenfordes men hade uppon them ther lordes lyuery,..whiche was a sterre withe stremys. *c* **1530** *Crt. of Love* 849 Now am I caught..With persant stremes of your yën clere. *a* **1536** *Songs, Carols* etc. (E.E.T.S.) 7 The streme shon over Bedlem bryght. **1596** Dalrymple tr. *Leslie's Hist. Scot.* II. 90 A maruellous gret Comet, quhilk toward the south schot fyrie stremes terrabillie. **1680** Luttrell *Brief Rel.* (1857) I. 60 The late comett was seen in other parts,..the starr was but small, yet the stream near 40 degrees in length. **1681** R. Knox *Hist. Rel. Ceylon* 60 In the year 1666 in the month of February, there appeared in this Countrey another Comet or stream in the West. *a* **1700** Evelyn *Diary* 20 Aug. 1682, This night I saw another comet, neere Cancer, very bright, but the stream not so long as the former.

†**8.** A streamer, pennant. *Obs.*

c **1440** *Ipomydon* 1938 With shippis and sayles manyfolde, There stremes were of fyne golde. **1585** T. Washington tr. *Nicholay's Voy.* ii. xi. 46 b, [We] put out all the flags, banners, streames, & gailliadets of our gallies. **1608** Willet *Hexapla Exod.* 643 The violet and purple colour of the amethyst betokened their shipping, sailes and streames. **1626** Capt. Smith *Accid. Yng. Seamen* 18 Out goeth his flag and pendance or streames, also his Colours.

9. *attrib.* and *Comb.* **a.** simple attrib., as ***stream-bank, -bed, -gravel, -ground, -head, -name, -side, -water.***

1619 Atkinson *Gold Mynes Scot.* (Bannatyne Club) 15 To frame or make a long sowgh, or scowring place, into which they bringe the streame water. *c* **1630** Milton *Let.* in Birch *Wks.* 1738 I. Life p. v, And here I am come to a streame-head, copious enough to disburden itselfe like Nilus at seven Mouthes into an Ocean. **1778** W. Pryce *Min. Cornub.* 134 The additional trouble of removing back the soil in heaps, and levelling the Stream ground to receive it, is so little. **1807** J. Barlow *Columb.* v. 39 The sandy streambank and the woodgreen plain. **1844** Mrs. Browning *Rom. Swan's Nest* i, Little Ellie sits alone..By a stream-side, on the grass. **1857** M. Arnold *Rugby Chapel* 95 The stream-bed descends In the place where the wayfarer once Planted his footstep. **1870** Morris *Earthly Par.* III. iv. 410 That day he needs must leave the stream-side road. **1871** Kingsley *At Last* xi, A coarse low fern on stream-gravel. **1901** *Q. Rev.* July 22 The country [Uganda] is almost like a succession of gigantic furrows, and in nearly every furrow there is a 'sponge', swamp, or stream-head. **1922** E. Ekwall *Place-Names of Lancashire* 25 It *might* be an old stream-name.. and might have given name to the forest. **1960** P. H. Reaney *Orig. Eng. Place-Names* v. 81 It is also possible that this (and other names) may contain a stream-name *ec(c)les*, as in Ecchinswell.

b. objective, parasynthetic, etc., as ***stream-bordering, -cut, -embroidered, -illumed, -like*** adjs. Also ***stream-cutting*** *vbl. sb.*

1626 Sandys *Ovid's Metam.* x. 198 Streame-bordering Willow. *c* **1630** Quarles *Solomons Recant.* Solil. ii. Wks. (Grosart) II. 175/1 The green-breasted, stream-embroydred Plaines. **1820** Shelley *Prometh. Unb.* ii. iii. 26 Dim twilight-lawns, and stream-illumèd caves. **1820** Wordsw. *Misc. Sonn.* iii. ii. 13 The stream-like windings of that glorious street. **1957** G. E. Hutchinson *Treat. Limnol.* I. i. 47 Since there is little or no stream-cutting below such lakelets, they may persist longer than do the lakes dammed by the main mass of the slide. **1970** R. J. Small *Study of Landforms* ix. 314 Pediments form not at the bases of fault-scarps but beneath the retreating walls of stream-cut valleys. **1973** *Nature* 2 Mar. 40/1 In a streamcut channel, the Ganurgarh shales intercalated with limestone have been exposed.

c. Special comb.: **stream-anchor**, an anchor intermediate in size between the bower and the kedge, used to moor a ship in a sheltered position, and for warping; **stream-cable**, the cable or hawser of the stream-anchor; **stream-current** (see quots.); **stream-flow** orig. *U.S.*, flow of water in streams and rivers; the rate or amount of this in any one stream or from any particular area; **stream function** *Physics*, a mathematical function of position defined so that lines along which it has a constant value are the streamlines of a flow or the lines of force of a field; **stream-gold**, gold in alluvial deposits; **stream-ice**, pieces of drift ice joining each other in a continuous ridge and following the line of current; **stream-lake** (see quot. 1867); †**stream-net**, a net for fishing in running water; **stream-ore**, ore in alluvial deposits; **stream-tide**, a spring tide; **stream-tin**, tin ore found in pebble-like lumps in alluvial beds; hence **stream-tinner**, one who works this ore; †**stream-toll**, a toll paid for the use of a stream; **stream-tube** (see quot. and streamline *sb.*); **stream-way**, (*a*) the main current of a river; (*b*) the shallow bed of a stream, a watercourse; **stream-wheel** (see quot.); **stream-work(s**, the operation of washing detrital deposits for metal, esp. tin; a place where this is done.

1627 Capt. Smith *Sea Gram.* vii. 29 There is also a *streame Anchor not much bigger [than a kedger], to stemme an easie stream or tide. **1784** J. King *Cook's 3rd Voy.* v. iv. III. 67 We carried out a stream anchor, to enable us to haul the ship abreast of the town, in case of an attack. **1883** *Man. Seamanship for Boys* 192 A stream anchor..is used for warping on, in a tideway or calm. **1618** in J. Charnock *Hist. Mar. Archit.* (1801) II. 227 Till of late none but the great shipps weare allowed *stream cables. **1644** Manwayring *Seamans Dict.* 103 *Streame-Cabell* is a small cabell, which we ride withall in streames, as rivers, or in faire-weather, when we stop-a-tide. **1805** in Nicolas *Disp. Nelson* VII. 195 *note*, At daylight got the end of the stream-cable on board the prize, and made sail with her in tow. *a* **1830** J. Rennell *Currents Atlantic Ocean* (1832) 21 *note*, I distinguish two kinds of currents. The one *drift* or *drift current*, is the mere effect of a constant or very prevalent wind on the surface-water... The other..is the **stream* current, formed of the accumulated waters of the drift current. **1875** *Encycl. Brit.* III. 19/1 A current thus directly impelled by wind is termed a 'drift-current', whilst a current whose onward movement is sustained by the *vis a tergo* of a drift-current is called a 'stream-current'. **1902** W. P. Mason *Water-Supply* (ed. 3) vi. 269 The forest acts as a 'governor' of *stream flow, rather than as a means of increasing precipitation. **1922** Glazebrook *Dict. Appl. Physics* I. 498/2 It has been possible..to deduce the total run-off or stream flow from a drainage area from the difference of rainfall and the computed evaporation over that area. **1971** *Sci. Amer.* Sept. 142/3 The cooling water required by power plants already constitutes 10 percent of the total U.S. streamflow. **1979** *Bull. Amer. Meteorol. Soc.* LX. 560 (*heading*) A method for assessment of effects on streamflow by orographic cloud seeding in the Colorado Rocky Mountains. **1879** H. Lamb *Treat. Math. Theory Motion of Fluids* iv. 67 If P move about in such a manner that the value of ψ does not alter, it will trace out a curve such that no fluid anywhere crosses it, *i.e.* a stream-line. Hence the curves $\psi =$ const. are the stream-lines, and ψ is called the '*stream-function'. **1937** S. L. Green *Hydro- & Aero-Dynamics* ii. 19 When $w = \phi + i\psi$ is a function of $z = x + iy$ the conditions $\phi x = \psi y$, $\phi y = -\psi x$ are satisfied, and these conditions are exactly the same as those satisfied by the velocity potential and the stream function for an irrotational motion in two dimensions. **1979** Bertin & Smith *Aerodynamics for Engineers* ii. 44 The existence of a stream function is a necessary condition for a physically possible flow. **1875**

Ure's Dict. Arts III. 298 The gold of alluvial districts, called *stream-gold or placer-gold. **1856** KANE *Arct. Expl.* I. vi. 54 We stood on, boring the loose *stream-ice. **1867** SMYTH *Sailor's Word-bk.*, **Stream-lake*, one which communicates with the sea by means of a river. **1662** *Act 14 Chas. II*, c. 28 §1 With any Drift Net Trammel or *Stream Net. **1850** ANSTED *Elem. Geol., Min.* etc. 365 Among the minerals of importance obtained from Tertiary deposits, we may mention the *stream-ores of gold, platinum, and other rare metals found with these. **1789** J. WILLIAMS *Min. Kingd.* II. 198 A *stream-tide and a strong fresh meeting one another, would throw some of this sediment pretty high. **1854** H. MILLER *Sch. & Schm.* xiii. (1860) 136 The common oyster ..is sometimes found in the Gairloch..in beds laid bare by the ebb of stream-tides. **1778** W. PRYCE *Min. Cornub.* 65 It is more profitably used for melting of *Stream Tin. **1853** URE *Dict. Arts* II. 859 This variety, called 'stream tin', produces the highest price in the market. **1839** DE LA BECHE *Rep. Geol. Cornwall* etc. xiii. 403 Confused mass of mud, sand, clay, and stones, which has been much disturbed by the *stream-tinners. **1189–99** in *Cal. Charter Rolls* IV. 63 Cum *stramtol et watertol et hamsochne. **1892** MINCHIN *Hydrostatics* etc. 371 If at any point, *A*,..we describe a very small closed curve and at each point on the contour of this curve we draw the stream line, such as *AP*, and produce it indefinitely, we obtain a *stream tube. **1911** *Encycl. Brit.* XXIV. 940/1 The surface formed by all the stream lines passing through a small closed contour is termed a 'stream tube'. **1822** SCOTT *Nigel* xxvi, They got into the *stream-way accordingly, and, although heavily laden, began to move down the river with reasonable speed. **1904** *Surrey Comet* 17 Sept. 6/7 There would be barges moored alongside the wharf, and there would be a demand for a mooring in the streamway. **1905** HOLMAN-HUNT *Pre-Raph.* II. 324 Near at hand I came upon the little stream-way. **1875** KNIGHT *Dict. Mech.*, **Stream-wheel*, an undershot or current wheel. **1586** CAMDEN *Brit.* 69 Horum autem stannariorum, siue metallicorum operum duo sunt genera. Alterum Lode-works, alterum *Streame-works, vocant. **1602** CAREW *Cornwall* I. 8 Which [scattered ore] being sought and digged, is called Streamworke. **1823** BUCKLAND *Reliq. Diluv.* 219 The gold mine that was worked a few years since in the county of Wicklow was simply a stream-work, in which the gold was dispersed in the form of small pebbles and sand, through a bed of gravel. **1882** RHYS *Celtic Brit.* ii. 48 Some stream-works of the Bronze Age are known to have been carried out in localities.

stream (striːm), *v.* Forms: 3, 6–7 **streame**, 4–6 **streme**, 7– **stream**. [f. STREAM *sb.*]

I. Intransitive senses.

1. a. Of a body of liquid: To flow or issue in a stream; to flow or run in a full and continuous current. Also with advs., as *away, down, out, forth.*

Formerly sometimes of a river (merely = *flow*).

a **1225** *Ancr. R.* 188 (MS. T.) Blodi strundes streamden & leafden his swete bodi. **1375** BARBOUR *Bruce* XII. 500 Quhill throu the byrneiss brist the blud, That till the erd doune stremand ȝeed. **1526** *Pilgr. Perf.* (W. de W. 1531) 302 b, So sore they dyd thryst them on thy heed yᵗ the blode stremed downe by thy blessed chekes. **1591** G. FLETCHER *Russe Commw.* ii. 6 The eight [river is] Ocka, that..streameth into Volgha. *c* **1630** RISDON *Surv. Devon* §247 (1810) 259 The river Ock streameth by Stow. **1667** MILTON *P.L.* VIII. 467 A Rib, with cordial spirits warme, And Life-blood streaming fresh. **1759** JOHNSON *Rasselas* vii, The clouds broke on the surrounding mountains, and the torrents streamed into the plain on every side. **1849** MACAULAY *Hist. Eng.* vi. II. 72 She suffered the tears to stream down her cheeks unconcealed.

fig. **1579** TOMSON *Calvin's Serm. Tim.* 341/1 Let euery one of vs know..that vnlesse hee were stayed vp from an high by the vertue of the holie Ghost, he should finde him selfe to streame away as the water doth.

b. of a glacier.

1860 TYNDALL *Glac.* I. xiv. 98 Not a trace of vegetation could be seen along the whole range of the bounding mountains: glaciers streamed from their shoulders into the valley beneath.

c. of a road, or of land which seems to move in the opposite direction to one who passes along it.

1833 TENNYSON *Dream Fair W.* Introd., As when a man, that sails in a balloon, Downlooking sees the solid shining ground Stream from beneath him. **1864** —— *Voyage* 50 O hundred shores of happy climes, How swiftly stream'd ye by the bark! **1882** BRET HARTE *Flip* i, Just where the red track of the Los Gatos road streams on and upward.

2. *transf.* and *fig.* **a.** Of light, air, vapour, immaterial effluences, etc.: To be carried or emitted in a full and continuous current.

a **1300** *E.E. Psalter* lxi. 11 Welthes if þai stremen smert [Vulg. *si affluant*], Nil þou set on þam þi hert. **14..** *Beryn* 2468 Part of sapience Stremyd in-to his hert, for his eloquence. **1578** H. WOTTON *Courtlie Controv.* 59 Vntill the fountaine of loue, streaming from their eyes, gaue libertye vnto restrained speeche. **1601** SHAKS. *All's Well* II. iii. 82 And to imperiall loue, that God most high, Do my sighes streame. **1661** POWER *Exp. Philos.* (1664) Pref. b 4 b, They are all porous, and the ætherial Matter is continually streaming through them. **1794** MRS. RADCLIFFE *Myst. Udolpho* xxvi, She observed the rays of the lamp stream through a small opening. **1852** H. ROGERS *Ecl. Faith* (1853) 244 The morning sun was streaming in at the window. **1871** L. STEPHEN *Playgr. Eur.* (1894) iv. 98 The clouds.. streamed out from their shelter into the current of the gale. **1875** CLARK RUSSELL *John Holdsworth* xx, Amid the clanking of spoons in glasses,..the conversation streamed into milder channels. **1897** S. CRANE *Third Violet* i. 4 Dust streamed out behind the vehicle. **1897** *Allbutt's Syst. Med.* III. 81 In a short time neuralgic pangs stream along the limbs.

b. Of a star or meteor: To form a continuous trail of light as it moves in its course. (Cf. 6.)

1838 EMERSON *Lit. Ethics* Wks. (Bohn) II. 206 Over him [the scholar] stream the flying constellations. **1884** R. S. BALL in *Nature* 4 Sept. 455/1, I looked up just in time to see a superb shooting star stream across the heavens.

3. a. Of a flag, or the like: To wave or float outwards in the wind.

1560 PHAER *Æneid* IX. (1562) Dd iij, Thou sawest..how his helmet crest did streaming stare? **1667** MILTON *P.L.* I. 537 Th' Imperial Ensign..Shon like a Meteor streaming to the Wind. *Ibid.* V. 590 Ten thousand thousand Ensignes high advanc'd..Streame in the Aire. **1846** MRS. A. MARSH *Father Darcy* II. xx. 346 His own man, pale with terror, his hair streaming in the wind, came rushing..through the wood. **1853** LYTTON *My Novel* XII. xxxii, Flags stream, and drums beat.

indirect passive. **1907** E. GOSSE *Father & Son* 157 Dark rocks..streamed over by silken flags of royal crimson and purple.

b. Of hair, a garment, etc.: To hang loose and waving; to lie in undulating curves; to trail *out, behind.*

1784 COWPER *Task* IV. 541 Her head, adorn'd with lappets pinn'd aloft, And ribbands streaming gay. **1820** KEATS *Hyperion* I. 214 His flaming robes stream'd out beyond his heels. **1822** W. TENNANT *Thane of Fife* V. xlv, Stream'd from her cinctur'd waist her long cymar behind. **1883** S. C. HALL *Retrospect* II. 155 His loose grey hair streamed over his shoulders.

c. *indirect passive*, with *upon*: To be ornamented *with* (a profusion of jewels).

1837 LADY GRANVILLE *Lett.* (1894) II. 225 A white tissue floating about her like clouds, looped up and streamed upon with jewels.

4. a. Of persons (or animals): To move together continuously in considerable numbers; to flock. Often with adv., as *out, in, down, up, away.*

1735 DYCHE & PARDON *Dict.*, *Stream* v., to walk, move, or go along soberly or gently with the Current, &c., also to loiter about idly. **1815** SCOTT *Guy M.* xiii, People.. streamed to it from all quarters. **1837** CARLYLE *Fr. Rev.* III. I. vii, Recruits stream up on him. **1853** KANE *Grinnell Exp.* xlix. (1856) 464 We began to observe too flocks of little Auk streaming south. **1863** KINGSLEY *Water-Bab.* viii. 343 The sea-birds sang as they streamed out into the ocean. **1879** FROUDE *Cæsar* xix. 323 Horse and foot were streaming along the roads.

b. *spec.* of the hounds going after the fox in open country.

1853 R. S. SURTEES *Sponge's Sp. Tour* ix. 45 From the summit..they see the hounds streaming away to a fine grass country below. **1883** E. PENNELL-ELMHIRST *Cream Leicestersh.* 146 A fine big fox away, with the pack streaming after him. **1897** *Encycl. Sport* I. 583/1 (Hunting, fox) *Streaming*, going across open country, spread out.

c. Without the notion of large numbers: To go with a rush. *rare.*

1848 THACKERAY *Van. Fair* xv, It was scarcely out of his mouth when Mrs. Firkin and Miss Briggs had streamed up the stairs, had rushed into the drawing-room [etc.].

5. To pour off or exude liquid in a continuous stream; to run, drip, overflow with moisture. Of the eyes: To overflow *with* (tears); also with *over*. Of the body: To run *with*, †*on* (blood or sweat).

[*c* **1374** CHAUCER *Troylus* IV. 247 Hys eyen two, for pite of his herte, Out stremeden as swyfte welles tweye.] *a* **1375** *Joseph Arim.* 560 He seiȝ a child strauȝt þer-on, stremynge on blode. **1693** EVELYN *De La Quint. Compl. Gard.*, *Cult. Orange-trees* 15 Whilst the Clod is thus streaming, should one put it into a new Earth'd Case, it would make it all into a Mortar. **1735** SOMERVILLE *Chase* IV. 90 The smoking Litter..seek the pouting Teat, That plenteous streams. **1736** tr. *Rollin's Anc. Hist.* XVIII. II. iii. VIII. 426 Every part of the city streamed with blood. **1791** MRS. RADCLIFFE *Rom. Forest* i, With supplicating eyes that streamed with tears. **1812** BYRON *Ch. Har.* I. xiii. Song viii, Fresh feeres will dry the bright blue eyes We late saw streaming o'er. **1841** DICKENS *Barn. Rudge* xlviii, Still Lord George, streaming from every pore, went on with Gashford. **1850** [see STREAMING *ppl. a.* 1]. **1875** JOWETT *Plato* (ed. 2) III. 18 The day was hot and he was streaming with perspiration. **1878** MEREDITH *Love in Valley* xii, Streaming like a willow grey in arrowy rain.

6. a. Of a luminous body: To emit a continuous stream of beams or rays of light. Also *spec.* of a comet, with reference to its 'tail': To issue in a widening stream of light.

a **1400–50** *Wars Alex.* 5286 With stoute starand stanes þat stremed as þe son. *c* **1420** LYDG. *Ballad, Commend. Our Lady* 68 Lauriat coroun, stremand as a sterre. **1592** SHAKS. *Rom. & Jul.* II. ii. 21 Her eye[s] in heauen, Would through the ayrie Region streame so bright, That Birds would sing, and thinke it were not night. **1608** TOPSELL *Serpents* 277 About their backes there are many little shining spots like eyes..streaming like starres. **1617** L. DIGGES tr. *Claudian's Rape Proserpine* I. D 3 b, A Comet..streaming o're the world with bloudy light. **1842** TENNYSON *Farew.* 13 A thousand suns will stream on thee. **1908** [Miss E. Fowler] *Betw. Trent & Ancholme* 68 The Comet's tail streams and widens upward.

b. With a blending of sense 5: To be suffused *with* (radiant light).

1830 T. S. HUGHES *Trav. Sicily* (ed. 2) I. iv. 119 As he ascended in the sky the mountain tops began to stream with golden light. **1856** KANE *Arct. Expl.* I. xviii. 223 A gorge that was streaming at noonday with the southern sun.

II. Transitive senses.

7. a. To cause to flow; to pour forth, discharge, or emit in a stream (a liquid, rays of light, etc.). Also with adv., as *out, forth, down.*

1388 WYCLIF *Prov.* v. 16 Thi wellis be stremed forth [Vulg. *deriventur fontes tui foras*]. **1493** *Dives & Paup.* (W. de W. 1496) I. ii. 33/2 His hondes were nayled to the crosse and stremed out blood. **1570** DEE *Math. Pref.* b ij, The true Sonne of rightwisenesse..hath so abundantly streamed into our hartes, the direct beames of his goodnes, mercy, and grace. **1596** SPENSER *Hymne Hon. Beautie* 26 It may so please, that she at length will streame Some deaw of grace into my withered hart. **1600** FAIRFAX *Tasso* II. xx, That light'ning ray Which her sweete beautie streamed on his face. **1601** SHAKS. *Jul. C.* III. i. 201 Had I as many eyes, as thou hast wounds, Weeping as fast as they streame forth thy blood. **1641** J. JACKSON *True Evang. T.* II. 115 S. Peter.. streamed downe upon the Church such abundance of sincere milk, as himselfe styleth it. **1789** POLWHELE *Engl. Orator* IV. 380 She [Religion] sits..Streaming cherubic Effluence o'er her Heaven Of spotless Azure. **1823** SCOTT *Quentin D.* iv, He took a large purse from his bosom,..and streamed a shower of small silver pieces into the goblet. **1868** *Model Stream Eng.* 19 If now cold water from a sponge be streamed over the bottom of the flask, boiling will recommence. **1880** C. R. MARKHAM *Peruv. Bark* 143 The moon streamed its floods of light over the forest. **1891** 'MAX O'RELL' *Frenchm. in Amer.* 268 The firemen streaming floods of water over the roof and through the windows.

†*fig.* **1607** HIERON *Wks.* I. 420 The best which he [*sc.* man] hath in him is corrupt: he is streamed out of an infected fountain. **1608** WILLET *Hexapla in Exod.* 641 Royall power, streaming glorie and princely dignitie.

b. Of a river, a fountain: To have its stream composed of (an alien liquid); to run with (blood, etc.).

1613 PURCHAS *Pilgrimage* V. i. (1614) 454 A golden world, where meale was as plentifull as dust, and fountaines streamed milke, hony, wine, and oyle. **1615** G. SANDYS *Trav.* 209 The riuer of Adonis, which is said by Lucan [*ed. 3 correctly* Lucian] to haue streamed bloud.

c. *to stream out*: to exhaust by unrestricted flow. Also *fig.*

1628 FELTHAM *Resolves* I. xv. 43 Themistocles, that streamed out his youth, in Wine, and Venery. **1894** E. A. MINCHIN tr. *Bütschli's Investig. Microsc. Foams* 79 To find out whether..one can produce new streamings in drops which have streamed themselves out.

8. To suffuse or overspread (a surface) *with* flowing moisture. Also *fig.*

1526 *Pilgr. Perf.* (W. de W. 1531) 302 b, With..pale visage, all stremed with blode. **1806** G. PINCKARD *Notes W. Indies* III. 207 From using only moderate exercise, I am so streamed with perspiration as to make it necessary to change my clothes four or five times in the course of the day. **1897** F. THOMPSON *New Poems* 17 While his being is Streamed with the set of the world's harmonies.

†**9.** To ornament with flowing lines or rays. *Obs.*

c **1430** LYDG. *Min. Poems* (Percy Soc.) 8 Stremyd with sonnes were alle her garmentis. **1611** FLORIO, *Irrigare*, to streame any thing by lines. *a* **1626** BACON *New Atlantis* 23 The Heralds Mantle is streamed with Gold.

10. To cause (a flag) to float outwards in the wind; to wave (a handkerchief).

1593 SHAKS. *Rich. II*, IV. i. 94 Streaming the Ensigne of the Christian Crosse, Against black Pagans, Turkes, and Saracens. **1787** POLWHELE *Engl. Orator* II. 654 Some Bark Streaming the well-known Pendant. **1823** SCOTT *Quentin D.* xiv, As they streamed towards him their kerchiefs, in token of encouragement.

11. *Naut.* ***to stream the buoy***: to throw the anchor-buoy overboard before casting anchor.

1769 FALCONER *Dict. Marine* (1780) s.v. *Buoy*. **1840** R. H. DANA *Bef. Mast* x. 23 After the topsails had been sheeted home,..and the buoys streamed, and all ready forward for slipping. **1882** NARES *Seamanship* (ed. 6) 162 Stream the buoy, and heave the anchor over.

12. *Mining.* To flush (a detrital deposit) with a stream of water, in order to carry off the earthy matter, and leave the ore exposed. Usually *absol.* ***to stream for*** (tin, copper, etc.).

1778 W. PRYCE *Min. Cornub.* 132 Nothing else remains than to describe the manner of Streaming. **1787** GROSCHKE tr. *Klaproth's Observ. Fossils Cornw.* 11 The manner of streaming or collecting the tin rubbles..is briefly the following. **1796** *Trans. Soc. Arts* XIV. 166 On streaming or searching for tin,..another stratum was discovered. **1866** KINGSLEY *Herew.* iii, Past the ugly dykes and muddy leats, where Alef's slaves were streaming the gravel for tin ore. **1877** *Encycl. Brit.* VI. 425/2 Copper, which lies deeper in the earth, and consequently cannot be 'streamed' for. **1899** BARING-GOULD *Bk. West* II. *Cornw.* 61 Hardly a gully has not been streamed, every river-bed has been turned over. **1907** *Proc. Soc. Antiquaries* 456 For the purpose of streaming for wolfram, or tungsten.

13. *Dyeing.* To wash (silk fabric) in running water, before putting in the dye.

1883 R. HALDANE *Workshop Rec.* Ser. II. 40/2 After which it [the woven silk] is removed to be streamed in running water, and beaten, till thoroughly clean and ready for dyeing.

14. *Educ.* In a school, to divide (pupils) into streams (sense 6 e); to place (a pupil) in a stream.

1957 *Listener* 12 Dec. 997/1 The Russians..neither stream nor select their children... All are expected to reach a common standard. **1966** J. PARTRIDGE *Middle School* iii. 41 The boys are thus streamed according to recognized ability. **1973** *People's Jrnl.* (Inverness & Northern Counties ed.) 4 Aug. 9/2, I suppose they had their problems trying to get me 'streamed'. **1980** *Times* 7 May 15/3, I got myself streamed at Manchester Grammar towards the sciences.

streamed, *a.* [f. STREAM *sb.* (senses 6 e, 7) + -ED².] † **1.** Emitting streams of light; (of a comet) furnished with a 'stream' or tail. Also, ornamented with flowing lines (cf. STREAM *v.* 9). *Obs.*

c **1440** LYDG. *Secrees* 1003 This stoon of Colour is Sumtyme Cytrynade lyk the sonne stremyd in his kynde. **1593** NASHE *Christ's T.* 27 Ouer the Temple..was seene a Commet most coruscant, streamed & tayled forth, with glistering naked swords. **1641** *Invent. Goods C'tess. Arundel* in *Burlington Mag.* (1912) Jan. 235/1 Nyne streamed Tafeta Curtaines. *Ibid.* 235/2 A streamed silke Curtaine.

2. *Educ.* Of a school, esp. a comprehensive school: organized in classes of pupils of like rather than mixed ability. Also of pupils: grouped according to ability.

1962 *Guardian* 30 Mar. 10/5 There are some very good streamed schools. **1968** *Listener* 4 July 8/3 In streamed comprehensive schools.. all advantages lie with the children of middle-class parents. *a* **1974** R. CROSSMAN *Diaries* (1977) III. 391 She has got four different streamed groups and a fifth group of backward children. **1978** *Times* 28 July 4/8 The bottom classes of streamed schools.. often.. get the worst teachers.

streamer ('striːmə(r)), *sb.* Forms: 3-7 stremer(e, 4-5 stremour (6 *Sc.* stremowr), 6 streemer, stremar (*Sc.* streamar), streymer (straymer), 6- streamer. [f. STREAM *v.* + -ER[1].]

1. A flag streaming or waving in the air; *specif.* a long and narrow pointed flag or pennon.

1292 in Champollion-Figeac *Lettres des Rois* (1839) I. 397 Lesqueles banères sount appelés baucans, et la gent d'Engleterre les appelent stremeres. **1295** *Acc. Exch. K.R.* 5/8 m. 13 Et v.s. vj.d. in .j. Stremer empto de Hugone Kelinge Et xij.d. in .j. Phane empto ad Mast. **13..** *Sir Beues* 3042 Vpon þe hiȝeste mast is top þere He let sette vp a stremere Of his fader armure. *a* **1400** *Isumbras* 224 Those schippes sawe thay ryde With toppe castelles sett one lofte, ... Stremours fro thame ferre gane glyde. **1500** *Inv. Ch. Goods Canterb.* in *Gentl. Mag.* (1837) Dec. 571/2, j stremer, of rede bokeram, wt a dragon of Saynt George therin, and a rode baner staff 'longyng thereto. *a* **1548** HALL *Chron.*, *Hen. VII*, 53 b, Barges garnished with standardes, stremers and penons. **1602** MARSTON *Antonio's Rev.* III. i, *Ant.* Where stands my fathers hearse? *2nd Pa.* Those streamers beare his armes. **1631** WEEVER *Anc. Funeral Mon.* 596 A little Streamer worne on the top of a lawnce by a Horseman. **1671** MILTON *Samson* 718 Like a stately Ship.. With all her bravery on, and tackle trim, Sails fill'd, and streamers waving. **1704** PRIOR *Let. to M. Boileau Despreaux* 74 What Poet would essay To count the Streamers of my Lord Mayor's Day? **1721** STRYPE *Eccl. Mem.* II. I. xxxii. (271) Whose Streamers and Cognizances hang still up in the said Church. **1784** COWPER *Task* II. 255 Now hoist the sail, and let the streamers float Upon the wanton breezes. **1841** DICKENS *Barn. Rudge* xlviii, He shall carry.. the gayest silken streamer in this valiant army.

fig. **1648** HERRICK *Hesper.*, *Mrs. Eliz. Wheeler, Lost Shepardesse* 12 In yond' Carnation goe and seek, There thou shalt find her lip and cheek:.. In bloome of Peach, and Roses bud, There waves the Streamer of her blood. **1784** COWPER *Task* v. 330 Your self-denying zeal, that holds it good.. to hang His thorns with streamers of continual praise. **1860** HAWTHORNE *Transform.* xlviii, [To him] the Corso was but a narrow and shabby street of decaying palaces; and even the long, blue streamer of Italian sky, above it, not half so brightly blue as formerly.

2. *transf.* **a.** *gen.* Something long and narrow, that hangs loose in the manner of a streamer.

1810 SCOTT *Lady of L.* I. xi, The brier-rose fell in streamers green. **1853** MRS. GORE *Dean's Dau.* xxxvii. III. 183 'My maid pointed out to me.. this morning half-a-dozen grey hairs in these miserable streamers,' replied Lady Emily, passing her hand lightly through the long, fair ringlets. **1889** *Repent. Paul Wentworth* III. 228 Tying up a bouquet.. with long streamers of pale yellow ribbon. **1908** [MISS E. FOWLER] *Betw. Trent & Ancholme* 286, I have seen long streamers of dark pink roses swinging over the Red Sandstone walls of Melrose.

†**b.** Some kind of decoration for pastry. *Obs.*

1710-11 SWIFT *Jrnl. to Stella* 6 Jan., Great cakes frothed with sugar, and stuck with streamers of tinsel. **1717** PRIOR *Alma* I. 388 He must be an idle dreamer, Who leaves the pie, and gnaws the streamer.

c. A long flowing ribbon, feather, etc. attached to some article of dress.

1838 W. C. HARRIS *Narr. Exped. S. Africa* xii. 106 A collection of skin streamers like the tails of a lady's boa attached to a thin waistcord, being the nearest approach to an habiliment amongst them. **1841** DICKENS *Barn. Rudge* xxxi, The obliging care of his martial friend had decorated his hat with sundry parti-coloured streamers. **1853** C. BRONTE *Villette* xx, A lady's head-dress—a most airy sort of blue and silver turban, with a streamer of plumage on one side. **1862** THACKERAY *Philip* xxviii, Her own battered, blowsy old *chapeau*, with its limp streamers.

d. A long exserted feather streaming away from the rest of the plumage of certain birds.

[Cf. 1869-73 in sense 8 a.]

1879 A. NEWTON in *Encycl. Brit.* X. 712/1 In this [species] the remigial streamers do not lose their barbs. **1899** A. H. EVANS *Birds* 548 The extraordinary *Pteridophora alberti* possesses a wonderful streamer behind each eye, twice as long as the body.

e. A long narrow strip of vapour, snow, etc.

1871 L. STEPHEN *Playgr. Eur.* (1894) viii. 176 Fragments of vapour.. clustered in long streamers upon the mountain sides. **1874** SYMONDS *Sk. Italy & Greece* (1898) I. i. 27 Streamers of snow may be seen flying from the higher ridges. **1895** R. W. CHAMBERS *King in Yellow* (1909) 253 Long streamers of clouds touched with rose swept low on the western sky.

f. A long narrow strip of coloured paper used as a festive decoration or rolled up to unwind when thrown (at a celebration, etc.).

1857 C. M. YONGE *Dynevor Terrace* I. xvi. 262 The [Christmas] tree became more laden, and the streamers and glass balls produced a more brilliant effect. **1918** A. BENNETT *Jrnl.* 14 Nov. (1932) II. 242 The feature of last night was girls with bunches of streamers which they flicked in your face as you passed. **1930** E. RICE *Voyage to Purilia* xii. 155 The room was gay, with streamers of coloured paper and with large gas balloons. **1959** M. SHADBOLT *New Zealanders* 239 She.. found herself waving farewell to her tearful parents from the deck of a ship. Only then, as the tangling streamers snapped across the widening water, did she remember to be surprised at herself. **1980** *Daily Tel.* 25 Nov. 15/6 This useful company also supplies carnival and party novelties including balloons.., dance streamers,.. lucky dip prizes and stocking fillers.

g. = BANNER *sb.*[1] 2 c. Also *transf.*

1909 G. R. CHESTER *Making of Bobby Burnet* xix. 230 Use two-inch streamers clear across the page. **1922** U. SINCLAIR *They call me Carpenter* 88 The headlines flamed before my mind's eye—streamer heads, all the way across the sheet. **1938** F. D. SHARPE *Sharpe of Flying Squad* xxv. 254 Then a very good crime reporter called a portico thief a cat-burglar and the story got a streamer headline. **1957** [see BANNER *sb.*[1] 2 c]. **1963** *Times* 19 Apr. 8/5 Invitations to browse in these places, moreover, occasionally decorate the discreet vans of the Stationery Office. But this form of streamer on the van is technically known as a 'filler', which means that it is used only when the space is not required for boosting some new publication.

h. *Angling.* A fly with feathers attached, which simulates a small fish; also, the feathers so employed. Freq. *attrib.*, chiefly as ***streamer fly***. orig. and chiefly *U.S.*

1919 D. CARROLL *Fishing, Tackle & Kits* 265 The white bucktail with the red feather streamers in the shape of a tail made the trout strike. **1929** *Field & Stream* June 65/3 (Advt.), Dixie Wiggler.. different colored streamers. **1930** Forest & Stream Mar. 202/2 A lure which is justly famous in a few restricted localities.. is the Streamer Fly... This fly is tied in more or less conventional hackle style with a two- or three-inch streamer feather as a tail. **1952** J. VENIARD *Fly Dressers' Guide* xiii. 140 *Streamer Flies.* This type of fly is immensely popular in America, but its possibilities in the United Kingdom have never been seriously considered. The nearest approach we have to it is the 'lure', which consists usually of two or three hooks in tandem with a long wing. The idea is very much the same.. the main difference being that many of the 'streamers' are tied to represent the small fish on which game fish feed, whereas most of the lures are just brightly coloured 'attractors'. **1971** K. DRAPER *Trout Flies in N.Z.* ii. 41 One of the most popular types of tie is the Parson's Glory style of streamer. This fly is closely allied to the American streamer fly which is tied in much the same manner except that the long neck or saddle hackles 'stream' free. **1975** D. J. COLLYER *Fly-Dressing* xi. 167 Seven years ago I received.. two very interesting flies, both streamers.. designed by Lew Oatman, an American, to imitate small fish.

3. †**a.** A luminous heavenly body emitting a continuous stream of light. *Obs.*

1513 DOUGLAS *Æneis* XII. Prol. 21 The twinkling stremowris of the orient Sched purpour sprangis with gold and asure ment, Persand the sabill barmkyn nocturnall. **1594** NASHE *Terrors Nt.* Wks. 1904 I. 354 Sundry times wee behold whole Armies of men skirmishing in the Ayre, Dragons, wilde beasts, bloody streamers, blasing Comets, firie strakes, with other apparitions innumerable. **1647** J. HALL *Poems* 71 O who so stupid that would not Resolve to Atoms, for to play 'Mong th' golden streamers he shall shut, While he prolongs one endlesse day?

b. Formerly, †the tail of a comet. In mod. use, a long, thin component or appendage of the tail of some comets.

1621 QUARLES *Esther* Introd. B 4 b, With mighty streamers came these blazing starres, Portending Warres. **1665** *Phil. Trans.* I. 39 It was not by far so bright, nor its streamer shining as this hath appeared. **1710** N. BLUNDELL *Diary* (1895) 85 My Wife and I saw ye Strange Starr.. the Streamer of it seemed to be fully four yards long. **1909** G. F. CHAMBERS *Story of Comets* iii. 23 Although comets usually have but one tail, 2 are not uncommon, whilst even that number is often increased by the presence of slender streamers, which are virtually independent tails. **1931** [see JET *sb.*[2] 4 c (i)]. **1972** D. C. KNIGHT *Comets* 13 The tail of Donati's comet of 1858 was some 50 million miles long.. and was split into two or three streamers.

c. A ray proceeding from the sun; esp. *pl.*, the radiation of the sun's corona seen in eclipses.

1697 DRYDEN *Æneis* VII. 35 When the rosie Morn began to rise, And wav'd her Saffron Streamer thro' the Skies. **1708** *Brit. Apollo* No. 108. 2/2 Your Rayes so extensive, And Lust'ring Streamers. **1878** PROCTOR *Myst. Time & Space* (1883) 110 The Sun's long streamers. *Ibid.* 119 The theory that such meteor systems may explain coronal streamers seen during total eclipses of the sun.

d. *pl.* The Aurora Borealis; rarely *sing.* (*poet.*), one of the darting rays or flashes forming this phenomenon. Cf. STREAMING *vbl. sb.* b.

1735 BYROM *Rem.* (1855) I. II. 519 Mr. C. had a coach, in which I rode to Gray's Inn; there were streamers in the air very remarkable. *a* **1774** GOLDSM. *Surv. Exp. Philos.* (1776) I. 64 The Aurora Borealis.. which the vulgar call streamers. **1775** L. SHAW *Hist. Moray* III. 148 In the Winter Nights, the Aurora Borealis (from its desultory motion, called Merry-dancers and Streamers) affords no small light. **1801** J. LEYDEN *Elfin-King* xxx, When high over head fall the streamers red. **1842** TENNYSON *Morte d'Arth.* 139 The great brand.. flashing round and round, and whirl'd in an arch, Shot like a streamer of the northern morn. *a* **1861** A. CLOUGH *Mari Magno* v. 329 While the arctic streamers bright Rolled from the clouds in waves of airy light. **1873** SYMONDS *Grk. Poets* viii. 250 His splendour is like that of northern streamers in its lambency.

e. A streaming jet or tongue of flame.

1758 REID tr. *Macquer's Chem.* I. 265 From time to time this streamer darts out to the length of seven or eight inches, snapping and emitting sparks of fire.

f. A filamentary luminosity sometimes seen to extend from an electrode in a gas when the potential difference is not great enough to produce a spark or arc; a similar feature that extends from a cloud or something on the ground prior to a stroke of lightning along the same path.

1910 *Encycl. Brit.* V. 883/1 Bright curved streamers starting from the negative terminal. **1934** *Physical Rev.* XLVI. 101/2 The breakdown in argon is similar to that in helium except that no glow discharge is observed and no anode streamer forms. **1935** *Proc. R. Soc.* A. CLII. 597 The leader to the first stroke consists of a series of streamers moving downwards in a step-by-step manner. **1953** MEEK & CRAGGS *Electr. Breakdown of Gases* iii. 159 In a 6-cm. gap with a 0·05-mm. point, the streamers gradually lengthen, as the voltage is raised, to 1·1 cm. and then breakdown occurs. **1972** *Jrnl. Physics D* V. 2179 Photomultiplier investigations .... have shown that the streamers are weakly luminous channels, and that almost all the ionization phenomena are concentrated at their tip. **1979** J. G. NAVARRA *Atmosphere, Weather & Climate* ix. 298 When the leader stroke approaches the ground, a discharge streamer is extended from the ground up to the leader and completes the channel.

†**4.** A rider or supplementary addition to a document. *Obs.*

1696 S. SEWALL *Diary* 2 Dec. (1878) I. 439 Capt. Byfield brings in a long Bill from the deputys for a Fast and Reformation, written by Mr. Cotton Mather, to which a Streamer was added expressing that Partiality in Courts of Justice was obvious.

5. The geometrid moth *Anticlea derivata*.

1775 M. HARRIS *Eng. Lepidoptera* 45 Streamer... White moth, having a bar of brown near the thorax and another waving like a narrow flag near the tip. **1832** J. RENNIE *Butterfl. & Moths* 123 The Streamer (*Anticlea derivata*). **1869** E. NEWMAN *Brit. Moths* 166.

6. *Mining.* One who washes detrital deposits to procure the ore they contain.

1619 in W. Macfarlane *Geogr. Collect.* (S.H.S.) III. 34 John Gibson.. who.. now is a Washer or streamer for Gold. **1758** BORLASE *Nat. Hist. Cornw.* 214 A streamer there, found native gold immersed in the body of a blue sandy slat. **1769** *Phil. Trans.* LIX. 49 Some streamers.. brought in a parcel of tin ore. **1865** ESQUIROS *Cornw.* 41 Streamers, that is to say, men who obtain tin by washing the deposits found by the disaggregation of the primitive rocks.

7. *Educ.* [f. the sb.] With a categorizing letter prefixed: a child belonging to that stream in a school, or one whose abilities are adapted to such a stream; esp. ***C-streamer***, a child of little academic ability.

1966 *Guardian* 4 Apr. 6/1 C-stream children in a competitive society have the makings of failure before they start... Let us take it that eventually the C-streamer has been taught to read. **1967** *Punch* 20 Dec. 952/3 These.. riddles will hold ten-year-olds enthralled until *next* Christmas—or even, in the case of certain C-streamers, the one after. **1970** *Sunday Times* (Colour Suppl.) 18 Jan. 8/1 They are C-streamers, from poor homes.

8. *attrib.* and *Comb.* **a.** In general use.

1534 in Sharp *Cov. Myst.* (1825) 196 Paid to þe stremer-berers xvj d. **1869-73** T. R. JONES *Cassell's Bk. Birds* II. 131 The Streamer-bearing Night Jar.. (*Cosmetornis vexillarius*). **1871** NESBITT *Catal. Slade Coll. Glass* 75 Green and red streamer points. **1883** *Encycl. Brit.* XVI. 688/1 Drawn out to streamer-like dimensions. **1899** MEREDITH *Poems, Night-walk* 3 Awakes for me and leaps from shroud All radiantly the moon's own night Of folded showers in streamer cloud.

b. *Physical Chem.* Applied to a type of molecular orbital possessing a single nodal plane and formed out of identical atomic orbitals of the same phase from each of the atoms in the ring or chain backbone of the molecule.

1966 PHILLIPS & WILLIAMS *Inorg. Chem.* II. xxvii. 348 The lowest benzene π (aromatic) orbitals of the 'streamer' kind, one from each benzene, have nodes only in the planes of the benzene rings, and taken in combination are therefore either of the A_{1g} or A_{2u} type symmetry. **1974** GILL & WILLIS *Pericyclic Reactions* iv. 117 The lowest hexatriene level (ψ_1) is the typical 'streamer' orbital (i.e. $\pm\ \pm\ \pm\ \pm\ \pm\ \pm$) which is of *A* symmetry with respect to C_{2y} and of *S* symmetry with respect to the mirror plane σ_{yz}.

streamer ('striːmə(r)), *v.* [f. STREAMER *sb.*] *trans.* To furnish or fill with streamers. Hence **'streamered** *ppl. a.*, **'streamering** *vbl. sb.*

1814 SCOTT *Ld. of Isles* I. xv, Lord Ronald's fleet swept by, Streamer'd with silk, and trick'd with gold. **1818** HOGG *Brownie of Bodsbeck* I. ii. 21 After the last rays of day had disappeared, and again in the morning before they had begun to streamer the east, the song of praise was sung. **1824** MOIR in *Blackw. Mag.* XVI. 283 The streamer'd flags of far-spread realms shall meet. **1834** J. WILSON *Ibid.* XXXVI. 5 The air is streamered with flags. **1837** CARLYLE *Fr. Rev.* II. VI. iii, We have a bright Sun; and all is marching, streamering, and blaring. **1902** ELIZ. BANKS *Newspaper Girl* 143 She had secretly donned the despised streamered cap.

†**'streamful**, *a. Obs. rare*[−1]. [f. STREAM *sb.* + -FUL.] Full of streams or currents.

1596 DRAYTON *Legends, Piers Gaveston* cv, Like a Ship.. Shoou'd by the Wind against the streamfull tyde.

streamie ('striːmɪ), *sb. Sc.* [See -IE.] A poetical diminutive of STREAM *sb.*

1789 BURNS *To Dr. Blacklock* v, Ye.. dainty damies, Wha by Castalia's wimplin' streamies, Lowp, sing, and lave your pretty limbies.

streaming ('striːmɪŋ), *vbl. sb.* [f. STREAM *v.* + -ING[1].] **a.** The action of the verb in various senses; an instance of this.

1398 TREVISA *Barth. De P.R.* VIII. xxviii. (1495) x vj, Arystotle sayth that lyghte is noo body, nother stremynge oute of a body. **1607** HIERON *Wks.* (1614) I. 206 In a conuenient season, the veines of the earth are opened, and the dryed spring returneth to his former streaming. **1624** GEE *Foot out of Snare* xv. 97 This streaming of my pen from the fountaine of my heart. **1655** GURNALL *Chr. in Armour* I. 45 The streamings forth of divine grace. *a* **1716** SOUTH *Serm.* (1842) III. 601 We should deal with these first streamings out of sin, as the Psalmist would have the people of God deal with the brats of Babylon. **1887** BESANT *The World went* xv. II. 24 The women.. who can afford it have ribbons round their hats, the streaming of which in the breeze greatly gratifies them.

†**b.** The Aurora Borealis. *Obs.* Cf. STREAMER *sb.* 3 d.

1694 *Acc. Sev. Late Voy.* II. (1711) 214 Nor should I much doubt to affirm, that it [this light] is that which is sometimes seen in England, and especially in the Northern parts, call'd Streaming. **1727** DERHAM *Lumen Boreale* in *Phil. Trans.* XXXIV. 245 There are two sorts of Streamings,..one, by way of Explosion from the Horizon; the other, by opening and shutting, [etc.].

c. *Her.* (See quot.)

1725 J. COATS *Dict. Her.* (1739) 319 *Streaming* is the Term us'd to express the Stream of Light darting from a Comet, or Blazing Star, vulgarly call'd the Beard.

d. *Mining.* The washing of ore (usually tin-ore) from the detritus with which it is associated.

1778 W. PRYCE *Min. Cornub.* 134 It did not require any great degree of penetration, to have comprehended Streaming and Draining under one idea. **1802** PLAYFAIR *Illustr. Huttonian Theory* 110 Hence the streaming, as it is called, or washing of the earth to obtain the tin-stone from it. **1853** URE *Dict. Arts* (ed. 4) II. 859 The greatest quantity of tin has been produced by 'streaming' (as washing the debris in the valleys is termed).

e. *Biol.* A peculiar flowing motion or 'rotation' of protoplasm in a cell.

1875 BENNETT & DYER tr. *Sachs' Bot.* 38 In the sacs of the Characeæ the nucleus disappears altogether when the streaming (Strömung) of the protoplasm begins. **1880** BESSEY *Bot.* 6 In their plasmodia..many kinds of movements may be observed, the commonest of which is streaming. **1894** E. A. MINCHIN tr. *Bütschli's Investig. Microsc. Foams* 122 The so-called rotational streaming of the protoplasm.

f. *Educ.* The practice of dividing pupils in a school into streams (sense 6e). Also, the allocation of pupils to different schools according to ability.

1954 *Brit. Jrnl. Psychol* XLV. 147 Present methods of streaming in primary and secondary schools do not give the more backward as good a chance to make up. **1961** *New Left Rev.* Jan.–Feb. 6/2 A streaming system..with secondary modern, technical and grammar-type schools. **1966** D. JENKINS *Educated Society* v. 200 An argument for turning all Secondary schools into Comprehensive schools with a strong streaming system. **1971** *Where* Sept. 262/2 The practice of streaming—classifying children according to their abilities in reading, writing and arithmetic—is gradually becoming suspect. **1980** *Daily Tel.* 10 Dec. 16/6 The proposals include phasing out of church schools, single sex schools, and streaming.

streaming ('striːmɪŋ), *ppl. a.* [-ING².] That streams, in senses of the verb.

1. a. Of a liquid, a river, etc.: Flowing copiously. Of a source, surface, etc.: Overflowing, running, or dripping with moisture.

1579 SPENSER *Sheph. Cal.* Nov. 61 Let streaming teares be poured out in store. **1590** —— *F.Q.* III. iv. 17 And with his streaming gore Distaines the pillours and the holy grownd. **1600** FAIRFAX *Tasso* XIII. lxxvii, The streaming showres.. which heau'n shed on the thirstie lands. **1655** J. S. *Bonarelli's Filli di Sciro* III. ii. 52 That little streaming Brook. **1697** DRYDEN *Virg. Georg.* IV. 784 From the slain Victims pour the streaming Blood. **1797** HT. LEE *Canterb. T., Frenchm. T.* (1799) I. 263 Constance..fixed her streaming eyes upon him. **1828** *Lights & Shades* II. 256 With clasped hands and streaming cheeks she implores us to give up our design. **1850** TENNYSON *In Mem.* lxxii. 4 Blasts that..lash with storm the streaming pane.

transf. and *fig.* **1784** COWPER *Task* VI. 150 Laburnum, rich In streaming gold. **1856** EMERSON *Eng. Traits* i. Wks. (Bohn) II. 6 With a streaming humour, which floated everything he looked upon.

b. Of a cold: accompanied by copious running of the eyes and nose.

1923 W. R. INGE *Lay Thoughts* (1926) III. vii. 229 Persons ..suffering from streaming colds, which are quite as infectious as..mumps or chicken-pox. **1982** *Guardian Weekly* 26 Dec. 22/1 One is sorry for foreigners, both as a Christian duty and because they tend to have streaming colds.

2. Of light or other effluence: Issuing in a full stream. Of a luminous body: Emitting a stream of rays or beams.

13.. *E.E. Allit. P.* A. 115 Stremande sternez. *a* **1400–50** *Wars Alex.* 3796 As ai stremand sternes stared all þaire wedis. **1513** BRADSHAW *St. Werburge* II. 1656 Anone a stremyng sterre appered sodaynlye. **1600** TOURNEUR *Transf. Metam.* lxxxv. D vj, Her streaming rayes haue pierc'd the cloudie skies. **1634** MILTON *Comus* 340 Som gentle taper.. visit us With thy long levell'd rule of streaming light. **1735** SOMERVILLE *Chase* IV. 73 If haply then he cross the streaming Scent, Away he flies vain glorious. **1757** W. WILKIE *Epigoniad* I. 4 As, from the setting skies, At ev'n's approach, a streaming meteor flies. **1887** BOWEN *Virg. Æneid* III. 151 Clear in the streaming light they showed.

3. Of a flag, hair, etc.: see STREAM *v.* 3, 3 b.

1567 TURBERV. *Epit.*, etc. 40 b, In steade of streaming sayles hee Wishes hanges aloft. **1575** FENTON *Gueuara's Golden Epist.* (1582) 14 Thou mayest see in mine [house] many streaming ensignes. **1781** GIBBON *Decl. & F.* xix. II. 143 Their streaming banners of silk..waved round the person of the emperor. **1792** S. ROGERS *Pleas. Mem.* I. 214 The mild Tupia..Long watch'd the streaming signal from the mast. **1836** C. WORDSWORTH *Athens* ii. (1855) 11 Their braided hair falls over the back in two long streaming folds. **1855** *Poultry Chron.* II. 519 The male bird..with his white streaming feathers.

4. Of persons or animals: Moving in a continuous stream.

1852 TENNYSON *Ode Death Wellington* 9 Here, in streaming London's central roar. **1895** M. HEWLETT *Earthwork out of Tuscany* 38 Streaming processions of virgins and young boys. **1900** *Westm. Gaz.* 12 Jan. 3/1 A fox ..went away..with the streaming pack on fairly good terms.

5. That 'streams' for tin: see STREAM *v.* 12.

1778 W. PRYCE *Min. Cornub.* 132 When a Streaming Tinner observes a place favourable in situation, he takes a lease..of the land owner or lord of the fee.

6. *Biol.* Of protoplasm: cf. STREAMING *vbl. sb.* e.

1894 E. A. MINCHIN tr. *Bütschli's Investig. Microsc. Foams* 124 The structural relations of the streaming protoplasm of the vegetable cell.

Hence **'streamingly** *adv.*

a **1500** *Medulla Gram.*, *Coactim*, stremyngly. **1585** HIGINS *Junius' Nomencl.* 404/2 At the burning of Corinth the veins of copper, brasse, golde, and siluer did runne streamingly together, and become mixed. *a* **1608** DEE *Relat. Spir.* I. (1659) 362 Now goeth fire out of his mouth streamingly. **1677** COLES *Eng.-Lat. Dict.*, Streamingly, *profluenter.* **1710** FULLER *Pharmacop.* 152 This of Turbith.. brings off..thin Lympha..plentifully and streamingly.

streamless ('striːmlɪs), *a.* [f. STREAM *sb.* + -LESS.] **a.** Of water: Having no current. **b.** Of a ditch or river-bed: Having no water. **c.** Of a district: Having no streams.

1863 BATES *Nat. Amazons* x. (1864) 288 The picturesque hilly country of the Tapajos, and its dark streamless waters. **1868** DILKE *Greater Brit.* II. 33 The Murray in February is a streamless ditch. **1888** A. H. KEANE in *Encycl. Brit.* XXIV. 758/2 Such a bleak, arid, and almost streamless land.

streamlet ('striːmlɪt). [f. STREAM *sb.* + -LET.] A small stream; a brook, rill, or rivulet.

a **1552** LELAND *Itin.* (1907) II. 145 The streates have streamlettes of springes almost yn every one renning. **1610** HOLLAND *Camden's Brit.* I. 330 The river Medway branching itself into five streamlets. **1729** SAVAGE *Wanderer* I. 313 And hence the Streamlets seek the terrass Shade. **1799** WORDSW. *Fountain* 21 No check, no stay, this Streamlet fears; How merrily it goes! *c* **1820** S. ROGERS *Italy, Feluca* 15 A streamlet, clear and full, ran to the sea. **1865** LIVINGSTONE *Zambesi* x. 210 Our path..crossed several streamlets.

transf. and *fig.* **1855** BAILEY *Mystic* 5 Time's sand-dry streamlet through its glassy straits Flowed ceaseless. **1862** SMILES *Engineers* III. 263 Horizontal tubes, through which the heated air passed in streamlets. **1867** PROCTOR in *Intell. Observer* Aug. 2 The Milky Way again subdivides, a branch running off at an angle of 20°, and losing itself in a narrow streamlet. **1871** SIR W. W. HUNTER in Skrine *Life* (1901) 196, I found great difficulty in getting at the streamlet of fact in a desert of verbiage. **1874** C. A. DAVIS in Spurgeon *Treas. David* IV. 350 The streamlet of practical daily effort.

streamline, *sb.* Also **stream-line.**

1. *Hydrodynamics* and *Aerodynamics.* **a.** (See quot. 1906.) In mod. use, a line such that, at any instant, the direction of the tangent at any point is the direction of the flow of fluid at that point. (This definition is equivalent to that in quot. 1906 for the special case of steady flow.)

1868 W. J. RANKINE in *Engineer* 16 Oct. 285/1 A stream-line is the line, whether straight or curved, that is traced by a particle in a current of fluid. **1873** J. C. MAXWELL *Electr. & Magn.* §648 II. 260 If ϕ is constant for any curve, there is no current across it. Such a curve is called a Current-line or a Stream-line. **1882** MINCHIN *Unipl. Kinematics* 151 When the motion becomes steady, each line of flow becomes the actual path of a fluid particle, which is called a stream-line. **1906** HOR. LAMB *Hydrodynamics* (ed. 3) 17 A 'line of motion' or 'stream-line' is defined to be a line drawn from point to point, so that its direction is everywhere that of the motion of the fluid. *Footnote*, Some writers prefer to restrict the use of the term 'stream-line' to the case of steady motion. **1945** R. VON MISES *Theory of Flight* ii. 23 In the case of an unsteady flow the streamlines, *i.e.*, the curves whose tangents have the velocity direction are, in general, not the pathways of the particles. **1971** G. M. HIDY *Waves* iv. 47 Streamlines generally bear no relation to particle paths because different fluid elements form different streamlines at given times. **1980** BOBER & KENYON *Fluid Mech.* iv. 124 If the flow is steady then a fluid particle will move along a streamline.

b. *attrib.* (*a*) Designating motion of a fluid that is free from turbulence, so that it can be represented by a pattern of streamlines that either is constant or changes steadily with time.

1898 HELE-SHAW in *Rep. Brit. Assoc.* 136 Stream-line Motion of a Viscous Film. **1916** H. BARBER *Aeroplane Speaks* 62 To secure a stream-line motion of the air free from eddies. **1957** G. E. HUTCHINSON *Treat. Limnol.* I. v. 251 The only simple way of observing regular streamline or laminar flow is adjacent to some smooth surface over which a slow current is passing. **1979** A. L. LYDERSEN *Fluid Flow & Heat Transfer* i. 2 This type of motion, where the velocity at a certain point is constant and independent of time, is termed laminar flow. It is sometimes called streamline flow or viscous flow.

(*b*) Having or being a shape such that the flow of a fluid round it is smooth, and there is no separation of streamlines from the surface; more widely, shaped so as to reduce air or water resistance; ***streamline wire***, a wire of elongated cross-section.

1907 F. W. LANCHESTER *Aerodynamics* i. 20 In an actual fluid, bodies of other than streamline form experience resistance apart from that directly due to viscosity. *Ibid.* iii. 102 In the hydrodynamic theory of an inviscid fluid, every conceivable body is of stream-line form. **1909** C. C. TURNER *Aerial Navig. To-day* viii. (1910) 131 Bodies having 'streamline' form present the least resistance to the air. Pure streamline form is, roughly speaking, pear-shaped, the blunt end foremost. **1914** *Automobile Topics* 30 May (Advt., back cover), That beautiful stream-line Car. **1918** W. L. COWLEY *Aeronautics* iv. 93 The following table gives the resistance coefficients of aeroplane stream line wires, of fineness ratio 3:1. **1919** G. WHALE *Brit. Airships* 160 The remaining two engines are carried in a small streamline car situated amidships. **1928** E. CADBURY in C. F. S. Gamble *Story North Sea Air Station* xxii. 408, I..seized a scarf, goggles and helmet, tore off my streamline coat, and semi-clothed..took a running jump into the pilot's seat. **1929** *Jrnl. R. Aeronaut. Soc.* XXXIII. 360 In aeronautical nomenclature a 'streamline body' is one about which the flow of a real fluid..approximates very closely to a steady flow of the hypothetical inviscid fluid, except in a very thin layer called the 'boundary layer', surrounding the exposed surfaces. *Ibid.* 361 The ideally streamline aeroplane cannot exist. **1936** J. C. CORLETT *Rigging & Airframes* v. 108 On the final inspection of streamline wires they must be checked for 'safety'. **1953** M. RAUSCHER *Introd. Aeronaut. Dynamics* vi. 259 The theory of the ideal fluid comes very close to representing the actual flow conditions about a streamline body in a fluid of low viscosity.

(*c*) *fig.*

1933 S. SPENDER *Poems* 44 Where only a low streamline brightness Of phosphorus on the tossing hills is white. **1942** *R.A.F. Jrnl.* 2 May 21 The camp is the last word in streamline modernity. **1967** B. J. BANFILL *Pioneer Nurse* xi. 129 Snow, in long streamline drifts, covered the now familiar objects.

c. Used predicatively as *adj.* in preceding senses.

1907 F. W. LANCHESTER *Aerodynamics* i. 27 If..we assume continuity as hypothesis, then all bodies must be streamline. **1922** *Daily Mail* 3 Nov. 2 The body of the car is streamline according to British practice. **1929** *Jrnl. R. Aeronaut. Soc.* XXXIII. 366 The b.h.p. required..should not be seriously influenced by interference, provided that the interference does not cause the flow to cease being streamline. **1936** B. JONES *Elem. Pract. Aerodynamics* vii. 115 Wherever possible the airplane parts that would cause parasite drag are made streamline in shape. **1971** J. W. IRELAND *Mech. of Fluids* viii. 234 Oil of specific gravity 0·9 and viscosity 1 poise is pumped through a 5 cm diameter pipe at the rate of 280 litres/min. Show that the flow is streamline.

d. A contour of a body that is coincident with a streamline of flow round it; *loosely*, a smooth, flowing outline.

1917 D'A. W. THOMPSON *Growth & Form* xvi. 673 The naval architect learns a great part of his lesson from the investigation of the stream-lines of a fish; and the mathematical study of the stream-lines of a bird..has helped to lay the very foundations of the modern science of aeronautics. **1936** B. JONES *Elem. Pract. Aerodynamics* vii. 117 Any non-streamlined body can have its resistance or drag greatly reduced merely by the addition of a blunt nose and a tapered tail. If the contour is also a continuous curve the shape approaches the ideal streamline. **1943** KOESTLER *Arrival & Departure* ii. 41 He was able to re-draw in his mind the curve of Odette's knees.., the streamlines of her jumper. **1944** W. FORTESCUE *Mountain Madness* xxiv. 162 If my curls were grey, at least I had kept my stream-line.

2. (See quot.)

1885 TAIT *Prop. Matter* iv. §83. 70 The line of steepest slope at any point of a surface is represented on the map by the shortest line which can be drawn to the nearest contour line. Thus it cuts the contour lines at right angles, and is the path along which a drop of water would trickle down. It is therefore called a Stream-line.

'streamline, *v.* Also **stream-line.** [f. the sb.]

1. *trans.* To give a streamline form to. Chiefly as STREAMLINED *ppl. a.*, STREAMLINING *vbl. sb.*

1918 H. BARBER *Aeroplane Speaks* (ed. 6) 61 From the designer's point of view it always pays to stream-line detrimental surface. **1927** HALDANE & HUXLEY *Anim. Biol.* xiii. 316 The air-sacs..are used to stream-line the body. **1927** *Daily Tel.* 27 Sept. 9/5 It appears that Flight-Lieut. Kinkead came down because the spinner, a metal fitting streamlining the propeller boss, came off.

2. *fig.* **a.** To slim; to remodel on smooth, uncluttered lines. Also *absol.*

1935 P. B. HAWK (*title*) Streamline for health. **1937** *Denver Post* 27 Jan. (Mag. Section) 9 (*heading*) Streamline your dance frock.

b. To simplify, esp. in order to make more efficient or better organized.

1936 *Sun* (Baltimore) 2 Nov. 13/5 Those who watch financial fashion observe a tendency to streamline capital set-ups for tax purposes. **1947** *Hansard Commons* Written Answers 2 Dec. 46, I am anxious to do all I can to streamline controls. **1950** A. HUXLEY *Let.* 16 Mar. (1969) 620 Chapters might be 'streamlined'. **1957** *New Yorker* 26 Oct. 60/2 The producers got panicky and decided to 'streamline' the production, stressing professional finish. **1958** *Post Office Mag.* Apr. 117/2 The Ministry are co-operating with us all ..on streamlining general building methods. **1974** *Whitaker's Almanack 1975* 812/1 Through its advisory services, it helps its member governments to..streamline health services.

streamlined ('striːmlaɪnd), *ppl. a.* Also **stream-lined.** [f. prec. + -ED¹ (early uses derived from the sb.).] **1.** Having a streamline form; designed so as to reduce air or water resistance.

1913 *Aeroplane* 30 Oct. 480/1 Its [*sc.* an aeroplane's] small span and carefully streamlined body. **1916** [see CLEAN *a.* 13 c]. **1928** C. F. S. GAMBLE *Story North Sea Air Station* 10 Her two stream-lined gondolas..were designed to be capable of sustaining severe impact loads when alighting on water. **1930** *Observer* 16 Feb. 17/5 She has oval, instead of stream-lined funnels. **1948** M. LASKI *Tory Heaven* iv. 58 I'd thought of..one of the old Lagondas..but I believe everything's streamlined these days. **1968** O. S. NOCK *Railway Enthusiast's Encycl.* 279 From 1923 onwards, the 'Cheltenham Flyer' of the G.W.R. claimed the honours until the advent of the L.N.E.R. streamlined trains. **1977** C. MCCULLOUGH *Thorn Birds* xvii. 439 Nowadays even the ocean liners were streamlined, hulls shaped like destroyers to get there faster.

2. *fig.* **a.** Having smooth, flowing, or elongated lines; slender.

1934 H. READ *Art & Industry* 3 'Streamlined' is popularly, if inaccurately, used as a term of approval for the design of any object in daily use. **1935** *Amer. Speech* X. 194/1 Terminology from other fields aids the fashion editors... The *streamlined* silhouette came in with the new automobile. **1937** *Nation* 15 May 559/2 The cows came from their stables down a runway into a streamlined building. **1944** A. HOLMES *Princ. Physical Geol.* v. 63 The effects of shearing or flowage give the rocks a new structure, due to the stream-lined arrangement of the platy and elongated minerals. **1951** M. MCLUHAN *Mech. Bride* (1967) 96/1 Streamlined, synthetic blondes—these are at once abstract and exciting. **1966** WODEHOUSE *Plum Pie* 75 Dieting continues to be all the go.. and the number of those who hope to become streamlined by pushing their plates away untasted increases daily. **1976** *Country Life* 1 Apr. 805/2 The two aspects of the ubiquitous Deco that have caused such confusion in recent terminology, the one still curved and flowing (Streamlined Moderne), the other angular and machine-style (Zig-Zag Moderne).

b. Efficient; simplified, having inessentials removed.

1937 *Words* May 100/1 Our streamlined professors. **1942** E. PAUL *Narrow St.* xvii. 128 Clever women.. manipulated high statesmen, financiers and stream-lined executives as if the men were marionettes. **1947** A. HUXLEY *Let.* 9 Mar. (1969) 568 We might think in greater detail about.. a stream-lined construction for the revised Goldsmith. **1957** L. F. R. WILLIAMS *State of Israel* ix. 156 This.. end is secured by an ingenious, stream-lined, procedure which makes the guillotine unnecessary. **1971** *Daily Tel.* 15 Jan. 15/5 A streamlined, yet cosy, kitchen overlooks a tiny paved garden. **1979** *Tucson* (Arizona) *Citizen* 20 Sept. 3 c/2 The majority's reasons for dissolving the former trustees included a desire.. to make 'more streamlined' decisions regarding control of health care costs and treatment of indigents.

'streamliner. [f. as prec. + -ER[1].]

a. A stream-lined train.

1938 *Times* 14 Oct. 15/6 One of the latest streamliners to be put into operation is that of the Reading Line between New York and Philadelphia. **1946** D. C. PEATTIE *Road of Naturalist* v. 55 To read the country while you run is possible even from a streamliner. **1958** J. KEROUAC *On Road* ix. 229 A hundred and ten miles an hour straight through, an arrow road, sleeping towns, no traffic, and the Union Pacific streamliner falling behind us in the moonlight. **1967** O. WYND *Walk Softly* v. 72 The Fuji is a great train, a streamliner, everything shiny and new. **1982** WHITEHOUSE & ALLEN *E. Treacy—Railway Photographer* 85 A streamliner takes the 5.25 to Euston past Wavertree.

b. One who streamlines.

1943 F. L. WRIGHT *Autobiogr.* IV. 321 Invention.. looking for salvation to the engineer, the streamliner, and the elevator, has been trying to.. hold the profits of superconcentration.

c. *gen.* Something streamlined.

1968 *Church Times* 13 Sept. 18/3, I hear you have sold your old house and are looking for a streamliner.

†**'streamling**[1]. *Obs. rare.* Also 7 **streamlin.** [f. STREAM *sb.* + -LING[1].] = STREAMLET.

1598 SYLVESTER *Du Bartas* II. i. IV. *Handicrafts* 515 In two square creases of unequall sises To turn to yron streamlings he devises. **1615** BRATHWAIT *Strappado* 213 Wipe, wipe, those eyes with briny streamelings drownd. **1621** —— *Nat. Embassie*, etc. (1877) 210 Hadst thou seene.. What crimson streamlins flow'd from either of vs.

†**'streamling**[2]. *Obs. rare.* [Formed as prec., after Sw. *strömling, strömming* (MSw. *strömlinger, strömminger*); cf. MLG. *stromelink*, G. *strömling*.] A kind of small herring found in the Baltic and the Swedish lakes.

1694 [BP. J. ROBINSON] *Acc. Sueden* i. 9 These.. Lakes.. are not ill stored with varieties of Fish,.. of which the most plentiful is the Streamling. **1799** W. TOOKE *View Russian Emp.* III. 169 The streamlings, a degenerate species of herring, are everywhere found in the.. Baltic.

'streamlining, *vbl. sb.* [f. STREAMLINE *v.* + -ING[1].]

1. a. Streamlined shape or design. **b.** The action of giving something a streamlined shape.

1918 H. BARBER *Aeroplane Speaks* (ed. 6) 61 The weight of the stream-lining is always paid for many times over by the greater velocity and consequent increase of lift due to the decreased drift. **1921** *Discovery* Apr. 98/1 This probably is partly due.. to the careful streamlining of the machine [*sc.* an aircraft] and the sensible distribution and installation of the engines. **1932** D. L. SAYERS *Have his Carcase* vi. 76 The car glided away amid the reverent murmurings.. of persons gathered.. to admire its streamlining. **1936** *Discovery* Feb. 40/1 To diminish air-resistance by the streamlining of both engine and train. **1950** *Times* 5 May 5/6 A large engine does not necessarily mean a large wash. Bad streamlining and excessive speed create the wash. **1955** *Sci. Amer.* Mar. 90/3 The streamlining of birds of course is the envy of all aircraft designers. **1965** H. HOOD in R. Weaver *Canad. Short Stories* (1968) 2nd Ser. 219 'That's quite a car, Mister.' 'Yes, that's what they call streamlining.' **1980** *Daily Tel.* 24 Sept 12/2 The drag factor of a car is becoming an increasingly significant item... It is, loosely, what used to be referred to as the streamlining effect.

2. *transf.* and *fig.* **a.** The action or result of giving smooth, flowing lines to something.

1934 *Punch* 19 Dec. 691/1 This 'streamlining' bunkum is spreading from the sordid realms of mere mechanics to those of everyday life, even to human physiognomy. **1937** G. FRANKAU *More of Us* vi. 70 '*I* find these modern figures far too arty,' Continued Sophie, obviously not repining Tho' hers had long since faltered from streamlining. **1940** GRAVES & HODGE *Long Week-End* xi. 181 The use of streamlining as a modern style in domestic objects.

b. Simplification of procedures, an organization, or the like to improve efficiency.

1959 *Daily Tel.* 24 July 5/7 (*heading*) Railway streamlining to be speeded. **1965** *Listener* 3 June 822/2 The streamlining of the administrative and financial planning structure was as urgent as was the physical planning in 1961. **1970** *Daily Tel.* 18 Mar. 2/5 As a result of a streamlining operation the weekly expenses had been cut from £1,200 to £700. **1978** R. LEWIS *Inevitable Fatality* ii. 42 If there's to be a *streamlining* .. some heads will have to roll.

stream of consciousness. [f. STREAM *sb.*]

1. *Psychol.* An individual's thoughts and conscious reaction to external events experienced subjectively as a continuous flow. Also *loosely* (influenced by sense 2), an uncontrolled train of thought or association.

1855 A. BAIN *Senses & Intellect* 359 The concurrence of Sensations in one common stream of consciousness,—in the same cerebral highway. **1890** W. JAMES *Princ.* Psychol. I. ix. 239 Consciousness.. does not appear to itself chopped up in bits... A 'river' or a 'stream' are the metaphors by which it is most naturally described. In talking of it hereafter, let us call it the stream of thought, of consciousness, or of subjective life. **1908** W. MCDOUGALL *Introd. Social Psychol.* i. 15 Psychology must not regard the introspective description of the stream of consciousness as its whole task. **1928** D. H. LAWRENCE *Lady Chatterley's Lover* xiv. 253 The quiver was going through the man's body, as the stream of consciousness again changed its direction, turning downwards. **1942** M. MCCARTHY *Company She Keeps* vi. 251 Damn my stream of consciousness, her mind said. **1959** PENFIELD & ROBERTS *Speech & Brain Mechanisms* iii. 47 Ganglionic patterns that preserve the record of the stream of consciousness. **1975** C. FREMLIN *Long Shadow* xx. 142 Cynthia's stream-of-consciousness soon meandered obediently back to the matter in hand. **1979** K. R. POPPER in Popper & Eccles *Self & its Brain* III. 157 When we—actively—try to be passive, there may be something like a stream of consciousness; but normally we are active, and then there is.., rather, organized procedures of problem-solving.

2. *Lit. Criticism.* A method of narration which depicts events through this flow in the mind of a character; an instance of this.

[**1918** M. SINCLAIR in *Little Rev.* Apr. 6 In identifying herself with this life which is Miriam's stream of consciousness Miss Richardson produces her effect of.. getting closer to reality than any of our novelists.] **1939** S. S. O'CASEY *Let.* Apr. (1975) I. 792, I differ from you.. in your contention that my 'dream fantasies & streams of consciousness' are 'foreign to my best style'. **1961** W. C. BOOTH *Rhetoric of Fiction* III. xi. 324 The deep plunges of modern inside views, the various streams-of-consciousness that attempt to give the reader an effect of living thought and sensation, are capable of blinding us to the possibility of our making judgments not shared by the narrator or reflector himself. **1964** M. MCLUHAN *Understanding Media* xxix. 296 Here [*sc.* in *David Copperfield*] was the stream of consciousness, perhaps, in its original form before it was adopted by Proust and Joyce and Eliot. **1971** B. MALAMUD *Tenants* 162 Bill took on a sort of stream-of-consciousness and heavily overworked association. **1978** I. B. SINGER *Shosha* xiii. 233, I had also read in a literary magazine about the kind of literature called the 'stream of consciousness'.

3. *attrib.* (freq. with hyphens).

1931 *N. & Q.* 1 Aug. 74/1 This is in part a development from the 'stream of consciousness' method. **1942** *Q. Jrnl. Speech* Feb. 4/2 *This Lonely Heart*, a stream-of-consciousness play. **1955** L. P. HARTLEY *Perfect Woman* iii. 24 Do you think the stream-of-consciousness method has come to stay, or have Joyce and Virginia Woolf exhausted it? **1958** *Listener* 16 Oct. 603/2 The late Dorothy M. Richardson was one of the earliest exponents of the 'stream-of-consciousness' novel. **1975** B. GARFIELD *Death Sentence* (1976) iii. 22 He darted from topic to topic... He wasn't a stream-of-consciousness talker. **1982** *Times* 7 Apr. 9/8 A stream-of-consciousness chess match.

streamy ('striːmɪ), *a.* [f. STREAM *sb.* + -Y[1].]

1. Abounding in or full of running streams.

†**a.** of the bottom of the sea. *Obs.*

14.. *Sailing Directions* (Hakl. Soc. 1889) 21 Betwene Cille and Huschant there is grete stremy grounde with white shellis. **1574** W. BOURNE *Regim. Sea* 60 You shall finde streamie ground, and dentes in the talow. **1625** PURCHAS *Pilgrims* I. v. vii. 647 From Linga vnto this place we had.. twentie fathom, as wee supposed, streamy ground.

b. of a district, country.

a **1718** PRIOR *1st Hymn of Callimachus* 23 Arcadia, (However streamy now) adust and dry, Deny'd the Goddess Water. **1799** CAMPBELL *Pleas. Hope* II. 103 His path shall be where streamy mountains swell Their shadowy grandeur o'er the narrow dell. **1806** J. GRAHAME *Birds Scot.* 1 Fair Scotia's streamy vales. **1833** *Blackw. Mag.* XXXIII. 689 Beauty.. holds her court in the streamy wilderness.

2. Of water, etc.: Flowing in a stream, running.

c **1586** C'TESS PEMBROKE *Ps.* XCVIII. iii, You streamy rivers clapp your swymming hands. **1825** BROCKETT *N.C. Gloss.*, *Slack*, a long pool in a streamy river.

fig. **1731** A. HILL *Advice to Poets* iii, No—like thy own Ulysses, make no Stay: Shun Monsters—and pursue thy streamy Way. **1804** COLERIDGE *Anima Poetae* (1895) 65 The streamy nature of the associative faculty.

b. Of hair, etc.: Flowing.

1813 W. TAYLOR in *Monthly Mag.* XXXVI. 332 With streamy golden hair. **1817** KEATS *Sleep & Poetry* 127 A car And steeds with streamy manes.

3. Of the nature of, having the appearance of, or issuing in, a stream. Also, emitting streams (of light).

1718 POPE *Iliad* XIII. 1014 His nodding Helm emits a streamy Ray. *a* **1720** J. HUGHES *Poems, Ecstasy* ix, The nightly-wakeful swain.. marks no stars, but o'er his head Beholds the streamy twilight spread, Like distant morning in the skies. *a* **1814** *Gonzanga* IV. vi. in *New Brit. Theatre* III. 139 Blaze on, ye streamy flames of vivid glare! **1842** *Penny Cycl.* XXIII. 106/1 The result is a streamy or imperfectly concentric stratification. **1869** PROCTOR *Ess. Astron.* xxv. (1872) 320 On a closer inspection, however, we recognise in the northern cluster [of nebulæ] a decidedly streamy character.

Hence **'streaminess.**

1869 PROCTOR *Ess. Astron.* xxv. (1872) 319 The northern map accords better with this view than the southern; but even in the former there is an irregularity in the clustering, an occasional evidence of streaminess, [etc.].

streap(e, var. ff. STRIPE *sb.*[2] *Sc.*, rivulet.

strease, obs. Sc. pl. STRAW *sb.*[1]

†**streat,** *sb. Obs.* Forms: 5 **streete, strete,** 6 **streate, streitte, streicte, streyte, strette.** [Aphetic variant of ESTREAT *sb.*] = ESTREAT *sb.* 1 and 2. Also *attrib.* as ***streat-office.***

c **1440** *Promp. Parv.* 480/1 Streete catchepol bok to gader by mercymentys. **1451** *Paston Lett.* Suppl. 34 Blake wate atte London on Thursday and herd no word of the stretes. **1467** in *Eng. Gilds* (1870) 400 Alle suche issues so forfet by defaute to be written out in stretys. **1479** *Ibid.* 421 Ther-upon the seide Toune clerk to make vp his Stretys vnto the Baillifs. **1507** in *Sel. Cases Star Chamber* (Selden Soc.) 257 He.. retaynyth the Court Rolls.. and also the Streittes of the same Courtes. **1538** in *Reg. Priory St. Bees* (Surtees) 486 All mercyamentes and fynys in ye strettes of ye graves marcyell in ye courtes of sanct Bees. *a* **1547** in J. R. Boyle *Hedon* (1875) App. 73 The maiore or chamberlains or any other officer that hathe anye streictes, rentalles, or bookes. *c* **1550** *Ibid.* App. 85 All accyons that comes to your handes ye shall enttare and make owt your streytes of the same. *a* **1601** SIR T. FANSHAWE *Pract. Exch.* (1658) 93 He certifieth into the Clerke of the Streate office Yearly in the Exchequer, all the Kings moities recovered.

†**streat,** *v. Obs.* Also 7 **streit.** Aphetic form of ESTREAT *v.*

a **1601** SIR T. FANSHAWE *Pract. Exch.* (1658) 53 The Lord Treasurors Remembrancer.. hath his Office cheifly established upon the execution of the originall, save for the great accounts, the Customers, controllers and searchers, that is yearly streated to him out of the Chancerie. **1605** *Southampton Crt. Leet Rec.* (1907) I. 427 Manie thinhabitants.. were absent at the lawdaye... [Margin adds] To be streited. **1808** W. HERBERT *Ella Rosenberg* I. 136 'No!' exclaimed the count... 'I will remain in my castle. If I perish here, at least they will not streate my castle from my posterity!'

streat(e, streatch: see STREET, STRETCH *v.*

†**streave,** *a. Obs. rare*[−1]. [? Altered form of STRAY *a.* Cf. STRAIF.] ? Stray, casual.

1598 BP. HALL *Sat.* v. i. 55 What, did he counterfait his Princes hand, For some braue [*Corrections* (*end of book*) straue; *ed.* 1599 streaue] Lord-ship of concealed land?

streaw, obs. form of STREW *v.*

streay, streayte: see STRAW *sb.*[1], STRAIT *a.*

strecch(e, strech(e, obs. forms of STRETCH.

streche, obs. form of STRITCH, a strickle.

strecht, obs. Sc. form of STRAIGHT.

streck, *a. Obs.* exc. *dial.* In 4 **streke.** [Belongs to root *strak- of STRETCH *v.* Cf. OE. *stræc, strec* (? *strǽc, strēc*) rigorous, severe.] Straight.

c **1375** *Sc. Leg. Saints* xviii. (*Mary Egypt*) 225 Hayre scho had, quhyt and streke, Rekand na forthire na hir neke. *a* **1864** R. B. PEACOCK *Lonsdale Gloss.*, *Streck*, adj., straight. **1898** B. KIRKBY *Lakeland Words* 142 Streck as a seave.

Hence **'streckly** *adv.* (in 4 **strykly**) = next.

1340 HAMPOLE *Pr. Consc.* 3288 Sum.. Sal wend strykly til heven blis. **1876** *Mid-Yorks. Gloss.* s.v., Go thy ways streckly, now.

streck, *adv. Obs.* exc. *dial.* Forms: 4 **strik,** 4–5 **streke,** 4–6 **strek,** 8–9 **strick,** 9 **streck.** [f. STRECK *a.*] In a straight course, directly; immediately, straightway. Also with *away*. Also ***streck up,*** in an upright posture.

13.. *Gosp. Nicod.* 867 (Sion MS.) Tille þe temple held þai streke þe way. **1340** HAMPOLE *Pr. Consc.* 2623 Þe synful saul þan gas strik to helle. *Ibid.* 3378 He sal noght.. Wend strek to purgatory. *a* **1400–50** *Wars Alex.* 3854 Þan come he streke on a staunke. **1513** DOUGLAS *Æneis* III. ii. 128 The followand wynd blew strek in our taile. **1790** MRS. WHEELER *Westmld. Dial.* (1802) 103 We went tae see th giants,.. I think they wod net stand strick up ith heeghst hause ith parish. **1885** *Spec. Westmld. Dial.* III. 6 (E.D.D.) Sooa a teeak em streck awae to Willie Hartley's.

strecour, obs. form of STREAKER.

strecte, obs. form of STRAIT *a.*

stred, strede: see STREET, STRIDE.

stree(a, obs. and dial. forms of STRAW *sb.*[1]

streek, streak (striːk), *v.* Now *Sc.* and *dial.* Pa. t. and pa. pple. streeked. Forms: 3–6 **streke,** 4 **streck,** 4–5 **streek,** 5 **striek, streyk(e,** 5–9 **streik,** 6–9 **streek;** 4–5, 9 **strike,** 5–7, 9 **stryke;** 6–7 **streake,** 7, 9 **streak,** 9 **straik.** *Pa. t.* and *pa. pple.* 4 **streked, strekyd,** 4–6 **strekit, -yt,** etc. [Northern ME. *strēk-*, corresp. to southern ME. *strĕch-* (mod. dial. *streach*), a present-stem generalized from the non-geminate forms in the conjugation of OE. *stręccan* STRETCH *v.* (imper. *stręce*, 3 sing. *stręceð*). The northern form of this present-stem early gave rise to a pa. t. and pa. pple. *strēked*, but down to the 16th c. the forms descending from OE. *streaht*, *streahte* (and their variants) also continued in use in dialects which in the present tense used *strēke* (either exclusively or beside *stretch*); in this Dict. the forms *straucht*, *streght*, etc. are treated only under STRETCH *v.*

Although the word is in early and in present use almost exclusively northern, it is used in the 16–17th c. by several writers—Gascoigne, Chapman, Marston, Bp. Hall—whose language is in general free from northern characteristics.]

1. a. *trans.* To stretch (oneself), thrust out or extend (one's limbs), in a recumbent posture. Also in *pass.*, to lie thus stretched. Also with adv., as *down*, *out*. Cf. STRETCH *v.* 1.

c **1330** R. BRUNNE *Chron. Wace* (Rolls) 12703 Gapyng he lay at erþe al streked. **1414** BRAMPTON *Penit. Ps.* (Percy Soc.) 30 For stark, my lemys I may not streke. *c* **1480** HENRYSON *Fox, Wolf & Cadger* 185 Baith heid, and feit, and taill ȝe man streik out. **1576** GASCOIGNE *Steele Gl.* Ep. Ded., I have lien streaking me (like a lubber) when the sunne did shine. **1598** MARSTON *Sco. Villanie* I. iii. C 8 b, Shall Curio streake his lims on his dayes couch, In Sommer bower? **1615** CHAPMAN *Odyss.* IX. 416 Along his den, amongst his cattell downe He rusht, and streakt him. *a* **1774** FERGUSSON *Farmer's Ingle* Poems (1845) 38 Where the guidman aft streeks him at his ease. **1815** SCOTT *Antiq.* xxi, I wad e'en streek mysell out here.

b. *intr.* To fall prostrate; to lie *down* at full length. Cf. STRETCH *v.* 1 e.

c **1250** *Gen. & Ex.* 481 Caim.. Grusnede, and strekede, and starf wið-ðan. **1598** BP. HALL *Sat.* VI. i. 206 When Lucan streaked on his Marble-bed To thinke of Cæsar, and great Pompeys deed. **1728** RAMSAY *Monk & Miller's Wife* 71 There's braw ait strae; Streek down upon 't, my lad. **1814** SCOTT *Wav.* xxx, Many an honester woman's been set upon it than streeks doon beside ony whig in the country. **1820** CLARE *Rural Life* (ed. 3) 60 I'd just streak'd down.

c. Of the limbs: To be stretched (*out*); to be extended or expanded. Of a person: To stretch oneself, stretch one's limbs. Cf. STRETCH *v.* 3 b.

a **1400** *Signs of Death* 13 in *Pol. Rel. & L. Poems* (1903) 253 His feet shullen streken. **1586**, **1608** [see STREEKING *vbl. sb.* 1]. **1648** J. BEAUMONT *Psyche* VI. ccv, He began to streak, and nod, and yawn. **1728** RAMSAY *Monk & Miller's Wife* 140 Mill-knaves.. Whase kytes can streek out like raw plaiding.

2. *trans.* To lay prostrate; to lay out (a corpse). Also with *out*. Cf. STRETCH *v.* 1 b.

1303 R. BRUNNE *Handl. Synne* 944 Furþ, for ded, men gan hym streke. *c* **1585** MONTGOMERIE *Misc. P.* xxxvi. 4 Suppl. Vol. 247 So daithe at last sell straik þe stark. **1787** BURNS *To W. Creech* xi, May I be.. streekit out to bleach In winter snaw. **1815** SCOTT *Guy M.* liii, I may be streekit here or night. There will be few, few at Meg's lykewake. **1858** R. CRAIG in J. Brown *Horæ Subs., Locke & Sydenham* etc. 426 A female relative.. saying that she would come and streek him after he died. **1859** H. KINGSLEY *Geoff. Hamlyn* xliv, Mrs. Buckley and the women were down at Mrs. Mayford's, streaking the bodies out. **1896** CROCKETT *Grey Man* v. 35 The maid washed and streeked him.

3. To stretch (one's limbs) in order to exercise the muscles. ***to streek one's shanks, wame***, to take a walk, step out. Cf. STRETCH *v.* 3 c.

1456 SIR G. HAYE *Gov. Princis* Wks. (S.T.S.) II. 120 Quhen thou rysis in the mornyng, thou suld.. strek and rak thy membris suetely and softly and evinly. **1788** PICKEN *Poems* 65 Sae, now, I e'en maun streek my wame, An' see gin things be right at hame. *Ibid.* 111, I never whisky us't, nor snuff, To streek the legs o' fancy. *a* **1810** TANNAHILL *Poems* (1846) 60 Wha mony a mile wud streek his shanks, To ha'e a crack wi' Josie Banks. **1827** J. WILSON *Noct. Ambr.* Wks. 1855 I. 327 Sair gien to gauntin, and the streekin out o' ane's airms.

4. a. To extend from the body, hold *out* or *up*, stretch *forth* (one's arm, hand, etc.) in order to touch, grasp, etc. Cf. STRETCH *v.* 4.

a **1300** *Cursor M.* 5817, I bidd þe strek þi hand þe fra. *c* **1375** *Sc. Leg. Saints* xi. (*Simon & Judas*) 258 We sal gyf þam leyf to speke, bot nane a fowt furth to streke [*sed ambulare non posse*]. *c* **1400** *Apol. Loll.* 69, I schal streke out my hand on him. *c* **1425** WYNTOUN *Cron.* I. 717 Þan þat fute vp þai streik, þat it fra þaim þe weddyr brek. *c* **1440** *Promp. Parv.* 479/1 Streykyn owte, *protendo, extendo.* **1513** DOUGLAS *Æneis* XIII. Prol. 150 Be my richt hand streikit vp in hy. *a* **1578** LINDESAY (Pitscottie) *Chron. Scot.* (S.T.S.) I. 60 He fell doune wpoun his knies and streikit forth his craig to the sword. **1615** CHAPMAN *Odyss.* XII. 148 She lurkes in midst of all her denne: and streakes From out a ghastly whirle-poole, all her necks. **1901** G. DOUGLAS *Ho. Green Shutters* 311 Think of your mother.. streeking out her auld hand for charity.

transf. *a* **1340** HAMPOLE *Psalter* lxxix. 12 *Extendit palmites suos vsque ad mare...* Sho streikis hir brawnchis til the see.

†**b.** To put forth, hold out, launch (a weapon, etc.). Also *fig.* *Obs.*

1513 DOUGLAS *Æneis* II. ix. 41 With grundin lance at hand so neir furth strykit [*rime-word* arrekit]. *c* **1585** MONTGOMERIE *Misc. P.* xlix. 29 Go to than, shirs, and let vs streik a sting.

†**c.** Of a heavenly body: To emit, project (beams of light). *Obs.* Cf. STRETCH *v.* 7.

1375 BARBOUR *Bruce* IV. 704 Sum ar less, sum othir mair, Eftir as thair bemys strekit air, Owthir all evin, or on wry. *c* **1375** *Sc. Leg. Saints* xviii. (*Egipciane*) 1319 þe sone cane fare bemys strek.

5. a. *intr.* To go or advance quickly; to go at full speed; to decamp. Also with *away*, *off*, etc. Cf. STRETCH *v.* 10. (The verb is, in this sense, now regarded as part of STREAK *v.*[2] 6).

c **1380** *Sir Ferumb.* 1265 Doun in the pyt sche strekes. ? *a* **1400** *Morte Arth.* 2085 Thane strekez the steryne, and streynys his brydylle. *c* **1510** DOUGLAS *K. Hart* II. 335 Than Jelosie come strekand vp the stair. *c* **1730** RAMSAY *Horace to Virgil* 39 Dedalus must.. upward streek. **1768**, etc. [see STREAK *v.*[2] 6 a]

b. *transf.*, e.g. of the sun in its course. Of a river: To flow, stream.

1598 FLORIO, *Irrigare*.. to streame or streake along. **1622** DRAYTON *Poly-olb.* xxii. 27 Ouze.. varying her cleere forme a thousand sundry wayes, Streakes through the verdant Meads. **1642** H. MORE *Song of Soul* II. I. ii. 30 So doth the gentle warmth of solar heat Eas'ly awake the centre seminall, That makes it softly streak on its own seat, And fairly forward force its life internall. **1821** CLARE *Vill. Minstr.* I. 175 How swift the sun streaks down the western sky.

c. To walk along, stroll, saunter (E.D.D.).

1819 W. TENNANT *Papistry Storm'd* (1827) 10 While younksters, by the sea-side streikin', Gaed paidlin' in without a breik on.

†**d.** *trans.* ? To urge on (an animal), cause to go quickly. *Obs. rare.*

c **1500** *Lancelot* 3082 His hors he strekith our the larg gren.

†**6. a.** *intr.* To extend or reach (in a specified direction or for a specified distance). *Obs.* Cf. STRETCH *v.* 13.

1375 BARBOUR *Bruce* XVIII. 130 Apon the cawse That wes betuix thame and the toune, That strekit lang in a randoune. *c* **1375** *Sc. Leg. Saints* ix. (*Berthol.*) 220, & of his hewyd þe lochtris of hare til his fete strekand ware. **1388** in Sir J. H. Ramsay *Bamff Charters* (1915) 22 Begynnand on the west part of the Lowssy law, strekand west by the land of Tyny. *a* **1400-50** *Wars Alex.* 5063 Betwene þa styes.. þat strekis þurȝe þe mountis. *c* **1425** WYNTOUN *Cron.* I. 553 Fra north on south þe streme it strekis In till þe Red Seye quhill it reikis. **1513** DOUGLAS *Æneis* VI. v. 1 Fra thine strekis the way profound anon Deip onto hellis flude of Acheron. **1535** STEWART *Cron. Scot.* II. 74 All the landis that la in the south Fra Forth streikand recht on to Eskis mouth. **1594** BLUNDEVIL *Exerc., Cosmogr.* II. xix. (1597) 199 A perpendicular shadow, which streeketh right downe from head to foote. **1602** *Reg. Mag. Sig. Scot.* 476/1 Begynnand at the Hammer-pule-fute, and strykand langis the watersyde of Air to [etc.]. *c* **1680** J. MORISONE in W. Macfarlane *Geogr. Collect.* (S.H.S.) II. 211 Upon the west syde of the Countrie there are no harbouring for shipps except the Loch of Carluvay, streeking in almost in the middest of the countrie.

b. *fig.* *Obs.*

1375 BARBOUR *Bruce* XVII. 929 Micht he haf lifit quhill he had beyne Of perfit elde, withouten weyne, His renoune suld haf strekit fer. *c* **1375** *Sc. Leg. Saints* xxvii. (*Machor*) 1120 Ne manis wit ma strek þartill, to consawe it thru kindly skill. *c* **1400** *Apol. Loll.* 61 Boþ of lawe of kind, and of law writun, and law of grace, he is þe first begining.. and to wam al laws strekyn.

7. a. *trans.* To stretch out, extend (a rope, etc.); †to pitch (a tent). Cf. STRETCH *v.* 12 b, c.

a **1340** HAMPOLE *Psalter* ciii. 3 *Extendens celum sicut pellem* .... Strekand heuen as a skyn. *Ibid.* cxxxix. 6 *Funes extenderunt in laqueum*, strengis þai strekid in snare. ? *a* **1400** *Morte Arth.* 1229 Furthe stepes that steryne, and strekez his tentis One a strenghe by a streme.

†**b.** To stretch on a rack or on a cross. *Obs.* Cf. STRETCH *v.* 17.

c **1375** *Sc. Leg. Saints* iii. (*Andrew*) 688 þane one þe croice but howne þai strekyt and band hym sone with cordis. *Ibid.* xlii. (*Agatha*) 168 He gert strek hire in a frame, & torment hir in syndry vyse.

c. To pull (a boot) *on* one's leg.

1815 SCOTT *Guy M.* xi, He had as gude a pair o' boots as a man need streik on his legs.

d. ***to streek a tow***, also *intr.* ***to streek in a halter***: to be hanged, 'swing'. Cf. STRETCH *v.* 18 a, c.

1796 J. LAUDERDALE *Poems* 80 (E.D.D.) May I in a halter streek If I hae Latin, French, or Greek. **1895** CROCKETT *Men of Moss Hags* ii. 22 But ye shall all streek a tow for this.

8. To cause to reach across a space. In quot. with *over*. Cf. STRETCH *v.* 12 a.

1787 BURNS *Brigs of Ayr* 92 Ance ye were streekit owre frae bank to bank!

9. To put (an implement) in action. ***to streek the plew***: to draw the first furrow after harvest.

c **1480**, **1555** [see STREEKING *vbl. sb.* 2]. **1577** GRANGE *Golden Aphrod.* I ij b, I.. thinke dame Pallas streaked mine oare as well in this cace, as did Vlisses preuaile thorow hyr counsell against the Syrenes. **1790** D. MORISON *Poems* 109 (Jam.) Ae day last week.. She happ'd by chance to streek the wheel. *Ibid.* 131 Gae streek the rake.

streek(e, obs. ff. STREAK, STRICK, STRIKE.

streeker ('striːkə(r)). *dial.* [f. STREEK *v.* + -ER[1].] A layer-out of the dead.

1876 *Whitby Gloss.*, *Streeaker*, a stretching board for a corpse. Also a layer out of the dead. **1898** WATTS-DUNTON *Aylwin* XI. ii, She's bin a streaker in her day.

'streeking, *vbl. sb.* [f. STREEK *v.* + -ING[1].]

1. The action of stretching or extending.

a **1340** HAMPOLE *Psalter* xxi. 17 The strekynge of his body in the tre myght noght haf ben bettere dyscryed. *c* **1440** *Promp. Parv.* 479/1 Streykynge [*MS. K.* strekyng], or spredynge owute,.. *extencio, protencio.* **1586** BRIGHT *Melanch.* xxvi. 150 In streaking the muscles are contracted. **1608** BP. HALL *Charac. Vertues & Vices* II. 120 After some streaking and yawning [he] calles for dinner. **1828** CARR *Craven Gloss.*, *Streaking*, stretching.

b. *spec.* The laying out a corpse. Also *attrib.*

1777 BRAND *Pop. Antiq.* 23 The Ceremonies used.. in what we call laying out or streeking in the North. *Ibid.* note, A Streeking-Board is that on which they stretch out and compose the Limbs of the dead Body. **1815** SCOTT *Guy M.* xxvii, He's a bonny corpse,.. and weel worth the streaking. **1896** BARRIE *Sentim. Tommy* xxvii. 317 'Do you know what straiking is?' 'Arraying the corpse for the coffin, laying it out, in short, is it not?' 'Ay, ay.'

2. The action of setting (a plough or other implement) to work. ***streeking-time***, plough-ing-time.

c **1480** HENRYSON *Fables, Fox, Wolf & Husbandman* 4 Swa happynnit him in streiking tyme of ȝeir Airlie in the morning to follow furth his feir, Vnto the pleuch. **1555** *Charters* etc. *Peebles* (1872) 218 At the streking of the plewis yerelie, betwix Sanct Lucas day and Mertymes, and at harrowis streking. **1678** SIR G. MACKENZIE *Crim. Laws Scot.* I. xxxi. §iv. (1699) 157 The season of labouring,.. from the time of streiking, to upseed time.

'streeking, *ppl. a.* [f. STREEK *v.* + -ING[2].] That extends; that is stretched out.

c **1425** WYNTOUN *Cron.* II. 432 Ryngis fyrst he gert men were, þa he gert on mydfynger ber, For fra þat to þe hart, he saide, Ane ewyn strekande wayne was laide. **1572** GASCOIGNE *Hund. Flowres, Gascoignes good nyghte* 23 The streking [1575 stretching] arms, the yauning breath, which I to bedward vse. **1577** GRANGE *Golden Aphrod.* I ij b, Then is it no masterie for me (Lady) with streaking armes to swimme in a sea of honny. **1600** HOLLAND *Livy* IV. xix. 152 He ouerthrew him backward with the bosse of his target, and laid him streaking along.

streel (striːl), *v.* Chiefly *Anglo-Irish.* Also **streal**. [Cf. Irish *straoillim*, to trail, drag along the ground.] *intr.* To trail on the ground; to stream, float at length. Also of persons, to stroll, wander aimlessly.

1805 E. CAVANAGH *Let.* 20 Aug. in Londonderry & Hyde *Russian Jrnls.* (1934) II. 182 In walk'd a Grenadier of a Man ....& after him streal'd in at his heels a Girl. **1839** CARLETON *Fardorougha* i. 13 It's on your knees you ought to be this same night,.. an' not grumblin' an' sthreelin' about the place. **1848** THACKERAY *Van. Fair* xx, She had earrings like chandeliers; you might have lighted 'em up, by Jove —and a yellow satin train that streeled after her like the tail of a comet. **1892** JANE BARLOW *Irish Idylls* iii. 66 Everybody else thought that.. they would have him streeling home again in a couple of days. **1943** J. STUART *Taps for Private Tussie* iv. 57 It was after four o'clock when Aunt Vittie and Grandma came strealin up the Turnpike from town.

Hence as *sb.*[1], a straggling, untidy procession of persons; **'streeler**, a disreputable, idle person; **''streeling** *ppl. a.* and *vbl. sb.*

1841 *Fraser's Mag.* XXIV. 216 No great, long, strealing tails of periods,—no staring peonies and hollyhocks of illustrations. *c* **1874** D. BOUCICAULT in M. R. Booth *Eng. Plays of 19th Cent.* (1969) II. 202, I was thrying to get away from him.. but he was at my heels all the way, and Tatthers at his heels. A nice shtreel we made along the road. **1884** *Harper's Mag.* Oct. 713/2 The streeling lines of flapping wings and their rasping bronchial note accorded well. **1885** "LUCAS MALET" *Col. Enderby's Wife* IV. iv, Across the lawn there drifted one of those streeling milk-white gossamers. **1907** J. M. SYNGE *Playboy* II. 48 An ugly young streeler with a murderous gob on him. **1927** E. BOWEN *Hotel* xvi. 184 Miss Fitzgerald's party going forward in the leisurely and spread-out manner called in Ireland 'strealing'. **1937** G. FRANKAU *More of Us* ii. 30 Remembered she her own pre-ducal streelings: Some boy she had filched from her own mother dear; When all the world that either knew was Ealing's? **1971** T. KILROY *Big Chapel* ix. 177 She never went anywhere without a streel of children.

streel (striːl), *sb.*[2] Chiefly *Anglo-Ir.* Also **sthreal**, **shtreel**. [ad. Ir. *s(t)raoill(e)* untidy or awkward person; cf. *straille* wench or untidy girl and prec.] A disreputable, untidy woman; a slut.

1842 S. LOVER *Handy Andy* xliii. 322 To marry a thrampin' shtreel like that—a great red-headed Jack. **1909** G. B. SHAW *Press Cuttings* 36 Not out o bed yet! Go and pull her out be the heels, the lazy shtreel. **1919** —— *O'Flaherty V.C.* in *Heartbreak House* 185, I thought that covetious sthreal in there was a walking angel; and now if ever I marry at all I'll marry a Frenchwoman. **1922** JOYCE *Ulysses* 354 She did look a streel tugging the two kids along with the flimsy blouse.. like a rag on her back and a bit of her petticoat hanging like a caricature. **1936** M. FRANKLIN *All that Swagger* xx. 188 That streel must have gone off with James Fullwood. **1961** 'F. O'BRIEN' *Hard Life* i. 11 A streel of a girl with long lank fair hair arrived to look after myself and the brother. **1970** D. M. DAVIN *Not Here, not Now* I. i. 8 She certainly kept the house in trim, even if she always looked a bit of a streel. **1978** D. MURPHY *Place Apart* iv. 78 Jimmy wouldn't like a streel.

Hence **'streelish** *a.*; **'streelishness**.

1936 M. FRANKLIN *All that Swagger* xxii. 218 Belike she has picked up some of me brogue as well as some civilised habits, if she doesn't fall back into her streelishness. **1974** E. O'BRIEN in *New Review* Apr. 35/2 We saw this wild creature coming... Her costume was streelish.

streen(e, obs. forms of STRAIN.

streepje, var. STREPIE.

street (striːt), *sb.* Forms: 1–2 **strǣt**, **strét**, (2–5 **strate**), 3 **stræt(e**, (**stred**), 3–4 **stret**, 3–6 **strete**, 4–6 **strett(e**, **streit(e**, 6 **streitt**, **streyt(e**, **streat(e**, 4–7 **streete**, 4– **street**. [OE. *strǣt* str. fem. = OFris. *strête* (WFris. *striette*), OS. *strâta*, MLG., MDu. *strâte* (mod.Du. *straat*), OHG. *strâȥa* (mod.G. *strasse*), ON. (from OE.) *strǣti* str. neut. (Da. *stræde*), MSw. *strâta* fem. (mod.Sw. *strât* masc.) from MLG.; MSw. had also *sträte* fem. from OE. The word is a Com.

WGer. adoption of late L. *strāta* (fem. pa. pple. of *sternĕre* to lay down, to pave: cf. STRATUM) used ellipt. for *via strata* paved road; represented in Rom. by Pr., Sp., Pg. *estrada*, OF. *estrée*, It. *strada*. The OIrish *sráth* (mod.Irish *sráid*, Gael. *sràid*) was adopted from late Latin.]

†**1. a.** A paved road, a highway. *Obs.*, but preserved in the proper names of certain ancient roads (chiefly Roman), as Watling Street, Ermine Street, Icknield Street.

Beowulf 320 Stræt wæs stanfah, stiȝ wisode gumum ætgædere. **847** *Charter* xx. in *O.E. Texts* 434 Ðonon on ða lytlan burȝ westewearde ðonon to stræte. *c* **1205** LAY. 4839 Þat wha swa i þen stræten [*c* 1275 stredes] braken grið þe king him wolde bi-nimen his lif. *c* **1250** *Owl & Night.* 962 Wenestu þat wise men forlete Vor fule venne þe rihte strete. **1297** R. GLOUC. (Rolls) 172 Fram þe souþ tilþ to þe norþ erninge stret, & fram est to þe west ykenilde stret. *c* **1330** R. BRUNNE *Chron. Wace* (Rolls) 13311 He passed hilles, wode, & playn, Til þey com þer þe stret lay hey. **1377** LANGL. *P. Pl.* B. XII. 105 And riȝt as syȝte serueth a man to se þe heighe strete. *c* **1405** *Bidding Prayer* in *Lay Folks Mass Bk.* (1879) 65 For thaim that brigges and stretes makes and amendes. **1564** *Yorks. Chantry Surv.* (Surtees) 264 Being one thoroughffare towne of the Kinges strete ledyng from London to Karliel. **1578** LYTE *Dodoens* I. lxvii. 98 The Male knot grasse groweth in fieldes about wayes and pathes, and in streates. **1606** in *N. Riding Rec.* (1884) I. 50 The Kinges Maties street called Nunhouse Lane. **1610** HOLLAND *Camden's Brit.* (1637) 397 The publike Street commonly called Watlingstreet. **1903** CONRAD & HUEFFER *Romance* I. i. 5 Just beside the Roman road to Canterbury; Stone Street—the Street—we called it.

b. Used vaguely for: A road, way, path. *lit.* and *fig.* ***to wend one's street***: to go one's way.

c **950** *Lindisf. Gosp.* Matt. xiii. 4 Mið ðy saues ðorlease ȝefeollon neh *vel* æt stræt *vel* woeȝ [L. *secus viam*]. *a* **1200** *Moral Ode* in *Lamb. Hom.* 179 Laete we þe brode stret, and þe wei bene. *a* **1300** *Cursor M.* 6182 Ar philistiens suld wit þam mete And lett þam for to wend þair strete. *a* **1340** HAMPOLE *Psalter* xxii. 3 He led me on þe stretis of rightwisnes [Vulg. *super semitas iusticiæ*]. *a* **1352** MINOT *Poems* (1897) vi. 56 A bare now has him soght..þat es ful wele bithoght To stop Philip þe strate. *c* **1366** CHAUCER *A.B.C.* 70 Than makest thou his pees with his sovereyn, And bringest him out of the crooked strete. **1481** CAXTON *Reynard* (Arb.) 55 Tho wente he his strete, tho flewe I doun. **1535** COVERDALE *Prov.* xv. 10 He that forsaketh yᵉ right strete, shalbe sore punyshed. *c* **1510** *Lyt. Geste Robin Hood* 81 But as they loked in Barnysdale By a derne strete Then came there a knyght rydynge. *a* **1547** SURREY *Æneis* II. (1557) Djb, For while I ran by the most secret stretes.. From me catif, alas, bereued was Creusa then my spouse.

c. In alliterative association with *sty*, *stile*.

c **1205** LAY. 16366 Bi stiȝen & by straten. *a* **1300** in Wright *Anecd. Lit.* (1844) 96 Love hath his stivart by sti and by strete. *c* **1425** *Cast. Perseverance* 353 Werldis wele, be strete & stye, Faylyth & fadyth, as fysch in flode. *Ibid.* 404 Cum a-gayn be strete & style! *c* **1460** *Towneley Myst.* ii. 365 And where so any man may me meyte, Ayther bi sty, or yit bi strete.

2. a. A road in a town or village (comparatively wide, as opposed to a 'lane' or 'alley'), running between two lines of houses; usually including the side-walks as well as the carriage way. Also, the road together with the adjacent houses.

c **1000** *Ags. Gosp.* Matt. vi. 5 Standende on ȝesomnungum & stræta hyrnum [L. *in angulis platearum*]. *c* **1200** ORMIN 7358 Þurrh þatt te Kalldewisshe folc oppnedenn þeȝȝre maddmess, Nohht i þe stræte, acc i þatt hus þatt Crist wass borenn inne. **13..** *E.E. Allit. P.* A. 1043 Such lyȝt þer lemed in alle þe stratez Hem nedde nawþer sunne ne mone. *c* **1382** WYCLIF *Luke* xiv. 21 Go out soone in to grete stretis and smale streetis of the citee [Vulg. *in plateas et vicos civitatis*]. *c* **1400** MAUNDEV. (Roxb.) xxxiv. 152 Þe stretez er paued with swilk maner of stanes. *c* **1412** HOCCLEVE *De Reg. Princ.* 534 Now hath þis lord but litil neede of broomes To swepe a-way þe filthe out of þe street. *c* **1450** CAPGRAVE *St. Gilbert* xxvii. 101 Þe smale townes had no dwelleres, þe wallis were falle down and stretes distroyed. **1500–20** DUNBAR *Poems* lxxxii. 37 Tailyouris, soutteris, and craftis vyll, The fairest of ȝour streitis dois fyll. *a* **1533** BERNERS *Huon* lxviii. 235 They lodged in the strete next to the palays. **1575** CHURCHYARD *Chippes* (1817) 136 And no sooner entring the towne, but our whole powre kept themselues in order to cleere the streates and commaund the inhabitants the better. **1598** SHAKS. *Merry W.* IV. v. 32 My Master..sent to her seeing her go thorough the streets, to know (Sir) whether [etc.]. **1598** B. JONSON *Ev. Man in Hum.* IV. i. (1601) I 1, I slidde downe by a bottome of packthread into the streete, and so scapt. **1611** *Proclam. Building Lond.* 3 Aug., At the least the forefront..thereof..looking towards the street or streetes [to] bee wholly built of Bricke. **1660** F. BROOKE tr. *Le Blanc's Trav.* 308 When they come to the crossing of a street, the Corps stayes. **1758** JOHNSON *Idler* No. 53 ¶3 A convenient house in a street. **1798** *Monthly Mag.* Mar. 181/2 Broadway is undoubtedly the handsomest street in America. **1834** LYTTON *Pompeii* I. ii, The two young men sauntered through the streets. **1877** *Law Rep.*, *3 Exch. Div.* 9 They clearly supposed they were entitled..to take the popular sense of the word 'street,' as meaning not only a roadway over which passengers and vehicles might pass, but also that which in popular language is part of the street, namely the houses on both sides. **1880** DISRAELI *Endym.* xv, It is the very best time for hiring a house. What I have set my heart upon is the Green Park... I am sure I could not live again in a street. **1885** *Act 48 Vict.* c. 17 §13 The lists of voters may be made out either alphabetically or by streets. **1889** *Act 52 & 53 Vict.* c. 44 §17 The expression 'street' includes any highway or other public place, whether a thoroughfare or not.

b. With prefixed word, forming the proper name of a street. Abbreviated *St.*, *st.*

In early examples these appellations were originally descriptive, as in *the Broad street*, *the* HIGH STREET. (In some towns, a name of this type still retains the definite article.) In modern nomenclature, the choice of the prefixed word is often arbitrary.

Modern usage is divided as to the writing of these names with hyphen or as two words. (In the 16–17th c. they were not unfrequently written as one word, e.g. 'Limestreete', Stow *Surv.* ed. 1603, p. 152.) It is to be observed that names ending in *street* are always stressed on the prefixed element, while those ending in *road* or *lane* have level stress: cf., e.g., *'Park-street* with *'Park-'lane*, *'Park-'road*.

?*c* **1275** in *Trans. Shropsh. Archæol. Soc.* Ser. I. (1878) I. 351, ij denar' annui reddit' de domo in le Brode stret q'm emi de Susanna moil. **1457** *Cal. Anc. Rec. Dublin* (1889) 296 For Seynt Thomas ys stret. **1513** MORE *Rich. III* Wks. 53/1 Crosbies place in Bishops-gates strete. **1531** TINDALE *Expos. 1 John* (1537) 60 Though thou were anoynted with al the oyle in teames strete. **1842** *Civil Engin. & Arch. Jrnl.* V. 200 St. James's Street, at 660 feet from Piccadilly, is 1 in 27.

¶ ***Mars' street***: mistranslation of ὁ Ἄρειος πάγος AREOPAGUS (*Bible* 1611 'Mars' Hill').

1526 TINDALE *Acts* xvii. 19 They..brought hym into Marce strete. **1579** W. WILKINSON *Confut. Fam. Love* 29 Standing in the middest of the Mars streate he [St. Paul] openly inueighed agaynst the superstition of that worthy Citye.

c. ***street of houses*** or ***shops***: a number of houses or shops built in a double line with a road in the middle, forming a street. Also *transf.* as ***street of booths***, ***ships***.

1613 PURCHAS *Pilgrimage* IV. xviii. (1614) 435 It seemed to bee, as it were, a continued street of Shippes. **1662** TRENCHFIELD *Chr. Chym.* 109 A certain person that had sold a street of houses, and laid out the money in costly apparrel, came to Court, [etc.]. *a* **1700** EVELYN *Diary* 1 Jan. 1684, The weather continuing intolerably severe, streetes of booths were set upon the Thames. **1725** DE FOE *Tour Gt. Brit.* III. I. 191 Stopping a terrible Fire which otherwise had endangered burning the whole Street of Houses on the City Side of the Bridge. **1855** DICKENS *Out of Town* Repr. Pieces (1868) 217 We..built a street of shops, the business of which may be expected to arrive in about ten years.

d. Used for: The inhabitants of the street; also, the people in the street.

14.. *Chance of Dice* in Skeat *Chaucer Canon* 126 Lord! so merily crowdeth then your crokke That all the streete may heare your body clokke. **1568** GRAFTON *Chron.* II. 382 Then roase the streete, namely the youth, and they woulde haue had him out of the Bishoppes house. **1620** MIDDLETON *Chaste Maid* v. 66 All the whole Street will hate vs, and the World Point me out cruell. **1712** ARBUTHNOT *John Bull* II. iv. 17 If the Coach swung but the least to one side, she used to shriek so loud, that all the Street concluded she was overturn'd. **1856** *Chamb. Jrnl.* 12 Jan. 26/1 There was a mystery about him which the whole street had tried its skill in fathoming. **1894** A. MORRISON *Tales of Mean Streets* 121 The street had the news the same hour.

e. *transf.* A passage between continuous lines of persons or things.

c **1430** LYDG. *Min. Poems* (Percy Soc.) 4 The meyer.. Made hem hove in rengis twayne, A strete betwene eche party lyke a walle, Alle clad in white, [etc.]. **1598** BARRET *Theor. Warres* IV. iv. 113 The shot..arriuing, do open, making a lane or streete, betwixt the which the Pikes do enter. **1802** C. JAMES *Milit. Dict.* s.v. *Camp*, The tents are placed in rows..with spaces between them, called streets. **1826** DISRAELI *Viv. Grey* III. viii, I was ushered through an actual street of servitors..into a large and crowded saloon. **1829** SHIPP *Mem.* II. 133 To do honour to the reception of such a personage, the two flank companies of the 87th Regiment..formed a street to the general's tent. **1883** *Daily News* 5 Sept. 5/6 If..a hundred thousand of them could be marshalled in Hyde Park, the artillery of the Government would make streets through them.

f. ***the street***: some particular street to which the merchants or financiers of a city resort for business intercourse. In mod. use primarily *U.S.* (with cap.), applied to Wall Street, New York. Hence, the money market; the body of persons who conduct transactions in stocks and shares. Also, in London, ***in the street*** is said with reference to business done or prices quoted after the hour of closing of the Stock Exchange.

1555 EDEN tr. *P. Martyr's Decades* III. 149 That they had cities fortified with waules,..and common places whyther marchauntes resort as to the burse or streate. [L. *plateas etiam, stratasque uias ordine composito, ubi negocientur, haberent.*] **1563** GRESHAM in Burgon *Life* (1839) II. 26 By the reason, this plague tyme, there is noe money nor creadit to be had in the streat of London [*editor explains as* Lombard-street]. **1746** P. FRANCIS tr. *Horace*, *Ep.* I. i. 77 This maxim echoes through the bankers' street. **1863** KIMBALL *Undercurrents* 131 (Flügel) Sufficient of the two millions [could be] launched on the street. **1883** *Nation* (N.Y.) 16 Aug. 132/1 'The Street' begins to play a larger and larger part in the financial world, owing to the enormous amounts of American capital it holds and of foreign capital it distributes. **1888** C. MILLS in *N. Amer. Rev.* Jan. 50 Then it was that the Street began to suspect that money would not always remain at four per cent. **1895** *Daily News* 11 Jan. 7/1 After a weak opening South African shares improved,..and ..the tone in the 'Street' this evening appeared firm. **1912** *Daily Tel.* 19 Dec. 2/3 Americans were idle throughout, with a slightly firmer appearance in the street.

(*b*) Also, = ***Fleet Street*** s.v. FLEET *sb.*² 2 b.

1932 *News Chron.* 11 Feb. 6/3 A year ago he was coming back as Editor to the Street. **1963** L. MEYNELL *Virgin Luck* v. 101 The Street isn't the best place to come looking for a job at the moment. **1976** 'J. WELCOME' *Grand National* viii. 123 Things were bad on the street... Two dailies were.. expected to be unable to survive.

g. *Physics.* More fully ***vortex street*** [tr. G. *wirbelstrasse*]. An arrangement of vortices in which they form two parallel lines with clockwise rotation in one and anticlockwise rotation in the other; similarly ***cloud street***.

1927 *Proc. R. Soc.* A. CXVI. 170 These vortex bands.. roll up and form what is commonly known as a vortex street. **1929** *Aircraft Engin.* I. 124/3 Vortices in a 'street' of two rows. **1936** *Proc. R. Soc.* A. CLIV. 68 For any given street the distance between consecutive vortices remains remarkably constant. **1954** [see *cloud street* s.v. CLOUD *sb.* 12]. **1956** A. A. TOWNSEND *Struct. Turbulent Shear Flow* vii. 144 For higher Reynolds numbers, either the vortex street forms very close to the cylinder or the circulation is itself unstable. **1973** *Times* 29 Jan. 14/4 As a fish swims it produces a turbulent 'vortex street' of whirling water behind it. **1978** R. S. SCORER *Environmental Aerodynamics* ix. 340 Cloud streets occur over land temporarily in the morning, and occasionally in the evening. *Ibid.* 341 Streets are common over the sea, particularly where the air stream is being slowly warmed.

h. ***the street***: the streets regarded *loosely* as the realm of the common people, and esp. as the source of popular political support.

1931 [see NAZI *sb.*]. **1954** B. & R. NORTH tr. *M. Duverger's Pol. Parties* I. i. 38 The Storm troops wrested from the Communist and Socialist crowds their dominance of the street. **1969** *Listener* 24 Apr. 555/3 This was the street taking over a modern state in a way which hasn't happened, I think, at any other time in our history. It was as if this country had been taken over by the Black and Tans.

i. ***the street*** (U.S. slang): the world outside prison or other confinement, freedom.

[**1931** G. IRWIN *Amer. Tramp & Underworld Slang* 185 *Streets*, freedom, and so called by prisoners in confinement.] **1935** J. HARGAN *Gloss. Prison Lang.* 8 *Street, hit the*, to be released. **1956** B. HOLIDAY *Lady sings Blues* (1973) xviii. 144, I was too busy thinking about 'the street' all the time and the life I'd left. **1966** J. MILLS *Panic in Needle Park* xix. 184 It is no accident that our patients refer to the world outside [the hospital] as 'the street': they cherish their mobility, the opportunity to escape difficult relationships, very highly. **1977** E. LEONARD *Unknown Man No. 89* iv. 35 The jury believed Robert Leary and he was allowed to return to the street.

3. Phrases. **a.** ***in the street(s)***: outside the house, out of doors; also, out of doors in a town or city. So (chiefly *Sc.* and *U.S.*) ***on*** or ***upon the street(s)***.

c **1200** [see 2]. *a* **1300** *Cursor M.* 2772 He praid þam..þai wald to gestening com hame,..and þai said nai, bot in the stret þar duell wald þai. **1340** HAMPOLE *Pr. Consc.* 4546 Þan sal þair bodys..In þe stretes ligg stille thre days And an half, ..For na man sal þam dur biry. *a* **1430** *Sev. Sages* (Cott. Galba) 1556 Þe dore ful stalworthly he sperd..And lete his whif stand in þe strete. *c* **1450** *Mirk's Festial* 193 Anoþer tyme, as he walkyd yn þe strete, he herd a womon cry trauelyng on chyld. **1581** PETTIE *Guazzo's Civ. Conv.* I. (1586) 26 Diogenes..being asked why he eate openlie in the streete, answered because he was hungered in the streete. **1582** ALLEN *Martyrdom Campion* (1908) 118 He was apprehended in the streats of London ready to goe over to the seminarie at Remes. **1752** A. STEWART in *Scots Mag.* (1753) Sept. 447/1 The deponent..met William Stewart upon the street. **1827** CARLYLE *Germ. Rom.* II. 160, I have seen him on the street. **1837** —— *Fr. Rev.* III. I. v, He recognized me on the streets and spoke to me, seven months after. **1861** *Two Cosmos* III. ii. I. 280 This town-officer has stopped me on the street, pretending that I owe an account to Mr. Donald Caird. **1866** SALA *Trip to Barbary* 89 The concourse thinned not on the streets or in the Port. **1883** C. D. WARNER *Roundabout Journ.* 37 The young women are on the street with babies; the old ones sit by the doors of their little shops or their houses and knit. **1883** JEAFFRESON *Real Ld. Byron* I. 260 On leaving parties, to which she had not been invited, he found her waiting for him in the street. **1883** *Harper's Mag.* Aug. 338/2 Cymric was heard commonly on the street.

b. ***on the street***: (*a*) *U.S. slang*, outside prison, at liberty; (*b*) *slang*, by illicit trafficking (with reference to the acquisition of drugs): (*c*) *colloq.*, out of work, unemployed.

1935 N. ERSINE *Underworld & Prison Slang* 73 *Street*, *n.*, figuratively, freedom. 'Another year will see him on the street.' **1951** W. FAULKNER *Requiem for Nun* III. 251 They worked their fines out on the street. **1977** *New Yorker* 24 Oct. 64/3 A number of men who are heterosexual on the street practice homosexuality in prison. **1979** *Guardian* 30 Oct. 8/5 We have either an extremely successful therapeutic service, or people are obtaining the drugs which they want 'on the street'. **1980** J. WAINWRIGHT *Venus Fly-Trap* 12 It's *my* living, too... If I upset that crowd, I could be on the street.

c. ***on the streets*** (Sc.): turned out of doors, homeless.

1852 J. ANDERSON in *Literary Gaz.* 3 Jan. 12/2 The door of the church..opened, and there issued forth Chalmers and Welsh,..and the Church of Scotland was on the streets, and free.

d. ***to be on the streets***: to be a prostitute. Hence, ***the street(s)*** as designating a life of prostitution.

[**1728**: see f.] **1750** JOHNSON *Rambler* No. 12 ¶10 She told me, that having a respect for my relations, she was willing to keep me out of the street, and would let me have another week. **1754** SHEBBEARE *Matrimony* (1766) II. 227 By Heavens! I would rather hear of her being on the Streets of London, than married to so vile a Fellow. **1802** H. MARTIN *Helen of Glenross* III. 82 To be..accompanied by any woman, not absolutely on the streets, is a point to her, whom scarce one does not feel unwilling to appear publicly with. **1851** MAYHEW *Lond. Labour* I. 60 Two girls, who..had been forced to go upon the streets to gain a living. **1885** *Daily News* 3 Nov. 6/3 This little girl had a sister who was on the streets and who was in the house of this bad woman. **1886** BARING-GOULD *Court Royal* xiii, They went into service, and when they found that they were expected to dust chairs and wash up breakfast things they went on the streets. **1905** MISS BROUGHTON *Waif's Progr.* i. 6 'If we refuse the girl, what is the alternative?' 'None, apparently, but the streets.'

e. ***up street***, ***down street*** (vulgar): in or towards the upper or lower part of the street.

1876 Miss Braddon *J. Haggard's Dau.* xxiii, A retired miller who had died of dropsy 'up street'. **1890** W. A. Wallace *Only a Sister?* 115 We've some chaps bad down street after that little kick up at the Irish affairs meeting.

†**f.** ***to weep full a street***: 'to fill a street with one's tears', to weep immoderately. *Obs.*

c **1374** Chaucer *Troylus* iv. 929 What helpeth it to wepen ful a strete, Or though ye bothe in salte teres dreynte?

g. ***to walk the street***(*s*: to go about on foot in a town. Also with reference as in c.

1606 N. B[axter] *Sydney's Ourania* K 3 b, Each swaggering Ruffin now that walk's the streetes, Proud as Lucifer, stabbeth whom he meetes. **1709** Hearne in *Lett. Eminent Persons* (1813) I. 193 There has been a person in Oxford, who saw her walk the street since this amazing accident. **1714** Budgell tr. *Theophrastus* xxiv. 69 When he walks the Streets, he never Condescends to look about him, or to know any one he meets. **1728** Pope *Dunc.* I. 230 While all your smutty sisters walk the streets. **1735** —— *Sat. Donne* II. 73 For you he walks the streets thro' rain or dust. **1753** Jane Collier *Art of Tormenting* I. ii. 54 How likely is it, that ..you would be deserted by those base wretches your seducers! You know I have often wept,..lest you should come to walk London Streets. **1858** O. W. Holmes *Aut. Breakf.-t.* viii. (1883) 195 When a lady walks the streets.. she knows well enough that the street is a picture-gallery, where pretty faces..are meant to be seen, and everybody has a right to see them. **1908** S. E. White *Riverman* xvii, The remainder of the time he spent walking the streets and reading in the club rooms.

h. ***the man in*** (also *U.S.* ***on***) ***the street***: the ordinary man, as distinguished from the expert or the man who has special opportunities of knowledge. Similarly ***the woman in the street.*** Also (with hyphens) *attrib.*

1831 Greville *Mem.* 22 Mar. (1874) II. 131 The other [side affirms] that the King will not consent to it, knowing, as 'the man in the street' (as we call him at Newmarket) always does, the greatest secrets of kings. **1854** Emerson *Lett. & Soc. Aims, Eloquence* Wks. (Bohn) III. 192 The speech of the man in the street is invariably strong, nor can you mend it by making it what you call parliamentary. **1860** —— *Conduct Life, Worship* ibid. II. 398 Certain patriots in England devoted themselves for years to creating a public opinion that should break down the corn-laws and establish free trade. 'Well,' says the man in the street, 'Cobden got a stipend out of it.' [Frequent in Emerson.] **1868** Whyte Melville *White Rose* xlvii, 'Jerry', said he, 'I didn't come here at early dawn only to tell you what "the Man in the Street" says.' **1898** Bodley *France* II. III. v. 259 It is the man in the street and the democracy generally that the fall of a Ministry fails to move. **1900** Fairbairn in *Examiner* 21 June 327/2 The man in the street..may be a very excellent person, but his very ordinariness puts a long way between him and an ample and distinguished manhood. **1926** Galsworthy *Silver Spoon* III. xi. 305 She had the political cynicism of the woman in the street. **1928** *Amer. Speech* IV. 134 The American newspaper man..speaks a patois bewildering to the man on the street. **1942** G. Greene *British Dramatists* 20 We notice the quality which reached its height in the great comedies..a kind of man-in-the-street poetry. **1962** A. Nisbett *Technique Sound Studio* vii. 130 A sort of convention has arisen whereby 'man-in-the-street' interviews are cut together by simple editing. **1964** R. K. Goldsen in I. L. Horowitz *New Sociol.* 89 We must endeavor to make sociological knowledge as inescapable for men-on-the-street as are..the virtues of the latest detergent. **1973** *Observer* (Colour Suppl.) 4 Feb. 15/4 He really wanted to please the man on the street and the man on the street knew it. **1977** E. W. Hildick *Vandals* I. ii. 17 Taperecorded man- and woman-in-the-street interviews.

i. colloq. or slang. ***not to be in the same street with***: to be far behind in a race, to be far inferior to. ***to be streets ahead, better***: to be far ahead in a race, to be far superior. ***not the length of a street***: no great interval. ***by a street***: by a wide margin (esp. of a sporting victory).

1883 Mrs. E. Kennard *Right Sort* xx, Nevertheless, though not in the same street with King Olaf, it won't do to estimate Singing Bird's chance too lightly. **1884** G. Moore *Mummer's Wife* (1887) 162, I don't pretend to be able to teach singing, but were you under my grandfather a year or so, I am..certain that Beaumont wouldn't be in the same street with you. **1893** *Kennel Gaz.* Aug. 213/2 Kitty of Coleshill was just the best of the bunch [of setters], but there was not the length of a street between her and Sister Gabrielle. **1898** *Westm. Gaz.* 1 Feb. 6/3 The English are better photographers than the Americans, but as regards mechanical ingenuity..the latter are streets ahead. **1912** *Throne* 7 Aug. 227/1 The race will be over by the time these notes appear in print, but..I do not think Pinks will finish in the same street as the holder. **1917** *Times* 27 Jan. 9/5 The man who takes a glass of tawny port and a biscuit at 11 a.m. is streets better off than the man who takes a whisky and soda and a cigarette. **1962** *Times* 5 Nov. 4/1 Oxford..could have won by a street before half time. **1971** *Daily Tel.* 28 Sept. 30/1 He already knew what most of us had already calculated —that Bodell had won by a street. **1977** *Time Out* 17–23 June 65/5 The Scots should win the drinking by a street. **1982** *Age Monthly Rev.* (Melbourne) Mar. 11/3 Any label embracing such a wide range of usage is too wide by a street.

j. ***to be up*** (***down***, †***in***) ***one's street***: to be suited to someone's taste or ability.

1903 Farmer & Henley *Slang* VII. 10/1 *Street*.., a capacity, a method; a line: *e.g.* 'That's not in my street' = 'I am not concerned' or 'That's not my way of doing', etc. **1929** *Publishers' Weekly* 21 Dec. 2813/2 A great many of the books published today are, as the saying is, right up her street. **1937** *Forward* 13 Nov. 1/2 We Labour people can the more easily say these things because some of his activities were 'up our street'. **1945** E. Waugh *Brideshead Revisited* II. iv. 259 She is a jolly attractive girl, the sort of girl any chap would be glad to have—terrific, too, just down your street. **1955** Knight & George *Advice to Student of French* 67 The historical line of enquiry is outside your scope, but the analysis of the book or books is right down your street. **1960** L. Cooper *Accomplices* I. vi. 55 John Pollard got me the job and..I loved it... It was right up my street. **1977** *It* May 28/1 If you like Miles Davis's 'In a Silent Way' then Don Cherry has a new release which is just up your street.

k. ***to play*** or ***work both sides of the street*** (orig. and chiefly *U.S.*): to ally oneself with both sides, to behave inconsistently and opportunistically.

1938 *Sun* (Baltimore) 8 Sept. 1/2 Our friends of the New Deal have the devil's own nerve when it comes to working both sides of the street... Mr. James A. Farley..can reel off a speech as pious as the heart could wish and he can play the part of Jobmaster General with all the ruthlessness of the Tammany school of politics. **1951** E. Kefauver *Crime in Amer.* xvii. 202 He played both sides of the street and made contributions to candidates of both major parties. **1969** *Listener* 13 Feb. 196/3 Amnesty International has to play both sides of the political street in seeking to obtain the release of political prisoners... Information usually comes either from the press or through prisoners' friends, but known domestic or foreign opponents of a regime are not.. necessarily the best channel for bringing influence to bear.

4. ***attrib.*** and ***Comb.*** **a.** Simple attrib., with the senses 'of or pertaining to the streets', 'exercising one's calling in the streets', 'transacted or taking place in the streets', as in ***street accident, band, battle, beggar,*** †***-beggary, bookie, -bookmaker, -bookmaking, clothes, -crier, -cry, decoration, fair, game, gang, -life, market, meeting, music, -musician, -noise, -orator, organ, party, patrol, photographer, piano, preacher, riot, -rioter, -robber, robbery,*** †***-scuffler, -seller, -shrine, -singer, -singing, song, -talk, theatre, trade, -trader, -trading, vendor, violence, warfare.***

1892 Kipling *Many Inventions* (1893) 164, I heard Keller saying, as though he were watching a *street accident, 'Give him air. For God's sake, give him air.' **1980** J. Hone *Flowers of Forest* I. i. 14 An essential witness in a street accident. **1838** Dickens *Nicholas Nickleby* (1839) ii. 6 *Street bands are on their mettle in Golden Square. **1977** *New Statesman* 2 Sept. 292/1 The traditional Trinidadian street bands and dancers. **1936** *New Yorker* 7 Mar. 29/1 In 1923..the Commissioner..in a *street battle routed the brownshirts. **1978** 'A. Stuart' *Vicious Circles* 21 Last night's riots in Milan where fascists had fought communists in a running street battle. **1713** Steele *Guardian* No. 144 ¶1 Our very *Street Beggars are not without their peculiar Oddities. **1976** *Birmingham Post* 16 Dec. 5/5 Patrick Haplin, a street beggar, will celebrate Christmas in prison—for the tenth consecutive year. **1625** Donne *Serm.* lxv. (1640) 659 That *street-beggery, which is become a Calling. **1939** *John o' London's Weekly* 2 June 320/2 He gets himself..into minor social difficulties, finding himself one day..in the police cells in Kennington, accused of being a *street-bookie. **1980** G. M. Fraser *Mr. American* xxiv. 479 Unless ultimately he could break them, he might as well go back to catching street bookies. **1939** H. Hodge *Cab, Sir?* xvi. 238 We [*sc.* cabmen] have come to look on the police-court dock as a normal trade risk—just as *street-bookmakers and prostitutes do. **1981** R. Samuel *East End Underworld* xiv. 179 They kept a big cat's meat shop, but his real money came from *street bookmaking. **1908** M. Morgan *How to dress Doll* vii. 63 (*heading*) *Dolly's *street clothes.* Here is Dolly dressed for a walk. **1981** M. C. Smith *Gorky Park* I. 10 In his street clothes Arkady was slovenly. **1847** Lever *Knt. Gwynne* xxxv, With the sing-song intonation of a *street-crier. **1858** *Punch* XXIV. 103 The value of the houses..is daily diminishing by reason of the *Street Cries, which render the place uninhabitable. **1874** *All Year Round* 14 Feb. 372 The London street cries which we find recorded in old books. **1911** *Encycl. Brit.* XXIX. 759/2 *Street decoration. **1969** *Guardian* 18 Dec. 9/1 There are fewer street decorations.. store displays are less lavish. **1872** B. Jerrold *London* xix. 158 These *street-fairs are held chiefly on Saturday nights and Sunday mornings. **1982** 'E. McBain' *Beauty & Beast* viii. 130 Calusa's street fairs during..March and April, when the tourists were thickest. **1890** *Public Ledger* (Philadelphia) 9 Dec. 6/5 Mr. Stewart Culin..recently delivered a lecture in Brooklyn, on children's *street games. **1969** I. & P. Opie *Children's Games* p. vi, There is no town or city known to us where street games do not flourish. **1942** E. Waugh *Put out More Flags* i. 32 A Glasgow millionaire.. who had started life in a *street gang. **1979** *Amer. Speech* 1976 LI. 61 Their speech is closer to standard than is that of the adolescent street-gang members. **1851** Mayhew *Lond. Labour* I. 327 This is a trade associated with *street-life rather than forming an integrant part of it. **1884** Phillipps-Wolley *Trottings of Tenderfoot* 210 Which to me were the great feature of the town's street-life. **1870** D. J. Kirwan *Palace & Hovel* xxxiv. 507 The roughest audience.. wandered right and left..to..choke the thoroughfare to buy in the *street market, which was now—eleven o'clock —at the height of commercial prosperity. **1922** V. Woolf *Jacob's Room* viii. 157 The street market in Soho is fierce with light. **1982** *Listener* 16 Dec. 34/3 Beware street-market tapes at silly prices, even if they have well-known brand names. [**1923** R. Macaulay *Told by Idiot* I. xii. 46 She attended street labour meetings in the east [end].] **1933** 'G. Orwell' *Down & out in Paris & London* xxv. 183 There were *street meetings... In the East India Dock Road the Salvation Army were holding a service. **1982** R. Manheim tr. *Grasse's Headbirths* vi. 85 Street meeting in the pedestrian zone. **1829** *Harlequin* 20 June 48 *Street music is on the march... At Ascot, some glee-singers received two sovereigns for singing before the Royal Stand. **1841** C. Knight *Lond.* I. 141 De la Serre..is enthusiastic in his praises of the *street music of London. **1839** *Act 2 & 3 Vict.* c. 47 §57 To require any *Street Musician to depart from the Neighbourhood of the House. **1841** C. Knight *Lond.* I. 129 *Street noises. **1780** *Ann. Reg.* II. 23 At Rome, those *street-orators sometimes entertain their audience with interesting passages of real history. **1849** E. Ruskin *Let.* 28 Oct. in M. Lutyens *Effie in Venice* (1965) I. 54 This Milan is a most wonderful place for *street organs. **1964** G. Mitchell *Death of Delft Blue* i. 15 If you go there [*sc.* Amsterdam], be sure to look out for the street organs, the barrel-organs, you know. **1953** *Times* 3 June 8/1 The most popular events were the *street parties. In some 30 or 40 streets the inhabitants had clubbed together to hold parties, starting, as a rule, with tea for the children. **1977** *New Yorker* 27 June 52/1 London's celebrations of the Queen's Silver Jubilee seemed like one mammoth street party. **1976** *Guardian* 12 Apr. 20/7 All good police officers know that the *street patrol on foot ..is the classic champion over the scourge of street crime. **1945** E. Waugh *Brideshead Revisited* I. vi. 132 Here..is a group taken by a *street photographer. **1981** 'S. Caudwell' *Thus was Adonis Murdered* xviii. 230 The street photographers and sellers of souvenirs continued about their business. **1857** *Punch* XXXII. 40 All music sounds alike to him, whether it be the Handel of the organ-loft or the handle of the *street piano. **1903** [see plunk *v.* 1 b]. **1978** L. Deighton *SS-GB* xix. 166 Douglas stopped to give a penny to an old man at the handle of a street piano. **1878** *Golden Hours* X. 85/2 Moxy looked up quickly into the face of an old black 'mammy' who..had paused for a moment to listen to the words of the *street preacher. **1916** G. B. Shaw *Androcles & Lion* p. xii, The horror of the High Priest was perfectly natural: he was a Primate confronted with a heterodox street preacher uttering what seemed to him an appalling and impudent blasphemy. **1977** J. Gillis *Killers of Starfish* (1979) v. 35 He pretended he was a street preacher once and people put pennies and dimes in his hat to save the sinners. **1980** L. St. Clair *Obsessions* i. 16 Perhaps there would be no more *street riots and shooting. **1900** Kipling *Let.* 24 July in C. Carrington *Rudyard Kipling* (1955) xiii. 314 We advanced against 'em [*sc.* the Boers] as if they were *street-rioters that we didn't want to hurt. **1728** [De Foe] *Street-Robberies* 25 Shoplifters, House-breakers and *Street-Robbers. *Ibid.* 59 Another Reason of the Frequency of *Street Robberies, is the Remissness or Corruption of the Watch. **1772** Nugent tr. *Grosley's Tour Lond.* I. 87 The state of nature, a state with which the *street-scufflers of London are closely connected. **1827** Hone *Table Bk.* I. 685 The man..was a *street seller of hobbyhorses. **1911** J. Ward *Roman Era Brit.* vii. 119 The Pompeian *street shrines were as varied as the domestic. **1789** C. Burney *Hist. Mus.* III. 64 It seems to have been the wish of illiterate and furious reformers, that all religious offices should be performed by field-preachers and *street-singers. **1841** C. Knight *Lond.* I. 144 The street-singers of Paris. **1624** Heywood *Captives* II. ii. in Bullen *O. Pl.* IV, Hee had too handsome *streete-singing-fact lasses in his companye. **1958** E. Routley *Eng. Carol* 228 Television probably accounts in part for the decline of street-singing. **1891** R. Fry *Let.* 4 Mar. (1972) I. 129 There is a good deal of spontaneous music in the Italians... Their *street songs are perfect of their kind. **1959** W. R. Bird *These are Maritimes* x. 274 There were street songs brought out over the years from the old country. **1826** Lamb *Pop. Fallacies* xii, The casual *street-talk between a poor woman and her little girl. **1959** G. Wickham *Early Eng. Stages* I. iii. 51 Specially erected platforms..in market squares or other open spaces..are usually known by such names as 'booth theatres', *théâtres de la foire*, or simply '*street theatres'. **1977** *Spare Rib* May 16/1 I'd like to do street theatre, but it's not that easy in a place like Sheffield. **1841** C. Knight *Lond.* I. 139 Of the *street trades that are past and forgotten, the smallcoal-man was one of the most remarkable. **1870** D. J. Kirwan *Palace & Hovel* xxvi. 395 These dog-sellers are the keenest *street-traders to be found in London. **1979** S. Brett *Comedian Dies* i. 17 [He] spoke with the brash confidence of an East End street-trader. **1903** *Act 3 Edw. VII* c. 45 §2 Any local authority may make byelaws with respect to *street trading by persons under the age of sixteen. **1977** J. Thomson *Case Closed* viii. 99 They'd kept their street-trading licence and..they'd go round the local markets selling clothing. **1872** B. Jerrold *London* ii. 23 Stopped by *street vendors of all descriptions. **1978** N. Longmate *Hungry Mills* vii. 100 His heart went out to the inexperienced street-vendors he encountered. **1977** *Times* 22 Jan. 4/4 The two days of *street violence [in Cairo] which took more than 60 lives. **1830** in *Times* (1982) 7 June 14/7 Locomotive Carriages might be used with great advantage in cases of Riot and *Street Warfare. **1938** 'G. Orwell' *Homage to Catalonia* x. 174 Few experiences could be.. more nerve-racking than those evil days of street warfare.

b. attrib. with the sense 'of or pertaining to a street or streets', as ***street architecture, -corner, -crossing, -directory, -end, island, -lamp, -length, map, -name, plan, -side.*** Also ***street-like*** adj., ***street-wise*** adv.

1933 J. Betjeman *Ghastly Good Taste* vi. 99 The true eighteenth century tradition, which lavished adornment on the interior and did not worry as much about *street architecture. **1978** *Architectural Design* 5 June 314/2 Shaw's Albert Hall Mansions of 1879–81..are excellent as street architecture. **1836** Dickens *Sk. Boz* 2nd Ser. ii. 22 The policeman at the *street corner. **1841** —— *Barn. Rudge* xxvi, They alighted at the street-corner. **1909** C. Elsee *Neoplatonism* Pref. p. v, The crowd that listens to the street-corner preacher of materialism. **1944** [see feel *v.* 9 e]. **1978** J. Wainwright *Jury People* xxxvi. 118 Yobbo types, tearaways, bully-boys, street-corner louts. **1875** 'Mark Twain' in *Atlantic Monthly* May 571/1 Go on until you know every *street-crossing, the character, size, and position of the crossing stones, [etc.]. **1956** D. Gascoyne *Night Thoughts* 26 Street-crossing islands stand becalmed. **1977** R. L. Wolff *Gains & Losses* II. iii. 243 The virtuous street urchin who has never heard of Christ..raises himself ..to the proprietorship of a muddy street-crossing as a sweeper. **1817** A. Johnstone (*title*), The London commercial guide and *street directory. **1864** Burton *Scot Abr.* I. iii. 109 Names familiar to us now..in street-directories had been found among the dead at Poitiers. **1890** Kipling *Life's Handicap* (1891) 79 A lamp at a *street-end. **1904** A. C. Benson *House of Quiet* xiii. (1907) 77 The constant presence, in these London pictures, of straight framing lines, contributed by house-front and street-end. **1919** J. Buchan *Mr. Standfast* x. 187 A hundred yards away a bomb fell on a *street island. **1934** *Sun* (Baltimore) 31 May 5/3 A hard-driving taxi driver ignored a red signal, threatened the traffic policeman's knees, missed the street island by a hair [etc.]. **1799** C. B. Brown *Arthur Mervyn* I. iv. 33 [The room's] height and spaciousness were imperfectly discernible..by gleams from a *street lamp. **1870–74** J. Thomson *City Dreadf. Nt.* I. vi, The street-lamps always burn. **1874** Longf. *Sonn., Summer day by Sea* 6 From the dim headlands many a lighthouse gleams, The street-lamps of the ocean. **1910** *Spectator* 9 July 51/2 They may be *street-lengths from it, but it is sure to find them. **1595** E. C. *Emaricdulfe* Sonn. xxi. in *Lamport Garl.* (Roxb.), Through *street-like straight hie-waies I did attempt. **1964** L. DEIGHTON *Funeral in Berlin* vii. 52 Spectacles produced a *street map and..began marking circles here and there. **1978** T. ALLBEURY *Lantern Network* x. 141 The street map showed it as a small road off the Brighton Road. **1861** *Chamb. Jrnl.* 30 Nov. 337 (*art.*) *Street Names. **1970** J. McN. DODGSON *Place-Names Cheshire* I. p. xliv, As a rule, street-names not recorded before 1700 are excluded. **1929** *Woolley's Ludlow Guide* (ed. 18) 44 (*caption*) *Street plan of Ludlow. **1978** W. J. BURLEY *Wycliffe & Scapegoat* iii. 55 Wycliffe studied the street plan. 'Here we are. Albert Terrace.' **1463** *Bury Wills* (Camden) 22 The gate be the *strete syde. **1538–9** *Act Comm. Counc.* in Calthrop *Rep. Cases*, etc. (1670) 177 That strong Grates of Iron along the said Water-side, and also by the Street-side,..be made by the Inhabitants of every Ward. **1911** J. WARD *Roman Era Brit.* vii. 116 Along the street-side were the remains of a narrow building. **1974** *New Yorker* 29 Apr. 47/1 The odd oarsman..looks forlorn seen from the bridges or the streetsides. **1977** *Antiquaries Jrnl.* LVII. 251 The building extended only for the width of the streetside room..from the street frontage. **1911** WEBSTER, **Streetwise, adv.*, after the manner of a street.

c. objective, as ***street-cleaner***, ***-cleaning***, ***-layer***, ***-lighting***, ***-pacing*** adj., ***-sweeper***, ***-sweeping***.

1898 'MERRIMAN' *Roden's Corner* xi. 111 A few *street-cleaners were leisurely working, a few milkmen were hurrying from door to door. **1896** *Harper's Mag.* June 149/1 What do you think of the new *Street-Cleaning Department? *a* **1893** W. BURNS THOMSON *Remin.* (1895) 78 He had been much exposed from his calling as a *street-layer. **1916** G. B. SHAW *Androcles & Lion* p. lxxii, The sportsmen, the musicians, the physicists, the biologists will get their apparatus for the asking as easily as their bread or, as at present, their paving, *street lighting, and bridges. **1979** *Time* 8 Jan. 23/2 In 1975 Gacy became a trustee of the Norwood Park Township Street Lighting District. **1784** COWPER *Tiroc.* 217 There waiter Dick..His counsellor and bosom-friend shall prove, And some *street-pacing harlot his first love. **1848** THACKERAY *Van. Fair* lxv, If she..made a curtsey to a *street-sweeper. **1871** RUSKIN *Arrows of Chace* (1880) II. 174, I mean, on 1st January next, to take three street-sweepers into constant service. **1843** *Builder* 18 Feb. 21/3 [Description of the] Patent Self-Loading Cart, or *Street-Sweeping Machine. **1849** A. R. WALLACE *My Life* (1905) I. xviii. 273 Piassaba (the coarse stiff fibre of a palm, used for making brooms for street-sweeping).

d. locative, with the sense 'in the streets', as ***street wanderer***; ***street-bred***, ***-sold*** adjs.

1722 DE FOE *Col. Jack* i, Sharp as a *street-bred boy must be, but ignorant and unteachable from a child. **1892** KIPLING *Barrack-room Ballads* 174 The poor little street-bred people that vapour and fume and brag. **1851** MAYHEW *Lond. Labour* I. 326 At the National Gallery, the *street-sold catalogues are 1d., 3d., and 6d.; in the hall, the authorised copy is sold at 4d. and 1s. **1828** MISS MITFORD *Village* III. 254 A 'palpable obscure,' which..threatens to extinguish the lamps and lanthorns, with which the poor *street-wanderers strive to illumine their darkness.

e. *attrib.* passing into *adj.*, with reference to the streets as the focus of modern urban life, esp. among the poor and contrasted with polite society. Often with the implication of illegal dealings (esp. drug-trafficking), or the sharp-wittedness needed to survive 'on the streets'. orig. *U.S.*

1967 'T. WELLS' *Dead by Light of Moon* xiii. 126 A street merchant is a con artist who pretends to sell stolen goods. **1967** *Trans-Action* Apr. 5/1 Street culture exists in every low income ghetto. It is shared by the hustling elements of the poor, whatever their nationality or color. **1972** *N.Y. Times* 24 Dec. IV. 6 Murphy called a news conference to announce that 57 pounds of heroin with an estimated street value of more than $10-million had been stolen. **1973** D. BARNES *See the Woman* (1974) 73 His name is Frederick L. Pepper... He's got a street name of 'Red Pepper'. **1976** R. CONDON *Whisper of Axe* I. xv. 87 The street price for one kilogram of heroin is one million two hundred thousand dollars. **1979** W. J. FISHMAN *Streets of East London* 74/1 A street culture based on the pub. **1980** *Brit. Med. Jrnl.* 6 Dec. 1511/1 Phencyclidine is now a class 2 controlled substance in the United States—and after marijuana has become the most widely abused 'street drug' in North America. **1982** R. LEIGH *Girl with Bright Head* ii. 12 She wasn't street tough but neither was she a runaway kid up from the provinces.

f. Special comb.: **street-Arab** (also written with small *a*), a homeless vagrant (usually a child) living in the streets (see ARAB *sb.* 3); **street-ballad**, a ballad composed to be sung by street-singers; **street-boy**, a homeless or neglected boy who lives chiefly in the streets; **street-breakfast** (see quot.); † **street-chair**, ? a sedan chair; **street-child**, a homeless or neglected child who lives chiefly in the streets; † **street-coach**, a hackney-coach; **street cred** *slang*, abbrev. of *street credibility* and *street credible* adj. below; **street credibility** *slang*, popularity with, or accessibility to, ordinary people, esp. those involved in urban street culture; the appearance or fact of being 'street-wise'; hence, (apparent) familiarity with contemporary trends, fashions, social issues, etc.; also **street credible** *a.*, possessing street credibility; **street crime** *U.S.*, a crime such as robbery, assault, etc., committed on the streets; **street-dirt** = *street-manure*; **street-dog**, an ownerless dog living in the streets; **street-farer** *nonce-wd.*, one who passes through the streets; **street fighting**, fighting conducted in the streets, esp. on a large scale for political or revolutionary ends; so **street fight**, **street fighter**; **street-firing**, discharge of musketry in order to defend or scour a street; **street floor** *U.S.* = GROUND-FLOOR; **street furniture**, objects such as post-boxes, road-signs, litter bins, etc., placed in the street for public use or assistance (orig. a planners' term); † **street-gadder**, one who 'gads' about the streets; **street girl**, a homeless or neglected girl who lives chiefly in the streets; a prostitute; **street-grid**, an arrangement of streets crossing at right angles to each other; **street hockey** *N. Amer.*, a variety of ice hockey played on the street; **street jewellery**, painted enamel advertising plates considered as collectors' items; **street kid** = *street child* above; **street-legal** *a.*, applied to a motor vehicle which satisfies the legal requirements for roadworthiness; **street level**, (*a*) ground-floor level; (*b*) *fig.*, the level of direct contact with the public or of operation on the streets; **street-light**, † (*a*) a window opening on the street; (*b*) a street lamp; **street-manure**, horse-dung and road-scrapings used for manure; **street name** *U.S.* [after WALL STREET], the name of a stock-brokerage firm, bank, or dealer in which stock is held on behalf of the purchaser; † **street-parlour**, a sitting-room on the ground-floor, fronting the street; **street people** orig. and chiefly *U.S.*, (*a*) homeless or vagrant people who live on the streets, esp. as a protest against the conventional values of society; (*b*) people involved in petty crime in the urban underworld; (*c*) *spec.* people dealing in the illicit supply of drugs 'on the street'; **street-porter**, a porter employed to lift or carry heavy packages in the street (in early use = *ticket-porter*); **street price** *Stock Exchange*, see quot. 1893; **street-railway**, a tramway; † **street-raking** *a. Sc.*, that wanders about the streets; **street-refuge** = REFUGE *sb.* 3; **street rod** orig. *U.S.* (see quot. 1954); hence **street rodding** *vbl. sb.*; **street-room**, sufficient space in the streets; **streetscape**, a view or prospect provided by the design of a (city) street or streets; **street scene**, the spectacle of life in the streets; **street-smart** *a. U.S. slang* = *street-wise* adj. (*b*) below; also **street-smarts**, the ability to live by one's wits in an urban environment; **street-soil** (? *obs.*) = *street-manure*; † **street-thread** = *street-web*; **street-to-street** *a.*, of fighting: taking place in the streets; **street tree**, a tree planted at the side of a street to enhance the view; **street urchin**, a mischievous little street-boy; **street village**, a long, narrow village formed of buildings along either side of a main street; **street warden**, (*a*) an air-raid warden assigned to a particular street or streets; (*b*) a warden selected to look out for certain social problems in a particular street or streets; **street-web** (now *dial.*), see quot. 1854; **street-wise** *a. slang* (orig. and chiefly *U.S.*), (*a*) familiar with the outlook of ordinary people in an urban environment; (*b*) cunning in the ways of modern urban life; **street worker** orig. *N. Amer.*, a social worker whose concern is with juvenile delinquents; **street-yarn** *U.S.* = STREET WORKER.

1859 G. A. SALA *Twice round Clock* 388 *Street Arabs, threw 'cart-wheels' into the midst of the throng. **1865** LITTLEDALE *Cath. Ritual Ch. Eng.* 8 How can we most easily get a half-savage street-Arab..to understand that there is [etc.]. **1875** *Punch* 6 Mar. 108/2 Irregular crossing-sweepers, unlicensed boot-cleaners, and street-Arabs generally. **1892** MRS. H. WARD *David Grieve* II. vii, He strode on just in time to avoid a flight of street-arabs. **1924** LAWRENCE & SKINNER *Boy in Bush* 49 The children..were singing..with a sort of street-arab abandon. **1759** DILWORTH *Pope* 80 Such as the lowest political pamphlets, the meanest *street-ballads glancing at state-affairs or the church established. **1851** D. JERROLD *St. Giles* ii. 9 A voice was heard..droning a street-ballad of the day. **1854** DICKENS *Hard Times* I. xvi. 127, I was a ragged *streetboy. **1862** BURTON *Bk. Hunter* 31 He opens the door, and fetches in the little stranger. What can it be? a street-boy of some sort? **1834** DICKENS *Sk. Boz, Steam Excurs.*, At the corner of a by-street, near Temple-bar, was stationed a '*street-breakfast'. The coffee was boiling over a charcoal fire [etc.]. *a* **1712** FOUNTAINHALL *Decis.* (1759) II. 347 Dame Anna Macmorran..pursues her daughter..for paying her 4000 merks for her mournings..having put a room or two in black, covered her *street-chair, and cloathed two servants, a page, &c. **1863** DICKENS *Mrs Lirriper's Lodgings* i, in *All Year Round* Extra Christmas No. 3 Dec. 8/2 You must allow me to inform you..that my grandson is *not* a *street-child. **1959** I. & P. OPIE *Lore & Lang. Schoolch.* xii. 232 The street-child today with his soot-blackened face and red-daubed nose, rattling a tin, is a much more demure creature than his predecessors. **1982** G. WAGNER *Children of Empire* vii. 123 Three-quarters of his young life had been spent in the workhouse, yet technically he was a 'street child'. **1818** SCOTT *Hrt. Midl.* xxxv, 'No, sir,' said Jeanie; 'a friend brought me in ane o' their *street coaches—a very decent woman'. **1981** *Guardian Weekly* 6 Sept. 4/5 A couple of expressions have only come my way in the last month or so. One is 'street wise' and the other '*street cred'. **1985** *Sunday Times* 11 Aug. 17/7 Neil Kinnock, the Labour leader, lives in a 'street cred' west London semi. **1985** *Internat. Musician* June 9/4, I know that walking down main street with an oboe in hand does nothing for the street cred. **1986** *Sunday Tel.* 2 Feb. 11/8 You need to have 'street cred.'..You need to have done something which makes you popular for people to let you do the projects you want. **1979** *Sounds* 1 Dec. 33/1 Levine has real *street credibility (not like some wimp who wears Mary Quant's latest range, went to public school and then tells the world he's as street level as the Cockney Rejects). **1980** *Washington Post* 24 Nov. B11/2 Springsteen's street credibility is the core of his effectiveness. His striking working-class imagery is within everyone's experience, or at least within their reach. **1985** *Observer* 20 Oct. 18/7 The two parties..were organised by people whose claim to fame is their knowledge of society, street credibility and social organisation. **1984** *Daily Tel.* 11 Sept. 16/4, I await with baited breath the arrival of 'caring-profession', '*street-credible' and 'yuppie' in the next volume. **1986** *Sunday Express Mag.* 9 Nov. 36/1 Talking Heads are sufficiently street-credible in three-quarters of the known universe. **1973** *Listener* 20 Sept. 364/1 You'd expect..New York to take a highly sophisticated view of the drug problem, for it is more subtle in its operations here,.. and responsible for more *street crimes—robberies and rapes—than in any other State. **1978** *Chicago* June 162/2 The states attorney's office..must prosecute virtually all local street crime, leaving meager resources for long, complex investigations. **1765** *Museum Rust.* IV. 373 He has seen it [coleseed] yield good crops on a dry chalky soil, on which *street-dirt had been laid. **1873** LELAND *Egypt. Sketch-Bk.* 228 Nobody looked at it but I and a *street-dog. **1911** *Contemp. Rev.* July 27 We have got rid of the street dogs in Constantinople. **1880** W. WATSON *Prince's Quest* (1892) 51 As one who cared no-wise to make fast his ears Against the babble of the *street farers. **1851–61** MAYHEW *Lond. Labour* III. 29 The result of some *street-fight. **1930** E. POUND *XXX Cantos* ix. 35 And he fought in Fano, in a street fight. **1976** *Sunday Mail* (Glasgow) 26 Dec. 1/2 Late-night revellers were terrified when several running street fights broke out. **1970** K. PLATT *Pushbutton Butterfly* (1971) ix. 102, I promised my mother I would only marry a *street fighter. **1832** F. MACERONI (*title*) Defensive instructions.. on..*street and house fighting. **1900** W. S. CHURCHILL in *Morning Post* 12 July 7/7 The cavalry halted on the hills for a while, the general being desirous of obtaining the formal surrender of Heilbron, and so preventing street-fighting or bombardment. **1981** *Times* 6 July 13/1 Within a few months there have been three major eruptions of street fighting, all of which have included an ethnic element. **1763** *Brit. Mag.* IV. 543 About a mile and a half from the fort we had orders to form into platoons, and, if attacked in the front, to fire by *street-firings. **1790** BEATSON *Nav. & Milit. Mem.* I. 97 The grenadiers..having, with very little loss, received two fires from the enemy, they began a street firing. **1837** CARLYLE *Fr. Rev.* I. v. iii, Neither have the Gardes Françaises, the best regiment of the line, shown any promptitude for street-firing lately. **1927** DOUBMAN & WHITAKER *Organization & Operations of Department Stores* vii. 162 The first or *street floor of a store is the most desirable for selling. **1972** H. KEMELMAN *Monday the Rabbi took Off* xxvi. 170 Why would he take an apartment on a street floor here? **1944** J. C. RIDDELL *Rep. Post War Housing* 11 In all future planning there should..be the closest co-operation between all departments and services responsible for the erection of *street furniture and small buildings. **1976** *Cumberland & Westmorland Herald* 27 Nov., We don't want to waste officers' time..on more street furniture which costs a fortune today. **1577** HELLOWES *Gueuara's Fam. Ep.* 309 His wife is a seeker of kinred, a gossip, a *streete gadder. **1907** G. B. SHAW *Major Barbara* I. 206 You have had the education of a lady... Don't talk like a *street girl. *a* **1911** [see MOST *adv.* 4]. **1979** *Maledicta* III. 11 For a budding sexologist I must have been uncommonly naive, but I swear that I didn't catch on that these were street girls' joints till it dawned on me, while sorting out my notes, that I seemed to have a disproportionate number of sexual idioms. **1948** *Antiquity* XXII. 173 The wide road leading to its main entrance from the east is plainly out of alignment with the *street grid on the west side of the Forum block. **1964** *Listener* 27 Aug. 300/2 The avenue slices diagonally across the basic street-grid. **1964** *Globe & Mail* (Toronto) 15 Dec. 41/8 He brought a fresh approach to *street hockey when he began trying to teach Frank how to shoot a puck. **1976** *New Yorker* 26 Apr. 90/3 Meynell and I played marbles, mumblety-peg, running games, street hockey, primitive baseball, stoop ball, games of imagination. **1978** BAGLEE & MORLEY *Street Jewellery* 9 *Street jewellery, flashing in the winter sunlight, gleaming in gaslight..—the enamel sign. **1982** *Arts North* June 9 (*caption*) Street jewellery—one of the saucier enamel signs from the fascinating exhibition at the Dorman Museum. **1929** E. WILSON in *New Republic* 17 Apr. 256/2 The money with which the *street-kids have been playing craps. **1977** *Rolling Stone* 5 May 55/1 You could go to New Delhi or Calcutta, there are thousands of street kids there. **1976** *Casper* (Wyoming) *Star-Tribune* 29 June 19/1 (Advt.), Yamaha 125. *Street legal. Good condition. **1980** *Dirt Bike* Oct. 58/3 The rear fender is plastic, which is a rarity on street legal bikes. **1934** *Archit. Rev.* LXXV. 214/3 The storey built above, the *street-level floor was called a solar. **1963** 'J. LE CARRÉ' *Spy who came in from Cold* xv. 140 Branch Secretaries with..a good record of stimulating mass action at street level. **1974** 'E. LATHEN' *Sweet & Low* xi. 114 He reached street level. **1976** *Times* 6 Sept. 2/3 Plans are advanced to open..an office in Belfast.. accessible to both communities. An effort will be made to concentrate organization at street level. **1982** G. F. NEWMAN *Men with Guns* ix. 69 Kohn avoided contact with street-level hoods... Now he was a respectable businessman. *a* **1625** FLETCHER *Wom. Pleased* II. iii, For you Lady, Ile have your Lodgings farther off, and closer, Ile have no *street-lights to you. **1906** B'NESS VON HUTTEN *What became of Pam* 212 The street-lights burst like great flowers into the dusk. **1955** E. BLISHEN *Roaring Boys* iii. 128 The street lights..were on early. **1969** L. MICHAELS *Going Places* 27 Streetlights glowed in a receding sweep. **1844** STEPHENS *Bk. Farm* II. 676 That stable-dung is the most heating,..that byre-dung is cooler,..and that *street-manure is very inferior to the other two in every respect. **1930** C. F. HODGES *Wall Street* 383 When a security is registered in the name of a recognized brokerage firm, usually members of the Exchange, it is said to be in a '*Street Name'. **1933** *North Western Reporter* CCXLVI. 660/1 The court properly instructed as to the 'street name' custom of the exchange.. submitted to the jury the question of fact [etc.]. *Ibid.* 664/2 Evidence sustained finding that customer's repudiation of broker's purchase of stock in 'street name', instead of customer's name, was made within reasonable time. **1976** E. STEWART *Launch!* (1977) 35 'And I want to know how much the brokerage houses are holding in street names.' All the brokerage houses had street-name accounts, stock bought and traded for clients in the broker's name. **1760–72** H. BROOKE *Fool of Qual.* (1809) IV. 39 The earl sat in the *street-parlour. **1967** *Trans-Action* Apr. 5/1 In Los Angeles, members of.. street groups sometimes call themselves '*street people', 'cool people', or simply 'regulars'. **1969** *Guardian* 24 May 1/3 The precincts inhabited by Berkeley's hippies and 'street people'. **1972** *National Observer* (U.S.) 27 May 7/2 There's evidence that methadone has become almost as popular as heroin among addicts. Street people say so. **1976** *Billings* (Montana) *Gaz.* 4 July 2-B/3 'At first, we got mostly street people,' said Nyberg. 'Lately our patients have begun to be from the higher social levels.' **1606** *Street-porter [see TACKLE-HOUSE 1 b]. **1801** *Farmer's Mag.* Jan. 32 If such meat can be digested by the.. infirm in an alms-house, it could surely do no damage to the stronger organs of a street-porter. **1840** CARLYLE *Heroes* iii. (1841) 128 If, as Addison complains, you sometimes see a street-porter staggering under his load on spindleshanks. **1889** *Pall Mall Gaz.* 12 Nov. 3/1 'Do you give '*street' prices?'—'No, we never do that. After the official prices close at half past three we continue to give the unofficial prices up to four o'clock, but never after the doors of the Exchange are closed.' **1893** CORDINGLEY *Guide Stock Exch.* 23 Some business, too, is usually effected outside the Exchange, after the doors are closed; this is quoted in the newspapers as 'In the Street', or 'Street Prices'. **1861** *Chamb. Jrnl.* 29 June 416/1 The *street railways of the American cities. **1862** D. W. MITCHELL *Ten Yrs. U.S.* 265 A crowded street-railway car. **1818** SCOTT *Hrt. Midl.* xviii, What signifies what we were, ye *street-raking limmer! **1884** *St. James's Gaz.* 11 Jan. 5/2 A new *street-refuge should be constructed. **1954** *Amer. Speech* XXIX. 103 **Street rod* (*job, roadster*, etc.), *n.* A hot rod suitable for street use, one of the competition types. The 'street rod' is distinguished from the 'track car', which is intended primarily for drag-strip or lakes racing. **1972** *World of Wild Wheels* (Custom Car) 58/1 Street rods don't have to be American based—just tinged with American thought. **1977** *New Society* 3 Mar. 436/2 Custom-car cruisers, in their glistening, overpowered improvisations... The monthly influx of around 250 'street rods' causes a solid traffic jam. **1976** *Panorama* (Austral.) Dec. 4 One of Australia's fastest-growing sports is *street rodding—turning pre-1948 cars into sparkling, high-performance vehicles which belie their age. **1711** ADDISON *Spect.* No. 127 ¶7 Our publick Ways would be so crowded that we should want *Street-room. **1924** *Glasgow Herald* 8 Mar. 9 Where aerial invaders left ugly.. scars in the *streetscape noble new buildings have already appeared. **1979** *Jrnl. R. Soc. Arts* Nov. 770/2 Giorgio Grassi and others have designed housing blocks as long arcaded streetscapes. **1870** D. J. KIRWAN *Palace & Hovel* xxvi. 407 The great.. attraction among the multifarious *street scenes of London, is the Punch and Judy show. **1979** *N.Y. Times Mag.* 30 Sept. 37/2 The girls' mother, Ada, is down on the stoop, watching the street scene as if it were television. **1976** *National Observer* (U.S.) 1 May 5/1 Rizzo is tough, *street-smart, charming in his own special way. **1976** *N.Y. Times* 9 Aug. 30 To be free, however, requires street-smarts, the cunning of the survivor. **1978** *Time* 3 Apr. 61 Norris also sought out local black leaders and followed their street-smart advice. **1978** *New Yorker* 20 Nov. 113 They thought always about winning, and, one way or another, they almost always did win. Like the A's, these Yankees have street-smarts. **1983** *Underground Grammarian* VII. III. 7/2 Frank will be demoted to the lowliest rank in education, teacher, so that those adaptable street-smart kids can go and apply their skills in *her* classroom. **1766** ENTICK *Lond.* IV. 17 A wharf used for a laystall, to which the rakers carry *street-soil. *a* **1661** FULLER *Worthies, Kent* (1662) 58 Many idle women who now onely spin *Street-thread (going tatling about with tales). **1945** *Finito! Po Valley Campaign* (15th Army Group) 33 *Street-to-street battles. **1976** *Southern Even. Echo* (Southampton) 12 Nov. 10/3 She recalls the street-to-street fighting that became an everyday feature. **1911** W. SOLOTAROFF *Shade-Trees in Towns & Cities* p. ix, This book treats particularly of the planting and care of *street-trees. **1981** *Garden* CVI. 443/2 They [*sc.* local authorities] might be persuaded to plant street trees. **1849** LEVER *Con Cregan* I. viii. 96 What a fellow am I.. to discourse in this strain to a *street urchin. **1977** Street urchin [see *street-crossing*, sense 4 b]. **1978** J. KRANTZ *Scruples* vi. 168 Jake.. had a droll and artful street-urchin look to him and typically Black Irish coloring. **1949** *Ann. Assoc. Amer. Geographers* XXXIX. 261 **Street Villages* (*Strassendörfer*), the name being used only for those villages which were founded on an existing route. **1974** C. TAYLOR *Fieldwork in Medieval Archaeol.* vi. 142 Caxton.. is now a long street village on either side of the Old North Road. **1940** N. LAST *Diary* Oct. *Nella Last's War* (1983) 78 Our *street warden called tonight... He wanted to know if we had buckets, stirrup-pumps, blankets, bandages, [etc.]. **1973** *Daily Tel.* 8 Jan. 2/2 Mrs Green said her organisation wanted street wardens whose job 'for perhaps £1 a week' would be to call on old people each morning. **1980** *Church Times* 11 Apr. 6/4 Much is said about almost every activity that laypeople can undertake—forming a 'Jesus gang', personal witness, acting as street wardens, helping the bereaved, befriending the elderly. **1614** SYLVESTER *Bethulia's Rescue* IV. 135 Nor trip from feast to feast, nor *Street-webs span, To see, and to be seen of every, man. **1854** MISS BAKER *Northampt. Gloss., Spinning street-webs*, walking about idly, gossiping from house to house. 'She has nothing better to do than spinning street-webs.' **1965** *New Yorker* 27 Mar. 78 A [social] worker therefore had to be wary as well as trustful, be security minded as well as loving, and be '*street-wise' as well as compassionate. **1971** *N.T. Times* 18 June 37 Take a dirt-poor Sicilian peasant kid fresh out of steerage. Make him scrappy and street-wise. **1977** H. FAST *Immigrants* v. 321 Al Smith, street-wise Catholic from New York. **1980** *Times Lit. Suppl.* 1 Aug. 867/5 The learned men on the council of the SPR were not, as we would say now, 'street-wise'. **1981** *Daily Tel.* 27 Nov. 16/2 Their [*sc.* young blacks'] values place a premium on being 'street-wise',.. that is, being able to survive in the rough and tough world of the streets. **1964** *Maclean's Mag.* 25 Jan. 23 Almost all of them have quit school. The *street-worker has become so friendly with them that he can sometimes return stolen goods before the police are even aware of the theft. **1973** 'J. PATRICK' *Glasgow Gang Observed* xxi. 219 Adolescents.. did not know how to react to the non-evaluative, non-judgmental approach of the street worker. **1855** MRS. WHITCHER *Widow Bedott Papers* xiv. (1883) 54 They say when she ain't a spinnin' *street yarn, she don't dew nothin' but write poitry.

street (striːt), *v.* [f. STREET *sb.*] *trans.* To furnish or provide with streets, to lay out in streets. Also *to street out*, to lay out as a street or road.

1555 WATREMAN *Fardle Facions* I. iv. 46 The chiefe citie.. strieted with tentes and pauilions placed in good ordre. *c* **1645** HOWELL *Lett.* (1655) I. I. xii. 18 There are few places this side the Alps better built, and so well Streeted as this. **1760** in *Weekly Reporter* (1877) XXV. 470 The said [allottees] shall street out the same way leading through their said respective allotments so that the same shall be made and ever after remain eleven yards broad at the least.

Hence **'streeted** *ppl. a.*; **'streeting** *vbl. sb.*

1876 MORRIS *Sigurd* III. 201 Though a house of the windy battle their streeted burg be grown. **1889** *Pall Mall Gaz.* 13 Apr. 1/3 The absence of any direct line.. between Holborn and the Strand is the greatest blot in the present streeting of Central London.

streetage ('striːtɪdʒ). *U.S.* [f. STREET *sb.* + -AGE.] A charge or toll for the use of a street or street facilities.

1866 *Maryland Law Rep.* XXV. 72 The defendants.. charged in addition to the usual freight for transportation between those points a further compensation for streetage to the foot of 6th Street in the latter City. **1884** *Reading* (Pa.) *Morning Herald* 17 Apr., The Washington avenue tracks are.. owned by the Pennsylvania company, and for years there has been charged but a nominal sum on the Reading's business for streetage.

street-car. 1. *N. Amer.* A passenger car, running through the streets, usually on rails; a tram-car.

1862 A. TROLLOPE *N. Amer.* I. 185 Omnibuses, or street cars working on rails run hither and thither. **1872** HOWELLS *Wedd. Journ.* (1892) 29 The street-cars that slowly tinkled up and down. **1887** *Grip* (Toronto) 5 Feb. 6/2 Toronto law is plain and hard—no streetcars out on Sunday. **1915** D. R. CAMPBELL *Proving of Virginia* 108 So I shall bid you good-by and take a street car home. **1929** M. DE LA ROCHE *Whiteoaks* iv. 58 They boarded a street car and stood together, swaying, hanging by the straps,.. oblivious of the other passengers. **1931** W. G. MCADOO *Crowded Years* iv. 44 The street cars went like sleepy tortoises; they were pulled by mules. **1947** *Partisan Rev.* XIV. 366 They returned in a streetcar, although Jasper wanted to take a taxi. **1947** T. WILLIAMS (*title*) A streetcar named Desire. **1968** *Globe & Mail* (Toronto) 15 Jan. 17/1 Bus companies reported delays and power failure contributed to the problems of city street cars. **1974** *Plain Dealer* (Cleveland, Ohio) 26 Oct. 5-D/1 The people who came to the Barons-Rangers game that night long ago came by streetcar and bus and by shank's mare as well as by auto. **1978** *Detroit Free Press* 16 Apr. (Record) 9/4 The Warsaw street cars stop sixty or seventy meters from the gates of the ghetto.

attrib. **1875** KNIGHT *Dict. Mech.* 1858/1 Dean and Coleman's street-car rail. **1888** PENNELL *Sent. Journey* 20 Here we turned from river and street-car track to walk to the other end of the town.

2. A shell. *Mil. slang.*

1920 C. R. HERR *Company F Hist.: 319th Infantry* 22 The air was filled with the sounds of the shells as they lazily went on their way towards the back lines of both sides. 'Street cars'.. the boys called them. **1950** R. CHANDLER *Let.* 18 May (1966) 78 Doesn't he [*sc.* Partridge] overlook some of the most commonly used words of soldier-slang? E.g... 'street cars' or 'tram cars' for heavy long range shells.

street-door. The chief external door of a house or other building, giving immediate access to the street.

1563–70 FOXE *A. & M.* (ed. 2) 2124/2 One knockt at the street doore. **1671** WOODHEAD *St. Teresa* II. xxxv. 252 We found the good Lady at the street-door, where she received us with many tears. **1778** MISS BURNEY *Evelina* xlviii, I went to the street-door, where I stood some time. **1837** DICKENS *Pickw.* xxxvi, Mr. Weller left the room, and immediately afterwards was heard to shut the street door. **1870** MISS BRIDGMAN *R. Lynne* II. xi. 226 There came a.. rat-tat at the street-door.

b. *attrib.* and *Comb.*

1716 N. BLUNDELL *Diary* (1895) 141 Our Street Doar Lock was picked and yᵉ Doar opened. **1729** SWIFT *Direct. Serv.* Wks. 1751 XIV. 48 The Street-Door Key. **1802** G. COLMAN *Br. Grins, Elder Bro.* (1819) 115 A street-door bell. **1862** *Catal. Internat. Exhib., Brit.* II. No. 6105, Street-door latches.

streetful ('striːtfʊl). Pl. **streetfuls** (less correctly **streets-full**). [f. STREET *sb.* + -FUL.] As much or as many as a street will hold.

1837 CARLYLE *Fr. Rev.* III. i. ii, The dull street-lamps disclose only streetfuls of haggard countenances. **1846** DICKENS *Pict. Italy, Rome* 177 The carriages.. showing, the whole street-full, through the storm of flowers. **1901** A. BIRRELL in *N. Amer. Rev.* Feb. 252 Majuba Hill made Tories in streetfuls. **1914** J. C. COX in *Antiquary* (1915) XI. 17/2 The University and Library [of Louvain were] obliterated, and streets-full of houses destroyed by wanton and deliberate incendiaries.

street-keeper. A parish or district official appointed to keep order in the streets. See also quot. 1858.

1728 J. CHAMBERLAYNE *St. Gt. Brit.* II. (ed. 29) 159 Thomas Cowdell, Robert Davis, Street-Keepers. **1837** DICKENS *Pickw.* xli, I think I can see him now, a coming up the Strand between the two street-keepers, a little sobered by the bruising, [etc.]. **1858** SIMMONDS *Dict. Trade, Street-keeper*, a street-ward; a beadle having the charge of a private street or thoroughfare. **1887** *Pall Mall Gaz.* 10 Oct. 7/2 The Wandsworth District Board of Works has confirmed the appointment of the street-keeper for a further period of three months.

streetless ('striːtlɪs), *a.* [-LESS.] Destitute of streets, having no street or streets.

1883 *Sat. Rev.* 28 Apr. 529 The main body of the old town [Yarmouth] is absolutely streetless.

streetlet ('striːtlɪt). [f. STREET *sb.* + -LET.] A diminutive street.

a **1552** LELAND *Itin.* (1769) VII. 106 Selwood.. had thought to have reedified the Townelet with mene Houses.. whereof yn deade he made but one Streatelet. **1855** *Fraser's Mag.* LI. 575 There were enough of them in that streetlet alone to rig out all Paris. **1890** *Temple Bar* Oct. 159 The narrow streetlets are full of.. Easterns.

streetman ('striːtmən). [f. STREET *sb.* + MAN *sb.*]

†**1.** An official appointed for the good government of the streets of London. *Obs.*

1720 STRYPE *Stow's Surv.* v. xviii. II. 286/1 [The Court of Common Council in 1665 ordered] the said President and Governors [of Christ's Hospital] to have Power.. to nominate and appoint Streetmen,.. to be Overseers of the said Carmen; to see and take care, that Merchants and other Citizens Goods be well and faithfully delivered at the Rates and Prices, without any Exactions, Hindrance or Disturbance. **1766** ENTICK *Lond.* IV. 179 They have also three servants, which they call street-men, that see to the well government of the carts of London.

2. a. A man working in the street.

1894 *Critic* (U.S.) 15 Sept. p. iv/3 Full history of Tree and sample Jumping Bean to Agents or Streetmen 25 Cents.

b. A petty criminal who works 'on the street', esp. as a pickpocket or drug pedlar. *U.S. slang.*

1908 'O. HENRY' *Gentle Grafter* 161 I'd like to shake hands with Parley-voo Pickens, the greatest street man in the West. **1974** *Publishers Weekly* 21 Jan. 80/3 He is playing partner to the pusher whose street man is keeping the girl hooked. **1981** W. H. HALLAHAN *Trade* ii. 41 They were the perfect team, the tough street man and the elegant boardroom manipulator.

stree'tology. *Obs. rare.* [f. STREET *sb.* + -OLOGY.] Science or knowledge of the streets of a town. Hence **streeto'logical** *a.*, of or pertaining to streetology.

1837 (*title*) Streetology of London. *Ibid.* 9 The collector of these streetological sketches. **1845** FORD *Handbk. Spain* I. 246 The streetology is difficult, the town is a labyrinth of lanes each of which resembles the other.

street-orderly. A street-sweeper or scavenger. Also *Comb.*, as ***street-orderly boy, system***; **street-orderly bin**, an iron box erected by the side of the street, for the reception of refuse.

1851 MAYHEW *Lond. Labour* II. 257 The street-orderly system of scavaging. *Ibid.* 259 The first appearance of the street-orderlies in the metropolis was in 1843. **1894** Street-orderly bin [see ORDERLY *a.* 5]. **1907** *Westm. Gaz.* 22 Oct. 10/2 The street-orderly boys are to undergo a medical examination before being placed on the establishment.

Hence **street-orderlyism**, the system of employing street-orderlies for scavenging.

1851 MAYHEW *Lond. Labour* II. 257 The system called Street-Orderlyism.

street-walker.

1. One who walks in the street.

1618 MYNSHUL *Ess. Prison* 29 The Maister of a Prison is the *primum mobile*, in that euerlasting motion (a Iayle) and those key-turners, and street-walkers, are the petty and necessary slauish wheeles. **1673** [R. LEIGH] *Transp. Reh.* 33 To follow our Street-walker with a full Cry of Boys and Women at his heels. **1737** SWIFT *Proposal Badges Beggars* Wks. 1738 VI. 161 But all Street-walkers, and Shop-keepers, bear an equal Share in this hourly Vexation. **1872** W. READE *Martyrdom Man* 497 Athens, where the milestones are master-pieces, and the street-walkers poets and philosophers.

2. *spec.* A common prostitute whose field of operations is the street.

1592 GREENE *Discov. Coosenage* C 3 b, They shold see how these street walkers wil iet in rich garded gowns. **1721** AMHERST *Terræ Fil.* No. 28. 150 Common strumpets, and mercenary street-walkers. **1762** JOHNSON *Let.* 21 Dec. in *Boswell*, Mr. Levet has married a street-walker. **1828** LANDOR *Imag. Conv., Richelieu, Cotes*, etc., Wks. 1846 I. 301 Lady Fosset.. had been a street-walker, a kept mistress, and an actress. *a* **1870** BUCHANAN *Poems, Pan* Epil. 31 On rainy nights thy breath blows chill In the street-walker's dripping hair. **1894** STEAD *If Christ came to Chicago* 368 Where arbitrary power of arrest is given.. the street-walker proves a great revenue to the policeman.

Similarly **street-walking** *vbl. sb.* and *ppl. a.*

1752 FIELDING *Amelia* I. ii, The Justice.. declaring she was guilty within the statute of Street-walking, ordered her to Bridewell for a month. **1767** WILKES *Corr.* (1805) III. 144, I spoke of street-walking publishers, whom it would be ridiculous in government to take up. *c* **1770** in *Satir. Songs Costume* (Percy Soc.) 248 For so much as the street-walking hussies They will have their hair drest you see. **1824** SCOTT *Redgauntlet* ch. xiv, Jess Cantrips.. had the honour to be transported to the plantations, for street-walking and pocket-picking.

†**street-ward**, *sb. Obs.* [f. STREET *sb.* + WARD *sb.*] The office of guarding the streets; the market-dues payable to the holder of this office.

1202 in *Cal. Charter Rolls* (1903) I. 257 Quieti de geldis.. et de shirys et hundredis, et de sectis eorum infra burgum et extra, et de stretwardis, et de omnibus placitis. **15..** in Dugdale *Monast. Angl.* (1661) II. 187/2 Præterea idem Comes dedit præfato Nigello Constabulario suo, le Strete-ward in nundinis Cestriæ & Marketzell in omni terra pertinente ad honorem de Haulton. *Ibid.*, Et valent per annum le Streteward & le Marketzeld xviii.s. & ob.

streetward ('stri:twəd), *a.* and *adv.* [f. STREET *sb.* + -WARD.] **a.** *adv.* Towards the street. Also in phr. †*to the streetward.* **b.** *adj.* Facing or opening on the street.

1596 *Manch. Court Leet Rec.* (1885) II. 116 No Inhabitante.. shall make or suffer any myddinge within this towne to the streetewarde. **1642** HOWELL *For. Trav.* (Arb.) 25 Let his Chamber be street ward. **1656** HEYLIN *Surv. France* 70 The buildings.. are.. very handsomely and uniformely set out to the street-ward. **1864** TENNYSON *En. Arden* 170 Their little streetward sitting-room. **1866** MISS G. JEWSBURY in *Carlyle's Remin.* (1881) II. 301 He.. made for the streetward entrance into the Park. **1873** MORRIS *Love is enough* 22 He gained the gate that gave streetward.

streetway ('stri:tweɪ). A paved road or highway, the roadway of a street. Now only *poet.*

1610 HOLLAND *Camden's Brit.* I. 64 These causeys or Street-waies, the Romanes called Vias Consulares &c. **1686** PLOT *Staffordsh.* 401 There remains in the Lane upon the north side of the street-way some small fragments of a wall. **1735** J. PRICE *Stone-Br. Thames* 4 The Foot-way to be.. paved with Perbeck Squares, and the Coach, or Street-way, with the best Pebbles. **1871** TENNYSON *Last Tourn.* 140 Down a streetway hung with folds of pure White samite.

streety ('stri:tɪ), *a.* [f. STREET *sb.* + -Y.] Of, pertaining to, or characteristic of the streets. Cf. EARTHY *a.* 6.

1857 DICKENS *Dorrit* I. vi, His son began.. to be of the prison prisonous and of the street streety. **1887** F. W. ROBINSON *In Bad Hands* I. 25 A street figure that was very streety.

Strega ('streɪgə). The proprietary name of a kind of Italian liqueur flavoured with orange; a drink or glassful of this.

1910 *Trade Marks Jrnl.* 19 Jan. 104 Liquore Strega. Liqueurs. The firm trading as Ditta Giuseppe Alberti. **1920** D. H. LAWRENCE *Lost Girl* xvi. 358 Pancrazio took her to the place where she could drink coffee and a strega. **1922** —— *Aaron's Rod* xiv. 203 The waiter rattled off a list, beginning with Strega and ending with cherry brandy. **1938** E. AMBLER *Cause for Alarm* iv. 63, I found.. an empty Strega bottle. **1948** W. S. MAUGHAM *Here & There* 25, I ordered coffee and strega, which is the best liqueur they make in Italy. **1974** K. CLARK *Another Part of Wood* v. 179 The only penalty was that the meal traditionally ended with quantities of Strega, which gave one a sore head the next day.

streght(e, strehte: see STRAIGHT, STRAIT, STRETCH *v.*

†**streiche**, *a. Sc. Obs. rare*⁻¹. [? repr. OE. *stræc* rigid.] Stiff, affected.

1500-20 DUNBAR *Poems* xviii. 32 And be I ornat in my speiche Than Towsy sayis, I am so streiche, I speik not lyk thair houss menȝie.

streict(e, obs. ff. STRAIT.

streight(e: see STRAIGHT, STRAIT, STRETCH.

streigne, streignour: see STRAIN, STRAINER.

streiht(e: see STRAIGHT, STRAIT, STRETCH.

strein(e, obs. forms of STRAIN.

†**streinant.** *Obs. rare.* [app. a. OF. *estraignant* (one example), denoting some kind of musical note.] App. a musical note written with two stems; a breve. Cf. STRENE *sb.*²

c **1325** in *Rel. Ant.* I. 292 Ʒet ther is a streinant [*printed* streiuant] witz to longe tailes.

streinght, streinþ(e, obs. ff. STRENGTH.

†**streit**, *a. Obs. rare*⁻¹. [ad. L. *strictus*, pa. pple. of *stringĕre* to draw (a sword).

The form is due to the confusion of this L. *strictus* with the etymologically distinct *strictus* bound, drawn tight, which was known to be represented by *streit*, STRAIT *a.*]

Of a sword: Drawn.

c **1386** CHAUCER *Nun's Pr. T.* 537 Whan Ylion Was wonne, and Pirrus with his streite [*v.rr.* streyte, streighte, streiȝt, streiht] swerd Whan he hadde hent kyng Priam by the berd And slayn hym.

streit(e, streith, obs. ff. STRAIGHT, STRAIT.

streitch, obs. form of STRETCH.

strek(e: see STREAK, STRECK, STREEK, STRIKE.

strelitz ('strɛlɪts). *Hist.* Forms: *sing.* 7 strelits, 7, 9 strelitz, often incorrectly as pl.; *pl.* 7 strelsey, strelsies, strelitzi, 7, 9 strelitzes. [a. Russian *strⁱeˈlets*, archer (pl. *strⁱeltsy*), agent-n. f. *strⁱelyatⁱ* to shoot with the bow, f. *strⁱela* arrow.] A soldier belonging to a body of Russian troops composed of infantry raised by the Tsar Ivan the Terrible (1533–84) and abolished by Peter the Great in 1682. Also *attrib.*

1603 R. JOHNSON *Kingd. & Commw.* 155, 5000 attend aboute the citty of Mosco, or where the emperour shall abide, and two thousande, Stremaney Strelsey, or gunners at the stirroppe, aboute his owne person. **1662** J. DAVIES tr. *Olearius' Voy. Ambass.* 7 Our Musketiers, or Strelits. *Ibid.* 78 The Strelitz, who are spying up and down. *a* **1670** [S. COLLINS] *Pres. St. Russia* (1671) 111 With these he [the Czar] pays his Strelsies or Janzaries. **1799** W. TOOKE *View Russian Emp.* II. 471 Without mentioning the strelitzes. **1833** R. PINKERTON *Russia* 300 The officers and common soldiers of the Strelitzi. **1841** *Penny Cycl.* XX. 259/1 The first acts of his [*sc.* Ivan IV, 1533–84] reign were the institution of the corps of Strelitzes (archers), the first regular army of Russia. **1841** MOTLEY *Corr.* (1889) I. iv. 112 Peter the Great disbanded and annihilated the Strelitz or Russian janissaries. **1904** WHISHAW *Tiger of Muscovy* xxxi, A Strelitz soldier lay sleeping at the door leading to the corridor... To the Strelitz the Tsar said: 'Go quickly,.. and follow the Boyar Nagoy.'

Strelitzia (strəˈlɪtsɪə). Also **strelitza.** [f. *Strelitz* (after Charlotte of Mecklenburg-Strelitz, queen to Geo. III) + -IA.] A genus of herbaceous plants (N.O. *Musaceæ*), natives of S. Africa; also a plant of this genus.

1789 AITON *Hortus Kewensis* I. 285 Strelitzia... Canna-leav'd Strelitzia. Nat. of the Cape of Good Hope. Introd. 1773, by Sir Joseph Banks, Bart. **1836** A. F. GARDINER *Journ. Zoolu Country* i. 17 We slept well under the shade of some strelitza trees (very similar to wild banana). **1902** *Pall Mall Mag.* June 252/1 Occasional tree ferns and strelitzias.. are a reminder that.. the country is in the tropics.

streme, stremer, obs. ff. STREAM, STREAMER.

strenable, -bylle, obs. ff. STRAINABLE.

strend(e, var. ff. STRIND, generation.

†**strene**, *sb.*¹ *Obs. rare.* [Origin and meaning obscure.]

1531 *Privy Purse Exp. Hen. VIII* (1827) 151 Paied to one that brought a strene to the vyne fro pexhalles house, xl s.

†**strene**, *sb.*² or *a. Mus. Obs.* [? Corruption of STREINANT.] *strene note*: a term applied to the breve.

In the figure subjoined to the passage quoted, the breve has the form of a black slanting oblong with a stem pendent from each end. Cf. the quot. s.v. STREINANT.

1550 MARBECK *Bk. Com. Praier noted* A ij, The first note is a strene note and is a breue. The second a square note, and is a semy breue. The iii. a pycke and is a mynymme... The iiii. is a close.

strene, *v. Obs.* exc. *north.* Forms: 1 (**ʒe-)streónan, striénan, strénan, strínan, (ʒe)strýnan,** 2 **(i)streonen, (ȝe)strenen, (ȝe)strienen,** 2–4 **strenen,** 3–4 **streonen,** (3 **streonien),** 4 **strene,** 9 *dial.* **strain, strene.** [OE. (*ʒe*)*striénan*: see STRAIN *sb.*¹]

†**1.** *trans.* To beget, procreate (offspring). Also with *forth*: To propagate (one's kind). *Obs.*

In OE. also to gain, acquire, which seems to be the primary sense.

c **893** ÆLFRED *Oros.* IV. i. §3 Þa.. sceoldon be heora wifum bearna strienan. *c* **1000** *Ags. Gosp.* Matt. i. 6 Iudas ʒestrynde phares. *a* **1175** *Cott. Hom.* 225 Heo and his wif þa bearn ȝestriende. *c* **1200** *Trin. Coll. Hom.* 19 Ure helende crist is his onlepi sune noht after chesunge ac after strene for þan he him strende, alse þe sunne streneð liht. *c* **1200** *Ormin* 28 Forr all follc wass þatt illke streon þatt Adam haffde strenedd. *c* **1205** LAY. 2502 [Locrine] þe streonede Abren vppen Astrild. *c* **1220** *Bestiary* 609 in *O.E. Misc.* 19 And behinden he hem sampnen ðanne he sulen oðre strenen. *a* **1225** *Ancr. R.* 210 Þeo þet.. ei þing dude hwarðuruh no childe ne schulde beon of hire istreoned. *a* **1300** *Havelok* 2983 Him stondes wel þat god child strenes. *c* **1320** *Cast. Love* 1380 Hou he is Fader ȝe schullen i-heren, And hou we alle of him i-streoned weren. **1393** LANGL. *P. Pl.* C. XIV. 172 And whan þe pocok caukede þer-of ich took kepe, How vn-corteisliche þe cok hus kynde forth strenede.

fig. a **1225** *Ancr. R.* 234 Sikernesse streoneð ȝemeleaste.

†**b.** *absol. Obs.*

c **1175** *Lamb. Hom.* 133 Nis na stude to istreone bicumelic butan ða þe istreonieð beon bispused rihtliche to gedere. *c* **1300** *E.E. Psalter* lxxii. 27 Þou forlest alle saufe to be þat strenen with-outen þe [L. *perdidisti omnes, qui fornicantur abs te*]. **13..** *K. Alis.* 7057 Withoute lost of synne they streoneth. *c* **1315** SHOREHAM *Poems* I. 2006 Ac ȝyf þat on þoþren warneþ hys flesch, Ne myȝt[e] hy naut strene.

2. *intr.* Of dogs, etc.: To copulate. Also *trans.* (see quot. 1728). (See *Eng. Dial. Dict.*)

a **1728** WHITE KENNETT (E.D.D.) A dog streneth a bitch. [Durham.] **1820** WILBRAHAM *Chesh. Gloss.* 63 *Strain v.* expressive of the union of the sexes in the canine race. **1847** HALLIWELL, *Strain*, to copulate, said of the cat. *Ibid.*, *Strene*, to copulate, said of a dog. *Durh.*

Hence **'strening** *vbl. sb.*

c **1230** *Hali Meid.* 47, I þe streonunge þrof, is on earst hire flesch wið þat fulðe ituked. *c* **1315** SHOREHAM *Poems* I. 2003 Þat oþer godnesse hys strenyng, þer me may children wene. *c* **1320** *Cast. Love* 1389 Adam.. Fleschliche streoned vs euerichon, Ac þulke fleschliche streonynge Beere vs bale.

streng, obs. or dial. f. STRING; dial. f. STRONG *a.*

†**'strenger**, *a.* and *adv. Obs.* Forms: 1 **strengra, (strencra, strængra),** 3 **strengre,** 3–5 **strenger,** 4–5 **-ere,** 4 **strengor.** [OE. *strẹngra* (neut. *-re*):—OTeut. **straŋgizon-* compar. of **straŋgo-* STRONG *a.*] **A.** *adj.* Stronger (in various senses: see STRONG *a.*).

c **888** ÆLFRED *Boeth.* xxiv. §3 We wenað ðæt mon bio þy strencra [*Bodl. MS.* strængra] þe he bið micel on his lichoman. *Ibid.* xxxii. §1 Þeah ðu nu wære.. strengra þonne leo. *a* **1225** *Ancr. R.* 326 Þe wunde þet euer wurseð an hond, & strengre is forte helen. *a* **1300** *Cursor M.* 4298 Hert o stele, and bodi o brass, Strenger þen euer sampson was. *a* **1400** *Minor Poems fr. Vernon MS.* l. 523 Ofte we seon the strengor falle Thorw him that feblore was. **1426** LYDG. *De Guil. Pilgr.* 8260, I am nat strengere than dauyd was.

B. *adv.* More strongly.

1340 *Ayenb.* 170 Þe ilke þet.. is.. ine þise viȝtinge: heþ more strenger to done.. him-zelue to werie. **1382** WYCLIF *Exod.* xxxix. 19 That the coope and the breest broche streyt myȝten be knyt togidere to the girdil, and with rynges strengere cowplid.

Hence †**'strengerly** *adv.*, more strongly.

a **1390** *Prol. Job* in *Wyclif Bible* II. 671 As if thou woldest an eel.. holde with streite hondis, how myche strengerli thou thristis, so myche the sunnere it shal sliden awey.

†**'strengest**, *a. Obs.* [OE. *strẹngest*:—OTeut. **straŋgisto-*, superl. of **straŋgo-* STRONG *a.*] Strongest (see the senses of STRONG *a.*).

c **893** ÆLFRED *Oros.* III. x. (Sweet) 138 Feower þa strengstan þeoda. *a* **1225** *Ancr. R.* 280 Heo [*sc.* humility] is .. þinge strengest. *a* **1450** *Knt. de la Tour* xxxiv. 34 And thanne he required hem that the strengest hore of hem shulde smite furst the stroke. **1471** FORTESCUE *Wks.* (1869) 534 This is the strengyst argument that is made in the said boke. *c* **1489** CAXTON *Sonnes of Aymon* ix. 208 Ye made hym the castel of Mountalban vpon the strengest grounde that is wythin your royame. *c* **1500** *Melusine* vi. 33, I neuer sawe hym syn that the chasse was at the strengest.

†**strengh**, *sb. Obs.* Forms: 1 **strengo, strengu,** 3 **strenge,** 3–5 **strengh(e,** 5 **stryngh(e.** [OE. *strẹngu* wk. fem. = OS. (*megin*)*strengi*, OHG. *strengî*, *strangî* (MHG., mod.G. *strenge*):—OTeut. type **straŋgîn-*, f. **straŋgo-* STRONG *a.*] = STRENGTH *sb.*, in various senses.

1. The quality of being strong, whether in physical or immaterial senses.

Beowulf 1533 Wearp ða wundenmæl.. strenge ʒetruwode mundgripe mæʒenes. *Ibid.* 2540 Strengo ʒetruwode anes mannes. *c* **825** *Vesp. Psalter* xxxvii. 11 Heorte min ʒedroefed is in me & forleort mec strengu min. *c* **1205** LAY. 26690 Þa atstoden Rom-leoden mid ræȝe strenȝe [*sic*; *c* 1275 strengþe]. *c* **1250** *Gen. & Ex.* 714 Quor deades strenge warp him dun. *Ibid.* 3728 [God's] milce is mikel, is strenge is strong. *a* **1275** *Prov. Ælfred* 561 in *O.E. Misc.*, Gif.. þu ne moȝe mid srenghe þe selwen steren. *c* **1400** tr. *Secreta Secret., Gov. Lordsh.* 117 Brodnesse of thees and heles, bytoknys stryngh of body. *a* **1420** *Aunters of Arthur* 266 (Thornton MS.) Ʒoure kynge es to couetous..; Maye no mane stere hym of strenghe, whilles þe whele standis. **14..** in Parker *Dom. Archit.* (1859) III. 42 Then the strenghe of the streme astoned hem stronge.

b. Force, violence.

a **1300** *Cursor M.* 19323 Bot strengh nan did þai þam till, For þai come wit þaim al wit will. *c* **1300** *Leg. Gregory* (Schulz) 238 Sche swore, sche schuld hir neuer ȝeld, Bot he wiþ strenge hir wonne.

2. *concr.* **a.** An armed force. **b.** A fortified place.

?*a* **1400** *Morte Arth.* 2242 Thane the conquerour tuke kepe, and come with his strenghes To reschewe the ryche mene of the Rounde Table. *Ibid.* 1475. **1489** HEN. VII in *Paston Lett.* III. 358 The garnson of the towne of Concarnewe, which is oon of the grettest strenghes of all Bretayn, was besieged.

†**strengh**, *v. Obs.* Forms: 3–5 **streng(e, strengh(e,** (4 **strenghi),** 5 **strynghe(e.** [OE. **strẹngan* (cf. *ætstrẹngan* to deforce, withhold wrongfully):—prehistoric **strangjan*, f. *strang* STRONG *a.*

If the word had survived it would normally have become *stringe* in the south and *streng* or *string* in the north.]

trans. To make strong or stronger (in material or immaterial sense); to strengthen, confirm; to fortify, to reinforce.

a **1175** *Cott. Hom.* 237 And elc of ham [*sc.* laws] ȝestrenð & fulfellþ oðre. *c* **1200** *Ormin* 2614 For þild birrþ ben wiþþ iwhillc mahht To beoldenn itt & strengenn. *a* **1225** *St. Marher.* 14 Þis beoð þe wepnen.. þat strengeð ham stale-wardlukest aȝein me. *a* **1225** *Leg. Kath.* 717 Þeos meiden.. stod, þurh þeos steuene starcliche istrenget. *a* **1300** *Cursor M.* 18930 Þe fire es god to strengh þe tile. *c* **1315** SHOREHAM *Poems* I. 701 For bred strengeþ þe herte of man. *a* **1340** HAMPOLE *Psalter* xvii. 20 He reft me out fra my faes stalworthest,.. for þai ere strenghid [*confortati sunt*] abouen me. *Ibid.* lxvii. 31 Strenghi in the and conferme in vs.. that thou wroght in vs. *c* **1400** *Melayne* 1365 He comes at hande With men of armes a sexty thowsande, To strenghe with ȝone Cite. *c* **1400** tr. *Secreta Secret., Gov. Lordsh.* 82 Some þing strynghys and fattys þe body, some makys it megre and feble. *c* **1435** *Torr. Portugal* 113 Now god, þat Dyed appon a Rode, Strengithe hym bothe bone and blod, The fyld for to haue! *c* **1440** *Ps. Penit.* (1894) 18 Thei strenghed hem that my sowle sought.

Hence †**'strenghing** *vbl. sb.*

a **1300** *Cursor M.* 18678 Bot þair mistrouth.. Es strenghing of vr trouth to dai. **1535** in *Lett. Suppress. Monasteries* (Camden) 31 That ye had brought that tale unto him more for the strenghing and confirmation of your opinion then for any other thing els. *a* **1578** LINDESAY (Pitscottie) *Chron. Scot.* (S.T.S.) I. 62 So inordinatlie to promove his freindis to landis and lordschipis ffor the strenghen of his awin house.

†'**strenghfully**, *adv. Obs.* [f. STRENGH *sb.* + -FUL² + -LY².] With might or power.

13.. *Gosp. Nicod.* 155 Sykyr men haf þai soght at stere þam strenghefully [*Addit. MS.* myghtily].

strengite ('strɛŋaɪt). *Min.* [a. G. *strengit* (named after A. Streng): see -ITE.] Hydrous phosphate of iron, found as a drusy incrustation of a red colour.

1881 WATTS *Dict. Chem.* VIII. II. 1827. **1883** *Encycl. Brit.* XVI. 405/1.

strengle, obs. or *dial.* form of STRANGLE.

†'**strengly**, *adv. Obs.* Also 5 strengely. [Alteration of STRONGLY *adv.*, due to the influence of STRENGERLY.] = STRONGLY *adv.*

a **1425** tr. *Arderne's Treat. Fistula*, etc. 22 It byhoueþ noȝt to cure þe pacient with no cure bot cuttyng with yren, or fretyng with a threde strengely yfestned. **1435** MISYN *Fire of Love* 117 Oft-tyme we fall þat, be many casys taghtt, strenglyar we suld stand.

strength (strɛŋθ), *sb.* Forms: 1 strengðu, -o, strengð, strængð, strenð, strencð, *oblique cases* strengðe *etc.*, 2-3 strengðe, 2 streongðe, streangðe, 2-5 strengþe, 2-6 strengthe, 2 streinðe, 2 (5 *Sc.*) streinþe, 3 strencðe, strenncþe (*Orm.*), strenðe, 3-4 strencþe, strencth, 3-5 strenkþe, 3-7 strenth, 4 strenþe, strinth(e, (strennthe, streinþ, streinthe), 4-6 strenthe, 4 strenȝt, 4-5 strenkith, -keþ, (4 strenket, 5 strenkit, -kyght, 4, 6 *Sc.* strynth, (4 -the), 4-6 strenght, (4 strengheth), 5 strengþ, streynth(e, streynght, stryngth(e, (strengyth, strentht, streyngthe, strayngth, streyint, strynt), 5-6 strenghth, (6 stranghth, streinght, strycht, *Sc.* strainth, stryntht), 3- strength. [OE. *strengðu* str. fem. = OHG. *strengida*:—OTeut. type **straŋgiþō*, f. **straŋgo-* STRONG *a.*: see -TH¹ b.]

1. The quality or condition of being strong.

a. Power of action in body or limbs; ability to exert muscular force.

In 15-18th c. the plural was often used after a plural possessive.

a **1000** *Ags. Ps.* (Spelm.) cxlvi. 11 Na on strengðe horses willan habbað. **1297** R. GLOUC. (Rolls) 6136 Edmond vor is strengþe [*v.r.* strenge] was ycluped yrensyde. **1303** R. BRUNNE *Handl. Synne* 3047 3yf þou for strenkþe be mysproute, And hast bostful wrdys and loude. **1340** HAMPOLE *Pr. Consc.* 5898 Þe gudes of kynd er bodily strenthe,.. And delyvernes and bewte of body. *c* **1386** CHAUCER *Prol.* 84 Of his stature he was of euene lengthe And wonderly delyuere and of greet strengthe. *c* **1400** *Parce michi* 101 in *26 Pol. Poems* 146 Sampson loste hys streyngthe therfore. **14..** *Lat. & Eng. Prov.* (MS. Douce 52) 27 Strenghth mowes down þe medow. *c* **1470** *Gol. & Gaw.* 346 War al your strenthis in ane, In his grippis and ye gane, He wald ourcum yow ilkane. **1471** CAXTON *Recuyell* (Sommer) 242 He put hem a backe by naturell strength and force many tymes. **1577** GOOGE tr. *Heresbach's Husb.* I. 14 Some woorkes require strength more then skill. **1590** SPENSER *F.Q.* II. ii. 17 More huge in strength, then wise in workes he was. **1592** *Soliman & Pers.* I. iii. 5 Put Lambe-like mildenes to your Lyons strength. **1633** T. JAMES *Voy.* 49 We heaued to the vttermost of our strengths. **1661** BOYLE *Style of Script.* 248 The self same Nail must enter Lesse or Deeper according to the Strength of the Hand that Drives it in. **1719** DE FOE *Crusoe* I. (Globe) 123 Getting one [*sc.* a block of wood] as big as I had Strength to stir, I rounded it. **1732** B. ROBINSON *Anim. Oecon.* 101 A frequent Increase of this Force in Muscles much moved must of Necessity increase both their Magnitudes and Strengths. **1736** BUTLER *Anal.* I. iii. Wks. 1874 I. 62 Possibly the sum of the whole strength of brutes may be greater than that of mankind. **1817** SHELLEY *Rev. Islam* 2785 She grasped me with the strength Of madness. **1832** BREWSTER *Nat. Magic* x. 246 Dr. Desaguliers was convinced that his feats were exhibitions of skill and not of strength. **1868** *Field* 4 July 14/3 London rowed in very good form, but lacked strength and dash. **1888** F. HUME *Mme. Midas* I. Prol., You have strength, I have brains.

b. Bodily vigour in general; efficiency of the bodily powers; esp. in contrast with the weakness due to illness, fatigue, age, immaturity, etc.

†Also *collect. pl.* for *sing.*: cf. L. *vires*.

c **1000** ÆLFRIC *Hom.* II. 76 Swa swa se fulfremeda wæstm bið on fulre strencðe þeonde. **1362** LANGL. *P. Pl.* A. VIII. 83 Olde Men and hore þat helples beoþ of strengþe. *c* **1375** *Sc. Leg. Saints* xxi. (*Clement*) 438 Þe fadyr þane strynth cane tyne. In swonyng þane he fel flat brad. *Ibid.* xxxi. (*Eugenia*) 274 Fevrys.. þat trawalit hir hard & hat, & of strinthis mad hyr mat. **1490** CAXTON *Eneydos* xxviii. 108 Dydo.. thre tymes made her effort to reyse her self vpon her elbowe. But her strengthes.. myght not therto suffyse. **1544** BETHAM *Precepts War* I. clxiv. H vj b, Sparyng nothynge, yᵗ they may be healed and may haue theyr strength restored. **1597** SHAKS. *2 Hen. IV*, III. i. 42 It is but as a Body, yet distemper'd, Which to his former strength may be restor'd, With good aduice, and little Medicine. **1618** W. LAWSON *New Orch. & Gard.* (1626) 16, I haue knowne a tree tainted in setting, yet grow, and beare blossomes.. and yet for want of strength could neuer shape his fruit. **1662** J. DEGRAVERE *Thesaurus Remed.* (ed. 2) 35 The full Dose is the whole Medicine, for Men and Women of strength. **1725** N. ROBINSON *Th. Physick* 173 At last, after many Fits and much enduring, the Hands tremble, the Strength fails, and Spirits sink. **1748** in *Nairne Peerage Evid.* (1874) 125 You may.. assure Mrs. Brown that her son is recovering strength daily. **1776** *Trial of Nundocomar* 32/2 He has not strength to undergo any examination, after the fatigue of bringing him to court. **1860** TYNDALL *Glac.* I. xi. 79 My strength was gone, and.. I required to rest once more.

c. Power in general, whether physical, mental, or due to the possession of resources; ability for effective action; efficiency, vigour (of mental faculties, etc.).

a **1000** *Cædmon's Gen.* 950 (Gr.) Ac se weard [of Eden] hafað miht & strengðo. *a* **1225** *Leg. Kath.* 1014 Þat tu mahe stihen to understonden in him godes muchele strencðe. *c* **1320** *Cast. Love* 534 We [the Trinity] beoþ on in one fulnesse, In miht, in strengþe and in heiȝnesse. **138.** WYCLIF *Sel. Wks.* III. 478 Þer wittes ben þinne, þer strynthe littel, þer tyme schort, to study and teche holy writte. **1551** T. WILSON *Logic* Dj, The natural strength, is an aptnes of nature, geuen either to the body, or to the mynd. **1561** HOBY *Castiglione's Bk. Courtier* I. (1900) 28 To laye uppon me a burden that passeth my strengthe. **1562** *Aberd. Kirk. Sess. Rec.* (Spalding Club) 5 Quhow God suld be lowit,.. wirshipped allanerlie, with the haill man, saull, hart, mynd, mycht, and stryncht. **1616** B. JONSON *Devil an Ass* I. i. 24 Foolish feind, Stay i' your place, know your owne strengths, and put not Beyond the spheare of your actiuity. **1662** GUNNING *Lent Fast* 51 As Nazianzen above attemperating his example to our strength. **1759** JOHNSON *Rasselas* viii, Discovering in me great strength of memory and quickness of apprehension. **1779** *Mirror* No. 19 The natural strength of his understanding. **1838** DICKENS *Nich. Nick.* xxii, You could write us a piece to bring out the whole strength of the company. **1859** J. MARTINEAU *Ess.* (1866) I. 73 So far we think Mr. Mill's strength as great here as elsewhere. **1894** LIDDON *Life Pusey* I. i. 32 His strength lay in accurate verbal scholarship rather than in philosophy.

d. Capacity for moral effort or endurance; firmness (of mind, character, will, purpose); power to resist temptation or fulfil a difficult duty; †fortitude as one of the cardinal virtues. Freq. in phr. ***strength of character***.

in one's own strength: in reliance on oneself and not on divine grace.

c **900** *Bæda's Hist.* I. ix. [xii.] (1890) 46 Achi.. lærdon þæt hi him.. modes strengðo naman. *c* **1000** ÆLFRIC *Hom.* I. 44 Þa wearð se eadiȝa Stephanus mid Godes ȝife, and mid micelre strencðe afylled. *c* **1175** *Lamb. Hom.* 155 Ah ure drihten.. ȝeue us mihte and streinðe. *c* **1200** ORMIN 5519 Þe feorþe ȝife off Haliȝ Gast Iss strenncþe ȝæn þe deofell. *c* **1320** *Cast. Love* 801 Foure vertues cardinals [þat] beoþ; þat is, strengþe and sleihschupe, Rihtfulnesse and worschupe. *a* **1350** *S. Lucy* 155 in Horstm. *Altengl. Leg.* (1881) 18 Swilk strenkith god sent to hir. *c* **1374** CHAUCER *Boeth.* I. pr. iv. (1868) 13 Þo I þat hadde gadered strenkeþ in my corage answerede and seide [etc.]. *c* **1386** —— *Pars. T.* 728 Agayns this horrible synne of Accidie.. ther is a vertu, that is called fortitudo or strengthe. **1526** *Pilgr. Perf.* (W. de W. 1531) 138 The more perfytly the lyght of goostly strength shall shyne in vs. **1552** ABP. HAMILTON *Catech.* (1884) 8 Of hoip in our awin strenth. **1567** *Gude & Godlie Ballatis* (S.T.S.) 34 Faithfull is God, and on ȝow hes pietie, And will not thole ȝow temp[t]it for to be, Aboue ȝour strenth. **1592** SHAKS. *Rom. & Jul.* IV. i. 72 If.. Thou hast the strength of will to slay thy selfe. **1636** B. JONSON *Discov.* init., He knows not his own strength, that hath not met adversity. **1675** J. OWEN *Indwelling Sin* x. (1732) 116 This therefore ought a Believer diligently to attend unto, namely, That every thing he doth to God, be done in the Strength of Christ. **1779** COWPER *Human Frailty* 19 A stranger to superior strength, Man vainly trusts his own. **1836** J. H. NEWMAN *Parochial Sermons* III. i. 3 Of course men who make such sacrifices, often evidence much strength of character in making them. **1855** TENNYSON *Will* 11 But ill for him who, bettering not with time, Corrupts the strength of heaven-descended Will. **1863** N. HAWTHORNE *Our Old Home* I. 74, I have not found reason to suppose that the English dowager of fifty has actually greater courage, fortitude, and strength of character than our woman of similar age. **1902** VIOLET JACOB *Sheep-Stealers* xiii, Her overwrought mind was beginning to feel the influence of his quiet strength of purpose. **1919** G. B. SHAW *Heartbreak House* II. 52 You know, Ellie has remarkable strength of character. I think it is because I taught her to like Shakespear when she was very young. **1957** *Oxf. Dict. Chr. Ch.* 583/2 It was owing to Gregory, in whom firmness and strength of character were tempered by gentleness and charity, that many of these evils were conquered. **1975** *Economist* 15 Mar. 38/3 Mike Denness had the job sewn up after his batting performances against India last summer... His batting efforts.. show his strength of character.

pl. **1653** JER. TAYLOR *Serm. Golden Grove, Winter* v. 65 [Want of attendance to the sense and intention of our prayers] is only so remedyed as our prayers are made zealous, and our infirmities passe into the strengths of the Spirit.

e. Power of contending in warfare; now chiefly, military power derived from numbers, equipment, or resources.

a **1122** *O.E. Chron.* (Laud. MS.) an. 1106, Ac seo streongðe & se siȝe wearð þæs cynges. *c* **1175** *Lamb. Hom.* 13 Ah ic eou ȝife siȝe and streinþe. *a* **1200** *Vices & Virtues* 27 Ac ne mai non senne ne non dieuel habben strengþe aȝean ðessere gode ileaue. *c* **1250** *Owl & Night.* 1713 For mony mon myd speres orde haueþ lutle strengþe & mid his schelde, Ah naþeles in one felde [etc.]. *a* **1400-50** *Wars Alex.* 1013 [The old knights say] We may noȝt stand now in stede oure strenth is [to] febill. *c* **1400** MAUNDEV. (Roxb.) xv. 69 By cause of ȝour ill liffing.. and noȝt of oure strenth Godd has giffen it intill oure handes. *c* **1425** *Eng. Conq. Ireland* (1896) 96 Men that.. yn so fele Anguysshes with vs hath your streynth assayed, cometh forth, men! **1474** CAXTON *Chesse* IV. ii. (1883) 168 For yf he [*sc.* the king] be taken or ded or ellis Inclusid and shette vp alle the strengthes of alle other faylle and alle Is fynyshid and loste. *c* **1511** *1st Eng. Bk. Amer.* (Arb.) Introd. p. xxxiii/2 For if they sholde come out by there strength and hardynesse the[y] wolde conquere all the worlde. **1525** BERNERS *Froiss.* II. ccxi. 270 b, They were desyrous to proue their strengthes agaynst the Christen men. **1592** KYD *Span. Trag.* I. iv. 15 Their fight was long,.. Their strength alike, their strokes both dangerous. **1598** GRENEWEY *Tacitus, Ann.* XI. v. (1622) 146 Declaring that the ancient liberty of Germany was taken from them, and that the Roman strength mastered all. **1792** *Anecd. W. Pitt* III. xxxix. 51 If our people are united.. we have an internal strength sufficient to repel any foreign invasion. **1818** J. T. JONES *Acc. War Sp. & Portugal* 423 Buonaparte was yet in strength to make face against the united armies of the remainder of Europe.

f. In a fortification, fortified place, etc.: Power of withstanding assault or capture.

c **1375** *Sc. Leg. Saints* xxxiii. (*George*) 67 He entre mycht nocht, for gret strinth & hicht of wal & gret ȝemesel of ȝettis al. **1523** BERNERS *Froiss.* I. cccxciii. 274 Within the towne there was a mynster.. the whiche they of the countrey had fortefyed, and there in they were, in trust of the strenght of yᵉ place. **1562** WINȜET *Cert. Tractatis* Wks. (S.T.S.) I. 37 Quhat strenth had his armour of defence thair. **1585** T. WASHINGTON tr. *Nicholay's Voy.* I. viii. 9 Enquiring of him what strength the tower might be of. **1591** SHAKS. *1 Hen. VI*, III. iv. 7 This Arme, that hath reclaym'd To your obedience .. seuen walled Townes of strength. **1617** MORYSON *Itin.* II. 20 To the natural strength of the place is added the art of interlacing the low bowes, and casting the bodies of trees acrosse the way. **1794** MRS. RADCLIFFE *Myst. Udolpho* xxxi, 'But they know not,' thought she, 'its strength, or the armed numbers within it' [the castle]. **1820** SCOTT *Monast.* xxxv, He questioned him.. concerning the Baron of Avenel's probable forces—the strength of his castle [etc.]. **1842** BORROW *Bible in Spain* xxxiv, Llanes is an old town, formerly of considerable strength.

g. In things, material or immaterial: Operative power; capacity for producing effects.

c **1000** *Sax. Leechd.* I. 114 Wið attres strenðe ȝenim þas wyrte. *a* **1225** *Leg. Kath.* 649 Lauerd.. ȝef swuch mahte & strengðe i mine wordes þat þeo.. moten missen þrof. *c* **1400** MAUNDEV. (Roxb.) xxvi. 125 My worde sall be of als grete strenth, and als scharpe and scherand, as my swerde. *c* **1440** *Generydes* 6821 In strenthe or [? *read* of] erbys that ben profeitable, In them I knowe the vertu that is sure. **1569** UNDERDOWN *Ovid's Invect. Ibis* Pref. A v b, There is no poyson, to the poyson of a Serpente, no strength, to the strength of Gunpouder. **1590** SHAKS. *Mids. N.* III. ii. 250 Thy threats haue no more strength then her weak praise [*Theobald* prayers]. **1611** —— *Wint. T.* IV. iv. 124 Pale Prime-roses, That dye vnmarried, ere they can behold Bright Phœbus in his strength. **1680** MOXON *Mech. Exerc.* xii. 205 And by the force and strength of the Wedge, the whole Drill-bench is drawn down, and fastned athwart the Cleeks of the Lathe. **1695** WOODWARD *Nat. Hist. Earth* VI. (1723) 294 The Sun.. (to speak in the Phrase of the Vulgar, ..) hath gain'd a greater Strength. **1732** POPE *Ess. Man* II. 67 Most strength the moving principle requires; Active its task, it prompts, impels, inspires. **1781** COWPER *Flatting Mill* 4 When a bar of pure silver.. is.. roll'd In an engine of utmost mechanical strength. **1817** SHELLEY *Rev. Islam* 1569 Great is the strength Of words. **1882** G. M. MINCHIN *Unipl. Kinematics* vi. 167 The time rate of supply of liquid through the source is called the strength of the source.

†**h.** Validity, legal force. *to bear strength*: to be in force. *to stand in its strength*: to remain valid. *Obs.*

c **1418** LYDG. *Troy-bk.* IV. 342 But wher so be þat he be lef or loth, þer is no more; but in conclusioun, In his [= its] strengþe stood þe eleccioun. **1423** *Rolls of Parlt.* IV. 256/1 That this ordynaunce stretche and bere strenketh also wel wyth in Chesshire. **1439** *E.E. Wills* (1882) 122 Annuites.., wiche he will that thei stande yn their strenketh. **1448** in Willis & Clark *Cambridge* (1886) II. 9 Then the forseid obligacion.. stand in non strenketh nor effect, and elles yef hit be not fulfilled that then hit stand in strenketh and vertu. **1450** *Rolls of Parlt.* V. 186/2 That oure Graunt.. be not prejudiced nor hurt, but stande in his strenght. **1538** *Extracts Aberd. Reg.* (1844) I. 159 And this my petitioune, be way of reconuentioune to haf the strynth of ane borght, gyf neid beis. **1579** TOMSON *Calvin's Serm. Tim.* 2/2 This rule.. whiche shal remaine of strength vnto the worldes end. **1690** in *Nairne Peerage Evid.* (1874) 27 The haill.. provisions.. are declared to stand.. in their full force strenth and effect.

i. Power to sustain the application of force without breaking or yielding.

c **1384** CHAUCER *H. Fame* 1980 And loo thys hous of which I write.. Alle was the tymber of no strengthe Yet hit is founded to endure. **1667** MILTON *P.L.* I. 427 Spirits.. Not ti'd or manacl'd with joynt or limb, Nor founded on the brittle strength of bones. **1727** CHAMBERS tr. *Le Clerc's Treat. Archit.* 23 Were we only to have regard to the Laws of Strength and Weakness, we shou'd diminish the Entablements of Columns that have Pedestals, rather than those which have none. **1763** MILLS *Pract. Husb.* IV. 217 The bass used for this, or for any other binding, should be taken from a sound mat, and be soaked in water for some hours, to increase it's strength. **1839** *Penny Cycl.* XV. 48/2 The strength of materials in resisting the strains to which they are subject. **1841** *Civil Engin. & Arch. Jrnl.* IV. 79 Tables.. to facilitate the computation of the strength and dimensions of Girders, Bressummers, [etc.]. **1842** GWILT *Archit.* §1624 The primitive horizontal or transverse Strength of Oak is taken at 1000; its supporting or primitive vertical Strength at 807; and its cohesive or absolute Strength at 1821. **1876** VOYLE & STEVENSON *Milit. Dict.* 427/2 Tensile strength as applied to iron, is its power to resist being torn asunder by a force exerted.. in the direction of its length. **1883** M. P. BALE *Saw-Mills* 191 The strength of best oxhide belts, used for belting, has been calculated at about 3,086 lbs. per square inch of section. **1884** SARGENT *Rep. Forests N. Amer.* 252 The specimens tested for the purpose of determining the strength of the wood produced by the different trees.

fig. **1662** STILLINGFL. *Orig. Sacræ* I. i. §20 If Procopius his pillar hath strength enough to bear such a conjecture.

j. Intensity and active force (of movement, wind, fire, a stream, current of electricity, or the like); intensity (of a physical condition, colour, sound, etc.). In *Telecommunications* also with following numeral, indicating signal strength as shown on a meter. † ***with strength***: violently.

c **1275** *Passion of our Lord* 499 in *O.E. Misc.* 51 He schef hit [*sc.* the spear] myd strenkþe þat to his heorte hit com. **1340** HAMPOLE *Pr. Consc.* 3106 For þe fire here, of strenth es les þan þe fire of purgatory es. *c* **1430** *Hymns Virgin* (1867) 120 Thorowe the strength off þe wynd Into the Welken hitt [the sea] schall slynge. *c* **1440** *Alphabet of Tales* (1904) 96

With strenthe of hur lowpyng þe bote drownyd. **1480** *Rob. Devyll* 334 in Hazl. *E.P.P.* I. 232 So swyfte with strenght Robert dyd come, That hys speare ran thorowe the knyghtes bodye. *a* **1593** MARLOWE *Ovid's Eleg.* I. ii. 11, I saw a brandisht fire encrease in strength. **1705** H. BLACKWELL *Engl. Fencing-Master* 8 For if a Thrust come to be forced, or with any Strength, the Parry is so narrow, that no Parade can be made. *a* **1719** ADDISON *Disc. Learning* Misc. Wks. 1914 II. 463 Thus has Time mellowed the Works of Antiquity, by qualifying, if I may so say, the Strength and Rawness of their Colours. **1727** P. WALKER *Semple* Biog. Presbyt. (1827) I. 159 He entred in, and the Strength of Water carried him and his Horse beneath the Foord. **1815** J. SMITH *Panorama Sci. & Art* II. 267 If the strength of the shock is found to give uneasiness, it may be moderated by [etc.]. *Ibid.* 757 The colour thus prepared produces a fine crimson, .. its strength may be increased by adding more of the oxide of gold. **1832** BREWSTER *Nat. Magic* vi. 138 The strength of the image of the Castle so far obscured the background, that it made no sensible impression on the observers. **1866** *Chamb. Encycl.* VIII. 7/2 The strength of the pulse depends chiefly on the force with which the blood is driven from the heart. **1873** J. C. MAXWELL *Electr. & Magn.* II. vii. 206 It is a homogeneous function of the second degree with respect to the strengths of the [electric] currents. **1914** *Rep. Brit. Assoc. Adv. Sci. 1913* 132 These instructions would include directions for simultaneous observations of .. the strength of the time-signals .. and the average strength and frequency of strays. **1923** *Radio Times* 28 Sept. 2/1 We can take the following as useful ranges from one of the main broadcasting stations for good strength on the head telephones. **1968** J. SANGSTER *Touchfeather* xvi. 188 He finally got the message, strength five. 'What do you want?' **1979** P. NIESEWAND *Member of Club* i. 6 'I've got them, but they're only hearing me strength two.'.. 'How do you hear them?' 'Strength five.'

k. Vigour, intensity (of feeling, conviction, etc.). Also, emphasis, positiveness (of refusal).

1550 COVERDALE *Spir. Perle* xxviii. (1560) 271 Faith.. receiueth increasement and more strength, through patience. **1596** SHAKS. *Merch. V.* v. i. 198 If you did know .. You would abate the strength of your displeasure. **1596** —— *1 Hen. IV.* I. iii. 25 Those Prisoners in your Highnesse [name] demanded Were .. not with such strength denied As was deliuered to your Maiesty. **1781** COWPER *Conversat.* 88 Opposition gives opinion strength.

l. Intensity of the specific property, or proportionate quantity of the active ingredient in a substance; potency (of drugs, liquors). Also, in particularized sense, a definite degree of strength.

1588 KYD *Househ. Philos.* Wks. (1901) 272, I speake of choyse wynes which get strength with age. **1653** T. BRUGIS *Vade Mecum* (ed. 2) 134 If you will put in gummes, .. you must boyle them very gently least they burn, and the strength vanish away. **1697** DRYDEN *Virg. Georg.* IV. 155 T'allay the Strength and Hardness of the Wine. **1790** *Act 30 Geo. III*, c. 37 §2 Spirits of any greater or higher Degree of Strength than that of One in Six under Hydrometer Proof. **1843** *Penny Cycl.* XXVII. 459/1 A wine is prepared which is green, and which becomes deeper by time, while the strength increases so much, that [etc.]. **1851-3** TOMLINSON *Cycl. Useful Arts* (1867) II. 29/2 A mixture of lime and water of 3 or 4 different strengths. **1904** *Knowledge* Mar. 43/2 This difference of price is due to the greater 'strength' of the flour .. meaning by 'strength' the capacity to make more and larger loaves for equal weights of flour used. **1907** J. A. HODGES *Elem. Photogr.* (ed. 6) 151 A developer of normal strength.

m. Of soil: Firmness.

1573-80 TUSSER *Husb.* (1878) 49 The straw and the eare to haue bignes and length, betokeneth land to be good and in strength. **1707** MORTIMER *Husb.* 42 Ploughs .. must be great or small according to the depth and strength of the Soil you Plow. **1794** VANCOUVER *Agric. Cambridge* 73 Westwardly of this, the soil again improves in strength, and staple. **1892** *Speaker* 3 Sept. 289/1 Half a hundred acres of thistly land, from which savour and strength had long departed.

n. Demonstrative force or weight (of arguments, evidence); amount of evidence for (a case).

1593 SHAKS. *3 Hen. VI*, III. i. 49 Whiles Warwick tels his Title, smooths the Wrong, Inferreth arguments of mighty strength. **1725** WATTS *Logic* IV. ii. (1726) 351 Afterwards mention the Objections distinctly in their full Strength, and give a distinct Answer to them. **1814** CHALMERS *Evid.* ii. 65 Consider the strength even of heathen testimony to the facts of the gospel history. **1818** HALLAM *Mid. Ages* viii. III. (1819) III. 48 In this consists, I think, the sole strength of the opposite argument. **1895** *Law Times* XCIX. 544/1 The litigant should as speedily as can be learn something of the strength of his opponent's case.

o. Energy or vigour of literary or artistic conception or execution; forcefulness (of delineation, versification, expression).

1687 MIEGE *Gt. Fr. Dict.* II. s.v., The strength (or energy) of a Discourse, *la force d'un Discours.* **1695** [R. GRAHAM] *Short Acc. Painters* in *Dryden's Du Fresnoy's Art Paint.* 314 He had indeed an admirable Colouring, and great strength in all his Works. **1709** POPE *Ess. Crit.* 361 And praise the easy vigour of a line, Where Denham's strength, and Waller's sweetness join. **1710** FELTON *Diss. Classics* (1718) Pref. 17 We should see more and more into the Property, Strength, and Compass, and all the hidden Beauties of the Greek and Latin Tongues. **1715** POPE *Iliad* I. Pref. C 4, He consider'd these [dialects] as they had a greater Mixture of Vowels or Consonants, and accordingly employ'd them as the Verse requir'd either a greater Smoothness or Strength. **1752** GRAY *Stanzas to Mr. R. Bentley* 13 Ah! could they catch his strength, his easy grace, His quick creation, his unerring line. **1777** POTTER *Æschylus, Prometh. Chain'd* Foreword, There is in this remaining drama a sublimity of conception, a strength, a fire, a certain savage dignity peculiar to this bold writer. **1802** *Edin. Rev.* Oct. 86 Dr. Rennel's first sermon, upon the consequences of gaming, is admirable for its strength of language, its sound good sense, [etc.]. **1906** *Lit. World* 15 Nov. 519/2 The pictures are notable for a proper mingling of strength and delicacy.

p. *Cards.* Of a hand (or the player holding it): Effectiveness due to the value of the cards held; also, the condition of being strong or abundant *in* (a specified suit). Of a suit: Number and value of the cards held by a player.

1862 'CAVENDISH' *Whist* (1864) 22 Both these ends are advanced by choosing for your original lead the suit in which you have the greatest numerical strength. **1900** J. DOE *Bridge Man.* 32 The test of very many doubtful No Trumpers lies in the strength or weakness of the Spades.

q. *Billiards.* (See quot. 1896.)

1788 J. BEAUFORT *Hoyle's Games Impr.* 194 [Billiards.] This game [*i.e.* the losing game] depends greatly upon particular strengths. **1896** W. BROADFOOT *Billiards* iii. (Badm. Libr.) 106 Strength is the measure of force used to make a stroke, which is said to be soft or hard according to the strength.

r. *Comm.* Firmness, absence of lowering tendency, in prices.

1891 *Daily News* 15 Apr. 2/7 No strength is yet felt in the market for home trade yarns. **1912** *Standard* 20 Sept. 8/7 Prices showed some degree of strength at the opening. **1913** *Times* 9 Aug. 17/2 The South African market showed strength.

2. Phrases. †**a.** ***by*** or ***with strength of***: by force of. Cf. FORCE *sb.*[1] 16. *Obs.*

13.. *Minor Poems fr. Vernon MS.* xlix. 424 He þat may fulli conquerre Al a cuntre bi strengþe of were. **1555** *Instit. Gentl.* E ij, When as they winning by strength of armes yᵉ cuntrie of Asia.. did frely geue [etc.]. **1585** T. WASHINGTON tr. *Nicholay's Voy.* I. v. 4 We rowing with strength of oares towardes the saide citie. *Ibid.* II. xi. 46 With strength of rowing we coasted along. **1598** W. PHILLIP tr. *Langenes' Voy. Ships Holland E. Ind.* 27 They entered into their boate, and by strength of oares rowed from vs.

†**b.** ***no strength***: no matter (= *no force*, FORCE *sb.*[1] 20). *Obs.*[−1]

1340 *Ayenb.* 51 And yef he him damnede be him zelue: þer-of no strengþe.

†**c.** (***to hunt***) ***with strength***: by way of regular chase. Cf. FORCE *sb.*[1] 22 a. *Obs.*

c **1369** CHAUCER *Dethe Blaunche* 351 And al men speke of huntynge How they wolde slee the hert with strengthe. *c* **1400** *Master of Game* (MS. Digby 182) xxv, Whan þe kynge .. will hunte for þe herte with strength, þe maister of þe game moste haue [etc.].

d. ***on the strength of***: †(*a*) with the strength derived from, fortified by (food or drink) (*obs.*); (*b*) encouraged by, relying on, or arguing from.

Cf. 1 Kings xix. 8 'in the strength of that meat', which is literal from the Hebrew.

1625 MASSINGER *New Way* II. ii, Here; drinke it off, the ingredients are cordiall... You may ride on the strength of this till to morrow morning. **1708** ADDISON *Pres. St. War* 24 The Allies after a successful Summer are too apt upon the Strength of it to neglect their Preparations for the ensuing Campaign. **1717** PRIOR *Alma* III. 243 Was ever Tartar fierce or cruel, Upon the Strength of Water-Gruel? *a* **1734** NORTH *Life Ld. Kpr. Guilford* (1742) 53 Sir William Jones, who, upon the Strength of the Duke of Bucks, set his Lordship so hard for the Solicitor General's Place. **1780** *Mirror* No. 92, I have known a lady here contrive to make a figure for half the winter, on the strength of a plume of feathers, or the trimming of a petticoat. **1806-7** J. BERESFORD *Miseries Hum. Life* (1826) iii. §39 Going to see a party of strolling players on the strength of an encouraging report. **1845** DICKENS *Chimes* iii. 110 [He] had considerably improved his acquaintance with Sir Joseph Bowley on the strength of his attentive letter. **1865** EMERSON in *Harper's Mag.* (1884) Feb. 461/2 On the strength of your note, I am working away at my last pages. **1885** *Manch. Exam.* 13 July 5/2 He makes a careful selection of instances, on the strength of which he asks us to accept the conclusion at which he has arrived. **1890** D. C. MURRAY *John Vale* xxv, You have [made a discovery], have you?.. And you want half-a-crown for a drink on the strength of it?

e. ***the strength of***: the point or meaning of, the essential facts about (*ellipt.* in quot. 1958). Esp. in phr. ***that's about the strength of it***: that is what it amounts to (cf. *that's* (*about*) *the size of it* s.v. SIZE *sb.*[1] 10 f); ***to get the strength of***: to understand. *colloq.* (orig. and chiefly *Austral.* and *N.Z.*).

1908 H. FLETCHER *Dads & Dan: between Smokes* 112 'So yous thinks I'se wore out, .. an' past patchin' an' mendin'?' 'That's about ther strength of it.' **1916** C. J. DENNIS *Moods of Ginger Mick* 63 Then, bit be bit, Mick gits the strength uv it. **1926** K. S. PRICHARD *Working Bullocks* xv. 136 Now .. I'll just give you the strength of Red Burke... They say there never was a good Burke. **1943** N. MARSH *Colour Scheme* v. 93, I don't get the strength of it myself. He wouldn't say much. **1946** K. TENNANT *Lost Haven* (1947) ix. 129 If it hadn't been for her engine .. you might just as well have left her on the sandbar to go to pieces... That's about the strength of it. **1958** F. NORMAN *Bang to Rights* I. 10 The strength was that he'd got nicked for ponceing off his old woman. **1965** A. PRIOR *Interrogators* x. 188 'Just passing and you saw the door was open?' He laughed. 'Well, yes, that's just about the strength of it.' **1969** *Advertiser* (Adelaide) 12 May 5/4 Get the strength of this: You [*sc.* Australians] talk about bankos and trunks—is that English? **1974** J. CLEARY *Peter's Pence* vi. 178 'What's the strength of all this?' 'Strength?' Kessler's English didn't run to Australian colloquialisms. 'What's the point, the meaning?'

f. ***give me strength***: used as an expression of exasperation.

1967 'S. WOODS' *And shame Devil* 251 'Give me strength,' said O'Brien helplessly. 'I'll try to explain.' **1970** K. BENTON *Sole Agent* xviii. 194 'You make all my plans sound so drab and sordid.' 'Oh give me strength!'

3. Used for: A source of strength; that which makes strong. (Not now in *pl.*)

Often in Biblical language (literally from Heb.), esp. as predicated of God.

c **1000** *Ags. Ps.* (Th.) lix. 6 And Effrem ys æðele strengþu heafdes mines. *a* **1300** *Cursor M.* 7208 His wijf wald noght fin.. Til sco þe soth had gert him sai, In quat stede al his strencth lai. *a* **1340** HAMPOLE *Psalter* xxx. 4 For my strenght and my fleynge ert thou. *c* **1386** CHAUCER *Monk's T.* 68 For alle hise strengthes in hise heeres weere. *a* **1400** *Minor Poems fr. Vernon MS.* xxiii. 234 Heil vr Ioye of worþinesse, And vr strengþe þerto. **1615** E. S. *Britain's Buss* in Arber *Eng. Garner* III. 648 Our shipping and mariners, sea towns, and coasts, which .. should be the walls and strength of this Islandish Monarchy. **1630** R. JOHNSON *Kingd. & Commw.* 220 Both of them are wonderfull strengths, eases, and riches to his Countrey. **1630** M. GODWYN tr. *Bp. Godwyn's Ann. Eng.* 21 Our chiefe strength were our Archers. **1667** MILTON *P.L.* x. 921 [Eve to Adam] Bereave me not, Whereon I live, .. My only strength and stay. **1678** BP. SPRAT *Serm.* 7 Nov. (1710) 130 What they boaded would be a Mischief to us, you are providing shall be one of our principal Strengths. **1738** WESLEY *Psalms* LI. vii, And all my Powers shall join to bless The Lord, my Strength and Righteousness. **1855** PRESCOTT *Philip II* I. v. I. 69 The strength of his army lay in his Spanish veterans. **1883** *Manch. Exam.* 24 Oct. 4/6 The strength of Conservatism was that it appealed to men of all classes and positions .. who desire to maintain the Constitution as it is.

†**4.** Superior power exerted for conquest, outrage, or compulsion; force; wrongful force, violence; *pl.* acts of violence. ***to make strength***; to resort to force. *Obs.*

c **1000** *Apollonius of Tyre* (1834) 2 He.. ða ongean-winnendan fæmnan mid micelre strengðe earfoðlice ofercom. *a* **1122** *O.E. Chron.* (Laud MS.) an. 1119, Sume þa castelas he mid strengðe ȝenam. **1154** *Ibid.* an. 1137, §6 Landes þat rice men hefden mid strengthe. *a* **1200** *Moral Ode* 168 in *O.E. Hom.* I. 169 Ne scal him na mon mene þer of strengþe ne of wronge. *c* **1200** *Trin. Coll. Hom.* 179 And ȝif þe louerd net his underlinge to ȝiuene, þat beoð strengðe, and refloc. *c* **1250** *Gen. & Ex.* 673 Nembrot nam wið strengðhe ðat lond, And helde ðe tur o babel in his hond. **1297** R. GLOUC. (Rolls) 4166 Some he mid strencþe nom & al quic hom vret. *c* **1300** *K. Horn* 1084 (Laud) Mody Myd strencþe hyre hadde And in to toure ladde. *c* **1300** *Leg. Gregory* (Schulz) 621 Þo was þe douke wiþ strengþe ytake, And brouȝt to þe conteise sone. **13..** *Cursor M.* 19323 (Edin.) To þe tempil þan þai giede, þa postlis to þair curte to lede, bot strenþes nane did þai þaim til. **1390** GOWER *Conf.* I. 240 And that thing mai I noght fulfille, But if I scholde strengthe make. *c* **1400** MAUNDEV. (1839) v. 37 On that was clept Guytoga.. made him Soudan be strengthe. *c* **1400** *Brut* lix. 54 Þai hade descomfitede him biforn-hand, and dryuen him out by strengþ. *c* **1400** *Pride of Life* 332 in *Non-Cycle Myst. Plays* 99 Med is mad a demisman, Streyint betit þe lau. **1463** *Stat. Roll Irel. 3 Edw. IV* (1914) 187 To resist the malicieux pourposes might and strayngth of your forsaid Irishe Enemyez.

†**5.** A power, faculty; an active property. *Obs.*

c **1000** *Sax. Leechd.* I. 116 Ðenim þas ylcan wyrte & ele & swinen smero do tosomne þonne hæfð hit ða strængðe hyne to ȝewyrmenne. **1387-8** T. USK *Test. Love* III. vi. (Skeat) l. 67 Instrument of willing is thilke strength of the soule, whiche that constrayneth to wilne. *c* **1400** tr. *Secreta Secret., Gov. Lordsh.* 96 Vche sawle is a spirituell stryngthe, .. and it hauys two stryngthes rennynge to-gedre yn þe body, .. oon of þe stryngthes is a tokenynge, þe oþer ys wirkand, þat glorious god hauys inlightyd of vij stryngthes; of stryngthe attractyue, and retractyf, of stryngthe digestyf, and purgatyf, of strengthe nutrityf, and infirmatyf, and sustantyf. *c* **1440** *Gesta Rom.* xcvi. 427 (Add. MS.) Therfore I am holdyn to serue hym with all my strengthes And membres. **1508** DUNBAR *Tua Mariit Wemen* 264 Be dragonis baith and dowis, ay in double forme, And quhen it nedis ȝow, onone, note baith ther stranthis. **1525** tr. *Brunswyke's Handywork Surg.* xv. D j b, That the powder [shall] haue in hym selfe suche strength that when it towcheth the vayne, that it therwith may close, which strength is namyd stiptica. *Ibid.* lxviii. O iv b, Lay thervpon this plaster, whyche hathe the strengthe to cause all bowed bones to come out agayn.

†**6.** A feat of strength; an act requiring strength. ***to make no strength of***: to find no difficulty in.

c **1290** *Alban* 62 in *S. Eng. Leg.* 69 Huy comen to an vrninde brok: þere huy mosten ouer wade: þe tormentores woden ouer al a-brod: and no strencþe þar-of ne maden. **1375** BARBOUR *Bruce* XVI. 646 Thar did ane Ynglis man, perfay, A weill gret strynth, as I herd say. **1579-80** NORTH *Plutarch, Crassus* (1612) 573 These bowmen [Parthians] drew a great strength, and had big strong bowes.

†**7.** The force, tenor, or import (of a document); the power, phonetic value (of a letter of the alphabet). *Obs.*

c **1425** *Eng. Conq. Ireland* (1896) 90 The forme of thay preuyleges, as thay wer endyted .. a latyne, ne myght I nat comly setten yn Englyshe, & þerfor I hyt leue; bot the meste streynth ys thys. **1447** *Rolls of Parlt.* V. 132/1 That it be doone after the strengthe, fourme and effecte of this Petition. *c* **1450** *Godstow Reg.* 348 Aftir the strengthe, forme, and effecte, of theire charter therof made. **1602** [J. WILLIS] *Art Stenogr.* B 5, In these wordes, H, hath the strength of a thicke Aspiration, as if they [*sc.* Ah, Oh] were thus written, Agh, Ogh.

†**8.** Strengthening, reinforcement, confirmation.

c **1420** *Brut* cxxxviii. 144 He passede þe see, and come into Engeland, þrouȝ conseil & strengþ & helpe of meny grete Lordes of Engeland. *c* **1450** *Mirk's Festial* 52 Soo, for þis man was so yturnet from all wyckednesse ynto all goodnesse, yn gret strengþe and helpe to holy chyrch. *Ibid.* 228 For ryght as a castell hath a depe dych yn strengyth of hyt, soo hath our lady a dyche of mekenes. *c* **1450** *Godstow Reg.* 95 Into witnesse and strengthe of all thingis he made his seale. *Ibid.* 206 Yf nede were the sewters of the forsaid court shold come fully to the strengthe of the courte for the kyngis breef or writte ther to be demed at that tyme.

†**9.** Legal power; authority. (Cf. 1 h.) *Obs.*

1414 *Rolls of Parlt.* IV. 58/1 By strengthe and colour of the forseide Statut so generally mad.. the forseide Priour and Chanons hav us .. by enquestes enbraced as for her bonde boremen. **1480** CAXTON *Cron. Eng.* ccviii. 190 He..axed the keyes of the yates of the Cyte thurgh vertue and strengthe [*Brut* strengh] of his commyssyon. **1501** *Will of John Bawde* in *Bury Wills* (Camden) 84, I charge my feffours that they delyuer strengthe jn as moche londe as jt most redyest mony to be had for to my executours. **1530** *Will of John Bewchyr*, ibid., *note*, I gyve all my strength that my mother gaue me ..I gyve nowe all my strength to John Wallgore for to gyve or sell all the goods, houses [etc.]. *c* **1600** SHAKS. *Sonn.* xlix. 13 To leaue poore me, thou hast the strength of lawes, Since why to loue, I can alledge no cause. **1689** in *Acts Parlt. Scot.* (1875) XII. 63/2 By causeing persewand forfault seuerall persones upon strenthes of old and absolute lawes.

10. a. A stronghold, fastness, fortress. Now *arch.* or *Hist.*, chiefly with reference to Scotland.

a **1225** *Ancr. R.* 270 Auh þis heie sacrament..unwrihð his wrenches, & brekeð his strencðes. *c* **1330** R. BRUNNE *Chron. Wace* (Rolls) 7142 Alle þe strengþes he gan to sese..he had alle þys forceresses. **1375** BARBOUR *Bruce* v. 469 Thai held the strynthis of the land. **1387** TREVISA *Higden* (Rolls) II. 449 Codrus..entrede in to þe strengþe of his enemyes [L. *castra hostium ingreditur*]. **1390** GOWER *Conf.* III. 55 Ther let he make of lym and sond A strengthe where he wolde duelle. **1393** LANGL. *P. Pl.* C. IV. 238 Meny hardy men that hadden wil to fyghte, To brennen and to bruten, to bete a-doun strengthes. *c* **1420** *Contin. Brut* ccxlv. 386 And so þe King gat and conquered alle the tounez and Castelles, Pilez, Streynthis, and Abbeyez, vnto Pountlarge. **1513** DOUGLAS *Æneis* VI. xiii. 42 Sum in the hillis hie sall set wp syne The strenthis and the castellis Collatyne. **1542** *Acc. Ld. High Treas. Scot.* VIII. 109 Utheris to kepe thair housis and strengthis un the bordouris. **1568** GRAFTON *Chron.* II. 118 In conclusion, he toke money sayth Reynulph and yeelded vp his Castelles and strengthes which he helde. **1598** BARRET *Theor. Warres* V. i. 121 The Generall of the Artillerie is to prouide for all the forts and strengths of the realme. **1643** CHAS. I. *Conc. Treaty Oxf.* Wks. 1662 II. 320 If any Prince seize upon any Strength that belongs to His stronger Neighbour. **1661** J. D[AVIES] *Civil Warres* cviii. 370 To lay down their Arms, and surrender Chester and other strengths. **1667** MILTON *P.L.* VII. 141 This inaccessible high strength, the seat Of Deitie supream. **1748** SMOLLETT *Rod. Random* xxxiii, Our sailors at the same time become masters of all the other strengths near Boca Chica. **1807** G. CHALMERS *Caledonia* I. I. ii. 91 There was once a subterraneous communication, between these two British strengths, on Barry-hill. **1815** SCOTT *Antiq.* xxviii, Auld Elspeth's like some of the ancient ruined strengths and castles that ane sees amang the hills. **1870** BURTON *Hist. Scot.* lix. (1873) V. 351 If we suppose it clear..that King James was to be taken to that lonely strength, it is..an absolute mystery how he was to be treated when he was there.

†**b.** A defensive work, munition, fortification. Also *fig.* *Obs.*

1377 LANGL. *P. Pl.* B. XIX. 362 Conscience comaunded þo al crystene to delue, And make a muche mote þat myȝte ben a strengthe, To helpe holycherche. **1382** WYCLIF *Isa.* xxxiii. 16 The strengthys of huge stones his heȝte [Vulg. *munimenta saxorum sublimitas ejus*]. *c* **1400** *Beryn* 239 The knyȝt..went to se the wall, And þe wardes of the town..; Devising ententifliche þe strengthis al a-bout. **1500** *Reg. Privy Seal Scot.* I. 791 To big a tour..and mak thairapon irn ȝettis, machcolyn,..and al uther strenthis. **1609–10** *Act 7 Jas. I*, c. 20 §2 For the making..keeping and mainteyninge of Peres, Wals, Jettes, Pyles, Strengthes, Fortificacions, Defences, and other thinges whatsoever to withstand and breake the rage and violent beating of the Sea. **1636** B. JONSON *Discov.* (1640) 92 That there was a Wall or Parapet of teeth set in our mouth..that the rashnesse of talking should..be fenced in, and defended by certaine strengths, placed in the mouth it selfe, and within the lips. **1661** *Reg. Privy Counc. Scot.* Ser. III. I. 6 To cause demolish and slight the wallis, strenths and fortificationes of the Citiedale of Inuernesse.

†**c.** One's strong position; the place within which one is most secure; *spec.* in *Wrestling* (see quot. 1714). *Obs.*

1375 BARBOUR *Bruce* III. 44 Tharfor me thynk maist awenand To withdraw ws,..Till we cum owt off thar daunger. For owr strenth at our hand is ner. **1436** *Rolls of Parlt.* IV. 498/1 Ye Parysh Kirk of Bidstone in ye same Countee of Chestre, within his awne strenght. *c* **1440** *Bone Flor.* 497 All that were lefte onslayne, Fledd unto ther strenkyth agayne. **1464** in *Archæologia* XLVII. 191 Be it kend..me Alexander Hom..be these present letters assouver..Thomas Burghe..safly to pass agan in Ingland to thar own st[r]enth. **1513** MORE *Rich. III*, Wks. 57/2 Then thought the protectour,..while yᵉ lordes of the realme wer about him out of their owne strenghtis,..it wer best hastly to pursue his purpose. **1612** HAYWARD *Ann. Eliz.* (Camden) 52 They kept themselves so within their strength, that only two of their horsemen and one of their footemen [were] slayne. *a* **1674** CLARENDON *Hist. Reb.* IX. §100 The counter-scuffle at Petherton-bridge, when two of his own parties.. fought with each other, whilst the enemy retired to their own strengths. **1714** PARKYNS *Inn-Play* (ed. 2) 57 Stand straight and wide, but not out of your strength with your Toe out.

†**11. a.** *collect. sing.* Troops, forces. *Obs.*

1154 *O.E. Chron.* an. 1140, Þa hi þær inne wæren þa com þe Kinges cuen mid al hire strengthe. **1297** R. GLOUC. (Rolls) 8793 So þat a Misselmasse eue, mid hor ost hii come To gadere mid gret strengþe, & þe bataile nome. *c* **1420** *Contin. Brut* ccxli. 351 The King..made hym redy with his streynthe, and rode yn-to Essex. **1461** *Paston Lett.* II. 59 And yet..he wolde send me with strengthe of men as a presoner. *c* **1482** J. KAY tr. *Caoursin's Siege of Rhodes* (1870) ¶ 11 Therfor the lord mayster putted also strenght of men into the walles of Rhodes whiche were beten downe with bombardes. **1560** DAUS tr. *Sleidane's Comm.* 51 That we shold sende our strength and souldiours unto straungers [L. *subministrare videlicet copias, et militem nostrum aliis*]. *Ibid.* 137 b, He fortifieth it with workes and strength of men [L. *opere praesidioque munit*]. **1642–4** VICARS *God in Mount* 163 In expectation of some more strength either from Glocester-shire, or else from the Lord Generall. **1649** DAVENANT *Love & Hon.* V. i. 16 Vasco, it is the Dukes command that you Assemble straight some strength from the cast regiments To guard the pallace yard. *a* **1700** EVELYN *Diary* Apr. 1646, Within is another fort and spacious lodgings for the souldiers... No accommodation for strength is wanting. **1703** BURCHETT *Mem. Transactions at Sea* 288 All that the Admiral could do was to protect the Trade, till such time as the additional Strength expected from England joined him.

b. A body of soldiers; a force. *Obs.*

a **1500** in Kingsford *Chron. Lond.* (1905) 177 Quene Margaret came owte of ffraunce in to Scotland wᵗ a strength of people; and so entred into England and made opyn warr. **1544** BETHAM *Precepts War* II. lxiv. L vj b, Wherfore we must all wayes fyght wyth fresshe men, newe strengthes, and plentye of vytayles. **1565** COOPER *Thesaurus*, *Decurias hominum inducere*, to bryng in a strength of men. **1597** SHAKS. *2 Hen. IV*, I. iii. 76 That he should draw his seuerall strengths together And come against vs in full puissance. **1599** HAYWARD *1st Pt. Hen. IV*, 18 The king..sent a strength of men with charge, either to set vpon the earle of Arundell where he did lie, or [etc.]. **1617** MORYSON *Itin.* II. 210 The Forces in Garrison at Carrickfergus, out of which Sir Arthur Chichester was to draw a competent strength to come by water and meete the Lord Deputie. **1627** DRAYTON *Mis. Q. Marg.* xcix, Yorke..With his deare Nevils, Counsels what to doe, For it behou'd him, to make good his Guard With both their strengthes and all to little too.

12. *Mil.* and *Naval.* **a.** The number of men on the muster-roll of an army, a regiment, etc.; the body of men enrolled; the number of ships in a navy or fleet. ***under strength***: having less than the standard or normal number.

1601 SHAKS. *All's Well* IV. iii. 181 Demaund of him of what strength they are a foot. *c* **1610** *Let.* in *Daily News* (1896) 24 Nov. 8/1 His strength is as followeth: When he goeth in person to the wars, he hath not less than 300,000 men armed with lances and swords. *a* **1700** EVELYN *Diary* 7 Nov. 1691, The relation he gave of the strength of the French King..was very wide from what we fancied. **1711** SWIFT *Cond. Allies* 40 And as they [the Dutch] increase their Trade, it is obvious they will enlarge their Strength at Sea. **1718** LADY M. W. MONTAGU *Let. to Abbé Conti* 31 July, His strength at sea now [is] very small. **1802** C. JAMES *Milit. Dict.* s.v., In all returns which are made of corps, strength implies the number of men that are borne upon the establishment, in contradistinction to effective force, which means the number fit for service. **1809** *Lond. Chron.* 8 Aug. 130 Strength of the Garrison. Two captains, [etc.]... Total 127. **1849** MACAULAY *Hist. Eng.* v. I. 580 Orders were given that the strength of every company of infantry and of every troop of cavalry should be increased. **1859** *Musketry Instr.* 82 [Rules for 'Monthly Progress Return'] 1st. *Strength, &c.* —Under this head are to be shown the effectives of each company,—that is, every man of the company, whether present or absent, on the last day of the month, minus regimental staff-serjeants, drummers, and recruits in a musketry sense. **1894** 'J. S. WINTER' *Red Coats* 26 But outside the fighting strength of the regiment Colonel de Crespigny was *not* liked. **1896** *Daily News* 9 Feb. 3/3 At present the Brigade of Guards was under strength.

b. ***on the strength***: entered on the rolls of a regiment. Also said of those soldiers' wives whose marriage has been approved by the authorities, and who have therefore a recognized position; opposed to ***off the strength***.

1864 WHYTE MELVILLE *Brookes of Bridlemere* ii, The coloured clothes denoting that the wearer was a bâtman, or officer's servant, though on the strength of the regiment as a trooper in its ranks. **1889** *Eng. Illustr. Mag.* Apr. 533/2 The colonel had put the widow woman 'on the strength' —she was no longer an unrecognized waif, but had her regimental position. **1890** *Pall Mall Gaz.* 6 Sept. 7/2 Only the wives of the men on the married strength proceed, at the expense of the Government,..but those married without leave go at their own expense. **1897** COL. FORREST in *United Serv. Mag.* Nov. 147 Married soldiers are of two categories, those married 'on the strength' and those married 'off the strength'.

13. A sufficient number (of persons or things) for some purpose. Now *dial.*

1607 MARKHAM *Caval.* I. 75 When the colt is haltered, you shall prouide, that good strength of men take hold vpon the end of the chase halter. **1640** J. TAYLOR (Water P.) *Differing Worships* 2 His Worships Altar's Crown'd with Glorious strength Of Massie Plate. **1717** BOLINGBROKE *Let. to Sir W. Windham* (1753) 69 When..she took the resolution of laying him aside, there was a strength still remaining sufficient to have supported her government. **1748** *Anson's Voy.* II. ii. 128 Without the help of their crews he had no longer strength enough to navigate the ship. **1765** A. DICKSON *Treat. Agric.* (ed. 2) 316 These two plowings may be performed with the same strength, and in the same time with one clean plowing. **1769** G. WHITE *Selborne, To Pennant* 2 Jan., Half-a-dozen gentlemen, furnished with a good strength of water-spaniels. **1875** W. ALEXANDER *Sk. Life* 140 Maister Mutch has stren'th o' men an' beasts to be mair nor maister o' a' the wark upo' the fairm. **1878** *Cumbld. Gloss.*, *Strenth o' men and pitchforks*, power, influence.

†**14.** The aggregate resources (of a nation). *Obs.*

1695 C. DAVENANT *Ess. Ways & Means* Wks. 1771 I. 62 In taxing the people we have hitherto gone chiefly upon land, and foreign trade, which are about ⅘d part of the strength of England. **1708** ADDISON *Pres. St. War* 6 The Woollen Manufacture is the British Strength, the staple Commodity and proper Growth of our Country. **1711** SWIFT *Cond. Allies* 8 No Monarch..did ever engage beyond a certain Degree; never proceeding so far as to exhaust the Strength and Substance of their Country by Anticipations and Loans.

15. Strongest part. †**a.** *gen.* *Obs.*

c **1530** *Judic. Urines* II. xiii. 42 b, Ilica passio... Ile is the pyth and the strenth of a thyng. **1585** HIGINS *Junius' Nomencl.* 143/1 *Pulpa*,..the hart, or strength of timber. **1725** POPE *Odyss.* II. 427 Then studious she prepares the choicest flour, The strength of wheat, and wines, an ample store.

b. *Fencing.* = FORTE *sb.* 2. *Obs.*

1705 H. BLACKWELL *Engl. Fencing-Master* 10 You must engage your Adversary with the Strength of your Foile on the Feeble of his. **1711** Z. WYLDE *Engl. Master of Defence* 5 From the Shell to the middle, I call the Fort or Strength of the Weapon.

c. The strongest part (of a stream or current).

1807 O. W. ROBERTS *Voy. Centr. Amer.* 258 Keeping generally in the strength of the current, which..carried us down with great velocity. **1867** SMYTH *Sailor's Word-bk.*, *Strength of the tide*, where it runs strongest, which in serpentine courses will be found in the hollow curves.

16. A mighty company, a power. *nonce-use.*

1842 TENNYSON *Ulysses* 66 We are not now that strength which in old days Moved earth and heaven.

17. ***strength through joy*** [tr. G. *kraft durch freude*]: a movement founded in Germany by the National Socialist Party in 1933 to promote physical and cultural recreational activities among working people. Also *transf.* and *fig.* (Freq. with capitals and hyphens.)

1935 G. DIMITROV *Working Class against Fascism* in *Rep. 7th World Congress* (1936) 43 In the Hitler Youth Leagues, in the sports organizations, in the *Kraft durch Freude* organisations (*Strength Through Joy*). **1939** *Ann. Reg. 1938* iii. 201 During the first days after the 'Anschluss', 10,000 [Austrian] workers..inclined to Communism and Socialism, had been invited for a fourteen-day trip to Germany where they found a hearty welcome and were shown the institutions of the *Kraft durch Freude* (strength through joy) movement. **1943** *Tribune* 4 June 19/1 The strength-through-joy brigades you will have met Whose mouths are baggy and whose hair is scented. **1962** L. R. BANKS *End to Running* II. iv. 177 Full of an awful sort of phoney strength-through-joy. **1967** T. STOLPER tr. *G. Stolper's German Economy* v. 152 Annual paid vacations, inexpensive theaters and concerts, and all the other activities of the party's leisure time organization—'Strength through Joy' (*Kraft durch Freude*). **1973** 'G. BLACK' *Bitter Tea* x. 156 The girl..looked as if she had graduated from one of Lee Kuan Yew's strength-through-joy courses. **1975** *Listener* 16 Jan. 71/3 Physical fitness was a Nazi fetish..bronzed young Germans cultivating 'strength-through-joy'. **1979** J. GARDNER *Nostradamus Traitor* xv. 86 'They sent me up to Scotland.' It was a toughening-up course at a Strength Through Joy Camp... Survival. Living off the land.

18. *attrib.* and *Comb.*, as ***strength-constant***, ***-return***, ***test***; ***strength-(to-)weight ratio***; objective, as ***strength-giver***; ***strength-conferring***, ***-decaying***, ***-giving***, ***-increasing***, ***-inspiring***, ***-restoring***, ***-sapping***, ***-showing***, ***-sustaining***, ***-testing*** adjs.

1720 POPE *Iliad* XIX. 168 Built anew with *Strength-conferring Fare. **1881** *Q. Jrnl. Geol. Soc.* XXXIX. 139 On the Elasticity and *Strength-constants of Japanese Rocks. By Thomas Gray..and Prof. John Milne. **1600** *Weakest goeth to Wall* F 3 *Strength-decaying age. **1890** *Spectator* 3 May, They could settle..what the value of the potato really is as a *strength-giver. **1845** J. R. LOWELL in *Amer. Rev.* Aug. 137, I saw them in all higher moods, and durst Face their *strength-giving eyes. **1880** C. R. MARKHAM *Peruv. Bark* 144 The strength-giving, invigorating coca. **1655** MARQ. WORCESTER *Cent. Invent.* Index p. iij, A *Strength-increasing Spring. **1799** CAMPBELL *Pleas. Hope* I. 101 Thy *strength-inspiring aid. **1852** BAILEY *Festus* 524 Another holy day..hath now slid Into the passive *strength-restoring night. **1893** BOWDLER tr. *von Pfeil's Exper. Prussian Officer* iii. 31 Prince Charles..compared the figures shown on the *strength-returns of some Russian troops with the actual numbers. **1961** *Times* 6 Dec. 3/4 Both boxers kept up a *strength-sapping pace. **1939** N. DE V. HART *Bridge Players' Bedside Bk.* 133 North's Two Spades is a true *strength-showing reverse, because South has to raise the bidding level to three in order to put North back to clubs. **1967** *Bridge Players' Encycl.* 490/1 *Strength-Showing Bids*, in some special situations a suit bid can be used to show strength rather than length or control. *c* **1624** CHAPMAN *Hymn to Hermes* 665 Because he beares Of *strength-sustaying youth, the flaming yeares. **1898** *Engin. Mag.* XVI. 154/2 *Strength Tests of Swedish Iron and Steel. **1898** *Daily News* 12 Apr. 3/7 *Strength-testing machines. **1978** *Jrnl. R. Soc. Arts* CXXVI. 682/1 The primary incentive for the development of titanium was without doubt its *strength-to-weight ratio and the potential of this property in aircraft construction. **1945** F. S. STEWART *Airframe Materials* i. 2 The *strength-weight ratio of materials used in airframes is of such great importance.

†**strength**, *v.* *Obs.* Forms: see STRENGTH *sb.*; also 4 **strengþi.** [f. STRENGTH *sb.*]

1. *trans.* To give strength to, to make strong or stronger, to strengthen, fortify, confirm.

c **1160** *Hatton Gosp.* Luke i. 80 Soðlice se cnape weox & wæs on gaste ȝe-stræncþed. *a* **1225** *Ancr. R.* 140 Heo temeð wel hire fulitowene fleschs, & strenðeð & deð menske hire wurðfule soule. **1297** R. GLOUC. (Rolls) 4720 Hii.. strengþede castles. **13..** *Cursor M.* 22366 (Gött.) Þai sal.. strinth þaim al gain þat fight. *c* **1375** *Sc. Leg. Saints* v. (*John*) 384 Þan mad he byschoppis ay-quhare, to strinth and vpehald goddis lare. **1382** WYCLIF *Prov.* xx. 18 Thoȝtis bi counseilis ben strengthid. **1414** *26 Pol. Poems* xiii. 108 Strengþe ȝoure marche, and kepe þe see. *c* **1425** *Eng. Conq. Ireland* (1896) 68 The lond of Irland..whyche he had y-cast for to streynth with castell. **1450–80** tr. *Secreta Secret.* 82 Thynges þat stryinghtes and makys fat þe body. *c* **1450** *Godstow Reg.* 104 And leste that the same Rauf or his heires shold rynne into harme thereof afterwarde by hym or by his heires, he strengthed þis writyng with his seale. **1483** CAXTON *Golden Leg.* 308/1 They be sent for to strengthe in us all our perfection unto the ende. **1526** *Pilgr. Perf.* (W. de W. 1531) 12 God is as redy to here hym, & with his grace to helpe & strength hym. **1534** MORE *Comf. agst. Trib.* I. Wks. 1140/1 To stable and strength the walles of our heartes agaynste the gret sourges of this tempesteous sea. **1562** WINȜET *Cert. Tractatis* Wks. (S.T.S.) I. 25, I strenthit not my purpose with ma sufficient ressonis and auctoriteis. **1573–80** TUSSER *Husb.* (1878) 46 Marsh wall too slight, strength now, or god night. **1610** MASON *Turke* G 2 Twas loue and state Gaue thee this time of life to strength my fate. **1614** J. TAYLOR (Water P.) *Water-worke* B 4 b, Those Marchants..more to strength their power, ioynd with the Pope.

2. To force, compel.

1340 *Ayenb.* 86 Ne alle þe dyeulen of helle ne moȝen mannes wyl strengþi to do one zenne wyþ oute his wylle.

3. *refl.* To summon up one's strength.

c **1489** Caxton *Sonnes of Aymon* iii. 109 Whan Bayarde wyst hymselfe lade wyth two knyghtes, he strengthed hym selfe so strongly that it semed to Reynawde that he was more ioyouse.

Hence † **strengthed** *ppl. a.*; † '**strengthing** *vbl. sb.* the action of the verb, also *concr.*

c **1375** *Sc. Leg. Saints* xiii. (*Mark*) 197 To þe strinthinge of haly kirk. **1382** Wyclif *4 Kings* xxiv. 10 The cyte is enuyround with streynthyngis. *Ibid., Isa.* xxxvi. 1 Alle the strengthid cities of Iuda. **1472** in *Charters*, etc. *Edinb.* (1871) 135 To help..to the said fortressing and strenthing of our said Burgh. **1528** Paynell *Salerne's Regim.* Djb, The streingthynge therof is nat sufficient to digest great repletions of meates. **1574** in P. Cunningham *Extr. Acc. Revels* (Shaks. Soc.) 84 Tape for tyenge and strengthing, vij s.

strengthen ('strɛŋθ(ə)n), *v.* Also 3-4 **strenþin**, 4-5 **strenkþen**; *pa. t.* 5 *Sc.* **stryngthnit**. [f. STRENGTH *sb.*; cf. STRENGTH *v.* and -EN[5].]

1. *trans.* To give moral support, courage, or confidence to (a person); to encourage, hearten, inspirit, fix in resolution.

The first example may belong to STRENGTH *v.*, as the inflected inf. does occur, though rarely, in the text quoted.

a **1300** *Cursor M.* 22366 (Edin.) He sale..strenþin [*Cott.* strength] þaim ogain þat siȝte [? *read* fiȝte]. *c* **1450** *Mirk's Festial* 285 Þe wheche bred ȝe schull pray our gostly Fadyr forto ȝeue you..þat ȝe mowe ete þat in your hert yche day aftyr yn your labour, and soo strenkþen your soule þerwyth þat [etc.]. **1557** N. T. (Geneva) *Luke* xxii. 32 Therfore when thou art conuerted, strengthen thy brethren. **1582** N. T. (Rheims) *Luke* xxii. 43 There appeared to him an Angel from heauen, strengthening him [so **1611**]. **1593** Shaks. *3 Hen. VI*, ii. vi. 7 Impairing Henry, strength'ning misproud Yorke. **1611** Bible *Deut.* iii. 28 But charge Ioshua, and encourage him, and strengthen him. **1628** Feltham *Resolves* i. xxiv. (1636) 84 The good mans goodnesse, lies not hid in himselfe alone: hee is still strengthening of his weaker Brother. **1651** Hobbes *Leviath.* ii. xxviii. 162 The Subjects did not give the Soveraign that right; but onely in laying down theirs, strengthened him to use his own as he should think fit. **1760–72** H. Brooke *Fool of Quality* (1792) II. 170 A little resentful haughtiness arose in his mind, and strengthened it against the violence of the reproofs that he expected. **1830** Tennyson *Ode to Mem.* 5 Strengthen me, enlighten me! **1856** Froude *Hist. Eng.* II. viii. 247 A country strengthened in hostility by the means which has been used to subdue it. **1861** J. A. Alexander *Gosp. Christ* xxxi. 412 Brethren, Christ strengthens us by his example.

b. To confirm (a person *in* an opinion).

1833 John Davidson *Embalming* 17 There is one leading peculiarity which strengthens me in the opinion I have offered, viz. [etc.]. **1860** Tyndall *Glac.* i. x. 67, I was strengthened in this opinion by the fact [etc.].

2. a. To give physical strength to, make stronger or more robust (a person, his body or members); to increase the functional vigour of (a bodily organ or its powers).

1585 T. Washington tr. *Nicholay's Voy.* ii. xxi. 58 b, [It doth] comfort your sinewes and strengtheneth your members. **1604** Marston *Malcontent* ii. iv. D 1 b, It purifieth the blood,..strengthneth the vaines, mundifieth the teeth. **1665–6** Boyle *Let.* 9 Mar., Wks. 1772 I. *Life* p. lxxxii, Lemons..have..the power to..strengthen the stomach. **1725** N. Robinson *Th. Physick* 309 Lastly, in strengthning and restoring the digestive Faculty of the Stomach. **1750** tr. *Leonardus' Mirr. Stones* 134 The opal sharpens and strengthens the sight. **1789** W. Buchan *Dom. Med.* (1799) 423 Wine..taken in moderation..strengthens the stomach, and promotes digestion. **1856** Kane *Arctic Expl.* II. iii. 45 See..how the back has been strengthened to its increasing burden. **1908** [Miss E. Fowler] *Betw. Trent & Ancholme* 173 The doctor had recommended him beer, to strengthen him.

b. *to strengthen the hand(s of*: fig. to enable (a person or body of persons) to act with greater effect. (Orig. a Hebraism.)

1535 Coverdale *1 Sam.* xxiii. 16 Jonathas wente vnto Dauid..and strengthned his hande in God. **1734** R. Trevor *Let.* in *10th Rep. Hist. MSS. Comm.* App. i. 251 The late Proceedings of Parliament for strengthening the King's hands. **1779** C'tess Carlisle in Jesse *Selwyn & Contemp.* (1844) IV. 200 The Opposition say they will do anything to strengthen the hands of Government at this juncture. **1827** Hallam *Const. Hist.* (1876) I. ii. 101 A new scheme of ecclesiastical laws was drawn up,..rather calculated to strengthen the hands of the spiritual courts than to withdraw any matter from their cognisance. **1884** W. E. Norris *Thirlby Hall* xi, What strengthened my hands and completely took the wind out of his sails was a most opportune letter from my uncle.

c. To increase the strength of (the mind or its faculties).

1828 Lytton *Pelham* xv, If we strengthen their [*sc.* children's] minds, instead of weakening them. **1862** Sir B. Brodie *Psychol. Inq.* II. ii. 41 The faculties of the mind generally..are strengthened by exercise.

3. To give defensive strength to (a town, etc.), to make strong against attack, to fortify; in mod. use, to increase the strength of (a fortified place, a frontier).

1452 *Extracts Aberd. Reg.* (1844) I. 20 The toune salbe stryngthnit and fortifiit with walles and strynthes in all gudeli haste. *c* **1595** Capt. Wyatt *Dudley's Voy.* (Hakl. Soc.) 29 Another sconce..having the other side soe strengthned with wood that it was impossible to be assaultid. **1610** Holland *Camden's Brit.* (1637) 675 A proper Castle, strengthned with high Towres. **1611** Bible *1 Macc.* ix. 50 These [cities] did he strengthen with high wals, with gates, & with barres. **1841** W. Spalding *Italy & It. Isl.* III. 193 Frederic II., wishing to strengthen his frontier towards Rome, planned the city. **1884** *Manch. Exam.* 4 June 5/1 He is already taking steps, by strengthening Herat, to guard against any inroad upon his territories.

4. To make stronger in influence, authority, or security of position.

1579 Fenton *Guicciard.* i. 25 They sought..to strengthen first with colers lawful & after to set out their fortune with most ample titles. **1588** Shaks. *Tit. A.* i. i. 214 (Qo. 1600) My faction if thou strengthen with thy friend[s], I will most thank-full be. **1593** —— *3 Hen. VI*, iv. i. 37 To haue ioyn'd with France, in such alliance Would more haue strength'ned this our Commonwealth 'Gainst forraine stormes. *c* **1645** Howell *Lett.* i. xvii. (1650) I. 28 The Favourit Luines strengthneth himself more and more in his minionship. **1823** Scott *Quentin D.* xii, The Boar of Ardennes,..strengthened by the possession of that fair lady's lands, castles, and seigniory. **1830** Greville *Mem.* (1874) II. 45 In the meantime the Duke does nothing here towards strengthening his Government, and he will probably meet Parliament as he is. **1863** Geo. Eliot *Romola* Introd., He loved to strengthen his family by a good alliance. **1885** *Sat. Rev.* 3 Jan. 4/1 Proposing measures for the purpose of strengthening the House of Lords.

5. To reinforce (some material thing) by an additional support, added thickness, or covering.

1611 Bible *Isa.* liv. 2 Lengthen thy cords and strengthen thy stakes [of a tent]. **1687** Miege *Gt. Fr. Dict.* ii. s.v., To strengthen the Foundation of a House. **1748** *Anson's Voy.* iii. x. 415 The sails are made of matt, strengthened every three feet by an horizontal rib of bamboo. **1879** *Cassell's Techn. Educ.* III. 151 Sometimes the bows of iron ships are strengthened by breast-hooks formed of plates and angle-irons. **1882** Caulfeild & Saward *Dict. Needlework* 305 To strengthen Heels, they are often knitted with double thread. **1888** Mrs. Custer *Tenting on Plains* xvii. (1893) 358 In order to strengthen the tents against these hurricanes, he had ordered poles at each corner sunk deep into the ground.

6. To add strength or intensity to, to augment, intensify.

a **1586** Sidney *Arcadia* ii. xv. (1912) 246 Ever remembring to strengthen the suspition of his estate with private jelousie of her love. **1597** Hooker *Eccl. Pol.* v. lxvi. §9 A distinction of grace..planted in them at the first by Baptisme, after cherished, watred, and..strengthned as by other vertuous offices which pietie and true Religion teacheth. **1601** Shaks. *Jul. C.* ii. i. 248 So I did, Fearing to strengthen that impatience Which seem'd too much inkindled. **1736** Butler *Anal.* i. v. Wks. 1874 I. 89 Practical habits are formed and strengthened by repeated acts. **1789** Polwhele *Eng. Orator* iv. 74 The listless Lectures thou hastidly heard Strengthen the false Idea. **1799** *Trans. Soc. Arts* XVII. 299 Strengthen the shadows, making them..as dark as they are intended to be. **1857** Trollope *Barchester T.* x, Looking as she did, so beautiful.., with the pure brilliancy of her white dress brought out and strengthened by the colour beneath it, [etc.]. **1900** *Jrnl. Sch. Geog.* (U.S.) Apr. 133 The demand for a water route was strengthened by danger that the growing commerce of the Genesee country would be diverted [etc.]. **1907** J. A. Hodges *Elem. Photogr.* (ed. 6) 114 To strengthen the weak image.

7. To increase the strength or force of (reasons, obligations); to support (a case, an opinion) by additional evidence; to give increased strength or vigour of style to (a composition).

1600 E. Blount tr. *Conestaggio* 15 Strengthning their reasons with many examples. **1651** Hobbes *Leviath.* iii. xl. 249 Nor was there any Contract, that could adde to, or strengthen the Obligation, by which they..were bound naturally to obey God Almighty. **1712** *Spectator* No. 548 ¶1, I have however drawn up some additional Arguments to strengthen the Opinion which you have there delivered. **1882** Pebody *Engl. Journalism* xvi. (1882) 124 His revisions, alterations, and suppressions generally strengthened and improved an article.

8. To make more effective or powerful by reinforcement of numbers or resources.

1677 Miege *Dict. Eng.-Fr.* s.v., He strengthned his Army with a Recruit of six thousand men. **1820** Belzoni *Egypt & Nubia* ii. 260 My purse was but light..and though it had been a little strengthened by the two statues I lately disposed of.., my whole stock did not amount to two hundred pounds. **1838** Thirlwall *Greece* xliii. V. 313 The number now added to it was 4000, and 150 cavalry with eighteen galleys to strengthen the fleet. **1862** 'Cavendish' *Whist* (1864) 29 You must do your best to assist or strengthen your partner by leading high or strengthening cards. **1913** *Times* 14 May 6/2 The directors have deemed it advisable to strengthen the insurance fund by the transfer of £100,000 to that fund.

9. To make (a substance, a solution) stronger in the proportion of its active ingredient. Also with *up*.

1882 Paton in *Encycl. Brit.* XIV. 382/2 By some the weak and exhausted oozes..from the pits are strengthened up by renewed leaching.

10. *intr.* To become strong or stronger; to grow in strength or intensity.

1610 Shaks. *Temp.* v. i. 227 These are not naturall euents, they strengthen From strange, to stranger. **1662** Gurnall *Chr. in Arm.* iii. verse 17. lviii. 532 Thus as the days lengthen, so the cold strengthens. **1680** Otway *Orphan* i. i. (1691) 7 Oh men for flattery and deceit renown'd!..As your years increase, that strengthens too, T' undo poor Maids. **1732** Pope *Ess. Man* ii. 136 The young disease, that must subdue at length, Grows with his growth, and strengthens with his strength. **1792** Jefferson *Writ.* (1830) IV. 472 A year, even, was a great gain to a nation strengthening as we were. **1825** Scott *Talism.* xxviii, The sun's rays, now strengthening fast, seemed [etc.]. **1825** —— *Betrothed* xiv, As this conviction strengthened on Rose's mind. **1883** Jeaffreson *Real Ld. Byron* I. 255 Byron's journals show how steadily his tender concern for Miss Milbanke deepened and strengthened. **1906** Belloc *Hills & Sea* (1913) 169 The wind had strengthened by about half-past eight, so that it was very strong indeed.

Hence '**strengthened** *ppl. a.*

a **1586** Sidney *Ps.* xviii. x, Unto my strengthned stepps, thou didst enlardge the way. **1604** Marston *Malcontent* ii. v. D 4 Lets be once drunke together, and so vnite a most vertuously strengthened friendship. **1763** Churchill *Conference* 86 Hence to Yon Mountain which outbraves the sky, And dart from pole to pole thy strength'd eye. **1859** Geo. Eliot *Adam Bede* xxx, Adam's words..also carried a meaning which sickened her with a strengthened foreboding.

strengthener ('strɛŋθ(ə)nə(r)). Also 6-8 **strengthner**. [f. STRENGTHEN *v.* + -ER[1].] One who or something which strengthens.

1579 J. Jones *Preserv. Body & Soul* i. xi. 24 Exercise..is the preseruer of mans life,..strengthner of the partes, death of disseases. **1635** Jackson *Creed* viii. xxix. 340 But vinegar, ..mingled with hyssop, is a strengthener. **1645** G. Smith *Englands Pressures* 14 These have beene the strengthners of the hands of the Enemies. **1733** Cheyne *Eng. Malady* ii. iv. §3 (1734) 144 There is not a more wonderful Strengthner of the Solids..than the Jesuits Bark. **1768–74** Tucker *Lt. Nat.* (1834) II. 235 The grand strengthener of faith and every other virtue is a behaviour conformable thereto. **1805** Wordsw. *Prelude* v. 422 Simplicity in habit, truth in speech, Be these the daily strengtheners of their minds. **1825** L. Hunt *Redi's Bacchus in Tuscany* 120 Tea is highly commended..as a strengthener to the head and stomach. **1845** G. Dodd *Brit. Manuf.* IV. 152 If we open a piano-forte ..we shall see bars and rods and strengtheners of various kinds. **1872** O. W. Holmes *Poet Breakf.-t.* v, They go for weakness whenever they see it, with stimulants and strengtheners.

strengthening ('strɛŋθ(ə)nɪŋ), *vbl. sb.* [-ING[1].]

1. The action of the vb. STRENGTHEN, in various senses; an instance of this.

1535 Coverdale *1 Macc.* vi. 18 They..sought euer styll to do them harme, for the strengthenynge of the Heithen. *c* **1595** Capt. Wyatt *Dudley's Voy.* (Hakl. Soc.) 32 This letter..gave..better respect unto themselves for the strengthninge of our fortification. **1660** Fuller *Mixt Contempl. Better T.* ii. l. 74 Charles the Second..when a Childe was much troubled with a weaknesse in his Legs, and was appointed to weare Steel-bootes, for the strengthning of them. **1723** Chambers tr. *Le Clerc's Archit.* I. 23 The greater Solidity, and the further strengthning of the Building. **1870** J. F. Smith *Ewald's Introd. Hebr. Gram.* 162 A peculiar strengthening of the two preceding moods is attained by suffixing [etc.]. **1882** Caulfeild & Saward *Dict. Needlework* 307 *Strengthening*..is done by working doubled threads into the heels or toes of stockings.

2. *concr.* Something that strengthens, a source or means of strength.

1583 Golding *Calvin on Deut.* ii. 10 Is not yͤ knowledg of such doctrine an excellent strengthening to vs, when we see that [etc.]? *c* **1613** Middleton *No Wit like Woman's* ii. iii. 141 Out flies your moneys for restoratives and strengthenings. **1663** Gerbier *Counsel* 44 The peeres of Brick or Stone..will..be of a fit width to be a strengthening to the building. **1773** Hawkesworth *Cook's 1st Voy.* ii. x. III. 462 Thwarts..were securely lashed on each side, as a strengthening to the boat. **1879** *Cassell's Techn. Educ.* III. 151/1 Such supplementary strengthenings..are, however, not nearly so much required in iron as in wood ships.

strengthening ('strɛŋθ(ə)nɪŋ), *ppl. a.* [-ING[2].]

1. That strengthens or makes stronger.

1646 P. Bulkeley *Gospel Covt.* iv. 317 Faith is a strengthening grace. **1660** F. Brooke tr. *Le Blanc's Trav.* 74 They use themselves to very violent exercises,..feeding on strengthning foods onely. **1786** J. Hunter *Treat. Venereal Dis.* vi. iv. (1810) 563 In such cases I would recommend strengthening diet, and strengthening medicines. **1842** Loudon *Suburban Hort.* 633 Such a wall..may be made.. with stakes to serve as strengthening piers. **1848** J. T. White *Xenophon's Anab.* ii. iii. §18 *notes* (1872) 111 Observe here the strengthening force of *καί*. It is often employed in this way, when something stronger is subjoined to what had just preceded, and answers to the English *and..too*.

b. *Card-games.* Of a card or course of play: That strengthens one's hand.

1862 'Cavendish' *Whist* (1864) 34 When you have led a strengthening card, and it wins the trick. **1864** W. Pole *Th. Whist* (1870) 18 *Strengthening play* is getting rid of high cards in any suit, the effect of which is to give an improved value to the lower cards of that suit still remaining in, and so to strengthen the hand that holds them. **1900** J. Doe *Bridge Man.* 73 In leading what you may be pleased to consider a strengthening card, you are opening the very suit which your adversaries are secretly praying that they may be able to establish.

2. That grows or becomes stronger.

1855 Lynch *Rivulet* xlv. i, All the marvels have begun That wait upon the strengthening sun. **1906** M. Sellers *Eastland Co.* (Camden) Introd. 76 The manifestation of a slowly strengthening feeling in favour of a policy of less general restriction.

strengthful ('strɛŋθfʊl), *a.* [f. STRENGTH *sb.* + -FUL.] Full of or characterized by strength.

1382 Wyclif *2 Sam.* i. 19 What maner wise fellen the strengthful [Vulg. *fortes*]? *c* **1450** *Mirour Saluacioun* 2547 Bot crist prayed with swete teres and strengthfulle voice crying. **1584** Cogan *Haven Health* ccxl. 236 To make butterd Beere..Some put in the yolk of an egge or two.., and so they make it more strengthfull. **1604** Marston *Malcontent* ii. iii. 146 We are of Medicis; Florence our friend; in court my faction Not meanly strengthful [etc.]. **1830** Lamb *Let. to Ayrton* 14 Mar., All which fancies, redolent of middle age and strengthful spirits, come across us ever and anon in this vale of deliberate senectitude. **1866** [Miss Thackeray] *Village on Cliff* xii, Therein did her healthy and strengthful nature reassert itself, battling with these invisible foes.

Hence '**strengthfulness**.

1846 in Worcester (citing *Westm. Rev.*). **1855** in Ogilvie Suppl.

strengthily ('strɛŋθɪlɪ), *adv. rare.* Also 5 *Sc.* **strenthily,** 6 *Sc.* **strenthelie.** [f. STRENGTHY + -LY².] Strongly.

1456 SIR G. HAYE *Law Arms* (S.T.S.) 130 The band spirituall..byndis mare strenthily na temporale or carnale bandis. **1561** WINȜET *Four Scoir Thre Quest.* Wks. (S.T.S.) I. 55 Thai desyrit thir questionis mair trimlie and strenthelie to be set furth with ma large auctoriteis. **1883** *Daily News* 17 Sept. 2/3 The mare..is so strengthily made that her apparent lack of size will not cause the hammer to flag much when she has been walked once or twice round the ring.

strengthless ('strɛŋθlɪs), *a.* [f. STRENGTH *sb.* + -LESS.] Destitute of strength.

c **1200** ORMIN 12530 Þe deofell wennde aweȝȝ anan Forshamedd off himm sellfenn, Off þatt he wass all strenncþelæs Onnȝæn þatt newe kemmpe. **1311** *Pol. Songs* (1839) 255 That lond is streintheles. **1548** UDALL etc. *Erasm. Par. John* xvi. 29–33 The tyme is full nyghe that ye shall declare howe strengthelesse ye are of your selfes. **1594** WILLOBIE *Avisa* (1880) 99 You are the chieftaine, that haue layd This heauie siege to strengthlesse fort. *a* **1603** T. CARTWRIGHT *Confut. Rhem. N.T.* (1618) 155 A vaine and superstitious feare of the Popes strengthlesse curse. **1836** HARE *Guesses* (1859) 229 The laws we have imposed on ourselves, knowing now baseless and strengthless they are, we are impatient to throw off. **1857** BORROW *Romany Rye* (1858) I. 166 A time would come when my eyes would be bleared,..my arms.. strengthless and sapless. **1883** MISS M. BETHAM-EDWARDS *Disarmed* xvi, The listener sank back in his chair, white and strengthless, as if stricken with a blow.

Hence **'strengthlessly** *adv.* **'strengthlessness.**

1666 BUNYAN *Grace Ab.* ¶ 292 (1900) 384 At which times I should have such a strange faintness and strengthlessness seize upon my body that my legs have scarce been able to carry me. **1833** J. ROBERTSON *Let.* in *Life* iv. (1887) 52 With the exception of some considerable strengthlessness, which makes the chariot wheels drag on accordingly, I may call myself quite well. **1877** J. HAWTHORNE *Garth* II. VII. liv. 291 The fingers of one hand were fumbling strengthlessly at a grey twist of silky material. **1879** FARRAR *St. Paul* II. 83 The corruption, the indignity, the strengthlessness of the mortal body, into which at birth the soul is sown.

† **'strengthly,** *adv. Sc. Obs.* In 4 **strenthly.** [f. STRENGTH *sb.* + -LY².] Strongly. **a.** With force. **b.** So as to be strong.

1375 BARBOUR *Bruce* III. 769 (Edin.) Thai our possessioune Haldis strenthly [*Camb. MS.* IV. 541 with strinth], agayn resoun. **1573** *Diurn. Occur.* (Bannatyne Club) 331 On the north syid..lay the cannoune ryell, and tua cannounis, forthit strenthlie with gabiouns.

† **strength silver.** *Sc. Obs.* App. a sum of money which the tenant of a 'steelbow' farm received from his landlord on entering, on the same conditions as the farming stock.

1640 [see STEELBOW²].

strengthy ('strɛŋθɪ), *a.* Chiefly *Sc.* and *north.* Forms: 4 **strenkithi, -y, strenghti, -þi,** 4–6 **strenthy,** 6 **strenthie, strynthy,** 8– **strengthy.** [f. STRENGTH *sb.* + -Y.]

† **1.** Of a person: Strong to act or to withstand attack, mighty, powerful. *Obs.*

13.. *Gosp. Nicod.* 1317 (MS. Galba) [The devils say of Jesus] He es a strenkithi swayn. *a* **1340** HAMPOLE *Psalter* xxx. 4 Nourewhare i fele me strenghti and sykere bot of þe. **1340** —— *Pr. Consc.* 5075 And strenthy men, and bond and fre, In caves þai wald þan hyde ilkan. *c* **1470** HENRY *Wallace* x. 570 Allace! My best brothir in warld that euir I had!.. My faith, my help, strenthiast in stour! **1520** M. NISBET *N.T. in Scots* Apocal. xviii. 8 For God is strenthie [*Wycl.* strong], that sal deme hir. **1549** *Compl. Scot.* xvii. 151 He vas strynthy ande auful in ane battel contrar the enemeis of alexander. *a* **1578** LINDESAY (Pitscottie) *Chron. Scot.* (S.T.S.) I. 243 Thair was nane that mycht war him at na tyme bot he wan the lady frome thame all for he was verie puissant and strenthie on horsback.

† **b.** Of a position or structure: Strong against assault. *Obs.*

1513 DOUGLAS *Æneis* VIII. x. 19 Duke Tharcon, and the Tuscanis..intill a strenthy place Thayr palȝeonis all had plantit. **1535** W. STEWART *Cron. Scot.* II. 47 The strenthis all, baith castell, tour and toun,..He hes gart big far strenthear agane. **1596** DALRYMPLE tr. *Leslie's Hist. Scot.* (S.T.S.) II. 16 The Balie fortifiet all castellis in the Realme estemet strenthiest.

† **c.** Of action, etc.: Formidable to contend with, difficult to overthrow. *Obs.*

1533 BELLENDEN *Livy* (S.T.S.) II. 127 This aduersite cumin to þe ciete maid þe actioun of tribunis mare strenthy þan afore. *a* **1560** ROLLAND *Crt. Venus* I. 514 Lufe is sa perrellous, To all gude deid it is ane strenthie bar. **1561** WINȜET *Four Scoir Thre Quest.* Wks. (S.T.S.) I. 60 This tractate..micht be maid..in sentence fer mair strenthy and difficill to our aduersaris to mak anssuer thairto. **1563** J. DAVIDSON *Answ. Tract. Kennedy* (1844) 208 Na examinatione can subvert the veritie, bot make it the mair strenthy and the mair manifest to the warlde. **1573** J. TYRIE *Refut. Answ. Knox* To Rdr. †ij b, So destitute of iugement.. that we can nocht perceaue, quhat difference thair be betuix the simple and strenthie defence of ane iust caus, and the craftie coloring of ane lesing.

2. Physically or muscularly strong. Now *rare* exc. *dial.*

1456 SIR G. HAYE *Law Arms* (S.T.S.) 118 Gif hardynes, or cowardis cum of a stark or strenthy corps. **1568** G. SKEYNE *Descr. Pest* viii. (Bannatyne Club) 32 For as natural facultie, & it quhilk is callit animalis facultas, ar maist strenthy & best at eis, the vitale faculte becummis the mair feble. **17..** *Hardyknute* in Maidment *Scottish Ballads* (1868) I. 24 Right strengthy arms forfeebled grew. **1828** J. WILSON in *Blackw. Mag.* XXIV. 275 Look at him now, a straight and strengthy stripling..springing over rock-ledge after rock-ledge. **1896** *Daily Chron.* 1 Sept. 10/6, 6 active, useful, strengthy cart and van horses.

† **strenk,** *v. Obs. rare.* [Early ME. *strenken,* of obscure origin. Cf. *strenkle* STRINKLE *v.*] *trans.* To sprinkle.

c **1200** ORMIN 1099, & toc himm þa þatt illke bold..& warrp itt tær wiþþ strenncless,..& siþþen ȝede he þeþenn ut To strennkenn i þe kirrke. *Ibid.* 1771 þatt blod tatt þurrh þe bisscopp wass þær o þa þingess strennkedd. *Ibid.* 1789.

strenket(h, -kit(h, -kyght, obs. ff. STRENGTH.

strenkle, var. STRINKLE *sb.* and *v.*

strenlyng, var. STRANDLING *Obs.*

strenth(e, obs. ff. STRENGTH.

strenuity (strɪ'njuːɪtɪ). Now *rare.* Also 5–6 **strenuite,** 6 **-uyte, strenewite,** 7 **strenuitie.** [ad. L. *strēnuitās,* f. *strēnu-us*: see STRENUOUS *a.* and -ITY.] The quality of being strenuous, strenuousness.

1436 *Libel Eng. Policy* in *Pol. Poems* (Rolls) II. 200 Thus nere I leve the kynge wyth his nobelesse, Henry the fifte.. for aboute in the see No better was prince of strenuité. **1500–20** DUNBAR *Poems* lxxxviii. 19 London, thou art of townes A per se...Strong Troy in vigour and in strenuytie. **1525** *St. Papers Hen. VIII,* VI. 413 The valiant acquitaile, vertue, and strenuite of the faithfull and good capitans, in the honorable defence of Italye. *c* **1611** CHAPMAN *Iliad* xv. 649 And thus, vnlike affects Bred like strenuitie in both. **1681** H. MORE *Exp. Dan.* vi. 163 His dominion..not having that strenuity and greatness of parts, nor that strength; his entire Empire being thus divided into four Kingdoms. **1905** J. OXENHAM *White Fire* iv. 46 His white, set face and blazing eyes looked out at her in that agonised strenuity of appeal which had..stirred her to the depths.

strenuosity (strɛnjuː'ɒsɪtɪ). [f. STRENUOUS *a.*: see -OUS and -ITY.] Strenuousness (somewhat disparaging in use).

1886 *Academy* 30 Jan. 73/1 The author..may be reminded that strenuosity in style is not quite the same thing as strength, and recommended to be sparing of quotations [etc.]. **1904** *Morning Post* 18 Apr. 9/1 In every place he [Roosevelt] has filled,..he has displayed that strenuosity which must always be associated with his name. **1915** E. V. LUCAS *In Gentlest Germany* ix. 70 The watchword of the nation [Germany] is strenuosity.

strenuous ('strɛnjuːəs), *a.* [f. L. *strēnu-us* brisk, active, vigorous (related to Gr. στρηνής strong, hard, rough, στρῆνος haughtiness, arrogance) + -OUS. Cf. It. *strenuo,* Sp. *estrénuo.*

App. first used by Marston; one of the words ridiculed, as pedantic neologisms, by Ben Jonson in his attack on Marston in *Poetaster* (1601), where (v. iii. 302) Marston's line is almost literally quoted.]

1. Of persons or their dispositions: Vigorous in action, energetic; 'brave, bold, active, valiant' (J.). Now usually with stronger notion: Unremittingly and ardently laborious.

1599 MARSTON *Ant. Rev.* v. i. (1602) I 2, The fist of strenuous vengeance is clutcht. *c* **1611** CHAPMAN *Iliad* XVII. 495 He..tooke one Podes, that was heire, to old Eetion, A rich man, and a strenuous [Gr. ἀγαθός]. **1631** WEEVER *Anc. Funeral Mon.* 254 A strenuous and an expert Souldier. **1632** LITHGOW *Trav.* VII. 326 Our Ship..did carry..foure score strong and strenuous Saylers. **1656** BLOUNT *Glossogr.,* *Strenuous,* valiant, stout, hardy, active. **1670** MILTON *Hist. Brit.* IV. 181 Offa the Mercian, a strenuous and suttle King. **1718** POPE *Iliad* III. 91 Like Steel, uplifted by some strenuous Swain. **1849** MACAULAY *Hist. Eng.* vii. II. 162 His attention had been confined to those studies which form strenuous and sagacious men of business. **1877** MRS. OLIPHANT *Makers Flor.* xii. 301 Faith was more strenuous and robust in those days. **1899** J. L. WILLIAMS *Stolen Story,* etc. 128 The city editor, who had his fingers on the pulse of the strenuous metropolis.

b. Zealous, earnest, 'strong' as a partisan or opponent. *Obs.* exc. as contextual use of sense 1.

1713 SWIFT in *Buccleuch MSS.* (Hist. MSS. Comm.) I. 359 Lord Hintchingbrook..is grown a strenuous Tory. **1735–6** —— *Let. to Pope* 7 Feb, I hear he resolves to be strenuous for taking off the Test. **1759** DILWORTH *Pope* 67 So strenuous a member of the Romish Church was Mr. Pope. **1774** PENNANT *Tour Scot. in 1772,* 92 A strenuous supporter of Mary Stuart. **1775** BURKE *Corr.* (1844) II. 26, I have been a strenuous advocate for the superiority of this country. **1792** A. YOUNG *Trav. France* 127 Mons. l'Abbé de —— was particularly strenuous for what is called the regeneration of the kingdom. **1822** HAZLITT *Men & Manners* Ser. II. iii. (1869) 75 He was as open to impressions as he was strenuous in maintaining them. **1860** TYNDALL *Glac.* II. xvi. 312 The idea attached to Professor Forbes's words by some of his most strenuous supporters. **1892** LADY F. VERNEY *Verney Mem.* I. 41 Sir Ralph was as strenuous as ever for Edward IV in the city.

2. † **a.** Of inanimate things: Strong, powerful in operation; also, physically robust. *Obs.*

1632 QUARLES *Div. Fancies* II. xxv. 66 The Sun shines alwaies strenuous and faire, But, ah, our sins, our Clouds benight the ayre. **1633** T. ADAMS *Exp. 2 Pet.* iii. 3. II. 1140 Heaven and earth are of a strenuous composition, compact together with more powerfull sinewes and ligaments.

b. Of voice, etc.: Powerful, loud. *arch.*

1680 H. MORE *Apocal. Apoc.* 181 He..pronounceth the sentence against the great Whore with a strong and strenuous voice. **1748** *Anson's Voy.* III. viii. 372 They expressed their approbation, according to naval custom, by three strenuous cheers. **1817** KIRBY & SP. *Entomol.* xxiv. (1818) II. 379 The wasp and hornet also are strenuous hummers. **1850** GROTE *Greece* II. lx. (1862) V. 292 He was seen..marshalling the troops,..and addressing them with a voice louder, more strenuous, and more commanding than was his wont. **1876** MORRIS *Sigurd* III. 180 Forth go their hearts before them to the blast of the strenuous horn.

3. Of action or effort: Vigorous, energetic; now with stronger sense, persistently and ardently laborious. Of conditions, periods, etc.: Characterized by strenuous exertion.

strenuous idleness (= L. *strenua inertia,* Hor. *Ep.* I. xi. 28): busy activity to no useful purpose.

1671 MILTON *Samson* 268 But what more oft in Nations grown corrupt,..Then to love Bondage more then Liberty; Bondage with ease then strenuous liberty. **1681** FLAVEL *Meth. Grace* xxviii. 481 Languishing consumptive persons are very unfit to be employed in difficult and strenuous labours. *a* **1700** EVELYN *Diary* 14 Aug. 1654, Belvoir Castle ..is famous for its strenuous resistance in the late civil warr. **1728** MORGAN *Algiers* II. iv. 265 One [galley] by meer Dint of strenuous Rowing..escaped. **1742** YOUNG *Nt. Th.* I. 149 A soul immortal, spending all her fires, Wasting her strength in strenuous idleness. **1760–72** H. BROOKE *Fool of Qual.* (1809) IV. 156 He..seized upon him with a strenuous embrace. **1785** COWPER *Task* I. 388 Himself derives..From strenuous toil his hours of sweetest ease. **1794** MRS. RADCLIFFE *Myst. Udolpho* xxxiii, He..was conveyed to a place of confinement, whither the most strenuous inquiries of his friends had been unable to trace him. **1810** SOUTHEY *Kehama* VI. iii, Soaring with strenuous flight above, He bears her to the blessed Grove. **1829** WORDSW. '*This Lawn, a carpet all alive*' 6 Worldlings revelling in the fields Of strenuous idleness. **1846** GROTE *Greece* I. I. vi. 153 He is one of the few Grecian princes who..is found in a strenuous and honoured old age in the midst of his children and subjects. **1849** MACAULAY *Hist. Eng.* vi. II. 10 But for their strenuous opposition to the Exclusion Bill he would have been a banished man. **1851** CARLYLE *Sterling* III. iii. (1872) 186 On this *Tragedy of Strafford*..he expended many strenuous months. **1871** L. STEPHEN *Playgr. Eur.* (1894) xiii. 321 The hours of labour, divided into minutes..of strenuous muscular exertion. **1899** ROOSEVELT *Sp.* 10 Apr. in *Strenuous Life* (1902) 1, I wish to preach, not the doctrine of ignoble ease, but the doctrine of the strenuous life, the life of toil and effort, of labor and strife.

strenuously ('strɛnjuːəslɪ), *adv.* [f. STRENUOUS *a.* + -LY².] In a strenuous manner.

The first example is merely in ridicule of Marston's use of the adj.: see note s.v. STRENUOUS.

1601 B. JONSON *Poetaster* II. i. 14, I am most strenuously well, I thank you, sir. **1631** WEEVER *Anc. Funeral Mon.* 257 He had strenuously gouerned his Church the space of 26. yeares. **1662** A. COOPER *Stratologia* VII. 150 Their Mines and Batteries strenuously they ply'd. *a* **1708** BEVERIDGE *Thes. Theol.* (1710) II. 276 These works we ought to do,.. strenuously, or with our might. **1766** GOLDSM. *Vic. W.* xiii, My wife very strenuously insisted upon the advantages that would result from it. **1856** MACAULAY *Biog., Johnson* (1860) 85 His marriage made it necessary for him to exert himself more strenuously than he had hitherto done. **1857** DICKENS *Lett.* (1880) II. 7, I still strenuously believe that I did so. **1875** JOWETT *Plato* (ed. 2) III. 253, That God being good is the author of evil to any one, is to be strenuously denied.

strenuousness ('strɛnjuːəsnɪs). [f. STRENUOUS *a.* + -NESS.] The quality of being strenuous.

a **1649** in *N. & Q.* Ser. I. X. 357 Strenuousnes must be added, if he find resistance, amongst other virtues which compleate a judge. **1727** BAILEY vol. II, *Strenuousness,* Vigorousness, Earnestness, Laboriousness. **1819** CHALMERS *Serm. Tron Ch.* iv. 121 The man has put forth all his strenuousness to the task of accomplishing all that he is able for. **1909** R. LAW *Tests of Life* v. 69 This the writer maintains with unexampled strenuousness and rigour.

streny(e, obs. ff. STRAIN *v.*¹

streon(e, -(i)en: see STRAIN *sb.*¹, STRENE *v.*

† **strep**¹. *Mining. Obs.*⁻¹. Corruption of or mistake for STRAKE *sb.*³

1778 [see STRAKE *sb.*³ a].

strep² (strɛp), colloq. abbrev. of (*a*) STREPTOCOCCUS (freq. *attrib.*); (*b*) STREPTOMYCIN.

(*a*) **1927** *Amer. Speech* II. 313/2 A streptococcus infection of the throat becomes a 'strep throat'. **1941** R. CHANDLER *Let.* 1 Feb. (1981) 19 Awfully sorry to hear you had been sick. I know what the streps can do to a person. **1956** [see STAPH]. **1962** A. LURIE *Love & Friendship* iv. 68 There's germs flying round in the air.., pneumonia and bronchitis and strep. **1966** H. KEMELMAN *Saturday the Rabbi went Hungry* iv. 25 It's a strep infection, the doctor says. **1974** [see SHET, SHED]. **1980** *Daily Tel.* 6 Oct. 14/6 Strep infections can cause breathing disorders, shock, bleeding and meningitis in newborn babies.

(*b*) **1959** J. BRAINE *Vodi* vi. 85 They'd tried strep. and P.A.S. **1961** C. COCKBURN *View from West* i. 6 Hallucinated myself by the effects of streptomycin—we soon all got very matey with this potent drug and called it strep.

strepe, obs. form of STRIP *sb.* and *v.*

strepent ('strɛpənt), *a. rare* [ad. L. *strepentem* pr. pple. of *strepĕre* to make a noise.] Noisy.

1750 SHENSTONE *Rural Elegance* 287 Peace to the strepent horn! Let no harsh dissonance disturb the Morn. **1801–2** CAMPBELL *Mobiade* 9 No strepent goose at Christmas-tide Hissed in the strangler's hand. **1817** KIRBY & SP. *Entomol.* xxiv. (1818) II. 384 He..had called many to witness the vibrating and strepent wings of this trumpeter humble-bee. **1830** W. L. BOWLES *Life Ken* I. iv. 59 Ten thousand strepent horns of pamphleteering fury.

† **strepe'rosity.** *Obs. rare*⁻¹. [f. next: see -OUS and -ITY.] High-sounding language.

1772 [T. NUGENT] tr. *Isla's Hist. Friar Gerund* I. I. vii. 175 The blessed Domine..ravished with the streperosity [orig. Sp. *con el estrepitoso sonido*] of pentacontarch, captain, soldiers, and stipendiary, told his scholars [etc.].

† **'streperous**, *a. Obs.* [f. med.L. *streper-us* (f. *strepĕre* to make a noise) + -OUS. Cf. OBSTREPEROUS.] Noisy, harsh-sounding.

1637 HEYWOOD *Lond. Spec.* B 3 b, Triton with his pearly trumpets blew A streperous blast. **1637** —— *Dial.* i. 7 He.. with a voice strep'rous and loud (That all they in the ship might heare him) vow'd To set before that Saint a waxen Light. **1646** SIR T. BROWNE *Pseud. Ep.* II. vi. 100 In a streperous eruption it [the bay-tree] riseth against Fire. **1688** CUDWORTH *Immut. Mor.* (1731) 182 The streperous Noise of a Single Fiddle. **1822** T. TAYLOR *Apuleius* II. 39 Scarcely had the streperous song of the crested cohort proclaimed a truce to night.

Hence †**'streperously** *adv.*, †**'streperousness.**

1727 BAILEY vol. II, *Streperousness*, Noisiness. **1822** T. TAYLOR *Apuleius* IV. 72 They play clamorously, they sing streperously.

strephosymbolia (ˌstrɛfəʊsɪm'bəʊlɪə). *Psychol.* [mod.L., f. Gr. στρέφειν to turn, twist + σύμβολ-ον (see SYMBOL *sb.*[1]) + -IA[1].] (See quot. 1937.)

1925 S. T. ORTON in *Arch. Neurol. & Psychiatry* (Chicago) XIV. 610 The term 'congenital word-blindness' because of its association with the acquired condition and the implications therefrom, does not seem to be properly descriptive of this disability, and I would therefore like to offer the term 'strephosymbolia'.. as a descriptive name for the whole group of children who show unusual difficulty in learning to read. **1937** —— *Reading, Writing & Speech Problems in Children* 214 *Strephosymbolia*, a delay or difficulty in learning to read.. characterized by confusion between similarly formed but oppositely oriented letters, and a tendency to a changing order of direction in reading. **1968** E. J. KAHN *Harvard* xiv. 223 There are students who should be exempt from language requirements because they suffer from strephosymbolia—an affliction that makes it difficult.. to see the ends of written words in unfamiliar languages.

strepie ('striːpɪ). *S. Afr.* Also **streepie, streepje.** [a. Afrikaans, f. *streep* STRIPE *sb.*[3] + -IE.] A small fish, the striped karanteen, *Sarpa salpa*. Cf. KARANTEEN.

1913 [see *bamboo-fish* s.v. BAMBOO *sb.* 2]. **1945** *Cape Argus* 27 Jan. 4/8 Half an inch of her wool.. tied to a 'streepie' hook, caught about a dozen small fish. **1957** S. SCHOEMAN *Strike!* iii. 89 The strepie, with its beautiful gold and silver colouring, is the favourite prey of the elf. **1974** *Stand. Encycl. S. Afr.* X. 320/1 Strepie.. is one of the most beautiful and best-known bait fishes in southern Africa.

strepitant ('strɛpɪtənt), *a.* [ad. L. *strepitant-em*, pr. pple. of *strepitāre*: see next.] Making a great noise, noisy.

1855 BROWNING *Master Hugues* xvi, Three makes rejoinder, expansive, explosive; Four overbears them all, strident and strepitant. **1861** F. HALL in *Jrnl. Asiatic Soc. Bengal* 209 A hue as of the smoke associated with the fire of the poison of strepitant snakes.

Hence **'strepitantly** *adv.*, boisterously.

1913 *Engl. Rev.* Oct. 465 The autumn season has begun strepitantly.

† **'strepitate**, *v. Obs.*$^{-0}$ [f. L. *strepitāt-*, ppl. stem of *strepitāre* to make a repeated noise, frequentative of *strepĕre* to make a noise: see -ATE.] *trans.* (See quot.)

1656 BLOUNT *Glossogr.*, *Strepitate*,.. to make a noise often, to make a great noise, to rusle.

strepitation (strɛpɪ'teɪʃən). *rare.* [f. prec.: see -ATION.] A repeated noise, clattering.

1913 *Nation* 12 July 560/2 To listen in the gathering darkness to the strepitation of Apollyon's wings.

‖**strepitoso** (strepi'toso), *a.* (*adv.*, *sb.*) *Mus.* [It., lit. 'noisy, loud'.] A direction indicating that a composition be played in a spirited or boisterous manner. Also as *sb.*, a piece designed to be played in this manner.

1801 T. BUSHY *Compl. Dict. Mus.*, *Strepitoso*.., a word signifying that the movement to which it is prefixed is to be performed in an impetuous, boisterous style. **1876** STAINER & BARRETT *Dict. Mus. Terms* 410/1 *Strepitoso* (*It.*), noisy, impetuous. **1946** E. BLOM *Everyman's Dict. Mus.* 596/2 *Strepitoso* (It. = noisy), a direction suggesting a forceful and spirited perf., but more often used in the sense of a climax growing in force and speed. **1966** *Listener* 17 Feb. 256/3 The first act finale of both operas ends with a canonic *andantino* in A flat leading to a prolonged *strepitoso* in C major.

strepitous ('strɛpɪtəs), *a.* [ad. mod.L. type **strepitōsus*, f. L. *strepitus* noise, clatter, f. *strepĕre* to make a noise. Cf. It. *strepitoso* (used chiefly as musical term).] Noisy, accompanied with much noise. (Now used chiefly in musical criticism.)

1681 NEVILE *Plato Rediv.* 119 A poor Gentleman, who by means of the Harangue of a Strepitous Lawyer, was found guilty of Murder. **1854** S. DOBELL *Balder* vii. 40 In louder progress strepitous so came The great approach. **1893** *Guardian* 8 Mar. 382/3 The overture is very long, very ambitious, very strident, and—as the analyst would say—very 'strepitous'. **1903** A. B. WALKLEY *Dram. Crit.* 100 These are the people who are for ever talking as though action must be something external and strepitous.

† **strepsinema.** *Cytology. Obs.* [f. Gr. στρεψι-, comb. form of στρέφειν to twist + νῆμα yarn.] A condition of the nucleus during cell division, characterized by pairs of chromosomes twisted around one another or in the form of twisted rings; in most cases applied to diplotene nuclei.

1900 H. H. DIXON in *Proc. R. Irish Acad.* VI. 2 In the next stage (fig. 2) the nucleus is in what I would suggest to call the 'strepsinema' condition. The chromatin appears in much the same condition as in the preceding stage, except that in many places it may be seen that the two portions of the thread are more or less loosely twisted together. **1911** *Q. Jrnl. Microsc. Sci.* LVII. 15 The onset of synizesis coincides with the entrance of the nucleus into strepsinema. **1925** E. B. WILSON *Cell* (ed. 3) ii. 126 A noteworthy peculiarity of the spireme sometimes seen is a twisting of the longitudinal halves about each other to form a strepsinema; but this is much less common in the somatic mitoses than in meiosis.

strepsipterous (strɛp'sɪptərəs), *a. Ent.* [f. mod.L. *Strepsiptera* neut. pl. (f. Gr. στρεψι-, comb. form of στρέφειν to twist + πτερόν wing) + -OUS.] Belonging to the order *Strepsiptera* of insects (named by Kirby from the twisted front wings).

1817 KIRBY & SP. *Entomol.* xxiii. II. 327 The strepsipterous genera, *Stylops*, K. and *Xenos*, R. **1835** WESTWOOD in *Trans. Entom. Soc.* (1836) I. 173 Description of a new Strepsipterous Insect recently discovered in the Island of Mauritius. **1870** ROLLESTON *Anim. Life* p. cxi.

Also **strep'sipteral** *a.*; **strep'sipteran** *a.*, also *sb.* an insect of the order *Strepsiptera*.

1842 BRANDE *Dict. Sci.*, etc., *Strepsipterans.* **1877** HUXLEY *Anat. Inv. Anim.* 451 The Strepsipteral larva.

† **strepsitene.** *Cytology. Obs.* [ad. F. *strepsitène* (V. Grégoire 1907, in *La Cellule* XXIV. 372), f. STREPSINEMA: see -TENE.] = STREPSINEMA.

1911 *Q. Jrnl. Microsc. Sci.* LVII. 14 Following immediately after the bouquet is the strepsitene or diplotene stage, in which the conjugants which were temporarily united in the pachytene loops separate again. **1925** E. B. WILSON *Cell* (ed. 3) vi. 544 Sooner.. or later.., the threads are plainly longitudinally double (diplonema): and the two threads, especially in the later stages, are often spirally twisted about each other to form the strepsinema or strepsitene. These various conditions cannot as yet be very logically separated as distinct stages.

strepto- ('strɛptəʊ), before a vowel **strept-**, combining form of Gr. στρεπτός twisted (f. στρέφειν to turn, twist); used in many scientific terms, as **strep'taster** [Gr. ἀστήρ star], a form of sponge-spicule (see quot. 1888). **ˌstreptoba'cilli** [BACILLUS] *sb. pl.*, bacilli arranged in chains. **streptobac'teria** [BACTERIUM] *sb. pl.*, bacteria linked together like a chain. **streptoco'ccolysin**, also (in shortened form) **strepto'colysin**, 'a hemolysin destructive to streptococci, formed when virulent streptococci are grown in blood serum' (Dorland *Med. Dict.* 1913). **'streptocyte** [-CYTE], an amœbiform body occurring in bead-like strings from the vesicles of foot-and-mouth disease. **strep'tolysin** [LYSIN] = *streptococcolysin*. **ˌstrepto'neural, -'neurous** *adjs.*, belonging to or characteristic of the *Streptoneura*, a branch of Gastropoda in which the loop of visceral nerves embracing the intestine is twisted into a figure-of-eight. **ˌstrepto'phiurid** *a.*, pertaining to or connected with the *Streptophiuræ*, a subdivision of Ophiuroidea; *sb.* an individual of this subdivision. **'streptospon'dylian, -'spondyline, -'spondylous** *adjs.*, pertaining to the genus *Streptospondylus* of fossil crocodiles, in which the vertebral articulations are apparently reversed. **strepto'stylic, -'stylicate** *adjs.* [ad. G. *Streptostylica*, name of a group (H. Stannius 1856, in von Siebold & Stannius *Handb. der Zootomie* (ed. 2) II. 45), Gr. στῦλος pillar], orig., pertaining to or connected with the *Streptostylica*, that one of the two main divisions of Reptiles (in Stannius' classification) in which the quadrate bone is freely articulated with the skull; now used with reference to the free articulation of the quadrate bone with the squamosal rather than to any taxonomic group; so **'streptostyly**, streptostylic condition. Also used as comb. form of STREPTOCOCCUS, STREPTOCOCCAL *a.*, as in STREPTODORNASE, and of *Streptomyces* (see STREPTOMYCETE), as in STREPTOVARICIN.

1888 W. J. SOLLAS in *Challenger Rep.* XXV. p. lxiii, The asters are divided into two subsections, the true asters or euasters, and the *streptasters or those in which the actines do not proceed from a centre, but from a longer or shorter axis, which is usually spiral. **1900** E. A. MINCHIN in *Ray Lankester's Treat. Zool.* II. *Sponges* 134. **1903** THAYER *Schmaus' Path. & Pathol. Anat.* 202 Bacilli. Long or short rods, propagate by fission or spores; the former by fission or crosswise, the younger forms separating or connected (*streptobacilli). **1883** *Streptobacteria [see *diplococci* s.v. DIPLO-]. **1891** G. S. WOODHEAD *Bacteria* 31 In the rod-shaped bacteria this division takes place.. and when it is imperfect or incomplete it gives rise to chain-bacteria or Strepto-bacteria. **1897** *Allbutt's Syst. Med.* II. 688 Schottelius found in the contents of foot-and-mouth vesicles peculiar bodies which he termed *streptocytes. **1904** *Brit. Med. Jrnl.* 10 Sept. 571 The neutralization curves of.. bodies and their antibodies: the rennet.., the vibriolysin, the staphylolysin, and the *streptolysin. **1883** *Encycl. Brit.* XVI. 646/2 The *Streptoneurous condition of the visceral loop in Zygobranchia. **1888** ROLLESTON & JACKSON *Anim. Life* 111 Certain streptoneurous *Gastropoda Anisopleura*. **1892** *Proc. Zool. Soc.* 183 *Ophiobyrsa hystricis*. The largest *Streptophiurid found within the British area is the species so named by Mr. Lyman. **1849** A. G. MELVILLE in *Phil. Trans.* CXXXIX. 286 The *Streptospondylian form of the body of a vertebra. *Ibid.*, The Streptospondylian type is not.. persistent. **1892** *Proc. Zool. Soc.* 179 *Ophioteresis* is a *streptospondyline Ophiurid. **1901** *Nature* 14 Mar. 462/2 The *streptostylic types appear first in the Jurassic as Lacertilia. **1933** *Univ. Calif. Publ. Zool.* XXXVII. 524 A comparison of the streptostylic condition in these salamanders with that in certain reptiles.. shows great differences in both skeleton and muscles, such that no homology is possible. **1980** *Nature* 21 Feb. 779/1 Streptostylic quadrates are found in fossil lizards before the appearance of mesokinesis and occur in animals with limited mesokinetic potential such as *Uromastix* and *Ctenosaura*. **1887** E. D. COPE *Orig. Fittest* xi. 337 The existing *streptostylicate orders have advanced beyond their Permian ancestors. **1925** J. S. KINGSLEY *Vertebrate Skeleton* (ed. 2) 335/2 (Index), *Streptostyly. **1933** *Univ. Calif. Publ. Zool.* XXXVII. 521 In a study of some Pacific coast salamanders, it was found that at least three species.. possess a pivoting squamosal... Streptostyly, so far as the writer has been able to learn, is otherwise unknown in Amphibia. **1973** *Nature* 11 May 72/2 The articulation of the maxillae with the nasals and premaxillae reveals how streptostyly was associated with an akinetic skull in *Hesperornis*.

‖**Streptocarpus** (strɛptəʊ'kɑːpəs). Also Anglicized **'streptocarp.** [mod.L., f. Gr. στρεπτός (see STREPTO-) + καρπός fruit.] A genus of African Gesneraceous plants bearing pistils or fruits spirally-twisted towards the point; a plant of this genus, esp. the Cape Primrose (see PRIMROSE 2 b).

1828 J. LINDLEY in *Bot. Reg.* XIV. 1173 (*heading*) Cape Streptocarpus. **1846** LINDLEY *Veg. Kingd.* 672 Gesneraceæ. .. Genera.. *Streptocarpus, Lindl. **1882** *Garden* 25 Nov. 462/3 The whole surface is completely covered with large mauve-tinted blossoms, not much smaller than those of ordinary Gloxinias, to which the Streptocarpus is related. **1895** *Daily News* 22 May 7/3 Choice varieties of streptocarpus, gloxinias, [etc.]. **1904** *Daily Chron.* 10 Aug. 4/7 An exhibit of pentstemons and streptocarps.

‖**streptococcus** (strɛptəʊ'kɒkəs). *Bacteriology.* Pl. **-cocci** (-'kɒksaɪ). [mod.L. (Billroth), f. Gr. στρεπτό-ς twisted (see STREPTO-; taken by Billroth to mean 'chain') + κόκκος berry.] A form of bacterial organism in which the cocci are arranged in chains or chaplets.

1877 tr. *Billroth's Lect. Surg. Pathol.*, etc. I. 137 These streptococci are sometimes moving ones. *Ibid.* 138 In a state of absolute rest the streptococcus may form long threads running parallel with the surface. **1891** G. S. WOODHEAD *Bacteria* 31 Chain-cocci or strepto-cocci.

attrib. **1897** *Allbutt's Syst. Med.* III. 636 Streptococcus infection. **1900** *Brit. Med. Jrnl.* 20 Jan. 142 No streptococcus colonies were found.

Hence **streptococcal** (-'kɒkəl), **-coccic** (-'kɒksɪk), **-coccous** (-'kɒkəs), *adjs.* pertaining to or produced by streptococcus.

1897 *Brit. Med. Jrnl.* 13 Mar. 655 It was important for surgeons to distinguish between streptococcal peritonitis.. and peritonitis due to the colon bacillus. **1897** *Trans. Amer. Pediatric Soc.* IX. 90 The streptococcic cases are very dangerous. **1902** *Encycl. Brit.* XXXI. 558/1 The statement .. is in direct contradiction to all our knowledge of the behaviour of the blood in streptococcous infections.

streptodornase (strɛptəʊ'dɔːneɪz). *Pharm.* and *Biochem.* [f. STREPTO(COCCAL *a.* + D(E)O(XY)-R(IBO)N(UCLE)ASE.] A deoxyribonuclease, or a group of such enzymes, produced by some streptococci and used in conjunction with streptokinase to bring about the dissolution of purulent and fibrinous exudates.

1949 S. SHERRY et al. in *Jrnl. Clinical Investigation* XXVIII. 1094/1 The word 'Streptodornase' has been employed in this article as an abbreviation of streptococcal desoxyribose nuclease. **1977** *Proc. R. Soc. Med.* LXX. 571/1 Skin testing to streptokinase-streptodornase, candida and phytohaemagglutinin proved negative.

streptokinase (strɛptəʊ'kaɪneɪz). *Pharm.* [f. as prec. + KINASE.] An enzyme produced by hæmolytic streptococci which activates plasminogen to form plasmin and is given intravenously to dissolve intravascular blood clots.

1944 CHRISTENSEN & MACLEOD in *Jrnl. Gen. Physiol.* XXVIII. 581 Streptococcal fibrinolysin, also a misnomer in the light of present knowledge, may be termed 'streptokinase', analogous to 'enterokinase' or 'mold kinase'. **1969** *Brit. Med. Jrnl.* 29 Mar. 812/1 Nine patients with arteriographically proved pulmonary embolism have been treated by a 36-hour infusion of streptokinase. **1978** F. X. HASSELBERGER *Uses of Enzymes* x. 122 A controlled experiment.. confirmed the superiority of streptokinase over heparin (a chemical anticoagulant) in reducing deaths due to acute myocardial infarction.

streptomycete (strɛptəʊ'maɪsiːt). *Bacteriology.* [f. mod.L. *Streptomycetes*, pl. of *Streptomyces*, generic name (Waksman & Henrici 1943, in *Jrnl. Bacteriol.* XLVI. 339), f. STREPTO- + Gr. μύκης fungus.] A bacterium of the genus *Streptomyces*, which belongs in the family like bacteria and comprises aerobic forms that grow as branching filaments, form spores in chains, and occur chiefly as saprophytes in soil.

1956 CARTER & SMITH *Microbiol. & Pathol.* (ed. 6) xxxii. 494 The streptomycetes are of medical importance because they are the source of the antibiotics, streptomycin, [etc.]. **1961** *Lancet* 12 Aug. 377/2 A large variety of mould products have been reported effective in cancer in man, from myxomycetes to streptomycetes. **1977** R. W. THOMA *Industr. Microbiol.* 51 Rigorous proof for genetic recombination via transduction or transformation among streptomycetes is still lacking. **1978** *Nature* 31 Aug. 844/2 C. Stuttard..reported the isolation of virulent transducing phage in a chloramphenicol-producing streptomycete.

streptomycin (strɛptəʊ'maɪsɪn). *Pharm.* [f. prec.: see -MYCIN.] An antibiotic, $C_{21}H_{39}N_7O_{12}$, produced by the soil bacterium *Streptomyces griseus*, which was the first drug to be successful against tuberculosis but is now used chiefly in conjunction with other drugs because of its toxic effects. Also *Comb.*

1944 A. SCHATZ et al. in *Proc. Soc. Exper. Biol. & Med.* LV. 67/1 Because of its similarity to streptothricin, this substance may be designated as streptomycin, derived from the generic name that has recently been given to the aerial-mycelium producing and sporulating group of actinomycetes, namely *Streptomyces.* **1948** 'G. ORWELL' *Let.* 4 Feb. in *Coll. Ess.* (1968) IV. 404 We are now sending for some new American drug called streptomycin which they say will speed up the cure. **1961** *Lancet* 29 July 247/2 Streptomycin-resistant strains [of gonococci] remained.. susceptible to penicillin. **1973** *Sci. Amer.* Sept. 130/2 Streptomycin and isoniazid have diminished the need for state tuberculosis sanatoriums. **1974** M. C. GERALD *Pharmacol.* xxvi. 457 Streptomycin binds to the ribosome in such a manner that incorrect amino acids are laid down, thus resulting in the formation of a nonfunctional protein. **1978** *Antimicrobial Agents & Chemotherapy* XIII. 430 Combinations of penicillin and gentamycin have been shown to be synergistic against all strains of enterococci, including those resistant to penicillin and streptomycin.

streptosolen (strɛptəʊ'səʊlən). [mod.L. (J. Miers 1850, in *Ann. Mag. Nat. Hist.* 2nd Ser. V. 208), f. STREPTO- + Gr. σωλήν pipe.] A climbing evergreen shrub, *Streptosolen jamesonii*, of the family Solanaceæ, which is native to Colombia and Ecuador and bears clusters of orange flowers.

1938 J. S. DAKERS *Mod. Greenhouse* vii. 105 Streptosolen ..has orange scarlet flowers produced in bunches. **1952** R. GENDERS *Greenhouse* xv. 150 Streptosolen..is a grand evergreen plant for covering a wall of a lean-to house. **1976** *Homes & Gardens* Aug. 75/2 At the minimum heat mentioned, little more than that needed to keep out winter frost, climbers one can grow include..blue plumbago, orange streptosolen, [etc.].

streptothricin (strɛptəʊ'θrɪsɪn, -'θraɪsɪn). *Biochem.* [f. mod.L. *streptothric-*, STREPTOTHRIX + -IN[1].] Each of a group of related antibiotic but toxic compounds, $C_{13}H_{21}N_6O_7(C_6H_{12}N_2O)_n$, produced by the soil bacterium *Actinomyces lavendulæ.*

1942 WAKSMAN & WOODRUFF in *Proc. Soc. Exper. Biol. & Med.* XLIX. 207 A new substance can now be added to this list of antibiotic agents. This substance has been obtained from a soil *Actinomyces*, and is designated as *streptothricin*, derived from the early generic designation *Streptothrix*, given to this group of organisms. **1955** *Sci. News Let.* 21 May 326/3 Two other antibiotics, streptothricin and noformicin,..are effective against Newcastle disease virus in the test tube. **1963** BARBER & GARROD *Antibiotic & Chemotherapy* vi. 89 This first antibiotic of any value resulting from this investigation was streptothricin, which ..was subsequently found to be too toxic for clinical use. **1972** *Jrnl. Antibiotics* XXV. 501 All the available preparations of antibiotics of this type were mixtures of six streptothricins differing in the number of L-β-lysine residues (1 in streptothricin F, 2 in streptothricin E and so on to 6 in streptothricin A). **1978** *Res. in Vet. Sci.* XXV. 110 The number of worms remaining in the infected dogs after one or more treatments with this streptothricin complex.

streptothricosis (ˌstrɛptəʊθrɪ'kəʊsɪs). *Vet. Sci.* Also -trichosis. [f. as prec. + -OSIS.] A usu. chronic, sometimes fatal disease caused by actinomycetes and producing scabs on the skin of cows and other farm animals, esp. in the wet season in tropical regions.

1927 *Ann. Rep. Veter. Dept., Northern Provinces, 1926* (Nigeria) 10 Contagious Impetigo or Streptothricosis... This disease made its appearance in the Government herd [of cattle] at Vom. **1971** D. L. DOXEY *Veter. Clinical Path.* xiv. 267 Although formerly classed as of differing aetiology, cutaneous streptothricosis in cattle, mycotic dermatitis in cattle, sheep, goats and horses, and strawberry foot rot of sheep, are all caused by the same organism, *Dermatophilus congolensis.* **1973** AINSWORTH & AUSTWICK *Fungal Dis. Animals* (ed. 2) 135 Dermatophilosis, especially in cattle (streptotrichosis) and sheep (mycotic dermatitis, strawberry foot-rot), occurs in many tropical and temperate countries as acute local infections of the skin following damage by prolonged soaking, insolation, tick bites or other agencies.

Streptothrix ('strɛptəʊθrɪks). *Bacteriology.* Pl. -thrices (-'θraɪsiːz). [mod.L., f. Gr. στρεπτό-ς twisted (see STREPTO-) + θρίξ hair.] A genus of bacteria, comprising organisms having branching filaments growing in interlacing masses; a micro-organism of this genus or type.

1891 G. S. WOODHEAD *Bacteria* 41 Cylindrical colourless filaments—streptothrix. **1899** T. BOWHILL *Man. Bacteriol. Technique* 4 By Streptothrix [we understand] organisms that ..resemble at one time the thread fungi, and at other times the bacteria. *Ibid.* 102 The Streptothrices.

attrib. **1898** *Allbutt's Syst. Med.* V. 262 The streptothrix form of the bacillus tuberculosis. **1899** *Ibid.* VIII. 904 Streptothrix infections of the skin.

Hence **strepto'thricial** *a.*, of or relating to streptothrix.

1903 *Lancet* 18 Apr. 1102/1 Examination of the pus revealed the presence of abundant streptothricial growth.

streptovaricin (strɛptəʊ'værɪsɪn). *Pharm.* [f. mod.L. *Strepto-myces* (see STREPTOMYCETE) + VARI(OUS *a.* + -MY)CIN.] Each of a group of related antibiotics produced by the bacterium *Streptomyces spectabilis.*

1957 P. SIMINOFF et al. in *Amer. Rev. Tuberculosis* LXXV. 582 A new antimicrobial complex, streptovaricin, is produced by *Streptomyces spectabilis*, n. sp. The complex consists of at least five microbiologically active, closely related components which have been named streptovaricins *A, B, C, D,* and *E*, respectively. **1972** *Accounts Chem. Res.* V. 60/1 The streptovaricins all contain an identical carbon skeleton and..they differ from one another in the degree of oxygenation and degree of acetylation.

streptozotocin (strɛptəʊ'zɒtəsɪn). *Pharm.* [f. as prec. + *-zoto-*, of unkn. origin + -MY)CIN.] An antibiotic substance obtained from *Streptomyces achromogenes* that damages insulin-producing cells and is used to induce diabetes in laboratory animals.

1960 J. J. VAURA et al. in *Antibiotics Ann. 1959–60* 234 Streptozotocin is a new antibiotic produced by a streptomycete isolated from the soil. **1972** *Jrnl. Pharm. Sci.* LXI. 491/1 Chemically streptozotocin is a *N*-methyl-*N*-nitrosourea derivative..of D-glucosamine. **1976** A. MARBLE et al. in G. S. Avery *Drug Treatment* xv. 421/1 Streptozotocin, another hyperglycaemic drug, has been similarly used in cases of malignant insulin-secreting tumour. **1980** *Nature* 3 Jan. 100/1 Proinsulin mRNA was purified from rat B-cell tumours induced with streptozotocin and nicotinamide.

Strepyan ('strɛpɪən), *a. Archæol.* Also **Strepyian.** [ad. F. *Strépyien*, f. *Strépy*, name of a town (the type site) in Belgium: see -AN.] Of or belonging to a palæolithic culture of Europe supposed to have existed before the Chellean. Freq. *absol.*

[**1904** A. RUTOT in *Bulletin Société d'Anthropologie de Bruxelles* XXIII. Mém. I. 15 Les industries éolithiques quaternaires et des pièces qui se rapportent absolument à notre transition de l'Éolithique au Paléolithique ou du Mesvinien au Chelléen, c'est-à-dire au Strépyien.] **1910** J. MCCABE *Prehistoric Man* i. 12 It is usual to admit three stages in the earlier Paleolithic, the names of which are taken from the French sites where we find them best exhibited... Advanced students, like M. Rutot, add an earlier stage (the Strepyian). **1911** W. J. SOLLAS *Ancient Hunters* v. 112 The distinctive character of the Strepyan industry, according to M. Rutot, is that all the implements retain a considerable part of the original crust of the flint nodule. **1914** J. GEIKIE *Antiquity of Man in Europe* ii. 43 The 'Strepyan', on the other hand, is marked by the presence not only of simple flakes but of primitive forms of the Chellean *coup de poing.* **1927** PEAKE & FLEURE *Apes & Man* vi. 90 The Strépyan, more often termed by others pre-Chellean, are accepted under the latter name by most archaeologists as being merely a very early type of Chellean. **1948** A. L. KROEBER *Anthropology* xvi. 631 Rutot's Mesvinian stage of the Eolithic is recognized as probably a Belgian facies of the oldest Levalloisian or Pre-Mousterian, his Strepyan as being Chellean—all of them Palaeolithic and Pleistocene. **1961** L. D. STAMP *Gloss. Geogr. Terms* 532 *Acheulian*,..a cultural stage..characterized by a certain type of chipped stone implements. The more usually accepted stages are:.. Eolithic, Strepyan, pre-Chellean.

stress (strɛs), *sb.* Forms: 4–6 **stres**, 4–7 **stresse**, 5 **stresce, strest**, 6 *Sc.* **straisse**, 6– **stress.** [Prob. an aphetic form of DISTRESS *sb.*, which occurs earlier in all the older senses; in ME. *destresse* and *stresse* often appear as variant readings. It is, however, not unlikely that this formation has coalesced, esp. in sense 1, with an adoption of OF. *estrece* narrowness, straitness, oppression :—popular L. **strictia*, f. L. *strictus*, whence OF. *estreit* STRAIT *a.* It is further possible that some of the senses or shades of meaning may be derived from STRESS *v.*]

I. † 1. a. Hardship, straits, adversity, affliction. *Obs.* Cf. DISTRESS *sb.* 2.

1303 R. BRUNNE *Handl. Synne* 5004 Þat floure ys kalled 'aungelys mete' þat God ȝafe þe folke to ete Whan þey were yn wyldernes Forty wyntyr, yn hard stres. *a* **1400** *Salut. to our Lady* 51 in *Minor Poems fr. Vernon MS.* 135 Heil distruyere of eueri stresse. **1556** LAUDER *Tractate* 469 O Lord..help the pure that ar in stres Opprest and hereit mercyles. **1568** T. HOWELL *Arb. Amitie* (1879) 39 O get my graue in readinesse, Faine would I die to ende this stresse. **1588** A. KING tr. *Canisius' Catech., Of Conf.* 5 Sinnes done aganes the fift commandement... 9. To be sorie for oure nychtbours prosperitie, and glaid of thair straisse. **1590** SPENSER *F.Q.* III. xi. 18 With this sad hersall of his heauy stresse The warlike Damzell was empassiond sore. **1704** *Collect. Voy. & Trav.* III. 597/2 [He] began to be reduced to the utmost stress.

b. *to do to stress, do* (a country) *stress*: to reduce to straits, overcome. *to make stress*: to effect ravages. *Obs.*

1338 R. BRUNNE *Chron.* (1810) 29 Constantyn he [*sc.* Athelstan] reymed, & did vnto stresse. *Ibid.* 321 Saue kyng Athelstan, þat wastid alle Catenesse, Siþen was no man, þat so fer mad stresse. *c* **1450** *St. Cuthbert* (Surtees) 7839 Þai did þe contre ouer grete stresse.

c. *in stress*: (of an animal) hard pressed. *Obs.*

14.. in *Rel. Ant.* I. 152 If it be a best in strest or in chace.

d. *to call to stress*: to summon to undergo trial. *Obs.*

1338 R. BRUNNE *Chron.* (1810) 138 Bot if he [*sc.* an escaped felon] to þer baylifes mak his sikernesse, þat þei will him maynp[r]is, if he wer cald to stresse [Fr. *kaunt serra chalengé*].

e. Bodily suffering or injury. *Obs.*

1533 BELLENDEN *Livy* I. x. (S.T.S.) I. 57 This horiciane happynnyt (as þan) to be haill, but ony stress or hurte of body.

† 2. a. Force or pressure exercised on a person for the purpose of compulsion or extortion. Cf. DISTRESS *sb.* 1. *Obs.*

1303 R. BRUNNE *Handl. Synne* 2798 Ȝyf þou madest awhere any vowe..Ȝyf þou dedyst hyt with þy gode wylle, with-oute stress [*v.r.* out distresse] or ouþer ylle. *Ibid.* 8344 A-nother vyleynye thyr ys To do a womman synne thurgh stres. **1338** —— *Chron.* (1725) 281 His dedes ere to alowe, for his hardynesse. He did many on bowe in þat lond þorgh stresse. *c* **1420** *Prose Life Alex.* 32 We went into þe weste Marches, whare all þe folkes þat duellez thare..ȝalde þam vn-till vs wit-owtten stresse. *c* **1440** *York Myst.* xx. 188 Ȝoure neghbours house, whilkis ȝe haue hele, The ix[te] [*sc.* commandment] biddis take noȝt be stresse. **1655** *Nicholas Papers* (Camden) II. 334, I cannot beleeve that Maynard for a fee would hazard losse of money or liberty, and his conscience never yet putt him to that stresse.

b. *to do* or *make* (a person) *stress*: to put force or compulsion upon; to press hardly upon; to oppress. *Obs.*

1303 R. BRUNNE *Handl. Synne* 3939 Ȝyf þou make one so hard stresse þat hys godnesse wexe þe lesse. *Ibid.* 8232 For ȝyf she lyued yn wykkednes, þan myȝte we do to here sum stres. *c* **1300** —— *Chron. Wace* (Rolls) 16276 Perauenture he haþ som syknesse Or oþer greuaunce þat makeþ hym stresse.

c. Strain upon endurance. *Obs.*

1534 MORE *Comf. agst. Trib.* III. Wks. 1262/1 Not desyring to be brought vnto ye peril of persecucion (for it semeth a proude high mind to desyre martyrdom) but desyring helpe and strength of god, if he suffer vs to come to the stresse. **1692** R. L'ESTRANGE *Josephus, Wars* VII. xxix. (1733) 801 The Children stood the same Stress with the rest, and when they had suffer'd all that Malice or Invention could inflict upon them, not so much as one Soul of them would own Caesar to save his Life.

3. a. The overpowering pressure *of* some adverse force or influence. Chiefly in *stress of weather.* Cf. DISTRESS *sb.* 1 b.

1513 DOUGLAS *Æneis* X. xii. 140 The Orodes the hard rest doith oppres, The cauld and irny slepe of deidis stres. **1665** in *Extr. S.P. rel. Friends* III. (1912) 236 Which shipp had beene at Sea three Monthes and bett back by stress of weather. **1691** RAY *Creation* II. (1692) 130 It hath quite outdone the Chymists, effecting that by a gentle Heat, which they cannot perform without great stress of Fire. **1699** DAMPIER *Voy.* III. I. 155 When the stress of the Weather was over, we set our Sails again. **1715** *Lond. Gaz.* No. 5379/1 A..Frigate..was driven ashore..by Stress of Weather. **1785** COWPER *Task* II. 551 Perverting often, by the stress of lewd And loose example, whom he should instruct. **1821** JOANNA BAILLIE *Metr. Leg., Lady G. Baillie* iv, She saw.. hope's fresh touch undoing lines of care Which stress of evil times had deeply graven there. **1850** LONGF. *Building of Ship* 42 Broad in the beam, that the stress of the blast.. Might not the sharp bows overwhelm. **1874** GREEN *Short Hist.* vii. §7. 422 The stress of poverty may have been the cause which drove William Shakspere..to London and the stage. **1895** *Law Times Rep.* LXXIII. 157/1 Owing to stress of weather, the master decided to run back for Holyhead harbour. **1895** M. HEWLETT *Earthwork out of Tuscany* 39 Pious virgins, under stress of these things, swoon. **1918** *Times* 1 Feb. 9/3 Man's pensioners and even Nature's are feeling the stress of the war.

† b. *upon a stress*: at a pinch. *Obs. rare.*

1672 R. MONTAGU in *Buccleuch MSS.* (Hist. MSS. Comm.) I. 513, I..let them know that upon a stress we did reckon that his Christian Majesty must..supply us beyond what is stipulated.

† c. The brunt, severest pressure. *Obs.*

1618 BOLTON *Florus* III. x. (1636) 205 The whole stresse of the Warre [L. *tota belli moles*] was about Gregovia.

d. A condition of things compelling or characterized by strained effort. Sometimes coupled with *storm.* (For *storm and stress* see STORM *sb.* 3 d.)

1637 RUTHERFORD *Lett.* lxxxv. (1862) I. 217 But God be thanked that Christ in His children can endure a stress and a storm, howbeit soft nature w[d] fall down in pieces. **1845–6** TRENCH *Huls. Lect.* Ser. II. i. 160 When the stress comes we can withdraw. **1883** *Fortn. Rev.* May 734 This age of stress and transition. **1909** C. G. LANG *Parab. Jesus* 118 Resolute and brave-hearted service brings into the very midst of toil and stress a deep sense of joy. **1911** MARETT *Anthropol.* viii. 216 The Todas..have retired out of the stress of the world into the fastnesses of the Nilgiri Hills.

† e. A strong blast of wind. *Obs.*

1666 *Lond. Gaz.* No. 91/4 But the Wind blew such a stress, that they were in no possibility of Engaging.

f. *Sc.* A pressing demand.

1822 GALT *Provost* vii, A flock of fleets and ships frae the East and West Indies came in a' thegither; and there was sic a stress for tide-waiters, that [etc.].

g. *Psychol.* and *Biol.* An adverse circumstance that disturbs, or is likely to disturb, the normal physiological or psychological functioning of an individual; such circumstances collectively. Also, the disturbed state that results.

1942 *Endocrinology* XXXI. 420 When the normal animal is subjected to stress the adrenal cortices show hypertrophy. **1953** Fruton & Simmonds *Gen. Biochem.* xxxvii. 843 Similar reduction in the adrenal ascorbic acid and cholesterol is observed when normal animals are subjected to a variety of stress [*sic*] (injury, cold, heat, drugs, toxins, lack of oxygen, etc.). **1955** H. Basowitz et al. *Anxiety & Stress* i. 7 Anxiety has been defined in terms of an affective response; stress is the stimulus condition likely to arouse such response. **1959** *New Scientist* 12 Nov. 927/1 Some examples of the diseases thought to result from stress are high blood pressure, peptic ulceration and coronary thrombosis. **1968** Passmore & Robson *Compan. Med. Stud.* II. xxxvi. 8/1 Parenthood itself can be a stress for the immature adult. **1973** R. M. May *Model Ecosystems* iii. 60 Equation (3.21) tends to require that each species encounters greater competitive stress from its own, rather than from the other, species. **1976** *Sci. Amer.* July 55/1 The familiar human experience described as stress (caused by many factors, including fear, physical trauma, severe heat or cold or even extreme joy) has as a common denominator an increased secretion of adrenal steroids. **1978** S. Levine et al. in H. Ursin et al. *Psychobiol. of Stress* i. 4 When the psychologically threatening or arousing aspects of a situation were altered, classical stresses such as fasting and heat no longer activated the pituitary-adrenal system. **1979** *McGraw-Hill Yearbk. Sci. & Technol.* 374/1 Cacti suffering from water stress become fully rehydrated within 24 hr following a heavy rain.

4. Strained exertion, strong effort. Now *rare.*

1690 Norris *Beatitudes* (1692) 107 Such a desire as carries with it the full bent and Stress of the Soul. **1697** Dryden *Æneis* xi. 845 Then, press'd by Foes, he stemm'd the stormy Tyde; And gain'd, by stress of Arms, the farther Side. *c* **1698** Locke *Cond. Und.* §28 Though the faculties of the mind are improved by exercise, yet they must not be put to a stress beyond their strength. **1789** Polwhele *Engl. Orator* iv. 131 They know not to pursue, With Stress of mental Faculties, a Train Of Argument. **1857** Longf. *Sandalphon* iii, The Angels of Wind and of Fire Chaunt only one hymn, and expire With the song's irresistible stress.

5. a. Physical strain or pressure exerted upon a material object; the strain *of* a load or weight. Now *rare* exc. in scientific use: see c. †Phr. ***to lay stress upon, put stress to, put to stress.***

c **1440** *Promp. Parv.* 480/1 Stresse, or streytynge, *constriccio, constrictura.* *a* **1547** Surrey *Eccles.* iv. 66 The single twyned cordes May no such stresse indure, As cables brayded threfould may, Together wrethed suer. *a* **1578** in T. Procter *Gorg. Gallery* F iv b, As tender Flaxe can beare no stresse, before that it bee sponne. **1578** H. Wotton *Courtlie Controv.* 317 The which [door] fleeing open with small stresse, caused them to enter in thereat. **1601** Holland *Pliny* xvii. xiv. I. 518 In this businesse there is an opinion, that two hands togither are put to smaller stresse [L. *minus nituntur*]..than one alone. **1630** Bp. Hall *Occas. Medit.* §136 (1633) 335 If it [*sc.* the cart] be soundly laden..all the frame of it is put unto the utmost stresse. **1662** R. Venables *Exper. Angler* i. 6 The whole stress or strength of the fish is born or sustained, by the thicker part of the Rod, which [etc.]. **1681** Flavel *Meth. Grace* xx. 350 The world is full of hope without a promise, which is but as a spider's web, when a stress comes to be laid upon it. **1682** Wheler *Journ. Greece* vi. 466 Against which the whole stress and fall of the Waters seems to lean. **1688** Keepe *Narr. Finding Crucifix* 10 There was also in the Coffin white-Linnen,..that look't indifferent fresh, but the least stress put thereto shew'd it was well nigh perish't. **1797** *Encycl. Brit.* (ed. 3) VI. 670/1 Gravers.. should be..small towards the point, but stronger upwards, that they may have strength enough to bear any stress there may be occasion to lay upon them. **1805** R. W. Dickson *Pract. Agric.* I. Plate xi, A Wheel-Harrow..by which the stress on the horses is rendered less. **1829** *Chapters Phys. Sci.* 143 Let the strength allowed be more than fully competent to the stress to which the parts can ever be liable. **1831** J. Holland *Manuf. Metal* I. 185 The amazing stress, which a large ship riding at anchor in foul weather exerts upon the cable. **1847** Yeowell *Anc. Brit. Ch.* ii. 11 Jesus Christ himself being the chief corner-stone—who holds the several parts together, and supports the whole stress of the edifice.

†**b.** *Naut.* Strain on a cable, due to violence of wind; a time when the cable is strained. Phrase, *to ride a stress. Obs.*

1633 T. James *Voy.* 23 We came to an Anker, and rid a good stresse all night. *Ibid.* 47 The Cable and Anker induring an incredible stresse. **1644** Manwayring *Seamans Dict.* 103 This is not safe rideing in a stresse.

c. A force acting on or within a body or structure and tending to deform it; now usu. the intensity of this, the force per unit area.

As orig. defined by Rankine the stress was the equal and opposite reaction of the body to the force, rather than the force itself (see quots. 1855, 1856).

1855 W. J. M. Rankine *Misc. Sci. Papers* (1881) 120 In this paper, the word 'Strain' will be used to denote the change of volume and figure constituting the deviation of a molecule of a solid from that condition which it preserves when free from the action of external forces; and the word 'Stress' will be used to denote the force, or combination of forces, which such a molecule exerts in tending to recover its free condition, and which, for a state of equilibrium, is equal and opposite to the combination of external forces applied to it. **1856** Thomson in *Phil. Trans.* CXLVI. 481 A stress is an equilibrating application of force to a body. *Ibid. note,* It will be seen that I have deviated slightly from Mr. Rankine's definition of the word 'stress,' as I have applied it to the direct action experienced by a body from the matter around it, and not, as proposed by him, to the elastic reaction of the body equal and opposite to that action. **1873** R. H. Bow *Economics of Construction* 45 *note,* The term *stress* expresses the condition of a part of the structure to the extremities of which are applied compressing or extending forces; the amount of the stress is measured by the magnitude of the force acting on either extremity; the *strain* is the change of length from elasticity which the part undergoes when subjected to the stress. **1873** Maxwell *Electr. & Magn.* I. 59 The nature of this stress [in dielectrics] is..a tension along the lines of force combined with an equal pressure in all directions at right angles to these lines. **1876** *Encycl. Brit.* IV. 285/2 There are three kinds of stress, due to tension, compression, and shearing. *Ibid.* The ultimate strength of the material is measured by the maximum intensity of stress which it can bear, or in other words, by the stress which the unit area of cross section can bear. **1896** Greener *Gun* (ed. 6) 545 The stresses upon a gun are a radial stress or 'pressure'; a tangential stress, or hoop tension..; a longitudinal stress. **1911** J. A. Ewing in *Encycl. Brit.* XXV. 1007/2 Stress is the mutual action between two bodies, or between two parts of a body, whereby each of the two exerts a force upon the other... A body is said to be in a state of stress when there is a stress between the two parts which lie on opposite sides of an imaginary surface of section. **1925** J. Case *Strength of Materials* i. 2 When we wish to give the stress a numerical value it is desirable..to refer to the stress in relation to the area of the cross section... The total force acting on a section, divided by the area of that section, is called the stress intensity or, more often, simply the stress. [*Note*] In future when we use the word 'stress' without qualification it must be understood to mean 'intensity of stress'. **1938** Laurson & Cox *Mech. of Materials* i. 2 Total stress is a force... Intensity of stress, however, is expressed in units of force divided by units of area. **1960** H. K. Preston *Practical Prestressed Concrete* i. 3 The same beam ..is prestressed by a force of 54,000 lb... This force creates a uniform compressive stress of + 1,000 psi over the entire cross section of the beam. **1979** *Nature* 23 Aug. 670/1 Arctic sea-ice breaks under wind stress throughout the year, exposing leads of open water.

d. Strain upon a bodily organ or a mental power.

1843 R. J. Graves *Syst. Clin. Med.* xx. 229 The stress thrown upon the air cells and passages gives rise to emphysema. **1899** *Allbutt's Syst. Med.* VIII. 135 Neurasthenia is indeed often the product of stresses upon the functions of the mind.

e. ? *Anglo-Irish.* (See quot.) ? *Obs.*

1814 W. S. Mason *Statist. Acc. Irel.* I. 584 Many of them [the poor], particularly females, die in their youth, of what they call stresses, that is violent heats from hard work.

6. Phr. ***stress(es) and strain(s)*** (with reference to senses 3 and 5; cf. *strain and stress* s.v. STRAIN *sb.*[2] 11).

1854 C. Patmore *Angel in House* I. viii. viii. 118 Puzzled and fagg'd by stress and strain. **1856** *Phil. Trans. R. Soc.* CXLVI. 481 (*heading*) Elements of a mathematical theory of elasticity... Part I. On stresses and strains. **1935** *Discovery* Sept. 259/1 The interdependent mechanical stresses and strains. **1952** *Sat. Rev.* (U.S.) 20 Sept. 38/2 There never are stresses in government, but *stresses* and *strains.* **1959** M. Steen *Tower* i. vi. 85, I realised what the last few years, with their stresses and strains, had done to us both. **1960** *Times* 13 Jan. 15/2 Wrestling once again with unknown aeronautical quantities and resolving new propositions in stress and strain. **1979** *Jrnl. R. Soc. Arts* CXXVII. 363/2 New stresses and strains in the relationships between.. Britain and the remaining territories.

†**7. a.** Testing strain or pressure on a support or basis; weight (of inference, confidence, etc.) resting upon an argument or piece of evidence; amount of risk ventured on some assurance; degree of reliance. Chiefly in phrase *to lay* (occas. *put, place*) *stress on* or *upon,* to rely on, rest a burden of proof upon. *Obs.*

The phrase is now used with changed meaning: see 8.

1651 Baxter *Inf. Bapt.* 250 You lay the main stress of your cause on it. *a* **1676** Hale *Prim. Orig. Man.* i. ii. (1677) 69 When all is done, I lay the great stress of my Conclusion upon the first sort of Evidences. *c* **1680** Beveridge *Serm.* (1729) II. 107 The main stress of our salvation lying upon our performing this duty. **1690** Norris *Beatitudes* (1694) 25 He does not lean upon any created Good with any Stress. **1712** Addison *Spect.* No. 399 ¶7 We should not lay too great a Stress on any supposed Virtues we possess that are of a doubtful Nature. **1720** De Foe *Capt. Singleton* xiii. (1840) 220, I always put a great deal of stress upon his judgment. **1722** —— *Relig. Courtsh.* i. i. (1840) 25 I can lay no stress on anything she said. **1735** Dyche & Pardon *Dict.* s.v., *To lay a Stress,* to depend or rely upon a Person or Thing. **1736** Butler *Anal.* ii. i. (1798) 187 Mankind are for placing the stress of their religion any where, rather than upon virtue. **1765** Goldsm. *New Simile* 13 The stress of all my proofs on him I lay.

b. Weightiest or most important part, essential point (of a business, argument, question). *Obs.*

1668 Hale *Rolle's Abridgm.* Pref. 2 He was a strict Searcher and Examiner of businesses, and a wise discerner of the weight and stress of them wherein it lay, and what was material to it. **1676** H. Phillippes *Purch. Patt.* (ed. 5) B 1 b, Now the stress of the question is, what number of years may be allowed and taken in this case? **1679** Coles *Eng.-Lat. Dict.* (ed. 2), The Stress of the business, *rei momentum, cardo controversiæ.* **1687** R. L'Estrange *Answ. Diss.* 7 But I am for speaking Plain, Home, and in Few Words, to the Stress of the Subject in hand. **1736** Butler *Anal.* ii. vii. (1798) 309 In these things the stress of what I am now observing lies. **1791** Wesley *Serm. God's Love* 6 The stress of the argument lies on this very point.

c. Argumentative force; also, impressiveness, telling effect (of a composition). *Obs.*

1653 tr. *J. Stegmann's Diss. de Pace* ix. 45 They [*sc.* the Socinians] conceive that the Holy Fathers, and the consent of so many ages, do adde more dignity and veneration, then stress to the doctrine of the Trinity. **1737** *Gentl. Mag.* VII. 363/1 All the Stress of the Poem, all the Magnanimity and Heroism of Leonidas entirely depend on this Oracle. **1754** W. Goodall *Exam. Lett. Mary Q. of Scots* I. 49 As the whole stress, in a manner, of the cause depends fundamentally upon this declaration. **1784** Cowper *Tiroc.* 803 And some perhaps,..Will need no stress of argument t' enforce Th' expedience of a less advent'rous course.

8. Exceptional insistence on something; attribution of special importance; emphasis. Chiefly in phrase *to lay* (occas. *place, put*) *stress upon* (formerly used with different meaning: see 7 a).

1756 C. Lucas *Ess. Waters* II. 61 On the nitrous.. qualities..he seems to lay no small stress. *a* **1763** Shenstone *Ess.* 33 It is requisite to lay some stress yourself, on what you intend should be remarked by others. **1789** Belsham *Ess.* I. xiv. 270, I place but little stress upon.. external accomplishments and graces. **1796** Jane Austen *Pride & Prej.* ii, Do you consider the forms of introduction, and the stress that is laid on them, as nonsense? **1846** W. R. Birt in *Rep. Brit. Assoc.* i. 132, I do not place any stress upon these deductions. **1857** Buckle *Civiliz.* I. vii. 313 Hooker, though he shows much respect to the Councils, lays little stress upon the Fathers. **1860** Tyndall *Glac.* ii. xiv. 300, I do not want to lay more stress than it deserves upon a conjecture of this kind. **1883** *Manch. Exam.* 22 Nov. 5/2 A ..questioning habit inevitably inclines us to lay more stress upon the miseries than on the blessings of our lot.

9. Relative loudness or force of vocal utterance; a greater degree of vocal force characterizing one syllable as compared with other syllables of the word, or one part of a syllable as compared with the rest; stress-accent. Also, superior loudness of voice as a means of emphasizing one or more of the words of a sentence more than the rest.

1749 *Power & Harmony Pros. Numbers* 25 The Accents.. were designed very probably at first to regulate the Tone or Key of the Voice, not the Stress or Force of it. **1785** J. Walker *Rhet. Gram.* (1801) 8 The Secondary Accent is that stress we may occasionally place upon another syllable, besides that which has the principal accent. *Ibid.* 162 An injudicious reader of verse would be very apt to lay a stress upon the article *the* in the third line. **1785** *Ess. Punctuation* 153 The syllables, which require a particular stress of the voice in pronunciation. **1824** L. Murray *Eng. Gram.* (ed. 5) I. 345 In the word *presúme,* the stress of the voice must be on the letter *u,* and second syllable, *sume,* which take the accent. **1847** Malden in *Proc. Philol. Soc.* III. 95 That which is commonly called accent, but which it will be more convenient in the present inquiry..to call stress. **1862** Mrs. H. Wood *Channings* iv. 27 There was a stress on the word 'to-night,' and Hamish marked it. **1879** H. Nicol in *Encycl. Brit.* IX. 633/2 Stress in the French of to-day is independent of length (quantity) and pitch (tone). **1893** Bridges *Milton's Prosody* 33 Two kinds of line, one the eight-syllable line with rising stress (so-called iambic), the other the seven-syllable line with falling stress (so-called trochaic).

II. 10. *Law.* A distraint; also, the chattel or chattels seized in a distraint: = DISTRESS *sb.* 3, 4. Phrase, to *take* (*a*) *stress, to take stresses* = to distrain. *Obs.* exc. *dial.*

c **1440** *Promp. Parv.* 480/1 Stresse, or wed take be strengthe and vyolence, *vadimonium.* **1464** *Mann. & Househ. Exp.* (Roxb.) 276, I payd..to the ij. men of Wensche that helpe to brenge home the strese howete of Warweke scheyer, of Dalbyes, fore theyer reward, iiij.s. iiij.d. **1479** *Engl. Gilds* (1870) 321 John Brendon the yonger werned stresse to the Master and Wardons,..for he come nott to derge that same euen. **1487** *Paston Lett.* III. 340 Sir John Howard, Knyght,..gederith grete feloship of men, purposyng on Monday next comyng to take stresses of the Lady Roos. *c* **1500** *Colin Blowbol's Test.* 193–5 (Lehmeyer) And of this rent, yf that he doith faile, I gyve hym powre to ..take an stresse,..Vpon the grounde, one, two, or thre. And with hym home his stressis for to cary. **1510** *Sel. Cases Crt. Star Chamber* (Selden Soc.) 206 The baylis..and.. sergiaunttes of the said towne..toke awaye Fro the abbottes tenaunttes then..Certen stresses be Cause the said tenaunttes willnot appere at the towne Courte. **1544** in *Sel. Cases Crt. Requests* (Selden Soc.) 97 The said Olyuer..to deliuer vnto theym all stresses lately taken from theym. **1546** J. Heywood *Prov.* (1867) 39 Their landlorde came to their house to take a stresse For rent. **1601** Bp. Andrewes *Serm.* (Matt. xxii. 21) (1629) ii. 93 We must offer it as it were a Gift, voluntarily, willingly, cheerfully,..though Hophni had no flesh-hook, though Cæsar had no Publican to take a stresse. **1606** Holland *Suetonius* 7 After his goods were arrested and stresses taken,..him he clapt up in prison. **1613** *MS. Acc. St. John's Hosp. Canterb.,* Ther wass a stress taken owt of Slewes shopp being a bare of yourne for a yearly newellty of iiijd a yeare. **1886** *W. Somerset Word-bk.* s.v., Mr. Jones 've a-tookt a stress vor dree quarters' rent.

III. 11. *attrib.,* as (senses 3 c, d) *stress area, -memorial;* (sense 3 g) *stress reaction, situation, symptom;* (senses 5 a, c) *stress-axis, -component, -difference;* (senses 5 c, 9) *stress-pattern;* (sense 9) *stress-accent, -difference, -point, -prosody, -rhythm, -shift, -syllable;* **stress analysis** *Engin.,* the theoretical or experimental study of the stresses within a mechanical structure in relation to its function; hence **stress analyst; stress-breaker** *Dentistry,* a device attached to or incorporated in a partial denture to reduce the occlusive forces that have to be borne by the underlying tissue and the teeth to which the denture is attached; so **stress-breaking** *vbl. sb.* and *ppl. a.;* **stress-broken** *ppl. a.;* **stress concentration** *Engin.,* a local increase in the stress inside an object; also, a stress raiser; **stress contour** *Phonetics,* a sequence of varying levels of stress within an utterance; **stress corrosion** *Metallurgy,* the development of cracks as a result of the combined effects of stress and corrosion; freq. *attrib.;* **stress diagram** *Mech.,* a diagram that represents graphically the stresses within a framed structure; **stress-dilatancy** *Physics*, dilatancy that occurs as a result of applied stress; **stress disease**, a disease that occurs as a result of continual exposure to stress; **stress fracture** *Med.*, a fracture of a bone caused by the repeated application of a high load; **stress-free** *a.*, pertaining to or possessing freedom from mechanical or biological stress; **stress grading** *vbl. sb.*, the grading of timber according to its strength, as estimated from the number and distribution of knots and other visible defects; so **stress grade** *sb.* and (with hyphen) *v. trans.*; **stress-graded** *ppl. a.*; **stress-group** *Phonetics*, a group of syllables forming a rhythmic unit with one primary stress; †**stress house**, ? a house of detention, lock-up; **stress incontinence** *Med.*, a condition found chiefly in women in which a (usu. small) escape of urine occurs when the intra-abdominal pressure increases suddenly, as in coughing or lifting; **stress interview**, an interview in which there is a deliberate attempt to subject a candidate to stress by the nature of the questioning; **stress mark**, (*a*) *Phonetics*, a symbol or a diacritical mark indicating that a syllable carries stress; (*b*) *Photogr.*, a mark on a photographic print caused by friction or pressure on the film surface; hence **stress-marked** *a.*; **stress maximum** *Phonetics*, the tonic accent; **stress mineral** *Petrol.*, a mineral whose formation in metamorphic rocks is believed to be dependent on shearing stress; **stress-neutral** *a. Linguistics*, designating a derivational or inflectional suffix which plays no part in the placing of stress within a word; hence **stress-neutrality**; **stress phoneme** *Linguistics*, a phoneme whose contrastiveness consists in a distinctive degree of stress; **stress raiser** *Engin.*, a feature in the shape or composition of an object that gives rise to a local increase in stress; **stress relaxation** *Engin.*, a decrease of stress occurring in a material when the associated deformation remains constant; **stress relief** *Metallurgy*, the reduction of residual stress in a material by thermal treatment; also **stress-relieve** *v. trans.*, **-relieved** *ppl. a.*, **-relieving** *vbl. sb.* (freq. *attrib.*); **stress-strain** *adj. phr. Engin.*, pertaining to or depicting the relation between mechanical stress and the strain it produces; **stress-timed** *a. Phonetics*, designating or pertaining to a language in which primary stresses occur at approximately equal intervals, irrespective of the number of unstressed syllables in between; hence **stress-timing**.

1880 RUSKIN *Elem. Eng. Prosody* Pref. p. vi, I believe the *stress-accent on English words will be found always to involve delay as well as energy or loudness of pronunciation. **1926** PIPPARD & BARROW in *Building Res. Board Techn. Paper* No. 1. 1 The bow girder..presents an interesting problem in *stress analysis. **1980** *Strain* XVI. 132/2 The stress analysis of turbine components for the new hydroelectric pumped storage system. **1950** M. HETÉNYI *Handbk. Exper. Stress Analysis* p. v, Several principal methods and literally hundreds of individual tools and artifices constitute the 'arsenal' of the experimental *stress analyst. **1976** B. JACKSON *Flameout* (1977) ii. 32 His career as stress analyst with Lockheed Aircraft. **1973** *Times* 17 Apr. 1/2 His brief will be to review the functions and relationship of the two bodies to enable them to make the most effective contribution in strengthening the voluntary housing movement in *stress areas. **1881** G. H. DARWIN in *Phil. Trans.* CLXXIII. 191 To find the magnitude and direction of the principal *stress-axes at any point. **1930** H. P. BOOS in I. G. Nichols *Prosthetic Dentistry* xxxvii. 600 *Stress-breakers can be used in conjunction with the tube successfully. **1955** J. OSBORNE *Dental Mech.* (ed. 4) x. 215 (*caption*) Split casting type of stress breaker. **1930** L. M. FARNUM in I. G. Nichols *Prosthetic Dentistry* xxxvi. 593 *Stress-breaking construction is indicated where there are no posterior abutments on one or both sides of the mouth. **1963** C. R. COWELL et al. *Inlays, Crowns, & Bridges* xi. 118 This form of bridge incorporates a stress-breaking device, which allows limited movement at one of the joints between pontic and retainer. **1973** D. H. ROBERTS *Fixed Bridge Prostheses* ix. 152 The dovetail and slot introduces a certain degree of 'stress-breaking' between the two parts of the bridge, and because of this the retainers..are far less likely to fail. **1955** J. OSBORNE *Dental Mech.* (ed. 4) ix. 150 In cases when the teeth are periodontally affected, *stress-broken designs may be employed. **1856** THOMSON in *Phil. Trans.* CXLVI. 496 The concurrences of the *stress-components used in interpreting the differential equation of energy with the types of the strain-coordinates. **1925** TIMOSHENKO & LESSELLS *Appl. Elasticity* i. 10 A semi-circular groove in a strip subjected to tension..also produces very high *stress-concentration. **1936** [see *stress raiser* below]. **1977** E. J. HEARN *Mech. of Materials* xviii. 477 If..stress concentrations such as notches, keyways, holes, etc., are present in the bar, these will result in local stress increases. **1958** A. A. HILL *Introd. Linguistic Struct.* 28 *Stress contours differ from pitch contours in that two phrases are never united into a single stress contour. **1971** *Language* XLVII. 269 It appears that the stress contours of English sentences are determined in a simple and regular way by their underlying syntactic structures. **1931** *Jrnl. Iron & Steel Inst.* CXXIV. 723 *Stress corrosion of metals. **1967** A. H. COTTRELL *Introd. Metallurgy* xxiii. 467 In stress-corrosion cracking there is usually very little overall corrosion. **1973** A. PARRISH *Mech. Engineers' Ref. Bk.* (ed. 11) v. 77 The higher Mo bearing steels offer more resistance to stress corrosion cracking than 18/8; stress relief treatment (two hours at 870°C) after fabrication considerably reduces the risk of cracking. **1873** J. G. MEDLEY *Roorkee Treat. Civil Engin. in India* (ed. 3) I. xxv. 550 Loads on Roofs naturally divide themselves into two sets... Hence two distinct *Stress-diagrams must be drawn, one for each system of load. **1919** PIPPARD & PRITCHARD *Aeroplane Structures* viii. 72 Probably the most satisfactory method of determining the forces in the individual members of a structure is by means of the stress diagram. **1965** G. M. MILLS *Theory of Structures* ix. 168 The variation of stress along a given axis may be shown graphically by means of a stress diagram. **1881** G. H. DARWIN in *Phil. Trans.* CLXXIII. 199, I shall refer to the difference between the greatest and least principal stresses as 'the *stress-difference'. **1924** O. JESPERSEN *Philos. Gram.* xvii. 231 The old compound *mankind* (now stressed on the second syllable) comprises all human beings, but the younger *mankind* (stressed on the first syllable) is opposed to *womankind*. (The stress-difference, as made in N.E.D., is not, however, recognized by everybody.) **1971** *Language* XLVII. 261 The analysis given..correctly predicts the existence of a stress difference associated with the two readings of sentences like *The parable shows what suffering men can create.* **1944** G. W. S. BLAIR *Survey Gen. & Appl. Rheol.* iii. 31 The exceptions [to this rule] are..(*c*) Materials whose consistency is increased by increasing the stress (as distinct from the strain) applied to them. This phenomenon has been little studied, but may be referred to as '*stress-dilatancy'. **1962** *Proc. R. Soc.* A. CCLXIX. 500 (*heading*) The stress-dilatancy relation for static equilibrium of an assembly of particles in contact. **1979** *Geotechnique* XXIX. 341 Rowe's (1962) stress-dilatancy relation..allows indirect measurement of this angle [*sc.* of interparticle friction] based on triaxial compression tests on dense..samples. **1948** *Observer* 13 June 5/5 Absenteeism which arises..from those once..despised causes which passed under names such as neurasthenia and described to-day as *stress diseases. **1966** G. E. EVANS *Pattern under Plough* viii. 96 It is more enlightened and scientific in psychosomatic and stress diseases for medicine to address itself as much to the man as to the actual disease. **1952** R. WATSON-JONES *Fractures* (ed. 4) I. xv. 343 (*heading*) Fatigue or *stress fractures. **1983** *Brit. Med. Jrnl.* 12 Nov. 1449/1 Stress fractures are widely recognised in running. **1946** *Nature* 5 Oct. 475/1 After discussing the effect of swelling on the sorption isotherm he proceeded to derive a *stress-free isotherm. **1961** *Economist* 21 Oct. 249/1 A stress-free cruising speed of 70–75 mph. **1978** D. BLOODWORTH *Crosstalk* xxiv. 188 Stress-free mice are far better performers. **1944** *Grading rules for Stress-graded timber (B.S.I.)* 4 The present revision has been undertaken..to provide for *stress grades higher than 800 lb. f. **1971** *Timber Trades Jrnl.* 21 Aug. 23/3 The timber for all the main structural components was visually stress-graded to a minimum of 50 grade before use. **1973** *Materials & Technol.* VI. i. 27 In Britain, four basic stress grades are specified for sawn softwood, and three for laminated timber. **1944** (*title*) Grading rules for *stress-graded timber. (B.S.I.) **1941** *Grading Rules for Structural Timber (B.S.I.)* 2 A further standard for the compressive *stress grading of these species for use in compression and tension members..is being prepared. **1971** *Timber Trades Jrnl.* 21 Aug. 26/2 Typical yields of sawn timber have been ..graded by the stress-grading machine installed by Timber-lab at Princes Risborough. **1973** *Materials & Technol.* VI. i. 27 Visual stress grading is not a difficult operation, but requires considerable experience. **1876** H. SWEET in *Trans. Philol. Soc. 1875–6* 473 We find..that every sentence can be analyzed into smaller groups characterized by one predominant stress-syllable, round which the others group themselves... In our first sentence there are two such stress groups... A word is, phonetically speaking, a *stress-group. **1959** J. T. PRING *Colloq. Eng. Pronunc.* 56 A stress-group is formed by a strongly stressed, prominent syllable, together with any unstressed, nonprominent syllables which cluster about it. **1505** *Nottingham Rec.* III. 100, j. aliam clavem pro le *stres hous dore. **1935** A. W. BOURNE *Midwifery for Nurses* ii. 24 *Stress incontinence is due to a weakening of the supports of the bladder. **1972** LAW & FRIEDMAN *Midwifery* xiv. 334 The patient is then asked to strain down and any tendency to prolapse of the vaginal walls is noted. She is then asked to cough to determine whether any stress incontinence is present. **1955** *Explorations* Feb. 7, I examined *stress interviews as well as non-directive ones. **1978** *Jrnl. R. Soc. Arts* CXXVI. 270/1 Whilst stress interviews in which the interviewer sets out to be provocative or rude may have been appropriate for the selection of American Special Services personnel during the war, I would not recommend them for civilian use. **1888** H. SWEET *Hist. Eng. Sounds* 8 The *stress marks are put before the element on which the stress begins. **1918** *Photo Miniature* Mar. 41 *Stress marks*, scummy appearance or black lines on a bromide or D.O.P. print, caused by..the sensitive paper being rubbed against the negative or other sheets of paper, or any sharp pressure. **1919** *Brit. Jrnl. Photogr. Alm.* 251 Free from tendency to give rise to stress or abrasion marks. **1961** *Amer. Speech* XXXVI. 221 Tone patterns illustrated by Kingdon's tonetic stress marks in ascending order of complexity. Indicates the force of each pattern on basic grammatical constructions. **1968** L. A. MANNHEIM tr. *Fritsche's Faults in Photography* III. 331 Most enlarging papers are largely protected against stress marks by an emulsion supercoating. **1964** R. H. ROBINS *Gen. Linguistics* iv. 138 In a word stressed on a non-initial syllable, in *stress-marked languages, the stressed articulation usually begins on the consonant. **1969** *Computers & Humanities* III. 136 The next step in this project is to replace orthographic entries with phonetic entries... Then, *stress maxima will be determined and various features of meter tabulated and analyzed. **1971** *Language* XLVII. 588 Thus in *the mangy dog*, the stress on the first syllable of *mangy* is a stress maximum. **1830** CARLYLE *Richter Again* Ess. 1840 II. 326 The *stress-memorials and siege-medals of Poverty. **1918** A. HARKER in *Q. Jrnl. Geol. Soc.* LXXIV. p. lxxvii, Shearing stress manifestly favours the production of sericite and the chlorites, of albite [etc.]... These may conveniently be styled *stress-minerals. **1952** H. RAMBERG *Origin Metamorphic & Metasomatic Rocks* 119 It has yet to be proved..that any of the suggested stress minerals really are such. **1965** G. J. WILLIAMS *Econ. Geol. N.Z.* x. 158/1 The chief constituent of all specimens he examined is a variety optically identical with the stress-mineral antigorite. **1971** *Language* XLVIII. 269 If word stress is assigned prior to syntactic transformations, then it follows automatically that transformationally attached affixes are *stress-neutral. **1972** *Ibid.* XLVIII. 336 He [*sc.* Lakoff] suggests that the NSR [*sc.* Nuclear Stress Rule] might precede the assignment of word-stress; this destroys the principle of the phonological cycle, and again fails to explain the *stress-neutrality of transformationally placed affixes. **1954** S. ROBERTSON *Devel. Mod. Eng.* (rev. ed.) iv 77 In English, any word of two or more syllables has its own *stress-pattern. **1968** R. A. LYTTLETON *Myst. Solar Syst.* vi. 193 Tektites reveal series of dark and light bands associated with the internal stress-pattern. **1980** *Early Music* July 403/2 Freed from the obligations of setting a poetic text, from the need to conform to text stress-patterns and changes of poetic mood, a composer might indulge in the exploration of thematic material to the full. **1933** L. BLOOMFIELD *Language* xvii. 295 In modern English verse..the author shapes his wording so that *stress-phonemes at certain intervals. **1968** CHOMSKY & HALLE *Sound Pattern Eng.* 26 He [*sc.* the speaker] need not make a choice among various 'stress phonemes'. **1932** D. JONES *Outl. Eng. Phonetics* (ed. 3) xxviii. 223 The lengths separating the '*stress-points' or 'peaks of prominence' of the syllables. **1956** *Kenyon Rev.* XVIII. 466 Mr. Chatman has shown the metrical stress-points in each line, but in my judgment he has misplaced them in lines 2, 12 and 14. **1893** BRIDGES *Milton's Prosody* 69 Here was..a definite statement of the laws of a *stress prosody. **1936** *Trans. Amer. Inst. Mining & Metall. Engineers* CXX. 32 Yet another field in which correlation of metallographic and mechanical methods is needed is the study of the relative seriousness of 'inherent' and 'imposed' sources of stress concentration—'*stress raisers', as Gillett has aptly called them. **1978** R. J. GRAY in McCall & French *Metallogr. in Failure Analysis* 240 The surfaces must be free of machining marks that could serve as stress raisers where a fissure and subsequent fracture could occur. **1966** LAZARUS & OPTON in C. D. Spielberger *Anxiety & Behavior* x. 227 The second phase involved the plan to manipulate 'ego-defense' processes so as to reduce *stress reactions while subjects watched a stressful film. **1979** D. A. BAKAL *Psychol. & Med.* iii. 86 The capacity of any situation to produce stress reactions depends on the characteristics of individuals. **1943** *Jrnl. Chem. Physics* XI. 127/1 As a result of their studies of *stress relaxation..of polyvinyl acetate held at constant elongation these authors conclude that the polymer is composed of a netted system of chains through which interpenetrates a system of relatively free chains. **1959** *Jrnl. Iron & Steel Inst.* CXCII. 198/3 Stress relaxation tests at a constant total strain of 0·15% for times exceeding 20 000 h on three low-alloy steels. **1979** R. P. BROWN *Physical Testing of Rubbers* xi. 200 Stress relaxation is the measurement of change of stress with time under constant strain. **1935** *Symp. Welding Iron & Steel* (Iron & Steel Inst.) II. 42 *Stress relief by heat treatment reduced the stresses to approximately 10 per cents of those existing in the plates as welded. **1973** [see *stress corrosion* above]. **1980** *Metallography* XIII. 69 A stress-relief treatment at 600–650°C results in the transformation of ferrite primarily to $M_{23}C_6$ carbide. **1935** *Symp. Welding Iron & Steel* (Iron & Steel Inst.) II. 47 The whole member was now *stress-relieved in the furnace and delivered to the machine shop for completion of the work. **1980** *Metallography* XIII. 59 Large components are invariably stress relieved to reduce the residual stresses generated in welding. **1935** *Symp. Welding Iron & Steel* (Iron & Steel Inst.) II. 46 The *stress-relieved grid was next planed on a planer and planed top and bottom. **1980** *Metallography* XIII. 59 (*heading*) Microstructural transformations in stress relieved type 316 stainless steel weld metal. **1938** D. K. BULLENS et al. *Steel & its Heat Treatment* (ed. 4) I. v. 140 Finish machining is then done and a final *stress-relieving draw given..at 1050°, holding 48 hr. at temperature and furnace cooling. **1956** *Jrnl. Iron & Steel Inst.* CLXXXIII. 99/2 Stress relieving of 11-ft. dia. electrically welded steel duct. **1980** *Jrnl. Nucl. Materials* XCI. 189 The stress-relieving treatments [of Zircalloy-4] were made at..773,793 and 813 K, during 1 and 2 hr. **1901** BRIDGES *Milton's Prosody* (ed. 2) 88 On the rules of the common lighter *stress-rhythms. **1888** H. SWEET *Hist. Eng. Sounds* 124 This law of *stress-shift in weak diphthongs explains the lNorth. *am* = *eom*: weak *eom* became first *eam*.., then *eám*, and finally, by dropping the almost inaudible *e*, *am*. **1930** T. SASAKI *On Lang. R. Bridges' Poetry* 91 It has been the rule in the English blank verse since Chaucer not to tolerate stress-shift (or inversion of accent) in the fifth foot. **1972** M. L. SAMUELS *Linguistic Evol.* iii. 36 Later in Germanic stressing on the root-syllable was generalised, and because of this stress-shift the voiced allophones..were no longer in complementary distribution, [etc.]. **1959** *New Scientist* 12 Nov. 927/2 Much was still to be understood of the intermediate steps between the *stress situation and the decrease in circulating eosinophils. **1972** 'T. COE' *Don't lie to Me* xviii. 149 That premonition of something being wrong that sometimes strikes people in stress situations. **1886** K. PEARSON in I. Todhunter *Hist. Theory Elasticity* I. 503 There exist certain materials for which even in a state of ease the *stress-strain relation is not linear; that is to say the stress-strain curve..is not a straight line even for very small elastic strains. **1923** GLAZEBROOK *Dict. Appl. Physics* V. 56/2 This will be the most convenient place in which to treat of the stress-strain relations of a doped fabric. **1956** *Nature* 24 Mar. 561/1 Papers..dealt with the measurement of residual stresses in cold-drawn tubes;..and stress-strain characteristics of metal at high rates of strain. **1973** J. G. TWEEDDALE *Materials Technol.* I. iv. 79 Having derived the respective stress and strain values it is possible to study the tensile characteristics of a material from a graph comparing these values..a stress-strain diagram. **1847** *Proc. Philol. Soc.* III. 101 The *stress-syllable may be made the more acute, or the more grave, at the discretion of the speaker. **1910** G. HENDERSON *Norse Infl. Celtic Scot.* v. 110 The tone falls on the stress syllable with grave accent. **1958** *Times Lit. Suppl.* 17 Oct. 596/4 A cold in the head is more often than not a *stress-symptom with which one must learn to live. **1977** P. DICKINSON *Walking Dead* I. i. 24 At a certain point of over-crowding..[rats] manifest stress symptoms. **1946** K. L. PIKE *Intonation Amer. Eng.* III. 35 Many non-English languages..tend to use a rhythm which is more closely related to the syllable than the regular *stress-timed type of English. **1956** [see ISOCHRONIC *a.* 3]. **1980** *English World-Wide* I. 1. 108 RP is stress-timed, with primary stress recurring at roughly even intervals through a sentence. **1964** M. A. K. HALLIDAY et al. *Linguistic Science* iii. 72 The English type of rhythm is known as '*stress-timing'.

stress (strɛs), *v.*[1] Forms: 4 **stres, stresce**, 6 *Sc.* **straisse**, 4–6 **stresse**, 6– **stress.** [In early use prob. a. OF. *estrecier* = It. †*strizzare*:—popular L. **strictiāre*, f. *strictus*: see STRAIT *a.* In later use f. STRESS *sb.*]

†**1. a.** *trans.* To subject (a person) to force or compulsion; to constrain or restrain; to compel *to* (do something). *Obs.*

1303 R. BRUNNE *Handl. Synne* 3726 ȝyf þou for yre bygynne wykkednes þat no man may lette þe, ne stres. *c* **1450** *Gesta Rom.* xxvii. 103 It is displesing to me þat I have grevid god so muche, for the whiche I am stressid to come heþere. **1581** A. HALL *Iliad* v. 90 They leaue not thee, but vs also, who here are come not strest In thy quarrell to spend our bloud.

b. To abridge the liberty of; to confine, incarcerate. *Obs.*

1340 HAMPOLE *Pr. Consc.* 8001 Þe dampned bodyse salle fredom mys; For þai salle be stresced in helle als thralle. **1530** PALSGR. 738/2, I stresse, I strayght one of his liberty or thrust his body to guyther, *je estroysse. Ibid.*, The man is stressyd to soore, he can nat styrre him. **1556** J. HEYWOOD *Spider & F.* lxxxii. 23 At time of this graunt, I was (as who say,) Stressed by you: your prisoner (as it were).

†**2. a.** To subject to hardship; to afflict, distress, harass, oppress; in passive, to be 'hard up'. *Obs.*

1535 STEWART *Cron. Scot.* I. 124 In that storme so stranglie tha war straist, Mony war lost and mycht no langer lest. **1559** ALYMER *Harborowe* P 1, These Romaines..being stressed and almoste brought to the last cast. **1563** *Mirr. Mag., Henry Duke Buckhm.* xxxix, The dread wherewyth him selfe was strest. **1653** E. WATERHOUSE *Apol. Learning* 155 If the Magistrate be so stressed that he cannot protect those that are pious and peaceable, the Lord help. **1824** SCOTT *St. Ronan's* x, I wad say naething mair than that I was stressed for the penny money.

b. To tax or burden (one's pecuniary resources). *Obs.*

1584 LODGE *Hist. Forbonius & Prisceria* G ij, Lead by couetousnesse, for that he woulde not stresse his coffers.

3. a. To subject (a material thing, a bodily organ, a mental faculty) to stress or strain; to overwork, fatigue. Now chiefly *Sc.*

1545 ASCHAM *Toxoph.* II. (Arb.) 126 Bycause they shoote wyth a softe lowse, and stresses not a shaft muche in the breste where the weyghte of the bowe lyethe. **1548** PATTEN *Exped. Scot.* Peroration P ij b, I..thearfore [was] dryuen to stresse my memorie yᵉ more for callinge the same too mind again. **1551** RECORDE *Cast. Knowl.* (1556) 53 So that the Meridiane maye entre iustlye into those socketts, and turne in them without stressynge. **1704** F. FULLER *Med. Gymn.* (1718) 135 The Nerves are quite stress'd with a Load of Wine. **1715** RAMSAY *Christ's Kirk Gr.* II. xviii, Some were like to tine their sight, Wi' sleep and drinking strest. **1722** WODROW *Corr.* (1843) II. 638 Let me know how your eyes are. Dont stress them. **1756** MRS. CALDERWOOD in *Coltness Collect.* (Maitland Club) 260 The Capucines are commonly imployed to preach, but the method here is not to stress themselves by saying too much at once. **1815** SCOTT *Guy M.* xxiii, 'I could gar him show mair action', said his master, 'but..it would be a pity to stress Dumple'. **1894** P. H. HUNTER *James Inwick* vi. 74 Them wha had kent him a' his days said that he had ne'er stressed himsel' wi' wark.

b. *intr.* for *refl.* ? *Sc.*

1901 G. DOUGLAS *Ho. Green Shutters* 5 A horse the feet of which struck sparks from the paved ground as they stressed painfully on edge to get weigh on the great waggon.

c. *Mech.* (cf. STRESS *sb.* 5 c).

1883 THOMSON & TAIT *Nat. Phil.* §832 (ed. 2) I. II. 423 When a solid is stressed, the state of stress is completely determined when the amount and direction of the three principal stresses are known. **1892** *C.T.C. Monthly Gaz.* June 179/1 It is a well known fact amongst engineers that a metal structure..must not be stressed more than one-third of its ultimate breaking stress.

d. In contexts of *Biol.* and *Psychol.*: cf. STRESS *sb.* 3 g.

1973 *Country Life* 7 June 1859/2 The transfer to a new environment stresses the calves, and it is now that latent infection will show itself. **1975** *Verbatim* Sept. 5/2 An analysis of the tapes will show exactly how stressed he was, stated the author of a book on certain intelligence methods. **1979** *Sci. Amer.* Nov. 65/1 When the reovirus-infected mice were stressed by injection with a large dose of glucose, however, it became quite clear that their ability to metabolize glucose had become impaired.

4. a. To lay the stress or emphasis on, emphasize (a word or phrase in speaking); to place a stress-accent upon (a syllable).

1859 MEREDITH *R. Feverel* ii, Stressing the epithet to increase the defiance. **1892** S. A. BROOKE *E. Eng. Lit.* I. Pref. p. xi, I used alliteration whenever I could, and stressed as much as possible the alliterated words. **1893** BRIDGES *Milton's Prosody* 74 If a boy were told..that it saved the monotony of a pentameter to stress the penultimate.

b. *fig.* To lay stress on, emphasize, bring into prominence (a fact, idea, etc.). Chiefly *U.S.*

1896 *Mod. Lang. Notes* XI. 78/2 A sketch of the history of the Troy legend was outlined, and its popularity in medieval literature stressed, as the theme for numerous romances. **1901** G. B. HALSTED in *Science* 8 Nov. 705 In the Columbus report I particularly stressed the work of two authors. **1906** W. H. FLEMING *Slavery* 34 Physical facts, stressed by an ineradicable race pride, bar the way against assimilation.

†**5.** *intr.* Of tears: To burst forth, gush. *Obs.*

c **1450** *St. Cuthbert* (Surtees) 2128 Ay when he sang his messe, þe teres oute of his eyen stresse.

Hence '**stressing** *vbl. sb.*

1540 PALSGR. *Acolastus* IV. vi. V iv b, Is the strength and lustinesse..of my body..nothyng worne (by excedyng or ouer moch stressyng of nature?). **1915** *Nation* (N.Y.) 6 May 487/1 If..the offending film..stirred his heart to mutiny and rage, the potentialities for evil in less-balanced minds need no stressing.

stress, *v.*[2] *Obs.* exc. *dial.* [Aphetic f. DISTRESS *v.*] *trans.* To levy a distress upon, distrain. Also *absol.*

c **1380** WYCLIF *Wks.* (1880) 234 ȝif here rente be not redily paied here bestis ben stressid & þei pursued wiþouten mercy. **1483** *Cath. Angl.* 368/2 To Stresse, *distringere.* **1876** *Whitby Gloss.* s.v., 'They're boun te stress for 't', to force the payment by law. **1886** *W. Somerset Word-bk.* s.v., Well, I be zorry vor to zee a widow umman a-stress'd; but her can't never 'spect to bide there, not if her don't pay no rent.

stressable ('strɛsəb(ə)l), *a. Linguistics.* [f. STRESS *v.*[1] + -ABLE.] Capable of being stressed. Also **stressa'bility**.

1964 W. S. ALLEN in D. Abercrombie et al. *Daniel Jones* 6 In verse, as in the language, not every heavy syllable is stressed; it is only *stressable.* **1964** *English Studies* XLV. 495 He investigates its relation to Latin phonology, which in the realm of accent is characterized by the category of stressability. **1972** *Language* XLVIII. 295 The statement 'B is stressable' is to rule out cases like anaphoric noun phrases, which are not stressable. **1977** *Ibid.* LIII. 28 We agree that the stressability of prepositions is to be handled by the rules of the grammar rather than poetry, but we differ substantially on the specific analysis.

stressed (strɛst), *ppl. a.* [f. STRESS *v.*[1] + -ED[1].]

†**1.** Distressed, afflicted. Also *absol. Obs.*

1559 AYLMER *Harborowe* B 3 b, With a certain choise and judgement to giue passage and safetie to the stressed. **1590** SPENSER *F.Q.* II. x. 37 Stird with pitty of the stressed plight Of this sad realme. *c* **1590** J. STEWART *Poems* (S.T.S.) II. 88 The stressit knycht all stupefact did stand. **1632** LITHGOW *Trav.* VII. 328 Stress'd Saylers.

2. Marked with a stress, emphasized.

1885 MEREDITH *Diana* i, The stressed repetition of calculated brevity while a fiery scandal was abroad concerning the lady. **1913** A. C. CLARK *Prose Rhythm in English* 18 Rhythm in poetry depends upon the recurrence of longs and shorts, or stressed and unstressed syllables, in a regular order.

3. *Engin.* Subjected to mechanical stress; *spec.* = PRESTRESSED *ppl. a.*; ***stressed skin***, an outer covering of an aircraft or other structure that bears a significant part of the stresses and contributes to the overall strength and stiffness; usu. *attrib.*

1930 *Flight* 11 Apr. 411/2 Recently a monoplane of orthodox aerodynamic design was completed by the company, employing the stressed-skin type of wing construction. **1951** *Archit. Rev.* CX. 342/1 The roof is of stressed-skin plywood construction formed by two skins of exterior ply panel grade on an internal timber framework. **1954** [see DIAGRID]. **1966** *Daily Tel.* 10 Aug. 18/2 American steel was being bought for the 'highly stressed' parts of future British-built nuclear submarines. **1968** *Punch* 13 Nov. 688/3 British Railways 'revolutionary gas-turbine advanced passenger train with stressed-skin, aircraft-type construction'. **1979** *Jrnl. Magnetism & Magn. Materials* XI. 76 Uniaxially stressed semiconductors.

stressful ('strɛsfʊl), *a.* [f. STRESS *sb.* + -FUL[2].] Causing or inclined to cause stress; full of, or subject to, stress or strain.

1853 MISS E. S. SHEPPARD *Ch. Auchester* II. 206, I could not bear the stressful brightness. **1886** LINSKILL *Haven under Hill* I. ii. 28 The stressful days of labour and care. **1952** *Psychosomatic Med.* XIV. 311/2 Characteristically in the patient with chronic fatigue, the stressful activity is implicit rather than explicit. **1966** O. NORTON *School of Liars* vi. 104 'How do you protect a man like him from stress?'.. 'By not being stressful yourself.' **1972** C. M. PARKES *Bereavement* iii. 32 Situations that tend to produce alarm are regarded as *stressful.* **1978** *Detroit Free Press* 5 Mar. D4/4 Are you always changing things in your life, changing jobs, changing residences?.. If so, subtract two years. Too much change is stressful.

Hence '**stressfully** *adv.*

1890 *Harper's Mag.* Apr. 809/1 [Her poetry] is often too stressfully subjective. **1902** *Q. Rev.* Apr. 367 Flaubert.. preached, and laboured stressfully to put into practice, his conviction that great art is 'scientific and impersonal'.

stressless ('strɛslɪs), *a.* [f. STRESS *sb.* + -LESS.] Having no stress, unstressed. Hence '**stresslessness**.

1885 *Encycl. Brit.* XVIII. 788/2 In originally stressless syllables long vowels were shortened and short vowels dropped. **1892** FENNELL *Stanford Dict.* Introd. p. ix. Nor is it implied that all syllables marked as unaccented have precisely the same stresslessness.

stressman ('strɛsmən). *Engin.* Pl. **stressmen.** [f. STRESS *sb.* + MAN *sb.*[1]] = *stress analyst* s.v. STRESS *sb.* 11.

1935 C. G. BURGE *Compl. Bk. Aviation* 260/2 The 'stressman' may be able to suggest practical methods of lightening the weight. **1954** VEALE & RADFORD *Aircraft for All* iv. 62 Stressmen..check the strength of every major part. **1960** *Times* 1 Apr. 2/3 (Advt.), Hunting Aircraft Limited have vacancies for..aerodynamicists, stressmen, design draughtsmen. The work programme embraces both high and low speed military and civil aircraft. **1979** *Offshore Engineer* Sept. 134/1 There is provision for override so that when needed the system can operate continuously—say during a period of bad weather or, as Desmond Thurgood, Seatek's chief stressman, points out, during installation.

stressor ('strɛsə(r)). *Psychol.* and *Biol.* [f. STRESS *sb.*, *v.*[1] + -OR.] A single condition or agent that constitutes a stress for an organism (see STRESS *sb.* 3 g).

1950 H. SELYE *Physiol. & Path. of Exposure to Stress* 9 The expression systemic stress is used here to denote a condition in which..extensive regions of the body deviate from their normal resting state. In accordance with the common usage of the word 'stress', the term 'systemic stress' is sometimes loosely employed also to denote the stimuli which cause systemic stress. In this sense, it is preferable however, to speak of alarming stimuli or 'stressors'. **1958** *Proc. 10th Internat. Congr. Entomol.* IV. 727 (*heading*) Crowding as a stressor [in insects]. **1962** *Lancet* 27 Jan. 200/2 It has long been known that the response of schizophrenic patients to stressor agents is dulled. **1969** *Nature* 4 Oct. 18/2 Stress results from a threat, real or apparent, to the biological integrity of the animal. More simply—a 'stressor' can be defined as any stimulus or situation which causes maladaptive behaviour. **1972** C. M. PARKES *Bereavement* i. 4 Loss of a close relative is normally a major stressor.

stressy ('strɛsɪ), *a. rare.* [f. STRESS *sb.* or *v.*[1] + -Y[1].] Characterized by stress, *spec.* in the prosody of G. M. Hopkins; in which stress is conspicuous.

1880 G. M. HOPKINS *Lett. to R. Bridges* (1955) 107, I think you have missed the clue. You take the rhythm for three triple time, iambs and anapaests say, and four feet to a line (except the refrain). But to get this you have to skip.. a whole foot as marked and stressy as any other foot. **1961** *Times Lit. Suppl.* 18 Aug. 549/4 Neither of these versions reveals the bold, thoroughgoing 'stressy' flexibility of genuine sprung rhythm.

†**strestell, -tulle,** corrupt forms of TRESTLE.

1531 *Rec. St. Mary at Hill* (1905) 40 Item, a tabull and a payre of strestells, ij s. **1563** *Stanford Churchw. Acc.* in *Antiquary* (1888) Apr. 168 For mending the Screene & strestulles in the churche howse, xij d.

stret, obs. and dial. variant of STRAIT *a.*

stretch (strɛtʃ), *sb.* Also 6 **stretche**, 7 **strech**, *Sc.* **streitch, streach.** [f. STRETCH *v.*]

1. The action or an act of stretching physically; the fact of being stretched.

a. Forcible extension or dilatation; *occas.* degree or amount of this.

1600 ROWLANDS *Lett. Humours Blood* D 6, Or else heele haue it with fiue and a reach, Although it cost his necke the Halter stretch. **1691** RAY *Creation* II. (1704) 332 To secure them from disruption, which..they [the bones] would be in some danger of, upon a great and sudden stretch or contortion, if they were dry. **1705** ELSTOB in *Hearne's Collect.* 30 Nov. (O.H.S.) I. 109 He gagg'd him to ye fullest stretch. **1883** S. CHAPPEL *Sewing Machine* 24 You will find when you want to work the machine that the belt, owing to the continued stretch, is too slack. **1898** *Allbutt's Syst. Med.* V. 472 The amount of distension of the ventricle, in other words, the degree of stretch in the muscle fibres. **1907** O'GORMAN *Motor Pocket Bk.* (ed. 2) 598 In adjusting the stretch of side chains by the turn-buckle.., care must be taken to [etc.].

b. Stretching out or extension of the limbs; extent or measure of stretching out.

1696 R. H. *Sch. Recreat.* 80 (Fencing) And when you are at your full stretch, keep your Left-hand stretched, and ever observe to keep a close Left-foot, which [etc.]. **1697** DRYDEN *Æneis* x. 967 Sometimes he thought to swim the stormy Main, By stretch of Arms the distant Shore to gain. **1700** —— *Fables, Ceyx & Alcyone* 482 At all her stretch her little wings she spread. **1710** FELTON *Diss. Classics* (1718) 12 What is Excellent is placed out of ordinary Reach, and Your Lordship will easily be persuaded to put forth Your Hand to the utmost Stretch, and reach whatever You aspire at. **1830** A. FONBLANQUE *Eng. under Seven Administr.* (1837) II. 35 The knight.., lifting his battle-axe to the utmost stretch of his arm, dashed the edge with all his might upon the forehead of the giant. **1854** SPENCER in *Brit. Q. Rev.* July 139 Amongst other ancient measures were the orgyia or stretch of the arms, the pace, and the palm.

c. A resting with outstretched limbs. † ***at full stretch***: reclining at full length.

1700 T. BROWN *Amusem. Ser. & Com.* Wks. 1719 III. 14 He lolls at full Stretch within, and half a dozen brawny Bulk-begotten Footmen behind [his coach]. **1856** *Chamb. Jrnl.* 12 Jan. 27/2 Punter never gets above four hours' sleep in his bed; but he makes up for that deficiency..by a two hours' stretch on the bench in the afternoon.

†**d.** ***upon one's last stretch***: in one's death-agony. *Obs.*

1680 R. L'ESTRANGE *20 Select Colloq. Erasm.* 258 Observing the Woman to Yawn and just upon her last Stretch, he put [etc.].

e. An act of drawing up the body and extending the arms, indicating weariness or languor.

1712 STEELE *Spect.* No. 320 ¶5 Our Salutation at Entrance is a Yawn and a Stretch, and then without more Ceremony we take our Place at the Lolling Table. **1856** MISS YONGE *Daisy Chain* I. viii, He gave a yawn and a stretch.

f. An act of 'stretching one's legs'; a walk taken for exercise. (Cf. 6 c.)

a **1761** [S. HALIBURTON & HEPBURN] *Mem. Magopico* viii. (ed. 2) 24 A good stretch, in a morning, over heath, and hills, and ditches,..will make a man eat a good breakfast. **1871** GLADSTONE in Morley *Life* VI. viii. (1903) II. 378, I have had a twelve-miles stretch to-day, almost all on wild ground. **1887** *Old Man's Favour* II. II. vii. 37 'Were you detained at the office?' 'No; I went for a stretch after.'

g. The condition of being stretched; state of tension. Phrases, ***on, upon the stretch***; ***to bring to the stretch.***

1673 BOYLE *New Exper. Efficacy Air's Moisture* 11, I suppos'd, that after a time this unusual stretch of the Rope would cease. **1679** DRYDEN *Troil. & Cress.* Pref. b 1 b, What melody can be made on that Instrument, all whose strings are screw'd up at first to their utmost stretch, and to the same sound? **1737** BRACKEN *Farriery Impr.* (1757) II. 153 The Blood-vessels in the Legs are more upon the Stretch. **1748** *Anson's Voy.* I. vi. 66 They..strain the two thongs in contrary directions.., keeping the thongs still upon the stretch. **1753** J. BARTLET *Gentl. Farriery* (1754) 356 E, a strap fixed to the pad,..to keep the tail on the stretch at pleasure. **1781** COWPER *Truth* 384 An instrument, whose cords, upon the stretch,..Yield only discord in his Maker's ear. **1786** J. PEARSON in *Med. Commun.* II. 97 The ligament was on the stretch. **1793** SMEATON *Edystone L.* §274 The chains being introduced and brought to a stretch. **1816** CRABB *Engl. Syn.* 177 s.v. *Breeze*, The mariner has favourable gales which keep the sails on the stretch. **1827** D. JOHNSON *Ind. Field Sports* 73 The string..is kept at its stretch by means of a stiff piece of stick. *c* **1860** H. STUART *Seaman's Catech.* 27 The rigging must be got on a stretch. *fig.* **1702** VANBRUGH *False Friend* IV. i, Sure Villainy and Impudence were never on the Stretch before: This Traytor has wreckt 'em till they Crack.

h. Capacity for being stretched.

1875 KNIGHT *Dict. Mech.* 2415/2 It is called the straining, because the stretch is taken out of it by repeated wettings and stretchings. **1887** *Wheeling* 6 July 208/1 The leather used for the seats has been subjected to sufficient pressure to take all the stretch out of it. **1894** *Times* 15 Aug. 11/1 The Vigilant cold not sail owing to the stretch not having been taken out of her new main rigging.

i. *Baseball.* An action used in pitching (see quots.).

1939 E. J. NICHOLS *Hist. Dict. Baseball Terminol.* 75 *Stretch*,..a pitcher's straightening of his arms above his head preliminary to delivering the ball. **1951** H. TURKIN *Official Encycl. Baseball* 572 The pitching delivery can be broken down and analyzed to reveal six distinct actions: windup, stretch, leg lift, stride, body pivot and follow through... The stretch brings the pitching arm behind the head. **1976** *Webster's Sports Dict.* 428/2 *Stretch*,..a movement a pitcher uses instead of a windup when there are runners on base. *Ibid.* 429/1 The stretch, with its integral pause, allows the pitcher to throw to the base to try to pick off the runner or to keep him close to prevent his stealing without interrupting the pitching motion and making a balk.

j. *Aeronaut.* Modification of an existing aircraft design to increase its capabilities, esp. by lengthening the fuselage; capacity for this allowed for in a design.

1954 *Economist* 11 Sept. 2/2 However much 'stretch' may have been designed into the two machines—and the evidence suggests it was not too great—these changes in elements outside the designer's control mean modifications ..delays. **1960** *New Scientist* 30 June 1640/1 The modifications involved in stretch are chiefly concerned with stress and control parameters. **1976** *Farnborough Internat. Exhibition* (Official Programme) 46/2 The Lynx design is capable of considerable 'stretch', says Westland.

2. In immaterial sense: A stretching or straining something beyond its proper limits.

†**a.** An act exceeding the scope of one's authority or commission, or the bounds of strict law or justice; a strained or unfair argument or representation; also, an act of 'stretching a point', a deviation from one's accustomed rule or principle. Chiefly *Sc. Obs.*

1541 WYATT *Let. to Privy Counc.* Poems (1858) p. xxiv, If these be the matters that may bring me into suspect, me semeth..that the credit than an Ambassador hath, or ought to have, might well discharge as great stretches as these. **1689** EARL OF CRAWFORD in *Leven & Melv. Papers* (Bannatyne Club) 319 Mr. Aird, who is represented as a man of great piety, and turned out by a streach. *a* **1714** G. LOCKHART in *L. Papers* (1817) I. 212 Such a proposal had actually been made; and even supposing it were otherwise, it was not the first time they had made greater stretches with a design that good might come of it. **1715** BURNET *Own Time* (1766) II. 29 It was an unheard of stretch, to oblige men to be bound for others in matters of Religion. **1717** WODROW *Corr.* (1843) II. 264 Though it was urged in his defence, that by 'natural powers' was meant only such as hearing, reading, going to ordinances,..yet these stretches did not satisfy. **1722** —— *Hist. Suff. Ch. Scot.* II. 398 Then the Probation is summed up with much Cunning, and many Stretches. *c* **1730** BOSTON in Morrison *Mem.* xii. (1899) 381 Mr. Gordon returning to Edinburgh,..desired an interview. Where-upon I made a stretch, and went thither. **1742** KAMES *Decis. Crt. Sess. 1730–52* (1799) 61 It is therefore a stretch beyond the common law, to support a man's nomination of tutors to his children. **1776** PAINE *Com. Sense* (1791) 63 The unwarrantable stretch, likewise, which that house made in their last sitting, to gain an undue authority over the Delegates of that Province, ought to warn the people at large, how they trust power out of their own hands.

b. More explicitly: An unwarranted exercise *of* power, prerogative; a straining *of* the law.

1689 in *Acts Parlt. Scot.* (1875) XII. 64/2 The causeing perseu and forfault severall persones upon streitches of old and absolute Lawes. **1693** *Apol. Clergy Scot.* 25 A stretch of Arbitrary Power, never heard of in Scotland. **1718** HICKES & NELSON *Kettlewell* II. xliii. 145 None could be more zealous in putting the King upon the Stretch of his Prerogative. **1757** HUME *Hist. Gt. Brit., Chas. II*, ii. II. 187 His ministers..could not forbear making very extraordinary stretches of authority. **1759** BP. HURD *Moral Dialogues* iv. 133 Her [Q. Eliz.] parliaments were disposed to wave all disputes about the stretch of her prerogative, from a sense of their own and the common danger. **1766** BLACKSTONE *Comm.* II. v. 69 Neither himself [Chas. I] nor his people seemed able to distinguish between the arbitrary stretch, and the legal exertion, of prerogative. **1771** GOLDSM. *Hist. Eng.* IV. 14 These stretches of power naturally led the lords and commons into some degree of opposition. **1818** CRUISE *Digest* (ed. 2) V. 449 The determination of the Judges.., so far from being considered as an unwarrantable stretch of their authority, must on the contrary be acknowledged to have been a measure of great public utility. **1849** HT. MARTINEAU *Hist. Peace* IV. xii. (1877) III. 95 Public sympathy was with them, as with men punished by a stretch of law for a nominal offence. **1874** GREEN *Short Hist.* viii. §5. 510 As daring a stretch of the prerogative superseded what was known as Knox's Liturgy.

c. An exaggerated statement. *on the stretch* (nonce-phrase): using exaggeration, 'drawing the long bow'.

1710–11 SWIFT *Jrnl. to Stella* 1 Jan., That's a d——ned lie of your chimney being carried to the next house with the wind... My Lord Hertford would have been ashamed of such a stretch. **1782** MRS. COWLEY *Which is the Man?* IV ii, Hyperbole! What's that? Why, that's as much as to say, a stretch. **1834** MARRYAT *P. Simple* xxxi, It a'n't that I might not stretch now and then,..but..he's always on the stretch. .. He never tells the truth except by mistake.

d. An exercise of imagination, understanding, etc. beyond ordinary limits. Now freq. in phr. *by any* (or *no*) *stretch of the imagination*.

1781 MME. D'ARBLAY *Diary* June, [His] supposed enmity to Merlin is, indeed, a stretch of that absurd creature's imagination. **1803** *Med. Jrnl.* IX. 26 It requires no great stretch of understanding to know that the same practice will not answer in all climates. **1828** LYTTON *Pelham* lxx, Every day the ministers are filling up the minor places, and it requires a great stretch of recollection in a politician to remember the absent. **1839** J. MARTINEAU *Stud. Christianity* iii. (1858) 111 But this was a stretch of charity too great for any Hebrew. **1841** DICKENS *Barn. Rudge* i, Indeed it needed no very great stretch of fancy to detect in it other resemblances to humanity. **1862** *Sporting Mag.* Nov. 329 It required no great stretch of intellect to acquit the officers honourably on the evidence. **1942** T. BAILEY *Pink Camellia* xv. 122 Peter could not, by any stretch of the imagination, be compared to that Satan of the Scriptures who came so inopportunely to the Garden. **1957** *Pract. Wireless* XXXIII. 573/2 Most neutral leads..have registered between 5 and 25 volts R.M.S., voltages which cannot, by any stretch of the imagination, be called lethal. **1977** A. ECCLESTONE *Staircase for Silence* iv. 77 The church they belong to seems hopelessly stuck fast in a way of life that by no stretch of the imagination can be described in terms of leaven or salt or light.

e. An undue extension of scope or application. *stretch of language*: the use of words or expressions with undue latitude of meaning.

1849 GROTE *Greece* II. xxxix, (1862) III. 412 This bold stretch of exegetical conjecture. **1860** TYNDALL *Glac.* II. App. 431 With reference to this hypothesis, I will only say that it is a bold stretch of analogies. **1875** W. K. CLIFFORD *Lect. & Ess.* (1879) I. 229 It is only by a stretch of language that we can be said to desire that which is inconceivable. **1905** MISS BROUGHTON *Waif's Progr.* xiv. 164 It could not, by any stretch of language, be considered a good thing for any young woman to be taken under the..wing of Lady Tennington.

3. a. *furthest, utmost stretch*: the utmost degree to which a thing can be extended. Now *rare* or *Obs.*

1558 in Feuillerat *Revels Q. Eliz.* (1908) Table I, For castinge and ymployeinge of the stuffe to the furdeste stretche of service. **1687** ATTERBURY *Answ. Consid. Spirit Luther* 45 Quotations..which, in their utmost stretch, can signify no more then that Luther lay under severe agonies of mind. **1712** GRANVILLE *Unnatural Flights Poetry* 65 This is the utmost Stretch that Nature can, And all beyond is fulsome, false, and vain. **1713** *Guardian* No. 147 ¶2 He did not exceed, but went to the utmost stretch of his Income. **1715** POPE *Iliad* I. Pref. B 1, The utmost Stretch of human Study, Learning, and Industry,..can never attain to this. **1741** RICHARDSON *Pamela* (1824) I. 199 She shall know it all, said he; and I defy the utmost stretch of your malice.

†**b.** Utmost degree, acme. *Obs.*

1742 RICHARDSON *Pamela* III. 182 [It] was the very Stretch of shameless Wickedness.

4. Strain or tension of mental or bodily powers; strained exertion. (Figurative use of 1 g.) Chiefly in phrases.

†**a.** *on the stretch, on her stretches* (said of a hawk): making a long swooping flight. *Obs.*

1622 FLETCHER *Prophetess* IV. iv, And scatter 'em, as an high towring Falcon on her Stretches, severs the fearfull fowl. **1636** MASSINGER *Bashful Lover* III. ii, See with what winged speed they climb the hill Like Falcons on the stretch to seise the prey.

b. † *at the full stretch* (obs.), *upon full stretch, on the stretch*: with strain of the physical powers; chiefly, making full speed.

1697 DRYDEN *Æneis* v. 259 They row At the full stretch, and shake the Brazen Prow. **1711** ADDISON *Spect.* No. 56 ¶3 He saw the Apparition of a milk-white Steed, with a young Man on the Back of it, advancing upon full Stretch after the Souls of about an hundred Beagles. **1768** J. BYRON *Narr. Patagonia* (ed. 2) 221 While their horse is upon full stretch. **1797** S. JAMES *Narr. Voy.* 175 To return to our own ship. We were now on the stretch for Europe. **1839** *Laws of Coursing* in *Youatt's Dog* (1845) App. 262 She [a hare] turns of her own accord to gain ground homeward, when both dogs are on the stretch after her. **1893** STEVENSON *Catriona* xvi, About fifty seconds after two I was in the saddle and on the full stretch for Stirling.

c. *on the* (†*full*) *stretch*: in a state of mental strain, making intense effort; so *to put, set upon the* (*full*) *stretch*. Now chiefly *at full stretch*: to capacity; working fully or as hard as possible.

1683 DRYDEN *Life Plutarch* 24 His memory was always on the stretch to receive..their discourses. **1691** NORRIS *Pract. Disc.* (1716) II. 98 We cannot live always upon the Stretch; our Faculties will not bear constant Pleasure any more than constant Pain. **1692** ATTERBURY *Serm.* (Ps. l. 14) (1726) I. 23 The Praise and Admiration of God..sets our Faculties upon their full Stretch. **1711** STEELE *Spect.* No. 38 ¶1 You might see his Imagination on the Stretch to find out something uncommon. **1722** DE FOE *Col. Jack* (1840) 318 This set all..heads upon the stretch, to inquire. **1768–74** TUCKER *Lt. Nat.* (1834) II. 361 Craft and cozenage..put our faculties to the stretch, and lay the foundation of prudence. **1771** WESLEY *Wks.* (1872) V. 272 He is on the full Stretch to save their Souls. **1778** SIR J. REYNOLDS *Disc.* viii. (1876) 443 The writers of every age and country, where taste has begun to decline,..are always on the stretch; never deviate..a moment from the pompous and the brilliant. **1796** *Ann. Reg., Hist.* 108 His thoughts were uninterruptedly on the stretch. **1862** STANLEY *Jew. Ch.* (1877) I. xiv. 277 The inmates of Sisera's harem..are on the stretch of expectation for the sight of..their champion. **1866** A. HALLIDAY in Dickens etc., *Mugby Junction, Engine-driver* 26/2 Me and my stoker were on the stretch all the time, doing two things at once—attending to the engine and looking out. **1884** H. A. TAINE in *Contemp. Rev.* Oct. 521 His business keeps his mind on the stretch. **1934** G. B. SHAW *On Rocks* I. 221, I am an overworked..man,..having to keep my mind at full stretch all the time struggling with problems. **1955** *Times* 1 June 10/1 United States tire manufacturers are still working at full stretch. **1977** *Evening Post* (Nottingham) 27 Jan. 4/5 Wilford power station, Nottingham, has been at full stretch to meet heavy demand.

d. Exhausting effort or strain of mind. Now *rare*.

1791 BOSWELL *Johnson* I. Advt. ¶2 The stretch of mind and prompt assiduity by which so many conversations were preserved. **1814** JANE AUSTEN *Mansf. Park* ix, The greater length of the service, however, I admit to be sometimes too hard a stretch upon the mind. *c* **1815** —— *Persuas.* (1818) II. viii. 148 The horror and distress you were involved in—the stretch of mind, the wear of spirits. **1859** BOYD *Recreat. Country Parson* iii. 117 Mental work is much the greater stretch; and it is strain, not time, that kills.

†**5.** *to give stretch to*: to allow to act unchecked. *Obs.*

1777 BURGOYNE *Proclam.* in *Gentl. Mag.* XLVII. 360/2, I have but to give stretch to the Indian forces under my direction,..to overtake the hardened enemies of Great-Britain.

6. Extent in time or space.

a. An unbroken continuance of some one employment, occupation, or condition, during a period of time; an uninterrupted 'spell' of work, rest, prosperity, etc. Chiefly in phrase *at one* or *a stretch, upon* or *on a stretch*, rarely *at the stretch*: without intermission, continuously (during the time specified or implied); [cf. G. *in einer strecke*].

1689 *Lond. Gaz.* No. 2451/3 So [we] continued Battering upon a Strech till five in the Afternoon. **1693** NORRIS *Pract. Disc.* (1711) III. 134 God will then proceed to the highest actuation of the Soul..so that her whole Life shall be but one constant Stretch of Thought. **1774** GOLDSM. *Nat. Hist.* III. 163 They will trot..between fifty and sixty English miles, at one stretch. **1799** J. KING in *Corr. W. Fowler* (1907) 32 We are much in at Sunderland. We are eight nights in upon a stretch, out of twenty one. **1818** SCOTT *Hrt. Midl.* ix, The halt's gane now, unless he has to walk ower mony miles at a stretch. **1825** WATERTON *Wand. S. Amer.* I. (1903) 2 Sometimes you see level ground on each side of you, for two or three hours at a stretch. **1834** MARRYAT *P. Simple* vii, He can snore for fourteen hours on a stretch. **1841** THACKERAY *Gt. Hoggarty Diamond* i, We always played seven hours on a stretch. **1851** MACAULAY in Trevelyan *Life & Lett.* (1880) II. 215, I read the last five books at a stretch. **1857** TROLLOPE *Barchester T.* xiii, I saw her talking to him for half an hour at the stretch. **1879** 'OUIDA' *Cecil Castlemaine* 7 His rider had been in boot and saddle twenty-four hours at the stretch. **1885** *Law Times* LXXIX. 206/1 He was unable..to walk more than five miles at a stretch. **1887** JESSOPP *Arcady* vii. 214 He..gave us..accounts of the number of hours he had kept on working at a stretch. **1900** *Law Rep., App. Cases* 405 The net remains fixed for periods as long as six hours at a stretch.

b. An extent in duration; a (more or less long) period of time.

1698 NORRIS *Pract. Disc.* (1707) IV. 216 Could I lengthen out my span to an Antediluvian stretch, what should I be the better? **1865** DICKENS *Mut. Fr.* IV. xiv, If you..had been fretted out of..your mind, for a stretch of months together. **1892** E. REEVES *Homeward Bound* 102 We now have a stretch of eleven days before us, in which..we shall cross the Equator..and reach a new world at Colombo. **1905** TREVES *Other Side of Lant.* II. xvii. (1906) 118 To be still unforgotten after a stretch of years.

c. A continuous journey or march. Now *colloq.*

1699 BENTLEY *Phal.* 441 To go from Syracuse to Alexandria and back again in a Morning, and on foot too over the Sea, is a stretch something extraordinary. **1715** ADDISON *Freeholder* No. 3 ¶2 Upon this alarm we made incredible stretches towards the South, to gain the Fastnesses of Preston. **1819** SCOTT *Leg. Montrose* xviii, I made a stretch of four miles with six of my people in the direction of Inverlochy. **1840** DICKENS *Old C. Shop* i, 'A long way, wasn't it, Kit?' said the little old man. 'Why then, it was a goodish stretch, master,' returned Kit.

d. *Naut.* A continuous sail on one tack.

1675 H. TEONGE *Diary* (1825) 42 All the last night wee were becalmed, but this morning a fayre gale, which carrys us smoothly over this longe stretch. **1688** in *Third Collect. Papers Pres. Junct. Affairs* 2 Next day, upon Tide of Ebb, they made a Stretch, and made a Watch above a League, and then stood Westward. **1823** W. SCORESBY *Jrnl.* 131 In the evening, we made a stretch toward the land. **1840** R. H. DANA *Bef. Mast* xxxvi, Two long stretches..brought us into the roads. **1845** J. COULTER *Adv. Pacific* iv. 31 Having made a stretch off the coast about forty miles, we had a fine view of the tops of the Andes, covered with snow. **1883** CLARK RUSSELL *Sailors' Lang.* s.v., A long stretch is to sail a long distance on one tack.

e. Extent in length; a continuous length or distance; a continuous portion of a journey, of the length of a road, river, or the like.

1661 HICKERINGILL *Jamaica* 36 Some of them (I have seen) six or seven yards long, but their usual stretch, may bate the half. **1791** NEWTE *Tour Eng. & Scot.* 294 The canal is carried on in almost a straight line for 2000 toises, all cut through a rock, which occasioned so great an expence, that in this stretch of the canal, they found themselves obliged to restrict the breadth of the upper surface of the water to five toises. *Ibid.* 297 This arch was thrown over in three stretches, having only a centre of thirty feet, which was shifted on small rollers from one stretch to another. **1872** 'MARK TWAIN' *Roughing It* xviii. (1882) 99 It was nothing but a watering depot in the midst of the stretch of sixty-eight miles. **1876** HARDY *Hand of Ethelberta* xxxi, There was, as the crow flies, a stretch of thirty-five miles between the two places. **1885** BRET HARTE *Maruja* iii, Dead leaves of roses.. lay thick on the empty stretch of brown verandah. **1908** G. CORMACK *Egypt in Asia* ii. 18 This range [Lebanon] has an unbroken stretch of a hundred miles.

f. An expanse of land or water (usually, of uniform character).

1829 SCOTT *Anne of G.* xv, You will see a species of thicket, or stretch of low bushes. **1850** D. G. MITCHELL *Reveries Bachelor* 151, I see a broad stretch of meadow. **1851** WHITTIER *In Peace* 9 A slumberous stretch of mountain-land. **1873** BLACK *P'cess Thule* i. 3 He may have recalled mechanically the names of these stretches of water. **1885** *Manch. Exam.* 16 June 4/6 To dwell at Windsor, with its wide stretches of park and woodland and river. **1898** 'H. S. MERRIMAN' *Roden's Corner* xxxii. 337 The wide stretch of sand was entirely deserted when they emerged from the narrow streets. **1912** J. L. MYRES *Dawn of Hist.* ix. 203 Macedon and Thrace, which also offer some stretches of pasture.

g. *Linguistics.* A definable extent (of text or speech).

1961 M. A. K. HALLIDAY in *Word* XVII. 250 Language is patterned activity. At the formal level, the patterns are patterns of meaningful organization: certain regularities are exhibited over certain stretches of language activity. **1964** *English Studies* XLV (Suppl.). 56 It certainly seems worth while trying to bring more system into stretch-of-speech analysis in general by studying the potentialities and realities of absence of sound, sound zero. **1967** D. G. HAYS *Introd. Computational Linguistics* x. 171 As the text is being prepared, each stretch between unit boundaries is compared with the contents of the exclusion list. **1972** J. McH. SINCLAIR *Course in Spoken Eng.: Grammar* 3 Strict grammatical relationships need only be made across stretches of language a few words long. **1973** A. H. SOMMERSTEIN *Sound Pattern Anc. Greek* i. 1 The final chapter.. contains a summary.. of the rules of the part of Greek phonology that I have investigated, a stretch of text written in the form it would have before the application of these rules, [etc.].

7. *slang.* **a.** A yard (measure).

1811 *Lex. Balatron.* **1812** J. H. VAUX *Flash Dict.* s.v., Five or ten stretch signifies five or ten yards.

b. A term of hard labour; twelve months as a term of imprisonment. Also *loosely*, a prison sentence (freq. with preceding numeral signifying the number of years). Also *transf.*

1821 *Life D. Haggart* (ed. 2) 138, I was then sentenced to lag for seven stretch. **1857** 'DUCANGE ANGLICUS' *Vulgar Tongue* 21 *Stretch*, hard labour, in prison. *Th[ieves].* *Stretch*, twelve months hard labour. *Th.* **1888** 'R. BOLDREWOOD' *Robbery under Arms* iv, There's a lot of law! How did I learn it? I had plenty of time in Berrima Gaol—worse luck—my first stretch. **1949** 'M. INNES' *Journeying Boy* ix. 109 If we were getting him a stretch, we could go to bed feeling we had done something useful. **1951** P. BRANCH *Lion in Cellar* xx. 222 He's in Joe Gurr again. He got nicked in Cardiff on a snout gaff... It's only a two stretch and a lot of the Boys had their collars felt. **1957** G. THOMAS *Gazooka* 42, I owed it to him now to see that he would not be saddled with another stretch under the probation officer or in a reform school for an offence which was not.. immoral. **1960** S. CLAYDON *Lesson in Murder* v. 75, I was going to serve my stretch, come out, and get a job. **1967** J. MORGAN *Involved* 40 What do you think he'll get for this lot, guv'nor, ten? I suppose a ten stretch is the least he can expect. **1976** K. BONFIGLIOLI *Something Nasty in Woodshed* ix. 106 'Porridge'.. means penal servitude. There is a legend.. that if.. on the last morning of your 'stretch', you do not eat up all your nice porridge, you will be back in durance vile within the year.

8. Chiefly *U.S.* **a.** *Racing.* (See quot. 1895.) Also *attrib.* (esp. = 'home-stretch') as ***stretch run, turn.***

1895 G. J. MANSON *Sporting Dict.*, *Stretch*, the straight or nearly straight sides of a course as distinguished from the curves or bends. **1903** *Publ. Ledger* (Philad.) 24 June 13/9 Mexoana.. took command in the stretch and won by two lengths from the favorite. **1934** D. RUNYON in *Collier's* 3 Mar. 42/3 Gallant Godfrey comes to the conclusion that Westrope is working on him in a stretch run. **1944** *Sun* (Baltimore) 14 Apr. 14/1 Backers of Sollure had no worries all through the stretch run. **1949** *Time* 10 Oct. 42/2 They had less reason to thank their own bats than the batty stretch-run performance of the Cardinals. **1972** *N.Y. Times* 4 June v. 1/4 Shortly after the field hit the stretch turn, Run the Gantlet moved into the lead position. **1978** *Detroit Free Press* 2 Apr. 2E/1 Craig's Corner, a 7-year-old gelding, won the Carolina Cup steeplechase at Camden, S.C., with a strong stretch run before a race record crowd of 30,000-plus. **1979** *Internat. Herald Tribune* 31 Oct. 23/3 It would be the clubhouse turn in the United States, but this was the Vaal Racing Club in the Orange Free State of South Africa, where the horses run clockwise, so it was really the stretch turn.

b. ***home-stretch***: see HOME-STRETCH. ***back stretch = back-straight*** s.v. BACK- B.

1839 *Picayune* (New Orleans) 2 Apr. 2/2 He went to work himself, soon passed the old black, made all sorts of a brush while rounding the last turn and commencing the back stretch. **1868** H. W. WOODRUFF *Trotting Horse Amer.* xii. 122 On the back-stretch.. Mr. Duffy asked me if I could ride it out without tiring. **1903** A. ADAMS *Log of Cowboy* xv. 237 He was speeding her on the back stretch. **1931** *Daily Express* 21 Sept. 11/5 Box stalls were built around the walls, while in other parts of the ballroom were reproduced in miniature the back stretch and the home stretch of the track. **1933** *Boys' Mag.* XLVII. 119/2 He shot by a little group of runners, and in the backstretch was hard upon the heels of the four leaders. **1948** *Life* 21 June 32 (*caption*) Dewey, Taft and Stassen will get away fast, but watch out for Dark Horse Vandenberg on the backstretch. **1970** *Toronto Daily Star* 24 Sept. 21/4 The jock had to check her twice on the backstretch.

c. *transf.* and *fig.*

1949 *Sun* (Baltimore) 9 Aug. 14/3 Baseball's 1949 stretch is now only a few furlongs away. Oddly enough, conditions in the two leagues have been somewhat reversed since last April. **1957** *Baseball Digest* Jan.–Feb. 15 Despite Joss' great work in the stretch, the season ended with the Indians in second place. **1972** *Publishers' Weekly* 12 June 9 (Advt.), Put your money on *Miss Elizabeth Arden* to win in the stretch. **1976** *Billings* (Montana) *Gaz.* 20 June 1E/3 Friday when he led the second round by one shot, Mahaffey expressed disappointment that shoddy putting down the stretch prevented him from running away from the field. **1976** *National Observer* (U.S.) 6 Nov. 5/1 Ford, at the very last, was doing something right. Most of the polls showed he was closing fast on Jimmy Carter, who was limping badly down the stretch.

9. *Mining* and *Geol.* Course or direction of a seam or a stratum with regard to the points of the compass: = STREAK *sb.*[1] 5, STRIKE *sb.* 8.

1799 KIRWAN *Geol. Ess.* 294 The stretch or course of seams of coal, and of their attendant strata, is commonly between E. and W. or N.E. and S.W. **1805** JAMESON *Min. Descr. Dumfries* 37 If we wish to discover the general stretch and dip of the strata of an extensive district.

10. *Spinning.* The length of spun yarn which is wound on the spindles at each journey of the mule-carriage towards the roller-beam: = DRAW *sb.* 6.

1835 URE *Philos. Manuf.* 312 The mule.. makes in general three stretches in a minute. **1891** R. MARSDEN *Cotton Spinning* (ed. 4) 197 This wheel is an intermittent spinning wheel, spinning a 'draw' or 'stretch', so called, probably, from its being the length obtainable by the outstretching of the spinster's arm.

stretch (stretʃ), *v.* Forms: 1 streccan, 3 strecchen, 3–6 strec(c)he, 4 strecce, strechche, 4–5 strech, 4–7 stretche, 5 strac(c)he, 5–6 stratche, 6 stratch, streych, 6–7 streache, streatch, 7 streach, 4– stretch. *Pa. t.* α. 1 strehte, 3 stræhte, streahte, strehte, streiȝhte, streþte, 3–4 streihte, 4 streiȝt(e, streyght(e, streyt, 4–5 streight(e, streyȝt(e, streght(e; β. 3–4 strahte, 4 straughte, strawght, strawhte, strawte, 4–5 straght(e, strauȝt(e, strauhte, strawȝte, 4, 6–7 straucht, 5 strawcht, 5, 7 straught; γ. 4 stretchide, 4–5 stretchid, 5 stratched, strechid, 6 streched, 6–7 strecht, 6–8 stretcht, 5– stretched. *Pa. pple.* α. 2–3 istreiht, 3 ystreith, 4 streyhte, 4–5 (i)streiȝt, 4–5 streight(e, streiht, 5 streght, ystreight, (*Sc.* strecht); β. 2–4 istraht(e, 3–5 straught, 4 straȝt, (i)straut, strawght, 4–5 (i)strauȝt, 5 *Sc.* straucht, 6 strauth; γ. 4 strecchid, stretchid, 5 stracched, 6–7 stretcht, 5– stretched. See also I-STRETCH, STREEK *vbs.* [Com. WGer.: OE. *stręccan* = OFris. *strekka*, MLG., MDu. *strecken* (mod.Du. *strekken*), OHG. *strecchen* (MHG., mod.G. *strecken*); the MSw. *sträkkia* (mod.Sw. *sträcka*), Norw. *strekkja, strekka*, Da. *strække* are from LG. The WGer. type is **strakkjan*, f. **strakko-* straight, rigid, stiff (MLG., MDu., mod.Du. *strak*, OHG. *stracch*, mod.G. *strack*), whence **strakkǣjan* (OHG. *stracchēn*) to have extension, be spread out. The root may be a metathetic var. of that found in STARK *a.*; the OE. *stræc, strec, strǽc*, severe, harsh, is perh. unconnected.]

I. To place at full length.

1. a. *trans.* To prostrate (oneself, one's body); to extend (one's limbs) in a reclining posture; *refl.* to recline at full length. Also with †*along*, †*down* (obs.), *out*. Phrase, ***to stretch one's length.***

c **900** *Bæda's Hist.* IV. xxi, He.. hine wæs in ȝebed streccende [L. *prosternens se*] æt lichoman þæs Godes weres. *c* **1200** *Vices & Virtues* 63 Ðat he lið istreiht upe ðare bare ierðe. *c* **1205** LAY. 25994 He.. adun lai bi þan fure & his leomen strahte. *c* **1325** *Chron. Eng.* (Ritson) 756 So schert he [the stone coffin] was ywroht, Istraht ne myhte he ligge noht. **1387–8** T. USK *Test. Love* II. xiv. (Skeat) 99 And these wordes sayd, she streyght her on length, and rested a whyle. *c* **1480** HENRYSON *Fox, Wolf & Cadger* 100 He.. strawcht him doun in middis of the way, As he wer deid he feinȝeit him. **1481** CAXTON *Godfrey* cciv. 300 They fylle doun flat and stratched in the chirches they kyssed.. therthe. **1597** SHAKS. *2 Hen. IV*, III. i. 10 Why rather (Sleepe) lyest thou in smoakie Cribs, Vpon vneasie Pallads stretching thee. **1600** —— *A.Y.L.* III. ii. 253 There lay hee stretch'd along like a Wounded knight. **1697** DRYDEN *Virg. Past., Ecl.* i. 5 Stretch'd at Ease you sing your happy Loves. *a* **1700** EVELYN *Diary* 10 Nov. 1644, There is a chayre to sleepe in with the leggs stretcht out. **1750** GRAY *Elegy* 103 There at the foot of yonder nodding beech.. His listless length at noontide would he stretch. **1766** GOLDSM. *Vicar* xxviii, While I was stretched on my straw. **1794** MRS. RADCLIFFE *Myst. Udolpho* l, On the hearth were several dogs stretched in sleep. **1799** WORDSW. *Poet's Epit.* 59 Here stretch thy body at full length. **1809** MALKIN *Gil Blas* VI. i. (Rtldg.) 213 We stretched our length upon the grass, and soon fell fast asleep. **1840** DICKENS *Old C. Shop* v, Daniel Quilp.. climbed on to the desk.. and stretching his short length upon it went to sleep. *a* **1852** M. ARNOLD *Lines Kensington Gard.* 22 Scarce fresher is the mountain sod Where the tired angler lies, stretch'd out. **1874** L. STEPHEN *Hours in Library* (1892) I. vii. 237 He was generally to be found stretched.. upon a rug before the fire. **1908** R. BAGOT *A. Cuthbert* vii. 77 He stretched himself on his desk-chair.

b. To lay (a person) flat. Also (now *dial.*), to straighten the limbs (of a dead person); to 'lay out' for burial (= STREEK *v.* 2); (*slang*), to kill (a person). Cf. LAY *v.*[1] 56.

a **1225** *Juliana* 26 (Royal MS.) þe reue.. grede: strupeð hire steort naket & strecheð hire on þe eorðe. *c* **1275** *Signs of Death* 8 in *O.E. Misc.*, On flore me þe strecheþ And leyþ þe on bere. *c* **1275** *Serving Christ* 6 Ibid., And þolede dom vor his duþe, þat he wes ded strauht. *a* **1375** *Joseph Arim.* 519 þe stiward of Eualak.. lai streiht on þe feld, striken to þe eorþe. **1612** SHELTON *Quix.* III. i. (1620) 117 Striking me downe on the place where I yet lie straught. **1697** DRYDEN *Æneis* v. 495 And by the Stroak of his resistless Hand, [he] Stretch'd the vast Bulk upon the yellow Sand. **1757** W. WILKIE *Epigoniad* III. 67 Andremon first,.. Of life bereft, lay stretch'd upon the sand. **1839** CARLETON *Fardorougha* vi, Confusion to the ring he'll ever put an her! I'd see her stretched [*foot-n.* dead] first. **1847** PRESCOTT *Peru* IV. v. (1850) II. 341 The struggle lasted for some minutes, till both of Pizarro's pages were stretched by his side. **1902** S. E. WHITE *Blazed Trail* xxx, He rushed on Dyer, and with one full, clean in-blow stretched him stunned on the dock. **1902** KIPLING *Traffics & Discoveries* (1904) 11 He said if you stretched a man at his prayers you'd have to hump his bad luck before the Throne as well as your own. **1907** J. H. PATTERSON *Man-Eaters of Tsavo* v. 51, I.. found seven badly injured men lying stretched out on the ground. **1953** M. GILBERT *Fear to Tread* viii. 107 Once.. Annie had a husband. She got tired of him, so she 'stretched him with a bottle'.

†**c.** To spread out on the ground; to make (a bed). *Obs.*

a **1000** *Ags. Gosp.* Mark xi. 8 Maneȝa hyra reaf on þone weȝ strehton [L. *straverunt*]. *c* **1175** *Lamb. Hom.* 3 Heo nomen heore claþes.. and strehiten [? *read* streihten] under þa assa fet. *c* **1475** *Partenay* 1005 Forth anon the bede [was] straight And made redy.

†**d.** ***long streight, straught***: extended at length.

? *a* **1366** CHAUCER *Rom. Rose* 1021 Hir tresses yelowe, and longe straughten, Unto hir heles doun they raughten. *c* **1374** —— *Troylus* IV. 1163 He rist him up, and long streight he hir leyde. *a* **1400** *Octouian* 959 Thus they shall lye long straught Or that they go. **1609** J. DAVIES (Heref.) *Holy Rood* A 4 b, Thinke that thou seest him on his face longe straught In Praier, and in Passion sweating Bloud. **1611** —— *Sco. Folly* clxvi. 79 O Sweete, deere sweete,.. Quoth Citheris (long straught) vnto her deere.

†**e.** *intr.* for *refl.* To fall to the ground; also, to lie *down* at full length. *Obs.*

c **1400** *Song Roland* 769 Stedes in that stound strechid to ground. **1828** SCOTT *F.M. Perth* xxiv, Stretch down in the stern of that boat, and let me wrap this cloak about thee.

2. a. To extend (the arms) laterally; to expand (the wings), esp. for flight.

c **1205** LAY. 28007 Arður þa up aras and strehte his armes. *a* **1240** *Ureisun* in *O.E. Hom.* I. 185 Hwi nam ich in þin earmes. In þin earmes swa istrahte and isprad on rode. **1382** WYCLIF *3 Kings* vi. 27 Forsothe the cherubyn strauȝten out her weengis. *c* **1430** *Pilgr. Lyf Manhode* IV. xxxv. (1869) 194 And hadde wynges redy streiht for to flee to þe skyes. **1692** PRIOR *Ode Imit. Hor.* III. ii. 107 Let Fear look back, and stretch her hasty Wing, Impatient to secure a base Retreat. **1742** R. SEAGRAVE *Hymn*, Rise, my Soul, and stretch thy Wings. **1814** CARY *Dante, Purg.* xi. 39 That ye have power To stretch your wing, which e'en to your desire Shall lift you.

b. Of a tree: To extend (its branches).

1382 WYCLIF *Ecclus.* xxiv. 22, I as a terebynt streiȝte out [**1388** stretchide forth] my braunchis. *c* **1386** CHAUCER *Knt.'s T.* 2058 The fyr.. That.. twenty fadme of brede the armes straughte. **1815** SHELLEY *Alastor* 562 A pine, Rock-rooted, stretched athwart the vacancy Its swinging boughs.

3. a. *refl.* To straighten oneself; to rise to full height (†also with *up*); also, to draw up the body, as from a stooping, cramped, or relaxed posture; to straighten the body and extend the arms, as a manifestation of weariness or langour (chiefly coupled with *yawn*).

c **1325** *Chron. Eng.* (Ritson) 772 And a cripel eke anon Ther him strahte ant myhte gon. *c* **1384** CHAUCER *H. Fame* 1373 She Hir tho so wonderliche streighte, That with hir feet she therthe reighte, And with hir heed she touched hevene. **1470–85** MALORY *Arthur* XX. xxi. 836 Than he stratched hym vp & stode nere syr Gauwayn. **1509** HAWES *Past. Pleas.* xxxv. (Percy Soc.) 182 He stretched hym up and lyft his axe a lofte. **1550** LYNDESAY *Sqr. Meldrum* 374 He lap vpon his Cursour wicht, And straucht him in his stirroppis richt. **1563** SACKVILLE *Induct. Mirr. Mag.* xix, I strecht my selfe, and strayt my hart reuiues. **1590** *Cobler Canterb.* 69 At length the Farmar awoke, and stretching himself, finding he was naked, [etc.]. **1602** W. VAUGHAN *Direct. Health* (1626) 165 First of all in the morning when you are about to rise, stretch your selfe strongly. **1639** S. DU VERGER tr. *Camus' Admir. Events* 3 Wrastlers, who stretch themselves up on their feet, so much the stronglier.. by how much their adversary is tall. **1714** MANDEVILLE *Fable Bees* (1733) II. 340 Stretching ourselves before others, whilst we are yawning, is an absolute breach of good manners. **1829** SCOTT *Anne of G.* x, Yawning and stretching himself like one whose slumbers had been broken by no welcome summons. **1858** LYTTON *What will he do?* III. iv, Mop [the dog].. rose and stretched himself. **1888** 'R. BOLDREWOOD' *Robbery under Arms* xxii, Jim soon woke up and stretched himself.

b. *intr.* for *refl.*

a **1586** [see STRETCHING *vbl. sb.*[1]]. **1614** J. TAYLOR (Water P.) *Nipping Abuses* D 1, The seuenth was Sloth,.. Who being cald, did gape, and yawne, and stretch. **1704** CIBBER *Careless Husb.* v. 62 And by that time you stretcht, and Gap'd him Heartily out of Patience.

c. ***to stretch one's legs***: to straighten the lower limbs from a sitting position; usually, to relieve by walking the stiffness or fatigue caused by sitting; to take a walk for exercise.

1607 A. GORGES in Purchas *Pilgrims* x. xiv. (1625) IV. 1951 [We] went ashoare, to stretch our legs in the Isle of Flores. **1632** LITHGOW *Trav.* v. 205, I would often fetch a walke, to stretch my legs, that were stifled with a stumbling beast. **1653** WALTON *Angler* i. 1, I have stretch'd my legs up Totnam Hil to overtake you. **1779** G. KEATE *Sketches fr. Nat.* (ed. 2) II. 208, I was glad after so long a confinement, to stretch my legs, and determined to walk home. **1838** DICKENS *Nich. Nick.* v, Mr. Squeers got down at almost every stage—to stretch his legs, as he said. **1872** EARL OF PEMBROKE & G. H. KINGSLEY *S. Sea Bubbles* i. 36 About every hour we stopped to change horses, when we took the opportunity to stretch our legs. **1899** RODWAY *In Guiana Wilds* 30 Allan..began to feel cramped from remaining so long in one position; he wanted to stretch his legs.

†**d.** *intr.* To strut. In quot. with *it*. *Obs.*

1619 H. HUTTON *Fellies Anat.* D 4, Cornuted Phœbe, in her coach, doth prance: Bacchus..doth stretch it on the stage.

II. To put forward, protrude.

4. a. *trans.* To put forth, extend (the hand, an arm or leg, the neck, head); †to extend, hold out (a weapon, a staff). Also (now almost always) with adv., *forth*, *out*, *forward*.

a **1000** *Ags. Gosp.*, *John* xxi. 18 þonne þu eald est þu strecst [L. *extendes*] þine handa. *c* **1205** LAY. 21227 He stræhte scait stærcne. *a* **1225** *Leg. Kath.* 2233 Streche forð þine swire scharp sweord to underfonne. **1375** BARBOUR *Bruce* II. 348 Thai straucht thar speris. *c* **1380** WYCLIF *Sel. Wks.* II. 198 Stretche out þin hond. **1382** —— *Exod.* x. 13 And Moyses strau3te out the 3erde vpon the loond of Egipte. **1390** GOWER *Conf.* I. 195 And thanne hire handes to the hevene Sche strawhte. *c* **1430** *Pilgr. Lyf Manhode* III. xxxvii. (1869) 155 She..a yens me strauhte hire handes. **1577** KENDALL *Flowers of Epigr.* 107 His snout was stretched forth. **1579** GOSSON *Sch. Abuse* (Arb.) 50 God..that stretcheth out his armes from morning to euening to couer his children. *c* **1611** CHAPMAN *Iliad* VII. 164 He stretcht his hand, and into it, the Herald put the lot. **1696** R. H. *Sch. Recreat.* 68 [Fencing] To Elonge. This is to Streach forward your Right Arm and Leg, and [etc.]. **1777** POTTER *Æschylus, Prometh. Chain'd* 62 To stretch my supplicating hands. **1784** COWPER *Task* II. 825 So when the Jewish leader stretch'd his arm,..a race obscene..came forth Polluting Egypt. **1804** ABERNETHY *Surg. Observ.* 189 He stretched out his right arm when required. **1812** H. & J. SMITH *Rej. Addr., Playho. Musings* 27 These stretch'd forth a pole From the wall's pinnacle. **1812** BYRON *Ch. Har.* II. lxviii, The Suliotes stretch'd the welcome hand, Led them o'er rocks and past the dangerous swamp. **1837** CARLYLE *Fr. Rev.* I. II. vi, Swindlery and Blackguardism have stretched hands across the Channel. **1838** DICKENS *Nich. Nick.* xiv, The guests..stretched their necks forward and listened attentively. **1847** W. C. L. MARTIN *Ox* 132/2 The animal staggers.., its flanks heave, the head is stretched out. **1851** THACKERAY *Eng. Hum.* i. (1876) 153 His hand was constantly stretched out to relieve an honest man. **1860** TYNDALL *Glac.* I. xi. 79, I stretched my hand towards him. **1904** KATH. C. THURSTON *J. Chilcote* iii. (1912) 29 Moving straight forward, he paused by the grate and stretched his hands to the blaze.

b. *absol.* To extend one's hand, reach *for* something.

a **1375** *Joseph Arim.* 544 Sone þenne he starte vp and strei3te to his hache. **1775** GOLDSM. tr. *Scarron's Com. Romance* II. 149 Whenever they stretched for the holy water, a thousand hands made tenders of their service.

†**c.** *intr.* Of an arm: To be extended. *Obs.*

c **1350** *Will. Palerne* 2957 Of 3our ri3t arm þat ouer rome streyt, I se wel þe signifiaunce. **1765** ANGELO *Sch. Fencing* 7 When the arm stretches forth in order to thrust, the foot must follow at the same time.

5. a. To hold out, hand, reach (something). Now only *Naut.* in phrase (see quot. 1644).

c **1450** *Merlin* xxxii. 639 Than he drough oute a letter.. and straught it to the Kynge. **1644** MANWAYRING *Seamans Dict.* 103 When they goe to hoyse a yard, or hale the sheate, they say, stretch fore-ward the Hilliards, or the sheates: that is deliver along that part (which they must hale by) into the mens hands. **1849** LYTTON *K. Arthur* VI. xlix, 'Sir Host,' said Gawaine, as he stretched his platter, 'I'll first the pie discuss, and then the matter.'

†**b.** *fig.* (*a*) To direct (one's hope, trust) to an object. (*b*) To hold out, extend (relief) to a person. *Obs.*

c **1000** ÆLFRIC *Hom.* I. 252 Strece ðærto þinne hiht. *c* **1400** *Apol. Loll.* 91 þei þat were helid were not helid sympli bi þe touching, but for þe trust þat þei strechid finaly in to God. **1711** in *10th Rep. Hist. MSS. Comm.* App. v. 184 The potentats of that religion have stood idle..without stretching the least relief.

†**6.** To set *up* (a standard). *Obs.*

c **1400** *Sege Jerus.* 21/385 (E.E.T.S.) He strey3t up a standard. *c* **1400** *Melayne* 1185 All [nyghte on]e þe bent þay bade With standardes euen vp streghte.

†**7.** To emit (rays, streams); also *intr.* of a light, to be emitted in a certain direction. *Obs.*

c **1205** LAY. 17886 þe leome þa strehte west riht a seouen bæmen wes idiht. *Ibid.* 17978 þe oðer leome þe strahte [*c* **1275** streahte] west wunder ane lihte þat bið a dohter. *c* **1400** *Destr. Troy* 915 And as he [*sc.* the dragon] tilt out his tung with his tethe grym, He straght fro hym stremes all of styth venym. *c* **1400** *Brut* I. 64 By þe beem þat stracchet towarde Irland, is bitokenede þat 3e shul bigete a dou3ter þat shal be quene of Irland.

III. To direct a course.

†**8. a.** To direct (one's course). Also *refl.* of a person. *Obs.*

a **1225** *St. Marher.* 9 He [the dragon] strahte him ant sturede toward tis meoke meiden. *c* **1350** *Will. Palerne* 3279 He..strei3t him in-to the stabul þere þe stede stod. **1390** GOWER *Conf.* II. 296 He seith noght ones 'grant merci', Bot strauhte him forth to the cite. *Ibid.* III. 313 Towardes Tharse his cours he straghte.

b. To direct the course of (a ship, etc.); *absol.* to steer. *Obs.*

c **1205** LAY. 2887 Brecon þa strenges þe he mid strahte & he feol to folde. *Ibid.* 9750 To Tottenas heo come, strahten scipen to þan londe & eoden uppen stranden.

9. *intr.* To make one's way (rapidly or with effort). In later use coloured by sense 20 b.

c **1205** LAY. 27589 His cnihtes..mid muchelere strengðe þurh þat feht stræhten. **13..** *E.E. Allit. P.* A. 971 To strech in þe strete þou has no vygour. *Ibid.* B. 905 Loke 3e stemme no stepe, bot strechez on faste. *c* **1350** *Will. Palerne* 1113 Strecches forþ wiþ 3our ost, stinteþ no lenger. **1390** GOWER *Conf.* II. 258 The Sail goth up, and forth thei strauhte. *c* **1400** *Destr. Troy* 1354 Thai..Streght into stretis and into stronge houses. *c* **1430** *Chev. Assigne* 220 The grypte eyþur a staffe in here honde & on here wey straw3te. **1697** DRYDEN *Virg. Georg.* I. 496 Crying Cormorants forsake the Sea, And stretching to the Covert wing their way. **1735** SOMERVILLE *Chase* II. 13 Then o'er the Lawn he [the Roe-buck] bounds, o'er the high Hills Stretches secure. **1810** SCOTT *Lady of L.* III. xiii, Stretch onward in thy fleet career! **1860** THACKERAY *Lovel* iv. (1861) 156, I stretch over Putney Heath, and my spirit resumes its tranquillity. **1861** WHYTE MELVILLE *Good for N.* xxvi. II. 2 Stretching away at the best pace a wiry little Australian horse..can command, rides an Englishman in the normal state of hurry peculiar to his countrymen.

†**10.** Of a stream: To run, flow swiftly. *Obs.*

c **1205** LAY. 27476 Stræhten after stretes blodie stremes.

11. *Naut.* To sail (esp. under crowd of canvas) continuously in one direction. Also with advs.

1687 *Lond. Gaz.* No. 2251/4 The headmost..stretched to Windward, and there lay pecking at us, whilest his Companion was doing the same a Stern. **1726** SHELVOCKE *Voy. round World* 388, I stretched over for California. **1719** DE FOE *Crusoe* I. (Globe) 142 Just as I had set my Mast and Sail, and the Boat began to stretch away, I saw [etc.]. **1776** COOK *2nd Voy.* III. iii. II. 27 Then we tacked and stretched in for the island till near sun-set. **1809** COLLINGWOOD in *Naval Chron.* XXII. 502 Our boats stretched out. **1832** MARRYAT *N. Forster* v, They were stretching off the land. **1845** J. COULTER *Adv. in Pacific* xv. 244 In a few days we put to sea, and stretched away to the northward of this group [of islands]. **1884** 'H. COLLINGWOOD' *Under Meteor Flag* 4 We stretched off the land, close-hauled upon the starboard tack.

IV. To (make to) reach; to give or have a certain extent.

12. *trans.* To place (something) so as to reach from one point to another, or across an interval in space.

a. with obj. something rigid. *Obs.* exc. *techn.*

a **1225** *Juliana* 56 (Royal MS.) þat axtreo stod istraht on twa half in te twa stanene postles. *a* **1300** *Cursor M.* 3779 In slepe he say a ladder strau3t Fro his heed to þe sky hit rau3t. **1776** G. SEMPLE *Building in Water* 50 On those set-off's stretch your Plates.

b. To extend (something flexible, e.g. a cord or curtain) from one point to another or across a space, by drawing it out more or less straight.

This may be regarded as a weakening of sense 16, from which it is often indistinguishable.

c **1430** *Pilgr. Lyf Manhode* IV. xxviii. (1869) 191 And aboue was þe mast of þe ship dressed wher vpon heeng þe seyl ystreight. **1481** CAXTON *Godfrey* clxxvii. 261 They toke the hydes of the beestes that deyde and stratched them vpon thengynes for to kepe & defende them fro fyre. **1535** COVERDALE *Isa.* xl. 22 That he spredeth out the heauens as a coueringe, that he stretcheth them out, as a tent to dwell in. **1697** DRYDEN *Virg. Georg.* I. 381 Then Weavers stretch your Stays upon the Weft. **1818** SCOTT *Br. Lamm.* xiv, I ought to have torn away the veil which interested persons had stretched betwixt us. **1832** BREWSTER *Nat. Magic* iv. 87 A black cloth should be stretched at some distance behind them. **1854** tr. *Hettner's Athens & Peloponnese* 56 The dancers take hands and form a circle; to widen which they sometimes stretch handkerchiefs from hand to hand. **1867** SMYTH *Sailor's Word-bk.*, *Stretch along a brace*, to lay it along the decks in readiness for the men to lay hold of. **1884** J. MARSHALL *Tennis Cuts* 85 We invented gloves; then we lined those gloves. After that, we stretched gut-strings across the gloves. **1907** J. A. HODGES *Elem. Photogr.* (ed. 6) 87 A piece of clothes line, stretched across the room.

†**c.** To pitch (a tent). Also with *out*. *Obs.*

1382 WYCLIF *Gen.* xxxi. 25 And now Jacob hadde strau3te [Vulg. *extenderat*; **1388** stretchid forth] a tabernacle in the hil. *c* **1475** *Partenay* 869 Tentes And pauilons streght and pight freshly Besyde a ualey, enmyddes a plain. **1536** *Stories & Proph. Scripture* F iv b Moche wyder hath youre bryde the holy cherche stretched out and piched hyr tente. **1587** D. FENNER *Song of Songs* i. 6 For why should I become like vnto one of those Which doeth stretch out his Tent fast by the flockes of thy fellowes?

†**d.** To draw out in a straight line. *Obs.*

1542 UDALL tr. *Erasm. Apoph.* 7 b, Yf thou stretch y[e] walkynges that thou vsest at home, & laye theim on length by the space of fiue or sixe dayes together y[u] shalt easyly reache to Olympia.

13. a. †*refl.* (obs.) and *intr.* (rarely *passive*). To have a specified extent in space; to be continuous to a certain point, or over a certain distance or area. Also with *away*, *out*, *off*.

In mod. use ordinarily implying a large extent; where this notion is not present the synonym *extend* is now preferred.

refl. **1423** *Coventry Leet Bk.* (1907) 50 A feld of Wylliam Wymeswold stretchyng hym-selff vnto a comyn hy3e-way, þat is callyd the Deed-lane... The said way, þat is callyd Deed-lane, þat strechithe hym-selff fro the Span-brooke toward the Hill-Crosse. *c* **1460** *Oseney Reg.* 181 And j. Rodde of londe the wich strecchith hit-Selfe In lambescotestrete By the londe of William Sweyne. **1607** T. RIDLEY *View Civ. & Eccles. Law* Contents A 1, That the second part hath eight books... That the third part stretcheth it selfe into eight bookes.

intr. **1387** TREVISA *Higden* (Rolls) II. 107 þe kyngdom of Deyra tillede and strei3te [L. *extendebatur*] from þe ryuer of Humber anon to þe ryuere of Tyne. **1390** GOWER *Conf.* I. 137 A tree..Whos heihte straghte up to the hevene. *c* **1400** MAUNDEV. (Roxb.) vi. 22 Araby strechez fra þe end of Caldee to þe last end of Affric. **1434** *Coventry Leet Bk.* (1907) 157 þe weye that stretcheth fro Cheylesmore Grene vnto Somerlesowe. **1542–3** *Act 34 & 35 Hen. VIII* c. 12 §1 Allso oone litle Lane streatching from the saide waie to the Signe of the Bell at Drewrye Lane ende. **1585** T. WASHINGTON tr. *Nicholay's Voy.* I. iii, Minorque hath in length 60. miles, & in circuit 150. & to the East stretcheth from Maiorque 30. miles. **1603** J. DAVIES (Heref.) *Microcosmos, Extasie* 238 Her nether Vesture strecht but her calfe, Yet lower rought then that aboue, by halfe. **1608** TOPSELL *Serpents* 41 The place must be seared with a hot yron, so farre as the venom stretcheth. *a* **1700** EVELYN *Diary* 28 Jan. 1645, Pursuing the same noble [Appian] way..we found it to stretch from Capua to Rome itselfe. **1748** *Anson's Voy.* I. vi. (ed. 4) 97 The Andes which skirt it, and stretch quite down to the water. **1788** MME. D'ARBLAY *Diary* 13 Feb., Their green benches..stretched..along the whole left side of the Hall. **1848** DICKENS *Dombey* v, The dreary perspective of empty pews stretching away under the galleries. **1852** THACKERAY *Esmond* I. iii, The London road stretched away towards the rising sun. **1858** ETHERIDGE *Life A. Clarke* I. viii. (ed. 2) 128 The minister's family were to reside in the apartments on the ground-floor, the school-room stretching over all above. **1860** TYNDALL *Glac.* I. vii. 47 A steep slope stretches down to the Mer de Glace. **1894** BLACKMORE *Perlycross* xviii. 149 Southward stretched the rich Perle valley.

passive. **1652** NEDHAM tr. *Selden's Mare Cl.* 39 Whatsoever is stretcht forth on this side and within Mount Amanus, is the Territorie of Israel. **1867** LADY HERBERT *Cradle L.* viii. 223 On one side is stretched the great plain of Esdraelon.

b. To have its length in a specified direction. ? *Obs.*

c **1400** MAUNDEV. (Roxb.) xxxiii. 150 þe walle..strechez fra þe south toward þe north. **1449** in *Cal. Proc. Chanc. Eliz.* (1830) II. Pref. 54 The same hous by ground shall have a parclose walle, strecchyng along north and south duryng the seid length of lxvj fete. **1598** W. PHILLIP tr. *Langenes' Voy. Ships Holland E. Ind.* 11 We put out with a North wind, the Bay stretching Northeast and Southwest. **1697** DRYDEN *Æneis* XI. 486 A Tract of Land..Along the Tyber, stretching to the West.

c. *transf.* with reference to time. *nonce-uses.*

1606 SHAKS. *Ant. & Cl.* I. i. 46 There's not a minute of our liues should stretch Without some pleasure now. **1868** STANLEY *Westm. Abb.* iv. 263 Three statesmen stretch across the first half of the eighteenth century. **1898** JEAN A. OWEN *Hawaii* iii. 53 The influence of these enterprising navigators is seen stretching on for some hundreds of years.

14. *fig.* †**a.** To have a specified measure in amount, degree, power, etc.; to be adequate for some purpose. *Obs.*

refl. *c* **1386** CHAUCER *Melib.* ¶ 3015 Youre liberal grace and mercy strecchen hem ferther in-to goodnesse, than doon oure outrageouse giltes and trespas in-to wikkednesse.

intr. *c* **1374** CHAUCER *Troylus* II. 341 If ye be swich, your beautee may not strecche To make amendes of so cruel a dede. *c* **1386** —— *Can. Yeom. Prol. & T.* 534 As ferforth as my konnyng may strecche. **1418** *E.E. Wills* (1882) 43 He will that..his brother..fynde his fadir..with the profitz of the place, as ferre as they wille strecche. **1466** in *Somerset Medieval Wills* (1901) 210 And if my goodes will streche thereto I will than an honest preest have 9 marcs for a hoole yere to syng. *c* **1572** I. B. *Let. to R.C.* A ij, Some..whose vnderstanding can not stretche to a matter of so greate aduice. **1581** MULCASTER *Positions* xxxvii. (1887) 143 You would haue your childe learned, but your purse will not streatch. **1596** SHAKS. *1 Hen. IV*, I. ii. 62 *Fal.* Thou hast paid al there. *Prin.* Yea and elsewhere, so farre as my Coine would stretch. *a* **1648** LD. HERBERT *Hen. VIII* (1683) 372 We will take such Commons as they have at Oxford; Which, yet, if our Purse will not stretch to maintain, for our last refuge we will go a Begging.

†**b.** To go a certain length in action. *Obs.*

refl. *c* **1374** CHAUCER *Troylus* I. 903 For vertue streccheþ not hym self to shame.

intr. **1550** HARINGTON tr. *Cicero's Bk. Friendship* (1562) 26 Let vs firste see this poinct, howe farre oughte loue to stretche in freendshyp [L. *quatenus amor in amicitia progredi debeat*].

†**c.** To have a specified extent or range of action or application. *Obs.*

refl. *c* **1449** PECOCK *Repr.* v. ii. 490 Tho textis strecchen hem to viciose persoones being out of religioun, as weel as to viciose persoones in religioun. **1559** *Homilies, Charity* II. L ij b, Howe charitie stretcheth [*earlier edd.* extendeth] it selfe, both to God and man, frend and foe.

intr. *c* **1380** WYCLIF *Sel. Wks.* III. 420 þis charite of freris schulde streeche to alle gode men. **1423** *Rolls of Parlt.* IV. 256/1 That this ordynaunce stretche and bere strenketh also wel wyth in Chesshire. *c* **1449** PECOCK *Repr.* III. i. 278 Into ferther purpos than in to this purpos now here seid strecchith not eny of the textis now bifore alleggid. **1461** *Little Red Bk. Bristol* (1900) II. 128 That thes acte strecche not to any mannes wyfe of the Crafte of Wevers nowe levyng. **1531** tr. *St. German's Dial. Doctor & Stud.* xlii. 84 If a man..banyshed be restored by the prynce, whether shall that restitucion stretche to the goodes. **1568** GRAFTON *Chron.* II. 13 He would there should no such power stretch to his successours, therefore he made no mention of them. **1621** ELSING *Debates Ho. Lords* (Camden) 125 L. Chamberlaine thinkes the priviledge dothe not stretche to goodes, and they are not to be delivered. **1625** SIR H. FINCH *Law* (1636) 25 A Statute that maketh it felony to receiue.. one that committeth such and such an offence..stretcheth not to a woman that receiueth..her husband in such a case. **1659** MILTON *Civil Power Eccl. Causes* 27 The other.. makes himself supream lord or pope of the church as far as his civil jurisdiction stretches.

passive. *c* **1380** WYCLIF *Sel. Wks.* III. 343 For siþ vertue of a kyng mut be strecchid by al his rewme, myche more þe vertue of Crist is comuned wiþ al his children. *a* **1586** SIDNEY *Apol. Poetrie* (Arb.) 58 But I honor philosophicall instructions,..so as they be not abused, which is likewise stretched to Poetrie.

†**15.** To tend, be serviceable (to some object).

c **1400** *Destr. Troy* 9207 Hit semith me vnsertain, all serchyng of wayes Ys stokyn vp full stithly, shuld streche to my hele! *c* **1412** HOCCLEVE *De Reg. Princ.* 4836 For Cristes sake, so yow gyeth ay, As þat may strecche to your peples ese. **1491** *Act 7 Hen. VII*, c. 1 §1 His offence stretchith to the hurt and jopardie of the King. **1587** A. DAY *Daphnis & Chloe* (1890) 11 And for that her care stretched that the girle ..might the sooner be taken and reputed for hers, she.. called her Chloe. **1621** *True Relat. Exec. Prague* A3, The Iudgement..should not be executed, but in such a sort as might..stretch to the reputation and authority of the Emperours Maiesty.

V. To tighten by force, to strain.

16. a. *trans.* To pull taut; to bring (e.g. a rope, piece of cloth) to a rigid state of straightness or evenness by the application of tractive force at the extremities; to strain; to remove the curl from (hair).

1387 TREVISA *Higden* (Rolls) III. 211 ȝif þe streng is i-strauȝt endelonges [L. *chorda extensa*] uppon þe holownesse of a tree. *c* **1530** *Judic. Urines* II. vii. 30 b, Diafragma... And therfore it is strauth and taught and raeyched oute as it were a testure of clothe. *a* **1535** FISHER *Serm.* Wks. (1876) 394 Neuer anye Parchement skynne was more strayghtlye stratched by strength vpon the tentors. **1579** GOSSON *Sch. Abuse* (Arb.) 57 It behoooueth your Honour..too play the Musition, streatch euery string till hee breake. **1590** LODGE *Rosalynde* (1592) B, The meane is sweetest melodie, where strings high stretch[t], eyther soone cracke, or quickly grow out of time [? *read* tune]. **1705** TATE *Warriour's Welcome* xxxiv, Then try your Skill: a well-prim'd Canvass stretch. **1735** SOMERVILLE *Chase* II. 268 Each eager Hound exerts His utmost Speed, and stretches ev'ry Nerve. **1763** J. BROWN *Poetry & Music* v. 67 Mercury was the Inventor of the Lyre; which had but four Strings, and these were stretched on a Turtle's Shell. **1815** J. SMITH *Panorama Sci. & Art* II. 698 For the convenience of keeping the paper stretched and smooth,..a drawing-board is used. **1883** M. P. BALE *Saw-Mills* 185, Considerable trouble is often found in stretching or tightening large belts on to their pulleys. **1963** W. SOYINKA *Lion & Jewel* 9 Her hair is stretched Like a magazine photo. **1971** C. ACHEBE *Girls at War* (1972) 58 Now Abigail was a lady; she could sew and bake..put on powder and perfumes and stretch her hair.

†**b.** To take *out* (wrinkles) by stretching. *Obs.*

a **1541** BARNES *Wks.* (1573) 254 Her wryncles bee streatched out.

c. intr. *to stretch out*: to be made even by straining.

1838 in *Newton's Lond. Jrnl.* Conj. Ser. XVI. 68 The cloth is then folded back tightly over the tension rod *e*, and stretches out smooth in the opposite direction.

17. To pull (a person's) limbs lengthwise; esp. to torture by so doing, to rack. In early use, to place with extended limbs on a cross. Also with *out*.

a **1225** *Ancr. R.* 362 Nes Seinte Peter & Seinte Andrew, þereuore, istreiht o rode, and Seint Lorenz oðe gredil. *a* **1375** *Joseph Arim.* 560 þenne he..on þe cros biholdes; He seiȝ a child strauȝt þer-on stremynge on blode. **1526** *Pilgr. Perf.* (W. de W. 1531) 257 Beholde..those blessed armes.. whiche were so stretched on the crosse, now all starke and styffe. **1585** T. WASHINGTON tr. *Nicholay's Voy.* II. xxi, After they [the bath-men] haue well pulled and stretched your armes..in such sort that he wyll make your bones too cracke. **1603** SHAKS. *Meas. for M.* v. 316 The Duke dare No more stretch this finger of mine, then he Dare racke his owne. **1605** —— *Lear* v. iii. 315 He hates him, That would vpon the wracke of this tough world Stretch him out longer. **1611** G. H. tr. *Anti-Coton* 41 If hee [this Jesuit] were but a little stretcht by the fingers, a man might learne strange misteries of him. **1665** DRYDEN *Ind. Emp.* v. ii. (1668) 57 Fasten the Engines; stretch 'em at their length. **1669** —— *Tempest* IV. (1670) 51, I feel my self as on a Rack, stretch'd out, and nigh the ground, on which I might have ease, yet cannot reach it. **1888** 'R. BOLDREWOOD' *Robbery under Arms* xxiii, If a man..was being stretched on the rack.

18. †**a.** *to stretch a halter, rope*: to be hanged.

1592 GREENE *Black Bk's. Messenger* Wks. (Grosart) XI. 22, I at last resolutely vowed in my selfe to haue it though I stretcht a halter for it. **1657** BILLINGSLY *Brachy-Martyrol.* xxxii. 123 One man for saying he'd believe the Pope No sooner then the devil, stretch'd a rope. *a* **1708** T. WARD *England's Reform.* IV. (1710) 72 We our selves..Were in fair way to stretch a Halter.

†**b.** *to stretch* (a person, his neck): to hang.

1595 *Locrine* II. ii. 81 Here, good fellow; take it at my command, Vnlesse you meane to be stretcht. *a* **1652** BROME *Queen & Concubine* IV. iii. (1659) 82 For fear the Rusticks may presume again To stretch their penitent necks with halter strain. **1700** CIBBER *Love makes a Man* IV. iv, *D. Du.* But pray, Sir, were you as intimate at both Play-houses? *Clo.* No, stretch 'em! **1775** *N.Y. Jrnl.* 9 Feb. in F. Moore *Diary Amer. Rev.* I. 19 'Pray, Mr. ——, what is a Tory?' He replied, 'A Tory is a thing whose head is in England, and its body in America, and its neck ought to be stretched.' *c* **1800** *Irish Song*, The night before Larry was stretch'd The boys they all paid him a visit.

†**c.** *intr.* To be hanged.

1576 *Common Conditions* 202 (Brooke) If hee could haue taken me I know that I should stretch. **1596** H. MOUNTAGU in *Buccleuch MSS.* (Hist. MSS. Comm.) I. 231 Two of his charge gave the slip; it was well for them; they might else have stretched with the rest of their companions. **1676** D'URFEY *Mme. Fickle* v. ii, Ay, ay, you need not fear, you are a Lord, you'll come off well enough, 'tis we shall stretch for 't.

19. *to stretch a point* = to strain a point: see STRAIN *v.* 11 f. Also, in the same sense, †*to stretch string* (cf. quot. 1579 in 16).

In the first quot. app. used with somewhat different sense.

1565 COOPER *Thesaurus* s.v. *Neruus*, *Intendere neruos in re aliqua*, to strayne a sinew: to stretche a poy[n]cte: to indeuour to the vttermost of his power. *a* **1566** R. EDWARDS *Damon & Pithias* (facs.) G ij b, Wyll you not stretche one poynt: to bringe me in fauour agayne? **1575** GASCOIGNE *Glasse of Govt.* II. iii. (1910) 37 Might not a man entreat master Eccho to carry her a present if neede were? *Eccho.* Sir there is never a gentleman in this citie, shall make Eccho stretch a string sooner then your selfe, but [etc.]. **1576** A. HALL *Acc. Quarrel w. Mallerie* etc., Misc. Antiq. Angl. (1816) I. 96 If for affection you stretch a string, you cannot be excused. **1687** ATTERBURY *Answ. Consid. Spirit Luther* 22 Yet these same Schoolmen do not stretch the point so far, as to say the Pope has an absolute limited power over these Vows. **1814** SCOTT *Wav.* liii, I am not likely, I think, to ask any thing very unreasonable, and if I did, they might have stretched a point. **1861** H. KINGSLEY *Ravenshoe* xlii, It would be stretching a point to say that Cuthbert was a handsome man.

20. †**a.** *fig.* To exert to the utmost, strain (one's powers). *Obs.*

1612 in *Capt. J. Smith's Wks.* (Arb.) II. 422 Their men women, and children..kindly welcommed vs,..stretching their best abilities to expresse their loues. *a* **1660** *Faithful Friends* III. iii, Till my veins And sinews crack, I'll stretch my utmost strength.

b. *refl.* and *intr.* To strain, press forward, use effort. Also with *on*.

c **1350** *Will. Palerne* 219 þemperour..folwed as stiffuly as is stede miȝt strecche on to renne. **1526** TINDALE *Phil.* iii. 13, I forget that which is behynde me, and stretche my silfe [Gr. ἐπεκτεινόμενος] vnto that which is before me. **1551** T. WILSON *Logic* C viij, If by labour and earnest trauaile, they will stretche to attein that whereunto thei are apt. **1738** WESLEY *Hymn*, 'When shall thy lovely Face be seen?' IV, And every Limb and every Joint Stretches for Immortality.

c. *to stretch to the oar, to the stroke* (rarely trans. *to stretch one's oars*): to put forth one's strength in rowing; also *fig.* Also, *to stretch out*.

1697 DRYDEN *Æneis* v. 172 To bear with this, the Seamen stretch their Oars. *Ibid.* 247 Tug the lab'ring Oar; Stretch to your Stroaks, my still unconquer'd Crew. **1725** POPE *Odyss.* XII. 265 Their oars they seize, Stretch to the stroke, and brush the working seas. **1820** SCOTT *Let.* 30 Mar. in *Lockhart* (1837) IV. xi. 373 He must stretch to the oar for his own credit as well as that of his friends. **1835** DICKENS *Sk. Boz, River*, Why don't your partner stretch out? **1840** R. H. DANA *Bef. Mast* xviii. 51 [We] were returning, stretching out well at our oars. **1846** A. YOUNG *Naut. Dict.* 328 *Stretch out!* an order to a boat's crew to pull strong.

d. Of a horse, etc. *to stretch out into a gallop*, *to be stretched out at a gallop*.

1890 'R. BOLDREWOOD' *Col. Reformer* xix, The roused animal commenced to stretch out into a gallop. **1896** 'H. S. MERRIMAN' *Sowers* i, His little Cossack horse..was stretched out at a gallop.

VI. To lengthen or widen by force.

21. a. *trans.* To lengthen or widen (a material thing) by force; to pull out to greater length or width; to enlarge in girth or capacity by internal pressure. Also in figurative context.

Now the most prominent sense; in early use rare and perh. contextual (cf. 16), chiefly with advs. *abroad*, *out*.

1398 TREVISA *Barth. De P.R.* XI. ii. (1495) 385 A stronge blaste of wynde..blowyth and stretchyth bledders by entrynge. **1530** PALSGR. 738/2, I stretche out a length, *jalonge*. Stretche out this corde a lengeth. **1552** HULOET, Stretche abrode, *dilato*. **1613** SHAKS. *Hen. VIII*, II. iii. 33 And which guifts..the capacity Of your soft Chiuerell Conscience, would receiue, If you might please to stretch it. **1632** MARMION *Hollands Leaguer* II. v. F2, Gentlemen, You'l breake your wits with stretching them. **1680** DRYDEN *Ovid's Epist.* Pref. (1716) a4, I suppose he [a translator] may stretch his Chain to such a Latitude, but by innovation of Thoughts, methinks he breaks it. **1687** ATTERBURY *Answ. Consid. Spirit Luther* 32 He is a very Procrustes in his way: what-ever he meets of other men's, he unmercifully either stretches, or curtails, till he has made it exactly of a size with his own notions. **1691** HARTCLIFFE *Virtues* 69 If the Stomach be stretched beyond its..true extent, it will [etc.]. **1762** *Mead's Med. Wks.* (1775) 395 Her belly was so vastly stretched with water, that I pronounced the case incurable. **1843** HOLTZAPFFEL *Turning* I. 421 Little risk of stretching the plates, if the work be delicately performed. **1843** in *Newton's Lond. Jrnl.* Conj. Ser. XXV. 373 Machinery or apparatus..for stretching certain fibrous materials. **1860** RUSKIN *Unto this Last* i. (1862) 4 It might be shown, on that supposition, that it would be advantageous to roll the students up into pellets, flatten them into cakes, or stretch them into cables. **1889** *Harper's Mag.* Mar. 623/2 My business..is to stretch new boots for millionaires.

b. To open wide (the eyes, mouth, nostrils).

1599 SHAKS. *Hen. V*, II. ii. 55 If little faults..Shall not be wink'd at, how shall we stretch our eye When capitall crimes ..Appeare before vs? *Ibid.* III. i. 15 Now set the Teeth, and stretch the Nosthrill wide. **1605** *1st Pt. Jeronimo* I. i. 56 Then let him..Stretch his mouth wider with big swolne phrases. **1823** SCOTT *Quentin D.* viii, Looking as if he were stretching his eyes to see into futurity.

c. *colloq.* To eke out (food), esp. to serve a greater number of people than originally intended.

1923 *Chambers's Jrnl.* Christmas 858/2 The problem of how to stretch a supper made for two to fit three. **1951** H. MACINNES *Neither Five nor Three* xiii. 184 She began worrying how far she could stretch the beef stew now simmering on the stove. **1974** N. FREELING *Dressing of Diamond* 80 She had made stuffing for the trout, to stretch them a bit. **1977** C. MCCARRY *Secret Lovers* viii. 98 She wondered if I was free to have dinner at her house... They were having something that the cook could stretch for three.

d. *Cinemat.* To adapt (a silent film) for projection on sound equipment by duplicating alternate frames so that the speed of action is not distorted.

1953 L. J. WHEELER *Princ. Cinematogr.* v. 145 Many occasions arrive when it is desirable to 'stretch' an original negative, that is, assuming an old, silent negative, is required to be printed into a sound film. **1965** *Listener* 11 Feb. 231/3 If a silent film (sixteen frames/sec.) is projected on a sound projector (twenty-four frames/sec.), the action appears too fast. To rectify this, silent films are sometimes 'stretched' by making a special print in which every other frame is printed twice. **1969** *Observer* 26 Jan. 7/4 The technique of stretching them [*sc.* silent films] to run at 24 or 25 frames a second..has been known and used for very many years. **1976** *Oxf. Compan. Film* 664/2 Makers of compilation films often incorporate old footage without stretching it, with the result that modern audiences have come to regard all silent film as comic.

e. *Engin.* To increase the capability or power of (an aircraft, power plant, etc.).

1960 *New Scientist* 30 June 1640/1 Engine power again was an essential factor in stretching the Viscount. **1967** *Economist* 8 July p. xxvi/3 The newest Gardener engine now runs at 1,800 rpm to give 180 bhp—still with remarkable fuel economy. This is near the far limit to which the engine can be stretched without supercharging. **1979** *Nature* 19 July 187/3 Why is it necessary to scale up to 1,300 MW? Doesn't the ability to replicate and perhaps stretch the 250 MW Dounreay prototype fast reactor give sufficient insurance against the risk of long-term uranium scarcity?

22. *fig.* **a.** To enlarge or amplify beyond proper or natural limits; to extend unduly the scope or application of (a law, rule, etc.) or the meaning of (a word).

1553 *Primer or Bk. Priv. Prayer* P v b, That they [*sc.* landlords] remembryng them selues to be thy tenauntes, may not racke and stretche oute yͤ rentes of their houses and landes. **1580** SPENSER *Let. to Harvey* Poet. Wks. (1912) 611/2 Heauen, beeing vsed shorte as one sillable, when it is in Verse, stretched out with a Diastole, is like a lame Dogge that holdes vp one legge. **1581** J. BELL *Haddon's Answ. Osorius* 415 b, The speech of Peter in this whole Epistle, ought not in any wise be stretched to the paynes of Purgatory. **1631** *Star Chamber Cases* (Camden) 8 Then he delivereth over the goods..they were stretched in value already. **1670** SOUTH *Serm.* (1698) III. 154 To Love an Enemy is to stretch Humanity as far as it will go. **1746** H. WALPOLE *Let. to Mann* 15 Apr., The judge..told her he wished he could stretch the law to hang her. **1764** GOLDSM. *Trav.* 382 When contending chiefs blockade the throne, Contracting regal power to stretch their own. **1848** J. S. MILL *Pol. Econ.* III. xxiii. §3 II. 183 In speculative times, money-dealers..are inclined to extend their business by stretching their credit. **1878** O. W. HOLMES *Motley* ii. 15 The rules of the Phi Beta Kappa Society..were stretched so as to include him. **1899** *Allbutt's Syst. Med.* VIII. 471 This reflex hypothesis has been stretched to explain cases following tonsillitis or disturbances of other organs. **1915** HARTLAND in *Man* XV. 126 Thus, to refer to *mana* as 'divine energy' is stretching the word unwarrantably.

b. *absol.* To stretch one's ordinary rule, 'launch out'.

1766 GOLDSM. *Vicar* xxx, He bespoke also a dozen of their best wine,..adding with a smile, that he would stretch a little for once.

†**c.** To extend the duration of. *Obs.* (? *nonce-use.*)

1568 T. HOWELL *Arb. Amitie* 10 b, I cursse eche lingring howre of day, by bloudie woundes to stratch.

d. To exaggerate in narration; chiefly *absol.* (colloq.)

1674 *Govt. Tongue* xi. 200 What an allay do we find to the credit of the most probable event, that it is reported by one who uses to stretch? **1678** D'URFEY *Trick for Trick* I. i. 10 But I must confess t'ee, under the Rose here, I did stretch a little, as a good teller of a Story shou'd. **1711** SWIFT *Jrnl. to Stella* 1 Dec., The fifteen images that I saw were not worth forty pounds, so I stretched a little when I said a thousand. **1883** *Harper's Mag.* Apr. 658/2 They call anything that is 'stretched' a Yankee story. **1884** 'MARK TWAIN' *Huck. Finn* i, There was things which he stretched, but mainly he told the truth.

(*b*) In colloq. phr. *to stretch it* (or *things*): to go too far, to go beyond the limits of credibility; to exaggerate.

1965 M. ALLINGHAM *Mind Readers* xx. 212 Rightie ho. If you say so. Any friend of yours is a friend of mine but that's stretching it. **1974** M. HASTINGS *Dragon Island* xi. 96 'I can't believe that by some chance Jones found himself with *two* people in whom he had special interest.' 'That would be stretching it.' **1975** R. STOUT *Family Affair* ix. 83 Everyone in Washington is connected..with Watergate. That's stretching it, but not much. **1980** R. HILL *Killing Kindness* v. 46 It's stretching things a bit... Still, it's worth checking.

e. *colloq.* To cause (someone) to exert himself to the utmost of his talents or abilities, esp. with regard to learning or employment.

1951 C. MORGAN *Breeze of Morning* I. v. 25, I had found that he always 'stretched' me in the way I liked, and gave me confidence by having such unswerving confidence in himself. **1960** C. DAY LEWIS *Buried Day* i. 23 Under such conditions, an only child may become precocious, stretching himself unnaturally to meet the adult world on its own terms. **1968** *Guardian* 21 Nov. 10/5 He is satisfied by being a bishop; he says he felt a need to be stretched by some equally big job. **1978** D. DEVINE *Sunk without Trace* iv. 36, I hear good reports of your work... I fear, however, we're not stretching you enough. **1983** *Times* 8 Jan. 3/8 Local education authorities..could ensure..that the curriculum suited and stretched all children.

23. a. *intr.* To be or admit of being forcibly lengthened or dilated without breaking.

1485 CAXTON *Chas. Gt.* 236 The vaynes of hys necke braken a sondre, and the synewes of his body stratcheden. *c* **1537** DE BENESE *Measurynge Lande* A iij, A corde or a lyne ..wyl.. somtyme streche longer by long dryeth. **1558** WARDE tr. *Alexis' Secr.* 30 Ye shall cause the skinne to stretche, and come to his place, as it was before. **1597** E. S. *Discov. Knts. Poste* B 4 b, Conscience,..I tell you their consciences are like chiuerell skins, that will stretch euery way. **1660** BOYLE *New Exper. Spring of Air* xxiv. 191 The inner Membrane that involv'd the several Liquors of the Egge, because it would stretch and yield, remain'd unbroken. **1871** B. TAYLOR *Faust* (1875) II. I. iii. 31 Think, the thread won't stretch forever! Have a care! it might be broken. **1872** W. POLE *Iron* 60 If we attach one end of a bar of iron to the ceiling, and hang a weight to the other end, the bar will stretch.

b. *Jazz.* To play without restraint, esp. in a solo. Const. *out*.

1961 *N.Y. Times Mag.* 25 June 39/3 When a cat stretches out, he can make the moon on his own thrust or horn. **1962**

Down Beat 5 July 35/3, I heard this group in person, at the Village Gate, and they stretched out. **1968** *Crescendo* June 12/2 Everybody really had a chance to stretch out and play what and how they wanted to.

VII. 24. a. *Comb.* **stretch-bench** *Leather-manuf.*, a bench on which the stretching of hides is performed; **stretch forming** *vbl. sb. Mech.*, a process in which sheet metal under tension is shaped by the pressure of a punch to the required contour; hence **stretch-form** *v. trans.*; **stretch-gut** (see quot.); †**stretch-halter**, one who deserves to be hanged, a gallows-bird; †**stretch-hemp** = prec.; †**stretch-leg**, that which lays prostrate, Death; **stretch mark**, a linear mark on the skin (esp. of the stomach or thighs) when it has been distended by pregnancy or obesity; = STRIA 2 e; †**stretch-mouthed** *a.*, wide-mouthed, *fig.*; †**stretchneck** [tr. AL. *collistrigium*], a pillory; **stretch receptor** *Physiol.*, a sensory receptor that responds to the stretching of tissue; **stretch reflex** *Physiol.*, a reflex contraction of a muscle resulting from the stretching of the same muscle; †**stretch-rope**, one who stretches a rope (applied to a bellringer); **stretch spinning** (see quot. 1957); **stretch-wood**, an apparatus for stretching gloves; a wooden hand upon which a glove is stretched to dry in dyeing.

1897 C. T. DAVIS *Manuf. Leather* xli, (ed. 2) 543 The stretching is also performed by hand on the *stretch-bench. **1951** G. SACHS *Princ. & Methods Sheet-Metal Fabricating* v. iii. 470 In most instances a part is *stretch-formed from a rectangular blank. **1973** J. G. TWEEDDALE *Materials Technol.* II. iv. 85 (*caption*) Stretch forming a curved shape. **1942** *Iron Age* 4 June 49 (*heading*) *Stretch-forming contoured sheet metal aircraft parts. **1951** *Archit. Rev.* CIX. 166/1 It can be spun into a bell-like shape, or it can be shaped on a stretch-forming machine, which pulls it into shape over a former. **1973** J. G. TWEEDDALE *Materials Technol.* II. iv. 85 Stretch forming uses a principle that involves applying a uniaxial tension to a thin plate,..and then pushing a controlled shape progressively into the surface of the tensioned sheet. **1673–8** LITTLETON *Lat.-Eng. Dict.*, *Saturio*, a *stretch-gut, an over-eater. **1583** GOLDING *Calvin on Deut.* cxxiii. 759 Thou villaine, thou *stretchehalter. **1606** HEYWOOD *2nd Pt. If you know not Me* (1609) D 2 b, I know this is the shop by that same stretch-halter. **1532** *Stretch hempe [see HEMP *sb.* 3]. **1566** DRANT *Horace, Sat.* II. vii. I ij, Thou stretche hempe [*furcifer*]. *c* **1560** *Most Fruitf. Treat. Chr. Man* I. xxxix. 150 Learne to beware by yᵉ example of other men, vpon whom *stretche legge came sodenly and slewe them. **1960** F. W. GOODRICH *Maternity* iii. 59 The development of '*stretch marks' in the skin of the abdomen and thighs is not unusual. **1970** D. MARLOWE *Echoes of Celandine* viii. 143 'The marks you see ..are not stretch-marks even though I have had three children.'.. She then turned around..revealing scars.. across her thighs. **1972** G. BOURNE *Pregnancy* vi. 110 Stretch marks may occur at puberty on the buttocks and also on the breasts, especially if a girl is overweight. **1980** *Family Med. Guide* (R. Soc. Medicine) ix. 210/1 Cushing's syndrome is characterized by..thinning of the skin which may lead to large stretch marks, and a tendency to bruise easily. **1611** SHAKS. *Wint. T.* IV. iv. 196 Some *stretch-mouth'd Rascall. **1543** tr. *Ordin. Bakers* etc. [*c* 1300] c. 3 Euery pyllory or *stretche-necke [L. *collistrigium*] must be made of conuenyent strength. **1890** CONAN DOYLE *White Company* xxi, Some of you may find yourselves in the stretchneck, if you take not heed. **1936** C. L. EVANS *Starling's Princ. Human Physiol.* (ed. 7) xxxvii. 906 The lung evidently possesses *stretch receptors similar in their responses to those of muscle. **1961** *Listener* 23 Nov. 858/1 If the animal [*sc.* an octopus] cannot use information from internal stretch receptors in its muscles, it will not be able to define the relative positions of the sense organs on the suckers that is uses to pick up an object. **1969** J. H. GREEN *Basic Clin. Physiol.* ix. 52/2 As one breathes in, the lungs expand, and stretch receptors in the lungs send sensory information up the vagus nerve to the respiratory centre cutting short inspiration. **1916** C. ASAYAMA in *Q. Jrnl. Exper. Physiol.* IX. 278 Quick stretching of tibialis anticus by a sharp pull on its tendon..elicits a reflex contraction of the muscle... It may be termed a *stretch-reflex. **1978** B. W. PAYTON in G. ROSS *Essentials Human Physiol.* ix. 478 Stretch reflexes occur in all muscles but are particularly obvious in those involved in maintaining posture. **1634** HEYWOOD & BROME *Lanc. Witches* III. i. E 3, 'Tis some merry conceit of the *stretch-ropes the Ringers. **1925** *U.S. Patent 1,528,219* This extract..prevents adhesion of the filaments in multiple spinning, and thereby greatly promotes '*stretch spinning'. **1957** *Textile Terms & Definitions* (Textile Inst.) (ed. 3) 96 *Stretch spinning*, a process of spinning whereby the filaments are substantially stretched at some stage between extrusion and collection. **1883** R. HALDANE *Workshop Rec.* Ser. II. 235/2 The glove [is] then allowed to dry on the *stretch-wood.

b. Used *attrib.* or as *adj.* to designate various (usu. synthetic) fibres or fabrics which are elastic or capable of stretching, and garments, etc. (which may stretch to provide close fitting) made from them. Occas. *absol.* as *sb.*

1956 *Jrnl. Textile Inst.* XL. 280 A stretch yarn in which the deformation is produced by suitable combinations of heat-setting and twisting. **1957** *Times* 18 Nov. 11/4 Ties.. by Jacques Fath with matching nylon stretch socks. **1959** *Times* 12 Jan. 11/3 Courtauld's process to obtain resilient stretch-nylon yarn. **1961** *Listener* 16 Nov. 825/2 My favourite example comes from a very modish American magazine... 'As contemporary..as C. P. Snow and stretch-pants.' **1962** *Guardian* 23 Feb. 8/5 Until recently I had never found a fine stretch which did not ladder quickly. **1963** *Harper's Bazaar* Jan. 50 Stretch slacks and cardigan in gold and silver. **1963** *Daily Mail* 24 Aug. 5/1 (Advt.), 100% Nylon Stretch Tights. **1963** *Economist* 7 Sept. 840/2 The most promising..growth area..is..in 'stretch' fabrics. **1964** *Woman* 18 Jan. 13 Keep your stretch pants slender. **1968** *Vogue* 15 Apr. 60 Snug-topped bubble dress..of sun red stretch. **1972** *Times* 22 May 10/2 Too-tight stretch nylon socks cause many foot troubles. **1977** J. FRASER *Hearts Ease in Death* xiv. 166 The chair..was fitted with one of those cheap stretch covers with a large floral pattern. **1978** J. GORES *Gone, no Forwarding* xiii. 76 A wide-hipped woman in red stretch slacks. **1980** *Times* 19 Feb. 8 The now obligatory stretch fabrics.

stretchaˈbility. [f. STRETCHABLE *a.*: see -BILITY.] Capability of being stretched.

1940 H. R. MAUERSBERGER *Matthews's Textile Fibers* (ed. 5) xx. 863 On cold-drawing, nylon becomes exceedingly strong and elastic. But elasticity means more than 'stretchability'. The degree to which a stretched material recovers its original length is a measure of true elasticity. **1959** POTTER & CORBMAN *Fiber to Fabric* (ed. 3) iv. 60 Stretch yarns..when subjected to certain methods that use heat to set crimp in thermoplastic filament yarns..increase their stretchability. **1962** *Listener* 22 Mar. 510/2 What he does..is to measure the 'strength' of a flour..by measuring the 'stretchability' of the dough it makes. **1967** E. CHAMBERS *Photolitho-Offset* i. 9 It [*sc.* zinc] also stretches more before breaking—this stretchability being sometimes useful to correct mis-register. **1978** *Detroit Free Press* 5 Mar. 30 (Advt.), We tested it for launderability, durability, stretchability and shape retention.

stretchable (ˈstrɛtʃəb(ə)l), *a.* [f. STRETCH *v.* + -ABLE.] Capable of being stretched.

1398 TREVISA *Barth De P.R.* v. xxv. (1495) 135 Yf they [*sc.* fowl] haue longe neckes and strechable [*Bodl. MS.* streccheable: L. *abile ad declinandum*] they bynde theym as it were foldynge in pleyghtes whan they flee. **1862** CARLYLE *Fredk. Gt.* XII. xii. III. 388 Strenuous Siege; which, had.. the Laws of Nature and the rigours of Arithmetic..been stretchable entities, might have succeeded better! **1889** A. JAMES *Diary* 16 Nov. (1965) 56 She seems as large a joke as ever, an embodiment of the stretchable, a purely transatlantic and modern possibility. **1975** L. BLUE *To Heaven with Scribes & Pharisees* iv. 39 Jewish cooking.. inclines to casseroles and stews, which are infinitely stretchable.

ˈstretchant, *a. Her. rare.* [f. STRETCH *v.* + *-ant*, after *couchant* and the like.] (See quot.)

1828–40 BERRY *Encycl. Her.* I, *Stretchant*, beasts upon their legs, but stretching themselves out, which they often do after lying down.

stretched (strɛtʃt), *ppl. a.* [f. STRETCH *v.* + -ED¹.]

1. Extended to the full length, not bent or flexed. Of a limb: Thrust out from the body. Also with *out*, *forth*.

1518 H. WATSON *Hist. Oliver of Castile* (Roxb.) Q 1, He.. ranne to hym with stratched armes and embraced hym. **1535** COVERDALE *Ps.* cxxxv. 12 With a mightie hande and a stretched out arme. *a* **1566** R. EDWARDS *Damon & Pithias* (1571) D iv b, A pledge you did require.., For which, with heart and stretched handes, most humble thankes I geue. **1656** FLECKNOE *Diarium* 28 Now Chantecleer with stretcht-out wings, The glad approach of Phœbus sings. **1692** SIR W. HOPE *Fencing-Master* 148 Keep a streight point towards his face with a stretched arme. **1697** DRYDEN *Æneis* III. 320 At length rebuff'd, they leave their mangled Prey, And their stretch'd Pinions to the Skies display. **1760** R. LLOYD *Actor* 97 The sudden whirl, stretch'd leg, and lifted staff, Which please the vulgar. **1846** TRENCH *Miracles* 459 The stretched forth hands are the hands extended upon either side on the transverse bar of the cross. **1847** TENNYSON *Princess* II. 356 Jewels five-words long That on the stretch'd forefinger of all Time Sparkle for ever. **1856** MISS WARNER *Hills Shatemuc* vi, He yielded his brother's [letter] again to her stretched-out hand.

2. Of the neck, throat: Extended or expanded unduly or abnormally. Also with *out*.

1557 PHAER *Æneid* VII. (1558) V viiij, As swannes..With stretchid neckes, their melody they yelde. **1659** W. CHAMBERLAYNE *Pharonnida* III. i. 306 An ill-boding Note Sent from a fatal Ravens stretcht-out Throat. **1666** W. SPURSTOW *Spiritual Chym.* 89 Gospel Mysteries, which Angells with stretched out necks have more desire to pry into, then ability perfectly to understand. **1780** COWPER *Progr. Error* 380 The gosling pair, With awkward gait, stretch'd neck, and silly stare. **1845** BROWNING *How they brought the good News* vi, For one heard the quick wheeze Of her chest, saw the stretched neck and staggering knees.

3. a. Of material, a line, etc.: Extended, spread out, drawn out so as to be tight. Hence *fig.* of a receptacle: Strained in capacity, filled to the utmost.

? **1605** DRAYTON *Poems, To Virginian Voy.* 10 Britans.. quickly aboard bestowe you, And with a merry gale swell your stretch'd sayle. *c* **1681** DUKE *Review* 96 [He] Swell'd his stretch'd coffers with o'er-flowing gold. **1832** BREWSTER *Nat. Magic* viii. 193 If..we strew the sand over a stretched membrane, the sand will form itself into figures. **1840** in *Newton's Lond. Jrnl.* Conj. Ser. XVI. 361 When India rubber is introduced, it is in the stretched or non-elastic state. **1889** BRINSMEAD *Hist. Pianoforte* 40 The vibrations of stretched strings. **1906** *Westm. Gaz.* 28 July 6/3 You walk the stretched rope.

b. Of the senses: Tense.

1800 HT. LEE *Canterb. T.* (ed. 2) III. 34 That profound stillness under which the stretched senses seem to ache.

4. a. Of language, ideas, prerogative, etc.: Strained beyond natural or proper limits.

c **1600** SHAKS. *Sonn.* xvii. 12 So should..your true rights be termd a Poets rage, And stretched miter of an Antique song. **1674** N. FAIRFAX *Bulk & Selv.* 71 If this answer seems harsh or stretched, we shall easily slacken and soften it by a clearer Instance. *a* **1711** KEN *Psyche* Poet. Wks. 1721 IV. 225 Say, if your stretch'd Imaginations find More horrid Monsters than foul human kind. **1790** BURKE *Fr. Rev.* 95 They therefore take up, one day, the most violent and stretched prerogative, and another time the wildest democratic ideas of freedom. **1833** LAMB *Elia*, *Product. Mod. Art*, They satisfy our most stretched and craving conceptions of the glories of the antique world.

b. Of life: Drawn *out* beyond the normal period.

1606 SHAKS. *Tr. & Cr.* I. iii. 61 And thou [Nestor] most reuerend for thy stretcht-out life.

5. Of an aircraft, engine, etc.: increased in size or operating capacity; based on a smaller or less powerful design. Cf. STRETCH *v.* 21 e.

1960 *New Scientist* 30 June 1639/2 The Super-VC 10, which BOAC has just ordered off the drawing-board, is an example of a 'stretched' aeroplane. **1966** *Wall St. Jrnl.* 13 Jan. 1 Their orders of 'stretched' jets—conventional models expanded to carry more passengers—will also have to be carefully considered. **1967** *Economist* 8 July p. xxvi/3 Operators are suspicious of 'stretched' engines. **1972** *Daily Tel.* 26 Sept. 6/7 The car is a stretched version of the latest Daimler Double-Six, itself developed from the Jaguar XJ12. **1978** *Ibid.* 23 Feb. 6/8 Improvements in technology mean that the British Hovercraft Corporation's 'stretched' SRN-4 is likely to be used on some of the established 100–150 mile European routes.

†**ˈstretchen,** *a. Obs. rare.* [As if strong pa. pple. of STRETCH *v.*] Extended.

1642 H. MORE *Song of Soul* II. II. ii. 15 If stretchen corporeity Longs to the soul, then Augmentation Must likewise thereto appertain. *Ibid.* III. ii. 11 For in his instantaneous removes He in them all at once doth fairly shine, Nor that large stretchen space his freenesse can confine.

stretcher (ˈstrɛtʃə(r)), *sb.* Also 5 strecher, 8 streacher. [f. STRETCH *v.* + -ER¹.]

I. One who or something which stretches.

1. One who stretches; *spec.* a worker employed in various industries to stretch fabrics.

c **1420** ? LYDG. *Assembly of Gods* 674 There were bosters, braggars, & brybores, Praters, fasers, strechers, & wrythers. **1615** CHAPMAN *Odyss.* XXI. 135 Yet his hopes enstild His strength, the stretcher of Vlysses string. **1721** WODROW *Hist. Ch. Scot.* (1829) II. II. iv. 126 When things are stretched too far, they break to the hurt of the stretcher. **1820** J. BROWN *Hist. Brit. Churches* I. vii. 213 Arminian stretchers of the royal prerogative were caressed and preferred. **1823** SCOTT *Quentin D.* vii, The scraper of chins hath no great love for the stretcher of throats. **1861** *Internat. Exhib. 1862, Alph. Lists Trades* 39 Stretchers. **1881** *Instr. Census Clerks* (1885) 54 Carver, Gilder:..Stretcher (Canvas). *Ibid.* 60 Woollen Cloth Manufacture:..Stretcher. *Ibid.* 67.

2. An exaggerated story or yarn; chiefly *euphemistically* or *jocularly*, a lie.

1674 [J. PATRICK] *Refl. Devot. Rom. Ch.* 416 Any story of a Cock and a Bull, will serve their turns to found a Festival upon,..though the circumstances are never so improbable. This of removing the Rock is a pretty stretcher. **1677** S. HERNE *Acc. Charterhouse* v. 29 Now listen to a visible Stretcher. **1825** BROCKETT *N.C. Gloss.*, *Stretcher*, an untruth; a softer term for a falsehood. **1840** E. E. NAPIER *Scenes & Sports For. Lands* II. vi. 215 This may, perhaps, be a stretcher; but, however, it is certain that [etc.]. **1855** OGILVIE Suppl., *Stretcher*, a notorious lie. (Local.) **1889** J. K. JEROME *Three Men* xii. 196 When the pipes are lit, and the boys are telling stretchers about the dangers they have passed through.

II. Technical senses.

†**3.** *Falconry.* A toe of a hawk or falcon. *Obs.*

1486 *Bk. St. Albans, Hawking* a viii, The Clees that are uppon the medyll strecheris ye shall call the loong Sengles. **1575** TURBERV. *Falconrie* 55 She hath no great scales upon hir legges, unlesse it be a fewe that beginne behinde the three stretchers. **1677** N. COX *Gentl. Recr.* II. 207 The Haggard... A large wide Foot, with slender Stretchers. *Ibid.* 208 Of the Barbary-Faulcon..with long Talons and Stretchers.

4. a. An instrument or appliance for expanding material, making it taut, removing its wrinkles, and the like.

1532 MORE *Confut. Barnes* VIII. Wks. 1557. 800/1 Stretchyng oute hys wryncles with the stretching them vppon the stretcher or tenter hookes of the crosse. **1774** in *Abridgm. Specif. Patents, Music* (1871) 9 [The silk strings] are then to be put on a stretcher that they may dry in a proper tension. **1825** J. NICHOLSON *Oper. Mech.* 382 The cotton, or..roving, is taken out and wound upon a bobbin, and..carried to a machine called a stretcher. **1838** in *Newton's Lond. Jrnl.* Conj. Ser. (1840) XVI. 65 Having determined the figure or design to be produced, the cloth.. is spread..in lengths..over a stretcher of canvas, which stretcher is placed in a frame. **1862** *Catal. Internat. Exhib., Brit.* II. No. 5130, Marking-ink, linen stretcher, &c., with specimens.

b. A frame upon which an artist's canvas is spread and drawn tight by means of corner-pieces or wedges. See also quot. 1875.

1847 *Man. Oil-Paintng* 48 There are, however, certain sizes [of canvas] which are always kept on hand at the shops, ready mounted on stretchers. **1867** TROLLOPE *Chron. Barset* II. lx. 177 The rent canvas fell and fluttered upon the stretcher. **1875** KNIGHT *Dict. Mech.*, *Stretcher*, a corner-piece for distending a canvas frame.

c. *Leather-manuf.* (*a*) = STAKE *sb.*¹ 5 b; (*b*) a hand-tool used in finishing leather.

1839 URE *Dict. Arts* 767 [The skins] are dried with the fleece outermost,..and are finished upon the stretcher. **1872** *Saddlers' Gaz.* 1 Dec. 212/1 The hide..is then turned over and the hair side moistened with water and rubbed with a copper stretcher until it is nearly dry.

d. An instrument for easing the fit of boots, gloves, hats, etc.

1858 SIMMONDS *Dict. Trade, Stretcher*,..an instrument for easing boots or gloves. **1885** *Harper's Mag.* Feb. 449/2 She was manipulating the..pair of stretchers.

5. A bar serving as a stay or brace.

a. A buttress in masonry; a tie-beam in joinery; in trench timbering, a temporary strut.

1774 GOSTLING *Walk Canterb.* xxxi. 136 There seems to have been some failing in the south-west pillar, and..care has been..taken to prevent any ill consequences of it by adding stretchers of stone-work on all sides to stiffen it... The stretchers are very substantial and deep walls of stone pierced in such patterns as make them..an ornament: They are carried on arches from this pillar to two other principal ones. *a* **1805** ROBISON *Syst. Mech. Philos.* (1822) I. 669 The struts which carry the king-post spring from those points of the stretcher where it rests on the strut below. **1869** C. KNIGHT *Mechanician* 67 The class of columns represented by Fig. 130 are used also as stays, and in the horizontal position; they are in such cases named stretchers, and should be forged as nearly as possible to the intended form.

b. A bar or rod used as a tie or brace in the framework of an article; esp. a cross-piece between the handles of a plough or the legs of a chair.

1844 H. STEPHENS *Book of Farm* I. 413 The stretchers which support and retain the handles [of the plough] at their due distance apart. **1846** HOLTZAPFFEL *Turning* II. 725 There is a central rod or stretcher [to the frame saw], to which are mortised two end pieces that have a slight power of rotation on the stretcher. **1882** CAULFEILD & SAWARD *Dict. Needlework* 196 The ordinary [Embroidery] Frames are made of four pieces of wood, the two upright pieces of which are called Bars,..and two horizontal pieces, called Stretchers. **1902** [see *stretcher bar* (c) in 12]. **1905** C. G. HARPER *Oxf. Road* I. 125 Four men thus working will 'get out' the timber [beech] and turn it into legs or rails—'stretchers' as they call them in the trade—at the rate of four gross a day.

c. A bar which keeps apart the traces between every two horses in a team.

1828 CARR *Craven Gloss.* **1852** C. W. HOSKYNS *Talpa* xvi. (1854) 136 The fore-horse..turned suddenly..into the high-road, grazing Mr. Greening's unspurred foot with the point of the leader's stretcher.

d. *Naut.* (See quot.)

1867 SMYTH *Sailor's Word-bk., Stretchers*... Also cross-pieces placed between a boat's sides to keep them apart when hoisted up and griped.

e. *Mining.* A prop or sprag.

1883 GRESLEY *Gloss. Coal-Mining* 244.

6. A bar or rod used to expand and to keep expanded something collapsible.

a. A jointed or sliding rod used to spread the head or legs of a thing, esp. each of the rods pivoted at the ends to the ribs and the sleeve which slides upon the stick of an umbrella.

1833 *Reg. Deb. Congr. U.S.* 22nd Congr. 1 Sess. App. p. xli, [Duty] on square wire used for the manufacture of stretchers for umbrellas..twelve per centum ad valorem. **1843** HOLTZAPFFEL *Turning* I. 136 Whalebone is now principally used for the stretchers for umbrellas. **1857** *Repert. Patent Invent.* June 511 Samuel Fox,..for heating..ribs and stretchers of umbrellas and parasols. **1886** ROCK in *Abridgm. Specif. Patents Opt.* etc. *Instrum.* (1875) 515 For tripod stands I employ three elongating stretchers converging to a point in the middle (when the legs are spread); they are formed of brass tubes sliding one within the other. **1875** KNIGHT *Dict. Mech., Stretcher*... 5. (*Vehicle.*) A jointed rod by whose extension the carriage bows are separated and expanded, so as to spread the canopy or hood.

b. A stick or each of the sticks used to keep a fishing net expanded.

1823 J. F. COOPER *Pioneers* xxiii, Benjamin prided himself greatly on his skill in throwing the net... At length a loud splash in the water, as he threw away the 'staff', or 'stretcher'..announced that the boat was returning. **1884** G. F. BRAITHWAITE *Salmonidæ of Westmorld.* vi. 23 Lighter sticks or stretchers are attached to the top and bottom cord which keep the net extended.

c. A piece of wood or metal used to spread the clews of a hammock.

In recent Dicts.

7. A foot-rest in a rowing-boat. (See quots. 1769, 1898.)

1609 DEKKER *Ravens Alm.* B 2, Any Sculer, whose legs get his liuing by a Stretcher, will not deny it. **1697** DRYDEN *Æneis* x. 417 They tug at ev'ry Oar; and ev'ry Stretcher bends. **1769** FALCONER *Dict. Marine* (1780), *Stretcher*, a sort of staff fixed athwart the bottom of a boat, for the rower to place his feet against, in order to communicate a greater effort to his oar. **1834** MARRYAT *P. Simple* xxxi, Swinburne appeared.. followed by the rest of the boat's crew, armed with the boat's stretchers. **1898** *Encycl. Sport* II. 298/1 (Rowing) *Stretcher*, a board placed slopingly at a right angle across the boat in front of the oarsman, upon which he braces his feet.

8. A kind of litter composed of two poles separated by cross-bars upon which canvas is stretched, used to transport sick or wounded persons.

1845 *Ann. Reg.* 380/1 After the body was discovered Fletcher went for the stretcher. **1875** *Encycl. Brit.* I. 668/2 The ambulance conveyances authorised for use in the British army are..1. Conveyances carried by the hands of bearers, called stretchers; 2. Conveyances wheeled by men, wheeled stretchers, [etc.]. **1892** BIERCE *In Midst of Life* 129 Two were hospital attendants and carried a stretcher.

9. a. A folding bed or bedstead chiefly for camp or hospital use; also (chiefly *Austral.* and *N.Z.*), a camp-bed used as a spare bed in a house, etc. Also *pl.* the trestles for a bed.

1841 MARRYAT *Poacher* xlv, They sat down on the stretchers upon which the bed had been laid [in the prison cell] during the night. **1893** SELOUS *Trav. S.E. Africa* 56 He gave me..a stretcher to sleep on in one of the empty chambers. **1943** *Amer. Speech* XVIII. 86 A common article of furniture [in New Zealand] is a *stretcher*—a folding camp bed or cot, often used to provide temporary sleeping accommodation in a house. **1974** *Weekend Mag.* (Montreal) 18 May 21/1 All summer cottages in those days had two or three camp cots or 'stretchers', with flat wire springs and small mattresses, which could be folded up and stuffed under beds for use when unexpected or surplus guests arrived. **1980** B. MASON *Solo* 30 Tim, I got the stretcher out. It's quite sound. Needs a dust, that's all. I'm giving you three blankets. That should be enough.

b. A flat board on which a corpse is laid out preparatory to coffining. ? *Sc.*

1850 OGILVIE; and in some later Dicts.

10. Something laid lengthways.

a. *Building.* A brick or stone laid with its length in the direction of the wall. Also *Fortif.*, a sod laid in a similar positon.

1693 MOXON *Mech. Exerc.* (1703) 360 If the Header on one side of the Wall, toothed as much as the Stretcher on the other side, it would be a stronger Toothing. **1693** J. HOUGHTON *Collect. Improv. Husb.* No. 74 ¶3 A Brick-wall of a Foot and half thick is commonly made by Stretchers and Headers. **1725** [see HEADER 5]. **1791** SMEATON *Edystone L.* (1793) §82 The long pieces or Stretchers were retained between two Headers or bond pieces. **1839** *Civil Engin. & Arch. Jrnl.* II. 430/2 The front is to be of..stone, laid header and stretcher alternately. **1851, 1884** [see HEADER 5].

b. ? A horizontal branch (see quots.).

1733 W. ELLIS *Chiltern & Vale Farm.* 162 Great Plantations of Hazel, that..are also of vast Service to the Thatcher, by its Stretchers, Sprays, and Withs. **1886** *W. Somerset Word-bk.* s.v., In 'making' a hedge certain growing stakes are chopped half through, laid down lengthwise on the hedge, and fastened down with a crook. Earth is then thrown upon them, and they root afresh. These are the stretchers.

11. *Angling.* The artificial fly at the extremity of a casting line to which two or more flies are attached.

1837 J. KIRKBRIDE *Northern Angler* 3 The first dropper ought to be about a yard from the stretcher, or tail-fly. **1885** *Outing* (U.S.) Oct. 77/1 The trout..were lusty, vigorous fellows, and with a 'Silver Doctor' as a stretcher, I managed to forget myself..completely. **1938** W. C. PLATTS *Mod. Trout Fishing* vii. 59 Two flies—a stretcher, or tail fly, and one dropper—is rather risky. **1963** A. N. MARSTON *Newnes Encycl. Angling* 249/1 *Stretcher*, the bottom fly on a wet-fly cast made up of two or more flies. Usually called a tail fly.

III. attrib. and Comb.

12. *attrib.* and *Comb.*, as (sense 5 b) ***stretcher-bolt, -tube***; **stretcher-bar**, (*a*) the bar which is set across a level as a support for a rock-drill; (*b*) *Leather-manuf.*, an appliance for stretching hides transversely; (*c*) (see quot. 1902); **stretcher-bearer** (see quot.); **stretcher-bed, -bedstead**, a folding bed, chiefly for camp or barrack use (cf. 9); **stretcher-brick** (see 10 a); **stretcher case**, an injured or sick person needing conveyance on a stretcher; **stretcher-fly** (see 11); **stretcher-iron** *Leather-manuf.* = STAKE *sb.*[1] 5 b; **stretcher-man** = *stretcher-bearer*; **stretcher-mule** (see quot.); **stretcher-party** *Mil.*, a party of men equipped with stretchers and appliances for assisting and removing the wounded; **stretcher-pole**, a pole of an ambulance stretcher; **stretcher strain** *Metallurgy*, a furrowed marking on the surface of a metal produced by local deformation.

1883 *Encyl. Brit.* XVI. 448/1 In driving a level with the Darlington drill it is usual to fix the *stretcher bar horizontally across the level so as to command the upper part of the face. **1897** C. T. DAVIS *Manuf. Leather* xli. (ed. 2) 544 A stretcher-bar of suitable form for stretching the hides transversely. **1902** *Lockwood's Dict. Mech. Engin.* (ed. 3), *Stretcher Bar*, or *Stretcher*, a long bar or bolt shouldered near each end, and used for the purpose of maintaining A frames and side frames at a fixed distance apart and perfectly rigid. **1876** VOYLE & STEVENSON *Milit. Dict.* 412/1 **Stretcher Bearers*, men..whose special duty..is to carry the wounded from the battle-field, to the ambulance wagons. **1842** MRS. GORE *Fascin.* 21 In a gloomy inner room stood a common *stretcher-bed. **1888** *Daily News* 5 June 6/2 The life of the emergency men in camp..is luxurious... They have stretcher beds and blankets to cover them. **1895** *Army & Navy Co-op. Price-list* 442 Barrack Furniture and Camp Equipment. Folding *Stretcher Bedstead, Iron frame and legs. **1844** H. STEPHENS *Book of Farm* I. 420 The right handle [of the plough] is formed in one bar,..and it is connected to the left handle by the *stretcher-bolts. **1867** MUSGRAVE *Nooks & Corners Old France* I. 80 A perilous mode of scamping off their work, which among fifty *stretcher bricks, exhibited not two headers. **1917** 'CONTACT' *Airman's Outings* v. 118 On this occasion there was good reason for the delay, as we ceded the right of way to a hospital ship and waited while a procession of ambulance cars drove along the quay and unloaded their *stretcher cases. **1978** R. V. JONES *Most Secret War* xxxvi. 310 The Navy would not take him because as a stretcher case he would occupy as much space on board ship as four men standing up. **1883** *Century Mag.* July 379/1 A bass rose and snapped the *stretcher fly before it fully settled on the water. **1839** URE *Dict. Arts* 768 The clean skins after being dried, are finished first on the *stretcher-iron, and then on the herse or stretching frame. **1875** BEDFORD *Sailor's Pocket Bk.* vii. (ed. 2) 247 If a couple of spare limbers are available the S.A.A. might be placed upon them and drawn by the spare-ammunition and *stretcher-men. **1875** KNIGHT *Dict. Mech.*, **Stretcher-mule*, a mule adapted to stretch and twist fine rovings of cotton. **1884** *Mil. Engineering* I. II. 112 The strength of the *stretcher party will be determined by the principal medical officer. **1892** KIPLING *Barrack-room Ballads, Oonts*, We socks 'im with a *stretcher-pole. **1931** *Metal Progress* Sept. 90/1 *Stretcher strains (or more appropriately 'worms') are the shop names for the phenomenon known as the 'Lines of Lüder', after Lüder of Magdeburg, who first described them in 1860. **1971** *Steel in U.S.S.R.* I. 899 (*heading*) Causes of the formation of strain lines (stretcher strains) when drawing stainless-steel tubes. **1844** H. STEPHENS *Book of Farm* I. 668 The beam and handles are further connected by *stretcher-tubes and bolts.

stretcher ('strɛtʃə(r)), *v.* [f. the sb.] *trans.* To carry *off* or convey (an injured or sick person) on a stretcher.

1976 *Daily Mirror* 15 Mar. 30/6 The sickening blow of seeing Gary Locke stretchered off in only the seventh minute. **1978** J. UPDIKE *Coup* (1979) i. 7 The beer-crazed mob of American boobs cheers..the crunched leg of the unhome-team left tackle as he is stretchered off the field. **1980** K. ROYCE *Third Arm* v. 52 He did not himself feel shock until after Adams had been stretchered from the car. **1982** *Times* 11 June 6/4 Casualties..were stretchered to a field hospital.

'stretchiness. [f. STRETCHY *a.* + -NESS.] The quality of being stretchy; elasticity.

1963 *Economist* 7 Sept. 840/2 A slight stretchiness can be woven into two directions. **1976** A. FARRER *Interpretation & Belief* 208 In this way I stretch my terms and I do not know how much they ought to be stretched. At this point the stretchiness of terms in my descriptions to myself of my own experience comes into play.

stretching ('strɛtʃɪŋ), *vbl. sb.* [f. STRETCH *v.* + -ING[1].] **a.** The action or an act of the verb. Also with advs., *forth, out.*

c **1375** WYCLIF *Serm.* Sel. Wks. I. 127 A þousand ȝeer ben to him as ȝisterday; and, shortly, al þing þat was or ever shal be hereafter is present unto him, ffor streeching of his longe beying. **1398** TREVISA *Barth. De P.R.* v. xxiii. (1495) 131 By stretchynge of the Iowes the frogge makyth his noyse. *c* **1449** PECOCK *Repr.* IV. iii. 431 Not so that the thing or gouernaunce wirchith or makith bi his kinde eny strecching into the yuel, but that [etc.]. **1560** BIBLE (Genev.) *Isa.* viii. 8 And the stretching out of his wings shall fil the breadth of thy lande. *a* **1586** SIDNEY *Arcadia* IV. (1598) 399 With a painfull stretching, and forced yawning. **1609** HOLLAND *Amm. Marcell.* XXIX. iv. 357 After they had been maimed and lamed before with stretching upon the racke. **1835** HEBERT *Engin. & Mech. Encycl.* I. 407 Previously to the rovings receiving their last reduction on the spinning frame, they undergo a process called stretching. **1838** DICKENS *Nich. Nick.* xxii, The Masters Crummles..evinced, by various half-suppressed yawns and stretchings of their limbs, an obvious inclination to retire for the night. **1855** DUNGLISON *Med. Lex.* s.v. *Pandiculation*, In the state of health, stretching occurs before and after sleep; especially when we are fatigued. **1897** C. T. DAVIS *Manuf. Leather* xxvi. (ed. 2) 409 The above process..acts as a preservative and stops all further stretching, one of the disadvantages of new belts.

†**b.** ***stretching out***: extent. *Obs.*$^{-0}$

1530 PALSGR. 277/1 Stretchyng out of a thyng, *estendue*.

c. *attrib.* and *Comb.*, as ***stretching-force, -frame, -machine, -pulley, -roller, -string***; **stretching-board**, (*a*) a board used to lie upon in callisthenic exercises; (*b*) a flat board upon which a corpse is laid out before being placed in a coffin; (*c*) *Leather-manuf.* = *stretch-bench* s.v. STRETCH *v.* 24; **stretching-bond**, a bond (see BOND *sb.*[1] 13 *a*) in which stretchers only (and not headers) are used; **stretching-carriage**, a tenter in the form of a carriage; **stretching-course**, a course of bricks or stones laid with their length in the direction of the wall; **stretching-iron** = STRETCHER *sb.* 4 c; **stretching-mule** = STRETCHER-*mule*; **stretching-room**, space in which to stretch (the limbs); †**stretching-sticks**, a glove-stretcher; **stretching-stone** *Building*, a stone set in the position of a stretcher; †**stretching-torture**, torture upon the rack.

1825 JAMIESON, *Streiking-Burd*, **Stretching-Burd*. **1843** THACKERAY *Ravenswing* iv, Who knows but at that moment Lady Bell was at work with a pair of her dumb namesakes, and Lady Sophy lying flat on a stretching-board? **1847** H. MILLER *First Impr.* xiii. (1857) 221 He had become as true a corpse as the one whose stretching-board he had usurped. **1976** T. WALKER *Spatsizi* v. 47 He taught me how to skin, showing me how to turn the hides fur side out before they were quite dry and then pull them back on the stretching board. **1805** in *Civil Engin. & Arch. Jrnl.* (1838) I. 330/1 *Stretching bond is where the longitudinal direction of the bricks is parallel with the face of the wall. **1876** in *Textile Colourist* III. 207 The series of tenters or *stretching carriages may..be so arranged that the fabric is stretched..by any given number of the tenters. **1693** MOXON *Mech. Exerc.* (1703) 261, I would advise in the *Stretching courses, wherein you lay stretching on both sides the Wall next the Line, so also to lay stretching in the middle of the Wall. **1783** *Phil. Trans.* LXXIV. 14 The steening [of the well].. consisted of two stretching courses of bricks. **1973** L. RUSSELL *Everyday Life Colonial Canada* v. 60 Each layer of bricks was called a course; the parallel arrangement was a stretching course and the transverse a heading course. **1900** *Jrnl. Soc. Dyers* XVI. 11 Such a *stretching force as has been hitherto customary. **1825** J. NICHOLSON *Oper. Mech.* 383 Although this is called the *stretching-frame, the yarn is not stretched, but merely undergoes a further process of drawing and spinning. **1896** *Peterson Mag.* (Philad.) N.S. VI. 242/2 The stretching frame [for the canvas of a picture], 9 ft. by 14 ft. **1839** URE *Dict. Arts* 377 The *stretching iron, is a flat plate of iron or copper, fully a fourth of an inch thick at top, and thinning off at bottom in a blunt edge. **1851–54**

Tomlinson's Cycl. Useful Arts (1867) II. 37/2 The stretching or softening iron..is an upright plate..mounted upon an upright beam. **1839** URE *Dict. Arts* 1190 **Stretching machine.* Cotton goods and other textile fabrics,..are prepared for the market by being stretched in a proper machine, which lays all their warp and woof yarns in parallel positions. **1835** —— *Philos. Manuf.* 40 The fine bobbin and fly-roving frame..can do a certain part of the work formerly done by the *stretching mule. **1805** R. W. DICKSON *Pract. Agric.* I. Plate xiv, This..machine..is set a-going, or stopped, at pleasure, by a *stretching pulley. **1835** URE *Philos. Manuf.* 196 The tension or *stretching-roller has its axle mounted in the segment-racks. **1895** M. HEWLETT *Earthwork out of Tuscany* 10 Twenty-four legs, and urgent need of *stretching-room [in the railway-carriage] as the night wore on. **1688** HOLME *Armoury* III. 360/2 In the Sinister side, are the Glovers *stretching Sticks in Salter. **1833** LOUDON *Encycl. Archit.* §981, *a* is the..heading stone; and *b*, the..*stretching stone. **1585** HIGINS *Junius' Nomencl.* 195/2 *Fidiculæ*,..the *stretching stringes or cords of the racke. **1599** NASHE *Lenten Stuff* 67 The strapado and the *stretching torture.

stretching (ˈstrɛtʃɪŋ), *ppl. a.* [f. STRETCH *v.* + -ING[2].] That stretches, in the senses of the verb. ***stretching gallop***, a gallop in which the legs of the horse are fully extended.

a **1547** SURREY *Æneid* IV. 258 (1557) Eij, An hundred hugie great temples he built, In his farre stretching realmes, to Jupiter. **1594** CHAPMAN *Shadow of Nt.* Ej b, And in the stretching circle of her eye All things are compast. **1697** DRYDEN *Æneis* x. 297 A hundred sweep, With stretching Oars at once the glassy deep. **1794** MRS. RADCLIFFE *Myst. Udolpho* xliii, Stretching plains, And peopled towns. **1815** *Sporting Mag.* XLVI. 116 Bring [the horse] by degrees to take regular stretching gallops. **1872** *Routledge's Every Boy's Ann.* 2/2 To have a stretching canter on a good horse. **1887** *Pall Mall Gaz.* 17 Jan. 2/2 It depends upon the nature of the country, whether it is dense forest or stretching park land. **1897** MARY KINGSLEY *W. Africa* 653 You..want..a conscience made of stretching leather to deal with the Kruboy in the African climate, and live.

b. stretching beam, a tie-beam or brace used in building.

1776 G. SEMPLE *Building in Water* 70 Be careful, that your stretching Beams lie firm and solid upon all your Caps. **1838** *Civil Engin. & Arch. Jrnl.* I. 178/2 Stretching beams or braces are framed across to each of the ribs.

stretchless (ˈstrɛtʃlɪs), *a.* [f. STRETCH *sb.* or *v.* + -LESS.] Incapable of being stretched.

Used in the leather belting trade to designate belting from which the 'stretch' has been taken out (see STRETCH *sb.* 1 h).

† **ˈstretchling.** *nonce-wd.* [f. STRETCH *sb.* or *v.* + -LING[1].] A minute quantity of space.

1674 N. FAIRFAX *Bulk & Selv.* 110 [An atome] not being a stretchling or *quid quantum*, any more than a now is an onwardling or *quid successivum.*

ˈstretch-out. Chiefly *N. Amer.* Also unhyphened. [f. STRETCH *v.* + OUT *adv.*]

1. A practice of requiring workers, esp. in textile industries, to do extra work or operate extra machines for little or no additional pay.

1933 *Sun* (Baltimore) 30 June 12/1 The 'stretch-out' is a scheme for getting more work done in the textile mills with less labor. **1933** E. CALDWELL *God's Little Acre* v. 84 The mill can't get us back unless they shorten the hours, or cut out the stretchout, or go back to the old pay. **1934** *Sun* (Baltimore) 17 Aug. 1/3 Wage increases, shorter hours, differentials in the higher wage brackets, and an end to the 'stretch-out' are objectives to be sought in the strike. **1943** *Ibid.* 14 June 10/7 A managerial stretch-out which prostrates war workers is intolerable.

2. A practice of slackening production schedules as an economy, so that a set quantity will be produced over a longer period; a postponement of the date of fulfilment of orders or contracts, etc.

1946 [see sense 3 below]. **1952** *N.Y. Times* 16 Aug. (Late city ed.) 14/1 The North Atlantic defense program, already handicapped by a 'stretch-out'. **1959** *Wall St. Jrnl.* 14 Jan. (Eastern ed.) 2/4 The stretchout is understood to apply to the date at which the two aircraft were to go into flight and become 'operational'. **1960** *Times* 21 Nov. (Canada Suppl.) p. xiii/3 Stretch-out of deliveries has been broadly accepted by the industry. **1969** *Look* 29 Apr. 57/3 Support on the part of so many in the diocese made this patient waiting over weeks of time much easier. But the long stretch-out freed us. **1979** *Aviation Week & Space Technol.* 13 Aug. 9 Neither the abandonment of the B-1 by the current Administration nor its stretchout of the MX missile..speeded up SALT.

3. *attrib.*

1934 *Sun* (Baltimore) 1 Sept. 2/4 It has failed to do anything about solving the 'stretch-out' problem. **1946** *Ibid.* 10 May 15/3 A 'stretch-out' plan, under which those employed will work less hours weekly, will be adopted soon. **1960** *Times* 21 Nov. (Canada Suppl.) p. xiii/2 The viability of a satisfactory stretch-out arrangement depends on the transfer of contracts from the weaker to the stronger mining operations. **1967** *Canad. Ann. Rev. 1966* 75 The Prime Minister announced a major increase in the amounts allocated to vocational and technical training in the stretch-out period.

ˈstretchy, *a. colloq.* [f. STRETCH *v.* + -Y.]

1. Having the quality of stretching; elastic.

1854 *Poultry Chron.* I. 503 The marvellous stretchy tightness of their feathers. **1902** ELIZ. L. BANKS *Newspaper Girl* 164 Would that we had some of the same stretchy kind [of rules] in America!

b. Liable to stretch unduly.

1885 *Harper's Mag.* Jan. 282/2 A workman with a true eye can often counteract 'stretchy stock,' and cover up the deficiencies of the stitcher so that the upper [of the boot] will be a 'snug fit'.

2. Inclined to stretch oneself or one's limbs.

1872 'MARK TWAIN' *Roughing It* xxvii. (1882) 151 In the night the pup would get stretchy and brace his feet against the old man's back.

strete, aphetic f. ESTREAT; obs. f. STREET.

‖ **stretta** (ˈstrɛtta). *Mus.* [It., fem. of *stretto* adj.: see next.] = STRETTO b.

1876 STAINER & BARRETT *Dict. Mus.* s.v., The conclusion of the chorus in Haydn's *Creation*, 'The heavens are telling,' is a *stretta.*

‖ **stretto** (ˈstrɛtto), *adv.* and *sb. Mus.* Pl. stretti (ˈstrɛtti), also **strettos.** [It. = narrow: see STRAIT *a.*] **A.** *adv.* A direction to perform a passage, esp. a final passage, in quicker time.

1740 J. GRASSINEAU *Mus. Dict.* 240 *Stretto*, shortened, is often used to signify that the measure is to be short and concise, therefore quick. **1753** *Chambers' Cycl.* Suppl., *Stretto*, in the Italian music, is sometimes used to signify that the measure is to be short and concise, and consequently quick. In this sense it stands opposed to *largo.* **1801** BUSBY *Dict. Mus.* **1883** GROVE *Dict. Mus.* III. 739/2.

B. *sb.* **a.** (See quot. 1869.) Also *transf.*

1854 *Cherubini's Counterpoint* 65 The stretto is..one of the essential requisites of a fugue. **1869** OUSELEY *Counterpoint* xxi. 166 In a fugue the stretto is an artifice by which the subject and answer are, as it were, bound closer together, by being made to overlap. **1898** G. B. SHAW *Perf. Wagnerite* 3 In classical music..there are fugues, with counter-subjects, strettos, and pedal points. **1962–3** *Sight & Sound* Winter 19/1 Finally, there are the flashbacks and then the stretto of flashbacks, as if, at the end, Colin Smith were still attempting to make up his mind. **1963** J. WIESENFARTH *H. James* v. 104 The *coda* begins in Chapter XII and ends with Chapter XIV in a *stretto.* **1979** *UCT Studies in English* (Univ. Cape Town) Sept. 38 Pope mimics the convention: *The Rape of the Lock* is threaded with premonitory phrases which he gathers into a *stretto* as the climax draws near.

attrib. **1887** BANISTER *Mus. Anal.* 133 Alternating such fragments, or bringing them together, *stretto* fashion.

b. ***stretto maestrale*** [cf. MAESTRALE] (see quot. 1946).

1876 STAINER & BARRETT *Dict. Mus. Terms* s.v. *Maestrale*, *Stretto maestrale*, a term sometimes applied to the stretto of a fugue when in canon. **1910** E. PROUT *Anal. J. S. Bach's Forty-Eight Fugues* 13 As the subject appears in a complete form in all the groups of the entries now under notice,..we have here an example of a stretto maestrale. **1946** E. BLOM *Everyman's Dict. Mus.* 672/1 *Stretto maestrale*,..a S[tretto] in which the fugal subject not only appears in close, overlapping entries, but is carried through from beginning to end at each entry. **1948** G. OLDROYD *Technique & Spirit of Fugue* ix. 143 It is a specimen of '*stretto maestrale*' in which a phrase in its full length is repeated in canon throughout all the strands. **1959** J. V. COCKSHOOT *Fugue in Beethoven's Piano Mus.* v. 68 This four-fold entry foreshadows the final section, with an effect of *stretto maestrale.*

streu, obs. form of STRAW.

streught, streum: see STRAIGHT, STREAM.

streusel (ˈstrɔɪzəl, ˈstruːzəl, ‖ˈʃtrɔʏzəl). Chiefly *U.S.* [Ger., f. *streuen* to sprinkle.] A crumb-like topping for cakes and pastries made from fat, flour, cinnamon, and sugar; a confection with such a topping. Freq. *attrib.*, esp. as ***streusel cake, kuchen.***

1909 L. MEIER *Art of German Cooking & Baking* xvii. 335/2 (*heading*) Streusel Coffee Cake. Preparation of the Streusel. **1910** M. MALZBENDER *Pract. Man. for Confectioners, Pastrycooks & Bakers* (rev. ed.) iii. 66/2 Streusel Kuchen. Proceed same as No. 6 only put streusel on top before baking. **1952** L. J. MITCHELL *Lüchow's German Cookbk.* xi. 183 (*heading*) Apple crumb cake (Apfel Streuselkuchen). *Ibid.*, For the Streusel, coarsely mix ⅝ cup butter, the flour, sugar and cinnamon with a pastry blender. **1957** M. E. SHOWALTER *Mennonite Community Cookbk.* i. 27 (*heading*) 'Streusel Kuchen' *Raised Coffee Cake*... Let rise 1½ hours. Sprinkle with streusel crumbs. **1960** 'A. KNOX' *Cooking Austrian Way* (rev. ed.) 202 (*heading*) Streusel Cake *Streuselkuchen*... This is a cake with a yeast dough and a streusel mixture on top. **1966** W. S. RAMSON *Austral. Eng.* viii. 161 Some unrecorded borrowings from German may be in local use in parts of South Australia. Price noted ..*streuselkuchen*, 'cake', [etc.]. **1976** *Woman's Day* (U.S.) Nov. 104, no. 14 Mashed Potatoes/Peach Streusel/Gingerbread. **1977** C. MCFADDEN *Serial* (1978) xx. 46/1 Sam wanted to buy a Sara Lee streusel cake.

streuth, var. 'STREWTH.

streven, -in, -yn: see STRIVE *v.*

strew (struː), *sb. rare.* [f. STREW *v.*] A number of things strewed over a surface or scattered about.

1578 BANISTER *Hist. Man* I. 28b, Brachiale..is to be vnderstanded the whole strewe, and packe of bones [L. *totam eam ossium struem intelligi*], intersited betwene the cubit, and Postbrachiale. **1657** BP. H. KING *Exequy* Poems (1843) 34 And for sweet flowres to crown thy hearse, Receive a strew of weeping verse. **1891** W. WHITMAN *Autobiog.* (1892) 204 There being quite a strew of printer's proofs and slips, and the daily papers. **1907** 'BARBARA BURKE' *Barbara goes to Oxford* 255, I have been sitting in a perfect strew of books and pamphlets and pictures.

strew (struː), *v.* Also (now *arch.* and *dial.*) **strow** (strəʊ). Pa. t. and pa. pple. **strewed, strowed;** pa. pple. also **strewn, strown.** Forms: α. 1 **strewian, streowian, streawian,** 3–7 **strewe,** 6–7 **strue,** 7 **streaw,** 6– **strew.** β. 4 **strouwe,** 4–7 **strowe,** 5 **strowhe,** 6 **stroe,** *pa. t.* **strouit,** 6– **strow.** γ. 6 **stroye,** 7 **stroy.** See also STRAW *v.*[1] [Com. Teut. weak verb: OE. *stręwian, streowian, streawian*, corresponds (exc. for differences of conjugation) to OFris. *strewa*, OS. pa. t. pl. *strôidun, streidun* (MLG. *strôien, streien*), MDu. *strôien* (mod.Du. *strooien*), OHG. *strouwen, strewen* (MHG. *ströuwen*, mod.G. *streuen*), ON. *strá* (but MSw. *ströa*, Sw. *strö*, Da. *strø*, are from MLG.), Goth. (**straujan*) pa. t. *strawida*, f. OTeut. root **strau-*; the ulterior relations are uncertain, but most scholars assume some kind of connexion with the Indogermanic root **ster-* (extended **strā-*) in L. *sternĕre*, pa. pple. *strātus*: see STRATUM.

The OE. forms representing the orig. Teut. conjugation are: **striegan*, etc. (see STRAY *v.*[1]) = Goth. *straujan*, and pa. t. *strędwe* = Goth. *strawida*. The original pres.-stem. in OE. (as in some other Teut. langs) was superseded by a new-formation after the pa. t. Owing to the influence of the following *w*, the umlaut -*ę* became diphthongized, producing the forms *streow-, streaw-*. The OE. forms with *ę* or falling diphthong are represented by the α forms above, while *streow-* pronounced with a rising diphthong gave rise to the β forms. According to modern usage, the two spellings correspond to the two pronunciations; formerly, the spelling *strew* was often used where the rime was a word like *so*, and conversely *strow* riming with *new* etc.

The rare γ forms *stroy(e* are app. borrowed from or influenced by Du. *strooien.*

The pa. pple. is now most commonly *strewn* or *strown* in passive tenses, esp. where there is no distinct reference to an agent; and *strewed, strowed* in active tenses.]

1. *trans.* To scatter, spread loosely; to scatter (rushes, straw, flowers, etc.) on the ground or floor, or over the surface of something; to sprinkle (something granulated or in powder) over a surface.

α. **971** *Blickling Hom.* 71 Sume naman þa twiȝu of þæm treowum, & streowodan on þone weȝ. *a* **1300** *E.E. Psalter* Ps. cxlvii. 16 Cloude als aske spredes [*MS. E.* strewes] he. *c* **1320** *Sir Tristr.* 2195 Meriadok dede floure bring And strewed it bi tvene. **1382** WYCLIF *Matt.* xxi. 8 Ful muche cumpanye strewiden her clothis in the wey. *c* **1400** MAUNDEV. (Roxb.) xviii. 84 Þai take alde peper and stepez it and strewez apon it spume of siluer. **1592** KYD *J. Brewen* 105 Shee powred out a measse for him, and strewed secretly therein part of the poyson. **1601** SHAKS. *Twel. N.* II. iv. 61 Not a flower, not a flower sweete, On my blacke coffin let there be strewne [*rime* throwne]. **1608** SYLVESTER *Du Bartas* II. iv. IV. *Decay* 1153 One gobbet here, another there they streaw. **1656** J. SMITH *Pract. Physick* 128 The powder is strued into the Eye. **1675** HANNAH WOOLLEY *Gentlew. Comp.* 140 Strew some Nutmeg thereon. **1773** BOSWELL *Johnson* 19 Oct. (Tour Hebrides), Some good hay was strewed at one end of it [*sc.* the barn], to form a bed for us. **1826** *Art of Brewing* (ed. 2) 162 If a few cloves..be strewed over the liquid sulphur. **1841** DICKENS *Barn. Rudge* xxxix, The newspapers which were strewn upon the table. **1860** TYNDALL *Glac.* I. v. 38 The roof strewed itself in ruins upon the floor.

β. *c* **1385** CHAUCER *L.G.W.* 101 [= 207], I bad hem strowe [*v.r.* strewe] flouris on myn bed. **1402** *Pol. Poems* (Rolls) II. 110 The presciouse perlis ȝe strowun to hogges. **1530** PALSGR. 741/1, I strowe spyces apon meates, or floures apon a place..*je surseme.* **1551** TURNER *Herbal* I. 5 This herbe.. strowene in the bedde,..driueth serpentes awaye. **1584** COGAN *Haven Health* xc. 81 *marg.*, Damask powder..to stroe among clothes. **1634** SIR T. HERBERT *Trav.* 197 A small Altar..on which they strow flesh and flowres. **1697** DRYDEN *Virg. Georg.* IV. 428 Sweet Flow'rs are strow'd Beneath his Body. **1727** SWIFT *Desire & Possess.* 36 Possession kept the beaten Road; And gather'd all his Brother strow'd. **1815** BYRON *Destr. Sennacherib* ii, Like the leaves of the forest when Autumn hath blown, That host on the morrow lay wither'd and strown. **1864** TENNYSON *En. Arden* 501 These be palms Whereof the happy people strowing cried 'Hosanna in the highest!' **1870** BRYANT *Iliad* II. 517 When they had prayed And strown the salted meal.

absol. **1535** COVERDALE *Matt.* xxv. 24 Thou..gatherest where thou hast not strowed. [*Ibid.* 26 Where I strawed not.]

b. with *adv.*, as *on, in, about, †abroad, around.*

c **1440** *Promp. Parv.* 480/2 Strowyn a-brode, or scateryn, *spergo.* *c* **1440** *Pallad. on Husb.* XII. 589 Strowe on origan. **1560** DAUS tr. *Sleidane's Comm.* 461 b, *marg.*, Libelles strowed about in London. **1591** A. W. *Bk. Cookrye* 33 Then strew on sugar vpon it. **1697** DRYDEN *Virg. Past.* vii. 76 And lavish Nature laughs, and strows her Stores around. *a* **1756** ELIZA HAYWOOD *New Present* (1771) 47 Strew in a little salt and pepper. **1820** SCOTT *Monast.* viii, Looking at the leaves which lay strewed around. **1870** DICKENS *E. Drood* ii, Their fallen leaves lie strewn thickly about.

c. *transf.* and *fig.*

1382 WYCLIF *Isa.* xiv. 11 Vnder thee strouwed shal be a moȝte [Vulg. *subter te sternetur tinea*]. **1535** COVERDALE *Ezek.* xx. 23 That I wolde scatre them amonge the Heithen, and strowe them amonge the nacions. **1602** CHETTLE *Hoffman* III. (1631) E 1, The cleare moone strowes siluer in our path. **1603** SHAKS. *Meas. for M.* I. iii. 15 For so I haue strewd it in the common eare, And so it is receiu'd. **1731–8** SWIFT *Pol. Conversat.* Introd. 23 Excepting a small Number [of cant words] strewed here and there in the Comedies of that Age. **1750** GRAY *Elegy* 83 And many a holy text around she strews. **1823** B'NESS BUNSEN in Hare *Life* I. vi. 210 The torches were so thinly strewed, that..the procession seemed to be groping its way in the dark. **1837–42** TENNYSON *St. Agnes' Eve* 28 All heaven bursts her starry floors, And strows her lights below. **1848** T. RICKMAN *Styles Archit. Eng.* 212 The Tudor flower..profusely strewed over the roofs, &c. of rich late buildings.

†**d.** To spread out to view, display. *poet. Obs.*

1579 SPENSER *Sheph. Cal.* July 75 Of Synah can I tell thee more,..But little needes to strow my store, Suffice this hill of our.

2. To cover (the ground, a floor, any surface) with something loosely scattered or sprinkled.

13.. *K. Alis.* 1026 (Laud MS.) Of Olyue, & of muge floures Weren ystrewed halle & boures. **1375** BARBOUR *Bruce* XIV. 304 Of wapnys, armyng, and ded men The feld wes haly strewit then. **1382** WYCLIF *Mark* xiv. 15 He schal shewe to ȝou a greet souping place strewid [Vulg. *cenaculum grande stratum*]. **1480** in *Berks, Bucks & Oxon Archæol. Jrnl.* (1913) Oct. 84 For strewyng the church for ii yeres.., iij s iiii d. **1594** CHAPMAN *Shadow of Nt.* B iij, My funerall bed, Strewed with the bones and relickes of the dead. **1667** MILTON *P.L.* XI. 439 The Inwards and thir Fat, with Incense strew'd. *c* **1770** MRS. GLASSE *Compl. Confectioner* 11 Strew it with fine powder sugar. **1788** COWPER *Negro's Compl.* 34 Wild tornadoes, Strewing yonder sea with wrecks. **1852** MRS. STOWE *Uncle Tom's C.* xxxii, The floor was already strewn with weary sleepers. **1885** MISS BRADDON *Wyllard's Weird* I. i. 13 He had strewed the carriage with newspapers and magazines.

β. **13..** *Coer de L.* 3735 Ladyes strowe here boures With rede roses, and lylye flowres. **1375** BARBOUR *Bruce* XVI. 633 All the feldis strowit war Of Ingliss men that slayn wes thar. **1426** LYDG. *De Guil. Pilgr.* 14673 Placys ful off old ordure I kan strowhe with Rosshys grene, That ther ys no ffelthe sene. *c* **1450** *Merlin* xviii. 294 All the feilde was strowed full of deed men and horse. **1530** PALSGR. 741/1 Strowe al your chamber with carpettes agaynst the kyng come. **1667** MILTON *P.L.* VI. 389 All the ground With shiverd armour strow'n. **1697** DRYDEN *Æneis* VI. 1225 Let me with Fun'ral Flowers his Body strow. **1711** ADDISON *Spect.* No. 44 ¶5 It is indeed very odd, to see our Stage strowed with Carcases in the last Scene of a Tragedy. **1855** MACAULAY *Hist. Eng.* xi. III. 62 The mightiest enemy that had threatened our island since the Hebrides were strown with the wrecks of the Armada. **1859** TENNYSON *Enid* 874 The marble threshold.. strown With gold and scatter'd coinage.

γ. **1647** HEXHAM I. s.v. *Rush*, To stroy with rushes, *met biesen bestroyen*.

b. with *over*.

1540 PALSGR. *Acolastus* II. iii. L j, The soppe made of breade..strowyd ouer wyth harde chese and pepper. **1604** MARSTON *Malcont.* II. iv. D 1 b, Indian Eringos, strow'd ouer with the powder of Pearle of America. **1611** SHAKS. *Wint. T.* IV. iv. 129 O, these I lacke, To make you Garlands of, and my sweet friend, To strew him o're and ore. **1627** HAKEWILL *Apol.* (1630) 390 The very floore was strowed over with saffron. **1640** T. BRUGIS *Marrow of Physicke* II. 153 Strewe it over with powdered Sugar. **1844** H. H. WILSON *Brit. India* II. 28 In the course of three days the place was strewn over with the killed.

c. *transf.* and *fig.*

1390 GOWER *Conf.* II. 103 The chambre is strowed up and doun With swevenes many thousendfold. **1671** MILTON *P.R.* IV. 334 All our Law and Story strew'd With Hymns. **1714** MACKY *Journ. Eng.* (1724) I. 52 Between those Towns and Newberry the Country is finely strow'd with Gentlemen's Seats. **18..** R. JEBB *Law* in *Encycl. Metrop.* (1845) II. 703/1 His path, at every turn, has been strewed with multi-form difficulties. **1879** A. R. WALLACE *Australasia* xi. 219 The coast is thickly strewn with islands.

†**d.** *to strew out*: ? to intersperse *with*. *Obs.*

1626 B. JONSON *Staple of N.* III. ii, I was bespeaking but a parcell of newes, To strewe out the long meale withall. *a* **1637** —— *Underwoods* lxv, I have no portion in them, nor their deale Of newes they get, to strew out the long meale.

3. To be spread or scattered upon (a surface).

α. **1596** SPENSER *Prothal.* 40 The snow which doth the top of Pindus strew, Did neuer whiter shew. *a* **1618** SYLVESTER *Hymn of Alms* 518 The fresh and fruitfull Deaw, Which every morning Flora's Buds doth streaw. **1697** DRYDEN *Æneis* IX. 906 Heaps of spent Arrows fall; and strew the Ground. **1792** S. ROGERS *Pleas. Mem.* I. 17 The mouldering gateway strews the grass-grown court. **1816** BYRON *Siege Corinth* xiii, Where thousand sleepers strew'd the strand. **1850** HANNAY *Singleton Fontenoy* III. vii, The latest magazines and novels..strewed the table. **1893** D. J. RANKIN *Zambesi Basin* viii. 135 The boulders that strewed the mountain-side.

β. **1513** DOUGLAS *Æneis* VIII. xii. 110 Befor the altaris.. The brytnit beistis strowit all the ground. **1587** MARLOWE *1 Tamb.* III. iii. 1313 Their bodies strowe the field. **1667** MILTON *P.L.* I. 302 Thick as Autumnal Leaves that strow the Brooks In Vallombrosa. **1733** POPE *Ess. Man* III. 37 Is thine alone the seed that strows the plain? **1786** BURNS *Raving Winds* 2 Yellow leaves the woodlands strowing. **1880** W. WATSON *Prince's Quest* (1892) 104 The light o' the stars that strow the Milky-way.

†**b.** Of an individual: To lie dead upon (the ground). *poet. Obs.*

c **1611** CHAPMAN *Iliad* XIII. 742 Thou, (If thou dar'st stand this lance) the earth before the ships shalt strow.

4. a. To spread (a cloth or the like) as a covering. **b.** To cover (a bed) *with* a coverlet. **c.** To make or lay (a bed). *rare.*

1615 CHAPMAN *Odyss.* XIV. 69 Of Osiers [he] spred A thickned hurdle; on whose top, he strow'd A wilde Goats shaggy skin. **1698** FRYER *Acc. E. India & P.* 18 A Cott or Bed strewed with a Quilt. **1810** SCOTT *Lady of L.* I. xxxi, Hands unseen thy Couch are strewing.

5. To level with the ground, lay low, throw down, prostrate. Also with *down*. Chiefly *poet.*

c **1460** *Towneley Myst.* vii. 194 Shall nothyng here in erth be kend, Bot it shall be strewyd and brend, All waters and the see. **1513** DOUGLAS *Æneis* XII. vi. 47 Down strowand eik vnder fut in the plane Diuers otheris ȝit thrawand and half slane. **1621** BRATHWAIT *Time's Curtain drawn* B 1, Yet would that God of hosts, thy power confound, And strow thy slaughterd corps vpon the ground. *a* **1639** SIR H. WOTTON *Parall. Essex & Buckhm.* (1641) 12 About sixescore of their two hundred horse [were] strewed upon the Sand. **1663** BUTLER *Hud.* I. ii. 917 He spying Hudibras lye strow'd Upon the ground, like log of Wood. **1785** BURNS *To Mouse* iv, Thy wee-bit housie, too, in ruin! It's silly wa's the win's are strewin! **1847** TENNYSON *Princess* VI. 26 They mark'd it with the red cross to the fall, And would have strown it, and are fall'n themselves.

†**b.** *refl.* To spread out one's limbs. *poet. Obs.*

1610 G. FLETCHER *Christ's Vict.* II. ii, Soone did the Ladie to her Graces crie, And on their wings her selfe did nimbly strowe.

6. To level, calm (stormy waves); to allay (a storm). *poet.* Cf. L. *sternere aequor*.

1594 LODGE & GREENE *Looking-Gl. Lond.* (1598) A 4, Neptune on the Seas, Whose frowne stroyes [*Dyce* strows] all the Ocean with a calme. **1875** TENNYSON *Q. Mary* I. v, God lay the waves and strow the storms at sea..! **1884** —— *Freedom* ix, How long thine ever-growing mind Hath still'd the blast and strown the wave.

Hence **strewed, strewn** *ppl. adjs.*

Chiefly in comb. as *health-strewed, leaf-strewn*.

1603 E. FAIRFAX *Eclogue* IV. 1 in Mrs. Cooper *Muses Libr.* (1737) I. 364 The rough and Heath-strewed Wilderness. **1697** DRYDEN *Æneis* XI. 98 The Body on this rural Hearse is born, Strewd Leaves and Funeral Greens the Bier adorn. **1730–46** THOMSON *Autumn* 955 These now the lonesome Muse, Low-whispering, lead into their leaf-strown walks. **1837** CARLYLE *Fr. Rev.* I. III. v, Monsieur..is met with vivats and strewed flowers. **1847** DISRAELI *Tancred* IV. iv, The twilight descended over the rocky city,..and its strewn remains of palaces and theatres. **1890** 'R. BOLDREWOOD' *Miner's Right* xliv, Endless flower-strewn plains.

strewage ('struːɪdʒ). [f. STREW *v.* + -AGE.] = STREWING *vbl. sb.* b.

1902 J. H. SKEINE *Pastor Agnorum* 266 The waking of that Syrian refugee..after his sleep among the great strewage of rocks on a down of Canaan. **1929** R. BRIDGES *Test. Beauty* III. 894 Vestiges of his stony asceticism imbue all time, thick as the strewage of his flinty tools, disseminate wheresoe'er he hath dwelt. **1940** C. F. C. HAWKES *Prehist. Found. Europe* ii. 13 The basement-beds below it, formed of the strewage of older land-surfaces.

strewbery, obs. form of STRAWBERRY.

strewer ('struːə(r)). Also **strower** ('strəʊə(r)). [f. STREW *v.* + -ER[1].] One who strews.

a **1593** *Exam. H. Barrowe* B iij, He said, I was a strower of errors. **1710** J. CHAMBERLAYNE *St. Gt. Brit.* (ed. 33) 545/2 Strewer of Herbs. **1716** LADY G. BAILLIE *Househ. Bk.* (S.T.S.) 48 For Apoticars man, strewer 5 waterman 1s. shoemakers 2s., 0 8 0. **1820** W. TAYLOR in *Monthly Rev.* XCIII. 532 When the strowers of grain had repeated their office, the birds again burst screaming on the flood.

strewine, obs. Sc. pa. pple. of STRIVE *v.*

strewing ('struːɪŋ), *vbl. sb.* Also (now *arch.*) **strowing** ('strəʊɪŋ). [f. STREW *v.* + -ING[1].] The action of the verb STREW.

c **1440** *Promp. Parv.* 480/2 Strowynge, or dede of strowynge, *sternicio*. **1692** BENTLEY *Boyle Lect.* v. 28 Whatsoever should result from the strowing of those loose Letters. **1865** G. MACDONALD *A. Forbes* 15 The strewing of the caltrops on the field of Bannockburn.

b. *concr.* Something strewed; a layer or bed of strewed material; esp. *pl.* flowers, leaves, etc., scattered on a grave. Now *rare* or *Obs.*

c **1000** *Lamb. Psalter* cxxxi. 3 ȝif ic astiȝe on bedde aþeninge minre *vel* strewunge [*in lectum strati mei*]. **1388** WYCLIF *Gen.* xxxi. 34 Sche..hidde the idols vndur the strewyngis of the camel [Vulg. *subter stramenta cameli*]. *c* **1440** *Promp. Parv.* 480/2 Strowynge, or mater to strowe wythe, *stramentum*. **1578** H. WOTTON *Courtlie Controv.* 7 Throwing one at an another handfuls of roses,..wherof they made such lauishe expence, as the ground was almost couered with the strowing therof. **1611** SHAKS. *Cymb.* IV. ii. 285 The hearbes that haue on them cold dew o' th' night Are strewings fit'st for graues. **1648** HERRICK *Hesper.*, *To Perilla* 15 Let some weekly-strewings be Devoted to the memory of me. **1660** *Tales & Jests Mr. H. Peters* 12 The Parson seeing the Turf, was well pleased, supposing it was laid there onely as strowings to adorn his seat. **1726** LEONI *Alberti's Archit.* II. 114 b, Strew the bottom of your Cistern with good round Pebbles..: and the higher you make this strewing, your water will be the more limpid. **1728** E. SMITH *Compl. Housew.* (ed. 2) 173 Put a row of Flowers, and a strowing of Sugar, till the Pot is full. **1823** W. TAYLOR in *Monthly Mag.* LVI. 125 Be content to let another inherit thy strewings of palm-leaves.

c. *attrib.*, as *strewing-herb*.

1571 in Feuillerat *Revels Q. Eliz.* (1908) 140 Bayes & strewing erbes. **1573–80** TUSSER *Husb.* (1878) 95 Strowing herbes of all sortes. **1593** NASHE *Christ's T.* 26 Happy is that Sister, that (for strewing-hearbes) may scatter her discheueld Mayden-hayre, on her dead Brothers trunck. **1877** *Encycl. Brit.* VI. 82 The coarsest variety [of ground smalts], known as strewing blue.

†**'strewingly**, *adv. Obs. rare*[−1]. [f. *strewing* pr. pple. of STREW *v.* + -LY[2].] Dispersedly.

1578 BANISTER *Hist. Man* VII. 92 b, The flesh of Muscles ..is for the most part one kynde [of fibre], and those more strewyngly set.

strewment ('struːmənt). *rare.* [f. STREW *v.* + -MENT.] Something strewed or for strewing; *pl.* flowers, etc. strewed on a grave.

1602 SHAKS. *Ham.* V. i. 256 Yet heere she is allowed her Virgin Rites, Her Maiden strewments, and the bringing home Of Bell and Buriall. **1834** J. WILSON in *Blackw. Mag.* XXXVI. 409 You all know..Raleigh..who spread his fine purple cloak on the mire... But here is a sweeter strewment. **1857** *Chamb. Jrnl.* VII. 368 Oh, minster gray!.. I come to thee with strewments.

strewn, *ppl. a.*: see after STREW *v.*

strewn field. *Geol.* Also **strewnfield.** [f. STREWN *ppl. a.* + FIELD *sb.*] A part of the earth's surface over which tektites of a similar age are found.

1937 *Proc. R. Soc. Victoria* XLIX. 167 There are no records of the discovery of australites in towns within the australite 'strewn field'. **1961** *Sci. Amer.* Nov. 63 (*caption*) Estimates of ages of tektites in strewn fields are based on ages of rocks with which they are found. **1973** *Nature* 16 Feb. 431/1 Tektites..are apparently limited to four large areas (strewnfields) and four corresponding ages.

'strewth. *vulgar.* Also **streuth, strewth, 'strooth, 'struth, struth.** Short for *God's truth*, used as an oath. See 'S.

1892 KIPLING *Barrack-room Ballads* 20 Mad drunk and resisting the Guard—'Strewth, but I socked it them hard! **1913** A. J. REES *Merry Marauders* ix. 149 'Strooth! he's looked up all our lines. **1915** [see KING-PIN 2]. **1925** [see GARN *int.*]. **1933** M. LOWRY *Ultramarine* ii. 75 Gawd strewth, you're some fellow, you are! **1938** P. LAWLOR *House of Templemore* xvii. 186, I have made a string bookshelf just like you had. Streuth! So you have. **1954** A. SETON *Katherine* xiv. 235 ''Struth,' said Edmund... 'High time I got me *some* wife.' **1975** P. G. WINSLOW *Death of Angel* iv. 86 Strewth, they've made a mess of this office. **1977** *Sunday Sun* (Brisbane) 30 Jan. 29/1 Struth! What next? says Sam.

strey: see STRAW *sb.*[1], STRAY *sb.*

streyght(e: see STRAIGHT, STRAIT, STRETCH *v.*

streyint, streynth(e: see STRENGTH.

streyk(e, obs. ff. STREAK *v.*[1], STREEK *v.*

streym(e, obs. forms of STREAM.

streyt(e: see STRAIGHT, STRAIT, STRETCH *v.*, STREET.

streyves (*pl.*): see STRAIF.

‖**stria** ('straɪə). Pl. **striæ** ('straɪiː). [L. *stria* a furrow, flute of a column. Cf. F. *strie*.]

1. *Arch.* A fillet between the flutes of columns, pilasters, and the like.

The accepted sense among architects, both French and English; but app. due to misunderstanding of Vitruvius, who uses the word for a flute of a column, or a facet of a column of polygonal section.

1563 SHUTE *Architect.* D j b, The fifth parte is for Striæ, which are also called Femora. **1664** EVELYN tr. *Freart's Parallel Archit.* etc. 130 The Striæ..are those plain spaces between the Flutings in the Ionic, Doric, Corinthian and Composed Orders. *Ibid.*, The Stria being commonly a third or fourth part of the widness of the Flutings, and diminishing with the Contraction of the Scapus, unless the Shaft be very high. **1771** W. NEWTON tr. *Vitruvius' Archit.* IV. iii. (1791) 78 The columns are to be wrought in twenty striæ, which, if made flat, form twenty angles, but, if they are hollowed, they are to be thus performed. **1836** PARKER *Gloss. Archit.* (1850) I. 449.

2. a. Chiefly in scientific use. A small groove, channel, or ridge; a narrow streak, stripe, or band of distinctive colour, structure, or texture; *esp.* one of two or of a series.

1673 RAY *Journ. Low C.* 341 Rayes or ribs of stone (answering to the ridges or *striæ* of a cochle-shell). **1681** GREW *Musæum* I. §5. iii. 113 The Scales..of the same Fish ..have a great many exceeding small *Striæ*. **1698** T. MOLYNEUX in *Phil. Trans.* XX. 220 Nor can there be observed Rays, Furroughs, *Striæ* or any manner of Lines running along its [Giant's Causeway stone] Superficies. **1728** WOODWARD *Nat. Hist. Fossils* I. I. 229 Three Crusts of an Hæmatites, adhering to each other, and cross'd with fine small *Striæ*. **1731** MILLER *Gard. Dict.* s.v. *Malva*, Each little Lodge appears most artificially jointed within the corresponding *Striæ* or Channels. **1783** M. CUTLER in *Life, Jrnls. & Corr.* (1888) II. 208 This vapor was of a bright color, without any tincture of red, and striated with very fine striæ. **1815** STEPHENS in *Shaw's Gen. Zool.* IX. I. 31 Neck on both sides with two striæ. **1823** W. PHILLIPS *Introd. Min.* (ed. 3) p. xcv, The slight channels occasionally observable on the planes of crystallized minerals are termed striæ. **1860** TYNDALL *Glac.* I. vii. 56 The dirt upon the surface of the ice was arranged in striæ. **1873** T. H. GREEN *Introd. Pathol.* (ed. 2) 55 In hearts less affected, striæ of fat will be seen lying amongst the muscle. **1875** BENNETT & DYER *Sachs' Bot.* 29 The one system, consisting of parallel striæ, is always cut by the other system, which also consists of parallel striæ.

b. *Path.* A linear hæmorrhagic macula.

1855 DUNGLISON *Med. Lex.*, *Vibices*,..*Striæ*,..large purple spots, like the marks produced by the strokes of a whip, which appear under the skin in certain malignant fevers.

c. *Glass-manuf.* An imperfection in the form of a streak or band.

1832 G. R. PORTER *Porcelain & Glass* 248 Striæ are undulating appearances, perfectly vitrified, and equally transparent with any other part of the glass; they..result from a want of congruity in the composition of the particles which make up the substance. **1867–77** G. F. CHAMBERS *Astron.* VII. viii. 723 Air-bubbles, sand-holes, striæ, scratches [in the lens] are no doubt undesirable.

d. *Electr.* Each of the alternate bright and dark bands observed in vacuum-tubes (Geissler tubes) upon the passage of an electrical discharge.

1859 *Phil. Trans. R. Soc.* CXLVIII. 3 The discharge did not exhibit the uniform white light of the Torricellian vacuum, but striæ in confused or irregular forms. **1881** SPOTTISWOODE in *Nature* 6 Oct. 549/2 When the pressure is considerably reduced, these blocks are replaced by the beautiful system of flakes or 'striæ' delineated. *Ibid.* 550/2 As the exhaustion proceeds the striæ become more and more separated... At first mere flakes of light, they gradually increase in thickness. **1883** [see STRIATED *ppl. a.* 1 e]. **1893** SLOANE *Electr. Dict.* 496 In Geissler tubes the light produced by the electric discharge is filled with striæ, bright bands alternating with dark spaces; these may be termed electric striæ.

e. *Med.* Also ***stria atrophica*** [mod.L. *atrophica* (see ATROPHIC *a.*)]. A stretch mark;

stria gravidarum [L., gen. pl. of *gravida* pregnant woman], one on a pregnant woman, usu. darker than the surrounding skin; ***stria albicans*** (pl. ***albicantes***) [L., pres. pple. of *albicāre* to make or be white], a former stria gravidarum that has become light-coloured following delivery.

1867 *Jrnl. Cutaneous Med.* I. 142 None of the early writers have alluded to any other cause of the striae atrophicae than over-distension. **1880** *Trans. Amer. Gynecol. Soc.* IV. 141 These cicatrices are usually described as red or white shining striæ, marking the skin..of pregnant and multiparous women. **1884** R. & F. BARNES *Syst. Obstetric Med. & Surg.* I. viii. 294 Striæ gravidarum. **1906** T. W. EDEN *Man. Midwifery* I. 51 *Striæ gravidarum* appear on the abdominal wall... They are pearly..when recent, but afterwards they become pale and silvery (*striæ albicantes*). **1968** D. C. BETHEA *Introd. Maternity Nursing* iii. 25 Thin, red streaks, called striae gravidarum, occur on the breasts of some pregnant women. **1970** C. LERCH *Maternity Nursing* v. 61/2 In subsequent pregnancies new striae appear in addition to the silvery white markings of the previous pregnancy.

striack, obs. form of STIRK.

striæform (ˈstraɪɪfɔːm), *a.* [f. *striæ* genit. sing. of STRIA + -FORM.] Having the form or structure of striæ.

1822 J. PARKINSON *Outl. Oryctol.* 223 Rays small, close, striæform, equal. **1840** *Penny Cycl.* XVII. 359/2 Shell.. marked with numerous very narrow, striæform..rays.

striatal: see STRIATUM.

striate (ˈstraɪeɪt), *a.* [ad. mod.L. *striāt-us*, f. L. *stria*: see STRIA and -ATE². Cf. F. *strié*.]

1. Marked or scored with striæ, showing narrow structural bands, striped, streaked, furrowed.

The earliest examples relate to the hypothesis of Descartes, as to the 'striate' or channelled condition of the constituent particles of matter.

1678 CUDWORTH *Intell. Syst.* 684 Though Cartesius would needs imagine this Earth of ours once to have been a Sun, and so it self the Centre of a lesser Vortex; whose Axis was then Directed after this manner, and which therefore still kept the same Site or Posture, by reason of the Striate Particles, finding no fit Pores or Traces for their passage thorough it, but only in this Direction. *a* **1706** EVELYN *Hist. Relig.* (1850) I. 15 Des Cartes..will have God contribute nothing more to the creation of the world, than the whirligig of innumerable vortices, globes, and striate particles. **1760** J. LEE *Introd. Bot.* I. xiv. (1765) 37 Striate, streaked. **1777** ROBSON *Brit. Flora* 263 *Equisetum fluviatile*... Stem striate. **1805** [S. WESTON] *Werneria* 26 This stone..is in texture foliate, And partly striate. **1822–29** GOOD *Study Med.* (ed. 3) I. 346 The long thread worm is..beneath, smooth; finely striate on the fore-part. **1870** HOOKER *Stud. Flora* 94 Trifolium hybridum... Standard twice as long as the calyx, striate. **1876** J. G. JEFFREYS in *Ann. & Mag. Nat. Hist.* Ser. IV. XVIII. 252 The rest of the lower valve is free and concentrically striate.

2. *Anat.* Epithet of the striatum (esp. in sense a) and the blood vessels supplying it.

1890 BILLINGS *Med. Dict.* 599/2 *Striate arteries*, small twigs from anterior and middle cerebral arteries that.. supply corpus striatum. **1902** D. J. CUNNINGHAM *Textbk. Anat.* 837 An inferior striate vein descends on each side from the substance of the corpus striatum. **1907** *Arch. Neurol.* III. 42 Homonymous visual defects are due to disease and destruction of the striate cortex. **1921** TILNEY & BASSETT *Form & Functions Central Nerv. Syst.* xliv. 805 In its process of evolution from the lower vertebrates to mammals, the primordial portion of the striate body corresponds to the globus pallidus. **1948** A. BRODAL *Neurol. Anat.* iv. 73 The striate body, the corpus striatum, consists of large grey nuclear masses..subdivided by fibre strands into different portions. **1968** PASSMORE & ROBSON *Compan. Med. Stud.* I. xxiv. 52/2 The striate area..contains extra fibres which widen the outer lines of Baillarger into a broad white band. *Ibid.* 72/1 The striate artery..supplies the medial part of the head of the caudate nucleus and putamen and the anterior part of the internal capsule. **1978** *Nature* 3 Aug. 423/1 Posteriorly, the striate cortex is so distinct and uniform that its borders are visible, in histological sections, even to the naked eye.

striate (ˈstraɪeɪt), *v.* [ad. mod.L. *striāt-*, ppl. stem of *striāre*, f. *stria*: see STRIA and -ATE³.] *trans.* To mark or score with striæ, to furrow, streak. Also *fig.*

1709 *Phil. Trans.* XXVI. 378 This melted Matter..fix'd in a Regulus-like, friable Mass, and appear'd some-times lightly striated, or shot into sharp Points like Needles. *a* **1776** J. ELLIS *Zoophytes* (1786) 3 Its body is striated lengthways with thousands of little glands. **1814** SOUTHEY *Roderick* XVI. 96 The rocky vale..Bare here, and striated with many a hue, Scored by the wintry rain. **1862** G. P. SCROPE *Volcanos* 409 Such sudden floods..striate and polish its hardest rocks. **1979** D. HOFFMANN in *Harvard Guide Contemp. Amer. Writing* xii. 579 Clarity and strength striate the poems of Charles Edward Eaton.

striated (ˈstraɪeɪtɪd), *ppl. a.* [f. prec. + -ED¹.]

1. a. In scientific use: Marked or characterized by striæ, furrowed, streaked; = STRIATE *a.* Also *fig.*

1646 SIR T. BROWNE *Pseud. Ep.* II. ii. 58 Whether these effluviums do flye by streated [*sic*; **1658** striated] Atomes and winding particles as Renatus des Cartes conceaveth; or [etc.]. **1705** PETIVER in *Phil. Trans.* XXV. 1954 This is a deep, thin,..finely striated Shell. **1753** *Chambers' Cycl.* Suppl. s.v. *Leaf, Striated Leaf*, one with a number of longitudinal furrows on its surface. **1871** DARWIN *Desc. Man* II. xvi. 184 Young cross-bills..in their immature striated plumage..resemble the mature redpole. **1923** H. CRANE *Let.* 2 Mar. (1965) 129 Striated with nuances, nervosities, that we are heir to.

b. In specific names of animals, birds, etc. Also ***striated ipecacuanha***: see IPECACUANHA 3.

1753 *Chambers' Cycl.* Suppl. s.v. *Trumpet-shell*, The striated buccinum, with oblong tubercles. **1771** PENNANT *Syn. Quadrupeds* 231 Striated Weesel. **1781** —— *Hist. Quadrupeds* I. 209 Striated Monkey. **1783** LATHAM *Gen. Synopsis Birds* II. I. 142 Striated Grosbeak. **1827** GRIFFITH tr. *Cuvier* v. 228 *Mus Striatus* (the Striated Mouse). **1831** J. DAVIES *Man. Mat. Med.* 439 Striated ipecacuanha. *Psychotria emetica.* **1840** MACGILLIVRAY *Brit. Birds* III. 86 *Picus striolatus.* The Striated Woodpecker. **1845** J. E. GRAY *Catal. Lizards Brit. Mus.* 23 The Striated Spine-tail. *Acanthopyga striata.*

c. *Min.* ***striated fracture*** (see quot.).

1796 KIRWAN *Elem. Min.* (ed. 2) I. 35 The Striated Fracture..consists of long narrow separable parts laid on or beside each other.

d. Of muscle: = STRIPED *ppl. a.* 1 c.

1846 W. B. CARPENTER *Man. Physiol.* iii. 199 When the striated Muscular Fibre is examined still more closely, it is found to contain an assemblage of very minute elements. **1851** CARPENTER *Man. Phys.* (ed. 2) 204 When the striated Muscular Fibre is examined still more closely. **1866** HUXLEY *Physiol.* xii. (1872) 291 Muscle is of two kinds striated, or striped, and smooth, plain, or unstriated. **1959** W. ANDREW *Textbk. Compar. Histol.* ii. 48 The muscular tissue in man and other vertebrates is of three chief types: (1) smooth, (2) cardiac, and (3) skeletal. The last two types frequently are referred to as striated because of the cross-striations on the fibers. **1982** [see SKELETAL *a.* b].

e. Of an electric discharge: exhibiting striæ (sense 2 d).

1852 *Phil. Trans. R. Soc.* CXLII. 100 In a well-exhausted receiver containing a small piece of phosphorus, the discharge is throughout its course striated by transverse non-luminous bands. **1883** *Rep. Brit. Assoc. Adv. Sci.* *1882* 31 A stria, with its attendant dark space, forms a physical unit of a striated discharge. **1942** J. D. STRANATHAN *'Particles' Mod. Physics* iii. 71 Small amounts of impurity in the gas affect the striated positive column greatly. **1973** J. YARWOOD *Electricity & Magnetism* xiv. 503 For a striated positive column, the number of ions per unit volume is least at the bright edge of the striation.

2. *Arch.* Chamfered, channelled, grooved.

1727 BAILEY, vol. II. **1771** W. NEWTON tr. *Vitruvius' Archit.* IV. iv. (1791) 80 Two columns..one being striated, the other not. **1842** GWILT *Archit.* Gloss.

3. Constituting striæ.

1854 FAIRHOLT *Dict. Terms Art, Striated*, disposed in ornamental lines, either parallel or wavy. **1899** *Allbutt's Syst. Med.* VIII. 608 Little hard papules..secondarily complicated with striated excoriations.

striation (straɪˈeɪʃən). [n. of action f. STRIATE *v.*: see -ATION.]

1. Striated condition or appearance.

1851 RUSKIN *Stones Venice* (1874) I. viii. 94 Longitudinal furrowing or striation on the original single shaft. **1866** HUXLEY *Physiol.* xii. (1872) 291 This contractile substance ..presents a..transverse striation. **1877** M. FOSTER *Physiol.* I. ii. (1878) 81 Striation is characteristic of muscles whose contraction is rapid. **1883** CHAMBERLIN in *3rd Ann. Rep. U.S. Geol. Surv.* 318 Glacial movements... Striation. **1914** CONAN DOYLE *Capt. Pole Star* 40 This weapon is said to exhibit a longitudinal striation on the steel.

2. a. One of a set or system of striæ, a streak, a marking; esp. *Geol.* one of the grooves or glacial marks found on rock-surfaces; *Min.* (*pl.*) the fine parallel lines on a crystalline face.

1849 DANA *Geol.* App. I. (1850) 710 A fragment from Harper's Hill contains 25 to 27 striations in half an inch. **1888** P. L. SCLATER *Argentine Ornith.* I. 97 *Agelæus thilius.* .. Beneath paler, cineraceous white with black striations.

b. *Electr.* = STRIA 2 d (in *sing.*).

1902 *Encycl. Brit.* XXVIII. 47/2 The bright parts of the striations are slightly concave to the positive electrode. **1942** J. D. STRANATHAN *'Particles' Mod. Physics* iii. 67 As the pressure is still further reduced..the striations become more coarse and indistinct, and the Crookes dark space lengthens. **1973** [see STRIATED *ppl. a.* 1 e].

striato- (straɪˈeɪtəʊ), used in *Zool.* and *Bot.* as combining form of mod.L. *striātus*, prefixed to adjs. in the sense 'striate and ——', as ***striato-crenulate, -echinulate, -nervose, -punctate, -reticulate, -rugose, -tubular***.

1850 W. KING *Permian Fossils* 9 Arborescent plants, having stems with a large pith encircled by a narrow striato-tubular (ligneous?) cylinder. **1871** W. A. LEIGHTON *Lichenflora* 91 Striato-nervose. *Ibid.* 92 Striato-rugose. *Ibid.* 111 Striato-crenulate. **1881** H. B. BRADY in *Jrnl. Microsc. Sci.* Jan. 46 Surface, striatopunctate, i.e. with minute pits or depressions in close, regular, parallel lines from one end of the test to the other. **1893** G. BROOK *Catal. Madrep. Corals* I. 40 Wall striato-reticulate when thin. *Ibid.* 76 Wall striato-echinulate.

striatum (straɪˈeɪtəm). *Anat.* Pl. **striata.** [mod.L., neut. of *striātus* STRIATE *a.*] **a.** The corpus striatum, a body of grey matter within each cerebral hemisphere comprising the lentiform nucleus (i.e. the globus pallidus and the putamen) and the caudate nucleus; some writers also include the claustrum. **b.** (Now the more usual use.) = NEOSTRIATUM, i.e. the putamen and the caudate nucleus only.

[**1803** C. BELL *Anat. Human Body* III. I. iii. 87 The corpora striata are smooth, cineritious convexities... These bodies are called striata, from the intermixture of the medullary matter, which gives the appearance of striæ when they are cut.] **1889** J. LEIDY *Elem. Treat. Human Anat.* (ed. 2) xv. 751 The striatum, or corpus striatum, appears in the body of the lateral ventricle as a smooth, convex gray eminence projecting from its outer wall. **1948** A. BRODAL *Neurol. Anat.* iv. 73 The putamen and the caudate nucleus together constitute the neostriatum (often collectively called on account of their similarities the striatum). **1971** N. G. SUTTON *Anat. Brain & Spinal Medulla* vii. 102 The claustrum is often considered part of the striatum, that is a detached part of the putamen, but it has also been thought to be an included portion of the cortex of the insula. **1978** *Nature* 23 Feb. 767/1 The rats were decapitated and the corpus striatum ipsilateral to the lesion, the contralateral unlesioned striatum and striata from unlesioned animals were assayed.

Hence **striˈatal** *a.*, of or pertaining to the striatum.

1926 *Jrnl. Nerv. & Mental Dis.* LXIV. 9 All kinds of striatal tremors..are action-tremors. **1937** *Arch. Neurol. & Psychiatry* (Chicago) XXXVIII. 737 One can infer that hippocampal activity..through the striatal connections regulates attitudes of emotional expression. **1974** D. & M. WEBSTER *Compar. Vertebr. Morphol.* xi. 268 It is not definitely established whether some or all of the bird's striatal structures are related to the mammalian striatum.

striature (ˈstraɪətjʊə(r)). [ad. L. *striātūra* (Vitruv.), f. L. *stria* (see STRIA).] Disposition of striæ, striation; also, one of a set of striæ. Also *fig.*

1728 WOODWARD *Nat. Hist. Fossils* I. I. 230 Hæmatitæ shewing several Varieties in the Crusts, Striature, Texture, and Constitution of this Body. **1771** W. NEWTON tr. *Vitruvius' Archit.* IV. iii. (1791) 78 Thus the Doric column will have its proper kind of striature. **1846** DANA *Zooph.* (1848) 374 The exterior striatures of the calicles. **1918** F. HACKETT *Ireland* xiii. 362 This striature of Catholics and Protestants, nationalists and anti-nationalists, Irish and Scotch-Ulstermen, is by no means so insufferable as the tenor of argument may indicate.

stric, obs. form of STREAK *sb.*

†**strich.** *Obs. rare.* Also 6 **stryche, stritche.** [Prob. a formation suggested by *scrich-(owl)* and L. *strix*.] The screech-owl.

1552 HULOET, s.v. *Owle*, A stryche owle. *Ibid.*, Stritche owle, *Strix*. **1590** SPENSER *F.Q.* II. xii. 36 The ruefull Strich, still waiting on the bere.

strich, var. STRITCH².

strichel(l, obs. forms of STRICKLE *sb.*

stricht, obs. Sc. form of STRAIGHT.

strick (strɪk), *sb.* Forms: 5 **stric, strek, stryche,** 5–7 **strik,** 5, (9 *Sc.*) **streek,** 6 **streeke, strycke,** 6–7 **stricke,** 6– **strick.** [f. **strik-* wk.-grade of the root of STRIKE *v.* Cf. OF. *estrique* (= sense 3), Pg. *estriga* (= sense 1).]

1. A bundle of broken hemp, flax, jute, etc. for heckling. Cf. STRIKE *sb.* 2.

14.. *Nom.* in Wr.-Wülcker 696/12 *Hic linipolus*, a stric of lyne. *c* **1440** *Promp. Parv.* 479/2 Streek, of flax (*Kylw. A.P. linipulus*). **1616** SURFL. & MARKHAM *Country Farm* V. xviii. 568 So you shall beate this flaxe till it handle as soft as any silke, then vnplat the strickes againe, and heckle it through the second heckle. **1673** A. WALKER *Lees Lachrymans* 8 The Blaze, a lock or strik of Flax, which gives but one flash, and dyes. **1688** HOLME *Armoury* III. 106/2 A Head of Flax, is twelve Stricks tied up to make a Bunch. A Strick, is about ten handfulls [of hemp or flax] made up together in a head. **1847** *Jrnl. R. Agric. Soc.* VIII. II. 385 It is considered best to divide the labour of cleaning each strick of flax among three different stands. **1852** A. ROBB *Poems & Songs* 115 A streek o' lint I canna pu'. **1881** *Spons' Encycl. Industr. Arts* etc. IV. 1243 Each stone [of 14 lb.] contains 5–8 'stricks' or handfuls of finished flax, and each strick is composed of two 'fingers', two of the small lots that have been treated at one operation in the scutching-process.

b. In *Silk-manuf.* A bunch of silk fibre.

1887 *Encycl. Brit.* XXII. 63/1 When the spikes are sufficiently filled [with silk fibre], the lap is cut.., and so stripped from the drum it forms a definite number of 'stricks'.

2. A measure of capacity for corn, coal, etc.; also the measuring vessel. Cf. STRAIK *sb.*¹ 2, STRIKE *sb.* 4. Now *dial.*

1421 *Coventry Leet Book* 27 He schall haue a strik of corne for his labour. **1530** in Phillipps *Wills* (*c* 1830) 177, I bequethe to..our Lady at Bretforton a strycke of barley. **1569** *Nottingham Rec.* (1889) IV. 135 Payd..for makyng of a sealle to sealle stryckes wyth alle xij d. **1576–77** *Ludlow Churchw. Acc.* (Camden) 165 Item, for half a strick of coales, ij d. **1600** in T. North *Bells Lincs.* (1882) 512 Item pd to Anthony harte for a stricke of mawlt..iijs. iiijd. **1893–4** *Northumbld. Gloss.*, *Streek*,..applied occasionally to the measure of corn itself, a streek being understood for a bushel.

3. A piece of wood with which surplus grain is struck off level with the rim of the measure. Cf. STRICKLE *sb.* 1, STRIKE *sb.* 3 a. Now *dial.*

14.. *Lat. Eng. Voc.* in Wr.-Wülcker 588/13 *Hostorium*, a stryche. *c* **1440** *Promp. Parv.* 479/1 Strek, of a mesure as of a buschel or other lyke, *hostorium*. **1585** HIGINS *Junius' Nomencl.* 256/1 *Radius*,..that which Bakers vse to make their meale measures euen: a streeke or strichell. *Ibid.* 341/1 *Hostorium*,..a stritchill: a stricke: a..peece of wood.. wherewith measures are made euen.

Comb. **1886** *W. Somerset Word-bk.* s.v. *Strick* 2, So 'strick-measure' means level, in distinction from 'heap-measure', as peas, potatoes, fruit, &c. are sold.

strick (strɪk), *v.* Also 5 **stryche.** [f. STRICK *sb.*]

1. *trans.* To strike off (corn, etc.) level with the brim of the measure.

14.. *Lat.-Eng. Voc.* in Wr.-Wülcker 588/12 *Hostio*, to stryche. **1651** N. Bacon *Disc. Govt. Eng.* II. vii. 65 The price must be the same with the true Market price; the measure according to the common measure stricked. **1692** *Capt. Smith's Seaman's Gram.* II. xxi. 134 Thrust your Ladle into the same [*sc.* the budge-barrel], filling it full of Powder, and then strick it with a Ruler.

2. To prepare (lint) for heckling; also, to heckle (flax, etc.).

1808 Jamieson *s.v.*, *To strick lint*, to tie up flax in small handfuls, in preparing it for being milled. **1894** *Times* 12 Mar. 13/5 [Flax Machinery.] By means of this breaker the middle operation of 'stricking' is dispensed with.

strick, *a. Sc.* Chiefly in form strict. [perh. related to STRIKE *v.* 1 c, to flow.] Of running water: Swift, rapid.

1629 Z. Boyd *Last Battell* 1075 Furnish him with strength, whereby he may row against the strictest streams of all temptations. *a* **1808** *State, Leslie of Powis v. Fraser of Fraserfield* 60 (Jam.) That the said dike..stems and calms the water where the shot is felled, while otherwise it would be a strict current. **1808** Jamieson *Strict* [ed. 1879 *Strick, strict*], rapid. *The stream's very strict*, it runs rapidly. **1812** J. J. Henry *Campaign against Quebec* 34 Some strict water interfered, but in a few days we came to the first pond.

absol. **1825** Jamieson, *Strick o' the watter*, the most rapid part of any stream.

strick(e, obs. forms of STREAK *sb.*[1], STRIKE *v.*

stricken (ˈstrɪk(ə)n), *pa. pple.* and *ppl. a.* [pa. pple. of STRIKE *v.*]

A. *pa. pple.* in special sense. (For other uses see STRIKE *v.*) ***stricken in years*** (earlier † ***stricken on, in age, in elde***): advanced in years. *arch.* (See also STRUCK, STRUCKEN.)

The pple. in these phrases belongs to STRIKE *v.* in the intransitive sense 'to go'. Cf. the equivalent *stepped* (*stape, stopen*) *in years* (STEP *v.* 4).

c **1380** *Sir Ferumb.* 3481 Sirs, ȝe knoweþ wel þat y am sumdel stryken on age. *c* **1400** *Sc. Trojan War* (Horstm.) 2621, I ame now so strikine in elde, That I þe kynryk may nocht welde. **1535** Coverdale *Gen.* xviii. 11 And Abraham and Sara were both olde, & well stryken in age. **1542** Udall tr. *Erasm. Apoph.* 37 b, He learned to plaie on the harpe after y^t he was well striken in age. *a* **1586** Sidney *Arcadia* I. iii. (1912) 19 He being already well striken in yeares, maried a young princes, named Gynecia. **1662** J. Davies tr. *Olearius' Voy. Ambass.* 133 A man well stricken in years. **1709** Steele *Tatler* No. 98 ¶2 Though you are stricken in years, and have had great experience in the world. **1819** Scott *Leg. Montrose* xxiii, A matron somewhat stricken in years. **1839** Lane *Arab. Nts.* I. 84 At length there arrived..a great sage, stricken in years, who was called the sage Doobán.

B. *ppl. a.*

1. Of a deer (occas. of other animals): Wounded in the chase. †Also of a person: Hurt by a pointed instrument.

1513 Douglas *Æneis* IV. ii. 40 Our all the cetie enragit scho..Wandris, as ane strikin hynd. **1540** Palsgr. *Acolastus* IV. iii. Tj b, I beinge a stryken fysher, waxe wyse .i. whan a fisher man hath hurte his hande with a hoke, [etc.]. **1590** Spenser *F.Q.* I. ii. 24 A virgin widow, whose deepe wounded mind With loue, long time did languish as the striken hind. *Ibid.* II. i. 12 That shall I shew (said he) as sure, as hound The stricken Deare doth chalenge by the bleeding wound. **1603** Shaks. *Ham.* III. ii. 282 (Qo. 1) What, frighted with false fires? Then let the stricken [1604 Qo. 2 strooken; 1623 *Fol.* strucken] deere goe weepe, The Hart vngalled play. **1784** Cowper *Task* III. 108, I was a stricken deer, that left the herd Long since. **1885** *Riverside Nat. Hist.* (1888) V. 202 A stricken whale has been known to stay an hour below the surface.

2. Struck with a blow.

1538 Elyot *Dict.*, *Pulsatus*, striken as a harpe or other instrument is, whyche hath strynges. **1803** Visct. Strangford *Poems of Camoens* (1810) 107 The stricken flint its fires betray'd! **1815** Scott *Waterloo* xx. 24 O! when thou ..mark'st the matron's bursting tears Stream when the stricken drum she hears. **1847** Tennyson *Princess* v. 484 Into fiery splinters leapt the lance, And out of stricken helmets sprang the fire. **1893** S. Gee *Auscult. & Percussion* iii. (ed. 4) 60 A secondary object [in percussion] is to discover the degree of resistance or the density of the stricken spot.

b. Of a sound, musical note: Produced by striking a blow. ***stricken hour*** (*arch.*): a full hour as indicated by the striking of the clock.

1820 Scott *Monast.* x, And without interruption or impatience, to listen for a stricken hour to his narration. **1855** Hawthorne *Eng. Note-Bks.* (1807) I. 365 General —— made us a call..and sat talking a stricken hour or thereabouts. **1873** Mrs. Whitney *Other Girls* xxxiv, A sudden stop, in speech as in music, is sometimes more significant than any stricken note.

3. Of a person, community: Afflicted with disease or sickness; overwhelmed with trouble or sorrow, and the like. Of the face: Marked with or exhibiting great trouble.

Frequent in comb., as *fever-* (1818), *panic-* (1814), *pestilence-* (1819), *poverty-* (1844), *sorrow-* (1809) *stricken*: see those words.

[**1611** Bible *Isa.* liii. 4 Yet we did esteeme him striken, smitten of God, and afflicted.] **1846** Lytton *Lucretia* I. vii, He rather heightened than removed the picture which haunted Mainwaring—Susan, stricken, dying, broken-hearted! **1873** Burton *Hist. Scot.* VI. lxx. 209 The generous assistant of the stricken or oppressed. **1875** H. James *Roderick Hudson* xxvi, Roderick's stricken state had driven him..higher and further than he knew. **1896** Mrs. Caffyn *Quaker-Grandm.* 222 The woman shuddered, and shrank away. Presently she lifted up a drawn, stricken face. **1904** *Verney Mem.* II. xlvii. 269 It should have reached him the summer of the great plague, when there was but little intercourse between the ships and the stricken city [Aleppo].

b. Of the mind, heart, soul: Afflicted with frenzy, madness, grief, or the like.

1795 Southey *Joan of Arc* I. 58 To place her with some pious sisterhood, Who..may likeliest remedy The stricken mind, or frenzied or possess'd. **1845-6** Trench *Huls. Lect.* Ser. I. iii. 42 The good Samaritan that bound up the wounds of every stricken heart. **1897** Watts-Dunton *Aylwin* XIII. iii, Those..know little or nothing..of the stricken soul that looks out on man..through the light of an intolerable pain.

c. *jocularly.* 'Smitten' with love. Cf. *love-stricken.*

1840 Dickens *Old C. Shop* viii, A stricken market-gardener.

4. Of a measure: Having its contents levelled with the brim of the measuring vessel, as distinguished from *heaped*. Cf. STRIKED *ppl. a.*

1495 *Act 11 Hen. VII*, c. 4 §2 Be it also enacted that ther be but only viij busshelles rased and streken to the quarter of Corne. **1641** Best *Farm. Bks.* (Surtees) 103 Wee have allwayes of a stricken bushell of corne, an upheaped bushell of meale. **1778** [W. Marshall] *Minutes Agric.* 27 Nov. 1775, I have employed an itinerant Chaff-cutter, at 1s. the quarter of sixteen striken-bushels. *Ibid.* 21 May 1776, Nine cart-horses eat thirty quarters of chaff..about three double quarters (of sixteen bushels equal to stricken measure) a-team a-week.

5. Of a sail: Lowered.

1593 *Sidney's Arcadia* II. (1598) 125 The cunningest mariners were so conquered by the storme, as they thought it best with striken [ed. 1 (1590) *reads* striking] sailes to yeeld to be gouerned by it.

6. ***stricken field*** (rarely ***battle***): a joined engagement between armed forces or combatants; a pitched battle.

A Sc. use, restored to literary currency by Scott. Cf. the phrases *to strike a battle, field* s.v. STRIKE *v.* 35 b.

?*a* **1700** *Old Ballad* in Scott *Waverley* Note 2 E, The Highlandmen are pretty men For handling sword and shield, But yet they are but simple men To stand a stricken field. **1820** Scott *Abbot* xviii, I never had the good fortune to see a stricken field. **1828** Macaulay *Misc. Writ.* (1860) I. 252 He was vanquished on fields of stricken battle. **1864** Burton *Scot Abr.* I. iii. 134 As if there had been an actual stricken field, with all the able-bodied men on both sides engaged in it.

Hence ˈ**strickenly** *adv.*, †ˈ**strickenness**.

1599 A. M. tr. *Gabelhouer's Bk. Physicke* 26/1 A precious water for the strickennes, & fallinge Sicknes... For strickennes. Take Assesbloode [etc.]..and this with God his ayde will recovere agayne his speeche. **1880** Mrs. C. Reade *Brown Hand & White* I. viii. 192 She marvels, and each succeeding year more strickenly, at the exceeding beauty of the young world. **1881** D. C. Murray *Joseph's Coat* II. xxv. 268 'This is a queer start', said the bewildered reader, staring strickenly at Joe.

strickle (strɪk(ə)l), *sb.* Forms: α. 1 stricel, -il, 5 strik-, strykylle, -elle, strykkell, 6-7 strikle, 7 strickle, 7- strickle. β. 6 strichell, stritchill, 7-8 stritchel(l, 7-9 strichel. γ. 7-8 stricklace, 8-9 strickless, 9 stric(k)les, -liss, strecless, strikeless. [OE. *stricel* (? also **stricels*) = Flem. *strekel* masc. (Kilian, De Bo), mod.Fris. *strikkil* strickle for a scythe (= sense 2 below), f. Teut. **strik-*: see STRIKE *v.*

The OE. word is recorded (see Bosworth-Toller) only in the senses 'Pulley, small wheel', and 'teat', which did not survive into ME.; they seem, like the senses explained below, to be referable to known senses of the verbal root. The β forms are due to a different ablaut-grade of the suffix; the γ forms seem to represent an OE. **stricels*.]

1. A straight piece of wood with which surplus grain is struck off level with the rim of the measure. Sometimes applied to the amount so measured.

14.. *Nom.* in Wr.-Wülcker 726/4 *Hoc os*[*t*]*orium*, a strikylle. **1483** *Cath. Angl.* 369/2 A Strykylle, *hostorium*. A Strylkell [*sic*: ? *read* strykkell] for A buschelle, *hostimentum*. **1585** Higins *Junius' Nomencl.* 256/1 *Radius*,..that which Bakers vse to make their meale measures euen: a streeke or strichell. *Ibid.* 341/1 *Hostorium*,..a stritchill: a strike: a long & round peece of wood like a rolling pinne (with vs it is flat) wherewith measures are made euen. **1641** Best *Farm. Bks.* (Surtees) 103 When wee goe to take up corne for the mill, the first thing wee doe is to looke out poakes, then the bushell and strickle. **1790** W. H. Marshall *Rur. Econ. Midl.* II. 443 *Strickless*; striker of a bushel, &c. **1800** W. Pitt in S. Shaw *Hist. Staff.* (1801) II. I. 207/1 The grosser articles are heaped, but grain is stricken off, with the strait edge of a strip of board, called a strickless: this level measure of grain is here provincially termed strike, and strickless. **1887** *Kent Gloss.*, *Strickle*, a striker, with which the heaped-up measure is struck off and made even. The measure thus evened by the strickle is called race measure, *i.e.* razed measure.

b. Applied to various instruments used for similar purposes in casting or moulding: see quots.

1688 Holme *Armoury* III. 326/1 The third [plumbers' instrument] is the Strickle; it is a slender Sparr, rabated in the ends answerable to the breadth of the Casting Frame,.. by this he beats down the Sand in the Frame,..and when the Lead is cast over..the Plummer followeth the Lead with this Instrument, to drive it forwards, and keep it..all of a thickness. **1831** J. Holland *Manuf. Metal* I. 69 The box is now filled up [with sand], and having been levelled with a strickle, is turned over. **1843** Holtzapffel *Turning* I. 363 A semi-circular piece of wood, called a strickle, is used for working and smoothing the half core. **1885** [Horner] *Pattern Making* 154 The sand within the frame is scraped out with a strickle, shouldered to the same depth as the thickness of the plate. **1888** *Lockwood's Dict. Mech. Engin.*, *Strickle*,..Any piece of wood cut to a special shape and used to impart a special contour to a bed of foundry sand, and thus save expense in pattern making.

2. A tool with which a reaper whets or sharpens his scythe = STRAIK *sb.*[1] 4. Also a mechanical grinder (see quot. 1846).

1641 Best *Farm. Bks.* (Surtees) 32 The tooles that mowers are to have with them, are sythe, shafte, and strickle,..the best stricles are those that are made of..oake. **1764** *Museum Rust.* II. viii. 32 The fixing of the strickle or whetstone at the extremity of our [scythe-] shafts gives a very advantageous balance to the whole machine. **1828** Carr *Craven Gloss.*, *Strickle*, a piece of wood besmeared with grease and strewed with sand to sharpen scythes. **1846** Holtzapffel *Turning* II. 913 The edges of the eight blades [of revolving shears for shearing cloth] are ground..by a grinder or strickle fed with emery, passed to and fro on a slide. **1859** F. S. Cooper *Ironmongers' Catal.* 70 Emery Strickles. **1908** [Miss E. Fowler] *Betw. Trent & Ancholme* 372 The sharpening strickle on the scythe or the reaping-hook.

strickle (ˈstrɪk(ə)l), *v. Founding.* [f. STRICKLE *sb.*] *trans.* To strike *off* with a strickle (the superfluous sand) in moulding; to shape (a core) or form (a mould) by means of a strickle. Also *absol.*

1885 [Horner] *Pattern Making* 153 A level bed would be made on the sand, the frame laid upon it, and the sand rammed round flush with its top edge, and strickled-off level. *Ibid.*, The curb ring facing, boss, and bed are strickled in the bottom by a board working round a core-bar. *Ibid.* 154 The sand within the frame is strickled over level with its upper face. *Ibid.*, In making tank-plates in quantity,..it is usually considered cheaper to make the pattern solid, and so save the cost of strickling each time of moulding. **1927** *Jrnl. Inst. Metals* XXXVII. 25 Red-hot sand was used to fill this space and strickled off level with the top of the mould. **1934** *Proc. Inst. Brit. Foundrymen 1932–1933* XXVI. 548 It [*sc.* stucco] is a splendid material and can be swept or strickled to very fine limits.

Hence ˈ**strickling** *vbl. sb.*

1888 *Lockwood's Dict. Mech. Engin.*, The strickling is effected by means of a strickle or striking board and a guide of some form or another.

†ˈ**strickling,** *adv. Obs. rare*[−1]. [f. *strick*, STRECK *a.* + -LING[2].] Stiffly.

1641 Best *Farm. Bks.* (Surtees) 9 The best way to make sheepe goe of in a markett is to..cutt of all the shaggie hairy woll which standeth stricklinge up; by which meanes they make them seeme more snodde, and of a better stapple.

†**strickman.** *Sc. Obs. rare*[−1]. Meaning uncertain: ? a dummy, puppet.

a **1578** Lindesay (Pitscottie) *Chron. Scot.* (S.T.S.) II. 274 And so he was bot ane strickman in that caus.

strict (strɪkt), *a.* Forms: 6 stryckt, 6-7 strickt, stricte, 7 (8-9 *dial.*) strick, 6- strict. [ad. L. *strict-us* drawn together, tight, severe, rigid, pa. pple. of *stringĕre* to draw or bind tight. Cf. F. *strict* (18th c.), and see STRAIT *a.*]

I. Physical senses. Cf. STRAIT *a.* I.

1. †a. Drawn or pressed tightly together; tight, close. *Obs.*

1592 Shaks. *Ven. & Ad.* 874 She wildly breaketh from their strict imbrace. **1615** Crooke *Body of Man* 925 Their [the Bones] Articulations and Compositions many dissolute and laxe, many strict and close. **1694** in *Phil. Trans.* XVIII. 17 Her Thighs, Leggs, and Feet were..so extreamly elevated with a watry Humour, that upon a strict impress I could have buried three or four Fingers. *Ibid.* 43 A fresh Flux of Blood happened, and strict Bandage was applied. **1712** Arbuthnot *John Bull* III. App. iii, The fatal Noose perform'd its Office, and with most strict Ligature, squeez'd the Blood into his Face. **1781** Cowper *Retirement* 234 As woodbine weds the plant within her reach,..Strait'ning its growth by such a strict embrace.

quasi-*adv.* **1650** Bulwer *Anthropomet.* iv. (1653) 86 The Russian Ladies tie up their Foreheads so strict with fillets.

b. Stretched taut. *rare*[−1].

1858 W. H. Russell *Diary India* (1860) II. 207 We sat and listened to the rain falling on the strict canvas of the tents till dinner-time.

2. †a. 'Strung up', tense; not slack or relaxed. *Obs.*

1578 Banister *Hist. Man* VI. 86 This coate of the Testicle ..sheweth the nature of a certaine strict, and long Muscle. **1731** Arbuthnot *Aliments* vi. (1735) 157 We feel our Fibres grow strict or lax, according to the State of the Air.

b. Of frost: Keen, hard. *rare*[−1].

1893 Stevenson *Catriona* xxviii, Late in the night, in a strict frost, and my teeth chattering, I..considered [etc.].

3. a. Restricted as to space or extent; narrow, drawn in. Cf. STRAIT *a.* 2-4. Now *rare* or *Obs.*

1597 A. M. tr. *Guillemeau's Fr. Chirurg.* 50 b, The Breaste being anguste and stricte. **1603** B. Jonson *Entert. Queen & Prince at Althorpe* 13 And when slow Time hath made you fit for war, Looke ouer the strict Ocean, and thinke where You may but leade us forth. **1612** Woodall *Surg. Mate* Wks. (1653) 214 In ulcers and fistula's scarce a better medicine is found, to enlarge a strict orifice. **1675** R. Burthogge *Causa Dei* 36, I am apt to think that Hell is of a Vast Extent, and that the bounds and limits of it, are not so strict and narrow, as the most imagine. **1828** Wordsw. *Power of Sound* i, Strict passage, through which sighs are brought. **1897** F. Thompson *New Poems* 68, I, the boundless strict savannah Which God's leaping feet go through.

†b. Of handwriting: Compressed. *Obs.*

1648 E. Sparke *Shute's Sarah & Hagar* Ep. Ded., Penned in so diminutive a Letter, writ in so strict an Hand, (the wonder of Youth to read, much more of Age to write it).

4. Straight and stiff. *Obs.* exc. *Bot.* and *Zool.* (see quots.).

1592 R. D. *Hypnerotomachia* 27 The Chapters which stood vpon their strict and vpright Antes. [**1793** MARTYN *Lang. Bot., Strictus*, stiff and straight. Strict will not do in English, and I do not recollect that we have any one word to express this idea.] **1857** A. GRAY *First Less. Bot.* 232 *Strict*, close and narrow; straight and narrow. **1870** HOOKER *Stud. Flora* 328 Euphorbia exigua..branches 6–15 in., erect and strict, or prostrate curved and ascending. **1891** *Century Dict.* s.v., The strict stem of some corals.

II. Figurative senses.

5. a. Of personal relations, alliance, etc.: Close, intimate. Now *rare* or *Obs.*

1600 MARSTON etc. *Jack Drums Entert.* III. (1601) F 2 b, By that strickt bond of loue that lincks our hearts. **1611** SIR D. CARLETON *Let.* 7 Sept. in *10th Rep. Hist. MSS. Comm.* App. I. 533 There is now notoriously discovered a stricte intelligence between yᵉ Spaniards and the Albanesi. **1677** SIR R. SOUTHWELL in *Essex Papers* (Camden) II. 110 A new address to his Majesty for entring into a stricter Confederation with the Allies. **1719–20** STEELE *Theatre* No. 12 ¶6 There never was a more strict friendship than between those Gentlemen. **1834** DE QUINCEY *Autob. Sk.* Wks. 1854 II. 345 My intercourse with him was at no time very strict. **1845** SARAH AUSTIN *Ranke's Hist. Ref.* I. 541 The ill concealed hostile disposition in which Don Juan Manuel had found the court of Rome..had been converted into the strictest union by his efforts.

†**b.** Of a council: Secret, privy. After F. *conseil estroit* (Cotgr.). *Obs.*

1606 B. BARNES *Offices* I. 2 As at this day in Fraunce; where *Les generalx des finances, & les presedents des accomptes*, haue a prioritie..before both the Counsels strict and at large.

6. Of correspondence, agreement, or connexion between facts, ideas, etc.: Close, exactly fitting.

1715 ATTERBURY *Serm.* (Matt. xxvii. 25) (1734) I. 124 Some Circumstances which shew how strict a Correspondence there was between their Crime and their Punishment. **1762** KAMES *Elem. Crit.* i. (1833) 20 Where ideas are left to their natural course, they are continued through the strictest connections. **1860** PUSEY *Minor Proph.* 38/2 The strictest explanation is the truest.

Comb. (quasi-*adv.*) **1787** POLWHELE *Engl. Orator* III. 675 Like the abstruser Rules Of Logic link'd by strict-connecting Chain.

†**7.** Restricted or limited in amount, meaning, application, etc. *Obs.*

1597 HOOKER *Eccl. Pol.* v. lviii. §2 Definitions, whether they be framed larger to augment, or stricter to abridge the number of sacraments. **1611** SHAKS. *Cymb.* v. iv. 17 To satisfie If of my Freedome 'tis the maine part, take No stricter render of me, then my All. **1620** T. GRANGER *Div. Logike* 336 Here the predicate is more strict in signification then the subiect. **1737** WATERLAND *Eucharist* 42 The Word *Sacrament* is of great Latitude, and capable of various Significations, (some stricter and some larger).

8. a. Accurately determined or defined; exact, precise, not vague or loose. †Of particulars: Enumerated or described in exact detail.

1631 MILTON *Sonn.* ii. 10 It shall be still in strictest measure eev'n To that same lot. **1658** SIR T. BROWNE *Hydriot.* ii. 6 Though we meet not with such strict particulars of these parts, before the new Institution of Constantine. **1692** ATTERBURY *Serm.* (Ps. l. 14) (1726) I. 13 According to the strict Import of the Word. **1760** *Cautions & Adv. to Officers of Army* 130 He may in a stricter Sense be called, *The Officer of the Day* than *of the Guard*. **1818** HALLAM *Mid. Ages* viii. III. (1819) III. 273 These [lieutenancies] do not however bear a very close analogy to regencies in the stricter sense, or substitutions during the natural incapacity of the sovereign. **1837** CARLYLE *Fr. Rev.* I. I. ii, If the very Rocks and Rivers (as Metaphysic teaches) are, in strict language, *made* by those Outward Senses of ours. **1875** E. WHITE *Life in Christ* IV. xxiv. (1876) 394 Public legislative documents, in which important words are to be always taken in their strictest and most direct definition.

b. With defining word: Restricted to the exact use or definition indicated by the word.

1842 LOUDON *Suburban Hort.* 23 The fruit, in a strict botanical sense, is the mature pistillum. **1891** *Century Dict.*, *Strict* 8. Restricted; taken strictly, narrowly, or exclusively: as, a strict generic or specific diagnosis.

c. Of a calculated or measured result: Precise, exact; opposed to *approximate*.

1791 SMEATON *Edystone L.* (1793) §261 *note*, The masons were employed in reducing the whole area of the work to a strict level.

d. *Law.* ***strict settlement***: see quot. 1841.

1710 T. VERNON *Chanc. Cases* (1728) II. 659 By Proof it appears a strict Settlement was intended. **1791** C. FEARNE *Contingent Remainders* (ed. 4) I. 129 The limitation to her [the wife] for life, and a subsequent one to the heirs of her body by the husband have been decreed to operate by way of strict settlement. **1835** *Tomlins' Law Dict.* II. 3 Q. s.v. *Remainder*, In these strict settlements, the estate is unalienable till the first son attains the age of twenty-one. **1841** H. J. STEPHEN *Comm. Laws Eng.* I. vii. I. 307 When land is settled..by a limitation to the parent for life, and after his death to his first and other sons in tail, and trustees are interposed to preserve the contingent remainders, this is called a *strict settlement*.

e. *Logic.* ***strict implication***: a relationship holding between propositions in which it is impossible for the antecedent to be true and the consequent false. Cf. *material implication* s.v. MATERIAL *a.* 2 b.

1912 C. I. LEWIS in *Mind* XXI. 526 Intensional disjunction bears the same relation to inferential or 'strict' implication that extensional disjunction bears to the algebraic or 'material' implication. **1933** C. A. MACE *Princ. Logic* iv. 68 This is clearly a different sense of implies, and is sometimes called strict implication. **1947** H. REICHENBACH *Elem. Symbolic Logic* viii. 379 The calculus of strict implication..constitutes a system of this kind. **1977** *Fontana Dict. Mod. Thought* 206/1 The systems of strict implication are the basis of contemporary modal logic.

9. Of confinement or imprisonment: Rigorous; severely restricted in regard to space or liberty of movement.

1667 MILTON *P.L.* II. 321 To remaine In strictest bondage. **1685** in *Verney Mem.* (1907) II. 400 'Tis true our confinement is not strict. **1756–7** tr. *Keysler's Trav.* (1760) I. 397 Your brother shall be kept in strict custody. **1869** A. HARWOOD tr. *Pressensé's Early Yrs. Christ.* II. ii. 166 The captivity of the apostle became increasingly strict.

10. Of watch and ward, authority, discipline, obedience, etc.: Rigorously maintained, admitting no relaxation or indulgence.

1602 SHAKS. *Ham.* I. i. 71 This same strict and most obseruant Watch. **1613** BEAUM. & FL. *Philaster* II. i, What maister holds so strickt a hand ouer his boy, That he will part with him without one warning. **1667** MILTON *P.L.* IV. 783 Uzziel, half these draw off, and coast the South With strictest watch. **1692** R. L'ESTRANGE *Fables* liii. 54 A Prince's Leaving his Bus'ness Wholly to his Ministers without a Strict Eye over them in their Respective Offices. **1706** E. WARD *Wooden World Diss.* (1708) 72 He keeps so strict a Hand over his Crew, that he won't suffer them to Keep one Holy-Day. **1748** SMOLLETT *Rod. Random* xxix, [He] gave the second mate a caution to keep a strict guard over his tongue. **1838** THIRLWALL *Greece* xlii. V. 205 He..every where maintained strict discipline among his troops. **1855** MACAULAY *Hist. Eng.* xiii. III. 341 His temper was under strict government.

11. a. Of a law, ordinance, etc., or its execution: Stringent and rigorous in its demands or provisions, allowing no evasion.

1578 WHETSTONE *2nd Pt. Promos & Cass.* II. v, Their crafte, they colour so, As styll they haue, stryckt lawe vpon their side. **1580** E. KNIGHT *Trial Truth* 5 There shall neede no such strickt order to mooue them therunto. **1667** MILTON *P.L.* IX. 903 Rather how hast thou yeelded to transgress The strict forbiddance..? **1699** EVELYN *Diary* 24 Nov., To punish offenders and put the laws in more strict execution. **1789** W. BUCHAN *Dom. Med.* (1790) 499 During ..the second stage of the disorder, though so strict a regimen is not necessary as in the first or inflammatory state, yet intemperance of every kind must be avoided. **1834** JAMES *J. Marston Hall* xi, The Duke had given him strict orders to follow my commands implicitly. **1835** THIRLWALL *Greece* vii. I. 290 From the beginning of their eighteenth year they were subjected to a stricter rule. **1913** J. H. MORRISON *Trail Pioneers* xiv. 65 This purdah system is strictest in the north, ..but its baneful influence is felt all over India.

b. Of a legal instrument or provision: Stringent.

1739 J. RICHARDS *Annuities on Lives* 96 This is often the Case, let the Covenants of the Lease be ever so strict and binding.

c. quasi-*adv.*

1721 RAMSAY *Scribblers Lashed* 191 We order strict, that all refrain.

d. ***strict liability***: a liability which does not depend upon intent to commit an offence.

1896 *Rep. Cases N.Y. Court of Appeals* CLI. 142 The weight of the argument..is in favor of the rule of strict liability which requires a public official to assume all risks of loss. **1926** *Law Q. Rev.* XLII. 51 The description of the rule in *Rylands* v. *Fletcher* as an example of absolute liability in tort is unhappy in view of some half dozen exceptions which are admitted as qualifications of it. 'Strict liability' seems to be a better term. **1935** *California Law Rev.* May 431 Liability on the ground of nuisance should not be confused with the doctrine of absolute or strict liability for certain classes of lawful acts. **1945** W. T. S. STALLYBRASS *Salmond's Law of Torts* (ed. 10) ii. 20 A period of strict liability, an 'unmoral period, is succeeded by a period of fault liability, a moral' period. **1953** *N.Y. Univ. Law Rev.* XXVIII. 1076 The courts have made no inroads upon strict liability for damage done by animals ferae naturae, nor upon scienter liability. **1979** *Internat. Jrnl. Sociol. of Law* Feb. 54 In short, by substantially removing the issue of intention from the crimes of employers, the 1844 Act took a substantial step towards the doctrine of strict liability.

12. a. Of an art or science, its procedure, etc.: Characterized by rigid conformity to rules or postulates.

1638 JUNIUS *Paint. Ancients* 31 Wee should not too much accustome our selves to a strict course of Imitation. *a* **1677** BARROW *Expos. Creed* (1697) 43 Which is a most reasonable proceeding and conformable to the method used in the strictest sciences. **1777** PRIESTLEY *Matt. & Spir.* (1782) I. xx. 259, I do not..find the strict immaterial system in any writer earlier than our Sir Kenelm Digby. **1796** KOLLMANN *Ess. Mus. Harmony* xv. 114 Of strict or free Imitation. **1834** MRS. SOMERVILLE *Connex. Phys. Sci.* xiv. 109 It is proved.. by strict mathematical reasoning, that [etc.]. **1861** PALEY *Æschylus* (ed. 2) *Persians* 43 The penult should perhaps be long in strict prosody. **1869** OUSELEY *Counter-point* ii. 6 The only concords recognized in strict counter-point are the perfect octave [etc.]. **1873** H. C. BANISTER *Music* (1889) 177 Imitation may be only of the general form of a passage..Or the intervals may be exactly imitated, which is termed Strict Imitation. **1880** E. GURNEY *Power of Sound* xix. 430 Greek iambic verse was less strict in this respect.

b. ***strict tempo***: in Music, a strict and regular rhythm; freq. used *attrib.* with reference to a kind of ballroom dancing to music with such a rhythm.

1936 F. G. HAWKES *Studies in Time & Tempo* vi. 35 If the proper rhythmical effect..is to be secured, the observance of accurate and strict *tempo* becomes an absolute necessity. **1958** P. GAMMOND *Decca Bk. Jazz* xxv. 320 The vacuities of 'strict tempo' and the morbid sex neurosis of the modern 'sob' song. **1959** F. NEWTON *Jazz Scene* xiii. 230 'Strict tempo' dancing, the foundation of the mass ballroom vogue among the British working class,..grew in a direction diametrically opposed to jazz. **1961** *Listener* 23 Nov. 887/2 A champion strict-tempo dancer. **1978** F. MULLALLY *Deadly Payoff* vi. 81 Strict-tempo ballroom dancing: the slow foxtrot, the quickstep, the waltz. **1982** WARNER & SANDILANDS *Women beyond Wire* ii. 19 The strict-tempo orchestra which reeled off foxtrots and quicksteps.

13. a. Of a quality or condition, an attitude or line of action: Maintained to the full, admitting no deviation or abatement; absolute, entire, complete, perfect. (Cf. 15 b.)

1588 SHAKS. *L.L.L.* IV. iii. 165 O me, with what strict patience haue I sat, To see a King transformed to a Gnat? **1593** —— *Rich. II*, II. i. 80 The pleasure that some Fathers feede vpon, Is my strict fast, I meane my Childrens lookes. **1607** —— *Timon* III. v. 24 You vndergo too strict a Paradox, Striuing to make an vgly deed looke faire. **1663** PATRICK *Parab. Pilgr.* xxxix. (1687) 521 But that is no more than strict Justice exacts. **1753** RICHARDSON *Grandison* (1754) II. iii. 21 All this shall be mentioned to Lady D. in strict confidence. **1822** SHELLEY *Faust* ii. 262 In turth, I generally go about In strict incognito. **1855** MACAULAY *Hist. Eng.* xix. IV. 265 In his public acts he observed a strict neutrality. **1858** CARLYLE *Fredk. Gt.* I. iii. I. 39 A pleasant attractive physiognomy; which may be considered better than strict beauty. **1860** TYNDALL *Glac.* I. x. 67 A man of the strictest prudence. **1898** 'H. S. MERRIMAN' *Roden's Corner* xiv. 152, I should recommend a strict reticence on this matter. **1907** J. A. HODGES *Elem. Photogr.* (ed. 6) 27 The observance of strict cleanliness.

b. Of truth, accuracy, etc.: Exactly and rigidly observed; exactly answerable to fact or reality.

1748 MELMOTH *Fitzosborne Lett.* lxi. (1749) II. 109, I may venture, however, to assert..that the Muses are, in strict truth, of heavenly extraction. **1821** SCOTT *Kenilw.* i, I would not have you think all I said of him, even now, was strict gospel. **1849** MACAULAY *Hist. Eng.* vi. II. 80 Two prerogatives, of which the limits had never been defined with strict accuracy.

14. a. Rigorous and severe in rule and discipline, in administering justice, etc.; not lax or indulgent.

1596 SHAKS. *Merch. V.* IV. i. 204 (Qo.) This strict Court of Venice must needes giue sentence gainst the Merchant there. **1603** —— *Meas. for M.* I. ii. 186 Implore her in my voice, that she make friends To the strict deputie. **1621** FLETCHER *Thierry & Theod.* I. i, A Monasterie, A most strickt house; a house where none may whisper. **1697** DRYDEN *Æneis* VI. 582 Minos, the strict Inquisitor, appears. **1828** SCOTT *F.M. Perth* ix, The King..ought to have been ..liberal in rewarding services, strict in punishing crimes. **1832** HT. MARTINEAU *Hill & Valley* iii. 31 Who was not remembered to have been particularly strict..about having the whole establishment in good order. **1850** H. MELVILLE *White Jacket* I. xxix. 191 Three of these officers..were strict disciplinarians. **1904** F. D. How *Six Great Schoolm.* 253 He was extremely strict with the Masters in spite of the sympathy and kindness he showed them.

b. of fate, necessity.

1608 SHAKS. *Per.* III. iii. 7 O your sweet Queene! that the strict fates had pleas'd, you had brought her hither to haue blest mine eies with her! **1667** MILTON *P.L.* VI. 869 But strict Fate had cast too deep Her dark foundations, and too fast had bound. *Ibid.* x. 131 But strict necessitie Subdues me, and calamitous constraint. **1700** DRYDEN *Cock & Fox* 528 Not forc'd to Sin by strict necessity.

15. a. Of persons: Holding a rigorous and austere standard of living; stern to oneself in matters of conscience and morality.

[**1578**: cf. STRICTNESS 3.] **1614** W. B. tr. *Philos. Banq.* (ed. 2) 105 They abstained from all flesh and wines..; nay, so strict they were, they seldom eate Bread. **1634** MILTON *Comus* 109 Strict Age, and sowre Severity. **1648** FAIRFAX, etc. *Remonstr.* 21 Consciencious, strickt in manners, sober, serious. **1662** in *Verney Mem.* (1907) II. 173 My sister says the queen is very hansom, and I hear very stricte in her carage. **1770** LANGHORNE *Plutarch, Cato Ynger.* V. 49 The whole course of his life was strict and austere. **1837** CARLYLE *Fr. Rev.* I. IV. iv, With a strict painful mind. **1860** THACKERAY *Lovel* vi. (1861) 237 My mother and sisters are dissenters, and very strict. I couldn't ask a party into my family who has been [on the stage]. **1894** 'MARK RUTHERFORD' *Cath. Furze* I. vi. 98 On many points their 'views' were 'strict' —whatever that singular phrase may have meant.

Comb. **1837** CARLYLE *Fr. Rev.* I. IV. iv, A strict-minded, strait-laced man!

b. of virtue, chastity, etc. (Cf. 13.)

1589 WARNER *Albion's Eng., Æneidos* 153 Greater is the wonder of your strickt chastity. **1591** SHAKS. *1 Hen. VI*, V. iv. 67 Is all your strict precisenesse come to this? **1671** MILTON *Samson* 319 Against his vow of strictest purity. **1705** MRS. CENTLIVRE *Gamester* III. (1708) 30 A Gentleman that plays is admitted every where—Women of the strictest Vertue will converse with him. **1905** F. HARRISON *Chatham* iv. 56 Pitt..was the statesman who finally established strict honour in the public service.

16. Undeviating in adherence to the principles or practice implied by the designation.

c **1660** in J. Morris *Troub. Catholic Forefathers* Ser. I. (1872) vi. 257 A good devout Sister, and very strict in regular observance. **1661** in *Extr. St. Papers rel. Friends.* Ser. II. (1911) 125 Persons of most exemplar regular Course of life..yet extreame strict to the rules of there profession. **1666** E. MOUNTAGU in *12th Rep. Hist. MSS. Comm.* App. v. 8 If the young Lord was a strict and a grounded Papist. **1718** PRIOR *Poems* Ded. (1905) p. xx, He was so strict an Observer of his Word, that no Consideration whatever, could make him break it. *a* **1721** —— *Vicar of Bray & Sir T. More* (1907) 259 This Strict adherence to Truth. **1801** J. THOMSON *Poems Sc. Dial.* 81 To leave the Kirk ye surely mean, An' turn a strict Seceder clean. **1853** LYTTON *My Novel* I. ix, The Hazeldeans..were great sportsmen and strict preservers. **1861** *Contrib. Eccl. Hist. Connecticut* 280 The new churches, called Separates, or, as they preferred, Strict Congregationalists. **1868** FREEMAN *Norm. Conq.* (1877) II. App. 653 The feeling on the subject among strict churchmen comes out very forcibly. **1884** EARL MALMESBURY *Mem. Ex-Minister* I. 14 Mr. Bowle was..a strict observer of saints' days and dates. **1888** BRYCE *Amer. Commw.* I. I. v. 62 Every vote given by the members of the Commission was a strict party vote.

17. a. Of inquiry, investigation, inspection, observation, calculation, and the like: Characterized by close and unrelaxing effort, so as to let nothing escape notice.

1596 SHAKS. *1 Hen. IV*, III. ii. 149 And I will call him to so strict account, That he shall render euery Glory vp. **1617** L. DIGGES tr. *Claudian's Rape Proserpine* I. C 4, The god, vnto this vnexpected newes Gaue strict attention. **1696** TATE & BRADY *Ps.* cxxxix. 1 Thou, Lord, by strictest search hast known My rising up and lying down. **1699** *Flying Post* 6–9 May 2/1 The Coroners Jury have.. upon strict Inquiry found it was accidental. **1710** SWIFT *Examiner* No. 17 ¶2 Is he not severely us'd by the Ministry or Parliament, who yearly call him to a strict Account? **1725** DE FOE *Voy. round World* (1840) 317 To take the strictest observation they could of the plain. **1726** SWIFT *Gulliver* II. i, Upon a strict review, I blotted out several passages. **1755** J. ELLIS *Corallines* 52 The Vesicles, on the strictest Examination, appear to have no Opening into them. **1839** DICKENS *Nich. Nick.* viii, Mrs. Squeers.. instituted a stricter search after the spoon. **1855** *Orr's Circ. Sci., Inorg. Nat.* 45 The knowledge of this fact soon leads to the more strict investigation of the nature of the deposits thus noticed.

b. with an agent-noun.

1668 HALE *Rolle's Abridgmt.* Pref. 2 He was a strict Searcher and Examiner of businesses.

strict: see STRICK *a.*

strictarian (strɪk'tɛərɪən), *sb.* and *a. rare.* [f. STRICT *a.*: see -ARIAN.] **A.** *sb.* One holding rigidly conformist views. **B.** *adj.* Characteristic of a strictarian.

1867 [see -ARIAN]. **1926** *Chambers's Jrnl.* Mar. 153/1, I was not churlish enough or strictarian enough to decry that acceptance. **1931** A. L. ROWSE *Politics & Younger Generation* ix. 251 These are points in Marxism, particularly in the orthodox, strictarian interpretation of it, that are open to criticism.

‖**stricti juris** ('strɪktaɪ 'dʒʊərɪs, 'strɪktiː 'juərɪs), *adv. phr. Law.* Also **stricti iuris**. [L., lit. 'of strict law'.] Strictly according to the law; according to law as opposed to equity. Also as quasi-*sb.*, the practice of strict interpretation of the law.

1684 G. MACKENZIE *Institutions Law of Scotland* IV. i. 342 Some actions are stricti juris; in which the Judge is to follow the strict prescript of the Contract upon which the Action is raised. **1704** T. WOOD *New Inst. Imperial or Civil Law* IV. iii. 327 Some *stricti juris*, where the Judge cannot depart from the strict terms of the Contract. **1845** H. BROOM *Sel. Legal Maxims* v. 242 Defences which were not admissible or valid *stricti iuris*. **1971** R. D. BAKER *Judicial Rev. in Mexico* vii. 185 The rule of *stricti iuris* (*estricto derecho*) requires the courts to confine their attention to and base their decisions exclusively on those conclusions of law. **1977** A. WATSON *Society & Legal Change* ii. 12 *Stipulatio*.. was a unilateral formal contract of strict law (*stricti iuris*) but the formalities were far from complicated.

striction ('strɪkʃən). [ad. L. *strictiōn-em*, n. of action f. *stringĕre* to draw tight, strain.]

1. The action of straining. *rare*$^{-1}$.

1889 *Engl. Mechanic* 27 Dec. 355/2 There is.. a kind of elongation by striction, which in the case of a direct pull, is produced with a constant load applied at a rate accelerated up to the point of rupture.

2. *Geom.* In a skew surface, ***curve*** or ***line of striction***: see quots.

1875 P. FROST *Solid Geom.* (ed. 2) I. 297 The curve which is the limit of the polygon formed by joining *a, b, c, d*,.. at which the imagined membranes would have the greatest density, is called *the curve of greatest density*; it is also called the *line of striction*. **1889** CAYLEY *Math. Papers* I. 234 The curve *pqr*.. is said to be the minimum distance curve (or curve of striction). **1892** *Ibid.* XIII. 233 Supposing the distances PQ_1, P_1Q_2, P_2Q_3, &c. to be all of them infinitesimal, we have a skew surface containing upon it a curve $P_1P_2P_3$, &c., which is the line of striction, viz, this is the locus of the point on a generating line which is the nearest point to the consecutive generating line.

†**'strictive**, *a. Obs.* [ad. L. *strictīvus*, f. *strict-*, *stringĕre* to bind, also (a different word) to gather (flowers, etc.). In classical Latin the adj. has only sense 2.]

1. Astringent, styptic.

a **1400–50** *Stockh. Med. MS.* 10 For to makyn surripe þat is stryctyf. **1569** R. ANDROSE tr. *Alexis' Secr.* IV. II. 16 Cause hem to drinke of the rennet of an Hare or of an Hart in strictiue water. **1580** T. NEWTON *Approved Med.* 54 All parts of the Oake tree be stryctiue and byndinge.

2. (See quot.) *rare*$^{-0}$.

1656 BLOUNT *Glossogr.*, *Strictive*, gathered or cropped with the hand.

Hence †**'strictiveness**, astringency.

1580 T. NEWTON *Approved Med.* 26 Incense is dry in the first degree, and hath a certayne bynding or strictiuenesse.

†**strictland.** *Obs. rare*$^{-1}$. [f. STRICT *a.* (in the sense 'narrow') + LAND *sb.*[1]] An isthmus.

1577 HARRISON *England* I. ix. [xii.] 22/2 in *Holinshed*, Beyonde the which I find a narrow going or stricktland leading from the poynte to Hirst Castle.

strictly ('strɪktlɪ), *adv.* [f. STRICT *a.* + -LY[2].]

†**1.** In physical sense: Tightly, closely. *Obs.*

1641 G. SANDYS *Paraphr. Song Sol.* VIII. i. 29 Thy left Arme for my Pillow plac'd, And stricktly with thy right embrac'd. **1714** YOUNG *Force of Relig.* II, Her lord and father, for a moment's space, She strictly folded in her soft embrace. [**1871** TENNYSON *Last Tourn.* 653 The vow that binds too strictly snaps itself.]

Comb. (*fig.*) **1648** J. BEAUMONT *Psyche* XXI. lii, Nothing is lac'd so strictly-strait into It self, as this immeasurable Nature.

2. With reference to confinement or custody, watch or guard, a siege, etc.: Closely, narrowly, rigorously, vigilantly.

1608 SHAKS. *Per.* II. v. 8 She hath so strictly Tyed her to her Chamber. **1638** MAYNE *Lucian* (1664) 170 The gates were strictlier kept, and no man was any more permitted to enter into the house. *a* **1700** EVELYN *Diary* 16 Feb. 1649, Paris being now strictly besieged by the Prince de Condé. **1764** H. WALPOLE *Otranto* iii, He ordered some of his attendants to carry Theodore to the top of the Black Tower and guard him strictly. **1892** LADY F. VERNEY *Verney Mem.* I. i. 4 A door less likely to be strictly guarded than the other issues.

3. a. With reference to commands, obligation, etc.: Rigorously, stringently; with insistence on exact performance, execution, or obedience. Cf. STRAITLY *a.* 5.

1487 *Plumpton Corr.* (Camden) 54, I therfore on the kinges behalfe strictly charg you,.. that ye [etc.]. **1594** SHAKS. *Rich. III*, IV. i. 17, I may not suffer you to visit them, The King hath strictly charg'd the contrary. **1710** FELTON *Diss. Classics* (1718) 41 For which Reason the Celebrated Dr. Busby strictly forbad the Use of Notes. **1828** FOSTER in *Life & Corr.* (1846) II. 149, I am strictly ordered to keep out of the evening damp and cold. **1833** H. COLERIDGE *Biog. Borealis, Marvell* 12 The publication of debates was at that time.. really and strictly forbidden.

b. With strict provisions; by strict enactment.

1651 G. W. *Cowel's Inst.* 189 He who hath a Fee-tail in his owne, or Fee-simple in anothers Right,.. is tied a little more strictly. **1706** T. VERNON *Chanc. Cases* (1728) II. 552 In a Court of Equity the Trust ought to have been strictly pursued. **1827** W. F. CORNISH *Ess. Doctr. Remainders* 19 The court will generally order the lands to be settled strictly. **1907** J. H. PATTERSON *Man-Eaters of Tsavo* xviii. 191 The whole of this country.. is now a strictly protected Game Reserve.

4. With reference to punishment, judgement, rule, etc.: Rigorously, unsparingly, severely.

1602 W. S. *Thomas Ld. Cromwell* I. iii. 41 And to deale strictly with such a one as he, Better seuere then too much lenitie. **1607** BEAUM. & FL. *Woman-Hater* IV. i, I wish those of my bloud that doe offend, Should be more strictly punish, then my foes. **1625** MILTON *Death fair Infant* 33 Could Heav'n for pittie thee so strictly doom? **1849** MACAULAY *Hist. Eng.* vi. II. 98 These laws, though they had not, except when there was supposed to be some peculiar danger, been strictly executed. **1876–89** BRIDGES *Growth of Love* xx, God's love to win is easy, for He loveth Desire's fair attitude, nor strictly weighs The broken thing.

5. With rigid and exact adherence to a plan, regulation, etc.; with complete and literal observance of a rule or enactment. Also, according to a strict standard of life, obligation, etc.

1597 HOOKER *Eccl. Pol.* v. lxii. §19 It is.. meete that the strength of mens deedes and the instruments which declare the same should strictlie depend vpon diuers solemnities. **1651** JER. TAYLOR *Serm. Golden Grove, Summer* xxvi. 338 But while they talk as if they did not need to live strictly, many of them live so strictly as if they did not beleeve so foolishly. **1712** STEELE *Spect.* No. 298 ¶2 Many of the most strictly virtuous. **1805** WORDSW. *Ode to Duty* 32 But thee I now would serve more strictly, if I may. **1826** *Art Brewing* (ed. 2) 87 Cases may occur, when.. the admixture of chalybeate tonics.. ought to be strictly avoided. **1849** MACAULAY *Hist. Eng.* ii. I. 174 Not only were the intentions of the court strictly concealed, but [etc.]. **1854** *Poultry Chron.* I. 213/2 Unless these regulations be strictly complied with.

6. a. With unrelaxed care or attention to detail; without letting particulars escape notice; narrowly, closely, exactly.

1632 LITHGOW *Trav.* IX. 390 [He] sent a Guide with me.. to view the Mountayne more strictly. **1655–60** STANLEY *Hist. Philos., Periander* (1687) 49/1 Periander said, it was not possible but that he should say something more, and pressed him more strictly. *a* **1700** EVELYN *Diary* 12 Sept. 1641, Where our names were taken and our persons examin'd very strictly. **1720** DE FOE *Capt. Singleton* xv. (1840) 258 One of our men looking a little more strictly than the rest, thought he saw the head of one of the Indians. **1751** EARL ORRERY *Remarks Swift* (1752) 122 It is preceded by an explanatory advertisement, that was either dictated, or strictly revised by the Dean himself. **1796** MME. D'ARBLAY *Camilla* II. 360 Tell me, and ask yourself strictly, would you change with Indiana? **1837** P. KEITH *Bot. Lex.* 54 It is evident that Ferns must be excluded from the cellular department, if structure is to be strictly attended to.

b. Qualifying an adjective, adverb, or equivalent phrase: In the strict sense of the word (or words).

1764 DODSLEY *Leasowes* in *Shenstone's Wks.* (1777) II. 294 A.. wild and romantic appearance of water, and at the same time strictly natural. **1799** HT. LEE *Canterb. T., Poet's T.* (ed. 2) I. 48 [He was] not strictly handsome, yet winning. **1839** DICKENS *Nich. Nick.* iv, This was strictly true. **1849** MACAULAY *Hist. Eng.* iii. I. 365 They governed strictly according to law.

c. Qualifying a predication or assertion as a whole = *strictly speaking* (see 8).

1680 MOXON *Mech. Exerc.* xiv. 238 This whole Member is called the Moving Collar, though the Collar strictly is only the round Hole at *a*. **1736** BUTLER *Anal.* I. v. Wks. 1874 I. 88 It is only these inward principles exerted, which are strictly acts of obedience, of veracity, [etc.]. **1818** CRUISE *Digest* (ed. 2) IV. 344 This sort of acquisition of.. an estate tail.. is not strictly a descent. **1834** K. H. DIGBY *Mores Cath.* v. v. 132 For which purpose there was a multitude of minor clerks employed who had not strictly orders. **1885** *Stand. Nat. Hist.* V. 371 The genus *Helarctos*.. strictly embraces but one species, *Helarctos malayanus*.

7. With respect to resemblance, correspondence, adaptation, and the like: Precisely, exactly; without discrepancy or exception.

1763 J. BROWN *Poetry & Mus.* xii. 213 Our sacred Poetry, sung in the Cathedrals, is transcribed strictly from the holy Scriptures. **1777** PRIESTLEY *Philos. Necess.* iv. 31 As far as we can judge, motives and actions do strictly correspond to each other. **1831** SCOTT *Ct. Robt.* iii, The first, which strictly resembled her own chair in size and convenience. **1892** *Photogr. Ann.* II. 570 The parts are made strictly interchangeable. **1909** E. R. TENNANT in *Expositor* Aug. 117 The sinful is strictly correlative with the guilty.

8. With exact use of words; exactly, precisely. Often in the parenthetic phr. ***strictly speaking*** or ***to speak strictly***.

1601 B. JONSON *Poetaster* v. ii. 39 Horace hath (but more strictly) spoke our thoughts. **1639** W. SCLATER *Worthy Commun.* 66 That speech.. is to be understood in Trope, or sacred Figure, not strictly, and abstractively. **1673** *S'too him Bayes* 92 If this (strictly speaking) be no Quibble. *a* **1722** FOUNTAINHALL *Decis.* (1759) I. 11 A fictitious and umbratile kind of treason, and to speak strictly, no treason at all. **1837** P. KEITH *Bot. Lex.* 397 Plants have no digestive apparatus strictly so called. **1849** MACAULAY *Hist. Eng.* i. I. 13 During the century and a half which followed the Conquest, there is, to speak strictly, no English history. **1912** *Eng. Hist. Rev.* Oct. 762 What he describes as the Amorian period, though this name strictly applies only to the last forty-seven years.

9. *colloq.* (chiefly *U.S.*). Definitely; exclusively. Phr. ***strictly for the birds***: see BIRD *sb.* 5 d.

1938, 1945 [see MICKEY MOUSE 2]. **1947** [see MODEL *sb.* 7 e]. **1951** [see *man-hungry* s.v. MAN *sb.*[1] 20]. **1977** *Amer. Speech 1975* L. 67 *Strictly*.., absolutely, honestly, sincerely, definitely. 'My teacher is handsome, strictly!'

strictness ('strɪktnɪs). [-NESS.] The quality or condition of being strict.

†**1.** In physical senses: Narrowness, straitness; tightness, close compression. *Obs.*

1604 R. CAWDREY *Table Alph.*, *Strictnes*, narrownes or smalnes. **1605** in *10th Rep. Hist. MSS. Comm.* App. v. 372 That strictnes of the gate that leadeth into blisse. **1620** VENNER *Via Recta* viii. 193 They are repleated with grosse humors with a naturall strictnes of the veines. **1709** *Phil. Trans.* XXVII. 73 When their Force is inhibited by the strictness of the Pores, they are unable to remove.

†**2.** Closeness (of friendship or intimacy). *Obs.*

c **1614** CORNWALLIS in Gutch *Collect. Cur.* I. 138 He desired as great a strictness, and nearness of amity and alliance, as might be, between the Crowns of England, and Spain.

3. Severity of life or behaviour; inflexibility of principle or virtue.

1578 LYLY *Euphues* Wks. 1902 I. 315 Thou hast therefore .. great cause to reioyce, that God by punishment hath compelled thee to stricktnesse of lyfe. **1611** BEAUM. & FL. *Maid's Trag.* II. i. (1619) D 3 b, *Evad.* Alas Amintor thinkst thou I forbeare To sleepe with thee, because I haue put on A maidens strictnesse. **1650** HUBBERT *Pill Formality* 52 They can change their habits of strickness into a habit of looseness and profaneness. **1756** MRS. CALDERWOOD in *Coltness Collect.* (Maitland Club) 175 All the nuns are English, of the order of the Recolly, who are but a degree above the Capucines for strickness. **1800** MRS. HERVEY *Mourtray Family* 37 The governess was a French woman, strongly recommended for the strictness of her principles. *a* **1901** W. BRIGHT *Age of Fathers* (1903) I. ii. 18 A genuine enthusiasm for Christian strictness.

4. Severity, rigour, stringency (of laws, enactments, obligation, judgement, discipline, etc.).

1602 ROWLANDS *Greene's Ghost* (1872) 9 They will vrge the strictnesse of their oath, and the danger of the law in such cases of concealement. **1660** WOOD *Life* (O.H.S.) I. 359 The strictness of the Lord's day was mitigated. **1699** T. BAKER *Refl. Learn.* iii. 22 Priscian himself.. notwithstanding his strictness in giving Rules.. has much ado to preserve himself from Barbarism. *a* **1716** SOUTH *Serm.* (1727) VI. 430 They never understood the fiery Strictness of the Law, nor the Spirituality of the Gospel. **1861** PATTISON *Ess.* (1889) I. 47 Peace and order were maintained by police regulations of German minuteness and strictness. **1909** *Blackw. Mag.* Mar. 311/2 The strictness of the Jain observances varies a great deal, according to the sect.

5. Closeness of watch or scrutiny.

1806 *Med. Jrnl.* XV. 510 In consequence of this intimation, Pierre Landart was watched with the greatest strictness.

6. Rigorous accuracy or precision in statement, interpretation, investigation, and the like.

1638 SANDERSON *Serm., Ad Aulam* vii. (1681) II. 97 Divine (especially Prophetical) expressions, are not ever tied to such strictnesses. **1726** SWIFT *Gulliver* II. vii, I.. gave to every point a more favourable turn, by many degrees, than the strictness of truth would allow. **1787** J. MITFORD *Plead. Suits Chanc.* (ed. 2) 232 In pleading there must in general be the same strictness in equity as at law. **1885** *Law Rep.*, 28 Chanc. Div. 97 A clause which this Court has always been in the habit of construing with the greatest strictness.

b. Phr. ***in strictness***: taken or understood strictly; according to a strict conception, definition, or interpretation. More explicitly ***in strictness of speech***, ***of law***, etc.

1641 WILKINS *Math. Magick* II. i. (1648) 145 But in its strictnesse and propriety, it is onely appliable unto fresh inventions. **1660** R. COKE *Power & Subj.* 135 In cases wherein things in conscience ought to be done, yet for want of some formalities or niceties they cannot in strictness of law be exacted. *a* **1691** BOYLE *Chr. Virtuoso* II. Wks. 1772 VI. 748, I chose to take in.. several that perhaps did not in strictness belong to the *Christian Virtuoso*. **1692** ATTERBURY *Serm.* (Ps. l. 14) (1726) I. 7 Praise and Thanksgiving do, in Strictness of Speech, signify things somewhat different. **1794** G. ADAMS *Nat. & Exper. Philos.* IV. xliv. 188 Dr. Herschel even goes so far as to suppose that there is not, in strictness of speaking, one fixed star in the heavens. **1849** MACAULAY *Hist. Eng.* v. I. 639 She was undoubtedly guilty of what in strictness is a capital crime. **1863** LYELL *Antiq.*

Man 6 The term Post-pliocene ought in strictness to include all geological monuments posterior in date to the Pliocene. **1870** FREEMAN *Norm. Conq.* (ed. 2) I. App. R. 595 Neither of these Kings were, in strictness of speech, deposed.

† **'strictory.** *Obs.* [ad. med.L. *strictōrium*, f. L. *strict-*, *stringĕre* to bind: see -ORY.] A medicated compress.

a **1425** tr. *Arderne's Treat. Fistula* etc. 96 Aboue þis emplastre..putte a strictorie of white of eiren and mele of whete and lynnen cloutez y-dipped þerin. **1430–40** LYDG. *Bochas* I. xx. (1554) 36 b, They haue strictories to make their skin to shine, wrought subtilly of gommes and of glaire.

‖ **stricto sensu** ('strɪktəʊ 'sɛnsuː). Also *erron.* **strictu sensu.** = SENSU STRICTO.

1931 [see FOLSOM]. **1972** *Mod. Law Rev.* XXXV. I. 55 In the case of custom *stricto sensu* lack of consensus enhances the importance of the consolidating effect of time. **1976** *Times Lit. Suppl.* 17 Sept. 1176/3 'A philosophical analysis of the feasibility' of the structuralist enterprise *stricto sensu.* **1979** *Nature* 22 Feb. 599/1 Thus 'mosaic' RNAs produced by splicing are *strictu sensu* recombinant molecules in that they contain data drawn from different parts of the genome.

strictural ('strɪktjʊərəl), *a.* [f. STRICTURE *sb.*[1] + -AL[1].] Pertaining to or of the nature of a stricture.

1886 J. M. DUNCAN *Dis. Women* xii. (ed. 3) 95 There is no strictural obstruction to the progress of the fæces.

stricture ('strɪktjʊə(r)), *sb.*[1] Also 5 strictture. [a. L. *strictūra*, f. *strict-*, *stringĕre*, really two etymologically distinct verbs of coincident form in Latin: the one (whence branch I below) with the sense to bind tightly, draw tight, strain; the other (whence branch III) with the senses to touch lightly, to gather (flowers), to draw (a sword). Cf. F. *stricture* (16th c. in Littré) = sense 1 below.]

I. A binding, tightening.

1. a. *Path.* A morbid narrowing of a canal, duct, or passage, esp. of the urethra, œsophagus, or intestine.

c **1400** *Lanfranc's Cirurg.* 199 If þere be ony þing to take awei þerof as akynge ouþer ony strictture, ouþer ony byndyng, þan remeue awey þat first [etc.]. **1797** M. BAILLIE *Morb. Anat.* (1807) 340 The most ordinary diseased appearance of the urethra is stricture. **1804** ABERNETHY *Surg. Observ.* 209 A similar plan of conduct is very suitable to strictures of the œsophagus. **1846** J. MILLER *Pract. Surg.* 269 Stricture of the Windpipe. *Ibid.* 407 Stricture of the Rectum. **1887** *Encycl. Brit.* XXII. 575/2 Stricture of the Pylorus.

b. *Phonetics.* Partial or complete closure of the air-passage in the articulation of speech sounds.

1943 K. L. PIKE *Phonetics* vii. 120 At the time in the production of some sound when any moveable part of the vocal apparatus causes any *stricture* (the partial or complete closure of an air passage) it becomes an *articulator.* **1962** B. M. H. STRANG *Mod. Eng. Structure* 31 Articulated sounds may further be differentiated by the variable shape of the articulators and strictures involved in their production. **1964** J. C. CATFORD in D. Abercrombie et al. *Daniel Jones* 26 The articulatory stricture *generates* turbulent airflow. *Ibid.* 32 These five major phonatory stricture types.

2. *gen.* in various occasional uses: The action of binding or encompassing tightly; tight closure; restriction. *rare.*

1649 JER. TAYLOR *Gt. Exemp.* II. Disc. ix. 116 Christ came to knit the bonds of government faster by the stricture of more religious tyes. **1726** POPE *Odyss.* XXII. 186 Within the stricture of this palace wall To keep inclos'd his masters till they fall. **1731** ARBUTHNOT *Aliments* vi. (1735) 158 For the lateral Vessels, which lie out of the Road of Circulation, let gross Humours pass, which could not if the Vessels had their due degree of Stricture. **1812** J. J. HENRY *Camp. agst. Quebec* 103 Bred at home under the strictures of religion and morality. **1821** SCOTT *Kenilw.* xviii, I defy chemistry..and every other occult art, were it as secret as hell itself, to unloose the stricture of my purse-strings. **1822** WORDSW. *Eccl. Sonn.* I. *Seclusion* 12 Like ivy, round some ancient elm, they twine In grisly folds and strictures serpentine. **1849** D. G. MITCHELL *Battle Summer* (1852) 103 Old strictures are removed, and what managers will, is put upon the scene. **1889** STEVENSON *Master of Ballantrae* v, A windless stricture of frost had bound the air. [Cf. quot. 1686 in 4.]

† **II. 3.** A spark, flash of light. *lit.* and *fig. Obs.*

[The L. *stricturæ* in Virg. *Æn.* viii. 421 was formerly interpreted 'a spark from the anvil'; hence this use, which when figurative blended with sense 4.]

1627 J. DOUGHTY *Serm. Divine Myst.* (1628) 4 Flashes and strictures of lightning doe indeed enlighten the eye, but..they doe also hurt it. **1651** MANTON *Comm. James* iii. 9. 379 Yea in the Body there were some rays and strictures of the divine Glory and Majesty. **1656** BLOUNT *Glossogr.*, *Stricture*, a spark that flies from a piece of iron red hot, when it is beaten. **1666** SPURSTOWE *Spir. Chym.* (1668) 17 Those two tapers which enlighten the same room, do not shine with a Divided..light,..and yet the Eye..cannot difference the raies and strictures that flow from them. **1674** tr. *Scheffer's Lapland* Pref., Amidst the barbarity and darkness which reign in Lapland, there appear strictures of light which will entertain the eie of the most knowing observer.

III. A touching slightly or in passing.

† **4.** A touch, slight trace. *Obs.*

a **1672** WILKINS *Nat. Relig.* II. i. (1675) 289 In the actions of many brute creatures, there are discernable some footsteps, some imperfect strictures and degrees of Ratiocination. **1674** W. BATES *Harmony Div. Attrib.* iv. 55 There are some weak strictures of Truth in lapsed Man, but they dye in the Brain, and are..ineffectual as to the Will. *a* **1676** HALE *Prim. Orig. Man.* (1677) 63 Whatever may be said of other matters, certainly the first draughts and strictures of Natural Religion and Morality are naturally in the Mind. **1686** GOAD *Celest. Bodies* II. iv. 198 We need not wonder at some stricture of Frost occurring. **1695** J. EDWARDS *Perfect. Script.* 573 They surpass all humane wisdom, yet..they have strictures of all arts and sciences.

5. An incidental remark or comment; now always, an adverse criticism.

1655 HAMMOND *Acc. Cawdrey's Triplex Diatribe* 289 What now followes §35, is so far from having any weight in it, that I must not allot any solemn answers to it, the lightest strictures will be more proportionable. **1664** H. MORE *Myst. Iniq.* II. xi. 401 These are the chiefest strictures that do occurre to my minde in the Prophetick Visions that are applicable to this second member of Antichristianism. **1722** WOLLASTON *Relig. Nat.* ix. 218 At the foot of the page I have in some places subjoind a few little strictures principally of antiquity, after the manner of annotations. **1779** JOHNSON *L.P., King* (1781) II. 276 He bestowed some strictures upon Dr. Kennet's adulatory sermon at the funeral of the duke of Devonshire. **1781** —— *Let. to Mrs. Thrale* 20 Oct., We may now and then add a few strictures of reproof. **1790** *Cook's 3rd Voy.* V. 1658 Here ends Mr. Anderson's strictures on Otaheite, and its neighbouring islands. **1804** L. MURRAY *Gram.* Advt. to 9th Ed. *note*, The author conceives that the occasional strictures, dispersed through the book, and intended to illustrate and support a number of important grammatical points, will not..appear to be dry and useless discussions. **1831** D. E. WILLIAMS *Life & Corr. Sir T. Lawrence* II. 383 His profession had a right to expect from him a series of strictures upon the works of the great masters. **1878** STUBBS *Const. Hist.* III. xviii. 101 Beaufort ...was unsparing in his strictures. **1910** *Q. Rev.* Apr. 321 Her strictures on some sightseers in Berlin reveal some knowledge of art.

† **'stricture,** *sb.*[2] *Obs. rare*$^{-1}$. [f. STRICT *a.* + -URE.] Strictness.

1603 SHAKS. *Meas. for M.* I. iii. 12 A man of stricture and firme abstinence.

stricture ('strɪktjʊə(r)), *v. rare.* [f. STRICTURE *sb.*[1]] *trans.* To criticize, censure.

1851 HELPS *Comp. Solit.* v. (1874) 59, I had been..stricturing, perhaps too severely, some recent acts of government.

strictured ('strɪktjʊəd), *ppl. a.* [f. STRICTURE *sb.*[1] + -ED[2].] Affected with stricture.

1801 *Med. Jrnl.* V. 224 Fæces..bearing marks of having passed some strictured part of the intestine. **1879** *St. George's Hosp. Rep.* IX. 420 The walls of the strictured portion were much softened. **1886** J. M. DUNCAN *Dis. Wom.* xxviii. (ed. 3) 251 The ileum being strictured.

transf. **1838** LYTTON *Alice* v. ii, Sir John Merton—very civil, very pompous, and talking, at strictured intervals, about county matters, in a measured intonation, savouring of the House-of-Commons jerk at the end of the sentence.

stricturotomy (strɪktjʊə'rɒtəmɪ). *Surg. rare*$^{-0}$. [f. STRICTURE *sb.*[1] + -(O)TOMY.] (See quot. 1898.)

1876 DUNGLISON *Med. Lex.*, *Stricturotomy*, Urethrotomy. **1898** *Syd. Soc. Lex.*, *Stricturotomy*, a cutting operation for the relief of stricture.

strictu sensu, ¶ var. STRICTO SENSU.

strid (strɪd). [app. repr. OE. *stride*: see STRIDE *sb.*] The proper name of the narrowest part of the channel of the Wharfe between level rocks at Bolton Priory; hence, any similar gorge or chasm.

[**1807** WORDSW. *Force of Prayer* 21 The striding place is called The Strid.] **1863** KINGSLEY *Water-Bab.* iii. 116 On through narrow strids and roaring cataracts, where Tom was deafened and blinded for a moment by the rushing waters. **1895** MEREDITH *Amazing Marr.* xli, Any pauses occurring, he was the one guilty of them; she did not allow them to be barrier chasms, or 'strids' for the leap with effort.

striddle ('strɪd(ə)l), *sb.* [f. the verb.] A stride.

1721 RAMSAY *Elegy Patie Birnie* xi, How pleasant was 't to see thee diddle And dance sae finely..With nose forgainst a lass's middle,..With cutty steps to ding their striddle, And gar them fag. **1835** D. WEBSTER *Sc. Rhymes* 42 (E.D.D.) Losh! he lamps at the rate o' four yards at a striddle.

striddle ('strɪd(ə)l), *v. Obs.* exc. *dial.* [Back-formation from STRIDDLING *adv.*]

1. *intr.* To stand with the legs wide apart; to straddle.

1530 PALSGR. 732/2, I stande a strydling with my legges abrode, *je me esquarquille.* **1570** LEVINS *Manip.* 128/12 To striddil, *varicari.* *a* **1585** MONTGOMERIE *Flyting* 19 Strydand and stridland like Robin red-brest. *c* **1640** *Gramercie Good Scot* in Maidment *Scot. Ballads* (1868) I. 340 Where are our proud Prelates that strideled so wide. **1825** BROCKETT *N.C. Gloss.*, *Striddle*, to straddle.

2. To stride.

1785 BURNS *2nd Epist. J. Lapraik* ix, Sin' I could striddle owre a rig. **1821** SCOTT *Pirate* iv, It's nae pleugh of the flesh that the bonny lad-bairn..sall e'er striddle between the stilts o'—it's the pleugh of the spirit.

3. *Comb.* **striddle-legs** *adv.*, astride.

1825 BROCKETT *N.C. Gloss.*, *Striddle-legs*, astride. **1900** 'R. GUTHRIE' *Kitty Fagan* 84 One man..sat 'striddle-legs' on the chimney, to the huge delight of the juveniles.

Hence **'striddling** *ppl. a.*

1638–9 *Caveat for Scot.* in Maidment *Scot. Pasquils* (1868) 65 With Gallaway Tam: that squint-eyed stridling asse.

striddling(s ('strɪdlɪŋ(z)), *adv. dial.* Forms: 5–6 **strydlingis,** 7, 9 **stridling,** 9 **stridelins, stridlin(g)s** (see *Eng. Dial. Dict.*). [f. *strid-* wk. stem of STRIDE *sb.* or *v.* + -LING, -LINGS.]

Astride.

c **1440** *Alphabet of Tales* 392 And onone þe devull come & sett hym stridlyngis on hys bakk. **1528** LYNDESAY *Dreme* 89, I bure thy grace vpon my bak, And, sumtymes, strydlingis on my nek. **1632** LITHGOW *Trav.* IX. 395 The women ride here stridling in the sadle. **1822** GALT *Sir A. Wylie* xl, I didna mean that she was to gallop, stridling on a horse, wi' you in a pock before her.

stride (straɪd), *sb.* Also 4–5 **stryde,** 5 **strede.** [Two formations: (1) OE. *stride* str. masc. (corresp. to MLG. *strede*), f. *strid-* wk.-grade of the root of STRIDE *v.* The ME. spelling *stride, stryde* may sometimes represent this formation (with short *i*), which, with regular dialectal development of the vowel appears also in the 15th c. form *strēde*; the latter, however, might also possibly represent OE. (north.) *strǣde*, f. the same root. (2) The surviving word, f. the pres.-stem of the vb., is attested already *a* 1300 in the *Cursor Mundi* (line 10592) by the rhyme with *biside.*]

1. a. An act of striding; a long step in walking. Phrase ***at*** or ***in a stride.***

c **1200** *Trin. Coll. Hom.* 111 He steh to heuen-liche heh settle, and wiche strides he makede dunward, and eft uppard, þat seið sanctus salomon þe wise. *c* **1440** *Promp. Parv.* 480/1 Stryde, *clunicatus.* **1518** WHITINTON *De Heteroclitis Nom.* B iij, *Passus*, a stryde. **1545** ASCHAM *Toxoph.* II. (Arb.) 146 Some wyll gyue two or iii. strydes forwarde, daunsing and hoppynge after his shafte, as long as it flyeth. **1548** *Elyot's Dict.*, *Grallatorius gradus*, a great or longe stride, suche as one taketh that goeth on styltes. **1596** SHAKS. *Merch. V.* III. iv. 68 Ile..turne two minsing steps Into a manly stride. **1609** HEYWOOD *Brit. Troy* XII. xcii. 324 Accootred thus, strong Aiax with huge strides Stalkes in the field before the best of men. **1667** MILTON *P.L.* II. 676 The Monster moving onward came as fast, With horrid strides. **1741** RICHARDSON *Pamela* (ed. 3) I. 240 There was first the horrible Colbrand, running with his long Legs, well nigh two Yards at a Stride. **1837** DICKENS *Pickw.* xxiv, Mr. Pickwick had taken a few strides to and fro. **1860** TYNDALL *Glac.* I. xiv. 99 We went downwards with long swinging strides. **1906** CHARL. MANSFIELD *Girl & Gods* xxiv, The sexless females..whose strides disgrace their petticoats.

b. *transf.* and *fig.* Esp. in phr. ***to take*** or ***make strides:*** to make progress.

1600 J. CHAMBERLAIN *Lett.* (Camden) 97 Mrs. Pranell is like to make a wide stride from that she was, to be Countesse of Hartford. **1658** SIR T. BROWNE *Hydriot.* Ep. Ded., Simplicity flies away, and iniquity comes at long strides upon us. **1756** MRS. CALDERWOOD in *Coltness Collect.* (Maitland Club) 189, I said I had never heard of one taking such a stride at once, as from the top of the kirk of Scotland to the top of the church of Rome. **1791** W. HUTTON *Hist. Derby* 285 Having now got into the political world,..he made rapid strides towards preferment. **1815** SCOTT *Guy M.* xi, Our narration is now about to make a large stride, and omit a space of nearly seventeen years. **1880** KINGLAKE *Crimea* VI. x. 384 The newly split stones..had scarce been yet worn down to smoothness when already the stride of a railway began to cover the ground. **1914** *Blackw. Mag.* Nov. 580/2 Stride by stride the village has closed in on the modest manor. **1926** J. S. HUXLEY *Essays in Pop. Sci.* 21 Great strides have been taken in this field too during the last twenty years. **1934** *Discovery* Dec. 362/2 Photography for all purposes has made immense strides latterly. **1956** J. B. WILSON *Lang. & Pursuit of Truth* i. 14 The development of a good system of notation made it possible to take great strides in our mathematical knowledge. **1976** *Field* 18 Nov. 979/1 Great strides have been made in short term forecasting in the last five years.

c. The distance covered by a stride; the normal length of a stride used as a measure of distance. Phr. ***to lengthen*** (or ***shorten***) ***one's stride,*** (*U.S.*) ***to lengthen*** (or ***shorten***) ***stride.***

c **725** *Corpus Gloss.* (Hessels) P 134 *Passus*, faeðm *uel* tuegen stridi. **13..** *K. Alis.* 4433 (Laud MS.), Ne miȝtten men a stride go Bot men stepped on ded men. *a* **1320** *Sir Tristr.* 1488 No ȝede he bot ten stride, His speche les he þar. *cc* **1380** *Sir Ferumb.* 4644 And nowar myȝte he passe be-syde, For þe roche was heȝ an hundred stryde. **1470–85** MALORY *Arthur* IV. x. 131 Syre Arthur..gaf hym..suche a buffet that he went thre strydes abak. **1471** CAXTON *Recuyell* (Sommer) 256 And as for shotyng a ferre, he passid the ferthest on the felde .xxiiii. stredes. **1590** SPENSER *F.Q.* II. vii. 24 Betwixt them both was but a litle stride. **1663** WOOD *Life* (O.H.S.) I. 482 A part of the quadrangle, containing 30 of my strides in square. **1670** COVEL in *Early Voy. Levant* (Hakl. Soc.) 163 The first tent..was 15 strides long and 12 broad. **1706** PHILLIPS (ed. Kersey), *Stride*, two Steps, or a Measure of five Foot. **1824** SCOTT *Redgauntlet* ch. xvi, I am to carry you to old Father Crackenthorp's, and then you are within a spit and a stride of Scotland, as the saying is. **1925** E. F. NORTON *Fight for Everest: 1924* 32 On April 8 we lengthened our stride and covered 12 miles. **1978** *Washington Post* 24 Mar. B6/2 Her many backers had some anxious moments as she shortened stride after a clear lead at the head of the stretch. **1980** H. D. WESTACOTT *Walker's Handbk.* (ed. 2) iv. 60 On level ground use your natural stride and resist any temptation to lengthen it. On a gradient the stride should be shortened.

d. Extent of reach. *nonce-use.*

1703 SWIFT *Sid Hamet's Rod* 53 Sid's Rod was of a larger stride, And made a circle thrice as wide.

† **e.** One of a flight of steps. *Obs. rare*$^{-1}$.

a **1300** *Cursor M.* 10592 þis maiden..was..on þis grece..On þe neþermast stepp don, Bot sco þan clamb an oþeir son; Þþat quils þai locked [= looked] þam biside Sco was won to þþe heist stride.

2. a. A striding gait; a manner of progression by long steps.

1671 MILTON *Samson* 1067, I know him by his stride. c1705 POPE *Imit. Dorset, Artemisia* 18 Her voice theatrically loud, And masculine her stride. 1813 SCOTT *Trierm.* I. xvii, While she aped a martial stride. 1853 C. BRONTE *Villette* x, I recognized his very tread: it was the same firm and equal stride I had followed under the dripping trees. 1893 *Outing* XXII. 154/2 Green was slightly crotch-bound, and had in consequence a 'digging stride'.

†**b.** An energetic walking tour. ? *nonce-use.*

1767 S. PATERSON *Another Trav.* I. 112 He chose to take great strides upon the continents of Europe and Asia.

c. A distance traversed by a striding walk.

1834 PRINGLE *Afr. Sk.* xiii. 376 *note*, The usual mode of measuring..was for the *Veld-wagt-meester*..to stride or pace the ground; and half an hour's stride in each direction from the centre..was the regulated extent of the farms.

3. a. An act of progressive movement of a horse, or occasionally of other quadrupeds, completed when all the feet are returned to the same relative position which they occupied at the beginning; also, the distance covered by such a movement.

1614 MARKHAM *Cheap Husb.* I. i. 5 Be sure that he take a long stride with his feete, for..he which takes the largest strides goes at the most ease. 1846 *J. Baxter's Libr. Pract. Agric.* I. 415 Then, too, comes the art of the rider, to keep the horse within his pace, and..to add to the length of every stride. 1860 *Baily's Mag.* I. 301 The former [horse]..winning in the last stride by a head. 1861 *Sporting Rev.* June 414 Stride for stride he [the favourite] caught his horses; but still he did not go like a winner. 1875 W. PATERSON *Notes Milit. Surv.* (ed. 3) 80 Horse's stride in walking = about 1 yard. Ditto..galloping..about 2¼ yards.

b. *transf.* with reference to foot-racing.

1879 H. C. POWELL *Amateur Athletic Ann.* 19 [In the 100 yds. scratch race] It was only in the last few strides that he [the winner] could show at all in front. 1901 *Oxford Mag.* 24 Apr. 291/1 Brown overhauled Richards in the last stride.

c. The regular or uniform movement (of a horse) in a race. Hence *transf.* of rowers, their 'swing'. Freq. in phrases, as ***to get into one's stride, to hit one's stride, to put*** or ***throw*** (someone) ***out of*** (or ***off***) ***his stride.***

1883 PENNELL-ELMHIRST *Cream Leicestersh.* 356 Horses have been pulled out of their stride. 1901 *Daily News* 1 Apr. 5/6 The Dark Blues, however, almost immediately pulled themselves together, and got into their stride.

fig. 1890 S. WEBB *Let.* in J. MacKenzie *Victorian Courtship* (1979) viii. 104, I had a bad week... But I have 'got into my stride again' now. 1909 *Athenæum* 2 Jan. 9/3 The metre refuses to flow:..the reader loses his stride and has to return to the beginning of the line to get a fresh start. 1919 *Punch* 12 Mar. 210/1 The operator won the first game before I could get into my stride. 1933 A. POWELL *From View to Death* i. 19 Conversationally, Zouch was getting back into his stride and he knew that by the evening he would be in good form. 1941 E. S. GARDNER *Case of Haunted Husband* viii. 53 He threw me out of my stride for a whole half day. 1946 K. TENNANT *Lost Haven* (1947) xiv. 226 'Why, I had a talk with him only the other night.' 'Did you?' Dipper asked, put out of his stride. 1955 H. KURNITZ *Invasion of Privacy* (1956) xii. 77 It was late in the working day..but..Louis Stradling was just hitting his full stride. 1967 N. FREELING *Strike out where not Applicable* 85 'Who told you that?'.. The young man was thrown out of his stride. 1978 D. DEVINE *Sunk without Trace* xxii. 202 He was disappointed. He didn't think I'd let a man like Max Sapiro put me off my stride. 1983 *Listener* 27 Jan. 21/1 But when Mr. Maccoby gets into his stride of explaining the mechanisms of what has so often been the loathsome behaviour of so-called Christians to Jews, his book becomes of potent interest.

d. ***to take in his stride***: of a horse or his rider, to clear (an obstacle) without checking his gallop; *fig.* to deal with (a matter) incidentally, without interrupting one's course of action, argument, etc. Also (chiefly *U.S.*) without possessive adj.

1832 *Q. Rev.* XLVII. 239 Seven men, out of thirteen [fox-hunters], take it [the brook] in their stride. 1854 SURTEES *Handley Cr.* xxxv. (1901) I. 281 Cantering up, cracking his whip, as if he wanted to take it [*sc.* the fence] in stride. *Ibid.*, He rose in his stirrups and pounded while Charley took the fence in his stride.

fig. 1902 *Nature* 25 Dec. 171/1 Acting on this opinion, Ostwald has introduced physical theories, applicable to chemical facts, 'in his stride,' as it were. 1905 E. WHARTON *House of Mirth* xv, I'd want something that would look more easy and natural, more as if I took it in my stride. 1908 MISS BROUGHTON *Mamma* v, Her niece's talent for 'getting things' out of people..lay..in a brutal directness of inquiry, that took rebuffs in its stride. 1941 B. SCHULBERG *What makes Sammy Run?* iii. 48 It was funny to see him taking the Vendome [*sc.* an expensive restaurant] in stride too. 1974 *Publishers Weekly* 7 Jan. 49/2 Coach John Wooden..has taken it all in stride. 1976 *New Society* 3 June 521/1 Everyone understood what it meant to be photographed and took the request in stride.

4. a. Divergence of the legs when stretched apart laterally; straddle; also, the distance between the feet when the legs are stretched apart laterally to the utmost.

1599 T. STORER *Life & D. Wolsey* F 2 b, If once we fall, we fall Colossus-like,..They that betweene our stride their sailes did strike [etc.]. 1632 LITHGOW *Trav.* x. 455 My legs being put to the full stride, by a maine gad of iron aboue a yard long. 1681 COTTON *Wonders of Peak* 12 And yet above the Current's not so wide To put a Maid to an indecent stride. 1727 BAILEY vol. II, *Stride*, the greatest Distance between the Feet set wide. 1798 R. DODD *Port Lond.* 6 Through its arch will be seen sailing, gallant ships, like the ancient gallies through the stride of the great Colossus in the isle of Rhodes.

b. *transf.*

1791 W. GILPIN *Rem. Forest Scenery* I. 106 When two shoots [of an oak] spring from the same knot, they are commonly of unequal length; and one with large strides generally takes the lead. 1850 BECKETT-DENISON *Clock & Watch-m.* 47, 20° between them [*sc.* the rollers of the pendulum] would give them a sufficiently wide stride for a firm bearing and add hardly anything to the pressure.

c. *Tailoring.* (See quot. 1806-7.)

1806-7 J. BERESFORD *Miseries Hum. Life* xx. No. 33 (1826) 257 A pair of pantaloons so constructed with regard to what taylors call the stride as to limit you to 3 or 4 inches per step. 1922 JOYCE *Ulysses* 344 A navy threequarter skirt cut to the stride showed off her slim graceful figure to perfection. 1939 *Country Life* 11 Feb. p. xxxiii/2 (Advt.), There is plenty of stride; the knees are well formed; the lines and run of seams are perfectly executed.

d. *pl.* Trousers. Also occas. breeches; jeans. *slang.*

1889 A. G. MURDOCH *Scotch Readings* (Ser. 3) 26 His two legs, which were encased in a pair of all but skintight 'strides'. 1889 CLARKSON & RICHARDSON *Police!* xxv. 346 If the 'Peter' (cash-box) can be found, that is at once appropriated, as also are a man's 'strides' (trousers). 1914 JACKSON & HELLYER *Vocab. Criminal Slang* 81 *Strides*,..a pair of trousers. 1924 *Truth* (Sydney) 27 Apr. 6 *Strides*, trousers. 1932 L. MANN *Flesh in Armour* 291 His tunic and light coat were of the ultra fashionable style, and his strides would not have disgraced an officer of the Guards. 1947 D. M. DAVIN *For Rest of our Lives* xxxviii. 196 Trying to get his strides up. 1950 'N. SHUTE' *Town like Alice* ix. 261 Could you get into a pair of my strides? 1960 'A. BURGESS' *Doctor is Sick* xxvi. 211 He handed a crumpled bundle to Edwin, saying: 'You'll 'ave to take my strides.'.. The trousers, Edwin found, were too short. 1973 M. AMIS *Rachel Papers* 186 The Oxford University candidate was to be seen in T-shirt and khaki strides. 1980 B. MASON *Solo* 91, I wiped damp hands on my serge strides.

5. The action of bestriding. *rare*$^{-1}$.

a1616 BEAUM. & FL. *Wit at sev. Weapons* II. i, *Lady.* So, what Saddle have I? *Pris.* Mounsieur Laroon's... *Lady.* That agen, You know so well it is not for my stride, How oft have I complain'd on't?

†**6.** ? A foot-bridge. *Obs.*

1791 *Rep. Commiss. Thames-Isis Navig.* 15 At the lower End of this Channel there is a Pen formed by a Swing Stride and Flood Gates.

7. Ellipt. for *stride piano* (see sense 8 b below).

1956 PANASSIÉ & GAUTIER *Guide to Jazz* 260/2 *Stride*, a piano style much in use by soloists about 1930. 1969 *Listener* 6 Feb. 186/3 Peterson stands at the end of a long and honourable tradition of jazz piano playing originally known as 'Harlem stride'. The stride refers to a left-hand vamping method using alternating tenths and note clusters at least an octave apart. 1975 *New Yorker* 19 May 6/2 Jaki Byard, who displays a confident feel for ragtime, stride, and more modern piano styles, has fun with bassist Major Holley.

8. a. *Comb.*: **stride-high** *a.*, placed at such a height as to be reached by a stride; **stride-leg(s** *adv.* (*Sc.* and *north.*), astride, 'straddle-legs'; **stride-legged** *a.*, riding astride; *adv.* astride; **strideways** *adv.*, astride.

1906 *Pall Mall Gaz.* 16 Apr. 2/1 Smooth steps projecting, *stride-high, from the breasts of the rough masonry. 1809 T. DONALDSON *Poems* 150 He sat down *stridelegs on a stane. 1828 *Ann. Reg.* 378/1 Burke stood stride legs over her. 1894 CROCKETT *Raiders* xx. 180 Yet it was an amazing sight—Dee Bridge that night, with..men stride-leg on the parapet of it. 1688 HOLME *Armoury* III. 310/2 A like Torture ..is for an Offender to sit *stride-legged over a great Gun, and so to have it Fired. 1879 STEVENSON *Trav. Cevennes* (1895) 30 A pair of mounted stride-legged women..dashed past me at a hammering trot. 1859 MEREDITH *R. Feverel* xxiii, I wish they'd let us ride our ponies *stride-ways.

b. *Jazz.* Used *attrib.* to designate a style of piano-playing in which the left hand alternately plays a single note and a chord that is an octave (or more) higher; *esp.* in ***stride piano*** (hence ***stride pianist***); also ***stride accent, bass, tempo***, etc.

c1938 N. E. WILLIAMS *His Hi de Highness of Ho de Ho* 35/2 'Gut tempo' and 'stride tempo' usually are intelligible only to our own musicians. 1950 BLESH & JANIS *They all played Ragtime* x. 192 He could play the ragtime stride bass, but it bothered him because his stomach got in the way of his arm, so he used a walking bass instead. 1952 B. ULANOV *Hist. Jazz in Amer.* iv. 29 'Stride piano', the particular pride and joy of Fats Waller and, before him, of innumerable ragtime pianists, comes from the blues. *Ibid.* 30 The blues is usually played in unaccented four/four time or with stride accents. 1955 L. FEATHER *Encycl. Jazz* 289 His lacy, charming melodies sometimes contrast with 'stride' passages of great intensity. 1959 *Jazz Rev.* June 14/1 He [*sc.* James P. Johnson]..developed the New York style of 'stride' piano from the rags of Scott Joplin and the southern Negro cotillion and set dances. 1978 *Listener* 29 June 841/2 An exhilarating two hours of Fats Waller numbers.. accompanied on stage by the celebrated stride pianist, Luther Henderson. 1983 *Listener* 20 Jan. 10/2 Its earliest landmark was James P. Johnson's stride-piano showpiece 'Carolina Shout'.

stride (straɪd), *v.* Pa. t. **strode** (strəʊd), pa. pple. **stridden** (strɪd(ə)n), (*colloq.*) **strode**. Forms: 1 **strídan**, 3 **striden**, 4 **strid**, (*3rd pers. sing.* **strit**), 4-6 **stryd(e**, 5 **strydyn**, 4- **stride**. *Pa. t.* 4-9 *north.* **strade**, 5 *Sc.* **straid**, 5, 7 **strad**, 6 *Sc.* **straide**, 6 **stryd**, 7 **strid**, 7-9 **strided**, 5- **strode**. *Pa. pple.* 6 **stridde**, 7 **strid**, 9- **stridden**. [OE. *strídan* str. vb. (once only, but cf. *bestrídan*, found once in pa. t. *bestrád*: see BESTRIDE *v.*) = (M)LG. *strîden* str. vb., to set the legs wide apart, straddle, to take long steps; cf. LG. *bestriden* to bestride (a horse). The vb. is not found elsewhere in Teut. with similar sense, but is formally coincident and prob. identical with the str. vb. meaning to strive, quarrel: OFris. *strîda*, (M)Du. *strijden*, MLG. *strîden*, OHG. *strîtan* (MHG. *strîten*, mod.G. *streiten*); of the same or similar meaning are the weak verbs, OS. *strîdian* (MLG. *strîden*), ON. *stríða* (Norw., Sw. *strida*; Da. *stride* is now conjugated strong); cf. OFris., OS. *strîd*, Du. *strijd*, OHG. *strît* (mod.G. *streit*) masc. strife, quarrel, ON. *stríð* neut. strife, grief, affliction (Norw., Sw., Da. *strid*), *stríða* fem. adversity, severity, *stríð-r* stubborn, severe (Norw., Sw., Da. *strid*).

The primary meaning of the Teut. root **strîd-* is commonly assumed to be 'contention' or 'strong effort'. On this view the Eng. sense of the vb., 'to take long steps' (sense 2 below), would be a development from the continental sense 'to strive'. This would in itself be possible, but sense 1 would remain unexplained. The assumption of a primary sense 'to diverge' (cf. Skr. *sridh* to go astray) would account plausibly on the one hand for the sense 'to quarrel', and on the other hand for the sense 'to straddle', from which the sense 'to take long steps' would be a natural development.

The later examples show much uncertainty with regard to the conjugation. Perhaps (though this is far from certain) most people would give *strode, stridden* in answer to a grammatical question; but in actual speech and writing there is often hesitation as to the correct form. The pa. pple. rarely occurs; our material includes hardly any 19th or 20th c. examples of *stridden*, and not many of *strided*. In the pa. t. *strode* is certainly the usual form; but where the reference is to a single act and not to a manner of progression there seems to be a tendency to say *strided* ('I strided over the ditch').]

†**1. a.** *intr.* To stand or walk with the legs widely diverging; to straddle. *Obs.* in literal sense; cf. b.

c700 *Epinal Gloss.* 1086 *Varicat*, stridit [So *Erfurt* and *Corpus*; Leiden *stridæd*]. a1310 in Wright *Lyric P.* xxxix. 110 Mon in the mone stond ant strit. 14.. *Lat.-Eng. Voc.* in Wr.-Wülcker 579/8 *Distrigio*, to stryde. 1530 PALSGR. 738/2, I stryde, I stond a stridlyng with my legges, *je me escarquylle*. Stryde and I will dryve thes schepe betwene thy legges. 1577 B. GOOGE *Heresbach's Husb.* III. 115 b, If wee assaye to take vp a thing from the ground, stryding, and not with our legges together, wee take it vp with more ease and strength. a1585 MONTGOMERIE *Flyting* 394 Some, on steid of a staig, ouer a starke monke straide. 1590 SPENSER *F.Q.* II. vii. 40 The gate was open, but therein did wait A sturdy villein, striding stiffe and bold. 1598 STOW *Surv.* 69 When the great fenne or Moore..is frozen, many young men play vpon the yce, some stryding as wide as they may, doe slide swiftly. 1623 COCKERAM II, To Stride wide in going, *diuaricate*. 1638 W. LISLE *Heliodorus* x. 180 Then [he] strid, and strongly pight His feet on chosen ground, with armes out-right, Backe, necke, and shoulders bent.

b. *transf.* (Often said of an arch.)

1598 SYLVESTER *Du Bartas* II. ii. IV. *Columnes* 201 Because th' acute, and the rect-Angles too, Stride not so wide as obtuse Angles doe. 1650 FULLER *Pisgah* v. xix. 176 How many, but especially how high must the arches therein be, to stride over so vast a concavity? 1787 BURNS *Written Kenmure Inn* 15 The arches, striding o'er the new-born stream. 1791 CUMBERLAND *Observer* No. 143 V. 197 The bridge of Toledo, which proudly strides with half a dozen lofty arches over a stream scarce three feet wide. 1858 HAWTHORNE *Fr. & It. Jrnls.* (1871) II. 238 An arched gateway..that..looked like a great short-legged giant striding over the street. 1863 —— *Our Old Home, Pilgr. Boston* I. 243 A Roman arch which..has been striding across the English street ever since the latter was a faint village path.

2. a. To walk with long or extended steps; to stalk.

Often with implication of haste or impetuosity, of exuberant vigour, or of haughtiness or arrogance.

c1200 *Trin. Coll. Hom.* 111 Here he cumeð stridende fro dune to dune, and ouer strit þe cnolles. a1300 *Cursor M.* 10235 Ioachim..tilward þe auter can stride. a1400-50 *Wars Alex.* 2194 (Dubl. MS.), þen tenyd þe tebe folke..And withstode his strenth & strode to þe walles. c1475 *Rauf Coilȝear* 32 His steid aganis the storme staluartlie straid. 1650 FULLER *Pisgah* v. xix. 178 The going up to the Altar was not divided into steps..but that it heightened it self by insensible degrees,..so that the Priests, not striding, but pacing up there-on, were not necessitated to any divarication of their feet. 1667 MILTON *P.L.* II. 676 The Monster moving onward came as fast, With horrid strides, Hell trembled as he strode. 1697 DRYDEN *Æneis* III. 880 But when our Vessels out of reach he found, He strided onward. 1735 SOMERVILLE *Chase* III. 276 The stately Elephant from the close Shade With Step majestick strides. a1790 BURNS '*My Harry was a gallant gay*' i, My Harry was a gallant gay Fu' stately strade he on the plain. 1791 BOSWELL *Johnson* an. 1768, He then rose up, strided to the fire, and stood for some time laughing and exulting. 1825 CROKER *Fairy Leg. Irel.* I. 153 With an air of becoming consequence he strided out of the stable-yard. 1829 J. STERLING *Ess.* etc. (1848) I. 78 He would have stridden among them without belonging to either faction. 1842 TENNYSON *Morte d'Arthur* 181 But the other swiftly strode from ridge to ridge,..looking, as he walk'd, Larger than human on the frozen hills. 1848 THACKERAY *Van. Fair* xxx, The hypocrite was..striding about the room, upsetting the chairs,..and showing other signs of great inward emotion. 1862 MISS BRADDON *Lady Audley* ix, Mr. Talboys strode out of the room, banging the door after him. 1951 R. LYND *Essays on Life & Lit.* I. 27 But a *gauche* big farmer's son in a white coat..had strode past her roughly. 1972 *Observer* (Colour Suppl.) 24 Sept. 23/2 The clear mental picture of the battlefront with which he had so boldly strode into Samsonov's headquarters.

b. with various advs. ***to stride out***: to go with vigorous strides.

1581 PETTIE *Guazzo's Civ. Conv.* III. (1586) 159 His sonne in law..used a slow and mincing pace, like a woman: his daughter..stryd out lustelie like a man. 1697 DRYDEN *Æneis* XII. 126 Striding on, with speedy Pace. 1798 JOANNA BAILLIE *Tryal* IV. iii. *Plays on Passions* (1821) I. 274 Come away, uncle, and see him go down the back walk,.. I'll warrant you he'll stride it away most nobly. **1837** DICKENS *Pickw.* ii, The officer whistled a lively air as he strode away. **1843** CARLYLE *Past & Pr.* II. x, Striding prosperously along. **1853** LYTTON *My Novel* XII. vi, Randal stood still for a few moments as Harley strided on. **1915** *Daily Tel.* 5 May 7/4 The going has seldom been better, and judging by the way the horses strode out they appreciated it in every way. **1980** *New Yorker* 24 Mar. 127/1 (Advt.), No consumer advocate has yet strode forth to defend and protect the interests of those who can afford a $30,000 sport coupe.

c. *transf.* and *fig.*

c **1205** LAY. 17982 þe leome gon striden a ueire seoue strengen. *c* **1400** *Destr. Troy* 4105 Fifté shippes full shene strode fro þe depe. **1839** LYTTON *Richelieu* I. i. 37 Midst Richelieu's foes I'll find some desperate hand To strike for vengeance, while we stride to power. **1884** *Harper's Mag.* Feb. 393/2 The long low barns with great windmills striding through the air. **1886** CORBETT *Fall of Asgard* I. 268 Five ships, each with forty oars swinging like music, were striding over the fjord. **1936** 'R. WEST' *Thinking Reed* iii. 89 From youth he had strode through the twenty-four hours at the pace of a Marathon race.

¶ **d.** To step, tread. *nonce-use.*

1596 SPENSER *F.Q.* IV. viii. 37 They.. kept on their readie way, With easie steps so soft as foot could stryde.

3. a. To take a long step; to advance the foot beyond the usual length of a step; to pass *over* or *across* an obstacle by a long step or by lifting the feet. Also in figurative context.

a **1310** in Wright *Lyric P.* xxxix. 111 Sete forth thyn other fot, stryd over sty. *a* **1320** *Sir Tristr.* 151 Ouer bord þai strade Al cladde. *c* **1440** *Promp. Parv.* 480/1 Strydyn (or steppyn ovyr a thynge) *clunico, patento, strigio.* **1530** PALSGR. 738/2, I stryde over a brooke or the canell or any fowle place as I am goyng, *je jamboye.* **1610** HOLLAND *Camden's Brit.* (1637) 199 To stride over the rivelet there. **1611** BEAUM. & FL. *Philaster* IV. iv. (1620) 51 When my fortunes eb'd, that men strid o're them carelesse, She did showre her welcome graces on me, And did swell my fortunes. **1634–5** BRERETON *Trav.* (Chetham Soc.) 45 The lowest of these hedges higher than any man can stride over. **1642** FULLER *Holy & Prof. St.* V. xi. 400 They that stride so wide at once will go farre with few paces. *c* **1643** LD. HERBERT *Autobiog.* (1824) 64 To teach men how far they may stretch out their Feet when they would make a Thrust.. lest they either overstride themselves, or not striding far enough fail to bring the point of their weapon home. **1818** MAGINN in *Blackw. Mag.* IV. 321 A Gulliver chap such as I, That could stride over troops of their tribes. **1899** J. MILNE *Romance of Pro-consul* ix. 89 The larger quarter-deck on to which Sir George Grey had stridden, much needed cleaning up.

b. With cognate obj.

a **1300** *Cursor M.* 5194 Israel wit þis vplepp þat moght noght forwit strid a step. **1661** CHILDREY *Brit. Baconica* 28 Ordulphus.. was a Giant-like man, that (if William of Malmesbury say true) would break open the bars of Gates, and stride 10 foot. **1859** TENNYSON *Marr. Geraint* 376 The Prince,.. fain To follow, strode a stride, but Yniol caught His purple scarf.. and said, 'Forbear!'

†**c.** To mount (*on* a horse, *into* a stirrup). *Obs.*

a **1300** in Wright *Anecd. Lit.* (1844) 96 Love is stalewarde and strong for to striden on stede. *a* **1400–50** *Wars Alex.* 778 Ilk a hathill to hors hiȝis him be-lyue, Stridis into stele-bowe stertis apon loft. *Ibid.* 2880 He.. Strad vp him-selfe on a stede in starand wedis, And on a cursoure þe kniȝt with a collt foloȝes. *c* **1400** *Destr. Troy* 10205 Achilles.. wan to his armys, Strode on a stith horse, stroke into batell. *c* **1470** *Gol. & Gaw.* 616 On twa stedis thai straid.

†**d.** To put the foot down *upon*; to tread *upon*. *Obs. rare.*

1581 A. HALL *Iliad* VI. 104 But for to plucke his Iaueline out, he forced was to stride Vpon the carcasse [Gr. λὰξ ἐν στήθεσι βάς].

4. *trans.* To step over with a stride.

c **1572** GASCOIGNE *Fruites Warre* cx, Where blockes are stridde by stumblers at a strawe. **1611** SHAKS. *Cymb.* III. iii. 35 A Debtor, that not dares To stride a limit. **1682** CREECH *Lucretius* (1683) 167 That Man of such vast force and limbs did rise, That he could stride the Ocean. **1709** CONGREVE tr. *Ovid's Art of Love* III. Wks. 1730 III. 310 Another, like an Umbrian's sturdy Spouse, Strides all the Space her Petticoat allows. **1821** CLARE *Vill. Minstr.* II. 110 A hedge to clamber or a brook to stride.

transf. **1906** *Westm. Gaz.* 25 Sept. 7/1, I would place two wheels at the front and two at the rear, with a considerable gap under the middle of the engine. This gap would permit it to stride a curve if I may put it that way.

5. To walk about (a street, etc.) with long steps; to pace; hence, to measure by striding.

1577 GRANGE *Golden Aphrod.* etc. R j, I stryde the streetes both long and wyde, A stealed sight of hir to haue. **1834** [see STRIDE *sb.* 2 c]. **1850** H. MELVILLE *White Jacket* II. xviii. 111 'Call all hands!' roared the Captain. 'This keel sha'n't be beat while I stride it.' **1853** LYTTON *My Novel* VIII. xii, Riccabocca.. with a firm step strode the terrace, and approached his wife. **1915** *Blackw. Mag.* Feb. 229/1 The brave ghosts who stride these fields and live in the people's mind are Englishmen.

6. To bestride.

13.. *K. Horn* 753 (Harl. MS.) His stede he bigan stryde. **1599** *George a Greene* B 1, They haue othe, Not to leaue one aliue that strides a launce. **1602** CHETTLE *Hoffman* IV. (1631) H 3 b, Some got on Rafts..; many strid the mast, But the seas working was soe violent, That [etc.]. **1605** SHAKS. *Macb.* I. vii. 22 Pitty, like a naked New-borne Babe, Striding the blast, or Heauens Cherubin, hors'd Vpon the sightlesse Curriors of the Ayre, Shall [etc.]. **1607** —— *Cor.* I. ix. 71, I meane to stride your Steed. **1657** BILLINGSLY *Brachy-Martyrol.* II. vii. 171 The old man strides his horse, and rides to look him. **1735** DYCHE & PARDON *Dict.*, *Stride*,.. to throw the Legs over the two Sides of a Thing, as a Horse, a Camel. **1820** SHELLEY *Prometh. Unb.* IV. 421 The tempest is his steed, he strides the air. **1868** J. G. HOLLAND *Kathrina* II. (1869) 103 E'en the prophet's ass Had better eyes than he who strode his back.

7. *Jazz.* To play stride piano (see STRIDE *sb.* 8 b).

Found only in the gerund or participial form *striding*.

1944 *Metronome* Nov. 17/3 Alberta Simmons, from down in the Jungles, could beat the average man 'striding'. **1958** P. GAMMOND *Decca Bk. of Jazz* xv. 187 Nobody else has compounded so many pianistic devices—the delayed note, the tremolo, the dazzling run, the striding bass—into such a homogeneous quiddity.

†**'stridelong**, *adv. Obs. rare*⁻¹. [f. STRIDE *sb.* + -LONG. Cf. STRIDDLING *adv.*] With the legs wide apart.

1609 HOLLAND *Amm. Marcell.* XIV. 16 The militarie men ..with hairie cords bound fast to his legges, drew him stride-long [L. *divaricatum*] without any intermission as farre as to the Præfects Prætorium.

stridence ('straɪdəns). [f. STRIDENT: see -ENCE.] The fact of being strident.

1890 S. P. THOMPSON in *Nature* (1891) 15 Jan. 252/1 For compound tones corresponding to the whole series, odd and even, there is, in every case, minimum intensity, brilliancy, and stridence with $\delta = \frac{3}{4}$, and maximum with $\delta = \frac{1}{4}$.

stridency ('straɪdənsɪ). [f. STRIDENT: see -ENCY.] The quality of being strident.

1865 *Even. Standard* 6 June, A peculiar stridency characterised the voice of the assailant. **1883** BESANT *All in Garden Fair* II. i, The piano.. required now the most delicate fingering to keep down the stridency of age. **1968** CHOMSKY & HALLE *Sound Pattern Eng.* 329 Stridency is a feature restricted to obstruent continuants and affricates. **1976** *Word 1971* XXVII. 220 This appearance of the Stridency distinction among Stops and Continuants evidently does not generalise immediately to the affricates. **1979** *Canad. Jrnl. Linguistics* XXIV. I. 20 It incorporates both articulatory (anteriority-coronality) and acoustic (stridency) features.

strident ('straɪdənt), *a.* (and *sb.*) [ad. L. *strīdentem*, pr. pple. of *strīdĕre*, to creak. Cf. F. *strident.*]

1. a. Making a harsh, grating or creaking noise; loud and harsh, shrill.

1656 BLOUNT *Glossogr.*, *Strident*, crashing or making a noise, creaking. **1721** BAILEY. **1848** THACKERAY *Van. Fair* li, 'Brava! brava!' old Steyne's strident voice was heard roaring over all the rest. **1860** FARRAR *Orig. Lang.* iv. 76 Strident consonants evidently formed from the hiss of certain serpents. **1875** H. JAMES *R. Hudson* xxv. (1879) III. 231 His strident accent. **1905** J. B. FIRTH *Highw. Derbysh.* xxvi. 394 The rush and rattle of strident wheels.

b. *Phonetics.* Of the articulation of a consonantal sound: characterized by friction that is comparatively turbulent. Also as *sb.*, a consonant articulated in this way.

1956 JAKOBSON & HALLE *Fundamentals of Lang.* 31 Strident/mellow: acoustically—higher intensity noise *vs.* lower intensity noise; genetically—rough-edged *vs.* smooth-edged. *Ibid.* 42 Mellow constrictives, opposed to strident constrictives, or strident plosives (affricates) opposed to mellow plosives (stops proper) do not appear in child language before the emergence of the first liquid. **1965** *Amer. Speech* XL. 9 *T* cannot follow a dental stop or *S* follow a strident (sibilant). **1968** CHOMSKY & HALLE *Sound Pattern Eng.* 329 Strident sounds are marked acoustically by greater noisiness than their nonstrident counterparts. **1976** *Word 1971* XXVII. 220, /s/.. [and] /f/.. also embody the Strident vs. Mellow distinction and are both + Strident.

2. *transf.* and *fig.*

1876 F. HARRISON *Choice Bks.* (1886) 413 All this is not to be disposed of by a somewhat strident scorn in the name of a somewhat mysterious gospel. **1907** *Athenæum* 25 May 641/1 The.. picture.. is free from the strident colour which he has sometimes fallen into of late.

Hence **'stridently** *adv.*

1859 BOYD *Recreat. Country Parson* (1862) 36 There lies the large blue quarto,.. there the massive foolscap,.. then the ivory stridently cuts it through. *a* **1894** STEVENSON *St. Ives* xxvi. (1908) 194 The whole enclosure continuously and stridently resounded with the rain.

strider ('straɪdə(r)). [f. STRIDE *v.* + -ER¹.]

1. One who strides.

1856 [H. H. DIXON] *Post & Paddock* i. 11 They [Shropshire horses] are.. quick striders through dirt. **1876** BLACKMORE *Cripps* xxxii, Hardenow came almost daily, having put his class of striders under a deputy six-leaguer. **1895** *Outing* Sept. 457/1 He is a wonderful strider, having occasionally taken two instead of three steps between the hurdles. **1895** MARG. STOKES *Three Months in Forests of France* 174 The stalwart strider by the side of the green-hooded waggons.

2. *U.S.* = *pond-skater* s.v. POND *sb.* 4.

1974 A. DILLARD *Pilgrim at Tinker Creek* xi. 189, I read that striders are attracted to any light. **1978** *Sci. Amer.* Apr. 134/1 When the strider stands on the surface film, it is supported by its long, slender middle and hind legs.

striding ('straɪdɪŋ), *vbl. sb.* [f. STRIDE *v.* + -ING¹.] The action of the vb. STRIDE.

c **1440** *Promp. Parv.* 480/1 Strydynge, *patentacio, stragiatus, pantagium.* **1677** COLES *Dict. Eng.-Lat.*, A striding over, *interceptio passis cruribus facta.* **1856** EMERSON *Eng. Traits, Lit.* Wks. (Bohn) II. 113 No hope, no sublime augury, cheers the student, no secure striding from experiment onward to a foreseen law. **1905** VACHELL *The Hill* ix. 187 A nod of the head, a keen look, and a striding off elsewhere.

Comb. **1807** WORDSW. *Force of Prayer* 21 The Striding-place is called The Strid.

striding ('straɪdɪŋ), *ppl. a.* [f. STRIDE *v.* + -ING².] That strides. Also *fig.*

1538 ELYOT *Dict.*, *Varicus*, an aduerbe, whyche sygnyfyethe strydynge. **1665** D. LLOYD *State-Worthies* (1670) 27 Men of quick and large striding minds loving to walk together. **1818** KEATS *Endym.* II. 24 What care, though striding Alexander past The Indus with his Macedonian numbers? **1891** N. GOULD *Double Event* xix, He meant to give the horse a good striding gallop as soon as it was light. **1909** ELIZ. BANKS *Myst. Frances Farrington* 101 The somewhat striding walk of a tall woman.

b. *striding level*: a spirit-level supported at both ends so as to straddle over intervening projections. So *striding stand*.

1878 LOCKYER *Stargazing* 332 Place a striding level on the pivots. **1890** W. F. STANLEY *Surv. Instrum.* 222 In the construction of the striding level,.. the two striding stands *SS* are carried down from the ends of the casing tube *B* of the spirit level.

stridingly ('straɪdɪŋlɪ), *adv.* [f. STRIDING *ppl. a.* + -LY².] In a striding manner.

1548 THOMAS *Ital. Gram., Dict.* (1550) F iv, *Cauascione*, stridynglie. **1677** MIEGE *Dict. Eng.-Fr.*, Stridingly, *en élargissant ses jambes.* **1842** *Tait's Mag.* IX. 289 He stepped timidly, and yet almost stridingly, towards me.

stridor ('straɪdə(r)). Also 7 stridour. [a. L. *strīdor*, f. *strīdĕre*: see STRIDENT *a.* Cf. F. *strideur.*]

1. A harsh, high-pitched sound, a shrill grating or creaking noise.

1632 W. LITHGOW *Trav.* x. 439 Least.. for the stridor of his teeth his charges be redoubled. **1649** BULWER *Pathomyot.* II. i. 90 That hated stridor that is so offensive to the Eares of those. **1697** DRYDEN *Æneis* XII. 1258 Juturna.. knew th 'ill Omen, by her screaming Cry, And stridour of her Wings. **1778** W. PRYCE *Min. Cornub.* 69 Bend a piece of pure Tin, or bite it hard, and it will give a crashing noise or stridor. **1846** LANDOR *Imag. Conv., Southey & Landor* Wks. 1853 II. 65/2 Now there never was an arrow in the world that made a horrible stridor in its course. **1880** A. H. SWINTON *Insect Variety* 152 Thus, if two males be confined, they maintain incessant stridor. *a* **1894** STEVENSON *Lay Morals* etc. (1911) 290 The listener heard in his memory.. the stridor of an animated life.

2. *Path.* A harsh, vibrating noise produced by some bronchial, tracheal, or laryngeal obstruction. (*Syd. Soc. Lex.*)

1876 BRISTOWE *Theory & Pract. Med.* (1878) 559 The patient suffers from more or less stridor of the breath sounds. **1898** *Allbutt's Syst. Med.* V. 280 The tracheal stridor and brassy cough. *Ibid.* VI. 376 The peculiar importance of laryngeal stridor with dyspnœa is not merely diagnostic.

stridulant ('strɪdjʊlənt), *a.* [ad. mod.L. *strīdulantem* (neut. pl. *Stridulantia*, the name of a group of insects), pr. pple. of *strīdulāre*: see next.] That stridulates.

1843 *Zoologist* I. 31 A stridulant little creature to which I frequently listened during the silent watches of the night.

stridulate ('strɪdjʊleɪt), *v.* [f. mod.L. *strīdulāt-*, *strīdulāre*, f. L. *strīdul-us*: see STRIDULOUS.] *intr.* To make a harsh, grating, shrill noise: said *spec.* of certain insects.

1838 tr. *Goureau* in *Entom. Mag.* V. 98, I am inclined to believe these insects mute,.. because I have never heard them stridulate. **1854** BADHAM *Halieut.* 101 Women are obliged to stridulate louder at each other as the wind rises and threatens to drown their voices. **1871** DARWIN *Desc. Man* x. (1874) 303 Some species stridulate very loudly. **1895** *Natural Sci.* Jan. 49 The spider stridulates to warn animals that would prey upon it of its deadly nature.

b. *Path.* (See quot.)

1898 *Syd. Soc. Lex.*, *Stridulate*, to suffer from stridor.

Hence **'stridulating** *vbl. sb.* and *ppl. a.*

1861–2 LE CONTE *Classif. Coleoptera N. Amer.* I. Introd. p. xx, Stridulating organs.. exist in various families. **1871** DARWIN *Desc. Man* ix. (1874) 273 The males of several species of Theridion have the power of making a stridulating sound. **1880** A. H. SWINTON *Insect Variety* 167 The Stridulating Locust (*Pachytylus stridulus*).

stridulation (strɪdjʊ'leɪʃən). [a. F. *stridulation* (Goureau 1837), agent-n. f. mod.L. *strīdulāre*: see STRIDULATE *v.*] The action of the vb. STRIDULATE; the stridulous noise produced by certain insects.

1838 tr. *Goureau* in *Entom. Mag.* V. 92 The male alone possesses the power of stridulation; he makes use of it to attract and please the female. *Ibid.* 94 The combination of all these little sounds produces the general sound or stridulation. **1871** DARWIN *Desc. Man* ix. (1874) 274 The stridulation serves.. to call.. the female. **1872** —— *Emotions* xiv. 350 Even insects express anger, terror, jealousy, and love by their stridulation.

stridulator ('strɪdjʊleɪtə(r)). [f. STRIDULATE *v.* + -OR.] **a.** An insect that stridulates. **b.** A stridulating apparatus.

1880 A. H. SWINTON *Insect Variety* 152 Others, as the Mole-crickets are evening stridulators. **1895** *Natural Sci.* Jan. 49 A small and feeble spider, which.. could in no sense profit, as the large spiders do, from the possession of a stridulator unless there were something terrifying or repellent in the sound pure and simple.

stridulatory ('strɪdjʊlətərɪ), *a.* [f. STRIDULATE *v.* + -ORY².] Pertaining to, causing, or caused by stridulation; also, capable of stridulating.

1838 tr. *Goureau* in *Entom. Mag.* V. 93 It is sufficient to cut off one of the elytra; we shall then see the cricket execute the stridulatory movement without producing any sound. *Ibid.* 97 The stridulatory sound. *Ibid.* 363 All the stridulatory insects hitherto mentioned. **1874** DARWIN *Desc. Man* x. (ed. 2) 288 The females have rudiments of the stridulatory organs proper to the male.

†**'stridulency.** *Obs. rare.* [f. L. *strīdul-us* (see STRIDULOUS) + -ENCY.] Stridulousness.

1657 REEVE *God's Plea* 21 High phrased bablings, Pharisaicall boastings and stridulencies.

stridulent ('strɪdjʊlənt), *a.* [f. L. *strīdul-us* (see next) + -ENT. Cf. STRIDULANT *a.*] = next.

1874 COUES *Birds N.W.* 118 They..have a not displeasing stridulent sound, from mingling of the weak chirrups from so many throats. **1880** RUSKIN in *19th Cent.* June 957 Coarse, stridulent, and, in the ordinary sense of the phrase, 'broad' forms of utterance, are not dialects at all.

stridulous ('strɪdjʊləs), *a.* [f. L. *strīdul-us* (f. *strīd-ēre*: see STRIDENT *a.*) + -OUS.]

1. Emitting or producing a shrill grating sound.

1611 CHAPMAN *Iliad* III. Comm. 48 But where they were graue and wise Counsellors, to make them garrulous, as Grashoppers are stridulous; that application holdeth not in these old men. *a* **1634** BP. HALL *Serm. Beauty & Unity Ch.* Wks. II. 369 The Church then is a Dove.., not a stridulous Jay. **1663** BOYLE *Usef. Exp. Nat. Philos.* II. v. xiv. 250 A servant sometimes complained to me,..that when he was put to whet a knife, that stridulous motion of the air was wont to make his gummes bleed. **1819** H. BUSK *Vestriad* IV. 767 Stridulous guitar with wiry twang. **1864** G. A. LAWRENCE *Maurice Dering* II. 32 That..stridulous young person, who..screams when she talks, and squalls when she sings. **1878** LONGF. *Ovid in Exile* II. 30 Nor as before o'er the Ister Comes the Sarmatian boor driving his stridulous cart.

2. Of voice, sound: Harsh, shrill, grating.

1646 SIR T. BROWNE *Pseud. Ep.* II. vi. 95 A small and stridulous noyse. **1778** BP. LOWTH *Transl. Isaiah* Notes 153 A feeble stridulous sound. **1779** G. WHITE *Selborne* II. xlvi. *To Barrington* (1789) 252 The shrilling of the field-cricket, though sharp and stridulous,..marvellously delights some hearers. **1790** COWPER *Iliad* II. 268 In piercing accents stridulous. **1873** MORLEY *Rousseau* I. 229 Rousseau.. sought new life away from the stridulous hum of men.

3. *Path.* Pertaining to or affected with stridor.

1822–29 GOOD *Study Med.* (ed. 3) I. 609 *Laryngismus stridulus.* Stridulous constriction of the larynx. **1877** F. T. ROBERTS *Handbk. Med.* (ed. 3) I. 360 More or less dyspnoea is usually felt, while the breathing may be stridulous.

Hence **'stridulously** *adv.*; **'stridulousness.**

1727 BAILEY vol. II, Stridulousness. **1831** *Blackw. Mag.* XXX. 317 The old dotard..is heard feebly and stridulously proclaiming, 'Take notice! I will' [etc.].

strie: see STRAY *v.*[1], STRY.

strie, strier, obs. forms of STROY *v.*, STROYER.

strief, striek: see STRIFE, STREEK *v.*

†**strif.** *Obs.* Also 5 **stryf, strift.** [Error of some kind for MDu. *schreve*, a use of *schreve* line, mark (mod.Du. *schreef*).] A measure for Rhenish wine, one-24th of the ohm or aam.

1495 HALYBURTON *Ledger* (1867) 22 A stek off Ryne vyne hald 3 ham and 1 strif, the rowd cost 15 li. 15 s. **1496** *Ibid.* 25 A stek of Ryns wyne haldand 4 ham 12 strift. *Ibid.* 90 A stek of Rynis wyne..haldand 4 ham 18 stryf.

strif, obs. form of STRIVE *v.*

strife (straɪf). Forms: 3–5 **strif, stryf,** 3–7 **strive,** 4 **strijfe,** 4–5 **strijf, striif,** 4–6 **striff(e, stryff(e, stryve,** 4–7 **stryfe,** 5–6 **stryif(f,** 6 **strief,** *Sc.* **strywe,** 4– **strife.** Pl. 4–6 **stryves** (4–5 **-is, -ys**), 4–7 **strives;** 4 **strifs,** 5 **stryfs,** 4–5 **stryfes, -ys, strifis,** 6– **strifes.** [a. OF. *estrif*, related to *estriver*: see STRIVE *v.*]

1. a. The action of striving together or contending in opposition; a condition of antagonism, enmity, or discord; contention, dispute.

a **1225** *Ancr. R.* 200 þe uormest is Cheaste, oðer Strif. *c* **1250** *Gen. & Ex.* 373 Nið, and strif, and ate, and san, Sal ben bitwen neddre and wimman. *a* **1300** *Cursor M.* 28196 Wit flitt, wit brixil, striue and strut. *c* **1350** *Leg. Rood* iii. 838 A fell woman and full of strife. **1471** CAXTON *Recuyell* (Sommer) 74 They desired nothing but stryf & debate. **1535** COVERDALE *Ps.* liv. 9 For I se vnrightuousnes & strife in ye cite. **1546** J. HEYWOOD *Prov.* II. ii. (1867) 47 The diuell hath cast a bone..to set stryfe Betweene you. **1601** SHAKS. *Jul. C.* III. i. 263 Domesticke Fury, and fierce Ciuill strife. **1692** PRIOR *Ode Imit. Hor.* viii, When bound in double Chains poor Belgia lay, To foreign Arms, and inward Strife a Prey. **1750** GRAY *Elegy* 73 Far from the madding crowd's ignoble strife. **1867** SMILES *Huguenots Eng.* vi. (1880) 90 The unemployed sought to remove to some foreign country less disturbed by party strife.

b. An act or instance of contention or antagonism; a contest or conflict, a quarrel or dispute.

a **1225** *Leg. Kath.* 735 Comen alle strikinde..for to heren þis strif. *a* **1300** *Cursor M.* 18568 þan bigan a neu strif Son bituix þam and min kynghtes. *c* **1380** WYCLIF *Sel. Wks.* I. 218 Suche diuisioun is cause of bateilis and strives among men. **1474** CAXTON *Cheese* IV. iv. (1883) 173 To appese alle stryues and contencions. **1484** —— *Fables of Alfonce* iv, They fylle in a grete dyfferent or stryf. **1568** GRAFTON *Chron.* II. 111 Strifes increased in the land euery where. **1570** LEVINS *Manip.* 152/31 A striue, *certamen.* **1600** FAIRFAX *Tasso* I. xxx, These striues..And discords. **1671** TRENCHFIELD *Cap Gray Hairs* (1688) 43 He that blows the Coals in other strifes, shall be sure to have the sparks fly in his mouth. **1844** H. H. WILSON *Brit. India* I. 217 The counsels of the elders of the tribe..arrested the strife upon the eve of its occurrence. **1846** SUMNER *Scholar, Jurist,* etc. 69 With-drawing from the strifes of the world. **1875** JOWETT *Plato* (ed. 2) IV. 259 His simple and noble thoughts..soon degenerated into a mere strife of words.

c. *transf.* and *fig.* Now *rare.*

1398 TREVISA *Barth. De P.R.* v. xxxi. (1495) 142 Also it happeth that..wynde is gadred and closed wythin the smalle skynnes of the rybbes and by the stryf therof is brede sore pryckynge and ache. *c* **1400** *Destr. Troy* 10105 Pollexene the pert with hir pure loue..stoppet the strif of his strong hert. *c* **1491** *Chast. Goddes Chyld.* 12 That is somtime for a stryfe betwene the spirite and the flesshe. **1773** JOHNSON (ed. 4), *Strife*..4. Natural contrariety; as, the strife of acid and alkaly. **1797–1809** COLERIDGE *Three Graves* III. 378 He reach'd his home, and by his looks They saw his inward strife. **1822** BYRON *Heaven & Earth* iii, While safe amidst the elemental strife, Thou sitt'st within thy guarded ark! **1826** HOOD *Mermaid of Margate* 69 And whilst he stood, the watery strife Encroach'd on every hand. **1901** *Macm. Mag.* Apr. 450/2 The north wind blew up the crests of the waves in the race as when we were in the strife of it.

d. A subject of contention. *rare.*

1535 COVERDALE *Ps.* lxxix. [lxxx.] 6 Thou hast made vs a very strife vnto our neghbours. **1662** H. NEWCOME *Diary* (Chetham Soc.) 118 But I have ever yet beene made the strife of tongues. [Cf. Ps. xxxi. 20 (1535 Coverdale and 1611).] **1738** WESLEY *Psalms* lxxx. vii, A Strife we are to All around.

†**e.** *occas.* (for rime). Trouble, toil, pain, distress. *Obs.*

c **1250** *Gen. & Ex.* 268 Fro swinc, and sorwe, and deades strif. *Ibid.* 778 Ðe king ðholede sorȝes strif. **1390** GOWER *Conf.* III. 10 Mi joie is torned into strif. **1567** *Gude & Godlie Ball.* (S.T.S.) 28 The flesche man die, with paine and striue.

f. *Austral. colloq.* Trouble, disgrace, difficulties. Freq. in phr. *in strife.*

1963 A. LUBBOCK *Austral. Roundabout* 45 'By cripes!' said the landlord, 'I bet you was in strife after that.' **1966** *Sunday Mail Mag.* (Brisbane) 9 Jan. 2/2 He's having trouble with his irrigation. His sudax is coming along all right but he's often in strife priming his pump. **1966** P. MATHERS *Trap* 15, I reckon she needs..a bloody flogging... She'll get us all in strife, he finished. **1969** 'A. GARVE' *Boomerang* iv. 147 'Keep close on my tail,' he called. 'If you get in any strife, bang on your horn.'

2. *Phr.* †**a.** *in strife*: in a state of discord or contention. *Obs.* (See also sense 1 f.)

a **1300** *Cursor M.* 14544 þir Iues þat him hild in strijf, þai hatted na man mare on lijf. **1398** TREVISA *Barth. De P.R.* VI. xviii. (1495) 204 A good lorde..acordyth theym that ben in stryffe. *c* **1470** HENRY *Wallace* I. 194 For he with thaim hapnyt richt offt in stryff. **1544** BETHAM *Precepts War* I. cxxxii. Gvb, And chefely when thy kingdom is in stryfe. **1590** SHAKS. *Mids. N.* v. i. 228 If I should as Lion come in strife Into this place.

b. *at strife*: at variance. †Also, *at a strife.*

c **1470** HENRY *Wallace* I. 237 The ȝong captane has fallyn with me at stryff. **1508** DUNBAR *Poems* v. 25 Scho..held Sanct Petir at stryfe. **1579–80** NORTH *Plutarch, Romulus* (1595) 25 Romulus and Remus..fell sodainely at a strife together about the place where the citie should be builded. **1593** SHAKS. *3 Hen. VI,* I. ii. 4 Why how now Sonnes, and Brother, at a strife? **1670** DRYDEN *Tyr. Love* v. i. 52 My lab'ring thoughts are with themselves at strife. **1746** P. FRANCIS tr. *Horace, Ep.* I. i. 141 If my judgment, with itself at strife, Should contradict my general course of life. **1861** PATTISON *Ess.* (1889) I. 34 The crown of England, always at strife, and often at open war, with its own barons. **1878** BROWNING *La Saisiaz* 35 Why are right and wrong at strife?

†**c.** *without strife*: without demur; without doubt, indisputably, unquestionably. Sometimes app. a mere tag, for rime. Also, *thereof no strife*: that is not disputed. *Obs.*

1297 R. GLOUC. (Rolls) 6417, & wan Edmond made is eir of is lond wiþoute striue. *a* **1300** *K. Horn* 407 'Horn', heo sede, 'wiþute strif þu schalt haue me to þi wif'. *a* **1300** *Cursor M.* 4622 'Do wai,' he said, 'þer-of na strif.' *c* **1380** *Sir Ferumb.* 1892 Noþeles woldy of þe fayn wyte wyþ-oute strif, Wat maner man ys Charlemayn. **1375** in Horstm. *Altengl. Leg.* (1878) 124/2 And bad hem boþe wiþoute stryf Naȝt eten of þe tre of lyf. *c* **1407** LYDG. *Reson & Sens.* 6831 Alceste.. ches to goon vn-to hir grave Wilfully, without[e] stryve.

†**d.** *by* or *with strife*: by force or violence. *Obs.*

c **1330** *Arth. & Merl.* 6493 What bi loue & what bi striif, He forlay þe stewardes wiif. *c* **1400** *Destr. Troy* 174 And wo this wethur shuld wyn bude wirke as I say, Ayre euyn to þe Oxen, entre hom in yoke, With striffe or with stroke till þai stonde wolde.

†**e.** *to have, hold, make, take strife*: to contend, quarrel (*with*). *Obs.*

c **1374** CHAUCER *Boeth.* I. pr. iv. (1886) 9, I took stryf [L. *certamen suscepi*] ayeins the prouost of the pretorie for comune profit. *c* **1375** *Sc. Leg. Saints* xxxvi. (*Baptist*) 721 Cese, þare-for, & hald na strife. *c* **1385** CHAUCER *L.G.W.* 595 For which he tok with rome & Cesar stryf. *c* **1400** *Rule St. Benet* (Verse) 650 And mak no strif with old no ȝing. **1430–40** LYDG. *Bochas* VIII. i. (1558) 2 b, The tyraunt Decius agayn them toke a stryfe. *a* **1450** *Knt. de la Tour* xiv. 20 Faire doughters, kepe you that ye take no striff with no comberous folke. *c* **1600** SHAKS. *Sonn.* lxxv. 3 And for the peace of you I hold such strife, As twixt a miser and his wealth is found.

f. *to make strife*: to cause dissension.

1303 R. BRUNNE *Handl. Synne* 1192 Take no wyfe For to make betwyxe ȝou stryfe. *c* **1400** MAUNDEV. (1839) ii. 11 Thei seyd, that he made Discord and Strif amonges hem. **1822** BYRON *Heaven & Earth* iii, Get thee hence, son of Noah; thou makest strife.

3. Competition, emulation; an effort or exertion of rivalry, a contest of emulation. †*to make strife*: to contend or compete (*for*). †*by strifes*: in emulation or rivalry.

1530 PALSGR. 277/1 Stryfe bytwene two, *brigue. Ibid.* 277/2 Stryfe who shall do best, *estriue a lestriuee. Ibid.* 630/1, I make stryfe to gette an offyce that gothe by election, *je brigue.* **1556** T. HOBY *Castiglione's Courtyer* (1561) Ep. Transl. A iiij, With an honest strife of matching others. **1592** SHAKS. *Ven. & Ad.* 291 His Art with Natures workmanship at strife, As if the dead the liuing should exceed. **1593** —— *Lucr.* 1791 Then sonne and father weep with equall strife, Who shuld weep most for daughter or for wife. **1623** B. JONSON in *Shaks. Wks.* To Rdr., Wherein the Grauer had a strife with Nature, to out-doo the life. **1630** R. N. *Camden's Hist. Eliz.* I. 56 The wealthier Inhabitants also of the Sea-coasts..built them ships of warre by striues who should exceede. **1697** DRYDEN *Virg. Past.* vii. 23 Great was the strife betwixt the Singing Swains. **1709** J. JOHNSON *Clergym. Vade-M.* II. p. cx, In those Ages, when..the Laity did as it were by strifes run into Monasteries. *a* **1710** CONGREVE *To Earl Godolphin* 105 Thus Gods contended, (noble Strife! Worthy the heavnly Mind) Who most should do to soften anxious Life. **1836** THIRLWALL *Greece* xv. II. 305 Let us still be rivals: but let our strife be, which can best serve our country.

4. The act of striving; strong effort. *rare.*

1601 SHAKS. *All's Well* v. iii. 338 Which we will pay, With strife to please you, day exceeding day. **1603** —— *Meas. for M.* III. ii. 246 One, that aboue all other strifes, Contended especially to know himselfe. **1642** D. ROGERS *Naaman* 136 We know what strife a man useth in his trade, who hath no inward principle of skill to enable him. **1687** tr. *Sallust* (1692) To Rdr., As if these Mystic Authors made it their strife to imitate Nature. **1827** KEBLE *Chr. Yr., 2nd Sund. Advent* vi, Be your strife To lead on earth an Angel's life.

5. *attrib.* and *Comb.*, as ***strife-fellow***, †***-race***; objective, as ***strife-maker***, ***-monger***; ***strife-hatching***, ***-stirring***, ***-torn*** ppl. adjs.; ***strife-weary*** adj.

1875 MORRIS *Æn.* v. 108 But some were dight amid the games their strife-fellows to be. **1598** SYLVESTER *Du Bartas* II. ii. IV. *Columnes* 32 Men's strife-hatching, haut ambition. **1552** HULOET, Stryfe maker, *litistonsor, rixosus, contumeliosus.* **1909** *Edin. Rev.* Oct. 466 The solemn warning to strife-mongers with which he concludes. **1647** TRAPP *Comm., Heb.* xii. 1 Ἀγῶνα.. The strife-race, for we must run, and fight as we run, strive also to outstrip our fellow-racers. **1591** SYLVESTER *Ivry* 315 Our strife-stirring Quils. **1972** R. D. WALSHE in G. W. Turner *Good Austral. Eng.* xi. 227 The ego ceases to be a shifting strife-torn no-man's-land between the armies of the id and the superego. **1983** *Times* 30 Mar. 7/2 She flies there today on her third tour of the strife-torn Brahmaputra valley state in the past 10 weeks. **1949** KOESTLER *Promise & Fulfilment* III. i. 302 Millions of war-worn, strife-weary people longing to find peace.

strife, obs. form of STRIVE *v.*

strifeful ('straɪfful), *a.* Forms: 4 **striffful,** 5 **stryffule, -fulle,** 6 **strifull, strivefull, stryf(f)ul(l,** 6–8 **strifefull,** 8– **strifeful.** [f. STRIFE *sb.* + -FUL.] Full of strife; contentious.

1382 WYCLIF *Ecclus.* viii. 14 Stonde thou not aȝen the face of the striffful. **14..** in *Walter of Henley's Husb.* etc. (1890) 148 That in no wyse be in the howseholde, men debatefulle or stryffulle. **1590** SPENSER *F.Q.* III. ii. 12 Her list in strifull termes with him to balke. **1591** —— *M. Hubberd* 1021 Th' Ape was stryfull, and ambicious. **1621** G. SANDYS *Ovid's Met.* I. 102 Nor Swords, nor Arms were yet:..nor strifefull Trumpets sound. **1726** POPE *Odyss.* XXI. 410 Eumæus, thus incourag'd, hastes to bring The strife-full bow. *a* **1835** WORDSW. *Misc. Sonn.* II. '*Four fiery Steeds*', Soldiers..sick at heart of strifeful Christendom. **1850** *Tait's Mag.* XVII. 762/2 We are no apologists for the violence committed..in those strifeful days. **1890** W. MORRIS in *Eng. Illustr. Mag.* July 762 They are a strifeful race.

strifeless ('straɪflɪs), *a.* [f. STRIFE *sb.* + -LESS.] Free from strife.

1621 G. SANDYS *Ovid's Met.* I. 24 With strifeless peace. **1858** J. M. NEALE *Rhythm of Bern. de Morlaix* (1864) 17 Peace, endless, strifeless, ageless, The halls of Syon know. **1906** S. W. MITCHELL *Pearl* 30 The strifeless bourne of Paradise.

strifer, strifing, obs. ff. STRIVER, STRIVING.

striff(e, obs. forms of STRIFE.

striffen ('strɪfən). *Sc.*, *Ulster*, and *U.S. local.* Also 9 **striffion, striffan, -in,** etc. (see *Eng. Dial. Dict.*). [Of obscure origin.] A thin membranous film; a thin skin or membrane.

a **1612** LOWE *Chirurg.* (1634) 142 The fourth [membrane] is called Arnoides, it is very white and delicate, like unto the thinne striffen of an ynzoin or Spiders webbe. **1802** M. CUTLER *Life, Jrnls. & Corr.* (1888) II. 71 A pie called macaroni, which appeared to be a rich crust filled with the striffions [*printed* strillions] of onions. **1824** MACTAGGART *Gallovid. Encycl.* 397 Low poor fallow now ye be, Wi' striffan white drawn owre thy e'e. **1836** *Shetld. Jrnl.* in *Chamb. Edin. Jrnl.* 31 Dec. 388/2 The interior membrane, or, to speak in our own dialect, the black striffin, left in the lugs of the fish.

†**strift.** *Obs.* Also 4 **strijft,** 7 **strifte.** [f. STRIVE *v.* + -T[3] a, after *drift*, *thrift*, etc.

In the first quot. the true reading is prob. *þrift*, but the erroneous reading perh. indicates that the word was in existence at the date of the Göttingen MS.]

The action of striving; an instance of this; also, contention, strife.

The word seems to have survived to some extent in the traditional religious phraseology of the Society of Friends; the use of it in the *Epistle* of 1893 (see quot. below) gave rise to much discussion in the Society.

[*a* **1300–1400** *Cursor M.* 4439 (Gött.) He ferd ay wid sua mekil strijft [*Cott.* thrift] þat all was done as he wald scift.] **1612** BRINSLEY *Lud. Lit.* v. 50 This same strift for these Masteries, and for rewards of learning, is the most commendable play. *Ibid.* xiv. 195 This exercise is..a stirrer vp of inuention and of good wits to strift and emulation. **1615** CROOKE *Body of Man* 195 Hippocrates saith, that the onely cause of the strifte of the Infant in the byrth is the want of Nourishment. **1619** W. WHATELY *God's Husb.* I. (1622) 112 Hee is busie in labouring to obey, and a man that liues with him, may euen perceiue in him..a strift this way. *a* **1656** USSHER *Ann.* (1658) 868 Exhibiting shews in the theatre, all kinds of musicall ostentations or strifts, and other variety of pleasures. **1674** N. FAIRFAX *Bulk & Selv.* 119 So neither has the first spring of motion any thing of onwardness or stirring, but only a pend or earnest strift fromwards, which we call springsomness or bearing. *Ibid.* 124 The spring or strift to stir. **1710** PRIDEAUX *Orig. Tithes* v. 276 Those [laws]..which they would never have made that strift for..had they been put in Execution upon them. *Ibid.* 281 In the Reigns of King Stephen..and King John when the greatest strift was about these Laws. **1815** J. J. GURNEY in Brathwaite *Mem.* (1854) I. 107 Overcome by a violent apoplectic attack, and in the strift of death. **1828** *Ibid.* 374, I think there is good reason to suppose a period of some strift and considerable loss to be at hand. **1845** MRS. ELIZ. FRY in Fry & Cresswell *Mem.* (1847) II. 518 [Her dying words] Pray for me—It is a strift, but I am safe. **1893** *Epistle Yearly Meeting Soc. Friends* 2 Take comfort from the thought that others have passed through as great a strift, and have come forth into peace and happy trustfulness.

strift: see STRIF *Obs.*, a measure for wine.

strig (strɪg), *sb.* Also 6 **strigge**. [Of obscure origin.]

1. The stalk of a leaf, fruit, or flower; a petiole, peduncle, or pedicel. Also, the stem of the hop cone.

1565 J. HALLE *Hist. Expost. Table* 114 Certayne tender strigges of *Iuncio palustris*..the marshe rushe. **1572** in Feuillerat *Revels Q. Eliz.* (1908) 156 Strigges of bay Leaves for twigg heades at vi[d] the peece. **1577** B. GOOGE *Heresbach's Husb.* IV. 187 Perfume them with *Galbanum*, Reazins, or olde strigges of Grapes. **1578** LYTE *Dodoens* VI. xvi. 678 The roote [of Heath] is tender..and putteth foorth in diuers places many newe twigges or strigges. **1674** RAY *S. & E.C. Words* 76 (*bis*) The *Strig*: the footstalk of any fruit. Petiolus. Suss[ex]. **1682** WHELER *Journ. Greece* IV. 309 A quadrangular Stalk, set at several distances with Leaves, upon a long strig or stem. **1881** WHITEHEAD *Hops* 13 One fault in the flower cones of the old fashioned Grape hops is that they have a thick strig or stem. **1891** *Jrnl. R. Agric. Soc.* 852 The central stem, or 'strig' of the hop cones. **1901** *Times* 2 Sept. 6 [Birds] will strip a currant-bush of its fruit so effectively as to leave nothing but the bare strigs.

2. A long thin appendage in various tools; the tang of a sword-blade (*Cent. Dict.*); the stem of a marking-gauge; or the like. Also, the projection under the bowl of a tobacco-pipe.

1703 [R. NEVE] *City & C. Purchaser* 195 The Scraper..is ..of Steel, in the form of an Equilateral Triangle, in the middle of which is fixed an Iron Strig, on the end of which is fixed a Wooden-knob, or Handle. **1805** R. W. DICKSON *Pract. Agric.* II. 596 The earthing up may be accomplished with facility by the above implement, merely by fixing a small piece of wood on the strig of it. **1844** *Florist's Jrnl.* (1846) V. 159 From the base of the two lower ones the strig or tail is fastened, which is thrust into the earth to support and retain the label in its place. **1875** SEATON *Fret-Cutting* 83 The marking gauge is composed of two pieces, the gauge block, through which passes the bar or strig on which is fixed the iron point that marks the work.

Hence **strig** *v. trans.*, to remove the strig or stalk from (currants, etc.); **'strigging** *vbl. sb.* (*attrib.* in ***strigging machine***).

1887 *Kentish Gloss.* 165 Will you help me strig these currants? **1899** *Jrnl. R. Agric. Soc.* Ser. III. X. 46 Some Dutch black currants..were being put through a patent stigging machine.

‖**striga** ('straɪgə). Pl. **strigæ** ('straɪdʒiː). [L. *striga* furrow, swath of hay or corn, flute of a column (= *stria*).]

†**1.** *Arch.* = STRIA 1. *Obs.*

1771 W. NEWTON tr. *Vitruvius' Archit.* III. iii. (1791) 64 The strigæ of the columns are in number twenty-four.

2. *Bot.* A row of stiff bristles; now, a stiff bristle (chiefly *pl.*).

1760 J. LEE *Introd. Bot.* III. xviii. (1765) 213 *Strigæ*, with their stiff Bristles, are of use to prevent Plants from being bruised and destroyed by Vermin. **1796** WITHERING *Brit. Plants* (ed. 3) I. 85 *Strigæ*, strong spear-shaped bristles, or thorns. **1829** T. CASTLE *Introd. Bot.* 109 The bristles of plants have also received other denominations..a. Striga, or stiff-bristles—that variety of the awl-shaped, which are seen in the common borage. **1840** PAXTON *Bot. Dict.*, *Strigæ*, little upright, unequal, stiff hairs, swelled at their bases.

3. *Ent.* (See quots.)

1826 KIRBY & SP. *Entomol.* xlvi. IV. 290 Striga (*Striga*). A narrow transverse streak. **1836** SHUCKARD tr. *Burmeister's Man. Entom.* 25 Striga (*striga*) a transverse band.

strigate ('straɪgeɪt), *a. Ent.* [ad. L. *strigāt-us*, f. L. *striga*: see STRIGA and -ATE[2].] = STRIGOSE *a.*[2] 2.

1891 *Century Dict.*

strigated (straɪ'geɪtɪd), *a.* [f. L. *strigāt-us* (see prec.) + -ED[1].] Having a channelled surface. **a.** *Min.* **b.** *Zool.* (in specific name of a snake).

1728 WOODWARD *Nat. Hist. Fossils* I. I. 147 Spar of a strigated or ridg'd Form. **1849** J. E. GRAY *Catal. Snakes Brit. Mus.* 10 The Strigated Trimesurus. *Trimesurus strigatus.*

‖**striges** ('straɪdʒiːz), *pl.* [L. *strigēs* (Vitruv.), synon. with *striæ*, *strigæ*: if the word be not a misreading, the sing. would normally be *strix*.] The channels of a fluted column.

1563 SHUTE *Archit.* D iij b, If this piller be garnished and filled with Canaliculi, and Striges. **1664** EVELYN tr. *Freart's Parallel Archit.* etc. 130 To the..Shafts of some Columns appertain Striges, which..are those excavated Channells, by our Workmen call'd Flutings. **1789** P. SMYTH tr. *Aldrich's Archit.* I. iii. 13 Those channellings in the shaft of the column, which are called by the several names of *Striæ*, *Striges*, or..*Strigiles*. **1842** GWILT *Archit.* Gloss. 1038.

striggle ('strɪg(ə)l). *colloq.* [perh. f. STR(AGGLE *v.*[1] + W)IGGLE *sb.*] A wavy line.

1906 W. DE MORGAN *Joseph Vance* xxx. 286 I've got him [*sc.* a fly out of the milk]! But he's brought a long striggle of cream out with him. **1963** V. NABOKOV *Gift* iv. 220 This old diary, which was written in an even hand with little striggles and was in a home-made code.

stright, obs. Sc. form of STRAIGHT.

strigil ('strɪdʒɪl). [ad. L. *strigilis*, f. *strig-*, *stringĕre* to touch lightly (see STRICTURE *sb.*).

The cognate pop.L. **strigula*, curry-comb, is represented by It. *stregghia*, OF. *estrille* (mod.F. *étrille*); it was adopted in OHG. as *strigil* (mod.G. *striegel*).]

1. *Ant.* An instrument with a curved blade, for scraping the sweat and dirt from the skin in the hot-air bath or after gymnastic exercise. Also applied *transf.* to a flesh-brush or other instrument used for the same purpose.

1581 MULCASTER *Positions* xxxiv. (1887) 123 Certaine scrapers called Strigiles. *a* **1700** EVELYN *Diary* June 1645, Being rubbed with a kind of strigil of seal's-skin, put on the operator's hand like a glove. **1775** R. CHANDLER *Trav. Asia M.* (1825) I. 63 We were rubbed with a mohair-bag fitted to the hand, which, like the ancient strigil, brings away the gross matter perspired. **1843** *Civil Engin. & Arch. Jrnl.* VI. 96/1 One day Hadrian recognized an old companion in arms in poverty, scraping himself with a tile instead of the strigil. **1854** FAIRHOLT *Dict. Terms Art*, *Strigil*, an instrument of bronze, curved, and hollowed like a spoon, used by the Romans to scrape off perspiration from the body after bathing. **1887** D. MAGUIRE *Art of Massage* ii. 19 Our masseurs of to-day use an instrument similar to the strigil made of box or any other hard wood, and call it sometimes strigil or *raclette*. **1894** J. STURGIS *Bk. Song* 8 Or naked Lysis, fresh from eager game, Draws down the strigil light o'er breast and limbs aflame.

2. *Ent.* (See quot.)

1873 F. B. WHITE in *Entomol. Monthly Mag.* X. 60, I found that the males of certain species [of *Corixa*] were provided with a curious structure... As this structure bears some resemblance to a 'curry-comb' it may be styled..the 'strigil' or 'strigiliform organ'. **1910** G. H. CARPENTER *Hemiptera* in *Encycl. Brit.* XIII. 261/1 The sixth segment [of the male *Corixa*] bearing on its upper side a small stalked plate (*strigil*)..furnished with rows of teeth.

3. *Comb.*

1870 ROLLESTON *Anim. Life* 23 The strigil-shaped first phalanx of the index digit.

strigilate ('strɪdʒɪleɪt), *a.* [ad. mod.L. *strigilātus*, f. L. *strigil-is*: see STRIGIL.] (See quot.)

1826 KIRBY & SP. *Entomol.* xlvi. IV. 330 Strigilate (*Strigilata*). When on the inner side of the first joint of the hand or palm the segment of a circle is taken out at the base opposite to the spur, the sinus being often pectinated with spines.

†**'strigilate**, *v. Obs.*[—0] [f. mod.L. *strigilāt-*, f. *strigil-is* STRIGIL.] *trans.* (See quot.) Hence **strigi'lation**.

1623 COCKERAM I, *Strigillate*, to currie a horse. **1656** BLOUNT *Glossogr.* **1658** PHILLIPS, *Strigilation*,..a currying of a horse.

strigiliform ('strɪdʒɪlɪfɔːm), *a.* [ad. mod.L. type *strigiliformis*, f. *strigili-s*: see STRIGIL and -FORM.] Having the form of a strigil.

1873 F. B. WHITE in *Entomol. Monthly Mag.* X. 60.

strigillose ('strɪdʒɪləʊs). *Bot. rare.* [f. mod.L. *strigilla*, dim. of STRIGA.] Finely strigose.

1857 A. GRAY *First Less. Bot.* 232 *Strigillose*, *Strigose*: beset with stout and appressed, scale-like or rigid bristles.

†**'strigment.** *Obs.* [ad. L. *strigmentum*, f. *strig-* root of *stringĕre*: see STRIGIL.] The dirt and perspiration scraped off the skin with a strigil or otherwise. Hence **strigmen'titious** *a.*, of the nature of 'strigment'.

1646 SIR T. BROWNE *Pseud. Ep.* II. v. 85 [Certain physicians] who beside the strigments and sudorous adhesions from mens hands, acknowledge that nothing proceedeth from gold in the usuall decoction thereof. **1745** R. JAMES *Med. Dict.* III. s.v. *Strigmentum*, Strigments absterged in the Baths are of a healing, mollifying, and discutient Quality. *Ibid.*, The strigmentitious Sordes of the *Palæstra*, which have a Mixture of Dust, discuss Collections of Matter about the Joints.

†**'strigose**, *a.*[1] *Obs.* [ad. L. *strigōsus*, lean, lank, meagre, f. *striga*: see STRIGA and -OSE.] Meagre, sapless. Also *fig.*

1708 BERKELEY *Commonpl. Bk.* Wks. 1871 IV. 478 In short, the dry, strigose, rigid way will not suffice. **1710** T. FULLER *Pharm. Extemp.* 231 The Juices of Herbs..correct a dry strigose Habit with mollifying Moisture.

strigose ('straɪgəʊs), *a.*[2] [ad. mod.L. *strigōsus*, f. L. *striga* (in mod.Latin uses): see STRIGA and -OSE.]

1. *Bot.* Covered with strigæ or stiff hairs. Also of hairs: Having the character of strigæ.

1793 MARTYN *Lang. Bot.*, *Strigosum folium*, a Strigose leaf ..set with stiff lanceolate bristles. **1832** LINDLEY *Introd. Bot.* I. ii. 42 The adjective term *strigose* is..occasionally still employed to express a surface covered with stiff hairs. **1866** *Treas. Bot.* 1104/1 *Strigose*, covered with strigæ. Linnaeus considered this word synonymous with Hispid. **1887** W. PHILLIPS *Brit. Discomycetes* 215 Covered with a very dense coat of rigid, fasciculate,..strigose hairs.

2. *Ent.* Having strigæ, streaked.

1826 KIRBY & SP. *Entomol.* xlvi. IV. 290 Strigose (*Strigosa*). Painted with several such streaks [*sc.* strigæ]. **1847** *Proc. Berw. Nat. Club* II. v. 256 Elytra..very minutely and strigose punctulate.

Hence **'strigosely** *adv.*

1866 *Treas. Bot.* 689/1 (*Lithospermum*) They are rough strigosely hairy herbs or undershrubs.

strigous ('straɪgəs), *a. Bot. rare.* [ad. mod.L. *strigōsus*: see STRIGOSE and -OUS.] = STRIGOSE *a.*[2] 1 (in quot. 1877 *transf.*).

1776 J. LEE *Introd. Bot.* Explan. Terms 385 *Strigosum*, *strigous*, armed with lance-shaped Prickles. **1877** COUES & ALLEN *N. Amer. Rod.* 115 The ears..are hirsute—almost strigous—with rather long and stiffish straight hairs, that form a slight fringe.

strigulated ('strɪgjʊleɪtɪd), *a.* [f. mod.L. *strigula*, dim. of *striga* (see STRIGA) + -ATE[2] + -ED[1].] = STRIGILLOSE *a.*

1899 *Novitates Zool.* Dec. 307 *Gonodela obliquilineata*. *Forewings*: white, speckled with olive-fuscous; the costa strigulated with fuscous.

striif, strijf(e, obs. forms of STRIFE, STRIVE *v.*

strik, obs. form of STIRK, STRICK *sb.*

strikable ('straɪkab(ə)l), *a.* [f. STRIKE *v.* + -ABLE.] **a.** That may be struck. **b.** Of an issue: that may provoke an industrial strike.

1904 J. P. MANNOCK *Billiards Expounded* I. i. 23 The various 'strikable faces' of a ball. **1977** *Washington Post* 18 May c2 The idea of 5-day mail service is a 'strikeable issue'.

strike (straɪk), *sb.* Forms: 4-6 **strik, stryk**, 4-7 **stryke**, 4- **strike**. [f. STRIKE *v.* (In senses 2-4 perh. a. MLG. derivatives of the same root: cf. STRICK *sb.*)

In early instances it is sometimes doubtful whether the word is this or STRICK *sb.* or STREAK *sb.*[1], as the spelling *strik*, *stryk*, *strick* does not always indicate a short vowel, and conversely the spelling *strike*, *stryke* does not always imply that the vowel is long.]

†**1.** A distance. *Obs.*

From the rimes the word seems to be *strike*, not *strick*.
c **1330** R. BRUNNE *Chron. Wace* (Rolls) 1052 He dyde make for fens a dyk Aboute þe castel a gret stryk. *Ibid.* 1420 In-to þe se of Aufryke þey comen, & passed a gret stryke.

2. a. A bundle or hank of flax, hemp, etc.: = STRICK *sb.* 1. [Cf. Pg. *estriga*.]

c **1386** CHAUCER *Prol.* 676 This Pardoner hadde heer as yelow as wex, But smooth it heeng as dooth a strike of flex. **1530** PALSGR. 277/2 Stryke of flaxe, *poupee de filace*. **1615** MARKHAM *Eng. Housew.* II. iii. 96 Then you shall say it [the hemp or flax] is brak't enough, and then tearming that which you called a baite or bundle before, now a strike, you shall lay them together. **1669** WORLIDGE *Syst. Agric.* 276 A Strike of Flax, so much as is Heckled at one handful. **1743** R. MAXWELL *Sel. Trans. Soc. Improv. Agric.* 336 When the Flax is well scutched, take a moderate Handful of it, fold it in the Middle, plet it like a Rope, but loosely... After you have beat it for some time, open the Strike. **1794** A. YOUNG *Agric. Suffolk* 49 The buyer heckles it [*sc.* hemp]..; he makes it into two or three sorts: long strike, short strike, and pull tow.

b. ? A handful of corn-stalks.

1817 COLERIDGE *Three Graves* III. ii, On the hedge-elms in the narrow lane Still swung the strikes [so *Sibyll. Leaves*; *earlier version* spikes] of corn.

3. a. = STRICKLE *sb.* 1, STRICK *sb.* 3.

c **1425** *Voc.* in Wr.-Wülcker 664/14 *Hoc ostorium*, stryke. **1474** *Stat. Winch.* in *Coventry Leet Bk.* 396, viij Buysshelles makith a Quarter, striken with a Rasid stryke, and neyther hepe nor Cantell. **1538** ELYOT *Dict.*, *Hostorium*, the staffe wherwith all measures be made euen, a stryke. **1557** *Cal. Anc. Rec. Dublin* (1889) 467 In every myll ther shalbe a toll dysshe..cheyned with a cheyne of iron, and a stryke of iron fast to the cheyne. **1639** HORN & ROB. *Gate Lang. Unlocked* xxxii. §400 Bread-corne..being measured is strick'd even with a strike (strickle). **1758** in *Rep. Comm. Ho. Commons* II. 431 (Weights & Meas.) The Bushel is striked, and to strike it they use a round circular Strike, which is of the same Diameter from one End to the other. **1844** H. STEPHENS *Bk. Farm* II. 280 In connection with the bushel is the *strike* for sweeping off the superfluous corn above the edge of the bushel. **1859** BARTLETT *Dict. Amer.* (ed. 2) 457.

b. An instrument, usually a rod or narrow board, used in various trades (e.g. brickmaking, casting, plumbing, gardening) for levelling a surface by striking off the superfluous material.

1683 J. HOUGHTON *Collect. Lett. Improv. Husb.* II. vi. 188 We also have upon the Table..a little Trough,..and in it a Strike to run over the Mould, to make the Bricks smooth: this Strike is usually made of Firr, nine inches long, an inch and a half broad, and half inch thick. **1825** J. NICHOLSON *Oper. Mech.* 631 A kind of rake, called a *strike*, which consists of a board about 5 inches broad. **1839** *Penny Cycl.* XIII. 372/1 An instrument called a strike is..provided to regulate the thickness of the sheet [of lead], and to spread the melted metal evenly over the table. **1840** *Florist's Jrnl.* (1846) I. 198 A strike, which is made of wood, about two feet longer than the width of the bed. **1850** E. DOBSON *Bricks & Tiles* I. 27 After which the superfluous clay is striken with a strike. *Ibid.* 71 The strike is not used at Nottingham. **1885** P. J. DAVIES *Pract. Plumbing* I. 28 The Strike..is rather an important tool, made as follows.

c. Measurement by the use of the 'strike' (sense 3 a): Struck or levelled, as opposed to heaped measure. Now *rare* or *Obs.*

1674 JEAKE *Arith.* (1696) 70 Usage in some places hath continued Measure by heap, although some Statutes order it by Strike. **1821** *Acc. Peculations Coal Trade* 5 The Newcastle chaldron..by measure is 24 bolls strike... The London chaldron is 36 bushels heaped.

4. A denomination of dry measure in various parts of England (but not officially recognized since the 16th c.); usually identical with the bushel, but in some districts equal to a half-bushel, and in others to two or four bushels. Also, the cylindrical wooden measuring vessel containing this quantity. Cf. STROKE *sb.* 22.

First recorded in AF. form *estrike*. The word is believed to have been originally used for a measure 'struck' or levelled with a strickle, not heaped.

[**1284** *MS. Acc. Exch. K.R.* Bd. 97 No. 3 m. 11 In .vij. estrikes et .j. pecke auene. **1350–1** *Rolls of Parlt.* II. 230/2 Et q̃ les Estrikes soient auxi bien enseales, come Bussels & autres Mesures.] **13..** *Propr. Sanct.* (Vernon MS.) in *Archiv Stud. neu. Spr.* LXXXI. 318/16 Men takeþ not of a lanterne þe liht And put vndur a strik vnriht Bote on a Candelstikke on hiȝ. *c* **1440** *Pallad. on Husb.* XI. 104 Salt let screue On hem, iij stryk on x strike [L. *per decem modios*] of olive. **1467** *Coventry Leet Bk.* 334 Also they have ordenyd that the wardens Make ij strikis, ij halfe strykis, ij hopes, & let the salters have hem with-owt eny money. **1523–34** FITZHERB. *Husb.* §12 Two London busshelles of pease, the whyche is but two strykes in other places. **1540** *Nottingham Rec.* III. 378 A cordyng to the Kynges Standard, after viij' gallans to the stryke. **1598** BP. HALL *Sat.* IV. vi. 27 Altho he buy whole Haruests in the spring And foist in false strikes to the measuring. **1609** HOLLAND *Amm. Marcell.* Annot. d ij, A measure with us called a strike, or London bushell would have cost 4.s. **1636** SIR R. BAKER *Cato Variegatus* 28 Hees no good Husbandman, that will mislike: To sowe a Pynte where he may reape a strike. **1680** W. WALKER *Idiomat. Anglo-Lat.* 452 He measures his money by strikes, *Nummos modio metitur.* **1681** in *Reliquary* (1862) III. 100 Paid for gathering 208 Strikes of acornes, 03 09 06. **1707** [E. WARD] *Hudibras Rediv.* VI. 11 In Shape most like That Measure which we call a Strike. **1759** R. BROWN *Compl. Farmer* 57 A strike, which is a bushel measure fill'd only to the edges. **1811** P. KELLY *Univ. Cambist* I. 259 A Last contains..40 Strikes or 80 Bushels. **1868** PEACOCK *Myrc* Notes 81 In the Isle of Axholme,..a bushel is not, as elsewhere, one-eighth of a quarter, but double that measure. The *strike* or half-bushel represents there the legal bushel of eight pecks.

†**5.** The unit proportion of malt in ale or beer. Also (? erroneously) ***of the first strike*** = of the highest strength: said of ale. *Obs.* Cf. STRAIK *sb.*[1] 2.

1610 BEAUM. & FL. *Scornf. Lady* V. iii, Thou miserable man, repent, and brew three strikes more in a hogshed. **1702** FLOYER *Cold Bathing* iv. 129 We must use..more moderate vinose Liquors, Beer of three or four Strike at Meals. **1819** SCOTT *Ivanhoe* xl, Our cellarer shall have orders to deliver to thee a butt of sack,..and three hogsheads of ale of the first strike, yearly. **1820** —— *Monast.* xviii, An hogshead of ale at Martlemas, of the double strike.

6. An act of striking.

a. An act of striking a blow; of a snake, the act of darting at its prey.

1587 W. FOWLER *Wks.* (S.T.S.) I. 69 Sche suddenlye hir visage did from his [*sc.* Cupid's] strykes so hyde, that [etc.]. **1638** SIR A. JOHNSTON (Ld. Wariston) *Diary* (S.H.S.) 325 The Almighty..hes many arroues in his quyver to peirce the at the heart if the first stryk in thy flesch move the not. **1859** H. KINGSLEY *Geoff. Hamlyn* xxviii, She [the dog] had drawn herself ahead, and made a bold strike at the kangaroo, but missed him. **1879** ATCHERLEY *Trip to Boërland* 50 This brute [a snake]..made a strike at my boot as I was in the very act of taking it off. **1902** 'M. FAIRLESS' *Roadmender* 7 With the snake there is the swift, silent strike, the tiny, tiny wound, then sleep and a forgetting.

fig. **1888** STEVENSON *Black Arrow* III. iv, It had been determined..to make one bold strike that evening, and, by brute force, to set Joanna free.

b. The striking of a clock, or of the clapper of a bell.

1871 ELLACOMBE *Belfries & Ringers* (ed. 3) 38 The way to cure a clapper of rearing, or doubling its strike, is to lengthen the flight. **1903** B. HARRADEN *Kath. Frensham* 47 We go on adjusting our lives and emotions to the strike of the parish clock.

†**c.** ***strike of day***: daybreak. *Obs.* or *spurious.*

[If genuine, perh. referring to the striking of the hour. But possibly a mistake of Grose (followed by Dickens) for *shrike of day* (SKRIKE *sb.* 2). Cf. STREAK *sb.*[1] 3.]

1790 GROSE *Prov. Gloss.* (ed. 2) Suppl., *Strike of Day*, break of day. **1854** DICKENS *Hard T.* II. iv, I could sen nommore if I was to speak till Strike o' day.

d. Infestation of a sheep or cow with flies whose larvæ burrow into the skin; an occurrence of this. Freq. with preceding sb.

1933, etc. [see *blow-fly strike* s.v. BLOW-FLY b]. **1933**, etc. [see MULES]. **1934** *Bulletin* (Sydney) 26 Sept. 22/1 The C.S.I.R. regards dipping in the light of only 'perhaps rendering the sheep less favorable for strike, but a measure not to be relied upon'. **1937**, etc. [see *fly-strike* s.v. FLY *sb.*[1] 11]. **1952** I. E. NEWSOM *Sheep Dis.* vi. 140 In South Africa ..*L[ucilia] cuprina* is thought to be responsible for 90 per cent of the strikes either alone or in combination with other flies. **1972** *TV Vet Sheep Bk.* xlviii. 143/1 In Britain strike usually starts when the lambs start scouring. **1975** *N.Z. Jrnl. Agric.* Sept. 65/1 One measure for blowflies' resistance to insecticides is the time that it takes, after a spray or dip, for implanted larvae to establish a strike. **1977** *Bulletin* (Sydney) 22 Jan. 16/3 The blowfly costs rural industry $70 million a year in sheep and cattle strike.

e. A sudden military attack concentrated on selected targets; also occas. *concr.*, the force used in such an attack. Also (chiefly with reference to the use of nuclear weapons) preceded by a qualifying word, as ***first-strike, pre-emptive strike, second strike***: see under the first elements.

1942 [see *strike patrol*, sense 20 below]. **1943** T. DUDLEY-GORDON *Coastal Command at War* ii. 16 When the Admiralty desires a special reconnaissance or strike to be 'laid on'. **1943** *Yank* 19 Nov. 3 But, when the last strike returned, there were no bullet holes, no torn fabric and the pilots climbed out unhurt. **1945** [see *air strike* s.v. AIR B. III. 2]. **1963** *Ann. Reg. 1962* 520 The purpose of these bases can be none other than to provide a nuclear strike capability against the Western hemisphere. **1972** *Newsweek* 10 Jan. 1/1 Described by the Pentagon as 'protective-reaction' strikes, the bombings in fact signaled to the world the continuing U.S. interest in Southeast Asia. **1979** H. KISSINGER *White House Years* xxiii. 983 The Son Tay raid was accompanied by a two-day strike by 200 airplanes against North Vietnamese supply installations.

f. ***bird-strike***: see BIRD *sb.* 9.

7. *Fishing.* †**a.** ? A place where salmon are speared. *Obs. rare*⁻¹.

a **1828** BEWICK *Mem.* (1862) 222, I was frequently sent by my parents to purchase a salmon from the fishers of the 'strike' at Eltringham ford.

b. The jerk by which the angler secures a fish that is already hooked.

1840 J. YOUNGER *River Angling* (1860) 88 [This motion is wrongly named: it is] rather a retentive hold than a start, or a strike. **1892** *Field* 19 Mar. 402/1 Once the salmon has gone down head foremost with the fly, there is no reason to delay the strike.

c. A large capture (of fish).

1887 HALL CAINE *Deemster* x, No 'strike' was made. **1894** R. LEIGHTON *Wreck Golden Fleece* 36 The best strike of herrins be always at the moon-risin'. **1905** *Daily Chron.* 3 Oct. 4/5 When there is a 'strike,' and the movement of the buoys that support the nets show that a shoal has become enmeshed [etc.].

8. *Mining* and *Geol.* The horizontal course of a stratum; direction with regard to the points of the compass. Cf. STREAK *sb.*[1] 5, STRETCH *sb.* 9.

Prob., as stated in a footnote to the first passage quoted below, a recent adoption from German. The Ger. word is *streichen*, the inf. of the vb. corresponding to STRIKE *v.*

1829 A. SEDGWICK & MURCHISON in *Trans. Geol. Soc.* Ser. II. III. 337 The range or strike of this series is from E.N.E. to W.S.W. **1833** LYELL *Princ. Geol.* III. 346 In Europe the strike of the beds is not always parallel to the direction of the chain. **1850** ANSTED *Elem. Geol., Min.* etc. 291 The direction of the bed is called, in Geological language, the *strike*, and the inclination, the *dip.* **1888** TEALL *Brit. Petrogr.* 448 *Strike* —The strike of a bed is the direction (expressed by reference to the points of the compass) of the line formed by the intersection of the plane of the bed with the plane of the horizon.

transf. **1883** *Nature* 22 Feb. 395/2 The main strike of the auroræ is magnetic east-west.

9. a. A concerted cessation of work on the part of a body of workers, for the purpose of obtaining some concession from the employer or employers. Formerly sometimes more explicitly ***strike of work.*** Cf. STRIKE *v.* 24, 24 b. Phrase, ***on strike***, also (*U.S.*) ***on a strike.*** Freq. with preceding qualifying word, as ***general, outlaw, selective, sit-down, stay-away (-down, -in), sympathetic, wildcat strike***: see under the first elements. Also *fig.*

The sb., together with the related sense of the vb., has been adopted into several European langs.: G. *streik*, Du. *strijk*, Sw. *strejk*.

1810 *Docum. Hist. Amer. Industrial Soc.* (1910) III. 370 The Society, in November 1809, ordered a general strike. **1815** *Ibid.* IV. 42 It appeared there was a strike for higher wages. **1825** *Edin. Rev.* XLIII. 14 Combinations and strikes of work may be necessary..to bring things sooner to their proper level. **1830** *Poor Man's Guardian* 31 Dec. 8/1 It has been determined at a meeting of delegates, appointed by the spinners in the different parts of the country, that a general strike shall take place on Monday, the 27th instant, of all spinners who are receiving less that 4s. 2d. per 1000 hanks. **1850** *Athenæum* 7 Dec. 1282/3 Three hundred men on strike have taken a mill! **1881** *Chicago Times* 14 May, The employés of the Grand Trunk car shops are on a strike for an advance in wages. **1899** C. PLUMMER *Saxon Chron.* II. 289 Simeon of Durham..represents the enactment as causing a sort of clerical strike. **1907** R. DUNN *Shameless Diary of Explorer* xv. 201 Miller's stomach went on strike after we washed in the glacier stream.

b. *transf.* A concerted abstention from a particular economic, physical, or social activity on the part of persons who are attempting to obtain a concession from an authority or to register a protest; esp. in ***hunger strike, rent strike*** (see HUNGER *sb.* 4, RENT *sb.*[1] 4 c).

1889, etc. [see *hunger strike* s.v. HUNGER *sb.* 4]. **1911** G. B. SHAW *Getting Married* 220 Ive told our last four Prime Ministers that if they didnt make our marriage laws reasonable there would be a strike against marriage. **1934** *Sun* (Baltimore) 8 Nov. 10/4 People with fixed incomes necessarily buy less. There are indignation meetings and 'buyers' strikes'. **1937** *Ibid.* 30 Aug. 8/1 The falling birth rate indicates that 'mankind cannot be forced or bribed to produce children'... The present 'birth strike' will continue until necessary social readjustments are effected. **1938** *Ibid.* 28 Jan. 22/1 Forty-eight tenants of an apartment building.. started a 'strike' January 1, demanding rent reductions. **1965** B. PEARCE tr. *Preobrazhensky's New Economics* 167 A consumers' strike is the limit which arises to state planning whenever the state's prices exceed the level acceptable to the private market. **1970**, etc. [see *rent strike* s.v. RENT *sb.*[1] 4 c]. **1976** *Gramophone* Dec. 1052/1 The Lysistrata plot about the women stopping a war by going on sexual strike.

10. A last ploughing before the sowing. *local.*

1823 E. MOOR *Suffolk Words, Strike* is also a mode of plowing. We call it *back-striking*. **1844** *Jrnl. R. Agric. Soc.* V. I. 6 First year making the fallow, three whole tilths, and one strike, at 8*s.*, 1*l.* 8*s.* 0*d.*

11. An act of 'striking oil' (see STRIKE *v.* 68 d); a discovery of a rich vein of ore in mining. Similarly, the sudden discovery of an accumulation of natural gas. Also *fig.* a stroke of success. orig. *U.S.*

1852 L. CLAPPE *Shirley Lett. Calif. Mines* (1922) 131 They are always longing for big strikes [of gold]. **1855** H. HELPER *Land of Gold* 296, I may make a 'strike', but that is mere speculation. **1864** [see *oil strike* s.v. OIL *sb.*[1] 6 e]. **1883** *Century Mag.* July 330/1 A restless, speculative person,.. now making a lucky strike, and now sinking all his available means in a dry hole. **1895** *Daily News* 13 Sept. 2/5 Langlaagte Estate Gold... The supervising director writes that the strike at the sixth level is really grand. **1901** *Munsey's Mag.* XXIV. 841 Mr. Grau made a strike with his first novelty, 'La Bohème'.

12. In certain games. **a.** *Ten-pins* and *Ninepins.* The knocking down of all the pins with the first bowl. Also *fig. U.S.*

1859 *Atlantic Monthly* Nov. 641 Strike: terms of the game of nine-pins. **1866** LOWELL *Biglow P.* Ser. II. Introd., To make a strike is to knock down all the pins with one ball, hence it has come to mean fortunate, successful. **1884** [see SPARE *sb.*[1] 4]. **1939** H. MILLER *Cosmological Eye* 219 *Of Human Bondage* was a great book, he thought. I thought so too and I scored another strike for the constable on my mental blackboard. **1958** [see FRAME *sb.* 11 g]. **1974** *Cleveland* (Ohio) *Plain Dealer* 13 Oct. c. 8/3 Marge opened her third game with nine strikes in a row, but left the 5-9 pins on her first ball in the 10th frame on the way to her 275 game and 614 series.

b. *Baseball.* (*a*) An act of striking at the ball, characterized as a ***fair*** or ***foul strike*** (see quot. 1874); three 'foul strikes' cause the batsman to be put out. (*b*) A 'foul strike', or any act or shortcoming on the batsman's part which incurs the same penalty. Hence, a pitched ball recorded against the batter; esp. as one of three counts against the batter.

1841 *Picayune* (New Orleans) 25 May 2/2 If 'Edith' wishes to see 'a great strike'.., let her walk down Water street..and see *the* 'bachelors' make the ball fly. **1845** in *Appletons' Ann. Cycl. 1885* (1886) X. 77/2 Players must take their strike in regular turn. **1856** *Spirit of Times* 22 Nov. 197/2 The striker should also be compelled to run on such occasions, strike or no strike. **1867** *Ball Players' Chron.* 4 July 6/2 Their batting was of a superior character, two of their players..each makng some powerful strikes. **1868** H. CHADWICK *Base Ball Player's Bk. Reference* 75 Mills called 'one strike' on him. **1874** CHADWICK *Base Ball Man.* 105 A fair strike. The batsman, when in the act of striking at the ball, must stand within the lines of his position... A foul strike. Should the batsman, when in the act of striking at the ball, step outside the lines of his position, the umpire must call 'foul strike'. **1891** N. CRANE *Baseball* 76 Every ball that is not hit by the batsman must be a 'strike' or a 'ball'. **1896** KNOWLES & MORTON *Baseball* 103 Strike.—When the batsman tries and fails to hit a ball delivered to him by the pitcher, or refuses to strike at a fair ball. **1912** C. MATHEWSON *Pitching* 12 It put me in the hole with the count two balls and one strike. **1942** *Sun* (Baltimore) 3 Apr. 18/7 The machine will throw 75 per cent more strikes in a given number of pitches than a human. **1974** *Anderson* (S. Carolina) *Independent* 19 Apr. 4B/7 The Citadel scored on a missed third strike and two errors.

(*c*) *fig.* Usu. preceded by a numeral or enumerative adj. and const. *against* or †*on.* Something to one's discredit, a black mark.

1938 *New Republic* 26 Jan. 336/1 All movements for social good will..have two strikes on them before they start. *a* **1939** in E. J. Nichols *Hist. Dict. Baseball Terminol.* (Unpublished Ph.D. thesis, Pennsylvania State College) Appendix I, p. iv, You therefore are starting with two strikes against him. It's up to you to hit one into the bleachers and send yourself home. **1943** *Official Rep. Deb. House of Commons Canada* 31 May 3196/2, I am a little afraid that a man who approaches that board claiming exemption as a conscientious objector goes to bat with three strikes against him. **1956** B. HOLIDAY *Lady sings Blues* (1973) xxi. 169 The only evidence they've got is on me. I've got one strike against me. **1962** J. GLENN in *Into Orbit* 16, I knew that I might have a couple of small strikes against me... I was not a college graduate... Also..I was probably a little older than most of the men NASA was considering. **1968** *Globe & Mail Mag.* (Toronto) 13 Jan. 3/2 The student council also did nothing. Strike one for student power. **1975** *Listener* 13 Feb. 204/1 One of the main strikes against Ted Heath was that he did not 'come over' on the box. **1979** 'S. WOODS' *This Fatal Writ* 129 The discovery of your man, injured, would have been an additional strike against him.

c. *Cricket.* The right of the batsman to receive the next ball. Also without article.

1886 *Cricket* 20 May 137/1 Seeing over sixty runs scored, he, strange to relate, did not succeed in getting a strike. **1955** [see FARM *v.*[2] 6]. **1963** A. ROSS *Australia 63* iii. 83 He played McKenzie fine of Harvey at cover, called euphorically, in an effort to keep the strike, for a second, and was run out. **1976** J. SNOW *Cricket Rebel* 57 Geoff Boycott took first strike leaving 'Ollie' [Milburn] at the non-striker's end.

d. *U.S. Football.* A forward pass, straight into the hands of the receiver.

1947 *Richmond* (Va.) *Times-Dispatch* 9 Nov. B7/7 Brown threw a perfect 'strike' to Elliott on the 10-yard ribbon, but the lanky freshman end dropped the ball. **1972** J. MOSEDALE *Football* v. 72 To this strike-tossing forward passer..went the plaudits of the nation.

13. *U.S. Political slang.* (See quots.)

1885 *Century Mag.* Apr. 824/2 When a member introduces a bill hostile to some moneyed interest, with the expectation of being paid to let the matter drop... [This proceeding is] technically called a 'strike'. **1888** BRYCE *Amer. Commw.* II. xliv. II. 163 *note.* **1894** H. C. MERWIN in *Atlantic Monthly* Feb. 247/1 A 'strike' is a measure brought forward simply for purposes of blackmail.

†**14.** *slang.* 'Twenty shillings' (Grose *Dict. Vulgar T.*, ed. 2, 1788).

15. *Printing.* (See quots.)

1871 *Amer. Encycl. Printing* (ed. Ringwalt) 149 Drives are also sometimes called strikes, or the originals of matrices.

1888 [see DRIVE *sb.* 15]. **1888** JACOBI *Printers' Vocab.* 134 *Strikes*, a term for type matrices struck from the original punches. **1900** H. HART *Cent. Typogr.* p. viii, Nowadays a type-founder.. would be able.. to buy 'strikes', which when justified would become matrices—the punches being left in the hands of the proprietor for the production of more 'strikes'.

16. *Sugar-making.* See quot. 1864. (Cf. STRIKE *v.* 21 b.)

1847 W. J. EVANS *Sugar-Planter's Man.* 152 The time required for taking off a strike containing fourteen moulds of fifty pounds each was two hours. **1864** WEBSTER, *Strike of sugar*, (*a*) the act of emptying the teache, or last boiler, in which the cane-juice is exposed to heat, into the coolers; (*b*) the quantity of the sirup thus emptied at once. **1887** *Century Mag.* Nov. 114/1 When sufficiently boiled, the thick syrup is called the 'masse cuite'. The 'strike' is now done, air is admitted to the pan, and the contents are run off into the 'mixer'.

17. *Coining.* 'The whole amount struck at one time.'

1891 *Century Dict.*

18. *Soap-making.* The proper crystalline or mottled appearance of a soap, indicating complete saponification.

1884 A. WATT *Soap-making* 50 The leys are made from.. black ash, the impurities in which give the mottled or marbled 'strike' for which this variety of soap is famed. **1885** W. L. CARPENTER *Manuf. Soap & Candles* 12 The appearances known as 'grain' or 'strike' in a hard soap.. are due to the crystalline character of soap.

†**19.** ? A strip or band (of metal). *Obs. rare*$^{-1}$.

Possibly the word may belong to STREAK *sb.*[1], or may be misprinted. The passage (copied by Weever and some other authors) is the origin of the sense 'stanchion or pale in a fence or gate' given by some Dicts.

1603 STOW *Surv.* (1908) I. 322 There were 9. Tombes of Alabaster and Marble, inuironed with strikes of Iron in the Quire, and one Tombe in the body of the Church, also coped with iron.

20. *attrib.* and *Comb.*, as (sense 3 c) ***strike bushel, measure***; (sense 6 e) ***strike aeroplane, aircraft, carrier, Command, patrol, power, trainer, wing***; also ***strike-attack, -reconnaissance*** attrib. phrases; (sense 8) ***strike-fault, -joint, vein; strike-faulting*** vbl. sb.; (sense 9) ***strike action, benefit, call, committee, fund, leader, meeting, money, movement, notice, record, wave, weapon; strike-free, -happy, -prone, -ridden, -torn*** adjs.; (sense 16) ***strike-heater, -pan***. Also †**strike-block** [= Du. *strijkblok*] *Carpentry* (see quot. 1678); **strike-bound** *a.*, immobilized by a strike; **strike-breaker**, a workman who consents to work for an employer whose workmen are on strike, thus contributing to the defeat of the strike; **strike-breaking** *vbl. sb.*, the action of a strike-breaker; also as *ppl. a.*; hence (as back-formation) **strike-break** *v. intr.*; **strike force**, (*a*) a military force equipped to deliver a (nuclear) strike; (*b*) a police unit organized for rapid and effective action against crime; **strike-furrow plough** = *strike plough* below; †**strike iron**, ? malleable iron; **strike pay**, the periodical payment made by a trade-union for the support of men on strike; **strike plough** (see quot. 1856); **strike-slip** *Geol.* (orig. *U.S.*), the component of the slip of a fault in a horizontal direction, parallel to the strike; also as *adv.*; freq. *attrib.*, esp. in ***strike-slip fault***, a fault in which motion was predominantly parallel to the strike; **strike zone** *Baseball*, an imaginary rectangle 17 inches wide, stretching from the height of the batter's armpits to that of his knees, within which the pitcher must throw the ball for the pitch to be called a strike.

1949 *Britannica Bk. of Year* 606/2 Minority groups.. threatening and, from time to time, taking *strike action by way of protest. **1977** M. EDELMAN *Polit. Lang.* vii. 131 Wage demands their fellow workers would otherwise be free to back with strike action if necessary. **1965** *New Scientist* 22 Apr. 217/1 The Hawker Siddeley Buccaneer naval *strike aeroplane might be modified to suit the RAF. **1957** *Times* 22 Aug. 6/6 The supersonic *strike aircraft which Hawker Aircraft are developing as a private venture. *Ibid.*, The fact that it is described as a strike aircraft indicates that it can be used as a bomber as well as a fighter. **1980** *Daily Tel.* 24 Sept. 4/8 Iraqi transport aircraft have been withdrawn to the safety of bases in Jordan, beyond the reach of Iran's strike aircraft. **1977** *R.A.F. News* 11–24 May 1/5 The two squadrons operate in the same maritime *strike attack role. **1896** *Rep. Proc. Internat. Typogr. Union N. Amer.* 22/1, $48,087.18.. [were] paid during the two years in *strike and lockout benefits. **1678** MOXON *Mech. Exerc.* iv. 66 The *Strike-Block.. is a Plain shorter than the Joynter,.. and is used for the shooting of a short Joynt. **1823** P. NICHOLSON *Pract. Build.* 245 The Strike-Block Plane. **1949** *Britannica Bk. of Year* 687/1 **Strike-bound*, prevented from moving, travelling, sailing etc. by a strike or strikes. **1956** *B.B.C. Handbk.* 1957 121 The editors of strike-bound national dailies and periodicals. **1982** *Daily Tel.* 3 Aug. 22/4 Strike-bound Sealink ships have.. moored at the two Holyhead berths. **1961** *Economist* 6 May 525/1 Individual exporters and importers should be allowed to send their own staff in to get their own goods on and off the ships, if their staff will agree to *strike-break in this way. **1904** *N.Y. Even. Post* 4 Aug. 2 [Half of] the *strike breakers are men who, having been idle for a time, simply wanted a chance to make a little ready money. **1905** *Daily Chron.* 4 May, The strikers made repeated attacks on the 'strike-breakers'. **1905** *Amer. Mag.* May 107/2 It is quite a new profession, this *strike breaking, a curious evolution of modern industrial methods. **1920** *Manch. Guardian News Bull.* 10 Sept. 2/1 A direct incitement to strike-breaking. **1978** S. BRILL *Teamsters* x. 362 The police sent an armed convoy to escort a strikebreaking truck. **1858** TROLLOPE *Three Clerks* I. i. 12 Young Tudor had produced a very smart paper on the merits—or demerits—of the *strike bushel. **1862** ANSTED *Channel Isl.* IV. App. A. 567 It may be worth stating that the Guernsey heaped bushel is nearly equivalent to the imperial strike bushel. **1976** *Strike call [see *stay-away* s.v. STAY *v.*[1] 31]. **1966** *Daily Tel.* 18 Aug. 1/4 'Straight Laced' is the first multinational *strike-carrier exercise for some years. **1968** *Ann. Reg.* 1967 27 The White Paper envisaged.. the merging of the RAF's Fighter and Bomber Command into a new *Strike Command. **1949** *Britannica Bk. of Year* 210/2 The men's allegiance to the *strike committee outweighed their loyalty to the union. **1879** *Encycl. Brit.* X. 303/1 Faults.. are classified as dip-faults and *strike-faults. **1894** TARR *Econ. Geol. U.S.* 50 When the horizontal direction of a fault plane is in the direction of the dip of the strata, the fault is a dip fault; when at right angles to this, a strike fault. **1925** N. E. ODELL in E. F. Norton *Fight for Everest: 1924* 299 There is considerable evidence of *strike-faulting which would explain this. **1965** G. J. WILLIAMS *Econ. Geol. N.Z.* iii. 30/2 Some ore was won from a 390 ft shaft, but both strike- and cross-faulting seem to have disrupted the lode. **1961** *Listener* 14 Dec. 1011/2 The development of nuclear *strike forces by Britain and France. **1973** *Black Panther* 1 Sept. 11/2 Federal and local strike forces smashed into homes and offices in a series of pre-dawn raids. **1947** *Sun* (Baltimore) 2 Jan. 17/1 If operations are *strike-free, enough steel can be turned out to restore within a few months a balance between supply and demand. **1982** *Times* 23 Mar. 8/7 The reductions in strike-free days. **1906** *Daily Chron.* 17 May 4/7 The earliest mention of a *strike fund occurred in the strike of the Parisian stocking-weavers in 1724. **1846** KEIGHTLEY *Notes Virg.*, Terms Husb. 353 When the plough was prepared for seed-sowing, the *aures* were put to it, so that it then resembled our *strike-furrow plough. **1955** *Times* 26 May 11/5 We are being placed on a par with other '*strike-happy' industries. **1903** *Longman's Mag.* Nov. 76 After repeated skimming and filtration, the juice is ready for the strike-pans, whence it is discharged by valves into the *strike-heaters—double-lined cauldrons supplied with steam enough to keep the sugar hot until crystallisation is reached. **1814** *Sporting Mag.* XLIII. 269 A large quantity of these shears made out of *strike iron. **1879** *Encycl. Brit.* X. 297/1 The former set is known as dip-joints,.. the latter is termed *strike-joints. **1913** W. OWEN *Let.* 19 Oct. (1967) 201 You should set up as Suffragette, Dublin-*Strike-Leader, or Schoolmistress, so that you would be *obliged* to speak for seven hours a day. **1978** P. BOARDMAN *Worlds of Patrick Geddes* vii. 246 The strike leader had the reputation of being a dangerous man. **1766** *Museum Rust.* VI. 264 More frequently a fraud, in the construction of measures of that kind, where heap, and not *strike measure, is the custom. **1926** *Brit. Gaz.* 12 May 1/7 Large crowds of them congregated in the streets, while some abortive *strike meetings were held in the squares. **1913** D. H. LAWRENCE in *Westm. Gaz.* 13 Sept. 2/2 *Strike-money is paid in the Primitive Methodist Chapel. **1932** *Sun* (Baltimore) 13 Sept. 8/3 The certain futility of the '*strike' movement. **1926** *Brit. Gaz.* 12 May 2/2 *The Weston Mercury*, Weston-super-Mare, reports that after *strike notices had been received the local branch of the Typographical Association decided to return to work. **1903** *Strike-pan: see *strike-heater*. **1942** *Strike patrol [see ROVER[1] 3 e]. *a* **1878** in G. Howell *Confl. Capital & Labour* vii. 344 The men who receive what is called '*strike pay'. **1891** *Spectator* 13 June, Whether these conditions are satisfied, it is not for us to say, though.. the scale of strike-pay does not suggest an overflowing exchequer. **1789** *Trans. Soc. Arts* I. 123, I took a common *strike plough. **1856** MORTON *Cycl. Agric.* II. 726/1 *Strike-plough* (Sussex), double-mould board plough. **1959** *Time* 23 Feb. 22/3 U.S. *strike power is clearly supreme now. **1961** *Daily Tel.* 22 Apr. 9/2 The *strike-prone motor industry. **1963** *Times* 2 Feb. 9/2 Adopting American nuclear warheads for its *strike-reconnaissance aircraft missiles defending the North American continent. **1938** *Encycl. Brit. Bk. of Year* 614/1 In 1936 there were but 156 strikes..; a rather typical *strike record for Canada. **1967** *Spectator* 8 Dec. 706/2 Two of our favourite illusions are that we are among the most *strike-ridden nations on earth, and that every strike brings chaos in its wake. **1913** W. LINDGREN *Mineral Deposits* ix. 121 The *strike-slip is the component of the slip parallel with the fault slip. *Ibid.* 126 The expressions 'normal' and 'reverse' may be used in connection with oblique and dip faults, even when these are strike-slip or oblique slip faults. **1932** C. R. LONGWELL et al. *Textbk. Geol.* I. xii. 315 (*caption*) Broken lines show the displacement (slip), and its three components—throw, heave, and strike-slip—measured along axes at right angles to each other. **1964** W. C. PUTNAM *Geology* vi. 146/2 Ordinarily, in order to establish whether or not movement has been strike-slip or dip-slip, it is necessary to have layered rocks with strongly differing dips cut by the fault. *Ibid.* 147/1 The actual movement as demonstrated by the outcrop was strike-slip. **1971** I. G. Gass et al. *Understanding Earth* xxiii. 327/2 The San Andreas is called a strike-slip fault. **1977** *Sci. Amer.* Apr. 36/2 In Mongolia most earthquakes are associated with strike-slip faulting. **1977** *Belfast Tel.* 28 Feb. 7/9 The crisis at *strike-torn Leyland deepened. **1967** *Observer* 26 Nov. 2/6 The Jaguar *strike-trainer which was born.. in the Anglo-French agreement of 1965. **1877** RAYMOND *Statist. Mines & Mining* 241 The *strike-vein is north and south. **1957** *Encycl. Brit.* XXI. 469/1 The *strike waves that accompanied the Russian revolutions of 1905 and 1917. **1955** *Times* 26 May 11/5 The apparently indiscriminate use of the *strike weapon. **1944** *Hansard Commons* 7 Mar. 1910 In conjunction with the *strike wings of Coastal Command and R.A.F. fighters our Light Forces have constantly attacked enemy convoys in the Channel. **1948** *Sporting News Dope Bk.* 119 The umpire shall rule it a ball even though it passed over the heart of the plate within the *strike zone. **1950** *Official Baseball Rules* ii. 17 The strike zone is that space over home plate which is between the batter's armpits and the top of his knees when he assumes his natural stance.

strike (straɪk), *v.* Pa. t. **struck**; pa. pple. **struck**; also *arch.* exc. *U.S.* (esp. in legal use) **stricken**. Forms: *Inf.* and *Pres. stem.* 1 **strícan**, 3–7 **strik**, 4–6 **stryke**, 4–7 **stryk**, 4 *Sc.* **stirk(e**, 5–7 **stricke**, 6 **stryck(e**, 6–8 **strick**, 7 *Sc.* **streck**, 3– **strike**. *Pa. t. sing.* α. 1 **strác**, 2–3 **strac**, 3–5, 6–8 *Sc.* **strak**, 7 *Sc.* **strack**, 4–8 **strake**, 5 **straak**, 5–6 *Sc.* **straik**, 6 *Sc.* **strayk**; β. 4–7 **strok**, **stroke**, 5 **strocke**, 5–7 **stroak(e**, 5–9 **strook**, 6–7 **strooke**, 6 **stroock**, **stroucke**, *Sc.* **struke**, **struik(e**, 7 **strucke**, 7– **struck**; γ. 4 **strek**, 5 **streke**; δ. 7 **stricke**; ε. *weak forms* 4 **striked**, 4–6 **stryked**, 6 **stryckt**. *Pa. t. pl.* 1 **stricon**, 2–3 **striken**. *Pa. pple.* α. 1 **stricen**, 4 **strikyn**, 4–6 **stryken**, **-yn**, (4 **-yne**), 4–7 **striken**, 5 **strikon**, **strynken** (*sic*), **strikyne**, *Sc.* **strikine**, 5–6 **strikin**, **strykin**, 6 **strykowen**, **stirkin**, *north.* **streikenne**, *Sc.* **strakin**, 7 **strake**; β. 4 **y-strike**, 3–4 **strike**, 5 **stryke**; γ. 4 *Sc.* **strekine**, 4–6 **streken**, 5–6 **strekyn(e**, (5 **stregun**), 6 **strek(k)in**; δ. 5 **strikkyn**, **stryckyn**, 5–6 **strikken**, **-in**, 6 **ystricken** (*arch.*), **strycken**, **strickin**, **-yn**, 6– **stricken**; ε. 6 **strycke**, **stricke**; ζ. 5 *Sc.* **strukkin**, 6 *Sc.* **struiken**, **stru(c)kne**, **strukin**, **strukned**, **strokin**, 6–7 **stroken**, **strooken**, **struken**, **strocken**, (6 **strockin**), 7 **stroaken**, **stroocken**, 6–9 **strucken**, (6 **-in**); 6–7 **stroke**, **strook(e**, 6 **strock**, 7 **stroake**, **strucke**, 7– **struck**; η. 4–6 **striked**, 5 **stryked**. [A Com. WGer. strong verb: OE. *strícan*, pa. t. *strác*, pl. *stricon*, pa. pple. *stricen*, corresponds to OFris. *strîka*, MLG. *strîken*, (M)Du. *strijken*, OHG. *strîhhan* (MHG. *strîchen*, mod.G. *streichen* str. vb.; the weak vb. *streichen* corresponds to STROKE *v.*) to pass lightly over a surface, to go, rove, wander, to stroke, rub, beat, f. OTeut. **strīk-* (:—**straik-*: **strik-*; for examples of these grades of the root see STROKE *sb.*, STREAK *sb.*[1], STRICKLE):—Indogermanic **streig-* (:—**stroig-*: **strig-*) found in L. *stringĕre* to touch lightly, graze (radically distinct from *stringĕre* to bind, tighten), *strigilis* STRIGIL, OSl. *strigą* I shear (Russ. *strigu*, inf. *strič'*).

A distinct, but prob. ultimately connected root of similar meaning, OTeut. **streuk-* (: **strauk-*: **struk-*):—Indogermanic **streug-*: **stroug-*: **strug-*, is found in ON. *strjúka* str. vb. (Sw. *stryka*, Da. *stryge*) to stroke, rub, OHG. *strûhhôn*, *strûhhên* (MHG. *strûchen*) to strike against something, stumble. It has been suggested by Hirt that the parallel roots may have arisen from ablaut modification of an original **streyeweg*.]

I. 1. *intr.* To make one's way, go. In early use chiefly *poet.* In later use, chiefly with adv. (*forth, forward, over*) or phrase indicating the direction. *Obs.* exc. *arch.*

c **1200** ORMIN 14804, & Godess follc strac inn anan Uppo þe driȝȝe sandess, To flen fra Faraon þe king. *c* **1205** LAY. 9318 Hamun him to strac. *a* **1225** *Leg. Kath.* 732 Comen alle strikinde, þe strengest te swiðest of eauer euch strete. **1362** LANGL. *P. Pl.* A. VI. 67 Twei stokkes þer stondeþ but stunt þou not þere,.. stryk forþ bi hem boþe. **1377** *Ibid.* B. Prol. 183 A mous.. Stroke forth sternly and stode biforn hem alle. *a* **1400** *King & Hermit* 83 3yff i stryke into a pytte, Hors and man myȝht spylle. *a* **1400–50** *Wars Alex.* (Dubl.) 826* To poliponenses hase he passed.. And so was strykyn or he styntyd in-to þe strange realm. *c* **1440** *Sir Degrev.* 1640 The stede stert over a fosse And strykys astray. *c* **1460** *Vrbanitatis* 49 in *Babees Bk.*, To þe beste morselle þou may not stryke Thowȝ þou neuur so welle hit lyke. **1481** CAXTON *Reynard* (Arb.) 66 Neuertheles he.. stryked forth thurgh alle the folke til he cam in to the place where the Kynge him self was. **1582** N. T. (Rhem.) *Luke* viii. 22 And he went vp into a boate, and his disciples, and he said to them, Let vs strike ouer the lake. **1599** *George a Greene* IV. iv. 951 *George.* But what are these come trasing here along? *Bettris.* Three men come striking through the corne, My loue. **1608** WILLET *Hexapla Exod.* x. 13. 118 [It was extraordinary] for them [*sc.* locusts].. to come in the spring,.. whereas they vsually do strike ouer into other countries in haruest. **1641** TATHAM *Distracted State* IV. i. (1651) 20 When you have done the Deed Strike towards the Back stairs. **1699** MAUNDRELL *Journ. Jerus.* (1714) *Journ. to Euphrates* 4 Their way to cross is, by drawing up the Boat.. and then with wretched Oars stricking over. **1883** STEVENSON *Silverado Sq.* (1886) 43 The Jews were not long of striking forward.

†**b.** of inanimate things. Also with *up*. *Obs.*

a **1000** *Boeth. Metr.* xx. 140 [Se rodor] stríceð ymbutan [i.e. revolves round the earth] ufane & neoðane, efenneah ȝehwæþer. *a* **1225** *Juliana* 59 Ha bigon to broken al as þat istelede irn strac hire in ouer al. **13..** *E.E. Allit. P.* A. 125 Al songe to loue þat gay Iuelle, þe steuen moȝt stryke þurȝ þe vrþe to helle. *a* **1400–50** *Wars Alex.* 1415 Strykis vp of þe stoure stanes of engynes. **1456** SIR G. HAYE *Law Arms* (S.T.S.) 26 The reik that strake vp in the aire.

†**c.** Of a stream (of water, blood, tears): To run, flow. Also with *down, adown*. *Obs.*

a **1225** *Leg. Kath.* 2479, & strikeð a stream ut of þat stanene þruh þat ha in resteð. *a* **1225** *St. Marher.* 5 The let blod barst ut ant strac adun of hire bodi. *a* **1240** *Ureisun* in *O.E. Hom.* I. 189 þe ilke fif wallen þet of þi blisfulle bodi sprungen and strike dun strondes of blod. *c* **1320** *Castel of Love* 729 A welle.. Wiþ foure stremes þat strikeþ wel, And erneþ vppon þe grauel. *c* **1386** CHAUCER *Prioress' T.* 222 (Corpus MS.) His salte teeres stryked doun as reyn. *a* **1450** *Octavian* (Camb. MS.) 426 A welle feyre welle there they sye Come strykyng ouyr a stone.

†**d.** In immaterial sense: To go, pass (into a condition). *Obs.*

to be stricken in years: see STRICKEN *pa. pple.* and *ppl. a.* *c* **1350** *Will Palerne* 2981 þere þat semli ladi.. strek in-to a styf studie of hire sterne sweuen. *Ibid.* 4038.

2. To proceed in a new direction; to make an excursion; to turn in one's journey *across, down, over, into, to*, etc. Also with *aside, in, off, out.*

1615 G. SANDYS *Trav.* 202 To avoid them, we strucke out of the way. **1669** N. MORTON *New Eng. Mem.* (1910) 32 They recovered themselves, and having the flood with them, struck into the harbour. **1681** R. KNOX *Hist. Ceylon* 162 We left the Road, and struck into the Woods. **1698** FRYER *Acc. E. India & P.* 3 Here we began to drop the rest of our Company, some striking East for the Streights. **1700** S. L. tr. *Fryke's Voy. E. Ind.* 230 A French Privateer came up the English Road, and passed by our Fleet, narrowly viewing it, and struck in to Sea again. **1709** MRS. MANLEY *Secret Mem.* I. 20 Let us strike down that Walk, and it brings us to the Palace. **1711** SWIFT *Jrnl. Stella* 7 July, It began raining, and I struck into Mrs. Vanhomrigh's, and dined. **1785** MISS FIELDING *Ophelia* II. xvii, I should.. go.. into Oxfordshire, and then strike into the western road. **1845** DARWIN *Voy. Nat.* xiv. (1879) 294 At Chonchi we struck across the island, following intricate winding paths. **1872** JENKINSON *Guide Eng. Lakes* (1879) 106 When the wall begins to descend, strike to the right along a green path. **1872** BLACK *Adv. Phaeton* x. 144 Instead of going by Pershore, we had struck away northward. **1877** MISS A. B. EDWARDS *Up Nile* x. 279 Leaving the tombs, we now strike off towards the quarries. *fig.* **1575** GASCOIGNE *Philomene* Ep. Ded., I changed my copy, and stroke ouer into the *Deprofundis* which is placed amongst my other Poesies. **1618** in Foster *Eng. Factories India* (1906) 9 He stricks into another course and embargues all the hearbe into his hands. **1748** MELMOTH *Fitzosborne Lett.* lvi. (1749) II. 78 A strange disposition.. to tread the same paths that have been traversed by others, or to strike out into the most devious extravagancies. **1837** CARLYLE *Fr. Rev.* III. I. viii, The hapless course they struck into. **1863** COWDEN CLARKE *Shaks. Char.* iii. 66 He even strikes off into a wild levity and startling humour at times.

b. of inanimate things, esp. of a road, or stream.

1584 B. R. tr. *Herodotus* II. 94 b, Albeit there be another way also tendinge to the same place, strykinge ouer by the Neb of Delta. **1815** KIDD *Geol. Ess.* xxii. 218 The Gulph Stream.. strikes off to the E. and S.E. towards Africa. **1883** 'HOLME LEE' *Loving & Serving* II. vii. 118 A bridle road.. struck into the fields. **1894** *Speaker* 2 June 610/1 Other roads striking off on every side into the forest. *fig.* **1850** *Tait's Mag.* XVII. 78/1 Their hostility strikes out into many ramifications, but it is not difficult to trace all these to the parent root.

c. Of a boundary, path, mountain-range, etc.: To take a (specified) direction, esp. with reference to the points of the compass.

1456 *Regist. de Aberbrothoc* (Bannatyne Club) II. 89 The boundis.. syne strikand north our betwen the proper landis of Arbroth and the commoun. **1585** *Reg. Mag. Sig. Scot.* 415/1 Passand.. linallie thairfra as the commoun gait strikis ewin eist to the calsay and brig of the Bow. **1833** JAS. DAVIDSON *Brit. & Rom. Rem. Axminster* 73 That branch of the Fosse-way which, striking off at Watergrove, advances in a south-westerly direction. **1839** MURCHISON *Silur. Syst.* I. xxxvi. 493 A narrow quartzose ride.. extends.. in a line striking from 15° W. of N., to 15° E. of S. **1881** *Proc. R. Geog. Soc.* (N.S.) III. 31 To the west of the Town, a range of hills strikes southerly.

d. trans. ***to strike a line*** or ***path***, to take a direction or course of movement.

1867 *Jrnl. R. Agric. Soc.* Ser. II. III. II. 666 They struck a line across the estuary of the Wash. **1890** A. GISSING *Village Hampden* II. x. 213 They struck their path across the fields. **1892** *Field* 26 Nov. 805/3 We decide to strike a bee line across country.

II. To stroke, rub lightly, smooth, level.

3. *trans.* To go over lightly with an instrument, the hand, etc.; to stroke, smooth; to make level. Also with *down, out, over.* Also *absol.* Now *dial.* (see *Eng. Dial. Dict.*).

c **1000** *Sax. Leechd.* III. 30 Mid wætere ne þwea ac strice hy mid claðe clæne. *c* **1330** R. BRUNNE *Chron. Wace* (Rolls) 11192 þenne come chaumberleyns & squiers, Wiþ riche robes.. To folde, to presse, & to pyke, & somme to hange, & som to strike. *c* **1380** *Sir Ferumb.* 244 þat gode hors blessede he þo & louely strek ys mane. *c* **1460** J. RUSSELL *Bk. Nurture* 280 Youre hed ne bak ye claw.., ne youre heere ye stryke. **1481** CAXTON *Reynard* (Arb.) 38 Where his footspore stood, there stryked he with his tayl and make it smothe with his mouth that noman shold espye it. **14..** in *Archæologia* IV. 312 The warderoper to delyver the second sheete unto two yomen, they to crosse it over theyr arme, and to stryke the bedde as the ussher shall more playnly shewe unto theym. **1494** in *Househ. Ord.* (1790) 122 And the esquires to gather the sheete round together in their hand on eyther side the bedd, and goe to the bedd's head and strike downe the same twice or thrice as they come downe. **15..** in *Dunbar's Poems* (1893) 308 Sum strykis down a threid bair cheik For luve. **1525** tr. *Brunswyke's Handywork Surg.* lxv. O iij, Take hede that yᵉ.. foote stande vp ryght, and you with your flat hande ouer the fracture stryke so that ye about nor vnder fele none vneuen place. **1530** PALSGR. 739/2, I stryke, I make smothe, *japlanis.* Stryke over this paper. *Ibid.*, I stryke ones heed, as we do a chyldes whan he dothe well. **1548** HALL *Chron., Hen. VIII*, 226 b, He hauyng a great gray beard, striked out his beard and sayd to the hangman [etc.]. **1558** PHAER *Æneid* VIII. (1562) Ccj b, A she wolfe.. them swetely lyckt reforming soft their limmes, & soft wᵗ tong them smothly stryckt. **1573–80** TUSSER *Husb.* (1878) 81 More stroken and made of when ought it doo aile, More gentle ye make it, for yoke or the paile. **1579** RICE *Invect. agst. Vices* I ij b, He shall strike your heades, and make very muche of you.

†**b.** To shave. *Obs.*

c **1205** LAY. 20303 Balduf lette striken [*c* **1275** strike] to þan bare lichen his bærd and his chinne.

c. To rub gently, stroke (a diseased part), by way of charm, or with the application of a salve. *Obs.* exc. *dial.* (see *Eng. Dial. Dict.*). Also, † ***to strike one's hand over*** (a part).

1400 *Brut* 229 And a drope of dry bloode and smal sande cleued on his honde, and þerwiþ he striked his eyne. **1611** BIBLE *2 Kings* v. 11 He will.. strike [1885 (*Revised*) wave] his hand ouer the place, and recouer the leper. **1886** *W. Somerset Word-bk.* s.v., The ordinary specific for a stye in the eye is 'to strike it three times with a wedding-ring'. **1892** *Cornhill Mag.* Sept. 236 People came to her to have their swellings struck.

†**d.** To scrape or skim off. Also, ? to skim (a liquid). *Obs.*

c **1430** *Two Cookery-bks.* I. 27 Take þan a clene canvas, & caste þe mylke vppe-on, & with a platere stryke it of þe cloþe. **1587** HARRISON *England* II. vi. 169/2 in *Holinshed*, She returneth the middle woort vnto the furnace, where it is striken ouer. *Ibid.* 170/1 She.. seetheth againe with a pound and an halfe of new hops,.. & when it hath sodden.. she striketh it also.

†**4.** To smear (soap, blood, etc.) on a surface; also to spread (a surface) with (something); to coat (a surface) *over* with oil, a wash, etc. *Obs.*

14.. in *Rel. Ant.* I. 108 To make murrour bryȝt. Stryke wel theron blak sope. **1525** tr. *Brunswyke's Handywork Surg.* lxi. O j, Take powder as hereafter foloweth medled with yᵉ whyte of an egge, and stryke it vpon a clothe lyke a plaster. *Ibid.* lxv. O iij b, The clothe must be wel stryken on the one syde with the salue. **1530** PALSGR. 739/1, I hade as lefe stryke my breed with butter as with hony. **1535** COVERDALE *Exod.* xii. 7 And they shal take of his bloude, and stryke it on both the syde postes of the dore. [So **1611**; Heb., LXX, and Vulgate have simply 'put'; Luther *bestreichen*, which Coverdale prob. followed.] **1577** HARRISON *England* II. x. 84 b/2 in *Holinshed*, Whyte lime.. wher-with we stricke ouer our clay workes & stone walles, in Cities. **1596** THOMASIUS *Dict.* (1606), *Moretum*, A kinde of pudding; also any thing that may be striked, as butter. **1640** T. BRUGIS *Marrow of Physicke* II. 141 Take it [your Marmalade] from the fire, and fill your Boxes, and with a feather strike it over with Rosewater. **1687** J. SMITH *Art Painting* xix. (ed. 2) 89 With a Pencil dipt in clear Wallnut-Oyl.. let the printed Paper be struck clean over on both sides. **1793** SMEATON *Edystone L.* §328 A couple of men with brushes, struck over the surface.. with raw Linseed oil. **1799** G. SMITH *Laboratory* I. 265 Take smooth-planed pear-tree wood, strike it over with aqua fortis.

5. To make (grain, etc.) level with the rim of the measure by passing a strickle over it. Also with object the measure. Also ***to strike off.***

14.. *Tretyce* in *Walter of Henley's Husb.* (1890) 50 Se pᵗ yoʳ corne be mesured withe.. a trewe bushell & þat euery bushell be strekyn. **1474** [see STRIKE *sb.* 3]. **1543** tr. *Act 25 Edw. III* Stat. 4 c. 10, 32 And euery measure of corne shalbe stryked without hepe. **1641** BEST *Farm. Bks.* (Surtees) 104 When wee sende our corne to mill, wee allwayes strike all cleane of; yett the use is in most places to handwave it..; but the millers will say that they had as leave have corn stricken, as soe handwaved. **1669** STURMY *Mariner's Mag.* v. xii. 68 Strike off the heaped Powder. **1697** *View Penal Laws* 338 If Head Officers of Cities.. wilfully suffer any to sell Corn.. by other Measure, or Strucken in other manner. **1878** *Act 41 & 42 Vict.* c. 49 §17 In using an imperial measure of capacity, the same shall not be heaped but either shall be stricken with a round stick,.. or [etc.]. **1892** *Field* 2 Apr. 469/3 The somewhat delicate operation of gently filling the bushel measure, striking it, and then weighing the oats.

b. To level (sand) in moulding. Also with *up.*

1779 *Ann. Reg., Projects* 103/1 The sand should be struck smooth with an hollow rule. **1885** [HORNER] *Pattern Making* 40 The moulder.. stikes over a bed of hard rammed sand representing the top of the boss. *Ibid.* 67 Being plastic when in the wet state it [foundry loam] can be 'struck up', or made to assume any shape that may be required.

†**6.** To mould (wax, a taper, candle, etc.). *Obs.*

1485 *Churchw. Acc. St. Dunstan's, Canterb.*, For strykyng of the pascall and the font taper ijs. iij d. For strykyng of x li of olde torche waxe x d. **1492–3** *Rec. St. Mary at Hill* 188 Payd to Roger Mydylton for strekyng of xiijˣˣli and xvj of waxe. **1526** *Churchw. Acc. Dunmow* (MS.) fol. 4 b, Item, for strykynge of the lyght.. att the hy alter. **1527** *Ibid.* 6 b, Item, for strekynge of the Rode lyght, xiiid. **1546** in *Archæol. Cant.* (1874) IX. 225 Payd to Holnesse for strekyng of the crosse lygth & the paschall & for strekyng of ij li. of small candles, iij s. iiij d. **1547** *Ibid.* 226 Item payd for strycking of the olde & new waxe at Ester, xv d. *Ibid.*, Item payd for strykynge of ij li. of small candyll that wase of the passkoll, ij d. **1555** *Ibid.* 231 Item ffor strikinge of the same waxe, iiij d.

7. To mould (a brick or tile).

1683 J. HOUGHTON *Collect. Lett. Improv. Husb.* II. vi. 188 With the Earth he forms a Brick, strikes it, and lays it upon the Pallat. **1736** NEVE *Build. Dict.* (ed. 3) s.v. *Brick* G 2 b/2 The mould [of a stock-brick] is put on a Stock, after the Manner of moulding, or strikeing of Tiles. *Ibid.*, And so they continue to strike and place them on the Stage.

8. *Bricklaying.* To level up (a joint) with mortar; to spread (mortar) along a joint. (Cf. 4.)

1668 LEYBOURN *Build. Guide* II. 109 And here note, That the Barge Courses in any Building must be struck with Lime and hair Mortar. **1703** T. N. *City & C. Purchaser* 169 Pointing, (which is striking Mortar under the lower ends). **1833** LOUDON *Encycl. Archit.* §1596 Strike the joints inside of the schoolrooms flush and fair for lime-whiting.

b. To cut off the superfluous mortar from the edges of (tiling).

1693 MOXON *Mech. Exerc.* (1703) 248 A piece of Lath.. with which they strike, or cut off the Morter at the britches of the Tiles. *Ibid.*, A Broome, to sweep the Tyling after 'tis strooke. **1842** GWILT *Encycl. Archit.* §1908.

9. *Tanning.* To smooth and expand (skins). Also ***to strike out.***

1764 *Museum Rust.* III. 54 Mr. Brookfield, tanner, reported, the specimens exhibited were well tanned, and thoroughly struck. **1845** DODD *Brit. Manuf.* Ser. v. 193 The goat-skins, after being thoroughly washed, are.. 'struck', that is scraped and rubbed out as smooth as possible. *Ibid.*, The drying in the loft has had the effect of shrivelling the skins.. to obviate which, the skins are wetted, and 'struck out', or smoothed again. **1897** C. T. DAVIS *Manuf. Leather* xxiii. (ed. 2) 364 The skins.. are next 'struck out' on mahogany tables... A steel 'slicker' is used for this operation.

10. *Carpentry.* To fashion (moulding) with a plane: = STICK *v.*¹ 18 c. [So Du. *strijken.*]

1842 GWILT *Archit.* Gloss., *Striking*... Another application of the word occurs in the practice of joinery, to denote the act of running a moulding with a plane. **1854** *Jrnl. R. Agric. Soc.* XV. II. 456 A beaded moulding to be struck on each of the angles of the under sides of rafters.

III. To mark with lines, draw a line.

Cf. OE. *bestrícan* 'to make a stroke round' (B.-T. Suppl.).

†**11.** To mark (a surface) with a line or lines. Also ***to strike out, through.*** *Obs.*

1539 *Acc. Ld. High Treas. Scot.* VII. 218 Item, for calk to strik the treis witht. *c* **1710** CELIA FIENNES *Diary* (1888) 122 They new washe and plaister their houses wᵗʰ in and without wᶜʰ they strike out in squares like free stone. **1656** EARL MONM. tr. *Boccalini's Advts. fr. Parnass.* II. xxiii. (1674) 171 An exquisite Card whereby to sail.. struck through with lines on all parts.

†**b.** *fig.* To mark, stigmatize. *Obs.*

1594 J. KING *On Jonas* xiii. (1599) 177 Sylla: whose name shall bee striked with the blackest cole of infamie in all the ages of the worlde.

12. To draw (a straight line) esp. by mechanical means; to draw (a circle, an arc) with compasses. In wider sense, †to make (a stroke, written mark).

1611 HOPTON *Speculum Topogr.* xxvii. 71 Placing the one foote of your compasse in g,.. with the other strike the portion of the circle h i k l. **1614** T. BEDWELL tr. *Schoner's De Num. Geom.* 33 First with the iage, I strike two parallel lines. **1662** FAITHORNE *Graving & Etching* xiv. 15 Accustome your self to strike your strokes firm and bold. **1687** P. AYRES *Lyric Poems* (1906) 272 Since my dull pen trembles to strike a line. **1688** HOLME *Armoury* III. 413/2 Dashes.. which serve for the cutting off or shortning of words,.. which all of them are strucken downwards to the foot of the Letter. **1737** BRACKEN *Farriery Impr.* (1756) I. 268 The nearer the Line struck from the Perpendicular approaches to a right Angle. **1770** LUCKOMBE *Hist. Printing* 229 None can strike two letters of the same signification, so as.. to have the same likeness. **1856** R. FERGUSON *Northmen Cumbld. & Westmld.* 199 *Strike*, to make a straight line by means of a string. **1875** SEATON *Fret Cutting* 65 Take your compasses, put on a pencil point, and with it strike the semicircle as above directed. **1881** CHILTON-YOUNG *Ev. Man his own Mech.* §375 By aid of the chalk line and reel, a perfectly straight line could be struck from E to F. **1885** [HORNER] *Patternmaking* 7 In striking special pairs of wheels, of course it is not necessary to use the same describing circle throughout.

†**b.** ? To interline in a list. *Obs.*

1639 FULLER *Holy War* v. xxi. (1647) 265 The Reader, as he lighteth on more, at his leisure may strike them into this catalogue [of Princes].

13. To cancel or expunge with or as with the stroke of a pen. Const. *from, off, out (of)*, rarely † *away*; also (*U.S.*) without const., esp. in legal contexts, and *colloq.*, in the *imp.*, annulling or reversing what the speaker has just said. Also ***to strike*** (a name, a person) ***off*** or (now rarely) ***out of*** a list. Cf. ***strike off*** (82 a), ***strike out*** (83 a), ***strike through*** (84).

The pa. pple. form *stricken* is common in the legal examples of this sense.

to be struck off the rolls: see ROLL *sb.*¹ 3 c.

c **1386** CHAUCER *Friar's T.* 66 Thanne wolde he seye, freend, I shal for thy sake Do striken hire out of oure lettres blake. **1549** OLDE *Erasm. Par. Eph.* 6 Christ.. stroke away al the difference of circumcised, and not circumcised. **1601** SHAKS. *All's Well* v. iii. 56 That thou didst loue her, strikes some scores away From the great compt. **1746** H. WALPOLE *Let. to Mann* 15 Apr., Vernon is struck off the list of admirals. **1794** MRS. RADCLIFFE *Myst. Udolpho* xlvii, O! could I strike from my memory all former scenes. **1829** *Rep. Supreme Court Tennessee* (1832) IX. 229 That an attorney may be stricken from the roll for good cause, none can doubt. **1839** THACKERAY *Fatal Boots* Jan., He has struck Thomas out of his will. **1849** MACAULAY *Hist. Eng.* vi. II. 36 His name was struck out of the list of privy councillors. **1873** P. V. SMITH *Hist. Eng. Inst.* III. viii. 214 A person tried for his life might.. challenge and strike off the panel as many as thirty-five. **1883** MISS M. BETHAM-EDWARDS *Disarmed* ii, The first person who flouts her shall be struck off my visiting list. **1891** *Field* 7 Nov. 701/3 [List of] Horses struck out of their engagements. **1906** *Federal Reporter* (1907) CXLVII. 451 All of the testimony given by the witness.. is withdrawn and stricken out of this case. **1915** *Southwestern Reporter* CLXXV. 661/1 No further steps.. were taken in the case until the February term, 1904, of the Magoffin circuit court, when it was stricken from the docket. **1938** *Congress Rec.* 24 May 7405/2 That the Committee do.. report the bill back to the House with the recommendation that the enacting clause be stricken out. **1973** *N.Y. Law Jrnl.* 19 July 4/2 The Convention.. voted 132 to 49, to strike that section from the Constitution.

1957 *Reports Supreme Court Kansas* (1958) CLXXXI. 623 In our opinion the reply was erroneously stricken. **1965** *Pacific Reporter* CCCCIV. 230/2 Where.. a second clause appears which expresses a different intent and declares a life estate plus a remainder which is void under the rule, the qualifying clause will be stricken. **1973** *N.Y. Law Jrnl.* 31 Aug. 19/2 Motion to strike the statement of readiness is granted. **1978** *N.Y. Times* 29 Mar. B3/4 Over strong objections from the prosecutor, Sybil R. Moses, Judge William J. Arnold ordered the question stricken.

1963 R. I. MCDAVID *Mencken's Amer. Lang.* xi. 754 In television we might note *mark it* and *strike it*, directions to stage hands to chalk out the position for scenery and then rub out the mark for the next set. **1976** R. M. STERN *Will* I. ii. 17 Do you.. believe that the crash was not an accident? Strike that. We will look into it with an open mind. **1977** H. GREENE *FSO-1* ii. 16, I don't give a damn what the congressman says. Strike that: I *do* give a damn.

b. Phr. ***to strike*** (a medical practitioner, etc.) ***off the register***: to remove (that person's name) from the register of qualified practitioners and thereby forbid him or her to practise. Usu. *pass.*

1911 G. B. SHAW *Doctor's Dilemma* p. xciii, Execute the doctor, if necessary, *as* a doctor, by striking him off the register. **1936** A. CHRISTIE *Cards on Table* xvi. 157, I heard him say he'd get Dr. Roberts struck off the—Medical Register, would it be? **1951** 'E. CRISPIN' *Long Divorce* xvi. 199 We can and shall get him struck off the register.

14. To form (a jury) by cancelling a certain number of names from the list of persons nominated to serve; similarly, to form (a committee), to make (a new register of voters).

1715 *Lond. Gaz.* No. 5389/2 The Clerk of the Crown was required to strike a Jury for his Tryal. **1768** BLACKSTONE *Comm.* III. vi. 83 That twelve freeholders of that hundred, qualified to serve on juries, and struck by the sheriff, shall be summoned to appear at such court by rotation. **1821** *Examiner* 321/1 Let us suppose the Jury to be struck with perfect fairness and impartiality. [**1823** *Ibid.* 323/1 Out of the 48 persons first nominated, each party, after due inquiry, strike twelve—leaving 24, of whom the first 12 called (who attend) form the actual jury.] **1877** COX *Cases Crim. Law* (1878) XIII. 646 The case was tried by a special jury of the city of Dublin, struck under the old system. **1892** *Graphic* 9 Apr. 455/2 If the General Election fell at any date after the 31st of July, when the new Register is struck. **1896** *Daily News* 17 Dec. 4/7 The Committee was struck late in the summer, and did not meet till the 15th of August.

15. To make or cut (a tally). See TALLY *sb.*[1] 1 b.

1626 [see TALLY *sb.*[1] 1 b]. **1634** B. JONSON *Loves Welcome Bolsover* Wks. 1640 II. 284 We ha' cleft the bough, And struck a tallie of our loves, too, now. **1644** *Docq. Lett. Patent at Oxf.* (1837) 392 To deliuer back the Tallies strucken for the same as aforesaid vncancelled. *c* **1645** HOWELL *Lett.* VI. xxxii. (1650) I. 220, I reconcile my self to my Creator, and strike a tally in the Exchequer of Heaven for my *quietus est*, ere I close my eyes. **1695–6** *Act 7 & 8 Will. III*, c. 30 §38 Several Tallies..have been also levied or stricken att the Receipt of the Exchequer upon His Majesties said Revenue ariseing in the General Letter-Office.

16. *Agric.* To mark off (land, a ridge) by ploughing once up and down the field (also with *down, up*); to make (furrows) in this manner (also with *out*); also *absol.*

1573–80 TUSSER *Husb.* (1878) 128 Thry fallow once ended, go strike by and by. **1707** MORTIMER *Husb.* 45 You must not let it lie long before you strick, size, or plow it up into small Ridges. **1789** *Trans. Soc. Arts.* I. 123 To striking said fields, seventeen acres. **1834** D. LOW *Elem. Pract. Agric.* 146 The first operation in the forming of ridges is striking the furrows. **1844** H. STEPHENS *Bk. Farm* I. 465 The first process in ridging up land from the flat surface is called *feering* or *striking* the ridges. **1844** *Jrnl. R. Agric. Soc.* V. I. 5 These [ridges]..are..struck down with two furrows. **1845** *Ibid.* VI. II. 287 Cost of cultivation [of hops]..Striking up and furrowing, 0 5 0. **1846** *Ibid.* VII. I. 41 This land..is again ploughed across..in the manner we term striking, or back-bouting. This is done by turning one furrow to the land, and in returning to turn over this furrow, and the furrow or earth on which it was laid.

b. To make (a row of holes) with a dibble.

1797 A. YOUNG *Agric. Suffolk* (ed. 2) 48 A man, walking backwards on the flag,..with a dibber of iron..in each hand, strikes two rows of holes..on each flag. **1805** R. W. DICKSON *Pract. Agric.* I. 475 A one-horse roll then follows to level the flag, or furrow, for the dibblers, who strike only one row upon each.

IV. To lower (sails, masts), and derived senses.

[Sense 17 is in (M)LG. and (M)Du. and in mod.G.; it therefore cannot be a derivative from branch V, which is specially English. The actual development is uncertain; possibly the sense may be pre-Teut.: cf. L. *stringĕre* to strip off (leaves, etc.).]

17. *Naut.* To lower or take down (a sail, mast, yard, etc.); esp. to lower (the topsail) as a salute and (more rarely) as a sign of surrender in an engagement. Phrase, ***to strike sail***. ***to strike a hull*** (see A-HULL 1867). Also ***to strike down***.

a **1300** *K. Horn* 1013 (Camb.) Hi strike seil & maste & Ankere gunne caste. **1399** LANGL. *Rich. Redeles* IV. 80 For ne had þei striked a strake and sterid hem þe better, And abated a bonet or þe blast come. *c* **1440** *Bone Flor.* 1864 Then beganne the storme to ryse,.. They stroke the sayle. **1524** *Inform. Pilgr. Holy Land* (Roxb.) c iv b, So they saylled forth ..& neuer stryked sayle tyll they came to port Iaffe. **1590** SPENSER *F.Q.* I. xii. 42 Now strike your sailes ye iolly Mariners, For we be come vnto a quiet rode. *c* **1594** WYATT *R. Dudley's Voy. W. Ind.* (Hakl. Soc.) 13 By that they had some 3 peeces bestowed on them they stroke saile, yealdinge themselves unto the mercie of our Generall. **1601** WEEVER *Mirr. Mart.* B vj b, They vaile their bonnet low, And strike their top-saile in submissiue dutie. **1611** BIBLE *Acts* xxvii. 17 They vsed helps,..and fearing lest they should fall into the quicke-sands, strake saile, and so were driuen. **1626** CAPT. SMITH *Accid. Yng. Seamen* 28 Strike your top masts to the cap. **1627** —— *Sea Gram.* xii. 56 He must..strike a Hull that you may not descry him by his sailes. **1630** WADSWORTH *Pilgr.* ii. 8 The Marriners stroke Saile and submitted. **1644** MANWAYRING *Seamans Dict.* 104 So when we take downe the top-masts, they say, Strike them downe. **1745** P. THOMAS *Jrnl. Anson's Voy.* 296 Both Ships struck their Yards and Top masts. **1762–9** FALCONER *Shipwr.* II. 257 Now some, to strike top-gallant-yards attend. **1768** *Ann. Reg.* 92 A body of sailors..proceeded..to Sunderland.., and at the cross there read a paper, setting forth their grievances... After this they went on board the several ships in that harbour, and struck (lowered down) their yards, in order to prevent them from proceeding to sea. **1814** SCOTT *Ld. of Isles* III. xii, Fain to strike the galley's yard, And take them to the oar. **1840** R. H. DANA *Bef. Mast* xxii, The royal-yards were then struck. **1890** CLARK RUSSELL *Ocean Trag.* II. xxi. 181 His maintopmast was struck, that is, sent down on deck. **1894** C. N. ROBINSON *Brit. Fleet* 179 The custom of 'striking' or lowering a sail [as a salute] has almost died out.

in figurative phrases. **1509** BARCLAY *Shyp of Folys* (1570) 117 Nowe would I of my boke haue made an ende, And with my ship drawen to some hauen or port, Striken my sayle. **1593** SHAKS. *3 Hen. VI*, III. iii. 5 Now Margaret Must strike her sayle, and learne a while to serue, Where Kings command. **1680–90** TEMPLE *Ess. Pop. Discont.* Wks. 1731 I. 270 To this, all differing Opinions, Passions and Interests should strike Sail. **1733** POPE *Sat. Donne* IV. 231 He boarding her, she striking sail to him.

b. To haul down (a flag), esp. as a salute or as a sign of surrender. Chiefly in the phrases ***to strike (the) flag, to strike one's colours***. Also ***to strike*** one's ***flag*** (said of an admiral): see FLAG *sb.*[4] 2.

1628 DIGBY *Voy. Mediterr.* (Camden) 42 Because I did not strike flag nor do other ceremonies of dutie. **1666–7** PEPYS *Diary* 4 Mar., He hears that the Dutch..will have a promise of not being obliged to strike the flag to us before they will treat with us. **1676** *Lond. Gaz.* No. 1077/4 Three Ostend Privateers..fired several Guns at him,..to make him strike his Colours. **1692** *Capt. Smith's Seaman's Gram.* I. xvi. 77 *To lower or strike the Flag*, is to pull it down upon the Cap, and in Fight is a token of yielding; but otherwise of great respect. **1747** J. LIND *Lett. Navy* (1757) I. 31 If an admiral be killed, the instructions forbid his flag to be struck, for fear of discouraging the fleet. **1799** *Hull Advertiser* 6 July 1/4 Admiral Lord Bridport struck his flag last evening. **1802** C. JAMES *Milit. Dict.* s.v., *To strike the colours*. This is properly a naval term, but it may be applied to military matters on some occasions. **1867** J. T. HEADLEY *Farragut & Nav. Commanders* 492 He..on the 12th of next month struck his flag as admiral of the South Atlantic Blockading Squadron.

fig. **1861** WHYTE MELVILLE *Good for N.* xiii. I. 162, I thought he seemed very much smitten with the young lady. You know he is not very susceptible, so when he *does* strike his flag, it is all the greater compliment. **1875** F. T. BUCKLAND *Log-Book* 141 The mouse..would have to fight and not strike his colours to a scorpion as he would to a cat.

c. *absol.* To lower sail, haul down one's flag; esp. to lower the topsails or haul down the flag or colours as a sign of surrender or as a salute.

1390 GOWER *Conf.* III. 338 Thei hadden wynd at wille tho, With topseilcole and forth they go, And striken nevere, til thei come To Tyr. **1449** *Paston Lett.* I. 85, I cam abord the Admirall, and bade them stryke in the Kyngys name of Englond. *a* **1578** LINDESAY (Pitscottie) *Chron. Scot.* (S.T.S.) I. 185 The day befoir the schip strak in the raid of Leyth. **1617** in J. S. Corbett *Fighting Instr.* (1905) 39 If you give chase and being near a ship you shall shoot to make her strike. **1769** FALCONER *Dict. Marine* s.v. *Sail* (1780) Kk 2 b, All foreign vessels strike to an English man of war in the British seas. **1814** *Niles' Weekly Reg.* 19 Nov. 174/2 The Avon had not struck, but was reported to have had her colors nailed to the mast. **1836** MARRYAT *Midsh. Easy* xxx, The second lieutenant was deputed to pull alongside of the frigate to ascertain if she had struck. **1886** HENTY *Yarns on Beach* 84 Captain Ball..reported that the fort with which he was engaged had struck.

fig. **1593** SHAKS. *Rich. II*, II. i. 266 We see the winde sit sore vpon our sailes, And yet we strike not, but securely perish. **1601** B. JONSON *Poetaster* III. iv, What, will he saile by, and not once strike, or vaile to a Man of warre? ha? **1749** SMOLLETT *Gil Blas* v. i. (1782) II. 161, I thought myself the first man in the world, but truely I strike to you. **1886** STEVENSON *Dr. Jekyll* i, He would have clearly liked to stick out; but there was something about the lot of us that meant mischief, and at last he struck.

18. *trans.* **a.** *Naut.* To lower (a thing) into the hold by means of a rope and tackle. Chiefly ***to strike down*** (also *absol.*). Also, ***to strike out***, to hoist out from the hold and lower to the dock.

1644 MANWAYRING *Seamans Dict.* 104 When we lower any thing into the howld with the tackles or any other roape, we call it Striking-down into Howld. **1748** *Anson's Voy.* I. v. 56 Each Captain had orders..to strike down some of their great guns into the hold. **1850** H. MELVILLE *White Jacket* I. xxxvii. 242 To the..consternation of the sailors, an order now came from the quarter-deck to 'strike the strangers down into the main-hold!' *c* **1860** H. STUART *Seaman's Catech.* 71 The fore hatchway, for striking down or hoisting up stores in the fore part of the ship. **1867** SMYTH *Sailor's Word-bk., Strike down!* the order to lower casks, &c., into the hold. **1890** CLARK RUSSELL *Ocean Trag.* II. xxi. 181 He had struck the long gun forward down below.

†**b.** *gen.* To lower, let down with a rope.

1547 in J. R. Boyle *Hedon* (1875) App. 135 Item, for strykyng the greatte stee, ij. d. **1595** *Strange Things R. Hasleton* in Arber *Garner* VIII. 380 And by it [*sc.* the rope] did I strike myself over the wall into the town ditch.

†**c.** To let down the rope or chain of (a crane). Also ***to strike down*** (see quot. 1778). *Obs.*

1530 PALSGR. 739/2, I stryke, I let downe the crane, *je lache*... Stryke lowe. **1778** PRYCE *Min. Cornub.* Expl. Terms 329/1 *Strik*, to strik or streeck down, or strike down; is to let a man down in a Shaft by the windlass.

19. *Building.* **a.** To remove (scaffolding); in trench-work, to remove (the timbers with which the sides have been secured). **b.** To remove (the centre or centering of an arch).

a. **1694** EVELYN *Diary* 5 Oct., The choir, now finish'd as to the stone work, and the scaffolds struck both without and within, in that part. **1768–74** TUCKER *Lt. Nat.* (1834) II. 107 If we consider religion only as the scaffolding of reason;..any one..may see that it is much too early to strike the scaffolding yet. **1821** *Corr. W. Fowler* (1907) 406 The angels ..will want painting..that may be done at any time with a ladder if you must strike the scaffold before they are ready. **1868** MILMAN *St. Paul's* xiv. 347 On striking the scaffolding, part of the south transept..came down.

b. **1739** LABELYE *Short Acc. Piers Westm. Bridge* 43 The.. Arches..would have been in..Danger of falling the Moment the Centers that supported them..should be struck. *Ibid.* 45 They attempted to strike down the Centers, on which they had turned the Arches. **1838** *Civil Engin. & Arch. Jrnl.* I. 127/1 Upon striking the centering the arches followed from 1 inch and ⅝ to 2 inches and ⅝. **1883** *Specif. Alnwick & Cornhill Rlwy.* 4 The string courses..are not to be put on until the centres are struck.

20. *Shipbuilding.* To cause (a vessel) to slide *down, off* (the slipway); to release (a boat from the cradle).

a **1647** in *Archæologia* XII. 259 Being ready to have the ship strucken down upon her ways, I caused twelve of the choice master carpenters..to be sent for from Chatham. **1892** *Field* 26 Nov. 825/2 She is hauled up on their large patent slipway and struck off the cradle.

21. To discharge (a load); to empty (a vessel) of its load.

1627 CAPT. SMITH *Sea Gram.* vii. 33 When you let any thing downe into the Howle, lowering it by degrees, they say, Amaine; and being downe, Strike. **1797** CURR *Coal Viewer* 12 The modes I have invented of striking, or landing and emptying them [*sc.* corves]. **1901** *Law Jrnl. Rep.* LXX. Chanc. Div. 680/2 The operation known as striking the casks—that is, discharging the vans with the load.

absol. **1702** *Post Man* 12–14 Mar. 2/2 Advt., Lost on the Key, or by error delivered a Pipe of..Wine..which is wanted out of a parcel of Wines taken up by Josiah Bishop, ..who ordered the Carmen to strike in Cullumstreet near Ipswich Arms.

b. *Sugar-boiling.* To empty (the liquor, the tache).

1793 B. EDWARDS *Hist. Brit. Col. W. Indies* v. ii. II. 235 This operation is usually called *striking*; i.e. lading the liquor, now exceedingly thick, into the cooler. **1839** URE *Dict. Arts* 1203 The thermometer..can by no means be regarded as a sure guide, in determining the proper instant for striking the teache. **1882** *Spons' Encycl. Industr. Arts* etc. v. 1891 If, after a moment's cooling, the sling can be formed into a ball which does not stick to the fingers,..the correct period has arrived for striking.

22. To let down (a tent) for removal; to remove the tents of (a camp or encampment).

1707 *Lond. Gaz.* No. 4337/2 The Enemy..struck their Tents, and form'd in Line of Battle. **1825** SCOTT *Talism.* xxii, The pavilion which they had left, was..struck with singular dispatch. **1829** C. ROSE *Four Yrs. S. Africa* 167 At the first dawn of day, all was in motion;..some striking the tent, yoking the oxen, and saddling the horses. **1854** F. A. GRIFFITHS *Artil. Man.* (ed. 6) 148 To strike the Encampment..at the word *Strike Tents, and Pickets*, the pickets are struck at once; the tents and marquees prepared for striking... At the word *Down*, the whole are lowered together. **1891** *Field* 26 Dec. 973/2 Next morning we struck camp and turned homewards.

23. To unfix, put out of use.

1793 *Ann. Reg., Chron.* 53 Bath. This day the whole body of chairmen..struck their poles, and proceeded in a mutinous manner to Guildhall, respecting the granting of their licenses. [**1821–6**: see 24 b.] **1840** DICKENS *Old C. Shop* xxvi, The steps [of the caravan] being struck by George and stowed under the carriage, away they went. **1851** W. BOLLAND *Cricket Notes* iv. 67 Arrange, before your game commences, the hour for dinner, and striking wickets.

b. *Theatr.* To remove (a scene); to remove the scenery, etc. of (a play); to turn down (a light).

1889 *Daily Tribune* (N.Y.) 14 July, (*Cent. Dict.* s.v. SET[1] 9) An elaborate scene is 'set' when it is arranged upon the stage, and 'struck' when it is removed. **1891** *Pall Mall Gaz.* 5 Dec. 1/3 It took twelve hours of work by a very large staff to 'strike' 'Ivanhoe' and mount 'La Basoche'. **1893** *Black & White* Christm. No. 7/1 Stage suddenly dark. Gas ballens and limes slowly up. Strike all gas lengths.

c. *Hawking.* (See quot.) Cf. UNSTRIKE *v.*

1891 HARTING *Bibl. Accipitr.* 230 *Strike the hood*, to half open it, so as to be in readiness to hood off the moment the hawk is to be flown.

24. *intr.* Of an employee: To refuse to continue work; esp. of a body of employees, to cease working by agreement among themselves or by order of their society or union.

For the origin of this sense cf. quot. 1768 in sense 17 and quot. 1793 in sense 23.

1768 *Ann. Reg.* 107 [May 9th] This day the hatters *struck*, and refused to work till their wages are raised. **1793** G. DYER *Compl. Poor People Eng.* 74 The poor..seldom strike, as it is called, without good reason... The colliers had struck for more wages. **1801** *Times* 3 Aug., A number of Journeymen Biscuit-bakers..struck from their work for an increase of wages. **1840** *Civil Engin. & Arch. Jrnl.* III. 32/2 They 'struck', as it is termed, because their employer infringed, as they considered, upon their privileges. **1857** HUGHES *Tom Brown* I. viii, The fifth form would fag us, and I and some more struck. **1892** *Sat. Rev.* 2 Jan. 10/1 The London omnibus men struck in a body.

b. More explicitly ***to strike work***, †***tools*** (cf. sense 23). Also with particular kind of work as obj.

1803 SCOTT *Let.* in *Lockhart* (1837) I. xi. 376, I never heard of authors striking work, as the mechanics call it, until their masters the booksellers should increase their pay. **1820** CROKER in *C. Papers* (1884) I. vi. 176 The regiment intended to strike work, as the tradesmen would say. **1821–6** CHALMERS *Wks.* (*c* 1840) XVI. 69 If..the artisans of any establishment should strike their tools. **1837** CARLYLE *Fr. Rev.* II. vi. i, Thus do Cabinet-ministers themselves, in extreme cases, strike work. **1878** TROLLOPE *Is he Popenjoy?* III. xix. 251 She had on one occasion threatened to strike lecturing. **1891** *Law Times' Rep.* LXV. 580/1 The secretaries called off their respective union men, who in obedience to the call struck work.

transf. **1806–7** J. BERESFORD *Miseries Hum. Life* (1826) x. lxi, The machinery of the window sash abruptly striking work. **1897** *Allbutt's Syst. Med.* IV. 56 The liver can 'strike work' and refuse to secrete bile.

c. *trans.* Of a workmen's society or union: To order a strike of workmen against (a firm); to order (a body of workmen) to strike. Also in wider but analogous contexts. Now only *N. Amer.*

1891 *Daily News* 31 Dec. 6/3 Pending the outcome, no fresh firms will be struck. **1892** *Bury Guardian* 23 Apr. 5/5 The secretary of the Weavers' Association struck the mill on an entirely new question. **1930** J. Dos Passos *42nd Parallel* I. 117 She'd worry Mac about striking his boss for more pay. **1941** *Sun* (Baltimore) 23 Sept. 12/2 Now the affected union, the Seafarers' International Union of the AFL, serves formal notice that it will strike every ship on which it has contracts. **1946** *Ibid.* 16 Jan. 4-0/1 They [*sc.* students] held a mass meeting, staged a snake dance, struck their classes, and otherwise asserted themselves, in protest over the resignation of..a football coach at the university. **1950** Patterson & Conrad *Scottsboro Boy* II. vii. 137 Right here we struck the whole squad. No one would do any work till the question of slowing down the work was settled. **1968** *Globe & Mail* (Toronto) 1 Feb. B10/3 The union will strike company plants in five U.S. cities. **1978** *N.Y. Times* 29 Mar. A20/4 Photoengravers voted 177 to 0 yesterday to strike The New York Times and The Daily News.

d. To leave off (work), e.g. at the close of the day, at meal-times. Also *absol.*

1890 Conan Doyle *Firm of Girdlestone* xxx, The work went on until six, when all hands struck and went off to their homes. **1891** Mary E. Mann *Winter's Tale* II. 259 Another good hour's digging was due..before his day-labourer was justified in striking work and betaking himself homeward.

V. To deal a blow, to smite with the hand (*occas.* another limb), a weapon or tool.

The construction with cognate obj. (*to strike a stroke, a blow*) is common to most of the senses in this branch that admit of absolute or intransitive use. See blow *sb.*[1], stroke *sb.*

25. *trans.* To deal (a person, an animal) a blow; to hit with some force either with the hand or with a weapon. Also with double obj. *to strike* (a person) *a blow*.

a **1300** *Cursor M.* 12429 Þe maister..Gaf iesu wit hand a strak; For he him strak wit na resun, Ded in þe place þar fell he dun. **1377** Langl. *P. Pl.* B. xii. 14 Al-þough þow stryke me with þi staffe with stikke or with ȝerde. **1432–50** tr. *Higden* (Rolls) III. 283 Socrates walkenge in a cite, and strynken [*sic*; *Trevisa* evel i-smete on the heed; L. *colapho percussus*] of a symple felowe. **1556** in W. H. Turner *Select. Rec. Oxford* (1880) 255 Thomas Cartwright..offered to stricke with the mase certen of the defendants. **1582** N. T. (Rhem.) *Matt.* xxvi. 68 And other smote his face with the palmes of their hands, saying, Prophecie vnto vs O Christ: who is he that strooke thee? *c* **1590** Marlowe *Faustus* 896 (Brooke) Cursed be hee that strooke his holinesse a blowe on the face. **1700** S. L. tr. *Fryke's Voy. E. Ind.* 140 Laying 'em flat on their Belly, and stricking them with a Rope across the Breech. **1725** Ramsay *Gentle Sheph.* I. i, 'Till he yowl'd sair she strak the poor dumb tyke. **1824** *Examiner* 539/2 [He] struck the boy a violent blow. **1848** Thackeray *Van. Fair* xlix, You may strike me if you like, sir, or hit any cruel blow. **1891** Farrar *Darkn. & Dawn* xxxviii, Glanydon..forgetting that he was a captive, had once struck in the face a Prætorian officer who insulted him.

b. *absol.* and *intr.* To deal or aim a blow with the fist, a stick, etc. Const. *at.* Also *to strike back, out.*

1509 Hawes *Past. Pleas.* xxxv. (Percy Soc.) 182 He stroke at me with many strokes rude. **1530** Palsgr. 739/1, I stryke at the gaynest, or at all adventures, as one dothe that is in afraye and taketh no hede where or howe he stryketh. **1579–80** North *Plutarch, Themistocles* (1595) 129 Strike and thou wilt, said he, so thou wilt heare me. **1644–66** J. Caryl *Expos. Job* xii. 5, 6 (1676) I. 1118 Many are striking at thy heels, but they cannot strike them up, while God holds thee up. **1678** Sir G. Mackenzie *Crim. Laws Scot.* I. xi. §xv. (1699) 66 If by our Law, he who stricks with his Fist, or a Batton..be punishable by death. **1798** Wordsw. *Peter Bell* I. 195 And the blows fell with heavier weight As Peter struck—and struck again. **1859** Tennyson *Marr. Geraint* 413 His dwarf..Struck at her with his whip. **1894** E. A. Haggard *Drummer Boy* vii, [He] was hot-blooded enough, and quite ready to strike back if struck.

26. *trans.* To hit, smite (a material, an object) with an implement, esp. with one designed for the purpose. Also with cogn. obj.

†In early use also with phrase expressing the result, as *to strike to powder*.

1340 Hampole *Pr. Consc.* 7018 Þe devels..with hamers gyf swa gret dyntes, þat alle to powdre moght stryke hard flyntes. **1572** *Sat. Poems Reform.* xxx. 163 As Quheit is strukin for [*read* fro] the stra besyde. **1585** Higins *Junius' Nomencl.* 297 *Flagellum*,..a battledarre wherwith the ball is striken. **1602** Dolman *La Primaud. Fr. Acad.* III. (1618) 732 Fire..is forced out of the flint being stroken with a gad of steele. **1680** Cotton *Compl. Gamester* (ed. 2) 19 [Billiards.] Wooden Boxes for the hazards..are nothing near so commendable as the former [*i.e.* nets], because a Ball struck hard is more apt to flie out of them when struck in. *Ibid.*, If the head [of the cue] happen to be loose, you will never strike a smart stroke. **1744** in 'Bat' *Cricketer's Man.* (1851) 31 If a ball is nipped up and he Strike her again Wilfully..its out. **1827** Faraday *Chem. Manip.* v. (1842) 153 Substances should be made red hot, and struck in that state, until they are sufficiently cracked. **1866** 'Capt. Crawley' *Billiard Bk.* iv. 43 A ball struck moderately hard will traverse the table three or four times from end to end.

fig. **1781** Cowper *Table-T.* 663 Wit now and then, struck smartly, shows a spark, Sufficient to redeem the modern race From total night and absolute disgrace.

b. *absol.* and *intr.* To make a stroke with a hammer or other implement; spec. in *Smithing.*

Phr. *to strike while the iron is hot*: to make one's effort while opportunity serves. Also *allusively*.

1340 Hampole *Pr. Consc.* 7013 And als smyths strykes on þe yren fast. **1530** Palsgr. 740/2 The poore smyth ryseth at foure of the clocke to stryke with his hammer upon his anvelde. *a* **1566** R. Edwards *Damon & Pithias* (1571) C iij b, I haue plied the Haruest, and stroke when the Yron was hotte. [**1575** Gascoigne *Glasse Govt.* Wks. 1910 II. 40 Play you now the wise man, and strike the Iron whiles it is hot.] **1577** B. Googe *Heresbach's Husb.* III. 122 b, Strike upon the head of euery nayle with the hammer. **1593** Shaks. *3 Hen. VI*, v. i. 49 Strike now, or else the Iron cooles. **1615** Chapman *Odyss.* XII. 487 He..of my present absence tooke His fit aduantage, and their iron strooke At highest heate. **1744** Love *Cricket* (1754) 20 The Champion strikes. When scarce arriving fair, The glancing ball mounts upwards in the air. *a* **1841** T. Hook *Ned Musgrave* i, Taking the poker in his right hand, and striking at a large coal placed on the summit of the grate, [etc.]. **1866** 'Capt. Crawley' *Billiard Bk.* iii. 27 Between the thumb and forefinger you place the Cue, in taking aim before you strike. **1890** W. E. Norris *Misadventure* II. x. 138 She struck while the iron was hot.

c. trans. *to strike* (a prisoner) *in the boots*: to crush the limbs by driving wedges between them and the iron boots as a form of torture (cf. boot *sb.*[3] 3). *Obs.* exc. *Hist.*

a **1715** Burnet *Own Time* III. (1724) I. 583 When any are to be struck in the boots, it is done in the presence of the Council. **1855** Macaulay *Hist. Eng.* xiii. III. 291 They..directed the magistrates of Edinburgh to strike the prisoner in the boots.

27. With complementary adv. or phrase: To remove or drive (a thing) with a blow of an implement or the hand. Cf. *strike down* 79 a.

Now somewhat *rare*; formerly common in contexts where some other vb., as *knock*, would now be used.

1450 *Extracts Burgh Rec. Edin.* (1869) I. 12 The lede tane vp, and the bodome strukken owt. **1499** *Ibid.* 75 It is statute that na persoun sell nor tap derrer beir than for xvj d. the galloun, vnder the payne of strikken furth of the heid of the barrell. *a* **1533** Berners *Huon* lv. 188 He..strake out braynes with the pomell of his swerd. **1567** Harman *Caveat* 64 After halfe a dosen blowes, he strycks his staffe out of his hande. **1601** Bp. W. Barlow *Defence* 217 After his sole and onely eie was stroken out. **1612** Peacham *Minerva Brit.* 113 The Tennis-ball, when strucken to the ground, With Racket,..doth back againe rebound. **1622** Mabbe tr. *Aleman's Guzman d'Alf.* II. 357 Hee commanded my irons to bee strooke off. **1657** Billingsly *Brachy-Martyrol.* xiv. 45 Then were his teeth struck out. **1677** Moxon *Mech. Exerc.* iii. 51 You may strike a nail in at the hole. **1678** *Ibid.* v. 90 You may stiffen it by striking a wooden wedge between the Mortess and the Staff. **1680** *Reg. Privy Counc. Scot.* Ser. III. VI. 389 Udney..caused strick two old pewes out of their hinges. **1744** in 'Bat' *Cricketer's Man.* (1851) 31 If in running a Notch ye Wicket is struck down by a Throw..its out. *Ibid.*, He that catches ye Ball must strike a Stump out of ye Ground Ball in Hand. **1797** Ht. Lee *Canterb. T.*, *Old Woman's T.* (1799) I. 392 [They] now prepared to strike the weapon from his hand. **1855** Kingsley *Westw. Ho!* ix, Strike their swords down, Raleigh, Mackworth! **1910** J. McCabe *Prehist. Man* iii. 40 The..knife (a long flake of flint, struck off the core at one blow).

In figurative context. *c* **1520** Skelton *Magnyf.* 1933 *Adversyte*... Of some of theyr chyldren I stryke out the eye. **1706** T. Boston *Mem.* viii. (1899) 177 The Lord struck the bottom out of my discouragement. **1814** Scott *Let.* in *Lockhart* (1837) III. iii. 118 The huge bulk of his power..was obviously to sink when its main props were struck away. **1853** Lynch *Self-Improv.* vi. 154 The tasted cup is stricken from us ere we have done more than taste.

b. *fig.* To remove suddenly as with a blow, to dash.

1599 T. Storer *Life & D. Wolsey* F 3 b, No strokes of Musickes sound could strike away, High thoughts by night, nor deepe conceits by day. **1823** Scott *Quentin D.* xxviii, I shall love to see the sense of approaching death strike the colour from that ruddy cheek. **1891** *Strand Mag.* II. 483/1, I began to laugh at this, but the laugh was struck from my lips at the sight of his face.

28. To stamp with a stroke.

a. To impress (a piece of metal, coin), stamp (a medal) *with* a device by means of a die; to coin (money); †also *absol.* Also *to strike off.*

1449 *Sc. Acts Jas. II* (1814) II. 37/1 Ande at nane tak one hande to strik in tym to cum bot þai þat has or sal haf commandment of the king vnder his grete sele. **1451** *Ibid.* 39/1 Þai think it expedient..at þar be strikyn in þis realme new mone conformyt ewin in wecht to the mone of Inglande. **1463** *Stat. Irel. 3 Edw. IV*, c. 32 To make and strike..iiij. peces of brasse or coper rennyng at j.d. of oure said siluer. *c* **1520** in Gutch *Collect. Cur.* (1781) II. 295 Item iij gilte Boolls withe a Cover strekin withe Martletts. **1526** *Ibid.* 325. **1551** Sir J. Williams *Accompte* (Abbotsf. Club) 86 Grotes stricken withe harpes. **1609** Skene *Reg. Maj.*, *Stat. David II*, 44 Ane notable signe salbe vpon it, quhereby it may be evidently knawen fra all other money alreadie striken. **1687** H. Slingesby *Let.* 11 Oct. in Pepys *Diary* (1879) VI. 157 The medalls made by Roettiers, of which I had an opportunity to chuse the best struck off. **1736** Lediard *Life Marlborough* II. 42 A fine Medal was struck..on Occasion of the Victory. **1775** *Lond. Chron.* 18–20 May 474/3 Giles Forrester, Dereham, and Williams were charged with striking half-pence. *Ibid.*, They seized eight shillings and four-pence halfpenny, with the dies for striking. **1855** Macaulay *Hist. Eng.* xxi. IV. 620 Till the reign of Charles the Second our coin had been struck by a process as old as the thirteenth century. **1879** H. Phillips *Notes Coins* 3 This medal appears to have been chased by hand and not to have been struck from a die.

fig. **1841** D'Israeli *Amen. Lit.* II. 172 These scriptural plays..seem struck in the same mint.

b. To impress (a device) *upon*; also to impress (a die, etc.) with a device.

1551 Sir J. Williams *Accompte* (Abbotsf. Club) 77 For..strickinge the kinges armes vpon the plates in the busholles of a paier of pottes parcell gilte. **1639** in *Fabric Rolls York Minster* (Surtees) 120 To Mr. Horsley for strikeing my Lord Deputyes coate on the organs, 4 s. **1820** T. Hodgson *Ess. Stereotype Printing* 102 The page..composed with these types..would become..one complete matrice, with which the plates, in relief and in reverse, could be struck. *Ibid.* 107 The operation of striking the matrices.

c. To impress or print by means of type, an engraving or the like; to print. *Obs.* exc. in *to strike off.*

1759 Franklin *Ess.* Wks. 1840 III. 217 The assembly..finding both to be such as required an extension of their paper currency..unanimously resolved to strike an additional sum of twenty thousand pounds. **1776** *Pennsylvania Even. Post* 13 Mar. 142 Since a few of this day's papers were struck off, we hear the above ship is a man of war. **1790** Gouv. Morris in Sparks *Life & Writ.* (1832) II. 108 They can make use of that gentle means of striking paper to satisfy their demands. **1838** Mrs. Carlyle *Lett.* I. 105 New title-pages can be struck off at a trifling expense. **1866** J. P. Collier in *Athenæum* 3 Nov. 571/3 These few extra copies I have always had struck off by the printer. **1892** *Temple Bar* Sept. 53 Send it to the printer to strike off a certain number of proofs.

d. To stamp (velvet, etc.).

1701 *Lond. Gaz.* No. 3754/8 A Stuff Gown of Red and Blue Chequer-work, lined with a Norwich Stuff struck with Blue and dark-colour. **1789** Mrs. Piozzi *Journ. France* I. 30 Nothing..can compare with the beauty of these velvets, or with the art necessary to produce such an effect, while the wrong side is smooth, not struck through.

e. *fig.* To imprint on the mind. ? *Obs.*

1615 J. Taylor (Water P.) *Fair & Foul Weather* A 4, I wish my Verse should such Impression strike, That what men Read off, they should thinke the like. **1651** in M. Sellers *Acts Eastland Co.* (Camden) Introd. 47 If there were but a motion of this remotion, I doubt not but it would strike a sad impression into their minds. **1690** Locke *Hum. Und.* II. x. §5 There seems to be a constant decay of all our Ideas, even of those which are struck deepest. **1709** Shaftesb. *Charac.* (1733) II. 395 Those Beautys which strike a sort of Melancholy.

f. *Cinemat.* To make (another print) *from* a motion picture film.

1970 A. Fowles *Dupe Negative* xiv. 192 I've got four hundred feet of 35 mm. ECO original here... How long will it take to strike a master positive? *Ibid.* 196 The piece of film that actually runs through the camera is called the original..from which all subsequent prints are struck.

29. Without the notion of great force: To tap, rap, knock. Also with cognate or double object, and *intr.* with *on, upon.*

c **1470** Henry *Wallace* VI. 237 Wallace..Straik at the dure with his fute hardely. *a* **1577** Sir T. Smith *Commw. Eng.* (1633) 49 When any man is made a Knight, hee kneeling downe is strooken of the Prince with his sword naked. **1596** Spenser *F.Q.* v. v. 18 Tho with her sword on him she flatling strooke, In signe of true subiection to her powre. **1605** Shaks. *Macb.* II. i. 32 Goe bid thy Mistresse, when my drinke is ready She strike vpon the Bell. **1613** —— *Hen. VIII*, III. ii. 117 He..Strikes his brest hard, and anon, he casts His eye against the Moone. **1699** Dampier *Voy.* II. I. 75 There is one that strikes on a small Gong, or a wooden Instrument, before every stroke of the Oar. **1732** Pope *Epit. Gay* 12 The Worthy and the Good shall say, Striking their pensive bosoms—*Here* lies Gay. **1754** Erskine *Princ. Sc. Law* (1809) 169 If he get not access to the house, he must strike six knocks at the gate. **1843** *Penny Cycl.* XXV. 446/1 Tutenag..is very sonorous when struck. **1844** Eliz. Sewell *Amy Herbert* I. xii. 214, I do think if I had but a fairy's wand, I should strike them all as they came into the house, and change them into boys. **1889** Amelia E. Barr *Feet of Clay* ix. 159 He struck the table a blow. **1897** *Pall Mall Mag.* XIII. 40, I struck sharply upon the glass of the window.

indirect passive. **1653** H. Cogan tr. *Hist. Diod. Sic.* v. ii. 177 A huge brazen table, which being strucken upon, yeelded..a dreadfull sound.

†**b.** To beat (time). *Obs. rare.*

1663 J. Spencer *Prodigies* (1665) 136 This harmony would not last long, did not the Chief Musician strike time and measure.

c. To beat or sound (a drum, etc.), esp. in order to 'beat up' for recruits or as a signal to march; to sound (an alarm) on a drum (said also of the drum). Also, *to strike up.* Also *absol. Obs.* exc. *Hist.*

1572 *Charters* etc. *Peebles* (1872) 342 The counsale..Ordanis the haill inhabitantis..to be in ane reddynes, quhen the swische strykis..to pas with thair baillies quhair thai pleis. **1577** *Reg. Privy Council Scot.* II. 641 Licence to stryke drummis, display handsenzies, and lift and collect the saidis cumpaneis of futemen. **1579** Gosson *Sch. Abuse* (Arb.) 16, I may seeme well ynough too strike vp the drumme, and bring all my power to a vaine skirmishe. **1593** Shaks. *3 Hen. VI*, IV. vii. 50 Drummer strike vp, and let vs march away. **1598** R. Bernard tr. *Terence, Eunuch* IV. vii. 167 From whence I will strike vp alarme to shew when you shall beginne. **1612** Coverte *True Rep.* 24 They strooke vp their drums and were in Armes, taking vs to be Portugales. **1819** Scott *Leg. Montrose* xiv, Neither did they strike kettle-drums again at the head of that famous regiment until they behaved themselves so notably at the field of Leipsic. **1849** Macaulay *Hist. Eng.* x. II. 661 The kettledrums struck up: the trumpets pealed.

d. To touch (a string, a musical note; *poet.* to play upon (a harp, lyre, etc.). Also †*intr.* const. *upon.*

1565 Cooper *Thesaurus*, s.v. *Pulsus*, *Nervi in fidibus pulsi*, stringes stroken. **1587** Golding *De Mornay* xxv. 446 A passion that fadeth away like the sound of a Lute, when the player ceasseth to strike. **1594** Hooker *Eccl. Pol.* I. iii. §3 He that striketh an instrument with skill, may cause notwithstanding a verie vnpleasant sound, if the string whereon he striketh chaunce to be vncapable of harmonie. **1611** Shaks. *Wint. T.* v. iii. 98 Musick; awake her: Strike. *a* **1650** *King Estmere* lviii. in Child *Ballads* II. 54/2 He stroake upon his harpe againe. **1677** F. North *Philos. Ess. Mus.* 18 A great string struck near the Bridge with a Bow..will whistle and break into chords above; which if it were struck by the thumb..would give the true Tone. **1708** Pope *Ode St. Cecilia's Day* 63 But hark! he strikes the golden lyre! **1795** Southey *Joan of Arc* IV. (1853) 41 Meantime the Trouveur struck the harp.

fig. **1579** J. Melvill *Diary* (Bannatyne Club) 60 They dwelt verie commodiuslie togidder,..all strak on a string and soundet a harmonie. **1599** Marston *Ant. & Mel.* III. (1602) E 3 b, I will warble to the delicious concaue of my Mistresse eare: and strike her thoughts with The pleasing touch of my voice. **1630** Donne *Serm.* ix. (1640) 90 That soule, who, whatsoever string be strucken in her base or treble, her high or her low estate, is ever tun'd toward God. **1828** *Mirror* V. 102/2 My muse shall strike a loftier string. **1831–3** E. Burton *Eccl. Hist.* iii. (1845) 51 They struck upon a chord which vibrated to the heart of every Israelite.

30. To produce by percussion.

a. (*a*) To produce (fire, a spark) by percussion, esp. by the percussion of flint and steel. Chiefly in the phrase ***to strike fire***. Also, *to strike out*.

c **1450** *St. Cuthbert* (Surtees) 823 þan of flynt fyre þai strake, And made a fyre. **1578–9** in *Fabric Rolls York Minster* (Surtees) 117 For an yron to stryke fyer with in the revestrie, 3d. **1599** MARSTON *Antonio's Rev.* II. ii, Showers of dartes may darke Heavens ample browe, but not strike out a sparke. **1604** E. G. tr. *Acosta's Hist. Ind.* III. ii. 119 The manner to strike fire in rubbing two stones one against another, as some Indians vse. **1755** YOUNG *Centaur* (1757) I. i. 129, I must observe, that no man can strike fire with a feather. **1810** SCOTT *Lady of Lake* v. xviii, Blair-Drummond sees the hoofs strike fire. **1862** *Temple Bar* VI. 169 The fire which is struck out of a flint. **1865** MEREDITH *R. Fleming* xvii, Two flints strike fire.

absol. **1604** SHAKS. *Oth.* I. i. 141 Strike on the Tinder, hoa: Giue me a Taper.

transf. and *fig.* **1601** SHAKS. *Jul. C.* I. ii. 177, I am glad that my weake words Haue strucke but thus much shew of fire from Brutus. **1637** R. ASHLEY tr. *Malvezzi's David Persecuted* 103 That light, which untill it be stricken out doth never appeare. **1687** DRYDEN *Hind & P.* I. 75 My pride struck out new sparkles of her own. **1742** YOUNG *Nt. Th.* I. 39, 40 O Thou! whose word from solid Darkness struck That spark, the sun; strike wisdom from my soul. **1891** A. GISSING *Moorland Idyll* III. vi. 107 His words struck kindred sparks within herself. **1893** *Eng. Illustr. Mag.* X. 277/1 Gleams of moonlight..struck a glitter from standing rain-pools.

(*b*) *transf.* (in recent use). To cause (a match) to ignite by friction. Also *intr.* of a match: To admit of being struck.

The corresponding use of G. *streichen* is an application of the sense 'to rub' (cf. 3 above), and only accidentally coincides with this use.

1880 SPURGEON *Serm.* XXVI. 653 They may strike their matches and light their candles if they will. **1892** *Black & White* 30 July 116/1 Matches that strike only on the box. **1957** 'R. WEST' *Fountain Overflows* i. 14 And I think the matches are wet, they won't strike. **1962** J. BRAINE *Life at Top* ii. 31, I heard a match strike and smelled cigar smoke.

(*c*) Phr. ***to strike a light***: to produce a flame with flint and steel or by the friction of a match. Also (chiefly *Austral.* and *N.Z.*) *imp.* as a mild imprecation (cf. sense 46 c).

1684 BUNYAN *Pilgr.* II. 184 Wherefore he strook a Light (for he never goes also without his Tinder-box). **1794** MRS. RADCLIFFE *Myst. Udolpho* l, A light being struck, a fire was kindled. **1820** SCOTT *Monast.* xxviii, The means of striking light were at hand in the small apartment. **1892** *Temple Bar* Apr. 471 He felt for his matches and struck a light.

fig. **1704** NORRIS *Ideal World* II. viii. 381 If we were not to see but by striking a light to ourselves, we must for ever be in the dark.

imp. **1936** A. RUSSELL *Gone Nomad* vi. 44 'Strike a light!' he broke in suddenly. 'See them?' **1960** I. CROSS *Backward Sex* ii. 39 'Strike a light,' he hissed.. 'Get over here, quick,' he said. 'Have a bloody look, man.'

b. To produce (music, a sound, note) by touching a string or playing upon an instrument; hence *gen.* to sound (a particular note). Also said of the instrument. Cf. *strike up*, 87 c.

1597 MORLEY *Introd. Mus.* 95, I greatlie mislike..your causing the treble strike a sharpe eight to the base. ? **1599** A. HUME *Poems* vii. 217 Nor famous lute of cunning Amphion, Struike neuer note so pleasant to the eir. **1610** DOWLAND *Var. Lute-lessons* C 1 b, The Note following though it be measured with a new measure, must be strooke with the fore-finger. **1629** MILTON *Hymn Nativ.* 95 Such musick sweet..As never was by mortall finger strook. **1787** WOLCOT (P. Pindar) *Ode upon Ode* Wks. 1816 I. 310 Didst ever see this lady striking *A* Upon her harpsichord, with bending ears? **1885** 'MRS. ALEXANDER' *At Bay* i, Her reply was to strike a few chords, and begin a sweet, wild, plaintive air. **1892** *Graphic* 9 Apr. 468/2 With one hand we strike three or four notes simultaneously.

fig. **1827** SCOTT *Chron. Canongate* Introd. App., Whatever note he [Shakespeare] takes, he strikes it just and true, and awakens a corresponding chord in our own bosoms. **1908** R. BAGOT *A. Cuthbert* iv. 30 What did, perhaps, strike an incongruous note was the presence of various implements of sport.

c. To make (a door *through*), to open *out* (a window) by knocking a hole through a wall. *Sc.*

1652 LAMONT *Diary* (Maitl. Club) 40 She caused also a doore to be struken throughe the wall of her chamber, for to goe to the wine cellar. **1827** [see STONE *sb.* 16 g].

31. To pierce, stab, or cut (a person. etc.) with a sharp weapon. Also with double object. Also with compl. ***to strike dead, to*** (***the***) ***death. to strike through***, to transfix. Also, †to cut (a gash).

Now *rare* exc. as a contextual variety of sense 25; the verb would now hardly be used with reference to a thrust or stab, unless inflicted by a downward movement.

a **1300–1400** *Cursor M.* 18018 (Gött.) Mine eldrin folk of iuen lede Haue I done rise againes him, To strike him wid a spere ful grim. *a* **1375** *Joseph Arim.* 567 A whit kniht.. Baar him doun of his hors..strok him stark ded. *c* **1400** *Destr. Troy* 6258 If any stert vpon stray, strike hym to dethe! **1461** *Paston Lett.* II. 42 It is talkyd here how that..on of Howard's men schuld a' strekyn yow twyess with a dagere. **1515** *Extracts Burgh Rec. Edin.* (1869) I. 156 He was adiugeit to be had to the trone and thair strikkin throw the hand. **1568** GRAFTON *Chron.* II. 655 The Lorde Clyfforde.. putting of his Gorget, sodaynely wyth an arrowe..was striken into the throte. *a* **1586** SIDNEY *Arcadia* II. xxi. (1912) 288 She ranne to her sonnes dagger, and..strake her selfe a mortall wound. **1622** CALLIS *Stat. Sewers* (1647) 19 That is Lacyes Case, where one was stricken on the Seas, and dyed on the Land, that the Common Law could not try this murther. **1642** FULLER *Holy St.* v. xvi. 423 He strook a deep gash into his own thigh. **1745** R. JAMES *Med. Dict.* III. s.v. *Styptica*, Trials were made..by stricking a Cock through the Head [etc.]. **1825** SCOTT *Talism.* xxviii, The Templar struck him to the heart with a Turkish dagger. **1837** LOCKHART *Scott* I. iii. 105 The maid-servant, in a sudden access of insanity, struck her mistress to death with a coal-axe. **1893** *Longm. Mag.* June 114 What is to prevent me striking you through where you stand?

b. *fig.* Of a feeling, etc.: To pierce (a person *to* the heart, *to* the quick).

c **1400** *Apol. Loll.* 2 Wan þe heldar gifiþ ensaumple to þe ȝong to deþ, þer is he to be stregun [St. Gregory *feriendus est*] wiþ scharp blamyng. **1534** MORE *Comf. agst. Trib.* III. iii. (1553) O ij, The sodayn dreade of euery bodely payne woundeth vs to the hearte and striketh our deuocion starke dead. *a* **1540** BARNES *Wks.* (1572) 328/2 The which thyng, when S. Gregory saw, stroke hym sore to the hart. **1599** MARSTON *Antonio's Rev.* I. iv, Strike me quite through with the relentlesse edge Of raging furie. **1674** Fox in *Jrnl. Friends' Hist. Soc.* (1914) July 100 When shee hard of my being stoped by ther impresen mee it strok her to the hart that shee died. **1697** COLLIER *Ess. Mor. Subj.* II. (1703) 117 Humility disarms envy and strikes it dead. **1712** R. F. tr. *Du Bos' Hist. League Cambray* II. 111 The News of the loss of Bologna, struck Pope Julius the 2d to the Heart. **1833** TENNYSON *Pal. Art* 220 She fell, Like Herod, when the shout was in his ears, Struck thro' with pangs of hell.

c. With complementary adv. or phrase: To remove or separate with a cut. Now *rare* exc. in *strike off* (82 b).

c **1320** *Sir Beues* 637 And sum he strok of þe swire. *c* **1375** *Sc. Leg. Saints* i. (*Petrus*) 362 þan Nero bad a man suld ga, and strik symonis nek intwa. *c* **1420** *Liber Cocorum* (1862) 44 And heke hedes þou take with stalk in fere, þat is in peses þou stryke. *c* **1440** *Generydes* 6375 Downe by the cheke his ere away he strake. *c* **1480** HENRYSON *Mor. Fab.* II. (*Town & C. Mouse*) xvi, Muttoun and beif strukkin [*v.r.* strikin] in tailyeis greit. *c* **1489** CAXTON *Sonnes of Aymon* xix. 415 His brother richarde wolde have stryked the hede fro the body of hym. *c* **1614** SIR W. MURE *Dido & Æneas* III. 222 The anchore roape, With shyning sword vnsheath't, in twaine he stroake. **1646** DRUMM. OF HAWTH. *Answ. Objections agst. Scots* Wks. (1711) 213 That Nation, who stroke the Head from the Grandmother, may make small Reckoning to do the same to the Grandchild. **1831** *Examiner* 711/2 The soldier..struck the head from the body. **1831** SCOTT *Cast. Dang.* xvii, Turnbull..struck from a neighbouring oak-tree a branch.

32. *absol.* and *intr.* (also with cognate object). To deliver a cut or thrust with a sharp weapon. Also said of the weapon. Const. *at*, †*to*, †*unto*.

Phrase †***without*** (***a***) ***stroke*** (or ***a blow***) ***stricken*** (and variants), without any fighting. Cf. F. *sans coup férir*.

1340 HAMPOLE *Pr. Consc.* 7346 þe devils ay omang on þam salle stryke. **1375** BARBOUR *Bruce* VI. 234 He smertly raiss, And, strikand, rowm about him mais. *c* **1400** *Destr. Troy* 8760 A meruelous ymage..with a noble sword..Vp holdand on high as he þat wold stryke. *c* **1430** *Chev. Assigne* 333 Thenne he stryketh a stroke..Euen his sholder in twoo. *c* **1430** *Syr Tryam.* 774 And sykurly can they stryke and threste. **1518** *Sel. Cases Star Chamber* (Selden Soc.) II. 137 They met hym agen..and stroke at hym one of them wyth a knyffe. **1598** GRENEWEY *Tacitus, Ann.* XII. x. (1622) 171 By the comming of the Parthians, the Hiberi were driuen out without stroke striking [L. *sine acie*]. **1607** SHAKS. *Cor.* IV. ii. 19 To banish him that strooke more blowes for Rome Then thou hast spoken words. **1611** CHAPMAN *Iliad* III. 369 This said, he shooke, and threw his lance; which strooke through Paris shield. **1622** R. HAWKINS *Voy. S. Sea* xlv. 113 Pillage ..all winked at and vnpunished, although such prizes haue beene rendred without strooke stricken. **1632** SIR T. HAWKINS tr. *Mathieu's Unhappy Prosperitie* 222 The offer.. had assured him of the whole Iland without a blow strucken. **1677** EARL CASTELHAVEN in *Essex Papers* (Camden) II. 92 With-out a stroke striking all the greate townes will submit unto him. **1700** DRYDEN *Pal. & Arc.* II. 245 Like Lightning flam'd their Fauchions..; so strong they strook, There seem'd less Force requir'd to fell an Oak. **1719** DE FOE *Crusoe* II. (Globe) 372 The Fellow..struck at the Spaniard with his Hatchet. **1769** BLACKSTONE *Comm.* IV. ix. 125 Assaulting a judge, sitting in the court, by drawing a weapon, without any blow struck, is punishable with the loss of the right hand. **1843** MACAULAY *Horatius* xxxviii, Herminius struck at Seius, And clove him to the teeth. **1861** *Temple Bar* II. 120 Shot down before I could strike a blow. **1891** FARRAR *Darkn. & Dawn* xlii, Even the soldier who had raised his hand to strike stood amazed, and delayed his blow.

in fig. context. **1735** POPE *Prol. Sat.* 203 Willing to wound, and yet afraid to strike.

b. *fig.*, esp. in ***to strike at***, to aim at the overthrow, destruction, or defeat of.

c **1400** *Apol. Loll.* 3 He ouercam hunger in desert,..he strak ageyn veyn glorie vp on þe temple. **1470–85** MALORY *Arthur* II. viii. 84 Thou shalt stryke a stroke most dolorous that euer man stroke. *a* **1500–20** DUNBAR *Poems* lxxii. 98 Methocht Compassioun, vode of feiris, Than straik at me with mony ane stound. **1513** MORE *Rich. III* in Hall *Chron.* (1548) 28 b, It strake to her harte, like the sharpe darte of death. *a* **1586** SIDNEY *Arcadia* III. xxii. (1912) 484 And hate, & spare not, for your worst blow is striken. **1593** SHAKS. *3 Hen. VI*, II. iii. 6 Smile gentle heauen, or strike vngentle death. **1605** —— *Lear* II. ii. 124 It pleas'd the King his Master very late To strike at me vpon his misconstruction. **1642** CHAS. I *Answ. to Printed Bk.* 29 The Regall Power was never before this time strucken at. **1645** W. JENKYN *Stil-destroyer* Ep. Ded. A 3, The sin I here strike at, is very improperly called self-seeking. *a* **1700** EVELYN *Diary* 22 Dec. 1680, Parliament which was now assembl'd, and which struck at the succession of the Duke of York. *a* **1720** SEWEL *Trans. Hist. Quakers* (1795) I. IV. 283 This book struck chiefly against the Quakers. **1764** GOLDSM. *Trav.* 394 When first ambition struck at regal power. **1777** POTTER *Æschylus, Persians* 474 Thy words strike deep, and wound the parent's breast. **1829** SIR J. MACKINTOSH *Sp. Ho. Comm.* 1 June in *Hansard* 1601 A measure which would..strike the death-blow to whatever attempts might be made on the part of other states. **1845** MCCULLOCH *Taxation* III. ii. (1852) 445 It obviously strikes at the very foundation of the principle of accumulation. **1892** *Sat. Rev.* 14 May 581/2 The Revolution ..began to strike at Church and King. **1908** R. BAGOT *A. Cuthbert* xxiii. 298 Every fresh proof of Anthony's love for her struck like a knife into her heart.

c. Phr. ***to strike at the root*** or ***foundation***: to attempt or tend to the utter destruction or overthrow (*of* something).

1550 LATIMER *Serm.* B viij, So we Preachers..haue drawen our swerdes of Gods word, and stryken at the rootes of all euyll, to haue them cut downe. **1661** W. LOWTHER in *Extr. St. Papers rel. Friends* Ser. II. (1911) 118 To disowne all Magistracy, and soe by dangerous consequence strike att the foundation of his Majestyes power. **1793** J. BOWLES *Ground War w. France* (ed. 5) 71 Principles which strike at the root of all established Government.

d. ***to strike short, wide.*** (*lit.* and *fig.*)

1602 SHAKS. *Ham.* II. ii. 491 Anon he findes him, Striking too short at Greekes. *Ibid.* 494 Pyrrhus at Priam driues, in Rage strikes wide. **1745** WESLEY *Answ. Church* 39 You strike quite wide of me still. I never said so of what I do. **1820** *Examiner* 414/1 It appears to us then that this excellent and able actor struck short of the higher and imaginative part of the character.

33. In various specific uses of sense 31.

a. *trans.* To prick (a horse) *with* the spur. *Obs.*

1375 BARBOUR *Bruce* VI. 226 Than vith the spuris he strak his steide. **1813** SCOTT *Rokeby* VI. xxxii, His charger with the spurs he strook.

b. To kill or wound (deer) with an arrow or spear, or with a gunshot. Said also of the weapon.

a **1400–50** *Wars Alex.* 1069 þe stede þar þis stith man strikis þis hert, Sagittarius forsoth men gafe it to name. **1530** PALSGR. 739/1, I stryke a dere or any other wylde beest, as a huntar dothe..*je enferre.* **1568** in *Archæologia* XXXV. 206 A forreste..where my Lord strake iij. stagges with his gonne. **1590** SPENSER *F.Q.* II. iii. 32 Didst not thou see a bleeding Hind, Whose right haunch earst my stedfast arrow strake? **1611** SHAKS. *Cymb.* III. iii. 74 He that strikes The Venison first, shall be the Lord o' th' Feast. **1820** SCOTT *Monast.* xix, The huntsman-like fashion in which you strike your game.

c. To spear (a turtle), harpoon (a whale, etc.).

1697 DAMPIER *Voy.* I. 33 Our Moskito men went in their Canoa, and struck us some Manatee, or Sea-cow. **1827** O. W. ROBERTS *Voy. Centr. Amer.* 94 The spear with which the Indians strike the turtle, is made of very hard wood.

†**d.** To lance or cut (a vein). Also *absol.* *Obs.*

1580 LYLY *Euphues* (Arb.) 329 A white vaine beeing striken, if at the fyrst there springe out bloud, it argueth a good constitution of bodye. **1607** TOPSELL *Four-f. Beasts* 409 Hauing striken [1658 stricken] it with a fleame, thrust out the ielly with your finger. **1639** T. DE GREY *Compl. Horsem.* 350 The cure is eyther to stricke with your fleame [etc.].

†**e.** To broach (a cask). *Obs.*

1606 SHAKS. *Ant. & Cl.* II. vii. 103 Strike the Vessels hoa. Heere's to Cæsar. **1717** PRIOR *Alma* iii. 426 L'Avare.. Strikes not the present Tun, for fear The Vintage should be bad next Year.

f. *Angling.* To cause the hook to pierce the mouth of (a fish) by a jerk or sudden movement of the tackle; to hook. Also said of the hook or the rod. Also, to cause (a hook) to pierce the mouth. Also *absol.* In 16–17th c. often *fig.*

1580 LYLY *Euphues* (Arb.) 333 Philautus, who euer as yet but played with the bait, was now stroke with the hooke. **1611** SHAKS. *Cymb.* v. v. 168 That hooke of Wiuing, Fairenesse, which strikes the eye. **1647** DIGGES *Unlawf. Taking Arms* §4. 157 They are contented to give Him line enough, being confident they can strike Him when they please. **1651** JER. TAYLOR *Serm. for Year* Summer x. 129 The hook hath strook their nostrils and they shall never escape the ruine. **1660** DRYDEN *Astræa Redux* 171 He like a patient Angler er'e he strooke, Would let them play a while upon the hook. **1662** R. VENABLES *Exper. Angler* iv. 44 If you strike a large Trout, and she..break hook or line. **1688** [see *spring-hook* s.v. SPRING *sb.*[1] 25]. **1760** SIR J. HAWKINS *Walton's Angler* 171 note, You are to strike as soon as he has taken it [*sc.* the bait]. **1881** *Sportsman's Year-bk.* 69 To try a roach rod's integrity to strike truly, place the rod on a table, and [etc.]. **1892** *Field* 19 Mar. 402/1 The troutlings have to be struck sharply... High authorities say that salmon should not be struck at all.

34. To hit with a missile, a shot, etc. Also said of the missile. Also with adv. or phrase (expressing the result). Now somewhat *rare*.

1377 LANGL. *P. Pl.* B. XII. 77 With stones men shulde hir stryke and stone hir to deth. *a* **1400–50** *Wars Alex.* 804 Many starand stanes strikis of þaire helmes. *c* **1400** *Destr. Troy* 12151 Scho..with stonys in þe strete strok hom to ground. **1557** W. TOWRSON in Hakluyt *Voy.* (1589) 114 We found 2 Elephants which we strooke diuers time with harquebusses. **1587** T. SAUNDERS *Discr. Voy. Tripolie* B ij b, And the second shot he strake vs vnder water. **1589** HAKLUYT *Voy.* 773 With one of our great shot their Master gonners shoolder was stroken away. **1662** A. COOPER *Stratologia* VI. 118 A Cannon bullet stroke off Sandies head. **1822** *Examiner* 215/1 Ali himself was struck down by a bullet. **1863** W. C. BALDWIN *Afr. Hunting* vi. 210 P. fired, striking him in the centre of the chest and killing him. **1865** RUSKIN *Sesame* i. §41 A group of schoolboys have piled their little books upon a grave, to strike them off with stones.

fig. **1592** SHAKS. *Ven. & Ad.* 462 Or like the deadly bullet of a gun: His meaning struck her ere his words begun.

b. *Curling.* To hit (an opponent's stone) *away*, *off* with one's own. Also *absol.*

1811 *Acc. Game Curling* 8 He attempts to strike away the stone of his antagonist. *Ibid.*, To guard the stone of his partner..or to strike off that of his antagonist. *a* **1870** D. THOMSON *Musings among Heather* (1881) 20 Keen curlers.. draw, an' guard, an' wick, an' strike.

c. *intr.* Of a missile: To make a hit. ? *Obs.*

1589 BIGGES *Summarie Drake's W. Ind. Voy.* 43 The first shot..strake through the Ensigne. **1627** MAY *Lucan* VI. K 5 b, In the left eye Of Scæua strucke the shaft. **1669** STURMY *Mariner's Mag.* v. xii. 70 If the first Shot had struck under the Mark.

35. *intr.* To use one's weapons: to fight. Also with cognate obj. Const. *for* (a cause, one's king or country, etc.). Also, † *to strike it out*.

1579 Gosson *Sch. Abuse* (Arb.) 58 The stoutest Souldier, when the Trumpet sounds, strikes fiercest. **1581** A. Hall *Iliad* viii. 137 Both sides so soundly stroke it out, right doubtful was the fray. **1601** Shaks. *All's Well* ii. iii. 308 His present gift Shall furnish me to those Italian fields Where noble fellowes strike. **1601** R. Johnson *Kingd. & Commw.* (1603) 39 They were never known..to mutine or to strike stroke amongst themselves. **1825** Scott *Talism.* ix, He despairs of the security of Palestine..since the arm of Richard of England hath ceased to strike for it. **1842** W. C. Taylor *Anc. Hist.* xii. §1. (ed. 3) 312 [Cleomenes] followed by a few friends rushed through the streets of Alexandria, exhorting the multitude to strike for freedom. **1847** Marryat *Childr. N. Forest* xxi, I should indeed like to strike one blow for the King, come what will. **1889** S. Walpole *Life Ld. J. Russell* II. xxviii. 314 Austria, though too angry to be silent, was too timid to strike.

b. *trans.* To fight (a battle). Also, *to strike up*. Chiefly *Sc.* Cf. stricken *ppl. a.* 6.

1375 Barbour *Bruce* xiii. 152 Thar wes the battell strikyn weill. *c* **1470** Henry *Wallace* x. 245 Quhen Bruce his battaill apon the Scottis straik. **1524** Wolsey in *St. Papers Hen. VIII*, VI. 281 If bataile be not striken before the receipte of thies letters..ye shal [etc.]. **1535** Coverdale *2 Macc.* xv. 1 When Nicanor knewe that Iudas was in..Samaria, he thought with all his power to strike a felde with him vpon a Sabbath daye. **1544** *Acc. Ld. High Treas. Scot.* VIII. 292 Item, to ane barbour in Glasqw, eftir the feild strikkin on the mure of the samyn. **1570** Foxe *A. & M.* (ed. 2) 372 b/1 And so the battaile beyng strocken vp, the armyes began to ioyne. **1599** Shaks. *Hen. V*, ii. iv. 54 When Cressy Battell fatally was strucke. **1606** Holland *Sueton.* 88 Claudius Pulcher.. thereupon strucke a battaile at Sea. **1710** Sibbald *Fife & Kinross* i. vii. 28 This Battel was struck with great Art and Skill upon either side. **1821** Scott *Kenilw.* xii, 'The battle of Bosworth,' said Master Mumblazen, 'stricken between Richard Crookback and Henry Tudor.' **1834** H. Miller *Scenes & Leg.* xi. (1857) 160 The day the battle of Killiecrankie was stricken.

c. *intr.* To engage *together* in combat.

a **1400–50** *Wars Alex.* 785 Now athire stoure on þar stedis strikis to-gedire. *c* **1440** *Generydes* 2793 Generides ther mette..The Kyng Ruben, Redy with spere and sheld, And ther they strake to geder in the feld. **1470–85** Malory *Arthur* iii. vii. 107 [They] stroke to gyders myghtely.

d. *Mil.* To make an offensive blow, to attack. Const. with *at*. Also *trans.* to attack (in flank, etc.): cf. sense 68.

1606 Shaks. *Ant. & Cl.* iii. viii. 3 Strike not by Land, Keepe whole, prouoke not Battaile Till we haue done at Sea. **1802** C. James *Milit. Dict.* s.v., *To strike at*, to attack; to endeavour to destroy, directly or indirectly. **1839** Marryat *Diary Amer.* Ser. i. II. 231 To strike means to attack. 'The Indians have struck on the frontier.' **1866** Sir T. Seaton *Cadet to Colonel* II. iii. 85 Lord Canning thought it advisable to strike a blow at Barrackpoor before the mutiny at Lucknow should become known. **1892** *Sat. Rev.* 2 Jan. 10/2 [He] divided his forces, struck where there was no use in striking, failed to strike at the essential point. **1893** *Pall Mall Mag.* II. 302 The French centre..was marching to strike it in flank.

36. *trans.* With transferred object.

a. To deliver a blow with (the hand or something held in the hand), to bang, slap (the fist, hand), to stamp (the foot) *on, upon, against*. Also, to strike a horse with (the spur). Const. *to, against* (cf. 50).

a **1548** Hall *Chron., Hen. VI*, 160 [He] entered into London,..strykyng his sworde on London stone, saiyng: now is Mortymer lorde of this citie. **1595** Shaks. *John* iv. i. 2 When I strike my foot Vpon the bosome of the ground, rush forth. **1597** —— *2 Hen. IV*, i. i. 44 (Qo. 1600) He.. strooke his armed heeles Against the panting sides of his poore iade, Vp to the rowell head. **1678** Moxon *Mech. Exerc.* v. 76 If with often striking the Pricker against the Tongue [of the Square] it becomes ragged. **1820** Scott *Monast.* xxv, The Baron, striking his hand against the table, as if impatient of the long unbroken silence. **1862** *Temple Bar* V. 70 He struck the stock of his gun violently upon the ground. **1884** *Graphic* 25 Oct. 438/3 'That's a thing I'll think about', rejoined the Baronet, as he struck spurs to his hack.

†**b.** To drive or thrust (a weapon, a tool); to make a cut or thrust with. Const. *into, through*.

c **1470** Henry *Wallace* ii. 99 A felloun knyff fast till his hart straik he. **1556** *Rec. Inverness* (New Spald. Club) I. 1 James Patyrson messenger strykis ane broch on Hendre Kar elder. **1590** Webbe *Trav.* (Arb.) 33 And stricke their sworde into their flesh like vnto a Scabbard. *c* **1614** Sir W. Mure *Dido & Æneas* iii. 387 The cursed blaide..Which in her breast vnto the hilts she strak. **1737** Bracken *Farriery Impr.* (1756) I. 296 Unskilfully striking the Fleam into a Horse's Neck. **1748** [see fleam *sb.*[1] 2].

transf. and *fig.* **1598** Brandon *Octavia* iii. D 3, In these respects, perhaps I could be brought, To strike reuenge as deepe as any could. **1641** J. Jackson *True Evang. T.* iii. 209 The Bitturn lying under, strikes his bill upward through the Hawkes gorge.

c. To cause (a tool, etc.) to make the required stroke. In *Bookbinding*, To cause (a hot tool) to make an impression in tooling (Webster 1911).

1600 Sir W. Cornwallis *Ess.* i. xi. G 4 b, A Clocke, whose hammer was stricken by an Image like a man. **1845** *Jrnl. R. Agric. Soc.* VI. ii. 255 The workman strikes the instrument towards the standing corn. **1877** De Vinne *Invent. Printing* (ed. 2) 517 It required great force..to strike the punch truly.

†**d.** To thrust (something pointed) *in, into* (a surface). *Obs.*

1570–6 Lambarde *Peramb. Kent* 282 Yet God (I say) styre vp some Edgar, to strike nayles in our cuppes. **1605** Shaks. *Lear* ii. iii. 15 Bedlam beggers, who with roaring voices, Strike in their num'd and mortified Armes, Pins, Wodden-prickes, Nayles, Sprigs of Rosemarie. **1631** Weever *Anc. Funeral Mon.* 345 Hee strake his staffe into the dry ground. **1660** F. Brooke tr. *Le Blanc's Trav.* 10 Pegs struck into the ground.

†**e.** *pass.* To be struck *full of* (nails). *Obs.*

1610 Healey *St. Aug. Citie of God* i. xiv. 24 Shutting him in a narrow barrell, strucken all full of sharpe nayles.

** Said of an animal.

37. Of a serpent or other venomous animal: To wound (a person) with its fangs or sting. Also *absol.* †Of a basilisk: To kill or injure (a person), dart out (venom) by its glance.

c **1375** *Sc. Leg. Saints* x. (*Mathou*) 67 þai cuth, be þare enchawnment, ger serpentis strik men ful sare. **1539** Taverner *Erasm. Prov.* (1552) 3 A certayne fysherman.. chaunced to take up..a Scorpyon, which forthwith strake hym. **1592** Greene *Philomela* Wks. (Grosart) XI. 152 He stood as mortified as if hee had beene strocken with the eye of a Baselisk. **1594** Shaks. *Rich. III*, i. ii. 151 Would they were Basiliskes, to strike thee dead. **1608** Topsell *Serpents* 44 If that anie person hath either been wounded or strooken of any venomous liuing thing. **1617** Bp. Hall *Quo Vadis?* §15 How many haue wee knowne stroken with these aspes, which haue died sleeping! **1621** Quarles *Esther* xii, Whose ..visage sternly strikes Worse venime to mine eyes, than Basilisks. **1635–56** Cowley *Davideis* iv. 601 If..either King Fall wounded down, strook with some fatal sting. **1837** [Miss Maitland] *Lett. fr. Madras* (1843) 163 Their music seems to irritate the snakes and incite them to strike. **1893** *Eng. Illustr. Mag.* X. 285/1 A hideous snake..had uplifted its triangular head to strike.

38. To wound or attack with the heels, horns, tusks, claws, or any natural weapon. Also *absol.* Now *rare*.

1538 Elyot *Dict.*, *Recalcitro*, to stryke with the heele, to kicke. **1600** E. Blount tr. *Conestaggio* 307 Sanches d'Auila died, being stroke with a horse. **1621** Burton *Anat. Mel.* i. iii. i. iii. (1624) 170 A wild boare, that by chance stroke him on the legge. **1705** Dalton *Country Justice* cxlv. 344 If a man hath an Horse of that property, that he will strike such as come near him. **1716** W. Hawkins *Pleas of Crown* i. xxix. §12. 74 He..who kills another..by going deliberately with a Horse used to strike..among a Multitude of People. **1722** Hearne *Collect.* (O.H.S.) VII. 386 Having lost his Life by being struck by a Cow. **1883** Fenn *Middy & Ensign* lvi, The tiger had struck the Malay down. **1892** M. C. F. Morris *Yorksh. Folk-Talk* 382 Cu' by, or else t'hoss'll mebbe strike tha.

b. *intr.* To aim a blow with a natural weapon; to lash *out* (with the feet, etc.).

1565 Cooper *Thesaurus*, *Calcitro*, a horse that flingeth or striketh. **1667** Dk. Newcastle *New Method to dress Horses* 184 Or when..he offers to Bite or Strike, then the Spurrs will Divert him. **1774** Goldsm. *Nat. Hist.* (1776) VI. 378 They strike with their claws, they bite each other. **1803** Shaw *Zool.* IV. i. 128 If accidentally trodden on, it strikes backwards..and endeavours to wound the aggressor with the spines of its first dorsal fin. **1822** D. Johnson *Ind. Field Sports* 107 Not long before this, he [the tiger] must have struck at a porcupine, as several of the quills were still remaining between the joints of one of his fore feet. **1893** *Pall Mall Mag.* II. 88 The giraffe has, too, a nasty habit.. of striking out with its fore feet.

39. *trans.* †**a.** Of a bird of prey, esp. a falcon: To dart at and seize (its quarry or prey). Also *intr.* to dart *at*.

a **1500–20** Dunbar *Poems* xxxiii. 99 The egill strong at him did stryke. **1632** Holland *Cyrupædia* 53 An Ægle.. having espied the Hare running, made wing, strake her, caught her up, and away. **1687** Norris *Misc.* 101 So th' eager Hawk makes sure of's prize, Strikes with full might, but overshoots himself and dyes. **1736** Hale *Pleas of Crown* I. 432 As laying an infant in an orchard,..whereby a kite strikes it. **1738** Albin *Nat. Hist. Birds* III. 1 The Vulture.. is a fierce bold Bird, and will strike at any thing that comes near him. **1879** Miss Yonge *Cameos* IV. vii. 83 His hawk was striking the quarry.

b. Of a greyhound: To seize (the hare) in coursing. Cf. striker 2 f.

1861 H. Kingsley *Ravenshoe* xiii, But Ruin! you should see him lie behind the other dog all the run, and strike the hare at last.

c. *intr.* Of a fish: To seize the bait.

1891 *Field* 21 Nov. 774/2 Then another fish struck, but only to graze and kill the bait. **1902** S. E. White *Blazed Trail* xviii, He whipped the fly lightly within six inches of a little suction hole; a fish at once rose and struck.

*** Said of mechanism or the like.

40. *intr.* Of a piece of mechanism: To make a stroke, hit or beat something.

1610 Shaks. *Temp.* i. ii. 281 Where thou didst vent thy groanes As fast as Mill-wheeles strike. **1725** T. Thomas in *Portland Papers* (Hist. MSS. Comm.) VI. 103 A very large fire engine for draining the coal pits..strikes (as they term it) or makes a discharge fourteen times in one minute. **1839** Ure *Dict. Arts* 883 These..finish the grooving..at a single blow, by striking against each other, with the head of the needle between them. **1892** J. Wilkins *Autobiog. Gamekeeper* 330 Particular attention should be paid to the striking of the trap, which ought to strike high, and strike quickly. **1907** J. H. Patterson *Man-Eaters of Tsavo* viii. 87 On extracting the unexploded cartridge, I found that the needle had not struck home.

b. *trans.*

1787 Burns *Death & Dr. Hornbook* xxxi, The auld kirk-hammer strak the bell Some wee, short hour ayont the twal.

41. *intr.* and *trans.* with cognate obj. Of a clock: To make one or more strokes on its sounding part. Hence *trans.* to indicate (the hour of day) by a stroke or strokes; also with object a numeral designating the hour. Rarely with *out*.

1417 *York Memor. Bk.* (Surtees) I. 184 Efter xij of the clok be strekyn at the cathiderall church. **1509** Hawes *Past. Pleas.* xxix. (Percy Soc.) 140 Passyng the tyme..Tyll that the clocke did strike aleven. **1529** *Extracts Burgh Rec. Edin.* (1871) 7 Quhill xij houris be struikin. **1562** J. Heywood *Prov. & Epigr.* (1867) 111 Thy tong should be a clocke.., For than would it strike but once in one hower. **1590** Shaks. *Com. Err.* i. ii. 45 The clocke hath strucken twelue vpon the bell. **1617** Bacon *Sp.* Resusc. (1657) 86 Every Tuesday.. after nine a Clock strucken. **1629** Wadsworth *Pilgr.* iii. 18 Till the clocke and our stomackes strike supper time. **1675** J. S[mith] *Horol. Dial.* i. ii. 10 A moving wheel..indented ..according to the number of strokes at each time to be strucken. **1742** Young *Nt. Th.* i. 54 The bell strikes One. **1837** Carlyle *Fr. Rev.* III. vii. vii, Four of the afternoon is struck. **1860** Sala *Baddington Peerage* I. v. 100 The neighbouring church clock struck out twelve slowly. **1864** Mrs. Carlyle *Lett.* III. 234 A clock made to strike fourteen every hour. **1878** *Bye-gones* Dec. 147/1 Striking the day of the month. This practice, according to the *Gents: Mag:* for Sep. 1816, was in vogue in Pembroke at that period. **1892** *Argosy* Mar. 180 It struck four. **1902** R. Bagot *Donna Diana* xxvi. 331 Counting the hours as the clocks struck in the different quarters of the city.

b. *intr.* in passive sense. Of the hour: To be indicated by the striking of the clock.

a **1417** *York Memor. Bk.* (Surtees) I. 224 Fra evynsang ryng..on to the morne that prime stryke at the mynster. **1613** Shaks. *Hen. VIII*, v. i. 1 *Gard.* It's one a clocke Boy, is't not. *Boy.* It hath strooke. **1787** Mrs. Inchbald *Midnt. Hour* iii. i. (1788) 28, I will sit up 'till twelve strikes. **1850** H. Melville *White Jacket* I. xxiii. 146 Two bells struck; and soon after, all who could be spared from their stations hurried to the half-deck.

c. *fig.*

Phrase. *to strike twelve the first time* or *all at once* (see twelve 2 b).

1589 *Pasquil's Ret.* B iiij, The Preachers of England begin to strike and agree like the Clockes of England. **1605** *1st Pt. Jeronimo* i. i, This day my years strike fiftie. **1606** Heywood *2nd Pt. Know not me* i. i, A merchants tongue Should not strike false. **1610** Shaks. *Temp.* ii. i. 13 Looke, hee's winding vp the watch of his wit, By and by it will strike. **1628** Earle *Microcosm., Stayed Man* K 3 b, One whose Tongue is strung vp like a Clocke till the time, and the strikes, and sayes much when hee talkes little. **1684** Norris *Poems* 5 That Hour is come, The unerring Clock of Fate has struck. **1893** *Pall Mall Mag.* II. 201 He would have his time of danger after striking sixty. **1912** G. W. E. Russell *Politics & Pers.* iii. i. (1917) 201 Princess Victoria had now struck sixteen.

d. *intr.* Of a bell: To sound its note.

1677 Stedman *Campanalogia* 32 By delaying its [*sc.* the treble's] striking untill the Second Bell has struck, it may by that means strike next after it. **1901** H. E. Bulwer *Gloss. Techn. Terms Ch. Bells* 36 When two or more bells are 'striking' in succession.

e. *causatively.* To cause (a clock, a repeating watch) to sound the time; to cause (bells) to sound *together*.

1675 J. S[mith] *Horol. Dial.* ii. v. 55 To do this strike your Clock gradually from eight to nine, and then from nine to ten, [etc.]. **1748** Chesterf. *Let. to Son* 22 Feb., Wear your learning, like your watch, in a private pocket; and do not pull it out, and strike it, merely to show that you have one. **1854** Surtees *Handley Cr.* xxxix. (1901) II. 19 'Wants twenty minutes to six,' observed Mr. Marmaduke, striking the repeater. **1893** *National Observer* 18 Nov. 17/1, I struck my repeater again, and found that midnight was past by two hours. **1901** H. E. Bulwer *Gloss. Techn. Terms Ch. Bells* etc. 37 *Firing*, striking all the bells together at successive pulls. *Ibid.*, The bells were 'clammed' or struck together by successive pairs.

42. *intr.* Of the pulse, heart: To beat, pulsate, throb. *rare.*

1590 Barrough *Meth. Physick* i. xv. (1639) 24 Their pulse is great and striketh seldome. **1666** G. Harvey *Morbus Angl.* ix. (1672) 20 And the mind all that while so disturbed..that the heart strikes five hundred sorts of Pulses in an hour. **1891** Meredith *One of our Conq.* III. xiv. 295 His heart struck heavily when the house was visible.

**** Of natural or supernatural agencies.

43. *trans.* Of lightning, thunder, a thunderbolt: To descend violently upon and blast (a person or thing). Freq. in pass, constr. *by, with*, rarely *of*. Also *to strike down*.

c **1375** *Sc. Leg. Saints* xli. (*Agnes*) 312 He gert thonnir & fire-slacht stirk done þe payanis þar stracht. *c* **1400** Maundev. (Roxb.) xxxi. 140 We ware oft tymes striken doune to þe erthe with grete hidous blastez. **1563** Fulke *Goodly Gallery Meteors* (1571) 28 The thonder bolt.. stryketh downe steples, and hyghe buildynges. **1586** Lupton *Thous. Notable Th.* (1675) 122 Bodies that are strucken with Lightening do remain uncorrupt. **1605** B. Jonson *Volpone* iii. vii. (1607) H 2, Some *serene* blast me, or dire lightning strike This my offending face. **1663** Bayfield *Treat. De Morb. Capitis* 67 Cardanus reports of eight Mowers, which supping under an Oak were struck with thunder. *a* **1718** Prior *Engraven on a Column* Poems (1905) 206 Tho' Lightning strike the Dome again. **1808** *Med. Jrnl.* XIX. 121 The house had been struck with lightning. **1865** Swinburne *Poems & Ball.*, *Satia te Sanguine* 37, I wish you were stricken of thunder.

fig. **1588** Greene *Metam.* Wks. (Grosart) IX. 102 Till I be strooken to death with loues thundering bolt.

b. with compl. *to strike dead, blind*.

1598 Yong *Diana* 261 Stroken dead with a fearefull thunderclap. **1750** Franklin *Wks.* (1840) V. 237 Lightning has often been known to strike people blind. **1890** Clark Russell *Ocean Trag.* III. xxxiii. 205 That flash..had struck me blind.

c. *absol.* and *intr.*

1750 Franklin *Wks.* (1840) V. 236 Electrified clouds passing over hills or high buildings at too great a height to strike, may be attracted lower. **1815** J. Smith *Panorama Sci. & Art* II. 231 Which may result from the lightning striking upon a house not properly secured. **1884** *Science* 4 Jan. 3/1 There are no data for determining the..violence of lightning..or for discovering its possible preference for one or another..geological district when it 'strikes'.

44. *trans.* Of God: To visit with lightning, esp. as a punishment. Also, *to strike dead.*

1577 HANMER *Anc. Eccl. Hist., Euseb.* VII. xvii. 133 Therefore God strooke Iulianus image from heauen with lightening and rent it in peeces. 1594 SHAKS. *Rich. III,* I. ii. 64 Either Heau'n with Lightning strike the murth'rer dead: Or Earth gape open wide, and eate him quicke. 1647 R. STAPYLTON *Juvenal* 188 Then for his crown th' old trembling souldier took An helmet, and at great Jove's altar strook, Fell like an ox. 1697 DRYDEN *Æneis* VI. 804 But he, the King of Heav'n,..launching from the Sky His writhen Bolt,..Down to the deep Abyss the flaming Felon strook.

b. Of a storm, earthquake, etc.: To 'visit' (a district, crop).

1570 *Satir. Poems Reform.* xvii. 172 Swa mony stormes at onis Struke neuer land sa sair. 1613 SPELMAN *De non Temer. Eccl.* (1646) 30 When thy fruit and thy vineyard are strucken with haile. 1830 LYELL *Princ. Geol.* I. 438 The island of St. George was struck by an earthquake. 1904 *Sun* (N.Y.) 23 Aug. 1 The storm twister struck Willow Lakes about 9 o'clock. 1976 *Daily Mirror* 16 July 13/3 Earthquakes killed 275 people and injured 2,000 early yesterday as they struck Indonesia's tropical holiday island of Bali.

45. To bring suffering or death upon (a person, etc.) as with a blow; to afflict suddenly (*with, by* sickness, infirmity, death), esp. as a punishment. Also, *to strike down.* (Said chiefly of God or a deity.)

c 1375 *Sc. Leg. Saints* xxxii. (*Justin*) 287 [The master devil said] sic lustful het sal be hir in, & eftyr hyr stirke sal I nere wodnes & frenesy. 1530 PALSGR. 739/1 You shall se God stryke them when he seys hys tyme. 1549–62 STERNHOLD & H. *Ps.* lxxviii. 66 With Emrods in the hinder parts he strake his enimies all. 1563 WINȜET *Four Scoir Thre Quest.* Wks. (S.T.S.) I. 127 Ananias and Saphira wes strukin be ane word of Petir to the deth. 1580 TUSSER *Husb.* (1878) 83 For lamb, pig and calfe..tithe so as thy cattle the Lord doo not strike. *a* 1591 H. SMITH *Serm.* (1594) 333 When God stroke Zacharias, he made him dumbe, but not deafe. *c* 1610 *Women Saints* 82 God in defence of his spouse [St. Frideswide] stroke them with blyndnes. 1611 SHAKS. *Cymb.* V. i. 10 Gods,..so had you saued The noble Imogen, to repent, and strooke Me (wretch) more worth your Vengeance. 1711 in *10th Rep. Hist. MSS. Comm.* App. v. 123 He strikes..where the sinner least dreames to be strucken. J. BRUCE *Gideon* iii. 59 Heavily the hand of the Lord had stricken him.

absol. *a* 1500–20 DUNBAR *Poems* lxx. 33 Lord! hald thy hand, that strikken hes so soir. 1604 SHAKS. *Oth.* V. ii. 22 This sorrow's heauenly, It strikes, where it doth loue. *a* 1605 MONTGOMERIE *Sonn.* vii. 7 Quhen ȝe sulde stryk, I wald ȝe vnderstude; Quhen ȝe suld spair, I wish ȝe were bening.

b. Of a disease, etc.: To attack or afflict (a person) suddenly; to make infirm, lay low. Chiefly *pass.* To be attacked *by, with* (a disease). Also, *to strike down.*

1530 PALSGR. 739/2 He was stryken with the plage as he stode in his dore. 1601 W. LEIGH *Soules Solace* (1617) 21 It may be some goe to bed who neuer rise, strooken with a deadly sleepe or lethargie. 1607 SHAKS. *Cor.* IV. i. 13 Now the Red Pestilence strike al Trades in Rome. 1653 H. MORE *Antid. Ath.* III. vii. §9 (1712) 107 She was so struck in her fits that six men or more could not hold her. 1789 *New Lond. Mag.* Oct. 510/2 The Earl was struck with death while drinking his coffee. 1837 CARLYLE *Fr. Rev.* I. v. v, Hot old Marquis Mirabeau lies stricken down, at Argenteuil. 1860 *Jrnl. R. Agric. Soc.* XXI. II. 554 About 60 out of 280, chiefly shearlings, were struck with a chill. 1878 R. H. HUTTON *Scott* xvii. 174 The climate struck him down, and he died at Teheran. 1891 E. PEACOCK *N. Brendon* II. 199 The Duke had been stricken by paralysis.

c. *transf.*

1509 BARCLAY *Shyp of Folys* (1570) 236 And though thou now be stricke with couetise That vice shall slake in thee if thou arise, [etc.]. 1639 S. DU VERGER tr. *Camus' Admir. Events* 66 They are strucken with that pleasant folly of the Athenian who imagined all the riches..to be his. 1875 MANNING *Mission H. Ghost* viii. 212 Such, in the sight of God, is a soul which is struck by sin. 1891 *Speaker* 11 July 36/2 The fear is..that public life may be stricken with sterility in consequence of this veto.

d. In *passive.* Of a crop, of cattle: To be tainted or infected with a disease.

1750 W. ELLIS *Mod. Husbandm.* IV. i. 45 Wheat mildewed, blighted, or what we, in Hertfordshire, call struck. *Ibid.* IV. ii. 124 (E.D.S.) What we call striking, or, in plainer terms, the glutinizing of the green ears [of wheat], by the fall of..honey-dew. 1784 *Young's Annals Agric.* II. 65 (E.D.D.) [On the Weald of Kent] They have a distemper [in sheep] which they call struck with the blood. 1840 *Jrnl. R. Agric. Soc.* I. III. 327 They [lambs] have been struck with the fly late in the season. 1842 *Ibid.* III. II. 199 In a bad case of mildew I have seen a large field of these early swedes struck in July. 1877 E. LEIGH *Gloss. Chesh., Struck with iron,* an apoplectic seizure to which sheep and cows (gen. previous to their calving) are liable. They turn black.

46. To deprive (a person) suddenly of life, or of one of the faculties, as if by a physical blow. Often with compl., as *to strike dead, blind, deaf, dumb.* Said of God, †of a planet (*obs.*: cf. PLANET-STRICKEN, -STRUCK), of witchcraft, etc., and of physical agencies, e.g. the sun, blinding light, or deafening noise. Also in *passive,* without implication of any definite agency: To become suddenly *blind, dumb,* etc.

1534 MORE *Comf. agst. Trib.* I. iv. (1553) A viij, Sainct Paule was himselfe sore agaynst Chryst, tyll Christ..strake him starke blynde. 1595 *Problems of Aristotle* etc. M 2, Why are children strooken with a planet in the summer? 1595 T. EDWARDS *Narcissus* (Roxb.) 51 So was I gazing on this Orient Sunne Stroke blinde. 1598 B. JONSON *Ev. Man in Hum.* IV. vii, Sure I was strooke with a Plannet then, for I had no power to touch my weapon. 1600 W. WATSON *Decacordon* (1602) 356 He [Peter] stricke them both [Ananias and Sapphira] dead at his feet. 1626 BACON *Sylva* §276 It is an old Tradition, that those that dwell near the Cataract of Nilus are strucken deaf. *a* 1628 DABORNE *Poor-man's Comf.* I. (1655) B 3, *Osw.* Some dismall planet strike you ever mute. *Ibid.* III. E 1 b, *Luc.* Some Planet strike him dead. 1636 H. BURTON *Div. Tragedie* 18 And before he had done ringing, he was strucke sicke, and a while after dyed. 1667 MILTON *P.L.* IX. 1064 Confounded long they sate, as struck'n mute. 1712 ARBUTHNOT *John Bull* III. x, He'd got a great cold that had struck him deaf of one ear. 1737 BRACKEN *Farriery Impr.* (1756) I. 144 A young Fellow..was struck blind all of a sudden.

absol. 1602 SHAKS. *Ham.* I. i. 162 The nights are wholsome, then no Planets strike,..nor Witch hath power to Charme.

fig. 1592 NASHE *P. Penilesse* Wks. 1904 I. 190 They, being but lightly sprinckled with the iuyce of the Hop, become sencelesse, and haue their reason strooken blind. 1600 MARSTON etc. *Jack Drum's Entert.* II. C 4, Yet calme husht sleepe Strikes dumbe the snoring world. 1638 JUNIUS *Paint. Ancients* 209 The rule of eloquence being once corrupted was strooke dumbe. 1837 CARLYLE *Fr. Rev.* II. i. viii, Let the concentrated flash of your Patriotism strike stealthy Scoundrelism blind, paralytic, as with a *coup de soleil.*

b. *hyperbolically,* expressing the temporary effect of fear, amazement, etc., *to strike †dead, dumb,* etc.

1533 BELLENDEN *Livy* I. v. (S.T.S.) I. 36 Þis wncouth sicht movit..baith þe armes with sa petuus commiseratioun, þat baith þe hostis wer strikin dvm. 1591 SHAKS. *Two Gent.* II. ii. 21 Alas, this parting strikes poore Louers dumbe. 1598 GREENWEY *Tacitus' Ann.* XIV. ii. (1622) 201 Nero stroken dead with feare [L. *pavore exanimis*]. 1607 CHAPMAN *Bussy D'Ambois* IV. i, *Mons.* Sweet heart: come hither, what if one should make Horns at Mountsurry? would it strike him iealous Through all the proofes of his chaste Ladies vertues? 1775 SHERIDAN *Duenna* II. ii, Her beauty will certainly strike me dumb. 1837 CARLYLE *Fr. Rev.* II. II. iv, Next day marching it back again, through streets all struck silent. 1865 DICKENS *Mut. Fr.* II. iv, Fascination Fledgeby and Georgiana..struck each other speechless.

c. Vulgarly used in jocular forms of imprecation, as *strike me blind, dumb, lucky* (*if, but* —), and various nonce-phrases. *strike me pink*: see PINK *a.* 8. Also (*Austral.* and *N.Z.*) *ellipt.* as *strike!*

1696 VANBRUGH *Relapse* I. iii, Well, 'tis an unspeakable Pleasure to be a man of Quality—Strike me dumb. 1704 CIBBER *Careless Husb.* II. i. 19 Right, Charles: And strike me Blind, but the Women of Virtue are now grown such Ideots in Love..that [etc.]. 1835 DICKENS *Sk. Boz., Charac.* ix, Whereupon the two gentlemen swore, 'strike 'em wulgar if they'd stand that'. *Ibid., Tales* x, Strike me bountiful if you ain't one of the modest sort! 1849 CUPPLES *Green Hand* i. (1856) 9 Well, strike me lucky, mates all, if the whole affair warn't a complete trap! 1861 WHYTE MELVILLE *Market Harb.* i, The very place!.. Strike me ugly, if I won't go to Market Harborough! 1896 *Punch* 25 Apr. 197/1 The caddie nearest me said 'Strike me', under his breath, and another caddie said 'S'elp me'. 1915 C. J. DENNIS *Songs of Sentimental Bloke* (1916) 43 'Ah, strike!' she sez. 'I wish that I could die!' 1960 B. CRUMP *Good Keen Man* 116 Strike, he went crook! Who the hell was responsible? Had we been blasting fish?

d. To turn as by enchantment *into.*

1609 B. JONSON *Sil. Wom.* I. ii, Strooke into stone, almost, I am here, with tales o' thine vncle! 1641 BROME *Joviall Crew* III. Wks. 1873 III. 396 O let us not Acteon-like be strook..into the shape of Stags. 1853 MRS. GORE *Dean's Dau.* xlii. III. 300 She looked stricken into stone.

e. In *pa. pple.* Bewitched; affected by the evil eye. Also *struck so,* suddenly rendered motionless (as if by enchantment) in a particular attitude or grimace. *dial.* and *vulgar.*

1839 J. KEEGAN *Leg. & Poems* (1907) 165 Whenever a child is suspected to be 'struck', it is thought useless to apply to a medical person. 1851–61 MAYHEW *Lond. Labour* III. 65/2 Keeping their toes turned out, as if they had been 'struck so', while taking their first dancing-lesson. 1862 T. C. CROKER *Fairy Leg. S. Irel.* (ed. 2) 39 Just then she got a pain in the small of her back, and out through her heart, as if she was struck. 1881 W. S. GILBERT *Patience* II, *Maj.* I can't help thinking we're a little stiff at it. It would be extremely awkward if we were to be 'struck' so. 1891 FARMER *Slang* II. 163 *To be Struck Comical* (popular), to be astonished. 1912 CHESTERTON *Manalive* 234 Dr. Cyrus Pym had remained for an unprecedented time with his eyes closed and his thumb and finger in the air. It almost seemed as if he had been 'struck so', as the nurses say.

47. To prostrate mentally; in weaker sense, to shock, depress. *Obs.* exc. in *to strike all of* (†*on*) *a heap* (colloq.): see HEAP *sb.* 5 e.

1598 BASTARD *Chrestol.* III. vi. 56 The newes of Spanish wars, how woondrously, It strooke our heartes. 1628 EARLE *Microcosm.* (Arb.) 26 Anotomies and other spectacles of Mortalitie haue hardened him, and hee's no more struck with a Funerall then a Grauemaker. 1631 WEEVER *Anc. Funeral Mon.* 144 Being struncken and fearfully affrighted at this strange..spectacle. *a* 1715 BURNET *Own Time* I. ii. (1897) I. 45 This struck many of the enthusiasts of the king's side as much as it exalted the Scots. 1786 MRS. DELANY *Autob. & Corr.* (1862) III. 392 He informed her of the whole affair. The Queen stood struck and motionless for some time. 1791 W. GILPIN *Forest Scenery* II. 282 On running to him, he was struck with finding he had killed one of the best horses of his own team.

†**b.** To cause (a person) to fall suddenly *in, into, on, to* (grief, perplexity, anger, amazement, etc.). Also with compl. as *to strike sad* (freq. in Shaks.), *to strike astound. Obs.*

c 1440 *Alphabet of Tales* 166 A man of Egipte was stryken in-to a luste with his neghbur wyfe. 1542 UDALL *Erasm. Apoph.* 282 b, He was stricken in fear of ye courageous stomake of the freashe young manne. 1553 T. WILSON *Rhet.* 37 But altogether stricken in a dumpe, you seke to be solitarye. 1563 FOXE *A. & M.* 14/1 Which when Hildebrandus harde, he was stroken in suche a fury, that scharsly he could kepe his hands of him. 1582 N. T. (Rhem.) *Matt.* xvii. 23 And they were stroken sadde exceedingly. 1593 SHAKS. *Lucr.* 262 Which strooke her sad,..Vntill her husbands welfare shee did heare. 1606 N. B[AXTER] *Sydney's Ourania* M 3, Whose suddaine view, strook him to such amaze, As marueling a while did naught but gaze. 1640 J. GOWER *Ovid's Festiv.* IV. 82 The wonder strikes them all astound. 1682 BUNYAN *Holy War* (1905) 285 At this they were all of them struck into their dumps, and could not tell what to say. 1711 in *10th Rep. Hist. MSS. Comm.* App. v. 143 This loss of the artillery struck the Prince..into a great fury. 1853 LYTTON *My Novel* XII. xxvii, The brave man saw before him..that crime of a coward; and into cowardice he was stricken.

c. To cause (a person) to be overwhelmed or seized *with* (terror, amazement, grief; *rarely* delight, love). Also of the feeling: To seize.

In 16th c. sometimes of a deity (cf. 46); usually of incidents, things seen or heard.

1533 BELLENDEN *Livy* I. xxi. (S.T.S.) I. 120 Throw quhilk þe king was strikin [*v.r.* stirkin] haistelie with na les fere þan hevy thocht. 1542 UDALL *Erasm. Apoph.* 189 b, Alexander beeyng rauyshed with the sight of her, was soodainly striken with hotte burnyng loue. 1611 SHAKS. *Cymb.* I. vi. 118 O deerest Soule: Your Cause doth strike my hart With pitty, that doth make me sicke. 1616 W. BROWNE *Brit. Past.* II. v. 130 Amazement strucke the multitude. 1671 MILTON *Samson* 1644 Such other tryal I mean to shew you of my strength..As with amaze shall s^trike all who behold. 1726 SWIFT *Gulliver* III. x. 129, I freely own my self to have been struck with inexpressible Delight upon hearing this Account. 1774 BURKE *Sp. Amer. Tax.* Wks. 1842 I. 164 Any of these innumerable regulations, perhaps, would not have alarmed alone;..the multitude struck them with terrour. 1777 POTTER *Æschylus, Prometh. Chain'd* 18 It is a sight that strikes my friends with pity. 1816 SCOTT *Old Mort.* xxxix, He was struck with shame at having given way to such a paroxysm. 1848 THACKERAY *Van. Fair* xxxi, Rebecca's appearance struck Amelia with terror.

d. To cause (a feeling, etc.) to fall or come suddenly. Const. *into,* †*in,* †*to.*

1583 STUBBES *Anat. Abus.* C ij, The maiestrats also..may were..costlie ornaments..to dignifie their callings..therby to strike a terroure & feare into the harts of the people. 1591 SHAKS. *1 Hen. VI,* II. iii. 24 It cannot be, this weake and writhled schrimpe Should strike such terror to his Enemies. 1594 O. B. *Quest. Profit. Concern.* 18 b, This would haue stroken such a present ioy into his heart, to heare me give sentence on such impenitent castawaies. 1611 *Sec. Maiden's Trag.* 2444 Her Constancy strikes so much firmnes in vs. 1651 tr. *Wotton's Panegyr. K. Chas.* Reliq. W. 142 Afterwards at a solemn Tilting, I became uncertain whether you strook into the beholders more Ioy or Apprehension. 1659 W. CHAMBERLAYNE *Pharonnida* V. v. (1820) 92 Which ..through the sad spectator's eye Struck such a terror. 1736 LEDIARD *Life Marlborough* I. 199 [He] struck Terror and Amazement, throughout the whole Empire. 1859 GEO. ELIOT *Adam Bede* ii, He..might at any moment show himself to them in some way that would strike anguish and penitence into their hearts. 1875 JOWETT *Plato* (ed. 2) I. 83 His appearance will strike terror into his enemies.

VI. To make a vigorous movement (as if striking a blow).

48. *intr.* To make a stroke with the limbs in swimming. Also *to strike forward, out.* Also *trans.* in *to strike a stroke.*

1660 R. WILD *Iter Bor.* 9 [He] Flings out his arms and strikes some strokes to swim. 1719 DE FOE *Crusoe* I. (Globe) 45 Finding the Water had spent it self,..I strook forward against the Return of the Waves. 1745 POCOCKE *Descr. East* II. I. ix. 36 It bore me up in such a manner, that when I struck in swimming, my legs were above the water. 1851 MRS. BROWNING *Casa Guidi Wind.* I. x. 80 Through the blue Immense, Strike out all swimmers! 1861 HUGHES *Tom Brown at Oxf.* ii, His first impulse on rising to the surface.. was to strike out for the shore. 1888 'SARAH TYTLER' *Blackhall Ghosts* II. xxi. 183 He..struck out, and swam for a few yards.

fig. 1880 GOLDW. SMITH *Pessimism* in *Atlantic Monthly* Feb. 210 Good men striking out against the everflowing current of evil and indifference.

b. To make a stroke with one's oar. †Also *trans.*

1725 POPE *Odyss.* XIII. 95 At once they bend, and strike their equal oars. 1789 *New Lond. Mag.* Sept. 462/2 The boatmen..struck their oars and pushed on. 1892 *Sporting Life* 26 Mar. 7/5 At this point a spurt of 8 strokes was indulged in, the rate of striking being 37 to the minute.

49. Of a horse: To put down his fore feet *short, close,* etc.

1683 *Lond. Gaz.* No. 1844/8 [He] strikes but little on a pace, but trots and gallops well. 1691 *Ibid.* No. 2727/4 Lost .., a dark-brown Gelding,..strikes close before apt to cut. 1850 'H. HIEOVER' *Pract. Horsemanship* 51 He will find his horse occasionally 'strike short', i.e. put down his fore-feet perhaps a yard short of his usual stroke or stride.

b. *trans.* Of a horse: To alter his pace into (a faster movement). Also *intr.* To quicken his pace *into.* Also *causatively* to put (a horse) *into* a quicker pace.

1816 SCOTT *Old Mort.* iii, No sooner had the horses struck a canter than [etc.]. 1823 *Examiner* 416/1 He struck his horses into a gallop. 1861 *Temple Bar* II. 71 The horses had struck into a quick sharp trot.

50. *trans.* To thrust (the hand, etc.) with a sudden movement; to impel as with a blow. Cf. 36 a. Also *to strike out, together.* Also *intr.*

1607 TOPSELL *Four-f. Beasts* 478 [The lion] laying downe his eares, and striking his taile betwixt his legges, like a curre-dogge. 1827 SCOTT *Surg. Dau.* i, So saying, he struck the forefinger of his right hand against a paper which he held. 1865 MEREDITH *Rhoda Fleming* xxxii, He struck out his right arm deprecatingly. 1885 E. F. BYRRNE *Entangled* I. I. viii. 128 The colonel struck his fingers together. 1892 *Temple Bar* Mar. 314 He struck a quick hand through a thick bundle of papers.

51. *intr.* To move quickly, dart, shoot. Also *fig.*

1639 S. DU VERGER tr. *Camus' Admir. Events* 175 Hee doubted no more of that truth which strooke into his eyes. **1719** YOUNG *Busiris* IV. i, A sudden pain..struck across my heart. **1789** MRS. PIOZZI *Journ. France* I. 307 Some unaccountable sparks of fire seemed to strike up and down the hedges. **1855** LYNCH *Rivulet* XV. iii, Upward the growing twilight strikes, The morning has begun.

†**b.** To pass suddenly, 'burst', *into* (a condition). *Obs.*

1674 *Govt. Tongue* iii. 14 Atheism..has struck on a sudden into such reputation, that it scorns any longer to sculk.

c. To start suddenly *into* (a song, tune).

1819 SCOTT *Ivanhoe* xl, The Jester next struck into another carol. **1892** STEVENSON & L. OSBOURNE *Wrecker* vii. 109 The musicians..struck into a skittish polka.

d. To thrust oneself suddenly or vigorously *into* (a quarrel, debate, a joint action).

1828 SCOTT *F.M. Perth* ii, He sees no brawl but he must strike into the midst of it. **1850** CARLYLE *Latter-d. Pamph.* i. (1872) 39 Here is work for you; strike into it with man-like, soldierlike obedience. **1879** MCCARTHY *Own Time* III. xxxix. 190 He could not strike into a debate actually going on. **1883** FRANCES M. PEARD *Contrad.* xvii, Atherton.. struck into the conversation again.

e. *trans.* (= *strike into*) in certain phrases. ***to strike an attitude***: see ATTITUDE 2. †***to strike a bustle***: to make a commotion.

1825 COBBETT *Rur. Rides* 187, I got up, struck a bustle, got up the ostler, set off, [etc.]. **1840** DICKENS *Old C. Shop* lvi, At the end of this quotation in dialogue, each gentleman struck an attitude.

52. *intr.* **a.** Of light: To pierce *through* (a medium), break *through* (clouds, darkness). Also *fig.*

1563 FULKE *Goodly Gallery Meteors* (1571) 36 Ye sunn striking through a sixe pointed stoone, called Iris. **1641** MILTON *Reform.* I. 6 The bright and blissfull Reformation ..strook through the black and settled Night of Ignorance and Anti-christian Tyranny. **1797** HT. LEE *Canterb. T.*, *Frenchm. T.* (1799) I. 295 As moonlight struck through the breaks, she put her head out of the window. **1908** [MISS E. FOWLER] *Betw. Trent & Ancholme* 43 When a lowering sun strikes through the blooms, and enhances their glories.

b. Of cold: To go *through*, penetrate *to*. *lit.* and *fig.* Also of the wind, something damp or cold, ***to strike chill, damp***, etc.; also *trans.*

1569 W. HUBBARD *Ceyx & Alcione* A iij, There strake: A chilnes straight vnto hir hart. **1656** COWLEY *Misc.* Pref., The cold of the Countrey had strucken through all his faculties. **1841** BROWNING *Pippa Passes* I. Poems (1905) 168/2, I rather should account the plastered wall A piece of him, so chilly does it strike. **1844** *Jrnl. R. Agric. Soc.* V. I. 101 In frosty weather the cold strikes through the slates. **1863** W. C. BALDWIN *Afr. Hunting* vii. 279, I swam five rivers in pursuit, having on a pair of goatskin trousers, which struck me icy cold. **1887** G. M. ROBINS *False Position* III. i. 9 May felt as if the cold were striking to her heart. *Ibid.* III. ix. 171 His cold voice struck miserably into her heart. **1889** RIDER HAGGARD *Col. Quaritch* xli, The..damp of the place struck to his marrow. **1894** A. ST. AUBYN *Orchard Damerel* III. ii. 44 [The rooms] struck damp and chilly like a vault.

c. Of a disease: To pass *inwards* (leaving the surface or extremities). Cf. *strike in*, 81 d.

1843 R. J. GRAVES *Syst. Clin. Med.* xxviii. 363 When ostitis occupies the external table of the cranium, it seldom strikes inwards. **1865** DICKENS *Mut. Fr.* II. ix, But as long as they [the measles] strikes out'ards, sir..they ain't so much. It's their striking in'ards that's to be kep off.

53. *trans.* **a.** To cause to penetrate, impart (life, warmth, dampness), *to*, *into*, *through*.

1611 SHAKS. *Cymb.* III. iii. 97 The yonger Brother.. Strikes life into my speech, and shewes much more His owne conceyuing. **1712** J. JAMES tr. *Le Blond's Gardening* 203 Vapours..strike a very great Dampness to the Walls of the Building. **1721** BRADLEY *Philos. Acc. Wks. Nat.* 194 A Coat of Horse-Dung..for about six Weeks strikes a Warmth through the Boards. **1749** FIELDING *Tom Jones* xv. ii, You have struck a damp to my heart which has almost deprived me of being. **1890** MRS. H. WOOD *House of Halliwell* II. ii. 24 The east wind had struck inflammation to the chest of a lovely child. **1890** CONAN DOYLE *Firm of Girdlestone* xli, His voice..struck a chill into the girl's heart.

†**b.** ? To send out or forth (a beam of light); to cause to impinge *on* (cf. 62 b). *lit.* and *fig.* *Obs.*

1697 DRYDEN *Virg. Georg.* IV. 419 In this, four Windows are contriv'd, that strike To the four Winds oppos'd, their Beams oblique. **1697** —— *Æneis* VIII. 35 So when the Sun by Day, or Moon by Night, Strike, on the polish'd Brass, their trembling Light. **1704** NORRIS *Ideal World* II. iii. 246 To strike a through light into this whole matter at once.

c. To force (heat) *into*.

1677 MOXON *Mech. Exerc.* i. 8 Wet the outside of the Fire to damp the outside, as well to save Coals, as to strike the force of the Fire into the inside.

54. Of a plant, cutting, etc.: To send down or out (its roots); to put forth (its root or roots).

1707 MORTIMER *Husb.* 133 The best experienced Planters prefer October..that then the Hops will settle and strike Root against Spring. **1733** W. ELLIS *Chiltern & Vale Farm.* 87 The hollow Earth..will..receive, nourish, and cause the same [seed] to strike its Radicle into it. **1851** *Jrnl. R. Agric. Soc.* XII. II. 296 Grasses which strike their roots deep in the ground. **1859** JEPHSON *Brittany* v. 57 The tree which strikes its roots and fibres most widely into the soil produces the most abundant fruit and foliage. **1886** *Encycl. Brit.* XX. 174/1 The danthonia and sparobolus strike deep roots.

fig. **1711** ADDISON *Spect.* No. 261 ¶5 The Passion should strike Root, and gather Strength before Marriage be grafted on it. **1893** TRAILL *Social Eng.* Introd. 45 The art of painting ..had all the tenderness of an exotic. It struck no roots into our chilly soil.

b. *intr.* Of a plant, seed, cutting, piping, layer, etc.: To put forth roots. Of a root: To penetrate the soil. Also with advs. *in*, *down*.

1682 GREW *Anat. Plants* 59 Some [roots] run Level,.. Some strike down, but a little way,..others grow deep. **1766** *Complete Farmer* s.v. *Saintfoin*, There is some seed of which not one in ten will strike. **1800** *Trans. Soc. Arts* XVIII. 372 The cuttings of jasmine..strike with wonderful facility. **1841** *Florist's Jrnl.* (1846) II. 51 The pipings or layers.. otherwise..will have become hard, and not strike quite so easily. **1841** *Jrnl. R. Agric. Soc.* II. I. 55 The roots..will strike down several feet. **1847** *Ibid.* VIII. I. 210 The roots will strike in deeper in search of nutriment. **1892** *Cassell's Mag.* Nov. 718/1 The chrysanthemum strikes so easily that, in order to get a dwarf plant, we merely take off the tops and strike them. *Ibid.* 718/2 In a very few days your young cuttings will have struck and commenced their growth.

fig. **1769** *Junius Lett.* xxxi, Believe me, sir, the precedent strikes deep. **1825** *New Monthly Mag.* XIII. 94 The impression, if it takes root, strikes deep. **1892** *Sat. Rev.* 30 Jan. 132/1 The taint strikes deeper.

c. *transf.* Of a young oyster: (see quot.).

1881 INGERSOLL *Oyster-Industr.* (Hist. Fish. Industr. U.S.) 249 *Strike*, to become tenanted by living oysters; or when infant oysters attach themselves to any object they are said to 'strike'. (Staten Island.)

d. *trans.* To cause (a cutting, etc.) to root; to propagate (a plant) by means of a cutting, etc.

1842 LOUDON *Suburban Hort.* 251 In the case of plants which are not difficult to strike, a portion of the young shoot is cut off. **1891** *New Rev.* Oct. 384 She says she can strike one of the flowers and make it grow into a plant.

55. To change the colour of (a substance) by chemical action *into* (a specified colour); to produce or assume (a specified colour) by this means.

1664 POWER *Exp. Philos.* I. 74 If into the Infusion of Violets you put..the oyl of Tartar..it will presently strike it into a green Tincture. **1670** W. SIMPSON *Hydrol. Ess.* 69 Artificial alom will not with galls strike a purple colour. **1682** GREW *Anat. Plants* v. 277 There are very few Flowers that will strike into a Blew by any Liquor. **1686** PLOT *Staffordsh.* 106 The water of the Well..though it will not turn milk, or strike with Galls, yet it takes not Soap. **1765** MORRIS *Somersham Water* in *Phil. Trans.* LVI. 23 The water..still preserved its property of striking a blue and purple with galls. **1826** *Art of Brewing* (ed. 2) 87 Salt of steel..causes a fine mantling head to the porter, and strikes a fine nut-brown colour over the froth. **1857** MILLER *Elem. Chem.*, *Org.* 280 A neutral solution of perchloride of iron strikes with morphia a very characteristic blue colour. **1862** C. O'NEILL *Dict. Calico Printing & Dyeing* 24/2 A..method of dyeing by means of bichromates..by which the logwood is 'struck' of an intense black and fixed. **1879** *Cassell's Techn. Educ.* IV. 359 We have met with some [well-water] which struck a decided brown tinge after..contact with the nitrate.

b. *transf.* Of a young turkey: ***to strike the red*** (see quot.).

1867 *Jrnl. R. Agric. Soc.* Ser. II. III. II. 526 It is a critical time for young turkeys when the fleshy tubercles begin to appear on the head, generally termed striking the red.

56. a. *trans.* To cause (a colour, dye) to take or sink in. **b.** *intr.* Of a dye: To sink in; also, to spread, run.

a. 1769 MRS. RAFFALD *Eng. Housekpr.* (1805) 40 Put a lump of butter in a cloth, and rub it [*sc.* a boiled lobster] over; it will strike the colour and make it look bright. **1839** URE *Dict. Arts* 642 [It] will enable the oxygen of the atmosphere to strike the dye more perfectly..into the materials.

b. *c* **1790** IMISON *Sch. Arts* II. 88 To stain Wood Red. Take archal one pound, add 1-4th oil of vitriol,..to make it strike deeper, add a little more oil of vitriol. **1835** HANNETT *Bibliopegia* 91 Each colour should be allowed to properly strike into the leather before another is used. **1873** SPON *Workshop Rec.* Ser. I. (1885) 321/2 Wash the shawl..in this [scouring] mixture... Next rinse it in salt and water, in order to prevent the colours striking.

57. *trans.* To cause (herrings) to become impregnated with salt or (pork) with saltpetre in curing.

1780 YOUNG *Tour Irel.* I. 230 Vessels for striking the herrings, that is, putting them in salt for 10 or 12 days. **1850** *Jrnl. R. Agric. Soc.* XI. II. 589 The latter..is sometimes found a formidable difficulty in the way of good curing, or, as it is technically termed, striking the meat and taking the salt, the former term applying to saltpetre, and the latter to the common salt used.

VII. To impinge upon.

58. *intr.* Of a moving body: To impinge upon or come into collision or contact with something else. Const. *on*, *upon*, *against*.

[*c* **1340**, *c* **1375**: see *strike together*, 85.] **1626** BACON *Sylva* §957 There would be Triall also made, of holding a Ring by a Threed in a Glasse, and telling him that holdeth it, before, that it shall strike so many times against the side of the Glasse, and no more. **1690** LOCKE *Hum. Und.* III. iv. §10 The Cartesians tell us, that Light is a great number of little Globules, striking briskly on the bottom of the Eye. **1737** BRACKEN *Farriery Impr.* (1756) I. 88 Objects compress or strike upon the Extremities of the Nerves by their Motion. **1827** FARADAY *Chem. Manip.* vi. (1842) 183 If, in passing through the funnel, some of the powder has struck against and adhered to the inside of the neck of the flask. **1858** LARDNER *Hand-bk. Nat. Philos.* 102 When a liquid strikes upon a solid surface in an oblique direction. **1891** EMILY & DOR. GERARD *Sensitive Plant* III. III. xx. 204 The arm which had struck against the bridge was swollen. **1901** *Scotsman* 10 Sept. 7/1 There is a close connection between lunar darkness and the number of birds killed striking [against the glass of a lighthouse].

fig. **1846** T. T. LYNCH *Lett. to Scattered* (1872) 546 Cold words of argument strike upon the face, like a sleet shower.

†**b.** said of a moving shadow. *Obs.*

1669 STURMY *Mariner's Mag.* II. xvi. 93 Hold up the Center until the Shade of the Brass-Pin strikes on the Sight and Line of E.

†**c.** ***to strike upward***: to rebound. *Obs.*$^{-0}$

1530 PALSGR. 740/2, I stryke upwarde, I rebounde... Whan a thyng falleth strayght out of the ayre, it wyll stryke upwarde whan it falleth to the yerthe.

59. *trans.* To come into forcible contact or collision with.

1626 BACON *Sylva* §9 All Liquors strucken make round Circles. **1636** COWLEY *Sylva* 411 As when soft westwinds strooke the garden Rose. **1697** DRYDEN *Æneis* V. 683 She [the dove] leaves her Life aloft, she strikes the Ground. **1774** GOLDSM. *Nat. Hist.* (1824) I. xxx. 244 This air strikes and affects the auditory nerves, which carry the sound to the brain. **1866** 'CAPT. CRAWLEY' *Billiard Bk.* iv. 46 Here you will see how a ball may be made to strike all six cushions. **1867** SMYTH *Sailor's Word-bk.*, *Struck by a Sea*, said of a ship when a high rolling wave breaks on board of her. **1882** *Encycl. Brit.* XIV. 385/2 The drum is made to revolve.., the blunt edges and external angles of the knives thereby striking the surface of the leather. **1892** *Longm. Mag.* July 272 The wind striking the face of the mountain. **1899** W. C. MORROW *Bohem. Paris* 49 His stool-legs were so loosened that when he sat down he struck the floor with a crash.

b. *fig.* (chiefly after Latin *ferire cælum, sidera*).

1605 SHAKS. *Macb.* IV. iii. 6 Each new Morne, New Widdowes howle, new Orphans cry, new sorowes Strike heauen on the face, that it resounds [etc.]. **1625** T. H[AWKINS] *Horace, Odes* I. i. (1638) 2 But let me stand a Lyrick mongst the rest, I'le strike the starry vault with raised crest. **1712–14** POPE *Rape L.* v. 42 Heroes' and Heroines' shouts confus'dly rise, And bass, and treble voices strike the skies. **1819** WIFFEN *Aonian Hours* 73 A loud shout thrice strikes the golden stars.

†**c.** With adv. or phrase expressing the result. Also, to make (a hole) by impact. *Obs.*

1530 PALSGR. 739/2, I stryke ones foote out of joynt, *je mets son pied hors du moulle*. **1594** SHAKS. *Rich. III*, I. iv. 19 Me thought that Glouster stumbled, and in falling Strooke me (that thought to stay him) ouer-boord. **1601** *Strange Rep. Sixe Notorious Witches* A iij, He had such a fal, that the huckle bone of his thigh was stroken out of ioynt. **1632** LITHGOW *Trav.* II. 62 A great lake [= leak] was stricken into our Ship. **1751** *Affecting Narr. H.M.S. Wager* 20 One of our Men..had the Misfortune to be struck over-Board in handing the Fore-Sail.

60. *spec.* Of a ship: **a.** *intr.* To hit (*on* or *upon* a rock, etc.), to collide with a rock, run aground.

1518 H. WATSON *Hist. Oliver of Castile* (Roxb.) E 3 b, Vpon the thyrde daye theyr shyp stroke on grounde, by so grete force that it claue in two pyeces. **1612** COVERTE *Voy.* 23 And presently the ship strooke, which I presently went vp and told him of. **1669** DRYDEN *Tempest* I. (1670) 4 *Trinc.*.. There's a Rock upon the Star-board Bow. *Steph.* She strikes, she strikes! **1743** BULKELEY & CUMMINS *Voy. S. Seas* 17 The Ship struck abaft on a sunken Rock. **1769** FALCONER *Dict. Marine* (1780) s.v., To *Strike*, to run ashore, or to beat upon the ground in passing over a bank or shallow. **1890** CLARK RUSSELL *Ocean Trag.* III. xxviii. 89 The yacht had struck bow on.

b. *trans.* To hit or run upon (a rock, the ground, a mine).

1587 JANES in Hakluyt *Voy.* (1589) 792 This day we stroke a rocke. **1870** MORRIS *Earthly Par.* III. 512 My sight clears, and I see his black bows strike The hidden skerry. **1913** *Times* 14 May 5/5 The Portuguese cruiser..struck a rock near Dumbell Island.

61. Naut. ***to strike ground, soundings***: to reach the bottom with a sounding line. Also *transf.* of a swimmer: To touch (bottom).

1726 SHELVOCKE *Voy. round World* 66, I stood right in, the greatest part of the day, with intent to strike ground upon them [i.e. the shoals]. **1748** *Anson's Voy.* II. vii. 214 We struck ground with sixty-five fathom of line. **1846** A. YOUNG *Naut. Dict.* 289 To strike soundings, is to find bottom with the deep-sea-lead on coming in from sea. **1890** CLARK RUSSELL *Ocean Trag.* III. xxxiv. 238 Scarce had we struck soundings,..when a whole gale of wind blew down upon us.

transf. **1875** *Scribner's Monthly* XXX. 735/1 Their steeds ..now swimming, again striking bottom, and so until the hoofs of their leader struck the shore.

b. *intr.* Of water: To have (a specified depth) when sounded.

1858 *Merc. Marine Mag.* V. 322 A..clear..channel appeared open, and..did not strike less than 6½ fathoms.

62. *trans.* Of a beam or ray of light or heat: To fall on, catch, touch.

a **1586** SIDNEY *Arcadia* III. xxvi. (1912) 504 The beames thereof so strake his eyes..that [etc.]. **1598** R. HAYDOCKE tr. *Lomazzo* II. 154 By reason of the reflexion of the parte strooken with the light. **1789** D. DAVIDSON *Thoughts on Seasons* 69 In yon distant glade The Sun, refulgent, strikes the pearly stream. **1812** CARY *Dante, Parad.* ix. 66 In splendour glowing, Like choicest ruby stricken by the sun. **1903** G. H. LORIMER *Lett. Self-made Merch.* xiii. 184 So he leads the nag out into the middle of a ten-acre lot, where the light will strike him good and strong.

b. *intr.* Of light: To fall, impinge *on*.

1662 GERBIER *Princ.* 34 The Lights of the Stable strikes on the Horse their backs. **1690** LOCKE *Hum. Und.* II. viii. §19. 58 Hinder light, but from striking on it, and its Colours vanish. **1808** SCOTT *Marmion* IV. xxi, Full on his face the moonbeam strook. **1831** BREWSTER *Optics* iii. 20 Having marked the point at which the ray from S strikes. **1892** H. R. MILL *Realm of Nature* vii. 110 Light from the Sun.. strikes on the upper atmosphere.

63. *trans.* Of a sound, report, etc.: To fall on, reach, or catch (the ear). †Also (? *nonce-use*) of an odour: To affect (the nostrils).

1596 DRAYTON *Legends, Matilda* 122 Hauing his Eare oft strooke with this Report. **1603** FLORIO *Montaigne* I. xii. 22 If the cracke of a musket do sodainly streeke mine eares, in a place where I least looke for it. **1611** SHAKS. *Wint. T.* I. ii. 421 Turne then my freshest Reputation to A sauour, that may strike the dullest Nosthrill Where I arriue. **1650** SIR H.

NEWTON in *Verney Mem.* (1904) I. 464 The sound of your sadnesse first struck my eares at Flushing, but heere it strikes my heart to know the truth of it. **1741** WATTS *Improv. Mind* I. i. 25 So that the glance of an eye, or a word striking the ear.. shall conduct you to a train of happy sentiments. **1805** WORDSW. *Fidelity* 15 Nor shout, nor whistle strikes his ear. **1891** *Strand Mag.* II. 512/1 [A] scraping sound struck his quick ear.

absol. **1816** BYRON *Ch. Har.* III. xxi, But hush! hark! a deep sound strikes like a rising knell!

b. *intr.* with *on, upon.*

1848 DICKENS *Dombey* lvi, The words.. will strike upon my ears like a knell. **1850** *Tait's Mag.* XVII. 270/2 A sound struck on his ear.

64. *trans.* Of a thought, an idea: To come into the mind of, occur to (a person). Freq. in the phr. ***it strikes*** (or ***it struck***) ***me that*** —.

1606 SHAKS. *Ant. & Cl.* I. ii. 87 He was dispos'd to mirth, but on the sodaine A Romane thought hath strooke him. **1712–13** SWIFT *Jrnl. to Stella* 14 Jan., I said something in his praise, when it struck me immediately that I had made a blunder in doing so. **1775** SHERIDAN *Duenna* I. iv, Hold.. a thought has struck me! **1827** SCOTT *Highl. Widow* v, The first idea that struck him was, that the passenger belonged to his own corps. **1867** FREEMAN *Norm. Conq.* (1876) I. App. 754 It strikes me that the scribe confounded these laws. **1891** *Murray's Mag.* X. 732 A happy thought struck Lady Betty.

65. To impress or arrest (the eye, view, sight).

1700 DRYDEN *Fables* Pref. *A 2 b, Words, indeed, like glaring Colours, are the first Beauties that arise, and strike the Sight. **1737** *Gentl. Mag.* VII. 30/1 The first Thing intended to have struck the Eye, was to have been a grand and stately Statue. **1759** JOHNSON *Rasselas* xxx, When the eye or the imagination is struck with any uncommon work. **1779** J. MOORE *View Soc. Fr.* (1789) I. ii. 12 Whose appearance always strikes the eye with delight. **1837** P. KEITH *Bot. Lex.* 196 Habit.. is that sort of resemblance which strikes the eye of the beholder at first sight, without putting him to the trouble of enquiring in what it specifically consists. **1892** *Cornh. Mag.* July 36 That is the only object that strikes our eyes.

66. Of something seen or heard: To impress strongly (a person); to appear remarkable to.

1672 VILLIERS (Dk. Buckhm.) *Rehearsal* IV. ii. (Arb.) 109 [*Volscius* recites.] *Bayes.* Ah! I gad, that strikes me. **1711** ADDISON *Spect.*, No. 50 ¶ 1 Being wonderfully struck with the Sight of every thing that is new or uncommon. **1764** DODSLEY *Leasowes* in *Shenstone's Wks.* (1777) II. 318 On the entrance into this shrubbery, the first object that strikes us is a Venus de Medicis. **1802** MAR. EDGEWORTH *Moral T., Forester* xvi, Those arguments.. struck him.. with all the force of conviction. **1823** SCOTT *Quentin D.* xxvi, His attendant was struck by the unusual change in his deportment. **1839** CARD. WISEMAN *Anglican Claim Apostolic Succession* (1905) 89 We have been struck how the Donatists, while they did not relish this name, had no objection to the national appellation of Africans. **1888** BURGON *Lives 12 Gd. Men* II. x. 263 The absence in him of prejudice and partisanship.. was what used to strike us most.

absol. **1717** POPE *Ep. Jervas* 44 Thence endless streams of fair Ideas flow, Strike in the sketch, or in the picture glow. **1732** BERKELEY *Alciphr.* IV. § 15 Things which rarely happen strike; whereas frequency lessens the admiration of things. **1779** JOHNSON *L.P., Milton* (1781) I. 204 The style [of his *History of England*] is harsh; but it has something of rough vigour, which perhaps may often strike, though it cannot please. **1830** J. G. STRUTT *Sylva Brit.* 6 A forest is more calculated to strike by the greatness of its aggregate. **1869** J. PHILLIPS *Vesuvius* i. 4 The first passage which strikes in Latin authors is that written by Pliny.

b. *intr.* To make an impression (*on* the mind, senses, observation).

1732 POPE *Ess. Man* II. 128 All spread their charms, but charm not all alike; On diff'rent senses, diff'rent objects strike. **1848** KEBLE *Serm.* Pref. 23 A plain and palpable case, and would strike on pure minds with a force like mathematical demonstration. **1887** E. F. BYRRNE *Heir without Heritage* I. ix. 161 The obvious truth in her mother's sayings struck on her sense of the fitting.

c. *trans.* To impress in a specified way; ***to strike one as*** —, to appear to one as —, to give one the impression of being —. †Also *absol.* (obs.).

a **1701** MAUNDRELL *Journ. Jerus.* (1732) 137 That it strikes the Mind with an Air of Greatness. **1749** FIELDING *Tom Jones* VIII. xiv, It has often struck me, as the most wonderful thing I ever read of. **1777** STORER in *Jesse Selwyn & Contemp.* (1844) III. 198, I know the same thing strikes different people in many ways, but thus he seemed to me. **1779** SHERIDAN *Critic* I. i, Now, Mrs. Dangle, didn't you say it struck you in the same light? **1802** W. TAYLOR in Robberds *Mem.* (1843) I. 410 The style of building [at Calais] strikes as being more roomy and gentlemanlike. **1858** HAWTHORNE *Fr. & It. Note-bks.* (1872) I. 6 The French cathedral strikes one as lofty. **1888** LADY DUFFUS HARDY *Dang. Experiment* II. v. 82 Her beauty struck him in a new light. **1902** BRIDGES *To Burns* xv. Poems (1912) 388 The good man's pleasure 'tis to do 't; That's how it strikes him.

d. To impress or catch (the senses, fancy, imagination, notice, curiosity, etc.).

1697 DRYDEN *Æneis* XI. 520 Such Truths, O king, said he, your Words contain, As strike the Sence, and all Replies are vain. **1698** COLLIER *Short View Eng. Stage* 160 We ought not to.. Fly out at every Thing that strikes the Fancy. **1728** POPE *Dunc.* I. 65 There motly images her fancy strike, Figures ill pair'd, and Similes unlike. **1781** C. JOHNSTON *Hist. J. Juniper* II. 228, I could not help staring at her, in such a way, as struck her notice. **1781** J. MOORE *Italy* II. xlviii. (1790) 63 No ceremony can be better calculated for striking the senses. **1784** TYERS in *Gentl. Mag.* LIV. II. 908/1 He talked much of travelling into Poland, to observe the life of the Palatines, the account of which struck his curiosity very much. **1890** *Hardwicke's Sci. Gossip* XXVI. 71 Any moss, which.. may strike the finder's fancy should be lifted.. and planted in a.. pot.

e. To catch the admiration, fancy, or affection of (one of the opposite sex); in pass., to be favourably impressed by (an idea, suggestion, etc.). In pass., constr. *by, with*, also (vulgarly) ***to be struck on***. Now *colloq.*

1599 MARSTON *Ant. & Mel.* III. (1602) E 4, I haue put on good cloathes, and smugd my face, Strook a faire wench, with a smart speaking eye. **1638** COWLEY *Love's Riddle* III. i. 37 You'd aske how many shepheards she hath strooken? **1796–7** JANE AUSTEN *Pride & Prej.* iii. (1813) 10 He seemed quite struck with Jane as she was going down the dance. **1838** DICKENS *Nich. Nick.* xxiii, Miss Ledrook.. joked Miss Snevellicci about being struck with Nicholas. **1893** *Fam. Herald* 131/1 'I'm glad you're struck on her', said Bob. **1899** J. K. JEROME *Three Men in Boat* i. 17 The only one who was not struck with the suggestion was Montmorency. **1938** C. P. CONIGRAVE *Walk-About* ix. 50, I don't think he's too struck on my going back to Rosewood. **1940** 'N. SHUTE' *Old Captivity* iv. 110, I don't know that I'm so struck on this, sir.

67. *intr.* To hit or light *on, upon.*

1616 J. HEALEY tr. *Cebes* 166 You strike on truth in all things, sir. **1839** LONGF. *Hyperion* I. vii. (1852) 44 [These literary men] often strike upon trains of thought, which stand written in good authors some century or so back... But they know it not; and imagine [etc.].

68. *trans.* To come upon, reach (a hill, river, path, etc.) in travelling; to come to (a place) in the course of one's wanderings. Also of a line: To hit, come upon (a specified point). orig. chiefly *U.S.* and *Colonial.*

1798 *Mass. Mercury* 30 Oct. (Thornton *Amer. Gloss.*) Thence south, such a course as will strike William Negro's house. **1808** PIKE *Sources Mississ.* (1810) II. 134 In about five miles we struck a beautiful hill, which bears south on the prairie. **1824** *Excurs. U.S. & Canada* 182 My host.. put me into the proper direction for 'striking' the path leading to Cat's Ferry. **1830** LYELL *Princ. Geol.* I. 324 A line drawn through the Grecian archipelago,.. Southern Italy, Sicily, Southern Spain, and Portugal, will, if prolonged westward through the ocean, strike the volcanic group of the Azores. **1879** S. C. BARTLETT *Egypt to Pal.* x. 221 We continued the sharp ascent, and struck a path winding.. round the hill. **1890** 'R. BOLDREWOOD' *Col. Reformer* xxiii, They struck the river within a day's ride of Rainbar. **1896** BADEN-POWELL *Matabele Campaign* vi, At length we successfully struck the spoor. **1901** ALLDRIDGE *Sherbro* xxvi. 293 At 10.50 we struck the boundary line of the Limba Sehla country. **1915** *Nation* 30 Oct. 175 Born of pioneer parents, who struck Iowa just before the Civil War.

b. ***to strike town***: to go into town from camp. Chiefly *N. Amer.*

1902 S. E. WHITE *Blazed Trail* xxvi, When the boys struck town, the proprietors and waitresses [of the saloons] stood in their doorways to welcome them. **1910** G. H. LORIMER *Old Gorgon Graham* ii, Binder got a pretty warm welcome when he struck town.

c. To come across, meet with, encounter (a person or thing) unexpectedly; also, to hit upon (the object of one's search). Chiefly *U.S.*

1851 MAYNE REID *Scalp Hunt.* xxx, The third day I struck a town o' sand-rats. **1877** J. F. RUSLING *Great West* 39 On Wild-Cat Creek.. we struck a Mr. Silvers. **1892** *Harper's Mag.* Aug. 404/1 That's an introduction to the editor,.. and you'll strike him at the office just now, if you'd like to see him. **1893** *Black & White* 25 Feb. 234/1 He calculated upon getting across the Bay of Biscay and striking warm, safe weather in June. **1890** F. R. STOCKTON *The 'Merry Chanter'* xii. 114, 'I did 'nt strike the stairs at first,' whispered the butcher, 'and I went too far along that upper hall.'

d. To come upon, find (a pocket, vein, or seam of mineral, a stratum of water, oil, etc.) in prospecting, boring, etc. ***to strike a bonanza*** (cf. BONANZA 1). ***to strike it rich***: to find a rich mineral deposit. Also in similar *fig.* phrases. ***to strike oil***: see OIL *sb.*[1] 3 f.

1835 C. F. HOFFMAN *Winter in West* II. 47, I hear that he has lately struck a lead. **1852** L. CLAPPE *Shirley Lett. Calif. Mines* 216 When a company wish to reach the bedrock as quickly as possible, they sink a shaft.. until they 'strike it'. **1854** *California Daily Chron.* 19 May 3/7 Messrs. Emory & Bacon, just above the claim of Messrs. Meredith & Co., have also struck it rich. **1862** 'MARK TWAIN' *Let.* (1917) I. iii. 76 Well, if you haven't 'struck it rich—' that is, if the piece of rock you sent me came from a *bona fide ledge*—and it looks as if it did. *c* **1863** T. TAYLOR *Ticket-of-Leave Man* III. 47 He.. had to bolt to Australia—struck an awfully full pocket at the diggings, and is paying off his old ticks like an emperor. *a* **1864** GESNER *Coal, Petrol.*, etc. (1865) 33 He [the oil-well borer] cannot tell to a certainty that he will 'strike oil'. **1872** 'MARK TWAIN' *Innoc. at Home* xvi. (1882) 361 At the end of two months we had never 'struck' a pocket. **1875** *Eagle Mag.* (St. John's Coll. Camb.) IX. 340 He started 'prospecting', struck gold, entered his claim. **1885** *Manch. Exam.* 22 Sept. 4/7 A seam of coal 6 ft. thick has been struck at depths of 441 and 444 yards. **1885** *Harper's Mag.* Apr. 698/1 Courage and hope are kept up by the expectation of 'striking it rich'. **1887** F. FRANCIS Jun. *Saddle & Mocassin* 56 He said.. that as soon as he 'struck a Bonanza', he meant to sit around.. on week-days too. **1892** *Harper's Mag.* May 906/2 Water is struck at from 600 to 1200 feet.

transf. and *fig.* **1884** 'MARK TWAIN' *Huck. Finn* xxi. 208 We struck it mighty lucky. **1884** *Milnor* (Dakota) *Teller* 18 July, Mr. B. is very enthusiastic over his location, and thinks he has struck it rich. **1895** *Pall Mall Mag.* Nov. 329 Ef I'd a smart pad.. we might strike a lead of luck. **1953** [see *pay-dirt* s.v. PAY- 2]. **1975** *Sydney Morning Herald* 15 Nov. 55 West Indies batsmen struck pay dirt aplenty in the SCG yesterday. **1977** A. C. H. SMITH *Jericho Gun* vi. 85 He didn't mind a penny. It was what he had always thought he would do when he struck it.

e. *intr.* Colloq. phr. ***to strike lucky***, to hit a vein of good fortune.

1951 *Sport* 6–12 Apr. 17/1 Birmingham struck lucky because several London clubs refused to give Graham Warren a trial. **1984** *Financial Times* 31 Jan. 17/7 The Bush strikes lucky more often than any fringe theatre has a right to.

VIII. Senses of uncertain position.

69. ***to strike hands*** (said of two parties to a bargain): To take one another by the hand in confirmation of a bargain; hence, to ratify a bargain *with* (another). Hence † ***to strike one's truth***, to pledge one's truth by 'striking hands'; † ***to strike hearts*** (nonce-use).

c **1440** *Sir Eglam.* 246 'Ȝys,' seyde the erle, 'here myn honde!' Hys trowthe to hym he strake. **1530** PALSGR. 739/2, I stryke handes, as men do that agre apon a bargen or covenant, *je touche la.* **1560** BIBLE (Geneva) *Esther* Apocr. xiv. 8 They haue stroken hands with their idoles, That thei wil abolish the thing that thou.. hast ordained. **1606** BP. W. BARLOW *1st Serm. Hampton Crt.* (1607) D 2, The Apostle Paul receiued not his function by hands either imposed or strooken, but by especiall reuelation,.. The hands imposed Acts 13. were commendatiue, the right handes strooken, Gal. I were stipulative. **1652** SHIRLEY *Brothers* I. i, I'll find a portion for her, if you strike Affectionate heartes. **1682** BUNYAN *Holy War* (1905) 210 This Son of Shaddai, I say, having stricken hands with his Father, and promised that he would be his servant to recover his Mansoul again, stood by his resolution. **1745** *De Foe's Eng. Tradesm.* xi. (1841) I. 85 Three things every tradesman ought to consider before he 'strikes hands with a stranger', that is, before he is bound for another. **1823** 'JON BEE' *Dict. Turf* 167 Bargains in Smithfield are confirmed by the striking of hands—the palms together. **1885** *Times* 10 Mar. 4/1 The parties had 'struck their hands together' in the usual Yorkshire fashion, but before the delivery of the calves. **1915** *Nation* (N.Y.) 10 June 642/1 Stories about McKinley or Roosevelt having struck hands in the dark with France and England.

†**b.** ***to strike*** (a person) ***luck***: to give him a 'luck-penny' on making a bargain. *Obs.*

1599 NASHE *Lenten Stuffe* F 1 b, The consistorians or setled standers of Yarmouth.. gather about him as flocking to hansell him and strike him good luck. *a* **1616** BEAUM. & FL. *Scornf. Lady* II. iii, *Capt.* Take it, h'as overbidden by the Sun: bind him on his bargain quickly. *Young Lo.* Come strike me luck with earnest, and draw the writings. **1664** BUTLER *Hud.* II. i. 540 But if that's all you stand upon; Here, strike me luck, it shall be done. **1677** W. HUGHES *Man of Sin* II. viii. 128, I.. dare not venture to make a Bargain, and strike them luck.

70. [Partly from sense 69; partly after L. *ferire fœdus.*] To settle, arrange the terms of, make and ratify (an agreement, a treaty, covenant, truce; †marriage, †peace); esp. in phrase ***to strike a bargain.*** See also *strike up*, 87 d.

1544 BETHAM *Precepts War* I. lxxii. D vij b, Yet he denyed not to stryke truce wyth hym. **1581** A. HALL *Iliad* VIII. 143 A noble Nimphe, with hir good king in Thrace did mariage strike. **1600** S. NICHOLSON *Acolastus' After-witte* H 3 b, While Leacherie and Lucar strike a match, Making a compound of two deadly sinnes. **1624** QUARLES *Job Militant* vii, The Beasts shall strike with thee eternall Peace. **1646** HAMMOND in *Copy of some Papers* (1647) 96 The Gospel.. or second Covenant, stricken with us in Christ. **1711** in *10th Rep. Hist. MSS. Comm.* App. v. 172 The Confederat Princes will be compelled.. to strike a peace with France. **1749** FIELDING *Tom Jones* IX. iv, Between these two.. a league was struck. **1766** BLACKSTONE *Comm.* II. xxx. 448 As soon as the bargain is struck, the property of the goods is transferred to the vendee. **1865** PARKMAN *France & Eng. in N. Amer.* I. vii. (1876) 89 The compact struck, Menendez hastened to his native Asturias. **1883** F. M. CRAWFORD *Mr. Isaacs* i, I struck a bargain with an old *marwarri* over a small stone. **1892** *Good Words* Oct. 658/2 We struck a truce.

b. To form (acquaintance) *with.* ? *Obs.* exc. in *strike up*: see 87 e.

1595 W. W[ARNER] *Plautus' Menæcmi* II. i. (1779) 124 If they can by any meanes strike acquaintance with him.

c. To fix (a price) by agreement.

to strike the (sheriff-) fiars, to strike the (fiar-) prices (Sc. 1723–1887): see FIARS.

1526 in *Househ. Ord.* (1790) 215 That to be done within six dayes after the striking of the said prices.

†**d.** *intr.* To agree (*to* articles or terms). *Obs.*

1706 E. WARD *Wooden World Diss.* (1708) 14 Batter him with Gold once, and he shall strike instantly to the most scandalous Articles that Hell can offer.

71. *trans.* To balance (a book or sheet of accounts); ***to strike a balance***: see BALANCE *sb.* 17 b. Also, to reach (a figure, loss, or profit) by balancing an account.

1539–40 in *Househ. Ord.* (1790) 229 And the said.. Bookes, to lye vpon the Green cloth dayly, to the intent the Accomptants.. may take out the solutions.., whereby they may strike their Lydgers. **1855** *Poultry Chron.* III. 284 In striking the balance sheet, [he] found himself in consequence of the experiment, *minus* over 1000 dollars. **1880** *Tax Cases* I. 500 In striking their annual profits so as to fix the sum divisible as dividend, the Railway Company have gone upon actual expenditure, and not upon a mere estimate of probable wear and tear. **1932** *Economist* 16 Jan. 127/2 For years past the banks have been building up contingency reserves by appropriations made before and after striking their net profits. **1955** [see *clearing-bank* s.v. CLEARING *vbl. sb.* 8]. **1980** *Daily Tel.* 30 July 1/4 Last year's loss.. was struck after allowing for depreciation of £87 million and interest payments of £188 million.

72. To determine, estimate (an average, a mean).

1729 A. DOBBS *Trade Irel.* 37 The Number of Years upon which each Medium is struck. **1853** *Jrnl. R. Agric. Soc.* XIV. I. 68 A difference in value of full 20 per cent. is often struck in the London market between the produce of contiguous dairies. **1862** *Temple Bar* V. 269 When a sufficient number of records have been kept, the average is struck. **1884** *Manch. Exam.* 30 Sept. 5/6 One has to strike a mean between the glowing accounts of fortunate settlers and the pessimistic views of its detractors. **1888** BRYCE *Amer. Commw.* ciii. III. 480, I think, that so far as it is possible to strike an average, both the pecuniary and the social position of the American clergy must be pronounced slightly better.

73. *to strike a docket*: see DOCKET *sb.*[1] 6.

†**74.** To throw (a die) in some particular fraudulent manner. *Obs.*

1586 T. NEWTON tr. *Daneau's Dice-play* F 4 b, If there bee any cogging Panion..that by sleight..goeth about to help the chaunce, or strike the Dyce [L. *casum aleæ moderari, aut regere conetur.*] **1680** COTTON *Compl. Gamester* (ed. 2) 11 Fourthly by Knapping, that is, when you strike a Dye dead that it shall not stir.

75. *slang.* †**a.** *trans.* To steal (goods), rob (a person); also *absol.* and with cognate object.

1567 HARMAN *Caveat* (1869) 86 Now we haue well bousd, let vs strike some chete. Nowe we haue well dronke, let us steale some thinge. **1591** GREENE *Notable Discov. Coosnage* Wks. (Grosart) X. 38 In Figging Law..The Act doing, striking. **1591** —— *2nd Pt. Conny-catching* Ibid. X. 110 The young toward scholler although perhaps he had striken some few stroks before, yet seeing [etc.]. *Ibid.* X. 112 While hee was busie about that, the Nippe had stroken the purse. **1611** MIDDLETON & DEKKER *Roaring Girl* v. i. L 1 b, 1 *Cut[purse]*. Shall we venture to shuffle in amongst yon heap of Gallants and strike? **1622** FLETCHER *Beggars' Bush* III. iii, To mand on the pad, and strike all the cheats. *a* **1700** B. E. *Dict. Cant. Crew.*

†**b.** *intr.* To borrow money. *Obs.* **c.** To beg; also in phr. *to strike it.*

1618 MYNSHUL *Ess. Prison* 47 To borrow money is called striking, but the blow can hardly or neuer be recouered. **1655** SHIRLEY *Gent. Venice* I. i, I must borrow money, And that some call a striking. *a* **1700** B. E. *Dict. Cant. Crew*, *Strike*, to Beg, to Rob; also to borrow Money. **1898** M. DAVITT *Life & Progr. Australia* xxxv. 192 To 'strike it' is to beg.

d. *trans.* To make a sudden and pressing demand upon (a person *for* a loan, etc.). Also *absol.* or *intr.*

1751 FIELDING *Amelia* VIII. vi, The gentleman, who in the vulgar language, had struck, or taken him in for a guinea. **1766** GOLDSM. *Vicar* xx, The moment a nobleman returns from his travels..I strike for a subscription. **1893** *Scribner's Mag.* Aug. 263/2 It would be vastly better for him to shelve his books and go down and strike his Uncle Munday for a job. **1899** JESSE L. WILLIAMS *Stolen Story* etc. 291 There's Billy Woods..look out, let's hurry by or he'll strike us for the price of a drink.

e. *U.S. polit. slang.* 'To induce (a person) to pay money on the promise of getting him votes, legislative favors, etc.' (*D.A.E.*).

1859 G. W. MATSELL *Vocabulum* 87 *Strike*, to get money from candidates before an election, under the pretense of getting votes for them. **1883** M. DE L. LANDON *Wit & Humor of Age* 345 He had a way of striking the politicians who wanted a favor out of the Governor. **1894** H. C. MERWIN in *Atlantic Monthly* Feb. LXXIII. 248/2 A legislator 'strikes' a corporation, as I have indicated, when he introduces some bill calculated to injure it directly or indirectly; his purpose being, not to have the bill pass, but to compel the corporation to buy him off.

76. a. *Electr.* (See quot. 1891[1].) Also, †of an electric charge, to pass as a spark (cf. sense 43 a); of an electric discharge, to come into being; also *transf.* of the tube containing it.

1777 T. CAVALLO *Compl. Treat. Electr.* III. iii. 163 When the jar is charging, and the charge is become so high as to strike through half an inch of air. **1827** *Phil. Mag.* I. 344 If the distance be greater than that over which the charge can *strike* in the form of a spark, or with explosion. **1891** '*Electrician' Primers* (ed. W. R. Cooper), *Gloss.* (1906) 31 When the carbons of an arc lamp separate and form an arc the lamp is said to 'strike', or the arc to be 'struck'. *Ibid.* No. 44. 1 In spite of this, arc lamps sometimes start or 'strike' violently and repeatedly..on first being switched on. **1929** *Phil. Mag.* VIII. 1100 The uncertain delay which occurs between the instant at which the requisite voltage is applied to the lamp and that at which the discharge strikes. **1962** J. H. & P. J. REYNER *Radio Communication* v. 237 Once the tube has struck, however, the current can be maintained with a somewhat lower anode potential.

b. *Electroplating.* To produce the beginning of (a deposit of metal).

1894 J. W. URQUHART *Electro-plating* vi. (ed. 3) 160 For 'striking' the first deposit [of nickel] two or more [batteries] are usually employed.

c. *trans.* To bring (an arc) into being. Cf. sense 30 a.

1891 [see sense 76 a]. **1930** *Engineering* 7 Feb. 173/2 Oil.. played an important part in quenching the arc which was struck when those contacts were separated. **1950** GILL & SIMONS *Mod. Welding Technique* xi. 129 On occasion it may be found difficult to strike an arc. **1976** C. BRADSHAW *Metall. for Schools* xi. 143/1 An arc is struck between the electrode and the workpiece.

77. *intr.* In the United States army: To perform menial services for an officer; to act as an officer's servant. (*Cent. Dict.* 1891.) Cf. STRIKER 6 b.

b. *U.S. Naut.* (See quot. 1952[1].)

1952 J. V. NOEL *Naval Terms Dict.* 212 *Strike*..to work for, as in..'he is striking for chief'. *Strike for*..to learn the trade of. **1952** *MSTS Bull.* May 9/1 Few and far between are those who don't 'strike' for a rating during their short or long Navy career.

IX. With adverbs.

†**78. strike by.** *trans.* To consign to oblivion. *Sc. Obs.*

1457 *Dunfermline Reg.* (Bannatyne Club) 344 All thingis concernynge þe said mater o tyme bygane strekyn by and fullely remyttyt foreuermare.

79. strike down. a. *trans.* To fell (a person or animal) to the ground with a blow.

1470–85 MALORY *Arthur* VII. xxiii. 249 With his grete force he stroke doune that knyghte. *a* **1500** *Chevy Chase* 62 (Ashm. MS.), Many sterne the strocke done streght. **1593** SHAKS. *Lucr.* 217 Or what fond begger, but to touch the crowne, Would with the scepter straight be stroken down? **1771** SMOLLETT *Humph. Cl.* 4 July (1815) 221, I was so exasperated by the pain of my ear..that, in the first transport, I struck him down. **1890** CONAN DOYLE *Firm of Girdlestone* xxi, Burt..struck him down with a life-preserver. **1892** *Temple Bar* Nov. 355 The Constitutionalists..saw the sword of a conqueror ready to strike them down.

fig. **1593** SHAKS. *2 Hen. VI*, IV. ii. 28 Then is sin strucke downe like an Oxe. **1881** GARDINER & MULLINGER *Study Eng. Hist.* I. iv. 74 The hope of England seemed to be struck down with Earl Simon. **1976** *National Observer* (U.S.) 9 Oct. 7/4 A new trend in comics has stricken down many of the old taboos.

†**b.** To precipitate (dregs). *Obs. rare.*

1594 PLAT *Jewell-ho.* I. 79 Dissolue some Sal Armoniacke, in some good Aquafortis, whose fæces..haue beene first striken down with some fine siluer.

†**c.** *intr.* To fall (on the knees). *Obs. rare.*

1616 J. LANE *Contn. Sqr.'s T.* v. 332 Th' whole armie veild their pikes, soldiers and officers on knees down strikes, while hee rode vp and downe.

d. Of the sun: To send down its heat oppressively.

1907 J. H. PATTERSON *Man-Eaters of Tsavo* App. I. 321 The sun strikes down very fiercely towards midday.

e. *trans.* To hold invalid (chiefly in legal contexts). *U.S.*

1894 *Congress. Rec.* 12 Dec. 267/1, I do not care who strikes down class legislation in this country. **1951** *Federal Reporter* (1952) CXCIII. 250/2 The court's opinions make abundantly clear its intention to strike down the entire arrangement. **1964** *Mod. Law Rev.* XXVIII. III. 343 Their main agreement had been struck down by the Restrictive Practices Court. **1979** *Tucson* (Arizona) *Citizen* 3 Oct. 4c/2 The decision..struck down a..Superior Court ruling.

80. strike home. (See HOME *adv.* 4, 5.) *intr.* To make an effective stroke or thrust with a weapon or tool. Said also of a weapon or stroke.

1590 *Cobler Canterb.* 10 Because my wife is so idle and will not strike home [with a flail], I stand with my whip to whet hir on. **1598** SYLVESTER *Du Bartas* II. iii. IV. *Captaines* 913 Courage (saith she) brave Souldiers,..Strike, & strike home, lay on with all your mights. *a* **1628** DABORNE *Poorman's Comf.* III. (1655) E 2, Who strikes a Lion must be sure strike home. **1695** *Fletcher's Bonduca* III. i, Britains, Strike Home: Revenge your Country's Wrongs. **1822** CAMPBELL *Song of Greeks* 39 Strike home! and the world shall revere us As heroes descended from heroes. **1891** *Black & White Christm. No.* 20/2 The arrow struck home.

fig. **1604** MARSTON *Malcontent* IV. iii. F 3 b, For he that strikes a great man, let him strike home.

b. Of words, etc.: To tell powerfully; to produce a strong impression.

1694 F. BRAGGE *Disc. Parables* vii. 234 Go and do thou likewise. Which words struck home upon his conscience. **1879** DOWDEN *Southey* vi. 174 The title 'Satanic School' struck home. **1885** *Manch. Exam.* 5 June 5/4 Mr. Bartley's letter asking the Conservative leaders to define a policy appears to have struck home.

81. strike in. †**a.** *intr.* To join *with* (a person or party) as a co-worker, confederate, partisan, etc.; to fall in agreement *with* (an opinion, project, etc.). *Obs.*

a **1637** B. JONSON *Underwoods, Execr. Vulcan* 200 Would you had..Strooke in at Millan with the Cutlers there. **1668** DRYDEN *Dram. Poesie* 18 A Servant or Slave, who has so much wit to strike in with him, and help him to dupe his Father. **1699** BENTLEY *Phalaris* Introd. 22 A shifting Adversary, that to avoid a thing which presses him, will strike in with any opinion. **1710** HEARNE *Collect.* (O.H.S.) III. 36 Men that will strike in with all Governments purely for the sake of Preferment. *a* **1732** T. BOSTON *Crook in Lot* (1805) 117 Strike in with humbling providences, and fight not against them while ye have them. **1793** R. HALL *Apol. Freedom of Press* 78 Ministers of that description..will be disposed on all occasions to strike in with the current of the court.

†**b.** Of a thing: To fit in (*with*), agree (*with*).

1704 NORRIS *Ideal World* II. xii. 490 These expressions.. strike in no less surprisingly..with this Ideal Hipothisis. **1712** ADDISON *Spect.* No. 415 ¶6 Every thing that is Majestick imprints an Awfulness and Reverence on the Mind of the Beholder, and strikes in with the Natural Greatness of the Soul. **1714** R. FIDDES *Pract. Disc.* II. 9 Sin strikes early in with our tempers and inclinations.

†**c.** To enter a competition *for.* (Cf. *go in*, GO *v.* 81.) *Obs.*

1632 BROME *North. Lass* III. ii, If he be mad, I will not be foolish, but strike in for a share. *a* **1700** EVELYN *Diary* 18 June 1660, I propos'd the Ambassy of Constantinople for Mr. Henshaw, but my Lord Winchelsea struck in. **1711** SWIFT *Jrnl. to Stella* 12 Sept., He advises me to strike in for some preferment now I have friends.

d. Of an eruption, disease: To disappear from the surface or the extremities with internal effects. †Also *trans.*, to drive (a disease, sweat) inwards.

1584 COGAN *Haven Health, Sickn. Oxf.* 280 If men did take cold outwardly, it stroke the sweate in, and immediately killed them. **1716** HEARNE *Collect.* (O.H.S.) V. 280 The small Pox..being struck in upon him by wet & Carelessness, after they were come out. **1767** BICKERSTAFFE *Love in the City* III. vii. (ed. 2) 60 *Miss M.* These are vapours, I was once troubled with them myself on the striking-in of a rash. **1858** O. W. HOLMES *Aut. Breakf.-t.* vi. (1891) 134 It is very bad to have thoughts and feelings, which were meant to come out in talk, *strike in*, as they say of some complaints which ought to show outwardly. **1887** A. BIRRELL *Obiter Dicta* Ser. II. 43 He lived on till Sunday..when the gout..struck in and he died.

e. To interpose actively in an affair, a contention, quarrel, etc.

a **1715** BURNET *Own Time* III. viii. (1900) II. 154 Upon this the English struck in again: and the King talked so high as if he would engage anew into the war. **1823** SCOTT *Quentin D.* vi, Lindesay—Guthrie—Tyrie, draw, and strike in! **1891** *Cornh. Mag.* Dec. 644, I can see the pennons of..many others who struck in against us for Charles of Blois. **1892** *Leisure Hour* June 525/1 Its editor has therefore been able to strike in in great problems..with an effect almost unexampled in journalism.

f. To interpose in a discussion or conversation with a remark, an expression of opinion, etc.

1791 BOSWELL *Johnson* (1904) I. 41 He..sat silent, till upon something which occurred in the course of conversation, he suddenly struck in and quoted Macrobius. **1823** SCOTT *Quentin D.* xxxiii, But ere he could proceed farther, Louis arose, and struck in with a tone of..dignity and authority. **1865** MEREDITH *R. Fleming* xlvi, 'Mark that', Sedgett struck in. **1892** *Temple Bar* Sept. 130 A hesitating voice..strikes in with a timid remark.

g. To thrust in the scythe in mowing. Also *trans.*

1845 *Jrnl. R. Agric. Soc.* VI. II. 256 The mower has a cradle fixed to a scythe, and strikes in towards the standing corn. **1893** *Scribner's Mag.* Sept. 371 When will the reapers Strike in their sickles?

h. (See quot.)

1888 *Sci. American* 9 June 352/2 A dispatch from Newfoundland says that the caplin have 'struck in'. This means that the cod..has arrived on the banks.

82. strike off. a. *trans.* To cancel by or as by a stroke of a pen; to remove from a list or record. Also *fig.*, †to cancel, remit (an obligation). *to strike off with a shilling* (*Sc.*) = cut off (see CUT *v.* 56 i).

1597 HOOKER *Eccl. Pol.* v. lxxvi. §10 To the end it might thereby appeare that we owe to the guides of our soules euen as much as our soules are worth, although the debt of our temporall blessings should bee stricken off. **1606** SHAKS. *Tr. & Cr.* III. iii. 29 Her presence Shall quite strike off all service I have done. **1662** *Ir. Act 14 & 15 Chas. II*, c. 2 §59 You are to strike off and deduct all fractions of odd acres, roods and pearches. **1690** E. GEE *Jesuit's Mem.* 7 Striking off such Scandalous Writers out of the rank of Historian. **1732** POPE *Ep. Cobham* 160 Strike off his Pension. **1822** *Examiner* 628/1 Strike off nearly a third from the nine millions. **1848** ARNOULD *Mar. Insurance* I. 127 The loss is then said to be settled or 'struck off'. **1894** A. ROBERTSON *Nuggets* 98 If I thocht ye had ever been in a playhouse,..I'd strike ye off wi' a shillin'.

(*b*) *spec.* in *pass.*, of a medical practitioner, solicitor, etc.: to be struck off the register (see sense 13 b above).

1937 A. J. CRONIN *Citadel* IV. xxi. 424 You remember the case of Jarvis, the manipulator, several years ago, when he got some cad of a doctor to anaesthetise for him. *He* was struck off, instanter. **1958** J. CANNAN *And be Villain* i. 20 He'd be struck off if he was the least bit naughty. **1965** A. CHRISTIE *At Bertram's Hotel* xvi. 153 We still call him Dr. Stokes although he's been struck off. **1983** *Times* 12 Oct. 3/4 Mr Parsons is asking Mr Justice Vinelott to order that Mr Davies be struck off.

b. To cut off with a stroke of a sword, axe, etc.

1375 BARBOUR *Bruce* XVII. 870 [He] on the hill besyde the toune Strake of his hede but ransoune. **1456** SIR G. HAYE *Law Arms* (S.T.S.) 110 Sanct Petir..strake of Malcus ere. **1583** MELBANCKE *Philotimus* Bb j b, The adders tayle, whiche being stricke of will skippe vp and downe. **1626** BACON *Sylva* §400 An Emperor of Rome, did shoot a great Forked Arrow at an Estrich,..and strook off her head. **1839** LANE *Arab. Nts.* I. 96 The King gave orders to strike off his head. **1842** LOUDON *Suburban Hort.* 139 The branch should not be larger than $1\frac{1}{2}$ in. in diameter.., otherwise it cannot be so readily struck off at one blow.

c. To produce (a picture, literary composition, etc.) quickly or impromptu; also to delineate exactly, 'hit off'.

1821 *Examiner* 235/2 A scene of unsophisticated..nature ..is struck off with an unusually bold and broad pencil. **1876** TREVELYAN *Macaulay* I. iii. 134 Striking off puns.. which followed each other in showers like sparks from flint. **1879** J. C. SHAIRP *Burns* v. 120 A burst of inspiration which came on him in the fall of 1790, and struck off at one heat the matchless *Tale of Tam o' Shanter.*

d. To mark off as enumerated.

1881 J. PAYN *From Exile* II. xxxiii. 251 She held up her plump little hand, and struck off the two items on her fingers.

e. *intr.* Of a peal of bells: To begin ringing.

a **1843** SOUTHEY *Comm.-pl. Bk.* (1851) IV. 391, 10*s.* 6*d.* to the ringers to ring one peal of grand bobs, which was to strike off while they were putting him into his grave.

f. To set off, contrast.

1884 G. GISSING *Unclassed* II. IV. i. 109 She exaggerated the refinement of her utterance that it might all the more strike off against the local twang.

83. strike out. a. *trans.* To cancel or erase by or as by a stroke of a pen; to remove from a record, text, list, etc.; also, †to erase, to rub or wipe out.

Cf. *to strike out of*: see 13.

1530 PALSGR. 740/1, I stryke out, or blotte out with a penne..*joblittere.* **1535** J. MASON in Ellis *Orig. Lett.* Ser. II. II. 59 The ignorant preist..wolde not suffer the name of Satanas in the Masbook, butt strake itt owte and putt God in the place of itt. **1693** DRYDEN *Persius* I. Note 18 (1697) 421 Floors..were strew'd with Dust or Sand; in which the Numbers and Diagrams were made and drawn, which they might strike out again at Pleasure. **1830** A. DE MORGAN *Elem. Arith.* 48 Strike out as many figures from the right of the dividend as there are ciphers at the right of the divisor. **1853** *Congr. Globe* 15 Feb. 627/2 Its only effect will be to strike out the salary of the Superintendent. **1861** *Ibid.* 18 Feb. 947/2, I will read the words to be stricken out. **1892**

Law Times XCIII. 414/2 The memorandum of association ..should be altered by striking out certain paragraphs and substituting others therefor.

fig. **1863** *Baily's Mag.* Apr. 159 Sir Tatton had so repeatedly baulked the memoir men of the newspapers by his recoveries when he had been reported to be 'struck out'. **1883** *Ch. Times* 9 Nov. 813/2 Calvin did not strike out asceticism entirely from his system as Luther..did.

b. *Mining.* (See quot.)

1778 PRYCE *Min. Cornub.* Expl. Terms 329/1 When a Lode by any Flookan..[etc.] is interrupted or cut out, they say also, 'She is struck out,' or, 'She is lost.'

c. To produce or elicit as by a blow or stroke. Also *intr.* for *refl.*

1720 STEELE *Consc. Lovers* III. i, We must strike out some pretty Livelyhood for our selves, by closing their Affairs. **1741** RICHARDSON *Pamela* I. 143 He can't have thought of *every* thing! And something may strike out for me there. **1748** J. MASON *Elocution* 26 Every Word is emphatical, and on which ever Word you lay the Emphasis,..it strikes out a different Sense. **1779** J. MOORE *View Soc. Fr.* (1789) I. viii. 53 Difficulties and dangers often strike out particles of genius. **1874** BLACKIE *Self-Cult.* 11 The true magician's wand for striking out the most important results is induction.

d. To produce by a stroke of invention (a plan, scheme, fashion, etc.).

1735 LD. HARRINGTON *Let.* 9 Oct. in *10th Rep. Hist. MSS. Comm.* App. I. 261 But might not a third way be struck out founded upon your Idea of Security for the Succession of Tuscany? **1821** *Examiner* 9/2 He..struck out a speculation in oil that in one year brought him an enormous sum. **1842** MIALL in *Nonconf.* II. 329 Plans hastily struck out by a little knot of individuals. **1859** LEVER *Dav. Dunn* lxxvi. 669 He'd strike out a new scheme, and say carelessly, 'Call the capital one million.' **1879** PATTISON *Milton* xiii. 170 Of this difference Wordsworth was conscious when he struck out the phrase, 'In his hand the thing became a trumpet.'

e. To represent in a working drawing or plan. Also, to sketch rapidly.

1678 MOXON *Mech. Exerc.* v. 82 So shall the bounds of your Mortess be struck out on the Quarter. **1753** F. PRICE *Brit. Carpenter* (ed. 3) 45 Which not only shews the use of the pitch-board, in striking out the string-board, the newels, and rails, but [etc.]. **1860** RUSKIN *Mod. Paint.* V. IX. xi. 325 *note*, A hasty drawing throughout,..he has struck out the broken fence..with a few impetuous dashes of the hand. **1885** [HORNER] *Pattern Making* 28 For the working drawing we strike out a sectional view.

f. To open up, make for oneself (a path, course, line). Chiefly *fig.*

1712 HUGHES *Spect.* No. 554 ¶3 He began to strike out new Tracks of Science. **1823** THOMASINA ROSS *Bouterwek's Hist. Sp. Lit.* I. 229 Herrera..evinced undaunted resolution in pursuing the new path which he had struck out for himself. **1881** GARDINER & MULLINGER *Study Eng. Hist.* I. iii. 49 Thought..had no tendency to strike out new and untrodden paths. **1884** *Graphic* 22 Nov. 554/1, I have struck out my own line, and made a reputation under another name. **1892** *Chamb. Jrnl.* 2 July 426/2, I tried to strike out a course in the world for myself.

g. *intr.* To go energetically.

1847 MARRYAT *Childr. New Forest* xi, He..struck out in the direction in which it [the pitfall] lay. **1890** CLARK RUSSELL *Ocean Trag.* II. xvii. 78 He struck out as though walking for a wager.

h. To hit violently, to lay about one (with the fists, a weapon, etc.).

1859 *Habits of Gd. Society* v. 191 Strike out, strike straight, strike suddenly; keep one arm to guard, and punish with the other. **1885** E. F. BYRRNE *Entangled* III. II. xxi. 197 It was this..that prompted him to strike out murderously at her. **1891** D. RUSSELL *Secret of River* I. xi. 239 Striking out at the tall reeds by the river with his stick.

i. In various games. (See quots.) Also *fig.*

1853 *Oregonian* (Portland) 2 July 1/5 No doubt they will find that strikers have struck out. **1866** *N. Y. Herald* 28 Aug. 8/2 Pennington was third man at the bat, and struck out. **1874** CHADWICK *Base Ball Man.* 56 When the batsman strikes at a fair ball three times, and fails to hit it, and the ball be caught, or it be sent to first base in time to put the player out, he 'strikes' out. **1897** *Encycl. Sport* I. 254/1 (Croquet) *Strike out*, to hit the winning post after passing through the hoops in order. **1937** *New Yorker* 19 June 30 The senator had his hopes, but he struck out on three wide 'ha's'. **1974** *Los Angeles Times* 13 Oct. III. 10/2 Garvey grounded to short. Ferguson struck out.

j. To draw out the scythe in mowing.

1840 *Jrnl. R. Agric. Soc.* I. IV. 444 In using the scythe.. the great art is to leave a short..ridge of stubble,..which is done by setting in and striking out, about five inches from the soil.

k. *trans.* Of a pitcher in Baseball, to put (a batter) out by pitching three strikes to a batter. *U.S.*

1939 E. J. NICHOLLS *Hist. Dict. Baseball Terminol.* (Unpublished Ph.D. thesis, Pennsylvania College) 75 *Strike-out king*, a pitcher who is noted for the large number of times he strikes out opposing batters. **1968** *Washington Post* 4 July C1/8 It was the third time in the game that he struck out the side. **1975** *New Yorker* 14 Apr. 92/2 He struck out two of the first three Yankee batters, without really trying his fastball.

84. strike through. *trans.* To cancel (writing) by drawing a line through it.

1898 *Encycl. Laws Eng.* VIII. 207 The initialling of the memorandum is struck through, and the loss is then 'struck off' or settled in account.

85. strike together. a. *intr.* To come into collision. **b.** *trans.* To bring into collision.

a. 1340 HAMPOLE *Pr. Consc.* 7355 Þe noyse salle be swa hydus þare, Omang devels and þase þat salle com þider, Ryght als heven and erth strake togyder. *c* **1375** *Sc. Leg. Saints* xlii. (*Agatha*) 261 Þe erde steryt sa felloun[l]y, þat al þe cyte in til hy schuke & to-giddire strake.

b. 1398 TREVISA *Barth. De P.R.* v. lvii. (1495) 173 Yf the bones of lyons ben strongly stryken togyders, fyre shall.. come oute of theym. **1578** H. WOTTON *Courtlie Controv.* 155 As two flints striken togither disburse the fier hidden in their intrayles.

86. strike under. *intr.* To give in. *Sc.*

c **1730** RAMSAY *Daft Bargain* 14 [He] lootna on till Rab strak under. **1812** P. FORBES *Poems* 79 (E.D.D.) To match wi' you I maunna fa', Sae I maun just strike under.

87. strike up. †**a.** *trans.* To break or burst open. *Sc. Obs.*

1467 in *Anc. Laws Burghs Scot.* (1910) II. 31 Nor that na gudis be schorne nor strikin vp in na wise in to the maisteris defalt. **1529** *Extracts Burgh Rec. Edin.* (1871) II. 8 That na ..man nor woman that bringis ony meill to this merket.. stryk vp the samyne quhill ix houris befor none. **1541** *Ibid.* 109 With certificatioun to thame and thai failyie thairin thai will strik vp thair girnellis. **1579** *Ibid.* (1882) IV. 134 Thatt the merchandis gudes to be laid to thair schippis be weill and discreitlie handlit and nocht strykin vp without speciall consent of the merchand.

†**b.** To draw or pull up, raise (a curtain, the hose, sleeves, etc.). *Obs.*

a **1400–50** *Bk. Curtasye* 451 in *Babees Bk.* 313 He strykes hom [the curtains] vp with forket wande. **1530** PALSGR. 377b, I stryke vp, as a man dothe his hosen, *Ie amonte.* *c* **1563** *Jack Juggler* (Roxb.) 13 Woll the horesoon fyght.. See how he beginnith to strike vp his sleues.

c. (*a*) To begin to play or sing (a piece of music, a song); (*b*) *intr.* (or *absol.*) To begin playing or singing; (*c*) *intr.* Of music: To begin to be played. Cf. 29c.

(*a*) **1562–75** *Gammer Gurton* Prol. 20 With a pot of good nale they stroake vp theyr plauditie. **1567** DRANT *Horace, Art of Poetry* A v, That when the Epilogue is done we may with franke intent, After the plaudite stryke vp our plausible assente. **1599** MARSTON *Antonio's Rev.* I. ii, I spent three spur roials on the fidlers for striking up a fresh hornepipe. **1789** *New Lond. Mag.* Nov. 560/2 The band struck up *God save the King*. **1856** MRS. STOWE *Dred* I. xxiii. 303 Come, father Bonnie, come forward, here, and strike up the hymn. **1890** F. BARRETT *Betw. Life & Death* II. xxvi. 157 The enthusiastic Greeks strike up a chant.

(*b*) **1549–62** STERNHOLD & H. *Ps.* lxxxi. 2 (1566) 202 Strike vp with harpe and lute so sweete. **1599** SHAKS. *Much Ado* v. iv. 130 Strike vp Pipers. **1769** G. WHITE *Selborne, To Pennant* 2 Jan., This bird..[begins] its song..so exactly, that I have known it strike up..just at the report of the Portsmouth evening gun. **1824** *Examiner* 242/2 The band strikes up, the regiment presents arms. **1872** EARL OF PEMBROKE & G. H. KINGSLEY *S. Sea Bubbles* i. 16 Roaming from choir to choir as each struck up in turn.

(*c*) **1829** *Examiner* 454/1 'The Rogue's march' presently struck up. **1885** 'MRS. ALEXANDER' *At Bay* v, The waltz for which Glynn had been longing struck up.

d. To conclude, to make and ratify (an agreement, a treaty, bargain, etc.): = sense 70. In recent use slightly disparaging.

1646 EARL MONM. tr. *Biondi's Civ. Warres* VI. 12 This match was agreed upon..and Monsieur de Dammartin was sent into England to strike it up with Edward. **1658** *Whole Duty Man* viii. §10 Bargains being most conveniently to be struck up at such meetings. **1661** *P'cess Cloria* I. 75 And so the present bargain was struck up between them, which she thought commodious, in respect it procured her a reprieve. **1737** WATERLAND *Eucharist* 438 God struck up a Covenant with the People of the Hebrews. **1760–72** H. BROOKE *Fool of Qual.* (1809) III. 120, I have just struck up a most advantageous bargain with our neighbour. **1885** *Manch. Exam.* 5 June 5/4 The Fourth Party is endeavouring to strike up an alliance with the Irish members. **1889** *Spectator* 14 Dec. 831 The reason being an alliance he had struck up with the Somalis.

e. To start, set afoot (a friendship, an acquaintance, a conversation, trade, etc. *with* another).

1711 SWIFT *Jrnl. to Stella* 4 May, We have struck up a mighty friendship. **1833** *Q. Rev.* L. 156 M. d'Haussez was ..unreasonable in expecting that Miss Scott should have struck up conversation with him. **1858** TROLLOPE *Three Clerks* viii, Undy Scott had struck-up an acquaintance with Alaric Tudor. **1882** STEVENSON *Fam. Studies* 48 We hear of his facility in striking up an acquaintance with women. **1891** B. HARTE *First Fam. Tasajara* I. i. 22 In the mornin' you may be able to strike up a trade with somebody else.

†**f.** *intr.* To associate or ally oneself (*with* others). *Obs.*

1714 G. LOCKHART *Mem. Scot.* (ed. 3) 383 Taking the Advantage of the Discords betwixt the Treasurer and the Whigs, [he] struck up with the latter. **1716** [DARRELL] *Gentl. Instr.* (ed. 6) 491 He spurr'd to London... Here he struck up with Sharpers, Scourers, and Alsatians.

g. *to strike up the heels of*: to overthrow.

1599 MARSTON *Ant. & Mel.* I. Wks. 1856 I. 16 Now gustie flawes strook up the very heeles Of our maine mast. **1604** [? CHETTLE] *Wit of Woman* E 2b, Stage-dir., He leades him a Lauolta, and strikes vp his heeles, and there leaues him. **1696** VANBRUGH *Relapse* IV. vi, I..strikes up his Heels, binds him Hand and Foot,.. and commits him Prisoner to the Dog-kennel.

†**h.** To cause to spring up (heat, light). *Obs.*

1596 SHAKS. *1 Hen. IV*, I. iii. 139 Who strooke this heate vp after I was gone? **1620** I. C. *Two Merry Milk-maids* IV. iii. N 2, Your bloud moues slow and cold, and all the fire That strikes vp any heat, is in desire. **1625** BACON *Ess., Of Building* (Arb.) 550 Let the Court not be paued, for that striketh vp a great Heat in Summer, and much Cold in Winter. **1627** H. LESLY *Serm.* 25 The Lord strickes vp new lights in the minde.

i. *intr.* To rise up quickly, dart or spring up.

† *to strike up into the head*: 'to fly to the head', intoxicate.

1711 SWIFT *Jrnl. to Stella* 30 Sept., Don't mind politics, young women..; they are not good after the waters;..they strike up into the head. **1837** CARLYLE *Fr. Rev.* II. IV. vii, The respected Travelling Party..will perhaps please to rest itself..till the dawn strike up! **1857** J. HAMILTON *Less. fr. Gt. Biog.* (1859) 157 Just then a squall struck up. **1861** *Temple Bar* II. 261 An aromatic fragrance strikes up on my face from some passing boat. **1889** G. M. FENN *Crown & Sceptre* v, The faint grey light..seemed to strike up from below.

j. *trans.* To pitch (a tent).

1755 AMORY *Mem.* (1769) I. 155 We immediately landed, and the tents were struck up.

k. *U.S.* in *pass.* (*a*) To be bewildered. (*b*) To be fascinated *with* or 'gone' *on* (a person of the opposite sex).

1844 'JONATHAN SLICK' *High Life N. York* I. 116, I couldn't have helped it, I was so struck up in a heap at seeing her in sich a fix. *Ibid.* 152, I was so struck up with the room and the table that it was more than a minit afore I found out [etc.]. **1885** HOWELLS *Silas Lapham* (1891) I. 49 Did..that young man..seem struck up on Irene? asked the Colonel.

l. (See quot.)

1875 KNIGHT *Dict. Mech.*, *Striking-up Press*..A press for striking-up or raising sheet-metal in making dishes, pots, pans, cups, etc.

m. To cause (the lettering of a coin) to stand out.

1883 P. GARDNER *Types Gr. Coins* I. iii. 21 Sometimes the type is quite at the edge of the coin, sometimes it is confused and not fairly struck up.

X. 88. *Comb.* in phrases used as substantives or adjectives, as **strike-a-light**, a flint used for striking fire; **strike-anywhere** *a.*, that may be struck on any surface; **strike-back**, used *attrib.* to designate the capacity of making a retaliatory nuclear strike; **strike-fire** *slang*, gin; **strike me blind** *slang* (see quots.); **strike-me-dead** (*Naut. slang*), small beer; **strike-or-silent** (see quot.); **strike-out**, an out in baseball, called when a batter has made three strikes; also *attrib.* and *fig.*; **strike-over** *U.S.*, the typing of a character on a spot occupied by a character typed previously; **strike through** *Printing* (see quots.).

1870 E. T. STEVENS *Flint Chips* 588 Of the articles called '*strike-a-light' there is a small quantity annually exported to the East. **1870** *Spectator* 13 Aug. 976 Flakes..unfit for the manufacture of gun-flints are made into 'strike-a-lights,' for the use of the tinder-box. **1878** SOUTHALL *Epoch of Mammoth* xv. 272 M. de Mortillet..took the ground that ordinarily the flints found in Merovingian graves were either 'strike-a-lights' (pierres à feu) or amulettes. **1898** *Daily News* 4 June 7/2 Yellow phosphorus is absolutely necessary in the manufacture of '*strike anywhere' matches. **1962** *Listener* 29 Mar. 539/2 It was clear that we would soon ..have a sufficiently invulnerable *strike-back nuclear capacity. **1966** SCHWARZ & HADIK *Strategic Terminology* 44 *Strike-back capability*, nuclear forces which could survive an enemy first strike and then be used against him in a second strike. **1725** G. SMITH *Compl. Body Distill.* I. 49 Geneva hath..different names and titles..: as..Tittery, Collonia, *Strike-fire, &c. **1901** S. H. KING *Dog-Watches at Sea* 146 Rice was known as '*strike me blind'. **1936** B. M. ADAMS *Ships & Women* viii. 180 The dish..called 'strike-me-blind'. Boiled rice, with black-strap molasses. **1824** in *Spirit Publ. Jrnls.* (1825) 285 He had a taste for every species of fluid, from inferior '*strike me dead,' to the superlative grog. **1875** KNIGHT *Dict. Mech.*, **Strike-or-silent* (*Horology*), a piece in a clock which sets the striking parts in or out of action [etc.]. **1911** J. B. FOSTER *How to Pitch* 72 It happens to be a pitcher..of the *strike-out kind. **1922** E. J. LANIGAN *Baseball Cycl.* II. 39/1 Another top-notcher joined them in the person of Thomas Ramsey, eminent strike-out king. **1937** *Philadelphia Rec.* 23 Mar. 15/1 Mr. Roosevelt has.. grown into the stature of a strike-out king. **1967** *Boston Sunday Herald* 14 May II. 3/3 Six of his strikeouts came in those innings. **1978** M. PUZO *Fools Die* xvi. 170 After Pfc. Hiller was recalled, his case would be evaluated by a Regular Army board. Another strikeout. **1950** *Richmond* (Virginia) *Times-Dispatch* 3 Oct. 1/8 A patent on typewriter type designed to permit *strikeovers on letters in about 11 per cent of common typing errors. **1978** W. WHITE *W. Whitman's Daybooks & Notebooks* I. p. xxii, Corrections, strike-overs, inserted words..I have transcribed exactly the way Whitman has left them. **1958** T. LANDAU *Encycl. Librarianship* 290/2 **Strike through*, penetration of the type impression from the verso to the recto of a page due to improper pressure or faulty makeready. **1979** G. A. GLAISTER *Gloss. Bk.* (ed. 2) 464/1 *Strike through*, a fault caused when the oily medium in printing ink soaks into and through the paper, making it translucent.

strike: see STIRK, STREAK *sb.*[1], STREEK *v.*

[**strike**, *sb.* error for *stike*, STICK *sb.*[2]

1674 JEAKE *Arith.* (1696) 66. **1694** E. CHAMBERLAYNE *St. Eng.* III. ii. (ed. 18) 385. **1891** *Century Dict.*, *Strike*, *n.* 18, same as Stick[3] 10.]

†**strike-balk**, *v.* *Agric. Obs.* [Formation not clear: perh. orig. a phrase, STRIKE *v.* 16 + BALK *sb.*[1] 3; but cf. BALK *v.*[1] 1.] See quot. 1736: = REST-BALK *v.* (Young's explanation is app. due to misapprehension).

1736 J. LEWIS *I. of Tenet* (ed. 2) 39 *Strike-baulk*, to plough one Furrow, and leave another. **1784–1815** *Young's Annals Agric.* I. 308 (E.D.S.) Strike-balking. **1807** RUDGE *Agric. Glouc.* (1813) 110 In the neighbourhood of Stow..it is the practice, in dry seasons, to plough one furrow and leave one; which is called 'risbalking', or 'strike balking'.

striked (straɪkt), *ppl. a.* [f. STRIKE *v.* + -ED[1].] Of a bushel or other measure: Levelled with a strike or strickle: opposed to *heaped*.

1581 LAMBARDE *Eiren.* IV. iv. (1588) 435 If any such Purveior..have taken corne by any other measure then by the striked bushel. **1674** JEAKE *Arith.* (1696) 70 Meal in some places sold by Measure. In 1 Bushel 12 Gallons striked. **1725** *Bradley's Family Dict.* s.v. *Bushel*, Meal, Corn, and other Grain are now measured with strik'd Bushels, and without any Grain above the edges. **1844** H.

STEPHENS *Bk. Farm* III. 980 The heaped measure of the summer will tell out in an equal number of bushels of striked measure in spring. **1894** R. S. FERGUSON *Hist. Westmorld.* 137 Two old peck measures, one containing eight and the other ten striked quarts.

strikeless, dial. f. STRICKLE *sb.*

striker ('straɪkə(r)). [f. STRIKE *v.* + -ER[1].]

I. Designating a person.

†**1. a.** One who 'strikes' or roams as a vagrant. Cf. G. *landstreicher* vagrant. *Obs.*

1393 LANGL. *P. Pl.* C. x. 159 Lolleres lyuyng in sleuthe and ouer-londe strykers. *c* **1410** *Lanterne of Liȝt* 54 Strong staff-beggers & strikars ouere þe lond.

b. A footpad. *Obs.*

1596 SHAKS. *1 Hen. IV*, II. i. 82, I am ioyned with no Foot-land-Rakers, no Long-staffe six-penny strikers. **1611** *Second Maiden's Tragedy* 960 (Malone Soc.) One that robbes the mynde twenty tymes worse then any hywaie striker.

2. A person (or animal) that strikes (in various senses of the vb.). **a.** *gen.*

1581 SIDNEY *Apol. Poetrie* (Arb.) 50 Musick,..the most diuine striker of the sences. **1596** DALRYMPLE tr. *Leslie's Hist. Scot.* I. 123 Quhen Nout [cattle] fechtis togither ane be strukne to deid, na man knaweng the stryker, the beist that is hommil amang thame Judge giltie of the slachtir. *c* **1616** in Sprott *Scott. Liturgies Jas. VI* (1901) 18 That so blessing the hand of Thee the Striker, Thou that humblest, may in Thy own appointed time raise again. **1686** BLOME *Gentl. Recr.* II. 278/2 It is a Maxim [in Cock-fighting], That he that is a close sitter, is ever a narrow striker. **1742** JARVIS *2nd Pt. Quix.* II. x. II. 146 Don Quixote, seeing Sancho so evil intreated, made at the striker with his launce. **1810** BENTHAM *Packing* (1821) 199 'Two Juries' were struck: and 'in striking them, the official striker' was, 'to a certain extent'..influenced by this principle. **1876** EMERSON *Lett. & Soc. Aims* vii. 178 Against which no blow can be struck but it recoils on the striker. **1890** HENTY *Lee in Virginia* 30 Before the whip could again fall..Vincent..wrested it from the hands of the striker.

b. One addicted to striking; one who is ready to resort to blows. *nonce-use.*

1582 N. T. (Rhem.) *Tit.* i. 7 A Bishop must be..not giuen to wine, no striker [so **1611** and **1881**; Wycl. *smiter*, other versions *fighter*; Vulg. *percussorem*, Gr. πλήκτην].

†**c.** *Sc.* One who coins (money). *Obs.*

1449 *Sc. Acts Jas. II* (1814) II. 37/1 All falss strikaris of gold & siluer & of falss grotis & pennys. **1451** *Ibid.* 40/2 Al þe yrnis of þe kingis strikaris bathe of gold & siluer. **1678** SIR G. MACKENZIE *Crim. Laws Scot.* II. xii. §ii. (1699) 207 They should apprehend..the strikers of false Coyn.

†**d.** In indecent sense. Hence, a fornicator.

1593 *Passionate Morrice* in *Tell-trothes N.Y. Gift*, etc. (1876) 80 He cannot see a wench out-start the bounds of modestie, but straight he hollowes the sight of a striker, thinking it vnpossible that if shee want maidenly behauiour, shee can haue womanly honestie. **1596** NASHE *Saffron-Walden* T 1, In some Countreys no woman is so honorable as she that hath to doo with most men, and can giue the lustiest striker oddes by 25. times in one night. **1635** GLAPTHORNE *Lady Mother* IV. i. in Bullen *Old Pl.* II. 169 These are immodest devills that make modest ladyes become strickers. **1665** NEDHAM *Med. Medicinæ* 64 Which should be sad News to all the Strikers of both Sexes.

e. A horse given to kicking. *rare*[−1].

1693 *Ling. Rom. Dict., Eng.-Lat.*, A striker or striking horse, *calcitro.* **1970** J. H. GRAY *Boy from Winnipeg* 69, I also first got to know horses that were strikers.

f. *Coursing.* A dog trained to 'strike' the hare.

1861 H. KINGSLEY *Ravenshoe* xiii, Ruin is the quickest striker we have ever bred.

3. In certain industries.

a. A maker or moulder of bricks or tiles.

1585 Tyle-stricker [see TILE *sb.*[1] 6]. **1610** in *Engl. Hist. Rev.* (1898) XIII. 524 A Brick Striker. **1703** *Art's Improv.* I. 4 A Molder or Striker of Bricks with his Attendants, can strike about 9000 of Bricks in a Day.

b. One who 'strikes' fish with a spear or harpoon (also †*striker-out*). Also *U.S.* (see quot. 1891).

1697 DAMPIER *Voy.* I. 39 We..kept our Moskito-men, or strikers out, which brought aboard some half-grown Tortoise. **1764** C. BIDDLE *Autob.* (1883) 16 We touched at the Mosquito Shore, and hired one of the Indians they call a striker, that is, a man to supply the crew with fish, turtle [etc.]. **1827** O. W. ROBERTS *Voy. Centr. Amer.* 47 The natives are excellent hunters and strikers of fish. **1891** *Century Dict.*, *Striker*, In the menhaden-fishery (*a*) The man who manages the striker-boat. (*b*) A green hand who works at low wages while learning the business, but is one of the crew of a vessel.

c. *Mining.* (See quot.)

1824 MANDER *Derbysh. Miner's Gloss.* 70 *Striker*, the man who lands the Kibble or Corf of Ore, &c. at the Shaft-top.

d. In metal-working, the assistant operator who wields the heavy sledge-hammer.

1831 J. HOLLAND *Manuf. Metal* I. 140 By two hammer-men, a maker and a striker, they [the bars for rolled spades] are drawn out on the anvil. **1886** *Pall Mall Gaz.* 15 July 6/2 A blacksmith uses what influence he possesses over his striker, a bricklayer uses his over his labourer. **1887** HALL CAINE *Deemster* xxx. 195 The smith was hooping a cart-wheel, and his striker set down his sledge and tied up his leather apron to look on and listen.

e. One who 'strikes' corn, etc. off a measure.

1867 SIMMONDS *Dict. Trade* Suppl., *Striker*,..the man whose business it is to strike off the superfluous quantity from the top of a measure.

f. *Tanning.* One who smooths and stretches skins either by hand or by means of a machine. Also *striker-out.*

1921 *Dict. Occup. Terms* (1927) §338 *Striker, striker-out*, (i) lays wet hide or skin on a slate or marble slab or table, and rubs it with a hard 'slicker' tool, of stone or steel, to stretch it, drive out excess of moisture, smooth it, and to close grain; (ii) sets rollers of a machine..in motion..and passes skin or hide between revolving rollers. **1972** *Classification of Occupations* (Dept. Employment) III. 24/2 *Finishing machine operator*... Other titles include..Striker.

4. In various games: The player who is to 'strike'; *occas.* the player who has made a stroke. In *Assoc. Football* and *Hockey*, a forward whose main function is to seek to score goals. In *Rugby Football* = HOOKER[1] 6. Also *striker-out* in *Real Tennis*, etc. the one who plays the ball when first served.

1699 E. S——CY *Country Gentl. Vade M.* 55 (Tennis) Squire A. is a good Striker-out, but Squire B. is a better Back-hand. **1744** J. LOVE *Cricket* (1770) 5 Stiff Spectators quite inactive stand, Speechless, attending to the Striker's Hand. **1773** in *Waghorn's Cricket Scores* (1899) 95 Simmons standing so near the strikers, greatly intimidated the Hampshire gentlemen. **1816** [see PLAY *v.* 17 f]. **1862** *Sunday Mercury* (N.Y.) 13 July 6/2 The Excelsiors led off, Young being their first striker, and he sent the ball flying to left field. **1866** 'CAPT. CRAWLEY' *Billiard Bk.* iii. 18 In making your stroke, an instantaneous glance will be sufficient—a glance that rises from the Striker's-ball to the Object-ball. **1874** CHADWICK *Base Ball Man.* 52 The striker at the bat is called the batsman or 'striker' until he has hit a fair ball. **1884** *J. Marshall's Tennis Cuts* 14 The Server may not take a bisque after a fault; but the Striker-out may do so. **1891** W. G. GRACE *Cricket* viii. 235 It is the striker's duty to call [for a run] if the ball is hit in front of the wicket. **1963** J. GREAVES *Soccer* vii. 73 If John White or another Spurs' player is bringing the ball up..I move into a position ready to race through and be first to the ball when he pushes it forward. It is the ball goal-strikers dream of. *Ibid.* 74 Remember, the striker never takes it for granted..he goes after the ball on every occasion. **1973** *Daily Mail* 24 July 27/1 John White, Bristol's 30-year-old reserve hooker,..replaces ex-Coventry striker John Gray. **1974** M. WEIR *Women's Hockey for Seventies* 96 Before the ball is hit the right striker is sprinting out to the right wing and the right wing is cutting into the space she has made. *Ibid.* 8 It is confusing for a defence to have to cater for elusive strikers. **1974** *Encycl. Brit. Macropædia* 257/2 The striker does not have to run after he has hit the ball. **1980** *Daily Tel.* 20 Mar. 34/3 Wales, without Chester striker Ian Rush, could not break down the Irish defence.

5. A workman who is 'on strike'.

1850 *Athenæum* 7 Dec. 1282/3 A vast change must have come over the factory population ere a man possessing mill-property could dream of letting it out to strikers. **1865** in *Docum. Hist. Amer. Industr. Soc.* (1910) IX. 101 These two congresses might adopt the same rule respecting strikers, runaway apprentices, and trades' unions.

6. *U.S.* **a.** *Polit. slang.* One who seeks to effect a strike. Cf. STRIKE *sb.* 13 and *v.* 75 e.

1883 *Nation* (N.Y.) 6 Sept. 200/1 If he can elect such a ticket..he will take the field after election as a 'striker', and will offer his electoral votes to whichever candidate will give the highest 'terms'. **1884** *American* VIII. 99 Bracketing together the political 'strikers and heelers' with the commercial respectables.

b. *Mil.* An officer's batman or servant.

1867 CUSTER in Mrs. Custer *Tenting on Plains* (1888) 529 (Thornton) The Dutchman and Englishmen and the rest of the strikers. *Note*, Striker was the name of a soldier servant. **1898** *Harper's Mag.* Apr. 700/2 My 'striker' had just left me, with instructions to have my horse fed. **1929** B. DAVIS *Truth about Geronimo* 107 Geronimo's son demanded the post of striker (servant) to me. **1948** *Time* 14 June 9/3 He takes the same attitude toward Congress as he would to a striker who fails to put the proper polish on his boots.

c. A hired ruffian.

1836 *Spirit of Times* 9 July 162/2 An awkward looking *striker* of old Thompson's holding her by the cheek of the bridle. **1853** 'P. PAXTON' *Stray Yankee in Texas* 335 To a few he [*sc.* John Murel] confided the extent of his design, and to each of these gave the authority to enlist all the minor villains of their acquaintance. The latter were termed Strikers and used but as tools. **1859** BARTLETT *Dict. Amer.* (ed. 2) 457 *Striker*, a bruiser; a ruffian. *a* **1872** *Country Merchant* 317 (Schele de Vere) He was one of the most accomplished strikers, or barkers, as they are called, in the employ of the hells. **1873** J. H. BEADLE *Undevel. West* xi. 184, I had published a severe criticism of this Judge Smith. His 'strikers' now had me at Court as defendant. **1883** 'MARK TWAIN' *Life Mississippi* xxix. 315 [Murel's gang of robbers] was composed of two classes: the Heads or Council ..[and] the active agents..termed strikers.

d. An engineer's apprentice on a steamboat. Also in extended use: see quots. 1944, etc.

Cf. also quot. 1891 at sense 3 b.

1872 [see *mud-clerk* s.v. MUD *sb.*[1] 5]. **1875** 'MARK TWAIN' in *Atlantic Monthly* XXXV. 70/2 He turned up as apprentice engineer or 'striker' on a steamboat. **1944** K. D. MCCRACKEN *Baby Flat-Top* 53 In the Navy a striker is a seaman or fireman who is working particularly hard in order to convince his superiors that he ought to become a petty officer of some kind. **1955** C. S. FORESTER *Good Shepherd* 104 An electrician's mate and his striker stood behind him. **1963** *Amer. Speech* XXXVIII. 45 *Striker*, a [truck] driver's helper. **1970** *National Fisherman* Aug. 21-A/1 Emery Brown as rigman or 'striker' [on a shrimp boat]..testified in person during this trial.

II. A thing that strikes or is used for striking.

7. *gen.*

1644 DIGBY *Nat. Bodies* xii. (1645) 124 The missives.. must be so heavy that the aire may not break their course; and yet so light, that they may be within the command of the stroke which giveth them motion; the striker must be dense, and in its best velocity. **1901** ALLDRIDGE *Sherbro* xxvi. 289 To these again are attached little rings, and as the hands work the strikers, these jingling irons make a pleasant tinkling sound. **1911** E. BEVERIDGE *N. Uist* x. 325 Although the writer was able to obtain an ornamented steel 'striker' —for use with a flint..—the tinder-box seems quite unknown.

†**8.** A farrier's instrument (see quot.). *Obs.* (Cf. STRIKE *v.* 33 d.)

1688 HOLME *Armoury* III. 324/2 A Blooding stick or Striker..is a heavy piece of Wood, wherewith the Fleme is smitten or driven into the Horse Neck Vein, when he is Blooded.

9. a. = STRICKLE *sb.* 1 a. **b.** = STRICKLE *sb.* 1 b.

a. 1714 BUDGELL tr. *Theophrastus* xi. 38 He has a Measure of a particular make for the use of his Domesticks, which he piles up very high, and is so dextrous at the management of it that with one sweep of the Striker he brushes off half their Dinner. **1828** CARR *Craven Gloss.*

b. 1693 MOXON *Mech. Exerc.* 248 A Striker..is only a piece of Lath..with which they strike, or cut off the Morter at the britches of the Tiles. **1764** CROKER, etc. *Dict. Arts* s.v. *Bricks*, The striker, or tool with which the moulder strikes off the superfluous earth in making bricks. **1842** GWILT *Encycl. Archit.* § 1908 The *striker*, a piece of lath about 10 inches long, for separating and taking away the superfluous mortar at the feet of the tiles.

10. A clock or watch that strikes. (Chiefly with qualifying adj.)

1778 BARRINGTON in *Archæologia* V. 426 Some of the watches used at this time seem to have been strikers. **1864** G. MUSGRAVE *Ten Days Fr. Parsonage* I. viii. 229 A large cased eight-day clock, the loudest striker I ever heard. **1869** MRS. H. WOOD *Roland Yorke* Prol. i, The clock of the old grey church struck twelve. A loud striker at all times, it sounded strangely so in the stillness of the night.

11. A harpoon. (Simmonds *Dict. Trade* 1858.)

12. A steam-hammer designed as a substitute for the blacksmith's 'striker' (see 3 d).

1869 C. KNIGHT *Mechanician* 91 Striker is a name given.. to substitutes and supersedes of hammermen, such as air-hammers and steam-hammers, whether vertical or horizontal. **1875** KNIGHT *Dict. Mech.*

13. The piece of mechanism in a gun, fuse, etc. which explodes the charge.

1824 COL. HAWKER *Instr. Young Sporstm.* (ed. 3) 74 The cock, or striker, should cover the nipple with a deep concave head. **1856** 'STONEHENGE' *Brit. Sports* I. I. viii. 70/2 The striker explodes this tube, just as the flint set fire to the powder in the pan of the old flint-gun. **1882** J. H. WALSH *Sportsman's Gun & Rifle* I. 263 Strikers. This necessary part of the hammerless gun is either of one piece with the tumbler,..or jointed to it,..or entirely detached.

14. That part of a bell, clock, etc. which strikes.

1872 ELLACOMBE *Ch. Bells Devon* Suppl. i. 196 The clapper or striker [of a bell]. **1897** *Westm. Gaz.* 29 Apr. 10/2 The striker [of the clock] was prevented from working.

15. The automatic regulator of the striking of the pens of a ruling machine.

1875 KNIGHT *Dict. Mech.* 2001/2 s.v. *Ruling-machine.* **1888** JACOBI *Printers' Voc.*, *Striker*, the apparatus attached to a machine for 'striking on', or putting it in motion. **1909** *Daily Chron.* 26 June 8/5 Machine Ruler wanted for double striker.

16. A hardened mould upon which a softened steel block is struck to receive a concave impression.

1843 HOLTZAPFFEL *Turning* I. 232 A solid mould, core or striker, exactly a copy of the work to be produced, is made. **1875** KNIGHT *Dict. Mech.*

17. A preparation for 'striking' or fixing a dye; a mordant.

1884 *Health Exhib. Catal.* 38 The colour is then made fast with what is known as a 'striker', a chemical preparation suited to the colour.

III. **18.** *attrib.* and *Comb.*, as ***striker hand***, ***-machine*** (sense 15); **striker-boat** *U.S.*, in menhaden fishing = DRIVE-*boat*; hence ***striker boatsman***; **striker-plate** = *striking plate* (see STRIKING *vbl. sb.* 3).

1884 KNIGHT *Dict. Mech.* Suppl., Striker Plate. **1891** Striker boat [see sense 3 b]. **1898** *Daily Chron.* 24 Sept. 10/6 Machine Ruler..wanted..; must be used to striker machines. **1902** *Ibid.* 28 Oct. 10/7 Machine Ruler.—Good striker hand. **1950** *Richmond* (Va.) *Times-Dispatch* 23 July (Mag. Section) 5/1 When a bunch [of fish] is spotted, a striker boat, manned by a striker boatsman, is sent out to indicate the direction in which the fish are moving.

striking ('straɪkɪŋ), *vbl. sb.* [f. STRIKE *v.* + -ING[1].]

1. a. The action of STRIKE *v.*, in various senses.

c **1400** *Laud Troy Bk.* 7389 Of his scheld a ful quartere He carff a-wey at that strikyng. **1485** *Naval Acc. Hen. VII* (1896) 22 His wages vj[s] viij[d] workyng about the said Ship.. preparyng the strikyng of her mast. **1572** *Charters* etc. *Peebles* (1872) 341 The counsale ordanis Robert Thomsone ..to vse the stryking of the swische nychtlie to the wauche. **1592** SHAKS. *Ven. & Ad.* 250 Strucke dead at first, what needs a second striking? **1631** B. JONSON *New Inn* I. iii, It should not come, me thinkes, Vnder your cap, this veine of salt, and sharpnesse! These strikings vpon learning, now and then! **1668** DRYDEN *Dram. Poesie* 43 [Jonson] has allow'd a very inconsiderable time, after Catiline's Speech, for the striking of the battle, and the return of Petreius, who is to relate the event of it to the Senate. **1820** T. HODGSON *Ess. Stereotype Printing* 104 Herhan applied this machine to the striking of his types. **1874** A. J. ELLIS *Early Eng. Pronunc.* IV. xi. 1329 An *r* made by a striking of the tongue against the teeth, gums, or roof of the mouth. **1897** *Encycl. Sport* I. 264/2 (Curling) *Striking*, hitting with a stone another placed on the tee with sufficent force to drive it out of the circle.

b. with *adverbs.*

1530 PALSGR. 277/2 Strykyng agayne, *repercussion.* Strykyng togyder, *collision.* **1582** T. WATSON *Centurie of Love* To Rdr., Virgill in expressing the striking downe of an oxe, letteth the end of his hexameter fall withall. **1619** ABP. ABBOT in Rushw. *Hist. Collect.* (1659) I. 12 Our striking-in will comfort the Bohemians. **1721** MORTIMER *Husb.* (ed. 5) I. 388 The Price for plowing of Land with us is four

Shillings an Acre, for each striking of it over, two Shillings an Acre. **1865** DICKENS *Mut. Fr.* II. i, 'I don't like that', said Bradley Headstone. His pupil was a little surprised by this striking-in with so sudden..an objection.

†**c.** An assault. *Obs.*

1541 *Act 33 Hen. VIII*, c. 12 §1 Murders, manslaughters and other malicious strikinges..commytted within the lymittes of the Kinges palace.

d. *Building, Carpentry*, etc. (See quot. 1842.)

1735 J. PRICE *Stone Br. Thames* 8 To facilitate the striking of the Centers to each Arch. **1842** GWILT *Archit.* Gloss., *Striking*, a term used to denote the draught of lines on the surface of a body;..also..the drawing of lines on the face of a piece of stuff for mortises, and cutting the shoulders of tenons... [Also].. the act of running a moulding with a plane. The striking of a centre is the removal of the timber framing upon which an arch is built, after its completion. **1898** *Daily News* 17 May 2/6 The striking of the centering round the north light was the cause of the accident.

e. *Tanning.* The process of smoothing and stretching skins. Also ***striking-out***. Freq. *attrib.*

a **1877** KNIGHT *Dict. Mech.* III. 2429/1 Striking-machine. **1882** *Encycl. Brit.* XIV. 385/2 For striking or pinning by hand the hide is dampened with water, thrown over a beam, and worked all over the grain side with a striking pin. *Ibid.*, Striking machines are now very generally used for the operation. **1897** C. T. DAVIS *Manuf. Leather* (ed. 2) 378 The 'striking out' was performed on mahogany tables. **1920** *Conquest* Nov. 38/3 Stretching and smoothing [hides] with a striking-pin (a two-handled tool triangular in sections). **1942, 1953** [see SETTING *vbl. sb.*[1] 13 a].

2. †**a.** ? A paralytic stroke, paralysis. *Obs.*

1599 A. M. tr. *Gabelhouer's Bk. Physic* 26/2 Water of Mayflowers for the strickinge. *Ibid.*, An excellente.. Confectione, for the strikinge of the hande of God.

b. A disease in calves; also ***blood-striking*** [= G. *blutschlag*].

1776 *Compl. Grazier* (ed. 4) 21 To prevent Stricking of Calves. **1861** *Jrnl. R. Agric. Soc.* XXII. I. 145 Blood-striking, or quarter-ill, is hardly known. **1887** *Field* 19 Feb. 260/1 Quarter-ill or Striking.

3. *attrib.* and *Comb.*, as ***striking force***; in designations of mechanism concerned in producing the striking of a clock, as ***striking barrel, part, -pin, train, -weight, -wheel, -work***; in names of tools or appliances used for striking (in various senses), as ***striking-bar, -board, -hammer, staff, wedge***. Also **striking-box**, the metal box on a door-jamb which receives the end of the bolt of the lock when the door is locked; **striking-circle** *Hockey* (see quots.); **striking distance**, (*a*) the distance within which it is possible to strike a blow; (*b*) *Electr.* (see quot. 1893); **striking-earth** *Agric.*, soil for roots to strike in; **striking force**, (*a*) the force with which a projectile strikes; (*b*) a military force held in readiness for sudden attack; **striking gear**, in a saw-mill (see quot.); **striking-house**, (*a*) *Mining* (see quot.); (*b*) *Agric.* a house in which seeds, etc. are placed to 'strike', before they are planted out; **striking-iron**, a kind of harpoon; **striking knife**, †(*a*) a heavy knife for kitchen use; (*b*) *Leather-manuf.*, a triangular steel knife for scraping hides (Knight *Dict. Mech.* 1875); (*c*) *Carpentry*, a knife for marking or scribing (cf. sense 1 d); **striking-line**, a harpoon line; **striking magnet** *Electr.* (see quot.); **striking-plate**, (*a*) the metal plate against which the end of a spring-lock bolt strikes, when the door or lid is being closed; (*b*) (see quot. *a* 1877); **striking platform** *Archæol.*, a flat area on a core of flint or stone on which a blow is struck to detach a flake; **striking-plough** (see quot. 1805); **striking price** *Stock Exch.* (see quots. 1973, 1982); **striking-reed** *Mus.*, a percussion reed (Stainer & Barrett); **striking-ring** *Billiards*, the D or half-circle in which a player whose ball is in hand must place it to make a stroke; **striking-tache** *Sugar manuf.* (see TACHE *sb.*[3] 1).

1850 DENISON *Clock & Watch-m.* 131 A pin in the *striking barrel. **1885** [HORNER] *Pattern Making* 68 The first *striking board, C, notched to correspond to the semi-diameter of the flange, minus half the diameter of the *striking bar, D,..will be swept over this surface. **1896** A. MORRISON *Child Jago* xxxiii. 308 Josh..forced the *striking-box of the lock off its screws. **1890** F. S. CRESWELL *Hockey* 11 No goal can be scored unless the ball be hit by one of the attacking side from within the *striking circle. **1906** *Official Handbk. Hockey Assoc.* 120 In front of each goal shall be drawn a white line 4 yds. long, parallel to, and 15 yds from, the goal line. This line shall be continued each way to meet the goal line by quarter-circles having the goal posts as centres. The space enclosed by these lines and the goal lines, including the lines themselves, shall be called the striking circle. **1961** F. C. AVIS *Sportsman's Gloss.* 219/1 *Striking circle*, in Hockey the space immediately in front of goal, really a rough *semi*-circle, 15 yards from the goal line. **1751** B. FRANKLIN *Exper. & Observations Electricity* 62 A needle ..will draw the fire from the scale silently at a much greater than the *striking distance. **1767** —— *Of Lightning* etc. Wks. 1840 V. 415 The distance at which a body charged with this fluid will discharge itself suddenly, striking through the air into another body that is not..so highly charged, is different according to the quantity [etc.]... This distance, whatever it happens to be between any two bodies, is called their striking distance, as, till they come within that distance of each other, no stroke will be made. **1804** T. JEFFERSON *Writ.* (1830) IV. 20 While fortune then places us within striking distance, let us avail ourselves of it. **1870** *Daily News* 20 Dec., The north-westward movement of Chanzy brought him within striking distance of the German Corps at Chartres. **1893** SLOANE *Electr. Dict.* 496 *Striking distance*, the distance that separates two conductors charged with electricity of different potential, when a spark starts between them. **1863** *Jrnl. R. Agric. Soc.* XXIV. I. 224 It may then be laid about 2 feet deep, and 6 inches of loose *striking-earth spread upon it. **1881** GREENER *Gun* 182 The various calculations respecting the *striking force of rifles. **1917** T. E. LAWRENCE *Lett.* (1938) 230 Force 3 is our striking force (of perhaps 6,000 not bad men) and may be able to rush Deraat, or at least should cut off the garrison there. **1944** [see *air strike* s.v. AIR *sb.*[1] B. III 2)]. **1965** J. A. MICHENER *Source* (1966) 793 The well-trained Jews of the Palmach—an abbreviation for the Plugat Machatz, 'striking force', organized in 1941 to resist the threatened German invasion. **1883** M. P. BALE *Saw-mills* 336 **Striking gear*, known also as belt gear, is an arrangement of levers for stopping or starting machinery by throwing the driving belt off or on the driving pulley. **1865** H. KINGSLEY *Hillyars & Burtons* v, My father stepped across to the [blacksmith's] shop for a trifle of a *striking hammer, weight eighteen pounds. **1824** MANDER *Derbysh. Miner's Gloss.* 70 **Striking-house*, a sheltered place where the Striker stands, either at the top or middle length of an engine. **1863** *Jrnl. R. Agric. Soc.* XXIV. I. 221 In order to test the goodness of some yellow globe-seed,..I had ordered some to be..raised in a striking-house. **1817** *Q. Rev.* Oct. 217 Harpoons and *striking-irons. **1578** *Knaresb. Wills* (Surtees) I. 133 In the kitching..one *striking knyfe, one flesh axe. **1901** J. BLACK *Carp. & Build., Home Handicr.* 15 In place of a pencil many prefer to mark the stuff across with a 'striking knife' (fig. 4) and try square. **1827** O. W. ROBERTS *Voy. Centr. Amer.* 57 The fishing Indians of the coast..use them as *striking lines for securing turtle, &c. **1897** *Outing* XXIX. 470/1 The striking-line ordinarily used on the coast is three-sixteenths, medium-laid, white cotton line. **1898** SLOANE *Electr. Dict.* (ed. 2) 622 **Striking magnet* (*a*) An electro-magnet used in an arc lamp to separate the carbons..so as to form or 'strike' the arc. (*b*) An electro-magnet used to ring a bell, by having a hammer attached to its armature. **1675** J. S[MITH] *Horol. Dial.* I. ii. 10 *Striking part. **1825** J. NICHOLSON *Oper. Mech.* 497 The striking part of this clock. **1696** W. DERHAM *Artific. Clock-m.* ii. 34 The Pin-wheel is 78, the *Striking-pins are 13. **1837** HEBERT *Engin. & Mech. Encycl.* II. 108 The patentees cause this part [*sc.* the bolt] to drop into a notch in the *striking plate after it has been elevated by passing over an inclined plane upon it. **1856** G. PRICE *Fire & Thief-proof Depositories* etc. 811 Spring locks are those in which the bolt locks itself out by coming in contact with the striking-plate. *a* **1877** KNIGHT *Dict. Mech.* III. 2429/2 *Striking-plate*, the device by which the wooden centering of an arch is lowered when the arch is completed. **1913** *Proc. Prehistoric Soc. E. Anglia* I. III. 311 The flaking..is of a very high order, dexterous vertical blows, with well-masked cones of percussion, and *striking platforms being supplemented by the most regular and fine edge-work. **1949** K. P. OAKLEY *Man Tool-Maker* 25 Each blow is delivered obliquely downwards near the edge of some conveniently placed flattish area (the striking platform), usually the scar of a flake previously struck off. **1977** L. L. JOHNSON in Hill & Gunn *Individual in Prehistory* x. 218 Collapsed platforms were noted only where there was no retouch on the striking platform. **1805** R. W. DICKSON *Pract. Agric.* I. 470 In some parts of Kent..an implement is often employed which they term a **striking plough*, by which little drills or channels are formed in the ground for the reception of the seed, about ten inches distant from each other. **1961** K. S. MOST *How to make Money on Stock Exch.* iii. 35 Suppose I have a..well-founded belief that Woolworths' shares are going to rise in price..I shall have to pay out £335 plus purchase costs for every 100 shares. I may not have this money available..so I arrange to give the price of a call option, say, 5s. per share, for the right to buy 100 Woolworths' shares at any time during the next twelve weeks at a price of, say, 66s., being the '*striking price' at the end of the previous Account. **1973** N. SEARLE *Successful Investments* 85 *Striking price*, the price at which the holder of an option has the right to effect a purchase or sale. **1982** *Times* 9 Nov. 19 With a tender offer for sale, investors tender at the price they are prepared to pay. The issuing house works down the list to the lowest price at which the issue is totally subscribed. This becomes the 'striking price'. **1875** A. J. ELLIS *Helmholtz' Sensat. Tone* App. 712 The harshness of the *striking reed is obviated in the English method of voicing. **1814** C. JONES *Hoyles' Games Impr.* 378 [Billiards.] In stringing, the striker must place his ball within the *striking ring. **1697** DAMPIER *Voy.* I. 35 His *striking staff ..is about 8 foot long, almost as big as a mans Arm, at the great end, in which there is a hole to place his Harpoon in. **1830** G. R. PORTER *Sugar Cane* vii. 83 The cane liquor..is transferred to the third boiler, and so on to the last,..which is called the *striking teache. **1884** F. J. BRITTEN *Watch & Clockm.* 249 Connection is made between the *striking train and the *striking work by the gathering pallet. **1834–6** BARLOW in *Encycl. Metrop.* (1845) VIII. 95/1 This acting upon the surface of the *striking wedges equal to 540 square feet gives a pressure of 140 pounds per square inch. **1844** *Civil Engin. & Arch. Jrnl.* VII. 246/2 The striking-wedges were of seasoned oak, well greased. **1845** G. DODD *Brit. Manuf.* IV. 189 In the Limehouse clock the going-weight is about sixty pounds, whereas the *striking-weight is a mass of iron weighing five hundred pounds. **1704** J. HARRIS *Lex. Techn.* I, **Striking-Wheel*, in a Clock, is that which by some is called the *Pin-wheel*. **1876** *Encycl. Brit.* IV. 311/2 Figure 55 shows the *striking plates* and *wedges* by which the centre is lowered after the completion of the arch.

striking ('straɪkɪŋ), *ppl. a.* [f. STRIKE *v.*[1] + -ING[2].] That strikes.

1. *gen.*

c **1611** CHAPMAN *Iliad* xv. 654 Not a shaft, nor farre-of striking dart, Was vsde through all. **1676** MACE *Musicks Mon.* 109 When you would perform This Grace, it is but to strike your Letter,..with one of your Fingers, and immediately clap on your next striking Finger, upon the String which you struck. **1875** A. J. ELLIS tr. *Helmholtz' Sensat. Tone* I. v. 144 Formerly, striking vibrators or reeds were employed, which on each oscillation struck against their frame.

†**b.** Of a horse: Addicted to kicking. *Obs.*

1661 LOVELL *Hist. Anim. & Min.* 257 The decoction helps striking Horses.

2. Of a clock or watch: **a.** Constructed so as to be capable of striking.

[**1611** FLORIO, *Horologio*, any kind of clock, horologe, or striking-houre instrument.] **1625** in Rymer *Fœdera* XVIII. 238/1 A high Salte of Goulde..with a striking Clocke in the Cover. **1659** TORRIANO, *Horologiografia*, a description of striking-clocks or horologes. **1665** HOOKE *Microgr.* 134, I have heard of a striking Watch so small, that it serv'd for a pendant in a Ladies ear. **1862** *Catal. Internat. Exhib., Brit.* II. No. 3316, Eight-day turret striking clock, with four faces. **1873** NELTHROPP *Watch-work* 87 A striking watch, by Marwick, of London. A.D. 1680.

b. That is in the act of striking.

1732 FIELDING *Covent-Gard. Trag.* II. vii, Twice and once I've told the striking Clock's increasing Sound, And yet unkind Stormandra stays away. **1905** R. BAGOT *Passport* xi. 100 At length, however, a striking clock had roused Monsieur d'Antin.

3. That strikes the attention of an observer; producing a vivid impression on the mind; telling, impressive, unusually remarkable.

Prob. imitated from the similar use of F. *frappant*.

1752 SIR H. BEAUMONT *Crito* 7 Tho' Colour be the lowest of all the constituent Parts of Beauty, yet is it vulgarly the most striking, and the most observed. **1755** JOHNSON, *Striking*, affecting, surprising. **1759** —— *Rasselas* x, Or whether,..the first writers took possession of the most striking objects for description. **1765** *Museum Rust.* IV. 99 This gentleman..has written the following very striking passage. **1788** *New Lond. Mag.* Mar. 142 Account of Mr. Alderman Bell. Embellished with a striking Likeness. **1818** SCOTT *Rob Roy* xix, The principal street was..of an architecture rather striking than correct in point of taste. **1820** *Q. Mus. Mag.* II. 19 The Fugata itself forms a striking contrast with the succeeding movement by Leal and Rego. **1858** J. BLACKWOOD in Mrs. G. Porter *Ann. Publishing Ho.* (1898) III. 47 The story is a very striking one, and I cannot recollect anything at all of the same kind. **1859** JEPHSON *Brittany* viii. 114 The dress of the peasants is striking.

Comb. **1855** D. COSTELLO *Stories fr. Screen* 116 Alfred Washball was one of the most striking-looking..members of the profession. **1894** CONAN DOYLE *Mem. Sherlock Holmes* 218 She was a striking-looking woman.

4. *Naut.* Of a mast: Capable of being struck or lowered.

1677 *Lond. Gaz.* No. 1192/4 The *Dolphin* of *Ostend*,..a striking Top-mast, a square Stern, and an open Vessel. **1861** SMILES *Engineers* II. 270 Coasters and even colliers, with striking masts, might then be able to navigate the whole extent of the City westward.

5. Of a workman, etc.: That is on strike.

1894 *Westm. Gaz.* 11 June 3/2 Presently some men come in, with..the badge of the striking cabby..pinned on their coats. **1898** HAMBLEN *Gen. Manager's Story* xiv. 229 No striking employee would be allowed to trespass on the company's property during the continuance of the strike.

Hence '**strikingness**.

1818 TODD. **1839** *Fraser's Mag.* XX. 701 If strikingness of character be at all an object worth attending to. **1889** *Spectator* 28 Dec., Oratorical power, be it eloquence, as with Mr. Gladstone, or strikingness of phrase, as with Lord Beaconsfield.

strikingly ('straɪkɪŋlɪ), *adv.* [f. STRIKING *ppl. a.* + -LY[2].] In a striking manner or degree.

1752 W. DODD *Beauties Shaks.* (1757) I. 114 Caliban's Exultation..has something in it very strikingly in Character. **1817** MALTHUS *Popul.* III. 166 The reasonings of the foregoing chapter have been strikingly confirmed by the events of the last two or three years. **1854** GRACE GREENWOOD *Haps & Mishaps* 129 The scenery of Ayr is not grand, surely, nor strikingly picturesque; but [etc.]. **1888** W. J. SOLLAS in *Challenger Rep.* XXV. 212 The canal system presents a strikingly open appearance.

strikle, obs. variant of STRICKLE.

†**strim-stram.** *Obs.* [Echoic; cf. STRUM-STRUM, and *strim-strum* (in *Eng. Dial. Dict.*).] A rude stringed instrument of the guitar kind.

c **1730** RAMSAY *Gentleman in Country* 82 Your strim-strams and your jingling bells. **1771–2** *Ess. fr. Batchelor* (1773) I. 55 The nerves of the one, like the strings of a fiddle, vibrate on the slightest touch; whilst the other's, like the cords of a Strim-stram, scarce bend under the rough hand of a porter.

strincate, ? earlier form of TRINKET *sb.*[1]

1489 *Extracts Aberd. Reg.* (1844) I. 45 His tresour, strincates, and artalzery.

strinc(k)le: see STRINKLE *sb.* and *v.*

†**strind**[1]. *Obs.* In later use only *Sc.* Forms: 1 (ȝi)strýnd, 3 strund, strend, 5–6 strynd(e, 3–6 strind, 7, 9 strine, 9 stryne, streind. See also STRAND *sb.*[3] [OE. (Anglian) strýnd fem., also *ȝestreónd, ȝistrýnd*, f. (*ȝe*)*strienan* to produce, beget: see STRENE *v.* Cf. STRAIN *sb.*[1]]

1. Generation, descent, lineage; a race, breed, stock; offspring, progeny; = STRAIN *sb.*[1] 4–7.

c **900** *Bæda's Hist.* v. vii. (1890) 406 Se wæs eac of ðære cynelican strynde [L. *de stirpe regia*]. *c* **950** *Lindisf. Gosp.* Matt. xix. 28 Sittes ȝie ofer seatla tuelf doemende twoelf strynda israeles. *c* **1000** *Rit. Dunelm.* (Surtees) 29 *Progeniem*, soð ȝistrynd. *c* **1205** LAY. 2736 Swiðe riche cnihten of Troinisce cunne þa weoren in Lumbardie of heore strund. *a* **1225** *Juliana* 55 Wel bi semeð þe..to beo streon of a swuch strunde. *a* **1300** *E.E. Psalter* ix. 27 [x. 6] Fra strend in strende [L. *a generatione in generationem*]. *c* **1425** WYNTOUN *Orig. Cron.* I. vii. 332 In Egipt.. Giandis grew, and of þat strynd Come Anachyn. **1513** DOUGLAS *Æneis* VI. x. 47 Heir was the noble kyn and ancyant strynd, The maist dochty lynage sprang be kynd Fra king Teucer. **1570** *Sat. Poems Reform.* xxiv. 13 Degenerat Stewartis of ane Hieland strynde. **1603** *Proph. of Merlin* (Bannatyne Club) 12 That commed are of strodlings strynd.

2. An inherited quality or disposition; individual nature or character; = STRAIN *sb.*[1] 8.

1508 DUNBAR *Flyting* 55 Thy trechour tung hes tane ane heland strynd. **1513** DOUGLAS *Æneis* VIII. viii. 129 Ne war that of the blude of this ilk land Admixit standis he, taikand sum strynd, Apone his moderis syd, of Sabyn kynd. *a* **1568** A. SCOTT *Poems* (S.T.S.) iii. 5 For, knew ȝe wemenis natur, course, and strynd, ȝe wald nocht be so trew to thair vntrewth. **1710** RUDDIMAN *Gloss. Douglas' Æneis* s.v., The word *strynd* or *strain* is Metaphorically used for the resemblance of the features of the body, or of the dispositions of the mind. As we say, He has a strynd or strain of his Grand-Father, i.e. resembles him. [Jam. 1808 adds: It is also said, He takes a streind of such an one.] *a* **1807** J. SKINNER *Amusem. Leis. Hours* (1809) 95 And do't he will, I ken his stryne, As far 's he can.

3. (In form *strine*.) = STRAIN *sb.*[1] 3.

a **1667** SKINNER *Etymol.*, A cocks *Stride*, vel, ut melius in agro Linc. efferunt, a cocks *Strine*, Aristot. χάλαζαι seu Grandines. **1886** *S.W. Linc. Gloss.*, *Strine*.

† **strind**[2]. *Obs.* Forms: 3 strunde, 4–5 strynde, 5 strind, (9 *dial.* strine). See also STRAND *sb.*[2] [Early ME. *stründe*.

The word has the appearance of a ppl. derivative from the root of STREAM *sb.*; but it is found in no other Teut. lang.]

A stream, rivulet.

a **1225** *Ancr. R.* 188 Þe blodi streames [*v.rr.* strundes, strunden] urnen adun. *a* **1240** *Ureisum* in *O.E. Hom.* I. 187 Þe strunden þe striken adun of þine deorwurþe fet. **13..** *E.E. Allit. P.* C. 311 Þy stryuande stremez of stryndes so mony. *c* **1400** *Sc. Trojan War* I. 263 The stryndes in dyuerse places were Rynnand throw gravaile quhyt & clene. *c* **1450** *St. Cuthbert* (Surtees) 6675 It takes name of a watir strynde, Þe whilk þat tyme was calde lynde. **1456** SIR G. HAY *Bk. Knighthood* Wks. (S.T.S.) II. 6 A faire well of water.. quhilk in divers stryndis past throu the herber till othir gardynis. **1456** [see SINK-HOLE[1]]. [**1841** HARTSHORNE *Salop. Ant.* Gloss., *Strine*, a ditch. **1879** MISS JACKSON *Shropsh. Word-bk.*, *Strine*, a water-channel.]

† **strind**[3]. *Obs.*[−1] (Sense obscure; ? corrupt.)

c **1250** *Owl & Night.* 242 (Cott. MS.) By daie þu art stare-blind þat þu ne siehst ne boȝ ne strind [*secunda manu* ne bov ne rind; *Jesus MS.* bouh of lynd].

† **strind**[4]. *Obs.*[−1] In 6 strynde. [? related to STRAIN *sb.*[3] or STRAND *sb.*[4]] A streak, vein.

1523–34 FITZHERB. *Husb.* §55 If he [a sheep] be ruddy, and haue reed stryndes [*c* 1545 stringes] in the white of the eye, than he is sounde; and if the eye be white, lyke talowe, and the stryndes darke-coloured, thanne he is rotten.

Strindbergian (strɪnd'bɜːgɪən), *a.* [f. the name of the Swedish dramatist Johan August *Strindberg* (1849–1912) + -IAN.] Of, pertaining to, or characteristic of Strindberg or his writings.

1913 G. B. SHAW *Quintessence of Ibsenism* (Completed ed.) Pref. p. xiii, An eminent bacteriologist filled three columns of The Times with a wild Strindbergian letter. **1934** C. LAMBERT *Music Ho!* iv. 265 It [*sc.* Soupault's *Death of Nick Carter*] reads.. like an elaborate stage direction from some super-Strindbergian play. **1954** *Encounter* May 51/1 [The Swedes] are inclined to examine themselves with a touch of Strindbergian introspection. **1966** J. FOWLES *Magus* xliv. 281 Brought up, like bacilli in a test-tube, on a culture of such pure Strindbergian melancholia. **1974** R. RENDELL *Face of Trespass* viii. 70 An old Swedish film full of pale Strindbergian people.

† **strindle.** *Obs.* In 6 stryndle. Corrupt form of TRINDLE.

c **1500** *Durham Acc. Rolls* (Surtees) 251 Repar. le stryndle et muri lapidei molendini.

Strine (straɪn), *a.* and *sb. joc.* (orig. *Austral.*). Also 'strine. [imit. of alleged Austral. pronunc. of *Australian*, coined by Alistair Morrison in 1964 under the pseudonym 'Afferbeck Lauder' (Strine pronunc. of 'alphabetical order').]

A. *adj.* Australian. **B.** *sb.* **a.** An Australian. **b.** The English language as (allegedly) spoken by Australians.

1964 A. MORRISON in *Sydney Morning Herald* (Sat. Mag.) 19 Dec., (*heading*) New light on the Strine language, by Afferbeck Lauder, Professor of Strine Studies, University of Sinny. *Ibid.*, Selected translations of everyday words will be of interest.. also to overseas vistas and to the many New Strines in our mist. **1965** 'A. LAUDER' (*title*) Let stalk Strine. **1965** *Listener* 2 Sept. 340/1 While I was there they discovered a new dialect or speech pattern called Strine. Strine is simply the way the word 'Australian' sounds if you slur and twist it enough. **1967** *Daily Express* 6 May 13/6 He said in a broad Strine accent: [etc.]. **1973** E. MCGIRR *Bardel's Murder* iv. 93 Iced beer stops up the nose which is why you Yanks and also the Strines talk so funny. **1974** *Times* 21 Dec. 10/6 'The *legs*, Ealing, go for the *legs*!' she exhorted in a strong 'strine accent. **1980** [see ROOMETTE].

string (strɪŋ), *sb.* Forms: 1–6 streng, (*pl.* 3 strengen, -us, 3–6 strenges), 4 streing, strenge, 4–6 strynge, 4–7 stringe, 5–6 stryng, 5– string. [OE. *stręng* masc. = MLG. *strenk*, *strenge*, MDu. *strenghe*, *stringhe* (mod.Du. *streng* fem.), ON. *streng-r* masc. (Da. *streng*, Sw. *sträng*):—OTeut. type **straŋgi-z*; another declensional form is found in MLG. *strank*, *strange* masc., OHG. *stranc* masc. (MHG. *stranc*, *strange* masc., fem., mod.G. *strang* masc.):—OTeut. type **straŋgo-z*, f. **straŋg-* :—pre-Teut. **stroŋk-*: **streŋk-*.

The pre-Teut. root **streŋk-* appears not to be known in this form, but a parallel form **streŋg-* is represented by Irish (and Sc. Gaelic) *sreang* cord, string, M. Irish *srincne* navel-string, Gr. στραγγάλη halter, L. *stringĕre* to bind, draw tight. Connexion with STRONG *a.* is doubtful.]

I. A line, cord, thread.

1. A line for binding or attaching anything; normally one composed of twisted threads of spun vegetable fibre.

†**a.** In early use sometimes a rope or cord of any thickness (applied, e.g. to a cable, a rope forming part of the rigging of a ship, a bell-rope, etc.). In 16–18th c. applied jocularly to the hangman's rope. *Obs.*

The expression 'to go to heaven in a string' (to be hanged) referred originally to the Jesuits who were hanged in the reign of Elizabeth.

a **900** ÆLFRED *Blooms* in Cockayne *Shrine* (1864) 175 Þeah þæt scyp si ute on ðære sæ.. hyt byþ ȝesund.. ȝyf se streng [*cf.* ancerstreng *above*] aþolaþ. *a* **1000** *Andreas* 374 Streamas styredon, strengas gurron. *c* **1330** R. BRUNNE *Chron. Wace* (Rolls) 8649 Octa had don, in stede of streng, Aboute his nekke a chayne heng,.. & seide, Sire kyng! Mercy! **1506** in T. North *Bells Lincs.* (1882) 506 Item payd for a stryng to the Sants bell, *ob.* **1542** UDALL *Erasm. Apoph.* 71 b, βρόχος is in latin *laqueus*, in englyshe an halter or a streng. *c* **1560** *Interl. John Evang.* (facs.) C2b, If he do here thy exclamacyon He wyll make the to stye. *Actio.* Not in a strynge I trowe. **1588** *Wills & Invent. Durham* (Surtees) II. 330, vj yockes, girded, 4s. ij cowpe waines, with stringes, 8s. 8d. **1592** GREENE *2nd Pt. Conny-catching* B2b, The quest went vpon him and condemned him, and so the priggar went to heauen in a string. *a* **1625** FLETCHER *Bloody Brother* III. ii, Three merry boyes are we, As ever did sing in a hempen string, under the gallow-tree. *a* **1708** T. WARD *England's Reform.* II. (1710) 47 Then may he boldly take his Swing, And go to Heaven in a String. *c* **1793** BURNS *Epist. Esopus* 10 Where tiny thieves not destin'd yet to swing, Beat hemp for others, riper for the string. **1840** BARHAM *Ingol. Leg.* Ser. I. *Execution*, To see a man swing At the end of a string, With his head in a noose.

¶ Literal rendering of Vulg. *funiculus* (a mistranslation; see the mod. Eng. Bibles).

a **1300** *E.E. Psalter* civ. (cv.) 11, I sal give þe þe land of Chanaan, Stringe of þine heritage on-an. *Ibid.* cxxxviii. (cxxxix.) 3 Mistie and mi stringe in-stepped þou nou. *a* **1340** HAMPOLE *Psalter* xv[i]. 6 Strengis fel til me in fulbryght.

b. Chiefly applied, and gradually restricted, to a line of smaller thickness than that connoted by *rope*. In modern use: a thin cord or stout thread.

1154 *O.E. Chron.* (Laud MS.) an. 1137, Me dide cnotted strenges abuton here hæued. *c* **1200** *Vices & Virtues* 45 Þat ure ropes ne to-breken, þe bieð ibroiden mid þrie strænges. *c* **1290** *St. Edmund* 167 in *S. Eng. Leg.* 436 Heo [*sc.* a hair shirt] nas i-sponne ne i-weoue ake i-broide strengus longue. **1297** R. GLOUC. (Rolls) 9353 Þe streng brac & he [*sc.* the pyx] vel adoun suche signe nas noȝt god. *c* **1440** *Promp. Parv.* 480/1 Strynge, *cordula*, *instita*, *funiculus*. **1631** H. C[ROOKE] *Expl. Instrum. Chirurg.* 15 But the Seton or string which is in the wound must be gently drawne to and againe. **1726** SWIFT *Gulliver* III. ii, Like the scraps of paper fastened by school-boys at the end of the string that holds their kite. **1908** [MISS E. FOWLER] *Betw. Trent & Ancholme* 82 A string, pretty strong, with loop for the hand.

c. In generalized sense, as a material: Thin cord or stout thread used for tying parcels and the like: = TWINE *sb.*[1] 1.

1827 FARADAY *Chem. Manip.* i. (1842) 21 Matches, string, and bladder are necessary. **1859** DICKENS *T. Two Cities* II. xxi, Lo, Miss Pross, in harness of string, awakening the echoes, as an unruly charger, whip-corrected. **1892** GREENER *Breech-loader* 77 It is best to balance the gun on thin string.

d. †A cord used as a whip-lash (*obs.*). Also *U.S.* 'A common name among teamsters for a whip' (Bartlett).

c **1000** *Ags. Gosp.* John ii. 15 And he worhte swipan of strengon. **1576** GASCOIGNE *Philomene* Wks. 1910 II. 181 She bare a skourge, with many a knottie string. **1579** GOSSON *Sch. Abuse* (Arb.) 28 Musick replyes, that Melanippides,.. and such fantasticall heades, haue.. with manye stringes, geuen her so many woundes that [etc.]. **1839** MRS. KIRKLAND *New Home* i. 12 Until by unwearied chirruping and some judicious touches of 'the string' the horses are induced to struggle as for their lives.

e. A cord used as a snare. *rare.*

c **1325** *Gloss. W. de Bibbesw.* in Wright *Voc.* 166 Un oysel ke est dist becaz Près du rivere est pris en laz [*glossed* streing]. *a* **1340** HAMPOLE *Psalter* cxxxix. [cxl.] 6 And strengis [Vulg. *funes*] þai strekid in snare. **1837** CARLYLE *Fr. Rev.* III. VI. i, We walk in a world of Plots; strings universally spread, of deadly gins and fall-traps.

f. A cord for leading or dragging along a person or an animal; a leading-string, a leash. Also in figurative phrases (especially common in 17–18th c.), esp. ***to lead in a string***, ***to have in*** (or ***on***) ***a string*** = to have under control, to be able to do what one likes with.

a **1300** *Deb. Body & Soul* in *Map's Poems* (Camden) 339 An hundred develes.. with stringes him drowen, unthanc his, Til he kome to that lodli lowe, ther helle was. **1583** MELBANCKE *Philotimus* I j, Those that walke as they will,.. perswading themselues that they haue the worlde in a string, are like the ruffian Capaney, who [etc.]. **1590** NASHE *1st Pt. Pasquils Apol.* C 4 b, He perceiueth not in all this, that I haue his leg in a string still. **1616** R. C. *Times' Whistle* vi. 2383 The country parson may, as in a string, Lead the whole parish vnto anything. **1681** H. MORE *Exp. Dan.* 162 He [Alex. the Great] had the world in a string, as our English Proverbial Phrase is. **1682** *Wit & Drollery* 77 My Dog in a String doth lead me,.. For to the Blind, All Men are kind. **1697** VANBRUGH *Relapse* II. i, By this means a Lady may.. lead Twenty Fools about in a String, for two or three Years together. **1706** E. WARD *Wooden World Diss.* (1708) 36 He's the Captain's humble Pig in a String. **1748** RICHARDSON *Clarissa* VII. 324 They govern me as a child in strings. **1791** COWPER *Let. to W. Bagot* 26 Feb., He either suffered prejudice to lead him in a string whithersoever it would, or [etc.]. **1823** 'JON BEE' *Dict. Turf* 167 'Got him in a string,' is when a man is made to believe one thing, several others follow as matter of course. **1894** F. BARRETT *Justif. Lebrun* viii. 66 When they believed they had the world on a string. **1897** MARY KINGSLEY *W. Africa* 352 He.. took me down the Woermann Road.. as it were on a string. **1901** *Westm. Gaz.* 18 Sept. 8/2 Mr. H. said he was not a candidate on a string; he had his own convictions.

(*b*) *fig.* (orig. *U.S.*), a limitation, condition, or restriction attached to something. Freq. in phr. ***no strings attached*** (cf. *no strings* s.v. NO *a.* 5 d); also (with hyphen) as adj. phr.; hence ***strings-attached*** *a.* (*rare*).

1888 in *Dict. Amer.* (1951) II. 1665/1 Bob Ingersoll says there is a string to it. **1930** *Randolph Enterprise* (Elkins, W. Va.) 19 Dec. 4/2 All the propositions with a string to them remind us of the.. First of April joke. **1948** G. E. KIRK *Short Hist. Middle East* viii. 242 The masses are accustomed to poverty and will listen to their own political leaders rather than to foreigners who offer them opulence with a political 'string' attached. **1951** in M. McLuhan *Mech. Bride* (1967) 90/1 It has for its elements.. imagination with no strings attached. **1953** S. PLATH *Johnny Panic & Bible of Dreams* (1977) II. 151 Would he ask her out.. just for herself, no strings attached? **1960** *Washington Post* 16 Nov. A16/2 Much has been said about the desirability of aid without strings, and a strong case can be made for this in some areas where the need is economic. Certainly any strings ought to be obvious. **1969** *Daily Tel.* 12 Dec. 1/1 The Government is to give a new £7 million loan to Upper Clyde Shipbuilders. .. The new loan would not carry any 'strings'. **1971** *Nature* 16 Apr. 420/2 A 'substantial' effort will be made in the category called *l'aide au développement*, a strings-attached arrangement whereby state loans proffered for industrial development must be repaid if the project proves successful and profitable. **1976** *Women's Rep.* Sept./Oct. 2/1 The feminist-run clinics in Australia.. who persuaded the government to fund them (no strings attached). **1980** *Forest Products News* (Wellington, N.Z.) XVII. I. 2/2 As a gesture of goodwill, NZFP has given 'no-strings-attached' aid to an experimental forestry venture in Northland. **1981** J. B. HILTON *Playground of Death* v. 58, I could aspire to be his assistant editor... He was very proud of the *Examiner's* freedom from strings.

g. A thread on which beads, pearls, etc. are strung. (See 12.)

1612 DONNE *Progr. Soul, 2nd Anniv.* 208 And as these starres were but so many beads Strung on one string. **1676** STILLINGFL. *Def. Disc. Idol. Ch. Rome* I. i. §13. 119 They.. say their prayers exactly with their Beads, of which they have 180 on a string. **1830** SCOTT *Monast.* Introd., As the string of a necklace links the beads, which are otherwise detached. **1867** MORRIS *Jason* XVII. 1170 Nor on one string are all life's jewels strung.

†**h.** A fishing-line. *Obs.*

1585 T. WASHINGTON tr. *Nicholay's Voy.* I. xvi. 17 b, Eeles.. haue so sharpe teeth, that there cannot be a string so good, but they will bite it asunder. **1615** E. S. *Brit. Buss* in Arber *Eng. Garner* III. 642 Strings, for each man, six... Every string must be fifty fathom long.

i. A cord for actuating a puppet. Also *fig.*, esp. in ***to pull the strings***, to control the course of affairs, to be the concealed operator in what is ostensibly done by another; ***to pull strings***, to exert influence privately. Cf. *string-pulling* vbl. sb., sense 33 below.

1860–70 STUBBS *Lect. Europ. Hist.* I. i. (1904) 11 A king who pulled the strings of government so exclusively himself. **1868** BRIGHT *Sp. Irel.* 1 Apr. I. 426 Persons.. who pull the strings of the Catholic world in the city of Rome. *c* **1880** *Our Own Country* II. 257 Some men.. who pulled the strings that influenced the mob. **1888** BRYCE *Amer. Commw.* lx. II. 421 The same men continuing to serve year after year, because they hold the strings in their hands. **1924** M. KENNEDY *Constant Nymph* III. xvi. 213 With half a dozen strings within her reach, she had not made up her mind which to pull. **1938** M. ALLINGHAM *Fashion in Shrouds* xxii. 404 I've been trying to pull a few strings myself.. but there's an ominous frigidity on all sides. **1955** G. GREENE *Loser takes All* I. v. 26 Rice is still short, but I'm certain Aunt Marion can pull strings with the grocer. **1960** *News Chron.* 30 Jan. 3/8 She admits she will pull any strings to get things done. **1979** R. JAFFE *Class Reunion* (1980) II. viii. 265 He couldn't be dumb or they wouldn't have accepted him at Le Rosay. On the other hand, his father had strings to pull everywhere.

j. A bell-pull (? *obs.*); a check-string.

1748 RICHARDSON *Clarissa* VI. 66 He pulled the string... The coachman stopp'd. **1825** T. HOOK *Sayings* Ser. II. *Passion & Princ.* vi, The door [of his bedroom was] without a lock, and the bell without a string.

k. Each of the rudder-lines of a boat.

1852 R. B. MANSFIELD *Log Water Lily* 43 Coxswain could only lay down in the boat, and pull whichever string he was directed.

l. *Weaving.* (See quot.)

1891 *Labour Commission* Gloss., *String in length*, is three yards three inches of warp. It is a method of measurement of work in the weaving trade to be paid by the piece at so much per string.

m. Figurative phrases. † ***to draw by one string***: to be in accord, 'pull together'. † ***to hang*** (***together***) ***on*** or ***in a string***: (of persons) to be united in purpose; (of things) to be closely connected. ***at one's string's end*** (dial.): see quot. 1854.

1558 W. FORREST *Grysilde Seconde* (Roxb.) 159 Of thy noble Counselours the truthe to saye, Neauer hathe beene seene to drawe by one strynge More stedfastely sure then nowe at this daye. **1679** *Hist. Jetzer* 23 The Bishop being able to get nothing out of them who all hung together on a string, commanded them however to proceed no further in so slippery a business. **1697** in Perry *Hist. Coll. Amer. Col.*

Ch. I. 47 *By.* That is another subject. *C.* But it hangs all in a string. **1802–12** BENTHAM *Ration. Judic. Evid.* (1827) II. 153 A judge, not nominated, and employed by either party, would certainly not.. hold himself warranted in going out of his string to act the part of Daniel. **1854** MISS BAKER *Northampt. Gloss.* s.v., 'He's got to his string's end,' meaning he's either got to the end of his purse or the end of his story.

(*b*) In phrases (freq. *attrib.*) with *sealing-wax*, used to denote the unpretentious apparatus with which great discoveries may be made.

1962 *Daily Tel.* 5 Mar. 20/5 The traditional British method of scientific research with 'string and sealing wax' will pay rich dividends. **1969** *New Scientist* 28 Aug. 422/2 Systems which are.. still in the string and sealing-wax stage of development. **1972** *Physics Bull.* July 393/1 The individual with his sealing wax and string has been replaced by the battalion with a multimillion pound particle accelerator. **1975** *Nature* 2 Oct. 349/1, I have been told that it is impossible to 'put the clock back'. The assumption is that the age of string, sealing wax and enthusiasm has gone for ever. **1976** *Sci. Amer.* Oct. 138/2 Blackett's world was no longer Rutherford's string-and-sealing wax one.

n. A hoax or trick. Cf. STRING *v.* 15, STRINGER 9. *U.S. slang.*

1851 T. A. BURKE *Polly Peablossom's Wedding* 92 Of course Mabe was innocent of the 'string'. **1937** E. H. SUTHERLAND *Professional Thief* iii. 69 Many other shortcon games have been played, including the gold-brick,..the strap, the string (a variation of the string). [*sic*: ? *read* strap].

o. A fashion shade of the natural colour of string, a light greyish-brown. Also *attrib.* or as *adj.* Cf. *string-colour, -coloured*, sense 32 b.

1914 *Queen* 24 Oct. 2 (Advt.), Colours—champagne, silver, Wedgwood, sky, string. **1923** *Daily Mail* 7 June 6 In Ivory, String, Beige, Light Grey. **1949** *Dict. Colours Interior Decoration* (Brit. Colour Council) III. 26/1 *String*, a colour standardised by B.C.C. in 1934. A similar colour is here shown under the name of String Beige. **1963** *Harper's Bazaar* May 17 (Advt.), In navy, string, cedar, nut brown or black calf... In cardinal, white or string calf. **1972** *Vogue* June 13/1 A kind of warm biscuit shade that some paint-makers bluntly term 'string'.

p. (See quot. 1964). Usu. *attrib.* (see *string underwear, vest*, sense 33 below) or as *adj.*

1964 *Which?* Apr. 123/1 There are four main types of knit for men's underwear—*plain*; *interlock*; *cellular, mesh* or *eyelet*; and *string*... String fabrics are mesh fabrics, but of a very open structure—the holes may be nearly one inch across, and the fabric is usually in the form of thick strands joined together. This type originated in Norway, where the fishermen used to cut up their old fishing nets and wrap them round their bodies to keep warm when fishing in icy weather. **1966** 'A. YORK' *Eliminator* viii. 156 His underwear was Norwegian string. His coat was a Burberry.

2. *transf.* A natural string or cord.

a. In an animal body: A ligament, tendon, nerve, etc.; an elongated muscle or muscular fibre; the frænum of the tongue. Cf. EYESTRING, HEARTSTRINGS.

Exc. in *string of the tongue*, the sense is now *rare*. The word is occas. applied to a tough piece of fibre in meat or the like. (Cf. STRINGY *a.* 1.)

c **1000** *Sax. Leechd.* III. 102 Ceorf þane streng under þara tunga. *c* **1340** *Nominale* (Skeat) 32 *Dentz foreynz lange et filet* Forteth tunge and strynge. **1398** TREVISA *Barth. De P.R.* v. xxiii. (Bodl. MS.), þe instrumentes of þe voice.. beþ longen, strenges [L. *arteriæ*; cf. ARTERY 1], þe þrote [etc.]. **1525** tr. *Brunswyke's Handywork Surg.* lxxiv. P iv, Seldom is broken the bone of the calfe, for it is an harde bone, and is defendyd with the strynges & synewes. **1526** TINDALE *Mark* vii. 35 The stringe off hys tounge was loosed [so later versions]. **1541** R. COPLAND *Guydon's Quest. Chirurg.* D j, Of what nature are the cordes? Answere. The strynges ben almoste as all of one nature.. but yet the cordes more than the strynges. For lyke as the strynges be meane amonge the cordes and the bones, so be the cordes meane amonge yᵉ strynges & the synewes. **1577** B. GOOGE *Heresbach's Husb.* IV. 159 b, You must in no wise shake them [*sc.* eggs].. leste you breake the stringes of lyfe [L. *vitales fibras*] that are but newely begun. **1585** HIGINS *Junius' Nomencl.* 21/2 *Ligamentum*,.. the ligatures or strings of yᵉ bones. **1614** W. B. *Philos. Banquet* (ed. 2) 3 The braine, and Strings thervnto offitiall. **1621** LODGE *Summary Du Bartas* I. 280 The Tendons, proceeding from the Muskles,.. which the Physicions.. haue called Synderique Nerues or Strings. **1686** BLOME *Gentl. Recreat.* II. 61 Instead of cutting off the Stern [of a young Spaniel], it is better to twist it off... And if thus pulled off, there is a string that comes out with it which doth hinder their madness. *a* **1722** LISLE *Husb.* (1757) 315 Whilst he draws the stones with his teeth, he has his two hands at liberty to hold back the strings of the stones that they are not drawn away; for the strings run up into the loins and backbone. **1757** W. THOMPSON *R.N. Adv.* 20 The Flesh .. will be nothing better than the Strings or Husk of Flesh. **1842** T. WEBSTER *Encycl. Dom. Econ.* §4839. 860 In young mutton, that fat readily separates; in old, it is held together by strings of skin. **1890** COUES *Ornith.* 329 These threads.. are called *chalazæ*; they are the 'strings', rather unpleasantly evident in a soft-boiled egg.

†*fig.* *c* **1440** *Gesta Rom.* (1878) 235 She was hiliche greuid in alle the strenges of hir herte. **1592** LYLY *Gallathea* III. i. 57 My wanton eyes which conceiued the picture of his face, and hangd it on the verie strings of my hart. **1606** SHAKS. *Ant. & Cl.* III. xi. 57 Egypt, thou knew'st too well, My heart was to thy Rudder tyed by' th' strings.

b. In certain fishes. ? *Obs.*

1611 COTGR., *Cordé*, Corded,.. also, out of season; (a Metaphor from Lampreyes, which being out of season, haue a hard string in their backes). **1668** WILKINS *Real Char.* 140 Lamprey.. considerable for having.. Two pair of finns; either that which is the biggest of this tribe, having two very long strings from the upper jaw, and four shorter from the lower jaw [etc.]. **1675** V. ALSOP *Anti-Sozzo* iii. §2. 155 A vein of his old thredbare Fallacy discovers it self, which I now perceive (like the poysonous string in the Lamprey,) he resolves shall run through his whole Discourse. **1725** SLOANE *Jamaica* II. 289 The Old-Wife... There is no Prickles in this Fish's Fins only long Strings.

c. In plants: A cord, thread, or fibre; a 'vein' of a leaf; the tough piece connecting the two halves of a pod (in beans, etc.); a root-filament.

1398 TREVISA *Barth. De P.R.* XVII. i. (Bodl. MS.) In euerich rote manye maner knottes and stringes. **1573** BARET *Alv.* S. 866 To pull of the small stringes of rootes, *fibras radicum euellere*, Cic. **1585** HIGINS *Junius' Nomencl.* 113/1 *Neruus*,.. the nerue, sinew or string of a leafe, as in plantaine. **1657** COLES *Adam in Eden* cxxxiii, The Roots [of Avens] consist of many brownish strings, or Fibres, smelling some-what like unto Cloves. **1707** MORTIMER *Husb.* 239 If you will pull it [*sc.* Broom] up you are apt to leave strings behind, the least of which will grow. **1733** TULL *Horse-Hoeing Husb.* xxiii. 379 It may be objected, that the fore-part of these hinder Sheats might not be oblique enough to raise up the Strings of Roots or Stubble, which might come across them in their Way. **1842** LOUDON *Suburban Hort.* 671 They [*sc.* cardoons] are then to be carefully deprived of the slime and strings which will be found to cover them. **1880** BESSEY *Bot.* 16 There may almost always be seen in plant-cells bands or strings of protoplasm which lie in or between the vacuoles. **1884** *Implement & Mach. Rev.* 1 Dec. 6710/2 A rate of production equal to 47,000 strings of rhea per day. **1904** *Nature* 18 Aug. 392/2 The vascular strings of the sugar-cane.

fig. **1605** BACON *Adv. Learn.* II. xx. §6 The Enquirye concerning the Rootes of Good and euill, and the strings of those Rootes. **1685** BUNYAN *Seventh-day Sabbath* v. 118 Luther.. had yet work hard enough to get his Conscience clear from all those roots and strings of inbred errour.

d. A tendril (of hops, vine, pea); a runner (of the strawberry, the potato). ? Now *dial.*

1585 HIGINS *Junius' Nomencl.* 146/1 *Capreolus*,.. the strings that wind about and fasten the vine to the perches or polles: they be called tendrilles. **1675** EVELYN *Fr. Gard.* 255 When your Strawberries shoot their strings, you must castrate them. **1707** MORTIMER *Husb.* 131 If the Haum and Strings of the Hops be burnt every year. *a* **1722** LISLE *Husb.* (1757) 105 Peas.. never thrive well till they can take hands with one another, that is, by their strings. **1805** R. W. DICKSON *Pract. Agric.* II. 622 After the potatoe plants have begun to throw out their wires or strings.

3. a. A cord or line (composed of vegetable fibre, gut, or fine wire) adapted to produce a musical sound when stretched and caused to vibrate.

a **1000** *Ags. Ps.* (Th.) cxliii. 10 Mid tyn strengum ʒetoʒen hearpe. *c* **1000** *Voc.* in Wr.-Wülcker 311/16 *Fidis*, streng. *a* **1300** *E.E. Psalter* xxxii. 2 In harpe and sautre Of ten stringes to him sing yhe. **1398** TREVISA *Barth. De P.R.* XII. ii. (1495) A iiij b, Strenges made of wulfes guttes.. corrumpyth strenges made of shepes guttes yf.. they be sette amonge theym as in lute or in harpe. **1471** CAXTON *Recuyell* (Sommer) 256 The strenges of the harpe. **1585** HIGINS *Junius' Nomencl.* 351/2 *Hypate*,.. a basse or base string: that string that maketh the base sound. **1667** MILTON *P.L.* VII. 598 All sounds on Fret by String or Golden Wire Temper'd soft Tunings. **1748** HUME *Enq. Hum. Und.* VII. ii, We say.. that the vibration of this string is the cause of this particular sound. **1811** BUSBY *Dict. Mus.*, *String*, any wire, or preparation of sheep or catgut, used in musical instruments. **1825** T. HOOK *Sayings* Ser. II. *Passion & Princ.* viii. III. 110 The sweet tones of a harp, whose strings were swept with a master's hand, sounded through the adjoining saloon. **1879** STAINER *Music of Bible* 74 The most primitive material used for strings was, probably, twisted grass; next in time, the guts of animals; lastly, wire or silk. **1898** 'H. S. MERRIMAN' *Roden's Corner* vii. 73 Cornish remembered that he had been specially told to get a new bass string for the banjo.

b. *fig.* and in fig. context. Cf. CHORD *sb.*[1] 2 b.

to harp on one (*the same*, etc.) *string*: see HARP *v.* †*to stretch a string*: see STRETCH *v.* 19.

1583 H. HOWARD *Defensative* E j, We read.. of a certaine .. custome among the false prophets.. to meete together:.. at which times, I doubt not, but they tuned euery string with such a cunning wrest, as none could trippe them in theyr tale. **1636** MASSINGER *Gt. Duke Flor.* II. iii, Ever touching Upon that string? **1638** R. BAKER tr. *Balzac's Lett.* (vol. II.) 14 You touch the right string of my inclination, when you pray me to praise.. that Prince. **1655** LD. NORWICH in *Nicholas Papers* (Camden) III. 217 But why touch I this string agayne? **1705** COLLIER *Ess. Mor. Subj.* III. *Pain* 19 This is scruing up the Strings too high in all Conscience. **1718** POPE *Let. to Jervas* 12 Dec., But I must own, when you talk of Building and Planting, you touch my String. **1741** RICHARDSON *Pamela* (1824) I. 278 The dear man makes me spring to his arms, whenever he touches this string. **1748** THOMSON *Cast. Indol.* I. xxxi, But how shall I attempt such arduous string? **1789** MME. D'ARBLAY *Diary* 6 Jan., No sooner did the King touch upon that dangerous string, the History of Music, than all else was forgotten! **1852** DICKENS *Bleak Ho.* xxxvii, I asked Mr. Vholes if he would like to live altogether in the country? 'There, miss,' said he, 'you touch me on a tender string.' **1854** *Poultry Chron.* II. 320 What, another song to the old tune,—another play on the old string.

c. *Pl.* Stringed instruments; now only, such as are played with a bow. Also, in mod. use, the players on stringed instruments (in an orchestra or band). Cf. the attrib. use in 32 a.

a **1340** HAMPOLE *Psalter* cl. 4 Louys him in strenges & orgyns [**1535** *Coverdale* vpon the strynges; Vulg. *in chordis*]. **1820** *Q. Mus. Mag.* II. 414 The peculiar appropriateness of wind instruments to that element [water], and their decided preference over strings. **1880** *Academy* 24 Dec. 467/1 Herr Joachim introduced last season his sextet for strings. **1884** *Girl's Own Paper* Nov. 20/1 By the 'strings' of an orchestra, we are always to understand merely such instruments as are played with a bow. **1887** *Daily Tel.* 14 Mar. (Cassell), With the orchestra little fault could be found beyond the weakness of the strings.

4. a. A bowstring; †a cord similarly used in a catapult, etc.

Beowulf 3117 þonne stræla storm strengum ʒebæded scoc ofer scild-weall. *c* **1205** LAY. 1454 He leadde an his honde enne bowe stronge & he þene streng up braid. *c* **1386** CHAUCER *Sompn. T.* 359 He took his bowe in honde And vp the streng he pulled to his ere. **1420** in *York Memor. Bk.* II. (Surtees) 123 Et quod lez strynges pro arcubus, qui inventi erunt defectivi, sint forisfacti. **1523–34** FITZHERB. *Husb.* §142 Bowe, arrowes, sworde, bukler, horne, leisshe, gloues, stringe, and thy bracer. **1535** COVERDALE *Ps.* xx[i]. 12 With thy stringes thou shalt make ready thine arowes agaynst the faces off them. **1609** HOLLAND *Amm. Marcell.* XV. x. 50 As if they were bolts and darts discharged violently from the writhed and wrested strings of a brake or such like engine. **1611** BIBLE *Ps.* xi. 2 They make ready their arrow vpon the string. **1795** COLERIDGE *Lines in Manner of Spenser* 30 When twang'd an arrow from Love's mystic string. **1849** LYTTON *K. Arthur* II. xcix, He did but pause, with more effect to wing The stone that chance thus fitted to his string. **1870** BRYANT *Iliad* IV. 149 On the string He laid that fatal arrow.

b. In fig. phrase, *to have two* (*many*, etc.) *strings to one's bow*: to have two (etc.) alternative resources.

1524 WOLSEY in *St. Papers Hen. VIII*, IV. 103 Ne totally to grounde you upon the said Quenes doinges, but to have 2 stringes to your bowe, specially whan the oone is wrought with a womans fingers. **1546** J. HEYWOOD *Prov.* I. xi. (1867) 30 Ye haue many stryngis to the bowe. **1579, 1678, 1812** [see BOW *sb.*[1] 4 c]. [**1644** R. BAILLIE *Lett. & Jrnls.* (Bannatyne Club) II. 262 Allaster McDonnell wes the smallest string in his bow.] **1877** SPURGEON *Serm.* XXIII. 113 She had three strings to her bow.

c. Hence *second string*, a second resource available if the first should fail. Freq. (with hyphen) *attrib.*

1643 *Plain English* 28 It would be a good second string in case the Parliament should.. miscarry.

1911 MARETT *Anthropol.* iv. 113 They found them a people of hunters and fishers, it is true, but with agriculture as a second string. **1943** J. B. PRIESTLEY *Daylight on Saturday* xxxi. 245 He was one of that select.. group of second-string personages for whom the party.. had always to provide. **1958** *People* 4 May 19/1 The man who may take over as second string to Tony Lock is Mike Allen, of Northampton. **1965** *Times Lit. Suppl.* 25 Nov. 1058/3 Moore was a kind of second-string Clarence Darrow. **1977** C. MCCULLOUGH *Thorn Birds* iv. 80 The big Queensland blue brute that led the dog pack took a slavish fancy to the priest and followed him without question, meaning Frank was very definitely the second-string man.

d. *Sporting.* Said of a racehorse. Also of an athlete (see quot. 1897) and a team. Hence occas. without prefixed ordinal.

1863 *Baily's Mag.* Mar. 102 Still Jennings has a very dangerous 'second string' in Valentine. **1884** *Sat. Rev.* 12 Apr. 469/1 La Touche.. had won the [mile] race at Cambridge in about 4 min. 27 sec... while the Oxford first string, Pratt, had occupied nearly 13 sec. more in covering the ground. **1893** *Daily News* 22 Apr. 5/3 He ran a dead heat with the other Oxford string for first place in the One Hundred Yards Race. **1897** *Encycl. Sport* I. 62/2 (Athletics) *Strings*.. (2) 'First,' 'second,' and 'third' strings are the first, second, and third men chosen to represent a club in any event. **1934** *Times* 14 Feb. 6/3 In the first string match P. Q. Reiss (R.A.F. Club) just beat S. N. Capel-Cure by three games to two. *Ibid.* 3 Mar. 6/4 The match was decided on the last fight, that between the first-string welter-weights. **1951** *Sport* 27 Jan.–2 Feb. 3/1 On Saturday, 'Archie' kept goal for the Rochdale second string. **1972** J. MOSEDALE *Football* iii. 32 Walter Camp named him a second-string All-American. **1976** *Norwich Mercury* 19 Nov. 10 Terry Medwin's finest moment so far as Norwich City Reserves' coach was in defeat. The second string went down 3–2 in September at Tottenham.

†**5.** *transf.* in *Geom.* = CHORD *sb.*[1] 4. *Obs. rare.*

1594 BLUNDEVIL *Exerc.*, *Arith.* (1597) 48 b, *Sinus Rectus* is the one halfe of a Chord or string of any Arke which is double to the Arke that is giuen or supposed. **1695** ALINGHAM *Geom. Epit.* 51 Many other useful Practises mecanicks perform by this Theo. as the finding the length of strings.

6. a. A piece of cord, tape, ribbon, etc. (often used in pairs) for tying up or fastening some portion of dress, for securing a hat or bonnet by being tied under the chin, for binding the hair, for closing a bag or purse.

13.. *K. Alis.* 208 (Laud MS.) Her ȝelewe her was faire atired Mid riche strenges of golde wyred. **1564** *Reg. Privy Council Scot.* I. 308, lxxxxvi stringis to hattis of diverse cullouris. **1588–9** *Shuttleworths' Acc.* (Chetham Soc.) 50 For mottlaye to be a cloke bagge and for stringes to the same, vijᵈ. **1604** SHAKS. *Oth.* I. i. 3 Thou.. who hast had my purse, As if yᵉ strings were thine. **1674** in *Jrnl. Friends Hist. Soc.* (1914) 30 Beare slypt out the runing string of his drawers and tyed it about his necke. **1737** in *Sixth Rep. Dep. Kpr. Rec.* App. II. 120 A new invented Hoop Petticoat, with.. strings for contracting the compass of a Petticoat from four yards in circumference to two yards. **1829** SCOTT *Anne of G.* xxvii, Our purses, my Lord Duke, are our own—we will not put the strings of them into your Highness's hands, unless [etc.]. **1838** DICKENS *Nich. Nick.* xvii, Kate's.. duties being limited to holding articles of costume until Miss Knag was ready to try them on, and now and then tying a string, or fastening a hook-and-eye. **1848** —— *Dombey* xi, The Doctor was a portly gentleman in a suit of black, with strings at his knees, and stockings below them. **1878** HARDY *Ret. Native* V. iii, Her little hands quivered so violently as she held them to her chin to fasten her bonnet that she could not tie the strings. **1885** 'MRS. ALEXANDER' *At Bay* v, She wore just such a velvet string as this through the lace of her dress.

†**b.** In *plural*, the short cords, ribbons, or leather straps, formerly often attached (in pairs) to the edges of book-covers, to be tied in order to keep the book closed. *Obs.* (now usually called *ties*).

1583 in *Dee's Diary* (Camden) 71 [A book] In paste-bords, with strings. **1585** DANIEL tr. *P. Jovius' Disc. Imprese* C v b, A Booke of accomptes, with leather stringes and buckles. **1641** MILTON *Reform.* I. 39 Many of those that pretend to be great Rabbies in these studies have scarce saluted them from the strings, and the titlepage. **1646** CRASHAW *Steps to Temple, On Mr. G. Herbert's Bk.* 5 When your hands untie these strings, Think yo' have an Angell by the wings. **1663** WOOD *Life* (O.H.S.) I. 470 Both which [books] for strings and covers cost me 1*s.* 7*d.*

c. A very scanty bikini (see quot. 1974[1]).

1974 *W* 14 June 17/2 The latest—The String—looks like a winner on the beaches of other countries too... Held by thin strings, it's just two tiny triangles—front and back—worn with a mini-bra. **1974** *Times* 13 Aug. 5/6 The String, a sort of cache-sexe sized bathing suit from Brazil which is now sweeping America. **1977** *Courier-Mail* (Brisbane) 5 Nov. 1/4 They were what we call 'strings'—just a string holding them up.

7. A cord or ribbon worn as a decoration; the ribbon of a knightly order. ? *Obs.*

1660 F. BROOKE tr. *Le Blanc's Trav.* 60 These Bramins.. wear next to their flesh certain strings, the badge of their order. **1700** PRIOR *Carmen Sec.* 386 Round Ormond's Knee Thou ty'st the Mystic String, That makes the Knight Companion to the King. **1733** SWIFT *On Poetry* 468 When on thy Breast and Sides Herculean, He fixt the Star and String Cerulean. **1753** FOOTE *Englishm. Paris* I. Wks. 1799 I. 34 Belike they had been sent to Bridewell, hadn't a great gentleman in a blue string come by and releas'd them. **1814** BYRON *Ode to Napoleon* xviii, The gewgaws thou wert fond to wear, The star, the string, the crest.

†**8.** *Anglo-Irish.* ? A stretched cord for laying out the boundaries of land: in phrase *by lot and string*. Hence, a document recording allotments of land. *Obs.*

1658 in T. A. Larcom *Down Surv.* (1851) 246, 9thly. Your petitioners desire that the County of Kildare may be set out unto them by lott and string. **1666** in Prendergast *Cromw. Settlem.* (1870) 199 *note*, The claymants produce a string whereby the lands were sett out.. Mr. Petty swears that the paper signed was the original..that these strings had as much force as injunctions—that they took possession under them.

†**9. a.** The cord or chain wound on the barrel of a watch. **b.** A chain or a cord for carrying a watch. *Obs.*

1646 SUCKLING *Aglaura* II. i, Like the string of a Watch Wound up too high. **1675** J. S[MITH] *Horolog. Dial.* II. i. 38 You must first wind it [a watch] up rightly;.. not too hastily, least you force the stop, and break the string. *a* **1676** HALE *Prim. Orig. Man.* IV. iv. (1677) 324 If I should see a curious Watch,..and should observe the exact disposition of the Spring, the String, the Wheels, the Ballance, the Index, [etc.]. **1680** *Lond. Gaz.* No. 1499/4 A silver Watch with a String. **1701** *Ibid.* No. 3692/4 Lost.., a Watch with a double Case.., a Green and Silver String with 2 Seals.

†**10.** = SLING *sb.*[2] 3c. *Obs.*

1718 F. HUTCHINSON *Ess. Witchcraft* vii. 104 After him Blew brought his Arm in a String.

†**11.** = SCROLL *sb.* 3b. *Obs.*

1797 MRS. BERKELEY *Poems of G. M. Berkeley* Pref. p. cccclxviii, Mr. Berkeley's [motto]..'*Vivat post funera virtus*'; which he engraved in the strings of his crest.

II. A number of objects strung on a thread; hence, a series, succession.

12. a. A thread or file with a number of objects strung upon it; a number (of beads, pearls, etc.) strung on a thread; a 'rope' of onions (ROPE *sb.*[1] 6); a number of herrings or other fish strung on a thread passed through the gills. Also, a number of things (e.g. sausages) linked together in a line.

1488–92 *Acc. Ld. High Treas. Scot.* I. 84 Ane string of grete perle contenand fyfti and a perle, and stringis of small perle. **1578** *Invent. R. Sc. Wardr.* (1815) 263 A string of cornellingis sett in gold. **1620** SHELTON *2nd Pt. Quix.* l. 335, I haue sent you..a string of Corall Beads. **1687** A. LOVELL tr. *Thevenot's Trav.* I. 124 These Pouseragues are Wheels, with a Rope hanging round them like a string of Beads without an end. **1732** EARL OF OXFORD in *Portland Papers* (Hist. MSS. Comm.) VI. 153 We had herrings for dinner caught that very morning, and was the first string they had this year. **1737** *Ochtertyre House Bk.* (S.H.S.) 27 For two strings of flounders and a letter, 0 0 7. **1819** KEATS *Otho* IV. i, Fetch me a missal, and a string of beads. **1830** JAMES *Darnley* iv. I. 60 Endless strings of sausages. **1834** MARRYAT *P. Simple* xxviii, The steward came down..loaded with cabbages, baskets of eggs, strings of onions, [etc.]. **1874** H. H. COLE *Catal. Ind. Art S. Kens. Mus.* 173 Bracelet. Six strings of pink glass beads. **1891** *Field* 7 Mar. 344/1 A movement is making amongst the fish, several nice strings of codling having fallen to different boats. **1903** MRS. H. TAYLOR *Pastor Hsi* vi. 43 He had no money to draw upon, and no means left of raising even a few strings of cash.

b. *Lumber-trade.* A number of logs fastened together to be carried down by a river.

1878 *Lumberman's Gaz.* 5 Jan., One string of lumber went over the falls on Friday afternoon of last week. **1880** *Ibid.* 14 Jan., With this decrease in the size of the logs, comes the constant increase in the number of strings into which the company are required to tie the logs.

c. *Billiards.* (See quots. 1879, 1891.) *U.S.*

1848 B. A. BAKER *Glance at New York* 11, I have beat Miss Wilson one string. **1855** J. HOLBROOK *Ten Years among Mail Bags* 60 Just allow me twenty on a 'string'. **1871** G. W. PECK *Adventures of Terence McGrant* iii. 22 I'd do it to him half a string. **1879** WEBSTER Suppl., *String*, the number of points made, in a game of billiards. **1891** *Century Dict.*, *String* 9 (*a*) A number of wooden buttons strung on a wire to keep the score or tally of the game. There is a string for each player or side. (*b*) The score, tally, or number of points scored by either player or side at any stage of a game: as, he made a poor string at first, but won. **1924** *Billiards Mag.* June 46/1 Kreshel beat the coast's amateur three-cushion titlist, 80–44. The score of the first block was 40–14, with the string completed in 110 innings.

13. a. A number of animals driven in single file tied one to the other; a train of animals, vehicles, or persons one behind the other.

1686 PLOT *Staffordsh.* 352 They generally plough with their Oxen in pairs, but with their Horses in a string, to prevent poching the land. **1717** LADY M. W. MONTAGU *Let. to Miss Thistlethwayte* 1 Apr., The drivers take care to tie them [*sc.* camels] one to another with strong ropes, fifty in a string, led by an ass, on which the driver rides. **1820** *Sporting Mag.* VI. 79 The long string of carriages.. increased the animation..of the scene. **1823** 'JON BEE' *Dict. Turf* 167 Dealers fasten the halter of one horse to the halter and tail of another, and so on to the amount of sixteen, twenty, or more, and either is a string. 'Several strings of good horses entered Smithfield to-day.' **1830** COLERIDGE *Table-T.* 5 Oct., I call these strings of school boys or girls which we meet near London—walking advertisements. **1842** DARWIN in *Life & Lett.* (1887) I. 320 Smugglers and their strings of pack-horses. **1849** F. B. HEAD *Stokers & Pokers* iii. (1851) 41 A string of empty carriages..[to be] formed into the next departure train. **1885** RUDLER & CHISHOLM *Europe* 175 A steam-tug with a long string of rafts or a heavily-laden barge in tow. **1902** S. E. WHITE *Blazed Trail* iii, The train consisted of a string of freight cars. **1910** G. F. WRIGHT in *The Fundamentals* II. I. 10 Strings of captives with evidently Jewish features.

b. A flock (of birds) flying in single file.

In quot. 1889 perh. confused with SPRING *sb.*[2] 15.

1801 J. THOMSON *Poems Sc. Dial.* 12 Just like to wild geese in a string, When aff they flee. **1813** HAWKER *Diary* (1893) I. 89 Not one string of birds came low enough to be fired at. **1889** F. A. KNIGHT *By Leafy Ways* 70 We talk of a covey of partridges, a pack of grouse, a string of teal.

14. a. A set or stud of horses, beasts of draught or burden, †slaves.

a **1734** R. NORTH *Life Sir D. North* (1744) 59 He procured him a String of Slaves out of his *Chiurm*, with a *Capo*, to work in his Building. **1764** *Museum Rust.* II. 163 This circumstance of seeing his highness's string of mules, it was first induced me to think of breeding them. *a* **1809** HOLCROFT *Mem.* I. xi. (1852) 36 Johnstone..had a string of no less than thirteen famous [race-]horses..under his care. **1814** HEYNE *Tracts on India* 274, I learnt that a gentleman of my acquaintance was encamped near the town with a string of elephants. **1883** J. GILMOUR *Among Mongols* xviii. 230 He had flocks of sheep, herds of cattle, droves of horses, and strings of camels. **1889** BADEN-POWELL *Pigsticking* 120 A man to whom money is no object will naturally complete his 'string' with Arabs or small thoroughbred Walers.

†**b.** A set (of persons); a band, a faction. *Obs.*

1579–80 NORTH *Plutarch, Publicola* (1595) 108 Brutus.. had maried their own sister, and had many children by her. Of the which the Vitellians had drawen to their string, two of the eldest of them. **16..** *Rob. Hood & Maid Marian* xii. in Child *Ballads* III. 219/1 'O hold thy hand,'..said Robin Hood, 'And thou shalt be one of my string.' **1699** BENTLEY *Phalaris* 484 All of that String, Bacchylides, Simonides, Pindar, got their livelyhood by the Muses.

†**c.** *Sc.* = FILE *sb.*[2] 7. *Obs.*

1627 SIR T. KELLIE *Pallas Armata* 125 Stand right in your Ranks and your Stringes.

d. *transf.* = STABLE *sb.*[1] 2b. *U.S. slang.*

1913 G. J. KNEELAND *Commercialized Prostitution in N.Y. City* iv. 77 A single girl, at times a 'string' of girls, 'working' for them [*sc.* pimps] on the street or in houses. **1946** *Amer. Mercury* Sept. 272/2 Promoters of commercialized prostitution look to two main sources for replenishing their 'stables' or 'strings' of girls. **1982** L. BLOCK *Eight Million Ways to Die* (1983) x. 87 She wants out of my string of girls.

15. a. A number of things in a line; a row, chain, range.

1683 [R. NORTH] *Discourse Fish & Fish-ponds* vi. (1713) 17 The third Pond may be a Work of another Year; and if the Ground lies fair for it,..I would not be without it; for it will ..fill up a Range or String of Waters, which two doth not. **1788** GIBBON *Decl. & F.* lv. V. 544 A long sea-coast, [Croatia] indented with capacious harbours, covered with a string of islands. **1796** MORSE *Amer. Geog.* I. 166 Eastward of this lake, lie several small ones, which extend in a string to the great carrying place. **1843** LEFEVRE *Life Trav. Phys.* III. III. viii. 184 A string of houses built after the model of the peasants' habitations. **1862** G. P. SCROPE *Volcanos* 365 Thence radiate several elevated embranchments or strings of conoidal hills.

b. Orig. (more fully *string of tools*), the drilling bit and weights that occupy the hole in drilling for oil, etc.; in mod. use, the entire drilling assembly in the hole (so *drilling string*); also, the coupled lengths of drill pipe or of casing in the hole.

1895 W. T. BRANNT *Petroleum* vii. 182 The string of tools —the bit, the auger-stem and jars, with the sinkerbar—are [*sic*] more than sixty feet long. **1929** BABBITT & DOLAND *Water Supply Engin.* vii. 160 The only tools on the string in spudding are usually the auger stem and the spudding drill. **1939** D. HAGER *Fund. Petroleum Industry* viii. 181 A string of cable tools consists of the bit, stem, jars, sinker bar or sub, and rope socket. The parts of the string are all joined by tool joints and fastened to the drilling cable or line by means of the rope socket. **1947** *Richmond* (Va.) *Times-Dispatch* 12 Mar. 11/2 Pacific Western's well contains the longest 'string' of casing ever run into a well—16,406 feet. **1963** G. SELL *Petroleum Industry* iii. 53 The swivel is so designed as to allow the drilling string to rotate freely on roller bearings. **1976** M. MACHLIN *Pipeline* xxvii. 318 Can you imagine old Wilbur all touted out in greasy coveralls, working the string on some well up in the slope? **1979** R. PIPER *Story of Oil* vi. 23 When boring for oil, a separate engine, apart from the one that raises and lowers the drill string, is needed to turn the drill stem.

c. *Math.*, etc. A sequence of symbols or linguistic elements in a definite order.

1932 LEWIS & LANGFORD *Symbolic Logic* iii. 49 Propositions are not strings of marks, or series of sounds, except incidentally. **1940** W. V. O. QUINE *Math. Logic* vii. 284 Now *x* is a string of accents, symbolically Ac *x*, if every initial segment of *x* ends in an accent. **1954** *Jrnl. Assoc. Computing Machinery* I. 120/2 A finite, possibly null, sequence of members of the alphabet is called a string. **1955** N. CHOMSKY *Logical Struct. Linguistic Theory* (microfilm, Mass. Inst. Technol.) viii. 356 There are cases where similar strings have intuitively quite different interpretations, but where we can discover no grounds..for assigning different markers to them. **1958** [see IDENTIFIER 2c]. **1970** J. LYONS *Chomsky* 58 The ambiguity of such strings as *old men and women*. **1977** *Word 1972* XXVIII. 91 The surface string of such sentences indeed looks perfectly straightforward—an adjective with comparative inflection and a comparative marker. **1979** *Sci. Amer.* Oct. 138/3 It was hoped that by transforming the statements of mathematics into strings of meaningless symbols to be combined according to the rules of logic, whatever unavowed principles of reasoning had given rise to the paradoxes would be revealed.

d. *Computers.* A linear sequence of records or data.

1956 *Jrnl. Assoc. Computing Machinery* III. 147 Areas are set aside for shuttling strings of control fields back and forth until a completely sorted sequence is obtained. **1964** C. DENT *Quantity Surveying by Computer* iii. 34 After the second pass tapes *A* and *B* contain the data in strings of four items. **1979** PAGE & WILSON *Introd. Computational Combinatorics* iii. 49 Two strings of r, s items respectively are each in ascending order in the main store of a computer.

16. a. A continuous series or succession (e.g. of stories, questions, incidents, historical personages).

1710 FELTON *Diss. Classics* (1718) 19 If this [*sc.* the ballad theory of the Homeric poems] be true, they are the completest String of Ballads I ever met with. **1713** *Guardian* No. 42 ¶6 Sir Harry hath what they call a String of Stories, which he tells over every Christmas. **1772** *Ann. Reg.* 52/2 He then read to the House a string of resolutions under thirteen heads. **1797** BURNEY *Let. to Mme. D'Arblay* 28 Sept., I had a string of questions ready to ask. **1839** HAWKER *Diary* (1893) II. 165 Made a string of indispensable visits, that I could not catch a moment to do before. **1843** S. R. MAITLAND *Dark Ages* xv. (1890) 286 The brief records of whole strings of abbots, priors, &c. **1859** HELPS *Friends in C.* Ser. II. II. i. 10 The man..who masters long strings of facts. **1867** FREEMAN *Norm. Conq.* (1876) I. App. 712 We now come to the long string of English writers who accuse Eadric. **1884** *Law Times Rep.* L. 278/1 Lyell administered to Kennedy a long string of interrogatories. **1902** S. E. WHITE *Blazed Trail* vi, The reptilian gentleman let out a string of oaths.

†**b.** *Oxford slang.* (See quots.) *Obs.*

1721 AMHERST *Terræ Fil.* No. 20. 104 These commodious sets of syllogisms are call'd strings and descend from undergraduate to undergraduate,..so that, when any candidate for a degree is to exercise his talent in argumentation, he has nothing else to do but to enquire amongst his friends for a string upon such or such a question, and to get it by heart, or read it over in his cap... I have in my custody a book of strings upon most or all of the questions discussed in a certain college. **1780** *Gentl. Mag.* L. 277 Every undergraduate [at Oxford]..has in his possession certain papers, which have been handed down from generation to generation, and are denominated *strings*. [*Footnote*, In our Sister University called *arguments*.].. These strings consist of two or three arguments, each on those subjects which are discussed in the schools.

c. A continuous utterance, a 'screed'. *contemptuous.*

1766 GOLDSM. *Vicar W.* xiv, Did he not talk a long string of learning about Greek? **1858** HAWTHORNE *Fr. & Ital. Note-bks.* (1871) I. 5 It sounds like a string of mere gabble. **1870** E. PEACOCK *Ralf Skirl.* III. 236 The fox sang a string of doggerel.

d. The 'thread', sequence (of a narrative). *rare.*

1833 J. S. SANDS *Poems* 105 (E.D.D.) Whiles the soul Is apt to tak a rigmarole; And o' her tale to lose the string. **1860–70** STUBBS *Lect. Europ. Hist.* I. ix. (1904) 116 Events.. not of great interest as touching the string of Charles's history. **1876** —— *Early Plantag.* v. 86 We must now return to the direct string of the story.

e. A continuous series of successes or of failures. orig. and chiefly *U.S.*

1890 BARRÈRE & LELAND *Dict. Slang* II. 313/2 A common expression in America is 'to get in a *string*', applied to any kind of fortunate series. **1898** H. M. BLOSSOM *Checkers* 170 Well, I've had my hard luck, and 'played out the string'. **1967** *Boston Herald* 8 May 16/5 Womack preserved the victory that ended a four-game losing string for New York. **1968** *Globe & Mail* (Toronto) 15 Jan. 19/1 The victory stretched the Canadiens' unbeaten string to nine games. **1973** *Times* 17 Apr. 14/6, I try to take it in my stride and relax, and not get too nervous about continuing a string. **1976** *Billings* (Montana) *Gaz.* 27 June 1-F/2 The Mustangs stretched their scoreless string to 12 innings before finally connecting in the fourth inning.

f. *Sport.* (See quot. 1961.) Also *spec.* in *Bowling*, a succession of strikes. *N. Amer.*

1961 WEBSTER, *String*, a fixed or standard number of turns at play in a game or competition. **1970** *Globe & Mail* (Toronto) 28 Sept. 21/4 Fred Harrison failed to win any.. prize money in the Ace Bowling Centre's men's open five pin tournament but he..included a perfect 450 game in his 10-game string. **1979** RITGER & ALLEN *Compl. Guide Bowling Spares* 228/1 *String*, a number of continuous strikes. Also, in some areas, one game of bowling.

17. a. *Printing.* (*U.S.*) See quot. 1891.

1875 *Chicago Tribune* 23 Nov. 7/3 [She] always had a full string at measuring-time. **1889** *Current Lit.* Apr. 314/1 Presently his week's 'string' averaged twelve thousand a day. **1891** *Century Dict.*, *String*... A piece-compositor's aggregate of the proofs of types set by him, pasted on a long strip of paper. The amount of work done is determined by the measurement of this string. **1898** *Milwaukee Sentinel* 11 Jan. 3/1 Printers..who found it no unusual thing to 'paste up' 'strings' that averaged more than 1,500 an hour.

b. (See quots.)

1892 *Dialect Notes* I. 207 When he [*sc.* a correspondent] comes to make up his bill, he takes all the articles he has written for a given period and pastes them together, end to end. This he calls his *string*. **1913** W. G. BLEYER *Newspaper Writing & Editing* iii. 55 On some papers the correspondents clip out all of their news stories and paste them together in a 'string' which they send in once a month, so that the telegraph editor may pay them according to the length of the 'string'.

III. In various transferred uses.

†**18.** A ray, line of light. *Obs.*

c **1205** LAY. 17983 Þe leome gon striden a ueire seoue strengen.

†**19.** A length of wire. *Obs.*

1435 *Coventry Leet Bk.* I. 181 And then that wire that the mayster suppositthe wille be cherisshed atte gurdell, he shall com to his girdulmon and sey to hym 'Lo, here is a stryng or ij, that hathe ben mysgouerned atte herthe.'

†**20.** (See quot.) *Obs.*

1545 ELYOT *Dict.*, *Canterii* be the pieces, whiche do lye vnder a piece of tymber whan it is sawen, which som do call strynges.

21. *Mining.* A thin vein of ore or coal; a ramification of a lode.

1603 G. OWEN *Pembrokesh.* (1892) 91 The stringe is a smale narowe vayne sometymes ij iij or iiij foote in biggnes. **1619** S. ATKINSON *Discov. Gold Mynes Scot.* (Bannatyne Club) 37 From Short-clough water he removed unto Long-cloughbrayes,.. to seeke gold in solidd places: where he discovered a small stringe thereof. **1653** MANLOVE *Lead Mines Derbysh.* 270 (E.D.S.) Stickings and stringes of oar. **1747** HOOSON *Miner's Dict.* s.v. *Break-Off*, But if it happen that it break into several Leadings or Strings. **1855** LEIFCHILD *Cornwall* 98 Some of the copper veins in Herland mine.. eventually passed away east and west in mere strings, scarcely thicker than paper. **1867** MURCHISON *Siluria* ii. (ed. 4) 27 The frequent recurrence of thin strings of copper-ore.

†**22.** A rail, bar of iron or wood on which something slides or runs. *Obs.*

1778 W. HUTCHINSON *Northumb.* II. 417 Wheels of iron, the fellies or rims of which are hollow, so as to run upon strings of wood adapted thereto, with which the roads are laid. **1790** W. MARSHALL *Midl. Co.* I. 143 On this bar or string of iron, a ring, with a chain passing to the wheels, plays freely from end to end.

23. †**a.** = STRINGHALT. *Obs.*

1650 BULWER *Anthropomet.* 205 A Gelding (that was proud of a string). **1823** PURSGLOVE *Pract. Farriery* 204 The string, or spring halt.. is termed by some authors the blind spavin.

†**b.** A form of constipation in cattle. *Obs.*

1776 *Compl. Grazier* (ed. 4) 40 The Hind Spring or String is when they [*sc.* kine] become bound in their body, and cannot dung.

c. *Sc.* In *plural*: see quot. 1798.

1798 R. DOUGLAS *Agric. Roxb. & Selkirk* 149 Calves.. are sometimes seized with an inflammation in the intestines, provincially called *liver-crook*, or *strings*. **1802** G. V. SAMPSON *Statist. Surv. Londonderry* 214 Calves are liable to a disorder, called the strings.

†**24.** A narrow ridge on the surface of a flint.

a **1728** WOODWARD *Nat. Hist. Fossils* I. (1729) I. 53 The Flint constituting the Body of the Stone, of the Cylinder, and the String about it, is all of the same Colour and Substance.

25. *U.S.* A line of fencing.

1794 WASHINGTON *Lett.* Writ. 1892 XIII. 20, I was led to form the plan of having but one public road through my Mount Vernon tract,.. along the string of fence that divides the upper from the lower fields. **1854** *Trans. Mich. Agric. Soc.* VI. 177 The strings of fence will average eight and three-quarter rails high. **1903** A. ADAMS *Log of Cowboy* 17 On the Mexican side there was a single string of high brush fence.

26. *Carpentry.* **a.** = *string-board* (see 33); often with qualifying word or words; **b.** = *rough string* (ROUGH *a.* 21).

1711 W. SUTHERLAND *Shipbuild. Assist.* 65 A pair of winding Stairs, having a Nuel in the Center, and a Side or String for the Circumference. **1737** W. SALMON *Country Builder's Estimator* (ed. 2) 25 Of Stair-Cases... 1. Steps of common Stairs, Strings and String-boards, and Bearers included, of Oak, 8*d.* per Foot. **1812** P. NICHOLSON *Mech. Exerc.* 184 Sometimes the risers [are] mitred to brackets, and sometimes mitred with quaker strings. **1849** [P. NICHOLSON] *Carpentry* II. 3 Those pieces which support the ends of the steps are called strings.—That against the wall is called the wall string; the other, the outer string. **1886** MORSE *Jap. Homes* iv. 197 [The staircase] has two side-pieces, or strings, in which the steps, consisting of thick plank, are mortised.

27. *Shipbuilding.* (See quots.)

1711 W. SUTHERLAND *Shipbuild. Assist.* 164 Strings; parts used to strengthen; and what are called Clamps in the lower parts, are termed Strings upward. **1750** BLANCKLEY *Naval Expos.* 165 *String* is that strake of Plank within Side of the Ship that is wrought over the upper Deck Ports in the Wast. *c* **1850** *Rudim. Navig.* (Weale) 154 *String*, one or two planks withinside, next under the gunwale, answering to the sheer-strakes withoutside.

28. *Arch.* = *string-course* or *-moulding* (see 33).

1809 T. D. W. DEARN *Bricklayer's Guide* 101 This projection frequently occurs, and in many instances serves as an agreeable relief to the eye, if of no other use; it is sometimes called a *string*. **1817** RICKMAN *Archit.* 50 A plain string is also sometimes used as a cornice. **1842** *Ecclesiologist* I. 199 Ancient lancets have not, indeed, invariably strings underneath them. **1850** INKERSLEY *Inq. Styles Romanesque & Pointed Archit. France* 323 A moulded inclined plane above a flowered string.

29. *the String of Lorn*: see quot. 1678.

a **1678** in *Highland Papers* (S.H.S.) II. 85 The mountain betwixt Lochow and Lorn called the String. **1889** in Ld. A. Campbell *Waifs & Strays Celtic Tradit.* I. 28 She fled with the precious deeds across the String of Lorn.

30. *Shetland.* A strong tidal current in a narrow channel. [ON. *strengr.*]

1884 C. RAMPINI *Shetld. & Shetlanders* ii. 80 Even in crossing a string of tide the fishermen always betook themselves to their oars. **1888** JESSIE SAXBY *Lads of Lunda* 131, I am sure we could not cross that string of tide in safety.

31. *Billiards.* A string-line, a baulk-line. *U.S.*

1857 *Spirit of Times* 30 May 200/1 The player in hand can play at any ball, the largest half of which lies outside the string. **1872** 'MARK TWAIN' *Roughing It* 336 Cheese it, pard; you've banked your ball clean outside the string. **1964** SULLIVAN & CRANE *Young Sportsman's Guide to Pocket Billiards* viii. 77 Through the head spot is drawn the 'head string'. This is a line that passes through the head spot and the two center diamonds on the opposing side rails (near the head end of the table). There are comparable designations —'foot spot' and 'foot string'—at the opposite end of the table. **1974** *Rules of Game* 80/1 Each player takes a cue ball, and plays it against the foot cushion from behind the head string.

IV. *attrib.* and *Comb.*

32. Obvious comb. **a.** In sense 'made or consisting of string', as ***string bag, ball, netting, rug***; 'containing string', as ***string box, case***; *Mus.* (see 3 c), as ***string band, instrument, man*** (*obs.* exc. *Hist.*), †***minstrel, music, musical instrument, player, quartet, trio***; **b.** similative, as ***string colour***; ***string-coloured, -like, -tailed*** adjs. **c.** instrumental, as ***string-soled, -tied*** adjs.

1901 B. PAIN *Another Englishwoman's Love-Lett.* xxvi. 116 A *string-bag full of parcels. **1891** KIPLING *Light that Failed* (1900) 232 Dick.. played aimlessly with the tins and *string-ball on the counter. **1860** SALA *Baddington Peerage* I. xvi. 290 There was a *string-band and a wind-band at the Apollo Belvidere. **1839** DICKENS *Nicholas Nickleby* xxxvii. 354 Paper, pens, ink, ruler, sealing-wax, wafers, pounce-box, *string-box, fire-box.. all had their accustomed inches of space. **1852** —— *Bleak Ho.* x, Mr. Snagsby has dealt.. in string boxes, rulers, inkstands,.. ever since he was out of his time. **1926–7** *Army & Navy Stores Catal.* 120/2 Household string box.. containing a ball of fine, medium, and coarse brown string. **1980** R. ADAMS *Girl in Swing* xix. 255 She came back with the other two saucepans, the lemon-squeezer, the string-box and two brown-paper parcels. **1899** *Pall Mall Gaz.* 26 Dec. 3/2 *String-cases in red morocco. **1899** *Daily News* 20 Mar. 8/7 The creamy lace.. will be deep enough in tint to be beige, or even *string-colour. **1898** *Ibid.* 19 Feb. 3/3 With collars and sleeves of *string-coloured guipure. **1705** ADDISON *Italy, Rome* 321 There is not One *String-Instrument that seems comparable to our Violins. **1859** *Habits of Gd. Society* vi. 232 The zither, one of the sweetest and most touching of string instruments. **1882** VINES tr. *Sachs' Bot.* 120 Mosses, which have *string-like cell-groups in the stem. *c* **1470** in J. P. Collier *Engl. Dram. Poetry* (1879) I. 39 Mynstrells.. wherof some use trumpetts, some shalmes, some small pipes: some are *stringmen. **1971** *Country Life* 23 Dec. 1776/3 The peacock for the most distinguished person at the high table was carried into the dining-hall with pompous ceremony on a gold or silver-gilt charger by the most elegant lady of the assembled company, attended by trumpeters, pipers and string-men. **1498** in R. Henry *Hist. Gt. Brit.* (1793) VI. 724 Item, for three *stryngmynstrels wages, 5 li. **1712** ADDISON *Spect.* No. 361 ¶3 He added, that the Cat had contributed more to Harmony than any other Animal; as we are not only beholden to her for this Wind-Instrument, but for our *String Musick in general. **1686** PLOT *Staffordsh.* 300 He.. makes.. all sorts of *string-musical instruments. **1882** CAULFEILD & SAWARD *Dict. Needlework* 464 **String Netting* .. is made to cover glass bottles.., the network formed by the string protecting the more fragile object that it covers. **1923** *Daily Mail* 6 Feb. 7 All the *string-players pulled their weight. **1979** *Jrnl. R. Soc. Arts* CXXVII. 385/2 The Council has approved this year's awards of scholarships to enable young string players and singers to undertake advanced studies. **1875** J. BISHOP tr. *Otto's Violin* iv. (ed. 4) 52 A *string quartett, made by A. Engleder, of Munich,.. possessed the following peculiarity of form. The upper half of each instrument was [etc.]. **1876** STAINER & BARRETT *Dict. Mus. Terms, String quartet*, (1) A composition in four parts, for two violins, viola and violoncello. (2) The group of stringed instruments in a band. **1882** CAULFEILD & SAWARD *Dict. Needlework* 464/2 **String rugs*.. are made from odds and ends of coarse Berlin or fleecy wool, which are either knitted up with string or worked into coarse canvas in loops. **1924** *Blackw. Mag.* Oct. 556/2 We steal softly on our *string-soled shoes down the stairs. **1893** E. H. BARKER *Wand. Southern Waters* 64 *String-tailed, goggle-eyed, meagre cats that seize your dinner. **1925** J. GREGORY *Bab of Backwoods* xxiii. 285 There was a *string-tied canvas bag, as long as her open palm. **1960** *Farmer & Stockbreeder* 2 Feb. 5/3 Hay from £9 10s to £10, loose in stack; in bales, string-tied, £10 to £10 10s. **1874** OUSELEY *Musical Form* 52 Thus are constructed symphonies and sonatas; *string-trios, quartetts.

33. Special comb.: **string analysis** *Linguistics*, a method of analysing sentences as linear strings; **string art** *U.S.*, the art of making decorative pictures by winding yarn round nails driven into a flat surface; **string-bark (tree)** *Austral.*, = STRINGY-BARK; **string bass** *Jazz*, a double-bass; also *transf.*, the player of a double-bass; **string-bean**, (*a*) *U.S.*, the French or kidney bean; (*b*) *U.S. colloq.*, a tall thin person; also *transf.*; **string bed**, the Indian charpoy; **string bikini** = sense 6 c above; **string-binder**, a reaping-machine which ties the corn in sheaves; similarly **string-binding** *ppl. a.*; **string-block**, in a wooden-frame pianoforte, a block of wood holding the studs to which the fixed ends of the strings are looped; **string-board**, a board which supports the ends of the steps in a wooden staircase; also *collect. sing.*; **string bog** *Physical Geogr.*, a boggy area containing long, high banks of silty material; **string correspondent** = STRINGER 11; **string cot** = *string bed* (cf. COT *sb.*[4] 1); **string-course** (see quot. 1910); **string drum**, a musical instrument, consisting of a rectangular box over which strings are stretched, and played by striking the strings with a stick; **string figure**, a figure made by passing a length of string round the fingers of both hands (cf. CAT'S-CRADLE); so **string game**; **string-galvanometer**, a galvanometer consisting of a fine conducting fibre, for measuring rapidly-fluctuating currents; **string-gauge** (see quot.); **string glove**, a glove knitted or crocheted of coarse mercerized cotton yarn; †**string-hough** *v. trans.*, to hamstring; †**string hound**, ? a leash-hound; **string-jack**, a jumping-jack; **string-line**, †(*a*) = CHORD *sb.*[1] 4; (*b*) *Billiards* (*U.S.*), the baulkline; **string-maker**, one who makes string or strings; †also with reference to sense 16 b; **string man** = STRINGER 11 (see also sense 32 a); †**string-metal**, ? metal for making wire strings for musical instruments; **string-moulding**, a moulding carried horizontally along a wall; **string organ** (see quot.); **string-pea** *U.S.*, a pea with edible pods; **string-piece**, (*a*) a long piece of timber serving to connect and support a framework (e.g. a floor, bridge); a longitudinal railway-sleeper (*U.S.*); a heavy squared timber carried along the edge of a wharf-front; †(*b*) (see quot. 1842); **string-pin** = HITCH-PIN; **string-plate**, the metal plate into which the hitch-pins are inserted; **string point, proof**: in sugar manufacture, a degree of concentration at which the boiled sugar may be drawn out in the form of a thread; **string-pulling** *vbl. sb.*, the act of exerting influence, esp. behind the scenes; cf. WIRE-PULLING *vbl. sb.*; hence **string-puller**; **string puppet**, a puppet actuated by means of strings, a marionette; also *fig.*; **string slum** *U.S.*, a row of unsightly buildings along the side of a road (see quot. 1939[2]); **string tie** orig. *U.S.*, a very narrow necktie worn as a bow; **string-tone** *Mus.*, the sound of bowed stringed instruments; hence **string-toned** *a.*; †**string-torments**, a rendering of L. *fidiculæ* (pl.), an instrument of torture consisting of a number of thin cords; **string vest**, a man's vest or singlet made from an open-knit fabric (cf. sense 1 p above); also ***string underwear***; †**string-watch**, ? a watch having a string fitted to the fusee and barrel instead of a chain (cf. 9 a above); **stringwood**, a small tree of St. Helena, *Acalypha rubra*, now extinct, named from its pendent spikes of reddish sterile flowers (*Treas. Bot.* 1866).

[**1960** *Language* XXXVI. 63 Positively, it leads to the development of a string constituent analysis in which grammatical strings are discovered and described.] **1962** Z. S. HARRIS (*title*) *String analysis of sentence structure. **1972** HARTMANN & STORK *Dict. Lang. & Linguistics* 221/2 A string analysis of the sentence *Today we heard three shots in the park* would be as follows: *We heard shots* is the elementary sentence; *today* is an adjunct to the left of the elementary sentence; *in the park* is an adjunct to the right of the elementary sentence; *three* is an adjunct to the left of the word *shots*. **1972** *Creative Crafts* Aug. 21/1 Our ship bounding over gleaming silver waves is an excellent example of fascinating *string art, the fool-the-eye craft which makes curves from straight lines. **1975** *String Art Encycl.* 41 (*caption*) A traditional fruit display looks different.. when you stitch it using the string-art technique. **1845** J. O. BALFOUR *Sk. N.S. Wales* 37 The *string bark tree is also useful. **1862** W. ARCHER *Products of Tasmania* 39 (Morris) Gum-topped String-bark, sometimes called white gum (*Eucalyptus gigantea*, var.). **1927** *Melody Maker* Aug. 771/2 Their instrumentation.. which, when playing on Sundays, is a combination of piano, flute, 'cello, violin, *string bass and tymps. **1930** *Ibid.* Jan. 27/1 The pianist and string bass must be particularly complimented on the steadiness of their playing. **1956** M. STEARNS *Story of Jazz* (1957) xvii. 205 The string-bass began to 'walk', or play melodic figures instead of pounding away at one or two notes. **1977** J. WAINWRIGHT *Do Nothin'* iii. 39 'Occupation?' 'Musician... String bass.' *Ibid.* xi. 197, I turn to the string-bass man. **1759** E. HOLYOKE *Diary* 11 July in G. F. Dow *Holyoke Diaries* (1911) 20 First *Str[ing] Beans y^e^. year. **1801** *Spirit of Farmers' Museum* 244 Her neck-beef sausage, and her tough string beans. **1842** HAWTHORNE *Amer. Note-bks.* (1868) II. 99 It was a very pleasant moment when I gathered the first string-beans. **1936** WODEHOUSE *Laughing Gas* xi. 114 'Gee!' he said. 'Are you one of those English Oils?' 'I am. Or, rather, I was.' 'I always thought they were string-bean sort of guys without any chins.' **1975** R. H. RIMMER *Premar Experiments* (1976) i. 70 Ellen, I know you can't help it, but you remind me of a starving, stringbean kitten that wandered into our house when I was a kid. **1977** *New Yorker* 3 Oct. 80/2 'Did Germany need living space?' Hellmann asked, translating the stringbean's German word. **1895** MRS. CROKER *Village Tales* 16 We were presently conducted to an empty hut, provided with broad *string beds. **1911** H. BEGBIE *Other Sheep* i. 9 The priest.. insisted upon my having a charpoy, or string-bed, for the night. **1974** *McCall's* Nov. 10/1 Winter vacation time is coming and the *string bikini is still with us—better, if not bigger, than ever. **1976** 'E. MCBAIN' *Guns* (1977) vii. 194 The tall sleek blonde in the white string bikini. **1891** *Daily News* 10 Oct. 3/1 It is not so long since the master was entirely at the mercy of his labourers in harvest time... The *string-binder has altered all that. **1910** P. M'CONNELL *Farm Equipm.* 75 The modern string-binder was simply this machine plus a mechanical tier. **1882** *Essex Herald* No. 4269/3 This is the second harvest in Australia in which *string-binding reapers of American manufacture have been used. **1851** W. POLE in

Rimbault *Pianoforte* (1860) 163 The strings were looped at one end upon studs driven into a solid block of wood, which we may call the *string-block. **1703** R. Neve *City & C. Purchaser* 252 Stairs, with Rails, Ballasters, *String-boards, Posts. **1825** J. Nicholson *Oper. Mech.* 604 The price of string-board is regulated by the foot superficial. [**1956** *Contrib. Gray Herbarium Harvard Univ.* CLXXVIII. 62 These bog ridges are the strings of the *Strangmoor* of European authors.] **1959** *Geogr. Jrnl.* CXXV. 145 A particularly well defined form [of patterned ground feature] are the *string bogs, or *strängmoore*, which occur particularly in eastern Canada. **1973** A. L. Washburn *Periglacial Processes & Environment* iv. 151 Although string bogs or closely similar features have also been observed far north of tree line and well within the zone of continuous permafrost.., most investigators agree they are not necessarily indicative of permafrost. **1960** *Spectator* 24 June 920 Later he became a '*string correspondent' sending items to all the local papers, and he also sold jokes at a dollar apiece. **1969** B. Moore *Workers in World News* i. 6 To return to our Paris correspondent, as well as the news coming to him through the newspaper in whose office he worked, he would probably have his own 'stringers'—or string correspondents—in the different provincial centres. **1895** Kipling *Day's Work* (1898) 178 Scott..laid himself down to rest on a *string cot in a bare room. **1960** R. P. Jhabvala *Householder* ii. 83 A string-cot had been put up for her in the living-room. **1825** Fosbroke *Encycl. Antiq.* vi. 123* **String-courses* are those from which buildings begin to narrow upwards. **1833** Loudon *Encycl. Archit.* §451 A string course, or horizontal band. *a* **1878** Sir G. Scott *Lect. Archit.* I. 228 The sill always well sloped, to throw off the water, and having usually a string-course below, to prevent it from running down and discolouring the walls. **1910** C. H. Gregory *Gloss. Build. Constr.* 42 String course. A distinctive horizontal course, projecting or flush, carried round a building, usually at floor level, to roughly mark the division of a building into floors. **1940** *Amer. Speech* XV. 125 'Ionisation', written for percussion instruments and piano, requires the use of *bongos, sirens.., guiro, claves, maracas, tarole*, and **string-drum*. **1976** D. Munrow *Instruments Middle Ages & Renaissance* v. 33/4 Various names have been used for the string drum... The thick gut strings are stretched over an oblong sound box and tuned to the key-note and fifth of the pipe so as to provide a drone accompaniment. All the strings are struck at the same time with a small stick held in the right hand. **1902** *Man* II. 146 Many travellers have stated that various peoples, more or less primitive, amuse themselves by making *string figures to which the general term of 'cat's cradle' is usually applied. **1963** K. Vonnegut *Cat's Cradle* v. 20 His fingers made the string figure called a 'cat's cradle'. **1909** *Westm. Gaz.* 13 May 5/2 The Einthoven *string galvanometer,..by means of which the beating of the heart can be measured with the greatest accuracy. **1879** *Jrnl. Anthropol. Inst.* IX. 26 Now as to the origin of the *string games among these Malays (Dayaks) and Polynesians, it is evident that they did not learn them from Europeans. **1910** *Encycl. Brit.* X. 601/2 In particular it is found that the string game called 'cat's cradle' in various forms is of very wide diffusion, being found even in Australia. **1876** Stainer & Barrett *Dict. Mus. Terms*, **String-gauge*, a small instrument for measuring the thickness of strings for violins, guitars, etc. **1949** 'J. Tey' *Brat Farrar* xxiv. 217 Did I put my *string gloves in the locker? **1978** A. Morice *Murder by Proxy* iii. 32 His coat, cap and string gloves..were neatly arranged on a chair. **1605** Willet *Hexapla Gen.* 447 Some read they *string-haughed a bull. **1631** in *Househ. Ord.* (1790) 350 The Master of the Bows and *String Hounds. **1863** 'Holme Lee' *A. Warleigh* II. 205 Sinclair..stood like a *string-jack, his arms outstretched. **1551** *Stryngline [see chord *sb.*[1] 4]. **1897** in R. F. Foster *Compl. Hoyle* 585 A ball whose centre is on the string line must be regarded as within the line. **14..** *Nom.* in Wr.-Wülcker 686/32 *Hic cordex*, a *stryngmaker. **1721** Amherst *Terræ Fil.* No. 20. 104 From whence it appears, that this Richard P——e was a great string-maker. **1833** Fardely tr. *Otto's Treat. Violin* 60 The Neukirch string-makers. **1943** C. Hollingworth *German just behind Me* ix. 150 By means of bribing his assistant I got a telephone call to my own '*string man' in Belgrade in order that my paper should know I was alive. **1968** M. Allingham *Cargo of Eagles* viii. 98 I'm the string man in these parts... I..write for the *Gazette* at Nine Ash and keep a watching brief for the *Globe* in town. It's called stringing. *a* **1626** Bacon *Physiol. Rem. Baconiana* (1679) 96 Statua Metal, and Bell Metal, and Trumpet Metal, and *String Metal. **1833** Loudon *Encycl. Archit.* Gloss., *String mouldings. **1837** *Civil Engin. & Arch. Jrnl.* I. 57/2 An elegant three-light Gothic window, having a neat label and string mouldings. **1876** Stainer & Barrett *Dict. Mus. Terms*, **String organ*, a new musical instrument, the sounds of which are produced by the association of a free reed and wire string. **1891** *Century Dict.* s.v. *Pea*, The pods of the sugar-pea, skinless pea, or *string-pea are eaten, as in the case of 'string-beans'. **1789** W. Jessop *Rep. Thames & Isis* 22 Flat Stones set edgeways [inside a Lock], with a *String piece of Elm at the Foot. **1802** G. V. Sampson *Stat. Surv. Londonderry* 323 The piers [of the bridge]..are bound together by 13 string-pieces, equally divided, and transversely bolted; on the string-pieces is laid the flooring. **1840** H. S. Tanner *Canals & Rail Roads U.S.* 261 *String pieces*, wooden rails upon which the iron bars of rail-roads are placed. **1842** Gwilt *Archit.* Gloss., *String* or *String Piece*, that part of a flight of stairs which forms its ceiling or sofite. **1898** *Scribner's Mag.* May 573 He just fell in off the stringpiece of the dock. **1889** Brinsmead *Hist. Pianoforte* 181 The Brinsmead system of tuning requires no wood either to fasten the *string-pins or support the iron frame. **1827** Broadwood *Patent* in *Newton's Lond. Jrnl.* Ser. II. (1830) IV. 132 A metallic plate ..to be called the *string plate, into which the hitch pins are set, for the ends of the strings to be fastened to. **1909** Jones & Scard *Manuf. Cane Sugar* vii. 198 The highly concentrated juice is boiled to '*string' or crystallising point. .. The admission and subsequent discharge of the juice are so regulated, that by the time the latter has reached the point of withdrawal, it has been concentrated to 'string' point. **1909** H. C. P. Geerligs *Cane Sugar* 214 The consistency of the liquid being such that a sample can be drawn out in the form of a thread, the liquid is said to be boiled to 'string proof'. **1915** —— *Pract. White Sugar Manuf.* 80 String-proof boiling should entirely be discarded. **1961** *Guardian* 27 Sept. 10/4 International *string-pullers still try to make the Congo dance to their tunes. **1977** D. Ramsay *You can't call it Murder* I. 51 Judith contrived, with the aid of a venerable string puller..to gain admittance. **1949** *Ann. Reg. 1948* 330 The same political manœuvres, corruption, and *string-pulling by moneyed interests..were discernible. **1970** E. R. Johnson *God Keepers* (1971) xiv. 146 The choice between public-opinion pressure and Lucchese string-pulling pressure. **1982** W. Buchan *John Buchan* x. 192 At Londonderry House..many believed, important political strings were pulled. The importance of that string-pulling was probably exaggerated. **1937** W. S. Lanchester (*title*) Hand puppets and *string puppets. **1970** G. F. Newman *Sir, You Bastard* iv. 126 The visit was nothing more than a test to see just how much the firm's man he was, to see how he would interpret the string-puppet role. **1980** S. Brett *Dead Side of Mike* iv. 39 Two Italian string-puppets in silver armour. **1939** *Sun* (Baltimore) 25 Mar. 8/2 A bill designed to halt the growth of *string slums along the public highways by conservative zoning has been pending before the Judiciary Committee of the State Senate for weeks. *Ibid.* 24 Oct. 12/1 The string slums walling in sections of the highways are composed of hot-dog stands, ramshackle overnight cabins, automobile graveyards, cheap dance halls, gaudy taverns and a host of other hideous business places. **1950** *Ibid.* 28 Apr. 18/3 Once string slums come into being, they stay. **1895** *Montgomery Ward Catal.* Spring & Summer 95/2 Men's folding *string ties. **1916** *Daily Colonist* (Victoria, B.C.) 22 July 12/6 (Advt.), Red, white and blue string ties. Made of a nice quality silk crepe de Chine. **1942** J. D. Carr *Seat of Scornful* xi. 152 He welcomed them.. wearing a shiny black alpaca suit and a string tie. **1976** L. Henderson *Major Enquiry* xvi. 108 He was dressed in a dark blue suit..pale blue shirt and string tie. **1928** J. P. Dunn *Student's Guide to Orchestration* xii. 54 *String tone permeates every orchestral movement of any length. **1968** A. Niland *Introd. Organ* ii. 30 Undulating stops..are usually of string tone. **1938** *Oxf. Compan. Mus.* 669/1 *Geigen Principal*.., a sort of slightly *string-toned diapason of 8- or 4-foot length and pitch. **1609** Holland *Amm. Marcell.* xxix. ii. 353 Then were the rackes stretched.., the *string-torments also and the whips put in readinesse. **1967** D. Pinner *Ritual* vii. 70 He shoved his nylon socks and *string underwear in the first drawer he found. **1951** *Catal. of Exhibits, South Bank Exhib., Festival of Britain* 96/1 Khaki trousers..*String vests..Long cashmere pants. **1983** *Listener* 3 Feb. 19/3 You can always..don your string vest and boxer shorts and bang hell out of a rowing machine. **1686** *Lond. Gaz.* No. 2120/8 An old *String-Watch (in two Silver Cases).

string (strɪŋ), *v.* Pa. t. and pa. pple. **strung.** Forms: 6 **stringe, strynge,** 6– **string.** *Pa. t.* 7 **stringed,** 9 *dial.* **strang,** 7– **strung.** *Pa. pple.* 6 **strong,** 7 **strunge,** 6– **strung;** 5 **y-strenged,** 6 **strynged,** 7–9 **stringed.** [f. string *sb.* Except for an instance of *ystrenged* (*c* 1400 in 1), the vb. first appears in the 16th c. The 'strong' conjugation in imitation of *sing* (cf. *ring*) has prevailed from 1590 onwards, though a few examples of the weak form *stringed* occur in the 16–19th c.]

1. *trans.* **a.** To fit (a bow) with its string; to 'bend' or prepare for use by slipping the loop of the bowstring into its notch, so that the string is drawn tight.

c **1400** *Laud Troy Bk.* 6537 With bowys gode wel y-strenged. **1545** Ascham *Toxoph.* II. (Arb.) 112 In stringynge youre bowe, you must loke for muche bende or lytle bende. **1697** Dryden *Æneis* x. 674 Then, as the winged Weapon whiz'd along; See now, said he, whose Arm is better strung. **1788** J. Hurdis *Village Curate* (1797) 96 He tipt his arrow, strung his bow, and shot. **1897** *Encycl. Sport* I. 43/1 (Archery) The next thing is to 'string' or 'bend' the bow.

b. To fit or furnish (a musical instrument) with a string or strings; to fix strings in. Also *poet.* to tighten the strings of (an instrument) to the required pitch; to tune.

1530 Rastell *Bk. Purgat.* II. xv. d 3 b, As the harper can not make nor shewe no melodye wyth his harpe, excepte yt be strynged and in tewne. **1591** Spenser *Virg. Gnat* 16 Playing on yuorie harp with silver strong. **1591** Shaks. *Two Gent.* III. ii. 78 Orpheus Lute was strung with Poets sinewes. **1676** Mace *Musick's Mon.* 42, I would..that the Scholar be taught to String his Instrument, with Good and True Strings. **1761** Sterne *Tr. Shandy* V. xv, Do you know whether my fiddle's in tune or no?.. 'Tis wickedly strung. **1812** Byron *Ch. Har.* I. xiii, He seized his harp, which he at times could string. **1827** J. Stewart in *Abridgm. Specif. Patents, Mus.* (1871) 101 Improvements in pianofortes and in the mode of stringing the same.

c. To fit (the bow of a violin, etc.) with horsehairs stretched from end to end.

1663 Butler *Hud.* I. ii. 126 His grizly Beard was long and thick, With which he strung his Fiddle-stick.

d. To fit (a racket) with strings and cross-strings of cord or catgut.

1884 [see stringing *vbl. sb.* 1].

e. To fit (a thing) with the necessary strings or ties to keep it firm or in place.

[**1805** *Edin. Bk. Prices* 61 Stringing or banding.] **1931** *Henley's ABC Gliding & Sailflying* 232 Having sewn up all the edges neatly, the next operation is 'stringing' the wing to keep the fabric tight to the ribs.

2. To furnish (the body) with nerves or sinews; *spec.* to furnish (the tongue) with its frænum. Chiefly used as in 3.

1632 *Lyly's Endimion* III. iii. 125 (Song), When his tongue Once goes, a Cat is not worse strung. **1632** Brome *North. Lasse* Ep. Ded., Though Art neuer strung her tongue; yet once it yeelded a delightfull sound. **1700** Dryden *Ovid's Met.* xv. 343 In time he vaunts among his Youthful Peers, Strong-bon'd, and strung with Nerves, in pride of Years. **1716** Gay *Trivia* III. 241 Has not wise nature strung the legs and feet With firmest nerves, design'd to walk the street? *fig.* **1697** Dryden *Æneis* Ded. (e) 2 Their Language is not strung with Sinews like our English. **1862** Merivale *Rom. Emp.* lxii. (1865) VII. 354 He lacked the tenacity of fibre which strung the old Roman and Sabine fabric.

3. *fig.* **a.** (often with direct allusion to 1). To make tense, brace, give vigour or tone to (the nerves, sinews, the mind, its ideas or impressions, etc.).

1599 Storer *Life & D. Wolsey* I 1 b, The peoples hearts of late are strung so hard, That they will breake before one note shall sound, Or so vntunable, that still they iar'de. **1699** Dryden *To John Driden* 89 Toil strung the Nerves and purifi'd the Blood. **1725** Pope *Odyss.* VIII. 568 He fights, subdues: for Pallas strings his arms. **1823** Scott *Quentin D.* xxxvii, The thought..strung his nerves with vigour, which defied fatigue. **1848–9** Lytton *K. Arth.* III. xiv, Strung by that sleep, the savage scowl'd around. **1871** Freeman *Hist. Ess.* Ser. I. viii. 229 The besiegers' hearts were strung by every motive which could lead men to defend themselves to the last. **1880** Meredith *Tragic Com.* I. v. 92 A turn of her fingers would string or slacken him.

b. with *up*.

1845 J. Coulter *Adv. Pacific* xvi. 247 The muscles of every one were strung up for the moment. **1888** 'R. Boldrewood' *Robbery under Arms* xxii, When a man's cold and tired, and hungry,..a good caulker of grog..strings him up and puts him straight. **1898** *Dubl. Rev.* Jan. 163 Perhaps this is an attempt to string up the human ideal too highly for everyday practice.

c. To brace *to*, rarely *for* (action) or *to* (do something). Also, to attune *to* (a frame of mind). Also (*Austral.* and *N.Z. slang*), to egg *on*.

1748 Gray *Alliance* 69 Need we the influence of the northern star To string our nerves and steel our hearts to war? **1881** A. Bathgate *Waitaruna* 142 A barmaid in one of its hotels..is popularly known as 'Goodall's stringer'... She makes herself agreeable to those who frequent the house, and so she 'strings them on' and induces them to spend their money there. **1888** Meredith *Reading of Earth* 10 Where Life is at her grindstone set, That she may give us edgeing keen, String us for battle, till [etc.]. **1888** 'R. Boldrewood' *Robbery under Arms* III. vi. 81 Mr. Hamilton waited for about an hour so as to be sure they weren't stringing him on to go into the open to be potted at.

d. With qualifying adv. (chiefly *pass.*): To bring to a (specified) condition of tension or sensitiveness. Cf. overstrung 1, *high-strung* s.v. high *adv.* 10 a.

1860 Mrs. Clive *Why Paul Ferroll* vi. 135 Elinor, finely strung to sounds. **1863** Mrs. Gaskell *Sylvia's Lovers* I. vii. 132 But Sylvia was too highly strung for banter. **1866** Ballantyne *Shifting Winds* ii. (1881) 11 A.. British tar.. whose nerves were tightly strung and used to danger.

†4. ? To furnish or adorn (a garment) with strings or ties. *Obs.*

a **1548** Hall *Chron., Hen. VIII*, 8 b, Garmentes of Crymosyn Satyn embroudered..with cloth of gold, cut in Pomegranettes and yokes, strynged after the facion of Spaygne. **1598** Florio, *Stringolare*, to point, to lace, or to string.

5. a. To bind, tie, fasten, or secure with a string or strings; †*spec.* to fasten (a book) with ribbons or cords (*obs.*); to tether (an animal).

1613 Chapman *Rev. Bussy d'Amb.* II. i. D 3, As the foolish Poet that still writ All his most selfe-lou'd verse in paper royall, Or Partchment..Bound richly vp, and strung with Crimson strings. **1641** Milton *Animadv.* 19 Set the grave councels up upon their shelvs again, and string them hard. **1805** Wordsw. *Prelude* v. 240 If..We had been followed, hourly watched, and noosed, Each in his several melancholy walk Stringed like a poor man's heifer at its feed. **1860** Geo. Eliot *Mill on Fl.* IV. iii, Bob took up the small stringed packet of books.

b. To bind (the handle of a cricket-bat) with twine wound tightly round.

1887 *St. James's Gaz.* 16 Feb. 5/1 Makers only string the bat for the purpose of concealing defects and selling the article at a higher price.

6. a. To thread or file (beads and the like) on or as on a string. Also *fig.* Also with *together*, etc.

1612 Donne *Progr. Soule, 2nd Anniv.* 208 As these starres were but so many beads Strung on one string. **1712** Addison *Spect.* No. 476 ¶2 Men of great Learning..often..chuse to throw down their Pearls in Heaps before the Reader, rather than be at the Pains of stringing them. **1783** Justamond tr. *Raynal's Hist. Indies* III. 177 The roots are afterwards strung upon little strings to dry them. **1832** Mrs. Child *Girl's Own Bk.* (ed. 4) 68 The hard red seed-vessels of the rose, strung upon strong thread, make quite a pretty necklace. **1836** Marryat *Midsh. Easy* vi, James was very busy stringing the fish through the gills upon a piece of osier. **1844** 'Jon. Slick' *High Life N. York* I. 46 There wasn't a gal ..could pull an even yoke with her a stringing onions. **1874** H. H. Cole *Catal. Ind. Art S. Kens. Mus.* App. 297 Necklace.., formed of gold pear-shaped drops strung together. **1901** *Jrnl. Exper. Med.* 1 Oct. 604 They contain much of the basophile substance in the form of fine granules, often strung along in rows.

b. To hang or suspend by a connecting string.

1890 Gunter *Miss Nobody* xxiii. (1891) 268 These [lights] are strung down the avenue and placed here and there through the gardens. **1907** J. H. Patterson *Man-Eaters of Tsavo* ii. 27 A rope by which two empty oil tins were strung across the donkey's neck.

c. *fig.* To compose, put together in connected speech. Sometimes with direct allusion to the literal sense (6). Also with *together, up*.

1605 *1st Pt. Jeronimo* I. i. 60 And well pickt out, knight Marshall; speech well strung. **1620** Shelton *2nd Pt. Quix.* xliii. 281 Threescore thousand Satans take thee and thy Prouerbs, this howre thou hast beene stringing them one vpon another. **1786** Burns *Vision* iv, Stringing blethers up in rhyme For fools to sing. **1830** H. Lee *Mem. Manager* I. iii. 81 Anecdotes and reminiscences which I am about to string together. **1856** *N. Brit. Rev.* XXVI. 223 On this thread of incident are strung the author's views of social life.

1884 *Manch. Exam.* 1 Nov. 5/1 It is easy to indulge in general assertions and to string platitudes together.

d. *to* ***string up***: to post up the name of (a person) in a list.

1854 SURTEES *Handley Cr.* xiv. (1901) I. 98 You can't do better nor follow the example o' the Leamington lads, who string up all the tradespeople with the amount of their [hunt-] subscriptions in the shops and public places.

7. a. To hang, kill by hanging. Usually with *up*.

1727 GAY *Begg. Op.* III. xiii, And if rich Men like us were to swing, 'Twou'd thin the Land, such Numbers to string Upon Tyburn Tree! **1786** BURNS *Author's Cry* xxii, Tho' by the neck she should be strung, She'll no desert. **1810** LAMB *Inconv. Being Hanged* Wks. 1903 I. 62 We string up dogs, foxes, bats, moles, weasels. Man surely deserves a steadier death. **1893** MCCARTHY *Red Diamonds* I. 71 They strung him up after a fair trial before Judge Lynch.

fig. **1747** W. HORSLEY *Fool* No. 76 (1748) II. 195 From this ..you may readily conclude the Reason why you are stringed up here, as a signal Instance of Folly.

b. *intr.* To be hanged. Also with *up*. *Sc.*

a **1714** LOCKHART *Mem. Scot.* (ed. 3) Pref. p. ix, My Accusations..are so well founded, that was there, (as we say in Scotland) a right sitting Sheriff, I would not doubt to see some Gentlemen string. **1715** PENNECUIK *Descr. Tweeddale*, etc. 139 You must, or you must string. **1817** SCOTT *Rob Roy* xxx, You have confessed yourself a spy, and should string up to the next tree. **1896** 'G. SETOUN' *R. Urquhart* xxvi. 280, I would ha'e strung for it willin'.

8. a. *trans.* To deprive (a thing) of its string or strings; to strip the 'string' from (a bean-pod); to remove the runners from (a strawberry-bed); to strip (currants) from the stalk.

1664 EVELYN *Kal. Hort., Mar.* (1679) 12 Mid-March dress up..and string your Strawberry beds. **1747** MRS. GLASSE *Cookery* (1767) 17 To dress French beans. First string them, then cut them in two. **1888** *Sheffield Gloss.* s.v., To string currants is to unstring them, i.e. to strip the berries off their stalks.

†**b.** *spec.* To remove the string from (a lamprey): see STRING *sb.* 2b. In quots. as a 'proper' term for carving the fish. *Obs.*

1508–13 *Bk. Keruynge* in *Babees Bk.* (1868) 265 Strynge that lampraye. **1694** N. H. *Ladies Dict.* 415/1 A Salmon, chine it; a Lamprey, string it; a Pike, splat it.

c. To pull off (bark) from a tree by champing it into strings or fibres.

1733 W. ELLIS *Chiltern & Vale Farm.* 124 The Deer greedily eat [the bark of the witch elm], and have so great a love for it, that they will string it with their Mouths to the last bit.

9. To furnish, equip, or adorn *with* something suspended or slung.

1845 J. COULTER *Adv. Pacific* iii. 24 We..shot a number of rabbits, and strung our rigging with geese. **1874** H. H. COLE *Catal. Ind. Art S. Kens. Mus.* 187 Brass and silver wires strung with green..beads. **1906** *Macm. Mag.* Sept. 844 A surly loon strung with a telescope.

10. To draw up in a line or row; to extend in a string or series; to post so as to form a series of detached or separated units. Also with *out, up*.

a **1670** SPALDING *Troub. Chas. I* (Bannatyne Club) I. 154 They stringed up their horse company on the other syde of the watter of Dee. **1875** W. T. SHERMAN *Mem.* I. vi. 163 Ships were strung for miles along the lower levee [of New Orleans]. **1901** CONAN DOYLE in *Wide World Mag.* VIII. 111/1 Ten thousand men, strung over a large extent of country. **1908** S. E. WHITE *Riverman* xxvi, The rowboats were dragged backward,..and strung out along the bank below.

(*b*) *spec.* to place (pipes) end to end along the line of a trench, in preparation for welding them together.

1949 *Our Industry* (Anglo-Iranian Oil Co. Ltd.) (ed. 2) v. 163 The pipes are strung out along the line of the trench and placed into position alongside or over it on temporary supports, and the lengths are then connected by electric welding. **1957** *Oil & Gas Reporter* VI. 1141 The service of 'stringing pipe' for oil and gas pipe lines does not, within and of itself, constitute a transportation of property. **1966** *Petroleum Handbk.* (Shell Internat. Petroleum Co.) (ed. 5) 266/2 The construction phases consist of: clearing and grading the right of way, hauling and 'stringing' the pipe, [etc.]. **1968** *Sunday Mail* (Brisbane) 29 Sept. 12/2 The first pipes will be 'strung out' this week.

11. a. To extend or stretch (something flexible of rigid) from one point to another. Also with *out*.

1838 THACKERAY *Yellowpl. Corr.* (1865) 4 While you were looking up to prevent hanging yourself with the ropes which were strung across and about. **1885** MCCOOK *Tenants Old Farm* 203 Young spiders often manage to string out structures that oddly resemble a bridge in miniature. **1908** S. E. WHITE *Riverman* xxvi, Old Heinzman..is stringing booms across the river—obstructing navigation. **1911** WEBSTER, *String v.t.* 6. To extend or stretch like a string; as, to string the cables of a suspension bridge.

b. *fig.* To stretch (something) *out* in order to make it last.

1867 'MARK TWAIN' *Sk. New & Old* (1875) 73 What is the use of stringing out your lives to a lean and withered old age? **1894** —— in *North Amer. Rev.* Apr. 447 It [*sc.* the story] is not strung out as I have strung it out, but it is all there. **1977** P. HILL *Fanatics* 125 They're just stringing it out, putting off the evil hour.

12. *intr.* **a.** To move or progress in a string or disconnected line; spec. in *Hunting*, of the hounds. Also with *adv.*, as *out, away, off, in*.

a **1824** *Old Song* in Mactaggart *Gallov. Encycl.* 257 String awa my crommies, to the milking loan. **1834** M. SCOTT *Cruise Midge* xx, As we strung along the narrow path in single file. **1875** WHYTE MELVILLE *Katerfelto* xxiv. (1876) 264 Twenty couple of powerful stag-hounds—stringing somewhat, it may be, as they passed in and out the gnarled substantial stems. **1888** W. B. LIGHTHALL *Young Seigneur* 4 The pedestrians are already stringing off along the road. **1905** *Blackw. Mag.* Jan. 86/2 Watch staghounds when they are laid on. However good the scent, they string out.

b. Of gun-shot: To travel with varying velocity, so that the pellets of one charge arrive at different times at a given point.

1892 GREENER *Breech Loader* 267 Having ascertained by actual experiment that at forty yards his shot was stringing from twenty to thirty feet.

c. To hang like a string, be stretched in a string or loose line, *from*.

1885 HOWELLS *Silas Lapham* (1891) I. 259 Her eldest daughter..lounged into the parlour..with her wrap stringing from her arm. **1898** SIR G. ROBERTSON *Chitral* xvi. 181 The British officers..blundered slowly through the torrent with a straggling line of Sepoys stringing from the ponies' tails.

d. To extend or continue. Const. *along, out.* ***to string along with***: to accompany, to agree with, to support or go along with (usu. without undue enthusiasm). Occas. without const. *colloq.* (orig. *U.S.*).

1869 'MARK TWAIN' *Lett. to Publishers* (1967) 21 So much of the 400 or 500 pages still left are reprint, and so will string out a heap. **1877** —— in *Atlantic Monthly* Nov. 591/1 Isaac knelt down and began to pray: he strung along, and strung along..till everybody had got tired. **1896** —— in *Harper's Mag.* Aug. 351/2 Well, the time strung along and along, and that fellow never come! **1927** *Vanity Fair* (N.Y.) Nov. 67/2 To this day the B. F. Keith chain call the small-time 'The Family Time' but the players still string along with the theatrical paper [*sc. Variety*]. **1937** J. STEINBECK *Of Mice & Men* 59 Funny how you an' him string along together. **1946** *Sun* (Baltimore) 31 May 15/1 The majority of the bettors decided to string along with Blind Path, a well bred youngster making his seasonal debut. **1950** 'S. RANSOME' *Deadly Miss Ashley* ix. 103 String along, won't you? Don't let me down. **1955** M. ALLINGHAM *Beckoning Lady* iii. 39 She had been..much younger than the crowd which had grown up with Minnie, but she had strung along with them. **1960** WODEHOUSE *Jeeves in Offing* vii. 75, I string along with that school of thought. **1972** L. P. DAVIES *What did I do Tomorrow?* ix. 114, I wasn't going to be taken in. I'll string along, I thought. **1978** A. GILCHRIST *Cod Wars* xi. 109 If at some particular moment, they were stringing along with those other departments and accepting..a continued tough line of policy, then my warning telegrams might seem tactless, tiresome, inept.

e. ***to string out***: to be under the influence of a drug. Cf. STRUNG *ppl. a.* 4c. *U.S. slang*.

1967 WENTWORTH & FLEXNER *Dict. Amer. Slang* Suppl. 706/1 *String out*, to use or be addicted to narcotics; to be 'high' on a drug. **1970** *Sunday Tel.* 20 Dec. 6/6 How long did you string out?

13. Of a viscous or glutinous substance: To form into strings, become stringy.

1839 URE *Dict. Arts* 1267 Let it [material for varnish] boil until it will string very strong. **1850** HOLTZAPFFEL *Turning* III. 1385 Let it boil until it strings freely between the fingers.

14. *Billiards.* †**a.** *trans.* See quot. and KING *sb.* 9d. *Obs.*

1680 COTTON *Compl. Gamester* (ed. 2) 23 If the Follower intend to hit his Adversaries Ball, or pass at one stroke he must string his Ball, that is, lay it even with the King. **1688** HOLME *Armoury* III. 262/2.

b. *intr.* See quot. 1896.

[**1788**: cf. *stringing-nail*, STRINGING *vbl. sb.* 3.] **1814** C. JONES *Hoyle's Games Impr.* 373 Rules...1. String for the lead and choice of balls. **1839** KENTFIELD *Billiards* 29 In commencing the game, string for the lead. **1896** W. BROADFOOT *Billiards* iii. (Badm. Libr.) 106 To string is to play from baulk to the top cushion so as to leave player's ball near the baulk-line or bottom cushion as may be selected. Before a match the players string simultaneously for choice of balls, and for the option of commencing the game.

15. a. *trans.* To fool, deceive, humbug. *slang* (now chiefly *U.S.*).

1812 J. H. VAUX *Vocab. Flash Lang.* in *Mem.* (1964) 251 To banter or jest with a man by amusing him with false assurances or professions, is also termed *stringing* him, or *getting* him *in tow.* **1846** *Swell's Night Guide* 133/1 *String, to*, to impose on a person's belief by some joke or lie. **1898** A. M. BINSTEAD *Pink 'Un & Pelican* v. 115 She strung him for fifty bob on an old tea-chest an' a jar o' pickled inyuns! **1901** *Munsey's Mag.* XXIV. 858/2 'Some one has been stringin' those reporters!' thought Dan. **1910** W. CHURCHILL *Mod. Chron.* I. ix. 114, I watched you last night when you were stringing the Vicomte. **1931** P. MACDONALD *Crime Conductor* I. i. 3 'It isn't!' said the Assistant Editor incredulously. 'You're stringing me!' **1959** 'R. MACDONALD' *Galton Case* xviii. 147 They were stringing you. They just don't want a woman in the way. **1982** H. ENGEL *Ransom Game* i. 5, I guess I don't have any reason to believe they'd string me.

b. *to string* (someone) *along*: to fool or deceive (someone); *spec.* to encourage (someone) to remain in a state of misplaced confidence. Cf. sense 3c. *colloq.* (orig. *U.S.*).

1902 G. H. LORIMER *Lett. Merchant* xviii. 270 Clytie had been stringing the old lady along, intending to produce Bud's spook as a sort of..climax. **1924** P. MARKS *Plastic Age* xviii. 206 I'm afraid that he's just stringing me along, trying to encourage me. **1933** D. L. SAYERS *Murder must Advertise* ix. 158 He told me to string him along. And afterwards, quite suddenly, he told me to give him the push. **1943** K. TENNANT *Ride on Stranger* viii. 84 'If he was taking you to lunch..you might work us in somewhere.' 'String him along, kid,' Douglas encouraged... 'We're with you.' **1959** H. HOBSON *Mission House Murder* xviii. 123 How do I know you're not stringing me along, just to get Sharon to go back? **1962** A. LURIE *Love & Friendship* xi. 208 Why not string Dr. Flory along? **1978** H. C. RAE *Sullivan* I. iii. 39, I don't appreciate being strung along by a contract employee.

16. *intr.* To work as a stringer (sense 11).

1960 G. EDINGER *Twain shall Meet* xv. 187 European journalists, stringing for papers in America or Britain. **1966** E. WEST *Night is Time for Listening* ii. 49 'It's not an assignment,' Darsoss said. 'I've been stringing.' **1972** *Maclean's Mag.* June 82/1 Fred Cleverly is a CBC news reporter in Winnipeg. He also strings for the Toronto *Star.* **1977** I. SHAW *Beggarman, Thief* III. ii. 202 An old newspaperman in Elysium, Ohio, who occasionally strings for us when there's anything of interest happening in that part of the world.

stringed (strɪŋd), *a.* [f. STRING *sb.* + -ED[2].]

1. Having a string or strings; *spec.* of musical instruments such as the violin and guitar. Also in parasynthetic comb., as ***ten-stringed***.

c **1000** *Lamb. Ps.* xci. 4 *In decachordo psalterio*, on tynstrængedum saltere. *a* **1300**, **1535** [see *ten-stringed* s.v. TEN D. 1]. **1552** HULOET, Strynged, *chordatus*. Strynged as a bowe is, *amentatus*. **1585** HIGINS *Junius' Nomencl.* 276/1 *Hasta amentata*,..a stringed or looped dart to fling with all. **1599–1843** [see THREE-STRINGED]. **1609** HOLLAND *Amm. Marcell.* xxx. ii. 380 The house rung againe with the sound of stringed and wynd instruments. **1742** BERKELEY *Lett.* Wks. 1871 IV. 284 A large four-stringed bass violin. **1871** D. COOK *Nts. at the Play* (1883) I. 177 The orchestra..is scarcely strong enough in stringed instruments to do full justice to Mr. Sullivan's music. **1873** LELAND *Egypt. Sketch-Bk.* 55 A one-stringed banjo.

b. *Her.* (See quots.)

1572 BOSSEWELL *Armorie* II. 123 Two bowes bente addorsed de Or, stringed Vert. **1864** BOUTELL *Her. Hist. & Pop.* xix. (ed. 3) 298 A Harp or, stringed argent. **1868** CUSSANS *Heraldry* (1893) 117 *Hunting-horn* or *Bugle*... It is usually blazoned as *Stringed*, which signifies that it depends from two strings, or ribbons, tied in a knot above.

c. Of a running-track: Divided by stretched strings into separate runs.

1897 *Encycl. Sport* I. 64/2 (Athletics) Sprint handicaps run over a stringed track.

2. *transf.* Produced by strings or stringed instruments; †made with a rosary or string of beads.

1629 MILTON *Hymn Nativ.* ix, Divinely-warbled voice Answering the stringed noise. **1655** [G. HALL] *Tri. Rome* v. 57 Such thraves and lasts of private Oraisons, which without the well-devised helps of stringed calculation, could never keep even reckoning. **1822** SHELLEY *Zucca* 72 Sounds of softest song Mixed with..stringèd melodies. **1837** CARLYLE *Fr. Rev.* II. I. xi, Three-deep these march; to the sound of stringed music. **1854** *Athenæum* 6 May 565/1 Two movements of a stringed Quartett, by Herr von Wilm.

stringency ('strɪndʒənsɪ). [f. STRINGENT *a.*: see -ENCY.] The quality of being stringent; strictness, rigour.

1844 KINGLAKE *Eothen* xxiii, He insisted on the stringency of the orders which he had received. **1856** FROUDE *Hist. Eng.* I. 55 Twice subsequently in the course of his reign he returned back upon the subject, insisting upon it with increasing stringency. **1885** *Law Jrnl.* 17 Jan. 36/2 Criticisms are sometimes passed on the stringency of the English laws of evidence.

b. Of reasoning: Compulsive force, convincingness.

1864 MAX MÜLLER *Chips* (1880) I. iv. 116 We see no stringency whatever in this argument. **1872** W. K. CLIFFORD *Lect. & Ess.* (1879) I. 156 As the known exactness of the uniformity became greater, the stringency of the inference increased.

c. *Comm.* 'Tightness' in the money-market.

1877 RAYMOND *Statist. Mines & Mining* 185 The stringency in the money-market aggravating the gloomy aspect of affairs. **1893** *Westm. Gaz.* 17 Oct. 6/1 In view of the money stringency at Chicago, they consider it unwise to recommend a larger distribution.

‖**stringendo** (strɪn'dʒɛndəʊ), *adv.* (*a.*) and *sb. Mus.* [It., gerund of *stringere*, to press, squeeze, bind together.] **A.** *adv.* (*a.*). A direction indicating that a composition be played with increasing speed and excitement. Also *transf.* and *fig.*

1853 GEO. ELIOT *Let.* 2 Dec. (1954) II. 129 Mrs. Pitt scolds the servants, *stringendo & fortissimo*, while I am dressing. **1894** G. B. SHAW in *World* 25 Apr. 24/2 Wagner thought it sufficient to indicate the necessary changes of tempo by such hints as 'ritenuto', 'stringendo', and the like. **1922** JOYCE *Ulysses* 207 *Stephen* (*Stringendo.*) He has hidden his own name, a fair name, William, in the plays, a super here, a clown there, as a painter of old Italy set his face in a dark corner of his canvas. **1959** *Times* 30 Oct. 4/7 A tendency to exaggerate the stringendo passages. **1977** *Gramophone* Nov. 837/1 His tempo for the funeral march is barely faster than Boult's, but it seems much more so thanks in part to his *stringendo* manner.

B. *sb.* (Pl. **stringendi.**) A passage played in this manner.

1937 R. JAQUES tr. *A. Cortot's Stud. Mus. Interpretation* 154 From the bars before the *stringendo* the upper C sharps of the left-hand part may be played by the right hand. **1978** *Gramophone* Feb. 1405/2 One finds the latter [*sc.* Karajan].. readier to indulge in *stringendi*, urging things on, where Giulini's combination of concentration and steadiness is compelling in quite a different way.

stringent ('strɪndʒənt), *a.* [ad. L. *stringentem*, pres. pple. of *stringĕre*, to draw together, bind tight, also to touch lightly, graze.]

1. Astringent, constrictive, styptic, esp. with reference to taste. Also *fig.*

1605 TIMME *Quersit.* III. 149 Vitriol [giveth] a stiptic or a stringent taste. **1614** W. B. *Philosopher's Banquet* (ed. 2) 72 Bitter Grapes are colde and stringent. **1642** H. MORE *Song of Soul, Antipsych.* III. iii. 20 What down doth dive Into the straitned Cuspis needs must strive With stringent bitternesse, vexation, Anxious unrest. **1858** TRENCH *Synon.* xiv. (1877) 46 Harsh and stringent to the palate, as..unripe fruit, and the like.

2. That draws or binds tight; tightly enfolding or compressing. *rare.*

1736 THOMSON *Liberty* IV. 188 The serpents, twisting round, their stringent folds Inextricable tie. **1849** KITTO *Daily Bible Illustr.* I. XII. ii. 395 The twisted bags were perhaps used to subject the grapes to a further and more stringent pressure, after being taken from the foot-press. **1886** STEVENSON *Dr. Jekyll* 135, I slept..with a stringent and profound slumber which not even the nightmares that wrung me could avail to break. **1898** MEREDITH *Odes Fr. Hist.* 39 Adding to slavery's chain the stringent twist.

3. Of reasoning: That compels assent, convincing.

1653 H. MORE *Antid. Ath.* II. vi. (1712) 58 But I have dwelt too long upon this Theory; we'll betake our selves to ....what is more unexceptionably stringent and forcing. **1706** PHILLIPS (ed. Kersey), *Stringent*, forcing, forceable, as *To maintain a Truth in a stringent Way.* **1866** GEO. ELIOT *F. Holt* xvii, Mr. Johnson's argument was not the less stringent because his idioms were vulgar.

4. a. Of regulations, procedure, requirements, obligations, etc.: Rigorous, strict, thorough-going; rigorously binding or coercive.

1846 F. W. NEWMAN *Let.* in Sieveking *Mem.* (1909) 142 Nothing less severe..would brace England up to the stringent remedies which alone can save that country [Ireland]. **1849** MACAULAY *Hist. Eng.* ii. I. 235 A more stringent test was now added. **1855** *Ibid.* xx. IV. 480 They imagined that they had devised a most stringent limitation of the royal power. **1868** M. PATTISON *Academ. Org.* iv. 106 The other professors are under more stringent requirements to teach. **1884** *Manch. Exam.* 2 May 4/7 It will need a stringent clause to guard against this abuse.

b. ? Rigorously urgent *upon*. *nonce-use.*

1862 CARLYLE *Fredk. Gt.* XIII. ii. III. 420 Readers may consider how stringent upon Friedrich that question now was, and how ticklish to solve.

5. Of the money-market: Tight. Cf. STRINGENCY.

1870 J. K. MEDBERY *Men & Mysteries Wall St.* v. 69 Money is 'very active', and the loan market 'stringent'. **1891** in *Century Dict.* And in later U.S. Dicts.

6. *Fort.* = RASANT. *Obs. rare.*

1673 SIR J. MOORE *Mod. Fortif.* 18 The Line coming from the Point of the Bastion..and drawn upon the face..to the Curtain..is called the *Line stringent*, and shews how much of the Curtain..will clear or scour the Face. **1711** *Milit. & Sea Dict.* (ed. 4) s.v. *Line*, Line Razant, Stringent or Flanking, or Second Flank.

Hence **'stringently** *adv.*; **'stringentness.**

1659 H. MORE *Immort. Soul* II. ii. 129 That the former part is false I shall now demonstrate, by proving more stringently, That [etc.]. **1727** BAILEY vol. II, *Stringentness*, binding Quality. **1866** GEO. ELIOT *F. Holt* viii, A clever, frank, good-natured egoist; not stringently consistent, but without any disposition to falsity. **1884** *Manch. Exam.* 2 Dec. 5/1 The principle of population has been applied more stringently than was at first proposed.

stringer ('strɪŋə(r)). Also 5 **strenger, strynger,** 6 **-ar.** [f. STRING *v.* and *sb.* + -ER[1].]

1. a. One who makes strings for bows. ? *Obs.*

1420 in *York Memor. Bk.* II. (Surtees) 122 Stryngers. Inprimis, pro bona regula..habenda in arte quadam, que vocatur stryngercrafte. **1541** *Act 33 Hen. VIII*, c. 9 §1 The Bowers, Fletchers, Stringers and Arrowehedmakers of this your Realme. **1545** ASCHAM *Toxoph.* II. (Arb.) 110 Now what a stringe ought to be made on, whether of good hempe ...., or of flaxe or of silke, I leaue that to the iugemente of stringers, of whome we muste bye them on. **1688** HOLME *Armoury* III. 106/1 The Crest of the Bow-String Maker, commonly called the Stringers of the City of Chester.

b. The workman who fits a musical instrument (now esp. a piano) with strings.

1842 *Penny Mag.* Apr. 173/1 The workmen called 'stringers' fix the proper strings to the proper pins. **1898** *Daily Chron.* 14 Oct. 10/6 Pianoforte.—Stringer and chipper-up wanted.

2. †**a.** One who winds thread on a bobbin. *Obs.*$^{-0}$ **b.** One who threads (beads and the like) on a string. *rare*$^{-0}$.

1598 FLORIO, *Accauigliatore*, a stringer of silke. **1850** OGILVIE, *Stringer*, one who arranges on a string, or thread; a bead or pearl stringer.

3. *fig.* One who strings words together. Also with *together*, *up.*

1774 *Univ. Mag.* Apr. 189/1 When the stringer up of a love-song condescends to take the pen. **1829** *Blackw. Mag.* XXVI. 915 Their great speakers were at best but stringers-together of good-for-nothing words. **1901** R. GARNETT *Ess.* xi. 313 A polisher and stringer of epigrammatic sayings.

†**4.** A fornicator, wencher. *Obs.*

App. the speaker's perversion of *striker*: see STRIKER 2 d.

1611 BEAUM. & FL. *Knt. Burning Pestle* I. (1613) B 4, *Wife.* A whoreson tyrant has ben an old stringer in's daies I warrant him.

5. *Build.*, etc. **a.** A horizontal member connecting uprights in a framework, supporting a floor, supporting or tying together a bridge, or the like; a tie or tie-beam.

1838 *Civil Engin. & Arch. Jrnl.* I. 150/1 These piles were connected on the inside by a pine stringer one foot square. **1893** *Scribner's Mag.* June 697/1 A plank sidewalk resting on the ordinary stringers. **1940** *Sun* (Baltimore) 24 May 19/5 The last span between piers 36 and 37 was closed today, engineers said, and work is being rushed on floor beams, stringers and decking. **1960** [see *cream-truck* s.v. CREAM *sb.*[2] 7]. **1976** *Columbus* (Montana) *News* 24 June 6/6 The best method to improve the bridges is to install more stringers.

b. *Shipbuilding.* An inside strake of planking or plating, secured to the ribs and supporting the ends of the beams.

1830 HEDDERWICK *Mar. Archit.* 130 *Stringers*, strakes of planks wrought round the inside at the height of the under side of the beams. **1842** *Civil Engin. & Arch. Jrnl.* V. 394/2 The iron gunwale stringer is formed of plate ⅛ in. thick. **1867** SMYTH *Sailor's Word-bk.*, *Stringers*, a name sometimes applied to shelf-pieces... Also, heavy timber similarly carried round a ship to fortify her for special heavy service, as whaling, &c. **1874** THEARLE *Naval Archit.* 331 Stringers are of two kinds, viz., hold and deck stringers.

attrib. **1869** SIR E. REED *Shipbuild.* ix. 161 All vessels to have stringer-plates upon the ends of each tier of beams. **1883** NARES *Constr. Ironclad* 6 Stringer plates are used to strengthen the ship longitudinally. These are iron plates laid along the end of the deck beams, and fastened to them and the frames.

c. *U.S.* A longitudinal railway sleeper.

1848 *Rep. Comm. Patents 1847* (U.S.) 72 One patent has been granted for improvements in the rail, and the manner of fastening it to the stringers. **1881** LE CONTE *Sight* 142 Parallel lines of all kinds, such as railway stringers, bridge timbers, &c. **1902** *Munsey's Mag.* XXVI. 601/2 The fuel consisted of parts of the Tarlac station house and some hard-wood stringers.

d. A string-piece supporting a staircase.

1883 *Law Rep. 8 Appeal Cases* 450 Cutting a groove in the ....wall, and inserting in it one of the wooden stringers supporting the stair.

e. The heavy squared timber carried along the edge of a wharf-front; cf. *string-piece* (STRING *sb.* 32).

1899 L. BECKE in *Pall Mall Gaz.* 26 Dec. 2/1 Tom sat down on a wharf stringer, dangling his feet.

f. *Aeronaut.* A spanwise member of a wing, parallel to the spars, used to give lateral stiffness to the ribs; also, a longitudinal member of a fuselage, serving to reinforce and stiffen the skin and assisting it to carry direct load.

1918 *Flight* 4 July 740/2 The main [wing] ribs consist of ply wood webs socketted into grooved spruce flanges, which are tapered off..except where they are met by a longitudinal stringer. **1920** *Ibid.* 12 Aug. 879/2 To this main [fuselage] structure is added stringers which bring the outside form up to a streamline shape. **1928** CHATFIELD & TAYLOR *Airplane & its Engine* xii. 212 As even the main ribs are very light, they must often be supported against tipping over sidewise. This is done by means of light wood stringers, which run parallel to the spars. **1932** M. LANGLEY *Metal Aircraft Construction* v. 113 The slightly curved contours of stringers may be achieved by rolling them to template immediately they come off the draw bench. **1945** *Aeroplane* 17 Aug. 185/2 The multiplicity of stringers forms an impressive skeleton upon which a preformed skin is laid in large panels of over 30 ft. in length. **1961** B. FERGUSSON *Watery Maze* vii. 160 This was *Bachequero's* first venture in anger since her conversion, and she was no doubt straining every plate and stringer to do herself credit. **1973** 'A. HALL' *Tango Briefing* ix. 111 The whole of the airframe began shivering as the stringers took the strain.

g. *Surfing.* (See quot. 1962.)

1962 T. MASTERS *Surfing made Easy* 65 *Stringers*, pieces of wood laminated into the surfboard foam for decoration and rigidity. **1965** J. POLLARD *Surfrider* ii. 21 Those strips of wood used in foam boards to add lateral strength are called "stringers". **1968** W. WARWICK *Surfriding in N.Z.* 16/3 Today about 50% of all surfboards are built with a centre stringer of either wood or fibreglass, whereas up to about 1966 nearly all boards had some kind of stringer.

6. *Mining* and *Geol.* A narrow vein of mineral traversing a mass of different material.

1874 RAYMOND *6th Rep. Mines* 32 This indicates that the present deposits are stringers or exflorescences [*sic*] of larger deposits. **1882** *Rep. Prec. Met. U.S.* 275 In the main vein is found a stringer of silver nearly pure.

7. *U.S.* A stick or switch used to string fish on.

1893 *Outing* XXII. 88/2 But, though he had several strikes, his stringer remained dry in his pocket.

8. *pl.* Handcuffs. *slang.*

1893 KIPLING *Many Invent.*, *My Lord the Elephant*, The corp'ril of the gyard..unlocked my stringers, an' he sez: 'If it comes to runnin', run for your life.'

9. = STRING *sb.* 1 n. *U.S. slang. rare.*

1851 T. A. BURKE *Polly Peablossom's Wedding* 89 He never lacked assistance from his acquaintances whenever he had concocted a 'stringer'.

10. *Metallurgy.* A microstructural feature consisting of a narrow vein of inclusion or alloy constituent oriented parallel to the direction of metal working.

1942 C. G. JOHNSON *Metallurgy* (ed. 2) x. 187 Fig. 103 illustrates a slag stringer in steel that caused failure in the hardening operation. **1959** *Jrnl. Iron & Steel Inst.* CXCI. 353/1 Forging draws out the carbides into long stringers running in the direction of hot working. **1976** *Sci. Amer.* Nov. 106/3 The most significant difference between bending and stretching is the role of microscopic impurities or inclusions that are not metallic... During hot-rolling they become elongated into 'stringers'.

11. A newspaper correspondent paid in proportion to the quantity of his published work (cf. STRING *sb.* 17 b). Hence, a correspondent employed part-time; *spec.* one employed to report on events in a particular place. Also *transf.* Freq. *attrib.* orig. *U.S.*

1952 *Time* 21 Jan. 7/1 Saporiti was in Portugal when he first started as a stringer (part-time correspondent) for *Time* in the spring of 1946. **1952** *Iowa Quest* 31 Jan. 3 (*heading*) 11 students hold 'stringer' jobs. **1956** *Sun* (Baltimore) 28 Aug. 4/6 Even the wire services used mainly stringer correspondents to cover trial. **1958** *Spectator* 31 Oct. 570/2 A free-lance reporter (formerly a stringer for *Confidential*). **1962** *Rep. Comm. Broadcasting 1960* 315/2 in *Parl. Papers 1961–2* (Cmnd. 1753) IX. 259 Organisation of independent television news: camera crews and 'stringer' cameramen. **1970** *Radio Times* 30 Apr. 10/4 Every weekday BBC radio puts out 5½ hours of news and current affairs programmes to Britain. It employs 17 full-time foreign corespondents and nearly 100 stringers, mostly newspapermen. **1973** H. TREVELYAN *Diplomatic Channels* vii. 116 They [*sc.* intelligence services] employ stringers to get caught and occasionally exchanged; but these are regarded by proper spies as an inferior form of life and are not admitted to the international spy confraternity. **1979** E. KOCH *Good Night Little Spy* viii. 65 He was a so-called 'stringer'; he was not attached to any one newspaper and freelanced for several of them.

†**stringere**, *v. Fencing. Obs.* Also 8 **stringer.** [? a. It. *stringere*, lit. to bind, clasp.] *trans.* ? To engage (the adversary, his weapon); to meet point to point. Hence quasi-*sb.*, the action of engaging. Also **'stringering** *vbl. sb.*

1688 HOLME *Armoury* III. xix. (Roxb.) 159/2 A Stringere, or stringering, is the touching of the adversaries point with thy point; which thou art to doe for to secure thy selfe on either side from a thrust. *Ibid.* 161/1 When a thrust is made without, do it by a Quarte, euer obserueing that after the thrust, stringere him on the same side thou did thrust in the recalling of thy body, not moueing the point from his. **1711** Z. WYLDE *Engl. Master of Defence* 15 Take notice, That if I join Touch, Engage, Embogne, Stringer, Bind, Caveat, or Rely upon your Weapon, 'tis all one and the same thing.

stringful ('strɪŋfʊl). [See -FUL 2.] As many as may be strung on a string; also *fig.*

1611 COTGR., *Cordée*, a string-full of. **1890** *Temple Bar* Nov. 420 So they may have a stringful of conquests to boast of. **1893** *Tablet* 18 Feb. 273 He..quoted a stringful of Biblical quotations.

stringhalt ('strɪŋhɔːlt). Also 6 **-halte, -hawlde,** 7 **-holt, -hault.** [app. f. STRING *sb.* + HALT *a.* and *sb.*[2] See also SPRINGHALT.] An affection of the hind legs of a horse which causes certain muscles to contract spasmodically.

1523–34 FITZHERB. *Husb.* § 108 The stryng-halte is an yl disease, and maketh hym to twyche vp his legge sodeynly. **1592** R. D. *Hypnerotomachia* 45, I might well perceiue that they [*sc.* the nymphs] had neither crampes nor stringhawldes or leaden heeles. **1639** T. DE GREY *Compl. Horsem.* 66 All manner of convulsions, cramps, numnesse, and stringholts. **1688** *Lond. Gaz.* No. 2353/4 He takes up his Legs behind when he walks, as if he had the String-halt. **1817** SCOTT *Rob Roy* xxvii, The stringhalt will gae aff when it's gaen a mile. **1888** W. WILLIAMS *Princ. Vet. Med.* (ed. 5) 11 Hereditary tendency.—Many diseases, such as curbs, spavin,..chorea or stringhalt, run in certain breeds of horses.

†**b.** as *adj.* Affected with stringhalt. *Obs.*

1675 *Lond. Gaz.* No. 983/4 A Grey Mare,..Stringhalt on the near Leg behind. **1703** *Ibid.* No. 3881/4 A brown-bay Nag,..much string-halt.

Hence **'stringhalted** (whence **stringhaltedness**), **-halty** *adjs.*, affected with stringhalt. **'stringhalter**, a horse affected with stringhalt.

1687 *Lond. Gaz.* No. 2224/4 The one [gelding] a grey,.. string-halted. **1853** SURTEES *Sponge's Sp. Tour* (1893) 61 A weedy string-halty chestnut.., high in bone and low in flesh. **1872** *Daily News* 18 Apr. 5/7 The roarers, wheezers, scramblers, star-gazers, stringhalters. **1889** F. C. PHILIPS *Ainslie's Courtship* I. vi. 62 There was also a distinct tendency towards string-haltedness.

†**string-hearth.** *Obs.* In 5 **stryngherth.** [? f. STRING *sb.*] The hearth or furnace at which iron was heated for its second working.

1409 *Durham Acc. Roll* in *Eng. Hist. Rev.* XIV. 520 Soluta pro i trowe empto pro le stryngherth. *Ibid.* 527 Et uxori ejusdem laboranti ad le stryngherth in fabricatione dictorum xii blomes, xiid.

stringily ('strɪŋɪlɪ), *adv.* [f. STRINGY *a.* + -LY[2].] So as to be stringy, so as to resemble string.

1940 G. FRANKAU *Self-Portrait* i. 19 My childhood acquired..a horror of macaroni, with which—cooked stringily à l'Anglais—we were compulsorily fed when we stayed for 'afternoon class'. **1976** SCOTT & KOSKI *Walk-In* (1977) ii. 17 One lonely and sullen girl in cut-offs and sweat shirt, hair hanging stringily to her waist.

stringiness ('strɪŋɪnɪs). [-NESS.] The quality of being stringy (see the adj.).

1699 EVELYN *Acetaria* 57 The bigger Roots..should..eat short and quick, without stringiness. **1842** LOUDON *Suburban Hort.* 665 The toughness and stringyness of the London asparagus. **1856** W. B. CARPENTER *Microsc.* 423 The bundles..which give 'stringiness' to various esculent vegetable substances. **1884** MCLAREN *Spinning* (ed. 2) 31 Then add 7½ gallons more lye of double the strength, and about 6 lbs. of pearl-ash, to prevent stringiness.

stringing ('strɪŋɪŋ), *vbl. sb.* [-ING[1].]

1. The action of the vb. STRING: **a.** in trans. senses.

1620 BACON *Let.* 30 Aug. *Lett. & Rem.* (1734) 112 The stringing of the harp, nor the tuning of it will not serve, except it be well plaied on from time to time. **1655** in *12th Rep. Hist. MSS. Comm.* App. v. 5 The polyphon is an instrument of so different a stringing and tuning that its impossible to play what is sett to it on any other hand instrument. **1862** *Catal. Internat. Exhib., Brit.* II. No. 3391, A new mode of stringing, adapted to instruments of all kinds. **1884** *Tennis Cuts* 69 All these results have been caused by the change in the stringing of rackets [etc.]. **1886** SYMONDS *Renaiss. It., Cath. React.* (1898) VII. ix. 82 The stringing together of words and ideas in triplets. **1914** S. GIBSON *Some Oxf. Libr.* vi. 78 The stringing and restringing of books..provided the Bodleian binders with much work.

b. in intr. senses.

1873 BENNETT & 'CAVENDISH' *Billiards* 477 The choice of balls and order of play shall..be determined by stringing. **1883** E. PENNELL-ELMHIRST *Cream Leicestersh.* 194 [The] party sail on..no tailing or stringing to-day, but the whole one compact and hurrying mass. **1892** GREENER *Breech-Loader* 267 The great stringing of the charge is due to the heavy charge of explosive used. The average stringing in a properly loaded gun is about ten feet at forty yards. **1952** *Iowa Quest* 31 Jan. 3/5 'Stringing' is interesting and has provided many aspiring journalists with valuable on-the-job training. **1970** A. FOWLES *Dupe Negative* iii. 23 I'd shot an interview with him..on a stringing job for the BBC. **1973** *Times* 3 July 18/7 Lyall then did more years in the editor's chair..before devoting himself to stringing.

2. *concr.* **a.** Strings collectively; †ornamentation of lace or fringe. *Obs.*

1722 RAMSAY *Three Bonnets* II. 15 And where gat ye that braw blue stringing, That's at your houghs and shuthers hinging? **1851-4** *Tomlinson's Cycl. Arts* II. 308/2 The stringing [in a pianoforte] was formerly much thinner than at present.

b. Material for the string-board of a staircase, or for string-courses on a building.

1833 LOUDON *Encycl. Archit.* §239. 125 Moulded nosings to the steps to be housed (let in) into the close stringing, which is to be one and a quarter inch thick, sunk. **1858** SKYRING *Builders' Prices* 91 In all copings, stringings, pilasters, cornices, and other solid works, find the cube quantity of stone as it comes from the banker to the building.

c. Straight or curved inlaid lines in cabinet-work.

1812 *MS. Letter*, I have purchased some veneer, but cannot get any stringing. **1842** G. FRANCIS *Dict. Arts.* **1843** HOLTZAPFFEL *Turning* I. 86 Holly..is used..for the stringings or lines of cabinet-work. **1846** *Ibid.* II. 737 The stringings, or the straight and circular lines combined with pearl buhl work, are mostly of white metal.

3. *Silk-dyeing.* The operation of twisting the hanks of silk after dyeing, in order to separate the fibres and impart lustre.

1885 HUMMEL *Dyeing Textile Fabrics* 55 Stringing or Glossing (Fr. *chevillage*).

4. *Comb.*: **stringing course**, a string-course; **stringing-deal** (see quot.); **stringing-machine** (see sense 3). †In *Billiards*: **stringing-line**, the baulk-line; **stringing nail**, each of two nails formerly used as 'spots' on the baulk-line; **stringing spot**, each of two 'spots' on the baulk-line.

1861 G. MUSGRAVE *By-roads* 179 Handsome farmhouses, built up in red brick with stone facings, labellings, and *stringing courses. **1881** RAYMOND *Mining Gloss.*, **Stringing-deals*, Eng. Thin planks, nailed to the inside of the curbs in a shaft, so as to suspend each curb from those above it. **1873** BENNETT & 'CAVENDISH' *Billiards* 6 The players led from the centre of the *stringing-line or baulk, which occupied a quarter of the table, instead of about a fifth as at present. **1885** HUMMEL *Dyeing Textile Fabrics* 55 The *stringing machine. **1788** J. BEAUFORT *Hoyle's Games Impr.* 195 *Stringing-nail is that part of the table from whence the player strikes his ball at first setting off, and is generally marked with two brass nails. **1808** C. JONES *Hoyle's Games Impr.* 338 A red ball is to be placed..between the stringing nails or spots. **1839** KENTFIELD *Billiards* 29 The player, in stringing for the lead,..must not place his ball beyond the *stringing spots.

stringless ('strɪŋlɪs), *a.* [-LESS.] Having no string; lacking strings.

1591 SYLVESTER *Du Bartas* I. vi. 322 [The porcupine] Who string-less shoots so many arrowes out. **1593** SHAKS. *Rich. II*, II. i. 149 His tongue is now a stringlesse instrument. **1826** A. A. WATTS *Poet's Den* 89 A broken, stringless lute. **1882** J. PAYN *Thicker than Water* iii, He had a frameless, stringless glass, which stuck in his eye with the tenacity of a limpet. **1894** BLACKMORE *Perlycross* xviii. 151 Her hat being stringless had flown far away.

†stringlet ('strɪŋlɪt). *U.S. Obs.* [f. STRING *sb.* + -LET, after *ringlet*.] A long wisp of hair.

a **1852** F. M. WHITCHER *Widow Bedott Papers* (1856) xv. 154 Them great long stringlets a danglin' down her cheeks. **1874** *Rep. Vermont Board Agric.* II. 600 Faded-out hair upon either side, with stringlets hanging halfway to the ground from hip and shoulder.

stringy ('strɪŋɪ), *a.* [f. STRING *sb.* + -Y[1].]

1. a. Resembling string or fibre; consisting of string-like pieces. Chiefly applied to vegetable or animal tissues, esp. meat when its fibres have become tough.

1669 W. JACKSON in *Phil. Trans.* IV. 1061 Mosses..are a kind of Moorish boggy ground, very stringy, and fatt. **1693** EVELYN *De La Quint. Compl. Gard.* II. 155 The Radishes that are sown on hot Beds..are more apt to grow hollow and stringy. *Ibid.* Dict., *Sticky* or *Stringy*, is said of Roots, when not kindly or running to Seed. **1748** *Anson's Voy.* II. i. 165 We usually preferred the tops of the turnips to the roots, which were often stringy. **1829** G. HEAD *Forest Scenes N. Amer.* 224 As to the woodpecker..His flesh was..lean and stringy. **1863** HAWTHORNE *Our Old Home, Glimpses Eng. Poverty* II. 189 Bits and gobbets of lean meat,..tough and stringy morsels. **1884** *Manch. Exam.* 12 Nov. 8/2 Dates which are rather stringy than sweet.

b. spec. of timber (see quot.).

1843 *Civil Engin. & Arch. Jrnl.* VI. 406/1 Deals that, when acted upon by the saw, do not form sawdust, but are torn into long strings or fibres, and, on that account, termed 'stringy'.

c. Designating defective cotton or wool, esp. cotton which has been imperfectly scutched.

1902 W. I. HANNAN *Textile Fibres Commerce* 115 The cotton which is struck off by the beater blades of the scutcher should be removed away from the beater's course immediately; any delay at this stage may cause the fibres to become contorted into very curious shapes, and such cotton is then termed *stringy*. **1932** E. MIDGELEY *Technical Terms Textile Trade* II. 215 *Stringy*, wool partially matted in fibre and drawn into a slightly ropy form. The stringing of wool is usually due to inefficient scouring. **1950** *Mercury Dict. Textile Terms* 481/1 *Stringy cotton.* This is a defective cotton produced by ginning wet or unripe seed cotton, or sometimes by a wrong adjustment of the brushes that take the lint from the ginsaws.

2. Of a person, the body, etc.: Thin; exhibiting sinew rather than flesh. Of hair: thin, tending to hang in strands. Also *Comb.*

1833 SIR F. B. HEAD *Bubbles Brunnen Nassau* (1834) 316 The stringy, weather-beaten features of the mountain peasant, were changed for countenances pulpy, fleshy, and evidently better fed. **1838** D. JERROLD *Men of Char.* I. II. iii. 48 A stringy little man of about fifty. **1879** MEREDITH *Egoist* xxi, Rather pale and stringy from his cold swim. **1956** J. CHEEVER in *New Yorker* 14 Jan. 26/1 Her light hair was long and stringy. **1981** P. THEROUX *Mosquito Coast* xviii. 234 The stringy-haired man.

3. Of liquid or viscous matter: Containing or forming glutinous thread-like parts; ropy.

1694 ADDISON *Virg. Georg.* IV. 49 For this they hoard up glew, whose clinging drops, Like pitch, or bird-lime, hang in stringy ropes. **1839** URE *Dict. Arts* 1266 (*Varnish*) Keep it boiling until it feels strong and stringy between the fingers. **1846** *Mechanics' Mag.* 31 Oct. 427/2 When the glass was disposed to be wavy (*ondé*) or stringy (*cordé*) an iron tool was introduced into it. **1875** J. PRIESTLEY in *Phil. Trans.* CLXVI. 509 A stringy mucus.

4. Of the voice: ? Resembling the tone of a stretched string.

1820 *Q. Mus. Mag.* II. 257 *note*, The effect of Mr. Bartleman's voice is often stringy, and of Mr. Braham's almost always either reedy or overbroke.

stringy-bark. *Austral.* **a.** A name for many species of *Eucalyptus* (e.g. *E. gigantea*), which have a tough fibrous bark. Also *attrib.*

1801 [see BLACKBUTT]. **1802** BARRINGTON *Hist. N.S. Wales* ix. 358 This [canoe] was formed of the Stringy bark. **1832** BISCHOFF *Van Diemen's Land* ii. 22 The stringy bark is perhaps one of the most useful trees in the island. **1859** CORNWALLIS *New World* I. 168 A short ascent through stringy-bark forest. **1885** HAYTER *Carboona* 4 She..made twine nets of the stringy-bark fibre.

b. The bark or wood of any of these trees.

1848 W. WESTGARTH *Australia Felix* vi. 73 These natives appear to like also the fruit of the pandanus, of which large quantities were found in their camps, soaking in water contained in vessels formed of stringy-bark. **1859** CORNWALLIS *New World* I. 191 Other sheets of stringy-bark were then bent over the platform. **1880** FISON & HOWITT *Kamilaroi* 196 Down to the waist they are all wound round with frayed stringybark in thick folds. **1901** M. FRANKLIN *My Brilliant Career* i. 3 The stringy bark roof of the salt-shed..protected the troughs from rain. **1928** 'BRENT OF BIN BIN' *Up Country* vi. 94 On that early journey when it rained they hove to under the drays, well-covered by tarpaulins supplemented by stringy-bark lean-tos. **1977** *Weekly Times* (Melbourne) 19 Jan. 39/2 The basic materials used are local gum and stringy bark.

c. An inhabitant of the outback, an uncouth person. Also as quasi-*adj.*, belonging to the 'bush' or uncultivated country.

1833 *N.S. Wales Mag.* I. 173 (Morris) The workmanship of which I beg you will not scrutinize, as I am but, to use a colonial expression, 'a stringy-bark carpenter'. **1836** J. F. O'CONNELL *Residence Eleven Yrs. New Holland* 49 Let us suppose the suitor an old 'stringy-bark', such being the soubriquet in which inland settlers rejoice. **1861** H. EARLE *Ups & Downs* 59 She would never have had the bad taste to prefer a stringy bark like me to such a fine-looking, first-class fellow as yourself. **1890** 'R. BOLDREWOOD' *Col. Reformer* xxiii, I'd give a tenner out of my own pocket they was all..back at Bowning or some other stringy-bark hole as is fit for 'em. **1892** H. NISBET *Bushranger's Sweetheart* iv. 30 He was a larikin of the larikins, this tiny Stringy Bark, who haunted my thoughts.

†'strinkle, 'strenkle, *sb. Obs.* Forms: α. 3 strenncle, strenkil, 5 strenkyl(le, 5-6 strencle, 6 strenkyll; β. 5 strynkylle, 6 strynkyll, strincle, strinkle; γ. 6 stryngel. [Related to STRINKLE *v.*] A holy-water sprinkler, an aspergillum.

α. *c* **1200** ORMIN 1095 Þatt blod tatt he þær haffde brohht, & warrp itt tær wiþþ strenncless. *Ibid.* 1707. *a* **1300** *E.E. Psalter* l. 8 Þou sal strenkil me ouer-alle With strenkil, and klensed be I salle. *c* **1440** *Promp. Parv.* 223/1 Haly water spryngelle, or strencle..*aspersorium. Ibid.* 479/2 Strenkyl, halywater styk, *aspersorium, isopus.* **1530** PALSGR. 277/1 Strenkyll to cast holy water, *uimpilon.* **1584** in J. Morris *Troubles Cath. Forefathers* (1877) 270 Certain Mass books, pictures, holy water with strencles.

β. *c* **1425** *Voc.* in Wr.-Wülcker 648/25 *Hoc aspersorium,* strynkylle. **1520** in J. Croft *Excerpta Ant.* (1797) 13 Item, paid for ij Strynkylls. **1533** in *Kal. & Inv. Exch.* (1836) II. 270 Item a holly waterstocke..crownyd wt a strincle and a small cheyne of golde. **1559** MORWYNG *Evonym.* 108 If part of this water..be..thrown into thair with a strinkle, it will make a great cloude.

γ. **1514** in E. Law *Hampton Crt. Pal.* (1885) 343 An holy waterstok of laton with a stryngel of laton.

strinkle ('strɪŋk(ə)l), **strenkle** ('strɛŋk(ə)l), *v. Obs.* exc. *Sc.* and *dial.* Forms: α. 3, 5 **strencle**, 4, 6 *Sc.* **strenkil**, 4-5 **-kyll(e**, 5 **strenkel**, **-kill(e**, **strengkyll**, 4, 9 **strenkle**, *Sc.* **strenkell**; β. 4, 6-9 *Sc.* **strinkle**, (6 *Sc.* **strynkle**, **strinkill**, 7 **strinckle**, 9 *Sc.* **strinkel**). [Possibly an altered form of SPRINKLE *v.* (which, however, is later in our quots.), due to association with *strew*.]

1. *trans.* To sprinkle (a person or thing *with* holy water) (*obs.* exc. *arch.*); to sprinkle or strew (a surface with something); also with *over.* Also *fig.*

α. *a* **1300** [see STRINKLE *sb.*, STRINKLING *vbl. sb.* 1]. *a* **1340** HAMPOLE *Psalter* l. 8 Ysope is a medicynall erbe,..whorwiþ who so is strenkild in penaunce, it purges him. *a* **1400-50** *Wars Alex.* 3224 (Dubl. MS.) Þat [wall of gold] was strengkyllyd [*MS. Ashm.* streken] full of sternez & strykyn with gemmys. *a* **1420** *Aunters of Arthur* 590 (Douce MS.) Stones of Iral þey strenkel and strewe. *c* **1460** *Towneley Myst.* xxviii. 108 Luf makys me, as ye may se strenkyllid with blood so red. **14..** *Promp. Parv.* 479/2 Strenkelyn, or sprenkelyn, MSS. *K., H., S. aspergo, conspergo.* *c* **1520** M. NISBET *Heb.* x. 22 And be our hartis strenkilit [*Wyclif* spreynt, spreined] fra ane euile conscience. **1819** W. TENNANT *Papistry Storm'd* (1827) 199 Strenkellin'..the fechtars' faces Wi' its out-waffin' water.

β. ? *c* **1330** R. BRUNNE *Chron. Wace* (Rolls) 11194 (Petyt MS.) Menyuere strinkled with gris. **1536** BELLENDEN *Cron. Scot.* (1821) II. 219 Bot Ilay..come with his ii sonnis, strinklit with dust and sweit o..attal. **1567** *Gude & Godlie Ball.* 123 With Isope Lord thow strinkill me, And than I sall be clene. **1733** P. LINDSAY *Interest Scot.* 153 The Ground is fallowed..; and at sowing it is all strinkled over with human Ordure. **1764** ELIZ. MOXON *Eng. Housew.* (ed. 9) 98 When they [*sc.* eels] are almost enough strinkle them over with a little shred parsley. **1819** W. TENNANT *Papistry Storm'd* (1827) 156 A streap o' blude..Strinkel't his ilka haffet.

2. To sprinkle, scatter, strew (something *on*, *upon*, *among*).

α. **13..** *E.E. Allit. P.* B. 307 [God speaks:] I schal strenkle my distresse & strye al togeder, Boþe ledez & londe & alle þat lyf habbez. *c* **1400** *Destr. Troy* 12145 Hir blod all aboute aboue hit was sched, And strawet in þe strete, strenklit full þik. **1850** T. BEWICK *Howdy & Upgetting* 10 Bring him..a shive oh Butter an Breed..an strenkle a leapyt ov sugar on't.

β. **1513** DOUGLAS *Æneis* IV. ix. 27 And to the walkryf dragon meit gaif sche,..Strynkland [L. *spargens*] to hym the wak hony sweit. *Ibid.* 80 And euir the wattir strinkles sche agane. **1581** N. BURNE *Disput.* 11 b, This christian man..did hallou valter,..and strinkle it vpon the lyme. **1607** MARKHAM *Caval.* III. 44 Giue him..a handfull or two of well sifted Oates, and a prety quantity of this scouring strinckled amongst them. **1721** WODROW *Hist. Ch. Scot.* (1830) II. II. xii. 354 They..had nothing but snow-water, strinkled upon some oatmeal, to drink. **1764** ELIZ. MOXON *Eng. Housew.* (ed. 9) 102 Strinkle in a little salt and mace. *Ibid.* 108 Strinkle at the top a little flour. **1829** BROCKETT *N.C. Gloss.* (ed. 2), *Strinkle*, to spread by scattering. **1877** *N.W. Linc. Gloss.* s.v., 'They've gotten a strange good cart at Brigg to strinkle watter aboot to lay th' dust.' 'Strinkle a bit o' Indian corn for them pigeons.'

Hence **†'strinkled** *ppl. a.*

c **1440** *Promp. Parv.* 479/2 Strenkelyd, or sprenkelyd (*Pynson* strenkled), *aspersus.*

strinkling, strenkling. *vbl. sb. Obs.* exc. *Sc.* and *dial.* [f. STRINKLE *v.* + -ING[1].]

1. The action of the verb.

a **1300** *Cursor M.* 28580 Of hali water þe strenkling. *c* **1440** *Promp. Parv.* 479/2 Strenkelynge, or sprenkelynge, *aspersio.*

2. A small quantity or amount sprinkled; also *fig.* a small proportion intermixed.

1660 H. MORE *Myst. Godl.* VII. ix. 316 He may also help himself something from those strinklings that are found in prophane Writers. *Ibid.* VIII. xiv. §11. 427 Men whose brains were seasoned with some strinklings at least of Madness and Phrensy. **1743** R. MAXWELL *Sel. Trans. Soc. Impr. Agric. Scot.* 83 If in the ensuing Spring, you harrow the Field, adding a strinkling of Clover..before harrowing. **1823** E. MOOR *Suffolk Words* s.v., 'A pretty strinkling of turnips,' means a goodish plant all over the field. **1883** *Almondbury & Huddersf. Gloss.* s.v., Thus a congregation might consist chiefly of women, with a strinkling of men.

strinth(e, obs. forms of STRENGTH.

strio- ('straɪəʊ), used as combining form of STRIA, in adjs. (*Anat.* and *Phys.*) with the sense 'pertaining to the striatum and something else', as ***strio-cerebral***; **strio'nigral** *a.*, epithet of nerve fibres running from the corpus striatum to the substantia nigra; **strio'pallidal** *a.*, epithet of nerve fibres running from the neostriatum to the globus pallidus (the palæostriatum).

1878 tr. *Ziemssen's Cycl. Med.* XIV. 700 We must speak only of spinal, bulbar, cerebellar, strio-cerebral, cerebro-cortical movements, &c. **1920** S. W. RANSON *Anat. Nerv. Syst.* xi. 164 The function of the substantia nigra is equally obscure... There terminates within it a bundle, consisting of both direct and crossed fibers from the corpus striatum, the strionigral tract. **1937** J. H. GLOBUS *Pract. Neuroanat.* I. 156 Through the red nucleus, the rubrospinal tract is brought in continuity with part of the striopallidal system. **1970** *Brain Res.* XVII. 125 As part of an analysis of the intrinsic and extrinsic connections of the caudate nucleus some information has been obtained on the termination of the strio-pallidal and strio-nigral fibres.

striola ('straɪəʊlə). *Biol.* Pl. **striolæ**. [mod.L., dim. of STRIA.] A small stria.

1903 *Ann. & Mag. Nat. Hist.* May 454 The disk bears numerous transverse striolæ.

striolate ('straɪəʊlət), *a. Biol.* [ad. mod.L. *striolātus*, f. STRIOLA: see -ATE[2].] Marked with striolæ.

1841 *Proc. Berw. Nat. Club* I. ix. 266 The whorls appear to be very finely striolate. **1899** *Proc. Zool. Soc.* 860 Abdominal integument punctured as well as striolate.

Hence **'striolated** *a.*, in the same sense.

1865 TRISTRAM *Land of Israel* (1876) 288 S. brought in several specimens of the striolated bunting. **1901** *Proc. Zool.*

Soc. II. 38 The 2nd and 3rd segments punctured and longitudinally striolated in the middle.

'striolet. *Ent. rare*⁻⁰. = STRIOLA.

1826 KIRBY & SP. *Entomol.* IV. xlvi. 302 Striolet, a short stria.

strioscopy (straɪ'ɒskəpɪ). *Physics.* [f. STRIO- (here of unkn. significance) + -SCOPY.] A form of electron microscopy in which the beam is focused on to the specimen as a hollow cone of particles, giving a bright image on a dark field.

1967 *Jrnl. Electron Microsc.* XVI. 11 The contrasts obtained by the contrast-stop method are better than those of strioscopy. **1974** *Physics Bull.* Sept. 397/2 Castaing contributes a chapter on the prism-mirror analyser, Fert on strioscopy. **1979** J. R. FRYER *Chem. Applications Transmission Electron Microsc.* ii. 62 Normal dark field technique either tilts the incident beam, or displaces an objective aperture, so that the primary beam does not contribute to the final image, whilst strioscopy physically stops the axial primary beam passing.

So **strio'scopic** *a.*

1972 P. W. HAWKES *Electron Optics* iii. 89 In a commercial instrument..that makes provision for strioscopic illumination, as this type of illumination is called, a third condenser..is provided below the annular aperture to match the latter exactly to the objective aperture. **1973** *Nature* 17 Aug. 412/1 Strioscopic methods are also of potential value for high resolution work.

strip (strɪp), *sb.*[1] *Law.* Now only *U.S.* Forms: 6 **stripe, stryppe, strepe,** 7– **strip.** [a. AF. *estrepe*, vbl. noun f. *estreper* ESTREPE *v.*]

= ESTREPEMENT.

1516 in *5th Rep. Hist. MSS. Comm.* (1876) 596/2 Jone my wyffe schalle make no stryppe ner waste in fellyng of tymbyr. **15..** *Modus tenend. Cur. Baron* (W. de W.) A 4, Yf ye knowe that ony tenaunt haue made ony strepe or waast vpon his bonde tenement. Strepe is to saye pullynge vp of trees or hedges, waste is to saye late houses fall downe for defaute of reperacyon. **1559** *Boke Presidentes* 30 N...shall haue..necessarie firebote, hedge bote [etc.]...duryng the sayd term, without stripe or wast. **1633** BP. HALL *Hard Texts, Isa.* vii. 20 In that day, the Lord shall by the hand of the Assyrians..make utter strip, & waste of Judah. **1662** GURNALL *Chr. in Arm.* III. verse 17. lx. [lxi.] 539 'Tis too bad if the tenant pays not his easie rent, but to make strip and waste of the trees on his Land-lords ground, this is more intolerable. **1682** tr. *Charter of Cinque Ports* 138 Strip or Estrepement is a Writ for taking Lands from him that strips and spoils them. **1701** in *Charters & Gen. Laws Massachusetts* (1814) 361 No woman that shall be endowed of any lands..as aforesaid, shall commit or suffer any strip or waste thereupon, but [etc.]. **1891** *Century Dict.*, *Strip*, destruction of fences, timber, etc.; waste. (U.S.)

strip (strɪp), *sb.*[2] Also 6 **strippe, stryppe,** 7 **stripp.** [a. or cogn. w. MLG. *strippe* strap, thong of a whip-lash, purse-string, etc., perh. f. Teut. root **strip-*: see STRIPE *sb.*[2]

The MLG. *strippe*, however, may be for **strüppe* cogn. with STROP *sb.*; if so, sense 3 may perh. be an adoption of an unrecorded continental use: cf. Du. *strop* collar, stock.]

1. a. A narrow piece (primarily of textile material, paper, or the like; hence *gen.*) of approximately uniform breadth.

pilaster strip (Arch.): see PILASTER.

1459 *Invent.* in *Paston Lett.* I. 478 Item, j pece of blak kersey with rosys... Item, ij. stripis of the same sute. *a* **1548** HALL *Chron., Hen. VIII*, 10 Strippes of black Veluet, euery strip set with a scalop shell. **1697** H. WANLEY in *Bodl. Q. Rec.* (1915) Jan. 107 That a little strip of Parchment be pasted to each Tract, with its number written upon it. **1706** PHILLIPS (ed. Kersey), *Strip*, a small piece of Cloth. **1756** C. LUCAS *Ess. Waters* III. 74 The glare of an egg..spread upon strips of paper. **1811** in *Rep. Comm. Publ. Rec. Irel.* (1815) 71 The Fees demandable by the Clerk of the Enrolments... For ingrossing every double strip of Enrolment, 0 1 7½. **1847** G. HARRIS *Life Ld. Hardwicke* III. xiv. 284 The following is in Lord Hardwicke's handwriting, on a small strip of paper. **1856** MISS YONGE *Daisy Chain* I. xviii, No carpet, except little strips by the bed. **1882** GASKELL in *Jrnl. Physiol.* IV. 51 A strip of muscular tissue is cut from the apex of the ventricle. **1907** J. A. HODGES *Elem. Photogr.* (ed. 6) 118 A strip of very fine muslin.

†**b.** *collect.* as a material.

1801 JANE AUSTEN *Lett.* (1884) I. 283 My mother has ordered a new bonnet, and so have I; both white strip, trimmed with white ribbon.

c. A long narrow tract of territory, of land, wood, etc.

1816 TUCKEY *Narr. Exped. R. Zaire* vi. (1818) 206 The banks [of the river here] have in some places low strips of soil and sand. **1841** W. SPALDING *Italy & It. Isl.* I. 27 The county of Nice and duchy of Genoa, which form a long narrow strip between the southern side of the mountains and the sea. **1842** W. AITON *Dom. Econ.* (1857) 284 The preceding minister..had planted a strip of firs..around the portion of the glebe on which the manse and offices were built. **1872** BLACK *Adv. Phaeton* vi. 74 This road is bordered by a strip of common. **1880** RUSKIN *On Old Road* (1885) II. 3 A narrow strip of untilled field.

d. A narrow piece of board, metal plate, etc.

1831 BREWSTER *Optics* xxviii. 240 The influence of compression and dilatation may be well exhibited by taking a strip of glass..and bending it by the force of the hands. **1860** J. HEWITT *Arms & Arm.* II. 120 Defences in which longitudinal strips appear, are of this [the 14th] century. These strips are placed contiguously, on the arms and legs: they sometimes form a mere ridge on the surface of a smooth armour. **1875** KNIGHT *Dict. Mech.* 2430 *Strip*, a narrow piece of board nailed over a crack or joint between planks. **1907** J. A. HODGES *Elem. Photogr.* (ed. 6) 41 Strips of wood about 2½ in. wide by 1 in. thick.

e. A narrow portion of a surface, bounded by parallel lines.

1882 G. M. MINCHIN *Unipl. Kinemat.* 185 To find the resistance of this area, we may consider it as broken up into ..an indefinitely great number of equipotential strips. **1892** CAYLEY *Math. Papers* (1897) XIII. 233 The skew surface is thus composed of rigid strips or elements, each included between two consecutive lines.

f. A sequence of small drawings telling a comic or serial story in a newspaper, etc. Freq. as ***comic strip.*** Also *transf.* orig. *U.S.*

1920 L. N. FLINT *Editorial* x. 229 In the paper..the week-day issues contain a preponderance of syndicate features—'comics', 'strips'..and continued stories. **1920** C. SANDBURG *Smoke & Steel* 47 The comic strips in the papers. **1928** *Daily Sketch* 7 Aug. 4/2, I keenly appreciate the qualities that make Pop the greatest comic strip in the world. No comic strip artist..has the same facile and generic lines the creator of Pop possesses. **1939** JOYCE *Finnegans Wake* 537 Such wear a frillick for my comic strip, Mons Meg's Monthly, comes out aich Fanagan's Weck. **1943** D. POWELL *Time to be Born* iv. 95 She had a curious impression of being in a Buck Rogers strip..and gazing into another planet. **1955** AUDEN *Shield of Achilles* ii. 38 Mild-looking middle class boys Who read the comic strips. **1967** *Listener* 21 Dec. 821/3 This feedback from strip to pop and back into strip again is very noticeable. **1979** *Tucson* (Arizona) *Citizen* 20 Sept. 7B/6 Why, you might wonder, would Universal and NBC risk an expensive space comic strip like 'Buck Rogers'?

g. = ***air-strip*** s.v. AIR *sb.*[1] B. III. 7. Also *fig.* See also ***fighter strip*** s.v. FIGHTER 4, ***landing-strip*** s.v. LANDING *vbl. sb.* 8.

1936 W. H. MCCORMICK *Mod. Bk. Aeroplanes* xi. 106 The strip extends across the landing-ground. **1944** *Yank* 14 Jan. 10 As a draftsman working for the Australian government, he helped plan both strips. **1958** 'N. SHUTE' *Rainbow & Rose* i. 9 This is the only strip in the vicinity? **1962** M. MCLUHAN *Gutenberg Galaxy* 64 Greek celature as a take-off strip for the medieval manuscript culture. **1977** *Whitaker's Almanack 1978* 756/2 Several flying strips are also in use by light aircraft [in Nigeria].

h. A street noted for its night-clubs, bars, gambling houses, etc. Freq. with def. article and capital initial (orig. with reference to *Sunset Strip* in Hollywood: see quot. 1974). *slang* (chiefly *N. Amer.*).

1939 *California* (Federal Writers' Project, Calif.) 193 Further west on Sunset Boulevard..is a section popularly known as 'the Strip'. **1941** B. SCHULBERG *What makes Sammy Run?* vii. 124 The wind sweeping down the Strip from the sea. **1957** *MacLean's Mag.* 6 July 33/1 The many-tongued enclave known as the Strip is cut off..by a near-Gothic stone pile that straddles the Avenue [*sc.* Spadina Avenue in Toronto] just north of College Street. **1967** W. MURRAY *Sweet Ride* vi. 89 The Place is located in the heart of the Strip. It..had once catered to a touristy clientele. **1968** *Globe & Mail* (Toronto) 3 Feb. 23/1 Visit the main floor bar of the Brown Derby at Dundas and Yonge, the crossroads of the Yonge Street 'strip' which includes seven bars within a block-and-a-half. **1971** *Guardian* 8 July 3/1 Bangkok has its own strip, the new Petchburi Road extension: miles of girlie bars, short time hotels, and soul food snack bars. **1974** *Encycl. Brit. Macropædia* XI. 109/2 Sunset Boulevard meanders 21 miles west from the state park..to the sea. A one-mile section of the boulevard becomes the 'Sunset Strip', or simply the 'Strip'. **1976** *Publishers Weekly* 21 June 62/2 Rush Street was a nightlife strip, virtually deserted during the day. **1978** S. BRILL *Teamsters* iv. 124 Just over to the right is the strip—a row of flickering neons wrapped around bold signs that advertise 'go-go girls' and 'live dancers'.

i. ***to tear*** (someone) ***off a strip, to tear a strip off*** (someone) and varr.: to upbraid or reprimand (someone); ***to lose a strip, to have a strip torn off,*** to be reprimanded or receive a dressing-down. *colloq.* (orig. *R.A.F. slang*).

1940 N. MONKS *Squadrons Up* ii. 56 For any breaches of discipline..he would 'tear a strip' off the luckless pilots. **1940** 'N. SHUTE' *Landfall* i. 25 Dickens tore me off a strip just now. **1942** T. RATTIGAN *Flare Path* I. 30, I didn't particularly like doing it, and I had the hell of a strip torn off about it afterwards. **1952** E. F. DAVIES *Illyrian Venture* iv. 71 Nicholls used to tear tremendous strips off Trayhorn. **1957** L. P. HARTLEY *Hireling* 42 If my wife saw me wearing one, she would tear me off a strip. *a* **1963** J. LUSBY in B. James *Austral. Short Stories* (1963) 225 It's all right... I've just lost a strip, too. **1967** *Listener* 31 Aug. 264/1 Mr Kosygin..tore great strips off almost every major industry for inefficiency, or shoddy work, or both. **1979** 'M. HEBDEN' *Death set to Music* ix. 99 He'd clearly suspected it might have been Nosjean's [idea] and had been hoping to be able to tear a strip off him.

j. A track used for motor-racing. See also ***drag strip*** s.v. DRAG *sb.* 1 f. *U.S.*

1941 *Sun* (Baltimore) 30 Aug. 13/1 Dick Pending has the racing strip in good condition and unless more rain comes tomorrow, the track will not be too bad. **1946** *Ibid.* 2 Oct. 16/5 The racing strip has been brought around slowly to peak form. **1977** *Custom Car* Nov. 5/4 The drivers of these American cars are also quite happy with the racing. They enjoy chasing the slower cars down the strip.

k. = ***strip light*** (*b*), sense 7 a below.

1970 R. CRAWFORD *Kiss Boss Goodbye* II. iii. 68 The basement was..warmed by wall-heaters and lit by softpearl strips. **1981** I. MCEWAN *Comfort of Strangers* x. 133 The room was small, windowless and heavily perfumed. It was lit by a fluorescent strip.

l. *Cricket.* The narrow band of ground lying between the wickets.

1976 J. SNOW *Cricket Rebel* 30 None of England's fast bowlers had been particularly menacing during the first Test on a typically sluggish Edgbaston strip. **1977** *Sunday Times* 9 Jan. 28/6 MCC's other team in Bengal found a better wicket for batting at Dacca than the mutilated strip at Calcutta.

†**2.** ? Some piece of armour. *Obs. rare*⁻¹.

Cf. the mod. application in quot. 1860 in 1 d, and in *strip-armour*.

c **1508** DUNBAR *Poems* xxvi. 37 Bostaris, braggaris, and barganeris..Al bodin in feir of weir, In iakkis, and stryppis and bonettis of steill.

†**3.** An ornamental article of attire worn, chiefly by women, about the neck and the upper part of the chest. *Obs.*

1598 BP. HALL *Sat.* IV. iv. 31 When a plum'd Fanne may shade thy chalked face, And lawny strips thy naked bosome grace. *Ibid.* IV. vi. 44 Tyr'd with pin'd Ruffes, and Fans, and partlet-strips And Buskes, and Verdingales about their hips. **1642** in Alice M. Earle *Two Cent. Costume Amer.* (1903) I. 205 [A Maryland gentleman left by will, with other attire, in 1642,] Nine laced stripps, two plain stripps, nine quoiffes, one call, eight crosse-cloths [etc.]. **1658** J. SMITH *Innov. Penelope & Ulysses* in *Wit Restored* 155 A stomacher upon her breast so bare, For Strips and Gorgets was not then the weare.

4. *Metallurgy.* **a.** An ingot prepared for rolling into plates.

1876 *Encycl. Brit.* IV. 217/2 The ingots [of brass] for rolling, termed 'strips', are in the cold state passed successively between rolls..of large size which squeeze them out and extend them lengthwise. **1879** C. HIBBS in *Cassell's Techn. Educ.* IV. 413/1 The ingots or 'strips' [of German silver] are then rolled into plates.

b. A narrow flat bar of iron or steel; hence, iron or steel in 'strips' (more fully ***strip iron, steel***).

Often with prefixed word denoting the purpose, as *gas, nail, rail, tube strip*.

1887 *Daily News* 16 May 2/3 Bedstead strip varies from £5 to £7 per ton..and gas strip £4 17s 6d to £5. **1893** *Ibid.* 5 June 2/4 Tube strip is £5 10s to £5 15s; the competition in thin strip and hoop iron..continues keen... Hoops and thin strips are being offered..at £6. Local makers ask £6 5s for steel strip. **1901** WATERHOUSE *Conduit Wiring* 8 The Conduits are made from selected steel strip.

5. *Mining.* (See quot.)

1875 KNIGHT *Dict. Mech.* 2430 *Strip* (*Mining*), an inclined trough in which ores are separated by being disturbed while covered by a stream of water descending the strip.

6. *colloq.* The clothing worn by and distinguishing a football team.

If the original sense is 'clothing to which a player strips down', this sense should properly be placed under STRIP *sb.*[3]

1974 *Evening News* (Edinburgh) 8 Oct. 16/3 Postal United, the East of Scotland League club, had their strip stolen from a car in the Hailesland Park area. **1977** *Shoot* 18 June 4/4 The national strip of Zambia is green jerseys, orange shorts, and black stockings. **1981** 'G. GAUNT' *Incomer* xiv. 87 The [football] team were..passing flagon bottles around. Frank & Bob were..in a corner, having changed into strip early, and managed to grab a bottle between them.

7. *attrib.*, as (sense 1 c) ***strip-holder, -holding, -owner***; (sense 1 f), ***strip advertisement, form, heroine***; (sense 1 g) ***strip landing ground***; (sense 4 a) ***strip-caster***; **strip-armour** *Hist.*, armour for the arms and legs, showing broad raised strips (see sense 1 d) alternating with sunken bands; **strip architecture** *U.S.*, the types of building or other features characteristic of strip development; **strip-built** *a. rare*⁻¹, that has been subjected to strip or ribbon development; **strip cartoon,** a sequence of cartoons (sense 2) telling a (comic) story; freq. *attrib.*; hence **strip cartoonist**; **strip chart, stripchart,** a long roll of (usu. graduated) paper on which the pen of an automatic recording device can trace changes of a measured quantity with time by moving the paper past the pen at a constant rate; usu. *attrib.*, designating recorders using such rolls; **strip-cropping,** (*a*) *U.S.*, a system of land cultivation in which crops of different types and habits of growth are sown alternatively in strips along the contours of a hill, etc., to prevent soil erosion (cf. *contour cropping* s.v. CONTOUR *sb.* 4); (*b*) the practice of growing crops in strips (cf. *strip farming* below); **strip-cultivation,** (*a*) = *strip farming* below; (*b*) *Archæol.*, the practice of using strip lynchets in farming; **strip development** *U.S.* = *ribbon development* s.v. RIBBON *sb.* 10 a; **strip-farm** *v. trans. U.S.*, to cultivate (land) in strips along the contours of a hill, etc., to prevent soil erosion (cf. *strip-cropping* (*a*) above); **strip farming** *Hist.*, a system of land cultivation in which the land was divided up into long narrow strips and allocated to different peasant-farmers; **strip-grazing** *Agric.*, a system of farm management in which strips of land are alternately grazed and kept empty; rotational grazing; hence **strip-graze** *v. trans.*, to graze (land or livestock) in this way; **strip-grazed** *ppl. a.*; **strip light,** (*a*) *Theatr.*, any device to provide diffused stage lighting by mounting several lamps in a row, as on a batten, in a trough, etc.; (*b*) a lighting device, now usu. in the form of a tubular fluorescent lamp, for providing a continuous line of light; also as *v. trans.*; hence **strip-lighted** *ppl. a.*; **strip-lighting** *vbl. sb.*; **strip line, stripline** *Electr.*, a MICROSTRIP; **strip-lit** *a.* = *strip-lighted* ppl. adj. above; **strip-loin** *U.S.*, a particular cut of the loin of beef; **strip-lynchet** *Archæol.*, a horizontal terrace used for cultivation; a long, narrow lynchet (sense 2 b); **strip map**, a long narrow map, showing the course of a line of road, and the places adjacent; **strip mill** *Metallurgy*, a rolling mill specially designed for the production of metal strip; **strip mine** *U.S.*, a mine worked by strip-mining; also as *v. trans.*, to obtain or exploit by strip-mining; **strip-mined** *ppl. a.*, **strip-miner**; **strip mining** *vbl. sb. U.S.*, a method of mining in which surface material is removed in successive parallel strips to expose the mineral, the spoil from each new strip being placed in the previously excavated one; **strip packaging**, a method of packaging small items, liquids, etc., in which individual sachets are formed (from plastic or metal foil), filled and heat-sealed in a single process; **strip park** orig. *U.S.*, a long, narrow park developed alongside a road, canal, etc. (cf. *strip development* above); **strip printer**, a photocomposing device which prints characters on a strip of paper or film; also, any device which prints on a narrow roll of paper; **strip steak** *U.S.* (see quot. 1962) (cf. *strip-loin*); **strip system** = *strip farming* above; **strip ticket**, a ticket for a journey by a public conveyance, printed with a number of similar tickets on a strip of paper; **strip-work**, (*a*) *Arch.* = *strap-work* (STRAP *sb.* 18); (*b*) = *strip-armour*; **strip-wound** *a.*, wound with strips, esp. of metal.

1938 *Strip advertisement [see BEFORE A. 5 c]. **1976** *New Yorker* 15 Mar. 27/3 '*Strip' architecture—the endless miles of trailer parks, gas stations, used-car lots, Taco Bells, etc., .. that fan out from every American metropolis—has its own validity. **1860** J. HEWITT *Arms & Arm.* II. 121 The manner of forming this *strip-armour is very exactly described. **1936** C. DAY LEWIS *Noah & Waters* 15 *Strip-built roads that stray Out like suckers to drain the country. **1936** *Discovery* Dec. 384/1 Shop-keeper's bill of the early 18th century. Note the smokers conversing about their tobacco, quite in the modern '*strip-cartoon' style. **1950** *Times* 2 Mar. 6/5 Separate or detachable sections or supplements comprised wholly or mainly of strip cartoons. **1967** E. SHORT *Embroidery & Fabric Collage* iii. 60 The coverlet tells the story of Tristan, in a series of scenes showing different incidents, in the manner of a strip cartoon. **1974** *Listener* 24 Jan. 118/1 Under the strip-cartoon image lies a message that is often puritanical. **1953** *New Internat. Yearbk. 1952* 47/1 J. C. Bancks, Australia's most popular *strip-cartoonist, was creator of Ginger Meggs. **1879** C. HIBBS in *Cassell's Techn. Educ.* IV. 413/1 The '*strip-caster' as he is termed. **1884** *B'ham Daily Post* 23 Feb. 3/5 Stripcaster.—Wanted, Steady Man, used to casting Brass for rolling. **1950** *Instruments* XXIII. 260/3 (Advt.), New 'Pneumatic Capacilog' air-operated *strip-chart recorder is completely self-contained. **1966** *N.Y. Times* 3 Feb. 33 The computer recorded wave variations that often are undetectable to the eye of a physician using the traditional strip chart. **1978** *Nature* 12 Oct. 520/2 The outputs are recorded on stripchart recorders, allowing a maximum resolution of 100 ms. **1936** *Sun* (Baltimore) 18 Aug. 3/5 This would be effected through .. a blending of 'soil depleting' crops with grasses by a system of '*strip-cropping'—a strip of crops and a strip of grass. **1949** MARTIN & LEONARD *Princ. Field Crop Production* v. 125 Strip cropping, now widely advocated, has been practiced for generations in sections of Pennsylvania. **1976** *S. Wales Echo* 26 Nov. 8/6 If you have plenty of cloches you could accomplish what is called strip cropping. This means that sowings are arranged in alternate strips so that cloches can be moved sideways from one strip to the next and back as required. **1932** KENDRICK & HAWKES *Archaeol. in England & Wales 1914–31* x. 173 The Celtic system .. lasted to reach its height in Roman times, and makes a striking contrast to the *strip cultivation of the Saxon and medieval open fields. **1974** C. TAYLOR *Fieldwork in Medieval Archaeol.* iii. 28 These terrace-like features [*sc.* strip lynchets] on hillsides are the remains of medieval strip cultivation. **1955** *Sun* (Baltimore) 7 Jan. 19/5 Shops in long-established business districts are predominantly in '*strip' developments; that is, strung out along principal highways that bisect the neighborhood. **1980** *Blair & Ketchum's Country Jrnl.* Oct. 68/1 The arrival of new kinds of people or a new industry or housing developments and strip developments loomed all the larger in many small towns. **1943** *Sun* (Baltimore) 8 Sept. 18/1 The corn rows follow the lay of the land on the contour and the land is *strip-farmed .. with the corn rows acting as dams to check losses of soil and moisture. **1913** A. D. HALL *Pilgrimage Brit. Farming* xiv. 103 The *strip farming .. prevails over all the land [of the Isle of Axholme] which we may suppose to have been dry in medieval times. **1962** H. R. LOYN *Anglo-Saxon England* i. 20 Pre-Saxon strip farming has been recognized at sites in Wessex .. and in Cumberland, Northumberland and South Scotland. **1949** *Radio Times* 15 July 17/2 Those inter-planetary adventures we find, in *strip form, in almost every comic. **1955** *Times* 6 June 4/5 Some farmers are such convinced believers in *strip grazing that in the larger fields they use two electric fences, one at the feeding face and one as a back fence to keep the animals off the grass that should be starting to grow again. **1975** *Country Life* 26 June 1702/3 Strip-grazing .. involves using two swards, one solely for grazing .. and used for a succession of years .. and the other sward used more often as a shorter ley for conservation. **1960** *Farmer & Stockbreeder* 12 Jan. 78/1 One part [of a herd] is housed and milked in a modern and double row cowshed and is *strip-grazed in summer. *Ibid.* 79/1 The kale is no longer strip-grazed. **1971** *Power Farming* Mar. 29/1 It was particularly useful for direct-drilling kale, which could then be strip grazed. **1976** *Burnham-on-Sea Gaz.* 20 Apr. 22/3 Although being .. strip grazed on a paddock system .. the herd has shown that it can milk well. **1960** *Farmer & Stockbreeder* 15 Mar. 133/1, I shall be going in for milk production. Please suggest a ration based on *strip-grazed beet tops, swedes, kale, hay, oats, barley and beet pulp. **1967** *Listener* 21 Dec. 822/1 The idea of a *strip-heroine for middle-aged onanists is surely a gloomy one. **1898** F. W. MAITLAND *Township & Borough* 64 Very often the office-holders were *strip-holders or at any rate belonged to families which had held strips. **1901** *Month* Dec. 603 The *strip-holding of arable land which was so universal in England. **1938** *Flight* 21 July 60/1 It is in fact a *strip landing ground with natural wind buffers. **1920** S. LEWIS *Main Street* xviii. 221 Sending to Minneapolis for .. a *strip light. **1927** *Proc. Inst. Civil Engin.* CCXXIV. 160 The manometer is illuminated by a 'strip light'. **1963** PARKER & SMITH *Scene Design & State Lighting* xvi. 292 One form of stage-lighting instrument that predates the invention of the incandescent lamp is the striplight, which produces the effect of a line of light by means of a number of sources. **1972** P. LIVELY *Driftway* i. 1 Big strip lights on the ceiling reached away almost as far as you could see. **1934** S. GOLD *Neon* xxii. 61 The question of *strip-lighting the building over the entire front is usually entertained only by cinemas. **1981** 'J. Ross' *Dark Blue & Dangerous* xx. 109 A corridor flanked with *strip-lighted offices. **1926** *Gloss. Terms Electr. Engin.* (Brit. Engin. Stand. Assoc.) 146 **Strip lighting*, a system of lighting in which a number of lamps, usually of tubular form, and installed in line with one another, so as to give the impression of a more or less continuous strip of light. **1934** S. GOLD *Neon* xxii. 61 A combination of colours in strip-lighting gives a charming effect to an otherwise straightforward display. **1976** L. DEIGHTON *Twinkle, twinkle Little Spy* iv. 39 The entrance hall .. was brightly lit by indirect strip-lighting set into the ceiling. **1952** *Proc. IRE* XL. 1658/2 In the case of *strip lines, the line conductor is a thin narrow ribbon of metal either cut from sheet or deposited. **1967** *Electronics* 6 Mar. 58/2 The military believes recent advances in stripline versions of Butler matrixes .. can produce faster memory units. **1974** *Physics Bull.* Apr. 153/3 The copper conductors .. are suitable for high resolution stripline and ground plane applications. **1960** *Guardian* 14 Apr. 9/3 Illuminated .. by .. *strip-lit shelves. **1973** M. AMIS *Rachel Papers* 131 Cat's crap on the strip-lit kitchen floor, musty wine-shop smells from the dining-room, objects tingled to flayed senses. **1884** *Harper's Mag.* July 299/1 Tenderloins, *striploins, sirloins. [**1928** *Antiquity* II. 172 Their .. observations .. of the .. long-strip lynchets of Saxon and medieval times.] **1929** *Ibid.* III. 174 The *strip lynchets .. on sloping ground, are made stable .. by the facing of masonry. **1975** J. G. EVANS *Environment Early Man Brit. Isles* vii. 168 Today, where ridge and furrow and strip lynchets are preserved they are generally under permanent pasture. **1983** *Out of Town* June 26/2 Bands of quite difficult ground are often stepped and striped by patterns of 'strip lynchets'... The strip lynchets .. were gradually bitten into the hillslopes by ploughs that were hauled (approximately) along the contours. **1903** *List New Publications* in *Daily Chron.* 30 July 3/2 'The Exeter Road.' *Strip map. 'The Liverpool and Manchester Road.' Strip map. 'The Carlisle Road'. Strip map. **1906** *Westm. Gaz.* 23 July 10/2 The Strip or Motor-Route Maps. **1910** H. P. TIEMANN *Iron & Steel* 286 Bar mills, also called merchant mills or, on account of the special product which they make .. rod mill, hoop mill or *strip mill. **1945** *Times* 26 Feb. 5/7 The strip mill for light sheet and tin plate, the continuous billet mill .. [etc.] all belong to this type. **1980** *Times* 19 Feb. 2/5 Wide sheet steel from the BSC's strip mills .. is widely used in the manufacture of domestic 'white goods'. **1934** *Coal Age* Oct. 376/3 The spread of trailer operation at Southwestern *strip mines reflects a number of advantages. **1976** *Billings* (Montana) *Gaz.* 1 July 2-A/4 The high court has dramatized the need for a national strip mine law so that everybody plays according to the same rules in extractable resource development. **1970** *New Scientist* 21 May 364/2 Nuclear explosions are also planned for *strip-mining large deposits of non-ferrous metals in the northern territories. **1978** *Peace News* 6 Oct. 7/2 Stewart Udall, Secretary of the Interior, gave approval to WEST to strip-mine vast areas of Indian land for coal. **1936** *Coal Age* Oct. 415/1 *Strip-mined coal, under early production conditions, .. generally sold at prices substantially under those for deepmined coal. **1980** *Sci. Amer.* Oct. 160/3 The reclamation of strip-mined land involves the relatively simple processes of flattening the piles of overburden, replacing the topsoil and replanting it. **1946** *Sun* (Baltimore) 19 Nov. 4/5 Mark McCauley, Davis (W. Va.) *strip miner convicted of first degree murder .. was sentenced to be hanged. **1977** *Economist* 23 Apr. 52/3 Despite the small proportion of stripminers in the United Mineworkers Union, the union as a whole has withdrawn its support for federal legislation. **1935** *Coal Age* Feb. 91/1 This first-and-second method of *strip mining cannot be employed economically with shovel equipment which must operate down in the cut. **1949** *Hansard Commons* 19 May 706 Strip-mining, as it is known in America, and opencast work in regard to gypsum .. or any .. base metal is essentially a mining problem. *Ibid.* There were .. technicians in the country .. familiar with American strip-mining methods. **1977** *Economist* 23 Apr. 52/2 The technique of stripmining —clearing the topsoil above a coal seam to scoop out the coal with bulldozers—once seemed an answer to low productivity. **1898** F. W. MAITLAND *Township & Borough* 6 The *strip-owners are for the more part colleges. **1969** L. S. MOUNTS in W. R. R. Park *Plastics Film Technol.* v. 140 Many products can be packaged in water soluble films with advantage. These include .. industrial and agricultural products like sprays, chemical additives and *strip packaging of seeds. **1975** C. F. ROSS *Packaging of Pharmaceuticals* i. 4 Sachets, filled automatically on suitable strip-packaging machines. **1938** *Sun* (Baltimore) 24 June 12/3 The financial operations .. seem likely to leave the Eastern United States with their third '*strip park', the others being the Shenandoah Skyway and the park at Natchez, Miss. **1972** *Times* 7 June 4/3 A number of smaller strip-parks, which people could walk to .. would be .. useful. **1962** *Amer. Lithographer* Apr. 90/3 An automatically-timed exposure light has been added to the *Strip Printer Photo Composing Machine Model 299. **1965** R. R. KARCH *Graphic Arts Procedures* (ed. 3) xiii. 331 The Strip Printer is used to produce lines of type in various sizes on paper or 35 mm. film. **1976** *Times* 8 June 10/5 By adding a simple keyboard and strip printer to a standard telephone, the telephone terminal could .. interact with a computer. **1962** J. N. WINBURNE *Dict. Agric. & Allied Terminol.* 769/2 **Strip steak*, the steak cut from the loin strip of a beef carcass. **1977** *Rolling Stone* 30 June 111/3 His guitar style is taut and as lean as a strip steak. **1954** J. KEITH *Fifty Yrs. Farming* xi. 125 Over a great part of Britain there developed the common-field and *strip system. **1965** R. WHITLOCK *Short Hist. Farming in Britain* i. 20 In conjunction with the pattern determined by the type of plough, arose the Saxon strip system of fields. **1908** *Daily Chron.* 7 Sept. 1/5 The experiment of substituting *strip tickets for season tickets on the Baker-street and Waterloo, Great Northern and Piccadilly, and Charing-cross, Euston, and Hampstead Railways comes into force on October 1. **1909** *Ibid.* 10 July 4/6 Our London tube strip-tickets. **1860** J. HEWITT *Arms & Arm.* II. 121 In both these sculptures the *strip-work is found on the arms and legs. **1893** *Reliquary* Jan. 16 The third stage has a large window in the south wall; this has decorated strip-work around it. **1907** HOBART & ELLIS *Armature Construction* xi. 265 Windings for a *strip-wound barrel type of armature. **1962** *Times* 26 Feb. (Canada Suppl.) p. vii/2 (Advt.), Hydraulic pressure cylinders in steel, stripwound, etc.

strip (strɪp), *sb.*[3] [f. STRIP *v.*[1]] **1.** *pl.* Tobacco-leaf with the stalk and midrib removed. Also ***strip-leaf***.

1844 *Rep. Sel. Comm. Tobacco Trade, Min. Evid.* 232 The consequence of the permission which is given to import strips at the same duty as leaf is, that the stalks are exported from America to the Continent. **1845** DODD *Brit. Manuf.* V. 133 'Strip-leaf' .. is the technical name for tobacco from which the stem of the leaf has been taken away before the latter is packed in the hogshead. **1904** *Daily Chron.* 6 May 6/3 His whole imports in March were 133 hogsheads of 'strips' and nineteen hogsheads of leaf tobacco.

2. *colloq.* (orig. *U.S.*). An act or the practice of removing one's clothes or of striptease. See also STRIP *v.*[1] 27 b.

1928 *Variety* 12 Dec. 46/3 Why do women principals try to do strip numbers against the competition of experienced runway specialists?.. Columbia, by the way, seems to be leery of the limit in strip at this telling. **1956** B. HOLIDAY *Lady sings Blues* (1973) v. 54 He kept on doing this slow elaborate strip. **1966** *Guardian* 9 July 8/3 Perhaps ten [clubs] provide regular striptease. Up to ten provide strip occasionally. **1971** R. PETRIE *Thorne in Flesh* vi. 86 Dahlia does a strip... I auction the things she takes off.

strip (strɪp), *sb.*[4] *Sc.* [Prob. a back-formation from *stript* var. of STRIPED *a.*] = STRIPE *sb.*[2]

In some dialects of Scotland the form *stripe* in this sense is unknown in genuine vernacular speech; 'strips' is the only word, e.g. for the stripes of a tiger or a zebra.

1789 J. WILLIAMS *Min. Kingd.* I. 80 The strips or streaks lie all of them exactly parallel to one another, and exactly parallel to the bed of the stone. **1843** J. BALLANTINE *Gaberlunzie's Wallet* 304 They wont be long in having sergeant's strips of their arms. **1914** *Brit. Mus. Return* 94 Green ewer with waved strip below the handle, found in Dora.

†**b.** *attrib.* or *adj.* Striped. *Obs.*

1666 in *Maitland Club Miscell.* (1840) II. 539 For six yeardis of strip silk stuff .. 015 08 00.

strip (strɪp), *v.*[1] Pa. t. and pa. pple. **stripped** (strɪpt), **stript**. Forms: 1 **-strýpan**, 3 **strupen**, 3–6 **stripe**, 4–6 **strype**, 4 **strepe**, **streepe**, **struype**, 4–6 **stryppe**, 4–7 **strippe**, 5 **streppe**, 7 **stripp**, 6– **strip**. *Pa. t.* 1 **-strýpte**, **-strípte**, 3 **strepte**, **streopte**, **strupte**, 5 **strypid**, **striput**, **strepid**, **strope**, 6 **stryp(p)ed**, 6– **stripped**, **stript**. *Pa. pple.* 1 **-strýped**, 3 **istruped**, 4 **i-strupt**, **i-stripte**, 5 **strypte**, **striped**, 6 **stryp(p)ed**, **striped**, 7 **strip'd**, 5– **stripped**, 6– **stript**. [ME. *stripe*, *strepe*, *strupe* (ü):—OE. **striepan*, **strépan*, **strýpan* (whence *be-strýpan* to plunder, despoil: see BESTRIP *v.*), corresp. to MLG., MDu. *strôpen* (mod.Du. *stroopen*), to plunder, strip, MHG. *ströufen* to skin, chastise (mod.G. *streifen* to strip off):—WGer. **straupjan*; the Teut. root **straup-*: **strup-* prob. occurs also in MHG. *strupfen* to strip off, and possibly in STROP *sb.*

The normal mod. form of the present-stem would be **stripe*; the shortening of the vowel prob. took place first before the two consonants in the pa. t. and pa. pple. *stript*, and hence extended to the pres.-stem.

The mod.Du. *strippen* to strip (tobacco), sometimes cited as cognate, is prob. from Eng.]

I. To unclothe, denude.

1. a. *trans.* To divest (a person, body) of clothing; to undress, make bare or naked. Often more definitely with compl. or phrase, ***to strip naked***, ***to strip to the skin***, (***to the buff***). Const. *of*, †*out of* (one's clothing); *down*, *off*, in *intr.* for *refl.* use.

a **1225** *Juliana* 16 He het hatterliche strupen hire steort naket. *c* **1386** CHAUCER *Clerk's T.* 807 Ye dide me streepe out of my poure weede And richely me cladden. **1387** TREVISA *Higden* (Rolls) VIII. 221 [Heo] was i-stripte and i-scourged [L. *exspoliata flagellaretur*]. *c* **1440** *Promp. Parv.* 480/1 Strypyn, or streppyn, or make nakyd, *nudo*, *denudo*. *c* **1450** *Mirk's Festial* 121 þay buffed hym and bobbyd hym, and aftyr striput hym naked. **1530–1** *Act 22 Hen. VIII*, c. 12 §2 They shall strype hym naked from the myddel upwarde & cause hym to be whypped. *a* **1586** SIDNEY *Arcadia* II. xix. (1912) 272 For there they began to strip her of her clothes, when I came in among them. **1592** TIMME *Ten Eng. Lepers* vii. Ij, Her husband .. might strip her out of her clothes, .. and beat her openly. **1657** BILLINGSLY *Brachy-Martyrol.* xxxii. 119 Strip, strip, man, woman, child, .. Leave not a rag on, turn them out of doors. **1697** DRYDEN *Æneis* II. 534 Thus Ripheus, Dymas, all the Trojan Train, Lay down their own Attire and strip the slain. **1825** SCOTT *Talism.* v, He beheld the anchorite stripping his shoulders with frantic haste of their shaggy mantle. **1891** FARRAR *Darkn. & Dawn* lxv, It meant stripping him naked, .. and then beating him to death with rods.

refl. *c* **1386** Chaucer *Merch. T.* 714 Anon he preyde hire strepen hire al naked. *c* **1450** *Gesta Rom.* xiii. 43 He strepid him, and shewid his woundis. **1600** Shaks. *A.Y.L.* iv. iii. 147 Who led me instantly vnto his Caue, There stript himselfe. **1662** J. Davies tr. *Mandelslo's Trav.* 27, I made some difficulty to accept of the profers they made me to strip themselves naked. **1720** Prior *Truth & Falshood* 23 The Nymph..Stript her self naked to the skin. **1839** Lane *Arab. Nts.* I. 78 He then stripped himself, and dived round the net. **1872** [see buff *sb.*[2] 3].

intr. for *refl.* **1687** A. Lovell tr. *Thevenot's Trav.* i. 31 Benches, where you sit down, and lay your cloaths after you have stript. **1725** De Foe *Voy. round World* (1840) 308 The other, being a good swimmer, stripped and put off to it. **1896** Housman *Shropshire Lad* lv, Now that other lads than I Strip to bathe on Severn shore. **1947** 'A. P. Gaskell' *Big Game* 22 You're not supposed to strip off but I had. **1962** D. Francis *Dead Cert* xi. 124 I'm glad it's you that's got to strip off and get soaked, and not me. **1976** D. Barnes *Yesterday is Dead* ii. 272 After taking a leak he'd strip down and jack off.

†**b.** *fig. phrase.* [Cf. Fr. 'se despouiller avant que se coucher' (Cotgr.).]

1675 South *Serm.* (1692) 571 Some fond, easy Fathers think fit to strip themselves before they lie down to their long sleep, and to settle their whole Estates upon their Sons.

c. *transf.* (jocular nonce-use).

1601 Shaks. *Twel. N.* iii. iv. 274 Therefore on, or strippe your sword starke naked.

d. To divest (a person, oneself) of outer garments, or of some specified outer garment. Const. *of*, †*out of*. Sometimes in phr. *to strip to*, †*into*, †*unto* (the shirt or other inner garment).

c **1422** Hoccleve *Jereslaus' Wife* 233 He strypid hir anoon left al delay, Vn-to hir smok. **1530** Tindale *Gen.* xxxvii. 23 They strypte him [Ioseph] out of his gay coote that was vpon him. *a* **1548** Hall *Chron., Hen. VIII*, 63 Diverse offenders ..came wel appareled to Westmynster & sodeynly stryped them into their shertes. *a* **1627** H. Shirley *Mart. Soldier* v. (1638) I 1 b, How comes she to this habite? Went she thus in? *Epid.* No Sir, mine owne hands stript her into rags. **1671** Milton *Samson* 1188 Then like a Robber [thou] stripdst them of thir robes. **1789** W. Buchan *Dom. Med.* (1790) 133, I have known mechanics frequently contract fatal diseases, by working stript at an open window. **1822** Byron *Juan* vii. lxxiii, An old man..besmear'd with dust, Stript to his waistcoat. **1831** Scott *Cast. Dang.* viii, Two or three archers showed themselves, stripped of their tunics, and only attired in their shirts and hose. **1865** Trollope *Belton Est.* xvi, He had already stripped himself of his wrappings, ..and..at once followed Clara to the squire's room.

fig. **1675** H. Teonge *Diary* (1825) 68 Ther fore our Admirall strips himself to his shirt; viz. he stays before the towne only with 3 shipps more.

e. *intr.* for *refl.* Also of an athlete, a pugilist, etc.: To take off one's ordinary wearing apparel in preparation for a contest. *to strip* (*well*, etc.): to have a good body, to have a pleasing appearance when stripped.

1688 Bunyan *Heavenly Footm.* (1724) 27 If thou intendest to win, thou must Strip, thou must lay aside every Weight. **1711** Steele *Spect.* No. 51 ¶5 [The author] in the *Rover*, makes a Country Squire strip to his Holland Drawers... The Pleasantry of Stripping almost Naked has been since practised..very successfully at Bartholomew Fair. **1815** T. Belcher *Art of Boxing* ix. 33 James Belcher..stripped remarkably well, and displayed much muscle. **1833** *Q. Rev.* XLIX. 391 Whether it be the prize-fighter who strips in the ring, or the race-horse at the starting-post. **1887** Shearman *Athletics* 73 A sprinter, too, to use a cant phrase of pedestrianism, 'strips big'—*i.e.* looks bigger stripped than he does in his clothes. **1932** D. L. Sayers *Have his Carcase* ix. 106 He strips better than I should have expected... Better shoulders than I realised, and, thank Heaven, calves to his legs. **1955** T. H. Pear *English Social Differences* ix. 201 Such boys, to use the drill-instructor's expression, 'strip better'.

f. *trans.* To deprive *of* armour, insignia, ornaments; also *fig.* Also const. †*out of.*

c **1386** Chaucer *Knt.'s T.* 148 To ransake in the taas of bodyes dede, Hem for to strepe of harneys and of wede. **1592** Stow *Ann.* 665 His souldiors were stripped out of their harnes, and let go. **1622** Fitz-Geffry *Elisha* 24 Doe they ake to bee..stripped [*printed* shipped] of their Jewels as the Israelites were? **1784** Cowper *Task* vi. 640 What heathen would have dar'd To strip Jove's statue of his oaken wreath, And hang it up in honour of a man? **1837** Carlyle *Fr. Rev.* I. ii. iv, Caron..regains his Lawsuit..; strips Reporter Goezman of the judicial ermine. **1866** Sir T. Seaton *Cadet to Colonel* II. iii. 86 The mutineers were stripped of their uniforms.

†**g.** To discharge (a liveried servant). *Obs.*

1756 Foote *Engl. ret. fr. Paris* i. Wks. 1799 I. 97 If you suffer that fellow to enter my doors again, I'll strip and discard you the very minute.

h. To remove the clothing of (a racehorse); also *intr.* of a horse, to undergo this process.

1730 Cheny *List Horse-Matches* 35 The three..run all on the wrong side a Post, at doing which *Sweetest when naked* broke away to the Place where they strip'd her. **1857** G. A. Lawrence *Guy Liv.* ix. 83 The bell for saddling rang, and the horses came out. The mare stripped beautifully, as fine as a star. **1860** *Baily's Mag.* I. 110 We have never seen a better-looking lot of two-year olds stripped at so early a period of the year. **1897** *National Police Gaz.* 26 May 14/2 It is fully expected that he will not only strip in much better fettle at Epsom than he did for the Guineas, but run a remarkably different horse altogether. **1973** *Times* 26 Feb. 12/8 Skymas runs in the Wills Premier Chase at Haydock this week, and will certainly strip fit.

i. *intr.* To perform a strip-tease act. *colloq.* (orig. *U.S.*).

1929 *Variety* 25 Sept. 53/3 She has the unadornment stuff to herself, since the other gals never strip beyond regulation soub garb. **1939** Joyce *Finnegans Wake* 68 She stripped teasily for binocular man. **1962** J. D. MacDonald *Girl, Gold Watch & Everything* vii. 86 I'm working a place, Rio's, up North Miami, singing and sort of stripping some, but not down to raw. **1976** 'E. McBain' *Guns* (1977) ii. 49 'Jocko said you used to be a stripper.' 'Yeah, but..I haven't been stripping for seven, eight years now.'

2. *fig.* **a.** To divest or dispossess (a person, oneself) of attributes, titles, rights, honours, offices, etc. Const. †*out of*, †*from*, *of.*

c **1320** *Castle of Love* 431 in *Minor Poems fr. Vernon MS.* 366 Ne helpeþ him no þing..þat his fo..I-strupt him al start-naked, Of miȝt and strengþe al bare I-maked. **1561** Hoby tr. *Castiglione's Courtier* ii. (1900) 117 The prince stripping himself of the person of a prince, and minglinge himself equallye with his underlinges. **1608** Shaks. *Lear* iv. iii. 45 (Qos.) His own vnkindnes That stript her from his benediction. **1610** Holland *Camden's Brit.* (1637) 621 Stephen afterwards stript him out of these Honours. **1663** Patrick *Parab. Pilgrim* x. (1687) 56 He ought to strip himself of all undue affections to the world. **1675** Bunyan *Saved by Grace* Wks. (1692) 561/1 Of his Godhead he could not strip himself. **1776** Gibbon *Decl. & F.* v. (1782) I. 148 Many cities of the east were stript of their ancient honours. **1851** Robertson *Serm.* Ser. ii. i. (1864) 2 He stripped the so-called religious party..of their respectability. **1849** Macaulay *Hist. Eng.* vi. II. 126 Queensberry was stripped of all his employments. **1880** Dixon *Windsor* III. xxiv. 245 The cardinal stripped him of his deanery. **1906** C. Bigg *Wayside Sk. Eccl. Hist.* iii. 81 Strip him of his mantle of Euphuism and you will find him always sensible and candid.

b. To denude or divest (a thing) of attributes.

1597 Hooker *Eccl. Pol.* v. lxv. §3 There is no necessitie of stripping sacraments out of all such attire of Ceremonies as mans wisedome hath at any time clothed them withall. **1690** Locke *Hum. Und.* iii. xi. §7 When I shall see any of those Combatants, strip all his Terms of Ambiguity and Obscurity,..I shall think him a Champion for Knowledge, Truth, and Peace. **1746** Hervey *Medit.* (1818) 272 Sometimes I have seen that resplendent globe, stript of her radiance. **1824** Scott *St. Ronan's* xxix, Your friend, sir, must at least strip his proposals of their fine gilding. **1856** *N. Brit. Rev.* XXVI. 39 The canonical writings have, in the process, been stripped of every claim to our regard. **1859** Jephson *Brittany* x. 161, I doubt the wisdom of stripping all social events of everything that appeals to the imagination. **1908** *Programme of Modernism* 223 The ecclesiastical authority..should strip itself of that external pomp which adorns it in the eyes of the public.

c. To expose the character or nature of (a person or thing).

1619 H. Hutton *Follies Anat.* B 7, Shutting my Muse in silence, least she strip This Saint-like creature with a Satyres whip. **1781** Cowper *Charity* 494 He hides behind a magisterial air His own offences, and strips others bare. **1781** —— *Expost.* 141 He stripp'd th' impostors in the noon-day sun; Show'd that they follow'd all they seem'd to shun.

3. To plunder, spoil; to deprive totally (whether justly or otherwise) of possessions, or of something specified; to render destitute.

†**a.** without const. *Obs.*

For slang uses see quot. *a* 1700.

a **1225** *Juliana* 62 Þu..deidest..ant stepe adun & struptest [*MS. Bodl.* herhedest] helle. *c* **1425** *Eng. Conq. Ireland* 144 Thay [the governors of Ireland]..pulled & strope ham that non harme dydde. **1612** S. Rid *Art of Jugling* C 4 b, He that hath the first dice, is like alwaies to stripp and rob all the table about. **1692** Luttrell *Brief Rel.* (1857) II. 530 They also brought off 50 wounded men, and divers of the dead with them, the enemy haveing not then stript the feild. *a* **1700** B. E. *Dict. Cant. Crew, Strip*, c. to Rob or Gut a House, to unrig any Body, or to Bite them of their Money. *Strip the ken*, c. to Gut the House. *Strip the Table*, c. to Winn all the Money on the Place.

b. const. *of.* Common in 17–18th c. and in the 20th.

1594 *Selimus* Greene's Wks. (Grosart) XIV. 216 We that haue fought with mighty Prester John, And stript th' Ægyptian soldan of his camp. **1598** R. Bernard tr. *Terence, Andria* iv. v. 86 *Despoliavit nos omnibus.* He hath not left vs a dish to eate our meat in. He hath stript vs of al. *a* **1656** Bp. Hall *Rem. Wks.* (1660) 143 Many a one here is borne to a fair estate, and is strip't of it. *a* **1716** South *Serm.* (1727) VI. 114 An endeavour to strip him of his Friends. **1726** *Whole Art Mod. Gaming* 27 It is about a thousand to one but he is so unlucky, as to come away clean stript of all his Money. **1727** [E. Dorrington] *Philip Quarll* (1816) 78 Yearly stripping the eagles of their eggs had prevented their increase. **1737** in *10th Rep. Hist. MSS. Comm.* App. i. 266 His fate was to be strip'd of all he had in Sweden. **1769** Robertson *Chas. V*, vii. Wks. 1851 IV. 200 [They] in the space of a few weeks, stripping him entirely of his dominions, drove him..to take refuge in the court of Bavaria. **1881** 'Mark Twain' *Prince & Pauper* xxxiii. 385 The pickpockets had stripped him of his last farthing. **1919** G. B. Shaw *Heartbreak House* ii. 81 Are you one of those who are so sufficient to themselves that they are only happy when they are stripped of everything, even of hope? **1936** J. Buchan *Island of Sheep* i. vii. 130 They had only to get hold of Haraldsen..to strip him bit by bit of his possessions. **1950** C. S. Forester *Midshipman Hornblower* 262 The last visit of Spanish ships of war had stripped the place of almost all its stores, and many of the dockyard hands had been pressed as seamen at the same time.

c. To deprive or rid (a substance or thing) *of.*

1675 G. Harvey *Dis. Lond.* xxiv. 265 The Basis whereof is Antimony stripped of its venenous Sulphur. **1796** Kirwan *Elem. Min.* (ed. 2) I. 491 Macquer first discovered, that Prussiated Iron, or Berlin blue, might be stripped of the tinging matter by digestion with alkalis. **1837** P. Keith *Bot. Lex.* 71 Plants are often stripped of their colours by the operation of the same agents through which they originally acquired them.

4. a. To denude (a thing) of its covering, esp. (a tree) of its bark, (a seed) of its skin, (a fruit) of its rind.

a **1225** *Ancr. R.* 148 Heo haueð bipiled mine figer—irend of al þe rinde, despoiled [*MS. C.* istruped] hire sterc naked. **1660** in *Verney Mem.* (1904) II. 99 A greate parcell of silke wch was that day to be delivered, and at the day of delivery we have a little trouble in weighing of itt, stripping of itt, and severall other things. **1727–46** Thomson *Summer* 688 Thou best anana,..Quick let me strip thee of thy tufty coat, Spread thy ambrosial stores, and feast with Jove! **1823** W. Cobbett *Rur. Rides* (1853) 163 They have been stripping trees (taking the bark off) about five or six days. **1841** *Penny Cycl.* XXI. 184/1 When the seed is stripped of its testa. **1883** *Hampsh. Gloss., Strip*, to bark the oak tree.

b. To pull off the winter growth of hair from (a dog); to pluck. Cf. stripping *vbl. sb.*[1] 1 a.

1930 E. C. Ash *Pract. Dog Bk.* xi. 197 Stripping a coat is in the varieties of Terriers most important. Powdered chalk is well rubbed into it. The long hair is then plucked out. **1931** *Daily Tel.* 21 May 1/3 Dogs stripped.

†**5.** To skin (an animal; in Hunting *spec.* a hare). *Obs.*

c **1400** *Master of Game* (MS. Digby 182) xxxiv, Þenne shulde she [*sc.* the hare] be stripped all, saue the heede. **1486** *Bk. St. Albans, Hunting* e iii b, Now to speke of the bestes when thay be slayne How many be strypte and how many be flayne. All that bere skyne and talow and Rounge leue me Shall be flayne safe the hare for he shall stripte be. **1530** Tindale *Lev.* i. 6 And let the burntofferynges be strypped and hewed in peces. **1575** Turberv. *Venerie* 100 An hart or a bucke is flayed, a hare strypped. **1677** N. Cox *Gentl. Recreat.* (ed. 2) 15 The Hare is Stripped or Cased. **1770** G. White *Selborne, Let. to Pennant* Mar., Understanding that it was not stripped, I proceeded to examine this rare quadruped [*sc.* a moose].

6. To deprive (a plant *of* its foliage or fruit); to remove (seed or grain *from* the straw).

1697 Dryden *Virg. Georg.* ii. 504 Crop luxuriant Straglers, nor be loath To strip the Branches of their leafy Growth. **1733** W. Ellis *Chiltern & Vale Farm.* 87 The Rook is a subtil Fowl, and will strip a Walnut Tree in a little time. **1759** Mills tr. *Duhamel's Husb.* i. ii. (1762) 3 We sometimes see trees strip'd by insects. **1837** P. Keith *Bot. Lex.* 74 If the upper part of a branch is stripped of its leaves. **1861** Smiles *Engineers* II. 110 The plan of stripping the corn from the straw by means of a scutcher.

7. a. To empty, make bare, clear out (a place, thing) *of* its contents, ornaments, etc.

1616 W. Browne *Brit. Past.* ii. iii. 59 The bowels of our mother were not ript For Mader-pits, nor the sweet meadowes stript Of their choise beauties. **1753** Challoner *Cath. Chr. Instr.* 220 Our Altars are also uncovered and stript of all their Ornaments. **1765** *Lond. Chron.* 14–17 Sept. 272/1 And while she went in a fright, to see if it was true, he [a thief] in the mean time stripped the room of things to the value of 30 shillings. **1826** Lamb *Pop. Fallacies* xi, His goodly shelves are one by one stript of his favourite old authors. **1828–32** Webster, *Strip*,..7. To deprive; to make bare by cutting, grazing or other means; as, cattle strip the ground of its herbage. **1894** Bridges *Feast of Bacchus* i. 112, I stripped the house for a sale. **1913** J. H. Morrison *On Trail of Pioneers* xxvi. 125 It was no loss when the islands were stripped of the fragrant wood.

b. *to strip up*: (see quot. 1893). Now *dial.*

1664 Evelyn *Sylva* xxvii. 72 Cutting all the rest away.. stripping up such as you spare from their extravagant Branches. **1893** *Wiltsh. Gloss., Strip up*, to shroud [*i.e.* trim] the lower part of a tree, as is usually done with hedge-row timber at intervals.

†**c.** Used with allusion to strip *sb.*[1] *Obs.*

1682 tr. *Charter of Cinque Ports* 138 Strip or Estrepement is a Writ for taking Lands from him that strips and spoils them. **1818** Cruise *Digest* (ed. 2) II. 409 This may excuse the trustees, if they..attempt to strip the estate of the timber.

d. ? To clear (land) of a crop.

1844 H. Stephens *Bk. Farm* II. 2 The reason for stripping turnips is to supply food to the sheep in the most convenient form. The portion of the turnip ground allotted to sheep is ..drawn or stript, that is, a certain proportion of the turnips is left on the ground, for the use of the sheep, and the other is carried away to the steading, to be consumed by the cattle. **1886** *Pall Mall Gaz.* 6 Apr. 14/1 Of this quantity 320,000 acres were not reaped..or what crop there was was mown for hay. This reduces the area actually stripped for wheat to 1,630,000 acres.

e. *slang* (orig. *U.S.*). To unpack or unload (a load, container, lorry, etc.).

[**1950** *Western Folklore* IX. 119 *Pulled, stripped*, or *gutted a load*, lost a load of logs]. **1963** *Amer. Speech* XXXVIII. 45 *Strip a load, v. phr.*, to unload a truck. **1968** *Wall St. Jrnl.* 27 Sept. 34/2 Management agreed to allow the dockworkers to strip and stuff containers in which mixed types of cargo had been packed. **1970** *Times* 16 Sept. (Road Haulage Suppl.) p. vii/9 The [overladen] container..should be devanned (or stripped, to use container parlance) and delivered on two vehicles. **1972** *Guardian* 8 May 20/2 According to the dockers' leader..those terms..are for.. the same guarantees over 'stuffing' (packing) and 'stripping' (unpacking) the containers. **1973** *Amer. Speech 1969* XLIV. 208 *Strip her*, unload a trailer.

8. To take away the accessories, equipment, or furniture of; to dismantle. Now freq. in contexts of the inspection or repair of motor vehicles, engines, etc. Also with *down*. Cf. stripped *ppl. a.* c.

1683 Moxon *Mech. Exerc., Printing* xiv. xxii. §2. 207 Thus the first Quarter is Stript..in order to be distributed. *Ibid.* xxiv. Dict. 391 Strip a Form. [Reference to prec. quot.] **1688** Holme *Armoury* iii. 125/2 [Printing] *Strip a Form*, is to take away all the Furniture from about it, and lett it so remain on the Letter board to be distributed. **1769** Falconer *Dict. Marine* (1780) s.v., To *Strip* the masts, is to unrig a ship, or deprive the masts of their machinery and furniture. **1798** in Nicolas *Disp. Nelson* (1846) VII. p. clvi, The Guerrier and Conquerant made a very inefficient resistance, the latter being soon stripped of her main and mizen-masts. **1807** Sir R. Wilson *Jrnl.* 24 Sept. in *Life* (1862) II. viii. 370 When the squall passed we attempted to hoist the sails again but again we were stripped. **1867** Smyth *Sailor's Word-bk., Stripped to the Girt-line*, all the standing-rigging and furniture having been cleared off the masts in the course of dismantling. **1881** Greener *Gun* 262 Stripping and repairing guns. To take to pieces a breech-loader for cleaning or repairs, first remove the fore-end and barrels. *Ibid.*, To strip breech-actions,..the first thing will be to remove the spring. *Ibid.* 263 To strip a muzzle-loader, first remove the lock. **1888** JACOBI *Printers' Vocab.* 134 *Strip a forme*, to take away the furniture from the pages of a forme, and thus leave it naked. **1937** *Discovery* May 164/1 Part of the necessary machinery could not be stripped down to parts small enough to be carried by mules over the narrow and difficult trails. **1958** *Listener* 13 Nov. 778/1 He drives the thing [*sc.* a car] straight into the repair shop at the back and has it stripped down. **1972** *Daily Tel.* (Colour Suppl.) 20 Oct. 10/4 At the end of 36,000 miles the engines were stripped and every component measured and meticulously examined. **1981** B. HINES *Looks & Smiles* 26 His bike..had also been stripped down to the frame.

II. To doff, take off, peel away.

9. To remove (the clothes, a garment, trappings, hair) from a person, body.

a. With adv. *off*, *away*, or with prep. *off*, *from*.

c **1290** *St. Francis* 11 in *S. Eng. Leg.* 54 He strepte of is cloþes of is rug and ȝaf þis pouere knyȝt. *c* **1290** *Beket* 2201 *ibid.* 169 Ase heo strepten of is cloþes, al a-boue heo founde Clerkene cloþes. **13..** *Coer de L.* 3399 And loke that hee her here off strype, Off hed, off berd, and eke off lyppe. *c* **1386** CHAUCER *Reeve's T.* 143 And to the hors he goth hym faire and wel, He strepeth of the brydel right anon. **1387** TREVISA *Higden* (Rolls) III. 173 Þis Cambises..made men stripe of þe skyn of a iuge, for he hadde i-ȝeue a false dome. **1660** F. BROOKE tr. *Le Blanc's Trav.* 220 This Prince..stript off his gorgious habilliments. **1797** HT. LEE *Canterb. T.*, *Old Woman's T.* (1799) I. 389 Stripping away his upper garment, and displaying the badge of knighthood upon his shoulder. **1895** R. W. CHAMBERS *King in Yellow*, etc. (1909) 255 As she spoke she stripped off her gloves.

fig. **1340** *Ayenb.* 98 Þet hi ous delyuri of þe zeue dyadliche zennes and hise strepe of al oure herten and ine hare stede zette..þe zeue uirtues. **1549** J. OLDE *Erasm. Par. Ephes.* Prol. ¶iiij b, Christe woulde not stycke cleane on our backes, onlesse olde Adam be stryped cleane of, wyth all his ragged rotten patches of infidelitie and sinfulnes. **1766** J. TOWERS *Brit. Biog.* I. 127 [Chaucer] discovered nature in all her appearances, and stripped off every disguise. **1780** COWPER *Progr. Err.* 583 Habits are soon assum'd: but, when we strive To strip them off, 'tis being flay'd alive. **1874** GREEN *Short Hist.* iii. § 1. 115 Picture after picture strips the veil from the corruption of the mediæval Church. **1884** L. J. JENNINGS *Croker Papers* I. i. 3 The immense correspondence of all kinds which he left strips away disguises.

b. without adv.: To divest oneself of. Chiefly *Sc.*

1760–2 GOLDSM. *Cit. W.* cii, [She] never once attempted to strip a single petticoat, or cover the board, as her last stake, with her head-clothes. **1837** CARLYLE *Fr. Rev.* III. vi. vi, The guests all stript their coats. **1855** *Poultry Chron.* III. 212 Aleck stripped his buckskins for the attempt. **1870** J. K. HUNTER *Life Studies* xliv. 273 They..had a consultation as to whether..one of them should strip his stockings and shoon and carry the other on his back.

fig. **1853** LYTTON *My Novel* XII. xxx, Strip the mask, Audley Egerton; let the world know you for what you are!

†**10.** To take as plunder or spoil. *Obs.*

c **1200** *Trin. Coll. Hom* 195 Erest he strepte of him his shep. **1599** SHAKS. *Hen. V*, I. i. 11 For all the Temporall Lands..Would they strip from vs. **1791** COWPER *Iliad* XVII. 102 He knew at once who stripp'd Euphorbus' arms.

11. a. To remove (an adhering covering of skin, bark, lead, paper, etc.); to pull off (leaves, fruit) from a tree, etc.; to remove (paint or varnish) from woodwork, etc. Also *to strip off*. Cf. STRIPPED *ppl. a.* b.

c **1430** *Two Cookery-bks.* 27 Take Almaundys..& strype of þe skyn. **1486** *Bk. St. Albans* b iij b, Take a knyfe..and stripe the skynne a way from the necke. **1688** HOLME *Armoury* III. 86/2 [Wett-Glover.] Pulling is stripping the Wool of the skin. *Ibid.* III. 97/1 [Cushion and Bed Terms.] Stripping the Feathers from the Quills. **1697** DRYDEN *Æneis* I. 295 Some strip the Skin, some portion out the Spoil. **1769** MRS. RAFFALD *Eng. Housekeeper* (1778) 363 Gather your currants when the sun is hot upon them, strip them from the stalks. *c* **1770** MRS. GLASSE *Compl. Confectioner* 26 Take young and thick stalks of angelica.., strip off the skins, and cut them into narrow slips. **1780** *Mirror* No. 93 ⁋8 The best china was set out... The covers were stripped from the worked chair-bottoms. **1836** *Philos. Mag.* Dec. 484 So perfect is the sheet of copper thus formed, that, on being stripped off, it has the polish and even a counterpart of every scratch of the plate on which it is deposited. **1849** *M. Taylor's Builder's Price-bk.* 63 Stripping and relaying ladies, countess, and duchess slating, per square, 0 10 0. **1854** *Poultry Chron.* II. 22 Directly the feathers are stripped from the poultry, throw them loosely in the corner. **1888** W. J. HARRISON *Hist. Photogr.* xiii. 112 In the same year (1855) the Frenchman, Galliard, coated collodion negatives with gelatine, and then stripped them from the glass. **1891** *Law Rep.*, *Weekly Notes* 78/2 The act of the defendants in stripping off the roof amounted to a forcible entry. **1908** P. N. HASLUCK *Cassell's House Decoration* 171/2 All the washing and stripping should be done first. The wallpaper must be removed, and the paint stripped. **1913** J. G. FRAZER *Psyche's Task* (ed. 2) iii. 30 When he has stripped the fruit [from the tree], the rascal restores the charm to its proper place. **1956** *Pract. Householder* July 596/1 A number of preparations..are intended to strip off only one coat at a time... I prefer the type which strips several coats. **1981** *New Homemaker* Apr. 90/1 (Advt.), Stripping isn't the soul-destroying job it used to be... Powerful Ronseal strips without scraping.

b. *intr.* Of bark, membrane: To lend or adapt itself to the process of peeling or decortication. Of a layer of metal: To become detached.

1877 JEFFERIES *Gamekeeper at H.* i. (1890) 15 In the spring, when the oak timber is throwed (because, you see, the sap be rising, and the bark strips then). **1899** *Allbutt's Syst. Med.* VII. 712 The leptomeninges stripping, on the contrary, with undue ease. **1905** *Electro-plating* (ed. P. N. Hasluck) 152 Silver will strip under the burnisher when it is deposited too fast or too slow.

12. To remove, roll up (a sleeve). Now only with *up*. Also *absol.*

1599 SHAKS. *Hen V*, IV. iii. 47 Then will he strip his sleeue, and shew his skarres. **1607** B. BARNES *Divils Charter* Prol. A 2 b, Presently the Pronotary strippeth vp Alexanders sleeue and letteth his arme bloud in a saucer. **1711** 'J. DISTAFF' *Char. Don Sacheverellio* 5 He stript up, and shew'd ..a most thundring Arm. *c* **1815** *Houlston's Juvenile Tracts* vii. 9 If his shirt sleeves were stripped up to his elbows.

13. To slip off (a jewel) from the arm, a ring from the finger.

1611 SHAKS. *Cymb.* II. iv. 101, I begge but leaue to ayre this Iewell... She stript it from her Arme. **1652** J. BURROUGHES *Exp. Hosea* ii. 186 Strip from your fingers your gold rings. **1865** A. CARY *Ball.*, *Lyrics & Hymns* 117 She stript from her finger the shining ring.

14. To remove entirely, clear off (vegetation). Also, to harvest (a crop).

1839 FR. A. KEMBLE *Resid. Georgia* (1863) 261 They have almost stripped the trees and thickets along the swamp road since I first came here. **1891** R. WALLACE *Rural Econ. & Agric. Austral. & N.Z.* i. 6 Twenty acres of grain can be stripped per day. **1938** *Sun* (Baltimore) 6 Sept. 2/7 The corn almost ready to strip. **1979** *Verbatim* Summer 8/1 In Queensland a wheat crop is *headed*, in Victoria *stripped*.

III. Technical uses.

15. *Tin-washing.* (See quot. 1674.) Also to wash out (gold).

1674 RAY *Prep. Tin* (E.D.S.) 12 Washing and sifting of it, which they call stripping of it. **1875** J. H. COLLINS *Metal Mining* 54 The tin gravel is 'stripped' at a cost of 3s. to 6s. per ton. **1871** SIMPSON *Recit.* 19 The wash dirt will be full of gold, ready to strip.

16. a. *Tobacco-manuf.* To remove the leaves from the stems of (tobacco). Also *absol.*

1688 HOLME *Armoury* III. xxii. (Roxb.) 274/1 Termes used by Tobacconists. Strip it, is take all the stalks away from the leaues. **1786** *Act 26 Geo. III*, c. 52 § 1 No.. Tobacco stalks stripped, nor Snuff manufactured from Tobacco so imported, shall be removed [etc.]. **1883** KILLEBREW *Rep. Culture & Curing Tobacco U.S.* 154 If there should happen to be no damp days when it is desired to strip, a few days in the cellar will impart the necessary moisture. *Ibid.* 186 In stripping tobacco, the leaves are pulled from the stalks and tied in bundles.

b. To remove the stalk and midrib from (tobacco-leaf). Cf. STEM *v.*[4] 3 a.

1844 *Rep. Sel. Comm. Tobacco Trade, Min. Evid.* 233 Tobacco could be stripped here at from 18*d.* to 2*s.* a cwt. **1881** *Spons' Encycl. Industr. Arts* IV. 1341 Cutting is the process by which the damped [tobacco-]leaves, whether stripped or not, are most extensively prepared for smoking in pipes and cigarettes.

17. a. *Mech.* To tear off (the thread from a screw or bolt, the teeth from a wheel).

1873 NELTHROPP *Watch-work* 21 The teeth of the scape-wheel will, by revolving against the jagged edge, be cut off; the wheel is then stript. **1875** KNIGHT *Dict. Mech.* 2430 *Strip* (Machinery), to tear the thread off a screw.

b. To rip off the screw thread of (a cannon-ball or bullet); to render incapable of receiving the rotatory direction from the rifling of the barrel.

1839 URE *Dict. Arts* 477 Instead of one quarter of a turn, which was the utmost that could be safely given in the old way, without danger of stripping the ball, a whole turn round the barrel, in its length, can be given to the two grooved rifles.

c. *intr.* for *refl.*

1854 *Chamb. Jrnl.* II. 202 If the charge of gunpowder be inordinately great, the ball may strip, to use the technical phrase; in other words, it may have its screw-thread rendered ineffective by the mere force of discharge. **1855** A. PIPER *Milit. & Nav. Dict.* s.v., A rifle bullet is said to strip when it passes out of the barrel of a rifle..without receiving the spiral motion on its axis. **1881** GREENER *Gun* 169 Immediately the barrel gets hot and expands, the bullets strip. **1978** D. BAGLEY *Flyaway* xxv. 230 I've got a spare differential... The bastards are always stripping so I've made it a habit to keep a spare.

18. *Mining.* To lay bare (a mineral deposit, etc.): see quot. 1839.

1839 URE *Dict. Arts* 842 If..the vein be quite distinct from the rock, the labour may be facilitated, as well as the separation of the ore, by disengaging the vein on one of its faces through a certain extent, the rock being attacked separately. This operation is called stripping the vein. **1839** MURCHISON *Silur. Syst.* I. xxxvi. 490 On 'stripping' the fault towards the trough, the limestone was found to be in contact with a seam of coal. **1887** *Times* (weekly ed.) 9 Dec. 1/4 Mr. Morgan has..now as the phrase goes, 'stripped the lode', so that many thousands of tons of stone, richly laden with gold, are ready to be stoped.

19. To smooth (a metal surface) by filing or the like; to smooth the surface of (a file-blank) preparatory to cutting the teeth; also see quot. 1880.

1831 J. HOLLAND *Manuf. Metal* I. 301 The file is now in a state either to be stripped or ground. **1855** FRANKE *Beil's Technol. Wörterb.* II. 521 To Strip a piece of work (to finish-off with a smooth file, or to smooth the surface with a hard file), *Abfeilen. Finir de limer.* **1880** *Encycl. Brit.* XI. 279/2 The [gun-]barrels are then 'stripped'—that is, turned down the whole length to correspond with the bore. **1898** J. SOUTHWARD *Mod. Printing* I. 96 [The leads are finished] by 'stripping', or 'shaving', in a stripping machine.

20. *Carding.* **a.** (See quot. 1835.) **b.** To remove fluff, etc. from the teeth of (a card).

1835 URE *Philos. Manuf.* 182 Which cylinder is employed as a stripper in place of a doffing-comb, to take off or strip the slivers of wool from the doffing cylinder. **1891** *Labour Commission* Gloss., *Stripper*, the man who strips the cards or leather combs of fluff.

21. *Cloth making.* (See quot. 1904.)

1896 W. M. GARDNER *Wool Dyeing* 32 This process is frequently resorted to for 'stripping' off the colour of dyed material previous to re-dyeing. **1904** *Eng. Dial. Dict.*, *Strip v.*,..A cloth-making term: to partially remove the colour from dyed material when the colour is found to be too 'full.'

22. *Metallurgy.* (See quot.)

1884 W. H. GREENWOOD *Steel & Iron* (ed. 2) § 642 Steel ingots, when newly stripped—that is, withdrawn from the moulds in which they have been cast—are far too hot in the interior for immediate rolling.

23. *Electrometallurgy.* To remove (the plating from a plated article, the metal from a positive pole, etc.) by electrolysis. Also *intr.* of a plating: To come off.

1877 A. WATT *Electro-Metallurgy* (ed. 6) 155 In coating steel or iron articles with nickel, deposition should not be allowed to take place too rapidly at first, otherwise the metal will be liable to strip. **1880** *Ibid.* (ed. 7) 114 Nickel-plated articles may be stripped in this solution by immersing them in it for a few moments. **1880** J. W. URQUHART *Electroplating* vi. 162 Deposits of nickel having a brilliant appearance on leaving the solution..are very apt to strip. **1898** THRELFALL *Laboratory Arts* iv. 306 The platinum foil testing cathode may also be 'stripped' by making it an anode.

24. *Physics.* **a.** To deprive (an atom or ion) *of* an electron, or (a molecule) *of* an atom. Also *absol.*

1933 O. H. BLACKWOOD et al. *Outl. Atomic Physics* xiv. 305 Throughout the interior of a star, atoms do not exist in what we consider their ordinary conditions... Near the center of the star they are assumed to be stripped of nearly all their planetary electrons. **1936** *Trans. Faraday Soc.* XXXII. 350 One empirical molar weight of $C_2H_4S_4$ in suspension in water is first 'stripped' of two sulphur atoms with sodium hydroxide. **1954** H. E. HUNTLEY *Nuclear Species* i. 4 By stripping the atoms which lay in its path of one or more of its orbital electrons the swiftly moving particle produced large numbers of positively charged ions and free electrons. **1969** *Times* 22 Apr. 6/3 Large amounts of energy are needed to strip the calcium atoms of their electrons before accelerating them into the target of plutonium atoms. **1970** *Sci. Amer.* Aug. 32/3 The ions are stripped not only in the terminal but also halfway down the positive acceleration column. **1978** L. VÁLYI *Atom & Ion Sources* i. 35 At low impact energies only the outer shell can be stripped of its electron.

b. To remove (an electron or other particle) *from* an atom, ion, nucleus, etc. Also const. *off*.

1935 B. JAFFE *Outposts of Science* ix. 349 This recoiling nucleus spends its energy of motion in stripping electrons from other atoms near it. **1947** *Physical Rev.* LXXII. 1003 A simple theory of neutron production, according to which the proton is 'stripped' from the deuteron by striking a target nucleus. **1958** *Ann. Physics* III. 275 In a deuteron stripping reaction, the rôle of the incident deuteron is to present at the target nucleus surface a neutron or proton ready to be captured (or 'stripped' off). **1979** *Sci. Amer.* Aug. 122/2 The star..becomes a white dwarf: a star with a core consisting of a highly compressed gas of atomic nuclei (mostly helium nuclei) and the electrons stripped from them.

25. a. *Oil Industry.* To separate (crude oil or gas) into fractions, to fractionate; to extract or recover (a light fraction) *from* a mixture.

1922 D. T. DAY *Handbk. Petroleum Industry* II. 324 The great bulk of crude handled was still stripped in batch stills. **1931** HOFFERT & CLAXTON *Motor Benzole* viii. 226 It is essential that the benzole should be stripped from the wash oil as completely as possible. **1938** A. E. DUNSTAN et al. *Sci. of Petroleum* II. II. xxv. 1559/2 The latent heat of vaporization of the components stripped from the oil is supplied by the sensible heat of the oil. **1979** *Liquefied Petroleum Gas* (Shell Internat. Petroleum Co.) 3 The aim of this scheme is to 'strip' the large amounts of associated gas which were previously flared and then separate LPG and other heavier gas liquids for export.

b. *Chem.* To extract or recover (a solute) *from* a solvent previously used in its extraction.

1962 COTTON & WILKINSON *Adv. Inorg. Chem.* xxxii. 906 The protactinium can be stripped from the solvent by aqueous acid fluoride solutions. **1980** *Sci. Amer.* Jan. 59/3 Both are recovered by using a complexing agent to dissolve the metal selectively into a dilute solution and then stripping the metal from the solution.

26. *Printing.* To mount (copy) in the correct position on a sheet for use in making a printing plate; freq. const. *in*. Also, to make (a flat) thus.

1937 R. W. POLK *Pract. of Printing* (ed. 2) xli. 291 If a number of pictures are to be used together, and the sizes of the originals are not in proper proportion to each other, separate exposures are made for each size, the necessary reductions made, and the resulting negatives are 'stripped' together in proper position on the composite negative plate. .. If the sizes are not in proper proportion, separate negatives must be made and stripped in on the plate. **1948** R. R. KARCH *Graphic Arts Procedures* viii. 232 After the negatives or positives of illustrations and type matter have been prepared.., the job must be stripped on a layout so that press plates may be made. *Ibid.* 233 Positives used for stripping flats for the deep-etch process are stripped on a piece of transparent acetate. **1964** R. W. & E. W. POLK *Pract. of Printing* (ed. 6) xl. 304 (*caption*) A masking sheet with negatives stripped in. *Ibid.* 306 Positioning and attaching films on a masking sheet is called stripping a flat. **1967** KARCH & BUBER *Offset Processes* v. 142 After the film is developed, the negative is washed and dried. It is then 'stripped' or placed in a predetermined position on a special type of paper for the plate maker who will expose the image onto the offset plate. **1975** J. BUTCHER *Copy-Editing* iv. 39 Combined line and half-tone may be used for a photograph that needs some lettering or a scale; this is usually done by stripping a line negative into a half-tone negative.

IV. 27. a. Comb.: **strip bush** *slang* (see quot.); **strip cell**, a cell in which a prisoner is subjected to sensory or physical deprivation; **strip-down**, (*a*) *U.S. colloq.*, a car which has been stripped down and reassembled so as to improve performance; (*b*) the dismantling or disassembly of an engine, etc. (cf. sense 8 above); **strip-jack-naked** *dial.* = *beggar-my-neighbour* (see BEGGAR *v.* 3); **strip-me-naked** *slang*, gin; **strip-poker** orig. *U.S.*, a game of poker in which a losing player sheds a garment as a penalty or forfeit; **strip-search**, a search of a prisoner during the course of which he is stripped naked; also as *v. trans.*; = *skin-search* s.v. SKIN *sb.* 16; **strip the willow**, a Scottish country dance performed by couples in longways sets.

1865 *Hotten's Slang Dict.* (ed. 2), *Strip-bush, a fellow who steals clothes put out to dry after washing. **1971** *New Society* 1 July 15/1 A *strip-cell. This contains only a mattress on a bare floor. **1973** *Black Panther* 7 July 9/2 If the guards wanted to they could turn on a light in the ceiling, but I was always kept in the dark, and nude. That is part of the deprivation, why the soul breaker is called a strip cell. **1950** *Sun* (Baltimore) 6 Oct. (B ed.) 7/4 Juveniles who have been racing the highways in stepped-up *strip-downs. **1963** *Times* 24 May (London Underground Suppl.) p. xii/5 The trains were withdrawn from service and sent to Acton, where they undergo a comprehensive strip-down. **1969** *Daily Tel.* 18 Feb. 5/5 Repair is in progress. A strip-down survey of the refinery is being undertaken. **1881** *Oxfordsh.* (*Suppl.*) *Gloss.*, **Strip Jack naked*, a game at cards sometimes called 'Byet (beat) my neighbour out of doors.' **1751** *Gen. Advertiser* 7 Mar. 1/2 (*N. & Q.* 5th Ser. VII. 69/2) *Strip-me-naked, or Royal Gin for Ever. **1756** [see GUNPOWDER 3]. **1929** M. LIEF *Hangover* i. 9 'How about a fast game of *strip-poker?' she suggested. **1935** G. GREENE *England made Me* II. 86 Two girls playing strip poker. **1961** *Times* 14 June 16/3 There had been a 'strip-poker' party that night. **1978** D. WILLIAMS *Treasure up in Smoke* xix. 169 'He .. suggested some kind of poker.'.. 'Strip poker?' **1947** *Strip-search [see RUNOVER 1]. **1970** G. F. NEWMAN *Sir, You Bastard* vii. 189 The arrested men were strip-searched and made to await the DI's pleasure. **1979** *Tucson* (Arizona) *Citizen* 3 Oct. 10C/5 A woman sentenced for drunken driving should not be strip-searched. *Ibid.*, Subjected to extreme trauma by a strip-search. **1924** *Scottish Country Dance Bk.* I. 16 *Strip the Willow or Drops of Brandy... Running step is used all through this dance. **1980** L. LEWIS *Private Life of Country House* xii. 166 'Strip the Willow', a country dance in which couples in turns came from the ends of two rows to perform some steps in the middle.

b. [Sometimes, f. STRIP *sb.*[3] 2.] In various *slang* or *colloq.* Combs. in sense 1 i, as ***strip act, bar, dancer, girl, party, show, song***; **strip club**, an establishment providing entertainment in the form of strip-tease; **strip joint** [JOINT *sb.* 14 a] *slang* = *strip club*.

1950 A. COOKE in *Manch. Guardian Weekly* 13 July 13/2 The all-American cult of the 'strip act'. **1963** R. I. MCDAVID *Mencken's Amer. Lang.* 728 Today the higher-priced girls are often connected with burlesque or work in strip-bars. **1975** D. LODGE *Changing Places* ii. 96 One of the South Strand strip bars. **1960** *Spectator* 12 Aug. 236 That strip clubs have been multiplying in London recently is generally known. **1962** *Ibid.* 7 Dec. 883 The strip-club owner who intends to fight .. on a campaign against entertainments tax. **1973** J. M. WHITE *Garden Game* 36 The neon lights of the strip-clubs and restaurants. **1946** D. RUNYON *Short Takes* 236 There were cut-outs of guys with their arms around hula dancers and around strip dancers. **1961** *Times* 21 Sept. 15/2 The strip-girl loved by a foolish, tiresome but engaging missionary. **1951** *Sun* (Baltimore) 27 June 30/3 Prince Georges County Sheriff Carlton Beall began a crackdown on what he called 'strip joints'. **1959** *Times Lit. Suppl.* 13 Mar. 148/4 Gambling rooms, saloons and strip joints. **1975** D. LODGE *Changing Places* ii. 95 He now stands gawping incredulously at the strip-joints that jostle each other all along Cortez Avenue. **1959** *Times* 19 June (Queen in Canada Suppl.) p. iv/5 Police are always cracking down on private strip parties. **1972** J. BROWN *Chancer* viii. 110 These strip parties—young business blokes—you know. **1967** *Listener* 5 Oct. 437/3 One of the old Windmill strip shows. **1971** *New Scientist* 10 June 641/2 Their dirty raincoats .. have been snapped up by strip-show patrons. **1937** *Hart & Kaufman You can't take it with You* III. 171 She kept singing a strip song while Mrs. Kirby undressed.

†**strip**, *v.*[2] *Obs.* Also 5 **strype**, 6 **strippe**. [Proximate origin obscure; f. Teut. root **strip*-: see STRIPE *sb.*[3]]

1. *intr.* To move or pass swiftly.

c **1400** *Rowland & O.* 560 And other stroke he to hym bere, And Doun by-fore hym it strypes there, his schelde a waye it reuede. **1579** GOSSON *Sch. Abuse* F 1 b, The swiftest Hound, when he is hallowed, strippes forth. **1616** BROWNE *Brit. Past.* II. iii. 119 Th' Eagle .. To countries farre remote would bend her flight, And with vnwearied wing strip through the skie. *Ibid.* II. v. 905 As the Westerne side shee stript along.

2. *trans.* To pass or surpass in running, flying, etc.; to pass by in travelling: = OUTSTRIP *v.*[1] (recorded from 1580).

c **1590** GREENE *Fr. Bacon* I. i. 4 Alate we ran the deere, and through the Lawndes Stript with our nagges the loftie frolicke bucks. ? **1605** DRAYTON *Poems Lyr. & Past., Man in Moone* H 7 b, She .. calls downe the Dragons that her chariot drawe, and .. mounteth thereon, in twinkling of an ey stripping the winds. **1613** BEAUM. & FL. *Honest Man's Fort.* I. i, Before he reacht it, he was out of breath, And then the other stript him. *c* **1624** CHAPMAN *Hymn to Apollo* 641 When first, they stript the Maleane Promont'rie: Toucht at Laconias soile, [etc.]. **1774** *Ann. Reg., Poetry* 211 But mark the beauteous Antelope! .. he strips the wind, And leaves them lagging, panting, far behind.

strip (strɪp), *v.*[3] [Cogn. w. STRIPE *sb.*[2]; cf. WFlem. *strippen* to draw (something) between the fingers or the teeth, in order to extract the contents or remove the leaves, etc.; also *strip* stream of milk from a teat.]

1. a. *trans.* To extract (the milk from a cow's udder). Now *spec.* to extract the milk remaining in the udder after the normal milking, esp. by a particular movement of the hand (see quot. 1844).

1610 FLETCHER *Faithf. Sheph.* I. ii. B 3 b, More white Then the new milke we strip before day light From the full fraighted bags of our faire flockes. **1788** W. H. MARSHALL *Yorksh.* II. 357 To *Strip*; to draw the aftermilkings of cows. **1791** W. BARTRAM *Trav.* 310 When the milkmaid has taken her share of milk, she looses the calf, who strips the cow. **1844** H. STEPHENS *Bk. Farm.* II. 454 Stripping consists of seizing the teat firmly near the root between the face of the thumb and the side of the fore-finger. **1863** MRS. GASKELL *Sylvia's Lovers* xv, Never were cows that required such 'stripping,' or were expected to yield such 'afterings' as Black Nell and Daisy that night.

b. ***strip cup*** (see quot. 1962).

1941 ROADHOUSE & HENDERSON *Market-Milk Industry* iv. 67 (*caption*) Strip cup used for detecting abnormal milk. The first stream of milk from each teat is milked into the strip cup through the fine mesh screen. **1950** *N.Z. Jrnl. Agric.* Mar. 265/1 Every cow should be tried, using a strip cup, before putting on the machines. **1955** J. G. DAVIS *Dict. Dairying* (ed. 2) 37 The routine use of strip-cups in the cowsheds will assist in the prevention of mastitis spreading. **1962** J. N. WINBURNE *Dict. Agric. & Allied Terminol.* 769/1 *Strip cup*, a small metal cup or vessel with a fine wire strainer or inner liner into which the first streams of milk from each teat are milked from the cow for examination to detect any indication of mastitis infection or any other abnormal condition of the milk or udder. **1975** CAMPBELL & MARSHALL *Sci. providing Milk for Man* xiv. 337 The California Mastitis Test (CMT) is much more sensitive in detecting inflamed quarters than is the strip cup.

2. To draw between the finger and thumb, through the closed hand, etc. In various technical uses: **a.** *Catgut-making.* (See quot.)

1883 R. HALDANE *Workshop Rec.* Ser. II. 320/1 [In preparing fiddle-strings] the gut .. is stripped through a ring .. or through a perforated brass thimble, the thumb being pressed upon the gut as it is passed through.

b. *Fish-culture.* To press out with the hand the ripe roe or milt from (a fish).

1884 DAY *Fishes Gt. Brit.* I. p. cix, The mode of spawning or stripping fish .. requires practice.

c. *Farriery.* (See quot.)

1908 *Animal Management* (War Office) 62 'Stripping' the ears, *i.e.* pulling them gently through the hand from base to apex .. should not be neglected.

strip (strɪp), *v.*[4] [f. STRIP *sb.*[2]] *trans.* To cut into strips. Hence **'stripping** *vbl. sb.*[3]; also *attrib.*

1885 W. L. CARPENTER *Manuf. Soap & Candles* 200 The first operation is to 'strip' the stock-soap, i.e. to cut it up into strips or shavings... After stripping, the soap is frequently dried somewhat, and it is then passed through the mill. **1885** *Harper's Mag.* Jan. 279/2 They buy the sides of leather, and cut them into 'strips' by means of a long straight knife, moved by a treadle or by steam, known as a 'stripping machine.'

stripe (straɪp), *sb.*[1] *Sc.* Also: α. 6 **strip**, 5–8 **stryp(e**, 7 **stryip**; β. 7 **streape**, 9 **streap**. [Prob. cogn. w. STRIP *sb.*[2], STRIPE *sb.*[3]; cf. WFlem. *strip* a running stream of liquid, e.g. of milk from a teat. Cf. OIrish *sribh* stream.] A small stream, a rivulet, rill.

c **1440** *Reg. Aberd.* (Maitland Club) I. 248 Ascendand þat lech til it cum to þe Karlynden and swa throw þe said den descendand a stripe til it cum to þe burn of Cortycrum. **1456–70** in *Acts Parlt. Scot.* (1875) XII. 27/1 Begynnand at the burne that gays fra Auchquhorty quhar that the strype fallys in the said burne. **1536** BELLENDEN *Cron. Scot., Descr. Albion* xiii. (1821) I. p. xlvi, Fra this fontane discendis ane litil burne, or strip. **1596** DALRYMPLE tr. *Leslie's Hist. Scot.* (S.T.S.) II. 118 As .. the water strype rinis to the fontane [L. *tanquam ad fontem rivulus*]. *a* **1598** ROLLOCK *Passion* i. (1616) 3 This Brooke Cedron .. was a little streape that ran when it was raine. **1598** [see SOUTH A. 5 a]. **1615** *Extracts Aberd. Reg.* (1848) II. 326 Ane great stryip callit the Banstickill burne. **1797** *Encycl. Brit.* (ed. 3) VII. 290/2 A very small stripe of water .. should always be running in and off from your pit. **1819** W. TENNANT *Papistry Storm'd* (1827) 33 Ilk laird's domain was clearly seen Defin'd wi' streaps o' silver sheen, That intervein'd the manors green. **1892** J. A. HENDERSON *Ann. Lower Deeside* 110 A hollow close by is still called the 'Bloody Stripe'.

stripe (straɪp), *sb.*[2] Also 5–6 **stryppe**, **strype**, 6 **strip**, 7 **stripp**. [Prob. from LG. or Du.: cf. mod.Du. *strippen* to whip, *strips* flogging (in *strips krijgen* to get a flogging), also mod.WFris. *strips*; but these words have not been found so early as the Eng. word. Cf. also MLG. *strippe* strap, whip-lash (see STRIP *sb.*[2]).

The common view that this word is a use of STRIPE *sb.*[3] would be plausible (on the assumption that sense 3 below is the original), but for the fact that STRIPE *sb.*[3] is not recorded till the 17th c., while this sb. occurs in the 15th c.]

†**1.** A blow or stroke with a staff, sword, or other weapon, with a missile, with the claws or hoofs of an animal, etc. Cf. HAND-*stripe*. *Obs.*

c **1475** *Songs & Carols* (Percy Soc.) 92 A strype ore ij. God myght send me, If my husbond myght her se me. **1530** PALSGR. 277/2 Stryppe, stroke or swappe, *coup*. **1530** TINDALE *Gen.* iv. 23, I haue slayne a man and wounded my selfe, and haue slayn a yongman, and gotte my selfe strypes. **1542** UDALL *Erasm. Apoph.* 11 b, If an Asse had geven me a strype with his heele. *Ibid.* 289 Receiuyng a stripe with a sweorde, he gaue but one sole grone, & [etc.]. **1544** BETHAM *Precepts War* I. lvi. D ij, And so either wil they suffre to take their cytye, or els they wyl fyght with the, and deale strypes. **1545** ASCHAM *Toxoph.* II. (Arb.) 123 The shaftes in Inde were verye longe, .. and therfore they gaue ye greater strype. *a* **1548** HALL *Chron., Hen. VI*, 128 b, Thei lefte woordes, and went to stripes. *a* **1552** LELAND *Itin.* (1769) V. 54 The Egle doth sorely assaut hym that distroith the nest, goyng doun in one Basket, and having a nother over his Hedde to defend the sore Stripe of the Egle. **1579–80** NORTH *Plutarch, P. Æmilius* (1595) 271 Perseus went from the battell .. because he had a stripe of a horse on the thigh the day before. **1580** TUSSER *Husb.* (1878) 129 Maides, mustard seede gather, for being too ripe, and weather it well, er ye giue it a stripe. **1596** SPENSER *F.Q.* V. xi. 27 With one stripe Her Lions clawes he from her feete away did wipe.

†**b.** A touch on the keys of an instrument; hence, measure, strain. *Obs.*

1590 GREENE *Never too Late* I. (1600) B 1 b, As in field this sheepheard lay, Tuning of his oaten pipe, Which he hit with many a stripe. **1592** —— *Vision* Wks. (Grosart) XII. 198 Tytirus .. Straigned ditties from his pipe, With pleasant voyce and cunning stripe. **1613–16** W. BROWNE *Brit. Past.* I. ii. 3 Now till the Sunne shall leaue vs to our rest, .. I shall goe on: and first in diffring stripe, The floud-Gods speech thus tune on Oaten pipe [Here the metre changes]. *Ibid.* II. iii. 731 And scarce one ended had his skilfull stripe, But straight another tooke him to his Pipe.

2. A stroke or lash with a whip or scourge. Now *arch.*, chiefly in *plural*.

c **1485** *Digby Myst., Mary Magd.* 1176 Stryppys on þi ars þou xall have. **1526** TINDALE *Luke* xii. 47 The servaunt that knowe his masters wyll, and prepared nott him silfe, .. shalbe beten with many strypes. **1580** E. KNIGHT *Trial Truth* 82 b, Euen as a good father or master that threateneth and shaketh the rod before hee layeth on the strypes. *c* **1623** LODGE *Poor Mans Talent* C 1, Sometimes the said paine commeth by a blow or stripp. **1692** J. WASHINGTON tr. *Milton's Def. People Eng.* ii. 33 The Hebrew Kings were liable .. to be punished with stripes, if they were found faulty. **1780** J. HOWARD *Prisons Eng.* 141 Keepers are punished for this .. by a fine for the first offence; and for the second by stripes. **1788** *Massachusetts Spy* 25 Sept. 3/3 On Thursday last, fifteen persons were publickly punished, .. William Nelson, 64 stripes. **1836** COBDEN in Morley *Life* (1881) I. iii. 53 The *backshish* kept the boat going, when stripes would have only made it stand. **1836** CAPT. BOLDERO *Sp. Ho. Comm.* 13 Apr. in *Hansard* 942 Colonel Evans also had commanded in many regiments, in which not a stripe had been inflicted for two or three years. **1839** FR. A. KEMBLE *Resid. in Georgia* (1863) 39 Labor exacted with stripes—how do you fancy that? **1887** HALL CAINE *Coleridge* i. 25 There is a tradition that Bowyer sometimes gave him an extra stripe of the birch 'because he was so ugly'.

fig. **1830** CARLYLE *Richter Again* Ess. 1840 II. 319 In regard to moral matters Leipzig was his true seminary, where, with many stripes, Experience taught him the wisest lessons. **1851** T. T. LYNCH *Lett. to Scattered* (1872) 202 Each passing day both gives to us and takes from us. It may give a stripe, a smile, a counsel, a reproach.

†**b.** A stroke of divine judgement. *Obs.*

1564–78 BULLEIN *Dialogue* 37 By what signe or token is this perilous plague or stripe of the pestilence best knowen emong the Phisitions? **1609** BIBLE (Douay) *Exod.* vii. Annot. 173 It ought to haue auailed Pharao to saluation, that Gods patience deferring his iust and deserued punishment, multiplied vpon him frequent stripes of miracles. **1623** LISLE *Ælfric on O. & N. Test.* Pref. 13 The least stripe that God giveth man after this life, is everlasting damnation.

†**c.** Said of a person: A 'scourge'. *Obs.*

1570 *Satir. Poems Reform.* xiii. 99 ȝe wer ay callit for ȝour tyrannie Strypis of the Schyre.

†**3.** The mark left by a lash; a weal. *Obs. rare.*

c **1440** *Promp. Parv.* 480/1 Stripe, or schorynge wythe a baleys, *vibex*. *c* **1475** *Pict. Voc.* in Wr.-Wülcker 791/23 *Hec vibex*, a strype. **1726–46** THOMSON *Winter* 373 Little tyrants .. At pleasure mark'd him with inglorious stripes.

†**b.** *fig.* A mark of disgrace. *Obs.*

1607 HEYWOOD *Wom. Killed w. Kindn.* IV. v. Wks. 1874 II. 140 Her spotted body Hath stain'd their names with stripe of bastardy.

stripe (straɪp), *sb.*[3] [Not found till the 17th c., but prob. much older. If not a back-formation from STRIPED *a.*, prob. a. MLG. or MDu. *strîpe* (early mod.Du. †*strijpe*), corresp. to OHG. **strîfo* (implied in the derivative *strîphaht* STRIPED *a.*), MHG. *strîfe* (mod.G. *streifen*) masc., Sw. *stripa*, Da. *stribe*, also ON., MSw. *strip* a striped fabric (cf. Icel. *striprendr* striped). Parallel synonymous forms, differing in ablaut-grade, are WFlem. *striepe*, MDu. *strêpe* (mod.Du. *streep* fem.); outside Teut. the OIrish *sríab*, stripe (:—**sreibā*), *srebnaid* striped, are believed to be cognate. The Teut. root **strīp*- (:**straip*-):—pre-Teut. **streib*- seems to have been nearly synonymous with **strĭk*-:—pre-Teut. **streig*- (see STRIKE *v.*), to which it may be ultimately related; the sense of the root is shown in the wk. verb OHG. **straifjôn* (MHG. *streifen*, *streipfen*, mod.G. *streifen*) to graze, pass over lightly, wander (the mod.G. *streifen* also represents MHG. *ströufen*: see STRIP *v.*[1]). For other cognates see STRIP *sb.*[2], STRIPE *sb.*[1], *sb.*[2], and *v.*[1]

There would seem to be some obscure relation between the Teut. roots **strip*- and **streup*- (see STRIP *v.*[1]) similar to that existing between **strĭk*- and **streuk*-: see STRIKE *v.*]

1. a. In textile fabrics, hence *gen.* (e.g. in the coat of an animal, a flower, a decorative pattern), a portion of the surface long in proportion to its breadth, or uniform width, and differing in colour or texture from the adjacent parts.

1626 BACON *Sylva* § 510 Carnation of seuerall Stripes. **1687** MIEGE *Gt. Fr. Dict.* II, The stripes of a striped Stuff, *les Raies* (*ou Barres*) *d'une Etoffe rayée*... To make white, or yellow stripes, *rayer de blanc, ou de jaune.* **1697** DAMPIER *Voy.* I. xix. 533 There is a very beautiful sort of wild Ass in this Country, whose body is curiously striped with equal lists of white and black: the stripes coming from the ridge of his Back. **1706** PHILLIPS (ed. Kersey), *Stripe*,..a streak in Silk Cloth, or Stuff. **1746** HERVEY *Medit.* (1748) I. 170 Some [flowers] are intersected with elegant Stripes, or studded with radiant Spots. **1774** GOLDSM. *Nat. Hist.* (1776) IV. 27 The little ground squirrel of Carolina, of a reddish colour, and blackish stripes on each side. **1782** E. WATSON *Men & Times Revol.* (1861) 202 The back-ground, which Copley and I designed to represent a ship, bearing to America the intelligence of the acknowledgment of Independence, with a sun just rising upon the stripes of the union, streaming from her gaff. **1802** C. JAMES *Milit. Dict.* s.v., Regimental sword knots are directed to be made of crimson and gold in stripes. **1833** T. HOOK *Parson's Dau.* III. xii, The Sir Timothy Wadd ..with..the Honourable John Company's stripes flying, had once the honour of being taken for an American seventy-four. **1859** DARWIN *Orig. Spec.* v. 164 In the north-west part of India..a horse without stripes is not considered as purely-bred. **1860** LD. W. LENNOX *Pict. Sporting Life* I. 209 Waistcoat, blue and yellow stripe, each stripe an inch in depth. **1868** W. B. MARRIOTT *Vestiarium Chr.* Introd. v. 37 Various grades of rank were distinguished at Rome..by the colour and by the relative width of the ornamental stripes worn upon the tunic by senators, and by knights. **1897** *Proc. Zool. Soc.* 545 A similar coloured short longitudinal stripe is also placed at the middle of each elytron. **1912** H. J. BUTLER *Motor Bodies* 108 The body panels are often striped. This may be either as a broad stripe, say an inch wide, or a series of, say, three fine lines occupying together one inch of panel.

b. (***Old***) ***Stripes***, a jocular name for a tiger.

1885 W. T. HORNADAY *2 Yrs. in Jungle* xiv. 157 There was Old Stripes in all his glory. **1909** *Ladies' Field* 28 Aug. 511/2 How I shot my first 'stripes.'

c. In the names of certain moths.

1775 M. HARRIS *Engl. Lepidoptera* 45 Phalæna... 315 Stripe, white. 316 Stripe, shoulder. 317 Stripe, yellow shoulder. 318 Stripe, cream dot. **1832** J. RENNIE *Consp. Butterfl. & Moths* 127 The Oblique Stripe. *Ibid.* 164 The Dark Silver Stripe. *Ibid.* 201 The Treble Gold Stripe.

d. *pl.* A prison uniform (with reference to the stripes with which it is patterned). *U.S. slang.*

1887 *Courier-Jrnl.* (Louisville, Kentucky) 29 Jan. 3/2 He changed his stripes for a suit of citizens' clothes. **1905** B. TARKINGTON *In Arena* 22 I'm going to clear this town of fraud, and if Gorgett don't wear the stripes for this my name's not Farwell Knowles! **1940** W. FAULKNER *Hamlet* III. ii. 212 He had never seen convicts' stripes before either. **1943** P. STURGES in Gassner & Nichols *Best Film Plays 1943–44* 279/1 He's going to be in jail, Trudy, for a long time. He can't do you any good in stripes, honey.

e. A narrow strip of magnetic material along the edge of a cine film on which the sound may be recorded.

1954 R. H. CRICKS tr. *Bau's How to make 8 mm. Films as Amateur* 169 The magnetic stripe is coated between the perforations and the edge of the film. **1972** *Amateur Photographer* 12 Jan. 65/3 Fujicascope SH1... Sound unit: Magnetic sound stripe, 6w amplifier. **1973** *Sci. Amer.* Dec. 49/1 Sights and sounds the camera records stay together on the super 8 film in synch during processing. Spoken comment can be added to the magnetic stripe during projection.

f. *U.S.* A line which forms part of the marking on a sports pitch or court. Cf. LINE *sb.*[2] 7 f.

1967 *Boston Herald* 1 Apr. 17/1 Kennedy led the visitors with 17 points, 11 from the foul stripe. **1974** *State* (Columbia, S. Carolina) 3 Mar. 1-D/7 We wanted to keep him off the foul line (Stewart made one of two from the stripe).

2. A narrow strip of cloth, braid, or gold lace, sewn on a garment of different colour. Popularly applied to the chevron worn on the upper part of the coat-sleeve by a non-commissioned officer to indicate his rank. Also applied to the similarly shaped badge worn on the sleeve by soldiers in recognition of good conduct; and (in more recent use) to the vertical badge on the left sleeve of a soldier who has been wounded. ***to pull stripes***: see PULL *v.* 20 h.

In the British army the lance-corporal wears one 'stripe', the corporal two, and the sergeant three.

An earlier name was 'slash' (C. James *Milit. Dict.* 1802).

1827 [MAGINN] *Milit. Sketch-bk.* I. 297 Ye speak your sentiments like a good sodger, and I hope afore long that ye'll have the stripes. **1848** J. GRANT *Adv. Aide-de-C.* xxxiv, Rings worn on the arms of the privates, called 'good-conduct stripes.' **1861** MAYHEW *Lond. Labour* III. 165/1 Although I used to wear the colonel's livery, yet I had the full corporal's stripes on my coat. **1876** VOYLE & STEVENSON *Milit. Dict.* 25/1 The good-conduct stripes worn on the arm by men of good behaviour are also called badges. **1892** KIPLING *Barrack-room Ballads, Danny Deever* 7 They've taken of his buttons off an' cut his stripes away. **1916** *Blackw. Mag.* Jan. 124/1 Private Tosh was 'offered a stripe,' too, but declined.

3. In glass, a streak differing in refractive power from the general mass.

1823 J. BADCOCK *Dom. Amusem.* 174 In making these pastes many precautions are necessary,..lest bubbles and stripes do supervene.

4. A striped textile fabric.

1751 *Rep. Comm. Linen Manuf.* (1773) II. 291 He imports Irish Yarn, which he manufactures into Cheques and Stripes. **1889** *Textile News* 5 Apr. 24/2 The chief goods in request are still the finer qualities of worsteds in stripes and checks.

5. *Geol.* A narrow band of rock interposed between strata of differing character.

1799 KIRWAN *Geol. Ess.* 302 Grey stone, with coal stripes. **1805** JAMESON *Min. Descr. Dumfries* 153 In sandstone, limestone, and salt, regular and very extensive stripes are sometimes observed, which have been confounded with true strata seams. **1849** MURCHISON *Siluria* ii. (1854) 24 These contorted, crystalline rocks..are associated with stripes or patches..of different palæozoic rocks of Silurian, Devonian, and Carboniferous age.

6. a. A long narrow tract of land (*occas.* of ice). Cf. STRIP *sb.*[2] 1 c.

1801 H. SKRINE *Rivers Gt. Brit.* iii. 46 The extraordinary stripe of romantic beauty which environs them [*i.e.* the baths] must create a peculiar interest in Matlock. **1802** HOME *Hist. Reb.* i. 4 A narrow stripe of land, between the hills and the German Ocean. **1807** J. HEADRICK *View Mineral.* etc. *Arran* 309 The cultivated land is occupied in run-rig, or in narrow stripes, called butts, with intervals betwixt them, whose possessors are changed every second or third year. **1817** M. BIRKBECK *Notes Journ. Amer.* (1818) 26 The country, from Richmond to Fredericksburg, is a barren sandy level, relieved occasionally by a stripe of better soil, on the banks of a rivulet. **1823** A. SMALL *Roman Antiq.* iii. 61 The very spot cannot be seen for a stripe of planting. **1823** SCORESBY *Jrnl.* 253, I reached a stripe of ice firmly frozen to the ground. **1860** TYNDALL *Glac.* I. xxi. 149 Narrow stripes of ice separated from each other by parallel moraines.

b. *Anglo-Irish.* (See quot.)

1888 *Times* 8 Dec. 5/3, I believe the holdings of tenants in the neighbourhood are called 'stripes'?—Yes.

7. A strip, shred; a narrow piece cut out.

1785 COWPER *Task* I. 40 Now came the cane from India..; sever'd into stripes That interlac'd each other, these supplied Of texture firm a lattice-work. **1799** *Hull Advertiser* 28 Dec. 3/2 Bankers have been in the habit of paying their notes..sometimes with a stripe in the middle taken out. **1814** SCOTT *Wav.* vi, He produced a letter, carefully folded, surrounded by a little stripe of flox-silk, according to ancient form. **1835** BROWNING *Paracelsus* IV. 200 Heap cassia, sandal-buds and stripes Of labdanum. **1843** CARLYLE *Misc., Dr. Francia* (1857) IV. 269 General Artegas was seen..sitting among field-officers, all on cow-skulls, toasting stripes of beef. **1875** DASENT *Vikings* I. 122, I will cut a red stripe out of each of your backs.

8. orig. *U.S.* **a.** A particular shade or variety of political or religious doctrine; in wider sense, a sort, class, type.

1853 *Congressional Globe* 11 Feb. 576/3 He has not been long in his present 'stripe' of politics. **1854** *Ibid.* 18 May 1206/2 Every member of the Democratic party, of whatever shade or stripe, is perfectly honest. **1863** *Battlefields of the South* I. vii. 93 Frank Blair pointed him out as 'of the right stripe'—the 'coming man'. **1875** STEDMAN *Vict. Poets* vii. (1887) 256 Various poems are of a democratic, liberal stripe, inspired by the struggle then commencing over Europe. **1890** HOSMER *Anglo-Sax. Freedom* 292 The religious faiths of the immigrants were various, not all or one stripe. **1943** L. ADAMIC *My Native Land* 137 Trubar scored a great cultural victory and set a national-linguistic precedent for men of his stripe. **1968** *Guardian* 9 Apr. 9/3 Negro organisers of all stripes, urging their footloose young 'to keep your cool'. **1979** *Daily Tel.* 6 Sept. 4/2 Guyana, led by a Socialist of another stripe.

b. = STREAK *sb.*[1] 6.

1860 O. W. HOLMES *Elsie Venner* iii, [The dog had] a projection of the lower jaw, which looked as if there might be a bull-dog stripe among the numerous bar-sinisters of his lineage.

9. black stripe = *black strap*: see BLACK *a.* 19.

1880 *Barman's & Barmaid's Man.* 55.

10. *Comb.* in parasynthetic adjs., chiefly *Zool.* and *Bot.*, as ***stripe-breasted***, ***-cheeked***, ***-necked***, ***-tailed***, ***-throated***; ***stripe-flowered***, ***-leaved***; also **stripe-shadowed** *nonce-wd.*, crossed by stripes of shadow.

1837 W. SWAINSON *Birds W. Africa* I. 267 *Stripe-breasted Bristle-neck. *Tricophorus strigilatus*, Swains. **1802** SHAW *Naturalist's Misc.* XIII. Pl. 517 Trochilus superbus. .. The *Stripe-cheeked Humming-bird. **1822** *Hortus Anglicus* II. 171 B[rassica] Eruca. *Stripe flowered Cabbage, or Garden Rocket. **1796** W. MARSHALL *Planting* II. 303 The English Oak admits of some Varieties:..There is one Variegation under the name of the *Stripe-leaved Oak. **1893** LYDEKKER *Roy. Nat. Hist.* I. 472 The *stripe-necked mungoose (*Herpestes viticollis*). **1878** MEREDITH *Love in the Valley* xvii. Poet. Wks. (1912) 234 In a breezy link Freshly sparkles garden to *stripe-shadowed orchard. **1812** SHAW *Gen. Zool.* VIII. 34 *Stripe-tailed Hornbill. **1837** SWAINSON *Birds W. Africa* (1861) II. 241 *Stripe-throated Lapwing. *Vanellus strigilatus*, Swains.

stripe (straɪp), *v.*[1] [Belongs to STRIPE *sb.*[2] Sense 2 is prob. a new formation on the sb.]

†**1.** *trans.* To beat, whip. *Obs.*

c **1460** [see *vbl. sb.* below]. **1530** PALSGR. 740/2, I strype, I beate, *je bats.* **1533** MORE *Apol.* xxxvi. 197, I caused a seruaunt of myne to strype [**1557** stryppe] hym lyke a chyld. *Ibid.* 198 They stryped [**1557** stripped] hym with roddys.

2. To punish with stripes. *rare.*

1843 CARLYLE *Past & Pr.* I. v. 37 We shall all be striped and scourged till we do learn it. **1870** MEREDITH *Odes Fr. Hist.* (1898) 64 Still the Gods love her..this good France, the bleeding thing they stripe.

Hence **'striping** *vbl. sb.*[1]

c **1460** *Promp. Parv.* 442 (Winch.) Strypynge, or scorgynge with abaleys: *vibex.* **1823** BENTHAM *Not Paul* 383 [Paul's] eight stripings and beatings.

stripe (straɪp), *v.*[2] Also 6 **stryppe**; *pa. t.* 6 **stripped**; *pa. pple.* 6 **stripped**, 7 **stript**. [f. STRIPE *sb.*[3] (in early examples perh. f. STRIP *sb.*[1])

It is possible that STRIPED *a.* may have been early adopted from LG. or Du., and that the verb is a back-formation.]

1. *trans.* To ornament (cloth, a garment) with narrow pieces of material or with stripes of colour.

In quot. 1471 perh. 'to border': cf. STRIP *sb.*[1] 1.

1471 *Paston Lett.* Suppl. (1901) 140, I pray zow that the welvet that levyt of my typet may be send hom a geyn, for I woold strype a dobelet ther with. **1547** in Feuillerat *Revels Edw. VI* (1914) 13, viij pere sloppes of changeable Taffita stripyd vpon with blewe golde dornix. **1558** in Feuillerat *Revels Q. Eliz.* (1908) 20 Redd cloth of gold with Roses and Scallope shells stripped down. **1583** *Rates Custom Ho.* A viij b, Canuas striped with silk. **1611** COTGR., *Brocar*, satin stript, or purfled, with gold. **1621** in Foster *Eng. Factories Ind.* (1906) 235 Some stript with blew for napkininge. **1905** *Westm. Gaz.* 25 May 4/2 A galloon effect, contrived either by tucking a strip of muslin or by striping a strip of muslin over with bars of narrow satin ribbon.

2. To mark with a narrow band or with bands of colour; to mark with alternate stripes of colour.

a. *Nat. Hist.* In *pa. pple.* Const. †*in*, *with.*

1597 A. M. tr. *Guillemeau's Fr. Chirurg.* 31/4 Those [leeches] which have the backe stripped, stroked with goulde-yellow strokes. **1645** G. DANIEL *Poems* Wks. (Grosart) II. 51 A goodly Tulip, Stript In Gold and Purple. **1660** F. BROOKE tr. *Le Blanc's Trav.* 184 The Girafe striped with white and red. **1859** DARWIN *Orig. Spec.* v. 165, I once saw a mule with its legs so much striped that [etc.].

b. *gen.*

1842 TENNYSON *Morte d'Arth.* 212 She..call'd him by his name, complaining loud, And dropping bitter tears against his brow Striped with dark blood. **1875** O. C. STONE in *Jrnl. R. Geog. Soc.* XLVI. 58 An heroic deed entitles a man to the distinguished privilege of striping his forehead. **1895** KIPLING *2nd Jungle Bk.* 209 As the sun rose they [*sc.* the morning mists]..churned off and let the low rays stripe the dried grass. **1908** *Nation* 13 June 374/1 Her husband stripes a toy canoe with red and black to please the fishing-spirit.

c. *intr.* Of a plant: To become variegated. Also *trans.* To produce variegation in (a plant).

1725 *Bradley's Family Dict.* s.v. *Stripe*, Cions of the Spanish Jessamine, whose Leaves had not been known to Stripe. **1731** MILLER *Gard. Dict.* s.v. *Variegated*, But whatever some Persons have affirm'd of striping Plants by Art, I could never observe it done by any.

d. To apply a magnetic stripe to (a cine film). Cf. STRIPE *sb.*[3] 1 e.

1954 R. H. CRICKS tr. *Bau's How to make 8 mm. Films as Amateur* 169 You then send your film to a suitable firm which 'stripes' it—i.e., coats a narrow strip of magnetic material along its whole length. Two methods of striping have been proposed. **1960** R. BATEMAN *Movie-Making as Pastime* ix. 58 A 'magnetic stripe' system is becoming more widely used... Experiments in 'striping' 8 mm film have been made.

3. To finish (a surface) with grooves or ridges (see quots.). Also *absol.*

1842 GWILT *Archit.* Gloss., *Droved and striped.* Work [in masonry] that is first droved and then striped. The stripes are shallow grooves done with a..chisel. **1882** W. J. CHRISTY *Joints* 206 Very coarse solder..would set quickly and be porous were it not glazed over by striping or overcasting.

†**4.** *intr.* ? To form a stripe. *Obs.*

1632 LITHGOW *Trav.* I. 40 The breadth in the planure is narrow, but stripeth larger among the hills and lakes.

5. *trans.* To divide (land) into strips or plots. *Anglo-Irish.* Cf. STRIPE *sb.*[3] 6 b.

1882 BAGENAL in *19th Cent.* Dec. 927 [The Irish tenant] stripes the worst and wildest portion and lets it out to the labourers. **1886** *Daily News* 13 Dec. 5/8 About 52 years ago the land reclaimed by their industry was striped, or apportioned, out among the tenants separately.

stripe (straɪp), *v.*[3] [var. of STRIP *v.*[3]]

1. *trans.* To thrust or draw (a thing, esp. a sword in order to cleanse or sharpen it) *through*, *over*. *Sc.* and *north.* Cf. STROKE *v.*[1] 2.

17.. *Clark Sanders* xv. in Child *Ballads* II. 159/1 Out he has taen a bright long brand, And he has striped it throw the straw. **17..** *Johnny Scott* xxviii. *Ibid.* 396/2 He's taen his broadsword in his hand, And stripd it oer a stane. **1895** CROCKETT *Men of Mosshags* v. 44 Wat, bending a little forward in his saddle and striping one long gauntlet glove lightly through the palm of the other hand.

†**2.** To draw the edge of an instrument sideways over (a surface). *Obs.*

1616 SURFL. & MARKH. *Country Farm* I. xxviii. 132 Another Groome shall take a piece of a Sword blade,..and ..he shall with the edge strype and wype downe the Horse.

stripe, obs. form of STRIP *sb.*[1]

striped (straɪpt), *ppl. a.* Also 8 *Sc.* **stripped**. [f. STRIPE *v.*[2] + -ED[1].

For earlier instances of *striped* (used predicatively, and therefore here treated as pa. pple.) see STRIPE *v.*[2] It is possible that the Eng. vb. may have been evolved from *striped* ad. Du. *strijpt* or MLG. *striped*; cf. OHG. *strîphaht* (MHG. *strîfeht*; mod.G. *gestreift*), MSw. *stripotter*.]

1. a. Marked with a stripe or stripes, having a band or bands of colour, streaked.

1617 MORYSON *Itin.* III. 174 The Greekes..weare Shasses, that is striped linnen (commonly white and blew) wound about the skirts of a little cap. *a* **1618** *Rates of Merchandizes* I 1 b, Stript or tufted Canuas. **1698** FRYER *Acc. E. India & P.* 24 Their Junks had three Masts, wearing an East-India strip'd Ancient. **1751** *Rep. Comm. Linen Manuf.* (1773) II. 293 Chequed and Striped Linen. **1752** D. STEWART in *Scots Mag.* (1753) July 343/2 Blue stripped trowsers. **1821** BYRON *Heav. & Earth* iii. 179 And the striped tiger shall lie down to die. **1832** LINDLEY *Introd. Bot.* 407 Striped (*vittatus*): when there are longitudinal stripes of one colour crossing another. **1860** TYNDALL *Glac.* I. ix. 62 The shining snow with its striped faults and precipices. **1874** H. H. COLE *Catal. Ind. Art S. Kens. Mus.* 261 Woven striped pattern of green, yellow, and red.. stripes alternating with bands of red.

b. In numerous specific names of animals, plants, and minerals (see quots.); also ***striped bass***, a large North American fresh-water or marine bass of the genus *Roccus*, esp. *R. saxatilis*; ***striped gopher***, a ground squirrel, *Citellus decemlineatus*, found in North America; ***striped mouse***, a mouse with one or more stripes along its back, found in Africa and belonging to the genus *Rhabdomys* or *Lemniscomys*; ***striped squirrel***, one of several small rodents with striped markings, esp. the North American chipmunk; ***striped tuna*** = *skipjack tuna* s.v. SKIPJACK 4.

1629 PARKINSON *Parad.* (1904) 593 The peare of Ierusalem, or the stript peare, whose barke while it is young, is as plainly seene to be stript with greene, red, and yellow, as the fruit it selfe is also. **1769** PENNANT *Brit. Zool.* III. 207 Striped wrasse. **1781** —— *Quad.* I. 250 The Striped Hyæna. **1783** LATHAM *Gen. Synop. Birds* II. I. 349 Striped Flycatcher. **1796** J. MORSE *Amer. Universal Geogr.* I. 203 The Striped Squirrel is still less than the [red squirrel]. **1815** AIKIN *Min.* (ed. 2) 244 Striped jasper. Occurs massive. **1818** *Amer. Monthly Mag.* II. 295 The striped bass..is another excellent salt-water fish. **1832** J. RENNIE *Consp. Butterfl. & M.* 25 The Striped Hawk (*Deilephila Livornica*). **1842** Z. THOMPSON *Hist. Vermont* I. 174 Striped Maple. *Acer Pennsylvanicum.* **1854** THOREAU *Walden* 323, I am on the alert for the first signs of spring, to hear..the striped squirrel's chirp. **1859** BARTLETT *Dict. Amer.* (ed. 2) 458 Striped bass. [**1900** H. A. BRYDEN *Animals Afr.* v. 48 The pretty little Striped Barbary Mouse..is a very different kind of animal.] **1901** H. SEEBOHM *Birds of Siberia* xxx. 308 The peasant had shot me a couple of striped squirrels. **1922** *Pacific Fisherman* Feb. 12/2 Striped tuna..is required to be designated with the qualifying adjective 'striped'. **1932** *Discovery* Nov. 364/2 Pythons are so sluggish that they have been nibbled to death by striped mice. **1941** E. T. SETON *Trail of Artist-Naturalist* 299 Gone..also the striped gopher, whose labyrinths are only four inches down. **1951** TRESSLER & LEMON *Marine Products of Commerce* (ed. 2) xx. 445 Skipjack..is also known as the striped tuna from the markings on the body. **1956** W. R. BIRD *Off-Trail in Nova Scotia* ii. 48 I've been after striped bass in many places up and down the coast of America but this is the best of them all. **1963** G. H. THOMSON *Crocus Country* xx. 133 At this time [*sc.* 1905] there were quite a few striped gophers left, though later they entirely disappeared, driven out, it was said, by their bigger grey cousins. **1973** *Stand. Encycl. S. Afr.* IX. 248/1 Some, like the striped mouse.., are diurnal. **1974** *Calhoun Times* (St. Matthews, S. Carolina) 18 Apr. 3/3 Some 200 striped bass are swimming through Lakes Marion and Moultrie with special tags attached.

c. Of muscular fibre: Divided by transverse bands into striations.

1850 *Phil. Trans. R. Soc.* CXL. 515 Muscles are now named according to their function, voluntary and unvoluntary; or according to their structure, striped and unstriped. **1854** *Orr's Circ. Sci., Organic Nat.* I. 48 One of these [kinds] occurs in the voluntary muscles, and is named, from conspicuous cross markings, the striped muscular fibre. **1880** GIBBES *Histol.* 73 Striped muscle is best shown in one of the large water beetles, Hydrophilus piceus.

d. *Masonry.* ***striped work***, chisel marks made across a stone at an angle of 45°.

1842 GWILT *Encycl. Arch.* §1914 Striped work must also be first droved and then striped.

e. Of a person: Entitled to wear a (good-conduct, etc.) stripe.

1890 *Pall Mall Gaz.* 12 June 5/2 in the E.C. district all the striped men were ordered to have their stripes forfeited.

f. ***striped trousers*** (typically worn by civil servants, businessmen, etc.), used allusively to indicate the wearer's status, and, by extension, bureaucracy, formality, etc.; by metonymy, a civil servant, etc.; so ***striped-trouser(ed)*** adj.; similarly (chiefly *U.S.*) ***striped pants***. Cf. PIN-STRIPE, PIN-STRIPED *a.*

1933 DYLAN THOMAS *Let.* Oct. (1966) 37 Oh to look.. different from the striped trouser lads. **1945** 'G. ORWELL' in *New Saxon Pamphlets* III. 38 The striped-trousered ones will rule, but so long as they are forced to maintain an intelligentsia, the intelligentsia will have a certain amount of autonomy. **1946** KOESTLER *Thieves in Night* 220 At the end emerged the striped-trousered finished product. **1958** S. HYLAND *Who goes Hang?* xxxiii. 140 He was almost in tears. Black tears with striped trousers. **1968** W. SAFIRE *New Lang. Politics* 398/2 The diplomatic niceties of 'striped-pants' diplomacy. **1972** M. GILBERT *Body of Girl* xxiv. 206 A crook in striped trousers turns my stomach. **1974** 'D. KYLE' *Raft of Swords* x. 97 They may be useful. So may the striped-trousers in the Foreign Secretary's entourage. **1976** G. MARKSTEIN *Man from Yesterday* xi. 59 'Who's had to apologize?' 'The gentlemen in striped pants.' **1977** *Time* 9 May 22/3 His youthful diplomatic appointee's aversion to striped-pants airs. **1977** 'J. LE CARRÉ' *Honourable Schoolboy* i. 24 Ring every damned striped-pants in the Colony! **1981** *New Standard* 1 Sept. 14/6 An old-fashioned striped-trouser diplomat.

g. Of cine film: having a magnetic stripe (STRIPE *sb.*[3] 1 e).

[**1956** J. J. ROSE *Amer. Cinematographer Hand Bk. & Ref. Guide* (ed. 9) 7 (Advt.), Your pre-striped film with magnetic sound lip-synchronized to your picture.] **1972** E. & D. SCHULTZ *How to make Exciting Home Movies* xi. 131 Your splicer can get magnetized when it's used on a film already striped.

2. *U.S.* ? = STREAKED *ppl. a.* 2.

1839 *Morning Post* (Boston) 4 July 2/2 She made a remark, which, if reported in full, would make one of O.F.M. [*sc.* Our First Men] feel decidedly striped. **1840** HALIBURTON *Clockm.* Ser. III. ix, That's the reason married folks are so everlastin' striped; they never romp.

3. In parasynthetic adjs. Cf. STRIPE *sb.*[3] 10.

1731 MILLER *Gard. Dict.* s.v. *Tilia*, The strip'd-leav'd Lime-tree. **1782** LATHAM *Gen. Synop. Birds* I. II. 563 Striped-bellied Woodpecker. **1783** *Ibid.* II. I. 275 Striped Headed Finch. **1829** GRIFFITH tr. *Cuvier* VII. 418 Striped-tailed or Angola Hornbill. **1859** WOOD *Illustr. Nat. Hist.* I. 482 The Banded Bandicoot, or Striped-backed Bandicoot.

stripeless ('straɪplɪs), *a. rare.* [f. STRIPE *sb.*[3] + -LESS.] Without a stripe or stripes.

1900 *Brit. Med. Jrnl.* 17 Mar. 656/1 So it comes about that cleaning windows..may be part of the duty of a stripeless man who enlists in the service of the Empire. **1906** *Daily Chron.* 30 June 6/5 Stripeless Mackerel... A fine mackerel ..which had not a single stripe on it.

striper ('straɪpə(r)). *colloq.* [f. STRIPE *sb.*[3] + -ER[1].]

1. Usu. as *two* (***two and a half, three, four***)-***striper***: an officer in the Royal Navy or U.S. Navy (from the stripes worn to denote rank). In later use, in the army, a lance-corporal (***one-striper***), corporal (***two-striper***), sergeant (***three-striper***).

1917 M. T. HAINSSELIN *Grand Fleet Days* xv. 118 But nowadays you find them lolling and sprawling in all the most comfortable armchairs, while the three-striper has to take a high chair or else go to his cabin! **1918** L. E. RUGGLES *Navy Explained* 146 *Two striper.* Instead of saying 'he was a lieutenant', many men say 'he was a two-striper', meaning that he wore two stripes on his cuff. If the officer was a lieutenant commander he would wear two-and-a-half stripes, hence 'he was a two-and-a-half striper'. **1920** *Blackw. Mag.* Mar. 320/2 A dapper two-and-a-half striper, R.N., dashed alongside in an obviously Navy gig, and scrambled aboard. **1936** *Nat. Geogr. Mag.* LXIX. 799/2 The three-striper looked me up and down. **1950** G. HACKFORTH-JONES *Worst Enemy* i. 20 It made me remember how I felt when some pompous four-striper came slumming or snooping on board my submarine. **1954** *Sun* (Baltimore) 11 Dec. 13/4 Some 250 other 'stripers' were named brigade officers for the period ending March 17. **1977** [see SPEC *sb.*[4]]. **1978** A. PRICE *'44 Vintage* iii. 41 A two-striper like himself. **1978** H. WOUK *War & Remembrance* i. 10 Bill, isn't that a three-striper slot?

2. = *striped bass* s.v. STRIPED *ppl. a.* 1 b.

1945 *Richmond* (Va.) *Times-Dispatch* 29 Aug. 22/1 It may be stated that in the West as in the North, the fish is called the striped bass or simply the striper. **1955** *Field & Stream* June 51/1 So far as is known, this is the first fresh-water lake in the entire country to be stocked with adult stripers. **1961** J. STEINBECK *Winter of our Discontent* xv. 292 Stripers come in sometimes. **1974** *Spartanburg* (S. Carolina) *Herald-Jrnl.* 21 Apr. B6/5 A hybrid is a cross between a striper and a white bass.

stripey ('straɪpɪ). [f. STRIPE *sb.*[3] + -Y[6] (in sense 2, ad. Afrikaans *strepie*): cf. STRIPY *a.*]

1. *Navy slang.* A long-service able seaman; one with good-conduct stripes.

1942 *Gen* 1 May 42/1 'What's the buzz, Stripey?'.. 'Dunno,' curtly responded the Bosun's Mate. **1945** 'TACKLINE' *Holiday Sailor* i. 8 Stripey was a small, middle-aged A.B. **1977** [see RATE *sb.*[1] 9 c].

2. *Afr.* Also **stripie.** = STREPIE.

1964 A. TREW *Smoke Island* viii. 133 Ezekiel was fishing in a deep pool; at his side were four or five mullet and as many 'stripeys'. **1969** *Guardian* 8 Mar. 7/6, I glimpsed his outstretched pectoral fins for a moment and saw the flash of purple. He was a stripie.

stripiness ('straɪpɪnɪs). [f. STRIPY *a.* + -NESS.] The condition of being stripy.

1958 tr. *Herberts' Artists' Techniques* III. 273 The tendency to stripiness can be avoided by stippling the paint on with a sponge. **1960** *Textile Terms & Definitions* (Textile Inst.) (ed. 4) 144 *Stripiness* (warp knitting), longitudinal defects caused by yarn variation or structural distortion in warp-knitted fabric.

striping *vbl. sb.*[1]: see STRIPE *v.*[1]

striping ('straɪpɪŋ), *vbl. sb.*[2] [f. STRIPE *v.*[2] + -ING[1].]

1. The action or process of making a stripe or of forming stripes.

1731 MILLER *Gard. Dict.* s.v. *Tulipa* 8 D/2 Though indeed, the Striping of Tulips doth never occasion so great Weakness in them. **1798** *Hull Advertiser* 8 Sept. 2/4 Fancy work..varnishing, gilding and striping. **1911** *Daily News* 2 Oct. 3/1 The holdings are ruthlessly rearranged among the tenants who remain—a process called 'striping'.

2. *concr.* **a.** A stripe or series of stripes of colour.

1677 PLOT *Oxfordsh.* 172 Where it [a striped Maple] flourishes still and retains its stripings. **1731** MILLER *Gard. Dict.* s.v. *Variegated*, It is a Distemper in the Plants, since whenever they become vigorous, this Striping is..rendered less visible. **1882** *Garden* 28 Jan. 67/1 The flowers present.. various kinds of striping and feathering. **1897** V. CORNISH in *Geogr. Jrnl.* IX. 293 The longitudinal striping (of sand) is reduced to a subordinate feature of the wind-ward slope of transverse dunes. **1900** *Pop. Sci. Monthly* Jan. 347 The detailed representations..showing in some respects a resemblance to the stripings of Mars.

striplet ('strɪplɪt). [f. STRIP *sb.*[2] + -LET.] A small strip. Also *attrib.*

1839 CAROLINE B. SOUTHEY in *Blackw. Mag.* XLV. 756 The rising flood came rushing on, Till not a sea-mark old was seen, Nor of the striplet islets green A speck of hard, dry sand. **1884** ANNIE S. SWAN *Mark Desb.* xiv. 122 The striplet of firm wet sand left by the ebbing tide.

stripling ('strɪplɪŋ). Also 4–6 **strepe-**, **stryplynge**, 5–6 **striplyng**, 6 **stripelyng**, **stryppplyng(e**, 6–7 **strippling** (6 **-yng**), 7, 9 **striplin**. [Prob. f. STRIP *sb.*[1] (though that word is not recorded before the 15th c.) + -LING[1].

The etymological notion seems to be 'one who is slender as a strip', one whose figure is not yet filled out.]

1. A youth, one just passing from boyhood to manhood.

1398 TREVISA *Barth. De P.R.* VI. i. (1495) 186 Adolescencia the aege of a yonge stryplynge duryth the thyrd vii yere. *c* **1400** MAUNDEV. (1839) xxvii. 278 The faireste ȝonge striplynges. *a* **1513** FABYAN *Chron.* v. civ. (1811) 79 Arthurus, the sone of Vter Pendragon, a strepelynge of .xv. yeres of Age. **1568** GRAFTON *Chron.* II. 139 Euery stripplyng of the age of .xii. yeres and aboue, before his Alderman in his warde was newly charged with the same othe. **1611** BIBLE *1 Sam.* xvii. 56 And the king said, Enquire thou whose sonne the stripling is. **1650** FULLER *Pisgah* IV. vi. 103 From a child he starts up a youth, and becomes a stripling. **1745** in *10th Rep. Hist. MSS. Comm.* App. I. 128 The only son I have left me, being but a stripling of fourteen years age. **1839** THIRLWALL *Greece* lii. VI. 262 He affected to speak slightingly of Alexander, as a stripling. **1878** BROWNING *Poets Croisic* ix, This proves mere Stripling's amusement.

transf. and *fig.* **1683** DRYDEN *Dk. Guise* II. ii, I'm but a Stripling in the Trade of War. **1693** *Humours Town* 32 A conceited School-master is but a stripling in Pedantry to him. **1879** STEVENSON *Trav. Cevennes* (1886) 19 An amiable stripling of a river. **1887** MOLONEY *Forestry W. Afr.* 230 My trees ran up so rapidly and such striplings that tornadoes blew down two or three.

2. *attrib.* (chiefly appositive) passing into adj.

1553 T. WILSON *Rhet.* 7 The stripelyng age, or spryng tide. **1598** SYLVESTER *Du Bartas* II. ii. II. *Babylon* 51 He tyranniz'd among his strippling-peers. **1645** MILTON *Colast.* 4 Having convers'd much with a stripling Divine or two of those newly fledge Probationers, that usually come scouting from the University. **1667** —— *P.L.* III. 636 A stripling Cherube. **1725** POPE *Odyss.* I. 194 Gay, stripling youths. **1795** SOUTHEY *Joan of Arc* VII. 107 Before his stripling arm Fled Warwick. **1853** M. ARNOLD *Scholar Gypsy* viii, Crossing the stripling Thames at Bab-lock-hithe.

strippable ('strɪpəb(ə)l), *a.* [f. STRIP *v.*[1] + -ABLE.] **1.** Of a coating: capable of being stripped off or removed.

1950 *Effects Atomic Weapons* (U.S. Sci. Lab., Los Alamos) x. 333 Another possibility in connection with protection against radioactive contamination..is to use strippable coatings. **1980** *Daily Tel.* 16 Dec. 11/4 The wallpapers are trimmed, washable and strippable.

2. *U.S.* Of a mineral deposit: capable of being strip-mined.

1975 *N.Y. Times* 24 Mar. 20/2 Their entrepreneurial thrust to exploit what industry spokesmen call the West's 'Persian Gulf' of strippable coal. **1978** *Time* 17 Apr. 74/3 When they do [legislate], Western strip-mine owners fear, up to 80% of the region's strippable tonnage will be ruled off limits.

strippado, obs. form of STRAPPADO.

strippage ('strɪpɪdʒ). *rare.* [f. STRIP *v.*[1] + -AGE.] Branches stripped from trees.

1873 BROWNING *Red Cott. Nt.-cap* I. 508 The leafy street-length through, decked end to end With August-strippage, and adorned with flags.

stripped (strɪpt), *ppl. a.* [f. STRIP *v.*[1] + -ED[1].]

a. That has been stripped, in senses of the vb. ***stripped gallop***, a gallop given a racehorse when 'stripped'.

1594 *Gd. Huswifes Handmaid Kitchin* 1 b, Then put in halfe a handfull of stripped Tyme. **1641** in *Archæologia* I. 99 Poor stript men, that had made their escapes from the rebels. **1683** MOXON *Mech. Exerc.* XIV. xxii. ¶3. 207 The Compositer..coming to his Stript Form, or Quarter of the Form he is to Destribute, he places [etc.]. **1714** E. WARD *Field-Spy* 26 Like a strip'd Gamester or a ruin'd Beau. **1844** *Rep. Sel. Comm. Tobacco Trade, Min. Evid.* 232 The stripped tobacco is an article which is manufactured by the extraction of the stalk. **1869** G. J. CHESTER *Transatl. Sk.* 264 Making indelicate remarks on the personal appearance of the stripped soldiers. **1896** *Daily News* 12 June 6/2 It was the first stripped gallop he ever had. **1898** J. SOUTHWARD *Mod. Printing* I. 97 The following table shews the usual number of improved—that is, shaved or stripped—leads to the pound.

(*b*) In senses 24, 25 of the vb.

1931 HOFFERT & CLAXTON *Motor Benzole* iv. 61 After the removal of the benzole in the scrubbers, the gas is usually referred to as stripped gas. **1933** O. H. BLACKWOOD et al. *Outl. Atomic Physics* xiv. 305 The electrons and the more or less stripped nuclei together are assumed to form a gas, which acts like a perfect gas even at hugh densities. **1947** *Physical Rev.* LXXII. 1008/2 It is just the narrowness of the cone which distinguishes the stripped neutrons from those produced by direct nuclear encounters. **1978** *Nature* 7 Sept. 41/2 Stripped iron nuclei in a hydrogen plasma under central solar conditions, according to the classical Debye-Hückel model, would undergo phase separation for concentrations well below the cosmic abundance value.

b. *spec.* Of wood (esp. pine) used for furniture or domestic woodwork, etc.: that has had the accretions of paint or varnish removed, so as to reveal the natural grain and colour.

1934 M. ALLINGHAM *Death of Ghost* ix. 105 The high narrow room with its top lights and stripped pine panelling. **1966** A. CHRISTIE *Third Girl* iv. 31 Long Basing..had two antique shops, one mostly consisting of stripped pine chimney pieces. **1976** *Listener* 15 July 49/2 He likes corner cabinets and stripped pine. **1976** *Lancs. Even. Post* 7 Dec. 14/5 (Advt.), Chairs include set eight stripped beech. **1981**

c. ***stripped-down*** adj., that has had all superfluous or extraneous parts removed; also *fig.* Esp. (orig. *U.S.*) applied to a motor vehicle so adapted in order to improve engine performance. Also of a machine: disassembled, dismantled. Cf. STRIP *v.*¹ 8.

1946 [see HOPPED *a.* 3]. **1958** *Times* 24 Nov. (Canada Suppl.) p. iv/4 In 1959, General Motors will introduce a small, stripped-down Chevrolet, which will be billed as a 'new' small car. **1961** R. B. LONG *Sentence & its Parts* 494 'Kernels.' This term is applied to stripped-down nucleuses [of sentences]. **1973** A. MACVICAR *Painted Doll Affair* vi. 66 A pimpled hairy youth in overalls wriggled out from underneath a stripped-down car. **1975** *New Yorker* 7 July 78/3 'Blue Lou' is short, stripped-down, and full of business. **1978** *Archit. Design* 5 June 310/2 The stripped-down classicism promoted by men [*sc.* architects] like Burnet and Richardson. **1979** J. GARDNER *Nostradamus Traitor* xlix. 237 They travelled in a stripped-down Heinkel 111. **1980** J. CARTWRIGHT *Horse of Darius* v. 66 He laid out the stripped-down Kalashnikov, the plasticine, the detonators.

Hence **'strippedness**, the quality or state of being stripped.

1856 MRS. CARLYLE *New Lett. & Mem.* (1903) II. 96 What is that quality in the skins of some women..which always suggests nakedness, striptness?

stripper¹ ('strɪpə(r)). [f. STRIP *v.*¹ + -ER¹.]

1. a. One who strips another; also one who strips or strips off some article or product, e.g. bark of a tree, tobacco, the accumulation of shoddy in a carding-machine.

1581 MULCASTER *Positions* xxxvii. (1887) 162 Preferment to degrees in schole..ought to be a mightier stripper of insufficiencie. **1611** COTGR., *Spoliateur*, a spoyler; stripper, despoyler. *a* **1722** LISLE *Husb.* (1757) 367 The greater the flush of sap..it makes the better bark, and is better both for the tanner and the stripper. **1859** FAIRHOLT *Tobacco* vi. 305 The 'stripper' performs her duties by folding the tobacco-leaf, and..cutting under both sides of the thick end of the stalk. **1876** SMILES *Sc. Naturalist* iii, 48 Each spinner had three boys under him—the wheeler, the pointer, and the stripper. **1886** LD. WALSINGHAM & PAYNE-GALLWEY *Shooting* I. 71 The stripper takes the gun to pieces down to the minutest detail, and carefully examines and regulates it in every way. **1890** *Melbourne Argus* 10 June 5/2 Had strippers been allowed to take out licenses to strip the wattles of their bark.

b. *colloq.* (orig. *U.S.*). A performer of strip-tease.

1930 *Variety* 3 Dec. 54/5 (*heading*) Detroit censor pinches four stock strippers. **1945** P. CHEYNEY *I'll say she Does!* ii. 42, I was a stripper one time... I had a feature spot in the programme. **1950** *Manch. Guardian Weekly* 13 July 13/2 A couple of famous strippers and a beloved Broadway comedian appeared in something called 'Wine, Women, and Song'. **1960** *New Left Rev.* Mar.–Apr. 45/2 The calculated obscenity of the stripper's act. **1972** C. WESTON *Poor, Poor Ophelia* v. 27 She unzipped her..mini-dress, and with the grace of a professional stripper, stepped out of it. **1980** *Times* 21 Oct. 12/6 (*caption*) Why should it only be male strippers who are subsidized?

2. a. A machine or appliance for stripping.

1835 [see STRIP *v.* 20]. **1856** P. KENNEDY *Banks of Boro* xli. (1867) 339 A..pair of strippers (curved chisels for stripping off bark). **1874** KNIGHT *Dict. Mech.* 842/2 A frame..which may be elevated to raise the stripper off the file through the instrumentality of a rock-shaft and a system of levers. **1875** *Ibid.* 2430/2 *Stripper* 2. (Carding) a device for lifting the top flats from the carding-cylinder. **1882** *Essex Herald* No 4269/3 A stripper is a labour saving machine used in.. Victoria... Its object is to strip the heads from the standing corn and thrash them at one operation. **1886** *Pall Mall Gaz.* 6 Apr. 14/2 One by one the [willow-] switches are placed in the mechanical stripper.

attrib. **1839** URE *Dict. Arts* 349 [Carding] This shaft drives the crank and lever mechanism of the stripper knife. **1908** *Westm. Gaz.* 12 Mar. 2/1 Sir William Lyne proposed to raise the duty from £12 to £16 for 'stripper harvesters'.

b. *Oil Industry.* A still for the fractionation of oil or oil products.

1930 H. S. BELL *Amer. Petroleum Refining* (ed. 2) xii. 222 Reboiling coils are sometimes used as strippers. **1938** A. E. DUNSTAN et al. *Sci. of Petroleum* II. II. xxv. 1559/2 Reheaters, when used, usually have been placed on the oil stream flowing from one of the lower plates of the stripper. **1961** D. PETRIE *Petroleum* xi. 64 In order to make the fractionation process even more exact, each fraction when it leaves the tower is led into another smaller fractionating tower called a 'side stripper'. **1975** W. G. ROBERTS *Quest for Oil* (rev. ed.) viii. 85 The purpose of the stripper is to remove small amounts of vapour from the liquid entering it.

c. *Physics.* In a particle accelerator, a section containing metal foil or gas at a high positive potential, which removes electrons from the ions passing through it. Also *attrib.*

1959 *Nuclear Instruments & Methods* IV. 123/2 The image size and beam divergence required at the object point for the accelerator are limited by the dimensions of the stripper tube. **1974** J. B. A. ENGLAND *Techniques in Nuclear Structure Physics* I. iii. 268 There is usually little to choose in final beam intensity between foil strippers and gas strippers for hydrogen and helium ions. **1979** *Sci. Amer.* Apr. 47/2 The aiming mechanism would first direct the negative-hydrogen beam at the target and then pass it through a gas 'stripper' for neutralization.

3. *pl. Gaming.* 'High cards cut wedge-shape, a little wider than the rest, so as to be easily drawn in a crooked game' (Farmer & Henley).

1843 J. H. GREENE *Exposure Arts & Miseries Gambling* (1845) 121 When cards are prepared as I have above described, they are called *strippers.* **1887** F. FRANCIS jun. *Saddle & Mocassin* 228 A tender-foot got in amongst the gamblers on board.., and what with 'strippers', and 'stocking', and 'cold decks',..and so forth, he hadn't the ghost of a show. **1894** MASKELYNE *Sharps & Flats* 222 The most commonly used form of cards, however, is that of the 'double-wedges' or 'strippers'.

4. a. A bleaching agent or solvent used to remove colour from fabrics before re-dyeing. Cf. STRIP *v.*¹ 21.

1909 A. MORRIS in Rothery & Edmunds *Mod. Laundry* II. xl. 150 Permanganic acid in the form of its potash or soda salt is a powerful oxidizing stripper. **1957** *Woman* 16 Nov. 25/4 Light over dark won't go, but if you want to try it you'll need a colour 'stripper'.

b. A chemical preparation used to remove paint, varnish, etc., from a surface; ***paint stripper***: see PAINT *sb.* 7.

1937 A. JONES *Cellulose Lacquers, Finishes & Cements* xii. 241 Wax has been objected to as a thickening agent as it settles out and the paint remover or stripper requires frequent and repeated shaking. **1949** C. H. HAYWARD *Woodworker's Pocket Bk.* 4 Many proprietary strippers are now available. **1979** C. CURZON *Leaven of Malice* ii. 22, I had bought..cleaning agents, strippers, filler for the cracks..in the plaster.

'stripper². [f. STRIP *v.*³ + -ER¹.] 'A cow not in calf, but giving very little milk' (*Eng. Dial. Dict.*).

1856 *Jrnl. R. Agric. Soc.* XVII. I. 266 The cows which I buy as strippers, for fattening, giving little milk. **1917** L. A. KLEIN *Princ. & Practice Milk Hygiene* i. 5 Cows in which lactation is about to cease are called 'strippers'.

stripper³ ('strɪpə(r)). *Oil Industry.* [? f. STRIPPER², by analogy with a low-yielding milk cow.] More fully, ***stripper well.*** An oil well in which production has dwindled to only a few barrels a day.

1930 *Oil & Gas Jrnl.* 18 Dec. 48/2 The proration committee is working out a plan safeguarding the interest of operators owning small and shallow producing wells... Nothing will be done that might cause the abandonment of the stripper wells. **1931** *Ibid.* 8 Jan. 26/1 There would apparently be nothing to do but to abandon these old strippers as having exceeded their useful life. **1976** *Watertown* (S. Dakota) *Public Opinion* 6 July 7/5 Throughout the United States marginally productive oil wells known as 'strippers' account for more than 13 percent of domestic production. **1980** *Fortune* 24 Mar. 64/1 Independents will also get a break on oil from 'stripper' wells, which produce ten or fewer barrels a day.

†'strippet. *Obs. rare*⁻¹. [f. STRIPE *sb.*¹ + -ET¹.] A small rill.

1577 HARRISON *Descr. Scot.* x. 12/2 in *Holinshed*, A fayre spring..from whence runneth a little brooke or strippet.

strippeuse (strɪ'pɜːz). *joc.* [An alteration of STRIPPER¹ 1 b, perh. after *danseuse.*] A (female) performer of strip-tease.

1939 *Life* 2 Jan. 15/2 Last year blonde Della Carroll was première strippeuse at New York's Paradise restaurant. **1960** [see IN *a.* 2 a]. **1962** *Times Lit. Suppl.* 26 Oct. 827/5 An eminent 'strippeuse' at Las Vegas.

stripping ('strɪpɪŋ), *vbl. sb.*¹ [-ING¹.]

1. a. The action of STRIP *v.*¹

1398 TREVISA *Barth. De P.R.* v. lxiv. (1495) 182 And that matere chaungyth and enfectith the skynne somtyme wyth scales..and somtyme wyth strippynge and pillynge. *a* **1400–50** *Wars Alex.* (Dubl. MS.) 781 What of stampyng of stedes & strippyng of baners, All demmyd þe dale & þe duste risez. *c* **1440** *Promp. Parv.* 480/1 Stryppynge, or makynge [*read* nakynge],..*denudacio.* **1653** W. JENKYN *Shock of Corn* (1654) 14 He who looks upon himself as possessing nothing in the world, fears not a stripping by death. **1713** ADDISON *Guardian* No. 109 ¶2 Having put a seasonable stop to this unaccountable humour of stripping, that was got among our British Ladies. **1845** J. COULTER *Adv. Pacific* vii. 76 As this spiral stripping of the blubber goes on, the body [of the whale] is kept turning. **1847** ELIZA GURNEY *Let.* 18 Sept., in A. J. C. Hare *Gurneys* (1895) II. xv. 252 This further stripping has afresh caused me to feel that 'I am bereaved', that life will soon contain but very few to bind me to it. **1899** *Allbutt's Syst. Med.* VII. 712 The pia [mater] on stripping is found to adhere to the cerebral cortex. **1952** W. H. KIRK *Sewell's Dogs & their Management* (rev. ed.) iv. 76 Proper trimming or stripping is a long, tedious, and continuous work. **1974** R. RENDELL *Face of Trespass* xiv. 134 Mr Greenberg doesn't have a surgery on Saturday afternoons. ..We're only open for clipping and stripping.

b. In technical senses.

1748 *Anson's Voy.* II. ii. 135 In the stripping of our fore-mast, we were alarmed by discovering it was sprung. **1837** WHITTOCK *Bk. Trades* (1842) 226 (File Maker) To prepare the files for cutting, is by making the surface to contain the teeth as level as possible; this process is called 'stripping'. **1853** URE *Dict. Arts* (ed. 4) II. 697 Interruptions occurred several times a day by the stripping of the main cylinder. **1875** J. H. COLLINS *Metal Mining* 54 The ore is got out by a kind of long-wall method called 'stripping'. **1886** A. WATT *Electro-Deposition* 252 It is usually the practice to remove what silver there may be upon old plated articles by the process termed 'stripping'. This consists in immersing the article in a hot acid liquid. **1922** D. T. DAY *Handbk. Petroleum Industry* II. 324 Stripping may be held to mean a complete removal of all light fractions down to those of lubricating value, and represents the initial refining process. **1943** *Ann. Reg. 1942* 364 Saha..suggested that both the stripping of the atoms and their high velocities are due to a nuclear reaction analogous to fission. **1949** MELCHER & LARRICK *Printing & Promotion Handbk.* 283/2 When two or more photographic negatives are used together to make one printing plate, the process of combining them is known as 'stripping'. **1955** [see DESORPTION]. **1972** *Physics Bull.* Mar. 145/1 After stripping the nitrogen ions..will behave like deuterons or alpha particles in the injection channel into the synchrotron. **1977** L. VÁLYI *Atom & Ion Sources* iv. 251 An alternative method for the production of multiply charged ions is the stripping of electrons in the interaction of singly charged positive ions. **1980** J. R. WALKER *Graphic Arts Fund.* vi. 116/1 (*caption*) Light table makes good work surface for stripping.

2. *concr.* Something stripped off or taken off in a thin layer.

1601 in *Househ. Ord.* (1790) 288 He [the yeoman of the Boyling House] hath for his fee the strippinges of beefe. **1835** BROWNING *Paracelsus* v. 486 And now the air is full of uptorn canes, Light strippings from the fan-trees. **1874** RAYMOND *6th Rep. Mines* 315 The layers of gravel passed through by the shafts in reaching the *mantas* or rich streaks are cast aside as of no value, and the surface of a Mexican placer is covered with heaps of these 'strippings'. **1883** GRESLEY *Gloss. Coal-mining* 245 *Stripping*, a web of coal worked off all along the face of a stall.

3. *attrib.* (chiefly technical), as ***stripping-acid, agent, -bath, bench, cement, column, desk, foil, -liquid, -machine, operation, -solution, still.*** Also **stripping-bill(e)**, a bladed implement or bill used in besom-making; **stripping-coat**, a coating of solvent used on the edges of double waterproof fabric in order to separate them for making a seam; **stripping-film**, a photographic 'plate' having a film which may be separated from its support after exposure; **stripping-knife**, (*a*) (see quot. 1875); (*b*) a knife used in the stripping of wallpaper or paint from surfaces; **† stripping law**, the 'art' of fleecing prisoners as practised by jailers (see quots.).

1905 *Electro-plating* (ed. P. N. Hasluck) 141 The *stripping acid is composed of sulphuric acid, nitric acid, and water. **1958** M. G. LARIAN *Fund. Chem. Engin. Operations* xiii. 495 In desorption dissolved gases are removed from a liquid by contacting the liquid with a suitable gas (the desorbing or *stripping agent), or a volatile liquid is separated from a relatively nonvolatile solvent. **1886** A. WATT *Electro-Deposition* 252 A *stripping-bath [for silver] is first made by pouring a sufficient quantity of strong oil of vitriol into a suitable stoneware vessel... To this must be added a small quantity of either nitrate of potash, or nitrate of soda. **1967** E. CHAMBERS *Photolitho-Offset* v. 51 A *stripping bench, layout and lining tables are essential... The former provides the illuminated working surface on which the various images can be positioned. **1968** J. ARNOLD *Shell Bk. Country Crafts* v. 97 The cuttings are prepared for use with chopping and *stripping-billes for the coarse and finer work. **1974** P. W. BLANDFORD *Country Craft Tools* ii. 38 The besom broom maker called his general-purpose tool a 'chopping bill' and had a lighter one with more curve to the point called 'stripping bill'. **1967** E. CHAMBERS *Photolitho-Offset* v. 50 With face-up stripping a *stripping cement is first applied to the base support. **1885** C. G. W. LOCK *Workshop Rec.* Ser. IV. 7/2 Such coatings are specially designated '*stripping-coats'. **1930** H. S. BELL *Amer. Petroleum Refining* (ed. 2) xii. 222 If withdrawn as a finished product, the light ends must be removed and this is usually accomplished in a separate small *stripping column. **1967** E. CHAMBERS *Photolitho-Offset* v. 55 (*caption*) Bench-type illuminated *stripping desk. **1885** C. G. W. LOCK *Workshop Rec.* Ser. IV. 395 *Stripping films. **1972** *Physics Bull.* Mar. 144/3 An aluminium *stripping foil of density 40 μg cm⁻² was therefore used at the high energy end of the Linac to convert the particles to ¹⁴N⁷⁺. **1875** KNIGHT *Dict. Mech.*, **Stripping-knife*, a tool for removing the blades of sorghum from the stalks, previous to grinding. **1927** W. DEEPING *Kitty* xx. 254, I could lend you a plank and a couple of step-ladders, and a stripping-knife. **1951** *Good Housek. Home Encycl.* 210/1 A paper-hanger's stripping knife, which is a flat, fairly flexible, steel-bladed knife. **1592** GREENE *Disput. Conny Catchers* D 1, The *stripping Lawe, wherein I will lay open the lewde abuses of sundry Iaylors in England. **1592** —— *Def. Conny Catching* Wks. (Grosart) XI. 104 The stripping Law..is the abuse offered by the keepers of Newgate to poore prisoners. **1846** *Mech. Mag.* XLV. 260/2 Silversmiths remove silver from copper by immersing the plated article in *stripping liquid, made of eight parts sulphuric acid and one part nitrate of potash. **1898** *Stripping machine [see STRIP *v.*¹ 19]. **1948** R. R. KARCH *Graphic Arts Procedures* viii. 232 (*heading*) The *stripping operation. **1980** J. R. WALKER *Graphic Arts Fund.* vi. 116/2 (*caption*) Stripping operations require sharp knives, scissors and brushes for opaquing pinholes. **1886** A. WATT *Electro-Deposition* 253 A Cold *Stripping Solution,..is made by [etc.]. **1931** HOFFERT & CLAXTON *Motor Benzole* viii. 225 The function of a modern *stripping still is to remove the remaining benzole from the hot oil leaving the preheater.

stripping ('strɪpɪŋ), *vbl. sb.*² [f. STRIP *v.*³ + -ING¹.] The action of STRIP *v.*³

1895 F. M. HALFORD *Making a Fishery* 194 Finding that she [the female fish] was not quite ripe for stripping he turned her on to a shallow. **1899** *19th Cent.* Sept. 399 The 'stripping' of the shad by the hatchery officials had only terminated the previous week.

b. *concr.* (*pl.*) = STROKING *vbl. sb.* 2.

1781 J. HUTTON *Tour to Caves* (ed. 2) Gloss. 97 *Stripings*, the last part of a cow's milk. **1808** J. C. CURWEN *Hints Feeding Stock* 145, I was doubtful of the accuracy of my own dairy, which stated a pound of butter to eight quarts of strippings. **1844** H. STEPHENS *Bk. Farm* II. 459 That which comes last, the afterings or strippings, as it is commonly called, is much the richer part of new milk.

c. *Comb.*: **stripping cow**, a cow which is going dry and requires to be 'stripped' in milking.

1894 *Times* 16 Apr. 4/4 Irish store cattle, consisting chiefly of heifers and stripping cows, continue to be imported.

stripping *vbl. sb.*³: see STRIP *v.*⁴

stripping ('strɪpɪŋ), *ppl. a.* [f. STRIP *v.*¹ + -ING².] That strips, in senses of the verb.

1681 OTWAY *Soldier's Fort.* I. i. (1683) 6 Be sure that they be lew'd, drunken, stripping Whores. **1713** ADDISON *Guardian* No. 118 ¶3 At a late meeting of the stripping Ladies,..it was resolved for the future to lay the modesty-piece wholly aside. **1809** MARY TITHERINGTON *Diary* in

Mem. 91 In the course of Christian experience we pass through such stripping times. **1913** MASEFIELD in *Engl. Rev.* Dec. 1 Till with a stripping crash the tree goes down.

strippy ('strɪpɪ), *a.* [f. STRIP *sb.*² + -Y.] Of the nature of a strip, made up of strips.

1822 *Examiner* 827/1 Intersected in every part with clashing colours, obtrusive lights, and strippy shapes and lines. **1963** *Times* 20 Apr. 11/6 Veneered with carefully matched figured or burr walnut,..with drawer fronts, fall flaps and door framing straight or herringbone cross-banded with strippy walnut. **1978** *Detroit Free Press* 16 Apr. (Detroit Suppl.) 20 (Advt.), Strippy, strappy stripes of canvas [sandals], wedged high, to put spring snap in your steps.

stript. [Variant of STRIPPED *ppl. a.* used as *sb.*] A trade-name of tobacco-leaf when 'stripped'.

1881 Spons' *Encycl. Industr. Arts* IV. 1341 Quantities of leaf-tobacco are shipped in a condition deprived of their stem and midrib, and are then known as 'stripts'.

strip-tease. *colloq.* (orig. *U.S.*). Also **strip tease, striptease.** [Back-formation from next.]

1. A kind of entertainment in which a female (occas. a male) performer undresses gradually in a tantalizingly erotic fashion before an audience, usu. to music; an instance of this.

[**1930** *Variety* 1 Oct. 49/4 Girls have the strip and tease down to a science.] **1936** *Variety* 2 Dec. 70/5 An undersea ballet, veil waving number and a mild strip tease by the entire chorus, which required little feeling, were nicely executed. **1937** *Daily Tel.* 29 Apr. 22/2 Can anything be said in defence of the present public interest in 'strip-tease' and nudist or semi-nudist displays on stage? **1943** *Scrutiny* XI. 286 The business-cum-Riviera set of which he is the representative in fiction (on the stage—strip-tease) were very pally with Goering and Co. **1960** *News Chron.* 23 Sept. 10/2 Strip-tease..can be banal. **1978** G. GREENE *Human Factor* II. iii. 75, I thought dinner in the Café Grill and afterwards a spot of strip-tease.

2. In *transf.* and *fig.* use.

1937 *Hansard Commons* 20 Apr. 1623 We had a display of what I believe is now known as 'strip-tease', in which we were kept in tantalising expectation of what was to come. **1956** E. LINKLATER *Dark of Summer* iv. 62 The whole female art of novel-writing—is an exquisitely prolonged strip-tease. **1969** I. & P. OPIE *Children's Games* 13 They snatch the girls' ties or hair ribbons and call it 'Strip Tease'. **1982** J. O'FAOLAIN *Obedient Wife* i. 26 'Do you feel I owe you a confidence?' 'No..if I come here to do a strip-tease, it doesn't mean *you* have to.'

3. In *attrib.* use. **strip-tease artist**, a performer of strip-tease.

1936 *N.Y. Post* 15 Sept. 13/1 Gypsy Rose Lee is at once the Bernhardt, the Duse and the Joan Crawford of Strip-Tease girls. **1939** A. HUXLEY *After Many a Summer* I. vi. 71, A strip-tease dancer in a Western mining-camp. **1944** 'G. ORWELL' in *Horizon* X. 237 A strip-tease act. **1947** H. A. SMITH *Low Man on Totem Pole* viii. 68 Miss Lee turned to a paragraph in the magazine in which Henry L. Mencken was represented as having coined a word to describe a strip-tease artist. **1953** C. DAY LEWIS *Italian Visit* i. 25 Whoever would master the truth by which your provocative, charming Strip-tease universe lives. **1958** N. MARSH *Singing in Shrouds* v. 101 That damn' spiritual striptease session. **1968** P. OLIVER *Screening Blues* vi. 251 As the strip-tease artist compares with the artist's model, so the seductive effects of slow unveiling are more stimulating erotically than the starkly naked. **1979** C. MACLEOD *Family Vault* xi. 71 Does it disgust you..that your..husband once made a fool of himself over a striptease dancer?

Hence as *v. intr.*, to perform a strip-tease act; **strip-teaseuse**, joc. alteration of STRIPTEASER (cf. CHANTEUSE, STRIPPEUSE, etc.); **strip-teasing** *vbl. sb.* and *ppl. a.*; **stripteuse** = *strip-teaseuse* above.

1937 G. FRANKAU *More of Us* 185 Dalliest thou, stripteasing and beachcombing, On some far southern beach of Gallic joy. **1937** *Variety* 31 Mar. 69/1 Kraus is accused by John S. Sumner, head of the vice society, of permitting strip-teasing in his show. **1941** *Sun* (Baltimore) 8 Mar. 20/2 (*caption*) Strip-teaseuses Betty Coette..and Winnie Garrett. **1942** *Time* 28 Sept. 40/3 Gipsy Rose Lee, stripteuse turned woman of letters. **1951** *Sun* (Baltimore) 27 June 30/3 A blond stripteuse was arrested at a Silver Hill night spot. **1957** *Times Lit. Suppl.* 11 Oct. 611/1 Little Rose Louise was..new to burlesque, and able to gasp at strip-teasing Flossie. **1958** *Listener* 18 Sept. 418/2, I..drove to a night club, where a girl stripteased while lashing a whip. **1960** *News Chron.* 22 Sept. 3/1, I have given up strip-teasing to be with my husband. **1962** *Guardian* 23 Feb. 9/4 A strip-teasing woman. **1977** J. MITFORD *Fine Old Conflict* vii. 118, I was temporarily in despair, hoping against hope that something would turn up. It did, in the shape of a former stripteaseuse whom I had met at a PW party.

strip-teaser. orig. *U.S.* [f. STRIP *v.*¹ + TEASER¹ 2 g.] A performer of strip-tease; an ecdysiast or stripper.

1930 *Variety* 26 Nov. 40/2 The main b[ox] o[ffice] lure is the girls, those known as 'strip teasers'. **1935** E. E. CUMMINGS *Let.* 29 Jan. (1969) 135, I recommend the Irving Place Burlesk (stripteasers in excelsis). **1952** *Chambers's Jrnl.* Feb. 71/1 There was not a pinpoint of light anywhere, not a glimmer from the long line of caravans parked round the square, where the Parisian Strip-teasers slept beside their watchful mothers. **1960** *News Chron.* 25 Feb. 5/8 They got Trixie Kent, our strip-teaser, to autograph one or two scraps of clothing. **1982** *Washington Post* 22 Jan. (Weekend section) 47/1 Despite its new soigné image, the essential pulse of Baltimore remains the rhythmic tic-toc of a stripteaser's tassels.

[**stripulose:** error in Dicts. for STUPULOSE.]

stripy ('straɪpɪ), *a.* [f. STRIPE *sb.*³ + -Y.] Having, marked with, or suggestive of stripes or bands of colour.

1513 *MS. P.R.O. Papers 5 Hen. VIII*, No. 4101 Itm' a standing bedde of dornix strypy. **1847** LEITCH tr. *C. O. Müller's Anc. Art* §324. 328 The undulated and stripy nature of light. **1891** M. MURIEL DOWIE *Girl in Karp.* ii. 12 There was a flutter of shutters and stripey awnings upon them. **1898** KIPLING *Day's Work* 107 His tiger..is supposed to be a clouded animal—not stripy, but blotchy.

strit (strɪt), *v. Obs.* exc. *dial.* [? Altered form of STRUT *v.*] *intr.* To walk proudly, strut.

1597 BP. HALL *Sat.* III. vii. 25 Yet for all that, how stifly strits he by, All trapped in the new-found brauerie. **1657** G. THORNLEY *Daphnis & Chloe* 100 The Goats stritting along with the Sheep. *Ibid.* 152. **1881** *Leicestersh. Gloss.*

strit, obs. 3rd pers. sing. of STRIDE *v.*

stritch¹ (strɪtʃ). *Obs.* exc. *dial.* Also 5 **stryche.** [? Shortened from *stritchel*: see STRICKLE *sb.*]

1. = STRICKLE *sb.* 1.

14.. *Lat.-Eng. Voc.* in Wr.-Wülcker 588/13 *Hostorium*, a stryche. **1825** JENNINGS *Observ. Dial. W. Eng.* 73 *Stritch*, a strickle: a piece of wood used for striking off the overplus from a corn measure.

2. = STRICK *sb.* 1, STRIKE *sb.* 4.

14.. *Lat.-Eng. Voc.* in Wr.-Wülcker 593/9 *Linipulus*, a streche of flaxe.

stritch² (strɪtʃ). [Origin uncertain.] Also **strich.** A musical instrument resembling a straightened alto saxophone. (Chiefly associated with the American jazz musician Roland Kirk, b. 1936.)

1960 *Downbeat* 4 Aug. 13/1 Kirk haunted music stores, examined all kinds of antique instruments, many of them remnants of the 19th century... When he found what he was looking for..they weren't saxophones at all... One was a stritch, the other a manzello. **1962**, etc. [see MANZELLO]. **1969** *Punch* 12 Mar. 393/2 The manzello and strich..sound fine as solo instruments or as sudden quasi-orchestral interludes in a tenor solo. **1977** *Time* 19 Dec. 53/1 Kirk played the manzello (a quasi-saxophone), the stritch (a horn resembling a dented blunderbuss) and the tenor sax together.

†**strite.** *Anglo-Irish. Obs.* Also 7 **streite, streyte.** [Perh. a form of STRAIT *sb.*] Some contrivance for intercepting fish in a river.

1537 *Ir. Act 28 Hen. VIII*, c. 22 (1621) 168 Divers wilful persons..have in divers places of the said rivers [Barrow, etc.] and waters made weres, purprestures, ingines, strites [1678 streites] and other obstacles... It shall be lawfull..to ....breake..all and everie such weres,..streytes and [etc.].

†**strithe.** *Obs.* In 4 **stryþ(þ)e.** [? A dial. form of STRIDE *sb.*, influenced by Scandinavian habits of articulation.] = STRIDE *sb.*

13.. *Gaw. & Gr. Knt.* 846 Sturne stif on þe stryþþe on stalworth schonkez. *Ibid.* 2305 þenne tas he hym stryþe to stryke, & frounses boþe lyppe & browe.

†**strivable**, *a. Obs. rare.* [a. OF. *estrivable*, f. *estriver*: see STRIVE *v.* and -ABLE.] Open to dispute, disputable.

c **1456** PECOCK *Bk. Faith* (1909) 187 The lay peple of the newe lawe is bound..for to receyve her feith..in ech doutable and strivable poynt therof.

strive (straɪv), *v.* Pa. t. **strove** (strəʊv), pa. pple. **striven** ('strɪv(ə)n). Forms: 3-8 **stryve**, 4 **strijf, strivi, striwe**, 4-5 **stryf**, 4, 6 **strif**, 4-6 **stryfe**, 4-7 **strife**, 5 **stryff**, 5-6 **stryffe**, 5-7 **strywe**, 7 **strivve**, 3- **strive**. *Pa. t.* α. *weak forms* 3 **strivede**, 3-9 **strived**, 4 **stryvede**, 6 **strivde, stryved**, *Sc.* **stryvit**, 7 **strivd**. β. *strong forms* 3-5 **strof**, 4 **stroove**, 4-5 **stroof**, 8 **struive**, 9 *dial.* **struv**, 4- **strove**; 4 **straff**, 4-6 *Sc.* **strafe, straif**, 5 *Sc.* **straiff**, 5-9 **strave**, 6 *Sc.* **straiv, straw(e**; also *pl.* 4-5 **stryue (i), streven.** *Pa. pple.* α. *weak forms* 4 **ystrived**, 4-9 **strived**. β. *strong forms* 4 **streven, -yn, strivin, stryve, stryven**, *Sc.* **strewine, striwine, -yn, strifine**, 6 **strevin**, 6-7 **stroven**, 7-9 **strove**, 7 **strivve**, 4- **striven**. [ME. *strīve-n* (13th c.), a. OF. *estriver* (early mod.F. *étriver*: still preserved in some dialects), to quarrel, contend: of disputed origin.

The verb is not found outside Fr., the alleged Pr. *estribar* cited by etymologists having no existence. It is commonly believed to be of Teut. etymology. According to some scholars, OF. *estriver* is f. *estrif* (whence STRIFE *sb.*), which is regarded as a modification of the older OF. (and Pr.) *estrit*, (= OIt. *strido, strio*), a. OTeut. **strīdo-* strife, combat, related to **strīdan* to fight: see STRIDE *v.* According to others, the OF. verb (of which, on this view, the sb. *estrif* is a derivative) is a. OTeut. **strīban* str. vb. (Mid. G. *strîben*, early mod.Du. *strijven*, though these are prob. of secondary origin), f. root **strīb-*, of which the ablaut-variant **strĭb-* is represented by the weak verb MLG. *streven* (mod. LG. *strewen*), (M)Du. *straven*, MHG., mod.G. *streben*, to endeavour, struggle (= sense 9 below), also (from LG.) Sw. *sträfva*, Da. *stræbe*. Both explanations present some unsolved difficulties; the former is more satisfactory with regard to sense, but the notions of 'conflict' and 'endeavour' easily pass the one into the other.

The strong conjugation (on the analogy of *drive* etc.) is found somewhat earlier than the weak conjugation which would be normal for a verb adopted from Fr., and has always been the more frequent of the two, though many examples of *strived* pa. t. and pa. pple. occur in writers of every period from the 14th to the 19th c. The Bible of 1611 has always *strove* in the pa. t.; the pa. pple. is *strived, striven* (one example each). The irregular pa. pple. *strove* (after the pa. t.; cf. the form *stroven* of the 16-17th c.) appears first in the 17th c., and remained somewhat common down to the middle of the 19th c., but is now confined to illiterate use.]

1. *intr.* To be in a state of variance or mutual hostility. ? *Obs.*

a **1225** *Ancr. R.* 84 þus ha beoð bisie i þisse fule mester, & eiðer mid oðer striueð her abuten. **1297** R. GLOUC. (Rolls) 623 þe king mi3te segge þat in a luþer time he striuede wiþ his wiue. **1338** R. BRUNNE *Chron.* (1810) 293 With his barons he striued, with him wild non go. A kyng þat striues with hise, he may not wele spede. **1340** HAMPOLE *Pr. Consc.* 1470 Now lofe we, now hate, now saghtel, now strife. **1340** *Ayenb.* 154 Vor þe scele ssel by ase a trewe arbytres be-tuene þþe goste and þe ulesse þet byeþ alneway striuinde. *c* **1386** CHAUCER *Sompn. T.* 278 And therfore Thomas, trowe me if thee leste, Ne stryue nat with thy wyf, as for thy beste. **1508** DUNBAR *Tua Mariit Wemen* 59 It is agane the law of luif, of kynd, and of nature, Togiddir hairtis to streine, that stryveis with vther. **1540** PALSGR. *Acolastus* IV. iv. T iv, We shal not fyghte herefore .i. we will not fall at bate or stryue for this matter, or here aboute. *a* **1628** LD. BROOKE *Of Humane Learning* cxxxiii. Poems (1633) 48 For earth, and earthynesse it is alone, Which envies, strifes, hates, or is malecontent. **1829** SCOTT *Anne of G.* xxxii, They say you cannot live in Rome and strive with the Pope.

2. To quarrel, wrangle. Now *rare* (*poet.*).

c **1290** *Infancy Jesus* 883-5 in Horstm. *Altengl. Leg.* (1875) 31 þis children bi gonne for to striue, And ech oþur þrettnede swiþe; So longue huy striueden with wicke mod, þþat euerech oþur vuele smot. **13..** *Solomon's Coronation* etc. 38 in *A. Davy's Dream* (E.E.T.S.) 97 3erne þai striueden & chid. **1382** WYCLIF *Lev.* xxiv. 10 A sone..of a womman of Yrael..hath streuen [Vulg. *jurgatus est*] in tentis with a man of Yrael. *a* **1450** *Knt. de la Tour* 126 The doughter of a senatour of Rome, that had so cruell hert that she straue & chidde in the plaine strete wit her neyghboures. **1461** *Paston Lett.* II. 42 It is talkyd here how that ye and Howard schuld a' strevyn togueder on the scher daye, and on of Howards men schuld a' strekyn yow twyess with a dagere. *a* **1533** BERNERS *Huon* lxxxiii. 262, I began to stryue with my brother so hyely that Gybouars myght here me. **1860** TENNYSON *Sea Dreams* 222 And still they strove and wrangled.

†**b.** To bandy words with a superior; to behave mutinously. Const. *with, against. Obs.*

1387 TREVISA *Higden* (Rolls) II. 323 þis is þe womman of Ethiopia for þe whiche Mary and Aaron stryue [L. *jurgati sunt*] with Moyses in desert. *c* **1400** *Rule St. Benet* iii. 7 þat nan folu þair ahen wille, ne nan bare þaim sua he3e, þat tay striue ogain þair abes. *c* **1430** *Diatorie* 52 in *Babees Bk.* (1868) 58 First with þi bettir be waar for to stryue. *c* **1440** *Alphabet of Tales* 153 þou sall se me correcte þis ill servand, && teche hym rather to be meke & speke fayr, þan for to flite or strife with his maister. *c* **1450** *Bk. Curtasye* 226 in *Babees Bk.* 305 Also, my chylde, a-gaynes þy lorde Loke þou stryfe with no kyn worde.

3. To contend, carry on a conflict of any kind; *esp.* to contend with another or each other *for* (the possession of) something or *for* (a cause or principle).

c **1290** *Beket* 1544 in *S. Eng. Leg.* 150 In þe churche of Caunterburi me þou3te i stod..And striuede for holi churche a3en þe kinge and his. *c* **1374** CHAUCER *Boeth.* II. pr. ii. (1868) 33 Stryf or plete wiþ me [L. *mecum contende*] by fore what iuge þat þou wilt of þe possessioun of rycchesse or of dignites. *c* **1375** *Sc. Leg. Saints* xxxvi. (*Baptista*) 720 We wil nocht for dignite strewe, ne quha sal gretare be. **1390** GOWER *Conf.* I. 334 For this thei tellen that ben wise, Wicke is to stryve and have the werse. *c* **1450** tr. *De Imitatione* III. iii. 66 Oþerwiles men striuen for o. peny ri3t shamfully. *c* **1485** *Digby Myst.* III. 1997 Than why shold I with my consyens st[r]yffe? **1530** PALSGR. 740/2, I stryve to gette an offyce that gothe by electyon, *je estrive*. **1567** R. BIRREL *Diary* (1798) 13 At this Parliament, the tounes of Dundie and Perth strave for the 2^d^ place amongst the burrowes. **1609** SIR J. HARINGTON *Nugæ Ant.* (1804) II. 258 There it seemes also the colledges strave for him, he removed so oft. **1626** [FEATLEY] *Pelagius Rediv.* To Rdr. A 2 b, The Doctrine so much strouen for, and so highly extolled by some, is it nothing but olde heresie new furbished ouer? **1697** DRYDEN *Virg. Georg.* IV. 93 If intestine Broils allarm the Hive, (For two Pretenders oft for Empire strive) The Vulgar in divided Factions jar. **1847** SARAH AUSTIN *Ranke's Hist. Ref.* III. 281 The old and bitter enemies with whom they had so long striven. **1905** J. B. BURY *St. Patrick* vi. 108 The story has a sequel which tells how Patrick strove with the other enchanter.

b. To fight against temptation or the like; to wage spiritual warfare.

c **1375** *Sc. Leg. Saints* xxxvi. (*Baptista*) 470 þe thrid is crone þat sal be giffine to marteris at here has wele striwine. **1399** LANGL. *R. Redeles* Prol. 82 þe story is of non estate þat stryuen with her lustus. **1598** SYLVESTER *Du Bartas* I. i. 769 While Jesus strove with Sathan's strong Temptations. *a* **1716** SOUTH *Serm.* (1727) VI. 314 It is the tempted Person's Duty..to fence, and strive, and oppose the Temptation with all his Art, as well as Resolution, that he can. **1816** J. WILSON *City of Plague* I. iii. 211 In vain I strove Against the Tempter. **1816** SCOTT *Old Mort.* xlii, Did ye never sleep in the same room wi' him, and hear him strive in his dreams with the delusions of Satan?

c. With cognate object. *rare.*

c **1375** *Sc. Leg. Saints* xxvii. (*Machor*) 1514 My strife I haf weile strifine. **1833** TENNYSON *Two Voices* 130 Waiting to strive a happy strife, To war with falsehood to the knife.

d. To struggle *with* disease or suffering.

1666 G. HARVEY *Morbus Angl.* xxxii. (1672) 101 Forestus knew another woman that strove eight years with a Consumption. **1686** tr. *Chardin's Trav. Persia* 18 M. de la Haye..strove with his distemper, and took a journey to Adrianople. **1786** BURNS *To Mountain Daisy* viii, Such fate to suffering worth is giv'n, Who long with wants and woes has striv'n.

†**e.** To struggle *with* hindrances. Const. *to* with *inf.* (Cf. sense 9.)

1594 SHAKS. *Rich. III*, v. iii. 104 Ile striue with troubled noise [*So* Ff; Qo. 1597 *and mod. edd.* thoughts], to take a Nap.

f. Of things: To be mutually opposed in action; to come into conflict *with*.

1387 TREVISA *Higden* (Rolls) I. 315 The fuyre..stryueþ wiþ þe ayer. *c* **1425** *Cast. Perseverance* 64 Envye, a-geyn Charyte strywyth ful ryth. **1560** DAUS tr. *Sleidane's Comm.* 63 This request is full of violence and robbery and striveth [L. *pugnat*] with the Gospell. **1592** KYD *Sp. Trag.* III. i. 8 So striueth not the waues with sundry winds. **1596** DALRYMPLE tr. *Leslie's Hist. Scot.* I. 1. 59 It swallyis vp hail schipis, and throuch the violence..of contrare workeng of the wais of the sey, quhen ilke streme stryues with vthir, droumes thame in the deip. *a* **1668** DENHAM *On Earl of Strafford's Trial & Death* 17 Now private pity strove with publick hate, Reason with Rage, and Eloquence with Fate.

†**4.** To contend in arms, fight *with*. *Obs.*

13.. *K. Alis.* 2870 How they stryveden for the kynriche. **1338** R. BRUNNE *Chron.* (1810) 40 For so hette S. Dunstan, he suld alle his lyue With werre his lond welde, & with his suerd stryve. **1340–70** *Alisaunder* 289 Philip enforceth hym now his folk for to gie;..Many mightfull menne made hee stryue. *c* **1400** *Destr. Troy* 3323 Your wille I moste wirke,..Syn weikenes of wemen may not wele stryve, Ne haue no might tawardes men maistries to fend. *c* **1470** *Gol. & Gaw.* 353 Wondir staluart and strang to striue in ane stour. **1470–85** MALORY *Arthur* Contents 10 How a knyght & a dwarf stroof for a lady. **1598** BASTARD *Chrestol.* VII. xlv. 183 Sakellus died striuing for the wall. *a* **1609** SIR F. VERE *Comm.* (1657) 38 Whilest it was hard stroven and fought on that side, I sent a Captain..to see what guard was held along the wall toward the Bay-ward. **1609** HOLLAND *Amm. Marcell.* 418 The Germans strove againe for their parts with the like obstinate resolution. **1697** DRYDEN *Æneis* XII. 57 Twice vanquish'd, while in bloody Fields we strive, Scarce in our Walls, we keep our Hopes alive. **1706** PRIOR *Ode to Queen* xxix, There Fleets shall strive by Winds and Waters tost.

†**5.** To contend in words, dispute. Chiefly followed by dependent question. *Obs.*

1320–30 *Horn Childe* in Ritson *Metr. Rom.* III. 306 Anon thai gun to strive rathe, Whether of hem him schuld have To duelle in her meinè. *c* **1325** *Metr. Hom.* 48 Wit sain Jon gan thai to strife, And said [etc.]. **138.** WYCLIF *Sel. Wks.* II. 147 Jewis and disciplis of Joon strooven. **1382** —— *Jude* i. 9 When Mychael,..disputinge with the deuel, stroof [Vulg. *altercaretur*] of Moyses body. *c* **1425** *Eng. Conquest Irel.* (1896) 32 Heruy..& Reymond vp dyuers domes strouen what men shold do wyth har pryson[er]s. **1471** CAXTON *Recuyell* (Sommer) 34 They argued and stroof to gyder that oon ayenst that other often tymes of this mater. **1535** COVERDALE *Job* xxxii. 1 So these thre men wolde stryue nomore with Iob, because he helde himself a rightuous man. **1567** *Gude & Godlie Ball.* 43 For cause thay knew him to depart, Thay straif quha suld be ouerest. **1600** HAKLUYT *Voy.* III. 438 Saying that they had strouen together who should haue him to his house.

†**b.** To debate, discuss. *Obs.*

a **1300** *Cursor M.* 13589 Þaa phariseus..Quen þai had striued þam emel..cuth na resun find, þai did þan bring again þat blind. **1340** *Ayenb.* 164 Þanne salomon huanne he hedde..of alle þinges and of foles and of wyse y-striued he zayde [etc.]. *c* **1350** *Will. Palerne* 4099 My wyf..striued stifli with hire-self as stepmoderes wol alle, bi what wise sche mi3t best þat bold barn spille.

†**c.** To cavil, dispute. Const. *of*. *Obs.*

13.. *Seuyn Sag.* 1850 Go forth and strif nowt therof. **1541** R. COPLAND *Galyen's Terap.* 2 C j b, It behoueth nat than thus miserably to stryue of the names. **1549** COVERDALE etc. *Erasm. Par. 1 Cor.* Argt. 1 b, Finallye they stryued among them selues of matrimonye, by reason that euen at that tyme some christian men styflye defended, that men should wholy abstayne from mariage.

†**6.** To contend in rivalry; to seek to surpass another or each other; to compete in a trial of strength or skill. Also *to strive a vie* (see A-VIE *adv.*). *Obs.*

c **1450** *St. Cuthbert* (Surtees) 732 Þai straue wha first to lande myght wynne. **1509** [see A-VIE *adv.*]. **1538** STARKEY *England* I. iii. 92 Euery towne semyd to me to stryue wyth other, as hyt had byn for a vyctory, wych schold be more beutyful & strong. **1586** LUPTON *1000 Notable Things* (1660) 75 A man..with swift running contended and strived with Dogs, and was hunted of them unhurt in the Woods. **1609** HOLLAND *Amm. Marcell.* XXVIII. viii. 339 They run all at once striving a vie who shall be formost. [Holland often uses the phrase.] *a* **1610** HEYWOOD & ROWLEY *Fortune by Land & Sea* III. iv, *Fost.* I have no money. *Phil.* But now you strived which man would lend me most. **1615** CHAPMAN *Odyss.* VIII. 179 When all had striu'd in these assaies their fill. **1619** SIR A. GORGES tr. *Bacon's Wisdom Anc.* xxvi. 124 Certaine games of Lampbearers, in which they that striued for the prize were wont to carie torches lighted. **1638** MAYNE *Lucian* (1664) 208 [They] smiled when they were rackt, and strived with their Tormentors who should be first tired. **1644** [see A-VIE *adv.*]. **1648** GAGE *West Ind.* 14 The Galley slaves strived who should sound their Waits and Trumpets most joyfully. **1697** DRYDEN *Virg. Georg.* III. 28 The Rival Chariots in the Race shall strive. **1725** POPE *Odyss.* IV. 241 There with commutual zeal we both had strove, In acts of dear benevolence, and love.

fig. **1605** SHAKS. *Lear* IV. iii. 18 Patience and sorrow strove [*So Pope and later edd.*; Qq. streme] Who should express her goodliest. **1636** BRATHWAIT *Rom. Emp.* 372 All vertues in him contentiously strived to imbellish him. *a* **1700** KEN *Hymnotheo* Poet. Wks. 1721 III. 318 The bowing Fruits strove which should first be crop'd.

†**b.** Const. *to* with inf. *Obs.* (cf. sense 9).

1520 BARCLAY *Sallust, Batt. Jugurth* liv. (Pynson) 78 b, They stryued [L. *certantes*] to ascende vnto the walles euery man couetyng to be before other. **1634** SIR T. HERBERT *Trav.* 52 The Kettle-drums and other their Iingling Instruments stroue to deafe vs. **1638** MAYNE *Lucian* (1664) 140 But when the fame of the Oracle once pierced Italy, and arrived at Rome, every one strived to be first.

†**c.** To vie, to be equal or comparable *with*.

a **1225** *Ancr. R.* 398 Asaeles swiftschipe, þet strof wið heortes ouervrn. *c* **1386** CHAUCER *Knt.'s T.* 180 That Emelye, þat fairer was to sene Than is the lylie..For with the Rose colour stroof hire hewe. **1509** [see A-VIE *adv.*]. **1540** PALSGR. *Acolastus* II. iii. M ij b, Holde or take this money, and prepare vs a supper, that may stryue with a pontifycal or bishops feaste. **1597** GERARDE *Herbal* I. xxxv. 50 The roote ..strieueth with the Florentine Iris in sweetnes. **1667** MILTON *P.L.* IV. 273 Nor that sweet Grove Of Daphne by Orontes..might with this Paradise Of Eden strive. **1697** DRYDEN *Æneis* v. 326 The Victor honour'd with a nobler Vest: Where Gold and Purple strive in equal Rows. **1700** —— *Meleager & Atalanta* 28 For Tusks with Indian Elephants he [the boar] strove.

7. To offer obstinate resistance, struggle *against*.

a **1300** *Cursor M.* 9306 For efter þat i es o-liue, Gains soth sal your eires striue. *c* **1300** *Havelok* 2271 Þer-yen ne wolde neuer on striue, þat he ne maden sone þat oth. **1362** LANGL. *P. Pl.* A. VII. 305 While Hunger was mayster heer wolde ther non chyde, Ne striue a3eyn the statutes. *c* **1400** tr. *Secreta Secret., Gov. Lordsh.* 41 No-þer ys non of hool mynde þat may stryf a3eyn þis sentence. **1500–20** DUNBAR *Poems* xxxv. 14 Thow suffer me to wirk gif thow do weill, And preiss the nocht to stryfe aganis my quheill, Quhilk every warldly thing dois turne and steir. **1530** PALSGR. 740/2 Thou stryvest agaynst a thyng that is evydent. **1560** DAUS tr. *Sleidane's Comm.* 136 b, They did not chaunge him wholy, which strove and defended his opinions stifly [L. *reluctantem suaque defendentem*]. **1597** BEARD *Theatre God's Judgem.* (1612) 66 The wonderfull judgements which the king of kings hath sent vpon those that..resisted and stroue against the truth. **1606** G. W[OODCOCKE] *Hist. Ivstine* IV. 22 Amongst the rest of these Tyrants, there was..one that striued against the cruelty of all the rest in the execution of Iustice. *c* **1709** PRIOR *2nd Hymn Callim.* 33 Against the Deity 'tis hard to strive. **1760–72** H. BROOKE *Fool of Qual.* (1809) II. 95 Vainly have I strove and struggled against you. **1858** H. SPENCER *Ess.* I. 308 The thing I desperately strove against as a misfortune did me immense good.

†**b.** with negative inf.

1623 BINGHAM *Xenophon* 101 Boiscus the Bœotian wrestler striued then, all he could, vnder pretence of sicknesse, not to carie his Target.

8. To struggle physically. *Obs.* exc. *dial.* of a horse: To be restive.

1398 TREVISA *Barth. De P.R.* XVIII. xv. (1495) 775 Whan the wylde oxe hath longe stryue and maye not delyuer hymself out of the bondes..thenne for indignacion he loowyth full lowde. **1561** T. HOBY tr. *Castiglione's Courtyer* III. (1577) Q ij b, And when she strived still more obstinatlye, at length with manye blowes and by force ouercame hir. **1562** T. COOPER *Answ. Def. Truth* xi. 83 The Deacon woulde not suffer so muche as the litle Infant to go without some parte [of the sacrament]: althoughe she striued against him, and scantely coulde force hir to take it. **1567** TURBERV. *Epit.* etc. 34 The Nymph..in hir armes the naked Noorie strainde: Whereat the Boy began to striue a good, But strugling nought auailed in that plight. **1645** GATAKER *God's Eye on Israel* 21 New named, and in stead of Jacob styled Israel, by the Angel, whom he had so strived and struggled with, at their parting. **1671** MILTON *P.R.* IV. 564 As when Earths Son Antæus..in Irassa strove With Joves Alcides. *a* **1824** *Ld. T. Stuart* xi. in Maidment *N.C. Garland* 3 The steeds they strave into [= in] their stables, The boys couldn't get them bound.

b. To struggle, endeavour to make one's way, against a natural force, e.g. winds, waves. Const. *with*, *against*.

The fig. phrase to *strive against the stream* (see STREAM *sb.* 2 f) is perh. imitated from German: see quot. 1535 below.

a **1300** *Cursor M.* 24855 Quen þai had striuen ai quils þai moght, again þat storm al was for noght. **1535** COVERDALE *Ecclus.* iv. 26 Withstande not yᵉ face of the mightie, and stryue not agaynst the streame [Luther *strebe nicht wider den Strom*]. **1537** CROMWELL in Merriman *Life & Lett.* (1902) II. 75 He that maketh you thus to stryve agenst the streame woll [etc.]. **1559** *Mirr. Mag., Dk. Glocester* xiv, To bridell the Prince of a Reame, Is euen..to striue with the streame. **1630** R. N. *Camden's Hist. Eliz.* I. 38 The Marquesse of Albeuf..hauing striued with the violence of a tempest vpon the coast of Holland, was with the losse of some shippes.. driuen back to Diepe. **1697** DRYDEN *Æneis* v. 37 We strive in vain against the Seas, and Wind.

9. To endeavour vigorously, use strenuous effort. Const. *to* with *inf.* (Cf. sense 6 b.).

Now the prevailing sense; the other senses, so far as they survive, are usually coloured by this.

a **1300** *Cursor M.* 11569 All for noght can he [*sc.* Herod] to striue, Might he noght iesu bring o liue. **1382** WYCLIF *2 Cor.* v. 9 And therfore we stryuen [Vulg. *contendimus*] whether absent, whether present, for to plese him. *a* **1547** SURREY *Eccles.* ii. 12 By princely actes thus straue I still, to make my fame indure. **1576** GASCOIGNE *Steele Gl.* Wks. 1910 II. 145, I..Gan cleere my throte, and strave to sing my best. **1582** BRETON *Flourish upon Fancy* (Grosart) 52/2 Although he striu'de, and tooke great pains, asmuch as in him lay. **1613** SHAKS. *Hen. VIII*, II. iv. 30 Which of your Friends Haue I not stroue to loue, although I knew He were mine Enemy? **1638** W. LISLE *Heliodorus* x. 181 Sith I cannot free you, though I strivve, Aske what I may doe for you, whilst you liue, And I shall grant it. **1643** SIR T. BROWNE *Relig. Med.* I. §19. 45 He striv'd to undermine the edifice of my faith. **1697** DRYDEN *Virg. Georg.* III. 574 Stags..strive in vain to make their way Through Hills of Snow, and pitifully bray. **1780** COWPER *Progr. Error* 582 Habits are soon assum'd; but when we strive To strip them off, 'tis being flay'd alive. **1821** SCOTT *Kenilw.* xxxix, Having strove in vain to restore it [the casket] either to Tressilian or the Countess. **1831** T. HOPE *Ess. Orig. Man* I. 34 This is what I have at least strived to do. I have tried to discard all preconceived opinions. **1843** LYTTON *Last Bar.* I. iv. 27 He strove to lift himself from the ground, and at length succeeded. **1848** DICKENS *Dombey* liii, It is our pride, not our trouble, to strive, John, and to strive together. **1865** RUSKIN *Sesame* ii. §72 She is to be taught to strive that her thoughts of piety may not be feeble in proportion to the number they embrace. **1880** MAHAFFY *Descartes* ii. 12 He ever strove to keep on good terms with the Order [of Jesuits]. **1885** 'MRS. ALEXANDER' *At Bay* viii, Her voice trembled; she strove to keep her self-control.

b. *transf.* of things.

a **1586** SIDNEY *Arcadia* II. x. (1912) 207 With that he groned, as if sorrow strave to breake his harte. **1597** DONNE *Lett. Ser. Pers., Storme* 60 Even our Ordinance plac'd for our defence, Strive to breake loose. **1598** BRANDON *Octavia* III. C 8 b, Looke how some proude hard harted mighty rocke ..Repell's the waters..Which mildely striue his body to imbrace. **1607** TOPSELL *Four-f. Beasts* 184 As if nature had only strouen to prouide sundry ready cures for this euill aboue all other. **1851** RUSKIN *Stones Ven.* (1874) I. Pref. p. vi, Modern Art is now striving to realize the promise of its poet. **1874** GREEN *Short Hist.* vi. §3. 294 A series of mercantile enactments strove to protect the growing interests of English commerce.

c. Const. *after*, *for*, †*to*, †*unto* (the object to be attained).

a **1300** *Cursor M.* 23571 Quar-to þan suld we for-þer striue, þan for to liue in santes liue? *a* **1591** H. SMITH *Serm.* (1594) 411 This is the state that a Christian should striue too, and neuer thinke that hee is sound at the heart til his thoughts be a kind of prayer. **1594** HOOKER *Eccl. Pol.* I. v. §2 The immutabilitie of God they [*sc.* all things] striue vnto, by working..after one and the same maner. **1605** A. WARREN *Poor Man's Pass.* C 2 b, Then Diuision striued for a store, To marre what golden Age had made before. **1849** LYTTON *K. Arthur* x. lxi, Thrice strove the King for speech, and thrice in vain. **1850** TENNYSON *In Mem.* li, He for whose applause I strove. **1856** MISS YONGE *Daisy Chain* I. xxvi, If I had striven for the temper, it would be worth having, but it is my nature. **1877** C. GEIKIE *Christ* lvi. (1879) 678 The priesthood had striven after kingly power and rank.

10. To make one's way with effort.

a **1586** SIDNEY *Arcadia* I. xv. §2 Now she brought them to see a seeled Dove, who, the blinder she was, the higher she strave. **1590** SPENSER *F.Q.* III. i. 18 But after the foule foster Timias did striue. **1813** BYRON *Corsair* III. xix, He..Strives through the surge, bestrides the beach, and high Ascends the path familiar to his eye. **1874** CARPENTER *Ment. Phys.* I. ix. 412 Ever striving upwards, so as..to reach..a still loftier elevation.

†**b.** Of a thing: To force its way. *Obs.*

1697 DRYDEN *Æneis* x. 1160 The purple Streams thro' the thin Armour strove, And drench'd th' imbroider'd Coat his Mother wove.

strive, obs. form of STRIFE.

†**strived,** *ppl. a. Obs.* [f. STRIVE *v.* + -ED[1].] In *strived-for* (nonce-use): see STRIVE *v.* 3.

1615 CHAPMAN *Odyss.* VIII. 633 The striu'd-for, for his worth, of worthy men.

striveling, obs. form of STERLING.

striver ('straɪvə(r)). Also 4 stryfer, 5 stryvar, 5–6 -er. [f. STRIVE *v.* + -ER[1].]

1. One who strives with others; a contender, competitor. †In early use also, one given to strife, a contentious person.

a **1400** *New Test.* (Paues) 1 Cor. xi. 16 3if þer be any of 3ow a stryfer. *c* **1400** tr. *Secreta Secret., Gov. Lordsh.* 115 A full fface..bytokyns a stryuer, a dyscordour. *c* **1440** *Promp. Parv.* 480/1 Stryvar, *litigator, rixator*. **1480** CAXTON *Chron. Eng.* VII. (1520) 81 b/2 Alexandre hadde stryfe 17 yere, and the foure stryvers that the Emperour set agaynst hym he overcame them and cursyd them. **1526** *Pilgr. Perf.* (W. de W. 1531) 98 It is not convenyent the seruaunt of god to be a stryuer or a brauler. **1658** J. DURHAM *Expos. Rev.* vii. 9 (1660) 391 The sealed ones were strivers; these are victors, Therefore must succeed them as victory doth to fighting. **1853** LYNCH *Self-Improv.* vi. 152 The case of the striver against Circumstance.

2. One who makes strenuous effort or endeavour.

1562 J. HEYWOOD *Prov. & Epigr.* (1867) 160 He strieuth agaynst the streme, by customs scoole That striuer is either a fishe or a foole. **1828** CARLYLE *Goethe's Helena* Misc. 1840 I. 198 In all his lofty aspirings, his strivings after truth.., it has never struck him to inquire how he, the striver, was warranted for such enterprises. **1865** M. ARNOLD *Ess. Crit., Marc. Aurel.* 275 This truly modern striver and thinker. **1887** *Pall Mall Budget* 27 Jan. 29/1 He was a diligent striver after perfection.

†**3.** ? Used jocularly for: A partner in the dance.

1609 BEAUM. & FL. *Scornf. Lady* II. (1616) D 2, Take thy striuer, and pace her till shee stew. *Sa.* Sure Sir, I cannot daunce with your Gentlewoman.

striviling, obs. form of STERLING *sb.*[1]

striving ('straɪvɪŋ), *vbl. sb.* [-ING[1].] The action of the verb STRIVE; an instance of this.

c **1205** LAY. 15561 Vmben ane stunde heo bigunnen striuinge. *c* **1290** *St. James* 284 in *S. Eng. Leg.* 42 Bi-twene þe fader and þe sone þe striuingue laste longue. *c* **1380** WYCLIF *Sel. Wks.* II. 250 Batailis and stryvyngis in plee shulden be forsaken of Cristene men. *a* **1425** tr. *Arderne's Treat. Fistula*, etc. 83 And forþi realgre is called of som men rede auripigment: of þe namez is no stryuyng so þat we vnderstond þe þingz. **1535** COVERDALE *Ps.* xvii[i]. 43 Thou shalt delyuer me from the stryuinges of the people. **1615** CHAPMAN *Odyss.* IV. 558 Hold him there, In spite of all his striuings to be gone. **1677** YARRANTON *Eng. Improv.* 13 When ever they give Notice they will take up a Sum of Moneys, there is great striving who can get in his first. **1718** ROWE *Lucan* VII. 513 The great deciding Hour at length is come, To end the Strivings of distracted Rome. **1851** MRS. BROWNING *Casa Guidi Wind.* II. 211 The fervid striving of the games. **1871** R. H. HUTTON *Ess.* II. 4 My ideas and higher strivings.

'striving, *ppl. a.* [-ING².] That strives (in senses of the verb).

13.. *E.E. Allit. P.* C. 311 þy stryuande stremez of stryndez so mony. *c* **1374** CHAUCER *Boeth.* II. pr. vii. (1868) 59 Somtyme þere was a man þat hadde assaied wiþ striuyng wordes an oþer man. **1530** PALSGR. 326/1 Stryvyng, full of stryfe or debate, *contentieux*. *a* **1566** R. EDWARDS *Damon & Pithias* (facs.) G iij b, Against the wind and striuinge streame I sayle. **1646** MAYNE *Serm. Unity* 20 Who..might have askt the same question which the striving Israelite askt Moses, Who made thee a Judge over us? **1697** DRYDEN *Æneis* I. 637 The striving Artists, and their Arts renown. **1868** NETTLESHIP *Ess. Browning* Introd. 7 The striving philosophy of 'Cleon'.

Hence **'strivingly** *adv.*

1382 WYCLIF *Deut.* xxxi. 27 Euermore stryuyngly ȝe diden [Vulg. *contentiose egistis*] aȝens the Lord. —— *Judg.* ix. 49 Stryuyngly [*certatim*]. **1552** HULOET, Stryuyngly, *rixose, velitatim*. **1563-87** FOXE *A. & M.* (1596) 72/2 The tyrant.. commanded euerie tenth man to be put to the swoord, where-to strivinglie and with great rejoising they committed their necks. **1598** FLORIO, *Agara*, striuingly, contending for the mastrie. **1677** MIÉGE *Dict. Eng.-Fr.*, Strivingly, *a l'envi*. **1890** W. JAMES *Princ. Psychol.* II. xxi. 315 The impulse to take life strivingly is indestructible in the race.

strivling, obs. form of STERLING *sb.*¹

†**'strivous,** *a. Obs. rare*⁻¹. [f. STRIFE *sb.* + -OUS.] Full of strife.

1382 WYCLIF *Jer.* viii. 5 With striuous turnyng awei [Vulg. *aversione contentiosa*]?

stro, obs. form of STRAW *sb.*¹

stroak(e, obs. forms of STROKE *sb.* and *v.*

stroake, obs. pa. t. and pa. pple. of STRIKE *v.*

stroaken, obs. pa. pple. of STRIKE *v.*

stroam, strome (strəʊm), *v. Obs.* exc. *dial.* [? Formed after *stroll* and *roam*.] *intr.* To walk with long strides. Also to wander about idly.

1796 MME. D'ARBLAY *Camilla* I. 174 A young Ensign.. stroamed into the ball-room, with the most visible marks of his unfitness for appearing in it. *Ibid.* II. 195 He..stroamed up and down the room, biting his knuckles. **1817** MAR. EDGEWORTH *Ormond* xiii. T. & N. 1848 IX. 330 One morning our young hero rose early,..and he walked out, or, more properly, he rambled, or he strolled, or *stroamed out*. *a* **1825** FORBY *Voc. E. Anglia*, *Strome*, to walk with long strides. **1840** SPURDENS *Suppl. to Forby* s.v., To 'stroam about': to wander idly without an object. **1878** S. H. MILLER & SKERTCHLY *Fenland* iii. 89 In Cambridgeshire we find the words—*cloof*, the hoof,..*stroming*, taking long strides.

transf. **1909** A. H. PATTERSON *Man & Nat. Tidal Waters* i. 21 What can lick a Norfolk wherry either for lines or the way she lays afore the wind stroming along.

stroam, variant of STRUM.

stroan, strone (strəʊn), *v. Sc. intr.* To make water, urinate.

a **1730** PENNECUIK etc. *Collect. Sc. Poems* (1756) 58 Te he, ..that's best, And we'll strone fine, among the rest. **1786** BURNS *Twa Dogs* 22 He wad stan't as glad to see him, And stroan't on stanes an' hillocks wi' him. **1890** SERVICE *Thir Notandums* viii. 43 Man, do ye no ken..that on Halloween the deil stroans on the haws?

stroap, Sc. variant of STROUP *sb.* gullet.

strobe (strəʊb), *a.* and *sb.* [f. first syllable of STROBOSCOPIC *a.* and related words.]

A. *adj.* **1.** = STROBOSCOPIC *a.*

1942 *Amer. Cinematographer* Sept. 422/3 Adjust the speed of the projector until the bars on the 'strobe' band corresponding to the number of blades in the projector shutter appear to stand still. **1949** H. LURAY *Strobe* viii. 110 (*caption*) A classic strobe shot. Drop of milk splashing on a plate covered by a thin layer of milk. **1962** *Amer. Jrnl. Physics* XXX. 925/2 Strobe photography is an area that has not been saturated at science fairs. **1966** *McGraw-Hill Encycl. Sci. & Technol.* XIII. 187/1 Stroboscopic or 'strobe' photography is generally understood to refer to pictures of both single and multiple exposure taken by flashes of light from electrical discharges. **1978** *Oceans* May-June 39/1 Flash bulbs or strobe (electronic flash) lighting is often used to restore lost colors and provide light for an exposure.

2. Special collocations: *strobe disc*, a disc with alternate light and dark sectors of equal size for checking the speed of rotation of something, its appearance being steady only when this speed is related in a definite way to the periodicity of the illumination; *strobe lamp, light*, an electric light that can be made to flash on and off rapidly and automatically; also (*U.S.*), an electronic flash for a camera; so *strobe-lighted, -lit* adjs.; *strobe pulse* (Electronics) (see quot. 1971).

1942 *Amer. Cinematographer* Sept. 423/1 Check the strobe disc for synchronization. **1967** *Nature* 23 Dec. 1173/1 The correct speed of a gramophone turn-table may be checked by viewing a strobe disk illuminated by electric light supplied by the a.c. mains. **1974** *Sci. Amer.* Aug. 108/3 The solution of the problem of stopping fast action lies in an electronic flash lamp. The duration of most 'strobe' lamps owned by amateurs is about 5 × 10⁻⁴ second, which is sufficiently brief for many events of interest. **1975** *Gramophone* Jan. 1297 (Advt.), Dots on the outer rim of the SR717 illuminated by the built-in strobe lamp. **1962** N. MAXWELL *Witch-Doctor's Apprentice* vi. 68 Augusto helped a lot, lugging the Strobe light and holding his flashlight so that I could check my camera settings. **1971** R. BUSBY *Deadlock* vii. 98 Pulsating strobe lights left Leric with a fragmented picture of girls. **1978** *Sci. Amer.* June 128/1 My best clue came from examining the floating drops under a strobe light set near the frequency of oscillation, so that the flashing light effectively slowed the vibration of the drops. **1979** *Listener* 18 Oct. 517/3 A strobe-lighted production number that sends images flashing around the vast auditorium. **1967** P. WELLES *Babyhip* ii. 36 It's not everyone who can have a strob-lit [*sic*] dream of love. **1972** *Listener* 23 June 845/1 Weird strobe-lit collages. **1946** *Jrnl. Inst. Electr. Engineers* XCIII. IIIA. 318/2 The operator had under his control a variable-range strobe pulse which he could bring into coincidence with the target echo. **1967** *Electronics* 6 Mar. 117/1 (*caption*) The level detector senses the moment when C_{int} reaches zero volts and generates a strobe pulse. **1971** *Gloss. Electrotechnical, Power Terms* (*B.S.I.*) III. vi. 18 *Strobe pulse*, a pulse, of duration less than the period of a recurrent phenomenon, used for scrutinizing a particular epoch of that phenomenon... In radar, a strobe pulse is sometimes made to follow automatically the echo from a moving object.

B. *sb.* **1.** = *strobe disc*, sense A. 2 above.

1942 *Amer. Cinematographer* Sept. 423/1 Watch the strobe for any changes in projector speed.

2. *Electronics.* = *strobe pulse*, sense A. 2 above.

1946 *Jrnl. Inst. Electr. Engineers* XCIII. IIIA. 319/1 In the A.I. Mark IV [radar] equipment, the search was a progressive outward movement of the strobe from zero to maximum range, followed by a rapid fly-back to zero. **1953** *Electronic Engin.* XXV. 191/1 Photographing a C.R.O. trace using a reference waveform as a strobe. **1959** *Ibid.* XXXI. 136/2 The *X* displacement may be dissociated from the phase of the strobe (time scale). **1980** D. G. GREEN *Digital Techniques & Systems* iv. 49 The strobe determines the times at which the *S* and *R* input signals should be effective.

3. a. = *strobe light*, sense A. 2 above. **b.** Stroboscopic photography.

1949 H. LURAY *Strobe* v. 73 You will know which size flash bulb your strobe approximates. *Ibid.* vii. 101 Strobe is used outdoors very much like flash. **1962** *Amer. Jrnl. Physics* XXX. 925/1 The strobe was flashing at three times the frequency of the wave. **1968** J. D. MACDONALD *Pale Grey for Guilt* (1969) xii. 153 Maybe the music got too loud... Maybe it was the strobes. **1975** J. RATHBONE *Kill Cure* II. vi. 48 For one brief moment she saw the man full face, caught in the jerky light of the strobe.

strobe (strəʊb), *v.* [f. prec.]

1. *trans. Electronics.* To gate (GATE *v.*¹ 2 a) by means of a strobe pulse.

1947 *Wireless World* Aug. 290/1 Work was also carried out on 'strobing' a portion of the time base. **1950** [see GATE *v.*¹ 2]. **1981** NASHELSKY & BOYLESTAD *Devices* xi. 391 The output remains high unless strobed.

2. *intr. Cinemat.* and *Television.* To exhibit or give rise to strobing.

1959 HALAS & MANVELL *Technique Film Animation* xix. 232 Fairly light colours do not strobe so much as white. **1965** *Punch* 12 May 684/1 Before my very first TV appearance the studio manager tried to get me to change clothes with him. .. He then explained that the black and white check I was wearing would 'strobe'—an optical illusion whereby the wearer of any pattern containing vertical or horizontal stripes appears to vibrate. **1982** *Observer* 12 Dec. 26/3 Don't blink, don't sniff, don't stick your chin up, don't slouch, don't wave your hands about, don't wear stripes (they 'strobe'), look at the person you're talking to, *smile*.

3. *fig.* (*intr.* and *trans.*) To flash.

1977 R. E. HARRINGTON *Quintain* vi. 53 Possible explanations flashed through his mind..thoughts strobing across his mind. **1980** J. MCNEIL *Spy Game* ix. 103 The fire strobed rosy light onto the burnished yew furniture.

Hence **strobed** *ppl. a.*

1980 D. C. GREEN *Digital Techniques & Systems* iv. 49 A clocked or strobed flip-flop will change only when a clock pulse is received.

strobic ('strɒbɪk), *a.* [a. Gr. type στροβικ-ός, f. στρόβ-ος a twisting or whirling round: see -IC.] That has a spinning motion. *strobic circles*: sets of concentric circles, toothed wheels, and the like, which appear to revolve when the surface on which they are inscribed is moved about.

1880 S. P. THOMPSON in *Brain* III. 293 If two such 'strobic circles' (as I have called them) are printed side by side.

strobil, variant of STROUBLE *v. Obs.*

strobila (strəʊ'baɪlə). *Zool.* Pl. strobilæ (-liː). [mod.L. *strobīla*, a. Gr. στροβίλη plug of lint twisted into the shape of a fir-cone.]

1. A stage in the development of certain Hydrozoa. Also *attrib.*

1842 *Encycl. Brit.* XXI. 1014/2 In a small volume published some years ago, this Swedish naturalist [Sars] described a new genus of Medusides under the name of *Strobila*, from its great similitude to a fir cone; but he now assures us that the Strobila is the young of Medusa aurita. **1857** CARPENTER *Microscope* (ed. 2) 504 Fig. 245 Successive Stages of Development of Medusa-buds from Strobila-larva. *Ibid.* 505 The progenitor of a new colony of Strobilæ. **1861** J. R. GREENE *Man. Anim. Kingd.*, *Cœlent.* 66 Sars.. observing the Scyphistoma at a still later stage,..gave it, from its resemblance to an artichoke, the name of Strobila. **1888** ROLLESTON & JACKSON *Anim. Life* 782 The *Scyphostoma* passes in late autumn into the *Strobila* stage.

2. A segmented tapeworm, consisting of a scolex and a chain of proglottides.

1864 T. S. COBBOLD *Entozoa* 105 Every cestode passes through several distinct phases during its life-history. In the ordinary colonial or tapeworm condition it has been termed the *strobila* (Van Beneden). **1888** ROLLESTON & JACKSON *Anim. Life* 225 The head and neck are often termed 'scolex', the joints, 'proglottides', and the whole Tapeworm, 'strobila'.

strobilaceous (strɒbɪ'leɪʃəs), *a. Bot.* [f. mod.L. *strobilāce-us*, f. STROBIL-US: see -ACEOUS.] Relating to, or resembling, a strobilus.

1802 R. HALL *Elem. Bot.* 183 Strobilaceous, *strobilaceus*, *s. strobiliformis*, having the form of a strobile. **1830** LINDLEY *Nat. Syst. Bot.* 248 The cones of..strobilaceous Cycadeæ.

strobilanthes (strəʊbɪ'lænθiːz). [mod.L. (K. L. Blume *Bijdragen tot de Flora van Nederlandsch Indië* (1826) 781), f. STROBILUS + Gr. ἄνθος flower, in reference to the shape of the young inflorescence.] A herb or subshrub of the genus *Strobilanthes*, belonging to the family Acanthaceæ, native to tropical Asia, and bearing clusters of blue or white tubular flowers.

1836 *Curtis's Bot. Mag.* LXIII. 3517 (*heading*) Mr. Sabine's strobilanthes. **1918** R. N. PARKER *Forest Flora Punjab* 386 In most floras all the Strobilanthes are described as shrubs but I have not found the Punjab species shrubby. **1944** J. CORBETT *Man-Eaters of Kumaon* (1946) 17 A bed of strobilanthes, the bent stalks of which were slowly regaining their upright position, showed where..the tigress had passed. **1979** A. J. HUXLEY *Success with House Plants* 375/1 A strobilanthes cannot tolerate temperatures below about 55°F.

strobilation (strɒbɪ'leɪʃən). *Zool.* [f. STROBIL-A + -ATION. Cf. STROBILIZATION.] The formation of strobilæ in Hydrozoa, tapeworms, etc.

1878 F. J. BELL *Gegenbaur's Comp. Anat.* 99 The strobilation of Scyphostoma and the consequent development of a number of Medusæ. **1881** LANKESTER in *Encycl. Brit.* XII. 553/2 The *Hydromedusæ* never produce medusæ by strobilation or transverse division of a hydriform person. **1896** F. W. GAMBLE *Flatworms* (Camb. Nat. Hist. II.) 76 The strobilation of a scyphistoma.

strobile ('strɒbaɪl, 'strəʊbaɪl, -bɪl). Also 8–9 strobil. [a. F. *strobile* or ad. L. *strobil-us*, Gr. στρόβῑλ-ος STROBILUS, also στροβῑλ-η STROBILA.]

1. *Bot.* = STROBILUS 1.

1777 ROBSON *Brit. Flora* 33 A *strobil* is a pericarpy formed of scales lying over one another, as in Pine or Birch. **1785** MARTYN *Rousseau's Bot.* xxi. (1794) 300 The fruit [of the magnolia] is a strobile or scaly cone of bivalvular capsules. **1836** J. M. GULLY *Magendie's Formul.* (ed. 2) 149 The strobiles of the hop. **1857** HENFREY *Bot.* §126 When the rachis bears large, persistent, imbricated scales, it forms a cone or strobile, as in the Firs and Pines.

2. *Zool.* = STROBILA 2.

1855 T. R. JONES *Anim. Kingd.* (ed. 2) 136 While the segments of the Strobile remain conjoined, they seem to enjoy a complete community of life and of movement. **1864** T. S. COBBOLD *Entozoa* 105 The separate joints of which the strobile is composed are denominated *proglottides* or zooids. **1870** ROLLESTON *Anim. Life* 137 (*Taenia*), The entire colony is called a 'strobile'.

strobiliform (strəʊ'bɪlɪfɔːm), *a. Bot.* [ad. mod.L. *strobiliform-is*, f. STROBIL-US: see -FORM. Cf. F. *strobiliforme*.] Shaped like a strobilus.

1830 LINDLEY *Nat. Syst. Bot.* 310 Cuneate scales.. collected into strobiliform heads. **1853** ROYLE *Mat. Med.* (ed. 2) 672 Spikes..strobiliform, formed of single-flowered, imbricated, acute bracts.

strobiline ('strɒbɪlaɪn), *a. Zool.* and *Bot.* [ad. Gr. στροβίλιν-ος of a fir-cone, f. στρόβῑλ-ος STROBILUS.] Relating to or of the nature of a strobila or strobilus; strobilaceous.

1842 *Encycl. Brit.* XXI. 1014/2 In its strobiline state, it [*Medusa aurita*] is composed of a series of circular pieces, with numerous tentacula, and the cone is surmounted by a cylindrical shaft. **1852-6** WRIGHT *Royal Dict. Cycl.* (1867), *Strobiline*, cone-shaped, growing on the cone of the fir.

strobilization (ˌstrɒbɪlaɪ'zeɪʃən). *Zool.* [f. STROBIL-A + -IZE + -ATION.] = STROBILATION.

1884 A. SEDGWICK & HEATHCOTE tr. *Claus' Zool.* I. 256 At first the *Scyphistoma* appears to multiply only by budding; the second mode of reproduction, the process of strobilization, begins later. **1914** MACBRIDE *Text-Bk. Embryol.* I. 72 By a repetition of the process the Scyphistoma comes to look like a pile of plates, and is called a Strobila. This process is known as strobilization.

strobill, variant of STROUBLE *v. Obs.*

strobiloid ('strɒbɪlɔɪd), *a. Zool.* and *Bot.* [f. STROBIL-A or STROBIL-US + -OID.] Resembling, or of the nature of, a strobila or strobilus.

1865 *Nat. Hist. Rev.* July 345 The *Cestoidea*, in their strobiloid stage, occur only within the alimentary canal. **1887** SOLLAS in *Encycl. Brit.* XXII. 415/1 (*Sponges*), Ascon type: simple, ex. *Ascetta*, Hk.; strobiloid, ex. *Homoderma*, Ldf. **1893** BOWER in *Phil. Trans.* B. CLXXXV. 493 The Lycopodineæ and Equisetineæ are strobiloid types. *Ibid.*, These strobiloid Pteridophyta.

strobilus (strəʊ'baɪləs). Pl. strobili (-laɪ). [a. L. *strobīlus* fir-cone, a. Gr. στρόβῑλος anything twisted up, fir-cone, etc.]

1. *Bot.* A fir-cone, or any fruit resembling a fir-cone; an inflorescence made up of imbricated scales, as that of the hop.

[**1706** PHILLIPS (ed. Kersey), *Strobilus*, the Artichoke-Plant; also a wild Pine-tree; or a Pine-apple.] **1753** *Chambers' Cycl.* Suppl., *Strobilus*, among botanists, a kind of pericarpium, formed of a number of vaginæ with contorted points applied close to one another. **1771** *Encycl. Brit.* III. 479/2 (*Pinus*). The calix of the female is a strobilus, containing two flowers. **1861** BENTLEY *Bot.* 325 The fruit of the Hop..is by some botanists considered as a kind of Cone with membranous scales, to which the name of Strobilus or Strobile has been given.

b. In cryptogams: An aggregation of sporophylls resembling a fir-cone.

1891 BOWER in *Proc. Roy. Soc.* L. 267 The sporophyte [of *Phylloglossum*] consists of two parts:—(i) the *protocorm*, with its protophylls and roots, and (ii) the *strobilus*, with sporophylls and sporangia. **1893** —— in *Phil. Trans.* B. CLXXXV. 511 The strobili have been cut radially, tangentially, and transversely.

2. *Zool.* = STROBILA 2.

1876 BRISTOWE *Th. & Pract. Med.* (1878) 707 The animal or rather colony of animals, in the form of a tape-worm or strobilus, occupies the alimentary canal.

strobing (ˈstrəʊbɪŋ), *vbl. sb.* [f. STROBE *v.* + -ING^1.] **1.** The action of STROBE *v.* 1.

1959 *Electronic Engin.* XXXI. 130/2 Strobing consists of sampling a repetitive waveform at what to all intents and purposes is an instant in the repetition period. **1981** NASHELSKY & BOYLESTAD *Devices* xi. 390 Figure 11.5 shows how a 311 comparator can be used with strobing.

2. a. *Cinemat.* Jerkiness in what should be a smooth movement on the screen. **b.** *Television.* An irregular movement and loss of continuity sometimes seen in lines and stripes in a television picture.

1959 HALAS & MANVELL *Technique Film Animation* xix. 231 When objects are panned through the screen area, strobing always appears to be worst (on standard 5 inch field) when the distance of movement is between ·125 and ·500 inch per frame. **1961** G. MILLERSON *Technique Television Production* iii. 52 Where..tiling, venetian blinds, etc., are seen at such a distance that their surface appears as close horizontal lines, line-beating or strobing will occur. **1973** R. DOUGALL *In & Out of Box* xxiii. 280 Ties..could be noisy or even loud, so long as they had no horizontal or diagonal patterns which caused 'strobing'. **1980** *Radio Times* 25 Nov.–5 Dec. 102/2 There are a few rules about television clothes... Some patterns can make the picture go all funny—what's known as strobing.

stroble, variant of STROUBLE *v. Obs.*

strobo- (ˈstrəʊbəʊ), formative element f. the first syllable of STROBOSCOPE, etc., as in **ˈstrobotorch**, a light source designed to give very brief flashes of light at a known rate; **ˈstrobotron** [-TRON], a gas-filled cold-cathode discharge tube used as a strobotorch, the flashing rate being determined by the frequency of the voltage applied to a control grid.

1951 *Electronic Engin.* XXIII. 187/3 It is..possible to link the flashing rate of the strobotorch to an electrical contractor ..fitted on the mechanism. **1970** *Nature* 15 Aug. 731/1 A sheet of white translucent plastic was placed between the geometrical figure and the strobotorch. **1937** GERMESHAUSEN & EDGERTON in *Electronics* Feb. 12/1 In this paper a tube, named the Strobotron, is described which has been developed primarily for producing stroboscopic light. **1949** *Jrnl. R. Aeronaut. Soc.* LIII. 460/1 The cathode ray tubes, amplifiers, and strobotron lamps, together with their power supplies, are built into one case. **1966** *McGraw-Hill Encycl. Sci. & Technol.* XIII. 190/1 A thyratron or a strobotron can be used as a trigger tube in place of the switch *S*.

stroboscope (ˈstrəʊbə-, ˈstrɒbəskəʊp). [f. Gr. στρόβο-ς a twisting or whirling round + -SCOPE.] **a.** A scientific toy which produces the illusion of motion by a series of pictures viewed through the openings of a revolving disc. **b.** An instrument for observing the successive phases of a periodic motion by means of light periodically interrupted.

a. 1836 [see STROBOSCOPICAL]. **1882** L. CAMPBELL *Life J. C. Maxwell* ii. 36 A scientific toy had recently come into vogue, an improvement on the thaumatrope, called variously by the names 'phenakistoscope', 'stroboscope', or 'magic disc'.

b. 1896 FR. A. WELBY tr. *Biedermann's Electro-Physiol.* I. 409 If two interrupters are used, one of which is connected with the capillary electrometer, the other with the stroboscope. **1903** *Engineering* 18 Dec. 837/1 A special differential stroboscope, in which the motor was illuminated only once in every two revolutions.

stroboscopic (strəʊbə-, strɒbəˈskɒpɪk), *a.* [f. prec. + -IC.] Relating to, of the nature of, the stroboscope. Also, involving or pertaining to rapid flashes of light.

1846 HOBLYN *Dict. Sci. Terms, Stroboscopic Plates*, an apparatus invented by Stampfer of Vienna, by which an impression is produced on the retina of an uninterrupted line of light by the rapid motion of a luminous object. **1873** DOLBEAR in Prescott *Telephone* (1879) 263 This was done by filling an organ bellows with smoke, and examining it through a stroboscopic disk while escaping from the pipe. **1874** *Pop. Sci. Rev.* XIII. 105 The Stroboscopic Determination of the Pitch of Tones. **1883** *Science* I. 72/1 A new stroboscopic method in which a fork is..kept in vibration by electro-magnets. **1949** H. LURAY *Strobe* i. 22 Real stroboscopic lighting equipment with ample light output can do wonderful things. **1959** L. A. MANNHEIM *Successful Flash Photogr.* 130 (*heading*) Stroboscopic shots. *Ibid.*, A stroboscopic flash outfit. **1971** *Nature* 11 June 397/2 Lately there has been a fad in this area for dances to be held under stroboscopic lighting. **1980** J. W. HILL *Intermediate Physics* iv. 35 Stroboscopic photography (where photographs are taken by a camera at intervals of fractions of seconds on the same film) shows this.

Also **strobo'scopical** *a.* = prec.; **strobo-'scopically** *adv.*, by means of a stroboscope or stroboscopic illumination.

1836 *R. D. & T. Thomson's Rec. Gen. Sci.* III. 114 Stroboscope.—Stampfer has invented some interesting stroboscopical tables, or glasses, founded upon a similar principle with the thaumatoscopical figures. **1877** *Catal. Spec. Collect. Sci. Apparatus S. Kens. Mus.* (ed. 3) 1046 Stroboscopical discs on the systems of Dove, Poggendorff, &c. **1919** *Proc. Nat. Acad. Sci.* V. 174 All measurements were made by the Michelson interferometer viewed stroboscopically. **1932** *Phil. Mag.* XIII. 163 The nature of the instability induced by sound in smoke jets has been examined stroboscopically and by means of photography. **1951** *Electronic Engin.* XXIII. 430/1 The valve structure may be observed stroboscopically while subjected to vibration and the offending portion detected visually. **1977** D. GOLDSTEIN et al. *Test System for Evaluations of Armors using Duplicate Fragments* (U.S. Patent 4,044,599), By using stroboscopically-controlled illumination, the high-speed flight of the fragments can be captured on one photograph.

stroboscopy (strəʊ-, strəˈbɒskəpɪ). [f. STROBOSCOPE + -Y^3.] **a.** The use of stroboscopic techniques or apparatus. **b.** Stroboscopic effects.

1932 *Sun* (Baltimore) 17 Sept. 16/4 Such effects are produced through the principle of stroboscopy, applications of which already make possible the photography of rapidly whirling objects. **1971** CHIN-WU KIM in W. O. Dingwall *Survey of Linguistic Sci.* 22 A slowed-down or stationary appearance in stroboscopy is due to an electro-mechanical apparatus of the stroboscope. **1980** S. L. LYONS *Exterior Lighting* ii. 31 A special effect of flicker is that termed stroboscopy in which rotating or rhythmically moving objects may give the illusion of being stationary.

stroc, obs. form of STROKE *sb.*^{1}

†**strocals.** *Glass-making. Obs.* Also (in Dicts.) 7–9 **strocal**, 8–9 **strokal**, 9 **strocle**, **strokle**, **strockle.** [Of obscure origin.] (See quot. 1662.)

1662 MERRETT *Neri's Art of Glass* App. 363 *Strocals* a long Iron instrument like a Fire-shovel to carry the Metall out of a broken into a whole Pot. **1670** BLOUNT *Glossogr.* (ed. 3), *Strocal.* **1708** KERSEY, **1721** BAILEY, **1755** JOHNSON, *Strokal.* **1858** SIMMONDS *Dict. Trade*, Strockle, in the glass trade, a shovel with a turned up edge, suited to filling the pots or moulds, from the chests or harbours of materials.

strochetts: see SCROCHAT.

1517 *Caldwell Papers* (Maitl. Club) I. 56, xxii. punds of strochetts, price of the pund xxviii d.

strock(e: see STROKE *sb.*^{1}, *v.*^{1} and STRIKE *v.*

†**strocke.** *Obs. rare*$^{-1}$. See quot.

Cf. *mulctrum* = new milk in Diefenbach.

1552 HULOET, Strocke or mylke, *mulctrum.*

strocken, -in, obs. ff. of pa. pple. of STRIKE *v.*

strockle, strocle: see STROCALS.

stroddle (ˈstrɒd(ə)l), *v.* Now *dial.* (see Eng. Dial. Dict.). Also 7 **strodle.** A variant of STRADDLE.

1607 Stroddle [see STATUARY *sb.*^{1}]. **1630** RANDOLPH *Aristippus, Pedler* 31, I haue strodled ouer three of the terrestrial globes with my Geometricall rambling. **1678** BUNYAN *Pilgr.* I. 71 Then Apollyon strodled quite over the whole breadth of the way. **1702** *Lond. Gaz.* No. 3867/4 Stolen.., a black Mare..straddles in her walk as if her Back was broke.

Hence **ˈstroddling** *ppl. a.* (in quot. *fig.*).

1647 *Maids' Petition* 1 To avoid all strodling or stragling intentions or actions on dayes consecrate.

strodir, variant of STROTHIR.

†**ˈstrodling.** *Sc. Obs.* Also 5 **stroddlyng.** [Of obscure origin.] A foundling.

c **1490** *Rathen Manual* (1905) 27 All thai that castis the barnis at kyrk duris or ony place, for the quhylk thai are callit stroddlyngis. **1603** *Proph. of Merlin* (Bannatyne Club) 12 They..that fel on face is faine to flee, That commed are of strodlings strynd.

stroe: see STRAW *sb.*^{1}, STREW *v.*

strof, obs. pa. t. of STRIVE *v.*

stroganoff (ˈstrɒgənɒf). Also **stroganov**, **strogonoff** and with capital initial. [a. Fr., f. the name of the 19th-cent. Russian diplomat Count Paul *Stroganov.*] A dish of strips of beef cooked in a sauce containing sour cream. In full, ***beef stroganoff***, ***bœuf stroganoff***.

1932 A. HEATH *Good Food* 30 Beef *Strogonoff*..slices from a fillet of beef..cut..into shortish, thin strips..onions and mushrooms..cook..in butter..add..thick sour cream. **1937** 'COUNTESS MORPHY' *Kitchen Library* IV. 50 (*heading*) Bœuf Strogonov (Russian). **1944** E. M. ALMEDINGEN *Dasha* vi. 235 All of it sounds as tidy as pieces of beef in the Strogonov dish. **1955** *Good Food Guide 1955–56* 341 Steak maison, tournedos Rossini and bœuf Stroganoff. **1961** *Listener* 28 Dec. 1107/2 In Leningrad's smartest restaurant I ordered beef strogonoff. **1964** 'D. SHANNON' *Death-Bringers* (1966) vi. 72 It's Beef Stroganov, and it's hot. **1969** D. LAMBERT *Angels in Snow* ii. 48 'What's for dinner?' Harry asked. 'Strogonoff,' said his wife. **1980** A. N. WILSON *Healing Art* xiv. 157 Did you get Gale to fix you..her strogonoff, followed by bilberry strudel?

strog(g)el(l, strog(g)le, obs. ff. STRUGGLE.

Stroh (strəʊ). The name of the inventor Charles *Stroh* (fl. 1901) used *attrib.* to designate stringed instruments (chiefly of the violin class) having an aluminium plate and horn attachment in place of a wooden body, formerly used for recording purposes.

1902 *Encycl. Brit.* XXXI. 766/1 The recent invention of the Stroh violin. **1923** [see PHONOFIDDLE]. **1934** C. LAMBERT *Music Ho!* iv. 257 The old pre-electric horn recording, with its euphoniums instead of 'cellos, and its handful of Stroh violins. **1947** F. W. GAISBERG *Music on Record* vi. 79 Stringed instruments we recorded by a subterfuge. We substituted the Stroh violin for violins and violas. **1979** *Oxf. Jun. Compan. Mus.* (ed. 2) 314/1 *Stroh violin*, a violin that has an aluminium plate and a trumpet bell instead of the normal wooden body. Invented in 1901 by Charles Stroh for use in the early recording studios, where primitive microphones could only pick up sound aimed directly at them (which..the trumpet bell could do). There are also Stroh violas, cellos, mandolins, and guitars.

stroil (strɔɪl). *s.w. dial.* Also **stroyl.** Couch-grass and other weeds with long creeping root-stocks.

1758 BORLASE *Nat. Hist. Cornw.* 87 Manures arising from putrefaction, burning the stroil, and the fæces of animals. **1796** W. H. MARSHALL *W. Eng.* I. 331 *Stroyl*: couch, or other weeds; or roots of weeds: especially what harrow up, or rake out of the soil; whether in the field, or the garden. **1845** *Jrnl. R. Agric. Soc.* VI. II. 425 The stroil, roots, and weeds are collected and burned.

strok, obs. pa. t. of STRIKE *v.*

strokal: see STROCALS.

stroke (strəʊk), *sb.*^{1} Forms: α. 3–4 **stroc**, 4–7 **strok**, 4–5 **strook**, 5–8 **strooke**, 6 **strocke**, 6–7 **stroake**, 6–8 **strock**, 7–8 **stroak**, 9 *dial.* **strauk**, 4– **stroke.** β. *Sc.* and *north.* 4–6 **strak**, 4–8 **strake**, *Sc.* 5–9 **straik**, 6 **strack**, **strek**, **strayk**, *pl.* **strax.** [ME. (late 13th c.) *strōk*, north. *strāk*, prob. repr. an unrecorded OE. **strác* = (M)LG. *strêk*, Du. *streek* masc., MHG., mod.G. *streich* masc. :—OTeut. **straiko-z*, f. **straik-* ablaut-var. of **strīk-*: see STRIKE *v.*]

1. An act of striking; a blow given or received.

a. A blow with the hand or a weapon (*occas.* with the paw of an animal, the claws or beak of a bird, etc.) inflicted on or aimed at a living being. Sometimes (now rarely) applied to the thrust of a pointed weapon.

to † ***smite, strike a stroke***: see those verbs. † ***to come to strokes*** = to come to blows. † ***within one's stroke***; within reach of one's weapon.

α. **1297** R. GLOUC. (Rolls) 4281 Sire wawein him biturnde & an stroc him ȝef, & al þat heued & þe breste al clanliche him to-clef. *a* **1320** *Sir Tristr.* 2335 Tvelue fete was þe wand þat vrgan wald wiþ play, His strok may no man stand. *c* **1380** WYCLIF *Sel. Wks.* II. 409 And so þer wordli liif, þat lettiþ sich service, is moche worse þanne a strooke upon þe cheke wiþ an hand. **1471** CAXTON *Recuyell* (Sommer) 259 They foyned with her speres eygrely, theyr strokes and foynes were grete. **1484** —— *Fables of Toge* viii, Fro wordes they came to strokes and cratchyng with naylys. *c* **1530** BERNERS *Arth. Lyt. Bryt.* (1814) 213 But Arthur put his shelde before hym, and the lyons stroke dashte theron so sore, that Arthur was all astonyed with the stroke. *a* **1533** —— *Huon* lv. 188 He slewe and bette downe..all that came within his stroke. **1590** SPENSER *F.Q.* II. vi. 29 Their mightie strokes their haberieons dismayld. **1625** SIR H. FINCH *Law* (1636) 411 An enditement that one strucke I.S. in one countie, of which stroke hee died in another Countie, is no good enditement. **1696** R. H. *Sch. Recreat.* 86 If your Adversary offers to answer your stroak, and go to the Parade, then your best way is [etc.]. **1741** in *Scott. Hist. Rev.* (1905) Apr. 303 The prisoner struck him and blooded him with the strock. **1760–72** BROOKE *Fool of Qual.* (1792) II. 137 Flying instantly at Harry, he gave him a smart stroke on the left cheek. **1806** WORDSW. *Horn of Egremont Castle* 43 And where'er their strokes alighted, There the Saracens were tamed. **1829** SCOTT *Anne of G.* Note A, In such parts of that country [Germany] as retain the old custom of execution by stroke of sword. **1849** JAMES *Woodman* I. iii. 53 He suddenly drew his sword from the sheath, and aimed a rapid and furious stroke at the woodman's head. **1863** GEO. ELIOT *Romola* xxii, [He] remained obstinately silent under all the strokes from the knotted cord. **1889** BADEN-POWELL *Pigsticking* 186 With the jobbing spear the arm should not be raised from the shoulder to deliver the stroke.

β. *a* **1300** *Cursor M.* 12428 Þe maister..Gaf iesu wit hand a strak. **13..** *Gosp. Nicod.* 419 Ane wane of fourty strakes with ȝerde he sal be smeten. *c* **1440** *Alphabet of Tales* 79 Saynt Benett strake þis yong monk with a wand..& so for ferd of þis strake of Saynt Benett þis fende..durst nevur after com & feche hym furthe. **1572–3** *Reg. Privy Council Scot.* II. 205 The said Stevin denyit the stryking of the said Jonet as is libellit, or that he offerit ony straikis to hir. **1607** *Sel. Rec. Regality Melrose* (S.H.S.) I. 33 Secundlie, gif thair be straikis without blude, ten pundis. **1635** *Reg. Privy Counc. Scot.* Ser. II. VI. 5 Johne..came..with ane pycked suord stalffe in his hand and.. gave her manie bauch and blae straiks upon the head [etc.]. **1818** HOGG *Brownie of Bodsbeck* I. iii. 42, I wheeled just round in a moment, sir, and drew a desperate straik at the foremost [pursuer]. **1820** SCOTT *Monast.* xxvi, It was a blithe time in Wight Wallace's day..when the pock-puddings gat naething here but hard straiks and bloody crowns.

¶ *stroke of grace*: Eng. rendering of *coup de grâce* (COUP *sb.*^{3} 5). *rare.*

1837 CARLYLE *Fr. Rev.* II. I. i, The victim having once got his stroke-of-grace.

†**b.** *pl.* = 'Stripes', blows as a punishment. *Obs.*

α. **1388** WYCLIF *Luke* xii. 48 He that knew not, and dide worthi thingis of strokis, schal be betun with fewe. **1593** *Tell-troth's N.Y. Gift* (1876) 5 A lesson learned with stroakes, staies with the scholler. **1699** TEMPLE *Introd. Hist. Eng.* Wks. 1720 II. 531 No Person was punished by Bonds, Strokes, or Death, without the Judgment..of the Druids.

β. **1552** ABP. HAMILTON *Catech.* I. x. (1884) 59, I sall.. punis thair wyckidnes with a wand, and thair synnis with strakis.

c. A blow struck at an inanimate object; e.g. with a hammer, axe, etc.

c **1400** *Rom. Rose* 3687 For no man at the firste stroke Ne may not felle doun an oke. *c* **1400** *Pilgr. Sowle* (Caxton 1483) IV. xxx. 78 Withouten strook of hamour ne may none impression be brought in to gold. **1539** TAVERNER *Erasm. Prov.* (1552) 26 With many strokes is an oke ouerthrowen. **1681** FLAVEL *Meth. Grace* Ep. Ded. 9 A true diamond will endure the smartest stroke of the hammer, but a false one will fly. **1697** DRYDEN *Æneis* VIII. 561 The Cyclops here their heavy Hammers deal; Loud Strokes, and hissings of tormented Steel Are heard around. **1799** G. SMITH *Laboratory* I. 25 Carry with your mallet an even and perpendicular stroke. **1799** WORDSW. *Lucy Gray* 26 With many a wanton stroke Her feet disperse the powdery snow. **1833** JAS. DAVIDSON *Brit. & Rom. Rem. Axminster* 82 A stroke of his pickaxe broke an urn which contained a number of Roman coins. **1842** MACAULAY *Horatius* vii, But now no stroke of woodman Is heard by Auser's rill. **1902** 'VIOLET JACOB' *Sheep-Stealers* xii, Rhys.. listened to the strokes of the pickaxe among the gooseberry bushes.

β. **1513** DOUGLAS *Æneis* XI. iii. 82 The heich eschis.. Down weltit ar with mony granand strakis.

d. In various games: An act of striking the ball; a hit or an attempted hit; in some games (e.g. tennis), a hit that satisfies certain conditions. Also, manner of striking.

α. **1744** J. LOVE *Cricket* III. 70 The strokes re-echo o'er the spacious ground. **1778** HOYLE *Games* 205 (Tennis) The lowest Odds given is a Bisque.., and is the Liberty of scoring a Stroke whenever the Player, who receives Advantage, chooses. **1806** J. BERESFORD *Miseries Hum. Life* iii. §22 Missing your cue at every stroke. **1879** *Encycl. Brit.* X. 767/2 (Golf) In Medal playing a ball may, under a penalty of two strokes, be lifted out of a difficulty of any description. **1884** *Lillywhite's Cricket Ann.* 104 Cantley has a good stroke off his legs. **1896** W. PARK Jr. *Game of Golf* 270 *Stroke*, any movement of the club which is intended to strike the ball. **1897** RANJITSINHJI *Cricket* 159 It is almost impossible to score off a genuine half-cock stroke. It is a mistake to play the stroke unless forced to do so. **1905** H. VARDON *Compl. Golfer* 251 A player whose handicap was several strokes removed from scratch.

β. **1811** H. MACNEILL *Bygane Times* 15 Is this the gate to gowf the ba', When by the straik ye're sure to fa'?

†**e.** The mark left by a blow; a bruise, wound, cut. *Obs.*

14.. *A.B.C. Poem* 28 in *Pol. Rel. & L. Poems* 272 With rede wondis & strokis blo He was dryue fro top to þe too. **1661** J. CHILDREY *Brit. Baconica* 143 One might see the stroaks of the Axe upon them. **1677** *Lond. Gaz.* No. 1204/4 Stolen.., a black Gelding six years old, with a large white snip on the top of the Nose,.. and had formerly a stroke upon the near Leg behind. **1686** BLOME *Gentl. Recr.* II. 25/1 For a Bite, or Stroak in the [Horse's] Eye. **1701** *Lond. Gaz.* No. 3723/4 His Mane half shorn, has had a Stroke in his right Eye.

†**f.** Discharge of an engine of war; a shot of a bow or gun; the impact of a missile. *Obs.*

α. *c* **1400** *Rom. Rose* 6278 Withouten stroke it mot be take Of trepeget or mangonel. *c* **1440** *Gesta Rom.* i. 3 Now hath he schote an arowe at the ymage; And for þat he failith of his strook, he makith moch sorowe. *c* **1482** J. KAY tr. *Caoursin's Siege of Rhodes* (1870) ¶10 [They] sayd, that they herde neuer strokes of bombardes so grete and so horryble as thylk were. **1544** BETHAM *Precepts War* II. xlii. K viij b, There is no breste plate, whyche is able to wythstand, and holde owte the stroke of the arrowes. **1665** MANLEY *Grotius' Low C. Wars* 313 The Third [governor],.. being kill'd with the stroke of a Stone, clearly made an end of his Government. **1678** R. L'ESTRANGE *Seneca's Mor.* (1702) 442 The Stroak of an Arrow convinc'd Alexander, that he was not the Son of Jupiter. **1695** SIBBALD *Autobiog.* (1834) 128 When the town was taken by storme my Father was hurt with a strock given him by a footman with a carabin. **1771** *Ann. Reg., Nat. Hist.* 91/2, The shot entered an inch above his eye, the animal fell under the stroke, and died almost instantly.

β. **1579–80** *Reg. Privy Council Scot.* III. 264 He wes sumquhat recoverit of his formar hurt ressavit be the strek of the first pistolett.

†**g.** Point of impact; place hit by a missile.

c **1450** *Mirk's Festial* 42 þen anothyr smot aftyr, and hut yn þe same stroke. **1669** STURMY *Mariner's Mag.* v. xii. 70 Observe how much the last stroke of the Shot is above the Mark.

h. †Shock or forcible impact of a moving body (*obs.*); impact or incidence of moving particles, light, etc. (now *rare*).

1534 BERNERS *Gold. Bk. M. Aurel.* (1546) F viij, With the stroke of metyng, the trumpettour was ouerthrawen with his hors. **1557** PHAER *Æneid* VII. (1558) V ij b, Full like a rocke in seas,.. Whom strokes of water strikes,.. and beates about. **1651** HOBBES *Leviath.* I. ii. 5 Many stroaks, which our eyes, eares, and other organs receive from externall bodies. **1660** STANLEY *Hist. Philos.* XI. *Democr.* ix. §8 (1687) 765/1 All Sensation is caused by a touch or stroak upon the Organ. **1661** BOYLE *Cert. Physiol. Ess.* (1669) 184 When the igneous Corpuscles have by their numerous and brisk strokes upon the vessel communicated by its means their agitation to the enclosed powder. **1681–6** J. SCOTT *Chr. Life* (1747) III. 116 Impressions.. such, as did as fully satisfy them that they were from God, as the Strokes of the Sun-beams on our Eyes do us that it is Day at Noon. **1860** TYNDALL *Glac.* I. vi. 42 The backs of the ridges.. meet the direct stroke of the solar rays.

2. Phrases.

†**a.** ***without*** (***any***) ***stroke*** (***of sword***): without fighting. Also ***without fighting a stroke***. (***to die***) ***without stroke***: otherwise than by violence. *Obs.*

For *without striking a stroke, without stroke stricken*, see STRIKE *v.* 32.

α. *c* **1400** MAUNDEV. (1839) xxv. 260 Thanne the Cristene men wenten.. and hire enemyes enclosed and confounded in Derknesse, with outen ony strok. *c* **1460** *Contn. Brut* 491 Many other townes in Normandie gafe þeme ouer with-out stroke or siege. *Ibid.* 507 At Bedford, on Ashtwesday, wer iij men murthred without strok, by falling doun of a steir. **1584** R. BIRREL *Diary* (1798) 23 Bot quhen he came, they yat ver vithin fled, sua yat hes Maiestie entred and tooke ye toune and castell vithout stroke of suord. **1645** R. BAILLIE *Lett. & Jrnls.* (Bannatyne Club) II. 262 A great many honest burgesses were killed,.. many were bursten in the flight, and dyed without stroak. **1670** MILTON *Hist. Brit.* II. 54 Suetonius writes that Claudius found heer no resistance, and that all was done without stroke: but this seems not probable. **1687** A. LOVELL tr. *Thevenot's Trav.* II. 159 This Murteza Basha, without stroke of Sword made himself master of Bassora. **1721** DE FOE *Mem. Cavalier* (1840) 266 We marched away without fighting a stroke.

β. **1533** BELLENDEN *Livy* (S.T.S.) II. 136 Fra þe wache was slane þe remanent war sone opprest and randerit but ony straik. **1535** STEWART *Cron. Scot.* (Rolls) II. 213 Tha tynt the feild but straik of sword or knyfe. *a* **1572** KNOX *Hist. Ref.* Wks. 1846 I. 88 Stout Oliver was without strack tackin, fleing full manfully. *a* **1670** SPALDING *Troub. Chas. I* (Bannatyne Club) I. 154 The lord Aboyne.. seeing their collours upon the Brig, takes the flight shamefully but straik of sword or any other kind of vassalage.

†**b.** ***stroke of battle***: active warfare. *Obs.*

1525 WOLSEY in *St. Papers Hen. VIII*, VI. 403 Putting theym unto the wors, not by stroke of batail.. but with consumyng of theym by long tract of tyme.

c. ***stroke and strife*** (altered from earlier *strot* or *sturt and strife*): lawless violence.

c **1510** *Lyt. Geste Robin Hood* 181 Or elles thou hast ben a sory housbande And leued in stroke and stryfe.

†**d.** ***the first stroke***: the beginning of a war.

c **1470** HENRY *Wallace* VI. 687 At the first straik with thaim he had nocht beyne. **1677** SIR R. SOUTHWELL in *Essex Papers* (Camden) II. 111, I cannot expect anything but ruin the very first stroke of the warr.

e. ***at one stroke, at a stroke***: with a single blow; *fig.* all at once.

c **1374** CHAUCER *Boeth.* v. pr. vi. (1868) 178 But he ay dwellynge comiþ byforn and enbraceþ at o strook [L. *uno ictu*] alle þi mutaciouns. *c* **1470** HENRY *Wallace* II. 60 And at a straik the formast has he slayne. **1556** J. HEYWOOD *Spider & Fly* xci. 102 The maide of the house with her brome: at a strake, Swepth downe those copwebs. **1709** T. ROBINSON *Vind. Mosaick Syst.* 16 Omnipotent Power might have created the whole World at one stroke, by an Imperious Fiat. **1879** FARRAR *St. Paul* (1883) 173 At one stroke he had lost all his old friends. **1884** BOSANQUET *Lotze's Logic* 236 It is not always possible to prove at one stroke that a proposition *T* holds good for all quantities, integral and fractional, positive and negative, [etc.].

3. *fig.* **a.** With conscious metaphor: An act which causes pain, injury, or death; often, an act of divine chastisement or vengeance.

α. **1340** *Ayenb.* 34 Efter alle þise zorȝuolle poyns of sleuþe him yefþ þe dyeuel þane strok dyadlych. *c* **1412** HOCCLEVE *De Reg. Princ.* 2029 Whan þat the colde stroke of deth My lyfe hath quenched, & me byraft my breth. **1484** CAXTON *Fables of Avian* xiii, Werse is the stroke of a tonge than the stroke of a spere. *c* **1520** SKELTON *Magnif.* 1882 The Stroke of God, Aduersyte, I hyght. **1611** BEAUM. & FL. *King & No K.* I. i, Sheele make you shrinke as I did, with a stroke But of her eye Tigranes. **1665** J. NORTH in *Extr. St. Papers rel. Friends* Ser. III. (1912) 234 By which false verdict the Murderer hath Escaped the stroke of Justice hitherto. **1667** MILTON *P.L.* x. 210 So judg'd he Man,.. And th' instant stroke of Death denounc't that day Remov'd farr off. **1689** *Extracts Rec. Convention Royal Burghs Scot.* (1880) IV. 100 By one strock of ane act of parliament.. we are outterly ruined in our trade. **1753** MISS COLLIER *Art Torment.* I. i. 37 All the pleasure of Tormenting is lost, as soon as your subject is become insensible of your strokes. **178.** BURNS *Highland Lassie* vi, Till the mortal stroke shall lay me low. **1858** RAWLINSON tr. *Herodotus* II. cxxix. II. 208 Mycerinus .. was acting as I have described, when the stroke of calamity fell on him. **1860** SALA *Baddington Peerage* I. xviii. 306 Not to be passed over in its portents any more than the first stroke of disease which attacks thrice before it kills.

β. **1560** ROLLAND *Seven Sages* 76 And thairefter to bide the straik of Law. **1590** R. BRUCE *Serm. Sacram.* iv. N 8, Therefore knawledge must go before the straik of the conscience. Thy hart can neuer feele that to be euil, quhilk thy mynde knawis not to be euill.

b. A calamitous event; †a 'blow' *to*, *upon* (a person, institution, etc.).

a **1700** EVELYN *Diary* 15 Apr. 1686, I looke on this as a greate stroke to the poore Church of England. *a* **1709** J. LISTER *Autobiog.* (1842) 50 On the Tuesday I laid him [*sc.* his son] in his grave at Kendall.. I feared this sad stroke would break my wife's heart, but.. she bore it with uncommon fortitude. **1762–71** H. WALPOLE *Vertue's Anecd. Paint.* (1786) II. 238 The tragic death of his royal protector was a dreadful stroke.. to Petitot. **1785** MARY MICHEL in *A. C. Bower's Diaries & Corr.* (1903) 25 The loss of an only son .. must be a very severe stroke upon her. **1852** MRS. STOWE *Uncle Tom's C.* xxix, Tom's whole soul was filled with thoughts of eternity; and while he ministered around the lifeless clay, he did not once think that the sudden stroke had left him in hopeless slavery.

†**c.** A hostile attack; an offensive movement in warfare. *Obs.*

1698 FRYER *Acc. E. India & P.* 337 He safely resides within, invulnerable from Foreign Strokes, and reigns in this his Capital City. **1700** S. L. tr. *Fryke's Voy. E. Ind.* 77 Yet were we wholly set upon pursuing the Stroke, and hoped that the night should prove rather more commodious and successful. **1777** WASHINGTON in W. Irving *Life* xcix. (1856) III. 806 A successful stroke on the Highlands.

†**d.** ***to have, bear, carry, strike a*** (***great***, etc.) ***stroke***: to have an influential or controlling share in an enterprise or action, to have great influence. ***to have, bear, carry, strike the stroke***: to prevail, rule, have authority; to be highest in excellence. ***to give, strike a good stroke***: to contribute largely, go far *to* effect some result. *Obs.*

1531 TINDALE *Expos. 1–3 S. John* (1538) 83 An yf.. we can fynde no shyfte, but that yᵉ byshop of Rome.. must thus mocke vs, what a stroke thynke ye hath Satan amonge vs? [Cf. *ante*, Then the deuell hath a greate swynge amonge vs.] **1538** BALE *Thre Lawes* 1514 Such a fellawe was he as of that age had the stroke. **1542** UDALL *Erasm. Apoph.* 168 All suche persones.. as beare any rewle, stroke, or autoritee in the commonweale. **1549** LATIMER *2nd Serm. bef. Edw. VI* (Arb.) 63 Thys byshoppe was a great man borne, and did beare such a stroke, that he was able to shoulder the Lord Protectour. **1564** *Brief Exam.* D iiij b, Which.. loue, if it beare stroke among vs, we shall be able.. to discomfyte the body.. of Antichrist. *a* **1569** KINGESMYLL *Comf. Afflict.* (1585) B iij, Hee knewe that whatsoever befell him, God had a stroke in it. **1600** HOLLAND *Livy* XXIX. xxix. 731 This Mezetulus having gathered a powre of.. paisants of the countrey (with whom he carried a great stroke). **1609** F. SHERWOOD in *Lismore Papers* Ser. II. (1887) I. 134 The advise you wisht me to geiue him.. gave a good stroke to perswade him. **1611** BEAUM. & FL. *Knt. Burn. Pestle* IV. (1613) I 2, *Wife.* Let him goe George, a shall not haue any countenance from vs, nor a good word from any i' th' Company, if I may strike stroke in't. **1611** BIBLE *Transl. Pref.* ¶11 The vintage of Abiezer, that strake the stroake: yet the gleaning of grapes of Ephraim was not to be despised. **1612** T. TAYLOR *Titus* ii. 14 (1619) 532 It is verie hard to say, whether nature or religion giveth the stroke to their actions. **1622** in Foster *Eng. Factories Ind.* (1908) II. 17 Captaine Fitzharbert opposed the resolutione, but the Admiralls double voice carried the stroke. **1634** SIR T. HERBERT *Trav.* Ep. Ded. A 3, Opinion strikes a great stroake in the iudgements and affaires of men. **1646** SIR T. BROWNE *Pseud. Ep.* VI. xii. 338 That the salts of naturall bodies doe carry a powerfull stroake in the tincture and vernish of all things, we shall not deny. **1659** in *Burton's Diary* (1828) IV. 444 The Jesuits have too great a stroke amongst them. **1687** BURNET *Contn. Reply to Varillas* 41 They had the main stroak in our Parliaments. **1697** COLLIER *Ess. Mor. Subj.* I. (1709) 246 We may plainly perceive, That the Prejudices of Education have a great Stroak in many of our Reasonings. **1702** *Engl. Theophrastus* 248 To stir up seditions and troubles the worst man commonly bears the stroke. **1731** T. BOSTON in Morrison *Mem.* iv. (1899) 34, I.. could never fall into the good graces of those who had the stroke in settling parishes.

†**e.** ***to come in the stroke***: to be part of one's task. *Obs.*

1617 HIERON *Penance for Sin* xx. Wks. 1619 II. 287, I speake not this.. by way of censuring.. any mans course; but I note this, (it comming in the stroke) according to my Text, to worke care in mine owne heart [etc.].

†**4.** Coinage, imprint of coin. *Sc. Obs.*

1449 *Sc. Acts Jas. II* (1814) II. 37/1 Of þe new strak to be maide & the cours þerof and of þe money þat now rynnis. **1493** *Sc. Acts Jas. IV* ibid. 233/1 Notwithstanding þe diuersitie of prentis of þe straikis of sundry cunȝeors. *a* **1578** LINDESAY (Pitscottie) *Chron. Scot.* (S.T.S.) II. 198 Vpone the thrid day of Julij the lordis.. tuik all the quenis siluir weschell and struik siluir quhilk straik was the xxx schilling peice. **1600** *Earl Gowrie's Conspir.* A 3, His answere was, that so farre as hee could take leisure to see of them, that they seemed to bee forraine.. strokes of coyne.

5. a. A damaging or destructive discharge (of lightning).

a **1542** WYATT *Poems*, '*The lively sparks*' 10 Muche lyke vnto the gyse Of one Istricken with dynt of lightening blynded with the stroke, erryng here & there. **1730** A. GORDON tr. *Maffei's Amphith.* (1735) 366 The Thunder, which.. has broken.. two large Pieces of the lowermost Stones;.. by the Nature of the Stroke.. it appears that the Direction of the Blow came from below upwards, [etc.]. **1810** SCOTT *Lady of L.* III. iv, Mingled with shivers from the oak, Rent by the lightning's recent stroke. **1889** *Science* 11 Oct. 257 The attempt to obtain information regarding lightning-strokes.. will result in a clearer understanding of the danger from these strokes to unprotected houses.

†**b.** An electric shock. *Obs.*

1766 *Ann. Reg., Chron.* 71 After applying the electrical strokes to several parts of her body, and at length to her mouth, she soon recovered her speech. **1799** HT. LEE *Canterb. T.* III. 95 An electric stroke could hardly have produced a more sudden effect on both his hearers than [etc.].

†**c.** A shock of earthquake. *Obs.*

1813 BAKEWELL *Introd. Geol.* (1815) 308 Earthquakes are most frequent in volcanic districts, but the strokes are not the most violent in the immediate vicinity of volcanoes.

6. An attack of disease.

a. An apoplectic or (now more usually) paralytic seizure. Formerly † ***the stroke of God's hand***.

1599 A. M. tr. *Gabelhouer's Bk. Physic* 25/2 An excellent Cinnamome water for the stroke of Gods hande. *a* **1700** EVELYN *Diary* 22 Nov. 1694, The Abp. of Canterbury, who a few days before had a paralytic stroke. **1762–71** H. WALPOLE *Vertue's Anecd. Paint.* (1786) IV. 11 He was seized with a stroke of apoplexy. **1780** JOHNSON *Let. to Mrs. Lucy Porter* 8 Apr., He has had a stroke, like that of an apoplexy. **1832** S. WARREN *Diary Physic.* II. ii. 85 Our inestimable friend, Mr. E——, had a sudden stroke of the palsy this afternoon. **1855** MACAULAY *Hist. Eng.* xvii. IV. 97 Soon after he had risen from table, an apoplectic stroke deprived him of speech and sensation. **1861** MRS. H. WOOD *East Lynne* III. xviii, Mr. Justice Hare's illness had turned out to be a stroke of paralysis. **1889** GRETTON *Memory's Harkback* 316 In his later years he had a partial stroke, which drew the muscles of his cheek a little on one side. **1898** J. HUTCHINSON in *Archives Surg.* IX. 382 The popular distinction between a stroke and a fit was well illustrated by a hemiplegic patient who asserted, 'I never had a fit; I never lost my senses; I only had a stroke'. **1905** *People's Doctor* 48 Apoplexy. This disease goes under quite a variety of names. The popular term is 'stroke'; doctors speak of cerebral hemorrhage; [etc.].

†**b.** *Falconry.* A disease in the eyes of hawks: = ***pin and web*** (PIN *sb.* 11). *Obs.*

1575 *Perf. Bk. Kepinge Sparhawkes* (1886) 31 Pyn and Web, or Stroke. Pyn or Web or other dymnes by strokes &c. must be spedely loked unto.

†**c.** A blight on wheat, honey-dew. *Obs.*

1750 W. Ellis *Mod. Husb.* II. i. 2 (E.D.S.) In the latter part of June,..green wheat is most liable to receive the stroke, as the farmer calls it; that is, the honey-dews.

7. The striking of a clock; the sound produced by each striking of the clapper or hammer upon a bell, or on the striking part of a clock. ***on*** or ***upon the stroke*** (***of*** a specified hour): on the point of striking.

1436 *Sc. Acts Jas. I* (1814) II. 24/1 Þat na man in burghe be fundyn in tauernys..efter the straik of ix houris. *a* **1558** in *Rep. Hist. MSS. Comm.* Var. Coll. IV. 129 Before the howre of ix of the cloke, at which time ther shalbe a bell to be towlde by the officers ther by xxti strokes. **1604** Marston *Malcontent* II. iii. C 4 b, *Piet.* What houre ist? *Celso.* Vpon the stroake of twelue. **1613** Purchas *Pilgrimage* (1614) 700 The King hath a Bell, the strokes whereof sound such terror into the heart of the fearefull theefe, that [etc.]. *c* **1616** Fletcher *Thierry & Theod.* III. i, His houres vpon the stroake. **1816** *Gentl. Mag.* Sept. 270/1 At Hatherleigh..a bell..announces, by distinct strokes, the number of the day of the month. **1832** Ht. Martineau *Hill & Valley* ix. 137, I used to like its stroke when it brought the work-people flocking from their cottages. **1847** C. Bronte *Jane Eyre* xi, It is on the stroke of twelve now. **1858** Trollope *Dr. Thorne* xxx, He dressed himself hurriedly, for the dinner-bell was almost on the stroke as he entered the house. **1874** Burnand *My Time* xxiii. 211 Straining my ears to catch the very first stroke of the hour. **1897** R. N. Bain tr. *Jókai's Pretty Michal* xxxii. 251 At the stroke of two she was already in the shop below. **1908** J. R. Harris *Side-Lights N.T. Research* ii. 55 The person who first succeeds in drawing the water after the stroke of midnight will find it turn to gold and silver.

†**8. a.** A touch on a stringed instrument; manner of playing a musical instrument; hence, a tune, strain. *Obs.*

1540 Palsgr. *Acolastus* III. i. O j, He can no more skille of the stroke of the harpe or lute, than a iay can. **1561** Hoby tr. *Castiglione's Courtier* I. I ij b, Afterward the musitien chaunging the stroke and his maner of tune [Alexander] pacified himself againe. **1586** W. Webbe *Eng. Poetrie* (Arb.) 61 Neither is there anie tune or stroke which may be sung or plaide on instruments, which hath not some poetical ditties framed according to the numbers thereof. **1600** Marston etc. *Jack Drum's Entert.* (1601) A 3, I had the best stroke, the sweetest touch, but now..I am falne from the Fidle. **1689** Ayres *Lyric Poems* (1906) 308 (To his Viol) Then to my soft and sweetest strokes I keep. **1721** A. Malcolm *Treat. Mus.* i. 18 The Notes of a Violin and all string'd Instruments that are struck with a Bow, whose Notes are made longer or shorter by Strokes of different lengths or Quickness of Motion. **1773** Barrington in *Phil. Trans.* LXIII. 261 Several nightingale strokes, or particular passages in the song of that bird.

†**b.** *Hunting.* A call played on the horn. Cf. strake *sb.*[4] *Obs.*

1688 Holme *Armoury* III. 76/2 [Hunting-lesson blown on the Horn] The Stroaks to the Field, *Ton-ton-tavern tone ton-tavern* [etc.].

9. A pulsation, beat (of the heart, pulse). Cf. 12 c.

1538 Elyot *Dict., Pulsus*..is more proprely the poulse or stroke that the arteries or beatyng vaines do make. **1737** Bracken *Farriery Impr.* (1756) I. 183 The Blood's Momentum or Stroke. **1800** *Med. Jrnl.* IV. 525 Her pulse usually beating from 120 to 130 strokes in the minute. **1843** R. J. Graves *Syst. Clin. Med.* xiv. 173 The pulse..changed its character from a short and small to a full soft stroke. **1859** Tennyson *Elaine* 716 Wroth, but all in awe, For twenty strokes of the blood,..Linger'd that other, staring after him. **1899** *Allbutt's Syst. Med.* VI. 390 The impulse communicated to an aneurysmal sac is of course repeated at each stroke of the heart.

10. a. A movement of beating time; a beat, measure; metrical ictus, rhythm. Now *rare* or *Obs.*

1576 G. Baker tr. *Gesner's Jewel of Health* 198 Distyll first with so softe a fyre, that foure musicall strokes may be made betweene droppe and droppe falling. **1586** W. Webbe *Eng. Poetrie* (Arb.) 62 The naturall course of most English verses seemeth to run vppon the olde Iambicke stroake. **1597** Morley *Introd. Mus.* 9 *Phi.* What is a stroke? *Ma.* It is a successiue motion of the hand, directing the quantitie of euery note & rest in the song, with equall measure..: this they make three folde, *more, lesse*, and *proportionate*. The *More* stroke they call, when the stroke comprehendeth the time of a Briefe. The lesse, when a time of a Semibriefe, and proportionate where it comprehendeth three Semibriefes. **1677** F. North *Philos. Ess. Mus.* 33 The due observance of time is gratefull for the same reason that I gave for the formality of a single Tune, because the subsequent strokes are measured by the memory of the former. **1891** J. C. Parsons *Engl. Versif.* 20 In iambic movement..the stroke or accent, which usually comes only on the last syllable, may, at times, come equally on the first syllable.

†**b.** ***to keep stroke***: to keep time. Cf. 13 b. *Obs.*

16.. G. Percy in Purchas *Pilgrims* (1625) IV. 1687 When they were in their dance, they kept stroke with their feet iust one with another.

11. a. In negative context: A minimum amount of work. **b.** In later use: A large or considerable amount *of* work, business, trade.

a. 1568 *Hist. Jacob & Esau* v. vi, I wrought not a stroke this day but led Isaac. **1791** Bentham *Panopt.* 69 Without either punishment, or interest given him in the profits of his labour,..how could you have insured a man's doing a single stroke of work? *a* **1843** Southey *Comm.-pl. Bk.* (1851) IV. 359 This fellow..never would strike a stroke of work afterwards. **1867** W. H. Dixon *New Amer.* II. 322 'Work!' said a stout young fellow in Tennessee..'thank God, I have never done a stroke of work since I was born.'

b. 1712 Steele *Spect.* No. 484 ¶4 The best Consolation that I can administer to those who cannot get into that Stroke of Business (as the Phrase is) which they deserve, is [etc.]. **1825** Brockett *N.C. Gloss.* s.v., A good stroke of business. **1838** Haliburton *Clockm.* Ser. II. xvii. 248 They carry on a considerable of a fishery here, and do a great stroke in the timber business. **1841** Hartshorne *Salop. Ant.* Gloss., *Stroke*, an unusual quantity of labor performed in a certain time. **1842** Thackeray *Fitz-Boodle's Prof.* i, A trade doing a stroke of so many hogsheads a week. **1853** C. R. Read *Austral. Gold Fields* 14 A little further on I met the carpenter of the ship I came out from England in, two years before; he told me he was doing a rattling stroke. **1861** Hughes *Tom Brown Oxf.* iv, One of those who do a good stroke of the work of the country without getting much credit for it. **1884** *Contemp. Rev.* Apr. 579 The mileage run and the stroke of work performed.

12. A movement like that of striking a blow. **a.** A single movement of the legs in walking or running, of the wings in flying, etc.

1618 Baret *Vineyard Horsem.* I. 20 Further he must handle his legges neatly,..with an equall largenesse of his stroke carrying an apt proportion according to the slownes or swiftnes of his pace. *a* **1642** Suckling *Goblins* IV. (1646) 39 How she..danc'd a stroak in, and a stroak out, Like a young Fillet [? *read* Filly] training to a pace. **1704** F. Fuller *Med. Gymn.* (1711) 29 Take the Bearings of a Running Horse, that is, measure the Extent of his Stroaks. **1865** A. L. Gordon *Poems, Ye Wearie Wayfarer* II. iv, I saw him shorten his horse's stroke As we splash'd through the marshy ground. **1869** Spencer *Princ. Psychol.* §91 (1870) I. 216 A gnat's wings make ten or fifteen thousand strokes per second. **1880** A. H. Swinton *Insect Variety* 175 In the pairing season..this music..is prolonged to ten or eleven strokes of the femora, lasting a quarter of a minute.

b. In swimming, the combined movement of the limbs forming a single impulse of progression; also, any particular manner of effecting this, as the breast-stroke, side-stroke.

c **1800** W. Hickey *Mem.* (1913) I. 158, I observed we were already too deep, asking the gunner whether he could swim, to which he answered: 'No, Sir, not a stroke'. **1863** Kinglake *Crimea* II. 220 There are however some deeps which would force a man to swim a few strokes. **1902** Buchan *Watcher by Threshold* 314 He found deep water, and in two strokes was in the grip of the tide.

c. A single complete movement in either direction of any piece of machinery having a reciprocating motion (e.g., of a piston, piston-rod, etc.); also, the amplitude or length of such a movement.

1731 Beighton in *Phil. Trans.* XXXVII. 11 If instead of sixteen Forcers they worked only eight, the Stroke might be five Feet in each Forcer. **1741** in *Sixth Rep. Dep. Kpr. Publ. Rec.* App. II. 120 A new pump, Engine or forcer for raising water with a perpendicular stroke. **1840** *Mechanics' Mag.* XXXIII. 157/1 A popular notion has for a considerable time past prevailed, that a long stroke engine is much superior to a short stroke engine. **1841** Whewell *Mech. Engin.* 185 The engine consumed 80 lbs. of coal per hour, working 18 strokes per minute. **1847** J. Bourne *Catech. Steam Eng.* 162 The engine should always be made to work full stroke. **1869** C. Knight *Mechanician* 109 The stroke of a slide-valve is the length of the path along which the valve moves. The stroke of a piston is the length of its travel or path. **1902** S. E. White *Blazed Trail* I. ii, The saw leaped back and forth a few strokes more.

13. *Rowing.* **a.** A single pull of the oar.

1583 H. Howard *Defensative* L iij b, Barges which are forced by the strength of oares, haue a kinde of gate or swinge when the stroke dooth cease. **1632** J. Hayward tr. *Biondi's Eromena* 40 The Galley-slaves..made her scoure little lesse than her full length betweene one stroake and the other. **1753** Miss Collier *Art Torment.* III. 221 You may scream at every stroke of the oar. **1836** Marryat *Midsh. Easy* xiii, So that they might dash on board of her with a few strokes of the oars.

†**b.** ***to keep stroke***: to keep time in rowing. Cf. 10 b.

1606 Shaks. *Ant. & Cl.* II. ii. 200 The Owers..to the tune of Flutes kept stroke. *a* **1619** Fotherby *Atheom.* II. xii. §2 (1622) 338 And he, that bending slowly brings his tarrying Oare to breast, His winding Armes keepe stroke with songs, while he the water beates. **1629** Wadsworth *Pilgr.* v. 38, I being unable to keepe stroake with the rest, was well beaten. **1652** *Hermeticall Banq.* 5 At Table, be sure that your Teeth labour like so many Gally slaves, keeping true stroke with the Hand.

c. Style of rowing, manner of handling the oars, esp. with regard to the length, speed, or frequency of the 'strokes' (see quot. 1898).

1870 *Field Q. Mag.* I. 202/2 Close came away at once, and, rowing a long easy stroke, won very easily by four lengths. **1877** *Oxf. & Camb. Undergrad. Jrnl.* 173/2 A journey to Ditton and back was essayed at a slow stroke. **1890** R. C. Lehmann *Harry Fludyer* 118 To-day we are going to work up our stroke, so as to be able to row forty [strokes to the minute]. **1898** *Encycl. Sport* II. 298/1 *Stroke*, (1) the number of dips of the oar in the water within a given time.

d. The oarsman who sits nearest to the stern of the boat, and whose 'stroke' sets the time for the other rowers (= *stroke-oar, -oarsman*, strokesman). Also quasi-*adv.* in ***to pull, row stroke***.

1825 Westmacott *Eng. Spy* (1907) I. 28 In a water party he was a stroke of the ten oar. [*Note.* A first rate water-man.] **1841** J. T. J. Hewlett *Peter Priggins* II. xiv. 306 Their talk was principally of boating,..with discussions on the merits of the 'strokes' of the different boats. **1845** in *Brasenose Ale* 77 Thus spake the prince, who set us all afloat, And pull'd first stroke in the old Brasenose boat. **1848** Thackeray *Van. Fair* xxxiv, He pulls stroke in the Boniface boat. **1868** *Field* 4 July 14/2 Hall's rowing as stroke was very different to his execution of the past two years. **1898** *Encycl. Sport* II. 298/1 (Rowing) *Stroke*, (2) the oarsman who sits nearest the stern of the boat and sets the work to the men behind him. The side upon which his oar projects is called 'stroke side' all the way up the boat.

e. The station occupied in a boat by the stroke-oarsman.

1901 *Oxford Mag.* 24 Apr. 291/2 University..with Huntley at stroke.

f. ***to put*** (someone) ***off*** (his) ***stroke***, to distract (someone) from his course of activity; to disconcert or disturb. *colloq.*

a **1914** Joyce *Stephen Hero* (1944) xx. 103 Besides girls praying put me off my stroke. **1922** —— *Ulysses* 285 Put you off your stroke. **1965** J. Gale *Clean Young Englishman* IV. 167 The note put me right off my stroke. I was trying to tell the audience what the war in Algeria was really like... But somehow I never finished what I wanted to say. **1977** R. Perry *Dead End* iii. 41 She must have..seen the bodies.. but it didn't put her off her stroke at all.

14. a. A vigorous attempt to attain some object; a measure, expedient, or device adopted for some purpose. Also ***stroke of policy*** (or †***politics***), ***of business*** (cf. 11 b).

1699 T. Baker *Refl. Learning* xiv. 166 Isidor's Collection was the great and bold Stroke, which [etc.]. **1732** Arbuthnot *Rules of Diet* in *Aliments* etc. 413 The greatest and most important Strokes for the Recovery of the Patient, must be made at the time of the Invasion, or first State of the Disease. **1769** Burke *Observ. Late St. Nat.* Wks. 1842 I. 102 He pays..some compliments to Lord Bute and Lord Despenser. But to the latter, this is, I suppose, but a civility to old acquaintance; to the former, a little stroke of politicks. **1822** Galt *Provost* xi, Before the Michaelmas I was..fully prepared to achieve a great stroke of policy for the future government of the town. **1850** Merivale *Rom. Emp.* iv. (1865) I. 185 This stroke of policy was not unsuccessful. **1865** Dickens *Mut. Fr.* II. iii, It is conceded by all, that that stroke of business on Brewer's part, in going down to the House that night to see how things looked, was the master-stroke. **1876** M. Arnold *Lit. & Dogma* 112 For us,.. Christianity [is] the greatest and happiest stroke ever yet made for human perfection.

b. ***stroke of state***: tr. Fr. *coup d'état* (see coup *sb.*[3] 5 a).

1783 Justamond tr. *Raynal's Hist. Indies* VIII. 115 If we destroy..the nature of any great body, those convulsive motions which are called strokes of state, will disturb the whole nation. **1865** Carlyle *Fredk. Gt.* XXI. v. (1872) X. 59 Her Son, the spirited King Gustav III., at Stockholm had made what in our day is called a 'stroke of state'. **1871** Browning *Pr. Hohenst.* 1367 He cannot but intend some stroke of state Shall signalize his passage into peace Out of the creaking. **1910** Rosebery *Chatham* xi. 238 Fortified by this treaty,..the Pelhams executed their stroke of state.

c. In a game: An effective move or combination.

1735 Bertin *Chess* Pref. p. iii, This noble Game abounds with a greater variety of fine strokes, than any other Games which depend upon design only. **1862** 'Cavendish' *Whist* (1864) 51 You almost preclude him from executing any of the finer strokes of play. **1913** *Illustr. Lond. News* 22 Feb. 264/3 P to Kt 5th The winning stroke, as White gains a passed Pawn.

d. ***to pull a stroke***, to play a dirty trick. Cf. pull *v.* 20 d. *slang.*

1970 P. Laurie *Scotland Yard* 293 *Pull a stroke, to*, to play a dirty trick. **1974** J. McVicar *McVicar* I. ii. 109 It would be wrong to let Charlie go... He's pulled too many strokes.

15. a. A feat, achievement; a signal display *of* art, genius, wit, etc. Cf. 18 c.

1672 Villiers (Dk. Buckhm.) *Rehearsal* III. ii. (Arb.) 75 There's a smart expression of a passion; O ye Gods! That's one of my bold strokes, a gad. **1677** Dryden *State Innoc.* Apol. Heroic Poetry b 3, The boldest strokes of Poetry, when they are manag'd Artfully, are those which most delight the Reader. **1692** R. L'Estrange *Fables* clii. 138 'Tis a Stroake of Art to Divert the Reproach, by Improving a Spitefull Word, or Thing, to a bodies Own Advantage. **1731** *Gentl. Mag.* I. 84 The statues about St. Paul's..are strokes of his masterly hand. **1757** Mrs. Griffith *Lett. Henry & Frances* (1767) III. 31 Perhaps 'tis this, by a Stroke of Simpathy, that hurries on the Reader at such a Rate. **1760–2** Goldsm. *Cit. W.* li, It is filled with strokes of wit and satire in every line. **1865** M. Arnold *Ess. Crit.* Pref. p. x, I had no notion, I protest, that this exquisite stroke of pleasantry was aimed at me. **1881** Ld. Acton *Lett. to Mary Gladstone* (1904) 74 One of the best strokes of wit I can remember in my time.

b. ***stroke of luck***: an unexpected piece of good fortune.

1853 C. B. Mansfield *Paraguay* etc. (1856) 420 The prisoner captain looked almost as much pleased as his capturer, who jumped for joy at this stroke of good luck. **1882** Pebody *Engl. Journalism* xxiii. 179 The *Times*, by a stroke of luck..was represented in that war by a man who [etc.]. **1885** 'Mrs. Alexander' *At Bay* x, That lynching business was a stroke of luck for Deering.

16. a. A movement of the pen, pencil, graver, etc., in writing, painting, drawing, etc.; a single movement of a brush, chisel, knife, file, etc. over the surface operated on. Phrase, ***with a stroke of the pen***: often said *hyperbolically*.

1668 Temple *Let.* Wks. 1720 II. 91 Your Excellency with a Stroak of your Pen, has brought to Light the most covered Designs of your Enemies. **1699** E. Ward *Lond. Spy* v. 4 Their Senses were Ravish'd with each Master'y stroak of the skillful Stone-Cutter. **1797** *Encycl. Brit.* (ed. 3) XVIII. 626/2 The varnish should be put on very quickly, making great strokes with the pencil or brush. **1804** *Revol. Plutarch* II. 305 In acting so, he changed with a stroke of the pen the general aspect of affairs, in such a manner that [etc.]. **1815** J. Smith *Panorama Sci. & Art* II. 745 Draperies are to be done with broad strokes of the pencil. **1875** Fortnum *Maiolica* 89 It would seem laid on purposely with a coarse brush the strokes of which are very apparent. **1885** 'Mrs. Alexander' *At Bay* viii, The money is in Spanish bonds..; it can be handed over to you with the stroke of a pen. **1889** Hasluck *Model Engin. Handybk.* 133 The file strokes should not all be made parallel one to another. **1907** J. A.

HODGES *Elem. Photogr.* (ed. 6) 106 The print should be cut with one stroke of the knife.

†**b.** Manner of handling the pencil, graver, etc.

1662 EVELYN *Chalcogr.* 69 The imitations of the graver.. are altogether admirable and inimitable, the stroke and conduct consider'd. **1699** WANLEY in *Lett. Lit. Men* (Camden) 282 The Print..is so well engraven, and the workman had so good a stroke, that I believe half the workmen in London cannot now do better. **1717** POPE *Ep. to Mr. Jervas* 38 Caracci's strength, Correggio's softer line, Paulo's free stroke, and Titian's warmth divine. *Ibid.* 64 Oh, lasting as those Colours may they shine, Free as thy stroke, yet faultless as thy line.

c. ***finishing stroke*** (lit. and fig.): see FINISHING *ppl. a.*

1695 PLOT in Aubrey *Lett. Eminent Persons* (1813) I. 74, I am heartily glad to hear Mr. Cook has given the finishing stroke to your fine chapel. **1800** *Asiatic Ann. Reg., Misc. Tracts* 16/2 Major Caillaud and the young Nabob crossed their troops over the Ganges, to put the finishing stroke to the affair. **1854** SURTEES *Handley Cr.* xxix. (1901) I. 218 On the Monday, he bespoke an audience with Mr. Jorrocks to put the finishing stroke to his arrangements. **1867** FREEMAN *Norm. Conq.* (1876) I. ii. 60 Æthelstan added the finishing stroke to the work of his father.

17. a. A linear mark; a mark traced by the moving point of a pen, pencil, etc.; a component line of a written character (cf. *up-stroke, down-stroke*); also, a dash (in writing or print).

1567 MAPLET *Gr. Forest* 2 [An agate] hauing strokes on eche side like to blew vaines. **1604** E. G[RIMSTONE] *D'Acosta's Hist. Indies* v. vii. 347 With the bloud they made a stroake on the dead mans face, from one eare to the other. **1673** DRYDEN *Marr. à la Mode* II. i, With strokes in ashes Maids their Lovers drew. **1688** HOLME *Armoury* II. 39/2 The Achate is variously coloured..: some have stroakes of blew, some with blood. **1693** J. EDWARDS *Author. O. & N. Test.* 201 The shadow..on the dial..went backward so many lines or stroaks. **1737** BRACKEN *Farriery Impr.* (1757) II. 32 The white Hoof is of a brittle Disposition; and those that have Strokes, or are ribbed as it were, with white, must be worse than the black Sort. **1745** P. THOMAS *Jrnl. Anson's Voy.* 243 A fourth Kind of Writing, the Strokes whereof being more joined, and less distinguished one from another, are made with more Ease and Expedition. **1815** J. SMITH *Panorama Sci. & Art* II. 19 The drawing of strokes by the eye with the black-lead pencil, charcoal, or chalk, will afford the most proper exercise. **1865** TROLLOPE *Belton Est.* xxvii. 326 Very careful in the perfection of every letter, and very neat in every stroke. **1885** SWEET *O.E. Texts* 132 The various readings are separated by a stroke, and come in the following order.

b. ***a stroke above***: = 'a cut above' (CUT *sb.* 17). *colloq. rare.*

1856 W. COLLINS *Wreck Golden Mary* ii. *Househ. Words* Christm. No. 14/2 She had had her schooling up in London ..so it was but nature she should be a stroke above the girls of the place. **1914** JOYCE *Dubliners* 153, I don't say Hynes. —No, damn it, I think he's a stroke above that.

c. *Bacteriology.* A line formed by drawing the point of an infected wire over the surface to be inoculated. Cf. *stroke-culture*, etc. in 26.

1893 M. CAMPBELL tr. *Migula's Introd. Pract. Bacteriol.* iv. 63 The colonies may confine themselves to the actual inoculating stroke, or they may spread themselves out.., until the whole surface of the nutrient medium is covered right up to the sides of the test-tube.

d. In *Telegraphy*, the name of the signal for an oblique stroke. Now usu. *colloq.*, a spoken representation of a solidus. Freq. used as *conj.* to indicate or stress alternatives: or else, alternatively.

1884 W. LYND *Pract. Telegraphist* i. 27 The oblique stroke is to be signalled 'stroke', thus—'FI three stroke five FF', meaning 3/5 (three shillings and fivepence). **1965** M. ALLINGHAM *Mind Readers* xv. 153, I have my own feel, of course, which would be 'glad stroke laughingat' in his case. **1971** J. YARDLEY *Kiss a Day keeps Corpses Away* ii. 39 The Truman stroke Eisenhower regime. **1974** G. MARKSTEIN *Cooter* xlvii. 171 ABPQ stroke 113 stroke 1. Ah yes. Is that your national registration number? **1977** N. J. CRISP *Odd Job Man* iii. 28 One dozen cardigans, stroke thirty-three, blue, for knitwear.

e. *spec.* in *Logic* = *Sheffer('s) stroke* s.v. SHEFFER.

1925 WHITEHEAD & RUSSELL *Principia Math.* (ed. 2) I. p. xvi, The symbol '*p/q*' is pronounced: '*p* stroke *q*'... All the usual truth-functions can be constructed by means of the stroke. **1952** R. L. WILDER *Introd. Found. Math.* ix. 220 Since P[rincipia] M[athematica] was first published, with its two undefined symbols (or 'logical constants')..it has been shown that *one* undefined symbol..[is] sufficient. The symbol referred to is / and is called 'stroke'. **1975** P. K. BASTABLE *Logic* 189 Later he [*sc.* Russell] preferred to become acquainted with implication through defining it as 'Either not *p* or *q*' or, like Sheffer and Nicod, in terms of the stroke functor.

†**18. a.** Lineament, line of a face or form. *Obs.*

1635-56 COWLEY *Davideis* IV. 526 Not bright Ahin'oam.. Had sweeter strokes, Colours more fresh and fair. **1638** JUNIUS *Paint. Ancients* 21 They..content themselves with the Imitation of visible things, following stroke after stroke.

†**b.** *fig.* A constituent feature; a characteristic; a trait of character. *Obs.*

1666 S. PARKER *Platonic Philos.* 41 In its main strokes it [*sc.* Plato's 'physiology'] accords with the Aristotelean Philosophie. **1710** FELTON *Diss. Classics* (1718) 49 Give me Leave, my Lord, to..draw out..some of the chief Strokes, some of the principal Lineaments, and fairest Features of a just and beautiful Style. **1729** LAW *Serious C.* xvi. (1732) 303 He is so very quick sighted that he discovers in almost every body, some Strokes of vanity. **1734** tr. *Rollin's Rom. Hist.* VI. (1827) III. 241 Two or three principal strokes of his character. **1780** A. YOUNG *Tour Irel.* II. 75 Many strokes in their character are evidently to be ascribed to the extreme oppression under which they live.

c. *fig.* A felicitous or characteristic expression or thought in literary composition; a 'touch' of description, satire, pathos, or the like. Cf. 15.

1666 DRYDEN *Ann. Mirab.* Pref., But when Action or Persons are to be described..how bold, how masterly, are the strokes of Virgil! **1697** *C'tess D'Aunoy's Trav.* (1706) 88 He wrote a Comedy which everybody likes, and the Queen ..found therein such moving and delicate Stroaks in it, that she would act a part in it herself. **1706** PRIOR *Ode to Queen* Pref., I have endeavor'd to imitate all the great Strokes of that Ode. **1725** COTES tr. *Dupin's Eccl. Hist. 17th C.* I. II. iii. 35 Not to mention many satyrical Strokes which are scatter'd throughout his History. **1770** JORTIN *Erasmus* II. 170 One can hardly excuse Erasmus intirely, for having put into the mouth of Folly some strokes, which seem to confound religious Truth with Folly. **1831** MACKINTOSH *Hist. Eng.* II. 16 A few strokes of Comines throw a more clear and agreeable light over our story than the scanty information of our own meagre and unskilful writers. **1876** TREVELYAN *Life & Lett. Macaulay* II. xi. 226 Macaulay.. thought..nothing whatever of reconstructing a paragraph for the sake of one happy stroke or apt illustration.

†**19.** ***to have a good stroke (at eating)***: to have a hearty appetite. (Cf. TWIST *sb.*[1] 18.) *Obs.*

1699 DAMPIER *Voy.* II. iv. 71 Neither can any man be entertain'd as a Soldier, that has not a greater stroke than ordinary at eating. **1731-8** SWIFT *Polite Conv.* ii. 150 *Lady Answ.* God bless you, Colonel; you have a good Stroke with you. *Col.* O Madam; formerly I could eat all, but now I leave nothing.

†**20.** A cut, slice (of meat). *Obs.*

1581 A. HALL *Iliad* IX. 157 Down he layes the spit, Wheron the strokes of flesh were brotcht.

21. *Agric.* (See quot. 1891.)

1765 *Museum Rust.* IV. 6 Give the land a stroke with the great harrow, and roll it as before. **1847** *Jrnl. R. Agric. Soc.* VIII. II. 449 When the seed is sown, it should be covered by two strokes of the light seed-harrow. **1891** MALDEN *Tillage* Gloss. s.v., Each time land is crossed with harrows it is said to have received a stroke or tine.

†**22.** = TRANSOM 2. *Obs. rare*$^{-1}$.

1684 STURMY *Mariner's Mag.* VII. xix. (ed. 2) 140 Chuse a convenient place in the Transum or Stroke of the Window.

23. A denomination of dry measure, varying in capacity according to locality: = STRIKE *sb.* 4.

1532 *Test. Ebor.* (Surtees) VI. 34 To have one stroke of peese. **1569** *Richmond Wills* (Surtees) 218, xx^{ti} stroke wheate, iiij li. **1681** O. HEYWOOD *Diaries* (1881) II. 286 A stroke of shilling [= shelled oats] standing on the table. **1744** *MS. Parish Bk. Pannal, Yorks.*, A strooke of Pottatoes 5 d. **1790** GROSE *Prov. Gloss.* (ed. 2) Suppl., *Stroke*, half a bushel. **1814** W. S. MASON *Statist. Acc. Irel.* I. 339 The measure, or stroke of potatoes 2 Bushels. **1862** C. C. ROBINSON *Dial. Leeds* 424 *Stroke*, a half-bushel, or two pecks; so called from the measure (when upheaped) being stroked off with a thin piece of wood.

24. *Geol.* = STRIKE *sb.* 8. *rare.*

1877 RAYMOND *Statist. Mines & Mining* 113 The stroke of the slates varies from north 25° west, south 25° east, to north 45° west, south 45° east.

25. *Basket-making.* A single movement analogous to a stitch in sewing or knitting; the result of this.

1912 T. OKEY *Art of Basket-Making* vii. 59 Where an even number of pairs of leagues or sticks is used, the centre strokes lie alternate, and not side by side. *Ibid.* 154 *Stroke*, any complete movement in basket-work: analogous to a stitch in needlework. **1960** E. LEGG *Country Baskets* iii. 29 And now for the strokes, which are comparable with 'stitches' in knitting... The strokes are indeed simple and few.

26. *attrib.* **a.** *Golf*, in terms relating to the method of scoring by strokes (sense 1 d) instead of by holes, as ***stroke-competition, -game, -play***; **b.** *Bacteriology* (sense 17 c), as ***stroke-cultivation, -culture, -inoculation***; **c.** special combinations, †**stroke-bias**, an obsolete game resembling 'prisoners' base'; †**stroke engraving**, a line engraving; **stroke-haul**, an apparatus used for illegal capture of fish, formed of three hooks joined back to back, and weighted with lead; hence **stroke-haul** *v.*, **stroke-hauling** *vbl. sb.*; **stroke-maker** *Cricket*, a batsman who plays attractive, attacking strokes; hence **stroke-making**; **stroke-oar**, (*a*) the oar nearest the stern of a rowing-boat; (*b*) the rower who handles this oar (= sense 13 d); **stroke-oarsman** = sense 13 d; **stroke-ornamented** *a. Archæol.* (see quot. 1970); **strokeplay** *Cricket*, the playing of attractive, attacking strokes; hence **stroke-player**; **stroke-side**, the side of a rowing-boat on which the stroke-oarsman sits; **stroke-stitch** *Needlework* (see quot.).

1700 J. BROME *Trav. Eng.* 264 The Kentish Men have a peculiar Exercise,..'tis called *Stroke-Biass. [Description follows.] **1904** in H. Vardon *Compl. Golfer* (1905) 274 Special Rules for *Stroke Competitions. **1890** W. W. CHEYNE tr. *Flügge's Micro-organisms* 177 *Stroke cultivations. **1893** M. CAMPBELL tr. *Migula's Introd. Pract. Bacteriol.* iv. 62 For the *stroke cultures we use the test-tubes. **1793** THOMSON in *Burns' Wks.* (1800) IV. 33 We intend presenting the subscribers with two beautiful *stroke engravings. **1896** *Westm. Gaz.* 8 Apr. 5/3 The match.. consists of the *stroke game to-day and play by holes to-morrow. **1850** *Act 13 & 14 Vict.* c. 88 §40 That it shall not be lawful..to use for the Purpose of taking Fish any Otter, Lyster, Spear, *Strokehaul, Dree Draw, or Gaff. **1912** *London Mag.* Sept. 97/2 They *stroke-hauled them in couples in the moonlight. **1860** C. SIMEON *Stray Notes Fishing* 37 This plan, with a large weighted treble hook, is sometimes adopted with destructive effect by poachers for salmon..it is then called '*stroke-hauling'. **1893** M. CAMPBELL tr. *Migula's Introd. Pract. Bacteriol.* iv. 62 The *stroke inoculation being completed. **1927** *Observer* 5 June 21/5 A beautiful *stroke-maker, he [*sc.* H. W. Austin] is pleasant to watch. **1976** J. SNOW *Cricket Rebel* 84 Nurse could be a brilliant and savage stroke-maker on his day, but could graft when necessary. **1956** R. ALSTON *Test Commentary* iii. 23 One of the features of the morning's play was the *stroke-making of..Van Geloven. **1977** *World of Cricket Monthly* June 87/1 He impressed the Lord's gathering with his crisp stroke-making. **1835** DICKENS *Sk. Boz, River*, After a great deal of changing and fidgeting, consequent upon the election of a *stroke-oar. **1848** THACKERAY *Van. Fair* xi, At College he pulled stroke-oar in the Christchurch boat. **1865** KINGSLEY *Herew.* xx, Winter steered the boat and Gwenoch took the stroke-oar. **1838** J. F. COOPER *Excurs. Italy* I. xvi. 302 The *stroke-oarsman of the boat advised me to pull in under the promontory. **1894** *Daily News* 3 July 8/3 One of the finest stroke oarsmen in England. **1925** V. G. CHILDE *Dawn Europ. Civilization* xii. 172 The second ware may..be called *stroke-ornamented pottery. Its forms are rather more angular than those of spiral-meander pottery. *Ibid.* xviii. 272 Hut foundations.. yielded sherds with curvilinear decoration and others recalling the Danubian stroke-ornamented ware. **1970** BRAY & TRUMP *Dict. Archaeol.* 222/1 *Stroke-ornamented ware*, pottery with zigzag patterns made by a series of distinct jabs rather than continuous lines. It was current during the centuries after 4000 BC in Bohemia, west Poland, Bavaria and central Germany. **1905** *Daily Chron.* 20 July 3/1 The old golf was Scotch, and was a match game. The new, English game, is *stroke play, with oneself as one's hardiest opponent. **1930** C. G. MACARTNEY *My Cricketing Days* ii. 14 Perhaps this sort of cricket was an aid to stroke play, perhaps not, but as far as I can see, it never did me any harm. **1979** *Daily Tel.* 19 May 29/1 Any doubts about his form or fitness were violently dismissed in a morning of rich strokeplay. **1935** *Times* 20 July 13/5 Some of the English cricketers now getting past their prime are still *stroke-players. **1963** A. ROSS *Australia 63* x. 183 There were, on the England side, three stroke-players capable of enhancing any Test, on the Australian side two. **1862** LD. W. LENNOX *Recreat. Sportsm.* I. 197 The terms in boating are as follows:—..*stroke side, the port, or right side. **1909** *Blackw. Mag.* May 613/2 Tell Jerry to get down a new strokeside oar, with a good six-inch blade. **1900** L. F. DAY & MARY BUCKLE *Art in Needlework* ii. (1901) 16 The mere work line—or '*stroke-stitch', not crossed, is a perfectly fair way of getting a delicate effect.

stroke, *sb.*[2] Also 7-8 **stroak**. [f. STROKE *v.*[1]]

1. A stroking movement of the hand, esp. for purposes of healing. Also, an act of stroking, esp. by way of caress.

1631 B. JONSON *New Inn* IV. ii, *Tip.* Hee'll borrow money on the stroke of his beard! Or turne off his Mustaccio. **1665** *Wonders if not Miracles V. Gertrux* title-p., Who Cureth all manner of Diseases with a stroak of his hand and Prayer. **1666** H. STUBBE *Mirac. Conformist* 6 Having..stopped the paine and effusion of blood by some strokes of his hand, he bad her put nothing to it but a linnen Cloth. **1697** DRYDEN *Æneis* x. 1229 Soothing his Courage with a gentle Stroke, The Steed seem'd sensible, while thus he spoke. **1728** CHAMBERS *Cycl.* s.v. *Stroaking*, But as to the particular Efficacy of the Stroak of particular Persons; we see little Foundation for it in Nature. **1953** H. E. BATES *Nature of Love* iv. 36 She gave her hair a long deep casual stroke with the brush.

2. An act of copulation. *slang. rare.*

1785 GROSE *Classical Dict. Vulgar Tongue* s.v., *Stroke. To take a stroke*, to take a bout with a woman. **1976** P. CAVE *High Flying Birds* ii. 19, I happened to be engaged upon a variation of the sexual act known as the 'Birmingham Stroke' at the time our little love-nest started rolling.

3. A comforting gesture of approval or congratulation (see also quot. 1964). Hence, a flattering or friendly remark, etc., esp. one made in order to help or manipulate another. Cf. STROKE *v.*[1] 1 e. Now chiefly *U.S. colloq.*

1964 E. BERNE *Games People Play* 15 By an extension of meaning, 'stroking' may be employed colloquially to denote any act implying recognition of another's presence. Hence a *stroke* may be used as the fundamental unit of social action. An exchange of strokes constitutes a *transaction*, which is the unit of social intercourse. **1969** T. A. HARRIS *I'm OK, You're OK* iii. 45 The Adult has something to work on: what must I do to gain their strokes, or their approval? **1973** *Houston* (Texas) *Chron. Texas Mag.* 14 Oct. 4/1 The popular saying around PDAP [*sc.* The Palmer Drug Abuse Program] is 'different strokes for different folks', and that's the basis of the program. **1978** M. PUZO *Fools Die* xi. 122 He started off dishing out some nice strokes. With an admiring smile he told me how smart I was, how honest, so absolutely reliable. **1981** *TV Picture Life* Mar. 12/3 Let's face it, everybody needs their strokes and that would be very ego-satisfying.

4. Special combinations: **stroke book**, a pornographic book; **stroke house** *U.S.*, a cinema where pornographic films are shown.

1972 *Pussycat* XXXIII. LIX. 10/1 For a stroke book, the quality of writing is astonishingly good. **1978** T. GIFFORD *Glendower Legacy* (1979) 73 I'm just going to pig out at home, look at a stroke book... As a matter of fact, I've taken to writing for stroke books. **1971** *Atlantic Monthly* July 52 He would camp in the 42nd Street stroke houses and come back with tales of what they were getting away with now.

†**stroke**, *sb.*[3] ? *Anglo-Irish. Obs. rare*$^{-1}$. (Sense obscure.)

Perh. a misprint for *noke*, NOOK *sb.* (where see senses 3 d, e).

1571 E. CAMPION *Hist. Irel.* 14/2 in *Holinshed* (1577), Styll erecting Castelles..so to mayster the Irishe, that with such maner of strengthes of Walles..had not as yet beene acquaynted, for tyll those dayes they knewe no defence but Woods, Bogs, or strokes.

stroke (strəʊk), *sb.*[4] *Obs.* exc. *dial.* Also 8 **stroak.** [Altered form of STRAKE *sb.*[1]] = STRAKE *sb.*[1] 1 a.

1688 HOLME *Armory* III. 332/1 The parts of a Wheel. The Nave,.. The Stroke, is the Iron Rim about the Felloes. **1773** W. EMERSON *Princ. Mech.* (ed. 3) 283 *Stroaks* or *straiks*, the iron going round the circumference of carriage wheels. **1904** *Eng. Dial. Dict.*

stroke (strəʊk), *v.*[1] Pa. t. and pa. pple. **stroked** (strəʊkt). Forms: α. 1 **strácian,** 6–7 **stroake,** 6–8 **stroak,** 7 **strocke, strooke,** 8–9 *dial.* **strock,** 3– **stroke.** β. *Sc.* and *north.* 5–6, 9 **strake,** 6 **straik(e, strayk(e,** 8–9 **straik.** [OE. *strácian*, corresp. to MLG., MDu. *strêken* (mod.Du. *streeken*), OHG. *streihhôn* (MHG., mod.G. *streichen*, which coalesced with *streichen*:—OHG. *strîhhan* STRIKE *v.*), f. Teut. **straik*-, ablaut-var. of **strīk*-: see STRIKE *v.*]

1. a. *trans.* To rub (a surface) softly with the hand or some implement; esp. to pass the hand softly in one direction over (the head, body, hair, of a person or animal) by way of caress or as a method of healing (cf. STROKE *sb.*[2], STROKER, also STRIKE *v.* 4 b).

α. *c* **897** ÆLFRED *Gregory's Past. C.* xli. 303 Swa [swa] wildu hors, ðonne we h[ie] æresð ȝefangnu habbað, we hie ðacciað & straciað mid bradre handa. *c* **1000** *Sax. Leechd.* III. 134 Myd swyþe driȝeon handum straca ȝeornlice þane innoþ. *c* **1290** *St. Francis* 367 in *S. Eng. Leg.* 64 He.. strokede heom [birds] with is longue sleue. **13..** *Gaw. & Gr. Knt.* 334 He stroked his berde. **1398** TREVISA *Barth. De P.R.* XVIII. xcvi. (1495) 842 Tame apes haue lykyng to be strokyd. **1530** PALSGR. 741/1, I stroke ones heed, as we do a chyldes by flatterynge, or whan he dothe well. **1575** TURBERV. *Falconrie* 100 Then muste you haue a little rownde stycke.. with the whiche you shall oftentymes stroke and handle your Falcon. **1603** KNOLLES *Hist. Turks* (1638) 302 Oftentimes stroking his white beard, as his manner was when he was thorowly angry. **1619** *Wonderf. Discov. Witchcrafts Marg. Flower* etc. (1837) 22 Wherevpon she brought downe a gloue and deliuered the same to her mother, who stroked Rutterkin her Cat with it. **1655** J. S. *Bonarelli's Filli di Sciro* II. i. 28 As they had Learnt to strooke each others cheekes. **1662** FAITHORNE *Graving & Etching* xxv. 41 Then take a piece of the whitest Virgin-wax and spread it thin over the plate, and with a smooth feather gently stroak it all over, to the end it may lie the more even and smooth. **1665** *Wonders if not Miracles V. Gertrux* 7 He likewise cures the Convulsion fits only by stroaking the persons afflicted with his hand. *a* **1700** EVELYN *Diary* 6 July 1660, The Chirurgeons cause the sick to be brought or led up to the throne, where they kneeling, the King strokes their faces or cheekes with both his hands at once. **1788** GIBBON *Decl. & F.* l. V. 183 His only gesture is that of stroking his beard. **1911** MAX BEERBOHM *Zuleika Dobson* xvi. 241 Softly she stroked the carpet with the palms of her hands.

β. **1786** BURNS *Epist. J. Rankine* viii, The poor wee thing was little hurt; I straiket it a wee for sport.

b. said of an animal.

1621 QUARLES *Hadassa* Introd. B 4 b, This [steed] stroaks the ground, that skorn's it with his heele. **1774** GOLDSM. *Nat. Hist.* IV. 56 It [the guinea-pig] strokes its head with the fore feet like the rabbit. **1913** *Oxf. Univ. Gaz.* 4 June 948/2 The male *Amauris egialea* stroking the brands of the hind wings with its anal tufts.

c. *absol.* (Proverbially contrasted with *strike*.)

c **897** ÆLFRED *Gregory's Past. C.* xxvi. 187 Sua se læce grapað, & stracað,.. ærðonðe he stingan wille. **1612** J. DAVIES (Heref.) *Muse's Sacrif.* (Grosart) 51/1 So, with remorse, reuenge to execute; So, stroke and strike at once. **1675** HANNAH WOOLLEY *Gentlew. Comp.* 128 When you have laid three or four layers one on the other, wet a feather in Rosewater and Musk, and stroke over it. **1699** THORESBY in *Phil. Trans.* XXI. 334 Where he stroked for Pains, he used nothing but his dry Hand. **1750** BERKELEY *Patriotism* §19 Wks. 1871 III. 456 A good groom will rather stroke than strike. **1757** W. WILKIE *Epigoniad* IV. 95 His weighty hands he laid On their soft backs, and, stroaking gently, said [etc.].

d. *to stroke against the hair, the wrong way* (*of the hair*): to rub (an animal) in the direction opposite to the natural lie of its hair; *fig.* to irritate, ruffle, cross (a person). Similarly *to stroke with the hair*, to soothe (*Sc.*).

c **1590** MONTGOMERIE *Sonn.* xxxiii. 6 In hir vnhappy hands sho held my heed, And straikit bakuard wodershins my hair. **1786** BURNS *Earnest Cry & Prayer* xviii, For God-sake, Sirs! then speak her fair, An' straik her cannie wi' the hair. **1816** SCOTT *Bl. Dwarf* viii, I'll speak him fair.. and stroke him wi' the hair. **1844** W. CROSS *Disruption* xi. (1846) 113, I hae a good deal o' the cuddy in me, when I'm straikit against the hair. **1860** TROLLOPE *Castle Richm.* I. xiii. 260 Somebody's been stroking him the wrong way of the 'air.

e. *transf.* and *fig.* †Formerly often, = to soothe, flatter, 'tickle'; also, to treat indulgently, cocker, make much of (cf. L. *mulcere*). Sometimes contrasted with *strike*. In recent use, to reassure (a child, etc.) by approval or congratulation (see also quot. 1964). Hence, to manipulate (another) by means of flattery, persuasion, etc.; to compliment. Cf. STROKE *sb.*[2] 3. Now chiefly *U.S. colloq.*, esp. in political contexts.

1513 DOUGLAS *Æneis* IV. Prol. 189 Venus henvifis.. That strakis thir wenchis hedis thaim to pleis. **1561** T. NORTON *Calvin's Inst.* II. i. §2 (1562) 70 There is nothing that mannes nature more coueteth, than to be stroked with flattery. **1600** EDMONDS *Observ. Cæsar's Comm.* VII. (1604) 126 If it be demaunded, what became of these great Princes and personages after the triumph, it will appeare that they did not stroke their heads, or make more of them then of miserable captiues. **1610** SHAKS. *Temp.* I. ii. 333 When thou cam'st first Thou stroakst me, & made much of me. **1616** B. JONSON *Epigr.* lxi, Thy praise or dispraise is to me alike, One doth not stroke me, nor the other strike. *a* **1637** —— *Underwoods, Eupheme* iv, The voice so sweet, the words so fair, As some soft chime had stroked the air. **1629** MAXWELL tr. *Herodian* (1635) 145 With these faire Promises he stroked the Senators. **1675** TRAHERNE *Chr. Ethics* To Rdr., The design of this treatise is, not to stroak and tickle the fancy, but to elevate the soul. **1742** YOUNG *Nt. Th.* IX. 2175 Sleep's dewy wand Has strok'd my drooping lids. **1898** HARDY *Wessex Poems* 94 They parted there as morning stroked the panes. **1964** [see STROKE *sb.*[2] 3]. **1969** T. A. HARRIS *I'm OK, You're OK* iii. 48 If a two-year-old concludes *I'm OK*, does this mean his *OK* is the product of 'self-stroking' and, if so, how does a small child stroke himself? **1973** T. C. HUSTON in L. Chester et al. *Watergate* iv. 43 Mr. Hoover should be called in privately for a stroking session at which the President [*sc.* Nixon] explains the decision he had made. **1975** *Atlantic Monthly* Mar. 44 It's Show Biz, man—a bunch a' egomaniacal people using a captive audience to stroked themselves. **1977** *Time* 17 Oct. 20/1 Carter also stroked the Jerusalem government by promising that the U.S. would never attempt to impose a Middle East settlement. **1978** *New Yorker* 9 Jan. 41 He tells his client, 'It's looking pretty good. We'll stay on top of it.' This is what is known as 'stroking' the client. **1981** *Observer* 11 Jan. 6/5, I think he's still a little kid from Hoboken, who likes to be stroked by Presidents.

f. *to stroke over*: = PERSTRINGE *v.*[2]

1822 BYRON *To Murray* 25 Dec., Since I have read the Quarterly, I shall erase two or three passages in the latter six or seven cantos, in which I had lightly stroked over two or three of your authors.

g. With adv. or similar extension: To bring into a specified position, condition, etc. by stroking. Also *fig.*

1594 NASHE *Unfort. Trav.* Wks. (Grosart) V. 73 Hee would take occasion to stroke vp his haire, and turne vp his mustachios twice or thrice ouer. **1615** CROOKE *Body of Man* 81 The Midwife after she haue stroaked down the bloud to nourish the Babe. **1639** FULLER *Holy War* II. viii. (1640) 54 The Pope.. stroked the angry Patriarch of Antioch into gentlenesse with good language. **1666** H. STUBBE *Mirac. Conformist* 29 Such consequents are usuall, when the Disease is not stroked out. **1675** SOUTH *Serm.* Judges viii. 34, 35 (1692) 581 He.. sees the folly of Endeavouring to stroke a Tyger into a Lamb. **1697** DAMPIER *Voy.* I. xv. 407 Letting it [their hair] grow very long, and stroking it back with their Hands curiously. **1764** GRAY *Jemmy Twitcher* 22 She strok'd up her belly, and strok'd down her band. **1770** LUCKOMBE *Hist. Printing* 360 With the back sides of the nails of his fingers to draw or stroke it [i.e. the paper to be printed] over the Point. **1859** *Habits of Gd. Society* xiv. 359 With his hands so full that he cannot even stroke out his splendid whiskers.

h. To express or testify by stroking. *rare.*

1648 J. BEAUMONT *Psyche* XIX. cclxxiii, And then she prais'd the steeds unwearied Pains, Stroking her thanks upon their ruffled Mains.

i. To pass (one's hand) gently *over* a surface.

1697 C. LESLIE *Snake in Grass* (ed. 2) 114 Stroaking his Hand over their Faces (as his Custom was) who kneel'd or fell prostrate before him.

2. To draw (a cutting instrument) along a surface in order to sharpen or whet it. Cf. STRAKE *v.*[3] 1 and G. *streichen. Obs.* or *arch.*

13.. *Gaw. & Gr. Knt.* 416 '.. Ta now þy grymme tole to þe, & let se how þou cnokez.' 'Gladly sir, for soþe', Quod Gawan; his ax he strokes. *a* **1800** *Bonny Birdy* xv. in Child *Ballads* II. 261 Then out the knight has drawn his sword, An straiked it oer a strae. **1885–94** BRIDGES *Eros & Psyche* July xv, She.. laid the knife, to mortal keenness stroked, Within her reach, where she was wont to lie.

†3. *fig.* To plight (one's troth). *Obs.* Cf. STRIKE *v.* 69.

a **1400–50** *Wars Alex.* 3192 Þire traitours on þis trechoure trowthis has strakid [*Dublin MS.* han stroken]. *a* **1776** *Sweet William's Ghost* ix. in Child *Ballads* II. 230 Up she has tain a bright long wand, And she has straked her trouth thereon.

4. To milk (a cow); esp. to draw the last milk from (a cow) by pressing the teat. Also *fig.* Cf. STROKING *vbl. sb.*; also STRAP *v.*[2], STRIP *v.*[3] 1.

1538 ELYOT *Dict.*, *Mulgeo*, to mylke or stroke. **1639** FULLER *Holy War* IV. xvii. (1640) 198 Some say.. that this onely was a trick to stroke the skittish cow to get down her milk. *a* **1658** LOVELACE *Lucasta, Posth. Poems* (1659) 83 No wonder if a Drawer Verses Rack,.. Whilst the Fair Barmaid stroaks the Muses teat, For milk to make the Posset up compleat. **1675** HAN. WOOLLEY *Gentlew. Comp.* 215 When you milk your Cattel, stroke them well, and in the Summer-time save those strokings by themselves, to put into your morning-Milk-cheese. **1746** *Exmoor Scolding* 47 Nif tha dest bet go down into the Paddick, to stroak the Kee. *Ibid.* 110 Thee hast a let the Kee go zoo vor Want o' strocking. **1886** *W. Somerset Word-bk.*, *Stroke*, to take part of the milk; to milk gently.

5. ? To whip (cream, a sillabub).

a **1639** WOTTON *Descr. Spring* 18, Reliq. W. (1651) 524 And now She trips to milk the Sand-red Cow; Where, for some sturdy foot-ball Swaine, Jone strokes a sillibub, or twaine. **1908** *Daily Chron.* 12 June 9/6 Chocolate Hands.—Wanted cream coverers, used to curl and stroke.

6. To smear (something) over a surface. *Obs.* exc. *Sc.* (Cf. STRAKE *v.*[3] 2.)

1586 LUPTON *1000 Notable Things* (1675) 88 Let.. the water thereof be dropped and stroaked about the Eyes. **1883** J. KENNEDY in D. H. Edwards *Mod. Sc. Poets* VI. 218 Now she's prappit near the ceiling, Straikin' whitening on the wa'. **1888** A. G. MURDOCH *Sc. Readings* Ser. II. (ed. 2) 33 Johnny himself was busy 'straiking' the melted solution roun' the inner edge of the rim of his hat with the point of his right fore finger.

7. *Masonry.* To work the face of (a stone) in such a manner as to produce a sort of fluted surface (Ogilvie 1850).

1842 GWILT *Archit.* §1911 In London, the squared stone used for facing buildings is usually stroked, tooled, or rubbed. **1910** [see STROKED *ppl. a.*[1]].

8. *Needlework.* To dispose (small gathers) in regular order and close succession by drawing the point of a blunt needle from the top of each gather downwards.

1875 [MRS. FLOYER] *Plain Needlework* 21 The top of the gathers above the thread should be stroked, to give them an even appearance. **1880** —— *Plain Hints Needlework* 48 Gather, stroke, and set in. **1909** *Even. Standard* 2 Aug. 11/4 In stroking gathers, the needle should be held in a sloping direction.

9. *Printing.* To move (a sheet) into place by a stroking-movement of the hand. Also *to stroke in.*

1888 [see STROKER 1 b].

10. To level (grain) in a measure; = STRAIK *v.*

1887 HALL CAINE *Deemster* v. 30 The bushel of the poor man was not to be stroked, but left in heaped-up measure.

Hence **stroked,** *ppl. a.*[1], **'stroking** *ppl. a.*

1619 B. JONSON *Masques, Pleas. reconciled to Virtue* (1640) 28 But with a minde as gentle as the stroaking winde runs ore the gentler flowers. **1620** QUARLES *Feast for Worms* G 3, A Yongling.. (Scarce weaned from his dandling mothers tet, Where he was cockerd with a stroking hand). **1693** DRYDEN *Ovid's Met.* I. 891 They stroke her Neck; the gentle Heyfar stands, And her Neck offers to their stroking Hands. **1890** *Nature* 9 Oct. 578/2 The method adopted.. consisted in determining the velocity of sound in the vapour by Kundt's dust-figures, from observation of the wave-length and the pitch of the note emitted by the stroked tube containing the vapour. **1898** A. LANG *Making of Relig.* i. 4 Such phenomena science has ignored, as it so long ignored the sparks from the stroked deer-skin. **1910** C. H. GREGORY *Gloss. Build. Constr.* 38 Striped or Stroked Work. Chisel marks made across a stone at an angle of 45°.

stroke (strəʊk), *v.*[2] [f. STROKE *sb.*[1]]

I. 1. *trans.* To mark with streaks or stripes. So **stroked** *ppl. a.*[2], striped. *rare.* Cf. STRAKE *v.*[4], STRAKED *ppl. a.*

1597 A. M. tr. *Guillemeau's Fr. Chirurg.* 31/4 Those [leeches] which have the backes stripped, stroked with gouldeyellow strokes. **1896** W. HARVEY *Kennethcrook* 35 (E.D.D.) If there's siccan things as spottit horses, what ails ye at strokit anes?

†2. To depict with strokes of the brush. *Obs.*

1624 WOTTON *Elem. Archit.* II. 84 Such a seeming softnesse in the Limbes, as if not a Chissell has hewed them out of Stone,.. but a Pensill had drawne and stroaked them in Oyle.

3. To draw the horizontal line across the upright of (the letter *t*); to cross. Also *fig.*: cf. T 1 b.

1894 MAX PEMBERTON *Sea Wolves* xi. (1901) 51 What I can spell right here is thirst, and stroke the t's, too! **1897** *Bookman* Jan. 120/1 So Landor dotted the i's, stroked the t's, put in qualifying words, and flat contradictions.

4. With *out* or *through*: To cancel by drawing a line or lines across; to cross out.

1885 EMILY D. GERARD *Waters of Hercules* xxv, Half of what I had written was stroked through. **1910** G. STEVENSON *Suppl. Montgomerie's Poems* (S.T.S.) 247 *note*, The name 'hay' has been stroked out.

5. Of a bell: to chime the strokes of (the hour, etc.). *poet. rare*[−1].

1902 HARDY *Poems of Past & Present* 132 As the hope-hour stroked its sum, You did not come.

†II. 6. *nonce-use.* To throw *into* (a palsy). Cf. STROKE *sb.*[1] 5.

1647 J. HALL *Poems* II. 78 In thine Eye Carrying an all-enraged Majesty; That shall the Earth into a Palsie stroke, And make the Clouds sigh out themselves in smoake.

III. 7. a. To row stroke in (a boat); to act as stroke to (a crew).

1866 *Morn. Star* 14 Feb., They are alternately stroked by Messrs. Brown and Senhouse. **1874** *Shotover Papers* I. No. xi. 172 They wanted Jones to stroke the Varsity boat. **1899** *Daily News* 16 Feb. 7/2 In the last two races he had the satisfaction of stroking his side to victory.

b. Of an oarsman or crew: to row at (a certain number of strokes per minute).

1928 *Times* 11 Aug. 5 The winner stroked an average of 28 to Gunther's 30. **1976** C. FREUD in *Webster's Sports Dict.* 431/1 With 500 yards to go, the Cairo Police, stroking 38, edged past Oxford.

8. *Sport.* To hit or kick (the ball) smoothly and elegantly; to score in this manner.

1960 J. FINGLETON *Four Chukkas to Australia* xvi. 136 He.. raved of the manner in which Cowdrey stroked the ball. **1962** [see CROSS *sb.* 22 e]. **1972** *Even. Telegram* (St. John's, Newfoundland) 24 June 1/1 Bernie Allen stroked his first home run of the season. **1976** *Wymondham & Attleborough Express* 3 Dec. 27/4 Wortwell fought back and were awarded a spot kick only for Webb to stroke the ball straight to the keeper.

stroke, *v.*[3] *rare.* Also 9 *Sc.* **straik.** [? related to STRAKE *v.*[1]] *intr.* To go quickly; to travel.

1735 SOMERVILLE *Chase* III. 445 The gen'rous Steed, that strokes along O'er rough, o'er smooth. **1823** TENNANT *Card. Beaton* I. iii. 28 We'el better slip awa' soon to our beds the night, that we may rise wi' the day-daw, if we're to straik down to the coast.

stroke, *v.*[4] *rare*[−1]. [? An artificial anglicizing of *straik*, Sc. form of STREEK *v.*] *trans.* To lay out (a corpse). Also with *out.*

1898 N. MUNRO *John Splendid* i. 4 My dear cousin, stroked out and cold under foreign clods at Velshiem. *Ibid.* xi. 116 We gathered and stroked our dead.

stroke, stroken: see STRIKE *v.*

strokel, obs. form of STRUGGLE *v.*

stroker ('strəʊkə(r)). [f. STROKE *v.*¹ and *sb.*¹ + -ER¹.]

1. One who strokes; *spec.* one who cures diseases by stroking.

1632 B. JONSON *Magn. Lady* IV. i, *Kee.* What you please, Dame Polish, My Ladies Stroaker. **1665** T. A. *Excell. Roy. Hand* 1 Divers persons.. boasting themselves the seventh Sons, Stroakers, and what not,.. promising by their manual Touch, the perfect Cure of those Swellings, commonly called by the name of the Kings Evil. **1666** *(title)* Rub for Rub; or, an Answer to a Physicians pamphlet, styled the Stroker Stroked. **1668** [GLANVILL] *Blow at modern Sadducism* 85 The great discourse now at the Coffee-Houses, and every where, is about Mr. G[reatrak], the famous Irish Stroker. **1851** MRS. BROWNING *Casa Guidi Wind.* I. 666 No man would be The stroker of his mane. **1886** *Folk-Lore Jrnl.* IV. 361 Erysipelas. This in Donegal is known as The Rose; it..can be cured by a Stroker. *Ibid.*, The women's friends brought in a 'stroker', who rubbed the nurse with bog-moss [etc.].

b. *stroker-in* in *Printing*: see quot. 1888.

1888 JACOBI *Printers' Vocab.* 134 *Stroker-in*, the layer-on who strokes in the sheets one by one to be printed. **1902** *Daily Chron.* 18 Aug. 9/7 Strokers-in (Smart) wanted for printing machine.

2. An implement used for some operation likened to stroking (see quots.).

1884 McLAREN *Spinning* (ed. 2) 161 As it revolves it is met by the stroker.., a wheel with sharp teeth projecting from it. .. This wheel revolves from left to right, and is used to stroke the wool which projects from the little circle, so as to turn the ends forwards. **1888** JACOBI *Printers' Vocab.* 134 *Stroker*, a small implement, generally made of wood and tipped with metal, for 'stroking in', or laying on sheets in a printing machine.

3. [f. STROKE *sb.*¹] One who make strokes in Polo.

1895 *Outing* XXVI. 389/1 The Iowa Clubs are now playing the regulation American game and they bring to it a formidable set of fearless riders and brilliant strokers.

strokesman ('strəʊksmən). [f. genit. of STROKE *sb.* + MAN *sb.*¹]

†**1.** A rubber or masseur. *Obs. rare*⁻¹.

1712 STEELE *Spect.* No. 332 ¶ 3 Though he would not willingly detract from the Merit of that extraordinary Strokes-Man Mr. Sprightly.

2. One who pulls the stroke-oar in a boat.

1769 FALCONER *Dict. Marine* (1780), *Strokesman*, the person who rows the hindmost oar in a boat, and gives the stroke, which the rest are to follow. **1805** *Naval Chron.* XIV. 280 A shot carried away the hand of the Strokesman. **1850** H. MELVILLE *White Jacket* I. xvii. 115 'Let him drown!' cried the strokesman; 'he's spoiled my watch below for me.' **1868** *Field* 4 July 14/3 The steady stroke rowed by Gulston, their strokesman, was deserving of all praise.

strokin, obs. Sc. pa. pple. of STRIKE *v.*

stroking ('strəʊkɪŋ), *vbl. sb.* [-ING¹.]

1. The action of STROKE *v.*¹, in various senses.

In the 17th c. often spoken of as a process of healing.

1587 MASCALL *Govt. Cattle, Sheepe* (1627) 206 Yee shall draw the Ewe a little, which the Heard men doe call stroking. **1626** SANDYS *Ovid's Met.* x. 198 A Stag..who.. well pleas'd, would stand The gentle strokings of a stranger's hand. **1632** J. HAYWARD tr. *Biondi's Eromena* To Rdr. (b) 1, I expect not the least stroaking of applause. **1633** WOTTON *Lett.* (1907) II. 343 The manner of his cure..is somewhat strange; he useth no bindings, but oils and strokings. **1666** H. STUBBE *Mirac. Conformist* Ep. Ded. 2 Upon his first stroaking the Patient should be worse, and cured by a second. **1713** GAY *Rural Sports* 94 When the big udder'd Cows with Patience stand, Waiting the Stroakings of the Damsel's Hand. **1842** GWILT *Archit.* §1910 This operation produces a sort of fluted surface, and is called stroking. **1880** [MRS. FLOYER] *Plain Hints Needlework* 19 The stroking should be done above the gathering thread, as well as below. **1899** *Allbutt's Syst. Med.* VIII. 489 A more or less forcible stroking of the skin with a pointed instrument.

2. *pl.* The last milk drawn from a cow; 'afterings'. Cf. STRAPPING *vbl. sb.*², STREAKING *vbl. sb.* (after STREAK *v.*¹), STRIPPING *vbl. sb.*² b.

1602 *Entert. Harefield* in *Lyly's Wks.* (1902) I. 492 You shall haue..stroakings, in good faith, redd cowes milk. **1658** *Compl. Cook* 76 Take a Gallon of Stroakings and a Pint of Creame as it comes from the Cow. **1748** SMOLLETT *R. Random* xl, The cook entertained me with choice bits, the dairy-maid with stroakings. **1844** H. STEPHENS *Bk. Farm* III. 913 The afterings or strokings are well known to be the richest part of the milk.

3. *Comb.*: †**stroking needle** [G. *streichnadel*], a touch-needle (see TOUCH-); **stroking pin**, a pin used to stroke gathers.

1683 PETTUS *Fleta Minor* I. i. 3 How..to make stroking or touching Needles, or Ingots of Silver for distinguishing the fine from the less fine Silver. **1880** [MRS. FLOYER] *Plain Hints Needlework* 46, 1 stroking pin.

strokle: see STROCALS.

stroky ('strəʊkɪ), *a. rare.* [f. STROKE *sb.* + -Y.] Consisting of, of the nature of, strokes (of a pen).

1847 *Tait's Mag.* XIV. 384 Contrast the Bs of the two writings... Take the As. In the one, they are full and bold; in the other, narrow and stroky. **1891** M. MURIEL DOWIE *Girl in Karp.* 215 Resembling in style Chinese and Japanese stroky pen-work.

stroll (strəʊl), *sb.* Also 7 stroule, strowle, 9 *rare* strole. [Belongs to STROLL *v.*; in sense 2 a new formation on the verb.]

1. = STROLLER. *Obs.* exc. *U.S.* (*rare*).

1623 MIDDLETON & ROWLEY *Sp. Gipsy* II. (1653) C 2 b, Wee'l entertaine no Mounty-bancking Stroule, No Piper, Fidler, Tumbler through small hoopes. *Ibid.* C 4 b, Y'are but a Country company of Strowles. **1641** BROME *Jovial Crew* v. (1652) N 1, I'll undertake that these Players..shall give your Guests much content, and move compassion in you towards the poor Strowles. **1900** J. L. ALLEN *Increasing Purpose* i. 21 They hired strolls to beat drums that we might not be heard for the din.

2. A walk or ramble taken leisurely, a saunter.

1814 JANE AUSTEN *Mansf. Park* vii, When the evening stroll was over. **1817** M. BIRKBECK *Notes Journ. Amer.* (1818) 55 In my stroll among the lovely inclosures of this neighbourhood, I called to enquire my way at a small farmhouse. **1860** SALA *Baddington Peerage* I. xvii. 294 Come, take my arm, and we will have a stroll; it's just the evening for a stroll.

stroll (strəʊl), *v.* Also 7 stroyle, 7–8 stroul, strowl(e, 8 strole. [Of uncertain origin.

Perh. this verb and the related STROLL *sb.* (which in our quots. appear early in the 17th c.) may be among the High German words introduced about that time by soldiers: cf. G. *strolch* vagabond, †*strolchen*, †*strollen* (18th c.) to wander as a vagrant.]

†**1.** *intr.* To roam or wander from place to place without any settled habitation. *Obs.* (but cf. STROLLING *ppl. a.*).

1603 DEKKER *Wonderf. Yr.* Wks. (Grosart) I. 100 He would..strowle (thats to say trauell) with some notorious wicked floundring company abroad. **1629** MASSINGER *Picture* II. i. (1630) D 4 b, You had a foolish itch to be an actor, And may strowle where you please. **1684–5** WOOD *Life* (O.H.S.) III. 123 He had been strouling beyond sea for some time to trail a pyke in the Low Countries. **1705** J. PHILIPS *Blenheim* 369 Dismay'd, unfed, unhous'd, The Widow, and the Orphan Strole around The Desart wide. **1729** SWIFT *Modest Proposal* 3 These Mothers instead of being able to work for their honest livelihood, are forced to employ all their time in Stroling, to beg Sustenance for their helpless Infants. **1756** J. MAIR tr. *Sallust* (1793) 20 The Trojans,..who flying their country, under the conduct of Æneas, strolled about, without any settled habitation. **1765** *Pet.* in McFarlane *v.* McNab 4 Absent sometimes for weeks together..., strolling about the country selling brandy.

2. a. To walk or ramble in a careless, haphazard, or leisurely fashion as inclination directs, often simply to take a walk.

1680 OTWAY *C. Marius* III. iii, Whilst Coxcombs strowl abroad on Holydays, To take the Air. **1703** *La Hontan's Voy. N. Amer.* I. 35 Unhappily one of the Iroquese,.. having stroul'd in the Night-time towards our Tents, overheard what we said, and so reveal'd the Secret. **1709** STEELE *Tatler* No. 3 ¶2 After the Play, we naturally stroll to this Coffee-house. **1734** POPE *Hor. Sat.* II. ii. 13 Your wine lock'd up, your Butler stroll'd abroad. **1782** MISS BURNEY *Cecilia* v. v, Cecilia..strolled to a window. **1827** LYTTON *Falkland* II. 99 They..then strolled along the sands towards the cliff. **1860** SALA *Baddington Peerage* I. xvii. 299 A policeman had strolled up during this parley, too late, however, to see the knife. **1865** TROLLOPE *Belton Est.* xi. 121 He again strolled down to the bridge. **1876** GEO. ELIOT *Deronda* I. xiv. 268 Some of the gentlemen strolled a little and indulged in a cigar.

transf. **1760** *Inform. Dk. Gordon v. Earls Murray & Fife* 10 A vagrant stream strolling [t]hrough chingle, unconfined by any thing that can be called a bank.

†**b.** Conjugated with *be*. *Obs.*

1722 DE FOE *Col. Jack* (1840) 199, I was strolled away that day to see the country about.

3. *trans.* To walk or pace along (a path) or about (a place). Chiefly *U.S.* in recent use.

1693 R. GOULD *Corrupt. Times by Money* 28 For thee the dirty Drab does strowl the Streets. **1720** SWIFT *Progr. Beauty* 87 So rotting Celia stroles the Street, When sober Folks are all a-bed. **1771–2** *Ess. fr. Batchelor* (1773) I. 249 After strolling the Green, arm in arm with L——d M——lt——on. **1810** *Splendid Follies* III. 119 [He] had been strolling the solitary path of the elm-walk. **1956** H. GOLD *Man who was not with It* (1965) vi. 50 Her laughter rang out as we strolled a business street of the suburb. **1974** *New Yorker* 3 June 76/3 (Advt.), Hike forest trails, stroll lovely gardens. **1977** *Gay News* 24 Mar. 23/1 They taxi to the Toilet and stroll the dock strip at 3 am.

quasi-*trans.* **1847** MRS. GORE *Castles in Air* xviii. II. 121 He left me to stroll my way back to my solitary dinner.

stroller ('strəʊlə(r)). [f. STROLL *v.* + -ER¹.] One who strolls.

1. A vagabond, vagrant; an itinerant beggar or pedlar. Now chiefly *Sc.*

1679 OLDHAM *Sat. Jesuits* II. (1681) 26 These are..Romes Strowlers, who survey each Continent, Its trinkets, and commodities to vent. **1694** N. H. *Ladies Dict.* 303/1 For she that is a Diver or Pick-pocket is an infallible Stroler or Night-walker. **1697** VANBRUGH *Relapse* IV. vi, I'm a Justice of the Peace, and know how to deal with Strolers. **1706** SWIFT *Baucis & Phil.* 11 Where, in the Strolers canting Strain, They begg'd from Door to Door in vain. **1796** H. HUNTER tr. *St. Pierre's Stud. Nat.* (1799) I. 61 The Patagonian is perpetually a stroller, for he lives entirely by hunting and fishing. **1818** SCOTT *Hrt. Midl.* xxxii, Who are you, young woman?..and what do you do in this country, and in such company?—We allow no strollers or vagrants here. **1855** [J. D. BURN] *Autobiog. Beggar Boy* (1859) 16, I can well remember the marked difference in the etiquette of the English and Scottish beggars; at that time, the manners and habits of these strollers were as different as it is well possible to conceive. **1856** P. KENNEDY *Banks Boro* xii. (1867) 48 We found the large fireplace provided with its retinue of labourers and servants, and a few of the half-witted strollers through the country.

transf. **1709** SWIFT *Advanc. Relig.* 32 The Men of Pleasure ..form their Idea's of the Clergy from a few poor Strolers they often observe in the Streets.

2. An itinerant actor; a strolling player.

1608 DEKKER *Lanth. & Candle-light* G 1, When they trauell thus on foote, they are no more call'd Rancke-riders, but Strowlers, a proper name giuen to Country-players, that ..trotte from towne to towne vpon the hard hoofe. **1681** DRYDEN *2nd Prol. Univ. Oxf.* 33 When Strollers durst presume to pick your purse, We humbly thought our broken Troop not worse. **1711** STEELE *Spect.* No. 48 ¶5 A Company of Strolers, who are very far from offending in the impertinent Splendor of the Drama. *a* **1774** GOLDSM. *Scarron's Com. Rom.* (1775) I. 9 The strolers, after drinking a few glasses a-piece,..retired to dress. **1806–7** J. BERESFORD *Miseries Hum. Life* xv. Introd. 41 What are you at now?.. spouting to yourself, like a mad stroller. **1855** MACAULAY *Hist. Eng.* xx. IV. 423 Two strollers personated Killegrew and Delaval. **1886** WILLOCK *Rosetty Ends* xi. (1887) 82 A puckle strollers reached oor place on their way to the toon frae some country fair they had been at.

attrib. **1840** DICKENS *Old C. Shop* xix, Vagabond groups assembled round the doors to see the stroller woman dance.

3. a. One who walks at leisure, a saunterer.

1834 L. RITCHIE *Wand. by Seine* 167 Nor are the Sunday strollers absent even here. **1868** B. J. LOSSING *The Hudson* 222 A lovely shaded walk invites the strollers on warm afternoons.

b. *transf.* A parasitic insect.

1705 [E. WARD] *Hudibras Rediv.* IV. 5 Besides the Legeons that they wear, In matted Locks of uncomb'd Hair, And listed Troops of eight-leg'd Strolers, That march from Wristbands to their Collars.

4. A casual traveller or visitor.

1738 WARBURTON *Div. Legat.* II. 222 Some Stroler out of Egypt into Greece. **1778** *Engl. Gazetteer* (ed. 2) s.v. *Glastonbury*, It was a receptacle for the strollers that came in pilgrimage to the abbey. **1837** CARLYLE *Fr. Rev.* II. I. iii, Nay how many come as vacant Strollers, aimless, of whom Europe is full, merely towards *something*!

†**5.** Of a plant: A 'sport' or new variety departing from the usual type. *Obs. rare.*

1723 P. BLAIR *Pharmaco-Bot.* I. 16 These [varieties] may justly be called Sporters or Strollers, so many *Lusus Naturæ* sporting themselves from more simple Colours [etc.].

6. A child's push-chair, esp. a collapsible buggy.

1920 *Sears, Roebuck & Co. Catal.* Fall 1049/2 Stroller Style Carriage... Body made of selected reeds finished in the natural shellac color. **1922** *Ibid.* Spring 590/2 Select your stroller or collapsible sulky from this page and you will be satisfied with service given. **1932** *Babies, just Babies* Dec. 63/3 (Advt.), Baby walker, stroller and gocart combined. **1954** W. McCULLOUGH *Illustr. Handbk. Child Care* vii. 144 We saw the Smithsonian Institute and art galleries today. So glad we brought along his stroller. We just fold it up and pack it in the car. **1962** J. R. BERNARD in *Southerly* XXII. II. 97 We keep stroller as meaning saunterer but we add the meaning of baby's push-cart. **1977** N. SAHGAL *Situation in New Delhi* i. 5 Young women in bright coats briskly pushing strollers carrying rosy bundled badies.

7. A casual shoe. Normally in *pl.*

1948 *Woman & Beauty* Oct. 118/2 For shoes I picked a pair of black suède strollers. **1953** R. CHANDLER *Long Good-Bye* xi. 64 On his feet were black moccasin type ties, the kind ..that are almost as comfortable as strollers. **1958** J. CANNAN *And be Villain* viii. 177 She stepped into her 'strollers'. **1970** *Washington Post* 30 Sept. B5/3 (Advt.), Softy suede stroller... Soft-walk into fall.

strolling ('strəʊlɪŋ), *vbl. sb.* [f. STROLL *v.* + -ING¹.] The action of the verb STROLL.

1717 PRIOR *Alma* II. 163 The am'rous Eyes thus always go A-stroling for their Friends below. **1725** POPE *Odyss.* XVIII. 409 Idly thus thy soul prefers to live, And starve by strolling, not by work to thrive. *c* **1755** in B. Ward *Hist. St. Edmund's Coll.* (1893) 303 All climbing of Trees,..all stroling out of Sight of ye Master are strictly forbid.

b. *attrib.*

1709 STEELE *Tatler* No. 8 ¶5 A Day, spent in the strolling Manner, which is usual with Men of Pleasure in this Town. **1712** T. BROWN etc. *Scarron's Wks.* 7 He would not suffer the miserable Remains of a scatter'd Company of Strollers to lodge in an Inn; but brought them to his own House, where the Carter having laid down the Strolling Furniture, return'd Home. **1817** COBBETT *Weekly Reg.* 25 Jan. 126 How they came to prevail upon him to take a part on their strolling boards is really a great mystery to me. **1821** SCOTT *Pirate* xxxiv, What! you call yourself a gentleman..why—your eyes! a tailor would make a better out of the worst suit of rags in your strolling wardrobe.

strolling ('strəʊlɪŋ), *ppl. a.* [f. STROLL *v.* + -ING².] That strolls; wandering, roving, itinerant. Chiefly in ***strolling actor, player***, an actor of a low class, who wanders about the country, giving performances in temporary buildings or hired rooms.

1621 B. JONSON *Masque Gypsies* Wks. (1640) 77 From a strolling Tinkers sheete, Or a payre of Carriers feet.. Blesse the Sov'raigne, and his smelling. **1641** BROME *Jovial Crew* v. (1652) N 3 b, But is there a Play to be expected, and acted by Beggars? *Cla.* That is to say, by Vagabonds; that is to say, by strowling Players. **1673** R. HEAD *Canting Acad.* 86 *Strowling-Morts* are such as pretend to be Widdows, travelling about from County to County, making laces upon [st]aves, as Beggars tape, or the like. **1676** *(title)* Scarron's Comical Romance: or, a facetious history of a company of strowling stage-players..turn'd into English. **1701** DE FOE *Trueborn Englishm.* 15 The Strolling Bands of banish'd Fugitives from Neighb'ring Lands. **1709** J. JOHNSON *Clergym. Vade M.* II. p. cvi, This Canon was designed against those strowling Scotch Bishops who Ordained any for Money. **1789** MRS. PIOZZI *Journ. France* etc. I. 432 It put me in mind of Hogarth's strolling actresses. **1823** SCOTT *Quentin D.* ii, The strolling spearman, half soldier, half brigand. **1837** DICKENS *Pickw.* iii, 'He is a strolling actor,' said the Lieutenant contemptuously. **1837** CARLYLE *Fr. Rev.* I. VII. xi, To lodge there, somewhat in strolling-player fashion. **1863** KINGLAKE *Crimea* (1876) I. xiv. 233 As though he were dealing with a mere troop of strolling players.

strom, obs. form of STORM *sb.*

13.. *Reinbrun* 107 in *Guy Warw.* (1891) 634 Swiche a strom hem cam upon, þat sore hem gonne drede. *Ibid.* 111.

strom, var. STRUM *sb.*[1]

‖**stroma** (ˈstrəʊmə). Pl. stromata (ˈstrəʊmətə). [mod.L. use of L. *strōma* bed-covering, a. Gr. στρῶμα 'anything spread or laid out for lying or sitting upon' (L. & Sc.), f. στρω- root of στρωννύναι to strew, spread, cogn. w. L. *strā-* (*sternĕre*): see STRATUM.]

1. a. *Anat.* The fibrous connective sustentacular tissue or substance of a part or organ. Also the framework containing the alveoli of cancer-cells.

1835–6 R. OWEN in *Todd's Cycl. Anat.* I. 356/2 The ova are imbedded in a stroma of delicate and yielding cellular substance. **1846** W. H. WALSHE *Cancer* 19 The stroma is closely set; the loculi are consequently small. **1873** T. H. GREEN *Introd. Pathol.* 159 The stroma varies considerably in amount, being much more abundant in some varieties of cancer than in others. It consists of a more or less distinctly fibrillated tissue, arranged so as to form alveoli of various forms and sizes, within which the cells are grouped. **1878** T. BRYANT *Pract. Surg.* I. 99 A tumour developed in the stroma of a fibrous structure will probably be fibrous.

b. The spongy colourless framework of a red blood corpuscle or other cell.

1872 THUDICHUM *Chem. Physiol.* 29 We further have in blood corpuscles a certain quantity of what is called stroma. **1873** RALFE *Phys. Chem.* 156 The stroma is the colourless portion of the living blood corpuscle.

2. a. *Bot.* A structure containing the substance in which perithecia or other organs of fructification are immersed.

1832 LINDLEY *Introd. Bot.* 209 *Stroma* is a fleshy body to which flocci are attached. **1836** M. J. BERKELEY *Sir J. E. Smith's Engl. Flora* V. II. 236 *Sphæria concentrica*.. easily known by its beautifully zoned stroma. **1857** HENFREY *Bot.* 171 A more or less distinct stroma or common receptacle. **1882** VINES tr. *Sachs' Bot.* 317 The stromata arise beneath the skin.

b. In vegetable physiology, the solid matter remaining after all the fluid has been expressed from protoplasm.

1885 GOODALE *Physiol. Bot.* vi. 198 To the solid matter [of the protoplasm], the name stroma is applicable. *Ibid.* x. 290 This spongy stroma, or 'trabecular mass'.

c. *Bot.* The colourless fluid surrounding the grana inside a chloroplast.

1914 M. DRUMMOND tr. *Haberlandt's Physiol. Plant Anat.* i. 37 In some cases the characteristic pigment [of chromoplasts] is suspended in a colourless protoplasmic matrix (or stroma). in the shape of minute globules or vesicles (grana). **1979** KRAMER & SCOTT *Cell Concept* iv. 80 The chemical changes in photosynthesis go on in the chlorophyll in the granules on the lamellae and are completed in the stroma.

3. *attrib.* and *Comb.*

1887 W. PHILLIPS *Brit. Discomycetes* 349 A stroma-like tubercle. **1898** *Syd. Soc. Lex.*, *Stroma fibrin*, Landois' term for fibrin formed directly from stroma instead of plasma. *Ibid.*, *Stroma plexus*, a plexus of axis-cylinders formed by the corneal nerves. **1905** *Brit. Med. Jrnl.* 1 July 19 The interstitial cells [of the ovary] are to be distinguished from the stroma cells.

stromal (ˈstrəʊməl), *a.* [f. STROMA + -AL[1].] Of, pertaining to, or of the character of the stroma or supporting tissue of an organ.

1846 W. H. WALSHE *Cancer* 13 The stromal substance.. divides the mass into minute loculi, lobules, and lobes. **1863** W. T. FOX *Skin Dis.* 42 The parasite.. is often present in its stromal form.

†ˈ**stromat.** *Obs. rare.* Anglicized form of STROMATEUS.

1803 SHAW *Gen. Zool.* IV. 108 Striped Stromat. *Ibid.* 111 The Stromats are destitute of ventral fins.

stromateoid (strəʊˈmætiːɔɪd), *a.* and *sb.* [f. STROMATEUS: see -OID.] **A.** *adj.* Of or having the characters of the *Stromateidæ*, a family of fishes of which the genus *Stromateus* is the type. **B.** *sb.* A fish of this family.

1884 G. B. GOODE *Nat. Hist. Aquatic Anim.* 332 The Stromateoid Fishes.

‖**Stromateus** (ˈstrəʊmətjuːs). *Ichth.* [mod.L. (Willughby *a* 1672), a. Gr. στρωματεύς, a patchwork bed-cover (f. στρῶμα: see STROMA), used as a name for a flat-fish of divers colours.] A genus of flat fishes, typical of the family *Stromateidæ*.

1753 *Chambers' Cycl.* Suppl. s.v., The stromateus is a broad, flat, and short sea-fish. **1774** GOLDSM. *Nat. Hist.* (1824) III. 64 The Stromateus. The body oblong; [etc.].

†**stroˈmatic**, *a.*[1] and *sb. Obs.* [f. Gr. Στρώματ-α (see below) + -IC.

Browne is really the sole authority for the word; the adj. was inferred by Blount from Browne's subst. use: Blount's reference to 'Ben Johnson' is presumably an error; it is omitted in the later edd.]

a. *adj.* (See quots. 1656, 1847–54.) *rare*⁻⁰. **b.** *sb.* In pl. *stromatics*, used by Browne to represent Gr. Στρώματα (more correctly Στρωματεῖς, lit. 'patch-work quilts'), the title of a work by Clement of Alexandria.

1646 SIR T. BROWNE *Pseud. Ep.* VI. i. 277 Clemens Alexandrinus.. in the first of his Stromaticks,.. collecteth [etc.]. **1656** BLOUNT *Glossogr.*, *Stromatick*.. belonging to strowings, or any thing spread on the ground, or under a thing. *Ben Johnson.* **1847–54** WEBSTER, *Stromatic*, miscellaneous; composed of different kinds.

stromatic (strəʊˈmætɪk), *a.*[2] [f. mod.L. *strōmat-* STROMA + -IC.] Of the nature of or resembling a stroma; stromatous.

1891 *Century Dict.* **1898** *Syd. Soc. Lex.*

stromatiform (ˈstrəʊmətɪfɔːm), *a.* [f. mod.L. *strōmat-* STROMA + -(I)FORM.] Having the form of a stroma, like a stroma.

1891 *Century Dict. (Bot.).* **1894** GOULD *Illustr. Dict. Med.* **1898** *Syd. Soc. Lex.*

stromatolite (ˈstrəʊmətəʊlaɪt). *Geol.* [ad. G. *stromatolith* (see next): see -LITE.] A laminated calcareous sedimentary structure built up by algae or bacteria. Cf. *oncolite* s.v. ONCO-.

1930 PEACH & HOME *Chapters on Geol. Scotl.* vi. 214 The structures referred to above as resembling the *Stromatolites* of Kallowsky [*sic*] are considered to be of the nature of a chemical deposit brought about by the action of organisms such as algae. **1957** *Prof. Papers U.S. Geol. Surv.* No. 294-D. 129/1 The present study discriminates between fossil algae and stromatolites. **1969** DUNBAR & WAAGE *Hist. Geol.* (ed. 3) viii. 182/2 Since these deposits preserve only the gross form of the colony, the algae cannot be identified biologically and the deposits are simply called stromatolites. **1979** D. ATTENBOROUGH *Life on Earth* i. 22 The blue-green pillars of Hamelin Pool are living stromatolites.

Hence **stromatoˈlitic** *a.*, of the nature of or pertaining to stromatolites.

1933 *Trans. Geol. Soc. S. Afr.* XXXV. 35 The main interest of the rocks is centred in the abundance amongst them of stromatolitic limestones. **1955** *Jrnl. Paleont.* XXIX. 723/2 (*heading*) Recent stromatolitic sediments from south Florida. **1978** *Sci. Amer.* Sept. 86/3 Microfossils have been identified in some 45 stromatolitic deposits.

stromatolith (ˈstrəʊmətəʊlɪθ). *Geol.* [f. mod.L. *stromat-* STROMA + -LITH.] †**a.** A laminated rock structure with a complex interleaving of igneous and sedimentary components. *Obs.* **b.** [a. G. *stromatolith* (E. Kalkowsky 1908, in *Zeitschr. der Deutsch. geol. Ges.* LX. 68).] = STROMATOLITE.

1916 W. G. FOYE in *Jrnl. Geol.* XXIV. 791 The noun 'Stromatolith' may be defined as a rock mass consisting of many alternating layers of igneous and sedimentary rocks in sill relationship. **1918** *Jrnl. Geol.* XXVI. 608 The stromatoliths are the sedimentary equivalent of the calcareous and siliceous 'sinter' of the hot springs. **1933** *Q. Jrnl. Geol. Soc.* LXXXIX. 415 These bodies—stromatoliths—are composed of chlorite or chlorite with zones of a brown or green-brown isotropic mineral. **1963** D. W. & E. E. HUMPHRIES tr. *Termier's Erosion & Sedimentation* xi. 223 The Cyanophyceae can give rise to carbonaceous substances (bogheads) in the form of 'waterblooms' and can also precipitate calcareous 'biscuits', stromatoliths and calcareous muds.

Hence **stromatoˈlithic** *a.*, of the nature of or pertaining to a stromatolith.

1916 W. G. FOYE in *Jrnl. Geol.* XXIV. 791 The term batholithic' does not describe the true character of these areas and the term 'stromatolithic' is suggested in its place. **1936** *Geogr. Jrnl.* LXXXVII. 534, I recognized.. a palaeozoic series which extends from the stromatolithic Cambrian to a lower carboniferous formation. **1963** D. W. & E. E. HUMPHRIES tr. *Termier's Erosion & Sedimentation* xvii. 343 The stromatolithic limestones of the Precambrian.

stromatoporid (ˌstrəʊmətəʊˈpɔərɪd). [ad. mod.L. *Stromatoporidæ* pl., f. *Stromatopora*: see STROMATOPOROUS and -ID.] = next *sb.*

1878 H. J. CARTER in *Ann. & Mag. Nat. Hist.* Ser. v. I. 306 The Stromatoporids. **1895** DANA *Man. Geol.* (ed. 4) 504 Hydrozoans are represented by Graptolites and Stromatoporids.

stromatoporoid (ˌstrəʊmətəʊˈpɔərɔɪd), *a.* and *sb.* [f. mod.L. *Stromatopora* (see next) + -OID.]

a. *adj.* Pertaining to or characteristic of the *Stromatoporidæ*. **b.** *sb.* A member of the *Stromatoporidæ*, a family of hydrocoralline corals of Paleozoic age, typified by the genus *Stromatopora*.

1877 H. A. NICHOLSON & MURIE in *Jrnl. Linn. Soc., Zool.* XIV. 189 A Stromatoporoid fossil. *Ibid.* 202 In studying the minute structure of any Stromatoporoid, it is necessary to make sections in two directions. **1896** S. F. HARMER *Polyzoa* (Camb. Nat. Hist. II.) 520 The Stromatoporoids.. have been variously referred to the Sponges, Hydrozoa, and Foraminifera, as well as to the Polyzoa.

stromatoporous (ˌstrəʊmətəʊˈpɔərəs), *a.* [f. mod.L. *Stromatopora* (f. *strōmat-* STROMA + *-pora* after *madrepora* MADREPORE) + -OUS.] Of or pertaining to the genus *Stromatopora* of hydrocoralline corals, typical of the family *Stromatoporidæ*.

1877 H. A. NICHOLSON & MURIE in *Jrnl. Linn. Soc., Zool.* XIV. 239 [These] forbid the idea of identity with *Clathrodictyon* or its Stromatoporous allies.

stromatous (ˈstrəʊmətəs), *a.* [f. mod.L. *strōmat-*, STROMA + -OUS.]

1. *Med.* Of or pertaining to stroma.

1889 J. M. DUNCAN *Dis. Women* xxiv. (ed. 4) 219 Interstitial or stromatous inflammation.

2. *Bot.* Bearing or producing a stroma.

1891 *Century Dict.* **1900** B. D. JACKSON *Gloss. Bot. Terms.*

stromb (strɒm). [Anglicized form of STROMBUS.] A gasteropod of the family *Strombidæ*, esp. a wing-shell of the genus *Strombus*.

1835 KIRBY *Hab. Inst. Anim.* I. ix. 282 The large strombs of the Caribbean sea have eyes furnished with iris and pupil. **1863** WOOD *Illustr. Nat. Hist.* III. 367 The Strombs form a large genus, containing about sixty species.

strombiform (ˈstrɒmbɪfɔːm), *a. Zool.* [ad. mod.L. *strombiformis*, f. L. *strombus*: see STROMBUS and -FORM. Cf. F. *strombiforme.*] Shaped like a stromb or strombus; belonging or related to the *Strombidæ*.

1843 *Penny Cycl.* XXVI. 446/1 Strombiform type.

strombite (ˈstrɒmbaɪt). [f. STROMB + -ITE.] A fossil stromb or some similar shell.

1811 PINKERTON *Petral.* II. 199 Tubercular strombites. **1828–32** WEBSTER, *Strombite*, a petrified shell of the genus Strombus. **1843** HUMBLE *Dict. Geol.* etc. (ed. 2) 246 Strombites are very rare.

stromboid (ˈstrɒmbɔɪd), *a.* and *sb.* [f. STROMB + -OID. Cf. F. *stromboïde.*] **a.** *adj.* Resembling or related to a stromb or strombus. **b.** *sb.* A stromb.

a. 1859 MAYNE *Expos. Lex.*, *Stromboides*.. resembling a *Strombus*,.. stromboid.

b. 1891 *Century Dict.* **1910** D. W. THOMPSON tr. *Aristotle's Hist. Anim.* 530b, This same property is common to all stromboids and to limpets.

Strombolian (strɒmˈbəʊlɪən), *a.* Also strombolian. [f. the name *Stromboli*, one of the Lipari Islands + -AN.] Of, pertaining to or characteristic of Stromboli, its volcano or volcanic eruptions. Hence applied to (the stage of) a volcanic eruption in which there are repeated or continuous explosions of moderate force with the ejection of gases and bombs of lava.

1897 I. C. RUSSELL *Volcanoes N. Amer.* i. 9 These two volcanoes belong to the explosive type,.. but illustrate two quite well marked phases of that type, which.. are termed the Strombolian stage and the Vesuvian stage,—the former characterized by long-continued but mild activity, the second by periods of rest broken by explosions of extreme violence. **1903** A. GEIKIE *Text-bk. Geol.* (ed. 4) I. 278 The second [phase of volcanic energy], known as the Strombolian, is shown by a continual eructatior of dust and stones. **1906** A. LACROIX in *Smithsonian Rep.* 224 This type of explosion I designate with Mercalli the Strombolian type. **1974** *Nature* 2 Aug. 385/1 Between these eruptions, activity on the volcano had been restricted to strombolian explosions and the extrusion of lava at the bottom of.. the summit crater. **1976** P. FRANCIS *Volcanoes* iii. 108 Strombolian activity.. is a bit noisier than Hawaiian, but it's still not particularly dangerous.

strombuliferous (ˈstrɒmbjʊˈlɪfərəs), *a. Bot.* [ad. mod.L. *strombulifer* f. **strombul-us*, dim. of L. *stromb-us* spiral shell: see STROMBUS and -FEROUS. Cf. F. *strombulifère.*] Bearing fruit spirally twisted.

1859 MAYNE *Expos. Lex.*, *Strombuliferus*. Bot., bearing fruit spirally contorted,.. strombuliferous. **1900** B. D. JACKSON *Gloss. Bot. Terms.*

strombuliform (ˈstrɒmbjʊlɪfɔːm), *a. Geol.* and *Bot.* [ad. mod.L. *strombuliformis* f. **strombulus*: see prec. and -(I)FORM. Cf. F. *strombuliforme.*] **a.** *Geol.* Shaped like a top. **b.** *Bot.* Twisted in a long spire, so as to resemble the convolutions of the shell *Strombus*.

1846 B. H. SMART Suppl., *Strombuliform*, shaped like a top. Geol. **1859** MAYNE *Expos. Lex.*, *Strombuliformis*. Bot., contorted like a screw, or spirally,.. strombuliform. **1866** *Treas. Bot.* 1104/2.

‖**Strombus** (ˈstrɒmbəs). *Zool.* [mod.L. use of L. *strombus* spiral shell, a. Gr. στρόμβος anything spirally twisted, a spiral snail-shell.] The typical genus of the family *Strombidæ* of gastropods, formerly conterminous with the family; a species or individual of this genus, a wing-shell or fountain-shell. Cf. STROMB.

1601 HOLLAND *Pliny* XXXII. x. II. 446 The wilks also or wrinkles called Strombi. **1706** PHILLIPS (ed. Kersey). **1777** PENNANT *Brit. Zool.* (ed. 4) IV. 122 Strombus. Its animal a Slug. **1802** G. SHAW *Naturalist's Misc.* XIII. Pl. 499 The Spindle Strombus is principally found about the American shores. *Ibid.* Pl. 519 The Wing Strombus. **1883** A. J. ADDERLEY *Fisheries Bahamas* 24 Mortimer.. had discovered the secret of the origin of the pearl, and by a clever contrivance aiding the Strombus in developing its treasure.

b. *Comb.* as ***strombus-like***, ***-shaped*** adjs.

1821 S. F. GRAY *Brit. Plants* I. 181 Cod.. Strombus-like. **1832** LINDLEY *Introd. Bot.* 373 Strombus-shaped.

strome, obs. Sc. form of STORM *sb.*

1528 LYNDESAY *Dreme* 80 With stalwart stormes [*v.r* stromes] hir sweitnes wes suprisit.

stromell, variant of STRUMMEL *sb.*[1], straw.

stromeyerine (ˈstrəʊmaɪərɪn). *Min.* [a. F. *stromeyerine* (Beudant, 1832), named after Fr.

Stromeyer, the German chemist who first analysed it: see -INE.] = next.

1843 E. J. CHAPMAN *Pract. Min.* 127 Stromeyerine Beud. **1856** DANA *Min.* (ed. 3) 95.

stromeyerite ('strəʊmaɪəraɪt). *Min.* [Named by Haidinger after Fr. *Stromeyer*: see prec. and -ITE.] Sulphide of silver and copper, of steel-gray colour and metallic lustre.

1835 SHEPARD *Min.* II. II. 211. **1849** J. NICOL *Man. Min.* 473. **1854** DANA *Syst. Min.* (ed. 4) II. 48.

strommel(l, var. forms of STRUMMEL *sb.*[1], straw.

stromming ('strɒmɪŋ). [ad. Sw. *strömming*, var. of *strömling* STREAMLING[2].] = STREAMLING[2].

1839 S. LAING *Tour Sweden* 162 Huddiksval, a very neat little town of 2000 inhabitants, principally engaged in the stromming fishery. *Ibid.* 163 The stromming is about the size of a sprat... They are cured like herrings, [etc.]. **1867** SIMMONDS *Dict. Trade* Suppl.

stromnite ('strɒmnaɪt). *Min.* [Named by T. S. Traill 1819, from *Stromness*, Orkney Isl., its locality: see -ITE.] A variety of strontianite, containing mechanically mixed barite.

1819 T. S. TRAILL in *Edin. Philos. Jrnl.* I. 381 This mineral,..for which the name Barystrontianite, or Stromnite, is proposed. **1854** DANA *Syst. Min.* (ed. 4) II. 531 Index, Stromnite v. Barystrontianite.

strompat, -ette, -it(t, -yd, obs. ff. STRUMPET.

stromperie, variant of STRUMPERY.

strond(e, obs. forms of STRAND *sb.*[1], *sb.*[2]

†**strone**[1]. *Anglo-Irish. Obs.* (Sense obscure.)

1453–4 *Cal. Anc. Rec. Dublin* (1889) I. 279 The suynerd of the towne shulde not suffre the swyne to cum into the strone of the said cite on the one party of the watir ne of the other.

†**strone**[2]. *Obs. rare.* [Of obscure origin.] In Martindale Forest, Westmorland, one of the tenants bound to assist the lord in hunting and turning back deer to the forest.

c **1670** MACHEL in H. Brierley *Hist. Martindale* (1907) 108 In the Forests there [Martindale] are tenants they call 'strones' bound to assist the Lord in hunting. **1777** J. NICOLSON & R. BURN *Hist. Westmorld. & Cumb.* I. 410 [citing Machel] Tenants..whom they call strones. **1864** MRS. LYNN LINTON *Lake Country* 312.

strone[3] (stron). *Sc.* Also **stron**. [? a. Gael. *sròn*, nose, promontory.] 'A hill that terminates a range, the end of a ridge' (Jam.).

1807 HOGG *Mtn. Bard, Mary of Moril Glen* 193 Swift came the maid ower strath and stron. **1813** —— *Queen's Wake* 213 Bold Tushilaw, o'er strone and steep, Pursues the roe and dusky deer.

strone, variant of STROAN *v.*

strong (strɒŋ), *a.* Forms: 1–2 **strang, strong**, 3–6, 4–9 *Sc.* and *north.* **strang**, 4–5 *Sc.* and *north.* **strange**, 4–6 **stronge**, (4 **stroong**, 5 **stronkg, stronke, strongge, strangg**), 3– **strong**. See also STRENGER, STRENGEST. [OE. *strang, strǫng*, corresponding to OS. *strang*, MDu. *stranc, strangh-* (cf. OHG. *strangô*, MHG. *strange*, strongly, severely), ON. *strang-r* strong, severe:—OTeut. type **straŋgo-*; a parallel type **straŋgjo-* is represented by OE. *stręnge* severe (found only once), MLG., MDu. *strenge* (mod.Du. *streng*), OHG. *strengi* (MHG. *strenge*, mod.G. *streng*), severe, strict; also (adopted from German) Sw. *sträng*, Da. *streng*. The two types prob. originated as declensional variants from an OTeut. **straŋgu-*: For the Teut. root **straŋg-* see STRING *sb.*

The umlaut form of the comparative and superlative (see STRENGER, STRENGEST) was common down to the 15th c., but the form without umlaut appears already in OE.]

1. a. Of living beings, their body or limbs: Physically powerful; able to exert great muscular force. ***the stronger sex***: the male sex.

c **888** [see STRENGER]. *c* **1205** LAY. 3547 Ich bi-tæche þe anne hængest godna & strongna. *a* **1300** [see STRENGER]. **1377** LANGL. *P. Pl.* B. XII. 161 Take two stronge men and in themese caste hem. **1471** CAXTON *Recuyell* (Sommer) 277 The strengeste man of troye had ynowh to doo to leye hit on his sholder. **1500–20** DUNBAR *Poems* xxxviii. 13 Thinking to grip ws in his clowss strang. **1535** COVERDALE *Ps.* cxliii. 14 That oure oxen maye be stronge to laboure. **1577** GOOGE tr. *Heresbach's Husb.* III. 119 b, It must be sene to, that they [*i.e.* the horses in a team] be euen matched, least the stronger spoyle the weaker. **1667** MILTON *P.L.* IX. 1059 So rose the Danite strong..and wak'd Shorn of his strength. **1782** COWPER *Gilpin* 154 So like an arrow swift he flew, Shot by an archer strong. **1819** BYRON *Juan* II. liii, The bubbling cry Of some strong swimmer in his agony. **1819** J. FOSTER *Contrib. Eclectic Rev.* (1844) I. 508 It was not..thought too much for persons of the stronger sex, to go and return many miles on foot. **1861** HUGHES *Tom Brown at Oxf.* xiv, He is as strong as a horse.

absol. *c* **1290** *St. Michael* 316 in *S. Eng. Leg.* 308 For mannes þoumbe strenguest is þare-fore he hatte 'þe strongue'. **13..** *K. Alis.* 7710 (Laud MS.), And Sampson also þe stronge [*Linc. MS.* theo fort]. **1697** DRYDEN *Æneis* X. 1054 Orses the strong to greater Strength must yield. **1817** SCOTT *Harold* I. ix. 13 With the deed of the brave, and the blow of the strong.

(*b*) ***strong man***: see as main entry below; also ***strong woman***, a designation for a woman who publicly exhibits feats of strength, as in a circus.

[**1936** J. S. CLARKE *Circus Parade* v. 46 Sandwina..was, until recently, the strongest woman in the world.] **1952** R. MANNING-SANDERS *Eng. Circus* xx. 284 Coming now to the *strong man* act, let us say at once that 'strong' men and 'strong' women, *are* strong men and women. **1953** K. TENNANT *Joyful Condemned* xx. 193 Stretched on the sofa lay Rene McGarty..looking like something between a lady wrestler and a circus strong woman. **1975** *Listener* 28 Aug. 275/3 Mildly humiliating experiences, such as being.. manhandled by a circus strongwoman.

b. *fig.*, as ***strong arm (of the law***, etc.) see STRONG ARM *sb.* 1.

†**c.** *Astrol.* (See quot.) *Obs.* (Cf. 5 f.)

1819 J. WILSON *Dict. Astrol.*, *Strong signs*, ♌, ♏, and ♒, because they are said to give strong athletic bodies.

d. Of an action: Performed with muscular strength.

1398 TREVISA *Barth. De P.R.* V. liv. (1495) 171 The fote [of a lion, etc.] is longe plane and holowe..and dystynguyth with toes for his stronge holdynge. **1471** CAXTON *Recuyell* (Sommer) 76 His strokes myght not be susteyned of men, they were so strong and puyssant. **1590** SPENSER *F.Q.* I. xi. 18 [He] with strong flight did forcibly diuide The yielding aire. **1590** SHAKS. *Com. Err.* V. i. 148 Anon I wot not, by what strong escape He broke from those that had the guard of him. **1697** DRYDEN *Æneis* IX. 1040 He joints the Neck: and with a stroke so strong The Helm flies off. **1816** BYRON *Pris. Chillon* viii. 47, I burst my chain with one strong bound.

e. Of a runner, swimmer, oarsman, etc.: Having great staying power. Hence, of his 'going' or pace: Maintained with vigour; that does not flag.

1854 *Poultry Chron.* II. 183 They are light on the wing, but not strong flyers. **1868** *Field* 4 July 13/1 Atter made the running at a strong pace. **1879** H. C. POWELL *Amateur Athletic Ann.* 13 A very strong runner. **1883** *Sat. Rev.* 24 Nov. 665/2 Too Good [a racehorse] took up the running and made it very strong to the Canal. **1886** RUSKIN *Præterita* I. xi. 379 He ran no risk but of a sound ducking, being, of course, a strong swimmer.

fig. **1863** KINGLAKE *Crimea* (ed. 3) I. iii. 38 Imagination, transcendent and strong of flight.

f. ***strong silent*** (***type***, etc.): see SILENT *a.* 1 a.

2. a. Physically vigorous or robust; capable of physical endurance or effort; not readily affected by disease; hale, healthy. Now often (predicatively) of one who has regained his normal health and vigour after illness.

†In legal enactments, said of a beggar: Able-bodied, fit for work, 'stout', 'sturdy'.

a **1225** *Ancr. R.* 6 Vor þi mot þeos riwle chaungen hire misliche efter euch ones manere, & efter hire efne. Vor sum is strong, sum is unstrong. **1340** *Ayenb.* 32 þou art yong and strang þou sselt libbe long. *c* **1400** *Rule St. Benet* xxvii. 22 Þa þat ere strang and hale. **1422** YONGE tr. *Secreta Secret.* 239 Men wyche haue the complexcion hote and stronge. **1530–1** *Act 22 Hen. VIII*, c. 12 §9 Whypped for a vagarant stronge begger. **1571** in Hudson & Tingey *Rec. Norwich* (1910) II. 344 Thexpulcinge of stronge beggers. **1588** KYD *Househ. Philos.* Wks. (1901) 239 A youth of eighteene or twenty yeeres of age,..tough sinewed, and of a strong constitution. **1656** EARL MONM. tr. *Boccalini's Advts. fr. Parnass.* I. lxxvii. (1674) 104 He was a man full of years, but of so fresh and strong a complexion, as he seemed likely to live yet many Ages. **1785** COWPER *Task* II. 705 His head..Bespoke him past the bounds of freakish youth, But strong for service still, and unimpair'd. **1785** in *Jrnl. Friends Hist. Soc.* (1918) 75, I find myself growing stronger. My cough is better. **1806** *Med. Jrnl.* XV. 26 A gentleman..who had always enjoyed good health, being of a strong and robust constitution. **1840** MARRYAT *Poor Jack* xxi, Old Nanny..was now quite strong again. **1888** 'R. BOLDREWOOD' *Robbery under Arms* xxiii, Starlight was none too strong... He wanted good keep and rest for a month.

transf. **1580** TUSSER *Husb.* (1878) 49 It signifieth land to be hartie and strong.

b. of the vital organs and their functions, the nerves, brain, †'spirits', etc.

1398 [see DIGESTION 2]. **1672** TEMPLE *Ess., Govt.* Wks. 1731 I. 97 In more temperate Regions the Spirits are stronger, and more active, whereby Men become bolder in the Defence or Recovery of their Liberties. **1833** *Cycl. Pract. Med.* I. 578/2 Persons, even with strong stomachs, are frequently under the necessity of taking some stimulant to assist its digestion. **1863** MISS BRADDON *John Marchmont* vi, That perpetual restlessness and disquietude which is cruelly wearying even to the strongest nerves. *Ibid.* viii, Mary Marchmont's story of a marriage arose out of the weakness of a brain, never too strong, and at that time very much enfeebled by the effect of a fever. **1905** E. CLODD *Animism* §9. 47 Even the strongest of nerve among us are not [etc.].

c. of a plant or its parts.

c **1420** *Pallad. on Husb.* I. 88 The treen..Not crokid, lene, or seek, but hool & stronge. **1719** LONDON & WISE *Compl. Gard.* viii. 118 In speaking of a strong Tree, is meant a vigorous Tree. **1765** *Museum Rust.* IV. 354 He has the same hundred and twenty acres in wheat as heretofore, and strong and hopeful. **1780** COWPER *Progr. Err.* 359 Plants rais'd with tenderness are seldom strong. **1822** SHELLEY *Zucca* ix, And light revived the plant, and from it grew Strong leaves and tendrils.

d. ***a strong head***: capacity for taking much drink without becoming intoxicated.

[**1814** SCOTT *Wav.* xii, The Baron proceeded: 'No, sir, though I am myself of a strong temperament, I abhor ebriety'.] **1822** LAMB *Elia* Ser. II. *Confess. Drunkard*, O pause, thou sturdy moralist, thou person of stout nerves and a strong head, whose liver is happily untouched.

3. a. Having great moral power for endurance or effort; firm in will or purpose; able to resist temptation; possessed of courage or fortitude; brave, resolute, steadfast.

c **897** ÆLFRED *Gregory's Past. C.* lxv. 465 Ic wende ðæt ic wære swiðe strong on manegum cræftum. *c* **1200** *Trin. Coll. Hom.* 185 *Estote fortes in bello*, et cetera. Beoð stronge on fihte and fihteð wið þe ealde neddre and ȝef ȝie ben strengere, ȝie shulle fon to mede þat endeles kineriche. *c* **1200** *Ormin* 13326 Symon..All harrd, & strang, & stedefasst,..To stanndenn ȝæn þe laþe gast. *c* **1315** SHOREHAM *Poems* I. 358 He þat ine saule is strang þat he wiþ-stent hi alle. *c* **1400** *Rule St. Benet* lxiv. 43 Sisters þat er strang and of gude lyuyng. **1422** YONGE tr. *Secreta Secret.* 226 Tho men wyche haue ouer lytill kneis they bene stronge of corage. **1526** *Pilgr. Perf.* (W. de W. 1531) 15 Lyke as god conforted the chyldren of Israel, and bad them to be stronge and not to drede. **1592** SHAKS. *Rom. & Jul.* IV. i. 122 Be strong and prosperous In this resolue. **1783** COWPER *Valed.* 61 [He] Should be.. Prepar'd for martyrdom, and strong to prove A thousand ways the force of genuine love. **1815** SHELLEY *Alastor* 181 His strong heart sunk and sickened with excess Of love. **1833** WORDSW. *Warning* 160 Be strong in faith, bid anxious thoughts lie still. **1861** HUGHES *Tom Brown at Oxf.* xiii, His face was quiet, but full of confidence... Tom felt calmer and stronger as he met his eye. **1861** F. W. ROBINSON *No Church* III. ix. II. 282 A heart strong to love. **1864** TENNYSON *En. Arden* 921 So past the strong heroic soul away.

b. Of actions or attributes.

c **1200** *Ormin* 7896 Forr cnapechild bitacneþþ uss Strang mahht i gode dedess. *c* **1450** *St. Cuthbert* (Surtees) 3678 Fewe wordes he spak, bot strange þai ware. **1490** CAXTON *Eneydos* i. 12 A grete multytude of noble companye, full of yougthe & of stronge corage. **1599** SHAKS. *Hen. V*, V. ii. 25, I haue labour'd With all my wits, my paines, and strong endeuors, To bring [etc.]. **1613** —— *Hen. VIII*, II. i. 145 This Secret is so weighty, 'twill require A strong faith to conceale it. **1671** MILTON *P.R.* I. 159 E're I send him forth To conquer Sin and Death..By Humiliation and strong Sufferance. **1819** SHELLEY *Mask* xlvi, 'Tis to be a slave in soul And to hold no strong control Over your own wills. **1905** 'G. THORNE' *Lost Cause* ix, The magistrates of London are quite ready to take a strong stand.

c. Of looks, voice, etc.: Indicative of strength of character.

1815 SOUTHEY *Roderick* xxi. 123 For he was troubled while he gazed On the strong countenance and thoughtful eye Before him. **1885** 'MRS. ALEXANDER' *Valerie's Fate* ii, Attracted by something kindly and strong in the tone of his voice. **1891** C. T. C. JAMES *Rom. Rigmarole* vii, The lady with the strong face, and the piercing grey eyes.

d. Of a statesman, judge, commander: That makes his authority felt; powerful by force of will and capacity.

1889 F. COWPER *Capt. of Wight* vi, As his appointment vested in his person the supreme civil as well as military command, his influence and authority were wide reaching —in other words, he was a 'strong' Captain. **1892** *Daily News* 10 May 3/3 He was emphatically what is called a strong Judge, and the mental force which he wielded impressed those who saw and heard him at his work.

4. a. Of the mind or mental faculties: Powerful. Of the memory: Tenacious, retentive.

1390 GOWER *Conf.* II. 33 Althogh mi wit ne be noght strong, It is noght on mi will along, For that is besi nyht and day To lerne al that he lerne may. **1398** TREVISA *Barth. De P.R.* V. iii. (1495) 107 Yf a man be a grete waker and stronge of minde [L. *memoria tenax*], it sygnefyeth dryenesse of the brayne. *c* **1440** *Alphabet of Tales* 293 And þan þis hermett with a strong wytt removid his cell v myle ferrer fro þe watir. **1664** POWER *Exp. Philos.* I. 80 A Person he was of those strong Parts and Hopes. **1731–8** SWIFT *Pol. Conversat.* Introd. 16 A strong Memory and constant Application.. will be highly necessary. **1749** CHESTERF. *Let. to Son* 10 Jan., A strong mind sees things in their true proportions: a weak one views them through a magnifying medium. **1781** COWPER *Retirem.* 698 Strong judgment lab'ring in the scripture mine. **1784** —— *Tiroc.* 137 Whose hum'rous vein, strong sense, and simple style, May teach the gayest, make the gravest smile. **1849** MACAULAY *Hist. Eng.* iv. I. 507 His writings and his life furnish abundant proofs that he was not a man of strong sense. *Ibid.* vii. II. 170 Where he loved, he loved with the whole energy of his strong mind.

b. Of occupations: Requiring exertion of mental power. ? *Obs.*

1759 JOHNSON *Rasselas* xxxix, 'The diversions of the women', answered Pekuah, 'were only childish play, by which the mind accustomed to stronger operations could not be kept busy.' **1817** G. TICKNOR *Life, Lett. & Jrnls.* I. vii. 152 With all these strong occupations [business cares and scientific studies, etc.], and tastes, and high qualities, he is the chief magistrate of the canton.

5. a. Having great controlling power over persons and things, by reason of the possession of authority, resources, or inherent qualities; able to enforce one's will.

Beowulf 1844 (Gr.) þu eart mægenes strang and on mode frod, wis wordcwida. *a* **1175** *Cott. Hom.* 231 Hit ȝelamp þat an rice king wes strang and mihti. *a* **1225** *St. Marher.* 12 Þa þu strong were he wes muchele strengre me to witene wið þis. *c* **1250** *Gen. & Ex.* 1846 Ðe strong god of ysrael. *a* **1300** *Cursor M.* 14404 God..liuerd þaim fra pharaon, Fra pharaon þat was sa strang þat þam in seruage held lang. **1590** SPENSER *F.Q.* II. x. 65 In the Realme ere long they [Hengist and Horsus] stronger arre, Then they which sought at first their helping hand. ? **1599** A. HUME *Poems, Ep. Mont-creif* 204 The pure quhome strang oppressors dois oppres. **1603** SHAKS. *Meas. for M.* III. ii. 198 What King so strong Can tie the gall vp in the slanderous tong? **1714** G. LOCKHART *Mem. Scot.* (ed. 3) 179 The Revolution Party only employ'd him.. out of Fear; and as soon as they found themselves strong enough without him, they kicked him out of Doors. **1841** F. E. PAGET *Tales of Village* (1852) 172 The Church of England, strong in the aid of antiquity, tradition, and apostolicity. **1850** TENNYSON *In Mem.* Prol. 1 Strong Son of God. **1858** *Sat. Rev.* 2 Jan. 6/2 Lord Palmerston boasts of having a strong Government, and he is determined to test and to parade its strength. **1860** [see SAVE *v.* 1 e].

b. *absol.* (and as postfixed epithet, ***the strong***).

c **825** *Vesp. Psalter* liii. 5 [liv. 3] & ða strongan [L. *fortes*] sohtun sawle mine. *c* **1205** LAY. 20872 Swa wes Childriche þan strongen & þan riche. *a* **1400–50** *Wars Alex.* 2381 And for Strasagirs þe strang he of his strenth prived. **1594** SHAKS. *Rich. III*, v. iii. 311 For Conscience is a word that Cowards vse, Deuis'd at first to keepe the strong in awe. **1598** SYLVESTER *Du Bartas* II. ii. II. *Babylon* 581 Th' ever-blessed soules Of Christ his champions.. Shall dance to th' honour of the Strong of strongs. **1697** DRYDEN *Æneis* III. 77 Who, when he saw the Pow'r of Troy decline, Forsook the weaker, with the strong to join. **1817** SHELLEY *Rev. Islam* Ded. iv, I grow weary to behold The selfish and the strong still tyrannise. **1820** SCOTT *Monast.* iv, It was a reign of minority, when the strongest had the best right. **1847** EMERSON *Poems, Initial*, etc. *Love* III. 51 By right or wrong, Lands and goods go to the strong.

†**c.** ***strong of friends*** or ***friendship***: possessed of powerful friends. *Obs.*

c **1386** CHAUCER *Doctor's T.* 135 Hym thoughte he was nat able for to speede ffor she was strong of freendes. **1444** *Rolls of Parlt.* V. 112 Suytz, triables in forein Shires, where thei be stronge of frendship.

d. Of things, sometimes personified.

a **1225** *Ancr. R.* 280 Þauh heo [humility] makie hire so lutel, & so meoke, & so smel, heo is þauh þinge strengest. **138.** WYCLIF *Sel. Wks.* III. 341 As o virtu is strengere if it be gedrid, þan if it be scatrid, so o malis is strenger whanne it is gederid in o persone. **1382** —— *Song Sol.* viii. 6 For strong is as deth looue. **1390** GOWER *Conf.* III. 146 The Kinges question was this; Of thinges thre which strengest is, The wyn, the womman or the king. **1423** JAS. I *Kingis Q.* 149 Fortune is most and strangest euermore Quhare lest foreknawing or intelligence Is in the man. **1606** SHAKS. *Ant. & Cl.* I. iii. 42 The strong necessity of Time, commands Our Seruices a-while. *a* **1656** HALES *Gold. Rem.* III. (1673) 48 Now humane Authority at the strongest is but weak, but the multitude is the weakest part of humane Authority. **1706** PRIOR *Ode to Queen* ix, Misguided Prince!.. Confess the Force of Marlbrô's stronger Star. **1789** BURNS *To Dr. Blacklock* 29 Ye ken, ye ken, That strang necessity supreme is. **1793** COWPER *Beau's Reply* 7 'Twas nature, Sir, whose strong behest Impell'd me to the deed. **1865** H. KINGSLEY *Hillyars & Burtons* xlix, The old Adam was too strong for her.

e. Having great financial resources, rich. In Anglo-Irish, *spec.* of a farmer.

1622 BACON *Hen. VII*, 161 The Merchant-Aduenturers likewise, (beeing a strong Companie at that time, and well vnderset with rich Men, and good order,) did hold out brauely. *a* **1700** B. E. *Dict. Cant. Crew, Squirish*, foolish; also one that pretends to Pay all Reckonings, and is not strong enough in the Pocket. **1726** SWIFT *Gulliver* II. vi. 113 He then desired to know.. Whether, a Stranger with a strong Purse might not influence the vulgar Voters. **1820** BELZONI *Egypt & Nubia* II. 260, I should have.. prepared the way for others stronger than myself in purse. **1845** MRS. S. C. HALL *Whiteboy* viii. 64 He and his wife.. have borne it [straw]—perhaps as a free gift from 'a strong farmer' —on their shoulders. **1873** O'CURRY *Manners & Cust. Anc. Irish* II. 35 The Bruighfer.. being what would now be called in Munster a 'strong farmer', he was to set an example to his neighbours. **1885** *Times* 3 Sept. 7/4 There must be a good deal of the article in the hands of 'strong people'—that is, people who can wait.. for a rise. **1888** *Pall Mall Gaz.* 24 Oct. 6/1 The merchants make their purchases in London, with the exception of some very strong firms, which import stones direct from the Cape.

†**f.** *Astrol.* (See quot.) Cf. 1 c. *Obs.*

1819 J. WILSON *Dict. Astrol.* 380 Planets are generally supposed to be strong when dignified either by house, exaltation, term, triplicity, or face, or by any accidental dignity.

6. a. Eminently able or qualified to succeed in something; well skilled or versed *in* some particular branch of knowledge or practice.

c **1000** ÆLFRIC *Saints' Lives* v. 6 He wæs.. strang foreþingere. *c* **1330** *King of Tars* 657 Thou hast assayed goddes thyn, Wolte that ich asaye myn, Whether be better leche? And leove sire, trouwe on this, And leef on hym that strengor is. *c* **1450** *Merlin* iv. 60 And Merlyn, that full of stronge arte was,.. shewed hym the voyde place. **1610** SHAKS. *Temp.* v. i. 269 His Mother was a Witch, and one so strong That could controle the Moone; make flowes, and ebs [etc.]. *a* **1628** PRESTON *Breastpl. Love* (1631) 188 Let that appeare by shewing thy selfe strong in thy actions. **1693** DRYDEN *Orig. & Progr. Satire* in *Juvenal* (1697) Ded. p. iii, Yet I was stronger in Prophecy than I was in Criticism. **1694** PENN *Rise & Progr. Quakers* i. 24 They were very Diligent, Plain and Serious; strong in Scripture, and bold in Profession. **1817** SHELLEY *Rev. Islam* XI. xxiv, Genius is made strong to rear The monuments of man beneath the dome Of a new Heaven. **1833** *Q. Rev.* XLIX. 399 Conolly [a jockey].. has a bad Irish seat, but he is very strong upon his horse, and his hand and head are good. **1852** THACKERAY *Esmond* III. xi, I am not very strong in spelling. **1857** BUCKLE *Let.* in Huth *Life* I. 138 The minor works of Fichte, which I could lend you if you find yourself strong enough in German to master them. **1885** *Manch. Exam.* 26 Aug. 3/2 We think Mr. Gough is much stronger as a *raconteur* than as a logician. **1889** W. H. POLLOCK etc. *Fencing* (Badm. Libr.) 105 A short man.. should be strong in the parry and riposte. **1905** *Athenæum* 30 Sept. 417/3 Advt., Wanted, Assistant Master [in a School of Art], strong in Design.

b. ***one's strong point***: see STRONG POINT 1.

c. In athletic contests, of a side, crew, etc.: Possessed of 'talent'; formidable as an opponent or competitor.

1860 *Baily's Mag.* Sept. 428 Mr. Dark had taken down a strong team [of cricketers]. **1861** HUGHES *Tom Brown at Oxf.* xiii, [Bumping races.] Brazen-nose isn't so strong as usual. We sha'n't have much trouble there. **1862** *Baily's Mag.* Oct. 199 We—England—are very strong, and, if we have the luck to go in first, shall, on that wicket, take a deal of getting out.

†**d.** ***to make oneself strong*** [= Fr. *se faire fort*]: to undertake; to affirm. *Obs.*

1477 CAXTON *Jason* 42 Put yow in my handes and cure, and I make me strong for to hele and make yow hole. *Ibid.* 120 b, I wil make me strong so to do if it be youre plaisir. *c* **1500** *Melusine* xxxvii. 296 And also other sayen, & make them strong that she is a spyryte of the fayry.

7. a. Powerful in arms; formidable as a fighting force (or as a commander) by reason of numbers, armament, position, etc.

a **1122** *O.E. Chron.* (Laud MS.) an. 975 Næs se flota swa rang ne se here swa strang. *c* **1205** LAY. 14463 Heo uareð in þine londe mid hære swiðe stronge. **1297** R. GLOUC. (Rolls) 354 Þo was þe compaynie strong & strengore þan it was er. *a* **1300** *Cursor M.* 15438 Þai armed þam þan al priueli, for to ma þam strang. *c* **1470** HENRY *Wallace* v. 23 A hundreth men chargit, in armes strang. **1535** STEWART *Cron. Scot.* I. 627 So strang power, sen weiris first began, Wes neuir sene ȝit with na levand man. **1590** SPENSER *F.Q.* II. x. 31 An army strong she leau'd, To war on those, which him had of his realme bereau'd. **1601** in Moryson *Itin.* II. (1617) 126 Wee resolved to leave the Northerne Garrisons very strong in foote and horse. **1606** SHAKS. *Ant. & Cl.* I. iv. 36 Pompey is strong at Sea. **1638** *Hamilton Papers* (Camden) 45 Your Ma[tti] should prouyd for itt by furnising of Beruick and Cayrlyll uith good and strong garnisones. **1761** HUME *Hist. Eng. to Hen. VII* (1762) I. ii. 49 Receiving in the spring a strong reinforcement of their countrymen. *a* **1774** GOLDSM. *Pref. & Introd. 7 Yrs. War* Misc. Wks. (1837) I. 520 They will find England strong at sea.

b. Of an individual: Powerful or formidable as a combatant. Also *fig.*

a **1450** *Le Morte Arth.* 1860 Was non so stronge that hym with-stode. **1553** PAYNELL tr. *Dares Phryg. Destr. Troy* Ej, Agamemnon consideryng that his moste strongest and moste valiaunt men were slayne, retired. **1563** WINȜET *83 Quest.* To Rdr. *Wks.* (S.T.S.) I. 62 [God] sall steir wp in his contrare strangar kempis.. than I am. **1864** TENNYSON *Aylmer's F.* 365 Where two fight The strongest wins.

c. Of a warlike operation: Performed or prosecuted with a powerful fighting force.

1560 DAUS tr. *Sleidane's Comm.* 37 Who lamentably complaining of the Turkes great crueltie, desyred stronge and continual aide. **1568** GRAFTON *Chron.* II. 88 The French king made strong warre in Normandy. **1590** SPENSER *F.Q.* III. iii. 52 King Vther now doth make Strong warre vpon the Paynim brethren. **1593** SHAKS. *2 Hen. VI*, III. iii. 22 Oh beate away the busie medling Fiend, That layes strong siege vnto this wretches soule. **1817** JAS. MILL *Brit. India* II. v. iv. 440 The enemy made a strong sally. **1870** *Pall Mall Gaz.* 23 Sept. 8/1 The enemy opened strong fire on us.

d. With prefixed numerical determination: Powerful to the extent of (a specified number of men, ships, etc.). Hence *gen.* of a body or assembly of persons: Having the specified number.

1589 GREENE *Menaphon* (Arb.) 83 He despatched letters to the Nobilitie.. with strait charge that they should bee in that place within three dayes with tenne thousand strong. **1592** *Soliman & Pers.* III. i. 48 Their fleete is weake; Their horse, I deeme them fiftie thousand strong. **1629** *Descr. S'hertogenbosh* 34 The Enemies came.. 150 ships strong. **1702** *Lond. Gaz.* No. 3831/2 The Body of French Forces.., being about 8000 strong. **1836** W. IRVING *Astoria* I. 253 A war party, three hundred strong, were prowling in the neighbourhood. **1847** GROTE *Greece* II. xxxv. IV. 402 The entire Phenician fleet, no less than 600 ships strong, co-operated on the coast. **1855** MACAULAY *Hist. Eng.* xvi. III. 638 The garrison, thirteen hundred strong, marched out unarmed. **1860** DICKENS *Uncomm. Trav.* ix, As a congregation, we are fourteen strong. **1879** B. TAYLOR *Germ. Lit.* 104 The Burgundians.. settled, eighty thousand men strong, between Geneva and Lyons.

¶ *transf.* in jocular nonce-uses.

1601 SHAKS. *Twel. N.* III. ii. 59, I haue beene deere to him lad, some two thousand strong, or so. **1719** D'URFEY *Pills* I. 356 A Wife that's fair and Young,.. and Forty Thousand strong.

e. Of a body of persons or things, a sect or party: Numerous. Also more explicitly ***strong in numbers***.

1617–18 J. CHAMBERLAIN in *Crt. & Times Jas. I* (1848) II. 62 Our East Indian fleet is setting out,.. They go stronger and more than ever heretofore. **1656** S. HOLLAND *Zara* (1719) 71 But behold Shakespear and Fletcher (bringing with them a strong party) appeared. **1816** SCOTT *Old Mort.* xxxvii, The Cameronians continued a sect strong in numbers and vehement in their political opinions. **1848** THACKERAY *Van. Fair* lxvii, A very strong party of excellent people consider her to be a most injured woman. **1854** SURTEES *Handley Cr.* iv. (1901) I. 28 The kennel was pretty strong in numbers. **1855** *Poultry Chron.* III. 302 Keep the stocks strong in numbers.

f. Abundantly supplied with persons or things of a specified kind. Const. *in*.

1621 in Foster *Eng. Factories Ind.* (1906) 337 Beinge thus strong in cash.. wee have concluded the present dispeede. **1711–12** SWIFT *Jrnl. to Stella* 16 Feb., The House of Lords is too strong in Whigs, notwithstanding the new creations. **1721** DE FOE *Mem. Cavalier* (1840) 108 The king was strong in horse. **1874** H. H. COLE *Catal. Ind. Art S. Kens. Mus.* App. 320 The India [Office] Museum.. is specially strong in arms and textile fabrics. **1885** *Truth* 28 May 848/2 Landscapes.. in which this year's Academy is unusually strong. **1886** *Manch. Exam.* 3 Nov. 3/1 The *Quarterly* for October is exceptionally strong in literary interest.

8. a. Of a fortress, town, country, or military position: Powerful for resistance; difficult to capture or invade; having powerful artificial or natural defences. Cf. STRONGHOLD.

c **1000** *Ags. Ps.* (Th.) lx. 2 [lxi. 3] Þu.. wære me stranga tor, stið wið feondum. *c* **1205** LAY. 6392 Þer he gon bulde castel swiðe strongne. *c* **1400** MAUNDEV. (1839) xxv. 259 The King of Abcaz hathe the more strong Contree: and he alle weyes vigerously defendethe his Contree. *c* **1440** *Promp. Parv.* 188/1 Garsone, stronge place, *municipium*. *c* **1450** *Merlin* xxii. 380 But litill thei founde in the contrey to take to, ffor all was turned from theire power into stronke fortresses. **1523** WOLSEY in *St. Papers Hen. VIII*, VI. 202 Bray was not, ne coude be, made in shorte space strong or tenyble. **1592** STOW *Ann.* (an. 1399) 508 Beawmareis was a strong Fortresse if it had byn manned and victualled. *Ibid.*, There is a Castell.. builded on a rocke, very strong by situation. *Ibid.* 509 The king was in Wales, which was a Countrey strong by reason of the Mountaines. **1667** MILTON *P.L.* XI. 655 Others to a Citie strong Lay Siege. **1673** TEMPLE *Observ. United Prov.* i. 44 This Countrey was strong by its nature and seat among the Waters that encompass and divide it. **1675–7** WARWICK *Mem. Chas. I* (1701) 233 Prince Rupert.. found a strong house on the road .. well mann'd, which gave him some short stop, before he clear'd it. **1711** SWIFT *Cond. Allies* 72 France was to deliver up several of their strongest Towns in a Month. **1794** MRS. RADCLIFFE *Myst. Udolpho* xli, The situation of Udolpho rendered it too strong to be taken by open force. **1831** SCOTT *Ct. Robt.* xxiv, [They] were gradually assembled, and placed in occupation of the strongest parts of the city. **1837** CARLYLE *Fr. Rev.* III. I. i, Longwi, our first strong-place on the borders, is fallen. *a* **1868** LD. BROUGHAM (Ogilvie), The hilly or strong country extended in those parts to no great distance from the towns. **1892** LADY F. VERNEY *Verney Mem.* I. 113 The king's position on the high ground was extremely strong.

in fig. context. **1638** CHILLINGWORTH *Relig. Prot.* I. Concl. 411 Which by so weak a Champion can overcome such an Achilles for error even in his strongest holds. **1823** SCOTT *Quentin D.* Introd., A subject which was strong ground to the Marquis.

b. Of a place of confinement, receptacle for valuables and the like: Difficult to escape from or break into. See also STRONG-BOX, STRONG ROOM.

c **1250** *Owl & Night.* 1082 He hire bilek in one bure þat hire was stronge & sure. *c* **1290** *Beket* 431 in *S. Eng. Leg.* 119 And he him sente word a-ȝen þat he scholde.. sethþe don him in strongue warde. **1436** *Rolls of Parlt.* IV. 498/1 Putte hir in a stronge chaumbre. **1508** DUNBAR *Flyting* 151 Ane thowsand kiddis, wer thay in faldis full strang. **1667** MILTON *P.L.* II. 434 Our prison strong. **1819** SHELLEY *Cenci* I. i. 115, I rarely kill the body, which preserves, Like a strong prison, the soul within my power. **1837** DICKENS *Pickw.* xxxiii, They could hear the shouts of the populace, who were witnessing the removal of the reverend Mr. Stiggins to strong lodgings for the night.

9. a. Of material things: Capable of supporting strain or withstanding force, whether by cohesion of substance or by thickness; not easily broken, torn, injured, or forced out of shape; solidly made, massive, stout.

c **1000** *Ags. Ps.* (Th.) cxl. 8 [cxli. 6] Æt strangum stane [Vulg. *juxta petram*]. *c* **1205** LAY. 1567 [He] igrap of onnes monnes honde ana wiæx swiðe stronge. *Ibid.* 12424 Heo bi-gunnen feorlic ane swiðe deope dich &.. ænne strongne stanene wal. *c* **1250** *Owl & Night.* 269 Ich habbe bile stif & strong & gode cleures scharp & longe. *a* **1300** [see STRENGER]. *c* **1375** *Sc. Leg. Saints* xii. (*Matthias*) 278 [He] went furtht & hyme-self can hynge with a cord bath styth & strange. *c* **1400** *Rom. Rose* 1726 He streight up to his ere drough The strong bowe. **1562** WINȜET *Last Blast* Wks. (S.T.S.) I. 37 Strang chenis of irne. **1590** *Cobler Canterb.* 3 His lims well set withall, Of a strong bone. **1588** KYD *Househ. Philos.* Wks. (1901) 240 Swifter then which [river] neuer ranne arrowe fro forth the strongest bow of Parthia. **1590** SIR J. SMYTHE *Disc. Conc. Weapons* 3 b, Strong short arming Swords. **1600** SHAKS. *Sonn.* lxv, When rocks impregnable are not so stoute, Nor gates of steele so strong but time decayes? **1613** —— *Hen. VIII*, v. iv. 8 Fetch me a dozen Crab-tree staues, and strong ones. **1697** DRYDEN *Æneis* II. 659 Himself.. with his Axe repeated Stroaks bestows On the strong Doors. **1707** MORTIMER *Husb.* 46 They use large round rowls which are stuck with strong Oaken pins. **1728** POPE *Dunc.* I. 150 There Caxton slept, with Wynkyn at his side, One clasp'd in wood, and one in strong cow-hide. **1765** *Museum Rust.* IV. 330 It hath been said that an elliptic is not equally strong as a semicircular arch. **1829** T. CASTLE *Introd. Bot.* 184 Plants .. whose fruit is covered with a strong rind or hard woody shell. **1834** M[c]MURTRIE *Cuvier's Anim. Kingd.* 57 Their hands are widened, armed with strong nails fitted to excavate the earth. **1861** PATTISON *Ess.* (1889) I. 44 Strong outer walls for defence were discarded. **1892** *Photogr. Ann.* II. 497 Sheets of strong blotting paper.

absol. **1390** GOWER *Conf.* I. 24 The fieble meynd was with the stronge, So myhte it wel noght stonde longe.

b. *fig.* and in fig. context.

c **1400** *Rule St. Benet* Prol. 1 Þe ryght strang & doghty armur of obedience. **1605** SHAKS. *Lear* IV. vi. 170 Plate sinne [*conj. Theobald*; *Fo.* Place sinnes; *Qo.* omits] with Gold, and the strong Lance of Iustice, hurtlesse breakes. **1712** POPE *Ep. Miss Blount* 67 This binds in ties more easy, yet more strong, The willing heart. **1818** SHELLEY *Julian* 181 How strong the chains are which our spirit bind. **1821** SCOTT *Kenilw.* xxvii, Doubting.. whether Amy's hopes.. rested on any thing stronger than a blinded attachment to Varney.

c. Of soil: Firm, tenacious, compact. Also, see quot. 1856.

c **1000** *Sax. Leechd.* I. 134 Ðeos wyrt.. bið cenned on fæstum landum & on strangum. **1591** G. CLAYTON *Mart. Discipl.* 45 Aduertising.. that the Pikemen.. doe holde the great ende of their pikes fastned harde in stronge earth, to the ende the Pike may haue the greater force. **1721** MORTIMER *Husb.* (ed. 5) I. 87 Peat-Marle or Delving-Marle, which is close, strong, and very fat. **1764** *Museum Rust.* IV. 31 Seemingly-opposite soils, viz. one set, shallow, light, gravelly; and the other, deep, strong, and rich. **1837** YOUATT *Sheep* xv. 498 Many a grazier has sustained considerable loss from having lambed his ewes thinly on strong land. **1842** LOUDON *Suburban Hort.* 54 Where a strong clayey soil is covered with a healthy vegetation. **1849** MACAULAY *Hist. Eng.* iii. I. 314 The wheat, which was then cultivated only on the strongest clay. **1856** MORTON *Cycl. Agric.* II. 726/1 *Strong* land, in Devons., is not clayey, but *rich*.

d. Of food: Solid, hard of digestion. Also *fig.* in phr. ***strong meat*** (alluding to Heb. v. 12: see quot. 1526), applied to something acceptable only to strong or instructed minds.

1526 TINDALE *Heb.* v. 12 Ye..are become soche as have nede off mylke, and no of stronge meate [Gr. στερεᾶς τροφῆς]. **1711** SWIFT *Jrnl. to Stella* 21 Apr., I ate but little to-day, and of the gentlest meat. I refused ham and pigeons, ..because they were too strong. **1836** A. COMBE *Physiol. Digestion* (ed. 2) 276 Instead..of oppressing a weakened stomach by administering stronger food than it has the power of digesting.

fig. **1837** [see MEAT *sb.* 1 b]. **1909** H. G. WELLS *Tono-Bungay* I. i. 26 Gulliver was there unexpurgated, strong meat for a boy perhaps. **1965** *Listener* 21 Oct. 640/2 *Nineteen Eighty-Four* was prefaced by a warning that it was not for nervous listeners. There was no such warning before Shirley Jenkins's *The Child*... Yet this too was..strong meat, dealing..with the thought stream of a woman on the point of giving birth.

e. Of moulding-sand: See quot. 1888.

1843 HOLTZAPFFEL *Turning* I. 332 A small portion of the strong facing-sand is rubbed through a fine sieve. **1888** *Lockwood's Dict. Mech. Engin., Strong Sand*, tenacious foundry sand, containing a large proportion of loam and horse dung.

f. *Mining.* (*a*) Of a vein: Thick, massive. (*b*) See quots. 1883, 1886.

1839 MURCHISON *Silur. Syst.* I. xiv. 177 In the same tract are strong courses of very pure concretionary limestone. **1877** RAYMOND *Statist. Mines & Mining* 159 The vein is very strong, and carries a very large proportion of quartz. **1883** GRESLEY *Gloss. Coal-mining* 245 *Strong*, a word having reference to the character of a bind or metal, meaning that the argillaceous is largely mixed with the arenaceous or siliceous material. **1886** J. BARROWMAN *Sc. Mining Terms* 65 *Strong*, hard; not easily broken, *e.g.*, *strong coal*.

g. *Iron-founding.* (See quot. 1888.)

1868 JOYNSON *Metals* 42 Mr. Glynn names [as the best mixture] one-third strong iron from South Wales, and two-thirds of the more fluid metal. **1888** *Lockwood's Dict. Mech. Engin., Strong Iron*, applied usually to mixtures of iron of various brands, together with scrap iron,..by which a definite grade of strength or toughness is obtained.

h. Of hair: Thick in fibre, coarse; stiff.

1726 SWIFT *Gulliver* II. vi. 103 Through these Holes I wove the strongest Hairs I could pick out. **1813** PRICHARD *Phys. Hist. Man* vi. §6. 310 Their hair is strong, of a shining black.

i. Of wool: Broad-haired or coarse-fibred; the opposite of *fine*. Also *Austral.*, of sheep, having such wool (W. 1911).

1885 F. H. BOWMAN *Struct. Wool Fibre* 219 If..the fleece was of a superior quality, such as a fine Kent selected for quality, it would make 'fine' matching..If, however, the fleece was a strong Lincoln or Gloucester, it would probably only be classed as 'neat' matching. **1886** *Colonial & Ind. Exhib., Catal. Exhibits N.S. Wales* (ed. 2) 20 Wool... Strong combing.

j. *Carpentry.* Of deals: see quot.

1843 *Civil Engin. & Arch. Jrnl.* VI. 406/1 When the saw has..reduced them to small dimensions, they warp and twist like a piece of whalebone. Deals of this character are termed by carpenters 'strong'.

†**k.** *absol.* as *sb.* = FORTE *sb.* 2.

1692 SIR W. HOPE *Fencing Master* 3 The Strong, Fort, or Prime of the Blade is Measured from the Shell..to the middle of the Blade.

10. Powerful in operative effect.

a. of a medicine, food or drink, poison, chemical reagent, etc.

c **897** ÆLFRED *Gregory's Past. C.* lxi. 455 Ongean swelce mettrymnesse mon beðorfte stronges læcedomes. *c* **1386** CHAUCER *Pard. T.* 539 This poyson is so strong and violent. *c* **1400** *Rule St. Benet* 1607 Wyne þat es myghty and strang. **1580** T. NEWTON *Approved Medicines* 67 That kynde [of water-lily] which hath the white roote is more stronger. **1593** SHAKS. *2 Hen. VI*, III. iii. 18 Giue me some drinke, and bid the Apothecarie Bring the strong poyson that I bought of him. **1626** BACON *Sylva* §45 Scotch Skinck, (which is a Pottage of strong Nourishment). **1697** DRYDEN *Æneis* Ded. (a) 2 b, Acute Distempers require Medicines of a strong and speedy operation. **1815** J. SMITH *Panorama Sci. & Art* II. 667 The seeds..are sown upon a strong hotbed. **1821** SCOTT *Kenilw.* v, I hate him like strong poison. **1843** R. J. GRAVES *Syst. Clin. Med.* xx. 233, I often diminish supersecretion from the lung by strong hydragogue cathartics. **1876** ABNEY *Instr. Photogr.* (ed. 3) 38 Always have a weak and a strong developer in the field. **1899** *Allbutt's Syst. Med.* VIII. 515 The above list gives them [i.e. astringent external applications] in order of their efficacy—from the weakest to the strongest.

b. of a mechanical agent.

1655 STANLEY *Hist. Philos.* II. (1687) 65/1 The Stars are impelled by the condensation of the Air about the Poles, which the Sun makes more strong by compressing. **1675** J. S[MITH] *Horolog. Dial.* 78 The spring is always strongest when first wound up. **1680** MOXON *Mech. Exerc.* x. 185 If the Pole prove too strong for their..Work, they will weaken it by cutting away part of the substance. **1824** COL. HAWKER *Instr. Yng. Sportsm.* (ed. 3) 42 The solid cock..will admit of mainsprings as strong as you please.

c. Of a lens: Having great magnifying power.

1887 *Proc. Zool. Soc.* 80 The punctuation much more distinctly visible anteriorly than posteriorly, where only traces of it can be seen under a strong lens.

d. Of a field of force.

1903 J. J. THOMSON *Conduction of Electricity through Gases* ii. 21 If we..apply a strong electric field between the plates. **1930** PAULING & GOUDSMIT *Structure of Line Spectra* ix. 159 The resultant magnetic moment of the atom in a very strong field, such that the spins and orbital moments of the individual electrons are quantized relative to the field. **1978** PASACHOFF & KUTNER *University Astron.* xxvii. 699 A related prediction of general relativity is that 'clocks' run slower in a stronger gravity field than they do in a weaker.

e. *Physics.* Applied to the strongest of the four known kinds of force between particles, which acts between nucleons and other hadrons when closer than about 10^{-13} cm. (so that protons in an atomic nucleus remain bound together despite the repulsive force due to their electric charge), and which conserves strangeness, parity, and isospin.

1947 *Nature* 4 Oct. 453/2 We refer to any particle with a mass intermediate between that of a proton and an electron as a meson... In using this term, we do not imply that the corresponding particle necessarily has a strong interaction with nucleons. **1953** *Physical Rev.* XCII. 833/2 Let us suppose that both..have interactions of three kinds: (i) Interactions that rigorously conserve isotopic spin. (We assume these to be strong.) (ii) Electromagnetic interactions... (iii) Other charge-dependent reactions, which we take to be very weak. **1954** *Progress Theoret. Physics* XII. 107/2 Contrary to the case of electric charge, *v*-charge is defined only for such particles that have strong nuclear interactions and its conservation is violated by the weak interactions responsible for decays. **1973** *Sci. Amer.* Aug. 34/2 All the particles discovered to date participate in strong interactions except the photon and the four weakly interacting leptons. **1975** *Nature* 5 June 453/1 The electromagnetic interaction is responsible for the force between charged particles, its strength is 1/137 that of the strong force. **1978** PASACHOFF & KUTNER *University Astron.* ix. 261 For nuclear fusion to begin, atomic nuclei must get close enough to each other so that the nuclear force, technically called the strong force, can play its part.

11. Severe, burdensome, oppressive. †**a.** Of laws, punishments, suffering, condition of life, etc.: Hard to bear, rigorous, grievous. ***strong death***: a violent or cruel death. *Obs.*

c **893** ÆLFRED *Oros.* v. xii. §9 Ealle þa ȝesetnessa þe þær to stronge wæron & to hearde he hie ealle ȝedyde leohtran & liþran. **971** *Blickling Hom.* 79 Wæs þæt wite swa strang, swa Godes ȝeþeld ær mycel wæs. *a* **1154** *O.E. Chron.* (Laud MS.) an. 1124, Se man þe æni god heafde him me hit beræfode mid strange ȝeoldes & mid strange motes. *c* **1205** LAY. 5271 For heom comen stronge tidinge from Belin þon Kinge. *a* **1225** *Ancr. R.* 362 Uolk to-limed & to-toren mid stronge liflode & mid herde. **1297** R. GLOUC. (Rolls) 1811 Cristen men þat he vond to stronge deþ he broȝte. *Ibid.* 2933 Hii smite harde & made moni an strange wounde. *a* **1300** *Cursor M.* 3416 Wit-outen child his wijf was lang, And þat thoght ysaac ful strang. *c* **1330** R. BRUNNE *Chron. Wace* (Rolls) 3321 Strong hit were for oure cite To be destruyed, & al þe contre. *c* **1400** *Brut* lii. (1906) 45 No man was so hardy for-to nempne God; & ho þat dede, anon he was put to strong deth. *a* **1450** *Le Morte Arth.* 1875 To bedde durste I ne noȝt dight, For drede ye hade som Aunter stronge. *c* **1450** *Mirk's Festial* 33 He..told of..the paynes of hell, how strong and how horribly þay wern. *c* **1485** *Digby Myst.*, *Mary Magd.* 1002 Yt ys In-tollerabyll to se or to tell, for ony creature, þat stronkg tourmentry. **1535** COVERDALE *2 Kings* xxv. 3 On yͤ nyenth daye of the fourth moneth was the honger so stronge in the cite, that the people of the londe had nothinge to eate. **1567** *Gude & Godlie Ball.* 44 He said, I thrist, with all my micht, To saif mankynde fra panis strang. **1592** SHAKS. *Rom. & Jul.* III. i. 195 But Ile Amerce you with so strong a fine, That you shall all repent the losse of mine.

†**b.** Of a storm, the weather, cold, etc.: Severe.

c **1000** *Sax. Leechd.* I. 326 Ðonne ne sceþþeð þe ne tunȝol ne haȝol ne strang storm. *a* **1122** *O.E. Chron.* (Laud MS.) an. 1115, Ðises ȝeares wæs swa strang winter mid snawe & mid forste, swa nan man þe þa lifode ær þan nan strengre ne ȝemunde. *c* **1250** *Owl & Night.* 524 Hwenne nyhtes cumeþ longe & bryngeþ forstes starke & stronge. *c* **1400** MAUNDEV. (1839) xxvi. 266 So is it fulle of Dragounes, ..that no man dar not passe, but ȝif it be strong Wyntre. *c* **1400** *Emare* 665 Myȝth y onus gete lond, Of þe watur þat ys so stronge. *c* **1425** *Eng. Conq. Irel.* 66 In thys tyme was the weder so stronge, & the wynd so aweyward, that [etc.]. *c* **1450** *St. Cuthbert* (Surtees) 1741 Þar felle a storme strange. **1671** T. HUNT *Abeced. Scholast.* 9 Let thy garments be long, When the cold is strong.

†**c.** Of a battle, fight, debate: Fierce, hotly contested. *Obs.*

c **900** *Bæda's Hist.* I. ix. (1890) 46 Wæs þis ȝefeoht wælgrimre & strengre eallum þam ærȝedonum. *c* **1205** LAY. 173 Wið Eneam he nom an feiht þæt wes feondliche strong. *c* **1250** *Owl & Night.* 5 Þat playd wes stif & starc & strong. *c* **1400** *Brut* cvj. 107 And þat batayle was wonder strong, for meny a man was þere slayn. *a* **1450** *Le Morte Arth.* 1583 Saugh nevir no man A strenger fyght. **1553** PAYNELL tr. *Dares Phryg. Destr. Troy* F v b, The whiche caused the war to be a great deale yͤ stronger & greater. **1613** [HAYWARD] *Lives 3 Norman Kings* 8 Hee was ouerthrowne in a strong battaile.

d. Of disease: Severe. ***strong apoplexy*** = mod.L. *apoplexia fortis* (Path.): the sanguineous as distinguished from the serous or 'weak' variety. Of convulsions, shuddering, palpitation: Violent.

c **1000** *Sax. Leechd.* II. 226 Oft strang fefer becymð on þa men þe þa adle habbað. **1389** in *Eng. Gilds* (1870) 30 No man schal ben excusyd of absence.., but it be for ye kyngges seruice er for stronge sekenesse. **1595** SHAKS. *John* III. iv. 110 Before the curing of a strong disease Euen in the instant of repaire and health, The fit is strongest. **1754** RICHARDSON *Grandison* IV. 150 In that space, Lady Clementina's absences [= attacks of delirium] were stronger, but less frequent than before. **1815** SCOTT *Guy M.* lv, A strong shuddering convulsed his iron frame for an instant. **1820** J. COOKE *Treat. Nervous Dis.* I. i. 168 *note*, In the strong paroxysm, persons are said to lie entirely deprived of sensation and motion. *Ibid.* 169 In the perfect, or strong apoplexy, the respiration of the patient is generally much impeded. **1821** SCOTT *Kenilw.* xl, Tressilian found himself, not without a strong palpitation of heart, in the presence of Elizabeth. **1825** —— *Betrothed* xiv, [She] fell into a strong shuddering fit. **1901** ALLDRIDGE *Sherbro* xxvi. 296 After a couple of hours I was attacked by a strong fever.

†**e.** Of a crime, evil quality, etc.: Gross, flagrant. Of a malefactor: Flagrantly guilty. *Obs.*

c **1290** *Beket* 1229 in *S. Eng. Leg.* 141 So strong þeof nis non in engelonde. *a* **1300** *Cursor M.* 4426 Suilk es tresun of ille womman In werld es stranger funden nan. **13..** *K. Horn* 1280 (Harl.), þou..seydest ich wes traytour strong. *a* **1400** *Minor Poems fr. Vernon MS.* xxxviii. 309 A þral..þat for his gult strong and gret Wiþ his lord was so I-vet. *c* **1400** *Laud Troy Bk.* 18638 And thus was Troye dryuen doun And y-lore thorow strong tresoun. *c* **1450** *Gesta Rom.* 390 She sayde, 'oute on the, stronge strompette!' *a* **1466** GREGORY *Chron.* in *Hist. Coll. Cit. Lond.* (Camden) 163 And that same yere there was a stronge thefe that was namyd Bolton was drawe, hanggyd, and i-quarteryde. **1518** *Sel. Cases Star Chamber* (Selden Soc.) II. 137 John Powre..pykyd a quarell to hym..and Callyd hym strong thefe and extorcyoner. **1575** *Gammer Gurton* III. iii. 35 Where is the strong stued hore? **1593** SHAKS. *2 Hen. VI*, IV. i. 108 Bargulus the strong Illyrian Pyrate. **1593** —— *Rich. II*, v. iii. 59 Oh heinous, strong, and bold Conspiracie. **1818** CRUISE *Digest* (ed. 2) VI. 554 When the abuse is so strong, gross, and complete, that every man of common sense, to whom it was stated, must exclaim against it.

f. Of a course of action, a 'measure': Extreme, high-handed.

1838 ARNOLD *Hist. Rome* I. xvi. 320 The Roman constitution of 306 was as short-lived..as some of the strongest measures of the long parliament. **1885** *Law Times' Rep.* LIII. 524/2, I think it would be rather a strong measure for me to decide now contrary to the authorities as there stated.

g. *colloq.* Of a payment, a charge: Heavy, 'stiff.'

1669 R. MONTAGU in *Buccleuch MSS.* (Hist. MSS. Comm.) I. 459 Five hundred is a very strong pension as things stand in our Court. **1838** THACKERAY *Yellowplush* i. (1865) 8 Fourteen shillings a wick was a *little* too strong for two such rat-holes as he lived in.

12. †**a.** Requiring great effort, arduous, difficult: chiefly const. *inf. Obs.*

c **1175** *Lamb. Hom.* 81 þes ilke Mon is strong to sermonen. *c* **1200** *Ormin* 6326 & tatt iss swiþe strang & harrd To forþenn her onn eorþe. **12..** *Moral Ode* 312 (Egerton MS.) in *O.E. Hom.* I. 179 It is strong to stonde longe, and liht it is to falle. *a* **1250** *Prov. Alfred* 145 Strong hit is to reowe a-yeyn þe séé þat floweþ. **1338** R. BRUNNE *Chron.* (1725) 240 In Wales it is fulle strong to werre in Wynter tide. **1422** YONGE tr. *Secreta Secret.* 216 Stronge is to fynde and know condycones and good vertues and maneris of Pepil wythout longe Prewe. **1430–40** LYDG. *Daunce of Machabree* in *Bochas* etc. (1554) 222 b, By many an hyll and many a strong vale I haue trauailed with many marchandise. **1474** CAXTON *Chesse* II. iv. (1883) 49 Ther is no thynge so stronge as for to mayntene loue vnto the deth.

†**b.** Of country: Thickly covered with undergrowth (*obs.*).

c **1400** *Master of Game* (MS. Digby 182) xxx, Eke in þe tyme þat þe heedes of þe hertes beth tendre..þei abyde amonge clere speyes and in hye wodes, for stronge cuntre shulde per auenture do hem harme to hir hedes.

(*b*) In more recent Canad. use, ***strong wood(s)*** [tr. Canad. Fr. *bois fort(s)*, a region of thick afforestation; freq. *attrib.* (see also quot. 1921).

1794 D. M'GILLIVRAY 12 Oct. *Jrnl.* (1929) 34 Soon after their departure 2 tribes of Assinoboines arrived..called Strong Wood &..Grand River Assiniboine [*sic*]. **1800** A. HENRY *Jrnl.* 5 Sept. in E. Coues *New Light Early Hist. Greater Northwest* (1897) I. iii. 83 We had a quarter of a mile of strong wood to pass through. **1861** *Canad. Naturalist* Dec. 438 The Strong-wood Reindeer inhabit the thickly wooded parts of the District. **1921** A. HEMING *Drama of Forests* 15 The several zones of the Canadian wilderness are locally known as the Coast Country—the shores of the Arctic Ocean and Hudson Bay; the Barren Grounds—the treeless country between Hudson Bay and the Mackenzie River; the Strong Woods Country—the whole of that enormous belt of heavy timber that spans Canada from east to west; the Border Lands—the tracts of small, scattered timber that lie between the prairies and the northern forests; the Prairie Country; the Mountains; and the Big Lakes. **1969** E. W. MORSE *Fur Trade Canoe Routes* II. iv. 45 The North Saskatchewan formed roughly the boundary of the 'strong woods' region where the furs were harvested.

13. Of movements or conditions: Intense.

a. Of a current of air or water, a wind, tide, stream: Having force of movement.

strong breeze, gale (*Naut.*): see quot. 1867.

c **950** *Lindisf. Gosp.* Matt. xiv. 30 ðesæh ec wind strong [L. *ventum validum*], ondreard. **1388** WYCLIF *Exod.* x. 19 The Lord..made a moost strong wynd to blowe fro the west. *a* **1420** *Anturs of Arth.* v, By þe stremys so strange, þat swyftly swoghes. *c* **1620** A. HUME *Brit. Tongue* I. v, Nether daer I, with al the oares of reason, row against so strang a tyde. **1697** DRYDEN *Æneis* v. 251 As when you stem'd the strong Malæan Flood. **1794** MRS. RADCLIFFE *Myst. Udolpho* xliv, The wind was strong, and the baron watched his lamp with anxiety. **1807** WORDSW. *Force of Prayer* 30 The river was strong, and the rocks were steep. **1841** DICKENS *Barn. Rudge* lviii, A stone-floored room, where there was..a strong thorough draft of air. **1855** MACAULAY *Hist. Eng.* xviii. IV. 239 At eight the next morning the tide came back strong. **1867** SMYTH *Sailor's Word-bk., Strong Breeze*, that which reduces a ship to double-reefed topsails, jib, and spanker. *Ibid., Strong Gale*, that strength of wind under which close-reefed topsails and storm-staysails are usually carried when close-hauled. **1913** M. ROBERTS *Salt of the Sea* x. 234 We ran on and on, faster and faster yet—for the tide was under her stronger and stronger, every minute.

transf. **1754** GRAY *Progr. Poesy* 8 Now the rich stream of music winds along Deep, majestic, smooth, and strong.

b. of the pulse, respiration.

1398 TREVISA *Barth. De P.R.* III. xxiv. (1495) 72 Strenger hete [in man] makyth stronger pulse. **1624** BURTON *Anat. Mel.* I. iii. II. ii. (ed. 2) 176 Short breath, hard winde, strange [1632 strong] pulse. **1785** COWPER *Task* IV. 348 While ev'ry breath, by respiration strong Forc'd downward, is consolidated soon Upon their jutting chests. **1876** BRISTOWE *Th. & Pract. Med.* (1878) 493 The pulse may be strong or weak, or in other words hard or soft. The former resists compression by the finger, the latter is easily obliterated by it.

c. Of fire, heat, an internal process, etc.: Intense, energetic, vigorously active.

c1290 *St. Christopher* 191 in *S. Eng. Leg.* 277 He let don þat oþur in strong fuyr. 1398 [see b]. 1608 SHAKS. *Per.* I. ii. 41 A sparke, To which that sparke giues heate, and stronger Glowing. a1626 BACON *New Atl.* 37 A Weake Heate of the Stomach will turne them into good Chylus; As well as a Strong Heate would Meate otherwise prepared. 1666 BOYLE *Orig. Forms & Qual.* 172 If, for instance, you expose a Sphære or Bullet of Lead to a strong fire, it will [etc.]. 1765 *Museum Rust.* IV. 405 Red Colour for the use of Enamel Painters, which will bear repeated and sufficiently strong fires without change. 1826 *Art of Brewing* (ed. 2) 60 By attenuating lower in summer, the beer does become.. disposed to fretting and staleness— the result of too strong a fermentation. 1857 MILLER *Elem. Chem., Org.* 144 By a stronger heat they are decomposed. 1874 W. GREGOR *Echo Olden Time N. Scot.* 111 If it [*sc.* the wort] fermented strongly, or, as it was expressed, if it was strong on the barm.

d. Of the voice, a sound: Powerful, loud and firm.

a1000 *Cædmon's Gen.* 525 (Gr.) Þonne ic siȝedrihten, mihtiȝne god mæðlan ȝehyrde strangre stemne. 14.. *Tundale's Vis.* 1145 He herde a strong dynne of þonder. 1422 YONGE tr. *Secreta Secr.* 231 And a grete hey and stronge voice tokenyth a stronge and an hardy man. 1594 HOOKER *Eccl. Pol.* IV. iv. §1 The eares of the people they haue therfore filled with strong clamour. 1764 in *Reliquary* (1860) I. 63 A Clergyman..whose voice is strong, and pronunciation distinct. 1788 COWPER *Dog & Water-lily* 25 But with a chirrup [to the dog] clear and strong,.. I thence withdrew. 1836 DUBOURG *Violin* ix. (1878) 273 His violoncellos.. are of the finest quality of tone—not so strong and fiery as old Forster's, but, sweetness and purity excelling them. 1908 R. BAGOT *A. Cuthbert* xxviii. 373 Her voice rang out clear and strong.

†**e.** Of sleep: Deep, sound. *Obs. rare.*

c1489 CAXTON *Sonnes of Aymon* xvi. 370 They beganne all to fall in a stronge slepe.

†**f.** Of a magnitude: Great, unusual. *Obs.*

c1400 *Destr. Troy* 1574 The Stretis were streght & of a stronge brede.

g. Of illumination, light, shadow, colour: Vivid, intense.

1658 W. SANDERSON *Graphice* 66 In what places, you will have those strong and high lights, and reflections to fall. 1665 *Phil. Trans.* I. 122 The Shaddows..seem to be stronger. 1704 NEWTON *Optics* I. II. v. (1721) 130 We are not to expect a strong and full white, such as is that of Paper, but some dusky obscure one. 1781 COWPER *Convers.* 331 The southern sash admits too strong a light. 1794 MRS. RADCLIFFE *Myst. Udolpho* xxxiii, The strong rays [of moonlight] enabled her also to perceive the ravages which the siege had made. 1815 J. SMITH *Panorama Sci. & Art* II. 724 All strong lights must be relieved by deep shades. 1820 BELZONI *Egypt & Nubia* III. 328 They [the fish] were of a strong blue silvered colour. 1831 BREWSTER *Nat. Magic* viii. (1832) 195 Two strong lights may be made to produce darkness! 1885 *Athenæum* 23 May 669/1 A foreground of whitish sun-blanched clay reflects the strong sungleam falling there.

fig. 1711 SWIFT *Examiner* No. 39 ¶9 The Shame of having their Crimes expos'd to open View in the strongest Colours. 1769 ROBERTSON *Chas. V,* IV. Wks. 1851 III. 573 He painted, in the strongest colours, the emperor's want of discernment. 1833 J. RUSH *Philos. Hum. Voice* xxxi. (ed. 2) 240 And this may serve to set the power of intonation in the strongest light.

h. Of effort, movement, pressure, etc.: Forcible.

1827 FARADAY *Chem. Manip.* xix. (1842) 533 It is better to make it [*sc.* the pressure] rather stronger when the glass is returned, than when drawn towards the body. 1837 CARLYLE *Fr. Rev.* I. v. i, You cannot without strong elbowing get to the counter. 1899 *Allbutt's Syst. Med.* VIII. 19 An architect.. putting in the details of a design by means of strong pressure with a hard pencil.

i. Of feeling, conviction, belief: Intense, fervid. Of party views or principles: Uncompromising, thoroughgoing.

c1200 *Ormin* 14461 Forr defless þewwess hafenn aȝȝ Strang niþ ȝæn Cristess þewwess. 1590 SPENSER *F.Q.* II. ii. 28 But her two other sisters..both their champions bad Pursew the end of their strong enmity. 1600 SHAKS. *A.Y.L.* I. iii. 28 Is it possible on such a sodaine, you should fall into so strong a liking with old Sir Roulands yongest sonne? 1610 —— *Temp.* II. i. 208 My strong imagination see's a Crowne Dropping vpon thy head. 1667 MILTON *P.L.* IX. 492 Hate stronger, under shew of Love well feign'd. 1794 MRS. RADCLIFFE *Myst. Udolpho* xxxiii, That there should be light in this chamber, and at this hour, excited her strong surprise. 1839 THACKERAY *Fatal Boots* Mar., The desire for the boots was so strong, that have them I must at any rate. 1849 MACAULAY *Hist. Eng.* vii. II. 200 A strong sense of duty. 1850 *Athenæum* 7 Dec. 1282/1 We confess to a strong interest..in the proposed change. 1881 MORLEY *Cobden* xxix. II. 243 M. Rouher, who was then Minister of Commerce, professed strong Free-trade views. 1902 'VIOLET JACOB' *Sheep-Stealers* xii, The sheep-stealer too was at all times a taciturn man with deep prejudices and strong loves and hates.

j. Of a person: Firmly convinced, decided in opinion; *colloq.* laying great stress *on* something. Often qualifying a party designation: Zealous, uncompromising, thoroughgoing.

1526 *Pilgr. Perf.* (W. de W. 1531) 276 In all maters stronge in theyr owne opinion. 1598 SHAKS. *Merry W.* IV. vi. 27 Her Mother, (euen strong against that match And firme for Doctor Caius). 1599 MARSTON *Ant. & Mel.* v, I was mightie strong in thought we should have shut up night with an olde comedie. 1625 BACON *Ess., Of Counsel* (Arb.) 329 In choice of Committees for ripening Businesse, for the Counsell, it is better to choose Indifferent persons, then to make an Indifferency, by putting in those, that are strong, on both sides. 1679 *Tryal R. Langhorn* 26, *L.C.J.* Is Anthony a Papist? *Mr. Bus.* Yes, a very strong Papist. 1711 ADDISON *Spect.* No. 126 ¶8, I find however that the Knight is a much stronger Tory in the Country than in Town. 1855 MACAULAY *Hist. Eng.* xix. IV. 350 For Bohun was as strong a Tory as a conscientious man who had taken the oaths could possibly be. 1858 SEARS *Athan.* III. iii. 274 The Essenes.. were strong anti-materialists. 1882 MORLEY *Cobden* xxix. II. 255 The Emperor was strong for a commercial treaty with England. 1859 MRS. STOWE *Minister's Wooing* xxx, 'Some folks say,' said Candace, 'that dreaming about white horses is a certain sign. Jinny Styles is very strong about that.' 1883 MRS. E. KENNARD *Right Sort* xxiv, I doubt very much if Mary, who is so strong on the proprieties, will consider you and Mr. McGrath sufficient chaperones.

k. Of a hold: Not easily dislodged, firm, tenacious. So *to take strong root.* Chiefly *fig.* (Cf. 9.)

1699 SOUTH *Serm.* (1727) IV. 517 Nothing has so strong and fast an Hold upon the Nature and Mind of Man, as that which delights it. 1821 SCOTT *Kenilw.* xxx, His friend's unusual finery had taken a strong hold of his imagination.

14. Having its specific property in a high degree.

†**a.** Of coin: Containing much precious metal.

1469 in *Archæologia* XV. 168 Whanne the seid money be founde atte the assaye..to stronge or to feble all only in weght or all only in allaye.

b. Of a liquor: Containing a large proportion of spirit or alcohol. See also STRONG DRINK, STRONG WATER 2.

to think strong beer of oneself: to have an unduly high opinion of oneself (*nonce-use.* Cf. SMALL BEER 1 c).

c1000 *Sax. Leechd.* I. 172 Ȝyf þu þas wyrte sylst þicȝean on strangon wine. 1530 TINDALE *Answ. More* Pref., Wks. (1572) 248/2 Ale & bere of the strongest. 1598 SHAKS. *Merry W.* III. v. 114 And then to be stopt in like a strong distillation with stinking Cloathes. 1618 *Owles Almanacke* 46 Small beere shall be for dyet-keepers, but strong twang shall proue as good as bagg-pudden. 1669 *Sir K. Digby's Closet opened* 126 To twenty Gallons of the Strong-wort he puts eight or ten pound..of honey. 1671 MILTON *Samson* 553-4 O madness, to think use of strongest wines And strongest drinks our chief support of health. 1707 MORTIMER *Husb.* 567 Which quantity will make a Barrel of Strong-Beer, and a Barrel and a half of Ale, and one Hogs-head and half of Small-Beer. 1762 BICKERSTAFF *Love in Village* III. ix, I tipsey brother!—I—that never touch a drop of any thing strong from year's end to year's end. 1837 SOUTHEY *Doctor* IV. Interch. xvi. 382, I am more inclined, as my Master insinuates, to think Strong Beer of myself. 1843 PEREIRA *Food & Diet* 422 Wines which contain a comparatively small quantity of it [*sc.* alcohol] are denominated light wines;.. while those which are rich in it are termed strong or generous wines.

c. Of an infusion, solution, etc.: Having a large preponderance of the solid ingredient or of the flavouring element; having little dilution.

1716 POPE *Basset-table* 108 The Tea's too strong. 1721 RAMSAY *Prospect of Plenty* 161 They'll..stow them [herrings] wi' strang brine. a1777 in *Jrnl. Friends' Hist. Soc.* (1904) Oct. 187 To these 2 Quarts of strong Jelly you may put a Pinte of Rhenish. 1827 FARADAY *Chem. Manip.* xxiv. (1842) 611 Put two ounces of acetate of potassa into a retort, with its weight of strong sulphuric acid. 1866 READE *Griffith Gaunt* II. xii. 195 Make him soup as strong as strong. 1873 T. H. GREEN *Introd. Pathol.* (ed. 2) 351 A drop of strong glycerine. 1899 *Allbutt's Syst. Med.* VII. 583 Antral and attic cavities washed out with strong antiseptic solution.

d. *strong of*: largely or greatly impregnated or flavoured with.

1617 MORYSON *Itin.* I. 26 These waters are so strong of brimstone, as the very smoake warmeth them that come neere. 1709 T. ROBINSON *Nat. Hist. Westmld. & Cumbld.* vii. 44 Upon the inside of this Fell, breaks out a Chalybiate Water, very strong of the Mineral. 1769 MRS. RAFFALD *Eng. Housekpr.* (1778) 215 When the water is strong of the apple, add to it the juice of a lemon. 1846 DICKENS *Pict. fr. Italy* 49 German sausages, strong of garlick. 1861 RAMSAY *Remin.* Ser. II. 124 'Oh, vera good, mem; it's just some strong o' the apple' (a common country expression for beer which is rather tart or sharp).

fig. 1745 YOUNG *Night-Thoughts* VIII. 15 Men, who think nought so strong of the romance, So rank Knight-errant, as a Real Friend. 1901 A. HOPE *Tristram of Blent* xxvi. 356 This situation was deliciously strong of the Tristrams.

e. Of a semi-liquid substance: Stiff, viscid.

1683 MOXON *Mech. Exerc., Printing* xxiv. ¶11 If it be small Letter.., the Inck must be Strong..: But if it be great Letter.., he makes Soft Inck serve. 1761 *Phil. Trans.* LII. 150, I had it varnished over several times with strong varnish, or japan. 1839 URE *Dict. Arts* 1266 (*Varnish*) Keep it boiling until it feels strong and stringy between the fingers.

f. Of flour (see quots.).

1844 H. STEPHENS *Bk. Farm* II. 349 When wheat is translucent..it is best suited to the common baker, as affording what is called *strong* flour; that is, flour that rises boldly with yeast into a spongy dough. 1905 *Westm. Gaz.* 16 Sept. 7/1 But the bakers want a 'strong' flour—one that holds more water and makes more bread.

15. Affecting the sense of taste or smell in a high degree.

a. Powerful in odour, strong-smelling; *spec.* having a powerful unpleasant smell. Also of an odour.

1340 HAMPOLE *Pr. Consc.* 6692 And yhit þe fire þat bryn þam sal, Sal gyfe a st[r]ang stynk with-alle. c1475 HENRYSON *Poems* III. (S.T.S.) 151 With reid nettill seid in strang wesche to steip. 1500-20 DUNBAR *Poems* lix. 9 That fulle dismemberit hes my meter, And poysound it with strang salpeter. 1567 in H. Campbell *Love-lett. Q. Scots* App. (1824) 61 The longer the dirt is hidden, it is the stronger. 1607 SHAKS. *Cor.* I. i. 61 They say poore Suters haue strong breaths. 1626 BACON *Sylva* §835 For those kinde of Smells, that we haue mentioned, are all Strong, and doe Pull and Vellicate the Sense. 1664 BUTLER *Hud.* II. i. 755 Which makes him have so strong a breath, Each night he stinks a Queen to death. 1728 POPE *Dunc.* II. 105 [He] from th' effluvia [of ordure] strong Imbibes new life. 1882 FLOYER *Unexpl. Baluchistan* 151 Bushire..contains more filth and strong smells in proportion to its size than any other town.

b. Powerful in flavour or taste; strong-tasting; rank. Also of a flavour or taste.

c1000 *Sax. Leechd.* I. 310 Þa [leaf] syndon stranges swæces. 1599 MASSINGER, etc. *Old Law* II. i, Tis like a cheese too strong of the Runnet. 1644 DIGBY *Nat. Bodies* xvii. §5. 149 They thought that paines well recompenced, by finding it in the tast to grow stronger and stronger. 1659 HOWELL *Lex. Tetragl., Eng. Prov.,* As strong as Mustard. 1719 LONDON & WISE *Compl. Gard.* IV. 66 Its Pulp is very buttery,..and Taste agreeable; the only fault is, that 'tis a little strong towards the Core. 1830 LYELL *Princ. Geol.* I. 202 The water is hot, has a strong taste. 1837 DICKENS *Pickw.* xxxii, The cheese went a great way, for it was very strong. 1893 R. LYDEKKER *Horns & Hoofs* 116 The flesh of other buck ibex is so strong as to be quite uneatable. 1908 R. BAGOT *A. Cuthbert* vii. 65 Commercial travellers..smoking the strongest of black cigars.

16. Having a powerful effect on the mind or will.

a. Of motives, impulses, temptations, etc.: Powerful; adapted to prevail; hard to resist. Of passions: Capable of great intensity; hard to control.

a1225 *Ancr. R.* 32 Habbeð reouþe of þeo þet beoth ine stronge temptaciuns. 1567 *Gude & Godlie Ball.* 66, I am compassit round about, With sore and strang temptatioun. 1600 SHAKS. *A.Y.L.* II. vii. 118 Let gentlenesse my strong enforcement be. 1598 B. JONSON *Ev. Man in Hum.* II. iii, When such strong motives muster, and make head Against her single peace. 1667 MILTON *P.L.* IX. 934 Inducement strong To us, as likely tasting to attaine Proportional ascent. *Ibid.* x. 265 Goe whither Fate and inclination strong Leads thee. 1692 ATTERBURY *Serm.* (1726) I. 13 By the Means of our Will, and that strong Bent towards Gratitude which the Author of our Nature hath implanted in it. 1779 *Mirror* No. 65 A man of warm affections and strong passions. 1815 SHELLEY *Alastor* 274 A strong impulse urged His steps to the sea-shore. 1823 F. CLISSOLD *Ascent Mt. Blanc* 20, I felt a strong inclination to sleep. 1849 MACAULAY *Hist. Eng.* v. I. 662 Both were impelled by the strongest pressure of hope and fear to criminate him. 1891 M. ROBERTS *Land-travel & Sea-faring* 57 In truth the nomadic instinct was always strong in me.

b. Of argument, evidence, proof, etc.: Powerful to demonstrate or convince; hard to confute or overthrow.

c1449 PECOCK *Repr.* v. viii. 527 Confirmacioun in strengist maner to this argument may be this: That Holi Writt [etc.]. 1471 [see STRENGEST]. 1565 SHACKLOCK tr. *Hosius* 8 b, Stronger obiections..then he was able to solute. 1601 SHAKS. *All's Well* IV. ii. 59 My reasons are most strong. 1608 —— *Per.* IV. ii. 38 Besides the sore tearmes we stand vpon with the gods, wilbe strong with vs for giuing ore. 1696 VANBRUGH *Relapse* II. i, You have many stronger Claims than that, Berinthia, whenever you think fit to plead your Title. 1742-3 *Johnson's Deb.* Wks. 1811 XIV. 390 Nor can any argument be offered for the present bill more strong than that. 1770 LUCKOMBE *Hist. Printing* 13 The fact is strong, and..passes for certain evidence of the age of books. 1784 SIR J. HAWKINS *Walton's Angler* (ed. 4) 107 *note,* The presumption therefore is very strong, that both were written by..Christopher Harvey. 1831 BREWSTER *Nat. Magic* v. (1832) 104 The shadow of the pin falling in the direction A B is a stronger proof to the eye that the light is coming from the right hand. 1857 MILLER *Elem. Chem., Org.* (1862) 236 A strong argument against the admission of the view that [etc.]. 1861 PALEY *Æschylus* (ed. 2) *Supplices* 764 *note,* There is a strong probability that they are right. 1892 *Law Times' Rep.* LXVII. 251/2 The evidence as to this is too strong to be discarded.

c. Of a case: Well-supported by evidence or precedent.

1698 in Sir H. Dalrymple *Decis.* (1792) 8 Which quadrates with the present case, which is yet stronger than it. 1737 *Gentl. Mag.* VII. 297 The Case..mentioned in *Coke* 4. *Inst.* 228. is by no Means so strong. 1863 COWDEN CLARKE *Shaks. Char.* xvi. 391 Shakespeare has made out a strong case for Shylock. 1885 *Law Rep.* 15 *Q.B.D.* 320 This seems to me a much stronger case than *Heaven* v. *Pender,* where it was held that the defendant was liable.

17. Having legal force. †**a.** Of a document: Valid (*obs.*). **b.** Of dispositions, sanctions, etc.: Effectual.

c1450 *Godstow Reg.* 145 Both partyes maade hit stronge by puttyng to þere seelys. 1544 tr. *Littleton's Tenures* III. v. 81 Yf he receyue the payment in any other place, thys is good ynoughe and as stronge for the feoffour, as yf [etc.]. 1593 SHAKS. *Rich. II,* IV. i. 235 There should'st thou finde one heynous Article,..cracking the strong Warrant of an Oath. 1600 —— *Sonn.* lviii, Be where you list, your charter is so strong, That you your selfe may priuiledge your time To what you will. 1741 *Cases Equity Time of Talbot* 181 The Nature of the Provision is strong enough for this Purpose, without any express Words. 1765 *Pet.* in *Walker* v. *Spence* 4 It would be quite inconsistent, that a right of hypothec should have stronger effects than a right of property. 1765 BLACKSTONE *Comm.* Introd §2. I. 54 Neither do divine or natural duties..receive any stronger sanction from being also declared to be duties by the law of the land. 1838 ARNOLD *Hist. Rome* I. xvi. 316 The old laws for the security of personal liberty were confirmed afresh, and received a stronger sanction.

18. Vividly perceptible, marked, definite.

a. of mental impressions.

1697 ADDISON *Dryden's Virg. Georg.* Ess. ¶¶1, We receive more strong and lively Ideas of things from his words, than we cou'd have done from the Objects themselves. 1748 MELMOTH *Fitzosborne Lett.* lvii. (1749) II. 84 While the impression of that national belief remained strong upon their minds. 1854 SURTEES *Handley Cr.* xxxix. (1901) II. 21 'We can't do with less,' replied the lady, the cares of dinner strong upon her. 1894 J. T. FOWLER *Adamnan* Introd. 56 The local traditions..are still very strong. 1897 P. WARUNG *Tales Old Regime* 139 The circumstances..are still strong in my recollection. 1902

'VIOLET JACOB' *Sheep-Stealers* xiv, 'Ah, I was younger then,' replied Harry, with all the wisdom of his twenty-five years strong upon him.

b. Of resemblance, contrast: Marked.

1796 MRS. INCHBALD *Nature & Art* xi. (1820) 26 A strong family resemblance appeared between the two youths. **1842** BORROW *Bible in Spain* xxxiv, Nothing could exhibit a stronger contrast to the desolate tracts..through which we had lately passed, than [etc.]. **1879** *Cassell's Techn. Educ.* IV. 1/2 It will not be necessary to describe any other lathes ..as there is a very strong family likeness amongst them. **1898** 'MERRIMAN' *Roden's Corner* ix. 98 Von Holzen was in strong contrast to the two Englishmen.

c. Of national or dialectal pronunciation: Strongly-marked, broad.

1818 SCOTT *Hrt. Midl.* xxi, A tattered cadie..exclaimed in a strong north-country tone, 'Ta deil ding out her Cameronian een.' **1842** SIR T. MARTIN in *Fraser's Mag.* Dec. 654/1 A strong Banffshire accent. **1859** *Habits of Gd. Society* 64 The ballads of Moore may gain much from a strong Irish brogue, but [etc.]. **1890** CONAN DOYLE *White Company* xxiv, 'I come,' he shouted.., with a strong Breton accent.

†**d.** Of the features: Coarse, ugly. *Obs.*

1794 MRS. RADCLIFFE *Myst. Udolpho* 1, Each was rendered more impressive by the grotesque habits and strong features of the guides and other attendants. **1817** J. EVANS *Excurs. Windsor*, etc. 48 Heidegger once laid a wager ..that..his lordship would not be able to produce so hideous a face in all London! A woman was found whose features, at first sight, were thought stronger than his.

e. Of a line: Broad, thick. Also, vivid in colour (cf. 13 g).

1731 *Art of Drawing & Paint.* 4 Then if the Print or Picture is done by a good Master, see which Lines are strong, and which are tender and soft: Imitate them. **1796** *Cavalry Instr.* Table, The strong Line denotes the Front. **1831** BREWSTER *Optics* x. 85 [Of Fraunhofer's lines] D is in the orange, and is a strong double line, easily seen..; E is in the green, and consists of several, the middle one being the strongest.

f. Of the outlines of an object in a landscape or picture: Bold, not faint. Also *fig.*

1818 SHELLEY *Julian & Maddalo* 106 The broad sun sunk behind it [a bell in a tower], and it tolled In strong and black relief. **1862** WHITTIER *Astræa at the Capitol* 63 On our ground of grief Rise day by day in strong relief The prophecies of better things.

g. *Photogr.* Of a negative: Having marked contrast of light and shade; dense.

1892 A. BROTHERS *Photogr.* 80 Strong, intense negatives are best printed by daylight.

h. That is in a high degree what is indicated.

1899 *Allbutt's Syst. Med.* VII. 415 According as the individuals in whom the lesions specified occur are 'visuals', or strong 'auditives'.

19. a. Of language, an expression, a word: Emphatic; signifying or implying much; not moderate. ***strong language***: see LANGUAGE *sb.*[1] 3.

1697 DRYDEN *Æneis* Ded. (a) 4, The work of Tragedy is on the Passions, and in Dialogue, both of them abhor strong Metaphors, in which the Epopee delights. **1796** JANE AUSTEN *Pride & Prej.* xxiv, I must think your language too strong in speaking of both. **1836** W. IRVING *Astoria* III. 245 He expressed his indignation in the strongest terms. **1845** THACKERAY *Cornhill to Cairo* v. Wks. 1878 VII. 597 The shabbiness of this place [Greece] actually beats Ireland and that is a strong word. **1884** E. YATES *Recoll.* II. 330 Exercising my power, I struck out some strong expressions. **1900** CHAMBERLAIN in *Daily News* 24 Sept. 2/4 Scandalous is a strong word, but weak people always use the strongest words.

b. Of a protest, recommendation, etc.: Emphatic, strongly-worded, urgent.

1733 BUDGELL *Bee* No. 2. I. 71 The Prussian Minister made the strongest Instances in favour of these Officers, but to no Purpose. **1768** BOSWELL *Corsica* ii. (ed. 2) 94 The prince of Wirtemburg..sent an express to the emperour, with a very strong letter. **1830** ELLENBOROUGH *Diary* (1881) II. 372 Told Lord Cleveland I had transmitted his letter with a strong recommendation. **1844** H. H. WILSON *Brit. India* II. 15 Strong remonstrances were addressed to the Court of Khatmandu. **1912** *Times* 19 Oct. 8/2 Strong protests were made by several members against Mr. Harper's proposal.

c. *Math.* Of a mathematical entity or concept: implying more than others of its kind; defined by more conditions.

1950 W. FELLER *Introd. Probability Theory* I. viii. 156 We shall prove a much stronger statement. **1955** M. LOÈVE *Probability Theory* 18 Now we can..use the supplementary requirement that the additive property of *P* remains valid for denumerable sums... This is the celebrated Borel strong law of large numbers. **1964** A. P. & W. ROBERTSON *Topological Vector Spaces* iii. 47 This topology is denoted by $\beta(E', E)$ and is sometimes called the strong topology on E'. **1971** G. GLAUBERMAN in Powell & Higman *Finite Simple Groups* i. 44 Here the condition of *p*-stability is too strong to be useful. **1979** *Proc. London Math. Soc.* XXXVIII. 338 We say that a linear operator L on $\mathcal{M}$ is a strong Feller operator if $Lf \in \mathcal{C}$ whenever $f \in \mathcal{M}k$.

20. Of literary or artistic work: Vigorous or forceful in style or execution.

1746 FRANCIS tr. *Horace, Art of Poetry* 422 Good Sense, that Fountain of the Muse's Art, Let the strong Page of Socrates impart. **1749** CHESTERF. *Let. to Son* 24 Nov., I should prefer moderate matter, adorned with all the beauties and elegancies of style, to the strongest matter in the world, ill-worded, and ill-delivered. **1822** *Q. Mus. Mag.* IV. 118 Mr. Horsley's [glee] is in his pure, strong, legitimate manner. **1905** *Daily Chron.* 16 Aug. 3/2 What the publishers call a 'strong' book. **1913** J. COLLIER in *19th Cent.* Mar. 603 He might have made a stronger picture, he could hardly have made a more beautiful one.

21. *Comm.* Of prices: Tending to steadiness or to a rise; not fluctuating or depressed.

1870 *Pall Mall Gaz.* 23 Sept. 9/2 The Home Funds are, if anything, rather stronger in tone. **1890** *Daily News* 6 Jan. 2/3 Coal is very strong in price. *Ibid.* 1 Sept. 2/5 Pig iron is strong at 43s. 6d. for cinder. **1895** *Ibid.* 14 Oct. 2/6 Producers have been stronger in their prices.

22. *Gram.* In various applications (opposed to *weak*). **a.** Of Teutonic sbs. and adjs., their inflexions, etc.: Belonging to any of those declensions in which the OTeut. stem ended otherwise than in *n*. **b.** Of Teut. verbs and their inflexions: Forming the pa. t. and pa. pple. by means of vowel-gradation in the root-syllable, as the Eng. *give*, *break*. Hence occas. used with reference to other Indo-Germanic langs., e.g. in ***strong aorist***, applied in Gr. grammar to the 'second aorist' (ἔλιπον) in contradistinction to the 'weak' or sigmatic aorist (ἔλειψα). Occas. *transf.* with reference to non-Teutonic languages. **c.** In Sanskrit grammar, applied to the unreduced form of noun-stems, and to those cases which are formed on the 'strong' stem.

In these uses *strong* and *weak* are translations of the G. *stark* and *schwach*, the grammatical senses of which are due to Jakob Grimm. The reason for the choice of these terms to denote the two classes of declension was prob. that in German the formal distinction of case is weakened in the *n* declensions by the disappearance of the original case-endings. (Some scholars, following the letter of Grimm's own definition, inconveniently restrict the term 'strong' to the vocalic stems, so that the stems ending in other consonants than *n* form a third class, neither 'strong' nor 'weak'.) The ablaut-verbs were designated as 'strong' because in them the form of the root sufficed to express past time without the adventitious aid of a tense-suffix.

a. 1841 LATHAM *Eng. Lang.* 58 In A.S...there is the Weak, or Simple Declension for words ending in a Vowel (as *Eage, Steorra, Tunga*), and the Strong, or Complex Declension for words ending in a Consonant (*Smið, Spræc, Leáf*).

b. 1833 *Philol. Museum* II. 385 No *weak* verb ever in process of time became *strong*, while strong verbs do become weak. **1841** LATHAM *Eng. Lang.* 277 The German Grammarians call the Tenses formed by a change of vowel, the Strong Tenses, the Strong Verbs, the Strong Conjugation, or the Strong Order. *Ibid.* 278 The Strong Præterites are formed from the Present by changing the vowel, as *sing, sang, speak, spoke.* **1871** EARLE *Philol. Eng. Tongue* §274 There is a slow continual tendency in these strong verbs to merge themselves gradually into the more numerous class of the weak verbs. **1946** BINCHY & BERGIN tr. *Thurneysen's Gram. Old Irish* 335 According to the way in which these stems are formed, two main classes of verbs can be distinguished, for which the terms 'strong' and 'weak' verbs are borrowed from the grammar of the Germanic languages. Strong verbs are without exception primary... Weak verbs are for the most part denominative. **1962** C. WATKINS *Indo-European Origins of Celtic Verb* II. 116 In the strong (non-derivative) verb..the present still exhibits numerous divergent formations.

c. 1863 BENFEY *Sansk. Gram.* §220 There are some nouns which have a strong and a weak form... Some have even three, a strong, a weak, and a weakest form.

¶ Incorrect use.

1858–9 G. P. MARSH *Lect. Engl. Lang.* (1860) 335 The strong inflections, or those consisting in a letter-change, as present *run*, past *ran*, singular *man*, plural *men*.

23. *Phonetics* and *Prosody*. Of a syllable: Bearing stress or metrical ictus. Of a consonant-sound: Characterized by force of utterance. Also in *Music*, accented.

1792 J. BURNET (Ld. Monboddo) *Orig. & Progr. Lang.* III. iii. VI. 237 Emphasis, by which one word in a sentence is sounded much louder and stronger than the other words. **1852** *Proc. Philol. Soc.* V. 153 A compound verse, composed of two parts, in each of which two dactyls..were followed by a long syllable, that is, a foot catalectic on the strong syllable, was alternated with the ancient epic verse. **1856** FARIS EL-SHIDIAC *Pract. Gram Arabic* 3 ص. The *true* sound of this letter must be learnt by the ear. It is like a strong *d*. **1869** OUSELEY *Counterp. Canon & Fugue* iii. 12 Every bar contains two beats, one down-beat, and one up-beat; or, as Cherubini and others name them, a strong or accented time, and a weak or unaccented time.

24. a. *Card-playing.* Of a player: Holding commanding cards (*in* a specified suit). Of a hand or suit: Composed of commanding cards. Of a card: Of high and commanding value.

1862 'CAVENDISH' *Whist* (1864) 59 It is conversely a disadvantage to trump a doubtful card when you are strong in trumps. **1864** W. POLE *Theory Whist* (1870) 18 A strong hand is difficult to define, further than as one likely to make many tricks; a weak one the contrary. *Ibid.* 34 It can only be warranted by very strong cards in all other suits. **1879** 'CAVENDISH' *Card Ess.* 184 If I only live long enough,.. perhaps some day my strong suit will be trumps! **1900** J. DOE *Bridge Man.* 31 The Dealer should go No Trumps with two very strong suits, one other suit weakly guarded, and the fourth not guarded at all. *Ibid.* 32 If his Spades are fairly strong he should leave the declaration to his partner.

attrib. **1886** 'CAVENDISH' *Whist* (ed. 16) App. 288 The original leader (a strong suit player), leads queen of a plain suit.

b. Hence *fig.*, as (one's) ***strong suit***: something at which one excels. Also ***strong card***, a particular advantage or forte. *colloq.*

1865 'MARK TWAIN' *Sketches New & Old* (1875) 33 Jumping on a dead level was his strong suit. **1884, 1898** [see SUIT *sb.* 20 a]. **1899** ADE *Fables in Slang* 138 Marie was a Strong Card. The Male Patrons of the Establishment hovered around the Desk long after paying their Checks. Within a Month the Receipts of the Place had doubled. **1936** E. M. FORSTER *Abinger Harvest* I. 16 As my husband points out, that is one of our strong cards. **1940** G. FRANKAU *Self-Portrait* lxiii. 388 Adaptability has always been one of my strong suits. **1970** R. LOWELL *Notebook* 140 Dating children with trash was your strong suit.

25. *Comb.* In parasynthetic adjs., as ***strong-armed, -backed, -brained***, etc. See also STRONG-BREATHED, -HEADED, -MINDED.

?*a* **1366** CHAUCER *Rom. Rose* 944 [Arrows] stronge poynted eueryschoon. *c* **1374** [see FAITHED *ppl. a.* 1]. **1412–20** LYDG. *Chron. Troy* I. 1252 A rial chef cite..Strong wallid & towred rounde aboute. *a* **1425** tr. *Arderne's Treat. Fistula* etc. 6 For that the pacient was strong herted, and suffrid wele sharp þingis. **1588** SHAKS. *L.L.L.* I. ii. 77 O well-knit Sampson, strong ioynted Sampson. **1592** —— *Ven. & Ad.* 111 Strong-temperd steele his stronger strength obayed. **1656** COWLEY *Pindar. Odes, Plagues Egypt* xi, The houses and strong-body'ed Trees it broke. **1657** *Whole Duty Man* (1755) 194 These stronger-brained Drinkers. **1677** *Lond. Gaz.* No. 1233/4 A bright bay Nag, very strong quartered. **1780** BURKE *Œcon. Reform.* Wks. III. 233 A man of a long-sighted and a strong-nerved humanity. **1785** BURNS *Addr. to Deil* iv, On the strong-wing'd Tempest flyin. **1785** Strong-bodied [see BAAS]. **1822** LAMB *Elia* Ser. II. *Bks. & Reading*, To be strong-backed and neat-bound is the desideratum of a volume. **1850** J. G. WHITTIER *Elliott* in *National Era* 10 Jan. 6/4 Strong-armed as Thor! **1858** HOMANS *Cycl. Comm.* 434/2 Fine, long, and strong-stapled cotton. **1863** TENNYSON *On Transl. Homer* I These lame hexameters the strong-wing'd music of Homer! **1868** RUSKIN *Pol. Econ. Art.* Addenda 200 A great deal may, indeed, be done..by a nation strong-elbowed and strong-hearted as we are. **1868** J. H. BLUNT *Ref. Ch. Eng.* I. 331 Then the stronger souled men betook themselves to preparation for violent deaths. **1899** LADY M. VERNEY *Verney Mem.* IV. 80 She came of a strong-willed family. **1907** *Munsey's Mag.* Dec. 309/1 The *piccola* looked up at the dark..strong-jawed face. **1922** JOYCE *Ulysses* 525 He wrote pencilled messages offering his nuptial partner to all strongmembered males. **1922** D. H. LAWRENCE *England, my England* (1924) 82 He looked so strong-blooded and healthy. **1926** —— *Plumed Serpent* vii. 130 White men sitting there would have been strong-muscled and frank. *a* **1930** —— *Etruscan Places* (1932) iii. 74 This sense of vigorous, strong-bodied liveliness is characteristic of the Etruscans. **1930** S. SPENDER *Twenty Poems* 3 Weapons men use, stone, sling, and strong-thewed bow He will not know. **1931** R. GRAVES *To Whom Else?* 11 With their strong-gutted and capacious bellies Digested stones and glass like ostriches. **1944** BLUNDEN *Shells by Stream* 31 Strong-elbowed and with wondrous beard, Whose statue's this? **1960** C. DAY LEWIS *Buried Day* ii. 44 My father..[had] the expression of an actor playing the part of a strong-charactered, resolute, if moody, man. **1978** W. F. BUCKLEY *Stained Glass* xvii. 169 He was strong-jawed, with a splotchy face that showed the ravages of frostbite.

26. Special comb.: **strong-back**, (*a*) any of several plants used in the West Indies to make medicinal infusions; (*b*) *Naut.* (see quot. 1867); also, a spar across boat-davits, to which the boat is secured at sea (*Cent. Dict.* 1891), and in extended uses, esp. a beam placed across an access cover to secure it in position; **strong bark**, a tree or shrub of the genus *Bourreria*, found in the West Indies and tropical America; **strong-eyed** *a.* chiefly *N.Z.*, of a sheep-dog: possessed of good powers of controlling sheep; hence **strong eye**, (*N.Z.*, a sheep-dog with) this ability; **strong house**, (*a*) a fortified house, a castle; (*b*) (see quot. 1797); **strong joint** *U.S. slang* (see quots. 1935, 1938); **strong-like** *a. Sc.*, having an appearance of strength; **strong-man's-weed**, the plant *Petiveria alliacea*, found in the West Indies and used there for its stimulating and sudorific properties; **strong stress** *Prosody*, accentuation which falls on syllables separated by a varying number of unstressed syllables, characteristic of certain poetic traditions, as Old English alliterative verse.

1738 *Phil. Trans.* XL. 350 *Pittoniæ similis* [*frutex*]. In the Bahama Islands it is called *Strong-back; a Decoction of the Bark is used there to strengthen the Stomach, and restore the Appetite. **1863** A. YOUNG *Naut. Dict.* 397 *Strong-back*, for the Chain Cable. **1867** SMYTH *Sailor's Word-bk.*, *Strong-back*, the same with Samson's post (which see). Also, an adaptation of a strong piece of wood over the windlass, to lift the turns of a chain-cable clear of it. **1927** M. W. BECKWITH *Notes Jamaican Ethnobotany* 28 Strong-back.. For a weak back drink a little as tea each day. **1927** G. BRADFORD *Gloss. Sea Terms* 176/2 *Strongback*, a steel (or wood) beam placed across a hatch to support the sections of the hatch covers... A spar lashed to and running between the old style davits to steady them and to aid in controlling and securing the boat. **1953** C. S. FORESTER *Hornblower & Atropos* xvi. 253 The next morning Hornblower watched launch and longboat start off with strongbacks erected in their sterns, and blocks and tackles rigged on them. **1953** *Caribbean Q.* III. I. 10 There are two or three kinds of strong-back (to make strengthening tea). **1970** M. SLATER *Caribbean Cooking for Pleasure* 21/2 In Jamaica, fish soup is 'Fish Tea' and sometimes called 'Strong Back', but this term is applied to anything nourishing 'make strong back'. **1977** *Austral. Sailing* Jan. 38/3 The strongback on which the mast is stepped is made as a complete trussed girder beam which is placed as a unit inside the shell. **1864** GRISEBACH *Flora Brit. W. Ind.* 788/1 *Strong-bark. **1884** SARGENT *Rep. Forests N. Amer.* 114 *Bourreria Havanensis*... Strong Bark. **1934** J. LILICO *Sheep Dog Mem.* 4 My father..taught me how to prevent the several faults that the *strong-eyed young dog will assuredly acquire if not taken in time. **1949** G. W. C. HARTLEY *Shepherd's Dogs* ii. 3 Excessively strong-eyed dogs. *Ibid.* 5 The pup is from a 'strong-eye' strain. **1952** *Arena* (N.Z.) XXXI. 2 Shepherding the stragglers would be Charlie's strong-eyes, Beau and Belle. **1977** *Field* 13 Jan. 55/2 A dog which can 'will' his sheep into submission requires what shepherds term a strong (or dominant) eye.

1649–50 CROMWELL *Let.* 15 Feb. in *Carlyle*, From thence I marched to a *Strong-house belonging to Sir Richard Everard. **1797** B. S. BARTON *New Views Orig. Tribes Amer.* p. xxxviii, The Senecas, Mohawks, Onondagos, Cayugas, and Oneidas, constitute the confederacy which has long been known by the name of the Five Nations. This confederacy, or compact, is called by the Indians themselves the Strong-House. **1875** W. MCILWRAITH *Guide Wigtownshire* 104 A strong-house was built here at an early date. **1926** MAINES & GRANT *Wise-Crack Dict.* 14/1 *Strong joint, unfair or cheater's game. **1935** N. ERSINE *Underworld & Prison Slang* 73 *Strong joint*, a crooked gambling house. **1938** F. CHESTER *Shot Full* xi. 98 A 'pick-out'. This is another form of 'strong-joint', or never-win game. **1963** Strong-joint [see *flat joint* s.v. FLAT *a.* 15]. **1782** J. BROWN *Nat. & Revealed Relig.* II. i. 139 He.. doth accomplish those promises.. which he had the *strongest-like reasons to shift. **1789** J. WILLIAMS *Min. Kingd.* I. 420 Some of these are dull and strong like. **1864** GRISEBACH *Flora Brit. W. Ind.* 788/1 *Strong-man's-weed. **1959** *PMLA* LXXIV. I. 588 The two main alternative principles of English meter.. are actually two kinds of stress—*strong stress (the Old English, the *Piers Plowman* tradition) and syllable stress (the Chaucer-Tennyson tradition). **1973** *Studies in Eng. Lit.: Eng. Number* (Tokyo) 22 There was no mention of Anglo-Saxon verse as a forerunner of sprung rhythm... There is.. little reason to suppose that Hopkins derived his sprung rhythm from strong-stress verse.

strong (strɒŋ), *adv.* Forms: 1, 4 **strange**, 1–5 **stronge**, 4– *north.* and *Sc.* **strang**, 4– **strong**. [OE. *strange*, *strǫnge* = OHG. *strango*: see STRONG *a.*]

1. a. Qualifying a verb or predication: = STRONGLY *adv. Obs.* exc. as in b, c. †*more stronger*: = A FORTIORI.

c **900** *Bæda's Hist.* I. xxvii. (1890) 68 þeah ðe þæt wiite hwene heardor & strongor don sy. *a* **1000** *Boeth. Metr.* vi. 15 Heo strange ȝeondstyred on staðu beateð. *a* **1250** *Owl & Night.* 254 þeos vle.. wes of teoned swiþe stronge. *a* **1300** *K. Horn* 304 (Camb.) Wel longe Ihc habbe þe luued stronge. *a* **1300** *Cursor M.* 24100 On mi sorou mai be nan end, It stikes me sua strang. **13..** *K. Alis.* 1609 (Laud MS.) þe fote men & þai on hors Trauaileden stronge her cors. *c* **1400** *Gamelyn* 397 Gamelyn þat stood y-bounde stronge. *c* **1425** *Seven Sag.* (P.) 197 This house that is so strange dyȝt. *c* **1489** CAXTON *Sonnes of Aymon* iii. 86 Soo stronge he spored his horse, that he wente ayenste Reynawde. **1532** *St. German's Dial. Laws Eng.* II. xxviii. 61 b, I suppose.. that more stronger he maye appoyntte at what age suche wylles as be made shalbe perfourmed. **1570** *Sat. Poems Reform.* xviii. 63 His Father [ye] wyrreit strang. **1641** J. JACKSON *True Evang. T.* II. 98 The more weary [the Oxe] is, the more strong doth he fixe his footings. **1679** MOXON *Mech. Exerc.* ix. 160 The stronger it is forced in, the faster the Hook sticks. **1697** DRYDEN *Æneis* XI. 1249 The Bow-string touch'd her Breast, so strong she drew. **1705** H. BLACKWELL *Engl. Fencing-Master* 34 If that Thrust be made at you, parry strong, and thrust at the same time. **1767** WARBURTON in W. & Hurd *Lett.* (1809) 407 G.S. was stronger engraved on your fancy than B.S. **1768–74** TUCKER *Lt. Nat.* (1834) II. 81 Whatever affects a man's private interests, touches him stronger than those of the community, or mankind in general. **1841** CATLIN *N. Amer. Ind.* i. (1844) I. 10 The reader will be disposed to forgive me for dwelling so long and so strong on the justness of the claims.

b. Used regularly with certain verbs, as *blow*, *flow*, *grow*, *run*, *smell*, etc. (Often indistinguishable from the complementary use of the adj.)

1422 YONGE tr. *Secreta Secret.* 174 The course of the ryuer So stronge and So styfe rane. *c* **1560** *Jack Jugler* (facs.) Ej, Many here smell strong but none so ranke as he. **1596** RALEGH *Discov. Guiana* 53 A slent of northerly wind that blew very strong. **1719** DE FOE *Crusoe* II. (Globe) 475 The Current setting strong to the E.N.E. *a* **1778** W. ANDERSON in *Cook's 3rd Voy.* III. ix. (1784) II. 143 This wind.. sometimes blows strong, though generally moderate. **1813** *Sporting Mag.* XLI. 85 His antagonist.. run strong in, leaving the other three hundred yards in the rear. **1855** MACAULAY *Hist. Eng.* xi. III. 110 The Whig peers.. mustered strong, and spoke warmly. *a* **1861** T. WOOLNER *My Beautiful Lady, Her Shadow* vi, Thro' pastures and thro' fields where corn grew strong.

c. In colloq. phrases. *to come it strong*: to go to great lengths; to display great activity, energy, boldness, etc.; to make statements which are hard to credit. *to come out strong*: to make a big display or impression; to 'launch out'; to declare or express oneself vigorously. *to come on strong* (orig. *U.S.*), to adopt or exhibit aggressive behaviour; to perform or contest successfully. *to go it strong*: to act vigorously or recklessly. *to go strong on*: to support or advocate energetically (? *obs.*). *to be going strong*: to be vigorous, thriving, or prosperous. *to pitch it strong*: to indulge in 'tall' talk; to make exaggerated or incredible statements.

1812, 1825- [see COME *v.* 28, 29]. **1837** T. HOOK *Jack Brag* xi, I can come it strong in that line. **1840** [see GO *v.* 46 c]. **1841** HOOD *Tale of Trumpet* 281 Unless the Managers pitch it strong. **1844** DISRAELI *Coningsby* II. vi, 'We go strong on the Church?' said Mr. Taper. **1844** DICKENS *Martin Chuz.* xlviii, He was a man as might have come out strong. **1850** THACKERAY *Pendennis* xxxvi, They've took a house in Grosvenor Place, and are coming out strong. **1853** MISS YONGE *Heir of Redclyffe* xliii, 'Over-worked, I suppose', said Charles, 'I thought he was coming it pretty strong these last few weeks.' **1860** *Players* I. 147 Many a fair lady must have lost her heart when she saw Mr. J. M. on his twentieth birthday, when he came out 'strong' at a fancy dress ball. **1861** MEREDITH *Evan Harrington* xiv, By Jove! this comes it strong. Fancy the snipocracy here—eh? **1863** READE *Hard Cash* xxxix, Well, I am thinking the 'Tiser is pitching it rather strong. **1866** A. HALLIDAY in Dickens, etc. *Mugby Junction, Engine-driver* 26/2, I used to make that journey to Brighton in fifty-two minutes. The papers said forty-nine minutes, but that was coming it a little too strong. **1879** *Oxf. & Camb. Undergrad. Jrnl.* 6 Nov. 65/1 A grand meeting in the Sheldonian.. at which Canon Farrar came out rather strong. **1898** *Punch* 22 Oct. 186/3 And though, just now, we're going strong, The brandy cannot last for long. **1913** *Daily Graphic* 26 Mar. 17/2 'Everybody's Doing It' and 'The Reaper's Dream' are still going very strong. **1970** H. E. ROBERTS *Third Ear* 5/2 *Come on strong*, to do something to a superlative degree, to an extreme; to 'pour it on'. **1976** *Honolulu Star-Bull.* 21 Dec. E-1/5 Young guys who've never had experience come on too strong and that's how a fight with a host starts. **1979** *Tucson* (Arizona) *Citizen* 28 Apr. B. 1/1 The Kings came on strong at the onset of the third period, outscoring the Suns, 15-6.

†**2.** Qualifying an adj.: Extremely, very. *Obs.*

c **1400** *Brut* cxxxiii. 138 When he saw þat he was so stronge sike. *c* **1450** *Merlin* iii. 52, I will tomorowe go to an Abbey, and feyne me stronge sike.

3. *Comb.* **a.** with pa. pples., as ***strong-built***, ***-knit***, ***-made***, ***-set***, etc.

c **1412** HOCCLEVE *De Reg. Princ.* 4305 Now, godė fadir, how mochil monye In your strong bounden chist is, we yow preye? **1577–87** HOLINSHED *Chron.* III. 1226/1 A big, broad, strong set fellow. *a* **1586** SIDNEY *Arcadia* III. xii. §10. (1912) 424 The unfaythfull armour yeelding to the swoordes strong-guided sharpenesse. **1591** SHAKS. *1 Hen. VI*, II. iii. 21 His strong knit Limbs. *a* **1592** MARLOWE *Jew of Malta* Prol. 22 A strong built Citadell. **1622** MABBE tr. *Aleman's Guzman d' Alf.* II. 308 Their strong-sowne pockets. *c* **1656** SIR H. CHOLMLEY *Mem.* (1787) 11 He was.. withal big and strong-made. **1690** *Lond. Gaz.* No. 2579/4 A very strong turn'd Gelding. **1757** DYER *Fleece* III. 382 To cast the strong-flung shuttle. **1776** BURNEY *Hist. Mus.* I. 59 There must have been other characteristic and strong-marked distinctions. **1820** HAZLITT *Lect. Dram. Lit.* 66 The same strong-braced tone of passionate declamation is kept up. **1823** SCOTT *Quentin D.* v, His firm and strong-set teeth. **1864** TENNYSON *En. Arden* 30 If they quarrell'd, Enoch stronger-made Was master. **1899** *Westm. Gaz.* 12 Sept. 5/3 It became apparent that the jockeys of the American horses did not want a strong-run race.

b. with pres. pples., as ***strong-beating***, ***-growing***, ***-smelling***, etc.

1598 SYLVESTER *Du Bartas* II. i. III. *Furies* 616 The Ram for Physick takes strong-senting Rue. **1619** A. NEWMAN *Pleasures Vision* D 7, In her [*sc.* woman's] strong-drawing fraile society. **1642** H. MORE *Song of Soul* I. i. 59 That large strong-beating flood That gars the Poet write. **1731** MILLER *Gard. Dict.* s.v. *Hyacinthus*, At which Time you must separate all the strong flowering Roots. **1761** GLOVER *Medea* III. vi. 52 The strong-constraining spell hath tam'd The restif blast. *c* **1770** MRS. GLASSE *Compl. Confectioner* 286 The aromatic, balsamic, oily, and strong-smelling plants. **1842** LOUDON *Suburban Hort.* 423 The stronger-growing plums, such as the Washington. **1848** THACKERAY *Van. Fair* xxx, He.. held her.. tight pressed against his strong-beating heart. **1880** 'BROOKSBY' *Hunting Countries* II. 212 Mounted on a bold, strong-jumping horse. **1898** J. A. GIBBS *Cotswold Vill.* 227 The hares in this district are remarkably big and strong-running.

strong, *v.* Forms: 1–2 **strangian**, **strongian**, 3 **strange-n**, 3–5 **stronge-n**. [OE. *strangian*, f. *strang* STRONG *a.* (OE. had also *ȝestrangian* intr. and trans.: see B.-T. Suppl.). Cf. OHG. *strangên* intr.] †**a.** *intr.* To become strong. *Obs.* **b.** *trans.* To make strong, strengthen. Also, to cause (one) to smell strong. Now only *U.S. local.* **c.** *to strong it*, to behave excessively, to exaggerate. *slang.*

a. *c* **825** *Vesp. Psalter* lxiv. [lxv.] 4 Word unrehtwisra strongadun [Vulg. *prævaluerunt*] ofer us. *c* **1000** ÆLFRIC *Gram.* xxvi. (Z.) 154 *Uigeo*, ic strangiȝe. *c* **1175** *Lamb. Hom.* 13 þet eower heorte erȝian swiðe and eower feond stronȝian.

b. *c* **971** *Blickling Hom.* 249 He þær wunode mid him seofon daȝas, lærende and strangenda hire heortan on ȝeleafan ures Drihtnes Hælendes Cristes. *c* **1000** ÆLFRIC *Saints' Lives* xxxiii. 255 Pafnuntius þa wearð micclan ȝestrangod þurh hire trymenesse. *c* **1205** LAY. 4461 þe castles heo nomen alle & strangede þa walles. *Ibid.* 8239 Androgeus forð rihtes nom alle his cnihtes.. & iwenden in to Kent to his ane castle & hine strongede wel. *c* **1315** SHOREHAM *Poems* I. 340 And wanne a man hit onderuangeþ, Ine saule hit hine strangeþ. *c* **1450** *Mirk's Festial* 229 For maydenhode ys lytyll helpe wyth, but yf hyt be strongyt wyth pacience.

1913 H. KEPHART *Our Southern Highlanders* xiii. 283 A verb will be coined from an adverb... Or from an adjective... Baby, that onion 'll strong ye! **1941** E. P. O'DONNELL *Great Big Doorstep* xviii. 250 The coffee gunna strong you soon, darling.

c. **1964** *New Statesman* 10 Apr. 555/2 'To strong it' means to overdo something, like taking more than 30 purple hearts in one night. **1970** G. F. NEWMAN *Sir, You Bastard* iii. 108 Don't you think that's stronging it?

strong, *sb. Austral. slang.* [f. the adj.] In the phr. *the strong of* (a person or thing) = *the strength of* s.v. STRENGTH *sb.* 2 e.

1916 A. WRIGHT *Under Cloud* 31 Don't yer want to own up? Some reason for wantin' to preserve yer incog, I suppose. What's th' strong of it? **1938** X. HERBERT *Capricornia* 566 What's the strong of you? What's the questioning for? I've done nuthin'. **1959** E. LAMBERT *Glory thrown In* 161 'What's the strong of this joint?' demanded Doc brusquely. 'Not an undertaker's is it?'

strong, obs. pa. pple. of STRING *v.*

strong arm, *sb.* (and *a.*) orig. *U.S.* **A.** *sb.*

1. Used *transf.* and *fig.* with reference to power, esp. in *strong arm of the law*. Cf. LONG *a.* 1 c.

1606 B. BARNES *Offices* I. 2 It [*sc.* riches] is the bone of that strong arme, by which the kingdome is in time of peace strengthened against all hostile attempts. **1822** GALT *Provost* xxiv, The five poor barks, that were warsling against the strong arm of the elements. **1873** B. HARTE *Fiddletown* 27 His abuse was confined to the police and limited by the strong arm of the law. **1911** MARETT *Anthropol.* vii. 181 To one who lives under civilized conditions the phrase 'the strong arm of the law' inevitably suggests the policeman.

2. With *the*: physical force or violence considered as a means of action, *spec.* in the course of robbery. Cf. STRONG HAND.

1836 M. HOLLEY *Texas* xiv. 322 This military council.. distributed lots to the inhabitants, contrary to all law, but that of the *strong arm*. **1903** A. H. LEWIS *Boss* 316 He was all for th' strong-arm, an' th' knock-about! It's a bad system. Nothin's lost by bein' smooth, Gov'nor. **1907** J. LONDON *Road* 169 Into the man's back goes his knee; around the man's neck.. passes his right hand, the bone of the wrist pressing against the jugular vein. Barber Kid throws his whole weight backward... It is the strong arm. **1948** *Daily Express* 2 Oct. 1/5 Modern youngsters.. get panicky and use the strong arm.

3. A criminal who resorts to violence; one who is employed or hired to use force against persons.

1907 J. LONDON *Road* 159 A world of rods and gunnels, blind baggages and 'side-door Pullmans'.. 'strong arms' and 'bindle-stiffs'. **1932** 'SPINDRIFT' *Yankee Slang* 60 *Strong arm*, bouncer or 'chucker out' for speakeasies and Honkytonks. **1978** N. J. CRISP *London Deal* ii. 21 He was a strong arm for an ambitious East End team which.. incurred the displeasure of the incumbent mob.

B. *attrib.* or as *adj.* (stress on first syllable).

1. Of a person: having or showing strength of arm; physically powerful; *spec.* of a criminal: resorting to violence, esp. for hire or in the case of robbery. Freq. in phr. ***strong-arm man***.

1897 ELDRIDGE & WATTS *Our Rival, the Rascal* ix. 281 The ordinary robber of to-day is frequently and familiarly styled by his 'pals', a 'strong arm man'. **1904** 'No. 1500' *Life in Sing Sing* 257/2 *Strongarm guy*, highway robber. **1931** *Times* 24 Sept. 11/2 A large force of gunmen and 'strongarm men'.. was soon effective in breaking down the resistance of the strikers. **1947** J. MULGAN *Report on Experience* x. 125 It comes down to cases with two strong-arm men who call round and offer a beating-up. **1953** J. PHELAN *Underworld* i. 21 A strong-arm chap is, roughly speaking, a bruiser, one who, for a pound or two, will punch some one on the nose, or start a fight in a pub, or even sometimes assault the police. **1973** D. WESTHEIMER *Going Public* ii. 27 Your strongarm boy won't always be around to save your skin.

2. Of an action: involving the use of physical violence. Also of policies, etc.: characterized by a display of (excessive) force; heavy-handed, oppressive, bullying.

1901 'J. FLYNT' *World of Graft* II. 18, I had been inclined to believe that the 'strong-arm' crimes were committed by men who were transients in the city. **1930** P. MACDONALD *Link* vii. 109 The law was in a pair, and with.. a little strong-arm stuff of their own, got the two apart. **1951** E. PAUL *Springtime in Paris* xi. 202 The Communists began strong-arm tactics to discourage the timid from seeing things at night. **1973** WODEHOUSE *Bachelors Anonymous* xii. 160 The strong-arm methods favoured by both counsellors might, of course, be resented, for he had no official knowledge that his love was returned. **1978** S. BRILL *Teamsters* vii. 288 The Vice-President has a record of strong-arm robbery.

Hence **'strong-arm** *v. trans.*, to treat roughly or manhandle (a person); to rob with violence, to coerce; to seize (something) by force; also *intr.*, to proceed in an aggressive, bullying manner; **'strong-arming** *vbl. sb.*

1903 *Monthly Maroon* (Chicago) June 444 If he refused, Phil.. was to strong-arm him while Tommy took away the badge. **1937** E. HEMINGWAY *To have & have Not* III. vii. 130 Don't try to strong arm it away from me. **1941** BAKER *Dict. Austral. Slang* 73 *Strongarm, to*, to act in a bullying fashion. **1948** LAIT & MORTIMER *New York* xi. 114 Mugging.. in old Chicago days called 'strong-arming'. **1954** D. DODGE *Lights of Skaro* vi. 215, I strong-armed my way out like a hero. **1965** D. FRANCIS *Odds Against* xiii. 179 He was strong-arming Brinton. **1969** *Daily Colonist* (Victoria, B.C.) 27 Feb. 35/1 A new trial was ordered by the B.C. Court of Appeals for a man jailed.. in connection with a Prince George strongarming. **1977** *Observer* (Colour Suppl.) 5 June 42/3 The OAS had financed themselves initially by strong-arming contributions from rich settlers, who usually shared their sympathies.

strong-box. A strongly made chest or safe for money, documents, or other valuables.

1684 *Lond. Gaz.* No. 1969/4 Lost out of the Dutchess of Portsmouth's Lodgings.. a little strong Box with several things in it. **1712** ARBUTHNOT *John Bull* II. iv. 16 She would rob her Father's strong Box, for Money to give the young Fellows that she was fond of. **1741** RICHARDSON *Pamela* (ed. 3) I. 196, I ask'd her for my Money; and she said it was above in her strong Box. **1851** D. JERROLD *St. Giles* xi. 105 Safe as his parchments in his strong-box. **1871** LONGF. *Wayside Inn* II. *Student's T., Cobbler of Hagenau* 108 A heavy strong-box.. Received, with a melodious sound, The coin that purchased Paradise.

fig. **1856** EMERSON *Eng. Traits* xi. *Aristocr.* Wks. (Bohn) II. 83 These are they who make England that strongbox and museum it is.

strong-breathed (ˈstrɒŋˈbrɛθt), *a.* ? *Obs.* [See BREATHED *ppl. a.* II; cf. LONG-BREATHED, SHORT-BREATHED.] Having a strong breath; vigorous of breath; also, having an offensive breath.

1620 J. TAYLOR (Water P.) *Pr. Hempseed* (1623) B 1 b, A learned Knight,.. A pamphlet of a Priuy did set forth, Which strong breath'd Aiax was well lik'd, because [etc.]. **1633** MASSINGER *Guardian* IV. ii, Wire-string and Cats-gut men, and strong-breath'd Hoboys. **1674** N. FAIRFAX *Bulk*

& *Selv.* 133 A strong breath'd and well set man for wayfaring.

strong drink. Intoxicating liquor, alcoholic liquors generally. Also, drink of more than ordinary alcoholic strength.

In all Bible translations from Tindale onwards used to render Heb. *shēkār* and Gr. *σίκερα*.

c **1386** CHAUCER *Pars. T.* 749 Whan that a man is nat wont to strong drynke. **1526** TINDALE *Luke* i. 15 He..shall nether drynke wyne ner stronge drynke. **1530** —— *Lev.* x. 9. *c* **1645** TULLY *Siege of Carlisle* (1840) 48 Ye Garrison was every where full of strong drink. **1798** R. JACKSON *Hist. & Cure Fever* 283 Men, who oppress the functions of the alimentary canal with strong drink and gross aliment. **1890** BESANT *Demoniac* ii. 25 The craving..for strong drink had seized him again.

b. With *a* and *pl.*

1555 EDEN *Decades* (Arb.) 292 Such stronge drinkes as are of force to inebriate. **1680** H. MORE *Let.* in R. Ward *Life* (1710) 355 It is..your constantly abstaining from all Strong Drinks, and using Moderate Drink, not too strong nor too small, that must contribute to the regaining of a due Temper of Body.

strongere, obs. f. STRANGER.

strongers ('strɒŋəz). *slang.* [f. STRONG *a.* + -ER[6].] **1.** = SOOGEE-MOOGEE a. *Naut.*

1929 F. BOWEN *Sea Slang* 135 *Strongers*, any strong cleaning preparation such as spirits of salt. **1961** F. H. BURGESS *Dict. Sailing* 202 *Strongers*, a compound cleaning mixture, caustic, etc., made up for use; also spirits of salts, acids, etc., undiluted.

2. = STRONG DRINK. *slang. rare.*

1939 JOYCE *Finnegans Wake* 58 Swiping rums and beaunes and sherries and ciders and negus and citronnades too. The strongers.

†'**strongful**, *a. Obs. rare*[−1]. [f. STRONG *a.* + -FUL.] Full of strength, very strong.

c **1400** *Laud Troy Bk.* 7995 So were the Troiens sore adred, For thei of Grece were so strongful, That [etc.].

Hence '**strongfully** *adv. arch.*

a **1400** *Laud Troy Bk.* 7584 Thei keped the Gregeys not-for-thi And stode a-ȝeyn strongfully. **1857** A. AINGER in Edith Sichel *Life & Lett.* (1906) 43 We look back on the Puritans, fighting strongfully and prayerfully in her defence.

strong hand. The exercise of superior power or strength; the use of force. Now *rare*; formerly common in phr. †*by, with strong hand*, by force, by (illegal) violence.

1382 WYCLIF *Exod.* iii. 19 The kyng of Egipte shal not ȝyue ȝow leue that ȝe goon, but bi strong hoond [Vulg. *per manum validam*]. *Ibid.* xxxii. 11 Thi puple, whom thow hast ladde out of the loond of Egipte..in a strong hoond [Vulg. *in manu robusta*]. **1386** *Rolls of Parlt.* III. 225/1 Nichol Brembre..with stronge honde..was chosen Mair. **1390** GOWER *Conf.* Prol. 716 Cesar Julius..With great bataile and with strong honde All Grece, Perse and eke Caldee Wan and put under. **1476** J. PASTON in *P. Lett.* III. 155 Robard Brandon and Colevyle have..enformyd my lady that ye wold have gotyn Caster fro hyr by stronge hand. **1561** T. NORTON *Calvin's Inst.* IV. xi. 73 b, And yet in a good cause he procedeth but thus farr, that if it come to violence and strong hande, he sayeth that he wyll geue place. **1590** SHAKS. *Com. Err.* III. i. 98 If by strong hand you offer to breake in .., A vulgar comment will be made of it. **1656–9** B. HARRIS *Parival's Iron Age* 205 They shut the Parliament house door, and kept the Speaker by strong hand in his Chair. **1713** SWIFT *Jrnl. to Stella* 23 Apr., I carried it with the strongest hand possible. **1799** DURNFORD & EAST *Cases K.B.* (1800) VIII. 357 The defendants..with force and arms, unlawfully, and injuriously, and with a strong hand, entered into a certain mill. **1888** *Times* 21 Aug. 7/3 When war is declared the law that obtains between belligerents is the law of the strong hand tempered..with humanity.

'**strong-'handed**, *a. rare.* [f. STRONG HAND + -ED[2].] †**1.** = STRONG *a.* 5 e. *Obs.*

1818 H. B. FEARON *Sk. Amer.* 224 The wealthy or 'strong-handed' farmer..owns five to twelve hundred acres.

2. Of a ship: well-manned. Also by synecdoche, of a ship's captain: in charge of a well-manned ship.

1827 J. F. COOPER *Red Rover* I. ii. 45 It is plain enough, by the manner in which his [a captain's] sails are furled, that he is strong-handed. **1844** —— *Afloat & Ashore* I. v. 129 He took us on board purely out of a national feeling, for his ship was strong-handed without us.

3. Forceful, imperious.

1949 I. DEUTSCHER *Stalin* vi. 178 Stalin..secured a more impressive abode for his Commissariat through a strong-handed intervention in a somewhat comic scramble between the commissars for accommodation.

'**strong'headed**, *a.*

1. Headstrong.

1603 FLORIO *Montaigne* II. vi. 216 One of my men.. mounted vpon a yong strong-headed horse. **1831** CARLYLE *Sartor Res.* II. iii, This young warmhearted, strongheaded and wrongheaded Herr Towgood. **1915** W. P. LIVINGSTONE *Mary Slessor* III. x. 83 They commiserated a Mother who was so strongheaded and wilful.

2. Endowed with strong intellectual faculties.

1849 MACAULAY *Hist. Eng.* vii. II. 222 Penn had never been a strongheaded man.

Hence ˌ**strong'headedness**, obstinacy.

1793 SIR M. EDEN in *Ld. Auckland's Corr.* (1862) III. 145 Their repeated losses were owing to their own strongheadedness in remaining scattered, against all advice, in small corps. **1862** BAGEHOT *Lit. Stud.* (1895) II. 250 Nature requites itself for the strongheadedness of several generations by the weakness of one. **1880** BARING-GOULD *Mehalah* xxi. (1884) 296 You will give way in the end—your weakness will yield to his strongheadedness.

stronghold ('strɒŋhəʊld). [f. STRONG *a.* + HOLD *sb.* (Originally *strong hold.*)]

A strongly fortified place of defence, a secure place of refuge or retreat, a fastness.

c **1425** *Cursor M.* 17342 (Trin.) Þei ladde Ioseph..To prisoun in to a strong holde [*Cott.* in a stalworth hald]. *a* **1466** GREGORY *Chron.* in *Hist. Coll. Cit. Lond.* (Camden) 149 The nombyr of an C townys and castellys, abbeys, and strong-holdys. *a* **1513** FABYAN *Chron.* v. lxxvii. (1811) 56 They wan frome yᵉ Almaynes dyuers Townes & stronge holds wᵗin Germania. **1524** WOLSEY in *St. Papers Hen. VIII*, VI. 249 To procede towardes Paris, in which waye is neither strong holde or river to empeche or let them. **1609** HOLLAND *Amm. Marcell.* XIV. ii. 5 This strong hold therefore they besieged round about for three dayes and three nights together. **1698** FRYER *Acc. E. India & P.* 42 They followed the rest to Policat, a Strong-Hold of theirs. **1799** SHERIDAN *Pizarro* I. i. 18 We know there is a secret path that leads to your strong-hold among the rocks. **1807–8** WORDSW. *White Doe* III. 205 Back therefore will they hie to seize A strong Hold on the banks of Tees. **1833** L. RITCHIE *Wand. by Loire* 158 It was here that, in..the thirteenth century, a famous robber had his stronghold. **1869** TOZER *Highl. Turkey* I. 147 Salonica..retained its importance as a strong-hold of resistance to the barbarians.

b. *transf.* and *fig.*

1535 COVERDALE *Ps.* lxxi. 3 Be thou my stronge holde. **1633** G. HERBERT *Temple, Nat.* i, O tame my heart; It is thy highest art To captivate strong holds to thee. **1690** LOCKE *Hum. Und.* IV. iv. §1 Such Castles in the Air will be as Strong Holds of Truth, as the Demonstrations of Euclid. **1825** JENNINGS *Observ. Dial. W. Eng.* 187 The South of Somersetshire, one of the strong holds..of the Anglo-Saxon dialect. **1830** *Westm. Rev.* XIII. 86 Except in a few strong holds where prejudice still fights against reason. **1856** FROUDE *Hist. Eng.* (1858) I. v. 389 The Northern counties.. were the stronghold of the papal party. **1880** 'BROOKSBY' *Hunting Countries* II. 199 Near Trafford Bridge are some good coverts, Warden Hill is a stronghold.

strongish ('strɒŋɪʃ), *a.* [f. STRONG *a.* + -ISH.] Somewhat strong (in various senses).

1799 A. YOUNG *View Agric. Lincoln.* 120 A practice lately introduced..is to baulk their turnip land on strongish soils. **1821** BYRON 8 Jan. in Moore *Lett. & Jrnls.* (1830) II. 402 It is a strongish post—narrow street, commanded from within —and tenable walls. **1854** SURTEES *Handley Cr.* xxx. (1901) I. 227 There was a strongish muster. **1890** 'R. BOLDREWOOD' *Col. Reformer* xviii, Mr. Neuchamp is restored by the exhibition of a strongish dram.

strongle ('strɒŋg(ə)l). [Illiterate pronunciation of STRONGYLE[1].] A thread-worm of the genus *Strongylus* (see STRONGYLE[1]) as a parasite causing disease in grouse: in quot. *collect.*

1884 T. SPEEDY *Sport Highl.* xi. 185 By the aid of the microscope, immense quantities of strongle were discernible in the inflamed parts.

strongle, obs. var. STRANGLE *v.*

strongly ('strɒŋlɪ), *adv.* Forms: see STRONG *a.* and -LY[2]. [OE. *stranglice*, f. *stranglic* adj., strong, robust, severe, f. *strang* STRONG *a.*: see -LY[1], -LY[2].

Formerly compared *stronglier*, *-est* (OE. *stranglicor*, *-ost*, early ME. *strongluker*, *-laker*, *-est*); now with *more*, *most*.]

1. In a strong manner.

a. Powerfully; with strong effect; forcibly.

c **1000** ÆLFRIC *On O.T.* (Gr.) 7/7 Dauid..stranglice rixode and bewerode þæt folc wið ða hæðenan leoda. *a* **1225** *Ancr. R.* 218 Sum ancre is þet weneð þet heo schule beon stronglukest iuonded iðe uormeste tweolf moneð þet heo bigon ancre lif, & iðen oðer tweolf þerefter. **1583** BABINGTON *Commandm.* ii. (1590) 74 Our natures are verie prone to the breach hereof, which by a negatiue is stronglier beate downe than by an affirmatiue. **1610** SHAKS. *Temp.* v. i. 17 His teares runs downe his beard..: your charm so strongly works 'em That if you now beheld them, your affections Would become tender. **1642** D. ROGERS *Naaman* 408 Whether thy lusts can draw thee stronglier then he. **1869** FREEMAN *Norm. Conq.* (1876) III. xii. 239 The districts most strongly marked with Breton characteristics.

b. So as to resist attack or displacement, firmly, solidly, securely.

c **897** ÆLFRED *Gregory's Past. C.* lviii. 443 To ðon ðæt he swa micle stranglicor [L. *solidius*] arise swa he hefiȝlicor afeoll. *c* **1175** *Lamb. Hom.* 9 Heo weren strongliche ibunden. **1597** MORLEY *Introd. Mus.* 71 To the end that what I haue shewed you..may the more stronglie sticke to your memorie, here is [etc.]. **1605** SHAKS. *Macb.* v. ii. 12 Great Dunsinane he strongly Fortifies. **1668** CULPEPPER & COLE *Barthol. Anat.* II. iv. 93 It hath its..outer [surface] more rough that it might be strongelyer fastned. **1678** HOBBES *Decam.* viii. 97 Those, whose smallest parts, naturally, without the force of Fire do strongliest cohere, are generally the heaviest. **1855** PRESCOTT *Philip II*, I. I. iii. 42 By this triumph over her enemies, Mary was seated more strongly than ever on the throne. **1856** W. IRVING *Life Washington* xcvi. III. 771 The American and British armies, strongly posted,..remained four days grimly regarding each other.

c. Violently, vehemently.

a **900** *O.E. Martyrol.* 5 May 76 He sæde þæt æȝhwelce ȝeare..þær to come þæs strongestan windes yste, ond þæt se swa stronglice hrure on þa circan, þæt [etc.]. *a* **1122** *O.E. Chron.* (Laud MS.) an 1016, Ða ȝewende se here sona to Lundene & þa burh uton besæton, & hire stranglice wið feaht. *a* **1300** *Havelok* 135 Quanne he hauede þis pleinte maked, þer after stronglike [he] quaked. **1340** *Ayenb.* 157 Þe dyeuel yziȝþ..þe stat of þe manne..and to huet vice he ys mest bouȝinde..and of þo half him asayleþ stranglakest. **1473** WARKW. *Chron.* (Camden) 6 Ther thei faughthe strongly togedere. **1610** FLETCHER *Faithf. Sheph.* II. ii. D 2, But hether am I come..To seeke you out, of whose great good the Aire Is full, and strongly labors. **1642–7** H. MORE *Song of Soul* II. iii. III. liii, Mid part is strongliest rouz'd, the Poles do sleep in rest. **1849** MACAULAY *Hist. Eng.* ii. I. 161 Bear-baiting..was the abomination which most strongly stirred the wrath of the austere sectaries.

d. Boldly, bravely, with fortitude.

c **1230** *Hali Meid.* 15, & eauer se þu strongluker stondest aȝain him, se he o tene & o grome wodeluker weorreð. **1382** WYCLIF *Judg.* xx. 41 The whiche beforehond feyneden fliȝt, turnede the face strongly withstoden. **1535** COVERDALE *2 Esdras* x. 15 Loke what happeneth vnto yᵉ, beare it strongly [Vulg. *fortiter fer*].

†**e.** With a strong military force. *Obs.*

1563–87 FOXE *A. & M.* (1596) 347 The archb. of Cant... gaue him aduertisement thereof, willing him more stronglier to go or else not to venter. **1587** GOLDING *De Mornay* xxxi. (1592) 496 The stronglier he had come, the lesse had beene his victorie. **1596** SPENSER *State Irel.* Wks. (Globe) 664/2 The which I knowe doe so stronglie commaund all the passages that waie as that none can passe from Ulster into Connaught, without their leave.

†**f.** With strength of reason. *Obs.*

1395 PURVEY *Remonstr.* (1851) 14 It sueth moche strongliere, that siche dymes and offringis shulen be withdrawe for these grevousere synnis. **1596** BACON *Maxims Com. Law* i. (1630) 2 The cause of deprivation, and more strongly of a resignation, moved from the partie himselfe.

g. Energetically, resolutely; emphatically.

1533 FRITH *Mirr. Baptism* B viij, Now wil I endeuour my self to..vtterly putte out the seconde erroure,..and that is of them whiche so stronglye steke vnto the weke ceremonyes. **1588** SHAKS. *L.L.L.* I. i. 309 Goe we Lords to put in practice that, Which each to other hath so strongly sworne. **1649** JER. TAYLOR *Gt. Exemp.* III. xv. 87 Whoever is accused strongly is never thought intirely innocent. **1680** BAXTER *Cath. Commun.* (1684) 35 And what man living hath written stronglier against it, than Dr. Isaac Barrow. **1849** MACAULAY *Hist. Eng.* ii. I. 157 His father had given a reluctant assent to a bill, strongly supported by Falkland. **1861** HUGHES *Tom Brown Oxf.* xxxiii, Most of whom would not scruple—as Mr. Brown strongly put it—to steal a copper out of a blind beggar's hat. **1879** *Cassell's Techn. Educ.* I. 183/2 We therefore strongly urge the student to work from the examples.

†**h.** In various obsolete uses: (to sleep) soundly; (to eat) heartily; (to gaze, etc.) intently; (to sound) loudly. *Obs.*

c **1450** *Merlin* xx. 323 And thei slepte strongeliche in the hoste ffor the tyme that relented. **1470–85** MALORY *Arthur* VI. xi. 201 Soo whan sir kay was vnarmed he asked after mete; soo there was mete sette hym, and he ete strongly. **1485** CAXTON *Paris & V.* 87 Vyenne byhelde the rynge so strongely. **1600** SURFLET *Country Farm* II. lxv. 409 By howe much you sound the stronglier, by so much they [*sc.* bees] mount the higher into the aire. **1675–7** WARWICK *Mem. Chas. I* (1701) 98 The eyes of the Nobility and Gentry being stronglyer fixt upon the Church-lands.

i. *Physics.* By means of the strong interaction (see STRONG *a.* 10 e).

1960 P. ROMAN *Theory Elementary Particles* v. 460 The K^-, but not the K^+, can react strongly with nuclear matter. **1977** *Sci. Amer.* Oct. 58/2 A strongly decaying hadron exists for only 10^{-23} second before it breaks up into less massive hadrons.

2. In a strong degree; with strength or intensity of the condition or quality predicated.

a. Qualifying a verb expressing a state or condition, emotion, belief, resemblance, or difference.

c **1400** *Brut* 294 Wherfore þe King, whan he herde of þis tydinge, he was stronglyche meued and þerwiþ an angred. *c* **1450** *Merlin* i. 13 When the gode man herde this he merveyled strongeliche. **1561** T. NORTON *Calvin's Inst.* II. vii. (1562) 108 b, The more that they hold back themselues, so much yᵉ stronglier within they are kindled. **1596** SHAKS. *1 Hen. IV*, II. ii. 113 The Theeues are scattred, and possest with fear so strongly, that they dare not meet each other. **1650** BAXTER *Saints' R.* II. iii. §1 (1653) 207 The stronger any mans Reason is, the stronglier is he perswaded that God is true. **1802** MAR. EDGEWORTH *Moral T.*, *Forester* xii, He was so strongly charmed by the sight of a watch-chain and seals, that [etc.]. **1818** ACCUM *Chem. Tests* 286 Heat the mixture strongly over a lamp, till a dry red mass is obtained. **1849** MACAULAY *Hist. Eng.* v. I. 659 It was strongly suspected that he had been in constant communication with the government. **1858** CARLYLE *Fredk. Gt.* I. iii. (1872) I. 28 In his Portraits as Prince-Royal, he strongly resembles her.

b. Qualifying an adj.

1491 CAXTON *Vitas Patr.* II. 278 b/2 A broder febled by sekenes sayd..that he was strongly seke [Fr. *q'il estoit fort malade*]. **1798** FERRIAR *Engl. Historians* 244 Superstition is strongly imitative. **1861** J. TULLOCH *Engl. Purit.* ii. 288 As we read it,..the ardour of local Puritanism becomes strongly intelligible. **1880** GEIKIE *Phys. Geog.* iii. 116 Sea-water is always strongly salt to the taste.

(*b*) *spec.* in *Math.*: cf. STRONG *a.* 19 e.

1955 M. LOÈVE *Probability Theory* ix. 442 Since..T is bounded and linear, every B_λ is..a strongly closed linear subspace of B. **1966** E. H. SPANIER *Algebraic Topology* ix. 510 Let X be a strongly simple space. **1979** *Proc. London Math. Soc.* XXXVIII. x507, K is said to be a spectral compact convex set if A and V are in spectral duality, and K is said to be strongly spectral if in addition [etc.].

3. *Comb.* With ppl. adjs., as ***strongly-bound, -drawing, -made, -marked, -scented, -shod, -worded***; also occas. with adjs. in -ED[2], forming combs. used as equivalent to parasynthetic formations on STRONG *a.*, as †***strongly-limbed***, †***necked***, †***opinioned***.

1890 *Hardwicke's Sci.-Gossip* XXVI. 155/2 The *strongly-bound and neatly got-up volumes of the Geological Survey of the United States. **1611** COTGR., *Rubrificatif*,..a plaister of..*strongly-drawing simples. **1598** SYLVESTER *Du Bartas* II. i. IV. *Handicr.* 315 Wise, active, valiant, *strongly-limb'd, and healthy. **1838** DICKENS *O. Twist* xlvi, He is tall,..and a *strongly made man. **1820** SCOTT *Monast.* xix, Traits which were rather *strongly marked than beautiful. **1892** *Rev. of Reviews* Apr. 332/2 Both were men of strongly-marked individuality. **1697** DRYDEN *Virg. Georg.* III. 88 The Mother Cow must wear a low'ring Look, Sour-headed, *strongly-neck'd, to bear the Yoke. **1615** T. ADAMS *Black Devil* 38 This is Satans first presumption; a *strongly-opinion'd trust in his owne strength. **1879** LUBBOCK *Sci. Lect.* ii. 64 The larva of Papilio machaon is..provided with *strongly-scented tentacles. **1831** SCOTT *Ct. Robt.* ii, A..*strongly-shod arrow. **1883** *Manch. Exam.* 30 Nov. 5/1 At a meeting held in the evening a *strongly-worded letter on the subject was read from Mr. P. A. Taylor, M.P.

strong man. **1.** A man of great physical strength; *spec.*, one who displays his strength professionally, as in a circus.

1699 *Flying Post* 14–16 Nov. 2/1 The strong Kentish Man, gave three Proofs of his extraordinary Strength before his Majesty. **1734** DESAGULIERS *Course Exper. Phil.* I. 259, I have observ'd the pretended Strong Man sometimes to have a short strong Stick [etc.]. **1734** in Fairholt *Eccentric Char.* (1849) I. 50 The strong man of Islington. **1745** *Ibid.* 54 Thomas Topham, Commonly called the Strong Man. **1841** THACKERAY *Loose Sk.* ii, in *Britannia* 15 May 315/3 A vast number of booths and exhibitions..no less than four companies of strongmen..'the Indian strong men'; 'the strong men with the fairy pony', &c. **1872** BROWNING *Fifine at Fair* 23 The Strong Man, whom..by-and-by You shall behold do feats. **1908** *Variety* 16 May 15 Blocksom and Burns, the 'strong' men,..have bookings at hand which, if accepted, will keep them busily playing in the west all summer. **1954** [see *beefcake* s.v. BEEF *sb.* 5]. **1977** C. WOOD *James Bond* xii. 99 He was..the product of a union between the strong man of a travelling circus and the Chief Wardress at the Women's Prison.

2. A dominating man; the man who exercises effective control of an organization; *spec.*, one who exercises absolute political power.

1859 MILL *Liberty* iii. 119, I am not countenancing the sort of 'hero-worship' which applauds the strong man of genius for forcibly seizing on the government of the world and making it do his bidding in spite of itself. **1879** *Nation* XXX. 1 (Cent.) He wants to show the party that he too can be a 'Strong Man' on a pinch. **1886** KIPLING *Plain Tales from Hills* (1888) 89 He called on the biggest and strongest man that the Government owned, and explained that he wanted an appointment at Simla on a good salary. The compound insolence of this amused the Strong Man. **1924** A. D. SEDGWICK *Little French Girl* II. ix. 165 They were both agreed on the necessity of a strong man for France and on many lopped heads. **1943** E. A. PEERS *Spain in Eclipse* I. ii. 39 The erstwhile 'strong man', President Azaña, emerged out of his silence. **1961** P. KEMP *Alms for Oblivion* ii. 29 Pluto had been nominated Minister Without Portfolio; Marshal Phibul, the 'Strong Man' of the country,..was under arrest. **1969** D. ACHESON *Present at Creation* (1970) xxi. 187 Colonel Juan Perón, the President and 'strong man' of Argentina. **1977** *Westindian World* 3–9 June 12/1 The other is Major General Ziaur Rahman, who became President of Bangladesh only a few weeks ago (though he had been the country's strongman for some time).

3. *attrib.*

1962 C. WALSH *From Utopia to Nightmare* ix. 122 A strong-man government. **1977** *Times* 12 July 14/3 Strongman rule has provided the region with comparative stability..and, in the case of South Korea and Singapore, phenomenal economic growth.

strong-minded (ˌstrɒŋˈmaɪndɪd), *a.*

a. Having a strong, vigorous, or determined mind.

1791 BOSWELL *Johnson* an. 1778 (1904) II. 252 A certain nobleman..was one of the strongest-minded men that ever lived. **1825** COLERIDGE *Aids Refl.* (1848) I. 166 That pious, learned, strong-minded, and single-hearted Jew. **1864** G. A. LAWRENCE *M. Dering* II. 245 Stronger-minded women than my little Georgie have gone down before the fascination that that unhappy man seemed able to exercise.

b. Applied (chiefly in the 19th c., and with disparaging implication) to women who have or affect the qualities of mind and character regarded as distinctively masculine, or who take up an attitude of revolt against the restrictions and disabilities imposed on their sex by law and custom.

1843 DICKENS *Mart. Chuz.* (1844) iv. 42 Then there was the widow of a deceased brother.., who being almost supernaturally disagreeable, and having a dreary face and a bony figure and a masculine voice, was..what is commonly called a strong-minded woman. **1854** MRS. GASKELL *North & S.* xlv, And then, what with Sholto playing with the fire, and the baby crying, you'll begin to wish for a strong-minded woman, equal to any emergency. **1862** MISS BRADDON *Lady Audley* xvi, I don't want a strong-minded woman, who writes books and wears green spectacles. **1878** BESANT & RICE *Celia's Arb.* vi, They had not become strong-minded; they did not sit on School Boards and sigh for Female Suffrage. **1887** R. N. CAREY *Uncle Max* xvi. 129 She had evidently got it into her head that I was a strong-minded young woman.

Hence **strong-ˈmindedness.**

1849 C. BRONTË *Shirley* II. xii. 294 With all her strictness, with all her 'strongmindedness', she could gain no command over them. **1859** MRS. CARLYLE *Lett.* III. 1 There is a growing taste for fastness, or, still worse, for strong-mindedness.

ˈstrongness. *Obs.* exc. as *nonce-use.* [f. STRONG *a.* + -NESS.] The quality of being strong.

c **1450** *Mirour Saluacioun* (1888) 72 Nowe Sampson it is to witt, for his grettest stroungnesse Prefigured oure lord crist. *a* **1578** LINDESAY (Pitscottie) *Chron. Scot.* (S.T.S.) I. 133 In bewtie more excellent and abone all men in strangnes and habilietie. *a* **1604** HANMER *Chron. Irel.* (1809) 245 When the fight is ended,..and all strongenesse of hostility set apart, then in a Noble man must humanity take place. **1650** GENTILIS *Consid.* 212 There is no such thing as insensibility of pain; if there be, it is not a strongnesse of heart but a weaknesse of the minde. **1916** *Blackw. Mag.* Feb. 197/1 Smoking is forbidden with a Teutonic strongness in the workshop.

strong point. **1.** *one's strong point*: that in which one excels, one's forte.

1840 J. S. MILL in *Westm. Rev.* XXXIII. 260 The strong points of each [*sc.* Bentham and Coleridge] correspond to the weak points of the other. *c* **1869** TAYLOR & DUBOURG *New Men & Old Acres* I. 22 Perhaps you didn't know Bunter was such a way... Humour is his strong point. **1875** MAX MÜLLER in *Contemp. Rev.* XXVII. 72, I sent my two eldest girls to be examined last year, chiefly in order to find out their weak and their strong points. **1889** T. A. GUTHRIE *Pariah* I. ix, Description was not Lettice's strong point.

2. *Mil.* [tr. G. *feste stellung*: see STRONG *a.* 8 and POINT *sb.*[1] A. 19.] A specially fortified position in a defence system. Also *transf.* and *fig.*

1915 E. DANE *Battles in Flanders* x. 183 An orchard, triangular in shape and bounded along each face by a road, which the Germans had fortified. This, one of the strong points of the German second line, the Devons carried by storm. **1931** *Times Lit. Suppl.* 30 Apr. 350/3 Billets, water-supply, roads, wiring, strongpoints, fighting. **1946** D. L. SAYERS *Unpopular Opinions* 100 Nobody was quite ready to coerce Britain into giving away her colonies, dependencies, and scattered strong-points. **1957** *Times* 16 Feb. 7/5 Its simple existence is a strong-point in the struggle to maintain our standards against the spread of the 'new illiteracy'. **1978** L. HEREN *Growing up on The Times* iii. 66 The Jewish Agency..had been determined to establish as many Jewish strongpoints as possible in an effort to extend its territorial claims. **1980** *Sci. Amer.* Mar. 56/1 Preserved under the city is a record of its development since the year of its founding in A.D. 71 as a strongpoint for the Roman Ninth Legion.

3. *R.A.F.* (See quots.)

1946 D. HAMSON *We fell among Greeks* i. 18 The strong-point is normally a powerful bolt and shackle fitted into the framework of the aircraft at the point of exit of the parachutist. To it are attached the static-lines from each man's parachute. **1951** *Gloss. Aeronaut. Terms* (*B.S.I.*) III. 15 *Strong point*, a fitting in an aircraft which is capable of transmitting a shock load and to which the static line or strop is attached. **1958** P. KEMP *No Colours or Crest* iii. 40 The sergeant clipped the static lines of our parachutes to the 'strong-point', a stout wire running along the fuselage beneath the roof.

strong room. A room made specially secure for the custody of persons or things; esp. a fire- and burglar-proof room in which valuables are deposited for safety, e.g. at the Mint, a bank, etc.

1761 FOOTE *Liar* II, Her father an Indian governor, shut up in the strong room [*i.e.* the 'Black Hole'] at Calcutta, left her all his wealth. **1818** SCOTT *Hrt. Midl.* vii, The persons we have mentioned remained in the strong-room of the prison. **1856** G. PRICE *Treat. Fire & Thief-proof Deposit.* viii. 94 The doors of fire-proof closets and strong-rooms are constructed in the same manner as the doors of safes. *Ibid.* 99 Portable strong rooms are made altogether of wrought-iron plates. **1863** READE *Hard Cash* xxxi, They took him to the strong-room, and manacled his ankles together.., and fastened his body down by broad bands of ticking. **1885** *Law Times' Rep.* LIII. 83/2 The plate..is now stowed away in the strong room of a bank.

attrib. **1862** *Catal. Internat. Exhib. Brit.* II. No. 6105, A model showing the arrangement of the bolts and locks as fixed on a strong-room door.

strong water. [Rendering of med.L. *aqua fortis.*]

†**1.** = AQUAFORTIS 1, 2. *Obs.*

1580 BLUNDEVIL *Curing Horses Dis.* cviii. 50 It shall be good..to wash all his taile with *Aqua fortis*, or strong water, made in this sort. **1604** E. G[RIMSTONE] *D'Acosta's Hist. Indies* IV. iv. 215 They refine it [gold] likewise with quicke-silver and strong water. **1626** BACON *Sylva* §800 Metalls themselues doe receiue in readily Strong-Waters; And Strong-Waters likewise doe readily pierce into Metalls, and Stones. **1694** SALMON *Bate's Dispens.* I. ix. 400/1 But if you dissolve apart in Strong-waters, you do two things at once.

2. Any form of alcoholic spirits used as a beverage. Now only in *pl.* (somewhat *arch.*).

a **1613** OVERBURY *Wife*, etc. (1638) 178 His new Trade of brewing Strong-Waters makes a number of mad-men. **1624** CAPT. SMITH *Virginia* IV. 160 After, with warme clothes and a little strong water, they had a little recouered him. **1687** *Relat. De Chaumont's Embassy Siam* 23 Eleven Barks full of Oxen, Sheep,..and Strong-water made with Rice. **1727** GAY *Begg. Op.* II. iv, Strong waters will in time ruin your constitution. **1790** *Act 30 Geo. III*, c. 38 §9 Any distilled Spirituous Liquors or Strong Waters. **1820** SCOTT *Monast.* xxxv, Usquebagh—a liquor strange to Halbert, for the strong waters known in the south of Scotland came from France. **1855** *Englishw. in Russia* 9 He gave so much strong waters.., that everybody became so drunk that they could not move.

†**3.** *attrib.* and *Comb.* *Obs.*

1654 *Burton's Diary* (1828) I. 181 Tobacco-shops, and strong-water houses. **1657** in Thurloe *St. Papers* (1742) VI. 315 This informant..searched in the house of Samuel Rogers, a strong-water-man,..and there found seven parcels of books. *Ibid.* vi. 318 Her master's shop, being a strong-water-shop. **1707** *Lond. Gaz.* No. 4391/4 Thomas Mathews, late of Newbery.., Strongwaterman.

strongyle[1] (ˈstrɒndʒɪl). See also STRONGLE. [ad. mod.L. *Strongylus*, ad. Gr. στρογγύλος round.] A thread-worm of the genus *Strongylus* (or the family *Strongylidæ*, of which this is the type), common as a disease-producing parasite in various animals.

1847 REDWOOD *S. F. Gray's Suppl. Pharmacop.* 187 *Strongylus gigas.* (Rudol.) The Large Strongyle. **1879** COBBOLD *Parasites* 377 In the Deangunid and Talybont districts these strongyles proved terribly fatal to mountain ponies. **1886** *Athenæum* 30 Jan. 171/3 *Strongylus axei*..also shows affinity with the grouse strongyle and with the stomach worm of lambs.

attrib. **1879** COBBOLD *Parasites* 338 Strongyle embryos.

strongyle[2] (ˈstrɒndʒɪl). *Zool.* Also in mod.L. form *strongyla.* [ad. Gr. στρογγύλη fem. (agreeing with ῥάβδος RHABDUS) of στρογγύλος round.] A sponge-spicule of the rhabdus type, rounded at both ends. Hence **ˈstrongylate, ˈstrongylote** *adjs.*, having the shape of a strongyle.

1887 S. O. RIDLEY in *Challenger Rep.* XX. p. xvi, Strongyla; here the spicule is not pointed at all, but the ends are evenly rounded off. *Ibid.* 36 Spicules.—Oxeote to strongylote, size variable. **1887** SOLLAS in *Encycl. Brit.* XXII. 416/2 (Sponges) Usually pointed (*oxeate*) at the ends, they [the spicular rays] are also frequently rounded off (*strongylate*), or thickened into knobs (*tylotate*), or branched (*cladose*). *Ibid.*, The rhabdus if pointed at both ends is known as an *oxea*; if rounded at both ends as a *strongyle.* **1900** E. A. MINCHIN in *Ray Lankester's Treat. Zool.* II. *Sponges* 137 Whether the extremities are sharp ('oxeote'),.. rounded ('strongylote'), knobbed ('tylote') [etc.].

strongylo- (ˈstrɒndʒɪləʊ), before a vowel **strongyl-**, used *Zool.* as combining form of STRONGYLE[2] in names for forms of sponge-spicule. **strongyˈlaster** [Gr. ἀστήρ star], a rhabdus strongylate at one extremity and star-shaped at the other. **ˈstrongyloclad, strongyˈloxea**: see quots.

1888 W. J. SOLLAS in *Challenger Rep.* XXV. p. lv, Strongyloclad, the esactine is strongylate, the ecactine cladose. *Ibid.*, Strongyloxea, a rhabdus with a strongylate esactine and oxeate ecactine. *Ibid.* 417 The microsclere when present is a spheraster or oxyaster or strongylaster.

strongyloid (ˈstrɒndʒɪlɔɪd), *a.* and *sb.* *Zool.* [f. mod.L. *Strongylus*: see STRONGYLE[1] and -OID.]

a. *adj.* Resembling a strongyle. **b.** *sb.* A strongyloid worm.

1879 COBBOLD *Parasites* 335 The growth and metamorphoses which I witnessed in strongyloid larvæ taken from earth-worms..were remarkably rapid. *Ibid.* 336 Leuckart supposes that all these strongyloids require a change of hosts before [etc.]. **1883** *Athenæum* 24 Mar. 381/3 Prof. Simonds regarded the worm as a species of *Strongylus.* .. It is found that what was at first regarded as the head turns out to be the tail, so that the supposed strongyloid character is incorrect.

Strongyloides (strɒndʒɪˈlɔɪdiːz). *Med.* and *Vet. Sci.* Also **strongyl-**. [mod.L. (B. Grassi 1879, in *Rendiconti R. Ist. Lombardo di Sci. e Lett.* XII. 233), f. *Strongyl-us* (see STRONGYLE[1]) + *-oides* (see -OID).] Nematode worms of the genus of the same name; also, = STRONGYLOIDIASIS.

1911 *Jrnl. Exper. Med.* XIV. 6 Most of the patients were admitted for malaria, so that the strongyloides were incidentally found as a result of the routine stool examinations. **1929** A. S. CHANDLER *Hookworm Dis.* vii. 287 Sandground himself, as the result of a light and brief *Strongyloides* infestation, apparently remained immune for at least 14 months. **1958** *Jrnl. Amer. Med. Assoc.* 22 Nov. 1651/2 Careful examination of serial sections of large intestine..failed to reveal any Strongyloides in this tissue. **1974** PASSMORE & ROBSON *Compan. Med. Stud.* III. xii. 56/1 In many British soldiers who acquired the infection when prisoners of war in the Far East, strongyloides has persisted for more than 25 years.

strongyloidiasis (ˌstrɒndʒɪlɔɪˈdaɪəsɪs). *Med.* and *Vet. Sci.* [f. STRONGYLOID(ES + -IASIS.] Infection with or a disease caused by nematode worms of the genus *Strongyloides* (family Rhabditidæ), esp. *S. stercoralis*, a threadworm infesting the human and the canine gut in tropical and subtropical regions, causing diarrhœa.

1930 E. C. FAUST *Human Helminthol.* xxxiii. 538 (*heading*) Strongyloidiasis. **1935** *Arch Path.* XIX. 782 In certain cases in which strongyloidiasis had been active for several months the presence of filariform, postfilariform and preadolescent worms in the respiratory passages suggested hyperinfection. **1977** *Lancet* 28 May 1121/2, 1 patient with strongyloidiasis had an increased total number of IgG-labelled cells in the lamina propria.

strongyloidosis (ˌstrɒndʒɪlɔɪˈdəʊsɪs). *Med.* and *Vet. Sci.* [f. as prec. + -OSIS.] = prec.

1911 *Jrnl. Exper. Med.* XIV. 7 Of 54 cases of strongyloidosis..none had been subject to diarrhea. **1957** SMITH & JONES *Vet. Path.* xiii. 494 It is generally believed that severe and fatal strongyloidosis is likely to occur only in man or animals debilitated from faulty nutrition or other factors. **1969** J. R. GEORGI *Parasitol. for Veterinarians* viii. 134 Canine strongyloidosis has been much feared in the past and demands respect in the future as a menace to human health. **1980** *Acta Parasitol. Polonica* XXVII. 89 Anatomical and pathological changes in animals that have died of the strongyloidosis consist mostly of changes in the respiratory and alimentary systems.

strongylosis (strɒndʒɪˈləʊsɪs). *Vet. Sci.* and *Med.* [f. mod.L. *Strongyl-us* (see STRONGYLE[1]) + -OSIS.] Infection with or a disease caused by nematode worms (strongyles) of the genus *Strongylus* or the family Strongylidae containing it, which are parasites of many domestic animals.

1892 O. FLEMING tr. *Neumann's Treat. Parasites* IV. ii. 580 (*heading*) Bronchial and pulmonary strongyloses. **1928** *Daily Tel.* 7 Aug. 9/4 Strongylosis, or grouse disease, is an infection produced by parasitic worms in the intestines, which are found to be present in almost all grouse. **1969** J. R. GEORGI *Parasitol. for Veterinarians* ix. 164 Although *Nematodirus* spp. infections are ordinarily not associated with clinical disease, serious outbreaks have been attributed to *N. battus*. This strongylosis is characterized by..very severe and debilitating diarrhea. **1981** *Equine Vet. Jrnl.* XIII. 35 (*heading*) Ischaemic myocardial fibrosis and aortic strongylosis in the horse.

stronke, stronkg, rare obs. ff. STRONG *a.*

†**'strontane.** *Chem. Obs.* [f. STRONT-IUM + -ANE.] Davy's name for strontium chloride, SrCl.

1812 SIR H. DAVY *Chem. Philos.* 345 From direct experiments I ascertained that 50 parts of strontane consisted of about 29 parts of metal and 21 of chlorine.

strontia ('strɒnʃ(ɪ)ə). *Chem.* [f. STRONTIAN *sb.*: see -IA.] One of the alkaline earths, the monoxide of strontium. Also *attrib.* in ***strontia water***, the aqueous solution of hydrate of strontium.

1802 CHENEVIX in *Phil. Trans.* XCII. 341 No precipitate took place from a mixture of barytes-water and strontia-water. **1802** *Sketch of Paris* II. lxix. 387 Crystallized sulphate of strontia, in the mines of Villefort. **1812** SIR H. DAVY *Chem. Philos.* 343 One combination of strontium with oxygene only is at present known; it is strontia, or strontites, the substance procured by burning strontium. **1884** *Health Exhib. Catal.* 19/2 Sugar, extracted from molasses by strontia. Samples of Strontia, in different stages.

strontian ('strɒnʃ(ɪ)ən), *sb.* Also 8 **strontion, strontean,** 8–9 **stronthian,** 9 **strontiane.** [The name of a parish in Argyllshire, where are the lead mines in which the mineral was discovered.] (Orig. †***strontian earth, lime, mineral, spar.***) Properly, native strontium carbonate, but more commonly applied loosely to strontia, sometimes to strontium. Not now in scientific use. †***strontian water*** = strontia water: see STRONTIA. ***strontian yellow***: a yellow colour produced by adding potassium chromate to a solution of a strontium salt.

1789 A. CRAWFORD in *Med. Commun.* II. 354 The Strontean mineral. **1793** T. C. HOPE in *Trans. R. Soc. Edin* (1798) IV. II. 6 When heat is applied to the Strontian spar, it crackles a little. *Ibid.* 23 The specific gravity of the Strontian far exceeds that of calcareous spar. **1794** KIRWAN in *Trans. R. Irish Acad.* V. 246 Equal parts quartz and Stronthian lime, melted [etc.]. **1794** SCHMEISSER in *Phil. Trans.* LXXXIV. 424 Another earth, which may be called *Strontion earth.* **1802** T. THOMSON *Syst. Chem.* I. 425 The solution, known by the name of strontian water. **1804** R. JAMESON *Min.* I. 598 Strontiane... Its most common colour is intermediate between asparagus and apple green. **1815** J. SMITH *Panorama Sci. & Art* II. 458 This mineral is the carbonate of strontian. **1832** BREWSTER *Nat. Magic* v. (1833) 113 The red might perhaps be procured in sufficient quantity from the nitrate and other salts of strontian. **1836** B. H. SMART, *Strontian*, a white earth, also called *Strontia.* **1854** FAIRHOLT *Dict. Terms Art, Strontian Yellow*, a solution of strontian, added to chromate of potash. It is a pale canary-yellow, and is a permanent colour. **1860** PIESSE *Lab. Chem. Wonders* 156 When it [the flame] is crimson, there is strontian. **1870** BARING-GOULD *In Exitu Israel* I. ix. 132 A vase, in which burned strontian and spirits of wine, casting a red glare into the water.

strontian ('strɒntɪən), *a. Min.* [f. STRONT-(IUM + -IAN 2.] Of a mineral: having a (small) proportion of a constituent element replaced by strontium.

1930 W. T. SCHALLER in *Amer. Mineralogist* XV. 573 Strontium—strontian. **1959** [see ELLESTADITE].

†**stronti'anic,** *a. Obs.* [f. STRONTIAN *sb.* + -IC.] ***strontianic earth*** = STRONTIA.

1811 PINKERTON *Petral.* I. Introd. p. xli, The alkaline earths, that is the calcareous, magnesian, barytic, strontianic.

strontianiferous ('strɒnʃ(ɪ)ə'nɪfərəs), *a. Geol.* [f. STRONTIAN *sb.* + -(I)FEROUS.] Containing strontian.

1888 *Lond.* etc. *Philos. Mag.* Ser. v. XXV. 238 The Strontianiferous marls of Meudon.

strontianite ('strɒnʃ(ɪ)ənaɪt). *Min.* [f. STRONTIAN *sb.* + -ITE.] Native strontium carbonate.

1794 KIRWAN in *Trans. R. Irish Acad.* V. 244 The first account I received of this substance, which I shall call Stronthianite, was from Dr. Crawford in the year 1790. **1794** SCHMEISSER in *Phil. Trans.* LXXXIV. 418 Account of a mineral Substance, called Strontionite. **1812** SIR H. DAVY *Chem. Philos.* 343 Strontianite, a mineral found at Strontian in Scotland. **1912** *Return Brit. Museum* 195.

strontic ('strɒntɪk), *a. Chem.* [f. STRONT-IUM + -IC. Cf. F. *strontique.*] Of or pertaining to strontium. (Said of salts: now superseded by the attrib. use of the sb.)

1883 *Science* I. 490/1 Strontic vanadate was prepared by fusion of the acid with sodic bromide and strontic bromide.

†**strontites** (strɒn'taɪtiːz). *Chem. Obs.* [f. STRONT-IAN + *-ites* (the ending was suggested by that of *barytes*, but assimilated in form to Gr. -ίτης: see -ITE).] = STRONTIA.

1793 T. C. HOPE in *Trans. R. Soc. Edin.* (1798) IV. II. 8, I shall..take the liberty of calling it by the name of Strontites; by which I wish to be understood to mean the earthy matter in a state of purity, in the same way as lime and barytes denote the pure earthy bases of calcareous spar and of aërated barytes. **1805** SAUNDERS *Min. Waters* 343 Nitrat of strontites. **1812** [see STRONTIA]. **1839** URE *Dict. Arts* 1192 Syrup possesses the property of dissolving alkaline earths, lime, magnesia, strontites, barytes.

†**stron'titic,** *a. Chem. Obs.* [f. STRONTIT-ES + -IC.] Pertaining to strontia.

1793 T. C. HOPE in *Trans. R. Soc. Edin.* (1798) IV. II. 10 These solutions are possessed of all the properties of Strontitic water above recounted. *Ibid.* 22 Strontitic spar. **1807** J. MURRAY *Syst. Chem.* III. 695 The natural species of the Strontitic Genus are those in which the earth is mineralized by sulphuric and by carbonic acids.

strontium ('strɒntɪəm, 'strɒnʃ(ɪ)əm). *Chem.* [f. STRONTIA: see -IUM.] The metallic base of strontia; a dark-yellow metal, fusible at red heat. Symbol Sr. Also *attrib.* and *Comb.*, as ***strontium chloride***, etc.; **strontium 90**, a radioactive isotope of strontium which is one of the chief products of the fission of uranium 235, can pass from fall-out into plants and animals and hence into human tissue (where it is concentrated in bones and teeth), and has been used in radiotherapy.

The salts of strontium are chiefly used for imparting a deep-red colour to flame.

1808 SIR H. DAVY in *Phil. Trans.* XCVIII. 346, I shall venture to denominate the metals from the alkaline earths barium, strontium, calcium, and magnium. **1868** ROSCOE *Elem. Chem.* 178 Copper is the only red-coloured metal known, whilst gold, strontium, and calcium, are yellow. **1892** *Photogr. Ann.* II. 447 [Price list enumerates:] Strontium acetate, bromide, carbonate, chloride, iodide, nitrate (pure, recrystallised), nitrate (commercial). **1916** *Med. Press & Circular* 10 May 419/2 Lactate of strontium 2 grammes a day, to control the albuminuria. **1955** *Sci. News Let.* 28 May 345/1 Strontium 90 is of particular interest because, being chemically similar to calcium, it may be deposited in human bone. **1961** *Lancet* 12 Aug. 366/1 Measurements of strontium 90 in human bone in the United Kingdom. **1978** *Jrnl. R. Soc. Arts* CXXVI. 257/1 Two fission products, Strontium 90 and Caesium 137 have particularly awkward half-lives of about 30 years.

stroock, -en, obs. ff. of pa. t. of STRIKE *v.*

stroof, obs. pa. t. and pa. pple. of STRIVE *v.*

strook(e, -en: see STRIKE *v.*, STROKE.

strool (strul). *Sc.* Also **strule.** [? ad. Sc. Gaelic **sruil* stream (*srùlach* abounding in streams).] A stream (of water or other liquid). Also *fig.*

1867 G. W. DONALD *Poems* 17 The water comes doon in perfect strools upon's. **1920** D. H. EDWARDS *Men & Manners* 236 There's juist a dreeble o' a strule at the burn spoot. **1922** JOYCE *Ulysses* 756 Sending me that long strool of a song out of the Huguenots to sing in French.

stroop, var. form of STROUP *dial.*

stroot(e, obs. forms of STRUT *v.*[1]

'strooth, var. 'STREWTH.

stroove, obs. pa. t. of STRIVE *v.*

strop (strɒp), *sb.* Forms: 4–5 **stroppe,** 5–6 **strope,** 1, 8– **strop.** [OE. *strop* (once only) = (M)Du., (M)LG. *strop*, OHG. *strupf* masc. (a derivative of the same meaning is MHG., mod.G. *strüpfe* fem., LG. *strippe*: see STRIP *sb.*[2]), prob. a WGer. adoption of L. *struppus, stroppus*, strap, band (? a. Gr. στρόφος), whence OF. *estrope* (mod.F. *estrope, étrope*), Pr. *estrop-s*, Catal. *estrop*, Pg. *estropo* rowlock-strap, It. *stroppa* strap, band.

In the 17th c. the dial. form STRAP *sb.* appears beside the original form; subsequently it appears in all senses, and in some of them is now the usual form.]

†**1.** A band, thong; a loop or noose of leather, etc. *Obs.* (Cf. STRAP *sb.* 1.)

In quot. *c* 1050, a thong or line for lashing an oar to a thole-pin.

c **1050** *Suppl. Ælfric's Voc.* in Wr.-Wülcker 181/42 *Struppus*, strop, *uel* arwiððe. **1481** CAXTON *Reynard* (Arb.) 33 Bynde the corde faste to the lynde, and make a rydyng knotte or a strope. **15..** *Ld. Fergus' Gaist* 83 in *Bannatyne MS.* (Hunter. Club) I. 326 And it wald play and hop, Abowt the heid ane stre strop. **1552** *Elyot's Dict., Amentum*, a thonge, or that whiche is bounden to the middes of a darte or iavelyn wherwith it is throwen, a strope or a loupe. **1723** *Pres. St. Russia* II. 378 A Strop of Leather tied about the Beast's Head like a Halter.

†**b.** *Surg.* A band used in setting a fractured limb. (Cf. STRAP *sb.* 7 a.) *Obs.*

1741 ETTRICK *Mach. for reducing Fractures of Thigh* in *Phil. Trans.* XLI. 565 The Leg is suspended by Bands, one of which is placed at the Ancle, from the Sides of which pass Two Strops, to join the inferior Knee-band.

2. A ring or band of hide or of rope with its ends spliced together, used upon a mast, yard, rope, etc., as a fastening or as a purchase for tackle; esp. a band of rope, iron, or chain fastened round a pulley or block. Chiefly *Naut.* (Cf. STRAP *sb.* 2.)

1357 in *Pipe Roll 32 Edw. III* m. 34/2, j. poleancre rope cum le stroppe. **1409** *Acc. Exch. K.R.* 44/11 (3) m. 3 In .xxij. lb. et di. de cordis..expenditis in factura del stroppes infra bargiam. **1417** in *For. Acc. 8 Hen. V*, G/1, ij Bowlynes j Stroppe..j Tooppe. **1485** *Naval Acc. Hen. VII* (1896) 36 Poleis with Stroppes..iiij. *Ibid.* 38 Stroppes of Russewale, ij. **1744** J. PHILIPS *Jrnl. Exped. Anson* 139 We also had one of the Strops of our Bobstay broke. **1769** FALCONER *Dict. Marine* (1780) *Strop*, a piece of rope spliced into a circular wreath, and used to surround the body of a block; so that the latter may be hung to any particular station about the masts, yards, or rigging... Strops are also used occasionally to fasten upon any large rope, for the purpose of hooking a tackle to the eye, or double part of the strop. **1789** *Trans. Soc. Arts* VII. 177 The line was fixed [to the harpoon] by a strop, made of fore-ganger, our wire-shackles being all broke. **1846** A. YOUNG *Naut. Dict.* 329 Any short piece of rope, with its ends spliced together, gets the name of a strop. Such strops are used for various purposes, as, for hooking a tackle to. **1860** G. S. NARES *Naval Cadet's Guide* 27 A single strop with a thimble seized in. **1875** CLARK RUSSELL *Wreck of Grosvenor* xvii, Clapping on strops to the collar of the mainstay. **1883** *Man. Seamanship for Boys* 32, *Q.* What are masthead pendants? *A.* Strops or short pieces of rope, fitted ..upon the heads of the lower masts, for applying tackles for staying the masts or setting up lower rigging. **1912** J. MASEFIELD in *Engl. Rev.* Oct. 340 The noisy half-deck rang with mirth, For two ship's boys were putting on the strop.

b. (See quot.)

1875 KNIGHT *Dict. Mech.*, *Strop* (Rope-making), a rope with an eye at each end, used in twisting strands.

3. A strip of leather (or of a special textile), or a strip of wood covered with leather or other suitable material, used for sharpening a razor; a razor-strop. (Cf. STRAP *sb.* 8 *dial.*)

1702 *Post Man* 3–5 Feb. 2/1 Strops for setting Razors, Pen-knives, &c. upon. **1822** SCOTT *Nigel* viii, You are wanted more than a strop for a blunt razor. **1844** DICKENS *Mart. Chuz.* xxix, He happened to have been sharpening his razors,..a huge strop dangled from the wall. **1887** F. FRANCIS Jun. *Saddle & Mocassin* 64 Three various strops were necessary to put an edge on the razor that was to execute me.

†**4.** A narrow band of metal; = STRAP *sb.* 9.

1573–4 in Swayne *Sarum Churchw. Acc.* (1896) 122 Mendinge of the stropes of iij belles, xij d. **1603–4** *Ibid.* 152 Iron stroppes and bolts and kayes for the belles.

5. *Comb.*, as ***strop-maker, strop-bound*** adj.

1736 *Gentl. Mag.* VI. 607/2 Soap-boilers, Razor-makers, Hone-makers, Strop-makers, &c. **1867** SMYTH *Sailor's Word-bk.*, *Strop-bound block*, a single block used in the clue of square-sails for the clue-lines to lead through.

strop, *a. dial.* ? *Obs.* [Cf. STROP *v.*[2]] ***strop milch cow*** = STRAPPER[2], STROPPER.

1781 in *Hist. Chesterfield* (1839) 339 For every strop milch cow, one penny.

strop (strɒp), *v.*[1] [f. STROP *sb.*]

1. *trans.* To sharpen or smooth the edge of (a razor) with a strop. Also *transf.* and *fig.*

1841 DICKENS *Barn. Rudge* xxv. The raven..after a long inspection of an epitaph, would strop his beak upon the grave to which it referred. **1850** HOLTZAPFFEL *Turning* III. 1155 The razor is always stropped backwards, and usually from heel to point. **1853** LYTTON *My Novel* II. ix, 'Well?' cried the Squire, suspending the operation of stropping his razor. **1944** 'PALINURUS' *Unquiet Grave* III. 72 The parrot stropping its beak on the bars of the cage. **1957** C. DAY LEWIS *Pegasus* 25 The river endlessly stropping its tides against the embankment. **1974** 'J. HERRIOT' *Vet in Harness* vii. 51 'I think a beef sandwich would go down rather nicely, Jim,' he murmured, as he stropped his carving knife on a steel.

2. *Naut.* To furnish (a block) with a strop. Cf. STRAP *v.*[1] 1.

c **1860** H. STUART *Seaman's Catech.* 29 How do you strop a block with a short splice?

Hence **stropped** *ppl. a.*; **'stropping** *vbl. sb.*: (*a*) the action of the verb; (*b*) *concr.* (*Naut.*) rope for making strops.

1850 HOLTZAPFFEL *Turning* III. 1156 A razor from continued use and stropping, has become dull. **1875** BEDFORD *Sailor's Pocket Bk.* x. (ed. 2) 362 Table of Size of Rope Stropping. **1882** NARES *Seamanship* (ed. 6) 75 An iron-stropped block. *Ibid.* 81 The..blocks..are iron stropped. **1883** *Fisheries Exhib. Catal.* 8 Internal Iron Stropped: External Iron Stropped: Wire Stropped: Rope Stropped. **1893** FORBES-MITCHELL *Gt. Mutiny* 287 As keen an edge as a well-stropped razor.

strop (strɒp), *v.*[2] *dial.* [Cf. STRAP *v.*[2], STRIP *v.*[3]] *trans.* = STRAP *v.*[2]

1884 STREATFEILD *Linc. & Danes* 367 *Strop*, to draw the last milk from the teats of a cow; *Stroppings*, the last milk that comes before the udder is empty.

†**strope,** *v. Obs. rare.* [? a. Du. *stroopen*: see STRIP *v.*[1]] *trans.* = STRIP *v.*[1]

1527 ANDREW tr. *Brunswyke's Distyll. Waters* I. xix. b v, Ye shal strope the herbes and leues from theyr steles and stalkes. *Ibid.* I. xx. b vj.

strope, obs. pa. t. of STRIP *v.*[1]

strophanthidin (strəʊ'fænθɪdɪn). *Pharm.* [f. next + -IDIN.] A poisonous steroidal aglycone, $C_{23}H_{32}O_6$, which is prepared by hydrolysis of strophanthin-K and is a stimulant of heart muscle.

1888 T. R. FRASER in *Proc. R. Soc. Edin.* XIV. 373 All mineral acids..resolve strophanthin, even in the cold, into glucose and a substance which I have named strophanthidin. **1962** H. L. KERN et al. in A. Pirie *Lens Metabolism Rel. Cataract* 394 The aglycone, strophanthidin, abolished the active transport of sugars..by intestine of hamsters. **1978** *Nature* 1 June 389/1 The aglycone strophanthidin was preferred to cardiac glycosides such as ouabain because its effects are more readily reversible.

strophanthin (strəʊˈfænθɪn). *Pharm.* [f. STROPHANTH(US + -IN[1].] Any or all of several polycyclic glucosides obtained from certain varieties of plants of the genera *Strophanthus* and *Acokanthera* and used as cardioactive drugs; ***G-*** or ***g-strophanthin*** (also ***strophanthin-G, -g***) [L. *g(rātus* agreeable], the primary active component, $C_{29}H_{44}O_{12}$, of the mixture obtained from *S. gratus*, *A. schimperi*, or *A. ouabaio*; also called *ouabane*; ***H-, h-strophanthin***, etc., [L. *h(ispidus* hairy], a mixture of the glucosides obtained from the seeds of *S. hispidus*; ***K-, k-strophanthin***, etc., [K(OMBÉ], $C_{36}H_{54}O_{14}$, the principle extract from *S. kombe*, also called KOMBÉ.

1873 *Pharm. Jrnl.* III. 524/2 From this extract [of seeds of *Strophanthus Hispidus*, D.C.] Dr. Fraser succeeded in separating a very powerful active principle, which he proposes should be named strophanthin. **1927** *Blackw. Mag.* May 582/1 Strophanthin, its [*sc.* strophanthus'] laboratory derivative is a drug commonly used by the medical profession. **1940** *Elsevier's Encycl. Org. Chem.* Ser. III. XIV. 270, h-Strophanthin is a mixt. of glycosides from the seeds of Strophanthus hispidus. **1960** J. J. LEWIS *Introd. Pharmacol.* xii. 356 Ouabain (G-strophanthin) is a crystalline glycoside obtained from *S. gratus*. **1962** H. L. KERN et al. in A. Pirie *Lens Metabolism Rel. Cataract* 389 The cardiac glycosides, gitalin and strophanthin K, produced effects [on the transport of potassium and anaerobic glycolysis in calf lens] comparable to ouabain. **1978** *Acta Physiol. Acad. Sci. Hungaricae* LI. 166 The therapeutic and toxic effects of strophanthin and digoxin on the heart were studied in the 6–7-week old human embryo.

‖**strophanthus** (strəˈfænθəs). [mod.L. (De Candolle 1802), f. Gr. στρόφ-ος twisted cord + ἄνθος flower.] **a.** *Bot.* A genus of plants of the N.O. *Apocynaceæ*, native of tropical Africa and Asia, having strongly poisonous qualities; a plant of this genus. **b.** A poisonous drug extracted from the seeds of various species of this genus, used by certain African tribes as a poison for arrows; in recent pharmacy used as a cardiac tonic.

1888 *Lancet* 11 Feb. 291/2 Fraenkel, Guttmann, and Langgaard have recently given the result of their experience with strophanthus. **1898** *Rev. Brit. Pharm.* 8 Two ounces of the extract of strophanthus is made from 1 oz. of seed. **1899** *Allbutt's Syst. Med.* VII. 751 The insomnia of heart disease is benefitted by digitalis, strophanthus, strychnine, [etc.]. **1906** ALICE WERNER *Natives Brit. Central Africa* viii. 189 The poison for spears and arrows is in most cases strophanthus. **1911** *Spectator* 11 Jan. 56/2 An arrow poisoned with the usual strophanthus &c. will kill the person wounded.

strophe (ˈstrəʊfiː). Pl. strophes (-fiːz), strophæ (ˈstrəʊfiː). Also 7 in L. form **stropha**. [a. Gr. στροφή, lit. 'turning', f. στροφ-, στρέφειν to turn. Cf. late L. *stropha*, Fr. *strophe*, Sp. *estrofa*, Pg. *estrophe*, It. *strofa*, *strofe*, stanza.]

1. In Greek choral and lyric poetry, and imitations of this: A series of lines forming a system the metrical structure of which is repeated in a following system called the ANTISTROPHE. Also, in wider sense, one of two or more metrically corresponding series of lines forming divisions of a lyric poem. Hence occas. (after Fr.) used with reference to modern poetry as equivalent to STANZA.

Originally the word στροφή, 'turning', was applied to the movement of the chorus from right to left, and ἀντιστροφή, 'counter-turn', to its returning movement from left to right; hence these terms became the designations of the portions of the choric ode sung during these movements respectively.

1603 HOLLAND *Plutarch's Mor.* 1257 By making turnes and winding cranks so strange In all his strophes, and those without the range Of harmony. **1622** [see ANTISTROPHE]. **1671** MILTON *Samson* Of Tragedy, The Measure of Verse us'd in the Chorus is of all sorts,..without regard had to Strophe, Antistrophe or Epod. **1755** GRAY *Let.* Poems (1775) 233 Neither am I quite of your opinion with regard to strophe and antistrophe;..methinks it has little or no effect on the ear, which scarce perceives the regular return of metres at so great a distance from one another. **1774** WARTON *Hist. Eng. Poetry* I. Diss. i. f 3 b, The bard extorted a speedy pardon..by producing the next day before the king at dinner an ode of more than thirty strophes. **1796** KOLLMANN *Ess. Mus. Harmony* xii. 85 It is not sufficient to observe the metre of the verse only according to the nature of its strophes, verses, and feet, with their subdivisions. **1823** THOMASINA ROSS *Bouterwek's Hist. Sp. Lit.* I. 243 Luis de Leon..discarded the prolix style of the canzone, and imitated the brevity of the strophes of Horace, in romantic syllabic measures and rhymes. **1837** CARLYLE *Fr. Rev.* III. v. iv, The Address we do not give; for indeed it was in strophes, sung *vivâ voce*, with all the parts. **1841** *Penny Cycl.* XX. 420/1 The Sapphic strophe consists of three Sapphic verses followed by a versus Adonicus. **1861** PALEY *Æschylus* (ed. 2) *7 agst. Thebes* 111 *note*, Hermann distributes the remainder of the chorus into strophae and antistrophae. **1886** RUSKIN *Præterita* I. 272 The balanced strophes of classic and Hebrew verse. **1895** M. HEWLETT *Earthwork out of Tuscany* 103 What a romance we should have had from Gautier,..what a strophe from Baudelaire half-obscene, half-mournful, wholly melodious. **1896** R. G. MOULTON *Lit. Study Bible* i. 58 The simplest case is where each antistrophe immediately follows its strophe.

fig. **1849** J. MARTINEAU *Ess., Rev.* etc. (1891) IV. 449 Law and love are but the strophe and antistrophe of the great chorus of redemption.

2. *Bot.* (See quot. 1866.) ? *Obs.*

1846 J. HUDSON tr. *Link* in *Rep. & Papers Bot.* (Ray Soc.) 348 The oblique lines which Schimper called spirals (wendel), and which our author terms 'Strophes'. **1866** *Treas. Bot.* 1105/1 *Strophe*, a term applied to the spirals formed in the development of leaves. **1900** B. D. JACKSON *Gloss. Bot. Terms. Strophes* pl. any spirals shown in phyllotaxy.

strophic (ˈstrɒfɪk, ˈstrəʊ-), *a.* *Prosody.* [f. STROPH-E + -IC. Cf. ANTISTROPHIC.]

a. Pertaining to strophes; consisting of strophes. **b.** Belonging to the strophe as distinguished from the antistrophe.

1848 *Class. Museum* V. 386 As regards Pindar, the fragments of the first dithyramb,..give evidence of strophic composition. **1861** PALEY *Æschylus* (ed. 2) *Supplices* 62 *note*, Either the strophic or the antistrophic verse must be altered. **1866** LYTTON *Lost Tales Miletus* Pref. x, The strophic metres of the ancients. **1896** R. G. MOULTON *Lit. Study Bible* i. 62 The reader must be on the watch to distinguish the 'strophic structure', where the stanzas may be unequal, from the 'antistrophic structure', in which the two stanzas of a pair are exact counterparts. **1906** *Expositor* June 565 [He] illustrates the ordinary parallelisms and strophic phenomena.

strophical (ˈstrɒfɪkəl), *a.* *Prosody.* [f. STROPHE + -ICAL.] = STROPHIC b.

1886 C. A. BRIGGS *Messianic Proph.* Pref. p. xii, There is a large amount of scepticism among Hebrew scholars as to..the strophical organization of Hebrew poetry. **1907** *Times Lit. Suppl.* 15 Mar. 82/1 Correction of errors, partly..by attention to the metre and strophical arrangement.

Hence ˈ**strophically** *adv.*

1848 *Class. Museum* V. 381 Songs strophically connected with each other.

strophiolate (ˈstrɒfɪələt), *a.* *Bot.* [ad. mod.L. *strophiolātus*, f. *strophiolum*: see STROPHIOLE and -ATE.] Furnished with a strophiole.

1821 S. F. GRAY *Brit. Plants* II. 667 Polygaleæ... Seed pendulous; hilum strophiolate or comose. **1830** LINDLEY *Nat. Syst. Bot.* 37 Seeds with a strophiolate apex, often winged.

strophiole (ˈstrɒfɪəʊl). *Bot.* [a. mod.L. *strophiolum* (Gærtner 1788; often incorrectly *strophiola*), a use of L. *strophiolum*, dim. of *strophium* chaplet, ad. Gr. στρόφιον, f. στροφ-, στρέφειν to turn, twist. Cf. F. *strophiole.*] An excrescence or tubercle surrounding the hilum of certain seeds.

1839 LINDLEY *Introd. Bot.* (ed. 3) 247 Mirbel has ascertained that in Euphorbia Lathyris the strophiole is the fungous foramen of the primine. **1861** BENTLEY *Man. Bot.* 342 Other botanists..instead of using the two terms strophioles and caruncles as synonymous with each other, apply the former term only when they proceed from the hilum, and the latter to those from the micropyle. **1870** *Henfrey's Bot.* §428 Turneraceæ... Seeds albuminous, with a strophiole or false aril. **1874** R. BROWN *Man. Bot.* 502 Strophiole.—Under the name of Strophiolæ, Gärtner has described certain cellular excrescences on the integument of various seeds.

strophoid (ˈstrɒfɔɪd). *Geom.* [ad. F. *strophoïde*, f. Gr. στρόφος twisted cord: see -OID.] (See quot. 1880.) Hence **stroˈphoidal** *a.* and *sb.*

1880 W. W. JOHNSON in *Amer. Jrnl. Math.* III. 320 The term Strophoid has been applied by French writers to a cubic curve, of which the symmetrical form has been discussed by Dr. James Booth under the name of the Logocyclic Curve... I have ventured to use the word in a more extended signification, and define the strophoid as the locus of the intersection of two straight lines which rotate uniformly about two fixed points in a plane. **1883** E. BARNES in *Johns Hopkins Univ. Circular* II. 145 A Note on the Strophoids. **1908** *Roy. Soc. Catal. Sci. Papers, Subj. Index* I. 535/1 Strophoid [several refs. to foreign periodicals]. *Ibid.* 535/2 Strophoidal curves of 3rd degree. *Ibid.* 631/2 Logocyclic curve..or strophoid. *Ibid.* 632/2 Strophoidals.

‖**strophulus** (ˈstrɒfjʊləs). *Path.* [mod.L. ('Reddegownde, *strophulus*' Huloet 1552, and later Lat.-Eng. Dicts.), app. a corruption of med.L. *scrophulus* 'redgownd' (*Promp. Parv.*), corruption of L. *scrōfulæ* (SCROFULA), misapplied to an eruptive disease.] A papular eruption on the skin of infants; it has several varieties, known popularly as *red-gum*, *white-gum*, *tooth-rash*, etc.

1808 WILLAN *Cutaneous Dis.* I. 16 The Strophulus is a papulous eruption, peculiar to infants, and exhibiting a variety of forms. **1822–7** GOOD *Study Med.* (1829) V. 565 The tooth-rash is the severest form in which strophulus shows itself. **1876** BRISTOWE *Th. & Pract. Med.* (1878) 348 Many attacks of so-called 'strophulus'..are really due to the operations of the above animals [*sc.* gnats, fleas, and bugs].

stroppado, obs. form of STRAPPADO.

stropper (ˈstrɒpə(r)), *dial.* [f. STROP *v.*[2] + -ER[1].] = STRAPPER[2].

1707 *Terrier of South Hykeham, Lincs.* (E.D.D.) For a new bare cow three pence, for a stropper three half-pence.

stroppy (ˈstrɒpɪ), *a.* *colloq.* [? abbrev. of OBSTREPEROUS *a.* with altered stem-vowel.] Bad-tempered, rebellious, awkward, obstreperous, unruly. Hence ˈ**stroppiness**.

1951 H. HASTINGS *Seagulls over Sorrento* II. i, in *Plays of Year 1950* IV. 76 There ain't nothing clever about answering him back and being stroppy. **1964** J. BURKE *Hard Day's Night* iv. 80 'Have you got a licence for it?' 'Oh, don't be so stroppy.' **1968** [see SHIT *sb.* 1 g]. **1969** *New Statesman* 31 Oct. 633/3 It anyhow seems to me (perhaps out of stroppiness) that the good toys aren't all necessarily the ones that teach how to count or measure. **1973** J. WAINWRIGHT *Devil you Don't* 116 All that balls about 'with respect'... Honesty. Stroppiness. **1977** *Guardian Weekly* 27 Feb. 5/4 Those who didn't know him well..missed the stroppy radicalism of his spirit. **1983** *Listener* 14 Apr. 37/1 Susan, on the other hand, is streetwise and stroppy.

†ˈ**strosser**. *Obs.* Also 6 **straser**. [Of obscure origin: the relation to TROUSER is uncertain. Cf. STROUSE.] = TROUSER.

1598 in *Malone's Shaks.* (1790) I. II. 301 Item, iij payer of red strasers and iij fares gowne of buckrome. **1599** SHAKS. *Hen. V*, III. vii. 57 Belike she was old and gentle, and you rode like a Kerne of Ireland, your French Hose off, and in your strait Strossers. **1609** DEKKER *Gull's Horn-bk.* i. 7 The Italians close strosser, nor the French standing coller. *c* **1613** MIDDLETON *No Wit like Woman's* II. i. 39 His son a-horse-back in cloth-of-gold breeches, while he himself goes to the devil a-foot in a pair of old strossers! **1637** I. JONES & DAVENANT *Brit. Triumphans* 15 His Squire apparell'd in a yellow Coat, with wide sleeves, and strossers cut in paines of yellow and watchet.

strost: see STRUST *v.* (= TRUST.)

strot, var. STRUT *sb.* *Obs.*

†**strothe**, ? *sb.* *Obs. rare*[−1]. [Perh. for **strode*, repr. OE. *strōd* marsh (cf. STROTHER); perh. metathetically a. ON. *storð* small wood (cf. *Storth*, *-storth* in Yorks. and Derbyshire place-names).] ? A marsh; ? a small wood.

13.. *Gaw. & Gr. Knt.* 1710 At þe last bi a littel dich he lepez ouer a spenné, Stelez out ful stilly bi a strothe rande.

†**strothe**, *a.* *Obs. rare*[−1]. (Meaning obscure.)

13.. *E.E. Allit. Poems* A. 115 A[s] stremande sternez quen stroþe men slepe.

†ˈ**strother**. *north. Obs.* Also 5 **strothre, stroudyr, strowder, strwder, struther, struder, -ire**, 5–6 **struthir**. [App. related to OE. *strōd* marsh: cf. the place-name *Strood*.] A marsh.

The *Peebles Charters* (ed. 1872) 1457–1569 frequently mention a piece of land called 'The common strother'.

? *a* **1300** *Feodarium Priorat. Dunelm.* (Surtees) 203 *note*, Ab ea cruce usque in mediam strother quæ proxima est versus Hoccale. **1479** *Hexham Priory, Black Bk.* (Surtees) II. 16 Inter moram de Stancrofte et le Syde usque le Langstrothre. *Ibid.* 17 Et sic a la Hac directe usque le strothre. **1486** *Reg. Mag. Sig. Scot.* 348 Cum una marresia vulgariter nuncupata a strudire juxta le Berresdikis. **1576** *Reg. Mag. Sig. Scot. 1586*, 297/1 Peciam terre vocatam the Cobstruthir extendentem ad 2 acras. **1832** MORTON *Mon. Annals Teviotdale* 116 Crailing..was granted by David I., with the crag in the same vill, and easements in the adjoining strother, in exchange for lands at Hardingesthorn.

†ˈ**strothir**. *Obs.* *rare.* Also **strodir**. [Contraction of OE. *stéor-róðor* steer-oar: see STEER *sb.*[2] and RUDDER.] A steering oar, helm, rudder.

[*c* **897** ÆLFRED *Gregory's Past. C.* lvi. 431 Ðæt hit wære swelce se stiora slepe on midre sæ, & forlure ðæt stiorroður.] **14..** *Beryn* 1580 And put in goddis gowernaunce, lyff, Shippe & strothir. *Ibid.* 1884 To sese both Shipp & strodir.

†ˈ**stroublance**. *Obs.* (In quots. *Sc.*) Forms: 5 **strublance, -ulance**, 5–6 **-lans**, 6 **-lens**. [Aphetic f. DISTROUBLANCE.] Disturbance, molestation.

1439 *Inchaffray Charters* (S.H.S.) 138 Meg..neuer sal agayn call it..na mak strublance to thaim in the said landis. **1496** *Extracts Aberd. Reg.* (1844) I. 59 Gyf euer the said Willame committis ony offense or strubulance to the said Thomas. **1543** *Ibid.* 190 Wm. Mathesone, fyscher, wes convict..for the strublens of John Valcar,..and strublens of all his bottis schipping. **1598** *Ibid.* II. 172 The strublans of this burgh, this day committit be Patrik Chein.

†**strouble**, *a.* *Obs. rare*[−1]. In 5 **strowbill**. [Cf. STROUBLE *v.* and TROUBLE *a.*] Troublous.

c **1470** HENRY *Wallace* VII. 138 In strowbill wer thou sall conteyne full lang.

†**strouble**, *v.* *Obs.* Also 4–5 **stroble, -il(l**, 4–6 **struble**, 5 **stroubel, -ulle, strowble**, (? **strabil**). [Aphetic f. DISTROUBLE *v.* Cf. STURBLE *v.*]

1. *trans.* To disturb, trouble.

c **1375** *Sc. Leg. Saints* xviii. (*Mary Egypt*) 948 Þa thochtis for to put me fra, my soroful corce þat stroblyt sa. **1382** WYCLIF *Micah* vii. 3 Thei strubliden [1388 sturbliden] to gydre it [Vulg. *conturbaverunt eam*]. *a* **1400–50** *Wars Alex.* 856 And Philip falne [was] sare seke & all þe fest strubled [*Dubl.* stroblet]. *c* **1425** *St. Mary of Oignies* I. viii. in *Anglia* VIII. 140/32 She knewe þe sleightes and wiles of þe enmy, þat gladly wolde strabil hir. *c* **1470** HENRY *Wallace* XI. 1072 The sayr bandys so strowblyt all his thocht. **1538** *Extracts Aberd. Reg.* (1844) I. 156 Als the saydis Robert and Johnn hed strublit..this guid towne, in stoping of dansing [etc.].

2. To make turbid or cloudy.

c **1375** *Sc. Leg. Saints* xl. (*Ninian*) 571 A cloud vondir blak ..stroublit þe ayre. *a* **1500** *Ratis Raving* II. 207 Thocht a day strublyt be the ayre, Ane vthir efter cumys faire.

Hence †**stroubling** *vbl. sb.* Also †**stroubler**.

a **1400** *Hampole's Prose Tr.* 22 With oute lettynge or strobillynge of worldely besynes. *c* **1460** *Promp. Parv.* (Winch.) 439/1 Stroblare, or troblare, *perturbator*. [The entry is in the alphabetical place of *Storb-*; cf. Way 477/2.] *a* **1500** *Wisd. Sol.* 652 in *Ratis Raving* (1870) 20 The strublyne of fulys crabis the visman.

strouce: see STROUSE *Obs.*

stroucke, obs. pa. t. of STRIKE *v.*

stroud (straʊd). ? *Obs.* Also 8 strowd. [? f. *Stroud* in Gloucestershire.]

1. A blanket manufactured for barter or sale in trading with the North American Indians. Also ***stroud blanket***.

1683 in C. H. Hunt *Life E. Livingston* (1864) 6 Four garments of Strouds. **1751** C. GIST *Jrnls.* (1893) 53 Six Strouds, two Match-Coats, and a String of Wampum. **1752** *Jrnl. Capt. Treat* 52 (Cent.) Be pleased to give to the son of the Piankasha king these two strowds to clothe him. **1809** A. HENRY *Trav.* 119 Before him, on a new stroud blanket, was placed a bason of water. **1812** J. J. HENRY *Camp. agst. Quebec* 133 A large, but coarse blue blanket, called a stroud. **1846** T. L. MCKENNEY *Mem.* I. i. 21 It was not so much a competition in blankets, and strouds, and calicoes..as in whiskey. **1858** SIMMONDS *Dict. Trade.* **1872** *Rep. Indian Affairs 1871* (U.S.) 459 Blankets, leggings, strouds, paints.

2. The material of which these blankets were made.

1759 *Ann. Reg.* 201, 12 pieces red stroud; 15 ditto, blue. **1805** PIKE *Sources Mississ.* (1810) 27 Five yards of blue stroud. **1844** G. DODD *Textile Manuf.* iv. 139 A kind of cheap cloth, called 'stroud' made from woollen rags, was exported to North American Indians.

3. *attrib.*

1683 in C. H. Hunt *Life E. Livingston* (1864) 7 Four Stroud-Coats and Two duffel-Coats. **1751** G. CROGHAN in *Pennsylvania Colonial Rec.* (1851) V. 531, I gave him a Strowd Shirt, Match Coat [etc.]. **1934** P. H. GODSELL *Arctic Trader* 39 A dozen other drivers, all clad in..blue stroud leggings and fur caps.

Hence **'strouding** *vbl. sb.* = prec. 2.

1814 BRACKENRIDGE *Jrnl.* in *Views of Louisiana* 201 The merchandise, which consisted of strouding, blankets,.. guns, beads, &c. **1886** *Century Mag.* Nov. 33/2 A few yards of blue strouding such as the Indians used for breech-clouts.

†**strough**, *v. Obs. rare*⁻¹. [? Corrupt var. of TROUGH *v.* (which, however, is not recorded in this sense).] *trans.* ? To subject (a mineral deposit) to a process by which the ore or metal is separated from other matter.

1618 S. ATKINSON *Gold Mynes Scot.* (Bannatyne Club) 2 Sufficient water..with which all sorts of earth are to be washed or scowred, else buddled, and so stroughed.

strougle, obs. form of STRUGGLE *v.*

Strouhal ('straʊəl, 'struːəl, ‖'strouhal). *Mech.* [The name of Čeněk (or Vincent) *Strouhal* (1850–1922), Czech scientist.] ***Strouhal number***: a dimensionless number used in the study of the vibrations produced in a body by a fluid flowing past it, defined as *vd/u* (or *u/vd*) where *u* is the fluid velocity, *v* the frequency of the vibration, and *d* the effective diameter of the body.

1949 *Proc. R. Soc.* A. CXCVIII. 175 The results are expressed in the form of Strouhal number: *S(R) = fd/Uo*, where *R = Uod/v*. **1975** *Offshore Engineer* Dec. 42/3 For an isolated stationary cylinder the Strouhal number is fairly constant for a wide range of Reynolds numbers.

strouit, obs. pa. t. of STREW *v.*

stroul(e, obs. forms of STROLL.

stroumpet, obs. form of STRUMPET.

strounde, obs. form of STRAND *sb.*¹

strounger, obs. form of STRANGER.

stroup (struːp). *Obs.* exc. *dial.* Forms: 4, 6 stroupe, 5, 7 strowpe, 6 strowp, 7 stroap, 7–9 stroop, stroup. [a. ON. *strúpe* (also *strjúpe*) = MSw., mod.Sw. *strupe*, Da. *strube*, throat.]

1. The throat; the gullet or the wind-pipe.

1338 R. BRUNNE *Chron.* (1810) 190 He smot him in þe helm, bakward he bare his stroupe. *a* **1400** *Celestin* 638 in *Anglia* I. 83 My weysaunt and my stroupe. *c* **1440** *Promp. Parv.* 480/2 Strowpe, of the throte, *epiglotus*. **1483** *Cath. Angl.* 369/2 A Strowpe, *lien.* **1661** *Reg. Privy Counc. Scot.* Ser. III. I. 21 They..went into the byre and cutted the stroaps of eight heid of bestiall. **1787** GROSE *Prov. Gloss.*, *Stroop*, the gullet. *a* **1825** FORBY *Voc. E. Anglia*, *Stroop*, the gullet, or the wind-pipe. It seems indifferently applied to both. **1878** S. H. MILLER & SKERTCHLY *Fenland* iv. 131 Stroop.

2. The spout of a pump, kettle, teapot, etc. Chiefly *Sc.*

1505 in J. Bain & C. Rogers *Liber Protocol. C. Simon* (1877) I. 335 [Two silver phials, one of which wanted] the strowp. **1672** G. SINCLAIR *Hydrostaticks* (1683) 292 This defect might be supplied by the blowing of Bellows from above ground, through a Stroop of Leather, or some other thing. **1828** J. WILSON *Noct. Ambr.* Wks. 1855 II. 74 That stroop's a gran' pourer. **1842** J. AITON *Domest. Econ.* (1857) 224 The stroup of an old tea-pot.

†**3.** ? A hood. *Obs.*

1579 in *Bk. Univ. Kirk Scot.* (1839) 187 The bruit was of same [*read* some] superstitious rites qwhilks ware prepared for the buriall, as ane qwhyte cross in the mortcloath, lang gownes with stroupes and torches. *Ibid.*, Who returnit with answer, that the Lords should cause cover the mortcloath with black velvet, and the stroupes should be removit.

Hence **strouped** *a.*, having a spout. **'stroupless** *a.*, having no spout.

1744 *Rec. Elgin* (1908) II. 339 A peuter strouped flaggon. **1802** *Medical Jrnl.* VIII. 176 It was received into a *strouped* decanter. **1823** GALT *Entail* lxxvii, I would na hae tied my talent in a napkin, nor hid it in a stroopless tea-pot.

stroupe, obs. form of STIRRUP.

†**strouse.** *Obs. rare.* Also strouce. = TROUSE *sb.*² Cf. STROSSER. *Obs.*

1600 *Sir J. Oldcastle* v. x. 124 *Irish.* Prethee, Lord shudge, let me haue mine own clothes, my strouces there. **1620** tr. *Boccacio's Decameron* VII. iii. 29 b, [Friar] Reynard being stript into his Trusse and straite Strouses.

†**strouse-man.** *Obs. rare*⁻¹. ?

1688 W. SCOT *Hist. Name Scot.* (1894) 45 The Keepers and the Strouse-men came, With Shouts from Hill to Hill, With Hound and Horn they rais'd the Deer.

strout(e, obs. forms of STRUT *v.*¹

strouter ('straʊtə(r)). *Newfoundland.* [Perh. f. dial. form of STRUT *sb.*²: cf. also STOUTER.] A heavy post used to support and strengthen the end of a fishing stage or wharf; = STOUTER.

1895 *Jrnl. Amer. Folklore* VIII. 31 *Strouters*, the outside piles of a wharf, which are larger and stronger than the inner ones. **1937** P. K. DEVINE *Folk Lore Newfoundland* 50 *Strouters*, the perpendicular posts at the front end of a fishing stage, jammed firmly into the sea bottom, and having rails nailed across to make the ladder for getting into and out of boats. **1973** *Even. Telegram* (St. John's, Newfoundland) 25 Oct. 3 You could hear a tin can bonking against the strouters or the rocks down there in the landwash. **1975** V. BUTLER *Little Nord Easter* 61 For the shores [of a wharf] there'd be strouters. They'd be called strouters and they'd be a little larger, probably seven or eight inches in diameter. **1975** *Canad. Antiques Collector* Mar.-Apr. 23/1 In the fishery we have such terms as:..strouters (perpendicular posts which support the front of a fishing-stage).

[**strow**, error for *frow*, FROUGH *a.*

1659 *Lady Alimony* II. v. D 4 b, The grass Too strow for fodder, and too rank for pasture. **1822** NARES; hence in recent Dicts.]

strow: see STREW *v.*

strowe, strowh, obs. forms of STRAW *sb.*¹

Strowger ('straʊgə(r)). *Teleph.* The name of Almon B. *Strowger*, U.S. telephone engineer, used *attrib.* with reference to an exchange switching system proposed by him in 1891 (U.S. Patent 447,918), involving successive step-by-step switches.

1900 K. B. MILLER *Amer. Telephone Pract.* (ed. 3) xxxiv. 459 The most important idea..in all of the Strowger automatic work, was that of simplifying the contacts for the different line wires. **1901** J. E. HOMANS *ABC of Telephone* xx. 268 A Strowger exchange in Atlanta, Ga., has as many as 500 subscribers. **1933** K. B. MILLER *Telephone Theory & Pract.: Automatic Switching* iii. 22 Of the three general types of automatic or machine-switching systems, 'step-by-step', 'power-driven', and 'all-relay', the former, also called the 'Strowger system', will be treated in this chapter. **1967** *Times Rev. Industry* July 19/1 There are three types of telephone exchange in use; one is the Strowger which has been the standard British equipment ever since we introduced the automatic exchange. **1973** *Nature* 16 Feb. 416/1 The antiquated Strowger step-by-step switching on which Britain's telephones deplorably now depend.

strowl(e, strowt(e: see STROLL, STRUT *v.*¹

†**stroy**, *sb. Obs.* [In sense 1, ? short for *stroy-all* or *-good*: see STROY *v.* b. In sense 2, aphetic f. DESTROY *sb.*]

1. One who destroys; a wasteful person. *dial.*

c **1440** *Promp. Parv.* 480/2 Stroy [*v.r.* stroye], or dystroyare, *destructor, dissipator*. *a* **1825** FORBY *Voc. E. Anglia*, *Stry, Stry-good, s.*, a wasteful person; a bad manager or economist.

2. Destruction. ***to make stroy of***, to make spoil of, pillage.

1682 BUNYAN *Holy War* (1905) 386 Nor did they partake or make stroy of any of the Necessaries of Mansoul, but that which they seised on against the Townsmens will. **1688** LD. DELAMERE *Adv. to Childr.* Wks. (1694) 25 To have your meat well drest does well, for there is not much difference betwixt a wilful stroy, and to have a great deal of meat spoiled in the dressing.

stroy (strɔɪ), *v. Obs.* or *arch.* Forms: α. 2–3 struȝe, 2–4 struie, 4 stru(e, strui, strwe, 4–5 struye. β. 4–5 strye, 4–6 strie, 5, 7, 9 *dial.* stry. γ. 4 stroȝe, 4– 5 stroie, 4–6 stroye, 4–9 stroy. [Aphetic f. DESTROY *v.*; cf. ASTROY *v.*] *trans.* To destroy.

c **1200** *Trin. Coll. Hom.* 51 Þat he sholde fare to þe burh of ierusalem and struȝen it. *Ibid.* 161 [The Devil] struieð rihte bileue. *a* **1300** *Cursor M.* 9203 In his time..Iurselem was struid [*Gött.* stroyd]. **13..** *Gaw. & Gr. Knt.* 2194 Hit is þe fende,..þat has stoken me þis steuen, to strye me here. **1377** LANGL. *P. Pl.* B. xv. 587 þei..studyeden to stroyen [*v.r.* struyen] hym and stroyden hemself. **1382** WYCLIF *Ecclus.* xxviii. 17 Wallid cites of riche men it stroȝede. *c* **1450** *St. Cuthbert* (Surtees) 4953 As clay of ways I sall þaim struye [Vulg. Ps. xvii. 43 *delebo*]. *c* **1450** *Mirk's Festial* 72, I woll strye hit [the world] wyth a flod. **1567** TURBERV. *Epit.* etc. 89 b, Though Tayler cut thy garment out of frame, And strie thy stuffe by sowing it amis. **1579** W. A. *Remedy agst. Love* (Roxb.) B iiij b, For take away the cause of every vice..You stroy theffect. **1603** J. DAVIES (Heref.) *Microcosmos* 49 Damn'd Nothing that hast such a some-thing stride, How wast begot? **1606** SHAKS. *Ant. & Cl.* III. xi. 54 What I haue left behinde Stroy'd in dishonor. *c* **1611** CHAPMAN *Iliad* XXII. 37 O Hector! flie, this man, this homicide, That strait will stroy thee. **1642** H. MORE *Song of Soul* II. I. iv. 6 They stroy one th' other in fell cankred mood. **1819** W. TENNANT *Papistry Storm'd* (1827) 189 As they look't up ilk lofty wa', Takin' their meiths for its downfa', That they may strike and stroy. *a* **1825** FORBY *Voc. E. Anglia*, *Stry*, to destroy; to waste.

†**b.** *Comb.*: **stroy-all, stroy-good**, a destructive or wasteful person.

1573–80 TUSSER *Husb.* (1878) 21 A giddie braine maister, and *stroyal his knaue, brings ruling to ruine and thrift to hir graue. **1540** PALSGR. *Acolastus* I. iii. F iij b, I reioyce..to be called Acolastus .i. a *stroygood, or a prodigal felow. **1567** GOLDING *Ovid's Met.* XI. (1593) 269 The cruell stroygood [L. *vastatorem*] with his bloodie mouth and heere. **1611** COTGR., *Bobancier*, an vnthrift, riotous waster, superfluous spender, immoderate stroy-good. *a* **1825** stry-good [see STROY *sb.* 1].

Hence †**'stroying** *vbl. sb.*

1396–7 in *Eng. Hist. Rev.* (1907) XXII. 303 Aborcife and stroying of kynde. ? *c* **1400** *Wyclif's Wycket* (1546) B j, Great stroyeng of the people of God. **1549** CHEKE *Hurt Sedit.* (1569) G iv, How many came to the campes from long labour to sodeine ease, and from meane fare to stroying of vittaile. **1573–80** TUSSER *Husb.* (1878) 106 If shepherd would keepe them from stroieng of corne.

†**'stroyer.** *Obs.* Also 4 struier, struyer, strier, 5 streier. [Aphetic f. DESTROYER.] A destroyer.

a **1300** *Cursor M.* 16703 Aha! þou struier [*Gött.* struyer] o þe temple. *c* **1380** WYCLIF *Wks.* (1880) 128 3yt þes possessioners ben þeues and so striers of clergye and of good lif in the people. *c* **1381** CHAUCER *Parl. Foules* 360 The drake, stroyer of his owne kinde. **1589** R. ROBINSON *Golden Mirr.* (Chetham Soc.) 18 He layes not gether poore men's grounds He is no countrey stroyer.

stroyl, stru: see STROIL, STROY *v.*

strub (strʌb), *v. s.w. dial.* [Of obscure origin: cf. STRIP *v.*] *trans.* To rob, strip. Also *absol.*

c **1680** in A. H. A. Hamilton *Quarter Sessions* (1878) 220 [Robert Coad was convicted of] being a night walker, and pilfering and strubbing in the night-time. **1867** ROCK *Jim & Nell* lxiv, But they've a-strubb'd vlower-knats an' heaths, And fudgeed up zum purty wreaths. **1870** PENGELLY in *N. & Q.* Ser. IV. VI. 72/1 [In East Cornwall thirty years ago] *to strub* was to strip or rob. Thus, we were said to *strub* a bird's nest (not the bird) when we took the eggs or young birds from it.

struble: see STROUBLE *v.*

†**strucion.** *Obs.* Forms: 3 strucion, 4 strucioun, struccon, 5 struccyon. Also in med.L. form 4 strucyo, 4–5 strucio, 6 struchio. [ad. med.L. *strūciōnem*, a miswriting of L. *strūthiōnem*, nom. *strūthio*, a. Gr. στρουθίων, f. στρουθός sparrow (ὁ μέγας σ. the ostrich).] The ostrich. (By some writers confused with the stork.)

a **1225** *Ancr. R.* 132 Þe steorc [MS. C. strucion, MS. T. ostrice]. *c* **1340** HAMPOLE *Prose Tr.* 9 Þay are lyke till a fowle þat es callede strucyo or storke. **1382** WYCLIF *Job* xxxix. 13 The fether of a strucioun [1388 ostriche] is lic to the fetheris of a ierfalcoun. —— *Micah* i. 8. **1388** —— *Lev.* xi. 16. **1387** TREVISA *Higden* (Rolls) III. 11 Salomon..closede Astructio his bryd in a glas, and þe struccon brouȝte a worme þat hatte Thamir out of wildernesse [**1432–50** *MS. Harl.* Strucio *in both places*; **1485** *Caxton* struccyon]. *c* **1400** *Three Kings Cologne* 46 þe which is clepyd strucio. *c* **1500** KENNEDY *Passion of Christ* 26 As struttioun [*MS. A* ? structioun] stif, as tigar tiranus. **1592** LODGE *Euphues Shadow* B 1, The birde Struchio [hath] a big body, but weake wings.

struck (strʌk), *pa. pple.* and *ppl. a.* [pa. pple. of STRIKE *v.*] †**A.** *pa. pple.* in special use = STRICKEN A, STRUCKEN A.

1594 SHAKS. *Rich. III*, I. i. 92 His Noble Queene [is] Well strooke [**1597** Qo. stroke] in yeares. **1629** QUARLES *Argalus & P.* III. 124 An old gray pilgrime, deeply strucke in yeares. **1787** *Minor* IV. ii. 206 A person struck in years, and of a noble deportment, approached.

B. *ppl. a.*

1. Subjected to a blow or stroke.

1627 MAY *Lucan* IV. F 5, Make the strooke earth to deluge peruious. **1693** J. O. tr. *Cowley's Hist. Plants* I. C.'s Wks. 1721 III. 272 As soon as Musick from struck Strings rebounds. **1821** JOANNA BAILLIE *Metr. Leg., Lady G. Baillie* xvii, Then from the struck flint flew the spark. **1851** W. POLE in Rimbault *Pianoforte* (1860) 185 The elasticity of the struck wire would send it [*sc.* the hammer] down with such force that it rebounded. **1875** A. J. ELLIS tr. *Heimholtz' Sensat. Tone* I. v. 108 The differences in the quality of tone of struck strings.

b. Wounded: = STRICKEN *ppl. a.* B. 1. *rare.*

1809 BYRON *Engl. Bards* 841 So the struck eagle..View'd his own feather on the fatal dart. **1819** SHELLEY *Cenci* I. ii. 12 Your image, as the hunter some struck deer, Follows me.

†**2.** Of a battle: = STRICKEN B. 6. *Obs.*

1618–19 BEAUM. & FL. *Bonduca* I. i, Ten struck Battels I suckt these honour'd scars from.

3. Marked, grooved.

1677 MOXON *Mech. Exerc.* iii. 47 Those wheels that have more than one Groove in them are called Two, Three, &c. Struck-wheels. **1678** *Ibid.* v. 83 You must not Saw just upon the struck line.

4. Of a jury: (See quot. 1856. Cf. STRIKE *v.* 14.)

1856 BOUVIER *Amer. Law Dict.*, *Struck Jury*, a special jury selected by striking from the pannel of jurors, a certain number by each party, so as to leave a number required by law to try the cause. **1902** LINN *Story of Mormons* 308 A struck jury was obtained.

b. ***struck-off***: of persons in certain professions, debarred from practising by having one's name deleted from the register of those qualified. Cf. STRIKE *v.* 13 b, 82.

1963 *Sunday Express* 27 Jan. 23/3 A struck-off doctor—now a dope addict. **1972** E. ROUTLEY *Puritan Pleasures of Detective Story* II. vii. 74 An unexpected meeting with a struck-off solicitor turned private detective. **1976** E. WARD *Hanged Man* xxix. 189 Are *you* really a doctor?.. You sound like a struck-off vet.

5. Of a measure: Levelled with a strickle. = STRICKEN B. 4, STRIKED.

1866 ROGERS *Agric. & Prices* I. x. 168 Nine struck bushels are reckoned as equal to eight heaped. **1883** GRESLEY *Gloss. Coal-mining* 245 *Struck*, level full; strickle measure.

6. Of a plant: That has put forth roots, rooted.

1856 DELAMER *Fl. Garden* (1861) 172 Pot off your struck chrysanthemums.

7. In various industrial arts.

a. Impressed with a device by means of a die.

1881 A. WATT *Mech. Industr.* 190 Another..branch of cheap jewellery manufacture consists in what is called 'struck' work. Thin sheet gold alloy of various qualities is struck by means of a die into any desired form, by which a hollow shell is obtained; this is then filled by fusing into it a quantity of silver solder. **1886** B. V. HEAD in *L. Jewitt's Eng. Coins & Tokens* 128 Modern casts made from ancient struck originals... The lettering and the types on cast coins are also less sharply defined than on struck coins.

b. *Electrometallurgy.* (See quot. 1881.)

1881 A. WATT *Scientific Industr.* II. 150 It is necessary that the article should be struck,..that is, receive an immediate coating directly after immersion, when deposition may be allowed to progress more slowly. **1909** *Century Dict.* Suppl. (citing Houston *Dict. Elect.*).

c. (See quot.)

1895 *Funk's Stand. Dict.*, *Struck fish*, fish saturated with salt and then smoked.

d. ***struck up***: (of tinware) raised or fashioned by means of a press.

1875 KNIGHT *Dict. Mech.* 2466/1 Other swages operate in drop or lever presses upon sheet-metal; forming the struck-up tinware, such as pie-pans, [etc.].

e. ***struck joint*** (Building): a joint in which the mortar between two courses of bricks is sloped inwards so as to be flush with the surface of one but below that of the other.

1876 *Notes Building Construction* II. xiii 219 Struck Joints should be formed by pressing back the upper portion of the joint while the mortar is moist, so as to form a sloping surface which throws off the wet. **1948** *Archit. Rev.* CIV. 20 (*caption*) Brick external walls are finished in buff face brick with struck joints. **1978** S. MARTIN *Build your own House* (ed. 7) v. 75 The flush joint and the struck weathered joint are formed with a trowel.

8. Of, pertaining to, or affected by an industrial strike. Chiefly *U.S.*

1894 S. & B. WEBB *Hist. Trade Unionism* ii. 80 Finding that the yarn was for a 'struck shop'. **1937** *N.Y. Times* 16 June 1/6 The Republic Steel Corporation..asked for a mandamus writ to compel Postmaster General Farley..to deliver to people in its struck plants 'all matter properly mailable'. **1939** *Sun* (Baltimore) 21 July 2/6, 60,000 butchers in retail shops would refuse to handle 'struck products'. **1947** *Ibid.* 14 Oct. 24/1 The league said it would withdraw its charges.., provided the union would delete its 'closed shop' and 'struck work' clauses. **1962** *Aeroplane* 12 Apr. 16/1 Since 1958 the same eight airlines..have had a mutual aid agreement whereby a 'struck' company receives from the others any excess revenues attributable to the strike, less additional expenses. **1968** *Globe & Mail* (Toronto) 3 Feb. B5/3 Men and women who make a living by working on struck newspapers. **1977** *Time* 27 June 35/2 Not since World War II, when President Roosevelt threatened to call out the armed forces to reopen struck mines, has the union played such an important role in the nation's well-being.

9. *Comb.*: † ***struck-blind*** adj.

c **1611** CHAPMAN *Iliad* v. 300 It..made th' Heroe stay His strooke-blind temples on his hand.

struck (strʌk), *sb.* [Subst. use of STRUCK *pa. pple.* and *ppl. a.*] A bacterial disease of sheep causing sudden convulsive death after few symptoms; orig. more loosely in *dial.* use.

[**1784**: see STRIKE *v.* 45 d]. **1903** *Jrnl. S.-E. Agric. College* XII. 86 First and most prominent is the disease commonly known as 'struck', or 'struck in the blood'. These terms appear to be somewhat loosely applied to any cases of sudden death in sheep... There is, however, especially in the marsh lands of Kent,..a disease in which few symptoms of a definite character are ever seen, owing to the rapid approach of death, and to which the term 'struck' is intended to be applied. [**1904** *Eng. Dial. Dict.* V. 827/1 Ken[t]. A sheep which dies suddenly of a disease akin to apoplexy is said to die 'struck'.] **1929** *Jrnl. Compar. Path. & Therapeutics* XLIII. 1 The term 'struck' is applied by the farming community [of Romney Marsh] to a rapid and fatal disease where post-mortem examination reveals an acute inflammatory condition in one or more of the following parts of the body: areas of muscular tissue, organs in the abdominal cavity, and organs in the thoracic cavity. **1966** T. DALLING *Internat. Encycl. Vet. Med.* I. 640 The classical type [of *Clostridium perfringens* Type C] was shown to be the cause of 'Struck' (Romney Marsh disease). **1972** *TV Vet Sheep Bk.* lxii. 169/1 All the clostridial diseases—enterotoxaemia, pulpy kidney, lamb dysentery, struck (blackleg),..can and should be prevented by vaccinating the ewe flock.

strucken (ˈstrʌk(ə)n), *pa. pple.* and *ppl. a. Obs.* exc. *Sc.* and *north.* [pa. pple. of STRIKE *v.*]

A. *pa. pple.* in special sense = STRICKEN A, STRUCK A.

1583–92 GREENE *Mamillia* II. O 1 b, Calling him which was well strooken in yeeres, & yet enamoured,..not an old louer, but a filthie foole. **1586** T. BRIGHT *Treat. Mel.* xix. 118 The aged, farre stroken in yeares, faile in the execution of externall actions. **1596** DALRYMPLE tr. *Leslie's Hist. Scot.* I. II. 154 Now Metellan weil strukne in ȝeiris, [etc.]. **1650** LAMONT *Diary* (Maitl. Club) 23 Old Inchdearnie.. depairted out of this life, being a man weill struken in yeares. **1768** FOOTE *Devil upon two Sticks* II. Wks. 1778 IV. 40 *Devil.* That was composing, indeed. *Last.* Ay, warn't it, master, for a man that is strucken in years.

B. *ppl. a.* = STRICKEN *ppl. a.* in various uses.

strucken blindness (nonce-use), the condition of being struck blind.

1596 DALRYMPLE tr. *Leslie's Hist. Scot.* I. I. 123 Lat him that strykes be called giltie, & the strukne absoluet. *Ibid.* I. II. 140 Afor him, in Albion was na vsse of strukne or cuinȝet money. **1612** J. DAVIES (Heref.) *Muse's Sacrif.* (Grosart) 81/2 Yet (like the strucken Fish) we are in hold. **1642** H. MORE *Song of Soul, Paraphr. Interpr.* P 7 b, I tune my strings..: some golden vein The strucken chords right sweetly shall resound. **1649** MILTON *Eikon.* Pref. B 2 b, That they..may have none to blame but thir owne folly, if they live and dye in such a strook'n blindness. **1661** FELTHAM *Resolves, Upon Eccles. ii. 11* (ed. 8) 382 A strucken Deer. **1901** G. DOUGLAS *House with Gr. Shutters* 297 John's asleep this strucken hour and mair.

† **ˈstructor.** *Obs. rare*$^{-1}$. [a. L. *structor*, agent-n. from *struĕre* to build.] A builder.

1634 SIR T. HERBERT *Trav.* 59 These Persians say one Iamshet was the structor [of the Palace of Persepolis].

structural (ˈstrʌktjʊərəl), *a.* [f. STRUCTURE *sb.* + -AL[1].] Of or pertaining to structure.

1. a. Of or pertaining to the art or practice of building. Chiefly in ***structural iron, steel***, iron or steel intended for building construction.

1867 BURTON *Hist. Scot.* ii. (1873) I. 53 The rise of structural skill in Scotland. **1895** *Current Hist.* V. 608 The great demand was for structural iron and steel. **1902** *Westm. Gaz.* 21 May 8/2 Structural steel.

b. *fig.* Pertaining to the art of literary construction. *rare.*

1870 LOWELL *Study Wind.* (1871) 188 Chaucer..had a structural faculty which distinguishes him from all other English poets, his contemporaries.

2. Of or pertaining to the structure of a building as distinguished from its decoration or fittings. ***structural load*** (see quot. 1888). ***structural engineering***, the branch of civil engineering concerned with large modern buildings and other structures; so ***structural engineer***.

1877 J. D. CHAMBERS *Div. Worship* 1 Structural and other requisites for Divine Worship. *a* **1878** SCOTT *Lect. Archit.* (1879) I. 69 It was my endeavour to illustrate the mechanical and structural portion of the process. **1879** *Cassell's Techn. Educ.* I. 183 The general rule, however, is that carpenters' work is structural, and connected with the carcase, whilst that of a joiner comprehends the finishings of the outside and inside of a building. **1886** CONDER *Syrian Stone-Lore* ii. (1896) 103 By careful examination I found that the arches near the great reservoir were not structural but false. **1888** *Lockwood's Dict. Mech. Engin.*, *Structural Load*, the load due to a structure itself, as distinguished from the imposed load. **1896** *Engineering Index 1892–5* II. 412 Structural engineering. Courses in —. See Engineering Education. **1912** T. D. ATKINSON *Cathedrals* 180 The great structural supports..Wykeham retained. **1912** *Register of Former Students* (Mass. Inst. Technol.) 65 Burleigh, Cha(rle)s R(andall)..structural engineer and chief draughtsman. **1924** *Times Trade & Engin. Suppl.* 29 Nov. 248/2 Structural engineers are irregularly employed. *Ibid.*, Some of the finest structural engineering in the world was done in the Black Country. **1943** A. RAND *Fountainhead* I. i. 15 Of course, no one denies the importance of structural engineering to a future architect. **1977** *Modern Railways* Dec. 488/1 The APT project placed a complex set of inter-related demands on the structural engineer.

fig. **1904** S. H. BUTCHER *Harvard Lect.* 200 The subject-matter of poetry is the universal—that which is abiding and structural in humanity.

3. Of or pertaining to the arrangement and mutual relation of the parts of any complex unity.

1870 YEATS *Nat. Hist. Comm.* 7 All raw substances contain within them structural evidences of the conditions under which they were developed. **1873** HAMERTON *Intell. Life* III. x. 129 We learn several languages by perceiving their structural relations, and remembering these. **1874** W. SPOTTISWOODE *Polarisation of Light* vi. 76 The mechanical strain has imparted to portions of the glass a structural character analogous..to that of a crystal. **1874** *Hartwig's Aerial World* ii. 24 Having obtained a knowledge of the various gaseous substances which compose the atmosphere, we will now cast a glimpse on their structural arrangement. **1884** tr. *Lotze's Logic* Introd. 7 If, again, a tool is to fit the hand, it must have such other structural properties as make it easy to grasp. **1887** *Athenæum* 8 Oct. 463/1 Singleton here ..passes at once from the attitude of the eye-witness to the attitude of the chronicler, and tells the story..by the historical method. Nor was there any structural need for him to do this; he could have [etc.].

4. In various scientific uses.

a. *Phys.* and *Path.* Of or pertaining to the organic structure of an animal or plant, or a portion of an animal or vegetable body.

1845 BUDD *Dis. Liver* 202 No structural lesion of the brain. **1862** SPENCER *First Princ.* II. xiii. §104. (1875) 302 The structural modifiability of an adult man is greater than that of an old man. **1863** HUXLEY *Man's Place in Nat.* ii. 103 The structural differences which separate Man from the Gorilla and the Chimpanzee. **1877** J. A. ALLEN *Amer. Bison* 488 In the structural character of the teeth themselves there is nothing that positively settles the question of their identity. **1880** BASTIAN *Brain* i. 21 The localization of the path of the stimulus leads to structural results of another kind. **1898** *Syd. Soc. Lex.*, *Structural disease*, one involving tissue and causing change visible to the naked eye or the microscope; also organic disease in contradistinction to functional disease.

Comb. **1901** *Amer. Jrnl. Psychol.* XII. 598 The structural-functional psychology question.

b. *Geol.* Pertaining to the structure of the earth's crust, of a rock, formation, mountain, or the like.

1855 *Orr's Circ. Sci.*, *Inorg. Nat.* 57 The phenomena just described are called structural, as affecting the intimate structure of the mass, and not merely its external form. **1862** DANA *Man. Geol.* IV. vi. 735 There are three elements at the base of the earth's features. First a geographical one..; the second, structural,—the system of cleavage-structure; the third dynamical. **1893** B. WILLIS in *13th Ann. Rep. U.S. Geol. Surv.* II. 224 In the Appalachian province there are four districts, each of which is distinguished from the others by a prevailing structural type.

c. Of a branch of a science: Concerned with the study of the structures of natural products.

structural botany: botany dealing with the structure and organization of plants. ***structural chemistry***: chemistry treating of the arrangement or order of attachment of atoms in the molecules of compounds. ***structural geology***: geology dealing with the method of the formation of the rocks that constitute the earth's crust; also called *geotectonic geology*.

1835 LINDLEY (*title*), A Key to structural, physiological, and systematic Botany. **1849** BALFOUR *Man. Bot.* 1 Structural Botany, or Organography, which has reference to the textures of which plants are composed, and to the forms of the various organs. **1882** GEIKIE *Text-bk. Geol.* IV. 474 Geotectonic (Structural) Geology, or the architecture of the earth's crust. **1907** *Nature* 24 Oct. 654/1 Structural chemistry, moreover, is slowly acquiring the mastery over cholesterin by making use of the experience afforded by the synthetic study of the hydroaromatic substances.

d. *Chem.* Of or pertaining to the arrangement of atoms in a molecule; ***structural formula***, a plane schematic method of representing the structure of a molecule by using punctuation (as $CH_3{\cdot}CH{:}CH_2$) or lines (as $CH_3—CH = CH_2$) to indicate the position and nature of the bonds between constituent atoms; ***structural isomerism***, a form of isomerism in which molecules having the same constituent atoms may have different structures, the atoms being joined in different sequences; so ***structural isomer***.

1872 *Phil. Mag.* XLIII. 241 (*heading*) On the relations between the atomic hypothesis and the condensed symbolic expressions of chemical facts and changes known as dissected (structural) formulæ. **1876** *Ibid.* II. 162 To so-called normal butylic alcohol is generally assigned the structural formula $CH_2(C_3H_7)OH$. **1926** J. READ *Textbk. Org. Chem.* xii. 215 The various kinds of isomerism encountered up to the present point are all included under the general title of structural isomerism. Structural isomers are substances possessing the same molecular formula but different structural formulæ. **1951** I. L. FINAR *Org. Chem.* I. i. 6 It is always desirable to show the arrangement (if known) of the atoms in the molecule, and this is done by means of structural formulæ or bonddiagrams. **1980** C. W. SPANGLER *Org. Chem.* I. i. 17 Such branching produces structural isomers, compounds having identical molecular formulas, but whose carbon backbones are arranged differently in three-dimensional space. *Ibid.* 18 If another atom (or group) is bonded to the carbon system (say, chlorine), positional isomerism as well as structural isomerism becomes possible. *Ibid.* 19 There are many different methods of writing structural formulas for organic molecules.

e. *Biol.* Of a gene: that specifies the aminoacid sequence of a polypeptide.

1959 PARDEE, JACOB, & MONOD in *Jrnl. Molecular Biol.* I. 177 The situation revealed with the present system, namely a genetic 'complex' comprising, besides the 'structural' genes (*z*, *y*) a repressor-making gene (*i*) whose function is to block or regulate the expression of the neighbouring genes is, so far, unique for enzyme systems. **1966** E. A. CARLSON *Gene* xxiv. 229 The repressor was assumed to be incomplete. Thus the structural genes would be transcribed and their enzymes would synthesize a metabolite. **1976** F. J. AYALA *Molecular Evolution* ii. 12 Substitutions in the DNA nucleotide sequence of a structural gene may result in changes in the amino acid sequence of the polypeptide encoded by the gene, although this is not always the case because of the degeneracy of the genetic code.

5. In the Social Sciences, Psychology, and other disciplines, such as Linguistics, connected with the analysis of social, mental, or linguistic organization. **a.** Of, pertaining to, involving, or resulting from those aspects of a system concerned with the formal laws and relations of its structure, as distinguished from function or phenomenon; also, relating to or connected with the 'deep' structures that are considered to generate 'surface' structures. Cf. *deep structure* s.v. DEEP *a.* IV. c; FUNCTIONAL *a.* 2 c.

1884 W. JAMES in *Mind* IX. 19 The contrast is really between two *aspects*, in which all mental facts without exception may be taken; their structural aspect, as being subjective, and their functional aspect, as being cognitions. **1890** O. T. MASON in *Ann. Rep. Smithsonian Inst.* (1891) 527 A complete syllabus of anthropology would include—first, what man is, and second, what man does. What man is may be denominated *structural anthropology*; what man does, *functional anthropology*. **1908** *Philos. Rev.* XVII. 651 The book is a very pronounced example of the structural type of psychology. **1917** *Internat. Jrnl. Amer. Linguistics* I. 177 The existence of phonetic shifts, and the presence of structural similarities are too numerous. **1932** M. FORTES tr.

Petermann's Gestalt Theory ii. 33 The concept leads to a theory of reactions..which is characterized by Köhler's key-word 'structural reaction'. **1940** C. C. FRIES in *Language* XVI. 199 (*heading*) On the development of the structural use of word-order in modern English. **1944** *Social Res.* XI. 99 A Beethoven symphony where from a part of the whole we could grasp something of the inner structure of the whole itself. The fundamental laws, then, would not be piecemeal laws but structural characteristics of the whole. **1952** C. C. FRIES *Structure of English* iv. 58 One of the basic assumptions of our approach here to the grammatical analysis of sentences is that all the structural signals in English are strictly formal matters that can be described in physical terms of forms, correlations of these forms, and arrangements of order. **1952** A. R. RADCLIFFE-BROWN *Structure & Function in Primitive Society* 11 When we are dealing with a structural system we are concerned with a system of social positions. **1958** *Eng. Jrnl.* XLVII. 479 Structural ambiguity, on the other hand, results from the arrangement of the words, that is, from the structure of the utterance. It is sometimes known as syntactic ambiguity and, in older logic books, as amphiboly. **1962** R. JAKOBSON *Sel. Writings* I. 654 An analysis of the structural laws which underlie language and its evolution necessarily leads us to ascertain a limited set of actually given structural types. **1963** JACOBSON & SCHOEPF tr. *Lévi-Strauss's Structural Anthropology* p. viii, Two papers..are published here for the first time in conjunction with fifteen others that seem to me to elucidate the structural method in anthropology. **1964** H. HARTMANN *Ego Psychol.* xiv. 289 The genetic viewpoint had to be supplemented by a structural approach, though Freud never quite explicitly stated this. **1974** *Howard Jrnl.* XIV. 37 Worsening structural inequalities... (We shall use the term 'structural' to refer to housing, education, employment, income and race.) **1974** I. ROSSI *Unconscious in Culture* 70 The same structural code is at work in mind, society, and physical reality. **1975** G. STEINER *After Babel* ii. 77 Hamann's opening statement..and his..dictum that theories of language and of economics will prove mutually explanatory..set out *in nuce* much of Lé vi-Strauss's structural anthropology. **1976** G. S. KLEIN *Psychoanal. Theory* 10 Basic tendencies that are often implied in the 'structural point of view' of contemporary psychoanalysis.

b. Special collocations: ***structural analysis***, analysis of a system in terms of its general characteristics or structure; hence ***structural analyst***; ***structural change*** (see quot. 1972); ***structural description*** = ***structural analysis*** above; ***structural-functional*** adj., that takes account of both structure and function; so ***structural-functionalism***, ***-functionalist*** adj. and sb.; ***structural grammar*** (see quot. 1975); ***structural integration***, a technique of deep massage developed by Ida P. Rolf (see ROLF); ***structural linguistics***, the study of a language viewed as a system made up of interrelated elements without regard to their historical development (cf. *descriptive linguistics* s.v. DESCRIPTIVE *a.* 3 b); hence ***structural linguist***; ***structural linguistic*** adj.; ***structural psychology***, an approach to the study of consciousness which relies on the introspective analysis of simple experience into elements; ***structural semantics***, the study of the sense relations that may be established between words or groups of words; hence ***structural semanticist***; ***structural-semantic*** adj.; ***structural unemployment***, unemployment resulting from reorganization in the structure of industry due to technological change, etc., rather than from fluctuations in supply and demand; ***structural word*** = ***empty word*** s.v. EMPTY *a.* and *sb.* C (cf. ***grammatical word*** s.v. GRAMMATICAL *a.* 2; ***structure word*** s.v. STRUCTURE *sb.* 8).

1898 E. B. TITCHENER in *Philos. Rev.* VII. 465, I believe ..that the best hope for psychology lies today in a continuance of structural analysis. **1901** H. OERTEL *Lectures on Study of Lang.* i. 45 We are here concerned with the method only of Humboldt's structural analysis. **1940** *Language* XVI. 216 This is the neglect of the method of structural analysis, i.e. of organized synchronic description. **1974** tr. *Wertheim's Evol. & Revol.* i. 91 Weber's views are more than once mentioned as having paved the way for structural analysis. **1979** F. KERMODE *Genesis of Secrecy* iv. 80 When the structural analysts have done their work, interpretation may take over. **1964** Structural change [see *SC* s.v. S 4a]. **1972** R. A. PALMATIER *Gloss. Eng. Transformational Gram.* 168 *Structural change*.., the generalization of the operation which a particular transformation performs..; the righthand side of a transformational rule. **1964** Structural description [see *SD* s.v. S 4a]. **1977** *Language* LIII. 15 The *ö* of *hösli* was not affected because, after all, phonetically it didn't meet the structural description of Lowering. **1947** T. PARSONS in Parsons & Henderson tr. *Weber's Theory Social & Econ. Organization* 20 A second type [of conceptual scheme].. may be called a generalized structural-functional system. **1977** J. D. DOUGLAS in Douglas & Johnson *Existential Sociol.* i. 6 The classical structural-functional paradigm of social theory grew out of and progressively diverged from this mechanistic model. **1958** *Listener* 28 Aug. 308/1 The first great proponent of structural-functionalism, Radcliffe Brown, failed to get beyond metaphor and analogy when he sought to explain his method. **1977** *Scott. Jrnl. Sociol.* I. 186 A sense that differs both from American structural-functionalism, in which structure is merely descriptive, and from French structuralism, in which it is 'reductive'. **1976** E. LEACH *Culture & Communication* i. 3 Others..offer structural-functionalist explanations. **1977** *Dædalus* Summer 64 Like many structural-functionalists, he regards as unproblematical the processes by which corporations and other 'surface structures' come into existence. **1949** W. O. BIRK (*title*) Structural grammar for building sentences. **1975** *Language for Life* (Dept. Educ. & Sci.) 594 *Structural grammar*, a grammar intended to explain the working of language in terms of the functions of its components and their relationships to each other without reference to meaning. **1963** *Systematics* I. 66 (*heading*) Structural integration. **1975** *Sat. Rev.* (U.S.) 22 Feb. 15/3 The body reformation methods called structural integration (commonly known as rolfing, after its developer Ida Rolf). **1949** *Archivum Linguisticum* I. 1. 89 The functional interpretations of language given by structural linguists are justified. **1951** *Language* XXVII. 8 We must remember the particular attention which structural linguists in the United States have bestowed upon non-culture languages. **1958** *New Statesman* 6 Sept. 288/3 The new advance guard, the Structural Linguists, round on the New Critics as amiable old pipe-smoking fuddy-duddies. **1954** U. WEINREICH in *Word* X. 389 Structural linguistic theory now needs procedures for constructing systems of a higher level out of the discrete and homogeneous systems that are derived from description. **1962** *New Yorker* 10 Mar. 158/2 For the scientific study of language the Structural Linguistic approach is superior to that of the old grammarians. **1940** *Amer. Speech* XV. 438/2 Harris, Zellig S. Rev. of L. H. Gray, Foundations of Language... Some useful remarks on 'structural' linguistics. **1941** A. W. DE GROOT in *Archives Néerlandaises de Phonétique Expérimentale* XVII. 71 (*title*) Structural linguistics and phonetic law. **1945** *Word* I. 58 With structural linguistics as the chief interest of some workers, area may be expected to play a more central role, —to be, in effect, a specialized point of departure. **1948** *Lingua* I. i. 23 'Structural linguistics' is a method, it is not a science and 'structuralism' is nothing but a collective name for general linguistic and explanatory grammatical examination of certain phenomena. **1959** J. C. CATFORD in Quirk & Smith *Teaching of English* vi. 168 Professor Quirk ..is talking about the approach to the scientific study of language which is known as 'structural linguistics'. **1972** D. LODGE *20th Cent. Lit. Crit.* 545 Structural linguistics goes beyond the description of any particular language to pursue the 'deep structures' that are common to all languages. **1898** E. B. TITCHENER in *Philos. Rev.* VII. 449 (*title*) The postulates of a structural psychology. **1933** J. C. FLUGEL *Hundred Yrs. Psychol.* IV. ii. 229 (*heading*) 'Structural' and 'functional' psychology. **1980** J. M. CARROLL (*title*) Toward a structural psychology of cinema. **1973** *Archivum Linguisticum* IV. 67 The structural-semantic category system of Soskin and John (1963). **1977** J. LYONS *Semantics* I. iv. 102 One of the points that Saussure and other structural semanticists have insisted upon is that each language has, not only its own stock of forms, but also its own system of meanings or concepts. **1962** D. H. HYMES in J. A. Fishman *Readings Sociol. of Lang.* (1968) 103 An ethnographic semantics..should be a structural analysis, achieving the economies of the rules of a grammar in relation to a series of analyses of texts. In the past generation Jakobson and his associates have done most to develop such a structural semantics. **1977** J. LYONS *Semantics* ix. 270 From its very beginnings structural semantics..has emphasized the importance of relations of paradigmatic opposition. **1932** A. H. HANSEN *Econ. Stabilization* ix. 148 By structural unemployment..we mean unemployment caused by changes in the structure of industry that are of a nonrecurring type. **1966** *Economist* 29 Jan. 407/2 The boom of the past years has brought jobs for Negroes and for the unskilled, in the teeth of cries that 'automation' and 'structural unemployment' meant that such people had no hope of finding work. **1979** *Guardian* 31 May 735/3 The spectre of 'structural unemployment'—the likelihood that some of today's young people will never have a job. **1940** BRYANT & AIKEN *Psychol. Eng.* iv. 38 A distinction is made between 'full' and 'empty' words, the latter being what are known as 'structural' words. **1966** J. DERRICK *Teaching Eng. to Immigrants* i. 8 If we take our first example again, 'The man is hitting the horse' we find we can substitute any one of a hundred or more different items for the words *man*, *hit* and *horse*... But if we try to do the same thing at one of the other places in the sentence, we find we can only substitute a limited set of words... The words in these places, where the choice is limited, are what writers have called the structural or grammatical words of the language, while the other words have been called content words or lexical items.

c. = STRUCTURALIST 2.

1953 *College Composition & Communication* IV. IV. 124 The structural objection to the traditional use of *language* is that the account of the mechanisms becomes distorted beyond reason. **1959** *Word* XV. 176 The newly established chair of General Linguistics and Phonetics (which was, incidentally, the first structural academic position to be established anywhere).

Hence **ˌstructuˈrality** *rare*$^{-0}$, structural quality or character.

1895 in *Funk's Stand. Dict.* **1909** *Century Dict.* Suppl.

structuralism (ˈstrʌktjʊərəlɪz(ə)m). [f. STRUCTURAL *a.* + -ISM.] **1.** *Psychol.* A method, connected esp. with the American psychologist E. B. Titchener (1867–1927), of investigating the structure of consciousness through the introspective analysis of simple forms of sensation, thought, images, etc.

1907 J. R. ANGELL in *Psychol. Rev.* XIV. 64 If you adopt as your material for psychological analysis the isolated 'moment of consciousness', it is very easy to become so absorbed in determining its constitution as to be rendered.. oblivious to its artificial character. The most essential quarrel which the functionalist has with structuralism.. arises from this fact. **1927** M. BENTLEY in C. Murchison *Psychologies of 1925* 390 However important or trivial we shall find the accomplishments of structuralism to be, we must recognize the gain in clear thinking which accrued to Titchener's sharply drawn distinction between the analytical psychology of structure and the descriptive psychology of mental operation and functional performance. **1930** *Times Lit. Suppl.* 19 Jan. 508/3 Modern schools of psychology, Structuralism, and Functionalism. **1968** *Internat. Encycl. Social Sci.* XV. 610 The movement called 'structuralism' which was founded in Germany by Wilhelm Wundt and transplanted to the United States by Edward B. Titchener of Cornell University.

2. Any theory or method in which a discipline or field of study is envisaged as comprising elements interrelated in systems and structures at various levels, the structures and the interrelations of their elements being regarded as more significant than the elements considered in isolation; also, more recently, theories concerned with analysing the surface structures of a system in terms of its underlying structure.

a. *gen.*

1951 *Mind* L. 270 Braithwaite evidently believes that the whole philosophy of structuralism breaks down over the question of a combining relation. **1968** *Sunday Times* 10 Mar. 52 Structuralism is a technique for analysing any kind of symbolic system. Its break with the past consists in refusing to take note of the appropriateness of symbols for the things they symbolise. **1969** P. ANDERSON in Cockburn & Blackburn *Student Power* 246 Namier's legacy to English historiography was thus inevitably equivocal. His structuralism was rapidly suppressed from memory. **1970** M. LANE *Structuralism* 31 Structuralism, then, is a method whose primary intention is to permit the investigator to go beyond a pure description of what he perceives or experiences..in the direction of the quality of rationality which underlies the social phenomena in which he is concerned. **1971** C. MASCHLER tr. *Piaget's Structuralism* i. 4 We come upon at least two aspects that are common to all varieties of structuralism: first, an ideal..of intrinsic intelligibility supported by the postulate that structures are self-sufficient. **1972** *Sci. Amer.* Sept. 50/3 Structuralism recognizes that information about the world enters the mind not as raw data but as highly abstract structures that are the result of a preconscious set of step-by-step transformations of the sensory input. **1973** *Film Comment* May/June 52/1 In recent years, structuralism and semiology have received much attention as methods for analyzing and interpreting film... Structuralism..attempts to analyze comparatively the deep structures, thus locating those distinctive features common to all of man's cultural and social expressions. **1975** *New Rev.* II. XIV. 55/1 (*title*) Is your structuralism really necessary? *Ibid.* 57/2 Is not the case for temporalism overwhelmingly stronger than the case for structuralism? **1978** *History Workshop* Autumn 3 British Marxist structuralism exalts theoretical practice to the point where it seems to become an end in itself. **1980** *London Rev. Bks.* 15 May 3/2 Structuralism is the philosophy of those in the universities and thereabouts who are not philosophers.

b. *Linguistics.* Applied to theories in which language is considered as a system or structure comprising elements at various phonological, grammatical, and semantic levels, esp. after the work of F. de Saussure (1857–1913).

1945 E. A. CASSIRER in *Word* I. 99 (*title*) Structuralism in modern linguistics. *Ibid.* 104 If the adherents and defenders of the program of linguistic structuralism are right, then we must say that in the realm of language there is no opposition between what is 'formal' and what is merely 'factual'. **1953** A. MARTINET in A. L. Kroeber *Anthropol. Today* 577/1 It would seem that the teaching of Ferdinand de Saussure has, directly or indirectly, influenced most of linguistic structuralism. **1964** *English Studies* XLV (Suppl.). 33 They intend..to stress the importance of semantic studies..(as a necessary counterpart to formal structuralism). **1968** J. LYONS *Introd. Theoret. Linguistics* x. 443 It is one of the cardinal principles of 'structuralism', as developed by de Saussure and his followers, that every linguistic item has its 'place' in a system and its function, or value, derives from the relations which it contracts with other units in the system. **1972** *Language* XLVIII. 419 Structuralism proper in linguistics began with phonology. **1976** *Archivum Linguisticum* VII. 152 With the rise of structuralism, linguistics turned back upon itself, so to say, and tended to abstract away from the social matrix of language.

c. *Anthrop.* and *Sociol.* The theories or methods of analysis concerned with the structure or form of human society or social life; also, following the work of the French anthropologist Claude Lévi-Strauss (b. 1908), theories concerned with the deeper structures of communication from which the surface structures or 'models' evolve.

1955 R. FIRTH in *Jrnl. R. Anthropol. Inst.* LXXXV. 1 All British social anthropologists are structuralists in their use of the analytical principles developed by this method. But the rigidity and limitations of a simple structuralism alone have come to be more widely perceived. **1969** A. G. FRANK *Latin Amer.* (1970) ii. 68 The pioneering service..of those latter students of economic development and cultural change is precisely that they drop all pretense and practice of social scientific structuralism. **1973** J. REX *Discovering Sociol.* ix. 118 French structuralism has to be sharply distinguished from the structuralism of Radcliffe-Brown with which it compares itself, and the structuralism of Simmel and Weber, of which it remains largely ignorant. **1978** J. Z. YOUNG *Programs of Brain* 299/1 *Structuralism*, a movement in social science originated by Claude Lévi-Strauss, which supposes that social structures depend upon certain basic characteristics of human brain programs.

structuralist (ˈstrʌktjʊərəlɪst), *sb.* (and *a.*) *Social Sci.* and *Humanities.* [f. STRUCTURAL *a.* + -IST.] **1.** An advocate or adherent of a structural approach (see STRUCTURAL *a.* 5 a) or of a theory of structuralism.

1907 J. R. ANGELL in *Psychol. Rev.* XIV. 67 Dwelling as the structuralist is supposed to do upon the problem of determining the irreducible elements of consciousness and their characteristic modes of combination. **1922** W. MCDOUGAL in *Amer. Jrnl. Psychiatry* Jan. 347 Mott and the other structuralists..would..dismiss the second alternative with contempt. **1949** *Archivum Linguisticum* I. 184 A survey of post-neogrammarian views on language, viz. those of Saussure..and the Danish 'structuralists'. **1965** *Economist* 25 Sept. p. xxvi/2 Some extreme structuralists argue that demand deflation is actually likely to increase cost inflation.

1975 G. STEINER *After Babel* ii. 83 More than a century before the modern structuralists, Humboldt notes the distinctive binary character of the linguistic process. **1982** *Listener* 18 Nov. 17/2 Structuralists and post-Structuralists maintain that the notion of the author as the creator of his works is merely a modern consolation prize.

2. *attrib.* or as *adj.*

1907 J. R. ANGELL in *Psychol. Rev.* XIV. 62 The most lucid exposition of the structuralist position still remains, so far as I know, Titchener's paper, 'The Postulates of a Structural Psychology'. **1929** W. B. PILLSBURY *Hist. Psychol.* xvi. 271 The structuralist school..holds that consciousness is directly observable and is composed of simple, definitely describable elements. **1955** *Jrnl. R. Anthropol. Inst.* LXXXV. 1 The air of enchantment which for the last two decades has surrounded the 'structuralist' point of view. **1955** *Times* 11 June 5/5 In contrast to much of to-day's painting..which is considered finished when it has reached the stage which, in any other epochs, would have been called the sketch, Structuralist painting is carried to completion in strict obedience to the scientific laws of colour-form structure. **1963** *Indian Econ. Rev.* Feb. 67 The monetarist-structuralist controversy is an argument over the remedy for inflation, the monetarist taking supply as given and recommending a contraction of demand, the structuralist..taking demand as given [etc.]. **1965** N. CHOMSKY *Aspects of Theory of Syntax* ii. 67 Such a system is apparently what is implicit in modern taxonomic ('structuralist') grammars. **1970** J. LYONS *Chomsky* 29 The 'structuralist' approach was by no means confined to Boas and his successors in America. **1970** *Sunday Times* 15 Nov. 32/2 Today when we go to Paris, we can read structuralist novels, look at structuralist paintings and hear structuralist music. Even newspaper cartoons and gourmet meals are subjected to structuralist interpretations. **1976** *Archivum Linguisticum* VII. 152 Even present-day transformational grammar, though quite remote from classical structuralist thought, singles out a 'fluent speaker' set apart from the disturbing influences of social variation. **1979** A. R. PEACOCKE *Creation & World of Science* i. 29 This more narrowly functionalist account of myth has given way, following the lead of Lévi-Strauss, to a 'structuralist' account.

structuralistic (ˌstrʌktjʊərəˈlɪstɪk), *a.* [f. STRUCTURALIST *sb.* + -IC.] Characteristic of a structuralist or of structuralism; structuralist.

1957 H. WHITEHALL in N. Frye *Sound & Poetry* 134 Both criticism and linguistics, in their modern phases, are structuralistic in attitude. **1972** *Jrnl. Social Psychol.* LXXXVII. 37 Mental imagery and image formation have recently become a topic of concern again, after avoidance of such structuralistic phenomena for 50 years or more. **1978** *Studies in Eng. Lit.: Eng. Number* (Tokyo) 134 Her idea of 'structure' is structuralistic, and this is no coincidence.

structuralize (ˈstrʌktjʊərəlaɪz), *v.* [f. STRUCTURAL *a.* + -IZE.] *trans.* = STRUCTURE *v.*; also, to apply structural theories or analysis to (something). So ˌ**structuraliˈzation**; ˈ**structuralized** *ppl. a.*; ˈ**structuralizing** *vbl. sb.*

1936 K. MANNHEIM *Ideology & Utopia* iii. 128 All that has become intelligible, understandable, rationalized, organized, structuralized, artistically, and otherwise formed, and consequently everything historical seems in fact to lie between these two extreme poles. **1953** C. E. BAZELL *Linguistic Form* iii. 29 Distributional criteria seldom provide grounds here for a narrower structuralisation. **1964** H. HARTMANN *Ego Psychol.* iii. 64 Once structuralization has taken place, they [*sc.* ego interests of the id] become partly independent in the service of the ego. **1965** *Canad. Jrnl. Linguistics* Spring 142 Once Kiowa was structuralized, however, it turned out that it made the same distinctions in vowel type that the Tanoan languages made. **1975** *Times Lit. Suppl.* 21 Nov. 1394 (*heading*) Structuralizing in Sumatra. **1977** *Dædalus* Fall 70 Far-reaching changes in the political regimes could affect the functioning of economic institutions and the structuralization of social hierarchies.

structurally (ˈstrʌktjʊərəlɪ), *adv.* [f. STRUCTURAL + -LY².] In structural respects; with regard to structure.

1839 HALLAM *Hist. Lit.* III. iii. §72 We do not know..the entire conditions of organic bodies (even structurally, not as living). **1849** *Sk. Nat. Hist., Mammalia* IV. 165 The Sloths ..are exclusively arboreal;..and for the trees alone are they structurally adapted. **1865** *Daily Tel.* 28 Dec. 5/3 St. Petersburg also is as marvellous a city, structurally speaking, as Amsterdam; its palaces, quays, and arsenals are all built on piles. **1869** *Daily News* 14 Oct., The question as to whether a counting-house which is not structurally severed constitutes a good qualification [to vote as a householder]. **1882** *Macm. Mag.* XLVI. 500 The houses are..structurally defective. **1915** *Edin. Rev.* Jan. 74 Dutch differs little structurally from Low German.

structurate (ˈstrʌktjʊəreɪt), *v. rare.* [f. STRUCTURE *sb.* + -ATE³.] *trans.*

= STRUCTURALIZE *v.* So ˈ**structurated** *ppl. a.*

1937 *Mind* XLVI. 512 The physical sciences are in a happy position, because their numerical world is mathematically structurated. **1978** *Eng. Jrnl.* Dec. 20/1 You say you've been grammaticized, transformalized, and structurated.

structuration (ˌstrʌktjʊəˈreɪʃən). [f. STRUCTURE *v.* + -ATION.] The condition or process of organization in a structural form.

1927 *Brit. Jrnl. Psychol.* XVIII. 6 After many such changes an image may represent a vast structure of meanings, and so 'structuration' may be attributed to it. **1934** *Mind* XLIII. 110 In man the main feature, because the *dynamic* feature, of his development consists in the structuration of his propensities into sentiments. **1952** W. SPROTT *Social Psychol.* iii. 52 All groups..tend towards structuration which is evidenced by..a role system, an ethos, a certain formalization of action-patterns. **1973** A. GIDDENS *Class Struct. Advanced Societies* xi. 201 The influence of paratechnical relations upon working-class structuration. **1973** *Screen* Spring/Summer 11 Semiology opens out that process in its disengagement of the heterogeneity of codes at work in the structuration of film. **1980** *Times Lit. Suppl.* 26 Sept. 1072/1 It might be more appropriate to speak of the differential structuration of life chances as constituting classes.

structure (ˈstrʌktjʊə(r)), *sb.* [ad. L. *structūra*, f. *struct-*, *struĕre* to build: see -URE. Cf. F. *structure*, Sp., Pg. *estructura*, It. *struttura*.]

1. The action, practice, or process of building or construction. Now *rare* or *Obs.*

c **1440** *Pallad. on Husb.* IX. 134 This doon, the sidis [of the tank] make vp with structure [L. *quo facto latera puteorum structura suscipiat*]. **1613** R. C. *Table Alph.* (ed. 3), *Structure*, building, setting in good order. **1624** WOTTON *Elem. Arch.* I. 48 This is yet a weake piece of Structure, because the Supporters are subiect to much impulsion. **1693** J. DRYDEN Jr. tr. *Juvenal* XIV. 116 His Son builds on, and never is content, Till the last Farthing is in Structure spent. *a* **1704** T. BROWN *Praise of Drunkenness* Wks. 1730 I. 32 If we look back into the primitive history of the first ages,.. from the very first structure of the world, we shall find [etc.]. **1726** LEONI *Alberti's Archit., Life* 5 A Florentine, who had worked for him..in the structure of the Choir. **1770** LUCKOMBE *Hist. Printing* 292 Presses of his structure became..general throughout the Low Countries. **1793** SMEATON *Edystone L.* Pref. p. v, A distinct account of the progress and structure of the Edystone Lighthouse. **1844** DISRAELI *Coningsby* VII. iii, The scarcity of brick and stone at the period of its structure.

2. Manner of building or construction; the way in which an edifice, machine, implement, etc. is made or put together.

1650 FULLER *Pisgah* III. ii. 317 The structure of this City was beautifull and high. **1695** tr. *Misson's Voy. Italy* II. 158 The structure of the Cathedral is not much unlike to that of the Church of Siena. **1706** E. WARD *Wooden World Diss.* (1708) 72 He can spy out the Faults in the Structure of a Boat, sooner than those of himself. **1772** PENNANT *Tours Scot.* (1774) 1 Chester; a city without parallel for the singular structure of the four principal streets, which are as if excavated out of the earth. **1826** *Art Brewing* (ed. 2) 149 There are variations in the structure of these mills—some are worked by hand, others by horse and water. **1837** CARLYLE *Fr. Rev.* II. III. iv, They..show purchased dirks, of an improved structure, made to order. **1908** *Animal Managem.* (War Office) 176 In speaking of the structure of the saddle.

3. The mutual relation of the constituent parts or elements of a whole as determining its peculiar nature or character; make, frame.

a. *gen.*

1615 CHAPMAN *Odyss.* IV. 1075 An Idoll, that Iphthima did present In structure of her euery lineament [*marg.* δεμας membrorum structura]. **1657** J. COOKE *Hall's Cures Englisht* 203 My Lady Rainsford beautifull and of a gallant structure of body. **1725** DE FOE *Voy. round World* (1840) 262 The admirable structure of this part of the Country. **1757** R. PRICE *Review Morals* i. (1769) 13 Then..it [morality] has no other measure or standard, besides every one's private structure of mind and sensations. **1774** GOLDSM. *Nat. Hist.* I. 51 Of the internal Structure of the Earth. **1803** BROUGHAM *Colon. Policy* I. 50 The structure of society..is the same in all those settlements. **1814** BREWSTER in *Phil. Trans.* CIV. 438 The interior part of the drop had a structure similar to that of fluid glass. **1839** CARLYLE *Chartism* iii. (1858) 12 With a feeling of thankfulness rather that there do exist men of that structure too. **1872** MORLEY *Voltaire* (1886) 2 Men.. became conscious of new fibre in their moral structure. **1880** HAUGHTON *Phys. Geog.* ii. 20 The structure of the Southern Hemisphere.

b. *Anat.*, *Biol.*, etc.

1615 H. CROOKE *Body of Man* VIII. iv. (1631) 730 Of the Vse, Figure and Structure of the Hand. **1725** N. ROBINSON *Th. Physick* 49 This imperfect Sketch,..concerning the Structure, Mechanism, Laws, Properties, and Motions of that System of Matter, that compose a human Body. **1774** GOLDSM. *Nat. Hist.* VIII. 11 Many philosophers..have.. minutely examined their [*sc.* caterpillars'] structure and internal conformation. **1814** SIR H. DAVY *Agric. Chem.* 56 Every plant examined as to external structure, displays at least four systems of organs. **1835** J. DUNCAN *Beetles* (Nat. Libr.) 142 An exotic group, very closely related to the Gyrini, but offering so many minute modifications of structure as to warrant their separation into a distinct genus. **1859** DARWIN *Orig. Spec.* v. (1873) 114 Variations of structure arising in the young or larvæ naturally tend to affect the structure of the mature animal. **1884** BOWER & SCOTT *De Bary's Phaner.* 88 The secretion of dermal glands ..always appears first in the walls of the cells, and gives them a peculiar structure.

c. *Geol.*, *Min.*, etc.

1813 BAKEWELL *Introd. Geol.* (1815) 27 Fragments of stone broken from simple rocks display the structure of the internal parts. **1822** CLEAVELAND *Min. & Geol.* (ed. 2) I. 58 The structure of a mineral undoubtedly depends on the shape, size, and arrangement of the minute parts, of which it is composed. **1879** A. GEIKIE in *Encycl. Brit.* X. 229/1 There are two leading types of structure among rocks— crystalline or massive, and fragmental.

d. With reference to a literary composition, a verse or sentence, a language, etc.

1746 FRANCIS tr. *Hor., Epist.* I. xix. 37, I fear'd to change the Structure of his Line. **1749** *Power & Harmony Prosaic Numbers* Pref. 3 A critical Regard to the Structure of their Periods. **1789** *New Lond. Mag.* July 361/1 A new farce..was presented last Saturday at this theatre. The structure is light and pleasant. **1814** KEBLE *Occas. Papers* (1877) 154 There remain two sorts of imitation instrumental to Poetry: indirect, by which the style and structure takes the colour of the subject; and direct. **1823** THOMASINA ROSS *Bouterwek's Hist. Sp. Lit.* I. 260 Combining the unity of ideas, which ought to distinguish that species of composition [*sc.* the sonnet], with the most elegant rounding and regularity of structure. **1833** J. RUSH *Philos. Human Voice* xlv. (ed. 2) 313 When the structure of a sentence is so much involved as to produce a momentary hesitation in an audience, about its concord or government. **1857** J. D. MORELL *Gram. Engl. Lang.* 49 The Structure of Words. 1. Roots and Derivatives. **1862** STANLEY *Jew. Ch.* (1877) I. xix. 371 The Apocalypse is ..thoroughly poetical in structure. **1887** *Spectator* 23 July 996/1 The story itself is in structure extremely simple.

(*b*) *spec.* in *Linguistics.* ***deep structure***: see DEEP *a.* IV. c; ***surface structure***: see SURFACE *sb.* 6 d.

1961 Y. OLSSON *On Syntax Eng. Verb* ii. 27 Both collocation and colligation operate syntagmatically... They are examples of *structures* constituted by *elements.* **1965** *Language* XLI. 73 The nested structures are phrase types which are in clear structural contrast in the language.

4. The coexistence in a whole of distinct parts having a definite manner of arrangement.

1873 SPENCER *Study Sociol.* iii. (1880) 63 Though structure up to a certain point [in the animal organism] is requisite for growth, structure beyond that point impedes growth. **1876** [see STRUCTURE *v.*].

5. *concr.* That which is built or constructed.

a. A building or edifice of any kind, esp. a pile of building of some considerable size and imposing appearance.

1615 BRATHWAIT *Strappado* 104 Her structures ruin'd are, and there doth grow, A groue of fatall Elmes. **1631** WEEVER *Anc. Funeral Mon.* 707 The bodies..were buried in the Abbey Church,..in Saint Peters, and in other religious Structures. **1664** H. MORE *Myst. Iniq.* 297 Dilichius..not onely mentions the seven Hills, but tells also what magnificent structures stand upon them. **1739** GRAY *Let.* Poems (1775) 69 A church..which is, indeed, a most stately structure. **1818** BYRON *Ch. Har.* IV. i, I saw from out the wave her structures rise As from the stroke of the enchanter's wand. **1853** PHILLIPS *Rivers Yorks.* viii. 202 Of these humble structures we have only the foundations. **1879** TOURGEE *Fool's Errand* viii. 34 This log house had in time given way to a more pretentious structure of brick.

transf. **1671** MILTON *Samson* 1239 [Spoken to the giant Harapha.] Go baffl'd coward, lest I run upon thee,..And with one buffet lay thy structure low.

b. *fig.*

1637 SALTONSTALL *Eusebius' Constantine* 49 Your contentions doe arise from points not concerning the maine structure of Religion. **1660** R. COKE *Power & Subj.* 269 The whole structure of his *civitas* might bee dissolved. **1694** PRIOR *Hymn to Sun* viii, Eternal Structures let Them raise, On William's and Maria's Praise: Nor want new Subject for the Song. **1892** WESTCOTT *Gospel of Life* 256 Christianity.. is not a structure of institutions.

c. Buildings collectively.

1671 MILTON *P.R.* III. 286 Ecbatana her structure vast there shews.

6. In a wider sense: A fabric or framework of material parts put together.

1677 T. JORDAN *Lond. Triumphs* title-p., Illustrated with many Magnificent Structures & Pageants. **1728** POPE *Dunc.* I. 247 Then [he] lights the structure with averted eyes, The rolling smoke involves the sacrifice. **1788** COWPER *Gratitude* 25 This moveable structure of shelves,..charg'd with octavos and twelves. **1841** WHEWELL *Mech. Engin.* 1 Combinations of material parts,..when constructed with a view to support weights, or to resist forces, without being moved,..are termed Structures. *Ibid.* 51 Structures are of various kinds, as Frames, which have their parts connected by pins or mortises; and Arches, in which the parts are connected only by contact. **1883** W. J. M. RANKINE in *Encycl. Brit.* XV. 750/1 The principles of the support of a floating structure form an important part of Hydromechanics.

7. An organized body or combination of mutually connected and dependent parts or elements. Chiefly in *Biol.*, applied to component parts of an animal or vegetable organism.

1830 J. G. STRUTT *Sylva Brit.* 6 Each stage of the existence of these wonderful vegetable structures. **1859** DARWIN *Orig. Spec.* vi. (1873) 140 When we see any structure highly perfected for any particular habit, as the wings of a bird for flight. **1876** SPENCER *Princ. Sociol.* §254 (1885) I. 526 The general law of organization..is that distinct duties entail distinct structures. **1882** VINES tr. *Sachs' Bot.* 1 The substance of plants is not homogeneous, but is composed of small structures, generally indistinguishable by the naked eye... These structures are termed Cells.

8. *attrib.* and *Comb.* ***structure-dependence***, ***dependency***, ***formula***, ***mill***, ***sensitivity***; ***structure-borne***, ***-dependent***, ***-independent***, ***-sensitive***, etc. adjs.; **structure-function** *attrib. phr.*, pertaining to both structure and function; **structure plan** *Local Government*, a plan drawn up by a local planning authority for the development, use, conservation, etc., of a prescribed area of land; hence **structure planning**, the preparation of such a plan; **structure word** = *structural word* s.v. STRUCTURAL *a.* 5 b.

1962 A. NISBETT *Technique Sound Studio* ii. 38 Structure-borne noises are almost impossible to eliminate and rebuilding work is complicated by the need to avoid all noisy work when nearby studios are recording. **1972** *Lebende Sprachen* XVII. 37/2 *Structure-borne noise*, a condition when the sound waves are being carried by a solid material. **1976** N. CHOMSKY *Reflections on Lang.* I. i. 33 The principle of structure-dependence is not learned, but forms part of the conditions for language learning. **1976** *Times Lit. Suppl.* 17 Dec. 1590/4 By structure dependency he [*sc.* Chomsky] means, and I mean, that the significance of any feature is determined by its position in a structure. **1965** Structure-dependent [see ANALYSABILITY]. **1978** *Logophile* VIII. 5/2 All syntactic operations in language are structure-dependent. **1879** *Amer. Jrnl. Sci.* May 405 On the Structure-formulas of Aromatic Compounds. **1963** *Canad. Jrnl. Linguistics* VIII. 59 (*heading*) A structure-function description of Terena phrases. **1977** *Dædalus* Fall 115 For the moment I want to draw the kind of structure-function distinction we might adopt, say, in discussing walking: what it is versus where it might take you. **1964** E. A. Power *Introd. Quantum Electrodynamics* i. 5 Also even the structure-independent radiation damping term depends on the arrow sign of time—unlike the fundamental equations themselves—because in calculating the radiation field boundary conditions at infinite time are involved. **1976** N. Chomsky *Reflections on Lang.* I. i. 33 Construct a structure-dependent rule, ignoring all structure-independent rules. **1860** Tyndall *Glac.* II. xxvii. 386 All the ice that forms the lower portion of this glacier has to pass through the structure-mill at the bottom of the fall, and the consequence is that it is all laminated. **1971** *Act 19 & 20 Eliz. II* c. 78 §7 The local planning authority shall..prepare and send the Secretary of State..a structure plan for their area. **1980** *Oxford Times* 12 Dec. 10/4 Policy E1 of the Structure Plan says that the Council will restrain growth of employment in the county as a whole. **1973** *Times* 8 Sept. 14/6 He made it plain that he did not expect an end to the structure planning process, the framework for regulating development which every local planning authority is expected to prepare. **1976** *Alyn & Deeside Observer* 10 Dec. 16/1 The strange spectacle of two Conservative councils locked in a fierce exchange over structure planning. **1936** *Jrnl. R. Aeronaut. Soc.* XL. 593 The strength of a crystal across a crystal plane is a structure-sensitive property. **1970** *Language* XLVI. 261 We demonstrate the use of transformational rules applied to the output of structure-free grammars as a means of generating symmetrical strings which are not only structure-sensitive but context-sensitive as well. **1976** *Times Lit. Suppl.* 17 Dec. 1590/4 My emphasis on structure sensitivity in 'natural' situations leads me to look for leads in linguistics. **1897** Mary Kingsley *W. Africa* 670 They..turn it bodily over and over, with structure-straining bumps to the boat, and any amount of advice..to each other. **1956** *Publ. Amer. Dial. Soc.* XXVI. 59 A listing by parts of speech brings out the numerical superiority of nouns, and the relatively small number of structure words borrowed. **1965** Structure-word [see functor 2].

structure (ˈstrʌktjʊə(r)), *v.* [f. prec. sb.: not common until the 20th c.]

a. *trans.* To build or form into a structure; to organize the parts or elements of (something) in structural form. Also, to establish a hierarchy of relationships or a pattern in (something). Hence *absol.* and *loosely*, to construct, form, or organize. So **ˈstructuring** *ppl. a.*

a **1693** *Urquhart's Rabelais* III. xliv. 361 In which dangerous Opposition, Equity and Justice being structured and founded on either of the opposite Terms, and a Gap being thereby opened for the ushering in of Injustice and Iniquity. **1876** Spencer *Princ. Sociol.* §186. (1885) I. 365 What degree of likeness can we find between a man and a mountain?..the one has little internal structure, and that irregular, the other is elaborately structured internally in a definite way. **1933** *Mind* XLII. 176 It is the architectonic (supreme and structuring) principle or spirit regulating in their mutual relations all other structuring activities. **1949** M. Mead *Male & Female* xv. 296 This has been an accurate picture of the way in which we have structured our society, with women as keepers of the house.., and men as keepers of women in the house. **1955** Auden *Shield of Achilles* I. 16 When, on some windless day Of dejection, unable To name or to structure. **1960** L. Pincus *Marriage* III. 221 An inhibited response structured by..these unconscious dilemmas. **1962** *Amer. Speech* XXXVII. 107 Bloomfield.. calls /r/ a 'vocaloid' and says it may be syllabic..but he has it function as a consonant when structuring the final consonant clusters of English. **1971** *Sci. Amer.* Aug. 91/1 Input/Output tables provide management..with a powerful new tool for forecasting and measuring the indirect as well as the direct inter-industry relationships that structure our industrial economy. **1974** R. Helms *Tolkien's World* v. 98 The parallel plot-lines of Book III..are both structured by the laws of providential control and of the cause-and-effect morality. **1978** *Guardian Weekly* 10 Sept. 17/4 A secret study memorandum..which helped structure Carter's decision last month to use trade restrictions. **1979** *Nature* 23 Aug. 652/1 The chemical exchanges among uplands, marshes and coastal waters are important in structuring these ecosystems.

b. To give (someone or something) a place in a structure; to absorb or integrate into a pattern or system.

1954 J. A. C. Brown *Social Psychol. Industry* vi. 174 Aggressiveness as a response to this has become structured into his basic personality. **1955** C. Cherry in B. I. Evans *Stud. in Communication* iii. 60 The individuals were to be structured into social coherence. **1959** M. Dolinsky *There is no Silence* iii. 44 You don't easily structure the unusual or the exotic. **1977** A. Giddens *Stud. in Social & Polit. Theory* i. 70 Criticism thus cannot be terminated within the sphere of science itself, but must concern itself with the standards or values which structure science as one mode of activity among others.

c. To present or manipulate (a situation, etc.) in such a way as to elicit desired responses or effects.

1966 *Listener* 10 Mar. 342/2 Parents who are trying to train their children make use of verbal explanations to structure the situation. **1971** J. B. Carroll et al. *Word Freq. Bk.* p. ix, His assistance was also essential in..structuring the survey to reflect curriculum divisions and publications diversity. **1973** *Howard Jrnl.* XIII. 282 Treatment..is a matter of so structuring the environment..that aversive consequences..follow unwanted or undesirable behaviour. **1975** *Language for Life* (Dept. Educ. & Sci.) x. 145 He must structure the learning so that the child becomes positively aware of the need for a complicated utterance.

ˈstructured, *ppl. a.* [f. structure *v.* + ed¹.]

1. That possesses structure or organization.

1873 Spencer in *Contemp. Rev.* XXII. 328 The changes by which this structureless mass becomes a structured mass. **1929** A. N. Whitehead *Process & Reality* 138 The enduring object..may be conceived as independent of the structured society. **1940** C. S. Sherrington *Man & his Nature* xi. 353 There is the difficulty that the outward process on analysis proves always to be 'granular', quantal, 'structured'; the inner process to be structureless, non-quantal. **1962** H. A. Gleason in Householder & Saporta *Problems in Lexicography* 91 Occasionally sets of language phenomena are observed which, though apparently structured, seem not to be so rigorously structured as this. **1968** *Guardian* 12 June 8/4 The taking of hallucinogenic drugs, where the objective is..to erase the influence of structured experience and organisation of perceptual material in order to explore some kind of world beyond the structures. **1980** P. Hill *Savages* iii. 46 The boys are not criminals... They need a structured group, a sense of belonging.

2. a. Organized or arranged so as to produce a desired result. Also *loosely*, formal, organized, not haphazard.

1959 *Listener* 17 Dec. 1079/1 The use of measured or structured arguments to get at the causes of such interesting phenomena as millionaires or strikes. **1968** *Brit. Med. Bull.* XXIV. 189/2 The computer can accept data only in a highly structured (digital) form. **1975** *Language for Life* (Dept. Educ. & Sci.) v. 59 In certain cases the object was to equip the mother with the ability to work through a structured programme with her child. **1976** *Ann. Rep. Manpower Services Comm. 1975–76* iv. 30/1 The review is intended to provide a framework within which choices can be made and resources allocated in a more structured way. **1977** *Cornish Times* 19 Aug. 8/7 It will provide all learning opportunities through the medium of formal teaching processes, planned excursions, structured and unstructured play and recreational experiences.

b. Of a computer program: organized in a logical way to facilitate debugging and modification; *spec.* composed of linked but distinct modules each having one entry point and one exit point, so that the program may be read straight through; so ***structured programming*** vbl. sb.

1966 *Information Processing 1965* II. 448/1 (*heading*) On solving large structured programs. **1972** *Bit* XII. I. 38 (*heading*) An experiment in structured programming. **1974** D. D. McCracken *Simplified Guide to Fortran Programming* vi. 110 This makes it possible to write the program without a go to... This..is one aspect of structured programming, which holds great promise of converting programming from a hit-or-miss craft into an engineering science. **1978** L. A. Leventhal *Introd. Microprocessors* vi. 250 In structured programming only single logic structures are used. Bohm and Jacopini showed that any program could be written by using only three structures. 1. A sequential structure... 2. A conditional structure of the if-then-else type... 3. A loop structure of the do-while type... The computer executes P repeatedly as long as A is true. **1983** *Personal Computer World* Sept. 216/2 If a program is badly structured..altering one part of the program may have unforeseen effects in a completely different part.

structuredness (ˈstrʌktjʊədnɪs). [f. structured *ppl. a.* + -ness.] The quality of being structured.

1966 S. Beer *Decision & Control* xiv. 350 He refers to the gain in structured-ness that accompanies the entropy change in a biological system as a gain in the *maturity* of that system. **1970** *Jrnl. Gen. Psychol.* July 69 The tasks of the Wechsler..are not composed of stimuli all of the same high degree of structuredness. **1974** *Lang. Sciences* Aug. 27/2, I am personally convinced that the focus on structuredness has been and will be as heuristic..in semantics as it has been in phonology and grammar. **1977** *Lancet* 22 Jan. 172/1 The data are too few at present to indicate whether the use of H.C.G. in addition to myelin or cancer basic protein will significantly improve the specificity of the M.E.M. test and the related test for the 'structuredness of cytoplasmic matrix' as means for detecting the presence of malignant disease.

structureless (ˈstrʌktjʊəlɪs), *a.* [f. structure *sb.* + -less.] Lacking organic structure.

1847–9 W. H. Walshe in *Todd's Cycl. Anat.* IV. 104/1 Granular matter lying in a structureless substance. **1856** Ruskin *Mod. Paint.* IV. v. xiii. §4 That structureless and massive rock which we have characterized by the term 'compact crystalline'. **1879** *Haeckel's Evol. Man* II. xv. 33 It is only in the case of Monera,—of structureless organizations without organs—that we can assume the hypothesis of spontaneous generation. **1896** *Tablet* 1 Feb. 161 The structureless creed of the Board schools.

Hence **ˈstructurelessness**.

1859 Huxley in *Todd's Cycl. Anat.* V. 476/1 The structurelessness of a homogeneous membrane. **1892** *Nation* (N.Y.) 7 Apr. 263/1 It is a fact which absolutely overthrows the whole theory of poetic structure or structurelessness implied in Whitman's volumes.

structurely (ˈstrʌktjʊəlɪ), *adv. rare*⁻¹. [badly f. structure *sb.* + -ly².] = structurally.

1867 Spencer *Princ. Biol.* §181. II. 14 These aggregates of the lowest order, each formed of physiological units united into a group that is structurely single, and cannot be divided without destruction of its individuality.

structurer (ˈstrʌktjʊərə(r)). *rare.* [f. structure *v.* + -er¹.] An architect, a builder or constructor.

1755 T. H. Croker *Orl. Fur.* xxxiv. liii, Stupendous work! Dedalian structurer, With us, what fabrick can to this aspire?

ˈstructuring, *vbl. sb.* [f. structure *v.* + -ing¹.] The action of the verb.

1951 M. McLuhan *Mech. Bride* (1967) 77/1 The emotional structuring which results..from affection that is tendered or withdrawn. **1958** *New Scientist* 25 Sept. 887/2 While apes and infants struggle towards some sort of structure-formation, the human artist of today struggles to free himself from all structuring or imagery. **1962** H. A. Gleason in Householder & Saporta *Problems in Lexicography* 92 Crossing grammatical structure in various ways are..other types of structurings, some of them, at least, so different in form as to be unrecognizable as structure by the methods of descriptive linguistics. **1965** H. I. Ansoff *Corporate Strategy* (1968) i. 19 One part of the administrative problem is concerned with organization: structuring of authority and responsibility relationships, work flows, information flows, [etc.]. **1970** T. Lupton *Managem. & Social Sci.* (ed. 2) ii. 35 The factors which influence the structuring of social relationships. **1977** M. Edelman *Polit. Lang.* v. 92 This kind of cognitive structuring exemplifies the selective perception of information to reinforce established beliefs. **1980** *Amer. Speech* LV. 42 A toponymic dialect would be shaped..also by other important factors:..by the structuring of onomastic fields.., by the sequence of naming, [etc.].

structurism (ˈstrʌktjʊərɪz(ə)m). [f. structure *sb.* + -ism.] The artistic theory or practice of a structurist (sense 2).

1963 *New Republic* 16 Feb. 26/3 Biederman..has written several books expounding Structurism as a future imperative. **1965** *Minneapolis Tribune* 21 Mar. (Arts Sect.) 1/4 His work evolved into the painted aluminium reliefs that represent his latest effort. These carried him through an attitude called constructionism to structurism. **1970** *Time* 26 Jan. 37 Biederman himself, having grandly declared that both painting and sculpture were obsolete, arrived at what he has come to call 'structurism'—reliefs that have the dimension of sculpture and the color of painting. **1973** *Phaidon Dict. Twentieth Cent. Art* 35/1 Biederman rejected Constructivism and termed his 'new art' Structurism—three-dimensional constructions in which small single-coloured rectangles are placed on a solid-coloured background, at right angles to the background and to each other.

structurist (ˈstrʌktjʊərɪst), *sb.* (and *a.*) [f. structure *sb.* + -ist.] **1.** A builder. *rare.*

1860 Worcester (citing *N. Brit. Rev.*).

2. An artist whose work emphasizes underlying structural forms and processes in nature; applied esp. to the U.S. artist Charles Biederman (b. 1906) and by him to earlier artists in whose work he perceived this tendency. Also *attrib.* or as *adj.*

1958 C. Biederman *New Cézanne* viii. 61 Monet alone is the great Structurist innovator for the 19th century. It is Cézanne who is the great Structurist innovator for the 20th century! *Ibid.* 77 The genuine Structurist is indifferent to the slick materials of industry. **1959** —— in *Structure* 2nd Ser. I. 16/1 Artists no longer found their art but only their method of art, not in the creations but only in the creative method of nature's structural process. I call this the Structurist direction of art. **1960** *Guardian* 2 Feb. 7/5 The post-cubist collage-makers and other pioneer abstract 'structurists'. **1967** *Times* 17 Mar. 12/5 The trustees [of the Tate Gallery] have also recently acquired 'Structurist Relief. Red Wing No. 20' 1954–65, by Charles Biederman. *Ibid.* Biederman's 'structurist' work developed from a study of Mondrian. **1970** *Sat. Rev.* (U.S.) 17 Oct. 54 He and others 'in curriculum development and teacher training have been guilty for years of structuring canvases and of choosing the brushes and paints'. And yet how many structurists are willing to abandon that on which they depend? **1976** J. van der Marck in *Charles Biederman* (Minneapolis Inst. Arts) 64 That gradual development, from the simple to the complex, which is a tenet of the Structurist philosophy.

structurization (ˌstrʌktjʊəraɪˈzeɪʃən). [f. structure *sb.* + -ization.] The process of giving a structure to something or of arranging material into an organized pattern.

1950 *Brit. Jrnl. Psychol.* Dec. 129 Do [rumours]..take their origin almost wholly from 'within' the mind... Or do they arise as 'constructions' or structurizations of the stimulus situation, produced by the peculiar attitude, which itself was formed under the influence of the special situation of a crisis? **1955** H. Read *Icon & Idea* iii. 60 Then, on the basis of this symbolic activity and of intuitive thought generally, a representational structurization of space becomes possible. **1958** C. Biederman *New Cézanne* viii. 62 Having failed, out of fear of the consequences of Cézanne's geometrical structurizations, they [*sc.* the Cubists] now switched their attention to the surface aspects of Cézanne. **1969** *New Scientist* 6 Nov. 304/3 For him [*sc.* Grèco],..the concept of structure and the process of structurization..are essential for the understanding of human intelligence.

structurize (ˈstrʌktjʊəraɪz), *v.* [f. structure *sb.* + -ize.] *trans.* To give a structure to (something), to organize structurally.

1958 C. Biederman *New Cézanne* iv. 37 The brush stroke structurizes color. *Ibid.* 48 Art is now directed towards a 'constant reality', structurized by 'constant relationships'. **1968** *Times* 18 Dec. 9 Research capacities are being structurized to the optimum in every single economic branch in order to meet the country's requirements of the scientific and technological revolution.

[**strude,** erroneous f. stud *sb.* (stock of mares).

1702 J. K. *New Eng. Dict.*; and in later Dicts.]

strudel (struːd(ə)l, ‖ʃtruːdəl). [a. Ger., lit. 'eddy, whirlpool'.] A baked sweet of Austrian origin, made of very thin layers of pastry with a filling, usu. of fruit. Also used *attrib.* to denote the kind of dough or pastry used in such confections. ***apfelstrudel***, ***apple strudel***: see apple *sb.* B. II.

1893 *Encycl. Pract. Cookery* II. 525/2 *Strudels*, a kind of pancake or fritter made in Germany. **1903** *Jewish Encycl.* IV. 257/2 The *strudel*, or single-layered jelly or fruit cake, takes the place of the pie for dessert. **1915** L. Kander *'Settlements' Cook Book* (ed. 7) xxi. 251 Prepare Strudel dough,..fill with kraut and other above ingredients. **1923**, etc. [see *apple strudel* s.v. APPLE *sb.* B. II]. **1932** [see LEKACH]. **1941** B. SCHULBERG *What Makes Sammy Run?* ix. 225 *Strudel*,.. still hot... Sammele used to say I made the best *strudel* in the whole world. **1950** *Here & Now* (N.Z.) Dec. 26/1 Whether visitors to Vienna went to the big expensive hotels..or ordered a quick meal in a coffee-house..they always kept haunting memories of *schnitzels, strudels* and cakes. **1960** [see SCHNITZEL]. **1972** F. B. MAYNARD *Raisins & Almonds* 31 She was baking while I watched..the miracle of the strudel. **1981** *Times* 19 Mar. 8/6 Feta cheese and phyllo or strudel pastry are..sold in shops specializing in Greek or Cypriot foods.

strue, obs. variant of STROY *v.*

'strue (struː), schoolboy's abbrev. of CONSTRUE *v.* and *sb.*

1903 FARMER & HENLEY *Slang* VII. 14/2 *Strue*, verb, (schools'), 'construe'. **1906** D. COKE *Bending of Twig* viii. 122 But mind, you've promised to sap out the 'strues, and 'strue them to me. *Ibid.* 125 Russell..made Lycidas extend his 'struing services to six more mornings' work.

struggle ('strʌg(ə)l), *sb.* Also 8 **strugle.** [f. STRUGGLE *v.*]

1. a. An act of struggling; a resolute contest, whether physical or otherwise; a continued effort to resist force or free oneself from constraint; a strong effort under difficulties.

1692 LOCKE *Consid. Lower. Interest* 115 The usual struggle and contest, as I said before,..is between the Landed Man and the Merchant. [Cf. *supra* 114 This pulling and contest is usually between the Landed Man and the Merchant.] *a* **1716** SOUTH *Serm.* (1727) VI. 180 Every Verse ..speaking nothing but the Horrors of an ungodly Soul, and the Struggles and Agonies of one sinking under the dismal Apprehensions of the divine Wrath. **1772** *Junius Lett.* lxviii. 341 There was a constant struggle between the legislature and the officers of justice. **1798** T. MORTON *Speed the Plough* v. i. (1800) 64 'Tis hard for the heart to forego, without one struggle, its only hope of happiness. **1827** SCOTT *Highl. Widow* v, Her demand was never refused, though granted in many cases with a kind of struggle between compassion and aversion. **1833** *Q. Rev.* XLIX. 407 These feather-weights.. sometimes ride a winning race; though if it comes to a struggle, as the term is, they are almost certain to be defeated by the experienced jockey. **1840** HOOD *Up Rhine* 217 The man..seized hold of the child's clothes in a very rough manner. A struggle immediately took place between the officer and the woman. **1849** MACAULAY *Hist. Eng.* vi. II. 159 The struggle which patriotism had for a time maintained against bigotry in the royal mind was at an end. **1867** RUSKIN *Time & Tide* i. §1 The immediate struggle between the system of co-operation and the system of mastership. **1918** *Times Lit. Suppl.* 28 Mar. 149/2 Zarathustra..anticipated that the final eschatologic struggle was at hand, when the sovereignty..of Ahura would be established.

b. A strong effort to continue to breathe, as in the death-agony or under conditions tending to produce suffocation.

1794 MRS. RADCLIFFE *Myst. Udolpho* vii, St. Aubert expired without a struggle or a sigh. **1809** *Med. Jrnl.* XXI. 138 This event [death] sometimes takes place..in a placid manner, without any struggle, and not unfrequently with a smile on the countenance. **1842** LOVER *Handy Andy* xi, Suddenly whipping the fish over the side into the boat, he began flapping it about as if it were plunging in the death struggle. **1845** J. COULTER *Adv. Pacific* vii. 87 [The whale] turned over in a few minutes without a struggle. **1854** SURTEES *Handley Cr.* i. (1901) I. 11 He died at the good old age of eighty without a groan or struggle. **1915** J. S. HALDANE in *Times* 29 Apr. 9/6 These men were lying struggling for breath... There was nothing to account for the..struggle for air, but the one fact that they were suffering from acute bronchitis.

†**c.** A conflict between material agents; *spec.* effervescence. (Cf. STRUGGLING *vbl. sb.* 2.) *Obs.*

1741 P. SHAW tr. *Boerhaave's Chem.* (ed. 2) I. 539 These salts rest after complete saturation, and then produce no struggle, upon the addition either of an alkali or an acid salt to the saturated mixture. **1796** KIRWAN *Elem. Min.* (ed. 2) I. 12 With magnesia it [*sc.* argill] can have no struggle. **1815** J. SMITH *Panorama Sci. & Art* II. 253 The earth, when dry, is a bad conductor, and will not receive the electricity from the clouds without a struggle.

d. *struggle for existence, for life*: in *Biology* used metaphorically to describe the relation between coexisting organic species when the causes tending to the survival of one tend to the extinction of another. Also *gen.*, an effort under difficulties to obtain the means of livelihood; a continued resistance to influences threatening destruction or extinction.

a **1827** in J. B. NORTON *Topics* (1858) 214 Madras..rose amidst poverty and many struggles for existence. **1832** LYELL *Princ. Geol.* II. 56 In the universal struggle for existence, the right of the strongest eventually prevails; and the strength and durability of a race depends mainly on its prolificness, in which hybrids are acknowledged to be deficient. **1859** DARWIN *Orig. Spec.* v. (1873) 118 In the struggle for life to which every animal is exposed, each would have a better chance of supporting itself, by less nutriment being wasted. **1875** JOWETT *Plato* (ed. 2) IV. 406 The struggle for existence is not confined to the animals, but appears in the kingdom of thought.

2. In generalized sense: Contention, determined effort or resistance.

1706 SIR D. HUME *Diary Parl. Scot.* (Bannatyne Club) 189 The Parliament..proceeded, and with very little struggle, approved Articles 9.-13. **1714** FORTESCUE-ALAND *Fortescue's Abs. & Lim. Mon.* Pref. 28 King John, after much struggle with his Barons, swears to restore the good Laws of his Ancestors. **1748** RICHARDSON *Clarissa* (1768) VIII. 138 A conscience, that is upon the struggle with thee, and like a cunning wrestler watches its opportunity to give thee another fall. **1833** HT. MARTINEAU *Briery Creek* iv. 89 Not only of week-day labour, but of struggle for subsistence. **1837** CARLYLE *Fr. Rev.* III. VI. i, Jacobinism is in uttermost crisis and struggle. **1879** JENNIE YOUNG *Ceramic Art* 276 After fifteen or sixteen years of unheard-of struggle and misery, this indomitable genius [Palissy] produced the long-sought enamel. **1881** P. BROOKS *Candle of the Lord* 353 Not till you make men..intelligent, and fond of struggle,..not till then have you relieved poverty. **1901** WATTS-DUNTON *Aylwin* Introd., Speculations..upon the gravest of all subjects—the subject of love at struggle with death.

3. *Comb.*, as **struggle-buggy** *U.S. slang*, a motor vehicle; *spec.* an old and battered one; **struggle meeting**, [tr. Chinese *dòuzhēng huì*], in Communist China: a meeting at which those who have aroused official or public disfavour are criticized or denounced.

1925 *College Humor* Sept. 20/2 I'll say you can park in my struggle buggy. **1946** Struggle-buggy [see RINKY-DINK *a.*]. **1966** F. SCHURMANN *Ideology & Organization in Communist China* v. 318 'Struggle meetings' were held throughout China in which offending cadres were attacked, and by mass demand removed from office. **1973** *Times* 21 Mar. (China Trade Suppl.) p. viii/5 Officials who have been through 'struggle meetings', because they were considered to be bureaucratic..are likely to be sufficiently shaken by the experience to avoid arousing such resentments in the future.

struggle ('strʌg(ə)l), *v.* Forms: 4-5 **strogel,** 5 **strogolyn, strogil (strokel),** 6 **strog(g)ell, stroggle,** 4-6 **strogle, strougle,** 4-7 **strugle, struggel,** 6- **struggle.** [ME. *strugle, strogel,* etc., a frequentative formation of obscure origin.

According to Skeat the root is that of ON. *strúg-r*, MSw. *strūgh-er*, ill will, Sw. dial. *strug*, contention, strife, reluctance, *struug*, revengeful, Norw. *stru*, refractory, Da. dial. *struende*, reluctantly. On this assumption, however, the formation of the ME. verb still requires explanation; there is no evidence of a Scandinavian type **struggla*. Others regard the word as cogn. w. Du. *struikelen*, G. *straucheln* (MHG. *strûcheln*, freq. of OHG. *strûhhên, -ôn*), to stumble. The change from (k) to (g) would not be a strong objection to this etymology, but the meanings of the Eng. and the continental verbs are widely apart. Possibly the word may be due to phonetic symbolism, the beginning being suggested by words like *strive, strong*; cf. TUGGLE *v.*, TOGGLE *v.*[2]]

1. *intr.* To contend (*with* an adversary) in a close grapple as in wrestling; also, in wider use, to make violent bodily movements in order to resist force or free oneself from constraint; to exert one's physical strength in persistent striving against an opposing force.

c **1386** CHAUCER *Merch. T.* 1130 As me was taught..Was no thyng bet to make yow to see Than strugle [*v.rr.* strogele, strogle, strougle] with a man vp on a tree. —— *Pard. T.* 501 And I shal ryue hym thurgh the sydes tweye Whil that thou strogelest [*v.rr.* strugglest, stroglest] with hym as in game. **1440** J. SHIRLEY *Dethe K. James* (1818) 19 And gretely the Kyng strogild with hem, for to have berevyd thame thare knyvys; by the which labur his handis wer all forkute. *c* **1440** *Promp. Parv.* 480/2 Strogolyn (*v.r.* strobelyn), *colluctor*. **1483** CAXTON *Golden Leg.* 211 b/1 A rechelles felaw stroglyd and wrestlyd wyth her and brake alle her egges. **1530** PALSGR. 741/1, I stroggell with my bodye, as one dothe that wolde nat be holden, *je me desrigle*. **1569** ROEST tr. *J. van der Noot's Theat. Worldlings* 5 b, Much like vnto the Hare, who being caught in the nette, the more he struggleth, the faster he maketh hym self. **1595** SHAKS. *John* IV. i. 77, I will not struggle, I will stand stone still. **1600** *Earl Gowrie's Conspir.* C 1, In this meane tyme, his maiesty, wyth struggeling and wrastling wyth the said maister Alexander had broght him perforce out of that study. **1603** KNOLLES *Hist. Turks* (1638) 120 In strugling with him for the knife, in wresting it out of his hand, hee hurt himselfe therwith in the forhead. **1611** BIBLE *Gen.* xxv. 22 And the children struggled together within her. **1687** A. LOVELL tr. *Thevenot's Trav.* I. 144 It is pleasant to see these Chickens, in one side some thrusting out their heads, others striving and struggling to get out their bodies. **1697** DRYDEN *Virg. Georg.* I. 291 The Boat's brawny Crew the Current stem, And, slow advancing, struggle with the Stream. **1787** BEST *Angling* (1822) 56 Then if he [*sc.* the pike] struggles again very much, give him line again. **1815** SCOTT *Guy M.* xl, The wind was adverse, attended by some rain, and they struggled against it without much assistance from the tide. **1825** BRYANT *Afr. Chief* 59 He struggled fiercely with his chain. **1842** TENNYSON *Dora* 100 So saying, he took the boy, that cried aloud And struggled hard. **1848** J. GRANT *Adv. Aide-de-C.* xl, I was struggling breathlessly in the water. **1848** THACKERAY *Van. Fair* lxiv, They..drank a great quantity of champagne at the buffet, where the people..struggled furiously for refreshments. **1856** KANE *Arctic Expl.* II. xv. 165 We struggled manfully to force our way through. **1905** ELIN. GLYN *Viciss. Evangeline* 222 'No, no', I said, struggling feebly to free myself.

b. To make violent efforts to breathe (usually, *to struggle for breath*); to be in the agony of death. Also (*nonce-use*) to pass *out of* (the world) with a struggle.

a **1674** CLARENDON *Surv. Leviath.* (1676) 281 There will at some time or other, before he struggles out of this world, be sadness to him in the consideration. *a* **1700** EVELYN *Diary* 4 Feb. 1685, Being now in much paine, and struggling for breath.

2. *fig.* To contend resolutely, esp. with an adversary of superior power; to offer obstinate resistance; to make violent efforts to escape from constraint. Const. *with, against, for.*

c **1412** HOCCLEVE *De Reg. Princ* 964 But in myn age wrastle with hardenesse, That with hym stroglid neuere in grennesse Of youthe, þat mutacion and chaunge..me seeme shulde al straunge. *c* **1425** *St. Christina* xii. in *Anglia* VIII. 124/30 Fro þen forþ þey sturglid [? *read* struglid] nor enforced no-thinge ageyne goddes wille. **1530** PALSGR. 741/1, I strogell, I murmure with wordes secretly, *je grommelle.* He stroggleth at every thyng I do. **1532** TINDALE *Expos. v-vii. Matt.* Prol. to Rdr. 6 b, Euen so is the spirite oppressed & ouer laden of the fleshe thorow custume, that she struggeleth and stryueth to get vp and to breake lowse in vayne. **1602** SHAKS. *Ham.* III. iii. 68 Oh limed soule, that strugling to be free, Art more ingag'd. **1642** FULLER *Holy & Prof. St.* v. vi. 381 With these and other arguments he struggles with his own conscience. **1771** *Lett. Junius* xlix. 254 A virtuous man, struggling with adversity, [is] a scene worthy of the gods. **1821** SCOTT *Kenilw.* viii, My father.. sits at home struggling with his grief. **1830** D'ISRAELI *Chas. I*, III. xii. 268 Whenever a party struggles for predominance in the State, it necessarily becomes a political body. **1849** MACAULAY *Hist. Eng.* I. i. 123 No sooner was the first pressure of military tyranny felt, than the nation..began to struggle fiercely. **1855** KINGSLEY *Misc.* (1859) I. 14 Close to our own shores, the Netherlands are struggling vainly for their liberties. **1856** *Ann. Reg., Chron.* 65/1 The counsel for the prisoner attempted to struggle against both the evidence and the prisoner's statement. **1857** BORROW *Rom. Rye* xxxi, There came over me the same feeling of horror that I had experienced of old. I struggled manfully against it. **1874** GREEN *Short Hist.* iii. §6. 146 It was with less success that the order struggled against the passion for knowledge. **1908** RIDER HAGGARD *Ghost Kings* i. 4 She and her people..had struggled against this South African scheme [of her husband's] even to the verge of open quarrel. **1918** *Times Lit. Suppl.* 14 Mar. 121/4 There are States to-day prepared to help Germany to a dictatorship, against which, if she were successful, they would have to struggle in the end.

b. Said of passions, qualities, forces, etc.

1619 FLETCHER *Knt. Malta* II. v, How nature and his honour struggle in him! **1663** PATRICK *Parab. Pilgr.* xxvii. (1687) 300 Two passions he felt strugling in him at the same point of time. **1681** DRYDEN *Abs. & Achit.* 314 Half loth and half consenting to the ill, For loyal blood within him struggled still. **1794** MRS. RADCLIFFE *Myst. Udolpho* xliv, Pride, and something very like fear, seemed struggling in his breast. **1810** SCOTT *Lady of Lake* VI. ii, The sunbeams.. struggling with the smoky air, Deaden'd the torches' yellow glare. **1837** CARLYLE *Fr. Rev.* III. III. viii, Hope and ruth, flickering against despair and rage, still struggle in the minds of men. **1858** A. LINCOLN in *Polit. Deb. with S. A. Douglas* 15 Oct. (1912) II. 268 Right and wrong..are the two principles that have stood face to face from the beginning of time, and will ever continue to struggle. **1906** PETRIE *Relig. Anc. Egypt* i. 5 This idea [of 'a jealous god'] struggled hard against polytheistic toleration.

3. quasi-*trans.* with adv. or phrase expressing the result of struggling. *lit.* and *fig.*

1633 BP. HALL *Hard Texts, Eccles.* vi. 10 Neither can hee thinke to struggle himselfe out from the mighty, and over ruling power of his Creator. **1639** FULLER *Holy War* II. ii. (1640) 45 Till after many changes he struggled himself again into the place. **1646** *Unhappy Game Scotch & English* 20 How they shufle and cut to strugle themselves out of the Bryers. **1660** INGELO *Bentiv. & Ur.* II. (1682) 170 When the light began to appear, the Ass had strugled her self out. **1889** STEVENSON *Master of Ballantrae* iv, He there struggled down the last of his emotion.

4. To make great efforts in spite of difficulties; to contend resolutely *with* (a task, burden); to strive *to do* something difficult. †Also const. *at.* *to struggle for existence*: cf. STRUGGLE *sb.* 1 d.

1597 HOOKER *Eccl. Pol.* v. lxvii. §12 They struggle with that which they cannot fully master. **1644** CHAS. I in Ellis *Orig. Lett.* Ser. I. III. 299 Besydes our taske is not litle that we strugle with. **1667** MILTON *P.L.* II. 606 They..wish and struggle, as they pass, to reach The tempting stream. **1687** ATTERBURY *Answ. Consid. Spirit Luther* 64 The Church of England..had struggl'd and heav'd at a Reformation, ever since Wicliff's dayes. **1759** JOHNSON *Rasselas* xxxv, Who that is struggling under his own evils will add to them the miseries of another? **1794** MRS. RADCLIFFE *Myst. Udolpho* xxxix, She struggled to overcome the pleadings of her heart. **1808** SCOTT *Marm.* I. xxviii, And when he struggled at a smile, His eye look'd haggard wild. **1820** W. IRVING *Sketch Bk.* I. 34 Such an opportunity as seldom occurs, of cheering a noble mind struggling under misfortunes. **1827** LAMB *Elia* Ser. II. *A Death-bed*, Where for years they have been struggling to raise a Girls' School with no effect. **1849** *Q. Rev.* Mar. 391 Long-horns [*sc.* cattle] which still struggle for a separate existence in a small district. **1855** *Poultry Chron.* II. 498, I saw a hungry little bantam cock struggling with a huge corn much too large for his gullet. **1856** MRS. MARSH *Ev. Marston* xxxv, Beds..where the same description of flowers were struggling for existence. **1862** CALVERLEY *Verses & Transl.* (ed. 2) 31, I hear that youth..struggling with the first few bars. And I do think the amateur cornopean Should be put down by law. **1885** 'MRS. ALEXANDER' *At Bay* i, While Glynn was struggling to answer the question..'Where have I seen that face?' **1897** HALL CAINE *Christian* x, When spoken to they would struggle to smile, but the smiles would break down after a moment. **1907** J. H. PATTERSON *Man-Eaters of Tsavo* xviii. 190 Along the baked banks of which [dry ravines] a few stunted trees—the only ones to be seen—struggle to keep themselves alive.

5. To make progress with difficulty *to, into, out of* (a place, a condition), *through* (something interposed). Also with adv., *along, forward, on.* *to struggle on*: occas. to maintain existence, or continue one's course of action, with difficulty.

a **1700** EVELYN *Diary* 18 Apr. 1686, The book will, I doubt not, struggle through this unjust impediment. **1820** W. IRVING *Sketch Bk.* II. 18 The light struggles dimly through windows darkened by dust. **1830** JAMES *Darnley* xvi, A bass-relief whose figures seemed struggling from the stone. **1837** CARLYLE *Fr. Rev.* III. VII. ii, Either way, the world must contrive to struggle on. **1841** DICKENS *Barn. Rudge* xxviii, Hugh, struggling into a sitting posture and gazing at him intently. **1844** E. WARBURTON *Crescent & Cross* (1846) I. i. 1 The town itself lay buried beneath an avalanch of snowy mist, through which a few spires scarcely struggled into sight. **1849** MACAULAY *Hist. Eng.* iv. I. 452 His looks and tones had inspired terror when he was merely a young advocate struggling into practice. **1860** TYNDALL *Glac.* I. §27. 212 My telescope..directed upon the men as they struggled through the snow. **1865** SEELEY *Ecce Homo* v. (ed. 8) 40 Christ did not struggle forward to a position in which he could found a new state, but simply founded it. **1880** A.

H. SWINTON *Insect Variety* 10 Here..still struggles on a remnant of a once rich coleopterous fauna of lacustrine aspect. **1885** 'MRS. ALEXANDER' *At Bay* vii, When he was slowly struggling back to life and strength. **1888** F. HUME *Mme. Midas* I. Prol., He struggled to his feet quickly. **1902** BUCHAN *Watcher by Threshold* 313 A moon was beginning to struggle through the windy clouds. **1908** E. M. GORDON *Indian Folk Tales* x. (1909) 98 For a while the medical work struggled along under great difficulties. **1910** MEREDITH *Celt & Saxon* xv. in *Fortn. Rev.* June 1061 His brown coat struggles out of the obscurity of the background [of the picture].

with cognate object. **1842** LOVER *Handy Andy* xx, All gentle feeling vanished, as he saw Scatterbrain struggling his way towards him. **1871** *Daily News* 6 Jan., The officers..were unable to struggle their way up to the inclosure in front of the altar.

†**6.** *trans.* To contest (a point) persistently. *Obs.*

1769 BLACKSTONE *Comm.* IV. xx. 280 The justices long struggled the point.

struggle-for-lifer. *slang.* [f. the phrase *struggle for life* (see STRUGGLE *sb.* 1 d) + -ER[1].

The word seems to have been first formed in Fr. as *struggle-for-lifeur*; in this form it was used in Alphonse Daudet's play *La Lutte pour la Vie* (1889). It had some currency in France (corrupted into *strugforlifeur*), and has often been used jocularly (occas. in the Fr. form) by English journalists.]

One who has a struggle to live; usually, one who is unscrupulous in his efforts to advance himself in the world.

1895 *Funk's Stand. Dict.*, *Struggle-for-lifer* (Slang, Eng.), a struggler for life, as against hopeless poverty. **1899** *Daily News* 11 Jan. 5/4 Some struggle-for-lifers have since carried seats there by sap, mine, and storm. **1905** *Pall Mall Gaz.* 22 Dec. 1 South Africa..will be edified by the manner in which its interests are employed to serve the tactical exigencies of a political 'struggle-for-lifer'.

struggler ('strʌglə(r)). [f. STRUGGLE *v.* + -ER[1].] One who struggles.

1554 T. MARTIN *Marr. Priests* Bbj, The Iewes were so hard hearted and malicious struglers against the Trueth, that [etc.]. **1598** BASTARD *Chrestol.* VI. xxix. 148 And was not death a sturdie strugler, In ouerthrowing Iames the iugler? **1677** MIEGE *Dict. Eng.-Fr.*, A Struggler, *qui se debat ou qui se demene.* *a* **1721** SHEFFIELD (Dk. Buckhm.) *Wks.* 1753 I. 107 Often she cast a kind admiring glance On the bold struggler for delight. **1825** SCOTT *Fam. Lett.* (1894) II. 298 An older woman..added, that we might give her an alms too, for she was an old struggler. **1871** MISS YONGE *Cameos* II. 295 Huss and many another struggler for truth, perished in the flames. **1884** YATES *Recoll.* I. 278 The unswerving kindness with which he supported me, an unknown struggler,..against a powerful clique. **1900** J. L. ALLEN *Increasing Purpose* xv. 211 Here is the hero in life! Among these easy-going people this solitary struggler.

struggling ('strʌglɪŋ), *vbl. sb.* [f. STRUGGLE *v.* + -ING[1].]

1. The action of STRUGGLE *v.*

c **1386** CHAUCER *Man of Law's T.* 823 For with hir struglyng wel and myghtily The theef fil ouer bord al sodeynly. **1398** TREVISA *Barth. De P.R.* VII. lv. (1495) 270 This skynne callyd Hernia is..slakyd somtyme by to grete traueylle of body as by grete strogelynge and wrastelynge. *c* **1440** *Bone Flor.* 1853 In hys armes he can hur folde, Hur rybbes crakyd as they breke wolde, In struglynge can they stryve. **1542** UDALL *Erasm. Apoph.* Pref. *viij b, And in places not a fewe I haue had muche strougleyng & wrastleyng with the faultes of enprientyng in yᵉ bookes. **1592** GREENE *3rd Pt. Conny catching* E 3, Both his handkercher with the chaine, and also his purse..were taken out of his pocket in this strugling. **1649** MILTON *Eikon.* xxvii. 211 It would..put us to another fatal struggling for libertie and life, more dubious then the former. **1702** ROWE *Tamerl.* I. i. 296 With strong Reluctance and Convulsive Struggling. **1830** CARLYLE *Richter Again* Ess. 1840 II. 300 No character of this kind..is to be formed without manifold..struggling with the world.

pl. **1615** CHAPMAN *Odyss.* XII. 242 They should with much more band Containe my struglings. **1690** T. BURNET *Theory Earth* III. xi. 96 Some Causes impelling the Waters one way, and some another, make intestine strugglings and contrary motions. *a* **1715** G. BURNET *Own Time* IV. (1724) I. 797 All the strugglings which that party have made ever since that time..did rise out of this. **1783** *Med. Commun.* I. 303 His strugglings were more violent. **1890** D. DAVIDSON *Mem. Long Life* ii. 29, I confess to some strugglings of the heart as we hurried past the scenes of my boyhood.

†**2.** Effervescence. (Cf. STRUGGLE *sb.* 1 c.) *Obs.*

1764 *Museum Rust.* II. 378 You may..try it with vinegar, where the effervescence, or struggling, will be much stronger than in water.

struggling ('strʌglɪŋ), *ppl. a.* [f. STRUGGLE *v.* + -ING[2].] That struggles. In recent use often: That has difficulty in making a livelihood.

1577 KENDALL *Flowers of Epigr.* 99 When stiffe, strong, struglyng, sturdie storms, began for to arise. **1590** SPENSER *F.Q.* III. xi. 12 There an huge heape of singultes did oppresse His strugling soule. **1599** MARSTON *Antonio's Rev.* IV. i, Now patience hoope my sides With steeled ribs, least I doe burst my breast With struggling passions. **1693** DRYDEN *Persius* v. 232 The strugling Greyhound gnaws his Leash in vain. **1697** —— *Æneis* v. 35 Sicilia..whose hospitable Shores In safety we may reach with strugling Oars. **1757** GRAY *Elegy* xviii, The struggling pangs of conscious truth to hide. **1817** C. WOLFE *Burial of Sir J. Moore* 7 By the struggling moon-beam's misty light. **1838** DICKENS *Nich. Nick.* xxiv, 'What do you mean to do for me, old fellow?' asked Mr. Lenville, poking the struggling fire with his walking stick. **1851** MAYHEW *Lond. Labour* I. 324 The rest of the class may be described as merely street-sellers; toiling, struggling, plodding, itinerant tradesmen. **1892** *Photogr. Ann.* II. 219 To the impecunious and struggling photographer..'copies', of course, mean considerable inconvenience.

absol. **1834** (*title*) Leigh Hunt's London Journal, to Assist the Inquiring, Animate the Struggling, [etc.]. **1837** CARLYLE *Fr. Rev.* I. v. vi, But, to the living and the struggling, a new, Fourteenth morning dawns. **1884** J. PAYN *Lit. Recoll.* 75 Their behaviour to the Young and Struggling.

strugglingly ('strʌglɪŋlɪ), *adv.* [f. STRUGGLING *ppl. a.* + -LY[2].] In a struggling manner.

1574 A. L. *Calvin's Foure Serm.* Epist., You see him some-tyme yeldingly stretch out, sometyme struglingly throw his weakened legges. **1596** NASHE *Saffron Walden* N 4 b, A dampe..in thick rouling clowds would strugglingly funnell vp. **1838** POE *A. Gordon Pym* Wks. 1864 IV. 165 A large black bird of the bittern species strugglingly and slowly arose above the shrubs. **1875** BROWNING *Aristoph. Apol.* 360 Sea claws at sand relinquished strugglingly.

strui(e, obs. forms of STROY *v.*

struik(e(n, struive: see STRIKE *v.*, STRIVE *v.*

struke(n, strukkin, etc.: see STRIKE *v.*

Struldbrug ('strʌldbrʌg). Also 8 (Swift) **-brugg**; *corruptly* 8–9 **Strulbrug**. [Arbitrarily formed.] In Swift's *Gulliver's Travels*, given as the native appellation of 'the immortals' in the kingdom of Luggnagg, who were incapable of dying, but after the age of eighty continued to exist in a state of miserable decrepitude, regarded as legally dead, and receiving a small pittance from the state. Hence in allusive uses.

1726 SWIFT *Gulliver* III. x. 127–8 Struldbrugs. 129 ff. Struldbrugg, -bruggs. **1773** MRS. ANNE GRANT *Lett. fr. Mountains* (1807) I. vii. 57 The sages here get a great deal of reverence and attention, not usually paid to the struldbruggs of other countries. **1784** H. WALPOLE *Let. to H. S. Conway* 25 June, I am very well content to be a Strulbrug, and to *exist* after I have done *being*. **1847** H. MILLER *First Impr. Eng.* xvi. 293 These [trees] are mere hollow trunks, of vast bulk, but stinted foliage..—mere *struldbrugs* of the forest. **1908** *Contemp. Rev.* Dec. 744 There is a danger lest the aged pensioner at home should sink into the condition of a Struldbrug.

attrib. **1844** DE QUINCEY *Greece under Romans* Wks. 1890 VII. 275 All the great Moslem nations being already in a *Strulbrug* state, and held erect only by the colossal support of Christian powers.

Hence **Struldbruggian** *a.*, of or pertaining to a Struldbrug. **Struldbrugism**, the condition or practice of a Struldbrug.

1778 H. WALPOLE *Let. to W. Mason* 15 May, I have long taken my doctor's degree in Strulbruggism, and wonder I concern myself about the affairs of the living. **1788** —— *Let. Lady Craven* 11 Dec., When any personage has shone as much as is possible in his or her best walk,..he should take up his strulbrugism, and be heard of no more. **1909** *Times Lit. Suppl.* 2 Sept. 314/1 Rescuing old authors from the dangers of the Struldbruggian state.

[**strull**, error for *strutt*, STRUT *sb.*

1831 LOUDON *Encycl. Agric.* (ed. 2) 1247 (Glossarial Index), *Strull*, a bar so placed as to resist weight, p. 498. (*In text*, a strutt). Hence **1860** WORCESTER; and in later Dicts.]

strum (strʌm), *sb.*[1] *Obs.* exc. *dial.* and *Naut.* Forms: α. 4, 7, 9 **strom**, 7 **stroam(e**, 8 **strawm**, 8–9 **stroom**. β. 5 **strumme**, 8–9 **strum**. γ. 9 **strung**, **strun**. [Of obscure origin.]

1. *Brewing.* An oblong basket of wicker work placed over the bung-hole within the mash-tub to prevent the grains and hops passing through when the liquor is drawn off.

1394–5 in *Cartul. Abb. Whiteby* (Surtees) 606 It. pro strom pro le brewhous, iiii d. **1483** *Cath. Angl.* 369/2 A Strumme, *qualus, statrum.* **1615** MARKHAM *Eng. Housew.* v. 121 Pluck vp your mashing stroame, and let the first liquour runne gently from the mault. **1674** RAY *N.C. Words* 47 A *Strom*: the instrument to keep the malt in the Fat. **1796** W. H. MARSHALL *Yorksh.* (ed. 2) II. 348 *Strum*; the hose used in brewing &c. to keep the tap free. **1854** MISS BAKER *Northampt. Gloss.*, *Stroom*, a wicker malt-strainer, used in brewing. **1865** W. S. BANKS *Wakefield Words*, *Strum* or *Strun*. **1866** BROGDEN *Prov. Lincs.*, *Strung*.

2. a. *Mining.* A kind of iron sieve placed round the suction-pipe of a pump to prevent obstruction.

1849 GREENWELL *Coal-trade Terms Northumb. & Durh.* (1851) 53 Strum. **1883** GRESLEY *Gloss. Coal-mining* 245 Strum. **1887** *Times* 9 Apr. 4/1 Some refuse..choking up the strum of the pipes leading to the pumps.

b. *Naut.* (See quots.) Also *strum-box*, *-plate*.

1894 H. PAASCH *From Keel to Truck* (ed. 2) 172/1 *Strainer*; *strum*; *strum-box*, terms applied to perforated plates, wire-clothes or any other objects fitted to allow the entry or exit of water or other fluids, but preventing the passing of any refuse matter. **1948** R. DE KERCHOVE *Internat. Maritime Dict.* 739/2 *Strum plate*, a plate fitted in pump suctions, deck scuppers, sea cocks, having a number of small holes in it to allow water to pass, but designed to stop foreign matter that would clog the piping. **1962** A. G. COURSE *Dict. Naut. Terms* 192 *Strum box*, a square metal box with perforated sides fitted round the bottom of a suction pipe in a ship's bilges. **1975** *B.S.I. News* July 21/2 Strum boxes for ships.

strum (strʌm), *sb.*[2] [Abbreviated form of STRUMPET.] A strumpet, prostitute.

a **1700** B. E. *Dict. Cant. Crew* s.v. *Strum*, *Rum-strum*,..a handsom Wench, or Strumpet. **1710** C. SHADWELL *Fair Quaker Deal* I. i. 2 The Whores you left here about ten Months since are Dead with Rottenness, and young Strums supply their Rooms. **1765** *Meretriciad* (ed. 6) 17 The awful Theatre of late's become A mere receptacle for ev'ry Strum. *a* **1825** FORBY *Voc. E. Anglia*, *Strum*, a battered prostitute.

†**strum**, *sb.*[3] *slang. Obs.* A periwig.

a **1700** B. E. *Dict. Cant. Crew*, *Strum*, a Periwig. *Rum-strum*, a long Wig. **1785** GROSE *Dict. Vulgar Tongue*.

†**strum**, *sb.*[4] *Obs. rare*[−1]. [? Confusion of THRUM *sb.*[2] and STRING *sb.*] (Sense not clear: see quot.)

1725 *Bradley's Family Dict.* s.v. *Catkin*, Catkins, the Male Blossoms of Nut-bearing..Trees, &c...; in the Hazel they are long Strums, composed of very small Flowers.

strum (strʌm), *sb.*[5] *Sc.* [Cf. STRUNT *sb.*[2]] A fit of ill-humour; esp. in phr. ***to take the strum*** or ***strums***.

1788 J. MACAULAY *Poems* 185 (E.D.D.) The petty lads hae ta'en the strum, Because we winna let them come. **1818** MISS FERRIER *Marriage* xxxv, Ye're..ay ready to tak the strums, an' ye dinna get a' thing yere ain wye.

Hence **strum** *v. intr.*, 'to be in a pettish humour' (Jam.).

1804 TARRAS *Poems* 132 (Jam.) Sinkin wi' care we aften fag, Strummin' about a gill we're lag, Syne drowsy hum. *Ibid.* Gloss., *Strumming*, glooming, looking sour.

strum (strʌm), *sb.*[6] [f. STRUM *v.*] The action of strumming or playing noisily and monotonously on a musical instrument.

c **1793** BURNS *Epist. Esopus* 51 Who christened thus Maria's lyre divine The idiot strum of vanity bemused..? **1840** MARRYAT *Olla Podr.* III. 143 There were four young ladies who were learning music. We now had our annoyance: it was strum, strum, all day long. **1845** ELIZA COOK *Poems* Ser. II. *Poem of Househ.* iii, There's more mirth in the jig and the amateur's strum, When the parchment-spread battledore serves as a drum.

strum (strʌm), *sb.*[7] *Mining. Sc.* [Of obscure origin.] (See quots.)

1880 J. NICOL *Poems & Songs* 75 They [*sc.* the miners] come To their daily task With powder flask And tinder, straw, and strum. **1886** J. BARROWMAN *Sc. Mining Terms* 65 *Strum*, safety fuse. **1895** *N.B. Daily Mail* 13 Nov. 5 The explosion..is supposed to have been caused by some careless miner leaving a ball of 'strum,' an explosive material used by them in the pits, in the vicinity of the fire. **1911** *Daily News* 3 Apr. 5 A piece of miners' 'strum' for blasting operations was also found.

strum (strʌm), *v.* [Echoic: cf. THRUM *v.*[3]]

1. *trans.* To play on (a stringed instrument) carelessly or unskilfully; to produce (notes, a tune, etc.) by such playing. Also with *out*, *over*.

Ash's explanation (quot. 1775) is badly expressed, and perh. implies a misunderstanding.

1775 ASH Suppl., *Strum* (*v.t. a droll word*), tuned as a stringed instrument in a clumsy manner. **1784** *New Spectator* No. xviii. 1 She has received what is called a genteel education, that is, she can strum a tune on a guitar, [etc.]. **1802** MRS. RADCLIFFE *Gaston de Blondeville* Posth. Wks. (1826) I. 86 Her mynstrells of music..began to blow upon their pipes, and to strum their stringed instruments with most sweet noise. **1845** FORD *Handbk. Spain* I. 30 In due time songs are sung, a guitar is strummed. **1850** THACKERAY *Pendennis* iv, Laura..had been strumming her music lessons for hours before. **1894** HALL CAINE *Manxman* ii. 53 He was sitting at the piano strumming a music-hall ditty. **1896** A. MORRISON *Adv. Martin Hewitt* Ser. III. 10, I turned to my little pianette and strummed over the notes, making my own time. *Ibid.* 28 He had got musicians to strum out the notes on all sorts of instruments. **1906** *Temple Bar* Jan. 76 The mate..sits on the booby hatch, and strums his banjo to the stars.

2. *intr.* To play carelessly or unskilfully on a stringed instrument. Also with *away*, *on*. Said also of an instrument: To sound when strummed upon.

1785 GROSE *Dict. Vulgar T.*, *Strum*,..to play badly on the harpsichord, or any other stringed instrument. *c* **1793** BURNS *Monody on Lady* 18 Here Vanity strums on her idiot lyre. **1840** LADY C. BURY *Hist. of Flirt* xii, Thelwal would strum away on the guitar. **1849** LYTTON *K. Arthur* VIII. lxxv, Fifes, viols, trumpets braying, screaming, strumming, Flatter his ears, and compliment his coming. **1875** BROWNING *Aristoph. Apol.* 186 You have been fouling that redoubtable Harp-player, twenty years, with what effect? Still he strums on, strums ever cheerily. **1914** J. L. PATON *J. B. Paton* xii. 202 Physical exercises..went with more go when the teacher..strummed on the piano by way of accompaniment.

3. quasi-*trans.* with adverbial extension.

1777 SHERIDAN *Sch. Scandal* II. i. Plays (1902) 160 To..be stuck down to an old Spinet to strum your father to sleep after a Fox Chase. **1787** WOLCOT (P. Pindar) *Ode upon Ode* (ed. 7) 41 [He] to his tent majestic strode to strum, And scrape his anger out on tweedle-dum. **1847** ANNE BRONTE *Agnes Grey* vii, The short half-hour of practising was horribly strummed through.

Hence **strummed** *ppl. a.*

1881 H. JAMES *Portr. Lady* xxi, Your conscience..will get out of tune, like a strummed piano.

‖**struma** ('struːmə). Pl. **strumæ**; also 6 **strumas**, 7 **-aes**, 7–8 **-a's**. See also STRUME. [mod.L. use of L. *strūma* scrofulous tumour.]

1. *Path.* **a.** = SCROFULA. Also applied to goitre or bronchocele, and to tubercular disease, esp. in mod.L. specific designations as ***struma aberrata***, ***adiposa***, etc.

1565 J. HALL *Lanfranc's Chirurg.*, *Expos. Table* 46 For if by melancholy they become scirrhous, he calleth them Scrophulas, but Galen nameth them Strumas. **1575** BANISTER *Chyrurg.* I. (1585) 92 Struma is called of the barbarous sort, Scrofula, and englished the Kinge's or Queenes euill. **1655** Culpeper, etc. *Riverius* x. iv. 290 Al the Mesaraick Veins..be stopped, as in Children who have the Struma, or Kings Evil. **1676** Wiseman *Surg. Treat.* iv. ii. 248 If this acid Humour be simple, the Disease is a simple *Struma*; if joined with a malignity, or any other Humour, it makes a mixt Tumour, as *Struma maligna, Phlegmonodes, Schirrhodes, Oedematodes*, &c. **1784** T. White (*title*) A Treatise on Struma or Scrophula, commonly called the King's Evil. **1843** R. J. Graves *Syst. Clin. Med.* xxix. 393 The constitution of the patient rapidly gives way under the continuation of struma. **1878** W. J. Walsham *Handbk. Surg. Pathol.* 41 Struma or scrofula manifests itself in bone either as a low form of chronic ostitis..or as a deposit of miliary tubercles.

b. A scrofulous swelling or tumour. Also, a goitre, bronchocele (*rare*).

1654 J. Webster *Acad. Exam.* 74 Great and dangerous sores, as the Lupus,..Elephantiasis, Strumaes. **1670** T. Brooks *Wks.* (1867) VI. 426 That one man dies..of an apoplexy in the head, another of a *struma* in the neck. **1676** Wiseman *Surg. Treat.* iv. ii. 249 When he wakened his Neck was full of *Strumæ* on both sides, some as big as Walnuts. *Ibid.*, iv. iv. 299 He had also a *Struma* ulcerated in each Arm. *Ibid.*, He had also in the Groin of the same side a Cluster of *Strumæ*. **1684** J. Browne (*title*) Adenochoiradelogia: or An Anatomick-Chirurgical Treatise of Glandules & Strumaes, or Kings-Evil-Swellings. **1693** Dryden *Juvenal* Ded. (1697) 28 A Bunch or Struma under the Chin. **1753** R. Russell *Diss. Sea Water* 142 Struma's are apt to rise again near their old Cicatrices.

c. ***struma lymphomatosa*** [mod.L., coined in Ger. (H. Hashimoto 1912, in *Arch. f. klin. Chir.* XCVII. 219)], = *Hashimoto's disease* s.v. Hashimoto; ***Riedel's struma*** [Riedel], a rare condition of uncertain status in which the thyroid becomes hard, nodular, and fibrotic.

1931 *Arch. Surg.* XXII. 548 Recent writers have stated that struma lymphomatosa is the early stage of Riedel's struma, despite the fact that Hashimoto..definitely rejected such a relationship. **1947** H. Selye *Textbk. Endocrinol.* 714/2 The etiology of struma lymphomatosa is unknown but its histologic characteristics are not typical of inflammatory lesions. **1966** [see Riedel]. **1974** S. L. Robbins *Path. Basis Dis.* xxix. 1328/1 In years past, Riedel's struma was thought to be the fibrotic end-stage of struma lymphomatosa.

2. *Bot.* A cellular dilatation on a leaf-stalk at the point where the petiole joins the lamina or where the midrib joins the leaflets of a compound leaf. See also quot. 1866.

1832 Lindley *Introd. Bot.* i. ii. 95 At the opposite extremity of the petiole, where it is connected with the lamina, a similar swelling is often remarkable..: this is called the *struma*, or, by the French *bourrelet*. **1861** Bentley *Man. Bot.* 174 A somewhat similar swelling may be also seen in many compound leaves at the base of each partial petiole, which is termed the *struma*. **1866** *Treas. Bot.*, *Struma*,..A protuberance at the base of the spore-cases of some urn-mosses.

strumatic (struːˈmætɪk), *a.* *rare*⁻⁰. [ad. late L. *strūmātic-us*, f. *strūma*: see prec. and -atic.] Suffering from struma. Hence **struˈmaticness**.

1656 Blount *Glossogr.*, *Strumatick*, that has the Impostume *Struma*. **1727** Bailey vol. II, *Strumaticknesss*, a being troubled with strumous Humours, or Swellings, that generally appear in the glandulous or kernelly Parts. **1883** Ogilvie, *Strumatic*. **1894** G. M. Gould *Illustr. Dict. Med.* etc., *Strumatic, Strumatous*, strumous, scrofulous.

ˈstrumatous, *a.* *rare*⁻⁰. [irreg. f. struma: see -ous.] = prec.

1894 [see strumatic *a.*].

strumbell, var. strummel *a.* and *sb.*²

†**strumble**, *v.*¹ *Obs.* *rare*⁻¹. [Cf. rumble *v.*] *intr.* ? To rumble.

1645 *Sacred Decretal* 9 Though..he be condemned as a Traitour and disturber of the publike Peace (for our gutts strumble at him every morning).

†**strumble**, *v.*² *Obs.* *rare.* [? Altered form of stumble *v.* Perh. a misprint; but cf. Du. †*strompelen* to stumble (Kilian).] *intr.* To stumble.

1681 Rycaut tr. *Gracian's Critick* vii. 127 He being lame with Age,..in a few paces, strumbled on his Crutches [orig. Sp. *tropeço en su misma muleta*] and fell.

strumble (ˈstrʌmb(ə)l), *sb.* *rare*⁻¹. [f. strumble *v.*¹] A rumble.

1938 Belloc *Sonnets & Verse* 180 Beneath His feet are implacable fate, and panic or night, and the strumble of the hungry river of death.

†**strumblowes**. *Obs.* *rare*⁻¹. Some kind of submarine vegetation (called in Pg. *tromba*).

1624 in Foster *Eng. Factories Ind.* (1909) III. 23 [In sailing to Surat] Mett with weeds called strumblowes, a good sine of neerness [to land].

†**strume**. *Obs.* [? a. F. *strume*, or ad. L. *strūma*.] = struma 1.

1559 Morwyng *Evonym.* 287 A marvelous water or oyll for strumes and swellinges of the throote. **1578** Lyte *Dodoens* ii. lxxxi. 258 The same..resolueth and scattereth the swelling about the necke called Strumes. **1630** Poeton *Chirurg. Closet* 20 It cures Strumes: It takes away proud and corrupt flesh in vlcers. **1635** Brathwait *Arcad. Pr.* 87 When Nonius that same scabbe Did of a Strume complaine. **1677** Coles, *Strume, -ma.* **1704** Cocker, *Strume* or *Struma*.

strumectomy (struːˈmɛktəmɪ). [f. struma + -ectomy.] Excision of a struma.

1894 Gould *Illustr. Dict. Med.* **1898** *Syd. Soc. Lex.*

struˈmiferous, *a.* *Path.* and *Bot.* [f. strum-a + -(i)ferous. Cf. F. *strumifère*.] Bearing a struma.

1860 Mayne *Expos. Lex.* **1894** Gould *Illustr. Dict. Med.* **1900** B. D. Jackson *Gloss. Bot. Terms.*

strumiform (ˈstruːmɪfɔːm), *a.* [ad. mod.L. *strūmiform-is*, f. *strūma*: see struma and -form.]

a. *Bot.* Having the appearance of a struma (*Treas. Bot.* 1866). **b.** *Path.* Resembling struma (Gould *Illustr. Dict. Med.* 1894).

strumitis (struːˈmaɪtɪs). *Path.* [f. strum(a + -itis.] Inflammation of a goitrous thyroid gland.

1889 *Buck's Handbk. Med. Sci.* VII. 96/1 Inflammation of the thyroid gland (thyroiditis, strumitis) is most commonly seen as the accidental or intentional result of remedial measures employed in the treatment of goitre. **1955** S. C. Werner *Thyroid* v. 745 Thyroiditis appears in acute, subacute, and chronic forms... If the acute disorders have their onset in pre-existing goiter, the disease is often termed strumitis.

strumme, obs. form of strum.

†**ˈstrummel**, *sb.*¹ *slang.* *Obs.* Forms: 6–7 **strommell**, 7 **stromell**, 7–8 **strommel**, 8 **stramel**, **strumil**, 8–9 **strammel**, 6–9 **strummel**. [perh. a. AF. **estramaille*, straw bedding, f. OF. *estramer*: see stramage.]

1. Straw.

1567 Harman *Caveat* (1869) 83 Strommell, strawe. *Ibid.* 85, I towre the strummel trine vpon thy nabchet and Togman. I see the strawe hang vpon thy cap and coate. **1622** Fletcher *Beggars' Bush* iii. iii, To..Twang dell's, i' the stiromell [*sic*]. **1641** Brome *Joviall Crew* ii. F 2 b, The Bratling's born, the *Doxey's* in the *Strummel*, Laid by an *Autum Mort* of their own Crew. **1719** D'Urfey *Pills* VI. 265 At Night he will tumble on Strumil or Hay. **1815** Scott *Guy M.* xxviii, You'll eat the goodman's meat, drink his drink, sleep on the strammel in his barn.

2. Hair.

1725 *New Cant. Dict.*, *Strommel*,..Hair, as, She hath good Store of Strommel on her Nob. **1812** J. H. Vaux *Flash Dict.*, *Strummel*, the hair of the head. To get *your strummel faked in twig*, is to have your hair dressed in style. **1834** Ainsworth *Rookwood* iii. v, With my strummel faked in the newest twig.

3. *Comb.*: **strummell-patch** *a.*, a contemptuous epithet for a person.

1599 B. Jonson *Ev. Man out of Hum.* v. v, The horson strummell patch, Goggle-ey'd Grumbledories.

†**ˈstrummel**, *a.* and *sb.*² *Obs.* *Sc.* Also 6 **strummall**, **strwmmill**, **strumbell**. [Of obscure origin and meaning; Jamieson identifies it with a mod.Sc. dial. *stumral* 'habituated to stumbling' (said of a horse), but the passages do not support this.] **a.** *adj.* A depreciatory epithet applied to a horse or a stirk. **b.** *sb.* A term of contempt for a person.

a. **1500–20** Dunbar *Poems* liii. 11 He stackerit lyk ane strummall awer, That hap schackellit war abone the kne. *Ibid.* lxxv. 54 Quod scho,..'My strwmmill stirk, ȝit new to spane.'

b. **1500–20** Dunbar *Poems* lx. 17 Stuffettis, strekouris, and stafische strummellis. *Ibid.* lx. 62 Ane pyk-thank..Fenȝeing the feiris of ane lord, And he ane strumbell.

strummer (ˈstrʌmə(r)). [f. strum *v.* + -er¹.] One who strums.

1785 Grose *Dict. Vulgar T.*, *Strummer of wire*, a player on any instrument strung with wire. **1808** J. Mayne *Siller Gun* iv. xxi, A cat-gut strummer. **1831** Macaulay in Trevelyan *Life* I. iv. 206 Pianoforte-strumming by the first pianoforte-strummer in England. **1872** Geo. Eliot *Middlem.* iv. xl, Thirty-five pounds a-year, and extra pay for teaching the smallest strummers at the piano. **1895** K. Grahame *Golden Age* 89 The pure, absolute quality and nature of each note in itself are only appreciated by the strummer.

strumming (ˈstrʌmɪŋ), *vbl. sb.* [-ing¹.]

1. The action of the verb strum.

1775 Ash Suppl., *Strumming*, the act of stringing or tuning in a clumsy manner. **1817** Byron *Beppo* ii, And there are songs and quavers, roaring, humming, Guitars, and every other sort of strumming. **1835** Westmacott *Eng. Spy* I. 362 The strumming of an ill-toned piano. **1887** Besant *The World went* xiii, As for tea, with the strumming of a harpsichord,..I cannot endure it. **1894** Jessopp *Random Roam.* ii. 75 We provide pianos for elementary schools, and encourage strumming.

2. *Sc.* 'A thrilling sensation, sometimes implying giddiness.' (Jam.)

1822 Hogg *Perils of Man* II. vii. 234 I'll never forget sic queer strummings as I had within me. Oh, I wad fain hae been at them! There was a kind o' yeuk, a kind o' kittling, a sort o' prinkling in my blood like.

strumming (ˈstrʌmɪŋ), *ppl. a.* *rare.* [f. strum *v.* + -ing².] Sounding like a strummed instrument.

1887 Hardy *Woodlanders* III. vii. 140 She fancied that she could hear, above the sound of her strumming pulse, the vehicle. *a* **1911** D. G. Phillips *Susan Lenox* (1917) II. xxv. 553 As a menace, as a prophecy, the old women and the hunchback and the strumming piano had gone forever.

strumose (ˈstruːməʊs), *a.* [ad. L. *strūmōs-us*, f. *strūma* struma: see -ose.]

1. *Bot.* Having a struma; strumiferous.

1841 Lindley *Elem. Bot.* 46 Filaments are sometimes..strumose, when a tubercle forms upon their face. **1849** Balfour *Man. Bot.* §398 In fig. 313, *a* represents such a staminiferous appendage found on the inner side of the base of the filament, *f*, which is hence called appendiculate, or sometimes strumose. **1864** M. G. Campbell in *Intell. Observ.* IV. 249 The capsule [of *Dicranium heteromallum*] is ..coloured of a reddish brown, with a somewhat, but never distinctly, strumose neck.

2. = strumous *a.* 1, 2.

1850 in Ogilvie. **1898** *Syd. Soc. Lex.*, *Strumose*, scrofulous; of, pertaining to, or affected by struma.

†**struˈmosity**. *Obs.* [ad. mod.L. *strūmōsitās*, f. *strūmōs-us*: see prec. and -ity. Cf. F. †*strumosité* (16–17th c.).] Strumous condition.

1674 *Phil. Trans.* IX. 114 Refuting withal the opinion of Riolan, who makes the glandals of the Mesentery the root of all strumosity.

strumous (ˈstruːməs), *a.* [ad. L. *strūmōsus*: see struma and -ous.]

1. Affected with struma; characteristic of or indicative of a scrofulous disposition.

1590 P. Barrough *Meth. Phys.* v. xxiv. (1634) 335 King Edward also..was wont marvellously to cure Strumous persons onely by touching them. *a* **1700** Evelyn *Diary* Apr. 1646, The men using more wine are not so strumous as the women. **1802** *Med. Jrnl.* VIII. 105 The brain I have given a description of was strumous. **1822** Miss L. M. Hawkins *Anecd.* I. 303 He had a pale strumous countenance. **1822–9** *Good's Study Med.* (ed. 3) I. 471 The first variety occurs.. in strumous or other weakly constitutions. **1867** J. Hogg *Microsc.* ii. i. (ed. 6) 298 With yeast already in a state of exhaustion, we have seen a crop of fungus produced in the head of a strumous boy. **1872** J. C. Jeaffreson *Woman in spite of Herself* i. vi, The son came in the form of a feeble, nervous, ricketty, strumous child. **1875** B. Meadows *Clin. Observ.* 67 A young lady, of strumous habit.

absol. **1891** *Sat. Rev.* 498 When Shakespeare spoke of holding the mirror up to Nature, he surely did not mean so holding it that it reflected only the base and strumous.

2. Of the nature of or caused by struma.

1590 P. Barrough *Meth. Phys.* v. xxiv. (1634) 333 Now these strumous tumours are greatly helped by using purging medicines. **1676** Wiseman *Surg. Treat.* iv. ii. 249 The similitude will hold good of our Strumous Acidity. *Ibid.* iv. iv. 298 He had a strumous Ulcer on the outside of his Ancle. **1748** tr. *Vegetius' Distempers of Horses* 160 Strumous Botches..or scrophulous Disorders infest the Throats of Horses. **1802** W. Heberden *Comm. Hist. & Cure Disease* (1806) 139 This disorder arises from a strumous swelling of the glands. **1859** J. Tomes *Dental Surg.* 71 The subject.. died exhausted by strumous abscesses. **1878** W. J. Walsham *Handbk. Surg. Pathol.* 41 Strumous ostitis is merely inflammation of bone occurring in an unhealthy or so-called 'strumous' subject. **1895** W. W. Cheyne *Tuberc. Dis. Bones & Joints* 18 In describing the morbid anatomy of tubercular diseases of bones and joints, I therefore describe the morbid anatomy of those affections known up till recently as 'strumous diseases'.

3. *Nat. Hist.* Having a natural protuberance on some part of the body. ***strumous lizard*** (see quot.).

1802 Shaw *Gen. Zool.* III. 224 Strumous Lizard. Lacerta Strumosa... Lizard with long round tail, and gibbose projecting breast... It is a native..of South America. **1846** Dana *Zooph.* (1848) 602 Anthelia strumosa. (Ehrenberg.).. Glaucous; polyps inflated below the mouth, strumous.

Hence **ˈstrumousness**, the state or quality of being strumous.

1883 Ogilvie.

†**strump**, *v.* *Obs.* *rare*⁻¹. [Back-formation from strumpet.] *intr.* Phr. ***to strump it***: to play the strumpet.

a **1553** C. Bansley *Treatise* (Percy Soc. 1841) 7 That is all theyr delyghte; To pleese theyr lewde lemmans all the daye, and to strumpe it well at nyght.

strumpat, obs. form of strumpet.

strumpell: see strumple.

†**ˈstrumpery**. *Obs.* Also 6 **stromperie**. [f. *strump* shortened form of strumpet + -ery.] The practice of harlotry or prostitution.

c **1470** Ashby *Active Policy* 533 And robbery lafte by that exercise, And strumpery als by this entreprise. *a* **1553** C. Bansley *Treatise* (Percy Soc. 1841) 9 Nowe fye vpon proude strumpery. **1565** T. Stapleton *Fortr. Faith* ii. v. 116 b, The roote whereof [*sc.* of that gospel] was the breache of virginitie, and an imfamous stromperie. **1573** G. Harvey *Letter-bk.* (Camden) 113 A sinke of strumperye.

strumpet (ˈstrʌmpɪt), *sb.* Forms: 4 **strumpat**, **strompat**, 4–6 **strompet**, 5–6 **-ett(e**, (5 **strompyd**, 6 **stroumpet**), 5–6 **strumpett(e**, (5 **-ytt**), 7 **strompit(t**, **strumpitt**, 4– **strumpet**. [Of obscure origin; for conjectures see Skeat.] A debauched or unchaste woman, a harlot, prostitute.

a **1327** *Pol. Poems* (Camden) 153 Uch a strumpet that ther is such drahtes wl drawe. *Ibid.* 155 That heo be kud ant knewe For strompet in rybaudes rewe. *c* **1374** Chaucer *Boeth.* i. pr. i. (1868) 6 þise comune strumpetis of siche a place þat men clepen þe theatre [L. *has scenicas meretriculas*]. **1382** Wyclif *Deut.* xxiii. 17 There shal be no strumpet [1388 hoore] of the douȝtres of Yrael. **1387** Trevisa *Higden* (Rolls) V. 299 He fonde seven children i-leyde bysides a pond, þat a strompat hadde i-bore at oon burþen. *c* **1440** *Alphabet of Tales* 3 Sho become þe moste common strompyd in all þe land. **1471** Ripley *Comp. Alch.* iv. x. in Ashm. (1652) 146 For seldome have Strumpetts Chyldren of them I bore. **1542** Udall *Erasm. Apoph.* 140 b, *marg.* Stroumpettes and paramoures. *a* **1548** Hall *Chron.*, *Edw. V*, 21 b, Shores wife a vile and abhominable strompet. **1556** *Chron. Gr. Friars* (Camden) 17 This yere the comyn strompettes that ware takene in London ware raye hoddes.

1601 SHAKS. *All's Well* II. i. 174 A strumpets boldnesse. **1604** in *Eng. Gilds* (1870) 434 If any man or woman call a wedded woman common strumpitt. **1631** DEKKER *Match Mee* IV. K, As I am thy wife Make not thy selfe a strompit of me. **1683** HEDGES *Diary* 11 Dec. I. 143 He regards nothing but to enjoy his little Seraglio of 6 Strumpets. **1712** STEELE *Spect.* No. 286 ⁋1 An innocent Creature who would start at the Name of a Strumpet, may think it pretty to be called a Mistress. **1864** E. A. PARKES *Pract. Hygiene* 451 The most degraded and dangerous strumpets are allowed to congregate round our barracks with-out hindrance. **1889** J. M. DUNCAN *Clin. Lect. Dis. Women* xxii. (ed. 4) 186 This is a disease of childhood, and the only exception to this I have seen was in a very young strumpet.

b. *fig.* and of things personified.

1545 BALE *Image Both Ch.* I. ix. (1550) K v, They knowe the open whoredome of the babylonicall strompet. **1547** BOORDE *Brev. Health* lxxiii. 21 b, I do say that an uryne is a strumpet, or an harlot, for it wyl lye, and the best Doctour of Phisicke of them all maye be deceyved in an uryne. **1563-83** FOXE *A. & M.* 799/2 John Houshold was charged to haue called..the Pope him selfe a strong strumpet, and a common baude vnto the world. **1595** SHAKS. *John* III. i. 61 France is a Bawd to Fortune, and king Iohn, That strumpet Fortune, that vsurping Iohn. **1602** —— *Ham.* II. ii. 515 Out, out, thou Strumpet-Fortune. **1663** PATRICK *Parab. Pilgrim* xxviii. (1687) 320 Those Divine Souls, who had converted the Muses, and of Courtesans and lewd Strumpets made them turn Religious and Saintly Creatures. **1727** P. WALKER *Vind. Cameron's Name* Biog. Presbyt. (1827) I. 315 That old Gray-headed Strumpet Prelacy. **1915** *Contemp. Rev.* Mar. 335 The Kaiser and his parasites have gone a-whoring after Bellona, the deadliest strumpet that ever wrecked the souls and bodies of men.

c. quasi-*adj.* That is a strumpet.

1596 SHAKS. *Merch. V.* II. vi. 16 The skarfed barke puts from her natiue bay, Hudg'd and embraced by the strumpet winde. *a* **1634** ? CHAPMAN *Alphonsus* V. i. 175 Will not your Grace dispatch the Strumpet Queen? **1812** COMBE *Syntax, Picturesque* XXIII, Oft have I said in words unkind, That strumpet Fortune's very blind.

d. *attrib.* and *Comb.*, as ***strumpet blood, flattery***; ***strumpet-like*** adj. and adv.; **strumpet-wise** *adv.*, after the manner of a strumpet.

1599 MARSTON *Antonio's Rev.* III. v, Disloyal to our Hymniall [*sic*] rites, What raging heat rains in thy *strumpet blood? **1641** MILTON *Ch. Govt.* II. Conclus. 64 But laying down his head among the *strumpet flatteries of Prelats, while he sleeps..they wickedly shaving off all those..tresses of his laws, and just prerogatives.., deliver him over [etc.]. **1574** J. BRADFORD *Two Notable Serm.* ii. K vj b, If thou doo not altogether consider Christes mynde, thou dealest vnhonestly & *strumpetlike with him. For it is the propertye of strumpets to consider the thynges geuen..them, rather then the loue..of the geuer. **1579** NORTHBROOKE *Dicing* 28 b, *Ludi Florales*, which were abhominable plaies in Rome, to the honour of their strumpetlike Goddesse *Flora*. **1647** STAPYLTON *Juvenal* 28 The more then strumpet-like impudence of these sarsenet judges. **1653** GATAKER *Vind. Annot. Jer.* 63 *Strumpet-wise fingring a lute, as the manner is,..where such are allowed, to invite customers to them.

Hence †'**strumpethood**, the condition of being a strumpet. †**strumpe'tier**, a whoremonger. **strumpe'tocracy** *jocular*, government by strumpets. †'**strumpetry**, harlotry (in quot. *fig.*).

1435 MISYN *Fire of Love* 54 þe couetus hart, for lufe of penys, to fendis strumpetry hys bosum opyns. *a* **1440** *Found. St. Bartholomew's* (E.E.T.S.) 55 And no more the ȝiftis of suche men plesith hym than the wagis of strompethode. **1633** T. ADAMS *Exp. 2 Peter* ii. 20. 1035 O that our luxurious Strumpetiers could reade in their diseased bodies the estate of their leprous soules. **1818** *Edin. Rev.* XXX. 425 In the *Strumpetocracy* of France, he had risen to this post by the most servile attention to Madame de Pompadour. **1833** CARLYLE *Misc. Ess., Diderot* (1888) 28 Where Denis (for heretical Metaphysics and irreverence to the Strumpetocracy) languishes in durance. **1899** H. S. WILSON in *New Cent. Rev.* V. 168 Zola wants to show in action the morals and manners..which developed the aristocracy of the Bourse and the strumpetocracy of Paris.

†'**strumpet**, *v. Obs.* [f. STRUMPET *sb.*]

1. *trans.* To bring to the condition of a strumpet.

1590 SHAKS. *Com. Err.* II. ii. 146 For if we two be one, and thou play false, I doe digest the poison of thy flesh, Being strumpeted by thy contagion. **1608** HEYWOOD *Lucrece* V. i. (1630) H 4, And by a stranger I am strumpeted, Rauisht, inforc'd. **1640** S. HARDING *Sicily & Naples* II. v. 30 Charintha's strumpetted; her name is rank't I' th vulgar breath, 'mongst common prostitutes. **1687** SETTLE *Refl. Dryden* 41 The King is aflicted for hearing his beloved Queen is strumpeted.

fig. *a* **1631** DONNE *Sat.* v. 69 Oh, ne'r may Faire lawes white reverend name be strumpeted, To warrant thefts. **1661** FELTHAM *Resolves* II. xxiii. (ed. 8) 229 Hee strumpets all his Businesse, that does disclose his secrets.

2. To repute as a strumpet; to debase (a woman's fame, name, virtue) to that of a strumpet.

c **1600** SHAKS. *Sonn.* lxvi. 6 And maiden vertue rudely strumpeted. **1632** MASSINGER *Maid of Hon.* III. iii, That proud man, that was Deny'd the honour of your bed, yet durst With his untrue reports, strumpet your fame. **1633** FORD *Broken Heart* IV. ii. H 2 b, To all memory, Penthea's, poore Penthea's name is strumpeted.

†**3.** intr. ***to strumpet it***, to play the strumpet.

1625 SANDERSON *Serm.* (1674) I. 119 When that God..shall see that people..to break the Covenant of Wedlock with him, and to strumpet it with the daughters and Idols of Moab.

Hence '**strumpeting** *vbl. sb.*

1656 BLOUNT *Glossogr.*, *Mechation*..fornication, Whoredom, strumpeting. *a* **1832** BENTHAM *Mem. & Corr.* Wks. 1843 X. 41 His life was one of gaming, drinking, and strumpeting.

†'**strumpetly**, *a.* and *adv. Obs. rare.* [-LY[1] and [2].] Like a strumpet.

a. **1614** tr. *Bp. Hall's No Peace with Rome* v. Wks. (1625) 640 Woe to thee thou Strumpetly Citie.

b. **1482** *Revel. Monk of Evesham* (Arb.) 43 The daye before she lefte her mortalle body in the whyche sche leuyd strompetly and vycyusly.

†**strumphusher.** *Obs.*[−1] [Of obscure origin.] (See quot.)

1631 LENTON *Charact.* C 5, A Pander..liues at all distances, and postures, one while Tapster, or Tobacco-seller, otherwise Strumphusher.

†'**strumple.** *Obs.* In 6 strumpell. [Alteration of STUMPLE (? influenced by STRUNT).] The fleshy stem of a horse's tail.

1598 R. HAYDOCKE tr. *Lomazzo* I. xx. 70 The truncke or strumpell is the beginning of the [horse's] taile. *Ibid.*, The taile which is fastned to the strumpell. **1879** MISS JACKSON *Shropsh. Word-bk.*, *Strumple sb.*, *obs.* ? the fleshy stump of a horse's tail left after 'docking'.

†'**strumstrum.** *Obs. rare.* [Echoic reduplication: see STRUM *v.*] A rude stringed instrument (see quots.).

1697 DAMPIER *Voy.* I. 127 The Strumstrum is made some-what like a Cittern; most of those that the Indians use are made of a large Goad cut in the midst, and a thin board laid over the hollow,..over which the strings are placed. **1728** *Capt. G. Carleton's Mem.* 279 Their Guitars..are their darling Instruments..: Tho' in my Opinion our English Sailors are not much amiss in giving them the Title of Strum Strums.

strumulose ('struːmjʊləʊs), *a.* [ad. mod.L. *strūmulōs-us*, f. *strūmula* dim. of *strūma*: see STRUMA and -OSE.] Having a small struma.

1866 *Treas. Bot.* **1900** B. D. JACKSON *Gloss. Bot. Terms.*

strund(e: see STRAND *sb.*[2], STRIND[1] and [2].

strung (strʌŋ), *ppl. a.* [pa. pple. of STRING *v.*]

1. Furnished or fitted with strings or a string. Cf. STRINGED *a.* 1, 1 b. Now *rare* or *Obs.*

1695 BLACKMORE *Pr. Arth.* IV. 65 Choice Instruments, some Strung, and some of Wind. **1714** GAY *Fan* II. 40 Ceres is with the bending Sickle seen, And the strung Bow points out the Cynthian Queen. **1754** BOYER *Gt. Theat. Honour* (ed. 2) 116 Strung, Adj. (is used to express the Strings of any thing), *Lié, Cordé, Cordonné.*

2. Threaded on a string.

1687 A. LOVELL tr. *Thevenot's Trav.* III. 29 He found twenty two Pound weight of strung Pearls. **1797** *Encycl. Brit.* (ed. 3) XV. 702/2 [*Pyrotechny*] Strung stars. **1901** ALLDRIDGE *Sherbro* xv. 145 None of the women wear any clothes, there is simply a sufficiency of strung beads around their waists. **1907** *Arbroath Guide* 15 June 2 The long line of 'strung' whitings overhead swing with the breeze.

3. ***strung out***: spread out in a straggling line. Also, extended, continuing in a long series.

1902 *Daily Chron.* 5 Mar. 7/4 The strung-out line of pursuers. **1914** *Blackw. Mag.* Nov. 588 Mahsud raiders had attacked the strung-out 'Kafila' on its way down the Gomul. **1978** *Language* LIV. 91 This falls short of accounting for strung-out MI correspondences where relative orderings remain the same.

4. In the sense of STRING *v.* 3. **a.** Of nerves, feelings, etc.: In a state of tension. Also ***strung-up***, and (*N. Amer. slang*) ***strung out*** (overlaps with sense c below). **b.** With prefixed adv., ***finely-***, ***highly-strung***: said of persons with reference to their nervous organization or condition.

1840 DICKENS *Old C. Shop* xiv, For, when your finely strung people are out of sorts, they must have everybody else unhappy likewise. **1853** MRS. GASKELL *Ruth* xvi, When there was nothing to decide upon,..Ruth's mind relaxed from its strung-up state. **1875** WHYTE MELVILLE *Katerfelto* xviii, On Waif's strung nerves and weary frame it jarred acutely. **1899** *Allbutt's Syst. Med.* VII. 855 We have already seen how highly strung and excitable the subjects of chorea usually are. **1900** *Daily News* 17 May 3/2 The strung thought, intense vision of statesmen. **1910** B. CAPES *Jemmy Abercraw* II. xvii, She stopped, and faced about, her eyes burning, strung passion in her attitude. **1933** M. DE LA ROCHE *Master of Jalna* xv. 198 She worries greatly over the child and that keeps her in a strung-up state. **1967** *N.Y. Times* 18 Aug. 22 'These are very strung-out kids with individual hang-ups,' said Jim Fouratt..describing the modern runaway. **1974** M. HASKELL *From Reverence to Rape* 208 Martha Vickers' spoiled, strung-out younger sister. **1979** K. M. PEYTON *Marion's Angels* ix. 137 You don't think she might Have——? Oh, Christ! She was strung up when she left me. We both were. **1980** *Globe & Mail* (Toronto) 20 Mar. T1/5 She takes to the streets daily in response to calls from tenants to investigate nuisance neighbours who might be strung out emotionally.

c. ***strung out***: weak or ill, esp. as a result of drug addiction; hence, addicted to, using, or 'high' *on* drugs. *slang* (orig. and chiefly *U.S.*).

1959 *Esquire* Nov. 70 *Strung Out*, in bad physical condition. **1960** *Jazz Rev.* Nov. 8/2 Unfortunately it was at this period he acquired the 'monkey' and frequently was strung out. **1965** *N.Y. Post* 3 Dec. 45/1 If one spends time talking to marijuana users, one can only conclude that the entire college population is 'strung out' thrice weekly. **1966** *San Francisco Chron.* 29 June 3 Acid does nothing for me...I love to get strung out on pot. **1973** *Black World* Aug. 59/1 The horns..lef' by some strungout junky musician. **1977** *Guardian Weekly* 30 Oct. 15/4 Young people get strung out on heroin.

strunt (strʌnt), *sb.*[1] Now *dial.* (*Sc.* and *north.*) [Cf. STRUNT *a.*; also Sw. dial. *strunt* stiff grass.] The fleshy part of the tail of an animal, esp. of a horse; also, rarely, that of a bird. Hence, also, the whole tail.

[**1577**: cf. STRUNT *a.*] **1610** MARKHAM *Masterp.* I. ciii. 205 Feele all downe the strunte of his taile with your hand. **1674** RAY *N.C. Words*, *Strunt*: the tail or rump. **1679** *Lond. Gaz.* No. 1413/4 A gray Nag..with a sprig tail, and his Strunt groweth crooked towards the right buttock. **1788** W. H. MARSHALL *Yorksh.* II. 357 *Strunt*; the dock of a horse, independant of the hair, also the tail of slaughtered cattle or sheep, when the skin is taken off. **1866** BROGDEN *Prov. Lincs.*, *Strunt*, the rump of a bird. **1884** G. S. STREATFEILD *Lincolnsh. & Danes* Gloss. 368 *Strunt*, the denuded tail of a quadruped or bird. **1886** *S.W. Linc. Gloss.*, *Strunt*, the bony, fleshy part of a horse's tail. 'It's strunt's so long; it's a pity but what it were docked.' 'The hair's cutten off close agen the strunt's end.' *a* **1930** D. H. LAWRENCE *Phoenix* (1936) 16 Wag thy [*sc.* a puppy's] strunt, then!

strunt (strʌnt), *sb.*[2] *Sc.* and *north.* [Cf. STRUM *sb.*[4], STUNT *sb.*[1] 3.] A fit of ill-humour or sulks; esp. in phr. ***to take the strunt***.

1721 RAMSAY *Richy & Sandy* 8 Wow man, that's unco' sad,—Is't that ye'r jo Has ta'en the strunt? **1776** C. KEITH *Farmer's Ha'* lv, Take tent, and nae wi' strunts offend. **1776** *Herd's Scott. Songs* (ed. 2) II. 222 Fare ye weel, my auld wife, The steerer up o' strunt and strife. *c* **1817** HOGG *Tales & Sk.* V. 287 The Marquess took the strunt, and would neither ratify some further engagement which he had come under, nor stand to those he had subscribed on oath. **1894** *Northumbld. Gloss.*, *Strunt*, a pique, pet. 'He's teyun the strunts.' **1895** P. H. HUNTER *James Inwick* iii. 31 The laird took the strunt on the heid o't, an' gied ower comin to the kirk.

strunt (strʌnt), *sb.*[3] *Sc.* [Of obscure origin.] Spirituous liquor.

1786 BURNS *Halloween* xxviii, Syne, wi' a social glass o' strunt, They parted aff careerin Fu' blythe that night. ? **1788** —— *Meg o' the Mill* 7 A dram o' gude strunt in a morning early.

†**strunt**, *a. north. Obs.* [Cf. STUNT *a.*] Stumpy.

1577 *Richmond Wills* (Surtees) 273, I geve and bequethe unto Christofer Wyvell..my dunne horse which was under strunte tayle maire. **1658** FRANCK *North. Mem.* (1694) 155 Let..your Hooks [be] well tempered..; their Points well drawn out, and as sharp as Needles, but their Birbs as stiff and as strunt as Bristles.

strunt (strʌnt), *v.*[1] [f. STRUNT *sb.*[1]] *trans.* To cut short, esp. to dock the tail of (a horse or sheep). Hence '**strunted** *ppl. a.*

1688 HOLME *Armoury* II. 176/2 Terms used by Shepheards... Strunted sheep, is when their Tails are cut off to keep them from Dunging them, and breeding of Maggots therein. **1703** THORESBY *Let. to Ray*, *Strunted* pp., cut off short. **1828** CARR *Craven Gloss.*, *Strunt*, to dock a horse's tail. **1889** *N.W. Linc. Gloss.* (ed. 2), *Strunt*, to dock the tail of a horse; sometimes, though very rarely, used with regard to sheep also.

strunt (strʌnt), *v.*[2] *Sc.* [Cf. STRUT *v.*; also Norw. *strunta* to walk stiffly as under a burden; to be haughty and stiff in manner (Ross).] *intr.* To move with a self-important air.

The ordinary version of *Muirland Willie* (see 1st quot.) runs: The wooer he stept up the house.

17.. *Old Song* (Jam. 1808) The wooer strunted up the house. **1786** BURNS *To a Louse* i, I canna say but ye strunt rarely, Owre gawze and lace. **1789** D. DAVIDSON *Seasons* 50 An to Strathfallan green burn-brae Fu' nimbly she [*sc.* a cow] did strunt.

struntain ('strʌntɪn). *Sc.* [Of obscure origin.] (See quot. 1858.)

1793 *Statist. Acc. Scot.* VII. 138 Before this period, the only manufacture was what is called Stow Struntain, made of the coarsest wool, and wrought by the women on a loom like a bed-heck. **1858** SIMMONDS *Dict. Trade*, *Struntain*, the name in Scotland for a kind of coarse worsted braid, less than an inch broad.

strunty ('strʌntɪ), *a. Sc.* and *north.* [f. STRUNT *a.* or *sb.*[1] + -Y.] Stunted, short.

1756 MRS. CALDERWOOD in *Coltness Coll.* II. (Maitland Club) 169 All the road we had to travell was a dead sandy desart, covered with a poor strunty heather. **1808** JAMIESON, *Strunty*, short, contracted; as a strunty gown. **1897** 'L. KEITH' *My Bonny Lady* xviii. 198 For a' he's sic a wee, strunty, little-boukit fella', he's got mair spunk in his pinkie than mony a man in his hail body.

strunzite ('strʌnzaɪt). *Min.* [ad. G. *strunzite* (C. Frondel 1957, in *Neues Jahrb. f. Min.: Monatshefte* 222), f. the name of K. Hugo *Strunz* (b. 1910), German mineralogist: see -ITE[1].] A hydrated basic phosphate of manganese and iron, $MnFe_2(PO_4)_2(OH)_2.8H_2O$, found as tiny yellow hair- or lath-like monoclinic crystals and produced by the weathering of manganese and iron phosphates.

1958 C. FRONDEL in *Naturwissenschaften* XLV. 38/1 Among the outstanding problems in the mineralogy of the hydrated phosphates of iron and manganese has been the identity of a straw yellow mineral first recognized in 1947...The writer takes pleasure in naming this mineral after Dr. Hugo Strunz, Professor of Mineralogy at Berlin. **1975** *Mineral. Record* VI. 71/2 Stewartite, strunzite, and cacoxenite, which in our specimens are confined to oxidized assemblage[s], are the products of weathering.

strupt(e, obs. pa. t. and pa. pple. of STRIP *v.*[1]

†**struse.** *Obs.* Also 7 **strusse.** [? repr. Russian *struzhok*, dim. of *strug* a kind of large boat (see quot. *c* 1581).] (See quots.)

[*c* **1581** C. BURROUGH in Hakluyt *Voy.* (1589) 441 Then the three stroogs or barks prouided to transport the said goods to Astracan..came ouer from Yeraslaue.] **1701** *Lond. Gaz.* No. 3727/3 Several large Boats of the Muscovite Built, called Strusses. **1782** P. H. BRUCE *Mem.* VII. 237 We met several strusses, or flat-bottomed vessels, carrying from eight to nine hundred tons, which go loaded from Astrachan to Moscow. **1858** SIMMONDS *Dict. Trade, Struse*, a long burdensome craft, used for transport on the inland waters of Russia.

†**strussioner.** *Obs. rare*[−1]. Meant to represent an illiterate corruption: ? for *destructioner*.

1553 *Respublica* 1779 Suche Strussioners as these have ofte made youe beleeve the Moone was a grene chese.

†**strust,** *v. Obs.* Also 5 **strost.** [An unexplained alteration of TRUST *v.*] *trans.* and *intr.* To trust. So †'**strusty** *a.* = TRUSTY.

a **1225** *Ancr. R.* 66 To sum gostliche monne þet ȝe beoð strusti uppen..god is þet ȝe asken red. *Ibid.* 380 Þeo hulles þet beoð lowure, þeo, ase þe lefdi seið, hire sulf ouerleapeð, ne strusteð heo so wel on ham, uor hore feblesce. **1450** *Paston Lett.* I. 102 The seid Duke of Suffolk being..strostid be you and alle your councellors to knowe the privite of your councell ther.

strut (strʌt), *sb.*[1] Forms: 3–4 **strutt,** 4 **strot,** 4, 9 *dial.* **strout,** 3–4, 7– **strut.** See also STURT *sb.* and A-STRUT. [The form *strout* prob. represents an OE. **strūt* = OHG., MHG. *strûz* masc., combat, strife (MHG. also *strûze* fem.; mod.G. dial. *strauss*):—OTeut. type **strūto-z*, f. root **strŭt-*, perh. orig. meaning to stand out, project, protrude; cf. ON. *strút-r* conical headdress, Norw. *strut* spout, snout, Da. *strud* end of a sausage, etc., Sw. *strut* cornet of paper. The forms *strut)t* and perh. *strot* appear to represent a different formation (from the weak grade of the root); see STRUT *v.*[1], and cf. Norw. *strutt* obstinate resistance.]

1. Strife, contention; a quarrel, wrangle, contest. *Obs.* exc. *dial.*

a **1300** *Cursor M.* 3461 Þair strut it was vn-stern stith. *Ibid.* 27617 O pride bicums vnbuxumnes, strif, and strutt, and frawardnes. *c* **1300** *Havelok* 1039 And he maden mikel strout Abouten þe alþerbeste but. **13..** *E.E. Allit. P.* A. 848 Among vus commez non oþer strot ne stryf. **1677** W. HUGHES *Man of Sin* II. i. 6 Could there be a strut, or fewd betwixt the two Apostles? *a* **1825** FORBY *Voc. E. Anglia, Strout*, a struggle; bustle; quarrel.

†**2.** Display, flaunting in fine attire. *Obs.*

1303 R. BRUNNE *Handl. Synne* 3347 But wlde þey þenke þat make swyche strut, yn what robe, yn erþe, þey shul be put.

strut (strʌt), *sb.*[2] Also 7–9 **strutt.** [Proximate origin obscure; from the root of STRUT *sb.*[1], *v.*[1] Cf. LG. *strutt*, rigid.]

1. A bar, rod, or built-up member, of wood, iron, etc., designed to resist pressure or thrust in a framework; e.g. a diagonal timber which acts as a brace to support a principal rafter.

1587 MASCALL *Bk. Cattle* II. (1596) 120 Preparing the cart... See the rath staues and struts be whole and sound. **1668** LEYBOURN *Platf. Purchasers* 132, K King-piece or Joggle-piece. L Strutts. **1688** HOLME *Armoury* III. 450/1 Struts, or Bunspars, pieces that go from either side the Kings piece to the Rafter of the Gable end to support them. **1755** HALES *Distillation* in *Phil. Trans.* XLIX. 314 Three or four small struts may be fixed to the sides of the air-box. **1845** *Civil Engin. & Arch. Jrnl.* VIII. 213/1 Mr. Adie introduced a series of arches or struts, traversing the railway at intervals of 15 feet from centre to centre. These struts consisted of two arches of rubble and rough ashlar masonry, placed back to back. **1854** MISS BAKER *Northampt. Gloss., Strut*, a pole or stick, with a spike at the end, to be let down from the shaft of a cart, to keep the weight off the horse's back when standing still with a heavy load. **1859** *Newton's Lond. Jrnl. Arts* 1 Feb. 114 A short iron strut or link is jointed to the thin end of each tongue-rail and to the end chair. **1879** *Cassell's Techn. Educ.* I. 107/2 Beyond that opening, how-ever, bridges are usually sustained by struts or tension-rods. **1886** *Encycl. Brit.* XXI. 819/2 The beam is required to act as a shore or strut, to prevent the sides of the ship from collapsing, and also as a tie to prevent their falling apart.

b. *attrib.*, as ***strut-brace***, †-***stower***; **strut-beam** = *strutting-beam* (see STRUTTING *vbl. sb.*[2] c).

1668 LEYBOURN *Platf. Purchasers* 132 Of the Roof... Coller-beam, Strutt-beam, Window-beam, or Top-beam. **17..** in F. Peck *Mem. O. Cromwell* etc. II. (1740) 58 [Alleged covenant of A.D. 1159] He shall deliver to you..ten stakes, eleven strut stowers & eleven yeathers, to be cut by you. **1869** RANKINE *Machine & Hand-tools* App. 26 The most efficient position for those ribs would be diagonal, like that of the strut-braces in a skeleton beam.

¶**2.** The alleged sense in quot. 1865 and subsequent Dicts. 'An implement of bone or wood formerly used to shape the folds of ruffs' is founded on quot. 1575, where *stroout* appears to be for *strouted* pa. pple. of *strout*, STRUT *v.*[1] (sense 2 c).

1575 LANEHAM *Let.* 47 Hiz shyrt..with rufs fayr starched, ..marshalld in good order: with a setting stik, & stroout y[t] euery ruf stood vp like a wafer. **1865** MRS. BURY PALLISER *Hist. Lace* xxiii. 286 The tools used in starching and fluting ruffs were called setting-sticks, struts, and poking-sticks; the two first were made of wood or bone.

strut (strʌt), *sb.*[3] Also 7 **strout.** [f. STRUT *v.*[1]]

a. A manner of walking with stiff steps and head erect, affecting dignity or superiority; a stiff, self-important gait.

1607 G. WILKINS *Mis. Enf. Marr.* IV. G 2, Curle vp your haire, walke with the best strouts you can. **1712** ADDISON *Spect.* No. 335 ¶2 Upon the entring of Pyrrhus, the Knight told me, that he did not believe the King of France himself had a better Strut. **1768** H. WALPOLE *Let. to Earl Strafford* 16 Aug., He has the sublime strut of his grandfather, or of a cock-sparrow. **1784** COWPER *Task* v. 74 The cock foregoes His wonted strut. **1847** DE QUINCEY *Sp. Mil. Nun* xii. Wks. 1853 III. 32 Mr. Urquiza entered first, with a strut more than usually grandiose.

b. *fig.*

c **1800** A. HAMILTON in F. S. Oliver *Life* (1906) 198 Real firmness is good for anything; strut is good for nothing. **1861** PEARSON *Early & Mid. Ages Eng.* xxvii. 330 A little more strut and bluster are required for the heroes who tread the stage of the world. **1877** MRS. OLIPHANT *Makers Flor.* vi. 167 That strut and crow of conscious superiority which is..so common among his class.

c. A type of slow and complicated dance or dance-step.

[**1917**: see SHIMMY *sb.*[2] 1]. **1937** [see *Big Apple* s.v. BIG *a.* B. 2]. **1970** C. MAJOR *Dict. Afro-Amer. Slang* 111 *Strut*.., a fancy-step slow dance. **1979** R. B. GILLESPIE *Crossword Mystery* i. 17 He..executed a few soft-shoe steps which merged into a strut.

strut (strʌt), *sb.*[4] [f. STRUT *v.*[2]] The act of strutting; deflexion (of the spoke of a wheel) from the perpendicular.

1880 *Encycl. Brit.* XI. 311/1 There is little strut, so that the lowest spoke is nearly vertical, and the tire forms a frustum of a cone, instead of being a cylinder.

†**strut,** *a. Obs.* In 8 *Sc.* **strute.** [Connected with STRUT *v.*[1]; perh. orig. the pa. pple.] So full as to be swollen or distended. Also *Sc.*, intoxicated, 'fou'. Also in comb. ***strut-bellied*** adj.

1577 tr. *Bullinger's Decades* III. iii. (1592) 313 The state of famished Lazarus..was farre better than the surfetting of the strut-bellied glutton. **1601** HOLLAND *Pliny* XI. xli. I. 348 Many [women] are so frim and free of milke, that all their breasts are strut and full thereof, even as farre as to their arme-holes. **1609** —— *Amm. Marcell.* 213 When hee beginneth now to returne with his bellie strut and full. **1715** RAMSAY *Christ's Kirk Gr.* II. xvii, When he was strute, twa sturdy chiels..Held up..The liquid logic scholar. **1724** —— *Wyfe of Auchtermuchty* xiv, The deil cut aff their hands .., That cramd your kytes sae strute yestrein.

strut (strʌt), *v.*[1] Inflected **strutted, strutting.** Forms: α. 1 **strútian,** 3–7 **stroute,** 4–7 **strowte,** 6–7 **strowt, stroot(e,** 6–9 **strout.** β. 3–5 **strut(e,** 6 **strutte,** 7 **strutt,** 6– **strut.** [The α forms represent OE. *strútian*, prob. f. **strút* STRUT *sb.*[1]; corresponding formations are mod.G. dial. *straussen* to wrangle, Da. *strude* to strut; also (with difference of conjugation), MHG. *striuzen* wk. v. to contend, struggle (mod.G. dial. *sträussen*). The β forms, though they may partly have arisen from contracted pa. pple. forms with shortened vowel, appear also to represent a distinct formation (not recorded in OE.) from the weak grade of the root, corresponding to MHG., mod.G. *strotzen* to swell out, bulge, Sw. *strutta* to hop, strut, Da. *strutte* to strut, Norw. *strutta* to offer obstinate resistance, *strotta* to sulk. Although the α and β types partly represent different formations, both are found in each of the senses; they are therefore here treated as variants of the same word.]

†**1.** *intr.* (Meaning somewhat uncertain.) ? To make a show of working; ? to struggle, make efforts. *OE. rare*[−1].

c **1000** ÆLFRIC *Saints' Lives* XXXII. 208 Swa þæt se halȝa wer [*sc.* the enshrined St. Eadmund] hi [*sc.* a band of robbers] wundorlice ȝeband, ælcne swa he stod strutiȝende mid tole [orig. *sanctus martyr eos ligat in ipso conamine*], þæt heora nan ne mihte þæt morð ȝefremman, ne hi þanon astyrian.

†**2. a.** To bulge, swell; to protrude on account of being full or swollen. Often with *out. Obs.*

α. *a* **1300** *Rel. Ant.* II. 15 Ne be þi winpil neuere..so stroutende. **1398** TREVISA *Barth. De P.R.* XIII. xxix. (Tollem. MS.) And ofte he bloweþ outt his wombe and makeþ it stroute. *c* **1440** *Promp. Parv.* 480/2 Strowtyn, or bocyn owte, *turgeo*. *c* **1611** CHAPMAN *Iliad* I. 464 The Misens strooted with the gale. **1612** DRAYTON *Poly-olb.* XIII. 402 The daintie Clouer..That makes each Vdder strout abundantly with milke. **1668** CULPEPER & COLE *Barthol. Anat.* I. xx. 51 Somtimes being full, it [the Bladder] does so strout in the belly, that it may be felt by the hand. **1854** MISS BAKER *Northampt. Gloss., Strout*, to protrude, to swell.

β. **1606** DEKKER *News fr. Hell* Wks. (Grosart) II. 124 Hauing..cheeks strutting out (like two footebals). **1609** HOLLAND *Amm. Marcell.* 373 Being for the nonce full of wine, till his skin strutted againe. **1678** MRS. BEHN *Sir P. Fancy* II. ii. 28 Lord how he's swoln? see how his Stomach struts? **1771** J. ADAMS *Diary* 5 June, Wks. 1850 II. 268 The cow, whose teats strut with milk, is unmilked till nine o'clock.

†**b.** *transf.* To be stuffed or filled *with. Obs.*

c **1611** CHAPMAN *Iliad* XXI. 540 When Troy, and all her towres, Strooted with fillers. *a* **1624** BP. M. SMITH *Serm.* (1632) 221 If the Exchequer doe stroute, and be stuft with siluer and gold.

†**c.** *trans.* To distend, cause to swell or bulge, make protuberant; to puff *out*. Also, to stuff or cram (*with*). *Obs.*

1540 PALSGR. *Acolastus* II. iv. M iv, That scrippe or bagge ..whiche is now..stroutted out with moche money. **1575** BANISTER *Chyrurg.* I. (1585) 17 When the veines are strowted out by the effusion of humor. **1613** PURCHAS *Pilgrimage* IX. iii. 700 Knitting their furrowed browes, and strouting out their goggle eyes to watch their treasure. **1648** HERRICK *Hesp., Paranæt. to M. J. Wicks* 21 And let Thy servant, not thy own self, sweat, To strut thy barnes with sheafs of Wheat. **1675** J. SMITH *Chr. Relig. Appeal* IV. 84, I have seen children, when they are strutted with the Milk, Play with the Breast. *c* **1730** RAMSAY *Boy & Pig* 9 The strait neck o't [*sc.* the pot] wadna suffer The hand..Sae struted, to return again. **1740** in Mrs. Delany *Autobiog. & Corr.* (1861) II. 72 His lady looked like a frightened owl, her locks strutted out and most furiously greased.

fig. *c* **1624** BACON *Consid. War with Spain* (1629) 33, I will make a briefe List of the Particulars themselues, in an Historical Truth, no wayes strowted, nor made greater by Language.

†**3.** *intr.* To contend, strive, quarrel, bluster. *Obs.*

a **1300** *Cursor M.* 829 Al bigan to strut and strijf [*G.* All bigan stour and strijf] Agains adam and his wijf. *c* **1300** *Havelok* 1779 Hwat are ye, þat are þer-oute, þat þus biginnen forto stroute? *c* **1330** *Arth. & Merl.* 233 Who so struted oȝainward, Anon þai ȝauen hem dintes hard. **1399** LANGL. *Rich. Redeles* III. 189 This makyth men mysdo more þan ouȝte ellis, And to stroute and to stare and stryue aȝeyn vertu. *c* **1400** *Beryn* 1840 What evir þow speke, or stroute, certis it wol nat be.

†**4. a.** To protrude stiffly from a surface or body; to stand *out*, jut *forth*. Also, to stick *up*. *Obs.*

α. *c* **1386** CHAUCER *Miller's T.* 129 Crul was his heer, and as the gold it shoon, And strouted as a Fanne, large and brode. **1566** ADLINGTON *Apuleius* XI. xlviii. 124, I carried.. a garlande of flowres upon my head, with palme leaves stroutinge out on every side. **1600** FAIRFAX *Tasso* IX. viii, Mustachoes strouting long.

β. **1676** T. GLOVER *Acc. Virginia* in *Phil. Trans.* XI. 635 Till such time as the leaves, that stood strutting out, fall down to the stalk. **1703** DAMPIER *Voy.* III. i. 24 They [guinea fowl] have a small red Gill on each side of their Heads, like Ears, strutting out downwards. **1705** tr. *Bosman's Guinea* 264 They are called Crown-Birds, from the great yellowish Tuft or Crown intermixed with speckled Feathers, strutting like Hogs Bristles. **1772** FOOTE *Nabob* II. Wks. 1799 II. 302 A tulip strutting up like a magistrate's mace. **1809** W. IRVING *Knickerb.* II. iv. (1849) 108 By the foot of a promontory, which strutted forth boldly into the waves.

†**b.** *trans.* To protrude, thrust forth, stick *out*, stretch *out* (an organ, part, growth). *Obs.*

1583 GOLDING *Calvin on Deut.* lxxii. 444 If wee will not bowe downe our neckes but strout them out as harde as if they were steele or brasse. **1599** BRETON *Will of Wit* etc. (Grosart) 57/2 If she stretch out a fine hande, hee strouteth out a straight legge. **1681** COLVIL *Whigs Supplic.* (1751) 41 Wild-Boars strouting out their bristles.

†**5. a.** *intr.* To behave proudly or vaingloriously; to flaunt, triumph, swagger. Often ***to strut it***, also ***to strut it out***. Also, to glory, exult *upon*, *over* (a possession). *Obs.* (exc. as in 7 c).

α. *c* **1570** *Buggbears* I. iii. 47 Thou woldst have me..hack & hew my clothes, & go stroot it like a tossepotte. **1579** GOSSON *Sch. Abuse* (Arb.) 36 Desirous to strowt it with the beste, yet disdayning too liue by the sweate of their browes. **1611** COTGR. s.v. *Paladin*, He swaggers, brags, or strouts it mightily. *a* **1643** J. SHUTE *Judgem. & Mercy* (1645) 90 Nebuchadnezar..when he was strouting upon his Babell, and bragged of his power.

β. **1611** COTGR., *Piaffer*,..to boast, or strut it vainely. **1675** T. BROOKS *Golden Key* 220 Those proud enemies of Christ, who now..strut it out against him. **1684** T. BURNET *Theory Earth* I. 297 He will many times strut and triumph, as if he had wrested the thunder out of Jove's right hand. **1754** RICHARDSON *Grandison* IV. 61 The one strutting over the beauties, in order to enhance the value of the present; the other, courtesying ten times in a minute, to shew her gratitude.

†**b.** *refl.* in the same sense as prec. (Cf. *boast, vaunt oneself*.) *Obs.*

1655 GURNALL *Chr. in Arm.* I. verse 13. vii. (1656) 364 Nebuchadnezzar strutting himself in his Palace with this bravado in his mouth, Is not this great Babylon that I have built? *a* **1716** SOUTH *Serm.* (1727) IV. 84 See Nebuchadnezzar also strutting himself upon the Survey of that Mass of Riches.

†**6. a.** *intr.* To raise oneself to one's full height; to thrust up one's head and stand erect; to perk *up*. Also *fig. Obs.*

1607 CHAPMAN *Bussy d'Ambois* I. i. 7 Vnskilfull statuaries, who suppose (In forging a Colossus) if they make him Straddle enough, stroote, and looke big, and gape, Their worke is goodly. **1612** DRAYTON *Poly-olb.* v. 288 And there-withall he [a mountain] struts, as though he scorn'd to show His head belowe the Heauen. **1614** GORGES *Lucan* III. 117 Then Lygdanus by chance did eye, Tyrrhenus mounted loftily, Strowting vpon a Gallion's puppe [L. *Stantem sublimi Tyrrhenum culmine proræ*]. **1662** GREENHALGH in Ellis *Orig. Lett.* Ser. II. IV. 19 At which they shewed great rejoicing, by strutting up, so that some of their veils flew about like morris dancers. **1791** BOSWELL *Johnson* (1904) I. 32 Johnson did not strut or stand on tiptoe: He only did not stoop. **1807** J. BARLOW *Columb.* I. 352 Taurus would shrink, Hemodia strut no more.

†**b.** *refl.* ? To stand erect, with feet firmly fixed on the ground. *Obs.*

1581 MULCASTER *Positions* viii. (1887) 51 Would any man beleue it,..that one Milo so strutted himselfe, so pitcht his feet, so peysed his bodie, as he remained vnremoueable from his place, being haled at..by a number of people.

†**c.** *intr.* Of the legs: To be firmly fixed or planted on the ground. *Obs.*

1681 DRYDEN *Span. Friar* III. 32 What are become of those two Timber-loggs that he us'd to wear for Leggs, that stood strutting like the two black Posts before a door?

7. a. To walk with an affected air of dignity or importance, stepping stiffly with head erect. Also with *it*, and with adv., as *about*, *off*. (The current sense.)

α. **1594** NASHE *Unfort. Trav.* K1, He ietteth strouting, dancing on hys toes with his hands vnder his sides. *a* **1624** BP. M. SMITH *Serm.* (1632) 170 They that carry their noses high into the wind,..and stroute in their gate, as though they went vpon stilts. **1640** C. HARVEY *Synagogue, Engines* vii. (1647) 31 Nor that, which giant-like before did strout, Be able with a pigmeys pace t'hold out.

β. **1518** *Galway Corporation Bk.* in O'Flaherty *West Connaught* (Irish Archæol. Soc. 1846) 35 *note*, That neither One Mac shall strutte ne swaggere thro' the streets of Gallway. **1598** SHAKS. *Merry W.* I. iv. 31 Do's he not hold vp his head (as it were?) and strut in his gate? **1638** W. LISLE *Heliodorus* x. 180 Full soone came in the gyant Æthiops, On tip-toe strutting. **1693** T. POWER in *Dryden's Juvenal* xii. 159 Pacuvius struts it, and triumphant goes In the dejected Crowd of Rival Foes. **1733** POPE *Ep. Cobham* 153 Tom struts a Soldier, open, bold, and brave. **1849** D. G. MITCHELL *Battle Summer* (1852) 242 Stiff little Republicans strut about as if in togas. **1887** BESANT *The World went* ii, He strutted proudly across the grass, regardless of his rags.

b. of a peacock or other fowl.

1591 SYLVESTER *Du Bartas* I. iv. 199 A Peacock, prickt with love's desire, To woo his Mistress, strouting stately by her. **1632** MILTON *L'Allegro* 52 While the Cock..Stoutly struts his Dames before. **1795** COWPER *Pairing Time* 39 Dick Redcap..strutting and sideling. **1840** DICKENS *Old C. Shop* xv, Plump pigeons skimming round the roof or strutting on the eaves. **1847** LONGF. *Ev.* I. i, And there, in his feathered seraglio, Strutted the lordly turkey.

c. *fig.*

1774 BURKE *Amer. Tax.* Sel. Wks. I. 103 In order meanly to sneak out of difficulties, into which they had proudly strutted. **1814** WORDSW. *Excurs.* III. 900 Big passions strutting on a petty stage. **1850** HAWTHORNE *Scarlet L.* Introd. (1879) 24 His voice and laugh..came strutting out of his lungs, like the crow of a cock.

d. quasi-*trans.* with cognate or adverbial object.

1605 SHAKS. *Macb.* V. v. 25 A poore Player, That struts and frets his houre vpon the Stage. **1749** FIELDING *Tom Jones* XV. xi, He..then strutted some turns about his room. **1824** MEDWIN *Convers. Byron* I. 122 Think how he would mouth such and such a sentence,..strut such and such a scene.

e. *trans.* To walk upon or over (a floor, space) with a strut.

1749 FIELDING *Tom Jones* XIV. i, Hence those strange monsters in lace and embroidery,..which, under the name of lords and ladies, strut the stage. **1810** *Splendid Follies* I. 170 No eastern princess, strutting the boards of a puppet-show, ever exhibited [etc.].

f. *to strut one's stuff*: to display one's ability. *U.S. slang.*

1926 C. VAN VECHTEN *Nigger Heaven* II. vi. 242 Some one cried, Strut your stuff, Lasca! **1935** [see ROLLER *sb.*[1] 18 d]. **1941** *Sun* (Baltimore) 30 Aug. 13/1 Rain today made the prospect for off-going for the first card, thus giving the 'mudders' an opportunity to strut their stuff. **1972** *N.Y. Times* 3 Nov. 28/1 The company is going to strut its stuff, with nothing more in mind than to entertain, in Washington Square, near the Arch. There will be singing and dancing and acting and acrobatics. **1977** *Rolling Stone* 30 June 121/1 (Advt.), Each run is equipped with a super, custom-designed sound system, so you can 'strut your stuff' or 'space walk' to your favorite tunes.

g. *intr.* To dance the strut. Cf. STRUT *sb.*[2] c.

1975 *Time Out* 8 Aug. 67/1 D'you wanna shake, strut, shimmy, jive, twist, waltz, mash potato, tango, tap or conga?

Hence †**'strutted** *ppl. a.*, distended, full-stored. (Cf. STRUT *a.*)

1648 EARL WESTMORLAND *Otia Sacra* (1879) 33 Are not my strutted Vessels full of Wine?

strut (strʌt), *v.*[2] Also 9 strutt. [f. STRUT *sb.*[2]]

1. *trans.* To brace or support by a strut or struts; to hold in place or strengthen by an upright, diagonal, or transverse support. Also with advs.

1828 CARR *Craven Gloss., Strut*, to brace, a term used in carpentry. **1838** *Civil Engin. & Arch. Jrnl.* I. 374/2 If the resistance piles are sufficiently braced and strutted not to yield by the driving of the wedges. **1845** *Civil Engin. & Archit. Jrnl.* VIII. 212/1 The toes of the walls will require to be strutted apart. **1869** SIR E. REED *Shipbuild.* i. 12 A ship rolling about with a heavy cargo will alter her form, as regards its transverse section, very much, if she is built of iron, and is not sufficiently strutted and tied with beams. *a* **1878** SIR G. SCOTT *Lect. Archit.* (1879) II. 225 In Henry VII's Chapel these great arches are visible only in the side vaults, which are strutted up from them with strong tracery. **1897** *Pall Mall Mag.* June 254 The old boat was no more than waterproof, and..Severn had to run a new stringer round her, to strut out the ribs. **1912** C. H. POWER *Eng. Mediæv. Arch.* II. 340 Flying Buttress to strut the Vault.

fig. **1832** *Examiner* 161/1 Employing, to boot, all tricky expedients to strutt up the tottering system.

2. *intr.* To be fixed diagonally or slantwise; to be bent so as to form a sharp turn or angle.

1841 W. TEMPLETON *Locomot. Eng.* 30 The best form of wrought iron wheels, is round arms strutting from the rim to the nave in a zig-zag form. **1853** SIR H. DOUGLAS *Milit. Bridges* 291 Braces, strutting considerably, were driven down as far as possible into the bottom of the river, at each end of the trestles.

'struth, var. 'STREWTH.

struther, variant of STROTHER *Obs.*

struthiin ('struːθɪɪn). *Chem.* Also 9 **strutheine.** [f. mod.L. (*Gypsophila*) *Struthi-um* the oriental soapwort, one of the sources of the substance (ad. Gr. στρουθίον soapwort): see -IN.] = SAPONIN.

1835 *R. D. & T. Thomson's Rec. Gen. Sci.* I. 203 Bley has obtained from the root of the *gypsophila struthium*..a substance which he terms Struthiin. **1852** BRANDE *Dict. Sci.* etc. Suppl., *Strutheine.* **1868** WATTS *Dict. Chem.* V. 438.

†**,struthio'camel(e, -ell.** *Obs.* [ad. L. *strūthiocamēlus*, incorrectly a. Gr. στρουθοκάμηλος, f. στρουθό-ς sparrow + κάμηλος camel.] An ostrich.

In quot. 1631 *struthiocameli* is the Latin genitive.

1607 WALKINGTON *Optic Glass* 79 The Struthio-camell or Ostridge..will concoct iron. **1624** F. WHITE *Repl. Fisher* 454 Concerning Stones, Iron, &c. I doe not thinke that these feed..Struthiocameles, &c. but onely coole or cleanse them. [**1631** MASSINGER *Emperor of East* IV. iv, This applied warme vpon the pained place, with a fether of Struthiocameli, or a bird of Paradise, shall expulse this tartarous..dolor.] **1684** J. P. tr. *J. Ludolphus' Hist. Ethiopia* (ed. 2) 63 The Struthiocamel or Ostrich.

struthioid ('struːθɪɔɪd), *a.* and *sb.* [ad. mod.L. type *strūthioīdēs*, f. L. *strūthio* ostrich: see STRUTHIOUS and -OID.] **a.** *adj.* Ostrich-like, struthious. **b.** *sb.* A struthious bird.

1879 LYDEKKER in *Rec. Geol. Surv. India* XII. 53 Fossil Struthioids. *Ibid.*, The only struthioid bones figured..are [etc.]. **1880** W. DAVIES in *Geol. Mag.* Jan. 18 Two distinct forms of Struthioid birds.

‖**'struthion.** *Obs.* [Gr. στρουθίον.] Soapwort.

1587 T. NEWTON *Herbal for Bible* x. 60 This herbe Borith or Struthion, which we heere cal Sopewort or fullers weed, doth [etc.]. **1706** PHILLIPS (ed. Kersey), *Struthion*,..a Plant call'd Fullers-herb.

struthious ('struːθɪəs), *a. Zool.* [f. L. *strūthio* ostrich (in mod.L. as generic name), a. Gr. στρουθίων.] Related to or resembling the ostrich.

1773 PENNANT *Genera of Birds* 38 Order VI. Struthious. *Ibid.*, Struthious is a new coined word to express this order; for these birds could not be used to any of the Linnaean divisions. **1835–6** *Todd's Cycl. Anat.* I. 271/1 The Struthious birds and Penguins, which cannot fly. **1841** R. E. GRANT *Outl. Comp. Anat.* 497 The two anterior branches..are..very small in strutheous [*sic*] birds. **1875** A. NEWTON in *Encycl. Brit.* III. 729/2 A large Bird, combining Dinornithic and Struthious characters. **1883** *Century Mag.* Jan. 415/2 If the pursued were acquainted with struthious tactics, he would lie down flat on the ground, where the bird finds it impossible to strike him.

struthir, variant of STROTHER *Obs.*

struthonian (struː'θəʊnɪən), *a.*, (*sb.*) *joc.* [Irreg. f. L. *struth-io*: see -IAN and STRUTHIOUS *a.*] Tending to 'hide one's head in the sand', like the ostrich (see SAND *sb.*[2] 2 d), and so to ignore unwelcome facts (Koestler's word). Also as *sb.*, one who does this. Hence **stru'thonianism.**

1963 A. KOESTLER in *Encounter* July 7/1 One need not be an economist to find these figures disconcerting. But there is a struthonian answer to them (from struthio the Latin for ostrich). Your Old Struthonian will start with some disparaging remarks about statistics in general, and..then explain that Britain started the Industrial Revolution, and that accordingly it is only natural..that other nations, which started later, should grow at a faster rate. **1966** *Listener* 18 Aug. 223/2 Housing, with doubtful justification, lags behind needs, and continues to take a lion-hearted and struthonian view of the climate. *Ibid.* 224/1 A fine piece of struthonianism is the failure to accept the fact that teenagers are now in practice sexually active. *Ibid.* 25 Aug. 279/1 It is unfortunate that Professor Wisdom should perpetuate Arthur Koestler's barbaric derivative struthonian... If *leonine*, then *struthionine*, or nothing.

†**'strutly**, *adv. Obs. rare*[−1]. [Cf. STRUT *a.*] ? Proudly.

c **1375** *Sc. Leg. Saints* xxv. (*Julian*) 676, & for his bred he send hym hay, & til hyme strutly can say [etc.].

strutter ('strʌtə(r)). In 4 strouter, 6 strowter. [f. STRUT *v.*[1] + -ER[1].] One who struts.

1399 LANGL. *R. Redeles* III. 269 To strie strouters þat sterede aȝeine rithis. *a* **1591** H. SMITH *Serm.* (1594) 227 They which will be strowters, shall not want flatterers. **1682** H. MORE *Annot. Glanvill's Lux Orient.* 12 What a meere nothing it is that this Strutter has pronounced with such sonorous Rhetorick. **1727** GAY *Fables* I. xl. 5 The Don, a formal, solemn strutter, Despises Monsieur's airs and flutter. **1804** EUGENIA DE ACTON *Tale without Title* II. 268 Those servile strutters in a great man's livery. **1824** MISS MITFORD *Village* I. 54 A brood or two of bantams..with a little ridiculous strutter of a cock at their head.

strutting ('strʌtɪŋ), *vbl. sb.*[1] [f. STRUT *v.*[1] + -ING[1].]

†**1.** The action of swelling with fullness, of projecting or sticking out, and the like. *Obs.*

1398 TREVISA *Barth. De P.R.* XVIII. ciii. (1495) 847 [Brockes] fynde sleyghte and manere by suche stroutynge oute of the skynne to eschewe and put of the bytynge of houndes. *c* **1440** *Promp. Parv.* 480/2 St[r]owtynge, *nominaliter, turgor.* **1573** BARET *Alv.* S 897 A stretching or strowtting out, *estendement.* **1622** T. STOUGHTON *Chr. Sacrif.* vii. 91 The Turkie cocke..maketh a great brustling and strouting with his wings. **1677** MIEGE *Dict. Eng.-Fr.*, A Strutting out, *bouffissure, enflement.* **1683** G. MARTINE *Reliq. Divi Andreae* (1797) 183 The chaple is built on the east of the steeple, and strutts and projects out upon it about two foot, which strutting..makes the chaple to be in length without the wall 31½ foot.

†**2.** The action of 'swelling' or looking big; contending, blustering; flaunting, swaggering. *Obs.*

1399 LANGL. *R. Redeles* III. 121 For ben þey rayed arith, þey recchith no fforther, But studieth all in stroutynge and stireth amys euere. **1629** H. BURTON *Truth's Triumph* 255 Without any strouting of arrogancy.

3. The action of walking with stiff bearing and self-important air.

1656 EARL MONM. tr. *Boccalini's Pol. Touchstone* 442 Spanish Dons..with their usual Castilian strutting, and with unsufferable Spanish ostentation. **1711** STEELE *Spect.* No. 156 ¶5 The Woman's Man expresses himself wholly in that Motion which we call Strutting: An elevated Chest, a pinched Hat, a measurable Step,..are the Marks of him. **1880** A. H. SWINTON *Insect Variety* v. 209 A love-call that reproduces..the strutting, wing-drumming, and rustling of the males of the turkey and grouse at the pairing time.

strutting ('strʌtɪŋ), *vbl. sb.*[2] [f. STRUT *v.*[2] + -ING[1].] **a.** The action of strengthening or supporting with a strut or struts. **b.** *concr.* Struts collectively.

1833 LOUDON *Encycl. Archit.* §1066 The joists to be..stiffened with herring-bone strutting. **1875** KNIGHT *Dict. Mech.* 2431 *Strutting*, diagonal braces between joists to prevent side deflection. **1896** *Daily News* 15 Dec. 2/3 The Committee ordered certain works to be done, including..the shoring and strutting of the gables and great northern arch.

c. *attrib.* **strutting-beam, piece**, a beam or piece that acts as a strut.

1753 F. PRICE *Brit. Carpenter* (ed. 3) 17 If the strutting-beam..be drove in very tight, it takes all the weight off from the rafters. **1833** LOUDON *Encycl. Archit.* §238 Pieces of timber driven fast between each pair of joists, with their ends butting against the groin of the joists; they are commonly called strutting pieces, and their use is to stiffen the floor.

strutting ('strʌtɪŋ), *ppl. a.* [f. STRUT *v.*[1] + -ING[2].]

†**1.** That swells or bulges with fullness. Also with *out*. *Obs.*

1398 TREVISA *Barth. De P.R.* XVIII. xcvi. (1495) 842 Some ape is callyd Spinga and ben rough and hery wyth stroutynge pappes and teetys. *c* **1440** *Promp. Parv.* 480/2 Strowtynge, *adjective, turgidus.* *c* **1590** GREENE *Fr. Bacon* III. iii. 1421 Fortie kine..With strouting duggs that paggle to the ground. **1620** VENNER *Via Recta* iv. 85 Turgid and strouting-out bellies.

β. **1565** COOPER *Thesaurus*, s.v. *Caper*, *Distentæ lacte capellæ*, hauyng struttyng teates. **1654** R. CODRINGTON tr. *Iustine* xliv. 519 A Hinde, who did offer her strutting dugs unto the little one. **1693** J. DRYDEN Jun. in *Dryden's Juvenal* xiv. 169 As thy strutting Bags with Money rise. **1711** ADDISON *Spect.* No. 127 ¶6 The strutting Petticoat smooths all Distinctions, levels the Mother with the Daughter. **1815** W. HERBERT *Helga* VI. 2084 Prosperous gales Already fill the strutting sails.

Comb. **1579** TWYNE *Phis. agst. Fortune* II. xiii. 187 Doe I not see thy bagges stroutyng full? **1610** HOLLAND *Camden's Brit.* I. 3 An infinite multitude there is of tame cattell with udders strutting-full of milke. **1652** BENLOWES *Theophila* XIII. x. 237 Next Close feeds many a strutting udder'd Cow. *a* **1661** HOLYDAY *Juvenal* ii. (1673) 21 The strutting-belly'd spindle, that does swell With slender yarn.

†**b.** That distends or causes to swell. *Obs.*

1567 TURBERV. *Epit.* etc. 14 For hee the emptie bagge with winde and strouting blast doth fill.

†**2.** That protrudes stiffly, sticks out, or juts forth. *Obs.*

1387 TREVISA *Higden* VII. 385 Þat tyme men usede stroutynge lokkes [L. *tunc fluxus crinium*]. **1398** —— *Barth. De P.R.* XIV. xxxii. (1495) E vij, The moost hyghe strowtyng partyes of cragges ben callyd Scopuli. **1598** CHAPMAN *Achilles Shield* To Vnderstander, Talke our quidditicall Italianistes of what proportion soeuer their strooting lips affect. **1650** BULWER *Anthropomet.* 77 The protuberating or strutting part of the Face. **1663** BUTLER *Hud.* I. i. 439 His strutting Ribs on both sides show'd Like furrows he himself had plow'd.

†**3.** *fig.* Swelling with pride or importance; wrangling, contending; flaunting, swaggering. *Obs.* exc. as in 5 b.

1577 KENDALL *Flowers of Epigr.* 41 Learne here ye mortalles all, what tis with stroutyng pride to swell. **1623** B. JONSON *Time Vind.* (1640) 97 These are fit freedomes For lawlesse Prentices, on a Shrovetuesday..; For drunken Wakes, and strutting Beare-baytings. **1677** MIEGE *Dict. Eng.-Fr.*, A Strutting fob,..*qui piafe, qui fait le brave.* **1725** RAMSAY *To Duncan Forbes* x, When strutting naethings are despis'd, With a' their stinking pride.

†**4.** That stands erect with the feet firmly planted and head high. Also *transf. Obs.*

a **1643** W. CARTWRIGHT *Ordinary* III. v. (1651) 52 Thy belly looks like to some strutting hill, O'r shadow'd with thy rough beard like a wood. **1693** DRYDEN *Juvenal* vi. 365 Behold the strutting Amazonian Whore, She stands in Guard with her right Foot before. **1710** SWIFT *Little Ho. Castleknock* 13 This is the little strutting pile, You see just by the church-yard stile.

5. That walks with a stiff erect gait and self-important air.

1606 SHAKS. *Tr. & Cr.* I. iii. 153 Like a strutting Player, whose conceit Lies in his Ham-string. **1610** —— *Temp.* I. ii. 385, I heare, the straine of strutting Chanticlere. **1635** QUARLES *Embl.* IV. iii. 16 My loftie strutting steps disdaine to tire. **1719** in W. W. Wilkins *Polit. Ballads* (1860) II. 193 In his embroider'd coat they found him, With all his strutting dwarfs around him. **1829** CUNNINGHAM *Brit. Painters* I. 162

Hogarth was a strutting consequential little man. **1912** C. N. & A. M. WILLIAMSON *Guests of Hercules* v. 54 Tables where people drank tea and fed the strutting pigeons.

b. *fig.*

1601 *2nd Pt. Return fr. Parnass.* III. iv. 1386 My high tiptoe strouting poesye. **1779** JOHNSON *L.P., Gray* Wks. 1825 VIII. 487 He [Gray in his Odes] has a kind of strutting dignity, and is tall by walking on tiptoe. **1785** COWPER *Let. to Newton* 10 Dec., All his persons..speak in an inflated and strutting phraseology. **1813** *Examiner* 15 Feb. 106/2 He was ..fond of strutting sentiments, and well-rounded declamation. **1852** M. ARNOLD *Urania* iv, Our petty souls, our strutting wits.

Hence **'struttingly** *adv.*

c **1440** *Promp. Parv.* 16/2 A-strut, or strutyngly, *turgide*. *Ibid.* 480/2 Strowtyngly, or asturt. **1576** NEWTON *Lemnie's Complex.* I. x. 80b, It is to bee noted that these complexioned personnes be..graunde paunched & stroutingly bellyed. **1681** W. ROBERTSON *Phraseol. Gen.* 1031 He walks proudly; struttingly. **1780** DAVIES *Garrick* (1781) I. iii. 25 In Tamerlane he [Bridgewater] was solemnly drowsy in speaking, and struttingly insignificant in action. **1827** LYTTON *Pelham* lxxix, Slowly and struttingly did the man of two virtues perform the whole pilgrimage of Oxford Street. **1902** SWINBURNE *Dickens* (1913) 31 The struttingly offensive father [Dombey].

struttle[1] ('strʌt(ə)l). *dial.* Corruption of *stuttle-(back)*, dial. var. of STICKLEBACK.

1821 CLARE *Vill. Minstr.* II. 74 Oft catching prickly struttles on their rout. **1851** STERNBERG *Northampt. Gloss.*

'struttle[2]. *nonce-wd.* [f. STRUT *sb.*[1] + -LE.] A petty strut or manner of strutting.

1829 E. ELLIOTT *Village Patriarch* III. ix, See, how magnificently he [the poacher] breaks down His neighbour's fence, if so his will requires! And how his struttle emulates the Squire's!

struv, dial. pa. t. of STRIVE *v.*

strüverite ('stryːvəraɪt). *Min.* [ad. G. *strüverit* (A. Brezina 1876) f. name of Prof. G. *Strüver*, of Rome: see -ITE.] **1.** A synonym of CHLORITOID.

1896 CHESTER *Dict. Names Min.* 261. **1912** *Return Brit. Museum* 194.

2. An oxide of titanium containing tantalum and ferric iron, found as black tetragonal crystals having a metallic lustre. [a. It. *strüverite* (F. Zambonini 1907, in *Rend. dell' Accad. d. Sci. fis. e matem.* (Napoli) XIII. 46).]

1907 *Mineral. Mag.* XIV. 411 Strüverite. **1908** *Ibid.* XV. 78 The mineral strüverite occurs as a rare accessory constituent of the pegmatite which is found in large detrital masses in the neighbourhood of Craveggia (Val Vigezzo, northern Piedmont). **1917** [see MOSSITE]. **1974** *Mineral. Abstr.* XXV. 236/1 Strüverite, tanteuxenite and tantalanatase from the pegmatites near the town of Chepelare, Central Rhodopes [Bulgaria].

struvite ('struːvaɪt). *Min.* [ad. G. *struvit* (G. L. Ulex 1846) f. name of *Struve*, Russian minister at Hamburg.] Hydrous phosphate of ammonium and magnesium, found in small yellowish-brown or greyish crystals.

1850 ANSTED *Elem. Geol., Min. etc.* 179. **1854** DANA *Syst. Min.* (ed. 4) II. 413 Struvite... Found in guano from Saldanha Bay, coast of Africa. **1870** *Amer. Jrnl. Sci.* Ser. II. L. 272 Struvite in crystals occurs in guano, in the Skipton Caves near Ballarat.

Struwwelpeter ('struːəlpiːtə(r), ‖'ʃtrʊvəl ˌpeːtər). Also *erron.* **Struwelpeter.** The name of a character in a children's book of the same name by Heinrich Hoffmann (1809–94), used *attrib.* to designate (a person with) long, thick, and unkempt hair. Also *transf.* Also *Comb.*, as ***Struwwelpeter-haired***. Hence **Struwwelpeterdom**, (of hair) the condition of being thick and untidy. Cf. *shockheaded Peter* s.v. SHOCK-HEADED *a.*

1909 W. J. LOCKE *Septimus* iii. 37 He passed his hand through his Struwelpeter hair. *Ibid.* xxii. 351 His hair.. reached the climax of Struwelpeterdom. **1920** E. SITWELL *Wooden Pegasus* 78 As he rides on his rocking-horse All Struwwelpeter-haired. **1927** 'G. DAVIOT' *Man in Queue* vii. 82 The artist's eyebrows disappeared in the Struwwelpeter hair. **1958** P. KEMP *No Colours or Crest* x. 228 The Commissar was a small, squat man with very bright eyes and a *Struwwelpeter* shock of black hair. **1959** C. SPRY *Favourite Flowers* xxv. 188 The flowers [of *Anemone alpina*] were over and I saw for the first time what Mr. Drake calls the 'Struwwelpeter' seed heads. **1973** R. W. CLARK *Einstein* xi. 269 William Rothenstein, making notes for his remarkable portrait of Einstein who is presented as a Struwelpeter character, smiling from an aureole of almost electrified hair.

struye(n, strwe, obs. forms of STROY *v.*

†**stry, strie.** *Obs.* Also 5 **stroye.** [a. OF. *estrie*:—L. *striga*.] A hag, beldam.

a **1300** *Havelok* 998 Of bodi was he mayden clene, Neuere ..Wit hire [*read* hore] ne wolde leyke ne lye, No more þan it were a strie. *c* **1440** *York Myst.* xxiv. 13 A! ffalse stod-mere and stynkand stroye! [*rime* abye.] *c* **1460** *Towneley Myst.* xvi. 348 Com hedyr, thou old stry!

stry, obs. form of STROY *v.*

stryche, variant of STRITCH.

strychnia ('strɪknɪə). *Chem.* [f. STRYCHN-OS: see -IA.] = STRYCHNINE.

1826 HENRY *Chem.* II. 302 Strychnia was detected by Pelletier and Caventou, in 1818, in the fruit of the *Strychnos Nux Vomica*, and *Strychnos Ignatia*. **1876** HARLEY *Mat. Med.* 515 Strychnia is a direct and powerful tonic to [etc.].

attrib. **1874** GARROD & BAXTER *Mat. Med.* (ed. 4) 239 The treatment of strychnia-poisoning.

strychnic ('strɪknɪk), *a. Chem.* [f. STRYCHN-OS + -IC.] Pertaining to strychnine. ***strychnic acid***: = IGASURIC *acid.*

1840 PEREIRA *Elem. Mat. Med.* II. 909 Strychnic or Igasuric acid.—Exists in the seeds of nux-vomica [etc.]. **1875** H. C. WOOD *Therap.* (1879) 297 Strychnic convulsions must be spinal, because they do not arise in any of the other possible methods. **1889** *Hardwicke's Sci.-Gossip* XXV. 176 A peculiar acid known as strychnic acid.

†**strych'nina.** *Chem. Obs.* = STRYCHNINE.

1838 T. THOMSON *Chem. Org. Bodies* 252 Strychnina was discovered, in 1818, by MM. Pelletier and Caventou.

strychnine ('strɪkniːn, -ɪn). *Chem.* [a. F. *strychnine* f. L. *strychn-os*: see STRYCHNOS and -INE[5].] A highly poisonous vegetable alkaloid, $C_{21}H_{22}N_2O_2$, obtained chiefly from *Strychnos Nux-vomica* and other plants of the same genus. It is used in medicine as a stimulant and tonic.

1819 *Edin. Philos. Jrnl.* I. 210 New vegetable Alkali called Strychnine.—This new alkali was discovered by MM. Pelletier and Caventou in the *Strychnos ignatia* and the *Strychnos nux vomiea*. **1861** *Brit. & For. Med.-Chirurg. Rev.* XXVII. 533 A case of poisoning by strychnine.

b. *attrib.* as in ***strychnine poisoning, tetanus***; **strychnine-plant**, *Strychnos Nux-vomica*; **strychnine-tree**, *S. psilosperma*.

1879 *St. George's Hosp. Rep.* IX. 688 Frogs, in whom strychnine tetanus had been produced. **1884** W. MILLER *Plant.-n.* 131 Strychnine-plant. **1885** LADY BRASSEY *The Trades* 129 The cottage was overshadowed by a strychnine-tree and a tamarind. **1898** FR. A. WELBY tr. *Biedermann's Electro-Physiol.* II. 423 The effect of strychnine poisoning ..is highly characteristic.

Hence **'strychnine** *v. trans.*, to poison by strychnine; **'strychnined** *ppl. a.*

1862 *Sporting Mag.* Apr. 288 We are informed that strychnined rabbits form the patent 'composing draught'. **1871** CARLYLE in *Mrs. Carlyle's Lett.* III. 11 Poor Nero, who had to be strychnined by the doctor. **1903** BOSW. SMITH in *19th Cent.* Mar. 441 Others..are willing to put down a strychnined egg for him [a raven].

strychninization (ˌstrɪknɪnaɪ'zeɪʃən). [f. as next + -IZATION.] The act of applying strychnine.

1898 in *Syd. Soc. Lex.* **1933** *Ann. Rep. London Co. Council* IV. III. 143 After strychninisation of the gyrus uncinatus and lobus pyriformis, fits could be induced by olfactory stimulation. **1951** J. F. FULTON *Frontal Lobotomy* ii. 47 Strychninization of the posterior hypothalamus activates the dorsomedial nuclei. **1974** *Proc. Soc. Exper. Biol. & Med.* CXLV. 979 (*heading*) Subcortical multiple unit activity.. during strychninization of the cerebral cortex in the female rat.

strychninize ('strɪknɪnaɪz), *v.* [f. STRYCHNINE + -IZE.] *trans.* To apply strychnine to.

1934 in WEBSTER. **1938** *Jrnl. Neurophysiol.* I. 69 The distribution of the spikes within the cytoarchitectonic area, of which a part has been strychninized. **1951** P. D. MACLEAN in J. F. Fulton *Frontal Lobotomy* ii. 57 Then we strychninized the nucleus. **1980** *Pavlovian Jrnl. Biol. Sci.* XV. 58/1 The response was made single by strychninizing a larger area of cortex.

Hence **'strychninized** *ppl. a.*

1938 *Jrnl. Neurophysiol.* I. 72 Farther away from the strychninized locus spikes are absent. **1978** H. TAKEUCHI in Chalazonitis & Boisson *Abnormal Neuronal Discharges* 161 The strychninized somatic abnormal biopotential was similarly subjected to temperature changes.

strychnism ('strɪknɪz(ə)m). *Path.* [f. STRYCHNIA + -ISM.] The condition induced by strychnine poisoning.

1857 DUNGLISON *Med. Lex.* s.v. *Strychnos*, When taken to such an extent as to induce toxical phenomena—Strychnism —it causes, at first..greatly augmented excitability of the spinal nervous system, [etc.].

strychnization (strɪknaɪ'zeɪʃən). [f. STRYCHN(IA + -IZATION.] = STRYCHNINIZATION.

1916 *Q. Jrnl. Exper. Physiol.* IX. 356 Slight strychnisation of the dorsal mechanisms..gives rise to a typical complex of symptoms. **1924** *Proc. R. Soc.* B. XCVI. 272 Local strychnization of the central nervous system..yields good results in investigations on the sensory mechanisms of the spinal cord.

strychnized ('strɪknaɪzd). [f. STRYCHNIA + -IZE + -ED[1].] Subjected to the action of strychnine.

1875 H. C. WOOD *Therap.* (1879) 249 Exposing the sciatic nerves of a strychnized frog.

Strychnos ('strɪknɒs). *Bot.* Also **strychnus**, pl. **strychni.** [mod.L. (Linnæus 1737) use of L. *strychnos* (Pliny), a. Gr. στρύχνος, a kind of nightshade.] A genus of plants (N.O. *Loganaceæ*), including the nux vomica (*S. Nux-vomica*), the St. Ignatius' bean (*S. Ignatia*), and other species. Also, a plant or a species of this genus.

[**1601** HOLLAND *Pliny* XXVII. viii. II. 280 Some..call this hearbe by another name, Strumus, and others give it the Greeke name Strychnos. **1706** PHILLIPS (ed. Kersey), *Strychnus* or *Strychnis*, an Herb which makes those mad that eat of it.] **1836** J. M. GULLY *Magendie's Formul.* (ed. 2) 1 In the year 1809 I presented to the senior class of the French Institute an account of a series of experiments which had led to the discovery that a whole vegetable family, the bitter strychni, possessed the property of stimulating the spinal marrow to an extraordinary developement of its functions. **1842** *Penny Cycl.* XXIII. 152/1 The genus Strychnos, consisting of about twelve species.

stryckt, obs. pa. t. of STRIKE *v.*

stryd, obs. pa. t. of STRIDE *v.*

stryddag ('streitdax). *S. Afr.* Pl. **stryddae.** [Afrikaans, lit. 'struggle day, day of battle'.] An Afrikaner political party rally. Also *transf.*

1950 *Cape Times* 26 July 1/3 Mr. C. R. Swart, Minister of Justice, told a Nationalist Party stryddag here yesterday that he was not prepared to reintroduce public hangings. **1961** *Ibid.* 11 Jan. 1/6 In Britain he will be able to give the moderately-phrased versions of *apartheid* far more expertly and convincingly than in heated debates in Parliament or during *stryddae* in the platteland. **1972** *Daily Dispatch* 14 Apr. 10 The day of the big stryddag is over. Those large crowds will never again drive across the veld to hear emotional appeals to the blood. **1978** *Pace* Dec. 51 On Sunday, Chief Buthelezi is going to..address an all-black *stryddag* in Soweto.

stryf(f)e, stryif(f: see STRIFE, STRIVE.

stryk(e: see STIRK, STREAK *sb.*[1], STREEK *v.*

stryking, variant of STRAIKEN *Obs.*

1536 *Test. Ebor.* (Surtees) VI. 53, ij payre of sheites of strykynges.

strykly, obs. form of STRECKLY *adv.*

stryncht, obs. form of STRENGTH.

stryne, obs. form of STRAIN *v.*

c **1374** CHAUCER *Boeth.* I. met. vi. 16 (Cambr. MS.).

stryne, variant of STRIND[1] *Obs.*

stryngest, variant of STRENGEST *a. Obs.*

1486 *Bk. St. Albans, Her.* a v b, Olibion was the stryngest and the manfullest man in his tyme.

stryngh(e, stryngth(e: see STRENGH, STRENGTH.

stryn(n)or, -our, strynt, -th(e, -tht, obs. ff. STRAINER, STRENGTH.

stryte, obs. form of STRAIT.

stryve, strywe, obs. forms of STRIFE, STRIVE.

stschi, var. SHCHI.

stu, obs. form of STEW *sb.*[1]

stuard(e, stuart, obs. forms of STEWARD.

Stuart ('stjuːət). Also formerly **Stewart.** The name of the British royal family from 1603 to 1688, used *attrib.* to designate that period of history and applied esp. to artefacts, buildings, etc., of that date or style.

1873 C. M. YONGE *Pillars of House* IV. xxxvi. 50 Here's the dining-room—This is the middle period, the Stewart style part. **1880** E. GLAISTER *Needlework* viii. 87 Some oak chairs, probably of early Stuart date. **1922** S. WEYMAN *Ovington's Bank* ix. 104 Long-backed Stuart chairs. **1937** *Discovery* Aug. 231/1 The penny of Tudor and Stuart times. **1973** *Country Life* 5 Apr. 909/2 He has treated the wainscot of the Stuart bedroom..in a similar manner to the Stuart staircase. **1981** V. GLENDINNING *Edith Sitwell* i. 12 Renishaw Hall..retained within its walls..most of its Stuart and Regency past.

stub (stʌb), *sb.* Forms: 1 **stubb, styb(b, (steb),** 3–7 **stubbe,** 4–9 **stubb,** 6 **stoubbe,** 4– **stub.** [OE. *stub(b* masc. = (M)LG., MDu. *stubbe* (early mod.Du., WFris. *stobbe*), ON. *stubb-r, stubbe*, rarely *stobbe* (MSw. *stubbe, stobbe*, SW., Norw. *stubbe, stubb*, Da. *stub*):—OTeut. types **stubbo-z, stubbon-*; OE. had also *stybb* masc.:—**stubjo-z* or **stubbjo-z*, which has coalesced with the other form. OE. had prob. a form **stob(b* with *o*-umlaut (cf. the duplicate ON. forms above), whence STOB *sb.*[1]; in the 14–16th c., however, *stob(b* may merely be a variant spelling for *stub*.

To the same root (**stŭb-*:—pre-Teut. **stŭp-*) belong ON. *stúf-r* stump (Norw. *stuv*), (see STOW *v.*[2]), MLG. *stûve* stump, fag-end, *stûf* blunt; outside Teut. cf. Gr. στύπος stump, stock, Lettish *stups* fag-end.]

1. a. A stump of a tree or, more rarely, of a shrub or smaller plant; the portion left fixed in the ground when a tree has been felled; also, †a trunk deprived of branches.

967 *Charter of Eadgar* in Kemble *Cod. Dipl.* No. 813. III. 10 Andlang dices on ðone stubb. *c* **1000** ÆLFRIC *Gloss.* in Wr.-Wülcker 108/5 *Stipes, stipitis*, treowwes steb. *c* **1000** —— *Gram.* ix. (Z.) 68 *Hic stirps* ðes stybb. **1301** *Acc. Exch. Q.R.* Bundle 147. No. 10 in G. J. Turner *Sel. Pleas Forest* (1901) 147/2 [Six] stubbs [sold for] 3*s.* 4*d.* **13..** *Gaw. & Gr. Knt.* 2293 Gawayn..stode stylle as þe ston, oþer a stubbe auþer. **1348–9** in *Blount's Law Dict.* (1691) s.v. *Zuche*, Rex concessit Thomæ de Colvile omnes Zoucheos aridos, vocat. Stubbes arborum succisorum, in Foresta de Galtres. **146.** *Plumpton Corr.* (Camden) 25 And it please to deliver unto Robert of Tymble a Stub, the which Mr. Controller granted unto his ward for him and his wife. **1519** HORMAN *Vulg.* 247b, We went by strayte pathes full of stoubbys, busshys, and bryers. **1590** SPENSER *F.Q.* I. ix. 34 Old stockes and stubs of trees, Whereon nor fruit nor leafe was euer seene.

1615 CHAPMAN *Odyss.* XII. 611 Yet, might my feete, on no stub fasten hold To ease my hands: the roots were crept so low Beneath the earth. **1621** LADY M. WROTH *Urania* 264 Then went shee a little further, and on a stub, which was betweene two trees, she sate downe. **1671** MILTON *P.R.* I. 339 We here Live on tough roots and stubs. **1760** R. BROWN *Compl. Farmer* II. 101 When it [rape] hath been cut, the stubs of it will sprout again. **1771** *Phil. Trans.* LXI. 138 In the forest of Kent,.. there still remains several large old chesnut stubbs. **1795** VANCOUVER *Agric. Essex* 152 The remaining stub of the thistle. **1799** COLERIDGE *Introd. Tale Dark Ladie* 64 How boughs rebounding scourg'd his limbs, And low stubs gor'd his feet. **1823** J. F. COOPER *Pioneers* iii, Unsightly remnants of trees that had been partly destroyed by fire were seen rearing their..columns..above the pure white of the snow. These,..in the language of the country are termed stubs. **1864** G. P. MARSH *Man & Nat.* 109 In the United States..dead trees..are often allowed to stand until they fall of themselves. Such stubs, as they are popularly called, are..often deeply cut by the woodpeckers. **1895** ZANGWILL *Master* II. xi. 268 The woodpeckers tapped on the hollow stubs. **1907** 'J. HALSHAM' *Lonewood Corner* 114 Before the stubs of the under-wood have sprouted again.

†**b.** *to buy* (brushwood, etc.) *on* or *at the stub*: to buy on the ground, growing. Hence (?), *to pay at the stub*: to pay ready money. *Obs.*

1532 *Lett. & Papers Hen. VIII*, V. 446 For thorns bought on the stubb... For edders and stakes bought likewise on the stub. **1573–80** TUSSER *Husb.* (1878) 78 In time go and bargaine..for fewell... To buie at the stub is the best for the buier. **1615** ROWLANDS *Melancholie Knt.* C 3, A very Cobler shall as welcome be That payes his readie money at the stub, As I that come a trust to worships dub. **1795** VANCOUVER *Agric. Essex* 62 The under woods are cut down at eleven years growth, and..they sell at the stub for 3 l. 10 s. per acre.

†**c.** The part of a tree-trunk close to the ground.

1558–9 *Act 1 Eliz.* c. 15 §1 No person..shall convert..to Coale or other Fuell for the making of Yron, any Tymber Tree..of the Breadthe of One Foot Square at the Stubbe. **1587** HARRISON *England* II. xvii. 200/1 in *Holinshed*, For what a thing it is to haue a ship growing upon the stub, and sailing on the sea within the space of fiue and fiftie daies? **1637** HEYWOOD in *Naval Chron.* III. 370 Timber,..ten feet at the stub or bottom.

†**d.** A stock for grafting upon. In quot. *fig.*

1587 HARRISON *England* II. i. 139/1 in *Holinshed*, You shall see no fewer deeds of charitie doone, nor better grounded vpon the right stub of pietie than before.

†**2.** *fig.* A blockhead; = STOCK *sb.*¹ 1 c. *Obs.*

1644 MILTON *Educ.* 3 Ye shall haue more adoe to driue our dullest and laziest youth, our stocks and stubbs from the infinite desire of such a happy nurture.

3. A short piece of a broken branch remaining on the stem.

c **1386** CHAUCER *Knt.'s T.* 1120 First on the wal was peynted a forest..With knotty knarry bareyne trees olde Of stubbes sharpe, and hidouse to biholde. *c* **1440** *Ipomydon* 1270 My palfrey..stumblyd..I toke this harme, A stubbe smote me þrow þe arme. **1712** J. JAMES tr. *Le Blond's Gardening* 159 A Parcel of Stubs [F. *chicots*], springing out of one Side and the other. **1796** C. MARSHALL *Garden.* xii. (1813) 163 Whether it is best to cut all spare shoots clean out, or to cut down to little stubs or false spurs is hardly yet determined. **1846** *J. Baxter's Libr. Pract. Agric.* (ed. 4) I. 164 Some cut superfluous fruit-shoots clean away; others leave a sprinkling of short stubs, cut very short if foreright. **1884** *Century Mag.* Dec. 222/1 His drum was the stub of a dry limb about the size of one's wrist.

4. a. = STUBBLE *sb.* Also *pl.* Now *dial.* [So Sw. *stubbe*, Da. *stub*.]

1250 *Owl & Night.* 506 Ȝet þu singst worse þon þe hei-sugge, [Þ]at fliȝþ bi grunde among þe stubbe. **1552** HULOET, Stubbe of corne, *stipula, stupa.* **1677** PLOT *Oxfordsh.* 246 If they are to sow wheat upon tillage, they choose wheat sown before upon bean stubs. **1811** T. DAVIS *Agric. Wilts* 266 *Stubs.* The stubble of all corn is usually called stubs, as wheat-stubs, barley-stubs, &c. **1820** CLARE *Poems Rural Life* (ed. 3) 95 But ill it suits thee in the stubs to glean.

†**b.** *pl.* The lower ends of cut stems of plants.

1764 *Museum Rust.* II. 81 It [*sc.* reaped coleseed] must not be turned, but raised up gently and laid lightly on the stubs.

†**c.** *in the stub*: said of growing flax. *Obs.*

1730 SWIFT *Answ. Craftsman* Wks. 1905 VII. 222 All the said commodities shall be sent in their natural state; the hides raw, the wool uncombed, the flax in the stub.

d. *pl.* Hair cut close to the skin. Now *dial.*

1607 R. TURNER *Nosce Te* D 1, A chinne as free from beard as any dogge, Saue stubbes more hard then brisles of a hogge.

5. a. A splinter or thorn in the flesh. Now *dial.*

1531 ELYOT *Gov.* II. xiii. (1557) 137 Out of whose foote a yong man had ones taken a stubbe. **1639** T. DE GREY *Compl. Horsem.* 160 To draw a thorne, stub, iron, splinter, naile.. out of the flesh of the horse. **1753** *Chambers' Cycl.* Suppl., *Stub*, in the manege, is used for a splinter of fresh-cut under-wood, that goes into a horse's foot as he runs. **1894** BLACKMORE *Perlycross* xxi. 197 Upon a truss of furze, with a flour-sack to shield him from the stubs and prickles.

†**b.** A stab or twinge of pain. Now *dial.*

1587 M. GROVE *Pelops & Hippod.* (1878) 86 Ixion nayled on the whirling wheele, Which hellish stubs & irksom pains doth feele.

6. a. A short thick nail (= STOB *sb.*¹ 4); a worn horseshoe nail, esp. in *pl.* old horseshoe nails and other similar scraps as the material for making stub-iron. Cf. *stub-nail*.

1394–5 in *Cartul. Abb. Whiteby* (Surtees) 615 It. pro viiiˣˣ cartnayle, x s. It. pro iᵐ stubs, ii s. **1595** *Strange Things R. Hasleton* in Arb. *Garner* VIII. 387 And immediately searching about, I found an old iron stub; with the which I brake a hole through the chamber wall. **1669** STURMY *Mariner's Mag.* v. xiii. 86 Fill it with Pibble-stones, Nails, Stubs of old Iron. **1720** DE FOE *Capt. Singleton* (1906) 256 He ordered that all the guns..should be loaded with musket balls, old nails, stubs [etc.]. **1820** W. SCORESBY *Acc. Arctic Reg.* II. 225 That kind which is of the most approved tenacity, is made of old horse-shoe nails or stubs. **1845** *Penny Cycl.* Suppl. I. 673 Horse-nails..which when worn out are collected with avidity as furnishing one of the best descriptions of scrap-iron, under the name of horse-nail stubs. **1846** GREENER *Sci. Gunnery* 107 An equal substance of the best steel ever invented or made, is less in tenacity than a mixture similar to stubs and steel. **1863** MRS. GASKELL *Sylvia's L.* xvi, Hammers beating out old iron such as horseshoes, nails or stubs into the great harpoons.

b. Short for *stub-barrel*: see 11.

1853 URE *Dict. Arts* I. 724 The barrels of musquets, birding-guns, etc. or what are called plain, to distinguish them from those denominated stubs or twisted barrels.

7. a. Something that looks stunted or cut short, e.g. a rudimentary tail or horn.

1670–1 NARBOROUGH *Jrnl.* in *Acc. Sev. Late Voy.* I. (1694) 33 They are shaped like English Hares..and instead of a Tail have a little stub about an inch long, without Hair on it. **1693** EVELYN *De La Quint. Compl. Gard.* II. 111 The Scutcheon cannot thrive, unless it be absolutely glued to the part to which it is apply'd; and consequently that part must be as smooth as the Scutcheon, which cannot be when a Scutcheon is apply'd upon an Eye, or Bud, which is an Elevated part, that forms a kind of Stub. *a* **1722** LISLE *Husb.* (1757) 377 There will remain a little stub at the end of the twig, which dries up. **1887** W. T. HORNADAY in *Smithsonian Rep.* II. 397 The horn [of the buffalo] at three months is about 1 inch in length, and is a mere little black stub.

b. A short thick piece of wood.

1833 W. H. MAXWELL *Field Bk.* 522 *Stub*,..a log. **1844** H. STEPHENS *Bk. Farm* I. 605 At the distance of a foot behind the coulter-box a strong stub of wood is mortised into the beam at *C. Ibid.*, The two stilts or handles are simply bolted to the stub. **1898** SLOANE *Electr. Dict.* (ed. 2) 622 *Stub, Anchor guy*, a short pole set securely in the ground to fasten a guy to.

c. (See quot.)

1884 KNIGHT *Dict. Mech.* Suppl. 869 *Stub*... 2. Short files for finishing in and around depressions.

d. *U.S. colloq.* A man of insignificant stature. Cf. STUB *a.*

1890 J. CURTIN tr. *Sienkiewicz' With Fire & Sword* xliv. (1892) 514, I have something to say to this little stub of an officer.

e. A short length of wire used in flower-arranging. Cf. *stub wire*, sense 11 below.

1951 R. A. BIRCH et al. *Mod. Florist* ix. 83 On the bench is fixed the wire tidy..a set of upright metal cylinders or holders into which the wires, or 'stubs', are placed. *Ibid.* 88 Next we come to 'invisible wiring' with ordinary stubs. **1960** V. STEVENSON in T. A. Price et al. *Retail Florist's Handbk.* iii. 66 Stem wires, often called stub wires (one assumes because they are stubbed into the design), vary from 3½ to 18 inches in length... Twenty gauge..is the most widely used wreath stub. **1963** M. SMITH *Arranging Flowers* viii. 83 With a very fragile stem it is best to lay a stub-wire against it..and to twist fuse-wire round both the stub and the stem to bind them together.

8. *Mech.* A stud or projection; *spec.* in a lock, a stationary stud which acts as a detent for the tumblers when their slots are in engagement with it.

1561 EDEN tr. *Cortes' Art Navig.* III. xi. 78 b, But for the Sea, you shall sother the Horizon two Axes, little stubbes, or endes commyng foorth. **1778** in *Abridgm. Specif. Patents Locks* etc. (1873) 2 An improvement on the tumbler and spring by means of a stub or projection so exactly fitted to a passage or opening in the bolt as not to permit the bolt to pass unless [etc.]. **1825** J. NICHOLSON *Oper. Mech.* 324 [Maudslay's lathes.] In the part C is an oblique slit *l l*, to receive a stub which projects from the bottom of the nut *n*, ..by this arrangement it is obvious that if the screw *m* is worked, the stub of the nut *n*, acting against the slide of the slit *l l*, as an inclined plane, will move it either backwards or forwards through the opening M.

9. a. The remaining portion of something (more or less cylindrical) that has been broken or worn down; a stump, fag-end; *spec.* the butt or stump of a cigar or cigarette.

c **1530** BERNERS *Arthur Lit. Brit.* (1814) 214 He gaue Arthur a grete stroke with the stubbe of his hurte arme. **1855** 'Q. K. P. DOESTICKS' *Doesticks, what he Says* xvi. 133 Perhaps they expect us to smoke 'stubs', like the newsboys. **1869** 'MARK TWAIN' *Innoc. Abr.* xvii. 116 You cannot throw an old cigar 'stub' down any where. **1873** J. H. BEADLE *Undevel. West* 787 Even little darkeys watch for the 'old stubs' as they are thrown away. **1898** HAMBLEN *Gen. Manager's Story* xii. 191 There lay a fellow at full length,.. smoking an old stub of a clay pipe. **1912** H. BELLOC *Four Men* 27 'It is to sharpen this pencil with', said the stranger, putting forth a stub of an H.B. much shorter than his thumb. **1914** B. M. BOWER *Flying U Ranch* 187 He spat upon the burnt end of his cigarette stub from force of the habit that fear of range fires had built. **1973** T. PYNCHON *Gravity's Rainbow* (1975) III. 309 The two of them sit there, passing a cigarette back and forth, till it's smoked down to a very small stub.

b. = *stub pen* (see 11). ? *Obs.*

1829 LAMB *Let. to B. W. Procter* in Ainger *Lett.* (1888) II. 219 The comings in of an incipient conveyancer are not adequate to the receipt of three twopenny post nonpaids in a week. Therefore after this, I condemn my stub to long and deep silence.

10. *U.S.* A counterfoil. (Cf. F. *souche* and STOCK *sb.* 42; also STUMP *sb.* 3 h.)

1876 *N. Amer. Rev.* CXXIII. 301 For which check stubs representing only small amounts were retained. **1884** *Harper's Mag.* June 61/2 Pay-rolls, check-book stubs, registers,..are here stowed away. **1916** A. B. REEVE *Poisoned Pen* 181 'Number 156' Herndon noted, as the collector detached the stub and handed it to her.

11. *attrib.* and *Comb.*, as (sense 1) ***stub-oak, -wood***; (sense 4) ***stub-thatched*** adj.; (sense 4 d) ***stub-bearded*** adj.; (sense 9 b) ***stub-pointed*** adj.; **stub-axle** (see quots.); **stub-barrel**, a gun-barrel made of strips of stub-iron; **stub-book** *U.S.*, a book containing only the counterfoils of cheques or other documents; **stub-bred** *a. Hunting* (see quot.); **stub Damascus**, a kind of stub-iron resembling Damascus iron; **stub-dig** *dial.* = *stub-hoe*; † **stub eel**, some variety of eel; **stub-end**, (*a*) the butt end of a connecting-rod, of a weapon, etc.; (*b*) *U.S.*, the unconnected end of a stub track; also ***stub-end track*** (see *stub track* below); (*c*) a cigarette stub (in quot. *fig.*); † **stub-faced** *a. slang* (see quot.); **stub-feather** (see quot. 1847); **stub-hoe**, an implement for grubbing up stubs; **stub-iron**, a tenacious kind of iron, originally made out of old horse-shoe nails; † **stub-money** (see quot.); **stub-mortise** (see quot.); **stub-mortised** *a.*, secured by a stub-mortise; **stub-nail** = sense 6; **stub-nail iron** = *stub-iron*; **stub-pen**, orig. a worn quill pen; hence a broad-pointed pen; **stub-rabbit** *dial.*, a rabbit that seeks shelter among stubs instead of going to ground; **stub-short, -shot** (see quot.); **stub-side**, the side of a swath which has the cut ends of the stems; **stub station** *U.S.*, a railway station at which the tracks terminate; **stub-switch** *U.S.* (see quot. 1911); **stub-tail**, (*a*) a partridge at a certain stage of growth; (*b*) see quot. 1867; also used of maize; (*c*) a short and thick or broad tail; also *fig.*; **stub-tenon** (see quot.); **stub-toed** *a.*, of a shoe: having a broad toe; **stub-tooth** *Mech.* (see quot.); **stub track** *U.S.*, a railway track, usu. at a terminus, connected to another at one end only; see also *stub-end track* above; **stub-twist**, a material for fine gun-barrels, composed of a ribbon of stub-iron twisted into a spiral shape; **stub wing** *Aeronaut.* (see quot. 1956); hence **stub-winged** *a.*; **stub wire** = sense 7 e above.

1875 KNIGHT *Dict. Mech.* 2431 **Stub-axle*, a short axle attached on the end of a principal axle-tree. **1907** O'GORMAN *Motor Pocket Bk.* (ed. 2) 505 The stub axle is the short axle which is so pivoted that the front (or steering) wheels can be deflected. **1833** J. HOLLAND *Manuf. Metal* II. 101 The Birmingham workmen, in preparing the material for *stub barrels, usually cut up strips of iron and steel,.. into bits like two inch nails. **1891** KIPLING *Light that Failed* xiv. 280 A *stub-bearded, bowed creature wearing a dirty magenta coloured neckcloth outside an unbrushed coat. **1886** *Rep. of U.S. Sec. of Treasury* 700 (Cent.) The filed *stub-books of stamps, now occupying a very large and rapidly increasing space in the files rooms. **1826** J. COOK *Fox-hunting* 57 *Stub bred foxes are thought to be the stoutest. **1897** *Encycl. Sport* I. 583/1 (Hunting, fox) *Stub-bred, Stump-bred.* Foxes which, in certain districts, make their lairs in bushes or stumps instead of underground; stubbed was the old term. **1845** *Penny Cycl.* Suppl. I. 673 **Stub Damascus* is a very beautiful kind of iron formed like the Damascus iron above described. **1862** *Catal. Internat. Exhib.* II. xi. 7 Double gun, stub Damascus barrels. **1837** *Boston Advertiser* 17 Jan. 2/2 Thomas Chapman..charged with stealing a *stub dig. **15..** in Dugdale *Monasticon* (1655) I. 81/2 Also to be sure of xij. *stubbe elles and lx. schafte eles to bake for the covent on shere thursday. **1545** *Rates Custom Ho.* bj, Elis called stubbe elis. **1582** *Ibid.* B vij b, Eeles called stub Eeles. **1875** KNIGHT *Dict. Mech.*, **Stub-end*, the large end of a connecting-rod, in which the boxes are confined by the strap. **1896** *Engineering News* XXXVI. 27/1 When a long stub-end track gets full of empties, the cars at the stub end are likely to remain for weeks and months. **1900** *Ibid.* XLIV. 377/2 Stub-end tracks should generally be in pairs, with crossovers near the ends, so that the engine of one incoming train can be got out without waiting for its train. **1903** W. M. CAMP *Notes Track Constr.* I. vi. 466 An arrangement that is sometimes provided where inbound, outbound and transfer houses are consolidated at one point is to have parallel stub tracks, with the inbound house on one side, the outbound house on the opposite side and the office between them, at the stub ends of the tracks. **1914** *Daily News* 7 Nov. 1 Even if he has nothing more formidable than an empty bully-beef can to rattle with the stub-end of his bayonet. **1932** AUDEN *Orators* III. 85 Stub-end of year that smoulders to ash of winter. **1788** GROSE *Dict. Vulgar T.* (ed. 2), **Stub-faced*, pitted with small-pox: the devil run over his face with horse stubbs (horse nails) in his shoes. **1847** HALLIWELL, **Stub-feathers*, the short unfledged feathers on a fowl after it has been plucked. **1889** *Cornh. Mag.* Apr. 376 It is a rare thing not to find stub feathers somewhere about a hawk or an owl. **1870** EMERSON *Soc. & Solit., Eloq.* Wks. (Bohn) III. 39 He is a graduate of the plough, and the *stub-hoe, and the bush-whacker. **1820** W. SCORESBY *Acc. Arctic Reg.* II. 225 Some manufacturers enclose a quantity of *stub-iron in a cylinder of best foreign iron. **1776** *Compl. Grazier* (ed. 4) 78 The woodward is allowed a shilling a range, as above, (called *stub-money) for his care in looking after the wood. **1846** WORCESTER (citing *Loudon*), **Stub-mortise*, a mortise that does not pass through the timber mortised. **1833** LOUDON *Encycl. Archit.* §1251 With an oak cap properly *stub-mortised. **1639** G. PLATTES *Discov. Subterr. Treas.* 41, I took 4. ounces of Iron in *stub nailes. **1683** MOXON *Mech. Exerc., Printing* xviii. ¶2 They chuse stub-Nails for the best Iron to Melt. **1802** C. JAMES *Milit. Dict.*, *Stub-Nails* are driven on the outside of the nave-hoops, to keep them in their places. **1839** URE *Dict. Arts* 471 The best modern barrels for fowling pieces are constructed of *stub-nail iron in this manner. **1880** BLACKMORE *Mary Anerley* xl, A thicket of *stub oak. **1891** *Century Dict.*, *Stub pen. **1897** *Westm. Gaz.* 13 Jan. 5/1 The first signature is 'Julian Pauncefote,' written with an extra broad-pointed steel stub pen. **1909** *Daily Chron.* 18 Sept. 10/6 advt., In this trial box of specially assorted pens you are offered a wonderful variety of fine, medium, and *stub-pointed pens to suit all hands. **1845** *Zoologist* III. 903 There is a variety..called..in the northern parts of the same county [Herts.] the *stub-rabbit. **1875** KNIGHT *Dict. Mech.*, **Stub-short*; *Stub-shot.* 1. The unsawed portion of a plank where it is split from the bolt or log. 2. (*Turning.*) The portion by which an object to be turned is grasped or chucked. **1733** TULL *Horse-Hoeing Husb.* xiv. 188 Tis best to raise up the Ear-sides first, and let the *Stub-side rest on the Ground in turning. **1916** J. A. DROEGE *Passenger Terminals* v. 104 The head or *stub station is an end-of-the-line station. *Ibid.*, Practically all the terminals in New York City are built on the stub station plan. **1929** *Amer. Railway Engineering Assoc. Man.* xiv. 960 The through and loop types of station are superior to the stub station from the standpoint of train operation. **1885** G. MORDECAI *Rep. Terminal Facilities* 6 The tracks are of good material, laid with *stub switches and railfrogs. **1903** W. M. CAMP *Notes Track Constr.* I. 292 The stub switch, with its open joint in winter and tight joint in summer, with a loose head block to be tampered with every few days. **1911** WEBSTER, *Stub switch*, Railroading, a switch in which the track rails are cut off squarely at the toe and the switch rails are thrown to butt end to end with the lead rails. **1686** BLOME *Gentl. Recr.* II. 37/1 Larg Partridges called *Stubtayls... There are several names or distinctions of Partridges; the first, when newly hatched, are called White-heads, the second Names are Chick-tayls, the third Stub-tayls. **1867** SIMMONDS *Dict. Trade* Suppl., *Stubtail, Stump-tail*, names in North America for flour made out of damaged wheat and good wheat ground together. **1873** *Spider & Fly* IV. i. 19 This corn is the Illinois growth of 1857, and is called 'stub-tail' because about one-third of it is rotten. **1938** L. MACNEICE *Zoo* 234 They [*sc.* bears] showed their stub-tails. **1973** *Times* 17 May 35/1 Compared with the 1100 it has a more streamlined bonnet curving down to a low radiator grille, and a stub tail somewhat reminiscent of the Hillman Avenger. **1875** KNIGHT *Dict. Mech.*, **Stub-tenon*, a short tenon at the foot of an upright, such as the scantling or studding of a partition or a floor-bearer. **1910** J. BARTLETT in *Encycl. Brit.* V. 387/2 A stub tenon or joggle (fig. 14) is used for fixing a post to a sill. **1872** J. G. MICHIE *Deeside Tales* (1908) 255 A little *stub-thatched cottage. **1930** J. DOS PASSOS *42nd Parallel* 134 He'd..clatter up and down stairs making a tremendous racket with his *stubtoed ironplated shoes. **1911** WEBSTER, **Stub Tooth*, a short gear tooth of great strength, with a large angle of obliquity. **1896** *Engineering News* XXXVI. 27/1 The empty car storage tracks on Mr. Derr's diagram are very long *stub tracks, which are objectionable. **1921** *Railway Engin. & Maintenance of Way Cycl.* 348/1 A freight terminal is commonly considered an important freight station served by stub tracks. **1956** *Railway Track & Structures Cycl.* (ed. 8) 425/2 Bumping posts are obstructions placed at the end of stub tracks. **1843** HOLTZAPFFEL *Turning* I. 221 The complex and ornamental figures for the barrels of fowling-pieces, described as '*stub-twist, wire-twist, Damascus-twist. **1931** *Flight* 2 Jan. 16/2 The lower *stub wings form part of the landing gear structure. **1956** W. A. HEFLIN *U.S. Air Force Dict.* 496/2 *Stub wing*,.. 1. A short wing, esp. as used on certain autogiros. 2. That part of a wing on certain airplanes that lies next to the fuselage, to which the rest of the wing, separately built, is attached... 3. Short for 'stubwing stabilizer.'.. *Stubwing stabilizer*, a hydro-stabilizer on a flying boat. **1958** *Times Rev. Industry* Aug. 39/2 The [Rotodyne] fixed stubwing..takes over the task of supporting the aircraft. **1957** *Times Survey Brit. Aviation* Sept. 2/6 Bristol are sending the *stub-winged twin-rotor Type 173. **1960, 1963** *Stub wire [see sense 7 e above]. **1976** *Eastern Even. News* (Norwich) 22 Dec. 4/8 (Advt.), Oasis (dry and wet). Dried flowers. Stub wires and a large selection of containers. **1770** *Phil. Trans.* LXI. 155 The woods..have great plenty of chesnut, both timber and *stub wood. **1787** W. H. MARSHALL *E. Norfolk* (1795) II. 389 *Stubwood*, all wood which grows in hedgerows and does not come under the denomination of 'timbers', 'pollards', or 'thorns', is called 'stubwood'.

stub (stʌb), *a. rare.* [f. STUB *sb.*] Of a person: Squat, stunted-looking.

1711 *Lond. Gaz.* No. 4928/4 The person suspected..is a short stub Fellow.

stub (stʌb), *v.*[1] Inflected **stubbed** (stʌbd), **stubbing.** Also 5 **stobe**, 5–6 **stubbe**, 7 **stube**, **stubb.** [f. STUB *sb.* Cf. Sw. *stubba*, Da. *stubbe.*]

1. a. *trans.* To dig up by the roots; to grub up (roots). Chiefly with *up.*

c **1400** *Jacob's Well* 26 Alle paryschenys, þat hewyn doun violently, or stubbyn, pullyn, or schredyn, or croppyn, ony treen in cherche-ȝerdes. **1555** WATREMAN *Fardle Facions* II. vii. 160 In the forenoone thei plante and graffe, digge vp settes, stubbe vp rootes. **1573–80** TUSSER *Husb.* (1878) 75 Go breake vp land, get mattock in hand, Stub roote so tough, for breaking of plough. **1574** in J. J. Cartwright *Chapters Hist. Yorks.* (1872) 75 Wyth lyberty to take and stubbe the trees and bushes. *a* **1631** DONNE *Eighty Serm.* 390 If one give me a timber tree for my house, I know not whether the root be mine or no, whether I may stub it by that gift. **1639** HORN & ROB. *Gate Lang. Unl.* xlviii. §529 A woodmonger felleth down trees, and stubes them up by the roots. *c* **1695** J. MILLER *Descr. New York* (1843) 9 He..may ..by stubbing up the trees and brushwood, have good arable land or pastures. **1706** SWIFT *Baucis & Phil.* 178 'Tis hard to be believ'd, How much the other Tree was Griev'd; Grew scrubb'd, dy'd at top, was stunted, So th' next Parson stubb'd and burnt it. **1791** R. MYLNE *2nd Rep. Thames Navig.* 10 Some Thorn-Bushes should be stubbed out of the Bank. **1865** TROLLOPE *Belton Est.* iii. 32 The roots want stubbing up horribly. **1889** JESSOPP *Coming of Friars* v. 238 He was found to have stubbed up a hedge which had been the boundary of the land.

b. *fig.* Now *rare.*

c **1440** *Jacob's Well* 77 He schal stubbyn þe vp, londe & roote, & cachyn þe out of þi dwellyng-place. **1571** CAMPION *Hist. Irel.* ix. (1633) 28 That these strangers would endeavor either to stub out that unruly generation, or to nurture them. **1651** FIRMIN *Serious Quest.* B 1, This Opinion will stub up all the Ordinances. **1662** *Jesuits' Reasons Unreas.* (1675) 128 Unless such Tenets be stubbed out of the heads..of your Preachers. **1876** FARRAR *Marlb. Serm.* xviii. 172 Beware that there be not—hidden deep under the soil of your heart—any sins and tendencies,..any vanities or lusts, which you have not as it were stubbed up.

†**2.** To dig *out* (gravel). *Obs.*

c **1440** *Jacob's Well* 265 But now schal I telle ȝow of þe howe or a pek-ex wherwyth ȝe muste stubbe out þe grauel.

3. To cut down (a tree, etc.) close to the root.

1594 NASHE *Unfort. Trav.* G 3 b, His horse was trapt in the earthie stringes of tree rootes, which though theyr increase was stubbed downe to the grounde, yet were they not vtterly deaded. **1750** W. ELLIS *Mod. Husb.* V. i. 86 (E.D.S.) Turneps may be houghed ill if the hougher stubs them, as we call it, *i.e.* if he houghs them so shallow as to only cut off the heads, and leave the roots in the ground. **1811** T. DAVIS *Agric. Wilts* I. x. 88 Young trees must be planted, part of which may be preserved for timber, and the remainder left to be stubbed off for underwood.

4. To remove the stubs from (land). Also, to clear (land) of trees, furze, etc. by uprooting. Chiefly with *up.*

1464 *Mann. & Househ. Exp.* (Roxb.) 455 [He] schal stobe me klen serten kloses wethe in Powenses. **1593** NASHE *Christ's T.* 29 b, Hee..pluckt downe Barnes and Store-houses, stubd vp Orchards and Vineyardes. *a* **1650** BOATE *Ireland's Nat. Hist.* (1860) 85 That land..produced nothing but moss, heath, and short low furze: which herbs are fired upon the ground and the ground stubbed, before it be plowed the first time. **1762** STERNE *Tr. Shandy* V. vii, We shall have a terrible piece of work of it in stubbing the Ox-moor. **1772** *Ann. Reg., Chron.* 75/2 Paterson stubbed up ten acres of furze or whin ground. **1847** C. G. ADDISON *Law of Contracts* II. i. (1883) 244 He must not convert arable land into pasture..or stub up a wood to make it pasture. **1864** TENNYSON *North. Farmer, Old Style* vii, An' I 'a stubb'd Thornaby waäste. **1889** *Harper's Mag.* Feb. 424/1 A large fenced-in field, well stubbed.

5. To remove the stub-feathers from (a fowl).

1875 PARISH *Sussex Gloss.*, *Stub*, to pluck chicken clean after their feathers have been pulled off. **1901** *Dundee Advertiser* 3 May 7 The fowl is at once plucked and 'stubbed,'..The plucking is done by men..and the stubbing, or the removal of the undeveloped feathers, by women.

6. To reduce to a stub or stump.

†**a.** To wear down (a quill pen). *Obs.*

1577 GRANGE *Golden Aphrod.* D ij, Yet wold their inke be dried vp, their paper spent, their pennes stubbed. **1589** NASHE *Anat. Absurd.* A iiij, What should I spend my yncke, waste my paper, stub my penne, in painting forth theyr vgly imperfections.

†**b.** To deprive *of* (a horn). In quot. *fig. Obs.*

1658 HARRINGTON *Prerog. Pop. Gov.* I. xii. 128 A Dilemma,..being a kind of argument that should not be stubb'd of one horne, but have each of equall length and danger.

c. To shorten and thicken by hammering.

1869 SANDBERG tr. *Styffe's Iron & Steel* 11 The author 'upset' or stubbed the bars at the ends.

7. To cause (a horse) to be wounded with a stub. Also *refl.* of the horse.

1686 *Lond. Gaz.* No. 2126/4 Lost.., a brown bay Gelding,..the near Leg behind stubb'd with Leaping. **1702** *Ibid.* No. 3850/4 Stolen or strayed.., a dun Nag.., was stub'd on the Fetlock Joint of one of the fore Legs. **1865** M. LEMON *Loved at Last* I. vi. 140 Pray keep on, sir, my horse has stubbed himself, I fancy. **1875** PARISH *Sussex Gloss.* s.v., To stub a horse is to lame him by letting him tread on stubs of underwood in a cover.

8. ? To crush, pulverize (marl, etc. for spreading over land, road-material); to fill up the ruts in (a road) with crushed stones, etc. Also *to stub in*: to crush (road-metal) into the ruts.

1765 *Museum Rust.* III. 287 If with stone of the farmers, a load of thirty bushels will do three rods, which costs one shilling and a halfpenny stubbing and picking. **1795** VANCOUVER *Agric. Essex* 141 The blue and white chalky clay ..should be stubbed and left exposed to the action of the air, sometime before it is carried out, and spread upon the land. **1800** *Little Cornard* (Suff.) *Highway Acc.* (MS.), Pd Robt. Sparrow for Stubbing the road from Parmers to Rowls pond, 0. 14. 5. **1805** R. W. DICKSON *Pract. Agric.* I. 165 The stones..are..dropped into the ruts, far better than a man can stub them in.

9. a. *to stub* (one's) *toe* (see quot. 1848.) Also *fig.* Formerly chiefly *U.S.*

1848 BARTLETT *Dict. Amer.* 339 'To stub one's toe', is to strike it against anything in walking or running; an expression often used by boys and others who go barefoot. *c* **1850** 'DOW JR.' in Jerdan *Yankee Hum.* (1853) 58 When I stubbed my toes. **1897** MARY KINGSLEY *W. Africa* 114 You are rather liable to what Captain Eversfield graphically describes as 'stub your toe' against lava-like rock. **1906** ALICE WERNER *Natives Brit. Centr. Afr.* vi. 140 The formation of a virulent ulcer every time a person stubbed a toe or barked a shin. **1957** *Economist* 19 Oct. 194/1 At a time when the Middle East has become more of a happy hunting ground for Russians seeking friends and influence than ever before, it is on Turkey that they are always stubbing their toe. **1967** [see GOOD *a.* C. 8]. **1976** 'J. ROSS' *I know what it's like to Die* xix. 126 It was a reputable organisation. At least, insofar as it hadn't stubbed its corporate toes on, or interfered with, anything under the supervision of the superintendent's own bailiwick.

b. *U.S. colloq. intr.* 'To walk along striking the toes against obstructions; go heedlessly; as, the boy *stubs* along to school' (*Funk's Stand. Dict.*). Also *transf.* and *fig.*

1875 C. B. LEWIS *Quad's Odds* 480 The writer will stub along through life with a heart full of joyfulness. **1878** B. F. TAYLOR *Between Gates* 241 An old whaler stubbing about estimated him [*sc.* a whale] at sixty barrels.

10. *trans.* To cover with stubs.

1878 W. C. SMITH *Hilda* 61 Last of a great pine forest that stubs the heath with its roots For miles.

11. *intr.* Of a tree: To send out branches from the 'stub' when cut down.

1791 *Trans. Soc. Arts* IX. 20 The Spanish Chestnut.. possesses a peculiar faculty of branching, provincially called stubbing, from the roots after being cut down.

12. *trans.* To extinguish (a cigarette) by pressing the lighted end of the stub against a hard object. Freq. with *out.* Also *fig.*

1927 *Daily Express* 28 Oct. 5 A new glass ash tray with cigarette rests has a glass stopper fitting in at the back which is used for stubbing one's smokes... On the stubber a Greek girl dancing, scarf in hand [is represented]. **1930** J. CANNAN *No Walls of Jasper* 116 He stubbed out his cigarette and smiled at her. **1955** P. LARKIN in *Listener* 8 Sept. 373/1, I lie Where Mr. Bleaney lay, and stub my fags On the same saucer-souvenir. **1962** J. BRAINE *Life at Top* xxvi. 277, I looked round for an ashtray and for the fifth time since nine o'clock stubbed out my cigarette on the floor. **1970** R. LOWELL *Notebk.* 214 A hand prepared to stub out liberty. **1974** 'E. FERRARS' *Hanged Man's House* xv. 149 There was always something that you could do with a cigarette, light it, draw on it, tip ash off it, stub it out. **1978** S. RADLEY *Death & Maiden* xi. 109 She stubbed out her cigarette with sudden vigour.

†**stub**, *v.*[2] *Obs. rare.* [Cf. STOB *v.*[1], STAB *v.*] *trans.* To thrust (a weapon) *into.*

1576 BEDINGFIELD tr. *Cardanus' Comf.* 37 b, When Iulius Cæsar..felte the daggers of diuers men stubbed into his body he [etc.].

stubbard ('stʌbəd). *s.w. dial.* Also **stubberd**, **stibbert.** [Perh. a surname: cf. quot. 1741.] An early codling apple. Also *attrib.*

1741 *Compl. Family-Piece* II. iii. 383 Apples. [July.].. Margaret Apple, Stubbard's Apple, and Codling. **1786** ABERCROMBIE *Gard. Assist.* Arrangem. p. xi, Principal varieties [of apples] are..Summer stubbard. **1826** *Horticult. Soc. Catal. Fruits* 148 Summer Stibbert. **1844** W. BARNES *Poems Rur. Life* 143 She gie'd me var a treat A lot o' stubberds var to eat. **1875** R. HOGG *Fruit Man.* (ed. 4) 144 Summer Stibbert ([*syn.*] Stubbard). **1880** HARDY *Trumpet-Major* I. ii. 26 In the large stubbard-tree at the corner of the garden was erected a pole of larch fir. **1893** 'Q.' (Quiller-Couch) *Delect. Duchy* 218 Thic' there's a stubbard apple you've got in your hand.

stubbed (stʌbd), *ppl. a.* [f. STUB *v.*[1] + -ED[1].]

1. a. Of trees: Cut down to a stub; cut off near the ground; also, deprived of branches or pollarded.

1575 GASCOIGNE *Posies, Hearbes* (1907) 343 Like a stubbed thorne. **1594** NASHE *Unfort. Trav.* G 3, After him followed the knight of the Owle, whose armor was a stubd tree ouer-growne with iuie. **1627** DRAYTON *Nimphidia* lvi, A paine he in his Head-peece feeles, Against a stubbed Tree he reeles. **1793** W. BLAKE *Amer.* 83 They cannot bring the stubbèd oak to overgrow the hills. **1819** KEATS *Otho* III. i. 35 What, man, do you mistake the hollow sky For a throng'd tavern, and these stubbed trees For old serge hangings? **1856** KINGSLEY *Misc.* (1859) II. 16 The trunk looking like an old stubbed oak.

b. Of ground: Having the stubs removed; grubbed up.

1573–80 TUSSER *Husb.* (1878) 73 In stubbed plot, fill hole with clot.

2. a. Short and thick, stumpy. ? *Obs.* exc. *dial.*

a **1529** SKELTON *E. Rummyng* 422 Her legges..were sturdy and stubbed. **1611** CORYAT *Crudities* 42 Their [*sc.* ostriches] heads are covered all with small stubbed feathers. **1630** R. JOHNSON *Kingd. & Commw.* 12 The Tartar is a stubbed squat fellow, hard bred, and such are their horses. **1658** EVELYN *Fr. Gard.* (1675) 164 Three years you must forbear to cut, that the plant may be strong, and not stubbed. **1687** MIEGE *Gt. Fr. Dict.* II, Stubbed, short and well set, *trapu, membru.* A stubbed Fellow, *un Trapu.* **1696** E. LHWYD in *Phil. Trans.* XXVII. 464 With Bills more stubbed and bigger than that of a Bull-finch. **1769** GRAY *Jrnl.* 13 Oct. *Poems* (1775) 375 The rock..rises perpendicular, with stubbed yew-trees and shrubs staring from its side. **1868** *Rep. U.S. Commissioner Agric.* (1869) 254 Trimming does thicken the surface of the hedge by causing a stubbed, stooling form of growth. **1883** S. C. HALL *Retrospect* II. 206 A short, thick, stubbed, ungainly and ungraceful form.

†**b.** *stubbed boy*: a 'hobbledehoy'. *Obs.*

16.. CHALKHILL *Thealma & Clearchus* (1683) 71 Memnon himself keeps home, attended on But by a stubbed Boy. **1722** *Hist. & Antiq. Glastonbury* Author's Pref. n 4 *note*, Saunders must be a stubbed Boy, if not a Man, at the Dissolution of Abbeys.

3. Reduced to a stub; worn down to a stub; (of hair) cut close to the skin, stubbly.

1621 SANDERSON *Serm., Ad Pop.* iv. (1674) I. 213 Thy new broom, that now sweepeth clean all discontents from thee, will soon grow stubbed. **1631** [MABBE] *Celestina* VII. 84 She did pull out seven teeth out of a fellowes head that was hang'd with a paire of pincers, such as you pull out stubbed haires withall. **1762** CHURCHILL *Ghost* II. 306 Hark! something scratches round the room! A Cat, a Rat, a stubb'd Birch-broom. **1802** *Trans. Soc. Arts* XX. 172 Effectually done..by a stubbed birch broom.

4. a. Blunted at the point.

1610 B. JONSON *Masque of Oberon* Wks. (1616) 977 To spight the coy Nymphes scornes, Hang vpon our stubbed hornes, Garlands, ribbands and fine poesies. **1675** A. BROWNE *Appendix Art Paint.* 26 Instead of the Rolls of Paper they make use of Stubbed Pencils; and some of them are stuffed with Cotton, and some others with Bombast. **1728** SWIFT *Pastoral Dial.* 3 While each with stubbed Knife remov'd the Roots That rais'd between the Stones their daily Shoots. **1854** MISS BAKER *Northampt. Gloss.*, *Stubbed* or *Stubby*, blunt-pointed, as the broad nib of a pen, thick, short. **1860** O. W. HOLMES *Elsie Venner* iii, The short, stubbed blade of his jack-knife.

†**b.** *fig.* Dull, not delicate or sensitive. *Obs.*

1744 BERKELEY *Siris* §105 The hardness of stubbed vulgar constitutions.

5. Abounding in stubs.

1855 BROWNING *Ch. Roland* xxv, Then came a bit of stubbed ground, once a wood. **1898** M. HEWLETT *Forest Lovers* vi, He urged his horse over the stubbed heath.

6. Chiefly, of a toe: injured by being struck against something. Cf. STUB *v.*[1] 9 a. orig. *U.S.*

1890 *Brighton* (Colorado) *Reg.* 11 Jan. 4/1 Montana is the 'stubbed-toe State'. **1958** J. G. MACGREGOR *North-West of 16* viii. 111, I don't suppose a city boy, or even a modern farm boy, knows what a stubbed toe is. Maybe that's just as well, because they were most painful. **1977** *Evening Gaz.* (Middlesbrough) 11 Jan. 4/5 None of the hair-raising stunts he performs for his TV series Some Mothers Do 'Ave 'Em led to any injury greater than a stubbed finger. **1978** B. BAINBRIDGE *Young Adolf* xviii. 101 Testily he kicked at the ..wood... Recoiling, he curled his stubbed toes within his boot.

7. ***stubbed-out***: of a cigarette, extinguished by being pressed against a hard object.

1975 O. SELA *Bengali Inheritance* xxv. 218 A single stubbed out Stuyvesant in the ashtray. **1979** *N.Y. Rev. Bks.* 8 Feb. 13/4 No other writer since Noël Coward can have so constantly punctuated dialogue and action with a ritual pattern of lighting-up, inhalation, smoke-rings, and stubbed-out butts.

Hence **'stubbedness**, 'a being short and thick'.

1727 BAILEY vol. II.

stubber ('stʌbə(r)). Also 6 stoobber. [f. STUB *v.*[1] + -ER[1].] **1.** One who stubs, in senses of the verb.

1481–90 *Howard Househ. Bks.* (Roxb.) 507 Item, payd to the stubber of Northffolk for xj. gret rotys stubbyng [etc.], v.s. **1562** J. HEYWOOD *Prov. & Epigr.* (1867) 161 But if stake stoobbers will not let stakis stand Blame not the stake. **1679** EVELYN *Sylva* xxxiv. (ed. 3) 245 Two of the Stubbers or Labourers..that were employ'd to clear the Ground. **1860** *All Year Round* 28 Apr. 66/2 The drainer, the leveller, the stubber-up of rotten stumps. **1908** *N. & Q.* Ser. x. X. 38/1 Scores of the roots taken out were 'crooked billets'—so called by the stubbers.

2. A contrivance against which a cigarette is stubbed out.

1927 [see STUB *v.*[1] 12].

stubbing ('stʌbɪŋ), *vbl. sb.* Also 5 stobenge, 8 *pl.* stubbens. [f. STUB *v.*[1] + -ING[1].] The action of the vb. STUB in various senses.

1445 tr. *Claudianus* in *Anglia* XXVIII. 277 Loondys which were vntilied..daies right many beforne [he] after his stubbyng staryth [? *read* storyth: L. *restituit*]. **1464** *Mann. & Househ. Exp.* (Roxb.) 455 He schal haue fore the stobenge of them..xxvi. viii d. **1574** in J. J. Cartwright *Chapters Hist. Yorks.* (1872) 75 The fencyng, stubbyng and dressyng of the ground. **1577** GRANGE *Golden Aphrod.* Ep. Ded. A iij b, It seemeth the nebbe of my penne is long, and that I lesse do feare the stubbing therof. **1607** MARKHAM *Cavel.* III. 6 In woody..grounds where a horse can neither conveniently make foorth his way, nor can tread without danger of stubbing. **1732** BERKELEY *Minute Philos.* I. 6 The mind of Man may be fitly compared to a piece of Land. What stubbing, plowing, digging and harrowing is to the one, that thinking..is to the other. **1770–4** A. HUNTER *Georg. Ess.* (1804) VI. 457 The tree itself possesses a peculiar faculty of branching provincially called stubbing. **1861** L. L. NOBLE *Icebergs* 312 An unlucky stubbing of my naked toes. **1887** J. A. PHILLIPS & BAUERMAN *Elem. Metall.* (ed. 2) 604 A few buckets of water are thrown into the hearth, in order..to cool it previous to the clearing or stubbing-out necessary before commencing another shift.

b. *attrib.*

1567 *Richmond Wills* (Surtees) 211 In the stubbing close one stake of hay. **1832** *Min. Evid. Comm. Factories Bill* 24 The cording and stubbing machinery.

stubble ('stʌb(ə)l), *sb.* Forms: *α.* 3–7 **stuble**, 4 **stubil(l**, 4, 6 **stubbil(l**, 4–5 **stobil(l**, **-yl(l**, **stobul(l**, 4–6 **stob(b)le**, 4–7 **stubbel(l**, 5 **-ull**, **-yll(e**, 5–6 **stubel(l**, 4, 6– **stubble**; *Sc.* 6 **stibill**, **stible**, 8, 9 **stibble**. *β.* 3 **stouple**, 5 **stopple**. [a. OF. *stuble*, *estuble*, *esteuble* (also *esteule* etc., see Godefr.; mod.F. dial. *éteuble*, *étouble*, *éteule*), = Pr. *estobla*, It. *stoppia*:—popular L. **stupla* = late L. *stupula*, class. L. *stipula*: see STIPULA.

The popular L. **stupla* was adopted in continental WGer.: hence OHG. *stupfala* (MHG., mod.G. dial. *stupfel*), (M)LG. *stoppel* (whence mod.G. *stoppel* fem.), MDu. *stoppele* fem. (mod.Du. *stoppel* masc.). It is possible that the word may have coalesced with a native word of similar meaning from the root of STUB *sb.*]

1. Each of the stumps or lower ends of grain-stalks left in the ground after reaping. Now only in pl.

1297 R. GLOUC. (Rolls) 4578 He smot of is heued as liȝtliche as it were a scouple [*v.rr.* a stouple, a lute stouple]. **1398** TREVISA *Barth. De P.R.* XI. vi. (1495) 393 Pestylence wastyth and dystroyeth stobles. **1569** G. B. in Farr *S.P. Eliz.* (1845) II. 388 In euerie place are stubbles and prickes, That stayes the feeble feete. **1577** *Extracts Burgh Rec. Glasgow* (1876) 63 That nane pull stibillis furth of ony landis about the toun. **1733** W. ELLIS *Chiltern & Vale Farm.* 319 Its Work is to plough up Stubbles, particularly in wet Weather. **1735** SOMERVILLE *Chase* II. 58 The gay Pack In the rough bristly Stubbles range unblam'd. **1836** EMERSON *Nat.* iii. Wks. (Bohn) II. 146 Every withered stem and stubble rimed with frost. **1884** H. SEEBOHM *Hist. Brit. Birds* II. 455 At this season the Partridge delights to 'jug' in the grass-fields, repairing to the turnips and the stubbles to feed. **1897** *Allbutt's Syst. Med.* VIII. 817 The crops of warts which attack the gums and palates of sheep feeding upon stubbles.

2. *collect. sing.* **a.** The stumps or lower parts of the stalks of wheat or other grain left in the ground by the sickle or reaping-machine.

a **1340** HAMPOLE *Psalter* xlix. 4 þan may þe cafe drede, and stubil. **1388** WYCLIF *Gen.* xli. 23 And othere seuene..camen forth of the stobil. **1398** TREVISA *Barth. De P.R.* XVII. clvii. (1495) 707 Stipula stobble is properly that strawe wyth leues and hosen that is lefte in the felde after that repers haue repen the corn wyth hokys and gadred it home. **1425** in *Rep. MSS. Ld. Middleton* (1911) 108 If any man tye his horse in any stubbull. **1523–34** FITZHERB. *Husb.* (1882) 35 In somme places they wyll shere theyr cornes hyghe, to the entente to mowe theyr stubble, eyther to thacke or to bren. **1615** CHAPMAN *Odyss.* XIV. 304 But I suppose, that you..Know by the stubble, what the Corne hath bene. **1720** SWIFT *Progr. Poetry* 1 The Farmer's Goose, who in the Stubble, Has fed without Restraint, or Trouble. **1765** A. DICKSON *Treat. Agric.* (ed. 2) 166 The stubble, or the roots, which the plough pushes before it, are sometimes intangled betwixt the coulter and sheath. **1848** THACKERAY *Van. Fair* xli, The sight of those fields of stubble and turnips, now his own, gave him many secret joys. **1887** *Spectator* 13 Aug. 1075 Carefully destroying the stubble of infested wheat and barley.

b. In various fig. or allusive contexts.

Often with allusion to 1 Cor. iii. 12.

a **1591** H. SMITH *2nd Serm. Song Simeon* (1602) D 5, But sinners are stubble, and their sentence is, Burne them. **1607** SHAKS. *Cor.* II. i. 274 This..suggested..Will be his fire To kindle their dry Stubble. **1624** BEDELL *Lett.* vii. 110 The stubble and errors of the Doctors. **1625** N. CARPENTER *Geog. Del.* II. vii. 128 This argument..is wittily spunne out by..Sr Humfry Gilbert, whose ability seemes to haue made a haruest out of the stubble. **1728** POPE *Dunc.* i. 254 No merit now the dear Nonjuror claims, Moliere's old stubble in a moment flames. **1748** RICHARDSON *Clarissa* VII. 5 Depend upon it, Mr. Belford..that one day you will be convinced, that what you call friendship, is chaff and stubble. **1773** BURKE *Sp. on Bill for Relief of Dissenters* Wks. X. 23 Fortunately her [the Church of England's] walls, bulwarks, and bastions, are constructed of other materials than of stubble and straw. **1846** J. C. HARE *Mission Comf.* (1850) 156 The very stubble of our old sins may run into our eyes and blind us. **1859** TENNYSON *Elaine* 731 So ran the tale like fire about the court, Fire in dry stubble a nine-days' wonder flared.

c. *transf.* A rough surface or short growth likened to the 'stubble' of grain, *esp.* the short bristly growth on a man's unshaven face.

a **1596** *Sir T. More* IV. iii. 56 Thou was wunt to blame My kissing when my beard was in the stubble. *a* **1660** *Prince d'Amour* etc. 128 The grim stubble eke On the Judges cheek. **1840** DICKENS *Old C. Shop* iii, His mouth and chin [were] bristly with the stubble of a coarse hard beard. **1873** HAMERTON *Intell. Life* VIII. ii. (1876) 291 On his chin, a black stubble of two days growth.

d. In sugar-planting, the sugar-cane in the field after the first year.

1846 *De Bow's Commerc. Rev.* II. 324 Fortunately the [sugar] cane is not an annual plant. Each year fresh shoots spring from the stubble which remains after cutting the crop.

3. The straw of grain-stalks, etc. gathered after the crop has been harvested.

1382 WYCLIF *Josh.* ii. 6 She made the men to stye vp into the soler of hir hows, and couerde hem with stuble of flaxe, that was there. **1483** CAXTON *Golden Leg.* 56/2 In no wyse gyue no more chaf to the peple for to make lome and claye but late them goo and gadre stopple. **1540–1** ELYOT *Image Gov.* 41 Beeyng bounden to a stake, with smoke made of greene stickes and wette stubbell, to be smouldred to death. *c* **1586** C'TESS PEMBROKE *Ps.* LXXXIII. vii, Torment them, Lord, as tossed balls; As stubble scatt'red in the aire. **1617** MORYSON *Itin.* III. 133 Where they have lesse store of wood within land there they burne straw, furres, and other kinds of stubble. **1760–72** H. BROOKE *Fool of Qual.* (1809) III. 91 One night as I lay on my bed of stubble. **1785** BURNS *To a Mouse* vi, That wee-bit heap o' leaves an' stibble, Has cost thee monie a weary nibble. **1846** MCCULLOCH *Acc. Brit. Empire* (1854) I. 179 The walls..are formed of a mixture of stubble and clay.

4. A field that has been reaped, and not yet ploughed again; a stubble-field. Chiefly in *plural.*

1792 A. YOUNG *Trav. France* 435 Sheep..are in most of the provinces fed upon straw, and what they can pick up on wastes and stubbles. **1859** JEPHSON *Brittany* iv. 41 The valleys..were of the deepest and richest green, which contrasted deliciously with the yellow stubbles and cornfields. **1908** *Outlook* 29 Aug. 279/1 The costly moors in the Highlands..must always be the privileged possession of the few, but the stubbles in September are available to the multitude.

5. *attrib.* and *Comb.* esp. attributive with the senses 'consisting of or covered with stubble' as ***stubble-beard*** (so ***-bearded*** adj.), ***-field***, ***-land***, etc., 'grown on the stubble' as ***stubble-clover***, ***-crop***, ***-turnip***, etc., 'used on the stubble' as ***stubble-plough***, ***-rake***, etc.; objective, as ***stubble-burner***, ***-burning***, ***-loving*** adj.; instrumental, as ***stubble-covered*** adj.; **stubble-butter** *Sc.*, butter made of the milk of cows fed on the stubble; **stubble-fed** *a.*, of poultry: fed on the stubble left in a reaped field; hence **stubble-feeding**; **stubble-fire**, fire made of stubble and so lasting but a moment; **stubble-grown** *a.* = *stubble-covered* adj. above; **stubble-jumper** *slang* (chiefly *Canad.*), a prairie farmer (see also quot. 1946); **stubble-quail**, a brown, black, and white quail, *Coturnix pectoralis*, native to southern Australia; **stubble-rig** *Sc.*, (*a*) a stubble-field; (*b*) the reaper who takes the lead; **stubble-time**, the time just after harvest; **stubble-turner** (see quot. 1875). Also STUBBLE-GOOSE.

1714 E. WARD *Field-Spy* 26 With *Stubble-Beard, about a Fortnight's growth. **1620** MELTON *Astrolog.* 36 A *stubble-bearded-Barister. **1980** *Sunday Times* 24 Aug. 1/7 Can *stubble-burners be controlled? **1973** *Times* 24 Aug. 2/5 The National Union of Agricultural and Allied Workers yesterday called for regulations to control *stubble burning. **1976** A. PRICE *War Game* I. ii. 48 There hadn't been so much stubble-burning this year, he noted approvingly. **1856** J. BALLANTINE *Poems* 167 The best *stibble butter taks langest o' churnin'. **1888** *Glasgow Even. Times* 15 Oct. 2/5 advt., Stubble butter. *a* **1722** LISLE *Husb.* (1757) 329 Fatting-sheep may be suffered to feed freely on the *stubble-clover. **1916** JOYCE *Portrait of Artist* (1969) ii. 61 Stephen often glanced with mistrust at his trainer's flabby *stubblecovered face. **1881** *Chicago Times* 11 June, The sugar districts in this state [i.e. Louisiana] report to the Planters' association..: *Stubble crop good. **1882** W. D. HAY *Brighter Britain!* I. 224 Cricket-fed turkey would shame any *stubble-fed bird altogether. **1928** *Daily Express* 6 Oct. 4/6 These stubble-fed geese are the best of all for eating. **1960** G. E. EVANS *Horse in Furrow* xii. 172 There were two kinds of shacking; *Lammas shack*..and *Michaelmas shack*, *stubble-feeding after the corn harvest. **1614** MARKHAM *Cheap & Good Husb.* II. xvi. 124 After they [the geese] haue in the *stubble fields, and during the time of haruest got into good flesh. **1786** BURNS *To Mountain Daisy* iv, But thou..Adorns the histie stibble-field, Unseen, alane. **1835** BROWNING *Paracelsus* I. 42 Which, look through near, this way, and it appears A stubble-field or a cane-brake. *a* **1618** SYLVESTER *Cup Consol.* 34 Whose brittle glosse and glory lasts and shines As *Stubble-Fire, and Dust before the Windes. **1697** DRYDEN *Virg. Georg.* III. 159 In vain he burns, like fainty Stubble Fires. **1801** *Farmer's Mag.* Apr. 176 No plough will choke in *stubble ground, if the crop is cut in a proper manner. **1916** JOYCE *Portrait of Artist* (1969) v. 227 Good evening, gentlemen, said the *stubblegrown monkeyish face. **1946** *California Folklore Q.* Apr. 164 'Top hands', 'sodbusters', 'hay stopers', '*stubble jumpers',..denote farmers who have turned to mining, and these terms are always opprobrious. **1961** *Sun* (Vancouver) 4 July 1/1 The prairie farmer, to those of us who don't know him well, is a stock comic character. Clod-hopper, we call him, and stubble-jumper. **1973** *Islander* (Victoria, B.C.) 19 Aug. 12/1 An authentic stubble-jumper from the prairies was looked upon as being at the very bottom rung of the social and employment ladder. **1596** SHAKS. *1 Hen. IV*, I. iii. 35 Like a *stubble Land at Haruest home. **1598** CHAPMAN *Hero & Leander* IV. 98 Who did of hollow bulrushes combine Snares for the *stubble-louing Grashopper. **1815** SCOTT *Field of Waterloo* iv, The bare extent of *stubble-plain Seems lately lighten'd of its grain. **1875** KNIGHT *Dict. Mech.*, *Stubble-plow. **1848** J. GOULD *Birds Austral.* V. plate 88 The name of *Stubble Quail has been given to it by the colonists of Van Diemen's Land, from the great numbers that visit the fields after the harvest is over. **1921** MATTHEWS & IREDALE *Man. Birds Austral.* I. 224 Stubble-quail... Head, neck, entire back and scapulars rufous-brown and black streaked with white. **1965** *Austral. Encycl.* VII. 316/1 The stubble-quail, which is closely allied to the quail of Europe, is confined to southern Australia and Tasmania. **1805** R. W. DICKSON *Pract. Agric.* II. 801 The stubble..being..raked together by means of a large horse *stubble-rake. **1785** BURNS *Halloween* xvi, Our *Stibble-rig was Rab M'Graen. ? **1780** in *Burns's Wks.* (Globe) 164/2 The stibble rig is easy plough'd, The fallow land is free. **1713** C'TESS WINCHILSEA *Misc. Poems* 77 A lowly Cottage..Fenc'd by a *Stubble-roof, from Rain and Heat. **1577** B. GOOGE tr. *Heresbach's Husb.* I. 11 b, Husbandry necessaries..whereof the smaller sort be these..*Stubble Sithes. **1486** *Bk. St. Albans* d ij, Ther be in a *stobull tyme Sordes of mailardes in the felde. **1875** KNIGHT *Dict. Mech.*, **Stubble-turner*, an attachment to a plow to turn over stubble and trash before the principal plow reaches it. **1819** *Rees' Cycl.* XXXII. 3 K 1/1 By..the use of *stubble turnips when necessary, the ewe and lamb-stock may be well supported through the severity of the season. **1844** J. T. HEWLETT *Parsons & W.* xxviii, The system of *stubble-turniping after wheat has proved very successful. **1549** LATIMER *1st Serm. bef. Edw. VI* (Arb.) 29 They walk not directely and playnly, but delite in balkes, and *stubble way.

†'stubble, *a. Obs.* Also 4 stubul, -el, 5 stubill, stubbill. [Prob. connected with STUB *sb.* ? Cf. STUBBORN *a.*]

a. ? Clumsy, awkward. **b.** ? Stoutly-built. ***stubble boy***: cf. *stubbed boy*, STUBBED *ppl. a.* 2 b.

a **1300** *Cursor M.* 23910 For-sak þou noght his stubul werc, For þof it rude and stubel be, It es in worscip wroght o þe. *c* **1480** HENRYSON *Two Mice* 92 In stubbill array throw gres and corne And vnder buskis preuilie culd thay creip. *c* **1475** *Rauf Coilȝear* 522 It is lyke..That sic ane stubill husband an wald stryke stoutly. **1562** LEGH *Armorie* Pref. ¶ iv, The third sort..are..very stubble curres, & be neither doers, sufferers, or wel speakers of honours tokens. **1598** R. BERNARD tr. *Terence, Andria* IV. v. 86 *Grandiusculus hinc profectus est.* He was a good stubble boy: a pretie baucket ladde and of a good stature when he went from hence. **1641** BEST *Farming Bks.* (Surtees) 133 Wee give usually 20s. to a good stubble boy for drivinge of the oxe plough.

Hence **†'stubbleness.**

1530 PALSGR. 277/2 Stubblenesse or sturdynesse, *lourdesse.*

stubble ('stʌb(ə)l), *v.* [f. STUBBLE *sb.*]

1. *trans.* To clear (land) of stubble. Also to remove stubble from (one's face).

1491 CAXTON *Vitas Patr.* (W. de W.) II. (1495) 256 b/1 How shall it be to me possyble to stubble & make clene this pyece of londe here. **1836** T. HOOK *G. Gurney* III. 128 He began stubbling his chin, as before.

b. To trample *down* into stubble.

1897 MARY KINGSLEY *W. Africa* 243 The grass is stubbled down into paths by hippos.

2. Cant. ***stubble it! stubble your whids!*** hold your tongue!

a **1700** B. E. *Dict. Cant. Crew*, Stubble-it. **1827** LYTTON *Pelham* lxxxii, Stubble it, you ben. **1830** —— *P. Clifford* xvi, Stubble your whids, You wants to trick I!

Hence **'stubbling** *vbl. sb.*

1872 *Daily News* 25 Sept., There is gleaning and stubbling, and then the two harvests of hay and corn.

†**'stubbled**, *a.*[1] *Obs. rare.* [Cf. STUBBLE *a.*; but perh. a misprint.] = STUBBED.

a **1529** SKELTON *E. Rummyng* 422 Her legges..were sturdy and stubbed [*v.r.* stubbled], Myghty pestels and clubbed.

stubbled ('stʌb(ə)ld), *a.*[2] [f. STUBBLE *sb.* + -ED[2].] Covered with stubble, stubbly.

a **1720** GAY *Epist.* iv. *To P. Methuen* 85 A crow was strutting o'er the stubbled plain. **1844** DICKENS *Mart. Chuz.* ii, The noiseless passage of the plough as it..wrought a graceful pattern in the stubbled fields. **1913** N. MUNRO in *Blackw. Mag.* Dec. 784/2 [He] felt at his stubbled chin, and took from his sack the razors.

stubble-goose. A goose fed on the stubble.

c **1386** CHAUCER *Cook's Prol.* 27 For of thy percely yet they fare the wors That they han eten with thy stubbel goos. **1584** COGAN *Haven Health* clxvi. 136 The greene goose is better [for digestion] than the stubble goose. **1612** *Benvenuto's Passenger* I. ii. 87 You are euen as wise as a stubble Goose. **1655** MOUFET *Health's Improv.* x. 87 A young stuble goose feeding it self fat in wheaten fields, is the best of all. **1708** W. KING *Art of Cookery* 77 So stubble Geese at Michaelmas are seen Upon the spit, next May produces green. **1816** W. TAYLOR in *Monthly Mag.* XLII. 37 Geese..are eaten young, under the name of *green* geese, ..They are eaten adult, under the name of *stubble* geese. **1842** BARHAM *Ingol. Leg.*, *Lay St. Cuthbert* 5 And the fat stubble-goose Swims in gravy and juice. **1844** STEPHENS *Bk. Farm* II. 720 Young geese are never seen at a Scottish farmer's table, though a stubble-goose at Michaelmas seems to be prized in England.

b. The grey-lag goose (*Anser cinereus*).

1885 SWAINSON *Prov. Names Birds* 147.

stubbly ('stʌblɪ), *a.* [f. STUBBLE *sb.* + -Y.]

1. Covered with stubble, stubbled.

1600 SURFLET *Country Farm* v. xviii. 692 Fasels grow in stubbly grounds. **1611** COTGR., *Chaumin*..Stubblie; made of, or, couered with, stubble. **1789** D. DAVIDSON *Thoughts Seasons* 130 An', o'er the stibbly plain, the nibbling rooks, In numbers spread. **1854** SURTEES *Handley Cr.* xxxix. (1901) II. 29 'Chi-e-l-dren,' continued our master, dry-shaving his stubbly chin, 'are certain cares' [etc.]. **1879** STEVENSON *Trav. Cevennes* 146 It led into a valley between fading hills, stubbly with rocks like a reaped field of corn.

2. Resembling stubble; *esp.* of hair, bristly.

1849 ALB. SMITH *Pottleton Legacy* xxx. 332 Two little stubbly tufts rising from his crown. **1864** *Realm* 25 May 3 The stubbly staple of Lord Russell's arguments is the material we have managed to convince Europe that the British Lion is stuffed with. **1885** RIDER HAGGARD *K. Solomon's Mines* xix, My stubbly hair came out of the treasure cave about three shades greyer than it went in.

Comb. **1891** *Daily News* 1 Sept. 3/1 Stubbly-chinned.

stubborn ('stʌbən), *a.* Forms: α. 4 stiborn(e, -(o)urne, styborn(e, 5 stiburn, styburne. β. 5–6 stoburne, 6 stobburne, stoberne, -orne. γ. 5 stuborn, 6 stubberne, -(o)urne, stuburne, 6–7 stubborne, (6 stouborne, -urne, 8 stouborn), 6– stubborn. [Of uncertain etymology.

The commonly assumed derivation from STUB *sb.* presents no great difficulty with regard to the sense ('as if immovable as a stub or stock'), but is not easy to justify morphologically. It has been suggested that the word represents an OE. *stybbor f. stybb STUB *sb.*, the final *n* being supposed to be due to a false analysis of *styburnesse*, *stobournesse* etc. (see STUBBORNNESS). But *-or* was not a living suffix in OE.; the words containing it are inherited from OTeut., and are not formed on noun-stems but on verbal roots. The early spelling of *stubbornness* with only one *n* is of no significance; more noteworthy, however, is the spelling *stoberlie* in our first example of the adv. The fluctuation in the vowel (see the Forms above) might be supposed to be an argument in favour of derivation from STUB *sb.* (OE. *stybb*, *stubb*, **stobb*); but it should be noted that a similar fluctuation appears in the forms of STUBBLE *sb.*, which is of Romanic origin.]

1. a. Of persons or animals: Pertinacious or dogged in refusing obedience or compliance; unyielding, inflexible, obstinate: chiefly in bad sense, unreasonably obstinate. In early use app. sometimes with stronger notion: †Untameable, implacable, ruthless, fierce.

c **1386** CHAUCER *Wife's Prol.* 456 And I was yong and ful of ragerye, Stibourne and strong and ioly as a pye. *Ibid.* 637 Stibourne I was as is a Leonesse. *c* **1430** LYDG. *Jack Hare* ii. Min. Poems (Percy Soc.) 52 This boy N. ful stuborn [*MS. Laud* styborne] of his bonys, Sluggy on morwe his leemys up to dresse, A gentil harlot chose out for the nonys, Sone and cheeff heir to dame Idilnesse. **1430** —— *Order of Fools* xiv. *Ibid.* 168 And he that holdithe a quarel agayn right, Holdyng hys purpos stiburn ageyn reson. *c* **1440** *Promp. Parv.* 475/1 Styburne, or stoburne (or sterne), *austerus*, *ferox*. **1508** FISHER *Ps.* cii. Wks. (1876) 194 Who is now soo stoburne and euyll wylled that his herte coude not melte and be kyndeled with the fyre of charyte. **1526** TINDALE *Rom.* i. 31 Beynge full of all vnrighteous doynge,..vnlovynge, stouborne [Gr. ἀσπόνδους, 1611 implacable] and merciles. **1530** —— *Exod.* xxxiv. 9 It is a stuburne [*Coverdale* (*lit. from Heb.*) hard-neckt, 1611 stiff-necked] people. **1538** ELYOT *Dict.*, *Peruicax*,..yll to intreate, stubbourne, obstinate. **1550** CROWLEY *Epigr.* 783 For syth thou arte a stout priest an example thou shalt be That all stouburne priestes may take warnyng by thee. **1594** in *Maitl. Club Misc.* I. 68 Johnne Kincaid..remaning stubburne to the citationis and admonitionis of the Kirk. **1634** MILTON *Comus* 434 Som say no evil thing that walks by night..Blew meager Hag, or stubborn unlaid ghost,..Hath hurtfull power o're true virginity. **1687** P. AYRES in *Minor Caroline Poets* (1906) II. 309 With Patience also will the country swain..make the stubborn heifer bow Its neck to th' yoke. **1702** YALDEN *Æsop at Court* vi. 28 But peevish Age,..Like Woman's Stouborn, Impotent and Loud. **1767** FORDYCE *Serm. Yng. Women* II. xiii. 255 A disputatious..and stubborn female will always offend. **1781** CRABBE *Library* 43 Books..soothe the grieved, the stubborn they chastise. **1843** LYTTON *Last Bar.* II. ii, The barons of England are a stubborn and haughty race. **1874** GREEN *Short Hist.* viii. §5. 503 The people were as stubborn as their King. **1901** T. R. GLOVER *Life & Lett. 4th Cent.* x. 240 'An exquisite poet but a most stubborn heathen' says Orosius of Claudian.

b. Of dispositions, resolves, speech or action: Characterized by obstinacy.

1526 *Pilgr. Perf.* (W. de W. 1531) 83 b, Yf thou speke ony false stubborne or foule worde. **1581** LAMBARDE *Eiren.* IV. xiv. (1588) 561 A punishment inflicted by the law, upon his contumacie and stubburne silence. **1611** BIBLE *Judges* ii. 19 They ceased not from their owne doings, nor from their stubborne way. **1667** MILTON *P.L.* XII. 193 The River-dragon..at length submits To let his sojourners depart, and oft Humbles his stubborn heart. *a* **1704** LOCKE *Ess. St. Paul's Epist.* (1707) Pref. p. xvii, All this..is to be had only from the Epistles themselves, and to be gather'd from thence with stubborn Attention, and more than common Application. **1750** JOHNSON *Rambler* No. 87 ¶2 This stubborn resistance of the most pathetic persuasion. **1809** SCOTT *Poacher* 151 Stout were their hearts, and stubborn was their strife. **1864** *Soc. Sci. Rev.* 399 We honour our brave soldiers, we glory in their stubborn deeds of daring. **1868** MISS YONGE *Cameos* I. xii. 80 His stubborn disposition was unchanged.

c. *transf.*

1612 *Two Noble K.* v. i. 13 Before the holy Altars..bow downe your stubborne bodies. **1663** BUTLER *Hud.* I. i. 17 A Wight was he,..That never bent his stubborn knee To any thing but Chivalry. **1688** PRIOR *On Exod. iii. 14* viii, Low, reverently low, Make thy stubborn Knowledge bow.

d. quasi-*sb.*

1871 *Chamb. Jrnl.* 23 Dec. 801/2 The 45th, or 'Sherwood Foresters',..is also known as the 'Old Stubborns'.

2. a. Of things; Refractory to treatment, intractable; difficult to subdue, work, cure, etc.

1514 BARCLAY *Cit. & Uplondyshman* (Percy Soc.) 17 Lyke as the grounde, is dull stony, and toughe,*Stubberne and hevy, rebellynge to the ploughe. **1541** COPLAND *Galyen's Terap.* 2 A iij, Some vlceres are stubburne and defycyle to be healed. **1588** SHAKS. *L.L.L.* IV. iii. 55, I feare these stubborn lines lack power to moue. **1615** CHAPMAN *Odyss.* xiii. 56 To whom, the black Oxe all day long hath turn'd The stubborne fallowes vp. **1718** POPE *Iliad* XVIII. 546 In hissing Flames huge silver Bars are roll'd, And stubborn Brass, and Tin, and solid Gold. **1747** WESLEY *Prim. Physick* (1762) 87 An old Stubborn Pain in the Back. **1757** GRAY *Elegy* vii, Their furrow oft the stubborn glebe has broke. **1820** HAZLITT *Lect. Dram. Lit.* 35 We are of a stiff clay, not moulded into every fashion, with stubborn joints not easily bent. **1865** RUSKIN *Sesame* i. §26 Most men's minds are indeed little better than rough heath wilderness, neglected and stubborn. **1899** *Allbutt's Syst. Med.* VIII. 605 The larger doses being reserved for local caustic effects in stubborn patches [of lichen].

Proverb. **1732** BUDGELL *Liberty & Property* II. 76 But as plain Matters of Fact are terrible stubborn Things, Mr. Walsingham does not at all meddle with any of these. **1733** *Copy Will of Matt. Tindal* 23 Matters of Fact, which as Mr. Budgell somewhere observes, are very Stubborn Things. **1799** *Med. Jrnl.* II. 270 Facts being stubborn things, it seemed necessary to examine these worms. *c* **1853** KINGSLEY *Misc.* (1859) I. 8 There is no more to be said about the matter, save that facts are stubborn things.

†**b.** Of wines: ? Not easily cleared. *Obs.*

1797 *Encycl. Brit.* (ed. 3) XVIII. 872/2 It sometimes happens that wines scuddy and stubborn will not fall with one or even two forcings.

3. Of material things: Hard, stiff, rigid. *Obs.* exc. of wood or stone (with some notion of sense 2).

1577 B. GOOGE *Heresbach's Husb.* III. 128 His hide not hard, or stubborne in feeling [L. *corium attactu non asperum ac durum*]. **1600** FAIRFAX *Tasso* xv. ii, They started vp, and euerie tender lim In sturdie steele and stubburne plate they dight. **1604** N. F. *Fruiterers Secr.* 14 Bee carefull to put the stubborne ends of the fearne cleane through the basket. **1609** HOLLAND *Amm. Marcell.* xxiv. ii. 242 All glittering with their bright helmets and terribly clad in stiffe and stubborne jacks. **1610** BEAUM. & FL. *Scornf. Lady* IV. i, For like strict men of order, they doe correct their bodies with a bench, or a poore stubborne table. **1630** DAVENANT *Just Ital.* v. i. I3, Ere long we must be cold,..and wrapp'd in stubborne sheets Of lead. **1681** R. KNOX *Hist. Relat. Ceylon* 16 This Skin is hard and stubborn like a piece of Board. **1697** DAMPIER *Voy.* I. 315, I observed their Cloath to be all of..equal fineness; but 'tis stubborn when new. **1770** LUCKOMBE *Hist. Printing* 256 Brown and stubborn paper that has not been well prepared for the Press. *a* **1789** G. WHITE *Selborne*, *To Pennant* iv, This rag is rugged and stubborn, and will not hew to a smooth face. **1796** MORSE *Amer. Geog.* I. 767 The trees were..of a wood so hard and stubborn, that [etc.]. **18..** *Marble-Worker* §35 (Cent.) Stubborn marble is that which, on account of its excessive hardness, is very difficult to work, and is apt to fly off in splinters. **1890** STANLEY *In Darkest Africa* (ed. 4) I. viii. 174 The bow is of stubborn hard brown wood, about three feet long.

4. *Comb.*: adverbial with another adj., as in ***stubborn-chaste***, ***-hard***, ***-stout*** (nonce-wds.); parasynthetic, as ***stubborn-hearted***, ***-shafted***.

1606 SHAKS. *Tr. & Cr.* I. i. 100 He's as teachy to be woo'd to woe, As she is stubborne, chast [*read* *stubborne-chast] against all suite. **1595** —— *John* IV. i. 67 Are you more *stubborne-hard, then hammer'd Iron. **1530** PALSGR. 326/1 *Stoburne herted, *fel.* **1635** JACKSON *Creed* VIII. II. 12 These ..did not so much affect the stubborne hearted Jews. *a* **1680** BUTLER *Sat.* Rem. (1759) I. 69 Enough to fright the stubborn'st-hearted Age. **1966** W. B. YEATS *Poems, 1899–1905* 55 Women are hard and proud and stubborn-hearted. **1859** TENNYSON *Enid* 969 A gloom of *stubborn-shafted oaks. **1608** SYLVESTER *Du Bartas* II. iv. IV. *Decay* 1114 Can you lesse piteous be To these Self-yeelders.. Than sternly-valiant to the *stubborn-stout.

stubborn ('stʌbən), *v.* Only *poet.* [f. prec.] *trans.* To make stubborn; to harden, make firm, render capable of resistance.

1820 KEATS *Hyperion* II. 17 Couches of rugged stone, and slaty ridge Stubborn'd with iron. **1874** D. GRAY *Poet. Wks.* 27 These twenty had themselves inured And stubborned to perfection. **1902** F. THOMPSON in *Academy* 12 Apr. 378/1 Who must call on the cannon to compact The hard Dutch-stubborned land.

stubbornly ('stʌbənlɪ), *adv.* Also 5 stoberlie. [f. STUBBORN *a.* + -LY[2].] In a stubborn manner.

c **1430** *Syr Gener.* (Roxb.) 2751 Malachias..threw Generides to the ground Ful herd and right stoberlie. **1528** MORE *Dyaloge* I. Wks. 149/2 Boldly and stubburnly defendyng, that sythe they had connyng to preache they were by God bounden to preach. **1591** SHAKS. *1 Hen. VI*, IV. i. 94 When stubbornly he did repugne the truth. **1651** HOBBES *Leviath.* III. xlii. 318 Hæretiques are none but private men, that stubbornly defend some Doctrine, prohibited by their lawfull Soveraigns. **1782** MISS BURNEY *Cecilia* IX. x, He retains stubbornly the prejudices which once have taken possession of him. **1873** M. ARNOLD *Lit. & Dogma* (1876) 324 The masses can no longer be relied on.. stubbornly to make clever men's extravagances and aberrations..of no avail. **1893** SIR R. BALL *Story of Sun* 290 It [carbon] will stubbornly remain solid even though exalted to an enormously high temperature. **1896** BADEN-POWELL *Matabele Campaign* xv, A small but determined party of the enemy..stubbornly opposed their advance.

stubbornness ('stʌbənnɪs). [f. STUBBORN *a.* + -NESS.] The quality of being stubborn.

c **1440** *Promp. Parv.* 475/1 Styburnesse, *austeritas*, *ferocitas*. **1467–8** *Rolls of Parlt.* V. 621/2 Because of the gretnesse and stobournesse of the same Wolle. **1530** PALSGR. 277/2 Stubbernesse, *contumace*. **1535** COVERDALE *Jer.* xiii. 17 Yf ye wil not heare me..I will mourne fro my whole herte for youre stubburnesse. *a* **1548** HALL *Chron.*, *Hen. V*, 56 b. Some for their stony stubbernes and mad obstinacy were adjudged to dye. **1600** SHAKS. *A.Y.L.* II. i. 19 Happy is your Grace That can translate the stubbornnesse of fortune Into so quiet and so sweet a stile. **1680** MOXON *Mech. Exerc.* x. 190 A thick String..having a strength and stubbornness proportionable to its size, it will not comply closely to a piece of Work of small Diameter. **1700** DRYDEN *To J. Dryden* 185 Patriots, in Peace, assert the Peoples Right, With noble Stubbornness resisting Might. **1757** HOME *Douglas* III. 31 Hard he seems And old in villainy. Permit us try His stubbornness against the torture's force. **1874** GREEN *Short Hist.* iv. §1. 162 The Prince [Llewelyn] held out in Snowdon with the stubbornness of despair. **1878** LECKY *Eng. in 18th C.* II. vii. 402 They were endowed with a full share of Scotch stubbornness, jealousy and self-assertion.

Stubbsian ('stʌbzɪən), *a.* [f. the surname *Stubbs* (see below) + -IAN.] **1.** Of, pertaining to, or characteristic of the English painter George *Stubbs* (1724–1806), or his work.

1960 *Times* 4 Nov. 16/7 Ferneley's brand of aristocratic elegance is splendidly represented, especially in the 'Five Hunters in the Park at Deene' (a Stubbsian subject with a better understanding of space than Stubbs). **1963** *Times* 1 May 5/7 Stubbs, of course, ranges over the whole field of conversation pieces, portraiture, wild life and land-scape as well as horse painting;..and there is a picture of almost Stubbsian quality by George Garrard.

2. Of or pertaining to William *Stubbs* (1825–1901), historian and Bishop of Oxford, or his historical opinions.

1979 *English Hist. Rev.* XCIV. 487 By 1934 Kenneth Pickthorn's study of *Early Tudor Government*..still framed its argument in Stubbsian terms by denying that the period had much of a constitution at all aside from the medieval idea of the supremacy of law.

stubby ('stʌbɪ), *a.* [f. STUB *sb.* + -Y.]

1. Of the nature of a stub; short and thick or broad. **a.** of a root, plant, etc.

1572 MASCALL *Plant. & Graff.* (1592) 16 If ye breake of the olde stubbie roote and set them lower, they will last a long time the more. **1664** EVELYN *Sylva* iii. 11 Abating only the tap-roots, which is that down-right, and stubby part of the Roots (which all Trees rais'd of Seeds do universally produce). **1681** GREWS *Museum* I. ii. 30 [A rhinoceros horn.] At the base,..surrounded with a Garland of black and stubby Bristles. **1755** JOHNSON, *Stubby*, short and thick, short and strong. **1851** I. J. MECHI *2nd Paper on Brit. Agric.* 32 There are millions of stubby pollards. **1863** W. C. BALDWIN *Afr. Hunting* vi. 180 The hackthorns..have low square tops, strong and very dense, with short stubby sharp thorns. **1881** *Chicago Times* 16 Apr., Short, stubby buffalo grass, which shed off what little rain that did fall. **1904** *Daily News* 8 July 5, A well-grown, 'stubby' plant..some-times has..27 trusses of bloom all expanded at once.

b. Of a person, beast, a limb, etc.: Short and thick-set in figure.

1831 TRELAWNY *Adv. Younger Son* II. 216 Her fat stubby finger. **1841** J. T. J. HEWLETT *P. Priggins* II. xiv. 318 A short stubby man. **1870** THORNBURY *Tour rd. Eng.* I. iv. 76 The poet..knocked his stubby little adversary down. **1891** *Daily News* 2 July 7/3 The lad is described as of medium height for his age, being a bit stubby. **1910** *Spectator* 10 Dec. 1026/1 The she-bear's short and stubby tail.

c. Of a thing: Short and thick or broad in make; also short and blunt as the result of wear.

1843 HOLTZAPFFEL *Turning* I. 447 A piece of cane the end of which is split into filaments to make a stubby brush. **1891** E. DAWSON *Fountain of Youth* iv. 39, I have still..his calculation of the amount..written with a stubby pencil. **1898** KIPLING *Fleet in Being* v. 48 From all three funnels of a high, stubby cruiser the smoke of a London factory insulted the clean air. **1899** DE VINNE *Pract. Typogr.* (1902) 30 The serif..in old-style lower-case letters..is a blunt spur or a stubby triangle. **1899** CONAN DOYLE *Duet* xx. 307 It was a worn, stubby old quill. **1905** J. B. FIRTH *Highw. Derbysh* xxviii. 422 The mill is an old one..with a stubby chimney.

2. Abounding in or full of stubs. Chiefly of the hair or beard: Composed of short, stiff bristles.

1604 R. CAWDREY *Table Alph.* (1613), *Knarry*, knotty, stubbie. **1847** ALB. SMITH *Chr. Tadpole* i, He was short and awkward, with stubby light hair and a low forehead. **1887** W. P. FRITH *Autob.* II. viii. 147 An air of breeding and refinement..that the prison-dress and the stubby beard could not efface. **1887** RIDER HAGGARD *Allan Quartermain* xxii, My grizzled stubby hair was turned snow-white.

3. Comb.: in parasynthetic adjs., as ***stubby-bearded, -chinned, -legged, -toed.***

1898 *Daily News* 1 Aug. 5/6 The *stubby-bearded weaver. **1870** *Ibid.* 5 Sept. 6/1 A slouching, undersized, *stubby-chinned ruffian. **1871** FURNIVALL *Capt. Cox's Ball.* etc. Introd. 76 *Stubby-legd Margery Mylkeducke. **1873** B. HARTE *Fiddletown* 9 The gallant Colonel was impelled to..trip away as smartly as his *stubby-toed high-heeled boots would permit.

Hence **'stubbiness.**

1855 in HYDE CLARKE *Dict.* In recent Dicts.

stubby ('stʌbɪ), *sb. Austral. slang.* Also **stubbie.** [f. STUBBY *a.*] **1.** A short, squat beer-bottle with a capacity of 375 ml. Also *Comb.*, as ***stubby beer bottle.***

1957 *Encycl. Brit.* IV. 106/2 A variety of standardized forms and sizes of bottles are in use, including the so-called Stubby, Steinie, Packie, Export and Single Trip bottles. **1966** *Sunday Truth* (Brisbane) 8 May 33/7 Well-known transport man generally likes to have a 'stubbie' of beer at home each evening. **1968** F. HARDY *Unlucky Australians* 49 He threw an empty stubby into the box and went to the refrigerator for a full one. **1969** *Sunday Truth* (Brisbane) 23 Nov. 37/7 Both as a safety measure and a fight against litter, I advocate the absolute banning of the stubby beer bottle. **1972** G. MORLEY *Jockey rides Honest Race* 165 Phil opened the freezer and pulled out four stubbies. **1977** *Mod. Boating* (Austral.) Jan. 88/1 Buy another stubby at the bar to gather strength to try again in half an hour.

2. Usu. *pl.* Shorts (see SHORT *sb.* 7 d).

1977 *Australian* 7 Apr. 3 Stubbies—the football shorts with pockets—have become an international fashion... Although the Stubby is a very Australian name—thought of in the context of short shorts to go with short bottles of beer—Mr Phillips is confident they will become as American as apple pie. **1982** *Guardian* 18 Dec. 11 'Stubbies', slang for both the shorts they wear..and the bottles from which they drink. *Ibid.* 11/4 (*caption*) 'Stubbies' (shorts) and pot bellies predominate on Australia's popular side.

‖**Stube** ('ʃtu:bə). Also **stube.** [Ger., lit. 'room, parlour'.] = BIERSTUBE.

1946 S. SPENDER *European Witness* 138 He invited me to join the other officers in going to a drinking Stube. **1956** E. BERCKMAN *Strange Bedfellow* vii. 66 The dimness and coolness of the village *Stube.* **1967** J. EASTWOOD *Little Dragon from Peking* xvii. 153 Hilde, the maid of all work, had already mopped the wooden floor of the *Stube.* **1969** A. GLYN *Dragon Variation* viii. 232 In a gasthof in the Maria-Josephastrasse, Jeff Falkner sat at a window, staring out at the snow. The others were downstairs playing chess in the stube. **1980** J. CARTWRIGHT *Horse of Darius* x. 149 A *stube* full of hearty people drinking beer.

stube, obs. form of STUB *v.*[1]

stuborn, -urne, obs. forms of STUBBORN.

stubwort ('stʌbwɜ:t). [f. STUB *sb.* + WORT. Cf. *stab-wort* STAB *sb.*[1] 5, STOB-WORT.] The Wood-sorrel, *Oxalis acetosella.*

1541 *Bk. Properties Herbs* A vj, This herbe Alleluya men call it wodsore or stubworte. **1583** L. M[ASCALL] *Prof. Bk. Remedies* 3 Take an hearbe called wood sorrel, or stubwort which..groweth in woods, in bushes & stubs of old trees. **1614** MARKHAM *Cheap & Gd. Husb.* Table for hard Words, Stubwort is an hearbe which growes in wooddy places, and is called wood-Sorrell. **1866** *Treas. Bot.* 1106/2 Stubwort, *Oxalis acetosella.*

stuc, stuck. Also 8 **stuke.** [a. F. *stuc*, ad. It. *stucco*: see STUCCO *sb.*] †**1.** = STUCCO 1 a. *Obs.*

1632 J. HAYWARD tr. *Biondi's Eromena* 42 Two of his pictures, the one limned and painted, the other made of stuck. **1702** J. K. *New Eng. Dict.*, *Stuke*, a kind of morter fit for imagery, made of chalk and marble well pounded together and sifted. **1703** tr. *Perrault's Abridgm. Vitruvius* I. ii. 16 The Cornishes..ought to be made of pure Stuck of Marble, without any Plaister. *Ibid.*, The Plaistering must be laid, Bed after Bed... The Ancients put six Lays, 3 of Mortar made of Lime, and 3 of Stuck. **1715** LEONI *Palladio's Archit.* (1721) I. I. xxii. 39 Others will have Compartments [of a ceiling] of Stuc [It. *di stucchi*] (which is a sort of hard Plaster). **1771** ROLAND LE VIRLOYS *Dict. Archit.* III. Vocab. 184 Stuke, *stuc.*

attrib. **1726** LEONI *Alberti's Archit.* I. 33 b, The..whitest [sort of Plaister of Paris] is used in Stuc Work [It. *opere di stucchi*] for Figures and Cornishes. *Ibid.* III. 28 Some finish their work..by adding to..the material;..those that work in wax, stuc or clay, whom we therefore call stuc-masters [It. *Maestri di stucco*]: others do it only by taking away,..these we call Sculptors.

2. = STUCCO *sb.* 1 b.

1932 T. CORKHILL *Conc. Building Encycl.* 207 *Stuc*, plasterwork to imitate stone. **1971** *Country Life* 14 Oct. 969/1 Its walls are of *stuc*, by M. Germain, an imitation of dressed Caen stone.

stuccador(e ('stʌkədɔə(r)). Also **stuccodore.** [irreg. ad. It. *stuccatore*; cf. Sp. *estucador.*] A worker in stucco. Cf. STUCCOER.

1952 *Archit. Rev.* CXI. 201/3 Its Tapestry Room with Floral Zephyrs by James 'Athenian' Stuart and a Saloon with walls marvellously decorated by Italian stuccadores. **1956** *Essays in Crit.* VI. 324 The iconography of other eighteenth-century arts (Tiepolo's painting, the interior plasterwork of Dublin stuccodores), is still that of the High Renaissance. **1972** *Canad. Antiques Collector* Mar.-Apr. 15/1 The interiors..are as exuberant and varied as the stuccodores through seventy years of changing taste (1730–1800) could make them. **1973** *Country Life* 10 May 1306/2 The Schmuzer family..whose activity as mason-stuccadors persisted right into the Rococo period. **1978** A. LAING in A. Blunt et al. *Baroque & Rococo* IV. 241/1 In Bavaria it was a Wessobrunner stuccador, Joseph Schmuzer (1683–1752), who was most successful in creating a local practice as the architect of parish churches, extending his competence from stucco to masonry.

† **'stuccature.** *Obs. rare*[−1]. [ad. It. *stuccatura*; f. *stuccare* to work in stucco, f. *stucco*: see next. Cf. G. *stuccatur.*] Stucco-work; also an ornament worked in stucco.

1715 LEONI *Palladio's Archit.* (1721) I. II. iii. 63 The Chambers..have been adorn'd with very fine Stuccatures [It. *di bellissimi stucchi*]. *Ibid.* 64 They have left nothing wanting..in the enriching of such a Building either for Stuccature or Painting [It. *come stucchi e pitture*].

stucche, stucchen: see STITCH *sb.*[2], STITCHEN.

stucco ('stʌkəʊ), *sb.* Also 8 **stocco, stocko.** [It.; believed to be ad. the Teut. word represented by OHG. *stukki* fragment, piece, also crust (mod.G. *stück* piece = (M)LG., (M)Du. *stuk*: see STICK *sb.*). The It. word has been adopted into several European langs.: F. *stuc* (see STUC), Sp. *estuque, estuco*, Pg. *estuque*, G. *stuck*, Du. *stuc* (from Fr.), Sw. *stuck*, Da. *stuk.*]

1. a. A fine plaster, esp. one composed of gypsum and pulverized marble, used for covering walls, ceilings, and floors, and for making cornices, mouldings, and other decorations.

1598 HAYDOCKE tr. *Lomazzo's Art Paint.* III. 94 There are yet remayning in Transtevero in Rome, certayne Children ..which so perfectly seeme to be made in Stucco, that they haue deceaved even divers good Painters. **1616–17** in *Crt. & Times James I* (1848) I. 465 Some heads, whereof, to my remembrance, there was but one of marble, the other of stucco or plaster. **1730** A. GORDON *Maffei's Amphith.* (1735) 305 In Rome..not only have the Remains of ancient Painting been seen, but other genteel Ornaments of Stucco also. **1787** BECKFORD *Lett. Italy* (1805) I. xv. 148 A parcel of naked boys over the doors, in white stucco. **1820** T. S. HUGHES *Trav. Sicily* I. iii. 75 The walls of the recesses are covered with a fine stucco, painted upon a vermilion ground with various colours and devices. **1856** STANLEY *Sinai & Pal.* Introd. 39 Halls and chambers..covered with white stucco, and this white stucco brilliant with colours, fresh as they were thousands of years ago. **1873** SPON *Workshop Rec.* Ser. I. 390/1 Stucco is a composition of slacked lime, chalk, and pulverized white marble tempered in water, designed to imitate different marbles used in the interior of buildings or [for] monuments. **1884** *Encycl. Brit.* XVII. 37 *Sgraffito*... The wall is covered with a coat of stucco made black..; over this a second very thin coat of white stucco is laid... The design is produced by cutting and scratching away the white skin.

b. A coarse plaster or calcareous cement used chiefly for covering the rough exterior surfaces of walls in imitation of stone; also called ***common stucco***; *spec.* the third or last coat of plastering.

bastard stucco (see quot. 1812). ***rough stucco***, stucco in which a large proportion of sand is used. ***trowelled stucco***, stucco set with a trowel to form a surface for painting.

1779 in *Repert. Arts & Manuf.* (1795) II. 289 My said invention of a water cement, or stucco, for building, repairing, and plastering walls. **1779** SHERIDAN *Critic* I. ii, Here is..[an article] 'a Detester of visible Brick-work, in favor of the new invented Stucco';..in the style of Junius. **1812** P. NICHOLSON *Mech. Exerc.* 306 Bastard Stucco, is three coat plaster,..but the finishing coat contains a little hair besides the sand, it is not hand floated, and the troweling is done with less labour than what is denominated troweled stucco. *Ibid.* 312 Stucco or Finishing is the third coat of three coat plaster... Rough stucco is only floated and brushed in a small degree with water: trowelled stucco is accounted the best. **1825** J. NICHOLSON *Oper. Mech.* 617 Common stucco, used for external work, consists of clean washed Thames sand and ground Dorking lime. **1862** MISS BRADDON *Lady Audley* xxxviii, A great mansion of white stucco. **1870** THORNBURY *Tour rd. Eng.* I. i. 26 We despise stucco now as false and flimsy. **1876** *Encycl. Brit.* IV. 507 It may not be amiss here to refer to some of the causes of the premature decay which takes place in stuccoes and cements. **1897** W. MILLAR *Plastering* iv. 101 The adoption in England of stucco externally to give brick houses the appearance of stone is due to Robert Adam.

fig. **1878** *Masque Poets* 261 Behind the stucco of this world's politeness I find some moral framework not amiss.

c. Plaster of Paris.

1839- [cf. 3 c]. **1868** ROSCOE *Elem. Chem.* (1869) 32 Fixing a thin piece of stucco on to one end of a glass tube. **1897** W. MILLAR *Plastering* ii. 35 Gypsum, from which plaster of Paris is made... In Italy it is known by the name of *gesso*; in Scotland it is called *stucco*;..and in the English trade ..*plaster.*

2. a. The process of ornamenting walls, ceilings, cornices, etc. with stucco; also, work or ornamentation produced by this process.

1697 EVELYN *Numism.* viii. 283 John de Udine Inventor or Restorer of the Art of Stucco. **1756** MRS. CALDERWOOD in *Coltness Collect.* (Maitl. Club) 141 The roofs in all the best rooms..are stucko, which was wrought by an Italian. **1782** PENNANT *Journ. fr. Chester* 345 The chancel has been very elegantly fitted up with stucco by the late duke.

b. A house plastered with stucco.

1976 C. WESTON *Rouse Demon* (1977) xi. 50 The Simmons house turned out to be a two-story Monterey-style stucco. **1981** P. MALLORY *Killing Matter* xvi. 167 A blue stucco at the corner of Delgado and Harding.

3. *attrib.* passing into *adj.* **a.** Made of stucco, ornamented with stucco-work.

a **1744** POPE *Hor. Sat.* II. vi. 192 Palladian walls, Venetian doors, Grotesco roofs, and stucco floors. **1756–7** tr. *Keysler's Trav.* (1760) I. 83 A stucco cabinet, so curiously wrought as to appear like the finest marble. **1799** *Hull Advertiser* 16 Feb. 2/1 With marble chimney-pieces and stucco cornice. **1884** *Encycl. Brit.* XVII. 37 The Moslem architects..made great use of stucco ornament. *Ibid.*, These stucco reliefs were, as a rule, further decorated with delicate painting.

b. Of a building, etc.: Plastered with stucco in imitation of stone. Of a locality: Abounding in such buildings.

1848 THACKERAY *Van. Fair* lx, 'Gardens' was a felicitous word not applied to stucco houses with asphalte terraces in front, so early as 1827. **1897** W. MILLAR *Plastering* i. 33 The brothers Adam introduced into England stucco façades and composition enrichments. **1897** WATTS-DUNTON *Aylwin* v. ii, After we had left behind us what he called the 'stucco world' of the West End. **1898** G. W. E. RUSSELL *Collect. & Recoll.* xxiv. 307 Our Ambassador in that city of stucco palaces [Berlin].

c. Of a matrix, ornament: Made of plaster of Paris; plaster.

1839 URE *Dict. Arts* 631 Gypsum is mixed with water to the consistence of cream, and poured into moulds by the manufacturers of stucco ornaments and statues. **1846** *Jrnl. Franklin Inst.* Jan. 67 The period varies from ten to twelve hours, liable to the breaking, splitting or warping of the stucco matrices. **1868** GEO. ELIOT *F. Holt* i, Her knowledge and accomplishments had become as valueless as old-fashioned stucco ornaments.

4. *attrib.* and *Comb.*, as ***stucco paint, plaster*** (hence ***plasterer***), ***work*** (hence ***worker***); instrumental, as ***stucco-adorned, -fronted, -moulded*** adjs.; †**stucco-paper,** ? a wall paper made to resemble stucco.

1864 *Reader* 3 Sept. 291/1 No flaunting *stucco-adorned town of yesterday. **1865** MISS A. B. EDWARDS *Half a Million* lxxxvi, A big *stucco-fronted many-windowed house. **1873** SPON *Workshop Rec.* Ser. I. 8/2 A frame of plain mouldings is more appropriate..than is a carved or *stucco-moulded frame. **1843** *Builder* 12 Aug. 323/1 Patent *Stucco Paint and Patent Stucco Paint Cement. **1750–1** LADY LUXBOROUGH *Let. Shenstone* 13 Feb., A common *stucco-paper. **1752** MRS. DELANY *Autob. & Corr.* (1861) III. 76, I think I should rather hang it with stucco paper. **1744** in *Sixth Rep. Dep. Kpr. Publ. Rec.* App. II. 121 [Specification for a Lime, *Stucco Plaster, Morter]. **1787** *Ibid.* 177 [Thomas Henderson, of the City of York, *Stucco Plaisterer]. **1686** AGLIONBY *Painting Illustr.* 326 He built himself a House, which he adorned with *Stucco Work. *Ibid.* 342 A New Pallace, which should be adorned with Stucco-Work paintings in Fresco. **1753** HANWAY *Trav.* I. II. xxxiv. 232 The rooms are lined with stocco work, painted in the Indian taste. **1908** R. BAGOT *A. Cuthbert* iv. 29 The rich carvings of the frieze and..the ornate stucco-work of the ceiling..had been executed in the sixteenth century, from Italian designs. **1897** W. MILLAR *Plastering* i. 26 During the reign of Henry VIII,..many Italian *stucco workers found their way into this country.

stucco ('stʌkəʊ), *v.* Inflected **stuccoed, stuccoing.** Also 8 **stucko.** [f. STUCCO *sb.*] *trans.* To coat or plaster (a cornice, wall, etc.) with stucco; to ornament with stucco-work. Also with *over.*

1726 LEONI *Alberti's Archit.* I. 48 b, A Cornice..ought to be firmly wrought and well stucco'd over to repel all the injuries of the weather. **1754** in Willis & Clark *Cambridge* (1886) I. 38 Agreed that instead of stuccoing the old court.. it be cas'd with Ketton Stone. **1774** G. GRENVILLE in *G. Papers* (1853) IV. 551 They have built it [a temple] entirely of marble, and stuccoed it over afterwards. **1782** PENNANT *Journ. fr. Chester* 307 The roof beautifully stuccoed.

b. In mod. building: To coat or plaster (a wall, building) esp. in imitation of stone-work.

1790 W. WRIGHTE *Grotesque Archit.* 11 It may be built of wood, and stuccoed. **1799** A. YOUNG *View Agric. Lincoln.* 26 If an old wall is to be stuccoed, all..vegetation must previously be removed. **1833** LOUDON *Encycl. Archit.* § 1587 Render float and set the walls in all the rooms..and stucco the committee-room. **1896** F. M. CRAWFORD *Corleone* v, Many of the houses [in Randazzo] on the main street have now been stuccoed and painted.

c. *transf.* and *fig.*

1774 GOLDSM. *Nat. Hist.* (1824) II. 78 The apartment at the end [of a marmot's hole] is very warmly stuccoed round with moss and hay. **1776** ANSTEY *Election Ball* (1808) 218 Ye must stucco and whitewash your faces. **1839** LADY LYTTON *Cheveley* (ed. 2) III. iii. 74 She was a great admirer of what the world stuccoes with the name of 'talent'.

Hence **'stuccoed** *ppl. a.*, **'stuccoing** *vbl. sb.*

a **1761** CAWTHORN *Taste* 75 Hence all our stucco'd walls, Mosaic floors. **1820** COMBE *Syntax, Wife* III. 206 In stucco'd eating room he dines. **1833** LOUDON *Encycl. Archit.* § 517 *Exterior Finishing* is the term applied to stuccoing, rough-casting, and plastering. **1842** *Penny Cycl.* XXIII. 166/2 As an imitation of stone, much wil depend upon the skill and care with which stuccoing is executed. **1856** LEVER *Martins of Cro' M.* ii, Fragments of carving, or pieces of stuccoed tracery, together with broken vases and uprooted shrubs, littered the garden. **1884** G. ALLEN *Philistia* II. 18 The noisy stuccoed modern watering-place.

stuccoer ('stʌkəʊə(r)). Also 9 **stuccoyer.** [f. STUCCO *v.* + -ER[1], -YER.] A modeller in stucco.

1818 SCOTT in *Lockhart* (1837) IV. 147 If there had been either limners or stuccoyers worth their salt in those days. **1848** R. N. WORNUM *Lect. Painting* Introd. 11 The Royal Academy of Munich..was established by three artists,—the painter Christian Wink, the sculptor Roman Boos, and the stuccoer F. X. Feichtmayr. **1887** *Dict. Archit.* (Arch. Publ. Soc.), *Stuccoer*, the artisan who worked in stucco.

stuccoist ('stʌkəʊɪst). = STUCCOER. Cf. STUCCADOR(E.

1945 J. LEES-MILNE *Jrnl.* 26 Sept. in *Prophesying Peace* (1977) 238 Lord Leigh assured me..that the plaster-work was by Cipriani, which I find hard to believe unless there was an earlier stuccoist of the same name as the well-known painter. **1969** M. WHINNEY *Home House* 19 In November 1775 Joseph Rose, Adam's principal stuccoist, was paid £603.10.0.

stuche, variant of STITCH *sb.*[2] *Obs.*

†**stuck**, *sb.*[1] *Obs. rare*[−1]. In 5 stuk. [? f. STUCK *a.*] (See quot.)

c **1440** *Promp. Parv.* 481/1 Stuk, or schort garment (*v.r.* stukkyd clothe), *nepticula.*

†**stuck**, *sb.*[2] *Fencing. Obs.* [? var. of STOCK *sb.*[3]] A thrust or lunge; = STOCK *sb.*[3] 2.

1601 SHAKS. *Twel. N.* III. iv. 303, I had a passe with him, rapier, scabberd, and all: and he giues me the stucke in with such a mortall motion that it is ineuitable. **1602** —— *Ham.* IV. vii. 162 If he by chance escape your venom'd stuck. **1614** G. H[ALE] *Priv. Sch. Defence* C 1, In single Rapier, and Rapier and Dagger, they teach all their Schollers as they call them, Stucks, otherwise Longe, to throw them into hit without disordering their aduerse Rapier.

†**stuck, stug**, *a. Obs.*[−1] In 5 stuk, stuke, 5, 7 stug. [? Connected with MDu. *stucke* piece, STITCH *sb.*[2]; cf. SCUT *a.* and *sb.*[3]] Short. Hence **stucked** *ppl. a.*, cut short; **'stuckness**[1], shortness.

c **1440** *Promp. Parv.* 448/1 Schort or stukkyd garment, *nepticula. Ibid.* 481/1 Stuk, short (*v.r.* stuke, stug, stukkid, schort) *curtus, brevis. Ibid.*, Stuknesse, *brevitas, curtitas.* *Comb.* **1699** *Banffsh. Document* (MS.), A stug-tailed horse.

stuck (stʌk), *ppl. a.* [Str. pa. pple. of STICK *v.*]

1. Of an animal: That has been stabbed or had its throat cut: = STICKED[1] b. Chiefly in proverbial phrase, ***to stare like a stuck pig.***

1702 YALDEN *Æsop at Crt.* iii. 29 Like a stuck pig the woman star'd. **1731-8** SWIFT *Pol. Conversat.* II. 162. **1782** MISS BURNEY *Cecilia* II. i, Ask for the rent-roll,—see how they'll look! stare like stuck pigs! **1812** *Sporting Mag.* XL. 66 Bleeding like a stuck pig. **1874** BURNAND *My Time* xxiii. 210 Staring at you..as if he was a stuck pig.

2. Unable to go further. Cf. STICKIT *a.* 2.

1885 *Revol. in Shorthand* 7, I studied Pitman's system.. for three or four months, but became a 'stuck' student. **1910** D. W. BONE *Brassbounder* 3 We come from our first voyage sick of it all... Would give up but for pride... Afraid to be called 'stuck sailors'.

3. *slang.* (See quot.)

1865 *Slang Dict.* 249 *Stuck*, moneyless.

4. *Joinery.* (Cf. STICK *v.* 18 c.)

1850 OGILVIE, *Stuck mouldings.* In *arch.*, mouldings formed by the planes instead of being wrought by the hand. **1910** C. H. GREGORY *Gloss. Build. Constr.* 64 Stuck Moulding. A moulding worked on the stuff itself.

5. With advs. forming adjs. with reference to attachment or sealing by adhesive, etc., as ***stuck-down, -on.***

1908 KIPLING *Actions & Reactions* (1909) 101 The Hive shook beneath the shattering thunder of a stuck-down quilt being torn back. **1940** *Chambers's Techn. Dict.* 815/2 *Stuck-on soles (Shoes)*, shoe soles in which the upper inner sole and the outer sole are attached together by means of strong cement; used for women's and children's shoes. **1960** *Farmer & Stockbreeder* 15 Mar. Suppl. 7 A whitewood bedside cabinet is given a stuck-on veneer finish. **1978** D. FRANCIS *Trial Run* xviii. 228 One of them handed me a stuck-down envelope.

stuck, dial. form of STOOK *sb.*[1] and *v.*

1813 RUDGE *Agric. Glouc.* 117 These [sheaves] are 'stucked', or placed upright, in parcels of ten.

stuck: see STUC *Obs.*, stucco.

stucken ('stʌkən). *Sc.* Also **stucking.** [? Cogn. w. STAKE *sb.*] A stake.

1844 N. PATERSON *Manse Gard.* 39 Let stuckings of peeled larch..be driven at the bottom of the wall. *a* **1870** RIDDELL *Poet. Wks.* (1871) I. 4 (E.D.D.) Syne for a stucken stout he felt.

†**'stuckle.** *Obs.* [dim. of STOOK.] A shock containing five sheaves of corn.

1682 R. DAVIES in *Hereford Dioc. Reg.* 1680-1-2, 18 Sept., Thomas Jones did demand one Stuckle of muncorne..due to him for tieth..and finding but 4 sheaves there, required one sheafe more to make up the said stuckle. **1736** AINSWORTH, A stuckle of corn, *mergitum strues.*

stuckling ('stʌklɪŋ). *dial.* [Of obscure origin: the sense 'small piece' (Sussex) might suggest formation on OE. *stycce* STITCH *sb.*[2]] (See quots.)

1674 RAY *S. & E.C. Words* 76 A Stuckling: an apple pasty. *Suss.* **1878** H. C. ADAMS *Wykehamica* 435 (Glossary) *Stuckling*, a sort of pudding composed of chopped meat and apple, flavoured with carraway. **1908** *Times* 29 July 13/4 [Winchester Domum Day] the usual ceremonies of eating stuckling and drinking hough were duly observed.

stuckness[1]: see STUCK *a.*

stuckness[2] ('stʌknɪs). [f. STUCK *ppl. a.* + -NESS.] The condition of being stuck or unable to move or progress.

1969 J. S. BRUNER in Elkind & Flavell *Stud. Cognitive Devel.* 225 Let me characterize that growth briefly as moving from a diffuse distractibility in the weeks immediately following birth to a stage of stuckness where attention has an 'obligatory character', to use Stechler's phrase. **1974** R. M. PIRSIG *Zen & Art of Motorcycle Maintenance* xxiv. 278 The first [problem] is stuckness, a mental stuckness that accompanies the physical stuckness of whatever it is you're working on.

stuck-up, *a. colloq.* [pa. pple. of *stick up*, STICK *v.*[1] 35.] Assuming an unjustified air of superiority, or pluming oneself unduly on real superiority; offensively pretentious.

1829 *Edin. Rev.* L. 245 At the first sight of the Elgin Marbles, we feel that..the ancient objects of our idolatry fall into an inferior class or style of art. They are comparatively..*stuck-up* gods and goddesses. **1839** DICKENS *Nickleby* ix, 'He's a nasty stuck-up monkey, that's what I consider him,' said Mrs. Squeers. **1844** 'JON. SLICK' *High Life N. York* II. 87 Does the stuck up varmint feel above riding with an honest Yankee, because he haint got no title? **1860** *Hotten's Slang Dict.* 230 *Stuck-up*, 'purse-proud' —a form of snobbishness very common in those who have risen in the world. **1861** SALA *Dutch Pict.* xvi. 252 Versailles is one of the dreariest,..most stuck-up places I know. **1863** KINGSLEY *Water-Bab.* i. 6 Tom..considered him a stuck-up fellow, who gave himself airs. **1869** TROLLOPE *He Knew* etc. xxxv. (1878) 196 She has no stuck-up ideas about herself. **1903** BRIDGES *Socialist in Lond.* 182 Poet. Wks. (1913) 430 The degrading pestiferous fuss Of stuck-up importance.

Hence **stuck'uppishness.**

1853 *Chamb. Jrnl.* XX. 307 We leave Ramsgate, then, with its 'stuckuppishness' and stiff and formal society. **1875** MISS BRADDON *Hostages* I. ii. 56 Thank heaven it is not a perky modern place, all stucco and stuckupishness.

stud (stʌd), *sb.*[1] Forms: 1 studu, stuðu (acc. stoðe, stuðe, -u, -o, dat. styde, styðe), 4 stod, stoode, 4-6 stode, 5-6 stodde, 5-7 studde, 6 stood, stude, 6-8 studd, 6- stud. See also STOOTH. [OE. *studu, stuðu* fem. (cons.-stem), also *stod* (? fem.) = MHG. *stud* fem., ON. *stoð* fem. (MSw. *stuþ* fem., neut., mod.Sw. *stöd* neut.):—OTeut. **stuð-*, **stuþ-*:—pre-Teut. **stut-*, prop, support. From the sb. are OHG. *studen* (MHG. *stüden*) to fix, settle, ON. *styðja* to prop, support, *stoða* to support, help, avail.

An extended form of the root (OTeut. **stutt-*:—pre-Teut. **stutn-*) appears in MLG., (M)Du. *stutten*, OHG. *stutzen* (MHG., mod.G. *stützen*) to prop, support, MLG., MDu. *stutte* (mod.Du. *stut*), MHG., mod.G. *stütze* fem., prop.

The meaning in branch II is not easy to account for, but there does not appear to be reason to doubt the etymological identity of the word.]

I. A post, prop.

1. a. †In early use *gen.*, a wooden post of any kind, an upright prop or support (*obs.*). Subsequently, one of the upright timbers in the wall of a building; now chiefly, one of the smaller uprights, of the height of a single story, interposed between the principal posts in the framing of a partition wall (= QUARTER *sb.* 19).

c **850** *Kent. Gloss.* in Wr.-Wülcker 63/30 *Et observat postes ostii mei*, & beȝemð stuðe [? *or* stoðe] minre dure. *c* **900** *Bæda's Hist.* III. x. (1890) 180 Aheng he þone sceat..on ane studu þæs waȝes [L. *in una posta parietis*]. *Ibid.* 182 Ac hit clæne forbarn, nemne seo studu aan [*MS. β*, butan þære anre styðe]. **1336-7** *Ely Sacrist Rolls* (1907) II. 78 In vij^xx et iiij stodes quercinis empt. apud Reche, 14 *s.* **1420** in Willis & Clark *Cambridge* (1886) II. 443 Item pro ij stodys angularibus oratorii iij*s*. **1481-90** *Howard Househ. Bks.* (Roxb.) 200 My Lord made comenaunt with Rychard Tornor to make his new wall..the space to be a fote and halffe betwene the stodes. **1486** *Nottingham Rec.* III. 253 For ij. studdes to þe same bothe. *c* **1568** in Swayne *Churchw. Acc. Sarum* (1896) 115, 3 dosen of stoddes 12d. **1577** HARRISON *England* II. x. 84 b, in *Holinshed*, In the open.. soyles they are inforced for want of stuffe to vse no studdes at all, but onlie raysines, groundselles,..and vpright principalles. **1578** BANISTER *Hist. Man* I. 17 b, The.. ridgbeame of a shyp..whereunto the chief studdes, or postes of the frame worke are mortised. **1617** in Willis & Clark *Cambridge* (1886) I. 205 The particians shall bee maide with..punchions and studds of oake. **1624** T. TAYLOR *Two Serm.* Ded. A 2 b, What were the two studs of the house in which Sampson played, that is, Religion and Iustice in the Common-wealth, if they be pulled downe.. the Church and Common-wealth fall together. **1656** *Artif. Handsom.* 11 It is a grosse mistake in Architecture, to think that every small stud bears the maine stresse and burthen of the building, which lies (indeed) upon the principall timbers. **1737** *Salmon's Country Builder's Estimator* (ed. 2) 7 The Studds, or Quarters, to stand twelve Inches asunder. **1792** A. YOUNG *Trav. France* (1889) 19 The houses and cottages of wood filled between the studs with clay or bricks. **1825** J. NICHOLSON *Oper. Mech.* 569 If to support girders, they [principal uprights in a partition wall] should be trussed, and afterwards filled in with parallel pieces, called studs. **1836** PARKER *Gloss. Archit.* (1850) I. 449 *Studs*, the intermediate posts in partitions or wood-work; they also are termed uprights and quarters. **1865** THOREAU *Cape Cod* ii. 22 The rows fully as straight as the studs of a building. **1915** *Antiquary* Nov. 426/2 A very rough floral design painted in black and white between the studs of a fifteenth-century cottage.

b. *collect. sing.* Laths to be used as the uprights in partition walls or the walls of lath-and-plaster buildings. Chiefly in combinations, as ***stud and mud, stud and plaster***, used attrib. to denote a mode of building in which the walls are of 'studs', interlaced with twigs or having laths nailed upon them, and covered with mud or plaster.

c **1535** in Dugdale *Monast. Angl.* (1825) V. 206 A litle chapell of our Ladie, which is coverd with tile and buylded with studde. **1580** TUSSER *Husb.* (1878) 73 Saue crotchis of wud, Saue spars and stud. **1613** MARKHAM *Eng. Husbandman* I. I. iv. (1635) 24 [A] house..intended..to be built of studde and plaster. **1788** *Archæologia* (1789) IX. 111 The buildings erected then were either of whole logs, or of timber uprights wattled, such as at this very day in the North is called *stud and mud.* **1854** MISS BAKER *Northampt. Gloss.*, *Stud and teer*, a rustic mode of building a wall with interwoven sticks instead of lath, plastered or teer'd with dirt instead of mortar.

†**2.** *fig.* A prop, or support. *Obs.*

a **1450** *Le Morte Arth.* 3621 There he hopyd it were beste For to gete hym som lyves stode. **1583** GOLDING *Calvin on Deut.* cli. 932 If we tread vpon such as haue no credite nor meane to defende themselues, nor any stud to leane vnto. *a* **1603** T. CARTWRIGHT *Confut. Rhem. N.T.* (1616) 576 The chiefe pillers and studds of Popery before 600 yeares after Christ. **1651** N. BACON *Disc. Govt. Eng.* II. iii. 27 The Lords were become Supporters to the Crown, Studds to the Throne, and a Reserve to the People, against the violent motions of an unbridled minde in their King. **1652** BENLOWES *Theoph.* VII. xxxi, Parent of Beings, Entities sole Stud.

3. *U.S.* The height of a room from floor to ceiling.

1850 MRS. HAWTHORNE in J. Hawthorne *N. Hawthorne & Wife* (1885) I. 369 You cannot think how pretty the room looks, though with such a low stud that I have to get acclimated to it, and still fear to be crushed. **1886** E. S. MORSE *Jap. Homes* ii. 63 These rooms were unusually high in stud.

4. †**a.** A stem, trunk (of a tree). *Obs.*

1579 SPENSER *Sheph. Cal.* Mar. 13 Seest not thilke same Hawthorne studde? **1591** —— *Virg. Gnat* 84 This with full bit doth catch the vtmost top Of some soft Willow, or new growen stud. **1621** G. SANDYS *Ovid's Met.* v. (1632) 187 Vpon a Sallow stud My robe I hung, and leapt into the flood.

b. A short branch, spur. *rare.*

1657 LIGON *Barbadoes* 76 Now there is an addition to her [*sc.* the palmetto tree's] beauty by two green studds, or supporters, that rise out of her sides,.. they are about three foot long, small at the place from whence they grow, but bigger upwards. **1797** COLERIDGE *Christening Friend's Child* 39 Ah, fond deceit! the rude green bud Alike in shape, place, name, Had bloom'd where bloom'd its parent stud, Another and the same! **1842** LOUDON *Suburban Hort.* 555 The fruit is generally produced on small spurs or studs, from half an inch to two inches in length, which proceed from the sides and ends of the two-year, three-year, and occasionally from the older branches.

II. Something fixed in and projecting from a surface.

5. a. In early use, an ornamental round knob of metal or amber on a girdle, bridle, or the like. In later use with wider sense, a boss or large nail-head standing out on a surface, for the purpose of decoration or protection.

[**1397**: see STOOTH 2.] **14..** *Metr. Voc.* in Wr.-Wülcker 623/3 *Bulla*, a stode, *i. nodus in cingulo.* **1420** *E.E. Wills* 46 A gurdyll..with a bocull and a pendaunt ad xxxiij. stodys of syluer and ouerguld. **1555** in Foxe *A. & M.* (1583) 1546/1 He vseth bridle wyth white studs & snaffle. **1577** B. GOOGE tr. *Heresbach's Husb.* III. 155 The shepheardes Mastie... To arme them agaynst the Woolfe..you may put brode collers about theyr neckes full of nayles, and iron studdes, lyning it with soft leather within. **1585** HIGINS *Junius' Nomencl.* 274/1 *Miliares clauiculi*,..the studs of a buckler. *a* **1593** MARLOWE *Passionate Sheph.* 18 A belt of straw and Iuie buds, With Corall clasps and Amber studs. **1596** SHAKS. *Tam. Shr.* III. ii. 63 And a womans Crupper of velure, which hath two letters for her name, fairely set down in studs. *c* **1598** DELONEY *Thomas of Reading* (1912) 220 The instruments whereon his seruants plaid, were richly garnished with studdes of siluer. **1603** STOW *Surv. Lond.* (1908) I. 57 They vsed Leather money, with a little stud or naile of siluer in the middest thereof. **1641** MILTON *Reform.* I. 27 Some of the nailes whereof hee put into his Helmet,.. others he fasten'd among the studds of his bridle. **1671** —— *P.R.* IV. 120 Crystal and Myrrhine cups imboss'd with Gems And studs of Pearl. **1706** PHILLIPS (ed. Kersey), *Stud*, a Nail imbossed in any thing. **1725** POPE *Odyss.* x. 375 Radiant with starry studs, a silver seat Receiv'd my limbs; a footstool eas'd my feet. **1753** HANWAY *Trav.* (1762) II. XIV. i. 342 *note*, These are the feathers of black herons stuck into a tube, supported by a stud of precious stones. **1756-7** tr. *Keysler's Trav.* (1760) II. 274 The studs used in the old mosaic-works are very large, and often covered either with silver or gold. **1784** COWPER *Task* v. 426 To wear out time in numb'ring to and fro The studs that thick emboss his iron door. **1818** KEATS *Endym.* I. 924 That time thou didst adorn, with amber studs, My hunting-cap. **1860** J. HEWITT *Arms & Arm.* II. 122 The brass of William de Aldeburgh, 1360, ..offers a variety, in the studs being quatrefoil instead of round. **1867** FREEMAN *Norm. Conq.* (1876) I. vi. 517 Each bore on his left arm a shield with gilded boss and studs. *a* **1890** D. DAVIDSON *Mem. Long Life* iii. 60 The gate..is.. of wrought brass, the studs being elaborately chased.

transf. and *fig.* **1591** SYLVESTER *Du Bartas* I. iv. 106 So those gilt studs in th' upper story driv'n, Are nothing but the thickest part of Heav'n. **1604** BRETON *Passionate Sheph.* (Grosart) 10/2 And for her teeth, no Granam studdes, Nor like the Knagges of Blacke-thorne buddes. **1694** N. H. *Ladies Dict.* 416/1 When Night has cast her Sable Mantle o're the World, the Face of Heaven..will be gay, by putting on her gaudy spots of Light, and Studs of Stars. **1821** CLARE *Vill. Minstr.* I. 48 There once were springs, when daisies' silver studs Like sheets of snow on every pasture spread.

†**b.** A coloured spot. *Obs.*

a **1728** WOODWARD *Nat. Hist. Fossils* I. (1729) I. 49 A Peble of a light brown Colour. In one part of it the Surface is somewhat depress'd; and there, upon a Plane, are several small oblong Studds, each near as big as a Rape-Seed, placed regularly in a Quincunx Order. **1751** G. EDWARDS *Nat. Hist. Birds* IV. 243 The great brown Caterpillar, with golden Studs.

c. *Arch.* A sculptured disk such as was used in the ornamentation of mouldings in the Late Norman period of English architecture.

1686 Plot *Staffordsh.* 360 [The Cathedral of Lichfield] being finely adorned with Studds and carved work. 1835 Whewell *Archit. Notes* (1842) 282 Here we have a great abundance of those things which are excluded from the supposed first Norman style. Zigzags large and small, frets lozenged and embattled, cable-mouldings, studs, &c. 1843 Bloxam *Princ. Gothic Archit.* iv. (ed. 5) 87 [Norman mouldings] The pellet or stud.

d. One of a series of small devices protruding slightly above the surface of a road and used to demarcate traffic lanes; *spec.* = cat's eye 5.

1935, etc. [see *road stud* s.v. road *sb.* 9b]. 1939 L. MacNeice *Autumn Jrnl.* viii. 33 The metal studs in the sleek macadam. 1943 *Ann. Reg. 1942* 386 A traffic stud insecurely fixed.. flew up and injured a cyclist. 1958 *Spectator* 8 Aug. 190/2 The road studs known as cat's eyes. 1975 R. Hoban *Turtle Diary* xxxii. 151 There were reflecting studs in the road. 1978 *Highway Code* 18 Coloured reflecting road studs may be used with white lines—white studs mark the lanes or centre of the road, while the edge of the carriageway may have red studs on the left-hand side and amber by the central reservation of dual carriageways. Green studs may be used across lay-bys and side roads.

e. = *ear-stud* s.v. ear *sb.*[1] 17.

[1873: see *ear-stud* s.v. ear *sb.*[1] 17.] 1968 J. Ironside *Fashion Alphabet* 172 *Stud*, a plain 'knob' on the ear. 1979 N. Freeling *Widow* xxiii. 143 Garnet studs in the pale fleshy lobes of the ears.

6. A kind of button (made of bone, ivory, mother-of-pearl or some imitation, or of metal, sometimes jewelled), which is passed through one or more eyelet-holes, either in order to fasten some article of dress, or merely for ornament. See also press-stud.

Quot. 1555 may belong to sense 5.

1555 *Instit. Gentl.* I vij b, The Frencheman.. vseth aggletes, studdes, perles embroderye, colors vpon colors. 1772 *Phil. Trans.* LXII. 135 The stud in his shirt sleeve. 1840 Hood *Up Rhine* 110 His shirt was fastened with mosaic studs, besides a complicated sort of brooch. 1854 Surtees *Handley Cr.* v. (1901) I. 40 He had.. an infinity of studs down an ill-fitting, badly-washed shirt.

7. *Machinery.* **a.** A lug or projecting socket to receive the end of an axle, pin, etc.

1683 Moxon *Mech. Exerc., Printing* x. ¶9 In the middle of these two Studs is made a.. Hole.. to receive the two round ends of an Iron Pin. 1688 Holme *Armoury* iii. 323/1 The end of the Spindle, which turns upon a Stud or Stand. 1825 J. Nicholson *Oper. Mech.* 314 This screw works in a stud M, which is screwed firmly upon the top of the stud F.

b. A short rod or pin fixed in or projecting from something, and serving as a support, axis, or stop.

1694 J. Smith *Horolog. Disquisit.* 50 Let him fix or drive into the back of the Case a strong Stud of Brass or Iron. 1815 in *Abridgm. Specif. Patents Locks*, etc. (1873) 20 In making the wards of the lock.. move or turn upon studs, pillars, or axes. 1843 Holtzapffel *Turning* I. 360 The ring for the outer case or cope is now laid down, and its position is denoted either by fixed studs or by marks. 1860 Rimbault *Pianoforte* 395 *Stud*, a metallic application to grand and other superior pianofortes, screwed into the wrest-plank to obtain an upward bearing of the string, instead of a downward one over the pin-bridge, by which clearness of tone is obtained. 1866 R. M. Ferguson *Electr.* 236 Morse's Recording Instrument.. By the attraction of A, the end *l* is lowered and brought against the stud *n*. 1871 Culley *Pract. Telegr.* (ed. 5) 215 The single current key may be made to send double currents by attaching a switch to the back-stop (the stud on which the key lies when at rest). 1873 Nelthropp *Watch-work* 21 Stud, a small piece of metal designed to hold some portion of the movement, as pendulum-stud, cap-studs, &c. 1879 *Cassell's Techn. Educ.* IV. 205/2 (*Carriage-building*) The plates are fitted to each other, and being forged to the required span are held in position by studs.

c. *Electric traction.*

1888 *Encycl. Brit.* XXIII. 496/1 The [electric railway] line is divided into short sections; each of these has an exposed conductor, which may be one of the rails, and this is placed in temporary contact with the insulated conductor as the train passes, by the pressure of the wheels on a flexible rail or stud. 1908 *Daily News* 14 Apr. 9 One of the principal defects has reference to the stud that supplies the current retaining its power some time after the car has passed. A 'live' stud will always be a source of danger.

d. *Gunnery.* One of a number of protuberances on the surface of a projectile to be fired from a rifled gun, placed spirally for the purpose of making the shot receive rotatory movement from the grooving of the gun.

1866 in *Parl. Papers* (1867) XLI. 809 In the last lot of 9-inch shot.. there are a considerable number that appear.. quite unfit for issue.. as some of the studs are shapeless blotches of gun metal, scarcely projecting at all from the surface of the shot. 1876 Will & Dalton *Artill. Hand-bk. Ref.* 228 For all projectiles for 7" M.L.R. guns and upwards the studs are made of an alloy of 10 parts of copper to 1 part of tin.

e. = *stud-bolt* (see 9).

1887 [see *stud-bolt* in 9]. 1908 McLaren *Mech. Engin.* 19 Studs are used where there is not room for a bolt-head.. or where it is undesirable to make a hole through both pieces of metal to be fastened together.

f. *Naut.* A transverse bar of cast-iron inserted in the middle of each link of a chain-cable.

1863 [see *stud-chain* in 9]. 1867 Smyth *Sailor's Word-bk.* 1876 *Encycl. Brit.* IV. 621/2 The stud [in chain cable] keeps the link from collapsing, and increases its strength considerably.

g. One of a number of metal pieces set into the tyre of a motor vehicle to improve roadholding in slippery conditions. *N. Amer.*

[1909 *Westm. Gaz.* 11 Nov. 5/2 Messrs. B. F. Goodrich will exhibit their all-rubber non-skids, in which the rubber studs form an integral part of the tread, as well as a new steel-studded tyre.] 1963 *Pop. Mechanics* Sept. 24 *PM* tried one version of Season Safety Stud tires on a glassy smooth skating rink and found performance impressive. 1976 *National Observer* (U.S.) 13 Nov. 10/4 In Illinois, Minnesota, and Wisconsin studded tires have been barred this year for the first time. In Michigan a new law permits studs only if they meet certain rigid—and some say impossible—specifications.

†**III. 8.** = *stud-rope*: see 9.

1336–7 *Acc. Exch. K.R.* 19/31 m. 4 In xv. petris cord' de canabo.. pro duobus stodes inde faciendis.

IV. 9. *attrib.* and *Comb.*, as (sense 7 c) *stud-shot*, (sense 7 d, with reference to electric traction) *stud-line, -tramway*, (sense 7 e) *stud-hole*, (sense 7 f) *stud-chain, -link*, (sense 6) *stud-maker*; also **stud-bolt**, a cylindrical bolt, threaded at both ends, one end to be screwed into a hole tapped in a casting or the like, while the other end passes through a hole in the cover-plate, which is secured by a nut; **stud-box**, a cylindrical tool for inserting stud-bolts, having at the lower end a tapped hole and at the upper end a square shank to be operated by a spanner; **stud centre**, a stud (sense 7 b) serving as an axis; †**stud-clay** *a.* = *stud and mud* (see 1 b); **stud-ear-ring** = *ear-stud* s.v. ear *sb.*[1] 17; cf. sense 5 e above; **stud-fish** *U.S.*, a kind of killifish (see quot.); **stud-partition**, a partition constructed of studs (sense 1); **stud-piece**, = sense 1; †**stud-rope** *Naut.*, a rope of some kind used on a ship; **stud-wall**, a wall built of lath and plaster; **stud welding**, a method of welding in which an arc is struck between a stud and the base metal, producing a pool of molten metal into which the stud is driven to form a weld; †**stud-wise** *adv.* (*nonce-wd.*) with a pattern of studs (mistransl. of L. *lato clavo*); **stud-work**, building in lath and plaster.

1887 D. A. Low *Machine Draw.* (1892) 18 Studs, or *stud bolts, are shown in figs. 15 and 16. 1894 Lineham *Mech. Engin.* 214 The stud hole being drilled and tapped.. the stud .. is entered, and a *stud box placed upon the opposite end. 1860 *Ure's Dict. Arts* III. 649 The pendent lower end of a bent lever, working on a *stud centre. 1863 A. Young *Naut. Dict.* 398 *Stud-chain. 1719 in Willis & Clark *Cambridge* (1886) II. 213 A *Stud-Clay-Wall which supported ye South end of that Stable. 1919–20 *T. Eaton & Co. Catal.* Fall & Winter 394/3, 14k *stud earrings, set with diamond. 1966 [see *ear-stud* s.v. ear *sb.*[1] 17]. 1973 E. Linington *Crime by Chance* i. 10 Sue.. put on makeup and small stud earrings. 1882 Jordan & Gilbert *Syn. Fishes N. Amer.* 337 *Fundulus stellifer*, Spotted *Stud-fish. 1894 *Stud-hole [see *stud-box*]. 1906 *Westm. Gaz.* 31 Jan. 3/2 This particular form of the *stud-line is.. being tried for the first time. 1876 *Encycl. Brit.* IV. 621/1 Cables are sometimes made of common chain, but the best.. are made of *stud-link chain. 1861 *Internat. Exhib. 1862, Alph. Lists Trades* 39 *Stud Makers. 1805 R. W. Dickson *Pract. Agric.* I. 90 Five square of *stud-partitions. 1886 Willis & Clark *Cambridge* II. 166 A passage.. separated from the dining-room by a stud-partition. 1799 A. Young *Agric. Lincoln.* 35 They are commonly built of.. stud and mud; the *stud-pieces as large as a man's arm. 1336 *Acc. Exch. K.R.* 20/20 De xij. petris cordarum de Canabo.. pro vno *Stodrop inde faciendo. 1867 *Jrnls. Ho. Comm.* 22 Feb. 69/2 The Report of the Commanding Officer of Artillery at Halifax, in respect to the Ordnance Select Committee's *Stud Shot sent to that Colony. 1598–9 in Willis & Clark *Cambridge* (1886) II. 477 The *studd wall that stood at the further ende. 1719 *Ibid.* II. 213 The lower part of that Stud-wall was.. pulled down. 1941 A. C. Davies *Sci. & Pract. Welding* iv. 298 (*heading*) *Stud welding or studding. 1962 *Engineering* 20 Apr. 527/1 Stud welding has the advantage that there is no distortion of the flanges of the steel beams. 1975 Bram & Downs *Manuf. Technol.* ii. 57 Stud welding is a form of electric-arc welding. 1600 Holland *Livy* xxvii. xix. 643 A coat embrodered with purple *stud-wise. 1789 T. Rawlins *Fam. Archit.* Introd. p. v, As all Persons that build are not willing to go to an equal Expence, some liking thick, others thin Walls, and some only *Stud-work. 1805 R. W. Dickson *Pract. Agric.* I. 91 Eight square and fifty feet of stud-work. 1859 Parker *Dom. Archit.* III. ii. vii. 211 The two stories over are of timber stud-work. 1897 *Archæologia* Ser. ii. V. 412 Subdivisions of lath and plaster or stud-work.

stud (stʌd), *sb.*[2] Forms: 1 stód, stood, 3 stude, 3–7 stode, 4–7 stod, 5 stoode, 5–6 studde, 5–7 *Sc.* stuid, 6 sstoode, stoude, stude, 7 stood, 7–8 studd, 7– stud. [OE. *stód* neut., corresponds (exc. in declension and gender) to MLG. *stôt, stôd-*, OHG. *stuot* fem. stud of horses (MHG. *stuot* stud, mare, mod.G. *stute* mare), ON. *stóð* neut. stud of mares (Da. *stod* stud of 12 horses; MSw. *stôþ* neut. stud of mares; mod.Sw. *sto* mare):—OTeut. **stōðo-m*, **stōðō*, f. root **stō-*: **sta-*: see stand *v.* Cf. OSl. *stado*, Lith. *stódas* stud of horses. The change of OE. *ó* before *d* into (ʌ) is paralleled in *blood, flood*.]

1. a. An establishment in which stallions and mares are kept for breeding. Also, the stallions and mares kept in such an establishment.

c 1000 Ælfric *Gloss.* in Wr.-Wülcker 119/39 *Equartium*, stood. *c* 1000 *Will of Ælfhelm* in Kemble *Cod. Dipl.* IV. 300 Ic ȝean minum wife healfes ðæs stodes æt Trostingtune and minum ȝeferan healfes ðe me mid ridað. *c* 1250 *Owl & Night.* 495 Þe sulue stottes yne þe stode Beþ boþe wilde and marewode. 1390 Gower *Conf.* III. 204 Unto his hors fulofte he yaf The men in stede of corn and chaf, So that the hors of thilke stod Devoureden the mennes blod. 1614 Sir R. Boyle in *Lismore Papers* (1886) I. 51 Given Dick Dalton a young gelding of my stood. 1710 *Lond. Gaz.* No. 4709/4 Richard Marshall, Esq; Master of her Majesty's Studd. 1725 *Bradley's Family Dict.*, *Studd*, a place where Stallions and Mares are kept to propagate their Kind; or else the Word signifies the Stallions and breeding Mares themselves. 1831 Sir J. Sinclair *Corr.* II. 212 A respectable Danish gentleman, Sir Frederick Nielson, who was the master of his Danish Majesty's Stud, came to Scotland, in 1824. 1851 'Cecil' *Stud Farm* 43 It may sometimes occur with blood stock that cannot race,.. that no occupation can be found for them, and thus they find their way into the stud. 1876 Voyle & Stevenson *Milit. Dict.* 412/2 *Stud*, a place where horses are bred or kept. In England, the government does not, under this name, possess any such establishment. 1898 Seton-Karr *Ld. Cornwallis* v. 115 A third [order] establishes a Government Stud in the district of Tirhút.

†**b.** A collection of mares (also, rarely, of stallions) kept for breeding. *Obs.*

c 1340 *Nominale* (Skeat) 770 *Vn harasse de poleyns*, A stode of coltes. *a* 1400 *Sir Perc.* 326 He sawe a fulle faire stode Offe coltes and of meres gude. *c* 1452 *MS. Egerton* 1995 in *Trans. Philol. Soc.* 1907–10, iii. 52 A Stoode of marys. *c* 1532 Du Wes *Introd. Fr.* in *Palsgr.* 916 Stoude of stalons, *haras destalons*. 1537 Darcy in *Lett. Suppress. Monast.* (Camden) 158 The kynges hyenes is att greatt charge with his sstoodes off mares att Thornbery and other placys. 1547 *Acts Privy Council* (1890) II. 86 The wages of divers persons having custodie of a studde or race of mares. 1607 Markham *Cavel.* i. 29, I.. would wish no.. man.. to preserue his Mares longer in his studd, then from three yeares old till ten.

†**c.** A breed, race (of horses); also *transf. Obs.*

c 1308 *Song on the Times* in *Pol. Songs* (1839) 201 Sei thou me, asse, wat hast i-do? Me thenchith thou cannist no gode. .. Thou come of lither stode. 1536 Bellenden *Cron. Scot.* (1821) I. p. cvi, (Proheme viii.) The awfull churle is of ane othir strind. Thoucht he be borne to vilest servitude, Thair may na gentrice sink into his mind,.. The bludy wolf is of the samin stude: He feris gret beistis, and ragis on the small. 1557 Phaer *Æneid* vii. (1558) Tij b, Coursers.. Engendryd of that race, whom Cyrces liuely did inuent To mixe with mortall studdes.

†**2.** Used for: Horses. *Obs.*

c 1305 *Land Cokaygne* 35 Þer nis schepe no swine no gote. .. Nother harate [*read* harace], nother stode. Þe lond is ful of oþer gode. *c* 1325 *Chron. Eng.* 840 in Ritson *Metr. Rom.* II. 305 For that tresoun that hy dude Hy were to-drawen wythe stude. 1422 Yonge tr. *Secreta Secret.* 204 Alle the most Inly.. tounes of leys, wyth moche of hare stode and har cornes,.. he braunt and destruyet.

3. a. In early use: The horses bred by and belonging to one person. In later use: A number of horses (esp. race-horses or hunters) belonging to one owner.

a 1661 Fuller *Worthies, Yorks.* (1662) 187 Whereas a Stud of Horses bred in foggy fenny ground.. have often a Fen in their feet, being soft and soon subject to be foundred. 1690 *Lond. Gaz.* No. 2588/4 The Stud or Breed of Horses, late belonging to Sutton Oglethorpe Esq;.. are now to be disposed of there. 1740 Richardson *Pamela* (1824) I. 104 After my master had dined, he took a turn into his stables to look at his stud of horses. 1814 Scott *Wav.* xxv, Sir Everard's letters.. seldom concluded without some allusion to our hero's stud. 1846 Ld. G. Bentinck *Let.* 18 Aug. in *Daily Tel.* (1883) 10 July, Mr. Mostyn has purchased my stud. 1858 Ld. J. Russell in Fitzmaurice *Life Granville* (1905) I. 321 There are various speculations as to Derby's selling his stud;.. the probable one is that his horses are not very good. 1863 W. C. Baldwin *Afr. Hunting* viii. 308 My stud is now reduced to three... All my Natal nags are dead. 1910 Goldw. Smith *Reminisc.* ii. 22 He kept a hunting stud to the last.

punningly. 1821 Lamb *Elia* Ser. i. *Witches & Night-fears*, I confess an occasional night-mare; but I do not, as in early youth, keep a stud of them.

b. *transf.* A collection of animals of a particular kind (esp. of dogs) belonging to one person; also sometimes jocularly applied to a staff or body of persons of some particular class or function. Also, in recent use, a number of motor-cars belonging to one person.

1798 J. Lawrence *Treat. Horse* II. 19, I am as fond of playing with my cat, as ever was.. Crebillion, who kept so large a stud of them. 1804 *Europ. Mag.* XLV. 365/2 This Gentleman.. has a stud of beauties the representatives of those of former times, Mary Queen of Scots, Ann Bulleyn, Fair Rosamond, [etc.]. 1813 *Sporting Mag.* XLI. 172 A gentleman in Hampshire,.. having a large stud of sows. 1828 *Ibid.* N.S. XXI. 187 The symmetry.. exhibited by some of the studs of greyhounds. 1833 Nyren *Yng. Cricketer's Tutor* (1902) 75 These four were our tip-top men, and I think such another stud was not to be matched in the whole kingdom, either before or since. 1854 *Poultry Chron.* I. 527, I had last year, a good stud of Partridge Cochins, which produced good chickens. 1899 *19th Cent.* May 816 Knowing the difficulties one meets with before one possesses a stud of reliable homers. 1907 *Motoring Illustr.* 16 Mar. 79/1 King Edward never goes on his travels unless accompanied by one or more of his numerous stud of motor-cars. 1908 *Advt.*, Fine stud of motor-cars for hire.

4. †**a.** [Short for stud-mare: cf. G. *stute*, Sw. *sto*.] A mare kept for breeding. *Sc. Obs. rare.*

c 1480 Henryson *Trial of Fox* xxix, Ga, mak ane message sone vnto that stuid. [Cf. *ante* xxviii, Thay said, 'Nane, except ane stuid gray meir.'] 1570 Buchanan *Admonit.* Wks. (1892) 31 Thay blamit opinlie the regent that reservit the quene.. as yai said.. to be ane stude to cast ma folis.

b. [Short for stud-horse.] A stallion. *U.S.*

1803 M. Cutler in *Life, Jrnl. & Corr.* (1888) II. 142 The famous white stud, an Arabian horse, called the Dey of Algiers, on the ground. 1807 P. Gass *Jrnl.* 201 Remained here all day and had a great deal of trouble with our horses, as they are all studs, and break almost every rope we can raise. 1891 C. Roberts *Adrift Amer.* 183 He was a stud, and as fine a horse of his class as I ever saw.

c. = stud-horse 2. Chiefly *U.S.*

[**1890** J. P. Quinn *Fools of Fortune* 188 Next to the banking games in the estimation of the betters comes poker, both 'draw' and 'stud'.] **1933** D. Runyon in *Collier's* 28 Jan. 8/1 A proposition may be only a problem in cards, such as.. how often a pair of deuces will win a hand in stud. **1942** W. Faulkner *Go down, Moses* 26 'Stud,' Mr Hubert said. 'One hand. You to shuffle, me to cut, this boy to deal.' **1979** Reese & Flint *Trick 13* 64 In seven-card stud a player who stays in the pot till the finish receives two cards face down, four face up, and one face down.

d. A man of (reputedly) great sexual potency or accomplishments; a womanizer, a habitual seducer of women. In weakened uses: as a familiar term of address among men; a boy-friend or escort.

Particularly common since *c* 1960.

1895 W. Rye *Gloss. E. Anglia* 217 *Stud*, a nickname given to a man from his love of venery (Wilton, 1877). **1909** *Dialect Notes* III. 377 *Stud (-horse)*, *n.*, a stallion. Also used as a term of familiar address among men. 'Hello, old stud, how are you?' **1955** *Amer. Speech* XXX. 305 [Wayne University slang] *Stud*, a ladies' man. **1959** C. MacInnes *Absolute Beginners* 165 The chick sits on cushions in the front part, with a brolly, and her stud heaves the thing along with a hop pole, just like gondolas. **1960** B. Moore *Luck of Ginger Coffey* iv. 88 Throwing her across this bed yesterday, pleased with yourself for being the great stud. **1964** S. Bellow *Herzog* 154 Still in fleeting moments the young and glossy stud—such as he really had never been. **1974** M. Haskell *From Reverence to Rape* 250 In the sixties we came to realize that the figure of the stud (the gamekeeper, the 'macho' Latin, the gigolo) is, like the sex-starved woman, largely a figment of male homosexual fantasy. **1981** S. Rushdie *Midnight's Children* iii. 395 A notorious seducer; a ladies'-man; a cuckolder of the rich; in short, a stud.

e. Hence (without explicit sexual significance): a man, a fellow, esp. one who is well-informed; a youth. *U.S. slang* (chiefly *Blacks'*).

1929 M. A. Gill *Underworld Slang* 10/2 *Stud*, man. **1944** D. Burley *Orig. Handbk. Harlem Jive* 70 If you're a hipped stud, you'll latch on. **1946** Mezzrow & Wolfe *Really Blues* (1957) 379 *Stud*, guy, man. **1963** E. J. Gaines in *Sewanee Rev.* Autumn 550, I mean a stud's going to drink eggnog, and he isn't going to put whiskey in it. **1967** W. Murray *Sweet Ride* x. 169 We're looking for a couple of studs.. Jimmy the Head and Jawbone. **1970** R. D. Abrahams *Positively Black* ii. 46 But who's this stud they call Billy?

5. *attrib.* and *Comb.*, as (sense 1) ***stud department***, ***-farm***, ***-fee***, ***-keeper***, ***-master***, ***-park***; denoting animals kept for breeding, as ***stud-greyhound***, ***-hound***, ***-sheep***, (sense 3) ***stud sale***. Also **stud-book**, a book giving the pedigree of thoroughbred horses; also, in recent use, a similar book relating to dogs or occasionally to other animals valued for pedigree; also *transf.* and *fig.*, a catalogue of aristocratic pedigree, esp. = Burke *sb.*, Debrett *sb.*; **stud-bred** *Anglo-Indian*, a horse bred in the government stud; †**stud-fold**, an enclosure in which brood-mares are pastured; **stud-groom**, the head groom attached to a stud; †**stud-herd**, the servant in charge of a stud; **stud-house**, a building for the accommodation of a stud; also, in England, the name of the official residence of the Master of the Horse at Hampton Court; **studman**, a servant attached to the stud; **stud-poker** = *stud-horse poker* (see stud-horse 2); (now the commonest form); **studsman**, a horse-breeder. Also stud-horse, stud-mare.

1803 (*title*) The General *Stud Book, containing pedigrees of race horses, &c. &c. from the restoration to the present time. **1888** Kipling *Story of Gadsbys* (1891) viii. 122 'Fraid you won't be entered in the Stud Book correctly unless you go Home? **1897** *Encycl. Sport* I. 210 *Stud Book*, the official registry of running and breeding greyhounds. **1906** (*title*) The United States Register and Studbook for Cats. **1933** D. L. Sayers *Murder must Advertise* xi. 198, I think I know the stud-book pretty well. I was not aware that you had a cousin Bredon. **1982** R. Barnard *Death & Princess* xii. 122 Lady Dorothy..can drone on endlessly about her family tree... She's a sort of walking stud-book. **1879** Mrs. A. E. James *Ind. Househ. Managem.* 69 These *stud-breds were then in good demand. **1886** Kipling *Departm. Ditties*, etc. (1899) 99 Ah! stud-bred of ill-omen. **1876** Voyle & Stevenson *Milit. Dict.* 413/1 Officers of the army specially appointed, belonging to the *stud department. **1833** *Q. Rev.* XLIX. 423 His lordship has also at his *stud-farm, in Derbyshire, the renowned horses Priam and Zinganee. **1922** Joyce *Ulysses* 540 What's our *studfee?.. You fee men dancers on the Riviera, I read. **1953** X. Fielding *Stronghold* 48 My stud-fee's as low as you like—I'd do it for nothing. *c* **950** *Boundaries of Baddanburh* in Kemble *Cod. Dipl.* VI. 213 Of ðam wylle on ðone *stodfald. **1558** *Exch. Rolls Scot.* XIX. 62 [48*s.*] de firmis domus tecte tegulis et stodfaldis. **1868** *Field* 4 July 21/2 Advt., *Stud Greyhounds. **1737** J. Chamberlayne *St. Gt. Brit.* ii. (ed. 33) 241 At Hampton Court, 2 *Studd Grooms. **1833** *Q. Rev.* XLIX. 385 Mr. Place, stud-groom to Cromwell, was a conspicuous character of those days. **1884** *Law Rep.*, *13 Q.B. Div.* 621 No one would think of requiring a stud-groom to groom cart horses. **1853** R. S. Surtees *Sponge's Sp. Tour* vi. (1893) 31 Leather..turned out in a very stud-groomish-looking, basket-buttoned, brown cut-away. **1458** *Mem. Fountains* (Surtees) 252 (Nomina famulorum) Rob. West, *studherd. **1826** J. Cook *Fox-hunting* 227 *Stud hounds. **1829** *Sporting Mag.* XXIV. 221 The great Ducal *stud-house at Florence is a fine and spacious building. **1911** *19th Cent.* Sept. 541 The King was dining with Lord and Lady Albemarle at the Stud House, Hampton Court. **1569** *Ir. Act 11 Eliz.* c. 7 (1621) 331 Nor shall as a Captaine..take or exacte for the finding of him or them their Horsemen, Footemen..*Stodekeepers, Officers, or adherentes..any kinde of Exaction. **1545** in *Lett. & Papers Hen. VIII* (1907) XX. ii. 515 Matt. de Mantua, *studman, 4*l.* 11*s.* 3*d.* **1937** E. Rickman *On & Off Racecourse* i. 3 Their best horses are placed at stud..or are sold to other *stud-masters. **1975** *N.Z. Jrnl. Agric.* Sept. 60/3 New Zealand studmasters have proved their ability through the years. **1875** R. H. R. *Rambles in Istria* 58 A *stud-park which the Emperor of Austria keeps in this part of his dominions. **1864** W. B. Dick *Amer. Hoyle* 167 **Stud poker*.., in all essential particulars, is like the other Poker games. **1882** *Poker; how to play it* 75 Stud Poker..is played in this manner. **1922** S. Lewis *Babbitt* xxv. 295 All the way north he pictured the Maine guides: simple and strong and daring, jolly as they played stud-poker in their unceiled shack. **1959** 'B. Mather' *Achilles Affair* i. i. 13 He and Finnessy were playing murderous stud poker. **1978** E. Tidyman *Table Stakes* ii. iii. 191 The best stud poker player who ever sat down among them. **1854** Surtees *Handley Cr.* lx. (1901) II. 145 Advertisements were inserted in all the papers,..headed 'Great *Stud Sale'. **1908** *Chamb. Jrnl.* Nov. 704/1 Australian flock-owners are willing to pay enormous prices for Tasmanian *stud-sheep. **1902** E. A. Woodruffe-Peacock *Thoroughbreds* 16 Few graziers and no *studsmen can recognise this dangerous fungus in their paddocks.

6. *attrib.* or *adj.* use of sense 4 d above: manly, displaying a masculine sexual character. Hence *loosely* in commendation: fine, excellent. Chiefly *U.S. slang.*

1944 Auden *Sea & Mirror* in *For Time Being* iii. 56 The stud contralto gargling through her maternal grief. **1969** *Sat. Rev.* (U.S.) 5 July 28 There's nothing like a head-shrinker..for putting you where you're at. That's stud. **1971** *Black Scholar* Sept. 45/1 He had learned the stories about stud broads..but he knew Christine 'used' to be a stud broad. **1977** *Amer. Speech 1975* L. 67 *Stud.* 1: *adj*, outstanding, having all the attributes approved of by the group.

stud (stʌd), *v.* Forms: 6 studd, 7 stood, styd, 7– stud. [f. stud *sb.*[1]]

1. *trans.* To supply with studs or upright timbers; to build with studs.

1505–6 in Swayne *Churchw. Acc. Sarum* (1896) 260 Pro bredyng & dabyng & studdyng murorum in diuersis stadiis. **1511** *Nottingham Rec.* III. 330 Settyng vp and studdyng of an other hous. **1849** Noad *Electricity* (ed. 3) 330 Within the walls are to be studded, to protect from cold and damp.

2. To ornament or cover with or as with studs, bosses, or nail heads.

1570 Levins *Manip.* 183/2 To studde, *baccis ornare*, *geminare* [read *gemmare*]. **1596** Shaks. *Tam. Shr.* Induct. ii. 44 Their harnesse studded all with Gold and Pearle. **1624** Gee *Foot out of Snare* v. 51 A gold Hat-band studded with letters or Characters. **1643** Baker *Chron., Hen. V*, 48 The King..appointed divers stakes studded with iron at both ends..to be pitched behinde the Archers. **1649** Jer. Taylor *Gt. Exemp.* ii. Disc. vii. 36 God hath studded all the Firmament, and paved it with starres. **1664** Power *Exp. Philos.* i. 4 The Common Fly..her body is as it were from head to tayl studded with silver and black Armour. **1675** Covel in *Early Voy. Levant* (Hakl. Soc.) 229 Severall round looking-glasses with gold frames..and stydded with pretious stones. **1715** tr. *Pancirollus' Rerum Mem.* I. ii. vi. 74 Their Gates were studded with Nails of the brightest Iron. **1735** Dyche & Pardon *Dict.*, *Stud* v., to fill or ornament any thing with Studs, or small Wire, &c. **1774** Goldsm. *Nat. Hist.* VIII. 140 Most travellers who have gone through sandy countries, must well remember the little shining sparks with which the ditches are studded on each side of the road. **1790** Cowper *Iliad* xix. 452 First to his legs his polish'd greaves he clasp'd Studded with silver. **1820** Scott *Monast.* i, A strong door of oak, studded with nails. **1823** Rutter *Fonthill* 41 The furniture of this room is entirely of ebony, studded with ivory. **1832–4** De Quincey *Cæsars* Wks. 1859 X. 231 His sandals were studded with pearls. **1837** Carlyle *Fr. Rev.* I. vi. iii, Leather girdles studded with copper nails. **1845** G. Dodd *Brit. Manuf.* Ser. iv. 105 From the designs the barrels are studded and thus made ready for the loom. **1891** *Leeds Mercury* 27 Apr. 4/7 The..sleeves studded thickly over with tiny glittering silver sequins.

3. To set (a surface) with a number of protuberant or conspicuous objects. Also with *over*.

1790 W. Wrighte *Grotesque Archit.* 6 The outside to be composed of..irregular stones, and studded with small pebbles. **1796** Withering *Brit. Plants* (ed. 3) IV. 300 [*Agaricus glandulosus*] Gills white, their sides studded with globular glands. **1804** C. B. Brown tr. *Volney's View U.S.* 71 The summit is..thickly studded with trees. **1835** Dickens *Sk. Boz, River*, The river is studded with boats of all sorts, kinds, and descriptions. **1843** R. J. Graves *Syst. Clin. Med.* xiv. 161 The chest, arms and hands studded with florid maculæ. **1847** C. Brontë *Jane Eyre* i, The coast of Norway, studded with isles from its southern extremity..to the North Cape. **1861** Reade *Cloister & H.* vii. (1896) 23 The windows and balconies were studded with wondering faces. **1877** Huxley *Physiogr.* 104 Mount Etna is remarkable for having its flanks studded with parasitic cones. **1885** *Law Times' Rep.* LIII. 385/1 The line of country through which they were going was studded with buildings and manufactories. **1898** *Allbutt's Syst. Med.* V. 1012 Both lungs were studded with tubercle.

b. *rarely* in immaterial sense.

1849 Miss Mulock *Ogilvies* xvii, Pennythorne's conversation was studded with execrable jokes. **1874** J. S. Blackie *Self-Cult.* 83 The method of teaching by concrete examples, with which the Scriptures are so richly studded.

4. Of things: **a.** To be fixed in (a surface) in the manner of studs. **b.** To be placed at intervals over (a surface).

1652 Benlowes *Theoph.* vii. xix, The stars..That stud the luminated sphere. **1682** N. O. *Boileau's Lutrin* i. 5 Her rich Face sparkling Rubies studded over. **1697** Dryden *Æneis* iii. 175 We pass the scatter'd Isles of Cyclades; That, scarce distinguish'd, seem to stud the Seas. *a* **1763** Shenstone *Odes* etc. (1765) 282 As when a shepherd.. surveys his less'ning flock In snowy groups diffusive, stud the vale. **1836** W. Irving *Astoria* I. 15 This..system of internal seas..was studded by the remote posts of the company. **1845** Gosse *Ocean* iv. (1849) 178 Of all the constellations that stud the sky of the southern hemisphere, there is none that more strikes a stranger than the Southern Cross. **1854** Surtees *Handley Cr.* x. (1901) I. 84 After passing the long line of villas that stud the road in the Mount Sion direction. **1906** Cornford *Defenceless Isl.* 71 Coaling-stations stud the ocean highways of the world. **1911** G. Elliot Smith *Anc. Egyptians* vi. 91 The Arab, having little or no moustache, removed the few hairs that studded his upper lip.

5. To insert or place (a number of things) at intervals over a surface.

1856 Stanley *Sinai & Pal.* i. (1858) 99 The little shrubs, which had more or less sprinkled the whole 'Arabah, were more thickly studded. **1881** 'Rita' *My Lady Coquette* iv, The stars are thickly studded in the dim deep blue of the sky. **1895** *Scott. Antiquary* X. 79 Around the firesides of the cottages, which were studded over the moor.

6. *Mech.* To secure with studs.

1911 Webster.

stud, obs. pa. t. of stand *v.*

studded (ˈstʌdɪd), *ppl. a.* [f. stud *v.* and *sb.*[1] + -ed.]

1. a. Set with or as with studs or large-headed nails.

1591 Percivall *Sp. Dict.*, *Tachonado*, studded, nailed, *Bullatus, clauatus.* **1592** Shaks. *Ven. & Ad.* 37 The studded bridle on a ragged bough, Nimbly she fastens. **1663** Cowley *Hymn to Light* xix. Verses & Ess. (1669) 37 A Crown of studded Gold thou bear'st. **1696** Mandey & Moxon *Mech. Powers* ix. i. (1699) 176 A Studded Wheel is, that in whose Periphery little Sphæres, or Convex Hemisphæres are disposed, or the Concaves are made hollow answering to the Convexes in the other Wheel. **1697** Dryden *Virg. Georg.* iii. 555 Swift Rivers are with sudden Ice constrain'd; And studded Wheels are on its back sustain'd. *a* **1776** J. Ellis *Zoophytes* (1786) 16 *Flustra bullata.* Studded Sea Matt. **1804** J. Grahame *Sabbath* 281 That house, with studded doors, And iron-visor'd windows. **1805** Scott *Last Minstr.* i. xvii, Orion's studded belt is dim. **1845** G. Dodd *Brit. Manuf.* Ser. iv. 106 The horizontal warp-threads, with the studded barrel..over them, form what we may term the permanent furniture of the carpet weaver's loom. **1860** J. Hewitt *Arms & Arm.* II. 122 Studded armour is found during this [the 14th] century.

b. Of a surface: Diversified by a number of prominent or conspicuous objects.

1823 Byron *Island* ii. xi, The lightly-launch'd canoe Which stemm'd the studded archipelago.

c. Of a tyre: provided with studs (stud *sb.*[1] 7 g).

1966 *Better Homes & Gardens* Jan. 14/2 Studded snow tires made their debut in many of the snow belt states last winter. **1970** *Toronto Daily Star* 24 Sept. 39/1 Studded tires were causing costly damage to city streets.

2. Built with studs or upright laths.

1805 R. W. Dickson *Pract. Agric.* I. 94 Five square of studded partitions.

3. *Arch.* Of a moulding: Ornamented with studs.

1843 Bloxam *Princ. Gothic Archit.* iv. (ed. 5) 87 [Norman mouldings] The studded trellis. **1855** *Man. Gothic Mouldings* 21 The studded patterns are of endless variety, the round studs receiving crosses, circles, or stars, according to the sculptor's pleasure. **1866** Parker *Concise Gloss. Terms Archit.* 151 The Star, the Billeted Cable, the Nebule, the Studded, the Indented, the Scolloped, [and other mouldings].

4. Of a projectile: Furnished with studs. (See stud *sb.*[1] 7 c.)

1870 *Pall Mall Gaz.* 24 Oct. 12 It is an easy and popular error to suppose that a lead-coated tightly fitting shot must shoot better than a studded shot.

5. *Naut.* Of the links of a chain: Strengthened with studs.

1901 J. Black *Scaffolding* 88 Crane chain, with short links, may be proved to fourteen tons, and cable chain, with studded links, to eighteen tons.

6. *U.S.* In parasynthetic adjs.: ***high-studded***, ***low-studded***, having a great or small 'stud' or vertical dimension. (See stud *sb.*[1] 3.)

1787 M. Cutler in *Life, Jrnls. & Corr.* (1888) I. 269 It is a very large chamber, and high studded. **1884** Howells *Silas Lapham* iii. 54 Certainly, have the parlours high-studded... Have the entrance-story low studded. **1891** *Harper's Mag.* Dec. 119/1 The roof of the house slanted from back to front, so that the two rooms were lower studded than the studio.

†**ˈstuddery.** *Obs.* [f. stud *sb.*[2] + -ery.] A place for keeping mares and stallions for breeding.

1587 Harrison *England* iii. i. 220/2 in *Holinshed*, King Henrie the eight erected a noble studderie and for a time had verie good successe with them.

studdie: see stithy, study.

studding (ˈstʌdɪŋ), *vbl. sb.* [f. stud *v.* + -ing[1].]

1. The woodwork of a lath and plaster wall or partition; also *pl.* wood cut into battens for use as studs.

1588 in *Archæologia* LXIV. 366 Lett to Fogg all the studding and particions over the hall as for xxs. **1823** P. Nicholson *Pract. Builder* App. 70 Deal Battenings or Studdings, as they are called in many parts of the kingdom, are of various descriptions. **1868** *Rep. U.S. Commissioner Agric.* (1869) 277 Walls..clapboarded on the outside of the studding. **1899** Kipling *Stalky* iii. 72 The rough studding of the lath and plaster wall under the dormer.

2. That with which a surface is studded.

1844 N. Paterson *Manse Gard.* iii. 236 The crocus..is.. perfectly beautiful as studding to a piece of smooth green sward. **1895** *Outing* XXVII. 217/2 All were lovely, with their studdings of islands and brightly-tinted shores.

3. *U.S.* The height (of a room) from floor to ceiling; = STUD *sb.*[1] 3.

1884 Howells *Silas Lapham* iii. 54 Lapham promptly developed his ideas of black walnut finish, high studding, and cornices.

studding sail. Also 6 *Sc.* **stoytene-**, 7 **studin-**, 8 **stutting-sail**; and see STUNSAIL. [Of obscure etymology.

The earliest recorded form seems to point to adoption from MDu. or MLG. *stôtinge*, but this word is known only as n. of action from *stôten* to push, thrust, collide. Cf. however Du. *stootlap* sail-lining, *stootkant* border, which have some affinity of sense with the Eng. word. It has been suggested that the synonymous OF. *estuinc*, *estoinc*, *estouin* (mod.F. †*estouine*, 18th c.) may be an adoption of the Teut. word, the medial dental disappearing according to phonetic law. This, however, is not certain; the ordinary F. word for studding-sail is *bonnette à étui*, which suggests a derivation of *estuinc* from *estui* (mod.F. *étui*). The Breton *misan a studincq*, studding-sail, is adopted from English.

The ordinary nautical pronunciation is STUNSAIL.]

A sail set beyond the leeches of any of the principal sails during a fair wind.

1549 *Compl. Scot.* vi. (1873) 42 The galliasse þat furtht hir stoytene sales. *a* **1618** Ralegh *Invent. Shipping* 16 To the courses we have devised studding Sayles, Top gallant Sayles [etc.]. **1627** Capt. Smith *Sea Gram.* vii. 31 There is also.. in a faire gaile your studding sailes, which are bolts of Canuasse.. wee extend alongst the side of the maine saile, and boomes it out with a boome or long pole. **1661** *St. Papers Dom. Chas. II* (P.R.O.) 6 May, No. 10, 2 studin sayles ould. **1687** A. Lovell tr. *Thevenot's Trav.* II. 2 Being fair before the Wind, so that no Sails but the Main and Main-Top-Sails could bear, we put out our Stutting Sails. **1779** W. King *Cook's 3rd Voy.* VI. viii. III. 392 At two, we set studding-sails, and steered West; but the wind increasing to a gale, soon obliged us to double reef the topsails. **1836** Marryat *Midsh. Easy* xxxiii, The Aurora was under way, with studding sails below and aloft, standing out of the roads. *c* **1860** H. Stuart *Seaman's Catech.* 20 When are studdingsails used? In fair and free winds.

attrib. **1743** Bulkeley & Cummins *Voy. S. Seas* 10 Got up a lower Studding-Sail-Boom of 40 Feet, & hoisted a Sail to keep the Ship to. **1834** Marryat *P. Simple* xxviii, He sent the topman down into the top for a tail-block and the studding-sail haulyards, made a whip, and lowered me on deck. **1840** R. H. Dana *Bef. Mast* i, The next day we were employed in preparations for sea, reeving studding-sail gear, crossing royal yards. **1867** Smyth *Sailor's Word-bk.*, *Studding-sail Yard*, the spar to which the head of the studding-sail is extended. **1874** Bedford *Sailor's Pocket Bk.* x. (ed. 2) 307 Studding-sail boom, *Bout de bonnette*.

studdle (ˈstʌd(ə)l), *sb.* Forms: 1 **stodl**, **stodle** (*or* **-la**), 4 **stoydel**, 5 **stedulle**, **stodul**, **studdul**, **-yll**, 6 **stodyll**, **studill**, **studle**, 7– **studdle**. [OE. *stodl* masc., *stodle* or *-la* wk. fem. or masc.; = ON. *stuðill* masc., prop, related to STUD *sb.*[1]]

†**1.** A post. *Obs.*

c **1050** *Voc.* in Wr.-Wülcker 280/14 *Postes*, durstodl. **1368** *Ely Sacrist Roll* in *Parker's Gloss. Archit.* (1850) I. 449 In 60 arboribus quercinis empt' pro stoydels et tignis, 25*s*.

†**2.** *Weaving.* One of the upright posts of a loom. *Obs.*

a **1100** *Gerefa* in *Anglia* IX. 263 He sceal fela tola.. habban.. stodlan. *c* **1440** *Promp. Parv.* 476/2 Stodul, or stedulle, of wevynge, *telarium*. **1562** *Richmond Wills* (Surtees) 156 A pece of clothe in studles, xiiij s. *Ibid.*, A pare of studles. **1615** Brathwait *Strappado* 193 One to the studdles goes, the next begins To rauell for new wefte.

3. *Mining.* (See quot. 1881.)

1757 Borlase *Earthquake* in *Phil. Trans.* L. 503 In Herland mine,.. the noise was heard 55 and 60 fathom deep, as if a studdle had broke, and the deads were set a running. **1875** J. H. Collins *Metal Mining* 38 Sometimes short corner pieces called 'studdles' are placed upright to keep the sets their proper distance apart. **1881** Raymond *Mining Gloss.*, *Studdles*, Corn. 1. Props supporting the middle of stulls. 2. Distance-pieces between successive frames of timbering.

†**4.** = STADDLE *sb.* 6 (? A misreading of that word.) *Obs.*

1635 L. Fox *N.-W. Fox* 216 We found the broad footing of Deere, and hard by them, the frame of a Tent standing, which had lately been made, with the studdle of a fire, the haire of Deere, and bones of fowle, left heere.

studdle (ˈstʌd(ə)l), *v. dial. trans.* To stir up (water) so as to make thick and muddy (Wilts. Gloss. 1893).

1852 Kingsley *Lett. & Life* (1877) I. 345 Some rascal's been 'studdling' the water.

studdy, stude: see STITHY, STUDY.

stude, obs. f. STEAD *sb.*; obs. pa. t. of STAND *v.*

studelfast, var. STATHELFAST.

a **1225** *Juliana* 74 þat stont studelfast.

studency (ˈstjuːdənsɪ). [f. STUDENT[1] + -CY.] = STUDENTSHIP 1.

a **1801** G. Wakefield *Mem.* (1804) I. 59 Dr. Jeffries,.. then a canon of Christ-church, kindly offered his assistance in procuring for me a studency in that house.

student[1] (ˈstjuːdənt). Forms: α. 4–5 **studiaunt**, 4–6 **studiant(e**, 5 **studyaunt(e**, *Sc* **-and**, 6 **steudiant**; 4–6 **studiente**, 4–8 **studient**, 5–6 **studyent(e**, 6 **stewdyent**. β. 5–6 **studente**, 5– **student**. [In the α forms, var. of ESTUDIANT, a. OF. *estudiant*, *estudient*, mod.F. *étudiant* (= Pr. *estudian*, Sp. *estudiante*, Pg. *estudante*, It. *studiante*, *studiente*), subst. use of pr. pple. of *estudier*, *étudier* to STUDY; in the mod. (β) form, ad. L. *student-em*, pr. pple. of *studēre*, to be eager, zealous, or diligent, to study; cf. It. *studente*, Du., G., Sw., Da. *student*.]

1. A person who is engaged in or addicted to study. Const. *of*, *in*, or with defining word prefixed, indicating the subject studied. Also with adj. of degree, as ***close***, ***deep***, †***good***, ***great***, ***hard student***.

α. **1398** Trevisa *Barth. De P.R.* VIII. xxvii. (Tollemache MS.) He [Mercurius] makeþ men studientes in science of numbris, and loueris þerof. **1450–80** tr. *Secreta Secret.* xxviii. 21 He that is a parfit studiaunt in that science. **1557** North *Gueuara's Diall Pr.* 98 We se it by experyence, that the greate studiantes are persecuted more wyth sycknes, then any others. **1601** Shaks. *Twel. N.* IV. ii. 9, I am not.. leane enough to bee thought a good Studient.

β. **1432–50** tr. *Higden* (Rolls) I. 13 Not vnprofitable to goode studentes [*non inutilem studiosis*]. **1529** More *Dyaloge* II. i. Wks. 178/1 No student in scripture should presume to trye examine, and iudge the catholike faith of Christes churche by the scripture. **1559** *Mirr. Mag.*, *Dk. Clarence* xxxviii, I know thou musest at this lore of mine, How I no student, should haue learned it. *a* **1568** Ascham *Scholem.* II. (Arb.) 129, I haue heard worthie M. Cheke many tymes say; I would haue a good student passe and iorney through all Authors both Greke and Latin. **1660** I. H *B. Valentine's Triumphant Chariot* 21 Moreover the courteous & favourable student of Art, ought to know the several sorts and kinds of Antimony. **1712** Steele *Spect.* No. 526 ¶3 Lest this hard Student should one time or other crack his Brain with studying. **1822** Shelley tr. *Calderon's Mag. Prodig.* i. 86, I see Both by your dress and by the books in which You find delight and company, that you Are a great student. **1857** J. Hullah *Rudim. Mus. Gram.* 2 The student should sing, or play.. this scale of *Do*, until he is thoroughly familiar with the sound of it. **1860** Tyndall *Glac.* I. v. 41 My position was in every way worthy of a student of nature. **1885** *Contemp. Rev.* Jan. 136 Guyard was well known in England by all Assyriological students.

2. a. A person who is undergoing a course of study and instruction at a university or other place of higher education or technical training. Also const. *of*, *in* (a subject); often with defining word prefixed, as ***art***, ***law***, ***medical student***.

α. *c* **1430** *Pilgr. Lyf Manhode* I. lxxxiv. (1869) 48 Now sey me.. if ther be many studyauntes, and how gret the citees ben. **1456** Sir G. Haye *Law Arms* (S.T.S.) 95 Quhethir a studyand may lefully be haldin in prisoun. **1509** Fisher *Funeral Serm. C'tess Richmond* Wks. (1876) 301 The studyentes of bothe the vnyuersytees to whome she was as a moder. **1547** *Househ. Bk. Edw. VI* in *Trevelyan Papers* (Camden) 195 Nicholas Bacon, studiant at the Lawe. **1564** J. Martiall *Treat. Crosse* title, By Iohn Martiall Bachiler of Lawe and Studient in Diuinitie. **1632** Lithgow *Trav.* x. 443 Flockes of Studientes, that ouer-swarme the whole land. *a* **1661** Fuller *Worthies*, *Norf.* (1662) 250 He was.. entered a Studient of the Municipal-law in the Inner-Temple. **1770** Luckombe *Hist. Printing* 61 William Rastall.. became a studient in Lincoln's Inn.

β. **1474** Caxton *Chesse* III. v. g vij, The Joly felawes that were students promysed to the woman a besaunte yf she myght or coude torne the corage of ypocras for to haue to doon wyth her. **1477** *Rolls of Parlt.* VI. 192/1 The studentes in the Universitees of Oxon and Cambrigge. **1553** T. Wilson *Rhet.* III. (1562) 83 b, When I was in Cambridge, and student in the kinges College. **1629** Wadsworth *Pilgr.* iii. 16 Now let vs come to the Collegiates or Students, and their diet. *a* **1700** Evelyn *Diary* an. 1637, Authors (it seems) desired by the students of divinity there [Balliol Coll.]. **1781** Gibbon *Decl. & F.* xvii. II. 40 After a regular course of education, which lasted five years, the students dispersed themselves through the provinces. **1845** W. B. S. Taylor *Hist. Univ. Dublin* 149 Provided the student be of two years' standing in the university. **1860** *N. Brit. Rev.* XXXIII. 78 The students at the Scottish universities.. usually reside either in furnished lodgings or are boarded in private families. **1886** C. Bigg *Chr. Platonists Alexandria* ii. 42 This was the famous Catechetical School... The students were of both sexes, of very different ages. **1895** Rashdall *Univ. Europe* II. II. 605 The medieval student in Arts was usually much younger than the modern undergraduate.

b. A scholar at an institute of primary or secondary education. orig. *U.S.*

1900 E. E. Brown in N. M. Butler *Monographs on Educ. in U.S.* 183 In these laboratories [high school] students perform representative experiments in the science they are pursuing. **1924** *Junior High School Clearing House* Mar. 6/1 It was felt.. that to single out the student who excelled in scholarship was usually to recognize native abilities but not necessarily serious effort. **1936** *Evening Citizen* (Glasgow) 29 Aug. 4/6 [In the United States] even schoolboys and schoolgirls are students. **1962** *Dict. Canad. English: Beginning Dict.* 644/2 *Student*... 2. a person who is studying in a school, college, or university: *That high school has 3,000 students.* **1976** *Times* 5 Aug. 14/7 We have primary school students, presumably working for BAs in Plasticine; the National Union of School Students; and graduation day for high school students... Formerly people were schoolboys or schoolgirls until they became undergraduates.

c. An inexperienced user of illegal drugs; *spec.* one who takes small or occasional doses. *U.S. drug-users' slang.*

1936 [see *joy-popper* s.v. JOY *sb.* 10]. **1949** [see JUNKIE]. **1951** [see SATURDAY NIGHT 1].

3. a. At Christ Church, Oxford: A member of the foundation, corresponding to the 'fellow' or 'scholar' of other colleges.

Since 1882 the title has been restricted to the senior members. Before that date the two groups were distinguished as ***Senior*** and ***Junior Students*** respectively.

1651 Langbaine *Found. Univ. Oxf.* 12 He [Henry VIII] established therein a Dean, 8 Canons, 3 publick Professors of Divinity, Hebrew, and Greek, 60 Students, eight Chaplains. *a* **1672** A. Wood *Life* (O.H.S.) I. 47 In the beginning of this yeare [1638] his eldest brother Thomas Wood.. became one of the students of Christ Church,.. he being then 14 yeares of age. *a* **1700** Evelyn *Diary* 24 Oct. 1672, Mr. Lock, an excellent learned gentleman and student of Christ Church. **1858** *Ordinances Oxf. Univ. Comm.*, *Ch. Ch.* §6 The Senior Students shall be persons of unblemished character. *Ibid.* §17 If in the judgment of the electors to open Studentships he shall not be in all respects fit to be a Student of the House.

b. A person who receives emoluments, during a fixed period, from a college or other institution, or from a special fund, to enable him to pursue his studies and as a reward of merit.

1800 *Camb. Univ. Cal.* 37 Gonvil or Caius College.. [4 names] Students in Physic. **1814** *Hist. Univ. Camb.* (ed. 2) 55 Gonville and Caius College... There are also four Studentships.. for students in physic: these students are required to take their degree of Bachelor in Physic as soon as they are of sufficient standing. **1888** *Camb. Univ. Cal.* 512 Gonville and Caius College.. Frank Smart Student [1 name].

†**4.** Const. *for*. One who strives after or studies to attain (an object or end). *Obs. rare.*

1545 Ascham *Toxoph.* I. (Arb.) 39 Wherein they both agre, that Musicke vsed amonges the Lydians is verie ill for yong men, which be studentes for vertue and learning. **1615** Chapman *Odyss.* XII. 467 So long, not a head Of all those Oxen, fell in any strife Amongst those students for the gut, and life [τόφρα βοῶν ἀπέχοντο λιλαιόμενοι βιότοιο].

5. a. *attrib.* and *Comb.*, as ***student activism***, ***activist***, ***body***, ***counselling***, ***demonstrator***, ***duel***, ***exchange***, ***grant***, ***hostel***, ***leader***, ***-life***, ***politics***, ***protest***, ***revolt***, ***revolution***, ***riot***, ***-song***, ***unrest***, ***violence***; appositive, as ***student-monk***, ***nurse***, ***-preacher***; ***student-like*** adj.

1977 *Hongkong Standard* 14 Apr. 4/4 The University of the Philippines, a hotbed of student activism before Mr Marcos declared martial law in September 1972. **1969** 'E. Lathen' *When in Greece* x. 114 He had almost forgotten his role as a student activist. **1906** W. James *Mem. & Stud.* (1911) xiv. 362 Above all things, offer the opportunity of higher personal contacts. A university provides these anyhow within the student body. **1979** A. Price *Tomorrow's Ghost* ii. 26 We're not infiltrating the delectable student body. *a* **1593** Marlowe *Massacre at Paris* 140 Paris hath full fiue hundred Colledges.. Besides a thousand sturdy student Catholicks. **1959** *Listener* 19 Mar. 515/1 This sort of thing must surely have been studied by university psychology departments before now—particularly in America, where 'student counselling' is respectable. **1889** *Hardwicke's Sci.-Gossip* XXV. 127 Mr. Ralfs has an abundant store of anecdotes relating to his student-days. **1968** 'J. le Carré' *Small Town in Germany* ii. 13 Student demonstrators.. overturned the American Ambassador's car. **1911** Student-duel [see MENSUR]. **1979** J. Leasor *Love & Land Beyond* iii. 48 Men.. take pride in bearing scars of student duels on their cheeks. **1971** K. Dick *Ivy & Stevie* 42 I've been to Potsdam, Amsterdam, Königsberg... Sort of student exchange holidays. **1965** *Students' Handbk. 1965* (Univ. Coll. London Union) 43 For years the Councils of the N.U.S... have reiterated a call for the abolition of the Means Test on parental incomes used in the assessment of student grants. **1974** Student grant [see *inflation-proofing* s.v. INFLATION 8]. **1960** *N.U.S. Year Bk.* 35 This year marks the eleventh in which the Union has maintained a student hostel in the Bloombsury area. **1977** R. Barnard *Blood Brotherhood* xvi. 182 It was the address of a student hostel. **1962** E. Snow *Red China Today* (1963) i. 20 Huang Hua, whom I knew as a student leader when I taught briefly at the American-supported Yenching University. **1841** W. Howitt (*title*) The Student-life of Germany:.. containing nearly forty of the most famous Student Songs. **1870** Ruskin *Lect. Art* v. 135 Not one [drawing] is weak or studentlike— all are evidently master's work. **1905** Holman-Hunt *Pre-Raph.* I. 49 Mulready was most painstaking and student-like. **1886** Willis & Clark *Cambridge* I. Introd. p. lxxxiii, Foundation of Gloucester House for student-monks. **1932** *Lancet Commission on Nursing* v. 46 Each 'student nurse', as they are called, is attached to a nursery class with part-time practical work with little children. **1956** K. Hulme *Nun's Story* xvii. 287 She listened deliberately now to the talk of her student nurses. **1954** P. Toynbee *Friends Apart* ii. 35, I used my freedom to become.. violently caught up in the excitement of student politics. **1912** G. W. E. Russell *Edward King* ii. 29 The student-preacher of a written sermon.. before the College [at Cuddesdon] had the right to dine at the Vicarage, and receive a detailed criticism after dinner. **1965** *Granta* Summer 9/1 The worst tactical mistake the SRC could make is not to dissociate itself from the old idea of 'student protest'. **1976** D. Clark *Dread & Water* vi. 133 We'd had a student protest at the gate. **1969** *Listener* 8 May 630/2, I said that western civilisation today was being challenged from within... The most obvious symptom is the outbreak of what is commonly called 'student unrest', or 'student revolt'. **1978** P. Boardman *Worlds of Patrick Geddes* xi. 403 In 1930, an event occurred which took the old and hardy critic of universities himself by surprise: a student revolt. **1968** *Punch* 31 July 168/1 When the student revolution intervened the group moved to England. **1968** *Listener* 4 July 1/1 'Student riots', 'student violence', 'the movement for student power'—these are phrases that have been used to cover a wide variety of actions and attitudes and opinions. **1966** J. Mitford in *Vogue* (U.S.) 15 Mar. 93/1 Campuses throughout the country, undergoing the 'wave of student unrest', are producing their share of women individualists. **1968** Student violence [see *student riot* above].

b. Special comb.: **student card**, a card or ticket issued to members of a student body, and usu. entitling the holder to certain privileges; **student interpreter**, a civil servant who is appointed to undergo a course of instruction in foreign languages in order to qualify for a post in the diplomatic or consular service; hence ***student interpretership***; **student power**, the exercise of authority within a school, college, or larger sphere by students (cf. POWER *sb.*^{1} 4 f); **student('s) lamp**, an argand lamp with an elevated reservoir which automatically controls the flow of oil; **student(s') union** = UNION *sb.*^{1} 10 c; also applied to a similar association or building at other centres of higher education, and *loosely*, to a national association of students, formed to promote the welfare and views of its members (cf. *N.U.S.* s.v. N II. 1); **student teacher**, a student of a university or training college who teaches in a school for a certain period, as part of the qualification for a teaching certificate (cf. PUPIL TEACHER); hence **student-teachership**; **student-teaching**; **student-teacher** *a.*, designating the relation between students at a school or college and their teacher or teachers (cf. *pupil-teacher* adj. s.v. PUPIL *sb.*^{1} 3 b).

1973 *Sat. Rev. Society* (U.S.) May 53/2 Cost of the 16-hour program: $50 ($30 for anyone with a *student card). **1975** P. THEROUX *Gt. Railway Bazaar* iii. 51 She was a student and..had a student card... A card got each one a 50 percent reduction on the ticket. **1872** *Parl. Paper* (title) Return of *Student Interpreters in China, Japan, and Siam: 1847–72. **1884** *(title)* Civil Service Commission. Open Competition for *Student Interpreterships in China and Japan. **1875** KNIGHT *Dict. Mech.*, *Student's Lamp. **1881** C. A. YOUNG *Sun* 249 Like the shade of a student-lamp. **1968** *Listener* 21 Mar. 365/3 He will go to any lengths to placate and excuse the brutally vocal ginger group of *Student Power. **1973** *Times* 15 Oct. 17/1 Student power alone would not have toppled the government unless circumstances were very much in their favour. **1891** *Students' Union [see UNION *sb.*^{1} 10 c]. **1916** J. BUCHAN *Power-House* v. 134 It had something to do with the Slav States of Austria and an Italian Students' Union, and it threatened..to be dangerous. **1967** M. KENYON *Whole Hog* i. 12 The student union cafeteria always had..fried, boiled or scrambled eggs. **1977** P. JOHNSON *Enemies of Society* xii. 171 It was Margaret Thatcher..who, in the winter of 1970–1, changed the wording of the official regulations to allow public money to be handed over to the Student Unions. **1982** A. TAYLOR *Caroline Minuscule* iii. 30 The forthcoming motion the Students' Union were planning.. deploring violence. **1909** *Rep. Board Educ. 1907–8* 57 During 1907 the new method of providing for the preliminary education of Elementary School Teachers, which is known as the 'Bursar System', has been brought into operation... The prospective Teacher either goes direct into a Training College..or..obtains an appointment as a *Student-Teacher. **1953** W. MOORE *Bring Jubilee* (1955) xiii. 122 That personal, face-to-face, student-teacher relationship. **1973** E. MCGIRR *Bardel's Murder* ii. 47 When I started..there was no difficulty in getting student teachers because they could use the rod. **1910** *Rep. Board Educ. 1908–9* 56 Upon..the passing of the necessary leaving examination, two alternative courses are immediately open to him—to proceed to a Training College or to proceed to *Student-Teachership. **1970** *Daily Tel.* 23 Oct. 13/8 In the 'bad old days' of student-teachership, despite our huge classes we knew how to deal with 'emotional and learning disorders' without the aid of drugs! **1929** MYERS & HARSHMAN *Training Secondary Sch. Teachers* 17 Regulations relative to prerequisites for *student-teaching.

Hence **'studentdom**, the community of students. **'studentess**, a female student. **'studenthood**, **'studentism**, the condition of being a student. **'studenting** *nonce-wd.* [-ING^1], studying; an object of study. **'studentless** *a.*, having no students.

18.. *Colburn's Mag.* (Flügel), The vices of *studentdom. **1899** *Scotsman* 2 June 4/5 Restrictions imposed by the authorities are such as to drive the whole of Russian studentdom into a common camp of protest. **1834** *Knickerbocker* IV. 120 The Collegiate Institute..was originally designed to afford its fair *studentesses all the advantages usually obtained by the best educated of the other sex. *c* **1870** STEVENSON *Let.* in *Westm. Gaz.* (1895) 13 July 10/1 Miss —— and the rest of our fellow-studentesses. **1904** *Contemp. Rev.* Mar. 367 His own [lectures] on Job, the Psalms,..and other Old Testament subjects drew only students and German and Russian studentesses. **1910** SIR H. JOHNSTON *Brit. across Seas, Africa* Pref. p. v, A concise history..which would not be too abstruse for young students,..nor yet too lacking in technical information to be of service to those who had left *student-hood behind. **1922** JOYCE *Ulysses* 739 That delicate looking student..nearly caught me washing through the window only for snapped up the towel to my face that was his *studenting. **1848** *Blackw. Mag.* LXIV. 530 Burghers and merchants..who, since the days of their *studentism, had fattened on tobacco and beer. **1899** J. C. SMITH *Wallace's Buchanan* vi. 129 St. Leonard's College..in the first year was *studentless.

Student^2 ('stju:dənt). *Statistics.* The pseudonym of William Sealy Gossett (1876–1937), English brewery employee, used *attrib.* and in the possessive to designate statistical concepts devised by him, as ***Student('s) (t-)distribution***, a statistical distribution which is that of a fraction whose numerator is drawn from a normal distribution with a mean of zero and whose denominator is the root mean square of *k* terms drawn from the same normal distribution (where *k* is the number of degrees of freedom); ***Student's (t) test***, a test for statistical significance that uses tables of this distribution.

1929 *Nature* 17 Aug. 267/1 This is not to say that the deviation from 'Student's' *t*-distribution..may not have a real application. **1935** R. A. FISHER *Design of Experiments* iii. 38 *(heading)* Student's *t* test. **1937** YULE & KENDALL *Introd. Theory Statistics* (ed. 11) xxiii. 440 We proceed to give one or two examples of the way in which the 'Student' distribution is generally used to test the significance of various results obtained from small samples. **1938** *Biometrika* XXX. 223 As the theory of mathematical statistics has developed, the significance of 'Student's' test has been elaborated from many angles and deeper meanings associated with it than its author had ever dreamed of. **1968** P. A. P. MORAN *Introd. Probability Theory* vii. 326 Since *t* is scale-invariant its distribution is independent of σ, and is known as 'Student's *t*-distribution with $n - 1$ degrees of freedom'. **1980** *Brit. Med. Jrnl.* 29 Mar. 890/2 The serial changes in mean daily volume, time taken, and flow were pooled and assessed with student's two-tailed *t* test.

studental (stju:'dɛntəl), *a. rare.* [f. STUDENT^1 + -AL^1.] Belonging to, resembling, characteristic of, a student.

1660 S. FISHER *Rusticks Alarm* Wks. (1679) 469 O ye Studental, more then truly Prudential searchers of the Scriptures. **1890** D. EMBLETON *Addr. Durham Coll. Med.* 5 The studental mind has been gradually expanding in power.

studential (stju:'dɛnʃəl), *a. rare*$^{-1}$. [f. STUDENT^1 + -IAL.] Of or belonging to a student.

1822 R. POLLOK in D. Pollok *Life* 132, I was free..from all studential fetters.

'studentish, *a.* [f. STUDENT^1 + -ISH^1.] Pertaining to, characteristic of, or resembling an (undergraduate) student; student-like, esp. in dress or opinion.

1934 *Times Lit. Suppl.* 9 Aug. 552/3 Her spectacles, her studentish clothes, her pride in her degrees..combine to make her an almost lovable character. **1979** *Church Times* 7 Dec. 7/3 Their very appearance was not studentish: 'puritans predominated, all with clean short hair, inexpensive shoes, mass-produced clothes well cared for'.

studentize ('stju:dəntaɪz), *v. Statistics.* Also **Studentize.** [f. STUDENT^2 + -IZE.] *trans.* To subject (data) to studentization; chiefly as **'studentized** *ppl. a.*, applied esp. to data that have been standardized by division throughout by their estimated standard deviation, and to quantities derived therefrom; **,studenti'zation** (see quot. 1957).

1938 *Suppl. Jrnl. R. Statistical Soc.* V. 80 This theory has been developed further, and quite a number of large-sample results have been 'studentized'. By this we mean that a statistic whose sampling distribution involves the unknown standard deviation of the population is modified so that its distribution involves only quantities calculated from the sample. **1939** *Biometrika* XXXI. 21 In a recent paper H. O. Hartley..has suggested a systematic method of obtaining probability levels for 'studentized' functions. **1957** KENDALL & BUCKLAND *Dict. Statistical Terms* 284 *Studentisation*, the process of removing complications due to the existence of an unknown parent scale-parameter by constructing a statistic whose sampling distribution is independent of it; especially by dividing a statistic which is of a certain degree in the observations by another statistic of the same degree. **1959** H. SCHEFFE *Analysis of Variance* ii. 28 In the next chapter we will apply the distribution of the Studentized range. **1972** *Biometrika* LIX. 165 Duncan's modification also starts with the studentized range test.

studentry ('stju:dəntrɪ). *rare.* [f. STUDENT^1 + -RY.] Students collectively; a body of students.

1830 W. TAYLOR *Hist. Surv. Germ. Poetry* III. 170 Here was..a considerable population to observe, and a manlier studentry to mingle with: and Schiller began to question many of his former points of view. **1853** KINGSLEY *Hypatia* xvi, The huge broad blade, at the ominous brown stains of which the studentry recoiled.

studentship ('stju:dəntʃɪp). [See -SHIP.]

1. A position, usually stipendiary, the holding of which constitutes a person a 'student': see STUDENT^1 3 a, b.

a **1782** T. NEWTON *Life & Anecd.* 18 Knowing the fellowships of Trinity College to be much more valuable than the studentships of Christ Church. **1814** *Hist. Univ. Camb.* (ed. 2) 55 Gonville and Caius College... There are also four Studentships..for students in physic. **1838** *Penny Cycl.* XII. 482/1 A studentship, worth about 100*l* a year, to be held for eight years, was founded by Christopher Tancred, Esq., for four students, to be educated in the study of the law at Lincoln's Inn. **1858** *Ordinances Oxf. Univ. Comm., Ch. Ch.* §2 In place of the hundred and one Studentships now existing..there shall be established and maintained within the House twenty-eight Senior Studentships and fifty-two Junior Studentships. **1882** *Nature* 26 Oct. 631/2 That the proceeds of the fund be applied to establish a studentship, the holder of which shall devote himself to original research in biology. **1883** *Pall Mall Gaz.* 14 Dec. 4/1 The medal carries with it a travelling studentship for travel and study abroad, of the value of £200 per annum, tenable for one year.

2. *gen.* The condition or fact of being a student.

1881 *Scribner's Monthly* XXII. 235 It was..during Lepage's studentship in the Latin Quarter that he was first attracted to Jean-François Millet. **1914** *Q. Rev.* Jan. 89 Hartleben..refused to outgrow the noisy youth of studentship.

†**studgi**, *v. Obs.* (only in the 'Katharine group'). [App. a variant of ME. *stude* (Y), STEAD *v.* The etymological import of the *-gi* is uncertain; it may be due to the analogy of verbs like OE. *blódgian*, *syngian* (q.v. under BLOODY *v.*, SIN *v.*).] *intr.* To stop, hesitate, delay. = STEAD *v.* 7.

a **1225** *Juliana* 72 Schendeð hire nuðen ant ȝeldeð hire ȝarewborh ne studgi ȝe neauer. *a* **1225** *Leg. Kath.* 1264 Hwi studgi ȝe nu, & steuentið se stille? *a* **1225** *St. Marher.* 9 Þe mone ant te steorren he walcnið biðe weolcne, ne stutteð ne studgeð.

'stud-horse. [f. STUD *sb.*^{2} + HORSE. Cf. ON. *stóðhross.*]

1. A stallion kept for breeding.

c **1000** *Sax. Leechd.* III. 176 Ðyf mon mæte þæt he feola stod horsa habbe. **1598** *Extracts Munic. Acc. Newcastle* (1848) 46 Paid for their stoude horses meate, 5*s.* **1833** *Q. Rev.* XLIX. 414 His lordship..at present has the stud-horse Lamplighter. **1891** C. ROBERTS *Adrift Amer.* 185 He ..challenged four stud-horses that belonged to us.

2. *U.S.* ***stud-horse poker***: a variety of the game of poker. Also *absol.* (The usual form is now STUD *sb.*^{2} 4 c or *stud-poker* s.v. STUD *sb.*^{2} 5.)

1879 *Rep. Cases at Law Supreme Court of State of Arkansas* (1881) XXXIV. 442 The proof..showed that he did bet chips, or checks, at a game played with cards, called 'stud', or 'stud-horse', poker; being somewhat different from other games called 'straight poker' and 'draw poker'. **1882** in *Colorado Q.* (1956) IV. III. 271 Brownie Lea is leading stud horse at Del Norte. **1891** C. ROBERTS *Adrift Amer.* 152 Every saloon had a gambling room, where poker, stud-horse poker, faro,..were usually hard at it. **1920** C. E. MULFORD *Johnny Nelson* ii. 19 He's a travelin' eddicator in th' innercent game of draw—or was it studhoss, Nelson?

studiable ('stʌdɪəb(ə)l), *a.* [f. STUDY *v.* + -ABLE.] Fit to be studied; capable of being studied or observed.

1858 CARLYLE *Fredk. Gt.* x. v. (1872) III. 254 This Voltaire-Friedrich Correspondence..now fallen drearily extinct—studiable by Editors only! **1971** *Jrnl. Gen. Psychol.* Jan. 172 The activities of single cells studiable by microelectrode techniques. **1982** *Times Lit. Suppl.* 23 Apr. 465/3 He does give a studiable picture of how Los Angeles may have sleep-walked into this unassimilable truth.

†**'studial.** *Obs. rare*$^{-1}$. [? f. STUDY *v.* + -AL^1.] ? A state of perplexity or uncertainty.

a **1513** FABYAN *Chron.* VII. ccxli. (1811) 283 Wherwithall the duke was put to such a studyall & fere, that he was forsed to seke meanys of treaty & of peace.

studiant, -aunt, obs. forms of STUDENT^1.

studie, obs. form of STITHY, STUDY.

studied ('stʌdɪd), *ppl. a.* Also 7 **studdied.** [f. STUDY *v.* + -ED^1.]

1. Resulting from, or characterized by, deliberate effort or intention; produced or acquired by study, carefully contrived or excogitated; designed, premeditated; deliberate, intentional.

1606 SHAKS. *Ant. & Cl.* II. ii. 140 Pardon what I haue spoke, For 'tis a studied not a present thought, By duty ruminated. **1611** —— *Wint. T.* III. ii. 176 What studied torments (Tyrant) hast for me? **1639** S. DU VERGER tr. *Camus' Admir. Events* 259 Her studdied countenance, her pleasing speeches. **1671** MILTON *Samson* 658 Consolatories writ With studied argument. **1676** MARVELL *Mr. Smirke* 10 Then which the Anim-adverter could never have invented a more notorious, studied, and deliberate Falshood. **1709** STEELE *Tatler* No. 128 ¶4 The studied Airs of a Lady's Fan. **1769** ROBERTSON *Chas. V*, IX. III. 173 Expressed..in terms of studied ambiguity. **1848** ALB. SMITH *Chr. Tadpole* xlvii. 408 As he came near Christopher he..made a studied bow, and bade him good morning. *a* **1859** MACAULAY *Hist. Eng.* xxiii. V. 50 During several days the ill humour of the Lower House showed itself by a studied discourtesy. **1908** U. SINCLAIR *Money-Changers* ii. 28 The magnate's inner sanctum..was plain with an elaborate and studied plainness.

b. with *for. rare*$^{-1}$.

1748 RICHARDSON *Clarissa* (1811) IV. 352 Notwithstanding my studied-for politeness and complaisance for some days past.

2. Of a person: Learned, deeply read, skilled, practised, versed. Const. *in* (a subject). ? *Obs.*

1530 TINDALE *Answ. More* Wks. (1573) 247/1 The naturall man..be he..neuer so well sene in the law, neuer so sore studied in the Scripture,..yet hee cannot vnderstand the thynges of the spirite of God. **1596** SHAKS. *Merch. V.* II. ii. 205 Vse all the obseruance of ciuillitie Like one well studied in a sad ostent To please his Grandam. **1602** F. HERING *Anat.* A 3, A Skilfull, well studyed, and approoued Lawyer. *a* **1662** HEYLIN *Laud* (1668) 529 So well was he studied in the Art of Dying. **1683** J. ILLINGWORTH in *Thoresby Corr.* (1832) I. 43, I wish sometimes the son had collected Lives instead of the father, finding him a studied and accurate man. *a* **1687** PETTY *Polit. Anat. Irel.* (1691) 71 All English Money..is quite carried away out of Ireland, and such Money brought instead of it, as these studied Merchants do from time to time bring in for their Advantage upon the Common People, their Credulity and Ignorance. **1760–72** H. BROOKE *Fool of Qual.* (1809) I. 89 You are equally studied and practised in turning any thing into nothing. **1806** J. BERESFORD *Miseries Hum. Life* vii. §71 As far as he is yet studied in the bills of fare. **1810** W. WILSON *Hist. Dissent. Ch.* III. 59 Mr. Smith was a learned, pious and well studied Divine. **1901** *Munsey's Mag.* XXV. 732/2 He could talk freely and well, with the knowledge of a traveled and a studied man.

†**b.** Prepared by study or cogitation (*for* doing or *to* do something). *Obs. rare.*

1606 SHAKS. *Ant. & Cl.* II. vi. 48, I..am well studied for a liberall thanks, Which I do owe you. **1657–8** *Burton's Diary* (1828) II. 382, I am not studied to answer all that that gentleman has said, but I shall give it this answer.

Hence **'studiedly** *adv.*, **'studiedness**.

1656 W. MONTAGU *Accomplish'd Woman* 113 If gracefulnesse then be described by doing all things by Nature, and not by studiedness. **1672** *Mede's Wks.* (ed. 3) Life p. xxxix, They should not forget to preach and press Charity; and this not in a slight perfunctory manner, but Studiedly and Digestedly to give the People the true Nature of it. **1828** D'ISRAELI *Chas. I*, II. ix. 226 The reception of Bassompiere..was studiedly uncivil. **1876** CLARK RUSSELL *Is he the Man?* III. 75 He made way for me studiedly. **1881** MAHAFFY *Old Grk. Educ.* ix. 109 We need only here call attention to the intense studiedness of Greek eloquence.

†**studient**, *a. Obs. rare*$^{-1}$. [ad. OF. *estudiant*, pr. pple. of *estudier*: see STUDENT^1.] Meditative, thoughtful.

1387–8 T. USK *Test. Love* III. vi. (Skeat) 137 Me thinketh ..by thy studient lokes, thou wenest in these wordes me to contrarien from other sayinges here-toforn in other place.

studient(e, obs. forms of STUDENT^1.

studier ('stʌdɪə(r)). Also 4–5 studyer, 5 -yare, stodiar, -yar, -ier(e, -yer. [f. STUDY *v.*^{1} + -ER^1. Cf. OF. *estudieor, -eur*.]

†**1.** A person who is addicted to or engaged in study; a student. *Obs.*

c **1380** WYCLIF *Wks.* (1880) 380 A lytille soler, a bedde, a borde, a chaire, and a kandilstek, þe whiche ben acordynge to a studier or a contemplatyfe man. **1387** TREVISA *Higden* (Rolls) I. 13 Profitable to good studiers and meke [*non inutilem studiosis*]. *c* **1440** CAPGRAVE *Life St. Kath.* I. 350 Solitary lyff to stodyers is comfort. *a* **1466** GREGORY *Chron.* in *Hist. Coll. Cit. Lond.* (Camden) 133 Collegys of studyers, and othyr collegys of Holy Chyrche.

2. One who studies a specified subject. Const. *of*, †*in*. Now *rare* or *Obs.*

1593 Q. ELIZ. *Boeth.* I. pr. iv. 8 Wisdom studiers [L. *studiosi sapientiae*]. **1607** T. SPARKE *Brotherly Persw. Vnitie* 25 The most diligent studier and searcher of ancient writers. **1671** J. WEBSTER *Metallogr.* xii. 161, I..am a continual reader of and studier in the best Authors. **1678** *Phil. Trans.* XII. 965 The first Studiers of Natural Philosophy commonly so called, were the Greeks. **1793** *Monthly Rev.* XII. 197 To the studier of Tacitus, it is amusing to observe the contrivances of different translators to vary from each other. **1797** JANE AUSTEN *Pride & Prej.* ix, I did not know before..that you were a studier of character. It must be an amusing study. **1820** W. IRVING *Sketch Bk.* x. (1859) 66 James flourished nearly about the time of Chaucer and Gower, and was evidently an admirer and studier of their writings.

3. Const. †*for*, *of*. One who strives after or pursues (an object or end). Now *rare*.

1597 J. PAYNE *Royal Exch.* 19 Happie be..the studiers for Godlines, and the lovers of God. *c* **1611** CHAPMAN *Iliad* XIII. 292 And these..will serue to fill the hand Of Hectors selfe, that Priamist, that studier for blowes. **1651** FULLER *Abel Rediv., Pareus* 580 He was a great studyer and promoter of the Churches peace. **1710** SHAFTESB. *Charac.* II. ii. (1737) II. 248 The merest Studier of Pleasure,..even Epicurus himself. **1833** T. HOOK *Love & Pride, Snowdon* x. III. 111 Although not a devoted studier of effect,..he could not help feeling that he should look very ridiculous, if [etc.].

†'**studify**, *v. Obs. rare*$^{-1}$. [f. STUDY *sb.* or *v.* + -FY; cf. *argufy*.] *intr.* To study, *illiterate*.

1775 T. BRIDGES *Dutchman* II. ii. 28 She's very busy reading... Yes, Mynheer, she often studifies very hard.

studio ('stju:dɪəʊ). [a. It. *studio*: see STUDY *sb.*]

†**1.** *Fine Art.* = STUDY *sb.* 10. *Obs. rare*$^{-1}$.

1819 SHELLEY *Let. to Peacock* 25 Feb., The most remarkable is the original studio by Michael Angelo of the 'Day of Judgment'.

2. a. The work-room of a sculptor or painter; also that of a photographer.

1819 *Edin. Rev.* XXXII. 322 The greatest work which proceeded from his [Cimabue's] *studio*, was his scholar Giotto. **1820** T. S. HUGHES *Trav. Sicily* I. x. 282 We had seen some beautiful casts from different figures of this sculpture in the studio of Monsieur Fauvel. **1837** LOCKHART *Scott* IV. xi. 363 Chantrey requested that Scott would come and breakfast with him next morning before they recommenced operations in the studio. **1881** *Spons' Encycl. Industr. Arts* IV. 1536 The 'studio' pertains to professional photography... It is..a well-lighted apartment in close proximity to the dark room. **1897** WATTS-DUNTON *Aylwin* III. ix, In the studios of artists she was in request as a face model of extraordinary value.

b. *transf.* ? *Obs.*

1854 THACKERAY *Newcomes* v, I would as soon have thought..of volunteering to take an arm-chair in a dentist's studio, and have a tooth out, as of entering into that awful precinct.

c. *Cinematogr.* A room in which a cinematographic film is shot. Hence, a film-making complex including film studios and attendant offices and premises (also in *pl.*); the company which runs this. Cf. *film studio* s.v. FILM *sb.* 7c.

1911 C. N. BENNETT et al. *Handbk. Kinematogr.* xiii. 102 Covered-in studios provided with expansive glass roofs for daylight work..are hardly among the first flights of commercial Kinematographic enterprise. **1923** *Variety* 15 Nov. 18 (*heading*) Hollywood studios moving to less costly locations. **1928** *Morning Post* 20 Oct. 4/3 The 'dedication' of Fox's new 8,000,000-dollar Movietone Studio at Los Angeles. **1937** A. HUXLEY *Let.* 12 July (1969) 423 With regard to the handling of my work, I am prepared to authorize you to take up the matter with film studios. **1956** H. KURNITZ *Invasion of Privacy* iii. 26 The actor was undoubtedly a handsome youngster... Five studios were squabbling over him now. **1971** *Guardian* 2 Dec. 11/2 The studio, Paramount, was 'not happy with it' [*sc.* a film] and failed to promote it.

d. *Radio* and *Television.* In a broadcasting station, etc.: a room from which items are broadcast live or in which they are recorded for subsequent transmission; the premises housing such a studio or studios. Also *pl.*

1922 J. REITH *Diary* 29 Dec. (1975) ii. 129 Newcastle... Here I really began my BBC responsibility. Saw transmitting station and studio place. **1923** *Radio Times* 5 Oct. 38/3 'Romeo and Juliet' is being..broadcast from our own studio. **1938** *Encycl. Brit. Bk. of Year* 633/2 The apparatus will operate satisfactorily either in natural or artificial light, the technique used in the television studio being somewhat similar to that in a film studio. **1968** M. BRAGG *Without City Wall* xxviii. 255 The television studios ..were on the edge of town. **1972** *Daily Tel.* 6 Jan. 1/2 Mr. Wilson, Leader of the Opposition, visited a television studio yesterday morning to pre-record his contribution to the programme.

e. A room used for recording and editing music, etc. to be reproduced on a gramophone record or similar medium.

1928 [see *recording studio* s.v. RECORDING *vbl. sb.* 5]. **1932** *Daily Mirror* 21 Oct. 10/3 It is good watching a record being made in a gramophone studio. **1955** L. FEATHER *Encycl. Jazz* 341 The bands of Andy Kirk, Count Basie, Hot Lips Page and Eddie Durham, the last two being studio-assembled combinations. **1977** *Rolling Stone* 24 Mar. 55/4 Ten months devoted to Fleetwood Mac's album has left Buckingham spindly and studio wan.

f. = *studio flat*, sense 3b below. orig. *U.S.*

1942 D. POWELL *Time to be Born* (1943) v. 100 Amanda's furnished 'studio'..was..a one-room apartment. **1962** P. MOYES *Death on Agenda* vi. 94 [The flat] was what is known on the Continent as a studio—that is to say, a one-room bachelor apartment with its own tiny hallway, off which led a box-sized kitchen and a dwarf bathroom. **1977** I. SHAW *Beggarman, Thief* IV. i. 365 Home was a nasty little one-room studio near the university.

3. a. *attrib.*

1891 KIPLING *Light that Failed* xiii. (1900) 226 Somebody hammered at the studio door. **1894** DU MAURIER *Trilby* II. I. 120 He..found studio French a different language altogether from the formal and polite language he had been at such pains to acquire. **1894** *Outing* XXIV. 31/1 When it blows great guns and the rain comes down..there is plenty of studio work to do, and plenty of fine old lofts with improvised studio windows to do it in. **1908** A. M. HIND *Engraving & Etching* 175 Two other large etchings have generally been regarded by recent criticism as studio productions. **1922** [see sense 2d above]. **1944** L. MACNEICE *Christopher Columbus* 16 The radio dramatist must..be studio-conscious, remembering what results can.. be obtained. **1956** B. HOLIDAY *Lady sings Blues* (1973) iii. 35 Benny [Goodman] was a radio-studio musician who talked a lot then about having his own band one day. **1972** P. BLACK *Biggest Aspidistra* I. iii. 28 The studio announcer introduced the band and the place, and wished the nation good night.

b. Special Combs. (senses 2c, d) ***studio audience, manager***; **studio apartment** *U.S.* = *studio flat* below; **studio bed, couch**, a couch which converts into a bed; **studio flat**, a flat containing a spacious room with large windows, which is or resembles an artist's studio; more recently, a small one-roomed flat; **studio party**, an informal party held in an artist's studio; also, a social gathering at a film studio; **studio portrait**, a posed photograph, as taken in a photographer's studio; **studio potter**, a potter (freq. one of a small group) who works in a studio producing hand-thrown pottery; hence **studio pottery**; **studio theatre**, (an) experimental theatre.

1903 *Archit. Rec.* July 240 The most economical way of combining a good high studio with an economical disposition of space would be to make the studio apartment two-storied in the service and living portions, and only one-storied in the space devoted to the studio. **1929** *Washington Post* 1 Sept. 6/5 Studio Apartment $100. **1949** *Archit. Rec.* Nov. 125 At the foot of the San Jacinto mountains, this small group of studio apartments is keyed to the needs..of a specific class of tenant—artists who spend part of the year in Palm Springs. **1978** J. IRVING *World according to Garp* xix. 428 Roberta went to..Duncan's live-in studio... Duncan's studio-apartment. **1932** *B.B.C. Year Bk. 1933* 20 Comedians probably most need the stimulus of the crowded hall, for which the 'studio audience' is a poor substitute. **1977** B. PYM *Quartet in Autumn* x. 90 The radio offered a choice of comedy, with a braying studio audience. **1963** M. MCCARTHY *Group* vi. 118 Across the room, a big lumpy studio bed was covered with a black velveteen spread. **1931** *Sears, Roebuck Catal.* Spring 662 New 'Sun Bed' Latest Style Couch... This new type davenport-bed or studio couch. **1977** A. SCHOLEFIELD *Venom* I. 3 His bedroom..had been designed..as a bed-sitter..and the bed itself was a studio couch. **1934** A. HUXLEY *Let.* 13 Oct. (1969) 385 We are in London for the winter—having found a studio flat, miraculously large. **1970** K. GILES *Death in Church* ii. 31 He had what they call a studio flat—bed, gas fire and tiny kitchenette. **1937** R. CHANDLER in *Black Mask* Jan. 19/1 The call letters of the station revolved in neon letters... I.. got to see a Mr. Dave Marineau, studio manager... 'We get one in the radio column about every second month. We're a small station still.' **1980** S. BRETT *Dead Side of Mike* i. 13 'I'm sorry, I don't speak BBC. What's an SM?' 'Studio Manager. Knob-twiddler..tape-machine starter and what you will.' **1909** E. NESBIT *Daphne in Fitzroy St.* xvii. 275 'Meals in studios are always rather like picnics.'..'Oh, yes,' she said. 'I've been to lots of studio parties. They're great fun, aren't they?' **1931** R. H. HEATON *Perfect Hostess* 110 (*heading*) Miss Eighteen borrows the Attic for her first Studio Party for her young friends from the Slade. **1974** A. MORICE *Killing with Kindness* viii. 59, I had met her..at a studio party. **1938** M. ALLINGHAM *Fashion in Shrouds* xviii. 329 The story had made..headlines on the front pages, most of which also carried studio portraits of Miss Adamson. **1978** F. OLBRICH *Desouza pays Price* xv. 93 A signed studio portrait of herself taken with a soft-focus lens. **1940** B. LEACH *Potter's Bk.* iii. 43 A potter's prime need is good clay. Whether he be industrial, peasant or studio potter the raw material of which pots are made is of fundamental importance. **1979** *China Now* Mar./Apr. 9/1 We saw the sort of simple country pots that we as studio potters (people actively engaged in making pots ourselves —by hand in a machine age) so much admire. **1959** J. & D. V. BAKER *Pottery Bk.* III. x. 59 At a studio pottery (generally a small pottery with perhaps half a dozen partners or employees..) machinery plays the least possible part. **1980** *Times* 11 Dec. 16/6 At Sotheby's Belgravia studio pottery was also making high prices. **1933** P. GODFREY *Back-Stage* xiii. 160 The studio or art theatre exists..to prevent dramatic art from being wiped out by the commercially minded. **1965** *Listener* 20 May 738/1 What we most lack today..is the type of experimental studio-theatre that flourished in Stanislavsky's lifetime. **1971** J. ELSOM *Theatre outside London* x. 172 There will be a high fly-tower, a studio theatre, fine foyers, a restaurant and good backstage facilities.

‖**studiolo** (studi'olo). [It., lit. 'small study'.] A private study hung with paintings.

1926 J. E. JEFFERY tr. *R. de la Sizeranne's Celebrities Ital. Renaissance* 180 She [*sc.* Isabella d'Este] heard that the decorations ordered for her *studiolo* at Mantua were not progressing, for Luca Liombeni, the painter, was a dawdler. **1958** *Times* 14 Nov. 16/4 Later developments, such as the '*Studiolo*' group, Pietro Candido, Salviati, and Tibaldi, are not represented. **1968** *N.Y. City* (Michelin Tire Corp.) 57 The major attraction of the Italian section is the 'studiolo', or private study, from the Ducal Palace at Gubbio (Umbria). **1978** M. GIROUARD *Life in Eng. Country House* vi. 166 The books..in the *trompe l'œil* paintings in the *studiolo* of Federigo Montefeltro at Urbino.

†**studi'osity.** *Obs. rare*$^{-1}$. [ad. F. *studiosité*, ad. med.L. *studiōsitās*, f. L. *studiōsus*: see next and -ITY.] The quality of being studious.

1578 FLORIO *1st Fruites* 72b, The daughters of Temperance .. are .. Shame, Honestie, .. Modestie, Studiositie, [etc.].

studious ('stju:dɪəs), *a.* Also 4, 6 studyouse, studiouse, 5–7 studyous, (6 stodious, studeous, studuous). [ad. L. *studiōs-us*, f. *studium*: see STUDY *sb.* and -OUS. Cf. OF. *estudieus*, mod.F. *studieux*, It. *studioso*, Sp., Pg. *estudioso*.]

1. Assiduous in study; devoted to the acquisition of learning. †Const. *in*, *of*.

1382 WYCLIF *2 Macc.* ii. 26 Sothely we curiden..that it were delectacioun, or lykyng, of ynwitt to men willynge for to reede; forsothe the studyouse [1388 to studiouse men], that thei miȝten liȝtlyer bytake to mynde; forsothe to alle men reedyng profit be ȝouen. **1390** GOWER *Conf.* III. 110 Under him [Mercury] who that bore is, In boke he schal be studious. *c* **1400** *Cato's Morals* 236 in *Cursor M.* App. IV. 1672 Heuy herted men, and stille studious men, vmbe-þing þe to fle. **1460** CAPGRAVE *Chron.* (Rolls) 6 The cause of this dyversite is assigned be studious men, that Moises counted nowt that hundred ȝere in whech Adam ded his penauns. **1528** MORE *Dyalogue* I. i. (1529) 3b/2 Master Tindall..was ..a man of ryght good lyuynge, studyouse & well lerned in scrypture. **1553** T. WILSON (*title*) The Art of Rhetorique, for the vse of all suche as are studious of Eloquence. **1588** KYD *Househ. Philos.* Wks. (1901) 243 It is well seene you are studious of Varro, not of Virgil onely. **1638** JUNIUS *Paint. Ancients* 29 Imitation was able to bring a studious Novice to such grounds of Art as had been put in practice by them that were before him. **1662** STILLINGFL. *Orig. Sacr.* II. ii. §6 For these..of a long time had been very studious of Geometry, as the Phœnicians of Arithmetick, and the Chaldæans of Astronomy. **1667** MILTON *P.L.* IX. 42 Mee of these Nor skilld nor studious, higher Argument Remaines. **1727** DE FOE *Syst. Magic* I. i. (1840) 36 The magicians being a race of honest studious Men, searching after wisdom. **1747** WESLEY *Prim. Physick* (1762) p. xix, For Studious Persons, about eight ounces of Animal Food..is sufficient. **1807** WORDSW. *White Doe* I. 295 And choice of studious friends had he Of Bolton's dear fraternity. **1827** CARLYLE *Misc. Ess., State Ger. Lit.* (1840) I. 81 These questions we must leave candid and studious inquirers to answer for themselves. **1847** EMERSON *Repr. Men, Montaigne* Wks. (Bohn) I. 338 The studious class are their own victims: they are thin and pale [etc.].

Comb. **1837** DICKENS *Pickw.* xxxviii, A studious-looking young gentleman in green spectacles.

absol. **1382** [see above]. **1565** ALLEN *Def. Purgatory* II. xii. 231b, But I would in this one example of praying for the deade, geue the studious a taste of all suche waies, as [etc.]. **1613** PURCHAS *Pilgrimage* III. xv. (1614) 319 Let the studious of these things search them in their proper Authors. **1693** DRYDEN *Persius* VI. Notes init., All the Studious, and particularly the Poets,..began to set themselves on Work. **1747** WESLEY *Prim. Physick* (1762) p. xxi, The Studious ought to have stated times for Exercise. **1783** J. C. LETTSOM *Fotheringill's Wks.* I. 103 To the studious therefore..I would recommend [etc.].

b. Of the nature of, pertaining to, or concerned with learning or study. †*studious consumption*: consumption induced by undue application to study.

1526 *Pilgr. Perf.* (W. de W. 1531) 233 Meditacyon is a profounde or studyous cogitacyon about ony certeyn thynge. **1590** SPENSER *F.Q.* II. iii. 40 Abroad in armes, at home in studious kind Who seekes with painfull toile, shall honor soonest find. **1644** MILTON *Areop.* 31 Pens and heads ..sitting by their studious lamps, musing, searching, revolving new notions and idea's. **1666** G. HARVEY *Morbus Angl.* x. (1672) 28 Of a Studious Consumption. **1667** MILTON *P.L.* VIII. 40 So spake our Sire, and by his count'nance seemd Entring on studious thoughts abstruse. **1695** LUTTRELL *Brief Rel.* (1857) III. 428 His physitians advise him to forbear all studious businesse because of a rheum fallen in his eye. **1816** SHELLEY *Hymn Intell. Beauty* 66 They have in visioned bowers Of studious zeal or love's delight Out-watched with me the envious night. **1832**

BREWSTER *Nat. Magic* iii. 50 With persons of studious habits, who are much occupied with the operations of their own minds, the mental pictures are much more distinct. **1844** MRS. BROWNING *Lost Bower* lx, Studious health and merry leisure.

c. Of a place: Devoted to or suited to study.

1591 SHAKS. *Two Gent.* I. iii. 10 Some to the warres, to try their fortune there;.. Some, to the studious Vniuersities. **1605–47** T. HABINGTON *Surv. Worcestershire* (1894) I. II. 238 The society of the learned Seriants and studyous Innes of Court and Chancery. **1632** MILTON *Penseroso* 156 But let my due feet never fail, To walk the studious Cloysters pale. **1671** —— *P.R.* IV. 243 Studious walks and shades. *a* **1806** H. K. WHITE *Time* 86 When the pale ray Of star-light penetrates the studious gloom. **1853** M. ARNOLD *Scholar Gipsy* xiv, And the grave Glanvil did the tale inscribe That thou wert wander'd from the studious walls To learn strange arts.

2. Giving careful attention; intent on a purpose or object, heedful, solicitous.

a. with agent-n.

c **1450** tr. *De Imitatione* II. ix. 50 The very trewe lover of crist and studyous folwer of vertu. **1599** B. JONSON *Cynthia's Rev.* III. iv, It is the pride of Arete to grace Her studious louers. **1655** STANLEY *Hist. Philos.* III. *Xen.* viii. (1687) 116/1 Xenophon was a studious Æmulatour of Herodotus, both in words and language. *a* **1700** EVELYN *Diary* init., My Father.. was a studious decliner of honours and titles.

b. const. *to* with inf., *of*, †*for* (rare), †*in*.

1526 TINDALE *Titus* iii. 8, I wolde thou shuldest certifie that they which beleve God, myght be stodious to go forwarde in goode workes. **1530** PALSGR. 64 In the often redyng of whiche boke if the lernar be studious. **1553** EDEN *Treat. New Ind.* Ded. (Arb.) 6 You haue bene euer studious for the commoditie of your countrey. **1555** —— *Decades* (Arb.) 80 The Spanyardes.. were more studious of sedition and newes, then desyrous of peace and quietnesse. **1576** FLEMING *Panopl. Epist.* 44 He was very circumspect and studious in his masters businesse. **1601** R. JOHNSON *Kingd. & Commw.* (1603) 90 The cittizens are more studious to build for vse, then for pompe. **1625** MASSINGER *New Way* I. i, You haue well aduis'd me. But.. you that are so studious Of my affaires, wholly neglect your owne. **1667** MILTON *P.L.* XI. 609 Studious they appere Of arts that polish Life. **1667** PEPYS *Diary* 20 Aug., I find I must provide some things to offer that I may be found studious to lessen the King's charge. **1697** DRYDEN *Virg. Georg.* IV. 258 Studious of Honey, each in his Degree, The youthful Swain, the grave experienc'd Bee. **1701** W. WOTTON *Hist. Rome* 23 He was studious of avoiding Bustle and Stir. **1725** POPE *Odyss.* II. 117 The work she plied; but studious of delay, By night revers'd the labours of the day. **1755** YOUNG *Centaur* vi. Wks. 1757 IV. 265 Though studious to do it justice, I have wronged my theme. **1779** *Mirror* No. 58 Nor was he less studious in forming her taste for company than for books. **1810** CRABBE *Borough* viii. 154 All he had suffer'd, every former grief, Made those around more studious in relief. **1850** MERIVALE *Rom. Emp.* (1865) I. ix. 370 Crassus was eminently studious of outward decorum. **1852** BLACKIE *Study Lang.* 35 Be studious to compare the idiom of one language with that of another. **1866** CARLYLE *Inaug. Addr.* 173 Kings.. who were anxious about the culture of their populations, and nobly studious of their best benefit.

c. Characterized by or exhibiting careful attention.

1532 TINDALE *Expos. Matt. v–vii.* (? 1550) C j b, The purenesse of the hertes is the consentinge and studyous purpose to kepe the law of God. **1560** DAUS tr. *Sleidane's Comm.* 171 b, He admonyshed them that they shulde acknowledge his studious desyre. *c* **1590** *Sir T. More* (Malone Soc.) 553 My studious thoughts shall tend the citties good. **1591** SHAKS. *1 Hen. VI*, II. v. 97 Thou art my Heire; the rest, I wish thee gather: But yet be wary in thy studious care. **1667** *Decay Chr. Piety* i. §11. 208 Those bodies, who by studious effeminacies and softness have superadded an artificial tenderness to the natural. *a* **1718** PRIOR *Henry & Emma* 129 With dutiful Respect, and studious Fear, Lest any careless Sound offend her Ear. **1798** SOPHIA LEE *Canterb. T., Young Lady's T.* II. 207 Both with tender, studious care promoted her every wish. **1879** FARRAR *St. Paul* I. 310 In carrying out his policy Agrippa paid studious court to the Jews. **1884** *Law Times* 24 May LXXVII. 62/1 Mr. Haynes has avoided monotony and intricacy of style with the most studious care.

d. Planned with care; studied, deliberate.

1750 JOHNSON *Rambler* No. 77 ¶14 For the frigid villany of studious lewdness, for the calm malignity of labored impiety, what apology can be invented? **1821** SCOTT *Kenilw.* vi, Observe.. the studious mystery with which the brightest jewel that England possesses is secluded from the admiring gaze. **1913** SIR F. POLLOCK *Revised Rep.* CXL. Introd. 6 The dissent [of two judges] is indicated with seemingly studious obscurity.

studiously ('stju:dɪəslɪ), *adv.* [f. prec. + -LY².]

1. With studied attention or care; carefully, solicitously, diligently.

a **1349** *Hampole's Wks.* (1895) I. 103 Graunte me, swete ladi, to haue & to holde þis passioun in mynde as hertili & as studiousli in al my lijf, as þou. **1408** tr. *Vegetius' Art War* (MS. Digby 233) 203 b/1 Thei that moost studiousliche haue ylerned of dedees of armes þei sei þat many mo perils fallen. *c* **1425** *St. Mary of Oignies* I. xi. in *Anglia* VIII. 147 Hir cloþes were in a mene, for desyred filthes & studiously soghte clennesse plesyd hir neuere. *c* **1450** *Myrr. Our Ladye* 21 All.. ar bydden.. to say or singe the seruyce of these vii houres studyously and deuoutly. **1561** T. NORTON tr. *Calvin's Inst.* I. ix. 20 b, We ought right studiously to apply the redyng & hearyng of the scripture. **1591** SHAKS. *1 Hen. VI*, III. i. 2 Com'st thou with deepe premeditated Lines? With written Pamphlets, studiously deuis'd? **1639** N. N. tr. *Du Bosq's Compl. Woman* II. 59 These Harlots sometimes seek more studiously the outward shewes of vertue. **1697** DRYDEN *Æneis* VII. 249 Sabinus,.. On a short Pruning-hook his Head reclines: And studiously surveys his gen'rous Wines. **1826** *Art of Brewing* (ed. 2) 99 Be at all times studiously attentive to flavour and complexion. **1839** DE QUINCEY *Recoll. Lakes* Wks. 1862 II. 175 From growing interest in the author, every copy of the small impression had been studiously bought up.

b. With careful design or intent; deliberately.

1658 SIR T. BROWNE *Hydriot.* v. 29 While some have studied Monuments, others have studiously declined them. **1694** S. JOHNSON *Notes on Pastoral Let.* I. 90 Men have studiously forgot it, and discharged their Memory of it. **1741** MIDDLETON *Cicero* II. x. 410 How studiously he had avoided every step. **1781** GIBBON *Decl. & F.* xix. (1787) II. 134 The troops, whose station lay along the public road, were studiously removed on his approach. **1838** W. C. HARRIS *Narr. Exped. S. Afr.* 19 He.. studiously absented himself from the house. **1856** FROUDE *Hist. Eng.* vi. (1858) II. 5 The language of this act was studiously guarded. **1884** *Manch. Exam.* 16 May 4/7 If he had studiously endeavoured to be unjust he could not have succeeded more completely. **1886** G. ALLEN *Darwin* i. 8 Buffon was careful to put his conjectural conclusions in a studiously guarded.. form.

c. qualifying an adj.

1856 FROUDE *Hist. Eng.* v. (1858) I. 400 To the English agents he had been studiously cold. **1862** WHYTE MELVILLE *Queen's Maries* II. 202 Maxwell by a studiously quiet.. demeanour, contrived to throw his gaoler completely off his guard. **1898** EARL SELBORNE *Mem.* I. II. xi. 229 Its tone was studiously respectful towards the United States; no pains were spared to avoid the use of any language which could wound [etc.].

2. With careful attention to learning or books; as a student.

a **1626** BACON *Elem. Com. Laws* (1630) (title-p.), Explicated for the more facile Introduction of such as are studiously addicted to that noble Profession. **1650** in *4th Rep. Hist. MSS. Comm.* 455/2 Wee.. doe certify that John Petty.. hath piously, soberly, and studiously demeaned himselfe in the same Colledge.

studiousness ('stju:dɪəsnɪs). [f. STUDIOUS *a.* + -NESS.] The state or quality of being studious.

1. Diligence in the pursuit of knowledge or learning; close application to study.

1530 PALSGR. 277/2 Studyousnesse, *studiosité*. **1551** T. WILSON *Logic* Ep. Ded. A v b, That all men.. maie be the more prouoked to folowe the examples of your Maiestie aswell in studiousnesse & desier of knowlege, as also in the exercise of all vertue. **1627** HAKEWELL *Apol.* I. III. §4. 33 Men are.. addicted.. sometimes to studiousnesse & learning, sometimes to ease and ignorance. **1718** HICKES & NELSON *J. Kettlewell* III. lii. 319 Those that knew him there have testified for Studiousness. **1755** JOHNSON, *Studiousness*, addiction to study. **1796** MME. D'ARBLAY *Camilla* I. 232 Though abstracted from outward objects, his studiousness was not of a solemn cast. **1838** DICKENS *Nich. Nick.* xix, The book fell from her hand. Lounging upon an ottoman close beside her was Sir Mulberry Hawk... 'What a delightful studiousness!' said this accomplished gentleman. *a* **1901** W. BRIGHT *Age of Fathers* xxix. (1903) II. 56 Ammonius.. was famed for his humility and self-discipline and also for his studiousness.

2. Careful attention or observance.

1628 WITHER *Brit. Rememb.* vi. 1173 Their Exercises were.. in studiousnesse Of piety, and of the Sciences, Which we terme liberall. *c* **1645** HOWELL *Lett.* (1650) II. lix. 87 In the interim I crave a candid interpretation of what is passed, and of my studiousnes in executing your Lordships Injunctions. **1670** EACHARD *Cont. Clergy* 39 They do it.. out of simple phantastick glory, and a great studiousness of being wonder'd at. **1713** *Lond. Gaz.* No. 5119/9 Your Studiousness of Your Peoples Goodness.

Studite ('stju:daɪt). [ad. med.L. *Studīta* (Eccl. Gr. *Στουδίτης*), f. *Studi-um* (Eccl. Gr. *Στουδιόν*), said to be named from its founder *Studius* (*Στουδιός*): see -ITE.] A monk of the order of Acœmeti ('the sleepless') established in the 5th cent. at the monastery of the Studium at Constantinople. Also *attrib.* and as adj.

1693 *D'Emilianne's Hist. Monast. Orders* 21 Of the Order of the Acæmetes or Studites. *Ibid.*, They were likewise called Studites, from one Studius, who founded for them, at Constantinople, the Monastery of St. John the Baptist. **1906** W. H. HUTTON *Ch. & Barbarians* xiv. 162 The age of the Iconoclast was the golden age of the Studite monks. *Ibid.* 163 For a while after his death there is silence over the history of the Studites. **1913** W. K. L. CLARKE *St. Basil* viii. 135 The monasteries were not all Studite, even after Theodore's influence had spread far and wide.

‖**studium** ('stju:dɪəm). *Hist.* [late L. (4th.-cent.) use of L. *studium* STUDY *sb.*] = STUDY *sb.* 9. Also, = next.

1610 HOLLAND *Camden's Brit.* I. 379 Those schooles of learning which wee call.. Universities, that age termed *Studia* that is, Studies. **1673** J. RAY *Observations Journey Low-Countries* 342 The *Studium*, called the *Sapienza*, where are the public Schools [in Siena]. **1834** [see next]. **1902** *Encycl. Brit.* XXXIII. 602/1 Immediately after 1168 allusions to Oxford as a *studium* and a *studium generale* begin to multiply. **1936** *Times Lit. Suppl.* 2 May 361/2 Out of such enterprises developed the medieval university. It grew and was not made. Later, of course, there was deliberate creation: there was the *studium* at Naples, brought into being by Frederick II. **1961** P. KIBRE *Scholarly Privileges Middle Ages* ii. 19 The measure requiring the rectors.. to take the oath that they would not seek the removal of the studium from the city [of Bologna] was retained.

‖**studium generale** ('stju:dɪəm dʒɛnɛ'reɪlɪ, -'ɑ:lɪ). *Hist.* Pl. **studia generalia** (-'eɪlɪə, -'ɑ:lɪə). [med.L.: f. as prec. + *generāle*, neut. sing. of *generālis* GENERAL *a.*] A medieval university which did not only receive scholars from its own locality (an earlier equivalent of the *universitas* UNIVERSITY); = *general study* s.v. STUDY *sb.* 9.

1834 *Edin. Rev.* Oct. 215 The oldest word for an unexclusive institution of higher education, was *studium*, and *studium generale*—terms employed in the twelfth and thirteenth centuries, and retained in those which followed. **1895** H. RASHDALL *Univ. Europe Middle Ages* I. 9 A Studium Generale meant a School of general resort, but in its origin the expression was a wholly popular and extra-legal one. *Ibid.* 10 In the latter half of the Thirteenth Century this unrestricted liberty of founding Studia Generalia gradually ceased. **1928** *Daily Tel.* 10 July 12/4 Where the liberal Arts and Sciences of a complete Studium Generale may be cultivated and practised. **1966** H. WIERUSZOWSKI *Medieval Univ.* I. i. 16 The term *studium generale* was used for schools of higher learning until late in the fifteenth century... Gradually.. the term 'university' replaced the word *studium*.

stud-mare. Also 1 stódmyre, 3–4 stod mere, 4 stode-mere, 5 studmer, stude mere, 6–7 *Sc.* stuid-meir, -mear. [f. STUD *sb.*² + MARE. Cf. ON. *stóðmerr.*] A mare kept for breeding purposes, a brood-mare. Cf. STUD *sb.*² 4 a.

a **1000** *Laws Ælfred* xvi, ȝif mon cu oððe stodmyran forstele, and folan oððe cealf ofadrife. *a* **1225** *Ancr. R.* 316 Ich am a ful stod mere. **1404** *Durham Acc. Rolls* (Surtees) 399, 1 studmer cum pullo. **1547** BOORDE *Introd. Knowl.* 147 Great studmares we bryng vp in Flaunders. **1594** *Reg. Mag. Sig. Scot.* 34 *note*, Pasturage of stuid-meiris, profits of each in foill 20 merks. **1634** *Ibid.* 43/1 Cum pastura 18 animalium et unius lie stuid-meir. **1709** *Ir. Act 8 Anne* c. 3 §34 Every papist or reputed papist may keep such stud-mares and stallions.

b. as an insulting epithet for a woman.

c **1440** *York Myst.* xxiv. 13 A! ffalse stodmere and stynkand stroye.

'**stud-sail.** [Of obscure etymology: see STUDDING-SAIL.] = STUDDING-SAIL.

18.. *Falconer's Shipwr.* I. 732 (1836) Now swelling stud-sails [1762, 1789, 1792 stu'n-sails] on each side extend. **1851** *B'ham. & Midl. Gardeners' Mag.* Oct. 192 With only a flying stud sail of green boughs at the end of it. **1857** *Merc. Marine Mag.* (1858) V. 9 In stud-sails and all small sails.

studuous, obs. form of STUDIOUS *a.*

study ('stʌdɪ), *sb.* Forms: 3–7 studie, 4–7 studye, 4 studi, 4–6 stude, 4–5 stodie, stody, 4–6 stodye, 5 stode, 6 studdi(e, (stiddie), 6–7 studdy, (6 studee), 4– study. [a. OF. *estudie* masc. (later *estuide*, *estude* masc. and fem., mod.F. *étude* fem.) = Pr. *estudi-s*, *estuzi-s*, Sp. *estudio*, Pg. *estudo*, It. *studio*, ad. L. *studium*, zeal, affection, painstaking, study, related to *studēre* to be zealous, seek to be helpful, apply oneself, study.

The etymology of the L. word is obscure: for conjectures see Walde.]

†**1.** In certain senses of L. *studium* (chiefly in translations from Latin): Affection, friendliness, devotion to another's welfare; partisan sympathy; desire, inclination; pleasure or interest felt in something. *Obs.*

c **1374** CHAUCER *Boeth.* IV. pr. ii (1868) 113 Al þe entencioun of þe wil of mankynde whiche þat is lad by diueise studies hastiþ to comen to blisfulnesse. **1483** CAXTON *Golden Leg.* 275/1 He had neuer studye in newe fabrykes ne buyldynges. **1537** tr. *Latimer's Serm. Convoc* B vj b, Therfore brothern, gather you, the disposition and study of the children, by the disposition and studye of the fathers. **1548–9** *Bk. Com. Prayer, Ordering of Priests*, Laying aside the study of the world and the fleshe. **1560** DAUS tr. *Sleidane's Comm.* Pref. A iij, What time the Princes electours chose this manne Emperour,.. the self same time Luther being prouoked came forthe to reason the matter, and disputed openly with Eckius at Lipsia, and than fell men to theyr study on ether side. **1561** tr. *Calvin's 4 Serm. Idol.* i. B ij b, To do all thing other wise then he [God] will, and cleane to be void of the studye and dutye which we owne vnto him. *a* **1619** FOTHERBY *Atheom.* I. x. §4. (1622) 106 Diuers of them, vpon vaine glory, or vpon studie of singularity,.. haue outwardly professed.. that There is no God. **1663** PATRICK *Parab. Pilgrim* xxx. (1687) 369 Pride and study to be admired in the World proclaim thee to us more than all that we see beside. **1697** DRYDEN *Virg. Georg.* III. 285 If to the Warlike Steed thy Studies bend, Or for the Prize in Chariots to contend.

†**2. a.** An employment, occupation, pursuit. *Obs.*

c **1374** CHAUCER *Boeth.* III. pr. ii. (1868) 64 Alle þe cures quod she of mortal folk whiche þat trauaylen hem in many manere studies gon certys by diuerse weies. **1484** CAXTON *Fable of Poge* iv, The studye of the huntynge and hawkynge is a slouful cure. *c* **1610** *Women Saints* 81 The diuell enuying hire these her vertuous studies, thought to supplant her.

†**b.** ? Ostensible function or character. *Obs.*

c **1380** WYCLIF *Wks.* (1880) 98 Prelatis also entren vnder colour & studie of cristis apostlis & lyuen & teche contrariously to hem.

†**3. a.** A state of mental perplexity or anxious thought. Sometimes with indirect question: Doubt *whether*, etc. *Obs.*

c **1290** *Beket* 1187 in *S.E. Leg.* 140 In gret studie he was i-brouȝt; He rounede in is wiues ere and tolde hire al is þouȝt. **1338** R. BRUNNE *Chron.* (1725) 58 Whan Edward perceyued, his herte was in studie, How þat werre bigan on him so sodanly. *c* **1450** *Mirk's Festial* 37 Þen stode þe Emperour yn full gret stude. *c* **1450** CAPGRAVE *St. Aug.* xi. 16 Fluctuacion calle we her whan a man is broute fro an euel entent, and ȝet þe same man stand in study wheithir he schal to þe good wey or nowt. *c* **1485** *Digby Myst.* (1882) III. 488 From stodyys and hevynes it woll yow relyff. *a* **1547** SURREY *Poems*, '*Laid in my quiet bed*', Laid in my quyett bedd, in study as I weare, I saw within my troubled hed, a heape of thoughtes appeare. **1582** N. LICHEFIELD tr. *Castanheda's Conq. E. Ind.* I. xxii. 57 Being therefore now in a studie what was best to be done. **1590** H. R. *Defiance to Fortune* H 3, Whome he found in a great studie, as one (as it might seeme) careful of that she had vndertaken. **1625** K. LONG tr. *Barclay's Argenis* IV. viii. 262

While the Mariners stand in a study, and sticke betweene two dangers, the Gallies which were sent out had enclosed them. **1689** R. MEEKE *Diary* 30 Nov. (1874) 18, I was at first in a study what to do, at last I promised.

b. A state of reverie or abstraction. *Obs.* exc. in BROWN STUDY.

13.. *Gaw. & Gr. Knt.* 2369 þat oþer stif mon in study stod a gret whyle. **1470–85** MALORY *Arthur* VIII. xxxi. 320 He was in suche a study he herd not what Gouernayle said. **1535** STEWART *Cron. Scot.* (Rolls) I. 554 Carthlyntus than into ane studie stude; Quhen that wes said spak nother ill no gude. **1582** STANYHURST *Æneis* IV. (Arb.) 119 In tears salt blubbring, in musing stiddye remayning, Shee fel on her mattresse. **16..** *Heir of Lin* 61 in *Percy Fol. MS.* I. 177 Still in a study there as he stood, he vnbethought him of [a] bill ..which his father had left with him. **1829** BROCKETT *N.C. Gloss* (ed. 2), *Study*, astonishment, amazement.

4. a. Thought or meditation directed to the accomplishment of a purpose; studied or deliberate effort or contrivance; also, the object or aim of (a person's) solicitous endeavour, one's 'concern'.

1390 GOWER *Conf.* II. 230 And he, which hadde noght foryete Of that belongeth to a clerk, His studie sette upon this werk. *c* **1430** LYDG. *Min. Poems* (Percy Soc.) 218 Lusty hertys in gladnesse them delite, Set al ther study on occupacioun, In joye and myrthe. **1445** *Claudian* in *Anglia* XXVIII. 269 Bothe pore and riche labouryd righte sore encrese to gete with studye. **1526** *Pilgr. Perf.* (W. de W. 1531) 145 b, Whan we be gyuen with all our study and diligence to clennesse of vertue & purite of lyfe. **1529** *Supplic. to King* (E.E.T.S.) 24 There is no study, striffe, nor laboure agaynst synne, but through faithe. **1545** BALE *Myst. Iniq.* 17 His great hot stodye is also to sett vp purgatorye againe. **1585** T. WASHINGTON tr. *Nicholay's Voy.* II. vii. 37 b, All their pleasure and studie is to attire and set out themselues. **1589** *Pasquil's Ret.* C iv, Spyders..spynne with great studie an vnprofitable webbe, good for nothing but to catch Flyes. **1594** CHAPMAN *Shadow of Nt.* E j, Thy glorious temple..That was the studie of all Asia, Two hunderd twentie somners to erect. *a* **1637** B. JONSON *Sad Sheph.* I. iv, No sought reliefe By all our studies can procure his peace. *a* **1700** EVELYN *Diary* 25 Jan. 1645, That never to be sufficiently admired gallery painted in deepe relievo, the worke of 10 years study for a trifling reward. **1764** DODSLEY *Leasowes* in *Shenstone's Wks.* (1777) II. 288 Far from violating its natural beauties, Mr. Shenstone's only study was to give them their full effect. **1803** BROUGHAM *Colon. Policy* I. 51 The indolence natural to their character is here thrown off; the acquisition of a fortune is the study of all. **1827** SCOTT *Surg. Dau.* xii, It was his study to sooth this ambitious and crafty female by blandishments.

†**b.** *of one's own study*: of one's own composition. *Obs. rare.*

1603 STOW *Surv. Lond.* (1908) I. 167 And that done, he was to make a sermon of his owne studie.

5. a. Application of mind to the acquisition of learning; mental labour, reading and reflection directed to learning, literary composition, invention, or the like.

c **1300** *St. Edmund* 217 in *E.E.P.* (1862) 76 He ne for-ȝat ..nomore þis oreisoun, For no studie ne for no neode, ne for þoȝt of lessoun. *c* **1386** CHAUCER *Prol.* 303 Of studie took he mooste cure and moost heede. **1393** LANGL. *P. Pl.* C. XVI. 181 Lettrure and longe studie letteþ ful menye. *c* **1450** in Aungier *Hist. Isleworth* (1840) 278 If there be an inuentory ..of the bokes of the library and how they and other bokes of study be kepte and repayred. **1540–1** ELYOT *Image Gov.* Pref., Beeyng almost fatigate with the longe studie about the correctyng and ampliatyng of my Dictionarie. **1564** HARDING *Answ. Jewel's Challenge* 10 b, Let them take paines to trauaile in studie, and they shall fynde by good auncient witnes..that [etc.]. **1567** TURBERV. *Epit.* etc. 46 But I was chiefly bent to Poets famous Art, To them with all my deuor I my studie did conuert. **1581** ALLEN *Apol.* 21 b, The persons which first put them selues together in the Vniuersitie of Duay the yere 1568, yelding to Collegial forme of studie and discipline vnder one President. **1598** GRENEWEY *Tacitus, Ann.* v. ii. (1612) 119 Vitellius..vnder colour of vsing it in his studie, asking for a penknife, lightly prickt a veine; and ended his life. **1611** BIBLE *Eccles.* xii. 12 Of making many bookes there is no end, and much studie [*marg.* Or, reading] is a wearinesse of the flesh. **1663** BAYFIELD *Treat. De Morb. Capitis* 67 Sitting and holding his pen, with his eyes open, and looking upon his Book, you would have thought he had been hard at study, till he was by calling..found to want all sense and motion. *a* **1700** EVELYN *Diary* 27 Jan. 1689, He was as earnest at his play as at his study. *a* **1732** GAY *Fables, Pack-horse & Carrier* 41 Learning by study must be won, 'Twan ne'er entail'd from son to son. **1737** POPE *Hor. Epist.* II. ii. 117 The Man, who, stretch'd in Isis' calm retreat, To books and study gives sev'n years complete. **1784** COWPER *Tiroc.* 822 See great commanders making war a trade, Great lawyers, lawyers without study made. **1810** CRABBE *Borough* xx. 267 Study to him was pleasure and delight. **1839** BAILEY *Festus, Village Feast* (1889) 158 When night hath set her silver lamp on high, Then is the time for study.

personified. **1362** LANGL. *P. Pl.* A. XI. 1 Þenne hedde wit A wyf was hoten dam Studie. *a* **1586** SIDNEY *Astroph. & Stella* i. 10 Inuention, Nature's childe, fledde step-dame Studie's blowes.

†**b.** *at (his) study*: as a student at a university or college. *Obs.*

1508 *Reg. Privy Seal Scot.* I. 235/1 To pas to Sanct Andres grafe besyde Napillis, and thairefter to remane in Italie at his study for..vj ȝeris. **1554** *Cal. Anc. Rec. Dublin* (1889) 439 Thomas Fitz Symon..being at the universite at Oxford at stude to acquir lernyng. **1577–87** HOLINSHED *Chron.* III. 1165/1 The kings maiestie..gaue him monie yeerelie out of his coffers, to find him honorablie at studie. *a* **1700** EVELYN *Diary* July 1645, Being resolved to spend some moneths here at study, especialy physic and anatomie, of both of which there was now the most famous professors in Europe.

†**c.** Acquirements, learning. *Obs.*

c **1374** CHAUCER *Boeth.* I. pr. iv. (1868) 16 Haþ my studie and my konnyng deserued þus [L. *nostræne artes ita meruerunt*]?

d. A department of study; the cultivation of a particular branch of learning or science. Often in *collect. plural*, a person's work as a student.

1477 EARL RIVERS (Caxton) *Dictes* 16 Ypocras..was the first fynder of the art of phisike whiche he shewed and taught to his children... And commaunded that they shulde dwelle in the middel habitacion of grece in iii. Isles. And ypocras rested in the Ile of Thau. And in the ij. other Isles the studye was lost in his dayes. **1500–20** DUNBAR *Poems* lxv. 4 To speik of science, craft, or sapience,..Off euerie study, lair, or discipline. **1538** STARKEY *England* II. iii. 203 The ordur of studys in vnyuersytys must..be amendyd. **1591** SHAKS. *Two Gent.* I. i. 67 Thou Iulia thou hast metamorphis'd me: Made me neglect my Studies, loose my time. **1594** R. ASHLEY tr. *Loys le Roy* 24 The learning of the Athenians was lost in Athens; only remaining in that towne the school or house of studies. **1597** BACON *Ess., Studies* (Arb.) 6 Studies serue for pastimes, for ornaments and for abilities. **1677** JOHNSON in *Ray's Corr.* (1848) 128 In the meantime wishing you success in your studies, I rest, &c. **1748** H. WALPOLE *Let. to G. Montagu* 11 Aug., These Veres have thrown me into a deal of this old study. **1756–9** A. BUTLER *Lives of Saints, S. Peter Damian*, He gave a considerable time to sacred studies. **1788** MRS. HUGHES *Henry & Isabella* III. 5 Is she persuaded to apply to any particular study, such as music, painting, &c. because her father is fond of it? **1841** *Penny Cycl.* XXI. 175/1 He began his studies at the gymnasium of Coburg in 1638. **1864** TENNYSON *Aylmer's F.* 394 Back would he to his studies, make a name. **1874** BLACKIE *Self-Cult.* 30 So far from rushing hastily into merely professional studies, a young man should rather [etc.]. **1892** LADY F. VERNEY *Verney Mem.* I. 122 Ralph still going on with his studies at Oxford.

6. a. The action of studying (something specified or implied); mental effort in the acquisition *of* (some kind of learning); attentive reading *of* (a book, etc.), or careful examination or observation *of* (an object, a question, etc.). Phrase, *to make a study of*, to study, observe carefully.

c **1300** *St. Edmund* 276 in *E.E.P.* (1862) 78 O tyme he was in grete studie of his lessoun a nyȝt. **1340–70** *Alisaunder* 637 Many thinges of man myght hee showe, By studie of þe stones in what state hee were. **1526** *Pilgr. Perf.* (W. de W. 1531) 232 b, The seconde parte of contemplacyon is study or redynge of holy scripture. **1584** POWEL *Lloyd's Cambria* 33 Who..trauelled to Athens, and bestowed there manie yeeres in the studie of the Greeke, Hebrue and Chaldie toongs. **1668** E. HOPKINS *Serm., Vanity* (1685) 10 God hath composed two books, by the diligent study of which we may attain to the knowledge of Himself: the Book of the creatures, and the book of the Scriptures. **1704** NORRIS *Ideal World* II. xii. 486 The study of the sciences is a natural abstraction of the mind from the creature. **1845** PATTISON *Ess.* (1889) I. 27 The volume of the canons which had formed the object of his study the preceding night. **1859** RUSKIN *Two Paths* i. §18 The study, however, of the effect of art on the mind of nations is one rather for the historian than for us. **1884** HUNTER & WHYTE *My Ducats* xxv. (1885) 374 Even in the midst of his own troubles, Lynn found himself engaged in making a study of Gertrude. **1895** M. HEWLETT *Earthwork out of Tuscany* 24 Never a chapel of them but is worth study and a stiff neck.

b. *Theat.* The action of committing to memory one's part in a play. Hence, *to have* or *be a quick, slow*, etc. *study*, to be quick, slow, etc. in learning by heart; also *transf.* in general contexts.

1590 SHAKS. *Mids. N.* I. ii. 69 *Snug.* Haue you the Lions part written? pray you if be, giue it me, for I am slow of studie. **1761** FOOTE *Liar* III. Wks. 1799 I. 316, I have a short scene to give you in study. **1822** H. MACKENZIE *Life Home* 95 Mrs. Siddons told me she never found any *study* (which, in the technical language of the stage, means the getting verses by heart) so easy as that of *Douglas*. **1838** DICKENS *Nich. Nick.* xxiii, I've got a part of twelve lengths here, which I must be up in to-morrow night..; I'm a confounded quick study, that's one comfort. **1857** READE *Course of True Love, Art* 128 Having what is called a very quick study, she was soon mistress of the twenty or thirty lines. **1882** ASHTON *Soc. Life Q. Anne* xxv. II. 21 Powell..was..a careless study, with a bad memory. **1900** J. K. JEROME *Three Men on Bummel* i. 13 Muriel is master of six pieces already, as perhaps you know; and all the other children are quick studies. **1954** M. EWER *Heart Untouched* ix. 164 She had learnt something in these last few days. She was a quick study. **1974** P. DE VRIES *Glory of Hummingbird* xiii. 197 We'll brush him up. He's a quick study. He's not a Neanderthal.

7. a. That which is studied; the object of one's study. Chiefly with *possessive*.

1535 COVERDALE *Ps.* cxix. 99, I haue more vnderstondinge than all my teachers for thy testimonies are my studye. **1595** *Phrases Lat. Aldi Manutii* 12 *Ad Ciceronem me contuli*, I haue giuen my selfe to Cicero: Tully is my whole studie. **1709** POPE *Ess. Crit.* 124 Be Homer's works your study and delight, Read them by day, and meditate by night. **1734** —— *Ess. Man* II. 2 The proper study [1733 The only Science] of mankind is Man. **1780** *Mirror* No. 97 ¶9 This gentleman.. discovered himself to be eminently skilled in the science of law, the study, as he boasted, of his earlier years. **1859** *Habits of Gd. Society* xi. 306 The man who makes dining a study..must go farther in the improvements of the room than we yet have. **1878** STEDMAN *Oxford: Soc. & Intell. Life* 238 There are several other commentaries, but they will not be found profitable study.

b. Something worth studying, or that requires to be studied; an object presenting effects of colour (and the like) attractive to an artist. Hence applied to the face registering an expression of incredulity, etc. (*colloq.*).

1766 FORDYCE *Serm. Yng. Women* (1767) I. ii. 53 The male heart is a study. **1779** *Mirror* No. 45 ¶9 A painter, who wished to express indignation, contempt, and pity, blended together, could not have found a finer *study*. **1817** HAZLITT *Pol. Ess.* (1819) 214 It is 'a psychological curiosity'; a study of human infirmity. **1853** MRS. STOWE *Uncle Tom's C.* xi, The various hats, in fact, were quite a Shakspearian study. **1856** KANE *Arct. Expl.* I. v. 45 Both it and Northumberland ..afforded studies of color that would have rewarded an artist. **1859** *Habits of Gd. Society* iv. 160 As a work of art, a well-dressed woman is a study. **1886** C. M. YONGE *Chantry House* II. xiv. 136 Emily's countenance was a study. **1891** E. PEACOCK *N. Brendon* I. 275 Basil was a curious study for her. **1894** *Yellow Bk.* I. 192 The harpist, whose nose is a study in purples. **1964** C. CHAPLIN *My Autobiogr.* x. 156 You should have seen his face watching you, it was a study! **1973** *Press & Jrnl.* (Aberdeen) 3 Aug. 7/3 We stopped for lunch at a little rustic inn. Specialite de la maison—chicken and chips with frozen peas on the side. Archie's face was a study.

8. a. A room in a house or other building, furnished with books, and used for private study, reading, writing, or the like. Often applied to 'the private room or office of the master of a house, however it may be used' (*Cent. Dict.*).

In Public Schools (and other large schools), the private room for study and other occupations of one or more boys.

1303 R. BRUNNE *Handl. Synne* 4745 Next hys chaumbre, besyde hys stody, Hys harpers chaumbre was fast þerby. *c* **1386** CHAUCER *Frankl. T.* 479 But in his studie ther as hise bookes be They seten stille. *c* **1430** *Life St. Kath.* (Roxb.) 14 He..passed from chambre to chambre tyle he come yn to hir secreet study where no creature vsed to come bot hir self allone. **1463** *Bury Wills* (Camden) 33, I yeve and be qwethe to the seid Jone my nece a lityl grene coffre for kerchys, stondyng in my stodye. **1490** CAXTON *Eneydos* Prol. 1, I sittyng in my studye where as laye many dyuerse paunflettis and bookys. **1507–8** *Acc. Ld. High Treas. Scot.* IV. 100 Item to Johne Forman for ane lok to the Kingis latron that standis in the Kingis studee, iiij s. **1560** DAUS tr. *Sleidane's Comm.* 316 A noble man of Spaire..kepeth the whole house to himself, and going into his studie [L. *bibliothecam*], searcheth all thinges. **1601** SHAKS. *Jul. C.* II. i. 7 *Luc.* Call'd you my Lord? *Brut.* Get me a Tapor in my Study, Lucius. **1609** B. JONSON *Sil. Wom.* IV. v, Doe you obserue this gallerie?.. Here are a couple of studies, at each end one. *a* **1632** L. HUTTEN *Diss. Antiq. Oxf.* (Hearne 1720) 347 That Tower which standeth upon the Bridge..is commonly called by the name of Frier Bacon's Study. **1641** *Commons Remonstr.* in *Wks. Chas. I* (1662) II. 62 Some Members of both Houses had their studies and cabinets, yea their pockets, searched. **1654** WHITLOCK *Zootomia* 180 Those that have counting Houses forget those that have Studies. **1798** SOPHIA LEE *Canterb. T., Yng. Lady's T.* II. 448 Crosby fitted up a large and retired parlour as a study. **1857** HUGHES *Tom Brown* I. v, 'And shall I have a study like this, too?' said Tom. **1868** WALCOTT *Sacred Archæol.* 117 *Carol*..(2) an enclosed study or reading-place in a cloister, used by the scribes or ordinary monks and regular canons. **1880** PAYN *Confid. Agent* I. 39 Your uncle and I are going to have a pipe in the study. **1904** DOR. P. HUGHES *Life H. P. Hughes* x. 240 When they came to consult him in his study.

transf. **1800** BLOOMFIELD *Farmer's Boy, Spring* 32 The fields his study, Nature was his book.

†**b.** A room or cupboard containing books, etc.

1538 ELYOT *Dict.*, *Armarium*, a study where bokes are laide, or a drye larder. *a* **1700** B. E. *Dict. Cant. Crew, Study*, a Closet of Books. **1711** HENLEY tr. *Montfaucon's Trav. Italy* v. 86 Having begun here to give an Account of Private Studies, or Closets, we have thought fit in this Place to speak of that of Tarvisiano.

†**c.** The books contained in a 'study' (sense 8, 8 b); a student's collection of books, etc.; a private library. Often a *study of books*. *Obs.*

1667 ASHMOLE *Diary* (1774) 333, I bought Mr. John Bookers study of books, and gave 140*l.* for them. *a* **1672** WOOD *Life* (O.H.S.) II. 178 Foulis..left behind him a larg studie of books; which being afterwards to be sold, A. W. did ..make a catalogue of them. **1682** WHELER *Journ. Greece* I. 41 He is of Candia, hath a good Study of Manuscripts which he brought from thence, and is called Pappa Agapito. **1722** HEARNE *Collect.* (O.H.S.) VII. 373 The Rev^{d}. M^{r}. Thomas Foulkes of Xt. Ch. hath bought the Study of my Friend. **1736** *Lett. Lit. Men* (Camden) 367 It is said also he was forced to sell his Study of Books.

†**d.** The office or place of business of a professional man. (= F. *étude.*) *Obs.*

1574 *Coventry Leet Bk.* 817, I gave a deed to be ingrossed with speed, and yt must be done very secretly in a Close studdie or parlour & not in the open shopp. **1581** PETTIE *Guazzo's Civ. Conv.* II. (1586) 106 He went hastelie to the studie of a brother of his who was a Doctor. *Ibid.* III. 145 Being not long since in an Aduocates studie, I heard [etc.].

†**9.** A seat of learning. *general study, study general* (= med.L. *studium generale*), a university.

1387 TREVISA *Higden* (Rolls) I. 177 In þis lond was somtyme þe studie and þe scole of Pallas and Minerua. *c* **1420** HOCCLEVE *Min. Poems* 221 He wente vn-to the studie general. **1456** SIR G. HAYE *Law Arms* (S.T.S.) 222 Charlis Maygne..transportit the study out of Rome and brocht it to Paris,..[and] has gevin to the study of Paris sa mony notable privileges that clerkis suld joys thare. *a* **1466** GREGORY *Chron.* in *Hist. Coll. Cit. Lond.* (Camden) 133 Alle maner chyrchys, unyversyteys, and studyys generalle. *a* **1470** HARDING *Chron.* CX. i, Martin bishop of Rome, graunted to king Alurede To found & mak a study..And an vniuersitee for clerkes in to reade the whiche he made, at Oxenford. **1499** *Reg. Privy Seal Scot.* I. 51/1 To pas to the partis beȝond sey to Paris or uther studeis. **1535** STEWART *Cron. Scot.* (Rolls) III. 498 This famous studie [*sc.* St. Andrews] in that ȝeir began. **1538** STARKEY *England* II. iii. 203 Thys thyng in studys and vnyuersytys ys neclectyd and despysyd. **1599** W. BAKER (*title*) The Fearfull Fansies of the Florentine Couper. Written in Toscane, by Iohn Baptist Gelli, one of the free Studie of Florence. **1673** O. WALKER *Educ.* I. x. 120 Oxford and Paris (the two onely general Studies for a long time on this side the Alps).

10. a. An artistic production executed for the sake of acquiring skill or knowledge, or to serve as a preparation for future work; a careful preliminary sketch for a work of art, or (more usually) for some detail or portion of it; an artist's pictorial record of his observation of some object, incident, or effect, or of something that occurs to his mind, intended for his own guidance in his subsequent work. Also, occas., a drawing, painting, or piece of sculpture aiming to bring out the characteristics of the object represented, as they are revealed by especially careful observation.

1769 REYNOLDS *Disc. R. Acad.* ii. Wks. 1797 I. 29 What, therefore, I wish to impress upon you is, that whenever an opportunity offers, you paint your studies instead of drawing them. **1822** H. MACKENZIE *Life Home* 92 Of this piece [*sc.* Douglas] there are extant..more fragments and original sketches, or, as a painter would call them, *studies*, than of any other of Mr. Home's productions. **1857** RUSKIN *Pol. Econ. Art* ii. §90 He will make a study of a picture he likes, for his own use, in his own way; but he won't and can't copy. **1871** HAMERTON *Etcher's Handbk.* 59 These two things, the pen study for line, and the sepia study for values of light and dark, are sufficient if properly done, and enough done, to educate an etcher. **1874** R. TYRWHITT *Sketching Club* 48 By a study I mean, generally speaking, a finished drawing of some part of a picture. **1883** RUSKIN *Art of Eng.* 10 The study of cattle on a Highland moor in the evening, by Mr. Davis. **1884** *Sat. Rev.* 7 June 745/2 M. Guignard exhibits a clever study of a calf being fed. **1911** *Act 1 & 2 Geo. V*, c. 46 §2 (1) Any..sketch, plan, model, or study made him for the purpose of the work.

b. A discourse or literary composition devoted to the detailed consideration of some question, or the minute description of some object; a literary work executed as an exercise or as an experiment in some particular style or mode of treatment.

1866 CARLYLE *Remin.* (1881) II. 240 It was by her address and invention that I got my sooterkin of a 'study' improved out of its worst blotches. **1877** SWINBURNE *Note C. Bronte* 29 A study in that kind as soft and true as Rousseau's, as keen and true as Browning's. **1911** A. G. HOGG *Christ's Message* 133 Recall the thought to which the two first Studies of this week led up.

11. *Mus.* (See quot. 1883.)

1875 STAINER & BARRETT *Dict. Mus. Terms, Study*, a term applied to an exercise for the pianoforte or other instrument. **1883** F. TAYLOR in *Grove's Dict. Mus.* III. 746/2 *Studies*, the name given to a large class of musical compositions,..having..the cultivation of the powers of execution for their chief object. Studies have been written for nearly every instrument, but..it will be sufficient here to speak of Pianoforte Studies, which form the great majority of all those in existence.

12. *attrib.* and *Comb.*, as (sense 5) ***study-book, -club, -day, †desk, †house, -leave, tour; study-bearing, -racked, -worn***, adjs.; (sense 8) ***study-bedroom, -cap, -chair, -door, -fagging, -fire, -lamp, †man, -table, window; study-bred*** adj. Also **study boy**, in some schools, a boy who, as being in an upper form, has a share of a 'study' (sense 8); **study circle**, a group that meets regularly to discuss a particular topic of study; **study group** = prec.; freq. an investigative committee formed by a political, industrial, or other body for this purpose; **study-hall** [= F. *salle d'étude*], in Roman Catholic colleges, a large room in which the pupils prepare their lessons; **study-place**, (*a*) = sense 8; (*b*) = *study-hall*.

1670 EACHARD *Cont. Clergy* 25 If..instead of such either of inferiour parts, or a feeble constitution,..there were pick'd out those that were of a tolerable ingenuity, of a *study-bearing body, and..as hence there is nothing to hinder our universities from being full, so [etc.]. **1930** *Times Educ. Suppl.* 26 July 332/2 *Study-bedrooms for 108 inmates. **1978** J. I. M. STEWART *Full Term* i. 15 Schools that are a bit lavish with study-bedrooms for senior boys. **1610** BOLTON *Elem. Armories* 49 Fitt Armes, and *study-books for whom. **1858** W. G. TRERY (*title*) A Study Book of Civil and Mechanical Engineering. **1893** STEVENSON *Catriona* xxiv, I..purchased a study-book in law. **1899** KIPLING *Stalky* vi. 181 The four long form-rooms in which all below the rank of *study-boys worked. **1899** J. A. HOBSON *Ruskin* 220 An abortive brood of *study-bred theories and researches. **1832** S. WARREN *Diary Physic.* II. ii. 59 He was in a brown dressing gown, and *study cap. **1848** B. F. WESTCOTT in A. Westcott *Life* (1903) I. ii. 102 In my inventory they call it a *study-chair! **1886** G. ALLEN *Maimie's Sake* xvii, He sat..in a red velvet-cushioned study-chair. **1938** L. MACNEICE *I crossed Minch* vi. 84 They've no team spirit, they won't take part In our *study circles and community art. **1979** B. G. SKINNER *Robert Exon* iv. 31 Study circles, Chapter meetings. **1910** *Universe* 26 Aug. 8 Its columns have in the past led to the formation of various groups and *study-clubs. **1730** T. BOSTON *Acc. My Life* xii. (1908) 286 For about 3 weeks, as my *study-day came about, I found my self unfitted for it. **1549** CHALONER *Erasm. Praise Folly* Q ij b, As though I had priuely piked our Maister doctors cunning out of their *studi deskes. **1585** DANIEL tr. *P. Jovius' Disc. Imprese* G vij, Of whom he [*sc.* Erasmus] demaunded what posie were fit to be set on his *Studie doore. **1853** MRS. GASKELL *Ruth* xxx, His study-door was but a step from that which led into the street. **1857** HUGHES *Tom Brown* I. viii, He..chose them for his fags, and excused them from *study-fagging. **1817** SCOTT *Harold* Introd., I love my *study-fire to trim, And con right vacantly some idle tale. **1926** *Scribner's Mag.* Sept. 8/2 The Foundation is accumulating a body of literature on Positive Health, for the use of individuals and organized *study groups. **1948** *Ann. Reg. 1947* 223 Before the conference came to an end thirteen of the participating countries decided to create a 'study group' to examine the possibility of creating a general European Customs union. *a* **1974** R. CROSSMAN *Diaries* (1975) I. 75 The only thing I need really mention is the dinner held at Arnold Goodman's house for my Rent Bill study group. **1891** *Tablet* 12 Sept. 415 You will not get it all in the *study-halls and in the class-halls. **1499** *Promp. Parv.* 65/2 (Pynson) Cell or *stody hows, *cella*. **1883** F. M. CRAWFORD *Dr. Claudius* i, He struck a match and lit his *study-lamp. **1961** *Times* 12 Oct. 13/7 The huge expansion of universities has..made it more difficult for them [*sc.* members of staff] to take *study-leave. **1982** M. DUKE *Flashpoint* vi. 44 A spell of study-leave before you take on the new job. **1657** J. WATTS *Scribe, Pharisee* etc. 266 Passing our times in speculative notions and contemplations, as some onely *Study-men, and not Pulpit-men do. **1563** SHUTE *Grounds Archit.* 3 b, Your *study places, where you wold write, draw or deuise..ought to receiue their light from the northe. **1667** in *Cath. Rec. Soc. Publ.* III. 71 They satt to gether in the study place. *c* **1755** in B. Ward *Hist. St. Edmund's Coll.* (1893) 301 At two o'clock on School Days all go to ye Study Place. **1812** W. TENNANT *Auster F.* VI. xlvi, Thy *study-rack'd, perplexed brains. **1857** HUGHES *Tom Brown* I. viii, Selling even his school-books, candlestick, and *study table. **1912** *Hibbert Jrnl.* Oct. 121 The dullard will be more happy and useful at the plough-tail than at the study-table. **1937** *John o' London's Weekly* 7 May 209/2 A tin to keep my damp cake of soap from coming into contact with the bristles of my toothbrush during *studytours. **1977** *Jrnl. R. Soc. Arts* CXXV. 519/2 Approximately 90 former Bursary winners made study tours abroad. **1871** LOWELL (*title*) My *Study Windows. **1897** 'TIVOLI' (H. W. Bleackley) *Short Innings* xv. 221 Dick hoisted himself through the study-window. **1843** D. POLLOK in *Life R. Pollok* 333 He..was pale, thin and *study-worn.

study ('stʌdɪ), *v.* Pa. t. and pa. pple. studied. Forms: 3–7 studie, 4 stidie, stude, 4–6 stodie, -y, studye, 5 studdie, (stedye), 5–6 stodye, (6 pres. pple. stoding), 7–8 studdy, 4– study. See also ESTUDY. [ME. *studie*, a. OF. *estudier* (mod.F. *étudier*) = Pr. *estudiar* (semi-popular *estuziar*), Sp. *estudiar*, Pg. *estudar*, It. *studiare*, ad. med.L. *studiāre*, f. *studium* STUDY *sb.*

The verb has always been the usual rendering of L. *studēre* (see STUDY *sb.*), which has influenced the sense-development.]

I. Intransitive uses.

1. a. To apply the mind to the acquisition of learning, whether by means of books, observation, or experiment. †Const. *in, on, upon* (a book, a branch of learning). See also sense 1 d.

c **1300** *St. Edmund* 279 in *E.E.P.* (1862) 78 He lynede adoun vpon his boc, þo he ne miȝte studie nomore. *c* **1320** *Sir Tristr.* 281 In bok, while he was þore, He stodieþ euer, þat stiþe. **1362** LANGL. *P. Pl.* A. XII. 6 The were lef to lerne but loth for to stodie. *c* **1375** *Sc. Leg. Saints* xxxi. (*Eugenia*) 34 þir twa ȝung men Ithandly studyt in philosophy. *c* **1386** CHAUCER *Prol.* 184 What sholde he studie, and make hymseluen wood Vpon a boke in Cloystre alwey to poure. *c* **1400** *Rule St. Benet* (Prose) xlviii. 33 When prime is sungen til vndern salle ye studie in lescuns. *c* **1430** LYDG. *Min. Poems* (Percy Soc.) 217 Eche thyng of kynde drawith to his nature, Som to profite in wysdam and science, Som also to studyen in Scripture. **1450–80** tr. *Secreta Secret.* xxviii. 21 The nobille Plato he stodied in the science of Astronomye. **1530** PALSGR. 741/2, I wolde fayne be a great clerke, but I love not to studye. **1661** H. NEWCOME *Diary* (Chetham Soc.) 9, I kept in all yᵉ afternoone and studdyed on another doct. on my text Act. xxiv. 25. **1709** HEARNE *Collect.* (O.H.S.) II. 245 [Harduin] maliciously asserts that the Cardinal's way of studying was to read Indexes. *a* **1721** PRIOR *Advice of Venus* 12 On female idleness his [Cupid's] pow'r relies, But when he finds us studying-hard he flies. **1746** FRANCIS tr. *Hor., Sat.* II. vii. 20 [He] Now rakes at Rome, and now to Athens flies; Intensely studies with the Learn'd and Wise.

b. quasi-*refl.* with complement.

1711 STEELE *Spect.* No. 132 ¶1 A Gentleman that had studied himself dumb. **1725** N. BAILEY *Fam. Colloq. Erasm.* (1733) 16, I approve well enough of studying hard, but not to study myself to Death. **1769** E. BANCROFT *Guiana* 227, I have not yet studied myself into a habit of investigating the Minutiae of Nature.

c. To follow one's educational or professional studies at a university, college, or the like; to be a student or learner of some science or art *under* a professor or master. †Const. *in*.

c **1450** CAPGRAVE *St. Aug.* xi. 17 Alipius, he seith, was at Cartage, stodying in rethorik. **1531** *N. Country Wills* (Surtees 1908) 127 Powr scolers..in eyther of thunyversites ..there studying in holy Dyvinitie. **1592** KYD *Span. Trag.* IV. i. 76 When in Tolledo there I studied It was my chance to write a Tragedie. **1617** MORYSON *Itin.* I. 6 Each man paid a Lubeck shilling for tribute, my selfe onely excepted, who had that priviledge because I went to study in the Universities. **1758** L. TEMPLE *Sketches* (ed. 2) 55 Vandyke studied under Rubens. **1780** *Mirror* No. 70 They had grown up at the same schools, and studied under the same masters. **1884** A. BAIN *Pract. Ess.* 204 In the current phrase, 'studying under some one,' there is a more express reference to being taught by a master, as in listening to lectures. **1898** A. SUTHERLAND in H. G. Turner & S. *Developm. Austral. Lit.* 132 Now he had a chance of studying at the hands of Tom Sayers, afterwards the pugilist hero of England.

d. To make a close study of (a subject), to 'bone' *up* (*on, in*), esp. in preparation for some display of knowledge (*intr.* use of sense 7 b). *U.S. colloq.*

1946 *Chicago Daily News* 25 June 31/3 Ah'll git a li'l closer, an' study up on him! **1956** R. ROBINSON *Landscape with Dead Dons* xiii. 114, I am sure that if you once studied up a little in psychology you would be as struck as I was. **1970** N. ARMSTRONG et al. *First on Moon* vi. 131 He had studied up on vineyards so he could tell wonderful stories about them. **1980** J. BALL *Then came Violence* ii. 10 'We know quite a lot about Pasadena,' he said. 'Have you been studying up?' the chief asked.

2. a. To think intently; to meditate (*about*, †*of*, *on, upon, in*); to reflect, try to recollect something or to come to a decision. Now *dial.* and *U.S. colloq.*

1340 *Ayenb.* 24 þet ech may betere y-zy yne him-zelue yef he wyle wel studie. *c* **1400** *Sc. Trojan War* (Horstm.) I. 64 All wrath ande angry ine hys hert Stude studeande a litill stert. *c* **1400** *Beryn* 1793 Beryn studied in the ches, al-þouȝe it nauȝt a-vailid. **1450–1530** *Myrr. our Ladye* I. xxiv. 63 But yf youre harte be set..to study aboute the stablynge of the mynde in god, ye can not..saye hys seruyce deuoutly. *c* **1489** CAXTON *Sonnes of Aymon* xii. 287 He loked dounwarde, & studyed a goode while that he sayd noo worde. **1514** BARCLAY *Cit. & Uplondyshm.* (Percy Soc.) 18 Yet let me stody, avoydynge perturbaunce So maye I call them unto my remembraunce. *a* **1533** BERNERS *Huon* liii. 179 They both began to study for yᵉ fyrst draught [*i.e.* move at chess]. *a* **1548** HALL *Chron., Hen. IV*, 20 When the kyng had long digested and studied on this matter he made aunswere and sayd. *c* **1563** *Jack Juggler* 310 And if I wold sit stoding this .vii. yere I shall not ells find how to saue me all clere. **1580** HESTER tr. *Fioravanti's Disc. Chirurg.* 31, I.. beganne to consider of the matter,..& so studying, it came in my memory, that the aire was cause of their death. **1610** SHAKS. *Temp.* II. i. 82 You make me study of that: She was of Carthage, not of Tunis. **1647** LIGHTFOOT *Harmony O.T.* 49 Moses feeding his sheep and studying upon God, hath a vision of Christ in a bush. **1672** DRYDEN *1st Pt. Conq. Granada* III. Stage-dir., He walks swiftly, and discomposedly studying. **1811** *Henry & Isabella* II. 5 He was not so spiritually engrossed, but that he had time to study a little upon temporal affairs. **1844** *Yorks. Comet* No. I. 1 Moare Ah studied aboot it an' war it pottered me. **1876** 'MARK TWAIN' *Tom Sawyer* xviii, 'Go on, Tom!' 'Just let me study a moment—just a moment. Oh, yes—you said you believed the door was open.' **1895** *Dialect Notes* I. 374 *Study*, talk, discuss, consider... 'I studied about her to my man when I got home.' **1940** W. FAULKNER *Hamlet* IV. i. 244, I was absent-minded one night when I was staking them out. Studying about something else and forgot how long the wire was. **1965** 'MALCOLM X' *Autobiogr.* (1966) xiii. 306, I studied about if I just *should* happen to say something to her—what would her position be?

†b. Phrase, *to study by* or *in oneself*. *Obs.*

c **1450** *St. Cuthbert* (Surtees) 1440 Cuthbert was gretly stonyed And be him selfe bisily stedyed. *c* **1450** *Merlin* ii. 28 Gretly stodied euery clerke be hym-self, but for all their labour thei cowde not fynde but oon thynge. *a* **1533** BERNERS *Huon* li. 171 He began to study in hymself whether he shulde shewe the trouthe or eles to lye.

†c. To be in doubt or perplexity; to 'take thought' anxiously. *Obs.*

1362 LANGL. *P. Pl.* A. VIII. 132 Mony tyme þis Metels han made me to studie For pers loue. *c* **1386** CHAUCER *Merch. T.* 711 Who studieth now but faire fresshe May? **1460** CAPGRAVE *Chron.* (Rolls) 25 This mad simple men to studye, supposing that he was a god. **1493** *Festivall* (W. de W. 1515) 139 b, Than came an aungel to Joseph & badde he sholde take Mary to his kepynge & study no more there-upon. **1546** J. HEYWOOD *Prov.* II. iv. (1867) 49 Husband (quoth she) ye studie, be mery now, And euen as ye thynke now so come to yow. *a* **1586** MONTGOMERIE *Misc. Poems* xxiv. 31, I, that som tyme solide wes and sage, Begouth to studie, stupefact and strange.

†d. With indirect question: To debate with oneself, deliberate, consider. *Obs.*

a **1300** *Cursor M.* 22166 þai sal be studiand in þair thoght, Queþer þat he be crist or nai. *Ibid.* 28013 And yee leuedis.. studis hu your hare to heu. *a* **1340** HAMPOLE *Ps.* xiii. 2 þai kast and studis how þai myght doe in dede þat þai haf wickidly thoght. **1390** GOWER *Conf.* I. 146 This king began to studie and muse, What strange matiere he myhte use The knyhtes wittes to confounde. *c* **1450** *Merlin* xii. 178 He..began to stodye howe he myght spede to go the kynge Arthur. *a* **1533** BERNERS *Huon* cl. 570 She stode styl and studyed what voyce it myght be. **1593** SHAKS. *Rich. II*, V. v. 1, I haue beene studying how I may compare This prison where I liue, vnto the world. **1600** FAIRFAX *Tasso* V. xcii, He studied how to feed that mightie host. **1694** ATTERBURY *Serm.* (1726) I. 184 Every Man is continually studying how to put a Trick upon his Neighbour. **1788** MRS. HUGHES *Henry & Isab.* III. 79 She determined..not to study what would best deceive her friends and the world; but [etc.].

†e. To ask oneself without answer, 'wonder' *why, what*, etc. *Obs.*

c **1480** HENRYSON *Mor. Fab.* x. (*Fox & Wolf*) v, I studdie, quhy ye suld stop me, Sen that I faltit neuer to you. *a* **1533** BERNERS *Gold. Bk. M. Aurel.* (1546) Dd vj b, I studye soore what hath meued the to leaue chyualrye.

†f. To search, 'cast about' *for*. *Obs.*

1551 ROBINSON tr. *More's Utopia* II. iii. (1895) 137 That no man..shall then afterwarde rather studye for [L. *excogitet*] reasons wherewyth to defende [etc.]. **1592** *Arden of Feversham* V. iii. 13 Study not for an answer; looke not down. **1609** ROWLANDS *Knave Clubs* (1872) 38 A greedy minded gripple Clearke, Had gathered store of gould, And studied for a place secure His hoorded heape to hould. **1613** T. ADAMS *White Devil* Ep. Ded., This Sermon beares so strange a Title in the forhead, that I durst not (a while) study for a Patronage to it. **1717–8** LADY M. W. MONTAGU *Let. to Lady ——* 16 Mar., I am in great danger of losing my English... I am forced to study for Expressions. **1732** SWIFT *Let. to Gay* 10 July, I found a Moral first and studied for a Fable. **1748** RICHARDSON *Clarissa* (1811) VII. 369 She must have studied for an expedient.

†3. To exercise oneself, employ one's thought or effort *in*. *Obs.*

1450–80 tr. *Secreta Secret.* Prol. 3 For euyr he was stodiyng in good and gracious thewes. **1456** SIR G. HAYE *Law Arms* (S.T.S.) 25 Otheris that studyit nocht in the keping of leautee, bot mare in the contrufing [*printed* contrusing] of falshede. **1474** CAXTON *Chesse* IV. i. (1883) 161 Whan the gouernours studye in wisedom.

4. a. With inf.: To endeavour, make it one's aim, set oneself deliberately *to do* something. *arch.*

1340 *Ayenb.* 232 Stude þou to bleue. *c* **1350** *Will. Palerne* 130 þan studied sche stifly as stepmoderes wol alle, to do dernly a despit to here stepchilderen. **1377** LANGL. *P. Pl.* B. xv. 587 þei..studyeden to stroyen hym and stroyden hemself. *c* **1450** CAPGRAVE *St. Gilbert* xiv. 80 þis very prest Gilbert stodied euery day to bere schidis to þe holy fyr whech brent in þe tabernacle. **1474** CAXTON *Chesse* III. vi. (1883) 132 We studye for to be lyke vnto belues of the see. *c* **1482** J. KAY tr. *Caoursin's Siege of Rhodes* (1870) ¶ i 1 They tourned theire fantasye and studyed wyth alle theire vertue and myghte to assaute the cyte. **1519** *Interl. Four Elem.* (Percy Soc.) 4 Yet amonge moste folke that man is holdyn Moste wyse, whiche to be ryche studyeth only. **1526** TINDALE *1 Thess.* iv. 11 We beseche you..that ye studdy to be quyet [so **1611**], and to medle with youre owne busynes. **1549** *Bk. Com. Prayer, Commun., Prayer for King*, That..he [the King] maye..study to preserue thy people,..in wealth, peace, and Godlynes. **1585** T. WASHINGTON tr. *Nicholay's Voy.* I. xvi. 17 b, They study to seek places coole & shadowous. **1639** N. N. tr. *Du Bosq's Compl. Woman* II. 59 The more lascivious study commonly to appeare most chast. *c* **1665** MRS. HUTCHINSON *Mem. Col. Hutchinson* (1846) 359 But Cromwell, who of late studied to give him neglects, passed him by. **1701** W. WOTTON *Hist. Rome* 312 He study'd to do as much Mischief as he could. *a* **1715** BURNET *Own Time* (1766) I. 115 No body did ever study to hurt him. **1798** WEBBE in Owen *Wellesley's Desp.* (1877) 10, I have not studied to exaggerate any part of this memorandum. **1823** SCOTT *Quentin D.* xxi, 'For whom are you?'..'For France—for France,' answered Quentin, studying to get away.

†**b.** With clause: To employ one's effort *that*.

1656 EARL MONM. tr. *Boccalini's Advts. fr. Parnass.* II. vi. (1674) 145 They should chiefly study, that..clemency might clearly be seen in the punishment.

†**5.** [After L. *studēre* with dat.] To be addicted *to*; to direct one's efforts *to*; to be solicitous *for*, *after*; to set one's mind *upon*. *Obs.*

1382 WYCLIF *Jer.* vi. 13 Alle to auarice studien. —— *2 Macc.* ii. 29 Forsothe grauntynge the trewthe of alle autours, bot we oure self studyinge to shortnesse. *c* **1430** *Pol. Rel. & L. Poems* 205 þou studiest after nyce aray. **1561** DAUS tr. *Bullinger on Apoc.* (1573) Pref. 19 Certeine thinges..I have not set forth in these my sermons, studieng much, for breuity. **1603** STOW *Surv. Lond.* (1908) I. 189 Their Prelates,..studying for mony, omitted the punishment limitted by law.

II. Transitive uses.

†**6. a.** To ponder over, meditate upon. *Obs.*

a **1300** *Cursor M.* 7128 þis [*sc.* Samson's riddle] it was quen þai had soght, And stodid thre dais al for noght. *c* **1380** WYCLIF *Sel. Wks.* II. 116 Studie þou þe dede of Crist, and knitt oo witt wiþ anoþer. **1474** CAXTON *Chesse* IV. viii. (1883) 186 To gyue hem cause to leue her pensifnes and sorowes In auysynge & studyynge this game.

b. *causatively.* To cause to muse; to perplex. *Obs.* exc. *dial.*

1654 T. WHALLEY in *Ussher's Lett.* (1686) 602 Your noting their defects..more studied me.

7. a. To apply one's mind to the acquiring of (a science, art, language, etc.).

1445 in *Anglia* XXVIII. 273 Aonias also, which crafte of musys studyed. **1516** *Kal. New Leg. Eng.* (Pynson) 28 b, As he was studyinge arythmetryke, his moder then latlye deed apperyd to hym. **1596** SHAKS. *Tam. Shr.* I. i. 40 In briefe sir, studie what you most affect. **1634** SIR T. HAWKINS *Pol. Observ.* 36 Happy he, who studieth prudence on anothers bookes. **1698** FRYER *Acc. E. India & P.* 263 Studying all the Arts of Thrift, will Travel for Fifty Shillings. *a* **1704** LOCKE *Educ.* §167 Wks. 1714 III. 74 If a Gentleman be to study any Language, it ought to be that of his own Country. **1715** ADDISON *Drummer* III. i, I warrant you he has study'd the black art. **1750** WARBURTON *Julian* Introd. p. xxxviii, That very Philosophy, which was then adopted to explain articles of Faith, was now studied only to instruct us in the history of the human mind [etc.]. **1788** MRS. HUGHES *Henry & Isab.* III. 28 Our heroine had not at all studied the rules of whist, and practised them very little. **1833** G. COMBE *Lect. Pop. Educ.* i. (1848) 14 They have wasted in studying—or in attempting to study—Greek and Latin, the only time which their pressing occupations left at their command. **1878** STEDMAN *Oxford: Soc. & Intell. Life* 280 Political Economy may be studied in Fawcett or Mill.

b. *colloq.* *to study up*: to study (a subject) in view of some special emergency, e.g. an examination; to 'get up'.

1880 'MARK TWAIN' *Tramp Abroad* 412 Studying up the subject of Alpine climbing. **1922** JOYCE *Ulysses* 728 He knows a lot..about the body and the insides..often wanted to study up that myself.

8. a. To be occupied with (a specific branch of learning) as the subject of one's educational course or professional training.

1569 UNDERDOWN *Ovid's Invect. Ibis* Pref. A vij, Ouid..was a gentleman of a good house,..who rather to please hys father, then for any loue he bare thervnto, studyed the lawe. But after his decease, he returned to his olde study of Poetry againe. **1611** G. H. tr. *Anti-Coton* 35 Being asked whether hee had studyed Diuinitie in the Colledge of Iesuites, he answered: Yea, [etc.]. **1700** EVELYN *Diary* 8 Dec., The Chancery requiring so little skill in deep law learning, if the practiser can talk eloquently in that Court, so that probably few care to study the law to any purpose. **1841** *Penny Cycl.* XXI. 184/1 The university of Göttingen, where Seetzen from 1785–88 studied medicine, the natural sciences, [etc.].

†**b.** In passive, To be educated. *Obs.*

a **1662** HEYLIN *Hist. Presbyt.* II. (1670) 54 The State of Avignion,..being visited with such of the French Preachers as had been studied at Geneva. **1662** STILLINGFL. *Orig. Sacræ* II. ii. §5 And after, speaking of their Kings being studied in their arts as well as others of the Priests, he adds, [etc.].

9. a. To read (a book, a passage, an author) with close attention.

1422 YONGE tr. *Secreta Secret.* 247 Good bokys to rede and study. **1526** *Pilgr. Perf.* (W. de W. 1531) 2 But rather I beseche all the reders so to study this present treatyse, that [etc.]. **1611** BIBLE *Transl. Pref.* ¶ 4 If we doe not studie them [the Scriptures]. **1701** DE FOE *Trueborn Eng.* 29 The Learned Men who study Aristotle. **1844** E. FITZGERALD *Lett.* (1889) I. 125 Think of the rococcity of a gentleman studying Seneca in the middle of February 1844 in a remarkably damp cottage. **1848** THACKERAY *Van. Fair* ix, At college..he prepared himself for public life..by studying the ancient and modern orators with great assiduity. **1865** M. ARNOLD *Ess. Crit.* Pref. p. viii, One cannot be always studying one's own works. **1881** P. BROOKS *Candle of Lord* 60 A text which we have once studied is like a star upon which we have once looked through the telescope. **1910** *Month* Jan. 2, I have read promiscuously in the *Miscellaneous Writings*, sampling nearly everything and studying some sections carefully. **1910** F. C. BURKITT *Earliest Sources Life Jesus* ii. 32 Their common matter may be studied and compared at a glance.

b. Of an actor: To commit to memory and exercise oneself in the rendering of (a part).

1601 SHAKS. *Twel. N.* I. v. 190, I can say little more then I haue studied, & that question's out of my part. **1602** —— *Ham.* II. ii. 566 You could for a need study a speech of some dosen or sixteene lines? **1778** MISS BURNEY *Evelina* (1791) I. x. 19, I could hardly believe he [*sc.* Garrick] had studied a written part, for every word seemed to be uttered from the impulse of the moment. **1779** *Mirror* No. 9 ¶ 2 The part of Lear was to be performed by an actor who had studied the character under the English Roscius.

10. a. To examine in detail, seek to become minutely acquainted with or to understand (a phenomenon, a state of circumstances, a series of events, a person's character, etc.); to investigate (a problem).

1600 E. BLOUNT tr. *Conestaggio* 131 Who had sent John de Noghera to the Vniuersitie of Coimbra, to studie the point of their pretended election. **1658** FLECKNOE *Enigm. Charac.* 76 In Grammer Schools, where they study Boyes so long, they are marr'd for ever studying men. *a* **1687** PETTY *Polit. Anat.* x. (1691) 70 So as it becomes a Trade to study and make Advantages of these Irregularities [in the value of coin]. **1807** OPIE *Lect.* iv. (1848) 321 In studying and copying the works of old and celebrated masters, it is proper, however, that [etc.]. **1830** R. KNOX *Beclard's Anat.* 42 The anatomist may study the human body in two different states. **1843** RUSKIN *Mod. Paint.* I. I. I. i. §2 The mindless copyist studies Raffaelle, but not what Raffaelle studied. **1845** PATTISON *Ess.* (1889) I. 14 The Church studying the barbarian temper for the purpose of winning it to Christ. **1849** MACAULAY *Hist. Eng.* vi. II. 105 Over the room which he occupied in the King's Bench prison lodged another offender whose character well deserves to be studied. **1885** 'H. CONWAY' *Family Affair* xxvii, The more he studied the situation, the more apparent it became that, to use his own words, he was in a cleft stick. **1907** A. W. STEWART *Stereochem.* 546 Brion studied the action of the animal organism upon the four tartaric acids. **1918** *Times Lit. Suppl.* 14 Mar. 126/2 It is through the writings of Tolstoy and others that the intelligent public has studied Russia.

b. To scrutinize (a visible object) in order to ascertain its nature or to be familiar with or interpret its appearance; *loosely*, to look at as if examining minutely.

1662 GURNALL *Chr. in Arm.* III. verse 18. lviii. 528 The curious Limner studies the face of the man before he makes his draught. **1700** DRYDEN *Fables* Ep. Ded. C 1, You have studied every Spot of Ground in Flanders, which..has been the Scene of Battles and of Sieges. **1802** MAR. EDGEWORTH *Moral T., Prussian Vase* (1816) I. 222 Many studied the countenance of the king, to discover what his wishes might be. **1844** KINGLAKE *Eothen* xiv, By seizing and studying the contents of my dearest portmanteaus. **1878** STEDMAN *Oxford: Soc. & Intell. Life* 286 Finally he will study the specimens in the Court with the aid of the Catalogues of the Oxford Museum. **1889** *Century Mag.* May 85/2 He was studying the toe of his foot visible through a rift in his well-worn brogan. **1908** R. BAGOT *A. Cuthbert* xxi. 257 She was engaged in studying her sister-in-law's figure and personality attentively.

11. To aim at, seek to achieve. Now only, to be solicitous of, aim at (some quality in one's own action).

1606 CHAPMAN *Gentl. Usher* v. ii. 22 Nor studiest eminence, and the higher place Amongst thy consorts, like all other Dames. **1611** BIBLE *Prov.* xxiv. 2 For their heart studieth destruction. *c* **1611** CHAPMAN *Iliad* VII. 55 Saturnius..(studying both our ils) Will neuer ceasse till Mars..his rauenous stomacke fils, With ruin'd Troy. **1658** SIR T. BROWNE *Hydriot.* v. 29 While some have studied Monuments, others have studiously declined them. **1667** MILTON *P.L.* IX. 233 For nothing lovelier can be found In woman, then to studie houshold good. **1719** DE FOE *Crusoe* II. (Globe) 355 The three Villains studied nothing but Revenge. **1738** SWIFT *Pol. Conversat.* Introd. 43, I most earnestly recommend to my male Readers, that they would please a little to study Variety. *Mod.* He seems to have studied brevity rather than lucidity.

†**12.** To meditate, purpose. *Obs.*

1669 DRYDEN *Tyr. Love* III. i. (1670) 27 He from your bed does study a Divorce.

13. To devise, excogitate. Now only with *out*.

1559 *Homilies* I. *Good Wks.* III. I iv, Suche as he hath commaunded in his holy Scripture, and not suche woorkes as menne haue studied out of their owne brayne. [**1549** I iv b *reads* haue immagined of their awne brayne.] **1611** BEAUM. & FL. *Maid's Trag.* v. (1619) L 1 b, Thou art some prating Fellow, One that hath studied out a tricke to talke And moue soft harted people. *a* **1637** B. JONSON *Sad Sheph.* I. iii, I will still study some revenge past this! **1782** WARTON *Ess. Pope* II. viii. 78 The temple itself is nobly and magnificently studied. **1845–6** TRENCH *Huls. Lect.* Ser. I. vi. 95 We might study out a system; but can we ever study out a person?

14. To exercise thought and deliberation in (an action, composition, etc.).

1668 EVELYN tr. *Freart's Idea Perf. Paint.* 120 Intelligent men, who finding nothing of rare and well studied in their Works..will be soon wearied with a transitory view of their Labors. **1710** FELTON *Diss. Classics* (1718) 171 His Words flowed rather from Nature than Art; and where they appear most to be studied, they appear at the same time to be most affected. **1852** MRS. STOWE *Uncle Tom's C.* xxvi, It was tied up with an evident eye to the contrast of colour, and the arrangement of every leaf had carefully been studied. **1857** TROLLOPE *Barchester T.* xxxii, The epistle to Mr. Towers was studied, and recopied, and elaborated at the cost of so many minutes, that [etc.].

15. To pay practical regard to, 'consider' (a person's wishes, feelings or interests); hence *colloq.* to be careful of the convenience or feelings of, to humour (a person).

1758 S. HAYWARD *Serm* xvii. 534 Where a person..is continually studding our advantage. **1798** SOPHIA LEE *Canterb. T. Young Lady's T.* II. 31 [He] soon studied her convenience. **1852** DICKENS *Bleak Ho.* ii, I [a tradesman] have been accustomed to study the leaders of my high connexion. **1858** MRS. CARLYLE *Lett.* II. 352 With no husband to study, housekeeping is mere play. **1861** F. W. ROBINSON *No Church* v. v. III. 258 Say that, to set her free, I have to ask the law to take you prisoner again, do you think for a moment I should study you in saving her? **1891** *Times* (weekly ed.) 1 Nov. 875/3 She was willing to study their wishes to a certain extent. **1895** *Law Times* XCIX. 545/2 We best serve our own interests in studying the interests of those for whom we act. **1909** *Spectator* 25 Sept. 451/1 They speak of a sensitive child who must be studied.

study, obs. var. STEADY, STITHY.

studyaunt(e, -ent(e, obs. forms of STUDENT[1].

studying ('stʌdɪŋ), *vbl. sb.* [f. STUDY *v.* + -ING[1].] The action of the verb STUDY.

1303 R. BRUNNE *Handl. Synne* 443 3yf þey [*sc.* dreams] com noght þurgh stodyyng [Fr. *de cogitacion*]. **1362** LANGL. *P. Pl.* A. IV. 143 Bote stareden for studiing and stooden as Bestes. **1423** JAS. I *King's Q.* viii, Myn eyën gan to smert for studying. *c* **1430** *Syr Gener.* (Roxb.) 1590 Stil he stoode in studiyng. **1534** MORE *Let. to Wilson* Wks. 1444/2, I determined with my self vtterly to discharge my mynde of any ferther studyinge or musinge on the matter. **1656** tr. *Hobbes' Elem. Philos.* (1839) 395 An earnest studying of one object, takes away the sense of all other objects for the present. **1697** FLOYER *Enq. Baths* iii. 64 Studying and Sleeping much is very injurious in the use of Baths. **1890** 'R. BOLDREWOOD' *Col. Reformer* xxiv, There's a deal of studying required..before a man comes to see the right thing at the right time.

b. *attrib.*

c **1440** *Promp. Parv.* 452/1 Selle, stodyynge howse, *cella*. **1628** T. BALL *Life Preston* (1885) 166 His preaching & studying labours were exceeding great. **1661** P. HENRY *Diaries & Lett.* (1882) 77 [Feb.] 9. Studying day... 10 Sabbath-subject, concerning Anger. *Ibid.* 80 [March] 9 Studying-day. **1661** J. WARD *Diary* (1839) 109 Wee saw him sitt..with his hat with silver lace about itt, and his studying gowne on. **1685** WILDING in *Colleet.* (O.H.S.) I. 262 For making my studding gown..00 02 00. **1708** CHAMBERLAYNE *Pres. St. Gt. Brit.* (1710) 303 All the Libraries in Oxford are Studying Libraries; and those of Cambridge..are Lending-Libraries. **1788** COWPER *Gratitude* 9 This wheel-footed studying chair.

'studyless, *a.* *rare*[−1]. [f. STUDY *sb.* + -LESS.] Not addicted to study.

1614 SYLVESTER *Little Bartas* 1009 School-lesse, Schollers; Learned, studi-lesse.

stue, obs. var. STEW *sb.*[1], *sb.*[2], *v.*[2], STOW *v.*[2]

1578 H. WOTTON *Courtlie Controv.* 32 Wee see for one braunche of a tree stued off, that nature planteth seauen scients vppon the same stocke.

stuer, var. STURE, a sturgeon.

stuerd(e, stuerne, obs. ff. STEWARD, STERN *a.*

‖**stufa** ('stufa). *rare.* [It. = next.]

1. = STUFE.

1832 GELL *Pompeiana* I. vi. 85 A heated *stufa*.

2. (See quot.)

1830 LYELL *Princ Geol.* (1835) I. II. iii. 304 In many volcanic regions, jets of steam, called by the Italians 'stufas,' issue from fissures, at a temperature high above the boiling point.

†**stu'fata.** *Obs.* *rare*[−1]. [Altered f. It. *stufato*, f. *stufare* to stew. Cf. STOFFADO.] Some kind of stew.

1771 SMOLLETT *Humph. Cl.* 11 Oct., He taught me..to cook several outlandish delicacies, such as *ollas*, *pepper-pots*, *pillaws*, *corys*, *chabobs*, and *stufatas* [many later edd. give *stuffatas*].

†**stufe**, *sb.* *Obs.* Also 6 **stuphe, stewfe, 7 stuph, stuffe.** [ad. It. *stufa*.] A hot-air bath: = STOVE *sb.*[1]

1533 ELYOT *Cast. Helthe* (1541) 72 b, Moderate sweatynge in hot bathes or stufes be to this complexion necessary. **1547** BOORDE *Brev. Health* §292 Vse than [for itching] purgacions and stuphes and sweates. **1549** THOMAS *Hist. Italie* 28 The Romaines vsed oftentime, to bathe theim selfes, wherfore..priuate men made them stewfes or hotehouses of theyr owne. **1631** JORDEN *Nat. Bathes* i. (1669) 2 Vapours [Baths] are Stuphs and Hot Houses. *a* **1697** AUBREY *Lives, Bacon* (1898) I. 78 There were two bathing-roomes or stuffes, whither his Lordship retired afternoons as he sawe cause.

attrib. **1598** FLORIO, *Stufaiuolo*, a bathe or stufe-keeper.

Hence †**stufe** *v.*

1598 FLORIO, *Stufare*, to stue meate, to stufe, or bathe in a whot house.

stufer, obs. f. STIVER.

stuff (stʌf), *sb.*[1] Forms: 4–5 **stof**, 5–6 **stoffe**, 4–7 **stuffe**, 5–6 **stuf**, 5–8 **stufe**, (6 **stoufe**), 4– **stuff**. [ME. *stoffe*, *stof*, a. OF. *estoffe* fem., material, furniture, provision (mod.F. *étoffe* material, stuff, esp. textile material) = Pr., Sp., Pg. *estofa*, cloth, quality, It. *stoffa* piece of rich textile fabric. From the OF. word are med.L. *estoffa*, *stoffa*, Du. *stoffe*, *stof* fem., G. *stoff* masc., matter, stuff, whence Sw. *stoff*, Da. *stof* neut.

The ultimate etymology is obscure. Diez conjectured that the Rom. *stoffa* and the related vb. *stoffare* (STUFF *v.*) are derived from the OHG. **stopfôn* (MHG., mod.G. *stopfen*) to plug with oakum, which (as explained s.v. STOP *v.*) represents a WGer. adoption of med.L. *stuppāre* to plug, stop up, f. *stuppa* tow, oakum. This is open to strong objections: the likelihood of a specifically HG. etymon for a Com. Rom. word is questionable, and the original sense of the Rom. verb appears to be, not 'to plug or stop up', but 'to garnish or store with something'. Whether the sb. is the source of the verb, or derived from it, is uncertain; the masc. form in It. *stoffo*, Pg. *estofo* quilted material, is undoubtedly a verbal noun.]

I. 1. Equipment, stores, stock.

†**a.** A body of soldiers; a garrison; an auxiliary force, reinforcement. Also ***stuff of people***. *Obs.*

1375 BARBOUR *Bruce* v. 258 Now takis Iames his viage.. Vith twa ȝhomen,.. That ves a sympill stuff to ta, A land or castell for to vyn! **1412-20** LYDG. *Troy-bk.* IV. 2119 Whanne he sawe his Grekis gonne faille And wexe feble to stonden in bataille For lak of stuf þat shulde hem recounforte. *c* **1425** WYNTOUN *Cron.* I. 124 Befor it set wes Cherubin, þat mai be vnderstandin richt A stuf of angellis blith and bricht. **1430-40** LYDG. *Bochas* II. xiv. (1554) 53 b, Up he rose and gan hymselfe tauance No stuffe about him but sergeauntes riotous. **1442** ROOS & BEKYNTON in *B's. Corr.* (Rolls) II. 213 Yf any stuf or pouaire of Englissh pouple had be there. *c* **1470** HENRY *Wallace* VI. 693 The ij captans sone mett thaim at Beggair, With the haill stuff of Roxburch and Berweike.

†**b.** In ME. poetry, the quilted material worn under the mail, or itself serving in place of armour. In later use: Defensive armour. *Obs.*

c **1330** R. BRUNNE *Chron. Wace* 10031 Vaumbras & rerbras, wyþ coters of stel, þer-opon an aketon wyþ stof & al sylk [Fr. *Hauberc et bon et bel vestu*], His cote of armes þer-on. **13..** *Gaw. & Gr. Knt.* 581, & syþen þe brawden bryne of bryȝt stel ryngez, Vmbe-weued þat wyȝ, vpon wlonk stuffe. *a* **1400-50** *Wars Alex.* 2980* Some arays þaim in rynggez some in rawe brenys, Some in stalwart stuffe & some in stele plates. *c* **1420** *Anturs of Arth.* xlv, He.. Thro the wast of the body wowundet him ille; The squrd styntet for no stuffe, he was so wele stelet. *c* **1470** HENRY *Wallace* IV. 663 With ire him straik on his gorgeat off steill, The trensand blaid to persyt euirydeill. Throu plaitt and stuff, mycht nocht agayn it stand. *c* **1470** *Gol. & Gaw.* 981 He.. Hakkit throw the hard weid, to the hede hynt; Throw the stuf with the straik.. He hewit attanis. **1535** STEWART *Cron. Scot.* (Rolls) II. 130 Thir wicht men weildit thair waponis so weill, That euerie straik out-throw thair stuf of steill Thay gart the blude brist out.

†**c.** The materials, stores, or supplies belonging to an army; munitions of war; more definitely ***stuffs of war***. *Obs.*

1375 BARBOUR *Bruce* XVII. 176 Wittaill thai fand in gret fusioune, And all that fell till stuff of toune. *c* **1440** *Promp. Parv.* 481/1 Stuffe, or stuffure, *staurum*. *c* **1450** *Brut* II. 428 He ordeynyd hym a newe retenewe of men of armys and archeris, with alle maner of othir stuffis that bylongid therto. *a* **1466** GREGORY *Chron.* in *Hist. Coll. Cit. Lond.* (Camden) 161 And he toke alle hyr ordynauns of gonnys and alle hyr vytayle, with alle the othyr stoffe that was at the sege, that is to saye, xiiij gonnys,.. and ij C pypys of brede and floure,.. and othyr stuffe of pavys and tentys. *a* **1500** *Bale's Chron.* in *Six Town Chron.* (1911) 116 Item this yere the duke of Somerset w^t a grete power ordenance and stuff moustred at portesmouth diverse tymes. *Ibid.* 152 W^t greet ordenannce of Gonnes and other stuffs of werre.

†**d.** The baggage of a soldier or an army; later *gen.* baggage, luggage. *Obs.*

? *a* **1400** *Morte Arth.* 735 Thus they stowe ine the stuffe of fulle steryne knyghtez. **1530** PALSGR. 277/2 Stuffe caryage, *aport, seruage*... Stuffe that is in a fardell, *fardage*. **1535** COVERDALE *1 Sam.* xxx. 24 Like as the porcion is of them that wente downe to the battayll, so shal ye porcion be of them also that abode with the stuffe. **1590** SHAKS. *Com. Err.* IV. iv. 153 Come to the Centaur, fetch our stuffe from thence. *a* **1625** FLETCHER *Noble Gent.* II. i, I see my folly, Pack up my stuffe, I will away this morne. **1653** H. COGAN tr. *Pinto's Trav.* i. 2 There I found a Carvel of Alfama, that was laden with the horses and stuff [Pg. *cavallos e fato*] of a Lord.

e. Stock or provision of food. *Obs.* exc. *Sc.* Cf. 6 c.

More definitely †*stuff of victual*. †*lent(en stuff*: fish procured as a provision for Lent.

1436 HEN. VI in *Rep. Hist. MSS. Comm.* Var. Coll. (1907) IV. 199 We..have notable purveyd for the defense and kepynge of hem, as well in sufficiaunce of nombre of men and in stuff of vitaille, artillerie and alle manere abillemens of werre as otherwyse. *c* **1506** *Plumpton Corr.* (Camden) 198 And your Lenten stoufe is to bey, & I wote not what to do. **1535** *Sc. Acts Jas. V* (1814) II. 347/1 Þat Nane forstallaris be fundin byand vittalis fische flesche or vþer stuff or þe samin be presentit to þe mercat.. vnder þe pane of presonyng of þare personis. **1580** TUSSER *Husb.* (1878) 126 Take shipping or ride, Lent stuffe to prouide. **1596** HARINGTON *Metam. Ajax* Prol. B 5 b, Lo stuffe for you good store, To gnaw, chew, bite and eate. *a* **1700** EVELYN *Diary* 23 Apr. 1667, Then was the banquetting stuff flung about the roome profusely. **1870** J. NICHOLSON *Idylls o' Hame* 113 O' Ne'r-day stuffs we're weel laid in, A sonsy cheese, jist like the mune, Wi' crumpy cakes.

f. Provision of corn; in full †***stuff of corn***; hence corn or grain in any state (see quot. 1825-82). *Obs.* exc. *Sc.*

1461-2 *Cal. Anc. Rec. Dublin* (1889) 311 Wher they fyndyth any maner of stof of corn grosyt, they to arest and take up all such stof. *c* **1470** HENRY *Wallace* III. 220 Quhen this was doyne, to thar dyner thai went, Off stuff and wyne. **1596** DALRYMPLE tr. *Leslie's Hist. Scot.* I. 6 In all kynde of stuffe, and cattell it abundes. **1635** D. DICKSON *Sel. Writ.* (1845) I. 94 He were an evil-skilled husbandman who should take a whole bing of stuff to be chaff, because there is much chaff in it. **1786** BURNS *Halloween* xv, The Simmer had been cauld an' wat, An' Stuff was unco green. **1825-82** JAMIESON, *Stuff*. It denotes grain in whatever state; whether as growing, cut down, in the barn, or in the mill.

g. Property, esp. movable property, household goods or utensils; furniture; more definitely ***stuff of money***, ***stuff of household***. *Obs.* exc. in HOUSEHOLD-STUFF *arch.*

1438 *E.E. Wills* (1882) 111 Item to my wyf, all my stuff beyng at the Fasterne. **1439** *Ibid.* 126 All his other godes and stuffes meveable that he leveth vnto hem. *c* **1442-55** DK. BUCKINGHAM in *Paston Lett.* I. 61 In gode faith, brother,.. I have but easy stuffe of money withinne me,.. so that I may not plese youre seid gode brotherhode. **1464** *Inv.* in *Turner's Dom. Archit.* (1859) III. iv. 113 A grete red standerd full of stuff, locked with 2 lockes. *c* **1490** CAXTON *Rule St. Benet* 136 Suche stuff that he hath not yeuen before to folke þat ben poore or other wyse, openly shall he thenne yeue to the monestary. **1501** *Bury Wills* (Camden) 84, I bequethe to Margarett my wyff all my stuff of hous-hold. **1538** in *Archæologia* XLIII. 210 Certeyne guddes or stuffe appertaynyng to the seid Monastery remayneth unsolde. **1596** H. CLAPHAM *Briefe Bible* I. 65 Joshuah giving in charge that no man take any execrable stuffe of Iericho. **1621** BURTON *Anat. Mel.* II. iii. III. 399 A poore man.. eates his meat in wooden spoones, wooden platters, earthen Vessels, and such homely stuffe. **1635-56** COWLEY *Davideis* III. 220 Some lead the groaning waggons, loaded high, With stuff, on top of which the Maidens ly. **1646** *Bury Wills* (Camden) 193 She shall not.. haue the vse of any of the goods, stuffe of houshold, chattells, personall estate, or thinges by me herein given to her.

†**h.** The furnishing proper to a place or thing; appurtenances, apparatus. *Obs.*

1406 HOCCLEVE *La Male Regle* 349 My thank is qweynt, my purs his stuf hath lore. **1427-9** *Wills & Inv. N.C.* (Surtees) II. 75 And I wyl yat ye stuffe of alle myn howses of offices as kychyn panetre and buttre.. remayne to my son. **1523-34** FITZHERB. *Husb.* (1882) 14 A carte made of asshe,.. and lyke stuffe to it as is to a wayne. **1530** PALSGR. 277/2 Stuffe for a bedde, *acoustrement de lit*. **1538** ELYOT *Dict.*, *Choragium*, stuffe, proprely wherwith that place is adorned, where as shall be enterludes or disguysynges. **1596** SHAKS. *Tam. Shr.* IV. iii. 87 Oh mercie God, what masking stuffe is heere? What's this? a sleeue? **1679-88** *Secr. Serv. Money Chas. & Jas.* (Camden) 160 To Francis Duddell.. for sev^{ll} provisions for church stuff for the chappel at Dublin, 267*li.* 4*s.* 10*d.* **1688** WOOD *Life* 26 Nov. (O.H.S.) III. 285 Common report that lord Delamere, who was about Northampton burning all popish chapel stuffs,.. would be at Oxon next day.

†**i.** *Cookery*. Materials for filling a pie or for stuffing. *Obs.*

c **1420** *Liber Cocorum* (1862) 51 For a pye... þy stuffe of fressh befe mynse þou schalle.. þen lay þy capon in coffyn fyne. *c* **1450** *Two Cookery Bks.* II. 76 Make faire rownde cofyns,.. fil hem full of the stuffe, and sette hem ayen in the oven. **1533** J. HEYWOOD *Johan* A iij, We made a pye.. The preest payde for the stuffe and the makyng. **1591** A. W. *Bk. Cookrye* 7 Then mingle all your stuf togither, and put it in your Rabets belly. **1598** *Epulario* I j, Take Marchpane stuffe .. prepare the paste.. then fill it with the stuffe.

j. Stock-in-trade. *Obs.* exc. *north.*

1560 DAUS tr. *Sleidane's Comm.* 118 b, There is not so lytle a corner any where, that they [*sc.* merchants] have not fylled full of theyr stuffe. **1630** BP. HALL *Occas. Medit.* xxx. (1633) 75 Each [street seller] tels what he hath,.. and yet (God wot) it is but poore stuffe that they set out, with so much ostentation. **1868** ATKINSON *Cleveland Gloss.* s.v., 'He's a deal o' stuff on hand, noo', a very large stock in trade.

II. That of which something is or may be made; material.

2. a. Material to work with or upon; substance to be wrought, matter of composition.

c **1440** *Pallad. on Husb.* I. 392 Of suche a stufe as esy is to fynde Is best.. to bilde. **1474** CAXTON *Chesse* III. v. (1883) 126 They that ben acustomed to make oynements they ought to make hyt proprely of true stuf and of good odoure. **1522** *Extracts Burgh Rec. Stirling* (1887) 17 And that tha [*sc.* the candles] be gud and sufficient stoufe. **1524** *Ibid.* 19 Johen Allan, talyour, was in amerciament for the occupyin of the furruris in furring of ane goune with new stoufe. **1585** HIGINS *Junius' Nomencl.* 347/2 *Fistula*,.. a pipe: a flute, whether it be of reede or other stuffe. **1594** HOOKER *Eccl. Pol.* I. iii. §3 Let Phidias haue rude & obstinate stuffe to carue,.. his worke will lacke that bewtie which otherwise in fitter matter it might haue had. **1621** DONNE *Serm.* xv. (1640) 147 In all the Potters house, is there one vessell made of better stuffe then clay? **1693** EVELYN *De la Quint. Gard.*, *Cult. Orange Trees* 9 A Shovel-full of Stuff [F. *matière*] is thrown from each of the two or three separated Heaps [of ingredients for a compost]. **1764** BURN *Poor Laws* 217 Hemp, wool, flax, or other stuff wrought, shall be sold.. either at some market or other place.

b. *collect.* Materials or requisites for a piece of work; esp. building materials.

c **1400** *Destr. Troy* 283 Now ordant was althing [*sc.* for the building of a ship] onestly þere, And abundantly broght þat hom bild might, With all stuff for þe stremes. **1442** *Rolls of Parlt.* V. 44/1 The makers of the seid new Brigge, to have free entry and issue, with their Tymbre, cariage, and othir stuffe. **1473-4** *Acc. Ld. High Treas. Scot.* I. 68 For a leueray colare..gevin to him..price of the colare, stuf and werkmanschip, xj li. viij s. iiij d. **1482** in *Eng. Hist. Rev.* (1910) XXV. 122 We fyndyng allemaner of stoffe as Bordes, Couerynges, Curreys, hookes, or Claspes, glewe, and flowre for paaste [for binding the books]. *c* **1489** CAXTON *Sonnes of Aymon* vi. 149 Whan all his stuff was redy, he made theym to buylde there a strong castell. *c* **1550** in *Turner's Dom. Archit.* (1859) III. iii. 79 V^c. marc or more to pay wekely pouer workemen, laborers stuff and cariage. *a* **1568** ASCHAM *Scholem.* Pref. (Arb.) 21 A small cotage, poore for the stuffe, and rude for the workemanship. **1630** R. N. *Camden's Eliz.* II. 106 The Queene by Proclamation prohibited any new dwelling houses to be built,.. vpon paine of imprisonment, and losse of the stuffe brought for the building. **1896** P. J. DAVIES *Pract. Plumbing* II. 801 *Stuff*, in plumbing, the lead and materials, such as is the stuff on the job.

†**c.** A manufactured material. Cf. sense 5. *Obs.*

1555 WATREMAN *Fardle Facions* I. v. 52 Thei did weare.. shoes of a certeine kinde of russhes, named *Papyrus*, whiche after became stuffe, to geue name to our paper. *a* **1626** BACON *New Atlantis* 38 Wee haue also diuerse Mechanicall Arts, which you haue not; And Stuffes made by them; As Papers, Linnen, Silks, Tissues; dainty Works of Feathers of wonderfull Lustre; excellent Dies, and many others.

3. *transf.* and *fig.* **a.** The substance or 'material' (whether corporeal or incorporeal) of which a thing is formed or consists, or out of which a thing may be fashioned.

1587 GOLDING *De Mornay* (1592) 127 God for the creating of the world needed neither stuffe nor newe advisement. **1604** SHAKS. *Oth.* I. ii. 2 Yet do I hold it very stuffe o' th' conscience To do no contriu'd Murder. **1610** —— *Temp.* IV. i. 156 We are such stuffe As dreames are made on. **1611** —— *Cymb.* v. iv. 49. **1612** *Two Noble K.* III. i. 49 Not finding in The circuit of my breast any grosse stuffe To forme me like your blazon. **1621** DONNE *Serm.* xv. (1640) 144 As soone as my soule enters into Heaven, I shall be able to say to the Angels, I am of the same stuffe as you, spirit, and spirit. **1648** BP. HALL *Breath. Devout Soul* xlviii. 81 When I look back upon the stuffe whereof it [my body] is made, no better then that I tread upon.. I have much adoe to hold good terms with so unequall a partner. **1709** T. ROBINSON *Vind. Mosaick Syst.* 14 The Platonick Hypothesis.. is to make God an Impotent Cause, not able to make this World with-out Matter and Stuff to work on. **1785** BURKE *Sp. Nabob Arcot's Debts* Wks. 1792 II. 502 The debt of the company from the rajah of Tanjore, is just of the same stuff with that of the nabob of Arcot. **1896** HOUSMAN *Shropshire Lad* xxxii, From far.. The stuff of life to knit me Blew hither: here am I. **1900** H. MACPHERSON *Herbert Spencer* v. 68 Now, in tracing the Universe, science can get no further back than the nebula, or world-stuff. **1914** A. F. GILES *Rom. Civiliz.* i. 7 We have to realize that human nature, which is the stuff of history, is much the same in all ages.

b. What a person is 'made of'; one's capabilities or inward character. Also, solid qualities of intellect or character; capacity for achievement or endurance; the 'makings' of future excellence.

1557 EDGEWORTH *Serm.* 305 b, He is a proud man he swelleth in the flesh and is not ful, but as a thing blowen vp and readie to burst, and yet is there no sure and permanent stuffe within him. **1597** MORLEY *Introd. Mus.* 120 He is a proper man, but he is no descanter.. there is no stuffe in him. **1601** SHAKS. *Jul. C.* III. ii. 97 When that the poore haue cry'de, Cæsar hath wept: Ambition should be made of sterner stuffe. **1613** —— *Hen. VIII*, I. i. 58 Surely Sir, There's in him stuffe, that put's him to these ends. **1785** COWPER *Task* IV. 636 Unapt to learn, and form'd of stubborn stuff, He yet by slow degrees puts off himself. **1792** R. CUMBERLAND *Calvary* v. 304 Is thy frail memory of that slippery stuff That a friend's sorrow washes out all trace Of a friend's features? **1820** BYRON *Morg. Maggiore* xxiv, For late there have appear'd three giants rough; What nation or what kingdom bore the batch I know not, but they are all of savage stuff. **1822** HAZLITT *Table-T.* Ser. II. ix. 212 There is stuff in him, and it is of the right practicable sort. **1853** LYTTON *My Novel* x. xxiv, Yet Frank Hazeldean has stuff in him—a good heart, and strict honour. **1858** HAWTHORNE *Fr. & It. Note-Bks.* I. 224 He was not naturally of the stuff that martyrs are made of. **1862** *Baily's Mag.* May 311 He [an oarsman] looks remarkably well, and is made of stuff to stand training. *Ibid.* Dec. 313 There is some good bowling stuff in him [*sc.* a cricketer]. **1879** *Times* 14 June 12/1 The Marquis.. has some of the stuff of a man in him, in spite of his self-indulgence and his follies.

c. Predicatively, with epithet, of a person or a horse. Esp. in phr. ***bit of stuff***: now chiefly in slang use, with or without epithet, of a woman or girl. Cf. BIT *sb.*[2] 4 f, h.

1553 *Respublica* I. iv. 376 Els will some of youe make good hanging stuff one daie. **1808** JAMIESON *s.v.*, It is said of one, who will not yield in reasoning, or in fighting, 'He is good stuff, or, a piece of good stuff'. **1828** *Subaltern's Log Bk.* II. 164, I entered the house in great spirits, fancying myself, to make use of a slang phrase, a very good bit of stuff. **1830** MARRYAT *King's Own* iv, He is real stuff—never winced. **1858** CARLYLE *Fredk. Gt.* II. vii. (1872) I. 95 Rudolf.. proved an excellent bit of stuff for a Kaiser. **1861** WHYTE MELVILLE *Market Harb.* i, 'Capital bit of stuff,' he repeats, dangling his feet out of the stirrups; 'as game as a pebble, and as neat as a pink.' **1863** W. C. BALDWIN *Afr. Hunting* vi. 175 He was as good a bit of stuff as ever was put together. **1909** in J. R. Ware *Passing Eng.* 31/1 He waited for a bit of stuff near the stage door of the Comedy Theatre. He was an elderly cove and he had great patience. **1971** B. W. ALDISS *Soldier Erect* 10 The infantry myth that one spent one's whole leave yanking it up some willing bit of stuff in a pub yard.

d. Material for literary elaboration; the matter or substance of a work, as distinguished from the form. Now *rare*. †*in stuff*: as regards the matter or substance.

c **1450** CAPGRAVE *St. Aug.* xlv. 60 Þis glorious doctour whom all cristen men ar bounde to do worchip, most specialy clerkys.. þat haue grete stuf oute of his bokes to her lernyng. *a* **1568** ASCHAM *Scholem.* II. (Arb.) 129 They busie not them selues with forme of buildyng: They do not declare, this stuffe is thus framed by Demosthenes, and thus and thus by Tullie. **1607** SHAKS. *Timon* v. i. 87 And for thy fiction, Why thy Verse swels with stuffe so fine and smooth, That thou art euen Naturall in thine Art. **1619** in *Eng. & Germ.* (Camden) 192 The inclosed writing.. being, as by perusall you will find, in stuffe the very same with that I had at Saltzburg. **1675** MARVELL *Corr.* Wks. (Grosart) II. 473 Having scarce stuffe enough for a letter to the Bench, I content myself with acquainting you [etc.]. **1684** ROSCOMMON *Ess. Transl. Verse* 44 Degrading Prose explains his meaning ill, And shews the Stuff, but not the Workman's skill. **1855** MOTLEY *Dutch Rep.* III. ix. II. 458 This great event [the siege of Harlem] constituted..the principal stuff in Netherland history, up to the middle of the year 1573.

4. In various operative trades, applied *spec.* to the kind of material used in the trade.

a. *Carpentry* and *Joinery*: Timber.

clear, free stuff: timber free from imperfections. ***quarter stuff***: see QUARTER *sb.* 31. ***thick stuff***: see quot. 1711.

1544 BETHAM *Precepts War* II. lv. L iv, Bycause stuffe doth somtyme want to make suche [wooden] brydges. **1678** MOXON *Mech. Exerc.* vi. 113 The Wood that Joyners work upon they call in general Stuff. **1711** W. SUTHERLAND *Shipbuild. Assist.* 48 Plank and thick Stuff for Ship-work. *Ibid.* 165 Thick-stuff; all Plank (as it may be termed) which is thicker than 4 Inches. **1799** *Hull Advertiser* 15 June 2/2 Timber. For sale... A variety of stuff suitable for camp buildings. **1812–16** J. SMITH *Panorama Sci. & Art* I. 118 The shoulder [of the square] is pressed against the edge of a rectangular piece of stuff, and a line drawn close to the blade. **1833** LOUDON *Encycl. Archit.* §83 The whole to be framed in a workmanlike manner, with the stuff (pieces of timber) sawed square of the several scantlings. **1879** *Cassell's Techn. Educ.* IV. 130/1 Panel stuff should be treated in a similar manner. **1883** *Encycl. Brit.* XVI. 453/2 The timbers are usually of 12-inch stuff square-hewn or sawn.

b. The material of which a beaver-hat is made. Cf. *stuff hat* (11 c).

1799 *Repert. Arts & Manuf.* X. 275 [Hat making.] The purpose of fulling being to form a dense compact stuff with hair.

c. *Paper-making.* (See quots.)

1745 DE COETLOGON *Hist. Arts & Sci.* II. 796/2 In these Mortars, the Rags being beaten.., they take them out with little Iron hooped Pails... This makes what they call the *first Stuff*... After this, the Stuff is again put into clean Mortars. **1766** Half-stuff [see HALF- 11 n]. **1840** *Penny Cycl.* XVII. 208/2 The pulp, or *stuff*, as it is technically called, is now ready to be made into paper. **1875** KNIGHT *Dict. Mech.*, *Stuff*, paper-stock, ground ready for use. When half ground it is known as half-stuff.

d. *Mining.* Material of rock, earth, or clay containing ore, metal, or precious stones.

1851 S. RUTTER *Hints to Gold Hunters* 12 The principal use of the washpan is in rewashing the partially washed stuff taken from the rocker. **1853** C. R. READ *Austral. Gold Fields* 15 Anxious, at all events, to have a look at the real stuff, I accompanied one down to see him wash out his tin dish. **1877** RAYMOND *Statist. Mines & Mining* 19 Fragments of a crimson-colored rock were found by the miners, intermixed with the gold-dust... This 'red stuff,' so called, bothered the honest diggers not a little, interfering with their operations much after the manner of the celebrated 'blue stuff'—the rich sulphurets of silver. **1885** RIDER HAGGARD *K. Solomon's Mines* xvi, I pointed to a series of worn flat slabs of stone..'if those are not tables once used to wash the "stuff", I'm a Dutchman.' **1887** J. A. PHILLIPS & BAUERMAN *Elem. Metall.* (ed. 2) 185 The [iron] ore remains about ten minutes in the drum, or about 10 tons of stuff are washed per hour.

5. a. Material for making garments; woven material of any kind.

1462 *Mann. & Househ. Exp.* (Roxb.) 150 Item, delyvaryd to Willyam off Wardrope ffor stoffe ffor my lordys doblett, xx.d. **1473** *Acc. Ld. High Treas. Scot.* I. 73 Veluous to purfel a govne to my Lady of blac satyne figory, of the Kingis awin stufe. **1551** ROBINSON tr. *More's Utopia* II. ix. (1895) 294 The priest is clothed in changeable coloures, whiche in workemanshyp be excellent, but in stuffe [L. *materia*] not verye pretious. **1596** SHAKS. *Tam. Shr.* IV. iii. 119 *Gris.* I gaue him the stuffe. *Tail.* But how did you desire it should be made? **1617** MORYSON *Itin.* I. 208 My selfe and my brother bought each of us a long coat of as course stuffe as we could find. **1713** BERKELEY *Ess. in Guardian* v. Wks. 1871 III. 161 My couches, beds, and window-curtains are of Irish stuff. **1801** STRUTT *Sports & Past.* I. ii. 34 Certain quantities of stuff for the purpose of making 'stalking coats, and stalking hose'. **1838** JAMES *Robber* i, A coarse sort of stuff used by the common people.

b. In particularized sense: A kind of stuff; a textile fabric.

1604 E. G[RIMSTONE] *D'Acosta's Hist. Ind.* IV. xli. 320 The Indians make stuffs of this wooll wherewith they clothe themselves. **1625** in Foster *Eng. Factories India* (1909) III. 62 'Neccanies, semeanes, dimittes, stuffs, gumlack, blood-stones, and the rest' will be sent as ordered. *a* **1627** MIDDLETON *Anything for Quiet Life* II. ii. (1662) D 1, But if you'd have a Petticoat for your Lady, here's a stuff. **1660** F. BROOKE tr. *Le Blanc's Trav.* 92 They make stuffes of the bark of a tree, to cover their nakednesse. **1756** NUGENT *Gr. Tour, Germany* II. 229 Leipsic has considerable manufactures of its own, as in stuffs. **1791** W. HAMILTON *Berthollet's Dyeing* I. Introd. 2 The stuffs..were immersed in vats, where they received various colours. **1838** LYTTON *Leila* I. iv, The walls were covered with the stuffs of the East. **1857** RUSKIN *Pol. Econ. Art* i. 10 Applying your labour rationally;..not..putting fine embroidery on a stuff that will not wear.

fig. **1601** SHAKS. *Twel. N.* II. iii. 53 Youths a stuffe will not endure.

c. *spec.* A woollen fabric (see quot. 1882).

c **1643** [cf. *stuff suit* 11 a]. **1712** STEELE *Spect.* No. 264 ¶1 He dresses himself according to the Season in Cloth or in Stuff. **1735** DYCHE & PARDON *Dict.*, *Stuff*, in Weaving, is any Sort of Commodity made of Woollen Thread, &c. but in a particular Manner those thin light ones that Women make or line their Gowns of or with. **1882** CAULFEILD & SAWARD *Dict. Needlework* 465 *Stuffs.* This term..may be applied to any woven textile,..but it more especially denotes those of worsted, made of long or 'combing wool'... Stuffs are distinguished from other woollen cloths by the absence of any nap or pile. **1896** C. K. PAUL tr. *Huysman's En Route* II. vii. 276 The Trappist is buried without a coffin, in his robe of stuff.

d. As the material for the gown worn by a junior counsel. Hence *rarely*, A 'stuff-gownsman', i.e. a junior counsel, as distinguished from a 'silk' (see SILK *sb.* 3 d).

For some years *c* 1900 'Silk and Stuff' was the heading of the column devoted to bar news in the *Pall Mall Gazette*.

1889 A. BIRRELL *Sir F. Lockwood* v. 82 In 1882 Lockwood whilst still in stuff defended..with great success, a woman who [etc.]. **1892** *Pall Mall Gaz.* 12 Oct. 6/1 He was appointed to the bench when he was a 'stuff' merely on the ground of professional merit.

III. Matter of an unspecified kind.

6. a. The general designation for solid, liquid, or (rarely) gaseous matter of any kind: used indefinitely instead of the specific designation, or where no specific designation exists. Often applied to a preparation or composition used for some special purpose.

1580–1 *Act 23 Eliz.* c. 9 *Preamb.*, A certeyne kinde of Ware or Stuffe called Logwood. **1617** MORYSON *Itin.* III. 165 They..delight to have their boots and shoos shine with blacking stuffe. **1617** *Shuttleworths' Acc.* (Chetham Soc.) 223 For stuffe to kille myce at Gawthropp, ij[s]. **1681** LANGFORD *Fruit-trees* 108 Some thin stuff out of a House of Office..hath been often used with good success. **1714** TYLDESLEY *Diary* (1873) 150 Gave Mrs. 6d. to by stufe ffor her tyeth. **1769** FALCONER *Dict. Marine* (1780), *Stuff*, any composition, or melted mass, used to smear or daub the masts, sides, or bottom of a ship. **1820** SHELLEY *Oedipus Tyr.* II. i. 123, I vote..that Purganax rub a little of that stuff Upon his face. **1882** W. HUGGINS in *19th Cent.* Aug. 275 We have found that one part of the cometary stuff is in the condition of gas. **1899** *Allbutt's Syst. Med.* VII. 819 The kidneys gradually finding greater and greater difficulty in getting out the toxic stuff.

¶ Although the Eng. word is not, like Ger. *stoff*, used for 'matter' in the scientific sense (as opposed to 'spirit' or to 'force' or 'energy'), it sometimes occurs in nonce-uses intended to illustrate the notion expressed by *matter* in this application.

1875 STEWART & TAIT *Unseen Univ.* iii. §93. 70 The conviction that there is something besides matter or stuff in the physical universe.

b. Applied to medicine, esp. liquid mixtures. More definitely ***doctor's stuff*** (see DOCTOR *sb.* 13). Now only *colloq.* or with disparaging implication.

1611 SHAKS. *Cymb.* V. v. 255, I..did compound for her A certaine stuffe, which being tane, would cease The present powre of life. **1636** in *Trans. Essex Archæol. Soc.* (1863) II. 213 Paid Mr. Stammer for a glasse of stuff sent to the sick folkes, 1s. od. **1779** WARNER in Jesse *Selwyn & Contemp.* (1844) IV. 298 Your very kind letter..did me more good, I think, than any of my doctor's stuff. **1819** MOORE *Tom Crib's Mem.* 17 Sandy tipp'd him a dose of that kind, that, when taken, It is n't the stuff, but the patient that's shaken. **1847** LEVER *Knt. Gwynne* xvii, The old doctor..tore a leaf out of his pocket-book to order me some stuff for the cough.

c. Applied to articles of food or drink. ***good stuff, the stuff***: colloq. whisky.

See also KITCHEN-STUFF, *sweet-stuff* (SWEET *a.* C. 1).

1597 SHAKS. *2 Hen. IV*, II. iv. 69 There's a whole Marchants Venture of Burdeux-Stuffe in him. **1678** in *Jrnl. Friends' Hist. Soc.* (1912) IX. 193 Who being gone from the fathers house where ther is Liueing bread enough, his owne Company are glad of his dry huskey stufe. **1706** E. WARD *Wooden World Diss.* (1708) 57 Wretched gripe-gut Stuff. **1712** ARBUTHNOT *John Bull* III. vi. 23 My Friend Nic and I, not being used to such heady Stuff [champagne], got bloody Drunk. **1825** T. C. CROKER *Fairy Leg. Irel.* xxxii. (1859) 269 Dropping the glass, and it full of the stuff too, I bolted out of the door. **1854** SURTEES *Handley Cr.* iv. (1901) I. 30 A farmer and brewer; and making pretty good stuff, 'Dobbs's Ale'. **1861** MEREDITH *Evan Harrington* xi, The guests had arrived at that stage when to reach the arm, or arrange the person, for a sip of good stuff, causes moral debates. **1886** D. C. MURRAY *Aunt Rachel* II. i. 12 Tek a shillin' and get a drop o' good stuff wi' it, an' warm up that old gizzard o' thine. **1895** BRAM STOKER *Watter's Mou'* i. 5 Despite of all vigilance, a considerable amount of 'stuff' finds its way to the consumers without the formality of the Custom House. **1896** HOUSMAN *Shropshire Lad* lxii, Ale, man, ale's the stuff to drink For fellows whom it hurts to think.

d. In certain operative trades, applied *spec.* to some particular composition or preparation used in the work. (*a*) *Plastering.* (See quot. 1812.) (*b*) *Baking.* (See quot. 1820.) (*c*) *Leather-manuf.* (See quot. 1875) = STUFFING.

red stuff (see RED *a.* 19). ***touching stuff*** (see TOUCHING *vbl. sb.* 4). ***white stuff***, a gilders' composition of size and whiting, used to form a surface over wood to be gilded. (*Cent. Dict.* 1891.)

(*a*) **1812** P. NICHOLSON *Mech. Exerc.* 307 *Fine Stuff* is made of lime slacked and sifted through a fine sieve, and mixed with a due quantity of hair, and sometimes a small quantity of fine sand. Fine stuff is used in common ceilings and walls, set for paper or colour. *Ibid.* 309 *Lime and Hair*, is a mixture of lime and hair used in first coating and floating. It is otherwise denominated coarse stuff.

(*b*) **1820** *Blackw. Mag.* III. 546 Other individuals furnish the baker with alum mixed up with salt, under the obscure denomination of *stuff*. **1843** PEREIRA *Food & Diet* 311 Notwithstanding that the law prohibits, under a penalty, the use of alum by bakers, it is very frequently employed under the name of 'stuff'.

(*c*) **1875** KNIGHT *Dict. Mech.*, *Stuff* (Leather) a composition of fish-oil and tallow for filling the pores of leather. Dubbing. **1897** C. T. DAVIS *Manuf. Leather* xv. (ed. 2) 216 It must always be remembered that stale goods will not carry the stuff as well as fresh ones.

e. Cultivated produce of a garden or farm; natural produce of land.

a **1687-** [see GARDEN-STUFF]. **1813** RUDGE *Agric. Glouc.* 246 In some coppices, the small stuff, called drift-wood, is sold..as high as 5s. the square perch. **1868** ATKINSON *Cleveland Gloss.*, 'There's a vast o' stuff on t' land, surely'; growth or produce. **1896** P. A. GRAHAM *Red Scaur* iii. 34 His judgment of live-stock was infallible, and he seldom let any real good stuff go past. **1901** J. H. HARRIS *Luck of Wheal Veor* xi. 162 The ducks, chickens, and goslings, and all the young stuff shaping 'keenly' for future sale.

f. In commercial and industrial use, often applied *spec.* to the particular commodity dealt in or produced.

1708 J. C. *Compl. Collier* (1845) 12 By sight of the Stuff taken out of the Wimble, or Scoop, you plainly discover of what Kind it is. **1881** *Good Words* 843/2 The iron rope.. which..brought up the tub..with the 'stuff' as it was dug out. **1883** GRESLEY *Gloss. Coal-mining* 245 *Stuff*, coals and slack, the produce of the mine. **1912** *World* 7 May 700/1 Most of the nitrate companies..are making a better showing in their reports. At anything over 7s. 3d. per quintal the stuff pays handsomely. **1913** *Standard* 14 July 3/1 British steel is affected by the cheap offers of foreign stuff.

g. Narcotics, 'dope'. Phr. ***on the stuff***, addicted to drugs, on drugs. *slang* (orig. *U.S.*).

1929 *Amer. Speech* IV. 345 *Stuff*, dope. **1934** [see MAINLINE *v.*]. **1935** A. J. POLLOCK *Underworld Speaks* 84/1 *On the stuff*, addicted to dope. **1952** *Sunday Times* 3 Feb. 5/4 There has lately been a lot of research into the sale of narcotics (or 'junk' or 'stuff') and their effects on addicts. **1959** 'F. NEWTON' *Jazz Scene* 292 Jive talk..contains all the fancy-dress devices of private languages..the never-ending substitution of new passwords into the group for new codes ..the use of neutral and general words for highly specific things (e.g. *on the stuff*, or simply *on* for drug addiction). **1965** *New Statesman* 20 Aug. 248/3 Addicts have a secret language, which changes like a code. The commonest current name for heroin is 'stuff'. **1973** L. HELLMAN *Pentimento* 290 'His room-mate's on the stuff.' This then new way of saying dope..was no surprise. Years before she had told me her son was on the stuff. **1976** H. FERGUSON *Confessions Long Distance Acid Head* 65 'Yes. You were the bloke who got done for someone else's stuff..weren't you?' It was a junkie whom I had met in Ashford.

7. *transf.* and *fig.* in non-physical senses.

a. Literary or artistic matter; compositions, productions. Now *rare* exc. with disparaging implication (cf. 8), and *colloq.* among journalists and professional authors = 'copy'.

1542 UDALL *Erasm. Apoph.* 12 Whiche booke perused, Euripides asked, what he thought of it. By Iuppiter (saied Socrates) that, that I haue been hable to vnderstand me thynketh to be ioyly good stuffe. **1562** TURNER *Herbal* II. 70 He pretendeth as thoughe he neuer saw Dioscorides of whom he hath conueyed so much learned stuf in his omnigatherum. *a* **1586** SIDNEY *Astroph. & Stella* lvi, But now that I, alas, doe want her sight, What, dost thou thinke that I can euer take In thy cold stuffe a flegmatike delight? *a* **1668** LASSELS *Voy. Italy* II. (1698) 76, I saw upon the wall some old painting,..pitiful stuff. **1693** DRYDEN *Persius* i. Argt. (1697) 400 To decry the Poetry then in Fashion; and the Impudence of those, who were endeavouring to pass their Stuff upon the World. **1711** SWIFT *Jrnl. to Stella* 3 Oct., I..then went in to the music-meeting..: but was weary in half an hour of their fine stuff, and stole out so privately that everybody saw me. **1883** F. M. CRAWFORD *Dr. Claudius* i, He had been reading serious stuff. **1898** *Scribner's Mag.* May 580 Some of the younger crowd could tell which was Linton's stuff, and what kind of a story he was best at. **1915** *Daily News* 24 Apr. 4 This does not mean that they had finished writing their 'stuff' (to use an expressive technical phrase) for the daily papers.

†**b.** Matter of thought. *Obs.*

1602 SHAKS. *Ham.* II. ii. 324 *Ham.*... Man delights not me; no, nor Woman neither; though by your smiling you seeme to say so. *Rosin.* My Lord, there was no stuffe in my thoughts.

c. Applied to a person: chiefly with qualifying word. See also HOT STUFF a.

1588 SHAKS. *L.L.L.* IV. iii. 276 *Kin.* No Diuell will fright thee then so much as shee. *Duma.* I neuer knew man hold vile stuffe so deere. **1604** MIDDLETON *Witch* IV. ii. (1778) 82 She goes here by the name on's wife: good stuff! **1607** —— *Michaelmas Term* III. i. E 4, *Sho.* How now? what peece of stuffe comes heere? *a* **1641** BP. MOUNTAGU *Acts & Mon.* (1642) 250 He was so besotted..upon that now broken stuffe, and Crone in yeares, the cast beauty of that woman [Cleopatra].

d. Fighting material. *colloq.*

1883 *Manch. Exam.* 24 Nov. 5/1 The army of Ibrahim included a good deal of tougher stuff than the ordinary fellah of Egypt. **1894** *Outing* Sept. 445/1 Good! that big stuff can't box a little bit.

e. ***to do one's stuff***: to do what is required or expected of one; to perform one's role. *colloq.*

Quot. 1663 may belong to another sense.

1663 G. FOX *Jrnl.* (1694) I. 266 A while after, when the priest had done his stuff, they came to the friends again. **1922** *Radio News* (U.S.) IV. 854/1 (*caption*) Take a look at S. M. Brown, Chief on the Mauretania, 'doing his stuff' in the saloon. **1930** T. E. LAWRENCE *Lett.* (1938) 677 That portable was good at Miranshah. I hope yours is doing its stuff. **1933** *Bulletin* (Sydney) 19 Apr. 29/4 Australia will be represented in this event by Alan Bruce, who has been doing his stuff in London. **1946** F. SARGESON *That Summer* 144 If you knew how to do your stuff you never could tell but what it mightn't end up in a date. **1959** [see ANTI-AIRCRAFT *a.*]. **1967** G. F. FIENNES *I tried to run a Railway* vi. 70, I go when I can for the fun of hearing Richard doing his stuff. **1972** WODEHOUSE *Pearls, Girls, & Monty Bodkin* ii. 27 The Bishop and assistant clergy and the bridesmaids shall be encouraged to line up and do their stuff. **1976** *Daily Times* (Lagos) 27 Aug. 30/2 Ghana's Johnny Francois and a few others did their stuff abroad and, gradually, the panel took root.

f. ***that's the stuff*** (***to give them*** or ***to give the troops***): that is what is particularly appropriate to the situation, that is what is required.

1923 'BARTIMEUS' *Seaways* vii. 98 George Grayson and his Flock of Fascinating Flappers presents a screaming farce: The Giddy Governess! That's the stuff to give the troops!

1927 *Daily Express* 13 Oct. 12 That, if one may be pardoned the colloquialism, was the stuff to give them. **1942** H. C. Bailey *Dead Man's Shoes* xiv. 63 'A new married man with a lovely wife spends half the night with a police inspector he meets by chance! That's not the stuff to give the troops.'.. 'No, it don't sound natural.' **1943** J. B. Priestley *Daylight on Saturday* vii. 46 'We're always glad to have suggestions from anybody.' 'That's the stuff,' said Mr. Ogmore. **1977** P. D. James *Death of Expert Witness* ii. i. 53 Inspector Blakelock.. was always ready for his tea... 'That's the stuff to give the troops,' he would invariably say.

g. ***to know one's stuff***: to be experienced or knowledgeable in one's subject, profession, etc. *colloq.*

1927 *Amer. Speech* II. 277 *Know your onions* or *know your stuff*, have grasp of your subjects. **1935** *Swing Music* June 111/1 The Little Man of the Rhythm Clubs did himself proud in this test paper. He knows his stuff. **1938** G. Greene *Brighton Rock* iii. i. 108 'This doctor,' she says, 'he knows his stuff?' **1945** R. A. Knox *God & Atom* x. 132 All I have written could have been written very much better by someone who, in an expressive modern phrase, knew his stuff. **1952** J. Steinbeck *East of Eden* xxxiii. 46 It's a lulu. Kate sure knows her stuff. **1967** M. Argyle *Psychol. Interpersonal Behaviour* ix. 166 His [*sc.* the supervisor's] influence will be accepted more readily if it is believed that he really knows his stuff. **1973** A. Christie *Postern of Fate* iii. vii. 174 'He gave me a lot of knowledge about planting things.' 'Yes, he knew his stuff, as you might say.'

8. What is worthless; rubbish. (Orig. a contextual use of sense 7, with disparaging epithet or other indication of aversion).

a. *gen.*

a **1668** Lassels *Voy. Italy* ii. (1670) 404 Here also they have every night in summer, a world of Montibanks, *Ciarlatani*, and such stuff. **1706** M. Henry *Expos. Gen.* xlv. 20 What they had in Canaan he reckoned but stuff.. the best of its [the world's] Enjoyments are but stuff, but lumber. **1720** Hearne *Collect.* (O.H.S.) VII. 120 Dr. Charlett.. went over.. to get some MSS. (I am told, very sorry ones) for the Publ. Library... The Persons that told me observ'd that a Library may soon be filled with such stuff. **1810** *Sporting Mag.* XXXVI. 187 A red curtain, a Grecian couch, or some such fashionable stuff. **1883** *Daily News* 14 Feb. 5/7 The brass dishes are poor stuff.

b. Worthless ideas, discourse, or writing; nonsense, rubbish. Often coupled with *nonsense* (chiefly ***stuff and nonsense***, †***nonsense and stuff***). Frequently in interjectional use.

1579 Gosson *Sch. Abuse* (Arb.) 66 Iuno crieth out in Seneca,.. Lets dwel in earth, for heauen is full of whores. What stuffe is this? wantons in heauen? **1606** Shaks. *Tr. & Cr.* i. iii. 161 At this fusty stuffe, The large Achilles.. laughes out a lowd applause. **1691–8** Norris *Pract. Disc.* IV. 415 Would not this be mere Stuff, wretched Trifling,.. and as much to the Purpose as if he had said just Nothing? **1701** Farquhar *Sir H. Wildair* iv. ii, Golden Pleasures! Golden Fiddlesticks.—What d'ye tell me of your canting Stuff? *Ibid.*, Stuff! stuff! stuff!—I won't believe a Word on't. **1749** Fielding *Tom Jones* vii. vi, Pooh, all stuff and nonsense. I tell thee, she shall ha' thee to-morrow. **1770** Foote *Lame Lover* i. 10 Pshaw! nonsense and stuff.—The eye! **1778** Johnson in *Boswell* (1904) II. 185 It is sad stuff, Sir, miserably written, as books in general then were. **1833** Coleridge *Table-t.* 28 Aug., Your art diplomatic is stuff:—no truly great man would negociate now upon any such shallow principles. **1851–61** Mayhew *Lond. Labour* II. 175/2 It's all stuff and nonsense, all this talk about dust-yards being unhealthy. **1852** Thackeray *Esmond* i. vi, 'Stuff! we must see Lady Castlewood,' says the lawyer, pushing by. **1860** Miss Yonge *Hopes & Fears* i. 181 'Only because I am not come out.' 'Stuff about coming out! I don't like my girls to be shy and backward.' **1887** T. E. Brown *Lett.* (1900) I. 125 Poor G. Sand! I am reading her *Amours de l'Âge d'Or*. Woe is me! what awful stuff! **1890** 'R. Boldrewood' *Col. Reformer* xxiv, 'Stuff!' said Miss Augusta.

†**c.** Indecent matter. *Obs.*

1749 Fielding *Tom Jones* xii. v, A grave matron told the master [of a puppet-show] she would bring her two daughters the next night, as he did not show any stuff.

d. *Phrase.* ——***and stuff***, and such-like useless or uninteresting matters. *colloq.*

? **1697** J. Lewis *Mem. Dk. Glocester* (1789) 66 She turned to me and said, 'Lewis, I find you pretend to give the Duke notions of the mathematics, and stuff.' **1729** Swift *Grand Question debated* 159 Your Noveds, and Blutraks, and Omurs and Stuff, By G——, they don't signify this Pinch of Snuff. **1774** Goldsm. *Retal.* 145 When they talk'd of their Raphaels, Corregios, and stuff. **1852** Thackeray *Esmond* iii. iv, And as for you, you want a woman.. to sit at your feet, and cry, 'O caro! O bravo!' whilst you read your Shakespeares and Miltons and stuff.

e. *gen.* Used *loosely* to denote any collection of things about which one is not able or willing to particularize (a weakened application of senses 6, 7); material, matter, business. *colloq.*

1922 [see sense 7 e above]. **1949** 'G. Orwell' *1984* ii. ii. 123 You thought I was a good Party member. Pure in word and deed. Banners, processions, slogans, games, community hikes—all that stuff. **1967** R. Brautigan *Trout Fishing in America* (1970) 83 One spring day she had me ascend to the attic and clean up some boxes of stuff and throw out some stuff and put some stuff back into its imaginary proper place. **1977** J. D. MacDonald *Condominium* xxxvii. 370 Once they left we were going to move his stuff out and change the locks.

f. Hence, with preceding epithet.

1929, etc. [see kid *sb.*[1] 6]. **1932** S. Gibbons *Cold Comfort Farm* xiii. 191 She had best not pull any Cinderella stuff on me. **1939** *Punch* 5 July 9/1 'Sam,' they said to him, 'what's wrong? You can bowl much better stuff than that.' **1948** *Sporting Mirror* 21 May 7/3 Jack Martin may also be available for fast stuff on occasions. **1974** *Times Lit. Suppl.* 26 Apr. 440/3 The principal message [of Hochhuth's comedy *Lysistrate und die NATO*] is largely straightforward feminist stuff. **1976** *National Observer* (U.S.) 9 Oct. 2/4 The threat of another oil embargo is always serious stuff here. **1978** D. Williams *Treasure up in Smoke* xiii. 120 What he said was pretty strong stuff... He fairly laid into Mr. O'Hara.

9. a. *U.S.* (See quot.) Cf. stuffy *a.* 4.

1787 J. Q. Adams *Diary* (1903) 66 She.. has rather too much temper, or as it is called in New-England, too much stuff.

b. *N. Amer.* In various sports, the spin or 'work' imparted to a ball in order to make it vary its course; the type of control which effects this. Also *fig.*

1905 *Sporting Life* (U.S.) 9 Sept. 1/1 If I tried some of the stuff that certain pitchers use and escape bumping, I have an idea that the fielders would never stop.. hitting. **1913** *Harper's Weekly* 13 Sept. 21/2 Weilman, the giant Brown, is another [pitcher] who has the 'stuff'. **1927** *Daily Tel.* 21 Feb. 13/6 T. A. Workman, their captain, was in wonderfully good form against Commander S. W. Beadle, finding an almost perfect length for an American service which had plenty of 'stuff' on it. Beadle could not do anything with it, and was kept on the defensive throughout. **1936** J. T. Farrell *World I Never Made* v. 68 The O'Neills are proud of their name, and they got as much stuff on the ball in the game of life as old Three-fingered Brown has when he toes the mound. **1947** *Sun* (Baltimore) 3 Apr. 20/1 He is only 20 years old, has a good arm and has much of the well known stuff on the ball. **1967** Varner & Harrison *Table Tennis* v. 51 These spinners are often one-ball hitters: they vary their 'stuff' until you yield a loose return, which they efficiently kill. **1970** J. H. Gray *Boy from Winnipeg* 152 That got us seats behind home plate where we could watch the stuff, mainly curves, that the pitchers were putting on the ball. **1981** *Washington Star* 30 Apr. c4/1 'I really had good stuff tonight,' the lefthander said in a post-game radio interview. 'My slider wasn't great at the beginning, but my fastball really was good.'

10. *slang.* **a.** Money, cash. Chiefly with article ***the stuff***.

1775 Sheridan *Rivals* i. i, But has she got the stuff, Mr. Fag; is she rich, hey? **1787** *Minor* 198 He made me an offer of some stuff—for such, you may recollect, is the epithet bestowed by all great philosophers on gold. **1823** 'Jon Bee' *Dict. Turf* s.v., 'Hand over the stuff,' give the money. **1896** J. F. B. Lillard *Poker Stories* 50 Those were the days, my boy—.. every sport with stuff in his pockets and lots of good clothes.

b. Stolen goods.

1865 *Daily Tel.* 3 Nov. 5/1 This particular parcel of 'stuff' was arrested, however, in mid course. **1894** *Daily News* 16 Oct. 2/5 Fitzpatrick at once confessed to complicity in the robbery, and said he would tell where 'the stuff' was.

c. Forbidden goods smuggled into a jail.

1904 A. Griffiths *50 Yrs. Publ. Service* xi. 154 We had news constantly of 'stuff' planted for cash in exchange.

11. Phr. ***not to give a stuff***, etc. = *not to give a fuck* s.v. fuck *sb.* 2. Cf. stuff *v.* 15 a. Chiefly *Austral.* and *N.Z. slang.*

1974 *Bookseller* 19 Jan. 117/3 A word or two of criticism: I don't give a stuff for your great managing director. **1976–7** *Sea Spray* (N.Z.) Dec./Jan. 62/1 Well, deep down inside I don't really give a stuff. **1977** *Bulletin* (Sydney) 22 Jan. 100/3 The list goes on and on and on and as it grows so does the feeling amongst the blokes in the bush that no one gives a stuff. **1979** N. Gordimer *Burger's Daughter* i. 42 In the end no one cares a stuff who's in jail or what war's on, so long as it's far away. **1980** B. Mason *Solo* 207, I don't give a stuff if it was or not. That spoke to me. Opened up my life, things I'd forgotten.

12. *attrib.* and *Comb.*

a. attrib. passing into adj.: Made of stuff or woollen cloth (see sense 5 c).

c **1643** Ld. Herbert *Autobiog.* (1824) 162 A.. person came to me apparelled in a black stuff suit. **1702** *Post Man* 17–19 Sept. 2/2 Sad coloured stuff Coat, and black Hat. **1718** *Freethinker* No. 13 ¶8 Were she to be reduced to a Stuff-Gown to-morrow, [she] could part with all her Jewels and Brocades, without a Sigh. **1730** *Inventory R. Woolley's Goods* (1732) 11, 3 Chairs with Stuff Seats. **1839** Macaulay *Gladstone* Ess. 1865 II. 65 To tell a barrister.. that he shall grow old in his stuff gown, while his pupils are seated above him in ermine. **1840** Barham *Ingol. Leg.* Ser. ii. *Bl. Mousquetaire* ii. 80 The fusty stuff gown of a *Sœur de la Charité*. **1856** *N. Brit. Rev.* XXVI. 248 He led the Northern Circuit in a stuff gown, many silks being obliged to keep their talents in abeyance. **1857** Hughes *Tom Brown* i. ii, The field thronged with country-folk, the men in clean white smocks.., and the women.. in new-fashioned stuff shawls. **1897** Voynich *Gadfly* i. iii, An old stuff frock that was too short for her.

b. Simple attrib., as ***stuff goods***, ***-manufacture***, ***mercer***, ***trade***; objective, as ***stuff-finisher***, ***-maker***, ***-manufacturer***, ***-seller***, ***-weaver***; ***stuff-weaving*** vbl. sb.; parasynthetic, as ***stuff-bottomed*** adj.

1816 Scott *Antiq.* x, The.. heavy *stuff-bottomed chairs. **1861** *Internat. Exhib. 1862, Alph. Lists Trades* 39 *Stuff Finishers. **1816** *Acts 14th Congr. U.S.* Sess. i. c. 107 §1 Blankets, woollen rugs and worsted or *stuff goods. **1780** *Indenture Clifton, Notts*, Bennet Thorpe, *stuffmaker. **1730** *Lett. to Sir W. Strickland* 11 The Callicoe-Act.. made on purpose to encourage our *Stuff-Manufacture. **1858** Simmonds *Dict. Trade*, **Stuff-manufacturer*, a maker of thin woollen cloth. **1723** *Lond. Gaz.* No. 6139/3 John Harrison and Richard Harrison,.. *Stuff-Mercers. **1711** *Ibid.* No. 4801/4 William Paine,.. *Stuff-seller. **1884** *Manch. Exam.* 12 Nov. 5/3 It was proclaimed.. that the *stuff trade had gone to the dogs altogether. **1706** *Lond. Gaz.* No. 4246/8 William Madlow,.. *Stuff-Weaver. **1832** Thackrah *Effects Arts* etc. *on Health* (ed. 2) Index 237 Stuff-weavers. **1702** E. Calamy *Abridgm. Baxter's Life & Times* iii. 34 Their Common Trade of *Stuff Weaving would find Work for all.

c. Special comb.: **stuff ball** (see quot.); **stuff-chest** *Paper-manuf.*, the vat or reservoir into which the pulps from the beating engine are run and mixed; **stuff engine** *Paper-manuf.*, the 'beating engine', a machine in which half-stuff is reduced to a fine pulp; **stuff gown**, a junior counsel (see 5 d above); so also **stuff gownsman**; **stuff hat** (see quot. 1839); **stuff heap**, a heap of coals and slack raised from a mine; **stuff mark**, a weaver's mark woven into goods for the purpose of identification or as attestation of their quality; **stuff-melter** *Soap-manuf.*, an operative who extracts the oils, fats, etc. from the raw materials; **stuff-over** *a.*, applied to chairs, etc., which are upholstered by having the material drawn over the frame of a fixed seat and secured beneath; also *absol.* as *sb.*, a stuff-over seat; **stuff-presser** *Woollen-manuf.*, a workman employed in pressing or finishing the cloth; **stuff shoes** (see quot. 1892); **stuff-shovel** (see quot.).

1880 Sir C. H. J. Anderson *Lincoln Pocket Guide* 176 Patronesses of the *Stuff Ball. Established in 1787 for the encouragement of native woollen manufacture... The ladies used to wear stuff gowns, and the gentlemen stuff coats [etc.]. [List of Patronesses, 1787–1879, follows.] **1799** *Hull Advertiser* 1 June 1/1 Paper-mill.. comprises.. four vatts, *stuff-chests and beaters. **1881** *Spons' Encycl. Industr. Arts* iv. 1497 Whence the mixed stuff flows on the sand-tables, to be again used to dilute fresh pulp from the stuff-chests. **1839** Ure *Dict. Arts* 924 The construction of the *stuff-engine is represented in figs. 785, 786. **1867** Woolrych *Bar & Serjeant-at-Law* 7 The promotions will be of a *Stuff Gown, as it is called, or of a learned Counsel of the Crown. **1852** *Fraser's Mag.* Feb. 129/1 A sagacious chancellor lifts a *stuff-gowns-man from the back row to the judgment-seat. **1839** Ure *Dict. Arts* 634 The materials used in making *stuff hats are the furs of hairs and rabbits freed from the long hair, together with wool and beaver. **1662** *Act 14 Chas. II*, c. 5 §15 Every Person.. shall weave his proper *Stuff Mark into every peice of Stuff which he shall weave. **1884** A. Watt *Soap-making* 28 Kitchen-stuff, as prepared by the '*stuff-melters,' is a very useful article for mottled soaps. **1915** R. S. Bowers et al. *Furniture Making* xxxi. 353 *Stuffover chair and settee. **1963** *Times* 2 Feb. 11 The slip-in seat is almost universal and the stuffover almost unknown in Portuguese Chippendale chairs. **1972** *Country Life* 1 June 1414/1 Regency mahogany dining chairs.. with stuffover seats. **1976** *Liverpool Daily Post* 11 Dec. (Advt.), For sale, stuff-over roll back (Chesterfield Settee in silk damask). **1831** Thackrah *Effects Arts* etc. *on Health* 72 *Stuff-pressers carry heavy plates of iron heated to redness. **1794** Waldron *Heigho for Husb.* i. ii. 3 We'll.. put on coarse linen gowns, and *stuff shoes; enrol ourselves at a register-office; get good places. **1892** *Labour Commission* Gloss., *Stuff Shoes*, shoes of which the tops or upper parts are made from 'lasting' [a woven worsted material], cashmere, or fancy cloth. **1858** Simmonds *Dict. Trade*, **Stuff-shovel*, an implement used by the paper-makers.

stuff (stʌf), *sb.*[2] Now *S. African.* Also 5 stuf. [a. Du. *stof* dust (cogn. w. G. *staub*): two independent adoptions.] Dust.

1481 Caxton *Reynard* xxxix. (Arb.) 107 Thenne wold he goo aboue the wynde and reyse the duste, that it made his eyen ful of stufs. **1863** W. C. Baldwin *Afr. Hunting* vi. 145 Herds.. scouring away before me.. amid such a cloud of stuff raised by their own tearing away that I never knew what I was firing at.

stuff (stʌf), *v.*[1] Forms: 4–5 stoff, 6 stof, 4–7 stuffe, 5–7 stuf, 4– stuff. [a. OF. *estoffer* (NE. dial. *stoffeir*: Anglo-Latin *stuffare*) to furnish, equip, garrison (mod.F. *étoffer*, to furnish with what is necessary, to supply material for) = Sp. *estofar*, to embroider in relief, Pg. *estofar*, to embroider, to quilt, to stuff (cushions, meat):—Rom. **stoffare*: for the ulterior etymology see stuff *sb.*[1]]

†**1. a.** *trans.* To furnish (a fortified town, stronghold, an army, a commander, etc.) with men, munitions, and stores; to garrison (a town). *Obs.*

13.. *E.E. Allit. P.* B. 1184 For þe borȝ was so bygge baytayled alofte, & stoffed wyth-inne with stout men to stalle hem þer-oute. **1375** Barbour *Bruce* xvii. 213 The king.. vald nocht brek doune the vall, Bot castell, and the toune with-all, Stuff weill with men and vith vittaill And alkynd othir apparaill. *Ibid.* 350 Wardis.. That war stuffit richt stalwardly With stanys, schot, and other thing. **1444** *Rolls of Parlt.* V. 74/1 Also to stuffe the Castelles, Tounes, and alle maner Forteresses. **1470–85** Malory *Arthur* i. 35 The kyng.. badde hym be redy and stuffe hym and garnysshe hym, for within xl dayes he wold fetche hym oute of the byggest castell that he hath. **1513** Douglas *Æneis* ix. iv. 4 The Troianis.. All thar deray beheld.. And baith wyth armour and with wappynnis brycht The tour hedis thai stuffit all that nyght. *Ibid.* xi. ix. 51 A party of the cietezanis, he said, Do stuf the entreis, and the portis defend. **1535** Stewart *Cron. Scot.* (Rolls) III. 314 He passit to Athell, And stuffit hes ilk castell that wes strang With men and meit. **1611** Speed *Hist. Gt. Brit.* ix. xvi. §10. 653 S. Iean, a Towne of Normandy.. which Edmund Duke of Somerset.. had lately fortified and stuft with souldiers. **1640** Yorke *Union Hon., Battles* 11 Hertford Castle.. like wise the Castle of Berkhampsteade, both which he stuffed with French Garrisons.

†**b.** To furnish (troops) with support; to reinforce; to support, aid (a war). ***to stuff a chase*** (*Sc.*), to provide men for, organize a pursuit. *Obs.*

c **1400** *Destr. Troy* 8284 Menelay with his men meuyt in swithe,.. Restorit hom stithly, stuffit hom anon. *c* **1470** Henry *Wallace* v. 277 To stuff the chas feyll frekis folowit fast. *Ibid.* v. 935, x. 268. **1513** Douglas *Æneis* x. ii. 89 Gif I evir into that weyr Minysterit dartis, wapynnys, or sic geyr? Or ȝit that bargane stuffyt or bet,.. With Cupidis blynd lust and subtilite? Than had bene [etc.]. **1533**

BELLENDEN *Livy* (S.T.S.) II. 77 To stuffe þis army..war ekit þe auld centurions. **1535** STEWART *Cron. Scot.* (Rolls) III. 170 Tha tuke haill purpois in that samin place, Efter king Edward for to stuffe ane chace. *c* **1560** ROLLAND *Seven Sages* (Bann. Club) 203 Ane Empreour..Quha had greit Kings into his companie,.. Doing seruice..Sum for pastime and sum to stuf his weir.

†**c.** To marshal (troops). *Obs.*

a **1375** *Joseph Arim.* 601 þe stiward of Tholomer stoffes hem to-gedere, and seis, [etc.].

†**2. a.** To supply or furnish (a person) with arms, provisions, money, etc. Const. *of*, *with*. *Obs.*

c **1375** BARBOUR *Bruce* XI. 47 Off tresour so stuffit is he, That he may vageowris haf plente. **1387-8** T. USK *Test. Love* I. x. (Skeat) 44 If thou laudest and joyest any wight, for he is stuffed with soche maner richesse, thou art in that beleeve begyled. **14..** *Sc. Acts Robt. I* (1844) I. 468/2 Ilk lord sal cum stuffyt & purvayt [L. *stuffatus*] to þe ost of caryage and vyttalis as he wil be servyt. **1430-40** LYDG. *Bochas* IX. xxxviii. (1554) 217, I, not expert, nor stuffed with language. **1432** *Rolls of Parlt.* IV. 410/1 The merchantes strangiers been stuffed so gretely therwith. *c* **1475** *Partenay* 6378 Thys lady..To all other lades exemplair, Well stuffed with all maner of goodnesse. **1551** EDW. VI *Jrnl.* (Roxb. Club) II. 327 Then, that she should be brought at her father's charge three monthes before she was twelf, sufficiently juelled and stuffed. **1592** SHAKS. *Rom. & Jul.* III. v. 183 A Gentleman..Stuft as they say with Honourable parts. **1656** *Burton's Diary* (1828) I. 198 This day hath brought you work enough for half a year, and another day will stuff you sufficiently.

†**b.** To arm and equip (a soldier). Alliterative phrase, ***stuffed in steel***. *Obs.*

?*a* **1400** *Morte Arth.* 1932 Whene any stirttez to stale, stuffe þame þe bettere, Ore thei wille be stonayede, and stroyede in ȝone strayte londez. *a* **1420** *Aunters of Arth.* 391 In stele was he stuffede, þat stourne vppone stede. *c* **1470** HENRY *Wallace* v. 266 Befor him come feyll stuffyt in fyne steill. *Ibid.* x. 22 The Sotheroun was rycht douchty in thair deid, To gydder straik, weyll stuffyt in steyll weid. *a* **1483** *Liber Niger* in *Househ. Ord.* (1790) 17 Every man stuffed and renned [*sic*] at the Kinges costes of suche defence as he coude best deale withall.

†**3. a.** To furnish (a place) with accessories, stock, inhabitants; to store with provisions, etc. *Obs.*

c **1386** CHAUCER *Clerk's T.* 208 Houses of office stuffed with plentee. *c* **1400** *Rom. Rose* 7065 So that the tour were stuffed wel With alle richesse temporel. **1430-40** LYDG. *Bochas* IV. ix. (1554) 107 In a caue..he made him to be throu, The place stuffed with good barking houndes. **1449** *Sc. Acts Jas. II* (1814) II. 36/2 Gif ony man..resettis ony þat ar conuict of tresone..or þat stuffis the housis of þaim þat ar conuict of tresone..[they] sal be punyst as tratouris. **1523** BERNERS *Froiss.* I. cxxiii. 148 They fledde away..and left their houses well stuffed, and graunges full of corne. **1530** PALSGR. 742/1, I stuffe, or store a grounde with thynges that growe and encrease, *je peuple*. **1546** *Supplic, Poore Commons* (E.E.T.S.) 79 Bringyng them [*sc.* children] vp other to bear wallettes, other eles, if thei be sturdy, to stuffe prisons, and garnysh galow trees. **1570-6** LAMBARDE *Peramb. Kent* 168 This Weald..was..not planted with Townes,..but stoared and stuffed with heardes of Deare. **1598** BARCKLEY *Felic. Man* II. 101 Hee buildeth his house with his sonnes money,..and stuffeth it handsomely. **1603-26** BRETON *Poste Mad Lett.* (Grosart) 42/1 Whose seruants better gouerned? whose house better stuffed and maintained?

†**b.** To store (goods) in a receptacle or place; to keep (flocks) in a place. *Obs.*

1567 *Bauldwin's Mor. Philos.* (Palfr.) III. (1600) 58 Princes liue more surely with the gathering to them men of good liuing & conuersation, then with treasures of mony stuffed in their chestes. **1596** SHAKS. *Tam. Shr.* II. i. 352 In Iuory cofers I haue stuft my crownes. **1605** *First Pt. Jeronimo* I. iii. 22 Farmers that crack barns With stuffing corne, yet starue the needy swarmes. **1606** *Nottingham Rec.* IV. 280 No person shall att any tyme hencefurthe stuffe, hould, or keepe any sheepe in or vpon any the sayd highwayes.

†**4.** To line (a helmet, a garment) with cloth, etc. *Obs.*

13.. *Gaw. & Gr. Knt.* 606 þe helme..þat was stapled stifly, & stoffed wyth-inne. *c* **1400** *Sege Jerus.* (E.E.T.S.) 422 Was noȝt, while þe nyȝt laste, bot nehyng of stedis, Strogelyng in stele wede & stuffyng of helmes. *c* **1470** *Gol. & Gaw.* 735 Thai stuffit helmys in hy, Breist-plait and birny. **1473-4** *Acc. Ld. High Treas. Scot.* I. 16 Gret braid clath to stuf ij doublatis to the King. **1552** *Ibid.* X. 70 Item, ane elne of quhite bukrame to stuff the hude and slevis. **1590** SIR J. SMYTH *Disc. Weapons* 46 Deepe steele skulles in very narrowe brimbd hats, well stuffed for the easines of their heades.

5. a. To line or fill with some material as a padding; to distend or expand with padding; esp. to fill (a bedtick, cushion, etc.) with packing in order to furnish a yielding support. Also with *out*, *up*.

c **1450** *Cov. Myst.* (Shaks. Soc.) 241 Cadace wolle or flokkys,..To stuffe withal thi dobbelet, and make the of proporcyon. **1480** *Wardr. Acc. Edw. IV* (1830) 125 For making and stuffing of a sadelle. *Ibid.* 130 Federbeddes stuffed with downe. **1494** *Act 11 Hen. VII*, c. 19 Quyltes mattres and cussions stuffed with horse here. **1530** PALSGR. 741/2, I stuffe a tycke of a bedde with fethers, *je emplume*. **1597** SHAKS. *2 Hen. IV*, v. v. 87 Giue me your Doublet, and stuffe me out with Straw. **1644** BP. HALL *Serm.* 21 July, Rem. Wks. (1660) 135 Many a one..hath found nothing but an image of clouts laid upon a bolster stuffed with Goats hair. *a* **1700** EVELYN *Diary* 4 Dec. 1679, The bound is made so exactly even, and the edges [of a billiard-table] not stuff'd. **1700** DRYDEN *Baucis & Ph.* 47 Two Cushions stuff'd with Straw, the Seat to raise. *a* **1716** SOUTH *Serm.* (1823) V. 140 Many of these [Plato's scholars] found it easier to imitate Plato's shoulders than his philosophy, and to stuff out their gowns than to furnish their understandings. **1784** COWPER *Task* VI. 674 For there [*sc.* in the theatre] some noble lord Shall stuff his shoulders with king Richard's bunch. **1827** SCOTT *Surg. Dau.* xiv, Horsemen..in a sort of defensive armour, consisting of rich silk dresses, rendered sabre proof by being stuffed with cotton. **1839** J. W. BURGON *Gresham* I. iii. 210 His breeches, which were stuffed out with cotton, were more useful than ornamental. **1891** FARRAR *Darkn. & Dawn* i, He had lingered on, chewing in his agony the tow with which his mattress was stuffed. **1908** *Animal Management* (Vet. Departm., War Office) 210 To stuff a collar under these circumstances means that it is too tight when the horse puts up muscle.

transf. and *fig.* **1633** G. HERBERT *Temple, Love Unknown* 48, I found that some had stuff'd the bed with thoughts, I would say, thorns. **1646** SIR T. BROWNE *Pseud. Ep.* I. vi. 22 A considerable part of Ancient times, was by the Greeks themselves termed μύθικον, that is made up or stuffed out with fables. **1648** GAGE *West Ind.* 122 Lying words of miracles, wherewith they stuffe up a whole houres preaching. **1699** BENTLEY *Phalaris* 296 His other Citations, with which his Margin is plentifully stuft out. **1781** COWPER *Hope* 105 No need, he cries, of gravity stuff'd out With academic dignity devout, To read wise lectures, vanity the text.

b. Of material: To serve as padding or stuffing.

c **1530** in *Archæologia* XXV. 503 For vj lb. of flock for to stuff cusshonys iiij d. **1599** SHAKS. *Much Ado* III. ii. 47 The Barbers man hath beene seen with him, and the olde ornament of his cheeke hath alreadie stuft tennis balls. **1607** —— *Cor.* II. i. 98 Your Beards deserue not so honourable a graue, as to stuffe a Botchers Cushion.

†**c.** To distend, expand (as if by padding). *Obs.*

1595 SHAKS. *John* III. iv. 97 Greefe fils the roome vp of my absent childe:..Stuffes out his vacant garments with his forme. **1605** *Hist. Capt. Stukeley* I 3, The ioyfull breath that issues from thy lips, Comes like a lusty gale to stuffe our sailes. **1631** FULLER *David's Sin* III. xxx. (1867) 238 Their very sighs might serve to stuff the sail. **1678** T. P[ORTER] *Fr. Conjurer* I. 4 Let his Breeches be made straight and stufft with Whalebone, to reduce his Limbs into a Spanish Posture.

†**d.** To convert (*into* something) by stuffing. *Obs.* (? *nonce-use*).

1724 SWIFT *Drapier's Lett.* v. (1730) 176, I have read..of an Eastern King who put a Judge to Death for an iniquitous Sentence, and order'd his Hide to be stuffed into a Cushion.

6. *Cookery.* To fill (the inside of a bird or animal, a piece of meat, etc.) with forcemeat, herbs, etc. as a stuffing.

c **1430** *Two Cookery-bks.* I. 32 Fyrste Stuffe þin chekons in þis wyse. *Ibid.* 40 þan stuffe hem as þou stuffyst a Pigge. **1530** PALSGR. 741/2, I stuffe a podyng or suche lyke, *je farce*. **1570** in Gutch *Collect. Cur.* (1781) II. 6 For a lege of mutton to be boyled and stofed with parshleye..viij d. **1591** A. W. *Bk. Cookrye* 12 To make puddings of a Swine..take the guts clean washed, and stuffe them with the aforesaid stuffe. **1596** SHAKS. *Tam. Shr.* IV. IV. 101 As shee went to the Garden for Parseley to stuffe a Rabit. **1623** MIDDLETON *More Dissemblers* IV. I. 154, I would they [the ducks] were all rotten rosted, and stuft with Onions. **1747** MRS. GLASSE *Cookery* ii. 26 To Stuff a Leg or Shoulder of Mutton. *Ibid.* 36 Take a Turky or Fowl, stuff the Breast with what Force-Meat you like. **1846** SOYER *Cookery* 255 Stuff the rabbits and roast them. **1855** [PHILP] *Pract. Housewife* 108 Tomatas, to stuff.—Take some fine tomatas and scoop the inside out, [etc.].

7. To fill out (the skin of a beast, bird, etc.) with material so as to resemble the living creature; *spec.* in *Taxidermy*, to fill the skin of (a bird or beast) with materials to preserve it and present it in its natural form.

1555 EDEN *Decades* (Arb.) 261 He causes them [*sc.* rebels] to be slene..: Then to bee stuffed with chaffe, and sette vppe. **1592** SHAKS. *Rom. & Jul.* v. i. 43 And in his needie shop a Tortoyrs hung, An Allegater stuft. **1617** MORYSON *Itin.* III. 163 The Cowes..will give no Milke till the skinne of the Calfe bee stuffed and set before them. **1727** [E. DORRINGTON] *Philip Quarll* (1816) 66 They carried away..the fine bird he had taken such pains to stuff. **1821** SCOTT *Kenilw.* xxx, Many birds have flown as high, that I have seen stuffed with straw, and hung up to scare kites. **1865** DICKENS *Mut. Fr.* III. vii, I was down at the water-side, looking for parrots brought home by sailors, to buy for stuffing. **1915** F. LEGGE *Forerunners of Christianity* II. xiii. 281 He was decapitated, and his skin stuffed with straw was suspended at the gate of the town.

8. a. To fill (a receptacle); esp. to fill by packing the materials closely together, to cram full. ***to stuff out***: to fill a receptacle so full that it bulges; to distend with filling.

c **1440** LYDG. *Hors, Shepe & G.* 616 When deth approchyth..The riche is shet with coloures & picture To hide his careyn stuffid with fowle ordure. **1515** BARCLAY *Egl.* IV. (1570) C vj, Some mery fit..Of perte of Norwiche,..Or buckishe Ioly well stuffed as a ton. **1596** SHAKS. *1 Hen. IV*, I. ii. 146 If you will go, I will stuffe your Purses full of Crownes. **1613** J. TAYLOR (Water P.) *Laugh & be Fat* Wks. (1630) II. 73/1 For as a candle's stuft with cotton weeke, So thou art cramm'd vp to the brim with Greeke. **1646** SIR T. BROWNE *Pseud. Ep.* II. v. 87 So a glasse stuffed with peeces of spunge. **1675** HOBBES *Odyss.* VIII. (1686) 98 The Horse of Wood..Stufft by Ulysses full of Warriours good. **1705** [E. WARD] *Hudibras Rediv.* IV. 11 In's Hand a Wallet stuff'd with Papers. **1766** GOLDSM. *Vic. W.* x. I. 84 At another time she imagined her daughter's pockets filled with farthings, a certain sign of their being one day stuffed with gold. **1781** COWPER *Conversat.* 310 But when unpack'd your disappointment groans To find it [a parcel] stuff'd with brick-bats, earth, and stones. **1827** SCOTT *Surg. Dau.* ii, His pockets stuffed out with bank-notes. **1830-60** W. HOLMES *Dorchester Giant* iv, Then he brought them a pudding stuffed with plums. **1855** KINGSLEY *Westw. Ho!* xi, As soon as Fortune stuffs your mouth full of sweetmeats, do you turn informer on her? **1899** *Allbutt's Syst. Med.* VIII. 855 The thickening of the hair is due to its being stuffed with fungus. **1904** B'NESS VON HUTTEN *Pam* I. iii, 'Well, Jane, and so here we are,' he began, stuffing his little meerschaum pipe from a leather bag.

b. Said of the filling material. ? *Obs.*

1664 POWER *Exp. Philos.* I. 25 The crustaceous Cornea of the Creckets Eye, which I have carefully separated from all the matter which stuff'd it within. **1697** DRYDEN *Æneid* II. 26 With inward Arms the dire Machine they load, And Iron Bowels stuff the dark Abode.

c. To crowd, cram (a vehicle, room *with* persons). Also *intr.* for *pass.* To be crammed. Now *rare*.

1571 in Hudson & Tingey *Rec. Norwich* (1910) II. 345 The victualling houses were stuffed with players and dronkerdes. **1799** SIR M. HUNTER *Jrnl.* 27 Feb. (1894) 138 On the wedding-day we assembled at ten o'clock, Jews and Christians; the room as full as it could stuff. **1829** C. ROSE *Four Yrs. S. Africa* 10 The long heavy waggon..hired for the day, and stuffed with black damsels.

d. *U.S.* 'To put fraudulent votes into (a ballot-box)' (W. 1911).

1872 SCHELE DE VERE *Americanisms* 272. **1906** *Q. Rev.* July 283 The interval had been devoted to stuffing the ballot-boxes.

e. To pack or load (a freight container). *slang.*

1965 R. B. ORAM *Cargo Handling* vi. 115 Containers can come into..a Consolidation Depot where they are stuffed with miscellaneous general cargo. **1968** [see STRIP *v.*[1] 7 e]. **1972** *Timber Trades Jrnl.* 13 May 44/1 The dockers threaten to continue the ban until their demands are met which include the exclusive right to stuff (pack) and unstuff (unpack) containers. **1972** *Nature* 11 Aug. 301/2 British dockers are..asking that members of their union should have a right to employment at the centres at which containers are stuffed with goods.

9. *fig.* **a.** To fill, crowd (speech, etc.) *with* something (usually something objectionable).

a **1568** ASCHAM *Scholem.* II. (Arb.) 112 Som man..is ouer full of words, sentences, and matter, and yet all his words be proper... His whole matter grownded vpon good reason, and stuffed with full arguments. **1576** FLEMING *Panopl. Epist.* 126 It shall not neede to stuffe my letter with particularities. **1591** SHAKS. *Two Gent.* IV. iv. 134, I will not looke vpon your Masters lines. I know they are stuft with protestations, And full of new-found oathes. **1610** HOLLAND *Camden's Brit.* (1637) 270 Stuffed hee [Nennius] hath that little booke with many a pretty lie. **1647** CLARENDON *Hist. Reb.* I. §11 Those accusations..are commonly stuffed with many odious generals, that the proofs seldom make good. **1682** DRYDEN *Medal* Ep. Whigs, Your Seditious Pamphlets are stuff'd with particular Reflexions on him. **1707** HEARNE *Collect.* 22 Apr. (O.H.S.) II. 8 His Discourse was stuff'd with Anglicisms. **1768** WALPOLE *Hist. Doubts* 123 John Rous..is an author to whom no credit is due, from the lies and fables with which his work is stuffed. **1817** JAS. MILL *Brit. India* III. i. 35 The absurdities, with which..a bill of indictment is frequently stuffed. **1876** F. HARRISON *Choice of Bks.* iv. (1886) 84 A book stuffed with curious facts.

b. To fill (a person, his mind, heart, etc.) with ideas, feelings, etc. Also with *up*.

1531 TINDALE *Expos. 1 John* (1537) 77 They be so full stuffed wyth lyes, that they can receaue nothyng els. *c* **1550** *Tottel's Misc.* (Arb.) 234, I see well..by the sighes that thou outthrowest, That thou art stuffed full of wo. **1585** T. WASHINGTON tr. *Nicholay's Voy.* II. xii. 47 b, Fortune..stuffed the hearte of the Athenians with..insatiable ambition. **1587** TURBERV. *Trag. T.* 74 The Queene perceiuing this In mockage to be ment Of Alboyne..Was stuft with raging rancour streight. **1595** SHAKS. *John* IV. ii. 133 Do not seeke to stuffe My head with more ill newes: for it is full. **1611** W. TRUMBALL *Let.* 17 Feb. in *10th Rep. Hist. MSS. Comm.* App. I. 563 These Provinces are no lesse stuffed with the unlikely newes of the King of Spaine's inclination to matche with yᵉ Lady Elizabeth then the Courte of Madrid. **1622** FLETCHER *Span. Curate* IV. v, Pray ye buy Books,..You have a learned head, stuff it with Libraries. **1640** FULLER etc. *Abel Rediv., Cowper* (1651) 562 These men were stuffed with such pride, self-conceit, disdain, and intolerable contempt, that [etc.]. **1642** D. ROGERS *Naaman* 110 They were stuft so full of their own skill and knowledge, that they scorned his simplicity. **1742** POPE *Dunciad* IV. 249 For thee we dim the eyes, and stuff the head With all such reading as was never read. **1876** TENNYSON *Harold* II. ii, I have often talk'd with Wulfnoth, And stuff'd the boy with fears that these may act On Harold when they meet. **1876** F. HARRISON *Choice of Bks.* i. (1886) 2 Now, to stuff our minds with what is simply trivial, simply curious..this is to close our minds to what is solid and enlarging. **1889** JEROME *Three Men in Boat* 7 Don't stuff up your head with things you don't understand.

c. *slang.* To 'cram', hoax, humbug (a person). Also with *up*.

1844 'JON. SLICK' *High Life N. York* I. 113, I wonder if these leetle coots think I'm soft enough to believe that [etc.]... They don't stuff me up that way, any how, if I did come from the country. **1859** *Hotten's Slang Dict.* 104 *Stuff*, to make false but plausible statements, to praise ironically, to make game of a person,—literally to stuff him with gammon or falsehood. **1885** *Harper's Mag.* Apr. 730/1 'That chatter-box Lenoir was joking,' he said; 'he was stuffing you to see how much you would both swallow.'

10. a. To fill (oneself, one's stomach, etc.) to repletion with food. Also said of the food.

a **1400-50** *Wars Alex.* 4436 Ȝoure mawis ȝe fill, With bakin mete..Stuffis so ȝour stomake with stullis & of wynes. *c* **1430** LYDG. *Min. Poems* (Percy Soc.) 155 The ryche man sit stuffyd at his stable [*read* table], The poore man stant hungry at the gate. **1585** T. WASHINGTON tr. *Nicholay's Voy.* III. xi. 91 Wines..wherof they do stuffe them selues so ful. **1600** *Weakest goeth to Wall* B 2 b, O for one pot of mother Bunches Ale,..it would cleare my sight, comfort my heart, and stuffe my veines. **1607** SHAKS. *Cor.* v. i. 53 When we haue stufft These Pipes, and these Conueyances of our blood With Wine and Feeding, we haue suppler Soules Then in our Priest-like Fasts. **1657** SPARROW *Bk. Com. Prayer* 156 Aerius and his followers..rising early to fill themselves with flesh and wine with which being full stuft they..scoff at the Catholick Christians folly. **1667** MILTON *P.L.* x. 601 Ravin..which here, though plenteous, all too little seems To stuff this Maw. **1749** FIELDING *Tom Jones*

XII. xii. (1806) III. 197 He was prevailed upon, not only to stuff himself with their food, but to taste some of their liquors. **1800** SHELLEY *On a Cat* i, It waits for some dinner To stuff out its own little belly. **1897** *Allbutt's Syst. Med.* II. 1043 The latter [i.e. an Indian]..has so to stuff his stomach three or four times a day, that dilatation of that organ..must necessarily ensue. **1903** G. H. LORIMER *Lett. Self-made Merch.* xvii. 249 [He] Stuffed himself till his hide was stretched as tight as a sausage skin.

b. To cause (a patient) to eat to repletion. Also, to treat (a disease) by feeding up the patient.

1789 W. BUCHAN *Dom. Med.* (1790) 145 Stuffing the patient with sweetmeats and other delicacies is likewise very pernicious. **1849** THOREAU *Week on Concord* Wed. *Writ.* (1893) I. 338 Stuff a cold and starve a cold are but two ways. **1899** *Allbutt's Syst. Med.* VIII. 163 A cure was effected simply by stuffing them with food.

†**c.** To satiate, glut. *Obs.*

1530 PALSGR. 741/2, I am as moche stuffed at the stomacke with the savour of this meate as if I had eaten a great meale: *je suis autant assouny en lestomac* [etc.]. **1603** DANIEL *Def. Ryme* H 6 b, Those continuall cadences of couplets..runne on, with..a kinde of certaintie which stuffs the delight rather then intertaines it.

d. *intr.* for *refl.* To gorge oneself with food.

1726 SWIFT *To a Lady in Heroic Style* 132 Let them neither starve nor stuff. **1728** [DE FOE] *Street-Robberies* 14, I..call'd for my Dinner, and stufft heartily. **1760–72** H. BROOKE *Fool of Qual.* (1809) III. 142 Gluttony stuffs till it pants, and unbuttons and stuffs again. **1794** J. WEBSTER *Agric. Galloway* 16 They go to the plough at 6 in the morning, and return at 2 in the afternoon; when they begin to feed, (or *stuff* which is their phrase). **1797** JANE AUSTEN *Sense & Sensib.* xxx, And such a mulberry tree in one corner! Lord! how Charlotte and I did stuff the only time we were there! **1840** BARHAM *Ingol. Leg.* Ser. I. *Bagman's Dog* 351 The Bagman bluff Continued to 'stuff', Of the fat, and the lean, and the tender and tough.

e. *trans.* To gorge (food). Also with *down*.

1743 MRS. E. MONTAGU *Corr.* (1906) I. 142 Wishing many good things to a boy who was stuffing a luncheon of bread and butter. **1775** J. JEKYLL *Corr.* (1894) 24 At six they stuff bread and cakes and wine. **1819** *Ibid.* 80 Lord Yarmouth again takes..a large party of us in the Admiralty barge next week to stuff whitebait at the 'Artichoke' beyond Greenwich. **1908** G. K. CHESTERTON *Man who was Thursday* 169 They paused for a few minutes only to stuff down coffee and coarse thick sandwiches at a coffee stall.

11. a. To fill (an aperture, cavity, etc.) by thrusting something tightly in; hence, to stop up, to plug; †to stop (a tooth). Also of a material: To fill *up* so as to block (an aperture).

1593 SHAKS. *Rich. II*, I. i. 44 Once more, the more to aggrauate the note, With a foule Traitors name stuffe I thy throte. **1683** *Sir K. Digby's Chym. Secrets* 139 The Ashes must be taken out..that they may not stuff up the place. **1724** SWIFT *Answ. to Dr. Delany* 39 Misc. 1735 V. 21 Which made my Grand-Dame always stuff-her-Ears. **1824** SCOTT *St. Ronan's* xxiv, I would rather..that my ears were stuffed with the earth of the grave than that they should again hear your voice! **1824** C. K. SHARPE *Corr.* (1888) II. 323 Had I not been under the hands of..the dentist, touching a diabolical tooth, which cannot be stuffed, and I am *sweer* to pull. **1833** J. RENNIE *Alph. Angling* 36, I found an old willow stump full of holes stuffed with clay. **1884** J. GILMOUR *Mongols* vi. 91 The hero..stuffing the mouth of the hole with his white bonnet.

b. To fill up (a joint or other space) by cramming something in; *spec.* in *Building*, to fill in the inside (of a wall) with concrete or rubble. ? *Obs.*

1601 R. JOHNSON *Kingd. & Commw.* (1603) 151 Commonly the wals of strong places are built of great beames stuffed with turffe or mosse, leauing loop-holes for their shot. **1726** LEONI *Alberti's Archit.* I. 46/1 Let them be ..as broad as the Wall, that there may be no need to stuff the middle with rubbish. *Ibid.* 47/1 The Ancients made it a rule in stuffing their Walls, not to continue the stuffing uninterrupted to the heighth of above five foot. **1776** G. SEMPLE *Building in Water* 78 He treats largely of..filling (or stuffing as he calls it) the inside with small Stones, and Lime-liquid.

†**12. a.** Of bodily humours: To clog, choke up (the body, its organs, vessels, etc.). Also with *up*. *Obs.*

c **1530** *Judic. Urines* III. ii. 48 Yf that parte of the hede be agreued & stuffed or stonyed, through euyll humours and fumosites. *Ibid.* III. vii. 51 b, Whan ye liuer is stopped & stuffed through mater of euyl humours. **1585** LUPTON *Thous. Notable Things* (1675) 180 Whosoever is stuffed in the Stomach with tough or hard flegm. **1618** LATHAM *2nd Bk. Falconry* xxviii. 131 Whensoeuer you shall..haue such a Hawke that is any whit stuft in the head. **1657** J. COOKE tr. *J. Hall's Sel. Observ. Engl. Bodies* 98 The stomach being stuffed and burdened with ill humors. **1710** FULLER *Pharmacopœia* (1719) 98 It..stuffs up the loaded Bronchia with a fresh Income of Filth. **1750** J. THEOBALD *Medulla Med. Univ.* 65 This Gargle..is to cleanse and scour the Glands of the Mouth from the Phlegmatic Matter, that stuffs and swells them.

†**b.** To cause stuffiness in (the head or nose).

1555 WATREMAN *Fardle Facions* II. i. 116 The plenty of swiete odours, and sauours in those quarters, doeth verely stuff ye smelling. **1599** SHAKS. *Much Ado* III. iv. 64 *Beat.* I am stuft cosin, I cannot smell. **1620** VENNER *Via Recta* ii. 39 The more bitter it be drunken, the more it filleth and stuffeth the head.

13. a. To thrust (something, esp. loose materials) tightly into a receptacle or cavity. Also *fig.* Also with *away*, *in*.

1579 W. WILKINSON *Confut. Fam. Love* 44 b, The Romanistes so cloyed the church with their fond festiuals, leud Legendes, and stuffed into the seruice of God such store of idle reuelations,..that [etc.]. **1626** BACON *Sylva* §365 Put them [the rose-leaves] into a Sweet Dry Earthen Bottle,..stuffing them close together. **1649** MILTON *Tenure Kings* (ed. 2) 57 They, in a cautious line or two here and there stuft in, are onely verbal against the pulling down or punishing of Tyrants. **1809** MALKIN *Gil Blas* VI. i. (Rtldg.) 213, I bought these dresses, into which we may stuff an inquisitor, a notary, and an alguazil, and play the parts. **1854** SURTEES *Handley Cr.* v. (1901) I. 42 With hands stuffed into his front pockets. **1878** *Chamb. Jrnl.* 19 Jan. 42/2 A woman was busy making a clearance of such articles as she could stuff away in corners and behind chairs. **1901** W. R. H. TROWBRIDGE *Lett. her Mother to Eliz.* xxi. 100 She stuffed her handkerchief into her mouth to keep from shrieking. **1904** BRIDGES *Demeter* 280 He, like a hurried thief, Stuffs his rich silks into too small a bag. **1907** J. H. PATTERSON *Man-Eaters of Tsavo* xxiv. 276 Courageously stuffing his left arm right into the great jaws.

b. To pack tightly (a person) in a confined space; to crowd (a number of persons *together*). Also with *down*, *up*.

1728 VANBR. & CIB. *Provok'd Husb.* II. i. 26 One has really been stufft up in a Coach so long, that—Pray Madam—could not I get a little Powder for my Hair? **1770** LANGHORNE *Plutarch, Pericles* (1879) I. 196/1 A number of people stuffed together..in small huts. **1785** MRS. INCHBALD *I'll tell you what* I. i. (1787) 10 If we are stuffed into a coach. **1900** ELIN. GLYN *Visits Eliz.* 195 There I was, taken off to a sofa..and stuffed down between Godmamma and the Marquis's mother.

intr. for *refl.* **1749–50** MRS. DELANY *Life & Corr.* (1861) II. 535, I cannot forgive Mrs. J. stuffing into your chariot.

14. *Leather-manuf.* To dress (a skin) with a coating of dubbing or stuffing.

1844 *Newton's Lond. Jrnl.* Conj. Ser. XXV. 247 When the skin or hide is taken out of tan..the patentees oil the grain with good clean oil, then stuff the fleshy side with a mixture of oil, tallow, and turpentine, and hang it up to dry. **1885** H. R. PROCTER *Tanning* 193 The process of currying consists in softening..the hides and skins..and in saturating or 'stuffing' them with fatty matters.

15. a. Used in coarse expressions of contempt or defiance. Cf. FUCK *v.* 2; STUFFED *ppl. a.* 6.

1955 P. LARKIN *Less Deceived* 30 Ah, were I courageous enough To shout *stuff your pension!* **1958** F. NORMAN *Bang to Rights* 168 The geezer just got up and told him to stuff his job. **1962** J. WAIN *Strike Father Dead* IV. 205 Very well, they could keep the whole outfit. And stuff it. I wasn't even going to stay in the same miserable country. **1965** 'T. HINDE' *Games of Chance* I. iii. 99 'Stuff you,' I said. **1973** J. PORTER *It's Murder with Dover* i. 2 He should have taken a stronger line... Told old Crouch to stuff it. **1976** W. TREVOR *Children of Dynmouth* xi. 204 She goes up to him and tells him to stuff himself and in a flat half-minute he's belting the old lorry up the London road. **1977** *Time* 28 Mar. 11/1 Stuff the criticism. He said what he was going to do. He won the election and now he's doing it.

b. *vulg. slang.* (With male subject) to copulate with (someone). Occas. *intr.*

1960 B. MOORE *Luck of Ginger Coffey* iv. 85 Trying to stuff another man's wife, is that your idea of being a friend? **1977** F. RAPHAEL *Cracks in Ice* (1979) 333 *Satura*..can also be applied, since it was originally adjectival, to a pregnant woman and to a sausage, both of which, in vulgar parlance, can clearly claim to have been stuffed. **1982** J. SCOTT *Uprush of Mayhem* vi. 63 You come all the way from the city..to stuff—to have intercourse with her. **1983** *Sunday Times* 16 Jan. 35/3 He was sacked from Eton for stuffing the boys' maids.

16. *Comb.*: **stuff-guts**, one who is addicted to gorging the stomach; in quot. *attrib.*

1875 BROWNING *Aristoph. Apol.* 112 In me, 't was equal-balanced flesh rebuked Excess alike in stuff-guts Glauketes Or starveling Chairephon.

†**stuff**, *v.*[2] *Obs.* [a. OF. *estofer* (mod.F. *étouffer*). = Pr. *estofar*: of obscure origin.]

1. *trans.* To stifle, suffocate.

1387 TREVISA *Higden* (Rolls) VI. 289 For aȝenst an hondred of Egbert his knyȝtes, þat were pale men and lene, come a þowsand þat were rody and fat, and were raþer i-stuffed [L. *suffocandi*] wiþ swoot þan with blood. *Ibid.* 449 A monke..fil doun of a brigge into a water, and was i-stufled [*v.r.* y-stoffed; L. *suffocatus est*]. **1398** —— *Barth. De P.R.* v. xxiv. (Bodl. MS.), And ȝif þe matere is colerike and woode it stuffeþ þe beest & sleeþ anon. *c* **1460** *Brut* cxxxiii. 138 (MS. Douce 323) Þere was grete hete..þat al stuffed [*c* 1400 stuffled: see STIFLE *v.* 1 b] was. **1530** PALSGR. 741/2, I stuffe a man with stynkynge savour, *je empunaysis*. *Ibid.*, I stuffe one up, I stoppe his breathe, *je suffoque*. I wyll take the ayre, I was almoste stuffed up in the prease. **1612** T. TAYLOR *Comm. Titus* i. 6 (1619) 107 He that hath beene in a noysome place is stuffed. **1636** FEATLY *Clavis Myst.* xl. 618 We all that have lived in the pleasures of sinne, have our senses stuffed and debilitated.

2. *intr.* To become out of breath. *Sc.*

c **1470** HENRY *Wallace* v. 285 His hors stuffyt, for the way was depe and lang. *c* **1470** *Gol. & Gaw.* 830 Quhen he is stuffit, than strike.

3. To render stifling.

1662 BOYLE *Def. Doctr. Spring Air* III. xviii. 81 [The Air] may thereby become sometimes more stufft, and sometimes more destitute of adventitious Exhalations.

†**stuff**, *v.*[3] *Obs. rare.* Var. of STOW *v.*[2]

1587 HOLINSHED *Chron.* I. 173/2 He commanded that such pledges as had beene deliuered to his father by certeine noble men..should haue their noses slit, and their eares stuffed [1577 stoued].

stuffado, var. STIFADO.

stuffage. [f. STUFF *sb.*[1] and *v.*[1] + -AGE.]

1. The act of stuffing or filling full; *concr.* the material with which a receptacle is stuffed.

1659 H. MORE *Immort. Soul* II. ii. (1713) 64 Upon any jog this Box receives, supposing all the stuffage thereof has Sense, it is evident, that the several things therein must be differently affected. **1685** —— *Cursory Refl. on Baxter* 5 Which is such an impertinent Stuffage of the Mind, that the Understanding is not thereby perfected, but burdened. **1690** NORRIS *Refl. Cond. Hum. Life* (1691) 51 It must needs be a very unedifying Stuffage of Mind. **1943** *Aeronautics* Jan. 34/1 An aeroplane should be stripped for action and not a stuffage of gadgets. **1963** C. ROBERTS *Buried Books* 13 The discarded papyrus MS used as stuffage for the binding cannot conceivably be later.

†**2.** *Path.* Obstructed condition, stoppage. *Obs.*

1761 *Phil. Trans.* LII. 264 Inflammatory fever, attended with..swelling and soreness, and stuffage of the nose.

†**stuffat, -et.** *Sc. Obs.* [? ad. F. *estafette*: see ESTAFETTE.] ? A groom, lackey; perh. only a vague term of abuse.

1500–20 DUNBAR *Poems* lx. 17 Stuffettis, strekouris, and stafische strummellis. **1550** LYNDESAY *Tragedy* 373 Bot not to rebaldis new cum frome the roste: Nor of ane stuffat stollin out of ane stabyll.

stuffata, incorrect form of STUFATA.

stuffe, obs. form of STIFF *a.*

stuffed (stʌft), *ppl. a.* [f. STUFF *v.*[1] + -ED[1].]

1. †**a.** Well stored or provided (*obs.*). **b.** In later use, of a receptacle: Filled full, crammed; also with *out*.

c **1440** *Promp. Parv.* 481/1 Stuffyd wythe stoore, *instauratus*. **1483** CAXTON *Cato* 2 b, A noble and well stuffed lybrary. **1596** SHAKS. *1 Hen. IV*, II. iv. 497 That huge Bombard of Sacke, that stuft Cloake-bagge of Guts. **1642** MILTON *Apol. Smect.* 11 His own stufft magazin, and hoard of slanderous inventions. **1837** CARLYLE *Fr. Rev.* II. VI. v, Men of Agio,..with stuffed purses. **1898** B. GREGORY *Side Lights* 495 Rescued..from the stuffed-out wallet of oblivion.

†**c.** ***stuffed man***: A wealthy man, a man of substance. *Obs.*

c **1400** *Beryn* 1730 The Burgeys was a stuffid man, þere lakkid noon deynte.

†**d.** *fig.* Full, complete. *Obs.*

1611 SHAKS. *Wint. T.* II. i. 185, I haue dispatch'd in post, ..Cleomines and Dion, whom you know Of stuff'd-sufficiency.

2. Of a garment, cushion, or the like: Filled out with some distending or stiffening material. Also with *out*.

1467 *Songs Costume* (Percy Soc.) 57 Leve your short stuffede dowblettes and your pleytid gownys. **1650** WELDON *Crt. Jas. I* (1651) 164 His Breeches in great pleits and full stuffed. **1828** LYTTON *Pelham* liii, One of N——'s best stuffed coats. **1856** OLMSTED *Slave States* 327 A stuffed easy-chair. **1858** J. BARON *Scudamore Organs* 53 The floor-sweeping and stuffed-out dresses of ladies, in juxtaposition with the short and scant garments of the poorer women. **1892** E. REEVES *Homeward Bound* 225 Our donkeys had no saddles: a stuffed sack was fastened on mine.

3. Of a dead animal, its skin: Filled with cotton, tow, etc., so as to preserve it and present the natural form of the living animal.

1595 SHAKS. *John* I. i. 141 And if..My armes [were] such eele-skins stuft. **1789** MRS. PIOZZI *Journ. France* I. 11 The great stuffed dog is a curiosity. **1818** SCOTT *Rob Roy* v, Huge antlers of deer,..interspersed with the stuffed skins of badgers,..and other animals of the chase. **1852** DICKENS *Bleak Ho.* xxxvii, Two stuffed and dried fish in glass cases.

4. Of a fowl, joint, fish, etc.: Filled with force-meat or minced seasoning before cooking. ***stuffed eggs***: see quot. 1883.

1729 H. CAREY *Poems* (ed. 3) 128 He gave her a Collation of Buns, Cheesecakes, Gammon of Bacon, Stuff'd-beef, and Bottled-Ale. **1852** R. B. MANSFIELD *Log Water Lily* 25 A stuffed goose and other delicacies. **1883** *Amer. Dishes* 193 Stuffed Eggs.—Cut six hard-boiled eggs in two. Take out the yolks and mash them fine. Add two teaspoonfuls of butter, one of cream... Mix all thoroughly. Fill the eggs from the mixture, and put them together.

5. Stopped up, obstructed; said esp. of a bodily organ when diseased. Of the head or brain: Oppressed by a feeling of obstruction. Also with *up*.

1584 COGAN *Hav. Health* cxi. 99 Almonde butter..good for a stuffed brest. **1711** SWIFT *Jrnl. to Stella* 1 Sept., My head is pretty well, only..sometimes it feels very stufft. **1772** LADY M. COKE *Jrnl.* 15 Jan. (1896) IV. 10 Her head was so stuff'd that She was obliged to hold her head over hot water. **1855** BROWNING *Andrea del Sarto* 80 In their vexed, beating, stuffed and stopped-up brain. **1904** SLADEN *Playing the Game* II. ix, Rich never could sing in tune, and he whistled like a stuffed-up dog-whistle.

fig. **1605** SHAKS. *Macb.* v. iii. 44 And with some sweet Obliuious Antidote Cleanse the stufft bosome, of that perillous stuffe Which weighes vpon the heart.

6. Phr. ***get stuffed***: used as a coarse imprecation. Cf. STUFF *v.*[1] 15 a, b.

1952 M. TRIPP *Faith is Windsock* x. 155 'Get stuffed,' he said savagely. **1968** M. RICHLER in R. Weaver *Canad. Short Stories* 2nd Ser. 188 'Why don't you tell Leopold to go get stuffed?' 'Because we need the foreign currency.' **1975** *Weekend Mag.* 1 Nov. 16/2 [He] told the Tories in so many words to get stuffed; he had no intention of telling them anything important, he proposed to deal only with the government. **1979** R. RENDELL *Make Death love Me* vii. 69 Who're you giving orders to? You can get stuffed.

7. Special collocations: **stuffed monkey**, a type of biscuit or cake made with almonds; **stuffed olive**, a stoned (usu. green) olive filled with pimento; **stuffed owl** [from the title of an anthology, ult. derived from Wordsworth's *Misc. Sonnets* III. xiii], used *attrib.* with reference to poetry which treats trivial or inconsequential subjects in a grandiose manner; hence **stuffed-owlish** *a.*; **stuffed pepper**, a cooked dish of green or red pepper (capsicum) de-seeded and filled with tomatoes, rice, meat, etc.; **stuffed shirt** *colloq.* (orig. *U.S.*), one who is pompous and conservative, but usu. ineffectual; hence **stuffed-shirted** *a.*; **stuffed-shirtedness**; **stuffed vine leaves**, an eastern (esp. Greek or Turkish) dish consisting of vine leaves wrapped round a savoury mixture of rice, onion, etc.

1892 I. ZANGWILL *Children of Ghetto* I. 14 The confectioners' shops, crammed with 'stuffed monkeys' and 'bolas'. **1943** A. L. SIMON *Conc. Encycl. Gastron.* IV. 127/2 *Stuffed Monkey* (S. Africa... Place the one half on a flat baking-sheet, cover with the filling or stuffing... Put the other half of the pastry over the filling; press the edges firmly together. **1962** *Listener* 11 Jan. 107/3 'Stuffed monkey' is a rich cake popular on the Continent. **1967** K. GILES *Death in Diamonds* iv. 78 Another cupper and a plate of stuffed monkeys. **1897** KIPLING *Captains Courageous* ix. 198 Try a stuffed olive. **1920** [see *angel('s)-food(-cake)* s.v. ANGEL *sb.* B. 2]. **1967** P. JONES *Fifth Defector* i. 4 He took a smallish savoury, a stuffed olive, and popped it into his mouth. [**1930** WYNDHAM LEWIS & LEE (*title*) The stuffed owl: an anthology of bad verse.] **1941** BLUNDEN *Thomas Hardy* xii. 264 Hardy's poems..have their share of stuffed-owl simplicities. **1957** R. A. KNOX *On Eng. Translation* 12, I will not entertain you..with choice specimens of really stuffed-owl renderings in this field; such as that famous translation from the Italian, about the medieval story of a woman who was turned into a horse. **1960** *Guardian* 13 May 6/7 Of the longer pieces, 'The Cruel Place' is the most stuffed-owlish. **1864** V. DAVIS *Let.* 8 Oct. in C. V. Woodward *Mary Chesnut's Civil War* (1981) xxvii. 663 Colonel Lubbock was funny about your breakfast—and your stuffed peppers. **1960** 'E. MCBAIN' *Killer's Payoff* ix. 89, I was going to call you for that stuffed-pepper recipe..you used for the last buffet. **1978** H. KAPLAN *Damascus Cover* vii. 69 Boys.. carried trays laden with soup and stuffed peppers. **1913** W. S. CATHER *O, Pioneers!* 144 He characterized Frank Shabata by a Bohemian expression which is the equivalent of stuffed shirt. **1939** C. DAY LEWIS *Child of Misfortune* III. iii. 287 These women and their stuff-shirt escorts. **1969** *Islander* (Victoria, B.C.) 23 Feb. 7/1 He had no time at all for the 'stuffed-shirt' types which were beginning to show in the north [of Canada]. **1976** *Country Life* 26 Feb. 496/3 The American President (a stuffed shirt) and two visiting Arab oil sheiks are held to ransom. **1977** A. J. AYER *Part of my Life* viii. 197 The head of the section, who disliked Cummings for his indifference to spit and polish and his preference for the company of the French cook and mechanics to that of the more stuffed-shirted Americans. **1981** 'J. ROSS' *Dark Blue & Dangerous* xxii. 127 You sounded so awfully priggish.. stuff-shirted..I do like you..in spite of your stuff-shirtedness. **1939** A. HEATH *Open Sesame* 120 Vine Leaves, Stuffed. **1978** H. KAPLAN *Damascus Cover* xv. 148 A man sitting on a straw stool eating stuffed vine leaves sunk in goat's milk.

stuffer ('stʌfə(r)). [f. STUFF *v.*[1] + -ER[1].]

1. A person who stuffs or fills; one whose trade it is to stuff (e.g.) dead animals or cushions.

1611 COTGR., *Embourreur*, a stuffer, bumbaster, or puffer vp of things with flockes, haire, &c. **1694** MOTTEUX *Rabelais* v. Prognost. v. 236 Stuffers and Bumbasters of Pack-saddles. **1862** JUKES *Stud. Man. Geol.* (ed. 2) 411 *note*, To speak of scientific men as 'mere beetle-hunters and bird-stuffers'. **1893** W. H. HUDSON *Idle Days Patagonia* xii. 185 In museums..the stuffer's work is endurable because useful. **1905** *Daily Chron.* 16 Mar. 8/7 Upholsterer.—Good stuffer wants Job.

2. A machine or implement used for stuffing.

1875 KNIGHT *Dict. Mech.*, *Stuffer*, a machine for packing or filling; as, 1. A machine for stuffing horse-collars. **1883** R. HALDANE *Workshop Rec.* Ser. II. 445/2 [The tomatoes] are fed by the 'stuffer', a cylinder worked by a treadle, into the cans. **1909** *Teachers' Assembly Herald* 13 Apr. 19/1 Other tools [for bird-stuffing]..long stuffers, bone-cutters.

3. An advertising leaflet or similar material enclosed with other literature, esp. when sent by post.

1942 [see FILLER[1] 2]. **1971** *Oxf. Univ. Gaz.* (Ann. Rep. Delegates Univ. Press) 5 The Promotion Department had to prepare, produce, and distribute 875,000 stuffers, 550,000 prospectuses. **1972** *Publishers Weekly* 31 Jan. 94/3 The prices they wish printed on the mailing piece, circular, stuffer, etc. **1976** *New Yorker* 12 Apr. 120/3 There was a program stuffer with a word-and-picture collage printed on one side and a full chronology of Tharp choreographies on the other.

stuffet: see STUFFAT.

stuffily ('stʌfɪlɪ), *adv.* [f. STUFFY *a.* + -LY[2].] In a stuffy manner; *fig.* in a manner that lacks freshness or interest.

1894 K. GRAHAME *Pagan Papers* 115 They spent the greater part of their time stuffily in-doors. **1902** S. E. WHITE *Blazed Trail* xv, The parlour..was a small square apartment carpeted in dark Brussels, and stuffily glorified in the bourgeois manner by [tasteless furniture]. **1912** *Nation* 20 Apr. 84/1 So he [a dull writer] goes stuffily on his way.

stuffiness ('stʌfɪnɪs). [-NESS.] The quality of being stuffy.

†**1.** Thickness or closeness of texture. *Obs.*

1611 COTGR., *Corps*..(in cloth, or stuffe) substance, tacke, stuffinesse.

2. The condition of being close or ill-ventilated.

1859 W. H. GREGORY *Egypt* II. 164 The smallness of the bedrooms, which we should consider conducive to much stuffiness. **1908** R. BAGOT *A. Cuthbert* vii. 65 Passengers who, like himself, preferred the fresh air on deck to the stuffiness of the saloon.

3. The state or sensation of stoppage and obstruction in the throat or nose.

1862 GEO. ELIOT in Cross *Life* II. xii. 279 As soon as one [cold] has departed with the usual final stage of stuffiness. **1884** M. MACKENZIE *Dis. Throat & Nose* II. 313 The patient almost always experiences a feeling of 'stuffiness' in the nose. **1898** *Allbutt's Syst. Med.* V. 289 A more or less general disagreeable stuffiness of the respiratory tract.

4. A formal or strait-laced attitude.

1926 GALSWORTHY *Silver Spoon* III. vi. 262 The book breaks through the British 'stuffiness' which condemns any frank work of art. **1933** *Times Lit. Suppl.* 9 Nov. 776/4 We see Angrove's clerical stuffiness gradually dispelled by the Greek sun and sea. **1975** J. R. L. ANDERSON *Death in North Sea* vi. 112 Mr. Wilson more than made up for his initial stuffiness... I took him into a small bar.

stuffing ('stʌfɪŋ), *vbl. sb.* [-ING[1].]

1. a. The action of STUFF *v.*[1], or the result of this action; †the strengthening of an army or military position (*obs.*); filling or cramming with material; gorging, eating to repletion.

1533 BELLENDEN *Livy* IV. i. (S.T.S.) II. 51 Þe Wolchis & equis brandisand in sa grete Ire for stuffing of verrigo aganis þame [L. *ob communitam Verruginem*]. *Ibid.* v. xvii. II. 206 Be stuffing of þe first batallis the myd batall was drawne furth thyn and waik. **1551–2** *Act 5 & 6 Edw. VI*, c. 23 An Acte for the true stuffynge of Featherbeddes, Mattresses, and Quyssheons. **1581** *Reg. Privy Council Scot.* III. 377 For the tressonable stuffing and withhalding of certane houssis and strenthis aganis his Hienes. **1594** KYD *Cornelia* v. 122 To purchase fame to our posterities, By stuffing of our tropheies in their houses. **1712–13** SWIFT *Jrnl. to Stella* 12 Mar., I cannot endure above one dish; nor ever could since I was a boy, and loved stuffing. **1820** SCOTT *Monast.* ix, These cowled gentry, that think of nothing but quaffing and stuffing! **1896** *Allbutt's Syst. Med.* I. 465 The supplementary stuffings at tuck shops are a fertile source of feeble health.

b. Obstruction of the throat, nose, or chest by catarrh; the sensation produced by this.

1601 HOLLAND *Pliny* XXVI. viii. II. 250 The same may bee taken..for the stuffing and other imperfections of the breast. **1618** LATHAM *2nd Bk. Falconry* xxix. 132 Of the Rye or stuffing in the Head. **1702** *Post Man* 13–15 Jan. 2/2 Advt., In a Cough or Cold..where there is Pain, and stuffing in the Head. **1843** R. J. GRAVES *Syst. Clin. Med.* xviii. 208 Blooded last night for cough and stuffing of chest.

c. The putting of fraudulent votes into a ballot-box. Also ***ballot stuffing***. Cf. STUFF *v.*[1] 8 d.

1976 *Birmingham Post* 16 Dec. 2/9 Special see-through ballot boxes were used to show that no pre-vote 'stuffing' had taken place. **1977** *Time* 3 Jan. 10/2 Apparently defeated in his first try for the state senate in 1962, he fought to prove ballot stuffing by the boss of Quitman County. **1979** *Internat. Jrnl. Sociol. of Law* Feb. 71 In actual fact, during the civilian rule, they occasionally employed illegal means.. and the stuffing or disappearance of ballot-boxes to help ruling party candidates.

2. a. The material with which a receptacle is stuffed or tightly filled.

1530 PALSGR. 277/2 Stuffyng of a saddell, *bourree*. **1575–6** *Act 18 Eliz.* c. 15 No Goldsmythe..shall..use..Sother Amell or other Stuffinges whatsoever..more then ys necessarie. **1628** tr. *Mathieu's Powerfull Favorite* 103 Meate being denied to Drusus, hee had eaten the stuffings of his bed. **1726** LEONI *Alberti's Archit.* I. 47 *a*, There are two sorts of Stuffing; the one..with which we fill the hollow.. between the two Shells, consisting of Mortar and broken.. Stone. **1748** RICHARDSON *Clarissa* VI. 157 Four old turkey-worked chairs,..the stuffing staring out. **1823** SCOTT *Quentin D.* xxxiv, In the stuffing of my saddle you will find a rich purse of gold pieces. **1842** J. AITON *Dom. Econ.* (1857) 166 A person with the scoop goes immediately before the one who puts in the stuffing [in a drain]. **1879** G. B. GOODE *Catal. Anim. Resources U.S.* 170 Preparation of curled hair for stuffings. **1897** *Allbutt's Syst. Med.* II. 532 Russian horse-hair which..had served as stuffing for an easy chair.

b. *Cookery.* Forcemeat or other seasoned mixture used to fill the body of a fowl, a hollow in a joint of meat, etc., before cooking.

1538 ELYOT *Dict.*, *Fartile*, stuffynge, or that wherewith any foule is crammed or franked. **1598** *Epulario* H j b, If you can deuise a better stuffing, you may: then fry them in oyle. **1675** HANNAH WOOLLEY *Gentlew. Comp.* 134 Make a farsing or stuffing of all manner of sweet Herbs minced very small. **1719** LONDON & WISE *Compl. Gard.* 192 The Leaves of this Plant are very good both in Pottage and in Stuffings. **1846** SOYER *Cookery* 129 Fill the belly of the fish with stuffing. **1887** *Spons' Househ. Man.* 460 Sauces, Butters, Gravies, Stuffings, &c.

†**c.** *fig.* (e.g. literary 'padding'). *Obs.*

1550 BALE *Engl. Votaries* II. (1551) 36 Muche good stuffynge is in thys bulle, whan it iudgeth marryage a fornycacyon. **1601** B. JONSON *Poetaster* v. i. 16 Hollow statues, which the best men are, Without Promethean stuffings reacht from heauen! **1641** MILTON *Ch. Govt.* II. 41 Men whose learning and beleif lies in marginal stuffings. **1804** *Ann. Rev.* II. 68/1 The doctor relates such daily occurrences, as would be esteemed too dull and unimportant for what is technically called, *stuffing*, in a garrison gazette.

d. ***to knock, beat, take the stuffing out of*** (an animal, person, etc.): to reduce to a state of weakness or flabbiness, take the strength or conceit out of. *colloq.*

1887 F. FRANCIS Jun. *Saddle & Mocassin* 123 Get up!—get up, or I'll beat the stuffing out of you! **1895** *Westm. Gaz.* 19 July 7/1 We will knock the stuffing out of the parties during the next ten years. **1906** 'L. MALET' *Far Horizon* v. 49 There is nothing to compare with a *mésalliance* for taking the stuffing out of anyone.

e. ***to put stuffing into***: to add strength or substance to. *colloq.*

1938 [see PAGE *v.*[1] c]. **1977** P. HARCOURT *At High Risk* III. v. 179 The whisky and wine I had drunk weren't making me rash..but they were putting some needed stuffing into me. **1979** J. SHERWOOD *Hour of Hyenas* iv. 44 She really puts the stuffing back into these women. Some of them even learn to cope with their dreadful husbands.

3. *Leather-manuf.* The process of rubbing with a mixture of fish-oil and tallow; the mixture used for this.

1851–4 TOMLINSON *Cycl. Usef. Arts* II. 35/2 When the skin is thoroughly cleansed,..the process of stuffing or dubbing..is performed. **1882** *Encycl. Brit.* XIV. 386/2 A stuffing, or dubbing, of cod oil and tallow is rubbed into both sides of the skin.

4. *attrib.* and *Comb.* as ***stuffing cloth***, ***work***; **stuffing-box** *Machinery*, a chamber packed with fluid-tight elastic material, through which a piston-rod or shaft is made to pass in order to prevent leakage at the orifice through which it leaves or enters a vessel; similarly ***stuffing-gland***, ***ring***; **stuffing drum** = *stuffing wheel*; †**stuffing stick** (see quot.); **stuffing wheel**, a revolving hollow drum in which leather is subjected to 'stuffing'.

1798 *Repert. Arts & Manuf.* (1799) X. 290 C, shews the *stuffing-box, through which the spindle must come, to work the chains. **1881** CAMPIN *Mech. Engin.* 115 The joint is made steam-tight by enclosing the extremity of the steam-pipe in a stuffing-box. **1522** in *Archæologia* XXV. 462 Item p[d] for *stuffyng clothe for the plyts [of a gown], xj d. **1897** C. T. DAVIS *Manuf. Leather* (ed. 2) 221 Freeman's *Stuffing Drum. **1885** LOCK *Workshop Rec.* Ser. IV. 102/1 The plunger is of stone-ware, accurately ground to fit the *stuffing-gland. **1797** CURR *Coal Viewer* 59 Pistons..should be $\frac{1}{8}$ or $\frac{3}{16}$ less than the cylinder, the *stuffing ring stands 4 inches from the side. **1688** HOLME *Armory* III. v. 273/1 The *Stuffing Stick..is..made of tough Wood or Iron, being a little bent at the end, with a nick in it; by the help whereof, all parts of the seat of a Cushion, Chair, or Stool, are equally filled. **1882** *Encycl. Brit.* XIV. 389/1 The currier's *stuffing wheel. **1726** LEONI *Alberti's Archit.* I. 55 *a*, Pumice Stone.. is..the properest..for the *stuffing work of Vaults.

'**stuffing**, *ppl. a.* [f. STUFF *v.*[1] + -ING[2].] In obs. sense: That stuffs or clogs the organs of breathing; that produces a sense of obstruction; oppressive to the head or lungs.

1579–80 NORTH *Plutarch*, *Sertorius* (1595) 631 When they should draw their breathes, this stuffing ayre and dust came in at their mouthes so fast, that they had much a do to hold out two dayes. **1653** CULPEPPER *Engl. Physic. enlarged* (1656) 98 The scent of the whole Plant [*sc.* Featherfew] is very strong, and stuffing. **1727** [DORRINGTON] *Philip Quarll* 19 Stale roasted Roots, which eat much pleasanter than the fresh, and are less stuffing.

'**stuffless**, *a.* [f. STUFF *sb.* + -LESS.] Wanting in 'stuff' or substance.

1896 BELLOC *Verses & Sonnets* 23 The tiny stuffless voices of the dark. **1913** J. E. FLECKER *Samarkand* 57 (*Don Juan*), That disastrous lie Which makes a god of stuffless Unity. **1932** W. DE LA MARE *Early Novels of Wilkie Collins* in J. Drinkwater *Eighteen-Sixties* 90 The best of them [*sc.* Collins' characters] are triumphantly in the round;..those in the background are somewhat stuffless in effect.

†'**stuffly**, *adv. Obs. rare*[−1]. [f. STUFF *sb.* + -LY[2].] With abundance of stuff or material.

1581 A. HALL *Iliad* IX. 162 The Egiptian Thebes..With people ful so stufly filde.

†**stuffure**. *Obs.* Also 5 -ur, -er. [a. AF. (*e*)*stuffure* = Anglo-L. (*e*)*stuffura*, OF. *estoffure*, material for ornament or outfit, f. *estoffer* STUFF *v.*[1]]

1. Material used for furnishing, supply, or outfit.

c **1440** *Promp. Parv.* 481/1 Stuffe, or stuffure, *staurum*, *instauracio*. **1463–4** *Rolls of Parlt.* V. 505/1 That noo Yoman ..use nor were in the aray for his body, eny bolsters nor stuffe of Wolle.., nor other stuffer in his Doublet, save lynyng. **1467–8** *Ibid.* 596/2 Keper of oure Stuffur' within oure Castell of Wyndesore. **1488** in *Lib. Cust. Villæ Northamptoniæ* (1895) 10 Arowe hedes silk wex ffethurs and other stuffures and necessaries.

2. *Cookery.* Stuffing, forcemeat.

c **1440** *Anc. Cookery* in *Househ. Ord.* (1790) 453 Qwhen hit is braiet smal take up the stuffure, and do hit in a chargeour. *c* **1450** *Two Cookery-bks.* II. 76 Take faire yonge beef, And suet of a fatte beste, or of Motton, and hak all this on a borde small;..then make a faire large Cofyn, and couche som of this stuffur in.

stuffy ('stʌfɪ), *a.* [f. STUFF *sb.*[1] + -Y.]

†**1.** Full of stuff or substance. *lit.* and *fig. Obs.*

1551–2 *Act 5 & 6 Edw. VI*, c. 6 §3 The good perfecte and stuffy makinge of the same Clothe. **1611** COTGR., *Substantieux*, substantiall, stuffie. **1620** T. GRANGER *Div. Logike* 69 By amplifications, and illustrations an oration is made stuffie, and fatted. **1642** FULLER *Holy & Prof. St.* v. xviii. (1652) 479 A mighty fire was made, and..(as if that pure Element of it self had been too fine and slender effectually to torment him) they made the flame more stiffe and stuffie, by the mixture of pitch and brimstone. *a* **1656** VINES *Lord's-Supp.* v. (1657) 64 This Sacrament of the Gospel is an after Supper *modicum*, full of spiritual signification, but not so stuffie for outward matter, that [etc.]. **1667** W. CAVENDISH *New Meth. Dressing Horses* 62 They..are to be Short from the Head to the Croup, and Stuffy.

2. a. Of a room, building, etc.: Ill-ventilated, close. Of the air: Wanting in freshness, oppressive to the lungs and head. Of persons: Addicted to living in stuffy conditions.

1831 LADY GRANVILLE *Lett.* 21 Feb. (1894) II. 89 In the evening I shall have a stuffy drum. **1853** LYTTON *My Novel* v. xi, I do believe the English are the stuffiest people! Look at their four-post bedsteads!..not a house with a ventilator! **1855** E. FORBES *Lit. Papers* vii. 190 He remains too long in the thick and stuffy atmosphere of town clubs and libraries. **1888** MRS. H. WARD *R. Elsmere* I. I. 10, I don't like stuffy cottages. **1904** F. LYNDE *Grafters* ii. 14 The stuffy little law office which had been his father's.

b. *transf.* Lacking in freshness, interest, or smartness.

1813 JANE AUSTEN *Pride & Prejudice* I. xvi. 173 They were superior to the broad-faced stuffy uncle Philips, breathing port wine, who followed them into the room. **1843** FROUDE *Nemesis of Faith* ii, Do not write me cold stuffy letters about my state of mind. **1900** C. HYNE *Filibusters* xxii. 318 In the waist below us, that stuffy little person the owner of the *Clarindella* was shedding tears of joy as his eyes gloated over his re-found treasure. **1904** [C'TESS. ARNIM] *Adv. Eliz. in Rügen* 132 In that sun-flecked place..how could I be seriously interested in stuffy indoor questions such as the equality of the sexes? **1909** MRS. H. WARD *Daphne* iii. 56 Listening to a stuffy debate in the Senate.

3. a. Of persons: Affected with a sensation of stoppage or obstruction in the organs of breathing, Said also of the sensation.

1847 FR. A. KEMBLE *Later Life* III. 290 If you are old and stiff, I am fat, stuffy, puffy, and old. **1871** C. GIBBON *Lack of Gold* xviii, Her head was stuffed, her nose was stuffed, and she felt altogether 'stuffy' and uncomfortable. **1898** *Allbutt's Syst. Med.* V. 287 At two or three in the morning he suddenly awakes with a stuffy feeling in his chest.

b. Of the voice: Muffled.

1889 *Harper's Mag.* Sept. 548/2 Her own stuffy voice, interspersed with the familiar coughs and gasps.

4. *U.S. colloq.* Angry, sulky.

1825 J. NEAL *Bro. Jonathan* I. 106 Don't care for you,.. with all your stuffy looks. **1898** KIPLING *Fleet in Being* vi. 77 They never growl at us or get stuffy.

5. Prim, formal, strait-laced, pompous; boring, conventional.

1895 KIPLING *Day's Work* (1898) 181 'You might have come to me to begin with,' said Scott stiffly... 'Well, you need't be stuffy about it.' **1904** E. NESBIT *Phoenix & Carpet* i. 11 It's awfully stuffy for a chap not to be allowed out in the evenings. **1922** J. CANNAN *Misty Valley* xv. 245 Cousin Innes was very stuffy about it when you got engaged. But all we wanted was for you to be happy, Claire. **1948** E. WAUGH *Let.* 24 Nov. (1980) 293, I went to one stuffy upper class dinner party on my first night & I go to another tonight. **1965** *Listener* 16 Sept. 418/2 Some of them have grasped the BBC's main dilemma, which is that it ought..to be in the widest, not in any 'stuffy' sense, an instrument of culture and education. **1979** R. JAFFE *Class Reunion* (1980) I. ii. 34 Every man I meet wants to go into business. They're all so stuffy.

stufre, obs. variant of STIVER.

1548 *Acts Privy Council* (1890) II. 159 Every floryne valued at xx Flemmisshe stufres.

†**stug**, *sb.*[1] *Obs. rare.* In 5 stugg(er)e. [Cf. STOCK *sb.*[1] 21.] A pig-trough.

c **1440** *Promp. Parv.* 481/1 Stugge [*Winch.* stuggere], hoggys trowghe, *siliquarium*,..vel *alveus porcorum*.

stug (stʌg), *sb.*[2] *Sc.* [Cf. STOG *sb.*[1]]

1. A stab, thrust.

1808 A. SCOTT *Poems* 98 (E.D.D. s.v. *Stog v.*[2]) Quo' he, let's sleely gie't a stug.

2. *Curling.* (See quot.)

1897 *Encycl. Sport* I. 264/2 (Curling) Stug, a shot gained by accident.

stug (stʌg), *v. Sc.* [Cf. STOG *v.*[1]] *trans.* To stab, pierce with a weapon.

1722 WODROW *Hist. Suff. Ch. Scot.* II. 173 They stugged all the Beds with their Swords. **1724** —— *Life J. Wodrow* (1828) 64 They stugged with their Swords the very bed my mother was lying on, jealousing he might be concealed there.

stug: see STUCK *a. Obs.*, short.

stuggy ('stʌgɪ), *a. dial.* [? Related to *stug*, STUCK *a.*

Cf. '*Stugged*, healthy, strong' (*Mrs. M. Palmer's Devon Dial.*, 1839, Gloss.).]

Of a person: Stocky, thick-set, sturdy. Also *transf.*

1847 HALLIWELL, *Stuggy*, thick and stout. *Devon.* **1864** BLACKMORE *Clara Vaughan* lxxxiii. (1872) 368 To use a Devonshire word, the farmer was too 'stuggy'. **1892** P. H. EMERSON *Son of Fens* viii. 74 She was stuggy and fat. **1945** P. WOODRUFF *Call Next Witness* II. 59 Quite as heavy a weight as his stuggy little brown mare was meant to carry. **1960** L. FIELDEN *Natural Bent* ix. 250 Ships with high noses and short noses, ships with long lines and stuggy lines.

stuid, stuile, stuill: see STUD *sb.*[2], STOOL.

stuipe, stuir, obs. ff. STOOP *sb.*[1], STOUR *a.*

stuiver: see STIVER.

stuk: see STOOK and STUCK *sb.*[1]

Stuka ('stu:kə, 'ʃ-). Also stuka. [Abbrev. of G. *sturzkampfflugzeug* dive-bomber.] A dive-bomber of the German air force, esp. as used in the war of 1939–45.

1940 *Sun* (Baltimore) 23 May 1/5 The awful destruction which German *Stukas* (dive bombers) wreak. **1942** *Ann. Reg. 1941* 12 On January 10 German Stuka dive-bombers.. made an attack..on a British convoy. **1942** *Daily Tel.* 23 Mar. 1/5 Fighters and stukas operate from the more forward flying ground at Tmimi. **1946** A. LEE *German Air Force* iii. 37 The Stuka pilot went straight to a specialist dive-bomber school. **1956** D. M. DAVIN *Sullen Bell* vii. 151 Sounds worse than a lot of screaming stukas. **1962** *Times* 7 June 16/5 After the drone of Stukas has died away. **1969** G. MACBETH *War Quartet* 21 So we would die..Picked into pulp by stukas. **1973** S. B. JACKMAN *Guns covered with Flowers* viii. 127 This was how the Stuka pilots must have seen it [*sc.* Warsaw], open and defenceless in the bomb-sights. **1980** *Daily Tel.* 16 Oct. 16/5 Sunset and sand. Stukas and sand. Food, flies, hospital, home—and sand.

Hence '**stuka** *v. trans.*, (*pass.*) to be attacked by Stukas.

1946 *Amer. Speech* XXI. 208, I served with the British Eighth Army in the desert.., but I never heard *sand happy*. *Bomb happy*, yes, when a bloke had been Stuka'd too often. **1977** N. FAULKS *No Mitigating Circumstances* vii. 80 On one lovely afternoon, I was sitting there with the G3 when we were Stuka'ed. **1980** *Daily Tel.* 16 Oct. 16/6 One moves from page to page, one moment 'brewing up', another being 'stuka-ed', to the cameo of a desert sunset.

stuke, stul: see STUC, STOOL.

†'**stulage, 'stuling.** *Sc. Obs. rare.* (Sense obscure: explained by editor as 'ballast'.)

1512 *Acc. Ld. High Treas. Scot.* IV. 289 To Thomas Bannatyne, skippar..for his haill victualing and haill necessaris xxv li. viij s., and for stuling xx li. *Ibid.* 307 Item, ..ressavit fourty twa celdris of met salt boght be Iohne Mowtray for stulage to the said schip.

stule, obs. Sc. form of STOOL.

stulko, var. of or error for STALKO *Anglo-Irish.*

1831 SCOTT *Jrnl.* 25 Mar. (1890) II. 389 Frank saw the necessity of doing something to keep himself independent, having, I think, too much spirit to become a Stulko.

stull (stʌl), *sb.*[1] *Obs.* exc. *dial.* [Cf. G. dial. *stollen* slice of bread.] A great piece or hunch (of anything edible).

a **1400–50** *Wars Alex.* 4436 þan as a Mare at a moghe ȝoure mawis ye fill,..Stuffis so your stomake with stullis & of wynes, þat vnethis haldis, be ȝe hoo þe hide of ȝow hale! **1674** RAY *S. & E. Country Wds.* 76* A *Stull*: a luncheon a great piece of bread, cheese or other Victuals, *Ess[ex]*. **1885** SPILLING *Daisy Dimple* 38 (E.D.D.) He kept taking great bites out of a thick stull of dirty-looking bread.

stull (stʌl), *sb.*[2] *Mining.* [Perh. a. G. *stollen* (OHG. *stollo*, MHG. *stolle*) a support, prop. The word has been adopted in a different sense as STULM.] A platform or framework of timber covered with boards to support workmen or to carry ore or rubbish; also, a framework of boards to protect miners from falling stones.

1778 PRYCE *Min. Cornub.* 150 Several of these pumps may be placed parallel upon different Stulls, Sallers, or Stages of the Mine. **1847** HALLIWELL. **1860** G. HARRIS in *Athenæum* (1861) 19 Jan. 83/1 And tin lay heap'd on stulls and level-plots. **1875** J. H. COLLINS *Metal Mining* 43 More timber is required for the construction of platforms, upon which the men stand while at work, 'stulls' as they are called.

b. *attrib.* and *Comb.*

1874 RAYMOND *Statist. Mines & Mining* 51, 3,829 feet of stull-timber. **1881** —— *Mining Gloss.*, *Stull*, Corn[wall]. A platform (stull-covering), laid on timbers (stull-pieces), braced across a working from side to side, to support workmen or to carry ore or waste. **1883** *Encycl. Brit.* XVI. 453/1 Stull-pieces... Stull-covering.

stull, obs. Sc. form of STOOL.

stulm (stʌlm). *Mining.* [? a. G. *stolln*, *stollen* of the same meaning.] An adit or level in a mine.

1684 *Copper Mines* ii. in *Phil. Trans.* XVII. 741 It hath a Stulm or Shaft to draw Water from the Mine. **1724** BAILEY (ed. 2), *Stulm*, a Shaft to draw Water out of a Mine. **1881** RAYMOND *Mining Gloss.*

stulp(e, var. ff. STOOP *sb.*[1]

†**stult.** *Obs. rare*$^{-1}$. ? A derisive name for a tailor.

1675 M. LOCKE *Engl. Opera* Pref. A3b, He who Composes for Voices, not considering their extent, is like a Botching Stult, who, being obliged to make Habits for men, cuts them out for Children.

stult, stulth: see STOUT *a.*, STOUTH.

†**stultificate**, *v. Obs. rare*$^{-0}$. [f. late L. *stultificāt-*, ppl. stem of *stultificāre*.] *trans.* = STULTIFY *v.* Only in **stultificating** *ppl. a.*

a **1693** *Urquhart's Rabelais* III. xxxiv. 288 So great was the stultificating Vertue of that..pulverized Dose.

stultification (ˌstʌltɪfɪ'keɪʃən). [n. of action f. STULTIFY *v.*: see -FICATION.] The action of the vb. STULTIFY, the state of being stultified; an instance of this.

1832 *Whistle-binkie* Ser. I. (1839) 95 Whilst others contrive with their speeches and songs, To complete her stultification, O. **1856** MISS YONGE *Daisy Chain* II. x, 'But as to the Market Cross, that came down a year before he was born.' 'It was the Town Council!' said Ethel. 'One of the ordinary stultifications of Town Councils?' **1901** 'LINESMAN' *Words by Eyewitness* xi. 225 Result as before, the daily arrival of refugees and a great stultification of the dominant Power.

stultificatory (ˌstʌltɪfɪ'keɪtərɪ), *a.* [f. STULTIFICATION: see -ORY[2].] = STULTIFYING *ppl. a.*

1931 *Times Lit. Suppl.* 21 May 400/2 Further penetration into the processes of the universe is self-stultificatory. **1972** D. BELL in Cox & Dyson *20th-Cent. Mind* I. vi. 180 A transcendental and intuitionist philosophy which Mill saw as internally inconsistent, obscurantist, and stultificatory of the progress of both science and philosophy.

stultify ('stʌltɪfaɪ), *v.* [ad. late L. *stultificāre*, f. *stult-us* foolish, fool: see -FY.]

1. trans. *Law.* To allege or prove to be of unsound mind: esp. *refl.*, to allege one's own insanity in order to evade some responsibility.

1766 BLACKSTONE *Comm.* II. xix. 291 It hath been said, that a *non compos* himself, though he be afterwards brought to a right mind, shall not be permitted to allege his own insanity in order to avoid such grant: for that no man shall be allowed to stultify himself, or plead his own disability. **1861** KENT *Comm. Amer. Law* (1873) II. xxxix. 451 The principle..that a man shall not be heard to stultify himself has been properly exploded.

2. To cause to be or appear foolish, ridiculous, or absurdly inconsistent; to reduce to foolishness or absurdity.

1809 *Europ. Mag.* LV. 19 This able senator..did not.. hesitate to tell his majesty's ministers, that..they had become completely stultified. **1810** WELLINGTON in *Croker Papers* 20 Dec., The licentiousness of the press..[has] gone near to stultify the people of England. **1850** KINGSLEY *A. Locke* xviii, I, to squash my convictions, to stultify my book for the sake of popularity, money, patronage! **1871** *Daily News* 24 Aug., This witness, however, stultified himself by admitting that he was too far off to hear what Clement said.

b. To render nugatory, worthless, or useless.

1865 *Daily Tel.* 27 Oct. 4/6 The Bermondsey guardians took upon themselves utterly to ignore and stultify this law. **1888** MISS BRADDON *Fatal Three* I. vi, The blind folly of his servants had stultified his efforts.

3. To regard as a fool or as foolish. *rare.*

1820 *Hazlitt Lect. Lit. Age Eliz.* i. (1884) 4 The modern sciolist stultifies all understanding but his own, and that which he conceives like his own.

Hence '**stultifying** *ppl. a.* Also '**stultifier** *rare*$^{-0}$, one who stultifies.

1826 KIRBY & SP. *Entomol.* III. xxx. 173 Affirming most absurdly, and under the most stultifying blindness of mind, that [etc.]. **1855** H. CLARKE *Dict.*, Stultifier. **1879** GEO. ELIOT *Theo. Such* xviii. 324 A stultifying inconsistency in historical interpretation.

stultiloquence (stʌl'tɪləkwəns). [ad. L. *stultiloquentia* (Plautus) f. *stultiloquus* speaking foolishly, f. *stult-us* foolish + *-loquus* that speaks.] Foolish or senseless talk, babble, bosh, twaddle.

1721 BAILEY, *Stultiloquence*, foolish talk. **1809** *Europ. Mag.* LV. 19 This sort of epithet..cannot fail to add..to the stultiloquence of every society. **1893** SWINBURNE *Stud. Prose & Poetry* (1894) 90 The blank and blatant jargon of epic or idyllic stultiloquence.

stul'tiloquent, *a. rare.* [f. L. *stultiloqu-us*: see prec. and -ENT.] Talking foolishly.

1845 S. JUDD *Margaret* I. v, 'Stultiloquent yarb-monger!' he [the schoolmaster] broke out. **1864** WEBSTER; and in later Dicts.

Hence **stul'tiloquently** *adv.* [-LY[2].]

1864 WEBSTER; and in later Dicts.

†**stulti'loquious**, *a. Obs. rare.* [f. L. *stultiloquium* (see next) + -OUS.] Talking foolishly.

1683 E. HOOKER in *Pordage's Myst. Div.* Pref. Ep. 15 What of..Punns and Flams, stultiloquious Dialogs?

stultiloquy (stʌl'tɪləkwɪ). [ad. L. *stultiloquium*, f. *stultiloqu-us*: see STULTILOQUENCE.] A speaking foolishly, a foolish babbling.

1653 JER. TAYLOR *Serm. Golden-Grove, Winter* xxiii. 301 What they call facetiousnesse and pleasant wit, is indeed to all wise persons a meer Stultiloquy, or talking like a foole. **1826** *Examiner* 190/1 A sort of unique stultiloquy governs some of the public deliberations of the owners and occupiers of land. **1867** DE MORGAN in *Athenæum* 21 Dec. 852/3 Such a self-destructive congeries of stultiloquies.

†**stul'titious**, *a. Obs.* [f. L. *stultitia* folly, f. *stultus* foolish; see -ITY and -OUS.] Foolish, ridiculous.

1547 BOORDE *Introd. Knowl.* ii. (1870) 127 In Wales..is vsed these two stulticious matters. **1632** LITHGOW *Trav.* I. 40 The Duke..espouseth the sea,..by casting a golden ring into it. Which Stultitious ceremony by Pope Alexander the third was graunted.

Hence †**stul'titiously** *adv. Obs.*

1536 BOORDE in Ellis *Orig. Lett.* Ser. III. II. 305 Then stultycyusly..I dyd as many of that Order doth.

†'**stulty**, *a. Obs. rare*$^{-1}$. [app. f. L. *stult-us* foolish + -Y.] Foolish, stupid.

1387–8 T. USK *Test. Love* II. iii. (Skeat) 106 Shal fyr ben blamed for it brende a foole naturelly, by his own stulty witte in steringe?

stum (stʌm), *sb.* Also 8 stumm, stume. [a. Du. *stom*, subst. use of *stom* dumb. Cf. F. *vin muet* in the same sense; also G. *stummer wein*, wine that tastes flat.]

1. Unfermented or partly fermented grape-juice, must; esp. must in which the fermentation has been prevented or arrested by fumigation with sulphur.

1662 CHARLETON *Myst. Vintners* (1675) 149 This Flower thus separated, is what they name Stum. **1665** *Oxf. Gaz.* No. 16/1 Another Vessel was..laden with Wine and Stum. **1705** ADDISON *Italy, Antiq. near Naples* 234 An unctuous clammy Vapour that arises from the Stum of Grapes. **1769** MRS. RAFFALD *Engl. Housekpr.* (1778) 329 To make Stum. **1802** PALEY *Nat. Theol.* xv. (ed. 2) 286 As necessary..as the fermentation of the stum in the vat is to the perfection of the liquor. **1845** T. Smeed *Wine Merchant's Man.* 59 Dissolve half a pound of white candy in a pint of Rhenish stum. **1858** Simmonds *Dict. Trade.*

pl. **1710** *Lond. Gaz.* No. 4681/4 There are about 50 Hdds ..of.. French Wines, some Stumes &c. **1731–3** P. Shaw *Chem. Lect.* x. (1755) 191 This is the common Method of matching Casks for Wines, but particularly for Stums.

transf. **1766** *Complete Farmer* s.v. *Mead* 5 M 2/1 The usual practice of making it so strong as to bear an egg, is very wrong. The liquor is thereby rendered a mere stum.

b. Must as used for renewing vapid wines. Also occas. applied to apple-juice similarly used.

1692 *B. Jonson's Leges Conviv.* v, Let our Wines without mixture, or Stum be all fine. **1693** Rymer *Short View Trag.* 78 Chaucer threw in Latin, French, Provencial, and other Languages, like new Stum to raise a Fermentation. **1731–3** P. Shaw *Chem. Lect.* x. (1755) 192 After the same manner a Stum is prepared in England from the Juice of Apples.

fig. **1679** Shadwell *True Widow* iii. 32 'Tis the stum of Love that makes it fret and fume, and fly, and never good. **1682** Dryden *Medal* 270 Thy bellowing Renegado Priests, That..with thy Stumm ferment their fainting Cause. **1707** *Refl. upon Ridicule* 168 Get rid of this stum in your Blood.

2. Vapid wine renewed by the mixture of stum.

1664 Butler *Hud.* ii. i. 569 I'll carve your name on Barks of Trees,..Drink every Letter on't, in Stum; And make it brisk Champaign become. **1746** Fielding *True Patriot* No. 24 ⁋7 We drank nine bottles a-piece of stum.

3. *attrib.* and *Comb.*

1675 Merrett in *Charleton's Myst. Vintners* (ed. 2) 219 Herring Roes preserve any Stum Wines. **1719** D'Urfey *Pills* V. 84 Who hate the stum Poison of Spain and France. **1753** *Chambers' Cycl.* Suppl. s.v. *Must*, The Rhenish Must ..made without boiling is only put up so close in the vessel, that it cannot work; this is called stumm-wine. **1769** Mrs. Raffald *Engl. Housekpr.* (1778) 329 Then put a quart of stum-forcing to it, which will..make it fine and bright.

stum (stʌm), *v.* Inflected **stummed, stumming.** Also 7 **stumb**, 8 **stoom.** [ad. Du. *stommen*, f. *stom* stum *sb.*]

1. *trans.* To renew (wine) by mixing with stum or must and raising a new fermentation.

1656 Flecknoe *Diarium* 26 Such trash in belly e're to put, As mungrel balderdash *Mine Heer*, Dutchman has stummed for us there. **1689** *Muses Farew. Popery* 88 Had a drunken Tom Tinker the Penance receiv'd, Or a Vintner for stumming his Wine, who'd have griev'd? **1775** Ash, *Stoom*, (v.t. with wine coopers), to impregnate wines by putting bags of herbs or other ingredients into them. *Ibid.*, *Stum* (v.t.), to renew wines by raising a fresh fermentation.

b. *fig.*

1661 C. W. in *A. Brome's Poems* To Author A 8, There strength of fancy, to it sweetness joynes, Vnmixt with water, nor stum'd with strong lines. **1676** Etherege *Man of Mode* iii. ii. 44 Nature has her cheats, stum's A brain, and puts sophisticate dulness often on the tastless Multitude for true wit and good humour. **1678** Oldham *Let. fr. Country* 204 As the poor Drunkard, when Wine stums his brains, Anointed with that Liquor, thinks he reigns. **1795** Burke *Let. to W. Elliot* 26 May, When that sad draught..was dashed and brewed, and ineffectually stummed again into a senatorial exordium in the house of lords.

¶ *to stum up*: ? to set going, work up. *rare*$^{-1}$.

The use may be due to some misapprehension.

1817 Keats *Let. to Haydon* 28 Sept., At Bailey's suggestion..we have stummed up a kind of contrivance whereby he will be enabled to do himself the benefits you will lay in his Path.

2. To fumigate (a cask) with burning sulphur, in order to prevent the contained liquor from fermenting; to stop the fermentation of (new wine) by fumigation.

1787 J. Croft *Wines Portugal* etc. 25 Most of the Spanish Wines are stoomed or matcht, as they term it, with brimstone, which also stops the fermentation. **1789** W. H. Marshall *Glouc.* II. 358 This expedient is termed 'stumming the [cider] casks'. **1860** Worcester; and in later Dicts.

Hence **stummed** *ppl. a.*, **'stumming** *vbl. sb.*

c **1645** Howell *Lett.* (1655) II. lv. 70 This is called stooming of wines. **1664** Sir P. Neile in *Evelyn's Pomona* 40 [Cider] cannot be unwholsome, upon the same measure that stummed Wine is so. **1666** G. Harvey *Morbus Angl.* xxviii. (1672) 77 A kind of crude dull stumb'd Burdeaux. *a* **1694** in C. Mackay *Songs Lond. Prentices* (Percy Soc.) 122 All loyal lads of true English race; That scorn the stum'd notion of Spain and France. *a* **1721** Prior *On Passage in Scaligeriana* 2 When you with High-Dutch Heeren dine, Expect false Latin, and stumm'd Wine. **1837** Richardson, Stummed casks are casks fumigated (with brimstone, to prevent the liquor from fermenting).

stuma: see stumer 3.

stumble ('stʌmb(ə)l), *sb.* Also 6 stomble. [f. stumble *v.*]

1. An act of stumbling.

a. A missing one's footing, a partial fall.

c **1645** Howell *Lett.* (1650) I. iii. xxxi. 92, I was told of a Spaniard, who having got a fall by a stumble, and broke his nose, rose up, and in a disdainfull manner said,..This is to walk upon earth. **1743** Wesley *Jrnl.* 20 Oct., Many endeavour'd to throw me down, while we were going down-hill on a slippery path to the town... But I made no stumble at all, nor the least slip 'till I was intirely out of their hands. **1825** Scott *Talism.* xxii, The horse of the knight made such a perilous stumble as threatened to add a practical moral to the tale. **1890** D. Davidson *Mem. Long Life* ix. 224 Douglas Graham's horse had stumbled in the soft bed of the nullah, and that stumble saved his rider's life.

fig. **1547** J. Harrison *Exhort.* in *Compl. Scot.* (1872) 222 This is a greete stomble at the thressholde of the dore: for it is plain by histories, that Lusitania, was not called Portyngale, almost by a M. yeres, after this supposed tyme. **1639** Fuller *Holy War* iv. xx. 203 A Prince, who in the race of his life met with many rubs, some stumbles, no dangerous falls.

†**b.** An ineffectual attempt. *Obs.*

a **1635** Corbet *Nonsence* Poems (1807) 221 Or lyke to rhyming verse that runs in prose, Or lyke the stumbles of a tynder box.

c. A blunder, slip.

1607 Harington *Nugæ Ant.* (1804) II. 49 Maister Vaghan examined him..and found him but shallow, and not very ready in the Roman tongue, his frend having been fayn to help him up, in two or three fowle stumbles, both of language and matter. *a* **1641** Bp. Mountagu *Acts & Mon.* (1642) 379 A prosecution of the former Paragraph, with a stumble of Baronius. **1687** Settle *Refl. Dryden* 68 By the damnable stumbles Mr. Notes makes in them, he is quite different from Aretine in his Preface. **1736** Hervey *Mem. Geo. II* (1848) I. 408 Sir Robert, finding the stumble his brother had made [in making this suggestion]..joined in the laugh against him. **1901** *Scotsman* 1 Mar. 7/4 The significant stumble made by the right hon. gentleman in his reply.

†**d.** A taking offence. *Obs.*

1674 Bunyan *Light for them in Darkness* (1675) 35 This their stumble might arise either; 1. From the cruelty of Herod: Or, 2 From their own not observing and keeping in mind the Alarum that God gave them at his Birth.

e. A moral lapse.

1702 *Engl. Theophrastus* 186 One stumble is oftentimes enough to deface the character of an honourable life. **1876** H. K. Wood *Highw. Salvation* v. 57 His stumbles and his transgressions are his sorrow.

f. A stumbling or coming by accident upon something.

1865 Holland *Plain Talk* iv. 122 There are exceptions to this rule in the lucky Stumbles that are made upon extraordinary deposits of the precious stones and metals.

2. In generalized sense: The action of stumbling.

1641 Milton *Ch. Govt.* i. 4 How much lesse can we believe that God would leave his..Church..to the perpetuall stumble of conjecture and disturbance. **1692** L'Estrange *Æsop's Fables* Life ix. 10 The Clown, after a little Stumble within himself,..says..If it be the Custome of the Family, 'tis not for me to be against it. **1880** Blackmore *Mary Anerley* I. x. 135 Buoys, nets, kegs,..lay about..here and there and everywhere, upon this half-acre of slip and stumble, at the top of the boat-channel down to the sea.

†**3.** A stumbling-block. *Obs.*

1651 H. More *Second Lash* To Rdr., in *Enthus. Tri.*, etc. (1656) M 2 b, And truly..that Book which hath proved so mischievous a scandal, I intended onely for a stumble to wake you.

stumble ('stʌmb(ə)l), *v.* Forms: 4 **stomble, stumbill, -bul,** 5 **stombel, -byl, stomel(e, stomle, stoomel, stumbylle, stumle, stummel,** 9 *dial.* **stummle,** 4– **stumble.** [Early 14th c. *stomble, stumble* (the *b* is euphonic; the original *stomle, stumle*, is not recorded till the 15th c.) corresponds to Norw. *stumla* to grope and stumble in the dark (Ross), Da. dial. *stumle*, Sw. dial. *stomla*; perh. repr. an unrecorded ON. **stumla*, synonymous with the cognate *stumra* to stumble (Norw. *stumra*): see stummer *v.* The root is an ablaut-variant of **stam-*: see stammer *v.*]

1. *intr.* To miss one's footing, or trip over an obstacle, in walking or running, so as to fall or be in danger of falling.

c **1325** *Gloss. W. de Bibbesw.* in Wright *Voc.* 143 Ke il ne ceste ne ne chece [*glossed* stumble ne falle] En la bowe ne messece. *c* **1330** R. Brunne *Chron. Wace* (Rolls) 12435 He [the giant] stombled, & gaf a cry. **1338** —— *Chron.* (1810) 55 A seruitour þer was, þat serued at þe mete, He stombled at a chance, & felle on his kne. *a* **1340** Hampole *Psalter* xix. 8 Proude horsis that will stumbill and gere vs breke oure neke. **1388** Wyclif *John* xi. 10 If he wandre in the niȝt, he stomblith [Vulg. *offendit*]. *c* **1450** *Brut* ii. 378 And þanne þeȝe Frenschmen come prikkyng doun as þei wolde haue ouyr-rydyn alle oure meyne; but God and our archers made hem sone to stomble. **1523–34** Fitzherb. *Husb.* §92 The cordes is a thynge that wyll make a horse to stumble, and ofte to fall. **1659** in *Verney Mem.* (1907) II. 147 The horse stumblinge threw them both. **1746** Francis tr. *Hor., Epist.* i. x. 63 Our Fortunes and our Shoes are near allied; We're pinch'd in strait, and stumble in the wide. **1810** Scott *Lady of L.* i. ix, But, stumbling in the rugged dell, The gallant horse exhausted fell. **1846** Mrs. A. Marsh *Father Darcy* II. xix. 321 A sort of broken gallop, as of horses forced forward, yet faltering and stumbling at every step, was now heard. **1900** Bp. W. How *Lighter Moments* 37 His horse stumbled in a lane and fell with him.

b. with const. *at, over.*

a **1450** *Le Morte Arth.* 115 His hors stomelyd at a stone. *c* **1450** Capgrave *Life St. Gilbert* xliii. 123 Sche stombeled at a blok whech was hid with straw and þus fel sodeynly. **1538** Elyot *Dict.*, *Offensaculum*, that which is layd in a mans waye, whereat he stumbleth. **1592** Shaks. *Rom. & Jul.* v. iii. 122 How oft to night Haue my old feet stumbled at graues. *a* **1707** Prior *Duke of Ormond's Pict.* 13 His steed..stumbles o'er the Heap. **1794** Mrs. Radcliffe *Myst. Udolpho* xxxiii, Give me the torch,..and take care you don't stumble over anything that lies in your way. **1824** Scott *Redgauntlet* ch. xv, Stumbling at every obstacle which the devotion of his guide, Richard, had left in the path, he [etc.]. **1833** Ht. Martineau *Briery Creek* iii. 58 As sure as one walks in the dark, one stumbles over a pig. **1845** Ford *Handbk. Spain* i. 52 Having stumbled over a stone. **1894** Alma-Tadema *Wings of Icarus* 158, I turned from the window and stumbled over something; I lighted a candle.

c. To fall in consequence of a stumble.

14.. *Sir Beues* (Pynson) 2454 There was a wel,..And Beuys stumbled ryght therin. **1907** *Connoisseur* Apr. 275/2 Here are men fighting.., there a horse is stumbling to his knees.

d. To knock or jostle *against* (a person or thing) involuntarily.

c **1440** *Promp. Parv.* 481/1 Stummelyn, or hurtelyn a-ȝen a stole, or clogge, or oþer lyke, *impingo.* **1822** Shelley *Faust* ii. 21 Every step One stumbles 'gainst some crag. **1835** *Politeness & Gd.-breeding* 28 This boy or girl..who never.. tries to vex your feelings, but if they happen so much as to stumble against you, or hurt you in any way, say immediately, 'I am sorry for it.' **1865** Kingsley *Herew.* xli, 'I am out,' quoth Hereward, as the man almost stumbled against him; 'and this is in.'

e. Of an inanimate thing: To strike unexpectedly *on.* ? *nonce-use.*

1702 *Secret Mercury* 23– 30 Sept. 2/1, I press'd her to discover her Lodgings, but in vain; for the Boat just stumbled on the Stones and parted us. **1822** Shelley tr. *Calderon's Mag. Prodig.* ii. 60 It [that sad ship] strikes—.. It stumbles on a jagged rock.

f. Phrase, ***to stumble at*** (***on***) ***the threshold.*** Chiefly *fig.*, to fail, take offence, meet with an ominous check at the beginning of an enterprise.

1377 Langl. *P. Pl.* B. v. 357 He stumbled [*So several MSS.; but see* thrumble *v.*] on the thresshewolde. **1579** Spenser *Sheph. Cal.* May 230 Tho went the pensife Damme out of dore And chaunst to stomble at the threshold flore. **1593** Shaks. *3 Hen. VI*, iv. vii. 11. **1699** T. Baker *Refl. Learn.* xvi. 200 This is no very great mistake, but it is always ominous to stumble at the threshold. **1725** N. Bailey *Erasm. Colloq.* (1733) 209, I lately began to read Seneca's Epistles, and stumbled, as they say, at the very Threshold. **1877** Froude *Short Stud.* (1883) IV. i. iv. 49 He stumbled on the threshold, and had almost fallen, but recovered himself.

2. *fig.* in various uses.

a. To trip morally.

1303 R. Brunne *Handl. Synne* 6521 Ful many on stumble vp and down Of þe greces of syre glotown. *a* **1340** Hampole *Psalter* xxv. 1, I shal not be seke [Vulg. *non infirmabor*] þat is, I shal noght stumbul. *c* **1400** *Destr. Troy* 2928 Soche stirrynges ger stumble, þat stidfast wold be. **1591** Shaks. *Two Gent.* i. ii. 3 *Jul.* Would'st thou then counsaile me to fall in loue? *Luc.* I Madam, so you stumble not vnheedfully. *a* **1692** Shadwell *Volunteers* i. i. (1693) 7 That Mother in Law of thine is..I believe given to stumble much; there is an odd fellow keeps her Company. **1851** Thackeray *Eng. Hum.*, *Swift* (1858) 31 They sinned and stumbled..with debt, with drink.

b. To make a slip in speech or action; to blunder through inadvertence or unpreparedness.

1450–1530 *Myrr. Our Ladye* 51 Yf yt happe..that any.. fayle or stomble, or be dystracte from saynge or hering of any worde, or verse, or psalme, etc. **1607** Rowlands *Diogines Lanth.* 44 T'is better stumble with thy feet Then stumble with thy tongue. **1611** Bible *Transl. Pref.* ⁋6 But yet as men they [the LXX] stumbled and fell, one while through ouersight, another while through ignorance.

c. To come *on* or *upon* by chance and unexpectedly; to come *in* or *into* (a place) by chance.

1555 Eden *Decades* (Arb.) 337 He that speaketh much shal sumtimes stumble on the truth. *c* **1575** G. Harvey *Letter-bk.* (Camden) 158 It was mie illuck to stumble on sutch company to Walden warde, that I could not possibely cumpas mie purpose, unles [etc.]. **1579** Gosson *Sch. Abuse* (Arb.) 30 Some Archplayer or other that hath read a litle, or stumbled by chance vpon Plautus comedies. **1592** Shaks. *Rom. & Jul.* ii. ii. 53. **1632** Lithgow *Trav.* i. 33 It was my lucke to stumble in here agaime. **1682** N. O. *Boileau's Le Lutrin* ii. 164 Thus trudg'd he nimble: Whom should he stumble next on, But that tough stick of Wood, Boirude the Sexton? **1706** E. Ward *Wooden World Diss.* (1708) 36 You shall sometimes stumble upon a Lieutenant..of a very different Make. **1781** Cowper *Conversat.* 280 He..had a world of talk With one he stumbled on, and lost his walk. **1815** Kirby & Sp. *Entomol.* xiii. (1818) I. 417 *note*, Some time after making this experiment I stumbled upon a passage in Redi. **1838** W. C. Harris *Narr. Exped. S. Africa* 17 In the course of our perambulations..we stumbled upon a waggon discharging a cargo of oranges. **1840** Dickens *Old C. Shop* xix, They were not the fittest companions she could have stumbled on. **1874** L. Stephen *Hours in Libr.* (1892) i. i. 10 The founders..appear to have stumbled upon their discovery by a kind of accident. **1877** Mrs. Oliphant *Makers Florence* viii. 211 The curiously accidental and fortuitous way in which real excellence sometimes stumbles into recognition. **1902** S. Squire Sprigge *Industr. Chevalier* vii. 165 Now and again they stumble upon prizes which they cannot appreciate.

d. To take offence; to find a stumbling-block or obstacle to belief. Chiefly with const. *at.*

1526 *Pilgr. Perf.* (W. de W. 1531) 11 b, Here perauenture the scrupulous persone wyll stomble, & say [etc.]. **1593** Bilson *Govt. Christ's Ch.* 410, I see no cause for others to stumble at it. **1647** N. Bacon *Disc. Govt. Eng.* i. xv. 46 In case the Prelacy for England should stumble at the Supremacy of Rome. **1687** J. Renwick in A. Shields *Life Biogr.* Presbyt. (1827) II. 287 Stumble not, because Religion is mocked at. **1782** Priestley *Corrupt. Chr.* I. i. 21 The circumstance at which mankind..stumbled the most. **1860** Pusey *Min. Proph.* 92 Those who rebel against the law of God, stumble, in divers manners, at the ways of God. They stumble at God Himself,..they stumble at His attributes; they stumble at His Providence, at His acts [etc.]. **1882** Pitman *Mission Life Greece & Palestine* 326 These two peoples stumble at one 'stumbling stone', even Christ.

†**e.** *Proverb.*

1530 Palsgr. 736/2 Thou lepest over a bloke and stomblest at a strawe. **1547** *Homilies, Works* D iv, They were of so blynd iudgemente, that they stombled at a strawe, & leped ouer a blocke. **1653** W. Ramesey *Astrol. Restored* To Rdr. 17 To skip over blocks, and stumble at straws.

3. To walk unsteadily and with frequent stumbles.

c **1435** *Torr. Portugal* 660 Stomlyng thurrow frythe and fen, Tyll he com to a depe glen. **1577** Grange *Golden*

Aphrod. N ij b, But who so bolde as blinde Bayarde? for he mistrusting nought, comes stumbling forth at will. **1627** MAY *Lucan* III. F i, He seeing his Sonne fall with trembling step Stumbling along came to that side the ship. **1667** MILTON *P.L.* III. 201 But..blind be blinded more, That they may stumble on, and deeper fall. **1697** DAMPIER *Voy.* I. xv. 408 By this unreasonable custom they [the Chinese women] do in a manner lose the use of their Feet, and instead of going they only stumble about their Houses. **1831** SCOTT *Cast. Dang.* ix, She kept talking all the while as she stumbled onward. **1869** TOZER *Highl. Turkey* I. 292 We stumbled along behind him by the light of the stars, over very rough places. **1878** BROWNING *La Saisiaz* 59 What a load he stumbles under through his glad sad seventy years. **1883** STEVENSON *Treas. Isl.* xx, And with a dreadful oath he stumbled off, ploughed down the sand,..and disappeared. **1902** S. E. WHITE *Blazed Trail* iv, He dressed, shivering, and stumbled down stairs to a round stove.

b. *transf.* Of an inanimate thing: To move by jolts or falls. *rare.*

1873 MISS THACKERAY *Old Kensington* ii. (ed. 2) 9 Staring ..at the luggage as it comes bumping and stumbling off the big ship.

c. *fig.* To proceed, speak, or act in a blundering or hesitating manner.

c **1394** *P. Pl. Crede* 591 Now mot a frere studyen & stumblen in tales. **1589** R. HARVEY *Plain Percival* Ded., As farre as Will Solnes stuttring pronunciation may stumble ouer at a breath. **1593** SHAKS. *2 Hen. VI*, III. ii. 316 My tongue should stumble in mine earnest words. **1598** MARSTON *Sco. Villanie* To iudiciall Perusers B 4 b, Yet both of them [Juvenal and Persius] goe a good seemely pace, not stumbling, shuffling. **1862** STANLEY *Jew. Ch.* (1877) I. xiii. 246 Through a succession of failures, they stumbled into perfection. **1868** TENNYSON *Lucretius* 123, I have forgotten what I meant: my mind Stumbles, and all my faculties are lamed. **1884** *Harper's Mag.* Nov. 912/2 I'll stumble through the driest scientific treatise you have. **1891** FARRAR *Darkn. & Dawn* xv, Seneca blushed, and his smooth tongue stumbled, as he attempted to express his gratification.

4. *trans.* (causatively).

a. To trip up, bring to the ground, overthrow. *lit.* and *fig.* ? *Obs.*

c **1330** R. BRUNNE *Chron. Wace* (Rolls) 13050 Stedes slayn, stumbled & failled. **1382** WYCLIF *Eccles.* x. 12 The lippis of the vnwise shuln stumblen hym doun [Vulg. *præcipitabunt eum*]. **1592** *Soliman & Pers.* IV. i. 222, I, now occasion serues to stumble him That thrust his sickle in my haruest corne. **1652** BROUGH *Sacred Princ.* (ed. 2) 449 Stumble not an Vpright foot, with a visible Block of offence.

b. To puzzle; to give pause or offence to; to embarrass, nonplus.

1605 L. HUTTEN *Aunswere* 5 But the Treatiser thought it more for his aduantage,..to set down his argument confusedly, the more to stumble the vnskilfull Reader. **1621** BURTON *Anat. Mel.* II. iv. I. i. (1624) 297 A common ague sometimes stumbles them all [*sc.* the apothecaries], they cannot so much as ease. **1653** W. RAMESEY *Astrol. Restored* 22, I think good for the clearing of all what hath been already said (least some may be stumbled thereat) to deliver my minde as touching their influence thus. **1669** S. SIMMONS *Milton's P.L.* To Rdr., A reason of that which stumbled many others, why the Poem Rimes not. **1682** BUNYAN *Holy War* 381 To question Election is..to stumble the faith of the Town of Mansoul. **1724** A. SHIELDS *Life J. Renwick* Biogr. Presbyt. (1827) II. 144 By these and the like Reproaches, many were stumbled at his Testimony. **1784** COWPER *Task* IV. 533 In days like these..when Virtue is so scarce, That to suppose a scene where she presides..stumbles all belief. **1893** W. G. COLLINGWOOD *Life Ruskin* I. 172 The proud possessor of a cut-and-dry creed will be stumbled by this new milestone in Mr. Ruskin's intellectual pilgrimage. **1901** *Church Quarterly* July 425 He [a Chinaman] is much stumbled that..the claims of a man's wife take precedence of those of his elder brother.

†**c.** To shake (a resolve, an opinion). *Obs.*

1607 MARKHAM *Cavel.* III. vii. 34 There is nothing dooth so much stumble mens mindes, and make them affraide of keeping hunting horses, as the verie remembrance and charge of keeping them. **1646** *Hamilton Papers* (Camden) 134 The small appearance he findes that his message will be satisfactory to you there hath much stumbled his resolution of sending it to London. **1651** N. BACON *Disc. Govt. Eng.* II. xxv. 192 Nor was it wisdome for Kings that sate loose in their Thrones, to stumble the good Opinions of so considerable [a] party towards them.

†**d.** To act as an obstacle to, to hinder, prevent.

1606 WARNER *Alb. Eng.* XVI. ciii. 406 What stumbleth our Banes-bidding, pra? cause Peg forsooth will be A Gentlewoman.

Hence **'stumbled** *ppl. a.*

1548 COOPER *Elyot's Dict.*, *Titubatus*, tripped, stumbled. **1848** S. WILBERFORCE in Ashwell *Life* (1880) I. xi. 499 Though to anonymous public slanderers I would give no answer, yet to a stumbled Christian friend I ought even to humble myself to reply to a surmise so degrading to my character even as this.

stumble-block, *v. nonce-wd.* [As if f. **stumble-block* = STUMBLING-BLOCK.] *trans.* To put stumbling-blocks in the way of.

1819 KEATS *Let. to Haydon* 3 Oct., If I ever do anything worth remembering the Reviewers will no more be able to stumble-block me than the Royal Academy could you.

stumblebum ('stʌmb(ə)lbʌm). Also **stumble bum, stumble-bum.** *slang* (orig. and chiefly *U.S.*). [f. STUMBLE *v.* + BUM *sb.*[4]]

a. A worthless, clumsy, or inept person; a 'down and out', a drunkard.

1932 E. HEMINGWAY *Death in Afternoon* 297 American word would be awkward bum, stumble-bum, flat-footed tramp. **1935** *Punch* 11 Dec. 652/3 An American gangster is stated to have begun his career by starting as a stumble-bum. **1936** [see PALOOKA]. **1940** G. FRANKAU *Self-Portrait* xxxi. 178 The good old English word for a posterior, which possesses a different meaning (cf. 'stumblebum'—a guy who comes home drunk) in America. **1954** *Sun* (Baltimore) 11 Feb. 1/4 He became a ragged stumble-bum, raging drunkenly through the village and selling mediocre poetry. **1955** D. KEENE *Who has Wilma Lathrop?* x. 93 He had a stubble of beard that made him look like a stumblebum. **1966** A. LA BERN *Goodbye Piccadilly* xii. 113 These stumble-bums may have stumbled across the real culprit. **1970** *Guardian* 25 Sept. 10/5 Iago is a red-necked farm boy... He's a stumblebum. **1981** *Times Lit. Suppl.* 11 Sept. 1042/1 The Eisenhower of the war years has lost much of his lustre, and the successful organizer of Montgomery, Bradley and Patton has been reduced by some writers to the level of a strategic stumble-bum.

b. *attrib.* or as *adj.* Also *fig.*

1940 *Topeka* (Kansas) *Daily Capital* 16 Jan. 4/4 Russia's stumblebum campaign in Finland. **1952** B. WOLFE *Limbo '90* (1953) VI. xxii. 372 It made its slapstick stumblebum way back and forth. **1975** N. FREELING *What are Bugles blowing For?* xii. 75 Airs and graces with plain stumblebum cops. **1981** *Washington Post* 23 July c9/4 Joe Benjamin has a nihilistic, stumblebum-drunk son (splendidly played by Michael Rothhaar).

stumbler ('stʌmblə(r)). [f. STUMBLE *v.* + -ER[1].]

1. One who, or something which stumbles; esp. a horse that is given to stumbling.

c **1440** *Promp. Parv.* 481/1 Stumlere (or stomelare) *cespitator.* **1562** J. HEYWOOD *Prov. & Epigr.* (1867) 150 Stumble at a strawe, and leape ouer a blocke, Such stumblers are blockeheads. **1613** *Uncasing of Machiav.* 26 Riding a stumbler hold fast the bridle. **1633** G. HERBERT *Temple, Ch. Porch* xxxvi, A stumbler stumbles least in rugged way. **1796** COLERIDGE *To an Infant* 5 Poor stumbler on the rocky coast of Woe. **1835** WILLIS *Pencillings* II. liv. 124 The horses were all sad stumblers. **1894** MEREDITH *Foresight & Patience* Poet. Wks. (1912) 418 Yet, happy for us when, their cause defined, They walk no longer with a stumbler blind.

2. A cause of stumbling; a 'poser'.

1863 P. DAVIDSON *Pentateuch Vind.* ii. 33 Here was a stumbler for the priests and a marrowbone for the infidels.

stumbling ('stʌmblɪŋ), *vbl. sb.* [-ING[1].] The action of the verb STUMBLE, in various senses.

a **1400–50** *Wars Alex.* 2623 Þare was stomling of stedis sticking of erles. **15..** *King & Barker* 106 in Ritson *Anc. Pop. Poetry* (1791) 64 With a stombellyng as he rode the thanner downe he [the horse] cast. **1568** GRAFTON *Chron.* II. 598 He tolde him also without anye stayeng or stomblyng,.. the names of all the colours that could be shewed him. **1611** BIBLE *1 John* ii. 10 Hee that loueth his brother, abideth in the light, and there is none occasion of stumbling in him. **1657** HOBBES *Marks Absurd Geom.* 4, I noted it only that you may be more merciful hereafter to the stumblings of a hasty Pen. **1818** KEATS *Endymion* I. 703 To entice My stumblings down some monstrous precipice. **1873** G. S. BADEN-POWELL *New Homes* 184 Stumblings and injuries to legs are of remarkably rare occurrence. **1892–3** FROUDE *Lect. Counc. Trent* vi. (1896) 134 There was stumbling again at the power of the keys, and at the splendour and assumptions of the hierarchy.

b. *Comb.*: **stumbling-shoe**, a horse-shoe devised to prevent stumbling; **stumbling-†stock, -stone** = STUMBLING-BLOCK.

1908 *Animal Managem.* (War Office) 367 *Stumbling shoes, 244 [In text: Shoes to obviate stumbling]. **1550** *Stumbling stock [see SISTER *sb.* 3 c]. **1569** ROEST tr. *J. van der Noot's Theat. Worldlings* 31 Christ is that stumbling stocke, and the stone of offense, whereat the world stumbled. *c* **1630** RISDON *Surv. Devon* (1714) II. 150 Richard Hooker..wrote a Book intitled *The Laws of Ecclesiastical Polity*, a great Stumbling-Stock to many, and not answered by any. **1841** BORROW *Zincali* II. ii. III. 156 Many of which have long been stumbling-stocks to the philologist. **1526** TINDALE *Rom.* ix. 33 Beholde I put in syon a *stomblynge stone and a rocke which shall make men faule [Gr. λίθον προσκόμματος καὶ πέτραν σκανδάλου]. **1567** *Sat. Poems Reform.* iii. 109 God he[t]is all that layis ane stumling stane, Quhilk may the cause be of our bretheringis fall. **1684** T. BURNET *Theory Earth* I. 294 The regularity of the universe was always a great stumbling-stone to the Epicuræans. ?**1780** COWPER tr. *Bourne, Glow-worm* 19 Nor crush a worm, whose useful light Might serve..To shew a stumbling stone by night. **1865** SWINBURNE *Chastelard* II. i. (1894) 47 Some scurril children that lurked near Set there by Satan for my stumbling-stone.

stumbling ('stʌmblɪŋ), *ppl. a.* [-ING[2].] That stumbles, in various senses of the verb.

c **1425** *Cast. Persev.* 1042 [*Avaricia loquitur:*] Þerfore, Pryde, good broþyr,..late Iche of vs take at othyr, & set Mankynde on a stomlynge stol. **1538** ELYOT *Dict.*, *Suffossus equus*, a stumblynge horse. **1579** SPENSER *Sheph. Cal.* May 231 Her stombling steppe somewhat her amazed. **1585** HIGINS *Junius' Nomencl.* 383/1 *Confragosus locus*,..a rough, rugged, rockie or stumbling ground: vphill and downehill. **1727** *Country-Post* xi. in *Swift's Miscell.* II. 290 There have died of the falling Sickness two stumbling Horses, as also one of their Riders. **1859** DICKENS etc. *Haunted Ho.* vii. 42/2 Then she heard him..go down stairs, with hurried, stumbling steps. **1859** *Habits of Gd. Society* xv. 372 The tearful, stumbling speeches of 'dear papa' after champagne [at the wedding breakfast]. *a* **1893** CHRISTINA G. ROSSETTI *Poems* (1904) 209/1 Is there a path to Heaven My stumbling foot may tread? **1905** TREVES *Other Side of Lant.* II. xxvii. (1906) 164 Everywhere is the figure of the devout offering his stumbling prayer.

stumbling-block. [f. STUMBLING *vbl. sb.*

Introduced by Tindale as a rendering of Gr. πρόσκομμα; later translators have preferred to use it to render σκάνδαλον. The phrase 'to stumble at a block' (i.e. a tree stump) is of earlier date: see quot. *c* 1450 under STUMBLE *v.* 1 b. Cf. *stumbling-stock, stone* (STUMBLING *vbl. sb.* b).]

Something to stumble at or over; a cause of stumbling. Chiefly *fig.*

a. An occasion of moral stumbling; a 'scandal', 'offence'.

1526 TINDALE *Rom.* xiv. 13 That no man putt a stomblinge blocke or an occasion to faule [Gr. πρόσκομμα ἢ σκάνδαλον] in his brothers waye. **1532** MORE *Confut. Tindale* Pref. Ee iij b, It wyll none otherwyse be, but that some stumblyng blokkys wyll allway be by malycyouse folke layed in good peoples way. **1651** HOBBES *Leviath.* I. xii. 58 All which doings, or sayings..be stumbling blocks, that make men to fall in the way of Religion. **1855** MACAULAY *Hist. Eng.* xiv. III. 489 To unite a scattered flock in one fold under one shepherd, to remove stumbling blocks from the path of the weak,..these were objects which might well justify some modification..of national or provincial usages. **1884** J. HALL *Chr. Home* xi. 166 If meat be a stumbling-block to a brother, then will he forego it (1 Cor. viii. 13).

b. An occasion of falling into calamity or ruin.

1535 COVERDALE *Ezek.* iii. 20 Yf a rightuous man go from his rightuousnesse,..I will laye a stomblinge blocke before him, and he shall dye. **1732** LEDIARD *Sethos* II. VIII. 247 Be upon your guard against this stumbling-block of heroes. **1829** SCOTT *Anne of G.* xvi, We are not men to be trodden on ..; those who have attempted it have found us stumbling-blocks.

c. An obstacle to belief or understanding; something repugnant to one's prejudices.

a **1593** MARLOWE & NASHE *Dido* IV. i. (Brooke) 1093, I see Æneas sticketh in your minde, But I will soone put by that stumbling-blocke. **1653** W. RAMESEY *Astrol. Restored* 271 Unless I here remove a seeming obstruction or stumbling block, perhaps some mistakes or errours might arise. **1714** ADDISON *Spect.* No. 592 ¶7 A Stumbling-Block to the whole Tribe of these rigid Criticks. **1721** WATERLAND *Case Arian-Subscr.* 32 The old Arians would have detested such Practises: The 'Ομοούσιον alone was such a Stumbling-Block to Them, that They could never get over it. **1857** KEBLE *Euchar. Ador.* 20 A most effectual stumbling block to those who were unwilling to believe. **1864** BOWEN *Logic* vii. 204 Baroko and Bokardo have been stumbling-blocks to the logicians. **1884** F. TEMPLE *Relat. Relig. & Sci.* viii. (1885) 244 Believers have thus prepared a stumblingblock for themselves.

d. An obstacle in the way of progress, or of the execution of a plan.

1593 SHAKS. *2 Hen. VI*, I. ii. 64 Were I a Man, a Duke, and next of blood, I would remoue these tedious stumbling blockes. **1658–9** *Burton's Diary* (1828) III. 398, I have heard that there are the greatest endeavours to put some obstruction in this business. Dutch and Dane are not wanting to lay stumbling-blocks. **1736** BUTLER *Anal.* II. vii. 354 Such a discovery might have been a stumblingblock in the way of Christianity. **1838** JAMES *Louis XIV*, I. 194 Nor did he ever quit his religion, though as a Hugonot it might have proved a great stumbling-block in his way. **1865** TROLLOPE *Belton Est.* xiii. 143 She..had come to fear that she might be an embargo on his prosperity, and a stumbling-block in the way of his success. **1912** *Nature* 21 Nov. 346/1 The cost of electrical power is the chief stumbling-block to the introduction of the manufacture on a large scale in this country.

e. In literal sense. *rare.* Also *attrib.*

1663 GERBIER *Counsel* 21 A good Surveyour shuns also the ordering of Doores with Stumbling-Block-Thresholds. **1893** *Law Times* XCV. 204/2 The cover projected about 1½ in. above the level of the road, and so formed a stumbling-block.

transf. **1859** HERSCHEL *Fam. Lect. Sci. Subj.* iii. §31 (1866) 119 Jupiter, in fact, is a regular stumbling-block in the way of comets.

stumblingly ('stʌmblɪŋlɪ), *adv.* [f. STUMBLING *ppl. a.* + -LY[2].] In a stumbling manner.

a **1586** SIDNEY *Apol. Poet.* (Arb.) 62, I know not, whether to meruaile more, either that he [Chaucer] in that mistie time, could see so clearely, or that wee in this cleare age, walke so stumblingly after him. **1879** BROWNING *Martin Relph* 95 A Man,..Who staggeringly, stumblingly, rises, falls, rises. **1915** *Chamb. Jrnl.* Aug. 491/2, I stumblingly descended the rugged bank.

'stumbly, *a.* [f. STUMBLE *v.* + -Y.]

a. Addicted to stumbling. **b.** Apt to cause stumbling.

1890 *Century Mag.* Aug. 570/2 The miserable horses of the peasants are awfully slow and very stumbly. **1898** G. W. STEEVENS *With Kitchener to Khartum* 114 It is an impenetrable, flesh-tearing jungle of mimosa-spears and dom-palm and stumbly halfa-grass.

stume, obs. form of STUM.

stumer ('stju:mə(r)). *slang.* Also **stumor.** [Of unknown origin.] **1. a.** A forged or dishonoured cheque; a counterfeit bank-note or coin; a sham. Also *attrib.*, as ***stumer cheque.***

1890 *Blackw. Mag.* June 793 'Stumer' is slang for a worthless cheque. *a* **1897** *Sporting Times* in Barrère & Leland *Slang Dict.* s.v., My collection of writs, pawn tickets, unreceipted bills, stumers [etc.]. **1897** HALL CAINE *Christian* IV. iv. 376 A 'thick'un'? Oh, that was a sovereign,..twenty-five pounds a 'pony', five hundred a 'monkey', flash notes were 'stumers'. **1911** A. G. C. *Through a College Keyhole* 13 For Maeterlinck's bird was a stumor, I've heard. **1912** L. WILLIAMS in *Daily News* 19 Dec. 7/4, I did pass a bad florin, guv'nor, but I did it innocent. I didn't know it was a stumer. **1926** F. M. FORD *Man could stand Up* II. iii. 140 Two [were] awaiting court-martial for giving stumer cheques. **1944** P. CHEYNEY *They never say When* i. 18 Tell him to get in touch with Effie and get that stumer cheque from her and issue a writ against Swayle. **1962** *Listener* 11 Jan. 98/1 People who cash stumer cheques. **1972** L. LAMB *Picture Frame* xvii. 149 Nice old Mr. Murgatroyd got your picture back from the man who gave you a stumer cheque.

b. *Austral.* Also **stoomer** (-u:-). (See quots.)

1898 *Bulletin* (Sydney) 17 Dec. (Red Page), *A stoomer* or *stumer* is a man without money. **1900–10** O'BRIEN & STEPHENS *Materials Dict. Austral. Slang* (MS.), *Come a stoomer*, stake a bet and lose everything. **1941** S. J. BAKER *Dict. Austral. Slang* 73 *Stumer*, (in gambling or racing) a bankrupt, a defaulter... *Come a stumer*, to crash financially, esp. in a racing bet.

2. *gen.* Something which is worthless; a failure, a 'flop', a 'dud'. Also used of persons.

1886–96 A. R. MARSHALL in Farmer & Henley *Slang* (1903) VII. 18/1 The merry stumer. **1902** *Sporting Times* 1 Feb. 3/1 He..had given her as security a 'stumer' in the shape of an unfinished history of Corsica. **1923** WODEHOUSE *Inimitable Jeeves* xii. 132 The agony of having put his little all on a stumer that hadn't finished in the first six. **1925** FRASER & GIBBONS *Soldier & Sailor Words* 273 *Stumer*, an expression used commonly to denote a shell that had failed to explode. **1928** GALSWORTHY *Swan Song* II. iv. 140 There is no good in me... You've pitched on a stumer. **1934** *Punch* 10 Jan. 50/1 *Myself*... No, drama. Young couple sightseeing in mine. Old Miner guide. Roof falls, water rises. *Daphne.* Sounds like a stumer. Are you going to give it a run? **1970** *Daily Tel.* 9 Feb. 15/1 While in the course of a year countless shares will establish new lows only half a dozen will turn out to be real stumers and eventually worthless. **1976** *Times* 21 Feb. 15/3 Eclecticism guarantees that in a period like this the [Tate] collection will come to include a fair proportion of stumers. **1980** R. HILL *Spy's Wife* iv. 25 Don't be such a stumer!.. Fetch them.

3. Also **stuma**. A state of agitation; a sweat or 'stew'.

1932 AUDEN in *Rev. Eng. Studies* (1978) Aug. 284 Poor old Ma in a perfect stuma. **1936** —— *Look, Stranger!* 36 Behind your simple sense of humour You hide the boss's simple stuma. **1941** S. J. BAKER *Dict. Austral. Slang* 73 *Stumer, in a*, in a 'stew', worried, angry.

stumle, stummel, obs. forms of STUMBLE *v.*

stumm, stummed: see STUM *sb.* and *v.*

stumm, var. SHTOOM *a.*

stummer (ˈstʌmə(r)), *v. Obs.* (? exc. *dial.*) [a. ON. *stumra*: see STUMBLE *v.*] *intr.* To stumble (*lit.* and *fig.*).

13.. *Old Age* in *Rel. Ant.* II. 211, I stunt, I stomere, I stomble as sledde. *c* **1470** *Gol. & Gaw.* 624 Thair stedis stakkerit in the stour, and stude stummerand. **1513** DOUGLAS *Æneis* v. vi. 80 He slaid and stummerit on the slydry ground. **1562** WINȜET *Cert. Tractates* Wks. (S.T.S.) I. 5 Hes not mony..mysknawin thair deuty..and sua in thair perfite beleif hes sairlye stummerit. *c* **1590** J. STEWART *Poems* (S.T.S.) II. 48 So I agains my will Dois stot and stummer in my mateir low. **1825** BROCKETT *N.C. Gloss.*, *Stummer*, to stumble.

stummick, repr. dial. and pop. pronunc. of STOMACH *sb.*

1888 KIPLING *Soldiers Three* (1890) 38 He was pegged out ..on his stummick, a peg to each arm an' leg. **1936** M. MITCHELL *Gone with Wind* xxii. 372 De Yankees is comin'! .. Dey'll run dey baynits in our stummicks! **1947** K. TENNANT *Lost Haven* x. 157 If I was ever *you*, Mollie, or if I ever developed scales on me stummick, which amounts to the same thing..I'd be able to wriggle under rocks. **1977** J. AIKEN *Five-Minute Marriage* v. 88 You didn't ought to go out giving lessons on an empty stummick.

stumming, *vbl. sb.*: see under STUM *v.*

stummock, obs. form of STOMACH.

†ˈ**stummy**, *a.* [f. STUM *sb.* + -Y.] = STUMMED *ppl. a.*

1770 CUMBERLAND *Brothers* Epil., The plodding Drudge shou'd here at Times resort, And leave his stupid Club and stummy Port. **1776** GRAVES *Euphrosyne* (1780) II. 159 Stummy wines.

stump (stʌmp), *sb.*[1] Forms: 4–6 **stompe**, 5 *Sc.* **stowmpe**, 5–7 **stumpe**, 6 **stoomp**, 6–7 **stumppe**, 6– **stump**. [First in 14th c.; a. or cogn. w. MLG. *stump* masc., *stumpe* fem., (M)Du. *stomp* masc., subst. use of MLG. *stump*, (M)Du. *stomp* adj., mutilated, blunt, dull; corresp. to OHG. (MHG., mod.G.) *stumpf* adj. and sb. masc.; the late ON. *stump-r* masc., MSw. *stumper* (mod.Sw. *stump*), Da. *stump* adj. and sb., are prob. from LG.

The senses of the word, in Eng. and other Teut. langs., show close parallelism with those of STUB *sb.* and its cognates, but etymological connexion is difficult to establish. On the other hand, there is no morphological objection to the view that the Teut. root **stump-* is an ablaut-variant of **stamp-* (see STAMP *v.*), but this is not supported by any striking similarity of sense.]

1. a. The part remaining of an amputated or broken-off limb or portion of the body.

to fight to the stumps: app. an allusion to quot. *c* 1600 below; cf. 3 b.

a **1375** *Joseph Arim.* 681 Þan Ioseph..bad þat mon knele, þe arm helede a-ȝeyn hol to þe stompe. *c* **1430** *Syr Tryam.* 1561 He [Tryamour] smote Burlond of be the kneys... Burlonde on hys stompus stode. *c* **1440** *Sir Eglam.* 739 Syr Egyllamowre,..Halfe the tonge [of the dragon] he stroke away, That fende began to ȝelle! And with the stompe that hym was levyd, He stroke the knyght in the hedd A depe wounde and a felle. *c* **1450** *Mirk's Festial* 223 Boþe hys hondys wern puld of by þe elboues,..and he wyth hys stompes stode soo. **1541** *Act 33 Hen. VIII*, c. 12 §3 The.. chief Surgeon..shalbe redye..to seare the stumpe when the hande is striken of. **1590** *Tarlton's News Purgatory* 24 He threatned to cut out her tongue, it is no matter for that knaue quoth she, yet shall the stump call thee prick-lowse. **1597** A. M. tr. *Guillemeau's Fr. Chirurg.* 37 b, [In an amputation] it is allwayes better to make the stumpe short, then longe. *c* **1600** *Chevy Chase* (later version) l. in Child *Ballads* III. 313 For when his leggs were smitten of he fought vpon his stumpes. **1615** CROOKE *Body of Man* 80 The nauell therefore is the stumpe of the vmbilicall vesselles, by which the Infant was nourished in the wombe. **1653** T. BRUGIS *Vade Mecum* (ed. 2) 143 They are very necessary..to cauterize the end or stump of a bone after dismembring. **1672** WISEMAN *Treat. Wounds* II. v. 30 Here your work is with a good Razor or Knife presently to plain the Stump, and pull up the Flesh, that you may saw off the end of the Bone as even as may be. **1766** H. WALPOLE *Let. to G. Montagu* 3 Mar., The stumps that beggars thrust into coaches to excite charity and miscarriages. **1822** SHELLEY *Chas. 1st* iii. 40 And hands, which now write only their own shame, With bleeding stumps might sign our blood away. **1853** LD. J. RUSSELL in *Life & Lett. 4th Earl Clarendon* (1913) II. xiii. 23, I feel sure that they [*sc.* the English people] would fight to the stumps for the honour of England. **1898** *Syd. Soc. Lex.*, *Stump of Eyeball*, the remainder of the globe after the excision of whole or part of the eyeball. **1905** *Brit. Med. Jrnl.* 1 July 15 The root of the appendix was..then amputated, the stump being buried by a purse-string suture of catgut.

b. A rudimentary limb of member, or one that has the appearance of being mutilated.

1555 EDEN *Decades* (Arb.) 232 This beast..hath in the place of armes, two great stumpes wherwith he swymmeth. **1611** CORYAT *Crudities* 54 A woman that had no hands but stumpes in stead thereof. **1635** SWAN *Spec. Mundi* viii. §2. (1643) 413 Out of their [*sc.* bees'] short feet or stumps, there grow forth as it were two fingers. **1664** POWER *Exp. Philos.* I. 32 The Sycomore-Locust... I could, near her shoulders, see the stumps of her growing wings. **1719** N. BLUNDELL *Diary* (1895) 158, I saw Matthew Buckinger who was born without Hands or Feet, I saw him writ very well with his Stumps. **1861** P. P. CARPENTER in *Rep. Smithsonian Instit.* 1860, 205 The eyes are on stumps at the base of the tentacles.

c. Jocularly used for: A leg. Chiefly in *to stir one's stumps*, to walk or dance briskly, †to do one's duty zealously.

c **1460** *Towneley Plays* xxx. 109 There I stode on my stumpe I stakerd that stownde. **1535** LAYTON in *Lett. Suppress. Monast.* (Camden) 76 His hore..bestyrrede hir stumpis towardes hir startyng hoilles. **1559** *Mirr. Mag.*, *Jack Cade* xx, But hope of money made him stur his stumpes, And to assault me valiauntly and bolde. **1583** STUBBES *Anat. Abuses* I. (1877) 147 Their pipers pipeing, drommers thundring, their stumps dauncing, their bels iyngling. **1596** COLSE *Penelope* (1880) 164, I doubt not but poore shepheards will stirre their stumps after my minstrelsie. **1603** B. JONSON *Ent. Althrope* (1604) 11 Come on Clownes, forsake your dumps, And bestir your Hobnaild stumps. **1619** H. HUTTON *Follies Anat.* B 4 b, Making his stumppes supporters to vp-holde This masse of guttes. **1682** N. O. *Boileau's Le Lutrin* ii. 16 Up starts amazed John, bestirs his Stump. *a* **1700** B. E. *Dict. Cant. Crew*, *Bustle about*, to be very Stirring, or bestir one's Stumps. *a* **1728** W. STARRAT *Epist. to A. Ramsay* 7, [I] Right tozylie was set to ease my Stumps. **1785** BURNS *Jolly Beggars* v, I'd clatter on my stumps at the sound of a drum. **1832** MARRYAT *N. Forster* x, Come this way, my hearty—stir your stumps. **1837** LYTTON *E. Maltrav.* IV. vi, Come, why don't you stir your stumps? I suppose I must wait on myself.

d. A wooden leg.

1679 J. YONGE *Currus Triumph.* 18 It being difficult..to use an artificial 'tump or supplemental Leg, till the Ulcer be cicatrized. **1740** SOMERVILLE *Hobbinol* I. 145 His [a one-legged fiddler's] single Eye Twinkles with Joy, his active Stump beats Time. **1771** SMOLLETT *Humph. Cl.* 5 May, At the same time [he] set his wooden stump upon my gouty toe.

2. a. The portion of the trunk of a felled tree that remains fixed in the ground; also, a standing tree-trunk from which the upper part and the branches have been cut or broken off. Cf. STUB *sb.*[1]

c **1440** *Promp. Parv.* 481/1 Stumpe, of a tree hewyn don, *surcus*. **1546** *Supplic. Poore Commons* (E.E.T.S.) 92 The old stompes of these fruitles trees. **1558** WARDE tr. *Alexis' Secr.* 29 b, Take *Polipodium* (whiche is an herbe, like vnto Ferne) growyng vpon the stumpe or stocke of a Chestnut tree. **1638** JUNIUS *Paint. Ancients* 68 Thick woods, graced between the stumpes with a pure and grasse-greene soile. **1697** DAMPIER *Voy.* I. 156 There are so many Stumps in the River, that it is very dangerous passing in the night. **1698** FRYER *Acc. E. India & P.* 41 On the top of a withered Stump perching a Chamelion. **1717** BERKELEY *Tour Italy* Wks. 1871 IV. 567 Hills on left almost naked, having only the stumps of trees. **1764** DODSLEY *Leasowes* in *Shenstone's Wks.* (1777) II. 291 A number of these extempore benches (two stumps with a transverse board). **1781** COWPER *Conversat.* 51 So wither'd stumps disgrace the sylvan scene, No longer fruitful, and no longer green. **1800** WORDSW. *Hartleap Well* 125 You see these lifeless stumps of aspen wood—Some say that they are beeches, others elms. **1836** [MRS. TRAILL] *Backw. Canada* 41 It would have broken my heart to have to work among the stumps, and never see..a well-ploughed field. **1860** TYNDALL *Glac.* I. xxvii. 213 Adjacent to my theodolite was a stump of pine. **1902** S. E. WHITE *Blazed Trail* xix, After you will come the backwoods farmer to pull up the stumps; and after him the big farmer and the cities.

transf. **1655** FULLER *Ch. Hist.* I. 23 The stumps of ruined Churches lately destroyed by Diocletian grew up into beautiful Buildings. **1899** BARING-GOULD *Bk. West* I. vii. 101 The main castle tower was..pulled down and left as a stump.

fig. **1580** LYLY *Euphues* (Arb.) 226 Philautus although the stumpes of loue so sticked in his mind..: yet [etc.]. **1583** MELBANCKE *Philotimus* R ij b, You say you cannot boote me, yet do stumps of old loue stick in your stomacke.

¶ The lofty and massive church tower of Boston, Lincs. (a conspicuous sea-mark), has long been known as 'Boston Stump', perh. as having no spire. This designation is mentioned in E. J. Wilson *Gloss. Gothic Archit.* (1823) 21.

b. The base of a growing tree. *to buy* (timber) *on the stump*; before felling. Cf. STUB *sb.* 1 b, c.

1902 S. E. WHITE *Blazed Trail* xiv, You originally paid in cash for all that timber on the stump just ten thousand dollars. *Ibid.* xxxiv, There ought to be about eight or ten million [feet of timber]..worth in the stump anywhere from sixteen to twenty thousand dollars. **1902** *Daily Chron.* 31 Dec. 6/3 Twenty-four hours from stump to saw-mill is a regular thing now in some of the eastern mills.

c. *up a stump*: perplexed, in difficulties (see also quot. 1834). Cf. *up a tree* s.v. TREE *sb.* 7. *slang* (orig. and chiefly *U.S.*).

1829 S. KIRKHAM *Eng. Gram.* 206 Hele [= he will] soon be up a stump. **1834** W. G. SIMMS *Guy Rivers* II. 241 Brooks ..in backwood parlance, was 'considerably up a stump'—that is to say, half drunk. **1880** 'MARK TWAIN' *Tramp Abroad* xxxvi. 402 The public reciter..would find himself 'up a stump' when he got to the church bell. **1924** GALSWORTHY *White Monkey* I. xii. 100 Look here, Uncle Soames, I'm up a stump. **1944** DUNCAN & NICKOLS *Mentor Graham* 147 For once in his life, work had him so up a stump that he could not snatch a moment for study or reading.

3. a. Something (e.g. a pencil, quill pen, cigar) that has been reduced by wear or consumption to a small part of its original length; a fag-end. = STUB *sb.* 9.

1516 *Will of R. Peke*, And then the stumpe to be put in on tapere with more stuffe in ytt. **1660** R. WILD *Iter Bor.* 4, I ..had gnaw'd my Goose-quill to the very stump. **1709** STEELE *Tatler* No. 9 ¶1 The Youth with broomy Stumps began to trace The Kennel Edge, where Wheels had worn the Place. **1809** SIR G. JACKSON *Diaries & Lett.* (1873) I. 16 A knife to improve the sorry stump that does duty for one [a pen]. **1829** G. HEAD *Forest Scenes N. Amer.* 49 A black stump of a tobacco-pipe was in his mouth. **1840** DICKENS *Old C. Shop* v, An inkstand with no ink and the stump of one pen. **1865** LE FANU *Guy Deverell* iv. I. 53 When he threw his last stump [*sc.* of a cigar] out of the window they were driving through Penlake Forest. **1911** MAX BEERBOHM *Zuleika Dobson* xiv. 218 'Yes, my Lord', said the boy, producing a stump of pencil. **1913** J. G. FRAZER *Golden Bough* (ed. 3) *Scapegoat* iii. 163 The fires are fed with stumps of old brooms.

fig. **1647** N. BACON *Disc. Govt. Eng.* I. lix. 176 He is contented with the stump of the Crown.

b. Phrase, *(to wear) to the stumps*. Chiefly *fig.* Very common in 16–18th c.; now *rare* or *Obs.*

a **1555** in Foxe *A. & M.* (1563) 1313/2 Though our soule priestes sing til they be bleare eyed, say tyl they haue worne theyr tongues to yᵉ stumpes, neither their singings nor their sayings shall bryng vs out of hel. **1602** T. FITZHERBERT *Apol.* 37 God wil..throw into the fyre, those rods of his wrath, when he hath worne them to the stumps. **1614** DAY *Festivals* x. (1615) 287, I have endeavoured to carke and care for them all, have spent my whole life, and worne my selfe to the very stumps. **1660** GAUDEN *Slight Healings* 63 The first reduceth a Nation to its stumps, and makes it a cripple a long time. **1679** *Hist. Jetzer* 10 When they had almost quite worn out their patience to the stumps. *c* **1680** BEVERIDGE *Serm.* (1729) II. 525 Thou may'st pray 'till thy tongue be worn to the stumps. **1716** M. DAVIES *Athen. Brit.* I. 148 Erasmus plainly shews, that Archbishop Lee had driven him to his Stumps. **1732** BERKELEY *Alciphr.* ii. §17 This man of pleasure, when, after a wretched scene of vanity and woe, his animal nature is worn to the stumps.

c. The part of a broken tooth left in the gum.

c **1430** LYDG. *Min. Poems* (Percy Soc.) 30 Thy mone pynnes bene lyche old yvory, Here are stumpes feble and her are none. **1601** HOLLAND *Pliny* XI. xxxvii. I. 338 He had a brother also who never cast his foreteeth, and therefore he wore them before, to the very stumps. **1613** SHAKS. *Hen. VIII*, I. iii. 49 Your Colts tooth is not cast yet? *L.San.* No my Lord, Nor shall not while I haue a stumpe. **1653** T. BRUGIS *Vade Mecum* (ed. 2) 144 A punch to force out a stump of a hollow tooth. **1777** *St. James's Chron.* 26–28 June 2/1 [Dentist's Advt.] Advice 1 l. 1 s. Taking out a Tooth or Stump, 1 l. 1 s. **1801** G. COLMAN *Poor Gentl.* IV. i. 57 My cousin Crushjaw, of Case-horton; who lugs out a stump with perfect pleasure to the patient. **1877** *Encycl. Brit.* VII. 99/1 The removal of roots and stumps as a preparatory step in the fitting of artificial teeth.

d. The part of a broken off branch that remains attached to the trunk.

1707 MORTIMER *Husb.* (1721) II. 83 If the Bough is large ..cut it off at some distance from the Tree..; but by no means leave any Stumps to stand out at any distance, because they cannot be covered by the Bark, 'till the Diameter of the Tree grows beyond it, and in the mean time the Stump will be continually rotting.

e. A docked tail.

1544 BETHAM *Precepts War* I. lxxxiii. E iv b, The weake man that laboured to plucke awaye [the horse's tail] heere by heere, made all bare to ye stompe. **1590** SPENSER *F.Q.* I. xi. 39 The knotty string Of his huge taile he quite a sunder cleft; Five ioynts thereof he hewd, and but the stump him left. **1770** CUMBERLAND *West Indian* II. ix, To hang the false tails on the miserable stumps of the old crawling cattle. **1885** RIDER HAGGARD *K. Soloman's Mines* iii, Still it does look odd to trek along behind twenty stumps [of oxen], where there ought to be tails.

f. *Naut.* The lower portion of a mast when the upper part has been broken off or shot away. Also = *stump mast* (see 19).

1725 N. BAILEY *Fam. Colloq. Erasm.* (1733) 187, I bethought my self of the Stump of the Mast. **1743** BULKELEY & CUMMINS *Voy. S. Seas* 10 Fitted a Capp on the Stump of the Mizen-Mast. **1745** P. THOMAS *Jrnl. Anson's Voy.* 44 We got down our Stumps, which are generally set up in bad Weather instead of Top gallant Masts. **1773** *Gentl. Mag.* XLIII. 321 A terrible storm arose, which obliged the Dolphin..to strike her top gallant-masts, and lie to in her stumps. **1800** in Nicolas *Disp. Nelson* (1845) IV. 219 *note*, Half past 6, shot away the main and mizen-masts: saw a man nail the French ensign to the stump of the mizen-mast.

g. *dial.* The remains of a hay-stack, most of which has been cut away. (*Eng. Dial. Dict.*)

1785 *Jackson's Oxf. Jrnl.* 15 Jan. 1/4 Two Hundred Tons of fine Old and New Hay, in several Ricks, Cocks, and Stumps. **1785** [see STADDLE *sb.* 8]. **1868** *Gloss. Sussex Wds.* in *Hurst's Horsham* (1899).

h. The remaining portion of a leaf cut out of a volume; the counterfoil of a cheque. Cf. STUB *sb.* 10, STOCK *sb.*[1] 42.

1887 ELLIS & SCRUTTON *Catal.* Feb. 5 It is conclusively shewn that the text is quite perfect, and that the eighth leaf of Sig. G. was a blank, of which there is still the stump remaining in this copy.

i. ***stump and rump*** adv. phrase: (Of destruction, removal, etc.) totally, completely. (See also RUMP *sb.*[1] 4.) Cf. STOUT AND ROUT. *dial.*

1825 BROCKETT *N.C. Gloss., Stump and rump*, entirely. **1828** CARR *Craven Gloss.* s.v., I's ruined stump and rump. **1901** R. BUCHANAN *Poems* 140 (E.D.D.) Geordie swallowed them 'stump an' rump.'

4. Applied to a person: A blockhead (cf. STOCK *sb.*[1] 1 c, STUB *sb.* 2); a man of short stumpy figure (cf. STUB *sb.* 7 d). †Sometimes as a term of contemptuous address: also ***stumps.***

1601 B. JONSON *Poetaster* I. ii, Come, bee not ashamed of thy vertues, old stumpe. **1605** *Tryall Chevalry* II. i. in Bullen *Old Pl.* (1884) III. 289 Stumps, I challenge thee for this indignity. **1825** BROCKETT *N.C. Gloss., Stump*, a heavy, thick-headed fellow. **1829** LYTTON *Disowned* ii, Come, Stump, my cull, make yourself wings. *a* **1835** HOGG *Tales & Sk.* (1837) VI. 352 He then sought out the common executioner, but he was a greatly, drumbly, drunken stump, and could tell him nothing. **1875** J. GRANT *One of Six Hundred* xxv. 201 Binnacle, the skipper, was a short, thick-set little stump of a fellow.

†**5.** A broken-off end of something. Also a splinter (cf. STUB *sb.* 5). *Obs.*

c **1400** *Laud Troy Bk.* 12539 He bare him thorow the scheld ymyddes, Thorow his plates In-to his brest; Opon the grounde ful stille he rest, For In his body lefft the stompe. **1625** T. GODWIN *Rom. Antiq.* 202 There came a fierce Lyon vnto him, moaning and grieuing, because of a stumpe of a tree which stucke fast in his foot.

6. a. The stalk of a plant (esp. cabbage) when the leaves are removed.

1819 SCOTT *Leg. Montrose* viii, Where no forage could be procured for his horse, unless he could eat the stumps of old heather. **1879** SALA in *Daily Tel.* 28 June, A very unlovely spot..presenting little beyond a prospect of empty baskets and cabbage stumps. **1882** *Garden* 18 Mar. 188/1 When the Cauliflowers or Cabbages were all cut, the stumps were cleared off. **1897** J. HOCKING *Birthright* iii. 52 Others pelting me [in the pillory] with cabbage-stumps and turnips. **1913** D. BRAY *Life-Hist. Brahui* v. 99 Three nights running must he take a draught of water in which the plant *charmāing* has been well boiled, leaves and stumps and all.

†**b.** *pl.* Stubble. *Obs.*

1585 HIGINS *Junius' Nomencl.* 107/2 *Stramentum*,..the strawe, stubble, or stumppes remaining in the grounde after the corne is rept.

c. *pl.* Hair cut close to the skin: cf. STUB *sb.* 4 c. Also, remains of feathers on a plucked fowl.

1584 B. R. tr. *Herodotus* II. 78 b, The Ægyptians at the decease of their friends suffer their hayre to growe, beeing at other times accustomed to powle & cut it to ye stumps. **1726** SWIFT *Gulliver* II. i, He said..that the Stumps of my Beard were ten times stronger than the Bristles of a Boar. **1845** ELIZA ACTON *Mod. Cookery* 261 To roast a Fowl. Strip off the feathers, and carefully pick every stump or plug from the skin. **1899** *Allbutt's Syst. Med.* VIII. 855 It [i.e. the ringworm patch] is studded with stumps of broken hairs. **1905** *Brit. Med. Jrnl.* 1 July 15 The scalp is carefully examined to see that no stumps are left.

7. a. A post, a short pillar not supporting anything.

a **1700** EVELYN *Diary* 12 Nov. 1644, In a little obscure place..is the Pillar or Stump at which they relate our Bl. Saviour was scourged. **1796** W. H. MARSHALL *Rur. Econ. Midl.* (ed. 2) II. 389 *Stump*; post; as 'gate stump'—stumps and rails. **1842** LOUDON *Suburban Hort.* 319 These short posts, or stumps, as they may be called, are formed of pieces of young larch-trees or oak branches, from which the bark has been taken. **1907** *Westm. Gaz.* 27 Aug. 10/2 The pillar yesterday was fulfilling the prosaic, but useful, functions of a clothes stump.

b. *Coal-mining.* (See quots.)

1881 RAYMOND *Mining Gloss., Stump*, Penn[sylvania]. A small pillar of coal, left at the foot of a breast to protect the gangway. **1883** GRESLEY *Gloss. Coal-mining* 245 *Stump*, the block of solid coal at the entrance to a breast, having a narrow roadway on either side.

†**c.** A peak, summit. (*Burlesque.*) *Obs.*

1664 [J. SCUDAMORE] *Homer à la Mode* 57 She [Thetis] spies Saturnius with sawcer eyes, On one oth' highest stumps alone, (For on that hill [Olympus] is many a one). [Cf. *Iliad* I. 499.]

8. a. A stake. ***to pull up one's stumps***: †(*a*) to break up camp, start again on the march (cf. STAKE *sb.* 1 e) (*obs.*); (*b*) to leave one's home, job, or settled way of life, to move; also without possessive pronoun; cf. *to pull up stakes* s.v. STAKE *sb.*[1] 1 e.

1530 PALSGR. 277/2 Stumpe a shorte stake, *estoc.* **1647** SPRIGG *Anglia Rediv.* II. i. 61 They marched that day but to Crookhorn,..but here Intelligence came that made them pull up their stumps, (as weary as they were). **1955** 'A. GILBERT' *Is she Dead Too?* xiii. 227 Seems to have pulled up his stumps now he's married again. Wonder if they left an address. **1974** M. BUTTERWORTH *Man in Sopwith Camel* I. i. 19 I've been trying to bully him into pulling up stumps and doing something with the rest of his life.

9. *Cricket.* **a.** Each of the three (formerly two) upright sticks which, with the bails laid on the top of them, form a wicket. ***to draw*** (***the***) ***stumps***: to pull up the stumps, as a sign of the discontinuance of play or of the termination of a match or game.

1735 in Waghorn *Cricket-Scores* (1899) 11 The stumps were immediately pitched. **17..** *Laws of Cricket* (1744), The Stumps must be 22 Inches long. **1744** J. LOVE *Cricket* III. (1754) 20 The Bail, and mangled Stumps bestrew the field. **1777** in Waghorn *Cricket-Scores* (1899) p. x, [June 4, the first match] to be played with three stumps, to shorten the game. **1833** NYREN *Yng. Cricketer's Tutor* (1902) 16 The stumps must stand twenty-seven inches above the ground. **1837** DICKENS *Pickw.* vii, The ball flew..straight and swift towards the centre stump of the wicket. **1862** *Baily's Mag.* Oct. 200 At half-past six the stumps were drawn. **1868** *Field* 4 July 11/1 When the stumps and the match also were drawn, four wickets were down for 96 runs.

b. *pl.* = *stump-cricket* (see 19).

1903 A. WESTCOTT *Life B. F. Westcott* I. vi. 322 My father ..himself occasionally joined us in a game of 'stumps'.

c. An act of stumping a batsman out. Also ***stump-out.*** Cf. STUMP *v.*[1] 8.

1859 *All Year Round* 23 July 305/2 All clever catches, and clever stumps too. **1871** 'THOMSONBY' *Cricketers in Council* 38 A stump-out may send the batsman back to his friends. **1912** A. A. LILLEY *Twenty-Four Years in Cricket* v. 61 Stover's wicket-keeping was remarkable... He..was always able to gather the ball with ease, and thus create for himself the maximum of certainty in..effecting a possible stump.

d. *pl.* Close of play, when stumps are drawn. Chiefly *Austral.*

1954 J. H. FINGLETON *Ashes crown Year* xxv. 268 England carried on to stumps. **1962** *Times* 3 Dec. 3/2 He looked to be coasting through to 'stumps' when Benaud bowled him. **1977** *World of Cricket Monthly* June 30/2 Bold tactics by Intikhab..carried the Pakistani score to 6-249 at stumps.

†**10. a.** The main portion of anything; the stock.

1634 T. JOHNSON *Parey's Wks.* XXIII. xii. 883 A. Sheweth the stump or stock of the woodden leg.

†**b.** ? The 'body' of a coat. *Sc. Obs.*

1506 *Acc. Ld. High Treas. Scot.* III. 313 For vj elne smal cammes to lyne the doublatis bodyis and stumpes of the cotis..ix s.

11. *Lock-making.* (See quot. 1856.) Cf. STUB *sb.* 8.

1808 in *Abridgm. Specif. Patents Locks* etc. (1873) 17 Which moves the stump on the same tumbler from a stump fixed under, or a groove cut in the bolt. **1852** *Tomlinson's Cycl. Usef. Arts* (1867) II. 95/1, *b* is the bolt into which is riveted the stump *s.* **1856** G. PRICE *Treat. Fire & Thief-proof Deposit., Locks & Keys* 259 The 'stump' of the bolt is that stud which projects at right angles from the face of the bolt, and which passes in and out of the 'slots' through the gating in the levers, or combinations, or other moveable obstructions contained in the lock.

12. Applied to animals of stumpy form or with a stumpy tail. **a.** *dial.* The stoat.

1854 *N. & Q.* Ser. I. IX. 385/1 A gamekeeper..told me that there are three kinds of the weasel tribe in the woods: the weasel, the stoat or stump, and the mousehunt. *Ibid.* X. 120/2 Hampshire Provincial Words... *Stump*, a stoat.

b. The name of a shell-fish: see quot.

1875 MELLISS *St. Helena* 203 *Scyllarus latus*, Latr.—A large shell-fish, called 'The Stump'.

13. A stump bedstead: see 19.

1875 *Carpentry & Join.* 84 The details are almost identical, whether the form is the old-fashioned and well-nigh obsolete four-poster or the half-tester or stump.

14. Originally *U.S.* **a.** In early use, the stump (sense 2) of a large felled tree used as a stand or platform for a speaker. **b.** Hence, 'a place or an occasion of political oratory' (*Cent. Dict.*). ***to go on the stump, to take the stump***: to go about the country making political speeches, whether as a candidate or as the advocate of a cause.

In the U.S. the word 'does not necessarily convey a derogatory implication' (*Cent. Dict.*). In Britain, though now common, it is still felt to be somewhat undignified.

a. 1775 *Broadside* (by a Boston Tory), Upon a stump he placed himself Great Washington did he. **1808** J. QUINCY *Sp.* 7 Dec. in *Deb. Congress* (1853) 766 This species of party insinuation was a mighty engine..on an election day, played off from the top of a stump, or the top of a hogshead, while the gin circulated. **1839** MRS. KIRKLAND *New Home* xliii. 287 He..mounted a stump, which had fortunately been left standing..and then and there gave 'reasons for my ratting.' **1842** *Congr. Globe* 29 Jan. 183/1 A stump orator in the West .., who, when he got down from the stump, said [etc.].

b. 1816 *Debates in Congress* (1854) 1169, I [a Virginian member] think his [a South Carolinian's] arguments are better calculated for what is called on this side of the river *stump*, than for this Committee. **1831** M. CAREY *New Olive Branch* 17 Declaimers in the forum, or on stumps, or in newspapers. **1838** L. BACON in *Ess. Chr. Minist.* (1841) 84/2 All artifice and trick—all the devices of the stage and of the stump. **1866** LOWELL *President on the Stump* Pr. Wks. 1890 V. 264 Mr. Johnson is the first of our Presidents who has descended to the stump. **1868** J. BRIGHT *Addresses* (1879) 76 We have seen the archbishops and bishops..doing what is described in America when they say a man has taken to the 'stump'. **1888** BRYCE *Amer. Commw.* lvi. II. 382 It is more by the stump than in any other way that an American statesman speaks to the people. **1892** *Daily News* 19 Dec. 2/3 If politicians took it up—'put the gold dollar on the stump,' as it is expressed—the trouble would be grievous. **1903** *Sat. Rev.* 7 Feb. 172 A Front Bencher goes on the stump in the provinces.

15. *Coffee-planting* (India). See quot.

1877 E. C. P. HULL *Coffee Planting* 274 This disease is there known as stump, from its being due to decay of the stump of a particular forest-tree peculiar to the district.

16. *slang.* See quot. Cf. STUMPY *sb.* 2.

1823 EGAN *Grose's Dict. Vulgar T., Stump*, money.

17. A stringed instrument of the lute family (see quots.). *Obs.* exc. *Hist.*

a **1623** in *R. Johnson's Compl. Works for Solo Lute* (1972) 22 (*music title*) Alman To the Stumpe. **1947** E. BLOM *Everyman's Dict. Mus.* 674/1 *Stump*, an obs. string instrument of the Cittern type invented *c.* 1600 by Daniel Farrant. **1961** A. BIRCH in A. Baines *Mus. Instr. through Ages* vii. 166 There were other instruments too, for accompanying the voice or for solo playing, 'stump', 'poliphant', 'penorcon', but little more than their names has survived. **1976** D. MUNROW *Instr. Middle Ages & Renaissance* ix. 83/4 Of the stump there are no surviving examples or descriptions though the name does suggest a small instrument. One piece of stump music is extant, however, entitled *Alman R. Johnson to the stump by F.P...* giving the impression that the stump was a wire-strung equivalent of the theorbo.

18. *attrib.* and *Comb.*, as (sense 2) ***stump-country, extracting, -extractor, fence, -hole, land, -wood; stump-dotted*** adj.; ***stump-like*** adj. and adv.; ***stump-wise*** adv.; (sense 3 c) ***stump-extractor, -puller***; (sense 14) ***stump campaign, oration, orator, oratory, oratress, speaker, speaking, speech.***

1888 BRYCE *Amer. Commw.* x. I. 132 The famous struggle of Mr. Douglas and Mr. Lincoln for the Illinois senatorship in 1858 was conducted in a *stump campaign. **1896** *Home Missionary* (N.Y.) July 129 Vast tracts of '*stump country' [in Michigan] are as truly virgin soil as if the region had just been discovered. **1902** S. E. WHITE *Blazed Trail* v, Sometimes he would look across the broad *stump-dotted plain to the distant forest. **1883** M. P. BALE *Saw-Mills* 295 Capstans are also used for *stump extracting. **1875** KNIGHT *Dict. Mech.* 2432/2 **Stump-extractor* 1. (Agriculture). A tool or machine for pulling the stumps of trees... 2. A dentist's instrument. **1883** M. P. BALE *Saw-Mills* 294 There are many other varieties of stump extractors amongst those used in America. **1845** S. JUDD *Margaret* I. xvi, The stile by which they crossed the *stump-fence into the herb-garden. **1897** *Daily News* 10 Sept. 8/3 The stump fence..consists of the gnarled roots of trees originally grubbed up from the land. **1828** P. CUNNINGHAM *N. S. Wales* (ed. 3) II. 166 It is long before grasses grow upon the places out of which stumps have been burnt... But it is astonishing to observe what a height of richness wheat will attain on these spots, every *stump-hole being easily reckoned in a field of wheat from this great luxuriance alone. **1889** *Hardwicke's Sci.-Gossip* XXV. 132 This tree attains a height of about six feet, and its branches spring from the gnarled top of the thick, *stump-like stem. **1831** *Constellation* (N.Y.) 12 Feb. 98/2 You see, sir, I want an office, for, as I told 'em in my *stump horation twict, the man..is the very one that ought to be awarded. **1813** T. JEFFERSON *Writ.* (1830) IV. 203 In the debates of Congress, of State legislatures, of *stump-orators. **1887** *Spectator* 19 Mar. 391/1 The shallowness and flippancy of stump-orators. **1811** E. FLETCHER *Let.* 11 Jan. (1965) 26 For you must know that the people in these parts get into office by '*Stump oratory' or praising and electioneering for themselves. **1854** H. MILLER *Sch. & Schm.* (1858) 496 Without any unnecessary display of stump-oratory. **1880** MCCARTHY *Own Times* IV. 380 Mr. Disraeli himself had taken to going round the country, doing what would be called in America stump oratory. **1852** HAWTHORNE *Blithedale Rom.* vi, She was made..for a *stump-oratress. **1884** KNIGHT *Dict. Mech.* Suppl. 870/1 *Stump pullers are of the lever and claw style, or [etc.]. **1848** *Let. fr. Washington* in *N.Y. Herald* 21 June (Bartlett), The Hon. W. R. Thompson,..one of the most popular *stump speakers of the day, addressed a large meeting of Whigs from the stoop of Barnum's Hotel, Baltimore. **1864** LOWELL *Lincoln* Pr. Wks. 1890 V. 187 All that was known of him was that he was a good stump-speaker. **1842** H. MANN *Boston Orat.* 4 July 46 The custom so prevalent at the West and South, of *stump speaking. **1888** BRYCE *Amer. Commw.* cxi. III. 604 They shine in stump speaking, properly so called —that is, in speaking which rouses an audience but ought not to be reported. **1820** J. FLINT *Lett. from Amer.* (1822) 251 The harangues are called *stump-speeches. **1839** PROFFIT in *Congr. Globe* 31 Dec. 72/2 He could make..a better stump speech himself. **1885** *Manch. Exam.* 16 May 6/1 Mr. Redmond rose and insisted on delivering a stump speech on the sentiments of the Irish and English people regarding royalty. **1884** PHILLIPPS-WOLLEY *Trottings of Tenderfoot* 208 If a constitution was to grow up strong, it didn't want forcing with a lot of *stump-spouter's rubbish. **1719** LONDON & WISE *Compl. Gard.* xix. 129 In those vigorous Trees, we must leave upon them..some Branches cut *Stump-wise. **1953** *Forestry Abstr.* XIV. 296/2 Miscellaneous notes are appended on: splitting *stumpwood with explosives.., and Spruce and Pine stumpwood for the manufacture of fibreboards. **1977** *Ibid.* XXXVIII. 44/2 (*heading*) Determining the volume of stumpwood and rootwood in *Picea abies.*

19. Special comb.: **stump bed, bedstead**, a bedstead without posts; **stump-bred** *a. Hunting* = *stub-bred*; **stump cricket** = SNOB *sb.*[2]; **stump embroidery** = *stump work*; **stump-end**, (*a*) the end of the stump of a tail; (*b*) the remnant of a cheque-book containing the 'stumps' or counterfoils; **stump foremast** (see *stump mast*); **stump-grubber**, a machine designed to excavate the stumps of trees after the trees have been felled (cf. *stump-machine*); **stump-grubbing**, the excavation of tree-stumps by manual or mechanical means; **stump joint** (see quot.); **stump-jump, -jumping** *adjs. Austral.*, designating a kind of plough by which land can be ploughed without clearing it of the stumps; also *absol.* as *sb.*; **stump jumper** *U.S.*, a countryman or hillbilly (cf. *stubble-jumper* s.v. STUBBLE *sb.* 5); **stump-machine** *U.S.*, a machine for extracting tree-stumps; **stump mast** (see quot.); **stump mortise** = *stub mortise* (W. 1911); †**stump nail** = *stub-nail*; †**stump pie**, a kind of meat-pie; **stump plant**, a cutting consisting of a short cut-back stem and roots which may or may not be pruned; **stump-shot** = *stub-short, -shot* (see STUB *sb.* 11); **stump-spire** *Arch.* (see quot.); **stump-tenon** = *stub-tenon* (W. 1911); **stump topgallant mast** (see *stump mast*); **stump tracery** *Arch.* (see quot.); **stump tree** *U.S.* (see quot. 1892); **stump water** *U.S.*, the rain-water which collects in the stumps of hollow-trees, associated esp. with folk remedies and charms; **stump word**, a word formed by abbreviating a single longer one, esp. by reducing it to a single syllable (freq. the first) or the minimum necessary for understanding; cf. CLIPPING *vbl. sb.*² 2 c; **stump-work**, a peculiar kind of raised embroidery practised in the 15–17th c. (see quot. 1904).

1841 *Penny Cycl.* XXI. 45/2 Under a *stump bed, immediately beneath, was a dog-kennel. **1823** J. SIMPSON *Ricardo* I. 235 Having never yet known a luxury beyond a *stump bedstead, and a flock bed. **1841** J. T. J. HEWLETT *Peter Priggins* I. i. 29 In one corner was a stump-bedstead, with a kind of dimity canopy. **1897** *Stump-bred [see *stub-bred* STUB *sb.* 11]. **1888** A. LANG in Steel & Lyttelton *Cricket* (Badm.) i. 1 There is a sport known at some schools as '*stump-cricket',..which is a degenerate shape of the game. **1907** C. B. FRY in *Daily Chron.* 10 Oct. 4/4 The old and renovated game of 'Le Bon Diable'..bears the same relation to Diabolo-Tennis as stump-cricket does to proper cricket. **1904** MRS. HEAD in *Burlington Mag.* IV. 173/1 Side by side with *stump-embroidery flourished two varieties of flat and semi-flat work. **1768** *Phil. Trans.* LX. 122 Tails..sewed together at the *stump-ends. **1894** 'J. S. WINTER' *Red Coats* 42 There were several stump-ends of old cheque-books there. **1897** KIPLING *Capt. Courageous* i. 20 Harvey heard a chuckle from Dan, who was pretending to be busy by the *stump-foremast. **1971** *Sylwan* CXV. x. 19 Investigation of the technical and economic efficiency of the Odyniec *stump-grubber. **1977** *Forestry Abstr.* XXXVIII. 580/1 The specifications of the stump-grubbers are tabulated, and data are given on stump-grubbing performance. **1938** M. RICHARDSON in B. A. Botkin *Treas. S. Folklore* (1949) III. i. 442 He went on the *stump-grubbing gang, soon as he got to the Farm. **1961** *Forestry Abstr.* XXII. 582/1 (*heading*) Using a vibratory shock method in stump-grubbing. **1977** Stump-grubbing [see *stump-grubber* above]. **1884** KNIGHT *Dict. Mech.* Suppl. 870/1 **Stump joint*, the form of joint used in the folding carpenter's rule. The ends or stumps of the parts when in line, abut against each other. **1896** *Waybrook Implement Co.* Advt. (Morris), This wonderful result [of the harvest] must in the main, be put down to the *Stump-jump Plough. **1898** MORRIS *Austral Eng.* 443 Stump-jump Plough. **1911** E. M. CLOWES *On Wallaby* xi. 297 Those people who..were once in undisputed possession of these mountains and forests—before the days of the axe and saw, the 'stump-jump', and the 'mallee roller'. **1936** J. H. STREET *Look Away* xiii. 87 That's the home of the hillbillies. Some folks call 'em '*stump-jumpers'. **1944** in H. Wentworth *Amer. Dial. Dict.* 606/2 She musta been one o' these West Virginia stump-jumpers. **1898** M. DAVITT *Life & Progr. Australia* xiii. 64 The most useful implement to the hardy settlers up here is the *stump-jumping plough. **1900** *Borough News* 11 Aug. 3/1 I'm breaking up that ten-acre field of *stump land. **1907** *Black Cat* June 21 Once outside the limits of the stump-land, Mehetabel made the best of her speed to the Knoll. **1868** LOSSING *The Hudson* 54 One of the *stump-machines stood in a field near the road. **1875** KNIGHT *Dict. Mech.*, **Stump-mast*, a lower mast without tops. Common in those steam-vessels which never depend wholly upon sails. **1704** in *Bagford Ballads* (1876) 64 The Lad..quickly fell to vomiting strange things, As bits of Glass, *stump Nails and crooked Pins. **1695** J. H. *Family Dict.* s.v., *Stump-Pye to Season: Take Veal or Mutton, mince it raw, [etc.]. **1953** *Brit. Commonw. Forest Terminol.* I. 36 *Cutting, root and shoot*, one consisting of a pruned tap-root and cut-back stem. Syn...*stump plant. **1960** *Forestry Abstr.* XXI. I. 31/1 Stump plants made from 1-year seedlings were planted in pots. **1812** J. SMYTH *Pract. Customs* (1821) 293 No other allowance is to be made, in taking the length of plank, for the *stump-shot, or split end. **1842** *Penny Cycl.* XXII. 356/2 If no better [name] can be found, we would suggest that of *Stump-spire for one whose height does not exceed two diameters at its base. *Ibid.* 357/2. **1804** in *Naval Docs. U.S. Wars with Barbary Powers* (U.S. Office Naval Rec.) (1942) IV. 346 You will know my ship by her having *stump top GI Masts. **1840** R. H. DANA *Bef. Mast* xx. 59 The ship, with her stump top-gallant masts and rusty sides. **1835** R. WILLIS *Archit. Mid. Ages* vi. 61 The After Gothic of Germany..has tracery in which the ribs are made to pass through each other, and are then abruptly cut off. This may be called *Stump Tracery. **1891** in *Century Dict.* (citing FALLOWS), *Stump tree. **1892** NEWHALL *Trees N.E. Amer.* 190 Kentucky Coffee Tree, Stump Tree (*Gymnocladus disicus*,..*G. Canadensis*). *Ibid.* 192 The fewness and abruptness of its large branches give to it in the winter a dead and stumpy look. **1892** J. C. HARRIS *Uncle Remus & Friends* 290 De way ter git rid er ha'nts wuz ter git some prickly-pear root en bile it in *stump-water en sprinkle it 'roun' de yard. **1972** J. S. HALL *Sayings from Old Smoky* 133 'His head is full of stump water.' That is, 'He don't use his brain.'.. Possibly 'stump water in the head' meant originally that the person had been affected by magic, that is, was 'teched in the head', or dazed. **1922** O. JESPERSEN *Language* II. ix. 169 We come to those changes which result in what one may call '*stump-words'... Words may undergo violent shortenings both by children and adults. **1963** *Amer. Speech* XXXVIII. 156 Other stump words or clipped forms such as *info, auto.* **1971** Stump word [see MELO]. **1904** MRS. HEAD in *Burlington Mag.* IV. 173/1 English *stump-work has..a definite individuality... Lace, brocade, satin,..peacock's feathers and human hair were all blended together by the finest and most elaborate of embroidery stitches, and raised on 'stumps' of wood, or wool pads, in the most fantastic of designs. **1938** *Burlington Mag.* Oct. 172/2 Stuart 'stump-work' embroidery. **1958** *Times* 25 Nov. 18/6 A highly important Venetian glass mirror with stumpwork panels. **1971** *Country Life* 10 June 1426/2 A mirror framed in stumpwork embroidery made in England three centuries ago.

stump (stʌmp), *sb.*² [Of obscure history.
The late appearance of the word suggests that it is an adaptation (influenced by STUMP *sb.*¹) of the far older Fr. synonym *estompe*, which, along with the related vb. *estomper*, †*estomber*, appears *c* 1700 in De la Hire *Traité de la Pratique de la Peinture*, published in *Mém. de l'Acad. Roy. des Sciences 1666–1699* (1730) IX. 658. De la Hire evidently regarded the words as established in use; he suggests that *estompe* may be a corruption of *étoupe* (earlier *estoupe*) tow, link. This is impossible; most etymologists regard the sb. as derived from the vb., which some believe to be ad. Du. *stompen* or *afstompen* to dull, blunt, though there seems to be no evidence that either of these vbs. was ever used in the sense of F. *estomper*.
The stump for crayon drawing is elaborately described, as an instrument used by Fr. pastellists, in A. Browne's *Appendix Art Painting* (1675), but without mention of either the English or the Fr. name. Browne says (in this copying W. Sanderson *Graphice* ii. 78, published 1658) that a 'stubbed pencil' (app. = 'brush', not 'crayon' or 'lead pencil'), sometimes 'stuffed with cotton or bombast', was employed by some artists for the same purpose. Obviously a 'stubbed pencil' could be called in English a 'stump' (STUMP *sb.*¹ 3); and the equivalent Du. *stompe* could be employed in the same way. On the whole, considering that in the 17th c. the art of crayon drawing received much improvement in Holland, the likeliest view seems to be that the word *stompe* was applied (with no intention of using a technical term) to the 'stubbed pencil' by Dutch artists working in French studios; and that in the adapted form *estompe* it became the Fr. name for the improved instrument invented in France. On this view the Eng. word would be an adaptation of the Fr., as the relative chronology suggests.]

A kind of pencil consisting of a roll of paper or soft leather, or of a cylindrical piece of indiarubber or other soft material, usually cut to a blunt point at each end, used for rubbing down hard lines in pencil or crayon drawing, for blending the lines of shading so as to produce a uniform tint, and for other similar purposes.

1778 *Encycl. Brit.* (ed. 2) III. 2293/2 When the head is brought to some degree of forwardness, let the back-ground be laid in, which must be treated in a different manner, covering it as thin as possible, and rubbing it into [the] paper with a leather-stump. **1811** *Self Instructor* 544 Blend your shadows..with a stump made of paper. **1859** GULLICK & TIMBS *Painting* 316 The tints are rubbed in, and blended for the most part with the finger, although 'stumps' (Fr. *estompes*), and the point of the crayon.. are also used. **1860** W. COLLINS *Woman in White* vii, Near it were some tiny jewellers' brushes, a washleather 'stump', and a little bottle of liquid, all waiting to be used in various ways for the removal of any accidental impurities which might be discovered on the coins. **1862** *Catal. Internat. Exhib., Brit.* II. No. 5483, Drawing stumps in paper, leather, and cork. **1869** EASTLAKE *Materials Hist. Oil Painting* II. 252 His love of gradation and of the imperceptible union of half-tints led him [*sc.* Correggio] to use the 'stump' of some similar mechanical means.

stump (stʌmp), *sb.*³ [f. STUMP *v.*¹]

1. A heavy step or gait, as of a lame or wooden-legged person.

1770 FOOTE *Lame Lover* I. Wks. 1799 II. 60, I hear his stump on the stairs. **1830** MISS MITFORD *Village* Ser. IV. 129 The old Brigade-Major,..lame of a leg,..was kept on the constant stump with explanatory messages.

b. Reiterated, with echoic intention. Also quasi-*adv.*, (to go, come) ***stump, stump***.

1690 *Pagan Prince* xii. 35 For a Prince to go Stump, Stump with a wooden Leg, is no way Majestical. **1854** SURTEES *Handley Cr.* xxvii. (1901) I. 204 Stump, stump, stump, creak, creak, creak, came old heavy-heels along the passage. **1862** BORROW *Wild Wales* xi. (1901) 63 She heard of a sudden a horse coming stump, stump, up to the door. **1890** D. DAVIDSON *Mem. Long Life* x. 261, I heard the stump, stump of a wooden leg behind me.

2. *U.S. colloq.* 'A dare, or challenge to do something difficult or dangerous' (W. 1911).

1871 MRS. WHITNEY *Real Folks* ii. 23 She understood life. It was 'stumps' all through... It was a stump when her father died, and her mother had to manage the farm... The mortgage they had to work off was a stump... It was a stump when her mother died and the farm was sold. **18..** *Electr. Rev.* (Amer.) XIV. 4 (Cent.) The reason for this little freak was a stump on the part of some musicians, because..it was not supposed he could handle a baton. He did it. **1894** *Advance* (Chicago) 18 Oct. 112/3 But me lad, the bravest thing ye did was to refuse to run the risk fer a mere stump!

stump (stʌmp), *a.* [Partly from the attrib. use of STUMP *sb.*¹, but perh. partly an original adj. corresponding to or adopted from Du., LG. *stomp.*]

1. Worn down to a stump.

1624 BURTON *Anat. Mel.* I. ii. III. xv. (ed. 2) 115 Like an Asse, he [a schoolmaster] weares out his time for prouender, and can shew a stumpe rod,..an old torne gowne, an ensigne of his infelicity. **1855** LEIFCHILD *Cornwall* 7 He cracked his stump whip.

2. Obtuse in outline, not pointed.

1676 *Lond. Gaz.* No. 1135/4 At Yarmouth, the Fortune of Dunkirk,..carrying four Guns, and 38 Men, with a Stump [*printed* Stamp] Head, Decks flush, Broad Stern, [etc.].

3. Said of mutilated or malformed limbs. ***stump foot***: a club foot. ***stump leg***: a leg without a foot or with a club foot.

1563–83 FOXE *A. & M.* 828/1 The goodman of yᵉ house hauing a stumpe foote. *a* **1568** ASCHAM *Scholem.* II. (Arb.) 127 Euen the best translation, is..but an euill imped wing to flie withall, or a heuie stompe leg of wood to go withall. *a* **1593** MARLOWE *Ovid's Elegies* II. xvii. 20 With his stumpe-foote he halts ill-fauouredly. **1678** *Lond. Gaz.* No. 1338/4 An iron grey Gelding Colt, a lame stump foot before, and two white feet behind. **1731** *Gentl. Mag.* I. 401 To apprehend several Vagrants with stump Hands, sore Arms, Legs and Faces. **1768–74** TUCKER *Lt. Nat.* (1834) I. 453 He did not skate with a stump leg,..but put out a broad foot with which he could have a good flat tread. **1898** *Syd. Soc. Lex.*, *Stump-foot*. Same as *Club-foot*.

4. Comb., as ***stump-fingered, -footed, -legged, -nosed, -rooted, -tailed*** adjs. Also **stump-foot** [= Du. *stompvoet*]: *sb.*, a stump-footed person; *adj.* = *stump-footed*; **stump-nose** *S. Africa* [after Du. *stompneus*] = STOMPNEUS; **stump-tail**, a stump-tailed dog; also *Austr.* a stump-tailed lizard (*Trachysaurus*).

1905 D. SMITH *Days of His Flesh* xlvi. 462 In the early Church Mark..was styled Mark the *Stump-fingered. **1593** *Tell-trothe's N.Y. Gift* (1876) 13 Ioane *Stoomp-foot and Tom Totty. **1602** *Invent.* in C. Wise *Rockingham Castle & Watsons* (1891) 206 Item one baie stumpefoote mare iijˡⁱ. **1612** J. TAYLOR (Water P.) *Sculler* E 1, The net the stump-foot Blackesmith made, Wherein fell Mars and Venus was betraid. **1602** BRETON *Wonders worth Hearing* (Grosart) 8/1 So was he faced like an olde Ape, *stumpe footed, and wry legged. **1691** WOOD *Life* (O.H.S.) III. 366 Solomon Nash. .. Stumpfooted. **1629** GAULE *Holy Madn.* 324 Bucklehamm'd, *Stump-legg'd. **1652** —— *Magastrom.* 186 The spindle-legd are fearful;..stump-legg'd, servile. **1838** *Stump-nose [see KLIPFISH 1]. **1878** T. J. LUCAS *Camp Life & Sport in S. Afr.* ii. 30 The harbour [near Cape Town] abounds in fish, amongst which 'Stump-nose,' 'Seventy-four,'..and other strangely named but well flavoured fish are pre-eminent. **1895** *Jrnl. Cutan. & Genito-Urin. Dis.* Nov. 466 Perhaps the old Peruvians were *stump-nosed. **1905** T. W. SANDERS *Vegetables* 170 The Shorthorn or *stump-rooted kinds [of carrot] will succeed on any light shallow soil. **1868** SIR J. RICHARDSON etc. *Mus. Nat. Hist.* II. 20 The curious-looking creatures called *Stump-tails (*Trachydosaurus*) natives of Australia. **1902** *Longman's Mag.* Oct. 514 Old Badger..the best stump-tail he ever had to help him. **1860** P. P. CARPENTER in *Rep. Smithsonian Instit.* 1859, 202 The *stump-tailed cats of the Isle of Man. *c* **1875** *Cassell's Nat. Hist.* IV. 296 The Stump-tailed Lizard. **1893** LYDEKKER *Roy. Nat. Hist.* I. 117 The brown stump-tailed monkey (*Macacus arctoides*).

stump (stʌmp), *v.*¹ Also 7 stompe, 5–6, 9 *dial.* stomp. [f. STUMP *sb.*¹]

†**1.** *intr.* To stumble over a tree-stump or other obstacle. Also, to walk stumblingly (in quot. *fig.*). *Obs.*

c **1250** *Owl & Night.* 1392 Ne beoþ heo nouht alle forlore þat stumpeþ at þe fleysses more. *Ibid.* 1424 If mayde luueþ derneliche, heo stumpeþ & falþ icundeliche. **1430–40** LYDG. *Bochas* IX. xxxviii. (1554) 217 b, Though I goe not vpright, but stomp and halt for lack of eloquence. **1607** TOPSELL *Four-f. Beasts* 78 If an oxe be wrinched and strayned in his sinnewes, in trauell or labour, by stumping on any roote or hard sharpe thing.

2. a. To walk clumsily, heavily, or noisily, as if one had a wooden leg.

1600 LANE *Tom Tel-troth's Message* 327 Some [dames] in their pantophels too stately stompe [*r.w.* pompe]. **1673** R. HEAD *Canting Acad.* 65 He..nimbly hops or stumps to a Coach side. *a* **1726** VANBRUGH *Journ. Lond.* I. i. (1728) 6 Here's John Moody arriv'd already; he's stumping about the Streets in his dirty Boots, and [etc.]. **1756** *Connoisseur* No. 103 ¶4 The maid-servants are continually stumping below in clogs or pattens. **1840** HOOD *Miss Kilmansegg* 1187 As the Giant of Castle Otranto might stump To a lower room from an upper. **1844** W. BARNES *Poems Rur. Life* 355 *Stumpy* or *Stump*, to walk with short firm steps as a short stout person. **1856** KANE *Arctic Expl.* I. xxxi. 431 Poor Wilson, just able to stump about after his late attack of scurvy. **1857** READE *Course of True Love, Clouds & Sunshine* iii. 204 The farmer stumped in, and sat down with some appearance of fatigue. **1874** *Punch* 11 Apr. 155/1 'He [a horse] seems,' I say, 'to rather stump on his near fore-leg.'

b. *slang.* 'To go on foot' (*Slang Dict.* 1859); also ***stump it*** (in quot. 1841 to be off, decamp).

1803 G. COLMAN *John Bull* IV. i. 41 Now, Sir, you and I'll stump it. **1841** LYTTON *Night & Morning* II. ii, Stump it, my cove; that's a Bow Street runner. **1909** A. N. LYONS *Sixpenny Pieces* xxii. 161 To the divil with cabs. Oi must stump ut. Stump ut on me ten old toes.

c. To knock on the floor in walking. *nonce-use.*

1872 BROWNING *Ring & Bk.* IX. 12 Stumping with his staff, Up comes an usher.

d. *trans.*

1890 W. CLARK RUSSELL *Ocean Trag.* I. vi. 117 Pendulously stumping the quarter-deck.

3. *trans.* To reduce to a stump; to truncate, mutilate; also, †to stunt, dwarf.

1596 NASHE *Saffron-Walden* Wks. 1910 III. 99 Whose pen..still splits and stumpes it selfe against olde yron. **1658** BROMHALL *Treat. Spectres* I. 148 He appeared a man that was stumped, or had his members cut off. **1658** EVELYN *Fr. Gard.* (1675) 166 It will stump your [Asparagus] plant. **1752** *Scotland's Glory* 24 That idol dagon prelacy We might have stumped tightly. **1829** *Examiner* 595/1 The only prudent course of the people of the United States is forthwith to cut off their legs, and stump themselves into concentration. **1872** MRS. A. GATTY *Bk. Sun-dials* Introd. p. xx, In the reign of Elizabeth the mortuary crosses were cut down, or stumped, in our churchyards. **1877** E. C. P. HULL *Coffee Planting* 93 These [coffee] plants..require, before being planted out on the estate, to be 'stumped', *i.e.* cut down to within some six inches above the roots.

4. To stub; to dig up by the roots. *colonial.*

1790 *Phil. Trans.* LXXX. 356 After which the [sugar] canes should be stumped out with care, and the stools burnt as soon as possible. **1828** P. CUNNINGHAM *N.S. Wales* (ed. 2) II. 62 You may hear people even now..relate their tales of..felling and stumping trees on spots where our best houses stand. **1897** *Outing* May 137/2 I've stumped every tree and root out'r that clearing.

5. To remove the stumps from (land). Also *absol.*

1796 C. MARSHALL *Garden.* iii. (1813) 34 The walks should be stumpt, keeping the tops of the stumps very level. **1828** P. CUNNINGHAM *N.S. Wales* (ed. 2) II. 164 In stumping land,..dry wood is piled over the stump, which..is set fire to. **1834** *Tait's Mag.* I. 418/1 Very good land, sir; and I was to pay a hundred pounds for it, for you know it was cleared but not stumped. **1915** W. P. LIVINGSTONE *Mary Slessor* v. ii. 269 She had as many as two hundred and fifty people engaged in cutting bush, levelling, and stumping.

6. ? To remove the stub feathers from (fowls): = STUB *v.* 5.

1822 LAMB *Let. to Miss Wordsworth* Xmas, She is to be seen in the market every morning,..cheapening fowls, which I observe the Cambridge poulterers are not sufficiently careful to stump.

7. *local.* To remove the ails from barley with a gridiron-shaped iron tool.

1787 WINTER *Syst. Husb.* 310 Barley should likewise be steeped the same as wheat, after being well shook in a sack by two men (stumping will bruise it) to be cleared from ailes. 1890 *Glouc. Gloss., Stump*, to dress the beards from barley.

8. *Cricket.* Of the wicket-keeper: To put (a batsman) out by dislodging a bail (or knocking down a stump) with the ball held in the hand, at a moment when he is out of his ground. Also with *out*.

1744 *Report of Kent & All Eng. Match* in Nyren *Yng. Cricketer's Tutor* (1833) 111 Bryan 12 s Kips. 1787 *Score of Match at Lord's* in H. Bentley *Cricket Matches* (1823) 20th June, Aylward 94 Run out 15 stumpt out. 1833 NYREN *Yng. Cricketer's Tutor* 29 Should you miss the ball, a clever wicket-keeper will surely stump you out. *Ibid.* 39 The wicket-keeper..should remove a little backward from the wicket..because by his doing so the catches will be much more easy, and he may stump as well. 1837 DICKENS *Pickw.* vii, In short, when Dumkins was caught out, and Podder stumped out, All-Muggleton had notched some fifty-four. 1859 *All Year Round* 23 July 305/2 He caught two of the town off my first 'over', stumped two in my second, and [etc.]. 1884 *Lillywhite's Cricket Ann.* 78 He caught three batsmen at the wicket and stumped one. 1897 *Encycl. Sport* I. 247/1 (Cricket) *Stump out*, to get the batsman out under Law 23.

†**9.** *intr.* (See quots.) *Obs. rare*$^{-0}$.

1721 BAILEY, *To stump*,..to brag or boast. 1735 DYCHE & PARDON *Dict., Stump v.*,..also to boast, brag, vaunt, or proudly value ones self upon some small Qualification, &c.

10. a. *trans.* = *stump up*, 17 b (*a*).

1841 HOOD *Tale of Trumpet* 260 Common prudence would bid you stump it;..It's the regular charge At a Fancy Fair for a penny trumpet.

b. *intr.* To pay up: = *stump up*, 17 b (*b*). Also with *out*.

1828 CARR *Craven Gloss., Stump*, to pay ready money,..to pay down on the nail. 1844 J. T. HEWLETT *Parsons & W.* xlvii, I'll stump handsome when we're spliced. 1854 LEVER *Dodd Family Abr.* xliv. 401 There is no salary at first, so that the Governor must 'stump out handsome'.

11. *trans. slang.* To render penniless. Chiefly in *passive*, to be 'stony broke'.

1828 CARR *Craven Gloss., Stump*,..2. to beggar. 1830 LOWER *Tom Cladpole* cxlviii, I..Paid the last tuppence I had got, An den I was just stump'd. 1836 T. HOOK *G. Gurney* III. 43 Haven't you heard, my dear fellow, we are stumped? 1900 'H. LAWSON' *Over Sliprails* 113 Going away from home with a few pounds in one's pocket and coming back stumped.

12. = *stump up*, 17 c.

1883 MRS. E. KENNARD *Right Sort* xvii, I stumped a couple of horses last week, and an extra rest will do them all the good in the world.

13. (*U.S. colloq.*) To strike (the toe) unintentionally against a stone or something fixed: = STUB *v.* 9.

1828–32 WEBSTER. 1857 A. LINCOLN in H. Binns *Life A. Lincoln* (1927) 181 Like the boy that stumped his toe..it hurt too bad to laugh. 1891 *Harper's Mag.* Feb. 364/2 Mus' be powerful sorrowful ter set at home an' shed tears lest he mought her stumped his toe on the road.

14. a. (orig. *U.S.*) To cause to be at a loss; to confront with an insuperable difficulty; to nonplus.

The primary reference was prob. to the obstruction caused by stumps in ploughing imperfectly cleared land.

[1807: implied in STUMPER 5.] 1833 [SEBA SMITH] *Lett. J. Downing* xii. (1835) 80 My Good Old Friend,—I'm stumped. I jest got a letter from the Gineral [etc.]. 1834 *Ibid.* xxxii. 218 This stumps me considerable. 1840 HALIBURTON *Clockm.* Ser. III. xvi. (1848) 132 Bein' stumpt is a sure mark of a fool. The only folks among us that's ever nonplushed, is them just caught in the woods. 1842 *Congr. Globe* 29 Jan. 183/1 He had been amazed—or, to use a Western phrase, he had been 'stumped' at the position occupied within these last few days by [etc.]. 1843 LOWELL *Lett.* I. 81, I met an Ohio abolitionist, who told me of his stumping a clergyman in a very neat manner. 1852 C. B. MANSFIELD *Paraguay*, etc. (1856) 72, I am..continually stumped in my speculations by the reflection, that [etc.]. 1854 'C. BEDE' *Verdant Green* II. xi, That beastly Euclid altogether stumps me. 1859 J. R. GREEN *Lett.* I. (1901) 30, I stumped him on a question which I had got up [etc.]. 1871 M. LEGRAND *Cambr. Freshman* 339 The papers I may do all right,..but the *viva voce* is safe to stump me. 1912 C. JOHNSTON *Why World laughs* 10 'But may I ask why this gay apparel?' The lady was stumped for an instant. Then she made reply.

b. ? To obstruct (progress).

1858 GEN. P. THOMPSON *Audi Alt.* II. lxvii. 5 The progress of sound knowledge..shall not be stumped to please lorn curates.

15. *U.S.* To challenge, 'dare' (a person) to do something.

1766 J. ADAMS *Diary* 8 Dec., Wks. 1850 II. 204 Keen, of Pembroke was warm, and stumped Soule, the moderator, to lay down the money and prevent a tax upon the poor. 1836 HALIBURTON *Clockm.* Ser. I. xxvi, I guess our great nation may be stumped to produce a more eleganter liquor than this here. 1853 LOWELL *Moosehead Jrnl.* Pr. Wks. 1890 I. 17 Our Uncle would..say, 'Wahl, I stump the Devil himself to make that ere boot hurt *my* foot'. 1890 *Amer. Jrnl. Psychol.* Jan. 66 In some games..younger children are commanded, or older ones stumped or dared, to do dangerous things.

16. (Chiefly *U.S.*)

a. *intr.* To make stump speeches; to conduct electioneering by public speaking. Also *to stump it*.

*a*1838 R. M. BIRD *Peter Pilgrim* (1839) I. 86, I stumped through my district, and my fellow-citizens sent me to Congress! 1847 WEBSTER s.v., *To stump it.* 1859 C. MACKAY *Life & Liberty Amer.* I. 159 *To stump*, to address public meetings in the open air. 1860 EMERSON *Cond. Life* ii. *Power* Wks. (Bohn) II. 340 Stumping it through England for seven years made Cobden a consummate debater. 1874 *Slang Dict.* 313 *Stump*, to go about speechmaking on politics or other subjects. 1878 *N. Amer. Rev.* CXXVI. 275 Down in Carolina, stumping for Grant.

b. *trans.* To travel over (a district) making stump speeches; to canvass or address with stump oratory.

1856 *N.Y. Hards* 5/1 Mr. Dickinson stumped the State. 1859 C. MACKAY *Life & Liberty Amer.* I. 159 *To stump a State*, to go on a tour of political agitation through a State. 1866 LOWELL *Seward-Johnson Reaction* Pr. Wks. 1890 V. 291 Furnishing the President with a pretext for stumping the West in the interest of Congress. 1885 *Manch. Exam.* 6 July 4/7 Those Tory orators who were stumping the country. 1892 KIPLING & BALESTIER *Naulahka* 17 Sheriff was stumping the district and was seldom at home.

17. stump up.

a. *trans.* To dig up by the roots.

1599 NASHE *Lenten Stuff* 60 Their imaginary dreame of Guilding crosse in theyr parish of S. Sauiours (now stumpt vp by the rootes). 1873 TRISTRAM *Moab* xviii. 362 The trees have been all stumped up or pollarded. 1899 *Jrnl. R. Agric. Soc.* Mar. 94 When the old hedgerow is stubbed or stumped up.

b. *slang.* (*a*) *trans.* To pay down, 'fork out' (money). (*b*) *absol.* or *intr.* (*c*) In extended use, const. *with*.

(*a*) 1833 T. HOOK *Parson's Dau.* II. ii, All I know is, Paxton, Trail, Cockerell, and Co. stumped me up the money. 1842 BARHAM *Ingol. Leg., Merch. Venice* 72 My trusty old crony, Do stump up three thousand once more as a loan. 1881 BLACKMORE *Christowell* xxi, Father has stumped up a five pound note. 1884 *Bath Jrnl.* 26 July 7/3 On returning to the yard at night he has to stump up ten shillings more.

(*b*) 1835 DICKENS *Sk. Boz, Mr. Watkins Tottle* ii, Why don't you ask your old governor to stump up? 1857 'DUCANGE ANGLICUS' *Vulgar Tongue* 21 *Stump-up*, pay your money or your share. 1862 MRS H. WOOD *Channings* viii, 'And it will be a very easy way of earning money.' 'Not so easy as making your mother stump up.' 1893 G. ALLEN *Scallywag* I. 30 The governor..fishes out his purse—stumps up liberally.

(*c*) 1956 'C. BLACKSTOCK' *Dewey Death* ii. 35, I hope the department will stump up with a decent wreath. 1958 *Listener* 9 Oct. 569/2 The Americans stumped up with *The Old Man and the Sea*.

c. *trans.* To wear out, exhaust (a horse, etc.) by excessive strain.

1853 J. PALLISER *Solitary Rambles* v. 126, I..reminded him how completely he had stumped me up that afternoon. 1875 REYNARDSON *Down the Road* 118 After a bit the new ploughs and harrows got old and required repairs, his horses got stumped up and old and required to be made into new ones. 1900 *Westm. Gaz.* 12 June 8/1 Year by year we see one or more of our best horses stumped up by the adamantine course.

d. In *passive* = sense 11 *pass.*

1854 *Househ. Words* VIII. 75/2 To say that a man is without money, or in poverty, some persons remark that he is down on his luck, hard up, stumped up, [etc.].

stump (stʌmp), *v.*^{2} *Drawing.* [App. ad. F. *estomper*, related to *estompe* STUMP *sb.*^{2} Cf. the following:

1802 C. JAMES *Milit. Dict., Stomper*, Fr. To sketch out a design, or to draw with colours that have been pounded into dust. Instead of the pencil or crayon, a roll of paper which is dipped into the coloured dust, serves to put on the different colours.]

trans. To tone or treat with a 'stump'.

1807 J. LANDSEER *Lect. Engraving* 125 Ryland..employed it [the chalk manner] so as rather to imitate such drawings as are done with crayons, or stumped, than such as are hatched with chalk. 1860 O. W. HOLMES *Elsie Venner* vii. (1887) 77 This must refer to her favorite monochrome, executed by laying on heavy shadows, and stumping them down into mellow harmony. 1868 BROWNING *Ring & Bk.* IX. 56 His notion of the Mother-Maid: Methinks I see it, chalk, a little stumped!

absol. 1820 C. HAYTER *Introd. Perspective* 169, I pay great attention to the model while stumping, so as to preserve all the lights.

stumpage ('stʌmpɪdʒ). *local U.S.* [f. STUMP *sb.*^{1} + -AGE.]

1. The price paid for standing timber; also, a tax charged in some States for the privilege of cutting timber on State lands.

1835 *Knickerbocker* V. 423 Such rough words as tariff jobbing, cuts, stumpage. 1848 BARTLETT *Dict. Amer.* 341 *Stumpage*, the sum paid to owners of land for the privilege of cutting the timber growing thereon. State of Maine. 1860 *Harper's Mag.* XX. 440 The timber tract is..purchased or a rate of stumpage agreed upon which is generally from \$2.50 to \$3.00 per thousand feet for all timber cut. 1891 E. ROPER *By Track & Trail* xxvii. 407 The settlers..have to pay to the Government one cent 'stumpage' for every tree cut down. 1902 S. E. WHITE *Blazed Trail* xxv, We must have that pine, even though we pay stumpage on it. Now what would you consider a fair price for it?

2. Standing timber considered with reference to its quantity or marketable value.

1854 SEBA SMITH *Way down East* 39 To sell stumpage to the loggers for the ensuing winter. 1857 THOREAU *Maine Woods* (1894) 164 He it is who..has not bought the stumpage of the township on which it stands. 1894 *Q. Rev.* July 185 We assume a pine stumpage of 5000 feet to the acre. 1902 S. E. WHITE *Blazed Trail* xiv, You owned five million feet of timber, which at the price of stumpage (standing trees) was worth ten thousand dollars.

stumped (stʌmpt), *ppl. a.*^{1} [f. STUMP *v.*^{1} + -ED^1.] Truncated; abruptly terminated, as if cut short.

1597 A. M. tr. *Guillemeau's Fr. Chirurg.* 31 b, They then imposed theron a smalle stumped Cauterye, well glowinge & redd hott. 1608 TOPSELL *Serpents* 247 This kinde of Spyder is..round as a ball, with very short stumped feete. 1642–7 H. MORE *Song of Soul* I. ii. 59 So standing wet and dry Around the stumped top soft mosse did grow. 1670 NARBOROUGH *Jrnl.* in *Acc. Sev. Late Voy.* I. (1694) 59 Their Coat is a downy stumped Feather. 1752 *Scotland's Glory* 55 This stumped idol still here stands Like Dagon in his temple.

stumped (stʌmpt), *ppl. a.*^{2} [f. STUMP *v.*^{2} + -ED^1.] Of a drawing: Produced by means of the stump.

1807 J. LANDSEER *Lect. Engraving* 126 People never stopt to consider whether even red-chalk or stumped drawings themselves were [etc.].

stumper ('stʌmpə(r)). [f. STUMP *v.*^{1} + -ER^1.]

†**1.** 'A boaster or bragger' (Bailey ed. 5, 1731).

2. One employed or skilled in stumping trees.

1828 P. CUNNINGHAM *N.S. Wales* (ed. 3) II. 279 Two..Dublin thieves, who went out with me, are now..first-rate 'fellers and stumpers' in a good clearing gang.

3. *Cricket.* One who stumps; a wicket-keeper.

1776 in Nyren *Yng. Cricketer's Tutor* (1833) 67, I had almost forgot..Little George, the long stop, and Tom Sueter, the stumper. 1833 in P. Norman *Scores & Annals W. Kent Cricket Club* (1897) 73 Herbert..is such a wonderous stumper. 1901 *Daily Mail* 19 Sept. 3/4 There are few better amateur stumpers than the Hampshire captain.

4. A horse which walks with a stiff leg.

1874 *Punch* 11 Apr. 155/1 If ever I saw a stumper with my own very dear eyes, that stumper is before me.

5. Something (e.g. a question, a task imposed, a reply) that 'stumps' one; a poser.

1807 *Salmagundi* (N.Y.) 20 Mar. 121 They happened to run their heads full butt against a new reading. Now this was a stumper. 1833 [SEBA SMITH] *Lett. J. Downing* xxii. (1835) 126, I'm afraid we'll git a stumper..one of these days, that will nock us all into kindlin-wood. 1855 J. LAWRENCE in Bosw. Smith *Life Ld. Lawrence* (1883) I. 470 One query in writing is often a stumper for a month or two. 1872 SCHELE DE VERE *Americanisms* 187 The American..speaks of a conclusive argument, or a difficult problem: 'That is a stumper.' 1899 E. PHILLPOTTS *Human Boy* vi. 137 We always noticed, at arithmetic times, that Browne, if he got a stumper, would put up the lid of his private desk and hide behind it.

6. *U.S.* A stump speaker.

1863 *Boston Sunday Herald* 30 Aug. 2/7 An Ohio stumper, while making a speech, exclaimed [etc.]. 1884 *Chr. Commw.* 6 Nov. 49/2 Oratorical stumpers are deceiving and bewitching the nation into the destruction of true polity. 1901 *Scotsman* 11 Nov. 9/2 The great majority of the Protestant..preachers are stumpers..for the Republican party.

'stumpie. *Sc.* [f. STUMP *sb.*^{1} + -IE.]

1. Playfully used for: The stump of a pen.

1785 BURNS *2nd Epist. J. Lapraik* vi, Sae I gat paper in a blink, An' down gaed stumpie in the ink. 1821 W. LIDDLE *Poems* 181, If I can do't afore I leave ye, Wi' ink and stumpie.

2. A person with a stumpy figure. Also, a small child.

1820 *Glenfergus* III. 142 These upstart stumpies, the Lumgaires, and their manœuvring mother, are determined to secure the coronet. 1866 J. SMITH *Merry Bridal* 7 Weel tether'd, weel gether'd, They 'gree'd like yowe an' lamb, Wi' meal-cogs an' kail-cogs For stumpies when they cam'.

stumping ('stʌmpɪŋ), *vbl. sb.*^{1} [f. STUMP *v.*^{1} + -ING^1.]

1. The action of the verb. **a.** The action of treading heavily, as with a wooden leg.

1805 WORDSW. *Waggoner* II. 60 What thumping—stumping—overhead! 1862 BORROW *Wild Wales* xi. (1901) 63 Both heard the stumping. 1905 A. T. SHEPPARD *Red Cravat* III. vi. 293 The tap of his cane, the stumping of his thick-soled boots.

b. *Cricket.*

1844 W. LILLYWHITE *Hand-bk. Cricket* 15 No byes, overthrows, stumping, or catching out behind wicket allowed. 1849 *Laws of Cricket* in 'Bat' *Cricket Man.* (1850) 57 The wicket-keeper shall not take the ball for the purpose of stumping until it has passed the wicket. 1895 *Westm. Gaz.* 4 May 5/2 This total of 1,397 wickets is made up of 611 clean bowlings, 698 catches, 37 stumpings, 48 leg-befores, and 3 hit wickets.

c. The action of delivering stump speeches.

1865 *Sat. Rev.* 18 Feb. 184/2 The babes and sucklings out of whose mouths political wisdom is to come seem to be commencing their 'stumping' in good time.

attrib. and *Comb.* 1884 *Boston* (Mass.) *Jrnl.* 6 Sept., In Windham county, the special stumping-ground of the Springfield Republican, the total Independent vote will not reach one hundred. 1884 *Manch. Exam.* 27 Aug. 5/2 The Leader of the Opposition would hardly go to Oban on a stumping expedition.

2. *concr.* (See quot.)

1883 GRESLEY *Gloss. Coal-mining* 245 *Stumping*, a kind of pillar and stall plan of getting coal.

3. *Comb.*, as **stumping machine** *N. Amer.* = *stump-machine* s.v. STUMP *sb.*^{1} 19; **stumping powder**, an explosive used for clearing land of tree stumps.

1871 G. EASTON *Trav. Amer.* xiii. 129 Until time has so destroyed the roots that, with the aid of a pair of oxen and a 'stumping machine', the stumps can be removed with comparative ease. 1906 *Daily Colonist* (Victoria, B.C.) 30

Jan. 5/5 An experiment in clearing Island lands by the aid of a steam stumping machine is shortly to be made in the vicinity of Duncan. **1973** L. Russell *Everyday Life Colonial Canada* ii. 31 Later a 'stumping machine' was used. It consisted of a very heavy wooden tripod, with a stout, vertical iron screw mounted at the apex. **1921** *Daily Colonist* (Victoria, B.C.) 6 Apr. 5/4 The regulations under which the Provincial Department of Agriculture will issue funds for the purchasing of cheap stumping powder to farmers have been approved. **1955** R. P. Hobson *Nothing too Good for Cowboy* i. 11 The cattle company..has exploded like a can of stumping powder.

'stumping, *vbl. sb.*^{2} [-ING^1.] The action of STUMP *v.*^{2} Also *attrib.*

1879 *Cassell's Techn. Educ.* II. 260 The crayon to be used for stumping is No. 2 or, for very dark shadows, No. 3. **1891** *Daily News* 14 May 6/1 M. Carrière overdoes the stumping-brush effect.

stumping ('stʌmpɪŋ), *ppl. a.* [f. STUMP *v.*^{1} + -ING^2.]

1. Treading heavily or clumsily.

1842 Borrow *Bible in Spain* xxvii. (Pelh. Libr.) 189 My reflections..were suddenly interrupted by a heavy stumping sound. **1862** —— *Wild Wales* xxxiv. (1901) 238, I heard the sound of stumping steps coming upstairs. **1865** Dickens *Mut. Fr.* IV. iii, The stumping approach of Wegg was soon heard.

2. Clumsily formed, stumpy. *colloq.* (Cf. *lumping.*)

1852 Mrs. Stowe *Uncle Tom's C.* iv, And look at my great black stumpin' hands.

stumpish ('stʌmpɪʃ), *a.* [f. STUMP *sb.*^{1} + -ISH.] Somewhat of the character of a stump.

1618 W. Lawson *New Orchard* viii. (1623) 22 Many trees haue more stumps than boughs, and most trees no well thriuing, but short, stumpish, & euill thriuing boughs. **1845** J. Keegan *Leg. & Poems* (1907) 218 He..delivered the stumpish whip and ragged ribbons into the hands of the driver.

†**stumple.** *rare*$^{-1}$. = STUMP *sb.*^{1} 3 e. Cf. STRUMPLE.

1686 Plot *Staffordsh.* 439 As soon as his [the bull's] horns are cut off, his Ears cropt, his taile cut by the stumple.

'stumpless, *a. rare*$^{-1}$. [f. STUMP *sb.*^{1} + -LESS.] Cleared of stumps.

1839 Mrs. Kirkland *New Home* xxiii. 148 Fields of grain, well fenced and stumpless, surrounded this happy dwelling.

'stumpling. *nonce-wd.* [-LING^1.] A little stump.

1786 Wolcot (P. Pindar) *Farew. Odes* i. 54 No poet's rage shall root our stumps and stumplings.

stumpy ('stʌmpɪ), *sb.* [f. STUMP *sb.*^{1} + -Y.]

1. A spritsail barge.

1881 *Standard* 22 June 3/7 The Committee boat, having steamed up to the stumpies.., gave an opportunity of witnessing a very interesting contest. **1889** Pask *Eyes Thames* 32 A craft that is known on the river as a 'stumpy', *i.e.* a barge without a top-sail.

2. *slang.* Money. Cf. STUMP *sb.*^{1} 16.

1828 *Lights & Shades* II. 7 He inquired whether I had any other dibbs, any more blunt or stumpy, any more money. **1835** Dickens *Sk. Boz., Last Cab-driver*, Till they was rig'larly done over, and forked out the stumpy. **1837** T. Hook *Jack Brag* ii, Send up the stumpy by to-night's post. **1844** J. T. Hewlett *Parsons & W.* xlii, I am short of ready stumpy. **1850** Kingsley *Alton Locke* ii, Down with the stumpy—a tizzy for a pot of half-and-half. **1859** *Hotten's Slang Dict.* 104 *Stumpy*, money.

stumpy ('stʌmpɪ), *a.* [f. STUMP *sb.*^{1} + -Y.]

1. Like a stump; short and thick. Of grass, etc. Full of stumps or short hard stalks.

1600 Surflet *Country Farm* IV. ii. 633 The haie..is full of stumpie stalkes,..and nothing pleasing [etc.]. **1669** Worlidge *Syst. Agric.* vii. (1681) 123 Once for all, the stumpy Graff will be found much Superior to the slender one, and make a much nobler and larger shoot. **1721** Mortimer *Husb.* (ed. 5) I. 157 They often burn the Stubble, it being so stumpy that they seldom plow it in. **1834** Beckford *Italy* II. 54 Festoons of luxuriant leaves and tendrils, not fastened to stiff poles and stumpy stakes as in France. **1836** T. Hook *G. Gurney* I. 198 A stout short-legged pony, with a thick neck and a stumpy tail. **1858** Carlyle *Fredk. Gt.* IV. iv. (1872) I. 295 Nose smallish, inclining to be stumpy. **1862** H. H. Dixon *Scott & Sebright* iii. 138 He was a thick short horse, got us little stumpy mares, we've very few of them. **1890** D. C. Murray *John Vale* iv, The stumpy bamboo cane which Mr. Macfarlane carried. **1899** *Allbutt's Syst. Med.* VI. 572 The hairs turn white, hypertrophy, become stumpy and brittle, or fall out. **1916** *Blackw. Mag.* Apr. 469/2 You may see a boat, her high receding bows surmounted by a stumpy beak.

Comb. **1865** Tylor *Early Hist. Man.* xii. 355 Both stories accounting..for the fact that bears and hyenas are stumpy-tailed. **1871** B. Taylor *Faust* (1875) II. III. 174 This pert throng Are only stumpy-winged and cackling..geese.

b. of a human figure.

1822 Galt *Provost* xliii. (1868) 125 This Mr. Peevie was, in his person, a stumpy man. **1856** F. E. Paget *Owlet of Owlst.* 78 That short stumpy woman in the cloak is Miss Creepmouse. **1862** Thornbury *Turner* II. 324 Turner was a stumpy, ill-dressed man, with a red face. **1866** Mrs. Gaskell *Wives & Dau.* xl, I was always afraid she'd be short and stumpy.

c. of a building.

1870 E. Peacock *Ralf Skirl.* II. 128 The stumpy towers of Ripon Minster. **1883** A. Dobson in *Eng. Illustr. Mag.* Nov. 76/2 The fine old Banqueting House..seems to overlook the stumpy Horse Guards much as a person with a pedigree might be supposed to survey a *nouveau riche.* **1896** Hare *Story My Life* I. ii. 57 Our high field, over which the stumpy spire of the church could be seen.

d. *Nat. Hist.*

1858 Baird *Cycl. Nat. Sci., Scarabæidæ*, Their forms are very varied, but generally short and stumpy. **1863** P. P. Carpenter in *Rep. Brit. Assoc.* I. 643 *Mytilus?* var. *glomeratus...* Short, stumpy, solid, crowded. **1886** J. J. Quelch *Coral-Reefs* in *Challenger Rep.* XVI. III. 66 Its thickened, short, stumpy and close branches and branchlets. **1896** Lydekker *Roy. Nat. Hist.* V. 20 Stumpy crocodile, a small and short-nosed crocodile (*Osteolæmus tetraspis*) from West Africa, in the neighbourhood of Sierra Leone.

2. Worn down to a stump.

1794 J. Williams *Crying Epist.* 15 Let them not force me to repair these slips: To fasten stumpy brooms upon my ships. **1840** Thackeray *Shabby-genteel Story* i, A stumpy pen, richly crusted with ink at the nib. **1883** R. Haldane *Workshop Rec.* Ser. II. 254/1 Rub the old colour up with a stumpy brush.

3. Of ground: Full of stumps. *U.S.*

1838 N. Hawthorne *Amer. Note-Bks.* (1883) 150 Climbing a rude, rough, rocky, stumpy, ferny height yesterday. **1879** J. Burroughs *Locusts & Wild Honey* 122 A little stumpy clearing. **1885** *Harper's Mag.* Mar. 536/2 Soil, whether..gravel, sand, stumpy, stony. **1897** *Outing* July 328/2 A few acres of stumpy pasture.

Hence **'stumpily,** *adv.*, **'stumpiness.**

1878 Sir G. Scott *Lect. Archit.* (1879) II. 107 Such stumpiness of proportion was not viewed as essential to the style. **1887** Ruskin *Præterita* II. 331 A stumpily made..good-natured simpleton.

stun (stʌn), *sb.* [f. STUN *v.*]

1. The act of stunning or dazing; a stunning effect; the condition of being stunned.

1727 Thomson *Summer* 488 [586] Till the stun [*later* sound] Of a near fall of water every sense Wakes. *a* **1734** North *Life Ld. Kpr. Guilford* (1742) 159 The People return'd their joyful Sense of the King's Safety..by numerous Addresses from all Parts of the Kingdom; which gave such a Stun to the rebellious Party..that little Sign of any Resurrection to Action appear'd in them. **1804** *Naval Chron.* XII. 397 He fainted from the stun. **1836** Ruskin *Ess. Lit.* Wks. 1903 I. 361 In the first stun of our astonishment. **1887** *Poor Nellie* (1888) 189 Before poor Adela could recover from the stun of a great astonishment.

2. A flaw on the surface of a piece of stone. Cf. STUN *v.* 5.

1850 Holtzapffel *Turning* III. 1198 The last marks to be eradicated in the smoothing are generally those called stuns, made in sawing the marble by coarse particles of sand getting between the side of the saw blade and the saw kerf.

stun (stʌn), *v.* Inflected **stunned, stunning.** Forms; 6 **stonne,** 7 **ston,** 4– **stun;** *pa. t.* and *pa. pple.* 4–7 **stund,** (4 **stunt**), 4–5 **stoned(e,** 5 **stonet, stonde,** 6–7 **stonnd, stonn'd.** [Aphetic a. OF. *estone-r* (mod.F. *étonner*): see ASTONE *v.*, of which this is a doublet. Cf. also STONY, STOYNE *vbs.*

It has been usual to regard this vb. as representing OE. *stunian*, to resound; but the sense differs essentially, and the OE. vb. app. did not survive into ME.]

1. a. *trans.* To deprive of consciousness or of power of motion by a blow, a fall, or the like.

a **1300** *Cursor M.* 12280 A child þar kest a-noiþer don Vte of þe loft vnto þe grund, Þe child to ded þar was he stund. *c* **1400** *Laud Troy Bk.* 10377 Bothe her swordis out thei drow And ffauȝt to-geder long y-now, Til thei were stoned hede and brayn. *c* **1420** *Avow. Arth.* xiii, His stode was stonet, starke ded. *c* **1475** *Partenay* 4700 With that stroke he was stoned manyfold. **1590** Spenser *F.Q.* III. vii. 42 Where-with he was so stund that he n'ote ryde, But reeled to an fro from East to West. **1662** J. Davies tr. *Olearius' Voy. Ambass.* 165 They kill it [a fish] by first stunning it with a knock with a mallet. **1794** Mrs. Radcliffe *Myst. Udolpho* xxxiv, At length Du Pont forced Verezzi to the floor, where he lay stunned by the violence of his fall. **1837** W. Irving *Capt. Bonneville* I. 271 The ball, which had been nearly spent before it struck him, had stunned instead of killing him. **1853** Mrs. Gaskell *Ruth* x, She was as one stunned into unconsciousness;..she hardly breathed.

fig. **1855** Macaulay *Hist. Eng.* xvi. III. 721 The faction which had been prostrated and stunned began to give signs of returning animation.

b. Applied to an inanimate or immaterial object.

1700 Dryden *Cymon & Iphig.* 341 The giddy Ship betwixt the Winds and Tides, Forc'd back and forwards, in a Circle rides, Stun'd with the diff'rent Blows. **1911** Sir H. Craik *Edw. Ld. Clarendon* II. 243 Public credit was shaken; commercial operations were stunned.

2. a. To daze or astound with some strong emotion or impression.

a **1300** *Cursor M.* 17288 + 443 Þen were þai stoned ilkone. No drede, he saide, has ȝe, Lokes side, hand, & fote. **1426** Audelay *Poems* (Percy Soc.) 78, I was adeuyd [*printed* adenyd] of that dynt, Hit stonede me. **1598** B. Jonson *Ev. Man in Hum.* IV. iv. (1601) H 3 b, Nay you haue stonnd me I fayth? **1654** Whitlock *Zootomia* 400 Salomons Wealth, it was of that vastnesse, it would..stun the Beliefe of one of our..Rich Misers. **1678** Bunyan *Pilgr.* I. (ed. 2) 264 At the sight therefore of this River, the Pilgrims were much stun'd [ed. 1 stounded]. **1802** Mar. Edgeworth *Forester, Catastrophe*, Lady Catherine was stunned by this distinct refusal. **1843** Macaulay *Ess., Mme. D'Arblay* (1897) 673 The multitude, unacquainted with the best models, are captivated by whatever stuns and dazzles them. **1886** Stevenson *Kidnapped* vi, I sat stunned with my good fortune.

†**b.** *intr.* To be amazed or astounded. *Obs.*

1533 Tindale *Supper of the Lord* 13 b, Thei beyng yet but feble of fayth..muste here nedis haue wondred, stonned and staggerd.

3. a. *trans.* To daze or bewilder with noise or din.

1621 Bp. H. King *Serm.* 25 Nov. 4 A man may heare so much that hee may ston the sense. **1660** Chas. II. in Julia Cartwright *Madame* (Henrietta of Orleans) (1894) 57 My head is so dreadfully stunned with the acclamations of the people. **1732** Pope *Ess. Man* I. 202 If nature thunder'd in his op'ning ears, And stunn'd him with the musick of the spheres. **1828** Scott *F.M. Perth* xii, Four half-stripped knaves stunned the neighbourhood with the clang of hammer and stithy. **1910** *Q. Rev.* July 100 The ear is stunned by the not unmusical roar of the Falls [of Niagara].

absol. **1723** Swift *Pethox* 76 The Britons, once a savage Kind,..With Limbs robust, and Voice that stuns. **1764** Goldsm. *Trav.* 412 Where..Niagara stuns with thund'ring sound.

b. hyperbolically.

1693 Dryden *Juvenal* i. 2 Still shall I hear, and never quit the Score, Stun'd with hoarse Codrus' Theseid, o're and o're? **1714** Budgell tr. *Theophrastus* vi. 22 You shall sometimes see him gather a Crowd round him,..and stun the People with a senseless Story of an Injury that is done him. **1816** Scott *Old Mort.* ii, An old drunken cavaliering butler, who..stunned the family nightly with his exploits at Kilsythe and Tippermoor. *a* **1818** M. G. Lewis *Jrnl. W. Ind.* (1834) 365 Complaints of all kinds stunned me from all quarters.

†**4.** To break or crush with heavy blows. *Obs.* Cf. STONY *v.* 5.

1470–85 Malory *Arthur* III. vii. 107 [They] clafe their sheldes and stoned their helmes and brak their hawberkes.

5. a. To bruise or loosen the surface of (stone, a mineral), so that it splinters or exfoliates. Also, to scratch or tear (a surface) in sawing. **b.** *intr.* Of stone, etc.: To exfoliate, peel off in splinters or laminæ.

1676 in *Phil. Trans.* XI. 755 The Mine-men do often strike such forcible strokes with a great Iron-crow, that that stuns the Diamond and so flaws it. **1811** Pinkerton *Petral.* II. 465 It..has numerous crystals and quadrilateral plates of felspar in perfect preservation, except that it has a dry aspect, and is *stunned* in some parts. **1843** [see STUNNING *vbl. sb.*]. **1890** *Funk's Stand. Dict.* **1911** Webster.

6. *Comb.* **stun gas,** a gas that incapacitates by causing temporary confusion and disorientation; **stun grenade,** a grenade that only stuns through its sound and flash; **stun gun,** a gun that fires shot which stuns without causing serious injury.

1968 *Punch* 21 Feb. 253 Here is a run-down of anti-crowd devices which other nations, notably America, are developing:..stun gas; gas which temporarily blinds. **1977** *Times* 19 Oct. 1/4 The 'stun' grenades which played such a vital part in enabling the West German commando unit to overcome the terrorists..were supplied by Britain. **1981** A. Winch *Blood Money* xxi. 236 The stun grenades..looked like unmarked beer cans and provided a deafening explosion, a blinding flash. **1971** *Sunday Times* 30 May 5 The stun gun has already been used effectively by the Alameda County Sheriff's Department who are called in whenever student riots at Berkeley become too much for the local police. **1975** *Nature* 13 Feb. 495/3 One hopes that the [polar bear tagging] expedition will be equipped with a supply of stun-guns.

stunay, var. STONY *v. Obs.*

stunch(e, obs. forms of STENCH.

stund, variant of STAND *sb.*^{2}

1664 Taylor in *Evelyn's Pomona* 49 Let your Vessels be very tight and clean wherein you put your Cider to settle: The best form is the Stund or Stand, which is set upon the lesser end, from the top tapering downwards.

stund(e: see STOUN *v.*, STOUND *sb.*^{1}, *v.*^{1}, *v.*^{2}

Stundism ('ʃtʊndɪz(ə)m, 'stʊndɪz(ə)m). [f. STUNDIST: see -ISM.] The teaching and practice of the Stundists.

1888 Stead *Truth about Russia* 362 The still more remarkable religious phenomenon which goes by the name of Stundism in the Southern provinces of Russia.

Stundist ('ʃtʊndɪst, 'stʊndɪst). [a. Russ. *štundist*, f. G. *stunde* hour, said to be used by the German settlers as the name for their religious meetings: see -IST.] A member of a large Evangelical sect (called *štunda*) which arose among the peasantry of South Russia about 1860, as a result of contact with German Protestant settlers, and in opposition to the doctrine and authority of the Orthodox Church.

1878 D. M. Wallace *Russia* xix. 301 Some of them are simply evangelical Protestants, like the 'Stundisti,' who have adopted the religious conceptions of their neighbours, the German colonists. **1888** Stead *Truth about Russia* 363 Deputations came to St. Petersburg from the Stundists, the Molokani, and the Baptists.

attrib. **1893** *The Stundists* 35 Ivan Golovtchenko, a Stundist preacher..was taken before the Court on a charge of propagating Stundist doctrines.

†**'stundum,** *adv. Obs.* [OE., dat. pl. of *stund* STOUND *sb.*] At times.

Beowulf 1423 Horn stundum song fuslic fyrd-leoð. *a* **1340** Hampole *Psalter* xliii. 11 Þou sall not out ga, as þou did stundum til þe iwes.

stung (stʌŋ), *ppl. a.* Also 3 **stungen,** 4 **stongyn,** 7 **stung'd.** [See STING *v.*] **1.** Wounded or hurt by a sting. *lit.* and *fig.*

c **1250** *Gen. & Ex.* 3901 Quat stungen man so saȝ ðor-on, ðat werk him sone al was vn-don. *a* **1400** *Stockholm Med. MS.* ii. 687 in *Anglia* XVIII. 324 Dragaunce is good To drynkyn for a stongyn man. **1600** Surflet *Country Farm* I. xii. 85 If any rat, spider,..or other venemous beast, by his sting or biting haue caused your flesh to rise..put vpon the stung place the dung of a cow or oxe very hot. **1605** Shaks.

Lear v. i. 56 Each iealous of the other, as the stung Are of the Adder. **1609** MARKHAM *Famous Whore* (1868) 31 My well stung'd conscience vrg'd me to repent. **1786** tr. *Beckford's Vathek* (1883) 84 The stung eunuch could scarcely preserve the semblance of respect. **1820** BYRON *Mar. Fal.* III. i. 102 When he, their last descendant chief, Stands plotting.. With stung plebeians. **1866** G. MACDONALD *Ann. Q. Neighb.* v. (1878) 63, I prayed God to keep me from feeling stung and proud.

2. *Austral. slang.* Drunk. Cf. STUNNED *ppl. a.* 2.

1919 W. H. DOWNING *Digger Dialects* 48 Stung,.. drunk. **1952** T. A. G. HUNGERFORD *Ridge & River* 62 The old bloke's stung already, and the pubs aren't even open yet! **1965** W. DICK *Bunch of Ratbags* 219 We had arrived at Doreen's sister's wedding-reception about an hour ago and by now we were all half stung. **1970** K. SLESSOR *Bread & Wine* 154 To a total abstainer, the line 'I am stung, stung to the heart of me' would convey, I suppose, nothing so coarse as the associations which I find in it.

'stunkard, *a. Sc.* Also ston-, stunkerd, stonkard, -art. [Of obscure origin.] Sulky, sullen.

1737 A. RAMSAY in *Gentl. Mag.* VII. 507/1 These stonkerd fellows Wha merit naithing but the gallows. **1814** *Saxon & Gael* I. 77 (Jam.), I was speerin' for you at my Lord, but he is sae stunkard and paughty. **1824** SCOTT *Redgauntlet* ch. ii, It's a sore thing to see a stunkard cow kick down the pail when it's reaming fou.

stunned, *ppl. a.* [f. STUN *v.* + ED[1].]

1. Rendered unconscious or dazed, as by a blow, etc.; astounded, bewildered.

1762 FALCONER *Shipwr.* III. 733 My stunned ear tingles to the whizzing tide. **1805** SOUTHEY *Madoc* II. xviii. 113 From his shield, The deadening force communicated ran Up his stunn'd arm. **1845** DICKENS *Chimes* iii. 96 Trotty.. turned his white face here and there, in mute and stunned astonishment. **1868–70** MORRIS *Earthly Par.* III. 456 And to her stunned heart came A flash of hope and pain.

2. *Austral.* and *N.Z. slang.* Drunk. Cf. STUNG *ppl. a.* 2.

1919 W. H. DOWNING *Digger Dialects* 48 *Stunned* (adj.), drunk. **1933** 'P. CADEY' *Broken Pattern* xii. 129 I'm afraid I got a bit stunned... I had one over the odd.

3. Phr. ***like a stunned mullet*** [MULLET[1]]: dull, stupefied. *Austral. slang.*

1953 BAKER *Australia Speaks* 267 [Similes] Dullness: (looking) like a stunned mullet. **1963** J. O'GRADY *Things they do to You* 147, I returned and lay on the bed like a stunned mullet. **1977** *Australian* 16 May 1 Mr. Hawke said yesterday the Federal Government had responded like a stunned mullet to his acceptance of the proposed Industrial Relations Bureau.

stunner ('stʌnə(r)). [f. STUN *v.* + -ER.]

1. Something that stuns or dazes; something that amazes or astounds.

1829 P. EGAN *Boxiana* 2nd Ser. II. 417 The blow was a *stunner*, and visible on his forehead. **1847** C. BRONTË *Jane Eyre* xxxiii, Here was a new stunner—I had been calculating on four or five thousand. **1847** LD. G. BENTINCK *Let.* 30 June in *Croker Papers* (1884) III. 128, I have read your article in the *Quarterly* and think it quite admirable.. a complete stunner for the Peel party. **1853** SURTEES *Sponge's Sp. Tour* (1893) 55 One tacked on two miles, another ten, and so it went on and on, till it reached the ears of the great Mr. Seedeyman.. as he sat in his den penning his 'stunners' for his market-day *Mercury*. **1872** 'ALIPH CHEEM' (Yeldham) *Lays of Ind* (1876) 56 He.. ordered the gunners To fire off some stunners, That the glory of France might be properly told.

2. *colloq.* A person or thing of extraordinary excellence or attractiveness.

1848 ALB. SMITH *Chr. Tadpole* xxix. 263 Watch the girl, Sir Frederick. Isn't she a stunner? **1855** THACKERAY *Newcomes* xlii, The cook.. was really a stunner for tarts. **1893** LELAND *Mem.* II. 278 He knew where to get one for a pound but £2. 10s. would buy a 'stunner'.

stunning ('stʌnɪŋ), *vbl. sb.* [-ING[1].] The action of the verb STUN; the state of being stunned.

c **1475** *Partenay* 1230 To hym A gret stonyng was it verily. **1804** ABERNETHY *Surg. Observ.* 175 The lad had recovered from the immediate stunning occasioned by the injury. **1847** J. RUSSELL *Remin. Yarrow* (1894) 296 Having recovered from the stunning, he was able to sit out the service.

b. *spec.* Exfoliation or scaling away of the surface of stone (see quot. 1843).

1843 BILLINGS *Durham Cath.* 15 There is a peculiarity about the stone, called by the workmen 'stunning', which is the peeling off (within a few years), from the effect of hammer and chisel, of a layer varying from one quarter to three eighths of an inch thick. **1884** BLUNT *Annot. Bk. Comm. Prayer* 429 *note*, The deficiencies now existing in the left-hand panel through the stunning of the stone on which they are sculptured.

stunning ('stʌnɪŋ), *ppl. a.* [-ING[2].]

1. That stuns or stupefies; dazing, astounding; deafening.

1667 MILTON *P.L.* II. 952 A universal hubbub wilde Of stunning sounds and voices all confus'd. **1702** C. MATHER *Magn. Chr.* VII. vi. (1852) 578 But the Stunningest wound of all given to them was when.. near four hundred of them were.. surprised at the house of Major Waldern. **1760** MRS. DELANY *Autob.* (1861) III. 614 The Rooms hot and stunning—I wish for balls as the quieter entertainment! **1818** SCOTT *Rob Roy* xxxvi, My father's arrival.. was a stunning blow to MacVittie and Company. **1863** READE *Hard Cash* I. ix. 249 The victorious crew raised a stunning cheer. **1911** *Expositor* July 61 His besetting sins received a stunning stroke.

2. *colloq.* Excellent, first-rate, 'splendid', delightful; extremely attractive or good-looking.

1849–50 DICKENS *Dav. Copp.* xi, 'Twopence-half-penny,' says the landlord, 'is the price of the Genuine Stunning ale.' **1850** THACKERAY *Pendennis* xxxix, Those regular stunning slap-up out-and-outers. **1856** F. E. PAGET *Owlet of Owlst.* 193 Laura Wydawake is the most stunning girl I ever set my eyes on. **1867** TROLLOPE *Last Chron. Barset* I. xl. 346 Fancy Polly with a house of her own! Won't it be stunning? **1883** FRANCES M. PEARD *Contrad.* xxiii, The new footman is a stunning hand.

b. quasi-*adv.* (intensifying the following adj.).

1851 MAYHEW *Lond. Labour* I. 36/2 A lad about fourteen informed me that 'brass buttons, like a huntman's.. looked stunning flash.' **1888** 'R. BOLDREWOOD' *Robbery under Arms* xxiv, The old woman cooked us a stunning good dinner.

Hence **'stunningly** *adv.*

1823 SCOTT *Quentin D.* xx, The noise.. became ten times more stunningly audible. **1854** DICKENS *Hard T.* II. i, Is the lady so very alarming?.. Repellently and stunningly clever? **1863** GEO. ELIOT *Romola* lxvii, Shouting, yelling, half-motiveless execration rang stunningly in his ears. **1889** *Temple Bar* Nov. 351 A pain that would have been fierce had it not been so stunningly dull.

stunny, stunnys: see STONY *v.*, STONISH *v.*

stunpoll ('stʌnpəʊl). *dial.* Also -pole. [? f. STONE *sb.* + POLL *sb.*[1]] A dolt, blockhead.

a **1794** MRS. M. PALMER *Devon. Dial.* (1839) 28 You dunder-headed stunpole. **1863** BARNES *Dorset Gloss.*, *Stunpoll*, stunhead, blockhead. **1879** HARDY *Ret. Native* I. iii, I saw myself as the next poor stunpoll to get into the same mess.

stunsail ('stʌns(ə)l). *Naut.* Also stu'n-sail, stun'-sail, stunsel. Contraction, representing the ordinary pronunciation, of STUDDING-SAIL.

1762 FALCONER *Shipwr.* I. 225 Now swelling stu'n-sails on each side extend. **1863** READE *Hard Cash* I. xi. 267 All hands set stunsels 'low and aloft! **1913** M. ROBERTS *Salt of the Sea* ix. 216 His ears [were] large and outstanding, like a couple of stunsails.

attrib. **1825** H. B. GASCOIGNE *Nav. Fame* 49 The Stunsail Booms they raise. **1850** H. MELVILLE *White Jacket* xlv, I.. was ordered to reeve anew the stun'-sail-halyards.

stunt (stʌnt), *sb.*[1] [f. STUNT *v.*[1]]

1. A check in growth; also, a state of arrested growth or development.

1795 *Trans. Soc. Arts* XIII. 166 If it [a tree] takes a stunt. *a* **1825** FORBY *Voc. E. Anglia*, *Stunt*, a check in growth. Ex. 'That tree has got a stunt.' **1864** LOWELL *Fireside Trav.* 143 The compressed nature struggles through at every crevice, but can never get the cramp and stunt out of it. **1894** G. M. GOULD *Illustr. Dict. Med.* etc., *Stunt*, a stunted or undeveloped state. *Ibid.*, s.v. *Cram*, *Cram-stunt*, arrest in mental development due to over-study. **1899** RIDER HAGGARD in *Longman's Mag.* Oct. 547 They suffer from mildew or stunt of one kind or another.

2. A creature which has been hindered from attaining full growth or development; *spec.* (see quot. 1858).

1725 DUDLEY *Whales* in *Phil. Trans.* XXXIII. 257 At two Years old, they [*sc.* whales] are called Stunts, being stunted after weaning. **1858** SIMMONDS *Dict. Trade*, *Stunts*, a name for young whales of two years old, which, having been weaned, are lean. **1894** *N. & Q.* 8th Ser. VI. 337/2 The streets are filled with stunts and runts.

3. *dial.* A fit of sulkiness or obstinacy; in phr. ***to take (the) stunt.***

This use of the phrase is perh. a fig. application of that in quot. 1795, sense 1. But cf. STUNT *sb.*[2]

1837 HOOD *Blue Boar* 34 Now at a line he gave a grunt, Now at a phrase took sudden stunt. **1862** C. C. ROBINSON *Dial. Leeds* 424 Tuke t' stunt an' went off wi'art speiking. **1890** *Sat. Rev.* 12 Apr. 446/2 The most probable explanation of his [Ld. Geo. Sackville's] inaction on that occasion [battle of Minden] is that he simply 'took stunts', as the Yorkshire phrase has it—a case of sheer sulkiness, not of cowardice.

stunt (stʌnt), *sb.*[2] *colloq.* [Of obscure origin.

Orig. belonging to the slang of American college athletics; not in the *Century Dict.* 1891 or in Webster 1897; our earliest quots. show that it seems to have been still current only among schoolchildren and college students. Its general colloquial currency, and its extension of application, seems to have begun early in the 20th c. In British use it was at first regarded as mainly a soldiers' word. It has been conjectured that the word may be a. G. *stunde*, lit. hour, or a variant of STINT *sb.*; neither of these suggestions seems impossible. A notion which is app. prevalent in the U.S. is that the word is a variant of STUMP *sb.*[3], but in spite of the remarkable affinity of meaning, etymological connexion between the words is very unlikely.]

1. a. A prescribed item in an athletic competition or display, an 'event'; a feat undertaken as a defiance in response to a challenge; 'an act which is striking for the skill, strength, or the like, required to do it; a feat' (W. *Suppl.* 1900); something performed as an item in an entertainment, a (theatrical, etc.) 'turn' and *spec.* in aerobatics. **b.** Hence, an enterprise set on foot with the object of gaining reputation or signal advantage. In soldiers' language often vaguely: an attack or advance, a 'push', 'move'. Also *spec.* in Advertising, Journalism, etc., a 'gimmick' or device for attracting attention.

1878 S. BUTLER *Let.* 7 Feb. (1955) 174 It was a stunt for advertising the books, so I sent them. **1892** R. H. DAVIS *West from Car Window* 13 They went about it as gleefully as schoolboys at recess doing 'stunts'. **1895** *Dial. Notes* (Amer. Dial. Soc.) I. VIII. 400 *Stunt* (stʊnt): one of those convenient words which may be used in almost any connection and the exact meaning of which must be determined largely by the context;.. 'It would be a great stunt to go to a dance without a girl' (*i.e.* an unpleasant thing to do). 'He performed various stunts for the prof.' (*i.e.* did things that would win him the professor's favor, give him a 'pull')... [*Editor's note*: Doing stunts is used in N.Y. City by boys in the sense of performing some feat in rivalry,—a long jump for instance,—one boy 'stumping' or challenging another.] **1897** *Outing* Aug. 440/2 A lamprey fastened upon a bare leg. That boy did more 'stunts' in five minutes than he would attempt now for five thousand dollars! **1899** JESSE L. WILLIAMS *Stolen Story* etc. 198 If I were you I'd have a mass meeting first, with horse speeches, and all the old Fresh-fire stunts, then a parade. **1901** *Westm. Gaz.* 31 Jan. 10/2 There will be many new 'stunts' of a vaudeville nature. **1904** J. A. RIIS *Theodore Roosevelt* ii. 29 [At College] he played polo, did athletic stunts with the fellows,.. having no end of good times in it. **1905** D. WALLACE *Lure of Labrador Wild* viii. 114 That snowshoeing trip would be a great stunt. **1909** *Daily Chron.* 25 Aug. 1/7 I've been in Texas about two years, doing broncho stunts. **1909** *Flight* 11 Sept. 552/2 He made the machine dart down as though it were going to pitch to earth head foremost, but when within about 20 feet of the ground, without effort he brought it horizontal again. These are what Americans style 'stunts'. **1915** W. E. DOMMETT *Submarine Vessels* viii. 88 Of course, nothing in the nature of 'stunts', such as are performed by airman, are tried. **1916** *Blackw. Mag.* Apr. 482/1 You remember it is time to get up, for there is a 'stunt on'. **1919** 'R. N. ETIENNE' *Strange Tales from Fleet* 27 The 'stunt' was over, and two brief hours had prevented the twelfth Cruiser Squadron from cutting off the enemy light forces. **1922** *Daily Mail* 13 Nov. 11 The plea for 'stipes' is a newspaper stunt. **1927** C. A. LINDBERGH *We* i. 13 We did a few stunts over the fair-grounds to get everyone's attention. **1930** *Lancet* 7 June 1264/1 It has even been whispered, Sir, that there are too many 'stunts' (if this word may appear in your columns), too little science, but this is just malicious gossip. **1942** *Sun* (Baltimore) 29 Dec. 13/2 It would be a good stunt for us fellows to learn all the tricks of the Coast Guard and then we could turn rum runners! **1968** J. R. ACKERLEY *My Father & Myself* vii. 61 My brother's assignment was what we called a 'stunt', a common affair, in this case important if only because the Brigadier had set his heart on it. **1975** *Sunday Times* (Colour Suppl.) 20 July 12/2 His bisexuality.. was attracting sensational publicity. How much of this was simply a stunt?

c. A stint, a task, an exercise. orig. *U.S.*

1880 *Hermean* (N.Y.) 256 Ye have heard it said by those of old time, 'A rolling stone gathers no moss,' but by reason perhaps of its having been used as a 'stunt' for our childhood in the copy books, we seldom realize how beautiful and full of wisdom is the adage. **1904** G. H. LORIMER *Old Gorgon Graham* 85 And you set the other at a twelve-hour stunt of making all the beds you've mussed. **1921** G. B. SHAW in G. C. Williamson *John Keats Memorial Vol.* 176 Milton can do a stunt of geniality, as in *L'Allegro*.

d. In wider use, a piece of business, an act, enterprise, or exploit.

1904 *Sun* (N.Y.) 8 Aug. 5 He took lessons in holding the life net.. and the other stunts firemen are taught. **1913** R. BROOKE *Coll. Poems* (1918) p. lxxxiv, Then I do my pet boyish-modesty stunt and go pink all over. **1920** C. BAX *Square Pegs* 21 *Hilda.* You'll drive me frantic If you're not just the teeniest bit romantic. *Gioconda.* It isn't done. You're absolutely wrong In asking me to do that stunt. So long! **1928** [see PEEP *sb.*[1] 2 b]. **1964** C. HASSALL *Rupert Brooke* vii. 277 'So of course you were frank and boyish?' said Mrs. Cornford, on hearing he [*sc.* Rupert Brooke] had just met Henry James. 'Oh yes,' he said, 'Of course I did the fresh, boyish stunt, and it was a great success.'

2. a. *attrib.*, as ***stunt artist, flying, pilot***, etc.

1904 W. H. SMITH *Promoters* iii. 75 He might have made a successful actor, of the modern 'stunt' sort. **1916** C. WINCHESTER *Flying Men* 112 Trick flying, or 'stunt' flying as it is colloquially called, can only be attempted with impunity by those aviators who have had some experience. **1922** H. L. WILSON *Merton of Movies* 174 Ain't I a good stunt actress? **1931** *Morning Post* 18 Feb. 6/4 (*heading*) 'Stunt' pilot's escape. **1931** *Everyman* 23 Apr. 388/2 We are on the eve of a reaction from the 'stunt Press', he believes—the Press of competitions and coupons and catchpenny sensations. **1938** M. MCCARTHY in *Partisan Rev.* Feb. 35 In the actual production of Gielgud's *Hamlet* and Welles's *Caesar*, the exploiter, that is, the stunt artist, wears a more successful disguise. **1971** *Flying* Apr. 46/3 He is in the stunt-flying business. **1976** M. MAGUIRE *Scratchproof* iv. 53 'Remember to stretch the line tight,' the stunt arranger emphasized. **1977** D. ANTHONY *Stud Game* vi. 37 After the war Dusty became a stunt pilot for the movies. **1981** *Times Lit. Suppl.* 13 Feb. 177/5 The black-and-white plates which illustrate the book.. reveal completely new aspects of the works of art reproduced, without ever verging on the stunt photography which so often distorts Baroque sculpture in books written by less scrupulous authors.

b. Special Comb.: **stunt-drive** *v. intr.*, to drive a car for stunts (sense 1 a), esp. for making dangerous film sequences; hence **stunt-driving** *vbl. sb.*; **stunt man**, one who performs dangerous feats, esp. as a stand-in for a film actor.

1966 J. CLEARY *High Commissioner* v. 96, I used to stunt-drive in the old Ealing comedies. **1975** *New Yorker* 21 Apr. 92/3 One can disregard obvious high-risk occupations, such as stunt-driving. **1930** *Aberdeen Press & Jrnl.* 23 Jan. 2/6 To those who wish to get plenty of excitement out of life our advice is—Be a movie stunt man. **1953** C. A. LINDBERGH *Spirit of St. Louis* II. vi. 275 We walked over to a group of pilots, mechanics, and stunt men. **1953** DYLAN THOMAS *Let.* (1966) 416, I cry to myself as I kick clear of the cling of my stuntman's sacking. **1968** P. GEDDES *High Game* viii. 101 He'd worked, off and on, as a stunt-man in movies. **1977** *New Yorker* 27 June 84/3 The successful stunt man explained that his plan had been to scale the tower a day earlier.

stunt, *a. Obs.* exc. *dial.* Also 3 stunnt (*Ormin*), 5 stont. [OE. *stunt* foolish, corresp. to MHG. *stunz* stubbed, short, ON. *stutt-r* (earlier **stunt-r* = MSw. *stunt-er*) short:—OTeut.

**stunto-* short, truncated, perh. repr. pre-Teut. **stṇdo-*, f. root **stem-*: cf. STUMP *sb.*

In OE. only in fig. sense (cf. 'short-witted'); the lit. sense may have existed unrecorded, but more prob. senses 2–4 are from Scandinavian. With sense 3 cf. SHORT *a.* 10.]

†**1.** Foolish, stupid. *Obs.*

c **960** *Rule St. Benet* (Schröer) vii. 30 Se stunta on lehtre his stefne ȝeuferað. *c* **1200** ORMIN 3714 Wiþþ mannkinn þatt wass stunnt, & dill, & skilllæs swa summ asse.

†**2.** Short in duration. *Obs.*

a **1450** *Knt. de la Tour.* i. (1906) 4 [He] yeuithe longe lyff and stont [Fr. *longue vie et courte*] in this terreyn.

3. Obstinate, stubborn; rudely or angrily curt or blunt. (Chiefly applied to persons.) Now only *dial.*

1581 A. HALL *Iliad* VII. 123 This speech so stunt and sodaine sayed yeelds all the troupe abasht. **1674** RAY *N.C. Words, Stunt*, Lincoln, stubborn, fierce, angry. **1788** W. H. MARSHALL *Yorksh.* II. 357 *Stunt*; stubborn; not easy to be bent; as, a 'stunt child', a stubborn child. *a* **1825** FORBY *Voc. E. Anglia, Stunt, Stunty*, short, blunt, crusty; unmannerly. **1869** TENNYSON *North. Farmer, New Style* v, Do'ant be stunt: taäke time; I knaws what maäkes tha sa mad.

4. Stunted. **a.** Short and thick. **b.** Dwarfed in growth.

a. 1788 W. H. MARSHALL *Yorksh.* II. 357 A 'stunt stick', a thick short stick. **1845** S. JUDD *Margaret* I. xvii. 147 The smoke of the stunt gray chimney.

b. 1819 KEATS *Fall of Hyperion* I. 293 Side by side we stood (Like a stunt bramble by a solemn pine). **1845** THACKERAY *Cornhill to Cairo* v. 48 A stunt district of olive trees is almost the only vegetation.

5. Of a turn, bend, end: Abrupt.

1851 MAYHEW *Lond. Labour* (1861) II. 431/2 In case we comes to a stunt end where there's a wall and no place for 'em to get away,.. they [*sc.* rats in a sewer] fly at us. **1886** *S.W. Linc. Gloss., Stunt*,.. blunt, abrupt: as a 'stunt turn', that is, an abrupt bend, one at right angles.

6. *Comb.*: **stunt-head** *Engineering*, the vertical timbered end of a trench which has been excavated for the purpose of laying a sewer or a water-main.

stunt (stʌnt), *v.*[1] [f. STUNT *a.*]

†**1.** *trans.* **a.** To irritate, provoke to anger. (Cf. STUNT *a.* 3.) **b.** To bring to an abrupt stand; to nonplus. *Obs.*

a. 1583 MELBANCKE *Philotimus* N j, The burning of his right eare stunted him likewise, for y^t^ it is one of ye parts which Saturne an euil planet gouerneth. *Ibid.* U iij, Y^e^ tender bloud, from whence thin rare spirites do breath.., enfeebles the body, and kepes it downe, whettes the wit and stunts the stomacke.

b. 1603 HARSNET *Popish Impost.* 55 It was sufficient.. that his girdle.. should at the first touch of the party possessed, stunt the deuils wits. **1614** LATHAM *Falconry* (1633) 40 For want of digesture.. she will be presently stunted by those obstructions. **1642** W. MONTAGU in *Buccleuch MSS.* (Hist. MSS. Comm.) I. 301 His going.. is the wonder of London, and stunts us all to apprehend either what was the cause or what will be the sequel of it.

2. To check the growth or development of (a person, plant, etc.); to decrease (growth or production); hence, to dwarf.

1678 EVELYN *Terra* (ed. 2) 333 It is ever advisable to Water whilst the Ground is a little moist, and not totally dry, especially during the growing seasons, for it stunts the Plant and interrupts its progress. **1712** ARBUTHNOT *John Bull* III. ii. 10 This Usage tho' it stunted the Girl in her Growth, gave her a hardy Constitution. **1740** CHEYNE *Regimen* 68 To stunt the growth of young Animals,.. they need only be frequently rubbed over, with Brandy. **1842** J. WILSON *Chr. North* (1857) II. 19 Not only was his stature stunted, but his whole frame was delicate in the extreme. **1845** *Florist's Jrnl.* (1846) VI. 97 They require to be kept rather dry, and to be stunted in the pots. **1881** WHITEHEAD *Hops* 27 Stimulating the plants is apt to weaken them, and stunt their growth afterwards. **1896** *Allbutt's Syst. Med.* I. 466 Exercise increases growth, while over-exercise stunts it.

b. *transf.* and *fig.*

1659 F. OSBORN *Miscell. Ess.* etc. 75 Such as succeed in their dear-bought Experiences.. become stunted in their Knowledge. **1796** BURKE *Let. Noble Lord* 30 When by a cold penury, I blast the abilities of a nation, and stunt the growth of its active energies, the ill I may do is beyond all calculation. **1819** J. FOSTER *Contrib. Eclectic Rev.* (1844) I. 509 Their minds were cramped, stunted, and irritated by a hyper-calvinistic cast of doctrine. **1849** MACAULAY *Hist. Eng.* i. I. 48 During the last three centuries, to stunt the growth of the human mind has been her [*sc.* the Church of Rome's] chief object. **1867** PUSEY *Eleven Addr.* ix. (1908) 108 It is a graver thing, if a duty, impressed on us in our very earliest childhood,.. remained stunted to its then measure. **1876** MOZLEY *Univ. Serm.* xiii. 238 There is a barrenness in their minds which stunts all the truths which they take up. **1893** J. EDGAR *Hist. Early Scot. Educ.* xiv. 175 However hostile critics may talk, their system does not necessarily cramp or stunt native genius.

3. *intr.* To become arrested in growth. ? *Obs.*

1706 LONDON & WISE *Retir'd Gard.* 20 Nor do our fruits stunt, chap, and drop off as they do with them [in France]. **1707** MORTIMER *Husb.* 379 [Of coppice wood] What is bit by the Cattle, will else stunt for several Years before it will take to its growth. **1750** W. ELLIS *Mod. Husbandm.* III. ii. 50 in Britten *Old Country Words* s.v., [Lambs] stunting or dying by the operation [of castrating]. *Ibid.* V. i. 78 ibid., [Turnips will] burn, stunt, and spoil [if they grow too thick]. **1796** C. MARSHALL *Gardening* viii. (1813) 101 Old fruit trees may sometimes succeed with good management, but they are liable to stunt, and dwindle off.

4. To become sullen or sulky. *dial.*

1877–89 *N.W. Linc. Gloss.* s.v., Doänt saay noht; I'd let her stunt it oot if I was thoo. Master Robad, O, how he stunt. **1886** *S.W. Linc. Gloss.* s.v., I spoke to him but he stunted directly.

stunt (stʌnt), *v.*[2] *Sc.* **a.** *trans.* To stamp (the feet). **b.** *intr.* To walk with a heavy tread. Cf. STUMP *v.* 2, STAMP *v.* 2 e.

1804 J. AIKMAN *Poems* (1816) 233 His feet he [*sc.* a horse] on the road fair stunted. **1901** G. DOUGLAS *House with Gr. Shutters* 45, I come stunting out in a bleeze of wrath and slam the yett ahint me!

stunt (stʌnt), *v.*[3] [f. STUNT *sb.*[2]] **a.** *intr.* To perform stunts (in quots. with reference to aerobatics). **b.** *trans.* To use (an aeroplane) for the performance of stunts.

1917 'CONTACT' *Airman's Outings* p. xxiii, They could turn, climb, and stunt quicker than any two-seater. **1928** *Daily Mail* 9 Aug. 7/1 The aeroplane was apparently 'stunting' at a height of between 2,000 and 3,000 feet. **1928** *Daily Tel.* 18 Sept. 11/4 There is no reason why the autogiro should not be stunted. **1953** C. A. LINDBERGH *Spirit of St. Louis* II. vi. 421 DHs aren't built like Jennies... And you can't stunt 'em like a Jenny either—no rolls or loops. **1970** L. DEIGHTON *Bomber* iv. 64 When the Luftwaffe was officially born in 1935 Peter Redenbacher was stunting a Bücker Jungmann biplane above the heads of Hitler, Göring, the foreign Press and a deliriously happy German crowd.

Hence **'stunter, 'stuntist**, one who performs or organizes stunts; **'stunting** *vbl. sb.*[2] and *ppl. a.*[2]

1914 G. HAMEL *Flying* 212 It [*sc.* the Royal Flying Corps] talks shop.. and indulges in rude health and proper pride, discouraging 'stunting' and heroics. **1922** *Daily Mail* 2 Nov. 5 Some of the members of the Committee.. went on the Council as economy 'stunters'. **1923** *Glasgow Herald* 14 July 7 Close on five o'clock the 'stunting' planes came to earth. **1925** *Public Opinion* 31 July 107/3 When the political stuntists saw fit to mobilise. **1927** C. A. LINDBERGH *We* vi. 94 The De Havilands were not considered safe for hard stunting. **1928** *Observer* 18 Mar. 17/2 Two officers.. who are considered to be the best 'stunters' in the force. **1940** G. FRANKAU *Self-Portrait* xlvi. 285 The stunt merchant, for all his stunting, had a creed. **1970** R. BLAKE *Conservative Party* viii. 253 The Conservatives, in spite of having a real point, incurred the charge of 'stunting' when they used such expressions as 'Gauleiter Laski'. **1978** *Detroit Free Press* 16 Apr. (Cartoon Suppl.) 1/2 (Advt.), Boys' deluxe MX motocross style bike... Not for stunting or off-road use.

stunt, error for or variant of STINT *sb.*[1] 4.

1691 MRS. D'ANVERS *Academia* 34 Because they have their stunt of Victuals, And that I'me sure, but very little's.

stunt(e: see STOUND *sb.*[1], STINT *v.*

stunted ('stʌntɪd), *ppl. a.* [f. STUNT *v.*[1] + -ED[1].]

1. Checked in growth or development; of growth, checked, arrested. Hence, diminutive, dwarf.

1719 LONDON & WISE *Compl. Gard.* p. xi, It can never be pleasing to see a stunted Tree. **1727** POPE *Macer* 11 Like stunted hide-bound Trees. **1776** ADAM SMITH *W.N.* I. I. xi. 234 That stunted breed [of cattle] which was common all over Scotland. **1821** SCOTT *Kenilw.* ix, A queer, shambling, ill-made urchin, who, by his stunted growth, seemed about twelve or thirteen years old. **1826** JEFFERSON *Writ.* (1830) IV. 427 The long succession of years of stunted crops. **1833** *Q. Rev.* XLIX. 407 Precocity of intellect in a stunted frame, is the grand desideratum in a Newmarket nursery. **1868** DARWIN *Anim. & Pl.* I. iii. 78 These pigs on the Paramos are small and stunted. **1875** C. C. BLAKE *Zool.* 21 The innermost digit is often stunted or absent. **1890** *Hardwicke's Science-Gossip* XXVI. 141/1 The florets at apex opened first and the lower ones last.. which gave the flower a stunted appearance.

b. of immaterial things.

1658 F. OSBORN *Mem. Eliz. & James* Epist. A 3, Scholars, who think it a sufficient excuse in the justification of a stunted Knowledge, to maintain an impossibility of transcending the Abilities of former Ages. **1864** TENNYSON *Aylmer's F.* 357, I lived for years a stunted sunless life. **1911** W. W. FOWLER *Relig. Exper. Rom. People* xii. 287 The old State religion remained, but in stunted form, and with paralysed vitality.

2. Of a thing: Shortened; †worn down (*obs.*); also, disproportionately or abnormally short.

1716 GAY *Trivia* II. 91 When waggish boys the stunted beesom ply To rid the slabby pavement. *c* **1844** ROSSETTI *Bürger's Lenore* Note (MS.), I have retained the German version.. thinking it more suited to the metre than the lengthy English word 'Leonora,' and by far less unpleasing to the ear than the stunted and ugly abbreviation 'Leonor'. **1845** *Ecclesiologist* IV. 89 A stunted chancel is affixed. **1898** C. HYNE *Through Arctic Lapland* ii. 24 He mounted on the stem-head of his steamer a stunted heavy-breeched gun.

b. In the names of animals or plants, the individuals of which are diminutive in form.

1827 GRIFFITH tr. *Cuvier* V. 38 *Simia Jacchus Vulgaris* (the Stunted Monkey or Jacchus). **1848** JOHNS *Week at Lizard* 271 Stunted Ox-eye Daisy. **1889** MAIDEN *Usef. Pl. Australia* 397 *Casuarina distyla*.. 'Stunted She-oak'.

Hence **'stuntedly** *adv.*; **'stuntedness**.

1740 CHEYNE *Regimen* 66 The Stuntedness, Punyness and Feebleness, so conspicuous among the better Sort. **1864** SALA in *Daily Tel.* 15 Aug., The pure Indians.. in the southern portion of Mexico are as a rule of very low stature, even to stuntedness. **1907** *Edin. Rev.* Oct. 439 The living organism within at last ceased struggling to extend itself, and stuntedly and pathetically took the shape prescribed.

stunting ('stʌntɪŋ), *vbl. sb.*[1] [f. STUNT *v.*[1] + -ING[1].] The action of the verb.

1835 URE *Philos. Manuf.* 23 That cramping of the faculties,.. that stunting of the frame,.. cannot.. occur under the equable distribution of industry. **1897** *Allbutt's Syst. Med.* III. 134 The chief question is the degree of bony deformity or stunting of structure which will remain. **1911** *Daily News* 3 May 3 The man whose education has been years of 'herding' in gigantic classes.. often has suffered from intellectual stunting.

stunting *vbl. sb.*[2]: see STUNT *v.*[3]

stunting ('stʌntɪŋ), *ppl. a.*[1] [f. STUNT *v.*[1] + -ING[2].] That stunts.

1902 R. BAGOT *Donna Diana* xx. 246 The atmosphere of ecclesiastical Rome is heavy—stagnant—stunting to all intellectual growth. **1907** A. C. BENSON *Altar Fire* 176 It is this ethical prudence which is always.. pulling up the plant to see how it grows, which is the weakening and the stunting thing.

stunting *ppl. a.*[2]: see STUNT *v.*[3]

†**stuntise.** *Obs. rare*[−1]. [? error for **stutise*, a. OF. *estoutise*, f. *estout* STOUT *a.*] ? Arrogance, violence.

a **1327** *Pol. Songs* (1839) 334 Hii brewen strut and stuntise there as sholde be pes.

†**'stuntly,** *a. Obs. rare.* In 1–2 **stuntlic.** [f. STUNT *a.* + -LY[1].]

1. Stupid, foolish.

c **1000** ÆLFRIC *Hom.* I. 472 Iob.. ne syngode mid his muðe, ne nan ðing stuntlices onȝean God ne spræc. *c* **1175** *Lamb. Hom.* 109 Hwet is eure.. swa stuntlic swa is þet þe alde mon nule his mod to gode awendan.

2. ? = STUNT *a.* 3.

1583 MELBANCKE *Philotimus* U iij, Lycurgus, not one clad with the stuntliest courage of all other, and far beyond Aereithous in strength.., slue him tho by sleight.

†**'stuntly,** *adv. Obs. rare.* In 1 **stuntlice.** [f. STUNT *a.* + -LY[2].]

1. Foolishly. *OE.* only.

c **1000** ÆLFRIC *Saints' Lives* xvii. 132 Sume men.. bringað heora lac to eorðfæstum stane.. And nellað under-standan hu stuntlice hi doð.

2. ? Arrogantly.

1581 A. HALL *Iliad* x. 174 Their state recite and eke their race, and doe not stuntly talke, Still with a lowe and courteous grace let there the speeches walke.

'stuntness. [f. STUNT *a.* + -NESS.]

†**1.** Foolishness, stupidity. *Obs.*

c **1000** ÆLFRIC *Saints' Lives* i. 228 þysses middan-eardes wysdom is stuntnis [L. *stultitia*] ætforan gode. *Ibid.* xvii. 23 Se rihtwisa soðlice ne þearf him ondrædan.. ȝif he him sylfum styrð fram eallum stunt-nyssum. *c* **1175** *Lamb. Hom.* 117 Fela stuntnesse beoð, þer nan steore ne bið.

2. Abrupt brevity.

1871 J. EARLE *Philol. Eng. Tongue* x. 497 Short sentences are prevalent in our language, as long ones are in German. In all things we incline to curtness and stuntness.

stunty ('stʌntɪ), *a.* [f. STUNT *a.* + -Y.]

1. Stunted in growth, short in stature.

1828 H. ANGELO *Remin.* I. 287 Two stock-broker's clerks, the one six feet two in height; the other, a stunty Jew, performed the parts of Pierre and Jaffier. **1868** *Cleveland Gloss., Stunty*, 1. Short in growth or stature; of Ling, or any other shrubby plant: of a person also, who is short in stature.

2. Sulky, obstinate; curt, blunt. *dial.*

a **1825** [see STUNT *a.* 3]. **1861** AGNES STRICKLAND *Old Friends* Ser. II. 69 Their hoss.. had kicked her own fetlock, and then she turned both lame and stunty (sulky stubborn).

3. Having the character of a stunt, extravagant, 'gimmicky'.

1981 *Daily Tel.* 27 Jan. 13/4 Cardin's minis do not look stunty or contrived.

Hence **'stuntiness**, the condition of being stunted.

Latham quotes from 'Cheyne *Philosophical Conjectures*' a passage identical with quot. 1740 s.v. STUNTEDNESS.

a **1878** SIR G. SCOTT *Lect. Archit.* (1879) II. 179 While walls and pillars might avail themselves to the full of this upward striving, it was hard that the arch should be condemned to unalterable stuntiness.

stuny, stunys: see STONY *v.*, STONISH *v.*

†**stuorie.** *Obs. rare*[−1]. [ad. It. *stuora* (in the orig.), repr. L. *storea*.] A mat.

1555 EDEN *Decades* (Arb.) 257 They founde the kyng in his pallaice sittynge vppon a floure or stuorie made of the leaues of date trees.

‖**stupa**[1] ('stju:pə). Also **stuppa.** [L. *stūpa*, more correctly *stuppa*, tow = late Gr. στύππη.]

1. = STUPE *sb.*[1] Only in Dicts.

1693 tr. *Blancard's Phys. Dict.* (ed. 2), *Stupea, seu stupa*, a piece of linnen dipt in a liquor, and applied to the part affected. *Ibid., Stuppa* or *Stupa*, the same with *Stupea*. **1706** PHILLIPS (ed. Kersey), *Stupa* or *Stupea*, the course part of Flax, Tow, Hards, Ockam to calk Ships with; also a Stupe us'd by Surgeons. **1875** KNIGHT *Dict. Mech., Stupa*, tow used as a pledget, compress, or as a wad in fomentations.

2. *Bot.* (See quots.) Only in Dicts.

1856 HENSLOW *Dict. Bot. Terms, Stupa*, a tuft or mass of hair or fine filament matted together. **1866** *Treas. Bot., Stupa*, tow; a tuft of long hairs. **1900** B. D. JACKSON *Gloss. Bot. Terms, Stupa* or *Stuppa*.

‖**stupa**[2] ('stu:pə). [Skr. *stūpa*.] A Buddhist monument; = TOPE *sb.*[5]

1876 FERGUSSON *Ind. & East. Archit.* I. iii. 57 The difficulty was met by assigning a portion [of the remains of Buddha] to each of the contending parties, who are said to have erected stupas to contain them. **1882** *Edin. Rev.* Oct. 356 Monasteries in ruins, and stupas in a dilapidated condition.

stupe (stju:p), *sb.*[1] Also 5 **stuppe**, 6 **stoupe**, 7 **stoup, stuphe**, 7–8 **stuph.** [ad. L. *stūpa, stuppa*:

see STUPA[1]. Cf. F. *étoupe* tow.] A piece of tow, flannel, or other soft substance, wrung out of hot liquor and medicated, for fomenting a wound or ailing part.

c **1400** *Lanfranc's Cirurg.* 53 Wiþinne þe wounde leie þe ȝelke of an ey, wiþ oile of rosis, with stupis, or ellis wiþ lint. *a* **1425** tr. *Arderne's Treat. Fistula*, etc. 87 Stuppez of lyne or coton. **1543** TRAHERON *Vigo's Chirurg.* 94 b, Applye it with stoupes moysted in water. **1612** WOODALL *Surg. Mate* Wks. (1653) 96 A large hot stupe wet in a good lixivium, and wrung out. **1634** T. JOHNSON *Parey's Chirurg.* XI. xii. (1678) 286 These stoups I stayed and held to the part with double cloaths. **1684** tr. *Bonet's Merc. Compit.* III. 76, I rolled up his head upon a Stuphe, dry wrung from the fomentation. **1743** tr. *Heister's Surg.* I. xv. (1768) 110 Foment the Eye with Stuphs wrung out of the Decoctions which we prescribed above. **1896** *Allbutt's Syst. Med.* I. 435 Fomentations and stupes are conveniently made of a length of flannel doubled.

stupe (stjuːp), *sb.*[2] (and *a.*) *colloq.* and *dial.* [Shortened f. STUPID.] A stupid person, a fool. Also as *adj.*

1762 BICKERSTAFFE *Love in Village* II. ii, Was there ever such a poor stupe! **1813** *Sketches of Character* (ed. 2) I. 11 How could they think of bringing that stupe of a Miss Newton? **1840** LADY C. BURY *Hist. Flirt* v, Of all the silent stupes, commend me to Captain Thelwal. **1876** BLACKMORE *Cripps* xxxv, 'What a stupe I must be,' she continued to herself, 'to imagine that the boy could be in love!' **1967** 'T. WELLS' *Dead by Light of Moon* (1968) i. 15 His assistant, a big stupe called Jersey Eng. **1967** E. MCGIRR *Here lies my Wife* v. 151 He carries on..all the time. He's stupe. **1977** *Time* 25 Apr. 46/3 She tells him that true love has washed away her sins and the pure and simple stupe embraces her.

stupe (stjuːp), *v.* Also 8 **stoop**. [f. STUPE *sb.*[1]]

† **1.** *trans.* To moisten (lint, tow, etc.) in some hot liquid so as to form a stupe. *Obs. rare*$^{-1}$.

c **1540** *Pract. Cyrurgyons* A i, Roulettes, stupes, or plagettes made of lynte,..stuped or dypped in hote Oyles.

2. To foment with a stupe or stupes.

1670 NARBOROUGH *Jrnl.* in *Acc. Sev. Late Voy.* I. (1694) 52 They use bathing and stuping those places. **1735** *Phil. Trans.* XL. 426 The Abdomen was stuped twice a Day with an emollient Fomentation. **1747** WESLEY *Prim. Physick* (1762) 100 Stoop it [a sprain] with one spoonful of Brandy, two of Vinegar and four of Water. **1843** in R. J. Graves *Syst. Clin. Med.* xxix. 390, I..stuped the part with warm water and laudanum. **1892** *Cassell's Fam. Mag.* Mar. 211/1 [She] developed a tiresome face-ache, which no amount of stuping with poppy-heads could bring into visiting shape.

stupe, obs. form of STOOP *v.*[1]

stupefacient (stjuːpɪˈfeɪʃənt), *a.* and *sb. Med.* Also 7 **stupi-**. [ad. L. *stupefacient-em*, pres. pple. of *stupefacĕre*: see STUPEFY *v.*]

A. *adj.* Stupefying, producing stupor. ? *Obs.*

1669 ROWLAND *Schroder's Chym. Disp.* I. xxx. 40 Stupefacient, Narcotick. **1675** GREW *Anat. Plants, Lect.* VI. i. 280 Stupifacient [is a kind of Taste] as in the Root of Black Hellebore. **1748** HARTLEY *Observ. Man* I. ii. §2. 155 Very nauseous and stupefacient Tastes may perhaps arise from violent and irregular Vibrations. **1849** in CRAIG; **1850** in OGILVIE; and in later Dicts.

B. *sb.* A medicine producing stupor. *rare*$^{-0}$.

1855 in OGILVIE Suppl. (and in later Dicts.). **1898** in *Syd. Soc. Lex.*

† **stupefact**, *v. Obs. rare*$^{-1}$. [f. L. *stupefact-*, ppl. stem of *stupefacĕre*.] *trans.* = STUPEFY.

1598 FLORIO, *Alloppiare*,..to stupefact ones sences.

† **stupefact**, *pa. pple. Obs.* Chiefly *Sc.* Also 6 **stupifact, stupe-, stupifak**. [ad. L. *stupefactus*, pa. pple. of *stupefacĕre*: see STUPEFY *v.*] Stupefied.

1513 DOUGLAS *Æneis* v. xi. 87 Of Troiane wemen the myndis worth agast, And all thair hartis sum deill stupifak. **1549** *Compl. Scot.* 6 Bot ȝit i vas lang stupefact ande timide, for falt of ane peremptoir conclusione. *a* **1578** LINDESAY (Pitscottie) *Chron. Scot.* (S.T.S.) I. 116 The king hearand this was stupefact in his mynd. **1590** BARROUGH *Meth. Physick* III. xi. (1596) 118 The senses be astonied and stupefact by cooling things.

stupefaction (stjuːpɪˈfækʃən). Also 7 **stupi-**. [a. F. *stupéfaction* (15–16th c.), or ad. mod.L. *stupefactiōn-em*: see STUPEFY *v.* and -FACTION.]

1. The action of stupefying or state of being stupefied; numbness, torpor, or insensibility, of body or mind.

1543 TRAHERON *Vigo's Chirurg.* II. xvi. 26 b, The extremitees of theyr bodyes..were reduced to suche colde, and congelation or stupefaction. **1677** tr. *Groeneveldt's Treat. Stone* 32 A stupefaction in the Thigh and Leg. **1756** BURKE *Subl. & B.* Introd., Wks. I. 103 Tobacco is the delight of Dutch-men, as it diffuses a torpor and pleasing stupefaction. **1865** DICKENS *Mut. Fr.* II. i, Half the pupils dropped asleep, or fell into a state of waking stupefaction. **1911** RIKER *Henry Fox Ld. Holland* viii. II. 98 The activity of Fox..seemed the result of long pent-up energy that had suffered stupefaction under an arbitrary over-lord.

¶ **b.** Used for STUPEFACIENT *sb.*

1651 WITTIE tr. *Primrose's Pop. Err.* 327 Stupefactions [L. *stupefacientia*] being applyed outwardly, doe [etc.].

2. Overwhelming consternation or astonishment.

1597 A. M. tr. *Guillemeau's Fr. Chirurg.* 52 b/2 This foresayed stupefactione and feare. **1634** SIR T. HERBERT *Trav.* 189 Which ceremony is so hideously acted that it raises no small stupefaction in the beholders. **1831** CARLYLE *Sartor Res.* III. viii, The deceptions, and wonder-hiding stupefactions, which Space practises on us. **1865** DICKENS *Mut. Fr.* III. vi, What was the stupefaction of the friendly movers when this object at last emerging proved to be a much-dilapidated dark lantern!

stupefactive (ˈstjuːpɪfæktɪv), *a.* and *sb.* ? *Obs.* Also 7 **stupi-**. [a. F. *stupéfactif*, *-ive* adj. (16th c.), ad. med.L. *stupefactīv-us*, f. L. *stupefact-*, ppl. stem of *stupefacĕre*: see STUPEFY *v.* and -IVE.]

A. *adj.* **1.** *Med.* Having the property of producing stupor or insensibility.

1527 ANDREW *Brunswyke's Distyll. Waters* c j b, The water of Nenufara floure..is half poyson or venym thrughe his great coldenes or stupefactyfe. **1543** TRAHERON *Vigo's Chirurg.* Interpret. Words, Stupefactiue: That, that hathe strength to astoynie, and take awaye felynge. **1626** BACON *Sylva* §98 Opium hath a Stupefactiue Part, and a Heating Part. **1649** E. REYNOLDS *Hosea* iii. 14 Some affections and motions of the heart..are of a cold stupefactive, and constringent nature. **1669** FLAVEL *Husb. Spiritual.* I. vi. 57 Opium and such-like stupifactive ingredients. **1789** W. BUCHAN *Dom. Med.* xlvi. (1790) 473 Those [*sc.* poisons] of the vegetable kind are generally of a narcotic or stupefactive quality. **1797** *London Compl. Art Cookery, Brewing* 219 Cocculus Indicus..is poisonous, stupefactive, and unlawful.

2. *gen.* Stupefying, astounding. *rare.*

1689 T. PLUNKET *Char. Good Commander* 45 What dire Catastrophe's impending are? What stupefactive things we daily hear?

B. *sb.* A stupefactive medicine.

1562 BULLEYN *Dial. Sorenes & Chir.* 33 b, Stuperfactiues or dedde things, as Opium. **1626** BACON *Sylva* §74 This we see in the Operation of Opium, and Stupefactiues, vpon the Spirits of liuing Creatures. **1668** E. REYNOLDS *Serm.* 24 Thereby teaching us..to refuse any Anodynes or Stupefactives which might take away the sense of sinne from us.

Hence **stupeˈfactiveness**. *rare*$^{-0}$.

1727 BAILEY, vol. II.

stupefiˈcation. *rare*$^{-1}$. In 7 **stupi-**. [f. STUPEFY *v.*: see -FICATION.] = STUPEFACTION.

1650 JOHN HALL *Paradoxes* 35 What other is this..but selfe stupification.

stupefied (ˈstjuːpɪfaɪd), *ppl. a.* [f. STUPEFY *v.* + -ED[1].] In senses of the verb.

1639 J. TAYLOR (Water P.) *Crabtree Lect.* 12 Goe, thou art a stupified Asse. **1664** POWER *Exp. Philos.* I. 70 Thirdly, in the return of the Spirits into the stupefied Leg, we plainly perceive by the prickling, what a slow motion the Spirits have. **1673** BUNYAN *Diff. Judgm. Water-Baptism* 44, I will not suppose you so much stupified. **1790** BURKE *Refl. Rev. France* Wks. 1792 III. 100 Several English were the stupified and indignant spectators of that triumph. **1825** MACAULAY *Milton* Ess. (1897) 27 To break the ties which bound a stupefied people to the seat of enchantment. **1908** C. BIGG *Orig. Christianity* xxi. (1909) 285 Herodian..speaks of Severus with an almost stupefied admiration.

Hence **ˈstupefiedness**.

c **1647** BOYLE *Disc. Swearing* Wks. 1772 VI. 6 We know that insensibility of pain may..proceed from the deadness and stupifiedness of the part.

stupefier (ˈstjuːpɪfaɪə(r)). [f. STUPEFY *v.* + -ER[1].] Something that stupefies; a medicine that produces stupor.

1684 tr. *Bonet's Merc. Compit.* VIII. 280 The violence of the Pain sometimes forces us of necessity to apply Stupefiers. **1735** BERKELEY *Querist* §348 Wks. 1871 III. 384 Whether the natural phlegm of this island needs any additional stupifier? **1831** J. DAVIES *Manual Mat. Med.* 43 Narcotics, soporifics or stupefiers.

stupefy (ˈstjuːpɪfaɪ), *v.* Also 7 **stupefie**, 7–8 **stupifie**, 6–9 **stupify**. [a. F. *stupéfi-er* (16th c.), ad. L. *stupefacĕre* to make stupid or senseless, f. *stupēre* to be struck senseless, be amazed: see -FY.

The spelling with *i* (cf. *liquify*) was common until the latter half of the 19th c. 'This word should..be spelled *stupefy*; but the authorities are against it' (Johnson).]

1. *trans.* To make stupid or torpid; to deprive of apprehension, feeling, or sensibility; to benumb, deaden.

? *a* **1600** in *Lyly's Wks.* (1902) III. 497 Twas not Tobacco stupifyed yͤ braine. **1611** SHAKS. *Cymb.* I. v. 37 Those [drugs] she ha's, Will stupifie and dull the Sence a-while. **1652** *Hermeticall Banquet* 69 This by the narcoticall Sulphur of the Opium, stupefied the Nerve. **1709** T. ROBINSON *Vindic. Mosaick Syst.* 56 That any one..should be so stupified by the Prevalency of his Lusts, as to deny the Being of that God, whose [etc.]. **1732** ARBUTHNOT *Rules of Diet* (1736) 365 Opiate and anodyne Substances which stupify and relax the Fibres. **1806–7** J. BERESFORD *Miseries Hum. Life* (1826) VI. xxx, Your fingers being..stupefied by the cold. **1849** MACAULAY *Hist. Eng.* v. I. 666 The prisoner, stupified by illness, was unable..to understand what passed. **1889** MRS. OLIPHANT *Poor Gentl.* xlv, His anxiety stupefied instead of quickening his senses.

fig. **1874** SPURGEON *Treas. David* lxxxi. IV. 26 No dulness should ever stupify our psalmody.

b. *absol.*

1691 HARTCLIFFE *Virtues* 81 As nothing doth restore us more to our selves, when we faint and are weary, than Sleep soberly taken, so nothing doth more stupifie, than its Excess. **1707** FLOYER *Physic. Pulse-Watch* 81 If the Bath be so long continu'd as to stupifie. *a* **1848** W. A. BUTLER *Serm.* ix. (1849) 149 Satan,..who deceives that he may destroy, stupifies that he may deceive.

2. To stun with amazement, fear, or the like; to astound. [So L.]

1596 SPENSER *F.Q.* v. iii. 17 With great amazement they were stupefide. **1622** MALYNES *Anc. Law-Merch.* 337 The apprehension of the continuance of intollerable Vsurie in England, is able to stupifie a mans senses. **1779** *Mirror* No. 11. ¶ 13 He sat, stupified with shame and remorse. **1796** MME. D'ARBLAY *Camilla* VI. iii. III. 175 'If she is not in the rooms to-night,' said Sir Sedley, 'I shall be stupified to petrifaction.' **1845** DARWIN *Voy. Nat.* viii. (1879) 171 The mind is stupified in thinking over the long, absolutely necessary, lapse of years. **1909** *Engl. Rev.* Feb. 602 All these people seem stupefied by the immensity of the calamity which has befallen them.

† **3.** To deprive (a material substance) of mobility. *Obs. rare*$^{-1}$.

a **1626** BACON *Physiol. Rem.* Baconiana (1679) 100 This stupifieth the Quick-silver that it runneth no more. *Ibid.* 122 When it..is not fluent, but stupified.

4. *intr.* To become stupid or torpid; to grow dull or insensible. Now *rare.*

a **1631** DONNE *Let. to Sir H. G.* v, Poems (1633) 365, I which live in the Country without stupifying, am not in darknesse, but in shadow. **1803** MARY CHARLTON *Wife & Mistress* III. 47 Do not go and stupify with such an old *illuminée* as the Dowager Lady Melville. **1844** SYD. SMITH in Lady Holland *Mem.* (1855) II. 523, I always fatten and stupefy on such diet; I want to lose flesh and gain understanding.

Hence **ˈstupefying** *vbl. sb.* and *ppl. a.*

1611 COTGR., *Noix vomique*..is of a poisonous, deadly, and stupifying qualitie. **1637** B. JONSON *Sad Sheph.* II. viii, The dead-numming Night-shade! The stupifying Hemlock! **1673** PENN *Chr. Quaker* xx. 585 The Stupifyings of Sin. **1731** MILLER *Gard. Dict.* s.v. *Wine*, The Effects they have upon the human Body are rather stupifying than inebriating. *a* **1768** SECKER *Serm.* (1770) IV. 27 The benumbing and stupefying of so important a Principle of their Nature. **1863** MARY HOWITT tr. *F. Bremer's Greece* II. xvi. 155 A cave, out of which..a stupefying exhalation ascended. **1916** *Blackw. Mag.* May 607/1 The views obtained are almost stupefying in their majesty and grandeur.

stupen, stuppin, dial. (Kent) ff. STEWPAN.

1617 in W. F. Shaw *Mem. Eastry* (1870) 227 Fowr brass potts three brass stupens. **1736** J. LEWIS *Hist. Isle Tenet* (ed. 2) 39 *Stuppin*, a Stew-pan or Skillet.

stupend (stjʊˈpɛnd), *a. Obs.* in serious use. [ad. L. *stupend-us*: see STUPENDOUS. Cf. *horrend*, *tremend*.] Stupendous.

1621 BURTON *Anat. Mel.* I. i. II. vii. 35 In time of sleepe this faculty is free, & many times conceaues strange, stupend, absurd shapes. *Ibid.* II. ii. II. 314 The Romanes had their publike Bathes, very sumptuous and stupend. **1676** *Doctrine of Devils* 25 That stupend miracle of Christ's Incarnation. **1702** C. MATHER *Magn. Chr.* III. II. xix. 122 The stupend Variety of Human Faces. **1864** LOWELL *Fireside Trav.* 127 A lobster..of experience so stupend, His claws were blunted at the end, Turning life's iron pages o'er.

Hence † **stuˈpendly** *adv.*

1621 BURTON *Anat. Mel.* III. iv. I. i. 717 The Brittaines are so stupendly superstitious in their ceremonies, that [etc.].

stupend (stjʊˈpɛnd), *v. rare.* [Back-formation from STUPENDOUS *a.*] *trans.* To amaze, dumbfound. (G. B. Shaw's word.)

1904 G. B. SHAW *Let.* 6 Dec. (1972) II. 470 You will be stupended at all meanness in this obvious & cheap retort. **1927** —— *Let.* 2 Feb. in *To a Young Actress* (1960) 113 The discovery that you actually wanted me to shew that daub to Charlotte has perfectly stupended me.

stupendiˈosity. *rare*$^{-1}$. [f. next, in imitation of *religiosity*, etc.: see -ITY.] Stupendousness.

1830 H. ANGELO *Remin.* I. 174 Gresse..could not patiently endure the least observations upon the stupendiosity of his figure.

† **stuˈpendious**, *a. Obs.* [irreg. f. L. *stupend-us* (see STUPENDOUS), after adjs. in *-ious*; cf. *tremendious*, vulgar form of *tremendous*.] Stupendous.

Our numerous instances show that this was the accepted form until the latter part of the 17th c., when the correct *stupendous* began to be used.

1547 BOORDE *Introd. Knowl.* 133 Yet in Ierland is stupendyous thynges; for there is neyther Pyes nor venymus wormes. **1591** HARINGTON *Orl. Fur.* Apol. Poetrie ¶ ij b, As witnes the huge Theaters, and Amphitheaters, monuments of stupendious charge. **1611** CORYAT *Crudities* 284 A most stupendious summe of money. **1667** MILTON *P.L.* x. 351 At sight Of that stupendious Bridge his joy encreas'd. **1712** STEELE *Spect.* No. 472 ¶ 7 That stupendious Machine [the Eye]. **1768** BOSWELL *Corsica* i. (ed. 2) 29 Craggy cliffs of so stupendious a height, that [etc.]. *a* **1800** PEGGE *Anecd. Eng. Lang.* (1814) 55 On the other hand, they [*sc.* Londoners] say *stupendious*, for *stupendous*.

Hence † **stuˈpendiously** *adv.*, **stuˈpendiousness**.

1630 PRYNNE *Anti-Armin.* 198 Can any elected persons heart be found so stupendiously obdurate, as to withstand this omnipotent working. **1656** EARL MONM. tr. *Boccalini's Advts. fr. Parnass.* I. v. 9 The stupendiousness of the Venetian liberty. **1662** H. MORE *Enthus. Tri.* 14 There may be such a due dash of Sanguine in the Melancholy, that the Complexion may prove stupendiously [*ed.* 1712 stupendously] enravishing. **1676** *Doctrine of Devils* 54 This is..an Axiomatical Truth among the Doctors of Demonology, That a Devil or Witch can, for stupendiousness of the work do as much as ever Christ did. **1711** in *10th Rep. Hist. MSS. Comm.* App. v. 113 The Jewes ..remained so stupendiously incredulous, that they putt him to death for an imposter.

stupendous (stjʊˈpɛndəs), *a.* [f. L. *stupend-us* 'that is to be wondered at, amazing', gerundive of *stupēre* to be struck senseless, be amazed at: see -OUS.] Such as to cause stupor or astonishment; amazing, astounding; marvellous, prodigious; amazingly large or great (now freq. in trivial use).

1666 PEPYS *Diary* 21 May, It is stupendous to see how favourably..my Lord Ashly carries himself to Mr. Yeabsly.

1669 GALE *Crt. Gentiles* I. I. iii. 22 The strength of these Anakims was stupendous. **1697** DRYDEN *Æneis* IX. 705 There stood a Tow'r..of stupendous height. **1732** POPE *Ess. Man* I. 267 All are but parts of one stupendous whole. **1798** SOPHIA LEE *Canterb. T., Young Lady's T.* II. 412 They reached the foot of that stupendous natural barrier, the Alps. **1863** COWDEN CLARKE *Shaks. Char.* x. 261 The man who thinks to outwit three women, who are aware of his purpose, must indeed be a stupendous ass. **1863** MISS BRADDON *Aurora Floyd* iii, The young officer laughed aloud at the stupendous joke. **1892** E. DOWSON *Let.* in *N. & Q.* (1962) Mar. 102/1, I have become the victim of the most stupendous cold which has ever occurred to me, & fear that I shall spend tomorrow in bed. **1914** *Eng. Hist. Rev.* Jan. 135 He is apt to attribute to his opponents stupendous oversights and elementary misunderstandings. **1939** *Airman's Gazette* Dec., All aircraft off duty being allowed to ..view the stupendous, side-splitting entertainment. **1942** E. PAUL *Narrow St.* ii. 15 The *marc* was undiluted—stupendous, in fact. **1959** C. L. WRENN *Word & Symbol* (1967) 35 That stupendous scholar, Max Förster.

Hence **stu'pendously** *adv.*, **stu'pendousness**.

1712 Stupendously [see STUPENDIOUSLY, quot. 1662]. **1727** BAILEY vol. II, *Stupendousness*, Astonishingness. **1742** *Lond. & Country Brew.* I. (ed. 4) 37, I have known some of the little Victualling Brewers, so stupendously ignorant, that [etc.]. **1743** J. ELLIS *Knowl. Div. Things* 219 Those very Works, which, from their Stupendousness, should have taught them the Greatness of the former. **1814** J. W. CROKER in *C. Papers* (1884) 7 Oct., Be..sure to make it [a column] stupendously high. **1848** DICKENS *Dombey* i, Her nose, stupendously aquiline. **1890** *Voice* (N.Y.) 17 July, This generation so familiar with stupendousness of all kinds.

†stu'penduous, *a. Obs.* [irreg. f. L. *stupend-us* (see STUPENDOUS), after adjs. in *-uous*: cf. *tremenduous*.] Stupendous.

1736 *Mrs. Manley's Secret Mem.* III. 17 Horatio, named *immortal* from his stupenduous [*ed.* 1720 III. 15 stupendous] Conquests in Iberia. **1760–72** H. BROOKE *Fool of Qual.* (1792) III. 241 Travellers..are apt to enquire by whom the stupenduous pile was erected. **1794** MORSE *Amer. Geog.* (1796) II. 12 A torrent, precipitating itself from stupenduous rocks.

stupent ('stju:pənt), *a. rare.* [ad. L. *stupent-em* pres. pple. of *stupēre* to be stupefied or astounded.] That is in a state of stupor or amazement.

1843 CARLYLE *Past & Pr.* III. viii, We stand speechless, stupent, and know not what to say! **1851** —— in Froude *C.'s Life in Lond.* (1884) II. xix. 68 Poor Simeon..sat stupent in the whirlpool of heterodox hail. **1912** G. B. SHAW *Pygmalion* II. (1916) 120 *Higgins* [*stupent*] Well!!! (*Recovering his breath with a gasp*) What do you expect me to say to you?

stupeous ('stju:pɪəs), *a. Zool.* and *Bot.* Also **stuppeous** ('stʌpɪəs). [f. L. *stūpe-us*, *stuppe-us* made or consisting of tow, f. *stūpa*, *stuppa*: see STUPE *sb.*[1] and -OUS.] Having, or covered with, matted or tufted hairs or filaments.

1826 KIRBY & SP. *Entomol.* IV. xlvi. 275 *Stupeous*, covered with long loose scales resembling tow. Ex. The *Palpi* of *Lepidoptera*. **1871** W. A. LEIGHTON *Lichen-flora* 104 Medulla stuppeous. **1900** B. D. JACKSON *Gloss. Bot. Terms*, *Stupeous*, woolly.

†stupex. *Obs.* App. a jocular improvement on STUPE *sb.*[2]

1853 SURTEES *Sponge's Sp. Tour* (1893) 338 'The little stupexes!' exclaimed Miss Glitters. **1864** MISS YONGE *Trial* I. 81 The light of nature would show that to any one but a stupex.

stuph(e, variant ff. STUFE *Obs.*, STUPE *sb.*[1]

stupid ('stju:pɪd), *a.* and *sb.* [ad. L. *stupid-us*, f. *stup-ēre* to be stunned or benumbed. Cf. F. *stupide* (Rabelais), Sp., Pg. *estúpido*, It. *stupido*.]

A. *adj.*

1. Having one's faculties deadened or dulled; in a state of stupor, stupefied, stunned; esp. *hyperbolically*, stunned with surprise, grief, etc. *Obs.* exc. *arch.* (*poet.*)

Very common in Dryden.

1611 SHAKS. *Wint. T.* IV. iv. 409 Is not your Father growne incapeable Of reasonable affayres? Is he not stupid With Age, and altring Rheumes? Can he speake? heare? Know man, from man? **1656** BLOUNT *Glossogr.*, *Stupid*, dismaid, abashed, astonied, amazed, senceless. **1675** *Machiavelli's Prince* xix. Wks. (1883) 123 These remained..stupid and astonished. **1697** DRYDEN *Æneis* VII. 1104 Men, Boys, and Women stupid with Surprise, Where ere she passes, fix their wond'ring Eyes. **1725** POPE *Odyss.* XVIII. 114 Down drop'd he stupid from the stunning wound. **1737** in H. T. Waghorn *Cricket Scores* (1899) 19 The latter..receiving..so smart a blow by the ball that he was knocked down and lay stupid for a long time. **1859** TENNYSON *Geraint & Enid* 753 And Enid could not say one tender word, She felt so blunt and stupid at the heart.

†b. Belonging to or characterized by stupor or insensibility. *Obs.*

1607 CHAPMAN *Bussy d' Ambois* v. 64 Reuiue those stupid thoughts, and sit not thus, Gathering the horrors of your seruants slaughter,..Into an idle fancie. **1697** DRYDEN *Virg. Georg.* III. 781 His Eyes are settled in a stupid peace. **1702** POPE *Sappho* 128 No sigh to rise, no tear had pow'r to flow, Fix'd in a stupid lethargy of woe. **1818** KEATS *Endymion* I. 678 My sweet dream Fell into nothing—into stupid sleep.

†c. Of a part of the body: Paralysed. *Obs.*

1638 A. READ *Chirurg.* xi. 82 Touch the stupid parts [of a paralytic person] with quick nettles.

d. *Path.* ? *Obs.*

1822–9 GOOD *Study Med.* (ed. 3) IV. 519 *Cephalæa gravans.* Stupid head-ache. Pain obtuse; with a sense of heaviness extending over the whole head.

†e. Emotionally or morally dull or insensible; apathetic, indifferent. Const. *to* [cf. F. *stupide à*].

1605 BACON *Adv. Learn.* II. xxii. §17 As for pleasure, wee haue likewise determined, that the minde oughte not to bee reduced to stupide, but to retayne pleasure. **1641** J. JACKSON *True Evang. T.* II. 148 The Stoicks..patience..was..onely a stupid senselessnesse, and wretched carelessnesse. **1653** H. MORE *Antid. Ath.* II. vi. §5 He is as stupid to these things [the beauties of nature] as the basest of Beasts. **1713** *Guardian* (1756) I. No. 19. 86 It was a cause of great sorrow and melancholy to me..to see a crowd in the habits of the gentry of England stupid to the noblest sentiments we have. **1758** S. HAYWARD *Serm.* xvii. 530 Oh stupid creatures that are not raised with the descriptions of his person! *a* **1770** JORTIN *Serm.* (1787) II. x. 199 Vice begets the dread of punishment, unless it be constantly attended with unbelief, and with a stupid carelessness about futurity.

†2. As the characteristic of inanimate things: Destitute of sensation, consciousness, thought, or feeling. *Obs.*

1626 BACON *Sylva* §98 Tangible Parts in Bodies are Stupide things; And the Spirits doe (in effect) all. **1642** H. MORE *Song of Soul* II. iii. III. 60 Yet if the Earth stand stupid and unmov'd, This needs must come to passe. **1660** BOYLE *New. Exp. Phys.-Mech.* xxxiii. 251 And as for the Care of the Publique Good of the Universe ascrib'd to dead and stupid Bodies; wee shall only demand, why [etc.]. *a* **1664** KATH. PHILIPS *Poems* (1667) 40, *In Mem. of F.P.* 14 Alas! in vain, in vain on thee I rave; There is no pity in the stupid Grave. *a* **1694** TILLOTSON *Serm.* (1743) IX. 4110 The stone is stupid, and is not in the least conscious of any of those impressions, does not perceive what is done to it. *a* **1718** PRIOR *2nd Hymn of Callimachus* 141 Euphrates..copious runs, but Muddy; And carries forward with his stupid Force Polluting Dirt. **1722** WOLLASTON *Relig. Nat.* v. 74 Matter is incapable of acting, passive only, and stupid. **1744** BERKELEY *Siris* §190 Were it not for this [fire], the whole wou'd be one great stupid inanimate mass. But this active element is supposed to be every where.

3. Wanting in or slow of mental perception; lacking ordinary activity of mind; slow-witted, dull.

1541 R. COPLAND *Galyen's Terap.* 2 B iij b, For the fyrste speake ouer lyghtly and to imprudently,..and the other are all togyther stupydes, sturdy, & lytygious. **1616** BULLOKAR *Eng. Expos.*, *Stupid*, blockish, without wit: dull. **1649** MILTON *Tenure of Kings* 8 No man who knows ought, can be so stupid to deny that all men naturally were borne free. **1667** —— *P.L.* XII. 116 O that men..should be so stupid grown While yet the Patriark liv'd, who scap'd the Flood, As to forsake the living God. **1692** DRYDEN *St. Euremont's Ess.* 290 But I esteem the Faith of a stupid Peasant, more than all the Lessons of Socrates. **1712** ADDISON *Spect.* No. 291 ¶8 A Man, who cannot write with Wit on a proper Subject, is dull and stupid. **1778** MISS BURNEY *Evelina* (1791) II. xxvii. 161 'Why is Miss Anville so grave?' 'Not grave, my Lord,' said I, 'only stupid.' **1819** SHELLEY *Peter Bell* VII. iii, His lordship stands and racks his Stupid brains. **1829** HOGG *Sheph. Cal.* Wks. (1865) 368/2 'What a stupid idiot I was!' exclaimed Wat. **1838** LYTTON *Alice* II. iii, How stupid in Caroline not to show it to you. **1842** LOVER *Handy Andy* xliii, She felt the pique which every pretty woman experiences who fancies her favours disregarded, and thought Andy the stupidest lout she ever came across. **1855** MACAULAY *Hist. Eng.* xv. III. 560 Anne, who, when in good humour, was meekly stupid, and, when in bad humour, was sulkily stupid. **1865** CARLYLE *Fredk. Gt.* XXI. viii. (1872) X. 160 He knew how to listen..which no stupid man was ever capable of. **1875** JOWETT *Plato* (ed. 2) I. 29, I remain as stupid as ever; for still I fail to comprehend. **1879** HARLAN *Eyesight* viii. 108 Children with astigmatism often appear stupid.

absol. **1692** R. L'ESTRANGE *Fables* xviii. 19 But Good Council is cast away, upon the Arrogant, the Self-conceited, or the stupid.

b. Of attributes, actions, ideas, etc.: Characterized by or indicating stupidity or dullness of comprehension.

1621 T. WILLIAMSON tr. *Goulart's Wise Vieillard* 131 Christians willingly lay downe their neckes vnder the light yoke..not with a stupid, or hastie mad braine-sicke, or fond toying ioy. **1687** A. LOVELL tr. *Thevenot's Trav.* I. 145, I went to that Burying-place on the Holy Friday of the Greeks ..that I might see what Ground they had for this stupid Belief. **1707** PATRICK *Disc. Prayer* II. xviii. 197 Let us not.. persist in such a stupid error. **1711** STEELE *Spect.* No. 2 ¶3 It is a stupid and barbarous Way to extend Dominion by Arms. *a* **1770** JORTIN *Serm.* (1771) IV. ix. 184 Great reason have we to be thankful that we are not educated in such stupid and inhuman principles. **1819** SHELLEY *Peter Bell* VI. xxxii, 'Twould make George Colman melancholy To have heard him, like a male Molly, Chanting those stupid staves. **1871** C. GIBBON *Lack of Gold* ii, This cursed frenzy makes me say and think the stupidest things. **1891** E. PEACOCK *N. Brendon* I. 122 Our stupid passion for snugness.

†c. Of the lower animals: Irrational. Also of an individual animal, its propensities, etc.: Lacking intelligence or animation, senseless, dull. *Obs.*

a **1680** BUTLER *Rem.* (1759) I. 203 And trains him up with Rudiments more false, Than Nature does her stupid Animals. **1774** GOLDSM. *Nat. Hist.* (1776) IV. 328 [The badger] is a solitary stupid animal. **1815** STEPHENS in *Shaw's Gen. Zool.* IX. I. 19 The birds of this genus [*Bucco*]..are a solitary stupid race. **1867** MORRIS *Jason* VIII. 64 A monstrous cage, Of iron bars, shut in the stupid rage Of those two beasts.

4. Void of interest, tiresome, boring, dull.

1778 MISS BURNEY *Evelina* (1791) I. xxxiii. 179 Of all the stupid places ever I see, that Howard Grove is the worst; there's never no getting nothing one wants. **1832** LYTTON *Eugene A.* I. iii, 'I am sorry, dear Ellinor, my awkwardness should occasion you so stupid an evening', answered Madeline. **1845** MISS G. JEWSBURY *Let. to Mrs. Carlyle* (1892) 161, I..was getting quite fat till within the last few days, when I caught cold on the stupid Rhine. **1854** WHYTE MELVILLE *Gen. Bounce* xviii, For the first time in her experience of a London season, Blanche begins to think it a 'stupid ball.' **1862** MISS BRADDON *Lady Audley* ii, We were quartered at a stupid sea-port town. **1884** M. CREIGHTON *Let.* 22 May, in L. Creighton *Life & Lett.* (1904) I. 269 If my letter is very stupid, forgive me. **1901** W. R. H. TROWBRIDGE *Lett. her Mother to Eliz.* xviii. 89 We went once to the Empire, but it was awfully stupid, and I never want to go again.

5. Obstinate, stubborn. *north. dial.*

1788 W. H. MARSHALL *Yorksh.* II. 357 *Stupid*; obstinate (the common epithet). **1829** BROCKETT *N.C. Gloss* (ed. 2), *Stupid*, obstinate, though possessing good talents. **1866** MRS. LYNN LINTON *Lizzie Lorton* xii, 'So Miss Lizzie, my dear, divn't be stupid'—she meant obstinate—'but let yersel be guided by them as knaws best.' **1877** *Holderness Gloss.*, *Stupid*, obstinate. 'As stupid as a mule.' **1893** J. K. SNOWDEN *Tales Yorksh. Wolds* 170 Kit Harpur were main stupid ower it.

6. *Comb.*, as ***stupid-looking*** adj.; adverbial with another adj., as ***stupid-honest***, ***-sure*** (nonce-wds.); **stupid-head**, a blockhead.

1838 DICKENS *O. Twist* xxxi, Think it's the same boy, *Stupid-head? **1877** TENNYSON *Harold* III. i, Be thou not *stupid-honest, brother Gurth! **1815** J. CAMPBELL *Trav. S. Africa* 502 How such a *stupid looking animal [as the turtle] finds out this speck of land [Ascension island]..is truly wonderful. **1877** TENNYSON *Harold* IV. iii, The people *stupid-sure Sleep like their swine.

B. *sb.* A stupid person. *colloq.*

1712 STEELE *Spect.* No. 468 ¶6 Thou art no longer to drudge in raising the Mirth of Stupids..for thy Maintenance. **1819** *Metropolis* I. 222 His loudest applauders were..stupids, like Sir G. W. who scarcely could speak a word of French. **1880** MRS. PARR *Adam & Eve* II. 17 Ain't there no place else for us to go to, eh, stupid? **1885** 'MRS. ALEXANDER' *Valerie's Fate* v, You do not know what a thoughtless, heartless stupid I have been.

†stu'pidious, *a. Obs.* [f. STUPID + -IOUS. Cf. STUPIDOUS.] Stupid, grossly unintelligent, dull. Hence **†stu'pidiously** *adv.*

1600 G. ABBOT *Jonah* 109 The Saracens and Turkes, who ..may not so much as dispute of any point of their religion, and so do beleeve in Mahomet, most grossly and stupidiously. **1615** J. TAYLOR (Water P.) *Taylor's Rev.* Wks. (1630) II. 144/2 Can you, O can your senses be stupidious And see your selues abused thus perfidious!

stupidish ('stju:pɪdɪʃ), *a.* [f. STUPID *a.* + -ISH.] Somewhat stupid.

1806 LOUISA GURNEY in A. J. C. Hare *Gurneys of Earlham* (1895) I. 153 On Monday we had a stupidish dinner at the Fellowes'. **1813** JANE AUSTEN *Lett.* (1884) II. 178 It was stupidish; Fanny did her part very well, but there was a lack of talk altogether. **1864** CARLYLE *Fredk. Gt.* XVI. xiii. IV. 463 Much can be done in that way with stupidish populations.

stupidi'tarian. *nonce-wd.* [f. STUPIDITY, after *humanitarian* etc.] One whose ruling principle is stupidity.

1846 WHIPPLE *Lit. & Life* (1851) 73 A heavy-headed stupiditarian in official station, veiling the sheerest incompetency in a mysterious sublimity of carriage!

stupidity (stju:'pɪdɪtɪ). [ad. L. *stupiditās*, f. *stupid-us*: see STUPID and -ITY. Cf. F. *stupidité*, It. *stupidità*.]

†1. Numbness, incapacity for sensation. *Obs.*

stupidity of the teeth = late L. *stupor dentium*: see STUPOR I.

1607 TOPSELL *Four-f. Beasts* 83 It is also good against the inflammation of the eares, the stupidity and dulnesse of the teeth. **1653** R. SANDERS *Physiogn.* 186 A dull stupidity of the head and sences. **1661** R. LOVELL *Hist. Anim. & Min.* 201 The signes of their wounds are great paine,..blacknesse, and stupidity of the part. **1702** FLOYER *Cold Bathing* I. (1709) 139 The Nature and Cure of a Torpor or Stupidity of the Limbs. **1737** BRACKEN *Farriery Impr.* (1757) II. 273 Those Things which take away Pain by causing a Stupidity.

†2. The condition of being deprived of the use of the faculties; a state of stupor. *Obs.*

1604 R. CAWDREY *Table Alph.*, *Stupiditie*, dulnesse: astonishment. **1608** WILLET *Hexapla Exod.* 267 Pharaoh was taken with such stupiditie that..hee had no power. **1615** CHAPMAN *Odyss.* VI. 252 As now thee To view (O Virgin) a stupiditie Past admiration strikes me. **1621** G. SANDYS *Ovid's Met.* V. (1626) 102 Stone-like stood Ceres at this heauy newes;..When griefe had quickned her stupiditie, Shee tooke her Chariot, and ascends the skie. **1622** WOTTON in L. P. Smith *Life & Lett.* (1907) II. 236 One of my gondoliers..was suddenly strucken with a silent stupidity, his feet going from him. **1627** DRAYTON *Agincourt* 39 The dreadfull bellowing..sounded like the dreadfull doome, And them with such stupidity benummes, As though [etc.]. **1684** tr. *Bonet's Merc. Compit.* VI. 169 Causing onely a gentle Sleep, in no wise a Stupidity. **1684** W. RUSSELL *Phys. Treatise* 117, I..found her drowsie, tho the Cold and Stupidity were some-what less. **1806** *Med. Jrnl.* XV. 381 The pain in her head became so acute, as to produce at times, actions of violence, which rendered confinement necessary, and the intervals were marked by stupidity. **1831** *Examiner* 764/2 'Locus' was a cant word to describe the act of putting a man in a state of stupidity.

†3. Incapacity for emotion; lack of feeling or interest, apathy, indifference. *Obs.*

1568 G. SKEYNE *Pest* (Bannatyne Club) 15 The cause quhairby few ar preseruit..is maist euident..the negligence & Stupiditie of mankynd, contemptioun of medicine, [etc.]. **1597** HOOKER *Eccl. Pol.* v. lxvii. §3 Shall I wish that men would more giue themselues to meditate with silence what we haue by the Sacrament, & lesse to dispute of the manner how? If any man suppose that this were too great stupiditie and dulnes, let vs see whether [etc.]. **1668** CLARENDON *Contempl. Ps.* Tracts (1727) 688 The stupidity of the heart alone is the cause of all desperate incogitance. *a* **1672** WILKINS *Nat. Relig.* 387 It supposes them to have..such a stupidity upon their consciences, as makes them past feeling. **1701** G. STANHOPE *Medit. St. Aug.* xl. (1720) 105 Awaken my stupidity, quicken my deadness. **1719** DE FOE *Crusoe* I. (Globe) 89 A certain Stupidity of Soul, without Desire of Good, or Conscience of Evil, had entirely overwhelm'd me. **1724** BOLINGBROKE *Let.* 12 Sept., in *Swift's Lett.* (1766) II. 37 It is neither sickness, nor journies, nor ill humours, nor age, nor vexation, nor stupidity, which has hindered me from answering sooner your letter. **1748** HARTLEY *Observ. Man* II. iv. §4. 412 If indeed a Man's Despair should make him..harden himself in a careless Stupidity with respect to his future Condition.

†**b.** Insensibility to pain or sorrow; blameable absence of resentment under injury or insult. *Obs.*

1627 DONNE *Serm.* xliv. (1640) 443 Without this [belief in the Trinity], all morall vertues are but diseases;..Active valour is but a fury, whatsoever we do, and passive valour is but a stupidity, whatsoever we suffer. **1661** COWLEY *Cromwell* Ess., etc. (1906) 362 The continuance of those oppressions upon the people, which will at last tire out their patience, though it be great even to stupidity. *a* **1673** STILLINGFL. *Serm.* vi. (1673) 110 Stupidity then under sufferings can be no part of the excellency of a man; which in its greatest height is in the Beings the most beneath him.

4. Dullness or slowness of apprehension; gross want of intelligence.

1541 R. COPLAND *Galyen's Terap.* 2 C ij b, Nowe we must esteme the stupydyte or audacyte of the man. I say the stupidite yf he thynke to saye well and the boldnes yf he fele hym selfe culpable to saye nothynge. **1598** B. JONSON *Ev. Man in Hum.* III. v, I forgive Mr. Stephen, for he is stupiditie it selfe! **1620** T. GRANGER *Div. Logike* 110 Stupiditie a naturall impotencie to vnderstand easily. **1675** in *Verney Mem.* (1907) II. 292 God watt his stupiditie will find it a hard Taske to learn one [*sc.* a trade]. **1690** LOCKE *Hum. Und.* II. x. §8. 67 It moves slowly, and retrieves not the Ideas, that it has, and are laid up in store, quick enough to serve the Mind upon occasions. This, if it be to a great degree, is Stupidity. **1759** GOLDSM. *Pres. St. Pol. Learn.* iv, But let the Germans have their due: if they are dull, no nation alive..better understands all the decorums of stupidity. **1774** H. WALPOLE *Let. to C'tess Upper Ossory* 14 June, Mr. Anstey..has published the most complete piece of stupidity I ever read. It is a satire on a parson who [etc.]. **1831** CARLYLE *Sartor Res.* II. vii, With Stupidity and sound Digestion man may front much. **1880** 'MARK TWAIN' *Tramp Abr.* viii. 58 'Have you engaged a hearse?' 'Bless my stupidity, I never thought of it!' **1896** *Law Times* CI. 516/1 On the average, stupidity in the Church gets better paid than brains at the Bar. **1913** WOODROW WILSON *New Freedom* iii. 70 In public affairs stupidity is more dangerous than knavery.

b. A stupid idea, action, etc.

1633 G. HERBERT *Temple, Ch. Militant* 153 Their hearts Are given over..To such Mahometan stupidities, As the old heathen would deem prodigies. **1707** *Curios. in Husb. & Gard.* 245 There..is an infinity of learned Men, who would think themselves Hereticks in Philosophy, if they..thought to search after Truth elsewhere... This is so great a Stupidity, that [etc.]. **1851** *N. Brit. Rev.* XV. 467 The dull stupidities and senseless flippancies of Roman architecture. **1868** E. EDWARDS *Ralegh* I. xxiii. 525 To..enlightened persons..such themes..are of course, mere obsolete stupidities. **1870** DASENT *Ann. Eventful Life* III. iv. 74 Of all our escapades and stupidities on the journey I decline to dwell. **1874** MICKLETHWAITE *Mod. Par. Churches* 115 One of the stock stupidities of modern times is belief in a *vista*.

5. Obstinacy. *dial.*

1886 *S.W. Linc. Gloss.*, *Stupidity*, obstinacy, not dullness. They understood it well enough; it was stupidity, and nowt else.

stupidly ('stjuːpɪdlɪ), *adv.* [f. STUPID *a.* + -LY[2].] In a stupid manner.

1. In a condition of stupor. Now *rare.*

1661 GLANVILL *Van. Dogm.* vii. 62 They that feel it not, are not less sick, but stupidly so. **1899** *Allbutt's Syst. Med.* VIII. 149 When ailing he sleeps long and stupidly.

†**b.** In consequence of stupefaction. *Obs.*

1667 MILTON *P.L.* IX. 465 That space the Evil One abstracted stood From his own evil, and for the time remained Stupidly good, of enmity disarmed.

†**2.** Apathetically, indifferently. *Obs.*

1647 CLARENDON *Hist. Reb.* II. §127 Their wariness and wisdom could not be great enough to preserve them, if they did not stupidly look on without seeming to understand what they could in no degree control or prevent.

3. With gross lack of intelligence; foolishly; in a manner indicative of stupidity.

c **1611** CHAPMAN *Iliad* XIV. 199 Comment., How stupidly soeuer all his interpreters would haue Hector (being strooke into a trembling, and almost dead) turne about like a whirle-wind. **1699** BENTLEY *Phalaris* 250 Would a person of Learning..be..so stupidly negligent as not to examin the Stone-Cutter's Work. **1700** DRYDEN *Fables* Ded. C 1, There was engraven on it, Plans of Cities, and Maps of Countries, which Ajax could not comprehend, but look'd on them as stupidly as his Fellow-Beast the Lion. **1719** DE FOE *Crusoe* II. (Globe) 445 They were all stupidly ignorant as to Matters of Religion. **1743** WESLEY *Jrnl.* 27 June, I preach'd at Awkborough, on the Trent-side to a stupidly-attentive congregation. **1819** SHELLEY *Peter Bell* VII. xxi, And every neighbouring cottager Stupidly yawned upon the other. **1851** W. WHEWELL *Let.* 26 Jan. in Mrs. Stair Douglas *Life* (1881) 414 We English are as stupidly servile in looking with reverence on all German philosophy, as we are stupidly conceited about our social institutions and manners. **1865** LECKY in Eliz. Lecky *Mem.* i. (1909) 39 The only printed review I have seen is an exceedingly stupidly written one. **1865** E. C. CLAYTON *Cruel Fortune* I. 259 It stared at her, stupidly, its round, chubby face streaked with tears and dirt. **1885** *Manch. Exam.* 25 Mar. 5/1 Nothing could be more stupidly false than such an impression.

4. Obstinately. *dial.*

1884 *Methodist Mag.* 52 Moffat stuck stupidly (this last word, in Lancashire, means resolute persistence in either a wise or foolish saying, or course) that he would go and hear Roby.

stupidness ('stjuːpɪdnɪs). Now *rare.* [f. STUPID *a.* + -NESS.] The quality of being stupid (in various senses of the adj.): = STUPIDITY.

a **1628** LD. BROOKE *Treat. Hum. Learning* lxiii, Therefore ..to refine Her stupidnesse, as well as ostentation, Let vs set straight that Industrie againe. **1645** MILTON *Tetrach.* 17 What a stupidnes then is it, that in Mariage,..wee should deject our selvs to such a sluggish and underfoot Philosophy, as to esteem the validity of Mariage meerly by the flesh. **1656** J. SMITH *Pract. Physick* 110 Stupidnesse in the Legs and the whole Body, that they can scarse feel the prick of a needle. **1689** SHERLOCK *Death* iii. §6 (1731) 139 We may be cut off by a sudden Stroke, or seized with Distraction or Stupidness. **1725** *Bradley's Family Dict.* s.v. *Lethargy*, A Person is threaten'd with this Distemper, when ..he grows sluggish, and percieves a Stupidness upon himself and is always inclin'd to Sleepiness.

†'**stupidous,** *a.* *Obs.* *rare*[−1]. [f. STUPID *a.* + -OUS.] = STUPID.

1597 A. M. tr. *Guillemeau's Fr. Chirurg.* f iii, We shewe our selves stupidouse and involuntary to helpe, the one the other.

†'**stupnet.** *dial. Obs.* In 7 stuppnett, ? stuppenet, stufnet. [? dim. of STUPEN: see -ET[1].] A saucepan.

1600 in W. F. Shaw *Mem. Eastry* (1870) 226 Two chafing dishes fower stuppuetts [? *read* stuppnetts] five brass candlesticks [etc.]. **1649** in *Archæologia Cantiana* XVI. 205 It' rec'd for a Brass Stugpenet [? *read* stuppenet] 00 02 00. **1674** RAY *S. & E. Country Wds.* 76 *Stufnet* [correctly placed, alphabetically, but erroneously printed *stusnet* (long f)]: a posnet or skillet. Suss. [Correctly printed in 1691.]

stupor ('stjuːpə(r); as scientific Latin ‖'stjuːpɔː(r)). Also 5, 7 stupour. [a. L. *stupor*, f. *stup-ēre*: see STUPID. Cf. F. *stupeur*, Sp., Pg. *estupor*, It. *stupore.*]

1. A state of insensibility or lethargy; spec. in *Path.*, a disorder characterized by great diminution or entire suspension of sensibility.

stupor of the teeth: tr. med.L. *stupor dentium*, the rendering, in the ancient translation of Galen, of Gr. αἱμωδία, 'a scorbutic affection of the gums' (L. & Sc.).

1398 TREVISA *Barth. De P.R.* VII. vii. (1495) 227 Stupor is a lettynge and stonyenge of lymmes and crokynge of the vtter partyes of the body for colde so that it semyth that the lymmes shrynke and slepe. **1656** tr. *Hobbes' Elem. Philos.* (1839) 395 For what is stupor but that which the Greeks call ἀναισθησία, that is, a cessation from the sense of other things? **1666** G. HARVEY *Morbus Angl.* x. (1672) 28 Various Diseases, as Catarrhs, stupors, [etc.]. **1678** GALE *Crt. Gentiles* IV. III. iii. 91 By the spirit of deep sleep, must be understood such a stupor of spirit as leaves men without al sense. **1746** R. JAMES *Moffet's Health Improv.* Introd. 12 Acid Eructations, which have in some Cases been so sharp as to induce a Stupor of the Teeth. **1752** *Phil. Trans.* XLVII. 413 There appear'd some signs of stupor from the medicine. **1822–9** GOOD *Study Med.* (ed. 3) IV. 500 The pricking pain like that of pins, or of a limb awaking from stupor. **1843** R. J. GRAVES *Syst. Clin. Med.* v. 71 An expergefaciant..was employed to rouse a patient from the lethargic stupor brought on by a large dose of opium. *a* **1849** POE *Tales, Oval Portrait* Wks. 1874 I. 281 The first flashing of the candles upon that canvas had seemed to dissipate the dreamy stupor which was stealing over my senses. *a* **1859** MACAULAY *Hist. Eng.* xxv. V. 289 James sank into a stupor which indicated the near approach of death. **1899** CONAN DOYLE *Duet* viii. 111 She had drunk herself into the stupor in which she had been found.

b. = DEMENTIA 1.

anergic stupor, a form of dementia in which the patient is quiet, listless, and non-resistant. *delusional stupor*, stuporous insanity or acute dementia. (Dorland *Med. Dict.* 1913.)

1899 *Allbutt's Syst. Med.* VIII. 297 Stupor, both in its melancholic and anergic varieties, is found much more frequently during the age of adolescence than in any other period of life.

2. A state of mental stupefaction; apathy or torpor of mind (now only, torpor or prostration of mind due to sorrow, painful surprise, or the like).

a **1672** WILKINS *Nat. Relig.* 267 That stupor and benummedness of spirit, whereby men are made unapprehensive of their afflictions. **1784** COWPER *Task* IV. 283 Laugh ye, who boast your more mercurial pow'rs, That never feel a stupor, know no pause, Nor need one. **1786** BURNS *Lament* x, Oh! scenes in strong remembrance set!.. Scenes, if in stupor I forget, Again I feel, again I burn! **1837** CARLYLE *Fr. Rev.* I. II. iii, Our Church stands..like a dumb ox..with dumb stupor, expecting its further doom. **1838** DICKENS *Nich. Nick.* xv, The back parlour sat with her mouth wide open, staring vacantly at the collector, in a stupor of dismay. **1841** ELPHINSTONE *Hist. Ind.* XII. iii. II. 633 The inhabitants of Delhi remained in a sort of stupor. They had not yet recovered the terror of the past. **1850** GROTE *Greece* II. lx. VII. 457 A downcast stupor and sense of abasement possessed every man. **1863** MRS. OLIPHANT *Salem Chapel* xxii, It was very different from the stupor of agony.

transf. **1772** BURKE *Let. to W. Dowdeswell* (1844) I. 346, I do not suppose that there was ever anything like this stupor in any period of our history. **1855** DISRAELI in G. E. Buckle *Life* (1916) IV. i. 23 There has been a great stupor over affairs since we parted,..but there are now indications of events. **1879** MORLEY *Burke* iv. 62 The war with the American colonies was preceded by an interval of stupor.

b. Admiring wonder. Also (after med.L. *stupor mundi*), the object of wonder, 'the marvel *of* (the world, etc.).

1482 *Monk of Evesham* (Arb.) 26 Yet beyng holde in a certeyn stupour and wondyr of mynde of suche thinges that he had seyne. **1599** *Broughton's Lett.* viii. 26 You Cynosura and Lucifer of nations, the stupor and admiration of the world. **1619** PURCHAS *Microcosmus* lxxiii. 727 What shall we say of Him,..the great Stupor and Wonder of Diuines? **1633** 'H. A.' (H. Hawkins) *Parthenia Sacra* 237 That Cæsar of Cæsars in captiuing..Caligula the Roman Monark, to the stupour and amazement of the world. **1706** PHILLIPS (ed. Kersey), *Stupor*,..Astonishment, Amazement;..Wonder, Surprise.

3. Stupidity, dullness of comprehension. *rare.*

1845 CARLYLE *Cromwell* (1871) III. 126 One stupid Annotator..says [etc.]; which is evidently downright stupor and falsehood.

4. *Comb.*

1823 SCORESBY *Jrnl.* 376 A dripping stupor-struck sailor, clinging by the weather-raill, comes aft at the moment. **1833** LAMB *Elia, Product. Mod. Art*, Bowed, bent down, so would they have remained, stupor-fixed, with no thought of struggling with that inevitable judgment.

†'**stuporific,** *a.* *Obs.* *rare*[−1]. [f. L. *stupōr-em* STUPOR + -IFIC.] That causes stupor.

1771 J. GILES *Poems* 169 Then she presents a stuporific draught.

‖**stupor mundi** ('stuːpɔː 'mʊndiː, 'stjuːpɔː 'mʌndaɪ). L. phr.: the marvel of the world; an object of admiring bewilderment and wonder. Cf. STUPOR 2 b.

The phrase was originally used by the thirteenth-century historian Matthew Paris to describe the Emperor Frederick II of Germany.

1879 *Encycl. Brit.* IX. 732/2 The general contemporary opinion regarding Frederick II is expressed in the words *stupor mundi*:.. wonder and perplexity are the predominant sentiments which..[the contemplation of his career] even yet awakens. **1946** R. LOWELL *Lord Weary's Castle* 5 Over the drum-beat of St. Stephen's choir I hear him, *Stupor Mundi.* **1980** J. A. T. ROBINSON *Roots of Radical* ii. 22 What is easier is to preen ourselves on our 'comprehensiveness' without realising that it is in every sense a *stupor mundi*, an object of incredulous disbelief to the world and even our fellow Christians.

stuporose ('stjuːpərəʊs), *a.* [ad. med.L. *stupōrōsus* (Diefenb.) f. L. *stupōr-em*: see STUPOR and -OSE.] = STUPOROUS *a.*

188. BUCK *Med. Handbook* V. 53 (*Cent. Dict.* Suppl.). **1899** *Allbutt's Syst. Med.* VIII. 297 The other 20 per cent. of the cases were mostly melancholic in character, seldom being deeply suicidal, but often tending to be stuporose. *Ibid.* 317 Chloral hydrate, if taken in very large doses, may cause stuporose dementia. **1901** *Brit. Med. Jrnl.* 29 June 1604 The amount of free hydrochloric acid was high when they were in a torpid and stuporose state.

stuporous ('stjuːpərəs), *a.* [ad. med.L. *stūpōrōsus*: see prec. and -OUS.] Affected with or characterized by stupor.

1892 E. C. SPITZKA *Insanity* II. v. 158 (Funk) Stuporous insanity consists in the simple impairment or suspension of the mental energies, unmarked by any emotional or other perversion. **1897** *Allbutt's Syst. Med.* III. 357 The stuporous form of melancholia, occurring in young adults. **1899** *Ibid.* VIII. 353 The patient is less responsive to questions and appears to be more profoundly stuporous.

stupose ('stjuːpəʊs), *a.* *Bot.* [ad. med.L. *stūpōsus, stuppōsus* (Diefenb.), f. L. *stūpa, stuppa* tow: see -OSE.] (See quots.)

1835 LINDLEY *Introd. Bot.* I. ii. 125 In Anthericum [the filament is] bearded or stupose. **1849** BALFOUR *Man. Bot.* §60 Bearded, or stupose,..when hairs occur in small tufts. **1900** B. D. JACKSON *Gloss. Bot. Terms*, *Stupose*, tow-like, with tufts of long hairs.

stuppenet, variant of STUPNET.

stuppeous: see STUPEOUS *a.*

stuppin: see STUPEN.

†**stupple.** *Obs.* *rare*[−1]. [Prob. related in some way to STEP *sb.*[1] and *v.*; cf. STOPEL.] ? A row of stepping-stones.

1611 CORYAT *Crudities* 89 [Vercellis] hath many faire streets through which diuers riuers doe runne, with many stupples to passe ouer from one side of the street to the other as in Sarisbury.

stuppnett, variant of STUPNET.

†'**stuprate,** *v.* *Obs.* Pa. pple. 6 *Sc.* stuprat. [f. L. *stuprāt-* ppl. stem of *stuprāre*, f. *stuprum*: see STUPRE and -ATE[3].] *trans.* To violate (a woman).

a **1548** HALL *Chron.*, *Rich. III*, 56 Richarde..hath.. compased all the meanes and waies y[t] he coulde inuent how to stuprate and carnally know his awne nece vnder the pretence of a cloked matrimony. *a* **1560** ROLLAND *Crt. Venus* III. 582 Sichem..Had hir stuprat. **1624** HEYWOOD *Gunaik.* III. 143 Sextus had stuprated the faire Lucretia. **1647** LILLY *Chr. Astrol.* xlix. 318 There may be just suspition..the Mother was stuprated.

Hence †'**stuprated** *ppl. a.*

1727 BAILEY vol. II, *Stuprated* [*stupratus*, L.] ravished.

†**stu'pration.** *Obs.* [a. OF. *stupration* or ad. L. *stuprātiōn-em* noun of action f. *stuprāre*: see STUPRATE *v.*] Violation (of a woman).

1533 BELLENDEN *Livy* III. xv. (S.T.S.) II. 2 The stupratioun and deforcement of lucres. **1535** STEWART *Cron. Scot.* (Rolls) II. 121 Stupr[at]ion to him wes sic plesour. **1646** SIR T. BROWNE *Pseud. Ep.* v. xxi. 270 Incest, adultery, or stupration. **1656** BLOUNT *Glossogr.*

† **stupre**, *sb. Obs. rare.* [a. OF. *stupre* (revived in 18th c.), ad. L. *stuprum.*] Defilement or violation (of a woman).

1382 WYCLIF *Gen.* xxxiv. 13 The sones of Jacob.. waxynge cruel for the stupre of the sister. *Ibid.* 27. **1563** BECON *Demands Script.* Wks. III. 457 Stupre, inceste, fornicacyon, and lyke abhominacyons.

† **stupre**, *v. Obs. rare*⁻¹. [a. OF. *stupre-r*, ad. L. *stuprāre*: see STUPRATE *v.*] *trans.* = STUPRATE *v.*

a **1548** HALL *Chron., Hen. VIII*, 172b, Thei violated Virgins, and stupred matrones.

† **'stuprous**, *a. Obs. rare*⁻¹. [ad. L. *stuprōsus*, f. *stuprum*: see STUPRE *sb.* and -OUS.] 'Corrupt, naught, given to adultery or whoredom, whoreish' (Blount *Glossogr.* 1656).

1603 FLORIO *Montaigne* II. xxxiii. 418 [Her father] seeing himselfe engaged in so stuprous a necessity [Fr. *en si villaine necessité*], resolved vpon an haughtie enterprize.

stupulose ('stjuːpjʊləʊs), *a. Ent.* [= mod.L. *stūpulōsus* (Kirby), f. **stūpula* dim. of L. *stūpa*, *stuppa*: cf. STUPOSE.] (See quot.)

1826 KIRBY & SP. *Entomol.* IV. xlvi. 276 *Stupulose*... Covered with coarse decumbent hairs. **1848** MAUNDER *Treas. Nat. Hist.* 807.

† **stur.** *Obs. rare.* Also 6 **sture**. [? subst. use of STOUR *a.* 7.] A hard variety of apple. Only in comb. ***stur-apple, -tree.***

1483 *Cath. Angl.* 370/2 A Sturtre, *Duracenus.* **1500** *Ortus Vocab.* (W. de W.) M ij, *Durascenus*, a sture tree. *Durascenum*, a sture appell.

stur, obs. form of STIR, STOUR, STURE².

† **sturb**, *v. Obs.* Also 4–5 **storb, stourb**, 5 **sturbe, stourbe**. [Aphetic var. of DISTURB *v.*] *trans.* To disturb, trouble, upset.

a **1225** *Ancr. R.* 428 Al so efter þe ancre cumplie uort midmorwen ne don no þing, ne ne siggen, hware þuruh hire silence muwe beon i-sturbed. **1382** WYCLIF *Gen.* xlii. 28 And thei stonyed al aboute and sturbed, seiden togideres, What forsothe is this that God hath doon to vs? *a* **1400–50** *Wars Alex.* 513 Þan was ser Philip of þat fare ferly mekill sturbid. *c* **1400** *Rule St. Benet* (1902) 34 Sho ne sal make noise for to sturbe the othir. *c* **1425** *Eng. Conq. Ireland* xlix. 124 (Dubl. MS.) Throgh that thynge, al the contrey forth ther-aftyr worth so I-storbet, that [etc.]. *a* **1450** MYRC *Par. Pr.* 686 We accursen al them that broken the pece of holy chirch or sturben hit. *Ibid.* 1459 Hast þou I-storbet prest or clerk þat were bysy in goddes werk? *a* **1450** in *Eng. Gilds* (1870) 448 And þat no brother presume to take vp-on him.. to lette, stourbe, ne geynseye, þat ellecciouN.

Hence † **'sturbing** *vbl. sb.*

a **1225** *Ancr. R.* 154 Heo fluwen monne sturbinge, & wenden bi ham one. *c* **1250** *Meidan Maregrete* 48 Wo þe hider sende, to maken stourbing. **13..** *Guy Warw.* 5751 (Auchinleck MS.) Gij werd him fast in þat sturbing.

† **'sturbance.** *Obs. rare.* In 5 **sturbans**. = DISTURBANCE.

c **1450** *Mirk's Festial* 185 Herod.. schapute.. how Ion myght be don to deth wythout sturbans of þe pepyll.

† **'sturblance.** *Obs. rare.* In 5 **sturbelans**. Aphetic form of DISTURBLANCE (cf. STROUBLANCE).

1435 MISYN *Fire of Love* I. xxiii. 50 And in [in]warldly rest, all sturbelans put bak, swetely to byde.

† **'sturble**, *v. Obs.* Also 5 **sturbyl, sturbel**. [Aphetic var. of DISTURBLE *v.* Cf. STROUBLE *v.*] *trans.* To disturb, trouble.

1303 R. BRUNNE *Handl. Synne* 4713 So was he sturbled with þe mynstral, þat he hadde no grace to sey with-alle His graces ryght deuoutely. *c* **1330** —— *Chron. Wace* (Rolls) 4764 When þe kyng þys chaunce herd seye, þe feste was sturbled & aweye. **1382** WYCLIF *Ezek.* xxvi. 18 And ylis in the see shulen be sturblid [1388 disturblid]. **1435** MISYN *Fire of Love* 97 Oftyms also odyr noys happyns þat gaynes & swetnes of lufars sturbyls. *c* **1440** *Promp. Parv.* 481/2 Sturbelyn, or turbelyn, *conturbo, turbo, perturbo.*

Hence † **'sturbling** *vbl. sb.* Also † **'sturbler**.

13.. *St. Marg.* 223 in Horstm. *Altengl. Leg.* (1881) 231 Who þe hider sent to make me sturbling. **1382** WYCLIF *Ezek.* xxi. 15 In alle the ȝatis of hem Y ȝaue togidre sturblynge [1388 disturbling] of swerd [Vulg. *conturbationem gladii*]. —— *Acts* xix. 23 Therfore ther was maad in that day a sturbling [1388 troubling, Vulg. *turbatio*] not leest, of the wey of the Lord. *c* **1440** *Promp. Parv.* 481/2 Sturbelare, or turbelare (or stroblare, sturblar or trowblar) *turbator, turbatrix. Ibid.*, Sturbelynge, or turbelynge, [sturblinge or troublynge] *turbacio, perturbacio.*

sturdied ('stɜːdɪd), *a.* [f. STURDY *sb.* + -ED².] Of sheep or cattle: Afflicted with 'sturdy'.

1807 *Prize Ess. & Trans. Highl. Soc.* III. 402, I catched every sturdied sheep that I could lay my hands on. **1822** SCOTT *Nigel* vi, I would as soon set out, with hound and horn, to hunt a sturdied sheep. **1844** H. STEPHENS *Bk. Farm* III. 877 The complaint may be cured, though it is seldom attempted, the sturdied hogg being killed whenever it is seen to be affected.

sturdily ('stɜːdɪlɪ), *adv.* Forms: see STURDY *a.*; also 4–6 **sturdely**. [f. STURDY *a.* + -LY².] In a sturdy manner; †with reckless daring (*obs.*); †ruthlessly, cruelly, violently (*obs.*); †surlily, rudely, harshly, mutinously, rebelliously (*obs.*); obstinately, unyieldingly, resolutely.

c **1374** CHAUCER *Compl. Mars.* 82 Til him fel a drede, Through Phebus, that was comen hastely Within the paleys-yates sturdely. **1375** BARBOUR *Bruce* II. 363 Thai.. Swappyt owt swerdis sturdyly. *c* **1440** *Partonope* 6154 The wind.. blew so sturdely. *c* **1470** HENRY *Wallace* II. 42 Full sturdely he could befor him stand. **1538** ELYOT *Dict.*, *Toruè*, sturdyly in looke. **1544** in *Sel. Cases Crt. Requests* (Selden Soc.) 107 The whiche to doo the said complaynaunte.. obstynatly and sturdyly then & there refusyd. **1549** CHEKE *Hurt Sedit.* (1569) Hij b, What say ye to the number of vagabonds and loytring beggers, which.. will.. stande sturdely in Cities, and begge boldly at euery dore. *a* **1674** CLARENDON *Hist. Reb.* x. §68 The Scots now begun again to talk sturdily. **1674** PRIDEAUX *Lett.* (Camden) 13, I assure you they dispute the case most sturdyly. **1810** SCOTT *Lady of Lake* IV. xxv, It was a stag, a stag of ten, Bearing his branches sturdily. **1858** FROUDE *Hist. Eng.* III. xvii. 456 Wyatt answered sturdily that Brancetor was his master's subject. **1893** J. EDGAR *Hist. Early Scott. Educ.* 211 The University of Aberdeen held out sturdily against the reformers. **1901** RASHDALL & RAIT *New College* vi. 115 The soul of the sturdily Protestant Bishop Horne was moved by the tidings which reached him from Oxford.

sturdiness ('stɜːdɪnɪs). Forms: see STURDY *a.*; also 4 **stordenesse**. [-NESS.] The quality or condition of being sturdy.

1. The condition (in animals) of being 'sturdy' or dizzy; *spec.* in sheep. = STURDY B. 1.

1552 HULOET, Sturdynes or desynes of a beast, ..*gangilion.* **1756** *Compl. Body Husb.* 695 Sturdyness.. is a kind of vertigo or giddiness in the Head of Sheep.

† **2.** Fierceness, violence; harshness, sternness.

1382 WYCLIF *2 Cor.* xii. 20 Sturdynessis [Vulg. *animositates*]. *c* **1386** [see STURDY *a.* 4]. *c* **1430** LYDG. *Min. Poems* (Percy Soc.) 198 Tempest on se, and wyndes sturdynesse.

† **3.** Refractoriness, rebelliousness, contumacy, obstinacy. *Obs.*

a **1400** *Gloss* in *Rel. Ant.* I. 7 *Contumacia*, a sturdynesse. *c* **1440** *Jacob's Well* 77 Þe laste cornere of wose in pride is sturdynesse, þat is, whanne þou excusyst þin opyn or pryue synne,..& wylt noȝt knowyn þi defawte, ne wylt noȝt suffryn to ben vndertakyn. *c* **1440** *Promp. Parv.* 481/2 Sturdynesse, *rebellio, inobediencia, contumacia.* **1544** BETHAM *Precepts War* II. xvii. Kiij, Of disobedience and sturdynesse. **1549** CHEKE *Hurt Sedit.* (1569) Cij b, What counsayle taketh place, where sturdinesse is lawe, and churlishe aunsweres be counted wisedome? **1673** *Ladies Calling* I. ii. §10 The stupid sturdiness of an asse has rendered it proverbial for folly.

4. Strength of character; firmness, resoluteness.

1675 J. SMITH *Chr. Relig. Appeal* I. 70 Their Nurture and Education.. had.. so much effeminated their innate sturdiness, as they were not able to sustain the sharpness of that War. *a* **1716** SOUTH *Serm.* (1727) VI. 273 The natural Sturdiness of some Tempers might be sufficient to enable some Persons to endure such exquisite Torments. **1727** BAILEY vol. II, *Sturdiness*, Lustiness, Resoluteness. **1768–74** TUCKER *Lt. Nat.* (1834) II. 287 What degree of sturdiness we can acquire, to maintain the determinations of our impartial judgment. **1822** HAZLITT *Table-t.*, *Knowl. Charac.* II. 346 All they want is imagination and sturdiness of moral principle! **1914** *Q. Rev.* Apr. 487 The virility and sturdiness of the Cretan Greeks.

5. Rough vigour of body; solidity of build. Also of things.

1863 GEO. ELIOT *Romola* xxx, His limbs had got back some of their old sturdiness. **1916** *Glasgow Herald* 1 Sept. 8 Craft that, despite their sturdiness, move in rough weather like buck-jumping ponies.

sturdy ('stɜːdɪ), *a.* and *sb.* Forms: 4 **stourdi, sturdi, (stourde)**, 4–6 **stourdy, stordy**, 6 **stourdie, sturdye**, 6–7 **sturdie**, 7 **stirdy**, 4– **sturdy**. [a. OF. *estourdi, estordi, esturdi*, stunned, dazed, reckless, violent (mod.F. *étourdi* featherbrained, thoughtless), = Pr. *estordit*, It. *stordito*, Sp., Pg. *aturdido*; pa. pple. of OF. *estourdir* (mod.F. *étourdir*) to stun, daze, = It. *stordire*, Sp., Pg. *aturdir* (? from Fr.):—vulgar L. **exturdīre*, of obscure origin.

Some scholars think that it is f. *ex-* (see EX-) + *turd-us* thrush (for the sense cf. the Fr. proverbial phrase *soûl comme une grive*, 'drunk as a thrush'); some regard it as a contraction of **extorpidīre* (L. *torpidus* TORPID) or of **exturbidīre* (L. *turbidus* TURBID). All these conjectures are open to grave objection; another hypothesis, of derivation from Teut. **sturtjan* to overthrow (see START *v.*), is on phonological grounds inadmissible.]

A. *adj.*

I. 1. In the primary etymological sense: Giddy. Said of sheep affected with the 'sturdy': see B. Now *dial.* (see *Eng. Dial. Dict.*).

1641 BEST *Farm. Bks.* (Surtees) 73 If there bee any of the hogges that bee sturdy, lame, weake.

II. † **2.** Impetuously brave, fierce in combat.

1297 R. GLOUC. (Rolls) 7936 Þe heyemen of engelond.. mid gret ost wende uorþ & mid stourdi [*v.r.* stourde] mode. *c* **1300** *K. Horn* 893 (Laud MS.) We neuere ne hente Of man so harde dunte Bute of þe king Mory þat was so swyþe stordy. **1375** BARBOUR *Bruce* v. 506* He sa sturdy wes and stout, That he wes the mast vorthy man That in-to Carrick liffit than. *c* **1425** *Engl. Conq. Ireland* xlvi. 116 The northeren men ben stordyer & smerter to fyght than other. *Ibid.* 118 Thegh he wer yn wepne vnmetly stordy, & sterne, out of wepne natheles, he was meke and sobre. **1630** R. JOHNSON *Kingd. & Commw.* 23 Able, and hardy bodies, and stout and sturdy stomacks. **1684** BUNYAN *Pilgr.* II. (1900) 258 They so belabored him, being sturdy men at Arms, that they made him make a Retreat.

† **b.** Of a battle: Fierce, violent. *Obs.*

c **1450** LOVELICH *Grail* xiii. 782 Therfore was that stour ful Stordy. **1579** E. K. *Gloss. to Spenser's Sheph. Cal.* Feb. 149 Sterne strife, said *Chaucer*, s. fell and sturdy.

† **3.** Recklessly violent, furious, ruthless, cruel.

1297 R. GLOUC. (Rolls) 3842 He adrou sire calibourne, is suerd..& anowarde þe helm, mid wel stourdy mod, þen oþer he smot. *c* **1374** CHAUCER *Boeth.* III. met. ii. (1868) 68 Þe liouns of þe contree of pene.. dreden her sturdy maystres [L. *trucem.. magistrum*] of whiche þei ben wont to suffren betinges. *a* **1513** FABYAN *Chron.* VII. (1811) 643 Lewys the .xi.. of Gaguinus is callyd the sturdy or fell Lewys. **1531** ELYOT *Gov.* III. ix. (1883) II. 272 So no violence or sturdye mynde lackynge reason and honestie is any parte of fortitude. **1589** PUTTENHAM *Eng. Poesie* I. iii. (Arb.) 22 To redresse and edifie the cruell and sturdie courage of man.

† **b.** Of waves, a stream, a storm, etc.: Violent, rough. *Obs.*

1375 BARBOUR *Bruce* III. 698 And entryt sone in-to the rase, Quhar that the strem sa sturdy was. **1426** LYDG. *De Guil. Pilgr.* 16670 Fordryven with many sturdy wawes off adversyte. **1569** T. NEWTON *Cicero's Old Age* 33 In the sturdy and nipping cold of winter. **1588** CHURCHYARD *Spark Friendship* Ep. Ded. A3b, The brute beastes that auoydes a sturdie storme, vnder the sauegard of a strong and flourishing tree. **1648** KENTISH *Serm. to Commons* 10 The highest Houses are subject to the sturdiest storms. **1660** RIDERS *Brit. Merlin* Oct., Sturdy storms of rain or snow, with extream ill weather, to the moneths end. **1823** COBBETT *Rur. Rides* (1885) I. 226 A pretty decent and sturdy rain began to fall.

† **c.** Of movement: Furious. Of a blow: Violent.

c **1386** CHAUCER *Sompn. T.* 454 And forth he gooth, with a ful angry chere.. A sturdy [*v.rr.* stourdy, stordy] paas doun to the court he gooth. **1579** SPENSER *Sheph. Cal.* Feb. 201 But to the roote [he] bent his sturdie stroke, And made many wounds in the wast Oake. **1603** KNOLLES *Hist. Turks* (1638) 40 With many wounds and sturdy blows both giuen and receiued.

† **4.** Of or with regard to countenance, speech, demeanour: Stern, harsh, rough, surly. *Obs.*

1297 R. GLOUC. (Rolls) 3287 After mete he nom is wif mid stourdi mod ynou, & wiþoute leue of þe kinge toward is contreye drou. *c* **1386** CHAUCER *Clerk's T.* 642 What koude a sturdy housbonde moore deuyse To preeue hire wyfhod or hir stedefastnesse, And he continuynge euere in sturdinesse? *c* **1440** *Partonope* 2573 And to my men dyspitous and sturdy. **1531** ELYOT *Gov.* I. vii. (1883) I. 40 Retaynyng his fiers and stourdie countenance. *Ibid.* II. v. II. 48 Litle and litle he withdrewe from men his accustomed gentilnesse, becomyng more sturdy in langage, and straunge in countenance, than euer before had ben his usage. **1552** HULOET, Sturdy, *superbus, superciliosus.* **1611** SPEED *Hist. Gt. Brit.* VIII. ii. §13 Their sturdy behauiour, and Lord-like carriage against the English.

† **5.** Hard to manage, intractable, refractory; rebellious, disobedient. *Obs.*

13.. *K. Alis.* 1332 Thider he wendith with gret pres, This stordy citeis for to dres. *c* **1400** *Master of Game* (MS. Digby 182) xv, Alauntes beeth inly fell and euyl vndrestondynge and more fooliche and more sturdy þan any oþer manere of houndes. *c* **1440** *Promp. Parv.* 481/2 Sturdy, vnbuxum, *rebellis, contumax, inobediens.* *c* **1440** *Jacob's Well* 296 To be sturdy to fadyr & modyr. **1514** BARCLAY *Cit. & Uplondyshman* (Percy Soc.) 17 The fyrste plowman and tyller of the grounde, Was rude and stordy, dysdaynynge to be bounde. **1603** DRAYTON *Bar. Wars* I. l, Sturdie to manage, of a haughtie Spright. **1604** F. HERRING *Mod. Defenee Caveat* 6 A sturdie horse requires a rough rider. **1611** SPEED *Theat. Gt. Brit.* II. xiii. 121 The ancient Inhabitants of this Country [Flint] were the Ordouices, a sturdy people against the Romans, but now most kinde and gentle towards the English. *c* **1635** in *Verney Mem.* (1907) I. 122 My sonn doth begine to be toe sturdie for my government. **1655** FULLER *Ch. Hist.* IX. 187 The most sturdy and refractory Non-conformists. **1688** PENTON *Guardian's Instruct.* (1897) 10 Beware of setting up that stirdy Resolution which some make, never to give off what they have once begun. **1781** COWPER *Hope* 182 Man is the genuine offspring of revolt, Stubborn and sturdy—a wild ass's colt.

† **b.** Obstinate, immovable in opinion. *Obs.*

1664 H. MORE *Myst. Iniq.* Apol. 522 If men would not bring their own sturdy Preconceptions, but listen to the easy and natural aire of the Text. **1680** *Tides* (MS. Bodl. Add. A. 202) 10 Seafareing men.. grow as sturdy and deafe to all the reason and argument that can be employed to undeceive them, as the Eliments wherein they converse. **1687** R. L'ESTRANGE *Answ. to Dissenter* 4 If they be not either too Sturdy, or too Stately, to Hearken to Reason. **1780** COWPER *Progr. Error* 539 Your blund'rer is as sturdy as a rock. **1781** —— *Expost.* 298 Where obstinacy takes his sturdy stand, To disconcert what policy has plann'd.

c. [With mixture of sense 7.] Epithet of beggars or vagabonds who are able-bodied and apt to be violent: see BEGGAR *sb.* 1 b., VALIANT *a.* 1 b. Also ***sturdy and valiant.***

1402 *Jack Upland* in *Pol. Poems* (Rolls) II. 96 For in many places thai damnen suche sturdy beggyng. **1535–6** *Act 27 Hen. VIII*, c. 25 §1 Suche poore creature or sturdie vacabund. **1556** in *Vicary's Anat.* (1888) 174 *note*, Sturdie & valiente Beggers. **1577** tr. *Bullinger's Decades* II. iii. (1592) 129 The sturdie roag vnworthie of almes. **1656** BEALE *Heref. Orchards* (1657) 39 Where Trade thrives not,.. all doors and highways are oppressed with idle and sturdy vagabonds. *a* **1680** BUTLER *Lady's Answ.* 43 Like sturdy Beggars, that intreat For Charity at once, and threat. *a* **1700** B. E. *Dict. Cant. Crew*, *Sturdy-beggers*, the fifth and last of the most ancient Order of Canters. **1789** J. WILLIAMS *Min. Kingd.* I. 202 When I reprove a sturdy beggar for being idle, he tells me roundly, that he cannot get employment.

6. Of material things: Refractory, defiant of destructive agencies or force; strong, stout.

c **1374** CHAUCER *Troylus* II. 1380 Þe sturdy ok On which men hakketh ofte for þe nones. *c* **1400** *Rom. Rose* 4155 Vpon the whiche also stode Of squared stoon a sturdy wall. **1575** *Gammer Gurton* I. ii. 16 Chwold rend it, though it were stitched wath sturdy pacthreede. **1577** B. GOOGE *Heresbach's Husb.* I. 41 b, Suche Grayne as hath the sturdiest strawe. **1600** FAIRFAX *Tasso* XV. ii, Euerie tender lim In sturdie steele and stubburne plate they dight. **1663** BUTLER

Hud. I. i. 305 His Doublet was of sturdy Buff. **1671** MILTON *P.R.* IV. 417 On the vext Wilderness, whose.. sturdiest Oaks Bow'd thir Stiff necks. **1697** EVELYN *Numism.* i. 10 Foliated with Silver upon this sturdy and inflexible Metal [Iron]. **1841** DICKENS *Barn. Rudge* xxxiii, A violent gust of wind and rain.. seemed to shake even that sturdy house to its foundation. **1858** HAWTHORNE *Fr. & It. Jrnls.* (1871) I. 141 The old triumphal arch of Drusus—a sturdy construction, much dilapidated [etc.]. **1870** BRYANT *Iliad* XIII. 359 Hasten thou And bring a sturdy javelin from the tent.

†**b.** Of wine: Rough or harsh to the taste. *Obs.*

c **1440** *Pallad. on Husb.* XI. 390 Also a man may in oon dayes while So trete a stordy wyn that hit shal smyle, And of a rough drynker be cleer and best.

†**c.** Of an ailment: Refractory to treatment. *Obs.*

1643 J. M. *Sov. Salve* 1 For a sturdy sore many plaisters are but sufficient. **1658** A. FOX *Wurtz' Surg.* III. viii. 239 The named remedies will availe nothing, because the Imposthumation is too sturdy for them.

d. Of a plant: Hardy.

1695 WOODWARD *Nat. Hist. Earth* VI. (1723) 296 The more sturdy and vigorous Vegetables. **1784** COWPER *Task* III. 530 Thence straight succeed The branches, sturdy to his utmost wish. **1853** CHRISTINA G. ROSSETTI *Poet. Wks.* (1904) 156/1 Lichen and moss and sturdy weed.

7. Of persons or animals; Characterized by rough bodily vigour; solidly built; stalwart, strong, robust, hardy.

c **1386** CHAUCER *Sompn. T.* 46 A sturdy harlot wente ay hem bihynde. **1456** SIR G. HAYE *Law Arms* (S.T.S.) 195 And he war stark and sturdy, and mycht wele bere armes. **1561** HOBY tr. *Castiglione's Courtyer* II. (1900) 120 Like as the armes of a smith that is weake in other thinges, because they are more exercised, be stronger then an other bodyes that is sturdy, but not exercysed to worke with his armes. **1580** BLUNDEVIL *Curing Horses Dis.* clxxxiv. 74 Weake, delicate, and tender Horses may not be purged in such sort, as those that be of a strong sturdie nature. **1705** *Lond. Gaz.* No. 4102/4 A short squat sturdy Lad. **1774** GOLDSM. *Nat. Hist.* (1776) IV. 325 The brown bear is made rather strong and sturdy, like the mastiff. **1784** COWPER *Tiroc.* 341 Great schools suit best the sturdy and the rough. **1837** KIRKBRIDE *Northern Angler* 55 His tackle must be strong; for lake-trout are in general rather sturdy customers. **1848** L. HUNT *Jar of Honey* x. 141 The sturdy youth, for the first time in his life, fainted away. **1875** JOWETT *Plato* (ed. 2) V. 267 A rugged land.. well fitted to produce a sturdy race.

b. Of movements: Displaying physical vigour. Also as epithet of health, vigour, etc.

1697 DRYDEN *Virg. Georg.* III. 639 And labour him with many a sturdy Stroak. **1710** PRIOR *Two Riddles* 14 With sturdy steps he walks. **1750** GRAY *Elegy* 28 How bow'd the woods beneath their sturdy stroke! **1861** STANLEY *East. Ch.* vi. (1869) 187 All were struck by the sturdy health and vigour of his frame. **1863** GEO. ELIOT *Romola* liii, His thickset frame had no longer the sturdy vigour which belonged to it.

8. *transf.* Of persons, their actions and attributes: Characterized by rough mental vigour; robust in mind or character; 'downright', uncompromising.

1775 JOHNSON *West. Isl.*, *Ostig* Wks. 1787 X. 464 A Scotch-man must be a very sturdy moralist, who does not love Scotland better than truth. **1802** MAR. EDGEWORTH *Forester* xiii, His sturdy principles of integrity could not bend to any of the arguments, founded on expediency, which [etc.]. **1828** HAZLITT *Self-Love & Benev.* Sk. & Ess. (1872) 77, I respect that fine old sturdy fellow Hobbes. **1866** KINGSLEY *Herew.* ix, They were distinguished.. for sturdy independence, and for what generally accompanies it—sturdy common sense. **1874** GREEN *Short Hist.* vii. §1. 344 The sturdy good sense of the man shook off the pedantry of the schools.

b. Of expressions: Vigorous, lusty.

1822 BYRON *Vis. Judgem.* lix, Here crash'd a sturdy oath of stout John Bull. **1856** EMERSON *Eng. Traits, Literature* Wks. (Bohn) II. 105 The more hearty and sturdy expression may indicate that the savageness of the Norseman was not all gone.

9. *Comb.*, as ***sturdy-chested***, ***-hearted*** adjs.; †**sturdy-boots** [see BOOTS[1] 3], jocularly, an obstinate person.

1531 ELYOT *Gov.* III. ii. (1883) II. 196 The infinite numbre of the sturdye harted Jues could neuer haue ben gouerned by any wisedome, if they had nat ben brideled with ceremonyes. **1762** BICKERSTAFF *Love in Village* I. x, Well said, sturdy-boots. **1836** DICKENS *Sk. Boz, Medit. Monmouth St.*, A stout, broad-shouldered, sturdy-chested man.

B. *sb.*

1. A brain-disease in sheep and cattle, which makes them run round and round; the turnsick.

1570 LEVINS *Manip.* 97/37 Ye sturdy, *vertigo.* **1598** *Fitzherbert's Husb.* II. xxvii. 63 Of the turne, otherwise called the sturdy. **1610** MARKHAM *Masterp.* I. xxx. 59 The horse will turne round like a beast that is troubled with the sturdy. **1718** RAMSAY *Christ's Kirk Gr.* III. xx, Fast frae the company he fled, As he had tane the sturdy. **1799** A. YOUNG *Agric. Surv. Lincs.* 329 The sturdy, or bladder on the brain. **1869** E. A. PARKES *Pract. Hygiene* (ed. 3) 187 The so-called 'gid', 'sturdy' or 'turnsick'.

b. A sheep afflicted with 'sturdy'.

1807 *Prize Ess. & Trans. Highl. Soc.* III. 402 A large parcel of lambs, whose bleating brought all the sturdies of the neighbourhood to them.

2. A name for darnel or some similar stupefying weed.

1683 R. DOBBS *Descr. Antrim* in *Antrim & Down Gloss.* s.v., A sort of Poyson.. called darnell, rises in the oats and other grain,.. ye country people call it sturdy, from the effects of making people light-headed. **1802** G. V. SAMPSON *Statist. Surv. Londonderry* 409 Another very injurious grain is thrown into the malt without reserve. It is called *sturdy*, and is the *lolium secalinum* of the botanists. *Ibid.* App. 15 *Bromus Secalinus*, field brome-grass; called by the farmers *sturdy.* **1824** MACTAGGART *Gallovid. Encycl.* 441.

3. A sturdy person.

1704 PENN in *Pennsylv. Hist. Soc. Mem.* IX. 305 Those sturdies will never leave off until they catch a Tartar. **1895** MEREDITH *Amazing Marr.* xxx. II. 339 The boy'll be a sturdy. She'll see he has every chance. He's a lucky little one to have that mother.

†**sture**[1]. *Obs.* Also 6 stuer, *Sc.* stuir. [? a. AF. **estuir*:—popular L. *sturio* (nom.); see STURGEON.] A sturgeon.

1456 SIR G. HAY *Gov. Princes* Wks. (S.T.S.) II. 137 The best fische has the maist hard skyn, as is gueddes,.. sturis and syk lyke. **1496** *Acc. Ld. High Treas. Scot.* I. 277 Item, the ix day of Junii, giffin to the man that brocht the sture fra Glasgo, vs. **1585** HIGINS *Junius' Nomencl.* 64/1 *Acipenser*,.. a stuer or sturgion. **1595** DUNCAN *App. Etym.* (E.D.S.), *Acipenser* a fish called the stuir. **1598** FLORIO, *Accipensero*,.. Some take it for the sturgion or elops, or stuer.

sture[2]. *Sc.* Also 7 stuir, 8–9 stur. Contracted form of STIVER. In Shetland used for: A penny.

1493 HALYBURTON *Ledger* (1867) 6 [He has] 700 ducatis, the quhilk makis 107 crounis and 5 sturis. **1575** *Reg. Privy Council Scot.* II. 473 The Commissaris of Burrowis.. hes.. grantit to Maister George Halkett, Conservatour of the privilegis of the Scottis natioun in Flanderis, sex sturis of every sek of gudis. **1606** in *Rec. Convent. Burghs Scot.* (1870) II. 227 Frae the merchand tuelf sturis and the skipper and schip thre stuiris for the sek. **1709** LADY G. BAILLIE *Househ. Bk.* (S.H.S.) 77, 16 gulders 3 sturs. **1892** G. STEWART *Shetl. Fireside Tales* (ed. 2) 252 Some evil thing wi' a face at first da size o' a copper stür.

sture, obs. form of STEER *v.*, STIR, STOWER.

sture, -ly, obs. forms of STOUR, STOURLY.

sturen, -li, obs. forms of STERN, STERNLY.

sturgeon ('stɜːdʒən). Forms: α. 3 sturgiun, 3–4 sturgun, 4 sturgin, sturgon(n, storgon, sturgeown, 5 storgeoun, sturgyn, storgyn, 5–6 sturgyon, 5–7 sturgion, (6 -ione), 6 strogyon, struggen, 6–7 sturgian, 7 sturgen, 4– sturgeon; β. 4 sturioun, sturion, 4–5 storion, 5 storjon, storyon, storioun, sturyon, sturione, -iowne. [a. AF. *sturgeon*, *esturgeoun* etc., OF. *sturg(i)un*, *esturgeon* (mod.F. *esturgeon*, †*éturgeon*), a Com. Rom. word = Pr. *esturjon*, *estorjon*, Sp. *esturion*, Pg. *esturião*, *esturjão*, It. *storione*:—popular L. *sturiōn-em* (nom. *sturio*), a. OTeut. **sturjon-*, whence OHG. *sturjo*, *sturo* (MHG. *stüre*, *störe*, mod.G. *stör*), MDu., MLG. *störe* (mod.Du. *steur*), OE. *styrȝa*, ON., mod.Norw. *styrja* (Sw. *stör*, Da. *stør*, are from LG.). Cf. STURE[1].

The origin of OTeut. **sturjon-* is obscure. If not a loanword, it may be f. the root of STIR *v.*]

1. A large fish of the family *Acipenseridæ*, having an elongated, almost cylindrical, body protected by longitudinal rows of bony scutes and a long tapering snout, found widely distributed in the rivers and coastal waters of the north temperate zone; esp. a fish belonging to either of the genera *Acipenser* and *Scaphirhynchops*, *A. sturio* being the common sturgeon of the Atlantic. It is a 'royal' fish (see FISH *sb.*[1] 2), esteemed as an article of food, and the source of caviar and isinglass.

α. *a* **1300** *Havelok* 753 He tok þe sturgiun, and þe qual, And þe turbut. *Ibid.* 1727 Lax, lampreys, and god sturgun. **134.** *Durham Acc. Rolls* (Surtees) 37 Et 7 pec. de sturgeon. *c* **1460** J. RUSSELL *Bk. Nurture* 627 in *Babees Bk.*, Then kut ye þe whelk asondur,.. and ley þe pecis þerof vppon youre sturgeoun. *c* **1475** *Pict. Voc.* in Wr.-Wülcker 765/20 *Hic rumbus*, a sturgyn. **1533** ELYOT *Cast. Helthe* (1539) 69b, Greatte fyshes of the see, as thurlepole, porpyse and sturgeon. **1591** SYLVESTER *Du Bartas* I. v. 143 Feast-famous Sturgeons. **1594** *Extracts Munic. Acc. Newcastle* (1848) 35 A cagge of struggen, 12*s.* **1618** J. SMYTH *Berkeleys* (1883) II. 435 All whale fishes, Sturgeons, and all other great and royall ffishes, in whatsoever free fishings within the river of Seavern. **1620** VENNER *Via Recta* iv. 78 Sturgion is a very acceptable dish. **1677** WOOD *Life* (O.H.S.) II. 378 A sturgeon of 8 foot long was taken up at Clifton ferry. **1711** SWIFT *Jrnl. to Stella* 5 Sept., I ate sturgeon, and it lies on my stomach. **1769** PENNANT *Zool.* III. 97 The sturgeon annually ascends our rivers. **1834** GRIFFITH tr. *Cuvier* X. 627 The sturgeon is much esteemed for food, and is said to eat like veal. **1836** YARRELL *Brit. Fishes* II. 360 *Acipenser Sturio*, Common Sturgeon. **1862** COUCH *Brit. Fishes* I. 150 The head of the Sturgeons is lengthened into a snout, which is slightly turned up. **1881** *Cassell's Nat. Hist.* V. 45 The Sturgeons form a small and natural group of fishes, distinguished by having a cartilaginous skeleton.

β. **13..** *Guy Warw.* 3895 Þilke lord þat.. in þe se made þe sturioun. **1390** *Earl Derby's Exped.* (Camden) 42 Jacobo Cremer pro ij barellis de sturion.., viij marc. viij scot. *c* **1425** *Voc.* in Wr.-Wülcker 642/7 *Hic rumbus*, storjon. *c* **1430** *Two Cookery-bks.* I. 13 Storion in brothe.—Take fayre Freysshe Storgeoun, an choppe it in fayre water.

b. With qualifying word indicating a particular species, as **black**, **lake**, **Ohio**, **red**, **rock**, **stone sturgeon**, *Acipenser rubicundus*, the sturgeon of the great lakes of N. America; **great white**, **isinglass**, **Russian sturgeon**, *A. huso*, the BELUGA or HUSO; **small** or **Ruthenian sturgeon** = STERLET.

1804 SHAW *Gen. Zool.* V. 375 Isinglass Sturgeon. *Acipenser Huso.* A larger fish than the common Sturgeon... Native of the Northern, Caspian, and Mediterranean seas.

2. Applied to other fishes.

1683 POYNTZ *Pres. Prosp. Tobago* 20 The Indian Sturgeon (so called by the English) frequents the Bays.

†**3.** ? A kind of cloth (? of the colour of a sturgeon). *Obs.*

1405 *Will of Culmer* (Somerset Ho.), Meam optimam togam videlicet de viride et de sturgeon parti[to] cum capicio partito de sturgeon & scarlet. **1420** *N.C. Wills* (Surtees) 29 Jupam meam nigram bene foderatam cum grey, et capicium de sturgon.

†**4.** (See quot. 1708.) *Obs.*

1708 *Brit. Apollo* I. No. 54. 3/2 There a Custom it was, A *Sturgion* to call, That same Animal, Which here for a Cods-head does pass. *Note.* A *Sturgion* is a Term they give one at *Dublin*, whom they think a fit Subject for Banter.

5. *attrib.* and *Comb.*, as ***sturgeon oil***, ***spawn***, ***tribe***; **sturgeon-boiler**, one who extracts sturgeon-oil; **sturgeon glue**, isinglass glue; **sturgeon-head** (see quot.); †**sturgeon lips** *jocular*, ? lips protruded like those of a sturgeon; **sturgeon-pickle**, a pickle for preserving sturgeon for food; †**sturgeon voyage**, ? a fishing-voyage for sturgeon.

1673 *Mass. Stat.* (1887) 210 The *sturgeon boyler or importer shall pay for the viewing and heading after 3s. 4d. p. score for all kegs and firkins. **1907** C. HILL-TOUT *Brit. N. Amer., Far West* vii. 128 The gum of the black pine was.. employed.. where the *sturgeon glue was not procurable. **1892** W. PIKE *Barren Ground N. Canada* 6 These inland boats.. are.. classified according to shape as York boats, *sturgeon-heads, and scows. **1599** NASHE *Lenten Stuff* 45 On his [Leander's] blew iellied *sturgeon lips, she was about to clappe one of those warme plaisters. **1881** *Spons' Encycl. Industr. Arts* IV. 1376 *Sturgeon-oil is prepared in Russia from the fat surrounding the intestines of the sturgeon. **1669** *Sir K. Digby's Closet opened* 254 Put it into pickle, like *Sturgeon-pickle. **1888** GOODE *Amer. Fishes* 37 *Sturgeon spawn or live minnows are used as bait. **1842** *Penny Cycl.* XXIII. 168/1 The *Sturionidæ*, or *Sturgeon tribe, have moreover but one opening to the gills. **1611** MIDDLETON & DEKKER *Roaring Girl* II. ii. E 1 b, You make as much hast as if you were a going vpon a *sturgion voyage.

Sturge-Weber (stɜːdʒ 'wɛbə(r)). *Path.* [The names of W. A. *Sturge* (1850–1919) and F. P. *Weber* (1863–1962), English physicians, who described the syndrome in 1879 and 1922 respectively.] ***Sturge-Weber syndrome*** or ***disease***: a congenital syndrome in which a diffuse malformation of blood-vessels on one side of the head produces port-wine nævus on the face and lesions of the brain, usually resulting in fits and mental retardation.

1935 H. BERGSTRAND in *Abstr. 2nd Internat. Neurol. Congr., London* 124 Sturge-Weber's disease is a syndrome comparable with von Recklinghausen's.. and Bourneville's diseases. **1974** J. H. MENKES *Textbk. Child Neurol.* x. 412/2 The coincidence of a facial vascular disease and seizures suggests Sturge-Weber disease.

†**sturgion.** *Obs.* = TORDION.

1579 J. JONES *Preserv. Body & Soul* I. xi. 22 Bargenets, Pauions, Galiardes, Sturgions and Roundes.

sturgion(e, -giun, -gon(n, -gun, -gyn, -gyon, obs. forms of STURGEON.

sturie, sturion(e, obs. ff. STIR, STURGEON.

sturine ('stjʊəriːn, -ɪn). *Biochem.* Also -in. [a. G. *sturin* (A. Kossel 1896, in *Zeitschr. f. physiol. Chem.* XXII. 180) f. pop.L. *sturiōnem* STURGEON: see -INE[5].] A protamine extracted from the testicles of fish of the genus *Accipenser*, esp. *A. sturio* and *A. guldenstadtii*, sturgeons of the Baltic and Caspian Seas.

1896 [see SALMINE]. **1960** *Adv. Protein Chem.* XV. 34 In the case of sturine, both procedures.. yield two NH_2-terminal amino acids, alanine and glutamic acid. **1977** *Bull. Exper. Biol. & Med.* LXXXIII. 710 The proportion of added DNA to be bound with spheroblasts untreated with sturine was 18%.

sturionian (ˌstjʊərɪ'əʊnɪən). [f. mod.L. *Sturiōnes* (see below; pl. of pop.L. *sturio* STURGEON) + -IAN.] A fish belonging to the *Sturiones*, a former order of fishes including the sturgeons (*Acipenseridæ*) and related families.

1835 KIRBY *Hab. & Inst. Anim.* II. xxi. 391 The Sturionians agree with the Ossean Fishes in their gills, but their skeleton is cartilaginous. **1842** BRANDE *Dict. Sci.* etc., *Sturionians*, the name of the family of Cartilaginous fishes of which the sturgeon is the type.

sturi'onic, *a. rare.* [f. popular L. *sturiōn-em* STURGEON + -IC.] Pertaining to the sturgeon.

1852 BADHAM *Halieut.* (1854) 467 In the rivers of Astrachan a.. flotilla sails yearly on the sturionic fishery.

sturioun, -iowne, obs. forms of STURGEON.

sturk(e, sturly, obs. forms of STIRK, STOURLY.

‖**Sturmabteilung** ('ʃtʊrmapˌtaɪlʊŋ). [Ger., lit. 'storm detachment'.] A paramilitary force forming part of the German National Socialist Party, founded in 1921 and deprived of power in 1934. Abbrev. S.A. (s.v. S 4 a).

1923 *Times* 22 May 11/1 At the headquarters of the [Nazi] organization near the Gärtnerplatz Theatre, the visitor is confronted in the main hall by the notice 'Sturm-Abteilung' (Storm-troop section). Newspaper correspondents.. are not very welcome. **1932** E. Lengyel *Hitler* x. 145 Germany is divided into five Sturm Abteilung inspections. **1977** M. Walker *National Front* i. 19 They [*sc.* Mosley's army] had neither the numbers nor the organization of Hitler's *Sturmabteilung* or Mussolini's *Squadristi*. **1977** [see *S.A.* s.v. S 4a].

‖**Sturmbannführer** (ˈʃtʊrmban,fyːrər). [Ger., = 'battalion leader'.] An officer in the *Schutzstaffel* (formerly part of the *Sturmabteilung*).

1955 J. Thomas *No Banners* xxv. 246 The *sturmbannführer* literally foamed at the mouth. **1965** M. Spark *Mandelbaum Gate* i. 13 Freddy..felt an urge to explain that he was not a mass-butcher and that he had never desired to become a *sturmbannführer*. **1978** T. Allbeury *Lantern Network* viii. 99 A fresh-faced blond German with the insignia of a Sturmbannführer.

†**sturme**, *v.* *Obs.* [OE. *styrman* = OHG. *sturman*, *-en* (MHG., mod.G. *stürmen*), ON. *styrma*:—OTeut. type **sturmjan*, f. **sturmo-z* storm *sb.* Cf. storm *v.*]

1. (*OE.* only.) *intr.* **a.** Of the weather: To storm, rage. **b.** To cry out loudly.

Beowulf 2552 (Gr.) Stearcheort styrmde. *c* **888** Ælfred *Boeth.* vii. §3 Styrmendum wedrum. *c* **900** *Bæda's Hist.* ii. x. [xiii.] (1890) 134 Hit rine & sniwe & styrme ute. *c* **1000** *Ags. Ps.* (Th.) cxli. 1 Min stefn to þe styrmeð, Drihten.

2. *trans.* To overwhelm as with a storm; to attack with overpowering force.

c **1205** Lay. 1670 Þa Freinsce weoren isturmede [*c* 1275 iwraþþed] & noðelas heo stal makeden. *Ibid.* 18327 Þat hæðene uolc þa ufere hond hafeden & mid muchelere strengðe sturmden [*c* 1275 sweinde] þa Bruttes.

Sturmer (ˈstɜːmə(r)). Also **sturmer**. The name of a village near Haverhill, on the Suffolk-Essex border, used *attrib.* or *absol.* in **Sturmer apple, Pippin** to designate a late-ripening dessert apple belonging to a variety developed there in the 1830s by S. and J. Dillistone (fl. 1827–50) and distinguished by yellowish-green skin, sometimes slightly russetted, and crisp, creamy-white flesh.

1831 *Catal. Fruits cult. in Garden* (Hort. Soc.) (ed. 2) 37 Apples... Sturmer Pippin. **1847** *Gardeners' Chron.* 27 Feb. 135/2 When the Nonpareil is getting over, the Sturmer Pippin, then in perfection, comes in to supply its place. **1851** R. Hogg *Brit. Pomology* 190 The Sturmer Pippin was raised by Mr. Dillistone, a nurseryman at Sturmer, near Haverhill, in Suffolk, and was obtained by impregnating the Ribston Pippin with the pollen of the Nonpareil. **1877** E. S. Dallas *Kettner's Bk. of Table* 35 Dessert Apples... February—Sturmer Pippin. **1950** *N.Z. Jrnl. Agric.* Aug. 191/1 Good sources of vitamin C include..sturmer apples. **1959** [see delicious *a.* 2b]. **1971** R. Petrie *Thorne in Flesh* x. 133 A flow of customers beyond the carefully stacked pyramids of Sturmers and Jonathans swelled and dwindled.

Sturmian (ˈstɜːmɪən), *a.* and *sb.* *Math.* [f. *Sturm* (see below) + -ian.] **a.** *adj.* Pertaining to or discovered by the Swiss mathematician, J. C. F. Sturm (1803–55), esp. with reference to his researches in the theory of equations. **b.** *sb.* = *Sturmian function* or *residue*.

1853 Sylvester in *Phil. Trans.* CXLIII. 483 Reverting now to the simplified Sturmian residues, since..these differ from the unsimplified complete residues required by the Sturmian method only in the circumstance of their being divested of factors, which are necessarily..positive, these simplified Sturmians may of course be substituted for the complete Sturmians for the purposes of M. Sturm's theorem. *Ibid.* 458 The Sturmian process. *Ibid.* 469 The simplified *i*th Sturmian residue R_i. *Ibid.* 473 The Sturmian convergents. *Ibid.* 483 The simplified Sturmian series given. *Ibid.* 485 My formulæ for the Sturmian functions. **1861** Cayley *Math. Papers* IV. 473 A discussion of the Sturmian constants for cubic and quartic equations.

‖**Sturm und Drang** (ʃtʊrm ʊnt draŋ): see *storm and stress* s.v. storm *sb.* 3d.

[**1844** F. L. J. Thimm *Lit. of Germany* 85 This period, so styled by Goethe, after the title of one of the dramas of Klinger, 'Sturm und Drang'.] **1857** C. Kingsley *Two Yrs. Ago* III. i. 29 One of the Sturm-und-drang party, of course; the express locomotive school, scream-and-go-ahead. **1873** Gostwick & Harrison *Outl. German Lit.* xvi. 228 That time of 'Sturm und Drang', when writing wild poetry was regarded as the object of life. **1925** L. P. Smith *Words & Idioms* iii. 105 In that wild period, which was called at the time *Genieperiode*, but has since acquired the name of *Sturm und Drang*, the great watchwords *Genius*, *Originality*, and *Creative* acquired a resonance..which they had certainly never possessed in England. **1950** M. J. C. Hodgart *Ballads* ix. 152 The philosophical and political obsessions which attracted the *Sturm und Drang* writers to folksong. **1973** *Listener* 28 June 862/3 The Romantic poets..loved the word 'storm' as a synonym for energy, in phrases like *Sturm und Drang*, 'storm and thrust'.

transf. **1885** H. Conway *Family Affair* III. v. 85 His *sturm und drang*, his emotional days, were well over... He had not bowed his knee to the intense, nor sacrificed on the altar of the incomprehensible. **1909** A. Nicolson *Let.* 24 Mar. in H. Nicolson *Sir Arthur Nicolson* (1930) xi. 305 When we have passed through the present 'Sturm und Drang' period, I should not be surprised if we were to find both France and Russia gravitating rapidly towards and Central Powers. **1938** E. Bowen *Death of Heart* i. v. 86 Eddie..wrote some pamphlets, which were printed by a girl who had a press in a loft. Arts and crafts had succeeded *Sturm und Drang*. **1962** J. Heller *Catch-22* iii. 29 Only when all the *Sturm und Drang* had been left far behind would he tip his flak helmet back wearily on his sweating head and stop barking directions to McWatt at the controls. **1978** H. Frank *Single* vi. 137 She wanted..mortification, punishment, Sturm und Drang.

†**sturmye.** *Cookery. Obs.*

c **1430** *Two Cookery-bks.* i. 26 Cxij. Sturmye. Take gode mylke of Almaundys y-drawe with wyne, [etc.].

S-turn: see S 2c.

sturne, obs. form of stern *a.*

sturnine (ˈstɜːnaɪn), *a.* *Ornith.* [ad. L. *sturnīn-us*, f. *sturn-us* starling.] Resembling a starling.

1809 Shaw *Gen. Zool.* VII. 470 Sturnine Grakle. *Gracula sturnina*. Grey Grakle,..Native of the Southern parts of Dauria,..building a nest similar to that of a Starling.

sturnoid (ˈstɜːnɔɪd), *a.* *Ornith.* [f. L. *sturn-us* starling + -oid.] Resembling the *Sturnidæ* or Starlings in form or characteristics.

1874 A. R. Wallace in *Ibis* Ser. iii. IV. 412 Sturnoid Passeres. **1879** E. P. Wright *Anim. Life* 264 The Sturnoid Perchers..are almost exclusively natives of the Old World.

sturope, obs. form of stirrup.

sturre, obs. form of star *sb.*[1], stir *sb.*[1] and *v.*

sturrop(p, obs. forms of stirrup.

sturt (stɜːt), *sb.*[1] Chiefly *Sc.* Also 5, 7 **sturte**, 6 **stourt.** [Metathetic form of strut *sb.*[1]]

1. Contention, violent quarrelling; contentious or violent behaviour.

Usually associated in the context with *strife*, esp. in the set phrase ***sturt and strife***.

[**1303** R. Brunne *Handl. Synne* 3743 3yf þou yn any strut, For Ire wundedyst a man, or hurt.] *c* **1375** *Sc. Leg. Saints* xliii. (*Cecilia*) 478 He sad til hire with sturt & schore: 'til ydolis þu mak sacryfice.' *a* **1500** *Ratis Raving* 3679 Oyss noght flityng, sturt, na stryf. **1500–20** Dunbar *Poems* xxvi. 31 Than Yre come in with sturt and stryfe; His hand wes ay vpoun his knyfe. *a* **1598** D. Ferguson *Sc. Prov.* (1785) 28 Sturt pays nae debt. **1786** Burns *Nature's Law* i, Let other heroes boast their scars, The marks of sturt and strife. **1831** J. Wilson *Noctes Ambr.* (1856) III. 337 Goodwife—without a' sturt or strife, Bring ben the siller bowl wi' care. **1832** Hogg *Queer Bk.* 15 And I will thrill thy frigid blood With marvellous tale of sturt and strife. **1881** *Blackw. Mag.* Mar. 399/1 He who..amid all the sturt and strife of his manhood, had composed a system of philosophy. **1891** R. Ford *Thistledown* xviii. 326, I liv'd aw my deyes, but sturt or strife.

†**2.** Disquiet of the mind, vexation of the spirit.

1513 Douglas *Æneis* ii. ii. 59 Dolorous my life I led in sturt and pane. *Ibid.* iv. Prol. 89 Lo, quhow from grace to all mischeif they flit, Fra weill to sturt, fra pane to deid! **1560** Rolland *Seven Sages* 83 The Emprice..For verie sturt in hir minde was richt wo. **1596** Dalrymple tr. *Leslie's Hist. Scot.* I. v. 279 In presoun, throw sturt and dule, he dies. *a* **1627** A. Craig *Pilgr. & Heremite* (1873) 8 But where thou wouldst seeme to salue all my sore, And by thy strait statutes to stay all my sturt. **1681** Colvil *Whigs Supplic.* (1751) 130 Fighting is a fool thing, What doth it else but sturt and dool bring. **1724** Ramsay *Tea-t. Misc.* (1733) I. 99 My heart take neither sturt nor wae For Meg, for Marjory or Mause, But be thou blyth.

†**sturt**, *sb.*[2] *Obs. rare*$^{-1}$. [? var. of start *sb.*[2]] A sudden impulse. Hence **sturt** *v.*[2] *intr.*, to start suddenly.

1674 N. Fairfax *Bulk & Selv.* 129 When we give a dartingness to outcasts, we betemme them but one or a few springs, which by often sturts and flashes of motion, cracker-like, weaken themselves. *Ibid.* 139, 140 A body having bequeath'd it one degree of sturt or yerk,..may upon taking in ten or twenty degrees of the same, in the next, sturt to many atoms in length.

sturt (stɜːt), *sb.*[3] *Tin-mining.* [Perh. identical with prec.] (See quots.)

1849–50 Weale *Dict. Terms*, *Sturt*, in mining: when a tributer takes a pitch at a higher tribute, and cuts a course of ore, he sometimes gets two, three, or five hundred pounds in two months: this great profit is called 'a sturt'. **1860** *Eng. & For. Mining Gloss.* 25 [Cornw. terms]. **1894** *Cornishman* 19 Sept. (E.D.D.) A good 'sturt'. At Levant mine, during the past month, tributers, who found a rich pocket of tin at the 278 f.m. level, have divided between them £101 13*s.* 4*d.*

Sturt (stɜːt), *sb.*[4] The name of Charles *Sturt* (1795–1869), Australian explorer, used *attrib.* or in the possessive in **Sturt('s) (desert) pea** to designate a plant collected by him in 1844, *Clianthus formosus*, a trailing perennial herb of the family Leguminosæ, native to desert regions of Western Australia and bearing racemes of red or white flowers blotched with black at the base.

1865 J. E. Tenison-Woods *Hist. Discovery & Exploration Austral.* I. i. 29 Some of the species are engraved in one account of his [*sc.* Dampier's] voyage, amongst which appears the beautiful clianthus, known to the colonists as Sturt's Desert Pea. **1911** W. R. Guilfoyle *Austral. Plants* 114 'Sturt's Desert Pea'..or 'Australian Glory Pea' (biennial), flowers scarlet. **1933** [see clianthus]. **1936** I. L. Idriess *Cattle King* iv. 27 The bluebush a sombre carpet splotched by scarlet patches of Sturt's desert pea. **1949** D. Walker *We went to Australia* xix. 183 The sturt pea is the most sensational [wild flower of West Australia]. **1966** *Times* 11 Nov. (W. Australia Suppl.) p. iv/2 There is the spectacular Sturt pea, sprawling crimson and black-hearted, on the red earth. **1977** *Caravan World* (Austral.) Jan. 37/3 The scarlet splash of Sturt's Desert Pea..mellowing the stark red earth. **1979** D. Bellamy in *Radio Times* 1–7 Dec. 5/1 Many Australian plants..have adapted to withstand bush fires... Sturt's Pea, the first plant to bloom after the ravages of fire.

†**sturt**, *a.* *Sc. Obs.* [? Belongs to sturt *sb.*[1]] (See quot.)

1726 R. Fleming *Fulfilling Script.* (ed. 5) Table of Scots Phrases, *Sturt*, turbulent, or contentious.

sturt (stɜːt), *v.*[1] *Obs.* exc. *Sc.* [f. sturt *sb.*[1]]

1. †**a.** *intr.* To contend, make trouble *with*. *Obs.*

c **1395** *Plowman's Tale* 868 Such beren yvell heven-kay They mowen..With trewe tillers sturte and stryve.

b. *trans.* To attack, trouble, molest, disturb. *Sc.*

1513 Douglas *Æneis* vii. vi. 40, I..nevir wald ceis, Quhen thai wer chasit of thair native land, To sturt thame on the streme fra hand to hand. **1786** Burns *Twa Dogs* 199 They mak enow themsels to vex them; An' ay the less they hae to sturt them, In like proportion, less will hurt them. **1892** G. Stewart *Shetl. Fireside Tales* (ed. 2) 247 She could staand at da briest o' wir hoose an' skyle wir lum withoot ever sturtin' her.

2. *intr.* To be startled or frightened. Cf. start *v.* 5.

1786 Burns *Halloween* xviii, He marches thro' amang the stacks, Tho' he was something sturtan. **1808** Jamieson, *Sturt*, to startle, to be afraid. **1850** in Ogilvie.

sturt *v.*[2]: see sturt *sb.*[2]

†**ˈsturtful**, *a.* *Sc. Obs.* [f. sturt *sb.*[1] + -ful.] Contentious.

c **1475** Henryson *Want of Wyse Men* 62 Poems (S.T.S.) III. 174 Sic sturtfull stering in to godis neiss it stinkis.

†**ˈsturting**, *ppl. a.* *Sc. Obs.* In 5 **sturtand**, 6 **sturtyn.** [f. sturt *v.*[1]] **a.** Of a person: Contentious. **b.** Of a thing: That causes vexation or disquiet.

a **1500** *Ratis Raving* 656 Mar is lowable to god with a.. pacient man na a Irfull, and a sturtand, quhilk makis reddy dyscord. **1513** Douglas *Æneis* viii. Prol. 15 Sturtyn study hes the steyr, distroyand our sport.

†**ˈsturtsome**, *a.* *Sc. Obs.* [f. sturt *sb.*[1] + -some.] Disturbing, troublesome, vexatious.

1570 *Satir. Poems Reform.* xi. 51 Throw the is raisit sturtsum stryfe. *a* **1585** Polwart *Flyting w. Montgomerie* 135, I..counsell thee For to eschew this sturtsome strife.

Hence †**ˈsturtsomeness.**

a **1586** in Pinkerton *Anc. Sc. Poems* (1786) 201 Scho list nocht at my layr to leyr: In all this land, forouttin dout, Of sturtsumnes scho hes no peir.

sturtup, variant of startup.

16.. in *Tarlton's Jests* (1844) Introd. 44 Hee..The counterfet expreste Of clowne, with cote of russet hew And sturtups with the reste.

sturty (ˈstʌrtɪ), *a.* *Sc.* [f. sturt *sb.*[1] + -y.] = sturtsome.

a **1807** J. Skinner *Christmas Ba'ing* xxviii. (Jam.), The lave their thumbs did blythly knack To see the sturty [ed. 1809 stalwart] strife.

sturun, sturyon, obs. ff. stern *a.*, sturgeon.

stuse, obs. pl. of stew *sb.*[1]

stushie (ˈstʌʃɪ, ˈstɪʃɪ). *Sc.* Also **stashie, stishie.** [Origin unknown.] A disturbance, uproar, row, fracas.

1824 G. Smith *Douglas Travestie* 12 Mony an aukward stashie was he in. **1840** G. Webster *Ingliston* xxviii. 289 The haill toun's been in a stushie about it. **1926** 'H. MacDiarmid' *Penny Wheep* 8, I lo'e the stishie o' Earth in space. **1959** M. Pugh *Chancer* 68 Big trouble from the film company... They're in a stushy. Some of the survivors started creating hell about the film. **1973** *People's Jrnl.* (Inverness & Northern Counties ed.) 24 Nov. 17/4 (*heading*) Army 'Samaritans' caused a stushie on the road to Durness. **1980** G. Hammond *Reward Game* vii. 96 Do you still want Briesland House, or did this morning's stishie put you off it for life?

stuss (stʌs, stʌʃ). *U.S.* [ad. Yiddish *shtos*, perh. a. G. *stoss* push, stack.] A form of faro.

1912 A. H. Lewis *Apaches of N.Y.* 35 Jigger owned a stuss-house in Forsyth Street. *Ibid.*, Between them they would divide the harvest of the stuss. **1913** [see *pipefiend* s.v. pipe *sb.*[1] 11b]. **1930** D. Runyon in *Sat. Even. Post* 5 Apr. 48/3, I do not wish to play stuss. *Ibid.* 72/1 It is what is called a stuss house, and many prominent citizens of the neighbourhood are present playing stuss. **1975** *Way to Play* 207/3 Stuss is also known as Jewish faro. It is a simplified form of faro, with a larger percentage in the house's favor.

stut (stʌt), *sb.* *Sc. local.* [Perh. a. or cogn. w. Du. *stut* (see etym. note s.v. stud *sb.*[1]); perh. a dial. var. of stud *sb.*[1]] A prop.

1559 *Extracts Aberd. Reg.* (1844) I. 325 Sum remeid to wphald the ruff of the northt yll with propis and stuttis [*printed* scuttis] for this wyntir sessoun, quhill fair wedder cum, to mend the samen. **1808** Jamieson, *Stut*, a prop, a support.

stut (stʌt), *v.*[1] *Obs.* exc. *dial.* Forms: 4–7 **stutte**, 6 **stutt**, (7 **stoott**), 6– **stut.** [ME. *stutte-n*, f. Teut. root **stut-*, ablaut-var. of **staut-* as in MLG. *stôten*, OHG. *stôzen* (mod.G. *stossen*) to knock, strike against, collide. Cf. stote *v.* 2.]

1. *intr.* To stutter.

1388 [see stutting *ppl. a.*[1]]. *c* **1400** *Destr. Troy* 3825 Neptolon..stutid full stithly, þat stynt hym to speke. *a* **1500** *Medulla Gram.*, *Blatio*, to stutt or stamer. **1516** *Life St.*

Birgette in *Kal. New Leg. Eng.* (Pynson) 120b, Nat stuttynge lyke the maner of other children that begynne to speke, she speke complete and full wordes. *a* **1529** Skelton *E. Rummyng* 339 Her felow did stammer and stut. **1529** Frith *Rev. Antichrist* 68 He offendeth also that doth stammer or stutte in the wordes of the canon. **1570** Levins *Manip.* 178/35 To stoote, stutte, *titubare*. **1571** Golding *Calvin on Ps.* v. 5, 13 After the manner of a broken speeche, according as the sainctes in praying doe oftetymes stutte. **1601** B. Jonson *Poetaster* iv. v, Hee lookes bigge and begins to stut, for anger. **1621** Burton *Anat. Mel.* i. iii. iii. i. 264 They stutte or faulter in their speech. **1626** Bacon *Sylva* §386 They that Stut, doe Stut more in the first Offer to speake, than in Continuance. **1638** Junius *Paint. Ancients* 315 They are deservedly laughed at, who going about to tell a tale doe nothing but stutte and stammer. *a* **1650** Calderwood *Hist. Kirk* (1843) III. 414 The King said blushing, and somwhat stootting: 'Least anie man sould [etc.].' **1688** Holme *Armoury* ii. 389/1 A Man..[doth] Stammer, Stut, when the Voice or Words come not freely, that hath an impediment in his Speech. **1797** *Gentl. Mag.* LXVII. 456 They [*sc.* cuckoos] stammer (or *stut*, as it is called in the North of England)..in the month of June. **1818** Wilbraham *Chesh. Gloss*, *Stut*, to stutter or stammer. **1825** Brockett *N.C. Gloss.*, *Stut*, to stutter.

b. *transf.* and *fig.*

1577 tr. *Bullinger's Decades* (1592) 965 The Lorde..hath a singular care of mans infirmitie, whereby hee framing him selfe to our capacitie, dooth after a sorte stut and stammer with us. **1613** Purchas *Pilgrimage* i. xi. 51 Megasthenes (whom Annius hath set out as truly as he hath done Berosus, saue that he stutted at the name and called him Metasthenes).

2. To stumble in walking.

1573 Baret *Alv.* S 905 To Stut: to stagger in speaking or going: to stumble, *titubo*. **1582** Stanyhurst *Æneis* ii. (Arb.) 89 In steps he stutted, apaled: And fixt his footing. **1583** Golding *Calvin on Deut.* xci. 563 It is as though such as haue not learned Gods Word do stut and stumble and go astray.

† **stut**, *v.*[2] *Sc. Obs.* Also 7 **stoot.** [f. STUT *sb.*; cf. MDu. *stutten* to prop.] *trans.* To prop up, support. Hence **'stutted** *ppl. a.*, **'stutting** *ppl. a.*[2]

1638 A. Cant *Serm.* 13 June (1699) 6 Noblemen, these Artificial and stooted Mountains [*sc.* the bishops], have over-toped you who are the Natural Mountains. *Ibid.* 12 These are the two Pillars whereupon our Mountain of Prelacie is Stooted. **1808** Jamieson, *Stut*, to prop, to support, with stakes or pillars. **1819** W. Tennant *Papistry Storm'd* (1827) 218 Frae her four stuttin' pillars stout Lumps of out batter't stane fell out.

stut(e: see STOUT, STUTTE *v.*

stuth, variant of STOUTH.

stuthe, variant of STOOTH.

1502 *Acc. Ld. High Treas. Scot.* II. 199 For brases and stuthes of lattoun to the harnessingis of thir sadilis. **1507** *Ibid.* III. 254 Item for 1 stuthes with ruffis callit ulȝeatis for the Kingis panses and mailȝeis. **1513** Douglas *Æneis* xii. xiv. 132 The fey gyrdill hie set dyd appeyr, With stuthis knaw and pendeis schynand cleyr. **1539–40** *Acc. Ld. High Treas. Scot.* VII. 287 Stuthis and bukelis to ane blak harnesing of the Kingis.

stuthe, variant of STOOTHE *v.*

1483 *Cath. Angl.* 370/2 To Stuthe [*v.r.* Stuche], *stipare*. **1501** *Acc. Ld. High Treas. Scot.* II. 27 Item, for vj dog collaris tane to the King, thre of thaim stuthit, vj s.

† **stutte**, *v. Obs.* Also 3 **stute, stitte.** Pa. t. **stutte.** [Early ME. *stutte-n* (ü), a. ON. *stytta* = OE. *styntan*: see STINT *v.* (Chiefly in texts of 'the Katherine group', the lang. of which, mainly southern, has some Scandinavian words.)]

a. *intr.* To stop, cease; to stay, remain. **b.** *trans.* To cease, desist from.

a. *a* **1225** *Leg. Kath.* 1529 Stute nu þenne, & stew þe, & stille þine wordes. *a* **1225** *Juliana* 70 As ha stutte oþe stude þer ha schulde deþ drehen, þa com þe ilke belial of helle þat [etc.]. *c* **1225** *Ancr. R.* 42 Hwo se wule mei a-stunten þeruppe [*v.r.* mei stutten þruppe]. *a* **1240** *Sawles Warde* in *Coll. Hom.* 267 þu schal[t] ful bliðeliche beon under-fon in as ofte as liues luue stutteð forto spekene. ? *a* **1300** *St. Kenelm* 239 in *E.E.P.* (1862) 54 Hi seȝe hire stitte [*MS. Laud* ——sitte] adai..Meteles stille in one stede.

b. *c* **1225** *Ancr. R.* 72 þeone kuðen heo neuere astunten hore cleppe [*v.r.* þa ne cuðen ha neauer stutten hare cleppen].

'stutter, *sb.*[1] *Obs.* exc. *dial.* [f. STUT *v.*[1] + -ER[1]. (Cf. STOTER *sb.*[1])] = STUTTERER.

1529 Rastell *Pastyme* (1811) 79 Lews the Stutter [= Louis the stammerer]. **1530** Palsgr. 277/2 Stuttar, *besgu*. **1547** Boorde *Brev. Health* xli. 21 If it [*sc.* stuttering] do come with beying in the company of a stutter or stamerer, a man must refrayne the company of a stutter. **1560** Bible (Geneva) *Isa.* xxxii. 4 The tongue of the stutters shalbe ready to speake distinctly. *a* **1618** Sylvester *Little Bartas* 988 The Spirit..Which..Gives Stutters Tongues, & makes the bash-full bold. **1626** Bacon *Sylva* §386 Many Stutters ..are vary Cholericke Men. **1825** Jamieson *Stuter*.

stutter ('stʌtə(r)), *sb.*[2] [f. STUTTER *v.*] An act or a habit of stuttering. Also *transf.*

1854 Surtees *Handley Cr.* iii. (1901) I. 20 After a long string of stutters, he [the would-be orator] slunk back into the crowd amid the laughter and applause of the company. **1883** S. C. Hall *Retrospect* I. 119 He had an awkward impediment of speech, not quite a stutter. **1886** Ruskin *Præterita* I. 253 Attempting even some stutter of apology which made matters worse. **1899** *Allbutt's Syst. Med.* VII. 451 Suddenly the stumbling-block is removed,..and the subsequent words tumble out rapidly..until checked by a fresh stutter. **1974** C. Ryan *Bridge Too Far* iv. vi. 263 As he neared the ground the stutter of machine guns and the dull thud of mortar bursts seemed to engulf him. **1981** M. E. Atkins *Palimpsest* ii. 12 The car engine—with..the merest apology of stutter—cut out completely.

attrib. **1878** tr. *von Ziemssen's Cycl. Med.* XIV. 836 Schulthess compared the stutter-spasm to the convulsive movements of photophobia and hydrophobia.

stutter ('stʌtə(r)), *v.* [Freq. f. STUT *v.*[1]: see -ER[5]. Equivalent forms in other Teut. langs. are MDu. *stoteren* (Du. *stotteren*), MLG. *stoteren* (mod.LG. *stötern*), mod.G. *stottern* (from LG.), Sw. dial. *stutra*, Norw. *stotra* (Ross).

The late date of the appearance of the word in Eng. is remarkable; possibly the frequentative formation was suggested by the Du. form.]

1. a. *intr.* To speak with continued involuntary repetition of sounds or syllables, owing to excitement, fear, or constitutional nervous defect; to stammer.

1570 Levins *Manip.* 79/7 To stutter, *titubare*. **1586** B. Young *Guazzo's Civ. Conv.* iv. 187b, All the companie laughed at this word (*Aripistus*) who stuttering, and against his will, hastelie spake it. **1598** Marston *Sco. Villanie* To Judicial Perusers B 4 b, I dare defend my plainnes gainst the veriuyce face of the crabbed'st Satyrist that euer stuttered. **1621** Burton *Anat. Mel.* i. ii. i. iv. 77 Those that stutter and are balde, will be soonest melancholy. **1686** *Lond. Gaz.* No. 2128/4 James Wybert, a well-proportioned tall man,.. stutters much in his speech,..went away..with a chestnut coloured Horse. **1711** J. Greenwood *Engl. Gram.* 31 He had taught..several of our own Countrymen who stutter'd extreamly. **1730** Swift *Traulus* i, And though you hear him stut-tut-tut-ter, He barks as fast as he can utter. **1764** Foote *Patron* ii. ii, This gentleman has..a small natural infirmity; he stutters a little. **1856** J. W. Croker in *C. Papers* (1884) I. 6, I..stuttered; for..I had a most distressing impediment in my speech. **1899** *Allbutt's Syst. Med.* VII. 452 Several patients always stuttered on the initial letter if the word subsequently contained an *r*, which they pronounced as *w*.

b. *transf.* and *fig.*

1831 Scott *Jrnl.* 5 Apr., I have a hideous paralytic custom of stuttering with my pen. **1911** [see STUTTERING *vbl. sb.*]. **1931** Nordhoff & Hall *Falcons in France* 236 Guns were stuttering faintly on every side. **1935** J. Steinbeck *Tortilla Flat* ii. 26 The lawyer..climbed into his Ford and stuttered down the hill. **1963** *Times* 11 Feb. 4/1 Meanwhile, the F.A. Cup stutters forward, step by step. **1976** *Scottish Rev.* Summer 8 Tractors stutter in and out of fields.

2. *trans.* To say or speak with a stutter. Also with *out* and *fig.*

c **1645** Howell *Lett.* (1655) IV. vii. 16 The Pagan Poet who stutter'd out this verse, that ther are but two good hours of any woman. **1709** [W. King] *Usef. Trans. Philos.* Mar. & Apr. 42 The Eloquence of the Vice-Roy..who stutters Gibberish of the Author's own Composing. **1849** James *Woodman* x, He attempted to stutter some vain excuses. **1855** Macaulay *Hist. Eng.* xvii. IV. 7 The nonsense stuttered by the tipsy nobles of the Empire. **1864** Burton *Scot. Abr.* II. ii. 178 The brave and reckless prince, who could not speak French, and only stuttered German. **1929** *Oxford Poetry* 12 And the map stutters inarticulate lines.

stutter, var. of STOTTER *v. dial.*, to walk hesitatingly or staggeringly.

1845 S. Judd *Margaret* ii. viii, I stuttered up to No. 4 yesterday arter the funeral. **1875** Jacque *Hope* etc. 194 And age took up its staff and stuttered out, To see what all the hubbub was about.

stutterer ('stʌtərə(r)). [f. STUTTER *v.* + -ER[1].] One who stutters.

1598 Marston *Sco. Villanie* iii. ix. G 8b, The vildest stumbling stutterer That euer hack'd and hew'd our natiue tongue. *c* **1643** Ld. Herbert *Autobiog.* (1824) 187 His words were never many as being so extreme a stutterer, that he would sometimes hold his tongue out of his mouth a good while before he could speak so much as one word. **1771** Smollett *Humphry Cl.* 10 June (1815) 152 The stutterer had almost finished his travels. **1822–9** Good *Study Med.* I. 566 Children..ought never to be intrusted in the company of a stutterer, till their speech has become steady and confirmed. **1899** *Allbutt's Syst. Med.* VII. 449 It is the difficulty of performing the necessary movements of the tongue and lips which usually obtrudes itself on a stutterer's attention.

stuttering ('stʌtərɪŋ), *vbl. sb.* [-ING[1].] The action of STUTTER *v.*

1594 Parsons *Confer. Success.* i. viii. 168 Luys the second, surnamed le begue, for his stuttering. *c* **1618** Moryson *Itin.* iv. v. v. (1903) 482 Nicknames, given them from the Colour of their haire, from lameness, stuttering, diseases or villanous inclinations, which they disdayne not. **1741** Mrs. Montagu *Lett.* I. 290 We must cure people of errors and lying, as they do of stuttering, by a long course of silence.

b. *transf.* and *fig.*

1665 Glanvill *Def. Van. Dogm.* 85 Yea, and.. persecuted them by his reproaches, calling the Philosophy of Empedocles, and all the Antients Stuttering. **1911** *19th Cent.* Jan. 126 In the case of some of the older carillons the apparent hesitation or 'stuttering' (to use the bell-maker's phrase), which is due to the imperfect mechanism, has a quaint and pleasing effect.

'stuttering, *ppl. a.* [-ING[2].] That stutters. Also *transf.* and *fig.*

1589 R. Harvey *Pl. Perc.* Ded., As farre as Will Solnes stuttring pronunciation may stumble ouer at a breath. **1594** Parsons *Confer. Success.* i. viii. 168 This Luys, the stuttering, left two bastard sonnes. **1598** Marston *Pygmal.*, Reactio 67 Who cannot stumble in a stuttering stile? And shallow heads with seeming shades beguile? *a* **1647** Boyle *Wks.* (1744) I. Life 6 Some children whose stuttering habitude he so long counterfeited that at last he contracted it. *a* **1721** Prior *Journ. Copt-Hall* 26 Wks. 1907 ii. 287 Sung to Stuttring Durfey's *Ge sol re*. **1786** Burgoyne *Heiress* i. i, Like a Miss at her stuttering harpsichord, with a nimble finger, but no ear. **1834** J. Forbes *Laennec's Dis. Chest* (ed. 4) 197 The intensity of the rhonchus..the stuttering sound of the pectoriloquy..are additional signs which in most cases leave no room for doubt. **1899** *Allbutt's Syst. Med.* VII. 450 Imitation, as from a stuttering nurse, is an occasional cause [of stuttering]. *a* **1918** W. Owen *Poems* (1963) 44 Only the stuttering rifles' rapid rattle Can patter out their hasty orisons. **1946** D. C. Peattie *Road of Naturalist* iv. 44 Turning out editorials of a rare charm and delicate fancy while the stuttering telegraph battered on his eardrums. **1980** L. Cody *Dupe* iii. 23 Even Selwyn's stuttering typewriter was silent.

Hence **'stutteringly** *adv.*

1563–83 Foxe *A. & M.* 2010/1 Then did the vnder Sheriffe bid him say the Lordes prayer, which he coulde not say neyther, but stutteringly. **1615** Crooke *Body of Man* 701 Those which be halfe deafe do speak but stutteringly. **1876** Meredith *Beauch. Career* III. xii. 229 Colonel Halkett argued stutteringly with the powerful man.

† **'stutting**, *vbl. sb. Obs.* [f. STUT *v.*[1] + -ING[1].] = STUTTERING *vbl. sb.*

c **1430** *Pilgr. Lyf Manhode* iii. xxxii. (1869) 153 Swich manere of langwetynge and of stutinge and turnynge vpsodoun þe wrong in to þe riht. **1483** *Cath. Angl.* 370/2 A Stuttynge, *balbicies*. **1547** Boorde *Brev. Health* xli. 21 As stuttynge that doth come by nature it can not be holpen except it be reformed in youth by some discrete tutor. **1571** Golding *Calvin on Ps.* v. 3 Under the first sort he betokeneth a confused stutting [L. *confusum strepitum*]. **1621** Burton *Anat. Mel.* i. iii. i. i. 231 Stutting, or tripping in speech, &c. hollow eyes, grosse veines, and broad lippes. **1626** Bacon *Sylva* §386 *marg.*, Experiment Solitary, touching Stutting. **1661** Lovell *Hist. Anim. & Min.* 359 Stutting and stammering from humidity.

† **'stutting**, *ppl. a.*[1] *Obs.* [f. STUT *v.*[1] + -ING[2].] = STUTTERING *ppl. a.*

1388 Wyclif *Isa.* xxxii. 4 The tunge of stuttynge men schal speke swiftli. **1575** Vautroullier *Luther on Ep. Gal.* iv. 3, 173 Banish this stutting and stammering Moises farre from thee, with his lawe. **1591** Sylvester *Du Bartas* i. vii. 68 If my dull, stutting, frozen eloquence May dare conjecture of his high intents. *a* **1603** T. Cartwright *Confut. Rhem. N.T.* (1618) 650 The stutting tongue of the lisping babe deserueth more favour then the gracious speech of the eloquent man.

Hence † **'stuttingly** *adv.*

1548 Cooper *Elyot's Dict.*, *Titubanter*, stameryngly, stuttyngly, vnconstantly.

stutting *ppl. a.*[2]: see STUT *v.*[2]

stutting sail: see STUDDING SAIL.

stuue, stuver: see STEW *sb.*[2], STIVER.

stuward, obs. form of STEWARD.

stuwe, obs. form of STEW *sb.*[1], *sb.*[2], and *v.*[2]

stuy, stuyll: see STEW *sb.*[1], STOOL.

stuyrne, obs. form of STERN *a.*

stuyue, stuyver: see STEW *sb.*[2], STIVER.

stw(e, obs. forms of STEW *sb.*[1], *sb.*[2], *v.*[2]

stwansyon, obs. form of STANCHION *sb.* (sense 2).

1481–90 *Howard Househ. Bks.* (Roxb.) 138 And to my Lord of Hely a stwansyon of seluer to pote in henke.

S-twist: see S 8.

stwle, stwyll, obs. Sc. forms of STOOL.

stwnys, stwrly: see STONISH *v.*, STOURLY *adv.*

† **sty**, *sb.*[1] *Obs.* Forms: 1 **stíȝ** (**stiiȝ**), 2, 4 **stiȝ**, 3 *Orm.* **stiȝhe, stih,** 3–4 **sti,** 4 **stighe** (**steghe, stieghe, stighte**), **styȝe,** 4–5 **stie, stye,** 4–6 **sty,** (6 *dial.* **stee**). [OE. *stíȝ* fem. = MDu. *stîge* (early mod.Du. *stijghe*), OHG. *stîga* (MHG. *stîge*):—OTeut. **stīȝō*; a parallel masc. form **stīȝo-z* is represented by MLG. *stîch*, *stîg-*, OHG., MHG. *stîc*, *stîg-* (mod.G. *steig*), ON. *stíg-r* (MSw. *stîgher*, mod.Sw. *stig*, Da. *sti*). From Teut. root **stīȝ-* to go, climb: see STY *v.*[1]

Synonymous words from other grades of the root are Goth. *staiga*, OHG. *steiga* (MHG. *steige*):—OTeut. **staiȝō*; MLG. *stech*, *steg-* (LG. *steg*); MDu. *stege* (mod.Du. *steeg* fem., path, *steg* masc., narrow bridge):—OTeut. **stiȝu-z*.]

A path or narrow way.

Beowulf 320 Stræt wæs stan-fah stiȝ wisode gumum ætgædere. *c* **725** *Corpus Gloss* 651 *Devia callis*, horweg [= orweȝ] stiȝ. [*c* **875** *Erfurt Gloss* 340 *Devia callis*, horuaeg stiiȝ.] *c* **1000** *Ags. Ps.* (Th.) cxviii [cxix]. 105 þæt ys þæt strange leoht stiȝe minre. *c* **1175** *Lamb. Hom.* 7 þe witeȝa het þet we sculde makien his stiȝes [rihte]; þenne make we ham rihte ȝef we haldet his beode. *c* **1200** Ormin 6208 Tatt narrwe stih þatt ledeþþ ȝunnc till heoffne. *c* **1250** *Gen. & Exod.* 3958 Balaam..bet and went it to ðe sti Bi-twen two walles of ston. *a* **1300** *Cursor M.* 4575, I folud siþen, me-thoght, a sti Vntil a feild. *c* **1330** R. Brunne *Chron. Wace* (Rolls) 14191 To Souþhamptone he tok þe sty. **1382** Wyclif *Job* xix. 8 My sty he heggide aboute, and I mai not gon ouer. *a* **1430** *Sev. Sage* (Cott. Galba) 3621 þan sho toke þe preue sty Into þe toure ful hastily.

b. Alliterative phrase, *by sty and street.*

c **1205** Lay. 16366 Ten þusend Scottes he sende bi-halues þe hæðene to imete bi stiȝen & by straten. *c* **1425** *Cast. Persev.* 364 Leue hym nowth, but cum with me, be stye & strete! *a* **1600** *Flodden F.* ii. (1664) 18 He brought them on by stee and street.

sty, *sb.*[2] *north. dial.* Forms: 3–4 sti, 5 stegh, stiȝe, 5–7 stye, 5, 6, 9 stie, 8 steeigh, sty, 9 stey, 5– stee. [a. ON. *stige*, *stege* wk. masc. (MSw. *stighi*, mod.Sw. *stege*, Da. *stige*), f. OTeut. root **stiȝ-*: see STY *v.*[1] Cf. OE. *stiȝe* str. masc., 'ascension', MLG. *stege* fem. step, staircase, OHG. *stega* fem. (MHG. *stege*) step, staircase, ladder.

The Eng. word has always been confined to northern dialects showing strong Scandinavian influence. The form *stee* shows that the original form had a short *i*.]

A ladder.

a **1300** *Cursor M.* 3779 In slepe he sagh stand vp a sti, Fra his heued right to þe ski. *a* **1400–50** *Wars Alex.* 1437 Sum stepis vp on sties to þe stane wallis. *c* **1440** *Alphabet of Tales* 309 Sho.. gatt a stye & clam vp at a hy wall to a wyndow of þe prison. *c* **1440** *York Myst.* xxxiv. 90 And sties also are ordande þore, With stalworthe steeles as mystir wore. Bothe some schorte and some lang. **1567–8** in *Fabric Rolls York Minster* (Surtees) 114 To Mr. Watson for a great long stie, 8s. **1641** BEST *Farm. Bks.* (Surtees) 137 Our longe styes lye allsoe under this helme all winter. **1674** RAY *N.C. Words*, A *Stee*: a ladder. *c* **1746** J. COLLIER (Tim Bobbin) *View Lanc. Dial* Wks. (1862) 44 We reeart th' Steeigh sawfly ogen th' Wough under th' Eawlhoyle. **1804** J. HODGSON in Raine *Life* (1857) I. 25, I could always frighten them well by going a few steps up the stee and showing my black head. **1881** *Cornh. Mag.* Jan. 126 Our Nancy's husband's brother fell off the stee.

b. *attrib.*

1483 *Cath. Angl.* 360/2 A Stee staffe, *scalare*.

sty (staɪ), *sb.*[3] Pl. sties (staɪz). Forms: 3 sti, 6, 7, 9 stie, 4– sty, stye. [OE. *stí* (in comb. *stí-fearh* 'sty-pig'), prob. identical with *stiȝ* (*ȝ* from *j*), ? hall (cf. *stiȝ-weard* STEWARD *sb.*); corresp. to ON. *stí* neut., once (*A'grip* 26, 12th c.) in comb. *svín-stí* 'swine-sty' (Da. *sti*, *svinsti*; Norw. *sti* flock of sheep or goats, also 'household work, esp. with regard to the feeding of the animals'; repr. OTeut. type **stijo-m*, f. root **sti-*: **stai-*). A parallel formation, OTeut. **stijōn-* wk. fem., is represented by ON. *stía* pen, fold, MSw. *stia* in *svína stia* (mod.Sw. *svinstiga*) and *stíogalder* 'sty-pig', MLG. *stege*, sty, MDu. *stije*, *swijn-stije* (mod.Du. *stijg*). Cf. also OHG. *stîga* (MHG. *stîge*, but also *stîje*) cattle-stall, which is perh. cognate, but influenced in form by derivatives of the root **stīȝ-*: see STY *sb.*[1], STY *v.*[1]]

1. An enclosed place where swine are kept, usually a low shed with an uncovered fore-court, a pigsty.

a **1225** *Ancr. R.* 128 Nout ase swin ipund ine sti uorte uetten. *c* **1386** CHAUCER *Sompn. T.* 121 He groneth lyk oure boor lith in oure sty. *c* **1400** MAUNDEV. (Roxb.) xxxiv. 154 Þai.. liffez in lust and lyking of þe flesch, as a swyne fedd in stye. **1573–80** TUSSER *Husb.* (1878) 32 Put bore in stie For Hallontide nie. **1577** B. GOOGE *Heresbach's Husb.* I. 13 There is also a thirde stie.. for the fatting of my Porkes. **1606** SHAKS. *Ant. & Cl.* IV. xiii. 62 Shall I abide In this dull world, which in thy absence is No better then a Stye? **1615** CHAPMAN *Odyss.* XIV. 21 Euery Sty Had roome and vse, for fifty Swine to lye. **1688** HOLME *Armoury* II. 181/2 A Stie is the out-courts, or limits of the Swine coat in which they walk and eat their Meat; but generally we call both the Cote and its outlet a Stie. **1725** POPE *Odyss.* X. 459 She.. hast'ning to the styes set wide the door, Urg'd forth, and drove the bristly herd before. **1864** MISS S. P. FOX *Kingsbridge Estuary* viii. 91 His wife went as usual to feed her pig... For some cause she entered the stye. **1882** JESSOPP *Arcady* ii. (1887) 33 The tottering old crone.. can give the alarm if the pig is in danger of breaking out of the sty.

2. *transf.* and *fig.* in opprobrious uses.

a. A human habitation (or sleeping-place) no better than a pigsty.

1598 SYLVESTER *Du Bartas* II. i. IV. *Handicrafts* 363 Some others yet more gross Their homely Sties in stead of wals inclose. **1684** OTWAY *Atheist* I. i, A foul-feeding Witch, that lived in a thatch'd Sty upon the neighb'ring Common. *a* **1687** SIR W. PETTY *Pol. Anat. Irel.* (1691) 14 Local Wealth I understand to be the building of 168,000 small Stone-wall Houses.. instead of the lamentable Sties now in use. **1712** MOTTEUX *Quix.* III. ii. (1749) I. 115 By this time Sancho.. was crept into his sty, where he did all he could to sleep. **1826** RENTON in *Trans. Med.-Chirur. Soc. Edin.* II. 376 The lower orders of the inhabitants, its principal victims, live huddled together in close and crowded sties.

b. An abode of bestial lust, or of moral pollution generally; a place inhabited or frequented by the morally degraded.

a **1400** *Fest. Church* 142 in *Leg. Rood* App. 215 Þenk on hellestynkyng stye, Where gosstis brenin bynde. **1599** SANDYS *Europæ Spec.* (1632) 36 On the one side of the Street a Cloyster of Virgins: on the other a stie of Courtizans. **1602** SHAKS. *Ham.* III. iv. 94. **1640** GRIMSTON *Sp. Impeachment Abp. Laud* (1641) 2 The Arch-Bishop of Canterbury.. is the stye of all Pestilent filth, that hath infected the State, and Government of the Church and Common-wealth. **1645** MILTON *Tetrach.* 11 What is this but to abuse the sacred and misterious bed of marriage to be the compulsive stie of an ingratefull and malignant lust. **1648** JENKYN *Blind Guide* i. 5 Could more be said for the removall of any stewes or stie of sin? **1790** BURKE *Refl. Fr. Rev.* (ed. 2) 238 The pavement booths and sordid sties of vice and luxury. **1849** MACAULAY *Hist. Eng.* iii. I. 403 But whatever our dramatists touched they tainted. In their imitations the houses of Calderon's stately and highspirited Castilian gentlemen became sties of vice. **1855** MOTLEY *Dutch Rep.* I. Introd. §14. 89 A people which had neither sunk to sleep in the lap of material prosperity, nor abased itself in the sty of ignorance and political servitude.

3. *Comb.*

1611 COTGR., *Bacquier*.. a stye-fed hog. **1864** TREVELYAN *Compet. Wallah* (1866) 33 No pork appears on a Calcutta table except such as has been sty-fed. **1917** *Times* 22 Mar. 7/2 French fields revive and the defilers flee Sty-ward driven back.

sty (staɪ), *sb.*[4] [Prob. a back-formation from STYANY (interpreted as *sty-on-eye*). But cf. early mod.Du. *stijghe* (Kilian), WFris. *stiich*, Norw. *stig*.] An inflammatory swelling on the eyelid.

1617 FLETCHER *Mad Lover* v. i, *Fool.* I have a Stye here, Chilax. *Chi.* I have no Gold to cure it. *a* **1667** SKINNER *Etymol. Ling. Angl.*, A Sty, (i.e.) Tumor Palpebræ Phlegmonodes. **1712** tr. *Pomet's Hist. Drugs* I. 191 It cures the Sty in the Eye-Lids. **1823** E. MOOR *Suffolk Words*, *Sty*—or *Styney*, a troublesome little excresence or pimple on the eye-lid. **1835** MARRYAT *J. Faithful* xvi, I hope your lordship's sty is better in your lordship's eye. **1902** W. W. JACOBS *Sunwich Port* v. 44 You've got a sty coming on your eye.

† **sty**, *v.*[1] *Obs.* Forms: see below; also with prefix 1 ȝe-, 2–3 i-. [OE. *stíȝan* (*stáh*, *stiȝun*, *stiȝen*), a Com. Teut. str. vb. corresponding to OFris. *stîga*, OS. *stîgan*, MDu. *stîghen* (mod.Du. *stijgen*), OHG. *stîgan* (MHG. *stîgen*, mod.G. *steigen*), ON. *stíga* (MSw. *stigha*, mod.Sw. *stiga*, Da. *stige*), Goth. *steigan*:—OTeut. **stīȝ-* (: **staiȝ-*):—Indogermanic **steigh-* (: **stoigh-* **stigh-*) to go, represented by Skr. **stigh* to step, stride, Gr. στείχειν to go, στοῖχος, στίχος a row, line, L. *ve-stīgium* footstep, trace.

Of the weak inflexion a doubtful trace appears in ONorthumbrian; otherwise it has not been found earlier than the 13th c.]

A. Inflexional Forms.

1. *Inf.* and *pres. stem.* 1 stíȝan, *North*, stíȝe, 2–5 stiȝe-n, (2–3 *Orm.* stiȝhenn), 3 stihe-n, 4–5 styȝe, 3–4 stighe, 4 stiyhe, *north.* steich, 5–7 stygh, 3 steo, ste-n, 3–4 stei(e, 5–6 stey, 5 stey-yn, 4–5 stegh, 4 steȝe, steye, stey3(e, (6 stee), 2–7 stie, 4–7 stye, 5–7 sty.

c **950** *Lindisf. Gosp.* Matt. xx. 18 Heonu we stiȝes vel we scilon stiȝe [Vulg. *ecce ascendimus*]. *c* **1200** *Trin. Coll. Hom.* 111 Siððen he is buuen alle heȝnesse hwider sholde he stiȝe. *Ibid.* 145 Ure drihten wolde.. deð þolien and arisen of deaðe and to heuene stie. *a* **1240** *Ureisun* in *O.E. Hom.* I. 201 Ne wene nomon to stihen wið este to þe steorren. *a* **1250** *Five Joys* in *Rel. Ant.* I. 49 [Þou] iseie him in to heuene sten. *c* **1250** *Long Life* 38 in *O.E. Misc.* 158 Weilawei deþ þe schal adun þrowe þer þu wenest heȝest to steo. **13..** *Bonaventura's Medit.* 208 He ros fro deþ to heuene to stye. *c* **1315** SHOREHAM *Poems* v. 252 Hi seȝ ihesus.. Op in-to heuene steȝe. *a* **1325** *Prose Psalter* cxxxviii. 7 [cxxxix. 8] 3if ich steiȝe to heuen þou art þer. *a* **1340** HAMPOLE *Psalter* xxiii. 3 Who sall stegh in þe hill of lord. *c* **1374** CHAUCER *Boeth.* III. met. ix. (1886) 69 O fadyr yiue thow to the thowht to styen vp in to the streyte sete. *c* **1440** *Promp. Parv.* 473/1 Steyyn vp, *scando, ascendo*. *c* **1450** *Mirk's Festial* 153 When þay seen hym.. bodyly stey vp wyth soo gret multitude of angeles. **1460–70** *Pol. Rel. & L. Poems* 229 Take þi crosse to þee, and folewe me, If þou wolt to my blis up stiȝe. ? *a* **1500** *Chester Pl.*, *Ascension* 96 You shall haue here my Blessinge for to heaven I must stye. **1593** G. HARVEY *Pierce's Super.* Wks. (Grosart) II. 234 Lightest phantasies that sty abooue the highest region of the cloudes. **1605** R. B. *Commend. Verses* in *Verstegan's Dec. Intell.*, Industrious then Verstiegan forwards stygh, Raise vp thy nations ancient woorthy fame.

b. *3rd pers. sing. pres.* 1 stíȝeþ, stíȝþ, stíhþ, 3 stiheð, stihð, styhð, 4 stegth, steþ, 4–5 styeþ, 6 stithe, 7 sties.

c **888** [see B 1]. *a* **1000** *Boeth. Metr.* xiii. 61 His [*sc.* the sun] ofer moncyn stihð á upweardes. *a* **1225** *Ancr. R.* 216 Uor stench stihð uppard. **13..** *Seuyn Sag.* (W.) 2288 Up to the halle rof he stegth. *c* **1320** *Cast. Love* 1490 Þat from heuene com, to heuene he steþ. ? *c* **1400** *Erthe upon Erthe* App. I. 42 Wanne eorthe ouer eorthe þorw prude styeþ. *a* **1535** MORE *Fortune* 111 in *Songs, Carols*, etc. (E.E.T.S.) 75 He holdeth faste, but vpward as he stithe, She whippeth her whele abowt, & þer he lieth. **1613** J. DAVIES (Heref.) *Muse's Tears* E 2 b, And, (as a Flame) she still, by Nature, sties Where her Originall reposed lies.

2. *Pa. t.* **a.** *sing.* *a.* 1 stáȝ, stáh, 2–3 stah, steah, steh, steȝ, steȝh, 3 stawe, 2–4 steiȝ, 3–5 stegh, stey, 4 steigh, steyȝ, steegh, steaȝ (*Kent.*), steeȝ, steghe, steye, steyȝe, stehe, steiȝe, steihe, styh, stih, sti, 4–5 stigh, 5 stygh, sty.

c **1000** *Ags. Gosp.* Luke xix. 4 He stah up on an treow. *c* **1200** *Trin. Coll. Hom.* 3 Seðen ure louerd ihesu crist steh to heuene. *Ibid.* 23 Þo he steah to heuene. *Ibid.* 165 Þreo siðes steȝh þis holie maiden. *c* **1200** ORMIN 5987 He stah upp till heoffne. *a* **1225** *Ancr. R.* 250 Þoa he steih into heouene. *c* **1275** *Five Joys* 26 in *O.E. Misc.* 88 Þo þi sone to heouene steyh. *a* **1300** *Fall & Pass.* 107 in *E.E.P.* (1862) 15 An after he steiȝ to heuen aboue. *a* **1300** *Cursor M.* 19009 (Edin.) Til heuin he steich. *Ibid.* 22723 Til heuin he stehe. **13..** *K. Alis.* 5827 The Kyng.. steigh [*Laud MS.* steeȝ] on the wal. *c* **1315** SHOREHAM *Poems* I. 50 Heron ihesus stawe vppe bifore. *a* **1325** *Prose Psalter* xlvi[i]. 5 God steȝ up in swete songe. **1340** *Ayenb.* 13 He.. steaȝ into heuene. *c* **1375** *Lay-Folks Mass-Bk.* (MS. B.) 225 He stegh til heuen. **1387** TREVISA *Higden* (Rolls) I. 113 Out of þat mount Crist steihe vp into heuene. **1390** GOWER *Conf.* I. 273 He styh up to his fader. *c* **1394** *P. Pl. Crede* 810 He steiȝ vp to heuene. *a* **1400** *Relig. Pieces fr. Thornton MS.* 4 He steye in till Heuen. *a* **1400** *Minor Poems fr. Vernon MS.* xxiv. 219 Þi sone in to heuene stih. **1400** GOWER *To Hen. IV* 176 in *Pol. Poems* (Rolls) II. 9 Er Crist.. stigh to hevene. *a* **1400–50** *Wars Alex.* 3467 He þat stiȝe to þe sternes. *c* **1400** MAUNDEV. (1839) viii. 96 Fro that Mount, steighe.. Jesu Crist to Hevene. *c* **1430** HOCCLEVE *New Ploughman's T.* 114 Shee vp to heuene ascendid up and sty. *c* **1440** *Floriz & Bl.* 892 Vp in to þe Toure he steyȝ. *a* **1450** MYRC *Par. Pr.* 518 Cryst.. Stegh in-to heuene.

β. weak forms. 1 *north.* ? stiȝade, 3–5 stide, 4–5 stiede, (4 sticht *Sc.*), 4 stiȝ-, styȝede, stighede, steȝede, steiȝed, -ide, styede, steiede, 5 steyt, 5 steyv(u)d, 5–6 steyyid, steyde, 6 steyed, 4–6 styed, 5–6 stied.

c **950** *Lindisf. Gosp.* John v. 4 Of dune staȝade [? *for* stiȝade]. *c* **1275** LAY. 10737 Þe eorl.. letten louke þe ȝates and stide to walle. *c* **1375** *Sc. Leg. Saints* l. (*Catherine*) 759, & sayand þis, he sticht in hewyn with mekill Ioy & angelis stewyne. **1382** WYCLIF *Prov.* xxi. 22 The wise man steȝede vp. —— *Matt.* xiv. 23 He steiȝide [**1388** stiede] vp in to an hill aloone for to preye. —— *Luke* xix. 4 And he rennynge bifore, stiȝede in to a sycamoure tree. *c* **1400** *Beryn* 1592 A marynere.. Styed in-to the topcastell. *c* **1436** *Libel Engl. Policy* in *Pol. Poems* (Rolls) II. 204 He that.. came frome hevyne, and stiede up with our nature. *c* **1450** *Mirk's Festial* 152 He.. steȝt vp ynto Heuen. *Ibid.* 154 Þus.. Crist steyd ynto Heuen. *c* **1450** *Godstow Reg.* 7 He stied to heuen. *c* **1460** *Play Sacram.* 423 How he styed by hys own powre. *c* **1485** *Digby Myst.* (1882) III. 1341 He steyyd to hevyn. **1492** RYMAN *Poems* xlvi. 7 in *Archiv Stud. neu. Spr.* LXXXIX. 213 He.. rose ayene.. and to blis steyde. *a* **1500** *Adrian & Epotys* 342 in *Brome Bk.* 36 He steyed to heuyn. *Ibid.* 446, 40 And yn to heuyn he steyyud [*printed* steyynd]. **1557** PHAER *Æneid* v. (1558) O iij, He spake, and thynne from sight as smoke, in skyes disperst he styed.

γ. 5 steut.

c **1450** *Mirk's Festial* 232 Yn to þe tyme þat he steut ynto Heuen.

b. *2nd pers. sing.* 3 stihe, stuhe, 4 stehe, stey, stei, 5 stiȝ.

a **1225** *Juliana* 62 Þu.. stihe [*Bodl. MS.* stuhe] abuuen þe steorren to þe heste heouene. *a* **1300** *Cursor M.* 25580 Þat ilk time til heuen stei [*Fairf. MS.* stey] þou,.. suete iesu! *a* **1310** in Wright *Lyric P.* xxv. 69 Jhesu, for love thou stehe on rode. *c* **1430** *Hymns Virg.* (1867) 102 Þou stiȝ to heuen in þi manhede.

c. *pl.* *a.* 1 stiȝon, -un, steoȝun, 2–3 stiȝen, 4 styȝe, stowe(n.

a **1000** *Cædmon's Gen.* 1375 Sæs up stiȝon ofer stæþweallas. *c* **1205** LAY. 26005 Ouer þan watere heo comen.. & stiȝen up þan hulle. **13..** *King Alis.* 1209 They into the walles stowe. **13..** *E.E. Allit. P.* B. 389 Summe styȝe to a stud & stared to þe heuen.

β. weak forms. 4 styeden, stiȝeden, stei-, steyden, 4–5 stieden, 5 stiden, 6 (as sing.).

1382 WYCLIF *Exod.* xiii. 18 And armed steyden vp [**1388** stieden] the sones of Ysrael. *c* **1400** *Destr. Troy* 4948 Two chere men.. Stiden vpon stithe horse. **1449** PECOCK *Repr.* II. xviii. 259 The vij kijn thynne and leene, whiche stieden up after tho. **1503** HAWES *Examp. Virt.* xiv. 288 To heuen we styed a place moost gloryous.

3. *Pa. pple.* *a. strong forms.* 1 stiȝen, 2–3 *Orm.* stiȝhenn, 3 i-stihe(n, 2–4 stoȝen, 3–4 stei (*north.* steich), 4 stiȝe, steie.

c **1175** *Lamb. Hom.* 107 For he mai findan fele þe beoð bet ipoȝen and istoȝen þene he. *c* **1200** ORMIN 8488 Affterr þatt daȝȝ þatt Crist himm sellf Wass stiȝhenn upp till heoffne. *a* **1300** *Cursor M.* 20908 (Edin.) Seix and xxx winter euin fra ihesu criste was steich [*Cott. MS.* stei] till heuin. *c* **1380** *Sir Ferumb.* 5027 By þat were stoȝen vp wyþ vygour An hundren Sarsyns oppon þe tour. **1387** TREVISA *Higden* (Rolls) VI. 227 Oo Kyng of bliss, Lord of vertues, þat.. art þis day i-steie up aboue alle hevenes.

β. weak forms. 4 steied(e, steyed, -id, stiȝed, styȝed, 5 steȝid, steyt, styet, steyut, (steuet), 5–6 styed, 4–6 stied.

c **1375** *Cursor M.* 20831 (Fairf.) Ofter [*sic*] hir sone til heiuen was steyed. *c* **1380** WYCLIF *Serm.* Sel. Wks. I. 25 Aftir þat Crist was steied to hevene. *c* **1400** *Three Kings Cologne* (1886) 31 Aftir tyme þat oure lord was styed vp into heuene. *c* **1450** *Mirk's Festial* 27 Whan Cryst was styet vp into Heuen. *Ibid.* 159 When our Lord Crist was steyut ynto Heuen, his dyscyples wern in care and mornyng. *Ibid.* 232 Aftyr þat hur sonne was steuet ynto Heuen. *Ibid.* 262 Tyll he was steyt vp ynto Heuen. **1583** MELBANCKE *Philotimus* R ij, When thou haste.. stied to the seate of my dignitie. **1587** GOLDING *De Mornay* i. (1592) 5 As from the Earth we haue styed up to the aire.

B. Signification.

1. *intr.* To ascend, mount up, rise or climb to a higher level. Said of persons and things. Also *fig.* Often with *up*, *upwards*.

Often used of the ascension of Christ or of Elijah (for examples see A). In the last quarter of the 16th c. the verb survived only as a literary archaism, and in the 17th c. it became wholly obsolete.

c **825** *Vesp. Psalter* lxvii. 19 Stiȝende in heanisse [L. *ascendens in altum*]. *c* **888** ÆLFRED *Boeth.* xxv, Eft heo [*sc.* the sun] secð hire ȝecynde & stiȝð on þa dæglan weȝas wið hire uprynæs. *c* **1175** *Lamb. Hom.* 5 Heo stiȝen uppeon þe godes cunnes treowe & nomen þa twigga. *c* **1200** *Trin. Coll. Hom.* 217 An ȝerd sal spruten of iesse more and an blosme stien of þare more. *c* **1200** ORMIN 10673, & forrþrihht alls he fullhtnedd wass He stah uppo þe strande. *Ibid.* 11827 Ȝiff aniȝ mann uss læreþþ, To stiȝhenn upp till haliȝ lif & upp till heȝhe mahhtess. *a* **1225** *St. Marher.* 13 Þe stench þæt of þi muð stiheð. *c* **1250** *Owl & Night.* 1405 Þe gost.. styhþ on heyh þur modynesse. **1297** R. GLOUC. (Rolls) 6579 It [*sc.* the tide] watte is brech al aboute & euere vpward it stey. *a* **1300** *Fall & Pass.* 9 in *E.E.P.* (1862) 13 Þo lucifer steiȝ in pride. **13..** *Bonaventura's Medit.* 635 Cryst Ihesu hys body vpp stey, By þat short ladder, þat cros an hy. *c* **1330** R. BRUNNE *Chron. Wace* (Rolls) 8341 Þe lowe was mikel, & vp-ward stey, So þat hit in to þe castel fley, & vp in to þe tour hit went. *c* **1374** CHAUCER *Boeth.* IV. pr. vi. (1868) 143 Whan þou art wel refresshed.. þou shalt ben more stedfast to stye in to heyere questiouns. *c* **1380** WYCLIF *Wks.* (1880) 191 But mannus foly & pride stieþ vp euere more & more in þis veyn nouelrie. **1387–8** T. USK *Test. Love* I. i. (Skeat) 45 Steyers to steye on is none. *c* **1400** tr. *Secreta Secret.*, *Gov. Lordsh.* 73 Moistures styen vp to þe croppys of trees and to þe heuedys of braunches. *c* **1450** *Godstow Reg.* 4 That we may stye and glorified be Where crist is kyng þat dyed on tre. **1450–1530** *Myrr. our Ladye* II. 172 And oute of the rowte therof shal stye vp a flowre. *c* **1530** *Judic. Urines* II. xiv. 45 b,

Coler . . styeth vp & puttet hym selfe in to the vterest partis of the body. **1545** RAYNALDE *Byrth Mankynde* 9 The womb passage . . takith his begynnyng at the passage port: and from thense styeth . . right vpward vnder yᵉ share bone. **1567** GOLDING *Ovid's Met.* v. 319 Till now that she [Pallas] did stie From Seriph in a hollow cloud. **1583** —— *Calvin on Deut.* xxiii. 135 Their wit styeth not high. **1590** SPENSER *F.Q.* I. xi. 25 The beast . . Thought with his winges to stye above the ground. **1590** —— *Muiop.* 42 From this lower tract he dar'd to stie Up to the clowdes. **1596** NASHE *Saffron Walden* Q 4 b, These great men . . had seperately contended to outstrip Pindarus in his Olympicis, and sty aloft to the highest pitch. **1599** PEELE *David & Bethsabe* xv. 125 The eagle . . is emboldened With eyes intentive to bedare the sun, And styeth close unto his stately sphere. **1601** VERSTEGAN *Odes Imit. Penit. Ps.* etc. 92 And as her feet did trauaile on the ground, Her inward mynde did vp to heauen stie. **1621** BP. MOUNTAGU *Diatribæ* 382 Led along, as some Creatures are, by the Noses, and voluntarily hood-winked: or like seeled Doues, stye vp, you know not whither, nor how farre. **1652** BENLOWES *Theoph.* VI. xxiii, That She might stye to th' Seat of Beatifick Mirth!

2. To climb *over* something.

c **1380** *Sir Ferumb.* 2388 'Maubyn,' saide þe Amyral 'wolt þou hit vndertake, To steȝe out ouer þe castel wal.' **1382** WYCLIF *1 Sam.* xiii. 23 Forsothe the stacioun of Philistym went out, for to stye ouer into aspijs to fiȝt.

3. With *down* adv., or other contextual indication: To descend. Also *gen.* to ascend or descend.

c **825** *Vesp. Hymns* iii. 21 Ða ofdune steoȝun in seað [L. *qui descendunt in lacum*]. *c* **1000** *Ags. Gosp.* Mark xiii. 15 Se þe is ofer þecone ne stiȝe he on his hus. *c* **1200** *Trin. Coll. Hom.* 111 Erest he steȝ neoðer and siðen on hegh. *c* **1200** ORMIN 16700 Wiþþutenn himm þatt stah forr menn Off heffne dun till erþe. *a* **1300** *E.E. Psalter* xxi. 30 In his sight sal be falland Alle þat doune stighen in land [Vulg. *qui descendunt in terram*].

4. *trans.* **a.** To ascend, climb up (a hill).

1491 CAXTON *Vitas Patr.* (1495) 129 Wherof some wold haue styed the mountayn.

b. To convey up hill.

1511 GUYLFORDE *Pilgr.* (Camden) 80 At the sayd Noualassa we toke moyles to stey us vp the mountayne.

sty (staɪ), *v.*[2] Also **stye.** [OE. *stiȝian*, f. *stiȝ*, *stí* STY *sb.* Cf. ON. *stía*.]

1. *trans.* To place or confine (swine) in a sty. Also with *up*.

a **1100** *Gerefa* in *Anglia* IX. 262 Swyn stiȝian. **1573–80** TUSSER *Husb.* (1878) 40 At Michelmas safely go stie vp thy Bore. **1614** MARKHAM *Cheap Husb.* v. xvi. 96 First, you shall stie vp those Swine which you intend to feede. **1655** MOUFET & BENNET *Health's Improv.* viii. 67 As for the common way of brawning Bores, by stying them up in so close a room that they cannot turn themselves round about. **1674** FLATMAN *Belly God* 76 The Hampshire Hog with Pease and Whey that's fed Sti'd up, is neither good alive nor dead. **1725** *Bradley's Family Dict.* s.v. *Swine*, In Champain Countries they must sty up thin Hogs. **1886** STEVENSON *Kidnapped* xvi, The inn . . was the most beggarly vile place that ever pigs were styed in. **1899** LUMSDEN *Edin. Poems* 108 The times wad be amiss When I styed here my soo.

b. *transf.* To confine as in a sty; to place in narrow and uncomfortable quarters; to pen *up*.

1610 SHAKS. *Temp.* I. ii. 342 And here you sty me In this hard Rocke, whiles you doe keepe from me The rest o' th' Island. **1622** MASSINGER & DEKKER *Virg. Mart.* v. i, Bandogs (kept three dayes hungry) worried 1000. British Rascals, styed vp, fat Of purpose. **1646** TRAPP *Comm. John* xxi. 2, 144 God dwels in the Assembly of Saints: shall we, like Stoicks stie up our selves, and not daily runne into their company?

2. *intr.* To share a sty *with*; to dwell as in a sty.

1748 RICHARDSON *Clarissa* (1768) VIII. 61 What woman . . did she know what miry wallowers the generality of men of our class are in themselves, and constantly trough and sty with, but would [etc.]. **1829** FONBLANQUE *Eng. under 7 Administr.* (1837) I. 283 See in your public estate too the havoc the pigs make, . . who . . devour your cabbages, . . stye in your house, and grunt in your Parliament. **1894** H. NISBET *Bush Girl's Rom.* 145 A nice piggery for successful squatters to sty in, I must say.

Hence **styed** *ppl. a.*, set in a sty.

1829 E. ELLIOTT *Village Patriarch* III. ix, Yet, unlike thee Is minion'd Erin's sty'd and root-fed clown.

sty, stye (staɪ), *int. Sc.* and *north.* Chiefly in *to say* (or *know*) *neither buff nor stye*: see BUFF *sb.*[5] A. b.

? *a* **1750–1824**: see BUFF *sb.*[5] A. b. **1823** GALT *Entail* li, He was clean dementit at that time, . . he would neither buff nor stye for father nor mother, friend nor foe. **1885** 'J. STRATHESK' *More Bits Blinkbonny* i. 5 Ye can neither make buff nor stye o' them.

styan ('staɪən). Now *dial.* Forms: 1 **stíȝend**, 6 **staying**, 7 **stian**, 9 **styan**, **stine**, etc. (see *Eng. Dial. Dict.*). [OE. *stíȝend* (lit. 'riser'), agent-n. (related to *stiȝende* pres. pple.) f. *stíȝan* STY *v.*[1]] = STY *sb.*[4]

c **1000** ÆLFRIC *Gloss.* in Wr.-Wülcker 114/10 *Ordeolus* stiȝend. **1597** LOWE *Chirurg.* (1634) 163 Hordelium . . In vulgar language, the Staying. **1601** HOLLAND *Pliny* XXVIII. xi. II. 324 A soveraigne liniment for the Stian or any other hard swelling in the eyelids. **1736** AINSWORTH *Lat. Dict.*, *Hordeolus*, . . a little swelling in the eye-lids, like a barley corn; a stian, or stithe. **1834** DE QUINCEY *Autob. Sk.* Wks. 1853 I. 70, I knew that a *styan* (as it is called) upon the eyelid could be easily reduced . . by the slight application of any golden trinket.

styany ('staɪənɪ). Now *dial.* Forms: 5 **styanie**, 6 **styonie**, **styony**, 8–9 **stiony**, 9 **styney**, **stine-eye**, **sty-on-eye**, etc. (see *Eng. Dial. Dict.*). [f. STYAN + EYE *sb.*; the etymological sense is therefore an eye with a 'styan' on it.] = STY *sb.*[4]

c **1440** *Promp. Parv.* 475/1 Styanye yn the eye, *egilopa*. **1552** HULOET, Styony, disease growyng within the eye lyddes, *sycosis*. **1570** LEVINS *Manip.* 102/24 Ye styonie, *sycosis*. **1572** HULOET (ed. Higins), Styony. **1706** PHILLIPS (ed. Kersey), *Stiony*, . . A Disease in the Eye-lids. **1823** Styney [see STY *sb.*[4]]. *a* **1825** FORBY *Voc. E. Anglia*, *Stiony*, a small itching and inflamed pimple among the eye-lashes. **1881** *Leicestersh. Gloss.*, Sty-on-eye.

†**stybill.** *Obs.*[−0] [Prob. an error for TWIBILL.] Some kind of axe.

c **1475** *Pict. Voc.* in Wr.-Wülcker 807/25 *Hic bipennus*, *Hic bidens*, a stybylle.

styborn(e, -urne, obs. forms of STUBBORN.

styca ('staɪkə). *Numism.* Also 8 **stica**, **sticca**, 9 **stika**, **styka**. [Assumed sing. from ONorthumb. *stycas*, dial. pl. of OE. *stycce* str. neut. (WS. pl. *styccu*) piece (of money): see STITCH *sb.*[2]

The sense 'piece of money' occurs only in the following passage, where it is applied to the 'widow's mite'. The OE. word was certainly never the distinctive name of a coin.

c **950** *Lindisf. Gosp.* Mark xii. 42 An widua ðorfend sende tuoȝe stycas þ is feorðung penniȝes.]

The name given in modern times to a small copper coin current in Northumbria in the seventh, eighth, and ninth centuries. The extant specimens weigh about 17 grains.

1705 FOUNTAINE in Hickes *Thesaurus* II. Diss. 164 Quod Styc vel Styca ab antiquis Anglis vocabatur. **1745** LEAKE *Engl. Money* (ed. 2) 14 They [Saxons] had Copper Stycas also, smaller than the Penny, having the King's Name on one Side [etc.]. **1753** *Scots Mag.* Apr. 200/2 Two small silver Saxon coins of a sort called *Sticaes*. **1756** *Gentl. Mag.* XXVI. 284 Mr. Thoresby says in relation to the *Sticas*, namely, that the three in his collection were all that were known at Oxford. **1778** *Engl. Gazetteer* (ed. 2) s.v. *Rippon*, A considerable number of Saxon coins were found here anno 1695, particularly the brass ones, called sticcas, eight whereof made a penny. **1844** LINGARD *Anglo-Saxon Ch.* (1858) II. App. O. 388 The *styca* was the one-fourth of a penny. **1845** *Proc. Berw. Nat. Club* II. No. xiii. 123 Mr. Donaldson Selby exhibited two Saxon Styca. **1851** D. WILSON *Preh. Ann.* 521 By far the greater number are stykas of Eadgar. **1915** *Proc. Soc. Antiq. Scot.* 201 The small disc referred to above . . is not a styca—for that it is too thick; possibly it has been a Roman minim.

stychling, var. STICHLING (see STICHLE *v.*).

styd, obs. form of STUD *v.*[1]

styd(e, obs. forms of STEAD *sb.*

styddie, styd(d)y, obs. forms of STITHY.

stye: see STY *sbs.*, *vbs.*, and *int.*

†'**styer.** *Obs.* Forms: 4 **steghere**, **steȝere**, **stier(e**, **steier**, **steyer**, **steyȝer**. [f. STY *v.*[1] + -ER[1].] One who ascends or mounts; in quots. a rider (tr. L. *ascensor*).

a **1340** HAMPOLE *Cant. Moses* (Exod. xv) 1 in *Psalter* 503 The hors and the steghere he kast down in the see. **1382** WYCLIF *Gen.* xlix. 17 An horned eddre . . biting the cleen of an hors, that the steyer [**1388** stiere] vp of hym falle bacward. **1382** —— *Isa.* xxi. 9 Lo! this cam, a man steȝere [**1388** stiere] of the carte of horse men.

styewe, obs. form of STEW *sb.*[1]

styf(e, styff(e, obs. forms of STIFF *a.*

styfer, obs. form of STIVER.

styful ('staɪfʊl). *rare.* [f. STY *sb.*[3] + -FUL.] As many (swine) as a sty will hold.

1875 BLACKMORE *Alice Lorraine* III. xx. 267 Mr. Bottler had designed . . to slay a large styful of pigs.

†'**Stygial,** *a. Obs.* [ad. L. *Stygiālis*, f. *Stygi-us*: see next and -AL[1]. Cf. F. *stygial*.] = next.

1523 SKELTON *Garl. Laurel* 1327 By the Stigiall flode, And the stremes wode Of Cochitos bottumles well.

Stygian ('stɪdʒɪən), *a.* and *sb.* Also 6 **Stygion**, 6–7 **stigian**, 7 **stigean**, (**stageoun**). [f. L. *Stygi-us* (a. Gr. *Στύγιος*, f. *Στυγ-*: see STYX) + -AN. Cf. F. *Stygien*.] **A.** *adj.*

1. Pertaining to the river Styx, or, in wider sense, to the infernal regions of classical mythology.

Stygian Jove, *Jupiter* (= L. *Juppiter Stygius*): Pluto, the god of the lower world.

1566 STUDLEY *Agam.* 545 Wher as the stygion porter doth aduaunce with lustye crakes. **1590** SPENSER *F.Q.* II. vii. 27 If euer he transgrest the fatall Stygian lawes. **1594** KYD *Cornelia* III. i. 138 It eyther turneth to the Stygian Lake, Or staies for euer in th' Elisian fields. **1602** *Narcissus* (1893) 658 Stray, soule . . vnto the Stingian [*sic*] strand. **1606** SHAKS. *Tr. & Cr.* III. ii. 10 Like a strange soule upon the Stygian bankes Staying for waftage. *c* **1610** SIR J. SEMPLE in *Sempill Ballatis* (1872) 242, I sweere . . by the stageoun stankes of hell, by which the gods do sweir. **1631** KNEVET *Rhodon & Iris* v. iii. H 3, Where . . Thou mai'st a thousand heroicke soules send packing Vnto the Stygian shore. **1667** MILTON *P.L.* III. 14 Thee [holy light] I re-visit now with bolder wing, Escap't the Stygian Pool, though long detain'd In that obscure sojourn. **1697** DRYDEN *Æneis* IV. 916 Thus will I pay my Vows, to Stygian Jove. **1827** HOOD *Ode to Melancholy* 49 Ay, let us think of Him a while, That, with a coffin for a boat, Rows daily o'er the Stygian moat. **1860** THACKERAY *Lovel* vi. (1861) 225 In that omnibus I had been carried over to t'other side of the Stygian Shore. I returned but as a passionless ghost. **1900** BRIDGES *Recoll. Solit.* 49 Ere ye the mournful Stygian river crost.

transf. and *fig.* **1600** W. WATSON *Decacordon* (1602) 46 As men inuolued in laberinths of errours, drowne themselues in the Stigean lake of their owne folly. **1802** BRITTON & BRAYLEY *Beauties Eng.* III. 111 The plain [near Solway Moss] that was covered by this stygian torrent, has since been reclaimed. **1879** FARRAR *St. Paul* I. II. vii. 119 Content to wallow, like natural brute beasts, in the Stygian pool of a hideous immorality.

b. Of an oath: Supremely binding, inviolable like the oath by the Styx, which the gods themselves feared to break.

1608 CHAPMAN *Byron's Trag.* v. ii. P 3, His vowes And othes so Stygian. **1647** H. MORE *Philos. Poems* 301 But O that envious Destinie, Or Stygian vow, or thrice accursed charm Should [etc.]. **1682** SIR T. BROWNE *Chr. Mor.* III. xvi. (1716) 104 They [astrologers] Kill us not with Stygian Oaths and merciless necessity, but leave us hopes of evasion. *Ibid.* xix. 107 But Honest Men's Words are Stygian Oaths, and Promises inviolable.

2. Infernal, hellish.

1601 YARINGTON *Two Trag.* IV. viii. in Bullen *O. Pl.* IV, We have such evidence, To ratifie your Stigian cruelty, That cannot be deluded any way. *a* **1627** MIDDLETON *Mayor Queenb.* v. ii, If this be not the man, whose Stygian Soul Breath'd forth that counsel to me. **1635** QUARLES *Emblems* I. x, Sometime they whoop, sometimes their Stygian cries Send their black-Santos to the blushing skies. **1648** JENKYN *Blind Guide* i. 3, I know not one . . left him to contend with for mastery in the . . art of lying . ., unlesse it be his stygian teacher. *a* **1652** J. SMITH *Sel. Disc.* ii. 32 The broad gates of hell are opened, the rivers of fire and Stygian inundations run down as a swelling flood. **1663** DRYDEN *Wild Gallant* I. ii, What a Stygian woman's this, to talk thus? **1667** MILTON *P.L.* x. 453 Amaz'd At that so sudden blaze the Stygian throng Bent thir aspect. **1784** COWPER *Task* III. 738 To be preferred to smoke, to the eclipse That Metropolitan volcanoes make, Whose Stygian throats breathe darkness all day long. **1876** HARDY *Hand Ethelberta* xxvii, But what Stygian sound was this? . . 'We are close to a kennel of hounds,' said Ethelberta.

3. Black as the river Styx; dark or gloomy as the region of the Styx.

1599 MARSTON *Antonio's Rev.* I. i, Will I not turne a glorious bridall morne Unto a Stygian night? **1634** MILTON *Comus* 134 Mysterious Dame, That ne're art call'd, but when the Dragon woom Of Stygian darknes spets her thickest gloom. **1742** YOUNG *Nt. Th.* VI. 80 Life In stronger thread of brighter colour spun . .; dipt by cruel fate In Stygian dye, how black, how brittle here! **1814** WORDSW. *Laodamia* 66 The conscious Parcæ threw Upon those roseate lips a Stygian hue. **1876** EMERSON *Lett. & Soc. Aims*, *Immortality* Wks. (Bohn) III. 277 Swedenborg . . announced many things true and admirable, though always clothed in somewhat sad and Stygian colours. **1910** *Bible in World* Jan. 28/1 Old prints show us the Irwell, whose stygian waters are now walled in . ., flowing through green fields and wooded banks.

†**4.** ***Stygian water, liquor*** [tr. mod.L. *aqua Stygia*]: in Old Chemistry, a name for nitrohydrochloric acid and other strong mineral acids. Also applied to virulent poisons. ***Stygian liquor*** (jocularly): a black nauseous drink. *Obs.*

1638 SIR T. HERBERT *Trav.* (ed. 2) 220 In the evening many Mussulmen assemble to sip a sort of Stigian liquour; a black, thick, bitter potion, brewed out of Bunchie or Bunnu berries. *a* **1661** BOYLE *Cert. Physiol. Ess.* iv. (1669) 140 Upon the mixture of these two Liquors there also obtrudes it self upon the Sense a very strong and offensive smell . . which perhaps occasion'd some Chymists to call a Menstruum (wherein that nitrous spirit and smell is predominant) the Stygian water. **1706** PHILLIPS (ed. Kersey), *Stygian Liquors*, are Acid Spirits, so call'd by Chymists, from their Power to destroy or dissolve Mixt Bodies. **1797** W. JOHNSTON tr. *Beckmann's Invent.* I. 100 The means Mr. Bell employed to analyse these stygian drops. *Ibid.* 101 That there are more kinds than one of this stygian water. *Ibid.* II. 44 The horns of a Scythian animal, in which the Stygian water that destroyed every other vessel could be contained.

B. *sb.* A dweller by the Styx. *nonce-use.*

1860 THACKERAY *Roundabout P.*, *Dessein's*, And so . . even among these Stygians this envy and quarrelsomeness . . survive?

styile, styill, obs. forms of STILE, STYLE.

†'**stying,** *vbl. sb.*[1] *Obs.* [f. STY *v.*[1] + -ING[1].] The action of ascending; an ascent.

c **1200** *Trin. Coll. Hom.* 167 Salomon þe wise . . sehȝ þese wunderliche stienge [*sc.* the three ascents of the Virgin Mary] alse suterliche alse he þis dai were. *a* **1340** HAMPOLE *Psalter* cxix [cxx]. 1 Sang of degres, that is, ioy of thoght in gastly steghynge. *c* **1380** WYCLIF *Wks.* (1880) 448 Aftir his steying to heuene. **1382** —— *Ps.* lxxxiii [lxxxiv]. 6 Steȝingus vp [**1388** stiyngis, Vulg. *ascensiones*] in his herte he disposide. *c* **1440** *Promp. Parv.* 473/2 Steyynge, *scansio*, *ascensus*. **1493** *Dives & Pauper* (W. de W. 1496) I. lvi. 97/1 Prayer is a styeng up of a mannes herte to god.

b. *concr.*

1382 WYCLIF *Cant.* iii. 10 His pileris he made siluerene, . . the steȝing vp [**1388** a stiyng, Vulg. *ascensum*] purpur. *c* **1440** *Promp. Parv.* 473/2 Steyle, or steyynge vp, *ascensus*, *scansile*.

stying ('staɪɪŋ), *vbl. sb.*[2] [f. STY *v.*[2] + -ING[1].] The placing of swine in sties.

1905 A. T. SHEPPARD *Red Cravat* II. ix. 149 The farmyard, where . . I once assisted in the stying of a refractory pig.

†'**stying,** *ppl. a. Obs.* [f. STY *v.*[1] + -ING[2].] That ascends.

1593 G. HARVEY *Pierces Super.* 8, I, that sought the winges of a mounting Pegasus, or a stying Phenix.

styk, styka: see STEEK *v.*³, STYCA.

styl, obs. form of STEEL, STILL.

ˌstylagal'matic, *a. rare. Arch.* (In Dicts. erron. -aic.) [f. Gr. στῦλος column + ἀγαλματ-, ἄγαλμα image + -IC.] Pertaining to, containing, or supported by, figures serving as columns.

1828 J. ELMES *Metrop. Improv.* 113 The stylagalmatic termini, which support the shop cornice. **1837** *Antiq. Athens* 45 The stylagalmatic portico of the Caryatides. [**1842** BRANDE *Dict. Sci.* etc. *Stylagalmaic.* **1846** B. H. SMART Suppl., *Stylogalmaic.*]

stylar ('staɪlə(r)), *a.* Also stilar. [f. mod.L. type *stylāris*, f. *stylus*: see STYLE *sb.* and -AR.]

†**1.** Pertaining to the 'style' or gnomon of a dial. *Obs.*

1614 E. WRIGHT *Dialling* xvi. E 2, Draw a right line out of the intersection of the line of contingence, and substilar perpendicularly ouerthwart the stilar line. **1668** MOXON *Mech. Dyalling* 12 Draw a Line from the Center through that number of Degrees for the Stilar Line. **1836** SMART.

†**2.** Pertaining to (literary) style. *Obs.*

1814 *Sporting Mag.* XLIV. 191 Stylar analogy between the preface and the text.

3. 'Having the character of or pertaining to a style for writing' (*Cent. Dict.* 1891).

stylary ('staɪlərɪ), *a. Zool.* [f. STYLE *sb.* + -ARY.] Pertaining to a style or stylet.

1885 H. O. FORBES *Nat. Wand. E. Archip.* 93 The rostellum..is not invaginated down to the stylary canal.

‖**Stylaster** (staɪ'læstə(r)). *Zool.* [mod.L. (Gray 1831), f. Gr. στῦλ-ος column + ἀστήρ star.] A genus of hydrozoa, closely related to the *Millepora*; a species or an animal of this genus, or of the family Stylasteridæ, of which it is the type. Hence **ˌstylaste'racean, sty'lasterid**, an animal of the family Stylasteridæ.

1831 J. E. GRAY (*title*) Description of a new genus (Stylaster) of Star-bearing Corals. **1872** DANA *Corals* (1875) 48 There are a number of genera in this Stylaster family, the Stylasteridæ. **1875** H. N. MOSELEY in *Phil. Trans.* CLXVI. 115, I examined a specimen of a Stylasteracean dredged by the 'Challenger'..with the same result. **1879** —— *Notes Nat. 'Challenger'* 530 In the case of another Stylasterid, *Allopora nobilis*, the development of regular systems of polyps is commenced. **1882** *Cassell's Nat. Hist.* VI. 277 The coloured Stylasters of the deep sea.

stylate ('staɪlət), *a.* [ad. mod.L. *stylātus*, f. *stylus*: see STYLE *sb.* and -ATE.] **a.** *Bot.* 'Having a persistent style' (*Treas. Bot.* 1866). **b.** *Zool.* Having a style or stylet. Also, having the form of a pen or pin, styliform, styloid.

(In recent Dicts.)

style (staɪl), *sb.* Forms: 4 **styele, styyl, stele**, 4–6 **still**, 5 **stiel, styll**, 5–6 **styill**, 6 **steill, stylle**, 6–7 **steele**, 4–9 **stile**, 4– **style**. [a. OF. *style, stile, stil, estile*, etc. (mod.F. *style*), ad. L. *stilus* (also incorrectly written *stylus*) a stake or pale, pointed instrument for writing, style of speaking or writing; f. root **sti-* (? to prick): cf. STIMULUS. Cf. Pr. *estil*, Sp., Pg. *estilo*, It. *stilo, stile*, G. *stil.*

The spelling *style*, originally a meaningless variant of *stile*, owes its modern currency, both in Fr. and Eng., to the erroneous notion that L. *stilus* is an adoption of Gr. στῦλος column. In senses 7 and 8, the early history of which is obscure, the word may possibly be ad. Gr. στῦλος; but without further knowledge it is impossible to say whether those who first used the word in these senses were thinking of the Gr. or the L. word; quite probably they regarded the two as identical. As these senses may quite easily have been developed from senses of the L. *stilus*, there is no sufficient reason against treating them as belonging to the present word.]

I. Stylus, pin, stalk.

1. a. *Antiq.* An instrument made of metal, bone, etc., having one end sharp-pointed for incising letters on a wax tablet, and the other flat and broad for smoothing the tablet and erasing what is written: = STYLUS 1. Also applied to similar instruments in later use.

1387 TREVISA *Higden* (Rolls) V. 297 Seinte Barnabe his body was founde in a den..wiþ þe gospel of Mathew þat he hadde i-write wiþ his owne stile. *c* **1470** HARDING *Chron.* LXIII. viii, Whiche me nede not with my stile auaunce. **1585** HIGINS *Junius' Nomencl.* 7/2 *Graphium*, a writing wyer, or a steele wherewith to write or note. **1621** G. SANDYS *Ovid's Met.* IX. (1626) 187 Then fits her trembling hands to write: One holds the wax, the style the other guides. **1710** HEARNE *Collect.* (O.H.S.) II. 395 *Liber Ceylonicus*, writ with a style upon the Leaves of Trees. **1766** *Complete Farmer* s.v. *Surveying*, A Welsh slate with a sharp stile..is more convenient at such a season, than pen, ink, and paper. **1840** ARNOLD *Hist. Rome* II. xxxii. 295 He had his tablets and his style in his hands, to record the votes. **1840** LARDNER *Geom.* 270 To trace a curve..by the continued motion of a pencil or stile. **1864** TICKNOR *Life Prescott* x. 134 The whole apparatus is called a noctograph. When it has been adjusted ..the person using it writes with an ivory style, or with a style made of some harder substance, like agate, on the upper surface of the blackened paper. **1885–94** BRIDGES *Eros & Psyche* Nov. x, All which he took his silver stile to write In letters large upon a waxèd board.

b. Used as a weapon of offence, for stabbing, etc.

1669 *Addr. Hopeful Yng. Gentry Eng.* 67 Methinks every point I direct my pen to should be the Sharp Execution of a Stile at their hearts. **1770** LANGHORNE *Plutarch, C. Gracchus* (1879) II. 892/1 They immediately killed Antyllius with long styles, said to have been made for such a purpose. **1845** LINGARD *Anglo-Sax. Ch.* II. xii. 246 *note*, A vague tradition that the boys, whom the sophist taught, provoked by his severity, had stabbed him with their styles for writing. **1856** MERIVALE *Rom. Emp.* xlviii. (1865) VI. 94 The senators fell upon the wretched man and stabbed him to death with their styles.

c. *fig.*, or as a symbol of literary composition.

1579 FENTON *Guicciard.* Ep. Ded., Suche as for the grauitie and fidelitie of their penne and style were cherished with the greatest Princes of those dayes. **1614** C. B. *Ghost Rich. III* (Shaks. Soc. 1844) 27 Crown'd be his stile with fame, his head with bayes. **1640** DENHAM *Cooper's H.* 132 But Princes swords are sharper then their styles. **1820** HAZLITT *Lect. Dram. Lit.* 329 Their swords and their styles carved out their way with equal sharpness. **1827** HOOD *Ode to Melancholy* 55 Where Death, with his keen-pointed style, Hath writ the common doom.

†**d.** Phrase. ***to turn one's style***: to change *to* another subject; also, to speak on the other side. [So *stilum vertere* in late L.] Similarly to ***address, bend, direct, dress, gye***, etc. ***one's style***. *Obs.*

a **1300** *Cursor M.* 13001 Leue we him a littel quille And turn we to sant Iohn vr still. *c* **1407** LYDG. *Reson & Sens.* 4890 To declare yt and expresse, A noon I wil my style dresse. *c* **1410** —— *Life Our Lady* lxvii. (1484) k iij, That thorow thyn helpe I may my style gye Somwhat to sey of thyn epyphanye. *c* **1412–20** —— *Chron. Troy* IV. 3362 Wher, for a tyme, I wil leue him dwelle, And to Grekis..directe ageyn my stile. **1420–22** —— *Thebes* 2124 Thus leue I hym ride forth a while, whilys that I retourne ageyn my style Vnto the kyng. *a* **1529** SKELTON *P. Sparowe* 772, I..cannot in effect My style as yet direct With Englysh wordes elect. **1535** STEWART *Cron. Scot.* I. 220 At this dewys I leif thame heir ane quhile, And to the Romanis turne I will my style. **1581** LAMBARDE *Eiren.* III. i. (1588) 333 Here let us.. addresse our stile to other statutes. **1605** BACON *Adv. Learn.* I. vii. §16 But saith hee, Turne your stile, and let vs heare what you can say against vs. **1639** DU VERGER tr. *Camus' Admir. Events* 159 This young man quite turning his stile when his Master had strayed from the right way of vertue, beganne to cry out against his inconstancy. *a* **1656** BP. HALL *Revelat. Unrevealed* §4 Reverend and holy Dionysius bent his style in two Books of the Promises of God. **1664** BUTLER *Hud.* II. iii. 202 Where, leave we Him and Ralph a while, And to the Conj'rer turn out stile. **1700** DRYDEN *Pal. & Arc.* II. 34 To gentle Arcite let us turn our Style.

2. An engraving-tool; a graver.

1662 EVELYN *Chalcogr.* (1906) 7 The γλυφεῖον Style, or Scalprum. **1682** DRYDEN *Medal* 22 The Style that copy'd every grace, And plough'd such furrows for an Eunuch face. **1785** COWPER *Task* I. 706 Nor does the chissel occupy alone The pow'rs of sculpture, but the style as much. **1801** FUSELI in Barry etc. *Lect. Paint.* (1848) 350 The outlines were traced with a firm but pliant style, which they called *cestrum.*

†**3.** A pointed instrument used for marking. *Obs.*

1659 TWYSDEN *S. Foster's Miscell.* xv. 12 With some stile or dent make a mark where the point of the Gnomon is reposed through the water, upon the side of the Vessel.

4. *Surg.* A blunt-pointed probe.

1631 H. C[ROOKE] *Expl. Instrum. Chirurg.* 7 Then it will be necessary to seare the Vlcer with a Style blunt at the end, and red hot running in a hollow pype. **1846** J. MILLER *Pract. Surg.* 98 To accomplish this, styles—or small bougies—are employed. **1895** *Arnold & Sons' Catal. Surg. Instrum.* 157 Style for Fistula Lachrymalis (Walton's), silver.

5. A hard point for tracing, in manifold writing; the marking-point in a telegraph or phonograph.

1871 CULLEY *Pract. Telegr.* (ed. 5) 205 A lever carrying a point or style, which embosses a mark upon a band of paper carried forward by wheelwork. **1878** M. FOSTER *Physiol.* III. iii. §1. 451 A very light style attached to the incus or stapes is made to write on a travelling surface. **1881** *Nature* 20 Oct. 582/2 A style concentric with the shaft presses lightly against a compound sheet of tracing and carbonised paper attached to the under side of the table.

6. *gen.* A fixed pointer, pin, or finger for indicating a point or position. Cf. STYLUS 4.

1555 EDEN *Decades* (Arb.) 390 We must tary vntyll the poynt or style of the clocke do exactly come to the poynt of sum houre. **1594** BLUNDEVIL *Exerc., Mercator's Globes* (1597) 209 A little round Squire of brasse,..the head or stile whereof is to shew the shadow of the Sunne being set vpon the Globe. **1646** SIR T. BROWNE *Pseud. Ep.* II. iii. 76 Placing therein two stiles or needles composed of the same steele, touched with the same Loadstone, and at the same point. **1664** EVELYN tr. *Freart's Parallel Archit.* etc. 152 The Style is a streight Ruler, one end whereof is fixt in the center of the said Circle, the other end moves about at pleasure, so as that it may be easily transfer'd and directed from one division of the Circle to another.

7. a. The pin, rod, or triangular plate which forms the gnomon of a sun-dial.

1577–87 HARRISON *England* II. vi. 171/1 in *Holinshed*, Among the Persians onelie the king dined when the sunne was at the highest, and shadow of the stile at the shortest. **1594** BLUNDEVIL *Exerc., Descr. Tables of Sines* (1597) 52 b, That shadowe is called *Vmbra versa*, which proceedeth from some right style or pearch being thrust into a wall or post standing right vp, and not leaning. **1651** J. WHITE *Rich Cabinet* (1677) 44 The Stile may be made of a thin Iron plate, and cemented in, or of a stiffe wire. **1764** J. FERGUSON *Lect.* 197 The edge of the plane by which the time of the day is found, is called the stile of the dial. **1834** MRS. SOMERVILLE *Connex. Phys. Sci.* xiii. 104 The shadow of the stile of a dial. **1868** LOCKYER *Elem. Astron.* §402. 193 In practice,..all we want is a projection called a style, parallel to the earth's axis,..and a dial.

b. defined as a *line.*

1690 LEYBOURN *Curs. Math.* 704 Draw the Line CF for the Axis, or Stile of your Dial. **1704** J. HARRIS *Lex. Techn.* I. *Style*, in Dyalling, is that Line whose Shadow on the Plane of the Dyal, shews the true Hour-Line. This is always supposed to be a part of the Axis of the Earth, and therefore must always be so placed, as that with its two extreme Points it shall respect the two Poles of the World, and with its Upper-end, the elevated Pole. This Line is the Upper-edge of the Cock, Gnomon, or Index.

8. *Bot.* A narrowed prolongation of the ovary, which, when present, supports the stigma at its apex.

1682 S. GILBERT *Florists Vade-Mecum* (1702) 122 The flowers..opening into five fair broad leaves, with a stile and small threds in the middle of a Saffron colour. **1691** RAY *Creation* I. (1692) 92 The figure of the Stile and Seed-vessel. **1784** J. KING *Cook's 3rd Voy.* VI. vi. III. 335 From the centre of the flower rises a style of a triangular form, and obtuse at the end. **1872** OLIVER *Elem. Bot.* I. i. 9 In many plants the stalk of the stigma is of considerable length,..whether long or short, however, it is called a style.

9. *Ent.* **a.** A slender bristle-like process in the anal region. **b.** The bristle or seta of the antenna of a dipter.

1826 KIRBY & SP. *Entomol.* III. xxxiii. 392 *Styli* (the Styles). Rigid, exarticulate, long and narrow anal organs. Ex. *Staphylinus.* **1895** D. SHARP *Insects* I. 238 The ninth pair [of abdominal appendages]..form the ventral styles. *Ibid.* II. 442 The part of the antenna beyond the scape is called the 'flagellum'; an appendage of the flagellum is called 'arista' when bristle-like, when thicker 'style'.

10. *Zool.* **a.** A small slender pointed process or part; a stylet.

1851 WOODWARD *Mollusca* 67 Octopodidæ:..shell represented by two short styles, encysted in the substance of the mantle. **1875** HUXLEY in *Encycl. Brit.* I. 762/1 There are five digits in the manus of the *Anura*; but the pollex is rudimentary, being represented only by a cartilaginous or more or less ossified style. **1876** —— in *Nature* 11 May 34/2 A horse-like animal..with three toes,..but having, in addition, a little style of bone on the outer side of the fore foot.

b. A sponge-spicule pointed at one end.

1879 H. N. MOSELEY *Notes Nat. 'Challenger'* 530 The 'style,' a rod of the calcareous skeleton, which in many genera of *Stylasteridæ* acts as a support to the mouth-bearing polyp within its pore. **1888** W. J. SOLLAS in *Challenger Rep.* XXV. p. lviii, When the single actine is strongylate at the origin and oxeate at the termination the term style is used without qualification.

¶**11.** A post, stake. *nonce-use* (tr. L. *stilus*).

1579 HAKE *Newes out of Powles* (1872) G ij, Entending.. to..seuer places by themselues, with styles and parting stakes. **1609** HOLLAND *Amm. Marcell.* XXIII. iii. 222 When as ..a round stone is put into the sling, foure lustie young men ..unfolding the barres whereto the ropes are incorporate, draw backe the style or standard up to the hooke.

II. [Developed in L. from sense 1.] Writing; manner of writing (hence also of speaking).

†**12. a.** A written work or works; literary composition; in later use occas. a composition spoken or sung. *Obs.*

a **1300** *Cursor M.* 21293 þe stile o matheu, water it was, And win þe letter o lucas. *c* **1430** LYDG. *Min. Poems* (Percy Soc.) 87 As seynt Jerom rehersithe in his style. **1500–20** DUNBAR *Poems* lxxxiv. 22 And sen thir clarkis hes writtin in thair stylis To ȝoungar folk and thair successioun. **1508** —— *Goldyn Targe* 68 Noucht thou, [H]omer, als fair as thou coud wryte, For all thine ornate stilis so perfyte. **1579** W. WILKINSON *Confut. Fam. Love* To Rdr. *iiij b, Against whose opinions my whole stile and writyng is especially directed. **1579** SPENSER *Sheph. Cal.* Jan. 10 Well couth he tune his pipe, and frame his stile. **1595** *Locrine* V. iv. 200 Addresse your eares to heare a mournfull stile!

†**b.** An inscription or legend. *Obs.*

c **1512** *Earl Northumb. Househ.-Bk.* (1770) 199 And a Still on the Hede of every Quarter of the Parcellis that is provided forre. **1640** SANDYS *Christs Passion* IV. 110 The Governour intreating to take down That glorious Stile [the superscription on the Cross]. **1689** LUTTRELL *Brief Rel.* I. 502 There is a new great seal made, with this stile round it: Willielmus 3. et Maria 2 [etc.].

†**c.** An entry, clause, or section in a legal document. Also ?the heading or introductory formula of a will, a writ, or other document. *Obs.*

1570–6 LAMBARDE *Peramb. Kent* (1826) 192 Without shewing for what auncient service..the same Rent grew due and payable, as in the first stile or entrie is expressed. **1619** *Depositions Bk. Archdeaconries Essex & Colchester* 103 b, Robert Wistocke..had begun to write the stile of the will, but went no farther. **1648–9** WHITELOCK *Mem.* (1853) II. 492 That the name of any one particular person should not be inserted as the style of any common writ.

13. a. The manner of expression characteristic of a particular writer (hence of an orator), or of a literary group or period; a writer's mode of expression considered in regard to clearness, effectiveness, beauty, and the like.

†*in frankis stile* (quot. 1330): in the French language.

c **1330** R. BRUNNE *Chron. Wace* (Rolls) 16705 (Petyt MS.) Pers of Langtoft..On frankis stile þis storie wrote. *c* **1386** CHAUCER *Clerk's T.* 1092 Therfore petrak writeth This storie, which with heigh stile he enditeth. **1412–20** LYDG. *Chron. Troy* I. 3090 After þe maner of my rude stile. *c* **1440** *Promp. Parv.* 475/2 Style, forme of indytynge, or spekynge or wrytynge, *stilus.* **1517** H. WATSON *Ship of Fools* Argt. A j, In facyle sentence and famylyer style. *a* **1548** HALL *Chron., Edw. IV.* 227 A letter of diffiance, bothe for the stile & the pennyng excellently endited. **1609** B. JONSON *Epicœne* II. ii, So shee may censure Poets, and Authors, and stiles, and compare 'hem. **1721** SWIFT *Let. Yng. Gentl. Holy Orders* Wks. 1898 III. 201 Proper words in proper places, make the true definition of a style. **1728** LAW *Serious C.* vii. (1732) 96 She will sometimes read a book of Piety..if it is much commended for stile and language. *a* **1817** T. DWIGHT *Trav.* (1821) I. 510 The Boston style is a phrase, proverbially used ..to denote a florid, pompous manner of writing. **1845** PATTISON *Ess.* (1889) I. 13 St. Gregory of Tours has no style, barely grammar. **1870** RUSKIN *Lect. Art* iii. 68 No man is worth reading to form your style, who does not mean what he says. **1889** SWINBURNE *Stud. B. Jonson* 174 The incomparable style of Mr. Ruskin.

b. Used for: A good, choice or fine style.

1589 *Pappe w. Hatchet* (1844) 17 All this is but bad English, when wilt thou come to a stile?

c. Proverbial phr. ***the style is the man***.

[**1624** R. BURTON *Anat. Melancholy* (ed. 2) 7 It is most true, *stylus virum arguit*, our stile bewrayes vs. **1753** G. BUFFON *Histoire Naturelle* VII. p. xvii, Le style est l'homme même.] **1901** G. B. SHAW *Caesar & Cleopatra* 208 Going to Caesar's books, and concluding that the style is the man. **1901** A. WHYTE *Bible Characters*: *Stephen to Timothy* civ. 72 If the style is the man in Holy Scripture also,..we feel a very great liking for Luke. **1942** H. F. HEARD *Reply Paid* (1943) ix. 141 Usually I don't like to have my style modified. 'The style is the man.' **1978** *Language* LIV. 284 In describing Achilles' speech, we have also been describing his character, since 'style is the man'.

14. In generalized sense: Those features of literary composition which belong to form and expression rather than to the substance of the thought or matter expressed. Often used for: Good or fine style.

1577 HARRISON *England* Ep. Ded., I neuer made any choise of stile, or picked wordes. *c* **1618** E. BOLTON *Hypercrit.* iv. §1 Language and Style, the Coat and Apparel of matter. **1713** STEELE *Englishm.* No. 7. 46 The Rules of Method, and the Propriety of Thought and Stile. **1749** CHESTERF. *Let. to Son* 24 Nov., Style is the dress of thoughts. **1840** DE QUINCEY *Lang.* Wks. 1858 IX. 93 It is certain that style, or..the management of language,..is able..to yield a separate intellectual pleasure quite apart from the interest of the subject treated. **1849** MACAULAY *Hist. Eng.* iii. I. 331 Some cultivated rhetoric with such assiduity and success that their discourses are still justly valued as models of style. **1875** JOWETT *Plato* (ed. 2) IV. 121 The Parmenides in point of style is one of the best of the Platonic writings.

15. A manner of discourse, or tone of speaking, adopted in addressing others or in ordinary conversation.

1567 TURBERV. *Epit.* etc. 77 Stop vp thine eares this Syren to beguile,..be sure To lend no eare vnto hir flattring stile. **1614** BACON *Charge touching Duels.* 28 No man tooke himselfe fowled by them [*sc.* reproaches], but tooke them but for breath, and the stile of an enemy. **1667–8** PEPYS *Diary* 23 Feb., But here talking, he did discourse in this stile: 'We', and 'We' all along, 'will not give any money' [etc.]. **1711** SWIFT *Cond. Allies* 32 This hath been the Style of late Years; which whoever introduced among us, they have taught our Allies to speak after them. **1722** WODROW *Hist. Suff. Ch. Scot.* II. 362 When Threats moved him very little, some others of them changed their Stile, and calmly asked him, What is the Reason you will not comply as your elder Brother hath done. **1791** BOSWELL *Johnson* an. 1768, May, He talked in his usual style with a rough contempt of popular liberty. **1807** CRABBE *Par. Reg.* III. 907 To a new style his reverence rashly took; Loud grew his voice, to threat'ning swell'd his look. **1832** GREVILLE *Mem.* (1874) II. 289 Able as he is, he has adopted a tone and style..unusual on the Episcopal bench. **1875** JOWETT *Plato* (ed. 2) V. 5 The Athenian talks to the two others..in the style of a master discoursing to his scholars.

†**16.** A form of words, phrase, or formula, by which a particular idea or thought is expressed.

1594 T. B. *La Primaud. Fr. Acad.* II. 571 Neuerthelesse wee meane according to the stile of the holy scriptures, that hee [etc.]. **1642** D. ROGERS *Naaman* 589 To use Saint Iames his stile..saying, If God will blesse it, it shall heale. **1649** JER. TAYLOR *Gt. Exemp.* II. Disc. viii. 60 Every sinner in the stile of Scripture is a fool. **1653** T. WATSON *Art Div. Contentm.* vii. (1668) 42 *Ipse dixit* was enough among Pythagoras his Scholars; *Be it enacted*, is the Royal Style. **1654** H. L'ESTRANGE *Chas. I* (1655) 4 In the stile of the Court he [James I.] went for Great Britain's Solomon. **1710** PRIDEAUX *Orig. Tithes* i. 9 The Stile and Phrase of the Text plainly speaks of it as such. **1736** BUTLER *Anal.* I. iii. 64 The eastern Stile would be literally applicable to him, that all People, Nations, and Languages should serve him.

17. a. *Scots Law.* The authorized form for drawing up a deed or instrument.

c **1480** HENRYSON *Sheep & Dog* 8 For by the vse, and cours, and commoun style On this maner maid his Citatioun. **1490** *Munim. de Melros* (Bannatyne Club) 600 In þe sikkyrast forme & styill of obligatioune wsyt..within the Realme. **1585** *Sc. Acts Jas. VI* (1814) III. 377/2 That euerie writtair subscribe his name on þe bak of þe signatour or lettre as allowit be him That it is writtin according to þe ordiner stile and forme. **1697** G. DALLAS (*title*) System of Stiles, as now Practicable within the Kingdom of Scotland. **1708** J. SPOTTISWOODE *Introd. Stile of Writs* (1727) 28 When the Bond of Provision is made by a Father, in favours of his whole Children, the Stile is thus. I A. for the paternal Love and fatherly Affection that I have and bear to B, C, &c. my lawful Children, by these Presents [etc.]. **1862** HENDRY (*title*) Styles of Deeds and Instruments..Second Edition.

b. In generalized sense: Legal technicality of language or construction; as in ***words*** or ***clauses of style***.

1743 KAMES *Decis. Crt. Sess. 1730–52* (1799) 75 The extent of the obligation is to be gathered from the nature of the transaction, rather than from clauses of style slightly or imperfectly framed. **1765–8** ERSKINE *Inst. Law Scot.* III. I. §1 Their *verborum obligatio*, to the forming of which it behoved both parties to utter certain *verba solennia*, or words of style. **1912** BLACK & CHRYSTAL *Life W. R. Smith* vi. 237 Libels were drawn up in the old ratiocinative form, bristling with words of style and verbosities of all kinds.

18. a. A legal, official, or honorific title; the proper name or recognized appellation of a person, family, trading firm, etc.; the ceremonial designation of a sovereign, including his various titles and the enumeration of his dominions.

a **1300** *Cursor M.* 16082 He es na godd ne godds sun, of him we knau þe stile. *c* **1412** HOCCLEVE *De Reg. Princ.* 2832 He þat noble is of blode, and a lorde In stile. **1414** *Dede is worchyng* 115 in *26 Pol. Poems* 59 To ffraunce kyng Edwarde had queryle, Hit was his kynde heritage; And ȝe han þe same style. *c* **1470** HENRY *Wallace* IX. 87 The Rede Reffayr thai call him in his still. **1543–4** *Act 35 Hen. VIII*, c. 3 (*title*) The Bill for the Kinges Stile. **1625** BACON *Ess.*, *Prophecies* (Arb.) 537 The Kings Stile, is now no more of England, but of Britaine. **1639** FULLER *Holy War* III. x. (1640) 126 King Richard, with some of his succeeding English Kings wore the title of Jerusalem in their style. **1667** MILTON *P.L.* II. 312 Or these Titles now Must we renounce, and changing stile be call'd Princes of Hell? **1758** *Payne's Universal Chron.* 29 July–5 Aug. 141/1 A Grant..of the dignity of an Earl of the said kingdom, by the name, stile and title of Earl of Wandesford, in the county of Kilkenny. **1796** MORSE *Amer. Geog.* I. 232 Articles of Confederation..in which they took the style of 'The United States of America.' **1849** MACAULAY *Hist. Eng.* x. II. 667 The title of king of France, assumed by the conqueror of Cressy, was not omitted in the royal style. **1863** H. COX *Instit.* III. viii. 715 Conferring the whole Admiralty jurisdiction..on one person, under the style of High Admiral. **1865** M. ARNOLD *Ess. Crit.* Pref. p. xiv, My native modesty is such, that I have always been shy of assuming the honourable style of Professor. **1886** *Law Rep.* Weekly Notes 198/1 The covenant was..that he would not use a particular name or style in trade. **1913** *Times* 13 Sept. 17/6 Partnerships Dissolved... P. Lawford and P. W. Billing,..under the style of A. S. Wilson and Co.

b. *gen.* Any distinguishing or qualifying title, appellation, or denomination. Now *rare* or *Obs.*

c **1400** *Pilgr. Sowle* IV. xx. (Caxton 1483) 67 And eke of moder hast thou lost the style. **1508** KENNEDIE *Flyting w. Dunbar* 282 Wallace..callit Corspatrick tratour be his style. *a* **1592** GREENE *Jas. IV*, I. i, The name of father, and the style of friend. **1605** BACON *Adv. Learn.* I. vi. §2 The one carrying the stile of a Manufacture, and the other of a lawe, decree, or Councell. **1611** MIDDLETON & DEKKER *Roaring Girl* K 4, A ruffler is my stile, my title, my profession. **1631** HEYWOOD *2nd Pt. Fair Maid of West* I. C 2 b, T' impose on me The hatefull stile and blot of pandarisme, That am a Gentleman. **1646** SIR T. BROWNE *Pseud. Ep.* I. iii. 10 Their soberest adversaries have ever afforded them the stile of fooles and mad men. **1673** PENN *Chr. Quaker* vii. Wks. 1726 I. 542 Which excellent Principles..do worthily deserve, in my Esteem, the Stile of Divinity. **1711** SWIFT *Cond. Allies* 30 The Style of *Maritime Powers*, by which our Allies, in a sort of contemptuous manner, usually couple us with the Dutch. **1742** YOUNG *Nt. Th.* IV. 788 A Christian is the highest stile of man.

III. Manner, fashion.

†**19. a.** A method or custom of performing actions or functions, esp. one sanctioned by usage or law. ***style of court***: see quot. 1726. *Obs.*

c **1430** *Pilgr. Lyf Manhode* III. xxxi. (1869) 152 But whan j wole, þe style j haue, and hippe a while bi lesinges and lyinge. **1530** PALSGR. 276/1 Style a processe, *stile*. **1535** STEWART *Cron. Scot.* II. 10 Tua legatis he hes send..To execute the law in Romane stylis. **1549** *Registr. Aberdon.* (Maitl. Club) I. 434 Togyddyr with seruice in ostijng and vthir generall raidis furneist þairto efter þe forme and styill of þe schyir. **1647** CLARENDON *Hist. Reb.* I. §20 According to the style of that Court and the slow progress in all things of ceremony. **1721** STRYPE *Eccl. Mem.* (1822) I. I. 145 He did an act against the custom and common style of the Court. **1726** AYLIFFE *Parergon* 193 The Style of Court is properly the Practice observ'd by any Court in its way of Proceeding. **1773** GOLDSM. *She stoops to Conq.* II. i, I like to give them a hearty reception in the old style at my gate.

†**b.** A particular manner of life or behaviour.

c **1412** HOCCLEVE *De Reg. Princ.* 4024 Allas! þat Kynges nobleye Turne schulde into style of tirannye! *Ibid.* 4516 [addressing a miser] Thus may thy style likned be to thefte.

†**c.** ? Outward demeanour. *Obs.*

1596 SPENSER *F.Q.* IV. ii. 29 Ne certes can that friendship long endure, How euer gay and goodly be the style, That doth ill cause or euill end enure.

†**20.** Condition with regard to external circumstances. *Obs.*

c **1450** HOLLAND *Howlat* 658 The stern Emprriouris Style thus staitly restord is. *Ibid.* 709 Quhar sic statis will steir, thar stylis till ostend, ȝe wait all worschip and welth dayly induris. *c* **1480** HENRYSON *Robene & Makyne* 57 Robene, I stand in sic a styll [*rimes* quhyle, begyle]; I sicht, and þat full sair.

21. a. A particular mode or form of skilled construction, execution, or production; the manner in which a work of art is executed, regarded as characteristic of the individual artist, or of his time and place; one of the modes recognized in a particular art as suitable for the production of beautiful or skilful work.

1706 *Art of Painting* (1744) 63 When a curious person has well consider'd the different pictures of a master, and has form'd a perfect idea of his stile. **1728** CHAMBERS *Cycl.*, *Style*, in Music, the manner of Singing and Composing. Thus we say, the Style of the Charissimi, of Lully, of Lambert; the Style of the Italians, the French, the Spaniards, &c. **1743** FRANCIS tr. *Hor.*, *Odes* III. i. 61 On Columns, rais'd in modern Style. **1763** J. BROWN *Poetry & Mus.* xii. 210 It [Modern Church Music] is infected with the same Puerility of Stile, with their Opera Airs. **1777** ROBERTSON *Hist. Amer.* (1778) II. VII. 286 The hardest Egyptian stile, stiff and imperfect as it was, is more elegant [than that of Mexican painting]. **1801** FUSELI *Lect. Paint.* ii. 69 Michael Angelo lived to see the electric shock which his design and style had given to art. **1812** CRABBE *Tales* v. 533 The shining tables, curiously inlaid, Were all in comfortless proud style display'd. **1832** G. DOWNES *Lett. Cont. Countries* I. 84 At Lausanne we only stopped for dinner (which we obtained in sufficiently bad style at the *Lion d'Or*). **1858** HINGESTON *Capgrave's Chron.* (Rolls) p. xxvi, The style of the writing corresponds very closely with that of those MSS. of Capgrave which are known..to have been written by his own hand. **1865** *Nat. Hist. Rev.* 338 The 'style' in which the book has been produced is excellent. **1910** *Encycl. Brit.* II. 28/1 British manufacturers are building [fishing-] rods after the American style.

b. In generalized sense. Often used for: Beauty or loftiness of style.

1801 FUSELI in Barry, etc. *Lect. Paint.* (1848) 381 The few nudities which he [Fra Bartolomeo] allowed himself to exhibit show sufficient intelligence and still more style.

c. A definite type of architecture, distinguished by special characteristics of structure or ornamentation. Often with prefixed designation, as the ***Grecian***, ***Gothic***, ***Italian***, ***Romanesque style***; the ***Norman***, ***Early English***, ***Decorated***, ***Perpendicular***, ***Tudor***, ***Renaissance***, ***Palladian style***; and the like.

1777 DALRYMPLE *Trav. Sp. & Port.* cxxxiii, A very handsome church..in the Gothic stile. **1817** RICKMAN *Styles Engl. Archit.* 46 The first or Norman style. *Ibid.* 56 The Second, or Early English Style. *Ibid.* 71 The Third, or Decorated English Style. **1838** *Civil Eng. & Arch. Jrnl.* I. 157 The beauties or defects of either the Egyptian, Grecian, Roman, or Gothic style. **1874** MICKLETHWAITE *Mod. Par. Churches* 251 A man can no more invent a new style than he can invent a new language. *a* **1878** SIR G. SCOTT *Lect. Archit.* I. 6 Each age had its architectural style distinctly and strongly marked.

d. *Printing.* The rules and methods, in regard to typography, display, etc., observed in a particular printing-office.

1871 *Amer. Encycl. Printing* (ed. Ringwalt) 451 It is highly important for a compositor to thoroughly familiarize himself with the style of the office in which he is employed, as well as the style adopted for any special work. *Ibid.*, After a compositor has been at an office for years, where, habituated to the style of the house, he sets up words in type as follows. **1894** *Amer. Dict. Printing*, etc. 530 Most printing-offices have their own particular method in the matter of display, spelling, &c., and this is known as the style of the house.

e. *Calico printing.* (*a*) See quot. 1844. (*b*) Any of the various methods in use for producing the coloured design.

1844 G. DODD *Textile Manuf.* ii. 58 Among calico-printers the term pattern is applied to disposition of forms, while style is applied to disposition of colours. **1874** CROOKES *Dyeing & Calico-Printing* 566 The madder styles have for a long time played the most important part in calico-printing. **1892** ARLIDGE *Dis. Occupations* 523 The art of dyeing is one characterised by very diverse methods, or, as they are called, 'styles'.

22. a. A kind, sort, or type, as determined by manner of composition or construction, or by outward appearance.

1794 MRS. RADCLIFFE *Myst. Udolpho* xxxii, Of the latter style of countenance..were those of the peasant and his wife. **1797** JANE AUSTEN *Sense & Sensib.* xxxiii, There was something in her style of beauty to please them [*i.e.* men] particularly. **1836** DICKENS *Sk. Boz*, *Visit Newgate*, The former [murderer]..exhibiting a style of head and set of features, which might have afforded sufficient moral grounds for his execution at any time. **1849** *N. Brit. Rev.* XI. 479 Emilia Wyndham is a complete example of the style of novel in which Mrs. Marsh is qualified to succeed. **1899** *Allbutt's Syst. Med.* VII. 659 The 'style' of the symptoms, as I am in the habit of calling it.

b. *transf.* Said predicatively of a person or thing: What suits (a person's) taste; the 'sort' that (a person or set of persons) would choose or approve.

1811 MISS L. M. HAWKINS *C'tess & Gertr.* I. 358 Had he continued to live *en garçon*, his own Chariot, little less weight than a farmer's loaded waggon, with gilt springs.. would have been his style. **1880** 'OUIDA' *Moths* I. 145 She is not the style of the day at all, you know.

†**c.** ***in a..style***. (*a*) Of a (specified) kind; (made) on a certain scale. (*b*) In a (good or bad) condition as regards health, mode of life, etc. *Obs.*

1772 *Test Filial Duty* II. 24 Every thing here is in a great stile; I shall hence forward look on the middle part of England as the miniature of nature. **1789** CHARLOTTE SMITH *Ethelinde* II. 269 By all accounts he's in a bad style. He was always, I thought, a giddy unpromising boy. *Ibid.* III. 5 Nor should I have thrown away a thought on this [lady], had not she had the reputation of an understanding in a superior style. *Ibid.* 264 My horses are all in a fine style.

23. a. Manner of executing a task or performing an action or operation. Often with reference to athletics, racing, games: The manner of action of a particular performer, racehorse, etc. Also *gen.*, one's characteristic manner of acting or reacting. Phr. ***to cramp one's style***: see CRAMP *v.* 5 c.

1774 BURKE *Sp. Amer. Tax.* Wks. 1792 I. 551 To repeal by a denial of our right to tax in the preamble..would have cut, in the heroic style, the Gordian knot with a sword. **1815** J. SMITH *Panorama Sci. & Art* II. 157 The bold adventurer ascended from Belvidere Grounds, Dublin,..and in a gradual and majestic style left the shores of Ireland. **1819** in *Lond. Gaz.* (1820) No. 17629. 1670/1 That the service entrusted to him has been executed in a stile most creditable to the professional skill of the Major-General himself. **1833** HT. MARTINEAU *Tale of Tyne* i. 11 A barge was coming up in fine style. **1833** *Q. Rev.* XLIX. 382 The style in which he [a horse] ran, his nose almost sweeping the ground. **1879** PROCTOR *Rough Ways* (1880) 159 They row in a style, which without being actually identical with that of the London waterman, resembles it in all essential respects. **1879** *Oxf. & Camb. Undergrad. Jrnl.* 13 Mar. 291/2 If his staying powers can be trusted he is perhaps the best man in the boat, his style being very good. **1891** B. HARTE *First Fam. Tasajara* x,

It was like you to..say all those mean, silly things to dad,.. in your regular looney style. **1937** C. ODETS *Golden Boy* I. iii. 47 Joe knows his own needs, as he says. Don't ask him to change his style. **1970** G. F. NEWMAN *Sir, You Bastard* viii. 247 It hadn't been his original intention to make her suffer, but he couldn't alter his style. **1978** S. BRILL *Teamsters* vi. 260 Lying low just isn't his style.

b. Used *absol.* for: Good or fine style.

1864 *Times* 21 Mar. 9/6 Mr. Hawkshaw, in speaking for the Cambridge crew, said they had been beaten by style.

24. a. A mode of deportment or behaviour; a mode or fashion of life, esp. in regard to expense, display, etc.

1770 C. JENNER *Placid Man* III. iv. I. 163 He found Lady Clayton in a very high stile of passion. *a* **1775** *Hobie Noble* xv. in Child *Ballads* IV. 3 Then Hobie Noble is that deer; I wat he carries the style fu hie! **1780** *New Newgate Cal.* V. 161 Living in the stile of a gentleman. **1788** MRS. HUGHES *Henry & Isab.* III. 66 An opportunity of marrying in such a manner as would enable her to live in a certain style, among a certain class. *c* **1789** GIBBON *Autobiog.* Misc. Wks. 1796 I. 117 Between the expensive style of Paris and of Italy it was prudent to interpose some months of tranquil simplicity. **1792** GOUV. MORRIS in Sparks *Life & Writ.* (1832) I. 374 The society is noisy and in bad style. **1798** SOPHIA LEE *Canterb. T., Young Lady's T.* II. 14 [He] had already brought home an immense fortune from the East, and was now to return in a high style. **1814** SCOTT *Wav.* lxii. ¶1 That gentleman..lived in what is called great style. **1816** *Remarks Eng. Manners* 87, I was convinced by their style that any overture on my part would be deemed an intrusion. **1825** LAMB *Lepus Papers* v. Wks. 1903 I. 278 What a style you *do* live in! what elegant curtains! **1847** C. BRONTË *Jane Eyre* xv, I began the process of ruining myself in the received style, like any other spoony. **1885** 'E. GARRETT' *At any Cost* xiii. 246, I don't say your Miss Chrissie did anything in that style, but she lost her place here through her carryings on. **1892** E. REEVES *Homeward Bound* 270 So we left in great style, with bands playing and soldiers presenting arms.

b. Used *absol.* for: Fashionable air, appearance, deportment, etc. Also, more generally, attractive or impressive quality; originality.

1807–8 W. IRVING *Salmag.* viii. (1860) 176 Style.. consists in certain fashions, or certain eccentricities, or certain manners, of certain people, in certain situations, and possessed of a certain share of fashion or importance. **1835** WILLIS *Pencillings* I. xxv. 175 A plain German city, with little or no pretensions to style. **1848** ALB. SMITH *Chr. Tadpole* xxvi. 233 An evident wish to throw a little style into their costume. **1885** HOWELLS *Ind. Summer* ii. 16 The refined and indefinite perfume which exhaled from the ensemble of her silks, her laces, and her gloves, like an odorous version of that otherwise impalpable quality which women call style. **1967** *Trans-Action* Apr. 11/1 Style is difficult to define as it has so many referents. It means to carry one's self well, dress well, to show class... A person with style must also show respect..for another's superior power. **1968** *Listener* 13 June 761/3 Jack, the prime Kennedy,..had a quality which practically everybody recognised as 'style'. **1979** R. JAFFE *Class Reunion* (1980) II. xi. 288 How much more dignified it would have been if Rusty could have trusted her... But Rusty had never had style.

c. *in style*: splendidly, showily, according to fashionable requirements. Also † *in a style*.

1781 W. BLANE *Ess. Hunting* (1788) 31 *note*, All other kind of Hounds are now entirely laid aside by those who affect to hunt in style. **1782** MISS BURNEY *Cecilia* IV. ii, We began with cotillons, and finished with country dances. It was the most elegant thing you ever saw in your life; everything quite in a style. **1807** *Sporting Mag.* XXIX. 23 Every gentleman who perambulates Bond-street and the Steyne in style. **1835** DICKENS *Sk. Boz, Publ. Dinners*, The driver.. —no doubt that you may do the thing in style—turns a deaf ear to your earnest entreaties to be set down at the corner. **1874** RUSKIN *Fors Clav.* IV. 39 This is what the modern British public thinks is 'living in style'.

d. *transf.* Attractive quality (in a thing).

1897 *Daily News* 18 Mar. 8/7 They found that the beer had 'more style,' as it was called, when there was a certain admixture of foreign barley.

25. A particular mode or fashion of costume.

1814 JANE AUSTEN *Mansf. Park* xxiv, A better style of dress. **1833** HT. MARTINEAU *Brooke Farm* viii, His daughters look very well in their better style of dress. **1860** *Draper & Clothier* I. 129/1 The dress is of the style called in Paris, the *robe Impératrice*. **1866** GEO. ELIOT *F. Holt* xvi, Got up, both inside and out, as candidates in the style of the period. **1891** *Truth* 10 Dec. 1240/2 The front was all white satin, made in Empire style.

26. A person's characteristic bearing, demeanour, or manner, esp. as conducing to beauty or striking appearance.

1826 DISRAELI *Viv. Grey* v. xv, Most amusing, delightful girl, great style! **1861** MRS. H. WOOD *Shadow of Ashlydyat* I. ii, I do not see much beauty in Charlotte Pain. I do not like her style. **1870** DICKENS *E. Drood* iv, Mr. Sapsea is very proud of this, and of his voice, and of his style. **1869** MRS. STOWE *Oldtown Folks* vi. (1870) 61 There are some very homely women who have a style that amounts to something like beauty.

IV. 27. a. A mode of expressing dates. *Chiefly*, Either of the two methods of dating that have been current in the Christian world since the introduction of the Gregorian calendar in 1582: viz., the ***New Style*** (abbreviated N.S.), which is the result of the Gregorian reform, and the ***Old Style*** (O.S.) which follows the unreformed calendar. The New Style is occasionally called the ***Roman Style***, and the Old Style the ***English Style***. In historical dates earlier than 1582, however, ***Roman Style***, as used by modern writers, means only that the year mentioned is to be understood as beginning on 1 Jan.

The Julian calendar was based on the assumption that the tropical year consisted of 365¼ days. In order that the average calendar year should have this length, it was provided that the normal year should contain 365 days, but every fourth year 366 days. Down to A.D. 1582 the Julian calendar continued to be used by all Christian nations. In calendars and almanacs, the year began on 1 Jan. (like the Roman consular year); but for ordinary purposes the time of beginning the year was different in different places; in England, after some fluctuations, the beginning of the legal year was fixed for 25 March. After the adoption of the Christian era, the leap years were those whose number A.D. (reckoned from 1 Jan.) was divisible by 4.

The Julian estimate of 365¼ days for the length of the tropical year was too great by about 11 minutes, an error which amounts to one day in about 128 years. Hence in 1581 the date of 21 March for the vernal equinox, assumed since the early 4th c. in the rule for computing Easter, was 10 days too late. To remedy this inconvenience, and to prevent its recurrence, Pope Gregory XIII, acting on the advice of the Jesuit Clavius and other eminent astronomers, ordained that in A.D. 1582 the day after 4 Oct. should be reckoned as 15 Oct., and that in future the years which had a number ending in two cyphers should not be leap years unless the number were divisible by 400. The Julian date of 1 Jan. for the beginning of the year was retained. The difference between the old and new calendars continued to be 10 days until 1700 (the first disputed leap-year), when it became 11 days; in 1800 it became 12 days, and in 1900 13 days, from which there will be no further increase till 2100.

The Gregorian calendar (so called from the name of the Pope) was speedily adopted in all Roman Catholic countries, while the other nations of Europe adhered to their traditional reckoning. In the 17th and 18th centuries, it was often found necessary to state whether a date was according to Old or New Style, or to give both datings. As the nations which accepted the reform usually began the year on 1 Jan., not, as in England, on 25 Mar., there was for the March quarter (in addition to the other difference) a discrepancy in the number of the year between the Old Style and New Style dates.

In England and Scotland the Gregorian calendar was established by the Act 24 Geo. II. c. 23 (1751), which provided that the year 1752 and all future years should begin on 1 Jan. instead of 25 Mar. (in Scotland this rule had been adopted in 1600), that the day after 2 Sep. 1752 should be reckoned the 14 Sep., and that the reformed rule for leap year should in future be followed. Ireland followed in 1788. The use of New Style is now universal throughout the Christian world with the exception of certain countries of the Greek Church; in Russia it was officially adopted by the revolutionary government in 1918.

The use of *stilus* for 'mode of dating' was current in med.L., as a specific application of the sense 'usage' (cf. 19 above). In France the expression New Style (*nouveau style*) had been current before the time of the Gregorian reform, with reference to the change in the beginning of the year from Easter to 1 Jan., which took place in that country in 1563.

[**1589**: cf. STILO NOVO]. **1590** WOTTON *Life & Lett.* (1907) I. 239 Written the xxv of September, 1590, style of England. **1615** COCKS *Diary* 18 June (Hakl. Soc.) I. 11, I receved a letter from Jorge Durois, dated in Langasaque, le 22nd of June, new stile. **1617** MORYSON *Itin.* I. 63 The ninth of September, after the old stile (for the new style is vsed in Poland) I tooke my iourney to Crakaw. **1625** *Docum. Impeachm. Buckhm.* (Camden) 160 The eight and twentieth day of this presente moneth of March, Old Stile of England. **1664** SIR R. FANSHAWE *Let.* in *Mem. Lady Fanshawe* (1829) 329 Madrid, Wednesday, the 15th June, 1664, English Style. **1674** MOXON *Tutor Astron.* II. (ed. 3) 84, I look in the Calender of Old Stile for June 1. **1678** *Trial of Coleman* 28 In the month of April old stile, May new stile. **1712** BUDGELL *Spect.* No. 395 ¶3 Telling me she looked upon the Month as then out, for that she had all along reckoned by the New Style. **1716** MAR *Jrnl.* in Patten *Hist. Rebell.* (1717) 269 It was about the middle of December (our Style) before he could reach Dunkirk. **1753** in Wilkins *Polit. Ballads* (1860) II. 311 In seventeen hundred and fifty three The Style it was chang'd to Popery. **1809** R. LANGFORD *Introd. Trade* 35 Russia is..the only country in which bills are dated by the Old Style. **1829** S. SHAW *Staffordsh. Potteries* vi. 137 At the time of altering the Style, in 1752. **1862** L. F. SIMPSON *Autob. Chas. V*, p. v, Where he was born on February 24, 1500, according to Roman Style. **1879** FROUDE *Cæsar* xxii. 387 The 9th of August, old style [*i.e.* according to the pre-Julian reckoning], or towards the end of May by real time, Cæsar had [etc.].

¶ **b.** *transf.* (in nonce uses).

1749 FIELDING *Tom Jones* XV. ii, Then they parted to dress, it being now past three in the morning, or to reckon by the old style, in the afternoon. **1755** J. SHEBBEARE *Lydia* (1769) II. 80 By which manner of computation he was but fifty in his style, and sixty in that of all others.

V. 28. *Comb.*, as ***style-like*** adj.; (in sense 8) ***style-flag, -flap***; (in sense 21 d) ***style manual, sheet***; **style analysis**, analysis of the characteristic style of an artist, writer, composer, etc., or of a school or period, on the basis of which attribution of a particular work can be made; **style-book**, (*a*) a book containing 'styles' of writs, etc., according to Scots law (see 17); (*b*) orig. *U.S.*, a book containing the methods and regulations observed in a particular printing-office (W. 1911); **style critic**, an expert in style analysis; **style-setter**, someone who or something which sets the fashion; so **style-setting** *ppl. a.*

1927 E. RICKERT *New Methods for Study of Lit.* 274/2 (Index), Subjectivity in *style analysis. **1953** M. SCHAPIRO in A. Kroeber *Anthropol. Today* 290/1 The refinement of style analysis has come about..through problems in which small differences had to be..described precisely. **1955** H. READ *Icon & Idea* vi. 112 Then are many other factors which can be used in style analysis..but though all these stylistic traits build up to an index of the painter's personality, they do not..indicate the painter's awareness of a self. **1969–70** *Computers & Humanities* IV. 41 These results, minor as they are, are of a nature that has not been achieved in any other use of the computer for style analysis in music. **1973** *Black World* Nov. 5/1 Conventional histories of music and style-analysis texts generally ignored the subject of the Black man's contribution to music. **1708** J. SPOTTISWOODE *Introd. Stile of Writs* Pref. (1727) a 6 b, I have thought fit to communicate the Scheme of a *Stile-book, form'd by James Hay of Carribber for the Use of the Gentlemen educated in his Writing-Chamber. **1873** BURTON *Hist. Scot.* V. lvii. 178 A narrative of the method of the deed has a certain old quaintness that may relieve it of the stiffness of the modern style-book. **1898** (*title*) Stylebook of the Chicago Society of Proofreaders. **1930** [see NEGRO 1 d]. **1981** K. WATERHOUSE *Daily Mirror Style* 5 In most newspaper offices there is to be found a manual known as the style-book which lays down.. the paper's rules on the usage of words and punctuation. **1959** *Times* 26 May 13/5 On that hypothesis David stays as the author of the 75 pictures,..finally reinstated by modern *style-critics. **1978** *Jrnl. R. Soc. Arts* CXXVI. 718/2 He may be the less inclined to indulge in wild or subjective speculation than the style critic. **1815** KIRBY & SP. *Entomol.* (1816) I. ix. 295 The petal-like expansion or *style-flag [in Iris]. **1907** SCOTT ELLIOT *Romance Pl. Life* 197 In Mimulus the *style-flaps close when touched. **1822** J. PARKINSON *Outl. Oryctol.* 72 A round, lamellated star, with a projecting *style-like axis in the centre. **1847–9** *Todd's Cycl. Anat.* IV. 11/2 Urocentrum..is furnished posteriorly with a sharp style-like process. **1922** (*title*) *Style manual of the Government printing office (U.S. Govt. Printing Office). **1964** E. D. SEEBER (*title*) A style manual for students. **1959** *News Chron.* 1 July 3/1, I have a feeling it is going to be a *style-setter. **1960** *Ibid.* 29 Feb. 6/7 Princess Margaret has always been a style-setter. **1955** KEEPNEWS & GRAUER *Pictorial Hist. Jazz* iii. 44 Earl Hines..quickly developed into an outstanding and *style-setting pianist. **1960** *Farmer & Stockbreeder* 1 Mar. 44/2 The Fordson Dexta with its proved style-setting three cylinder Diesel engine. **1924** H. L. MENCKEN *Let.* 7 Dec. (1961) 272 Have you such a thing as a *Style Sheet for The Atlantic? **1982** R. QUIRK *Style & Communication in Eng. Lang.* i. 16 This is not, of course, to say that the existence of the 'style sheet' mentality is always advantageous.

style (staɪl), *v.* Also 6–9 **stile**, 6 *Sc.* **styell**, 7 **still(e**, *Sc.* **stylle**, (8 *pa. pple.* **stilen**). [f. STYLE *sb.* F. *styler* means 'to train, practise, instruct'.]

1. a. *trans.* To give a name or style to; to call by a name or style. Const. with complement; †also with *for, with*.

1563–83 FOXE *A. & M.* 812/2 Howsoeuer it pleaseth.. Syr Tho. Moore..to stile Richard Hunne for a knowne and desperate heretique. *c* **1580** MONTGOMERIE *Misc. P.* l. 2 Luiffaris, leif of to loif so hie ȝour ladyes; and thame styell no mair, But peir, the erthlie A per se. **1607** HIERON *Wks.* (1613) I. 119 Hee..is therefore stiled, A murtherer from the beginning. **1614** RALEGH *Hist. World* I. II. xvii. §8. 491 So they [the Psalms] are intituled in the old Hebrew copies, though the vulgar and Septuagint..stile them otherwise. **1630** *Reg. Mag. Sig. Scot.* 1634, 13/2 Wmquhill Johnne lord Halyruidhous, then styllit Mr Johne Bothuell. **1648–9** WHITELOCKE *Mem.* (1853) II. 497 Now the commons styled what were before ordinances at this time *acts of parliament*. **1663** in *Verney Mem.* (1907) II. 229 Such strainge and unbeseeming titles I forbeare to stile you with. **1667** MILTON *P.L.* VI. 289 The strife which thou call'st evil, but wee style The strife of Glorie. *a* **1700** EVELYN *Diary* 12 Mar. 1686, One Hall, who styl'd himselfe his Majesty's printer. **1711** HEARNE *Collect.* (O.H.S.) III. 251 The present Queen (as she is styl'd). **1796** BURKE *Regic. Peace* ii. Wks. VIII. 251 That liberty was found, under Monarchies stiled absolute, in a degree unknown to the ancient commonwealths. **1829** CASSAN *Bps. of Bath & Wells* iii. 24 That from henceforward the Bishop should be stiled from both places. **1838** DE MORGAN *Ess. Probab.* 151 What we have called a fixed error is in fact a part of the phenomenon, styled an error because it is not a part of the result we wish to observe. **1855** BROWNING *Fra Lippo Lippi* 39 Yes, I'm the painter, since you style me so. **1894** LADY M. VERNEY *Verney Mem.* III. 95 The old man is still styled bailiff in 1639.

†**b.** Of a thing: To invest with a right to be called (so-and-so). *Obs.*

1634 SIR T. HERBERT *Trav.* 19 Both sexe goe naked, a linnen cloth only about their middles, which stiles them modest.

†**c.** To sign (a letter) with one's name and title. *Obs.*

1618 BOLTON *Florus* II. xii. (1636) 128 When hee wrote to the Roman Generall..and styled the letter, he put himselfe down in it by the name of 'King'.

†**2.** To name or address with honorific titles; to honour with a title. *Sc. Obs.*

1508 DUNBAR *Flyting* 3 Quhilk hes thame self aboif the sternis styld. *Ibid.* 103 Sen thow with wirschep wald sa fane be styld, Haill, souerane senȝeour. **1535** LYNDESAY *Satyre* 599 Howbeit I haif lang tyme bene exyllit, I traist in God my name suld ȝit be styllit. **1552** —— *Monarche* 4666 The pure Preist thynkis he gettis no rycht, Be he nocht stylit lyke ane Knycht, And callit 'schir' affore his name.

†**3.** To relate or express in literary form. With adv.: To express or phrase in a specified style. *Obs.*

1605 BACON *Adv. Learn.* II. iv. §1 In the later [sense] it [*sc.* poesy] is..one of the principall Portions of learning: and is nothing else but Fained History, which may be stiled as well in Prose as in Verse. **1605** *First Pt. Jeronimo* I. ii. 43 The phraise he vseth must be gently stylde, The king hath warned him to be smooth and mild.

†**4.** To order, direct to a purpose. *Obs.*

1584 HUDSON *Du Bartas' Judith* IV. (1608) 58 So wise Merari all his studie stilde, To facion well the maners of this childe.

5. To pierce with a stylet.

1736 BRACKEN *Farriery Impr.* (1757) II. 10 The Substance of the Ears should be..free from Flesh; and their Points when stiled or pricked should be nearer than their Roots.

6. To execute (a design) with a stylus on a prepared ground.
1864 MACLISE in *Builder* 27 Feb. 150/3 The cartoon to be punctured or styled on the wall and slavishly copied.
7. To design, arrange, make, etc., in a particular (esp. fashionable) style.
1934 J. RORTY *Our Master's Voice Advertising* 11 'Styling' clothes, kitchens, automobiles—everything, in the interest of more rapid obsolescence and replacement. **1936** H. L. MENCKEN *Amer. Lang.* (ed. 4) 194 The American liking for short cuts in speech, *e.g.* .. *to style* for *to cut in accord with the style.* **1958** J. CANNAN *And be a Villain* i. 25 The fashions of the day, styled to suit *gamines.* **1958** *Observer* 25 May 17/2 Mgr. Knox seems to have styled his translation to fit in with the least sufferable conceptions of this, really, stout-hearted young girl. **1976** 'Z. STONE' *Modigliani Scandal* III. iv. 137 Her hair had been styled by Sassoon.

style, obs. form of STEEL, STILE, STILL.

-style, *suffix*, forming adjs. and advbs.
1. Appended to adjs. **a.** Forming adjs. having the sense 'resembling or characteristic of something that is——'.
1934 *Discovery* June 174/1 He will have to put up at a Japanese style hotel. **1958** *Listener* 11 Sept. 368/1 He was dressed in European-style clothes. **1960** W. THORP *Amer. Writing in 20th Cent.* 296 A series of events .. convinced [them] that revolution, Russian-style, would never take place in America. **1966** [see SEDAN 1 c]. **1975** *Country Life* 20 Mar. 747/2 Elegant regency-style restaurant.
b. Forming advbs. with the sense 'in a manner that is——'. *colloq.*
1967 G. KELLY in *Coast to Coast 1965–6* 95 Bill Beatty leant across the table, his cigarette dangling casual style from his fingers. **1976** T. SHARPE *Wilt* (1978) vi. 61 We're here idyllicstyle, cruising down the river in the good old summertime.
2. Appended to sbs., forming advbs. and adjs. with the general sense '(in a manner) characteristic of or befitting——'.
The advb. use is highly colloq.
1944 W. SAROYAN *Human Comedy* xxiv. 166 He whistled, newsboy style. **1949** *Amer.-German Rev.* Apr. 10 Meals were served family-style. **1973** *Guardian* 31 Jan. 5/2 An election-style budget.

styled, *ppl. a.* [f. STYLE *v.* + -ED[1].]
†**1.** Having a certain style or designation. *Obs. rare.*
a **1625** GORGES in Farr *S.P. Jas. I* (1847) 315 When Tyme our styled yeare did end, And chaunge beganne your raigne, Then Time reft vs a soueraigne blisse, Which chaunge repay'de with gaine.
2. Of a person's hair: professionally arranged, cut, or set.
1958 *Spectator* 27 June 833/2 Another of the old gang in hacking jacket and styled hair mincing over to a seat. **1977** E. LEONARD *Unknown Man No. 89* ii. 13 His styled hair .. glistened.
3. With prefixed sb., adj., etc., forming combs. indicating the origin or provenance of the style.
1958 *Spectator* 11 July 56/2 Manhattan-styled clerical tuxedos. **1966** *Melody Maker* 15 Oct. 19 After an Alpert-styled 'Taste of Honey'.., he introduced a couple of new numbers. **1976** B. BOVA *Multiple Man* (1977) v. 64 Their Bavarian-styled paneled dining room.

styleless ('staɪllɪs), *a.* [f. STYLE *sb.* + -LESS.]
1. Devoid of style, in various senses. Hence **'stylelessness**.
1796 ANNA SEWARD *Lett.* (1811) IV. 196 An abode which, though a mansion .. spacious to my utmost wish, breathes of nothing above the level of mere common and stileless life. **1886** *Contemp. Rev.* July 106 The modern *styleless* Parisian images .. which are now the eyesore of most Roman Catholic churches. **1893** STEVENSON *Lett.* (1899) II. 314 The British pig returns to his true love, the love of the styleless, of the shapeless, of the slapdash and the disorderly. **1911** H. O. TAYLOR *Mediaeval Mind* II. VI. xxxi, The only trouble is stylelessness. In fine, an absence of quality characterizes Carolingian prose. **1912** *Nation* 20 Apr. 96/1 All his novels .. are styleless, formless, abounding in digressions.
2. *Bot.* Of an ovary: Having no styles.
1821 S. F. GRAY *Brit. Plants* I. 152 Ovary .. Style-less, *acephalum.* Not having any styles.

styler ('staɪlə(r)). [f. STYLE *v.* + -ER[1].]
1. = STYLIST 2 a, b. *rare.*
1960 *Lebende Sprachen* V. 35/2 [Clothing industry vocabulary] *Designer, styler, stylist,* Modellmacher, Modelleur (Bekleidung). **1972** *Classification of Occupations* (Dept. Employment) III. 257/2 Dolls' hair styler.
2. A device for styling hair.
1971 *Wall St. Jrnl.* (Eastern ed.) 1 Apr. 1/5 Bercy Industries .. has doubled its own forecast of men's hair styler sales... The response to stylers cheers retailers. **1976** *Honolulu Star-Bull.* 21 Dec. B-3/1 (Advt.), Save $5! women's 1200-watt styler-dryer.

stylet ('staɪlɪt). Forms: 7–9 stilet, 8 stillet, 9 stillette, 8– stylet. [a. F. *stylet*, ad. It. *stiletto*: see STILETTO.]
1. *Surg.* A slender probe. Also, a wire run through a catheter or canula in order to stiffen it or to clear it.
1697 *Phil. Trans.* XIX. 458, I thrust a Stilet or Probe into the Cavity of the Vertebres. **1722** *Ibid.* XXXII. 84 First, Pass the Catheter, .. then draw out the Stillet. **1806** *Med. Jrnl.* XV. 226, I found the instrument [a catheter] advance suddenly for the space of half an inch, but on with-drawing the stillette, nothing but a few drops of blood followed. **1846** BRITTAN tr. *Malgaigne's Man. Oper. Surg.* 271 Ware accidentally observed that when a metallic stylet is placed in the canal, the overflow of tears almost immediately ceases... His stylet is a metallic wire about an inch and a quarter long. .. The patient wears it all his life. **1864** *T. Holmes' Syst. Surg.* IV. 1047 In addition to these, the Surgeon should have a dozen elastic catheters, in graduated series, fitted with wire stilettes, and a few straight solid bougies. **1871** MEADOWS *Man. Midwifery* (ed. 2) 349 The first step to be taken is to puncture the membranes. This may readily be done by means of a stilet, or a common hair-pin. **1894** *Lancet* 3 Nov. 1033 If necessary, a stylet, passed through the puncture for stop, can be used for introduction. The fixation with two catheters, done in the first instance, is useful on emergency.
2. †**a.** *Bot.* = STYLE *sb.* 8.
1720 P. BLAIR *Bot. Ess.* i. 14 The Pistillum or Pestil, the Stylus or Stillet, the Apices or Tops. **1723** *Phil. Trans.* XXXII. 444 This Stylet ordinarily splits into 3 Parts, just opposite to the Top of the Stamina.
b. *Zool.* = STYLE *sb.* 9, 10.
1834 MCMURTRIE *Cuvier's Anim. Kingd.* 456 In Stratiomys .. the antennæ are much longer than the head, the first and last joint being greatly elongated; the latter is fusiform, .. consisting of at least five distinct rings, without an abrupt stilet at the extremity. **1838** *Penny Cycl.* XII. 492/2 In the Dragon-flies there are small flattened appendages .. which are called stylets. **1872** A. S. PACKARD *Guide Study Insects* (ed. 3) 58 The abdomen is now pointed at the extremity and divided into the rudiments of the two anal stylets, which form large, acute tubercles. **1889** *Hardwicke's Sci.-Gossip* XXV. 213/1, A crystalline stylet .. found in the stomach of some snails. **1899** *Allbutt's Syst. Med.* VIII. 944 This veneno-salivary gland is situated in the head of the mosquito, communicating by means of a long duct with the base of the middle stylet or lingula.
†**3.** = STYLE *sb.* 1, STYLUS 1. *Obs.*
1750 FREEMAN *Herculaneum* in *Phil. Trans.* XLVII. 139 A sort of standish, or inkhorn, in which were found many stylets or pens, with which they wrote in those days.
b. A kind of pencil for the use of the blind.
1819 tr. *Guillié's Ess. Blind* (1894) 97 The stilet, or pencil should be held with the thumb, the fore-finger, and the middle-finger... The blind, in general, have the fault of holding the stilet too close between their fingers. **1883** *Daily News* 17 May 2/3 Girls and lads .. writing their exercises with stylets with great rapidity... Others were taking notes with great rapidity by the familiar aid of the stylet and the brass perforated rule.
c. A pointed marking instrument; a graving tool.
1853 C. BRONTE *Villette* xx, The strong hieroglyphics graven as with iron stylet on his brow. *Ibid.* xli, Her eye grazing me with its hard ray like a steel stylet. **1872** S. MOSTYN *Perplexity* I. xiii. 260 Already I seem to trace the stylet of life in certain lines about my lineaments. **1874** J. GEIKIE *Gt. Ice Age* vi. 79 Stones used as chisels and stylets by the ice. **1902** *Westm. Gaz.* 23 Oct. 6/1 Sand was placed on the floor, and each time the pendulum passed over it a new track was marked by the stylet in regular deviation.
4. A stiletto, dagger.
1820 SCOTT *Abbot* iv, Whether it be a stilet, which we have borrowed from the treacherous Italian, or a dirk. **1842** BROWNING *In a Gondola* 108 While .. Gian pinions me, Him-self has past His stylet thro' my back; I reel. **1866** MEREDITH *Vittoria* viii, One sharp scar .. he owed to the knife of a friend, by name Sarpo, who had got things ready to betray him, and struck him .. but, striking, like a novice, on the bone, the stilet stuck there.
5. *Comb.*
1878 BRADY *Copepoda* I. 19 Artotrogidæ .. Mandibles stilet-shaped. **1880** *Ibid.* III. 12 Stylet-shaped.

stylewort ('staɪlwɜːt). *Bot.* [f. STYLE *sb.* (assumed to be equivalent to Gr. στῦλος, whence STYLIDIUM) + WORT *sb.*] Lindley's name for a plant of the genus Stylidium, or of the N.O. *Stylidiaceæ*, of which this is the type. Also *attrib.*
1846 LINDLEY *Veg. Kingd.* 696 Stylidiaceæ.—Styleworts. **1849** BALFOUR *Man. Bot.* §921 Stylidiaceæ, the Stylidium or Stylewort Family. **1887** BENTLEY *Man. Bot.* (ed. 5) 600 Stylidiaceæ, the Stylewort Order.

styliard, etc. obs. ff. STEELYARD[1].

‖**Stylidium** (staɪ'lɪdɪəm). *Bot.* [mod.L. (Swartz 1807), f. Gr. στῦλ-ος column + -ίδιον dim. suffix (here used loosely).] A genus of gamopetalous plants, native in Australia, India, and Sri Lanka, remarkable for the irritability of the column formed by the union of the stamens and style.
The genus had been named *Candollea* by Labillardière in 1805; this older name has been recently revived in accordance with the rule that the earliest botanical name given to a genus should be preserved. Hence the N.O. of which the genus is the type is now often called *Candolleaceæ* for the earlier *Stylidiaceæ* or *Stylidieæ.*
1829 T. CASTLE *Introd. Bot.* 154 A New Holland genus named stylidium. **1837** P. KEITH *Bot. Lex.* 340 The shrinking of the Mimosa, the collapsing of Dionæa, and the elastic spring of Stylidium [may be due to galvanism]. **1878** DARWIN *Life & Lett.* III. 287 As far as I know, Stylidium is the sole case of sensitive pistil. **1880** BESSEY *Bot.* 512 Species of Stylidium are grown in conservatories.

styliferous (staɪ'lɪfərəs), *a. Bot.* and *Zool.* [f. mod.L. *stylifer*, f. *styl-us* STYLE *sb.*: see -FEROUS.] Bearing a style or styles. **a.** *Bot.* (see STYLE *sb.* 8). **b.** *Zool.* (see STYLE *sb.* 10).
a. 1835 LINDLEY *Introd. Bot.* (1848) I. 387 The inferior opening of the styliferous canal. **1878** HOOKER *Stud. Flora* (ed. 2) 78 The styliferous and placentiferous axis.
b. 1826 KIRBY & SP. *Entomol.* IV. xlvii. 370 Anus styliferous. **1871** T. R. JONES *Anim. Kingd.* (ed. 4) 171 Nemertean Helminthozoa... Other glandular structures .. are in communication with the styliferous cavity.

styliform ('staɪlɪfɔːm), *a. Anat., Zool., Min.* [ad. mod.L. *styliformis*, f. *styl-us* STYLE *sb.*: see -FORM.] Shaped like a stylus.
1578 BANISTER *Hist. Man* I. 9 These stiliforme, or spurre-like processes are prominent. **1741** A. MONRO *Anat.* (ed. 3) 114 From near the Point .. a sharp-pointed Process is frequently produced downwards, which some call *Styliform.* **1819** SAMOUELLE *Entomol. Compendium* 292 Styliform joint of antenna. **1822** J. PARKINSON *Outl. Oryctol.* 71 The solid styliform axes projecting beyond the tubes. **1826** KIRBY & SP. *Entomol.* III. xxix. 167 They have no anal .. styliform appendages. **1828** STARK *Elem. Nat. Hist.* II. 433 Polypi... Gen. 30. Stylina, Lam. Stony, forming simple masses, .. axis styliform. **1839–47** T. R. JONES in *Todd's Cycl. Anat.* III. 961/2 A long styliform bone generally composed of two pieces. **1861** R. E. GRANT *Tabular View Rec. Zool.* 53 Rhipiptera... Mouth furnished with a pair of small styliform palpigerous mandibles. **1886** J. J. QUELCH *Coral-Reefs* in *Challenger Rep.* XVI. III. 56 The styliform prolongation of the columella generally absent.
Hence †**'styliformed** *a.*, in the same sense.
1578 BANISTER *Hist. Man.* I. 10 The fourth processe [of the temporal bone] .. beginnyng nere vnto the roote of the stiliformed. *Ibid.* III. 42 The stiliformed Processes of Hyoides.

styline ('staɪlaɪn), *a. Bot. rare.* [f. STYLE *sb.* + -INE.] Of or belonging to the style; stylar.
1866 *Treas. Bot.* 1107/2.

styling ('staɪlɪŋ). [f. STYLE *v.* + -ING[1].]
1. Ornament consisting of patterns traced by a style.
1867 *Morn. Star* 19 July, The ceilings .. are coloured pale blue, with panels of pink styling.
2. The action, process, or result of STYLE *v.* 7.
1928 *Publishers' Weekly* 9 June 2370 Recourse to art for investing conventional merchandise with fresh or added appeal has been the chief reliance of post-war sales strategy. It has been termed 'Styling' in some quarters. **1939** *Archit. Rev.* LXXXVI. 62/1 It is scarcely conceivable that any but an American designer would have designed such a building: it is 'styling' applied to architecture. One can only hope that this same 'styling' will not later be applied to Town Halls. **1958** *Observer* 25 May 11/3 The styling of clothes for small children has now passed out of the hands of British makers. **1959** *Daily Tel.* 27 Aug. 11/3 This same firm which now also makes Pilot [television] models with slightly different styling. **1966** *Listener* 17 Nov. 712/2 A new automobile... Engineering and 'styling' costs were $9,000,000. **1975** G. HOWELL *In Vogue* 206/2 Teddy Boys would go to a barber for 'styling'. **1980** *Times* 29 Feb. 23/4 Smooth, wedge-shaped styling makes for a distinctive appearance.

stylish ('staɪlɪʃ), *a.* Also †**stilish**. [f. STYLE *sb.* + -ISH.]
1. Of persons, their appearance or manners, also of dress, equipage, etc.: Noticeable for 'style' or conformity to the fashionable standard of elegance; showily fashionable.
1797 JANE AUSTEN *Sense & Sens.* xxx, A smart, stilish girl, they say, but not handsome. **1800** ELIZA SOUTHGATE BOWNE *Girl's Life Eighty Yrs. Ago* (1888) 23, I must either cut my hair or have one [a wig], I cannot dress it at all stylish. **1807–8** W. IRVING *Salmag.* (1824) 132 All who would be considered as admitted in the stylish arcana. **1815** CHALMERS in Hanna *Life* (1850) II. 8 My lodgings .. consist of a dining-room and bed-room, perhaps not so stylish as I could have wished, but [etc.]. **1831** O. W. HOLMES *My Aunt* 21 He sent her to a stylish school. **1847** C. BRONTE *Jane Eyre* xxi, Her dress .. looked as stylish as the other's looked puritanical. **1851** J. H. NEWMAN *Pres. Posit. Catholics* 16 They prowl about with handsome stocks and stylish waistcoats, and gold chains about their persons. **1883** *Manch. Exam.* 30 Oct. 8/4 A large farmer .. attired in good broad-cloth of stylish cut. **1884** LADY F. VERNEY *Peasant Properties* etc. (1885) II. 250 But 'stylish' is of the shop, shoppy, and belongs to the dialect of milliners' apprentices and waiting-maids alone .. in England. **1884** *Punch* 1 Nov. 215/1 Rather stylish to have a double-barrelled name. **1902** S. E. WHITE *Blazed Trail* lvii, Occasionally he might have noticed .. a besilvered pair champing before a stylish vehicle.
2. In occasional uses: Having 'style' (in various senses: see STYLE *sb.* 14, 23, 25 d).
1892 WALSH *Tea* 86 An exceedingly black, 'silky' and stylish leaf tea. **1895** *Daily News* 17 May 3/7 Hearne was bowled for a most patient and stylish innings of 65. **1900** *Athenæum* 7 July 12/1 He has produced .. a piece of lively and stylish writing.
Hence **'stylishly** *adv.*, **'stylishness**.
1798 JANE AUSTEN *Northanger Abb.* viii, Her air, though it had not all the decided pretension, the resolute stilishness of Miss Thorpe's, had more real elegance. **1879** MISS BRADDON *Vixen* III. 280 Why should you .. leave off dressing stylishly? **1898** *Daily Chron.* 8 Oct. 6/6 The plaintiff, a stylishly-dressed young lady.

stylism ('staɪlɪz(ə)m). [f. STYLE *sb.* + -ISM.] A stylistic device or effect; emphasis on style.
1928 H. CRANE *Let.* 5 Feb. (1965) 317, I am not as original in some of my stylisms as I had thought I was. **1942** [see

ABSTRACTIONAL]. **1958** *Times* 30 Sept. 3/1 The German company..proves to be a finely cast body of actors with an inevitably stronger feeling for classical stylism. **1971** R. APROBERTS *Trollope* i. 15 Both symbolic explanation and *stylism*, then, are overworked for fiction.

stylist ('staɪlɪst). [f. STYLE *sb.* + -IST. Cf. F. *styliste* (late 19th c.), G. *stilist.*] **1. a.** A writer who is skilled in or cultivates the art of literary style; a writer as characterized by his style.

1795 W. TAYLOR in *Monthly Rev.* XVIII. 522 He even delights in assisting the reader to trace his eternal allusions to their source; in pointing out..the stylist whose epithet he transplants, or the philosopher whose inference he impresses. *a* **1849** POE *Henry Cary* Wks. 1865 III. 68 A style that, as times go—in view of such stylists as Mr. Briggs for example—may be termed respectable. **1873** FITZEDWARD HALL *Mod. Engl.* 10 The latter [Addison] while notably distinguished, as a stylist, for ease,..combines with it the extreme of inexactness. **1882** M. PATTISON *Ess.* (1889) I. 127 Cotton's version 'orator' here misrepresents the French 'orateur,' which means 'stylist,' not speaker. **1882** JEBB *Bentley* 208 By his Latin compositions..Scaliger is connected with the Italian age of Latin stylists. **1882** *Pall Mall Gaz.* 2 June 5 She has evidently adopted for her model two great living stylists, Mr. Pater and Mr. J. A. Symonds. **1911** G. MACDONALD *Roman Wall Scot.* i. 15 Herodian..was too much of a stylist to live up to his own professions.

b. *transf.* In sport or music, one who plays with style.

1897 K. S. RANJITSINHJI *Jubilee Bk. Cricket* iii. 118 A young player of much promise—essentially a stylist, with brilliant strokes all round the wicket when set. **1898** —— *With Stoddart's Team* (ed. 3) i. 34 Hayward is essentially a stylist. **1969** *Listener* 3 Apr. 470/3 He's also perhaps the most original clarinet stylist in the British Isles. **1981** *Best of Karate '81* Spring 35/2 (*caption*) A Japanese stylist from Indiana, he has won virtually every major title available.

2. orig. *N. Amer.* **a.** In industry, esp. the retail clothing and car industries, one whose job is to create, co-ordinate, or promote the latest fashions or designs for a firm's commodities.

1928 *Daily Express* 18 July 12 The post of 'stylist' has been created during the last year in some of the better Canadian and American stores. The duties consist of linking departments,..informing the bag department of the trend of fashion in the shoe section, and the glove department what is happening in the costume department. *Ibid.* 24 Sept. 7 Harrods Fashion Buyers and Stylists. **1956** *Stanford Law Rev.* July 628 The General Motors stylist Harley Earl cannot be split into five pieces. **1958** *Spectator* 20 June 817/3 The quality and style of 'St. Michael' garments are the product of close collaboration between the Buying Executives, Stylists and Technologists. **1978** *Jrnl. R. Soc. Arts* CXXVI. 538/1 Mr. Nader caused a greater fundamental change to the appearance of cars than did a hundred stylists or engineers.

b. One who styles hair; = *hair-stylist* s.v. HAIR *sb.* 10.

1937 R. STOUT *Crime on her Hands* (1939) ii. 23, I could have got a job as a stylist, or..started a hat shop. **1962** *Times* 3 Feb. 9/4 Where are the barbers or even the hairdressers now? They have come stylists to a man or woman. **1968** [see CRIMPER[1] 1 b]. **1979** *West Lancs. Evening Gaz.* 10 Nov. 11 (Advt.), Wanted—all-round Stylist—male/female.

stylistic (staɪ'lɪstɪk), *a.* and *sb.* Also **stilistic**. [f. STYLE *sb.* + -IST + -IC; after G. *stilistisch* adj., *stilistik* sb.] **A.** *adj.* Pertaining to literary style.

1860 G. P. MARSH *Lect. Engl. Lang.* 82 Njála,..which, as an example of pure stylistic excellence, may fairly be pronounced altogether unsurpassed. **1864** CARLYLE *Fredk. Gt.* XVI. ix. IV. 380 Mere grammatical stylistic skin-deep work. **1877** E. W. GOSSE *North. Studies, 4 Danish Poets* (1890) 227 Paul Heyse..with his lyrical drama of *Amor and Psyche*, a work displaying stilistic gift of the first order. **1883** R. L. STEVENSON in *Mag. of Art* Nov. 26/2 The engendering idea of some works is stylistic; a technical preoccupation stands them instead of some robuster principle of life. **1888** *Jewish Q. Rev.* I. 77 Historical, linguistic, and stylistic peculiarities converge, he thinks, to prove this. **1911** H. O. TAYLOR *Mediaeval Mind* VI. xxxi. II. 152 The stylistic genius of Augustine and Jerome.

B. *sb.* The science of literary style; the study of stylistic features. Also (more commonly) **stylistics** [see -ICS].

[**1846** WORCESTER, *Stylistic*, the art of forming a good style in writing; a treatise on style.] **1882–3** SCHAFF *Encycl. Rel. Knowl.* II. 965 Giving proper place to New Testament stylistics and rhetoric. **1906** *Month* Feb. 215 A question of 'Stylistic,' to adopt a convenient, though to English ears an uncouth, German expression.

So **sty'listical** *a.* = STYLISTIC *a.* **sty'listically** *adv.*, with regard to literary or artistic style; also, in a stylized or conventional manner.

1889 A. J. EVANS in *Archæol. Rev.* II. 323 An ivory object ..so stylistically carved as to remind us of the treatment of some late Celtic bronze articles. **1889** *Class. Rev.* III. 87/2 The reproductions look pretty, but are far from being stylistically satisfactory. **1897** *Ibid.* XI. 284/1 Great numbers of stylistical peculiarities are required for correct inferences. **1911** H. O. TAYLOR *Mediaeval Mind* II. xiv. I. 346 Stylistically, these great church mosaics belonged to antique art. **1915** *Nation* (N.Y.) 10 June 650/1 Several glazed pieces, notably the Visitation, [etc.] seem stylistically to belong before 1440.

stylistician (staɪlɪ'stɪʃən). [f. STYLISTIC *a.* and *sb.* + -IAN.] One who studies stylistics.

1939 *Language* XV. 257 One misses the subtler approach of the 'stylisticians' of today. **1948** L. SPITZER *Linguistics & Lit. Hist.* iv. 136 In general, stylisticians have rather shied away from Diderot. **1957** *Archivum Linguisticum* IX. 148 He shares the weakness of other stylisticians, in claiming to have found the Philosopher's Stone. **1969** CRYSTAL & DAVY *Investigating English Style* 12 The stylistician is on precisely the same footing as anyone else. **1980** *Times Lit. Suppl.* 11 Jan. 28/1 He makes extensive use of the rhetorical device known to stylisticians as 'free indirect speech'.

stylite ('staɪlaɪt). *Eccl. Hist.* Also in Gr. form **stylites** (staɪ'laɪtiːz). [ad. Eccl. Gr. στυλίτης, f. στῦλ-ος pillar: see -ITE.] An ascetic who lived on the top of a pillar. Also *attrib.* or as *adj.*

a. *a* **1638** MEDE *Apostasy Later Times* (1641) 150 Peter à Metra, a famous Stylite, or Pillar-Monk. **1753** R. CLAYTON *Jrnl. fr. Cairo to Mt. Sinai* 12 Sept. 1722, The second [chapel is] of St. Simon the Stylite. **1831** K. H. DIGBY *Mores Cath.* (1845) I. II. ii. 114 St. Gregory, of Tours, relates his conversation with the monk Wulflaïch, who had lived the life of a Stylite in the diocese of Trèves. **1877** *Smith & Wace's Dict. Chr. Biog.* I. 14/2 In conjunction with a Stylite monk, Daniel, he placed himself at the head of the opposition to the Emperor Basiliscus. **1882–3** SCHAFF *Encycl. Rel. Knowl.* III. 2256 Stylites are mentioned as far down as the twelfth century. **1905** *Daily Chron.* 5 Jan. 4/6 Many as are the various eccentric sects that have appeared in America..no one seems to have thought of reviving the Stylite mode of life.

β. **1776** R. CHANDLER *Trav. Greece* lxii. 250 At Patræ was one of the living statues, then not infrequent; a madman standing on a column. To this Stylites did Luke minister for ten years. **1867** EMILY F. BOWDEN tr. *Ctess. Hahn-hahn's Fathers of Desert* 369 Another renowned Stylites was Simeon the younger, who died in 596, after he had stood for sixty-eight years upon columns.

Hence **stylitic** (staɪ'lɪtɪk) *a.*, pertaining to or characteristic of the Stylites. **stylitism** ('staɪlɪtɪz(ə)m), the mode of life or the ascetic principles of the Stylites.

1839 D. D. BLACK *Hist. Brechin* 268 These anchorites were called Stelites, from their living on pillars... The Styletic [*sic*] system began in the east in the year 460. **1843** CARLYLE *Past & Pr.* III. xv. 312 Stylitisms, eremite fanaticisms and fakeerisms. **1882** H. C. MERIVALE *Faucit of B.* II. II. v. 207 Your little tirade just now was a disguised farewell to the stylitic life, and to roots and water. You are tired of misanthropy as a profession.

stylize ('staɪlaɪz), *v.* [f. STYLE *sb.* + -IZE, after G. *stilisiren.*] *trans.* To conform (an artistic representation) to the rules of a conventional style; to conventionalize. Chiefly in pa. pple. Hence **'stylized** *ppl. a.*; also **styli'zation**.

1898 *Q. Rev.* July 97 The stylized and eclectic art of Tyre. **1901** A. J. EVANS in *Oxf. Univ. Gaz.* 12 Feb. 339/1 A highly stylized bull's leg of ivory, from a stool. **1904** *Q. Rev.* Apr. 428 The comparison of form in real objects and form as modified, 'stylised,' by art. **1908** A. J. EVANS in *Anthropol. & Classics* 12 The progressive degeneration and stylization of the heads of horses, goats, deer and oxen. **1912** H. G. SPEARING *Childh. of Art* v. 118 Stylisation..is now generally admitted to be a sort of degeneration, though some consider it only as a stage in the evolution of art to a higher plane.

styll, obs. form of STILE, STYLE.

styll(e, obs. forms of STILL.

styllathre, obs. form of STILLATORY *sb.*

stylleche, stylly(che, obs. ff. STILLY.

stylo ('staɪləʊ). Short for STYLOGRAPH (*pen*).

1890 *Stationery & Bookselling* 39 Apr. 111/2 The arrangements of the 'British Stylo' are such as to secure an immunity from that 'getting out of order' so common to the stylo when first introduced. **1902** *Daily Chron.* 29 July 3/1 All that is needed is a writing-pad and a stylo pen.

stylo- ('staɪləʊ), before a vowel **styl-**, used as combining form of Gr. στῦλος pillar in scientific words. **stylo'glossal** [Gr. γλῶσσα tongue], *a.* pertaining to the styloid process and the tongue; *sb.* = *styloglossus* (in recent Dicts.). ‖**stylo'glossus** (†-*glossum*), a muscle arising from the styloid process and inserted in the tongue. **styloman'dibular, styloma'xillary** *adjs.*, used to designate a ligament which connects the styloid process and the lower jaw-bone. **stylomma'tophorous** *a.* [Gr. ὀμματ-, ὄμμα eye, -φόρ-ος bearing] belonging to the suborder *Stylommatophora* of pulmonate gastropods (land-snails and slugs), which have eyes borne on the tips of a pair of retractile tentacles. **stylopha'ryngeal**, *a.* belonging to the styloid process and the pharynx; *sb.* = *stylopharyngeus* (in recent Dicts.). ‖**stylopha'ryngeus**, a muscle arising from the styloid process and separating the superior and middle constrictions of the pharynx. ‖**stylo'stemon** [Gr. στήμων: see STAMEN] (see quot.).

1671 PHILLIPS, *Styloglossum. **1684** *Blancard's Phys. Dict., Styloglossum*, is that pair of Muscles which lift up the Tongue. **1728** CHAMBERS *Cycl., Styloglossus*, a pair of Muscles, running off sharp and fleshy, from the *Processus Styloides*. **1831** R. KNOX *Cloquet's Anat.* 177 The styloglossus muscle. **1897** *Proc. Zool. Soc.* 376 The *stylo-mandibular ligament. **1831** R. KNOX *Cloquet's Anat.* 177 *Stylomaxillary Ligament. **1888** ROLLESTON & JACKSON *Anim. Life* 477 The *Stylommatophorous *Pulmonata*. **1684** tr. *Blancard's Phys. Dict.*, **Stylopharyngæus* is a pair of Muscles that dilate the Gullet. **1897** *Proc. Zool. Soc.* 377 The stylo-pharyngeus is always present though small. **1856** HENSLOW *Dict. Bot. Terms*, *Stylostemon, an epigynous stamen, originating in adhesion of the filament to the style.

stylobata (staɪ'lɒbətə). *Arch.* [a. L. *stȳlobata*, ad. Gr. στυλοβάτης, f. στῦλο-ς pillar + -βατης, f. βαίνειν to walk, step.] = next.

1563 SHUTE *Archit.* C ij b, If ye will set Stylobata, or Pedestal, vnder your pillor, thus ye shal begin. **1664** EVELYN tr. *Freart's Parallel Archit.* etc. 123 The Stylobata and Pedistals of Columns. **1771** W. NEWTON tr. *Vitruvius' Archit.* III. iii. (1791) 55 The stylobatæ should be wrought in such a manner, as to leave in the middle the adjection for the unequal scamilli. **1828–9** *Encycl. Metrop.* (1845) V. 311/2 Under each column in the range the stylobata is generally broken so that its face projects a little forward.

stylobate ('staɪləbeɪt). *Arch.* Also 9 **-bat**. [ad. L. *stȳlobata*: see prec.] A continuous basement upon which a row of columns is supported. See STEREOBATE.

1694 MOTTEUX *Rabelais* v. xliii, Its Stylobates or Foot-steps. **1823** P. NICHOLSON *Pract. Builder* 314 Fifty-two columns..standing on a circular stylobat. **1827** *Gentl. Mag.* XCVII. II. 11 A circular temple, raised on a stylobate of three steps. **1887** *Times* (weekly ed.) 9 Dec. 15/1 The temple rests on a stylobate, having a finely moulded base and surbase. **1902** A. J. EVANS in *Ann. Brit. Sch. Athens* 1901–2, 48 A raised base or stylobate which formed a division between the two halves of the Megaron.

stylograph ('staɪləgrɑːf, -æ-). [f. mod.L. *stylus*, incorrect form of L. *stil-us* STYLE + -GRAPH.] †**1.** (See quot.) *Obs. rare*$^{-1}$.

1866 J. HOGG in *Trans. R. Soc. Lit.* (1870) IX. 25 On a profane stylograph of the Crucifixion, at Rome. *Ibid.*, I venture to form the new title stylograph—signifying a sketch, or drawing, or writing, made with a style.

2. A stylographic pen. Also ***stylograph pen***.

1882 *Knowledge* 9 June 28/2 Glass stylographs. *Ibid.* 29/1 Most people who use mine think them superior to the ordinary stylographs. **1888** RYE *Records & Rec. Searching* 106 He must not use ink—not even from a stylograph. **1899** SOMERVILLE & ROSS *Exper. Irish R.M.* ii, I took out my stylograph pen and finished a letter to Philippa.

stylographic (staɪləʊ'græfɪk), *a.* [Formed as prec. + -GRAPHIC.]

1. Relating to stylography or writing with a style (see quots.). ? *Obs.*

1808 R. WEDGWOOD *Patent Specif.* No. 3110 An apparatus for producing several original writings or drawings at one and the same time which I call a Pennæpolygraph or pen and stylographic manifold writer. **1846** WORCESTER, *Stylographic, Stylographical*, relating to stylography. *Crosman.* **1847–54** WEBSTER, *Stylographic*, pertaining to or used in stylography; as, *stylographic cards*, cards which may be written upon with a style. *Stylographic pencil*, a pencil or style for this kind of writing.

2. ***stylographic pen***: a variety of fountain-pen, having no nib, but a fine perforated writing-point fed with ink from the reservoir in the stem; in this point is fitted a fine needle, which when pushed back in the act of writing opens a valve so as to permit the flow of the ink.

1880 *Harper's Monthly Mag.* LX. 624 A ream of paper, and a stylographic pen. **1892** G. & W. GROSSMITH *Diary of a Nobody* xviii, A new patent stylographic pen, which cost me nine-and-sixpence.

Hence **stylo'graphical** *a.* (Worcester 1846), **stylo'graphically** *adv.* (Webster 1864).

stylography (staɪ'lɒgrəfɪ). ? *Obs.* [Formed as prec. + -GRAPHY.] A method of writing, drawing, or engraving with a style (see quots.).

1840 SMART, *Stylography*, art of writing with a style. **1846** WORCESTER, *Stylography*... A name given to a new method of engraving or drawing, invented by Mr. J. C. Crosman, performed by the use of a style on a tablet. *Hale.* **1851** R. HUNT *Sci. Exhib.* in *Art Jrnl. Illustr. Catal.* IV. p. xvi*/1 'Stylography'—a [Danish] process bearing much analogy to our glyphography.

stylohyal (staɪləʊ'haɪəl), *a.* and *sb. Anat.* [f. STYLO- + HY-OID + -AL[1].] Epithet of one of the bones of the hyoid arch, constituting in man the styloid process of the temporal bone. Chiefly as *sb.* = stylohyal bone.

1846 OWEN in *Rep. Brit. Assoc.* I. 236 A slender styliform bone, the 'stylohyal'. **1880** GÜNTHER *Fishes* 64 A stylohyal process..may be distinguished. **1884** COUES *N. Amer. Birds* 186 A bone called stylo-hyal, or 'styloid process of the temporal'.

stylohyoid (staɪləʊ'haɪɔɪd), *a.* and *sb. Anat.* [ad. mod.L. *stylohyoid-eus* (see below), f. STYLO- + *hyoideus* (see HYOIDEAN and HYOID).] **a.** *adj.* Of or pertaining to the stylohyal and the hyoid bone. **b.** *sb.* The stylohyoid muscle or *stylohyoideus*, a muscle connecting the styloid process and the hyoid bone.

[**1710** J. HARRIS *Lex. Techn.* II, *Stylo-Hyoideus*, is a Muscle of the *Os-Hyoides*, arising..from near the middle of the *Processus Styliformis*.] **1840** E. WILSON *Anat. Vade M.* 377 The stylo-hyoid branch [of the facial nerve] is distributed to the stylo-hyoid muscle. **1873** G. FLEMING tr. *Chauveau's Comp. Anat. Dom. Anim.* 722 The stylo-hyoid nerve. **1897** *Proc. Zool. Soc.* 377 The typical carnivorous stylo-hyoid seems to consist of two parts, superficial and deep.

Hence **stylohy'oidean** *a.* = prec. (Cf. F. *stylohyoïdien.*)

1891 *Century Dict.* **1898** *Syd. Soc. Lex.*

styloid ('staɪlɔɪd), *a.* *Anat.* and *Zool.* [ad. mod.L. *styloid-es*, a. Gr. στυλοειδής (Galen) like a style, f. στῦλο-ς pillar: see -OID. Cf. F. *styloïde*.] Resembling a style in shape; styliform. Applied chiefly to several slender pointed processes of bone, e.g. the spine that projects from the base of the temporal bone.

[**1615** CROOKE *Body of Man* 917 Which runneth from the processe called Styloides vnto the fourth bone of the wrest. **1684** *Blancard's Phys. Dict.*, *Styloeides*, are Processes of Bone fashioned backward like a Pencil, fastened into the B·sis of the Skull itself.] **1709** *Phil. Trans.* XXVII. 143 Two Styloid Processes. **1822** J. PARKINSON *Outl. Oryctol.* 72 The styloid projecting axis rises from a depression in the centre. **1846** OWEN in *Rep. Brit. Assoc.* I. 237 A styloid piece of the os hyoïdes. **1873** G. FLEMING tr. *Chauveau's Comp. Anat. Dom. Anim.* 54 By its inferior extremity, the styloid bone is united either to the styloid nucleus or the styloid cornu. **1897** *Proc. Zool. Soc.* 377 *Styloglossus*.—This..is by far the best developed of all the styloid muscles in Carnivora.

stylolite (ˈstaɪləlaɪt). *Geol.* [f. Gr. στῦλο-ς pillar + -LITE.] (See quots.) Also *attrib.*

1866 LAWRENCE tr. *Cotta's Rocks Classified* 99 Stylolites are a very singular formation in certain limestones, dolomites, or marls; they consist of irregular and longitudinally striped cylinders standing at right angles to the rocks' stratification. **1882** A. GEIKIE *Text bk. Geol.* 313 The so-called 'lignilites,' 'epsomites,' and 'stylolites'..are cylindrical or columnar bodies varying in length up to more than four inches, and in diameter to two or more inches. **1888** *Proc. Boston Soc. Nat. Hist.* XXIII. 495 The stylolite structure often seen in massive limestones.

Hence **styloˈlitic** *a.*, of the nature of, or containing, stylolites.

1866 LAWRENCE tr. *Cotta's Rocks Classified* 289 Dolomite is seldom oolitic, slaty, fibrous, or stylolotic [*sic*].

stylomastoid (staɪləʊˈmæstɔɪd), *a.* *Anat.* [f. STYLO- + MASTOID.] Common to the styloid and mastoid processes of the temporal bone.

1797 *Encycl. Brit.* (ed. 3) I. 681/2 The stylo-mastoid hole, so called from its situation between the styloid and mastoid processes. **1840** E. WILSON *Anat. Vade M.* 369 The stylo-mastoid vein. **1877** W. TURNER *Introd. Hum. Anat.* II. 467 A stylo-mastoid branch, which enters the stylo-mastoid foramen.

stylometric (staɪləʊˈmɛtrɪk), *a.* [f. STYLE *sb.* + -O + -METRIC.] Of or pertaining to stylometry.

1935 H. W. B. JOSEPH *Essays in Anc. & Mod. Philos.* i. 1 The first book of Plato's *Republic*..may be earlier in date than those which follow. This view about it has strong support from 'stylometric' investigations. **1964** *Guardian* 17 June 9/3 Mr Thomson..determined..to use stylometric methods to investigate the Baconian controversy. **1971** *Computers & Humanities* V. 302 The goals are:..to establish stylometric criteria based on preferred sounds, to see if significant differences in phonemic and phonetic frequencies exist between prose and verse. **1982** *Times Lit. Suppl.* 26 Nov. 1322/2 Most unsettling is his claim, on stylometric grounds long invaluable in the study of Plato, that the so-called 'common books'..are Eudemian, not Nicomachean.

stylometry (staɪˈlɒmɪtrɪ). [f. as prec. + -METRY.] The technique of making statistical analyses of the features of a literary style, esp. by means of a computer. Hence **styˈlometrist**, one who practises this technique.

1945 R. G. COLLINGWOOD *Idea of Nature* 58 Scholars..have analysed the language of the Platonic dialogues statistically... Whatever view is taken of Platonic 'stylometry' in its more detailed development. **1953** *Classical Q.* XLVII. 80 This admission that only equal amounts of text should have been compared..had the effect of largely invalidating his own and most earlier attempts to order the dialogues by relative affinities of style. Stylometrists ignored the warning... The effect was..to discredit mechanical stylometry. **1972** *Ibid.* May 89 (*heading*) The new stylometry. *Ibid.*, Stylometry can be defined as the use of numerical methods for the solution of literary problems. **1979** *Sci. Amer.* Nov. 34/2 The 50,000 words of the 14 epistles attributed to St. Paul are a challenge to the stylometrist. *Ibid.* 34/3 Forensic stylometry is at least an inhibition to the temptation on the part of police officers to adjust the admissions they present in court.

stylopization (ˌstaɪləʊpaɪˈzeɪʃən). *Ent.* [f. as STYLOPIZED *pa. pple.* and *ppl. a.* + -IZATION.] The state of being or becoming stylopized.

1882 *Trans. Entomol. Soc. London* 228 The effects of stylopisation vary very much in different specimens. **1956** G. LAPAGE *Veterinary Parasitol.* xiv. 416 The Strepsitera are commonly known as 'stylops'. The bees and wasps in which they are parasitic undergo, as a result of their effects, changes known as 'stylopisation'. **1980** *Ann. Entomol. Soc. Amer.* LXXIII. 448/1 Morphological characters often modified as a result of stylopization include clypeal pigmentation, pollen-carrying hairs, and wing venation.

stylopized (ˈstaɪləʊpaɪzd), *pa. pple.* and *ppl. a.* [f. *stylop-s* (see def.) + -IZE + -ED[1].] Of a bee: Infested by a parasite of the genus *Stylops* or a kindred genus.

1850 *Zoologist* VIII. 2827, I have observed that Stylopized bees are the first to make their appearance in spring. **1899** D. SHARP *Insects* II. 26 A stylopised male bee.

stylopod (ˈstaɪləʊpɒd). *Bot.* Anglicized form of next.

1849 BALFOUR *Man. Bot.* §888 Ovary..crowned with a double disk or stylopod. **1888** HENSLOW *Orig. Floral Struct.* 72 It is this cord which constitutes the stylopod when the fruit is ripe.

stylopodium (staɪləʊˈpəʊdɪəm). *Bot.* Pl. -podia (-ˈpəʊdɪə). [mod.L. (Hoffmann), f. Gr. στῦλο-ς pillar (see STYLE *sb.* 8) + ποδ-, πούς foot.] The double fleshy disk from which the style of the *Umbelliferæ* arises.

1832 LINDLEY *Introd. Bot.* 137. **1868** ROYLE & HEADLAND *Mat. Med.* (ed. 5) 466 Narthex Assafœtida... Stylopodia urceolate and plicated.

stylospore (ˈstaɪləʊˌspɔə(r)). *Bot.* [a. F. *stylospore*, f. Gr. στῦλο-ς pillar (see STYLE *sb.* 8) + σπορά SPORE.] A name for the naked spores in certain fungals, which are produced at the tips of short thread-like cells. Hence **styˈlosporous** *a.*, pertaining to, of the nature of, a stylospore.

1851 tr. *Tulasne* in *Ann. & Mag. Nat. Hist.* Ser. II. VIII. 119 We may apply the name of stylospores to those which originate naked, that is to say, from linear stalk-like cells. *Ibid.* 120 The stylosporous *perithecia*. **1887** W. PHILLIPS *Brit. Discomycetes* 390 Stylosporous stage: *Ceuthospora phacidioides*. *Ibid.* 420 *Stylospores*, stalked spores.

stylostatistics (ˌstaɪləʊstəˈtɪstɪks). [f. STYLE *sb.* + -O + STATISTICS.] The application of statistical methods to the analysis of features of literary style.

1956 G. HERDAN *Language as Choice & Chance* i. 8 The main division [of the book] is according to the four main branches of quantitative linguistics: Stylostastics, Statistical Linguistics, Information Theory, and Linguistic Duality. *Ibid.* ii. 14 That the 'mood' of a text of considerable length should be reflected in the relative frequency of a linguistic form..,—this is precisely what stylostatistics claims to achieve. **1962** A. ELLEGÅRD *Who was Junius?* vi. 97 (*heading*) Identification by stylostatistics. **1964** G. HERDAN in H. G. Lunt *Proc. 9th Internat. Congr. Linguists* 323 Stylostatistics leads to establishing the general laws for the use of language as a necessary preliminary of the determination of divergencies from these laws in individual style.

‖**stylostegium** (staɪləʊˈstiːdʒɪəm). *Bot.* [mod.L., f. Gr. στῦλο-ς (see STYLOSPORE) + στέγ-η or στέγ-ος roof. (App. intended as a more correct substitute for STYLOTEGIUM.)] The inner corona enveloping the style in Stapelia and other asclepiads.

1856 HENSLOW *Dict. Bot. Terms*, *Stylostegium* (στυλος a style, στεγη a roof). A peculiar form of cucullus surrounding the style.

stylote (ˈstaɪləʊt), *a.* *Zool.* [f. STYLE *sb.* or STYLUS + -OTE.] Of sponge-spicules: Having the form of a style or stylus.

1886 *Proc. Zool. Soc.* 590 Spicules..tylostylote or stylote. **1887** S. O. RIDLEY in *Challenger Rep.* XX. 96 Megasclera stylote to tylostylote.

‖**stylotegium** (ˌstaɪləʊˈtiːdʒɪəm). *Bot.* [mod.L. f. Gr. στῦλ-ος pillar (regarded as the source of STYLE *sb.* 8) + τέγ-ος roof.] Earlier synonym of STYLOSTEGIUM.

1821 S. F. GRAY *Brit. Plants* I. 163 Hood, *Stylotegium*. A hollowing out of the united filaments of the stamens, covering the ovary like a hood. **1832** LINDLEY *Introd. Bot.* 121. **1866** *Treas. Bot.*

‖**stylus** (ˈstaɪləs). Also stilus. Pl. **styluses, styli.** [a. L. *stylus*, incorrect form of *stilus*: see STYLE *sb.*]

1. = STYLE *sb.* I.

1807 J. LANDSEER *Lect. Engraving* iii. 119 Lines drawn with a stylus or steel point (commonly called an etching needle) on copper. **1821** CRAIG *Lect. Drawing* etc. ii. 101 The early Babylonians had a practice of tracing out various figures, with a stylus or point. **1834** LYTTON *Pompeii* III. i, A stilus and tablets of no ordinary size. **1881** A. WATT *Mech. Industr.* 126 The next operation [in etching] is to employ the stylus, or point. **1882** *Chamb. Jrnl.* 4 Feb. 81 The pencil outlines are then cut sharply on the friable surface with a stylus. **1884** J. PAYN *Some Lit. Recoll.* (1885) 75 This delicate microscopic writing, looking as if it were done with a stylus.

2. a. A tracing-point used to produce the written record in a chart recorder, telegraph receiver, or the like.

1875 KNIGHT *Dict. Mech.* 2518/2 (*Telephone*), The other arm terminates in a stylus which normally rests upon an ink-ribbon over the bed of the receiving-table. **1879** G. PRESCOTT *Sp. Telephone* 295 The membrane carries a stylus, which also participates in the motion, and records it upon the blackened paper. **1966** *McGraw-Hill Encycl. Sci. & Technol.* XI. 382/1 By the use of a coated chart or an inked ribbon between the stylus and the chart, an intermittent record is made. **1971** MAGRAB & BLOMQUIST *Measurement Time-Varying Phenomena* v. 182 A voltage will be applied to the coils of the writing system which will cause the slider and writing stylus to move in proportion to the voltage, thus obtaining a recording.

b. = NEEDLE *sb.* 3 e.

1879 *Year-Bk. of Facts* 88/2 In that patent he [*sc.* Edison] describes a means of recording ordinary telegraph signals by a chisel-shaped stylus indenting a sheet of paper. **1892** W. GILLETT *Phonograph* 12 Instead of one stylus serving for the two purposes, there are now two; one, the recorder, having a very keen edge,..and the other, the reproducer, having a tiny knob highly polished. *Ibid.* 13 *note*, In some of Mr. Edison's recent instruments..two styluses are used. **1904** S. R. BOTTONE *Talking Machines & Records* 48 The recording stylus is now seldom made of steel, except only in the very commonest forms of recorders; but is usually made of..sapphire. **1943** *Gramophone* July 29/3 The stylus is a small sapphire carried on the toe of an L-shaped holder. **1960** *Practical Wireless* XXXVI. 370 (Advt.), Turnover sapphire styli. **1962** A. NISBETT *Technique Sound Studio* iv. 87 The hot-stylus method..helps to smooth the wall as the cutter moves on. **1975** *Times* 17 Sept. 16/3 Nowadays, you have a 'cartridge' with a 'stylus' in it, and the [gramophone] arm is called a 'pick-up'.

fig. **1936** DYLAN THOMAS *Coll. Poems* (1952) 37 The grooved land rotating, that the stylus of lightning Dazzle this face of voices on the moon-turned table.

3. The gnomon of a sun-dial; = STYLE *sb.* 7.

1796 MORSE *Amer. Geog.* I. 18 A species of sun-dial, having a stilus or gnomon erected perpendicularly upon an horizontal plane.

4. A pointer or finger; = STYLE *sb.* 6.

1884 *Manch. Exam.* 16 Sept. 6/2 A curious Kalender, with an astronomical volvelle of which the stylus had been preserved.

5. *Bot.* = STYLE *sb.* 8.

Used as mod.L. in Ray *Meth. Plant. Emend.* (1703) 202. **1728** J. DOUGLASS in *Phil. Trans.* XXXV. 570 They..fall to picking out the Filamenta Styli, or Chives, and together with them, a pretty long Portion of the Stylus itself, or String to which they are joined. **1771** *Encycl. Brit.* III. 457/1 Both have one stylus, and one long seed. **1856** HENSLOW *Dict. Bot. Terms*, *Stylus*. The style. Also the Ostiolum of certain Fungi.

6. *Zool.* A style or stylet.

1856–8 W. CLARK *Van der Hoeven's Zool.* I. 53 Trichodina.—Body oval, with vibratile cilia, without cirri or styli. **1887** SOLLAS in *Encycl. Brit.* XXII. 416/2 (*Sponges*) By the suppression of one of the rays of an oxea, an acuate spicule or stylus results. **1887** S. O. RIDLEY in *Challenger Rep.* XX. 84 Spicules.—Megasclera; long but very slender styli.

styly, obs. form of STILLY *adv.*

styme, stime (staɪm), *sb.* Chiefly *Sc.* and *north.* Forms: 3–4, 7– stime, 5– styme, (9 steyme, stim). [Of obscure origin.

The Icel. *skíma* ('Fra dagmálum til nóns sá ekki skímu úti heldr en menn væru blindir,' *Isl. Ann.* 254, *c* 1685) coincides in use with the Eng. word.]

1. In the phrase ***not to see a styme***: to be unable to see at all.

a **1300** *Cursor M.* 19652 Noþer he ete þaa thre dais time, Ne he iwiss moght se a stime. *c* **1475** HENRYSON *Poems* III. 86 To kene þe self a styme it [the spirit] may nocht se, For stammeris [*MS.* scammeris] on eftir effectioun. *a* **1568** A. SCOTT *Poems* xxxiii. 23 Thow [Cupid] markis quhair nevir styme thow seis, Bot hittis be gaiss. **1635** JACKSON *Creed* VIII. iv. 36 If a man cannot see (as we say) a *stime*, but with one eye, we account it no solecisme to say, hee hath lost the other. **1683** [G. MERITON] *Yorksh. Dial.* 8 My Neen..are seay Gummy and Furr'd up sometime. I can nut leauke at 'th Leet, nor see a stime. **1785** BURNS *There's naething like* ii, I've seen me daez't upon a time: I scarce could wink or see a styme. **1808** R. ANDERSON *Cumbld. Ball.* 142 Deil a wink cud I sleep, nay nor yet see a steyme. **1841** LEVER *C. O'Malley* cvii, The night was murthering dark; you could not see a stim. **1901** J. MOLLISON *Poems* 94 They feared that never again War their e'en tae see a stime.

2. A glimpse or glance; the least bit or quantity (of anything); a glimmer (of light); a moment (of time).

1776 *Herd's Coll. Sc. Poems* II. 150 And ne'er a blyth styme wad he blink, Until his wame was fou. **1794** *Har'st Rig* xxiii, To cut their fur, and tak their share O' their nane rig. But ony mair? The fient ae stime! *a* **1807** J. SKINNER *Amusem. Leis. Hours* (1809) 108 Else you may..wiss ye had ne'er seen a styme O' Louse nor Bonnet. **1888** BARRIE *Auld Licht Idylls* vii. (1892) 151 Even with three wicks it [the lamp] gave but a stime of light. **1895** JANE BARLOW *Strangers at Lisconnel* vi. 120 You've ne'er a stim of light to be workin' in, sittin' there in the corner. **1897** E. W. HAMILTON *Outlaws* ix. 102 There's never a styme to choose betwixt him and James Hepburn.

Hence **styme** *v.* *intr.* (see quot. 1808).

1808 JAMIESON, To *styme*, to open the eyes partially, to look as one does whose vision is indistinct. **1886** J. J. H. BURGESS *Shetl. Sk.* 66, I lookit an' stimed inta da black dark aroond me, but I could see naethin'.

stymie (ˈstaɪmɪ), *sb.*[1] *Sc.* In 7 *pl.* stymeis. [? f. STYME *v.* + -IE.] One who does not see well.

1616 in *Pitcairn's Crim. Trials* (Bannatyne Club) III. II. 588 Gif those howlattis and stymeis [*i.e.* the courtiers] war schote away. **1808** JAMIESON s.v. *Styme* v., It also denotes the aukward motions of one who does not see well. Hence a person of this description is vulgarly called *a blind stymie*.

stymie (ˈstaɪmɪ), *sb.*[2] *Golf.* Also **steimy, stimy.** [Of obscure origin: cf. prec. and STYME *sb.* and *v.*] An opponent's ball which lies on the putting green in a line between the ball of the player and the hole he is playing for, if the distance between the balls is not less than six inches; also, the occurrence of this; often in the phrase ***to lay a stymie***.

1834 *Rules of Musselburgh Golf Club* in C. B. Clapcott *Rules of Golf of 10 Oldest Golf Clubs* (1935) 66 With regard to Stimies the ball nearest the hole if within six inches shall be lifted. **1857** H. B. FARNIE in *Golfiana Misc.* (1887) 173 Wooden putters are used to play stimies when the intercepting ball is at some distance from that of the player. A curving-in motion is imparted to the ball, causing it to pass the stimy. **1862** *Remarks on Golf* 17 The iron is..used for lofting what are called steimies. A steimy occurs when your opponent's ball lies so directly in a line between the hole and your own ball that you cannot hole by putting. The only resource..is to take the iron and 'loft' your ball over the steimy and into the hole. It is not considered quite fair to play intentionally so as to lay a steimy. **1894** *Times* 28 Apr. 13/3 Mr. Ball left his opponent a stimie and Mr. Laidlay in trying to hole out sent his opponent's ball in. **1897** *Westm. Gaz.* 10 Dec. 9/3 His partner laid him a stimie.

attrib. **1857** H. B. FARNIE in *Golfiana Misc.* (1887) 172 These clubs are handled for stimy-playing on the same principle.

ˈstymie, *v.* [f. STYMIE *sb.*[2]]

1. *trans.* *Golf.* To put (one's opponent or oneself) into the position of having to negotiate a stymie; also *intr.* (of a ball) to intervene as a stymie.

1857 H. B. FARNIE in *Golfiana Misc.* (1887) 172 The ball stimying may be lifted if within six inches of that of the player, until the stroke is done. **1894** A. LANG in *Daily News* 5 July 5/2 A man often stimies himself, by a bad putt. **1896** R. B. MANSFIELD *New & Old Chips* 320 When he stimied me, I managed to play round him into the hole. **1901** *Scotsman* 5 Sept. 7/3 Mr. Worthington was stimied and in trying to loft, knocked Mr. Williamson's ball into the hole.

2. *fig.* To impede, obstruct, frustrate, thwart (a person, an activity, or a project).

1902 G. ADE *Girl Proposition* 70 In about 8 minutes he had the Regular Fellow stymied and Hazel was leaning against him. **1922** A. HADDON *Green Room Gossip* vii. 154, I looked like being stymied because I couldn't sing in tune. **1933** WODEHOUSE *Mulliner Nights* v. 183 There came the shrill cry of a Hunting Bishop stymied by a hat-stand. **1938** *East Liberty* (Pittsburgh) *Tribune* 26 Aug. 1/5 (*heading*) New recreation center at Mellon Field 'stymied'. **1946** J. W. DAY *Harvest Adventure* xvi. 274 Mr John Loverseed.. raised this whole question.. in spite of repeated attempts by the Ministry of Agriculture to stymie him. **1957** *Economist* 2 Nov. 389/1 It is hard to visualise Afghans and Albanians, Salvadoreans and Sudanese quickly triumphing over the very real difficulties that have stymied the five-power group. **1966** L. DURRELL in *Sat. Even. Post* 4 June 68/3 Coco was for selling her to a local clinic, but once more we were stymied by this public holiday. The clinic was shut. **1980** *Daily Tel.* 28 July 24/3 France's participation in the military force had merely been to stymie an intended intervention by troops from Pacific area countries.

Hence **ˈstymied** *ppl. a.* (also *fig.*)

1862 *Remarks on Golf* 17 Steimies.. frequently occur, and often cause the hole to be halved which the steimied man felt confident of winning. **1937** PARTRIDGE *Dict. Slang* 844/1 *Stymied*,.. awkwardly placed; nonplussed. **1974** P. DE VRIES *Glory of Hummingbird* vii. 97, I was worried about a stymied affair with a girl with whose parents I was getting on swimmingly.

stymmer, variant of STIMMER.

Stymphalian (stɪmˈfeɪlɪən), *a.* *Myth.* [f. L. *Stymphali-us* (f. *Stymphalus* or *-um*, a. Gr. Στύμφαλος) + -AN.] Of or belonging to Stymphalus, a district in Arcadia haunted by a species of odious birds of prey, the destruction of which was the sixth of the 'labours' of Hercules.

1653 H. COGAN tr. *Hist. Diod. Sic.* IV. xiii. 129 He [*sc.* Hercules] chaced away the Birds which infested all the Countrey about the Stymphalian Fen. **1704** SWIFT *T. Tub* iii. 78 A sort of dangerous Fowl, who have a perverse Inclination, to plunder the best Branches of the Tree of Knowledge, like those Stymphalian Birds that eat up the Fruit. **1888** A. H. SMITH *Catal. Engr. Gems Brit. Mus.* 152 Herakles kneeling to right, and drawing bow at Stymphalian birds (two) flying before him.

So **Stymphalid** *a.* [L. *Stymphalid-*, *-is*, Gr. Στυμφαλιδ-, Στυμφαλίς fem. adj.] = STYMPHALIAN *a.*; also *sb.*, a Stymphalian bird. †**ˈStymphalist** (see quot. 1595).

1560 B. GOOGE tr. *Palingenius' Zodiac* III. (1561) F vj b, He hath expelde the Stymphalides by force of valeant bowe. **1584** HUDSON *Du Bartas' Judith* v. (1608) 74 Ye Stymphalids, who with your youth vptaks, You rauens that from vs our riches raks. **1595** 'DANDO & RUST' *Maroccus Extat.* (Percy Soc.) 16 This stymphalist is hee, that with five or sixe tenements, and the retinue thereunto belonging, infectes the aire with stench and poisons that parish. **1620** SYLVESTER *Tobacco Batter.d* 775 Our Alcides.. Hath, as with Arrowes, from His sacred Sides, All-ready chac't These stinking Stymphalides. **1831** KEIGHTLEY *Mythol.* II. iv. (1854) 316 His sixth task was to drive away the Stymphalid birds.

stynch(e, styney: see STENCH, STYANY.

styng(k, styngill: see STINK *v.*, STINGLE.

styonie, -y, obs. ff. STYANY.

stypand, -end(e, obs. forms of STIPEND.

stype, stypell, obs. ff. STEEP, STEEPLE.

styphnate (ˈstɪfnət), *sb.* *Chem.* [f. STYPHN-IC + -ATE[1].] A salt of styphnic acid.

1857 MILLER *Elem. Chem., Org.* (1862) 663 The styphnates.. are decomposed with explosion, when gently heated.

styphnic (ˈstɪfnɪk), *a.* *Chem.* [f. supposed Gr. *στυφν-ός (a mistake for στρυφνός) astringent + -IC.

The name (G. *styphninsäure*) was given by the discoverers, Böttger and Will, *Liebig's Ann. der Chemie* 1846, LVIII. 269.]

styphnic acid, a dibasic astringent acid obtained by the action of nitric acid on asafœtida and other gum resins. Also called *oxypicric acid*.

1850 FOWNES *Chem.* (ed. 3) 524 To these may be added the styphnic acid recently described by MM. Boettger and Will.

stypium (ˈstɪpɪəm). *Pharm.* [quasi-L., f. Gr. στύπη tow.] A superior kind of carded oakum, used for surgical dressings.

1871 *Lancet* 17 June 826/2 Stypium is antiseptic, and has an agreeable odour. **1895** *Arnold & Sons' Catal. Surg. Instrum.* 726 Stypium, per lb., £0 1 0.

styple, styppyl, obs. ff. STEEPLE.

‖**stypsis** (ˈstɪpsɪs). *Med.* [late L. *stypsis*, a. Gr. στῦψις, n. of action to στύφειν (whence STYPTIC).] The application or use of styptics.

1890 BILLINGS *Med. Dict.* **1911** in WEBSTER.

styptic (ˈstɪptɪk), *a.* and *sb.* Forms: 5 **stiptik, -tyk**, 5–6 **styptyke**, 6–7 **-tike**, 5–7 **stiptike**, 6 **-tyke**, 5–8 **stiptick(e, styptique**, (7 **stiptict, stiticke**), 7 **stypticke**, 7–8 **styptick, stiptic**, 7– **styptic**. [ad. late L. *stypticus*, a. Gr. στυπτικός, f. στύφ-ειν to contract, have an astringent effect upon. Cf. F. *styptique*.] **A.** *adj.*

1. a. Having the power of contracting organic tissue; having an austere or acid taste; harsh or raw to the palate; having a binding effect on the stomach or bowels.

c **1400** *Lanfranc's Cirurg.* 98 Diete him with colde metis & stiptik. *c* **1425** tr. *Arderne's Treat. Fistula*, etc. 81 Al stiptik þingz bene repressiue of humours. *c* **1440** *Pallad. on Husb.* XI. 281 The stiptyk whyte [wine] a stomak that is laxe Wole helpe. **1477** NORTON *Ord. Alch.* v. in Ashm. (1652) 74 And so is Sowerish tast called Sapor Pontick, And lesse Sower allso called Sapor Stiptick. **1533** ELYOT *Cast. Helthe* II. vii. (1541) 18 b, Meates stiptike or rough on the tonge, byndeth and comforteth appetite. **1578** LYTE *Dodoens* VI. lxviii. 745 The gal [of the oak] is also very binding and stiptique. **1610** B. JONSON *Alchemist* II. v, What's that? A Lullianist? a Ripley?.. Know you the sapor pontick? sapor stiptick? **1620** VENNER *Via Recta* viii. 188 Take.. some stypticke thing after meale.. that may inhibit the ascending of vapors, by closing vp the mouth of the stomack. **1646** SIR T. BROWNE *Pseud. Ep.* VI. xii. 338 There is a sowre, stipticke salt diffused through the earth, which passing a concoction in plants, becommeth milder and more agreeable unto the sense. **1732** ARBUTHNOT *Rules of Diet* in *Aliments*, etc. (1735) 250 Austere, astringent, vegetable Substances..; as Several sorts of Plumbs,.. distinguishable by their rough styptick Taste... Pomegranates, which contain a Juice styptick, and extremely cooling. **1804** *Med. Jrnl.* XII. 30 Dogberry tree. .. The berries of this tree have a styptic quality, and are bitter to the taste. **1871** GARROD *Mat. Med.* (ed. 3) 88 An orange-brown solution, with a strong styptic taste.

b. Of a medicament, etc.: That arrests hæmorrhage. ***styptic pencil***, a stick of styptic substance used to stem the bleeding of small cuts.

c **1425** tr. *Arderne's Treat. Fistula*, etc. 27 Puluer of alum, zucarin combust, 'bole armenic', [etc.].. ar.. of þe same vertu in regeneracion of flesch an cicatrizacione and þat þai bene al stiptik. **1543** TRAHERON *Vigo's Chirurg.* III. xi. 100 b/2 Ye shal minister this.. which is stiptike, & consoundeth or ioyneth together, yͤ woundes in the guttes. **1658** A. FOX tr. *Wurtz' Surg.* II. xiii. 97 These Wounds.. ought to be healed with stiptick Plaisters. **1673** *Phil. Trans.* VIII. 6115 The Royal Styptique liquor was used in the last engagement against the Dutch by the Chirurgions. **1717** POPE *Iliad* XI. 983 A bitter root he bruised; The wound he wash'd, the styptic juice infused. **1745** R. JAMES *Med. Dict.* III. s.v. *Styptica*, I found that many little Trials were made there, also, with a Styptic Ball, mixed with French Brandy. **1872** F. G. THOMAS *Dis. Women* 107 Both these cases readily yielded to the recumbent posture, and the application of cold and styptic compresses. **1880** W. MACCORMAC *Antisept. Surg.* 167 Pure spirit is a good application; it is slightly styptic and quite antiseptic. **1908** *Sears, Roebuck Catal.* 799/2 Styptic Pencils. Used when shaving. Will instantly stop bleeding. **1936** G. GREENE *Gun for Sale* vii. 211 Plying his styptic pencil, sticking the cotton-wool on the longer wounds. **1961** I. FLEMING *Thunderball* i. 9 Bond dabbed with the blood-stained styptic pencil at the cut on his chin. **1978** *Observer* 26 Mar. 29/7 He had dropped his styptic pencil down the washbasin.

c. *fig.*

1583 STUBBES *Anat. Abus.* I. (1879) 98 Find the sawce sowre and stiptick enough in Hell. **1637** HEYWOOD *Dial.* ii. Wks. 1874 VI. 118 By her the Boy would be so much insenc'd, To aime a shaft in Stiptick poison dipt. **1641** MILTON *Ch. Govt.* II. iii. 56 Not medling with that restraining and styptick surgery which the law uses,.. against the eruptions and outermost effects thereof [malice]. **1648** J. BEAUMONT *Psyche* III. xcviii, That stiptic Word full in the Priest's face flew, And fastned mystic chains upon his Tongue.

d. In plant-names.

1847 DARLINGTON *Amer. Weeds* 110 *Cassia occidentalis*... Styptic Weed. **1864** GRISEBACH *Flora Brit. W. Ind.* 788/1 Styptic- or velvet-bur, *Priva echinata*.

†**2.** Of a person, etc., the bowels: Costive. *Obs.*

1582 HESTER *Secr. Phiorav.* III. lv. 77 This Diatartaro is good.. for those that are stiptike of bodie. **1607** TOPSELL *Four-f. Beasts* 381 A belly neither continually loose nor stiptike.

B. *sb.*

1. a. A substance having the power of contracting organic tissue.

a **1400** *Lanfranc's Cirurg.* 226 þou schalt avoide þe matere, & þou schalt comforte þe place [the mouth of the stomach] with stiptikis. **1638** tr. *Bacon's Life & Death* (1650) 37 This inconvenience is remedied.. by shutting the mouth of the Stomach strongly, with Stiptickes. **1712–14** POPE *Rape Lock* II. 132 Gums and Pomatums shall his flight restrain,.. Or Alum styptics with contracting pow'r Shrink his thin essence like a rivel'd flow'r. **1756** C. LUCAS *Ess. Waters* I. 13 That austere, rough styptic, called alum.

b. as a remedy for hæmorrhage.

c **1425** tr. *Arderne's Treat. Fistula*, etc. 74 Afterward [after phlebotomy] be þer done suffumigacion or fomentacion of gall, or of.. wormode, horsmynt, and sich oþer stiptikez. **1676** WISEMAN *Chirurg. Treat.* v. ix. 399 There was an effusion of bloud..: but having Dossils ready dipt in the Royal Stiptick, we applied them. **1755** MRS. DELANY *Life & Corr.* (1861) III. 322 Her nose.. has already bled 15 or 16 ounces: it is at present stopped by Eaton's Stiptic. **1825** SCOTT *Talism.* xiv, The physician.. withdrew from the wounded shoulder the fragment of the weapon, and stopped with styptics and bandages the effusion of blood which followed. **1842** *Penny Cycl.* XXIII. 180/2 Those astringents are alone entitled to be called styptics which can be applied directly to the bleeding orifice; and of these some act chemically, others vitally, and others merely mechanically. **1884** T. BRYANT *Pract. Surg.* (ed. 4) I. 481 Astringents or styptics are valuable agents in the arrest of bleeding... 'Cold' is a powerful styptic.

c. *fig.*

1785 GEO. A. BELLAMY *Apology* (ed. 3) VI. 119 Hope, celestial Comforter! that only Styptic for a bleeding heart. **1855** THACKERAY *Newcomes* II. xii. 120 Again the flow of words is checked by the styptic [*sc.* a kiss] previously applied. **1858** MRS. OLIPHANT *Laird of Norlaw* III. 92 Vulgar, needful business, the very elements of daily necessity—these are the best styptics for thrusts in the heart. **1879** DOWDEN *Southey* ii. 28 He had been squandering his emotions; he had been indulging in a luxury and waste of passion. Here was a tonic and a styptic.

†**2.** A mordant. *Obs. rare.*

1685 W. COLE in *Phil. Trans.* XV. 1281 The last and most beautifull colour.. will.. be.. of a fair bright Crimson..; which afterwards (notwithstanding there is no use of any Stiptic to bind the colour) will continue the same.

styptical (ˈstɪptɪkəl), *a.* ? *Obs.* [f. as prec. + -AL[1].] = STYPTIC *a.*

1528 PAYNELL *Salerne's Regim.* Q iiij, Prunes that be nat rype be stypticall. **1612** *Benvenuto's Passenger* I. ii. 205 Let vs take something sticall, without drinking therevpon, and those be Peares, Medlers, [etc.]. **1652** *Hermeticall Banquet* B 3, Aluminous and Pontick [Salts], which are Stegnoticall, Stypticall, and Corroborating the Retentive faculties. **1686** PLOT *Staffordsh.* 165 Every body knows what stiptical qualities, always attend ferrugineous bodies. **1762** B. STILLINGFLEET tr. *Beyerstein's Obst. to Impr. Physic* in Misc. Tracts (1791) 215 Thus watery mixed with dry,.. glutinous with stiptical,.. mutually weaken each other. **1820** SCORESBY *Acc. Arctic Reg.* I. 519 He has been observed to, .. as if conscious of the styptical effect of cold, apply snow with his paws to the wound.

Hence †**ˈstypticalness**, stypticity.

1528 PAYNELL *Salerne's Regim.* R ij, Medlars make one costife throughe their sowernes and stipticalnes. **1727** BAILEY vol. II, *Stipticalness*, stiptick Quality, or Aptness to stop Blood, &c.

stypticite (ˈstɪptɪsaɪt). *Min.* [f. Gr. στυπτικός STYPTIC + -ITE. Named by J. F. L. Hausmann in 1847.] An obsolete synonym of fibro-ferrite (see FIBRO-).

1854 DANA *Syst. Min.* (ed. 4) II. 388.

stypticity (stɪpˈtɪsɪtɪ). Forms: 5–6 **stipticite**, (6 **styp-**), 6–7 **stipticitie**, 7–8 **-ty**, 7 **stypticitie**, 7– **stypticity**. [ad. med.L. *stypticitās*, f. *styptic-us* STYPTIC *a.* Cf. F. *stypticité* (14th c. in Littré).]

1. Styptic quality; astringency.

c **1400** tr. *Secreta Secret., Gov. Lordsh.* 98 þe sensibilyte of þe tonge ys by way of tastynge & sauour, And þarof er ix maneres; Swetnesse, bitternesse,.. ponticite, stipticite, [etc.]. **1527** ANDREW *Brunswyke's Distyll. Waters* O j, Dronke of the same water [of crab-apples] stoppeth the laske with his styptycite. **1575** J. BANISTER *Treat. Chyrurg.* 134 b, Consolidatiua. By their stipticitie and drying they haue power to skinne and heale, equally incarnating fleshe and skinne. **1666** BOYLE *Orig. Forms & Qual.* 218 Qualities.. such as are Properties peculiar to it [Vitriol], as Greenness, easiness of Fusion, Stypticity of Tast. **1702** FLOYER *Cold Bathing* I. 22 Marle-Waters taste smooth, and have a little Stipticity. **1772** *Phil. Trans.* LXII. 462 The spring possesses some slight degree of stypticity, by means of a chalybeate impregnation. **1834** T. J. GRAHAM *Dom. Med.* (1844) 181 The gentle stypticity, or astringency in genuine claret, renders it.. the most wholesome of any strong liquor.

†**2.** Costiveness (of the stomach or bowels). *Obs.*

1620 VENNER *Via Recta* viii. 190 If it [the stomach] be subiect to laxitie, then a lesse portion of drinke; if to stypticitie, then a greater is to be assumed.

stypticize (ˈstɪptɪsaɪz), *v.* [f. STYPTIC *sb.* + -IZE.] *trans.* To dress or treat with a styptic.

1866 BLACKMORE *Cradock Nowell* xxxviii, Wena's tail was stypticized.

stypticness (ˈstɪptɪknɪs). ? *Obs.* [f. STYPTIC *a.* + -NESS.] = STYPTICITY.

c **1425** tr. *Arderne's Treat. Fistula*, etc. 81 [Zucaryne] mundifieth, forsoþ, with a stiptiknez. **1580** T. NEWTON *Approved Medicines* 58 b, The fruite with tartnes or stipticknesse hath a certayne waterishe sweetenesse. **1669** W. SIMPSON *Hydrol. Chym.* 82 Acidities.. may be turn'd.. to a spurious saltishness or stypticknes. **1727** BAILEY vol. II, *Stypticknes*, astringent or binding Quality.

†**b.** Costiveness (of the stomach or bowels). *Obs.*

1612 WOODALL *Surg. Mate* Wks. (1653) 145 Abstersive medicines.. leaving a certain stipticknesse behind them. **1620** VENNER *Via Recta* viii. 190 The drinke is to be increased, and diminished, according to the.. disposition of the stomack in.. loosenes, or stiptickenes.

†**ˈstyptive**, *a.* *Obs. rare.* [Alteration of STYPTIC: see -IVE.] = STYPTIC *a.*

1640 PARKINSON *Theatr. Bot.* 446 It [Rupturewort] hath a little stiptive or astringent taste.

Stypven (ˈstɪpvən). *Med.* Also **stypven**. [f. STYP(TIC *a.* and *sb.* + VEN(OM *sb.*] The dried and purified venom of Russell's viper for use in solution as a local hæmostatic and a blood coagulant; **Stypven time**, coagulation time measured when Stypven is added as a coagulant.

Stypven is a proprietary name in the U.S.

1940 *Lancet* 17 Aug. 195/1 This venom..is very efficient in bringing about the rapid formation of a strong clot when applied to a bleeding surface. It is supplied under the name of Stypven by Messrs. Burroughs Wellcome and Co. **1948** *Official Gaz.* (U.S. Patent Office) 20 Jan. 409/2 Burroughs Wellcome & Co. (U.S.A.) Inc., New York... *Stypven.* For dry viper venom... Claims use since 1937. **1955** *Lancet* 1 Oct. 692/1 'Stypven' times were estimated on all the samples as follows: To 0·1 ml. of warmed plasma was added 0·1 ml. of stypven... Immediately after, 0·1 ml. of calcium chloride was added, and the clotting-time was recorded. **1961** *Ibid.* 2 Sept. 503/1 In these men, the whole-blood clotting-time, silicone clotting-time, calcium clotting-time.., prothrombin-time, and 'Stypven' time were estimated in duplicate weekly for eight weeks. **1976** *Ibid.* 6 Nov. 995/2 The stypven time (Russell viper venom) of P.P.P. reflects the amount of available active phospholipids which may be dietary in origin.

styr, obs. form of STIR.

styracin ('staɪərəsɪn). *Chem.* Also **-ine**. [a. F. *styracine*, f. L. *styrac-* STYRAX: see -IN, -INE.] A crystalline substance obtained from storax and balsam of Peru.

1838 T. THOMSON *Chem. Org. Bodies* 522 When the balsam is treated with alcohol, about a fourth part remains undissolved, constituting a white crystalline mass. This is the substance which M. Bonastre has distinguished by the name of styracin. **1863** FOWNES *Chem.* (ed. 9) 563 This compound described respectively under the name of cinnamein (when oily), and styracin (when solid). **1871** GARROD *Mat. Med.* (ed. 3) 270 Styracin..or cinnamate of cinnyl.

styrage, styrer, obs. ff. STEERAGE, STEERER.

styrax ('staɪəræks). [a. L. *styrax*, a. Gr. στύραξ, storax, storax-tree.]

1. An aromatic gum; = STORAX 1.

1558 WARDE tr. *Alexis' Secr.* I. 45 Take..Ambergryse, ..*Styrax calamita*, [etc.]..And the Ambre, *Styrax*, and other thinges that remaine in the bottome of the sayd vessel, ..will be excedinge good to make muske or swete balles. **1621** BURTON *Anat. Mel.* II. ii. III. 336 Belzoin, Ladanum, Styrax, and such like gummes, which make a pleasant and acceptable perfume. **1783** *Phil. Trans.* LXXIII. 239 It is but too common to find it adulterated..with styrax or other resins. **1882** *Encycl. Brit.* XIV. 687/2 It is from the bark of this latter tree [*Liquidambar orientalis*] that the storax of the ancients.., the medicinal styrax of to-day, is prepared.

2. A styrax-tree (see 3). Cf. STORAX 2.

1832 MACGILLIVRAY *Trav. Humboldt* xxiii. (1836) 329 The truncated cone of Tolima..rises amidst forests of styrax.

3. *Comb.*, as ***styrax-flowing*** adj.; **styrax tree**, a tree of the genus *Styrax*, esp. *S. officinalis*.

1786 ABERCROMBIE *Gard. Assist., Arrang. Plants* 30 Liquidambar, or sweet gum tree *Styrax-flowing. **1579** NORTH *Plutarch, Lysander* (1595) 493 Not far from thence there grow great plenty of *Styrax [*printed* Styrap] trees. **1767** ABERCROMBIE *Ev. Man his own Gard.* (1805) 685/1 Styrax-tree, officinal.

styre, obs. f. STEER *sb.*[1] and *v.*[1]; var. STIRE.

styrene ('staɪəri:n). *Chem.* [f. STYR(AX + -ENE.]

1. A colourless, toxic, aromatic liquid, $C_6H_5{\cdot}CH{:}CH_2$, orig. obtained from the storax tree (hence called STYROL or S'TYROLENE) and now recovered as a by-product of petroleum. Also called *vinylbenzene* and *phenylethylene*.

1885 I. REMSEN *Introd. Study Compounds of Carbon* 343 Styrene... This hydrocarbon is contained in liquid storax. .. It is formed by distilling cinnamic acid with lime. **1926** H. G. RULE tr. *J. Schmidt's Text-bk. Org. Chem.* II. iii. 331 Styrene, phenyl-ethylene, vinyl-benzene, $C_6H_5{\cdot}CH{:}CH_2$, is the simplest representative of the olefine derivatives [of benzene]. **1947** *Sun* (Baltimore) 17 Apr. 2/5 Styrene was not explosive, Thomas said, but would burn as rapidly as gasoline. **1956** *Sci. News* XLII. 41 Hydrocarbons and low boiling organic compounds..are becoming increasingly important industrially owing to the development of petrochemicals,..which include polythene, styrene and synthetic rubber. **1978** J. R. HOLUM *Org. & Biol. Chem.* viii. 163 Polystyrene, made from styrene, has phenyl groups on alternate carbons of the main chain.

2. = POLYSTYRENE. Also *attrib.*

1938 *Encycl. Brit. Bk. of Year* 147/1 To the growing family of synthetic resins and plastics, 1937 saw added Styrene, characterized by clarity, low initial colour, and thermoplastic properties. **1969** *Islander* (Victoria, B.C.) 6 July 8/2 Keeping food hot or cold en route is important—a styrene foam chest has exceptional insulating ability. **1972** J. POTTER *Going West* 45 Every can was found to have a double bottom. Nuggets of gold lay embedded in white styrene between the two sheets of tin.

3. Special Combs.: **styrene-acrylonitrile**, the combination of styrene and acrylonitrile, esp. as copolymers in a rubber; usu. *attrib.*; **styrene-butadiene**, the combination of styrene and butadiene, esp. as copolymers in a rubber; usu. *attrib.*; **styrene monomer**, the monomeric form of styrene; = sense 1; **styrene oxide**, the toxic epoxide, $C_6H_5{\cdot}\underbrace{CH{-}CH_2}$; **styrene plastic**, any or all of the plastic materials that may be made using styrene; **styrene resin**, any compound formed by the polymerization of styrene.

1957 H. R. SIMONDS *Conc. Guide to Plastics* ii. 71 A styrene-acrylonitrile copolymer is available from Bakelite Co. **1977** R. A. DICKIE in M. O. W. Richardson *Polymer Engin. Composites* iii. 177 Results are presented..on several rubber-modified polystyrene and styrene-acrylonitrile copolymers. **1958** *Times Rev. Industry* Apr. 51/1 The synthetic S.B.R. (styrene-butadiene rubber) being tough and hard wearing, is good for tire treads. **1978** D. R. PAUL in Paul & Newman *Polymer Blends* II. xii. 59 A patent.. describes bonding an ethylene-propylenediene terpolymer rubber..to styrene-butadiene rubber..by a graft. **1947** I. THOMAS *Injection Moulding Plastics* iii. 168 The base material for polystyrene is styrene monomer. **1971** R. D. DEANIN in Tobolsky & Mark *Polymer Sci. & Materials* xiv. 335 These [polyesters] are mixed with about one-half their weight of styrene monomer. **1939** *Jrnl. Amer. Chem. Soc.* LXI. 997/2 The reaction of styrene oxide and hydriodic acid results in a primary alcohol. **1979** *Experientia* XXXV. 241/2 The observed differences in the metabolism of styrene oxide can be assigned theoretically to 2 possible factors. **1943** D. W. BROWN *Handbk. Engin. Plastics* ii. 27 (*heading*) Styrene plastics. **1947** *Brit. Catal. Plastics* 51/2 (*heading*) Methyl methacrylate and styrene plastics. **1937** R. S. MORRELL *Synthetic Resins* i. 16 The vinyl and styrene resins are used as lacquers and in nitro-cellulose finishes. **1959** E. C. BERNHARDT *Processing of Thermoplastic Materials* III. 628 (*heading*) Styrene resins.

Hence **'styrenated** *ppl. a.*, containing styrene in chemical combination; **styre'nation**, the process of chemically adding styrene.

1954 KIRK & OTHMER *Encycl. Chem. Technol.* XIII. 146 Styrenated drying oils, and styrenated alkyds as a base for many protective coatings..illustrate still further uses for styrene. *Ibid.* 177 The rate of the styrenation reaction and the clarity of the product are influenced by the kind and amount of unsaturation present in the oil. **1972** H. WARSON *Applic. Synthetic Resin Emulsions* v. 252 It is not readily possible to form a styrenated oil or alkyd in emulsion form directly. *Ibid.* 253 A maleinized oil is used as the basis for styrenation in the ammoniacal form.

styria, styriate(d, varr. STIRIA, STIRIATE(D.

Styrian ('stɪrɪən), *a.* and *sb.* [f. *Styria* (see below: in Ger. *Steier, Steiermark*) + -AN.]

A. *adj.* Of or belonging to Styria, a province of Austria, formerly a crownland and duchy of the Austrian empire.

1825 J. RUSSELL *Tour Germany* II. 345 An irruption of the Tartars had driven a Styrian priest to save himself by flight. **1890** D. DAVIDSON *Mem. Long Life* x. 246 The happy faces and picturesque costume of the Styrian peasantry. **1907** *Athenæum* 21 Dec. 794/3 An isolated mountain village in the Styrian Alps.

B. *sb.* An inhabitant of Styria.

1621 BURTON *Anat. Mel.* I. ii. II. i. 95, I. Aubanus Bohemius referres that Struma, or poke of the Bauarians & Styrians to the nature of their waters. **1867** H. P. LIDDON in J. O. Johnston *Life & Lett.* v. (1904) 105 The Tyrolese and Styrians.

styrk(e, styrlyng, styrn(e, obs. ff. STIRK, STARLING[1], STERN *a.*

Styrofoam ('staɪərəfəʊm). Chiefly *U.S.* Also **styro-**. [f. POLY)STYR(ENE + -O + FOAM *sb.*] A proprietary name for a variety of foam plastic.

1950 *Official Gaz.* (U.S. Patent Office) 11 July 403/1 Dow Chemical Co... *Styrofoam*... For irregular solid masses of multicellular expanded synthetic resinous material and granular masses of the same material comminuted. **1962** *Punch* 19 Dec. 881/1 How to make..lambs from glass fibre, angels from styrofoam. **1969** *Jane's Freight Containers 1968–69* 438/3 Insulated container. Rectangular, with styrofoam insulation between aluminium panels. **1971** *Islander* (Victoria, B.C.) 11 July 2/1 The styrofoam in the deckhead was wonderful in keeping it relatively cool below. **1973** R. HAYES *Hungarian Game* ii. 20 Each item was cradled in plush-lined styrofoam... Nothing could rattle. **1978** G. VIDAL *Kalki* vi. 135 Geraldine was referring to the top part of a huge Styrofoam statue of Vishnu. **1981** *Times Lit. Suppl.* 6 Mar. 254/2 A styrofoam beaker of instant coffee.

styrol ('staɪərɒl). *Chem.* Also **styrole**. [f. STYR-AX + -OL.] An oil obtained from storax and the resin of balsam of Peru; oil of storax.

1845 *Builder* 28 June 312/1 Styrole is a volatile oil, obtained by distilling the balsam styrax or storax, although only in small quantity, and has a general analogy to benzoin. **1871** GARROD *Mat. Med.* (ed. 3) 270 *Styrol* (C^8H^8), a colourless oil, of an aromatic odour.

styrolene ('staɪərəli:n). *Chem.* [f. prec. + -ENE.] = STYROL.

1881 WATTS *Dict. Chem.* 3rd Suppl. 1832 Styrolene, C^8H^8. Syn. with Cinnamene. **1891** J. E. MARSH tr. *van 't Hoff's Chem. Space* 33 Styrolene of Storax $C_6H_5.CH.CH_2$, reported active by Berthelot.

styrone ('staɪərəʊn). *Chem.* [f. STYR-AX + -ONE.] An alcohol in crystalline form obtained from the decomposition of styracin; used as an antiseptic and a bleaching agent.

1852 W. GREGORY *Handbk. Org. Chem.* (ed. 3) 296 The hydrated oxide of styryle, called also styrone, exists in two forms, as an oil and in a crystalline form. **1883–4** *Medical Ann.* 6/1 Styrone..one of the most powerful antiseptics known. **1893** W. R. DAWSON tr. *Schenk's Man. Bacteriol.* 244 Styrone, glycol, or equal parts of glycerine and ether are used as bleaching agents.

styrpe, styrre, obs. forms of STIRP, STIR.

styrrep, -op, etc., obs. ff. STIRRUP.

styryl ('staɪərɪl). *Chem.* Also **-yle**. [f. STYRAX + -YL.] A synonym of CINNYL. Also *attrib.*, as in ***styryl alcohol*** = STYRONE. Hence **sty'rylic** *a.*

1852 [see STYRONE]. **1877** WATTS *Dict. Chem.* V. 446–7.

stythe, styth (staɪð, staɪθ). *dial.* Also 8 **stith**, 9 **stithe**. [Of obscure origin; perh. altered from **stive* cogn. w. STIVE *v.*[3]]

1. Foul air in a mine; = CHOKE-DAMP.

1708 J. C. *Compl. Collier* (1845) 23 He may loose his Life by Styth, which is a sort of bad foul Air. **1765** *Phil. Trans.* LV. 240 The choak-damp, or stith, found in the coal-mines. **1818** W. PHILLIPS *Geol.* 101 The after-damp or stythe, which follows these blasts, is a mixture of the carbonic acid and azotic gases. **1863** *Tyneside Songs* 12 But did they face the deadly styth, where scarce a single breath Held life..! **1885** *Standard* 5 June 3/4 They have..succumbed to the effects of the stythe.

2. A suffocating smell.

1823 E. MOOR *Suffolk Words, Stithe.* Rhyming to *tithe*... 'The stithe is very oppressive.' **1850** T. BEWICK *Howdy & Upgetting* 15 She thout she wad ha' been skumfeesht wi the steyth. **1897** *Allbutt's Syst. Med.* II. 968 In burning off the old paint there is usually considerable stithe.

stythe, obs. form of STITHY.

styue, obs. form of STEW *sb.*[2], STIFF *a.*

styuye, obs. form of STEW *sb.*[1]

styward(e, stywerd(e, obs. ff. STEWARD.

stywe, stywye, obs. ff. STEW *sb.*[1] and *sb.*[2]

‖**Styx** (stɪks). *Myth.* In 4 **Stige**, 6 **Styxe**, 6–7 **Stix**. [L. *Styx*, a. Gr. Στύξ (Στυγ-) related to στυγεῖν to hate, στυγνός hateful, gloomy.] A river of the lower world or Hades, over which the shades of the departed were ferried by Charon, and by which the gods swore their most solemn oaths.

1390 GOWER *Conf.* II. 164 Be Segne and Stige he swor also, That ben the depe Pettes tuo Of helle the most principal. **1560** T. H. tr. *Ovid's Fable Narcissus* A iiij b, And when he was receyued, into that hyllye [*read* hellye] place be [*read* he] yeke wythin the ogly stype [*read* Styxe], beholde hys wretched face. **1588** SHAKS. *Tit. A.* I. i. 88 Why suffer'st thou thy Sonnes vnburied yet, To houer on the dreadfull shore of Stix? **1602** WARNER *Alb. Eng.* VI. xxx. 150 By Styx I vowe..Venus would be Vulcans, and he knowes I truely sware. **1614** RALEGH *Hist. World* v. iv. §8. 613 There is not any forme of oath, whereby such articles of peace can bee held inuiolable, saue onely *by the water of Styx*, that is, by Necessitie. **1642** H. MORE *Song of Soul* II. i. i. 5 That foul lore..and quill Steep'd in sad Styx, and fed with stinking gore. **1679** TRAPHAM *Disc. Health Jamaica* 27, I have observed it matter of Fact where such care hath been omitted, more lives then else-where have flooded into Styx. **1797** BURKE *Lett. Regicide Peace* iii. Wks. (1808) VIII. 280 This would be a never-failing source of true glory, if springing from just and right; but it is truly dreadful if it be an arm of Styx, which springs out of the profoundest depths of a poisoned soil. **1819** 'R. RABELAIS' *Abeillard & Heloisa* 197 To pass o'er Bot'ny Bays dread styx. **1852** THACKERAY *Esmond* II. ix, He told a falsehood as black as Styx.

DOMI MINA
NVS TIO
ILLV MEA